D0419264

DICTIONNAIRE

FRANÇAIS - ANGLAIS - / ANGLAIS - FRANÇAIS

FRENCH - ENGLISH / ENGLISH - FRENCH

DICTIONARY

2

ANGLAIS - FRANÇAIS

ENGLISH - FRENCH

GRAND DICTIONNAIRE

FRANÇAIS-ANGLAIS / ANGLAIS-FRANÇAIS

2

ANGLAIS FRANÇAIS

LAROUSSE - 17, RUE DU MONTPARNASSE - 75298 PARIS CEDEX 06

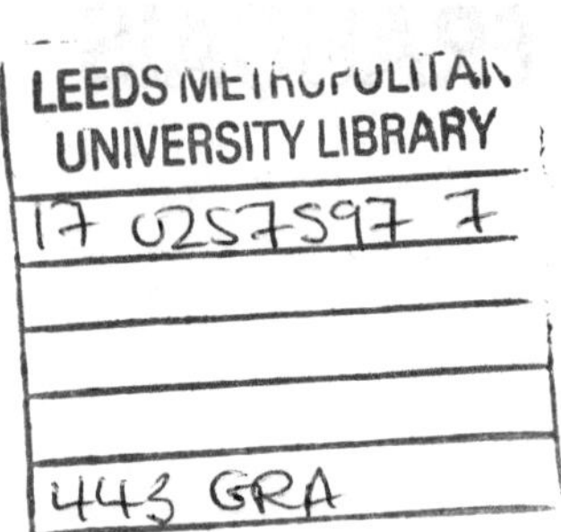

Distributeur exclusif au Canada : les Éditions Françaises Inc.

Photocomposition MAURY. - Malesherbes

IMPRIMERIE HÉRISSEY. - ÉVREUX.
Dépôt légal 1993-10. - N° de série Éditeur 17619.
IMPRIMÉ EN FRANCE *(Printed in France)*. - 401302 octobre 1993

ISBN 2-03-401300-X (édition complète)
ISBN 2-03-401302-6 (volume 2)

FRENCH - ENGLISH / ENGLISH - FRENCH

DICTIONARY

unabridged

2

ENGLISH
FRENCH

LAROUSSE - 17, RUE DU MONTPARNASSE - 75298 PARIS CEDEX 06

Réalisé par/Produced by
LAROUSSE BILINGUES
LONDON • EDINBURGH • PARIS

Direction de la rédaction/General Editor
FAYE CARNEY

Coordination éditoriale/Coordinating Editor
CLAUDE NIMMO

Rédaction/Editors
VALÉRIE KATZAROS
ROSE ROCIOLA
CLAUDE LE GUYADER
LAURENCE LARROCHE
MARTYN BACK
MICHAEL MAYOR
MARTIN CROWLEY
RUTH BLACKMORE

avec/with
CÉCILE VANWALLEGHEM
ANNE LECROART
SOPHIE MARIN
BERNARD GIRAUD
ANNE LANDELLE
CAROLE COEN
CATHERINE JULIA
SABINE CITRON
ISABELLE ROSSELIN
MARIE-PAULE PONCELET
NADINE MONGEARD
EDWIN CARPENTER
DAVID HALLWORTH
KAREN LAWSON
JANE ROGOYSKA
MARGARET JULL COSTA
STEPHEN CURTIS
CLAIRE EVANS
JANE GOLDIE
PATRICK WHITE
STEVE GARNER
PETER CROSS
PAUL DUFFY
SIMON FRASER

Comité de lecture/Advisory Panel
JACQUES VAN ROEY
JEAN-FRANÇOIS ALLAIN
GEOFFREY BREMNER
TREVOR PEACH

Suivi de la réalisation/Administration
SOPHIE JAQUET

Secrétariat d'édition/Copy Preparation
MARIE-NOËLLE TILLIETTE
EMMANUELLE DESRAMÉ
ALEXANDRA DALBIN
SANDRINE AVRIL

Correction sous la direction de/Proofreading coordinated by
ANNICK VALADE

Informatique éditoriale/Data Management
JOCELYNE REBENA
GABINO ALONSO
MARION PÉPIN
CLAUDE NIMMO

Composition/Typesetting
MICHEL VIZET

Maquette/Design
FRÉDÉRIQUE LONGUÉPÉE

Cartographie/Cartography
DOMINIQUE CORMIER
KRYSTYNA MAZOYER
CATHERINE ZACHAROPOULOU

Remerciements:
Nous tenons aussi à remercier tous ceux qui ont apporté leur collaboration à la phase initiale de la rédaction de cet ouvrage, en particulier David Jones, John Scullard, Hélène Houssemaine-Florent et Marie-Noëlle Lamy.

Acknowledgments:
We would like to thank all those who contributed to the early stages of this book, especially David Jones, John Scullard, Hélène Houssemaine-Florent and Marie-Noëlle Lamy.

Au Lecteur

Le Grand Dictionnaire Larousse de l'anglais est un ouvrage de référence essentiel pour l'angliciste, qu'il soit traducteur, universitaire, enseignant ou étudiant, journaliste ou tout simplement passionné d'anglais. Cet ajout à la grande gamme des ouvrages Larousse est le résultat d'une entreprise de longue haleine, menée par une équipe internationale de lexicographes travaillant à Londres, à Édimbourg et à Paris, avec le concours de spécialistes de plusieurs pays.

Cet ouvrage est conçu pour répondre au mieux aux trois critères principaux qui déterminent la qualité d'un dictionnaire: la richesse de la nomenclature et son adaptation aux besoins de l'usager, la convivialité de l'accès à l'information et la fiabilité de cette dernière.

Termes, sens, expressions et locutions ont été choisis pour répondre aux besoins des anglicistes d'aujourd'hui. La sélection de néologismes, d'abréviations, de sigles, d'acronymes et de noms propres a fait l'objet d'un soin tout particulier. Les domaines de l'informatique et du «business» ont également été privilégiés. Essentiel aujourd'hui, l'américain se voit accorder une place de choix: de nombreux ouvrages et publications ont été dépouillés systématiquement à cet effet; en outre, canadianismes, helvétismes et belgicismes contribuent à faire de cet ouvrage une référence véritablement internationale.

L'agencement des articles du dictionnaire ainsi que sa typographie ont reçu une attention particulière; ainsi, locutions et mots composés sont mis en relief et, dans certains cas, présentés comme entrées à part entière, afin d'aérer les articles les plus touffus. Nuances de sens et niveaux de langue sont clairement indiqués afin de faciliter l'accès à la traduction appropriée, elle-même recevant le cas échéant toute information, syntaxique ou autre, susceptible d'éclairer son emploi.

De nombreux exemples viennent illustrer l'usage et permettent d'introduire des traductions préférables dans tel ou tel contexte; le plus grand soin a été apporté à en assurer l'authenticité, ainsi qu'à fournir des traductions pertinentes et actuelles.

Mais un dictionnaire est aussi un pont entre les cultures et les sociétés, et nous avons voulu privilégier cette dimension afin de faciliter la compréhension de la langue et de la culture étrangères: de nombreuses gloses et notules s'efforcent d'expliquer lorsque traduire n'est pas possible, lorsqu'il faut aller au-delà du lexique.

Le Grand Dictionnaire Larousse de l'anglais s'inscrit dans un ambitieux programme éditorial dans le domaine bilingue. Cet outil de communication idéal entre le français et l'anglais, il faudra le faire vivre avec son temps, dans un souci d'innovation et d'amélioration constant; un dictionnaire est par définition perfectible: nous nous adressons à vous, lecteur, pour vous engager à participer à cette entreprise qui n'est jamais vraiment terminée, en nous faisant part de vos observations, de vos critiques, de vos suggestions.

L'Éditeur

To Our Readers

The Larousse Unabridged French-English English-French Dictionary is a major new reference work aimed at professional, academic, specialist and non-specialist users of French. Prepared over a period of several years by an international team of lexicographers based in London, Edinburgh and Paris, with contributions from consultants in several countries, this is the latest addition to a long-standing Larousse tradition of excellence in dictionary publishing.

Our aim throughout has been to meet the three basic criteria that make for quality in dictionaries: relevance and comprehensiveness of coverage, ease of use, and reliability.

Lexical items have been selected to reflect the particular needs of professional linguists and advanced students in today's world. Special attention has been paid to the coverage of new words and proper nouns, abbreviations and acronyms, and to essential fields such as business and computing. The text also reflects the international dimension of both languages: numerous Swiss, Belgian and Canadian French terms are included, and users of American English will find that American vocabulary and usage are particularly well represented.

The layout and typography of entries have been given much thought, with the aim of making set phrases and compounds easier to identify, both visually and linguistically. Nuances of meaning and register are clearly signposted, so that access to the appropriate translation is as straightforward as possible.

Every effort has been made to ensure that example sentences reflect authentic usage and that translations are accurate and up-to-date. Detailed glosses are provided wherever it is necessary to clarify usage or avoid confusion.

All of the above features are considered essential components of today's larger bilingual dictionaries. However the Larousse Unabridged French Dictionary goes one step further in recognizing that problems of communication and comprehension stem not only from the lexicon but also from cultural differences. Hence it places a unique emphasis on explaining 'culture-bound' vocabulary and historical references, using glosses and notes to help non-native speakers understand their implications and relevance.

Language evolves and so does lexicography, and any good dictionary strives to keep in step with the changing needs of its users. The Larousse Unabridged French Dictionary is part of an ambitious publishing programme which recognizes that the task of innovating and updating is continuous and long-term. No dictionary is ever perfect or complete, and so we invite you, as users, to take part in this venture by sending us your comments and criticisms. With your help we hope to set new standards in language reference.

The Publisher

Abbreviations used in this Dictionary
Abréviations utilisées dans ce Dictionnaire

abbreviation	*abbr/abrév*	abréviation
absolute – 'en usage abs' indicates a transitive verb used without a direct object: *il boit beaucoup*	*abs*	absolu – 'en usage abs' signale un verbe transitif employé sans complément d'objet: *il boit beaucoup*
adjective	*adj*	adjectif
phrase functioning as adjective	*adj phr*	locution ayant valeur d'adjectif
adverb	*adv*	adverbe
phrase functioning as adverb	*adv phr*	locution ayant valeur d'adverbe
African French	*Afr*	africanisme
American English	*Am*	américanisme
archaic	*arch*	archaïque
crime slang	*arg crime*	argot du milieu
drugs slang	*arg drogue*	argot de la drogue
military slang	*arg mil*	argot militaire
school slang	*arg scol*	argot scolaire
university slang	*arg univ*	argot universitaire
article	*art*	article
Australian English	*Austr*	anglais australien
auxiliary	*aux*	auxiliaire
before noun – indicates that an adjective is used attributively, i.e. directly before the noun which it modifies	*avant n*	avant le nom – souligne les cas où un adjectif est nécessairement antéposé
Belgian French	*Belg*	belgicisme
British English	*Br*	anglais britannique
countable noun – i.e. a noun which can exist in the plural and be used with 'a'	*C*	substantif comptable – désigne un substantif anglais qui peut être employé au pluriel et avec 'a'
Canadian English/French	*Can*	canadianisme
cardinal	*card*	cardinal
compound-forming noun – shows noun headword used as a noun modifier, e.g. *computer* in *computer course, law* in *law degree*	*comp*	substantif formant des composés – s'applique à un substantif employé en apposition: *computer* dans *computer course, law* dans *law degree*
comparative	*compar*	comparatif
conjunction	*conj*	conjonction
phrase functioning as conjunction	*conj phr*	locution ayant valeur de conjonction
continuous	*cont*	progressif
compounds	*cpds*	composés
crime slang	*crime sl*	argot du milieu
definite	*def/déf*	défini
demonstrative	*dem/dém*	démonstratif
determiner	*det*	déterminant
phrase functioning as determiner	*det phr*	locution ayant valeur de déterminant
dialect	*dial*	dialecte
diminutive	*dimin*	diminutif
direct	*dir*	direct
drugs slang	*drugs sl*	argot de la drogue
especially	*esp*	particulièrement
euphemism	*euph*	euphémisme
exclamation	*excl*	interjection
feminine	*f*	féminin
informal	*fam*	familier
figurative	*fig*	figuré
formal	*fml*	soutenu
generally, in most cases	*gen/gén*	généralement
Swiss French	*Helv*	helvétisme
humorous	*hum*	humoristique
impersonal	*impers*	impersonnel
indefinite	*indef/indéf*	indéfini
indicative	*indic*	indicatif

indirect	*indir*	indirect
informal	*inf*	familier
infinitive	*infin*	infinitif
offensive	*injur*	injurieux
inseparable – shows that the object of a phrasal verb cannot come between the verb and the particle, e.g. *I looked after him* BUT NOT *I looked him after*	*insep/insép*	inséparable – indique qu'un verbe anglais à particule ('phrasal verb') ne peut pas être séparé de sa particule, c'est-à-dire qu'un complément d'objet ne peut être inséré entre les deux, par exemple *I looked after him* ET NON *I looked him after*
exclamation	*interj*	interjection
interrogative	*interr*	interrogatif
invariable – applied to a noun, indicates that the plural and singular forms are the same, e.g. **garde-boue** (*des garde-boue*); **sheep** (*four sheep*). Applied to an adjective, indicates that feminine, masculine and plural forms are the same, e.g. **vieux jeu** (*ils sont/elle est vieux jeu*)	*inv*	invariable – avec un nom, signifie que la forme du pluriel est identique à la forme du singulier: **garde-boue** (*des garde-boue*); **sheep** (*four sheep*). Avec un adjectif, signifie que la forme du féminin et celle du pluriel sont identiques à la forme du masculin: **vieux jeu** (*ils sont/elle est vieux jeu*)
Irish English	*Ir*	anglais irlandais
ironic	*iro/iron*	ironique
literary	*lit/litt*	littéraire
phrase(s)	*loc*	locution(s)
phrase functioning as adjective	*loc adj*	locution ayant valeur d'adjectif
phrase functioning as adverb	*loc adv*	locution ayant valeur d'adverbe
phrase functioning as conjunction	*loc conj*	locution ayant valeur de conjonction
phrase functioning as correlative conjunction	*loc corrél*	locution ayant valeur de conjonction corrélative
phrase functioning as determiner	*loc dét*	locution ayant valeur de déterminant
phrase functioning as exclamation	*loc interj*	locution ayant valeur d'interjection
phrase functioning as preposition	*loc prép*	locution ayant valeur de préposition
phrase functioning as pronoun	*loc pron*	locution ayant valeur de pronom
masculine	*m*	masculin
military slang	*mil sl*	argot militaire
noun modifier – a noun functioning as an adjective and which can only be used attributively, i.e. before the noun it modifies	*modif*	substantif ayant valeur d'adjectif et devant obligatoirement être antéposé
noun	*n*	nom
negative	*neg/nég*	négatif
feminine noun	*nf*	nom féminin
feminine noun used in the plural	*nfpl*	nom féminin pluriel
masculine noun	*nm*	nom masculin
masculine or feminine noun – shows that a noun may be either masculine or feminine: *un architecte/une architecte*	*nmf*	nom masculin ou féminin – indique qu'un nom peut être masculin ou féminin: *un architecte/une architecte*
masculine and feminine forms – indicates a noun with a different form in the masculine and the feminine, e.g. *inspecteur/inspectrice*	*nm,f*	formes féminine et masculine – s'applique à un substantif ayant une forme différente au masculin et au féminin, par exemple *inspecteur/inspectrice*
masculine noun used in the plural	*nmpl*	nom masculin pluriel
proper noun	*npr*	nom propre
plural proper noun	*npr pl*	nom propre pluriel
plural noun	*npl*	nom pluriel
numeral	*num*	numéral
New Zealand English	*NZ*	anglais néo-zélandais
object	*obj*	objet
officially recognized term – some terms (especially borrowings from English) are considered substandard by the Académie française; terms marked 'offic' are recognized as acceptable alternatives for these, but are unlikely to be as widely used	*offic*	terme officiellement recommandé par l'Académie
onomatopoeia	*onomat*	onomatopée
ordinal	*ord*	ordinal
oneself	*o.s.*	
pejorative	*pej/péj*	péjoratif
personal/person	*pers*	personnel/personne

phrase(s)	*phr*	locution(s)
plural	*pl*	pluriel
plural proper noun	*pl pr n*	nom propre pluriel
possessive	*poss*	possessif
past participle	*pp*	participe passé
literal	*pr*	sens propre
predeterminer	*predet*	mot placé avant un déterminant et exprimant un degré ou une quantité
phrase functioning as predeterminer	*predet phr*	locution ayant valeur de 'predeterminer' (*voir* ci-dessus)
prefix	*pref/préf*	préfixe
preposition	*prep/prép*	préposition
phrase functioning as preposition	*prep phr*	locution ayant valeur de préposition
present	*pres/prés*	présent
proper noun	*pr n*	nom propre
pronoun	*pron*	pronom
phrase functioning as pronoun	*pron phr*	locution ayant valeur de pronom
proverb	*prov*	proverbe
past tense	*pt*	passé
	qqch	quelque chose
	qqn	quelqu'un
relative	*rel*	relatif
South African English	*SAfr*	anglais d'Afrique du Sud
someone, somebody	*sb*	
school slang	*school sl*	argot scolaire
Scottish English	*Scot*	anglais écossais
separable – shows that the object of a phrasal verb can come between the verb and the particle, e.g. *I let her in, he helped me out*	*sep/sép*	séparable – indique qu'un verbe anglais à particule ('phrasal verb') peut être séparé de sa particule, c'est-à-dire qu'un complément d'objet peut être inséré entre les deux: *I let her in, he helped me out*
takes singular verb	*sg*	employé avec un verbe au singulier
singular	*sing*	singulier
slang	*sl*	argot
formal	*sout*	soutenu
specialized term or usage	*spec/spéc*	terme ou sens spécialisé
something	*sthg*	
subjunctive	*subj*	subjonctif
subject	*subj/suj*	sujet
superlative	*superl*	superlatif
	tjrs	toujours
uncountable noun – i.e. an English noun which is never used in the plural or with 'a'; used when the French equivalent is or can be a plural, e.g. **applause** *n* (*U*) applaudissements *mpl*; **battement** *nm* beating (*U*)	*U*	substantif non comptable – désigne les substantifs anglais qui ne sont jamais utilisés au pluriel, lorsque l'équivalent français est un pluriel ou peut être mis au pluriel: **applause** *n* (*U*) applaudissements *mpl*; **battement** *nm* beating (*U*)
usually	*usu*	
link verb followed by a predicative adjective or noun – e.g. *tomber malade, être professeur*	*v attr*	verbe suivi d'un attribut – par exemple: *tomber malade, être professeur*
verb	*vb/v*	verbe
intransitive verb	*vi*	verbe intransitif
impersonal verb	*v impers*	verbe impersonnel
pronominal verb	*vp*	verbe pronominal
intransitive pronominal verb	*vpi*	verbe pronominal intransitif
transitive pronominal verb	*vpt*	verbe pronominal transitif
transitive verb	*vt*	verbe transitif

Symbols

❑ Separates expressions which are not set (given before the symbol) from more fixed expressions.

Sépare les emplois non figés (présentés avant le symbole) des expressions figées.

|| Indicates a shift of meaning within a sense category.

Indique un glissement de sens à l'intérieur d'une division sémantique.

≃ Indicates that the translation given is an approximate cultural equivalent.

Indique que la traduction est une équivalence culturelle approximative.

® Indicates that the item is a registered trademark.

Indique que le terme est une marque déposée.

▽ Warns the user that a lexical item or particular meaning is very colloquial, and thus should be used with caution by non-native speakers.

Avertit l'usager qu'un terme ou un sens est très familier et qu'il devra être employé avec prudence par le locuteur étranger.

▼ Warns the user that a lexical item or particular meaning is either vulgar or racist.

Avertit l'usager qu'un terme ou un sens est vulgaire ou raciste.

Trademarks

Words considered to be trademarks have been designated in this dictionary by the symbol ®. However, neither the presence nor the absence of this symbol should be regarded as affecting the legal status of any trademark.

Noms de marque

Les noms de marque sont désignés dans ce dictionnaire par le symbole ®. Néanmoins, ni ce symbole ni son absence éventuelle ne peuvent être considérés comme susceptibles d'avoir une incidence quelconque sur le statut légal d'une marque.

A Note on English Compounds

As in most modern dictionaries, we give lexicalized compounds (i.e. nouns consisting of more than one word) the same prominence as simplex headwords. This means that compounds that are considered as independent units of meaning appear as entries in their own right.

Les mots composés anglais

À l'instar de la plupart des dictionnaires actuels, nous accordons aux mots composés lexicalisés (c'est-à-dire aux substantifs composés de plus d'un mot) la même importance qu'aux mots simples. Ainsi, les composés anglais considérés comme des unités de sens autonomes font l'objet d'une entrée à part entière.

French Verbs

French verbs have a number (from [1] to [116]) which refers to the conjugation table given at the back of the dictionary. This number is not repeated for reflexive verbs when these appear as sub-entries.

Les verbes français

Les verbes français sont suivis d'une numérotation (de [1] à [116]) qui renvoie aux tableaux de conjugaison présentés à la fin de l'ouvrage. Ce chiffre n'est pas répété après les verbes pronominaux lorsque ceux-ci sont présentés en sous-entrées.

Field Labels		**Domaines**
acoustics	ACOUST	acoustique
administration	ADMIN	administration
aeronautics	AERON/AÉRON	aéronautique
agriculture	AGR	agriculture
anatomy	ANAT	anatomie
anthropology	ANTHR	anthropologie
antiquity	ANTIQ	antiquité
archeology	ARCHEOL/ARCHÉOL	archéologie
architecture	ARCHIT	architecture
arms	ARM	armement
astrology	ASTROL	astrologie
astronomy	ASTRON	astronomie
astronautics	ASTRONAUT	astronautique
cars	AUT	automobile
biology	BIOL	biologie
botany	BOT	botanique
chemistry	CHEM/CHIM	chimie
cinema	CIN	cinéma
civil engineering	CIV ENG	travaux publics
commerce	COMM	commerce
accounting	COMPTA	comptabilité
computing	COMPUT	informatique
construction	CONSTR	construction
sewing	COUT	couture
cooking	CULIN	cuisine
dentistry	DENT	dentisterie
ecology	ECOL/ÉCOL	écologie
economics	ECON/ÉCON	économie
electricity	ELECTR/ÉLECTR	électricité
electronics	ELECTRON/ÉLECTRON	électronique
teaching	ENS	enseignement
entomology	ENTOM	entomologie
horseriding	EQUIT/ÉQUIT	équitation
ethnology	ETHN	ethnologie
finance	FIN	finance
football	FTBL	football
geography	GEOG/GÉOG	géographie
geology	GEOL/GÉOL	géologie
geometry	GEOM/GÉOM	géométrie
grammar	GRAMM	grammaire
heraldry	HERALD/HÉRALD	héraldique
history	HIST	histoire
horticulture	HORT	horticulture
hunting	HUNT	chasse
printing	IMPR	imprimerie
industry	INDUST	industrie
computing	INF	informatique
jewellery	JOAILL	joaillerie
law	JUR	juridique
linguistics, language	LING	linguistique, langues
literature	LITERAT/LITTÉRAT	littérature
mathematics	MATH	mathématiques
mechanics	MECH/MÉCAN	mécanique
medicine	MED/MÉD	médecine
carpentry	MENUIS	menuiserie
metallurgy	METALL/MÉTALL	métallurgie

meteorology	METEOR/MÉTÉO	météorologie
military	MIL	militaire
mining	MIN	mines
mineralogy	MINER/MINÉR	minéralogie
music	MUS	musique
mythology	MYTH	mythologie
nautical	NAUT	nautique
nuclear physics	NUCL	physique nucléaire
wines and wine-tasting	ŒNOL	œnologie
optics	OPT	optique
ornithology	ORNITH	ornithologie
petroleum industry	PETR/PÉTR	industrie du pétrole
pharmaceuticals	PHARM	pharmaceutique
philosophy	PHILOS	philosophie
phonetics	PHON	phonétique
photography	PHOT	photographie
physics	PHYS	physique
physiology	PHYSIOL	physiologie
poetry	POET	poésie
politics	POL	politique
printing	PRINT	imprimerie
psychology	PSYCH	psychologie
radio	RAD	radio
religion	RELIG	religion
school	SCH	scolaire
science	SCI/SC	science
sewing	SEW	couture
sociology	SOCIOL	sociologie
stock exchange	ST. EX	bourse
technology	TECH	technologie
telecommunications	TELEC/TÉLÉC	télécommunications
textiles	TEX/TEXT	textiles
theatre	THEAT/THÉÂT	théâtre
transport	TRANSP	transports
civil engineering	TRAV PUBL	travaux publics
television	TV	télévision
typography	TYPO	typographie
clothing	VÊT	vêtements
veterinary science	VETER/VÉTÉR	médecine vétérinaire
viniculture	VINIC	viniculture
zoology	ZOOL	zoologie

PHONETIC TRANSCRIPTION

French vowels

[i] fille, île
[e] p**a**ys, ann**é**e
[ɛ] b**e**c, **ai**me
[a] l**a**c, p**a**pillon
[o] dr**ô**le, **au**be
[ɔ] h**o**tte, aut**o**mne
[u] **ou**til, g**oû**t
[y] **u**sage, l**u**ne
[ø] av**eu**, j**eu**
[œ] p**eu**ple, b**œu**f
[ə] l**e**, j**e**

Nasal vowels

[ɛ̃] **lim**be, m**ain**
[ɑ̃] ch**am**p, **enn**ui
[ɔ̃] **on**gle, m**on**
[œ̃] parf**um**, br**un**

Semi-vowels

[j] **y**eux, l**i**eu
[w] **ou**est, **ou**i
[ɥ] l**u**i, n**u**it

Consonants

[p] **p**rendre, gri**pp**e
[b] **b**ateau, ros**b**if
[t] **th**éâtre, **t**emps
[d] **d**alle, ron**d**e
[k] co**q**, **qu**atre
[g] **g**arder, épilo**gue**
[f] **ph**ysique, **f**ort
[v] **v**oir, ri**v**e
[s] **c**ela, **s**avant
[z] frai**s**e, **z**éro
[ʃ] **ch**arrue, **sch**éma
[ʒ] rou**ge**, **j**abot
[m] **m**ât, dra**m**e
[n] **n**ager, trô**ne**
[ɲ] a**gn**eau, pei**gn**er
[l] ha**ll**e, **l**it
[r] a**rr**acher, sab**re**

NOTES ON PHONETIC TRANSCRIPTION

FRENCH-ENGLISH

1. The symbol [’] has been used to represent the French ‘h aspiré’, e.g. **hachis** [’aʃi].
2. We have followed the modern tendency not to distinguish between the ‘a’ in **pâte** and the ‘a’ in **patte**. Both are represented in the text by the phonetic symbol [a].
3. Internal schwa
   In cases where the schwa [ə] is likely to be ignored in connected speech but retained in the citation form, the [ə] has been shown in brackets, e.g. **cheval** [ʃ(ə)val].

ENGLISH-FRENCH

1. Primary and secondary stress
   The symbol [ˈ] indicates that the following syllable carries primary stress and the symbol [ˌ] that the following syllable carries secondary stress.
2. Pronunciation of final ‘r’
   The symbol [ʳ] in English phonetics indicates that the final ‘r’ is pronounced only when followed by a word beginning with a vowel. Note that it is nearly always pronounced in American English.
3. British and American English
   Differences between British and American pronunciation have not been shown where the pronunciation can be predicted by a standard set of rules, for example where the ‘o’ in **dog** is lengthened in American English. However, phonetics have been shown at the more unpredictable cases of **schedule**, **clerk**, **cliché**, etc.
4. Alternative pronunciations
   Our approach being primarily functional rather than descriptive, we have avoided giving variant pronunciations unless both variants are met with equal frequency, e.g. **kilometre** [ˈkɪləmiːtəʳ, kɪˈlɒmɪtəʳ].
5. Strong and weak forms
   The pronunciation of certain monosyllabic words varies according to their prominence in a sentence, e.g. **the** when stressed is pronounced [ðiː]; when unstressed, [ðə] and before a vowel [ðɪ]. This information is presented in the text as follows: **the** [*weak form* [ðə], *before vowel* [ðɪ], *strong form* [ðiː]].

Transcription Phonétique

Voyelles anglaises

[ɪ] p**i**t, b**i**g, r**i**d
[e] p**e**t, t**e**nd
[æ] p**a**t, b**a**g, m**a**d
[ʌ] p**u**tt, c**u**t
[ɒ] p**o**t, l**o**g
[ʊ] p**u**t, f**u**ll
[ə] moth**er**, s**u**ppose
[i:] b**ea**n, w**ee**d
[ɑ:] b**ar**n, c**ar**, l**au**gh
[ɔ:] b**or**n, l**aw**n
[u:] l**oo**p, l**oo**se
[ɜ:] b**ur**n, l**ear**n, b**ir**d

Diphtongues

[eɪ] b**ay**, l**a**te, gr**ea**t
[aɪ] b**uy**, l**igh**t, **ais**le
[ɔɪ] b**oy**, f**oi**l
[əʊ] n**o**, r**oa**d, bl**ow**
[aʊ] n**ow**, sh**ou**t, t**ow**n
[ɪə] p**ee**r, f**ie**rce, id**ea**
[eə] p**ai**r, b**ea**r, sh**are**
[ʊə] p**oo**r, s**ure**, t**our**

Semi-voyelles

[j] **y**ou, span**ie**l
[w] **w**et, **wh**y, t**w**in

Consonnes

[p] **p**o**p**, **p**eo**p**le
[b] **b**ottle, **b**i**b**
[t] **t**rain, **t**ip
[d] **d**og, **d**i**d**
[k] **c**ome, **k**itchen
[g] **g**a**g**, **g**reat
[tʃ] **ch**ain, wre**tch**ed
[dʒ] **j**ig, fri**dge**
[f] **f**ib, **ph**ysical
[v] **v**ine, li**v**id
[θ] **th**ink, fif**th**
[ð] **th**is, wi**th**
[s] **s**eal, pea**ce**
[z] **z**ip, hi**s**
[ʃ] **sh**eep, ma**ch**ine
[ʒ] u**s**ual, mea**s**ure
[h] **h**ow, per**h**aps
[m] **m**etal, co**mb**
[n] **n**ight, di**nn**er
[ŋ] su**ng**, parki**ng**
[l] **l**itt**le**, he**l**p
[r] **r**ight, ca**rr**y

Notes sur la Transcription Phonétique

Anglais-Français

1. Accents primaire et secondaire
Les symboles [ˈ] et [ˌ] indiquent respectivement un accent primaire et un accent secondaire sur la syllabe suivante.
2. Prononciation du 'r' final
Le symbole [^{r}] indique que le 'r' final d'un mot anglais ne se prononce que lorsqu'il forme une liaison avec la voyelle du mot suivant; le 'r' final est presque toujours prononcé en anglais américain.
3. Anglais britannique et américain
Les différences de prononciation entre l'anglais britannique et l'anglais américain ne sont signalées que lorsqu'elles sortent du cadre de règles générales préétablies. Le 'o' de **dog**, par exemple, est généralement plus allongé en anglais américain, et ne bénéficie pas d'une seconde transcription phonétique. En revanche, des mots comme **schedule**, **clerk**, **cliché**, etc, dont la prononciation est moins évidente, font l'objet de deux transcriptions phonétiques.
4. Mots ayant deux prononciations
Nous avons choisi de ne donner que la prononciation la plus courante du mot, sauf dans les cas où une variante est particulièrement fréquente, comme par exemple le mot **kilometre** [ˈkɪləmi:tə^r, kɪˈlɒmɪtə^r].
5. Les formes accentuées et atones
La prononciation de certains mots monosyllabiques anglais varie selon le degré d'emphase qu'ils ont dans la phrase; **the**, par exemple, se prononce [ði:] en position accentuée, [ðə] en position atone, et [ðɪ] devant une voyelle. Ces informations sont présentées de la manière suivante dans le dictionnaire: **the** [*weak form* [ðə], *before vowel* [ðɪ], *strong form* [ði:]].

Français-Anglais

1. Le symbole ['] représente le 'h aspiré' français, par exemple **hachis** ['aʃi].
2. Comme le veut la tendance actuelle, nous ne faisons pas de distinction entre le 'a' de **pâte** et celui de **patte**, tous deux transcrits [a].
3. Prononciation du 'e' muet
Lorsque le 'e' peut ne pas être prononcé dans le discours continu, il a été mis entre parenthèses, comme par exemple pour le mot **cheval** [ʃ(ə)val].

ANGLAIS - FRANÇAIS
ENGLISH - FRENCH

a (*pl* a's OR as), **A** (*pl* A's OR As) [eɪ] ◇ *n* -**1.** [letter] a *m*, A *m*; 45 a [house, page number] 45 bis; A5 *Br* TRANSP ≃ route *f* nationale 5, RN *f* 5; from A to Z de A à Z; from A to B de A à B; from point A to point B d'un point A à un point B. -**2.** [in list]: I'm not going because a) I've no money and b) I've no time je n'y vais pas parce que primo je n'ai pas d'argent et secundo je n'ai pas le temps. -**3.** SCH: to get an A in French ≃ obtenir plus de 15 sur 20 en français. -**4.** MUS la *m*. -**5.** (*abbr of* ampere) A *m*.
◇ *adj* -**1.** MUS [string] de la. -**2.** *Br* TRANSP: A road route *f* nationale *(en Grande-Bretagne)*.

a [*weak form* ə, *strong form* eɪ] (*before vowel* an [*weak form* ən, *strong form* æn]) *det* -**1.** [before countable nouns] un, une; a book un livre; a car une voiture; I can't see a thing je ne vois rien; he has a broken leg il a une jambe cassée; a cup and saucer une tasse et sa soucoupe; would you like a coffee? voulez-vous un café?; an expensive German wine un vin allemand très cher ‖ [before professions]: she's a doctor elle est médecin; have you seen a doctor? as-tu vu un médecin? -**2.** [before numbers]: a thousand dollars mille dollars; a dozen eggs une douzaine d'œufs; a third/fifth un tiers/cinquième; a twentieth of a second un vingtième de seconde; an hour and a half une heure et demie ‖ [per]: £2 a dozen/a hundred deux livres la douzaine/les cent grammes; three times a year trois fois par an. -**3.** [before terms of quantity, amount]: a few weeks/months quelques semaines/mois; a lot of money beaucoup d'argent; a great many visitors de très nombreux visiteurs; have a little more wine reprenez donc un peu de vin; he raised a number of interesting points il a soulevé un certain nombre de questions intéressantes. -**4.** [before periods of time] un, une; I'm going for a week/month/year je pars (pour) une semaine/un mois/un an; we talked for a while nous avons parlé un moment. -**5.** [before days, months, festivals] un, une; the meeting was on a Tuesday la réunion a eu lieu un mardi; it was an exceptionally cold March ce fut un mois de mars particulièrement froid; we had an unforgettable Christmas nous avons passé un Noël inoubliable. -**6.** [in generalizations]: a triangle has three sides le triangle a trois côtés; a cheetah can outrun a lion le guépard court plus vite que le lion. -**7.** [before uncountable nouns]: a wide knowledge of the subject une connaissance approfondie du sujet; he felt a joy he could not conceal il éprouvait une joie qu'il ne pouvait dissimuler. -**8.** [before verbal nouns]: there's been a general falling off in sales il y a eu une chute des ventes. -**9.** [before personal names]: a Miss Jones was asking for you une certaine Miss Jones vous a demandé; he's been described as a new James Dean on le donne pour le nouveau James Dean; her mother was a Sinclair sa mère était une Sinclair ‖ [before names of artists]: it's a genuine Matisse c'est un Matisse authentique; there's a new Stephen King/Spielberg out next month il y a un nouveau Stephen King/Spielberg qui sort le mois prochain. -**10.** [after half, rather, such, what]: half a glass of wine un demi-verre de vin; she's such/rather an interesting person c'est quelqu'un de vraiment/d'assez intéressant; what a lovely dress! quelle jolie robe! -**11.** [after as, how, so, too + adj]: that's too big a slice for me cette tranche est trop grosse pour moi; how big a bit do you want? combien en veux-tu?; she's as nice a girl as you could wish to meet c'est la fille la plus gentille du monde.

a. *written abbr of* acre.

A-1 *adj* -**1.** [first-class, perfect]: everything's ~ tout est parfait. -**2.** [in health]: to be ~ être en pleine santé OR forme. -**3.** NAUT en excellent état.

A4 ◇ *n* [paper size] format *m* A4.
◇ *adj*: ~ paper papier *m* (format) A4.

AA [*n sense 2 pronounced* ˈdʌblˌeɪ] ◇ *adj abbr of* anti-aircraft.
◇ *pr n* -**1.** (*abbr of* Automobile Association) *automobile club britannique et compagnie d'assurances, qui garantit le dépannage de ses adhérents et propose des services touristiques et juridiques,* ≃ ACF *m*, ≃ TCF *m*. -**2.** (*abbr of* Alcoholics Anonymous) Alcooliques Anonymes *mpl*.
◇ *n* -**1.** *Am abbr of* Associate in Arts. -**2.** *Br dated* & CIN *film interdit aux moins de 14 ans (maintenant remplacé par «PG»)*.

AAA [*sense 1 pronounced* ˌθriːˈeɪz] *pr n* -**1.** (*abbr of* Amateur Athletics Association) *ancien nom de la fédération britannique d'athlétisme (remplacé en octobre 1991 par la British Athletics Federation)*. -**2.** (*abbr of* American Automobile Association) *automobile club américain,* ≃ ACF *m*, ≃ TCF *m*.

Aachen [ˈɑːkən] *pr n* Aix-la-Chapelle.

aardvark [ˈɑːdvɑːk] *n* oryctérope *m*.

Aargau [ˈɑːgaʊ] *pr n* Argovie *f*; in ~ en Argovie.

Aaron [ˈeərən] *pr n* Aaron.

AAUP (*abbr of* American Association of University Professors) *pr n syndicat américain des professeurs d'université*.

AB ◇ *n* -**1.** *Am* UNIV (*abbr of* Bachelor of Arts) *(titulaire d'une) licence de lettres*. -**2.** *Br* NAUT *abbr of* able/able-bodied seaman.
◇ *written abbr of* Alberta.

aback [əˈbæk] *adv*: to be taken ~ être pris au dépourvu, être interloqué ‖ NAUT être pris bout au vent.

abacus [ˈæbəkəs] (*pl* abacuses OR abaci [ˈæbəsaɪ]) *n* boulier *m*.

abaft [əˈbɑːft] NAUT ◇ *adv* à l'arrière.
◇ *prep* en arrière de.

abalone [ˌæbəˈləʊnɪ] *n* oreille-de-mer *f*, ormeau *m*.

abandon [əˈbændən] ◇ *vt* -**1.** [leave - person] abandonner; [- post, place] déserter, quitter; to ~ ship abandonner OR quitter le navire; we had to ~ the car in the snow nous avons dû abandonner la voiture dans la neige; they were ~ed to their fate on les abandonna à leur sort; to ~ o.s. to despair *fig* se laisser aller OR s'abandonner au désespoir. -**2.** [give up - search] abandonner, renoncer à; [- studies] renoncer à; [- idea, cause] laisser tomber; we ~ed the struggle nous avons renoncé à lutter; several runners ~ed the race plusieurs coureurs ont abandonné; the match was ~ed because of bad weather on a interrompu le match en raison du mauvais temps ❑ Abandon Hope, All Ye Who Enter Here laissez tout espoir vous qui entrez *(phrase tirée de l'Enfer de Dante, parfois utilisée ironiquement pour signaler un lieu prétendu dangereux)*. -**3.** [for insurance]: they ~ed the car to the insurance company ils ont cédé la voiture à la compagnie d'assurances.
◇ *n* -**1.** [neglect] abandon *m*; in a state of ~ laissé à l'abandon. -**2.** [lack of inhibition] désinvolture *f*, laisser-aller *m*; they leapt about with wild OR gay ~ ils sautaient de joie sans aucune retenue.

abandoned [əˈbændənd] *adj* -**1.** [person] abandonné, délaissé; [house] abandonné. -**2.** [dissolute - behaviour, person] débauché; [- life] de débauche. -**3.** [unrestrained - laughter, gaiety] sans retenue.

abandonment [əˈbændənmənt] *n* -**1.** [of place, project] abandon *m*. -**2.** [of right] cession *f*.

abase [əˈbeɪs] *vt*: to ~ o.s. s'humilier, s'abaisser.

abasement [əˈbeɪsmənt] *n* humiliation *f*.

abashed [əˈbæʃt] *adj* penaud; to be OR to feel ~ avoir honte.

abate [əˈbeɪt] ◇ *vi* [storm] s'apaiser; [pain] diminuer; [noise] s'atténuer.
◇ *vt* [tax] baisser, réduire.

abatement [əˈbeɪtmənt] *n* [of tax, rent] réduction *f*, abattement *m*; [of noise, strength] diminution *f*, réduction *f*.

abattoir [ˈæbətwɑːʳ] *n* abattoirs *mpl*.

abaxial [æbˈæksɪəl] *adj* BIOL désaxé.

abbess [ˈæbes] *n* abbesse *f*.

Abbevillian [ˌæbˈvɪlɪən] ◇ *adj* abbevillien.
◇ *n* abbevillien *m*.

abbey [ˈæbɪ] ◇ *n* abbaye *f*; the Abbey, Westminster Abbey l'abbaye de Westminster.
◇ *comp* [grounds] de l'abbaye.

abbot [ˈæbət] *n* abbé *m (dans un monastère)*.

abbr, abbrev -**1.** *written abbr of* abbreviation. -**2.** *written abbr of* abbreviated.

abbreviate [əˈbriːvɪeɪt] *vt* [text, title] abréger; "for example" is often ~d to "e.g." «par exemple» est souvent abrégé en «p. ex.».

abbreviation [əˌbriːvɪˈeɪʃn] *n* [of expression, title, word] abréviation *f*; Dr is an ~ for "doctor" Dr est l'abréviation de «docteur».

ABC ◇ *n* **-1.** [rudiments] rudiments *mpl*, B.A. Ba *m*; the ~ of woodwork le B.A. Ba de la menuiserie. **-2.** [alphabet] alphabet *m*; it's as easy as ~ c'est simple comme bonjour.
◇ *pr n* **-1.** (*abbr of* American Broadcasting Company) *chaîne de télévision américaine.* **-2.** (*abbr of* Australian Broadcasting Corporation) *chaîne de télévision australienne.*
◆ **ABCs** *npl Am* = **ABC** *n*.

ABD (*abbr of* all but dissertation) *n Am* UNIV *personne qui n'a plus qu'à rédiger sa thèse pour obtenir son doctorat.*

abdicate [ˈæbdɪkeɪt] ◇ *vt* **-1.** [right] renoncer à; [responsibility] abandonner. **-2.** [monarch]: to ~ the throne abdiquer.
◇ *vi* abdiquer.

abdication [ˌæbdɪˈkeɪʃn] *n* **-1.** [of throne] abdication *f*. **-2.** [of right] renonciation *f*; [of responsibility] abandon *m*; the Abdication *Br* HIST *abdication d'Édouard VIII d'Angleterre en 1936 devant l'opposition de l'Église anglicane à son mariage avec Wallis Warfield Simpson, Américaine deux fois divorcée.*

abdomen [ˈæbdəmen] *n* abdomen *m*.

abdominal [æbˈdɒmɪnl] *adj* abdominal.

abduct [əbˈdʌkt] *vt* enlever, kidnapper.

abduction [æbˈdʌkʃn] *n* rapt *m*, enlèvement *m*; 'The Abduction from the Seraglio' *Mozart* 'l'Enlèvement au sérail'.

abductor [əbˈdʌktəʳ] *n* **-1.** [of person] ravisseur *m*, -euse *f*. **-2.** PHYSIOL (muscle *m*) abducteur *m*.

abed [əˈbed] *adj* & *adv lit* dans son lit, au lit.

Abel [ˈeɪbl] *pr n* Abel.

Aberdeen Angus [ˈæbəˌdiːnˈæŋgəs] *n* [breed] aberdeen-angus *m*.

Aberdonian [ˌæbəˈdəʊnjən] ◇ *n* habitant *m*, -e *f* d'Aberdeen.
◇ *adj* d'Aberdeen.

aberrant [æˈberənt] *adj* [gen & BIOL] aberrant.

aberration [ˌæbəˈreɪʃn] *n* **-1.** [act, idea] aberration *f*; a mental ~ une aberration mentale; it's an ~ c'est aberrant. **-2.** ASTRON & OPT aberration *f*.

abet [əˈbet] (*pt* & *pp* abetted, *cont* abetting) *vt* [aid] aider; [encourage] encourager.

abeyance [əˈbeɪəns] *n fml* **-1.** [disuse] désuétude *f*; to fall into ~ tomber en désuétude; the law is in temporary ~ la loi a momentanément cessé d'être appliquée. **-2.** [suspense] suspens *m*; the question was left in ~ la question a été laissée en suspens; the final decision on the project is still in ~ la décision finale concernant le projet reste en suspens.

abhor [əbˈhɔːʳ] (*pt* & *pp* abhorred, *cont* abhorring) *vt* détester, avoir en horreur.

abhorrence [əbˈhɒrəns] *n fml* aversion *f*, horreur *f*; to have an ~ of sthg avoir horreur de qqch OR une aversion pour qqch, avoir qqch en horreur.

abhorrent [əbˈhɒrənt] *adj fml* **-1.** [detestable - practice, attitude] odieux, exécrable; I find their attitude ~, their attitude is ~ to me je trouve leur attitude détestable. **-2.** [contrary] contraire; [incompatible] incompatible; such economic considerations are ~ to socialism des considérations économiques de ce genre sont contraires au OR incompatibles avec le socialisme.

abide [əˈbaɪd] (*pt* & *pp* abode [əˈbəʊd] OR abided) ◇ *vi lit* **-1.** [live] demeurer, habiter; ~ with me RELIG restez avec moi. **-2.** [endure] continuer, durer.
◇ *vt* supporter; she can't ~ him elle ne peut pas le souffrir OR supporter; I can't ~ people smoking in restaurants je ne peux pas supporter les gens qui fument au restaurant.
◆ **abide by** *vt insep* [decision, law, promise] se conformer à, respecter; [result] supporter, assumer; will he ~ by the new regulations? respectera-t-il le nouveau règlement?

abiding [əˈbaɪdɪŋ] *adj* constant, permanent.

Abidjan [ˌæbɪˈdʒɑːn] *pr n* Abidjan.

ability [əˈbɪlətɪ] (*pl* abilities) *n* [mental or physical] capacité *f*, capacités *fpl*, aptitude *f*; he has great ~ il a beaucoup de capacités, il est très capable; to lack ~ manquer de capacités; do you feel you have the necessary ~ to run the project? croyez-vous avoir les capacités nécessaires pour gérer le projet?; children at different levels of ~/of different abilities des enfants de niveaux intellectuels différents/aux compétences diverses; I'll do it to the best of my ~ je le ferai du mieux que je peux, je ferai de mon mieux.
◆ **abilities** *npl* [special talents] capacités *fpl*, aptitude *f*; [artistic or musical] dons *mpl*, capacités *fpl*; her acting abilities remained unrecognized ses talents d'actrice sont restés méconnus.

abiotic [ˌeɪbaɪˈɒtɪk] *adj* abiotique.

abject [ˈæbdʒekt] *adj* [person, deed] abject, vil; [apology, flattery] servile; they live in ~ poverty ils vivent dans une misère noire.

abjectly [ˈæbdʒektlɪ] *adv* [act, refuse] de manière abjecte; [apologize] avec servilité, servilement.

abjure [əbˈdʒʊəʳ] *vt* [belief] renier; [religion] abjurer; [right] renoncer à; [alliance] refuser, renier.

ablation [æbˈleɪʃn] *n* ablation *f*.

ablative [ˈæblətɪv] ◇ *adj* ablatif.
◇ *n* ablatif *m*.

ablaut [ˈæblaʊt] *n* alternance *f* vocalique, ablaut *m*.

ablaze [əˈbleɪz] ◇ *adj* **-1.** [on fire] en flammes; the factory was already ~ when the firemen arrived l'usine était déjà en flammes lorsque les pompiers sont arrivés. **-2.** [luminous]: ~ with light brillant de lumière; the offices were ~ with light toutes les lumières brillaient dans les bureaux. **-3.** [face] brillant; [eyes] enflammé, pétillant; her eyes were ~ with anger ses yeux étaient enflammés de colère.
◇ *adv*: to set sthg ~ embraser qqch.

able [ˈeɪbl] (*compar* abler, *superl* ablest) *adj* **-1.** to be ~ to [to be capable of]: to be ~ to do sthg pouvoir faire qqch; I won't be ~ to come je ne pourrai pas venir; I wasn't ~ to see je ne voyais pas; she wasn't ~ to explain elle était incapable d'expliquer; I'll be ~ to visit you more often now je pourrai te rendre visite plus souvent désormais; I haven't been ~ to find out very much je n'ai pas pu savoir grand-chose; I'm not ~ to tell you je ne suis pas en mesure de vous le dire; she's better OR more ~ to explain than I am elle est mieux à même de vous expliquer que moi. **-2.** [competent] capable. **-3.** [talented] talentueux, de talent.

able-bodied *adj* robuste, solide.

able-bodied seaman, able seaman *n* NAUT matelot *m* breveté.

ablutions [əˈbluːʃnz] *npl* **-1.** *fml* [washing]: to do OR to perform one's ~ faire ses ablutions. **-2.** *mil sl* [building] lavabos *mpl*.

ably [ˈeɪblɪ] *adv* d'une façon compétente.

ABM (*abbr of* anti-ballistic missile) *n* ABM *m*.

abnegate [ˈæbnɪgeɪt] *vt* renoncer à.

abnegation [ˌæbnɪˈgeɪʃn] *n* abnégation *f*.

abnormal [æbˈnɔːml] *adj* anormal; ~ psychology psychopathologie *f*.

abnormality [ˌæbnɔːˈmælətɪ] (*pl* abnormalities) *n* **-1.** [quality] anormalité *f*, caractère *m* anormal. **-2.** [feature] anomalie *f*.

abnormally [æbˈnɔːməlɪ] *adv* anormalement.

abo▼ [ˈæbəʊ] (*pl* abos) *Austr n terme raciste désignant un aborigène.*

aboard [əˈbɔːd] ◇ *adv* à bord; to go ~ monter à bord; life ~ la vie à bord; all ~! NAUT tout le monde à bord!; RAIL en voiture!
◇ *prep* à bord de; ~ ship à bord du bateau.

abode [əˈbəʊd] ◇ *pt* & *pp* → **abide**.
◇ *n fml* demeure *f*; he took up his ~ in Tunisia il s'est installé en Tunisie; one's place of ~ JUR son domicile; to have the right of ~ in a country avoir le droit de séjour dans un pays.

abolish [əˈbɒlɪʃ] *vt* [privilege, slavery] abolir; [right] supprimer; [law] supprimer, abroger.

abolition [ˌæbəˈlɪʃn] *n* [of privilege, slavery] abolition *f*; [of law] suppression *f*, abrogation *f*.

abolitionism [ˌæbəˈlɪʃənɪzm] *n* abolitionnisme *m (dans un contexte américain, ce mot fait le plus souvent référence à l'abolition de l'esclavage aux États-Unis).*

abolitionist [ˌæbəˈlɪʃənɪst] ◇ *adj* abolitionniste.
◇ *n* abolitionniste *mf*.

A-bomb (*abbr of* atom bomb) *n* bombe A *f*.

abominable [əˈbɒmɪnəbl] *adj* **-1.** [very bad] abominable, lamentable, affreux; her handwriting is ~ son écriture est abominable. **-2.** [odious] abominable, odieux.

abominable snowman *n* abominable homme *m* des neiges.

abominably [əˈbɒmɪnəblɪ] *adv* **-1.** [write, spell] lamentablement, affreusement. **-2.** [as intensifier] extrêmement, abominablement; it's ~ difficult c'est abominablement difficile. **-3.** [act, behave] abominablement, odieusement.

abominate [əˈbɒmɪneɪt] *vt fml* détester, exécrer.

abomination [əˌbɒmɪˈneɪʃn] *n* **-1.** *fml* [loathing] abomination *f*; we hold such behaviour in ~ ce genre de comportement nous fait horreur OR nous horrifie. **-2.** *fml* [detestable act] abomination *f*, acte *m* abominable. **-3.** [awful thing] abomination *f*, chose *f* abominable; the building is an ~ l'immeuble est une abomination.

aboriginal [ˌæbəˈrɪdʒənl] ◇ *n* = **aborigine**.
◇ *adj* **-1.** [culture, legend] aborigène, des aborigènes. **-2.** BOT & ZOOL aborigène.

aborigine [ˌæbəˈrɪdʒənɪ] ◇ *n* **-1.** [original inhabitant] aborigène *mf*. **-2.** [in Australia] aborigène *mf* (d'Australie). **-3.** [language] langue *f* aborigène.
◇ *adj* aborigène, des aborigènes.
◆ **aborigines** *npl* BOT & ZOOL flore *f* et faune *f* aborigènes.

abort [əˈbɔːt] ◇ *vi* **-1.** [mission, plans] avorter, échouer; [flight] avorter; the controller gave the order to ~ l'aiguilleur du ciel a donné l'ordre d'abandonner OR de suspendre le vol. **-2.** MED avorter.
◇ *vt* **-1.** [mission, flight] interrompre, mettre un terme à; [plan] faire échouer. **-2.** MED avorter.
◇ *n* **-1.** [of mission, spacecraft] interruption *f*. **-2.** COMPUT abandon *m*.

abortifacient [əˌbɔːtɪˈfeɪʃnt] ◇ *adj* abortif.
◇ *n* abortif *m*.

abortion [əˈbɔːʃn] *n* **-1.** MED avortement *m*, interruption *f* (volontaire) de grossesse; to have an ~ se faire avorter. **-2.** [of plans, mission] avortement *m*.

abortionist [əˈbɔːʃənɪst] *n* **-1.** [practitioner] avorteur *m*, -euse *f*. **-2.** [advocate] partisan *m* de l'avortement (légal).

abortive [əˈbɔːtɪv] *adj* **-1.** [attempt] raté, infructueux. **-2.** [agent, organism, process] abortif.

aboulia [əˈbuːlɪə] = **abulia**.

abound [əˈbaʊnd] *vi* [fish, resources] abonder; [explanations, ideas] abonder, foisonner; the area ~s in OR with natural resources la région abonde en OR regorge de ressources naturelles; the city ~s with tourists at this time of year la ville grouille OR pullule de touristes à cette époque de l'année.

about [əˈbaʊt] ◇ *prep* **-1.** [concerning, on the subject of] à propos de, au sujet de; she's had a letter ~ the loan elle a reçu une lettre concernant le prêt; I'm worried ~ her je suis inquiet à son sujet; I'm not happy ~ her going ça ne me plaît pas qu'elle y aille; there's no doubt ~ it cela ne fait aucun doute, il n'y a aucun doute là-dessus; now, ~ your request for a salary increase... bon, en ce qui concerne votre demande d'augmentation...; what's the book ~? c'est un livre sur quoi?; it's a book ~ the life of Mozart c'est un livre sur la vie de Mozart; I don't know what all the fuss is ~ je ne sais pas ce que c'est que toute cette histoire; what do you want to see me ~? vous voulez me voir à quel sujet?; that's what life's all ~ c'est ça la vie; he asked us ~ the war il nous a posé des questions sur la guerre; she asked me ~ my mother elle m'a demandé des nouvelles de ma mère; you should do something ~ your headaches vous devriez faire quelque chose pour vos maux de tête; I can't do anything ~ it je n'y peux rien; what do YOU know ~ it? qu'est-ce que vous en savez, vous?; I don't know much ~ Egyptian art je ne m'y connais pas beaucoup en art égyptien; I didn't know ~ your accident je ne savais pas que vous aviez eu un accident; she talked to them ~ her holidays elle leur a parlé de ses vacances; tell me ~ your holidays parle-moi de tes vacances; what do you think ~ modern art? que pensez-vous de l'art moderne?; I was thinking ~ my mother je pensais à ma mère; I'd like you to think ~ my offer j'aimerais que vous réfléchissiez à ma proposition; I warned them ~ the political situation je les ai mis en garde en ce qui concerne la situation politique. -**2.** [in the character of]: what I like ~ her is her generosity ce que j'aime en OR chez elle, c'est sa générosité; what I don't like ~ the house is all the stairs ce qui me déplaît dans cette maison, ce sont tous les escaliers; there's something ~ the house that I don't like il y a quelque chose que je n'aime pas dans cette maison; there's something ~ the place that reminds me of Rome cet endroit me fait penser à Rome; there's something strange ~ her il y a quelque chose de bizarre chez elle. -**3.** [busy with]: while I'm ~ it pendant que j'y suis; be quick ~ it! faites vite!, dépêchez-vous! -**4.** [in phrasal verbs] partout; there were clothes lying all ~ the room des vêtements traînaient partout dans la pièce; you mustn't leave money lying ~ the house il ne faut pas laisser de l'argent traîner dans la maison; the children were running ~ the garden les enfants couraient dans le jardin. -**5.** *lit* [surrounding] autour de; there is a high wall ~ the castle un rempart entoure le château. -**6.** *fml* [on one's person]: he had a dangerous weapon ~ his person il portait une arme dangereuse.

◇ *adv* -**1.** [more or less] environ, à peu près; ~ a year environ OR à peu près un an; ~ £50 50 livres environ; ~ five o'clock vers cinq heures; that looks ~ right ça a l'air d'être à peu près ça; I've just ~ finished j'ai presque fini; I've had just ~ enough! j'en ai vraiment assez!; it's ~ time you started il serait grand temps que vous commenciez; that's ~ it for now c'est à peu près tout pour l'instant. -**2.** [somewhere, near] dans les parages, par ici; is there anyone ~? il y a quelqu'un?; there was no one ~ when I left the building il n'y avait personne dans les parages quand j'ai quitté l'immeuble; my keys must be ~ somewhere mes clés doivent être quelque part par ici. -**3.** [in all directions, places]: there's a lot of flu ~ beaucoup de gens ont la grippe en ce moment; watch out, there are pickpockets ~ méfie-toi, il y a beaucoup de pickpockets qui traînent; have you seen many of the new coins ~? tu as vu beaucoup de nouvelles pièces en circulation? || [in phrasal verbs]: there are some terrible rumours going ~ il court des rumeurs terribles; to run ~ courir dans tous les sens; don't leave your money ~ ne laissez pas traîner votre argent; they've been sitting ~ all afternoon ils ont passé tout l'après-midi assis à ne rien faire; stop fooling ~! *inf* arrête de faire l'imbécile!; she was waving her arms ~ elle agitait les bras dans tous les sens. -**4.** [in opposite direction]: to turn ~ se retourner.

◇ *adj* -**1.** [expressing imminent action]: to be ~ to do sthg être sur le point de faire qqch; I was just ~ to leave j'allais partir, j'étais sur le point de partir. -**2.** [expressing reluctance]: I'm not ~ to answer that kind of question je ne suis pas prêt à répondre à ce genre de question.

about-turn *Br*, **about-face** *Am* ◇ *interj*: ~! MIL [to right] demi-tour droite!; [to left] demi-tour gauche!

◇ *vi* -**1.** MIL faire un demi-tour. -**2.** faire volte-face.

◇ *n* -**1.** MIL demi-tour *m*; to do an ~ faire un demi-tour. -**2.** volte-face *f inv*; to do an ~ faire volte-face.

above [ə'bʌv] ◇ *prep* -**1.** [in a higher place or position than] au-dessus de; ~ our heads au-dessus de nos têtes; in the sky ~ us dans le ciel au-dessus de nous; smoke rose ~ the town de la fumée s'élevait au-dessus de la ville; ~ the equator au-dessus de l'équateur; ~ ground en surface; skirts are ~ the knee this year les jupes se portent au-dessus du genou cette année; they live ~ the shop ils vivent au-dessus du magasin; a village on the river ~ Oxford un village (situé) en amont d'Oxford; his name appeared three lines ~ mine son nom était trois lignes au-dessus du mien. -**2.** [greater in degree or quantity than] au-dessus de; ~ 40 kilos au-dessus de 40 kilos; it's ~ my price limit c'est au-dessus du prix OR ça dépasse le prix maximum que je me suis fixé; ~ average au-dessus de la moyenne. -**3.** [in preference to] plus que; he values friendship ~ success il accorde plus d'importance à l'amitié qu'à la réussite; he respected her ~ all others il la respectait plus que quiconque. -**4.** [beyond] au-delà de; the discussion was all rather ~ me la discussion me dépassait complètement; ~ and beyond the call of duty bien au-delà du strict devoir. -**5.** [morally or intellectually superior to]: she's ~ that sort of thing elle est au-dessus de ça; ~ suspicion/reproach au-dessus de tout soupçon/reproche; he's not ~ cheating il irait jusqu'à tricher; I'm not ~ asking for favours je ne répugne pas à demander des faveurs. -**6.** [superior in rank, quality to] au-dessus de; to marry ~ one's station se marier au-dessus de son rang; she's ranked ~ the other athletes elle se classe devant les autres athlètes ❑ to get ~ o.s. se monter la tête. -**7.** [in volume, sound] par-dessus; it's difficult to make oneself heard ~ all this noise il est difficile de se faire entendre avec tout ce bruit; a scream rose ~ the noise of the engines un cri se fit entendre par-dessus le bruit des moteurs. -**8.** MUS [in pitch] au-dessus de.

◇ *adj fml* ci-dessus, précité ADMIN; the ~ facts les faits cités plus haut; the names on the ~ list les noms qui figurent sur la liste ci-dessus.

◇ *adv* -**1.** [in a higher place or position] au-dessus; the stars ~ les étoiles là-haut; the people in the flat ~ les gens de l'appartement du dessus OR au-dessus; to fall from ~ tomber d'en haut; two lines ~ deux lignes plus haut. -**2.** [greater in degree or quantity]: aged 20 and ~ âgé de 20 ans et plus; £5 and ~ 5 livres ou plus. -**3.** [a higher rank or authority] en haut; we've had orders from ~ nous avons reçu des ordres d'en haut. -**4.** [in a previous place] plus haut; mentioned ~ cité plus haut OR ci-dessus. -**5.** [in heaven] là-haut, au ciel; the angels ~ les anges là-haut. -**6.** MUS [in pitch]: the note ~ un ton plus haut OR au-dessus.

◇ *n fml*: the ~ [fact, item] ce qui se trouve ci-dessus; [person] le susnommé *m*, la susnommée *f*; [persons] les susnommés; can you explain the ~? pouvez-vous expliquer ce qui précède?

◆ **above all** *adv phr* avant tout, surtout.

aboveboard [ə,bʌv'bɔːd] ◇ *adj* -**1.** [person] honnête, régulier. -**2.** [action, behaviour] franc, honnête.

◇ *adv* -**1.** [openly] ouvert, au grand jour. -**2.** [honestly] honnêtement, de façon régulière. -**3.** [frankly] franchement, cartes sur table.

above-mentioned [-'menʃnd] *fml* ◇ *adj* cité plus haut, susmentionné.

◇ *n*: the ~ [person] le susmentionné, la susmentionnée; [book] le livre mentionné plus haut.

above-named *fml* ◇ *adj* susnommé.

◇ *n*: the ~ le susnommé *m*, -e *f*.

abracadabra [,æbrəkə'dæbrə] ◇ *interj*: ~! abracadabra!

◇ *n* -**1.** [magical word] formule *f* magique. -**2.** [gibberish] charabia *m*.

abrade [ə'breɪd] *vt* -**1.** TECH user par abrasion OR par frottement. -**2.** [skin] érafler. -**3.** GEOL éroder.

Abraham ['eɪbrəhæm] *pr n* Abraham.

abrasion [ə'breɪʒn] *n* -**1.** TECH abrasion *f*. -**2.** [graze - on skin] éraflure *f*, écorchure *f*.

abrasive [ə'breɪsɪv] ◇ *adj* -**1.** TECH abrasif. -**2.** [character] rêche; [criticism, wit] corrosif; [voice] caustique.

◇ *n* TECH abrasif *m*.

abreact [æbrɪ'ækt] ◇ *vt* PSYCH libérer par abréaction.

◇ *vi* abréagir.

abreaction [,æbrɪ'ækʃn] *n* abréaction *f*.

abreast [ə'brest] *adv* -**1.** [march, ride] côte à côte, de front; the children were riding three ~ les enfants faisaient du vélo à trois de front. -**2.** [alongside] à la hauteur, au même niveau; their ship came OR drew ~ of ours leur navire est arrivé à la hauteur du nôtre. -**3.** [in touch]: to be ~ of sthg être au courant de qqch; to keep ~ of recent research rester informé OR au courant des recherches récentes; she likes to keep herself ~ of current affairs/the latest fashions elle aime se tenir au courant de l'actualité/de la dernière mode.

abridge [ə'brɪdʒ] *vt* [book] abréger; [article, play, speech] écourter, abréger; the ~d version of King Lear la version courte du Roi Lear.

abridg(e)ment [ə'brɪdʒmənt] *n* -**1.** [of book, speech] résumé *m*, abrégé *m*. -**2.** [act of abridging] réduction *f*, raccourcissement *m*.

abroad [ə'brɔːd] *adv* -**1.** [overseas] à l'étranger; to go ~ aller à l'étranger; to live/to study ~ vivre/faire ses études à l'étranger. -**2.** [over wide area] au loin; [in all directions] de tous côtés, partout; there are rumours ~ about possible redundancies le bruit court qu'il va y avoir des licenciements. -**3.** *lit* [out of doors] (au) dehors.

abrogate ['æbrəgeɪt] *vt fml* abroger, abolir.

abrogation [,æbrə'geɪʃn] *n fml* abrogation *f*.

abrupt [ə'brʌpt] *adj* -**1.** [sudden - change, drop, movement] brusque, soudain; [- laugh, question] brusque; [- departure] brusque, précipité. -**2.** [behaviour, person] brusque, bourru. -**3.** [style] haché, décousu. -**4.** [slope] abrupt, raide.

abruptly [ə'brʌptlɪ] *adv* -**1.** [change, move] brusquement, tout à coup; [ask, laugh] abruptement; [depart] brusquement, précipitamment. -**2.** [behave, speak] avec brusquerie, brusquement. -**3.** [fall, rise] en pente raide, à pic.

abruptness [ə'brʌptnɪs] *n* -**1.** [of change, movement] soudaineté *f*; [of departure] précipitation *f*. -**2.** [of behaviour, person] brusquerie *f*, rudesse *f*. -**3.** [of style] décousu *m*. -**4.** [of slope] raideur *f*.

Abruzzi [ə'brutsiː] *pl pr n*: the ~ les Abruzzes *fpl*.

ABS (*abbr of* **Antiblockiersystem**) *n* ABS *m*.

Absalom ['æbsələm] *pr n* Absalon.

abscess ['æbsɪs] *n* abcès *m*.

abscissa [æb'sɪsə] (*pl* **abscissas** OR **abscissae** [-siː]) *n* abscisse *f*.

abscond [əb'skɒnd] *vi fml* s'enfuir, prendre la fuite; to ~ from prison s'échapper de prison, s'évader; he ~ed with our money il s'est enfui avec notre argent.

absconder [əb'skɒndə^r] *n fml* [gen] fugitif *m*, -ive *f*; [from prison] évadé *m*, -e *f*.

abseil ['æbseɪl] ◇ *vi* descendre en rappel.

◇ *n* (descente *f* en) rappel *m*.

absence ['æbsəns] *n* -**1.** [state of being away] absence *f*; in OR during my ~ pendant mon absence ❑ ~ makes the heart grow fonder *prov* l'éloignement renforce l'affection. -**2.** [instance of being away] absence *f*; unexcused ~s from school absences injustifiées. -**3.** [lack] manque *m*, défaut *m*; in the ~ of adequate information en l'absence d'informations satisfaisantes, faute de renseignements. -**4.** JUR non-comparution *f*, défaut *m*; he was tried in his ~ il fut jugé par contumace.

absent [*adj* 'æbsənt, *vb* æb'sent] ◇ *adj* -**1.** [not present] absent; to be ~ from sthg être absent ❑ ~ friends *formule utilisée pour porter un toast aux absents*; to be OR to go ~ without leave MIL être absent sans permission, être porté manquant. -**2.** [lacking] absent; all signs of warmth were ~ from her voice il n'y avait aucune chaleur dans sa voix. -**3.** [inattentive - person] distrait; [- manner] absent, distrait.
◇ *vt*: to ~ o.s. (from sthg) s'absenter (de qqch).

absentee [,æbsən'tiː] ◇ *n* [someone not present] absent *m*, -e *f*; [habitually] absentéiste *mf*.
◇ *adj* absentéiste; ~ ballot vote *m* par correspondance; to vote by ~ ballot voter par correspondance; ~ landlord propriétaire *m* absentéiste; ~ rate taux *m* d'absentéisme; ~ voter électeur *m*, -trice *f* votant par correspondance.

absenteeism [,æbsən'tiːɪzm] *n* absentéisme *m*.

absently ['æbsəntlɪ] *adv* distraitement.

absent-minded [,æbsənt'maɪndɪd] *adj* [person] distrait; [manner] absent, distrait.

absent-mindedly [,æbsənt'maɪndɪdlɪ] *adv* distraitement, d'un air distrait.

absent-mindedness [,æbsənt'maɪndɪdnɪs] *n* distraction *f*, absence *f*.

absinth(e) ['æbsɪnθ] *n* absinthe *f*.

absolute ['æbsəluːt] ◇ *adj* -**1.** [as intensifier] absolu, total; what ~ nonsense! quelles bêtises, vraiment!; he's an ~ idiot c'est un parfait crétin OR imbécile; the whole thing is an ~ mess c'est un véritable gâchis OR un vrai fatras. -**2.** [entire - secrecy, truth] absolu. -**3.** [unlimited - power] absolu, souverain; [- ruler] absolu. -**4.** [definite, unconditional - decision, refusal] absolu, formel; [- fact] indiscutable; [- proof] formel, irréfutable; ~ veto véto *m* formel. -**5.** [independent, not relative] absolu; in ~ terms en valeurs absolues. -**6.** CHEM [alcohol] absolu, anhydre. -**7.** GRAMM [adjective] substantivé; [verb] absolu. -**8.** JUR [of court order, decree] définitif; the decree was made ~ le décret a été prononcé.
◇ *n* absolu *m*.

absolutely ['æbsəluːtlɪ] *adv* -**1.** [with adjective] vraiment; she's ~ adorable! elle est vraiment adorable! -**2.** [in expressing opinions] absolument, tout à fait; I ~ agree je suis tout à fait d'accord; it's ~ nothing to do with you cela ne vous regarde absolument pas; but he's an excellent teacher — oh, ~! mais c'est un excellent professeur — oh, absolument OR mais certainement!; do you agree? — ~ not! êtes-vous d'accord? — absolument pas! -**3.** [deny, refuse] absolument, formellement.

absolute majority *n* majorité *f* absolue.

absolute pitch *n* oreille *f* absolue.

absolute zero *n* zéro *m* absolu.

absolution [,æbsə'luːʃn] *n* [forgiveness] absolution *f*; RELIG absolution *f*, remise *f* des péchés; to grant sb ~ promettre à qqn l'absolution || [in liturgy]: the Absolution l'absoute *f*.

absolutism ['æbsəluːtɪzm] *n* POL absolutisme *m*; RELIG forme *f* intransigeante de prédestination.

absolve [əb'zɒlv] *vt* -**1.** [from blame, sin etc] absoudre; [from obligation] décharger, délier; to ~ sb from OR of all blame décharger qqn de toute responsabilité. -**2.** JUR acquitter; to ~ sb of sthg acquitter qqn de qqch.

absorb [əb'sɔːb] *vt* -**1.** *literal* & *fig* [changes, cost, light, liquid] absorber; [surplus] absorber, résorber; [idea, information] absorber, assimiler; black ~s heat le noir absorbe la chaleur; work on the book ~ed all my time j'ai été entièrement absorbée par ce livre sur lequel je travaillais; it's too much to ~ all in one day cela en fait trop à absorber pour une seule journée. -**2.** [shock, sound] amortir. -**3.** [incorporate - company] absorber, incorporer; [- group, people] absorber, assimiler; the newcomers were quickly ~ed into the community les nouveaux venus ont été rapidement intégrés OR assimilés à la communauté. -**4.** (*usu pass*) [engross] absorber; to be ~ed in sthg être absorbé par qqch; she was ~ed in what she was doing elle était absorbée par ce qu'elle faisait; he was utterly ~ed in the project/in his reading il était entièrement absorbé par son projet/sa lecture; the task completely ~ed our attention ce travail a complètement accaparé notre attention.

absorbency [əb'sɔːbənsɪ] *n* [gen] pouvoir *m* absorbant; CHEM & PHYS absorptivité *f*.

absorbent [əb'sɔːbənt] ◇ *adj* absorbant.
◇ *n* absorbant *m*.

absorbent cotton *n Am* coton *m* hydrophile.

absorbing [əb'sɔːbɪŋ] *adj* [activity, book] fascinant, passionnant; [work] absorbant, passionnant.

absorption [əb'sɔːpʃn] *n* -**1.** [of light, liquid, smell] absorption *f*; [of surplus] résorption *f*. -**2.** [of shock, sound] amortissement *m*. -**3.** [of company] absorption *f*, incorporation *f*; [of group, people] absorption, assimilation *f*. -**4.** [fascination] passion *f*, fascination *f*; [concentration] concentration *f* (d'esprit).

abstain [əb'steɪn] *vi* -**1.** [refrain] s'abstenir; to ~ from alcohol s'abstenir de boire de l'alcool. -**2.** [not vote] s'abstenir; ten members voted for the proposal and three ~ed dix députés ont voté pour le projet et trois se sont abstenus.

abstainer [əb'steɪnəʳ] *n* -**1.** [teetotaller] abstinent *m*, -e *f*. -**2.** [person not voting] abstentionniste *mf*.

abstemious [æb'stiːmjəs] *adj* [person] sobre, abstinent; [diet, meal] frugal.

abstemiousness [æb'stiːmjəsnɪs] *n* [of person] sobriété *f*, frugalité *f*; [of diet, meal] frugalité.

abstention [əb'stenʃn] *n* -**1.** [from action] abstention *f*; [from drink, food] abstinence *f*. -**2.** [in vote] abstention *f*.

abstinence ['æbstɪnəns] *n* abstinence *f*.

abstinent ['æbstɪnənt] *adj lit* [temperate] sobre, frugal; RELIG abstinent.

abstract [*adj* & *n* 'æbstrækt, *vb* æb'strækt] ◇ *adj* abstrait; ~ artist artiste *m* abstrait.
◇ *n* -**1.** [idea, term] abstrait *m*; in the ~ dans l'abstrait. -**2.** [summary] résumé *m*, abrégé *m*; an ~ of accounts FIN un extrait de comptes. -**3.** ART [painting, sculpture] œuvre *f* abstraite.
◇ *vt* -**1.** [remove] extraire. -**2.** *euph* [steal] soustraire, dérober. -**3.** [regard theoretically] abstraire. -**4.** [summarize] résumer.
◇ *vi* -**1.** [theorize] abstraire. -**2.** [summarize] résumer.

abstracted [æb'stræktɪd] *adj* -**1.** [preoccupied] préoccupé, absorbé; [absent-minded] distrait. -**2.** [extracted] extrait.

abstractedly [æb'stræktɪdlɪ] *adv* distraitement, d'un air distrait.

abstract expressionism *n* expressionnisme *m* abstrait.

abstraction [æb'strækʃn] *n* -**1.** [concept] idée *f* abstraite, abstraction *f*. -**2.** PHILOS abstraction *f*. -**3.** [act of removing] extraction *f*. -**4.** [preoccupation] préoccupation *f*; [absent-mindedness] distraction *f*; she wore her customary look of ~ elle avait son air distrait habituel. -**5.** ART [work of art] œuvre *f* abstraite.

abstractor [æb'stræktəʳ] *n* abstracteur *m*.

abstruse [æb'struːs] *adj* abstrus.

abstruseness [æb'struːsnɪs] *n* caractère *m* abstrus.

absurd [əb'sɜːd] ◇ *adj* [unreasonable] absurde, insensé; [ludicrous] absurde, ridicule; don't be ~! ne sois pas ridicule!; the idea is utterly ~ c'est une idée complètement ridicule OR idiote; I feel/I look ~ in this get-up je me sens/j'ai l'air ridicule dans cet accoutrement.
◇ *n* absurde *m*; he has a nice sense of the ~ il a un bon sens de l'absurde ❑ the theatre of the ~ le théâtre de l'absurde.

absurdity [əb'sɜːdətɪ] (*pl* absurdities) *n* absurdité *f*.

absurdly [əb'sɜːdlɪ] *adv* [behave, dress] de manière insensée; [as intensifier] ridiculement.

ABTA ['æbtə] (*abbr of* Association of British Travel Agents) *pr n association des agences de voyage britanniques*.

Abu Dhabi [,æbuː'dɑːbɪ] *pr n* Abou Dhabi.

abulia [ə'buːlɪə] *n* aboulie *f*.

abundance [ə'bʌndəns] *n* abondance *f*, profusion *f*; there was food in ~ il y avait à manger à profusion; she has an ~ of talent elle est bourrée de talent.

abundant [ə'bʌndənt] *adj* [plentiful] abondant; he gave ~ proof of his devotion il a largement fait la preuve de son dévouement; there's an ~ supply of food il y a des provisions (de nourriture) en quantité.

abundantly [ə'bʌndəntlɪ] *adv* -**1.** [profusely] abondamment; [eat, serve] abondamment, copieusement; [grow] à foison. -**2.** [as intensifier] extrêmement; it became ~ clear that we had been mistaken il devint tout à fait clair que nous nous étions trompés; she made it ~ obvious that I was not welcome elle me fit comprendre très clairement que j'étais indésirable.

abuse [*n* ə'bjuːs, *vb* ə'bjuːz] ◇ *n* -**1.** [misuse] abus *m*; such positions are open to ~ de telles situations incitent aux abus ❑ drug ~ usage *m* de la drogue. -**2.** (*U*) [insults] injures *fpl*, insultes *fpl*; to heap ~ on sb accabler qqn d'injures. -**3.** (*U*) [cruel treatment] mauvais traitements *mpl*; child ~ mauvais traitements à enfant; sexual ~ violences *fpl* sexuelles. -**4.** [unjust practice] abus *m*.
◇ *vt* -**1.** [authority, position] abuser de. -**2.** [insult] injurier, insulter. -**3.** [treat cruelly] maltraiter, malmener. -**4.** [masturbate]: to ~ o.s. *fml* se masturber.

abuser [ə'bjuːzəʳ] *n* -**1.** [gen]: ~s of the system ceux qui profitent du système. -**2.** [of child] *personne qui a maltraité un enfant physiquement ou psychologiquement*. -**3.** [of drugs]: (drug) ~ drogué *m*, -e *f*.

Abu Simbel [,æbuː'sɪmbl] *pr n* Abou-Simbel.

abusive [ə'bjuːsɪv] *adj* -**1.** [language] offensant, grossier; [person] grossier; to be ~ to sb être grossier envers qqn; an ~ phone call un coup de fil obscène. -**2.** [behaviour, treatment] brutal. -**3.** [incorrectly used] abusif, mauvais.

abusively [ə'bjuːsɪvlɪ] *adv* -**1.** [speak, write] de façon offensante, grossièrement. -**2.** [behave, treat] brutalement. -**3.** [use] abusivement.

abut [ə'bʌt] (*pt* & *pp* abutted, *cont* abutting) *vi fml*: to ~ on (to) sthg s'appuyer contre qqch.

abutment [ə'bʌtmənt], **abuttal** [ə'bʌtl] *n* -**1.** [point of junction] jointure *f*, point *m* de jonction. -**2.** ARCHIT [support] contrefort *m*; [on bridge] butée *f*.

abuzz [ə'bʌz] *adj* bourdonnant; ~ with activity en effervescence; ~ with conversation résonnant du bruit des conversations.

abysmal [ə'bɪzml] *adj* -**1.** [immeasurable] infini, abyssal; ~ ignorance une ignorance crasse. -**2.** *inf* [very bad] épouvantable, exécrable.

abysmally [ə'bɪzməlɪ] *adv* atrocement; we failed ~ nous avons échoué lamentablement.

abyss [ə'bɪs] *n* [chasm] abîme *m*, gouffre *m*; [in sea] abysse *m*; a great ~ seemed to open up between us *fig* il y avait comme un abîme entre nous.

abyssal [ə'bɪsəl] *adj* abyssal.

Abyssinia [,æbɪ'sɪnjə] *pr n* Abyssinie *f*; in ~ en Abyssinie.

Abyssinian [,æbɪ'sɪnjən] ◇ *adj* abyssinien, abyssin; ~ cat chat *m* abyssin; the ~ Empire l'empire *m* d'Éthiopie.
◇ *n* Abyssinien *m*, -enne *f*.

a/c (*written abbr of* account (current)) *Br* cc.

AC *n* -**1.** *Br abbr of* athletics club. -**2.** *abbr of* alternating current.

acacia [əˈkeɪʃə] *n* acacia *m*.

academe [ˈækədiːm] *n fml* & *lit* institution *f* universitaire.

academia [ˌækəˈdiːmɪə] *n* monde *m* universitaire.

academic [ˌækəˈdemɪk] ◇ *adj* -**1.** [related to formal study - book, institution, job] universitaire, scolaire; [- failure, system] scolaire; ~ **advisor** *Am* directeur *m*, -trice *f* d'études; ~ **dress** toge *f* d'étudiant; ~ **freedom** liberté *f* d'enseignement; ~ **rank** *Am* grade *m*; ~ **year** année *f* universitaire. -**2.** [intellectual - standard, style, work] intellectuel; [- person] studieux, intellectuel. -**3.** [theoretical] théorique, spéculatif; [not practical] sans intérêt pratique, théorique; **their speculations were purely ~** leurs spéculations étaient purement théoriques; **out of ~ interest** par simple curiosité; **whether he comes or not is all ~** qu'il vienne ou pas, cela n'a pas d'importance. -**4.** [conventional] académique; **an ~ painter** un peintre académique.
◇ *n* universitaire *mf*.

academically [ˌækəˈdemɪklɪ] *adv* [advanced, competent, talented] sur le plan intellectuel; [sound] intellectuellement; **to be ~ qualified** posséder les diplômes requis.

academicals [ˌækəˈdemɪklz] *npl* toge *f* et accessoires *mpl* d'universitaire.

academician [əˌkædəˈmɪʃn] *n* académicien *m*, -enne *f*.

academicism [ˌækəˈdemɪsɪzm], **academism** [əˈkædəmɪzm] *n* académisme *m*.

academy [əˈkædəmɪ] (*pl* academies) *n* -**1.** [society] académie *f*, société *f*. -**2.** [school] école *f*; [private high school] école *f* privée, collège *m*; **an ~ of music** un conservatoire de musique; **military ~** école *f* militaire ; **riding ~** académie *f* d'équitation.

Academy Award *n* oscar *m*.

Acadia [əˈkeɪdjə] *pr n* Acadie *f*; **in ~** en Acadie.

Acadian [əˈkeɪdjən] ◇ *n* Acadien *m*, -enne *f*.
◇ *adj* acadien.

acanthus [əˈkænθəs] (*pl* acanthuses OR acanthi [-θaɪ]) *n* acanthe *f*.

a cappella [ˌɑːkəˈpelə] ◇ *adj* a cappella; ~ **singing** chant *m* a cappella.
◇ *adv* a cappella.

acariasis [ˌækəˈraɪəsɪs] *n* acariose *f*.

acarid [ˈækərɪd] *n* acarien *m*.

ACAS [ˈeɪkæs] (*abbr of* Advisory, Conciliation and Arbitration Service) *pr n* *organisme britannique de conciliation et d'arbitrage des conflits du travail*, ≃ conseil *m* de prud'hommes.

accede [ækˈsiːd] *vi fml* -**1.** [agree] agréer, accepter; **to ~ to sthg** [demand, request] donner suite OR accéder à qqch; [plan, suggestion] accepter OR agréer qqch. -**2.** [attain] accéder; **to ~ to the throne** monter sur le trône; **to ~ to office** entrer en possession d'une charge; **to ~ to the directorship** accéder à la direction. -**3.** JUR: **to ~ to a treaty** adhérer à un traité.

accelerate [əkˈseləreɪt] ◇ *vt* [pace, process, rhythm] accélérer; [decline, event] précipiter, accélérer; [work] activer; ~**d classes** SCH & UNIV cours *mpl* OR niveaux *mpl* accélérés.
◇ *vi* -**1.** [move faster] s'accélérer. -**2.** AUT accélérer.

acceleration [əkˌseləˈreɪʃn] *n* [gen & AUT] accélération *f*.

accelerator [əkˈseləreɪtəʳ] *n* -**1.** AUT accélérateur *m*; **step on the ~!** appuie sur l'accélérateur! -**2.** PHYS accélérateur *m*.

accelerometer [ækˌseləˈrɒmɪtəʳ] *n* accéléromètre *m*.

accent [*n* ˈæksent, *vb* ækˈsent] ◇ *n* -**1.** [way of speaking] accent *m*; **she has** OR **she speaks with a Spanish ~** elle a l'accent espagnol; **she speaks French without an ~** elle parle français sans accent; **he has a strange ~** il a un drôle d'accent. -**2.** GRAMM & MUS [stress] accent *m*. -**3.** *fig*: **the ~ here is on team work** ici on met l'accent sur le travail d'équipe. -**4.** [written mark] accent *m*. -**5.** [contrasting detail] accent *m*; **the room is painted white with green ~s** la pièce est peinte en blanc avec des touches de vert.
◇ *vt* -**1.** [stress - syllable] accentuer, appuyer sur; [- word] accentuer, mettre l'accent sur. -**2.** [mark with accent] mettre un accent sur.

accentuate [ækˈsentjʊeɪt] *vt* -**1.** [word] accentuer, mettre l'accent sur. -**2.** [feature, importance] souligner, accentuer; **the thin dress only ~d her frailness** la robe légère ne faisait qu'accentuer OR que souligner son air fragile.

accentuation [ækˌsentjʊˈeɪʃn] *n* accentuation *f*.

accept [əkˈsept] *vt* -**1.** [agree to receive - apology, gift, invitation] accepter; [- advice, suggestion] accepter, écouter; COMM [- bill] accepter; [- goods] prendre livraison de; **he proposed and she ~ed (him)** il la demanda en mariage et elle accepta; **the machine only ~s coins** la machine n'accepte que les pièces. -**2.** [believe as right, true] accepter, admettre; **I can't ~ what he says** je ne peux accepter OR admettre ce qu'il dit; **I refuse to ~ that he's guilty** je me refuse à le croire coupable, je refuse de croire qu'il soit coupable; **it is generally ~ed that too much salt is bad for the heart** tout le monde sait que le sel en trop grande quantité est mauvais pour le cœur. -**3.** [face up to - danger] faire face à, affronter; [- challenge] accepter, relever; [- one's fate] se résigner à; **she hasn't really ~ed his death** elle n'a pas vraiment accepté sa mort; **you have to ~ the inevitable** il vous faut accepter l'inévitable; **we have to ~ the fact that war is imminent** nous devons accepter le fait que la guerre est imminente; **they refused to ~ the appalling working conditions** ils ont refusé de travailler dans des conditions aussi épouvantables. -**4.** [take on - blame, responsibility] accepter, prendre; [- job, task] se charger de, accepter. -**5.** [admit - to job, school] accepter, prendre; [- to club] accepter; **they ~ed her into the club** ils l'ont admise au club; **she's been ~ed at** OR *Am* **to Harvard** elle a été admise à Harvard.

acceptable [əkˈseptəbl] *adj* -**1.** [satisfactory] acceptable, convenable; [tolerable] acceptable, admissible; **her behaviour just isn't socially ~** son attitude est tout simplement intolérable en société; **they found her work ~** ils ont trouvé son travail convenable; **are these conditions ~ to you?** ces conditions vous conviennent-elles? -**2.** [welcome] bienvenu, opportun; **flowers always make an ~ gift** les fleurs sont toujours une bonne idée de cadeau OR font toujours plaisir.

acceptably [əkˈseptəblɪ] *adv* [suitably] convenablement; [tolerably] passablement; **he works ~ well** il ne travaille pas mal (du tout); **inflation has remained ~ low** l'inflation est restée assez faible.

acceptance [əkˈseptəns] *n* -**1.** [of gift, invitation] acceptation *f*; ~ **speech** discours *m* de réception. -**2.** [assent - to proposal, suggestion] consentement *m*; **his ~ of his fate** sa résignation devant son sort. -**3.** [to club, school, group] admission *f*. -**4.** [approval, favour] approbation *f*, réception *f* favorable; **his suggestion met with everyone's ~** tout le monde approuva sa suggestion; **the idea is gaining ~** l'idée fait son chemin. -**5.** [belief]: **there is general ~ now that smoking causes cancer** il est généralement reconnu maintenant que le tabac provoque le cancer. -**6.** COMM & FIN [of goods] réception *f*; [of bill of exchange] acceptation *f*; [bill of exchange] traite *f*; ~ **house** banque *f* d'escompte (d'effets étrangers) OR d'acceptation.

acceptation [ˌæksepˈteɪʃn] *n* [of term, word] acception *f*, signification *f*.

accepted [əkˈseptɪd] *adj*: ~ **ideas** les idées généralement répandues OR admises; **contrary to ~ belief** contrairement à la croyance établie; **it's an ~ fact that too much sun ages the skin** tout le monde sait que le soleil à haute dose accélère le vieillissement de la peau.

acceptor [əkˈseptəʳ] *n* accepteur *m*.

access [ˈækses] ◇ *n* -**1.** [means of entry] entrée *f*, ouverture *f*; [means of approach] accès *m*, abord *m*; JUR droit *m* de passage; **the kitchen gives ~ to the garage** la cuisine donne accès au garage; **how did the thieves gain ~?** comment les voleurs se sont-ils introduits?; '**~ only**' 'sauf riverains (et livreurs)' ❑ ~ **code** code *m* d'accès. -**2.** [right to contact, use] accès *m*; **I have ~ to confidential files** j'ai accès à des dossiers confidentiels; **he has direct ~ to the minister** il a ses entrées auprès du ministre; **the father has ~ to the children at weekends** JUR le père a droit de visite le week-end pour voir ses enfants ❑ ~ **rights** [to child] droits *mpl* de visite. -**3.** *Br lit* [bout - of illness] accès *m*, attaque *f*; [- of fever, anger] accès *m*; **in an ~ of despair** dans un accès de désespoir.
◇ *vt* accéder à.
◇ *comp* [port, route] d'accès; ~ **channel** TV canal *m* d'accès.

Access® [ˈækses] *pr n* *carte de crédit britannique*; **to put sthg on ~** payer qqch avec la carte Access.

accessary [əkˈsesərɪ] (*pl* accessaries) JUR = **accessory 2**.

accessibility [əkˌsesəˈbɪlətɪ] *n* accessibilité *f*.

accessible [əkˈsesəbl] *adj* -**1.** [place] accessible, d'accès facile; [person] accessible, abordable; **the teacher's very ~** ce professeur est facile à aborder OR d'un abord facile ‖ [available] accessible; **computers are now ~ to everyone** maintenant les ordinateurs sont accessibles à tous. -**2.** [easily understandable] à la portée de tous, accessible. -**3.** [open to, susceptible to] ouvert, accessible.

accession [ækˈseʃn] ◇ *n* -**1.** [to office, position] accession *f*; [to fortune] accession *f*, entrée *f* en possession; **Queen Victoria's ~ (to the throne)** l'accession au trône OR l'avènement de la reine Victoria; ~ **to an inheritance** entrée en possession d'un héritage. -**2.** [addition to collection] nouvelle acquisition *f*. -**3.** [increase] augmentation *f*, accroissement *m*; JUR [to property] accession *f*. -**4.** *fml* [consent] assentiment *m*, accord *m*; [of treaty] adhésion *f*.
◇ *vt* enregistrer.

accession number *n* numéro *m* de catalogue.

accessorize, -ise [əkˈsesəraɪz] *vt* accessoiriser.

accessory [əkˈsesərɪ] (*pl* accessories) ◇ *n* -**1.** (*usu pl*) [supplementary article] accessoire *m*; **car accessories** accessoires automobiles; **a suit with matching accessories** un ensemble avec (ses) accessoires coordonnés. -**2.** JUR complice *mf*; **an ~ after/before the fact** un complice par assistance/par instigation.
◇ *adj* -**1.** [supplementary] accessoire. -**2.** JUR complice.

accessory shoe *n* PHOT fiche *f* pour accessoires.

access road *n* [gen] route *f* d'accès; [to motorway] bretelle *f* d'accès OR de raccordement.

access time *n* temps *m* d'accès.

accidence [ˈæksɪdəns] *n* morphologie *f* flexionnelle.

accident [ˈæksɪdənt] ◇ *n* -**1.** [mishap] accident *m*, malheur *m*; [unforeseen event] événement *m* fortuit, accident *m*; **her son had a car ~** son fils a eu un accident de voiture; **she was killed in an ~** elle s'est tuée dans un accident; ~**s in the home** accidents domestiques. -**2.** [chance] hasard *m*, chance *f*; **it was purely by ~ that we met** nous nous sommes rencontrés tout à fait par accident; **any success we had was more by ~ than by design** notre réussite a été plus accidentelle qu'autre chose. -**3.** PHILOS accident *m*.
◇ *comp* [figures, rate] des accidents; ~ **insurance** assurance *f* (contre les) accidents; ~ **prevention** AUT la prévention des accidents, la prévention routière.

accidental [ˌæksɪˈdentl] ◇ *adj* -**1.** [occurring by chance - death, poisoning] accidentel; [- meeting] fortuit. -**2.** *fml* [nonessential] accessoire, extrinsèque; PHILOS accidentel. -**3.** MUS accidentel.
◇ *n* [gen & MUS] accident *m*.

accidentally [ˌæksɪ'dentəlɪ] *adv* [break, drop] accidentellement; [meet] par hasard; she ~ tore the page elle a déchiré la page sans le vouloir; he did it ~ on purpose *hum* il l'a fait «exprès sans le vouloir».

accident-prone *adj*: to be ~ être prédisposé aux accidents.

acclaim [ə'kleɪm] ◇ *vt* -**1.** [praise] acclamer, faire l'éloge de; [applaud] acclamer, applaudir. -**2.** [proclaim] proclamer.
◇ *n* acclamation *f*, acclamations *fpl*; his play met with great critical ~ sa pièce a été très applaudie par la critique.

acclamation [ˌæklə'meɪʃn] *n* acclamation *f*, acclamations *fpl*; to be elected by ~ être plébiscité; to win by ~ gagner par acclamation.

acclimate [æ'klɪmeɪt] *Am* = **acclimatize**.

acclimation [ˌæklɪ'meɪʃn] *Am* = **acclimatization**.

acclimatization [əˌklaɪmətaɪ'zeɪʃn] *n* [to climate] acclimatation *f*; [to conditions, customs] accoutumance *f*, acclimatement *m*.

acclimatize, -ise [ə'klaɪmətaɪz] ◇ *vt* [animal, plant] acclimater; to ~ sb to [climate] acclimater qqn à; [conditions, customs] habituer OR accoutumer qqn à.
◇ *vi* [to climate] s'acclimater; [to conditions, customs] s'habituer, s'accoutumer.

acclivity [ə'klɪvətɪ] *n* montée *f*.

accolade ['ækəleɪd] *n* -**1.** [praise] acclamation *f*, acclamations *fpl*; [approval] marque *f* d'approbation; [honour] accolade *f*; the prize is the highest ~ a writer can receive ce prix est le plus grand honneur qu'un écrivain puisse recevoir. -**2.** [in conferring knighthood] accolade *f*. -**3.** ARCHIT accolade *f*.

accommodate [ə'kɒmədeɪt] ◇ *vt* -**1.** [furnish lodging for] loger; [furnish with something needed] équiper, pourvoir; [furnish with loan] prêter de l'argent à; can you ~ me until the cheque comes through? pouvez-vous me prêter de l'argent OR me dépanner en attendant que je reçoive mon chèque? -**2.** [have room for - subj: car] contenir; [- subj: house, room] contenir, recevoir; the restaurant can ~ 150 people le restaurant peut recevoir 150 personnes; the cottage ~s up to six people dans la villa, on peut loger jusqu'à six (personnes). -**3.** [oblige] répondre aux besoins de; the management refused to ~ the union la direction a refusé de prendre en compte les exigences du syndicat; the bill is designed to ~ special interest groups cette loi vise à prendre en compte les besoins de groupes d'intérêts particuliers. -**4.** [adapt] accommoder, adapter; she soon ~d herself to the new working conditions elle s'est vite adaptée aux nouvelles conditions de travail.
◇ *vi*: to ~ to sthg s'accommoder OR s'habituer à qqch.

accommodating [ə'kɒmədeɪtɪŋ] *adj* [willing to help] obligeant; [easy to please] accommodant, complaisant.

accommodation [əˌkɒmə'deɪʃn] *n* -**1.** [lodging] logement *m*; [lodging and services] prestations *fpl*; the hotel has no ~ available l'hôtel est complet ❑ furnished ~ chambre *f* meublée, (logement *m*) meublé *m*; the high cost of rented ~ le prix élevé des locations; office ~ bureaux *mpl* à louer. -**2.** [facility] équipement *m*; sleeping ~ chambres *fpl*. -**3.** [settlement of disagreement] accord *m*, accommodement *m*; [compromise] compromis *m*. -**4.** *fml* [willingness to help] obligeance *f*; [willingness to please] complaisance *f*. -**5.** ANAT & PSYCH accommodation *f*. -**6.** COMM & FIN [loan] prêt *m* de complaisance.
◆ **accommodations** *npl Am* -**1.** [lodging, food and services] hébergement *m*. -**2.** [on boat, train] place *f*.

accommodation address *n Br* adresse *f (utilisée uniquement pour la correspondance)*.

accommodation agency *n* agence *f* de logement.

accommodation bill *n* effet *m* de complaisance.

accommodation bureau = **accommodation agency**.

accommodation ladder *n* échelle *f* de coupée.

accommodation road *n* route *f* de desserte.

accompaniment [ə'kʌmpənɪmənt] *n* -**1.** [gen] accompagnement *m*; he entered to the ~ of wild applause il entra sous un tonnerre d'applaudissements. -**2.** CULIN accompagnement *m*, garniture *f*. -**3.** MUS accompagnement *m*; guitar/piano ~ accompagnement *m* à la guitare/au piano.

accompanist [ə'kʌmpənɪst] *n* accompagnateur *m*, -trice *f*.

accompany [ə'kʌmpənɪ] (*pt* & *pp* accompanied) *vt* -**1.** [escort] accompagner, escorter; she was accompanied by her brother elle était accompagnée de son frère. -**2.** [supplement] accompagner; CULIN accompagner, garnir; she accompanied her advice with a warning ses conseils s'accompagnaient d'une mise en garde; her photos ~ the text ses photos accompagnent le texte. -**3.** MUS accompagner; he accompanies her on the piano il l'accompagne au piano.

accompanyist [ə'kʌmpənɪɪst] *Am* = **accompanist**.

accomplice [ə'kʌmplɪs] *n* complice *mf*; to be an ~ to OR in sthg être complice de qqch.

accomplish [ə'kʌmplɪʃ] *vt* -**1.** [manage to do - task, work] accomplir, exécuter; [- desire, dream] réaliser; [- distance, trip] effectuer; the talks ~ed nothing les pourparlers n'ont pas abouti; we hope to ~ a great deal during our discussions nous espérons obtenir des résultats durant ces débats. -**2.** [finish successfully] venir à bout de, mener à bonne fin.

accomplished [ə'kʌmplɪʃt] *adj* -**1.** [cook, singer] accompli, doué; [performance] accompli. -**2.** [successfully completed] accompli; an ~ fact un fait accompli.

accomplishment [ə'kʌmplɪʃmənt] *n* -**1.** [skill] talent *m*; speaking fluent French is just one of her many ~s elle parle français couramment, entre autres talents. -**2.** [feat] exploit *m*, œuvre *f* (accomplie). -**3.** [completion - of task, trip] accomplissement *m*; [- of dream] réalisation *f*.

accord [ə'kɔːd] ◇ *n* -**1.** [consent] accord *m*, consentement *m*; I'm in complete ~ with you je suis totalement d'accord avec vous; of one's own ~ de son plein gré; he left of his own ~ il est parti de son propre chef OR de son plein gré. -**2.** [conformity] accord *m*, conformité *f*; to be in ~ with sthg être en accord OR en conformité avec qqch. -**3.** [harmony] accord *m*, harmonie *f*. -**4.** *fml* [agreement] accord *m*; [treaty] traité *m*.
◇ *vt* accorder; to ~ sb permission accorder une autorisation OR une permission à qqn; he ~ed her a warm welcome il lui a réservé un accueil chaleureux.
◇ *vi* s'accorder, concorder; what he said did not ~ with our instructions ce qu'il a dit n'était pas conforme à nos instructions.
◆ **with one accord** *adv phr* d'un commun accord.

accordance [ə'kɔːdəns] *n* -**1.** [conformity] accord *m*, conformité *f*. -**2.** *fml* [granting] octroi *m*.
◆ **in accordance with** *prep phr*: in ~ with the law aux termes de OR conformément à la loi; her statement is not in ~ with company policy sa déclaration n'est pas dans la ligne de l'entreprise.

accordant [ə'kɔːdənt] *adj*: ~ with *fml* conformément à.

according [ə'kɔːdɪŋ]
◆ **according as** *conj phr fml* selon que, suivant que; ~ as they pass or fail the exam suivant OR selon qu'ils ont réussi ou échoué à l'examen.
◆ **according to** *prep phr* -**1.** [on the evidence of] selon, d'après; ~ to John, it's too late selon OR pour John, il est trop tard; ~ to what you say d'après ce que vous dites; ~ to the figures d'après les chiffres. -**2.** [in relation to]: arranged ~ to height placés OR disposés par ordre de taille; prices vary ~ to how long the job will take le prix varie selon le temps qu'il faut pour effectuer le travail. -**3.** [in accordance with] suivant, conformément à; ~ to instructions conformément aux OR suivant les instructions; everything went ~ to plan tout s'est passé comme prévu.

accordingly [ə'kɔːdɪŋlɪ] *adv* -**1.** [appropriately] en conséquence. -**2.** [consequently] par conséquent.

accordion [ə'kɔːdjən] *n* accordéon *m*.

accordionist [ə'kɔːdjənɪst] *n* accordéoniste *mf*.

accordion pleat *n* pli *m* (en) accordéon.

accost [ə'kɒst] *vt* [gen] accoster, aborder; [subj: prostitute] racoler.

account [ə'kaʊnt] ◇ *n* -**1.** [report] récit *m*, compte rendu *m*; her ~ differs from her husband's sa version diffère de celle de son mari, son récit diffère de celui de son mari; he gave his ~ of the accident il a donné sa version de l'accident; by his own ~ he had had too much to drink à l'en croire, il avait trop bu. -**2.** [explanation] compte rendu *m*, explication *f*; to bring OR to call sb to ~ demander des comptes à qqn; you will be held to ~ for all damages il vous faudra rendre des comptes pour tous les dommages causés. -**3.** [consideration] importance *f*, valeur *f*; a town of little ~ une ville de peu d'importance OR insignifiante; what you think is of no ~ to me ce que vous pensez ne m'intéresse pas; to take sthg into ~, to take ~ of sthg tenir compte de qqch; he took little ~ of her feelings il ne tenait pas compte OR faisait peu de cas de ses sentiments; does this estimate take all the costs into ~? est-ce que cette estimation prend en compte toutes ces dépenses?; the rising cost of living must also be taken into ~ il faut aussi prendre en compte l'augmentation du coût de la vie. -**4.** [advantage, profit] profit *m*; to put OR to turn one's skills to good ~ tirer parti de ses compétences; I started working on my own ~ j'ai commencé à travailler à mon compte. -**5.** [rendition] interprétation *f*, version *f*; the pianist gave a sensitive ~ of the concerto le pianiste a donné du concerto une interprétation d'une grande sensibilité; she gave a good ~ of herself in the interview elle a réussi à bien se définir au cours de cette entrevue. -**6.** COMM [in bank, with shop] compte *m*; to close/to open an ~ fermer/ouvrir un compte; we have an ~ at the garage nous avons un compte chez le garagiste; put it on OR charge it to my ~ mettez cela sur mon compte; I'd like to settle my ~ je voudrais régler ma note; to settle OR to square ~s with sb *fig* régler ses comptes avec qqn; to ~ rendered COMM suivant compte remis ❑ ~s payable comptes *mpl* fournisseurs; ~s receivable comptes *mpl* clients. -**7.** [detailed record of money] compte *m*; his wife keeps the ~s c'est sa femme qui tient les comptes. -**8.** [business, patronage] appui *m*; we were pleased to get their ~ nous étions contents d'avoir leur appui ‖ [in advertising] budget *m*; the agency secured the Brook ~ l'agence s'est assuré le budget Brook.
◇ *vt fml* estimer, considérer; she ~s herself my friend elle se considère mon amie.
◆ **by all accounts** *adv phr* aux dires de tout le monde, d'après ce que tout le monde dit.
◆ **on account** *adv phr* à crédit; we bought the car on ~ nous avons acheté la voiture à crédit; payment on ~ paiement à compte OR à crédit; I paid £100 on ~ j'ai versé un acompte de 100 livres.
◆ **on account of** *prep phr* à cause de; on ~ of the weather à cause du temps; don't leave on ~ of me OR on my ~ ne partez pas à cause de moi; we didn't go on ~ of there being a storm nous n'y sommes pas allés à cause de la tempête.
◆ **on no account** *adv phr* en aucun cas, sous aucun prétexte.

◆ **account for** *vt insep* **-1.** [explain] expliquer, rendre compte de; **there's no ~ing for his recent odd behaviour** il n'y a aucune explication à son comportement bizarre des derniers temps; **there's no ~ing for taste** les goûts et les couleurs, ça ne se discute pas. **-2.** [answer for] rendre compte de; **he has to ~ for every penny he spends** il doit rendre compte de chaque franc qu'il dépense; **all the children are ~ed for** aucun des enfants n'a été oublié; **two hostages have not yet been ~ed for** deux otages n'ont toujours pas été retrouvés. **-3.** [make up] représenter; **wine ~s for 5 % of all exports** le vin représente 5 % des exportations totales; **the North Sea ~s for a large proportion of our petrol** la mer du Nord produit une grande partie de notre pétrole. **-4.** *fml* [shoot, kill] abattre, tuer; [catch] attraper.

accountability [əˌkaʊntəˈbɪlətɪ] *n*: **the public wants more police ~** le public souhaite que la police réponde davantage de ses actes.

accountable [əˈkaʊntəbl] *adj* **-1.** [responsible] responsable; **she is not ~ for her actions** elle n'est pas responsable de ses actes; **I'm ~ to your mother for you** je suis responsable de toi devant ta mère; **they cannot be held ~ for the accident** on ne peut les tenir responsables de l'accident. **-2.** [explainable] explicable.

accountancy [əˈkaʊntənsɪ] *n* [subject, work] comptabilité *f*; [profession] profession *f* de comptable; **a degree in ~** un diplôme de comptabilité.

accountant [əˈkaʊntənt] *n* comptable *mf*.

account book *n* livre *m* de comptes.

account day *n* ST. EX jour *m* de liquidation.

account executive *n* responsable *mf* du budget.

accounting [əˈkaʊntɪŋ] *n* comptabilité *f*; **she does the ~** [for business] elle fait OR tient la comptabilité; [for the family] elle tient les comptes; **~ period** exercice *m*.

accoutre *Br*, **accouter** *Am* [əˈkuːtəʳ] *vt fml* équiper; **to be ~d with sthg** être équipé de qqch.

accoutrement [əˈkuːtrəmənt] *Br*, **accouterment** [əˈkuːtərmənt] *Am n* [equipment] attirail *m*; MIL équipement *m*.

Accra [əˈkrɑː] *pr n* Accra.

accredit [əˈkredɪt] *vt* **-1.** [credit] accréditer; **they ~ed the discovery to him** on lui a attribué cette découverte; **she is ~ed with having discovered radium** on lui attribue la découverte du radium. **-2.** [provide with credentials] accréditer; **ambassador ~ed to Morocco** ambassadeur accrédité au Maroc. **-3.** [recognize as bona fide] agréer.

accreditation [əˌkredɪˈteɪʃn] *n*: **to seek ~** chercher à se faire accréditer OR reconnaître.

accredited [əˈkredɪtɪd] *adj* **-1.** [idea, rumour] admis, accepté. **-2.** [official, person] accrédité, autorisé; **the ~ representative to the United Nations** le représentant accrédité aux Nations unies. **-3.** [recognized as bona fide] agréé; **~ dairy herds** troupeaux *mpl* tuberculinés; **~ schools** SCH & UNIV *établissements délivrant des diplômes reconnus par l'État*.

accretion [æˈkriːʃn] *n* **-1.** [growth - in size] accroissement *m*; [- of dirt, wealth] accroissement *m*, accumulation *f*. **-2.** [addition] addition *f*; **~ of property** JUR accumulation de biens. **-3.** GEOL concrétion *f*. **-4.** MED [adhesion] accrétion *f*; [deposit] concrétion *f*.

accrual [əˈkruːəl] *n fml* accumulation *f*; **~s** FIN compte *m* de régularisation (du passif).

accrue [əˈkruː] *fml* ◇ *vi* **-1.** [increase] s'accroître, s'accumuler; [interest] courir; **~d interest** intérêt *m* couru; **~d income** recettes *fpl* échues; **~d expenses** frais *mpl* à payer. **-2.** [benefit, gain]: **to ~ to** revenir à; **advantages accruing to property owners** les avantages revenant aux propriétaires fonciers.
◇ *vt* accumuler.

accumulate [əˈkjuːmjʊleɪt] ◇ *vt* accumuler.
◇ *vi* s'accumuler.

accumulation [əˌkjuːmjʊˈleɪʃn] *n* **-1.** [process] accumulation *f*. **-2.** [things collected] amas *m*, tas *m*. **-3.** FIN [of capital] accroissement *m*; [of interest] accumulation *f*.

accumulative [əˈkjuːmjʊlətɪv] *adj* cumulatif, qui s'accumule; FIN cumulatif.

accumulator [əˈkjuːmjʊleɪtəʳ] *n* **-1.** [battery] accumulateur *m*. **-2.** *Br* [bet] *pari dont les gains sont placés sur la course suivante*.

accuracy [ˈækjʊrəsɪ] (*pl* **accuracies**) *n* [of aim, description, report, weapon] précision *f*; [of figures, watch] exactitude *f*; [of memory, translation] fidélité *f*, exactitude *f*; [of judgment, prediction] justesse *f*.

accurate [ˈækjʊrət] *adj* [description, report] précis, juste; [instrument, weapon] précis; [figures, watch] exact; [estimate] juste; [memory, translation] fidèle; **the report was ~ in every detail** le compte rendu était fidèle jusque dans les moindres détails; **to be more ~, there were 15 of them** pour être plus précis, ils étaient 15; **she's very ~ in her calculations** elle est très précise dans ses calculs.

accurately [ˈækjʊrətlɪ] *adv* [count, draw] avec précision; [tell] exactement; [judge, estimate] avec justesse; [remember, translate] fidèlement.

accursed [əˈkɜːsɪd] *adj* [cursed] maudit; [hateful] maudit, exécrable.

accusal [əˈkjuːzl] *n* accusation *f*.

accusation [ˌækjuːˈzeɪʃn] *n* **-1.** [gen] accusation *f*; **to make an ~ against sb** porter une accusation contre qqn; **there was a note of ~ in her voice** sa voix prenait des accents un tant soit peu accusateurs; **she had no answer to the ~ that her fiscal policies had failed** elle n'avait rien à répondre aux accusations selon lesquelles sa politique fiscale avait échoué. **-2.** JUR accusation *f*, plainte *f*; **they brought an ~ of theft against him** ils ont porté plainte contre lui pour vol.

accusative [əˈkjuːzətɪv] ◇ *adj* **-1.** GRAMM accusatif. **-2.** = **accusatorial**.
◇ *n* accusatif *m*; **in the ~** à l'accusatif.

accusatorial [əˌkjuːzəˈtɔːrɪəl], **accusatory** [əˈkjuːzətrɪ] *adj* **-1.** [look, tone] accusateur. **-2.** JUR [system] accusatoire.

accuse [əˈkjuːz] *vt* accuser; **to ~ sb of (doing) sthg** accuser qqn de (faire) qqch; **he is** OR **he stands ~d of tax fraud** il est accusé de fraude fiscale.

accused [əˈkjuːzd] (*pl inv*) *n*: **the ~** l'accusé *m*, -e *f*, l'inculpé *m*, -e *f*.

accuser [əˈkjuːzəʳ] *n* accusateur *m*, -trice *f*.

accusing [əˈkjuːzɪŋ] *adj* accusateur.

accusingly [əˈkjuːzɪŋlɪ] *adv* de façon accusatrice.

accustom [əˈkʌstəm] *vt* habituer, accoutumer; **she's gradually ~ing herself to her new way of life** elle s'habitue peu à peu à son nouveau style de vie.

accustomed [əˈkʌstəmd] *adj* **-1.** [familiar] habitué, accoutumé; **to get** OR **to grow ~ to sthg** s'habituer OR s'accoutumer à qqch; **I'm not ~ to getting up so early** je n'ai pas l'habitude de me lever si tôt; **she's not ~ to being interrupted** elle n'a pas l'habitude qu'on l'interrompe. **-2.** [regular] habituel, coutumier.

AC/DC ◇ *written abbr of* alternating current/direct current.
◇ *adj inf* [bisexual]: **to be ~** marcher à voile et à vapeur.

ace [eɪs] ◇ *n* **-1.** GAMES [on card, dice, dominoes] as *m*; **the ~ of spades** l'as de pique ❑ **to have an ~ up one's sleeve, to have an ~ in the hole** avoir un atout en réserve; **to hold all the ~s** avoir tous les atouts dans son jeu; **to play one's ~** *literal* & *fig* jouer sa meilleure carte; **to come within an ~ of doing sthg** être à deux doigts de faire qqch. **-2.** [expert] as *m*; **she's an ~ at chess** c'est un as aux échecs. **-3.** [in tennis] ace *m*; **to serve an ~** servir un ace. **-4.** [pilot] as *m*.
◇ *adj inf* super, formidable; **she's an ~ skier, she's ~ at skiing** c'est une skieuse formidable; **the film was really ~!** le film était vraiment super!
◇ *vt* **-1. he ~d his opponent** [in tennis] il a servi un ace contre son adversaire; *fig* il n'a pas laissé une chance à son adversaire. **-2.** [in golf]: **to ~ a hole** faire un trou en un.

Ace bandage® [eɪs-] *n Am* bande *f* Velpeau®.

acellular [ˌeɪˈseljʊləʳ] *adj* acellulaire.

acephalous [ˌeɪˈsefələs] *adj* acéphale.

acerbic [əˈsɜːbɪk] *adj* [taste] acerbe; [person, tone] acerbe, caustique.

acerbity [əˈsɜːbətɪ] *n* [of taste] caractère *m* acerbe; [of person] aigreur *f*; [of tone] mordant *m*.

acetaldehyde [ˌæsɪˈtældɪhaɪd] *n* alcool *m* éthylique, éthanol *m*.

acetate [ˈæsɪteɪt] *n* acétate *m*.

acetic [əˈsiːtɪk] *adj* acétique.

acetic acid *n* acide *m* acétique.

acetone [ˈæsɪtəʊn] *n* acétone *f*.

acetylene [əˈsetɪliːn] ◇ *n* acétylène *m*.
◇ *comp* [burner, lamp, torch] à acétylène; **~ welding** soudure *f* acétylène.

ACGB *pr n abbr of* Arts Council of Great Britain.

ache [eɪk] ◇ *vi* **-1.** [feel pain] faire mal, être douloureux; **I ~ all over** j'ai mal partout; **my head/tooth ~s** j'ai mal à la tête/aux dents; **her heart ~d to see them so unhappy** *fig* elle souffrait de les voir si malheureux. **-2.** [feel desire] avoir très envie; **she was aching for them to leave** elle mourait d'envie de les voir partir.
◇ *n* [physical] douleur *f*; [emotional] peine *f*; **a dull ~** une douleur sourde; **~s and pains** douleurs, maux *mpl*.

achieve [əˈtʃiːv] *vt* [gen] accomplir, faire; [desire, dream, increase] réaliser; [level, objective] arriver à, atteindre; [independence, success] obtenir; **she ~d the impossible** elle a accompli l'impossible; **he'll never ~ anything in life** il n'arrivera jamais à rien dans sa vie; **we really ~d something today** on a vraiment bien avancé aujourd'hui; **the demonstration ~d nothing** la manifestation n'a servi à rien; **the plan ~d its objectives** le plan a atteint ses objectifs.

achievement [əˈtʃiːvmənt] *n* **-1.** [deed] exploit *m*, réussite *f*; **convincing her to come was quite an ~** c'est un véritable exploit d'avoir réussi à la convaincre de venir. **-2.** [successful completion] accomplissement *m*, réalisation *f*; **I felt a real sense of ~** j'ai vraiment eu le sentiment d'avoir accompli quelque chose. **-3.** SCH [performance]: **~ tests** tests *mpl* de niveau.

achiever [əˈtʃiːvəʳ] *n* fonceur *m*, -euse *f*.

Achilles [əˈkɪliːz] *pr n* Achille.

Achilles' heel *n* talon *m* d'Achille.

Achilles' tendon *n* tendon *m* d'Achille.

aching [ˈeɪkɪŋ] *adj* douloureux, endolori; **oh, my ~ head!** oh, ma pauvre tête!

achromatic [ˌækrəʊˈmætɪk] *adj* achromatique.

achy [ˈeɪkɪ] (*compar* **achier**, *superl* **achiest**) *adj* douloureux, endolori; **I feel ~ all over** je me sens toute endolorie.

acid [ˈæsɪd] ◇ *n* **-1.** [gen & CHEM] acide *m*. **-2.** *inf* [LSD] acide *m*.
◇ *adj* **-1.** [drink, taste] acide. **-2.** [remark, tone, wit] mordant, acide; [person] revêche, caustique. **-3.** CHEM acide.

acid drop *n* bonbon *m* acidulé.

acidhead▽ [ˈæsɪdhed] *n* drogué *m*, -e *f* au LSD.

acid house *n* MUS house *f*.

acidic [əˈsɪdɪk] *adj* acide.

acidify [əˈsɪdɪfaɪ] (*pt* & *pp* **acidified**) ◇ *vt* acidifier.
◇ *vi* s'acidifier.

acidity [əˈsɪdətɪ] *n* CHEM & *fig* acidité *f*.

acidosis [ˌæsɪˈdəʊsɪs] *n* acidose *f*.

acid-proof *adj* CHEM résistant aux acides.

acid rain *n* pluie *f* acide.

acid rock = **acid house**.

acid test *n* épreuve *f* décisive.

acidulous [əˈsɪdjʊləs] *adj* acidulé.

ack-ack [ˌæk'æk] *Br* ◇ *n* défense *f* contre avions, DCA *f*.
◇ *comp* de DCA, antiaérien; ~ **weapons** armes *fpl* de DCA; ~ **fire** tir *m* de DCA.

ackemma [ˌæk'emə] *adv dated* au matin.

acknowledge [ək'nɒlɪdʒ] *vt* -**1.** [admit truth of] reconnaître, admettre; [defeat, mistake] reconnaître, avouer; **we ~ (the fact) that we were wrong** nous admettons notre erreur; **she ~d her guilt** elle a avoué OR reconnu sa culpabilité; **the candidate ~d himself defeated** le candidat a reconnu OR admis sa défaite. -**2.** [show recognition of - person]: **he didn't even ~ my presence** il a fait comme si je n'étais pas là; **she ~d him with a nod** elle lui a adressé un signe de la tête; **they ~d him as their leader** ils l'ont reconnu comme leur chef; **he ~d her child (as his)** JUR il a reconnu l'enfant (comme étant le sien). -**3.** [confirm receipt of - greeting, message] répondre à; ADMIN [- letter, package] accuser réception de; **sign here to ~ receipt** signez ici pour accuser réception. -**4.** [express gratitude for] remercier (qqn) de OR pour, se montrer reconnaissant (envers qqn) de OR pour; **he ~d the cheers of the crowd** il a salué en réponse aux applaudissements de la foule; **I'd like to ~ the help and advice given me by my family** j'aimerais remercier ma famille pour l'aide et les conseils qu'elle m'a apportés.

acknowledged [ək'nɒlɪdʒd] *adj* [expert, authority] reconnu.

acknowledg(e)ment [ək'nɒlɪdʒmənt] *n* -**1.** [admission] reconnaissance *f*; [of mistake] reconnaissance *f*, aveu *m*. -**2.** [indicating confirmation of receipt] réponse *f*; **in ~ of your letter** en réponse à votre lettre; **~ of receipt** accusé *m* de réception. -**3.** [indicating gratitude] remerciements *mpl*; **he received a watch in ~ of his work** il a reçu une montre en reconnaissance OR remerciement de son travail. -**4.** [letter, receipt] accusé *m* de réception; [for payment] quittance *f*, reçu *m*.
◆ **acknowledg(e)ments** *npl* [in article, book] remerciements *mpl*.

ACLU (*abbr of* American Civil Liberties Union) *pr n ligue américaine des droits du citoyen*.

acme ['ækmɪ] *n* apogée *m*, point *m* culminant.

acne ['æknɪ] *n* acné *f*.

acolyte ['ækəlaɪt] *n* [gen & RELIG] acolyte *m*.

aconite ['ækənaɪt] *n* [plant] aconit *m*; [drug] aconitine *f*.

acorn ['eɪkɔːn] *n* gland *m*; ~ **cup** cupule *f*.

acoustic [ə'kuːstɪk] *adj* acoustique; ~ **engineer** ingénieur *m* acoustique.

acoustically [ə'kuːstɪklɪ] *adv* du point de vue acoustique.

acoustic coupler [-'kʌplə'] *n* coupleur *m* acoustique.

acoustic feature *n* trait *m* OR caractéristique *f* acoustique.

acoustic nerve *n* nerf *m* acoustique.

acoustic phonetics *n* phonétique *f* acoustique.

acoustics [ə'kuːstɪks] ◇ *n (U)* [subject] acoustique *f*.
◇ *npl* [of room, theatre] acoustique *f*; **to have bad/good ~** avoir une mauvaise/bonne acoustique.

acoustic tile *n* carreau *m* acoustique.

acquaint [ə'kweɪnt] *vt* -**1.** [inform] aviser, renseigner; **I'll ~ you with the facts** je vais vous mettre au courant des faits; **let me ~ you with the situation** laissez-moi vous mettre au fait de la situation; **she ~ed herself with their customs** elle s'est familiarisée avec leurs habitudes. -**2.** [familiarize] : **to be ~ ed with** [person, place, subject] connaître; [fact, situation] être au courant de; **she is well ~ed with the mayor** elle connaît très bien le maire; **we were just getting ~ed** on venait juste de faire connaissance; **I'm fully ~ed with the facts** je suis tout à fait au courant des faits.

acquaintance [ə'kweɪntəns] *n* -**1.** [person] connaissance *f*, relation *f*; **she's an ~ of ours** c'est une de nos relations; **he has a wide circle of ~s** il a des relations très étendues. -**2.** [knowledge] connaissance *f*; **pleased to make your ~** enchanté de faire votre connaissance; **on closer** OR **further ~ she seems quite intelligent** quand on la connaît un peu mieux, elle semble assez intelligente; **to have a nodding** OR **passing ~ with sb/sthg** connaître vaguement qqn/qqch.

acquaintanceship [ə'kweɪntənʃɪp] *n* -**1.** [relationship] relations *fpl*. -**2.** [people] relations *fpl*, cercle *m* de connaissances; **he has a wide ~** il a de nombreuses relations.

acquiesce [ˌækwɪ'es] *vi* acquiescer, consentir; **she finally ~d** elle a finalement acquiescé; **they ~d to our demands** ils ont consenti à nos exigences; **he ~d in the terms we had drawn up** il a consenti aux conditions que nous avions établies.

acquiescence [ˌækwɪ'esns] *n* acquiescement *m*, consentement *m*.

acquiescent [ˌækwɪ'esnt] *adj* consentant.

acquire [ə'kwaɪə'] *vt* -**1.** [advantage, experience, possession, success] acquérir; [reputation] se faire; **they have recently ~d the house next door** ils ont récemment acquis OR se sont récemment rendus acquéreurs de la maison d'à côté. -**2.** [information, knowledge, language] apprendre; **it took her years to ~ fluency in German** ça lui a pris des années pour apprendre couramment l'allemand. -**3.** [habit] prendre, contracter; **I've ~d a taste for champagne** j'ai pris goût au champagne.

acquired [ə'kwaɪəd] *adj* acquis; **an ~ taste** un goût acquis.

acquired characteristic *n* caractère *m* acquis.

acquired immune deficiency syndrome = **AIDS**.

acquirement [ə'kwaɪəmənt] *n* acquisition *f*.

acquisition [ˌækwɪ'zɪʃn] *n* acquisition *f*; **the ~ of knowledge** l'acquisition de connaissances; **she's the team's latest ~** elle est la dernière acquisition de l'équipe.

acquisitive [ə'kwɪzɪtɪv] *adj* [for money] âpre au gain; [greedy] avide; **he's a very ~ person** c'est une personne très avide.

acquit [ə'kwɪt] (*pt & pp* **acquitted**, *cont* **acquitting**) *vt* -**1.** [release - from duty, responsibility] acquitter, décharger; JUR acquitter, relaxer; **to ~ sb of sthg** acquitter qqn de qqch. -**2.** [behave]: **to ~ o.s.** se conduire; **he acquitted himself well during the trial** il s'est bien conduit pendant le procès. -**3.** [debt, duty] s'acquitter de.

acquittal [ə'kwɪtl] *n* -**1.** [of duty] accomplissement *m*. -**2.** JUR acquittement *m*. -**3.** [of debt, obligation] acquittement *m*.

acre ['eɪkə'] *n* ≃ demi-hectare *m*, acre *f*; **they have ~s of room** *fig* ils ont des kilomètres de place; **forty ~s and a mule** *'quarante acres de terre et une mule', minimum garanti par l'État américain aux esclaves affranchis au lendemain de la guerre de Sécession*.

acreage ['eɪkərɪdʒ] *n* aire *f*, superficie *f*; **how much ~ do you have here?** combien avez-vous d'hectares ici?

acrid ['ækrɪd] *adj* -**1.** [smell, taste] âcre. -**2.** [language, remark] acerbe, mordant.

Acrilan® ['ækrɪlæn] *n* Acrilan® *m*.

acrimonious [ˌækrɪ'məʊnjəs] *adj* [person, remark] acrimonieux, hargneux; [attack, dispute] virulent.

acrimoniously [ˌækrɪ'məʊnjəslɪ] *adv* avec amertume; **the meeting ended ~** la réunion s'est terminée dans l'amertume.

acrimony ['ækrɪmənɪ] *n* acrimonie *f*, hargne *f*.

acrobat ['ækrəbæt] *n* acrobate *mf*.

acrobatic [ˌækrə'bætɪk] *adj* acrobatique.

acrobatics [ˌækrə'bætɪks] *npl* acrobatie *f*; **to do** OR **to perform ~** faire des acrobaties OR de l'acrobatie.

acronym ['ækrənɪm] *n* acronyme *m*.

acrophobia [ˌækrə'fəʊbjə] *n* acrophobie *f*.

Acropolis [ə'krɒpəlɪs] *pr n* Acropole *f*.

across [ə'krɒs] ◇ *prep* -**1.** [from one side to the other of] d'un côté à l'autre de; **to walk ~ sthg** traverser qqch; **she swam ~ the lake** elle a traversé le lac à la nage; **I ran ~ the street** j'ai traversé la rue en courant; **they built a bridge ~ the lake** ils ont construit un pont sur le lac; **he lay ~ the bed** il était couché OR allongé en travers du lit; **she had a pain ~ her chest** une douleur lui a traversé la poitrine; **he's very broad ~ the shoulders** il est très large d'épaules. -**2.** [on or to the other side of] de l'autre côté de; **the house ~ the street** la maison d'en face; **we live ~ the street from them** nous habitons en face de chez eux; **he sat ~ the table from me** il s'assit en face de moi; **can you help me ~ the road?** pouvez-vous m'aider à traverser la rue?; **she glanced ~ the room at us** elle nous lança un regard de l'autre bout de la pièce. -**3.** [so as to cover]: **he leaned ~ my desk** il s'est penché par-dessus mon bureau; **a smile spread ~ her face** un sourire a éclairé son visage. -**4.** [so as to cross] en travers de, à travers; **the study of literature ~ different cultures** l'étude de la littérature à travers différentes cultures; **the lines cut ~ each other** les lignes se coupent. -**5.** [throughout]: **he gave speeches all ~ Europe** il a fait des discours dans toute l'Europe. -**6.** [on]: **he hit me ~ the face** il m'a frappé au visage.
◇ *adv* -**1.** [from one side to the other] d'un côté à l'autre; **the room is 3 metres ~** la pièce fait 3 mètres de large; **I helped him ~** je l'ai aidé à traverser. -**2.** [on or to the other side] de l'autre côté; **he reached ~ and picked the pen up** il a tendu le bras et a pris le stylo; **she walked ~ to Mary** elle s'est dirigée vers Mary; **I looked ~ at my mother** j'ai regardé ma mère. -**3.** [in crosswords] horizontalement; **what's 23 ~?** [clue] quelle est la définition du 23 horizontal(ement)?; [solution] qu'est-ce qu'il y a comme OR en 23 horizontal(ement)?
◆ **across from** *prep phr* en face de; **the man sitting ~ from me** l'homme qui était assis en face de moi; **the house ~ from ours** la maison située en face de la nôtre.

across-the-board ◇ *adj* général, systématique; **an ~ salary rise** une augmentation de salaire générale.
◇ *adv* systématiquement; **stock prices have fallen ~** le prix des actions a baissé de façon systématique.

acrostic [ə'krɒstɪk] *n* acrostiche *m*.

acrylic [ə'krɪlɪk] ◇ *adj* acrylique.
◇ *n* acrylique *m*.

act [ækt] ◇ *vi* -**1.** [take action] agir; **we must ~ quickly to stop her** nous devons agir rapidement pour l'arrêter; **they ~ed for the best** ils ont agi pour le mieux; **she has a good lawyer ~ing for her** elle est représentée par un bon avocat; **to ~ on behalf of sb, to ~ on sb's behalf** agir au nom de qqn. -**2.** [serve]: **to ~ as** servir de, faire office de; **she ~ed as my interpreter** elle m'a servi d'interprète; **the trees ~ as a windbreak** les arbres servent de barrière contre le vent. -**3.** [behave] agir, se comporter; **they ~ed very sensibly/responsibly** ils ont agi de façon très raisonnable/responsable; **she just ~s dumb** elle fait l'innocente; **you ~ed like a fool** vous vous êtes conduit comme un imbécile; **he ~s as though he were bored** il agit comme s'il s'ennuyait; **she's just ~ing like she's angry** elle joue à OR fait celle qui est en colère. -**4.** [perform a part] jouer; **he's been ~ing since he was a child** il joue depuis son enfance. -**5.** [produce an effect, work] agir.
◇ *vt* [part] jouer, tenir; [play] jouer; **he's ~ing (the part of) King Lear** il joue le rôle du Roi Lear ‖ *fig*: **he tries to ~ the dutiful husband** il essaie de jouer les maris parfaits; **stop ~ing the fool!** arrête de faire l'imbécile!; **~ your age!** sois raisonnable!
◇ *n* -**1.** [action, deed] acte *m*; **the Acts of the Apostles** les Actes des Apôtres; **an ~ of God**

un acte divin; an ~ of war un acte de guerre; to be caught in the ~ être pris sur le fait; to get in on the ~ être dans le coup. -**2.** [pretence] comédie *f*, numéro *m*; to put on an ~ jouer la comédie; it's all an ~ ce n'est que de la comédie; I'm not fooled by your worried mother ~! ton numéro de mère anxieuse ne prendra pas avec moi! -**3.** [in circus, show] numéro *m*; a comedy ~ un numéro de comédie ❑ to get one's ~ together *inf* se reprendre. -**4.** THEAT [part of play] acte *m*. -**5.** [law] loi *f*; an ~ of Congress/Parliament une loi du Congrès/Parlement; the Act of Supremacy l'Acte de suprématie; the Act of Union l'Acte d'union.

◆ **act on** *vt insep* -**1.** [advice, suggestion] suivre; [order] exécuter; she ~ed on the information we gave her elle a suivi les OR s'est conformée aux indications que nous lui avons données; ~ing on your instructions, we have cancelled your account selon vos instructions, nous avons fermé votre compte. -**2.** [chemical, drug] agir sur.

◆ **act out** *vt sep* [fantasy] vivre; [emotions] exprimer (par mime); [event, story] mimer.

◆ **act up** *inf vi insep* [person] faire l'idiot, déconner; [engine, machine] déconner.

◆ **act upon** = **act on**.

ACT (*abbr of* American College Test) *n examen de fin d'études secondaires aux États-Unis.*

Actaeon ['æktɪən] *pr n* Actéon.

acting ['æktɪŋ] ◇ *n* -**1.** [profession] profession *f* d'acteur, profession *f* d'actrice; I've done a bit of ~ [theatre] j'ai fait un peu de théâtre; [cinema] j'ai fait un peu de cinéma. -**2.** [performance] interprétation *f*, jeu *m*; the ~ was superb l'interprétation était superbe.

◇ *adj* -**1.** [temporary] provisoire, par intérim; ~ director/president directeur/président par intérim. -**2.** [lessons, school] de comédien.

actinic [æk'tɪnɪk] *adj* actinique.

actinide ['æktɪnaɪd] *n* actinide *m*.

actinium [æk'tɪnɪəm] *n* actinium *m*.

action ['ækʃn] ◇ *n* -**1.** [process] action *f*; it's time for ~ il est temps d'agir, passons aux actes; to go into ~ entrer en action; to take ~ prendre des mesures; we must take ~ to stop them nous devons agir pour les arrêter; to put sthg into ~ [idea, policy] mettre qqch en pratique; [plan] mettre qqch à exécution; [machine] mettre qqch en marche; she's an excellent dancer, you should see her in ~ c'est une excellente danseuse, vous devriez la voir en action; the car is out of ~ *Br* la voiture est en panne; the storm put the telephone out of ~ le téléphone est en dérangement à cause de l'orage; her accident will put her out of ~ for four months son accident va la mettre hors de combat pour quatre mois; freedom of ~ liberté d'action. -**2.** [deed] acte *m*, geste *m*, action *f*; she defended her ~ in dismissing him elle a défendu son geste en le congédiant; he's not responsible for his ~s il n'est pas responsable de ses actes; don't judge her by her ~s alone ne la jugez pas seulement sur ses actes ❑ ~s speak louder than words les actes en disent plus long que les mots. -**3.** [of chemical, drug, force] effet *m*, action *f*. -**4.** [activity, events] activité *f*; he wants to be where the ~ is *inf* il veut être au cœur de l'action; a man of ~ un homme d'action; ~! CIN silence, on tourne!; we all want a piece of the ~ *inf* nous voulons tous être dans le coup. -**5.** [of book, film, play] intrigue *f*, action *f*; the ~ takes place in a barber's shop l'action se situe OR se passe chez un coiffeur. -**6.** [movement - of person] gestes *mpl*; [- of animal] allure *f*; [- of heart] fonctionnement *m*. -**7.** [operating mechanism - of clock] mécanique *f*, mécanisme *m*; [- of gun] mécanisme *m*; [- of piano] action *f*, mécanique *f*. -**8.** JUR procès *m*, action *f* en justice; to bring an ~ against sb intenter une action contre qqn. -**9.** MIL [fighting] combat *m*, action *f*; to go into ~ engager le combat; he saw a lot of ~ il a vu de nombreux combats; killed in ~ tué au combat.

◇ *vt* [idea, suggestion] mettre en action OR en pratique; [plan] mettre à exécution.

◇ *comp* [film, photography] d'action.

actionable ['ækʃnəbl] *adj* [allegations, deed, person] passible de poursuites; [claim] recevable.

action-packed *adj* [film] bourré d'action; [holiday] rempli d'activités, bien rempli.

action painting *n* peinture *f* gestuelle.

action replay *n Br* TV *répétition immédiate d'une séquence.*

action stations ◇ *n* MIL postes *mpl* de combat.

◇ *interj*: ~! à vos postes!

activate ['æktɪveɪt] *vt* -**1.** [gen, CHEM & TECH] activer. -**2.** PHYS rendre radioactif.

activation [,æktɪ'veɪʃn] *n* activation *f*.

active ['æktɪv] ◇ *adj* -**1.** [lively - person] actif, dynamique; [- imagination] vif, actif. -**2.** [busy, involved - person] actif, énergique; [- life, stock market] actif; to be ~ in sthg, to take an ~ part in sthg prendre une part active à qqch; how much of the population is in ~ employment? quel pourcentage de la population a un emploi?; ~ minority minorité *f* agissante. -**3.** [keen - encouragement, interest] vif; the proposal is under ~ discussion la proposition fait l'objet d'une vive discussion; they took his suggestion into ~ consideration ils ont soumis sa proposition à une étude attentive; you have our ~ support vous avez notre soutien total. -**4.** [in operation - account] actif; [- case, file] en cours; [- law, regulation] en vigueur; [- volcano] en activité. -**5.** [chemical, ingredient] actif. -**6.** GRAMM actif; the ~ voice la voix active, l'actif *m*; in the ~ voice à l'actif. -**7.** MIL actif; to be on ~ service *Br* OR duty *Am* être en service actif; he saw ~ service in the Far East il a servi en Extrême-Orient; to be on the ~ list faire partie de l'armée active. -**8.** PHYS actif, radioactif.

◇ *n* GRAMM [voice] actif *m*; [verb] verbe *m* actif; a verb in the ~ un verbe à l'actif.

actively ['æktɪvlɪ] *adv* -**1.** [involve, participate] activement. -**2.** [disagree, discourage] vivement, activement.

activism ['æktɪvɪzm] *n* activisme *m*.

activist ['æktɪvɪst] *n* militant *m*, -e *f*, activiste *mf*.

activity [æk'tɪvətɪ] (*pl* activities) *n* -**1.** [of brain, person] activité *f*; [of place] mouvement *m*; economic/political ~ activité économique/politique. -**2.** [occupation] activité *f*; leisure activities des activités de loisir.

activity holiday *n Br* vacances *fpl* actives.

actor ['æktəʳ] *n* acteur *m*, comédien *m*; I'm a terrible ~ je suis un piètre comédien.

actress ['æktrɪs] *n* actrice *f*, comédienne *f*; she's a good ~ c'est une bonne comédienne.

actressy ['æktrɪsɪ] *adj pej* théâtral, cabotin *pej*.

ACTT (*abbr of* Association of Cinematographic, Television and Allied Technicians) *pr n ancien syndicat britannique des techniciens du cinéma et de l'audiovisuel, aujourd'hui remplacé par BECTU.*

actual ['æktʃʊəl] *adj* -**1.** [genuine] réel, véritable; [existing as a real fact] concret, positif; what were her ~ words? quels étaient ses mots exacts?; to take an ~ example prendre un exemple concret; the ~ result was quite different le résultat véritable était plutôt différent; the ~ cost was £1,000 le coût exact était de 1 000 livres; what's the ~ cash value of the car? quelle est la valeur réelle de la voiture? -**2.** [emphatic use] même; the ~ ceremony doesn't start until 10.30 la cérémonie même ne commence pas avant 10 h 30.

◆ **in actual fact** *adv phr* en fait.

actuality [,æktʃʊ'ælətɪ] (*pl* actualities) *n* -**1.** [reality] réalité *f*; in ~ en réalité. -**2.** [fact] conditions *fpl* réelles OR actuelles; the actualities of the situation les conditions réelles de la situation.

actually ['æktʃʊəlɪ] *adv* -**1.** [establishing a fact] vraiment; I haven't ~ read the book à vrai dire, je n'ai pas lu le livre; what did he ~ say? qu'est-ce qu'il a dit vraiment? -**2.** [emphatic use] vraiment; did you ~ say that? vous avez vraiment dit cela?; you mean she ~ speaks Latin! tu veux dire qu'elle parle vraiment le latin! -**3.** [contradicting or qualifying] en fait; she's ~ older than she looks en fait, elle est plus âgée qu'elle n'en a l'air; I don't agree, ~ en fait, je ne suis pas d'accord; ~, it's a bit more complicated than that en fait, c'est un peu plus compliqué que cela; I suppose you've never been there – I have, ~ je suppose que vous n'y êtes jamais allé – si, en fait. -**4.** [in requests, advice etc] en fait; ~, you could set the table en fait tu pourrais mettre la table.

actuarial [,æktjʊ'eərɪəl] *adj* actuariel.

actuary ['æktjʊərɪ] (*pl* actuaries) *n* actuaire *mf*.

actuate ['æktjʊeɪt] *vt* -**1.** [machine, system] mettre en marche, faire marcher. -**2.** *fml* [person] faire agir, inciter.

acuity [ə'kjuːətɪ] *n* [of hearing, sight] acuité *f*; [of person, thought] perspicacité *f*.

acumen ['ækjʊmen] *n* perspicacité *f*, flair *m*; business ~ sens *m* des affaires.

acupuncture ['ækjʊpʌŋktʃəʳ] ◇ *n* acupuncture *f*, acuponcture *f*.

◇ *comp* [needle, treatment] d'acupuncture.

acupuncturist ['ækjʊpʌŋktʃərɪst] *n* acupuncteur *m*, -trice *f*, acuponcteur *m*, -trice *f*.

acute [ə'kjuːt] ◇ *adj* -**1.** [hearing, sense] fin; [sight] pénétrant, perçant; an ~ sense of hearing l'ouïe fine; an ~ sense of smell l'odorat subtil OR développé. -**2.** [perceptive - mind, person] perspicace, pénétrant; [- intelligence] fin, vif; [- analysis] fin. -**3.** [severe - pain] aigu, vif; [- anxiety, distress] vif; [- shortage] critique, grave. -**4.** MED [attack, illness] aigu; ~ appendicitis appendicite *f* aiguë. -**5.** [angle] aigu. -**6.** GRAMM [accent] aigu; it's spelled with an "e" ~ ça s'écrit avec un «e» accent aigu.

◇ *n* accent *m* aigu.

acutely [ə'kjuːtlɪ] *adv* -**1.** [intensely - be aware, feel] vivement; [- suffer] intensément. -**2.** [extremely - embarrassing, unhappy] très, profondément. -**3.** [shrewdly] avec perspicacité.

acuteness [ə'kjuːtnɪs] *n* -**1.** [of hearing, sense] finesse *f*. -**2.** [of mind, person] perspicacité *f*, pénétration *f*; [of analysis, observation] finesse *f*. -**3.** [of anxiety, pain] violence *f*, intensité *f*; [of shortage] sévérité *f*, gravité *f*. -**4.** MED [of illness] violence *f*. -**5.** [of angle] caractère *m* aigu.

ad *inf* [æd] (*abbr of* advertisement) *n* [in newspaper] petite annonce *f*; [on TV] pub *f*; to put an ~ in the newspaper passer une annonce dans le journal.

AD ◇ *adv* (*abbr of* Anno Domini) apr. J.-C.; in 3 ~ en l'an 3 (après Jésus-Christ OR de notre ère).

◇ *n abbr of* active duty.

adage ['ædɪdʒ] *n* adage *m*.

Adam ['ædəm] ◇ *pr n* Adam; I don't know him from ~ je ne le connais ni d'Ève ni d'Adam.

◇ *adj* dans le style Adam *(style architectural créé par les Écossais Robert et James Adam au XVIIIᵉ siècle).*

adamant ['ædəmənt] *adj* résolu, inflexible.

adamantly ['ædəməntlɪ] *adv* résolument.

Adam's ale *n Br hum* flotte *f*, château-la-pompe *m hum*.

Adam's apple *n* pomme *f* d'Adam.

adamsite ['ædəmzaɪt] *n* diphénylaminechlorarsine *f*.

adapt [ə'dæpt] ◇ *vt* -**1.** [adjust] adapter, ajuster. -**2.** [book, play] adapter; the play was ~ed for television la pièce a été adaptée pour la télévision; ~ed from Shakespeare adapté de Shakespeare.

◇ *vi* s'adapter; she ~ed well to the change elle s'est bien adaptée au changement; children ~ easily les enfants s'adaptent facilement.

adaptability [ə,dæptə'bɪlətɪ] *n* [of person] faculté *f* d'adaptation, adaptabilité *f*.

adaptable [ə'dæptəbl] *adj* adaptable.

adaptation [ˌædæp'teɪʃn] *n* [of person, work] adaptation *f*; to make an ~ of a play for radio faire l'adaptation d'une pièce pour la radio.

adapter, adaptor [ə'dæptə^r] *n* -**1.** [person] adaptateur *m*, -trice *f*. -**2.** [device] adaptateur *m*; [multiple plug] prise *f* multiple.

ADC *n* -**1.** *abbr of* aide-de-camp. -**2.** *Am* (*abbr of* Aid to Dependent Children) *aide pour enfants assistés*. -**3.** (*abbr of* analogue-digital converter) CAN *m*.

add [æd] *vt* -**1.** [put together] ajouter; ~ her name to the list ajoute son nom à la liste ❑ to ~ fuel to the fire jeter de l'huile sur le feu; to ~ insult to injury dépasser les bornes, aller trop loin. -**2.** [say] ajouter; I have nothing to ~ je n'ai rien à ajouter. -**3.** MATH [figures] additionner; [column of figures] totaliser; ~ 4 and OR to 9 additionnez 4 et 9; it will ~ (on) another £100 to the cost cela augmentera le coût de 100 livres; they added (on) 10% for service ils ont ajouté 10 % pour le service.

◆ **add on** *vt sep* = **add 3**.

◆ **add to** *vt sep* ajouter à, accroître; inflation only ~ed to our worries l'inflation ne faisait qu'ajouter à nos soucis.

◆ **add up** ◇ *vt sep* [find the sum of - figures] additionner; [- bill, column of figures] totaliser; we ~ed up the advantages and disadvantages nous avons fait le total des avantages et des inconvénients.

◇ *vi insep* [figures, results] se recouper; these figures don't ~ up ces chiffres ne font pas le compte; the bill doesn't ~ up la note n'est pas juste; it just doesn't ~ up *fig* il y a quelque chose qui cloche OR qui ne marche pas.

◆ **add up to** *vt insep* -**1.** [subj: figures] s'élever à, se monter à. -**2.** *fig* [subj: results, situation] signifier, se résumer à; it all ~s up to our having to leave autrement dit, nous devons partir; his qualifications ~ up to an impressive CV ses qualifications constituent un CV impressionnant; what evidence we've got doesn't ~ up to much really les preuves dont nous disposons ne constituent pas vraiment grand-chose.

added ['ædɪd] *adj* supplémentaire; the tax is just an ~ financial burden l'impôt constitue simplement un fardeau financier supplémentaire.

addend [ə'dend] *n* nombre *m* OR nombres *mpl* à ajouter.

addendum [ə'dendəm] (*pl* addenda [-də]) *n* addendum *m*, addenda *mpl*.

adder ['ædə^r] *n* -**1.** [snake] vipère *f*. -**2.** [machine] additionneur *m*.

addict ['ædɪkt] *n* -**1.** MED intoxiqué *m*, -e *f*. -**2.** *fig* fanatique *mf*, fana *mf*; she's a film ~ c'est une fana OR mordue de cinéma.

addicted [ə'dɪktɪd] *adj* -**1.** MED adonné. -**2.** *fig*: to be ~ to sthg s'adonner à qqch, se passionner pour qqch; she's ~ to exercise/hard work c'est une mordue d'exercice/de travail.

addiction [ə'dɪkʃn] *n* MED dépendance *f*; *fig* penchant *m* fort, forte inclination *f*.

addictive [ə'dɪktɪv] *adj* MED qui crée une dépendance; those chocolates are positively ~ *inf* ces chocolats ont manifestement un goût de revenez-y.

adding machine ['ædɪŋ-] *n* calculatrice *f*, machine *f* à calculer.

Addis Ababa ['ædɪs'æbəbə] *pr n* Addis-Ababa, Addis-Abeba.

Addison's disease ['ædɪsnz-] *n* maladie *f* bronzée d'Addison.

addition [ə'dɪʃn] *n* -**1.** [gen & MATH] addition *f*. -**2.** [something added] addition *f*, ajout *m*; an ~ to the family: they're going to have an ~ to the family leur famille va s'agrandir; she's a welcome new ~ to our staff nous sommes heureux de la compter au sein du personnel; a last-minute ~ to the programme un ajout de dernière minute au programme. -**3.** *Am* [to house] annexe *f*.

◆ **in addition** *adv phr* de plus, de surcroît.

◆ **in addition to** *prep phr* en plus de.

additional [ə'dɪʃənl] *adj* additionnel; [supplementary] supplémentaire; ~ advantages des avantages supplémentaires; ~ postage tarif postal supplémentaire; there is an ~ charge on certain trains il y a un supplément à payer pour certains trains.

additionally [ə'dɪʃənəlɪ] *adv* -**1.** [further, more] davantage, plus. -**2.** [moreover] en outre, de plus.

additive ['ædɪtɪv] ◇ *adj* additif.

◇ *n* additif *m*.

addle ['ædl] ◇ *vt* embrouiller.

◇ *vi* -**1.** [person] s'embrouiller. -**2.** [egg] pourrir.

addled ['ædld] *adj* -**1.** [person] aux idées confuses, brouillon; [brain] fumeux, brouillon; [ideas] confus. -**2.** [egg] pourri.

add-on *n* ajout *m*; COMPUT périphérique *m*.

address [ə'dres] ◇ *vt* -**1.** [envelope, letter, package] adresser, mettre l'adresse sur; the letter is ~ed to you cette lettre vous est adressée. -**2.** [direct] adresser; ~ all complaints to the manager adressez vos doléances au directeur; his remarks were ~ed to you ses remarques vous étaient adressées. -**3.** [speak to] s'adresser à; [write to] écrire à; she stood up and ~ed the audience elle s'est levée et a pris la parole devant l'assistance; a judge should be ~ed as "your honour" on devrait s'adresser à un juge en disant «votre honneur»; to ~ the chair s'adresser au président. -**4.** [deal with - subject, theme] traiter, examiner; [- issue, problem] aborder; to ~ o.s. to a problem aborder un problème; to ~ o.s. to a task s'attaquer OR se mettre à une tâche. -**5.** [take position facing] faire face à.

◇ *n* -**1.** [of building, person] adresse *f*; we've changed our ~ nous avons changé d'adresse; have you notified him of any change of ~? lui avez-vous fait part d'éventuels changements d'adresse?; they left no (forwarding) ~ ils n'ont pas laissé d'adresse. -**2.** [speech] discours *m*, allocution *f*. -**3.** COMPUT adresse *f*. -**4.** *Br* POL [message to sovereign] adresse *f*. -**5.** *arch* [way of speaking] conversation *f*; [way of behaving] abord *m*. -**6.** *arch* (*usu pl*) [expression of affection]: ~es galanteries *fpl*; to pay one's ~es to sb faire la cour à qqn.

address book *n* carnet *m* d'adresses.

addressee [ˌædre'siː] *n* destinataire *mf*.

Addressograph® [ə'dresəgrɑːf] *n* Adressographe® *m*.

adduce [ə'djuːs] *vt* [explanation, proof, reason] fournir, apporter; [expert] invoquer, citer.

Adelaide ['ædəleɪd] *pr n* Adélaïde.

Adélie Land ['ædeɪlɪ-] *pr n* terre Adélie *f*; in ~ en terre Adélie.

Aden ['eɪdn] *pr n* Aden.

adenoidal [ˌædɪ'nɔɪdl] *adj* adénoïde.

adenoids ['ædɪnɔɪdz] *npl* végétations *fpl* (adénoïdes).

adept ['ædept] ◇ *adj* habile, adroit; to be ~ at doing sthg être adroit à faire qqch; she's ~ in mathematics elle est douée en mathématiques.

◇ *n* expert *m*.

adequacy ['ædɪkwəsɪ] *n* -**1.** [of amount, payment, sum] fait *m* d'être suffisant. -**2.** [of person] compétence *f*, compétences *fpl*, capacité *f*, capacités *fpl*; [of description, expression] justesse *f*.

adequate ['ædɪkwət] *adj* -**1.** [in amount, quantity] suffisant, adéquat; ~ supplies des réserves suffisantes. -**2.** [appropriate] qui convient, adapté; he proved ~ to the task il s'est révélé être à la hauteur de la tâche; this flat is hardly ~ for a family of six cet appartement ne convient guère à une famille de six personnes; this one is quite ~ celui-ci fera très bien l'affaire. -**3.** [just satisfactory] acceptable, satisfaisant.

adequately ['ædɪkwətlɪ] *adv* -**1.** [sufficiently] suffisamment. -**2.** [satisfactorily] convenablement.

adhere [əd'hɪə^r] *vi* -**1.** [stick] coller, adhérer; to ~ to sthg coller à qqch. -**2.** [join] adhérer, s'inscrire; to ~ to a political party s'inscrire à un parti politique. -**3.** [remain loyal]: to ~ to [party] adhérer à; [rule] obéir à; [plan] se conformer à; [belief, idea] adhérer à, souscrire à; they undertook to ~ to the agreement ils décidèrent de se conformer OR d'agir conformément à l'accord.

adherence [əd'hɪərəns] *n* adhésion *f*; ~ to a treaty/to a political party adhésion à un traité/un parti politique.

adherent [əd'hɪərənt] ◇ *adj* adhérent.

◇ *n* [to party] adhérent *m*, -e *f*, partisan *m*, -e *f*; [to agreement] adhérent *m*, -e *f*; [to belief, religion] adepte *mf*.

adhesion [əd'hiːʒn] *n* [attachment] adhérence *f*; PHYS adhésion *f*; MED adhérence *f*.

adhesive [əd'hiːsɪv] ◇ *adj* adhésif, collant; ~ tape [gen] ruban *m* adhésif, Scotch® *m*; MED sparadrap *m*.

◇ *n* adhésif *m*.

ad hoc [ˌæd'hɒk] ◇ *adj* [committee] ad hoc *(inv)*; [decision, solution] adapté aux circonstances, ponctuel; the board meets on an ~ basis le conseil se réunit de façon ad hoc.

◇ *adv* à l'improviste.

adieu [ə'djuː] (*pl* adieus OR adieux [ə'djuːz]) *n* adieu *m*; I bid you ~ *arch* je vous fais mes adieux.

ad infinitum [ˌædɪnfɪ'naɪtəm] *adv* à l'infini.

ad interim [ˌæd'ɪntərɪm] ◇ *adv* par intérim.

◇ *adj* [measures] provisoire.

adipose ['ædɪpəʊs] *adj* adipeux; ~ tissue tissu *m* adipeux.

adjacent [ə'dʒeɪsənt] *adj* -**1.** [sharing common boundary - house, room] contigu, voisin; [- building] qui jouxte, mitoyen; [- country, territory] limitrophe; their house is ~ to the police station leur maison jouxte le commissariat de police. -**2.** [nearby - street] adjacent; [- town] proche, avoisinant. -**3.** MATH adjacent.

adjectival [ˌædʒek'taɪvl] *adj* adjectif, adjectival.

adjective ['ædʒɪktɪv] *n* adjectif *m*.

adjoin [ə'dʒɔɪn] ◇ *vt* [house, land, room]: they had rooms ~ing mine leurs chambres étaient contiguës à la mienne.

◇ *vi* être contigu; the two buildings ~ les deux bâtiments sont contigus.

adjoining [ə'dʒɔɪnɪŋ] *adj* contigu, attenant; ~ rooms des pièces contiguës; at the ~ table à la table voisine.

adjourn [ə'dʒɜːn] ◇ *vi* -**1.** [committee, court - break off] suspendre la séance; [- end] lever la séance. -**2.** [move elsewhere] se retirer, passer; shall we ~ to the living room for coffee? passerons-nous au salon pour prendre le café?

◇ *vt* -**1.** [break off] suspendre. -**2.** [defer] ajourner, remettre, reporter; let's ~ this discussion until tomorrow reportons cette discussion à demain; the president ~ed the meeting le président a levé la séance.

adjournment [ə'dʒɜːnmənt] *n* [of discussion, meeting] suspension *f*, ajournement *m*; JUR [of trial] remise *f*, renvoi *m*; to call for an ~ demander un renvoi; to move the ~ demander la clôture.

adjt (*written abbr of* adjutant) adjt.

adjudge [ə'dʒʌdʒ] *vt fml* -**1.** [pronounce] déclarer. -**2.** JUR [judge] prononcer, déclarer; [award] adjuger, accorder; he was ~d guilty of the murder il a été déclaré coupable du meurtre; the court ~d damages in favour of the defendant le tribunal a accordé des dommages et intérêts au défendeur.

adjudicate [ə'dʒuːdɪkeɪt] ◇ *vi* -**1.** [give a decision] se prononcer. -**2.** [serve as judge] arbitrer.

◇ *vt* [claim] décider; [competition] juger.

adjudication [əˌdʒuːdɪ'keɪʃn] *n* -**1.** [process] jugement *m*, arbitration *f*; the matter is up for ~ l'affaire est en jugement. -**2.** [decision] jugement *m*, décision *f*; JUR arrêt *m*; ~ of bankruptcy JUR déclaration *f* de faillite.

adjudicator [ə'dʒuːdɪkeɪtə^r] *n* [of competition] juge *m*, arbitre *m*; [of dispute] arbitre *m*.

adjunct [ˈædʒʌŋkt] *n* -**1.** [addition] accessoire *m*. -**2.** [subordinate person] adjoint *m*, -e *f*, auxiliaire *mf*. -**3.** GRAMM adjuvant *m*.

adjure [əˈdʒʊəʳ] *vt fml* [appeal to] supplier; **to ~ sb to do sthg** supplier qqn de faire qqch.

adjust [əˈdʒʌst] ◇ *vt* -**1.** [regulate - heat, height, speed] ajuster, régler; [- knob, loudness] ajuster; [- brakes, machine, television] régler, mettre au point; [- clock] régler. -**2.** [alter - plan, programme] ajuster, mettre au point; [- length, size] ajuster; [- salary, wage] rajuster; **the government has ~ed prices downwards/upwards** le gouvernement a relevé/baissé les prix. -**3.** [correct] rectifier; **figures ~ed for inflation** chiffres en monnaie constante. -**4.** [position of clothing, hat] rajuster; **'please ~ your dress before leaving'** rajustez vos vêtements avant de sortir, SVP. -**5.** [adapt] ajuster, adapter. -**6.** [insurance]: **to ~ a claim** ajuster une demande d'indemnité.
◇ *vi* -**1.** [adapt] s'adapter; **the children ~ed well to their new school** les enfants se sont bien adaptés à leur nouvelle école. -**2.** [chair, machine] se régler, s'ajuster; **the cover ~s to fit all sizes** le couvercle se règle pour s'adapter à toutes les tailles.

adjustable [əˈdʒʌstəbl] *adj* [chair, height, speed] ajustable, réglable; [shape, size] ajustable, adaptable; [hours, rate] flexible; **~ spanner** clé *f* à molette OR anglaise.

adjusted [əˈdʒʌstɪd] *adj* équilibré.

adjustment [əˈdʒʌstmənt] *n* -**1.** [to heat, height, speed] ajustement *m*, réglage *m*; [to knob, loudness] ajustement *m*; [to brakes, machine, television] réglage *m*, mise *f* au point; [to clock] réglage *m*. -**2.** [to plan, programme] ajustement *m*, mise *f* au point; [to length, size] ajustement *m*; [to salary, wage] rajustement *m*. -**3.** [correction] rectification *f*. -**4.** [adaptation - of person] adaptation *f*; **a period of ~** une période OR un temps d'adaptation.

adjutant [ˈædʒʊtənt] *n* [assistant] assistant *m*, -e *f*, auxiliaire *mf*; MIL adjudant-major *m*.

adjutant bird *n* marabout *m*.

ad-lib [ˌædˈlɪb] (*pt & pp* **ad-libbed**, *cont* **ad-libbing**) ◇ *vi & vt* improviser.
◇ *adj* improvisé, impromptu.
◆ **ad lib** ◇ *n* [improvised performance] improvisation *f*, improvisations *fpl*; [witticism] mot *m* d'esprit.
◇ *adv* -**1.** [without preparation] à l'improviste. -**2.** [without limit] à volonté. -**3.** MUS ad libitum.

adman *inf* [ˈædmæn] (*pl* **admen** [-men]) *n* publicitaire *m*.

admass [ˈædmæs] ◇ *n Br* grand public *m*.
◇ *comp Br* [culture, society] de grande consommation.

admin *inf* [ˈædmɪn] (*abbr of* **administration**) *n* travail *m* administratif.

administer [ədˈmɪnɪstəʳ] ◇ *vt* -**1.** [manage - business, institution] diriger, administrer, gérer; [- finances, fund] gérer; [- country, public institution] administrer; [- estate] régir. -**2.** *fml* [dispense - blow, medicine, punishment, test] administrer; [- law] appliquer; [- justice] rendre, dispenser; **to ~ the last rites to sb** administrer les derniers sacrements à qqn; **to ~ an oath (to sb)** faire prêter serment (à qqn).
◇ *vi fml*: **to ~ to sb** subvenir aux besoins de qqn.

administrate [ədˈmɪnɪstreɪt] = **administer** *vt* **1.**

administration [ədˌmɪnɪˈstreɪʃn] *n* -**1.** [process - of business, institution] direction *f*, administration *f*, gestion *f*; [- of finances, fund] gestion *f*; [- of country, public institution] administration *f*; [- of estate] curatelle *f*; **you will need some experience of ~** vous devrez avoir une certaine expérience de l'administration. -**2.** [people - of business, institution] direction *f*, administration *f*; [- of country, public institution] administration *f*. -**3.** POL gouvernement *m*; **under the last ~** sous le dernier gouvernement. -**4.** [of help, justice, medicine, punishment] administration *f*. -**5.** [of oath] prestation *f*.

administrative [ədˈmɪnɪstrətɪv] *adj* administratif; **the ~ body** le corps administratif; **~ law** loi *f* administrative.

administrator [ədˈmɪnɪstreɪtəʳ] *n* [of business, institution] directeur *m*, -trice *f*, administrateur *m*, -trice *f*; [of area, public institution] administrateur, -trice; [of estate] curateur *m*, -trice *f*.

admirable [ˈædmərəbl] *adj* admirable, excellent.

admirably [ˈædmərəblɪ] *adv* admirablement; **she coped ~** elle s'en est tiré admirablement bien.

admiral [ˈædmərəl] *n* -**1.** NAUT amiral *m*; **~ of the fleet, fleet ~** ≃ amiral de France; **the Admiral's Cup** l'Admiral's Cup *f* (*course de voiliers en Angleterre*). -**2.** [butterfly] vanesse *f*.

admiralty [ˈædmərəltɪ] (*pl* **admiralties**) *n* amirauté *f*; **the Admiralty (Board)** *Br* ≃ le ministère de la Marine; **~ court/law** tribunal *m*/droit *m* maritime.

THE ADMIRALTY:
Ce nom désignait autrefois la Direction de la marine nationale britannique au ministère de la Défense. Aujourd'hui il désigne les bâtiments abritant le siège de la Fonction publique à Londres.

---

admiration [ˌædməˈreɪʃn] *n* -**1.** [feeling] admiration *f*. -**2.** [person, thing]: **she was the ~ of the entire class** elle faisait l'admiration de la classe entière.

admire [ədˈmaɪəʳ] *vt* admirer; **he ~d (her for) the way she dealt with the press** il admirait la façon dont elle savait s'y prendre avec la presse; **to ~ o.s. in the mirror** s'admirer dans le miroir; **you have to ~ his persistence!** on ne peut qu'admirer sa persévérance!

admirer [ədˈmaɪərəʳ] *n* admirateur *m*, -trice *f*; **he's one of her many ~s** il est un de ses nombreux admirateurs.

admiring [ədˈmaɪərɪŋ] *adj* admiratif.

admiringly [ədˈmaɪərɪŋlɪ] *adv* avec admiration.

admissibility [ədˌmɪsəˈbɪlətɪ] *n* [of behaviour, plan] admissibilité *f*; JUR recevabilité *f*.

admissible [ədˈmɪsəbl] *adj* [behaviour, plan] admissible; [document] valable; JUR [claim, evidence] recevable.

admission [ədˈmɪʃn] *n* -**1.** [entry] admission *f*, entrée *f*; **the ~ of Portugal to the EC** l'entrée du Portugal dans la CEE; **~ is free** l'entrée est gratuite; **'~ £1.50'** entrée £1.50; **'no ~ to minors'** 'entrée interdite aux mineurs'; **to gain ~ to a club** être admis dans un club; **he gained ~ to the minister's office** il a été admis dans le bureau du ministre; **they granted women ~ to the club** ils ont admis les femmes dans le club ‖ SCH & UNIV: **~s office** service *m* des inscriptions; **~s form** dossier *m* d'inscription. -**2.** [fee] droit *m* d'entrée. -**3.** [person admitted - to theatre] entrée *f*; [- to school] candidat *m* accepté; [- to club] membre *m* accepté. -**4.** [statement] déclaration *f*; [confession] aveu *m*; **an ~ of guilt** un aveu; **by OR on one's own ~** de son propre aveu. -**5.** JUR [of evidence] acceptation *f*, admission *f*.

admit [ədˈmɪt] (*pt & pp* **admitted**, *cont* **admitting**) *vt* -**1.** [acknowledge] admettre, reconnaître, avouer; **I ~ I was wrong** je reconnais que j'ai eu tort; **I must ~ it's more difficult than I thought** je dois admettre que c'est plus difficile que je ne pensais; **he admitted (that) he had failed** il a reconnu qu'il avait échoué; **she refused to ~ defeat** elle a refusé de reconnaître sa défaite; **no one would ~ doing it** personne ne voulait admettre l'avoir fait; **we had to ~ the validity of his reasoning** nous avons dû admettre la validité de son raisonnement; **it is generally admitted that women live longer than men** il est généralement admis que les femmes vivent plus longtemps que les hommes. -**2.** [confess] avouer; **he admitted taking bribes** il a reconnu avoir accepté des pots-de-vin. -**3.** [permit to enter - person] laisser entrer, faire entrer; [- air, light] laisser passer, laisser entrer; **'~ two'** [on ticket] 'valable pour deux personnes'; **he was admitted to (the) hospital** il a été admis à l'hôpital; **to be admitted to a university** être admis à l'université; **admitting office** *Am* [in hospital] service *m* des admissions. -**4.** [accommodate] (pouvoir) contenir OR recevoir. -**5.** *fml* [allow] admettre, permettre; **the facts ~ no other explanation** d'après les faits, il n'y a pas d'autre explication possible. -**6.** JUR [claim] faire droit à; [evidence] admettre comme valable.
◆ **admit of** *vt insep Br fml* admettre, permettre; **her behaviour ~s of no excuse** son attitude est inexcusable; **the text ~s of only one interpretation** le texte ne permet qu'une seule interprétation.
◆ **admit to** *vt insep* [acknowledge] admettre, reconnaître; [confess] avouer; **he ~s to having opened the letter** il a avoué avoir ouvert la lettre; **she did ~ to a feeling of loss** elle a effectivement avoué ressentir un sentiment de perte.

admittance [ədˈmɪtəns] *n* admission *f*, entrée *f*; **'no ~'** 'accès interdit au public'; **his supporters gained ~ to the courtroom/to the president** ses supporters ont réussi à entrer dans le tribunal/à s'approcher du président; **she was denied ~ to the club** on lui a refusé l'entrée au club.

admittedly [ədˈmɪtɪdlɪ] *adv*: **~, he's weak on economics, but he's an excellent manager** d'accord, l'économie n'est pas son point fort, mais il fait un excellent directeur; **our members, although ~ few in number, are very keen** nos membres, peu nombreux il faut le reconnaître, sont très enthousiastes.

admixture [ædˈmɪkstʃəʳ] *n fml* -**1.** [mixture] mélange *m*. -**2.** [ingredient] ingrédient *m*; **it's mainly comedy with an ~ of satire** *fig* c'est principalement de la comédie avec un élément de satire.

admonish [ədˈmɒnɪʃ] *vt* -**1.** [rebuke] réprimander, admonester; **he was ~ed for not having acted more promptly** il a été réprimandé pour ne pas avoir agi plus rapidement. -**2.** [warn] avertir, prévenir; JUR admonester.

admonition [ˌædməˈnɪʃn] *n* -**1.** [rebuke] réprimande *f*, remontrance *f*, admonestation *f*. -**2.** [warning] avertissement *m*; JUR admonition *f*.

ad nauseam [ˌædˈnɔːzɪæm] *adv literal* jusqu'à la nausée; *fig* à satiété; **she went on about her holiday ~** elle nous a raconté ses vacances à n'en plus finir.

adnominal [ədˈnɒmɪnəl] ◇ *adj* adnominal.
◇ *n* adnominal *m*.

ado [əˈduː] *n*: **without more OR further ~** sans plus de cérémonie OR de manières ❑ **'Much Ado About Nothing'** *Shakespeare* 'Beaucoup de bruit pour rien'.

adobe [əˈdəʊbɪ] ◇ *n* adobe *m*.
◇ *comp* [house, wall] d'adobe.

adolescence [ˌædəˈlesns] *n* adolescence *f*.

adolescent [ˌædəˈlesnt] ◇ *n* adolescent *m*, -e *f*.
◇ *adj* [boy, girl] adolescent; *pej* [childish] enfantin, puéril *pej*.

Adonis [əˈdəʊnɪs] *pr n* MYTH Adonis; **a young ~** *fig* un jeune Apollon.

adopt [əˈdɒpt] *vt* -**1.** [child] adopter. -**2.** [choose - plan, technique] adopter, suivre, choisir; [- country, name] adopter, choisir; [- career] choisir, embrasser; POL [- candidate] choisir; **he ~ed the suggestion as his own** il a repris la proposition à son compte. -**3.** [assume - position] prendre; [- accent, tone] adopter, prendre. -**4.** *fml* [approve - minutes, report] approuver; [- motion] adopter.

adopted [əˈdɒptɪd] *adj* [child] adoptif; [country] d'adoption, adoptif.

adoption [əˈdɒpʃn] *n* -**1.** [of child, country, custom] adoption *f*; **she's an American by ~** elle est américaine d'adoption. -**2.** [of candidate, career, plan] choix *m*. -**3.** *fml* [of bill, motion] adoption *f*.

adoptive [ə'dɒptɪv] *adj* [child] adoptif; [country] d'adoption, adoptif.
adorable [ə'dɔːrəbl] *adj* adorable.
adoration [ˌædə'reɪʃn] *n* adoration *f*; in ~ en adoration ❑ 'The Adoration of the Magi' 'l'Adoration des Mages'.
adore [ə'dɔːʳ] *vt* -**1.** RELIG adorer. -**2.** *inf* [like]: I ~ walking in the rain j'adore marcher sous la pluie.
adoring [ə'dɔːrɪŋ] *adj* [look] d'adoration; [smile] rempli d'adoration; a letter signed "your ~ daughter" une lettre signée «ta fille qui t'adore».
adoringly [ə'dɔːrɪŋlɪ] *adv* avec adoration.
adorn [ə'dɔːn] *vt fml* OR *lit* -**1.** [decorate - dress, hair] orner, parer; [- room, table] orner; ~ed with flowers orné de fleurs; she ~ed herself with jewels elle s'est parée de bijoux. -**2.** [story] embellir.
adornment [ə'dɔːnmənt] *n* -**1.** [act, art] décoration *f*. -**2.** [of dress, hair] parure *f*; [of room, table] ornement *m*.
ADP *n abbr of* automatic data processing.
adrenal [ə'driːnl] ◇ *n* surrénale *f*.
◇ *adj* surrénal.
adrenal gland *n* surrénale *f*.
adrenalin(e) [ə'drenəlɪn] *n* adrénaline *f*; it really gets the ~ flowing ça donne un bon coup d'adrénaline.
Adriatic [ˌeɪdrɪ'ætɪk] *pr n*: the ~ (Sea) l'Adriatique *f*, la mer Adriatique.
adrift [ə'drɪft] ◇ *adv* -**1.** NAUT à la dérive; their boat had been cut ~ leur bateau avait été détaché; his parents turned him ~ *fig* ses parents l'ont laissé se débrouiller tout seul. -**2.** *Br* [undone]: to come OR to go ~ se détacher, se défaire; the hem on my skirt has come ~ l'ourlet de ma jupe s'est défait; our holiday plans seem to have gone ~ il semble que nos projets de vacances soient tombés à l'eau.
◇ *adj* [boat] à la dérive; *fig* abandonné; she was (all) ~ elle divaguait complètement.
adroit [ə'drɔɪt] *adj* adroit, habile.
adroitly [ə'drɔɪtlɪ] *adv* adroitement, habilement.
ADT (*abbr of* Atlantic Daylight Time) *n heure d'été des Provinces Maritimes du Canada et d'une partie des Caraïbes*.
adulation [ˌædjʊ'leɪʃn] *n* flagornerie *f*.
adulatory ['ædjʊleɪtərɪ] *adj* adulateur.
adult ['ædʌlt] ◇ *n* adulte *mf*; 'for ~s only' 'interdit aux moins de 18 ans'.
◇ *adj* -**1.** [fully grown] adulte. -**2.** [mature] adulte; she's very ~ for her age elle est très sérieuse OR elle a beaucoup de maturité pour son âge; try and be a little more ~ about this essaie de faire preuve d'un peu plus de maturité. -**3.** [book, film, subject] pour adultes.
adult education *n* enseignement *m* pour adultes.
adulterate [ə'dʌltəreɪt] ◇ *vt* frelater; they ~d the wine with water ils ont coupé le vin (avec de l'eau).
◇ *adj fml* frelaté.
adulteration [əˌdʌltə'reɪʃn] *n* frelatage *m*.
adulterer [ə'dʌltərəʳ] *n* adultère *m (personne)*.
adulteress [ə'dʌltərɪs] *n* adultère *f*.
adulterous [ə'dʌltərəs] *adj* adultère.
adultery [ə'dʌltərɪ] *n* adultère *m (acte)*.
adulthood ['ædʌlthʊd] *n* âge *m* adulte.
adumbrate ['ædʌmbreɪt] *vt fml* -**1.** [outline] ébaucher, esquisser. -**2.** [foreshadow] faire pressentir. -**3.** [obscure] obscurcir, voiler.
advance [əd'vɑːns] ◇ *vt* -**1.** [date, object] avancer; the date of the meeting was ~d by one week la réunion a été avancée d'une semaine. -**2.** [further - project, work] avancer; [- interest, cause] promouvoir. -**3.** [suggest - idea, proposition] avancer, mettre en avant; [- opinion] avancer, émettre; [- explanation] avancer. -**4.** [money] avancer, faire une avance de; we ~d her £100 on her salary nous lui avons avancé 100 livres sur son salaire. -**5.** *fml* [increase] augmenter, hausser.
◇ *vi* -**1.** [go forward] avancer, s'avancer; to ~ on OR towards sthg avancer OR s'avancer vers qqch; the army ~d on Paris l'armée avançait OR marchait sur Paris. -**2.** [make progress] avancer, progresser, faire des progrès. -**3.** [time] avancer, s'écouler; [evening, winter] avancer. -**4.** *fml* [price, rent] monter, augmenter. -**5.** [be promoted] avancer, obtenir de l'avancement; MIL monter en grade.
◇ *n* -**1.** [forward movement] avance *f*, marche *f* en avant; MIL avance *f*, progression *f*; the enemy planned their ~ on the city l'ennemi a organisé son avance OR sa marche sur la ville; the ~ of old age *fig* le vieillissement. -**2.** [progress] progrès *m*; the great ~ in medicine le progrès OR les progrès en médecine. -**3.** [money] avance *f*; an ~ on his salary une avance sur son salaire; an ~ on royalties une avance sur droits d'auteur. -**4.** *fml* [in price, rent] hausse *f*, augmentation *f*.
◇ *comp* -**1.** [prior] préalable; ~ booking is advisable il est recommandé de réserver à l'avance; ~ booking office guichet *m* de location; ~ notice préavis *m*, avertissement *m*; ~ payment paiement *m* anticipé; ~ warning avertissement *m*. -**2.** [preceding]: ~ copy [of book] exemplaire *m* de lancement; [of speech] texte *m* distribué à l'avance; ~ group OR party [gen] groupe *m* de reconnaissance; MIL pointe *f* d'avant-garde; ~ man *Am* POL organisateur *m* de la publicité *(pour une campagne politique)*; ~ post MIL poste avancé.
◆ **advances** *npl* avances *fpl*; to make ~s to sb faire des avances à qqn.
◆ **in advance** *adv phr* [beforehand - pay, thank] à l'avance, d'avance; [- prepare, reserve, write] à l'avance; we had to pay two weeks in ~ il a fallu qu'on paie deux semaines d'avance; the agency asked for £50 in ~ l'agence a demandé 50 livres d'avance; he sent the messenger on in ~ [ahead] il a envoyé le messager devant; they arrived in ~ of their guests ils sont arrivés en avance sur OR avant leurs invités; their computer technology is far in ~ of anything we have ils sont très en avance sur nous en matière d'informatique.
advanced [əd'vɑːnst] *adj* -**1.** [highly developed - course, education] supérieur; [- child, country, pupil] avancé; [- research, work] poussé; [- equipment, technique, technology] avancé, de pointe; the system is very ~ technologically le système est très en avance au niveau technologique; he's ~ for his age il est avancé OR très en avance pour son âge ❑ ~ mathematics mathématiques *fpl* supérieures. -**2.** [afternoon, season] avancé; a woman of ~ years, a woman ~ in years une femme d'un âge avancé; the evening was already far ~ il était déjà tard dans la soirée.
Advanced level *Br* = **A level**.
advance guard *n* avant-garde *f*.
advancement [əd'vɑːnsmənt] *n* -**1.** [promotion] avancement *m*, promotion *f*. -**2.** [improvement] progrès *m*, avancement *m*.
advancing [əd'vɑːnsɪŋ] *adj* qui approche, qui avance; the ~ army l'armée en marche OR qui avance; the ~ tide la marée qui monte.
advantage [əd'vɑːntɪdʒ] ◇ *n* -**1.** [benefit] avantage *m*; her experience gives her an ~ over the other candidates son expérience lui donne un avantage sur les autres candidats; they have an ~ over us OR the ~ of us ils ont un avantage sur nous; the plan has the ~ of being extremely cheap le plan présente l'avantage d'être extrêmement bon marché; it's to your ~ to learn another language c'est (dans) ton intérêt d'apprendre une autre langue; that would be to their ~ cela leur serait avantageux, ils y auraient intérêt; she turned the situation to her ~ elle a tiré parti de la situation, elle a tourné la situation à son avantage; we took ~ of the holiday weekend to do some gardening nous avons profité du long week-end pour faire du jardinage; to take ~ of sb [make use of] profiter de qqn; [exploit] exploiter qqn; [abuse sexually] abuser de qqn; she uses her charm to great ~ elle sait user de son charme; that colour shows her eyes off to great ~ cette couleur met ses yeux en valeur; this lighting shows the pictures to their best ~ cet éclairage met les tableaux en valeur ❑ you have the ~ of me *Br* à qui ai-je l'honneur? -**2.** TENNIS avantage *m*. -**3.** [in team sports]: to play the ~ rule laisser jouer la règle de l'avantage.
◇ *vt* avantager.
advantaged [əd'vɑːntɪdʒd] *adj* favorisé, aisé.
advantageous [ˌædvən'teɪdʒəs] *adj* avantageux; to be ~ to sb être avantageux pour qqn, avantager qqn.
advantageously [ˌædvən'teɪdʒəslɪ] *adv* de façon avantageuse.
advent ['ædvənt] *n fml* OR *lit* [coming] venue *f*, avènement *m*.
◆ **Advent** *n* RELIG l'Avent *m*; Advent Sunday le premier dimanche de l'Avent.
Advent calendar *n* calendrier *m* de l'Avent.
adventitious [ˌædven'tɪʃəs] *adj* -**1.** *fml* [chance] fortuit. -**2.** BOT adventice.
adventure [əd'ventʃəʳ] ◇ *n* -**1.** [experience] aventure *f*; to have an ~ avoir une aventure; after many ~s après bien des péripéties. -**2.** [excitement] aventure *f*; he has no spirit of ~ il n'a pas le goût du risque; to look for ~ chercher l'aventure. -**3.** [financial operation] spéculation *f* hasardeuse.
◇ *vt* & *vi* = **venture**.
◇ *comp* [film, novel] d'aventures.
adventure playground *n Br sorte d'aire de jeux*.
adventurer [əd'ventʃərəʳ] *n* aventurier *m*; *pej* aventurier *m*, intrigant *m*.
adventuresome [əd'ventʃəsəm] *adj Am* aventureux, téméraire.
adventuress [əd'ventʃərɪs] *n* aventurière *f*; *pej* aventurière *f*, intrigante *f*.
adventurous [əd'ventʃərəs] *adj* [person, spirit] aventureux, audacieux; [life, project] aventureux, hasardeux.
adventurously [əd'ventʃərəslɪ] *adv* aventureusement, audacieusement.
adverb ['ædvɜːb] *n* adverbe *m*.
adverbial [əd'vɜːbjəl] *adj* adverbial.
adversarial [ˌædvə'seərɪəl] *adj* antagoniste, hostile.
adversary ['ædvəsərɪ] (*pl* **adversaries**) *n* adversaire *mf*.
adverse ['ædvɜːs] *adj* [comment, criticism, opinion] défavorable, hostile; [circumstances, report] défavorable; [effect] opposé, contraire; [wind] contraire, debout; the match was cancelled due to ~ weather conditions le match a été annulé à cause du mauvais temps.
adversely ['ædvɜːslɪ] *adv*: ~ affected: the harvest was ~ affected by late frosts la récolte a été très touchée par les gelées tardives.
adversity [əd'vɜːsətɪ] (*pl* **adversities**) *n* -**1.** [distress] adversité *f*; in the face of ~ dans l'adversité. -**2.** [incident] malheur *m*; they met with many adversities ils ont eu bien des malheurs.
advert[1] *inf* ['ædvɜːt] *n Br* [advertisement] (petite) annonce *f*; COMM annonce *f* publicitaire, pub *f*; the ~s TV la pub.
advert[2] [əd'vɜːt] *vi fml* se rapporter, se référer; he ~ed to the incident in his report il a fait allusion à l'incident dans son rapport.
advertise ['ædvətaɪz] ◇ *vt* -**1.** COMM faire de la publicité pour; I heard his new record ~d on the radio j'ai entendu la publicité pour son nouveau disque à la radio; I saw it ~d in a magazine j'ai vu une annonce là-dessus OR pour ça dans une revue. -**2.** [subj: individual, group] mettre une (petite) annonce pour; they ~d the job in all the nationals ils ont mis OR inséré une annonce pour le poste dans toute la presse; we ~d our house in the local paper nous avons mis OR passé une annonce pour vendre notre

maison dans le journal local. -**3.** [make known] afficher; don't go advertising the fact that we're thinking of leaving ne va pas crier sur les toits que nous pensons partir.
◇ *vi* -**1.** COMM faire de la publicité; to ~ in the press/on radio/on TV faire de la publicité dans la presse/à la radio/à la télévision; it pays to ~ la publicité paie. -**2.** [announce] mettre une (petite) annonce OR des annonces. -**3.** [make request] chercher par voie d'annonce; we ~d for a cook nous avons mis OR fait paraître une annonce pour trouver une cuisinière.

advertisement [əd'vɜːtɪsmənt] *n* -**1.** COMM [in all media] annonce *f* publicitaire, publicité *f*; TV spot *m* publicitaire; are the ~s effective? la publicité est-elle efficace?; she made a cup of tea while the ~s were on elle est allée se faire une tasse de thé pendant la publicité. -**2.** [for event, house, sale] (petite) annonce *f*; to put an ~ in the paper passer une annonce dans le journal; I got the job through an ~ j'ai eu le poste grâce à une annonce. -**3.** *fig* [example]: this company is a poor ~ for public ownership la situation de cette société OR entreprise ne plaide pas en faveur de la nationalisation.

advertiser ['ædvətaɪzəʳ] *n* annonceur *m* (publicitaire).

advertising ['ædvətaɪzɪŋ] ◇ *n* -**1.** [promotion] publicité *f*. -**2.** [advertisements] publicité *f*. -**3.** [business] publicité *f*; he works in ~ il travaille dans la publicité.
◇ *comp* [campaign, rates, revenues] publicitaire; ~ agency agence *f* de publicité; ~ jingle jingle *m*, sonal *m offic*; ~ medium média *m* OR support *m* publicitaire; Advertising Standards Authority *Br* ≃ Bureau *m* de vérification de la publicité.

advice [əd'vaɪs] *n* -**1.** *(U)* [counsel] conseil *m*; a piece of ~ un conseil; he asked his father's ~, he asked his father for ~ il a demandé conseil à OR a consulté son père; let me give you some ~ permettez que je vous donne un conseil OR que je vous conseille; acting on your ~, I called him, I took OR followed your ~ and called him suivant votre conseil, je l'ai appelé; to take legal/medical ~ consulter un avocat/un médecin. -**2.** [notification] avis *m*; ~ of delivery/payment avis de livraison/de paiement; as per ~ suivant avis ❑ ~ note, letter of ~ avis.

advisability [əd,vaɪzə'bɪlətɪ] *n* opportunité *f*, bien-fondé *m*; they discussed the ~ of performing another operation ils ont discuté de l'opportunité d'une nouvelle opération; I question the ~ of contacting the police je doute qu'il soit opportun de faire appel à la police.

advisable [əd'vaɪzəbl] *adj* conseillé, recommandé; it would be ~ to lock the door il serait prudent OR préférable que vous fermiez la porte à clé; I don't think it ~ that you go out je ne vous conseille pas de sortir; it would perhaps be ~ to warn them peut-être conviendrait-il de les prévenir; she thought it ~ to call him elle a cru bien faire en l'appelant.

advise [əd'vaɪz] *vt* -**1.** [give advice to] conseiller, donner des conseils à; [recommend] recommander; we ~d them to wait nous leur avons conseillé d'attendre; she ~d caution elle a recommandé la prudence; I ~d him against signing the contract je lui ai conseillé de ne pas signer le contrat; he ~d them against taking legal action il leur a déconseillé d'intenter une action en justice. -**2.** [act as counsel to] conseiller; she ~s the government on education elle conseille le gouvernement en matière d'éducation. -**3.** *fml* [inform] aviser, informer; we ~d them of our arrival nous les avons prévenus de notre arrivée, nous leur avons fait part de notre arrivée; keep me ~d of your progress tenez-moi au courant de vos progrès; she ~d him of the cost elle l'a informé du coût.

advised [əd'vaɪzd] *adj* [thought-out] réfléchi, délibéré; [judicious] judicieux.

advisedly [əd'vaɪzɪdlɪ] *adv* délibérément, en connaissance de cause.

advisement [əd'vaɪzmənt] *n Am*: the matter is still under ~ aucune décision n'a encore été prise.

adviser *Br*, **advisor** *Am* [əd'vaɪzəʳ] *n* conseiller *m*, -ère *f*; SCH & UNIV conseiller *m*, -ère *f* pédagogique.

advisory [əd'vaɪzərɪ] *adj* -**1.** [role, work] consultatif, de conseil; he's employed in an ~ capacity il est employé à titre consultatif ❑ ~ board OR body organe *m* consultatif; ~ opinion *Am* JUR avis *m* consultatif de la cour. -**2.** [informative]: ~ bulletin bulletin *m* de renseignements.

advocaat ['ædvəkɑː] *n* advocaat *m*.

advocacy ['ædvəkəsɪ] *n* soutien *m* appuyé, plaidoyer *m*; she speaks in ~ of educational reform elle prône OR préconise une réforme scolaire.

advocate [*vb* 'ædvəkeɪt, *n* 'ædvəkət] ◇ *vt* prôner, préconiser; he ~s reducing OR a reduction in defence spending il préconise une réduction des dépenses militaires.
◇ *n* -**1.** [supporter] défenseur *m*, avocat *m*, -e *f*; a strong ~ of free enterprise un fervent partisan de la libre entreprise; they are ~s of civil rights ils défendent les droits civiques. -**2.** [barrister] avocat *m* (plaidant), avocate *f* (plaidante).

advt *written abbr of* advertisement.

adze *Br*, **adz** *Am* [ædz] *n* herminette *f*.

AEA (*abbr of* Atomic Energy Authority) *pr n Br* ≃ CEA *f*.

AEC (*abbr of* Atomic Energy Commission) *pr n Am* ≃ CEA *f*.

AEEU (*abbr of* Amalgamated Engineering and Electrical Union) *pr n syndicat britannique de l'industrie mécanique*.

Aegean [iː'dʒiːən] ◇ *pr n*: the ~ la mer Égée.
◇ *adj* égéen; the ~ Sea la mer Égée; the ~ Islands les îles *fpl* de la mer Égée.

Aegina [iː'dʒaɪnə] *pr n* Égine.

aegis ['iːdʒɪs] *n fig* & MYTH égide *f*; under the ~ of the European Parliament sous l'égide du Parlement européen.

aegrotat ['iːgrəutæt] *n Br* UNIV *équivalence d'un diplôme accordée à un bon étudiant qui était malade lors des examens*.

Aeneas [ɪ'niːəs] *pr n* Énée.

Aeneid [ɪ'niːɪd] *pr n*: 'The ~' *Virgil* 'l'Énéide'.

aeolian [iː'əuljən] *adj* éolien.

aeolian harp *n* harpe *f* éolienne.

Aeolian Islands *pl pr n*: the ~ les îles *fpl* Éoliennes.

aeon ['iːən] *n* -**1.** [age] période *f* incommensurable; GEOL ère *f*; I haven't seen him in ~s *inf* je ne l'ai pas vu depuis une éternité. -**2.** PHILOS éon *m*.

aerate ['eɪəreɪt] *vt* -**1.** [liquid] gazéifier; [blood] oxygéner. -**2.** [soil] retourner.

aerial ['eərɪəl] ◇ *adj* -**1.** [in the air] aérien; ~ cable car, ~ railway téléphérique *m*; ~ combat combat *m* aérien; ~ photograph photographie *f* aérienne. -**2.** *lit* [imaginary] imaginaire. -**3.** *lit* [delicate] aérien, éthéré.
◇ *n* RADIO & TV antenne *f*.

aerialist ['eərɪəlɪst] *n Am* [tightrope walker] funambule *mf*; [trapeze artist] trapéziste *mf*.

aerial ladder *n Am* échelle *f* pivotante.

aerie ['eərɪ] *n Am* aire *f (d'aigle)*.

aerobatics [,eərəu'bætɪks] *n (U)* acrobatie *f* aérienne, acrobaties *fpl* aériennes.

aerobe ['eərəub] *n* aérobie *m*.

aerobic [eə'rəubɪk] *adj* aérobie.

aerobics [eə'rəubɪks] ◇ *n (U)* aérobic *m*; to do ~ faire de l'aérobic.
◇ *comp* [class, teacher] d'aérobic.

aerodrome ['eərədrəum] *n* aérodrome *m*.

aerodynamic [,eərəudaɪ'næmɪk] *adj* aérodynamique.

aerodynamics [,eərəudaɪ'næmɪks] *n (U)* aérodynamique *f*.

aero-engine ['eərəu-] *n* aéromoteur *m*.

aerogram ['eərəgræm] *n* -**1.** [letter] aérogramme *m*. -**2.** [radiotelegram] radiotélégramme *m*.

aerolite ['eərəulaɪt] *n* aérolithe *m*.

aeromodelling ['eərəu,mɒdlɪŋ] *n* aéromodélisme *m*.

aeronaut ['eərənɔːt] *n* aéronaute *mf*.

aeronautic(al) [,eərə'nɔːtɪk(l)] *adj* aéronautique.

aeronautics [,eərə'nɔːtɪks] *n (U)* aéronautique *f*.

aerophysics [,eərə'fɪsɪks] *n (U)* aérophysique *f*.

aeroplane ['eərəpleɪn] *n Br* avion *m*.

aerosol ['eərəsɒl] ◇ *n* -**1.** [suspension system] aérosol *m*. -**2.** [container] bombe *f*, aérosol *m*.
◇ *comp* [container, spray] aérosol; [hairspray, paint] en aérosol, en bombe.

aerospace ['eərəuspeɪs] ◇ *n* aérospatiale *f*.
◇ *comp* [industry, research] aérospatial.

aerostat ['eərəustæt] *n* aérostat *m*.

aerostatics [,eərəu'stætɪks] *n (U)* aérostatique *f*.

Aertex® ['eəteks] *n* Aertex® *m (tissu synthétique)*.

Aesop ['iːsɒp] *pr n* Ésope; '~'s Fables' 'les Fables d'Ésope'.

aesthete ['iːsθiːt] *n* esthète *mf*.

aesthetic(al) [iːs'θetɪk(l)] *adj* esthétique.

aesthetically [iːs'θetɪklɪ] *adv* esthétiquement.

aestheticism [iːs'θetɪsɪzm] *n* esthétisme *m*.

aesthetics [iːs'θetɪks] *n (U)* esthétique *f*.

aestivate ['iːstɪveɪt] *vi* estiver.

aestivation [,iːstɪ'veɪʃn] *n* estivation *f*.

aetiology [,iːtɪ'ɒlədʒɪ] (*pl* aetiologies) *n* étiologie *f*.

afar [ə'fɑːʳ] *adv lit* au loin, à (grande) distance.
◆ **from afar** *adv phr* de loin.

AFB *n abbr of* air force base.

AFC *n* -**1.** (*abbr of* automatic flight control) commande *f* automatique de vol. -**2.** (*abbr of* automatic frequency control) correcteur *m* automatique de fréquence.

AFDC (*abbr of* Aid to Families with Dependent Children) *n type d'allocations familiales, destiné tout particulièrement aux familles monoparentales*.

afear(e)d [ə'fɪəd] *adj arch*: to be ~ avoir peur.

affability [,æfə'bɪlətɪ] *n* affabilité *f*, amabilité *f*.

affable ['æfəbl] *adj* [person] affable, aimable; [conversation, interview] chaleureux.

affably ['æfəblɪ] *adv* affablement, avec affabilité.

affair [ə'feəʳ] *n* -**1.** [event] affaire *f*; the meeting was a noisy ~ la réunion était bruyante; it was a sorry ~ c'était une histoire lamentable ❑ the Dreyfus ~ l'affaire Dreyfus. -**2.** [business, matter] affaire *f*. -**3.** [concern] affaire *f*; whether I go or not is my ~ que j'y aille ou non ne regarde que moi; it's no ~ of his ça ne le regarde OR ne le concerne pas, ça n'est pas son affaire; don't meddle in my ~s ne vous mêlez pas de mes affaires, mêlez-vous de vos affaires. -**4.** [sexual] liaison *f*, aventure *f*; to have an ~ with sb avoir une liaison OR aventure avec qqn. -**5.** *inf* [thing] truc *m*; he was driving one of those sporty ~s il conduisait une de ces voitures genre sport.
◆ **affairs** *npl* [business, matter] affaires *fpl*; her financial ~s ses finances; I'm not interested in your private ~s je ne m'intéresse pas à votre vie privée; to put one's ~s in order [business] mettre de l'ordre dans ses affaires; given the current state of ~s étant donné la situation actuelle, les choses étant ce qu'elles sont; it's an embarrassing state of ~s la situation est gênante; this is a fine state of ~s! *iron* c'est du propre!; ~s of state affaires d'État.

affect [ə'fekt] ◇ *vt* -**1.** [have effect on - person, life] avoir un effet sur, affecter; [influence - decision, outcome] influer sur, avoir une incidence sur; how will these changes ~ you? en quoi serez-vous affecté OR concerné par ces changements?; I don't see how your decision ~s her je ne vois pas ce que votre décision change pour elle; she doesn't seem to be particularly ~ed by the noise elle ne semble

pas être particulièrement dérangée par le bruit; **these plants were badly ~ed by a late frost** ces plantes ont beaucoup souffert des gelées tardives; **the bad weather has ~ed sporting events this weekend** le mauvais temps a eu des répercussions sur les événements sportifs du week-end; **high interest rates are ~ing the housing market** le niveau élevé des taux d'intérêts affecte (le marché de) l'immobilier; **one of the factors that will ~ the outcome of the next election** l'un des facteurs qui influera sur le résultat des prochaines élections; **to what extent does price ~ your choice?** dans quelle mesure OR jusqu'à quel point le prix influence-t-il votre choix? -**2.** [concern, involve] toucher, concerner; **this new law ~s everyone** cette nouvelle loi concerne OR touche tout le monde; **they are directly ~ed** ce sont eux les premiers intéressés, ils sont directement concernés. -**3.** [emotionally] affecter, émouvoir, toucher; **he was deeply ~ed by her death** il a été très affecté OR touché par sa mort; **don't let it ~ you** ne vous laissez pas abattre par cela. -**4.** MED [subj: illness, epidemic] atteindre; [subj: drug] agir sur; **it has been proved that smoking ~s your health** il est prouvé que le tabac est nocif pour la santé; **thousands of people are ~ed by this incurable disease** des milliers de gens sont touchés OR concernés par cette maladie incurable; **it's a condition that particularly ~s young children** c'est une maladie qui affecte OR touche particulièrement les jeunes enfants; **a disease that ~s the kidneys** une maladie qui affecte les reins; **she has had a stroke, but her speech is not ~ed** elle a eu une attaque, mais les fonctions du langage ne sont pas atteintes. -**5.** *fml* [pretend, feign - indifference, surprise] affecter, feindre; [- illness] feindre, simuler; **he ~ed a strong foreign accent** il affectait un fort accent étranger; **she ~ed not to see him** elle fit semblant de ne pas l'avoir vu. -**6.** *arch* OR *lit* [be fond of] affectionner, avoir un penchant pour. -**7.** BOT & ZOOL [climate, habitat] être un habitué OR des habitués de, affecter.
◇ *n* PSYCH affect *m*.

affectation [ˌæfek'teɪʃn] *n* -**1.** [in behaviour, manners] affectation *f*, manque *m* de naturel; [in language, style] manque *m* de naturel; **without ~ simple**, sans manières. -**2.** [mannerism] pose *f*. -**3.** [pretence] semblant *m*, simulacre *m*; **with an ~ of interest/boredom** en simulant l'intérêt/l'ennui.

affected [ə'fektɪd] *adj* [person, behaviour] affecté, maniéré; [accent, dress, language] affecté, recherché.

-affected *in cpds* affecté par; **famine/drought~** affecté par la famine/sécheresse.

affectedly [ə'fektɪdlɪ] *adv* avec affectation, d'une manière affectée.

affecting [ə'fektɪŋ] *adj* touchant, émouvant.

affection [ə'fekʃn] *n* -**1.** [liking] affection *f*, tendresse *f*; **she has (a) deep ~ for him** elle a une profonde affection pour lui, elle l'aime profondément. -**2.** *(usu pl)* affection *f*; **to gain** OR **to win (a place in) sb's ~s** gagner l'affection OR le cœur de qqn; **she transferred her ~s to another man** elle a reporté son affection sur un autre homme. -**3.** MED affection *f*, maladie *f*.

affectionate [ə'fekʃnət] *adj* affectueux, tendre; **your ~ niece** [in letter] votre nièce affectionnée.

affectionately [ə'fekʃnətlɪ] *adv* affectueusement; **yours ~** [in letter] (bien) affectueusement.

affective [ə'fektɪv] *adj* [gen, LING & PSYCH] affectif.

affiance [ə'faɪəns] *vt lit*: **to become ~d to sb** se fiancer à OR avec qqn; **to be ~d** être fiancé.

affidavit [ˌæfɪ'deɪvɪt] *n* déclaration *f* sous serment *(écrite)*; **a sworn ~** une déclaration faite sous serment.

affiliate [*vb* ə'fɪlɪeɪt, *n* & *comp* ə'fɪlɪət]
◇ *vt* affilier; **the local group decided not to ~ (itself) to the national organization** la section locale a décidé de ne pas s'affilier au mouvement national.
◇ *n* [person] affilié *m*, -e *f*; [organization] groupe *m* affilié.
◇ *comp* [member, organization] affilié.

affiliated [ə'fɪlɪeɪtɪd] *adj* [member, organization] affilié; **an ~ company** une filiale.

affiliation [əˌfɪlɪ'eɪʃn] *n* -**1.** ADMIN & COMM affiliation *f*. -**2.** JUR attribution *f* de paternité; **~ order** jugement *m* en reconnaissance de paternité. -**3.** [connection] attache *f*; **his political ~s** ses attaches politiques.

affinity [ə'fɪnətɪ] (*pl* **affinities**) *n* -**1.** [connection, link] lien *m*, affinité *f*; BIOL affinité *f*, parenté *f*; CHEM affinité *f*; **the affinities between the English and German languages** la ressemblance OR la parenté entre l'anglais et l'allemand; **the artist's work shows a clear ~ to** OR **with that of his former teacher** on voit clairement le lien entre l'œuvre de cet artiste et celle de son maître. -**2.** [attraction] affinité *f*, attraction *f*; **he has little ~ for** OR **with modern art** il est peu attiré par l'art moderne; **she feels a strong sense of ~ with** OR **for him** elle se sent beaucoup d'affinités avec lui; **there is a strong ~ between them** ils ont beaucoup de choses en commun OR d'affinités. -**3.** JUR [relation] affinité *f*.

affirm [ə'fɜːm] *vt* -**1.** [state] affirmer, soutenir; **she ~s that it's the truth** elle affirme OR soutient que c'est la vérité; **"I will be there" he ~ed** «j'y serai» assura-t-il. -**2.** [profess - belief] professer, proclamer; **she ~ed her intention to sell** elle proclamait son intention de vendre.

affirmation [ˌæfə'meɪʃn] *n* affirmation *f*, assertion *f*; **to make a solemn ~** faire une déclaration solennelle.

affirmative [ə'fɜːmətɪv] ◇ *n* -**1.** GRAMM affirmatif *m*; **in the ~** à l'affirmatif, à la forme affirmative. -**2.** [in reply]: **the answer is in the ~** la réponse est affirmative; **to answer in the ~** répondre affirmativement OR par l'affirmative.
◇ *adj* affirmatif; **to give an ~ answer** répondre affirmativement.
◇ *interj*: **~!** affirmatif!

affirmative action *n Am (U)* mesures *fpl* d'embauche antidiscriminatoires *(en faveur des minorités)*.

affirmatively [ə'fɜːmətɪvlɪ] *adv* affirmativement.

affix [*vb* ə'fɪks, *n* 'æfɪks] ◇ *vt* [seal, signature] apposer; [stamp] coller; [poster] afficher, poser.
◇ *n* LING affixe *m*.

afflict [ə'flɪkt] *vt* affecter; **to be ~ed with a disease** souffrir d'une maladie.

affliction [ə'flɪkʃn] *n* -**1.** [suffering] affliction *f*; [distress] détresse *f*; **people in ~** les gens dans la détresse OR dans l'affliction. -**2.** [misfortune] affliction *f*, souffrance *f*; **blindness is a terrible ~** la cécité est une grande infirmité.

affluence ['æfluəns] *n* -**1.** [wealth] richesse *f*; **to live in ~** vivre dans l'aisance; **in times of ~** en période de prospérité. -**2.** *lit* [abundance] abondance *f*.

affluent ['æfluənt] ◇ *adj* -**1.** [wealthy] aisé, riche; **to be ~** vivre dans l'aisance; **the ~ society** la société d'abondance. -**2.** *lit* [abundant] abondant.
◇ *n* GEOG affluent *m*.

afflux ['æflʌks] *n* -**1.** *fml* [of visitors, traffic] affluence *f*, afflux *m*. -**2.** MED afflux *m*.

afford [ə'fɔːd] *vt* -**1.** [have enough money for] avoir les moyens de payer; **I can't ~ a holiday** je n'ai pas les moyens de prendre des vacances; **she couldn't ~ to buy a car** elle n'avait pas les moyens d'acheter OR elle ne pouvait pas se permettre d'acheter une voiture; **can you ~ it?** en avez-vous les moyens?, pouvez-vous vous le permettre?; **how much can you ~?** combien pouvez-vous mettre?, jusqu'à combien pouvez-vous aller?; **I can't ~ £50!** je ne peux pas mettre 50 livres! -**2.** [time, energy]: **the doctor can only ~ (to spend) a few minutes with each patient** le médecin ne peut pas se permettre de passer plus de quelques minutes avec chaque patient; **I'd love to come, but I can't ~ the time** j'aimerais beaucoup venir mais je ne peux absolument pas me libérer. -**3.** [allow o.s.]: **I can't ~ to take any risks** je ne peux pas me permettre de prendre des risques; **we can't ~ another delay** nous ne pouvons pas nous permettre encore un retard. -**4.** *lit* [provide] fournir, offrir; **this ~s me great pleasure** ceci me procure un grand plaisir; **the bell tower ~ed a panoramic view of the city** le clocher offrait une vue panoramique de la ville.

affordable [ə'fɔːdəbl] *adj* [commodity] (dont le prix est) abordable; **at an ~ price** à un prix abordable.

afforest [æ'fɒrɪst] *vt* boiser, reboiser.

afforestation [æˌfɒrɪ'steɪʃn] *n* boisement *m*.

affranchise [ə'fræntʃaɪz] *vt* affranchir.

affray [ə'freɪ] *n* échauffourée *f*.

affricate ['æfrɪkət] *n* affriquée *f*.

affright [ə'fraɪt] *arch* ◇ *vt* effrayer, terrifier.
◇ *n* effroi *m*, terreur *f*.

affront [ə'frʌnt] ◇ *n* affront *m*, insulte *f*; **to suffer an ~** essuyer un affront; **it was an ~ to her dignity** c'était un affront à sa dignité.
◇ *vt* [offend] faire un affront à, insulter, offenser; **to feel ~ed** se sentir offensé.

Afghan ['æfgæn] ◇ *n* -**1.** [person] Afghan *m*, -e *f*. -**2.** LING afghan *m*. -**3.** [dog] lévrier *m* afghan. -**4.** [coat] afghan *m*; *Am* [blanket] couverture *f* en lainage.
◇ *adj* afghan; **~ hound** lévrier *m* afghan.

Afghani [æf'gænɪ] GEOG & LING = **Afghan**.

Afghanistan [æf'gænɪstæn] *pr n* Afghanistan *m*; **in ~** en Afghanistan.

aficionado [əˌfɪsjə'nɑːdəʊ] (*pl* **aficionados**) *n*: **theatre ~s, ~s of the theatre** les aficionados OR les amoureux du théâtre; **a tennis ~** un mordu de tennis.

afield [ə'fiːld] *adv*: **to go far ~** aller loin; **people came from as far ~ as Australia** les gens venaient même d'Australie; **don't go too far ~** n'allez pas trop loin; **we didn't need to look very far ~** nous n'avions pas besoin de chercher très loin; **they travelled further ~ for their holidays this year** ils sont allés bien plus loin cette année pour leurs vacances; **this remark carried them even farther ~ from the subject under debate** *fig* cette remarque les fit s'éloigner encore plus du sujet.

afire [ə'faɪər] *lit* ◇ *adj* -**1.** [burning] en feu, embrasé. -**2.** *fig* [with emotion] enflammé; **she was ~ with passion** elle était enflammée par la passion.
◇ *adv*: **to set sthg ~** *literal* mettre le feu à qqch; *fig* embraser qqch.

aflame [ə'fleɪm] *lit* ◇ *adj* -**1.** [burning] en flammes, en feu. -**2.** [emotionally] enflammé; **to be ~ with desire/anger** être enflammé de désir/colère; **her cheeks were ~ with excitement** elle avait les joues rouges d'excitation, l'excitation lui enflammait les joues. -**3.** [in colour]: **the sky was ~ with colour** le ciel flamboyait de couleurs vives; **the countryside was ~ with autumn reds and yellows** la campagne était embrasée de rouges et de jaunes d'automne.
◇ *adv*: **to set ~** *literal* mettre le feu à; *fig* exciter, enflammer; **he set her heart ~** il a fait battre son cœur.

aflatoxin [ˌæflə'tɒksɪn] *n* aflatoxine *f*.

AFL-CIO (*abbr of* **American Federation of Labor and Congress of Industrial Organizations**) *pr n la plus grande confédération syndicale américaine*.

afloat [ə'fləʊt] ◇ *adj* -**1.** [swimmer] qui surnage; [boat] à flot; [cork, oil] flottant; *fig* [business] à flot. -**2.** [flooded] inondé; **the bottom of the boat was ~ with water** le fond du bateau était inondé.
◇ *adv* -**1.** [floating] à flot, sur l'eau; **we managed to get** OR **to set the raft ~** nous avons réussi à mettre le radeau à flot; **to stay ~** [swimmer] garder la tête hors de l'eau, surnager; [boat] rester à flot; **to keep ~** rester à flot; **to keep sthg/sb ~** maintenir qqch/qqn à flot || *fig*: **to get a business ~** [from start] mettre une entreprise à flot; [from financial difficulties] ren-

flouer une entreprise; **small businesses struggling to stay ~** des petites entreprises qui luttent pour se maintenir à flot; **to get** OR **to set a scheme ~** lancer un projet. **-2.** [on boat]: **holiday spent ~** [on barge] vacances en péniche; [at sea] vacances en mer.

aflutter [əˈflʌtər] ◇ *adj*: **to be (all) ~ with excitement** tressaillir d'excitation; **my heart was all ~** j'avais le cœur qui battait la chamade.
◇ *adv*: **she set my heart ~** elle fit battre mon cœur.

afoot [əˈfʊt] ◇ *adj* **-1.** [in preparation]: **there is something ~** il se prépare OR il se trame quelque chose; **there is a scheme ~ to build a new motorway** on a formé le projet OR on envisage de construire une nouvelle autoroute; **there is mischief ~** il va y avoir du vilain. **-2.** *lit & arch* [on foot] à pied.
◇ *adv lit & arch* à pied.

aforementioned [əˌfɔːˌmenʃənd] *adj fml* susmentionné, précité; **the ~ persons** lesdites personnes.

aforenamed [əˈfɔːneɪmd] *adj fml* susnommé, précité.

aforesaid [əˈfɔːsed] *adj fml* susdit, précité.

aforethought [əˈfɔːθɔːt] *adj fml* prémédité.

afoul [əˈfaʊl] *adv lit*: **to run ~ of sb** se mettre qqn à dos, s'attirer le mécontentement de qqn; **to run ~ of the law** avoir des démêlés avec la justice.

afraid [əˈfreɪd] *adj* **-1.** [frightened]: **to be ~** avoir peur; **don't be ~** n'ayez pas peur, ne craignez rien; **to make sb ~** faire peur à qqn; **she is ~ of the dark** elle a peur du noir; **there's nothing to be ~ of** il n'y a rien à craindre; **she was ~ (that) the dog would** OR **might bite her** elle avait peur OR elle craignait que le chien (ne) la morde; **he is ~ for his life** il craint pour sa vie; **she was ~ for her daughter** elle avait peur pour sa fille ❑ **'Who's Afraid of Virginia Woolf?'** *Albee* 'Qui a peur de Virginia Woolf?'. **-2.** [indicating reluctance, hesitation]: **he isn't ~ of work** le travail ne lui fait pas peur; **don't be ~ to speak** OR **of speaking your mind** n'ayez pas peur de dire ce que vous pensez; **I'm ~ (that) I'll say the wrong thing** je crains OR j'ai peur de ne pas dire ce qu'il faut. **-3.** [indicating regret]: **I'm ~ I won't be able to come** je regrette OR je suis désolé de ne pouvoir venir; **I'm ~ I can't help you** je regrette OR je suis désolé, mais je ne peux pas vous aider; **I'm ~ I cannot grant your request** je regrette de ne pas pouvoir accéder à votre requête; **I'm ~ to say...** j'ai le regret de dire...; **I'm ~ so** j'ai bien peur que oui, j'en ai bien peur; **I'm ~ not** j'ai bien peur que non, j'en ai bien peur.

afresh [əˈfreʃ] *adv* de nouveau; **we'll have to start ~** il va falloir recommencer OR reprendre à zéro.

Africa [ˈæfrɪkə] *pr n* Afrique *f*; **in ~** en Afrique ❑ **'Out of ~'** *Blixen* 'la Ferme africaine'.

African [ˈæfrɪkən] ◇ *n* Africain *m*, -e *f*.
◇ *adj* africain.

African American *n* Noir *m* américain, Noire *f* américaine.

Africanism [ˈæfrɪkənɪzm] *n* africanisme *m*.

Africanize, -ise [ˈæfrɪkənaɪz] *vt* africaniser.

African violet *n* saintpaulia *m*.

Afrikaans [ˌæfrɪˈkɑːns] *n* afrikaans *m*.

Afrikaner [ˌæfrɪˈkɑːnər] *n* Afrikaner *mf*.

Afro [ˈæfrəʊ] (*pl* **Afros**) ◇ *adj* [hairstyle] afro.
◇ *n* coiffure *f* afro.

Afro-American ◇ *n* Afro-Américain *m*, -e *f*.
◇ *adj* afro-américain.

Afro-Asian ◇ *n* Afro-Asiatique *mf*.
◇ *adj* afro-asiatique.

Afro-Caribbean ◇ *n* Afro-antillais *m*, -e *f*.
◇ *adj* afro-antillais.

aft [ɑːft] ◇ *adv* NAUT & AERON à OR vers l'arrière; **to go ~** aller à OR vers l'arrière.
◇ *adj* [deck] arrière.

AFT (*abbr of* **American Federation of Teachers**) *pr n syndicat américain d'enseignants*.

after [ˈɑːftər] ◇ *prep* **-1.** [in time - gen] après; [- period] après, au bout de; **~ breakfast** après le petit déjeuner; **~ dark** après la tombée de la nuit; **~ which she left** après quoi elle est partie; **it is ~ six o'clock already** il est déjà six heures passées OR plus de six heures; **shortly ~ midday/three** peu après midi/trois heures; **it's twenty ~ eight** *Am* il est huit heures vingt; **the day ~ tomorrow** après-demain *m*; **~ this date** ADMIN passé OR après cette date. **-2.** [in space] après; **the shopping centre is just ~ the church** le centre commercial est juste après l'église; **there ought to be a comma ~ "however"** il devrait y avoir une virgule après «however» ‖ [in series, priority etc] après; **Rothman comes ~ Richardson** Rothman vient après Richardson; **I would put Racine ~ Molière** pour moi Racine passe après Molière; **~ you** [politely] après vous (je vous en prie); **~ you with the paper** vous pouvez me passer le journal quand vous aurez fini. **-3.** [following consecutively]: **day ~ day** jour après jour; **time ~ time** maintes (et maintes) fois; **(for) mile ~ mile** sur des kilomètres et des kilomètres; **he's made mistake ~ mistake** il a fait erreur sur erreur; **generation ~ generation of farmers** des générations entières de fermiers; **it's been one crisis ~ another ever since she arrived** on va de crise en crise depuis son arrivée. **-4.** [behind] après, derrière; **close the door ~ you** fermez la porte derrière vous; **he locked up ~ them** il a tout fermé après leur départ OR après qu'ils soient partis; **don't expect me to clean up ~ you** ne croyez pas que je vais nettoyer derrière vous. **-5.** [in view of] après; **I'll never speak to him again, ~ what he said to me** je ne lui parlerai plus jamais après ce qu'il m'a dit; **~ the way I've been treated** après la façon dont on m'a traité; **~ what you told me** après ce que vous m'avez dit; **and ~ all I've done for them!** et après tout ce que j'ai fait pour eux! **-6.** [in spite of]: **~ all the trouble I took, no-one came** après OR malgré tout le mal que je me suis donné, personne n'est venu. **-7.** [in the manner of]: **~ Rubens** d'après Rubens. **-8.** [in search of]: **to be ~ sb/sthg** chercher qqn/qqch; **she's ~ you** elle te cherche; [angry with] elle t'en veut; [attracted to] tu l'intéresses; **the police are ~ him** la police est à ses trousses, il est recherché par la police; **their mother always seems to be ~ them** leur mère a l'air de ne jamais les laisser tranquilles; **he's ~ her money** il en veut à son argent; **what's he ~?** [want] qu'est-ce qu'il veut?; [looking for] qu'est-ce qu'il cherche?; [intend] qu'est-ce qu'il a derrière la tête?; **I know what she's ~** je sais où elle veut en venir. **-9.** [as verb complement]: **to ask** OR **to inquire ~ sb** demander des nouvelles de qqn; **to name a child ~ sb** donner à un enfant le nom de qqn; **to run ~ sb** courir après qqn; **they ran ~ him** ils lui ont couru après.
◇ *adv* après, ensuite; **the day ~** le lendemain, le jour suivant; **two days ~** deux jours après OR plus tard; **the week ~** la semaine d'après OR suivante; **for months ~** pendant des mois après; **soon ~** peu après; **to follow (on) ~** suivre.
◇ *conj* après que; **come and see me ~ you have spoken to him** venez me voir quand vous lui aurez parlé; **I came ~ he had left** je suis arrivé après qu'il soit parti; **~ saying goodnight to the children** après avoir dit bonsoir aux enfants; **was that before or ~ you'd signed the contract?** était-ce avant ou après que vous ayez signé le contrat?
◇ *adj* **-1.** [later]: **in ~ life** OR **years** plus tard dans la vie. **-2.** NAUT [cabin, mast] arrière.
◆ **afters** *inf npl Br* dessert *m*; **what's for ~s?** qu'est-ce qu'il y a pour le dessert OR comme dessert?
◆ **after all** *adv phr* **-1.** [when all's said and done] après tout; **~ all, she is very young** après tout, elle est très jeune; **that, ~ all, is why we came** après tout, c'est pour ça qu'on est venus; **it only costs £5 ~ all** ça ne coûte que cinq livres après tout. **-2.** [against expectation] après OR malgré tout; **so she was right ~ all** alors elle avait raison en fait.
◆ **one after another, one after the other** *adv phr* l'un après l'autre; **one ~ another they got up and left the room** l'un après l'autre, ils se levèrent et quittèrent la pièce; **he made several mistakes one ~ the other** il a fait plusieurs fautes d'affilée OR à la file.

afterbirth [ˈɑːftəbɜːθ] *n* placenta *m*.

afterburner [ˈɑːftəbɜːnər] *n* chambre *f* de postcombustion.

afterburning [ˈɑːftəbɜːnɪŋ] *n* postcombustion *f*, réchauffe *f*.

aftercare [ˈɑːftəkeər] *n* **-1.** MED postcure *f*. **-2.** [of prisoner] assistance *f (aux anciens détenus)*.

after-dinner *adj* [speaker, speech] de fin de dîner OR banquet; **an ~ drink** ≃ un digestif.

aftereffect [ˈɑːftərɪˌfekt] *n* [gen] suites *fpl*; MED séquelle *f*, séquelles *fpl*; **the ~s of war** les séquelles OR les répercussions de la guerre.

afterglow [ˈɑːftəgləʊ] *n* [of sunset] dernières lueurs *fpl*, derniers reflets *mpl*; *fig* [of pleasure] sensation *f* de bien-être *(après coup)*.

afterheat [ˈɑːftəhiːt] *n* chaleur *f* résiduelle.

after-hours ◇ *adv* [after closing time] après la fermeture; [after work] après le travail.
◇ *adj* [after closing time] qui suit la fermeture; [after work] qui suit le travail.

afterimage [ˈɑːftərˌɪmɪdʒ] *n* OPT image *f* récurrente OR consécutive; TV rémanence *f* à l'extinction.

afterlife [ˈɑːftəlaɪf] *n* vie *f* après la mort.

after-lunch *adj* qui suit le déjeuner; **to have an ~ nap** faire la sieste.

aftermath [ˈɑːftəmæθ] *n* **-1.** [of event] séquelles *fpl*, suites *fpl*; **in the ~ of the military coup** à la suite du coup d'État militaire; **in the immediate ~** tout de suite après, dans la foulée. **-2.** AGR regain *m*.

afternoon [ˌɑːftəˈnuːn] ◇ *n* après-midi *m inv or f inv*; **this ~** cet après-midi; **every ~** tous les après-midi; **all ~** tout l'après-midi; **tomorrow/yesterday ~** demain/hier après-midi; **in the ~** [in general] l'après-midi; [of particular day] (dans) l'après-midi; **on Friday ~s** le vendredi après-midi; **on Friday ~** [in general] le vendredi après-midi; [of particular day] vendredi après-midi; **in the early ~** tôt dans l'après-midi; **at 2 o'clock in the ~** à 2 h de l'après-midi; **on the ~ of May 16th** (dans) l'après-midi du 16 mai; **on a summer ~** par un après-midi d'été; **good ~** [hello] bonjour; [goodbye] au revoir; **have a nice ~!** bon après-midi!
◇ *comp* [class, train] de l'après-midi; [walk] qui a lieu dans l'après-midi; **~ performance** CIN & THEAT matinée *f*.
◆ **afternoons** *adv esp Am* (dans) l'après-midi.

afternoon tea *n thé pris avec une légère collation dans le cours de l'après-midi*; **to have ~** prendre le thé *(dans le cours de l'après-midi)*.

afterpains [ˈɑːftəpeɪnz] *npl* tranchées *fpl* utérines.

after-sales *adj* après-vente *(inv)*; **~ service** service *m* après-vente.

after-school *adj* [activities] extrascolaire.

aftershave [ˈɑːftəʃeɪv] *n*: **~ (lotion)** (lotion *f*) après-rasage *m*.

aftershock [ˈɑːftəʃɒk] *n* réplique *f* (d'un séisme).

aftertaste [ˈɑːftəteɪst] *n literal & fig* arrière-goût *m*.

after-tax *adj* [profits] après impôts, net d'impôt; [salary] net d'impôt.

afterthought [ˈɑːftəθɔːt] *n* pensée *f* après coup; **I had an ~** j'ai pensé après coup; **I only mentioned it as an ~** j'en ai seulement parlé après coup, quand l'idée m'est venue; **the west wing was added as an ~** l'aile ouest a été ajoutée après coup.

afterwards [ˈɑːftəwədz] *Br*, **afterward** [ˈæftərwərd] *Am adv* après, ensuite; **a long time ~** longtemps après; **I only realized ~** je n'ai compris qu'après coup OR que plus tard.

afterword [ˈɑːftəwɜːd] *n* [postscript] postface *f*; [epilogue] épilogue *m*.

afterworld ['ɑːftəwɜːld] *n* vie *f* après la mort.

again [ə'gen] *adv* **-1.** [once more] encore une fois, de nouveau; **it's me ~!** c'est encore moi!, me revoici!; **here we are back home ~!** nous revoilà chez nous!; **you'll soon be well ~** vous serez bientôt remis; **(the) same ~ please!** [in bar] remettez-nous ça OR la même chose s'il vous plaît!; **yet ~** encore une fois ‖ [with negative] ne... plus; **I didn't see them ~** je ne les ai plus revus; **not ~!** encore?; **not you ~!** encore vous? ❑ **~ and ~** maintes et maintes fois, à maintes reprises; **she read the passage through over and over ~** elle a lu et relu le passage. **-2.** [with verbs]: **to begin ~** recommencer; **to come ~** revenir; **to do ~** refaire; **if I had to do it ~** si c'était à refaire; **can you say it ~?** pouvez-vous répéter?; **don't make me have to tell you ~!** et que je n'aie pas à vous le répéter! **-3.** [indicating forgetfulness] déjà; **what's her name ~?** comment s'appelle-t-elle déjà?; **what did he say ~?** qu'est-ce qu'il a dit déjà? **-4.** [in quantity]: **as much** OR **many ~** encore autant; **half as much ~** encore la moitié de ça; **half as many pages ~** la moitié plus de pages; **it's as long/wide/far ~ as that** ça fait encore la même longueur/largeur/distance que ça. **-5.** [furthermore] d'ailleurs, qui plus est.

against [ə'genst] ◇ *prep* **-1.** [indicating position] contre; **he leant his bike (up) ~ the wall** il appuya son vélo contre le mur; **she had her nose pressed ~ the window** elle avait le nez écrasé au carreau; **put the chairs (back) ~ the wall** remettez les chaises contre le mur; **he was standing with his back ~ the wall** il était adossé contre le mur OR au mur ‖ [indicating impact] contre; **I banged my knee ~ the chair** je me suis cogné le genou contre la chaise; **the shutter was banging ~ the window** le volet claquait contre la fenêtre. **-2.** [in the opposite direction to - current, stream, grain] contre; [contrary to - rules, principles] à l'encontre de; **to go ~ a trend** s'opposer à une OR aller à l'encontre d'une tendance; **it's ~ the law to steal** le vol est interdit par la loi; **they sold the farm ~ my advice/wishes** ils ont vendu la ferme sans tenir compte de mes conseils/de ce que je souhaitais. **-3.** [indicating opposition to - person, proposal, government]: **the fight ~ inflation/crime** la lutte contre l'inflation/la criminalité; **to decide ~ sthg** décider de ne pas faire qqch; **to vote ~ sthg** voter contre qqch; **you're either for us or ~ us** tu dois être avec nous ou contre nous; **she's ~ telling him** elle trouve qu'on ne devrait pas le lui dire; **I advised her ~ going** je lui ai déconseillé d'y aller ❑ **what have you got ~ him/the idea?** qu'est-ce que vous avez contre lui/l'idée?; **what have you got ~ going?** pourquoi vous n'avez pas envie d'y aller?; **I've nothing ~ it** je n'ai rien contre. **-4.** [unfavourable to] contre; **conditions were ~ them** les conditions leur étaient défavorables; **his appearance is ~ him** son physique ne joue pas en sa faveur. **-5.** [in competition with] contre; **United ~ Everton** SPORT United contre Everton; **to run ~ sb** SPORT courir contre qqn; POL se présenter contre qqn; **a race ~ time** OR **the clock** une course contre la montre. **-6.** [indicating defence, protection, precaution etc] contre; **an injection ~ measles** une injection contre la rougeole; **to insure ~ accidents** [insurer] assurer contre les accidents; [client] s'assurer contre les accidents ‖ *fml* [in preparation for] en vue de, en prévision de; **to save money ~ one's retirement** faire des économies en prévision de OR pour la retraite. **-7.** [in contrast to] contre, sur; **to stand ~ the light** être à contre-jour; **the tall chimneys stood out ~ the sky** les hautes cheminées se détachaient sur le ciel; **yellow flowers ~ a green background** des fleurs jaunes sur un fond vert; **these events took place ~ a background of political violence** *fig* ces événements ont eu lieu dans un climat de violence politique. **-8.** [in comparison to, in relation to] en comparaison de, par rapport à; **they cost £10 here (as) ~ only £7 at the supermarket** ils coûtent 10 livres ici contre OR au lieu de 7 livres au supermarché; **the dollar fell ~ the yen** FIN le dollars a baissé par rapport au yen; **to plot the number of passengers ~ distance travelled** [in graph] relever le nombre de voyageurs par rapport à la distance parcourue. **-9.** [in exchange for] contre, en échange de; **cash is available ~ presentation of the voucher** ce bon peut être échangé contre de l'argent.
◇ *adv* contre; **are you for or ~?** êtes-vous pour ou contre?; **the odds are 10 to 1 ~** [gen] il y a une chance sur dix; [in horse racing] la cote est à 10 contre 1.

Agamemnon [,ægə'memnən] *pr n* Agamemnon.

agape [ə'geɪp] *adj* bouche bée *(inv)*.

agar(-agar) ['eɪgəʳ, ,eɪgə'eɪgəʳ] *n* agar-agar *m*, gélose *f*.

agaric ['ægərɪk] *n* agaric *m*.

agate ['ægət] *n* agate *f*.

agave [ə'geɪvɪ] *n* agave *m*.

age [eɪdʒ] ◇ *n* **-1.** [of person, animal, tree, building] âge *m*; **what ~ is he?** quel âge a-t-il?; **he is 25 years of ~** il est âgé de 25 ans; **at the ~ of 25** à l'âge de 25 ans; **when I was your ~** quand j'avais votre âge; **his wife is only half his ~** sa femme n'a que la moitié de son âge; **she's twice my ~** elle a le double de mon âge; **I have a son your ~** j'ai un fils de votre âge; **he lived to a ripe old ~** il a vécu jusqu'à un bel âge OR très vieux; **she doesn't look her ~** elle ne fait pas son âge; **I'm beginning to feel my ~** je commence à me sentir vieux; **act** OR **be your ~!** [be reasonable] sois raisonnable!; [don't be silly] ne sois pas stupide!; **he is of an ~ when he should consider settling down** il est à un âge où il devrait penser à se ranger; **the two of them were of an ~** ils étaient tous les deux à peu près du même âge; **to be of ~** JUR être majeur; **to be under ~** JUR être mineur ❑ **the ~ of consent** JUR *âge où les rapports sexuels sont autorisés par la loi britannique (16 ans pour les rapports hétérosexuels et 21 ans pour les rapports homosexuels)*; **they are below the ~ of consent** ils tombent sous le coup de la loi sur la protection des mineurs; **the ~ of discretion** *âge auquel une personne est jugée apte à prendre ses responsabilités*; **to come of ~** atteindre sa majorité, devenir majeur; **this way of thinking has at last come of ~** *fig* c'est un point de vue qui a fait son chemin. **-2.** [old age - of person] âge *m*, vieillesse *f*; [- of wood, paper, liquor] âge *m*; **bent with ~** courbé par l'âge; **to mellow with ~** [person] s'adoucir en vieillissant; [cheese] s'améliorer en vieillissant; **yellow** OR **yellowed with ~** jauni par l'âge ❑ **Age Concern** *association caritative britannique d'aide aux personnes âgées*. **-3.** [period - esp historical] époque *f*, âge *m*; GEOL âge *m*; **through the ~s** à travers les âges. **-4.** *(usu pl)* [long time] éternité *f*; **she was an ~ getting dressed, it took her an ~ to get dressed** elle a mis un temps fou à s'habiller; **I haven't seen you for** OR **in ~s!** cela fait une éternité que je ne vous ai (pas) vu!; **it took him ~s to do the work** il a mis très longtemps à faire le travail.
◇ *vi* vieillir, prendre de l'âge; **he's beginning to ~** il commence à se faire vieux; **to ~ well** [person] vieillir bien; [wine, cheese] s'améliorer en vieillissant; **he has ~d a lot** il a beaucoup vieilli.
◇ *vt* **-1.** [person] vieillir; **illness has ~d her** la maladie l'a vieillie. **-2.** [wine, cheese] laisser vieillir OR mûrir; **~d in the wood** vieilli en fût.

age bracket = **age group**.

aged [*adj sense 1* eɪdʒd, *adj sense 2* & *n* 'eɪdʒɪd]
◇ *adj* **-1.** [of the age of]: **a man ~ 50** un homme (âgé) de 50 ans. **-2.** [old] âgé, vieux; **my ~ aunt** ma vieille tante.
◇ *npl*: **the ~** les personnes *fpl* âgées, les vieux *mpl*.

age group *n* tranche *f* d'âge; **the 20 to 30 ~** la tranche d'âge des 20 à 30 ans; **the younger ~** les jeunes *mpl*.

ageing ['eɪdʒɪŋ] ◇ *adj* **-1.** [person] vieillissant, qui se fait vieux; [society] de vieux; [machinery, car] (qui se fait) vieux; **the ~ process** le processus du vieillissement. **-2.** [clothes, hairstyle] qui vieillit.
◇ *n* [of society, population] vieillissement *m*.

ageism ['eɪdʒɪzm] *n* âgisme *m*.

ageist ['eɪdʒɪst] ◇ *adj* [action, policy] qui relève de l'âgisme.
◇ *n personne qui fait preuve d'âgisme*.

ageless ['eɪdʒlɪs] *adj* [person] sans âge, qui n'a pas d'âge; [work of art] intemporel; [beauty] toujours jeune.

age limit *n* limite *f* d'âge.

agency ['eɪdʒənsɪ] (*pl* **agencies**) *n* **-1.** COMM [for employment] agence *f*, bureau *m*; [for travel, accommodation] agence *f*; **advertising ~** agence de publicité; **dating ~** club *m* de rencontres. **-2.** ADMIN service *m*, bureau *m*; **international aid agencies** des organisations d'aide internationale; **a government ~** une agence gouvernementale. **-3.** [intermediary - of person] intermédiaire *m*, entremise *f*; [- of fate] jeu *m*; **through her ~** par son entremise, grâce à elle; **by the ~ of direct sunlight** par l'action directe des rayons du soleil.

agenda [ə'dʒendə] *n* [for meeting] ordre *m* du jour; [for activities] programme *m*; **what's on today's ~, what's on the ~ (for) today?** [for meeting] quel est l'ordre du jour?; [for activities] qu'est-ce qu'il y a au programme pour aujourd'hui?; **it was top of the ~** *fig* c'était prioritaire ❑ **to set the ~** avoir l'initiative.

agent ['eɪdʒənt] *n* **-1.** COMM agent *m*, représentant *m*, -e *f*; [for travel, insurance] agent *m*; [for firm] concessionnaire *mf*; [for brand] dépositaire *mf*; **he acted as my local ~** il agissait en tant qu'agent local; **the firm are sole ~s for Pitkins** la société est agent exclusif de Pitkins; **where's the nearest Jaguar ~?** où est le concessionnaire Jaguar le plus proche? ❑ **election ~** agent *m* électoral; **I'm a free ~** je ne dépends de personne. **-2.** [for actor, sportsman, writer] agent *m*. **-3.** [spy] agent *m*. **-4.** [means] agent *m*, moyen *m*; **by the working of some outside ~** par l'opération de quelque agent extérieur; **her forceful nature turned out to be the ~ of her downfall** son naturel énergique fut aussi la cause OR à l'origine de sa chute. **-5.** CHEM & LING agent *m*.

agentive ['eɪdʒəntɪv] *n* agentif *m*.

Agent Orange *n* agent *m* orange *(défoliant utilisé par les Américains pendant la guerre du Viêtnam)*.

age-old *adj* séculaire, antique.

agglomerate [*vb* ə'glɒməreɪt, *n* & *adj* ə'glɒmərət] ◇ *vt* agglomérer.
◇ *vi* s'agglomérer.
◇ *n* aggloméral *m*.
◇ *adj* aggloméré.

agglomeration [ə,glɒmə'reɪʃn] *n* agglomération *f*.

agglutinate [*vb* ə'gluːtɪneɪt, *adj* ə'gluːtɪnət]
◇ *vt* agglutiner.
◇ *vi* s'agglutiner.
◇ *adj* agglutiné.

agglutination [ə,gluːtɪ'neɪʃn] *n* agglutination *f*.

agglutinative [ə'gluːtɪnətɪv] *adj* agglutinant.

aggrandizement [ə'grændɪzmənt] *n pej* agrandissement *m*; **personal ~** volonté *f* de se pousser en avant.

aggravate ['ægrəveɪt] *vt* **-1.** [worsen - illness, conditions] aggraver; [- situation, problem] aggraver, envenimer; [- quarrel] envenimer; JUR: **~d assault** coups *mpl* et blessures *fpl*; **~d burglary** cambriolage *m* aggravé de coups et blessures. **-2.** [irritate - person] agacer, ennuyer.

aggravating ['ægrəveɪtɪŋ] *adj* **-1.** [worsening - situation, illness, conditions] aggravant. **-2.** [irritating - person, problem] agaçant, exaspérant.

aggravation [,ægrə'veɪʃn] *n* **-1.** [deterioration - of situation, illness, conditions] aggravation *f*; [- of dispute] enveniment *m*. **-2.** [irritation] agacement *m*, exaspération *f*.

aggregate [*n* & *adj* 'ægrɪgət, *vb* 'ægrɪgeɪt]
◇ *n* **-1.** [total] ensemble *m*, total *m*; **in the ~, on ~** dans l'ensemble, globalement; **to win on**

~ SPORT gagner au total des points. -**2.** CONSTR & GEOL agrégat *m*.
◇ *adj* global, total; ~ income revenus *mpl* globaux.
◇ *vt* -**1.** [bring together] rassembler. -**2.** [add up to] s'élever à, se monter à.

aggression [əˈgreʃn] *n* agression *f*.

aggressive [əˈgresɪv] *adj* -**1.** [gen & PSYCH - person, behaviour] agressif. -**2.** MIL [action, weapon] offensif. -**3.** COMM [businessman] combatif, dynamique; [campaign] énergique.

aggressively [əˈgresɪvlɪ] *adv* [behave] agressivement, avec agressivité; [campaign] avec dynamisme.

aggressiveness [əˈgresɪvnɪs] *n* [gen] agressivité *f*; [of businessman] combativité *f*; [of campaign] dynamisme *m*, fougue *f*.

aggressor [əˈgresəʳ] *n* agresseur *m*.

aggrieved [əˈgriːvd] *adj* -**1.** [gen] affligé, chagriné; to feel ~ at OR about sthg être chagriné de OR par qqch. -**2.** JUR lésé.

aggro *inf* [ˈægrəʊ] *n Br (U)* -**1.** [violence, fighting] grabuge *m*, bagarre *f*; **there was a bit of ~ at the pub last night** il y a eu du grabuge OR ça a chauffé au pub hier soir. -**2.** [fuss, bother] histoires *fpl*; **people don't complain, because they don't want any ~** les gens ne se plaignent pas parce qu'ils ne veulent pas d'histoires; **there has been a lot of ~ at work recently** il y a eu pas mal d'histoires au boulot dernièrement.

aghast [əˈgɑːst] *adj* [astounded] interloqué, pantois; [horrified] frappé d'horreur, atterré; **she was ~ at the news** elle était atterrée par la nouvelle; **I stared at him ~** je l'ai regardé, atterrée.

agile [*Br* ˈædʒaɪl, *Am* ˈædʒəl] *adj* -**1.** [person, animal] agile, leste. -**2.** [brain, mind] vif.

agility [əˈdʒɪlətɪ] *n* -**1.** [physical] agilité *f*, souplesse *f*; **to move with great ~** se déplacer avec une grande agilité. -**2.** [mental] vivacité *f*.

Agincourt [ˈædʒɪnkɔːt] *pr n* Azincourt.

aging *etc* [ˈeɪdʒɪŋ] = **ageing**.

agio [ˈædʒɪəʊ] (*pl* agios) *n* agio *m*.

agiotage [ˈædʒətɪdʒ] *n* agiotage *m*.

agitate [ˈædʒɪteɪt] ◇ *vi* POL: **to ~ for/against sthg** faire campagne en faveur de/contre qqch; **they are agitating for better working conditions** ils réclament de meilleures conditions de travail.
◇ *vt* -**1.** [liquid] agiter, remuer. -**2.** [emotionally] agiter, troubler.

agitated [ˈædʒɪteɪtɪd] *adj* agité, troublé; **she was very ~** elle était très agitée OR dans tous ses états; **to become OR to get ~** se mettre dans tous ses états.

agitation [ˌædʒɪˈteɪʃn] *n* -**1.** [emotional] agitation *f*, émoi *m*, trouble *m*; **to be in a state of ~** être dans tous ses états. -**2.** [unrest] agitation *f*, troubles *mpl*; [campaign] campagne *f* mouvementée; **there was a lot of ~ in favour of nuclear disarmament** il y avait un fort mouvement de contestation pour réclamer le désarmement nucléaire. -**3.** [of sea] agitation *f*.

agitator [ˈædʒɪteɪtəʳ] *n* -**1.** POL [person] agitateur *m*, -trice *f*. -**2.** [machine] agitateur *m*.

agitprop [ˈædʒɪtprop] ◇ *n* agit-prop *f inv*.
◇ *comp* [art, theatre] de l'agit-prop.

aglow [əˈgləʊ] *adj* [fire] rougeoyant; [sky] embrasé; **to be ~ with colour** briller de couleurs vives; **his face was ~ with excitement/health** *fig* son visage rayonnait d'émotion/de santé.

AGM (*abbr of* **annual general meeting**) *n Br* AGA *f*.

agnate [ˈægneɪt] ◇ *n* agnat *m*, -e *f*.
◇ *adj* apparenté par les hommes de la famille.

agnostic [ægˈnɒstɪk] ◇ *n* agnostique *mf*.
◇ *adj* agnostique.

agnosticism [ægˈnɒstɪsɪzm] *n* agnosticisme *m*.

ago [əˈgəʊ] *adv*: **they moved here ten years ~** ils ont emménagé ici il y a dix ans; **how long ~ did this happen?** cela c'est produit il y a combien de temps?, il y a combien de temps que cela s'est produit?; **a long time ~, long ~** il y a longtemps; **as long ~ as 1900** en 1900 déjà, dès 1900.

agog *inf* [əˈgɒg] *adj* en émoi; **the children were all ~ (with excitement)** les enfants étaient tout excités; **I was ~ to discover what had happened** je brûlais d'impatience de savoir ce qui s'était passé; **the scandal set the whole town ~** le scandale a mis la ville entière en émoi.

agonize, -ise [ˈægənaɪz] *vi* se tourmenter; **to ~ over OR about a decision** hésiter longuement avant de prendre une décision; **don't ~ over it!** n'y passe pas trop de temps!; **to ~ over how to do sthg** se ronger les sangs OR se tracasser pour savoir comment faire qqch.

agonized [ˈægənaɪzd] *adj* [behaviour, reaction] angoissé, d'angoisse; [cry] déchirant.

agonizing [ˈægənaɪzɪŋ] *adj* [situation] angoissant; [decision] déchirant, angoissant; [pain] atroce; **we had an ~ half-hour** nous avons connu une demi-heure d'angoisse.

agonizingly [ˈægənaɪzɪŋlɪ] *adv* atrocement; **an ~ difficult decision** une décision atrocement difficile.

agony [ˈægənɪ] (*pl* agonies) *n* -**1.** [physical - pain] douleur *f* atroce; [- suffering] souffrance *f* atroce, souffrances *fpl* atroces; **to be in ~** souffrir le martyre; **to cry out in ~** crier de douleur; **it was ~ to stand up** je souffrais le martyre pour me lever ❑ **death ~** agonie *f* (de la mort). -**2.** [emotional, mental] supplice *m*, angoisse *f*; **to be in an ~ of doubt/remorse** être torturé par le doute/le remords; **it was ~ just listening to him** le seul fait de l'écouter était un vrai supplice.

agony aunt *n Br* responsable du courrier du cœur.

agony column *n* courrier *m* du cœur.

agoraphobia [ˌægərəˈfəʊbjə] *n* agoraphobie *f*.

agoraphobic [ˌægərəˈfəʊbɪk] ◇ *adj* qui souffre d'agoraphobie.
◇ *n* personne *f* souffrant d'agoraphobie.

agouti [əˈguːtɪ] (*pl inv* OR **agoutis**) *n* agouti *m*.

AGR (*abbr of* **advanced gas-cooled reactor**) *n* AGR *m*.

agrarian [əˈgreərɪən] ◇ *adj* agraire.
◇ *n* agrarien *m*, -enne *f*.

agree [əˈgriː] ◇ *vi* -**1.** [share same opinion] être d'accord; **I quite ~** je suis tout à fait d'accord (avec vous); **don't you ~?** n'êtes-vous pas d'accord?; **to ~ about sthg** être d'accord sur qqch; **I ~ about going on a holiday** je suis d'accord pour partir en vacances; **I think we ~ on OR about the basic facts** je pense que nous sommes d'accord sur l'essentiel; **to ~ with sb** être d'accord avec OR être du même avis que qqn; **I ~ with you about the decor** je suis d'accord avec vous pour ce qui est du décor; **they ~ with me that it's a disgrace** ils trouvent comme moi que c'est une honte; **I ~ with you entirely** je suis parfaitement d'accord OR en plein accord avec vous; **I couldn't ~ with you more** je partage entièrement votre avis. -**2.** [be in favour] être d'accord; **I don't ~ with censorship** je suis contre OR je n'admets pas la censure; **I don't ~ with people smoking in public places** je ne suis pas d'accord pour que les gens fument dans les lieux publics. -**3.** [assent] consentir, donner son adhésion; **to ~ to a proposal** donner son adhésion à OR accepter une proposition; **to ~ to sb's request** consentir à la requête de qqn; **her parents have ~d to her going abroad** ses parents ont consenti à ce qu'elle aille OR sont d'accord pour qu'elle aille à l'étranger; **they ~d to share the cost** ils se sont mis d'accord pour partager les frais; **they ~d to take a taxi** ils ont décidé d'un commun accord de prendre un taxi. -**4.** [reach agreement] se mettre d'accord; **the doctors couldn't ~ about the best treatment** les médecins n'arrivaient pas à se mettre d'accord sur le traitement à suivre; **to ~ on OR upon a date** convenir d'une date; **they ~d on Italy for the honeymoon** ils se sont mis d'accord sur l'Italie pour la lune de miel; **that was the price we ~d (on)** c'était le prix dont nous avions convenu OR sur lequel nous nous étions mis d'accord. -**5.** [correspond - account, estimate] concorder; **your statement doesn't ~ with hers** ta version OR ta déclaration ne correspond pas à la sienne, vos deux versions ne concordent pas. -**6.** [be suitable]: **the climate here ~s with me** le climat d'ici me réussit OR me convient très bien; **rich food doesn't ~ with me** la nourriture riche ne me réussit pas. -**7.** GRAMM s'accorder; **the verb ~s with the subject** le verbe s'accorde avec le sujet.
◇ *vt* -**1.** [share opinion]: **to ~ that** être d'accord avec le fait que; **we all ~ that he's innocent** nous sommes tous d'accord pour dire qu'il est innocent, nous sommes tous d'avis qu'il est innocent; **everyone ~s that the party was a success** tout le monde s'accorde à reconnaître que OR de l'avis de tous la fête était un succès; **I don't ~ that the police should be armed** je ne suis pas d'accord pour que la police soit armée. -**2.** [consent]: **to ~ to do sthg** accepter de OR consentir à faire qqch. -**3.** [admit] admettre, reconnaître; **they ~d that they had made a mistake** ils ont reconnu OR convenu qu'ils avaient fait une faute. -**4.** [reach agreement on] convenir de; **to ~ a date** convenir d'une date; **it was ~d to continue the next day** il a été convenu que l'on poursuivrait le lendemain; **we ~d to differ** nous sommes restés chacun sur notre position; **it was ~d that the money should be invested** il a été convenu que l'argent serait investi; **to ~ a price** se mettre d'accord sur un prix; **the budget has been ~d** le budget a été adopté; **unless otherwise ~d** JUR sauf accord contraire. -**5.** [accept - statement, plan] accepter.

agreeable [əˈgrɪəbl] *adj* -**1.** [pleasant - situation] plaisant, agréable; [- person] agréable. -**2.** [willing] consentant; **to be ~ to doing sthg** accepter de OR bien vouloir faire qqch; **I am quite ~ to his OR him going** je veux bien OR je suis d'accord pour qu'il y aille; **are you ~ to the proposal?** consentez-vous à la proposition?, êtes-vous d'accord avec la proposition?; **if you are ~** si cela vous convient, si vous êtes d'accord. -**3.** [acceptable] acceptable, satisfaisant; **I hope the terms are ~ to you** j'espère que les conditions vous conviennent.

agreeably [əˈgrɪəblɪ] *adv* agréablement; **I was ~ surprised** je fus agréablement surpris.

agreed [əˈgriːd] ◇ *adj* -**1.** [in agreement] d'accord; **is everyone ~?** est-ce que tout le monde est d'accord?; **it's ~ that we leave on Friday** il est entendu OR convenu que nous partons vendredi; **we are ~ on OR about the conditions** nous sommes d'accord sur les conditions. -**2.** [fixed -time, place, price] convenu; **as ~** comme convenu; **at the ~ time** à l'heure convenue.
◇ *interj*: ~! (c'est) d'accord OR entendu!

agreement [əˈgriːmənt] *n* -**1.** accord *m*; **to be in ~ with sb about sthg** être d'accord avec qqn sur qqch OR au sujet de qqch; **we are both in ~ on this point** nous sommes tous les deux d'accord OR du même avis à ce sujet; **to reach ~** parvenir à un accord; **by ~ with the management** en accord avec la direction. -**2.** COMM & POL accord *m*; **under the (terms of the) ~** selon les termes de l'accord; **to come to an ~** tomber d'accord, parvenir à un accord; **to break an ~** rompre un accord. -**3.** GRAMM accord *m*.

agribusiness [ˈægrɪˌbɪznɪs] *n (U)* agro-industries *fpl*.

agricultural [ˌægrɪˈkʌltʃərəl] *adj* [produce, machinery, land, society] agricole; [expert] agronome; [college] d'agriculture, agricole.

agricultural engineer *n* ingénieur *m* agronome.

agriculturalist [ˌægrɪˈkʌltʃərəlɪst] *n* [specialist] agronome *mf*; [farmer] agriculteur *m*, -trice *f*.

agricultural show *n* [national] salon *m* de l'agriculture; [local] foire *f* agricole.

agriculture [ˈægrɪkʌltʃəʳ] *n* agriculture *f*.

Agrigento [ˌægrɪˈdʒentəʊ] *pr n* Agrigente.

Agrippa [əˈgrɪpə] *pr n* Agrippa.

Agrippina [ˌægrɪˈpiːnə] *pr n* Agrippine.

agronomist [əˈgrɒnəmɪst] *n* agronome *mf*.

agronomy [ə'grɒnəmɪ] *n* agronomie *f*.

aground [ə'graʊnd] ◇ *adj* NAUT échoué; to be ~ toucher le fond, échouer.
◇ *adv*: to run OR to go ~ s'échouer.

ague ['eɪgju:] *n arch* fièvre *f*.

ah [ɑ:] *interj*: ~! ah!

aha [ɑ:'hɑ:] *interj*: ~! ah, ah!, tiens!

ahead [ə'hed] *adv* -**1.** [in space] en avant, devant; the road ~ la route devant nous/eux *etc*; there's a crossroads about half a mile ~ il y a un croisement à environ 800 m (d'ici); go/drive on ~ and I'll catch you up vas-y OR pars en avant, je te rattraperai; to push OR press ~ with a project poursuivre un projet. -**2.** [in time] à l'avance; the years ~ les années à venir; what lies ~? qu'est-ce qui nous attend?; looking ~ to the future en pensant à l'avenir; to plan ~ faire des projets; we must think ~ nous devons prévoir. -**3.** [in competition, race] en avance; three lengths/five points ~ trois longueurs/cinq points d'avance; it's better to quit while you're ~ *fig* mieux vaut te retirer du jeu pendant que tu as l'avantage.
◆ **ahead of** *prep phr* -**1.** [in front of] devant; there were ten people ~ of us in the queue il y avait dix personnes devant nous dans la queue. -**2.** [in time]: he arrived 10 minutes ~ of me il est arrivé 10 minutes avant moi; to finish ~ of schedule terminer plus tôt que prévu OR en avance; the rest of the team are two months ~ of us les autres membres de l'équipe ont deux mois d'avance sur nous; French time is one hour ~ of British time la France a une heure d'avance sur la Grande-Bretagne; to arrive ~ of time arriver en avance OR avant l'heure; to be ~ of one's time *fig* être en avance sur son époque. -**3.** [in competition, race]: he is five points ~ of his nearest rival il a cinq points d'avance sur son rival le plus proche, il devance son rival le plus proche de cinq points.

ahem [ə'hem] *interj*: ~! hum!

ahoy [ə'hɔɪ] *interj*: ~! ohé!, holà!; ship ~! ohé du navire!

AI ◇ *pr n* (*abbr of* Amnesty International) AI.
◇ *n* -**1.** (*abbr of* artificial intelligence) IA *f*. -**2.** *abbr of* artificial insemination.

AIB (*abbr of* Accident Investigation Bureau) *pr n commission d'enquête sur les accidents en Grande-Bretagne*.

aid [eɪd] ◇ *n* -**1.** [help, assistance] aide *f*; with the ~ of half a dozen helpers avec l'aide d'une demi-douzaine d'assistants; I managed to open the tin with the ~ of a screwdriver à l'aide d'un tournevis, j'ai réussi à ouvrir la boîte; to come to sb's ~ venir à l'aide de qqn; to go to the ~ of sb se porter au secours de OR porter secours à qqn. -**2.** POL aide *f*; food ~ aide alimentaire; overseas ~ aide au tiers-monde; the government gives ~ to depressed areas le gouvernement octroie des aides aux régions en déclin. -**3.** [helpful equipment] aide *f*, support *m*; teaching ~s supports OR aides pédagogiques; visual ~s supports visuels. -**4.** [assistant] aide *mf*, assistant *m*, -e *f*. -**5.** [for climber] piton *m*.
◇ *vt* -**1.** [help - person] aider, venir en aide à; [- financially] aider, secourir; to ~ sb with sthg aider qqn pour qqch; I refuse to ~ you in any illegal enterprise je refuse de vous aider dans une quelconque entreprise illicite; they ~ed one another ils se sont entraidés, ils se sont aidés les uns les autres. -**2.** [give support to - region, industry] aider, soutenir. -**3.** [encourage - development, understanding] contribuer à. -**4.** JUR: to ~ and abet sb être (le) complice de qqn; ~ed and abetted by her sister *fig* avec la complicité de sa sœur.
◆ **in aid of** *prep phr*: a collection in ~ of the homeless une collecte au profit des sans-abri; what are all these levers in ~ of? *inf Br fig* à quoi servent tous ces leviers?; what are the cakes in ~ of? les gâteaux sont en l'honneur de quoi?

AID ◇ *n* (*abbr of* artificial insemination by donor) IAD *f*.
◇ *pr n* (*abbr of* Agency for International Development) AID *f*.

aid climbing *n* escalade *f* artificielle.

aide [eɪd] *n* aide *mf*, assistant *m*, -e *f*.

-aided [eɪdɪd] *in cpds* -**1.** COMPUT assisté par; computer~ design conception *f* assistée par ordinateur, CAO *f*. -**2.** [financially]: grant~ [student] boursier; [industry] subventionné; [school] qui reçoit une subvention.

aide-de-camp [eɪddə'kɑ̃:] (*pl* aides-de-camp [ˌeɪdz-]) *n* aide *m* de camp.

aide-mémoire [ˌeɪdmem'wɑ:] (*pl* aides-mémoire ['eɪdz-]) *n* aide-mémoire *m inv*.

Aids, AIDS [eɪdz] (*abbr of* acquired immune deficiency syndrome) ◇ *n* sida *m*, SIDA *m*, Sida *m*.
◇ *comp* [sufferer] du sida; [clinic] pour sidéens *offic*; ~ research recherche sur le sida; ~ specialist sidologue *mf*; ~ patient sidéen *m*, -enne *f*; the ~ virus le virus du sida.

AIH (*abbr of* artificial insemination by husband) *n* IAC *f*.

aikido [aɪ'ki:dəʊ] *n* aïkido *m*.

ail [eɪl] ◇ *vt dial* OR *lit*: what ~s you? qu'avez-vous?, quelle mouche vous a piqué?
◇ *vi* être souffrant.

aileron ['eɪlərɒn] *n* aileron *m*.

ailing ['eɪlɪŋ] *adj* [person] souffrant, en mauvaise santé; [economy, industry] malade.

ailment ['eɪlmənt] *n* mal *m*, affection *f*; she has all kinds of ~s elle souffre de toutes sortes de maux.

aim [eɪm] ◇ *n* -**1.** [intention, purpose] but *m*, dessein *m*, objectif *m*; she came to the meeting with the ~ of causing trouble elle est venue à la réunion dans le but de faire des histoires; his ~ is to get rich quickly il a pour but OR il s'est donné comme but de s'enrichir rapidement; her ultimate ~ is to beat the world record son but final est de battre le record du monde; her ~ in going to London was to find a job elle était allée à Londres dans le but de trouver du travail; you need an ~ in life il faut un but dans la vie. -**2.** [with weapon]: to take ~ viser; to take ~ at sthg/sb viser qqch/qqn; to have a good ~ bien viser; your ~ isn't very good vous ne visez pas très bien; to miss one's ~ manquer la cible OR son but.
◇ *vt* -**1.** [gun] braquer; [missile] pointer; [stone] lancer; [blow] allonger, décocher; [kick] donner; he ~ed his gun at the man's head il a braqué son pistolet sur la tête de l'homme; he was ~ing stones at the tree il lançait des cailloux sur l'arbre; there are missiles ~ed at all the major cities des missiles ennemis sont pointés sur toutes les grandes villes; the man ~ed a kick at the dog l'homme donna un coup de pied au chien. -**2.** *fig* [criticism, product, programme] destiner; was that remark ~ed at me? est-ce que cette remarque m'était destinée?; the programme is ~ed at a teenage audience l'émission est destinée à un public d'adolescents.
◇ *vi* -**1.** [take aim]: to ~ at OR for sthg viser qqch; he ~ed at the target il visait la cible; she ~ed at OR for the post, but missed elle a visé le poteau, mais elle l'a manqué. -**2.** [have as goal]: she's ~ing to become a millionaire by the age of 30 son but, c'est d'être millionnaire à 30 ans; we ~ to arrive before midnight nous avons l'intention OR nous nous sommes fixés d'arriver avant minuit; he's ~ing at quick promotion il vise une promotion rapide; we're ~ing for Rouen before stopping nous nous sommes fixé Rouen comme but avant de nous arrêter; to ~ high viser haut.

aimless ['eɪmlɪs] *adj* [person] sans but, désœuvré; [life] sans but; [occupation, task] sans objet, futile.

aimlessly ['eɪmlɪslɪ] *adv* [walk around] sans but; [stand around] sans trop savoir quoi faire; he wandered ~ through the streets il errait dans les rues.

ain't *inf* [eɪnt] = **am not, is not, are not, has not, have not**.

Aintree ['eɪntrɪ] *pr n champ de courses en Grande-Bretagne*.

air [eər] ◇ *n* -**1.** [gen & PHYS] air *m*; sea ~ air de la mer, air marin; I need some fresh ~ j'ai besoin de prendre l'air; I went out for a breath of (fresh) ~ je suis sorti prendre l'air; to take the ~ *lit* prendre le frais; the divers came up for ~ les plongeurs sont remontés à la surface pour respirer; I need a change of ~ *fig* j'ai besoin de changer d'air ❑ Air Quality Index indice *m* de pollution de l'air. -**2.** [sky] air *m*, ciel *m*; the smoke rose into the ~ la fumée s'éleva vers le ciel; to throw sthg up into the ~ lancer qqch en l'air; seen from the ~, the fields looked like a chessboard vus d'avion, les champs ressemblaient à un échiquier; to take to the ~ [bird] s'envoler; [plane] décoller. -**3.** AERON: to travel by ~ voyager par avion; mail that is sent by ~ le courrier (envoyé) par avion. -**4.** RADIO & TV: to be on (the) ~ [person] avoir OR être à l'antenne; [programme] être à l'antenne; [station] émettre; to go on the ~ [person] passer à l'antenne; [programme] passer à l'antenne, être diffusé; you're on the ~ vous avez l'antenne; to go off the ~ [person] rendre l'antenne; [programme] se terminer; [station] cesser d'émettre. -**5.** [manner, atmosphere] air *m*; there is an ~ of mystery about her elle a un air mystérieux; she showed him the letter with a triumphant ~ elle lui montra la lettre d'un air triomphant; she smiled with a knowing ~ elle sourit d'un air entendu. -**6.** MUS air *m*.
◇ *vt* -**1.** [linen, bed, room] aérer. -**2.** [express - opinion, grievance] exprimer, faire connaître; [- suggestion, idea] exprimer, avancer. -**3.** *Am* RADIO & TV diffuser.
◇ *comp* [piracy] aérien; [travel, traveller] par avion.
◆ **airs** *npl*: to put on OR to give o.s. ~s se donner de grands airs; ~s and graces *Br* minauderies *fpl*.
◆ **in the air** *adv phr*: there's a rumour in the ~ that they're going to sell le bruit court qu'ils vont vendre; there's something in the ~ il se trame quelque chose; our holiday plans are still (up) in the ~ nos projets de vacances sont encore assez vagues; the project is still very much (up) in the ~ le projet n'est encore qu'à l'état d'ébauche OR est encore vague.

air alert *n* alerte *f* aérienne.

air bag *n* AUT air-bag *m*.

airbase ['eəbeɪs] *n* base *f* aérienne.

airbed ['eəbed] *n* matelas *m* pneumatique.

airborne ['eəbɔ:n] *adj* -**1.** [plane] en vol; to become ~ décoller. -**2.** [troops, division, regiment] aéroporté.

airbrake ['eəbreɪk] *n* AUT frein *m* à air comprimé; AERON aérofrein *m*, frein *m* aérodynamique.

air brick *n* brique *f* creuse.

airbrush ['eəbrʌʃ] ◇ *n* pistolet *m (pour peindre)*.
◇ *vt* peindre au pistolet.

air bubble *n* [in wallpaper, liquid] bulle *f* d'air; [in plastic, metal] soufflure *f*.

Airbus® ['eəbʌs] *n* Airbus® *m*.

air chamber *n* chambre *f* à air.

air chief marshal *n Br* général *m* de corps aérien.

air commodore *n Br* colonel *m* de l'armée de l'air.

air-conditioned *adj* [room, train] climatisé; fully ~ entièrement climatisé.

air-conditioner *n* climatiseur *m*.

air-conditioning *n* climatisation *f*.

air-cooled [-ku:ld] *adj* -**1.** [engine] à refroidissement par air. -**2.** *Am* [room] climatisé.

air corridor *n* couloir *m* aérien.

air cover *n* couverture *f* aérienne.

aircraft ['eəkrɑ:ft] (*pl inv*) *n* avion *m*.

aircraft carrier *n* porte-avions *m inv*.

aircraft(s)man ['eəkrɑːft(s)mən] (*pl* aircraft(s)men [-mən]) *n Br* MIL soldat *m* de deuxième classe *(dans l'armée de l'air)*.
aircraft(s)woman ['eəkrɑːft(s),wʊmən] (*pl* aircraft(s)women [-,wɪmɪn]) *n Br* MIL femme *f* soldat de deuxième classe *(dans l'armée de l'air)*.
aircrew ['eəkruː] *n* équipage *m (d'avion)*.
air current *n* courant *m* atmosphérique.
air curtain *n* store *m* d'air *(chaud ou froid)*.
air cushion *n* [gen] coussin *m* pneumatique; TECH coussin *m* OR matelas *m* d'air.
air cylinder *n* cylindre *m* à air comprimé.
airdrome ['eədrəʊm] *Am* = **aerodrome**.
airdrop ['eədrɒp] (*pt* & *pp* airdropped, *cont* airdropping) ◇ *n* parachutage *m*.
◇ *vt* parachuter.
air-dry *vt* sécher à l'air.
Airedale ['eədeɪl] *n*: ~ (terrier) airedale *m*, airedale-terrier *m*.
airfare ['eəfeəʳ] *n* prix *m* du billet (d'avion), tarif *m* aérien.
air ferry *n* avion *m* transbordeur.
airfield ['eəfiːld] *n* terrain *m* d'aviation, (petit) aérodrome *m*.
airfoil ['eəfɔɪl] *n Am* surface *f* portante, plan *m* de sustentation.
air force *n* armée *f* de l'air; ~ base base *f* aérienne.
airframe ['eəfreɪm] *n* cellule *f* (d'avion).
airfreight ['eəfreɪt] *n* [cargo] fret *m* aérien; [transport] transport *m* aérien; to send sthg by ~ expédier qqch par voie aérienne OR par avion.
airgun ['eəgʌn] *n* [rifle] carabine *f* OR fusil *m* à air comprimé; [pistol] pistolet *m* à air comprimé.
airhead *inf* ['eəhed] *n* taré *m*, -e *f*.
airhole ['eəhəʊl] *n* trou *m* d'aération.
airhostess ['eə,həʊstɪs] *n* hôtesse *f* de l'air.
airily ['eərəlɪ] *adv* avec désinvolture.
airiness ['eərɪnɪs] *n* -**1.** [of room] aération *f*, (bonne) ventilation *f*. -**2.** [of tone, manner] désinvolture *f*.
airing ['eərɪŋ] *n* -**1.** [of linen, room] aération *f*; this room needs an ~ cette chambre a besoin d'être aérée; give the sheets a good ~ secouez bien les draps. -**2.** *fig*: to give an idea an ~ agiter une idée, mettre une idée sur le tapis.
airing cupboard *n placard chauffé faisant office de sèche-linge*.
airlane ['eəleɪn] *n* couloir *m* aérien OR de navigation aérienne.
airless ['eəlɪs] *adj* -**1.** [room] qui manque d'air, qui sent le renfermé. -**2.** [weather] lourd.
air letter *n* aérogramme *m*.
airlift ['eəlɪft] ◇ *n* pont *m* aérien.
◇ *vt* [passengers, troops - out] évacuer par pont aérien; [- in] faire entrer par pont aérien; [supplies, cargo] transporter par pont aérien.
airline ['eəlaɪn] *n* -**1.** AERON ligne *f* aérienne. -**2.** [for compressed air] tuyau *m* d'air.
airliner ['eəlaɪnəʳ] *n* avion *m* de ligne.
airlock ['eəlɒk] *n* -**1.** [in spacecraft, submarine] sas *m*. -**2.** [in pipe] poche *f* OR bulle *f* d'air.
airmail ['eəmeɪl] ◇ *n* poste *f* aérienne; 'by ~' [on envelope] 'par avion'.
◇ *comp* [letter, parcel] par avion; ~ paper papier *m* pelure.
◇ *vt* expédier par avion.
airman ['eəmən] (*pl* airmen [-mən]) *n* -**1.** [gen] aviateur *m*. -**2.** *Am* MIL soldat *m* de première classe.
air marshal *n* général *m* de l'armée de l'air.
air mass *n* masse *f* d'air.
air mattress *n* matelas *m* pneumatique.
airmobile ['eəmə,biːl] *adj Am* aéroporté.
air pistol *n* pistolet *m* à air comprimé.
airplane ['eərpleɪn] *Am* = **aeroplane**.
airplay ['eəpleɪ] *n*: that record is getting a lot of ~ ce disque passe souvent OR on entend souvent ce disque à la radio.
air pocket *n* [affecting plane] trou *m* d'air; [in pipe] poche *f* d'air.
airport ['eəpɔːt] *n* aéroport *m*.
air pressure *n* pression *f* atmosphérique.
air pump *n* compresseur *m*, pompe *f* à air.
air raid *n* attaque *f* aérienne, raid *m* aérien.
air-raid shelter *n* abri *m* antiaérien.
air-raid warden *n* préposé *m*, -e *f* à la défense passive.
air-raid warning *n* alerte *f* antiaérienne.
air rifle *n* carabine *f* à air comprimé.
airscrew ['eəskruː] *n Br* hélice *f* (d'avion).
air-sea rescue *n* sauvetage *m* en mer *(par hélicoptère)*.
airship ['eəʃɪp] *n* dirigeable *m*.
air show *n* -**1.** COMM [exhibition] salon *m* de l'aéronautique. -**2.** [display] meeting *m* aérien.
airsick ['eəsɪk] *adj*: to be OR to get ~ avoir le mal de l'air.
airsickness ['eə,sɪknɪs] *n* mal *m* de l'air.
airsock ['eəsɒk] *n* manche *f* à air.
airspace ['eəspeɪs] *n* espace *m* aérien.
airstream ['eəstriːm] *n* courant *m* atmosphérique.
airstrike ['eəstraɪk] *n* raid *m* aérien, attaque *f* aérienne.
airstrip ['eəstrɪp] *n* terrain *m* OR piste *f* d'atterrissage.
air taxi *n* avion-taxi *m*.
air terminal *n* aérogare *f*.
airtight ['eətaɪt] *adj* hermétique, étanche (à l'air); I don't think his argument is completely ~ *fig* je ne crois pas que son argument soit totalement irréfutable.
airtime ['eətaɪm] *n* RADIO & TV: that record is getting a lot of ~ on entend souvent ce disque à la radio; the subject didn't get much ~ on n'a pas consacré beaucoup de temps au sujet pendant l'émission.
air-to-air *adj* MIL air-air *(inv)*, avion-avion *(inv)*.
air-to-surface *adj* MIL air-sol *(inv)*.
air-traffic control *n* contrôle *m* du trafic aérien.
air-traffic controller *n* contrôleur *m*, -euse *f* du trafic aérien, aiguilleur *m* du ciel.
air valve *n* soupape *f*.
airvent ['eəvent] *n* prise *f* d'air.
air vice-marshal *n Br* général *m* de brigade aérienne.
airwaves ['eəweɪvz] *npl* ondes *fpl* (hertziennes); on the ~ sur les ondes, à la radio.
airway ['eəweɪ] *n* -**1.** AERON [route] voie *f* aérienne; [company] ligne *f* aérienne. -**2.** MED voies *fpl* respiratoires; make sure the ~s aren't blocked assurez-vous que les voies respiratoires ne sont pas obstruées. -**3.** [shaft] conduit *m* d'air.
airwoman ['eə,wʊmən] (*pl* airwomen [-,wɪmɪn]) *n* -**1.** [gen] aviatrice *f*. -**2.** MIL (femme *f*) auxiliaire *f (de l'armée de l'air)*.
airworthy ['eə,wɜːðɪ] *adj* en état de navigation.
airy ['eərɪ] (*compar* airier, *superl* airiest) *adj* -**1.** [room] bien aéré, clair. -**2.** *fig* [casual - manner] insouciant, désinvolte; [- ideas, plans, promises] en l'air.
airy-fairy *inf adj Br* [person, notion] farfelu.
aisle [aɪl] *n* -**1.** [in church] bas-côté *m*, nef *f* latérale; her father led her up the ~ c'est son père qui l'a menée à l'autel; to walk up OR down the ~ [before ceremony] entrer dans l'église; [after ceremony] sortir de l'église. -**2.** [in cinema, supermarket] allée *f*; [on train, aeroplane] couloir *m* (central).
aitch [eɪtʃ] *n* H *m inv*, h *m inv*; he drops his ~es il ne prononce pas les h.
aitchbone ['eɪtʃbəʊn] *n* culotte *f (de bœuf)*.
ajar [ə'dʒɑːʳ] ◇ *adj* [door, window] entrouvert, entrebâillé.
◇ *adv*: the door stood ~ la porte est restée entrouverte.
Ajax ['eɪdʒæks] *pr n* Ajax.
AK *written abbr of* Alaska.
aka (*abbr of* also known as) *adv* alias, dit.
akimbo [ə'kɪmbəʊ] *adv*: with arms ~ les mains OR poings sur les hanches.
akin [ə'kɪn] *adj*: ~ to [like] qui ressemble à, qui tient de; [related to] apparenté à.
AL *written abbr of* Alabama.
Alabama [,ælə'bæmə] *pr n* Alabama *m*; in ~ dans l'Alabama.
alabaster [,ælə'bɑːstəʳ] ◇ *n* albâtre *m*.
◇ *comp* d'albâtre.
alack [ə'læk] *interj arch*: ~! hélas!
alacrity [ə'lækrətɪ] *n fml* empressement *m*; with great ~ avec grand empressement.
Aladdin [ə'lædɪn] *pr n* Aladin; '~, or the Wonderful Lamp' 'Aladin, ou la lampe merveilleuse'.
alalia [æ'leɪlɪə] *n* aphasie *f*.
Alamo ['æləməʊ] *pr n*: the ~ [fort] Fort Alamo; [battle] la bataille de Fort Alamo.

THE ALAMO:
Fort situé dans le Texas où, en 1836, pendant la guerre d'Indépendance de cet État contre le Mexique, une poignée d'Américains, parmi lesquels Davy Crockett, résistèrent jusqu'à la mort à l'assaut d'une troupe mexicaine. «Remember the Alamo» devint le cri de ralliement des Texans au moment de l'indépendance de leur État.

à la mode [ɑːlɑː'məʊd] *adj Am* [with ice cream] (servi) avec de la crème glacée.
alarm [ə'lɑːm] ◇ *n* -**1.** [warning] alarme *f*, alerte *f*; to sound OR to raise the ~ donner l'alarme OR l'alerte OR l'éveil. -**2.** [for fire, burglary] sonnette *f* OR sonnerie *f* d'alarme. -**3.** [anxiety] inquiétude *f*, alarme *f*; the news caused them some ~ la nouvelle leur a causé une certaine inquiétude; there is no cause for ~ il n'y a aucune raison de s'alarmer; the government viewed events with increasing ~ le gouvernement s'est montré de plus en plus inquiet face à ces événements. -**4.** = **alarm clock**.
◇ *comp* [signal] d'alarme; ~ bell sonnerie *f* d'alarme; to set (the) ~ bells ringing *fig* donner l'alerte; ~ call [to wake sleeper] réveil *m* téléphonique.
◇ *vt* -**1.** [frighten, worry - person] alarmer, faire peur à; [- animal] effaroucher, faire peur à; I don't want to ~ you unduly je ne veux pas vous alarmer sans raison. -**2.** [warn] alerter.
alarm clock *n* réveil *m*, réveille-matin *m inv*; he set the ~ for eight o'clock il a mis le réveil à sonner à 8 h OR pour 8 h.
alarmed [ə'lɑːmd] *adj* -**1.** [anxious] inquiet. -**2.** [vehicle, building] équipé d'une alarme; don't be ~ ne vous alarmez OR effrayez pas; to become ~ [person] s'alarmer; [animal] s'effaroucher, prendre peur.
alarming [ə'lɑːmɪŋ] *adj* alarmant.
alarmingly [ə'lɑːmɪŋlɪ] *adv* d'une manière alarmante.
alarmist [ə'lɑːmɪst] ◇ *adj* alarmiste.
◇ *n* alarmiste *mf*.
alas [ə'læs] *interj*: ~! hélas!
Alaska [ə'læskə] *pr n* Alaska *m*; in ~ en Alaska; the ~ Highway la route de l'Alaska.
Alaskan [ə'læskən] ◇ *n* habitant *m*, -e *f* de l'Alaska.
◇ *adj* de l'Alaska.
Alaskan pipeline *n*: the ~ *oléoduc traversant l'Alaska*.
Alaska Range *pr n*: the ~ la chaîne de l'Alaska.
alb [ælb] *n* aube *f (d'un prêtre)*.
Albania [æl'beɪnjə] *pr n* Albanie *f*; in ~ en Albanie.
Albanian [æl'beɪnjən] ◇ *n* -**1.** [person] Albanais *m*, -e *f*. -**2.** LING albanais *m*.
◇ *adj* albanais.
albatross ['ælbətrɒs] *n* -**1.** ZOOL & SPORT albatros *m*. -**2.** *fig* [handicap] boulet *m*; their past was an ~ round their necks ils traînaient leur passé comme un boulet.

albeit [ɔːl'biːɪt] *conj* bien que, encore que, quoique; an impressive, ~ flawed work of art une œuvre impressionnante bien qu'imparfaite OR quoiqu'imparfaite; we managed, ~ with great difficulty nous y sommes arrivés, quoiqu'avec grande difficulté.

Albert ['ælbət] *pr n*: the ~ Hall *salle de concert à Londres*; the ~ Memorial *monument à Londres érigé en l'honneur du prince Albert.*

THE ALBERT HALL:
Grande salle londonienne accueillant concerts et manifestations diverses, y compris sportives; elle a été nommée ainsi en l'honneur du prince Albert, époux de la reine Victoria.

Alberta [æl'bɜːtə] *pr n* Alberta *m*; in ~ dans l'Alberta.

Albigensian [,ælbɪ'dʒensɪən] ◇ *n* Albigeois *m*, -e *f*.
◇ *adj* albigeois; the ~ crusade la croisade des Albigeois.

albinism ['ælbɪnɪzm] *n* albinisme *m*.

albino [æl'biːnəʊ] *n* albinos *mf*.

Albion ['ælbjən] *pr n* Albion.

album ['ælbəm] *n* [book, LP] album *m*; photograph ~ album photo.

albumen ['ælbjʊmɪn] *n* -**1.** [egg white] albumen *m*, blanc *m* de l'œuf. -**2.** = **albumin**.

albumin ['ælbjʊmɪn] *n* albumine *f*.

albuminous [æl'bjuːmɪnəs] *adj* albumineux.

alchemist ['ælkəmɪst] *n* alchimiste *m*.

alchemy ['ælkəmɪ] *n* alchimie *f*.

Alcibiades [,ælsɪ'baɪədiːz] *pr n* Alcibiade.

alcohol ['ælkəhɒl] *n* alcool *m*.

alcoholic [,ælkə'hɒlɪk] ◇ *adj* [drink] alcoolisé; [person] alcoolique.
◇ *n* alcoolique *mf*.

Alcoholics Anonymous *pr n* Alcooliques *mpl* anonymes, ligue *f* antialcoolique.

alcoholism ['ælkəhɒlɪzm] *n* alcoolisme *m*.

alcove ['ælkəʊv] *n* [in room] alcôve *f*; [in wall] niche *f*; [in garden] tonnelle *f*.

aldehyde ['ældɪhaɪd] *n* aldéhyde *m*.

al dente [æl'dentɪ] *adj* al dente *(inv)*.

alder ['ɔːldəʳ] *n* aulne *m*, aune *m*.

alderman ['ɔːldəmən] (*pl* aldermen [-mən]) *n* -**1.** ADMIN alderman *m*, conseiller *m* municipal. -**2.** HIST ≃ échevin *m*.

ALDERMAN:
Ce mot désigne un haut magistrat de la City à Londres; jusqu'en 1974, il désignait également un conseiller municipal (sens qu'il a conservé aux États-Unis et au Canada).

Aldermaston ['ɔːldə,mɑːstən] *pr n village dans le Berkshire où se trouve l'agence de recherche sur l'armement nucléaire; il a été le siège de nombreuses manifestations antinucléaires (les 'Aldermaston marches').*

Alderney ['ɔːldənɪ] *pr n* Aurigny; ~ (cow) vache *f* d'Aurigny.

ale [eɪl] *n* bière *f (anglaise)*, ale *f*.

aleatoric [,ælɪə'tɒrɪk] *adj* aléatoire.

aleatory ['eɪlɪətrɪ] *adj* aléatoire.

alehouse ['eɪlhaʊs, *pl* -haʊzɪz] *n arch* taverne *f*.

Aleppo [ə'lepəʊ] *pr n* Alep.

alert [ə'lɜːt] ◇ *n* alerte *f*; to give the ~ donner l'alerte; to be on the ~ [gen] être sur le qui-vive; MIL être en état d'alerte; the sentries were told to be on the ~ for an attack les sentinelles avaient ordre de se tenir prêtes en cas d'attaque.
◇ *adj* -**1.** [vigilant] vigilant, sur le qui-vive; you should be ~ to the possible dangers soyez vigilants quant aux éventuels dangers. -**2.** [lively - child, mind] vif, éveillé.
◇ *vt* alerter, donner l'alerte à; the public should be ~ed to these dangers on devrait attirer l'attention du public sur ces dangers, on devrait sensibiliser l'opinion publique à ces dangers.

alertness [ə'lɜːtnɪs] *n* -**1.** [vigilance] vigilance *f*. -**2.** [liveliness] vivacité *f*, esprit *m* éveillé.

Aleutian Islands [ə'luːʃjən-] *pl pr n*: the ~ les îles *fpl* Aléoutiennes ; in the ~ aux îles Aléoutiennes.

A level (*abbr of* advanced level) *n* *Br* SCH: ~s, ~ exams ≃ baccalauréat *m*; he teaches ~ physics ≃ il est professeur de physique en terminale; to take one's ~s ≃ passer son bac.

A LEVEL:
Cet examen, qui ouvre l'accès aux études supérieures en Grande-Bretagne, est beaucoup plus spécialisé que le baccalauréat français; il ne comprend que deux ou trois matières (exceptionnellement quatre). D'autre part, les mentions sont très importantes pour pouvoir choisir l'université où l'on souhaite faire ses études.

Alexander [,ælɪg'zɑːndəʳ] *pr n*: ~ the Great Alexandre le Grand.

Alexandra Palace [,ælɪg'zɑːndrə-] *pr n salle d'exposition et de concert de Londres.*

ALEXANDRA PALACE:
Cet édifice de style victorien, situé à Alexandra Park au nord de Londres, abritait autrefois les studios de télévision de la BBC. C'est maintenant un centre d'expositions et de loisirs.

Alexandria [,ælɪg'zɑːndrɪə] *pr n* Alexandrie.

alexandrine [,ælɪg'zændraɪn] ◇ *adj* alexandrin.
◇ *n* alexandrin *m*.

alexia [ə'leksɪə] *n* alexie *f*, cécité *f* verbale.

alfalfa [æl'fælfə] *n* luzerne *f*.

Alf Garnett [,ælf'gɑːnɪt] *pr n personnage comique d'une série télévisée anglaise, stéréotype de l'ouvrier réactionnaire, raciste et sexiste.*

Alfred ['ælfrɪd] *pr n* Alfred; ~ the Great Alfred le Grand.

alfresco [æl'freskəʊ] *adj* & *adv* en plein air.

algae ['ældʒiː] *npl* algues *fpl*.

Algarve [æl'gɑːv] *pr n*: the ~ l'Algarve *f*.

algebra ['ældʒɪbrə] *n* algèbre *f*.

algebraic [,ældʒɪ'breɪɪk] *adj* algébrique.

Algeria [æl'dʒɪərɪə] *pr n* Algérie *f*; in ~ en Algérie.

Algerian [æl'dʒɪərɪən] ◇ *n* Algérien *m*, -enne *f*.
◇ *adj* algérien.

Algiers [æl'dʒɪəz] *pr n* Alger.

ALGOL ['ælgɒl] (*abbr of* algorithmic oriented language) *n* ALGOL *m*.

Algonkin [æl'gɒŋkɪn] (*pl inv* OR Algonkins), **Algonquin** [æl'gɒŋkwɪn] (*pl inv* OR Algonquins) ◇ *n* -**1.** [person] Algonkin *npr m*, Algonquin *npr m*. -**2.** LING algonkin *m*, algonquin *m*.
◇ *adj* algonquin.

algorithm ['ælgərɪðm] *n* algorithme *m*.

algorithmic [,ælgə'rɪðmɪk] *adj* algorithmique.

Alhambra [æl'hæmbrə] *pr n* Alhambra *f*.

alias ['eɪlɪəs] ◇ *adv* alias; Burke, ~ Brown Burke, alias Brown.
◇ *n* nom *m* d'emprunt, faux nom *m*; [of author] nom *m* de plume, pseudonyme *m*; he has several ~es il a plusieurs pseudonymes.

alibi ['ælɪbaɪ] ◇ *n* JUR alibi *m*; *fig* alibi *m*, excuse *f*.
◇ *vt inf Am* [person, action] trouver des excuses à.

Alice ['ælɪs] *pr n*: '~ in Wonderland' *Carroll* 'Alice au pays des merveilles'.

Alice band *n* bandeau *m (pour les cheveux)*.

alien ['eɪljən] ◇ *n* -**1.** ADMIN [foreigner] étranger *m*, -ère *f*. -**2.** [in science fiction] extraterrestre *mf*.
◇ *adj* -**1.** [foreign - customs, environment] étranger. -**2.** [contrary]: ~ to sthg contraire OR opposé à qqch; violence is completely ~ to his nature la violence n'est absolument pas dans sa nature. -**3.** [in science fiction] extraterrestre; ~ life forms d'autres formes de vie.

alienate ['eɪljəneɪt] *vt* [gen & JUR] aliéner; he has ~d all his former friends il s'est aliéné tous ses anciens amis; this tax will ~ the people avec cet impôt, ils vont s'aliéner la population; no government wishes to ~ votes aucun gouvernement ne souhaite perdre des voix.

alienated ['eɪljəneɪtɪd] *adj*: many young people feel ~ and alone beaucoup de jeunes se sentent seuls et rejetés.

alienation [,eɪljə'neɪʃn] *n* -**1.** [of support, friends] fait *m* de décourager OR d'éloigner. -**2.** JUR & PSYCH aliénation *f*.

alienist ['eɪljənɪst] *n Am* aliéniste *mf*, psychiatre *mf*.

alight [ə'laɪt] ◇ *vi* [bird] se poser; [person - from bus, train] descendre; [- from bike, horse] descendre, mettre pied à terre.
◇ *adj* [fire] allumé; [house] en feu; his face was ~ with happiness *fig* son visage rayonnait de joie.
◇ *adv*: to set sthg ~ mettre le feu à qqch; to catch ~ prendre feu.
◆ **alight on** *vt insep fml* [idea] avoir soudain; [information] apprendre par hasard; [lost object] trouver par hasard.

align [ə'laɪn] ◇ *vt* -**1.** [place in line - points, objects] aligner, mettre en ligne. -**2.** FIN & POL aligner; to ~ o.s. with sb s'aligner sur qqn. -**3.** TECH dégauchir; AUT régler le parallélisme de.
◇ *vi* [points, objects] être aligné; [persons, countries] s'aligner.

alignment [ə'laɪnmənt] *n* -**1.** [gen & POL] alignement *m*; to be in/out of ~ être/ne pas être dans l'alignement, être aligné/désaligné. -**2.** AUT parallélisme *m*; in/out of ~ [wheels] dont le parallélisme est bien/mal réglé; steering ~ parallélisme des roues avant.

alike [ə'laɪk] ◇ *adj* semblable; the two brothers are very ~ les deux frères se ressemblent beaucoup OR sont très semblables; no two are ~ il n'y en a pas deux pareils.
◇ *adv* [act, speak, dress] de la même façon OR manière; they look ~ ils se ressemblent; she treats them all ~ elle les traite tous de la même manière; two different words that sound ~ deux mots différents qui se ressemblent phonétiquement; this affects Peter and his brother ~ cela touche Peter aussi bien que son frère.

alimentary [,ælɪ'mentərɪ] *adj* alimentaire.

alimentary canal *n* tube *m* digestif.

alimentation [,ælɪmen'teɪʃn] *n fml* alimentation *f*.

alimony ['ælɪmənɪ] *n* pension *f* alimentaire.

A-line *adj* [skirt, dress] trapèze *(inv)*.

aliquot ['ælɪkwɒt] *adj* aliquote.

alive [ə'laɪv] *adj* -**1.** [living] vivant, en vie; he is still ~ il est toujours vivant OR en vie; while he was ~ de son vivant; to be burnt ~ être brûlé vif; to bury sb ~ enterrer qqn vivant; to keep ~ [person] maintenir en vie; [hope] garder; [tradition] préserver; they kept her memory ~ ils sont restés fidèles à sa mémoire; those ideas are still ~ and well amongst people in the country ces idées sont encore très vivaces OR répandues parmi la population rurale; to stay ~ rester en vie; he felt that he was the luckiest man ~ il se sentit l'homme le plus heureux du monde; no man ~ could endure such pain personne au monde ne pourrait endurer de telles souffrances; it's good to be ~ il fait bon vivre ❑ ~ and kicking: he's still ~ and kicking [not dead] il est toujours bien en vie; [lively] il est toujours d'attaque OR plein de vie. -**2.** [lively, full of life] plein de vie, vif, actif; she always comes ~ in the evening elle se réveille toujours le soir ❑ look ~! *inf* grouille-toi!, remue-toi! -**3.** [alert, aware] conscient, sensible; to be ~ to the dangers of sthg être conscient des OR sensible aux dangers de qqch; he was fully ~ to the risk he was taking il était pleinement conscient OR avait pleinement conscience du risque qu'il encourait. -**4.** [full, crowded]: the evening air was ~ with insects il y avait des nuées d'insectes dans l'air ce soir-là; the streets were ~ with people les rues fourmillaient OR grouillaient de monde.

alkali ['ælkəlaɪ] *n* alcali *m*.

alkaline ['ælkəlaɪn] *adj* alcalin.

alkalinity [,ælkə'lɪnətɪ] *n* alcalinité *f*.

alkaloid ['ælkəlɔɪd] *n* alcaloïde *m*.

alkie, alky *inf* [ælkɪ] (*pl* alkies) *n* poivrot *m*, -e *f*; ~ **cooking** *Am fabrication clandestine d'alcool.*

all [ɔːl] ◇ *det* -**1.** [the whole of] tout *m*, toute *f*, tous *mpl*, toutes *fpl*; ~ **the butter** tout le beurre; ~ **the beer** toute la bière; ~ **my life** toute ma vie; ~ **night** toute la nuit; ~ **day and** ~ **night** toute la journée et toute la nuit; ~ **five** tous/toutes les cinq; ~ **five women** les cinq femmes; ~ **six of us want to go** nous voulons y aller tous/toutes les six ‖ [every one of a particular type] : ~ **kinds of people** toutes sortes de gens; **for children of** ~ **ages** pour les enfants de tous les âges. -**2.** [the utmost] : **with** ~ **speed** à toute vitesse; **in** ~ **fairness (to sb)** pour être juste (avec qqn).
◇ *pron* -**1.** [everything] tout; **I gave** ~ **I had** j'ai donné tout ce que j'avais; **take it** ~ prenez tout; ~ **I want is to rest** tout ce que je veux c'est du repos; **that's** ~ **I have to say** c'est tout ce que j'ai à dire; ~ **will be well** tout ira bien; **will that be** ~ ? ce sera tout?; **it was** ~ **I could do not to laugh** j'ai eu du mal à m'empêcher de rire; **you men are** ~ **the same!** vous les hommes, vous êtes tous pareils OR tous les mêmes! ❑ ~ **or nothing** tout ou rien; ~ **in good time** chaque chose en son temps. -**2.** [everyone] tous; **good evening,** ~! bonsoir à tous!, bonsoir, tout le monde!; **don't** ~ **speak at once!** ne parlez pas tous en même temps!; **we** ~ **came** nous sommes tous venus; **they** ~ **made the same mistake** ils ont tous fait la même erreur; **the children were** ~ **hoping to go** les enfants espéraient tous y aller; ~ **who knew her loved her** tous ceux qui la connaissaient l'aimaient. -**3.** SPORT: **the score is 5** ~ le score est de 5 partout; **30** ~ [in tennis] 30 partout. -**4.** [as quantifier] : ~ **of** tout; ~ **of the butter/the cakes** tout le beurre, tous les gâteaux; ~ **of London** Londres tout entier; ~ **of it was sold** (le) tout a été vendu; **how much wine did they drink?** — ~ **of it** combien de vin ont-ils bu? – tout ce qu'il y avait; ~ **of you can come** vous pouvez tous venir; **listen,** ~ **of you** écoutez-moi tous; **she knows** ~ **of their names** elle connaît tous leurs noms ❑ **the book cost me** ~ **of £10** le livre m'a coûté rien moins que 10 livres; **it's** ~ **of five minutes walk away!** *hum* c'est AU MOINS à cinq minutes à pied! *hum.*
◇ *adv* -**1.** [as intensifier] tout, tout à fait; **she was** ~ **alone** elle était toute seule; **she was** ~ **dressed** OR **she was dressed** ~ **in black** elle était habillée tout en noir; ~ **along the road** tout le long de la route; ~ **around the edge** tout le long du bord; **the soup went** ~ **down my dress** la soupe s'est répandue partout sur ma robe; **the jacket's split** ~ **up the sleeve** la veste a craqué tout le long de la manche; **don't get your hands** ~ **dirty** *inf* ne va pas te salir les mains!; **the motor's** ~ **rusty inside** *inf* le moteur est tout rouillé à l'intérieur ❑ ~ **at one go** (tout) d'un seul coup; ~ **in one piece** [furniture] tout d'une pièce; *fig* [person] sain et sauf; **I'm** ~ **for it** moi, je suis tout à fait pour!; **she's** ~ **for giving children their freedom** elle est tout à fait convaincue qu'il faut donner aux enfants leur liberté; **it's** ~ **up with him** *inf* il est fichu. -**2.** [with comparative adjectives] : ~ **the better!** tant mieux!; **you will feel** ~ **the better for a rest** un peu de repos vous fera le plus grand bien; **it's** ~ **the more unfair since** OR **as he promised not to put up the rent** c'est d'autant plus injuste qu'il a promis de ne pas augmenter le loyer; ~ **the sooner** d'autant plus vite.
◇ *n* tout; **I would give my** ~ **to be there** je donnerais tout ce que j'ai pour y être; **the team gave their** ~ l'équipe a donné son maximum; **to stake one's** ~ tout miser.
◆ **all along** *adv phr* depuis le début; **that's what I've been saying** ~ **along** c'est ce que je dis depuis le début.
◆ **all at once** *adv phr* -**1.** [suddenly] tout d'un coup. -**2.** [all at the same time] à la fois, en même temps.
◆ **all but** *adv phr* presque; ~ **but finished** presque OR pratiquement fini; **I** ~ **but missed it** j'ai bien failli le rater, c'est tout juste si je ne l'ai pas raté.
◆ **all in** *inf* ◇ *adj phr* [exhausted] : **I'm** ~ **in** je suis mort.
◇ *adv phr* [everything included] tout compris; **the rent is £250 a month** ~ **in** le loyer est de 250 livres par mois tout compris.
◆ **all in all** *adv phr* tout compte fait.
◆ **all over** ◇ *adj phr* [finished] fini; **that's** ~ **over and done with now** tout ça c'est bien terminé maintenant; **it's** ~ **over between them** tout est fini entre eux.
◇ *prep phr* [everywhere in] partout; **there were toys scattered** ~ **over the floor** il y avait des jouets éparpillés partout sur le sol; **you've got ink** ~ **over you!** tu t'es mis de l'encre partout!; ~ **over the world** dans le monde entier; **we have agencies** ~ **over Europe** nous avons des agences dans toute l'Europe OR partout en Europe; **it'll be** ~ **over town tomorrow morning!** demain matin, toute la ville sera au courant! ❑ ~ **over the place** [everywhere] partout, dans tous les coins; [very erratic, inaccurate] pas au point *hum*; **their filing system's** ~ **over the place** leur système de classement n'est pas du tout au point; **he was** ~ **over her** il ne l'a pas laissée tranquille un instant; **he was** ~ **over us when he heard we were from the BBC** il ne nous a plus laissés tranquilles quand il a appris que nous étions de la BBC.
◇ *adv phr* [everywhere] partout; **painted green** ~ **over** peint tout en vert; **covered** ~ **over in blossoms** tout en fleur OR en fleurs ❑ **it was like being a child** ~ **over again** c'était comme retomber en enfance; **that's him** ~ **over!** *inf* ça c'est lui tout craché!
◆ **all that** *adv phr*: **it isn't** ~ **that difficult** OR **as difficult as** ~ **that** ce n'est pas si difficile que ça.
◆ **all the more** ◇ *det phr*: ~ **the more reason for doing it again** raison de plus pour recommencer.
◇ *adv phr* encore plus; **it makes her** ~ **the more interesting** ça la rend encore plus intéressante.
◆ **all the same** ◇ *adv phr* [nevertheless] tout de même, quand même; **he paid up** ~ **the same** il a payé quand même.
◇ *adj phr*: **it's** ~ **the same to me** ça m'est complètement égal, peu m'importe; **if it's** ~ **the same to you** si cela ne vous gêne pas.
◆ **all told** *adv phr* tout compris.
◆ **all too** *adv phr*: ~ **too soon** bien trop vite; **the holidays went** ~ **too quickly** les vacances ne sont passées que trop vite; **it's** ~ **too easy to forget that** c'est tellement facile de l'oublier.

all- *in cpds* entièrement; ~**male/female** entièrement masculin/féminin; **the first** ~**French baseball team** la première équipe de baseball entièrement française; **an** ~**singing,** ~**dancing spectacular** une grande comédie musicale.

Allah ['ælə] *pr n* Allah.

all-American *adj* cent pour cent américain; **the** ~ **boy** le jeune américain type.

all-around *Am* = **all-round**.

allay [ə'leɪ] *vt* [fear] apaiser; [doubt, suspicion] dissiper; [pain, grief] soulager, apaiser.

All Black *n*: **the** ~**s** les All Blacks *mpl (l'équipe nationale de rugby de la Nouvelle-Zélande).*

all clear ◇ *n* (signal *m* de) fin *f* d'alerte; **to sound the** ~ sonner la fin de l'alerte; **he received** OR **was given the** ~ **on the project** *fig* on lui a donné le feu vert pour le projet.
◇ *interj*: ~! fin *f* d'alerte!

all comers *npl*: **the British** ~ **100 m record** le record britannique de l'épreuve du 100 m ouverte à tous.

all-day *adj* qui dure toute la journée.

allegation [ˌælɪ'geɪʃn] *n* allégation *f.*

allege [ə'ledʒ] *vt* alléguer, prétendre; **he** ~**s that he was beaten up** il prétend avoir été roué de coups; **are you alleging police brutality?** est-ce que vous prétendez avoir été victime de violences policières?; **the incident is** ~**d to have taken place the night before** l'incident aurait eu lieu OR on prétend que l'incident a eu lieu la veille au soir.

alleged [ə'ledʒd] *adj* [motive, incident, reason] allégué, prétendu; [thief] présumé.

allegedly [ə'ledʒɪdlɪ] *adv* prétendument, paraît-il; **they** ~ **broke in and stole £300** ils seraient entrés par effraction et auraient volé 300 livres.

allegiance [ə'liːdʒəns] *n* allégeance *f*; **political** ~ allégeance politique; **to swear** ~ faire serment d'allégeance; **to switch** ~ changer de bord.

allegoric(al) [ˌælɪ'gɒrɪk(l)] *adj* allégorique.

allegorically [ˌælɪ'gɒrɪklɪ] *adv* sous forme d'allégorie, allégoriquement.

allegory ['ælɪgərɪ] (*pl* allegories) *n* allégorie *f.*

alleluia [ˌælɪ'luːjə] *interj*: ~! alléluia!

all-embracing [-ɪm'breɪsɪŋ] *adj* exhaustif, complet.

Allen key ['ælən-] *n* clé *f* (à vis) à six pans creux.

allergen ['ælədʒen] *n* allergène *m.*

allergic [ə'lɜːdʒɪk] *adj* [reaction, person] allergique; **I'm** ~ **to cats** je suis allergique aux chats; **he's** ~ **to hard work** *hum* il est allergique au travail.

allergist ['ælədʒɪst] *n* allergologiste *mf*, allergologue *mf.*

allergy ['ælədʒɪ] (*pl* allergies) *n* allergie *f.*

alleviate [ə'liːvɪeɪt] *vt* [pain, suffering] alléger, apaiser, soulager; [problem, difficulties] limiter, réduire; [effect] alléger, atténuer.

alleviation [əˌliːvɪ'eɪʃn] *n* apaisement *m*, soulagement *m.*

alley ['ælɪ] *n* -**1.** [street] ruelle *f*, passage *m*; [in park, garden] allée *f*; **that's right up my** ~ c'est tout à fait mon rayon. -**2.** *Am* [on tennis court] couloir *m*. -**3.** [for tenpin bowling, skittles] bowling *m*, prise *f* de jeu. -**4.** [marble] (grosse) bille *f*, calot *m.*

alley cat *n* chat *m* de gouttière.

alleyway ['ælɪweɪ] *n* ruelle *f*, passage *m.*

all-fired▽ *Am* ◇ *adj* infernal.
◇ *adv* vachement, super.

All Fools' Day *n* le premier avril.

all fours
◆ **on all fours** *adv phr* à quatre pattes; **to get** OR **to go down on** ~ se mettre à quatre pattes.

Allhallows [ˌɔːl'hæləʊz] *n* Toussaint *f*; ~ **Eve** la veille de la Toussaint.

alliance [ə'laɪəns] *n* alliance *f*; **to enter into** OR **to form an** ~ **with sb** s'allier OR faire alliance avec qqn.

allied ['ælaɪd] *adj* -**1.** POL [force, nations] allié. -**2.** [related - subjects] connexe, du même ordre; ECON & FIN [product, industry] assimilé; BIOL de la même famille. -**3.** [connected] allié; **his natural talent,** ~ **with his good looks, made him a star** son talent naturel allié à un physique agréable ont fait de lui une star.
◆ **Allied** *adj*: **the Allied forces in the Second World War** les forces alliées pendant la Seconde Guerre mondiale.

alligator ['ælɪgeɪtəʳ] ◇ *n* alligator *m.*
◇ *comp* [bag, shoes] en (peau d')alligator; [skin] d'alligator.

all-important *adj* de la plus haute importance, d'une importance primordiale OR capitale; **she found the** ~ **key** elle a trouvé la clé essentielle; **it is** ~ **that we get this contract** il est capital que nous obtenions ce contrat.

all-in ◇ *adj* -**1.** [price, tariff] net, tout compris, forfaitaire; [insurance policy] tous risques. -**2.** *inf* [exhausted] vanné, crevé; **I'm** ~! je n'en peux plus!, je ne tiens plus debout!
◇ *adv* tout compris; **the rent is £60 a week** ~ le loyer est de 60 livres par semaine tout compris OR net.

all-in-one *adj* tout-en-un *(inv).*

all-in wrestling *n* lutte *f* libre, catch *m.*

alliteration [əˌlɪtə'reɪʃn] *n* allitération *f.*

alliterative [ə'lɪtərətɪv] *adj* allitératif.

all-night *adj* [party] qui dure toute la nuit; [shop, restaurant] de nuit, ouvert la nuit; **an** ~ **sitting of Parliament** une session parlementaire de nuit ❑ ~ **pass** MIL permission *f* de (la) nuit; ~

showing CIN projection ininterrompue durant toute la nuit.

allocate ['æləkeɪt] *vt* -**1.** [assign - money, duties] allouer, assigner, attribuer; **funds ~d to research** des crédits affectés à la recherche. -**2.** [share out] répartir, distribuer. -**3.** JUR & FIN ventiler.

allocation [,ælə'keɪʃn] *n* -**1.** [assignment - of money, duties] allocation *f*, affectation *f*; [- of role, part] attribution *f*. -**2.** [sharing out] répartition *f*. -**3.** [share - of money] part *f*; [- of space] portion *f*. -**4.** JUR & FIN ventilation *f*.

allomorph ['æləmɔːf] *n* allomorphe *m*.

allopathy [ə'lɒpəθɪ] *n* allopathie *f*.

allophone ['æləfəʊn] *n* allophone *m*.

allot [ə'lɒt] (*pt* & *pp* allotted, *cont* allotting) *vt* -**1.** [assign - money, duties, time] allouer, assigner, attribuer; **in the allotted time** dans le délai imparti; **the farmers were allotted a few acres each** on a attribué aux fermiers quelques hectares chacun. -**2.** [share out] répartir, distribuer.

allotment [ə'lɒtmənt] *n* -**1.** [of money, duties, time] allocation *f*, attribution *f*. -**2.** *Br* [land] jardin *m* ouvrier OR familial.

allotrope ['ælətrəʊp] *n* variété *f* allotropique.

allotropy [æ'lɒtrəpɪ] *n* allotropie *f*.

all out *adv*: **to go ~ to do sthg** se donner à fond pour faire qqch.

◆ **all-out** *adj* [strike, war] total; [effort] maximum.

allover ['ɔːl,əʊvəʳ] *adj* qui s'étend sur toute la surface; **an ~ tan** un bronzage intégral.

allow [ə'laʊ] *vt* -**1.** [permit] permettre, autoriser; **to ~ sb to do sthg** permettre à qqn de faire qqch, autoriser qqn à faire qqch; **he wasn't ~ed to see her** il n'a pas été autorisé à la voir, il n'a pas eu le droit de la voir; **he was ~ed a final cigarette** on lui a permis (de fumer) une dernière cigarette; **we weren't ~ed in** on ne nous a pas permis d'entrer; **the dog is not ~ed in the house** on ne laisse pas le chien entrer dans la maison, l'accès de la maison est interdit au chien; **'smoking is not ~ed'** 'défense de fumer'; **she ~ed herself to be manipulated** elle s'est laissée manipuler; **he decided to ~ events to take their course** il a décidé de laisser les événements suivre leur cours; **I won't ~ such behaviour!** je ne tolérerai pas une telle conduite!; **~ me to make a suggestion** *fml* permettez-moi de faire une suggestion; **if I may be ~ed to make a point** si je peux me permettre (de faire) une remarque; **~ me!** vous permettez? -**2.** [enable] permettre; **the ramp ~s people in wheelchairs to enter the building** la rampe permet l'accès de l'immeuble aux personnes en fauteuil roulant. -**3.** [grant - money, time] accorder, allouer; [- opportunity] donner; [- claim] admettre; **three hours are ~ed for the exam** trois heures sont accordées pour l'examen; **he is ~ed £5 pocket money** on lui accorde OR donne 5 livres d'argent de poche; **she ~ed herself a cream cake as a special treat** comme petit plaisir, elle s'est offert un gâteau à la crème. -**4.** [take into account] prévoir, compter; **~ a week for delivery** il faut prévoir OR compter une semaine pour la livraison; **you need to ~ a few extra inches for the hem** il faut laisser OR prévoir quelques centimètres de plus pour l'ourlet. -**5.** *lit* [admit] admettre, convenir; **you must ~ that she is gifted** vous devez admettre OR reconnaître qu'elle est douée.

◆ **allow for** *vt insep* -**1.** [take account of] tenir compte de; **~ing for the bad weather** compte tenu du mauvais temps; **we ~ed for every possibility in our calculations** nous avons tenu compte de OR paré à toute éventualité dans nos calculs; **we must ~ for the fact that she has been ill** il faut tenir compte du fait qu'elle a été malade. -**2.** [make allowance or provision for]: **remember to ~ for the time difference** n'oublie pas de compter le décalage horaire; **we hadn't ~ed for these extra costs** nous n'avions pas prévu ces frais supplémentaires; **after ~ing for travel expenses** déduction faite des frais de voyage.

◆ **allow of** *vt insep fml* admettre, souffrir, autoriser; **the evidence ~s of no other conclusion** les éléments dont nous disposons n'autorisent aucune autre conclusion.

allowable [ə'laʊəbl] *adj* admissible, permis; **expenses ~ against tax** dépenses *fpl* fiscalement déductibles.

allowance [ə'laʊəns] *n* -**1.** ADMIN [grant] allocation *f*; [for housing, travel, food] indemnité *f*; [alimony] pension *f* alimentaire; [for student - from state] bourse *f*; [- from parents] pension *f* alimentaire; [pension] pension *f*; [income, salary] revenu *m*, appointements *mpl*; **his parents give him a monthly ~ of £100** ses parents lui versent une mensualité de 100 livres; **he gets a monthly ~ of £300** il touche 300 livres par mois; **she makes an ~ of £1,000 a year to her nephew** elle verse une rente OR une pension de 1 000 livres par an à son neveu ▫ **cost-of-living ~** indemnité de vie chère; **rent ~** allocation (de) logement. -**2.** [discount] rabais *m*, réduction *f*; **tax ~** [deduction] dégrèvement *m* fiscal; [tax-free part] revenu *m* non imposable; **trade-in ~** (valeur *f* de) reprise *f*. -**3.** *Am* [pocket money] argent *m* de poche. -**4.** *phr*: **to make ~** OR **~s for sthg** tenir compte de qqch, prendre qqch en considération; **we must make ~** OR **~s for the children's age** il faut tenir compte de OR il ne faut pas oublier l'âge des enfants; **you have to make ~s for inflation** il faut faire la part de l'inflation.

alloy [*n* 'ælɔɪ, *vb* ə'lɔɪ] ◇ *n* alliage *m*.

◇ *comp*: **~ steel** acier *m* allié OR spécial; **~ wheels** AUT roues *fpl* en alliage léger.

◇ *vt* -**1.** [metal] allier, faire un alliage de. -**2.** *fig* dévaloriser, souiller.

all-powerful *adj* tout-puissant.

all-purpose *adj* [gen] qui répond à tous les besoins, passe-partout *(inv)*; [tool, vehicle] polyvalent; **~ cleaning fluid** détachant *m* tous usages.

all right ◇ *adj* -**1.** [adequate] (assez) bien, pas mal; **the film was ~** le film n'était pas mal; **the money is ~, but it could be better** le salaire est correct, mais ça pourrait être mieux. -**2.** [in good health] en bonne santé; [safe] sain et sauf; **are you ~?** [not hurt] ça va?; **she's had an accident, but she's ~** elle a eu un accident mais ça va; **he was quite ill, but he's ~ now** il a été assez malade, mais ça va OR il est rétabli maintenant; **do you think the car will be ~?** tu crois que ça ira avec la voiture? ▫ **I'm ~ Jack** moi, ça va bien (et vous, je m'en fiche). -**3.** [okay]: **I hope they'll be ~ on their own** j'espère qu'ils sauront se débrouiller tout seuls; **is it ~ if they come too?** ça va s'ils viennent aussi?; **it's ~** [no problem] ça va; [no matter] ça ne fait rien, peu importe; **I've come to see if everything is ~** je suis venu voir si tout va bien; **it's ~ by me** moi, ça me va. -**4.** [pleasant] bien, agréable; [nice-looking] chouette; **the boss is ~** le patron est bien OR n'est pas trop mal; **she's ~** *inf* elle est plutôt sympa. -**5.** [financially] à l'aise, tranquille; **I'll see that you're ~** je veillerai à ce que vous ne manquiez de rien.

◇ *adv* -**1.** [well, adequately] bien; **the radio works ~** la radio marche bien; **they're doing ~** [progressing well] ça va (pour eux); [succeeding in career, life] ils se débrouillent bien; **everything went off ~** tout a bien marché. -**2.** [without doubt]: **it's rabies ~** pour être la rage, c'est la rage; **he was listening ~** ça, pour écouter, il écoutait.

◇ *interj*: **~!** [indicating agreement, understanding] entendu!, d'accord!; [indicating approval] c'est ça!, ça va!; [indicating impatience] ça va!, ça suffit!; [indicating change or continuation of activity] bon!

◆ **all-right** *inf adj esp Am*: **he's an ~ guy** c'est un type réglo; **it was an ~ film** le film n'était pas mal.

all-round *adj* -**1.** [versatile - athlete, player] complet; [- ability] complet, polyvalent. -**2.** [comprehensive - improvement] général, sur toute la ligne.

all round *adv*: **taken ~** à tout prendre.

all-rounder [-'raʊndəʳ] *n Br*: **he's a good ~** [gen] il est doué dans tous les domaines, il est bon en tout; SPORT c'est un sportif complet.

All Saints' Day *n* (le jour de) la Toussaint.

all-singing all-dancing *adj* dernier cri.

All Souls' Day *n* le jour OR la Fête des Morts.

allspice ['ɔːlspaɪs] *n* poivre *m* de la Jamaïque, tout épice *m*.

all square *adj* -**1.** [financially]: **we're ~ now** nous ne sommes plus en compte maintenant. -**2.** SPORT [level] à égalité.

all-star *adj* [show, performance] avec beaucoup de vedettes, à vedettes; **with an ~ cast** avec un plateau de vedettes.

all-time *adj* sans précédent, inouï; **sales have reached an ~ high/low** les ventes ont connu le niveau le plus élevé jamais atteint/sont tombées au niveau le plus bas jamais atteint; **this film is one of the ~ greats** ce film est un des meilleurs de tous les temps; **an ~ record** un record sans précédent; **an ~ best-seller** un best-seller jamais égalé.

all told *adv* en tout; **there were six of us ~** nous étions six en tout.

allude [ə'luːd] *vi*: **to ~ to sb/sthg** faire allusion à qqn/qqch.

allure [ə'ljʊəʳ] ◇ *vt* attirer, séduire.

◇ *n* attrait *m*, charme *m*.

alluring [ə'ljʊərɪŋ] *adj* séduisant, attrayant.

allusion [ə'luːʒn] *n* allusion *f*; **to make an ~ to sthg** faire allusion à qqch.

allusive [ə'luːsɪv] *adj* allusif, qui contient une allusion OR des allusions.

allusively [ə'luːsɪvlɪ] *adv* par allusion.

alluvial [ə'luːvjəl] *adj* [ground] alluvial; **~ deposits** alluvions *fpl*, dépôts *mpl* alluvionnaires.

alluvium [ə'luːvjəm] (*pl* **alluviums** OR **alluvia** [-vɪə]) *n* alluvion *f*.

all-weather *adj* [surface] de toute saison, tous temps; **~ court** [tennis] (terrain *m* en) quick *m*; **~ pitch** FTBL terrain *m* tous temps.

ally [*vb* ə'laɪ, *n* 'ælaɪ] (*pl* **allies**) ◇ *vt* allier, unir; **to ~ o.s. with sb** s'allier avec qqn; **Italy was allied with Germany** l'Italie était alliée avec OR à l'Allemagne.

◇ *n* [gen & POL] allié *m*, -e *f*; **the two countries were allies** les deux pays étaient alliés; **the Allies** HIST les Alliés.

Ally Pally *inf* [,ælɪ'pælɪ] *pr n surnom du 'Alexandra Palace'.*

Alma Mater, alma mater [,ælmə'mɑːtəʳ] *n* [school] *école ou université où l'on a fait ses études*; *Am* [anthem] *hymne d'une école ou d'une université*.

almanac ['ɔːlmənæk] *n* almanach *m*, agenda *m*.

almighty [ɔːl'maɪtɪ] ◇ *adj* -**1.** [omnipotent] tout-puissant, omnipotent. -**2.** *inf* [as intensifier - row, racket] formidable, sacré; **an ~ din** un vacarme de tous les diables, un formidable vacarme.

◇ *adv inf* extrêmement, énormément.

◆ **Almighty** RELIG ◇ *n*: **the Almighty** le Tout-Puissant.

◇ *adj*: **Almighty God, God Almighty** Dieu Tout-Puissant.

almond ['ɑːmənd] ◇ *n* -**1.** [nut] amande. -**2.** **~ (tree)** amandier *m*.

◇ *comp* [icing] d'amandes; [cake] aux amandes.

almond paste *n* pâte *f* d'amande.

almoner ['ɑːmənəʳ] *n* -**1.** HIST aumônier *m*. -**2.** *Br arch* [social worker] assistante *f* sociale *(dans un hôpital)*.

almost ['ɔːlməʊst] *adv* presque; **~ all the people** presque tous les gens, la quasi-totalité des gens; **it's ~ cooked/finished** c'est presque cuit/terminé; **he is ~ 30** il a presque 30 ans; **I can ~ reach it** j'arrive presque à l'atteindre; **I ~ cried** j'ai failli pleurer; **he was ~ crying with frustration** il pleurait presque de rage; **I ~ believed him** j'ai bien failli le croire, j'étais près de le croire.

alms [ɑːmz] *npl* aumône *f*; **to give ~ to sb** faire l'aumône OR la charité à qqn.

almshouse ['ɑːmz,haʊs, *pl* -,haʊzɪz] *n Br résidence pour personnes âgées ou défavorisées, gérée par l'Église ou par une association caritative*.

aloe ['æləʊ] *n* aloès *m*.

aloft [ə'lɒft] *adv*: (up) ~ [gen] en haut, en l'air; AERON en l'air; NAUT dans la mâture.

alone [ə'ləʊn] ◇ *adj* -**1.** [on one's own] seul; to be ~ être seul; I'm not ~ in thinking that it's unfair je ne suis pas le seul à penser que c'est injuste. -**2.** [only] seul; she ~ knows the truth elle seule connaît la vérité; time ~ will tell qui vivra verra; with the deep understanding of the situation that is his ~ avec cette faculté de saisir rapidement les situations qui le caractérise, avec cette fine perception des situations qui n'appartient qu'à lui; the frame ~ is worth £50 le cadre seul vaut 50 livres. -**3.** [lonely] seul; she felt very ~ elle se sentait très seule.
◇ *adv* -**1.** [on one's own] seul; he came ~ il est venu seul; she managed to open the box ~ elle a réussi à ouvrir la boîte toute seule; I'd like to speak to you ~ j'aimerais vous parler seul; to stand ~ [person] rester seul; [house] être situé à l'écart; she stands ~ as the most successful politician this century *fig* elle est la seule depuis le début du siècle à avoir aussi bien réussi politiquement OR en politique ❑ to go it ~ faire cavalier seul. -**2.** [undisturbed]: to leave OR to let ~ laisser tranquille; leave me ~ [on my own] laissez-moi seul; [in peace] laissez-moi tranquille, laissez-moi en paix; leave the bag ~! laissez le sac tranquille!, ne touchez pas au sac!; if I were you I would let well ~ si j'étais vous, je ne m'en mêlerais pas.
◆ **let alone** *conj phr* sans parler de; he's never been to London, let ~ Paris il n'a jamais été à Londres, sans parler de Paris; she can't even walk, let ~ run elle ne peut même pas marcher, alors encore moins courir.

along [ə'lɒŋ] ◇ *prep* [the length of] le long de; we walked ~ the road nous avons marché le long de la route; there were trees all ~ the road il y avait des arbres tout le long de la route, des arbres bordaient la route; the railway runs ~ the coast la voie ferrée longe la côte ‖ [at or to a certain point in]: could you move further ~ the row pourriez-vous vous déplacer vers le bout du rang?; her office is ~ here somewhere son bureau est quelque part par ici; the toilets are just ~ the corridor les toilettes sont juste un peu plus loin dans le couloir.
◇ *adv* -**1.** [in phrasal verbs]: I was driving/strolling ~ on a sunny afternoon, when... je roulais/me baladais par un après-midi ensoleillé, quand...; she was pulling a trolley ~ elle tirait OR traînait un chariot derrière elle; just then ~ came a policeman c'est alors qu'un policier est arrivé. -**2.** [indicating progress]: how far ~ is the project? où en est le projet?; we're further ~ than expected nous en sommes plus loin que prévu; things are going OR coming ~ nicely, thank you les choses ne se présentent pas trop mal, merci. -**3.** [indicating imminent arrival]: I'll be ~ in a minute j'arrive tout de suite; she'll be ~ later elle viendra plus tard; there'll be another bus ~ shortly un autre bus va passer bientôt.
◆ **along by** *prep phr* en passant par.
◆ **along with** *prep phr* avec; ~ with hundreds of others avec des centaines d'autres; I put the coat away ~ with the rest of my winter clothes j'ai rangé le manteau avec mes autres vêtements d'hiver.

alongshore [ə,lɒŋ'ʃɔːʳ] ◇ *adv* le long de la côte.
◇ *adj* [current, tide] côtier.

alongside [ə,lɒŋ'saɪd] ◇ *prep* -**1.** [along] le long de; to come OR to draw ~ the quay accoster le quai; the railway runs ~ the road la ligne de chemin de fer longe la route. -**2.** [beside] à côté de; the car drew up ~ me la voiture s'est arrêtée à côté de moi.
◇ *adv* -**1.** NAUT: to come ~ [two ships] naviguer à couple; [at quayside] accoster. -**2.** [gen - at side]: they're going to build a patio with a flower bed ~ ils vont construire un patio bordé d'un parterre de fleurs.

aloof [ə'luːf] *adj* distant; she is very ~ elle est très distante, elle est d'un abord difficile; to keep OR to remain ~ se tenir à distance; he keeps OR remains ~ from his colleagues il se tient à distance de ses collègues; I try to keep ~ from such matters j'essaie de ne pas me mêler à ces histoires.

aloofness [ə'luːfnɪs] *n* attitude *f* distante, réserve *f*.

alopecia [,ælə'piːʃə] *n* alopécie *f*.

aloud [ə'laʊd] *adv* [read] à haute voix, à voix haute, tout haut; [think] tout haut.

alp [ælp] *n* [mountain] montagne *f*; [pasture] alpage *m*, alpe *f*.

alpaca [æl'pækə] *n* alpaga *m*.

alpenhorn ['ælpənhɔːn] *n* cor *m* des Alpes.

alpenstock ['ælpənstɒk] *n* alpenstock *m*.

alpha ['ælfə] *n* -**1.** [Greek letter] alpha *m*; ~ and omega *fig* l'alpha et l'oméga, le commencement et la fin. -**2.** *Br* SCH ≃ mention *f* bien; ~ plus ≃ mention *f* très bien.

alphabet ['ælfəbet] *n* alphabet *m*.

alphabetic(al) [,ælfə'betɪk(l)] *adj* alphabétique; in ~ order par ordre OR dans l'ordre alphabétique.

alphabetically [,ælfə'betɪklɪ] *adv* alphabétiquement, par ordre alphabétique.

alphabetize, -ise ['ælfəbətaɪz] *vt* classer par ordre alphabétique.

alphameric [,ælfə'merɪk], **alphanumeric** [,ælfənjuː'merɪk] *adj* alphanumérique.

alpha particle *n* particule *f* alpha.

alpha ray *n* rayon *m* alpha.

alpha wave *n* rythme *m* alpha.

alpine ['ælpaɪn] ◇ *adj* -**1.** GEOG des Alpes. -**2.** [climate, landscape] alpestre; [club, skiing, troops] alpin; ~ plants [at low altitude] plantes *fpl* alpestres; [at high altitude] plantes *fpl* alpines.
◇ *n* [plant - at low altitude] plante *f* alpestre; [- at high altitude] plante *f* alpine.

alpinist ['ælpɪnɪst] *n* alpiniste *mf*.

Alps [ælps] *pl pr n*: the ~ les Alpes *fpl*; in the ~ dans les Alpes; the Southern ~ les Alpes du Sud.

already [ɔːl'redɪ] *adv* déjà.

alright [,ɔːl'raɪt] = **all right**.

Alsace [æl'sæs] *pr n* Alsace *f*; in ~ en Alsace.

Alsatian [æl'seɪʃn] ◇ *n* -**1.** [person] Alsacien *m*, -enne *f*. -**2.** LING alsacien *m*. -**3.** [dog] berger *m* allemand.
◇ *adj* [person] d'Alsace, alsacien; [wine] d'Alsace; ~ dog berger *m* allemand.

also ['ɔːlsəʊ] *adv* -**1.** [as well] aussi, également; she ~ speaks Italian elle parle aussi OR également l'italien; the other two books are ~ out of print les deux autres livres sont aussi OR également épuisés; he's lazy and ~ stupid il est paresseux et en plus il est bête. -**2.** [furthermore] en outre, de plus, également; ~, it must be pointed out that... en outre OR de plus, il faut signaler que..., il faut également signaler que...

also-ran *n* -**1.** SPORT [gen] concurrent *m* non classé; [in horse-race] cheval *m* non classé. -**2.** *fig* [person] perdant *m*, -e *f*.

Alta. *written abbr of* Alberta.

altar ['ɔːltəʳ] *n* autel *m*; to lead sb to the ~ *fig* conduire OR mener qqn à l'autel; to be sacrificed on the ~ of success *fig* être sacrifié sur l'autel du succès ❑ ~ cloth nappe *f* d'autel; ~ rail balustre *m (devant l'autel)*; at the ~ rail devant l'autel; the high ~ le maître-autel.

altar boy *n* enfant *m* de chœur.

altarpiece ['ɔːltəpiːs] *n* retable *m*.

alter ['ɔːltəʳ] ◇ *vt* -**1.** [change - appearance, plan] changer, modifier; this doesn't ~ the fact that you should have known cela ne change pas le fait que vous auriez dû être au courant; this ~s matters considerably cela change vraiment tout; to ~ course NAUT & AERON changer de cap OR de route. -**2.** SEW faire une retouche OR des retouches à, retoucher; the dress needs to be ~ed at the neck la robe a besoin d'être retouchée au col. -**3.** [falsify - evidence, facts, text] falsifier, fausser. -**4.** *Am euph* [castrate] châtrer.
◇ *vi* changer, se modifier; the town has ~ed a lot in the past few years la ville a beaucoup changé ces dernières années; to ~ for the better [situation] s'améliorer; [person] changer en mieux; to ~ for the worse [situation] s'aggraver, empirer; [person] changer en mal.

alteration [,ɔːltə'reɪʃn] *n* -**1.** [changing] changement *m*, modification *f*; [touching up] retouche *f*. -**2.** [change] changement *m*, modification *f*; [reorganization] remaniement *m*; [transformation] transformation *f*; to make an ~ to sthg modifier qqch, apporter une modification à qqch. -**3.** SEW retouche *f*; to make ~s to a dress faire des retouches à une robe. -**4.** [falsification - of figures, document] falsification *f*. -**5.** CONSTR aménagement *m*, transformation *f*; to have ~s done faire faire des aménagements; they've made major ~s to their house ils ont fait des transformations importantes dans leur maison.

altercation [,ɔːltə'keɪʃn] *n fml* altercation *f*; to have an ~ with sb se disputer OR avoir une altercation avec qqn.

alter ego *n* alter ego *m*.

alternate [*adj* & *n Br* ɔːl'tɜːnət, *Am* 'ɔːltərnət, *vb* 'ɔːltərneɪt] ◇ *adj* -**1.** [by turns] alterné; ~ spells of good and bad weather des périodes alternées de beau et de mauvais temps; we visit her on ~ weekends nous lui rendons visite un week-end sur deux. -**2.** [every other] tous les deux; on ~ days un jour sur deux, tous les deux jours. -**3.** BOT alterne. -**4.** GEOM alterne. -**5.** *Am* [alternative] alternatif.
◇ *vi* -**1.** [happen by turns] alterner; wet days ~d with fine days les jours pluvieux alternaient avec les beaux jours, les jours pluvieux et les beaux jours se succédaient. -**2.** [take turns] se relayer; two actors ~d in the leading role deux acteurs jouaient le rôle principal en alternance OR à tour de rôle. -**3.** [vary] alterner; she ~s between despair and elation elle est tour à tour désespérée ou enthousiaste, elle passe du désespoir à l'enthousiasme; an economy that ~s between periods of growth and disastrous slumps une économie où alternent la prospérité et le marasme le plus profond. -**4.** ELEC changer périodiquement de sens.
◇ *vt* (faire) alterner, employer alternativement OR tour à tour; AGR [crops] alterner.
◇ *n Am* remplaçant *m*, -e *f*, suppléant *m*, -e *f*.

alternately [ɔːl'tɜːnətlɪ] *adv* alternativement, en alternance, tour à tour.

alternating ['ɔːltəneɪtɪŋ] *adj* [gen] alternant, en alternance; ELEC & TECH alternatif; MATH alterné.

alternating current *n* courant *m* alternatif.

alternation [,ɔːltə'neɪʃn] *n* alternance *f*.

alternative [ɔːl'tɜːnətɪv] ◇ *n* -**1.** [choice] solution *f*, choix *m*; you have no other ~ vous n'avez pas d'autre solution OR choix; he had no ~ but to accept il n'avait pas d'autre solution que d'accepter; you leave me with no ~ vous ne me laissez pas le choix; what's the ~? quelle est l'autre solution?; there are several ~s il y a plusieurs possibilités; the country has chosen the democratic ~ le pays a choisi la solution démocratique. -**2.** PHILOS terme *m* d'une alternative.
◇ *adj* -**1.** [different, other - solution, government] autre, de rechange; you'll have to find an ~ solution il faudra trouver une autre solution; an ~ proposal une contre-proposition; an ~ route AUT un itinéraire bis OR de délestage. -**2.** [not traditional - lifestyle] peu conventionnel, hors normes; [- press, theatre] parallèle; ~ energy énergies *fpl* de substitution; ~ medicine médecine *f* douce; the ~ society la société alternative; ~ technology technologies *fpl* douces. -**3.** PHILOS alternatif.

alternatively [ɔːl'tɜːnətɪvlɪ] *adv* comme alternative, sinon; you could travel by train or ~ by bus vous pourriez voyager en train ou bien en autobus.

alternator ['ɔːltəneɪtəʳ] *n* alternateur *m*.

although [ɔːl'ðəʊ] *conj* **-1.** [despite the fact that] bien que, quoique; ~ **(he is) old, he is still active** bien qu'il soit vieux il est toujours actif; ~ **I have never liked him, I do respect him** bien que OR quoique je ne l'aie jamais aimé je le respecte, je ne l'ai jamais aimé, néanmoins je le respecte. **-2.** [but, however] mais; **I don't think it will work, ~ it's worth a try** je ne crois pas que ça va marcher, mais ça vaut la peine d'essayer; **the scar will become less visible, ~ it will never completely disappear** la cicatrice va s'estomper, mais elle ne disparaîtra jamais complètement.

altimeter ['æltɪmiːtəʳ] *n* altimètre *m*.

altitude ['æltɪtjuːd] ◇ *n* [gen & AERON] altitude *f*; [in mountains] altitude *f*, hauteur *f*; **to fly at an ~ of 8,000 metres** voler à une altitude de 8 000 mètres; **at high ~ OR ~s** en altitude, en hauteur; **at these ~s** à cette altitude, à ces hauteurs.
◇ *comp*: ~ **sickness** mal *m* d'altitude.

alt key [ælt-] *n* touche *f* alt.

alto ['æltəʊ] (*pl* altos) ◇ *adj* [voice - female] de contralto; [- male] de haute-contre; [instrument] alto *(inv)*; ~ **clef** clef *f* d'ut; ~ **saxophone/recorder** saxophone *m*/flûte *f* alto.
◇ *n* **-1.** [voice - female] contralto *m*; [- male] haute-contre *f*. **-2.** [instrument] alto *m*.

altogether [,ɔːltə'geðəʳ] ◇ *adv* **-1.** [entirely] tout à fait, entièrement; **I don't ~ agree with you** je ne suis pas tout à fait OR entièrement d'accord avec vous; **he isn't ~ reliable** on ne peut pas toujours compter sur lui; **it's ~ out of the question** il n'en est absolument pas question; **that's a different matter ~** c'est un tout autre problème. **-2.** [as a whole] en tout; **I owe him £100 ~** je lui dois 100 livres en tout; **taken ~** à tout prendre. **-3.** [in general] somme toute, tout compte fait; **~, it was an enjoyable evening** somme toute, c'était une soirée agréable.
◇ *n phr*: **in the ~** *inf Br hum* tout nu, à poil.

altruism ['æltrʊɪzm] *n* altruisme *m*.

altruist ['æltrʊɪst] *n* altruiste *mf*.

altruistic [,æltrʊ'ɪstɪk] *adj* altruiste.

ALU (*abbr of* **arithmetic and logic unit**) *n* UAL *f*.

alum ['æləm] *n* alun *m*.

aluminium [,æljʊ'mɪnɪəm] *Br*, **aluminum** [ə'luːmɪnəm] *Am* ◇ *n* aluminium *m*.
◇ *comp* [utensil] en aluminium.

alumna [ə'lʌmnə] (*pl* alumnae [-niː]) *n Am* SCH ancienne élève *f*; UNIV ancienne étudiante *f*.

alumnus [ə'lʌmnəs] (*pl* alumni [-naɪ]) *n Am* SCH ancien élève *m*; UNIV ancien étudiant *m*.

alveolar [æl'vɪələʳ] *adj* ANAT & LING alvéolaire; ~ **ridge** alvéoles *fpl* (dentaires).

alveolus [æl'vɪələs] (*pl* alveoli [-laɪ]) *n* alvéole *f*.

always ['ɔːlweɪz] *adv* toujours; **she ~ comes on Mondays** elle vient toujours le lundi; **has she ~ worn glasses?** a-t-elle toujours porté des lunettes?; **you can ~ try phoning** vous pouvez toujours essayer de téléphoner; **she's ~ complaining** elle est toujours en train de se plaindre.

alyssum ['ælɪsəm] *n (U)* alysse *f*.

Alzheimer's disease ['æltsˌhaɪməz-] *n* maladie *f* d'Alzheimer.

am [æm] → **be**.

a.m. (*abbr of* **ante meridiem**) *adv* du matin; **at 2 ~** à 2 h du matin.

AM *n* **-1.** *Am abbr of* **Master of Arts**. **-2.** (*abbr of* **amplitude modulation**) AM.

AMA (*abbr of* **American Medical Association**) *pr n ordre américain des médecins*.

amalgam [ə'mælgəm] *n* **-1.** [gen & METALL] amalgame *m*; **it is an ~ of several ideas** c'est un amalgame d'idées. **-2.** DENT amalgame *m*.

amalgamate [ə'mælgəmeɪt] ◇ *vt* **-1.** [firms, businesses] fusionner, unir. **-2.** [ideas, metals] amalgamer; **their findings were ~d with ours to produce the final report** leurs conclusions et les nôtres ont été réunies pour constituer le rapport final.
◇ *vi* **-1.** [firms] fusionner. **-2.** [races] se mélanger; [metals] s'amalgamer.

amalgamation [əˌmælgə'meɪʃn] *n* **-1.** COMM & ECON fusion *f*. **-2.** [of races] mélange *m*; [of metals] amalgamation *f*.

amanuensis [əˌmænjʊ'ensɪs] (*pl* amanuenses [-siːz]) *n fml* [secretary] secrétaire *mf*, sténographe *mf*; [transcriber, copyist] copiste *mf*.

amaranth ['æmərænθ] *n* amarante *f*.

amaryllis [,æmə'rɪlɪs] *n* amaryllis *f*.

amass [ə'mæs] *vt* [fortune, objects, information] amasser, accumuler.

amateur ['æmətəʳ] ◇ *n* [gen & SPORT] amateur *m*; **he's a keen ~** c'est un amateur enthousiaste.
◇ *adj* **-1.** [football, photographer] amateur; [painting, psychology] d'amateur; ~ **dramatics** théâtre *m* amateur; ~ **championship** championnat *m* amateur; **he has an ~ interest in psychology** il s'intéresse à la psychologie en amateur. **-2.** *pej* = **amateurish**.

amateurish [,æmə'tɜːrɪʃ] *adj pej* d'amateur, de dilettante.

amateurism ['æmətərɪzəm] *n* **-1.** SPORT amateurisme *m*. **-2.** *pej* [lack of professionalism] amateurisme *m*, dilettantisme *m*.

amatory ['æmətərɪ] *adj lit* [letter, verse] d'amour, galant *fml*; [feelings] amoureux.

amaze [ə'meɪz] *vt* stupéfier, ahurir; **you ~ me!** pas possible!; **I was ~d at OR by his courage** son courage m'a ahuri, j'ai été ahuri par son courage.

amazed [ə'meɪzd] *adj* [expression, look] de stupéfaction, ahuri, éberlué; [person] stupéfait, ahuri; **he was ~ to see her there** il était stupéfait de la trouver là.

amazement [ə'meɪzmənt] *n* stupéfaction *f*, stupeur *f*; **to our ~** à notre stupéfaction; **I watched in ~** j'ai regardé, complètement stupéfait.

amazing [ə'meɪzɪŋ] *adj* **-1.** [astonishing] stupéfiant, ahurissant; **it's ~ how fast they work** je ne reviens pas de la vitesse à laquelle ils travaillent; **that's ~!** je n'en reviens pas!; **'~ offer'** COMM 'offre exceptionnelle'. **-2.** [brilliant, very good] extraordinaire, sensationnel.

amazingly [ə'meɪzɪŋlɪ] *adv* incroyablement, extraordinairement; **he's ~ patient** il est d'une patience extraordinaire OR étonnante; **he was ~ good as Cyrano** il était absolument extraordinaire dans le rôle de Cyrano; **~ enough, she believed him** aussi étonnant que ça puisse paraître, elle l'a cru.

Amazon ['æməzn] *pr n* **-1.** [river]: **the ~** l'Amazone *f*. **-2.** [region]: **the ~ (Basin)** l'Amazonie *f*; **in the ~** en Amazonie; **the ~ rain forest** la forêt (tropicale) amazonienne. **-3.** MYTH Amazone *f*.
◆ **amazon** *n*: **she's a bit of an ~** *fig* [strong] c'est une grande bonne femme; [athletic] c'est une vraie athlète; [aggressive] c'est une vraie virago.

Amazonian [,æmə'zəʊnjən] *adj* amazonien.

ambassador [æm'bæsədəʳ] *n* POL & *fig* ambassadeur *m*; **the Spanish ~ to Morocco** l'ambassadeur d'Espagne au Maroc; **the ~'s wife** l'ambassadrice *f* ❑ **~-at-large** *Am* ambassadeur extraordinaire, chargé *m* de mission; **'The Ambassadors'** *James* 'les Ambassadeurs'.

ambassadorial [æmˌbæsə'dɔːrɪəl] *adj* d'ambassadeur.

ambassadorship [æm'bæsədəʃɪp] *n* fonction *f* d'ambassadeur.

ambassadress [æm'bæsədrɪs] *n* ambassadrice *f*.

amber ['æmbəʳ] ◇ *n* [colour, resin] ambre *m*.
◇ *adj* **-1.** [necklace, ring] d'ambre. **-2.** [dress, eyes] ambré; **~-(coloured)** ambré; **the (traffic) lights turned ~** *Br* le feu est passé à l'orange.

ambergris ['æmbəgriːs] *n* ambre gris *m*.

ambiance ['æmbɪəns] = **ambience**.

ambidextrous [,æmbɪ'dekstrəs] *adj* ambidextre.

ambience ['æmbɪəns] *n* ambiance *f*.

ambient ['æmbɪənt] *adj* ambiant.

ambiguity [,æmbɪ'gjuːətɪ] (*pl* ambiguities) *n* **-1.** [uncertainty] ambiguïté *f*, équivoque *f*; [of expression, word] ambiguïté *f*; **to avoid any ~** pour éviter tout malentendu. **-2.** [phrase] expression *f* ambiguë.

ambiguous [æm'bɪgjʊəs] *adj* ambigu, équivoque.

ambiguously [æm'bɪgjʊəslɪ] *adv* de façon ambiguë.

ambit ['æmbɪt] *n fml* [of regulation] étendue *f*, portée *f*; [of study] champ *m*; [of person] compétences *fpl*, capacités *fpl*.

ambition [æm'bɪʃn] *n* ambition *f*; **her ~ was to become a physicist** elle avait l'ambition OR son ambition était de devenir physicienne; **he has political ~s** il a des ambitions politiques; **to lack ~** manquer d'ambition.

ambitious [æm'bɪʃəs] *adj* ambitieux; **she's very ~ for her children** elle a beaucoup d'ambition pour ses enfants; **an ~ film** un film ambitieux; **as usual our holidays were nothing more ~ than a fortnight in Brighton** comme d'habitude, nos ambitions de vacances se sont bornées à aller passer quinze jours à Brighton.

ambitiously [æm'bɪʃəslɪ] *adv* ambitieusement.

ambivalence [æm'bɪvələns] *n* ambivalence *f*.

ambivalent [æm'bɪvələnt] *adj* ambivalent; **to be OR to feel ~ about sthg** être OR se sentir indécis à propos de qqch; **I have rather ~ feelings about him** j'éprouve des sentiments partagés à son égard.

amble ['æmbl] ◇ *vi* [person] marcher OR aller d'un pas tranquille; [horse] aller l'amble; **he ~d through the park** il a traversé le parc d'un pas tranquille; **we ~d home** nous sommes rentrés lentement OR sans nous presser; **she whistled as she ~d along** elle baguenaudait en sifflant.
◇ *n* [of person] pas *m* tranquille; [of horse] amble *m*; **to walk at an ~** marcher sans se presser.

ambrosia [æm'brəʊzjə] *n* ambroisie *f*.

ambulance ['æmbjʊləns] ◇ *n* ambulance *f*.
◇ *comp*: **~ driver** ambulancier *m*, -ère *f*; **~ man** [driver] ambulancier; [nurse] infirmier *m* d'ambulance; [stretcher carrier] brancardier *m*; **~ nurse** infirmier *m*, -ère *f* d'ambulance.

ambulance chaser *inf n Am pej avocat qui encourage les victimes d'accident à le consulter*.

ambulatory ['æmbjʊlətrɪ] (*pl* ambulatories) ◇ *adj* ambulatoire; **~ medical care** traitement ambulatoire.
◇ *n* ARCHIT déambulatoire *m*.

ambush ['æmbʊʃ] ◇ *vt* **-1.** [lie in wait for] tendre une embuscade à. **-2.** [attack] attirer dans une embuscade; **they were ~ed** ils sont tombés OR ils ont donné dans une embuscade.
◇ *n* embuscade *f*, guet-apens *m*; **the battalion was caught in an ~** le bataillon est tombé OR a donné dans un guet-apens.

ameba *etc* [ə'miːbə] (*pl* amebae [-biː] OR amebas) *Am* = **amoeba**.

ameliorate [ə'miːljəreɪt] *fml* ◇ *vt* améliorer.
◇ *vi* s'améliorer.

amelioration [əˌmiːljə'reɪʃn] *n fml* amélioration *f*.

amen [,ɑː'men] ◇ *n* amen *m inv*.
◇ *interj* RELIG: **~!** amen!; **~ to that!** *inf fig* bien dit!; **to say ~ to sthg** dire amen à qqch.

amenable [ə'miːnəbl] *adj* **-1.** [cooperative] accommodant, souple; **to be ~ to sthg** être disposé à qqch; **the boss is ~ to reason** le patron est raisonnable OR disposé à entendre raison; **the disease is ~ to treatment** la maladie peut être traitée; **~ to kindness** sensible à la bonté. **-2.** [accountable] responsable; **she is ~ for her actions to the committee** elle est responsable de ses actes devant le comité; **citizens ~ to the law** citoyens responsables devant la loi. **-3.** [able to be tested] vérifiable; **data ~ to analysis** données susceptibles d'être vérifiées par analyse.

amend [ə'mend] *vt* **-1.** [rectify - mistake, text] rectifier, corriger; [- behaviour, habits] réformer, amender *fml*. **-2.** [law, rule] amender, modifier; [constitution] amender.

amendment [əˈmendmənt] *n* -**1.** [correction] rectification *f*, correction *f*; [modification] modification *f*, révision *f*. -**2.** [to bill, constitution, law] amendement *m*; [to contract] avenant *m*; an ~ to the law une révision de la loi.

amends [əˈmendz] *npl* réparation *f*, compensation *f*; **to make ~ for sthg** [compensate] faire amende honorable, se racheter; [apologize] se faire pardonner; **we'll try and make ~** nous allons essayer de réparer nos torts; **I'd like to make ~ for my rudeness to you** j'aimerais réparer mon impolitesse envers vous.

amenity [əˈmiːnətɪ] (*pl* **amenities**) *n* [pleasantness] charme *m*, agrément *m*.
◆ **amenities** *npl* -**1.** [features] agréments *mpl*; [facilities] équipements *mpl*; **urban amenities** des équipements collectifs. -**2.** [social courtesy] civilités *fpl*, politesses *fpl*.

amenity bed *n Br dans un hôpital, catégorie de lits réservés aux malades qui paient pour avoir plus de confort et d'intimité.*

America [əˈmerɪkə] *pr n* Amérique *f*; **in ~** en Amérique.
◆ **Americas** *pl pr n*: **the ~s** les Amériques.

American [əˈmerɪkn] ◇ *n* Américain *m*, -e *f*.
◇ *adj* américain; **the ~ embassy** l'ambassade *f* des États-Unis ❑ **the ~ Dream** le rêve américain; **~ English** (anglais *m*) américain *m*.

Americana [əˌmerɪˈkɑːnə] *npl objets ou documents faisant partie de l'héritage culturel américain.*

American eagle *n* aigle *m* d'Amérique.

American football *n Br* football *m* américain.

American Indian *n* Indien *m*, -enne *f* d'Amérique, Amérindien *m*, -enne *f*.

Americanism [əˈmerɪkənɪzm] *n* américanisme *m*.

americanization [əˌmerɪkənaɪˈzeɪʃn] *n* américanisation *f*.

americanize, -ise [əˈmerɪkənaɪz] *vt* américaniser.

American League *pr n l'une des deux ligues professionnelles de base-ball aux États-Unis.*

American plan *n Am* pension *f* complète.

American Samoa *pr n* Samoa américaines *fpl*.

americium [ˌæməˈrɪsɪəm] *n* américium *m*.

Amerind [ˈæmərɪnd], **Amerindian** [ˌæmərˈɪndjən] ◇ *n* Indien *m*, -enne *f* d'Amérique, Améridien *m*, -enne *f*.
◇ *adj* amérindien.

amethyst [ˈæmɪθɪst] ◇ *n* -**1.** [stone] améthyste *f*. -**2.** [colour] violet *m* d'améthyste.
◇ *adj* -**1.** [necklace, ring] d'améthyste. -**2.** [colour] violet d'améthyste *(inv)*.

Amex [ˈæmeks] *pr n* (*abbr of* **American Stock Exchange**) *deuxième place boursière des États-Unis.*

amiability [ˌeɪmjəˈbɪlətɪ] *n* amabilité *f*.

amiable [ˈeɪmjəbl] *adj* aimable, gentil.

amiably [ˈeɪmjəblɪ] *adv* avec amabilité OR gentillesse, aimablement.

amicable [ˈæmɪkəbl] *adj* [feeling, relationship] amical, d'amitié; [agreement, end] à l'amiable; **to settle a dispute in an ~ way** régler un différend à l'amiable.

amicably [ˈæmɪkəblɪ] *adv* amicalement; **they welcomed me very ~** ils m'ont reçu très amicalement, leur accueil fut très amical; **let's try and settle this ~** essayons de régler ce problème à l'amiable.

amid [əˈmɪd] *prep* au milieu de, parmi; **~ all the noise and confusion, she escaped** dans la confusion générale, elle s'est échappée; **share prices fell ~ rumours of a change of government** le prix des actions a baissé face aux rumeurs selon lesquelles il allait y avoir un changement de gouvernement.

amidships [əˈmɪdʃɪps] *adj & adv* au milieu OR par le milieu du navire.

amidst [əˈmɪdst] = **amid**.

amino acid [əˈmiːnəʊ-] *n* acide *m* aminé, aminoacide *m*.

Amish [ˈɑːmɪʃ] ◇ *adj* amish.
◇ *npl*: **the ~** les Amish *mpl (communauté mennonite vivant en Pennsylvanie, austère et fidèle aux traditions)*.

amiss [əˈmɪs] ◇ *adv* -**1.** [incorrectly] de travers, mal; **to take sthg ~** mal prendre qqch; **don't take this criticism ~** ne prenez pas cette critique en mauvaise part. -**2.** [out of place] mal à propos; **a few words of explanation may not come ~ here** il conviendrait ici de donner une petite explication; **a little tact and diplomacy wouldn't go ~** un peu de tact et de diplomatie seraient les bienvenus OR ne feraient pas de mal.
◇ *adj* -**1.** [wrong]: **something seems to be ~ with the engine** on dirait qu'il y a quelque chose qui ne va pas dans le moteur; **there's something ~ with our calculations** il y a quelque chose qui ne va pas dans nos calculs. -**2.** [out of place] déplacé; **have I said something ~?** ai-je dit quelque chose qu'il ne fallait pas?; **would it be ~ to send her some flowers?** est-ce qu'il serait malvenu OR déplacé de lui offrir des fleurs?

amity [ˈæmətɪ] (*pl* **amities**) *n fml* [friendship] amitié *f*; [good relations] bonnes relations *fpl*, bons rapports *mpl*; **to live in ~ with one's fellow man** vivre en paix OR en bonne intelligence avec ses semblables *fml*.

Amman [əˈmɑːn] *pr n* Amman.

ammeter [ˈæmɪtəʳ] *n* ampèremètre *m*.

ammo *inf* [ˈæməʊ] *n (U)* munitions *fpl*.

ammonia [əˈməʊnjə] *n* [gas] ammoniac *m*; [liquid] ammoniaque *f*.

ammoniac [əˈməʊnɪæk] ◇ *adj* ammoniacal.
◇ *n* ammoniac *m*, gomme-ammoniaque *f*.

ammonite [ˈæmənaɪt] *n* -**1.** [mollusc] ammonite *f*. -**2.** [explosive] ammonal *m*.

Ammonite [ˈæmənaɪt] *n* Ammonite *mf*.

ammunition [ˌæmjʊˈnɪʃn] *n (U)* munitions *fpl*; **the letter could be used as ~ against them** *fig* la lettre pourrait être tournée contre eux.

ammunition belt *n* ceinturon *m*.

ammunition dump *n* dépôt *m* de munitions.

amnesia [æmˈniːzjə] *n* amnésie *f*; **to have** OR **to suffer (from) ~** être atteint d'amnésie, être amnésique.

amnesiac [æmˈniːzɪæk], **amnesic** [æmˈniːzɪk] ◇ *adj* amnésique.
◇ *n* amnésique *mf*.

amnesty [ˈæmnəstɪ] (*pl* **amnesties**) ◇ *n* amnistie *f*; **to declare an ~** déclarer une amnistie; **under an ~** en vertu d'une amnistie.
◇ *vt* amnistier.

Amnesty International *pr n* Amnesty International.

amniocentesis [ˌæmnɪəʊsenˈtiːsɪs] (*pl* **amniocenteses** [-siːz]) *n* amniocentèse *f*.

amnioscope [ˌæmnɪəʊˈskəʊp] *n* amnioscopie *f*.

amniotic [ˌæmnɪˈɒtɪk] *adj* amniotique; **~ fluid** liquide *m* amniotique.

amoeba [əˈmiːbə] (*pl* **amoebae** [-biː] OR **amoebas**) *n* amibe *f*.

amoebic [əˈmiːbɪk] *adj* amibien.

amoebic dysentery *n* dysenterie *f* amibienne.

amok [əˈmɒk] *adv*: **to run ~** *literal* être pris d'une crise de folie meurtrière OR furieuse; *fig* devenir fou furieux, se déchaîner; **the football fans ran ~** les supporters de foot se sont déchaînés; **defence spending has run ~** les dépenses militaires ont dérapé.

among(st) [əˈmʌŋ(st)] *prep* -**1.** [in the midst of] au milieu de, parmi; **I moved ~ the spectators** je circulais parmi les spectateurs; **she was lost ~ the crowd** elle était perdue dans la foule; **it was found ~ the rubble** on l'a trouvé parmi les gravats; **to be ~ friends** être entre amis; **murmurings of discontent arose ~ the students/the crowd** des murmures de mécontentement s'élevèrent parmi les étudiants/dans la foule. -**2.** [forming part of] parmi; **~ those who left was her brother** parmi ceux qui sont partis, il y avait son frère; **several members abstained, myself ~ them** plusieurs membres se sont abstenus, dont moi; **it is ~ her most important plays** c'est une de ses pièces les plus importantes; **that is only one ~ many possible options** ce n'est qu'une option parmi bien d'autres; **~ other things** entre autres (choses). -**3.** [within a specified group] parmi, entre; **it's a current expression ~ teenagers** c'est une expression courante chez les jeunes; **we discussed it ~ ourselves** nous en avons discuté entre nous; **I count her ~ my friends** je la compte parmi OR au nombre de mes amis. -**4.** [to each of] parmi, entre; **share out the sweets ~ the children** partagez les bonbons entre les enfants; **share the books ~ you** partagez les livres entre vous, partagez-vous les livres.

amontillado [əˌmɒntɪˈlɑːdəʊ] *n* amontillado *m*.

amoral [ˌeɪˈmɒrəl] *adj* amoral.

amorality [ˌeɪmɒˈrælətɪ] *n* amoralisme *m*, amoralité *f*.

amorous [ˈæmərəs] *adj* [person] amoureux, porté à l'amour; [glance] amoureux, ardent; [letter] d'amour; **~ advances** des avances.

amorously [ˈæmərəslɪ] *adv* amoureusement.

amorphous [əˈmɔːfəs] *adj* CHEM amorphe; [shapeless] amorphe; *fig* [personality] amorphe, mou; [ideas] informe, sans forme; [plans] vague.

amortization [əˌmɔːtɪˈzeɪʃn] *n* amortissement *m*.

amortize, -ise [əˈmɔːtaɪz] *vt* amortir.

amortizement [əˈmɔːtaɪzmənt] = **amortization**.

Amos [ˈeɪmɒs] *pr n* Amos.

amount [əˈmaʊnt] *n* -**1.** [quantity] quantité *f*; **great** OR **large ~s of money** beaucoup d'argent; **in small/large ~s** en petites/grandes quantités; **no ~ of talking can bring him back** on peut lui parler tant qu'on veut, ça ne le fera pas revenir; **I have a certain ~ of respect for them** j'ai un certain respect pour eux; **a modest ~** une quantité modeste; **any ~ of** des quantités de, énormément de; **that shop has any ~ of books** il y a des masses de livres dans ce magasin; **you'll have any ~ of time for reading on holiday** tu auras tout ton temps pour lire pendant les vacances. -**2.** [sum, total] montant *m*, total *m*; [of money] somme *f*; **do you have the exact ~?** avez-vous le compte (exact)?; **she billed us for the ~ of £50** elle nous a présenté une facture d'un montant de OR qui se montait à 50 livres; **you're in credit to the ~ of £100** vous avez un crédit de 100 livres; **please find enclosed a cheque to the ~ of $100** veuillez trouver ci-joint un chèque (d'un montant) de 100 dollars.
◆ **amount to** *vt insep* -**1.** [total] se monter à, s'élever à; **he left debts ~ing to over £1,800** il a laissé des dettes qui s'élèvent OR se montent à plus de 1 800 livres; **profits last year ~ed to several million dollars** les bénéfices pour l'année dernière se chiffrent à plusieurs millions de dollars; **after tax it doesn't ~ to much** après impôts ça ne représente pas grand-chose; **he'll never ~ to much** il ne fera jamais grand-chose. -**2.** [be equivalent to]: **it ~s to something not far short of stealing** c'est pratiquement du vol; **it ~s to the same thing** cela revient au même; **what his speech ~s to is an attack on democracy** en fait, avec ce discours, il attaque la démocratie.

amour [əˈmʊəʳ] *n lit* OR *hum* aventure *f* amoureuse, liaison *f*.

amp [æmp] *n* -**1.** = **ampere**. -**2.** *inf* [amplifier] ampli *m*.

ampere [ˈæmpeəʳ] *n* ampère *m*.

ampersand [ˈæmpəsænd] *n* esperluette *f*.

amphetamine [æmˈfetəmiːn] *n* amphétamine *f*.

amphibia [æmˈfɪbɪə] *npl* batraciens *mpl*, amphibiens *mpl*.

amphibian [æm'fɪbɪən] ◇ *n* -**1.** ZOOL amphibie *m*. -**2.** [plane] avion *m* amphibie; [car] voiture *f* amphibie; [tank] char *m* amphibie.
◇ *adj* amphibie.

amphibious [æm'fɪbɪəs] *adj* amphibie.

amphitheatre *Br*, **amphitheater** *Am* ['æmfɪ,θɪətəʳ] *n* amphithéâtre *m*.

amphora ['æmfərə] (*pl* amphorae [-riː] OR amphoras) *n* amphore *f*.

ample ['æmpl] *adj* -**1.** [large - clothing] ample; [- garden, lawn] grand, vaste; [- helping, stomach] grand; a woman of ~ proportions une femme forte. -**2.** [more than enough - supplies] bien OR largement assez de; [- proof, reason] solide; [- fortune, means] gros; he was given ~ opportunity to refuse il a eu largement l'occasion OR il a eu de nombreuses occasions de refuser; we have ~ reason to suspect foul play nous avons de solides OR de bonnes raisons de soupçonner quelque chose de louche; you'll have ~ time to finish vous aurez largement le temps de finir.

amplification [,æmplɪfɪ'keɪʃn] *n* -**1.** [of power, sound] amplification *f*. -**2.** [further explanation] explication *f*, développement *m*; the facts require no ~ les faits ne demandent pas plus d'explications.

amplifier ['æmplɪfaɪəʳ] *n* amplificateur *m*.

amplify ['æmplɪfaɪ] *vt* -**1.** [power, sound] amplifier. -**2.** [facts, idea, speech] développer.
◆ **amplify on** *vt insep* développer.

amplitude ['æmplɪtjuːd] *n* [breadth, scope] ampleur *f*, envergure *f*; ASTRON & PHYS amplitude *f*.

amplitude modulation *n* modulation *f* d'amplitude.

amply ['æmplɪ] *adv* amplement, largement; [person]: ~ built bien bâti; ~ rewarded largement récompensé; as has been ~ shown comme il a été amplement démontré.

ampoule *Br*, **ampule** *Am* ['æmpuːl] *n* ampoule *f (de médicament)*.

amputate ['æmpjʊteɪt] *vt* amputer; they had to ~ her arm ils ont dû l'amputer du bras; her right arm was ~d elle a été amputée du bras droit.

amputation [,æmpjʊ'teɪʃn] *n* amputation *f*.

amputee [,æmpjʊ'tiː] *n* amputé *m*, -e *f*.

Amsterdam [,æmstə'dæm] *pr n* Amsterdam.

amt *written abbr of* amount.

Amtrak® ['æmtræk] *pr n société nationale de chemins de fer aux États-Unis*.

amuck [ə'mʌk] = **amok**.

amulet ['æmjʊlɪt] *n* amulette *f*, fétiche *m*.

Amur [ə'mʊə] *pr n*: the (River) ~ l'Amour *m*.

amuse [ə'mjuːz] *vt* -**1.** [occupy] divertir, amuser, distraire; he ~d himself (by) building sandcastles il s'est amusé à faire des châteaux de sable; you'll have to ~ yourself this afternoon il va falloir trouver de quoi t'occuper cet après-midi. -**2.** [make laugh] amuser, faire rire; he ~s me il me fait rire; does the idea ~ you? l'idée vous amuse-t-elle?

amused [ə'mjuːzd] *adj* -**1.** [occupied] occupé, diverti; to keep o.s. ~ s'occuper, se distraire; the game kept them ~ for hours le jeu les a occupés pendant des heures. -**2.** [delighted, entertained] amusé; they were greatly ~ at OR by the cat's behaviour le comportement du chat les a bien fait rire; I was greatly ~ to hear about his adventures cela m'a beaucoup amusé d'entendre parler de ses aventures; she was not (at all) ~ elle n'a pas trouvé ça drôle (du tout); an ~ look/smile un regard/sourire amusé; she looked at him, ~ elle l'a regardé d'un air amusé ❑ we are not ~ très drôle! *iron (expression faisant allusion à une réflexion qu'aurait faite la reine Victoria pour exprimer sa désapprobation)*.

amusement [ə'mjuːzmənt] *n* -**1.** [enjoyment] amusement *m*, divertissement *m*; she smiled in ~ elle a eu un sourire amusé; I listened in ~ amusé, j'ai écouté; we've arranged a party for your ~ nous avons prévu une soirée pour vous divertir OR vous distraire; much to everyone's ~ au grand amusement de tous; there was much ~ at her untimely entrance son entrée intempestive a fait rire tout le monde. -**2.** [pastime] distraction *f*, amusement *m*; there are few ~s in small towns les petites villes offrent peu de distractions; what ~s do you have for the children? qu'est-ce que vous avez pour distraire les enfants? -**3.** [at a funfair] attraction *f*; to go on the ~s monter sur les manèges.

amusement arcade *n* galerie *f* de jeux.

amusement park *n* parc *m* d'attractions.

amusing [ə'mjuːzɪŋ] *adj* amusant, drôle.

amusingly [ə'mjuːzɪŋlɪ] *adv* d'une façon amusante.

amyl ['æmɪl] *n* amyle *m*.

an [*stressed* æn, *unstressed* ən] ◇ *indef art* → **a**.
◇ *conj arch* si.

ANA *pr n* -**1.** (*abbr of* American Newspaper Association) *syndicat américain de la presse écrite*. -**2.** (*abbr of* American Nurses Association) *syndicat américain d'infirmiers*.

Anabaptism [,ænə'bæptɪzəm] *n* anabaptisme *m*.

Anabaptist [,ænə'bæptɪst] ◇ *adj* anabaptiste.
◇ *n* anabaptiste *mf*.

anabolic [,ænə'bɒlɪk] *adj* anabolisant.

anabolic steroid *n* stéroïde *m* anabolisant.

anachronism [ə'nækrənɪzm] *n* anachronisme *m*.

anachronistic [ə,nækrə'nɪstɪk] *adj* anachronique.

anaconda [,ænə'kɒndə] *n* anaconda *m*.

anaemia *Br*, **anemia** *Am* [ə'niːmjə] *n* MED & *fig* anémie *f*; to suffer from ~ être anémique.

anaemic *Br*, **anemic** *Am* [ə'niːmɪk] *adj* -**1.** MED & *fig* anémique; to become ~ s'anémier. -**2.** [pale] anémique, blême.

anaerobe [æ'neərəʊb] *n* anaérobie *m*.

anaerobic [,ænə'rəʊbɪk] *adj* anaérobie; ~ exercise exercice *m* d'anaérobie.

anaesthesia *Br*, **anesthesia** *Am* [,ænɪs'θiːzjə] *n* anesthésie *f*; general/local ~ anesthésie générale/locale.

anaesthetic *Br*, **anesthetic** *Am* [,ænɪs'θetɪk] ◇ *n* anesthésique *m*, anesthésiant *m*; under ~ sous anesthésie; to give sb an ~ anesthésier qqn; local/general ~ anesthésie *f* locale/générale.
◇ *adj* anesthésique, anesthésiant.

anaesthetist *Br*, **anesthetist** *Am* [æ'niːsθətɪst] *n* anesthésiste *mf*.

anaesthetize, -ise *Br*, **anesthetize** *Am* [æ'niːsθətaɪz] *vt* MED anesthésier; *fig* anesthésier, insensibiliser.

anagram ['ænəgræm] *n* anagramme *f*.

anal ['eɪnl] *adj* -**1.** ANAT anal; ~ intercourse OR sex sodomie *f*. -**2.** PSYCH anal; he's so ~ *inf* il est vraiment coincé.

analgesia [,ænæl'dʒiːzjə] *n* analgésie *f*.

analgesic [,ænæl'dʒiːsɪk] ◇ *adj* analgésique.
◇ *n* analgésique *m*.

analog *Am* = **analogue**.

analogic(al) [,ænə'lɒdʒɪk(l)] *adj* analogique.

analogous [ə'næləgəs] *adj* analogue; to be ~ to OR with sthg être analogue à qqch.

analogue *Br*, **analog** *Am* ['ænəlɒg] ◇ *n* analogue *m*.
◇ *comp* [clock, watch] analogique; ~ device appareil analogique; ~ computer calculateur *m* analogique.

analogy [ə'nælədʒɪ] (*pl* analogies) *n* analogie *f*; the author draws an ~ between a fear of falling and the fear of death l'auteur établit une analogie entre la peur de tomber et la peur de mourir; by ~ with sthg par analogie avec qqch; reasoning from ~ raisonnement par analogie.

analysable *Br*, **analyzable** *Am* ['ænəlaɪzəbl] *adj* analysable.

analysand [ə'nælɪsænd] *n* patient *m* en analyse.

analyse *Br*, **analyze** *Am* ['ænəlaɪz] *vt* -**1.** [examine] analyser, faire l'analyse de; [sentence] analyser, faire l'analyse logique de. -**2.** PSYCH psychanalyser.

analysis [ə'næləsɪs] (*pl* analyses [-siːz]) *n* -**1.** [examination] analyse *f*; [of sentence] analyse *f* logique; in the final OR last OR ultimate ~ en dernière analyse, en fin de compte. -**2.** PSYCH psychanalyse *f*, analyse *f*; to be in ~ être en analyse, suivre une analyse.

analyst ['ænəlɪst] *n* -**1.** [specialist] analyste *mf*. -**2.** PSYCH analyste *mf*, psychanalyste *mf*.

analytic(al) [,ænə'lɪtɪk(l)] *adj* analytique; ~ language langue *f* analytique.

analytical geometry *n* géométrie *f* analytique.

analytical psychology *n* psychologie *f* analytique OR des profondeurs.

analytics [,ænə'lɪtɪks] *n (U)* analytique *f*.

analyze *etc Am* = **analyse**.

anamorphic [,ænə'mɔːfɪk] *adj* anamorphosique.

anamorphosis [,ænə'mɔːfəsɪs] *n* anamorphose *f*.

anaphora [ə'næfərə] *n* LING anaphorique *m*; [in rhetoric] anaphore *f*.

anaphoric [,ænə'fɒrɪk] *adj* anaphorique.

anarchic(al) [æ'nɑːkɪk(l)] *adj* anarchique.

anarchism ['ænəkɪzm] *n* anarchisme *m*.

anarchist ['ænəkɪst] *n* anarchiste *mf*.

anarchistic [,ænə'kɪstɪk] *adj* anarchiste.

anarchy ['ænəkɪ] *n* anarchie *f*.

anastigmatic [,ænəstɪg'mætɪk] *adj* anastigmate.

anathema [ə'næθəmə] *n* -**1.** *fml* [detested thing] abomination *f*; such ideas are ~ to the general public le grand public a horreur de ces idées; his books are ~ to her ses livres lui sont insupportables. -**2.** RELIG & *fig* anathème *m*.

anathematize, -ise [ə'næθəmətaɪz] *vt* RELIG anathématiser, frapper d'anathème; *fig* jeter l'anathème sur.

Anatolia [,ænə'təʊljə] *pr n* Anatolie *f*; in ~ en Anatolie.

Anatolian [,ænə'təʊljən] ◇ *n* Anatolien *m*, -enne *f*.
◇ *adj* anatolien.

anatomical [,ænə'tɒmɪkl] *adj* anatomique.

anatomically [,ænə'tɒmɪklɪ] *adv* anatomiquement; ~ correct [doll, model] réaliste du point de vue anatomique.

anatomist [ə'nætəmɪst] *n* anatomiste *mf*.

anatomize, -ise [ə'nætəmaɪz] *vt* MED & *fig* disséquer.

anatomy [ə'nætəmɪ] *n* -**1.** BIOL [of animal, person] anatomie *f*; *fig* [of situation, society] structure *f*. -**2.** *fig* [analysis] analyse *f*. -**3.** *hum* [body] corps *m*, anatomie *f hum*; every part of his ~ hurt il était plein de courbatures, il avait mal partout.

ANC (*abbr of* African National Congress) *pr n* ANC *m*.

ancestor ['ænsestəʳ] *n* [forefather] ancêtre *m*, aïeul *m*; *fig* [of computer, system] ancêtre *m*.

ancestral [æn'sestrəl] *adj* ancestral.

ancestress ['ænsestrɪs] *n* aïeule *f*.

ancestry ['ænsestrɪ] (*pl* ancestries) *n* -**1.** [lineage] ascendance *f*. -**2.** [ancestors] ancêtres *mpl*, aïeux *mpl*.

anchor ['æŋkəʳ] ◇ *n* -**1.** [for boat] ancre *f*; to lie OR to ride at ~ être à l'ancre; to cast OR to come to OR to drop ~ jeter l'ancre, mouiller; up OR weigh ~! levez l'ancre! -**2.** [fastener] attache *f*. -**3.** *fig* [mainstay] soutien *m*, point *m* d'ancrage; religion is her ~ in life la religion est son soutien dans la vie; many people need the ~ of family life beaucoup de gens ont besoin de la vie de famille comme point d'ancrage. -**4.** TV présentateur *m*, -trice *f*. -**5.** SPORT pilier *m*, pivot *m*.
◇ *vi* -**1.** [boat] jeter l'ancre, mouiller. -**2.** [fasten] s'ancrer, se fixer. -**3.** [settle] se fixer, s'installer; they remain firmly ~ed in tradition ils restent fermement ancrés dans la tradition.
◇ *vt* -**1.** [boat] ancrer. -**2.** [fasten] ancrer, fixer. -**3.** TV [programme] présenter.

anchorage ['æŋkərɪdʒ] *n* -**1.** NAUT [place] mouillage *m*, ancrage *m*; [fee] droits *mpl* de mouillage OR d'ancrage. -**2.** [fastening] ancrage *m*, attache *f*. -**3.** *fig* [mainstay] soutien *m*, point *m* d'ancrage.

anchorite ['æŋkəraɪt] *n* ermite *m*, solitaire *m*; RELIG anachorète *m*.

anchorman ['æŋkəmæn] (*pl* anchormen [-men]) *n* -**1.** TV présentateur *m*. -**2.** SPORT pilier *m*, pivot *m*.

anchorwoman ['æŋkə,wʊmən] (*pl* anchorwomen [-,wɪmɪn]) *n* TV présentatrice *f*.

anchovy [*Br* 'æntʃəvɪ, *Am* 'æntʃəʊvɪ] (*pl inv* OR anchovies) *n* anchois *m*; ~ **paste** pâte *f* d'anchois; ~ **sauce** sauce *f* aux anchois.

ancient ['eɪnʃənt] ◇ *adj* -**1.** [custom, ruins] ancien; [civilization, world] antique; [relic] historique; ~ **Greece** la Grèce antique ☐ ~ **history** histoire *f* ancienne; **their affair is** ~ **history now** *fig* leur liaison fait maintenant partie du passé OR est maintenant de l'histoire ancienne; ~ **monument** monument *m* historique OR classé; ~ **times** les temps *mpl* anciens, l'antiquité *f*; **'The Rime of the Ancient Mariner'** *Coleridge* 'la Chanson du vieux marin'. -**2.** *hum* [very old -person] très vieux; [- thing] antique, antédiluvien; **she drives an** ~ **Volkswagen** elle conduit une Volkswagen qui a fait la guerre; **her husband's absolutely** ~ son mari est vraiment très vieux.
◇ *n* -**1.** HIST: **the** ~**s** les anciens *mpl*. -**2.** *arch* OR *hum* [old person] vieillard *m*, vieille *f*.

ancillary [æn'sɪlərɪ] (*pl* ancillaries)
◇ *adj* -**1.** [supplementary] auxiliaire; **local services are** ~ **to the national programme** les services locaux apportent leur aide OR contribution au programme national; ~ **staff** [gen] personnel *m* auxiliaire; [in hospital] personnel *m* des services auxiliaires, agents *mpl* des hôpitaux; [in school] personnel *m* auxiliaire, auxiliaires *mfpl*. -**2.** [subsidiary - reason] subsidiaire; [- advantage, cost] accessoire.
◇ *n* -**1.** [helper] auxiliaire *mf*; **hospital ancillaries** personnel *m* des services auxiliaires, agents *mpl* des hôpitaux. -**2.** [of firm] filiale *f*.

Ancona [æŋ'kəʊnə] *pr n* Ancône.

and [ænd] ◇ *conj* -**1.** [in addition to] et; **brother** ~ **sister** frère et sœur; **get your hat** ~ **coat** va chercher ton manteau et ton chapeau; **he went out without his shoes** ~ **socks on** il est sorti sans mettre ses chaussures ni ses chaussettes; **he goes fishing winter** ~ **summer (alike)** il va à la pêche en hiver comme en été; **I have to interview** ~ **assess people as part of my job** mon travail consiste en partie à m'occuper des entretiens et à évaluer les capacités des gens; **you can't work for us** AND **work for our competitors** vous ne pouvez pas travailler ET pour nous ET pour nos concurrents; ~**/or** et/ou; **I'm Richard Rogers** – ~? je suis Richard Rogers – (et) alors? ☐ **there are books** ~ **books** il y a livres et livres; **there are champions** ~ **(there are) great champions** il y a les champions et (il y a) les grands champions. -**2.** [then]: **he opened the door** ~ **went out** il a ouvert la porte et est sorti; **I fell** ~ **cut my knee** je me suis ouvert le genou en tombant. -**3.** [with infinitive]: **go** ~ **look for it** va le chercher; **try** ~ **understand** essayez de comprendre. -**4.** [but] mais; **I want to go** ~ **he doesn't** je veux y aller, mais lui ne veut pas. -**5.** [in numbers]: **one hundred** ~ **three** cent trois; **five pounds** ~ **ten pence** cinq livres (et) dix (pence); **two hours** ~ **ten minutes** deux heures dix (minutes); **three** ~ **a half years** trois ans et demi; **four** ~ **two thirds** quatre deux tiers. -**6.** [indicating continuity, repetition]: **he cried** ~ **cried** il n'arrêtait pas de pleurer; **for hours** ~ **hours** pendant des heures (et des heures); **he goes on** ~ **on about politics** quand il commence à parler politique il n'y a plus moyen de l'arrêter ‖ [with comparative adjectives]: **fainter** ~ **fainter** de plus en plus faible; **louder** ~ **louder** de plus en plus fort. -**7.** [as intensifier]: **her room was nice** ~ **sunny** sa chambre était bien ensoleillée; **the soup is good** ~ **hot** la soupe est bien chaude; **he's good** ~ **mad** *inf* il est fou furieux. -**8.** [with implied conditional]: **one move** ~ **you're dead** un geste et vous êtes mort. -**9.** [introducing questions] et; ~ **how's your family?** et comment va la famille?; **I went to New York** – ~ **how did you like it?** je suis allé à New York – et alors, ça vous a plu? -**10.** [introducing statement]: ~ **now it's time for "Kaleidoscope"** et maintenant, voici l'heure de «Kaléidoscope»; ~ **another thing...!** ah! autre chose OR j'oubliais ‖ [what's more]: ~ **you still owe me money!** et tu me dois encore de l'argent!; ~ **that's not all...** et ce n'est pas tout...
◇ *n*: **I want no ifs,** ~**s or buts** je ne veux pas de discussion.
◆ **and all** *adv phr* -**1.** [and everything] et tout (ce qui s'ensuit); **the whole lot went flying, plates, cups, teapot** ~ **all** tout a volé, les assiettes, les tasses, la théière et tout. -**2.** ▽ *Br* [as well] aussi; **you can wipe that grin off your face** ~ **all** tu peux aussi arrêter de sourire comme ça.
◆ **and so on (and so forth)** *adv phr* et ainsi de suite.

Andalusia [,ændə'lu:zjə] *pr n* Andalousie *f*; **in** ~ en Andalousie.

Andalusian [,ændə'lu:zjən] ◇ *n* Andalou *m*, -se *f*.
◇ *adj* andalou.

andalusite [,ændə'lu:saɪt] *n* andalousite *f*.

Andean [æn'di:ən] *adj* des Andes, andin.

Andes ['ændi:z] *pl pr n*: **the** ~ les Andes *fpl*; **in the** ~ dans les Andes.

andesite ['ændɪzaɪt] *n* andésite *f*.

andiron ['ændaɪən] *n* chenet *m*.

Andorra [æn'dɔ:rə] *pr n* Andorre *f*; **in** ~ en Andorre; **the principality of** ~ la principauté d'Andorre.

Andorran [æn'dɔ:rən] ◇ *n* Andorran *m*, -e *f*.
◇ *adj* andorran.

andradite ['ændrədaɪt] *n* andradite *f*.

Andrew ['ændru:] *pr n*: **Saint** ~ saint André; **Saint** ~**'s Day** la Saint-André; **Prince** ~ le prince Andrew.

androcentric [,ændrəʊ'sentrɪk] *adj* androcentrique.

Androcles ['ændrə,kli:z] *pr n* Androclès.

androgen ['ændrədʒən] *n* androgène *m*.

androgynous [æn'drɒdʒɪnəs] *adj* BIOL & BOT androgyne.

android ['ændrɔɪd] ◇ *adj* androïde.
◇ *n* androïde *m*.

Andromache [æn'drɒməkɪ] *pr n* Andromaque.

Andromeda [æn'drɒmɪdə] *pr n* Andromède.

androsterone [æn'drɒstərəʊn] *n* androstérone *f*.

Andy Capp [,ændɪ'kæp] *pr n personnage de bande dessinée incarnant, sous une forme caricaturale, un ouvrier machiste, paresseux et irrévérencieux.*

anecdotal [,ænek'dəʊtl] *adj* anecdotique; ~ **evidence** preuve *f* OR témoignage *m* anecdotique.

anecdote ['ænɪkdəʊt] *n* anecdote *f*.

anecdotist ['ænɪkdəʊtɪst] *n* anecdotier *m*, -ère *f*.

anemia *etc Am* = **anaemia**.

anemometer [,ænɪ'mɒmɪtə'] *n* anémomètre *m*.

anemone [ə'nemənɪ] *n* anémone *f*.

anencephalic [,ænenke'fælɪk] *adj* anencéphale.

aneroid ['ænərɔɪd] *adj* anéroïde; ~ **barometer** baromètre *m* anéroïde.

anesthesia *etc Am* = **anaesthesia**.

anesthesiologist [ænɪs,θi:zɪ'ɒlədʒɪst] *n Am* anesthésiste *mf*.

anestrus *Am* = **anoestrus**.

aneurism ['ænjʊərɪzm] *n* anévrisme *m*, anévrysme *m*.

anew [ə'nju:] *adv lit* -**1.** [again] de nouveau, encore; **the fighting began** ~ le combat reprit. -**2.** [in a new way] à nouveau; **to start life** ~ repartir à zéro.

Anfield ['ænfi:ld] *pr n stade de football à Liverpool.*

angel ['eɪndʒəl] *n* -**1.** RELIG ange *m*; **an** ~ **of mercy** un ange de miséricorde ☐ **the Angel of Darkness** l'ange des ténèbres; **to be on the side of the** ~**s** être du bon côté; **to go where** ~**s fear to tread** s'aventurer en terrain dangereux. -**2.** [person] ange *m*, amour *m*; **be an** ~ **and fetch me a glass of water** sois gentil, va me chercher un verre d'eau. -**3.** *inf* THEAT [investor] commanditaire *mf*.

angel cake *n* ≃ gâteau *m* de Savoie.

Angeleno [ændʒə'li:nəʊ] *n habitant de Los Angeles.*

angelfish ['eɪndʒəlfɪʃ] (*pl inv* OR angelfishes) *n* [fish] scalaire *m*; [shark] ange *m*.

angelic(al) [æn'dʒelɪk(l)] *adj* angélique; **she looks absolutely** ~ elle a vraiment l'air d'un ange OR angélique.

angelica [æn'dʒelɪkə] *n* angélique *f*.

angelus ['ændʒələs] *n* [bell, prayer] angélus *m*.

anger ['æŋgə'] ◇ *n* colère *f*, fureur *f*; **she felt intense** ~ elle était très en colère; **in a fit** OR **a moment of** ~ dans un accès OR un mouvement de colère; **he later regretted words spoken in** ~ il regretta ensuite les mots prononcés sous l'empire de la colère; **his family reacted with** ~ **and disbelief at the verdict** sa famille a réagi avec colère et incrédulité à l'annonce du verdict; **she spoke with barely suppressed** ~ elle parla avec une colère à peine dissimulée OR en réprimant mal sa colère; **his remarks moved them to** ~ ses observations les ont mis en colère.
◇ *vt* mettre en colère, énerver; **he's easily** ~**ed** il se met facilement en colère, il s'emporte facilement, il est irascible.

angina [æn'dʒaɪnə] *n* angine *f*.

angina pectoris [-'pektərɪs] *n* angine *f* de poitrine.

Angkor ['æŋkɔ:'] *pr n* Angkor.

angle ['æŋgl] ◇ *n* -**1.** [gen & GEOM] angle *m*; **the roads intersect at an** ~ **of 90°** les routes se croisent à angle droit; **the car hit us at an** ~ la voiture nous a heurtés de biais; **she wore her hat at an** ~ elle portait son chapeau penché; **cut at an** ~ coupé en biseau; **the shop stands at an** ~ **to the street** le magasin est à l'angle de la rue. -**2.** [corner] angle *m*, coin *m*. -**3.** *fig* [point of view] angle *m*, aspect *m*; **seen from this** ~ vu sous cet angle; **he examined the issue from all** ~**s** il a étudié la question sous tous les angles; **from an economic** ~ d'un point de vue économique; **what's your** ~ **on the situation?** comment voyez-vous la situation?; **we need a new** ~ il nous faut un éclairage OR un point de vue nouveau. -**4.** *inf* [trick]: **she knows all the** ~**s** elle en connaît un bout OR un rayon. -**5.** *inf* [motive] raison *f*, motif *m*; **what's his** ~ **in all this?** qu'est-ce qu'il espère y gagner?
◇ *vt* -**1.** [move] orienter; **I** ~**d the light towards the workbench** j'ai orienté OR dirigé la lumière sur l'établi. -**2.** *fig* [slant] présenter sous un certain angle; **the article was deliberately** ~**d to provoke a certain response** l'article était rédigé de façon à provoquer une réaction bien précise.
◇ *vi* -**1.** [slant] s'orienter; **the road** ~**d (off) to the right** la route tournait à droite. -**2.** FISHING pêcher à la ligne; **to go angling** aller à la pêche (à la ligne) ‖ *fig*: **to** ~ **for sthg** chercher (à avoir) qqch; **stop angling for compliments!** arrête de chercher des compliments!; **he's always angling for an invitation/a job** il est toujours en train de chercher à se faire inviter/à se faire embaucher.

Angle ['æŋgl] *n* Angle *mf*.

angle bracket *n* crochet *m*.

angle plate *n* CONSTR cornière *f*, équerre *f*.

Anglepoise® ['æŋglpɔɪz] *n* lampe *f* architecte.

angler ['æŋglə'] *n* -**1.** FISHING pêcheur *m*, -euse *f* (à la ligne). -**2.** [fish] lotte *f* de mer, baudroie *f*.

Anglican ['æŋglɪkən] ◇ *adj* anglican; the ~ Communion la communion OR communauté anglicane.
◇ *n* anglican *m*, -e *f*.

Anglicanism ['æŋglɪkənɪzm] *n* anglicanisme *m*.

anglicism ['æŋglɪsɪzm] *n* anglicisme *m*.

Anglicist ['æŋglɪsɪst] *n* angliciste *mf*.

anglicize, **-ise** ['æŋglɪsaɪz] *vt* angliciser.

angling ['æŋglɪŋ] *n* pêche *f* à la ligne.

Anglo ['æŋgləʊ] (*pl* **Anglos**) *n* **-1.** *Am* Américain blanc *m*, Américaine blanche *f*. **-2.** *Can* Canadien *m*, -enne *f* anglophone.

Anglo- *in cpds* anglo-.

Anglo-American ◇ *adj* anglo-américain.
◇ *n* Américain *m*, -e *f* d'origine anglaise.

Anglo-Catholic *n anglican acceptant les préceptes de l'Église catholique sans pour autant se convertir.*

Anglo-French *adj* anglo-français, franco-anglais, franco-britannique.

Anglo-Indian ◇ *adj* anglo-indien.
◇ *n* **-1.** [person of mixed British and Indian descent] métis *m*, -isse *f* d'origine anglaise et indienne. **-2.** [English person living in India] Anglais *m*, -e *f* des Indes.

Anglo-Irish ◇ *adj* anglo-irlandais; the ~ Agreement *accord conclu en 1985 entre le Royaume-Uni et la république d'Irlande pour garantir la paix et la stabilité en Irlande du Nord.*
◇ *n* LING anglais *m* parlé en Irlande.
◇ *npl*: the ~ les Irlandais *mpl* d'origine anglaise.

Anglo-Norman ◇ *adj* anglo-normand.
◇ *n* HIST **-1.** [person] Anglais *m*, -e *f* d'origine normande. **-2.** LING anglo-normand *m*.

anglophile ['æŋgləʊfaɪl] *adj* anglophile.
◆ **Anglophile** *n* anglophile *mf*.

anglophobe ['æŋgləʊfəʊb] *adj* anglophobe.
◆ **Anglophobe** *n* anglophobe *mf*.

Anglo-Saxon ◇ *n* **-1.** [person] Anglo-Saxon *m*, -onne *f*. **-2.** LING anglo-saxon *m*.
◇ *adj* anglo-saxon.

Angola [æŋ'gəʊlə] *pr n* Angola *m*; in ~ en Angola.

Angolan [æŋ'gəʊlən] ◇ *n* Angolais *m*, -e *f*.
◇ *adj* angolais.

angora [æŋ'gɔːrə] ◇ *n* **-1.** [animal] angora *m*; ~ (cat/goat/rabbit) (chat *m*/chèvre *f*/lapin *m*) angora. **-2.** [cloth, yarn] laine *f* angora, angora *m*.
◇ *adj* **-1.** [cat, rabbit] angora *(inv)*. **-2.** [coat, sweater] en angora.

Angostura bitters® [æŋgə'stjʊərə-] *npl* bitter *m* à base d'angusture.

angrily ['æŋgrəlɪ] *adv* [deny, speak] avec colère OR emportement; [leave, stand up] en colère.

angry ['æŋgrɪ] (*compar* angrier, *superl* angriest) *adj* **-1.** [person - cross] en colère, fâché; [- furious] furieux; to be ~ at OR with sb être fâché OR en colère contre qqn; she's ~ about OR at not having been invited elle est en colère parce qu'elle n'a pas été invitée, elle est furieuse de ne pas avoir été invitée; they're ~ at the price increase ils sont très mécontents de l'augmentation des prix; I'm ~ with myself for having forgotten je m'en veux d'avoir oublié; to get ~ se mettre en colère, se fâcher; her remarks made me ~ ses observations m'ont mis en colère; his insolence made her very ~ son insolence l'a mise hors d'elle ❑ ~ young man jeune rebelle *m*; the Angry Young Men *Br jeunes écrivains britanniques protestataires des années 50*. **-2.** [look, tone] irrité, furieux; [outburst, words] violent; in an ~ voice d'un ton irrité OR furieux; he wrote her an ~ letter il lui a écrit une lettre dans laquelle il exprimait sa colère. **-3.** *fig* [sky] menaçant; [sea] mauvais, démonté. **-4.** [inflamed] enflammé, irrité; [painful] douloureux; she has an ~-looking scar on her cheek elle a une vilaine cicatrice sur la joue.

angst [æŋst] *n* angoisse *f*.

angstrom ['æŋstrəm] *n* angström *m*, angstroem *m*.

anguish ['æŋgwɪʃ] ◇ *n* [mental] angoisse *f*; [physical] supplice *m*; to be in ~ [worried] être angoissé OR dans l'angoisse; [in pain] souffrir le martyre, être au supplice; her indifference caused him great ~ son indifférence l'angoissait beaucoup.
◇ *vt* angoisser, inquiéter énormément.

anguished ['æŋgwɪʃt] *adj* angoissé; an ~ cry un cri d'angoisse OR angoissé.

angular ['æŋgjʊlə^r] *adj* **-1.** [features, room] anguleux; [face] anguleux, osseux; [body] anguleux, décharné. **-2.** [movement] saccadé, haché. **-3.** TECH [distance, speed] angulaire.

anhydride [æn'haɪdraɪd] *n* anhydride *m*.

anhydrite [æn'haɪdraɪt] *n* anhydrite *f*.

anhydrous [æn'haɪdrəs] *adj* anhydre.

aniline ['ænɪliːn] *n* aniline *f*; ~ dye colorant *m* à base d'aniline.

animadvert [ˌænɪmæd'vɜːt] *vi lit* critiquer, blâmer; to ~ on OR upon sthg critiquer OR censurer *lit* qqch.

animal ['ænɪml] ◇ *n* **-1.** ZOOL animal *m*; [excluding humans] animal *m*, bête *f*; man is a social ~ l'homme est un animal sociable; she's not a political ~ elle n'a pas la politique dans le sang. **-2.** *pej* [brute] brute *f*; he's like an ~ when he gets drunk c'est une brute lorsqu'il est ivre. **-3.** [thing] chose *f*; French socialism is a very different ~ le socialisme à la française est complètement différent; there's no such ~ ça n'existe pas.
◇ *adj* **-1.** [products] animal; ~ lover ami *m*, -e *f* des animaux OR des bêtes; ~ rights droits *mpl* des animaux ❑ 'Animal Farm' *Orwell* 'la Ferme des animaux'. **-2.** [desire, needs] animal, bestial; [courage, instinct] animal; ~ high spirits vivacité *f*, entrain *m*.

animal husbandry *n* élevage *m*.

animalism ['ænɪməlɪzm] *n* **-1.** [animal trait] animalité *f*. **-2.** [sensuality] animalité *f*, sensualité *f*. **-3.** [theory] animalisme *m*.

animal kingdom *n*: the ~ le règne animal.

animal magnetism *n* magnétisme *m*, charme *m*.

animate [*vt* 'ænɪmeɪt, *adj* 'ænɪmət] ◇ *vt* **-1.** [give life to] animer. **-2.** *fig* [enliven - face, look, party] animer, égayer; [- discussion] animer, stimuler. **-3.** [move to action] motiver, inciter. **-4.** CIN & TV animer.
◇ *adj* vivant, animé.

animated ['ænɪmeɪtɪd] *adj* animé; to become ~ s'animer.

animated cartoon *n* dessin *m* animé.

animatedly ['ænɪmeɪtɪdlɪ] *adv* [behave, participate] avec vivacité OR entrain; [talk] d'un ton animé, avec animation.

animation [ˌænɪ'meɪʃn] *n* **-1.** [of discussion, party] animation *f*; [of place, street] activité *f*, animation *f*; [of person] vivacité *f*, entrain *m*; [of face, look] animation *f*. **-2.** CIN & TV animation *f*.

animator ['ænɪmeɪtə^r] *n* animateur *m*, -trice *f*.

animism ['ænɪmɪzm] *n* animisme *m*.

animist ['ænɪmɪst] ◇ *adj* animiste.
◇ *n* animiste *mf*.

animosity [ˌænɪ'mɒsətɪ] (*pl* animosities) *n* animosité *f*, antipathie *f*; she felt great ~ towards politicians elle avait une grande animosité contre OR une antipathie profonde pour les hommes politiques; I sensed the ~ between them je sentais de l'antipathie entre eux.

animus ['ænɪməs] *n* **-1.** [hostility] = **animosity**. **-2.** [motive] animus *m*. **-3.** PSYCH animus *m*.

anion ['ænaɪən] *n* anion *m*.

anise ['ænɪs] *n* anis *m*.

aniseed ['ænɪsiːd] ◇ *n* graine *f* d'anis.
◇ *comp* à l'anis; ~ ball bonbon *m* à l'anis.

anisette [ˌænɪ'zet] *n* anisette *f*.

Ankara ['æŋkərə] *pr n* Ankara.

ankle ['æŋkl] ◇ *n* cheville *f*.
◇ *comp*: ~ boot bottine *f*; ~ sock socquette *f*; ~ strap bride *f*.

anklebone ['æŋkəlbəʊn] *n* astragale *m*.

ankle-deep *adj*: she was ~ in mud elle était dans la boue jusqu'aux chevilles; the water is only ~ l'eau monte OR vient seulement jusqu'à la cheville.

ankle-length *adj* qui descend jusqu'à la cheville.

anklet ['æŋklɪt] *n* **-1.** [chain] bracelet *m* de cheville. **-2.** *Am* [ankle sock] socquette *f*.

ankylosis [æŋkɪ'ləʊsɪs] *n* ankylose *f*.

Anna ['ænə] *pr n*: '~ Karenina' *Tolstoy* 'Anna Karénine'; '~ of the Five Towns' *Bennett* 'Anna des cinq villes'.

annalist ['ænəlɪst] *n* annaliste *mf*.

annals ['ænlz] *npl* annales *fpl*.

Annam [æn'æm] *pr n* Annam *m*.

Annamese [ˌænə'miːz] ◇ *adj* annamite.
◇ *n* Annamite *mf*.

Annapurna [ˌænə'pɜːnə] *pr n* l'Annapurna *m*.

Anne [æn] *pr n*: Saint ~ sainte Anne; ~ of Austria Anne d'Autriche; ~ Boleyn Anne Boleyn; ~ of Cleves Anne de Clèves.

anneal [ə'niːl] *vt* [glass] recuire; [metal] tremper, recuire.

annelid ['ænəlɪd] ◇ *adj*: ~ worm annélide *f*.
◇ *n* annélide *f*.

annex [*n* 'æneks, *vb* æ'neks] ◇ *n Am* = **annexe**.
◇ *vt* annexer.

annexation [ˌænek'seɪʃn] *n* [act] annexion *f*; [country] pays *m* annexé; [document] document *m* annexe, annexe *f*.

annexe *Br*, **annex** *Am* ['æneks] *n* [building, document] annexe *f*.

annihilate [ə'naɪəleɪt] *vt* **-1.** [destroy - enemy, race] anéantir, détruire; [- argument, effort] anéantir, annihiler. **-2.** *inf* [defeat] écraser.

annihilation [əˌnaɪə'leɪʃn] *n* **-1.** [destruction - of argument, enemy, effort] anéantissement *m*. **-2.** *inf* [defeat] défaite *f* (totale), pâtée *f*.

anniversary [ˌænɪ'vɜːsərɪ] (*pl* anniversaries) ◇ *n* anniversaire *m (d'un événement)*, commémoration *f*.
◇ *comp* [celebration, dinner] anniversaire, commémoratif.

Anno Domini [ˌænəʊ'dɒmɪnaɪ] *adv fml* après Jésus-Christ.

annotate ['ænəteɪt] *vt* annoter.

annotation [ˌænə'teɪʃn] *n* [action] annotation *f*; [note] annotation *f*, note *f*.

announce [ə'naʊns] ◇ *vt* annoncer; to ~ sthg to sb annoncer qqch à qqn; we are pleased to ~ the birth/marriage of our son nous sommes heureux de vous faire part de la naissance/du mariage de notre fils; a whistle ~d the arrival of the train un coup de sifflet annonça l'arrivée du train; management have ~d a cut in pay l'administration a annoncé une réduction des salaires.
◇ *vi Am*: to ~ for the presidency se déclarer candidat à la présidence.

announcement [ə'naʊnsmənt] *n* [public statement] annonce *f*; ADMIN avis *m*; [notice of birth, marriage] faire-part *m*.

announcer [ə'naʊnsə^r] *n* [gen] annonceur *m*, -euse *f*; RADIO & TV [newscaster] journaliste *mf*; [introducing programme] speaker *m*, speakerine *f*, annonceur *m*, -euse *f*.

annoy [ə'nɔɪ] *vt* ennuyer, agacer; is this man ~ing you? cet homme vous ennuie-t-il OR vous importune-t-il? *fml*; it's his constant boasting that ~s me ce sont ses fanfaronnades perpétuelles qui m'agacent; he only did it to ~ you il l'a fait uniquement pour vous ennuyer OR contrarier.

annoyance [ə'nɔɪəns] *n* **-1.** [displeasure] contrariété *f*, mécontentement *m*; with a look of ~ d'un air contrarié OR ennuyé; "no, I won't", she said with some ~ «non, je ne le ferai pas», déclara-t-elle d'un ton agacé; to my great ~ à mon grand mécontentement OR déplaisir. **-2.** [source of irritation] ennui *m*, désagrément *m*.

annoyed [ə'nɔɪd] *adj*: to be/to get ~ with sb être/se mettre en colère contre qqn; I felt really ~ with him j'étais vraiment en colère contre lui; she was very ~ elle était très mécontente.

annoying [əˈnɔɪɪŋ] *adj* [bothersome] gênant, ennuyeux; [very irritating] énervant, agaçant, fâcheux; the ~ thing is... ce qui est énervant dans l'histoire, c'est...

annoyingly [əˈnɔɪɪŋlɪ] *adv* de manière gênante OR agaçante; she remained ~ vague elle est restée si vague que c'en était agaçant.

annual [ˈænjʊəl] ◇ *adj* annuel; what's your ~ income? combien gagnez-vous par an?

◇ *n* -1. [publication] publication *f* annuelle; [of association, firm] annuaire *m*; [for children] album *m* (de bandes dessinées). -2. BOT plante *f* annuelle.

annual general meeting *n* assemblée *f* générale annuelle.

annualize, -ise [ˈænjʊəˌlaɪz] *vt* annualiser; ~d percentage rate taux *m* effectif global.

annually [ˈænjʊəlɪ] *adv* annuellement, tous les ans; he earns £20,000 ~ il gagne 20 000 livres par an.

annual report *n* FIN rapport *m* annuel.

annuity [əˈnjuːɪtɪ] (*pl* annuities) *n* [regular income] rente *f*; [for life] viager *m*, rente *f* viagère; [investment] viager *m*, rente *f* viagère; to purchase an ~ placer de l'argent en viager.

annul [əˈnʌl] (*pt* & *pp* annulled, *cont* annulling) *vt* [law] abroger, abolir; [agreement, contract] résilier; [marriage] annuler; [judgment] casser, annuler.

annular [ˈænjʊləʳ] *adj* annulaire.

annulment [əˈnʌlmənt] *n* [of law] abrogation *f*, abolition *f*; [of agreement, contract] résiliation *f*; [of marriage] annulation *f*; [of judgment] cassation *f*, annulation *f*.

Annunciation [əˌnʌnsɪˈeɪʃn] *n*: the ~ l'Annonciation *f*.

anode [ˈænəʊd] *n* anode *f*.

anodyne [ˈænədaɪn] ◇ *n* MED analgésique *m*, calmant *m*; *fig* baume *m*.

◇ *adj* -1. MED analgésique, antalgique; *fig* apaisant. -2. [inoffensive] anodin.

anoestrus *Br*, **anestrus** *Am* [ænˈiːstrəs] *n* interoestrus *m*.

anoint [əˈnɔɪnt] *vt* [gen] mettre un onguent sur; [in religious ceremony] oindre, consacrer par l'onction; to ~ sb with oil oindre qqn d'huile; they ~ed him king ils l'ont sacré roi; the ~ed King le roi consacré.

anointing [əˈnɔɪntɪŋ] *n* onction *f*.

anointment [əˈnɔɪntmənt] *n* -1. [action] onction *f*. -2. [ointment] onguent *m*, pommade *f*.

anomalous [əˈnɒmələs] *adj* [effect, growth, result] anormal, irrégulier; GRAMM anormal.

anomaly [əˈnɒməlɪ] (*pl* anomalies) *n* anomalie *f*.

anon [əˈnɒn] *adv arch* OR *lit* [soon] bientôt, sous peu; see you ~ *hum* à bientôt.

anon. (*written abbr of* anonymous) anon.

anonymity [ˌænəˈnɪmətɪ] *n* -1. [namelessness] anonymat *m*. -2. [unexceptional quality] banalité *f*.

anonymous [əˈnɒnɪməs] *adj* anonyme; to remain ~ garder l'anonymat.

anonymously [əˈnɒnɪməslɪ] *adv* [act, donate] anonymement, en gardant l'anonymat; [publish] anonymement, sans nom d'auteur.

anopheles [əˈnɒfɪliːz] (*pl inv*) *n* anophèle *m*.

anorak [ˈænəræk] *n* anorak *m*.

anorexia [ˌænəˈreksɪə] *n* anorexie *f*.

anorexia nervosa [-nɜːˈvəʊsə] *n* anorexie *f* mentale.

anorexic [ˌænəˈreksɪk] ◇ *adj* anorexique.

◇ *n* anorexique *mf*.

another [əˈnʌðəʳ] ◇ *det* -1. [additional] un... de plus, une... de plus, encore un, encore une; have ~ chocolate prenez un autre OR reprenez un chocolat; ~ cup of tea? vous reprendrez bien une tasse de thé?; ~ 5 miles encore 5 miles; can you wait ~ 10 minutes? peux-tu attendre encore 10 minutes?; ~ 5 minutes and we'd have missed the train 5 minutes de plus et on ratait le train; in ~ 3 weeks dans 3 semaines; without ~ word sans un mot de plus, sans ajouter un mot; and for ~ thing, he's ill et de plus il est malade. -2. [second] un autre, une autre, un second, une seconde; it could be ~ Vietnam ça pourrait être un second OR nouveau Viêt-nam. -3. [different] un autre, une autre; can't we do that ~ time? on ne peut pas remettre ça à plus tard OR à une autre fois?; let's do it ~ way faisons-le autrement; that's ~ matter entirely! ça, c'est une tout autre histoire!

◇ *pron* -1. [a similar one] un autre, une autre, encore un, encore une; a glass of milk and ~ of water un verre de lait et un verre d'eau; she finished one cigarette and lit ~ elle finit une cigarette et en alluma une autre; many ~ *lit* bien d'autres, beaucoup d'autres. -2. [a different one]: ~ of the girls une autre des filles; bring a dessert of one sort or ~ apportez un dessert (, n'importe lequel). -3. [somebody else] *arch* OR *lit* un autre, une autre; she loves ~ elle en aime un autre.

A. N. Other [ˌeɪənˈʌðəʳ] *n Br* monsieur X, madame X.

anoxia [ænˈɒksɪə] *n* anoxie *f*.

Ansaphone® [ˈænsəfəʊn] *n* répondeur *m* (téléphonique).

ANSI (*abbr of* American National Standards Institute) *pr n* ≃ AFNOR *f*.

answer [ˈɑːnsəʳ] ◇ *vt* -1. [letter, person, telephone] répondre à; [door] aller OR venir ouvrir; I ~ed an advertisement for the job j'ai répondu à une annonce pour le poste; he ~ed not a word *lit* il n'a pas répondu, il n'a pas soufflé mot; she ~ed with a shy grin pour toute réponse elle a souri timidement; I phoned earlier but nobody ~ed j'ai téléphoné tout à l'heure mais ça ne répondait pas; the maid ~ed the bell la bonne a répondu au coup de sonnette; to ~ a prayer exaucer une prière. -2. [respond correctly to]: he could only ~ two of the questions il n'a su répondre qu'à deux des questions; few of the students ~ed this question well peu d'élèves ont bien traité cette question. -3. [fulfil] répondre à, satisfaire; the computer ~s a number of requirements l'ordinateur répond à plusieurs fonctions. -4. [description] répondre à, correspondre à; a man ~ing this description was seen in the area un homme répondant OR correspondant à ce signalement a été aperçu dans la région. -5. JUR: the defendant ~ed the charge l'accusé a répondu à OR a réfuté l'accusation.

◇ *vi* répondre, donner une réponse.

◇ *n* -1. [reply - to letter, person, request] réponse *f*; [- to criticism, objection] réponse *f*, réfutation *f*; she made no ~ elle n'a pas répondu; he couldn't think of an ~ il n'a rien trouvé à répondre; in ~ to her question he simply grinned pour toute réponse à sa question, il a eu un large sourire; did you get an ~ to your letter? as-tu obtenu une réponse à ta lettre?; I rang the bell but there was no ~ j'ai sonné mais personne n'a répondu OR n'a ouvert; I phoned but there was no ~ j'ai téléphoné mais ça ne répondait pas; she won't take "no" for an ~ elle n'acceptera pas de refus; he has an ~ for everything il a réponse à tout; he's the ~ to our prayers il est notre sauveur; it's the ~ to all my prayers OR dreams! c'est ce dont j'ai toujours rêvé!; ~ to the charge JUR réponse à l'accusation. -2. [solution] solution *f*; the (right) ~ la bonne réponse; there's no easy ~ *literal* & *fig* il n'y a pas de solution facile. -3. [to exam question] réponse *f*; write your ~s on a separate sheet of paper notez vos réponses sur une feuille séparée. -4. [equivalent]: she's England's ~ to Edith Piaf elle est OR c'est l'Édith Piaf anglaise; it's the poor man's ~ to lobster c'est le homard des pauvres.

◆ **answer back** ◇ *vi insep* répondre (avec insolence), répliquer.

◇ *vt sep* répondre (avec insolence) à, répliquer à; don't ~ (your father) back! ne réponds pas (à ton père)!

◆ **answer for** *vt insep* -1. [be responsible for] répondre de, être responsable de; she'll ~ to me for his safety elle se portera garante envers moi de sa sécurité; this government has a lot to ~ for ce gouvernement a bien des comptes à rendre; you'll ~ for that! vous me le paierez! -2. [vouch for] garantir; I can't ~ for the quality of her work je ne peux pas garantir la qualité de son travail.

◆ **answer to** *vt insep* -1. [respond to]: the cat ~s to (the name of) Frankie le chat répond au nom de Frankie, le chat s'appelle Frankie. -2. [correspond to] répondre à, correspondre à; to ~ to a description répondre à une description.

answerable [ˈɑːnsərəbl] *adj* -1. [person] responsable, comptable; to be ~ to sb for sthg être responsable de qqch devant qqn, être garant de qqch envers qqn; politicians are ~ to their constituents for their actions les hommes politiques sont responsables de leurs actions devant leurs électeurs; you're ~ to the company for any damages vous êtes garant envers la société de toute avarie OR de tout dégât; he's ~ only to the president il ne relève que du président; I'm ~ to no one je n'ai de comptes à rendre à personne. -2. [question] susceptible de réponse, qui admet une réponse; [accusation, argument] réfutable.

answering machine [ˈɑːnsərɪŋ-] *n* répondeur *m* (automatique OR téléphonique).

answering service *n* permanence *f* téléphonique.

ant [ænt] *n* fourmi *f*; to have ~s in one's pants *inf* avoir la bougeotte.

ANTA *pr n abbr of* American National Theater and Academy.

antacid [ˌæntˈæsɪd] ◇ *n* (médicament *m*) alcalin *m*, antiacide *m*.

◇ *adj* alcalin, antiacide.

antagonism [ænˈtæɡənɪzm] *n* antagonisme *m*, hostilité *f*; there is considerable ~ towards the new tax il y a une opposition considérable au nouvel impôt.

antagonist [ænˈtæɡənɪst] *n* antagoniste *mf*, adversaire *mf*.

antagonistic [ænˌtæɡəˈnɪstɪk] *adj* [person] opposé, hostile; [feelings, ideas] antagoniste, antagonique; he's openly ~ to the policy il est ouvertement opposé OR hostile à la politique.

antagonize, -ise [ænˈtæɡənaɪz] *vt* rendre hostile; we can't afford to ~ the voters nous ne pouvons pas nous permettre de nous aliéner les électeurs; you'd best not ~ the boss tu ferais mieux de ne pas contrarier le patron OR de ne pas te mettre le patron à dos.

Antalya [ɑːnˈtɑːljə] *pr n* Antalya.

Antananarivo [ˈæntəˌnænəˈriːvəʊ] *pr n* Antananarivo.

Antarctic [æntˈɑːktɪk] ◇ *pr n*: the ~ (Ocean) l'Antarctique *m*, l'océan *m* Antarctique; in the ~ dans l'Antarctique.

◇ *adj* antarctique.

Antarctica [æntˈɑːktɪkə] *pr n* Antarctique *f*, le continent *m* antarctique.

Antarctic Circle *pr n*: the ~ le cercle polaire antarctique.

Antarctic Peninsula *pr n*: the ~ la péninsule antarctique.

ante [ˈæntɪ] ◇ *n* -1. CARDS mise *f*; a £3 ~ une mise de 3 livres; to up the ~ *inf* augmenter la mise. -2. *inf* [price] part *f*.

◇ *vi* CARDS faire une mise.

◆ **ante up**▽ *vt sep* & *vi insep Am* casquer; come on, ~ up! allez, allonge!

anteater [ˈæntˌiːtəʳ] *n* fourmilier *m*.

antebellum [ˌæntɪˈbeləm] *adj* d'avant la guerre; *Am* d'avant la guerre de Sécession.

antecede [ˌæntɪˈsiːd] *vt* précéder.

antecedence [ˌæntɪˈsiːdəns] *n* priorité *f*.

antecedent [ˌæntɪˈsiːdənt] ◇ *n* GRAMM, LOGIC & MATH antécédent.

◇ *adj* antérieur, précédent; ~ to sthg antérieur à qqch.

◆ **antecedents** *npl fml* [family] ancêtres *mpl*; [history] passé *m*, antécédents *mpl*.

antechamber ['æntɪˌtʃeɪmbəʳ] *n* antichambre *f*.

antedate [ˌæntɪ'deɪt] *vt* **-1.** [precede in time] précéder, dater d'avant. **-2.** [give earlier date to] antidater. **-3.** [set an earlier date for] avancer.

antediluvian [ˌæntɪdɪ'luːvjən] *adj lit* OR *hum* antédiluvien.

antelope ['æntɪləʊp] (*pl inv* OR antelopes) *n* antilope *f*.

ante meridiem [-mə'rɪdɪəm] *adj fml* du matin.

antenatal [ˌæntɪ'neɪtl] *Br* ◇ *adj* prénatal; ~ care soins *mpl* prénatals; ~ clinic service *m* de consultation prénatale.
◇ *n inf* consultation *f* prénatale.

antenna [æn'tenə] (*pl* antennae [-niː] OR antennas) *n* antenne *f*.

antepenult [ˌæntɪpɪ'nʌlt] *n* antépénultième *f*.

antepenultimate [ˌæntɪpɪ'nʌltɪmət] ◇ *adj* antépénultième.
◇ *n* antépénultième *f*.

anterior [æn'tɪərɪəʳ] *adj fml* antérieur; ~ **to this was the Pliocene (age)** le pliocène était antérieur à ça, avant ça il y eut le pliocène.

anteroom ['æntɪrʊm] *n* antichambre *f*, vestibule *m*.

anthem ['ænθəm] *n* [song] chant *m*; RELIG motet *m*.

anther ['ænθəʳ] *n* anthère *f*.

anthill ['ænthɪl] *n* fourmilière *f*.

anthologist [æn'θɒlədʒɪst] *n* anthologiste *mf*.

anthology [æn'θɒlədʒɪ] (*pl* anthologies) *n* anthologie *f*.

Anthony ['æntənɪ] *pr n*: **Saint** ~ saint Antoine; ~ **of Padua** Antoine de Padoue.

anthracite ['ænθrəsaɪt] ◇ *n* anthracite *m*.
◇ *adj*: ~ **(grey)** (gris *m*) anthracite *(inv)*.

anthrax ['ænθræks] *n* [disease] charbon *m*; [sore] anthrax *m*.

anthropocentric [ˌænθrəpə'sentrɪk] *adj* anthropocentrique.

anthropoid ['ænθrəpɔɪd] ◇ *adj* anthropoïde.
◇ *n* anthropoïde *m*.

anthropological [ˌænθrəpə'lɒdʒɪkl] *adj* anthropologique.

anthropologist [ˌænθrə'pɒlədʒɪst] *n* anthropologue *mf*.

anthropology [ˌænθrə'pɒlədʒɪ] *n* anthropologie *f*.

anthropomorphic [ˌænθrəpə'mɔːfɪk] *adj* anthropomorphique.

anthropomorphism [ˌænθrəpə'mɔːfɪzm] *n* anthropomorphisme *m*.

anthropomorphize, -ise [ˌænθrəpə'mɔːfaɪz] *vt* anthropomorphiser.

anthropomorphous [ˌænθrəpə'mɔːfəs] *adj* anthropomorphe.

anthropophagi [ˌænθrə'pɒfəgaɪ] (*sg* anthropophagus [-gəs]) *npl* anthropophages *mpl*.

anthropophagous [ˌænθrə'pɒfəgəs] *adj* anthropophage.

anthropophagy [ˌænθrə'pɒfədʒɪ] *n* anthropophagie *f*.

anti *inf* ['æntɪ] *adj*: **she's rather** ~ elle est plutôt contre; **he's a bit** ~ **all that kind of thing** il est un peu contre tout cela OR toutes ces choses.

anti- *in cpds* anti-; ~**American** antiaméricain; ~**British** antibritannique.

antiabortion [ˌæntɪə'bɔːʃn] *adj*: **the** ~ **movement** le mouvement contre l'avortement.

antiabortionist [ˌæntɪə'bɔːʃnɪst] *n* adversaire *mf* de l'avortement.

antiaircraft [ˌæntɪ'eəkrɑːft] *adj* [system, weapon] antiaérien; ~ **defence** défense *f* contre avions, DCA *f*.

antiapartheid [ˌæntɪə'pɑːtheɪt] *adj* antiapartheid.

antibacterial [ˌæntɪbæk'tiːrɪəl] *adj* antibactérien.

antibiotic [ˌæntɪbaɪ'ɒtɪk] ◇ *adj* antibiotique.
◇ *n* antibiotique *m*.

antibody ['æntɪˌbɒdɪ] (*pl* antibodies) *n* anticorps *m*.

anticathode [ˌæntɪ'kæθəʊd] *n* anticathode *f*.

Antichrist ['æntɪkraɪst] *n*: **the** ~ l'Antéchrist *m*.

anticipate [æn'tɪsɪpeɪt] ◇ *vt* **-1.** [think likely] prévoir, s'attendre à; **they** ~ **meeting some opposition, they** ~ **that they will meet some opposition** ils s'attendent à rencontrer une certaine opposition; **we had** ~**d a price increase** nous nous attendions à OR nous avions prévu une hausse des prix; **I didn't** ~ **leaving so early** je ne m'attendais pas à ce qu'on parte si tôt; **do you** ~ **visiting her?** pensez-vous lui rendre visite?; **faster than** ~**d** plus vite que prévu; **as** ~**d** comme prévu. **-2.** [be prepared for - attack, decision, event] anticiper, anticiper sur; [- needs, wishes] devancer, prévenir, aller au devant de; **we** ~**d our competitors by launching our product first** nous avons devancé la concurrence en lançant notre produit les premiers; **he** ~**d the fall in price and sold early** il a anticipé la baisse des prix et a vendu avant. **-3.** [act on prematurely - effect, success] escompter; [- profit, salary] anticiper sur; [- happiness] anticiper, savourer d'avance; [- pain] anticiper, éprouver d'avance. **-4.** [pay in advance - bill] anticiper. **-5.** [mention prematurely] anticiper, anticiper sur; **don't** ~ **the end of the story** n'anticipez pas la fin de l'histoire.
◇ *vi* anticiper; **just wait and see, don't** ~ attends de voir, n'anticipe pas; **do you think you'll get married? — I think you're anticipating a bit** penses-tu que tu vas te marier? — je crois que tu vas un peu vite.

anticipation [æn,tɪsɪ'peɪʃn] *n* **-1.** [expectation] attente *f*; **I was all kitted out in waterproofs in** ~ **of rain** pensant qu'il allait pleuvoir, je m'étais équipée d'un tas d'imperméables; **they raised their prices in** ~ **of increased inflation** ils ont augmenté leurs prix en prévision d'une hausse de l'inflation. **-2.** *fml* [readiness] anticipation *f*; **in** ~ **of your wishes, I've had the fire made up** pour aller au devant de OR pour devancer vos désirs, j'ai demandé qu'on fasse du feu; **thanking you in** ~ en vous remerciant d'avance, avec mes remerciements anticipés. **-3.** [eagerness] impatience *f*, empressement *m*; **fans jostled at the gates in eager** ~ les fans, ne tenant plus d'impatience, se bousculaient aux grilles d'entrée. **-4.** [premature experiencing - of inheritance, profits, success] anticipation *f*, attente *f*; [- of fear, pain] appréhension *f*.

anticipatory [æn,tɪsɪ'peɪtərɪ] *adj* d'anticipation.

anticlerical [ˌæntɪ'klerɪkl] ◇ *adj* anticlérical.
◇ *n* anticlérical *m*, -e *f*.

anticlericalism [ˌæntɪ'klerɪkəlɪsm] *n* anticléricalisme *m*.

anticlimactic [ˌæntɪklaɪ'mæktɪk] *adj* décevant.

anticlimax [æntɪ'klaɪmæks] *n* **-1.** [disappointment] déception *f*; **the opening ceremony was a bit of an** ~ la cérémonie d'ouverture a été quelque peu décevante; **what an** ~**!** quelle douche froide! **-2.** LITERAT chute *f* dans le trivial.

anticline ['æntɪklaɪn] *n* anticlinal *m*.

anticlockwise [ˌæntɪ'klɒkwaɪz] *Br* ◇ *adv* en sens inverse des aiguilles d'une montre.
◇ *adj*: **turn it in an** ~ **direction** tournez-le dans le sens inverse des aiguilles d'une montre.

anticoagulant [ˌæntɪkəʊ'ægjʊlənt] ◇ *adj* anticoagulant.
◇ *n* anticoagulant *m*.

anticonstitutional ['æntɪˌkɒnstɪ'tjuːʃənl] *adj* anticonstitutionnel.

anticonvulsant [ˌæntɪkən'vʌlsənt] ◇ *adj* antispasmodique.
◇ *n* antispasmodique *m*.

anticorrosive [ˌæntɪkə'rəʊsɪv] ◇ *adj* anticorrosif.
◇ *n* anticorrosif *m*.

antics ['æntɪks] *npl* [absurd behaviour] cabrioles *fpl*, gambades *fpl*; [jokes] bouffonnerie *f*, pitrerie *f*; **I'm fed up with her silly** ~ j'en ai assez de son cirque ridicule; **they're up to their (old)** ~ **again** les voilà repartis avec leurs pitreries.

anticyclone [æntɪ'saɪkləʊn] *n* anticyclone *m*.

anti-dazzle *adj Br*: ~ **headlights** phares *mpl* antiéblouissants.

antidemocratic ['æntɪˌdemə'krætɪk] *adj* antidémocratique.

antidepressant [ˌæntɪdə'presnt] ◇ *adj* antidépresseur.
◇ *n* antidépresseur *m*.

antidote ['æntɪdəʊt] *n* antidote *m*; **work is an** ~ **to** OR **for unhappiness** le travail est un antidote à OR contre la tristesse.

anti-Establishment *adj* anticonformiste.

antifreeze ['æntɪfriːz] *n* antigel *m*.

antifriction [ˌæntɪ'frɪkʃn] *n* antifriction *m*.

anti-G *adj* anti-g *(inv)*.

antigen ['æntɪdʒən] *n* antigène *m*.

antiglare ['æntɪgleəʳ] *adj*: ~ **headlights** phares *mpl* antiéblouissants.

Antigone [æn'tɪgənɪ] *pr n* Antigone.

Antigua [æn'tiːgə] *pr n* Antigua; **in** ~ à Antigua; ~ **and Barbuda** Antigua et Barbuda.

Antiguan [æn'tiːgən] ◇ *n habitant d'Antigua*.
◇ *adj* d'Antigua.

antihero ['æntɪˌhɪərəʊ] (*pl* antiheroes) *n* antihéros *m*.

antihistamine [ˌæntɪ'hɪstəmɪn] *n* antihistaminique *m*.

anti-imperialism *n* anti-impérialisme *m*.

anti-imperialist ◇ *adj* anti-impérialiste.
◇ *n* anti-impérialiste *mf*.

anti-inflammatory *adj* anti-inflammatoire.

anti-inflationary *adj* anti-inflationniste.

antiknock [ˌæntɪ'nɒk] *n* antidétonant *m*.

Antilles [æn'tɪliːz] *pl pr n* Antilles *fpl*; **in the** ~ aux Antilles; **the Greater/Lesser** ~ les Grandes/Petites Antilles.

antilog ['æntɪlɒg], **antilogarithm** [ˌæntɪ'lɒgərɪðm] *n* antilogarithme *m*.

antimacassar [ˌæntɪmə'kæsəʳ] *n* têtière *f*.

antimagnetic [ˌæntɪmæg'netɪk] *adj* antimagnétique.

antimatter ['æntɪˌmætəʳ] *n* antimatière *f*.

antimilitarism [ˌæntɪ'mɪlɪtərɪzm] *n* antimilitarisme *m*.

antimissile [ˌæntɪ'mɪsaɪl] ◇ *adj* antimissile *(inv)*.
◇ *n* missile *m* antimissile.

antimony ['æntɪmənɪ] *n* antimoine *m*.

anti-novel *n* nouveau roman *m*.

antinuclear [ˌæntɪ'njuːklɪəʳ] *adj* antinucléaire.

Antioch ['æntɪˌɒk] *pr n* Antioche.

antiparticle ['æntɪˌpɑːtɪkl] *n* antiparticule *f*.

antipathetic [ˌæntɪpə'θetɪk] *adj* antipathique; **he remains** ~ **to the cause** il reste hostile à la cause.

antipathy [æn'tɪpəθɪ] (*pl* antipathies) *n* antipathie *f*; **to feel** ~ **towards sb/sthg** avoir OR éprouver de l'antipathie pour qqn/qqch.

antipersonnel ['æntɪˌpɜːsə'nel] *adj euph* antipersonnel *(inv)*.

antiperspirant [ˌæntɪ'pɜːspərənt] ◇ *adj* déodorant.
◇ *n* déodorant *m*.

antiphon ['æntɪfən] *n* antienne *f*.

antiphony [æn'tɪfənɪ] (*pl* antiphonies) *n* chant *m* en contre-chant.

antiphrasis [æn'tɪfrəsɪs] (*pl* antiphrases [-siːz]) *n* antiphrase *f*.

antipodal [æn'tɪpədl] *adj* des antipodes.

antipodean [æn,tɪpə'dɪən] *adj* des antipodes.

antipodes [æn'tɪpədiːz] *npl* antipodes *mpl*.
◆ **Antipodes** *pl pr n*: **the Antipodes** l'Australie *f* et la Nouvelle Zélande.

antipope ['æntɪpəʊp] *n* antipape *m*.

antiproton ['æntɪˌprəʊtɒn] *n* antiproton *m*.

antipsychiatry [ˌæntɪsaɪ'kaɪətrɪ] *n* antipsychiatrie *f*.

antipyretic [ˌæntɪpaɪ'retɪk] ◇ *adj* antipyrétique.
◇ *n* antipyrétique *m*.

antiquarian [ˌæntɪˈkweərɪən] ◇ *adj* [collection, shop] d'antiquités; [bookseller, bookshop] spécialisé dans les livres anciens.
◇ *n* [collector] collectionneur *m*, -euse *f* d'antiquités; [researcher] archéologue *mf*; [merchant] antiquaire *mf*.

antiquary [ˈæntɪkwərɪ] (*pl* antiquaries) = **antiquarian** *n*.

antiquated [ˈæntɪkweɪtɪd] *adj* -**1.** [outmoded - machine, method] vieillot, obsolète; [- building, installation] vétuste; [- idea, manners] vieillot, suranné; [- person] vieux jeu *(inv)*; **you have such ~ ideas** tu es tellement vieux jeu. -**2.** [ancient] très vieux.

antique [ænˈtiːk] ◇ *adj* -**1.** [very old] ancien; [dating from Greek or Roman times] antique; **an ~ clock** une pendule ancienne OR d'époque. -**2.** *inf* = **antiquated**.
◇ *n* [furniture] meuble *m* ancien OR d'époque; [vase] vase *m* ancien OR d'époque; [work of art] objet *m* d'art ancien.
◇ *comp* [lover, shop] d'antiquités; **~ dealer** antiquaire *mf*.

antiquity [ænˈtɪkwətɪ] (*pl* antiquities) *n* -**1.** [ancient times] Antiquité *f*. -**2.** [building, ruin] monument *m* ancien, antiquité *f*; [coin, statue] objet *m* ancien; [work of art] objet d'art *m* ancien, antiquité *f*. -**3.** [oldness] antiquité *f*.

antiracial [ˌæntɪˈreɪʃl] *adj* antiraciste.

antiriot [ˌæntɪˈraɪət] *adj* antiémeutes.

anti-roll bar *n* barre *f* antiroulis.

antirrhinum [ˌæntɪˈraɪnəm] *n* muflier *m*, gueule-de-loup *f*.

antirust [ˌæntɪˈrʌst] *adj* antirouille *(inv)*.

anti-Semite *n* antisémite *mf*.

anti-Semitic *adj* antisémite.

anti-Semitism *n* antisémitisme *m*.

antisepsis [ˌæntɪˈsepsɪs] *n* antisepsie *f*.

antiseptic [ˌæntɪˈseptɪk] ◇ *adj* antiseptique.
◇ *n* antiseptique *m*.

antiserum [ˌæntɪˈsɪərəm] *n* antisérum *m*.

antiskid [ˌæntɪˈskɪd] *adj* antidérapant.

antislavery [ˌæntɪˈsleɪvərɪ] *adj* antiesclavagiste.

antislip [ˌæntɪˈslɪp] *adj* antidérapant.

antisocial [ˌæntɪˈsəʊʃl] *adj* -**1.** [behaviour, measure] antisocial. -**2.** [unsociable] sauvage; **don't be so ~** ne sois pas si sauvage.

antistatic [ˌæntɪˈstætɪk] *adj* antistatique.

antitank [ˌæntɪˈtæŋk] *adj* antichar; **~ grenades** grenades *fpl* antichars.

antitheft [ˌæntɪˈθeft] *adj* antivol; **an ~ device** un antivol, un dispositif contre le vol OR antivol.

antithesis [ænˈtɪθɪsɪs] (*pl* antitheses [-siːz]) *n* -**1.** [exact opposite] contraire *m*, opposé *m*; **he is the ~ of a forceful young manager** c'est tout le contraire du jeune cadre dynamique. -**2.** [contrast, opposition] antithèse *f*, contraste *m*, opposition *f*. -**3.** LITERAT antithèse *f*.

antithetic(al) [ˌæntɪˈθetɪk(l)] *adj* antithétique.

antithetically [ˌæntɪˈθetɪklɪ] *adv* par antithèse.

antitoxin [ˌæntɪˈtɒksɪn] *n* antitoxine *f*.

antitrust [ˌæntɪˈtrʌst] *adj Am* antitrust *(inv)*; **the Sherman Antitrust Act** *Am* HIST la loi antitrust Sherman.

THE SHERMAN ANTITRUST ACT:
Loi fédérale de 1890 interdisant la formation de monopoles aux États-Unis et provoquant le démembrement de sociétés telles que la «Standard Oil Company» et l'«American Tobacco Company».

---

antivivisectionist [ˈæntɪˌvɪvɪˈsekʃnɪst] *n* adversaire *mf* de la vivisection.

antiworld [ˈæntɪwɜːld] *n* monde *m* composé d'antimatière.

antler [ˈæntləʳ] *n* corne *f*; **the ~s** les bois *mpl*, la ramure.

antlike [ˈæntlaɪk] *adj* [movement] de fourmi; [activity] fourmillant.

ant lion *n* fourmi-lion *m*, fourmilion *m*.

antonomasia [ˌæntənəˈmeɪzɪə] *n* antonomase *f*.

Antony [ˈæntənɪ] *pr n*: (Mark) ~ (Marc) Antoine; **'~ and Cleopatra'** *Shakespeare* 'Antoine et Cléopatre'.

antonym [ˈæntənɪm] *n* antonyme *m*.

antonymous [ænˈtɒnɪməs] *adj* antonymique.

antsy *inf* [ˈæntsɪ] *adj Am* agité, nerveux; **I'm feeling ~** j'ai la bougeotte.

Antwerp [ˈæntwɜːp] *pr n* Anvers.

anus [ˈeɪnəs] *n* anus *m*.

anvil [ˈænvɪl] *n* enclume *f*.

anxiety [æŋˈzaɪətɪ] (*pl* anxieties) *n* -**1.** [feeling of worry] anxiété *f*, appréhension *f*; **rising interest rates have caused ~** la hausse des taux d'intérêt a suscité une vive anxiété; **I talked openly about my anxieties** j'ai évoqué franchement mes appréhensions; **a source of deep ~** une source d'angoisse profonde. -**2.** [source of worry] souci *m*; **her son is a great ~ to her** son fils lui donne énormément de soucis OR l'inquiète énormément. -**3.** [intense eagerness] grand désir *m*, désir *m* ardent; **in his ~ to please her, he forgot everything else** il tenait tellement à lui faire plaisir qu'il en oubliait tout le reste. -**4.** PSYCH anxiété *f*; **~ neurosis** anxiété névrotique.

anxious [ˈæŋkʃəs] *adj* -**1.** [worried] anxieux, angoissé, inquiet; **she's ~ about losing her job** elle a peur de perdre son travail; **an ~ smile** un sourire anxieux OR inquiet; **I'm ~ for their safety** je suis inquiète OR je crains pour leur sécurité; **she's a very ~ person** c'est une grande angoissée; **~ friends and relatives waited for news** amis et parents attendaient des nouvelles dans l'angoisse. -**2.** [worrying] inquiétant, angoissant; **these are ~ times** nous vivons une sombre époque; **we had one or two ~ moments** nous avons connu quelques moments d'anxiété OR d'inquiétude. -**3.** [eager] anxieux, impatient; **they're ~ to start** ils sont impatients OR pressés de commencer; **he was ~ for them to go** il attendait impatiemment qu'ils partent OR leur départ; **he was very ~ that we shouldn't be seen together** il tenait beaucoup à ce que l'on ne nous voie pas ensemble; **he's not exactly ~ to tell her** il n'a pas réellement envie de lui dire; **she's very ~ to please** elle est très désireuse OR anxieuse de plaire.

anxiously [ˈæŋkʃəslɪ] *adv* -**1.** [nervously] avec inquiétude, anxieusement. -**2.** [eagerly] impatiemment, avec impatience.

anxiousness [ˈæŋkʃəsnɪs] = **anxiety**.

any [ˈenɪ] ◇ *det* -**1.** [some - in questions]: **have you ~ money?** avez-vous de l'argent?; **did you see ~ lions?** avez-vous vu des lions?; **do they have ~ others?** en ont-ils d'autres?; **have ~ guests arrived?** des invités sont-ils arrivés?; **were you in ~ danger?** étiez-vous en danger?; **~ letters for me?** *inf* il y a du courrier pour moi?; **~ news about the application?** *inf* il y a du neuf pour la candidature? || [in conditional clauses]: **if there's ~ cake left, can I have some?** s'il reste du gâteau, est-ce que je peux en avoir?; **if you find ~ children's books, let me know** si jamais vous trouvez des livres pour enfants, dites-le moi; **if you have ~ free time, call me** si vous avez un moment, appelez-moi; **~ nonsense from you and you'll be out!** *inf* tu n'as qu'à bien te tenir, sinon, c'est la porte! -**2.** [in negative phrases]: **he hasn't ~ change/money/cigarettes** il n'a pas de monnaie/d'argent/de cigarettes; **you haven't ~ reason to complain** vous n'avez aucune raison de vous plaindre; **he can't stand ~ noise** il ne supporte pas le moindre bruit, il ne supporte aucun bruit; **it's impossible to say with ~ degree of certainty** on ne peut l'affirmer avec aucune certitude; **without ~ warning/fuss** sans le moindre avertissement/problème; **she's forbidden to do ~ work** tout travail lui est interdit; **hardly** OR **barely** OR **scarcely ~** très peu de. -**3.** [no matter which] n'importe quel, n'importe quelle; **ask ~ woman** demandez à n'importe quelle femme; **choose ~ colour you like** choisissez la couleur que vous voulez, choisissez n'importe quelle couleur; **at ~ time of day** à n'importe quel moment OR à tout moment de la journée; **~ one of these paintings is worth a fortune** chacun de ces tableaux vaut une fortune; **answer ~ two of the questions in section C** répondez à deux des questions de la section C ❑ **~ old cup will do** n'importe quelle vieille tasse fera l'affaire; **just give him ~ old thing** donnez-lui n'importe quel vieux truc; **she's not just ~ (old) pianist!** ce n'est pas n'importe quelle pianiste! -**4.** [all, every] tout; **give me ~ money you've got** donne-moi tout l'argent que tu as; **I'll accept ~ help I can get** j'accepterai toute l'aide qui me sera offerte; **~ latecomers should report to the office** tous les retardataires doivent se présenter au bureau; **~ public-spirited citizen would have done the same** tout citoyen ayant le souci du bien public aurait fait la même chose. -**5.** [unlimited]: **there are ~ number of ways of winning** il y a mille façons de gagner; **she has ~ amount** OR **number of friends to help her** elle a (une) quantité d'amis qui peuvent l'aider.
◇ *adv* -**1.** [with comparative - in questions, conditional statements]: **can you walk ~ faster?** peux-tu marcher un peu plus vite?; **can't you walk ~ faster than that?** tu ne peux pas marcher plus vite que ça?; **is she ~ better today?** va-t-elle un peu mieux aujourd'hui?; **if she isn't ~ better by tomorrow, call the doctor** si elle ne va pas mieux demain, appelez le médecin; **if the wind gets ~ stronger, we shan't be able to set sail** si le vent se renforce, nous ne pourrons pas partir; [- in negative statements]: **he won't be ~ (the) happier** il n'en sera pas plus heureux; **we can't go ~ further** nous ne pouvons aller plus loin; **it's not getting ~ easier to find good staff** c'est toujours aussi difficile de trouver de bons employés; **I can't get this floor ~ cleaner** je n'arrive pas à nettoyer le sol mieux que ça; **I can't put it ~ more plainly than that, can I?** je ne pourrais pas le dire plus simplement que ça, si? -**2.** [at all]: **you're not helping me ~** tu ne m'aides pas du tout; **has the situation improved ~?** la situation s'est-elle arrangée un tant soit peu?; **she wasn't ~ too pleased with the press coverage she got** elle n'était pas ravie de la publicité que lui ont faite les médias.
◇ *pron* -**1.** [in questions, conditional statements - some, someone]: **did you see ~?** en avez-vous vu?; **did ~ of them go?** est-ce que certains d'entre eux y sont allés?; **if ~ of you want to help, please phone** s'il y en a parmi vous qui veulent apporter leur aide, ils n'ont qu'à téléphoner; **if ~ of you wants them, do take them** si quelqu'un parmi vous OR si l'un d'entre vous les veut, il n'a qu'à les prendre; **few, if ~, of his supporters remained loyal** aucun ou presque aucun de ses supporters ne lui est resté fidèle. -**2.** [in negative statements - even one]: **he couldn't see ~ of them** il ne voyait aucun d'entre eux; **he won't vote for ~ of the candidates** il ne votera pour aucun des candidats; **there was hardly ~ of it left** il n'en restait que très peu; **she's learned two foreign languages, I haven't learned ~** elle a étudié deux langues étrangères, je n'en ai étudié aucune; **I have absolutely no money and don't expect to get ~** je n'ai pas un sou et je ne m'attends pas à en avoir; **if you don't eat supper now, you'll go to bed without ~** si tu ne manges pas immédiatement, tu iras au lit sans dîner ❑ **he's not having ~ (of it)** *inf* il ne marche pas. -**3.** [no matter which one] n'importe lequel, n'importe laquelle; **which chocolate shall I have? – take ~, they're all the same** quel chocolat est-ce que je vais prendre? – prends n'importe lequel, ils sont tous pareils; **which dress should I wear? – ~ but that one** quelle robe est-ce que je mets? – n'importe laquelle sauf celle-là; **study ~ of her works and you will discover...** étudie n'importe laquelle de ses œuvres et tu découvriras... || [every one, all] tout; **~ of the suspects would fit that description** cette description s'applique

à tous les suspects; **this applies to ~ of you who are married** ceci s'applique à tous ceux d'entre vous qui sont mariés.

anybody ['enɪˌbɒdɪ] *pron* -**1.** *(in questions, conditional statements)* [someone] quelqu'un; **has ~ lost their glasses?** est-ce que quelqu'un a perdu ses lunettes?; **if ~ asks, say I've gone abroad** si quelqu'un pose la question, dis que je suis à l'étranger; **(is) ~ home?** il y a quelqu'un?; **is ~ there?** [in seance] esprit, es-tu là?; **~ for more tea?** *inf* quelqu'un reveut du thé?; **she'll persuade them, if ~ can** si quelqu'un peut les convaincre, c'est bien elle. -**2.** *(in negative statements)* [someone] personne; **she's not accusing ~** elle n'accuse personne; **there was hardly ~ there** il n'y avait presque personne; **she left without speaking to ~** elle est partie sans parler à personne. -**3.** [no matter who, everyone]: **~ who wants can join us** tous ceux qui veulent peuvent se joindre à nous; **invite ~ you want** invitez qui vous voulez; **it could happen to ~** ça pourrait arriver à tout le monde OR n'importe qui; **I don't care what ~ thinks** je me fiche de ce que pensent les gens; **she's cleverer than ~ I know** c'est la personne la plus intelligente que je connaisse; **~ who saw the accident should come forward** ceux qui ont été témoins de l'accident sont priés de se faire connaître; **~ with any sense** OR **in their right mind would have...** toute personne un peu sensée aurait...; **please, ~ but him!** je t'en prie, pas lui!; **~ but him would have...** n'importe qui d'autre que lui OR tout autre que lui aurait...; **~ will do** n'importe qui OR le premier venu fera l'affaire; **~ would think you'd just lost your best friend** on croirait que tu viens de perdre ton meilleur ami ❑ **he's not just ~, he's my brother!** ce n'est pas n'importe qui, c'est mon frère!; **a couple of gin and tonics and you're ~'s** *hum* deux ou trois gin-tonics et on fait tout ce qu'on veut de toi. -**4.** [important person] quelqu'un (d'important OR de connu); **~ who's ~ will be there** tout le gratin sera là; **if you want to be ~, you've got to work** si tu veux devenir quelqu'un tu dois travailler.

anyhow ['enɪhaʊ] ◇ *adv* -**1.** = **anyway 1.** -**2.** [in any manner, by any means]: **you can do it ~, but just get it done!** tu peux le faire n'importe comment, mais fais-le!; **I had to persuade her somehow, ~** il fallait que je trouve un moyen de la convaincre, n'importe lequel. -**3.** *inf* [haphazardly] n'importe comment; **she threw her things down just ~** elle a jeté ses affaires en désordre par terre OR par terre n'importe comment.

◇ *adj*: **he left the room all ~** il a laissé la pièce sens dessus dessous.

any more *Br*, **anymore** *Am* [ˌenɪ'mɔːʳ] *adv*: **they don't live here ~** ils n'habitent plus ici; **I won't do it ~** je ne le ferai plus (jamais).

anyone ['enɪwʌn] = **anybody**.

anyplace *inf* ['enɪpleɪs] *Am* = **anywhere**.

anyroad ['enɪrəʊd] *Br dial* = **anyway**.

anything ['enɪθɪŋ] *pron* -**1.** [something - in questions] quelque chose; **did you hear ~?** avez-vous entendu quelque chose?; **is there ~ to eat?** est-ce qu'il y a quelque chose à manger?; **can we do ~?** est-ce qu'on peut faire quelque chose?; **can't we do ~?** est-ce qu'il n'y a rien à faire?; **are you doing ~ this weekend?** avez-vous quelque chose de prévu pour ce week-end?; **is there ~ in** OR **to what she says?** est-ce qu'il y a du vrai dans ce qu'elle dit?; **can we get ~ out of it?** peut-on en tirer quelque chose?; **have you heard ~ from them?** avez-vous eu de leurs nouvelles?; **did you notice ~ unusual?** avez-vous remarqué quelque chose de bizarre?; **is there ~ more annoying than just missing a train?** y a-t-il quelque chose OR rien de plus agaçant que de rater un train?; **~ good on TV tonight?** *inf* est-ce qu'il y a quelque chose de bien à la télé ce soir?; **~ the matter?** *inf* quelque chose ne va pas?; [- in conditional statements]: **if ~ should happen, take care of John for me** s'il m'arrivait quelque chose OR quoi que ce soit, occupez-vous de John; **if you should learn ~, let me know** si jamais vous apprenez quelque chose OR quoi que ce soit, dites-le moi; [- in negative statements] rien; **I didn't say ~** je n'ai rien dit; **you can't believe ~ he says** on ne peut rien croire de ce qu'il dit; **don't do ~ stupid!** ne fais pas de bêtise!; **I don't know ~ about computers** je ne m'y connais pas du tout OR je n'y connais rien en informatique; **I didn't know ~ about their divorce** je ne savais pas qu'ils avaient divorcé; **there's hardly ~ left** il ne reste presque rien; **she hasn't written ~ very much since last year** elle n'a pas écrit grand-chose depuis l'année dernière; **without saying ~** sans rien dire ❑ **she's not angry or ~** elle n'est pas fâchée ni rien; **do you want a book or ~?** voulez-vous un livre ou autre chose?; **if she feels sick or ~, call the doctor** si elle se sent mal OR si ça ne va pas, appelez le médecin. -**2.** [no matter what]: **just tell him ~** racontez-lui n'importe quoi; **~ you like** tout ce que vous voudrez; **~ will do** n'importe quoi fera l'affaire; **I'd give ~ to know the truth** je donnerais n'importe quoi pour savoir la vérité; **he won't read just ~** il ne lit pas n'importe quoi ❑ **~ goes!** tout est permis! -**3.** [all, everything] tout; **her son eats ~** son fils mange de tout; **I like ~ with chocolate in it** j'aime tout ce qui est au chocolat; **~ above 75/below 25 is a very good score** tout ce qui est au-dessus de 75/au-dessous de 25 est un très bon score; **she must earn ~ between £30,000 and £40,000** elle doit gagner dans les 30 000 à 40 000 livres; **you can use it to flavour ~ from jam to soup** vous pouvez l'utiliser pour parfumer n'importe quoi, de la confiture à la soupe. -**4.** [in intensifying phrases]: **he isn't ~ like his father** il ne ressemble en rien à son père; **it doesn't taste ~ like a tomato** ça n'a pas du tout le goût de tomate; **it isn't ~ like as good as his last film** c'est loin d'être aussi bon que son dernier film; **they aren't producing the goods ~ like fast enough** ils ne produisent pas la marchandise assez vite, loin de là; **I wouldn't miss it for ~** je ne le manquerais pour rien au monde; **it's as easy as ~** c'est facile comme tout; **to run like ~** courir comme un dératé; **he worked like ~** il a travaillé comme un fou; **they shouted like ~** ils ont crié comme des forcenés; **it rained like ~** il pleuvait des cordes.

◆ **anything but** *adv phr* tout sauf; **that music is ~ but relaxing** cette musique est tout sauf reposante; **is he crazy? — ~ but!** est-ce qu'il est fou? — bien au contraire! OR il est tout sauf ça!

anyway ['enɪweɪ] *adv* -**1.** [in any case - reinforcing] de toute façon; **it's too late now ~** de toute façon, il est trop tard maintenant; **what's to stop them ~?** de toute façon, qu'est-ce qui peut les en empêcher?; [- summarizing, concluding] en tout cas; **~, that's what I think** en tout cas, c'est mon avis OR ce que je pense; **~, in the end she left** toujours est-il qu'elle OR en tout cas, elle a fini par partir; **~, I have to go** [I'll be late] bon, il faut que j'y aille; [I don't have any choice] enfin, il faut que j'y aille. -**2.** [nevertheless, notwithstanding] quand même; **thanks ~** merci quand même; **we can invite them ~** on peut toujours OR quand même les inviter; **I don't care what you say, I'm going ~** tu peux dire ce que tu veux, j'y vais quand même. -**3.** [qualifying] en tout cas; **that's what we all think, well, most of us ~** c'est ce qu'on pense tous, ou presque tous en tout cas; **and that's the situation, to the best of my knowledge ~** et voilà où on en est, autant que je sache en tout cas. -**4.** [returning to topic] bref; **~, as I was saying...** bref, comme je disais...

anyways ['enɪweɪz] *Am* = **anyway**.

anywhere ['enɪweəʳ] ◇ *adv* -**1.** [in questions] quelque part; **have you seen my keys ~?** avez-vous vu mes clés (quelque part)?; **are you going ~ at Easter?** vous partez à Pâques?; **are you going ~ this evening?** est-ce que vous sortez ce soir? -**2.** [in positive statements - no matter where] n'importe où; **just put it down ~** posez-le n'importe où; **sit ~ you like** asseyez-vous où vous voulez; **the book could be ~** le livre pourrait être n'importe où; **~ you go it's the same story** où que vous alliez, c'est toujours pareil OR toujours la même chose; **I'd know her ~** je la reconnaîtrais entre mille || [everywhere] partout; **you can find that magazine ~** on trouve cette revue partout. -**3.** [in negative statements - any place] nulle part; **I haven't been ~ else today** je ne suis allé nulle part ailleurs aujourd'hui; **I can't find my keys ~** je ne trouve mes clés nulle part; **we didn't go ~** nous ne sommes allés nulle part; **look, this isn't getting us ~** écoute, tout ça ne nous mène à rien; **crying won't get you ~** pleurer ne te servira à rien. -**4.** [any number within a range]: **we might receive ~ between 60 and 600 applications** on peut recevoir entre 60 et 600 demandes; **the rate could be ~ from 10 to 20%** le taux peut aller de 10 à 20 %. -**5.** *phr*: **he isn't ~ near as quick as you are** il est loin d'être aussi rapide que toi; **are they ~ near completion?** ont-ils bientôt fini?

◇ *pron* [any place]: **do they need ~ to stay?** ont-ils besoin d'un endroit où loger?; **she's looking for a flat, but hasn't found ~ yet** elle cherche un appartement mais elle n'a encore rien trouvé; **they live miles from ~** ils habitent en pleine brousse.

anywheres *inf* ['enɪweəz] *Am* = **anywhere**.

anywise ['enɪwaɪz] *adv Am* [at all] en aucune façon, aucunement.

Anzac ['ænzæk] (*abbr of* **Australia-New Zealand Army Corps**) *n soldat néo-zélandais ou australien*.

ANZUS ['ænzəs] (*abbr of* **Australia, New Zealand, United States**) *pr n alliance entre l'Australie, la Nouvelle-Zélande et les États-Unis*.

aob, **AOB** (*written abbr of* **any other business**) *divers*.

A-OK *inf Am* ◇ *adj* excellent; **everything's ~** tout baigne; **he's ~** c'est un type bien.

◇ *adv* parfaitement.

aorist ['eərɪst] *n* aoriste *m*.

aorta [eɪ'ɔːtə] (*pl* **aortas** OR **aortae** [-tiː]) *n* aorte *f*.

Aosta [ɑː'ɒstə] *pr n* Aoste.

AP *n abbr of* **American Plan**.

apace [ə'peɪs] *adv lit* rapidement, vite.

Apache [ə'pætʃɪ] (*pl inv* OR **Apaches**) ◇ *n* -**1.** [person] Apache *mf*. -**2.** LING apache *m*.

◇ *adj* apache.

apart [ə'pɑːt] ◇ *adv* -**1.** [separated - in space]: **a couple of metres ~** à (une distance de) deux ou trois mètres l'un de l'autre; **the houses were about 10 kilometres ~** les maisons étaient à environ 10 kilomètres l'une de l'autre; **plant the seeds fairly far ~** plantez les graines assez loin les unes des autres; **cities as far ~ as Johannesburg and Hong Kong** des villes aussi éloignées l'une de l'autre que Johannesburg et Hong Kong; **he stood with his legs wide ~** il se tenait (debout) les jambes bien écartées; **they can't bear to be ~** ils ne supportent pas d'être loin l'un de l'autre OR séparés || [in time]: **the twins were born 3 minutes ~** les jumeaux sont nés à 3 minutes d'intervalle || *fig*: **we're miles ~ when it comes to politics** nous avons des points de vue politiques très différents; **how do you tell the two boys ~?** comment distinguez-vous les deux garçons l'un de l'autre? -**2.** [in pieces] en pièces, en morceaux; **to break ~** s'émietter. -**3.** [with verbs of motion]: **to push ~** éloigner (en poussant); **they sprang ~ when I entered the room** ils se sont écartés vivement l'un de l'autre quand je suis entré dans la pièce; **to grow ~ from sb** s'éloigner de qqn. -**4.** [isolated] à l'écart; **she stood ~ from the others** elle se tenait à l'écart des autres. -**5.** [aside] à part; **joking ~** trêve de plaisanterie; **that ~, did you enjoy yourselves?** à part ça, vous vous êtes amusés?

◇ *adj (after n)* [distinct and special] à part; **they regard it as a thing ~** ils considèrent que c'est quelque chose de complètement différent.

◆ **apart from** *prep phr* -**1.** [except for] à part; **~ from my salary, we have nothing** en dehors de

OR à part mon salaire, nous n'avons rien; it's fine, ~ from a few minor mistakes à part OR sauf quelques fautes sans importance, c'est très bien; but ~ from that, everything's fine! mais à part ça, tout va très bien! -**2.** [as well as] en plus de; she has many interests ~ from golf elle s'intéresse à beaucoup de choses à part le OR en plus du golf; quite ~ from the fact that it's too big, I don't like the colour outre (le fait) que c'est trop grand, je n'aime pas la couleur.

apartheid [ə'pɑːtheɪt] *n* apartheid *m*.

apartment [ə'pɑːtmənt] *n* -**1.** *Br (usu pl)* [room] pièce *f*; [bedroom] chambre *f*; the Royal ~s la résidence royale. -**2.** *Am* [flat] appartement *m*, logement *m*; a one-bedroom OR one-bedroomed ~ un deux-pièces.

apartment building *n Am* immeuble *m (d'habitation)*.

apartment house *n Am* immeuble *m (d'habitation)*.

apathetic [,æpə'θetɪk] *adj* apathique, indifférent.

apathetically [,æpə'θetɪklɪ] *adv* avec apathie OR indifférence.

apathy ['æpəθɪ] *n* apathie *f*, indifférence *f*.

APB (*abbr of* all points bulletin) *n Am message radio diffusé par la police concernant une personne recherchée*.

ape [eɪp] ◇ *n* -**1.** [monkey] grand singe *m*, anthropoïde *m spec*. -**2.** *pej* [person] brute *f*. -**3.** *inf Am*: to go ~ devenir fou; she went ~ over his new painting elle s'est emballée pour son nouveau tableau.
◇ *vt* singer.

ape-man (*pl* ape-men) *n* homme-singe *m*.

Apennines ['æpɪnaɪnz] *pl pr n*: the ~ l'Apennin *m*, les Apennins *mpl*.

aperient [ə'pɪərɪənt] MED ◇ *adj* laxatif.
◇ *n* laxatif *m*.

aperiodic [,eɪpɪərɪ'ɒdɪk] *adj* apériodique.

aperitif [əperə'tiːf] *n* apéritif *m*.

aperture ['æpə,tjʊə'] *n* -**1.** [opening] ouverture *f*, orifice *m*; [gap] brèche *f*, trouée *f*. -**2.** PHOT ouverture *f* (du diaphragme).

apex ['eɪpeks] (*pl* apexes OR apices ['eɪpɪsiːz]) *n* [of triangle] sommet *m*, apex *m*; to reach the ~ of one's career *fig* atteindre le point culminant OR le sommet de sa carrière.

APEX ['eɪpeks] *n Br* (*abbr of* advance purchase excursion): ~ fare tarif *m* apex.

aphasia [ə'feɪzjə] *n* aphasie *f*.

aphelion [æ'fiːljən] (*pl* aphelia [-ljə]) *n* aphélie *m*.

aphesis ['æfɪsɪs] (*pl* apheses [-siːz]) *n* aphérèse *f*.

aphid ['eɪfɪd] *n* puceron *m*.

aphis ['eɪfɪs] (*pl* aphides ['eɪfɪdiːz]) *n* aphididé *m*.

aphonic [eɪ'fɒnɪk] *adj* aphone.

aphorism ['æfərɪzm] *n* aphorisme *m*.

aphrodisiac [,æfrə'dɪzɪæk] ◇ *adj* aphrodisiaque.
◇ *n* aphrodisiaque *m*.

Aphrodite [,æfrə'daɪtɪ] *pr n* Aphrodite.

API (*abbr of* American Press Institute) *pr n association de journalistes américains*.

apiarist ['eɪpjərɪst] *n* apiculteur *m*, -trice *f*.

apiary ['eɪpjərɪ] (*pl* apiaries) *n* rucher *m*.

apical ['æpɪkl] *adj* apical; ~ consonant LING apicale *f*.

apices ['eɪpɪsiːz] *pl* → **apex**.

apiculture ['eɪpɪkʌltʃə'] *n* apiculture *f*.

apiece [ə'piːs] *adv* -**1.** [for each item] chacun *m*, -e *f*, (la) pièce; the plants are £3 ~ les plantes coûtent 3 livres pièce OR chacune. -**2.** [for each person] chacun *m*, -e *f*, par personne; we had two shirts ~ nous avions deux chemises chacun.

aplenty [ə'plentɪ] *adj lit*: she's always had money ~ elle a toujours eu beaucoup OR énormément d'argent.

aplomb [ə'plɒm] *n* sang-froid *m*, aplomb *m usu pej*.

apnoea *Br*, **apnea** *Am* [æp'nɪə] *n* apnée *f*.

APO (*abbr of* Army Post Office) *n service postal de l'armée*.

Apocalypse [ə'pɒkəlɪps] *n* Apocalypse *f*.

apocalyptic [ə,pɒkə'lɪptɪk] *adj* apocalyptique.

apocopate [*adj* ə'pɒkəʊpɪt, *vb* ə'pɒkəʊpeɪt]
◇ *adj* apocopé.
◇ *vt* abréger par apocope.

apocope [ə'pɒkəʊpɪ] *n* apocope *f*.

Apocrypha [ə'pɒkrɪfə] *npl*: the ~ les Apocryphes *mpl*.

apocryphal [ə'pɒkrɪfl] *adj* apocryphe.

apodosis [ə'pɒdəsɪs] (*pl* apodoses [-siːz]) *n* apodose *f*.

apogee ['æpədʒiː] *n* ASTRON & *fig* apogée *m*; to reach the ~ of one's career atteindre le sommet OR le point culminant de sa carrière.

apolitical [,eɪpə'lɪtɪkəl] *adj* apolitique.

Apollo [ə'pɒləʊ] *pr n* -**1.** MYTH Apollon. -**2.** [spacecraft] Apollo *m*; the ~ program le programme Apollo.

Apollonian [,æpə'ləʊnjən] *adj* apollinien.

Apollonius [,æpə'ləʊnjəs] *pr n* Apollonios.

apologetic [ə,pɒlə'dʒetɪk] *adj* -**1.** [person]: she was very ~ for being late elle s'est excusée plusieurs fois d'être arrivée en retard; he was most ~ il s'est confondu en excuses. -**2.** [letter, look, note, smile] d'excuse.

apologetically [ə,pɒlə'dʒetɪklɪ] *adv* [say] en s'excusant, pour s'excuser; [smile] pour s'excuser.

apologetics [ə,pɒlə'dʒetɪks] *n (U)* apologétique *f*.

apologia [,æpə'ləʊdʒɪə] *n* apologie *f*.

apologist [ə'pɒlədʒɪst] *n* apologiste *mf*.

apologize, -ise [ə'pɒlədʒaɪz] *vi* s'excuser; I ~d profusely je me suis confondu en excuses; there's no need to ~ inutile de vous excuser; he ~d to them for the delay il leur a demandé de l'excuser pour son retard; ~ to the lady demande pardon à la dame.

apology [ə'pɒlədʒɪ] (*pl* apologies) *n* -**1.** [expression of regret] excuses *fpl*; they were full of apologies ils se sont confondus en excuses; to make one's apologies to sb s'excuser auprès de qqn; I owe him an ~ je lui dois des excuses; we demand an ~ nous exigeons des excuses; please accept my sincere ~ je vous présente mes plus sincères excuses; the director sends his apologies le directeur vous prie de l'excuser; a letter of ~ une lettre d'excuses. -**2.** [defence] apologie *f*. -**3.** *Br pej* [poor example]: he's a mere ~ for a man c'est un nul.

apolune ['æpəluːn] *n* apolune *f*.

apoplectic [,æpə'plektɪk] ◇ *adj* apoplectique; to have an ~ fit avoir OR faire une attaque d'apoplexie.
◇ *n* apoplectique *mf*.

apoplexy ['æpəpleksɪ] *n* apoplexie *f*.

apostasy [ə'pɒstəsɪ] (*pl* apostasies) *n* apostasie *f*.

apostate [ə'pɒsteɪt] ◇ *adj* apostat.
◇ *n* apostat *m*, -e *f*.

apostatize, -ise [ə'pɒstətaɪz] *vi* apostasier.

apostle [ə'pɒsl] *n* RELIG OR *fig* apôtre *m*; the Apostles' Creed le Symbole des Apôtres.

apostolic [,æpə'stɒlɪk] *adj* apostolique.

apostrophe [ə'pɒstrəfɪ] *n* apostrophe *f*.

apostrophize, -ise [ə'pɒstrəfaɪz] *vt* apostropher.

apothecary [ə'pɒθəkərɪ] (*pl* apothecaries) *n* pharmacien *m*, -enne *f*, apothicaire *m arch*.

apothem ['æpəθem] *n* apothème *m*.

apotheosis [ə,pɒθɪ'əʊsɪs] (*pl* apotheoses [-siːz]) *n* apothéose *f*.

appal *Br*, **appall** *Am* [ə'pɔːl] (*pt* & *pp* appalled, *cont* appalling) *vt* [scandalize] choquer, scandaliser; [horrify] écœurer; she was appalled at OR by the very thought l'idée même l'écœurait.

Appalachia [,æpə'leɪtʃjə] *pr n* région *f* des Appalaches.

Appalachian [,æpə'leɪtʃjən] ◇ *pr n*: the ~s, the ~ Mountains les (monts *mpl*) Appalaches *mpl*.
◇ *adj* appalachien.

appall *Am* = **appal**.

appalled [ə'pɔːld] *adj* écœuré.

appalling [ə'pɔːlɪŋ] *adj* écœurant, infect.

appallingly [ə'pɔːlɪŋlɪ] *adv* -**1.** [badly] de façon écœurante. -**2.** [as intensifier] effroyablement; an ~ bad film un film effroyablement mauvais.

apparatchik [,æpə'rætʃɪk] *n* apparatchik *m*.

apparatus [,æpə'reɪtəs] (*pl inv* OR apparatuses) *n* -**1.** *(U)* [equipment] équipement *m*; [set of instruments] instruments *mpl*; ~ criticus, critical ~ LITERAT appareil *m* OR apparat *m* critique. -**2.** *(U)* [in gymnasium] agrès *mpl*; exercises on the ~, ~ work exercices *mpl* aux agrès. -**3.** [machine] appareil *m*; heating ~ appareil de chauffage. -**4.** ANAT appareil *m*; the digestive ~ l'appareil digestif. -**5.** [organization]: the ~ of government la machine administrative, l'administration *f*.

apparel [ə'pærəl] (*Br pt* & *pp* apparelled, *cont* apparelling, *Am pt* & *pp* appareled, *cont* appareling) ◇ *n* -**1.** *lit* OR *arch* [garb] costume *m*, mise *f*. -**2.** *Am* [clothes] habillement *m*, vêtements *mpl*; [industry] confection *f*.
◇ *vt lit* OR *arch* [dress] vêtir, habiller; [adorn] orner; he was apparelled in the robes of state il avait revêtu son costume d'apparat.

apparent [ə'pærənt] *adj* -**1.** [obvious] évident, apparent; the tension between them had become ~ to us all nous sentions tous désormais la tension qui existait entre eux; the need for better education facilities is becoming increasingly ~ il est de plus en plus évident qu'il faut améliorer le système éducatif; for no ~ reason sans raison apparente. -**2.** [seeming] apparent, supposé; I admire the ~ ease with which she does the work j'admire l'apparente facilité avec laquelle elle exécute le travail.

apparently [ə'pærəntlɪ] *adv* -**1.** [seemingly] apparemment, en apparence; she was ~ quite calm and collected elle paraissait assez calme et sereine. -**2.** [according to rumour] à ce qu'il paraît; he ~ quit his job il paraît qu'il a démissionné; is she leaving? — ~ not elle part? — on dirait que non; that's ~ the reason il paraît que c'est pour ça; ~, they had a huge row il paraît qu'ils se sont violemment disputés.

apparition [,æpə'rɪʃn] *n* apparition *f*.

appeal [ə'piːl] ◇ *n* -**1.** [request] appel *m*; she made an ~ on behalf of the victims elle a lancé un appel au profit des victimes; we made an ~ for money to help the refugees nous avons fait un appel de fonds pour aider les réfugiés; an ~ for help un appel au secours; an ~ for funds COMM & FIN un appel de fonds. -**2.** JUR appel *m*, pourvoi *m*; to enter OR to lodge an ~ interjeter appel, se pourvoir en appel; on ~ en seconde instance; notice of ~ infirmation *f*; right of ~ droit *m* d'appel; with no right of ~ sans appel. -**3.** [attraction] attrait *m*, charme *m*; travelling has lost its ~ for me je n'aime plus voyager, les voyages ne m'intéressent plus; the idea does have a certain ~ l'idée est bien séduisante.
◇ *vi* -**1.** [make request] faire un appel; [publicly] lancer un appel; [plead] supplier, implorer; she ~ed to me to be patient elle m'a prié d'être patient; they're ~ing for help for the victims ils lancent un appel au profit des victimes; to ~ for funds COMM & FIN faire un appel de fonds. -**2.** to ~ to sthg [invoke] faire appel à qqch; she ~ed to his sense of justice elle a fait appel à son sens de la justice. -**3.** [apply] faire appel; he ~ed to them for help il leur a demandé du secours; they ~ed to the management for better working conditions ils ont fait appel à la direction pour obtenir de meilleures conditions de travail; he ~ed against the decision il a fait appel contre cette décision. -**4.** JUR interjeter appel, se pourvoir en appel; to ~ against a sentence appeler d'un jugement. -**5.** [please] plaire; the programmes ~ most to children

ces émissions plaisent particulièrement aux enfants; the book ~s to the reader's imagination ce livre parle à l'imagination du lecteur; the idea ~ed to me l'idée m'a séduit; it doesn't really ~ to me ça ne m'attire pas vraiment, ça ne me dit pas grand-chose.

appeal court *n* cour *f* d'appel.

appealing [ə'pi:lɪŋ] *adj* -**1.** [attractive - dress, person] joli; [- idea, plan] intéressant. -**2.** [moving] émouvant, attendrissant; [imploring] suppliant, implorant; he had sad, ~ eyes il avait un regard triste et implorant.

appealingly [ə'pi:lɪŋlɪ] *adv* -**1.** [charmingly] de façon attrayante. -**2.** [beseechingly] d'un air suppliant OR implorant.

appear [ə'pɪəʳ] *vi* -**1.** [come into view - person, ghost, stars] apparaître; he suddenly ~ed round the corner il a soudain surgi au coin de la rue; the sun ~ed from behind a cloud le soleil est sorti de derrière un nuage; she ~ed to him in a vision elle lui est apparue dans une vision; she finally ~ed at about 8 o'clock elle est arrivée finalement vers 20 h. -**2.** [come into being] apparaître; [new product] apparaître, être mis sur le marché; [publication] paraître, sortir, être publié. -**3.** [feature] paraître, figurer; the father figure often ~s in his films le personnage du père figure souvent dans ses films. -**4.** [be present officially] se présenter, paraître; [in court] comparaître; to ~ before the court OR the judge comparaître devant le tribunal; he ~ed on a charge of murder il a été jugé pour meurtre; they ~ed as witnesses for the defence ils ont témoigné pour la défense; he ~ed for the accused il a plaidé pour l'accusé. -**5.** [actor] jouer; she ~ed as Antigone elle a joué Antigone; to ~ in a play jouer dans une pièce; to ~ on TV passer à la télévision. -**6.** [seem] paraître, sembler; she ~ed nervous elle avait l'air nerveux OR nerveuse; the baby ~ed quite content le bébé semblait plutôt satisfait; how does the situation ~ to you? comment voyez-vous la situation?; there ~s to have been a mistake il semble qu'il y ait eu erreur; it ~s she never received the letter il semble qu'elle n'ait jamais reçu la lettre; it ~s not il semble que non; so it ~s, so it would ~ c'est ce qu'il semble, on dirait bien; is she ill? – it ~s so est-elle malade? – il paraît (que oui); it would ~ that he was already known to the police il semble qu'il était déjà connu des services de police; it ~ed later that he had killed his wife il est ensuite apparu qu'il avait assassiné sa femme; there ~s to be a mistake in the bill on dirait qu'il y a une erreur dans la facture; it ~s the driver was drunk il semble que le conducteur avait bu; it ~s to me that he lied il me semble qu'il a menti.

appearance [ə'pɪərəns] *n* -**1.** [act of appearing] apparition *f*; the antibiotics help guard against the ~ of further infections les antibiotiques contribuent à éviter l'apparition de nouvelles infections; she made a brief ~ at the party elle a fait une brève apparition à la fête; the president made a personal ~ le président est apparu en personne; to put in an ~ faire acte de présence. -**2.** [advent] avènement *m*; [of new product] mise *f* sur le marché; [of publication] parution *f*. -**3.** [in court] comparution *f*; to make an ~ before a court OR a judge comparaître devant un tribunal. -**4.** [performance]: this was her first ~ on the stage c'était sa première apparition sur scène; she's made a number of television ~s elle est passée plusieurs fois à la télévision; offers have flooded in since her television ~ les propositions ont afflué depuis son passage à la télévision; in order of ~ par ordre d'entrée en scène. -**5.** [outward aspect] apparence *f*, aspect *m*; to have a good ~ [person] présenter bien; I tried to give the ~ that I cared j'ai essayé de donner l'impression que ça ne m'était pas indifférent; it has all the ~s of being a first-class show si l'on en juge par les apparences, ce devrait être un spectacle de premier ordre; to OR by all ~s he doesn't work very hard selon toute apparence, il ne travaille pas beaucoup; contrary to all ~s, against all ~s contrairement à toute apparence; ~s can be deceptive les apparences sont parfois trompeuses; don't judge by ~s ne vous fiez pas aux apparences, il ne faut pas se fier aux apparences; his parents tried hard to keep up ~s ses parents ont tout fait pour sauver les apparences; for ~s' sake pour la forme.

appease [ə'pi:z] *vt* apaiser, calmer.

appeasement [ə'pi:zmənt] *n* apaisement *m*; *pej* & POL conciliation *f*.

appellant [ə'pelənt] ◇ *adj* appelant.
◇ *n* partie *f* appelante, appelant *m*, -e *f*.

appellate [ə'pelət] *adj*: ~ court cour *f* d'appel.

appellation [,æpə'leɪʃn] *n* appellation *f*.

appellative [ə'pelətɪv] ◇ *adj* appellatif.
◇ *n* appellatif *m*.

append [ə'pend] *vt fml* [document, note] joindre; [signature] apposer.

appendage [ə'pendɪdʒ] *n* [gen & ZOOL] appendice *m*.

appendectomy [,æpen'dektəmɪ] (*pl* **appendectomies**) *n* appendicectomie *f*.

appendicectomy [ə,pendɪ'sektəmɪ] (*pl* **appendicectomies**) = **appendectomy**.

appendices [ə'pendɪsi:z] *pl* → **appendix**.

appendicitis [ə,pendɪ'saɪtɪs] *n* appendicite *f*; have you had ~? avez-vous eu l'appendicite?

appendix [ə'pendɪks] (*pl* **appendixes** OR **appendices** [-dɪsi:z]) *n* -**1.** ANAT appendice *m*; to have one's ~ out se faire opérer de l'appendicite. -**2.** [to book] appendice *m*; [to report] annexe *f*.

appertain [,æpə'teɪn] *vi fml* [belong]: to ~ to appartenir à; land ~ing to the Crown des terres appartenant à la Couronne; those islands ~ to the United States ces îles font partie des États-Unis ‖ [relate]: to ~ to relever de; the responsibilities ~ing to adulthood les responsabilités de l'âge adulte; duties ~ing to his position des devoirs qui incombent à ses fonctions.

appetite ['æpɪtaɪt] *n* appétit *m*; she has a good ~ elle a bon appétit; I've got no ~ je n'ai pas d'appétit; I've lost my ~ j'ai perdu l'appétit; don't have too many sweets, you'll spoil your ~ ne mange pas trop de bonbons, ça va te couper l'appétit; they've gone for a swim to work up an ~ ils sont allés se baigner pour s'ouvrir l'appétit OR se mettre en appétit; I have no ~ for that kind of thing *fig* je n'ai pas de goût pour ce genre de chose; he has an insatiable ~ for work *fig* c'est un boulimique du travail.

appetizer, -iser ['æpɪtaɪzəʳ] *n* [food] hors-d'œuvre *m inv*, amuse-gueule *m*; [drink] apéritif *m*.

appetizing, -ising ['æpɪtaɪzɪŋ] *adj* appétissant.

Appian ['æpɪən] *adj*: the ~ Way la voie Appienne.

applaud [ə'plɔ:d] ◇ *vi* applaudir.
◇ *vt* applaudir, approuver; his efforts are to be ~ed il faut applaudir ses efforts.

applause [ə'plɔ:z] *n (U)* applaudissements *mpl*, acclamations *fpl*; his performance won enthusiastic ~ from the audience son interprétation a été chaleureusement applaudie par le public; she left the stage to thunderous ~ elle quitta la scène sous un tonnerre d'applaudissements.

apple ['æpl] *n* [fruit] pomme *f*; [tree] pommier *m*; ~ blossom fleur *f* de pommier; ~ core trognon *m* de pomme; ~ tree pommier *m*; the ~ of discord *lit* & *fig* la pomme de discorde; he's a rotten ~ c'est un mauvais sujet; she's the ~ of his eye il tient à elle comme à la prunelle de ses yeux; don't upset the ~ cart *inf* ne fiche pas tout par terre; an ~ a day keeps the doctor away *prov* chaque jour une pomme conserve son homme *prov*.

applejack ['æpldʒæk] *n* eau-de-vie *f* de pommes.

apple pie *n* [covered] tourte *f* aux pommes; [open] tarte *f* aux pommes.

◆ **apple-pie** *inf adj* impeccable; in apple-pie order en ordre parfait ❑ apple-pie bed *Br* lit *m* en portefeuille.

apple sauce *n* -**1.** CULIN compote *f* de pommes. -**2.** *inf fig Am* & *Can* boniments *mpl*.

appliance [ə'plaɪəns] *n* -**1.** appareil *m*; [small] dispositif *m*, instrument *m*; domestic OR household ~s appareils électroménagers; electrical ~s appareils électriques. -**2.** [fire engine] autopompe *f*.

applicable ['æplɪkəbl] *adj* applicable.

applicant ['æplɪkənt] *n* -**1.** [gen, for patent] demandeur *m*, -euse *f*; [for a position] candidat *m*, -e *f*, postulant *m*, -e *f*; a job ~ un candidat à un poste, un postulant. -**2.** JUR requérant *m*, -e *f*.

application [,æplɪ'keɪʃn] *n* -**1.** [use] application *f*; the ~ of free market economics to communist systems l'application de l'économie de marché aux régimes communistes; the practical ~s of the research les applications pratiques de la recherche ‖ [of lotion, paint] application *f*; 'for external ~ only' MED 'réservé à l'usage externe'. -**2.** [request] demande *f*; a job ~ [spontaneous] une demande d'emploi; [in answer to advertisement] une candidature à un poste; I submitted my ~ for a scholarship j'ai fait ma demande de bourse; further information is available upon ~ des renseignements complémentaires sont disponibles sur simple demande; he made an ~ to the committee for a hearing il s'est adressé au comité pour obtenir une audition; we made an ~ for citizenship nous avons fait une demande de naturalisation. -**3.** [diligence] assiduité *f*; this student lacks ~ cet étudiant manque d'assiduité. -**4.** [relevance] pertinence *f*.

application form *n* formulaire *m*; [detailed] dossier *m* de candidature; UNIV dossier *m* d'inscription.

application program *n* programme *m* d'application.

applicator ['æplɪkeɪtəʳ] *n* applicateur *m*.

applied [ə'plaɪd] *adj* [gen, LING, MATH & SCI] appliqué; ~ arts arts *mpl* décoratifs.

appliqué [æ'pli:keɪ] ◇ *n* [decoration] application *f*; [decorative work] travail *m* d'application.
◇ *vt* coudre en application.

apply [ə'plaɪ] (*pt* & *pp* **applied**) ◇ *vt* -**1.** [use] appliquer, mettre en pratique OR en application; [rule, law] appliquer; we ~ the same rule to all students nous appliquons la même règle à OR pour tous les étudiants. -**2.** [pressure]: to ~ pressure to sthg exercer une pression OR appuyer sur qqch; she applied the brakes elle a appuyé sur le frein; the authorities applied pressure on the company to change its policy *fig* les autorités ont fait pression sur la société pour qu'elle change de politique. -**3.** [paint, lotion etc] appliquer, mettre; ~ antiseptic to the wound désinfectez la plaie; ~ the paint using a roller appliquez la peinture à l'aide d'un rouleau; to ~ heat to sthg exposer qqch à la chaleur; the doctor applied heat to her back le médecin lui a traité le dos par la thermothérapie. -**4.** [devote]: to ~ one's mind to sthg s'appliquer à qqch; she applied herself to her work elle s'est lancée dans son travail; he must learn to ~ himself il faut qu'il apprenne à s'appliquer.
◇ *vi* -**1.** [make an application] s'adresser, avoir recours; ~ to the personnel office adressez-vous au service du personnel; '~ within' 's'adresser à l'intérieur OR ici'; to ~ for a job/scholarship faire une demande d'emploi/de bourse; he applied to the Research Council for an award il s'est adressé au conseil de la recherche pour obtenir une bourse; she has decided to ~ for the job elle a décidé de poser sa candidature pour cet emploi; we applied for a patent nous avons déposé une demande de brevet; the right to ~ to the courts JUR le droit au recours juridictionnel. -**2.** [be relevant] s'appliquer; and that applies to you too! et ça s'applique aussi à toi!; this law applies to all citizens cette loi s'applique à tous

les citoyens; **this doesn't ~ to us** nous ne sommes pas concernés; **his criticism applies to all journalists** ses critiques s'appliquent à tous les journalistes.

appoint [əˈpɔɪnt] *vt* **-1.** [assign] nommer, désigner; **she was ~ed to the post of director** elle a été nommée directrice; **the members ~ed him president** les adhérents l'ont nommé président; **the president ~ed a committee** le président a constitué un comité ‖ [hire]: **we have ~ed a new cook** nous avons engagé un nouveau cuisinier. **-2.** [date, place] fixer, désigner; **we met on the ~ed day** nous nous sommes rencontrés au jour dit OR convenu; **let's ~ a time for the meeting** fixons une heure pour la réunion; **his ~ed agent** son agent attitré. **-3.** *Br fml* [furnish] aménager, installer; **a well-~ed house** une maison bien aménagée. **-4.** *arch* OR JUR [prescribe, ordain] ordonner, prescrire.

appointee [əpɔɪnˈtiː] *n* candidat *m* retenu, candidate *f* retenue, titulaire *mf*.

appointment [əˈpɔɪntmənt] *n* **-1.** [arrangement] rendez-vous *m*; **to make an ~ with sb** prendre rendez-vous avec qqn; **I made an ~ with the dentist** j'ai pris rendez-vous chez le dentiste; **they made an ~ to have lunch together** ils se sont donné rendez-vous pour déjeuner; **he has a 4 o'clock ~** il a un rendez-vous à 16 heures; **she only sees people by ~** elle ne reçoit que sur rendez-vous; **do you have an ~?** avez-vous (pris) rendez-vous?; **he had to cancel his ~s** il a dû annuler ses rendez-vous; **she has an important ~ to keep** elle doit aller à un rendez-vous important; **we have an ~ with the president** nous avons rendez-vous avec le président. **-2.** [nomination] nomination *f*, désignation *f*; [office filled] poste *m*; [posting] affectation *f*; **his ~ to the office of Lord Chancellor** sa nomination au poste de grand chancelier; **there are still some ~s to be made** il y a encore quelques postes à pourvoir; **by ~ to Her Majesty the Queen** COMM fournisseur *m* de S.M. la Reine ‖ [in newspaper]: '**~s**' 'offres *fpl* d'emploi'.

apportion [əˈpɔːʃn] *vt* [blame] répartir; [money] répartir, partager.

apposite [ˈæpəzɪt] *adj* juste, pertinent; **an ~ remark** une remarque très à propos.

apposition [ˌæpəˈzɪʃn] *n* apposition *f*; **a noun/phrase in ~** un nom/une expression en apposition.

appositive [əˈpɒzətɪv] *adj* en apposition.

appraisal [əˈpreɪzl] *n* appréciation *f*, évaluation *f*; **an official ~** une expertise ❑ **performance ~** [in company] évaluation.

appraise [əˈpreɪz] *vt* [object] estimer, évaluer (la valeur de); [importance, quality] évaluer, apprécier; **they ~d the damage after the fire** ils évaluèrent les dégâts après l'incendie.

appraising [əˈpreɪzɪŋ] *adj*: **she shot him an ~ glance** elle lui a lancé un coup d'œil pour le jauger.

appreciable [əˈpriːʃəbl] *adj* sensible, appréciable.

appreciably [əˈpriːʃəblɪ] *adv* sensiblement, de manière appréciable.

appreciate [əˈpriːʃɪeɪt] ◇ *vt* **-1.** [value] apprécier; [art] apprécier, goûter; [person] apprécier (à sa juste valeur); **they ~ good food** ils apprécient la bonne nourriture. **-2.** [be grateful for] être reconnaissant de, être sensible à; **I ~ your help** je vous suis reconnaissant de votre aide; **I would ~ a prompt reply to this letter** je vous serais obligé de bien vouloir me répondre dans les plus brefs délais; **I would ~ it if you didn't smoke in the car** je vous serais reconnaissant OR je vous saurais gré de ne pas fumer dans la voiture; **he greatly ~s this honour** il est très sensible à cet honneur. **-3.** [realize, understand] se rendre compte de, être conscient de; **he never ~d its true worth** il ne l'a jamais estimé à sa juste valeur; **I do ~ your concern but...** votre sollicitude me touche beaucoup mais...; **do you ~ how hard I try?** est-ce que tu te rends compte des efforts que je fais?; **we fully ~ the situation** nous nous rendons parfaitement compte de la situation. **-4.** [increase in value] accroître la valeur de.
◇ *vi* [increase in value - currency] monter; [- goods, property] prendre de la valeur.

appreciation [əˌpriːʃɪˈeɪʃn] *n* **-1.** [gratitude] reconnaissance *f*; **let me show my ~ for your help** laissez-moi vous témoigner ma reconnaissance; **she smiled her ~** son sourire témoignait de sa reconnaissance; **in ~ of what you have done** en remerciement OR pour vous remercier de ce que vous avez fait. **-2.** [assessment, understanding] évaluation *f*, estimation *f*; [of art, literature] critique *f*; **she wrote** OR **gave an ~ of the play** elle a fait une critique de la pièce; **he has a thorough ~ of the situation** il comprend très bien la situation. **-3.** [increase in value] hausse *f*, augmentation *f*.

appreciative [əˈpriːʃjətɪv] *adj* **-1.** [admiring] admiratif; **after a few ~ comments** après quelques remarques élogieuses; **an ~ look** un regard admiratif. **-2.** [grateful] reconnaissant; **I am very ~ of your help/concern** je te suis très reconnaissant de ton aide/ta sollicitude.

appreciatively [əˈpriːʃjətɪvlɪ] *adv* [with enjoyment] joyeusement; **he smiled ~** [gratefully] il eut un sourire reconnaissant; [admiringly] il eut un sourire appréciatif.

apprehend [ˌæprɪˈhend] *vt fml* **-1.** [arrest] arrêter, appréhender. **-2.** [understand] comprendre, saisir. **-3.** [fear, dread] redouter, appréhender.

apprehension [ˌæprɪˈhenʃn] *n* **-1.** [fear] inquiétude *f*, appréhension *f*; **there is no cause for ~** il n'y a pas de raison d'être inquiet. **-2.** *fml* [arrest] arrestation *f*. **-3.** *fml* [understanding] compréhension *f*.

apprehensive [ˌæprɪˈhensɪv] *adj* inquiet, craintif; **he is ~ about the interview** il appréhende l'entrevue; **I am ~ for your safety** je crains OR je suis inquiet pour votre sécurité.

apprehensively [ˌæprɪˈhensɪvlɪ] *adv* avec appréhension OR inquiétude.

apprentice [əˈprentɪs] ◇ *n* apprenti *m*, -e *f*; [in arts and crafts] élève *mf*; **she's an electrician's ~** elle est apprentie électricienne.
◇ *comp*: **an ~ toolmaker/butcher** un apprenti outilleur/boucher; **an ~ draughtsman** un élève dessinateur ❑ **the Apprentice Boys' Parade** *manifestation annuelle de jeunes protestants en Irlande du Nord.*
◇ *vt*: **to ~ sb to sb** mettre qqn en apprentissage OR placer qqn comme apprenti chez qqn; **he is ~d to a sculptor** il suit une formation chez un sculpteur; **she is ~d to a violin-maker** elle est en apprentissage chez un luthier.

apprenticeship [əˈprentɪʃɪp] *n* apprentissage *m*; **a two-year ~** un apprentissage de deux ans.

apprise [əˈpraɪz] *vt fml* informer, prévenir; **he was ~d of the danger** on l'a averti du danger.

appro *inf* [ˈæprəʊ] (*abbr of* approval) *n Br*: **on ~** à OR sous condition, à l'essai.

approach [əˈprəʊtʃ] ◇ *vt* **-1.** *literal* [person, place] s'approcher de, s'avancer vers; **as we ~ed Boston** comme nous approchions de Boston ‖ *fig* [state, time, quality] approcher de; **she is ~ing fifty** elle approche de la cinquantaine; **we are ~ing a time when...** le jour approche où...; **we have nothing ~ing that colour** nous n'avons rien qui se rapproche de cette couleur; **speeds ~ing the speed of light** des vitesses proches de celle de la lumière; **it was ~ing Christmas** Noël approchait; **a feeling ~ing hatred** un sentiment proche de la haine. **-2.** [consider] aborder; **let's ~ the problem from another angle** abordons le problème d'une autre façon; **that's not the way to ~ it** ce n'est pas comme cela qu'il faut s'y prendre. **-3.** [speak to] parler à; **to be easy/difficult to ~** être d'un abord facile/difficile; **a salesman ~ed me** un vendeur m'a abordé; **I ~ed him about the job** je lui ai parlé du poste; **they ~ed him about doing a deal** ils sont entrés en contact avec lui pour conclure un marché.
◇ *vi* [person, vehicle] s'approcher; [time, event] approcher, être proche.
◇ *n* **-1.** [of person, vehicle] approche *f*, arrivée *f*; **she heard his ~** elle l'a entendu venir; **the pilot began his ~ to Heathrow** le pilote commença sa descente sur OR vers Heathrow ‖ [of time, death] approche *f*, approches *fpl*; **the ~ of spring** la venue du printemps. **-2.** [way of tackling] façon *f*, approche *f*; **another ~ to the problem** une autre façon d'aborder le problème; **his ~ is all wrong** il s'y prend mal; **a new ~ to dealing with unemployment** une nouvelle conception de la lutte contre le chômage; **let's try the direct ~** allons-y sans détours; **this book adopts a non-scientific ~ to the subject** ce livre aborde le sujet d'une manière non scientifique. **-3.** [proposal] proposition *f*; **the shopkeeper made an ~ to his suppliers** le commerçant a fait une proposition à ses fournisseurs. **-4.** [access] voie *f* d'accès; **the ~es to the town** les approches *fpl* OR les abords *mpl* de la ville; **the ~ to the house/hotel is very impressive** les abords de la maison/l'hôtel sont très imposants; **the ~es to the beach** les chemins qui mènent à la plage; **the soldiers blocked all ~es to the camp** les soldats bloquèrent toutes les voies d'accès au camp; **the ~ to the summit** le chemin qui mène au sommet. **-5.** *fml* [approximation] ressemblance *f*, apparence *f*.

approachable [əˈprəʊtʃəbl] *adj* [place] accessible, approchable; [person] abordable, approchable.

approaching [əˈprəʊtʃɪŋ] *adj* [event] prochain, qui est proche; [vehicle] qui vient en sens inverse.

approach road *n Br* route *f* d'accès; [to motorway] voie *f* de raccordement, bretelle *f*.

approach shot *n* [in golf] approche *f*.

approbation [ˌæprəˈbeɪʃn] *n* approbation *f*, consentement *m*; **a nod/smile of ~** un signe de tête/un sourire approbateur.

appropriate [*adj* əˈprəʊprɪət, *vb* əˈprəʊprɪeɪt]
◇ *adj* [moment, decision] opportun; [word] bien venu, juste; [name] bien choisi; [authority] compétent; **the level of contribution ~ for** OR **to each country** la contribution appropriée à chaque pays; **music/remarks ~ to the occasion** de la musique/des propos de circonstance; **take the ~ action** prenez les mesures appropriées; **it wouldn't be ~ if she went** il ne serait pas convenable qu'elle y aille; **I am not the ~ person to ask** ce n'est pas à moi qu'il faut poser la question.
◇ *vt* **-1.** [take for o.s.] s'approprier, s'emparer de. **-2.** [set aside] affecter; **the funds ~d for** OR **to the school** l'argent affecté à l'école.

appropriately [əˈprəʊprɪətlɪ] *adv* convenablement; [speak] avec à-propos, pertinemment; [decide] à juste titre; **~ dressed** habillé comme il faut OR pour la circonstance; **the restaurant is ~ named** le restaurant porte bien son nom.

appropriateness [əˈprəʊprɪətnɪs] *n* [of moment, decision] opportunité *f*; [of remark] justesse *f*.

appropriation [əˌprəʊprɪˈeɪʃn] *n* **-1.** [taking for o.s.] appropriation *f*. **-2.** [allocation of money] dotation *f*; *Am* POL crédit *m* budgétaire; **allotment of ~s** répartition *f* des budgets ❑ **~s bill** projet *m* de loi de finances; **Appropriations Committee** *commission des finances de la Chambre des Représentants qui examine les dépenses.*

approval [əˈpruːvl] *n* **-1.** [favourable opinion] approbation *f*, accord *m*; **a gesture of ~** un signe approbateur; **the plan has your seal of ~, then?** alors tu donnes ton approbation pour le projet?; **to meet with sb's ~** obtenir OR recevoir l'approbation de qqn; **does the report meet with your ~?** êtes-vous satisfait du rapport? **-2.** [sanction] approbation *f*, autorisation *f*; **submit the proposal for his ~** soumettez la proposition à son approbation. **-3.** COMM: **to buy sthg on ~** acheter qqch à OR sous condition; **articles sent on ~** marchandises envoyées à titre d'essai.

approve [ə'pruːv] *vt* [plan, proposal etc] approuver; [agreement, treaty] ratifier, homologuer; **the plan must be ~d by the committee** il faut que le projet reçoive l'approbation du comité; **an appliance ~d by the authorities** un appareil agréé par les autorités.

◆ **approve of** *vt insep* approuver; [person] avoir une bonne opinion de; **I don't ~ of his ideas** je n'approuve pas OR je désapprouve ses idées; **they don't ~ of her going out with that man** ils n'apprécient pas du tout qu'elle sorte avec cet homme; **do you ~ of the proposal?** êtes-vous d'accord avec la proposition?; **she doesn't ~ of her son's friends** les amis de son fils ne lui plaisent pas.

approved [ə'pruːvd] *adj* -**1.** [method, practice] reconnu, admis. -**2.** [authorized] autorisé, admis.

approved school *n nom anciennement donné en Grande-Bretagne à un centre d'éducation surveillée (aujourd'hui appelé «community home»).*

approving [ə'pruːvɪŋ] *adj* approbateur, approbatif.

approvingly [ə'pruːvɪŋlɪ] *adv* d'une façon approbatrice; **she looked at him ~** elle l'a regardé d'un air approbateur; **he spoke ~** il a parlé d'un ton approbateur.

approx. (*written abbr of* **approximately**) approx., env.

approximate [*adj* ə'prɒksɪmət, *vb* ə'prɒksɪmeɪt]

◇ *adj* approximatif; **the ~ distance to town is 5 miles** il y a à peu près 5 miles d'ici à la ville; **he told the ~ truth** il ne disait qu'une partie de la vérité; **figures ~ to the nearest whole number** des chiffres arrondis au nombre entier le plus proche.

◇ *vi*: **to ~ to sthg** se rapprocher de qqch; **his answer ~d to a refusal** sa réponse était presque un refus.

approximately [ə'prɒksɪmətlɪ] *adj* à peu près, environ.

approximation [əˌprɒksɪ'meɪʃn] *n* approximation *f.*

appurtenance [ə'pɜːtɪnəns] *n* (*usu pl*) *fml* accessoire *m*; **the property and its ~s** [buildings, gardens etc] la propriété et ses dépendances; [legal rights & privileges] la propriété et ses circonstances et dépendances.

Apr. (*written abbr of* **April**) avr.

APR *n* -**1.** (*abbr of* **annualized percentage rate**) TEG *m.* -**2.** (*abbr of* **annual purchase rate**) taux *m* annuel.

après-ski [ˌæpreɪ'skiː] ◇ *n* après-ski *m.*

◇ *comp* [clothing, outfit] d'après-ski.

apricot ['eɪprɪkɒt] ◇ *n* -**1.** [fruit] abricot *m*; [tree] abricotier *m.* -**2.** [colour] abricot *(inv).*

◇ *comp* -**1.** [jam] d'abricots; [pie, tart] aux abricots. -**2.** [colour, paint, wallpaper] abricot *(inv).*

apricot tree *n* abricotier *m.*

April ['eɪprəl] *n* avril *m*; **~ Fools' Day** le premier avril; **an ~ fool** [person] *personne à qui l'on a fait un poisson d'avril*; [trick] un poisson d'avril; **~ fool!** poisson d'avril!; **~ showers** giboulées *fpl* de mars; **~ showers bring forth May flowers** *prov* les giboulées de mars apportent les fleurs du printemps *prov.*

APRIL FOOLS' DAY:
En Grande-Bretagne, le premier avril est l'occasion de farces en tous genres; en revanche, la tradition du poisson en papier n'existe pas.

---

a priori [ˌeɪpraɪ'ɔːraɪ] *adj* a priori.

apriorism [eɪ'praɪərɪzm] *n* apriorisme *m.*

apron ['eɪprən] *n* -**1.** [gen & TECH] tablier *m*; **he is tied to his mother's ~ strings** il est pendu aux jupes de sa mère. -**2.** AERON aire *f* de stationnement. -**3.** THEAT = **apron stage**.

apron stage *n* avant-scène *f.*

apropos ['æprəpəʊ] ◇ *adj* opportun, à propos.

◇ *adv* à propos, opportunément.

◆ **apropos of** *prep phr* à propos de.

apse [æps] *n* [in church] abside *f*; ASTRON apside *f.*

apt [æpt] *adj* -**1.** [person]: **to be ~ to do sthg** faire qqch facilement, être porté à faire qqch; **I am ~ to forget** j'oublie facilement; **people are ~ to believe the worst** les gens croient facilement le pire ‖ [things]: **to be ~ to do sthg** être susceptible de faire qqch; **it's the little things that are ~ to get forgotten** ce sont les petites choses sans importance que l'on oublie facilement; **buttons are ~ to get lost** les boutons se perdent facilement. -**2.** [suitable] convenable, approprié; [remark] juste, qui convient; **an ~ expression** une expression heureuse. -**3.** [clever] doué, intelligent.

apt. (*written abbr of* **apartment**) appt.

APT (*abbr of* **advanced passenger train**) *n Br train à grande vitesse,* ≃ TGV *m.*

aptitude ['æptɪtjuːd] *n* aptitude *f*, disposition *f*; **to have an ~ for sthg** avoir une aptitude à OR disposition pour qqch; **he has an ~ for languages** il a des dispositions OR un talent pour les langues; **she shows great ~** elle promet.

aptitude test *n* test *m* d'aptitude.

aptly ['æptlɪ] *adv* à OR avec propos, avec justesse; **the dog, Spot, was ~ named** le chien, Spot, portait OR méritait bien son nom; **as you so ~ pointed out...** comme tu l'as si bien fait remarquer...

aptness ['æptnɪs] *n* -**1.** [appropriateness] à-propos *m*, justesse *f.* -**2.** [tendency] tendance *f.* -**3.** [talent] aptitude *f*, disposition *f.*

Apulia [ə'pjuːljə] *pr n* Pouille *f*, Pouilles *fpl*; **in ~** dans les Pouilles.

AQ (*abbr of* **achievement quotient**) *n quotient d'aptitude obtenu en divisant l'âge d'aptitude par l'âge réel du sujet.*

aqualung ['ækwəlʌŋ] *n* scaphandre *m* autonome.

aquamarine [ˌækwəmə'riːn] ◇ *n* [stone] aigue-marine *f*; [colour] bleu vert *m inv.*

◇ *adj* bleu vert *(inv).*

aquanaut ['ækwənɔːt] *n* plongeur *m*, scaphandrier *m.*

aquaplane ['ækwəpleɪn] ◇ *n* aquaplane *m.*

◇ *vi* -**1.** SPORT faire de l'aquaplane. -**2.** *Br* [car] faire de l'aquaplanage *m.*

aquarium [ə'kweərɪəm] (*pl* **aquariums** OR **aquaria** [-rɪə]) *n* aquarium *m.*

Aquarius [ə'kweərɪəs] ◇ *pr n* ASTROL & ASTRON Verseau *m*; **it's the age of ~** c'est l'ère du Verseau.

◇ *n*: **he's (an) ~** il est (du signe du) Verseau.

aquatic [ə'kwætɪk] *adj* aquatique; [sport] nautique.

aquatics [ə'kwætɪks] *npl* sports *mpl* aquatiques.

aquatint ['ækwətɪnt] *n* aquatinte *f.*

aquavit ['ækwəvɪt] *n* aquavit *m*, akvavit *m.*

aqueduct ['ækwɪdʌkt] *n* aqueduc *m.*

aqueous ['eɪkwɪəs] *adj* aqueux.

aqueous humour *n* humeur *f* aqueuse.

aquifer ['ækwɪfə^r] *n* nappe *f* aquifère.

aquilegia [ˌækwɪ'liːdʒjə] *n* BOT ancolie *f.*

aquiline ['ækwɪlaɪn] *adj* aquilin; [nose] aquilin, en bec d'aigle.

Aquinas [ə'kwaɪnæs] *pr n*: **Saint Thomas ~** saint Thomas d'Aquin.

Aquitaine [ˌækwɪ'teɪn] *pr n* Aquitaine *f*; **in ~** en Aquitaine; **the ~ Basin** le bassin d'Aquitaine.

AR *written abbr of* **Arkansas**.

ARA (*abbr of* **Associate of the Royal Academy**) *n membre associé de la RA.*

Arab ['ærəb] ◇ *n* -**1.** [person] Arabe *mf.* -**2.** [horse] cheval *m* arabe.

◇ *adj*: **the ~-Israeli Wars** le conflit israélo-arabe; **the ~ League** la Ligue arabe; **the United ~ Emirates** les Émirats *mpl* arabes unis.

ARAB:
En anglais le mot «Arab» désigne l'ensemble des ressortissants des pays de culture arabe, et surtout de l'Arabie Saoudite. Il n'a pas le sens restreint de «Maghrébin» que l'on rencontre souvent en français: «the firm was bought by a wealthy Arab family».

---

arabesque [ˌærə'besk] *n* arabesque *f.*

Arabia [ə'reɪbjə] *pr n* Arabie *f.*

Arabian [ə'reɪbjən] ◇ *adj* arabe, d'Arabie; **the ~ Desert** le désert d'Arabie; **'the ~ Nights ('Entertainment)'** 'les Mille et Une Nuits'; **the ~ Peninsula** la péninsule d'Arabie; **the ~ Sea** la mer d'Arabie.

◇ *n* Arabe *mf.*

Arabic ['ærəbɪk] ◇ *n* arabe *m*; **written ~** l'arabe littéral.

◇ *adj* arabe; **~ numerals** les chiffres *mpl* arabes.

Arabist ['ærəbɪst] *n* [scholar] arabisant *m*, -e *f*; [politician] pro-Arabe *mf.*

arable ['ærəbl] *adj* arable, cultivable; [crops] cultivable; [farm] agricole; [farmer] qui cultive la terre; **~ farming** culture *f.*

Arachne [ə'ræknɪ] *pr n* Arachné.

arachnid [ə'ræknɪd] *n* arachnide *m.*

Aragon ['ærəgən] *pr n* Aragon *m*; **in ~** en Aragon.

arak ['ærək] = **arrack**.

Aral Sea [ɑːrəl-] *pr n*: **the ~** la mer d'Aral.

ARAM (*abbr of* **Associate of the Royal Academy of Music**) *n membre associé de la RAM.*

Aramaean, **Aramean** [ˌærə'miːən] *adj* araméen.

Aramaic [ˌærə'meɪɪk] ◇ *n* araméen *m.*

◇ *adj* araméen.

Aran ['ærən] *adj* -**1.** **the ~ Islands** les îles *fpl* Aran. -**2.** [sweater] Aran *(de grosse laine naturelle).*

arbiter ['ɑːbɪtə^r] *n* arbitre *m*, médiateur *m*, -trice *f*; **magazines act as ~s of modern taste** *fig* les magazines se font les juges OR les arbitres des goûts de notre société.

arbitrage [ˌɑːbɪ'trɑːʒ] *n* arbitrage *m.*

arbitrageur [ˌɑːbɪtrɑː'ʒɜː^r] *n* arbitragiste *mf.*

arbitrarily [*Br* 'ɑːbɪtrərəlɪ, *Am* ˌɑːrbə'trerəlɪ] *adv* arbitrairement.

arbitrariness ['ɑːbɪtrərɪnɪs] *n* [of decision, choice] côté *m* arbitraire.

arbitrary ['ɑːbɪtrərɪ] *adj* arbitraire.

arbitrate ['ɑːbɪtreɪt] ◇ *vt* arbitrer, juger.

◇ *vi* décider en qualité d'arbitre, arbitrer.

arbitration [ˌɑːbɪ'treɪʃn] *n* [gen & INDUST] arbitrage *m*; **both parties have gone to ~** les deux parties ont recouru à l'arbitrage; **they referred the dispute to ~** ils ont soumis le conflit à l'arbitrage; **settlement by ~** règlement *m* par arbitrage ❑ **~ court** OR **tribunal** instance *f* chargée d'arbitrer les conflits sociaux, tribunal *m* arbitral; **~ clause** clause *f* compromissoire.

arbitrator ['ɑːbɪtreɪtə^r] *n* arbitre *m*, médiateur *m*, -trice *f*; **the dispute has been referred to the ~** le litige a été soumis à l'arbitrage.

arbor ['ɑːbə^r] *n* -**1.** *Am* = **arbour**. -**2.** TECH arbre *m*, mandrin *m.*

arboreal [ɑː'bɔːrɪəl] *adj* [form] arborescent; [animal, technique] arboricole.

arboretum [ˌɑːbə'riːtəm] (*pl* **arboretums** OR **arboreta** [-tə]) *n* arboretum *m.*

arbour *Br*, **arbor** *Am* ['ɑːbə^r] *n* tonnelle *f*, charmille *f arch.*

arbutus [ɑː'bjuːtəs] *n* arbousier *m.*

arc [ɑːk] ◇ *n* arc *m.*

◇ *vi* -**1.** [gen] décrire un arc; **the ball ~ed up into the air** la balle décrivit un arc de cercle dans les airs. -**2.** ELEC projeter OR cracher des étincelles.

ARC [ɑːk] (*abbr of* **AIDS-related complex**) *n* ARC *m.*

arcade [ɑːˈkeɪd] *n* [set of arches] arcade *f*, galerie *f*; [shopping] galerie *f* marchande.

Arcadia [ɑːˈkeɪdjə] *pr n* Arcadie *f*; in ~ en Arcadie.

Arcadian [ɑːˈkeɪdjən] ◇ *n* Arcadien *m*, -enne *f*.
◇ *adj* arcadien, d'Arcadie.

Arcady [ˈɑːkədɪ] = **Arcadia**.

arcane [ɑːˈkeɪn] *adj* mystérieux, ésotérique.

arch [ɑːtʃ] ◇ *n* -**1.** ARCHIT arc *m*; [in church] arc *m*, voûte *f*. -**2.** [of eyebrows] courbe *f*; [of foot] cambrure *f*, voûte *f* plantaire; **to have fallen ~es** MED avoir les pieds plats OR *spec* un affaissement de la voûte plantaire.
◇ *vt* arquer, cambrer; **he ~ed his back** il a cambré le dos; **the cat ~ed its back** le chat fit le gros dos.
◇ *vi* former voûte, s'arquer.
◇ *adj* -**1.** [leading] grand, par excellence; **my ~ rival** mon principal adversaire; **he is an ~ traitor** c'est le traître par excellence; **the ~ villain in the play** le principal scélérat de la pièce. -**2.** [mischievous] coquin, espiègle; [look, smile, tone] malin, espiègle.

archaeology *etc Br* = **archeology**.

archaeopteryx [ˌɑːkɪˈɒptərɪks] *n* archéoptéryx *m*.

archaic [ɑːˈkeɪɪk] *adj* archaïque.

archaism [ˈɑːkeɪɪzm] *n* archaïsme *m*.

archangel [ˈɑːkˌeɪndʒəl] *n* archange *m*; **the Archangel Gabriel** l'archange Gabriel, saint Gabriel archange.

archbishop [ˌɑːtʃˈbɪʃəp] *n* archevêque *m*; **the Archbishop of Canterbury** l'archevêque de Cantorbéry; **the Archbishop of York** l'archevêque de York.

ARCHBISHOP:
L'archevêque de Cantorbéry est le chef spirituel de l'Église anglicane; l'archevêque de Westminster est le chef spirituel de l'Église catholique de Grande-Bretagne.

archbishopric [ˌɑːtʃˈbɪʃəprɪk] *n* archevêché *m*.

archdeacon [ˌɑːtʃˈdiːkən] *n* archidiacre *m*.

archdiocese [ˌɑːtʃˈdaɪəsɪs] *n* archidiocèse *m*.

archduchess [ˌɑːtʃˈdʌtʃɪs] *n* archiduchesse *f*.

archduchy [ˌɑːtʃˈdʌtʃɪ] (*pl* **archduchies**) *n* archiduché *m*.

archduke [ˌɑːtʃˈdjuːk] *n* archiduc *m*.

arched [ɑːtʃt] *adj* -**1.** [roof, window] cintré. -**2.** [back, foot] cambré; [eyebrows] arqué.

archenemy [ˌɑːtʃˈenɪmɪ] (*pl* **archenemies**) *n* pire ennemi *m*; **the Archenemy** RELIG Satan.

archeological [ˌɑːkɪəˈlɒdʒɪkl] *adj* archéologique.

archeologist [ˌɑːkɪˈɒlədʒɪst] *n* archéologue *mf*.

archeology [ˌɑːkɪˈɒlədʒɪ] *n* archéologie *f*.

archer [ˈɑːtʃəʳ] *n* archer *m*; **the Archer** ASTROL le Sagittaire.

archery [ˈɑːtʃərɪ] *n* tir *m* à l'arc.

archetypal [ˌɑːkɪˈtaɪpl] *adj* archétype, archétypique, archétypal.

archetype [ˈɑːkɪtaɪp] *n* archétype *m*.

archetypical [ˌɑːkɪˈtɪpɪkl] = **archetypal**.

Archimedes [ˌɑːkɪˈmiːdiːz] *pr n* Archimède; **~' principle** le principe d'Archimède; **~' screw** vis *f* d'Archimède.

archipelago [ˌɑːkɪˈpelɪgəʊ] (*pl* **archipelagoes** OR **archipelagos**) *n* archipel *m*.

archiphoneme [ˈɑːkɪˌfəʊniːm] *n* archiphonème *m*.

architect [ˈɑːkɪtekt] *n* architecte *mf*; *fig* artisan *m*, créateur *m*, -trice *f*.

architectonic [ˌɑːkɪtekˈtɒnɪk] *adj* architectonique.

architectonics [ˌɑːkɪtekˈtɒnɪks] *n (U)* architectonique *f*.

architectural [ˌɑːkɪˈtektʃərəl] *adj* architectural.

architecturally [ˌɑːkɪˈtektʃərəlɪ] *adv* au OR du point de vue architectural.

architecture [ˈɑːkɪtektʃəʳ] *n* [gen & COMPUT] architecture *f*.

architrave [ˈɑːkɪtreɪv] *n* architrave *f*.

archive [ˈɑːkaɪv] ◇ *n*: **the ~s** les archives *fpl* ‖ [repository] archives *fpl*, dépôt *m*; **a national ~ of photographs** des archives nationales de photographies.
◇ *comp* des archives; **the book uses a lot of ~ photographs** le livre contient beaucoup de photos d'archives.
◇ *vt* archiver.

archivist [ˈɑːkɪvɪst] *n* archiviste *mf*.

archly [ˈɑːtʃlɪ] *adv* d'un air espiègle OR malicieux.

archpriest [ˌɑːtʃˈpriːst] *n* archiprêtre *m*.

archway [ˈɑːtʃweɪ] *n* porche *m*; [long] galerie *f*, arcades *fpl*.

arc lamp, arc light *n* lampe *f* à arc; CIN & TV sunlight *m*.

ARCM (*abbr of* Associate of the Royal College of Music) *n membre associé du RCM*.

arctic [ˈɑːktɪk] ◇ *adj* -**1.** arctique. -**2.** *fig* [cold] glacial.
◇ *n Am* [overshoe] couvre-chaussure *m*.
◆ **Arctic** [ˈɑːktɪk] ◇ *pr n*: **the Arctic (Ocean)** l'(océan *m*) Arctique *m*; **in the Arctic** dans l'Arctique.
◇ *adj* arctique.

Arctic Circle *pr n*: **the ~** le cercle polaire arctique.

arctic skua *n* labbe *m* parasite.

arctic tern *n* sterne *f* arctique.

arc weld *n* soudure *f* à l'arc voltaïque.
◆ **arc-weld** *vt* souder à l'arc voltaïque.

arc-welding *n* soudure *f* à l'arc voltaïque.

ardent [ˈɑːdənt] *adj* [keen] ardent, passionné; **an ~ admirer** un fervent admirateur.

ardently [ˈɑːdəntlɪ] *adv* ardemment, passionnément.

ardour *Br*, **ardor** *Am* [ˈɑːdəʳ] *n* ardeur *f*, passion *f*.

arduous [ˈɑːdjʊəs] *adj* ardu, difficile; [work, task] laborieux, pénible; [path] ardu, raide; [hill] raide, escarpé.

arduously [ˈɑːdjʊəslɪ] *adv* péniblement, laborieusement.

arduousness [ˈɑːdjʊəsnɪs] *n* difficulté *f*.

are [*vb weak form* əʳ, *strong form* ɑːʳ, *n* ɑːʳ] ◇ → **be**.
◇ *n* are *m*.

area [ˈeərɪə] ◇ *n* -**1.** [surface size] superficie *f*, aire *f*; **the garden is 500 m^2 in ~, the garden has** OR **covers an ~ of 500 m^2** le jardin a une superficie de 500 m^2. -**2.** [region] région *f*; MIL territoire *m*; [small] secteur *m*, zone *f*; **we're staying in the New York ~** nous restons dans OR nous ne quittons pas la région de New York; **the Greater London ~** l'agglomération *f* de Londres; **a residential/shopping ~** un quartier résidentiel/commercial; **in the whole ~** [neighbourhood] dans tout le quartier; [political region] dans toute la région ❑ **a conservation ~** un site classé; **a protected wildlife ~** une réserve naturelle; **~ of outstanding natural beauty** *zone naturelle protégée*; **a disaster ~** *literal* une région sinistrée; *fig* un champ de bataille; **your sister's a walking disaster ~!** ta sœur est une vraie catastrophe ambulante! -**3.** [part, section] partie *f*; [of room] coin *m*; **living/eating ~** coin salon/salle à manger; **a large kitchen ~** une grande cuisine. -**4.** [of study, investigation, experience] domaine *m*, champ *m*; **in the foreign policy ~** dans le domaine de la politique étrangère.
◇ *comp* [manager, office] régional.

area code *n Br* code *m* postal; *Am* TELEC indicatif *m* de zone.

areaway [ˈeərɪəweɪ] *n* courette *f* en contre-bas.

areca [ˈærɪkə] *n* BOT: **~ (tree)** aréquier *m*; **~ nut** noix *f* d'arec.

arena [əˈriːnə] *n* arène *f*; **the challenger entered the ~** le challenger est descendu dans l'arène; **when he entered the electoral ~** *fig* quand il est entré en lice pour les élections; **the political ~** *fig* l'arène politique.

aren't [ɑːnt] = **are not**.

Arethusa [ˌærɪˈθjuːzə] *pr n* Aréthuse.

Argentina [ˌɑːdʒənˈtiːnə] *pr n* Argentine *f*; in ~ en Argentine.

Argentine [ˈɑːdʒəntaɪn] ◇ *n* Argentin *m*, -e *f*.
◇ *adj* argentin.

Argentinian [ˌɑːdʒənˈtɪnɪən] ◇ *n* Argentin *m*, -e *f*.
◇ *adj* argentin; **the ~ embassy** l'ambassade *f* d'Argentine.

argie-bargie *inf* [ˌɑːdʒɪˈbɑːdʒɪ] = **argy-bargy**.

argon [ˈɑːgɒn] *n* argon *m*.

Argonaut [ˈɑːgənɔːt] *n*: **the ~s** les Argonautes *mpl*.

argosy [ˈɑːgəsɪ] (*pl* argosies) *n lit* OR *arch* -**1.** [ship] galion *m* de commerce. -**2.** [fleet] flotte *f* de galions.

argot [ˈɑːgəʊ] *n* argot *m*.

arguable [ˈɑːgjʊəbl] *adj* -**1.** [questionable] discutable, contestable. -**2.** [plausible] défendable; **it is ~ that...** on peut soutenir que...

arguably [ˈɑːgjʊəblɪ] *adv* possiblement; **the Beatles are ~ the most popular group of all time** on pourrait dire OR on peut soutenir que les Beatles sont le groupe le plus populaire de tous les temps.

argue [ˈɑːgjuː] ◇ *vi* -**1.** [quarrel] se disputer; **they're always arguing about money** ils se disputent tout le temps à propos d'argent; **don't let's ~** ne nous disputons pas; **stop arguing!** arrêtez de vous disputer!; **she ~s with her sister almost constantly** elle se dispute presque constamment avec sa sœur. -**2.** [reason] argumenter; **she ~d for/against raising taxes** elle a soutenu qu'il fallait/ne fallait pas augmenter les impôts; **we ~d (about it) all day** nous (en) avons discuté toute la journée; **he ~d from the historical aspect** ses arguments étaient de nature historique; **the facts ~ for the evolutionary theory** les faits plaident en faveur de la théorie évolutionniste ‖ JUR témoigner; **everything ~s in her favour** tout témoigne en sa faveur; **the evidence ~s against him** les preuves sont contre lui.
◇ *vt* -**1.** [debate] discuter, débattre; **a well-~d case** une cause bien présentée OR défendue; **why do you always have to ~ the toss** *inf* OR **point?** pourquoi faut-il toujours que tu ergotes OR chicanes? -**2.** [person] convaincre; **he ~d me into/out of staying** il m'a persuadé/dissuadé de rester; **they ~d her into continuing her studies** ils l'ont convaincue OR persuadée de continuer ses études. -**3.** [maintain] soutenir, affirmer; **she ~s that war is always pointless** elle affirme OR soutient que la guerre ne sert jamais à rien. -**4.** *fml* [indicate] indiquer; **their attitude ~s a certain ignorance** leur attitude indique une certaine ignorance.
◆ **argue out** *vt sep* régler; **we'll have to ~ it out!** il va falloir nous mettre d'accord!

argument [ˈɑːgjʊmənt] *n* -**1.** [quarrel] dispute *f*; **they had another ~ about politics** ils se sont encore disputés à propos de politique; **he had an ~ with a lamppost** *hum* il a rencontré un réverbère. -**2.** [debate] discussion *f*, débat *m*; **for the sake of ~** à titre d'exemple; **it is open to ~ whether...** on peut s'interroger pour savoir si...; **you should listen to both sides of the ~** vous devriez écouter les deux versions de l'histoire; **she got the better of the ~** elle l'a emporté dans la discussion. -**3.** [reasoning] argument *m*; **I didn't follow his (line of) ~** je n'ai pas suivi son raisonnement; **their ~ was that the plan was too expensive** ils soutenaient que le projet était trop cher; **there is a strong ~ in favour of the proposal** il y a de bonnes raisons pour soutenir OR appuyer cette proposition. -**4.** [of book, play] argument *m*, sommaire *m*.

argumentation [ˌɑːgjʊmenˈteɪʃn] *n* argumentation *f*.

argumentative [ˌɑːgjʊˈmentətɪv] *adj* ergoteur, chicaneur; **she is extremely ~** elle a l'esprit de contradiction.

Argus [ˈɑːgəs] *pr n* Argos, Argus.

argy-bargy *inf* [ˌɑːdʒɪˈbɑːdʒɪ] (*pl* **argy-bargies**) *n (U) Br* chamailleries *fpl*; **there was a bit of ~ over who should do it** il y a eu des histoires pour savoir qui devait le faire.

argyle [ɑːˈgaɪl] ◇ *adj* à motifs de losanges.
◇ *n* chaussette *f* avec des losanges.

aria [ˈɑːrɪə] *n* aria *f*.

Ariadne [ˌærɪˈædnɪ] *pr n* Ariane.

Arian [ˈeərɪən] ◇ *n* Arien *m*, -enne *f*.
◇ *adj* arien.

Arianism [ˈeərɪənɪzm] *n* arianisme *m*.

ARIBA (*abbr of* **Associate of the Royal Institute of British Architects**) *n membre associé du RIBA*.

arid [ˈærɪd] *adj* **-1.** *literal* sec, desséché. **-2.** *fig* [of no interest] aride, ingrat; [fruitless] stérile.

aridity [æˈrɪdətɪ] *n literal & fig* aridité *f*, stérilité *f*.

Aries [ˈeəriːz] ◇ *pr n* ASTROL & ASTRON Bélier *m*.
◇ *n*: **I'm an ~** je suis (du signe du) Bélier.

aright [əˈraɪt] *adv* bien, correctement; **to set things ~** arranger les choses; **his explanation set matters ~** son explication a arrangé la situation OR l'affaire.

arise [əˈraɪz] (*pt* **arose** [əˈrəʊz], *pp* **arisen** [əˈrɪzn]) *vi* **-1.** [appear, happen] survenir, se présenter; **there arose a great cheer** *lit* des acclamations se firent entendre; **if complications should ~** si des complications survenaient; **a doubt arose in his mind** un doute est apparu dans son esprit; **if the need ~s** en cas de besoin; **if the occasion ~s** si l'occasion se présente. **-2.** [result] résulter; **a problem that ~s from this decision** un problème qui résulte OR découle de cette décision; **matters arising from the last meeting** des questions soulevées lors de la dernière réunion. **-3.** *lit* [person] se lever; [sun] se lever, paraître.

Aristides [ˌærɪˈstaɪdiːz] *pr n* Aristide.

aristocracy [ˌærɪˈstɒkrəsɪ] (*pl* **aristocracies**) *n* aristocratie *f*.

aristocrat [*Br* ˈærɪstəkræt, *Am* əˈrɪstəkræt] *n* aristocrate *mf*.

aristocratic [*Br* ˌærɪstəˈkrætɪk, *Am* əˌrɪstəˈkrætɪk] *adj* aristocratique.

Aristophanes [ˌærɪˈstɒfəniːz] *pr n* Aristophane.

Aristotelian [ˌærɪstɒˈtiːljən] ◇ *adj* aristotélicien.
◇ *n* Aristotélicien *m*, -enne *f*.

Aristotle [ˈærɪstɒtl] *pr n* Aristote.

arithmetic [*n* əˈrɪθmətɪk, *adj* ˌærɪθˈmetɪk] ◇ *n* arithmétique *f*; **mental ~** calcul *m* mental.
◇ *adj* arithmétique.

arithmetical [ˌærɪθˈmetɪkl] *adj* arithmétique.

arithmetician [əˌrɪθməˈtɪʃn] *n* arithméticien *m*, -enne *f*.

arithmetic progression *n* progression *f* arithmétique.

Arizona [ˌærɪˈzəʊnə] *pr n* Arizona *m*; **in ~** dans l'Arizona.

ark [ɑːk] *n* arche *f*; **this machine must have come out of the ~** *hum* cet appareil doit remonter au déluge OR est vieux comme Hérode ❑ **the Ark of the Covenant** l'arche d'alliance; **Noah's Ark** l'arche de Noé.

Arkansas [ˈɑːkənsɔː] *pr n* Arkansas *m*; **in ~** dans l'Arkansas.

arm [ɑːm] ◇ *n* **-1.** ANAT bras *m*; **he carried a book under his ~** il portait un livre sous le bras; **to hold sthg in one's ~s** tenir qqch dans ses bras; **to hold sb in one's ~s** étreindre OR tenir qqn dans ses bras; **with his wife on his ~** avec sa femme à son bras; **he offered her his ~** il lui a offert son bras; **she flung her ~s around my neck** elle s'est jetée à mon cou; **he put his ~ round her** il a passé son bras autour d'elle; **she put her ~ round my shoulders** elle a passé son bras autour de mes épaules; **he took her in his ~s** il l'a prise dans ses bras; **with ~s folded** les bras croisés; **he stood with his ~s wide apart** il se tenait les bras écartés; **to welcome sb/sthg with open ~s** accueillir qqn/qqch à bras ouverts; **within ~'s reach** à portée de la main; **at ~'s length** à bout de bras; **we kept him at ~'s length** nous l'avons tenu à bout de bras ❑ **a list as long as your ~** *fig* une liste qui n'en finit pas OR interminable; **the long ~ of the law** le bras de la justice; **I'd give my right ~ for that job** je donnerais cher OR n'importe quoi pour obtenir cet emploi; **the house cost them an ~ and a leg** *inf* la maison leur a coûté les yeux de la tête. **-2.** [of sea, machinery] bras *m*; [of clothing] manche *f*; [of spectacle frames] branche *f*; [of furniture] bras *m*, accoudoir *m*; [of record player] bras *m*. **-3.** [section] section *f*, branche *f*; **Sinn Fein is the political ~ of the IRA** Sinn Fein est la section politique de l'IRA.
◇ *vt* **-1.** [person, country] armer; **~ed with an umbrella** *fig* muni OR armé d'un parapluie; **to ~ o.s. with the facts/evidence** *fig* s'armer de faits/preuves. **-2.** [missile] munir d'une (tête d') ogive; [bomb, fuse] armer.
◇ *vi* s'armer, prendre les armes.
◆ **arm in arm** *adv phr* bras dessus bras dessous; **they walked along the street ~ in ~** ils marchaient dans la rue bras dessus bras dessous.

armada [ɑːˈmɑːdə] *n* armada *f*; **the Armada** l'Armada *f*.

armadillo [ˌɑːməˈdɪləʊ] (*pl* **armadillos**) *n* tatou *m*.

Armageddon [ˌɑːməˈgedn] *n* Apocalypse *f*; *fig* apocalypse *f*.

Armalite® [ˈɑːməlaɪt] *n* Armalite® *m*.

armament [ˈɑːməmənt] *n* **-1.** [fighting force] force *f* de frappe. **-2.** [weaponry] armement *m*, matériel *m* de guerre. **-3.** [preparation for war] armement *m*.
◆ **armaments** *npl* armement *m*.

armature [ˈɑːməˌtjʊəʳ] *n* [gen] armature *f*; [of magnet] armature *f*; [of motor] induit *m*; ZOOL carapace *f*.

armband [ˈɑːmbænd] *n* brassard *m*; [mourning] brassard *m* de deuil, crêpe *m*.

armchair [ˈɑːmtʃeəʳ] ◇ *n* fauteuil *m*.
◇ *adj* en chambre; **an ~ gardener/traveller** un jardinier/voyageur en chambre.

armed [ɑːmd] *adj* **-1.** [with weapons] armé; **they were ~ with knives** ils étaient armés de couteaux; **the minister arrived at the press conference ~ with pages of statistics** *fig* le ministre est arrivé à la conférence de presse armé OR muni de pages entières de statistiques ❑ **~ conflict** conflit *m* armé; **~ robbery** JUR vol *m* OR attaque *f* à main armée; **~ to the teeth** armé jusqu'aux dents. **-2.** [missile] muni d'une (tête d') ogive; [bomb, fuse] armé.

-armed *in cpds* aux bras...; **long~** aux bras longs; **one~** à un seul bras.

armed forces *npl* forces *fpl* armées; **to be in the ~** être dans les forces armées.

Armenia [ɑːˈmiːnjə] *pr n* Arménie *f*; **in ~** en Arménie.

Armenian [ɑːˈmiːnjən] ◇ *n* **-1.** [person] Arménien *m*, -enne *f*. **-2.** LING arménien *m*.
◇ *adj* arménien.

armful [ˈɑːmfʊl] *n* brassée *f*; **she had an ~ of flowers** elle portait une brassée de fleurs; **in ~s, by the ~** par pleines brassées, par brassées entières.

armhole [ˈɑːmhəʊl] *n* emmanchure *f*.

armistice [ˈɑːmɪstɪs] *n* armistice *m*.

Armistice Day *n* l'Armistice *m*.

ARMISTICE DAY:

La fête de l'armistice de la première guerre mondiale est maintenant célébrée le dimanche le plus proche du 11 novembre, qu'on appelle «Remembrance Sunday».

---

armlet [ˈɑːmlɪt] *n* [armband] brassard *m*; [bracelet] bracelet *m*.

armor *etc Am* = **armour**.

armorial [ɑːˈmɔːrɪəl] ◇ *adj* armorial; **~ bearings** armoiries *fpl*.
◇ *n* armorial *m*.

Armorica [ɑːˈmɒrɪkə] *pr n* Armorique *f*.

Armorican [ɑːˈmɒrɪkən] ◇ *n* Armoricain *m*, -e *f*.
◇ *adj* armoricain.

armour *Br*, **armor** *Am* [ˈɑːməʳ] *n* **-1.** HIST armure *f*; **in full ~** armé de pied en cap. **-2.** *(U)* MIL [plating] blindage *m*; [vehicles] blindés *mpl*; [forces] forces *fpl* blindées. **-3.** [of animal] carapace *f*.

armour-clad *Br*, **armor-clad** *Am adj* blindé; [ship] blindé, cuirassé.

armoured *Br*, **armored** *Am* [ˈɑːməd] *adj* **-1.** MIL blindé. **-2.** [animal] cuirassé, à carapace.

armoured car *n* voiture *f* blindée.

armourer *Br*, **armorer** *Am* [ˈɑːmərəʳ] *n* armurier *m*.

armour-piercing *adj* [mine, gun] antichar; [shell, bullet] perforant.

armour plate *n* blindage *m*; [on ship] cuirasse *f*.
◆ **armour-plate** *vt* blinder; **an armour-plated vehicle** un véhicule blindé.

armour plating = **armour plate**.

armoury *Br*, **armory** *Am* [ˈɑːmərɪ] (*Br pl* **armouries**, *Am pl* **armories**) *n* arsenal *m*, dépôt *m* d'armes; *fig* [resources] arsenal *m*; *Am* [arms factory] armurerie *f*, fabrique *f* d'armes.

armpit [ˈɑːmpɪt] *n* aisselle *f*.

armrest [ˈɑːmrəst] *n* accoudoir *m*.

arms [ɑːmz] *npl* **-1.** [weapons] arme *f*; **to ~! aux armes!**; **to bear ~** porter les armes; **lay down your ~!** déposez vos armes!; **to take up ~ against sb/sthg** s'insurger contre qqn/qqch ❑ **to be up in ~**: **the villagers are up in ~ over the planned motorway** la proposition de construction d'une autoroute a provoqué une levée de boucliers parmi les villageois; **the unions are up in ~ over the new legislation** les syndicats s'élèvent OR partent en guerre contre la nouvelle législation; **'Arms and the Man'** *Shaw* 'le Héros et le soldat'. **-2.** HERALD armes *fpl*, armoiries *fpl*.
comp: **~ control** contrôle *m* des armements; **~ dealer** armurier *m*; **~ manufacturer** fabricant *m* d'armes, armurier *m*.

arm's-length *adj* **-1.** [not intimate] distant, froid; **they have an ~ relationship** ils gardent leurs distances. **-2.** COMM: **~ price** *prix fixé dans les conditions normales de la concurrence*.

arms race *n* course *f* aux armements.

arm-twisting *inf* [-ˈtwɪstɪŋ] *n (U)* pressions *fpl*.

arm-wrestle *vi*: **to ~ with sb** faire une partie de bras de fer avec qqn.

arm wrestling *n* bras *m* de fer.

army [ˈɑːmɪ] (*pl* **armies**) ◇ *n* **-1.** MIL armée *f* (de terre); **to go into** OR **to join the ~** s'engager; **he was drafted into the ~** il a été appelé sous les drapeaux; **she is going into the ~** elle s'engage; **is he in the ~?** est-ce qu'il est militaire OR dans l'armée?; **an ~ of occupation** une armée d'occupation. **-2.** *fig* [multitude] foule *f*, multitude *f*; **an ~ of tourists descend on the town every summer** une armée de touristes envahit la ville tous les étés.
◇ *comp* [life, nurse, truck, uniform] militaire; [family] de militaires; **~ brat** *inf Am* gosse *mf* de militaire OR de militaires; **~ corps** corps *m* d'armée; **~ officer** officier *m* de l'armée de terre.

army ant *n* doryline *f*, fourmi *f* légionnaire.

Army List *n Br* annuaire *m* militaire OR des officiers de carrière *(de l'armée de terre)*.

A-road *n route nationale britannique*.

aroma [əˈrəʊmə] *n* arôme *m*; **an ~ of coffee** un arôme de café.

aromatherapy [əˌrəʊməˈθerəpɪ] *n* aromathérapie *f*.

aromatic [ˌærəˈmætɪk] ◇ *adj* aromatique.
◇ *n* aromate *m*.

aromatize, -ise [əˈrəʊmətaɪz] *vt* aromatiser.

arose [əˈrəʊz] *pt* → **arise**.

around [əˈraʊnd] ◇ *adv* **-1.** [in all directions] autour; **the fields all ~** les champs tout autour; **for 5 miles ~** sur OR dans un rayon de 5 miles. **-2.** [nearby] pas loin; **stay** OR **stick ~** restez dans les parages; **he's ~ somewhere** il n'est pas loin, il est dans le coin; will you be ~ this afternoon? tu seras là cet après-midi?; see you ~! à un de ces jours! -**3.** [in existence]: that firm has been ~ for years cette société existe depuis des années; he's one of the most promising actors ~ at the moment c'est un des acteurs les plus prometteurs que l'on puisse voir en ce moment; there wasn't much money ~ in those days les gens n'avaient pas beaucoup d'argent à l'époque; he won't be ~ long! il ne fera pas de vieux os! -**4.** [here and there] ici et là; to travel ~ voyager; to wander ~ faire un tour ❑ I don't know my way ~ yet je suis encore un peu perdu; he's been ~ *inf* [has travelled widely] il a pas mal roulé sa bosse; [is experienced] il n'est pas né d'hier. -**5.** = **round**.

◇ *prep* -**1.** [encircling] autour de; seated ~ a table assis autour d'une table; the people ~ us les gens qui nous entourent OR autour de nous; the area ~ Berlin les alentours *mpl* OR les environs *mpl* de Berlin; ~ the world in 80 days le tour du monde en 80 jours; the tree measures two metres ~ the trunk l'arbre mesure deux mètres de circonférence || *fig*: find a way (to get) ~ the problem trouvez un moyen de contourner le problème; my keys are somewhere ~ here mes clés sont quelque part par ici. -**2.** [through]: they travelled ~ Europe ils ont voyagé à travers l'Europe; we strolled ~ town nous nous sommes promenés en ville. -**3.** [approximately] autour de; ~ midnight autour de OR vers minuit; ~ 5 o'clock vers 5 h; ~ 1920 vers OR aux alentours de 1920; he's ~ your age il a environ OR à peu près votre âge.

around-the-clock *adj*: ~ protection/surveillance protection *f*/surveillance *f* 24 heures sur 24.

arousal [ə'raʊzl] *n* excitation *f*, stimulation *f*.

arouse [ə'raʊz] *vt* -**1.** [stimulate] stimuler, provoquer; the sound ~d their curiosity/suspicions le bruit a éveillé leur curiosité/leurs soupçons; his pleading ~d their contempt ses implorations n'ont suscité que leur mépris; sexually ~d excité (sexuellement). -**2.** [awaken] réveiller, éveiller; she ~d him from a deep sleep elle l'a tiré d'un profond sommeil.

arpeggio [ɑː'pedʒɪəʊ] *n* arpège *m*.

arrack ['ærək] *n* arak *m*, arac *m*, arack *m*.

arraign [ə'reɪn] *vt* traduire en justice; *fig* accuser, mettre en cause.

arraignment [ə'reɪnmənt] *n* ≃ lecture *f* de l'acte d'accusation.

arrange [ə'reɪndʒ] ◇ *vt* -**1.** [put in order] ranger, mettre en ordre; [clothing, room] arranger; [flowers] arranger, disposer; ~ the books in alphabetical order rangez les livres par ordre alphabétique; the room was ~d as an office la pièce a été aménagée en bureau. -**2.** [organize, plan] organiser, arranger; I can ~ a loan je peux m'arranger pour obtenir un prêt; I'll ~ a table for 8 o'clock je vais réserver une table pour 20 h; it has been ~d for us to travel by train il a été décidé OR convenu que nous voyagerions en train; let's ~ a time to meet fixons (une heure pour) un rendez-vous; the meeting is ~d for noon tomorrow la réunion est prévue pour demain midi; he has something ~d OR has ~d something for the weekend il a quelque chose de prévu pour le week-end; here is the first instalment, as ~d [money] voici le premier versement, comme convenu; don't worry, I'll ~ it ne vous en faites pas, je vais m'en occuper; everything is ~d tout est déjà arrangé; to ~ a marriage arranger un mariage; their marriage was ~d c'était un mariage arrangé. -**3.** [dispute] régler, arranger. -**4.** MUS & THEAT adapter; he ~d the concerto for guitar il a adapté le concerto pour la guitare.

◇ *vi* prendre des dispositions, s'arranger; I've ~d with the boss to leave early tomorrow je me suis arrangé avec le patron pour partir de bonne heure demain; he's ~d for the car to be repaired il a fait le nécessaire pour faire réparer la voiture.

arrangement [ə'reɪndʒmənt] *n* -**1.** (*usu pl*) [plan] disposition *f*, arrangement *m*; what are the travel ~s? comment le voyage est-il organisé?; I haven't made any ~s for the journey yet je n'ai pas encore fait de OR mes préparatifs pour le voyage; she made all the necessary ~s elle a pris toutes les dispositions utiles OR nécessaires; could you make ~s to change the meeting? pouvez-vous faire le nécessaire pour changer la date de la réunion?; he made ~s to leave work early il s'est arrangé pour quitter son travail de bonne heure; an ~ whereby you pay monthly un arrangement selon lequel vous effectuez des paiements mensuels. -**2.** [understanding, agreement] arrangement *m*; we can come to an OR some ~ on the price pour le prix, nous pouvons nous arranger; he came to an ~ with the bank il est parvenu à un accord avec la banque; a private ~ un accord à l'amiable. -**3.** [layout] arrangement *m*, disposition *f*; [of room] aménagement *m*; [of clothing, hair] arrangement *m*. -**4.** MUS & THEAT adaptation *f*, arrangement *m*.

◆ **by arrangement** *adv phr*: price by ~ prix à débattre; special designs by ~ autres modèles sur demande; by prior ~ we didn't tell her nous nous étions entendus pour ne rien lui dire; by ~ with the town hall avec l'autorisation de la mairie; he sold the stock by ~ with the company il s'est arrangé OR entendu avec la société pour vendre les actions; viewing by ~ with the owner pour visiter, prenez rendez-vous avec OR contactez le propriétaire.

arranger [ə'reɪndʒəʳ] *n* MUS arrangeur *m*, -euse *f*.

arrant ['ærənt] *adj* fini, parfait.

array [ə'reɪ] ◇ *n* -**1.** [collection] ensemble *m* impressionnant, collection *f*; a distinguished ~ of people une assemblée de gens distingués; there was a fine ~ of cakes in the window il y avait une belle sélection de gâteaux en vitrine || JUR, COMPUT & MATH tableau *m*; an ~ of data un tableau de données. -**2.** MIL rang *m*, ordre *m*; in battle ~ en ordre de bataille; in close ~ en rangs serrés. -**3.** [fine clothes] parure *f*, atours *mpl*; [ceremonial dress] habit *m* d'apparat.

◇ *vt* -**1.** [arrange] disposer, étaler; MIL [troops] déployer, disposer. -**2.** *lit* [adorn] habiller, revêtir; she was ~ed in silks elle était vêtue de soie.

arrears [ə'rɪəz] *npl* arriéré *m*; taxes in ~ arriéré d'impôts; I'm worried about getting into ~ j'ai peur de m'endetter; we're 6 months in ~ on the loan payments nous devons 6 mois de traites; your ~ now amount to over £2,000 vos arriérés s'élèvent maintenant à plus de 2 000 livres; ~ of work du travail en retard; to be paid a month in ~ être payé un mois après; she's in ~ with her correspondence elle a du retard dans sa correspondance.

arrest [ə'rest] ◇ *vt* -**1.** [police] arrêter, appréhender. -**2.** *fml* [growth, development] arrêter; [slow down] entraver, retarder; in an effort to ~ unemployment/inflation pour essayer d'enrayer le chômage/l'inflation; ~ed development MED [physical] arrêt *m* de croissance; [mental] atrophie *f* de la personnalité; to ~ judgment JUR surseoir à un jugement, suspendre l'exécution d'un jugement. -**3.** *fml* [attention] attirer, retenir.

◇ *n* -**1.** [detention] arrestation *f*; you're under ~! vous êtes en état d'arrestation!; he was put under ~ il a été arrêté; they made several ~s ils ont procédé à plusieurs arrestations || MIL: to be under ~ être aux arrêts; they put him under ~ ils l'ont mis aux arrêts ❑ open/close ~ arrêts *mpl* simples/de rigueur. -**2.** [sudden stopping] arrêt *m*, suspension *f*.

arrestable [ə'restəbl] *adj* [person] qui risque d'être appréhendé; [offence] répréhensible.

arrester [ə'restəʳ] AERON: ~ gear [on aircraft carrier] dispositif *m* d'appontage.

arresting [ə'restɪŋ] *adj* saisissant, frappant.

arrestingly [ə'restɪŋlɪ] *adv*: ~ beautiful d'une beauté frappante.

arresting officer *n policier qui a procédé à l'arrestation*.

arrival [ə'raɪvl] *n* -**1.** [of person, train, aeroplane etc] arrivée *f*; on OR upon ~ à l'arrivée; ~s and departures les arrivées et les départs *mpl*; the ~s board le tableau des arrivées; the ~s lounge le salon des arrivées. -**2.** [newcomer]: late ~s should report to reception les retardataires doivent se présenter à la réception; he's a new ~ c'est un nouveau venu; the new OR latest ~ in their family leur dernier-né OR dernière-née. -**3.** COMM [of goods] arrivage *m*. -**4.** [advent] avènement *m*; the ~ of the motor car l'apparition *f* OR l'avènement de l'automobile.

arrive [ə'raɪv] *vi* -**1.** [person, train, aeroplane etc] arriver; I've just ~d j'arrive à l'instant; as soon as you ~ dès votre arrivée, dès que vous arriverez; he ~d in the nick of time il est arrivé juste à temps; the first post ~s at 8 o'clock le premier courrier est à 8 h; the baby ~d three weeks early le bébé est arrivé OR né avec trois semaines d'avance; to ~ on the scene survenir; the time has ~d for us to take action, the time for action has ~d le moment est venu pour nous d'agir. -**2.** [achieve success] réussir, arriver; she finally ~d after years of singing in backstreet bars elle connut enfin le succès après avoir chanté pendant des années dans des bars miteux.

◆ **arrive at** *vt insep* [decision] arriver OR parvenir à; [perfection] atteindre; we finally ~d at the conclusion that... nous en sommes finalement arrivés à la conclusion que... || [price] fixer un prix; they finally ~d at a price ils se sont finalement mis d'accord sur un prix.

arrogance ['ærəgəns] *n* arrogance *f*, morgue *f*.

arrogant ['ærəgənt] *adj* arrogant, insolent.

arrogantly ['ærəgəntlɪ] *adv* de manière arrogante, avec arrogance.

arrogate ['ærəgeɪt] *vt fml* -**1.** [claim unjustly] revendiquer à tort, s'arroger; [victory] s'attribuer. -**2.** [assign unjustly] attribuer injustement.

arrogation [ˌærə'geɪʃn] *n* [claim] prétention *f* mal fondée; [act] usurpation *f*; ~ of the fortune usurpation de la fortune.

arrow ['ærəʊ] ◇ *n* flèche *f*; to loose OR to shoot OR to let fly an ~ décocher une flèche; the ball flew as straight as an ~ into the net la balle alla voler tout droit dans le filet.

◇ *vt* -**1.** [indicate - on list] cocher; [- on road sign] flécher. -**2.** [in editing] indiquer au moyen d'une flèche; to ~ a correction in indiquer l'emplacement d'une correction (au moyen d'une flèche).

arrowhead ['ærəʊhed] *n* fer *m*, pointe *f* de flèche.

arrowroot ['ærəʊruːt] *n* BOT marante *f*; CULIN arrow-root *m*.

arse▼ [ɑːs] *n Br* cul *m*; move OR shift your ~ pousse ton cul; you'd better get off your ~ tu ferais bien de te magner le cul; he's a pain in the ~ c'est un emmerdeur; it's a pain in the ~ c'est emmerdant; he fell OR went ~ over tit il est tombé cul par-dessus tête.

◆ **arse about▽**, **arse around▽** *vi insep Br* déconner.

arsehole▼ ['ɑːshəʊl] *n Br* trou *m* du cul; don't be such an ~ ne sois pas si con.

arse-licker▼ [-ˌlɪkəʳ] *n Br* lèche-cul *m inv*.

arse-licking▼ *Br* ◇ *n*: too much ~ goes on in this office! il y a un peu trop de lèche-culs dans ce bureau!

◇ *adj*: he's an ~ little bastard! c'est un salaud de lèche-cul!

arsenal ['ɑːsənl] *n* arsenal *m*.

arsenic ['ɑːsnɪk] ◇ *n* arsenic *m*; 'Arsenic and Old Lace' *Capra* 'Arsenic et vieilles dentelles'.

◇ *comp*: ~ poisoning empoisonnement *m* à l'arsenic.

arson ['ɑːsn] *n* incendie *m* criminel OR volontaire; to commit ~ provoquer (volontairement) un incendie.

arsonist [ˈɑːsənɪst] *n* incendiaire *mf*; [maniac] pyromane *mf*.

art [ɑːt] ◇ *arch* → **be**.
◇ *n* -**1.** art *m*; to study ~ étudier les beaux-arts; **she studies ~** elle fait les beaux-arts; ~ **for ~'s sake** l'art pour l'art; **African ~** l'art africain; **the ~ of ballet** l'art du ballet; **I'd love to go to ~ classes** j'aimerais beaucoup suivre des cours de dessin; **he was never any good at ~ at school** [school subject] à l'école il n'a jamais été très doué en dessin; **a work of ~** une œuvre d'art ❑ **~s and crafts** artisanat *m* (d'art). -**2.** [skill] art *m*, habileté *f*; **the ~ of survival** l'art de survivre; **she has got cooking down to a real** OR **fine ~** la cuisine chez elle, c'est du grand art. -**3.** [cunning] ruse *f*, artifice *m*; [trick] artifice *m*, stratagème *m*; **they used every ~ to persuade him** ils ont usé de tous les stratagèmes pour le convaincre.
◇ *comp* [collection, critic, exhibition] d'art; ~ **student** étudiant *m*, -e *f* en beaux-arts ❑ ~ **gallery** [museum] musée *m* d'art; [shop] galerie *f* d'art; ~ **school** ≃ école *f* des beaux-arts.
◆ **arts** ◇ *npl* UNIV lettres *fpl*; **Faculty of Arts (and Letters)** faculté *f* des lettres (et sciences humaines); **the Arts Council (of Great Britain)** *organisme public britannique de promotion des arts*.
◇ *comp* UNIV: **~s student** étudiant *m*, -e *f* de OR en lettres (et sciences humaines); **I have an ~s degree** j'ai une licence de lettres; **~s centre** ≃ musée *m* d'art.

Art Deco [-ˈdekəʊ] *n* Art *m* déco.

artefact [ˈɑːtɪfækt] = **artifact**.

Artemis [ˈɑːtəmɪs] *pr n* Artémis.

arterial [ɑːˈtɪərɪəl] *adj* artériel; ~ **road** *Br* route *f* OR voie *f* à grande circulation; ~ **line** *Br* RAIL grande ligne *f*.

arteriole [ɑːˈtɪərɪəʊl] *n* artériole *f*.

arteriosclerosis [ɑːˌtɪərɪəʊsklɪəˈrəʊsɪs] *n* artériosclérose *f*.

artery [ˈɑːtərɪ] (*pl* **arteries**) *n* artère *f*; [road] artère *f*, route *f* OR voie *f* à grande circulation.

artesian well [ɑːˈtiːzjən-] *n* puits *m* artésien.

art form *n* moyen *m* d'expression artistique.

artful [ˈɑːtfʊl] *adj* astucieux, habile; [crafty] rusé, malin; ~ **dodger** rusé *m*, -e *f*.

artfully [ˈɑːtfʊlɪ] *adv* [skilfully] habilement, avec finesse; [craftily] astucieusement, avec astuce.

artfulness [ˈɑːtfʊlnɪs] *n* [skill] habileté *f*, finesse *f*; [cunning] astuce *f*, ruse *f*.

arthritic [ɑːˈθrɪtɪk] ◇ *adj* arthritique.
◇ *n* arthritique *mf*.

arthritis [ɑːˈθraɪtɪs] *n* arthrite *f*.

arthropod [ˈɑːθrəpɒd] *n* arthropode *m*.

Arthur [ˈɑːθəʳ] *pr n* [king] Arthur.

Arthurian [ɑːˈθjʊərɪən] *adj* du roi Arthur; **the ~ legend** la légende du roi Arthur.

artic *inf* [ɑːˈtɪk] *n Br abbr of* **articulated lorry**.

artichoke [ˈɑːtɪtʃəʊk] *n* artichaut *m*; ~ **hearts** cœurs *mpl* d'artichauts.

article [ˈɑːtɪkl] ◇ *n* -**1.** [object] objet *m*; **an ~ of clothing** un vêtement; **~s of value** des objets de valeur ❑ **it's the genuine ~!** *inf* c'est du vrai de vrai! -**2.** [in press] article *m*. -**3.** JUR [clause, provision] article *m*; **the ~s of a contract** les stipulations d'un contrat ❑ ~ **of faith** article de foi; **the Thirty-Nine Articles** RELIG *les trente-neuf articles de foi de l'Église anglicane*; **~s of war** *Am* code *m* de justice militaire. -**4.** GRAMM article *m*. -**5.** COMM article *m*, marchandise *f*.
◇ *vt Br* [to trade] mettre en apprentissage; [to profession] mettre en stage; **to ~ sb to a tradesman** mettre qqn en apprentissage chez un commerçant.
◆ **articles** *npl Br* -**1.** COMM: **~s of association** statuts *mpl (d'une société à responsabilité limitée)*. -**2.** JUR: **~s of apprenticeship** contrat *m* d'apprentissage; **to do** OR **to serve one's ~s** faire son apprentissage.

articled clerk [ˈɑːtɪkld-] *n Br* clerc *m* d'avoué *(lié par un contrat d'apprentissage)*.

articular [ɑːˈtɪkjʊləʳ] *adj* articulaire.

articulate [*adj* ɑːˈtɪkjʊlət, *vb* ɑːˈtɪkjʊleɪt]
◇ *adj* -**1.** [person] qui s'exprime bien; [thought, sentence] clair, net. -**2.** [manner of speech] bien articulé, distinct. -**3.** ANAT & BOT articulé.
◇ *vt* -**1.** [words, syllables] articuler. -**2.** *fig* [wishes, thoughts] exprimer clairement. -**3.** ANAT & BOT articuler.
◇ *vi* articuler.

articulated lorry [ɑːˈtɪkjʊleɪtɪd-] *n Br* semi-remorque *m*.

articulately [ɑːˈtɪkjʊlətlɪ] *adv* [speak] distinctement; [explain] clairement.

articulation [ɑːˌtɪkjʊˈleɪʃn] *n* ANAT, BOT & LING articulation *f*.

articulator [ɑːˈtɪkjʊleɪtəʳ] *n* organe *m* articulatoire.

articulatory [ɑːˈtɪkjʊlətrɪ] *adj* articulatoire; ~ **phonetics** phonétique *f* articulatoire.

artifact [ˈɑːtɪfækt] *n* objet *m (fabriqué)*.

artifice [ˈɑːtɪfɪs] *n* -**1.** [trick] artifice *m*, ruse *f*; [scheme] stratagème *m*. -**2.** [cleverness] art *m*, adresse *f*.

artificer [ɑːˈtɪfɪsəʳ] *n* artilleur *m*.

artificial [ˌɑːtɪˈfɪʃl] *adj* -**1.** [man-made] artificiel; COMM synthétique, artificiel; ~ **fertilizer** engrais *m* chimique; ~ **flavouring** parfum *m* artificiel OR synthétique; ~ **flowers** fleurs *fpl* artificielles; **a wig made from ~ hair** une perruque en cheveux artificiels; **an ~ heart** un cœur artificiel; **an ~ leg** une jambe artificielle; ~ **light** la lumière artificielle; ~ **limb** prothèse *f*, membre *m* artificiel; **the current situation is an ~ one** *fig* la situation actuelle n'est pas naturelle OR est artificielle. -**2.** [affected - person] factice, étudié; **an ~ smile** un sourire forcé; ~ **tears** larmes *fpl* de crocodile. -**3.** JUR: ~ **person** personne *f* morale OR civique OR juridique.

artificial insemination *n* insémination *f* artificielle.

artificial intelligence *n* intelligence *f* artificielle.

artificiality [ˌɑːtɪfɪʃɪˈælətɪ] (*pl* **artificialities**) *n* manque *m* de naturel.

artificial kidney *n* rein *m* artificiel.

artificially [ˌɑːtɪˈfɪʃəlɪ] *adv* artificiellement; **the exchange rate is ~ high at the moment** le taux de change est artificiellement élevé en ce moment.

artificial respiration *n* respiration *f* artificielle.

artillery [ɑːˈtɪlərɪ] (*pl* **artilleries**) *n* artillerie *f*.

artilleryman [ɑːˈtɪlərɪmən] (*pl* **artillerymen** [-mən]) *n* artilleur *m*.

artisan [ˌɑːtɪˈzæn] *n* artisan *m*; **the ~s of Spain** les artisans espagnols.

artist [ˈɑːtɪst] *n* [gen & ART] artiste *mf*; *fig* spécialiste *mf*.

artiste [ɑːˈtiːst] *n* artiste *mf*.

artistic [ɑːˈtɪstɪk] *adj* artistique; [design, product] de bon goût, décoratif; [style, temperament] artiste; **she is an ~ child** cette enfant a des dons artistiques.

artistically [ɑːˈtɪstɪklɪ] *adv* avec art, artistiquement.

artistry [ˈɑːtɪstrɪ] *n* art *m*, talent *m* artistique.

artless [ˈɑːtlɪs] *adj* -**1.** [without deceit] naturel, ingénu; ~ **beauty** beauté *f* naturelle; **with an ~ smile** avec un sourire candide. -**2.** [without skill] grossier.

artlessly [ˈɑːtlɪslɪ] *adv* ingénument, innocemment.

artlessness [ˈɑːtlɪsnɪs] *n* ingénuité *f*, naturel *m*.

Art Nouveau [ɑːnuːˈvəʊ] *n* Art *m* nouveau, Modern Style *m*.

arts [ɑːts] → **art**.

artsy *inf* [ˈɑːtzɪ] (*compar* **artsier**, *superl* **artsiest**) = **arty**.

artsy-craftsy *inf* [ˌɑːtzɪˈkrɑːftzɪ] = **arty-crafty**.

artwork [ˈɑːtwɜːk] *n* -**1.** [illustration] iconographie *f*, illustration *f*. -**2.** TYPO documents *mpl*.

arty *inf* [ˈɑːtɪ] (*compar* **artier**, *superl* **artiest**) *adj pej* [person] qui se veut artiste OR bohème; [clothing] de style bohème; [object, film, style] prétentieux.

arty-crafty *inf* [ˌɑːtɪˈkrɑːftɪ] *adj pej* [person] qui se veut artiste OR bohème; [object, style] bohème, qui se veut artisanal.

arty-farty *inf* [ˌɑːtɪˈfɑːtɪ] *adj pej* [person] prétentieux, poseur; [play, film] prétentieux.

arum [ˈeərəm] *n* arum *m*; ~ **lily** calla *f*.

ARV (*abbr of* **American Revised Version**) *n traduction américaine de la Bible*.

Aryan [ˈeərɪən] ◇ *n* Aryen *m*, -enne *f*.
◇ *adj* aryen.

Aryanize, -ise [ˈeərɪənaɪz] *vt* germaniser.

as [əz] ◇ *conj* -**1.** [while] alors que; **the phone rang as I was coming in** le téléphone s'est mis à sonner alors que OR au moment où j'entrais; **I listened as she explained the plan to them** je l'ai écoutée leur expliquer le projet; **as a student, he worked part-time** lorsqu'il était étudiant, il travaillait à mi-temps; **as he advanced, I retreated** (au fur et) à mesure qu'il avançait, je reculais ‖ [when]: **take two aspirins as needed** prenez deux aspirines en cas de douleur. -**2.** [like] comme, ainsi que; **A as in Able** a comme Anatole; **as usual** comme d'habitude; **as shown by the unemployment rate** comme OR ainsi que le montre le taux de chômage; **as is often the case** comme c'est souvent le cas; **she is a doctor, as is her sister** elle est médecin comme sa sœur; **as I told you** comme je vous l'ai dit; **as you know, the inflation rate is up** comme vous le savez, le taux d'inflation a monté; **act as you see fit** faites comme bon vous semble; **leave it as it is** laissez-le tel qu'il est OR tel quel ❑ **to buy sthg as is** acheter qqch en l'état; **as you were!** MIL repos!; **my mistake! as you were!** c'est moi qui me trompe! faites comme si je n'avais rien dit! -**3.** [since] puisque; **let her drive, as it's her car** laissez-la conduire, puisque c'est sa voiture; **as you're the one in charge, you'd better be there** étant donné que c'est vous le responsable, il faut que vous soyez là. -**4.** [concessive use] *fml*: **old as I am, I can still keep up with them** malgré mon âge, j'arrive à les suivre; **try as they might, they couldn't persuade her** malgré tous leurs efforts, ils n'ont pu la convaincre; **powerful as the president is, he cannot stop his country's disintegration** quelque pouvoir qu'ait le président, il ne peut empêcher la ruine de son pays. -**5.** [with 'the same', 'such']: **I had the same problems as you did** j'ai eu les mêmes problèmes que toi; **at the same time as last week** à la même heure que la semaine dernière; **such a problem as only an expert can solve** un problème que seul un expert peut résoudre.
◇ *prep* en tant que, comme; **as her husband, he cannot testify** étant son mari, il ne peut pas témoigner; **he was dressed as a clown** il était habillé en clown; **I advised him as his friend, not as his teacher** je l'ai conseillé en tant qu'ami, pas en tant que professeur; **with Vivien Leigh as Scarlett O'Hara** avec Vivien Leigh dans le rôle de Scarlett O'Hara.
◇ *adv* [in comparisons]: **it's twice as big** c'est deux fois plus grand; **it costs half as much again** ça coûte la moitié plus; **as... as** aussi... que; **he's as intelligent as his brother** il est aussi intelligent que son frère; **he isn't as talented as you (are)** il n'est pas aussi doué que vous; **as often as possible** aussi souvent que possible; **not as often as I would like** pas aussi souvent que je voudrais; **they aren't as innocent as they look** ils ne sont pas aussi innocents qu'ils en ont l'air; **I worked as much for you as for me** j'ai travaillé autant pour toi que pour moi.
◆ **as against** *prep phr* contre; **he received 39 votes as against the 17 for his rival** il a obtenu 39 votes contre 17 pour son adversaire.
◆ **as and when** ◇ *conj phr*: **we'll buy new equipment as and when it's required** nous achèterons du nouveau matériel en temps voulu OR quand ce sera nécessaire.
◇ *adv phr inf* en temps voulu; **you'll be sent the money as and when** on vous enverra l'argent en temps voulu.
◆ **as for** *prep phr* quant à; **as for me, I don't intend to go** pour ma part OR quant à moi, je n'ai pas l'intention d'y aller; **as for your**

threats, they don't scare me in the least pour ce qui est de OR quant à vos menaces, elles ne me font pas peur du tout.

◆ **as from** *prep phr* = **as of**.

◆ **as if** *conj phr* comme si; **he carried on as if nothing had happened** il a continué comme si de rien n'était OR comme s'il ne s'était rien passé; **as if aware of my look, she turned** comme si elle avait senti mon regard, elle s'est retournée; **he moved as if to strike him** il a fait un mouvement comme pour le frapper; **it's not as if she were my sister** ce n'est quand même pas comme si c'était ma sœur; **as if it mattered!** comme si ça avait aucune importance!

◆ **as it is** *adv phr* -**1.** [in present circumstances] les choses étant ce qu'elles sont; **she's hoping for promotion, but as it is there's little chance of** that elle espère obtenir une promotion, mais dans la situation actuelle OR les choses étant ce qu'elles sont, il est peu probable que cela arrive. -**2.** [already] déjà; **you've got enough work as it is** vous avez déjà assez de travail, vous avez assez de travail comme ça; **as it is I'm an hour late** j'ai déjà une heure de retard.

◆ **as it were** *adv phr* pour ainsi dire.

◆ **as of** *prep phr* à partir de; **as of yesterday** depuis hier; **as of tomorrow** à partir de demain; **as of next week I'll be unemployed** je serai au chômage à partir de la semaine prochaine.

◆ **as such** *adv phr* -**1.** [properly speaking] véritablement, à proprement parler; **it's not a contract as such, more a gentleman's agreement** ce n'est pas un véritable contrat OR pas un contrat à proprement parler OR pas véritablement un contrat, mais plutôt un accord entre hommes de parole. -**2.** [in itself] même, en soi; **the place as such isn't great** l'endroit même OR en soi n'est pas terrible. -**3.** [in that capacity] à ce titre, en tant que tel; **I'm his father and as such, I insist on knowing** je suis son père et à ce titre j'insiste pour qu'on me mette au courant.

◆ **as though** *conj phr* = **as if**.

◆ **as to** *prep phr* -**1.** [regarding]: **I'm still uncertain as to the nature of the problem** j'hésite encore sur la nature du problème. -**2.** = **as for**.

◆ **as well** *adv phr* -**1.** [in addition] en plus, par-dessus le marché; [also] aussi; **I'd like one as well** j'en voudrais un aussi; **he bought the house and the land as well** il a acheté la maison et la propriété aussi; **and then the car broke down as well!** et par-dessus le marché la voiture est tombée en panne! -**2.** [with modal verbs]: **you may as well tell me the truth** autant me dire OR tu ferais aussi bien de me dire la vérité; **now that we're here, we might as well stay** puisque nous sommes là, autant rester; **shall we go to the cinema? – we might as well** et si on allait au cinéma? – pourquoi pas?; **she was angry, as well she might be** elle était furieuse, et ça n'est pas surprenant; **he has a few doubts about the job, as well he might** il a quelques doutes sur cet emploi, ce qui n'est guère surprenant; **he apologized profusely – as well he should!** il s'est confondu en excuses – j'espère bien!; **perhaps I'd better leave – that might be as well** peut-être vaudrait-il mieux que je m'en aille – je crois que ça vaut mieux; **it would be as well not to break it** ce serait mieux si on pouvait éviter de le casser; **I decided not to write back – just as well really** j'ai décidé de ne pas répondre – c'est mieux comme ça; **it would be just as well if you were present** il vaudrait mieux que vous soyez là; **it's just as well he missed his flight** c'est une bonne chose qu'il ait manqué l'avion.

◆ **as well as** *conj phr* [in addition to] en plus de; **so she's a liar as well as a thief** alors comme ça, c'est une menteuse en plus d'être une voleuse; **Jim looks after the children as well as helping around the house** Jim s'occupe des enfants en plus de participer au ménage.

◆ **as yet** *adv phr* encore; **I don't have the answer as yet** je n'ai pas encore la réponse; **an as yet undisclosed sum** une somme qui n'a pas encore été révélée.

AS ◇ *n abbr of* Associate in Science.
◇ *written abbr of* American Samoa.

ASA *pr n* -**1.** *Br* (*abbr of* Advertising Standards Agency) ≃ BVP *m*. -**2.** (*abbr of* American Standards Association) ASA *f*; **~/DIN exposure index** PHOT graduations *fpl* ASA/DIN; **an ~ 100 film, a 100 ~ film** une pellicule 100 ASA.

asap (*abbr of* as soon as possible) *adv* aussitôt OR dès que possible.

asbestos [æs'bestəs] ◇ *n* amiante *f*, asbeste *f*.
◇ *comp* [board, cord] d'amiante; **~ matting** plaque *f* d'amiante.

asbestosis [,æsbes'təʊsɪs] *n* asbestose *f*.

ascend [ə'send] ◇ *vi* monter; **she reached the bottom of the steps and started to ~ slowly** elle arriva en bas des escaliers et commença à monter lentement ‖ [in time] remonter; **to ~ (back) to sthg** remonter à qqch.
◇ *vt* [stairs] monter; [ladder] monter à; [mountain] gravir, faire l'ascension de; [river] remonter; **when Queen Elizabeth ~ed the throne** quand la Reine Elizabeth est montée sur le trône.

ascendancy, ascendency [ə'sendənsɪ] *n* -**1.** [position of power] ascendant *m*, empire *m*; **Japan has gained ~ over its competitors in the electronics market** le Japon domine ses concurrents sur le marché de l'électronique. -**2.** [rise] montée *f*; **their ~ to power** leur ascension jusqu'au pouvoir.

ascendant, ascendent [ə'sendənt] ◇ *adj* dominant, puissant; ASTROL ascendant.
◇ *n* ascendant *m*; **his star is in the ~** ASTROL son étoile est à l'ascendant; **his business is in the ~** *fig* ses affaires prospèrent.

ascender [ə'sendə^r] *n* -**1.** [in mountaineering] ascendeur *m*, autobloqueur *m*. -**2.** TYPO hampe *f* montante.

ascending [ə'sendɪŋ] *adj* -**1.** [rising] ascendant. -**2.** [increasing]: **in ~ order** en ordre croissant. -**3.** BOT montant.

ascension [ə'senʃn] *n* ascension *f*; **the Ascension** RELIG l'Ascension *f*.

Ascension Day *n* jour *m* OR fête *f* de l'Ascension.

Ascension (Island) *pr n* île *f* de l'Ascension; **on ~** à l'île de l'Ascension.

Ascensiontide [ə'senʃntaɪd] *n période entre l'Ascension et le dimanche de Pentecôte*.

ascent [ə'sent] *n* -**1.** [of mountain] ascension *f*. -**2.** [incline] montée *f*. -**3.** [in time] retour *m*; **the line of ~** l'ascendance *f*. -**4.** [in rank] montée *f*, avancement *m*.

ascertain [,æsə'teɪn] *vt fml* établir, constater; **the police ~ed their names and addresses** la police a vérifié leurs nom et adresse; **to ~ that sthg is the case** vérifier OR s'assurer que qqch est vrai; **he ~ed that it was safe to continue** il s'est assuré qu'on pouvait continuer sans danger.

ascertainable [,æsə'teɪnəbl] *adj fml* vérifiable.

ascetic [ə'setɪk] ◇ *adj* ascétique.
◇ *n* ascète *mf*.

ascetically [ə'setɪklɪ] *adv* [live] comme un/une ascète.

asceticism [ə'setɪsɪzm] *n* ascétisme *m*.

ASCII ['æskɪ] (*abbr of* American Standard Code for Information) *n* ASCII *m*; **in ~** en ASCII ❑ **~ file** fichier ASCII.

ascorbic acid [ə'skɔːbɪk-] *n* vitamine *f* C, acide *m* ascorbique *spec*.

Ascot ['æskət] *pr n champ de courses près de Windsor*.
◆ **ascot** *n Am* foulard *m (pour hommes)*.

> **ASCOT:**
> «Royal Ascot» est un événement hippique annuel qui entre dans le calendrier mondain de la haute société anglaise.

ascribable [ə'skraɪbəbl] *adj* attribuable, imputable; **his downfall is ~ to greed** sa chute est imputable à sa cupidité.

ascribe [ə'skraɪb] *vt* attribuer; [fault, blame] imputer; **heart attacks are often ~d to stress** les crises cardiaques sont souvent attribuées OR imputées au stress; **this painting is sometimes ~d to Millet** on attribue parfois ce tableau à Millet.

ascription [ə'skrɪpʃn] *n* attribution *f*, imputation *f*.

ASCU (*abbr of* Association of State Colleges and Universities) *pr n association des établissements universitaires d'État aux États-Unis*.

ASE (*abbr of* American Stock Exchange) *pr n deuxième place boursière des États-Unis*.

aseismic [,eɪ'saɪzmɪk] *adj* aséismique.

asepsis [,eɪ'sepsɪs] *n* asepsie *f*.

aseptic [,eɪ'septɪk] *adj* aseptique.

asexual [,eɪ'sekʃʊəl] *adj* asexué.

ash [æʃ] *n* -**1.** [from fire, cigarette] cendre *f*; **he dropped cigarette ~ on the carpet** il a laissé tomber de la cendre de cigarette sur le tapis; **the fire reduced the house to ~es** l'incendie a réduit la maison en cendres; **~es to ~es, dust to dust** RELIG tu es poussière et tu redeviendras poussière ❑ **~ bin** [for ashes] cendrier *m*; [for rubbish] poubelle *f*, boîte *f* à ordures. -**2.** [tree, wood] frêne *m*.
◆ **Ashes** *npl* [in cricket] *trophée fictif que se disputent l'Angleterre et l'Australie*.

ASH [æʃ] (*abbr of* Action on Smoking and Health) *pr n ligue antitabac britannique*.

ashamed [ə'ʃeɪmd] *adj* confus, honteux; **to be ~ (of oneself)** avoir honte; **he's ~ of his behaviour/of having cried** il a honte de sa conduite/d'avoir pleuré; **I'm ~ of you** j'ai honte de toi, tu me fais honte; **I'm ~ to say that...** j'avoue à ma grande honte que...; **you ought to be ~ of yourself** tu devrais avoir honte; **there is nothing to be ~ of** il n'y a pas de quoi avoir honte.

ashamedly [ə'ʃeɪmɪdlɪ] *adv* de façon honteuse.

ash blond ◇ *adj* blond cendré *(inv)*.
◇ *n* blond *m* cendré.

ash can *n Am* poubelle *f*.

ashen ['æʃn] *adj* -**1.** [ash-coloured] cendré, couleur de cendres; [face] blême, livide. -**2.** [for ashwood] en (bois de) frêne.

Ashkenazi [,æʃkə'nɑːzɪ] (*pl* Ashkenazim [-zɪm]) *n* Ashkénase *mf*.

ashlar ['æʃlə^r] *n* pierre *f* de taille.

ashore [ə'ʃɔː^r] ◇ *adv* à terre; **he swam ~** il a nagé jusqu'à la rive; **debris from the wreck was washed ~** des morceaux de l'épave ont été rejetés sur la côte; **to go ~** débarquer; **the ship put the passengers ~ at Plymouth** le navire a débarqué les passagers à Plymouth.
◇ *adj* à terre.

ashplant ['æʃplɑːnt] *n* canne *f* en bois de frêne.

ashram ['æʃrəm] *n* ashram *m*.

ashtray ['æʃtreɪ] *n* cendrier *m*.

Ash Wednesday *n* mercredi *m* des Cendres.

ashy ['æʃɪ] (*compar* ashier, *superl* ashiest) *adj* -**1.** [ash-coloured] cendré, couleur de cendre; [pale] blême, livide. -**2.** [covered with ashes] couvert de cendres.

Asia [*Br* 'eɪʃə, *Am* 'eɪʒə] *pr n* Asie *f*; **in ~** en Asie.

Asia Minor *pr n* Asie *f* Mineure.

Asian [*Br* 'eɪʃn, *Am* 'eɪʒn] ◇ *n* Asiatique *mf*.
◇ *adj* asiatique.

> **ASIAN:**
> Pour les Britanniques, «Asian» désigne le plus souvent les habitants de l'Inde et des pays limitrophes: ainsi, l'expression «the Asian community in Birmingham» fait référence aux personnes d'origine indienne, pakistanaise et bangladaise qui habitent Birmingham.
> Pour traduire «Asiatique», il est souvent préférable de choisir l'expression désignant l'habitant du pays en question: a Chinese person, a Japanese person etc.

Asian American ◇ *adj* américain d'origine asiatique.
◇ *n* Américain *m*, -e *f* d'origine asiatique.

Asian flu *n* grippe *f* asiatique.

Asiatic [*Br* ˌeɪʃɪ'ætɪk, *Am* ˌeɪʒɪ'ætɪk] ◇ *adj* asiatique.
◇ *n* Asiatique *mf*.

aside [ə'saɪd] ◇ *adv* de côté, à part; **these problems ~, we have been very successful** à part ces problèmes, ce fut un véritable succès; **she held ~ the curtains** elle écarta les rideaux; **I stepped ~ to let her pass** je me suis écarté pour la laisser passer; **he took her ~** il l'a prise à part; **we've been putting money ~ for the trip** nous avons mis de l'argent de côté pour le voyage; **would you put this dress ~ for me?** pourriez-vous me mettre cette robe de côté OR me réserver cette robe?; **the court set ~ the verdict** JUR la cour a cassé le jugement.
◇ *n* aparté *m*; **he said something to her in an ~** il lui a dit quelque chose en aparté.
◆ **aside from** *prep phr* -**1.** [except for] sauf. -**2.** *Am* [as well as] en plus de.

A-side *n* face *f* A *(d'un disque)*.

asinine ['æsɪnaɪn] *adj* [person, behaviour] stupide, sot; **that was an ~ thing to do!** là, tu as vraiment fait une bêtise!

ask [ɑːsk] ◇ *vt* -**1.** [for opinion, information]: **to ~ sb sthg** demander qqch à qqn; **I ~ed her the time** je lui ai demandé l'heure; **she ~ed him about his job** elle lui a posé des questions sur son travail; **may I ~ you a question?** puis-je vous poser une question?; **~ your mother!** demande à ta mère!; **if you ~ me** si vous voulez mon avis; **but how? I ~ you!** *inf* mais comment? je vous le demande!; **don't ~ me!** *inf* est-ce que je sais, moi?; **no one ~ed you!** *inf* on ne t'a rien demandé! -**2.** [request] demander, solliciter; **he ~ed them a favour** il leur a demandé un service; **he ~ed her hand in marriage** il l'a demandée en mariage; **to ~ sb to do sthg** demander à qqn de faire qqch; **I ~ed them to be quiet** je leur ai demandé de ne pas faire de bruit; **she ~ed to have the bags brought up** elle a demandé que les bagages soient montés; **he ~ed to be admitted** il a demandé à être admis; **she was ~ed to wait outside** on lui a demandé d'attendre dehors; **that's ~ing too much of me** c'est trop m'en demander ‖ COMM: **to ~ a price** demander un prix; **what are you ~ing for it?** combien en voulez-vous OR demandez-vous? -**3.** [invite] inviter; **they ~ed her to join them** ils l'ont invitée à se joindre à eux; **he ~ed her to the pictures** il l'a invitée au cinéma; **she ~ed us up** elle nous a invités à monter.
◇ *vi* demander; **he was ~ing about the job** il s'informait OR se renseignait sur le poste; **it's there for the ~ing** il suffit de demander; **I was only ~ing!** je ne faisais que demander!
◆ **ask after** *vt insep*: **she ~ed after you** elle a demandé de vos nouvelles; **I ~ed after her health** je me suis informé de sa santé.
◆ **ask along** *vt sep* inviter; **we ~ed them along (with us)** nous leur avons proposé de venir avec nous.
◆ **ask around** *vi insep* se renseigner; **I ~ed around about rents** je me suis renseigné sur les loyers.
◆ **ask back** *vt sep* [invite again] réinviter; [for reciprocal visit] inviter; **she ~ed us back for dinner** elle nous a rendu l'invitation à dîner.
◆ **ask for** *vt insep* demander; **they ~ed for some water** ils ont demandé de l'eau; **you're ~ing for the moon** vous demandez la lune; **she ~ed for her book back** elle a demandé qu'on lui rende son livre; **you're just ~ing for trouble!** tu cherches des ennuis! ❑ **he was ~ing for it!** il l'a cherché!; **she left him – he had ~ed for it** elle l'a quitté – il l'a voulu, il l'a eu!
◆ **ask in** *vt sep* inviter à entrer; **he ~ed us in for a drink** il nous a invités à (entrer) prendre un verre.
◆ **ask out** *vt sep* inviter à sortir; **they ~ed us out for dinner/to the theatre** ils nous ont invités au restaurant/au théâtre.
◆ **ask round** *vt sep* inviter (à venir); **we must ~ him round soon** nous devrions l'inviter un de ces jours.

askance [ə'skæns] *adv* du coin de l'œil; **he looked ~ at her** il l'a regardée d'un air méfiant.

askew [ə'skjuː] ◇ *adv* obliquement, de travers.
◇ *adj Am*: **something's ~ here** il y a quelque chose qui cloche.

asking price ['ɑːskɪŋ-] *n* prix *m* de départ OR demandé.

aslant [ə'slɑːnt] ◇ *prep* en travers de.
◇ *adv* de travers, de OR en biais.

asleep [ə'sliːp] *adj* endormi; **she's ~** elle dort OR est endormie; **to be fast** OR **sound ~** dormir profondément OR à poings fermés; **to fall ~** s'endormir; **you're half ~** tu dors à moitié, tu es à moitié endormi; **he's ~ on his feet** il dort debout.

ASLEF ['æzlef] (*abbr of* Associated Society of Locomotive Engineers and Firemen) *pr n syndicat des cheminots en Grande-Bretagne*.

A/S-level *n examen facultatif complétant les A-levels*.

ASM (*abbr of* air-to-surface missile) *n* ASM *m*.

asocial [ˌeɪ'səʊʃl] *adj* asocial.

asp [æsp] *n* -**1.** ZOOL aspic *m*. -**2.** BOT & *arch* tremble *m*.

asparagus [ə'spærəgəs] *n (U)* asperge *f*; **to eat ~** manger des asperges ❑ **~ fern** asparagus *m*; **~ tips** pointes *fpl* d'asperges.

aspartame [*Br* ə'spɑːteɪm, *Am* 'æspərteɪm] *n* aspartame *m*.

ASPCA (*abbr of* American Society for the Prevention of Cruelty to Animals) *pr n société protectrice des animaux aux États-Unis*.

aspect ['æspekt] *n* -**1.** [facet] aspect *m*, côté *m*; **we should examine all ~s of the problem** nous devrions étudier le problème sous tous ses aspects. -**2.** *lit* [appearance] air *m*, aspect *m*; **a young man of (a) serious ~** un jeune homme à la mine sérieuse. -**3.** [outlook] orientation *f*, exposition *f*; **a house with a northern/southern ~** une maison exposée au nord/sud. -**4.** GRAMM aspect *m*.

aspectual [æ'spektjʊəl] *adj* aspectuel.

aspen ['æspən] *n* tremble *m*.

asperity [æ'sperətɪ] (*pl* **asperities**) *n fml* -**1.** [of manner, voice] aspérité *f*; **"certainly not", she said with some ~** «certainement pas», dit-elle d'un ton sec. -**2.** [of person] rudesse *f*. -**3.** [hardship] rigueur *f*.

aspersion [ə'spɜːʃn] *n* médisance *f*; [untruthful] calomnie *f*; **to cast ~s on sb** dénigrer qqn; **he cast ~s on her honour** il a porté atteinte à son honneur.

aspersorium [ˌæspə'sɔːrɪəm] (*pl* **aspersoria** [-rɪə]) *n* [basin] bénitier *m*; [sprinkler] aspersoir *m*.

asphalt ['æsfælt] ◇ *n* asphalte *m*.
◇ *comp* [road, roof] asphalté.
◇ *vt* asphalter.

asphalt jungle *n* jungle *f* de la ville; **'The Asphalt Jungle'** *Huston* 'Quand la ville dort'.

asphodel ['æsfədel] *n* asphodèle *m*.

asphyxia [əs'fɪksɪə] *n* asphyxie *f*.

asphyxiant [əs'fɪksɪənt] ◇ *adj* asphyxiant.
◇ *n* agent *m* asphyxiant.

asphyxiate [əs'fɪksɪeɪt] ◇ *vi* s'asphyxier.
◇ *vt* asphyxier.

asphyxiating [əs'fɪksɪeɪtɪŋ] *adj* asphyxiant; **~ gases** gaz *mpl* asphyxiants.

asphyxiation [əsˌfɪksɪ'eɪʃn] *n* asphyxie *f*; **to die by** OR **of ~** mourir d'asphyxie.

aspic ['æspɪk] *n* gelée *f*; **eggs in ~** œufs *mpl* en aspic; **salmon in ~** aspic *m* de saumon.

aspidistra [ˌæspɪ'dɪstrə] *n* aspidistra *m*.

aspirant ['æspɪrənt] ◇ *n* ambitieux *m*, -euse *f*.
◇ *adj* ambitieux.

aspirate [*vb* 'æspəreɪt, *adj* & *n* 'æspərət]
◇ *vt* aspirer.
◇ *adj* aspiré; **an ~ h** un h aspiré.
◇ *n* aspirée *f*.

aspiration [ˌæspə'reɪʃn] *n* -**1.** [ambition] aspiration *f*; **young people with political ~s** des jeunes qui ont des aspirations politiques. -**2.** LING aspiration *f*.

aspirator ['æspəreɪtə^r] *n* aspirateur *m*.

aspire [ə'spaɪə^r] *vi* -**1.** aspirer; **he ~s to political power** il aspire au pouvoir politique; **she ~s to** OR **after higher things** elle vise plus haut, ses ambitions vont plus loin; **to ~ to fame** briguer la célébrité. -**2.** *arch* OR *lit* [rise] monter, s'élever.

aspirin ['æspərɪn] *n* aspirine *f*; [tablet] (comprimé *m* d') aspirine *f*.

aspiring [ə'spaɪərɪŋ] *adj* ambitieux; *pej* arriviste.

ass [æs] *n* -**1.** [donkey] âne *m*; **she-~** ânesse *f*; **an ~'s foal** un ânon. -**2.** *inf* [idiot] imbécile *mf*; **she's such an ~** elle est bête comme ses pieds; **he made a complete ~ of himself last night** il s'est conduit en parfait imbécile OR s'est parfaitement ridiculisé hier soir; **don't be such an ~** ne fais pas l'imbécile. -**3.** ▼ *Am* [behind] cul *m*; **my ~!** mon cul!; **you can bet your ~ I'll do it!** tu peux être sûr que je le ferai!; **to be on sb's ~** être sur le dos de qqn; **get your ~ out of here!** casse-toi!; **get your ~ over here!** amène-toi!; **to break one's ~** se crever le cul; **there's no need to bust your ~ to get it finished** pas la peine de te casser le cul pour le finir; **this weather is a pain in the ~** ce temps me fait vraiment chier; **they want your ~** ils veulent ta peau; **to be out on one's ~** ne pas avoir de pot. -**4.** ▼ *Am*: **a piece of ~** [sex] une baise; [woman] une fille baisable.

assail [ə'seɪl] *vt* attaquer, assaillir; *fig*: **he ~ed her with questions** il l'a harcelée de questions; **~ed by doubt** assailli par le doute.

assailant [ə'seɪlənt] *n* agresseur *m*, assaillant *m*, -e *f*.

Assam [æ'sæm] *pr n* Assam *m*; **in ~** en Assam.

Assamese [ˌæsə'miːz] (*pl inv*) ◇ *n* -**1.** [person] Assamais *m*, -e *f*. -**2.** LING assamais *m*.
◇ *adj* assamais.

assassin [ə'sæsɪn] *n* assassin *m*.

assassinate [ə'sæsɪneɪt] *vt* assassiner.

assassination [əˌsæsɪ'neɪʃn] *n* assassinat *m*.

assault [ə'sɔːlt] ◇ *n* -**1.** [attack] agression *f*; **he is accused of ~** il est accusé de voie de fait ‖ *fig*: **the music is an ~ on listeners' ears** cette musique est une agression pour les oreilles des auditeurs; **a brave ~ on widely held beliefs** une attaque courageuse contre des croyances très répandues ❑ **common ~** voie *f* de fait simple; **~ and battery** JUR coups *mpl* et blessures *fpl*. -**2.** MIL assaut *m*; **to lead an ~** se lancer à l'assaut; **they opened the ~ on enemy positions** ils ont donné l'assaut aux positions ennemies; **they made** OR **carried out an ~ on the camp** ils sont montés à l'assaut du camp. -**3.** [climbing] assaut *m*.
◇ *vt* -**1.** [gen] agresser; [sexually] violenter; **his rough language ~ed their sensibilities** *fig* son langage grossier blessait leur sensibilité. -**2.** JUR se livrer à des voies de fait sur; [sexually] se livrer à des violences sexuelles sur.

assault course *n* parcours *m* du combattant.

assay [ə'seɪ] ◇ *vt* -**1.** [analyse - metal] essayer. -**2.** *arch* [attempt] essayer, tenter.
◇ *n* essai *m*; **~ office** laboratoire *m* d'essais.

ass-backwards▽ *adv Am* à l'envers.

assegai ['æsəgaɪ] *n* sagaie *f*.

assemblage [ə'semblɪdʒ] *n* -**1.** [collection] collection *f*, groupe *m*; [of people] assemblée *f*. -**2.** [process] montage *m*, assemblage *m*.

assemble [ə'sembl] ◇ *vt* -**1.** assembler, amasser; [people] rassembler, réunir; [troops] rassembler. -**2.** [put together] monter, assembler; **factory ~d** monté en usine.
◇ *vi* se rassembler, se réunir.

assembler [ə'semblə^r] *n* assembleur *m*.

assembly [ə'semblɪ] (*pl* **assemblies**) *n* -**1.** [meeting - gen] réunion *f*, assemblée *f*; **a place of ~** un lieu de réunion; **the right of ~** la liberté de réunion. -**2.** POL assemblée *f*; **National Assembly** l'Assemblée *f* nationale. -**3.** SCH *réunion de tous les élèves de l'établissement*; **~ hall** SCH *hall où* *les enfants se réunissent le matin avant d'entrer en classe*. -**4.** MIL rassemblement *m*. -**5.** [building - process] montage *m*, assemblage *m*; [- end product] assemblage *m*; **the engine ~** le bloc moteur. -**6.** COMPUT assemblage *m*.

assembly language *n* langage *m* d'assemblage.

assembly line *n* chaîne *f* de montage; **to work on an ~** travailler à la chaîne.

assemblyman [ə'semblɪmən] (*pl* **assemblymen** [-mən]) *n Am homme qui siège à une assemblée législative*.

assembly point *n* point *m* de rassemblement.

assembly room *n* -**1.** [gen] salle *f* de réunion; [at town hall] salle *f* des fêtes. -**2.** [industrial] atelier *m* de montage.

assemblywoman [ə'semblɪ,wʊmən] (*pl* **assemblywomen** [-,wɪmɪn]) *n Am femme qui siège à une assemblée législative*.

assent [ə'sent] ◇ *vi* consentir, acquiescer; **they finally ~ed to the proposition** ils ont fini par donner leur assentiment à la proposition.
◇ *n* consentement *m*, assentiment *m*; **to give one's ~** to sthg donner son assentiment à qqch.

assentor [ə'sentəʳ] *n Br* POL *signataire à l'appui d'un candidat aux élections gouvernementales*.

assert [ə'sɜːt] *vt* -**1.** [proclaim] affirmer, maintenir; **she continues to ~ her innocence/good faith** elle ne cesse de protester de son innocence/de sa bonne foi. -**2.** [insist on] défendre, revendiquer; **we must ~ our right to speak** nous devons faire valoir notre droit à la parole ‖ [impose]: **to ~ o.s.** se faire respecter, s'imposer; **I had to ~ my authority** il a fallu que j'affirme mon autorité OR que je m'impose.

assertion [ə'sɜːʃn] *n* affirmation *f*, assertion *f*; [of rights] revendication *f*.

assertive [ə'sɜːtɪv] *adj* assuré, autoritaire; *pej* péremptoire.

assertively [ə'sɜːtɪvlɪ] *adv* fermement; *pej* de façon péremptoire.

assertiveness [ə'sɜːtɪvnɪs] *n* manière *f* assurée; *pej* arrogance *f*.

assertiveness training *n* stage *m* d'affirmation de soi.

assess [ə'ses] *vt* -**1.** [judge] estimer, évaluer; **I had to ~ the quality of their work** j'ai dû juger de la qualité de leur travail; **it is important to ~ public opinion on the subject** il est important de savoir ce qu'en pense l'opinion publique. -**2.** [value] fixer OR déterminer la valeur de; **to ~ a property for taxation** évaluer OR calculer la valeur imposable d'une propriété; **the court ~ed the damages at £200** la cour a fixé les dommages et intérêts à 200 livres. -**3.** [taxes] évaluer; **~ed income** revenu *m* imposable.

assessable [ə'sesəbl] *adj* imposable; **~ income** OR **profits** FIN assiette *f* de l'impôt.

assessment [ə'sesmənt] *n* -**1.** [judgment] estimation *f*, évaluation *f*; **I don't accept his ~ of our work** je ne suis pas d'accord avec son évaluation de notre travail; **what's your ~ of the situation?** comment voyez-vous OR jugez-vous la situation? -**2.** *Br* SCH contrôle *m* des connaissances; [on report card] appréciation *f* des professeurs; **methods of ~** méthodes *fpl* d'évaluation. -**3.** [valuation - of amount due] détermination *f*, évaluation *f*; [- of tax] calcul *m* (de la valeur imposable).

assessor [ə'sesəʳ] *n* -**1.** expert *m*; **~ of taxes** *Am* inspecteur *m* des contributions directes. -**2.** JUR (juge *m*) assesseur *m*.

asset ['æset] *n* avantage *m*, atout *m*; **she's a great ~ to our team** elle est un excellent atout pour notre équipe.
◆ **assets** *npl* [possession] avoir *m*, capital *m*; COMM, FIN & JUR actif *m*; **our total ~s** tous nos biens; **~s and liabilities** l'actif *m* et le passif; **the ~s amount to £5 million** l'actif s'élève à cinq millions de livres.

asset-stripper *n* dépeceur *m* d'entreprise.

asset-stripping [-,strɪpɪŋ] *n achat d'entreprises pour revente des actifs*.

asseverate [ə'sevəreɪt] *vt fml* déclarer; **he ~d his innocence** il a juré de son innocence.

asseveration [ə,sevə'reɪʃn] *n fml* déclaration *f*; [of good faith, innocence] protestation *f*.

asshole▼ ['æshəʊl] *Am* = **arsehole**.

assibilate [ə'sɪbɪleɪt] ◇ *vt* assibiler.
◇ *vi* s'assibiler.

assiduity [,æsɪ'djuːətɪ] (*pl* **assiduities**) *n* assiduité *f*, zèle *m*.

assiduous [ə'sɪdjʊəs] *adj* assidu.

assiduously [ə'sɪdjʊəslɪ] *adv* assidûment.

assign [ə'saɪn] ◇ *vt* -**1.** [allot] assigner, attribuer; **the room was ~ed to study groups** la salle fut affectée OR réservée aux groupes d'étude; **a date and place were ~ed for the exam** la date et le lieu de l'examen ont été fixés; **to ~ a duty/task to sb** assigner une responsabilité/tâche à qqn; **I ~ed her the task of writing the report** je l'ai chargée de la rédaction du rapport. -**2.** [appoint] nommer, désigner; **he's been ~ed to Moscow** il a été affecté à Moscou. -**3.** [ascribe]: **to ~ a reason for sthg** donner la raison de qqch; **we ~ a value to X** nous attribuons OR assignons une valeur à X; **the aqueduct has been ~ed to the Roman period** l'aqueduc a été attribué à l'époque romaine. -**4.** JUR céder, transférer; **the property was ~ed to his daughter** la propriété fut transférée au nom de sa fille; **she ~ed the copyright to the school** elle a fait cession du droit d'auteur à l'école.
◇ *n* cessionnaire *mf*.

assignation [,æsɪg'neɪʃn] *n* -**1.** [meeting] rendez-vous *m* clandestin; **to have an ~ with sb** *fml* OR *hum* avoir un rendez-vous secret avec qqn. -**2.** [assignment] attribution *f*; [of money] allocation *f*; [of person] affectation *f*. -**3.** JUR cession *f*, transfert *m*.

assignee [,æsaɪ'niː] *n* cessionnaire *mf*.

assignment [ə'saɪnmənt] *n* -**1.** tâche *f*; [official] mission *f*; SCH devoir *m*. -**2.** [appointment] attribution *f*; [of money] allocation *f*; [of person] affectation *f*. -**3.** JUR cession *f*, transfert *m*; **~ of a patent** cession d'un brevet; **~ of contract** *cession des droits et obligations découlant d'un contrat*.

assignor [ə'saɪnəʳ] *n* cédant *m*, -e *f*.

assimilate [ə'sɪmɪleɪt] ◇ *vt* -**1.** [food, information] assimiler. -**2.** [immigrants] intégrer; **they try very hard to ~ newcomers** ils font tout leur possible pour intégrer les nouveaux arrivants.
◇ *vi* s'assimiler, s'intégrer; **foreigners find it difficult to ~ into a new culture** les étrangers ont du mal à s'adapter OR s'intégrer à une autre culture.

assimilation [ə,sɪmɪ'leɪʃn] *n* [gen & LING] assimilation *f*.

assist [ə'sɪst] ◇ *vt* -**1.** [help] aider, assister; **he ~ed her up/down the stairs** il l'a aidée à monter/descendre l'escalier; **how may I ~ you?** comment puis-je vous être utile?; **the two groups ~ed each other with their research** les deux groupes se sont entraidés dans leur recherche; **a man is ~ing police with their enquiries** un homme aide la police dans ses investigations. -**2.** [with money]: **~ed by the town hall** avec le concours de la mairie; **~ed passage** billet *m* subventionné.
◇ *vi* -**1.** [help] aider, prêter secours; **she ~ed at the operation** elle a apporté son assistance pendant l'opération. -**2.** *arch* [attend] assister; **we ~ed at his funeral** nous avons assisté à ses obsèques.
◇ *n* SPORT *action qui permet à un coéquipier de marquer un point*.

assistance [ə'sɪstəns] *n* aide *f*, secours *m*; **may I be of ~ to you?** puis-je vous être utile?; **to come to sb's ~** venir au secours de qqn; **could you give me some ~ with these calculations?** pourriez-vous me venir en aide dans ces calculs?; **with the financial ~ of the university** avec le concours financier de l'université.

assistant [ə'sɪstənt] ◇ *n* assistant *m*, -e *f*, aide *mf*; **foreign language ~** SCH assistant *m*, -e *f* (en langue étrangère); UNIV lecteur *m*, -trice *f* (en langue étrangère); **non-teaching ~** SCH auxiliaire *mf*.
◇ *comp* [director, judge, librarian, secretary] adjoint; **~ manager** sous-directeur *m*, directeur *m* adjoint; **~ manageress** *Br* sous-directrice *f*, directrice *f* adjointe; **~ master**, **~ mistress** professeur *m (qui n'est pas responsable d'une section)*; **~ professor** *Am* ≃ maître-assistant *m*; **~ teacher** [primary] instituteur *m*, -trice *f*; [secondary] professeur *m (qui ne dirige pas de section)*.

assize [ə'saɪz] *n* réunion *f*; JUR assises *fpl*; **~ court**, **court of ~s** cour *f* d'assises.

assoc -**1.** *written abbr of* **association**. -**2.** *written abbr of* **associated**.

associate [*vb* ə'səʊʃɪeɪt, *n* & *adj* ə'səʊʃɪət] ◇ *vt* associer; **the problems ~d with nuclear power** les problèmes relatifs à l'énergie nucléaire; **I don't ~ you with that kind of activity** je ne t'imagine pas dans ce genre d'activité; **that kind of behaviour is often ~d with an unhappy childhood** ce type de comportement est souvent lié à une enfance malheureuse; **I don't want to be ~d with that scandal** je ne veux pas que mon nom soit mêlé à ce scandale; **he's ~d in the public's mind with that book** dans l'esprit du public, il est associé à ce livre-là.
◇ *vi*: **to ~ with sb** fréquenter qqn.
◇ *n* -**1.** [partner] associé *m*, -e *f*; JUR complice *mf*. -**2.** [of club] membre *m*, associé *m*, -e *f*; **an ~ of an institution** un membre d'une fondation ❑ **Associate in Arts (degree)** *(titulaire d'un) diplôme universitaire américain de lettres*; **Associate in Science (degree)** *(titulaire d'un) diplôme universitaire américain de sciences*.
◇ *adj* associé, allié; **I'm only an ~ member of the organisation** je suis seulement membre associé de l'organisation ❑ **~ judge** juge *m* assesseur; **Associate Justice** *Am* juge *m* de la Cour Suprême.

associated [ə'səʊʃɪeɪtɪd] *adj* associé.

associate professor *n Am* ≃ maître *m* de conférences.

association [ə,səʊsɪ'eɪʃn] *n* -**1.** [grouping] association *f*, société *f*; **the teachers have formed an ~** les enseignants ont constitué une association. -**2.** [involvement] association *f*, fréquentation *f*; **through long ~ with the medical profession** à force de fréquenter la profession médicale; **the police knew about his ~ with the underworld** la police savait qu'il fréquentait le milieu; **this programme was made in ~ with Belgian television** ce programme a été fait en collaboration avec la télévision belge. -**3.** [of ideas] association *f*; **by ~ of ideas** par association d'idées; **that trip has many unhappy ~s for me** ce voyage me rappelle bien des choses pénibles.

Association football *n Br* football *m* association.

associative [ə'səʊʃjətɪv] *adj* [gen & COMPUT] associatif; **~ storage** mémoire *f* associative.

assonance ['æsənəns] *n* assonance *f*.

assort [ə'sɔːt] ◇ *vt* classer, ranger.
◇ *vi* s'assortir; **to ~ with sthg** s'assortir à qqch.

assorted [ə'sɔːtɪd] *adj* -**1.** [various] varié, divers; **in ~ sizes** en différentes tailles. -**2.** [matched] assorti; **well-/ill-~** bien/mal assorti.

assortment [ə'sɔːtmənt] *n* assortiment *m*, collection *f*; [of people] mélange *m*; **there was a good ~ of cakes** il y avait un grand choix OR une bonne sélection de gâteaux; **she certainly has an odd ~ of friends!** ses amis forment un curieux mélange!

asst *written abbr of* **assistant**.

assuage [ə'sweɪdʒ] *vt fml* [grief, pain] soulager, apaiser; [hunger, thirst] assouvir; [person] apaiser, calmer.

assume [ə'sjuːm] *vt* -**1.** [presume] supposer, présumer; **let's ~ that to be the case** mettons OR supposons que ce soit le cas; **he's married, I ~** il est marié, je suppose OR présume; **he's ~d to**

be rich on le suppose riche; you ~ a lot! tu fais bien des suppositions! -**2.** [undertake] assumer, endosser; he ~d **management of the firm** il a pris la direction de l'entreprise. -**3.** [usurp - power] prendre; [- right, title] s'approprier, s'arroger. -**4.** [adopt] assumer, prendre; she ~d **a look of indifference** elle affectait un air d'indifférence; he ~d **the role of mediator** il a assumé le rôle de médiateur; **unemployment is assuming frightening proportions** le chômage commence à prendre d'inquiétantes proportions.

assumed [ə'sju:md] *adj* feint, faux; **with ~ indifference** avec une indifférence feinte; **~ name** nom *m* d'emprunt; **he travels under an ~ name** il se sert d'un nom d'emprunt pour voyager.

assuming [ə'sju:mɪŋ] *conj* en admettant OR supposant que; **~ he is alive** en admettant OR supposant qu'il soit toujours en vie.

assumption [ə'sʌmpʃn] *n* -**1.** [supposition] supposition *f*, hypothèse *f*; **our cultural ~s** nos présupposés; **on the ~ that he agrees, we can go ahead** en supposant OR admettant qu'il soit d'accord, nous pouvons aller de l'avant; **we're working on the ~ that what she says is true** nous partons du principe qu'elle dit la vérité. -**2.** [of power] appropriation *f*; **~ of office** entrée *f* en fonctions. -**3.** [of attitude] affectation *f*.
◆ **Assumption** *n* RELIG: **the Assumption** l'Assomption *f*.

Assumption Day [ə'sʌmpʃn-] *n* jour *m* OR fête *f* de l'Assomption.

assurance [ə'ʃʊərəns] *n* -**1.** [assertion] affirmation *f*, assurance *f*; [pledge] promesse *f*, assurance *f*; **she gave repeated ~s that she would not try to escape** elle a promis à plusieurs reprises qu'elle n'essaierait pas de s'enfuir; **he gave her a ring as an ~ of his love** il lui a donné une bague comme gage de son amour. -**2.** [confidence] assurance *f*, confiance *f* en soi; [overconfidence] arrogance *f*; **to lack ~** manquer de confiance en soi; **she said it with such ~, I believed her** elle l'a dit avec une telle assurance que je l'ai crue; **they set out with absolute ~ of their success** ils partirent, sûrs de leur réussite. -**3.** *Br* [insurance] assurance *f*.

assure [ə'ʃʊəʳ] *vt* -**1.** [affirm] affirmer, assurer; [convince] convaincre, assurer; [guarantee] assurer, certifier; **he ~d them of his sincerity** il les a assurés de sa sincérité; **they ~d her it was true** ils lui ont certifié que c'était vrai; **I can ~ you that your work was not in vain** je peux vous assurer que votre travail n'a pas été inutile; **we've never had anyone like that here, I can ~ you** je peux vous assurer que nous n'avons jamais eu quelqu'un comme ça ici; **she ~d herself (of) a good pension** elle s'est assuré une bonne retraite. -**2.** *Br* [insure] assurer.

assured [ə'ʃʊəd] ◇ *adj* -**1.** [certain] assuré, certain; **I am ~ of her loyalty** je suis convaincu OR certain de sa loyauté; **our success appeared ~** notre succès semblait assuré OR certain. -**2.** [self-confident] assuré, sûr de soi; [overconfident] arrogant, effronté. -**3.** *Br* [insured] assuré.
◇ *n* assuré *m*, -e *f*.

assuredly [ə'ʃʊərɪdlɪ] *adv* assurément, sûrement, sans aucun doute.

Assyria [ə'sɪrɪə] *pr n* Assyrie *f*; **in ~** en Assyrie.

Assyrian [ə'sɪrɪən] ◇ *n* Assyrien *m*, -enne *f*.
◇ *adj* assyrien.

AST (*abbr of* **Atlantic Standard Time**) *n heure d'hiver des Provinces Maritimes du Canada et d'une partie des Caraïbes.*

astable [ˌeɪ'steɪbl] *adj* instable.

astatic [ˌeɪ'stætɪk] *adj* [unstable] instable; PHYS astatique.

astatine ['æstətiːn] *n* astate *m*.

aster ['æstəʳ] *n* aster *m*.

asterisk ['æstərɪsk] ◇ *n* astérisque *m*.
◇ *vt* marquer d'un astérisque.

asterism ['æstərɪzm] *n* -**1.** TYPO *trois astérisques en triangle.* -**2.** ASTRON & MINER astérisme *m*.

astern [ə'stɜːn] ◇ *adv* à OR sur l'arrière, en poupe; **to go ~** [person] aller à l'arrière OR en poupe; [boat] faire machine arrière, battre en arrière, culer; **full speed ~!** en arrière toutes!
◇ *adj* à OR sur l'arrière.

asteroid ['æstərɔɪd] *n* astéroïde *m*.

asthenia [æs'θiːnjə] *n* asthénie *f*.

asthenosphere [əs'θiːnəˌsfɪəʳ] *n* asthénosphère *f*.

asthma ['æsmə] ◇ *n* asthme *m*; **she has ~** elle est asthmatique.
◇ *comp*: **~ attack** crise *f* d'asthme; **~ sufferer** asthmatique *mf*.

asthmatic [æs'mætɪk] ◇ *adj* asthmatique; **an ~ attack** une crise d'asthme.
◇ *n* asthmatique *mf*.

astigmatic [ˌæstɪg'mætɪk] ◇ *adj* astigmate.
◇ *n* astigmate *mf*.

astigmatism [æ'stɪgmətɪzm] *n* astigmatisme *m*.

astir [ə'stɜːʳ] *adj lit* -**1.** [out of bed] debout *(inv)*, levé. -**2.** [in motion] animé.

ASTMS ['æstiːmz, eɪestiːemes] (*abbr of* **Association of Scientific, Technical and Managerial Staffs**) *pr n ancien syndicat britannique des personnels scientifiques, techniques et administratifs.*

astonish [ə'stɒnɪʃ] *vt* [surprise] étonner; [amaze] stupéfier, ahurir; **we were ~ed that she had come** nous étions stupéfaits qu'elle soit venue; **she was ~ed to hear from him** OR **at hearing from him** elle était stupéfaite d'avoir de ses nouvelles; **no! you ~ me!** non! ce n'est pas vrai!

astonished [ə'stɒnɪʃt] *adj* surpris.

astonishing [ə'stɒnɪʃɪŋ] *adj* [surprising] étonnant; [amazing] stupéfiant, ahurissant; **it's ~ how he's changed** c'est stupéfiant comme il a changé; **with ~ speed** à une vitesse incroyable OR étonnante.

astonishingly [ə'stɒnɪʃɪŋlɪ] *adv* incroyablement; **she was ~ good at the piano** elle jouait incroyablement bien du piano; **~, they both decided to leave** aussi étonnant que cela paraisse, ils ont tous les deux décidé de partir.

astonishment [ə'stɒnɪʃmənt] *n* [surprise] étonnement *m*; [amazement] stupéfaction *f*, ahurissement *m*; **they stared in ~** ils avaient l'air stupéfait; **a look of ~** un regard stupéfait OR ahuri; **to our ~** à notre grand étonnement, à notre stupéfaction.

astound [ə'staʊnd] *vt* stupéfier, abasourdir; **we were ~ed to hear the news** la nouvelle nous a stupéfaits; **I was ~ed when she left like that** j'étais stupéfait qu'elle parte comme ça.

astounded [ə'staʊndɪd] *adj* stupéfait.

astounding [ə'staʊndɪŋ] *adj* stupéfiant, ahurissant.

astoundingly [ə'staʊndɪŋlɪ] *adv* incroyablement; **~ beautiful** d'une beauté incroyable; **~ enough, they'd already met** chose extraordinaire, ils s'étaient déjà rencontrés.

Astrakhan [ˌæstrə'kæn] *pr n* Astrakan, Astrakhan.
◆ **astrakhan** ◇ *n* astrakan *m*.
◇ *comp* [hat, jacket] d'astrakan.

astral ['æstrəl] *adj* astral.

astray [ə'streɪ] *adv* -**1.** [lost]: **to go ~** s'égarer; **the letter went ~** la lettre s'est perdue. -**2.** *phr*: **to lead sb ~** [mislead] détourner qqn du droit chemin; [corrupt] dévoyer qqn; **don't be led ~ by their so-called expertise** ne vous laissez pas tromper OR abuser par leur soi-disant compétence; **he's easily led ~** il se laisse facilement entraîner hors du droit chemin.

astride [ə'straɪd] *prep* à califourchon OR à cheval sur; **he sat ~ the fence** il était assis à califourchon sur la barrière.

astringent [ə'strɪndʒənt] ◇ *adj* -**1.** [remark] acerbe, caustique; [criticism] dur, sévère. -**2.** [lotion] astringent.
◇ *n* astringent *m*.

astrolabe ['æstrəleɪb] *n* astrolabe *m*.

astrologer [ə'strɒlədʒəʳ] *n* astrologue *mf*.

astrological [ˌæstrə'lɒdʒɪkl] *adj* astrologique.

astrologist [ə'strɒlədʒɪst] *n* astrologue *mf*.

astrology [ə'strɒlədʒɪ] *n* astrologie *f*.

astronaut ['æstrənɔːt] *n* astronaute *mf*.

astronautic(al) [ˌæstrə'nɔːtɪk(l)] *adj* astronautique.

astronautics [ˌæstrə'nɔːtɪks] *n (U)* astronautique *f*.

astronomer [ə'strɒnəməʳ] *n* astronome *mf*.

astronomic(al) [ˌæstrə'nɒmɪk(l)] *adj* ASTRON & *fig* astronomique.

astronomically [ˌæstrə'nɒmɪklɪ] *adv* astronomiquement.

astronomy [ə'strɒnəmɪ] *n* astronomie *f*.

astrophysicist [ˌæstrəʊ'fɪzɪsɪst] *n* astrophysicien *m*, -enne *f*.

astrophysics [ˌæstrəʊ'fɪzɪks] *n (U)* astrophysique *f*.

Asturias [æ'stʊərɪæs] *pr n* Asturies *fpl*; **the prince of ~** le prince des Asturies.

astute [ə'stjuːt] *adj* [person - shrewd] astucieux, fin, perspicace; [- crafty] malin, rusé; [investment, management] astucieux; **how ~ of you!** vous êtes malin!

astutely [ə'stjuːtlɪ] *adv* astucieusement, avec finesse OR perspicacité.

astuteness [ə'stjuːtnɪs] *n* finesse *f*, perspicacité *f*.

Asuncion [əˌsʊnsɪ'ɒn] *pr n* Asuncion.

asunder [ə'sʌndəʳ] *adj* & *adv lit* [apart] écartés, éloignés (l'un de l'autre); [in pieces] en morceaux; **to be torn ~** être mis en pièces.

ASV (*abbr of* **American Standard Version**) *n traduction américaine de la Bible.*

Aswan [æs'wɑːn] *pr n* Assouan; **the ~ (High) Dam** le barrage d'Assouan.

asylum [ə'saɪləm] *n* -**1.** [refuge] asile *m*, refuge *m*; **to give ~ to sb** donner asile à qqn; **to grant sb political ~** accorder l'asile politique à qqn. -**2.** [mental hospital] asile *m* (d'aliénés).

asymmetric(al) [ˌeɪsɪ'metrɪk(l)] *adj* asymétrique.

asymmetry [ˌeɪ'sɪmətrɪ] *n* asymétrie *f*.

asymptomatic ['eɪˌsɪmptə'mætɪk] *adj* sans symptômes.

asynchronous [ˌeɪ'sɪŋkrənəs] *adj* asynchrone.

asyndetic [ˌæsɪn'detɪk] *adj* asyndétique.

at [*weak form* ət, *strong form* æt] *prep* -**1.** [indicating point in space] à; **at the door/the bus stop** à la porte/l'arrêt de bus; **at my house/the dentist's** chez moi/le dentiste; **I'm at the airport** je suis à l'aéroport; **we're at the Savoy (Hotel)** [staying at] nous sommes au Savoy; **she's at a wedding/committee meeting** [attending] elle est à un mariage/en réunion avec le comité; **she was standing at the window** elle se tenait debout à la fenêtre; **turn left at the traffic lights/the Town Hall** tournez à gauche au feu/à la mairie; **change at Reading** RAIL prenez la correspondance à Reading; **where are you at with that report?** *Am* où en êtes-vous avec ce rapport? ☐ **this club is where it's at** *inf* ce club est très chic OR dans le vent; **that's not where it's at** *inf* [not fashionable] ça n'est pas dans le vent; *Am* [not the important thing] là n'est pas la question; **that's not where I'm at** c'est pas mon truc. -**2.** [indicating point in time] à; **at noon/6 o'clock** à midi/6 h; **I work at night** je travaille de nuit; **I like to work at night** j'aime travailler la nuit; **I'm busy at the moment** je suis occupé en ce moment; **at a time when...** à un moment où... || [indicating age]: **he started working at 15** il a commencé à travailler à (l'âge de) 15 ans. -**3.** [indicating direction] vers, dans la direction de; **look at this!** regarde ça!; **he shot at the rabbit** il a tiré sur le lapin; **she grabbed at the purse** elle a essayé de s'emparer du porte-monnaie; **don't shout at me!** ne me crie pas dessus! -**4.** [indicating activity] en train de, occupé à; **my parents are at work** mes parents sont au travail; **he was at lunch** il était allé déjeuner ☐ **get me some coffee while you're at it** *inf* prenez-moi du café pendant que vous y êtes; **she's at it again!** *inf* la voilà qui recommence!; **don't let me catch you at it again!** *inf* que je ne t'y reprenne pas! -**5.** [indicating level, rate] à, de; **the temperature stands at 30°** la température est de 30°; **at 50 mph** à 80 km/h; **he drove at 50 mph** il faisait du 80 (à l'heure); **the rise worked out at £1 an hour** l'augmentation correspondait à 1 livre de l'heure. -**6.** [indicating price] à; **it's a bargain at £5** à 5 livres, c'est une bonne affaire; **we sell it at (a price of) £1 a kilo** nous le vendons 1 livre le kilo. -**7.** [with superlative] à; **the water level was at its highest/lowest** le niveau d'eau était au plus haut/au plus bas; **she's at her most/least effective in such situations** c'est là qu'elle est le plus/le moins efficace. -**8.** [as adjective complement] en; **he's brilliant/hopeless at maths** il est excellent/nul en maths. -**9.** *phr*: to be (on) at sb harceler qqn; **he's always (on) at his secretary to arrive earlier** il n'arrête pas de harceler sa secrétaire pour qu'elle vienne plus tôt le matin; **his mother's always (on) at him to tidy his room** sa mère est toujours après lui OR le harcèle toujours pour qu'il range sa chambre.

◆ **at all** *adv phr*: **he's not at all patient** il n'est pas du tout patient; **thank you for your help — not at all** merci de votre aide — je vous en prie OR il n'y a pas de quoi; **nothing at all** rien du tout; **he comes rarely if at all** il vient très rarement, quand il vient; **if you had any feelings at all** si vous aviez le moindre sentiment; **if we had any money at all** si nous avions le moindre argent OR ne serait-ce qu'un peu d'argent; **if you do any travelling at all, you'll know what I mean** si vous voyagez un tant soit peu, vous comprendrez ce que je veux dire.

◆ **at once** *adv phr* -**1.** [immediately] tout de suite, immédiatement. -**2.** [simultaneously] en même temps; **they all came at once** ils sont tous arrivés en même temps; **don't all talk at once** ne parlez pas tous en même temps.

atavism ['ætəvɪzm] *n* atavisme *m*.

atavistic [ˌætə'vɪstɪk] *adj* atavique.

ataxia [ə'tæksɪə] *n* ataxie *f*.

ataxic [ə'tæksɪk] *adj* ataxique.

ATC ◇ *n abbr of* air traffic control.

◇ *pr n* (*abbr of* Air Training Corps) *unité de formation de l'armée de l'air britannique*.

ate [*Br* et, *Am* eɪt] *pt* → **eat**.

atelier [æ'telɪeɪ] *n* atelier *m*.

a tempo [ɑː'tempəʊ] *adj* & *adv* a tempo.

Athanasian Creed [ˌæθə'neɪʃn-] *n*: the ~ le symbole de saint Athanase.

atheism ['eɪθɪɪzm] *n* athéisme *m*.

atheist ['eɪθɪɪst] ◇ *adj* athée.

◇ *n* athée *mf*.

atheistic(al) [ˌeɪθɪ'ɪstɪk(l)] *adj* athée.

Athena [ə'θiːnə], **Athene** [ə'θiːniː] *pr n* Athéna *f*.

Athenian [ə'θiːnjən] ◇ *n* Athénien *m*, -enne *f*.

◇ *adj* athénien.

Athens ['æθɪnz] *pr n* Athènes; 'Timon of ~' *Shakespeare* 'Timon d'Athènes'.

athirst [ə'θɜːst] *adj lit* assoiffé; ~ **for revenge** assoiffé de vengeance.

athlete ['æθliːt] *n* [gen] sportif *m*, -ive *f*; [track & field competitor] athlète *mf*.

athlete's foot *n* *(U)* mycose *f*; **to have** ~ avoir une mycose.

athletic [æθ'letɪk] *adj* [sporty] sportif; [muscular] athlétique; **she's very** ~ elle est très sportive.

athletics [æθ'letɪks] ◇ *n (U)* athlétisme *m*.

◇ *comp* [club, meeting] d'athlétisme; [activity - track & field] athlétique; [- other sport] sportif; ~ **coach** *Am* SCH & UNIV entraîneur *m* (sportif).

athletic support(er) *n* suspensoir *m*.

at-home *inf n réception chez soi*.

athwart [ə'θwɔːt] *lit* ◇ *prep* -**1.** [across the path of] en travers de; NAUT par le travers de. -**2.** [in opposition to] contre, en opposition à.

◇ *adv* en travers; NAUT par le travers.

atishoo [ə'tɪʃuː] *onomat* atchoum.

Atlanta [ət'læntə] *pr n* Atlanta.

Atlantic [ət'læntɪk] ◇ *adj* [coast, community] atlantique; [wind] de l'Atlantique; **the ~ Ocean** l'Atlantique *m*, l'océan *m* Atlantique; **the ~ Charter** le Pacte atlantique; ~ **liner** transatlantique *m*; **the ~ Provinces** [in Canada] les Provinces *fpl* atlantiques.

◇ *pr n*: the ~ l'Atlantique *m*, l'océan *m* Atlantique.

Atlantis [ət'læntɪs] *pr n* Atlantide *f*.

atlas ['ætləs] *n* atlas *m*.

Atlas ['ætləs] *pr n* -**1.** GEOG: **the ~ Mountains** l'Atlas *m*; **the High ~** le Haut OR Grand Atlas; **the Middle ~** le Moyen Atlas. -**2.** MYTH Atlas.

atm. (*written abbr of* atmosphere) atm.

ATM (*abbr of* automatic telling machine) *n Am* GAB *m*.

atmosphere ['ætməˌsfɪə^r] *n* -**1.** [air] atmosphère *f*; **the smoky ~ bothered her** l'atmosphère enfumée la gênait. -**2.** [feeling, mood] ambiance *f*, atmosphère *f*; **there was an ~ of elation in the room** il régnait une joyeuse ambiance dans la pièce; **the place has no ~** l'endroit est impersonnel; **there's a really bad ~ at the office just now** il y a une très mauvaise ambiance au bureau en ce moment.

atmospheric [ˌætməs'ferɪk] *adj* -**1.** [pollution, pressure] atmosphérique. -**2.** [full of atmosphere]: **the film was very ~** il y avait beaucoup d'atmosphère dans ce film.

atmospherics [ˌætməs'ferɪks] *npl* parasites *mpl*.

atoll ['ætɒl] *n* atoll *m*.

atom ['ætəm] *n* -**1.** SCI atome *m*. -**2.** *fig*: **there's not an ~ of truth in what you say** il n'y a pas une once OR un brin de vérité dans ce que tu dis; **they haven't one ~ of common sense** ils n'ont pas le moindre bon sens.

atom bomb *n* bombe *f* atomique.

atomic [ə'tɒmɪk] *adj* [bomb, theory] atomique; **~-powered** (fonctionnant à l'énergie) nucléaire OR atomique ❑ ~ **age** ère *f* atomique; ~ **power station** centrale *f* nucléaire; ~ **warfare** guerre *f* nucléaire OR atomique.

atomic clock *n* horloge *f* atomique.

atomic cocktail *n mélange radioactif utilisé dans le traitement du cancer*.

atomic energy *n* énergie *f* nucléaire OR atomique.

Atomic Energy Authority *pr n commissariat à l'énergie nucléaire en Grande-Bretagne*.

Atomic Energy Commission *pr n commissariat à l'énergie nucléaire aux États-Unis*.

atomic heat *n* chaleur *f* atomique.

atomic mass *n* masse *f* OR poids *m* atomique.

atomic number *n* nombre *m* OR numéro *m* atomique.

atomic pile *n* pile *f* atomique, réacteur *m* nucléaire.

atomic power *n* énergie *f* atomique, réacteur *m* nucléaire.

atomic reactor *n* réacteur *m* nucléaire.

atomic structure *n* structure *f* atomique.

atomic volume *n* volume *m* atomique.

atomic weight *n* masse *f* OR poids *m* atomique.

atomize, -ise ['ætəmaɪz] *vt* -**1.** [liquid] pulvériser, atomiser, vaporiser; [solid] atomiser. -**2.** [bomb] atomiser.

atomizer ['ætəmaɪzə^r] *n* atomiseur *m*.

atonal [eɪ'təʊnl] *adj* atonal.

atonality [ˌeɪtəʊ'nælətɪ] *n* atonalité *f*.

atone [ə'təʊn] ◇ *vi*: **to ~ for**: **to ~ for one's sins** expier ses péchés; **how can I ~ for my past unkindness?** comment me faire pardonner ma méchanceté passée?; **to ~ for a mistake** réparer OR racheter une faute.

◇ *vt* [guilt, sin] expier.

atonement [ə'təʊnmənt] *n* [of crime, sin] expiation *f*; [of mistake] réparation *f*; **to make ~ for one's sins** expier ses péchés; **they made ~ for their past mistakes** ils ont racheté leurs erreurs passées ❑ **Day of Atonement** (fête *f* du) Grand Pardon *m*.

atonic [eɪ'tɒnɪk] *adj* -**1.** LING atone. -**2.** [muscle] atonique.

atony ['ætənɪ] *n* atonie *f*.

atop [ə'tɒp] *lit* ◇ *adv* en haut.

◇ *prep* en haut de, sur.

ATP (*abbr of* Association of Tennis Professionals) *pr n* ATP *f*.

Atreus ['eɪtrɪəs] *pr n* Atrée.

atrium ['eɪtrɪəm] (*pl* **atria** [-trɪə] OR **atriums**) *n* -**1.** [court] cour *f*; ANTIQ atrium *m*. -**2.** ANAT orifice *m* de l'oreillette.

atrocious [ə'trəʊʃəs] *adj* -**1.** [cruel, evil] atroce, horrible. -**2.** *inf* [very bad] affreux, atroce.

atrociously [ə'trəʊʃəslɪ] *adv* -**1.** [cruelly] atrocement, horriblement. -**2.** *inf* [badly] affreusement, atrocement.

atrocity [ə'trɒsətɪ] (*pl* **atrocities**) *n* atrocité *f*.

atrophy ['ætrəfɪ] (*pt* & *pp* **atrophied**) ◇ *n* atrophie *f*.

◇ *vi* s'atrophier.

◇ *vt* atrophier.

attaboy *inf* ['ætəbɔɪ] *interj Am*: ~! bravo! vas-y mon petit!

attach [ə'tætʃ] ◇ *vt* -**1.** [connect - handle, label] attacher, fixer; [- appendix, document] joindre; **the ~ed letter** la lettre ci-jointe. -**2.** [associate with]: **he ~ed himself to a group of walkers** il s'est joint à un groupe de randonneurs. -**3.** [be part of]: **the research centre is ~ed to the science department** le centre de recherche dépend du OR est rattaché au département des sciences. -**4.** [attribute] attacher, attribuer; **don't ~ too much importance to this survey** n'accordez pas trop d'importance à cette enquête. -**5.** [place on temporary duty] affecter; **she's ~ed to NATO** elle est attachée à l'OTAN. -**6.** JUR [person] arrêter, appréhender; [property, salary] saisir.

◇ *vi fml* être attribué, être imputé; **the benefits that ~ to this position are considerable** les avantages attachés à ce poste sont énormes; **no blame ~es to you for what happened** la responsabilité de ce qui s'est produit ne repose nullement sur vous.

attaché [ə'tæʃeɪ] *n* attaché *m*, -e *f*.

attaché case *n* mallette *f*, attaché-case *m*.

attached [ə'tætʃt] *adj* attaché; **he's very ~ to his family** il est très attaché OR il tient beaucoup à sa famille; **she's (already) ~** elle a déjà quelqu'un dans sa vie; **I was very ~ to that car** j'étais très attaché à cette voiture.

attachment [ə'tætʃmənt] *n* -**1.** [fastening] fixation *f*. -**2.** [accessory, part] accessoire *m*. -**3.** [affection] attachement *m*, affection *f*; [loyalty] attachement *m*; **she has a strong ~ to her grandfather** elle est très attachée à son grand-père. -**4.** [temporary duty] détachement *m*; **he's on ~ to the hospital** il est en détachement à l'hôpital. -**5.** JUR [of person] arrestation *f*; [of property] saisie *f*; ~ **of earnings** *saisie-arrêt du salaire, des biens ou des bienfaits d'un débiteur par un créancier*.

attack [ə'tæk] ◇ *vt* -**1.** [assault - physically] attaquer; [- verbally] attaquer, s'attaquer à; MIL attaquer, assaillir. -**2.** [tackle] s'attaquer à; **a campaign to ~ racism** une campagne pour combattre le racisme; **she ~ed the problem with enthusiasm** elle s'est attaquée au problème avec enthousiasme. -**3.** [damage] attaquer, ronger; **the disease mainly ~s the very young** la maladie atteint essentiellement les très jeunes enfants; **this apathy ~s the very roots of democracy** cette apathie menace les racines mêmes de la démocratie.

◇ *n* -**1.** [gen & SPORT] attaque *f*; MIL attaque *f*, assaut *m*; **~s on old people are on the increase** les agressions contre les personnes âgées sont de plus en plus nombreuses; **to launch an ~ on the enemy** donner l'assaut à l'ennemi; **yesterday the police launched an ~ on petty theft in the area** hier la police a lancé une opération contre les larcins dans le secteur; **the newspa-**

per launched an ~ on government policy le journal s'est attaqué à la politique gouvernementale; we made a new ~ on the problem nous avons abordé le problème d'une autre façon; the ~ on her life failed l'attentat contre elle a échoué; the ~ on drugs le combat contre la drogue; to return to the ~ revenir à la charge; to go on the ~ passer à l'attaque; the infantry was under ~ l'infanterie subissait un assaut OR était attaquée; to come under ~ être en butte aux attaques; she felt as though she were under ~ *fig* elle s'est sentie agressée; to leave o.s. wide open to ~ prêter le flanc à la critique. -**2.** [of illness] crise *f*; an ~ of malaria/nerves une crise de paludisme/de nerfs; an ~ of fever un accès de fièvre. -**3.** MUS attaque *f*.

attacker [əˈtækəʳ] *n* [gen] agresseur *m*, attaquant *m*, -e *f*; SPORT attaquant *m*.

attain [əˈteɪn] *vt* -**1.** [achieve - ambition, hopes, objectives] réaliser; [- happiness] atteindre à; [- independence, success] obtenir; [- knowledge] acquérir. -**2.** [arrive at, reach] atteindre, arriver à.

◆ **attain to** *vt insep*: to ~ to power arriver au pouvoir.

attainable [əˈteɪnəbl] *adj* [level, objective, profits] réalisable; [position] accessible; a growth rate ~ by industrialized countries un taux de croissance à la portée des OR accessible aux pays industrialisés.

attainment [əˈteɪnmənt] *n* -**1.** [of ambition, hopes, objectives] réalisation *f*; [of independence, success] obtention *f*; [of happiness] conquête *f*; [of knowledge] acquisition *f*. -**2.** [accomplishment] résultat *m* (obtenu); [knowledge, skill] connaissance *f*.

attempt [əˈtempt] ◇ *n* -**1.** [effort, try] tentative *f*, essai *m*, effort *m*; what do you think of my latest ~? que pensez-vous de mon dernier essai?; to make an ~ at doing sthg OR to do sthg essayer de faire qqch; she made an ~ at gardening elle a essayé le jardinage, elle s'est essayée au jardinage; we made our first ~ in January nous avons fait notre coup d'essai OR nous avons essayé pour la première fois en janvier; she made every ~ to put him at ease elle a tout fait pour le mettre à l'aise; he made no ~ to help il n'a rien fait pour (nous) aider; we made another ~ nous avons renouvelé nos tentatives, nous sommes revenus à la charge; no ~ will be made to stop you on n'essaiera pas de vous arrêter, on ne fera rien pour vous arrêter; he made an ~ on the record il a essayé de battre le record; he made a feeble ~ at a joke il a essayé de plaisanter sans y parvenir; he made it at the first ~ il a réussi du premier coup; I passed the test at my third ~ j'ai réussi l'examen la troisième fois; he was shot in an ~ to escape il fut tué lors d'une tentative d'évasion OR en essayant de s'évader; she gave up her ~ to convince him elle a renoncé à le convaincre; he went out without any ~ to conceal himself il est sorti sans chercher à se dissimuler. -**2.** [attack] attentat *m*; he survived the ~ on his life il a survécu à l'attentat perpétré contre lui.

◇ *vt* -**1.** [try] tenter, essayer; [undertake - job, task] entreprendre, s'attaquer à; he ~ed to cross the street, he ~ed crossing the street il a essayé de traverser la rue; she plans to ~ the record again in June elle a l'intention de s'attaquer de nouveau au record en juin; to ~ the impossible tenter l'impossible; he has already ~ed suicide once il a déjà fait une tentative de suicide. -**2.** [in mountaineering - ascent, climb] entreprendre; [- mountain] entreprendre l'escalade de.

attempted [əˈtemptɪd] *adj* tenté; ~ murder/suicide tentative *f* de meurtre/de suicide.

attend [əˈtend] ◇ *vt* -**1.** [go to - conference, meeting] assister à; [- church, school] aller à; will you be ~ing the meeting? assisterez-vous à la réunion?; she ~s the same course as me elle suit les mêmes cours que moi; I ~ed a private school j'ai fait mes études dans une école privée; the concert was well ~ed il y avait beaucoup de monde au concert. -**2.** [look after, care for] servir, être au service de; he was always ~ed by a manservant un valet de chambre l'accompagnait partout; a doctor ~ed the children un médecin a soigné les enfants. -**3.** *fml* [accompany] accompagner; serious consequences ~ such an action de telles actions entraînent de graves conséquences; the mission was ~ed by great difficulties la mission comportait de grandes difficultés.

◇ *vi* [be present] être présent; let us know if you are unable to ~ prévenez-nous si vous ne pouvez pas venir.

◆ **attend on** *vt insep* -**1.** [maid] servir, être au service de; [bodyguard] accompagner; [doctor] soigner; she ~ed upon her guests elle s'est occupée de ses invités. -**2.** *fml* [be consequence of] résulter de.

◆ **attend to** *vt insep* -**1.** [pay attention to] faire OR prêter attention à; she ~ed closely to the instructions elle a suivi les instructions attentivement. -**2.** [deal with - business, problem] s'occuper de; [- studies] s'appliquer à; [- customer] s'occuper de, servir; you'd better ~ to that wound vous feriez bien de (faire) soigner cette blessure; are you being ~ed to? [in shop] est-ce qu'on vous sert?, est-ce qu'on s'occupe de vous?

◆ **attend upon** = **attend on**.

attendance [əˈtendəns] ◇ *n* -**1.** [number of people present] assistance *f*; there was a record ~ of over 500 people il y avait plus de 500 personnes, ce qui est un record; a heavy OR large ~ une nombreuse assistance. -**2.** [presence] présence *f*; ~ at classes is obligatory la présence aux cours est obligatoire; his poor ~ made a bad impression ses nombreuses absences ont fait mauvaise impression; your ~ is requested vous êtes prié d'y assister; regular ~ assiduité *f*; will you be in ~? *fml* serez-vous là?, y assisterez-vous?; MED êtes-vous de service? -**3.** [service] service *m*; several servants were in ~ on her plusieurs domestiques l'escortaient OR l'accompagnaient.

◇ *comp* [record] d'appel; ~ sheet feuille *f* de présence.

attendance allowance *n Br allocation pour les handicapés.*

attendance centre *n Br maison de redressement où des délinquants assistent régulièrement à des réunions.*

attendant [əˈtendənt] ◇ *n* [in museum, park] gardien *m*, -enne *f*; [in petrol station] pompiste *mf*; [servant] domestique *mf*, serviteur *m arch*; the king and his ~s le roi et sa suite.

◇ *adj fml* -**1.** [person - accompanying] qui accompagne; [- on duty] en service; the salesman ~ on us was a Mr Jones le vendeur qui nous servait OR s'occupait de nous était un certain M. Jones. -**2.** [related]: there are some disadvantages ~ on working at home le travail à domicile comporte certains inconvénients; he talked about marriage and its ~ problems il parla du mariage et des problèmes qui l'accompagnent.

attention [əˈtenʃn] ◇ *n* -**1.** [concentration, thought] attention *f*; he wouldn't start until he had their full ~ il refusait de commencer tant qu'il n'avait pas toute leur attention; may I have your ~ for a moment? pourriez-vous m'accorder votre attention un instant?; we listened to him with close ~ nous l'avons écouté très attentivement; she knows how to hold an audience's ~ elle sait retenir l'attention d'un auditoire; they were all ~ ils étaient (tout yeux et) tout oreilles OR tout ouïe; to pay ~ prêter attention; he paid careful ~ to everything she said il a prêté une extrême attention à tout ce qu'elle disait; I paid little ~ to what she said j'ai accordé peu d'attention à OR j'ai fait peu de cas de ce qu'elle a dit; we paid no ~ to the survey nous n'avons tenu aucun compte de l'enquête; ~ to detail précision *f*, minutie *f*; she switched her ~ back to her book elle est retournée à son livre ❑ ~ span capacité *f* d'attention; children have a very short ~ span les enfants ne peuvent pas se concentrer longtemps. -**2.** [notice] attention *f*; he waved to attract OR catch our ~ il a fait un geste de la main pour attirer notre attention; the news came to his ~ il a appris la nouvelle; let me bring OR direct OR draw your ~ to the matter of punctuality permettez que j'attire votre attention sur le problème de la ponctualité; he drew ~ to the rise in unemployment il a attiré l'attention sur la montée du chômage; let us now turn our ~ to the population problem considérons maintenant le problème démographique; for the ~ of Mr Smith à l'attention de M. Smith; ~-seeking behaviour conduite dictée par le désir de se faire remarquer. -**3.** [care]: they need medical ~ ils ont besoin de soins médicaux; the furnace requires constant ~ la chaudière demande un entretien régulier. -**4.** MIL garde-à-vous *m inv*; to stand at/to come to ~ se tenir/se mettre au garde-à-vous.

◇ *interj*: ~! garde-à-vous!

◆ **attentions** *npl* attentions *fpl*, égards *mpl*; she felt irritated by his unwanted ~s elle était agacée par les attentions dont il l'entourait.

attentive [əˈtentɪv] *adj* -**1.** [paying attention] attentif; ~ to detail méticuleux. -**2.** [considerate] attentionné, prévenant; to be ~ to sb être prévenant envers qqn; she was ~ to our every need elle était attentive à tous nos besoins.

attentively [əˈtentɪvlɪ] *adv* -**1.** [listen, read] attentivement, avec attention. -**2.** [solicitously] avec beaucoup d'égards.

attentiveness [əˈtentɪvnɪs] *n* -**1.** [concentration] attention *f*. -**2.** [consideration] égards *mpl*, prévenance *f*.

attenuate [*vb* əˈtenjʊeɪt, *adj* əˈtenjʊɪt]

◇ *vt* -**1.** [attack, remark] atténuer, modérer; [pain] apaiser; attenuating circumstances des circonstances atténuantes. -**2.** [form, line] amincir, affiner. -**3.** [gas] raréfier.

◇ *vi* s'atténuer, diminuer.

◇ *adj* BOT atténué.

attenuation [əˌtenjʊˈeɪʃn] *n* -**1.** [of attack, remark] atténuation *f*, modération *f*; [of pain] atténuation *f*, apaisement *m*. -**2.** [of form] amincissement *m*.

attest [əˈtest] *fml* ◇ *vt* -**1.** [affirm] attester, certifier; [under oath] affirmer sous serment. -**2.** [be proof of] démontrer, témoigner de. -**3.** [bear witness to] témoigner; to ~ a signature légaliser une signature. -**4.** [put oath to] faire prêter serment à.

◇ *vi* témoigner, prêter serment; she ~ed to the truth of the report elle a témoigné de la véracité du rapport; to ~ to the honesty of sb se porter garant (de l'honnêteté) de qqn.

attestation [ˌæteˈsteɪʃn] *n fml* -**1.** [statement] attestation *f*; [in court] attestation *f*, témoignage *m*. -**2.** [proof] attestation *f*, preuve *f*. -**3.** [of signature] légalisation *f*. -**4.** [taking of oath] assermentation *f*, prestation *f* de serment.

attested milk [əˈtestɪd-] *n Br lait venant d'un cheptel certifié (comme ayant été tuberculinisé).*

attic [ˈætɪk] *n* [space] grenier *m*; [room] mansarde *f*.

Attic [ˈætɪk] ◇ *adj* attique.

◇ *n* LING attique *m*, dialecte *m* attique.

Attica [ˈætɪkə] *pr n* Attique *f*; in ~ en Attique.

Attila [ˈætɪlə] *pr n*: ~ the Hun Attila *m* roi des Huns.

attire [əˈtaɪəʳ] *fml* ◇ *n (U)* habits *mpl*, vêtements *mpl*; [formal] tenue *f*.

◇ *vt* vêtir, habiller, parer; she ~d herself in silk elle se vêtit de soie.

attitude [ˈætɪtjuːd] *n* -**1.** [way of thinking] attitude *f*, disposition *f*; what's your ~ to OR towards him? que pensez-vous de lui?; she took the ~ that... elle est partie du principe que...; an ~ of mind un état d'esprit; he has a very positive ~ of mind il a une attitude extrêmement positive; ~s towards homosexuality are changing les comportements à l'égard de l'homosexualité sont en train de changer. -**2.** [behaviour, manner] attitude *f*, manière *f*; I don't like your ~, young man je n'aime pas vos manières, jeune homme; **well, if that's your ~ you can go** eh bien, si c'est comme ça que tu le prends, tu peux t'en aller; **he's got an ~ problem** il a des problèmes relationnels. **-3.** *fml* [posture] attitude *f*, position *f*; **to strike an ~** poser, prendre une pose affectée. **-4.** *inf* [self-confidence] cran *m*.

attitudinize, -ise [ˌætɪ'tjuːdɪnaɪz] *vi pej* prendre des attitudes, poser.

attn (*written abbr of* for the attention of) attn, à l'attention de.

attorney [ə'tɜːnɪ] (*pl* attorneys) *n* **-1.** [representative] mandataire *mf*, représentant *m*, -e *f*. **-2.** *Am* [solicitor - for documents, sales] notaire *m*; [- for court cases] avocat *m*, -e *f*; [barrister] avocat *m*, -e *f*.

attorney-at-law *n Am* avocat *m*, -e *f*.

Attorney General (*pl* Attorneys General OR Attorney Generals) *n* [in England, Wales and Northern Ireland] *principal avocat de la couronne*; [in US] ≃ ministre *m* de la Justice.

attract [ə'trækt] ◇ *vt* **-1.** [draw, cause to come near] attirer; **the proposal ~ed a lot of attention/interest** la proposition a attiré l'attention/a éveillé l'intérêt de beaucoup de gens; **to ~ criticism** s'attirer des critiques; **we hope to ~ more young people to the church** nous espérons attirer davantage de jeunes à l'église. **-2.** [be attractive to] attirer, séduire, plaire; **she's ~ed to men with beards** elle est attirée par les barbus; **what is it that ~s you about skiing?** qu'est-ce qui vous plaît OR séduit dans le ski? ◇ *vi* s'attirer; **opposites ~** les contraires s'attirent.

attraction [ə'trækʃn] *n* **-1.** PHYS [pull] attraction *f*; *fig* attraction *f*, attirance *f*; **I don't understand your ~ for OR to her** je ne comprends pas ce qui te plaît chez OR en elle; **the idea holds no ~ for me** cette idée ne me dit rien. **-2.** [appeal - of place, plan] attrait *m*, fascination *f*; [- of person] charme *m*, charmes *mpl*; **it's the city's chief ~** c'est l'attrait principal de la ville; **the ~s of living in the country** les charmes de la vie à la campagne; **the main ~ of our show** le clou OR la grande attraction de notre spectacle; **a tourist ~** un site touristique.

attractive [ə'træktɪv] *adj* **-1.** [pretty - person, smile] séduisant; [- dress, picture] attrayant, beau. **-2.** [interesting - idea, price] intéressant; [- offer, opportunity] intéressant, attrayant. **-3.** PHYS [force] attractif.

attractively [ə'træktɪvlɪ] *adv* de manière attrayante; **to dress ~** s'habiller de façon séduisante; **the meal was very ~ presented** le repas était très agréablement présenté.

attractiveness [ə'træktɪvnɪs] *n* **-1.** [of person, smile] beauté *f*, charme *m*; [of dress, picture] beauté *f*. **-2.** [of idea, opportunity, price] intérêt *m*, attrait *m*. **-3.** PHYS attraction *f*.

attributable [ə'trɪbjʊtəbl] *adj* attribuable, imputable, dû; **the rise in price is entirely ~ to inflation** l'augmentation des prix est entièrement attribuable OR due à l'inflation.

attribute [*vb* ə'trɪbjuːt, *n* 'ætrɪbjuːt] ◇ *vt* [ascribe -accident, failure] attribuer, imputer; [- invention, painting, quotation] prêter, attribuer; [- success] attribuer; **to what do you ~ your success?** à quoi attribuez-vous votre réussite? ◇ *n* **-1.** [feature, quality] attribut *m*; [object] attribut *m*, emblème *m*. **-2.** LING & LOGIC attribut *m*.

attribution [ˌætrɪ'bjuːʃn] *n* attribution *f*.

attributive [ə'trɪbjʊtɪv] ◇ *n* attribut *m*.
◇ *adj* [gen & GRAMM] attributif.

attributively [ə'trɪbjʊtɪvlɪ] *adv* LING comme épithète.

attrition [ə'trɪʃn] *n* [wearing down] usure *f* (par friction); INDUST & RELIG attrition *f*.

attune [ə'tjuːn] *vt* MUS accorder; *fig* accorder, habituer; **her ideas are closely ~d to his** ses idées sont en parfait accord avec les siennes; **my ears are not really ~d to this modern music** mes oreilles ne sont pas vraiment habituées à cette musique moderne.

Atty. Gen. *written abbr of* Attorney General.

ATV *n* (*abbr of* all terrain vehicle) véhicule *m* tout terrain.

atypical [ˌeɪ'tɪpɪkl] *adj* atypique.

aubergine ['əʊbəʒiːn] *n Br* aubergine *f*.

aubretia [ɔː'briːʃə] *n* aubrietia *m*.

auburn ['ɔːbən] ◇ *adj* auburn *(inv)*.
◇ *n* (couleur *f*) auburn *m*.

auction ['ɔːkʃn] ◇ *n* (vente *f* aux) enchères *fpl*; **sold at OR by ~** vendu aux enchères; **to put sthg up for ~** mettre qqch en vente aux enchères; **they put the house up for ~** ils ont mis la maison en vente aux enchères.
◇ *vt*: **to ~ sthg (off)** vendre qqch aux enchères.

auction bridge *n* bridge *m* aux enchères.

auctioneer [ˌɔːkʃə'nɪəʳ] *n* commissaire-priseur *m*.

auction room *n* salle *f* des ventes.

audacious [ɔː'deɪʃəs] *adj* **-1.** [daring] audacieux, intrépide. **-2.** [impudent] effronté, impudent.

audaciously [ɔː'deɪʃəslɪ] *adv* **-1.** [boldly] audacieusement, avec audace. **-2.** [impudently] effrontément, impudemment.

audacity [ɔː'dæsətɪ] *n* **-1.** [daring] audace *f*, intrépidité *f*. **-2.** [impudence] effronterie *f*, impudence *f*; **he had the ~ to ask for a pay rise** il a eu l'audace de demander une augmentation (de salaire).

audibility [ˌɔːdɪ'bɪlətɪ] *n* audibilité *f*.

audible ['ɔːdəbl] *adj* [sound] audible, perceptible; [words] intelligible, distinct; **the music was barely ~** on entendait à peine la musique.

audibly ['ɔːdəblɪ] *adv* distinctement.

audience ['ɔːdjəns] ◇ *n* **-1.** [at film, match, play] spectateurs *mpl*, public *m*; [at concert, lecture] auditoire *m*, public *m*; [of author] lecteurs *mpl*; [of artist] public *m*; **someone in the ~ laughed** il y eut un rire dans la salle; **the ~ gave him a standing ovation** le public s'est levé pour l'ovationner; **was there a large ~ at the play?** y avait-il beaucoup de monde au théâtre?; **his books reach a wide ~** ses livres sont lus par beaucoup de gens. **-2.** RADIO auditeurs *mpl*, audience *f*; TV téléspectateurs *mpl*, audience *f*. **-3.** *fml* [meeting] audience *f*; **to grant sb an ~** accorder audience à qqn.
◇ *comp* [figures] de l'assistance, du public; **~ participation** participation *f* de l'assistance (à ce qui se passe sur la scène); **~ rating** indice *m* d'écoute; **~ research** études *fpl* d'audience.

audio ['ɔːdɪəʊ] ◇ *n* son *m*, acoustique *f*; **the ~ has gone** le son ne marche plus.
◇ *comp*: **~ cassette** cassette *f* audio; **~ equipment** équipement *m* acoustique; **~ recording** enregistrement *m* sonore; **~ system** système *m* audio.

audio frequency *n* audiofréquence *f*.

audiology [ˌɔːdɪ'ɒlədʒɪ] *n* audiologie *f*.

audiometer [ˌɔːdɪ'ɒmɪtəʳ] *n* audiomètre *m*.

audiophile ['ɔːdɪəʊfaɪl] *n* audiophile *mf*.

audio response *n* réponse *f* acoustique.

audiotyping ['ɔːdɪəʊˌtaɪpɪŋ] *n* audiotypie *f*.

audiotypist ['ɔːdɪəʊˌtaɪpɪst] *n* audiotypiste *mf*.

audiovisual [ˌɔːdɪəʊ'vɪzjʊəl] *adj* audiovisuel; **~ aids** supports *mpl* audiovisuels; **she teaches French using ~ methods** elle utilise l'audiovisuel OR des méthodes audiovisuelles pour enseigner le français.

audit ['ɔːdɪt] ◇ *n* vérification *f* des comptes, audit *m*.
◇ *vt* **-1.** [accounts] vérifier, apurer. **-2.** *Am* UNIV: **he ~s several courses** il assiste à plusieurs cours en tant qu'auditeur libre.

audition [ɔː'dɪʃn] ◇ *n* **-1.** THEAT audition *f*; CIN & TV (séance *f* d') essai *m*; **the director gave her an ~** THEAT le metteur en scène l'a auditionnée; CIN & TV le metteur en scène lui a fait faire un essai; **to hold ~s** THEAT organiser des auditions; CIN & TV organiser des essais; **to do an ~** passer une audition. **-2.** [hearing] ouïe *f*, audition *f*.
◇ *vt* THEAT auditionner; CIN & TV faire faire un essai à.
◇ *vi* THEAT [director] auditionner; [actor] passer une audition; CIN & TV faire un essai; **I ~ed for "Woyzeck"** THEAT j'ai passé une audition pour un rôle dans «Woyzeck»; CIN & TV j'ai fait un essai pour un rôle dans «Woyzeck».

auditor ['ɔːdɪtəʳ] *n* **-1.** [accountant] commissaire *m* aux comptes, auditeur *m*, -trice *f*, audit *m*. **-2.** *fml* [listener] auditeur *m*, -trice *f*. **-3.** *Am* [student] auditeur *m*, -trice *f* libre.

auditorium [ˌɔːdɪ'tɔːrɪəm] (*pl* auditoriums OR auditoria [-rɪə]) *n* **-1.** [of concert hall, theatre] salle *f*. **-2.** [large meeting room] amphithéâtre *m*.

auditory ['ɔːdɪtrɪ] *adj* auditif; **~ phonetics** phonétique *f* auditoire.

audit trail *n* COMPUT protocole *m* de vérification OR de contrôle.

AUEW (*abbr of* Amalgamated Union of Engineering Workers) *pr n ancien syndicat britannique de l'industrie mécanique, aujourd'hui remplacée par l'AEEU*.

au fait [ˌəʊ'feɪ] *adj*: **to be ~ with sthg** être au courant de qqch.

Aug. *written abbr of* August.

Augean [ɔː'dʒiːən] *adj* [filthy] crasseux, dégoûtant; [corrupt] corrompu; **the ~ stables** les écuries *fpl* d'Augias.

auger ['ɔːgəʳ] *n* [hand tool] vrille *f*; TECH foreuse *f*.

aught [ɔːt] *arch* OR *lit* ◇ *pron* ce que; **for ~ I know** (pour) autant que je sache; **for ~ I care** pour ce que cela me fait.
◇ *n* zéro *m*.

augment [ɔːg'ment] ◇ *vt* **-1.** [increase] augmenter, accroître; **her salary is ~ed by OR with gratuities** à son salaire s'ajoutent les pourboires. **-2.** MUS augmenter.
◇ *vi* augmenter, s'accroître.

augmentation [ˌɔːgmen'teɪʃn] *n* **-1.** [increase] augmentation *f*, accroissement *m*. **-2.** MUS augmentation *f*.

augmentative [ɔːg'mentətɪv] *adj* augmentatif.

augmented [ɔːg'mentɪd] *adj* augmenté.

augur ['ɔːgəʳ] ◇ *vi*: **this weather ~s ill/well for our holiday** ce temps est de mauvais/bon augure pour nos vacances.
◇ *vt* [predict] prédire, prévoir; [be omen of] présager; **the situation ~s nothing good** la situation ne présage rien de bon.
◇ *n* augure *m*.

augury ['ɔːgjʊrɪ] (*pl* auguries) *n* **-1.** [art] art *m* augural; [rite] rite *m* augural. **-2.** [omen] augure *m*, présage *m*; [prediction] prédiction *f*.

august [ɔː'gʌst] *adj lit* [dignified] auguste, vénérable; [noble] noble.

August ['ɔːgəst] *n* août *m*; **~ Bank Holiday** *jour férié tombant le dernier lundi d'août en Angleterre et au pays de Galles, le premier lundi d'août en Écosse*.

Augustan [ɔː'gʌstən] *adj* d'Auguste; **the ~ Period** LITERAT [Roman] l'époque *f* d'Auguste; [modern] l'époque néoclassique.

Augustine [ɔː'gʌstɪn] *pr n*: **Saint ~** saint Augustin.

Augustinian [ˌɔːgə'stɪnɪən] ◇ *adj* augustinien, de saint Augustin.
◇ *n* [follower] augustinien *m*; [monk] augustin *m*.

Augustus [ɔː'gʌstəs] *pr n* Auguste.

auk [ɔːk] *n* pingouin *m*.

Auld Lang Syne [ˌɔːldlæŋ'saɪn] *pr n chanson sur l'air de «ce n'est qu'un au revoir» que l'on chante à minuit le soir du 31 décembre en Grande-Bretagne*.

aunt [ɑːnt] *n* tante *f*.

auntie *inf* ['ɑːntɪ] *n Br* tantine *f*, tata *f*, tatie *f*; **~ Susan** tante Susan.
◆ **Auntie** *inf pr n Br surnom affectueux de la BBC, perçue comme une vieille tante détentrice des valeurs morales*.

Aunt Sally [-'sælɪ] (*pl* Aunt Sallies) *n Br* [at fairground] ≃ jeu *m* de massacre; *fig* [person] tête *f* de Turc.

aunty ['ɑːntɪ] (*pl* aunties) = **auntie**.
au pair [,əʊ'peəʳ] (*pl* au pairs) ◇ *n* (jeune fille *f*) au pair *f*.
◇ *adj* au pair.
◇ *adv*: to work ~ travailler au pair.
◇ *vi* travailler au pair.
aura ['ɔːrə] (*pl* auras OR aurae ['ɔːriː]) *n* -**1.** [of person] aura *f*, émanation *f*; [of place] atmosphère *f*, ambiance *f*; there's an ~ of mystery about her il y a quelque chose de mystérieux chez elle. -**2.** MED aura *f*.
aural ['ɔːrəl] *adj* -**1.** [relating to hearing] auditif, sonore; ~ comprehension compréhension *f* orale; ~ skills aptitudes *fpl* à la compréhension orale. -**2.** [relating to the ear] auriculaire.
aureole ['ɔːrɪəʊl] *n* auréole *f*.
auricle ['ɔːrɪkl] *n* -**1.** [of ear] pavillon *m* auriculaire. -**2.** [of heart] oreillette *f*.
auricular [ɔː'rɪkjʊləʳ] *adj* auriculaire.
aurochs ['ɔːrɒks] (*pl inv*) *n* aurochs *m*.
aurora [ɔː'rɔːrə] (*pl* auroras OR aurorae [-riː]) *n* aurore *f*.
◆ **Aurora** *pr n* MYTH Aurore.
aurora australis [-ɒ'streɪlɪs] *n* aurore *f* australe.
aurora borealis [-,bɔːrɪ'eɪlɪs] *n* aurore *f* boréale.
auscultation [,ɔːskəl'teɪʃn] *n* auscultation *f*.
auspices ['ɔːspɪsɪz] *npl*: under the ~ of the UN sous les auspices de l'ONU.
auspicious [ɔː'spɪʃəs] *adj* [event, start, occasion] propice, favorable; [sign] de bon augure; we made an ~ beginning nous avons pris un bon départ.
auspiciously [ɔː'spɪʃəslɪ] *adv* favorablement, sous d'heureux auspices; the meeting began ~ la réunion a bien commencé.
Aussie *inf* ['ɒzɪ] ◇ *n* Australien *m*, -enne *f*.
◇ *adj* australien.
austere [ɒ'stɪəʳ] *adj* -**1.** [person] austère, sévère; [life] austère, sobre, ascétique. -**2.** [design, interior] austère, sobre.
austerely [ɒ'stɪəlɪ] *adv* -**1.** [live] austèrement, avec austérité, comme un ascète. -**2.** [dress, furnish] austèrement, avec austérité, sobrement.
austerity [ɒ'sterətɪ] (*pl* austerities) ◇ *n* -**1.** [simplicity] austérité *f*, sobriété *f*. -**2.** [hardship] austérité *f*; a period of ~ une période d'austérité, des temps difficiles. -**3.** (*usu pl*) [practice] austérité *f*, pratique *f* austère.
◇ *comp* [budget, measure] d'austérité.
Australasia [,ɒstrə'leɪʒjə] *pr n* Australasie *f*; in ~ en Australasie.
Australasian [,ɒstrə'leɪʒn] ◇ *n* natif *m*, -ive *f* de l'Australasie.
◇ *adj* d'Australasie.
Australia [ɒ'streɪljə] *pr n* Australie *f*; in ~ en Australie; South ~ Australie-Méridionale *f*; Western ~ Australie-Occidentale *f*; the Commonwealth of ~ l'Australie.
Australia Day *n premier lundi suivant le 26 janvier (commémorant l'arrivée des Britanniques en Australie en 1788)*.
Australian [ɒ'streɪljən] ◇ *n* -**1.** [person] Australien *m*, -enne *f*. -**2.** LING australien *m*.
◇ *adj* australien; the ~ Alps les Alpes *fpl* australiennes.
Australian Antarctic Territory *pr n* Antarctique *f* australienne.
Australian Capital Territory *pr n* Territoire *m* fédéral de Canberra.
Australianize, -ise [ɒ'streɪljənaɪz] *vt* donner un caractère australien à.
Australian Rules (football) *n jeu ressemblant au rugby*.
Austral Islands ['ɔːstrəl-] *pl pr n*: the ~ les îles *fpl* Australes; in the ~ aux îles Australes.
Australoid ['ɒstrəlɔɪd] ◇ *adj* australoïde.
◇ *n* australoïde *mf*.
Austria ['ɒstrɪə] *pr n* Autriche *f*; in ~ en Autriche.
Austria-Hungary *pr n* Autriche-Hongrie *f*.
Austrian ['ɒstrɪən] ◇ *n* Autrichien *m*, -enne *f*.
◇ *adj* autrichien.
Austro-Hungarian [,ɒstrəʊ-] *adj* austro-hongrois.
AUT (*abbr of* Association of University Teachers) *pr n syndicat d'enseignants universitaires*.
autarchy ['ɔːtɑːkɪ] (*pl* autarchies) *n* -**1.** = **autocracy**. -**2.** [self-rule] autocratie *f*.
autarky ['ɔːtɑːkɪ] (*pl* autarkies) *n* -**1.** [system] autarcie *f*. -**2.** [country] pays *m* en autarcie.
authentic [ɔː'θentɪk] *adj* [genuine] authentique; [accurate, reliable] authentique, véridique; each document being ~ JUR chaque texte faisant foi.
authentically [ɔː'θentɪklɪ] *adv* de façon authentique.
authenticate [ɔː'θentɪkeɪt] *vt* [painting] établir l'authenticité de; [signature] légaliser.
authentication [ɔː,θentɪ'keɪʃn] *n* authentification *f*, certification *f*.
authenticity [,ɔːθen'tɪsətɪ] *n* authenticité *f*.
author ['ɔːθəʳ] ◇ *n* -**1.** [writer] auteur *m*, écrivain *m*; have you ever read this ~? avez-vous déjà lu des livres de cet auteur? -**2.** [of idea, plan] auteur *m*; [of painting, sculpture] auteur *m*, créateur *m*.
◇ *vt* être l'auteur de.
authoress ['ɔːθərɪs] *n* -**1.** [writer] *femme auteur d'ouvrages s'adressant au grand public*. -**2.** [of idea, plan] auteur *m*; [of painting, sculpture] auteur *m*, créatrice *f*.
authoritarian [ɔː,θɒrɪ'teərɪən] ◇ *adj* autoritaire.
◇ *n* personne *f* autoritaire; the boss is a strict ~ le patron est très autoritaire OR croit ferme à l'autorité.
authoritative [ɔː'θɒrɪtətɪv] *adj* -**1.** [manner, person] autoritaire. -**2.** [article, report] qui fait autorité. -**3.** [official] autorisé, officiel.
authoritatively [ɔː'θɒrɪtətɪvlɪ] *adv* avec autorité, de manière autoritaire *pej*.
authority [ɔː'θɒrətɪ] (*pl* authorities) *n* -**1.** [power] autorité *f*, pouvoir *m*; who's in ~ here? où est le patron?; she has ~ OR she is in ~ over all the staff elle a autorité sur tout le personnel; he made his ~ felt il faisait sentir son autorité; those in ~ in Haiti ceux qui gouvernent Haïti. -**2.** [forcefulness] autorité *f*, assurance *f*; "no!" he said with ~ «non!» dit-il avec autorité; her conviction gave ~ to her argument sa conviction a donné du poids à son raisonnement; his opinions carry a lot of ~ ses opinions font autorité. -**3.** [permission] autorisation *f*, droit *m*; who gave him (the) ~ to enter? qui lui a donné l'autorisation d'entrer?, qui l'a autorisé à entrer?; they had no ~ to answer ils n'étaient pas habilités à répondre; I decided on my own ~ j'ai décidé de ma propre autorité OR de mon propre chef; on his ~ avec son autorisation; without ~ sans autorisation. -**4.** (*usu pl*) [people in command] autorité *f*; the authorities les autorités, l'administration *f*; the proper authorities qui de droit, les autorités compétentes; the education/housing ~ *services chargés de l'éducation/du logement*; we'll go to the highest ~ in the land nous nous adresserons aux plus hautes instances du pays. -**5.** [expert] autorité *f*, expert *m*; [article, book] autorité *f*; he's an ~ on China c'est un grand spécialiste de la Chine. -**6.** [testimony]: I have it on his ~ that she was there il m'a certifié qu'elle était présente; we have it on good ~ that... nous tenons de source sûre OR de bonne source que.. -**7.** [permit] autorisation *f*.
authorization [,ɔːθəraɪ'zeɪʃn] *n* [act, permission] autorisation *f*; [official sanction] pouvoir *m*, mandat *m*; he has ~ to leave the country il est autorisé à quitter le pays; you can't do anything without ~ from the management vous ne pouvez rien faire sans l'autorisation de la direction.
authorize, -ise ['ɔːθəraɪz] *vt* -**1.** [empower] autoriser; she is ~d to act for her father elle a pouvoir de représenter son père, elle est autorisée à représenter son père. -**2.** [sanction] autoriser, sanctionner; to ~ a loan consentir un prêt; to ~ a drug for the market JUR homologuer un médicament.
authorized ['ɔːθəraɪzd] *adj* autorisé; ~ dealer COMM distributeur *m* agréé; ~ capital FIN capital *m* social OR nominal; duly ~ officer FIN & JUR représentant *m* dûment habilité.
Authorized Version *n*: the ~ *la version anglaise de la Bible de 1611 «autorisée» par le roi Jacques Ier d'Angleterre*.
authorship ['ɔːθəʃɪp] *n* -**1.** [of book] auteur *m*, paternité *f*; a work of unknown ~ un ouvrage OR une œuvre anonyme; they have established the ~ of the book ils ont identifié l'auteur du livre; he claimed ~ of the invention il a revendiqué la paternité de l'invention. -**2.** [profession] profession *f* d'auteur OR d'écrivain.
autism ['ɔːtɪzm] *n* autisme *m*.
autistic [ɔː'tɪstɪk] *adj* autiste.
auto *inf* ['ɔːtəʊ] *Am* ◇ *n* voiture *f*, auto *f*.
◇ *comp* d'auto, automobile; ~ accident accident *m* de voiture; ~ industry industrie *f* automobile; ~ parts pièces *fpl* détachées (pour voiture).
autobank ['ɔːtəʊ,bæŋk] *n* distributeur *m* automatique de billets (de banque).
autobiographic(al) ['ɔːtə,baɪə'græfɪk(l)] *adj* autobiographique.
autobiography [,ɔːtəbaɪ'ɒgrəfɪ] *n* autobiographie *f*.
autocade ['ɔːtəʊkeɪd] *n Am* cortège *m* d'automobiles.
autoclave ['ɔːtəʊkleɪv] *n* autoclave *m*.
autocracy [ɔː'tɒkrəsɪ] (*pl* autocracies) *n* autocratie *f*.
autocrat ['ɔːtəkræt] *n* autocrate *m*.
autocratic [,ɔːtə'krætɪk] *adj* autocratique.
autocross ['ɔːtəʊkrɒs] *n* autocross *m*.
Autocue® ['ɔːtəʊkjuː] *n Br* téléprompteur *m*.
auto-da-fé [,ɔːtəʊdɑː'feɪ] (*pl* autos-da-fé [,ɔːtəʊz-]) *n* autodafé *m*.
autodestruct [,ɔːtəʊdɪ'strʌkt] ◇ *vi* s'autodétruire.
◇ *adj* qui s'autodétruit.
autodidact ['ɔːtəʊdɪdækt] *n* autodidacte *mf*.
autoeroticism [,ɔːtəʊɪ'rɒtɪsɪzm], **autoerotism** [,ɔːtəʊ'erətɪzm] *n* autoérotisme *m*.
autogamous [ɔː'tɒgəməs] *adj* autogame.
autogenous [ɔː'tɒdʒənəs] *adj* autogène; ~ training training *m* autogène, autorelaxation *f*.
autogiro [,ɔːtəʊ'dʒaɪərəʊ] *n* autogire *m*.
autograph ['ɔːtəgrɑːf] ◇ *n* autographe *m*.
◇ *vt* [book, picture, record] dédicacer; [letter, object] signer.
◇ *comp* [letter] autographe; ~ album album *m* OR livre *m* d'autographes; ~ hunter *Br* OR hound *Am* collectionneur *m*, -euse *f* d'autographes.
autohypnosis [,ɔːtəʊhɪp'nəʊsɪs] *n* autohypnose *f*.
autoimmune [,ɔːtəʊɪ'mjuːn] *adj* auto-immun; ~ disease maladie *f* auto-immune.
autoimmunity [,ɔːtəʊɪ'mjuːnətɪ] *n* autoimmunisation *f*.
autoinfection [,ɔːtəʊɪn'fekʃn] *n* autoinfection *f*.
automat ['ɔːtəmæt] *n* [machine] distributeur *m* automatique; *Am* [room] cafétéria *f* équipée de distributeurs automatiques.
automata [ɔː'tɒmətə] *pl* → **automaton**.
automate ['ɔːtəmeɪt] *vt* automatiser.
automated ['ɔːtəmeɪtɪd] *adj* automatisé; ~ telling machine, ~ teller distributeur *m* automatique (de billets).
automatic [,ɔːtə'mætɪk] ◇ *adj* [machine] automatique; [answer, smile] automatique, machinal; ~ data processing COMPUT traitement *m* automatique des données; ~ pistol pistolet *m* automatique, automatique *m*.
◇ *n* -**1.** [weapon] automatique *m*. -**2.** AUT voiture *f* à boîte OR à transmission automatique; a Volkswagen ~ une Volkswagen à boîte OR à transmission automatique.

automatically [ˌɔːtəˈmætɪklɪ] *adv literal* automatiquement; *fig* automatiquement, machinalement; **teachers are ~ retired at age 65** les enseignants sont mis à la retraite d'office à l'âge de 65 ans; **~ void** JUR nul de plein droit; **I just ~ assumed he was right** j'ai automatiquement supposé qu'il avait raison.

automatic pilot *n* pilote *m* automatique; **on ~** en pilotage automatique; **I just went on to ~** *fig* j'ai poursuivi machinalement.

automation [ˌɔːtəˈmeɪʃn] *n* [process of making automatic] automatisation *f*; [state of being automatic] automation *f*; **factory** OR **industrial ~** productique *f*.

automatism [ɔːˈtɒmətɪzm] *n* automatisme *m*.

automatize, -ise [ɔːˈtɒmətaɪz] *vt* automatiser.

automaton [ɔːˈtɒmətən] (*pl* **automatons** OR **automata** [-tə]) *n* automate *m*.

automobile [ˈɔːtəməbiːl] *n Am* automobile *f*, voiture *f*.

automotive [ˌɔːtəˈməʊtɪv] *adj* **-1.** AUT [engineering, industry] (de l') automobile. **-2.** [self-propelled] automoteur.

autonomic [ˌɔːtəˈnɒmɪk] *adj* autonome.

autonomous [ɔːˈtɒnəməs] *adj* autonome.

autonomy [ɔːˈtɒnəmɪ] (*pl* **autonomies**) *n* **-1.** [self-government] autonomie *f*. **-2.** [country] pays *m* autonome.

autopilot [ˌɔːtəʊˈpaɪlət] = **automatic pilot**.

autopsy [ˈɔːtɒpsɪ] (*pl* **autopsies**) *n* autopsie *f*.

autosuggestion [ˌɔːtəʊsəˈdʒestʃn] *n* autosuggestion *f*.

autotimer [ˈɔːtəʊˌtaɪməʳ] *n* programmateur *m*.

autowinder [ˈɔːtəʊˌwaɪndəʳ] *n* avance *f* automatique du film.

autumn [ˈɔːtəm] ◇ *n* automne *m*; **in (the) ~** en automne.
◇ *comp* [colours, flowers, weather] d'automne, automnal; **~ leaves** [on tree] feuilles *fpl* d'automne; [dead] feuilles *fpl* mortes.

autumnal [ɔːˈtʌmnəl] *adj* automnal, d'automne.

Auvergne [əʊˈveən] *pr n* Auvergne *f*; **in ~** en Auvergne.

auxiliary [ɔːɡˈzɪljərɪ] (*pl* **auxiliaries**) ◇ *adj* auxiliaire, supplémentaire; **~ staff** [gen] le personnel auxiliaire, les auxiliaires *mpl*; *Br* SCH personnel *m* auxiliaire non enseignant.
◇ *n* **-1.** [assistant, subordinate] auxiliaire *mf*; **nursing ~** infirmier *m*, -ère *f* auxiliaire, aide-soignant *m*, -e *f*. **-2.** MIL: **auxiliaries** auxiliaires *mpl*. **-3.** GRAMM (verbe *m*) auxiliaire *m*.

auxiliary verb *n* (verbe *m*) auxiliaire *m*.

Av. (*written abbr of* avenue) av.

AV *n abbr of* Authorized Version.

avail [əˈveɪl] ◇ *n*: **of no ~**: **it is of no ~ to complain** il est inutile de se plaindre; **his efforts were of no ~** ses efforts n'ont eu aucun effet; **to no ~** sans effet; **they argued with her to no ~** ils ont essayé en vain de la convaincre; **to little ~** sans grand effet; **we tried but it was to little ~** nous avons essayé mais cela n'a pas servi à grand-chose.
◇ *vt*: **to ~ o.s. of sthg** se servir OR profiter de qqch; **I ~ed myself of the opportunity to thank her** j'ai profité de l'occasion pour OR j'ai saisi cette occasion de la remercier.
◇ *vi lit* servir; **nothing could ~ against the storm** rien ne s'avéra efficace contre l'orage.

availability [əˌveɪləˈbɪlətɪ] (*pl* **availabilities**) *n* **-1.** [accessibility] disponibilité *f*. **-2.** *Am pej* & POL [of candidate] caractère *m* valable.

available [əˈveɪləbl] *adj* **-1.** [accessible, to hand] disponible; **they made the data ~ to us** ils ont mis les données à notre disposition; **we tried every ~ means** nous avons essayé (par) tous les moyens possibles; **they're ~ in three sizes** ils sont disponibles en trois tailles. **-2.** [free] libre, disponible; **the minister in charge was not ~ for comment** le ministre responsable s'est refusé à toute déclaration; **were there any ~ men at the party?** est-ce qu'il y avait des hommes disponibles OR libres à la soirée? **-3.** *Am pej* & POL [candidate] valable *(à cause de son caractère inoffensif)*.

avalanche [ˈævəlɑːnʃ] ◇ *n literal* & *fig* avalanche *f*.
◇ *vi* tomber en avalanche.

avant-garde [ˌævɒŋˈɡɑːd] ◇ *n* avant-garde *f*.
◇ *adj* d'avant-garde, avant-gardiste.

avarice [ˈævərɪs] *n* avarice *f*, pingrerie *f*.

avaricious [ˌævəˈrɪʃəs] *adj* avare, pingre.

avatar [ˌævəˈtɑːʳ] *n* RELIG avatar *m*; *fig* manifestation *f*.

avdp. *written abbr of* avoirdupoids.

Ave. (*written abbr of* avenue) av.

Ave (Maria) [ˈɑːvɪ(məˈrɪə)] *n* Ave *m* (Maria) *(inv)*.

avenge [əˈvendʒ] *vt* venger; **he ~d his brother's death** il a vengé la mort de son frère; **he intends to ~ himself on his enemy** il a l'intention de se venger de OR de prendre sa revanche sur son ennemi.

avenger [əˈvendʒəʳ] *n* vengeur *m*, -eresse *f*; **'The Avengers'** [TV series] 'Chapeau melon et bottes de cuir'.

avenging [əˈvendʒɪŋ] *adj* vengeur; **an ~ angel** un ange exterminateur.

Aventine Hill [ˈævənˌtaɪn-] *pr n*: **the ~** le mont Aventin.

avenue [ˈævənjuː] *n* **-1.** [public] avenue *f*, boulevard *m*; [private] avenue *f*, allée *f (bordée d'arbres)*. **-2.** *fig* possibilité *f*; **we must explore every ~** il faut explorer toutes les possibilités.

aver [əˈvɜːʳ] (*pt* & *pp* **averred**, *cont* **averring**) *vi fml* affirmer, déclarer.

average [ˈævərɪdʒ] ◇ *n* **-1.** [standard amount, quality] moyenne *f*; **an ~ of 4 to 6 years** une moyenne de 4 à 6 ans; **above/below ~** au-dessus/au-dessous de la moyenne; **on (an** OR **the) ~** en moyenne; **we travelled an ~ of 100 miles a day** nous avons fait une moyenne de 100 miles par jour OR 100 miles par jour en moyenne; **the law of ~s** la loi de la probabilité. **-2.** MATH moyenne *f*.
◇ *adj* moyen; **of ~ intelligence/size** d'intelligence/de taille moyenne; **ask the ~ man in the street** demandez à l'homme de la rue; **the film was just ~** le film était moyen.
◇ *vt* **-1.** MATH établir OR faire la moyenne de. **-2.** [perform typical number of] atteindre la moyenne de; **the factory ~s 10 machines a day** l'usine produit en moyenne 10 machines par jour; **we ~ two letters a day** nous recevons en moyenne deux lettres par jour; **he ~d 100 km/h** AUT il a fait du 100 km/h de moyenne. **-3.** [divide up] partager; **the company ~s the profits among the staff** la firme distribue OR répartit les bénéfices entre le personnel.
◆ **average out** ◇ *vi insep*: **profits ~ out at 10%** les bénéfices s'élèvent en moyenne à 10 %; **factory production ~s out at 120 cars a day** l'usine produit en moyenne 120 voitures par jour.
◇ *vt sep* faire la moyenne de.

averse [əˈvɜːs] *adj*: **she's not ~ to the occasional glass of wine** elle boit volontiers un verre de vin de temps à autre; **he's not ~ to making money out of the crisis** ça ne le gêne pas de profiter de la crise pour se faire de l'argent.

aversion [əˈvɜːʃn] *n* **-1.** [dislike] aversion *f*; **to have an ~ to** avoir une aversion pour OR contre; **she has an ~ to smoking** elle a horreur du tabac; **I have an ~ to his brother** je ne supporte pas son frère, son frère m'est insupportable; **he has a strong ~ to travelling** il déteste voyager. **-2.** [object of dislike] objet *m* d'aversion; **my pet ~ is housework** *Br* ma bête noire OR ce que je déteste le plus, c'est le ménage.

aversion therapy *n* thérapie *f* d'aversion.

avert [əˈvɜːt] *vt* **-1.** [prevent] prévenir, éviter. **-2.** [turn aside - eyes, thoughts] détourner; [- blow] détourner, parer; [- suspicion] écarter; **I ~ed my gaze** j'ai détourné les yeux.

aviary [ˈeɪvjərɪ] (*pl* **aviaries**) *n* volière *f*.

aviation [ˌeɪvɪˈeɪʃn] ◇ *n* aviation *f*.
◇ *comp* [design, studio] d'aviation; **the ~ industry** l'aéronautique *f*; **~ fuel** kérosène *m*.

aviator [ˈeɪvɪeɪtəʳ] ◇ *n* aviateur *m*, -trice *f*, pilote *m*.
◇ *comp*: **~ glasses** lunettes *fpl* de sport.

aviculture [ˈeɪvɪˌkʌltʃə] *n* aviculture *f*.

avid [ˈævɪd] *adj* avide; **~ for revenge** avide de revanche; **~ to learn** avide d'apprendre.

avidity [əˈvɪdətɪ] *n* avidité *f*.

avidly [ˈævɪdlɪ] *adv* avidement, avec avidité.

avionics [ˌeɪvɪˈɒnɪks] ◇ *n (U)* [science] avionique *f*.
◇ *npl* [instruments] avionique *f*.

avocado [ˌævəˈkɑːdəʊ] (*pl* **avocados** OR **avocadoes**) *n* [fruit]: **~ (pear)** avocat *m*; [tree] avocatier *m*.

avocation [ˌævəˈkeɪʃən] *n Am* activité *f* de loisir.

avocet [ˈævəˌset] *n* avocette *f*.

avoid [əˈvɔɪd] *vt* **-1.** [object, person] éviter; [danger, task] éviter, échapper à; **she ~ed my eyes** elle évita mon regard; **we can't ~ inviting them** nous ne pouvons pas faire autrement que de les inviter; **they couldn't ~ hitting the car** ils n'ont pas pu éviter la voiture; **~ giving them too much information** évitez de leur donner trop d'informations; **don't ~ the issue** n'essaie pas d'éviter OR d'éluder la question; **to ~ (paying) taxes** [legally] se soustraire à l'impôt; [illegally] frauder le fisc ☐ **I ~ him like the plague** je le fuis comme la peste. **-2.** JUR [void] annuler, rendre nul.

avoidable [əˈvɔɪdəbl] *adj* évitable.

avoidance [əˈvɔɪdəns] *n*: **~ of work** le soin que l'on met à éviter le travail; **~ of duty** manquements *mpl* au devoir ☐ **tax ~** évasion *f* fiscale.

avoirdupois [ˌævədəˈpɔɪz] ◇ *n* **-1.** [system] avoirdupoids *m*. **-2.** *Am* [of person] embonpoint *m*.
◇ *comp* [ounce, pound] *conforme aux poids et mesures officiellement établis*; **~ ounce** once *f (28,35 grammes)*; **~ weight** avoirdupoids *m*.

avow [əˈvaʊ] *vt fml* [state] affirmer, déclarer; [admit] admettre, reconnaître, confesser; **he openly ~ed himself a communist** il a ouvertement reconnu qu'il était communiste.

avowal [əˈvaʊəl] *n* aveu *m*.

avowed [əˈvaʊd] *adj* déclaré; **she's an ~ feminist** elle avoue OR reconnaît être féministe.

avowedly [əˈvaʊɪdlɪ] *adv* de son propre aveu.

AVP (*abbr of* assistant vice-president) *n vice-président adjoint*.

avuncular [əˈvʌŋkjʊləʳ] *adj* avunculaire.

aw [ɔː] *interj Am*: **~!** oh!

AWACS [ˈeɪwæks] (*abbr of* airborne warning and control system) *n* AWACS *m*.

await [əˈweɪt] *vt* **-1.** [wait for] attendre; **a long-~ed holiday** des vacances qui se sont fait attendre; **mail ~ing delivery** courrier *m* en souffrance; **she's ~ing trial** elle est dans l'attente de son procès. **-2.** [be in store for] attendre, être réservé à; **a warm welcome ~ed them** un accueil chaleureux leur fut réservé; **who knows what may ~ us** qui sait ce qui nous attend OR est réservé.

awake [əˈweɪk] (*pt* **awoke** [əˈwəʊk], *pp* **awoken** [əˈwəʊkn]) ◇ *adj* **-1.** [not sleeping] éveillé, réveillé; **to be ~** être réveillé, ne pas dormir; **are you still ~?** tu ne dors pas encore?, tu n'es pas encore endormi?; **the noise kept me ~** le bruit m'a empêché de dormir; **I lay ~ all night** je n'ai pas fermé l'œil de la nuit; **his mother stayed ~ all night** sa mère a veillé toute la nuit; **he was wide ~** il était bien éveillé. **-2.** [aware] attentif, vigilant; **we're all ~ to the dangers of our situation** nous sommes tous conscients des dangers de notre situation; **is the minister ~ to the dangers inherent to the system?** le ministre a-t-il conscience OR se rend-il compte des dangers inhérents au système?
◇ *vi* **-1.** [emerge from sleep] se réveiller, s'éveiller; **I awoke from a deep sleep** je suis sorti OR je me suis réveillé d'un sommeil profond. **-2.** [become aware] prendre conscience, se ren-

dre compte; he finally awoke from his illusions il est enfin revenu de ses illusions.
◇ *vt* -**1.** [person] réveiller, éveiller. -**2.** *fig* [curiosity, suspicions] éveiller; [memories] réveiller, faire renaître; [hope] éveiller, faire naître.

awaken [əˈweɪkən] ◇ *vt* éveiller.
◇ *vi* s'éveiller.

awakening [əˈweɪknɪŋ] ◇ *n* -**1.** *literal* & *fig* [arousal] réveil *m*; it was a rude ~ c'était un réveil brutal OR pénible □ 'Spring Awakening' *Wedekind* 'l'Éveil du printemps'. -**2.** [beginning] début *m*, commencement *m*.
◇ *adj* naissant.

award [əˈwɔːd] ◇ *n* -**1.** [prize] prix *m*; [medal] médaille *f*; ~ for bravery décoration *f*, médaille *f*. -**2.** [scholarship] bourse *f*. -**3.** JUR [damages] dommages-intérêts *mpl* accordés par le juge; [decision] décision *f*, sentence *f* (arbitrale). -**4.** *Austr* & *NZ* [minimum wage]: ~ (wage) ≃ salaire *m* minimum interprofessionnel de croissance, SMIC *m*.
◇ *vt* [give - mark] accorder; [- medal, prize] décerner, attribuer; [- scholarship] attribuer, allouer; JUR [- damages] accorder.

award-winning *adj* qui a reçu un prix; he gave an ~ performance in... il a reçu un prix pour son rôle dans...

aware [əˈweəʳ] *adj* -**1.** [cognizant, conscious] conscient; [informed] au courant, informé; to be ~ of sthg être conscient de qqch; are you ~ of the problems? êtes-vous conscient des problèmes?; I am quite ~ of his feelings je connais OR je n'ignore pas ses sentiments; he's well ~ of the risks il sait très bien quels sont les risques; to become ~ of sthg se rendre compte OR prendre conscience de qqch; she made us ~ of the problem elle nous a fait prendre conscience du problème; as far as I am ~ autant que je sache; not that I am ~ of pas que je sache; without being ~ of it sans s'en rendre compte; politically ~ politisé; socially ~ au courant des problèmes sociaux. -**2.** [sensitive] sensible.

awareness [əˈweənɪs] *n* conscience *f*; a heightened ~ of colour une sensibilité plus aiguë à la couleur; political ~ politisation *f*.

awash [əˈwɒʃ] *adj* -**1.** *literal* & *fig* [flooded] inondé; ~ with oil inondé de pétrole. -**2.** NAUT à fleur d'eau, qui affleure.

away [əˈweɪ] ◇ *adv* -**1.** [indicating movement]: he drove ~ il s'est éloigné (en voiture); he walked ~ il s'est éloigné (à pied); they're ~! [at start of race] ils sont partis! ‖ [indicating position]: the village is 10 miles ~ le village est à 10 miles; ~ in the distance au loin, dans le lointain; ~ over there beyond the mountains là-bas, bien loin au-delà des montagnes ‖ [in time]: the holidays are only three weeks ~ les vacances sont dans trois semaines seulement; ~ back in the 20s il y a bien longtemps dans les années 20; ~ back in 1970 il y a longtemps déjà, en 1970. -**2.** [absent] absent; he feeds the cat whenever we're ~ il donne à manger au chat quand nous ne sommes pas là OR quand nous sommes absents; the boss is ~ this week [ill, on leave] le patron n'est pas là OR est absent cette semaine; [on business] le patron est en déplacement cette semaine; they're ~ on holiday/in Madrid ils sont (partis) en vacances/à Madrid. -**3.** [indicating disappearance, decline etc]: the water had boiled ~ l'eau s'était évaporée (à force de bouillir); we danced the night ~ nous avons passé toute la nuit à danser; government support gradually fell ~ le soutien de l'État a disparu petit à petit. -**4.** [continuously]: he was singing ~ to himself il fredonnait; she's working ~ on her novel elle travaille d'arrache-pied à son roman. -**5.** SPORT: the team is (playing) ~ this Saturday l'équipe joue à l'extérieur OR en déplacement samedi. -**6.** *phr*: ~ with *fml* assez de; ~ with petty restrictions! assez de restrictions mesquines!
◇ *adj* SPORT à l'extérieur; an ~ match un match à l'extérieur; the ~ team l'équipe (qui est) en déplacement.
◆ **away from** *prep phr* [indicating precise distance] à... de; two metres ~ from us à deux mètres de nous ‖ [not at, not in] loin de; somewhere well ~ from the city quelque part très loin de la ville; when we're ~ from home quand nous partons, quand nous ne sommes pas chez nous.

awe [ɔː] ◇ *n* effroi *m* mêlé d'admiration et de respect; to be OR to stand in ~ of être impressionné OR intimidé par; I stared at her in ~ je l'ai regardée avec la plus grande admiration.
◇ *vt*: the music ~d them into silence impressionnés par la musique, ils se sont tus; she spoke in an ~d whisper elle chuchotait d'une voix respectueuse et intimidée.

awe-inspiring *adj* [impressive] impressionnant, imposant; [amazing] stupéfiant; [frightening] terrifiant.

awesome [ˈɔːsəm] *adj* -**1.** = **awe-inspiring**. -**2.** *inf* [great] génial.

awe-stricken, awe-struck *adj* [intimidated] intimidé, impressionné; [amazed] stupéfait; [frightened] frappé de terreur.

awful [ˈɔːfʊl] ◇ *adj* -**1.** [bad] affreux, atroce; she was simply ~ to him elle a été absolument infecte avec lui; I feel ~ je me sens très mal; she looks ~ [ill] elle a l'air malade; [badly dressed] elle est affreusement mal habillée; what an ~ bore! [person] ce qu'il peut être assommant!; [task] quelle corvée!; you're ~! tu es impossible!; what ~ weather! quel temps affreux OR de chien! -**2.** [horrific] épouvantable, effroyable. -**3.** *inf* [as intensifier]: I have an ~ lot of work j'ai énormément de travail; they took an ~ chance ils ont pris un risque énorme OR considérable.
◇ *adv* *inf Am* = **awfully**.

awfully [ˈɔːflɪ] *adv* [very] très, terriblement; ~ funny/nice extrêmement drôle/gentil; he's an ~ good writer il écrit merveilleusement bien; I'm ~ sorry je suis vraiment OR sincèrement désolé; thanks ~ merci infiniment OR mille fois.

awfulness [ˈɔːfʊlnɪs] *n* -**1.** [of behaviour, treatment] atrocité *f*. -**2.** [of accident, crime] horreur *f*.

awhile [əˈwaɪl] *adv lit* (pendant) un instant OR un moment; let's think about it ~ réfléchissons-y un peu; not yet ~ pas encore, pas de sitôt.

awkward [ˈɔːkwəd] *adj* -**1.** [clumsy - person] maladroit, gauche; [- gesture] maladroit, peu élégant; [- style] lourd, gauche; he's ~ with his hands il n'est pas très habile de ses mains; the ~ age l'âge ingrat. -**2.** [embarrassed - person] gêné, ennuyé; [- silence] gêné, embarrassé; she felt ~ about going cela la gênait d'y aller. -**3.** [difficult - problem, situation] délicat, fâcheux; [- task] délicat; [- question] gênant, embarrassant; [- person] peu commode, difficile; it would be ~ if he met her cela serait fâcheux OR gênant s'il la rencontrait; it's an ~ time for me to leave cela me serait difficile de partir en ce moment; you've come at an ~ time vous êtes arrivé au mauvais moment; an ~ moment un moment inopportun; they could make things ~ for her ils pourraient lui mettre des bâtons dans les roues; he's an ~ customer *inf* il faut se le farcir; it's ~ to use ça n'est pas facile à utiliser; the table is at an ~ angle la table est mal placée ‖ [uncooperative] peu coopératif; he's just being ~ il essaie seulement de compliquer les choses.

awkwardly [ˈɔːkwədlɪ] *adv* -**1.** [clumsily - dance, move] maladroitement, peu élégamment; [- handle, speak] maladroitement, gauchement; an ~ phrased sentence une phrase lourde OR mal formulée; it's very ~ designed c'est très mal conçu. -**2.** [with embarrassment - behave] d'une façon gênée OR embarrassée; [- reply, speak] d'un ton embarrassé OR gêné, avec gêne; she grinned ~ elle a souri d'un air gêné.

awkwardness [ˈɔːkwədnɪs] *n* -**1.** [clumsiness - of movement, person] maladresse *f*, gaucherie *f*; [- of style] lourdeur *f*, inélégance *f*. -**2.** [unease] embarras *m*, gêne *f*; the ~ of the situation le côté gênant OR embarrassant de la situation.

awl [ɔːl] *n* alène *f*, poinçon *m*.

awning [ˈɔːnɪŋ] *n* -**1.** [over window] store *m*; [on shop display] banne *f*, store *m*; [at door] marquise *f*, auvent *m*; NAUT taud *m*, taude *f*. -**2.** [tent] auvent *m*.

awoke [əˈwəʊk] *pt* → **awake**.

awoken [əˈwəʊkn] *pp* → **awake**.

AWOL [ˈeɪwɒl] (*abbr of* Absent Without Leave) *adj*: to be/to go ~ *literal* & *fig* être absent/s'absenter sans permission.

awry [əˈraɪ] ◇ *adj* de travers, de guingois.
◇ *adv* de travers; to go ~ mal tourner, aller de travers.

axe *Br*, **ax** *Am* [æks] (*pl* axes) ◇ *n* [tool] hache *f*; to have an ~ to grind [ulterior motive] prêcher pour sa paroisse, être intéressé; [complaint] avoir un compte à régler; to get the ~ [person] être licencié OR viré; [programme, plan etc] être annulé OR supprimé; when the ~ falls quand le couperet tombe.
◇ *vt* -**1.** *literal* [wood] couper, hacher TECH. -**2.** *fig* [person] licencier, virer; [project] annuler, abandonner; [job, position] supprimer; many educational grants have been ~d un grand nombre de bourses d'études ont été supprimées.

axes [ˈæksiːz] *pl* → **axis**.

axial [ˈæksɪəl] *adj* axial.

axil [ˈæksɪl] *n* aisselle *f* BOT.

axiom [ˈæksɪəm] *n* axiome *m*.

axiomatic [ˌæksɪəˈmætɪk] *adj* axiomatique.

axis [ˈæksɪs] (*pl* axes [-iːz]) *n* [gen, ANAT, BOT & GEOM] axe *m*.
◆ **Axis** *n* HIST: the Axis l'Axe *m*.

axle [ˈæksl] *n* [gen] axe *m*; AUT essieu *m*; front/rear ~ essieu avant/arrière.

axle-box *n* boîte *f* d'essieu.

axle-pin *n* esse *f*, clavette *f* d'essieu.

axletree [ˈæksltriː] *n* essieu *m*.

ay [aɪ] = **aye** *interj* & *n*.

ayatollah [ˌaɪəˈtɒlə] *n* ayatollah *m*.

aye [*adv* eɪ, *interj* & *n* aɪ] ◇ *adv arch* OR *lit* toujours.
◇ *interj arch* OR *dial*: ~! oui; ~, ~ sir! NAUT oui, mon commandant!
◇ *n* oui *m* (*inv*); 25 ~s and 3 noes 25 oui et 3 non, 25 pour et 3 contre; the ~s have it les oui l'emportent.

aye-aye [ˈaɪaɪ] *interj Br*: ~! tiens donc!

AYH (*abbr of* American Youth Hostels) *pr n association américaine des auberges de jeunesse*.

AZ *written abbr of* Arizona.

azalea [əˈzeɪljə] *n* azalée *f*.

Azerbaijan [ˌæzəbaɪˈdʒɑːn] *pr n* Azerbaïdjan *m*; in ~ en Azerbaïdjan.

Azerbaijani [ˌæzəbaɪˈdʒɑːnɪ] ◇ *n* Azerbaïdjanais *m*, -e *f*.
◇ *adj* azerbaïdjanais.

Azeri [əˈzerɪ] ◇ *n* Azeri *mf*.
◇ *adj* azeri.

azimuth [ˈæzɪməθ] *n* azimut *m*.

Azores [əˈzɔːz] *pl pr n*: the ~ les Açores *fpl*; in the ~ aux Açores.

AZT (*abbr of* azidothymidine) *n* AZT *f*.

Aztec [ˈæztek] ◇ *n* Aztèque *mf*.
◇ *adj* aztèque.

azure [ˈæʒəʳ] *lit* ◇ *adj* azuré, d'azur.
◇ *n* azur *m*.

B

b (*pl* b's OR bs), **B** (*pl* B's OR Bs) [biː] *n* [letter] b *m*, B *m*; **B for Bob** B comme Bob; **6B Racine Street** 6ter, rue Racine.

b -**1.** *written abbr of* **billion**. -**2.** *written abbr of* **born**.

B -**1.** [indicating secondary importance]: **the B-side of a record** la deuxième face d'un disque; **we took the B-road** *Br* AUT nous avons pris la départementale; **B-movie, B-film, B-picture** film *m* de série B; **grade B meat** COMM viande de deuxième catégorie; **the B-team** SPORT l'équipe secondaire. -**2.** SCH & UNIV [mark] bien *(= 12 à 14 sur 20)*; **I got two Bs and an A** j'ai eu deux Bien et un Très Bien. -**3.** MUS [note] si *m*.

BA ◇ *n* (*abbr of* **Bachelor of Arts**) *(titulaire d'une) licence de lettres*.
◇ *pr n* -**1.** *abbr of* **British Academy**. -**2.** (*abbr of* **British Airways**) *compagnie aérienne britannique*.

baa [bɑː] ◇ *n* bêlement *m*; **~!** bêê!; **Baa, Baa, Black Sheep** *comptine enfantine anglaise*.
◇ *vi* bêler.

BAA (*abbr of* **British Airports Authority**) *pr n organisme autonome responsable des aéroports en Grande-Bretagne*.

baa-lamb *n baby talk* petit agneau *m*.

baba [ˈbɑːbɑː] *n* baba *m*; **rum ~** baba au rhum.

Babbitt [ˈbæbɪt] *n Am pej* bourgeois *m* borné.

babble [ˈbæbl] ◇ *vi* -**1.** [baby] gazouiller, babiller; [person – quickly] bredouiller; [– foolishly] bavarder, babiller. -**2.** [stream] jaser, gazouiller.
◇ *vt* [say quickly] bredouiller; [say foolishly] bavarder, babiller.
◇ *n* -**1.** [of voices] rumeur *f*; [of baby] babillage *m*, babil *m*; [of stream] gazouillement *m*, babil *m*. -**2.** [chatter] bavardage *m*.
◆ **babble away, babble on** *vi insep* -**1.** [baby] gazouiller, babiller; [person] jaser, jacasser. -**2.** [stream] jaser, gazouiller.

babbler [ˈbæbləʳ] *n* bavard *m*, -e *f*.

babbling [ˈbæblɪŋ] ◇ *n* -**1.** [of voices] rumeur *f*; [of baby] babillage *m*, babil *m*; [of stream] gazouillement *m*, babil *m*. -**2.** [chatter] bavardage *m*.
◇ *adj* babillard.

babe [beɪb] *n* -**1.** *literal* [baby] bébé *m*; *fig* [naive person] innocent *m*, -e *f*, naïf *m*, -ïve *f*; **~ in arms** *literal* enfant *m* au berceau; **she's a ~ in arms** *fig* elle est comme l'enfant qui vient de naître; **~s in the wood** de jeunes innocents OR naïfs. -**2.** *inf Am* [young woman] belle gosse *f*, minette *f*; **hey ~!** salut ma belle! -**3.** *inf Am* [term of endearment] chéri *m*, -e *f*.

babel [ˈbeɪbl] *n* brouhaha *m*.
◆ **Babel** *n*: **the tower of Babel** la tour de Babel.

baboon [bəˈbuːn] *n* babouin *m*.

babu [ˈbɑːbuː] *n Br* -**1.** [Indian term of address] monsieur *m*. -**2.** *pej* [clerk] employé *m* de bureau *(en Inde)*.

babushka [bəˈbuːʃkə] *n* foulard *m (porté par les paysannes russes)*.

baby [ˈbeɪbɪ] (*pl* **babies**, *pt* & *pp* **babied**)
◇ *n* -**1.** [infant] bébé *m*; **we've known her since she was a ~** nous l'avons connue toute petite OR bébé; **he's the ~ of the family** il est le plus jeune OR le benjamin de la famille; **don't be such a ~!** ne fais pas l'enfant! ❑ **~'s bottle** *Br* biberon *m*; **they left him holding the ~** il lui ont laissé payer les pots cassés, ils lui ont tout fait retomber dessus; **to throw the ~ out with the bathwater** jeter le bébé avec l'eau du bain, pécher par excès de zèle. -**2.** *inf Am* [young woman] belle gosse *f*, minette *f*; **hey ~!** salut ma belle! -**3.** *inf Am* [term of endearment] chéri *m*, -e *f*. -**4.** *inf* [project]: **the new library is the mayor's ~** la nouvelle bibliothèque est l'œuvre du maire; **that's his ~** c'est son bébé. -**5.** *inf Am* [machine] merveille *f*; **this ~ drives like a dream** cette voiture est une pure merveille à conduire.
◇ *vt* dorloter, bichonner.
◇ *adj* [animal] bébé, petit; [mushroom, tomato] petit; **~ cat** chaton *m*, petit chat *m*; **~ elephant** éléphanteau *m*, bébé *m* éléphant; **~ girl** petite fille *f*.
◇ *comp* [clothes, food] de bébé; **~ batterer** bourreau *m* d'enfants; **~ battering** *violences commises sur un bébé*; **~ changing area** relais-bébé *m*; **~ bottle** *Am* biberon *m*; **~ linen** layette *f*; **~ scales** pèse-bébé *m*; **~ seat** siège *m* pour bébés.

baby-blue ◇ *adj* bleu clair *(inv)*; **~ eyes** des yeux bleus OR bleu clair.
◇ *n* bleu clair *m*.

baby boom *n* baby boom *m*.

baby boomer [-ˌbuːməʳ] *n* enfant *m* du baby boom.

Baby-bouncer® *n* trotteur *m*, youpala *m*.

baby buggy *n* -**1.** *Am* = **baby carriage**. -**2.** *Br* [pushchair]: Baby buggy® poussette *f*.

baby carriage *n Am* voiture *f* d'enfant, landau *m*.

baby doll *n* poupée *f*.
◆ **baby-doll** *adj*: **baby-doll pyjamas, baby-doll nightdress** baby-doll *m*.

baby face *n* visage *m* de bébé.
◆ **baby-face** *adj* au visage de bébé.

baby grand *n* (piano *m*) demi-queue *m*.

babyhood [ˈbeɪbɪhʊd] *n* petite OR première enfance *f*.

babyish [ˈbeɪbɪɪʃ] *adj pej* [features, voice] puéril, enfantin; [behaviour] puéril, enfantin, infantile.

Babylon [ˈbæbɪlən] *pr n* Babylone.

Babylonia [ˌbæbɪˈləʊnjə] *pr n* Babylonie *f*; **in ~** en Babylonie.

Babylonian [ˌbæbɪˈləʊnjən] ◇ *n* -**1.** [person] Babylonien *m*, -enne *f*. -**2.** LING babylonien *m*.
◇ *adj* babylonien.

baby-minder *n* nourrice *f*.

baby-sit *vi* garder des enfants, faire du baby-sitting; **she ~s for them** elle garde leurs enfants.

baby-sitter *n* baby-sitter *mf*.

baby-sitting *n* garde *f* d'enfants, baby-sitting *m*.

baby sling *n* porte-bébé *m*, kangourou® *m*.

baby-snatcher *n* ravisseur *m*, -euse *f* de bébés.

baby-snatching [-ˌsnætʃɪŋ] *n* rapt *m* OR enlèvement *m* de bébés.

baby talk *n* langage *m* enfantin OR de bébé.

baby tooth *n* dent *f* de lait.

baby-walker *n* trotteur *m*.

babywipe [ˈbeɪbɪwaɪp] *n* lingette *f*.

baccalaureate [ˌbækəˈlɔːrɪət] *n* UNIV ≃ licence *f*.

baccarat [ˈbækərɑː] *n* baccara *m*.

Bacchae [ˈbækiː] *pl pr n*: **the ~** les Bacchantes.

bacchanal [ˈbækənl] ◇ *adj* bachique.
◇ *n* -**1.** [worshipper] adorateur *m*, -trice *f* de Bacchus; ANTIQ [priestess] bacchante *f*. -**2.** [reveller] noceur *m*, -euse *f*; [party] bacchanale *f*.

bacchanalia [ˌbækəˈneɪljə] *npl* [rite] bacchanales *fpl*; [party] bacchanale *f*.

bacchanalian [ˌbækəˈneɪljən] *adj* bachique.

Bacchic [ˈbækɪk] *adj* bachique.

Bacchus [ˈbækəs] *pr n* Bacchus.

baccy▽ [ˈbækɪ] *n Br* tabac *m*.

bachelor [ˈbætʃələʳ] ◇ *n* -**1.** [man] célibataire *m*; **confirmed ~** célibataire endurci; **he's a very eligible ~** c'est un beau OR bon parti. -**2.** UNIV ≃ licencié *m*, -e *f*; **~'s degree** ≃ licence *f*; **Bachelor of Arts/Science** [degree] ≃ licence *f* de lettres/de sciences; [person] ≃ licencié *m*, -e *f* ès lettres/ès sciences; **Bachelor of Education** [degree] ≃ licence *f* d'enseignement; [person] ≃ licencié *m*, -e *f* d'enseignement.
◇ *adj* [brother, uncle] célibataire; [life] de célibataire.

bachelordom [ˈbætʃələdəm] = **bachelorhood**.

bachelor flat *n* garçonnière *f*.

bachelor girl *n* célibataire *f*.

bachelorhood [ˈbætʃələhʊd] *n* [gen] célibat *m*; [of men] vie *f* de garçon.

bacillary [bəˈsɪlərɪ] *adj* [disease] bacillaire; [shape] bacilliforme.

bacillus [bəˈsɪləs] (*pl* **bacilli** [-laɪ]) *n* bacille *m*.

back [bæk] ◇ *adv* -**1.** [towards the rear] vers l'arrière, en arrière; **he stepped ~** il a reculé d'un pas, il a fait un pas en arrière; **I pushed ~ my chair** j'ai reculé ma chaise; **she tied her hair ~** elle a attaché ses cheveux; **he glanced ~** il a regardé derrière lui; **their house sits ~ from the road** leur maison est en retrait par rapport à la route. -**2.** [into or in previous place]: **we went ~ home** nous sommes rentrés (à la maison); **my headache's ~** j'ai de nouveau mal à la tête, mon mal de tête a recommencé; **they'll be ~**

on Monday ils rentrent OR ils seront de retour lundi; I'll be right ~ je reviens tout de suite; we expect him ~ tomorrow il doit rentrer demain; as soon as you get ~ dès votre retour; is he ~ at work? a-t-il repris le travail?; he's just ~ from Moscow il arrive OR rentre de Moscou; we went to town and ~ nous avons fait un saut en ville; he went to his aunt's and ~ il a fait l'aller et retour chez sa tante; the trip to Madrid and ~ takes three hours il faut trois heures pour aller à Madrid et revenir; meanwhile, ~ in Washington entre-temps, à Washington; ~ home there's no school on Saturdays chez moi OR nous, il n'y a pas d'école le samedi ❑ the ~-to-school sales les soldes de la rentrée. -**3.** [indicating return to previous state]: she wants her children ~ elle veut qu'on lui rende ses enfants; he went ~ to sleep il s'est rendormi; business soon got ~ to normal les affaires ont vite repris leur cours normal; miniskirts are coming ~ (in fashion) les minijupes reviennent à la mode. -**4.** [earlier]: six pages ~ six pages plus haut; ~ in the 17th century au 17e siècle; as far ~ as I can remember d'aussi loin que je m'en souvienne; ~ in November déjà au mois de novembre; ten years ~ *inf* il y a dix ans. -**5.** [in reply, in return]: you should ask for your money ~ vous devriez demander un remboursement OR qu'on vous rembourse; I hit him ~ je lui ai rendu son coup; she smiled ~ at him elle lui a répondu par un sourire; to write ~ répondre (par écrit).

◇ *adj* -**1.** [rear - door, garden] de derrière; [- wheel] arrière *(inv)*; [- seat] arrière *(inv)*, de derrière; the ~ legs of a horse les pattes arrière d'un cheval; the ~ room is the quietest la pièce qui donne sur l'arrière est la plus calme; the ~ page of the newspaper la dernière page du journal; the ~ nine GOLF les neuf derniers trous ❑ to put sthg on the ~ burner mettre qqch en attente; he got in through the ~ door [by having influence etc] il est entré par la petite porte; to take a ~ seat passer au second plan; she refused to take a ~ seat to her boss elle a refusé de céder le pas à son patron. -**2.** [quiet - lane, road] écarté, isolé; ~ street petite rue *f*; I grew up in the ~ streets of Chicago j'ai été élevé dans les mauvais quartiers de Chicago. -**3.** [not current] vieux; ~ issues OR copies of "Match" de vieux numéros de «Match». -**4.** [overdue] arriéré; ~ rent/taxes arriéré *m* de loyer/d'impôts; ~ pay rappel *m* (de salaire); ~ orders COMM commandes *fpl* en souffrance. -**5.** LING [vowel] postérieur.

◇ *n* -**1.** ANAT [of animal, person] dos *m*; she carried her baby on her ~ elle portait son bébé sur son dos; I fell flat on my ~ je suis tombé à la renverse OR sur le dos; we lay on our ~s nous étions allongés sur le dos; my ~ aches j'ai mal au dos; the cat arched its ~ le chat a fait le gros dos; I only saw them from the ~ je ne les ai vus que de dos; she sat with her ~ to the window elle était assise le dos tourné à la fenêtre; you had your ~ to me tu me tournais le dos ❑ they have the police at their ~s [in support] ils ont la police avec eux; [in pursuit] ils ont la police à leurs trousses; the decision was taken behind my ~ la décision a été prise derrière mon dos; he went behind my ~ to the boss il est allé voir le patron derrière mon dos OR à mon insu; to be flat on one's ~ [bedridden] être alité OR cloué au lit; get off my ~! *inf* fiche-moi la paix!; to have one's ~ to the wall être au pied du mur; the rich live off the ~s of the poor les riches vivent sur le dos des pauvres; to put sb's ~ up énerver qqn; to put one's ~ into something faire un gros effort; that's it, put your ~ into it! *inf* allez-y, un peu de nerf!; to put one's ~ out se faire mal au dos; I'll be glad to see the ~ of her je serai content de la voir partir OR d'être débarrassé d'elle. -**2.** [part opposite the front - gen] dos *m*, derrière *m*; [- of coat, shirt, door] dos *m*; [- of vehicle, building, head] arrière *m*; [- of train] queue *f*; at the ~ of the book à la fin du livre; we climbed in the ~ of the car nous sommes montés à l'arrière de la voiture; the garden is out OR round the ~ le jardin se trouve derrière la maison ❑ she's got a face like the ~ of a bus *inf* c'est un boudin. -**3.** [other side - of hand, spoon, envelope, cheque] dos *m*; [- of carpet, coin, medal] revers *m*; [- of page] verso *m*; I know this town like the ~ of my hand je connais cette ville comme ma poche. -**4.** [farthest from the front - of cupboard, room, stage] fond *m*; we'd like a table at the OR in the very ~ nous voudrions une table tout au fond ❑ in the ~ of beyond en pleine brousse, au diable vauvert; I've had it OR it's been at the ~ of my mind for ages j'y pense depuis longtemps, ça fait longtemps que ça me travaille. -**5.** [binding] dos *m*. -**6.** [of chair] dos *m*, dossier *m*. -**7.** SPORT arrière *m*.

◇ *vt* -**1.** [move backwards - bicycle, car] reculer; [- horse] faire reculer; [- train] refouler; I ~ed the car into the garage j'ai mis la voiture dans le garage en marche arrière; she ~ed him into the next room elle l'a fait reculer dans la pièce d'à côté. -**2.** [support financially - company, venture] financer, commanditer; [- loan] garantir; [encourage - efforts, person, venture] encourager, appuyer, soutenir; [- candidate] soutenir; we ~ed her in her fight against racism nous l'avons soutenue dans sa lutte contre le racisme; the Democrats ~ed the bill les Démocrates ont soutenu le projet de loi; to ~ a bill FIN avaliser OR endosser un effet. -**3.** [bet on] parier sur, miser sur ❑ to ~ a winner SPORT [horse, team] parier sur un gagnant; FIN [company, stock] bien placer son argent; *fig* jouer la bonne carte; to ~ the wrong horse *literal* & *fig* miser sur le mauvais cheval. -**4.** [strengthen, provide backing for - curtain, material] doubler; [- picture, paper] renforcer. -**5.** MUS [accompany] accompagner. -**6.** NAUT [sail] masquer.

◇ *vi* -**1.** [go in reverse - car, train] faire marche arrière; [- horse, person] reculer; the car ~ed into the driveway la voiture est entrée en marche arrière dans l'allée; I ~ed into a corner je me suis retiré dans un coin. -**2.** [wind] tourner en sens inverse des aiguilles d'une montre.

◆ **back and forth** *adv phr*: to go ~ and forth [person] faire des allées et venues; [machine, piston] faire un mouvement de va-et-vient; his eyes darted ~ and forth il regardait de droite à gauche.

◆ **back to back** *adv phr literal* & *fig* dos à dos; they're showing both films ~ to ~ ils montrent deux films l'un après l'autre.

◆ **back to front** *adv phr* devant derrière; you've got your pullover on ~ to front tu as mis ton pull devant derrière.

◆ **in back of** *prep phr Am* derrière.

◆ **back away** *vi insep* -**1.** [car] faire marche arrière. -**2.** [person] (se) reculer; she ~ed away from him elle a reculé devant lui; they have ~ed away from making a final decision *fig* ils se sont abstenus de prendre une décision définitive.

◆ **back down** *vi insep* [accept defeat] céder; he finally ~ed down on the issue of membership il a fini par céder sur la question de l'adhésion.

◆ **back off** *vi insep* -**1.** [withdraw] reculer; ~ off, will you! *inf* fiche-moi la paix!, lâche-moi les baskets! -**2.** *Am* = **back down**.

◆ **back onto** *vt insep* [have back facing towards] donner sur (à l'arrière); the house ~s onto the river l'arrière de la maison donne sur la rivière.

◆ **back out** *vi insep* -**1.** [car] sortir en marche arrière; [person] sortir à reculons. -**2.** *fig* [withdraw] se dérober, tirer son épingle du jeu; don't ~ out now! ne faites pas marche arrière maintenant!; they ~ed out of the deal ils se sont retirés de l'affaire; to ~ out of a contract se rétracter OR se retirer d'un contrat.

◆ **back up** ◇ *vi insep* -**1.** [car] faire marche arrière. -**2.** [drain] se boucher; [water] refouler.

◇ *vt sep* -**1.** [car, horse] faire reculer; [train] refouler. -**2.** [support - claim, story] appuyer, soutenir; [- person] soutenir, épauler, seconder; her story is ~ed up by eye witnesses sa version des faits est confirmée par des témoins oculaires; he ~ed this up with a few facts il a étayé ça avec quelques faits. -**3.** COMPUT sauvegarder. -**4.** TRANSP: traffic is ~ed up for 5 miles il y a un embouteillage sur 8 km.

backache ['bækeɪk] *n* mal *m* de dos.

backbench ['bækbentʃ] ◇ *n banc des membres du Parlement britannique qui n'ont pas de portefeuille*.

◇ *comp* [opinion, support] des «backbenchers».

backbencher [,bæk'bentʃəʳ] *n parlementaire sans fonction ministérielle.*

BACKBENCHER:
Les «backbenchers» sont assis aux derniers rangs de la Chambre des communes, tandis que les rangs de devant sont réservés aux ministres et aux membres du gouvernement fantôme.

backbend ['bækbend] *n* pont *m (en gymnastique)*.

backbiting ['bækbaɪtɪŋ] *n* médisance *f*.

backboard ['bækbɔːd] *n* [board] planche *f*, panneau *m*; [in basketball] panneau *m*.

backbone ['bækbəʊn] *n* -**1.** ANAT colonne *f* vertébrale; ZOOL épine *f* dorsale. -**2.** [of country, organization] pivot *m*, épine *f* dorsale; the working classes are the ~ of the economy la classe ouvrière est le pivot de l'économie. -**3.** *fig* [strength of character] fermeté *f*, caractère *m*; you haven't the ~ to do it tu n'as pas le courage de le faire; he has no ~ il n'a rien dans le ventre.

backbreaking ['bæk,breɪkɪŋ] *adj* éreintant; ~ work un travail à vous casser les reins.

backchat *inf* ['bæktʃæt] *n Br* impertinence *f*, insolence *f*; and I want none of your ~ et épargnez-moi votre insolence.

backcloth ['bækklɒθ] *n* THEAT toile *f* de fond; *fig* toile *f* de fond, fond *m*.

backcomb ['bækkəʊm] *vt* crêper.

back country *n Austr* & *NZ* campagne *f*, arrière-pays *m inv*.

backcourt ['bækkɔːt] *n* [in basketball] arrière *m* du terrain; [in tennis] fond *m* du court.

backdate [,bæk'deɪt] *vt* [cheque, document] antidater; the pay rise is ~d to March l'augmentation de salaire a un effet rétroactif à compter de mars.

back door *n* porte *f* arrière; to get in through OR by the ~ *fig* entrer par la petite porte.

◆ **backdoor** *adj* louche, suspect.

backdrop ['bækdrɒp] = **backcloth**.

-backed [bækt] *comb form* -**1.** [chair] à dos, à dossier; a high~ chair une chaise à dos OR dossier haut; silk~ à dos OR dossier en soie; a broad~ man un homme qui a le dos large. -**2.** [supported by]: US~ rebels des rebelles soutenus par les États-Unis.

back end *n* -**1.** [of car, bus] arrière *m*; [of train] queue *f*. -**2.** *Br dial* [autumn] arrière-saison *f*, automne *m*; the ~ of the year l'arrière-saison.

backer ['bækəʳ] *n* -**1.** [supporter] partisan *m*, -e *f*; [financial supporter] commanditaire *mf*, bailleur *m* de fonds. -**2.** SPORT [punter] parieur *m*, -euse *f*.

backfill ['bækfɪl] *vt* remplir.

backfire [,bæk'faɪəʳ] ◇ *vi* -**1.** [car] pétarader. -**2.** [plan] avoir un effet inattendu; the plan ~d on him le projet s'est retourné contre lui OR lui est retombé sur le nez.

◇ *n* -**1.** [noise] pétarade *f*; [explosion] retour *m* d'allumage. -**2.** [controlled fire] contre-feu *m*.

backflip ['bækflɪp] *n* [in gymnastics] culbute *f* à l'envers.

back formation *n* LING dérivation *f* régressive.

backgammon ['bæk,gæmən] *n* backgammon *m*.

background ['bækgraʊnd] ◇ *n* -**1.** [scene, view] fond *m*, arrière-plan *m*; [sound] fond *m* sonore; THEAT fond *m*, toile *f* de fond; yellow flowers on a green ~ des fleurs jaunes sur fond vert; in the ~ dans le fond, à l'arrière-plan; his wife remains very much in the ~ *fig* sa femme est très effacée OR reste à l'écart. -**2.** [of person -

history] antécédents *mpl*; [- family] milieu *m* socioculturel; [- experience] formation *f*, acquis *m*; [- education] formation *f*, bagage *m*; **people from a working-class ~** gens *mpl* de milieu ouvrier; **she has a good ~ in history** elle a une bonne formation en histoire; **what is the candidate's ~?** [social] à quel milieu social appartient le candidat?; [professional] quelle est la formation du candidat? -**3.** [of event, situation] contexte *m*, climat *m*; **the economic ~ to the crisis** les raisons économiques de la crise; **the talks are taking place against a ~ of political tensions** les débats ont lieu dans un climat de tensions politiques; **the report looks at the ~ to the unrest** le rapport examine l'historique de l'agitation.
◇ *adj* -**1.** [unobtrusive - music, noise] de fond. -**2.** [facts, material] de base, de fond; **~ information** éléments de référence OR de base; **~ reading** bibliographie *f*. -**3.** COMPUT: **~ processing** traitement *m* des données non prioritaires. -**4.** PHYS: **~ radiation** rayonnement *m* naturel.

backhand ['bækhænd] ◇ *n* revers *m*; **he has a wicked ~** il a un sacré revers; **keep serving to his ~** continue de servir sur son revers.
◇ *adj* [stroke] en revers; [volley] de revers.
◇ *adv* en revers.

backhanded ['bækhændɪd] *adj* -**1.** [blow, slap] donné avec le revers de la main; **~ stroke** SPORT revers *m*. -**2.** [compliment, remark] équivoque.

backhander ['bækhændəʳ] *n* -**1.** [blow, stroke] coup *m* du revers de la main; SPORT revers *m*. -**2.** [comment] remarque *f* équivoque. -**3.** *inf Br* [bribe] pot-de-vin *m*, dessous-de-table *m inv*.

backing ['bækɪŋ] *n* -**1.** [support] soutien *m*, appui *m*; [financial support] soutien *m* financier. -**2.** [material] renforcement *m*, support *m*. -**3.** MUS [accompaniment] accompagnement *m*.

backing group *n Br musiciens qui accompagnent un chanteur*.

back issue *n* vieux numéro *m*.

backlash ['bæklæʃ] *n* contrecoup *m*; **a ~ of violence** une réaction de violence.

backless ['bæklɪs] *adj* [dress] (très) décolleté dans le dos; [chair] sans dos, sans dossier.

backlog ['bæklɒg] *n* accumulation *f*, arriéré *m*; **a ~ of work** une accumulation de travail (en retard), un arriéré de travail; **a ~ of orders** COMM des commandes inexécutées OR en souffrance.

back number *n* vieux numéro *m*.

backpack ['bækpæk] ◇ *n* sac *m* à dos.
◇ *vi* faire de la randonnée; **to go ~ing** faire de la randonnée.
◇ *vt* transporter dans un sac à dos.

backpacker ['bækpækəʳ] *n* randonneur *m*, -euse *f*.

back passage *n* -**1.** [rectum] rectum *m*. -**2.** [alley] ruelle *f*.

backpedal [,bæk'pedl] (*Br pt* & *pp* **backpedalled**, *cont* **backpedalling**, *Am pt* & *pp* **backpedaled**, *cont* **backpedaling**) *vi* -**1.** [on bicycle] rétropédaler. -**2.** [change mind] faire marche arrière *fig*.

backrest ['bækrest] *n* dossier *m*.

back room *n* -**1.** [in house] pièce *f* de derrière; [in shop] arrière-boutique *f*. -**2.** [for research] laboratoire *m* de recherche secret.
◆ **backroom** *adj* [research, work] secret; **~ boys** [gen] ceux qui restent dans l'ombre OR dans les coulisses; [researchers] chercheurs *mpl* qui travaillent dans l'anonymat.

back-scratcher *n* [implement] gratte-dos *m inv*.

back seat *n* siège *m* arrière; **to take a ~** *fig* se tenir en retrait.

back-seat driver *n* [in car] *personne qui donne toujours des conseils au conducteur*; [interfering person] donneur *m*, -euse *f* de leçons.

backside *inf* [,bæk'saɪd] *n* derrière *m*; **he just sits around on his ~ all day** il reste assis toute la journée à ne rien faire.

backsight ['bæksaɪt] *n* [on rifle] cran *m* de mire; [in surveying] rétrovisée *f*.

back slang *n* ≃ verlan *m*.

backslapping ['bæk,slæpɪŋ] ◇ *n* [heartiness] (excessive) jovialité *f*; [congratulations] encensement *m*.
◇ *adj* jovial.

backslash ['bækslæʃ] *n* barre *f* oblique inversée.

backslide [,bæk'slaɪd] (*pt* **backslid** [-'slɪd], *pp* **backslid** [-'slɪd] OR **backslidden** [-'slɪdn]) *vi* retomber, récidiver; **no backsliding!** pas question de récidiver!

backslider [,bæk'slaɪdəʳ] *n* récidiviste *mf*.

backspace ['bækspeɪs] ◇ *vi* faire un retour arrière.
◇ *vt* rappeler.
◇ *n* espacement *m* OR retour *m* arrière.

backspin ['bækspɪn] *n* effet *m* contraire; **to put ~ on a ball** donner un effet contraire à une balle.

backstage [,bæk'steɪdʒ] THEAT & *fig* ◇ *n* coulisse *f*, coulisses *fpl*.
◇ *adv* dans la coulisse OR les coulisses, derrière la scène; **to go ~** aller dans les coulisses; **negotiations took place ~** *fig* les négociations ont eu lieu en coulisses OR en secret.
◇ *adj* secret, furtif.

backstairs [,bæk'steəz] ◇ *npl* [secondary] escalier *m* de service; [secret] escalier *m* secret OR dérobé.
◇ *adj* [secret] secret, furtif; [unfair] déloyal; **~ gossip** bruits *mpl* de couloirs.

backstitch ['bækstɪtʃ] ◇ *n* point *m* arrière.
◇ *vi* & *vt* coudre en point arrière.

backstop ['bækstɒp] *n* SPORT -**1.** [screen] panneau *m*. -**2.** [in baseball] attrapeur *m*.

back straight *n* ligne *f* (droite) d'en face.

backstreet ['bækstriːt] *adj* [secret] secret, furtif; [underhanded] louche; **~ abortionist** faiseuse *f* d'anges.

backstroke ['bækstrəuk] *n* [in swimming] dos *m* crawlé; **to do (the) ~** nager en dos crawlé.

backswept ['bækswept] *adj* rejeté en arrière.

backswing ['bækswɪŋ] *n* swing *m* (en arrière).

back talk *n Am* impertinence *f*.

back-to-back ◇ *adj literal* & *fig* dos à dos.
◇ *n*: **~s** [houses] *rangée de maisons construites dos à dos et séparées par un passage étroit, typique des régions industrielles du nord de l'Angleterre*.

backtrack ['bæktræk] *vi literal* revenir sur ses pas, rebrousser chemin; *fig* faire marche arrière; **he's already ~ing from** OR **on his agreement** il est déjà en train de revenir sur son accord.

backup ['bækʌp] ◇ *n* -**1.** [support] soutien *m*, appui *m*. -**2.** [reserve] réserve *f*; [substitute] remplaçant *m*. -**3.** COMPUT sauvegarde *f*. -**4.** *Am* MUS = **backing group**.
◇ *adj* -**1.** [furnace] de secours, de réserve; [plan] de secours; [supplies] supplémentaire, de réserve; [team] remplaçant; **~ troops** MIL réserves *fpl*. -**2.** COMPUT: **~ disk** sauvegarde *f*; **~ storage** mémoire *f* auxiliaire. -**3.** *Am* AUT: **~ light** phare *m* arrière.

backward ['bækwəd] ◇ *adj* -**1.** [directed towards the rear] en arrière, rétrograde; **without a ~ look** sans jeter un regard en arrière. -**2.** [late in development - country, society, child] arriéré. -**3.** [reluctant] hésitant, peu disposé; **he's not ~ about giving his opinion** il n'hésite pas à donner son avis; **she's not exactly ~ at coming forward** *hum* elle n'hésite pas à se mettre en avant.
◇ *adv Am* = **backwards**.

backward-looking *adj* [ideas] rétrograde.

backwardness ['bækwədnɪs] *n* -**1.** [of development - country] sous-développement *m*; [- person] retard *m* mental; [- of economy] retard *m*. -**2.** [reluctance] hésitation *f*, lenteur *f*.

backwards ['bækwədz] *adv* -**1.** [towards the rear] en arrière; **a step ~** *literal* & *fig* un pas en arrière; **I fell ~** je suis tombé en arrière OR à la renverse ☐ **to bend** OR **to lean over ~ to please sb** se mettre en quatre pour faire plaisir à qqn. -**2.** [towards the past] en arrière, vers le passé; **looking ~ in time** en remontant dans le temps. -**3.** [with the back foremost]: **to walk ~** marcher à reculons; **you've got your sweater on ~** tu as mis ton pull à l'envers OR devant derrière. -**4.** [in reverse] à l'envers; **now say it ~** dis-le à l'envers maintenant. -**5.** [thoroughly] à fond, sur le bout des doigts; **she knows her subject ~** elle connaît son sujet sur le bout des doigts.
◆ **backwards and forwards** *adv phr*: **to go ~ and forwards** [person] aller et venir; [machine, piston] faire un mouvement de va-et-vient; [pendulum] osciller; **we walked ~ and forwards along the beach** nous avons marché de long en large sur la plage; **she goes ~ and forwards between London and Paris** elle fait la navette entre Londres et Paris.

backwash ['bækwɒʃ] *n* sillage *m*, remous *mpl*; **caught in the ~ of war** *fig* pris dans les remous de la guerre.

backwater ['bæk,wɔːtəʳ] *n* [of river] bras *m* mort; *fig* [remote spot] coin *m* tranquille; *pej* coin *m* perdu; **a cultural ~** un désert culturel.

backwoods ['bækwudz] ◇ *npl* [forest] région *f* forestière *(peu peuplée)*; *fig* [remote spot] coin *m* tranquille.
◇ *adj* [remote] isolé; [backward] peu avancé.

backwoodsman ['bækwudzmən] (*pl* **backwoodsmen** [-mən]) *n literal* habitant *m* de la forêt; *pej* [uncouth person] rustre *m*.

back yard *n Br* [courtyard] cour *f* de derrière, arrière-cour *f*; *Am* [garden] jardin *m* de derrière; **in one's own ~** chez soi.

bacon ['beɪkən] *n* lard *m* (maigre), bacon *m*; **a slice** OR **rasher of ~** une tranche de lard; **~ and eggs** œufs *mpl* au bacon OR au lard; **~ slicer** coupe-jambon *m inv*; **to bring home the ~** *inf* [be the breadwinner] faire bouillir la marmite; [succeed] décrocher la timbale OR le gros lot.

bacteria [bæk'tɪərɪə] *npl* bactéries *fpl*.

bacterial [bæk'tɪərɪəl] *adj* bactérien.

bactericide [bæk'tɪərɪsaɪd] *n* (produit *m*) bactéricide *m*.

bacteriological [bæk,tɪərɪə'lɒdʒɪkl] *adj* bactériologique.

bacteriologist [bæk,tɪərɪ'ɒlədʒɪst] *n* bactériologiste *mf*.

bacteriology [bæk,tɪərɪ'ɒlədʒɪ] *n* bactériologie *f*.

bacterium [bæk'tɪərɪəm] (*pl* **bacteria** [-rɪə]) *n* bactérie *f*.

bad [bæd] (*compar* **worse** [wɜːs], *superl* **worst** [wɜːst]) ◇ *adj* -**1.** [unpleasant - breath, news, terms, weather] mauvais; [- smell, taste] mauvais, désagréable; **that's too ~!** [regrettable] c'est OR quel dommage!; [hard luck] tant pis pour toi!; **it's too ~ he had to leave** quel dommage qu'il ait été obligé de partir; **there was a ~ smell in the house** il y avait une odeur désagréable OR une mauvaise odeur dans la maison; **I have a ~ feeling about this** j'ai le pressentiment que cela va mal tourner; **I feel ~ about leaving you alone** cela m'ennuie de te laisser tout seul; **he felt ~ about the way he'd treated her** il s'en voulait de l'avoir traitée ainsi; **he's in a ~ mood** OR **~ temper** il est de mauvaise humeur; **she has a ~ temper** elle a un sale caractère, elle a un caractère de chien OR de cochon; **I'm on ~ terms with her** je suis brouillé avec elle; **to come to a ~ end** mal finir; **it's a ~ business** [unpleasant] c'est une sale affaire; [unhappy] c'est une triste affaire; **things went from ~ to worse** les choses se sont gâtées OR sont allées de mal en pis ☐ **it left a ~ taste in my mouth** *literal* cela m'a laissé un goût désagréable dans la bouche; *fig* j'en ai gardé un souvenir désagréable; 'Bad Day at Black Rock' *Sturges* 'Un homme est passé'. -**2.** [unfavourable - effect, result] mauvais, malheureux; [- omen, report] mauvais, défavorable; [- opinion] mauvais *(before n)*; **things look ~** la situation n'est pas brillante; **it happened at the worst possible time** ça ne pouvait pas tomber plus mal; **he's in a ~ way** [ill, unhappy] il va mal, il est dans un piteux état; [in trouble] il est dans de mauvais draps. -**3.** [severe - accident, mistake] grave; [- pain] violent, aigu; [- headache] violent; [- climate, winter] rude, dur; **I have a ~ cold** j'ai un gros rhume; she has a ~ case of flu elle a une mauvaise grippe. -**4.** [evil, wicked - person] méchant, mauvais; [- behaviour, habit] mauvais, odieux; they're a ~ lot ils ne sont pas recommandables; to call sb ~ names traiter qqn de tous les noms, injurier qqn; you've been a ~ girl! tu as fait la vilaine OR la méchante!; ~ boy! vilain! ❑ ~ language gros mots *mpl*, grossièretés *fpl*. -**5.** [harmful] mauvais, néfaste; smoking is ~ for your health le tabac est mauvais pour la santé; eating all these sweets is ~ for him c'est mauvais pour lui OR ça ne lui vaut rien de manger autant de sucreries. -**6.** [unhealthy - leg, arm, person] malade; [- tooth] malade, carié; your grandmother is ~ today ta grand-mère ne va pas OR ne se sent pas bien aujourd'hui; how are you? – not so ~ comment allez-vous? – on fait aller OR pas trop mal; he was taken ~ at the office *inf* il a eu un malaise au bureau; to have a ~ heart être cardiaque. -**7.** [poor - light, work] mauvais, de mauvaise qualité; [- actor, pay, performance, road] mauvais; that's not ~ for a beginner ce n'est pas mal pour un débutant; your painting isn't half ~ *inf* ton tableau n'est pas mal du tout; the salary isn't ~ le salaire est convenable; he speaks rather ~ Spanish il parle plutôt mal espagnol OR un espagnol plutôt mauvais; it would be ~ form OR manners to refuse ce serait impoli de refuser; I've always been ~ at maths je n'ai jamais été doué pour les maths, j'ai toujours été mauvais en maths; she's ~ about paying bills on time elle ne paie jamais ses factures à temps; ~ debt créance *f* douteuse OR irrécouvrable. -**8.** [food] mauvais, pourri; to go ~ [milk] tourner; [meat] pourrir, se gâter. -**9.** ▽ [very good] terrible; man, you're looking ~! mon vieux, tu as l'air super bien OR en super forme!

◇ *n* mauvais *m*; you have to take the ~ with the good il faut prendre les choses comme elles viennent, bonnes ou mauvaises; he's gone to the ~ il a mal tourné; we're £100 to the ~ nous sommes débiteurs OR nous avons un découvert de 100 livres; she got in ~ with her boss elle n'a pas la cote avec son patron.

◇ *npl* [people]: the ~ les mauvais *mpl*; 'The Bad and the Beautiful' *Minnelli* 'les Ensorcelés'.

◇ *adv inf*: he wants it ~ il en meurt d'envie; she's got it ~ for him elle l'a dans la peau; he was beaten ~ *Am* il s'est fait méchamment tabasser.

baddie *inf*, **baddy** *inf* ['bædɪ] *n* méchant *m*; he's the ~ c'est lui le méchant.

bade [bæd] *pt* → **bid**.

badge [bædʒ] *n* -**1.** [gen] insigne *m*; [of scout] badge *m*; MIL insigne *m*; a ~ of office un insigne de fonction. -**2.** *fig* signe *m*, marque *f*.

badger ['bædʒəʳ] ◇ *n* blaireau *m*; the Badger State *Am* le Wisconsin.

◇ *vt* harceler, persécuter; stop ~ing your mother with questions arrête de harceler ta mère de questions; she ~ed us into going elle nous a harcelés jusqu'à ce que nous y allions.

badlands ['bædlændz] *npl* bad-lands *fpl*; *fig* mauvais quartiers *mpl*.

badly ['bædlɪ] (*compar* worse [wɜːs], *superl* worst [wɜːst]) *adv* -**1.** [poorly] mal; ~ made/organized mal fait/organisé; ~ lit mal éclairé; things aren't going too ~ ça ne va pas trop mal; the candidate did OR came off ~ in the exams le candidat n'a pas bien marché à ses examens; we came off worst in the deal c'est nous qui nous en sommes le plus mal sortis dans l'affaire; his business is doing ~ ses affaires marchent OR vont mal, il fait de mauvaises affaires; I feel ~ about it [sorry] je le regrette beaucoup; [embarrassed] cela me gêne beaucoup; don't think ~ of him for what he did ne lui en voulez pas de ce qu'il a fait; she took the news ~ elle a mal pris la nouvelle; to be ~ off être dans la misère; we're ~ off for supplies nous manquons de provisions. -**2.** [behave - improperly] mal; [- cruelly] méchamment, avec cruauté. -**3.** [severely - burn, damage] gravement, sérieusement; [- hurt] gravement, grièvement; the town was ~ affected by the storm la ville a été sérieusement touchée par l'orage; she had been ~ beaten elle avait reçu des coups violents; the army was ~ defeated l'armée a subi une sévère défaite. -**4.** [very much] énormément; he ~ needs OR he's ~ in need of a holiday il a grand OR sérieusement besoin de (prendre des) vacances; we ~ want to see her nous avons très envie de la voir.

badman ['bædmæn] (*pl* badmen [-men]) *n* [crook] bandit *m*; [in movie] méchant *m*.

bad-mannered *adj* mal élevé.

badminton ['bædmɪntən] *n* badminton *m*.

Badminton Horse Trials *pr n prestigieux concours hippique en Angleterre*.

badmouth *inf* ['bædmaʊθ] *vt Am* médire de, dénigrer.

badness ['bædnɪs] *n* -**1.** [wickedness] méchanceté *f*; [cruelty] cruauté *f*. -**2.** [inferior quality] mauvaise qualité *f*, mauvais état *m*.

bad-tempered *adj* [as character trait] qui a mauvais caractère; [temporarily] de mauvaise humeur.

Baedeker ['beɪdekəʳ] *n* guide *m (livre)*.

Baffin Island ['bæfɪn-] *pr n* terre *f* de Baffin; in ~ en terre de Baffin.

baffle ['bæfl] ◇ *vt* -**1.** [puzzle] déconcerter, dérouter; the police are ~d les policiers sont déroutés. -**2.** [frustrate - effort, plans] faire échouer, déjouer; [- expectations, hopes] décevoir, tromper.

◇ *n* [deflector] déflecteur *m*; [acoustic] baffle *m*, écran *m*.

baffle board, **baffle plate** = **baffle** *n*.

bafflement ['bæflmənt] *n* confusion *f*.

baffling ['bæflɪŋ] *adj* déconcertant, déroutant; a ~ problem un casse-tête.

bag [bæg] (*pt* & *pp* bagged, *cont* bagging) ◇ *n* -**1.** [container] sac *m*; paper/plastic ~ sac en papier/en plastique; a ~ of sweets/groceries un sac de bonbons/d'épicerie ❑ tea ~ sachet *m* de thé; he's nothing but a ~ of bones c'est un vrai sac d'os, il n'a que la peau sur les os; he was left holding the ~ *inf Am* tout lui est retombé dessus; her promotion is in the ~ *inf* son avancement, c'est dans la poche OR dans le sac OR du tout cuit; to pull sthg out of the ~ sortir qqch du chapeau; the whole ~ of tricks *inf* tout le tralala. -**2.** [handbag] sac *m* (à main); [suitcase] valise *f*; ~s valises, bagages *mpl*; it's time to pack our ~s *fig* c'est le moment de plier bagage; they threw her out ~ and baggage *inf* ils l'ont mise à la porte avec toutes ses affaires. -**3.** [of cloth, skin] poche *f*; to have ~s under one's eyes avoir des poches sous les yeux. -**4.** HUNT prise *f*; did you get a good ~? avez-vous fait bonne chasse? -**5.** *inf pej* [woman]: old ~ vieille peau; stupid ~! espèce d'idiote! -**6.** ▽ [interest]: it's not my ~ ce n'est pas mon truc.

◇ *vt* -**1.** [books, groceries] mettre dans un sac. -**2.** *inf* [seize] mettre le grappin sur, s'emparer de; [steal] piquer, faucher; I ~s the cookies! *Br* les gâteaux sont à moi!; he bagged the best seat for himself il s'est réservé la meilleure place. -**3.** HUNT tuer.

◇ *vi* goder, faire des poches; his trousers ~ at the knees ses pantalons font des poches aux genoux.

◆ **bags** *inf* ◇ *npl Br* -**1.** [trousers] pantalon *m*, fute *m*. -**2.** [lots]: there are ~s of things to do il y a plein de choses à faire; we have ~s of time nous avons tout notre temps.

◇ *interj Br*: ~s I go! c'est à moi!; ~s I get the biggest one! le plus gros est pour moi!

bagasse [bə'gæs] *n* bagasse *f*.

bagatelle [ˌbægə'tel] *n* -**1.** [trinket] bagatelle *f*, babiole *f*; a mere ~ une simple bagatelle. -**2.** GAMES [board game] (sorte *f* de) flipper *m*; [billiards] billard *m* anglais. -**3.** MUS bagatelle *f*.

bagel ['beɪgəl] *n* petit pain *m* en couronne *(de la cuisine juive)*.

bagful ['bægfʊl] *n* sac *m* plein, plein sac *m*; a ~ of sweets un sac plein de bonbons; he ate a whole ~ of apples il a mangé un plein sac de pommes.

baggage ['bægɪdʒ] *n* -**1.** [luggage] valises *fpl*, bagages *mpl*; ~ car *Am* fourgon *m (d'un train)*; ~ room OR checkroom *Am* consigne *f*; ~ handler bagagiste *m*; ~ tag *Am* bulletin *m* de consigne. -**2.** MIL équipement *m* (portatif). -**3.** *inf dated* [saucy girl] coquine *f arch*; [prostitute] prostituée *f*, traînée *f*.

Baggie® ['bægɪ] *n Am petit sachet hermétique en plastique*.

baggy ['bægɪ] (*compar* baggier, *superl* baggiest) *adj* [clothing - too big] trop ample OR grand; [- loose-fitting] ample; ~ trousers un pantalon bouffant.

Baghdad [bæg'dæd] *pr n* Bagdad.

bag lady *n* clocharde *f*.

bagman ['bægmən] (*pl* bagmen [-mən]) *n* -**1.** *inf Br* [salesman] VRP *m*, voyageur *m* OR représentant *m* de commerce. -**2.** ▽ *Am* [racketeer] racketteur *m*.

bagpiper ['bægpaɪpəʳ] *n* joueur *m*, -euse *f* de cornemuse.

bagpipes ['bægpaɪps] *npl* cornemuse *f*.

bag-snatching [-ˌsnætʃɪŋ] *n* vol *m* à l'arraché.

bah [bɑː] *interj*: ~! bah!

Baha'i [bə'hɑːɪ] ◇ *n* adepte *mf* de la religion Bahaï.

◇ *adj* bahaï.

Bahaism [bə'hɑːɪzm] *n* bahaïsme *(religion)*.

Bahamas [bə'hɑːməz] *pl pr n* Bahamas *fpl*; in the ~ aux Bahamas.

Bahamian [bə'heɪmɪən] ◇ *n* habitant *m*, -e *f* des Bahamas.

◇ *adj* des Bahamas.

Bahrain [bɑː'reɪn] *pr n* Bahreïn, Bahrayn; in ~ à Bahreïn; the ~ Islands les îles *fpl* Bahreïn.

Bahraini [bɑː'reɪnɪ] ◇ *n* Bahreïni *m*, -e *f*.

◇ *adj* bahreïni.

Bahrein [bɑː'reɪn] = **Bahrain**.

Bahreini [bɑː'reɪnɪ] = **Bahraini**.

bail [beɪl] ◇ *n* -**1.** JUR [money] caution *f*; [guarantor] caution *f*, répondant *m*, -e *f*; [release] mise *f* en liberté provisoire sous caution; on ~ sous caution; the judge granted/refused ~ le juge a accordé/refusé la mise en liberté provisoire sous caution; she was released on £2,000 ~ elle a été mise en liberté provisoire après avoir payé une caution de 2 000 livres; to stand OR to go ~ for sb se porter garant de qqn; who put up ~? qui a payé la caution?; the prisoner jumped OR forfeited ~ le prisonnier s'est soustrait à la justice *(à la faveur d'une mise en liberté provisoire)*. -**2.** [in cricket] bâtonnet *m*.

◇ *vt* -**1.** JUR [subj: guarantor] payer la caution pour, se porter garant de; [subj: judge] mettre en liberté provisoire sous caution. -**2.** [water] vider.

◆ **bail out** ◇ *vt sep* -**1.** JUR = **bail** *vt* **1**. -**2.** [help] tirer OR sortir d'affaire; his parents usually ~ him out la plupart du temps, ses parents le tirent d'affaire OR le renflouent. -**3.** [boat] écoper; [cellar, water] vider.

◇ *vi insep* [parachute] sauter en parachute.

bail bond *n* JUR cautionnement *m*.

bailey ['beɪlɪ] *n* [wall] mur *m* d'enceinte; [courtyard] cour *f (à l'intérieur de l'enceinte)*.

bailiff ['beɪlɪf] *n* -**1.** JUR huissier *m*. -**2.** *Br* [on estate, farm] régisseur *m*, intendant *m*. -**3.** [official - in former times] bailli *m*.

bailiwick ['beɪlɪwɪk] *n* -**1.** JUR juridiction *f*, circonscription *f*. -**2.** *fig* [interest] domaine *m*.

bairn [beən] *n Br dial* enfant *mf*.

bait [beɪt] ◇ *n* FISHING & HUNT appât *m*, amorce *f*; *fig* appât *m*, leurre *m*; to rise to OR to take the ~ *literal* & *fig* mordre (à l'hameçon).

◇ *vt* -**1.** [hook, trap] amorcer. -**2.** [tease] harceler, tourmenter. -**3.** [badger, bear] lâcher les chiens sur. -**4.** [entice] tenter.

baize [beɪz] ◇ *n* [fabric] feutre *m*; [on billiard table] tapis *m*.

◇ *adj* [cloth, lining] de feutre; ~-covered feutré.

Bajan *inf* ['beɪdʒən] ◇ *n* habitant *m*, -e *f* de la Barbade.
◇ *adj* de la Barbade.

bake [beɪk] ◇ *vt* -**1.** CULIN faire cuire au four; she's baking a cake for me elle me fait un gâteau; ~d potatoes pommes *fpl* de terre au four. -**2.** [dry, harden] cuire; the land was ~d dry la terre était desséchée.
◇ *vi* -**1.** [person - cook]: she got busy baking [bread] elle s'est mise à faire du pain; [cake] elle s'est mise à faire de la pâtisserie. -**2.** [cake, pottery] cuire (au four); the ground was baking in the sun le sol se desséchait au soleil. -**3.** *inf* [be hot]: it's baking in here! il fait une de ces chaleurs ici!; I'm baking! j'étouffe!, je crève de chaleur!
◇ *n* -**1.** [batch of food] fournée *f*. -**2.** *Scot* [biscuit] (sorte *f* de) biscuit *m*. -**3.** *Am fête où l'on sert un repas cuit au four.*

baked Alaska *n* omelette *f* norvégienne.

baked beans *npl* haricots *mpl* blancs à la sauce tomate.

bakehouse ['beɪkhaʊs, *pl* -haʊzɪz] *n* boulangerie *f*.

Bakelite® ['beɪkəlaɪt] ◇ *n* Bakélite® *f*.
◇ *adj* en Bakélite®.

baker ['beɪkə^r] *n* boulanger *m*, -ère *f*; I'm going to the ~'s (shop) je vais à la boulangerie; a ~'s dozen treize à la douzaine.

bakery ['beɪkərɪ] (*pl* **bakeries**) *n* boulangerie *f*.

baking ['beɪkɪŋ] ◇ *n* -**1.** [process] cuisson *f* (au four). -**2.** [bread] pain *m*; [pastry] pâtisserie *f*, pâtisseries *fpl*.
◇ *adj* -**1.** [for cooking]: ~ potatoes pommes *fpl* de terre à cuire au four; ~ dish plat *m* allant au four; ~ tin [for cake, pie] moule *m*; ~ tray plaque *f* de four. -**2.** [hot - pavement, sun] brûlant; [- day, weather] torride.
◇ *adv*: a ~ hot afternoon un après-midi torride.

baking powder *n* levure *f* (chimique).

baking soda *n* bicarbonate *m* de soude.

baklava ['bɑːkləvɑː] *n* baklava *m*.

baksheesh [,bæk'ʃiːʃ] *n dated* bakchich *m*.

Baku [bæ'ku] *pr n* Bakou.

Balaam ['beɪlæm] *pr n* Balaam.

balaclava (helmet) [bælə'klɑːvə-] *n* passe-montagne *m*.

Balaclava [,bælə'klɑːvə] *pr n* Balaklava.

balalaika [,bælə'laɪkə] *n* balalaïka *f*.

balance ['bæləns] ◇ *n* -**1.** [of person - physical] équilibre *m*, aplomb *m*; [- mental] calme *m*, équilibre *m*; she tried to keep her ~ elle a essayé de garder l'équilibre OR son équilibre; I lost my ~ j'ai perdu l'équilibre OR mon équilibre; off ~ [physically, mentally] déséquilibré; he threw me off ~ *literal* il m'a fait perdre l'équilibre; *fig* il m'a pris par surprise. -**2.** [of situation] équilibre *m*; [of painting, sculpture] harmonie *f*; she tried to strike a ~ between the practical and the idealistic elle a essayé de trouver un juste milieu entre la réalité et l'idéal; ~ of nature l'équilibre de la nature; ~ of power [in government] balance OR équilibre des pouvoirs; [between states] balance OR équilibre des forces; he holds the ~ of power il peut faire pencher la balance, tout dépend de lui. -**3.** [scales] balance *f*; everything is still (hanging) in the ~ rien n'est encore certain; our future hangs OR lies in the ~ notre avenir est en jeu; his remark tipped the ~ in his favour sa remarque a fait pencher la balance en sa faveur. -**4.** [weight, force] poids *m*, contrepoids *m*; the ~ of evidence is against him la plupart des preuves lui sont défavorables; she acts as a ~ to his impulsiveness elle sert de contrepoids à OR elle contrebalance son impulsivité. -**5.** [remainder] solde *m*, reste *m*; COMM & FIN solde *m*; ~ due solde débiteur; I'd like to pay the ~ of my account j'aimerais solder mon compte ❑ bank ~ solde (d'un compte); a healthy (bank) ~ un compte sain; ~ of payments balance *f* des paiements; ~ of trade balance *f* commerciale.
◇ *vt* -**1.** [put in stable position] mettre en équilibre; [hold in stable position] tenir en équilibre; she ~d the book on her head elle a mis OR posé le livre en équilibre sur sa tête; to ~ the wheels AUT équilibrer les roues. -**2.** [act as counterbalance, offset] équilibrer, contrebalancer; we have to ~ the right to privacy against the public's right to know nous devons trouver le juste milieu entre le respect de la vie privée et le droit du public à être informé. -**3.** [weigh] peser; *fig* mettre en balance, comparer; you have to ~ its usefulness against the actual cost vous devez mettre en balance OR comparer son utilité et le coût réel. -**4.** [equation, finances] équilibrer; to ~ the budget équilibrer le budget; to ~ the books dresser le bilan, arrêter les comptes; to ~ one's chequebook faire ses comptes. -**5.** [settle, pay] régler, solder; to ~ an account solder un compte.
◇ *vi* -**1.** [remain in stable position] se maintenir en équilibre; [be in stable position] être en équilibre. -**2.** [act as counterbalance]: the weights ~ les poids s'équilibrent. -**3.** [budget, finances] s'équilibrer, être équilibré.
◆ **on balance** *adv phr* à tout prendre, tout bien considéré.
◆ **balance out** *vi insep*: the advantages and disadvantages ~ out les avantages contrebalancent OR compensent les inconvénients; the debits and credits should ~ out les débits et les crédits devraient s'équilibrer.

balance bridge *n* pont *m* basculant.

balanced ['bælənst] *adj* -**1.** [diet, scales, person] équilibré; the two teams were pretty well ~ les deux équipes étaient de force à peu près égale; a ~ view une vue impartiale OR objective. -**2.** [programme, report] impartial, objectif.

balance sheet *n* bilan *m*.

balance weight *n* contrepoids *m*.

balance wheel *n* balancier *m*.

balancing ['bælənsɪŋ] *adj* -**1.** [physical effort] stabilisation *f*; a ~ act un numéro d'équilibriste; it was a real ~ act keeping everyone happy *fig* il fallait jongler pour pouvoir satisfaire tout le monde. -**2.** FIN [account, books -equalizing] balance *f*; [- settlement] règlement *m*, solde *m*.

balcony ['bælkənɪ] (*pl* **balconies**) *n* -**1.** [of flat, house] balcon *m*. -**2.** THEAT balcon *m*.

bald [bɔːld] *adj* -**1.** [having no hair] chauve; he's going ~ il devient chauve, il perd ses cheveux; a ~ patch [on person] une calvitie; [on animal] un endroit sans poils ❑ as ~ as a coot *inf* OR as an egg chauve comme un œuf OR comme une boule de billard. -**2.** [carpet] usé; [mountain top] pelé; [tyre] lisse. -**3.** [unadorned] brutal; the ~ truth la pure vérité; a ~ statement une simple exposition des faits.

baldachin, baldaquin ['bɔːldəkɪn] *n* baldaquin *m*.

bald eagle *n* aigle *m* d'Amérique.

BALD EAGLE:
Cet oiseau est le symbole des États-Unis et figure sur le sceau officiel.

---

balderdash ['bɔːldədæʃ] *n* *(U) dated* âneries *fpl*, bêtises *fpl*.

bald-faced *adj Am* [liar, thief] effronté; [lie] flagrant.

bald-headed *adj* chauve.

balding ['bɔːldɪŋ] *adj* qui devient chauve.

baldly ['bɔːldlɪ] *adv* brutalement; to put it ~ pour parler franchement.

baldness ['bɔːldnɪs] *n* -**1.** [of person] calvitie *f*; [of animal] absence *f* de poils. -**2.** [of mountain top] aspect *m* pelé; [of tyre] usure *f*. -**3.** [of statement] brutalité *f*.

bale [beɪl] ◇ *n* -**1.** [of cloth, hay] balle *f*. -**2.** *arch* [evil] mal *m*.
◇ *vt* -**1.** [hay] mettre en balles; [cotton, merchandise] emballer, empaqueter. -**2.** = **bail** *vt* **2.**

Balearic Islands [,bælɪ'ærɪk-] *pl pr n*: the ~ les Baléares *fpl*; in the ~ aux Baléares.

baleful ['beɪlfʊl] *adj* -**1.** [menacing] menaçant; [wicked] sinistre, méchant; he looked at us with a ~ eye il nous a regardés d'un sale œil. -**2.** [gloomy] lugubre.

balefully ['beɪlfʊlɪ] *adv* -**1.** [menacingly - look] d'un sale œil; [- say] d'un ton menaçant. -**2.** [gloomily] d'une façon lugubre.

baler ['beɪlə^r] *n* ramasseuse-presse *f*.

Bali ['bɑːlɪ] *pr n* Bali; in ~ à Bali.

Balinese [,bɑːlɪ'niːz] (*pl inv*) ◇ *n* -**1.** [person] Balinais *m*, -e *f*. -**2.** LING balinais *m*.
◇ *adj* balinais, de Bali.

balk [bɔːk] ◇ *vi*: to ~ at sthg: the horse ~ed at the fence le cheval a refusé la barrière; he ~ed at the idea of murder il a reculé devant l'idée du meurtre.
◇ *vt* -**1.** [thwart] contrecarrer, contrarier. -**2.** [avoid] éviter.
◇ *n* -**1.** [beam] bille *f*; [of roof] solive *f*. -**2.** AGR billon *m*. -**3.** [hindrance] obstacle *m*. -**4.** [in baseball] feinte *f* irrégulière d'un lanceur.

Balkan ['bɔːlkən] *adj* balkanique; ~ States États *mpl* balkaniques, Balkans *mpl*; ~ Peninsula péninsule *f* balkanique, Balkans *mpl*.

balkanize, -ise ['bɔːlkənaɪz] *vt* balkaniser.

Balkans ['bɔːlkənz] *pl pr n* Balkans *mpl*; in the ~ dans les Balkans.

ball [bɔːl] ◇ *n* -**1.** [sphere] boule *f*; he rolled up the jersey into a ~ il a roulé le pullover en boule; the hedgehog was curled up in a ~ le hérisson était roulé en boule; a ~ of wool une pelote de laine; roll up the wool into a ~ mets la laine en pelote. -**2.** SPORT [small] balle *f*; [large] ballon *m*; [in snooker] bille *f*, boule *f*; [in croquet] boule *f*; the children were playing ~ les enfants jouaient au ballon; tennis/golf ~ balle de tennis/de golf; rugby ~ ballon de rugby. -**3.** [shot - in golf & tennis] coup *m*; [- in football & hockey] tir *m*; that was a difficult ~ c'était un tir difficile; a long ~ un coup qui est allé trop loin; it was a good ~ c'était bien joué. -**4.** ANAT: the ~ of the foot la plante du pied; the ~ of the thumb la partie charnue du pouce. -**5.** [dance] bal *m*; to have OR to hold OR to organize a ~ donner un bal ‖ *fig*: to have a ~ *inf* se marrer comme des fous; I'm having a ~ je me marre comme un fou, je m'éclate. -**6.** *phr*: the ~ is in his court now c'est à lui de jouer maintenant, la balle est dans son camp; to be on the ~ [capable] être à la hauteur de la situation; [alert] être sur le qui-vive; to keep the ~ rolling [maintain interest] maintenir l'intérêt; [maintain activity] assurer la continuité; [maintain conversation] alimenter la conversation; to start OR to set the ~ rolling [in conversation] lancer la conversation; [in deal] faire démarrer l'affaire; that's the way the ~ bounces! *inf Am* c'est la vie!
◇ *vi* -**1.** [wool] boulocher. -**2.** ▼ *Am* [have sex] baiser.
◇ *vt* -**1.** [wool] mettre en pelote; [fists] serrer. -**2.** ▼ *Am* [have sex with] baiser.
◆ **balls**▼ ◇ *npl* -**1.** [testicles] couilles *fpl*; they've got you by the ~s *fig* t'es bien baisé. -**2.** [courage]: to have ~s avoir des couilles au cul, en avoir; he lost his ~s il s'est dégonflé. -**3.** [rubbish]: what a load of ~s! c'est des conneries, tout ça!
◇ *interj*: ~s! quelles conneries!
◆ **balls up**▽ *Br*, **ball up**▽ *Am vt sep* foutre la merde dans; he completely ~ed OR ~sed up the job il a complètement salopé le boulot; we're really ~sed up now on est dans la merde jusqu'au cou.

ballad ['bæləd] *n* [song - narrative] ballade *f*; [- popular, sentimental] romance *f*; [musical piece] ballade *f*; 'The Ballad of Reading Gaol' *Wilde* 'Ballade de la geôle de Reading'.

ball-and-socket *adj* à rotule; a ~ joint un joint à rotule.

ballast ['bæləst] ◇ *n (U)* -**1.** [in balloon, ship] lest *m*; to drop ~ jeter du lest. -**2.** [in road] pierraille *f*; RAIL ballast *m*.
◇ *vt* -**1.** [balloon, ship] lester. -**2.** [road] empierrer, caillouter; [railway] ballaster.

ball bearing *n* bille *f* de roulement; ~s roulement *m* à billes.

ball boy *n* ramasseur *m* de balles.

ballbreaker▽ [ˈbɔːlˌbreɪkəʳ] *n* **-1.** [task] boulot *m* très difficile. **-2.** *pej* [woman] chieuse *f*.
ballcock [ˈbɔːlkɒk] *n* robinet *m* à flotteur.
ballerina [ˌbæləˈriːnə] *n* ballerine *f (danseuse)*.
ballet [ˈbæleɪ] *n* ballet *m*; **~ shoe** chausson *m* de danse.
ballet dancer *n* danseur *m*, -euse *f* de ballet.
ballet dress *n* robe *f* de ballet; [skirt] tutu *m*.
ball game *n* **-1.** SPORT [with small ball] jeu *m* de balle; [with large ball] jeu *m* de ballon; [baseball] match *m* de base-ball. **-2.** *inf fig* [activity]: **it's a whole new ~, it's a different ~ altogether** ce n'est pas du tout la même histoire; **we're talking about a different ~** ça n'a rien à voir avec notre sujet.
ball girl *n* ramasseuse *f* de balles.
ballistic [bəˈlɪstɪk] *adj* balistique.
ballistic missile *n* missile *m* balistique.
ballistics [bəˈlɪstɪks] *n (U)* balistique *f*.
ball joint *n* joint *m* à rotule.
ballocks [ˈbɒləks] = **bollocks**.
balloon [bəˈluːn] ◇ *n* **-1.** [toy] ballon *m*. **-2.** AERON ballon *m*, aérostat *m*; **to go up in a ~** monter en ballon; **hot-air ~** montgolfière *f*; **when the ~ goes up** *inf* quand ça démarre; **the ~ went up** *inf* l'affaire a éclaté. **-3.** [in comic strip] bulle *f*. **-4.** CHEM [flask] ballon *m*. **-5.** [brandy glass] (verre *m*) ballon *m*. **-6.** *Br* [shot - in tennis] lob *m*; [- in football] chandelle *f*.
◇ *vi* **-1.** AERON: **to go ~ing** faire une ascension OR des ascensions en ballon. **-2.** [billow - sail, trousers] gonfler. **-3.** *fig* [grow dramatically] augmenter démesurément; **unemployment has ~ed in recent months** le chômage a considérablement augmenté ces derniers mois.
◇ *vt Br* SPORT [ball] projeter très haut en l'air.
balloon glass *n* verre *m* ballon.
balloonist [bəˈluːnɪst] *n* aéronaute *mf*.
balloon sail *n* spinnaker *m*.
balloon sleeve *n* manche *f* ballon.
balloon tyre *n* pneu *m* ballon.
ballot [ˈbælət] (*pt & pp* **ballotted**, *cont* **ballotting**) ◇ *n* **-1.** [secret vote] scrutin *m*; **to vote by ~** voter à bulletin secret; **in the second ~** au deuxième tour de scrutin; **to take a ~** procéder à un scrutin OR à un vote. **-2.** [voting paper] bulletin *m* de vote.
◇ *vt* sonder au moyen d'un vote.
ballot box *n* **-1.** [for ballot papers] urne *f*; **~ stuffing** *Am* fraude *f* électorale. **-2.** *fig* système *m* électoral OR démocratique; **change cannot be achieved by the ~ alone** le système électoral à lui seul ne suffit pas à faire bouger les choses.
ballot paper *n* bulletin *m* de vote.
ball park *n* **-1.** [stadium] stade *m* de base-ball. **-2.** *inf* [approximate range] ordre *m* de grandeur; **his guess was in the right ~** il avait plutôt bien deviné.
◆ **ball-park** *comp inf*: **a ~ figure** un chiffre approximatif.
ballpoint [ˈbɔːlpɔɪnt] ◇ *adj* à bille; **~ pen** stylo *m* (à) bille.
◇ *n* stylo *m* (à) bille, Bic® *m*.
ballroom [ˈbɔːlrʊm] *n* salle *f* de bal.
ballroom dancing *n* danse *f* de salon.
balls [bɔːlz] → **ball**.
balls-up▽ *Br*, **ball-up**▽ *Am n* bordel *m*; **I made a real ~ of the interview** j'ai complètement merdé l'interview; **the trip was a complete ~** l'excursion a complètement foiré.
ball valve *n* robinet *m* à tournant sphérique.
bally *inf* [ˈbælɪ] *adj Br dated* sacré *(before n)*, satané *(before n)*; **~ fool!** espèce de crétin!
ballyhoo *inf* [ˌbælɪˈhuː] *n* [commotion] tapage *m*; [publicity] battage *m*.
balm [bɑːm] *n* **-1.** *literal & fig* baume *m*. **-2.** BOT mélisse *f* officinale; **lemon ~** citronnelle *f*.
Balmoral [bælˈmɒrəl] *pr n*: **~ (Castle)** *château situé dans le nord-est de l'Écosse et appartenant à la famille royale britannique*.
balmy [ˈbɑːmɪ] *adj* **-1.** [weather] doux. **-2.** [scented] embaumé, parfumé; BOT balsamique.
balneology [ˌbælnɪˈɒlədʒɪ] *n* science *f* de la balnéothérapie.
baloney *inf* [bəˈləʊnɪ] *n (U)* idioties *fpl*, balivernes *fpl*; **~, you don't know what you're talking about!** n'importe quoi, tu ne sais pas de quoi tu parles!
BALPA [ˈbælpə] (*abbr of* British Airline Pilots' Association) *pr n syndicat britannique des pilotes de ligne*.
balsa [ˈbɒlsə] *n* balsa *m*.
balsam [ˈbɔːlsəm] *n* **-1.** [balm] baume *m*. **-2.** [plant] balsamine *f*. **-3.** [turpentine] oléorésine *f*.
balsam fir *n* sapin *m* baumier.
balsam poplar *n* peuplier *m* baumier.
balsam spruce *n* épicéa *m* du Colorado, sapin *m* bleu.
balsawood [ˈbɒlsəwʊd] *n* balsa *m*.
Balt [bɔːlt] *n* [person] Balte *mf*.
Balthazar [bælˈθæzəʳ] ◇ *pr n* BIBLE Balthazar.
◇ *n* [bottle] balthazar *m*.
Baltic [ˈbɔːltɪk] ◇ *pr n*: **the ~ (Sea)** la Baltique.
◇ *adj* [port, coast] de la Baltique; **the ~ Republics** les républiques *fpl* baltes; **the ~ States** les pays *mpl* baltes.
Baltic Exchange *pr n*: **the ~** *bourse du commerce à Londres*.
Baluchi [bəˈluːtʃɪ] (*pl inv* OR **Baluchis**) *n* **-1.** [person] Baloutchi *mf*. **-2.** LING baloutchi *m*.
Baluchistan [bəˈluːtʃɪstɑːn] *pr n* Baloutchistan *m*, Béloutchistan *m*; **in ~** au Baloutchistan.
baluster [ˈbæləstəʳ] ◇ *n* balustre *m*; **the ~s** la rampe *(d'un escalier)*.
◇ *adj* [post, stem of glass] en forme de balustre.
balustrade [ˌbæləsˈtreɪd] *n* balustrade *f*.
Bamako [ˌbæməˈkəʊ] *pr n* Bamako.
bamboo [bæmˈbuː] ◇ *n* bambou *m*.
◇ *comp* [screen, table] de OR en bambou; **~ shoots** pousses *fpl* de bambou.
bamboo curtain *n* rideau *m* de bambou.
bamboozle *inf* [bæmˈbuːzl] *vt* **-1.** [cheat] avoir, embobiner; **they were ~d into signing the contract** on a fait pression sur eux pour qu'ils signent le contrat. **-2.** [confuse] déboussoler; **the game had him completely ~d** le jeu l'avait complètement déboussolé.
ban [bæn] (*pt & pp* **banned**, *cont* **banning**) ◇ *n* **-1.** [prohibition] interdiction *f*, interdit *m*; **they've put a ~ on smoking in the office** ils ont interdit de fumer dans le bureau; **the nuclear test ~** l'interdiction des essais nucléaires. **-2.** COMM [embargo] embargo *m*; [sanction] sanctions *fpl* économiques.
◇ *vt* interdire; **he was banned from going into town** on lui a interdit d'aller en ville; **they are banned from the club** ils sont exclus du club; **he was banned from driving for twelve months** il a eu une suspension de permis de conduire d'un an; **the Ban the Bomb movement** le mouvement contre la bombe atomique.
banal [bəˈnɑːl] *adj* banal.
banality [bəˈnælətɪ] *n* banalité *f*.
banana [bəˈnɑːnə] ◇ *n* [fruit] banane *f*; [plant] bananier *m*; **a bunch of ~s** un régime de bananes.
◇ *comp* de banane; **~ plantation** bananeraie *f*.
◆ **bananas** *inf adj* maboul, dingue; **she's completely ~s!** elle est complètement maboule!; **to go ~s** [crazy] devenir dingue; [angry] piquer une crise.
banana belt *inf n Can* région *f* chaude.
banana boat *n* bananier *m (bateau)*.
banana oil *n* nitrate *m* de cellulose.
banana republic *n pej* république *f* bananière.
banana skin *n* peau *f* de banane; **he slipped on a ~** *fig* il a fait une gaffe.
banana split *n* banana split *m*.
banco [ˈbæŋkəʊ] *interj*: **~!** banco!
band [bænd] ◇ *n* **-1.** [group of musicians - folk, rock] groupe *m*; [- brass, military] fanfare *f*; **drinks were free to members of the ~** les boissons étaient gratuites pour les musiciens. **-2.** [group] bande *f*, troupe *f*; **a ~ of dedicated reformers** une bande de réformateurs convaincus. **-3.** [strip - of cloth, metal] bande *f*; [- on hat] ruban *m*; [- of leather] lanière *f*. **-4.** [stripe - of colour] bande *f*; [- of sunlight] rai *m*; [- small] bandelette *f*. **-5.** [as binding - around wheel] bandage *m*; [- around books] sangle *f*; [- on cigar] bague *f*; [- on barrel] cercle *m*; **elastic** OR **rubber ~** élastique *m*. **-6.** MECH [drive belt] courroie *f* de transmission. **-7.** RADIO [range of frequency] bande *f*; OPTICS [in spectrum] bande *f*; COMPUT bande *f* magnétique. **-8.** *Br* [range - in age, price] tranche *f*; **people in this age ~** les gens dans OR de cette tranche d'âge. **-9.** [ring] anneau *m*; **wedding ~** alliance *f*.
◇ *vt (usu pass)* [stripe]: **a red wall ~ed with yellow** un mur rouge rayé de jaune.
◆ **band together** *vi insep* [unite] se grouper; [gang together] former une bande.
bandage [ˈbændɪdʒ] ◇ *n* **-1.** [strip of cloth] bande *f*, bandage *m*; **he wrapped the ~ around her hand** il a enroulé le bandage autour de sa main. **-2.** [prepared dressing] pansement *m*.
◇ *vt* [head, limb] bander; [wound] mettre un bandage sur; [with prepared dressing] panser.
◆ **bandage up** *vt sep* = **bandage** *vt*.
Band-Aid® [ˈbændeɪd] *n* sparadrap *m*.
bandan(n)a [bænˈdænə] *n* bandana *m*.
b and b, B and B (*abbr of* bed and breakfast) *n Br* chambres *fpl* d'hôte *(avec petit déjeuner)*; **we stayed in a ~ in Brighton** à Brighton, nous avons séjourné dans un bed and breakfast.
bandbox [ˈbændbɒks] *n* [for hats] carton *m* à chapeaux; [gen] boîte *f* cylindrique.
bandeau [ˈbændəʊ] (*pl* **bandeaux** [-dəʊz]) *n* bandeau *m (pour retenir les cheveux)*.
banderol(e) [ˈbændərəʊl] *n* [on ship] banderole *f*; ARCHIT & HERALD banderole *f*; [at funeral] drapeau *m*.
bandicoot [ˈbændɪkuːt] *n* péramèle *m*.
bandicoot rat *n* bandicoot *m*.
banding [ˈbændɪŋ] *n Br* SCH *répartition en groupes de niveau dans le primaire*.
bandit [ˈbændɪt] *n literal & fig* bandit *m*.
banditry [ˈbændɪtrɪ] *n* banditisme *m*.
bandleader [ˈbændˌliːdəʳ] *n* chef *m* d'orchestre; MIL chef *m* de fanfare; [of pop group] leader *m*.
bandmaster [ˈbændˌmɑːstəʳ] *n* chef *m* d'orchestre.
bandoleer, bandolier [ˌbændəˈlɪəʳ] *n* cartouchière *f*.
band saw *n* scie *f* à ruban.
bandsman [ˈbændzmən] (*pl* **bandsmen** [-mən]) *n* membre *m* d'un orchestre; MIL membre *m* d'une fanfare.
band spectrum *n* spectre *m* de bandes.
bandstand [ˈbændstænd] *n* kiosque *m* à musique.
bandwagon [ˈbændwægən] *n*: **to jump** OR **to climb on the ~** prendre le train en marche; *pej* suivre le mouvement.
bandwidth [ˈbændwɪdθ] *n* **-1.** RADIO largeur *f* de bande. **-2.** ACOUST bande *f* passante.
bandy [ˈbændɪ] (*pt & pp* **bandied**, *comp* **bandier**, *superl* **bandiest**) ◇ *vt* **-1.** [blows] échanger. **-2.** [ideas, witticisms, insults] échanger; **don't ~ words with me** ne discute pas avec moi.
◇ *adj* [person] aux jambes arquées; [leg - of animal, person] arqué.
◆ **bandy about** *Br*, **bandy around** *vt insep* [expression, story] faire circuler; **his name is often bandied about** on parle souvent de lui; **this is just one of the explanations being bandied around** c'est une des nombreuses explications qui circulent.
bandy-legged *adj*: **to be ~** avoir les jambes arquées.
bane [beɪn] *n* **-1.** [scourge, trial] fléau *m*; **it's/he's the ~ of my life** ça/il m'empoisonne la vie; **the tax has become the ~ of local government** l'impôt est devenu la bête noire des collectivités locales. **-2.** *lit* [poison] poison *m*.

banefully ['beɪnfʊlɪ] *adv lit* [influence] funestement.

bang [bæŋ] ◇ *n* -**1.** [loud noise - explosion] détonation *f*; [- clatter] fracas *m*; [- slam] claquement *m*; [- supersonic] bang *m*; she shut the door with a ~ elle a claqué la porte; there was a big ~ il y a eu une forte détonation OR une explosion ❑ to go over OR out with a ~ *Am*, to go with a ~ *inf* avoir un succès fou; the show went (off) with a ~ *inf* le spectacle a eu un succès fou. -**2.** [bump] coup *m* violent; he got a nasty ~ on the head il s'est cogné la tête assez violemment.
◇ *adv* -**1.** to go ~ [explode] éclater ‖ *fig*: ~ go my chances of winning! *inf* envolées, mes chances de gagner!; ~ goes another £10! et pan, encore 10 livres de parties! -**2.** [right] en plein; ~ in the middle au beau milieu, en plein milieu; the missile was ~ on target le missile a atteint sa cible en plein dans le mille; I walked ~ into him je suis tombé en plein sur lui; my desk is ~ against the wall mon bureau est contre le mur; his flat is ~ in the middle of town son appartement est en plein centre-ville.
◇ *onomat* [gun] pan!; [blow, slam] vlan!; [explosion] boum!
◇ *vt* -**1.** [hit - table, window] frapper violemment; he ~ed his fist on the table il a frappé la table du poing; I ~ed my head on the ceiling je me suis cogné la tête contre le OR au plafond; we're ~ing our heads against a brick wall *fig* nous perdons notre temps. -**2.** [slam - door, window] claquer; she ~ed the door shut elle a claqué la porte. -**3.** ▼ [have sex with] baiser.
◇ *vi* -**1.** [slam] claquer. -**2.** [detonate - gun] détoner.
◆ **bangs** *npl Am* frange *f*.
◆ **bang about** *inf Br*, **bang around** *inf*
◇ *vi insep* faire du bruit, faire du pétard.
◇ *vt sep* [books, crockery] cogner les uns contre les autres; [person] tabasser, cogner.
◆ **bang away** *vi insep* -**1.** [detonate - guns] tonner. -**2.** [keep firing - soldier] tirer sans arrêt; [keep hammering - workmen] faire du vacarme; *fig* [keep working] continuer à travailler; he was ~ing away on his typewriter il tapait sans arrêt sur sa machine à écrire.
◆ **bang down** *vt sep* [books] jeter violemment; [dish] poser brutalement; he ~ed the receiver down il a raccroché brutalement; she ~ed down the lid elle a violemment rabattu le couvercle.
◆ **bang into** *vt insep* [collide with] se cogner contre, heurter.
◆ **bang on** *inf vi insep Br*: he's always ~ing on about his personal problems il n'arrête pas de casser les pieds à tout le monde avec ses problèmes personnels.
◆ **bang out** *inf vt sep* [tune] jouer fort et mal; [article, book] pondre.
◆ **bang together** *vt sep* cogner l'un contre l'autre; I could have ~ed their heads together! j'aurais pu prendre l'un pour taper sur l'autre!
◆ **bang up**▽ *vt sep* [prisoner] boucler pour la nuit.

banger *inf* ['bæŋəʳ] *n Br* -**1.** [sausage] saucisse *f*; ~s and mash *inf* saucisses-purée. -**2.** [car] tacot *m*, vieux clou *m*. -**3.** [firework] pétard *m*.

Bangkok [,bæŋ'kɒk] *pr n* Bangkok.

Bangladesh [,bæŋglə'deʃ] *pr n* Bangladesh *m*; in ~ au Bangladesh.

Bangladeshi [,bæŋglə'deʃɪ] ◇ *n* Bangladais *m*, -e *f*, Bangladeshi *mf*.
◇ *adj* bangladais, bangladeshi.

bangle ['bæŋgl] *n* bracelet *m*.

bang-on *inf* ◇ *adv Br* -**1.** [exactly] pile; to hit sthg ~ frapper qqch en plein dans le mille. -**2.** [punctually] à l'heure.
◇ *adj*: his answers were ~ ses réponses étaient percutantes.

bang-up▽ *adj Am* formidable, génial.

banish ['bænɪʃ] *vt* [person] exiler; [thought] bannir, chasser; he was ~ed from Rome il a été exilé de Rome; ~ all worries from your mind chassez tout souci de votre esprit.

banishment ['bænɪʃmənt] *n* [of thoughts] bannissement *m*; [of person] exil *m*, bannissement *m*; after his ~ from the party après son exclusion du parti.

banister ['bænɪstəʳ] *n* rampe *f* (de l'escalier).

banjax▽ ['bændʒæks] *vt* -**1.** *Ir* [break] bousiller. -**2.** [hit - person] sonner.

banjo ['bændʒəʊ] (*Br pl* banjoes, *Am pl* banjos) *n* banjo *m*.

bank [bæŋk] ◇ *n* -**1.** FIN banque *f*; I asked the ~ for a loan j'ai demandé un crédit à ma banque; she has £10,000 in the ~ elle a 10 000 livres à la banque; what's the address of your ~? quelle est l'adresse de votre banque?; the ~ of issue la banque d'émission. -**2.** GAMES banque *f*; [in casino] *argent qui appartient à la maison de jeu*; to break the ~ faire sauter la banque; £10 isn't going to break the ~ 10 livres, ce n'est pas la fin du monde. -**3.** [reserve - of blood, data] banque *f*. -**4.** [of lake, river] bord *m*, rive *f*; [above water] berge *f*; [of canal] bord *m*, berge *f*; we ran along the ~ nous avons couru le long de la berge; the ~s of Lake Como les rives du lac de Côme; the Left Bank [in Paris] la rive gauche. -**5.** [embankment, mound - of earth, snow] talus *m*; [- on railway] remblai *m*; [hill] pente *f*; he ran up the ~ on to the road il a grimpé la pente en courant jusqu'à la route. -**6.** [ridge - on racetrack, road] bord *m* relevé; [- of sand] banc *m*; [- by sea] digue *f*. -**7.** EQUIT banquette *f* irlandaise. -**8.** [mass - of flowers, shrubs] massif *m*; [- of cloud, coal] amoncellement *m*; a ~ of fog lay ahead nous avions devant nous une épaisse couche de brouillard. -**9.** MIN [pithead] carreau *m*; [face of coal, ore] front *m* de taille. -**10.** AERON virage *m* incliné OR sur l'aile. -**11.** [row - of levers, switches] rangée *f*.
◇ *vt* -**1.** [enclose - railway, road] relever *(dans un virage)*; [- river] endiguer. -**2.** [heap up - earth, stone] amonceler; did you ~ the fire? as-tu couvert le feu? -**3.** AERON: to ~ an aeroplane faire faire à un avion un virage sur l'aile. -**4.** [cheque, money] déposer à la banque.
◇ *vi*: he ~s with the National Bank il a un compte à la Banque Nationale; where do you ~?, who do you ~ with? quelle est votre banque?
◆ **bank on, bank upon** *vt insep* [count on] compter sur; I'm ~ing on it je compte là-dessus; he's ~ing on us il compte sur nous.
◆ **bank up** ◇ *vt sep* -**1.** [road] relever *(dans un virage)*; [river] endiguer. -**2.** [fire] couvrir; [earth] amonceler.
◇ *vi insep* [cloud] s'amonceler.

bankable ['bæŋkəbl] *adj* bancable, escomptable; to be ~ *fig* être une valeur sûre.

bank acceptance *n* acceptation *f* bancaire.

bank account *n* compte *m* bancaire.

bank balance *n* solde *m* bancaire.

bankbook ['bæŋkbʊk] *n* livret *m* OR carnet *m* de banque.

bank card *n* carte *f* d'identité bancaire.

bank charges *npl* frais *mpl* bancaires.

bank clerk *n* employé *m*, -e *f* de banque.

bank discount *n* escompte *m* bancaire.

bank draft *n* traite *f* bancaire.

banker ['bæŋkəʳ] *n* -**1.** FIN banquier *m*; ~'s draft traite *f* bancaire; ~'s reference références *fpl* bancaires. -**2.** [in betting] banquier *m*.

banker's card *n* carte *f* d'identité bancaire.

banker's order *n Br* prélèvement *m* automatique.

bank holiday *n* -**1.** [in UK] jour *m* férié. -**2.** [in US] jour *m* de fermeture des banques.

banking ['bæŋkɪŋ] *n* (U) -**1.** FIN [profession] profession *f* de banquier, la banque; [activity] opérations *fpl* bancaires; international ~ opérations bancaires internationales. -**2.** [embankment - on river] berge *f*; [- on racetrack] bords *mpl* relevés. -**3.** AERON virage *m* sur l'aile.

banking hours *npl* heures *fpl* d'ouverture des banques.

banking house *n* établissement *m* bancaire.

bank manager *n* [head of bank] directeur *m*, -trice *f* d'agence; my OR the ~ [head of bank] le directeur de l'agence où j'ai mon compte; [in charge of account] le responsable de mon compte; I'll have to speak to my ~ *hum* il faudra que j'en parle à mon banquier.

bank note *n* billet *m* de banque.

bank rate *n taux officiel de l'escompte*.

bank robber *n* cambrioleur *m*, -euse *f* de banque.

bankroll *inf* ['bæŋkrəʊl] *Am* ◇ *n* fonds *mpl*, finances *fpl*.
◇ *vt* financer.

bankrupt ['bæŋkrʌpt] ◇ *n* JUR failli *m*, -e *f*; ~'s estate actif *m* de la faillite; ~'s certificate concordat *m*.
◇ *adj* JUR [insolvent] failli; *fig* [person] ruiné; to go ~ faire faillite; to be ~ être en faillite; the firm was declared ~ la firme a été déclarée OR mise en faillite ‖ *fig*: he is completely ~ of ideas il est complètement à court d'idées; morally ~ sans moralité.
◇ *vt* [company, person] mettre en faillite; *fig* [person] ruiner.

bankruptcy ['bæŋkrəptsɪ] *n* JUR faillite *f*; *fig* [destitution] ruine *f*; ~ proceedings procédure *f* de faillite; moral ~ *fig* ruine morale.

bankruptcy court *n Br* ≃ tribunal *m* de commerce.

bank statement *n* relevé *m* de compte.

banner ['bænəʳ] *n* [flag] étendard *m*; [placard] bannière *f*; *fig*: to march/to campaign under sb's ~ se ranger/faire campagne sous la bannière de qqn; she carried the ~ of women's rights elle brandissait l'étendard des droits des femmes.

banner headline *n* gros titre *m*; in ~s en gros titres.

bannister ['bænɪstəʳ] = **banister**.

banns [bænz] *npl* bans *mpl*; to publish the ~ (of marriage) publier les bans (de mariage).

banquet ['bæŋkwɪt] ◇ *n* [formal dinner] banquet *m*; [big meal] festin *m*.
◇ *vi* [dine formally] faire un banquet; [dine lavishly] faire un festin.
◇ *vt* [dignitary] offrir un banquet à; [treat lavishly] offrir un festin à.

banquette [bæŋ'ket] *n* -**1.** [seat] banquette *f* *(siège)*. -**2.** [footbridge] berme *f*.

bans [bænz] = **banns**.

banshee [bæn'ʃiː] *n personnage mythique féminin dont les cris présagent la mort*; the child was wailing like a ~ l'enfant hurlait comme un putois.

bantam ['bæntəm] *n* [hen] poule *f* naine; [cock] coq *m* nain; *fig* [small person] nain *m*, naine *f*.

bantamweight ['bæntəmweɪt] ◇ *n* [boxer] poids coq *m inv*.
◇ *adj* [boxer] poids coq *(inv)*.

banter ['bæntəʳ] ◇ *n* badinage *m*, plaisanterie *f*.
◇ *vi* badiner; to ~ with sb badiner avec qqn.

bantering ['bæntərɪŋ] *adj* [tone] de plaisanterie, badin.

Bantu [,bæn'tuː] (*pl sense 1 inv* OR Bantus) ◇ *n* -**1.** [person] Bantou *m*, -e *f*. -**2.** LING bantou *m*.
◇ *adj* bantou; ~ languages langues *fpl* bantoues.

banyan ['bænɪən] *n* banian *m*.

baobab ['beɪəʊbæb] *n* baobab *m*.

BAOR (*abbr of* British Army of the Rhine) *pr n forces britanniques en Allemagne*.

bap [bæp] *n Br pain rond que l'on utilise pour faire un sandwich*.

baptism ['bæptɪzm] *n* baptême *m*; ~ of fire *fig* baptême du feu.

baptismal [bæp'tɪzml] *adj* baptismal, de baptême; ~ font fonts *mpl* baptismaux; ~ name nom *m* de baptême.

Baptist ['bæptɪst] ◇ *n* -**1.** [member of sect] baptiste *mf*. -**2.** BIBLE: St John the ~ saint Jean-Baptiste.
◇ *adj* [sect]: the ~ Church l'église *f* baptiste.

baptist(e)ry ['bæptɪstrɪ] (*pl* baptistries OR baptisteries) *n* baptistère *m*; [font in Baptist church] fonts *mpl* baptismaux.

baptize, -ise [*Br* bæp'taɪz, *Am* 'bæptaɪz] *vt* RELIG & *fig* baptiser.

bar [bɑː] (*pt* & *pp* barred, *cont* barring) ◇ *n* -**1.** [pub] bar *m*, café *m*; [in hotel, club] bar *m*; [in station] café *m*, bar *m*; [counter] bar *m*; we sat at the ~ all night drinking on est restés à boire au bar toute la nuit. -**2.** [small shop - for coffee, tea] buvette *f*; [- for sandwiches] snack *m*; heel ~ talon-minute *m*. -**3.** [long piece of metal] barre *f*; [on grating] barreau *m*; [on door] bâcle *f*; ELEC [element] barre *f*; an iron ~ une barre de fer; behind the ~s of the cage derrière les barreaux de la cage; 'push ~ to open' [on exit doors] appuyer sur la barre pour sortir □ to be behind ~s être sous les verrous OR derrière les barreaux; they put him behind ~s ils l'ont mis sous les verrous. -**4.** [ban] interdiction *f*; there is no ~ on foreign athletes les athlètes étrangers sont autorisés à participer aux compétitions. -**5.** [bank - in lake, river] banc *m*; *Am* [alluvial deposit] barre *f*; sand ~ banc de sable. -**6.** [slab - of chocolate] tablette *f*; [- of gold] lingot *m*; a ~ of soap une savonnette, un pain de savon. -**7.** [stripe] raie *f*; a ~ of sunlight un rayon de soleil. -**8.** [in court] barre *f*; the accused stood at the ~ l'accusé était à la barre; the prisoner at the ~ l'accusé *m*, -e *f*. -**9.** [authority, tribunal] tribunal *m*. -**10.** *Br* POL *endroit au Parlement où le public peut venir s'adresser aux députés ou aux Lords*. -**11.** MUS mesure *f*; the opening/closing ~s les premières/dernières mesures. -**12.** MIL *Br* barrette *f (portée sur le ruban d'une médaille)*; *Am* galon *m*. -**13.** HERALD burelle *f*; [dividing shield] barre *f*. -**14.** [in jaw of horse] barre *f*. -**15.** [unit of pressure] bar *m*.
◇ *vt* -**1.** [put bars on - window] munir de barreaux; ~ the door mettez la barre OR la bâcle à la porte; they barred the door against intruders *fig* ils ont barré la porte aux intrus. -**2.** [obstruct] barrer; he barred her way OR her path il lui barra le passage; high interest rates are barring our way out of the recession *fig* le niveau élevé des taux d'intérêt empêche la reprise (économique). -**3.** [ban - person] exclure; [- activity] interdire; members of the sect were barred from entering the country l'entrée du pays était interdite aux membres de la secte; he was barred from the club il a été exclu du club. -**4.** [stripe] rayer.
◇ *prep* excepté, sauf; ~ accidents sauf accident, sauf imprévu; ~ none sans exception; ~ one sauf un, sauf une □ it's all over ~ the shouting l'affaire est dans le sac.
◆ **Bar** *n* JUR: the Bar *Br* le barreau; *Am* les avocats; to call sb to the Bar *Br*, to admit sb to the Bar *Am* inscrire qqn au barreau; she was called *Br* OR admitted *Am* to the Bar elle s'est inscrite au barreau.

-bar [bɑː] *in cpds*: a three~ gate une barrière à trois barreaux; a two~ electric fire un radiateur électrique à deux résistances.

Barabbas [bə'ræbəs] *pr n* Barabbas.

barb [bɑːb] *n* -**1.** [on fishhook] ardillon *m*; [on barbed wire] barbe *f*, pointe *f*; [on arrow] barbelure *f*; [feather] barbe *f*. -**2.** [dig, gibe] trait *m*, pointe *f*; that was a cruel ~ c'était un trait cruel. -**3.** [horse] cheval *m* barbe, barbe *m*.

Barbadian [bɑː'beɪdɪən] ◇ *n habitant de la Barbade*.
◇ *adj* de la Barbade.

Barbados [bɑː'beɪdɒs] *pr n* Barbade *f*; in ~ à la Barbade.

barbarian [bɑː'beərɪən] *n* [boor, savage] barbare *mf*.

barbaric [bɑː'bærɪk] *adj literal* & *fig* barbare.

barbarism ['bɑːbərɪzm] *n* -**1.** [state] barbarie *f*. -**2.** [in language] barbarisme *m*.

barbarity [bɑː'bærətɪ] *n* -**1.** [brutality] barbarie *f*, inhumanité *f*. -**2.** [atrocity] atrocité *f*; the barbarities committed by the enemy les atrocités commises par l'ennemi.

Barbarossa [,bɑːbə'rɒsə] *pr n* Barberousse.

barbarous ['bɑːbərəs] *adj* [language, manners, tribe] barbare.

barbarously ['bɑːbərəslɪ] *adv* [brutally] cruellement, inhumainement; [primitively] d'une façon barbare.

Barbary ['bɑːbərɪ] *pr n* Barbarie *f*, États *mpl* barbaresques; in ~ en Barbarie.

Barbary ape *n* singe *m* de Barbarie.

Barbary coast *pr n*: the ~ les côtes *fpl* de Barbarie.

barbecue ['bɑːbɪkjuː] (*pt* & *pp* barbecued, *cont* barbecuing) ◇ *n* [grill, meal, party] barbecue *m*; to have a ~ faire un barbecue; ~ sauce sauce *f* barbecue.
◇ *vt* [steak] griller au charbon de bois; [pig, sheep] rôtir tout entier.

barbed [bɑːbd] *adj* [arrow, hook] barbelé; [comment] acéré.

barbed wire *n* (fil *m* de fer) barbelé *m*; a ~ fence une haie de barbelés.

barbel ['bɑːbl] *n* [fish] barbeau *m*; [smaller] barbillon *m*; [spine on fish] barbillon *m*.

barbell ['bɑːbel] *n* barre *f* à disques.

barber ['bɑːbə^r] *n* coiffeur *m* (pour hommes); to go to the ~'s aller chez le coiffeur (pour hommes) □ 'The Barber of Seville' *Beaumarchais, Rossini* 'le Barbier de Séville'.

barbershop ['bɑːbəʃɒp] ◇ *n Am* salon *m* de coiffure (pour hommes).
◇ *adj* MUS [songs] *chanté en harmonie étroite*; ~ quartet *quatuor d'hommes chantant en harmonie étroite*.

barber's pole *n* enseigne *f* de coiffeur.

barbican ['bɑːbɪkən] *n* barbacane *f*.
◆ **Barbican** *pr n*: the Barbican (Centre) *centre culturel londonien*.

BARBICAN:
Le Barbican Centre réunit une salle de concert, un théâtre, un cinéma, un musée, une bibliothèque et des salles d'exposition.

Barbie doll® ['bɑːbiː-] *n* (poupée *f*) Barbie® *f*.

bar billiards *n Br version du jeu de billard, couramment pratiquée dans les pubs*.

barbitone ['bɑːbɪtəʊn] *n* véronal *m*.

barbiturate [bɑː'bɪtjʊrət] *n* barbiturique *m*; ~ poisoning barbiturisme *m*.

barbituric [bɑːbɪ'tjʊrɪk] *adj* barbiturique.

Barbour jacket® ['bɑːbə^r-] *n veste en toile cirée à col de velours souvent associée à un style de vie BCBG en Grande-Bretagne*.

barcarol(l)e [,bɑːkə'rəʊl] *n* barcarolle *f*.

Barcelona [,bɑːsɪ'ləʊnə] *pr n* Barcelone.

bar chart *n* histogramme *m*.

Barclaycard® ['bɑːklɪkɑːd] *n carte de crédit britannique*; to put sthg on ~ acheter qqch avec la Barclaycard®.

bar code ◇ *n* code-barres *m*; ~ reader lecteur *m* de code-barres.
◇ *vt* mettre un code-barres sur; ~d items des articles avec code-barres.

bard [bɑːd] ◇ *n* -**1.** [Celtic] barde *m*; [Greek] aède *m*; *lit* [poet] poète *m*; the Bard of Avon le Barde de l'Avon *(surnom de William Shakespeare)*. -**2.** CULIN barde *f* (de lard).
◇ *vt* barder.

bar diagram *n* histogramme *m*.

bardic ['bɑːdɪk] *adj* [poetry, privileges] du barde, des bardes.

bare [beə^r] (*compar* barer, *superl* barest) ◇ *adj* -**1.** [naked - body, feet] nu; they were ~ to the waist ils étaient nus jusqu'à la taille; he killed a tiger with his ~ hands il a tué un tigre à mains nues; to fight with ~ hands SPORT boxer à main nue. -**2.** [unadorned, uncovered] nu; ELEC [wire] dénudé; we had to sleep on ~ floorboards nous avons dû coucher à même le plancher; his head was ~ il était nu-tête; ~ wood bois *m* naturel; the tree was ~ of leaves l'arbre était dépouillé OR dénudé; the lawn was just a ~ patch of grass la pelouse consistait en un maigre carré d'herbe; a wall of ~ rock une paroi de roche nue; to lay ~ one's heart mettre son cœur à nu; to lay ~ a plot révéler un complot. -**3.** [empty] vide; the cupboard was ~ le garde-manger était vide. -**4.** [basic, plain] simple, dépouillé; I just told him the barest details je lui ai donné le minimum de détails; the ~ facts les faits bruts; the ~ bones of the story *fig* le squelette de l'histoire. -**5.** [absolute] absolu, strict; the house was stripped to the ~ essentials la maison ne contenait que le strict nécessaire; the ~ necessities of life le minimum vital; I took the barest minimum of cash j'ai pris le minimum d'argent. -**6.** [meagre]: a ~ 20% of the population is literate à peine 20 % de la population est alphabétisée; he earned a ~ £200 il a gagné tout juste 200 livres; they won by a ~ majority ils ont gagné de justesse; they manage to scrape a ~ living from the land ils arrivent tout juste à vivoter en travaillant la terre.
◇ *vt* -**1.** [part of body] découvrir; ELEC [wire] dénuder; [teeth] montrer; to ~ one's head se découvrir la tête; to ~ one's soul mettre son âme à nu. -**2.** [unsheath - dagger, sword] dégainer, tirer du fourreau.

bareback ['beəbæk] ◇ *adj* [rider] qui monte à cru.
◇ *adv* [ride] à nu, à cru.

barefaced ['beəfeɪst] *adj* [liar] effronté, éhonté; [lie] impudent.

barefoot ['beəfʊt] *adj* aux pieds nus.

barefoot doctor *n* aide-soignant *m*, -e *f*.

barefooted [,beə'fʊtɪd] ◇ *adj* aux pieds nus.
◇ *adv* nu-pieds, (les) pieds nus.

bare-handed ◇ *adv* [fight] à mains nues.
◇ *adj* aux mains nues.

bareheaded [,beə'hedɪd] ◇ *adv* nu-tête, (la) tête nue.
◇ *adj* nu-tête *(inv)*.

barelegged [,beə'legd] ◇ *adv* nu-jambes, (les) jambes nues.
◇ *adj* aux jambes nues.

barely ['beəlɪ] *adv* -**1.** [only just] à peine, tout juste; there was ~ enough to go around il y en avait à peine assez pour tout le monde; I had ~ arrived when I heard the news j'étais à peine arrivé que j'ai entendu la nouvelle. -**2.** [sparsely] très peu; [poorly] pauvrement.

bareness ['beənɪs] *n* -**1.** [nakedness - of person] nudité *f*. -**2.** [sparseness - of style] sécheresse *f*, dépouillement *m*; [- of furnishings] pauvreté *f*; [- of room] dénuement *m*. -**3.** [simplicity] dépouillement *m*.

Barents Sea ['bærənts-] *pr n*: the ~ la mer de Barents.

barf▽ [bɑːf] *vi Am* dégueuler.

barfly *inf* ['bɑːflaɪ] *n Am* pilier *m* de bistrot.

bargain ['bɑːgɪn] ◇ *n* -**1.** [deal] marché *m*, affaire *f*; you keep your end of the ~ and I'll keep mine vous respectez vos engagements et je respecterai les miens; we had a drink to seal the ~ nous avons pris un verre pour conclure le marché; it was a bad ~ c'était une mauvaise affaire; to strike OR to make a ~ with sb conclure un marché avec qqn; to drive a hard ~ marchander d'une façon acharnée. -**2.** [good buy] occasion *f*; it's a real ~! c'est une bonne affaire!, c'est une occasion!
◇ *comp*: ~ offer promotion *f*, offre *f* exceptionnelle; ~ price prix *m* avantageux; ~ sale soldes *mpl* exceptionnels.
◇ *vi* -**1.** [haggle] marchander; she ~ed with me over the price of the shoes elle a marchandé avec moi au sujet du prix des chaussures. -**2.** [negotiate] négocier; the unions are ~ing with management for an 8% pay-rise les syndicats négocient une hausse de salaire de 8 % avec la direction; I won't ~ with you je ne parlementerai pas avec vous.
◆ **into the bargain** *adv phr* par-dessus le marché.
◆ **bargain away** *vt sep* [rights] renoncer à, vendre.
◆ **bargain for** *vt insep* [anticipate] s'attendre à; I hadn't ~ed for this je ne m'étais pas attendu à ça; they got more than they ~ed for ils ne

s'attendaient pas à un coup pareil; things happened more quickly than he had ~ed for les choses sont allées plus vite qu'il n'avait pensé.

◆ **bargain on** *vt insep* [depend on] compter sur; I'm ~ing on it je compte là-dessus; I hadn't ~ed on this happening! je ne m'attendais pas à cela!

bargain basement *n* -**1.** [in shop] *dans certains grands magasins, sous-sol où sont regroupés les articles en solde et autres bonnes affaires.* -**2.** [in newspaper] *dans certains journaux, rubrique des petites annonces consacrée aux articles d'occasion.*

bargain-hunter *n* chercheur *m*, -euse *f* d'occasions.

bargaining ['bɑːgɪnɪŋ] *n* [haggling] marchandage *m*; [negotiating] négociations *fpl*; they have considerable ~ power ils ont beaucoup de poids dans les négociations.

bar game *n jeu pratiqué dans un pub.*

barge [bɑːdʒ] ◇ *n* -**1.** [on canal] chaland *m*; [larger - on river] péniche *f*; motor ~ chaland automoteur, péniche automotrice. -**2.** [ceremonial boat] barque *f*; the queen's ~ la barque de cérémonie de la reine; the admiral's ~ la vedette de l'amiral.

◇ *vi*: they ~ about as if they owned the place ils vont et viennent comme si l'endroit leur appartenait; he ~d into the room il fit irruption dans la pièce; she ~d past me elle m'a bousculé en passant; he ~d through the crowd il bousculait les gens dans la foule pour passer; she ~d across the room elle a traversé la pièce en trombe.

◇ *vt*: to ~ one's way into a room faire irruption dans une pièce; to ~ one's way through the crowd foncer à travers la foule.

◆ **barge in** *vi insep* [enter] faire irruption; I'm sorry for barging in like this excusez-moi de faire ainsi irruption ‖ [meddle]: he keeps barging in on our conversation il n'arrête pas de nous interrompre dans notre conversation.

◆ **barge into** *vt insep* [bump into - person] rentrer dans; [- piece of furniture] rentrer dans, se cogner contre.

bargee [bɑː'dʒiː] *n Br* batelier *m*, marinier *m*.

bargeman ['bɑːdʒmən] (*pl* **bargemen** [-mən]) *Am* = **bargee**.

barge pole *n* gaffe *f*; I wouldn't touch it with a ~ *Br* [disgusting object] je n'y toucherais pas avec des pincettes; [risky business] je ne m'en mêlerais pour rien au monde.

bar girl *n Am* [hostess] *inf* entraîneuse *f* de bar; *Br* [barmaid] serveuse *f* (de bar).

bar graph *n* histogramme *m*.

baric ['beərɪk] *adj* -**1.** CHEM [salt] barytique; [mineral, ore] barytifère; ~ oxide OR hydroxide baryte *f*. -**2.** METEOR de bars.

barite ['beəraɪt] *Am* = **barytes**.

baritone ['bærɪtəʊn] ◇ *n* [singer, voice] baryton *m*.

◇ *adj* [part, voice] de baryton.

barium ['beərɪəm] *n* baryum *m*.

barium meal *n* MED bouillie *f* de sulfate de baryum.

barium sulphate *n* barytine *f*, barytite *f*.

bark [bɑːk] ◇ *n* -**1.** [of dog] aboiement *m*; [of fox] glapissement *m*; *fig* [cough] toux *f* sèche; to give OR to let out a ~ [dog] aboyer, pousser un aboiement; [fox] pousser un glapissement; his ~ is worse than his bite il fait plus de bruit que de mal. -**2.** [of tree] écorce *f*; to take the ~ off a tree écorcer un arbre. -**3.** *Am* = **barque**.

◇ *vi* [dog] aboyer; [fox] glapir; *fig* [cough] tousser; [speak harshly] crier, aboyer; the dog ~ed at the postman le chien a aboyé après le facteur ❑ to be ~ing up the wrong tree se tromper de cible.

◇ *vt* -**1.** [order] aboyer. -**2.** [tree] écorcer; [skin] écorcher; to ~ one's shins s'écorcher les jambes.

◆ **bark out** *vt sep* [order] aboyer.

bark beetle *n* scolyte *m*.

barkeep *inf* ['bɑːkiːp] *n Am* barman *m*.

barker ['bɑːkə^r] *n* [in fairground] bonimenteur *m*.

barley ['bɑːlɪ] *n* -**1.** AGR [crop, grain] orge *f*. -**2.** [in cooking, distilling] orge *m*; [in soup] orge *m* perlé; [for whisky] orge *m* mondé.

barleycorn ['bɑːlɪkɔːn] *n* -**1.** [grain] grain *m* d'orge. -**2.** [barley] orge *f*.

barley sugar *n* sucre *m* d'orge.

barley water *n Br boisson à base d'orge.*

barley wine *n Br bière très forte en alcool.*

barm [bɑːm] *n* levure *f* (de bière).

barmaid ['bɑːmeɪd] *n* barmaid *f*, serveuse *f* (de bar).

barman ['bɑːmən] (*pl* **barmen** [-mən]) *n* barman *m*, serveur *m* (de bar).

bar mitzvah [,bɑː'mɪtsvə] *n* [ceremony] bar-mitsva *f inv*; [boy] garçon *m* qui fait sa bar-mitsva.

barmy *inf* ['bɑːmɪ] (*compar* **barmier**, *superl* **barmiest**) *adj Br* maboul, dingue.

barn [bɑːn] *n* -**1.** [for hay] grange *f*; [for horses] écurie *f*; [for cows] étable *f*; their house is a great ~ of a place *fig* leur maison est une énorme bâtisse. -**2.** [for railroad trucks] dépôt *m*.

Barnabas ['bɑːnəbəs] *pr n* Barnabé.

barnacle ['bɑːnəkl] *n* bernache *f (crustacé)*.

barnacle goose *n* ORNITH bernache *f*, bernacle *f*.

Barnardos [bə'nɑːdəʊz] *pr n association caritative britannique.*

BARNARDOS:
L'association, fondée par le docteur Barnado, gère des écoles et des centres pour orphelins et enfants défavorisés, notamment handicapés.

barn dance *n* [party] soirée *f* de danses paysannes; [dance] quadrille *m (des États-Unis)*.

barn door *n fig*: it's as big as a ~ c'est gros comme une maison.

barney *inf* ['bɑːnɪ] *n Br* engueulade *f*; to have a ~ avoir une engueulade OR une prise de bec.

barn owl *n* chouette-effraie *f*.

barnstorm ['bɑːn,stɔːm] *vi* -**1.** SPORT faire une tournée à la campagne; THEAT jouer sur les tréteaux. -**2.** *Am* POL *faire une tournée électorale (dans les circonscriptions rurales)*.

barnstormer ['bɑːn,stɔːmə^r] *n* -**1.** [actor] acteur *m* ambulant, actrice *f* ambulante; [acrobat] acrobate *m* ambulant, acrobate *f* ambulante. -**2.** *Am* [politician] orateur *m* électoral.

barnyard ['bɑːnjɑːd] ◇ *n* cour *f* de ferme.

◇ *adj* [animals] de basse-cour; *fig* [humour] rustre; ~ fowls volaille *f*.

barogram ['bærəgræm] *n* barogramme *m*.

barograph ['bærəʊgrɑːf] *n* barographe *m*.

barometer [bə'rɒmɪtə^r] *n* baromètre *m*; the ~ is showing fair le baromètre est au beau; the poll is a clear ~ of public reaction *fig* le sondage est un parfait baromètre des réactions du public.

barometric [,bærə'metrɪk] *adj* barométrique; ~ pressure pression *f* atmosphérique.

baron ['bærən] *n* -**1.** [noble] baron *m*. -**2.** [magnate] magnat *m*; a press ~ un magnat de la presse. -**3.** CULIN: a ~ of beef un double aloyau de bœuf.

baroness ['bærənɪs] *n* baronne *f*.

baronet ['bærənɪt] *n* baronnet *m*.

baronetcy ['bærənɪtsɪ] *n* [patent] titre *m* de baronnet; [position] rang *m* de baronnet.

baronial [bə'rəʊnjəl] *adj* de baron; ~ hall demeure *f* seigneuriale.

barony ['bærənɪ] *n* baronnie *f (terre)*.

baroque [bə'rɒk] ◇ *adj* baroque.

◇ *n* baroque *m*.

barostat ['bærəstæt] *n* barostat *m*.

barperson ['bɑː,pɜːsən] *n* serveur *m* de bar, serveuse *f* de bar.

barque [bɑːk] *n lit* barque *f*; NAUT [3 masts] trois-mâts *m inv*; [4 masts] quatre-mâts *m inv*.

barrack ['bærək] *vt* -**1.** [soldiers] caserner. -**2.** *Br* [heckle] chahuter.

◆ **barracks** *n* caserne *f*; infantry ~s quartier *m* d'infanterie; in ~s à la caserne; the school is a great ~s of a place *fig* l'école est une vraie caserne.

barracking ['bærəkɪŋ] *n* chahut *m*; he got OR they gave him a terrible ~ on l'a chahuté violemment.

barrack-room *adj* [humour, joke] de caserne.

barrack square *n* cour *f* de caserne.

barracuda [,bærə'kuːdə] *n* barracuda *m*.

barrage ['bærɑːʒ] *n* -**1.** MIL tir *m* de barrage. -**2.** *fig* [of punches, questions] pluie *f*, déluge *m*; [of insults, words] déluge *m*, flot *m*. -**3.** [dam] barrage *m*.

barrage balloon *n* ballon *m* de barrage.

barratry ['bærətrɪ] *n* -**1.** *Scot* JUR *délit commis par un juge qui se laisse suborner.* -**2.** JUR & NAUT baraterie *f*.

barred [bɑːd] *adj* [window, opening] à barreaux.

barrel ['bærəl] (*Br pt* & *pp* **barrelled**, *cont* **barrelling**, *Am pt* & *pp* **barreled**, *cont* **barreling**) ◇ *n* -**1.** [cask, unit of capacity - of wine] tonneau *m*, fût *m*; [- of cider] fût *m*; [- of beer] tonneau *m*; [- of oil, tar] baril *m*; [- of fish] caque *f*; they have a production capacity of 2 million ~s a day leur capacité de production est de 2 millions de barils par jour ❑ to have sb over a ~ *inf* tenir qqn à sa merci. -**2.** [hollow cylinder - of gun, key] canon *m*; [- of clock, lock] barillet *m*; [- of pen] corps *m*; to give sb both ~s *inf* passer un savon à qqn. -**3.** *inf* [lot]: we had a ~ of fun OR a ~ of laughs on s'est vachement amusés; he's a ~ of fun il est vraiment marrant.

◇ *vt* [beer] mettre en tonneau; [oil] mettre en baril.

◇ *vi inf Am*: to ~ (along) foncer, aller à toute pompe.

barrel-chested [-'tʃestɪd] *adj*: he is ~ il a le torse bombé.

barrelhouse ['bærəlhaʊs, *pl* -haʊzɪz] *n Am* bistrot *m*; ~ jazz jazz *m* de bastringue.

barrel organ *n* orgue *m* de Barbarie.

barrel roll ◇ *vi* AERON *exécuter une spirale dans la direction du vol.*

◇ *n* tonneau *m*.

barrel vault *n* voûte *f* en berceau.

barren ['bærən] ◇ *adj* -**1.** [land - infertile] stérile, improductif; [- bare] désertique; [- dry] aride; the Barren Lands OR Grounds la toundra canadienne. -**2.** [sterile - plant, woman] stérile. -**3.** [dull - film, play] aride; [- discussion] stérile; [- writing] aride, sec.

◇ *n* lande *f*; the pine ~s of Frankonia les landes de la Franconie.

barrette [bə'ret] *n Am* barrette *f (pour cheveux)*.

barricade [,bærɪ'keɪd] ◇ *n* barricade *f*.

◇ *vt* [door, street] barricader; they ~d themselves in ils se sont barricadés.

barrier ['bærɪə^r] *n* -**1.** [fence, gate] barrière *f*; [at railway station] portillon *m*. -**2.** [obstacle] obstacle *m*; lack of investment is a ~ to economic growth le manque d'investissement est un obstacle à la croissance économique; the language ~ le barrage de la langue; ~ method barrière *f* contraceptive.

barrier cream *n* crème *f* protectrice.

barrier reef *n* barrière *f* de corail.

barring ['bɑːrɪŋ] *prep* excepté, sauf; ~ rain the concert will take place tomorrow à moins qu'il ne pleuve, le concert aura lieu demain; ~ accidents sauf accident, sauf imprévu.

barrio ['bærɪəʊ] *n Am* quartier *m* latino-américain.

barrister ['bærɪstə^r] *n Br* ≃ avocat *m*, -e *f*.

barrister-at-law = **barrister**.

barroom ['bɑːrʊm] *n Am* bar *m (pièce ou bâtiment où l'on vend des boissons alcoolisées)*.

barrow ['bærəʊ] *n* -**1.** [wheelbarrow] brouette *f*; [fruitseller's] voiture *f* des quatre saisons; [for luggage] diable *m*; MIN wagonnet *m*; I wheeled OR carried the bricks in a ~ j'ai brouetté les briques. -**2.** [mound] tumulus *m*.

barrow boy *n Br* marchand *m* ambulant.
barrowload ['bærəʊləʊd] *n* brouettée *f*.
bar sinister = **bend sinister**.
bar snack *n repas léger pris dans un pub*.
Bart. *written abbr of* baronet.
bartend ['bɑːtend] *vi Am* être barman OR serveur (de bar), être barmaid OR serveuse (de bar).
bartender ['bɑːtendəʳ] *n Am* barman *m*, barmaid *f*, serveur *m* (de bar), serveuse *f* (de bar).
barter ['bɑːtəʳ] ◇ *n (U)* échange *m*, troc *m*; a system of ~, a ~ system une économie de troc.
◇ *vt* échanger, troquer; they ~ed animals for cloth ils ont échangé des animaux contre du tissu; he ~ed his freedom for money *fig* il a vendu sa liberté pour de l'argent.
◇ *vi* [exchange] faire un échange OR un troc; [haggle] marchander.
◆ **barter away** *vt sep* [rights] vendre; he's ~ed away his honour il s'est vendu.
Bartholomew [bɑː'θɒləmjuː] *pr n*: Saint ~ saint Barthélemy.
Bart's [bɑːts] *pr n surnom du Saint Bartholomew's Hospital à Londres*.
barycentre *Br*, **barycenter** *Am* ['bærɪˌsentəʳ] *n* barycentre *m*.
baryon ['bærɪɒn] *n* baryon *m*.
barysphere ['bærɪˌsfɪəʳ] *n* barysphère *f*.
barytes [bə'raɪtiːz] *n* barytine *f*.
barytone ['bærɪtəʊn] = **baritone**.
basal ['beɪsl] *adj* PHYSIOL basal; [gen] fondamental.
basalt ['bæsɔːlt] *n* basalte *m*.
bascule ['bæskjuːl] *n* bascule *f*.
bascule bridge *n* pont *m* à bascule.
base [beɪs] (*compar* **baser**, *superl* **basest**) ◇ *n* -**1**. [bottom - gen] partie *f* inférieure, base *f*; [- of tree, column] pied *m*; [- of bowl, glass] fond *m*; [- of triangle] base *f*; the bud grows at the ~ of the branch le bourgeon pousse à la base de la branche; the ~ came away from the rest la base OR la partie inférieure s'est détachée du reste. -**2**. [support] appui *m*, soutien *m*; she used the box as a ~ for her sculpture elle s'est servie de la boîte comme socle pour sa sculpture. -**3**. [of food, paint] base *f*; the stock forms the ~ of your sauce le fond constitue la base de votre sauce. -**4**. [basis - of knowledge] base *f*; [- of experience] réserve *f*. -**5**. ECON & POL base *f*; an industrial ~ une zone industrielle. -**6**. [centre of activities] point *m* de départ; MIL base *f*; the explorers returned to ~ les explorateurs sont retournés au camp de base; the visitors made central London their ~ les visiteurs ont pris le centre de Londres comme point de départ. -**7**. CHEM, COMPUT, GEOM & MATH base *f*. -**8**. [in baseball & rounders] base *f*; he's way off ~ *inf Am fig* il n'y est pas du tout; first ~ *Am* SPORT première base; to get to first ~ réussir la première étape; we didn't even get to first ~ on n'a pas fait le moindre progrès; to touch ~: I just thought I'd touch ~ je voulais juste garder le contact.
◇ *vt* -**1**. [found - opinion, project] baser, fonder; the project is ~d on cooperation from all regions le projet est fondé sur la coopération de toutes les régions. -**2**. [locate] baser; where are you ~d? où êtes-vous installé?; the job is ~d in Tokyo le poste est basé à Tokyo.
◇ *adj* [motive, thoughts, conduct] bas, indigne; [origins] bas; [ingratitude, outlook] mesquin; [coinage] faux.
baseball ['beɪsbɔːl] *n* base-ball *m*.
baseboard ['beɪsbɔːd] *n Am* CONSTR plinthe *f*.
base burner *n Am poêle où le charbon alimente le feu automatiquement*.
base component *n* LING composant *m* de base.
-based [beɪst] *in cpds* -**1**. [located]: the company is Tokyo~ le centre d'opérations de la firme est à Tokyo; a land~ missile MIL un missile terrestre. -**2**. [centred]: a science~ curriculum un programme basé sur les sciences; an oil~ economy une économie fondée sur le pétrole; an interview~ study une étude basée sur des entretiens. -**3**. [composed]: a water~ paint une peinture à l'eau.
Basel ['bɑːzl], **Basle** [bɑːl] *pr n* Bâle.
base lending rate *n taux de base du crédit bancaire*.
baseless ['beɪslɪs] *adj* [gossip] sans fondement; [suspicion] injustifié; [fear, superstition] déraisonnable.
baseline ['beɪslaɪn] *n* -**1**. [in tennis] ligne *f* de fond; [in baseball] ligne *f* des bases. -**2**. [in surveying] base *f*; [in diagram] ligne *f* zéro; ART ligne *f* de fuite. -**3**. [standard] point *m* de comparaison; ~ costs FIN coûts *mpl* de base.
base load *n* charge *f* minimum.
basely ['beɪslɪ] *adv* bassement, vilement.
basement ['beɪsmənt] *n* sous-sol *m*; in the ~ au sous-sol; a ~ kitchen une cuisine en sous-sol.
base metal *n* métal *m* vil.
baseness ['beɪsnɪs] *n* [of motives, outlook] bassesse *f*; [of conduct] ignominie *f*.
base rate *n* FIN taux *m* de base *(utilisé par les banques pour déterminer leur taux de prêt)*.
bash *inf* [bæʃ] ◇ *n* -**1**. [blow] coup *m*; [with fist] coup *m* de poing; he gave me a ~ on the nose il m'a donné un coup de poing sur le nez. -**2**. [dent - in wood] entaille *f*; [- in metal] bosse *f*, bosselure *f*; my car door got a ~ la porte de mon auto a été cabossée. -**3**. *inf* [party] fête *f*; we're having a bit of a ~ to celebrate nous organisons une petite fête pour fêter ça. -**4**. *inf* [attempt]: to have a ~ at sthg, to give sthg a ~ tenter le coup; go on, have a ~! vas-y, essaie!; I'm willing to give it a ~ je veux bien essayer.
◇ *vt* -**1**. [person, one's head] frapper, cogner; she ~ed him on the head elle l'a assommé. -**2**. [dent - wooden box, table] entailler; [- car] cabosser, bosseler; it's part of their campaign to ~ the unions *fig* leur campagne a en partie pour but d'enfoncer les syndicats.
◆ **bash about** *inf Br*, **bash around** *inf vt sep* -**1**. [hit - person] flanquer des coups à; [punch] flanquer des coups de poing à. -**2**. [ill-treat - person] maltraiter, rudoyer; [- car] maltraiter; the package has been bashed about OR around le paquet a souffert.
◆ **bash in** *inf vt sep* [door] enfoncer; [lid] défoncer; [car, hat] cabosser.
◆ **bash on** *inf vi insep Br* [with journey, task] continuer (tant bien que mal).
◆ **bash up** *inf vt sep* [car] bousiller; [person] tabasser.
-basher *inf* ['bæʃəʳ] *in cpds*: a union~ un anti-syndicaliste, une anti-syndicaliste; a bible~ un évangéliste à tous crins.
bashful ['bæʃfʊl] *adj* [shy] timide; [modest] pudique.
bashfully ['bæʃfʊlɪ] *adv* [shyly] timidement; [modestly] avec pudeur.
bashfulness ['bæʃfʊlnɪs] *n* [shyness] timidité *f*; [modesty] pudeur *f*.
-bashing *inf* ['bæʃɪŋ] *in cpds*: media~ dénigration *f* systématique des médias; they accused the government of union~ ils ont accusé le gouvernement d'anti-syndicalisme primaire.
basic ['beɪsɪk] *adj* -**1**. [fundamental - problem, theme] fondamental; [- aim, belief] principal; these things are ~ to a good marriage ces choses sont fondamentales OR vitales pour un mariage heureux. -**2**. [elementary - rule, skill] élémentaire; ~ English anglais *m* de base; a ~ knowledge of Greek une connaissance de base du grec; ~ vocabulary vocabulaire *m* de base; the four ~ operations MATH les quatre opérations *fpl* fondamentales. -**3**. [essential] essentiel; ~ foodstuffs denrées *fpl* de base; the ~ necessities of life les besoins *mpl* vitaux; ~ precautions précautions *fpl* élémentaires OR essentielles. -**4**. [primitive] rudimentaire; their flat is really ~ leur appartement est très rudimentaire. -**5**. [as a starting point - hours, salary] de base; this is the ~ model of the car voici la voiture dans son modèle de base. -**6**. CHEM basique; ~ salt sel *m* basique; ~ slag scorie *f* de déphosphoration.
◆ **basics** *npl*: the ~s l'essentiel *m*; let's get down to ~s venons-en à l'essentiel; I learned the ~s of computing j'ai acquis les notions de base en informatique; they learned to cook with just the ~s ils ont appris à faire la cuisine avec un minimum.
BASIC ['beɪsɪk] (*abbr of* beginner's all-purpose symbolic instruction code) *n* COMPUT basic *m*.
basically ['beɪsɪklɪ] *adv* au fond; they are both ~ the same au fond, ils sont tous les deux identiques; ~ I agree with you dans l'ensemble OR en gros je suis d'accord avec vous; she's ~ a very shy person, she's ~ shy c'est une personne foncièrement timide; ~, I think this war is wrong cette guerre me paraît fondamentalement injuste; ~, she doesn't know what to think dans le fond, elle ne sait pas quoi penser; ~, he only has to do two things en gros, il n'a que deux choses à faire.
basicity [beɪ'sɪsətɪ] *n* CHEM basicité *f*.
basic rate *n Br* taux *m* de base; most people are ~ taxpayers la plupart des gens sont imposés au taux de base.
basil ['bæzl] *n* BOT basilic *m*.
basilica [bə'zɪlɪkə] *n* basilique *f*.
basilisk ['bæzɪlɪsk] *n* MYTH & ZOOL basilic *m*.
basin ['beɪsn] *n* -**1**. CULIN bol *m*; [for cream] jatte *f*. -**2**. [for washing] cuvette *f*; [plumbed in] lavabo *m*. -**3**. GEOGR [of river] bassin *m*; [of valley] cuvette *f*. -**4**. [for fountain] vasque *f*; [in harbour] bassin *m*.
basinful ['beɪsnfʊl] *n* [of milk] bol *m*; [of cream] jatte *f*; [of water] pleine cuvette *f*; to have had a ~ *inf* en avoir ras le bol.
basis ['beɪsɪs] (*pl* bases [-siːz]) *n* -**1**. [foundation] base *f*; he can't survive on that ~ il ne peut pas survivre dans ces conditions-là; on the ~ of what I was told d'après ce qu'on m'a dit; the ~ for assessing income tax l'assiette de l'impôt sur le revenu. -**2**. [reason] raison *f*; [grounds] motif *m*; he did it on the ~ that he'd nothing to lose il l'a fait en partant du principe qu'il n'avait rien à perdre; there was no rational ~ for his decision sa décision n'avait aucun fondement rationnel. -**3**. [system]: on a worldwide ~ à l'échelle mondiale; employed on a part-time ~ employé à mi-temps; paid on a weekly ~ payé à la semaine; the centre is organized on a voluntary ~ le centre fonctionne sur la base du bénévolat.
bask [bɑːsk] *vi* -**1**. [lie]: a cat ~ing in the sunshine un chat se chauffant au soleil. -**2**. [revel] se réjouir, se délecter; he ~ed in all the unexpected publicity il se réjouissait de toute cette publicité imprévue.
basket ['bɑːskɪt] *n* -**1**. [container] corbeille *f*; [- for wastepaper] corbeille *f* à papier; [- for shopping] panier *m*; [- for linen] corbeille *f* OR panier *m* à linge; [- for baby] couffin *m*; [- on donkey] panier *m*; [- on someone's back] hotte *f*. -**2**. [quantity] panier *m*; a ~ of apples un panier de pommes. -**3**. [group] assortiment *m*; a ~ of European currencies un panier de devises européennes. -**4**. [in basketball - net, point] panier *m*; to score a ~ marquer un panier. -**5**. [on ski stick] rondelle *f* de ski.
basketball ['bɑːskɪtbɔːl] *n* basket-ball *m*, basket *m*; ~ player basketteur *m*, -euse *f*.
basket case▽ *n Am* -**1**. [invalid] grand invalide *m*, grande invalide *f*. -**2**. [nervous wreck] paquet *m* de nerfs.
basket chair *n* chaise *f* en osier.
basket clause *n* clause *f* fourre-tout.
basketful ['bɑːskɪtfʊl] *n* plein panier *m*.
basket maker *n* vannier *m*.
basketry ['bɑːskɪtrɪ] *n* vannerie *f*.
basket weave *n* TEX armure *f* nattée.
basketwork ['bɑːskɪtwɜːk] *n (U)* [objects] objets *mpl* en osier; [skill] vannerie *f*.
basking shark ['bɑːskɪŋ-] *n* requin *m* pèlerin, pèlerin *m*.
Basle [bɑːl] = **Basel**.

Basque [bɑːsk] ◇ *n* -**1.** [person] Basque *mf.* -**2.** LING basque *m.*
◇ *adj* basque.
Basque Country *pr n*: the ~ le Pays basque; in the ~ au Pays basque.
Basra, Basrah ['bæzrə] *pr n* Bassora.
bas-relief [,bæsrɪ'liːf] *n* bas-relief *m.*
bass[1] [beɪs] ◇ *n* -**1.** [part, singer] basse *f.* -**2.** [bass guitar] basse *f*; [double bass] contrebasse *f.* -**3.** ACOUST [on stereo] basses *fpl*, graves *mpl*; [knob] bouton *m* de réglage des graves.
◇ *adj* grave, bas; a part for a ~ voice une partie pour une voix de basse; a singer with a ~ voice un chanteur à la voix de basse, une basse.
bass[2] [bæs] *n* [freshwater fish] perche *f*; [sea fish] bar *m*, loup *m.*
bass clarinet [beɪs-] *n* clarinette *f* basse.
bass clef [beɪs-] *n* clef *f* de fa.
bass drum [beɪs-] *n* grosse caisse *f.*
basset ['bæsɪt] = **basset hound**.
basset hound *n* basset *m (chien)*.
bass guitar [beɪs-] *n* guitare *f* basse.
bassinet [,bæsɪ'net] *n* [crib] berceau *m.*
bassist ['beɪsɪst] *n* joueur *m*, -euse *f* de basse.
bassoon [bə'suːn] *n* basson *m.*
bass viol [beɪs-] *n* viole *f* de gambe.
bastard ['bɑːstəd] ◇ *n* -**1.** *lit* OR *pej* [child] bâtard *m*, -e *f*, enfant naturel *m*, enfant naturelle *f.* -**2.** ▽ *pej* [nasty person] salaud *m.* -**3.** ▽ [affectionate use]: you lucky ~! sacré veinard!; poor ~! pauvre type!; he's a silly ~! c'est un pauvre con! -**4.** ▽ [difficult case, job]: it's a ~ of a book to translate ce livre est vachement dur à traduire; this job's a real ~ ce boulot est une vraie vacherie.
◇ *adj* -**1.** *lit* OR *pej* [child] naturel, bâtard. -**2.** [language] corrompu. -**3.** TYPO [character] d'un autre œil.
bastardize, -ise ['bɑːstədaɪz] *vt* -**1.** [language, style] corrompre. -**2.** [child] déclarer illégitime OR naturel.
bastardy ['bɑːstədɪ] *n* bâtardise *f.*
baste [beɪst] *vt* -**1.** CULIN arroser. -**2.** SEW bâtir, faufiler. -**3.** [beat] rouer de coups, rosser.
basting ['beɪstɪŋ] *n* -**1.** CULIN arrosage *m.* -**2.** SEW bâtissage *m.* -**3.** [beating] raclée *f*, correction *f.*
bastion ['bæstɪən] *n* *literal* & *fig* bastion *m*; the last ~ of Stalinism le dernier bastion du stalinisme.
BASW (*abbr of* British Association of Social Workers) *pr n syndicat britannique des travailleurs sociaux.*
bat [bæt] (*pt* & *pp* batted, *cont* batting) ◇ *n* -**1.** [in baseball & cricket] batte *f*; [in table tennis] raquette *f*; he's a good ~ il manie bien la batte ❑ right off the ~ *inf Am* sur-le-champ; to do sthg off one's own ~ *Br* faire qqch de sa propre initiative. -**2.** [shot, blow] coup *m.* -**3.** ZOOL chauve-souris *f*; she's an old ~ *inf fig* & *pej* c'est une vieille bique OR chouette; to have ~s in the OR one's belfry *inf* avoir une araignée au plafond; to run/to drive like a ~ out of hell *inf* courir/conduire comme si l'on avait le diable à ses trousses. -**4.** ▽ *Am* [spree] fête *f*, bringue *f*; to go off on a ~ aller faire la bringue.
◇ *vi* [baseball player, cricketer - play] manier la batte; [- take one's turn at playing] être à la batte; he batted for Pakistan il était à la batte pour l'équipe pakistanaise; to go in to ~ aller à la batte; to go to ~ for sb *inf Am* intervenir en faveur de qqn.
◇ *vt* -**1.** [hit] donner un coup à. -**2.** [blink]: she batted her eyelids at him elle battit des paupières en le regardant; he didn't ~ an eyelid *fig* il n'a pas sourcillé OR bronché; she did it without batting an eyelid *fig* elle l'a fait sans broncher.
◆ **bat around** *inf vt sep Am*: to ~ sthg around parler de qqch à bâtons rompus.
batch [bætʃ] ◇ *n* [of letters] paquet *m*, liasse *f*; [of people] groupe *m*; [of refugees] convoi *m*; [of bread] fournée *f*; [of recruits] contingent *m*; COMM lot *m.*
◇ *vt* grouper.
batch processing *n* COMPUT traitement *m* par lots.
bate [beɪt] ◇ *vi lit* [abate] diminuer.
◇ *n Br dated* [temper] accès *m* de colère, crise *f.*
bated ['beɪtɪd] *adj*: we waited with ~ breath nous avons attendu en retenant notre souffle.
bath [bɑːθ] (*pl* baths [bɑːðz], *pt* & *pp* bathed) ◇ *n* -**1.** [wash] bain *m*; [tub] baignoire *f*; to give sb a ~ donner un bain à qqn; to take OR to have *Br* a ~ prendre un bain; she's in the ~ elle prend son bain, elle est dans son bain; to run OR *fml* to draw a ~ se faire couler un bain; a room with ~ une chambre avec salle de bains. -**2.** [for chemicals, dye] bain *m*; PHOT cuvette *f.*
◇ *vt* [baby, person] baigner, donner un bain à.
◇ *vi Br* prendre un bain.
◆ **baths** *npl* [swimming pool] piscine *f*; [public baths] bains-douches *mpl*; [at spa] thermes *mpl.*
bath bun *n petit pain rond aux raisins secs servi chaud et beurré.*
bath chair *n* fauteuil *m* roulant.
bath cube *n* cube *m* de sels de bain.
bathe [beɪð] (*pt* & *pp* bathed) ◇ *vi* -**1.** *Br* [swim] se baigner; we ~d in the sea/the river nous avons pris un bain de mer/dans la rivière. -**2.** *Am* [bath] prendre un bain.
◇ *vt* -**1.** [wound] laver; [eyes, feet] baigner; he ~d his eyes il s'est baigné les yeux. -**2.** [covered]: I was ~d in sweat j'étais en nage, je ruisselais de sueur; the hills were ~d in light les collines étaient éclairées d'une lumière douce; her face was ~d in tears son visage était baigné de larmes. -**3.** *Am* [bath] baigner, donner un bain à.
◇ *n* bain *m (dans la mer, dans une rivière)*; to have a ~ se baigner; we went for a ~ nous sommes allés nous baigner.
bather ['beɪðəʳ] *n* [swimmer] baigneur *m*, -euse *f.*
◆ **bathers** *npl Austr* [costume] maillot *m* de bain.
bathhouse ['bɑːθhaʊs, *pl* -haʊzɪz] *n* bains-douches *mpl (bâtiment)*.
bathing ['beɪðɪŋ] *n (U)* -**1.** *Br* [swimming] baignade *f*; 'not safe for ~' 'baignade interdite'. -**2.** [washing] bain *m.*
bathing beauty *n* belle *f* baigneuse.
bathing cap *n* bonnet *m* de bain.
bathing costume *n* maillot *m* de bain.
bathing hut *n* cabine *f* de bains.
bathing machine *n* cabine *f* de bains roulante.
bathing suit = **bathing costume**.
bathing trunks *npl Br* maillot *m* de bain.
bath mat *n* tapis *m* de bain.
bath oil *n* huile *f* de bain.
bathos ['beɪθɒs] *n (U)* LITERAT chute *f* du sublime au ridicule.
bathrobe ['bɑːθrəʊb] *n* -**1.** [for bathroom, swimming pool] peignoir *m* de bain. -**2.** *Am* [dressing gown] robe *f* de chambre.
bathroom ['bɑːθrʊm] *n* salle *f* de bains; to use OR to go to the ~ *euph* aller aux toilettes.
bath salts *npl* sels *mpl* de bain.
Bathsheba [bæθ'ʃiːbə] *pr n* Bethsabée.
bath towel *n* serviette *f* de bain.
bathtub ['bɑːθtʌb] *n* baignoire *f.*
bathwater ['bɑːθ,wɔːtəʳ] *n* eau *f* du bain.
bathyscaphe ['bæθɪskæf] *n* bathyscaphe *m.*
bathysphere ['bæθɪ,sfɪəʳ] *n* bathysphère *f.*
batik [bə'tiːk] *n* [cloth, technique] batik *m.*
batiste [bæ'tiːst] *n* batiste *f.*
batman ['bætmən] (*pl* batmen [-mən]) *n Br* MIL ordonnance *m* OR *f.*
baton ['bætən] *n* -**1.** [conductor's] baguette *f.* -**2.** [policeman's - in traffic] bâton *m*; [- in riots] matraque *f.* -**3.** SPORT témoin *m.*
baton charge *n* charge *f* à la matraque.
baton gun *n* fusil *m* à balles en plastique.
baton round *n* balle *f* en plastique.
bats *inf* [bæts] *adj* timbré, cinglé.
batsman ['bætsmən] (*pl* batsmen [-mən]) *n* SPORT batteur *m.*
battalion [bə'tæljən] *n* MIL & *fig* bataillon *m.*
battels ['bætlz] *npl* UNIV *compte d'un étudiant à Oxford.*
batten ['bætn] ◇ *n* [board] latte *f*; [in roof] volige *f*; [in floor] latte *f*, lame *f* de parquet; NAUT latte *f* de voile; THEAT herse *f.*
◇ *vt* CONSTR latter; [floor] planchéier; [roof] voliger.
◆ **batten down** *vt sep*: to ~ down the hatches *literal* fermer les écoutilles, condamner les panneaux; *fig* dresser ses batteries.
◆ **batten on, batten upon** *vt insep Br*: she immediately ~ed on me for help elle s'est immédiatement accrochée à moi comme une sangsue pour que je l'aide.
batten plate *n* CONSTR traverse *f* de liaison.
batter ['bætəʳ] ◇ *vt* -**1.** [beat - person] battre, maltraiter. -**2.** [hammer - door, wall] frapper sur. -**3.** [buffet]: the ship was ~ed by the waves le vaisseau était battu par les vagues; he felt ~ed by the experience *fig* il se sentait ravagé par l'expérience.
◇ *vi* [hammer]: to ~ at OR on the door/wall frapper à la porte/au mur à coups redoublés.
◇ *n* -**1.** TYPO [plate] cliché *m* endommagé; [print] tirage *m* défectueux. -**2.** CULIN pâte *f* à crêpes. -**3.** [in baseball] batteur *m.*
◆ **batter about** *vt sep* -**1.** [person] maltraiter, rouer de coups. -**2.** [ship] battre.
◆ **batter down** *vt sep* [vegetation] fouler; [wall] démolir; [tree] abattre.
◆ **batter in** *vt sep* [skull] défoncer; [door] enfoncer; [nail] enfoncer à grands coups.
battered ['bætəd] *adj* [building] délabré; [car, hat] cabossé, bosselé; [briefcase, suitcase] cabossé; [face - beaten] meurtri; [- ravaged] buriné; a ~ child un enfant martyr; a refuge for ~ wives un refuge pour femmes battues.
battering ['bætərɪŋ] *n* -**1.** [beating]: he got a bad ~ on l'a rossé sévèrement. -**2.** [hammering]: the building/city took a ~ in the war le bâtiment a été durement éprouvé/la ville a été durement éprouvée pendant la guerre; the team took a bad ~ l'équipe a été battue à plate couture.
battering ram *n* bélier *m.*
Battersea Dog's Home ['bætəsɪ-] *pr n centre d'accueil des chats et chiens abandonnés situé à Battersea, un quartier de Londres.*
battery ['bætərɪ] (*pl* batteries) *n* -**1.** ELEC [in clock, radio] pile *f*; [in car] batterie *f*, accumulateurs *mpl.* -**2.** [of guns, missiles] batterie *f.* -**3.** [barrage] tir *m* de barrage; a ~ of insults une pluie d'insultes. -**4.** JUR → **assault**. -**5.** AGR batterie *f.*
battery charger *n* chargeur *m.*
battery farming *n* élevage *m* intensif OR en batterie.
battery hen *n* poule *f* de batterie.
batting ['bætɪŋ] *n* -**1.** [wadding] bourre *f (pour matelas, couettes)*. -**2.** SPORT maniement *m* de la batte; he has a high ~ average il a un score élevé à la batte.
battle ['bætl] ◇ *n* -**1.** [fight] bataille *f*; he was killed in ~ il a été tué au combat; to do OR to give OR to join ~ livrer bataille ‖ *fig*: a ~ between the two companies une lutte entre les deux entreprises; a ~ for control of the government un combat pour obtenir le contrôle du gouvernement; the ~ between OR of the sexes la lutte des sexes; a ~ of wits une joute d'esprit ❑ the Battle of Britain la bataille d'Angleterre; Battle of Britain Day *jour commémoratif de la bataille d'Angleterre*; the Battle of the Boyne la bataille de la Boyne *(bataille qui mit fin au rôle politique des Stuart en Irlande (1690))*; the Battle of the Bulge la bataille des Ardennes. -**2.** [struggle] lutte *f*; the ~ for freedom la lutte pour la liberté; the ~ against poverty la lutte contre la pauvreté; the ~ of the bulge *hum* la lutte contre les kilos; life is one long ~ at the moment de nos jours la vie est un long combat; to do ~ for lutter pour; to do ~ against OR with lutter contre; we're fighting the same ~

nous nous battons pour la même cause; don't fight his ~s for him ne te bats pas à sa place ❑ it's half the ~ c'est presque gagné.
◇ *comp* [dress, zone] de combat; in ~ order en bataille.
◇ *vi* se battre, lutter; she ~d to save his life elle s'est battue pour lui sauver la vie; he's battling against the system il se bat contre le système; they ~d between themselves ils se battirent entre eux.
◇ *vt Am* combattre.

battleaxe *Br*, **battleax** *Am* ['bætəlæks] *n* -**1.** [weapon] hache *f* d'armes. -**2.** *inf pej* [woman] virago *f*.

battle cruiser *n* croiseur *m* cuirassé.

battle cry *n* cri *m* de guerre.

battledore ['bætldɔːʳ] *n* [racket] raquette *f*; [game]: ~ (and shuttlecock) jeu *m* de volant.

battledress ['bætldres] *n* tenue *f* de combat.

battle fatigue *n* psychose *f* traumatique.

battlefield ['bætlfiːld], **battleground** ['bætlgraʊnd] *n* MIL & *fig* champ *m* de bataille.

battlement ['bætlmənt] *n* [crenellation] créneau *m*.
◆ **battlements** *npl* [wall] remparts *mpl*; on the ~s sur les remparts.

battle royal *n fml* OR *lit* -**1.** [fight] bagarre *f*. -**2.** [argument] querelle *f*.

battle-scarred *adj* [army, landscape] marqué par les combats; [person] marqué par la vie; *hum* [car, table] abîmé.

battleship ['bætlʃɪp] *n* cuirassé *m*; 'The Battleship Potemkin' *Eisenstein* 'le Cuirassé Potemkine'.

batty *inf* ['bætɪ] (*compar* battier, *superl* battiest) *adj* [crazy] cinglé, dingue; [eccentric] bizarre.

batwing sleeve ['bætwɪŋ-] *n* manche *f* chauve-souris.

bauble ['bɔːbl] *n* [trinket] babiole *f*, colifichet *m*; [jester's] marotte *f*.

baud [bɔːd] *n* COMPUT & ELEC baud *m*.

baulk [bɔːk] ◇ *n* -**1.** [in snooker] *espace entre la bande et la ligne*. -**2.** = **balk**.
◇ *vi* & *vt* = **balk**.

baulk line *n* [in snooker] ligne *f* de départ; [in croquet] position *f* de départ.

bauxite ['bɔːksaɪt] *n* bauxite *f*.

Bavaria [bə'veərɪə] *pr n* Bavière *f*; in ~ en Bavière.

Bavarian [bə'veərɪən] ◇ *n* Bavarois *m*, -e *f*.
◇ *adj* bavarois; ~ cream CULIN bavaroise *f*.

bawbee [ˌbɔː'biː] *n Scot* sou *m*.

bawd [bɔːd] *n arch* [prostitute] catin *f*.

bawdiness ['bɔːdɪnɪs] *n* paillardise *f*.

bawdy ['bɔːdɪ] *adj* paillard.

bawdy house *n arch* maison *f* close.

bawl [bɔːl] ◇ *vi* -**1.** [yell] brailler; to ~ at sb crier après qqn. -**2.** [cry] brailler; the baby was ~ing le bébé braillait.
◇ *vt* [slogan, word] brailler, hurler.
◆ **bawl out** *vt sep* -**1.** [yell] = **bawl** *vt*. -**2.** *inf* [reprimand] passer un savon à; she really ~ed him out elle lui a passé un bon savon. -**3.** *phr*: the child was ~ing his eyes out *inf* l'enfant braillait à pleins poumons.

bay [beɪ] ◇ *n* -**1.** [on shoreline] baie *f*; [smaller] anse *f*; the Bay State *Am* le Massachussetts; the Bay of Biscay le golfe de Gascogne. -**2.** [recess] ARCHIT travée *f*; [window] baie *f*; RAIL voie *f* d'arrêt; loading ~ aire *f* de chargement; sick ~ infirmerie *f*. -**3.** BOT & CULIN laurier *m*. -**4.** HUNT & *fig*: to be at ~ être aux abois; to bring an animal to ~ amener un animal aux abois; to keep OR to hold sb at ~ tenir qqn à distance; to keep OR to hold hunger at ~ tromper la faim. -**5.** [horse] cheval *m* bai.
◇ *vi* [bark] aboyer, donner de la voix.
◇ *adj* [colour] bai.

bay leaf *n* feuille *f* de laurier.

Bay of Pigs *pr n*: the ~ la baie des Cochons.

THE BAY OF PIGS:
Tentative de coup d'État contre Fidel Castro par des Cubains exilés aux États-Unis, en 1961. Équipés et entraînés par la CIA, ils débarquèrent dans cette baie de La Havane, mais l'opération tourna au désastre.

---

bayonet ['beɪənɪt] (*pt* & *pp* bayoneted OR bayonetted, *cont* bayoneting OR bayonetting)
◇ *n* baïonnette *f*.
◇ *vt* passer à la baïonnette.

bayonet charge *n* charge *f* à la baïonnette.

bayonet joint *n* joint *m* à baïonnette.

bayonet point *n*: at ~ à la pointe de la baïonnette.

bayonet socket *n* douille *f* à baïonnette.

bayou ['baɪuː] *n Am* bayou *m*, marécages *mpl*.

bay rum *n sorte de lotion capillaire*.

bay tree *n* laurier *m*.

bay window *n* fenêtre *f* en saillie; *Am inf* [stomach] gros bide *m*.

bazaar [bə'zɑːʳ] *n* [in East] bazar *m*; [sale for charity] vente *f* de charité; [shop] bazar *m*.

bazooka [bə'zuːkə] *n* bazooka *m*.

BB ◇ *pr n abbr of* Boys' Brigade.
◇ *n* (*abbr of* double black) *sur un crayon à papier, indique une mine grasse*.

BBB (*abbr of* Better Business Bureau) *pr n organisme dont la vocation est de faire respecter la déontologie professionnelle dans le secteur tertiaire*.

BBC (*abbr of* British Broadcasting Corporation) *pr n office national britannique de radiodiffusion*; the ~ la BBC; ~1 *chaîne généraliste (sans publicité) de la BBC*; ~2 *chaîne à vocation culturelle de la BBC*; ~ World Service *émissions radiophoniques de la BBC diffusées dans le monde entier*; ~ English *l'anglais tel qu'il était parlé sur la BBC et qui servait de référence pour la «bonne» prononciation*.

BC ◇ *adv* (*abbr of* before Christ) av. J.-C; in the year 25 ~ en l'an 25 avant Jésus-Christ.
◇ *written abbr of* British Columbia.

BCD (*abbr of* binary-coded decimal) *n* DCB *m*.

BCG (*abbr of* bacille Calmette-Guérin) *n* BCG *m*; ~ vaccination vaccin *m* BCG.

B chromosome *n* chromosome *m* B.

BD (*abbr of* Bachelor of Divinity) *n (titulaire d'une) licence de théologie*.

BDS (*abbr of* Bachelor of Dental Science) *n (titulaire d'une) licence de chirurgie dentaire*.

be [biː] (*pres 1st sing* am [*weak form* əm, *strong form* æm], *pres 2nd sing* are [*weak form* ə, *strong form* ɑː], *pres 3rd sing* is [ɪz], *pres pl* are [*weak form* ə, *strong form* ɑː], *pt 1st sing* was [*weak form* wəz, *strong form* wɒz], *pt 2nd sing* were [*weak form* wə, *strong form* wɜː], *pt 3rd sing* was [*weak form* wəz, *strong form* wɒz], *pt pl* were [*weak form* wə, *strong form* wɜː], *pp* been [biːn], *cont* being ['biːɪŋ])
◇ *vi* -**1.** [exist, live] être, exister; I think, therefore I am je pense, donc je suis; to be or not to be être ou ne pas être; God is Dieu existe; once upon a time there was a prince il était une fois un prince; the greatest scientist that ever was le plus grand savant qui ait jamais existé OR de tous les temps; there are no such things as ghosts les fantômes n'existent pas; she's a genius if ever there was one c'est OR voilà un génie si jamais il en fut; as happy as can be heureux comme un roi; that may be, but... cela se peut, mais..., peut-être, mais... -**2.** [used to identify, describe] être; she is my sister c'est ma sœur; I'm Bill je suis OR je m'appelle Bill; she's a doctor/engineer elle est médecin/ingénieur; the glasses were crystal les verres étaient en cristal; he is American il est américain, c'est un Américain; be careful! soyez prudent!; to be frank... pour être franc..., franchement...; being the boy's mother, I have a right to know étant la mère de l'enfant, j'ai le droit de savoir; the situation being what OR as it is... la situation étant ce qu'elle est...; the problem is knowing OR is to know when to stop le problème, c'est de savoir quand s'arrêter; the rule is: when in doubt don't do it la règle c'est: dans le doute abstiens-toi; seeing is believing voir, c'est croire ❑ just be yourself soyez vous-même, soyez naturel. -**3.** [indicating temporary state or condition]: he was angry/tired il était fâché/fatigué; I am hungry/thirsty/afraid j'ai faim/soif/peur; my feet/hands are frozen j'ai les pieds gelés/mains gelées. -**4.** [indicating health] aller, se porter; how are you? comment allez-vous?, comment ça va?; I am fine ça va; he is not well il est malade, il ne va pas bien. -**5.** [indicating age] avoir; how old are you? quel âge avez-vous?; it's different when you're 50 ce n'est pas pareil quand on a 50 ans; you'll see when you're 50 (years old) tu verras quand tu auras 50 ans. -**6.** [indicating location] être; the cake was on the table le gâteau était sur la table; the hotel is next to the river l'hôtel se trouve OR est près de la rivière; be there at 9 o'clock soyez-y à 9 h; where was I? *literal* où étais-je?; *fig* [in book, speech] où en étais-je? -**7.** [indicating measurement]: the table is one metre long la table fait un mètre de long; how tall is he? combien mesure-t-il?; he is two metres tall il mesure OR fait deux mètres; the school is two kilometres from here l'école est à deux kilomètres d'ici. -**8.** [indicating time, date] être; it's 5 o'clock il est 5 h; yesterday was Monday hier on était OR c'était lundi; today is Tuesday nous sommes OR c'est mardi aujourd'hui; what date is it today? le combien sommes-nous aujourd'hui?; it's the 16th of December nous sommes OR c'est le 16 décembre. -**9.** [happen, occur] être, avoir lieu; the concert is on Saturday night le concert est OR a lieu samedi soir; when is your birthday? quand est OR c'est quand ton anniversaire?; the spring holidays are in March this year les vacances de printemps tombent en mars cette année; how is it that you arrived so quickly? comment se fait-il que vous soyez arrivé si vite? -**10.** [indicating cost] coûter; how much is this table? combien coûte OR vaut cette table?; it is expensive ça coûte OR c'est cher ‖ [add up to]: the phone bill is £25 la facture de téléphone est de 25 livres. -**11.** [with 'there']: there is, there are il y a, il est *lit*; there is OR has been no snow il n'y a pas de neige; there are six of them ils sont OR il y en a six; what is there to do? qu'est-ce qu'il y a à faire?; there will be swimming on nagera; there is nothing funny about it il n'y a rien d'amusant là-dedans, ce n'est pas drôle; there's no telling what she'll do il est impossible de prévoir ce qu'elle va faire. -**12.** [calling attention to]: this is my friend John voici mon ami John; here are the reports you wanted voici les rapports que vous vouliez; there is our car voilà notre voiture; there are the others voilà les autres; there you are! [I've found you] ah, te voilà!; [take this] tiens/tenez, voilà!; now there's an idea! voilà une bonne idée! -**13.** [with 'it']: who is it? — it's us! qui est-ce? — c'est nous!; it was your mother who decided c'est ta mère qui a décidé; it is I who am to blame *fml* c'est moi le responsable. -**14.** [indicating weather] faire; it is cold/hot/grey il fait froid/chaud/gris; it is windy il y a du vent. -**15.** [go] aller, être; she's been to visit her mother elle a été OR est allée rendre visite à sa mère; I have never been to China je ne suis jamais allé OR je n'ai jamais été en Chine; have you been home since Christmas? est-ce que tu es rentré (chez toi) depuis Noël?; has the plumber been? le plombier est-il (déjà) passé?; wait for us, we'll be there in 10 minutes attends-nous, nous serons là dans 10 minutes; there's no need to rush, we'll be there in 10 minutes inutile de se presser, nous y serons dans 10 minutes; he was into/out of the house in a flash il est entré dans/sorti de la maison en coup de vent; I know, I've been there *literal* je sais, j'y suis allé; *fig* je sais, j'ai connu ça ‖ [come] être, venir; she is from Egypt elle vient d'Égypte; your brother has been and gone votre frère est venu et reparti; someone had been there in her absence quelqu'un est venu pendant son absence ❑ he's only been and wrecked the car! *inf* il est allé casser la

voiture!; now you've been (and gone) and done it! *inf* et voilà, c'est réussi! *iron*. -**16.** [indicating hypothesis, supposition]: if I were you si j'étais vous OR à votre place; if we were younger, were we younger *fml* si nous étions plus jeunes; were it not for my sister *fml* sans ma sœur; were it not for their contribution, the school would close *fml* sans leur assistance, l'école serait obligée de fermer. -**17.** MATH faire; 1 and 1 are 2 1 et 1 font 2; what is 5 less 3? combien fait 5 moins 3?

◇ *v aux* -**1.** [forming continuous tenses] être en train de; he is having breakfast il prend OR il est en train de prendre son petit déjeuner; they are always giggling ils sont toujours en train de glousser; where are you going? où allez-vous?; a problem which is getting worse and worse un problème qui s'aggrave; I have just been thinking about you je pensais justement à toi; we've been waiting hours for you ça fait des heures que nous t'attendons; when will she ~ leaving? à quelle heure est-ce qu'elle part OR va-t-elle partir?; what are you going to do about it? qu'est-ce que vous allez OR comptez en faire?; why aren't you working? – but I am working! pourquoi ne travaillez-vous pas? – mais je travaille! -**2.** [forming passive voice]: she is known as a good negotiator elle est connue pour ses talents de négociatrice; the car was found la voiture a été retrouvée; plans are being made on fait des projets; what is left to do? qu'est-ce qui reste à faire?; smoking is not permitted il est interdit OR défendu de fumer; socks are sold by the pair les chaussettes se vendent par deux; it is said/thought/assumed that... on dit/pense/suppose que...; to be continued... à suivre...; not to be confused with à ne pas confondre avec. -**3.** *(+ infinitive)* [indicating future event]: the next meeting is to take place on Wednesday la prochaine réunion aura lieu mercredi; he's to be the new headmaster c'est lui qui sera le nouveau directeur; she was to become a famous pianist elle allait devenir une pianiste renommée; we were never to see him again nous ne devions jamais le revoir || [indicating expected event]: they were to have been married in June ils devaient se marier en juin. -**4.** *(+ infinitive)* [indicating obligation]: I'm to be home by 10 o'clock il faut que je rentre avant 10 h; you are not to speak to strangers il ne faut pas parler aux inconnus || [expressing opinion]: you are to be congratulated on doit vous féliciter; they are to be pitied ils sont à plaindre || [requesting information]: are we then to assume that taxes will decrease? faut-il OR doit-on en conclure que les impôts vont diminuer?; what am I to say to them? qu'est-ce que je vais leur dire? -**5.** *(+ passive infinitive)* [indicating possibility]: bargains are to be found even in the West End on peut faire de bonnes affaires même dans le West End; she was not to be dissuaded rien ne devait OR il fut impossible de lui faire changer d'avis. -**6.** *(+ infinitive)* [indicating hypothesis]: if he were OR were he to die *fml* s'il venait à mourir, à supposer qu'il meurt. -**7.** [in tag questions]: he's always causing trouble, isn't he? – yes, he is il est toujours en train de créer des problèmes, n'est-ce pas? – oui, toujours; you're back, are you? vous êtes revenu alors?; you're not leaving already, are you? vous ne partez pas déjà, j'espère? -**8.** [in ellipsis]: is she satisfied? – she is est-elle satisfaite? – oui(, elle l'est); you're angry – no I'm not – oh yes you are! tu es fâché – non – mais si!; it's a touching scene – not for me, it isn't c'est une scène émouvante – je ne trouve pas OR pas pour moi; I was pleased to see him but the children weren't (moi,) j'étais content de le voir mais pas les enfants. -**9.** [forming perfect tenses]: we're finished nous avons terminé; Christ is risen (le) Christ est ressucité; when I looked again, they were gone quand j'ai regardé de nouveau, ils étaient partis. -**10.** [as suffix]: the husband-to-be le futur mari; the father-to-be le futur père.

◆ **be that as it may** *adv phr* quoi qu'il en soit.

B/E *written abbr of* bill of exchange.

beach [biːtʃ] ◇ *n* [seaside] plage *f*; [shore - sand, shingle] grève *f*; [at lake] rivage *m*.

◇ *vt* -**1.** [boat] échouer. -**2.** [whale] *(usu pass)* échouer.

◇ *comp* [ball, towel, hut] de plage.

beach buggy *n* buggy *m*.

beach bum▽ *n* fana *mf* de la plage.

beachchair ['biːtʃˌtʃeə] *n Am* chaise *f* longue, transat *m*.

beachcomber ['biːtʃˌkəʊməʳ] *n* [collector] *personne qui ramasse des objets sur les plages*; [wave] vague *f* déferlante.

beachcombing ['biːtʃˌkəʊmɪŋ] *n ramassage d'objets sur les plages*; to go ~ aller ramasser des choses sur la plage.

beachhead ['biːtʃhed] *n* tête *f* de pont; to establish OR to secure a ~ mettre en place une tête de pont sur la plage.

beach umbrella *n* parasol *m*.

beachwear ['biːtʃweəʳ] *n (U)* [one outfit] tenue *f* de plage; [several outfits] articles *mpl* de plage.

beacon ['biːkən] *n* -**1.** [warning signal] phare *m*, signal *m* lumineux; [lantern] fanal *m*; AERON & NAUT balise *f*. -**2.** [bonfire on hill] feu *m* d'alarme. -**3.** [in place names] colline *f*.

bead [biːd] ◇ *n* -**1.** [of glass, wood] perle *f*; [for rosary] grain *m*; [necklace]: where are my ~s? où est mon collier? -**2.** [drop - of sweat] goutte *f*; [- of water, dew] perle *f*; [bubble] bulle *f*; ~s of sweat stood out on her forehead la sueur perlait sur son front. -**3.** [on gun] guidon *m*; to draw a ~ on sb *Br* viser qqn.

◇ *vi* [form drops] perler.

◇ *vt* [decorate] décorer de perles.

beaded ['biːdɪd] *adj* -**1.** [decorated] couvert OR orné de perles; a ~ evening bag un sac (à main) de soirée brodé de perles. -**2.** [with moisture] couvert de gouttelettes d'eau; ~ with sweat couvert de gouttes de sueur.

beading ['biːdɪŋ] *n* -**1.** ARCHIT astragale *m*; [in carpentry] baguette *f*. -**2.** SEW [trim] garniture *f* de perles; [over cloth] broderie *f* perlée.

beadle ['biːdl] *n* -**1.** RELIG bedeau *m*. -**2.** *Br* UNIV appariteur *m*.

beady ['biːdɪ] (*compar* beadier, *superl* beadiest) *adj* [eyes, gaze] perçant; a little old man with ~ eyes un petit vieux aux yeux perçants; I had to keep a ~ eye on the sweets il fallait que je surveille les bonbons de près; his ~ eyes never left the money il ne détacha pas ses yeux de fouine de l'argent.

beagle ['biːgl] ◇ *n* beagle *m*.

◇ *vi* chasser avec des beagles.

beagling ['biːglɪŋ] *n*: to go ~ aller à la chasse avec des beagles.

beak [biːk] *n* -**1.** [of bird] bec *m*. -**2.** *inf* [nose] nez *m* crochu. -**3.** ▽ *Br dated* [judge] juge *m*.

beaked [biːkt] *adj* [nose] crochu.

beaker ['biːkəʳ] *n* gobelet *m*; CHEM vase *m* à bec.

be-all *n*: the ~ and end-all la raison d'être.

beam [biːm] ◇ *n* -**1.** [bar of wood - in house] poutre *f*; [- big] madrier *m*; [- small] poutrelle *f*; [- in gymnastics] poutre *f*. -**2.** NAUT [cross member] barrot *m*; [breadth] largeur *f*; on the ~ par le travers; on the port ~ à babord; on the starboard ~ à tribord. -**3.** [of scales] fléau *m*; [of engine] balancier *m*; [of loom] ensouple *f*, rouleau *m*; [of plough] age *m*. -**4.** [ray - of sunlight] rayon *m*; [- of searchlight, headlamp] faisceau *m* lumineux; PHYS faisceau *m*; AERON & NAUT chenal *m* de radioguidage; to be off/on (the) ~ AERON ne pas être/être dans le chenal de radioguidage; to be on (the) ~ *inf Br* être sur la bonne voie; to be off (the) ~ *inf Br* dérailler; he's way off ~ *inf Br* il déraille complètement. -**5.** [smile] sourire *m* radieux; he greeted her with a ~ il l'accueillit avec un sourire radieux.

◇ *vi* -**1.** [smile]: faces ~ing with pleasure des visages rayonnants de plaisir; he ~ed when he saw us il eut un sourire radieux en nous apercevant. -**2.** [shine - sun] briller, darder ses rayons.

◇ *vt* RADIO & TV [message] transmettre par émission dirigée; the pictures were ~ed all over the world les images ont été diffusées dans le monde entier.

beam aerial *Br*, **beam antenna** *Am n* antenne *f* directive.

beam balance *n* balance *f* à fléau.

beam compass *n* compas *m* à verge.

beam-ends *inf npl*: on her ~ NAUT couché sur le flanc; to be on one's ~ *Br* tirer le diable par la queue.

beaming ['biːmɪŋ] *adj* radieux, resplendissant.

bean [biːn] ◇ *n* -**1.** BOT & CULIN haricot *m*; green ~s haricots verts; coffee ~s grains *mpl* de café. -**2.** *inf Am* [head] tête *f*, pomme *f*; [brains] cervelle *f*. -**3.** *inf phr*: to be full of ~s péter le feu; I haven't got a ~ je n'ai pas un rond; hello, old ~! *Br dated* OR *hum* salut, mon vieux!; that car isn't worth a ~ cette voiture-là ne vaut rien; he doesn't know ~s about it *Am* il n'y connaît rien.

◇ *vt Am*: to ~ sb frapper qqn (sur la tête).

beanbag ['biːnbæg] *n* [in game] balle *f* lestée; [seat] sacco *m*.

bean curd *n* pâte *f* de soja.

beanery *inf* ['biːnərɪ] (*pl* beaneries) *n Am* gargote *f*.

beanfeast *inf* ['biːnfiːst] *n Br* gueuleton *m*.

beanie ['biːnɪ] *n* [skullcap] calotte *f*.

beano *inf* ['biːnəʊ] *n Br* [meal] gueuleton *m*; [spree] bombe *f*; to have OR to go on a ~ faire la bombe.

◆ **Beano** *pr n magazine britannique de bandes dessinées pour enfants*.

beanpole ['biːnpəʊl] *n literal* rame *f*; *fig* (grande) perche *f*.

beanshoot ['biːnʃuːt], **beansprout** ['biːnspraʊt] *n* germe *m* de soja.

beanstalk ['biːnstɔːk] *n* tige *f* de haricot.

bear [beəʳ] (*pt* bore [bɔːʳ], *pp* borne [bɔːn]) ◇ *vt* -**1.** [carry - goods, burden] porter; [- gift, message] apporter; [- sound] porter, transporter; a convoy of lorries bore the refugees away un convoi de camions emmena les réfugiés; they bore him aloft on their shoulders ils le portèrent en triomphe; they arrived ~ing fruit ils sont arrivés, chargés de fruits; the wind bore the ship west le vent poussait le navire vers l'ouest; to be borne along by the crowd être emporté par la foule. -**2.** [sustain - weight] supporter; the ice couldn't ~ his weight la glace ne pouvait pas supporter son poids; the system can only ~ a certain amount of pressure *fig* le système ne peut supporter qu'une certaine pression. -**3.** [endure] tolérer, supporter; the news was more than she could ~ elle n'a pas pu supporter la nouvelle; she can't ~ the sight of blood elle ne supporte pas la vue du sang; I can't ~ to see you go je ne supporte pas que tu t'en ailles; I can't ~ that man je ne supporte pas cet homme; I can't ~ the suspense ce suspense est insupportable; she bore the pain with great fortitude elle a supporté la douleur avec beaucoup de courage. -**4.** [accept - responsibility, blame] assumer; they agreed to ~ the costs ils acceptèrent de supporter les frais. -**5.** [allow - examination] soutenir, supporter; his theory doesn't really ~ close analysis sa théorie ne supporte pas une analyse approfondie; his work ~s comparison with Hemingway and Steinbeck son œuvre soutient la comparaison avec Hemingway et Steinbeck; it doesn't ~ thinking about je n'ose pas OR je préfère ne pas y penser. -**6.** [show - mark, name, sign etc] porter; the glass bore the letters "TR" le verre portait les lettres «TR»; the letter bore the signatures of several eminent writers la lettre portait la signature de plusieurs écrivains célèbres; I still ~ the scars j'en porte encore les cicatrices; the crime bore all the signs of a professional job le crime avait tout du travail d'un professionnel; he ~s no resemblance to his father il ne ressemble pas du tout à son père; his statement bore no relation to the facts sa déclaration n'avait aucun rapport avec les faits; to ~ witness to sthg [person] attester qqch; [thing, quality] témoigner de qqch. -**7.** [give birth to] donner naissance à; she bore a child elle a donné naissance à un enfant; she bore him two sons elle lui donna deux fils. -**8.** [produce] porter, produire; the cherry tree ~s beautiful blossom in spring le cerisier donne de belles fleurs au printemps; all my efforts have borne fruit *fig* mes efforts ont porté leurs fruits; his investment bore 8% interest FIN ses investissements lui ont rapporté 8 % d'intérêt. -**9.** [feel] porter, avoir en soi; to ~ love/hatred for sb éprouver de l'amour/de la haine pour qqn; I ~ you no ill will je ne t'en veux pas; to ~ a grudge against sb en vouloir OR garder rancune à qqn; to ~ sthg in mind ne pas oublier qqch; thanks for the suggestion, I'll ~ it in mind merci de ta suggestion, j'en tiendrai compte. -**10.** [comport]: he bore himself like a man il s'est comporté en homme; she ~s her head high elle porte la tête haute. -**11.** ST. EX [market, security] chercher à faire baisser.

◇ *vi* -**1.** [move] diriger; ~ to your left prenez sur la gauche OR à gauche; we bore due west nous fîmes route vers l'ouest; they bore straight across the field ils traversèrent le champ en ligne droite ❑ '~ left ahead' *Am* 'tournez à gauche', 'filez à gauche'. -**2.** [tree - fruit] produire, donner; [- flower] fleurir. -**3.** [be oppressive] peser; grief bore heavily on her le chagrin l'accablait. -**4.** ST. EX jouer à la baisse. -**5.** *phr*: to bring to ~ braquer; to bring a gun to ~ on a target pointer un canon sur un objectif; to bring pressure to ~ on sb faire pression sur qqn; to bring one's mind to ~ on sthg s'appliquer à qqch.

◇ *n* -**1.** [animal] ours *m*, -e *f*; ~ cub ourson *m*; the Great/Little Bear ASTRON la Grande/Petite Ourse; he's like a ~ with a sore head *inf Br* il est d'une humeur de dogue. -**2.** *pej* [person] ours *m*. -**3.** ST. EX [person] baissier *m*, -ère *f*; ~ market marché *m* en baisse. -**4.** [toy] ours *m* (en peluche).

◆ **bear down** *vi insep* -**1.** [approach]: to ~ down on OR upon [ship] venir sur; [person] foncer sur; a lorry was ~ing down on me un camion fonçait sur moi. -**2.** [press] appuyer.

◆ **bear on** *vt insep* [be relevant to] se rapporter à, être relatif à; [concern] intéresser, concerner.

◆ **bear out** *vt sep Br* confirmer, corroborer; to ~ sb out, to ~ out what sb says corroborer ce que qqn dit; the results don't ~ out the hypothesis les résultats ne confirment pas l'hypothèse; he will ~ me out on this matter il sera d'accord avec moi sur ce sujet.

◆ **bear up** *vi insep Br* tenir le coup, garder le moral; she's ~ing up under the pressure elle ne se laisse pas décourager par le stress; ~ up! courage!

◆ **bear upon** = **bear on**.

◆ **bear with** *vt insep* [be patient with] supporter patiemment; if you'll just ~ with me a minute je vais vous demander une petite minute.

bearable ['beərəbl] *adj* supportable, tolérable.

bearbaiting ['beə,beɪtɪŋ] *n* combat *m* d'ours et de chiens.

beard [bɪəd] ◇ *n* -**1.** [on person] barbe *f*; [goatee] barbiche *f*; to have a ~ avoir la barbe; a man with a ~ un (homme) barbu; to grow a ~ se laisser pousser la barbe; he wears a full ~ il porte la barbe; a two-day ~ une barbe de deux jours. -**2.** [on goat] barbiche *f*; [on fish, oyster] barbe *f*; [on plant] arête *f*, barbe *f*. -**3.** TYPO talus *m*.

◇ *vt lit* [confront] affronter, braver; to ~ the lion in his den aller braver le lion dans sa tanière.

bearded ['bɪədɪd] *adj* barbu; ~ lady femme *f* à barbe.

beardless ['bɪədlɪs] *adj* imberbe, sans barbe; a ~ youth *lit* un jeunet.

bearer ['beərəʳ] ◇ *n* -**1.** [of news, letter] porteur *m*, -euse *f*; [of coffin] porteur *m*; [servant] serviteur *m*; I hate to be the ~ of bad tidings j'ai horreur d'annoncer les mauvaises nouvelles. -**2.** [of cheque, title] porteur *m*, -euse *f*; [of passport] titulaire *mf*. -**3.** CONSTR support *m*.

◇ *comp* FIN [bond, cheque] au porteur.

bear garden *n* pétaudière *f*; the place was like a ~ *Br* l'endroit était une véritable pétaudière, on se serait cru à la cour du roi Pétaud.

bear hug *n*: to give sb a ~ serrer qqn très fort dans ses bras.

bearing ['beərɪŋ] *n* -**1.** [relevance] rapport *m*, relation *f*; his comments have some OR a ~ on the present situation ses remarques ont un certain rapport avec la situation actuelle; the event had no ~ on the outcome of the war l'événement n'eut aucune incidence sur l'issue de la guerre. -**2.** [deportment] maintien *m*, port *m*; a man of distinguished ~ un homme à l'allure distinguée; her queenly ~ son port de reine. -**3.** [toleration]: it's beyond OR past all ~ c'est absolument insupportable. -**4.** [direction] position *f*; to take a (compass) ~ (on sthg) relever la position (de qqch) au compas; to take a ship's ~ NAUT faire le point; to get OR to find one's ~s *fig* se repérer, s'orienter; to lose one's ~s *fig* perdre le nord. -**5.** MECH palier *m*.

◆ **bearings** *npl* HERALD armoiries *fpl*.

-bearing *in cpds*: rain~ clouds des nuages chargés de pluie; oxygen~ water de l'eau riche en oxygène.

bearish ['beərɪʃ] *adj* -**1.** [person] *pej* comme un ours. -**2.** ST. EX [market] en baisse; [tendency] baissier.

bear pit *n* fosse *f* aux ours.

bearskin ['beəskɪn] *n* -**1.** [piece of fur] peau *f* d'ours. -**2.** MIL [hat] bonnet *m* à poil.

beast [biːst] *n* -**1.** [animal] bête *f*, animal *m*; the king of the ~s le roi des animaux; the Beast BIBLE l'Antéchrist, la bête de l'Apocalypse; he bears the mark of the Beast on his forehead il porte le signe de l'Antéchrist sur son front ❑ ~ of burden bête de somme; ~ of prey bête de proie. -**2.** [savage nature]: the ~ in man la bête en l'homme. -**3.** *pej* [person - unpleasant] cochon *m*; [- cruel] brute *f*; you ~! vous êtes dégoûtant! -**4.** [difficult task]: a ~ of a job un sale boulot.

beastie ['biːstɪ] *n* -**1.** *Scot* petit animal *m*. -**2.** *inf* [insect] bestiole *f*.

beastliness ['biːstlɪnɪs] *n* [of person] méchanceté *f*; [of act] bestialité *f*; [of language] obscénité *f*.

beastly *inf* ['biːstlɪ] *Br* ◇ *adj* [person, behaviour] bestial, brutal; [language] obscène; [sight, job] dégoûtant; what a ~ day! quelle journée infecte!; he's a ~ child c'est un enfant insupportable; he was ~ to her il a été infect avec elle.

◇ *adv* vachement; it's ~ cold! il fait vachement froid!

beat [biːt] (*pt* beat, *pp* beaten ['biːtn])

◇ *vt* -**1.** [hit - dog, person] frapper, battre; [- carpet, metal] battre; CULIN [eggs] battre, fouetter; to ~ sb with a stick donner des coups de bâton à qqn; to ~ sthg flat aplatir qqch *(en tapant dessus)*; to ~ sb black and blue battre qqn comme plâtre; he ~ the water with his hands il battit l'eau de ses mains; she ~ her breast *lit* elle se frappa la poitrine. -**2.** MUS: she ~ time to the music with her foot elle marquait le rythme de la musique avec son pied; to ~ a drum battre du tambour ❑ to ~ a drum for sthg *inf* faire du battage autour de qqch. -**3.** [move - wing] battre; the bird was ~ing its wings l'oiseau battait des ailes; the pigeon was ~ing the air with its wings le pigeon battait l'air de ses ailes. -**4.** [defeat] battre, vaincre; she ~ him at poker elle l'a battu au poker; Liverpool were beaten Liverpool a perdu; we ~ them to the railway station nous sommes arrivés à la gare avant eux; ~ the rush hour, travel early évitez l'heure de pointe, voyagez plus tôt; to ~ the system trouver le joint *fig*; we've got to ~ racism il faut en finir avec le racisme; to ~ the world record battre le record mondial; nothing ~s a cup of tea rien ne vaut une tasse de thé; she just ~ me to it elle m'a devancé de peu; you can't ~ the Chinese for inventiveness on ne peut pas trouver plus inventifs que les Chinois; the problem has me beaten OR ~ *inf* le problème me dépasse complètement ❑ to ~ the charge *inf Am* JUR échapper à l'accusation; to ~ the rap *inf Am* échapper à la tôle; if you can't ~ them, join them si on ne peut pas les battre, alors il faut faire comme eux OR entrer dans leur jeu; to ~ sb hollow *inf* OR hands down *inf Br*, to ~ the pants off sb *inf* battre qqn à plate couture; (it) ~s me *inf* cela me dépasse; it ~s me OR what ~s me is how he gets away with it *inf* je ne comprends pas OR ça me dépasse qu'il s'en tire à chaque fois; can you ~ it! *inf* tu as déjà vu ça, toi!; ~ that! *inf literal* voyons si tu peux faire mieux!; *fig* pas mal, hein?; that ~s the lot! *inf*, that takes some ~ing! *inf* ça, c'est le bouquet!; his answer takes some ~ing! *inf* [critically] c'est le comble!; [admiringly] on n'aurait pas pu mieux dire! -**5.** [path] se frayer; to ~ a way through the undergrowth se frayer un chemin à travers la végétation; the new doctor soon had people ~ing a path to his door *fig* très vite, les gens se pressèrent chez le nouveau docteur. -**6.** [retreat]: to ~ the retreat MIL battre la retraite; they ~ a hasty retreat when they saw the police arrive *fig* ils ont décampé en vitesse quand ils ont vu arriver la police. -**7.** HUNT: to ~ the woods/the moors battre les bois/les landes. -**8.** *phr*: ~ it! *inf* dégage!

◇ *vi* -**1.** [rain] battre; [sun] taper; [wind] souffler en rafales; to ~ on OR at the door cogner à la porte; the waves ~ against the sea wall les vagues venaient battre la digue; the rain was ~ing against the roof la pluie battait contre le toit ❑ he doesn't ~ about *Br* OR around *Am* the bush il n'y va pas par quatre chemins; so, not to ~ about *Br* OR around *Am* the bush, I've lost my job enfin bref, j'ai perdu mon emploi. -**2.** [heart, pulse, wing] battre; with ~ing heart le cœur battant; his heart was ~ing with terror son cœur palpitait de terreur; I heard the drums ~ing j'entendis le roulement des tambours. -**3.** NAUT: to ~ to windward louvoyer au plus près.

◇ *n* -**1.** [of heart, pulse, wing] battement *m*, pulsation *f*; [of drums] battement *m*; ACOUST battement *m*; to march to the ~ of the drum marcher au son du tambour. -**2.** MUS [time] temps *m*; a strong/weak ~ un temps fort/faible ‖ [in jazz and pop] rythme *m*; a funky ~ un rythme funky. -**3.** [of policeman] ronde *f*, secteur *m*; [of sentry] ronde *f*; we need more policemen on the ~ il faudrait qu'il y ait plus de policiers à faire des rondes; he saw the robbery when he was on his ~ il a été témoin du vol pendant qu'il effectuait sa ronde. -**4.** HUNT battue *f*. -**5.** ▽ [beatnik] beatnik *mf*.

◇ *adj* -**1.** *inf* [exhausted] crevé, vidé. -**2.** ▽ beatnik; a ~ poet un poète beatnik.

◆ **beat back** *vt sep* [enemy, flames] repousser.

◆ **beat down** ◇ *vt sep* -**1.** [grass]: the wind had beaten the grass down le vent avait couché les herbes; the horses had beaten down the crops les chevaux avaient foulé les récoltes. -**2.** *Br* [seller] faire baisser; I ~ him down to £20 je lui ai fait baisser son prix à 20 livres.

◇ *vi insep* [sun] taper; [rain] tomber à verse OR à torrents; the rain was ~ing down il pleuvait à torrents.

◆ **beat in** *vt sep* [door] défoncer; I'll ~ his head in je lui défoncerai le crâne.

◆ **beat off** ◇ *vt sep* [enemy, attack] repousser.

◇ *vi insep* ▼ *Am* se branler.

◆ **beat out** *vt sep* -**1.** [flames] étouffer. -**2.** [metal] étaler au marteau; to ~ one's brains out *inf fig* se creuser la cervelle; to ~ sb's brains out défoncer le crâne à qqn. -**3.** [rhythm] marquer; she ~ the rhythm out on a drum elle marquait le rythme OR elle battait la mesure sur un tambour.

◆ **beat up** *vt sep* -**1.** *inf* [person] tabasser, passer à tabac. -**2.** [eggwhite] faire monter; [cream, egg] fouetter, battre. -**3.** [drum up - help, volunteers] racoler, recruter.

beaten ['biːtn] ◇ *pp* → **beat**.
◇ *adj* -**1.** [gold] battu, martelé; [earth, path] battu; CULIN [eggs, cream etc] battu, fouetté; a ~ track *literal* un chemin OR sentier battu; off the ~ track *fig* hors des sentiers battus. -**2.** [defeated] vaincu, battu. -**3.** [exhausted] éreinté, épuisé.

beaten-up *adj* cabossé; a ~ old bus un vieux bus tout cabossé.

beater ['biːtəʳ] *n* -**1.** [manual] fouet *m*; [electric] batteur *m*. -**2.** TEXT peigne *m*; [for carpet] tapette *f*. -**3.** HUNT rabatteur *m*.

Beat generation *n*: the ~ *mouvement littéraire et culturel américain des années 50-60 dont les adeptes (les 'beatniks') refusaient les conventions de la société moderne*.

beatific [biːə'tɪfɪk] *adj* béat; a ~ smile un sourire béat.

beatifically [ˌbiːə'tɪfɪkəlɪ] *adv* avec béatitude.

beatification [biːˌætɪfɪ'keɪʃn] *n* béatification *f*.

beatify [biː'ætɪfaɪ] *vt* béatifier.

beating ['biːtɪŋ] *n* -**1.** [thrashing] correction *f*; to give sb a ~ donner une correction à qqn; to get a ~ recevoir une correction. -**2.** [defeat] défaite *f*; to take a ~ [gen & SPORT] se faire battre à plate couture. -**3.** [of wings, heart] battement *m*. -**4.** *(U)* [of metal] batte *f*; [of drums] battement *m*, roulement *m*; [of carpet] battage *m*. -**5.** HUNT battue *f*.

beating-up *inf n* passage *m* à tabac, raclée *f*.

beatitude [biː'ætɪtjuːd] *n* béatitude *f*.
◆ **Beatitudes** *npl*: the Beatitudes les béatitudes.

beatnik ['biːtnɪk] ◇ *n* beatnik *mf*.
◇ *adj* beatnik.

beat-up *inf adj* [car] bousillé, déglingué; *Am* [person] amoché.

beau [bəʊ] (*pl* beaux [bəʊz]) *n* [dandy] dandy *m*; [suitor] galant *m*.

Beaufort scale ['bəʊfət] *n* échelle *f* de Beaufort.

beaut *inf* [bjuːt] *n*: that's a ~ c'est super, c'est génial; (what a) ~! super!

beauteous ['bjuːtjəs] *lit* = **beautiful** *adj*.

beautician [bjuː'tɪʃn] *n* esthéticien *m*, -enne *f*.

beautiful ['bjuːtɪfʊl] ◇ *adj* -**1.** [song, person, dress] beau; a ~ woman une belle femme; a ~ baby/man un beau bébé/bel homme; what a ~ photo! quelle belle photo! -**2.** [splendid - weather, meal] magnifique, superbe; what a ~ shot! bien joué!, joli!
◇ *n*: fashions designed for the ~ and the rich des modes destinées aux gens beaux et riches ❑ 'The Beautiful and the Damned' *Fitzgerald* 'les Heureux et les Damnés'.

beautifully ['bjuːtəflɪ] *adv* -**1.** [sing, dress] admirablement, à la perfection. -**2.** [splendidly] : it was a ~ played shot c'était bien joué, c'était une belle balle; that will do ~ cela convient parfaitement. -**3.** [as intensifier - peaceful, light] merveilleusement.

beautify ['bjuːtɪfaɪ] (*pt* & *pp* beautified) *vt* embellir, orner; to ~ o.s. se faire une beauté.

beauty ['bjuːtɪ] (*pl* beauties) ◇ *n* -**1.** [loveliness] beauté *f*; a thing of ~ un objet d'une rare beauté; to spoil the ~ of sthg déparer qqch ❑ ~ is in the eye of the beholder *prov* il n'y a pas de laides amours *prov*; ~ is only skin-deep *prov* la beauté n'est pas tout *prov*. -**2.** [beautiful person or thing] beauté *f*; she's a/she's no ~ c'est une/ce n'est pas une beauté; this new bike's a real ~ *inf* cette nouvelle bicyclette est une vraie merveille; the beauties of nature les merveilles de la nature ❑ 'Beauty and the Beast' 'la Belle et la Bête'. -**3.** [attraction] : the ~ of the system is its simplicity ce qui est bien dans ce système, c'est sa simplicité; that's the ~ of it c'est ça qui est formidable.
◇ *comp* [cream, product, treatment] de beauté; ~ specialist esthéticien *m*, -enne *f*.

beauty competition, beauty contest *n* concours *m* de beauté.

beauty parlour *n* institut *m* de beauté.

beauty queen *n* reine *f* de beauté.

beauty salon = **beauty parlour**.

beauty shop *n Am* institut *m* de beauté.

beauty sleep *n*: I need my ~ *hum* j'ai besoin de mon compte de sommeil pour être frais le matin.

beauty spot *n* -**1.** [on skin] grain *m* de beauté; [artificial] mouche *f*. -**2.** [scenic place] site *m* touristique.

beaver ['biːvəʳ] ◇ *n* [animal] castor *m*; [coat] fourrure *f* de castor, castor *m*; [hat] chapeau *m* de castor, castor *m*.
◇ *comp* [coat, hat] de castor.
◆ **beaver away** *inf vi insep Br*: to ~ away at sthg travailler d'arrache-pied à qqch.

Beaverboard® ['biːvəˌbɔːd] *n* panneau *m* d'aggloméré.

bebop ['biːbɒp] *n* [music, dance] be-bop *m*.

becalm [bɪ'kɑːm] *vt (usu pass)*: to be ~ed être encalminé.

became [bɪ'keɪm] *pt* → **become**.

because [bɪ'kɒz] *conj* parce que; he came ~ it was his duty il est venu parce que c'était son devoir; if she won it was ~ she deserved to si elle a gagné, c'est qu'elle le méritait; it was all the more difficult ~ he was sick c'était d'autant plus difficile qu'il était malade; not ~ he was sad but ~ he was angry pas parce qu'il était triste mais parce qu'il était fâché; they only won ~ they cheated ils n'ont gagné que parce qu'ils ont triché; just ~ you're my sister, it doesn't mean you can boss me about ce n'est pas parce que tu es ma sœur que tu peux me donner des ordres; why can't I go? — ~ (you can't)! pourquoi est-ce que je ne peux pas y aller? — parce que (c'est comme ça)!
◆ **because of** *prep phr* à cause de; we couldn't move ~ of the snow nous étions bloqués par la neige; I couldn't go to work ~ of the tube strike je n'ai pas pu aller au travail à cause de la grève de métro; it was all ~ of a silly misunderstanding tout ça à cause d'un OR tout provenait d'un petit malentendu; he's ineligible ~ of his age il ne peut être élu à cause de son âge.

beck [bek] *n* -**1.** [stream] ruisseau *m*, ru *m lit*. -**2.** *phr*: to be at sb's ~ and call être constamment à la disposition de qqn; she has him at her ~ and call elle le fait marcher à la baguette, il lui obéit au doigt et à l'œil.

beckon ['bekən] ◇ *vi* faire signe; a glittering career ~ed for the young singer la jeune chanteuse avait devant elle une brillante carrière.
◇ *vt* -**1.** [motion] faire signe à; I ~ed them over to me je leur ai fait signe d'approcher; he ~ed me to follow him il m'a fait signe de le suivre. -**2.** [attract, call] attirer; the bright lights ~ed me to the city j'ai été attiré par les lumières de la ville.

become [bɪ'kʌm] (*pt* became [-'keɪm], *pp* become) ◇ *vi* -**1.** [grow] devenir, se faire; the noise became louder and louder le bruit est devenu de plus en plus fort OR a continué à augmenter; to ~ old vieillir; to ~ fat grossir; to ~ weak s'affaiblir; it became clear that we were wrong il s'est avéré que nous nous trompions; we became friends nous sommes devenus amis; she's becoming a dreadful nuisance elle est en train de devenir vraiment gênante. -**2.** [acquire post of] devenir; to ~ president devenir président; she's ~ an accountant elle est devenue comptable.
◇ *vt fml* -**1.** [suit - subj: hat, dress] aller à; that hat really ~s you ce chapeau vous va vraiment bien. -**2.** [befit] convenir à, être digne de; such behaviour doesn't ~ him une telle conduite n'est pas digne de lui.
◆ **become of** *vt insep (only following 'what', 'whatever')*: whatever will ~ of us? qu'allons-nous devenir?; what became of your black hat? où est passé ton chapeau noir?; I wonder what became of that young man je me demande ce qu'est devenu ce jeune homme.

becoming [bɪ'kʌmɪŋ] *adj fml* -**1.** [fetching] qui va bien, seyant; that's a very ~ hat ce chapeau vous va très bien. -**2.** [suitable] convenable, bienséant; such language is hardly ~ for a young lady! un tel langage n'est guère convenable pour une jeune fille!

becquerel [ˌbekə'rel] *n* becquerel *m*.

BECTU ['bektuː] (*abbr of* Broadcasting, Entertainment, Cinematograph and Theatre Union) *pr n syndicat britannique des techniciens du cinéma, du théâtre et de l'audiovisuel*.

bed [bed] (*pt* & *pp* bedded, *cont* bedding) ◇ *n* -**1.** [furniture] lit *m*; we asked for a room with two ~s nous avons demandé une chambre à deux lits; they sleep in separate ~s ils font lit à part; it's time to go to OR time for ~ il est l'heure d'aller au lit OR de se coucher; to get out of ~ se lever; did I get you out of ~? est-ce que je vous ai tiré du lit?; she got OR put the children to ~ elle a couché les enfants OR mis les enfants au lit; he took a walk before ~ il a fait une promenade avant de se coucher; to make the ~ faire le lit; they made me up a ~ ils m'ont préparé un lit; he was in ~ by midnight il était couché OR au lit avant minuit; he's in ~ with the flu il est au lit avec la grippe; she took to (her) ~ with pneumonia elle a dû s'aliter à cause d'une pneumonie; we gave them ~ and board nous les avons logés et nourris; she was brought to ~ of twins *arch* elle accoucha de jumeaux; to go to ~ with sb coucher avec qqn ❑ double ~ lit à deux places; single ~ lit à une place; ~ and board pension *f* complète; ~ and breakfast chambre *f* d'hôte OR chez l'habitant; they stayed in ~ and breakfasts ils ont pris des chambres chez des particuliers; '~ and breakfast' chambres avec petit déjeuner; to get out on the wrong side of (the) ~ se lever du pied gauche OR du mauvais pied; you've made your ~, now you must lie in it *prov* comme on fait son lit, on se couche *prov*. -**2.** [plot - of flowers] parterre *m*, plate-bande *f*; [- of vegetables] planche *f*; [- of coral, oysters] banc *m*; her life isn't a ~ of roses elle n'a pas la vie rose. -**3.** [bottom - of river] lit *m*; [- of lake, sea] fond *m*. -**4.** [layer - of clay, rock] couche *f*, lit *m*; [- of ore] gisement *m*; [- of ashes] lit *m*; CONSTR [- of mortar] bain *m*; ~ of nails lit à clous. -**5.** TECH [of machine] base *f*, bâti *m*; [of lorry] plateau *m*; TYPO [of printing press] marbre *m*, plateau *m*; to put a newspaper to ~ *Br* boucler un journal; the magazine has gone to ~ *Br* la revue est bouclée OR sur le marbre.
◇ *vt* -**1.** [embed] fixer, enfoncer; CONSTR asseoir. -**2.** HORT repiquer. -**3.** *lit* [have sex with] prendre *(sexuellement)*.
◇ *comp* [linen] de lit; ~ board planche *f* à mettre sous le matelas; ~ frame châlit *m*; the doctor recommended complete ~ rest le médecin lui a conseillé de garder le lit.
◆ **bed down** ◇ *vi insep* [go to bed] se coucher; [spend the night] coucher.
◇ *vt sep* -**1.** [children] mettre au lit, coucher; [animal] installer pour la nuit. -**2.** [embed] fixer, enfoncer; CONSTR asseoir.
◆ **bed out** *vt sep* repiquer.

BEd [ˌbiː'ed] (*abbr of* Bachelor of Education) *n (titulaire d'une) licence de sciences de l'éducation*.

bedaub [bɪ'dɔːb] *vt fml* [smear] enduire; [dirty] barbouiller; ~ed with mud barbouillé de boue.

bedazzle [bɪ'dæzl] *vt* [dazzle] éblouir, aveugler; [fascinate] éblouir.

bed bath *n* toilette *f (d'un malade)*.

bedbug ['bedbʌg] *n* punaise *f* des lits.

bedchamber ['bedˌtʃeɪmbəʳ] *n arch* chambre *f*.

bedclothes ['bedkləʊðz] *npl* draps *mpl* et couvertures *fpl*.

bedcover ['bedˌkʌvəʳ] *n* dessus *m* de lit, couvre-lit *m*.

-bedded [ˌbedɪd] *in cpds*: single~ room chambre *f* à un lit.

bedder [ˈbedəʳ] *n* -**1.** *Br* UNIV femme *f* de ménage *(qui fait les chambres à l'université de Cambridge)*. -**2.** HORT plante *f* à repiquer.

bedding [ˈbedɪŋ] ◇ *n* -**1.** [bedclothes] draps *mpl* et couvertures *fpl*; [including mattress] literie *f*; MIL matériel *m* de couchage. -**2.** [for animals] litière *f*.
◇ *adj*: ~ plant plante *f* à repiquer.

beddy-byes [ˈbedɪˌbaɪz] *n baby talk*: to go ~ (aller) se coucher.

Bede [biːd] *pr n*: the Venerable ~ Bède le Vénérable.

bedeck [bɪˈdek] *vt lit* orner, parer; a balcony ~ed with flowers un balcon orné de fleurs OR fleuri.

bedevil [bɪˈdevl] (*Br pt & pp* bedevilled, *cont* bedevilling, *Am pt & pp* bedeviled, *cont* bedeviling) *vt* -**1.** [plague - plans, project] déranger, gêner; [- person] harceler, tourmenter; bedevilled by OR with problems assailli par les problèmes; to be bedevilled by doubts être rongé par le doute. -**2.** [confuse] embrouiller. -**3.** [bewitch] ensorceler.

bedfellow [ˈbedˌfeləʊ] *n* -**1.** [bedmate]: he was my ~ when we were children nous avons partagé le même lit dans notre enfance. -**2.** [associate] associé *m*, -e *f*, collègue *mf*; they make strange ~s ils forment une drôle d'association OR de paire.

bedhead [ˈbedhed] *n Br* tête *f* de lit.

bed jacket *n Br* liseuse *f*.

bedlam [ˈbedləm] *n* chahut *m*, vacarme *m*; utter ~ broke out after her speech un véritable tumulte éclata après son discours; it's absolute ~ in town today! quelle anarchie aujourd'hui en ville!

bedmate [ˈbedmeɪt] *n* partenaire *mf*.

Bedouin [ˈbedʊɪn] (*pl inv* OR Bedouins) ◇ *n* Bédouin *m*, -e *f*.
◇ *adj* bédouin.

bedpan [ˈbedpæn] *n* bassin *m* (hygiénique).

bedpost [ˈbedpəʊst] *n* colonne *f* de lit; (just) between you, me and the ~ entre nous.

bedraggled [bɪˈdrægld] *adj* [clothing, person] débraillé; [hair] ébouriffé, échevelé.

bedridden [ˈbedˌrɪdn] *adj* alité, cloué au lit.

bedrock [ˈbedrɒk] *n* GEOL soubassement *m*, substratum *m*; *fig* base *f*, fondation *f*; to get down to ~ *Br* considérer l'essentiel.

bedroll [ˈbedrəʊl] *n* matériel *m* de couchage *(enroulé)*.

bedroom [ˈbedrʊm] ◇ *n* chambre *f* (à coucher).
◇ *comp* [scene] d'amour; ~ comedy THEAT comédie *f* de boulevard; ~ community *Am* cité-dortoir *f*; ~ eyes regard *m* sexy.

-bedroomed [ˌbedrʊmd] *in cpds*: two~ flat trois pièces *m*.

Beds *written abbr of* Bedfordshire.

bedsettee [ˌbedseˈtiː] *n Br* canapé-lit *m*.

bedside [ˈbedsaɪd] ◇ *adj* de chevet; ~ lamp/table lampe *f*/table *f* de chevet; ~ manner comportement *m* envers les malades; the doctor has a good ~ manner le médecin sait rassurer les malades.
◇ *n* chevet *m*; at OR by your ~ à votre chevet; to rush to sb's ~ courir au chevet de qqn.

bedsit [ˈbedˌsɪt], **bedsitter** [ˈbedˌsɪtəʳ], **bedsitting room** [ˌbedˈsɪtɪŋ-] *n Br* chambre *f* meublée.

bedsocks [ˈbedsɒks] *npl* chaussettes *fpl* (de lit).

bedsore [ˈbedsɔːʳ] *n* escarre *f*.

bedspread [ˈbedspred] *n* dessus-de-lit *m inv*, couvre-lit *m*.

bedsprings [ˈbedsprɪŋz] *npl* [springs] ressorts *mpl* de sommier; [frame] sommier *m* à ressorts.

bedstead [ˈbedsted] *n* châlit *m*.

bedtime [ˈbedtaɪm] ◇ *n* heure *f* du coucher; what's his ~? à quelle heure se couche-t-il?; it's your ~ il est l'heure d'aller te coucher; it's long past your ~ il y a longtemps que tu devrais être au lit; her mother reads to her at ~ sa mère lui lit une histoire avant qu'elle s'endorme.
◇ *comp*: ~ story histoire *f (qu'on lit à l'heure du coucher)*; I'll read you a ~ story je vais te lire une histoire avant que tu t'endormes.

Beduin [ˈbedʊɪn] (*pl inv* OR Beduins) = **Bedouin**.

bedwarmer [ˈbedˌwɔːməʳ] *n* bassinoire *f*.

bed-wetting [-ˌwetɪŋ] *n* incontinence *f* nocturne.

bee [biː] *n* -**1.** [insect] abeille *f*; he is a busy little ~ *inf* [energetic] il déborde d'énergie; [has a lot of work] il a énormément de choses à faire; to have a ~ in one's bonnet (about sthg) être obsédé (par qqch); it's the ~'s knees! *inf* c'est formidable OR super!; he thinks he's the ~'s knees *inf* il ne se prend pas pour n'importe qui. -**2.** *Am* [social event] réunion *f (de voisins ou d'amis pour des travaux en commun)*; quilting ~ atelier *m* de patchwork; spelling ~ concours *m* d'orthographe.

Beeb *inf* [biːb] *pr n Br*: the ~ *hum surnom courant de la BBC*.

beech [biːtʃ] (*pl inv* OR beeches) ◇ *n* [tree] hêtre *m*; [wood] (bois *m* de) hêtre *m*.
◇ *comp* [chair, table] de hêtre; ~ grove hêtraie *f*; ~ nut faine *f*; ~ tree hêtre *m*.

beech mast *n (U)* faines *fpl (tombées par terre)*.

beechwood [ˈbiːtʃwʊd] *n* [substance] (bois *m* de) hêtre *m*; [forest] bois *m* de hêtres.

beef [biːf] (*Br pl sense 2* beeves [biːvz], *pl sense 3* beefs, *Am pl* beefs) ◇ *n* -**1.** [meat] bœuf *m*; joint of ~ rôti *m* (de bœuf), rosbif *m*; roast ~ du rôti (de bœuf), du rosbif. -**2.** [animal] bœuf *m*. -**3.** *inf* [complaint] grief *m*; what's your ~? tu as un problème?; their main ~ is high taxation ils râlent surtout parce qu'ils trouvent les impôts élevés; to have a ~ with sb/sthg *Am* avoir des ennuis avec qqn/qqch. -**4.** *inf* [muscle]: put some ~ into it! allez, un peu de nerf!
◇ *comp* [sausage, stew] de bœuf; ~ cattle bœufs *mpl* de boucherie.
◇ *vi inf* râler; to ~ about sthg râler contre qqch.
◆ **beef up** *vt sep* [army, campaign] renforcer; [report, story] étoffer.

beefburger [ˈbiːfˌbɜːgəʳ] *n* hamburger *m*.

beefcake *inf* [ˈbiːfkeɪk] *n (U) hum* beau mâle *m*, beaux mâles *mpl*.

Beefeater [ˈbiːfˌiːtəʳ] *n surnom des gardiens de la Tour de Londres*.

beefsteak [ˈbiːfˌsteɪk] *n* bifteck *m*, steak *m*.

beef tea *n* bouillon *m* de bœuf.

beefy [ˈbiːfɪ] (*compar* beefier, *superl* beefiest) *adj* -**1.** [consistency, taste] de viande, de bœuf. -**2.** *inf* [brawny] costaud; [fat] grassouillet.

beehive [ˈbiːhaɪv] *n* -**1.** [for bees] ruche *f*; the Beehive State *Am* l'Utah *m*. -**2.** [hairstyle] *coiffure très haute maintenue avec de la laque*.

beekeeper [ˈbiːˌkiːpəʳ] *n* apiculteur *m*, -trice *f*.

beekeeping [ˈbiːˌkiːpɪŋ] *n* apiculture *f*.

beeline [ˈbiːlaɪn] *n* ligne *f* droite; he made a ~ for the kitchen [headed straight to] il s'est dirigé tout droit vers la cuisine; [rushed to] il s'est précipité OR a filé tout droit à la cuisine.

Beelzebub [biːˈelzɪbʌb] *pr n* Belzébuth.

been [biːn] *pp* → **be**.

beep [biːp] ◇ *n* [of car horn] coup *m* de Klaxon®; [of alarm, timer] signal *m* sonore, bip *m*.
◇ *vi* [car horn] klaxonner; [alarm, timer] sonner, faire bip.
◇ *vt*: to ~ one's horn klaxonner.

beer [bɪəʳ] ◇ *n* bière *f*; his life is not all ~ and skittles *Br* sa vie n'est pas toujours rose.
◇ *comp*: ~ barrel tonneau *m* à bière; ~ bottle canette *f*; ~ can boîte *f* de bière; ~ cellar, ~ garden *jardin d'un pub où l'on peut prendre ses consommations*; ~ glass verre *m* à bière, bock *m*; ~ gut▽, ~ belly *inf* brioche *f*, bide *m*; ~ tent *grande tente abritant la buvette lors des manifestations sportives de plein air en Grande-Bretagne*.

beery [ˈbɪərɪ] (*compar* beerier, *superl* beeriest) *adj* [atmosphere, smell, taste] qui sent la bière; [party] où l'on boit beaucoup de bière; [person] qui a bu beaucoup de bière.

beeswax [ˈbiːzwæks] ◇ *n* cire *f* d'abeille.
◇ *vt* cirer *(avec de la cire d'abeille)*.

beet [biːt] *n* betterave *f* (potagère); red ~ *Am* betterave *f* (rouge).

Beethoven [ˈbeɪtˌhəʊvn] *pr n*: Ludwig Van ~ Ludwig van Beethoven.

beetle [ˈbiːtl] ◇ *n* -**1.** [insect] scarabée *m*, coléoptère *m*. -**2.** GAMES *jeu de dés où l'on essaye de dessiner un scarabée*. -**3.** [hammer] mailloche *f*; [machine] mouton *m*.
◇ *vi inf Br* courir précipitamment; he ~d in/out of the house il est entré dans/sorti de la maison à toute vitesse; to ~ off filer; to ~ along filer à toute vitesse.
◆ **Beetle**® *n*: (Volkswagen) ~ AUT Coccinelle® *f*.

beetle-browed [-braʊd] *adj Br* [with bushy eyebrows] aux sourcils broussailleux; [scowling] renfrogné.

beetle drive *n Br fête où l'on joue au «beetle»*.

beetling [ˈbiːtlɪŋ] *adj* [cliff, crag] qui surplombe, surplombant; [brow] proéminent; [eyebrows] broussailleux.

beetroot [ˈbiːtruːt] *n* betterave *f* (potagère OR rouge); to go (as red as a) ~ devenir rouge comme une tomate.

beet sugar *n* sucre *m* de betterave.

beezer *inf* [ˈbiːzəʳ] *n* -**1.** *Br dated* [person] type *m*. -**2.** *Br dated* [nose] pif *m*. -**3.** *Scot* [extreme example] comble *m*.

befall [bɪˈfɔːl] (*pt* befell [-ˈfel], *pp* befallen [-ˈfɔːlən]) *fml* OR *lit* ◇ *vt* arriver à, survenir à; no harm will ~ her il ne lui sera fait aucun mal.
◇ *vi* -**1.** [happen] arriver, se passer. -**2.** [be due] échoir.

befit [bɪˈfɪt] (*pt & pp* befitted, *cont* befitting) *vt fml* convenir à, seoir à *fml*; as ~s a woman of her eminence comme il sied à une femme de son rang.

befitting [bɪˈfɪtɪŋ] *adj fml* convenable, seyant; in a manner ~ a statesman d'une façon qui sied à un homme d'État; with ~ modesty avec la modestie qui sied.

befog [bɪˈfɒg] (*pt & pp* befogged, *cont* befogging) *vt literal* envelopper de brouillard; *fig* [confuse - person] brouiller l'esprit OR les idées de, embrouiller; [- issue] obscurcir; his mind was befogged by whisky le whisky lui avait brouillé l'esprit.

before [bɪˈfɔːʳ] ◇ *adv* -**1.** [at a previous time] avant; you should have thought of that ~ tu aurais dû y penser avant; haven't we met ~? est-ce que nous ne nous sommes pas OR ne nous sommes-nous pas déjà rencontrés?; I have never seen this film ~ c'est la première fois que je vois ce film; I have/had seen it ~ je l'ai/l'avais déjà vu; he's made mistakes ~ ce n'est pas la première fois qu'il se trompe; such things have happened ~ c'est déjà arrivé; she carries on driving as ~ elle continue de conduire comme auparavant OR avant. -**2.** *lit* [ahead] en avant, devant.
◇ *prep* -**1.** [preceding - in time] avant; ~ the holidays avant les vacances; the day ~ the meeting la veille de la réunion; two days ~ your birthday deux jours avant OR l'avant-veille de votre anniversaire; the day ~ yesterday avant-hier; they arrived ~ us ils sont arrivés avant nous; the couch won't be delivered ~ next Tuesday le divan ne sera pas livré avant mardi prochain; it should have been done ~ now ça devrait déjà être fait ❑ that was ~ your time [you had not been born] vous n'étiez pas encore né; [you had not arrived, joined etc] vous n'étiez pas encore là. -**2.** [preceding - in order, preference] avant; her name was OR came ~ mine in the list son nom était avant le mien sur la liste; ladies ~ gentlemen les dames avant les messieurs; they put quality ~ quantity ils font passer la qualité avant la quantité; the welfare of the people comes ~ private con-

cerns le bien-être du peuple passe avant tout intérêt privé; ~ anything else, I would like to thank you avant tout, je voudrais vous remercier. -3. [in front of] devant; on the table ~ them *fml* sur la table devant eux; fields stretched away ~ us *fml* des champs s'étendaient devant nous; we have a difficult task ~ us *fig* nous avons une tâche difficile devant nous; ~ my very eyes sous mes propres yeux; to sail ~ the wind NAUT avoir le vent arrière OR en poupe; the troops fled ~ the enemy les troupes se sont enfuies devant l'ennemi. -4. [in the presence of] devant, en présence de; he said it ~ witnesses il l'a dit devant OR en présence de témoins; to appear ~ the court/judge comparaître devant le tribunal/juge; she appeared ~ the committee elle s'est présentée devant le comité. -5. [for the consideration of] devant; the problem ~ us la question qui nous occupe; the case ~ the court l'affaire portée devant le tribunal; to bring a case ~ the court saisir le tribunal d'une affaire; the matter went ~ the council l'affaire est passée devant le conseil.

◇ *conj* -1. [in time] avant de, avant que; she hesitated ~ answering elle a hésité avant de répondre; may I see you ~ you leave? puis-je vous voir avant que vous ne partiez OR avant votre départ?; get out ~ I call the police! fichez le camp avant que je n'appelle la police OR sinon j'appelle la police!; it'll be a long time ~ he tries that again il ne recommencera pas de sitôt, il n'est pas près de recommencer; we should be able to finish ~ the boss gets back nous devrions pouvoir terminer avant le retour du patron; it'll be summer ~ she plants the garden elle ne plantera pas le jardin avant l'été; it'll be two years ~ the school is built l'école ne sera pas construite avant deux ans; it was almost an hour ~ the ambulance arrived il a fallu presque une heure avant que l'ambulance n'arrive ❑ ~ you know it, ~ you can say Jack Robinson *inf* avant qu'on ait le temps de dire «ouf». -2. [rather than] plutôt que de; I'll die ~ I let him marry my daughter je mourrai plutôt que de le laisser épouser ma fille.

◇ *adj* d'avant, précédent; the day ~ la veille; the night ~ la veille au soir; the week ~ la semaine d'avant OR précédente; this summer and the one ~ cet été et celui d'avant OR le précédent.

beforehand [bɪ'fɔːhænd] ◇ *adv* auparavant, à l'avance; she had prepared her speech ~ elle avait préparé son discours au préalable OR à l'avance; if you're coming let me know ~ prévenez-moi si vous décidez de venir.

◇ *adj* [early]: you were a bit ~ with the congratulations! *hum* tu t'y es pris un peu tôt pour les félicitations!

before-tax *adj* brut, avant impôts; ~ income revenus *mpl* bruts.

befoul [bɪ'faʊl] *vt lit* souiller, salir.

befriend [bɪ'frend] *vt* [make friends with] donner son amitié à; [assist] venir en aide à, aider.

befuddle [bɪ'fʌdl] *vt* -1. [confuse - person] brouiller l'esprit OR les idées de, embrouiller; [- mind] embrouiller. -2. [muddle with alcohol] griser, enivrer; his mind was ~d with drink il était étourdi par l'alcool.

beg [beg] (*pt* & *pp* begged, *cont* begging) ◇ *vi* -1. [solicit charity] mendier; to ~ for food mendier de la nourriture; children begging (for money) in the subway des enfants qui mendient dans le métro; they live by begging ils vivent de charité OR d'aumône. -2. [ask, plead] supplier; to ~ for forgiveness/mercy demander pardon/grâce. -3. [dog] faire le beau. -4. *Br phr*: going begging: I'll have that last sandwich if it's going begging je prendrai bien ce dernier sandwich si personne d'autre ne le veut.

◇ *vt* -1. [solicit as charity] mendier; to ~ food mendier de la nourriture; she begged money from the passers-by elle mendiait auprès des passants. -2. [ask] demander, solliciter; [plead for] supplier; I begged the doctor not to say anything j'ai supplié le médecin de ne rien dire; she begged a favour of her sister elle a demandé à sa sœur de lui rendre un service; to ~ sb's forgiveness OR pardon demander pardon à qqn; I ~ your pardon [excuse me] je vous demande pardon; [I didn't hear you] pardon?; [indignantly] de grâce!, je vous en supplie! -3. *fml* [ask permission]: I ~ to differ je me permets de OR permettez-moi de ne pas être de votre avis; I ~ to inform you that... je tiens à OR j'ai l'honneur de vous informer que... -4. *Br phr*: to ~ the question [evade the issue] éluder la question; [assume something proved] considérer que la question est résolue.

◆ **beg off** *vi insep Br* se soustraire; our best player begged off pleading illness notre meilleur joueur s'est fait excuser pour cause de maladie.

began [bɪ'gæn] *pt* → **begin**.

beget [bɪ'get] (*pt* begot [-'gɒt] OR begat [-'gæt], *pp* begotten [-'gɒtn], *cont* begetting) *vt literal* [sire] engendrer; *fig* [cause] engendrer, causer.

beggar ['begəʳ] ◇ *n* -1. [mendicant] mendiant *m*, -e *f*; [pauper] indigent *m*, -e *f*; ~s can't be choosers *prov* nécessité fait loi *prov*; 'The Beggar's Opera' *Gay* 'l'Opéra du gueux'. -2. *inf Br* [so-and-so] type *m*; you lucky ~! sacré veinard!; poor ~! pauvre diable!; you naughty little ~! petit coquin!; jammy ~! veinard!

◇ *vt* -1. *fml* [impoverish] réduire à la mendicité, appauvrir. -2. *phr*: to ~ (all) description défier toute description.

beggarly ['begəlɪ] *adj* [conditions, life] misérable, malheureux; [meal] maigre, piètre; [salary, sum] misérable, dérisoire.

beggar-my-neighbour *Br* ◇ *n* [card game] bataille *f*.

◇ *adj* protectionniste; ~ policies politique *f* protectionniste OR du chacun pour soi.

beggary ['begərɪ] *n* misère *f*, mendicité *f*; they were reduced to ~ ils étaient réduits à la mendicité.

begging ['begɪŋ] ◇ *n* mendicité *f*.

◇ *adj*: ~ letter lettre *f* de requête *(demandant de l'argent)*.

begging bowl *n* sébile *f (de mendiant)*.

begin [bɪ'gɪn] (*pt* began [-'gæn], *pp* begun [-'gʌn], *cont* beginning) ◇ *vt* -1. [start] commencer; [career, term] commencer, débuter; [task] entreprendre, s'attaquer à; [work] commencer, se mettre à; to ~ to do OR doing sthg commencer à faire qqch, se mettre à faire qqch; I had begun to believe he was lying j'avais commencé à croire qu'il mentait; she began the essay [reading] elle commença à lire l'essai; [writing] elle commença à écrire son essai; the quotation beginning this chapter la citation qui ouvre ce chapitre; she began life as a waitress elle a débuté comme serveuse; he soon began to complain il n'a pas tardé à se plaindre; I began the day all wrong j'ai mal commencé la journée; the film doesn't ~ to compare with the book le film est loin de valoir le livre; he can't ~ to compete with her il ne lui arrive pas à la cheville; I can't ~ to explain c'est trop difficile à expliquer. -2. [start to say] commencer; "this is unforgivable", she began «c'est impardonnable», commença-t-elle. -3. [found - club, institution] fonder, inaugurer; [initiate - business, fashion] lancer; [- argument, fight, war] déclencher, faire naître; [- conversation] engager, amorcer; [- discussion, speech] commencer, ouvrir.

◇ *vi* -1. [start - person, career, concert, project, speech] commencer; work should ~ in the spring les travaux devraient commencer au printemps; the day began badly/well la journée s'annonçait mal/bien; to ~ again OR afresh recommencer (à zéro); ~ at the beginning commencez par le commencement; the night shift ~s at midnight l'équipe de nuit commence (le travail) à minuit; when does school ~? quand est la rentrée?; after the film ~s après le début du film; her career began in Hollywood sa carrière a débuté à Hollywood; he began in politics il s'est lancé dans la politique; let me ~ by thanking our host permettez-moi tout d'abord de remercier notre hôte; let's ~ with a song commençons par une chanson; her name ~s with B son nom commence par un B; the play ~s with a murder la pièce débute par un meurtre; I began with the idea of buying a flat au départ OR au début je voulais acheter un appartement ❑ well begun is half done *Br prov* ce qui commence bien est à moitié fait. -2. [originate - club, country, institution] être fondé; [- fire, epidemic] commencer; [- war] éclater, commencer; [- river] prendre sa source; [- fashion] commencer, débuter; the magazine began as a neighbourhood sheet la revue a débuté comme journal de quartier; the motorway ~s at Dijon l'autoroute commence à Dijon; that's when our troubles ~ c'est là que nos ennuis commencent.

◆ **to begin with** *adv phr* d'abord; to ~ with, it's too cold d'abord, il fait trop froid; to ~ with, the statistics are wrong pour commencer OR d'abord, les chiffres sont faux; everything went well to ~ with tout s'est bien passé au début OR au départ; the plate was cracked to ~ with l'assiette était déjà fêlée au départ.

beginner [bɪ'gɪnəʳ] *n* débutant *m*, -e *f*; I'm just a ~ at golf je ne suis qu'un débutant au golf; not bad for a ~ pas si mal pour un débutant; it's ~'s luck! on a toujours de la chance au début!; French for ~s français pour débutants.

beginning [bɪ'gɪnɪŋ] *n* -1. [start - of book, career, project] commencement *m*, début *m*; in OR at the ~ au début, au commencement; this is just the ~ of our troubles nos ennuis ne font que commencer; begin at the ~ commencez par le commencement; let's start again from the ~ reprenons depuis le début; at the ~ of the academic year au début de l'année universitaire; from ~ to end du début à la fin, d'un bout à l'autre; it's the ~ of the end c'est le début de la fin. -2. [early part, stage - of book, career, war] commencement *m*, début *m*; [- of negotiations] début *m*, ouverture *f*; the day had a good ~ la journée avait bien commencé; the ~ of the world l'origine OR le commencement du monde; since the ~ of time depuis la nuit des temps. -3. [origin - of event] origine *f*, commencement *m*; Protestantism had its ~s in Germany le protestantisme a pris naissance en Allemagne; his assassination signalled the ~ of the war son assassinat a marqué le déclenchement de la guerre.

begone [bɪ'gɒn] *vi lit*: ~! hors d'ici!

begonia [bɪ'gəʊnjə] *n* bégonia *m*.

begorrah [bɪ'gɒrə] *interj expression stéréotypée, souvent employée pour caricaturer la manière de parler des Irlandais*.

begot [bɪ'gɒt] *pt* → **beget**.

begotten [bɪ'gɒtn] *pp* → **beget**.

begrudge [bɪ'grʌdʒ] *vt* -1. [envy] envier; she ~s him his success elle lui en veut de sa réussite. -2. [give grudgingly] donner OR accorder à regret; he ~s every minute spent away from his family il rechigne à passer une seule minute loin de sa famille; I ~ spending so much on rent ça me fait mal au cœur de payer un loyer aussi cher.

beguile [bɪ'gaɪl] *vt* -1. [charm] envoûter, séduire. -2. [delude] enjôler, tromper; to ~ sb into doing sthg amener qqn à faire qqch; to ~ sb out of sthg obtenir qqch de qqn par la séduction. -3. [pass pleasantly]: to ~ (away) the hours faire passer le temps *(agréablement)*.

beguiling [bɪ'gaɪlɪŋ] *adj* charmant, séduisant.

beguine [bɪ'giːn] *n musique ou danse ressemblant au boléro*.

begum ['beɪgəm] *n* bégum *f*.

begun [bɪ'gʌn] *pp* → **begin**.

behalf [bɪ'hɑːf] *n*

◆ **on behalf of** *Br*, **in behalf of** *Am prep phr*: on ~ of sb [as their representative] de la part de OR au nom de qqn; [in their interest] dans l'intérêt de OR pour qqn; on ~ of everyone here, I thank you au nom de tous ceux qui sont ici présents, je vous remercie; I came on ~ of the president je viens de la part du président; she acted on his ~ when he was ill c'est elle qui l'a représenté quand il était malade; your lawyer acts on your ~ votre avocat agit en votre nom; the commission decided on their ~ la commission a décidé en leur nom; don't worry on my ~ ne vous inquiétez pas à mon sujet.

behave [bɪ'heɪv] ◇ *vi* -**1.** [act] se comporter, se conduire; why are you behaving this way? pourquoi agis-tu de cette façon?; to ~ badly/well mal/bien se comporter; he ~d badly towards her il s'est mal conduit envers elle; she's behaving very strangely elle se comporte de façon bizarre; she was sorry for the way she'd ~d towards him elle regrettait la façon dont elle l'avait traité. -**2.** [act properly] se tenir bien; will you ~! sois sage!, tiens-toi bien! -**3.** [function] fonctionner, marcher; she studies how matter ~s in extremes of cold and heat elle étudie le comportement de la matière dans des conditions de froid ou de chaleur extrêmes; the car ~s well on curves la voiture tient bien la route dans les virages.
◇ *vt* se tenir bien; ~ yourself! sois sage!, tiens-toi bien!

behaviour *Br*, **behavior** *Am* [bɪ'heɪvjəʳ] ◇ *n* -**1.** [of person] comportement *m*, conduite *f*; [of animal] comportement *m*; her ~ towards her mother was unforgivable la façon dont elle s'est comportée avec sa mère était impardonnable; to be on one's best ~ se tenir OR se conduire de son mieux; the child was on his best ~ l'enfant était d'une sagesse exemplaire. -**2.** [of atom, chemical, light] comportement *m*; [of machine] fonctionnement *m*.
◇ *comp* [modification, problem] du comportement; [pattern] de comportement.

behavioural *Br*, **behavioral** *Am* [bɪ'heɪvjərəl] *adj* de comportement, comportemental.

behavioural science *n* science *f* du comportement, behaviorisme *m*, comportementalisme *m*.

behaviourism *Br*, **behaviorism** *Am* [bɪ'heɪvjərɪzm] *n* behaviorisme *m*.

behaviourist *Br*, **behaviorist** *Am* [bɪ'heɪvjərɪst] ◇ *adj* behavioriste.
◇ *n* behavioriste *mf*.

behaviour therapy *n* thérapie *f* comportementale.

behead [bɪ'hed] *vt* décapiter.

beheld [bɪ'held] *pt* & *pp* → **behold**.

behemoth [bɪ'hiːmɒθ] *n* [monster] monstre *m*.

behest [bɪ'hest] *n fml* commandement *m*, ordre *m*; at the ~ of the Queen sur ordre de la reine.

behind [bɪ'haɪnd] ◇ *prep* -**1.** [at the back of] derrière; ~ the house derrière la maison; she came out from ~ the bushes elle est sortie de derrière les buissons; I sat down right ~ him je me suis assis juste derrière lui; lock the door ~ you fermez la porte à clé (derrière vous); his wife was ~ the bar that night sa femme était derrière le bar OR au bar ce soir-là. -**2.** [indicating past time] derrière; he has ten years' experience ~ him il a dix ans d'expérience derrière lui; your troubles are ~ you now vos ennuis sont terminés maintenant; you have to put the incident ~ you il faut que tu oublies cet incident. -**3.** [indicating deficiency, delay] en retard sur, derrière; she is ~ the other pupils elle est en retard sur les autres élèves; we're three points ~ the other team nous sommes à trois points derrière l'autre équipe; the trains are running ~ schedule OR ~ time les trains ont du retard (sur l'horaire). -**4.** [responsible for] derrière; who was ~ the plot? qui était derrière le complot OR à l'origine du complot?; what's ~ all this? qu'est-ce que ça cache? -**5.** [supporting]: we're right ~ you on this vous avez tout notre soutien dans cette affaire; the country is right ~ the new policies la population soutient tout à fait les nouvelles mesures.
◇ *adv* -**1.** [at, in the back] derrière, en arrière; look ~ regardez derrière; he attacked them from ~ il les a attaqués par derrière; they followed ~ ils arrivaient derrière, ils suivaient; disaster was not far ~ la catastrophe était imminente. -**2.** [late] en retard; I'm ~ in OR with my rent je suis en retard sur mon loyer; I'm ~ in OR with my work j'ai du retard dans mon travail; she's too far ~ to catch up with the others elle a pris trop de retard pour pouvoir rattraper les autres; our team is three points ~ notre équipe a trois points de moins; I'm all ~ today *inf* je suis en retard (dans mon travail) aujourd'hui.
◇ *n euph* derrière *m*, postérieur *m*.

behindhand [bɪ'haɪndhænd] *adv* en retard; we're ~ with the rent nous sommes en retard sur le loyer; I'm getting ~ with my work je suis en train de prendre du retard dans mon travail.

behind-the-scenes *adj* secret; a ~ look at politics un regard en coulisse sur la politique.

behold [bɪ'həʊld] (*pt* & *pp* beheld [-'held]) *vt arch* OR *lit* [see] regarder, voir; [notice] apercevoir; a sight to ~ un spectacle à voir; ~ your king voici votre roi; and ~, she actually agreed et chose étonnante, elle a accepté.

beholden [bɪ'həʊldən] *adj* redevable; I am deeply ~ to him je lui suis infiniment redevable.

behove *Br* [bɪ'həʊv], **behoove** *Am* [bɪ'huːv] *vt arch* OR *lit*: it ~s them to be prudent il leur appartient d'être prudents.

beige [beɪʒ] ◇ *adj* beige.
◇ *n* beige *m*.

Beijing [ˌbeɪ'dʒɪŋ] *pr n* Beijing.

being ['biːɪŋ] ◇ *pres p* → **be**.
◇ *n* -**1.** [creature] être *m*, créature *f*; a human ~ un être humain; a ~ from another planet une créature (venue) d'une autre planète. -**2.** [essential nature] être *m*; her whole ~ rebelled tout son être se révoltait. -**3.** [existence] existence *f*; already in ~ déjà existant, qui existe déjà; to bring OR to call sthg into ~ faire naître qqch, susciter qqch; they brought a new social policy into ~ ils ont établi une nouvelle politique sociale; the movement came into ~ in the 1920s le mouvement est apparu OR fut créé dans les années 20 ❑ 'Being and Nothingness' *Sartre* 'l'Être et le néant'; 'Being and Time' *Heidegger* 'Être et temps'.

Beirut [ˌbeɪ'ruːt] *pr n* Beyrouth; East ~ Beyrouth-Est; West ~ Beyrouth-Ouest.

bejewelled *Br*, **bejeweled** *Am* [bɪ'dʒuːəld] *adj* [person] paré OR couvert de bijoux; [box, purse] incrusté de bijoux.

bel [bel] *n* bel *m*.

belabour *Br*, **belabor** *Am* [bɪ'leɪbəʳ] *vt* [beat] rouer de coups; [criticize] injurier, invectiver.

Belarus [ˌbelə'ruːs] *pr n*: the Republic of ~ la république de Bélarus.

belated [bɪ'leɪtɪd] *adj* tardif.

belatedly [bɪ'leɪtɪdlɪ] *adv* tardivement.

belay [bɪ'leɪ] ◇ *vt* & *vi* -**1.** NAUT amarrer. -**2.** CLIMBING assurer.
◇ *n* assurance *f*.

belaying pin [bɪ'leɪɪŋ] *n* cabillot *m*.

belch [beltʃ] ◇ *n* renvoi *m*, rot *m*; to give a ~ éructer, roter.
◇ *vi* éructer, roter.
◇ *vt* [expel] cracher, vomir.

beleaguer [bɪ'liːgəʳ] *vt* -**1.** [harass] harceler, assaillir; reporters ~ed him with questions les journalistes le harcelèrent de questions; ~ed bureaucrats des bureaucrates assaillis OR harcelés. -**2.** [besiege - city] assiéger; [- army, group] encercler, cerner.

beleaguered [bɪ'liːgəd] *adj* -**1.** *literal* assiégé. -**2.** *fig* en difficulté.

belfry ['belfrɪ] (*pl* belfries) *n* [of church] beffroi *m*, clocher *m*; [of tower] beffroi *m*.

Belgian ['beldʒən] ◇ *n* Belge *mf*.
◇ *adj* belge.

Belgium ['beldʒəm] *pr n* Belgique *f*; in ~ en Belgique.

Belgrade [ˌbel'greɪd] *pr n* Belgrade.

Belgravia [bel'greɪvjə] *pr n quartier chic de Londres*.

belie [bɪ'laɪ] (*pt* & *pp* belied, *cont* belying) *vt fml* [misrepresent] donner une fausse idée OR impression de; [contradict - hope, impression] démentir, tromper; [- promise] démentir, donner le démenti à; her youthful figure ~d her age la jeunesse de sa silhouette démentait son âge.

belief [bɪ'liːf] *n* -**1.** [feeling of certainty] croyance *f*; ~ in God croyance en Dieu; I've lost any ~ I had in human kindness je ne crois plus du tout en la bonté humaine; contrary to popular ~ contrairement à ce qu'on croit; beyond ~ incroyable; he's lazy beyond ~ il est incroyablement paresseux. -**2.** [conviction, opinion] conviction *f*, certitude *f*; it's my ~ he's lying je suis certain OR convaincu qu'il ment; in the ~ that he would help them certains OR persuadés qu'il allait les aider; in the mistaken ~ that... persuadé à tort que...; to the best of my ~ autant que je sache. -**3.** [religious faith] foi *f*, croyance *f*; [political faith] dogme *m*, doctrine *f*. -**4.** [confidence, trust] confiance *f*, foi *f*.

believable [bɪ'liːvəbl] *adj* croyable.

believe [bɪ'liːv] ◇ *vi* -**1.** [be convinced of existence or truth of] croire; to ~ in miracles/in God croire aux miracles/en Dieu; seeing is believing voir c'est croire. -**2.** [be convinced in value of] croire; I ~ in free enterprise je suis partisan de la libre entreprise; they ~ in their president ils ont confiance en OR font confiance à leur président; he ~s in giving the public greater access to information il est d'avis qu'il faut donner au public un plus grand accès à l'information. -**3.** [have religious faith] être croyant, avoir la foi.
◇ *vt* -**1.** [consider as real or true] croire, donner foi à; don't ~ a word she says ne croyez pas un mot de ce qu'elle dit; I don't ~ a word of it je n'en crois rien OR pas un mot; don't you ~ it! détrompe-toi!; he's getting married! – I don't ~ it! il va se marier! – c'est pas vrai!; she's fifty, would you ~ it! elle a cinquante ans, figure-toi!; he couldn't ~ his ears/his eyes il n'en croyait pas ses oreilles/ses yeux; and, ~ it or not, she left et, crois-le si tu veux, elle est partie. -**2.** [accept statement or opinion of] croire; if she is to be ~d, she was born a duchess à l'en croire, elle est duchesse; and ~ (you) me, I know what I'm talking about! et croyez-moi, je sais de quoi je parle! -**3.** [hold as opinion, suppose] croire, supposer; I ~ he left je crois qu'il est parti; I don't ~ he left je ne crois pas qu'il soit parti; I ~ I've taken a wrong turning je crois que je me suis trompé de route OR que j'ai pris la mauvaise route; the jury ~s him guilty le jury le croit coupable; I don't know what to ~ je ne sais que croire, je ne sais pas à quoi m'en tenir; it's ~d that the prisoners have been killed on pense que les prisonniers ont été tués; she is, I ~, our greatest novelist elle est, je crois OR à mon avis, notre meilleure romancière; we have every reason to ~ he's telling the truth nous avons tout lieu de croire qu'il dit la vérité; he'd have her ~ it's an antique il voudrait lui faire croire que c'est un objet d'époque; I ~ not je crois que non, je ne crois pas; I ~ so je crois que oui, je crois; I wouldn't have ~d it of him je n'aurais pas cru cela de lui.

believer [bɪ'liːvəʳ] *n* -**1.** [supporter] partisan *m*, adepte *mf*; a ~ in socialism un partisan du socialisme; he's a great ~ in taking regular exercise il est convaincu qu'il faut faire régulièrement de l'exercice. -**2.** RELIG croyant *m*, -e *f*; are you a ~? êtes-vous croyant?

Belisha beacon [bɪ'liːʃə-] *n Br globe orange clignotant marquant un passage clouté*.

belittle [bɪ'lɪtl] *vt* rabaisser, dénigrer; he's always belittling her work il dénigre toujours son travail.

Belize [be'liːz] *pr n* Belize *m*; in ~ au Belize.

Belizean [be'liːzɪən] ◇ *n* Bélizien *m*, -enne *f*.
◇ *adj* bélizien.

bell [bel] ◇ *n* -**1.** [in church] cloche *f*; [handheld] clochette *f*; [on bicycle] sonnette *f*; [for cows] cloche *f*, clarine *f*; [on boots, toys] grelot *m*; [sound] coup *m* (de cloche); **there goes the dinner ~** c'est la cloche qui annonce le dîner; **has the first ~ for vespers gone?** a-t-on sonné le premier coup des vêpres?; **to sound ~s** NAUT piquer la cloche OR l'heure; **it sounded four/eight ~s** NAUT cela a piqué quatre/huit coups (de cloche) ❑ **saved by the ~!** sauvé par le gong!; **~, book and candle** instruments *mpl* du culte; **'For Whom the Bell Tolls'** *Hemingway* 'Pour qui sonne le glas'. -**2.** [electrical device - on door] sonnette *f*; **there's the ~** il y a quelqu'un à la porte, on sonne (à la porte). -**3.** *inf Br* [telephone call]: **I'll give you a ~** je te passe un coup de fil. -**4.** [of flower] calice *m*, clochette *f*; [of oboe, trumpet] pavillon *m*. -**5.** [of stag] bramement *m*; [of hound] aboiement *m*.
◇ *vi* -**1.** [stag] bramer; [hound] aboyer. -**2.** [bloat, distend] ballonner.

belladonna [ˌbelə'dɒnə] *n* belladone *f*.

bell-bottomed [-ˌbɒtəmd] *adj* à pattes d'éléphant.

bell-bottoms *npl* pantalon *m* à pattes d'éléphant.

bellboy ['belbɔɪ] *n* chasseur *m*, porteur *m*.

bell buoy *n* bouée *f* à cloche.

belle [bel] *n* belle *f*, beauté *f*; **the ~ of the ball** la reine du bal.

belletrist [bel'letrɪst] *n* écrivain *m* des belles-lettres.

bellflower ['belˌflaʊə^r] *n* campanule *f*.

bell glass *n* cloche *f* de verre.

bell heather *n* bruyère *f* cendrée.

bellhop ['belhɒp] *Am* = **bellboy**.

bellicose ['belɪkəʊs] *adj* belliqueux.

bellicosity [ˌbelɪ'kɒsətɪ] *n* bellicisme *m*.

belligerence [bɪ'lɪdʒərəns], **belligerency** [bɪ'lɪdʒərənsɪ] *n* belligérance *f*.

belligerent [bɪ'lɪdʒərənt] ◇ *adj* belligérant.
◇ *n* belligérant *m*, -e *f*.

bell jar *n* cloche *f* de verre; **'The Bell Jar'** *Plath* 'la Cloche de verre'.

bellow ['beləʊ] ◇ *vi* [bull] beugler, meugler; [elephant] barrir; [person] brailler; **he ~ed with pain** il a hurlé de douleur; **the crowd ~ed with laughter** la foule hurlait de rire.
◇ *vt*: **to ~ (out) sthg** brailler qqch.
◇ *n* [of bull] beuglement *m*, meuglement *m*; [of elephant] barrissement *m*; [of person] braillement *m*.

bellows ['beləʊz] *n pl* -**1.** [for fire] soufflet *m*; **a pair of ~** un soufflet. -**2.** [for accordion, organ] soufflerie *f*.

bellpull ['belpʊl] *n* [for servant] cordon *m* de sonnette; [on door] poignée *f* de sonnette.

bell push *n* bouton *m* de sonnette.

bell-ringer *n* sonneur *m*, carillonneur *m*.

bell-ringing *n* carillonnement *m*.

bell rope *n* [to call servant] cordon *m* de sonnette; [in belfry] corde *f* de cloche.

bell tent *n* tente *f* conique.

bell tower *n* clocher *m*.

bellwether ['belˌweðə^r] *n* [sheep] sonnailler *m*; *fig* [person] meneur *m*, -euse *f*, chef *m*.

belly ['belɪ] (*pl* **bellies**, *pt* & *pp* **bellied**)
◇ *n* -**1.** [stomach] ventre *m*; **a big ~** un gros ventre; **he only thinks of his ~** il ne pense qu'à son estomac. -**2.** [of plane, ship] ventre *m*; [of sail] creux *m*. -**3.** [of cello, guitar] table *f* d'harmonie. -**4.** CULIN: **pork ~** lard *m*. -**5.** *arch* [womb] ventre *m*.
◇ *vi*: **to ~ (out)** s'enfler, se gonfler.
◇ *vt* enfler, gonfler.

bellyache *inf* ['belɪeɪk] ◇ *n* -**1.** [pain] mal *m* au OR de ventre; **I've got (a) ~** j'ai mal au ventre. -**2.** [complaint] rogne *f*, rouspétance *f*.
◇ *vi* râler; **stop bellyaching!** arrête de râler!

bellyaching *inf* ['belɪˌeɪkɪŋ] *n* *(U)* ronchonnements *mpl*, rouspétances *fpl*.

belly button *inf n* nombril *m*.

belly dance ◇ *n* danse *f* du ventre.
◇ *vi* danser OR faire la danse du ventre.

belly dancer *n* danseuse *f* du ventre OR orientale.

belly flop *n*: **to do a ~** faire un plat.

bellyful *inf* ['belɪfʊl] *n* [of food] ventre *m* plein; *fig*: **I've had a ~** j'en ai jusque-là; **I've had a ~ of your complaints** j'en ai ras le bol de tes rouspétances.

belly-land *inf vi* & *vt* atterrir sur le ventre.

belly-landing *inf n* atterrissage *m* sur le ventre; **the plane made a ~** l'avion a atterri OR s'est posé sur le ventre.

belly laugh *inf n* gros rire *m*.

belong [bɪ'lɒŋ] *vi* -**1.** [be property]: **to ~ to sb** appartenir à OR être à qqn; **the dictionary ~s to her** le dictionnaire lui appartient OR est à elle; **the company ~s to a large conglomerate** l'entreprise appartient à un important conglomérat. -**2.** [be member]: **he ~s to a trade union** il fait partie OR il est membre d'un syndicat, il est syndiqué. -**3.** [be part] appartenir; **the field ~s to that house** le champ dépend de cette maison; **this key ~s to the car** cette clé est pour la voiture; **this jacket ~s with those trousers** cette veste va avec ce pantalon; **which species do they ~ to?** à quelle espèce appartiennent-ils?; **she ~s in another era** elle est d'une autre époque. -**4.** [have proper place] être à sa place; **the dishes ~ in that cupboard** les assiettes vont dans ce placard; **put the books back where they ~** remettez les livres à leur place; **the two of them ~ together** ces deux-là sont faits pour être ensemble; **these gloves ~ together** ces gants appartiennent à la même paire; **I don't ~ here** je ne suis pas à ma place ici; **go back home where you ~** rentrez chez vous; **she doesn't feel she ~s** elle ne se sent pas chez elle ici; **he ~s in teaching** sa place est dans l'enseignement; **these issues ~ in a court of law** ces questions relèvent d'un tribunal.

belonging [bɪ'lɒŋɪŋ] *n*: **a sense of ~** un sentiment d'appartenance.
◆ **belongings** *npl* affaires *fpl*, possessions *fpl*; **she packed the few ~s she had** elle a emballé le peu (de choses OR d'affaires) qu'elle avait; **personal ~s** objets *mpl* OR effets *mpl* personnels.

Belorussia *etc* [ˌbeləʊ'rʌʃə] = **Byelorussia**.

beloved [bɪ'lʌvd] ◇ *adj* chéri, bien-aimé; **he was ~ by** OR **of all his friends** il était cher à tous ses amis; **my ~ father** mon très cher père.
◇ *n* bien-aimé *m*, -e *f*, amour *m*; **dearly ~, we are gathered here today...** mes très chers amis, nous sommes ici aujourd'hui...

below [bɪ'ləʊ] ◇ *prep* -**1.** [at, to a lower position than] au-dessous de, en dessous de; [under] sous; **the flat ~ ours** l'appartement au-dessous OR en dessous du nôtre; **her skirt came to ~ her knees** sa jupe lui descendait au-dessous du genou; **~ the surface** sous la surface; **~ (the) ground** sous (la) terre. -**2.** [inferior to] au-dessous de, inférieur à; **temperatures ~ zero** des températures au-dessous de OR inférieures à zéro; **his grades are ~ average** ses notes sont au-dessous de OR inférieures à la moyenne; **~ the poverty line** en dessous du seuil de pauvreté; **children ~ the age of five** des enfants de moins de cinq ans; **the rank is just ~ that of general** le rang est juste au-dessous de celui d'un général. -**3.** [downstream of] en aval de. -**4.** [south of] au sud de.
◇ *adv* -**1.** [in lower place, on lower level] en dessous, plus bas; **we looked down onto the town ~** nous contemplions la ville à nos pieds; **down ~ in the valley** en bas dans la vallée; **the flat ~** l'appartement d'en dessous OR du dessous; **he could hear two men talking ~** il entendait deux hommes parler en bas; **seen from ~** vu d'en bas; **the title came first with her name immediately ~** le titre apparaissait en premier avec son nom juste en dessous ❑ **here ~** *arch* OR *lit* [on earth] ici-bas. -**2.** [with numbers, quantities] moins; **it was twenty ~** *inf* il faisait moins vingt; **children of five and ~** les enfants de cinq ans et moins. -**3.** [in text] plus bas, ci-dessous; **see ~** voir plus bas OR ci-dessous; **the address given ~** l'adresse mentionnée ci-dessous. -**4.** NAUT en bas; **to go ~** descendre dans l'entrepont; **she went ~ to her cabin** elle est descendue à sa cabine.

belt [belt] ◇ *n* -**1.** [gen & SPORT] ceinture *f*; MIL ceinturon *m*, ceinture *f*; **a leather ~** une ceinture en cuir; **he had a gun at his ~** il portait un revolver à la ceinture; **to give sb the ~** donner une correction à qqn; **a black/brown ~** SPORT une ceinture noire/marron ❑ **she now has a doctoral degree under her ~** elle a maintenant un doctorat en poche; **no hitting below the ~** *literal* il est interdit de porter des coups bas; *fig* pas de coups bas!; **that was a bit below the ~** c'était un peu déloyal comme procédé; **to pull in** OR **to tighten one's ~** se serrer la ceinture. -**2.** [of machine] courroie *f*. -**3.** [area, zone] région *f*; **~s of high unemployment** des régions à fort taux de chômage; **corn/cotton ~** région *f* de culture du maïs/du coton. -**4.** *inf* [sharp blow] coup *m*. -**5.** *inf* [of whisky] gorgée *f*.
◇ *vt* -**1.** [dress, trousers] ceinturer, mettre une ceinture à; **he had a gun ~ed to his waist** il avait un revolver à la ceinture; **a ~ed raincoat** un imperméable à ceinture. -**2.** [hit with belt] donner des coups de ceinture à; [as punishment] administrer une correction à. -**3.** *inf* [hit] donner OR flanquer un coup à; **I ~ed him (one) in the eye** je lui en ai collé un dans l'œil; **she ~ed the ball** elle a donné un grand coup dans la balle.
◇ *vi* *inf Br* filer; **they went ~ing along** ils fonçaient; **he ~ed into/out of the room** il est entré dans/sorti de la pièce à toute berzingue; **~ing down the motorway** fonçant sur l'autoroute.
◆ **belt down** *inf vt sep Br* [food] engloutir, enfourner; [drink] avaler, descendre.
◆ **belt out** *inf vt sep*: **she ~ed out the national anthem** elle a chanté l'hymne national à pleins poumons; **he ~ed out a song on the piano** il a joué un air entraînant au piano.
◆ **belt up** *vi insep* -**1.** [in car, plane] attacher sa ceinture; **~ up!** attachez votre ceinture! -**2.** *inf Br* [be quiet] la fermer, la boucler; **~ up!** boucle-la!

belt-driven *adj* actionné par courroie.

belting ['beltɪŋ] *n*: **to give sb a ~** [as punishment] donner des coups de ceinture OR administrer une correction à qqn; [in fight] rouer qqn de coups.

beltway ['beltˌweɪ] *n Am* (boulevard *m*) périphérique *m*.

belvedere ['belvɪˌdɪə^r] *n* belvédère *m*.

bemoan [bɪ'məʊn] *vt* pleurer, se lamenter sur; **he ~ed the loss of this freedom** il pleura la perte de sa liberté; **to ~ one's fate** pleurer sur son sort.

bemused [bɪ'mjuːzd] *adj* déconcerté, dérouté; **she seemed ~** elle semblait déconcertée; **he gave a ~ smile** il sourit d'un air OR il eut un sourire déconcerté.

ben [ben] *n Ir* & *Scot* sommet *m*, mont *m*.

Benares [bɪ'nɑːrɪz] *pr n* Bénarès.

bench [bentʃ] ◇ *n* -**1.** [seat] banc *m*; [caned, padded] banquette *f*; [in auditorium] gradin *m*; **park ~** banc public; **on the ~** SPORT en réserve. -**2.** *Br* [in Parliament] banc *m*; **the government ~es** les bancs du gouvernement. -**3.** [work table] établi *m*, plan *m* de travail. -**4.** JUR [seat] banc *m*; **the ~** [judge] la cour, le juge; **address your remarks to the ~** adressez-vous à la cour ‖ [judges as group]: **the ~** les juges, les magistrats; **she has been raised to the ~** elle a été nommée juge; **he serves** OR **sits on the ~** [permanent office] il est juge; [for particular case] il siège au tribunal; **what does the ~ feel about this?** qu'en pense la cour?
◇ *comp*: **~ lathe** tour *m* d'établi; **~ vice** étau *m* d'établi.
◇ *vt Am* SPORT retirer du jeu.

bencher ['bentʃə^r] *n Br* JUR ≃ membre *m* de l'ordre des avocats.

benchmark ['bentʃ,mɑːk] *n literal* repère *m*; [in surveying] repère *m* de nivellement; *fig* repère *m*, point *m* de référence; a ~ decision une décision de base OR de référence.

bench press ◇ *n banc sur lequel on s'allonge pour soulever des haltères.*
◇ *vt*: to ~ 50 kg soulever 50 kg *(allongé)*.

bench warrant *n Br* JUR mandat *m* d'arrêt.

bend [bend] (*pt* & *pp* bent [bent]) ◇ *vt* -**1.** [arm, finger] plier; [knee, leg] plier, fléchir; [back, body] courber; [head] pencher, baisser; they bent their heads over their books ils se penchèrent sur leurs livres; to ~ one's head in prayer baisser la tête pour prier; on ~ed knee à genoux; he went down on ~ed knee il se mit à genoux, il s'agenouilla; to ~ sb to one's will plier qqn à sa volonté ❑ he likes to ~ the elbow *inf Br* il sait lever le coude, il aime bien boire; to ~ sb's ear casser les oreilles à qqn. -**2.** [pipe, wire] tordre, courber; [branch, tree] courber, faire ployer; [bow] bander, arquer; to ~ sthg at right angles plier qqch à angle droit; she bent the stem slightly elle a courbé un peu la tige; he bent the rod out of shape il a tordu la barre ❑ to ~ the rules faire une entorse au règlement. -**3.** [deflect - light, ray] réfracter; [- stream] dériver, détourner. -**4.** *lit* [direct, turn] diriger; they bent their steps towards home ils se dirigèrent OR ils dirigèrent leurs pas vers la maison; he bent his attention OR his mind to solving the problem il s'appliqua à résoudre le problème; we bent all our efforts to fighting racism nous avons mis tous nos efforts dans la lutte contre le racisme; they bent themselves to the task ils se sont attelés à la tâche; all eyes were bent on the demonstration tous les yeux OR regards étaient fixés sur la démonstration. -**5.** NAUT [fasten - cable, rope] étalinguer; [- sail] enverguer.
◇ *vi* -**1.** [arm, knee, leg] plier; [person] se courber, se pencher; [head] se pencher; [rod, wire] plier, se courber; [branch, tree] ployer, plier; to ~ under the burden/the weight ployer sous le fardeau/le poids; she bent over the counter elle s'est penchée par-dessus le comptoir; he bent backwards/forwards il s'est penché en arrière/en avant. -**2.** [river, road] faire un coude, tourner; the road ~s to the left la route tourne à gauche. -**3.** [submit] céder; the people refused to ~ to the colonial forces le peuple a refusé de se soumettre aux forces coloniales; the government bent to pressure from the unions l'administration a cédé à la pression des syndicats.
◇ *n* -**1.** [in road] coude *m*, virage *m*; [in river] méandre *m*, coude *m*; [in pipe, rod] coude *m*; after I rounded the first ~ in the road après (avoir pris) le premier virage; the road makes a ~ to the right la route fait un coude vers la droite; '~s for 7 miles' 'virages sur 10 km' ❑ to drive sb round the ~ *inf* rendre qqn fou; he's completely round the ~ *inf* il est complètement cinglé. -**2.** [in arm] pli *m*, saignée *f*; [in knee] pli *m*, flexion *f*; she did a couple of forward ~s elle s'est penchée plusieurs fois en avant. -**3.** NAUT [knot] nœud *m* (de jonction).
◆ **bends** *npl* maladie *f* des caissons; to get the ~s être atteint par la maladie des caissons.
◆ **bend back** ◇ *vi insep* -**1.** [person] se pencher en arrière. -**2.** [blade, tube] se recourber.
◇ *vt sep* replier, recourber.
◆ **bend down** ◇ *vi insep* -**1.** [person] se courber, se baisser. -**2.** [branch, tree] plier, ployer.
◇ *vt sep* [branch, tree] faire ployer; [blade, tube] replier, recourber.
◆ **bend over** ◇ *vi insep* se pencher; to ~ over backwards to please (sb) se donner beaucoup de mal pour faire plaisir (à qqn).
◇ *vt sep* replier, recourber.

bender *inf* ['bendəʳ] *n* beuverie *f*; to go on a ~ faire la noce.

bend sinister *n* HERALD barre *f* de bâtardise.

bendy ['bendɪ] (*compar* bendier, *superl* bendiest) *adj* -**1.** [road] sinueux. -**2.** [flexible] souple, flexible.

beneath [bɪ'niːθ] ◇ *prep* -**1.** [under] sous; the ground ~ my feet le sol sous mes pieds; buried ~ tons of rubble enfoui sous des tonnes de gravats; the ship sank ~ the waves le navire a sombré sous les vagues. -**2.** [below]: the valley was spread out ~ us la vallée s'étalait sous nos pieds. -**3.** [unworthy of] indigne de; she thinks the work is ~ her elle estime que le travail est indigne d'elle. -**4.** [socially inferior to] inférieur *(socialement)*; he married ~ him il a fait une mésalliance *fml*, il n'a pas fait un bon mariage.
◇ *adv* [underneath] en bas; from ~ d'en dessous.

Benedict ['benɪdɪkt] *pr n*: Saint ~ saint Benoît.

Benedictine [*n sense 1* & *adj* ,benɪ'dɪktɪn, *n sense 2* ,benɪ'dɪktiːn] ◇ *n* -**1.** RELIG bénédictin *m*, -e *f*. -**2.** [liqueur] Bénédictine® *f*.
◇ *adj* bénédictin.

benediction [,benɪ'dɪkʃn] *n* -**1.** RELIG & *fig* [blessing] bénédiction *f*. -**2.** [service] salut *m*.

benefaction [,benɪ'fækʃn] *n* -**1.** [good deed] acte *m* de bienfaisance. -**2.** [donation] don *m*, donation *f*.

benefactor ['benɪfæktəʳ] *n* bienfaiteur *m*.

benefactress ['benɪfæktrɪs] *n* bienfaitrice *f*.

benefice ['benɪfɪs] *n* bénéfice *m*.

beneficence [bɪ'nefɪsns] *n* -**1.** [kindness] bienveillance *f*, bienfaisance *f*. -**2.** [good deed] acte *m* de bienfaisance, bienfait *m*.

beneficent [bɪ'nefɪsnt] *adj* [person, regime] bienfaisant, généreux; [change, effect] bienfaisant, salutaire.

beneficial [,benɪ'fɪʃl] *adj* -**1.** [good, useful] avantageux, profitable; legislation ~ to the self-employed des lois favorables aux travailleurs non-salariés; the holiday proved highly ~ les vacances ont été extrêmement bénéfiques; vitamins are ~ to health les vitamines sont bonnes pour la santé; ~ effects des effets salutaires. -**2.** JUR: ~ owner usufruitier *m*, -ère *f*; ~ legacy usufruit *m*.

beneficiary [,benɪ'fɪʃərɪ] (*pl* beneficiaries) *n* -**1.** [of insurance policy, trust] bénéficiaire *mf*; [of will] bénéficiaire *mf*, légataire *mf*. -**2.** RELIG bénéficier *m*.

benefit ['benɪfɪt] (*Br pt* & *pp* benefited, *cont* benefiting, *Am pt* & *pp* benefitted, *cont* benefitting) ◇ *n* -**1.** [advantage] avantage *m*; the ~s of a good education les avantages OR les bienfaits d'une bonne éducation; she is starting to feel the ~s of the treatment elle commence à ressentir les bienfaits du traitement; she did it for the ~ of the whole family elle a agi pour le bien-être de toute la famille; I'm saying this for your ~ je dis cela pour toi OR pour ton bien; for the ~ of those who arrived late pour les retardataires OR ceux qui sont arrivés en retard; the speech she made was all for his ~ le discours qu'elle a prononcé ne s'adressait qu'à lui; the holiday wasn't of much ~ to him les vacances ne lui ont pas fait tellement de bien; our discussion was of no ~ to me notre discussion ne m'a rien apporté; it's to your ~ to watch your diet il est dans votre intérêt de surveiller ce que vous mangez; this law is to the ~ of the wealthy cette loi favorise les gens aisés; with the ~ of hindsight, I now see I was wrong avec le recul OR rétrospectivement, je m'aperçois que j'avais tort; to give sb the ~ of the doubt laisser OR accorder à qqn le bénéfice du doute. -**2.** [payment] allocation *f*, prestation *f*; social security ~s prestations sociales; tax ~ *Am* dégrèvement *m*, allègement *m* fiscal. -**3.** [performance] spectacle *m (au profit d'une association caritative)*; ~ concert concert *m (au profit d'une association caritative)*; ~ match match *m (au profit d'une association caritative)*; ~ performance représentation *f* de bienfaisance.
◇ *vt* [do good to] faire du bien à; [bring financial profit to] profiter à.
◇ *vi*: he will ~ from the experience l'expérience lui sera bénéfique; no-one is likely to ~ by OR from the closures personne n'a de chance de tirer avantage des fermetures; the novel would ~ greatly from judicious editing le roman gagnerait beaucoup à être révisé de façon judicieuse; you would ~ from some time in the country un séjour à la campagne vous ferait du bien.

benefit society *n Am* société *f* de prévoyance, mutuelle *f*.

Benelux ['benɪlʌks] *pr n* Bénélux *m*; the ~ countries les pays du Bénélux; in the ~ countries au Bénélux.

benevolence [bɪ'nevələns] *n* -**1.** [kindness] bienveillance *f*, bienfaisance *f*. -**2.** [good deed] acte *m* de bienfaisance, bienfait *m*.

benevolent [bɪ'nevələnt] *adj* -**1.** [kindly] bienveillant, plein de bonté; his ~ attitude to OR towards children son attitude bienveillante envers les enfants. -**2.** [organization] de bienfaisance; ~ fund fonds *m* de prévoyance.

benevolently [bɪ'nevələntlɪ] *adv* avec bienveillance.

BEng [,biː'eŋ] (*abbr of* Bachelor of Engineering) *n (titulaire d'une) licence d'ingénierie.*

Bengal [,beŋ'gɔːl] *pr n* Bengale *m*; in ~ au Bengale; Bay of ~ golfe *m* du Bengale.

Bengali [beŋ'gɔːlɪ] ◇ *n* -**1.** [person] Bengali *mf*. -**2.** LING bengali *m*.
◇ *adj* bengali.

Bengal light *n Br* feu *m* de Bengale.

Bengal tiger *n* tigre *m* du Bengale.

benighted [bɪ'naɪtɪd] *adj lit* [ignorant - person] plongé dans (les ténèbres de) l'ignorance; [- mind] étroit; [- policy] aveugle.

benign [bɪ'naɪn] *adj* -**1.** [kind - person] affable, aimable; [- smile] affable, chaleureux; [- power, system] bienfaisant, salutaire. -**2.** [harmless] bénin; ~ illness maladie *f* bénigne; ~ tumour tumeur *f* bénigne. -**3.** [temperate - climate] doux, clément.

Benin [be'nɪn] *pr n* Bénin *m*; in ~ au Bénin.

Beninese [,benɪ'niːz] ◇ *n* Béninois *m*, -e *f*.
◇ *adj* béninois.

Benjamin ['bendʒəmɪn] *pr n* Benjamin.

Bennism ['benɪzm] *n politique de nationalisation de l'industrie en Grande-Bretagne (d'après Tony Benn, ministre travailliste en 1974).*

benny ['benɪ] (*pl* bennies) *n drugs sl* (comprimé *m* de) Benzédrine® *f*.

bent [bent] ◇ *pt* & *pp* → **bend**.
◇ *adj* -**1.** [curved - tree, tube, wire] tordu, courbé; [- branch] courbé; [- back] voûté; [- person] voûté, tassé. -**2.** [dented] cabossé, bosselé. -**3.** [determined]: to be ~ on (doing) sthg: he's ~ on becoming an actor il est décidé à OR veut absolument devenir acteur; she's ~ on winning elle est décidée à gagner; to be ~ on self-destruction être porté à l'autodestruction. -**4.** *inf Br* [dishonest] véreux. -**5.** ▽ *Br pej* [homosexual] homo, gay.
◇ *n* -**1.** [liking] penchant *m*, goût *m*; [aptitude] aptitudes *fpl*, dispositions *fpl*; they're of an artistic ~ ils sont tournés vers les arts; she has a natural ~ for music [liking] elle a un goût naturel pour la musique; [talent] elle a des dispositions naturelles pour la musique; he followed his (natural) ~ il a suivi son penchant OR son inclination. -**2.** *Br* [endurance] endurance *f*; to the top of one's ~ au meilleur de sa forme.

benthos ['benθɒs] *n* benthos *m*.

bentonite ['bentənaɪt] *n* bentonite *f*.

bentwood ['bentwʊd] *n* bois *m* courbé; a ~ chair une chaise en bois courbé.

benumb [bɪ'nʌm] *vt lit* engourdir, endormir; ~ed by the OR with cold [person] transi de froid; [fingers, toes] engourdi par le froid; her mind was ~ed with fear elle était transie de OR paralysée par la peur.

Benzedrine® ['benzədriːn] *n* Benzédrine® *f*.

benzene ['benziːn] *n* benzène *m*.

benzene ring *n* noyau *m* benzénique.

benzine ['benziːn] *n* benzine *f*.

benzoic [ben'zəʊɪk] *adj* benzoïque.

benzoin ['benzəʊɪn] *n* -**1.** [resin] benjoin *m*. -**2.** [tree] styrax *m* benjoin.

bequeath [bɪ'kwiːð] *vt* [pass on] transmettre, léguer; JUR [in will] léguer; **her father ~ed her his fortune** son père lui a légué sa fortune; **they've ~ed nothing to us but a ruined economy** ils ne nous ont légué qu'une économie en ruine.

bequest [bɪ'kwest] *n* legs *m*.

berate [bɪ'reɪt] *vt* réprimander; **he ~d them for being late** il leur a reproché d'être en retard.

Berber ['bɜːbəʳ] ◇ *n* -**1.** [person] Berbère *mf*. -**2.** LING berbère *m*.
◇ *adj* berbère.

bereave [bɪ'riːv] (*pt* & *pp* bereaved OR bereft [-'reft]) *vt* priver, déposséder; **the war ~d them of their two sons** la guerre leur a pris leurs deux fils, ils ont perdu leurs deux fils à la guerre.

bereaved [bɪ'riːvd] ◇ *adj* affligé, endeuillé; **a ~ mother** une mère qui vient de perdre son enfant; **he's recently ~** il a perdu quelqu'un récemment.
◇ *npl*: **the ~** ceux qui viennent de perdre un être cher.

bereavement [bɪ'riːvmənt] ◇ *n* [loss] perte *f*; [grief] deuil *m*; **she can't get over her recent ~** [husband's death] elle n'arrive pas à accepter la mort de son mari; **in his ~** dans son deuil.
◇ *comp*: **~ counselling** *service d'aide psychologique aux personnes frappées par un deuil*.

bereft [bɪ'reft] ◇ *pt* & *pp* → **bereave**.
◇ *adj* privé; **~ of all hope** complètement désespéré; **to be ~ of reason** avoir perdu la raison; **I feel utterly ~** je me sens totalement seul.

beret ['bereɪ] *n* béret *m*.

berg [bɜːg] *n* [iceberg] iceberg *m*.

Bergamo ['bɜːgəməʊ] *pr n* Bergame.

bergamot ['bɜːgəmɒt] *n* bergamote *f*.

Bergen ['bɜːgən] *pr n* Bergen.

beriberi [,berɪ'berɪ] *n* béribéri *m*.

Bering Sea ['berɪŋ-] *pr n*: **the ~** la mer de Béring.

Bering Strait *pr n*: **the ~** le détroit de Béring.

berk *inf* [bɜːk] *n Br* espèce *f* d'idiot *m*, -e *f*.

berkelium [bɜː'kiːlɪəm] *n* berkélium *m*.

Berks *written abbr of* Berkshire.

berlin [bə'lɪn] *n* -**1.** **~ (wool)** laine *f* à broder. -**2.** [carriage] berline *f*.

Berlin [bɜː'lɪn] *pr n* Berlin; **East ~** Berlin-Est; **West ~** Berlin-Ouest; **the ~ Wall** le mur de Berlin; **the ~ airlift** le pont aérien de Berlin.

Berliner [bɜː'lɪnəʳ] *n* Berlinois *m*, -e *f*.

berm(e) [bɜːm] *n* berme *f*.

Bermuda [bə'mjuːdə] *pr n* Bermudes *fpl*; **in ~** aux Bermudes; **the ~ Triangle** le triangle des Bermudes.

Bermudan [bə'mjuːdən], **Bermudian** [bə'muːdjən] ◇ *n habitant des Bermudes*.
◇ *adj* des Bermudes.

Bermudas [bə'mjuːdəz], **Bermuda shorts** *npl* bermuda *m*.

Bern [bɜːn] *pr n* Berne.

Bernese [,bɜː'niːz] ◇ *n* Bernois *m*, -e *f*.
◇ *adj* bernois.

berry ['berɪ] (*pl* berries, *pt* & *pp* berried) ◇ *n* baie *f*.
◇ *vi* -**1.** [bush] produire des baies. -**2.** [person] cueillir des baies; **to go ~ing** aller cueillir des baies.

berserk [bə'zɜːk] ◇ *adj* fou furieux.
◇ *adv* fou furieux; **to go ~** [person] devenir fou furieux; [crowd] se déchaîner.

berth [bɜːθ] ◇ *n* -**1.** [bunk] couchette *f*. -**2.** NAUT [in harbour] mouillage *m*, poste *m* d'amarrage; [distance] distance *f*. -**3.** *phr*: **to give sb a wide ~** *Br* éviter qqn (à tout prix); **I'd give him a wide ~ if I were you** je l'éviterais (à tout prix) OR je me tiendrais à distance si j'étais vous.
◇ *vi* [at dock] venir à quai, accoster; [at anchor] mouiller.
◇ *vt* [dock] amarrer, faire accoster; [assign place] donner un poste d'amarrage à.

beryl ['berəl] *n* béryl *m*.

beryllium [be'rɪljɪəm] *n* béryllium *m*.

beseech [bɪ'siːtʃ] (*pt* & *pp* beseeched OR besought [-'sɔːt]) *vt fml* OR *lit* -**1.** [ask for] solliciter, implorer. -**2.** [entreat] implorer, supplier; **he ~ed them to save him** il les a suppliés OR implorés de le sauver; **please, I ~ you** s'il vous plaît, je vous en supplie OR conjure.

beseeching [bɪ'siːtʃɪŋ] ◇ *adj* suppliant, implorant.
◇ *n* supplications *fpl*.

beseechingly [bɪ'siːtʃɪŋlɪ] *adv* d'un air OR ton suppliant.

beset [bɪ'set] (*pt* & *pp* beset, *cont* besetting) (*usu pass*) *vt* -**1.** [attack] assaillir, harceler; **I was ~ by** OR **with doubt** j'étais assailli par le doute; **the whole project is ~ with financial difficulties** le projet pose énormément de problèmes sur le plan financier; **they are ~ with problems** ils sont assaillis de problèmes. -**2.** [surround] encercler; **~ by the enemy** cerné par l'ennemi.

besetting [bɪ'setɪŋ] *adj*: **his ~ sin was greed** la cupidité était son plus grand défaut.

beside [bɪ'saɪd] *prep* -**1.** [next to] à côté de, auprès de; **walk ~ me** marchez à côté de moi; **he wanted to keep his family ~ him** il voulait garder sa famille auprès de lui; **a plate with a glass ~ it** une assiette avec un verre à côté; **a house ~ the sea** une maison au bord de la mer. -**2.** [as compared with] à côté de, par rapport à; **the results don't look very brilliant ~ last year's** les résultats n'ont pas l'air brillants à côté de OR par rapport à ceux de l'année dernière. -**3.** [in addition to] en plus que, outre; [apart from] à part, excepté. -**4.** *phr*: **to be ~ o.s. with rage/excitement/joy** être hors de soi/surexcité/fou de joie.

besides [bɪ'saɪdz] ◇ *prep* -**1.** [in addition to] en plus de, outre; **there are three (other) candidates ~ yourself** il y a trois (autres) candidats à part vous; **what other skills do you have ~ languages?** quelles compétences avez-vous à part OR outre les langues?; **that's ~ what you already owe me** c'est en plus de ce que tu me dois déjà; **~ being old, she's also extremely deaf** non seulement elle est vieille, mais elle est également très sourde; **~ which that book is out of print** sans compter que ce livre est épuisé. -**2.** [apart from] (*with negatives*) hormis, excepté; **nobody ~ me** personne à part moi; **she said nothing ~ what we knew already** elle n'a rien dit que nous ne sachions déjà.
◇ *adv* -**1.** [in addition] en plus, en outre; **and more ~** et d'autres encore; **he owns two flats and a country house ~** il est propriétaire de deux appartements ainsi que d'une maison à la campagne; **he knows the rudiments but little else ~** il connaît les rudiments mais pas grand-chose d'autre OR de plus. -**2.** [furthermore] en plus; **it's an excellent play and, ~, the tickets aren't expensive** la pièce est excellente et en plus, les billets ne coûtent pas cher; **~, I don't even like funfairs** d'ailleurs OR en plus, je n'aime pas les foires.

besiege [bɪ'siːdʒ] *vt* -**1.** [surround - town] assiéger; *fig* [- person, office] assaillir; **the tourists were ~d by beggars** les touristes étaient assaillis par des mendiants. -**2.** [harass] assaillir, harceler; **~d by doubt** rongé OR assailli par le doute; **we've been ~d by requests for help** nous avons été assaillis de demandes d'aide.

besieger [bɪ'siːdʒəʳ] *n* assiégeant *m*.

besmear [bɪ'smɪəʳ] *vt lit* [smear] barbouiller, salir; *fig* [tarnish] souiller; **to ~ sb's reputation** souiller OR ternir la réputation de qqn.

besmirch [bɪ'smɜːtʃ] *vt lit* [make dirty] salir, souiller *lit*; *fig* [tarnish] souiller; **~ed with mud** barbouillé de boue; **to ~ sb's name** souiller OR ternir le nom de qqn.

besom ['biːzəm] *n* [broom] balai *m*.

besotted [bɪ'sɒtɪd] *adj* -**1.** [infatuated] fou, épris; **to be ~ with sb** être fou OR follement épris de qqn. -**2.** [foolish] idiot; **~ with drink** abruti (par l'alcool), soûl.

besought [bɪ'sɔːt] *pt* & *pp* → **beseech**.

bespangle [bɪ'spæŋgl] *vt lit* pailleter; **~d with diamonds** pailleté OR parsemé de diamants.

bespatter [bɪ'spætəʳ] *vt lit* [splash] éclabousser; *fig* [tarnish] souiller, éclabousser.

bespeak [bɪ'spiːk] (*pt* bespoke [-'spəʊk], *pp* bespoke OR bespoken [-'spəʊkən]) *vt lit* -**1.** [be sign of] démontrer, témoigner de; **her action ~s kindness** son geste témoigne de sa bonté; **their hesitation ~s moral weakness** leur hésitation révèle une faiblesse morale. -**2.** [reserve - room, table] réserver, retenir; [- book, product] commander.

bespectacled [bɪ'spektəkld] *adj* qui porte des lunettes, à lunettes.

bespoke [bɪ'spəʊk] ◇ *pt* & *pp* → **bespeak**.
◇ *adj* [shoemaker, tailor] à façon; [shoes, suit] fait sur mesure.

bespoken [bɪ'spəʊkən] *pp* → **bespeak**.

besprinkle [bɪ'sprɪŋkl] *vt lit* [with sugar, talc] saupoudrer; [with liquid] asperger, arroser; **the grass was ~d with dew** l'herbe était couverte de rosée; **fields ~d with poppies** des champs parsemés de coquelicots.

Bessemer converter ['besɪməʳ-] *n* convertisseur *m* Bessemer.

Bessemer process *n* procédé *m* Bessemer.

best [best] (*pl inv*) ◇ *adj* -**1.** (*superl of* **good**) meilleur; **some of our ~ scientists will be there** certains de nos meilleurs chercheurs seront présents; **it's one of the ~ films I've ever seen** c'est un des meilleurs films que j'aie jamais vus; **she's my ~ friend** c'est ma meilleure amie; **may the ~ man win** que le meilleur gagne; **she gave him the ~ years of her life** elle lui a sacrifié les plus belles années de sa vie; **I'm doing what is ~ for the family** je fais ce qu'il y a de mieux pour la famille; **she knows what's ~ for her** elle sait ce qui lui va OR convient le mieux; **do as you think ~** faites pour le mieux; **they think it ~ not to answer** ils croient qu'il vaut mieux ne pas répondre; **it's ~ not to smoke at all** il est préférable de ne pas fumer du tout; **what's the ~ thing to do?** quelle est la meilleure chose à faire?; **the ~ thing (to do) is to keep quiet** le mieux, c'est de ne rien dire; **the ~ thing about it is that it's free/is that she didn't even realize** le mieux, c'est que c'est gratuit/c'est qu'elle ne s'en est même pas rendu compte; **~ of all** le meilleur de tout; **'~ before 1995'** COMM 'à consommer de préférence avant 1995' ❑ **it's the ~ thing since sliced bread** c'est génial. -**2.** [reserved for special occasions] plus beau; **she put out her ~ dishes** *Br* elle a sorti sa plus belle vaisselle; *Am* elle a sorti ses plus belles assiettes; **she was dressed in her ~ clothes** elle portait ses plus beaux vêtements. -**3.** *phr*: **the ~ part of sthg** la plus grande partie de qqch; **she spent the ~ part of the day working** elle a passé le plus clair de la journée à travailler; **I waited for the ~ part of an hour** j'ai attendu près d'une heure OR presque une heure.
◇ *adv* (*superl of* **well**) mieux; **he does it ~** c'est lui qui le fait le mieux; **Tuesday would suit me ~** le mieux pour moi serait mardi; **the ~-kept garden in the village** le jardin le mieux entretenu du village; **the ~-preserved Renaissance theatre in Italy** le théâtre Renaissance le mieux conservé d'Italie; **which film did you like ~?** quel est le film que vous avez préféré?; **I liked the Fellini ~** c'est le Fellini que j'ai préféré; **I comforted her as ~ I could** je l'ai consolée de mon mieux OR du mieux que j'ai pu ❑ **you had ~ apologize to her** vous feriez mieux de lui présenter vos excuses.
◇ *n* -**1.** [most outstanding person, thing, part etc] le meilleur *m*, la meilleure *f*, les meilleurs *mpl*, les meilleures *fpl*; **it/she is the ~ there is** c'est le meilleur/la meilleure qui soit; **he wants her to have the ~** il veut qu'elle ait ce qu'il y a de mieux, il veut ce qu'il y a de mieux pour elle; **the ~ of it is the paid holidays** le mieux OR ce qu'il y a de vraiment bien, ce sont les congés payés; **the ~ you can say about him is that...** le mieux qu'on puisse dire à son sujet c'est

que...; she can stand comparison with the ~ of them on peut la comparer avec les meilleurs d'entre eux/les meilleures d'entre elles; even the ~ of us can make mistakes tout le monde peut se tromper; to get OR to have the ~ of the bargain avoir la part belle ❑ she wants the ~ of both worlds elle veut tout avoir. -**2.** [greatest, highest degree] le mieux, le meilleur; they're the ~ of friends ce sont les meilleurs amis du monde; to the ~ of my knowledge/ recollection autant que je sache/je me souvienne; the ~ of luck! bonne chance!; even at the ~ of times même dans les meilleurs moments; she's not the calmest of people, even at the ~ of times ce n'est pas quelqu'un de très calme de toute façon; it was the ~ we could do nous ne pouvions pas faire mieux; it's journalism at its ~ c'est du journalisme de haut niveau; the garden is at its ~ in spring c'est au printemps que le jardin est le plus beau; he was at his ~ last night il était en pleine forme hier soir; I'm not at my ~ in the morning je ne suis pas en forme le matin; this is Shakespeare at his ~ voilà du meilleur Shakespeare; to do one's ~ faire de son mieux OR tout son possible; do your ~! faites de votre mieux!, faites pour le mieux!; do your ~ to finish on time faites de votre mieux pour finir à temps; to get the ~ out of sb/sthg tirer un maximum de qqn/qqch; to look one's ~ [gen] être resplendissant; she looks her ~ with short hair les cheveux courts l'avantagent; we'll have to make the ~ of the situation il faudra nous accommoder de la situation (du mieux que nous pouvons); to make the ~ of a bad bargain OR job faire contre mauvaise fortune bon cœur. -**3.** [nicest clothes]: they were in their (Sunday) ~ ils étaient endimanchés OR portaient leurs habits du dimanche. -**4.** [good wishes]: (I wish you) all the ~ (je vous souhaite) bonne chance; give your wife my ~ mes amitiés à votre femme. -**5.** [winning majority]: we played the ~ of three games le jeu consistait à gagner OR il fallait gagner deux parties sur trois.

◇ *vt arch* [get advantage over] l'emporter sur; [defeat] vaincre.

◆ **at best** *adv phr* au mieux; this is, at ~, a temporary solution c'est, au mieux, une solution temporaire; his performance has been at ~ mediocre ses résultats ont été, au mieux, médiocres.

◆ **for the best** *adv phr* pour le mieux; it's all for the ~ c'est pour le mieux; he meant it for the ~ il avait les meilleures intentions du monde.

best-case *adj* → **scenario**.

bestial ['bestjəl] *adj* bestial.

bestiality [ˌbestɪ'ælətɪ] (*pl* bestialities) *n* -**1.** [of behaviour, character] bestialité *f*. -**2.** [act] acte *m* bestial. -**3.** [sexual practice] bestialité *f*.

bestiary ['bestɪərɪ] (*pl* bestiaries) *n* bestiaire *m* (*recueil*).

bestir [bɪ'stɜːʳ] (*pt* & *pp* bestirred, *cont* bestirring) *vt*: to ~ o.s. s'activer.

best man *n* garçon *m* d'honneur.

BEST MAN:
Dans les pays anglo-saxons, le garçon d'honneur présente l'alliance au marié et prononce un discours lors de la réception de mariage.

bestow [bɪ'stəʊ] *vt fml* [favour, gift, praise] accorder; [award, honour] conférer, accorder; to ~ sthg on sb accorder OR conférer qqch à qqn.

bestowal [bɪ'stəʊəl] *n fml* [of favour, honour, title] octroi *m*.

bestrew [bɪ'struː] (*pt* bestrewed, *pp* bestrewed OR bestrewn [-'struːn]) *vt lit* joncher; the floor was ~ed with flowers le plancher était jonché de fleurs.

bestride [bɪ'straɪd] (*pt* bestrode [-'strəʊd], *pp* bestridden [-'strɪdn]) *vt lit* -**1.** [straddle - bicycle, horse] enfourcher; [- chair] se mettre à califourchon OR à cheval sur. -**2.** [span - river] enjamber, franchir; [- obstacle] enjamber.

best-seller *n* -**1.** [book] best-seller *m*, succès *m* de librairie; [hi-fi, record] article *m* qui se vend bien. -**2.** [author] auteur *m* à succès.

best-selling *adj* [book, product] à fort tirage; a ~ author un auteur à succès.

bet [bet] (*pt* & *pp* bet OR betted, *cont* betting) ◇ *n* pari *m*; do you want to make a ~? tu veux parier?; we accepted OR took the ~ nous avons accepté le pari; to win/to lose a ~ gagner/perdre un pari; he lay OR put OR placed a ~ on the race il a parié OR il a fait un pari sur la course; place your ~s! faites vos jeux!; they're taking ~s ils prennent des paris; it's a good OR safe ~ that they'll win *fig* ils vont gagner à coup sûr; your best ~ is to take a taxi *inf fig* tu ferais mieux de prendre un taxi; she's a bad/good ~ as a prospective leader *fig* elle ferait un mauvais/bon leader.

◇ *vt* parier; how much did you ~ on the race? combien as-tu parié OR misé sur la course?; I ~ her £5 he wouldn't come j'ai parié 5 livres avec elle qu'il ne viendrait pas; I'll ~ you anything you want je te parie tout ce que tu veux; I'm willing to ~ she's lying *inf* je suis prête à parier qu'elle ment; I ~ you won't do it! *inf* (t'es pas) chiche! ❑ I'll ~ my bottom dollar OR my boots he loses *inf* il va perdre, j'en mettrais ma main au feu; are you going to the party? – you ~! *inf* tu vas à la soirée? – et comment! OR qu'est-ce que tu crois?; I'll tell him off – I'll ~! *inf* [you will] je vais lui dire ses quatre vérités – j'en doute pas!; [you won't] je vais lui dire ses quatre vérités – mon œil!

◇ *vi* parier; to ~ against/on sthg parier contre/sur qqch; he ~s on the races il parie OR joue aux courses; which horse did you ~ on? quel cheval as-tu joué?, sur quel cheval as-tu misé?; to ~ 5 to 1 parier OR miser à 5 contre 1; he said he'd phone me – well, I wouldn't ~ on it! *inf* il a dit qu'il me téléphonerait – à ta place, je ne me ferais pas trop d'illusions!; I wouldn't ~ on getting your money back *inf* à mon avis, tu n'es pas près de revoir ton argent.

beta ['biːtə] *n* bêta *m inv*.

beta-blocker [-ˌblɒkəʳ] *n* bêtabloquant *m*.

betake [bɪ'teɪk] (*pt* betook [-'tʊk], *pp* betaken [-'teɪkn]) *vt lit*: to ~ o.s. to se rendre à; they betook themselves to the fair ils se rendirent à la foire.

beta wave *n* rayons *mpl* bêta.

betel ['biːtl] *n* bétel *m*.

betel nut *n* noix *f* d'arec.

betel palm *n* aréquier *m*, arec *m*.

bethel, Bethel ['beθl] *n lieu de recueillement pour les marins*.

Bethel ['beθl] *pr n* GEOG & BIBLE Béthel.

bethink [bɪ'θɪŋk] (*pt* & *pp* bethought [-'θɔːt]) *vt lit*: to ~ o.s. of sthg [consider] considérer qqch, songer à qqch; [remember] se rappeler qqch, se souvenir de qqch.

Bethlehem ['beθlɪhem] *pr n* Bethléem.

bethought [bɪ'θɔːt] *pt* & *pp* → **bethink**.

betide [bɪ'taɪd] *vi lit* advenir; woe ~ you if you are late! *hum* malheur à toi si tu es en retard!

betimes [bɪ'taɪmz] *adv arch* [early] de bonne heure, tôt; [in good time] à temps; [soon] bientôt.

betoken [bɪ'təʊkn] *vt fml* [indicate] être l'indice de, révéler; [augur] présager, annoncer.

betony ['betənɪ] (*pl* betonies) *n* bétoine *f*.

betook [bɪ'tʊk] *pt* → **betake**.

betray [bɪ'treɪ] *vt* -**1.** [be disloyal to - friend, principle] trahir; [- husband, wife] tromper, trahir; [- country] trahir, être traître à; my face ~ed me *fig* mon visage m'a trahi. -**2.** [denounce] trahir, dénoncer; [hand over] trahir, livrer; he ~ed the rebels to the police il a livré les rebelles à la police. -**3.** [confidence, hope] trahir, tromper; you've ~ed our trust vous avez trahi notre confiance. -**4.** [disclose - secret, truth] trahir, divulguer; [- grief, happiness] trahir, laisser voir; her voice ~ed her nervousness sa voix laissait deviner son inquiétude.

betrayal [bɪ'treɪəl] *n* -**1.** [of country, person, principle] trahison *f*. -**2.** [act] (acte *m* de) trahison *f*; it's a ~ of one's country c'est une trahison envers son pays. -**3.** [of confidence, trust] abus *m*, trahison *f*. -**4.** [of secret, truth] trahison *f*, divulgation *f*.

betrayer [bɪ'treɪəʳ] *n* traître *m*, -esse *f*.

betroth [bɪ'trəʊð] *vt arch* promettre en mariage.

betrothal [bɪ'trəʊðl] *n arch* fiançailles *fpl*; her ~ to the prince ses fiançailles avec le prince.

betrothed [bɪ'trəʊðd] *arch* ◇ *adj* fiancé, promis; she is ~ to our son elle est fiancée à OR avec notre fils.

◇ *n* fiancé *m*, -e *f*, promis *m*, -e *f*.

better ['betəʳ] ◇ *adj* -**1.** *compar of* good [superior] meilleur; the marks are ~ than I expected les notes sont meilleures que je ne m'y attendais; it's ~ than nothing c'est mieux que rien; that's ~! voilà qui est mieux!; I'm ~ at languages than he is je suis meilleur OR plus fort en langues que lui; he's a ~ cook than you are il cuisine mieux que toi; she's a ~ painter than she is a sculptor elle peint mieux qu'elle ne sculpte; I had hoped for ~ things j'avais espéré mieux; business is (getting) ~ les affaires vont mieux; things are (getting) ~ and ~! ça va de mieux en mieux!; it couldn't OR nothing could be ~! c'est on ne peut mieux!; he looks ~ without his glasses il est mieux sans lunettes; you get a ~ view from here on voit mieux d'ici; it's ~ if I don't see them il vaut mieux OR il est préférable que je ne les voie pas; it would have been ~ to have waited a little il aurait mieux valu attendre un peu; you're far ~ leaving now il vaut beaucoup mieux que tu partes maintenant ❑ to be all the ~ for having done sthg se trouver mieux d'avoir fait qqch; you'll be all the ~ for a holiday des vacances vous feront le plus grand bien; ~ off mieux; they're ~ off than we are [richer] ils ont plus d'argent que nous; [in a more advantageous position] ils sont dans une meilleure position que nous; she'd be ~ off in hospital elle serait mieux à l'hôpital; he'd have been ~ off staying where he was il aurait mieux fait de rester où il était. -**2.** *compar of* well [improved in health]: to get ~ commencer à aller mieux; now that he's ~ maintenant qu'il va mieux; my cold is much ~ mon rhume va beaucoup mieux; I'm feeling much ~ je me sens beaucoup mieux. -**3.** [morally]: she's a ~ person for it ça lui a fait beaucoup de bien; you're a ~ man than I am! *hum* mieux vaut toi que moi!; you're no ~ than a liar! tu n'es qu'un menteur! ❑ she's no ~ than she should be *euph* & *dated* elle n'est pas d'une vertu farouche. -**4.** *phr*: the ~ part of sthg la plus grande partie de qqch; I waited for the ~ part of an hour j'ai attendu presque une heure; we haven't seen them for the ~ part of a month ça fait presque un mois OR près d'un mois que nous ne les avons pas vus.

◇ *adv* -**1.** *compar of* well [more proficiently, aptly etc] mieux; he swims ~ than I do il nage mieux que moi; she paints ~ than she sculpts elle peint mieux qu'elle ne sculpte; they speak French ~ than they used to ils parlent mieux le français qu'avant; the town would be ~ described as a backwater la ville est plutôt un coin perdu; he held it up to the light, the ~ to see the colours il l'a mis dans la lumière afin de mieux voir les couleurs; all the ~ to hear you with c'est pour mieux t'entendre ❑ to go one ~ (than sb) renchérir (sur qqn). -**2.** [indicating preference]: I liked his last book ~ j'ai préféré son dernier livre; so much the ~ tant mieux; or ~ still ou mieux encore; the less he knows the ~ moins il en saura, mieux ça vaudra ❑ ~ late than never *prov* mieux vaut tard que jamais *prov*. -**3.** [with adj] mieux, plus; ~ looking plus beau; ~ paid/prepared mieux payé/préparé; she's one of Canada's ~-known authors c'est un des auteurs canadiens les plus OR mieux connus. -**4.** *phr*: you had ~ begin at the beginning tu ferais bien de commencer par le commencement; we'd ~ be going [must go] il

faut que nous partions; [would be preferable] il vaut mieux que nous partions; I'd ~ not wake him il vaut mieux que je ne le réveille pas; it'll be ready tomorrow – it'd ~ be! ce sera prêt demain – il vaudrait mieux!
◇ *n* -**1.** [superior of two] le meilleur *m,* la meilleure *f;* which is the ~ of the two? lequel des deux est le meilleur?; what do you think of this wine? – I've tasted ~ comment trouvez-vous ce vin? – j'en ai bu de meilleurs; there's been a change for the ~ in his health son état de santé s'est amélioré; the situation has taken a turn for the ~ la situation a pris une meilleure tournure ❑ for ~ or worse pour le meilleur ou pour le pire. -**2.** *(usu pl)* [person] supérieur *m,* -e *f.* -**3.** *phr:* to get the ~ of sb: curiosity got the ~ of me ma curiosité l'a emporté; we got the ~ of them in the deal nous l'avons emporté sur eux dans l'affaire. -**4.** [gambler] parieur *m,* -euse *f.*
◇ *vt* [position, status, situation] améliorer; [achievement, sales figure] dépasser; she's eager to ~ herself elle a vraiment envie d'améliorer sa situation.

betterment ['betəmənt] *n* amélioration *f;* JUR [of property] plus-value *f.*

better-off ◇ *adj* aisé, riche.
◇ *npl:* the ~ les riches *mpl.*

betting ['betɪŋ] ◇ *n* -**1.** [bets] pari *m,* paris *mpl;* the ~ was heavy les paris allaient bon train; what's the ~ they refuse to go? je suis prêt à parier qu'ils ne voudront pas y aller. -**2.** [odds] cote *f;* the ~ is 5 to 1 on Blackie (la cote de) Blackie est à 5 contre 1, la cote est à 5 contre 1 sur Blackie.
◇ *adj:* I'm not a ~ man je n'aime pas parier; ~ slip *Br* bulletin *m* de pari individuel.

betting office *n* ≃ (bureau *m* de) PMU *m.*

betting shop *n* bureau *m* de paris *(appartenant à un bookmaker).*

bettor ['betəʳ] *Am* = **better** *n* **4.**

between [bɪ'twiːn] ◇ *prep* -**1.** [in space or time] entre; the crowd stood ~ him and the door la foule le séparait de la porte; the distance ~ the two towns la distance entre OR qui sépare les deux villes; it happened ~ 3 and 4 a.m. cela s'est passé entre 3 h et 4 h (du matin); ~ now and this evening d'ici ce soir; I'm ~ jobs at the moment je suis entre deux emplois en ce moment; you'll have an hour ~ trains vous aurez une heure entre les deux trains; you shouldn't eat ~ meals tu ne devrais pas manger entre les repas OR en dehors des repas. -**2.** [in the range that separates] entre; it will cost ~ 5 and 10 million ça coûtera entre 5 et 10 millions; children ~ the ages of 5 and 10 les enfants de 5 à 10 ans; somewhere ~ a half and a third (quelque chose) entre une moitié et un tiers; something ~ a laugh and a groan quelque chose entre un rire et un grognement. -**3.** [indicating connection, relation] entre; a bus runs ~ the airport and the hotel un bus fait la navette entre l'aéroport et l'hôtel; it's a half-hour drive ~ home and the office il y a une demi-heure de route entre la maison et le bureau ‖ *fig:* a treaty ~ the two nations un traité entre les deux États; an argument ~ two experts une dispute entre deux experts; a contest ~ two heavyweight boxers un combat entre deux poids lourds; the difference/distinction ~ A and B la différence/distinction entre A et B; he drew a comparison ~ the two systems il a établi une comparaison entre les deux systèmes; he felt things weren't right ~ them il sentait que ça n'allait pas entre eux ❑ ~ you and me, ~ ourselves entre nous; ~ you, me and the gatepost OR bedpost *hum* entre nous. -**4.** [indicating alternatives] entre; I had to choose ~ going with them and staying at home il fallait que je choisisse entre les accompagner et rester à la maison. -**5.** [added together]: ~ us we saved enough money for the trip à nous tous nous avons économisé assez d'argent pour le voyage; they have 7 children ~ them à eux deux ils ont 7 enfants; the 5 groups collected £1,000 ~ them les 5 groupes ont recueilli 1 000 livres en tout; (in) ~ painting, writing and looking after the children, she was kept very busy entre la peinture, l'écriture et les enfants, elle était très occupée. -**6.** [indicating division] entre; he divided it ~ his children il l'a partagé entre ses enfants; they shared the cake ~ them ils se sont partagé le gâteau.
◇ *adv* = **in between.**
◆ **in between** ◇ *adv phr* -**1.** [in intermediate position]: a row of bushes with little clumps of flowers in ~ une rangée d'arbustes intercallés de petits bouquets de fleurs; he's neither right nor left but somewhere in ~ il n'est ni de droite ni de gauche mais quelque part entre les deux; she either plays very well or very badly, never in ~ elle joue très bien ou très mal, jamais entre les deux. -**2.** [in time] entretemps, dans l'intervalle.
◇ *prep phr* entre.

betweentimes [bɪ'twiːntaɪmz] *adv* dans l'intervalle, entre-temps.

betwixt [bɪ'twɪkst] *arch* ◇ *prep* = **between.**
◇ *adv:* something ~ and between quelque chose entre les deux.

BeV *(written abbr of* billion electron volts) GeV.

bevel ['bevl] *(Br pt & pp* bevelled, *cont* bevelling, *Am pt & pp* beveled, *cont* beveling) ◇ *vt* biseauter, tailler en biseau OR de biais.
◇ *n* -**1.** [surface] surface *f* oblique; [angle] angle *m* oblique; ~ (edge) biseau *m.* -**2.** = **bevel square.**

beveled *Am* = **bevelled.**

bevel gear *n* engrenage *m* conique.

bevelled *Br,* **beveled** *Am* ['bevld] *adj* biseauté.

bevel square *n* fausse équerre *f.*

beverage ['bevərɪdʒ] *n* boisson *f.*

bevvy ['bevɪ] *(pl* bevvies, *pt & pp* bevvied) *Br*
◇ *n dial* [drink] boisson *f* (alcoolisée); [drinking bout] beuverie *f.*
◇ *vi* boire de l'alcool.
◇ *vt:* to get bevvied▽ se soûler la gueule.

bevy ['bevɪ] *(pl* bevies) *n* [of people] bande *f,* troupeau *m pej;* [of quails] volée *f;* [of roe deer] harde *f;* a ~ of reports un tas de rapports.

bewail [bɪ'weɪl] *vt lit* pleurer; to ~ one's fate se lamenter sur son sort.

beware [bɪ'weəʳ] *(infinitive and imperative only)*
◇ *vi* prendre garde; ~ of getting lost prenez garde de ne pas vous perdre; ~ of married men méfiez-vous des hommes mariés; ~ of making hasty decisions gardez-vous de prendre des décisions hâtives; '~ of the dog!' 'chien méchant!'.
◇ *vt* prendre garde; ~ what you say to her prenez garde OR faites attention à ce que vous lui dites.

bewhiskered [bɪ'wɪskəd] *adj lit* [with side whiskers] qui a des favoris; [bearded] barbu.

bewilder [bɪ'wɪldəʳ] *vt* rendre perplexe, dérouter.

bewildered [bɪ'wɪldəd] *adj* perplexe; a ~ look un regard perplexe.

bewildering [bɪ'wɪldərɪŋ] *adj* déconcertant, déroutant.

bewilderingly [bɪ'wɪldərɪŋlɪ] *adv* de manière déconcertante OR déroutante.

bewilderment [bɪ'wɪldəmənt] *n* confusion *f,* perplexité *f;* "why?", she asked in ~ «pourquoi?», demanda-t-elle avec perplexité; to my complete ~ he refused à mon grand étonnement, il a refusé.

bewitch [bɪ'wɪtʃ] *vt* -**1.** [cast spell over] ensorceler, enchanter. -**2.** [fascinate] enchanter, charmer.

bewitching [bɪ'wɪtʃɪŋ] *adj* [smile] enchanteur, charmeur; [beauty, person] charmant, séduisant.

bewitchingly [bɪ'wɪtʃɪŋlɪ] *adv* d'une façon séduisante; she smiled at him ~ elle lui a adressé un sourire charmeur; ~ beautiful beau à ravir.

bey [beɪ] *n* bey *m.*

beyond [bɪ'jɒnd] ◇ *prep* -**1.** [on the further side of] au-delà de, de l'autre côté de; the museum is a few yards ~ the church le musée se trouve à quelques mètres après l'église; ~ the mountains lies China au-delà des montagnes se trouve la Chine; the countries ~ the sea les pays d'outre-mer OR au-delà des mers. -**2.** [outside the range of] au-delà, au-dessus de; do your duties extend ~ teaching? est-ce que vos fonctions s'étendent au-delà de l'enseignement?; ~ one's ability au-dessus de ses capacités; ~ belief incroyable; due to circumstances ~ our control dû à des circonstances indépendantes de notre volonté; his guilt has been established ~ (all reasonable) doubt sa culpabilité a été établie sans aucun OR sans le moindre doute; it's (gone) ~ a joke cela dépasse les bornes; ~ one's means au-dessus de ses moyens ❑ to be ~ sb: economics is completely ~ me je ne comprends rien à l'économie; why he wants to go there is ~ me je ne comprends pas pourquoi il veut y aller. -**3.** [later than] au-delà de, plus de; the deadline has been extended to ~ 1992 l'échéance a été repoussée au-delà de 1992; ~ 1995 that law will no longer be valid après OR à partir de 1995, cette loi ne sera plus applicable; don't stay out ~ midnight! rentre avant minuit! -**4.** [apart from, other than] sauf, excepté; I know nothing ~ what I've already told you je ne sais rien de plus que ce que je vous ai déjà dit.
◇ *adv* -**1.** [on the other side] au-delà, plus loin; the room ~ was smaller la pièce suivante était plus petite; they crossed the mountains and the valleys ~ ils ont traversé les montagnes et les vallées au-delà. -**2.** [after] au-delà; major changes are foreseen for 1992 and ~ des changements importants sont prévus pour 1992 et au-delà.
◇ *n* au-delà *m;* the (great) ~ l'au-delà.

Beyrouth [,beɪ'ruːt] = **Beirut.**

bezel ['bezl] *(Br pt & pp* bezelled, *cont* bezelling, *Am pt & pp* bezeled, *cont* bezeling)
◇ *n* -**1.** [face - of tool] biseau *m;* [- of gem] facette *f.* -**2.** [rim - for gem] chaton *m;* [- for watch crystal] portée *f.*
◇ *vt* biseauter, tailler en biseau.

bezique [bɪ'ziːk] *n* bésigue *m.*

bf ◇ *n inf (abbr of* bloody fool) *Br* crétin *m,* -e *f.*
◇ *(written abbr of* boldface) TYPO caractères *mpl* gras.

b/f *written abbr of* brought forward.

bhang [bæŋ] *n* cannabis *m.*

bhangra ['bæŋgrə] *n* MUS *sorte de musique pop indienne qui est une combinaison de musique traditionnelle du Pendjab et de musique pop occidentale.*

Bhopal [bəʊ'pɑːl] *pr n* Bhopal.

bhp *n abbr of* brake horsepower.

Bhutan [,buː'tɑːn] *pr n* Bhoutan *m.*

bi▽ [baɪ] ◇ *adj* bi *(inv).*
◇ *n* bisexuel *m,* -elle *f.*

Biafra [bɪ'æfrə] *pr n* Biafra; in ~ au Biafra.

Biafran [bɪ'æfrən] ◇ *n* Biafrais *m,* -e *f.*
◇ *adj* biafrais.

biannual [baɪ'ænjʊəl] *adj* semestriel.

bias ['baɪəs] *(pt & pp* biased OR biassed)
◇ *n* -**1.** [prejudice] préjugé *m;* there is still considerable ~ against women candidates les femmes qui se présentent sont encore victimes d'un fort préjugé; they are quite without ~ ils sont sans préjugés. -**2.** [tendency] tendance *f,* penchant *m;* the school has a scientific ~ l'école favorise les sciences. -**3.** SEW biais *m;* cut on the ~ taillé dans le biais. -**4.** [in bowls - weight] *poids ou renflement d'une boule qui l'empêche d'aller droit;* [- curved course] déviation *f.* -**5.** MATH biais *m.*
◇ *vt* [influence] influencer; [prejudice] prévenir; his experience ~ed him against/towards them son expérience l'a prévenu contre eux/en leur faveur; the course is ~ed towards the arts l'enseignement est plutôt orienté sur les lettres.
◇ *adj* en biais.
◇ *adv* en biais, de biais.

bias binding *n* biais *m (ruban).*

biased, biassed ['baɪəst] *adj* -**1.** [partial] partial. -**2.** [ball] décentré.

biathlon [baɪ'æθlɒn] *n* biathlon *m.*

bib [bɪb] *n* -**1.** [for child] bavoir *m,* bavette *f.* -**2.** [of apron, dungarees] bavette *f;* in one's best

~ and tucker *inf Br* sur son trente et un. -**3.** [of feathers, fur] tache *f*, touche *f*.

bibcock ['bɪbkɒk] *n* robinet *m* à bec courbe.

Bible ['baɪbl] ◇ *n* Bible *f*.

◇ *comp*: the ~ Belt *états du sud des États-Unis où l'évangélisme est très répandu*; ~ class [in school] classe *f* d'instruction religieuse; [Catholic church] catéchisme *m*; ~ school cours *m* d'instruction religieuse; ~ study étude *f* de la Bible.

◆ **bible** *n fig* [manual] bible *f*, évangile *m*; the fisherman's bible l'évangile des pêcheurs.

bible-basher *inf* = **bible-thumper**.

Bible paper *n* papier *m* bible.

bible-thumper *inf* [-,θʌmpəʳ] *n pej* évangéliste *m* de carrefour.

biblical, Biblical ['bɪblɪkl] *adj* biblique.

bibliographer [,bɪblɪ'ɒgrəfəʳ] *n* bibliographe *mf*.

bibliographic(al) [,bɪblɪə'græfɪk(l)] *adj* bibliographique.

bibliography [,bɪblɪ'ɒgrəfɪ] (*pl* **bibliographies**) *n* bibliographie *f*.

bibliophile ['bɪblɪəʊfaɪl] *n* bibliophile *mf*.

bibulous ['bɪbjʊləs] *adj lit* [person] adonné à la boisson.

bicameral [,baɪ'kæmərəl] *adj* bicaméral.

bicameralism [,baɪ'kæmərəlɪsm] *n* bicaméralisme *m*, bicamérisme *m*.

bicarb *inf* [baɪ'kɑːb] *n* bicarbonate *m* (de soude).

bicarbonate [baɪ'kɑːbənət] *n* bicarbonate *m*; ~ of soda bicarbonate *m* de soude.

bicentenary [,baɪsen'tiːnərɪ] (*pl* **bicentenaries**) *Br* ◇ *adj* bicentenaire.

◇ *n* bicentenaire *m*.

bicentennial [,baɪsen'tenjəl] ◇ *adj* bicentenaire.

◇ *n Am* bicentenaire *m*.

bicephalous [,baɪ'sefələs] *adj* bicéphale.

biceps ['baɪseps] (*pl inv*) *n* biceps *m*.

bichloride [,baɪ'klɔːraɪd] *n* bichlorure *m*.

bichromate [,baɪ'krəʊmeɪt] *n* bichromate *m*.

bicker ['bɪkəʳ] *vi* se chamailler; to ~ about OR over sthg se chamailler à propos de qqch.

bickering ['bɪkərɪŋ] ◇ *n* chamailleries *fpl*; stop your ~! arrêtez de vous chamailler!

◇ *adj* chamailleur.

bickie *inf* ['bɪkɪ] *n Br* [biscuit] petit gâteau *m*.

bicolour *Br*, **bicolor** *Am* ['baɪ,kʌləʳ] *adj* bicolore.

biconcave [,baɪ'kɒŋkeɪv] *adj* biconcave.

biconvex [,baɪ'kɒnveks] *adj* biconvexe.

bicultural [,baɪ'kʌltʃərəl] *adj* biculturel.

biculturalism [,baɪ'kʌltʃərəlɪzm] *n* biculturalisme *m*.

bicuspid [,baɪ'kʌspɪd] ◇ *adj* bicuspide.

◇ *n* prémolaire *f*.

bicycle ['baɪsɪkl] ◇ *n* vélo *m*, bicyclette *f*; I go to work by ~ je vais travailler à bicyclette OR à vélo; do you know how to ride a ~? sais-tu faire du vélo OR de la bicyclette?; he went for a ride on his ~ il est allé faire un tour à vélo.

◇ *vi* faire du vélo OR de la bicyclette; she ~s to work elle va travailler à bicyclette OR à vélo.

◇ *comp* [bell, chain, lamp] de vélo, de bicyclette.

bicycle clip *n* pince *f* de cycliste.

bicycle pump *n* pompe *f* à bicyclette OR à vélo.

bicycle rack *n* [for parking] ratelier *m* à bicyclettes OR à vélos; [on car roof] porte-vélos *m inv*.

bid [bɪd] (*pt & pp vi all senses and vt senses 1 and 2* **bid**, *pt vt senses 3, 4 and 5* **bade** [bæd], *pp vt senses 3, 4 and 5* **bidden** ['bɪdn], *cont vi and vt all senses* **bidding**) ◇ *vi* -**1.** [offer to pay] faire une offre, offrir; to ~ for sthg faire une offre pour qqch; they ~ against us ils ont surenchéri sur notre offre. -**2.** COMM [tender] faire une soumission, répondre à un appel d'offres; several firms ~ on the project plusieurs entreprises ont soumissionné pour le projet. -**3.** [make attempt]: he's bidding for the presidency il vise la présidence. -**4.** *phr*: to ~ fair to do sthg promettre de faire qqch; the negotiations ~ fair to succeed les négociations s'annoncent bien OR sont en bonne voie.

◇ *vt* -**1.** [offer to pay] faire une offre de, offrir; [at auction] faire une enchère de; what am I ~ for this table? combien m'offre-t-on pour cette table?; we ~ £300 for the statue nous avons fait une enchère de 300 livres pour la statue. -**2.** CARDS demander, annoncer. -**3.** *lit* [say] dire; he bade them good day il leur souhaita le bonjour; they bade him farewell ils lui firent leurs adieux; she bade them welcome elle leur souhaita la bienvenue. -**4.** *lit* [order, tell] ordonner, enjoindre; he bade them enter il les pria d'entrer; do as you are bidden faites ce qu'on vous dit. -**5.** *arch* [invite] inviter, convier.

◇ *n* -**1.** [offer to pay] offre *f*; [at auction] enchère *f*; I made a ~ of £100 [gen] j'ai fait une offre de 100 livres; [at auction] j'ai fait une enchère de 100 livres; a higher ~ une surenchère; they made a higher ~ ils ont surenchéri. -**2.** COMM [tender] soumission *f*; the firm made OR put in a ~ for the contract l'entreprise a fait une soumission OR a soumissionné pour le contrat; the State invited ~s for OR on the project l'État a mis le projet en adjudication. -**3.** CARDS demande *f*, annonce *f*; it's your ~ c'est à vous d'annoncer; to make a ~ of two hearts demander OR annoncer deux cœurs; I make no ~ je passe (parole); "no ~" «passe», «parole»; he raised the ~ il a monté OR enchéri. -**4.** [attempt] tentative *f*; they made a ~ to gain control of the movement ils ont tenté de prendre la tête du mouvement; the prisoners made a ~ for freedom les prisonniers ont fait une tentative d'évasion; a rescue ~ une tentative de sauvetage; Birmingham fails in ~ for next Olympics [in headlines] Birmingham n'est pas sélectionné pour recevoir les prochains jeux Olympiques.

◆ **bid in** *vi insep* enchérir OR surenchérir sur toute offre.

◆ **bid up** *vt sep* enchérir OR surenchérir sur.

biddable ['bɪdəbl] *adj* -**1.** CARDS demandable. -**2.** *Br* [docile] docile, obéissant.

bidden ['bɪdn] *pp* → **bid**.

bidder ['bɪdəʳ] *n* -**1.** [at auction] enchérisseur *m*, -euse *f*; there were no ~s il n'y a pas eu de preneurs, personne n'a fait d'offre; sold to the highest ~ vendu au plus offrant; the lowest ~ le moins offrant. -**2.** COMM soumissionnaire *mf*; the highest/lowest ~ le soumissionnaire le plus/le moins offrant.

bidding ['bɪdɪŋ] *n* -**1.** [at auction] enchères *fpl*; the ~ went against me on avait enchéri sur mon offre; to raise the ~ faire monter les enchères; ~ was brisk les enchères étaient vives; the ~ is closed l'enchère est faite, c'est adjugé. -**2.** COMM [tenders] soumissions *fpl*. -**3.** CARDS enchères *fpl*. -**4.** *lit* [request] demande *f*; [order] ordre *m*, ordres *mpl*; he did his mother's ~ il respecta les volontés de sa mère; at her brother's ~ sur la requête de son frère.

biddy ['bɪdɪ] (*pl* **biddies**) *n* -**1.** *Br dial* [chicken] poulet *m*; [hen] poule *f*. -**2.** *inf pej* [old woman] vieille bonne femme *f*; [gossip] commère *f pej*.

bide [baɪd] (*pt* **bided** OR **bode** [bəʊd], *pp* **bided**) *vt*: to ~ one's time attendre son heure OR le bon moment.

bidet ['biːdeɪ] *n* bidet *m*.

bid price *n prix auquel un acheteur accepte d'acheter des actions*.

Biel [biːl] *pr n* Bienne.

biennial [baɪ'enɪəl] ◇ *adj* -**1.** [every two years] biennal, bisannuel. -**2.** [lasting two years] biennal.

◇ *n* -**1.** [event] biennale *f*. -**2.** [plant] plante *f* bisannuelle.

bier [bɪəʳ] *n* [for corpse] bière *f*; [for coffin] brancards *mpl*.

biff *inf* [bɪf] ◇ *vt* flanquer un coup de poing à.

◇ *n* coup *m* de poing, gnon *m*; she gave him a ~ on the nose elle lui a flanqué son poing dans OR sur la figure.

bifid ['baɪfɪd] *adj* bifide.

bifocal [,baɪ'fəʊkl] *adj* bifocal.

◆ **bifocals** *npl* lunettes *fpl* bifocales OR à double foyer.

bifunctional [,baɪ'fʌŋkʃnəl] *adj* bifonctionnel.

bifurcate ['baɪfəkeɪt] ◇ *vi* bifurquer.

◇ *adj* à deux branches.

bifurcation [,baɪfə'keɪʃn] *n* bifurcation *f*.

big [bɪg] (*compar* **bigger**, *superl* **biggest**) ◇ *adj* -**1.** [in size - car, hat, majority] grand, gros; [- crowd, field, room] grand; [- person] grand, fort; the crowd got bigger la foule a grossi; to earn ~ money gagner gros; advertising is where the ~ money is la publicité rapporte gros; he has a ~ head *fig* il a la grosse tête; we're not ~ eaters nous ne sommes pas de gros mangeurs; he has a ~ mouth *inf fig* il faut toujours qu'il l'ouvre; why did you have to open your ~ mouth? *inf* tu ne pouvais pas la fermer, non?; to be ~ with child BIBLE & *lit* être enceinte, attendre un enfant ❑ she's too ~ for her boots OR her breeches *inf* elle ne se prend pas pour n'importe qui; the Big Three *les trois principaux constructeurs automobiles américains (General Motors, Ford, Chrysler)*; 'The Big Heat' *Lang* 'Règlement de comptes'; 'The Big Sleep' *Chandler, Hawks* 'le Grand Sommeil'. -**2.** [in height] grand; to get OR to grow bigger grandir; you're a ~ boy now tu es un grand garçon maintenant. -**3.** [older] aîné, plus grand; my ~ sister ma grande sœur. -**4.** *(as intensifier)* grand, énorme; he's just a ~ bully ce n'est qu'une grosse brute. -**5.** [important, significant - decision, problem] grand, important; [- drop, increase] fort, important; the ~ day le grand jour; he's ~ in publishing, he's a ~ man in publishing c'est quelqu'un d'important dans l'édition; we're onto something ~! nous sommes sur une piste intéressante! -**6.** [grandiose] grand; he has very ~ ideas about the future il a de grands projets d'avenir; he went into politics in a ~ way il est entré dans la politique par la grande porte; they entertain in a ~ way ils font les choses en grand quand ils reçoivent; ~ words! ce sont de bien grands mots! -**7.** [generous] grand, généreux; he has a ~ heart il a du cœur OR bon cœur; he's a ~ spender c'est un grand dépensier; that's ~ of you! *iron* quelle générosité! -**8.** *inf* [popular] à la mode; Japanese food is really ~ just now la cuisine japonaise est vraiment à la mode en ce moment. -**9.** *inf* [enthusiastic]: to be ~ on sthg adorer OR être fana de qqch; the company is ~ on research l'entreprise investit beaucoup dans la recherche.

◇ *adv* -**1.** [grandly]: he talks ~ il se vante, il fanfaronne; to think ~ voir grand. -**2.** *inf* [well]: their music goes over ~ with teenagers les adolescents adorent leur musique; they made it ~ in the pop world ce sont maintenant des stars de la musique pop.

bigamist ['bɪgəmɪst] *n* bigame *mf*.

bigamous ['bɪgəməs] *adj* bigame.

bigamy ['bɪgəmɪ] *n* bigamie *f*.

Big Apple *inf pr n*: the ~ New York *(la ville)*.

big band *n* big band *m (grand orchestre de jazz typique des années 40-50)*.

big bang *n*: the ~ le big-bang, le big bang.

big bang theory *n* la théorie du big-bang OR big bang.

Big Ben [-ben] *pr n* Big Ben.

BIG BEN:

Nom de la cloche de la Tour de l'horloge à Westminster, souvent donné à tort à la tour elle-même.

---

big-boned *adj* fortement charpenté.

Big Brother *pr n* Big Brother; ~ is watching you Big Brother vous regarde.

big business *n (U)* les grandes entreprises *fpl*.

big cat *n* fauve *m*, grand félin *m*; the ~s les fauves, les grands félins.

big cheese *inf n* gros bonnet *m*.

big deal *inf* ◇ *interj*: ~! tu parles!

◇ *n*: it's no ~ il n'y a pas de quoi en faire un plat!

Big Dipper *pr n Am* [constellation]: the ~ la Grande Ourse.

◆ **big dipper** *n* [in fairground]: the ~ les montagnes *fpl* russes.

big end *n Br* tête *f* de bielle.

big game ◇ *n* gros gibier *m*.
◇ *comp*: ~ hunter chasseur *m* de gros gibier; ~ hunting chasse *f* au gros gibier.

biggie *inf* ['bɪgɪ] *n* [success - song] tube *m*; [- film, record] succès *m*; **his next book/film should be a** ~ son prochain livre/film devrait faire un malheur.

big gun *inf n* gros bonnet *m*.

bighead *inf* ['bɪghed] *n* crâneur *m*, -euse *f*.

bigheaded *inf* [,bɪg'hedɪd] *adj* crâneur; to be ~ avoir la grosse tête.

bighearted [,bɪg'hɑːtɪd] *adj* au grand cœur; to be ~ avoir le cœur sur la main, avoir bon OR du cœur.

bighorn ['bɪghɔːn] (*pl inv* OR **bighorns**) *n* mouflon *m*.

bight [baɪt] *n* -**1.** [of shoreline] baie *f*. -**2.** [in rope - slack] mou *m*; [- coil] boucle *f*.

bigmouth *inf* ['bɪgmaʊθ, *pl* -maʊðz] *n* grande gueule *f*; she's such a ~ elle ne sait pas la fermer; shut up, ~! la ferme!

big name *n* grand nom *m*.

big noise *inf n Br* gros bonnet *m*.

bigot ['bɪgət] *n* [gen] sectaire *mf*, intolérant *m*, -e *f*; RELIG bigot *m*, -e *f*, sectaire *mf*.

bigoted ['bɪgətɪd] *adj* [gen - person] sectaire, intolérant; [- attitude, opinion] fanatique; RELIG bigot.

bigotry ['bɪgətrɪ] *n* [gen] sectarisme *m*, intolérance *f*; RELIG bigoterie *f*.

big shot *inf n* gros bonnet *m*.

big smoke *inf n Br*: the ~ [gen] la grande ville; [London] Londres.

big stick *n*: the ~ le bâton, la force.

big time *inf n*: to hit OR to make OR to reach the ~ arriver, réussir.
◆ **big-time** *adj* [actor, singer] à succès; [businessman, politician] de haut vol; [project] ambitieux, de grande échelle.

big-timer *inf n* gros bonnet *m*.

big toe *n* gros orteil *m*.

big top *n* [tent] grand chapiteau *m*; [circus] cirque *m*.

big wheel *inf*, **bigwig** *inf* ['bɪgwɪg] *n* gros bonnet *m*.

bijou ['biːʒuː] *adj Br pej* OR *hum* chic.

bike *inf* [baɪk] ◇ *n* [bicycle] vélo *m*, bicyclette *f*; [motorcycle] moto *f*; **to ride a** ~ [bicycle] faire du vélo OR de la bicyclette; [motorcycle] faire de la moto ❑ **on your** ~! *inf Br* [go away] dégage!; [don't be ridiculous] mais oui, c'est ça!
◇ *vi* [bicycle] faire du vélo; [motorcycle] faire de la moto.

biker *inf* ['baɪkəʳ] *n* motard *m*, motocycliste *mf*.

bikini [bɪ'kiːnɪ] *n* bikini *m*.

bikini line *n*: to have one's ~ done se faire épiler le maillot.

bilabial [,baɪ'leɪbjəl] ◇ *adj* bilabial.
◇ *n* bilabiale *f*.

bilateral [,baɪ'lætərəl] *adj* bilatéral.

bilaterally [,baɪ'lætrəlɪ] *adv* bilatéralement.

bilberry ['bɪlbərɪ] (*pl* **bilberries**) *n* myrtille *f*.

bile [baɪl] *n* -**1.** ANAT bile *f*. -**2.** *lit* [irritability] mauvaise humeur *f*, irascibilité *f*.

bilge [bɪldʒ] *n* -**1.** NAUT [hull] bouchain *m*, renflement *m*; [hold] fond *m* de cale, sentine *f*; [water] eau *f* de cale OR de sentine. -**2.** *inf fig* [nonsense] âneries *fpl*, idioties *fpl*; he talks a load of ~ il raconte un tas de bêtises.

bilge keel *n* quille *f* de bouchain.

bilge water *n* -**1.** NAUT eau *f* de cale OR de sentine. -**2.** *inf fig* [nonsense] âneries *fpl*, idioties *fpl*.

bilharzia [bɪl'hɑːtsɪə] *n* bilharzie *f*, bilharzia *f*.

bilharziasis [,bɪlhɑː'tsaɪəsɪs], **bilharziosis** [bɪl,hɑːtsɪ'əʊsɪs] *n* bilharziose *f*.

biliary ['bɪljərɪ] *adj* biliaire.

bilinear [baɪ'lɪnɪəʳ] *adj* bilinéaire.

bilingual [baɪ'lɪŋgwəl] *adj* bilingue; to be ~ in French and English être bilingue français-anglais.

bilingualism [baɪ'lɪŋgwəlɪzm] *n* bilinguisme *m*.

bilious ['bɪljəs] *adj* -**1.** MED bilieux; ~ attack crise *f* de foie; ~ disorder affection *f* hépatique. -**2.** [colour] écœurant. -**3.** [irritable] bilieux, irascible.

biliousness ['bɪljəsnɪs] *n* -**1.** MED affection *f* hépatique. -**2.** [of colour] aspect *m* écœurant. -**3.** [irritability] mauvaise humeur *f*, irascibilité *f*.

bilk [bɪlk] *vt Br*. -**1.** [thwart - person] contrecarrer, contrarier les projets de; [- plan] contrecarrer, contrarier. -**2.** [cheat] escroquer; **they** ~**ed her of her fortune** ils lui ont escroqué sa fortune.

bill [bɪl] ◇ *n* -**1.** [for gas, telephone] facture *f*, note *f*; [for product] facture *f*; [in restaurant] addition *f*, note *f*; [in hotel] note *f*; **may I have the** ~ **please?** l'addition, s'il vous plaît; **have you paid the telephone** ~? as-tu payé le téléphone?; **put it on my** ~ mettez-le sur ma note. -**2.** [draft of law] projet *m* de loi; **to introduce a** ~ **in Parliament** présenter un projet de loi au Parlement; **to vote on a** ~ mettre un projet de loi au vote. -**3.** [poster] affiche *f*, placard *m*. -**4.** THEAT affiche *f*; **to head** OR **to top the** ~ être en tête d'affiche OR en vedette. -**5.** [list, statement] liste *f*; ~ **of fare** carte *f* (du jour); ~ **of health** NAUT patente *f* (de santé); **the doctor gave him a clean** ~ **of health** *inf* le médecin l'a trouvé en parfaite santé; ~ **of lading** COMM connaissement *m*; **to sell sb a** ~ **of goods** *inf Am* rouler OR avoir qqn. -**6.** COMM & FIN [promissory note] effet *m*, traite *f*; ~**s payable** effets à payer; ~**s receivable** effets à recevoir ❑ ~ **of exchange** lettre *f* OR effet de change. -**7.** *Am* [banknote] billet *m* (de banque); **a ten-dollar** ~ un billet de dix dollars. -**8.** JUR: ~ **of attainder** décret *m* de mort civile; ~ **of indictment** acte *m* d'accusation; ~ **of sale** acte *m* OR contrat *m* de vente. -**9.** [beak] bec *m*. -**10.** GEOG promontoire *m*, bec *m*. -**11.** [weapon] hallebarde *f*. -**12.** = **billhook**.
◇ *vt* -**1.** [invoice] facturer; **he** ~**s his company for his travel expenses** il se fait rembourser ses frais de voyage par son entreprise; ~ **me for the newspaper at the end of the month** envoyez-moi la facture pour le journal à la fin du mois. -**2.** [advertise] annoncer; **they're** ~**ed as the best band in the world** on les présente comme le meilleur groupe du monde. -**3.** THEAT mettre à l'affiche, annoncer; **he is** ~**ed to appear as Cyrano** il est à l'affiche dans le rôle de Cyrano.
◇ *vi*: to ~ and coo [birds] se becqueter; [people] roucouler.

billabong ['bɪləbɒŋ] *n Austr* [pool] mare *f*; [of river] bras *m* mort.

billboard ['bɪlbɔːd] *n* panneau *m* (d'affichage).

bill broker *n* agent *m* OR courtier *m* de change.

billet ['bɪlɪt] ◇ *n* -**1.** [accommodation] cantonnement *m* (chez l'habitant); [document] billet *m* de logement. -**2.** ARCHIT billette *f*.
◇ *vt* [gen] loger; MIL cantonner, loger; **the captain** ~**ed his men on the mayor/on the town** le capitaine a cantonné ses hommes chez le maire/dans la ville.

billfold ['bɪlfəʊld] *n Am* portefeuille *m*.

billhook ['bɪlhʊk] *n* serpe *f*, serpette *f*.

billiard ['bɪljəd] *comp* de billard; ~ **ball/cue** boule *f*/queue *f* de billard; ~ **table/hall** (table *f*/salle *f* de) billard *m*.
◆ **billiards** *n* (*U*) (jeu *m* de) billard *m*; to play (a game of) ~ jouer au billard.

billing ['bɪlɪŋ] *n* -**1.** THEAT: to get OR to have top/second ~ être en tête d'affiche/en deuxième place à l'affiche. -**2.** *Am* [advertising]: to give sthg advance ~ annoncer qqch. -**3.** *literal* & *fig* [sound]: ~ and cooing roucoulements *mpl*.

billion ['bɪljən] (*pl inv* OR **billions**) *n* [trillion] billion *m*; *Br dated* [thousand million] milliard *m*.

billionaire [,bɪljə'neəʳ] *n* milliardaire *mf*.

Bill of Rights ◇ *n* déclaration *f* des droits de l'homme.
◇ *pr n*: the ~ *les dix premiers amendements à la Constitution américaine garantissant, entre autres droits, la liberté d'expression, de religion et de réunion.*

billow ['bɪləʊ] ◇ *vi* [cloth, flag] onduler; [sail] se gonfler; [cloud, smoke] tourbillonner, tournoyer.
◇ *n* -**1.** [of smoke] tourbillon *m*, volute *f*. -**2.** [wave] grosse vague *f*; the ~s *lit* les flots *mpl*.
◆ **billow out** *vi insep* [sail, cloth] se gonfler.

billowy ['bɪləʊɪ] *adj* [sea] houleux, agité; [wave] gros; [sail] gonflé; [skirt] tourbillonnant; ~ clouds of smoke de gros nuages de fumée.

billposter ['bɪl,pəʊstəʳ], **billsticker** ['bɪl,stɪkəʳ] *n* afficheur *m*, -euse *f*, colleur *m*, -euse *f* d'affiches.

billy ['bɪlɪ] (*pl* **billies**) *n* -**1.** *Am* [weapon]: ~ (club) matraque *f*. -**2.** *Br* & *Austr* [pan] gamelle *f*. -**3.** *inf* [goat] bouc *m*.

Billy Bunter [,bɪlɪ'bʌntəʳ] *pr n gros garçon gourmand (personnage d'une série de livres pour enfants en Grande-Bretagne).*

billycan ['bɪlɪkæn] *n Br* & *Austr* gamelle *f*.

billy-o(h) *inf* ['bɪlɪəʊ] *n Br*: he ran like ~ il a couru comme un dératé.

biltong ['bɪltɒŋ] *n SAfr* morceaux *mpl* de viande séchée.

bimbo *inf* ['bɪmbəʊ] (*pl* **bimbos** OR **bimboes**) *n pej jeune femme sexy et un peu bête.*

bimetallic [,baɪmɪ'tælɪk] *adj* bimétallique; a ~ strip un bilame.

bimetallism [,baɪ'metəlɪzm] *n* bimétallisme *m*.

bimonthly [,baɪ'mʌnθlɪ] (*pl* **bimonthlies**)
◇ *adj* [every two months] bimestriel; [twice monthly] bimensuel.
◇ *adv* [every two months] tous les deux mois; [twice monthly] deux fois par mois.
◇ *n* bimestriel *m*.

bimorph ['baɪmɔːf] *n* cristal *m* bimorphe.

bin [bɪn] (*pt* & *pp* **binned**, *cont* **binning**)
◇ *n* -**1.** *Br* [for rubbish] poubelle *f*, boîte *f* à ordures. -**2.** [for coal, grain] coffre *m*; [for bread] huche *f*. -**3.** *Br* [for wine] casier *m* (à bouteilles).
◇ *vt* -**1.** [coal, grain] mettre dans un coffre; *Br* [wine] mettre à vieillir. -**2.** *inf Br* [discard] flanquer à la poubelle.

binal ['baɪnəl] *adj* double.

binary ['baɪnərɪ] *adj* binaire; ~ **number/system** nombre *m*/système *m* binaire.

binary star *n* binaire *f*.

binaural [,baɪn'ɔːrəl] *adj* biaural, binaural.

bind [baɪnd] (*pt* & *pp* **bound** [baʊnd])
◇ *vt* -**1.** [tie] attacher, lier; ~ **him to his chair** attachez-le à sa chaise; to ~ sb hand and foot ligoter qqn; **he was bound hand and foot** il avait les pieds et les poings liés. -**2.** [encircle] entourer, ceindre; to ~ a wound bander OR panser une blessure. -**3.** [provide with border] border. -**4.** [book] relier; **the book is bound in leather** le livre est relié en cuir. -**5.** [stick together] lier, agglutiner; **add eggs to** ~ **the sauce** CULIN ajouter des œufs pour lier la sauce. -**6.** *fig* [bond, unite] lier, attacher; **they are bound by friendship** c'est l'amitié qui les unit; **the two companies are bound by commercial interests** des intérêts commerciaux lient les deux sociétés. -**7.** [oblige] obliger, contraindre; **we are bound to tell the truth** nous sommes obligés OR tenus de dire la vérité; **she bound me to my promise** elle m'a obligé à tenir ma promesse; **they bound him to secrecy** ils lui ont fait jurer le secret; **to be bound by oath** être lié par serment. -**8.** [apprentice] mettre en apprentissage.
◇ *vi* -**1.** [agreement, promise] engager; [rule] être obligatoire. -**2.** [sauce] se lier; [cement] durcir, prendre. -**3.** [mechanism] se gripper.
◇ *n* -**1.** [bond] lien *m*, liens *mpl*. -**2.** MUS liaison *f*. -**3.** *inf* [annoying situation] corvée *f*; **working at weekends is a real** ~! quelle corvée de devoir travailler le week-end!; **we're in a bit of a** ~ nous sommes plutôt dans le pétrin.
◆ **bind down** *vt sep* [tie, truss] lier, attacher.

◆ **bind over** *vt sep* -**1.** [apprentice] mettre en apprentissage. -**2.** *Br* JUR [order] sommer; they were bound over to keep the peace ils ont été sommés de ne pas troubler l'ordre public.

◆ **bind together** *vt sep literal* attacher, lier; *fig* lier, unir.

◆ **bind up** *vt sep* [tie - gen] attacher, lier; [- wound] bander, panser.

binder ['baɪndəʳ] *n* -**1.** [folder] classeur *m.* -**2.** [bookbinder] relieur *m,* -euse *f.* -**3.** [glue] colle *f;* TECH liant *m,* agglomérant *m.* -**4.** AGR [machine] lieuse *f.*

bindery ['baɪndərɪ] (*pl* **binderies**) *n* atelier *m* de reliure.

binding ['baɪndɪŋ] ◇ *n* -**1.** [for book] reliure *f.* -**2.** [folder] classeur *m.* -**3.** [for sewing] extrafort *m.* -**4.** [on skis] fixation *f.*

◇ *adj* -**1.** [law] obligatoire; [contract, promise] qui engage OR lie; the agreement is ~ on all parties l'accord engage chaque partie; it is ~ on the buyer to make immediate payment l'acheteur est tenu de payer immédiatement. -**2.** [food] constipant.

bindweed ['baɪndwiːd] *n* liseron *m.*

bin-end *n* fin *f* de série *(de vin)*.

binge *inf* [bɪndʒ] ◇ *n* -**1.** [spree]: to go on a ~ faire la bringue; they went on a shopping ~ ils sont allés dépenser du fric dans les magasins; an eating ~ une grosse bouffe. -**2.** [drinking bout] beuverie *f,* bringue *f.*

◇ *vi* -**1.** [overindulge] faire des folies. -**2.** [overeat] faire des excès *(de nourriture)*.

bingo ['bɪŋgəʊ] ◇ *n* ≃ loto *m.*

◇ *interj*: ~! ça y est!

BINGO:

Ce jeu d'argent très populaire en Grande-Bretagne consiste à cocher des chiffres sur une carte jusqu'à ce qu'elle soit remplie; il est souvent pratiqué dans d'anciens cinémas ou des salles municipales.

binman ['bɪnmæn] (*pl* **binmen** [-men]) *n Br* éboueur *m.*

binnacle ['bɪnəkl] *n* habitacle *m.*

binocular [bɪ'nɒkjʊləʳ] *adj* binoculaire.

◆ **binoculars** *npl* jumelles *fpl.*

binomial [,baɪ'nəʊmjəl] ◇ *adj* binomial.

◇ *n* binôme *m.*

bint▽ [bɪnt] *n Br pej* nana *f.*

binuclear [,baɪ'njuːklɪəʳ] *adj* binucléaire.

bio *inf* ['baɪəʊ] (*pl* **bios**) *n* biographie *f.*

bioactive [,baɪəʊ'æktɪv] *adj* bioactif.

bioassay [,baɪəʊə'seɪ] *n* essai *m* OR titrage *m* biologique.

biochemical [,baɪəʊ'kemɪkl] ◇ *adj* biochimique.

◇ *n* produit *m* biochimique.

biochemist [,baɪəʊ'kemɪst] *n* biochimiste *mf.*

biochemistry [,baɪəʊ'kemɪstrɪ] *n* biochimie *f.*

biocide ['baɪəsaɪd] *n* biocide *m.*

bioconversion [,baɪəʊkən'vɜːʃn] *n* bioconversion *f.*

biodegradable [,baɪəʊdɪ'greɪdəbl] *adj* biodégradable.

biodegrade [,baɪəʊdɪ'greɪd] *vi* biodégrader.

biodiversity [,baɪəʊdaɪ'vɜːsətɪ] *n* biodiversité *f.*

bioengineering ['baɪəʊ,endʒɪ'nɪərɪŋ] *n* bioingénierie *f.*

bioethics [,baɪəʊ'eθɪks] *n (U)* bioéthique *f.*

biofeedback [,baɪəʊ'fiːdbæk] *n* biofeedback *m.*

biogas ['baɪəʊgæs] *n* biogaz *m.*

biogen ['baɪədʒən] *n* protéine *f* biogène.

biogenesis [,baɪəʊ'dʒenɪsɪs] *n* biogenèse *f.*

biographer [baɪ'ɒgrəfəʳ] *n* biographe *mf.*

biographical [,baɪə'græfɪkl] *adj* biographique.

biography [baɪ'ɒgrəfɪ] *n* biographie *f.*

biological [,baɪə'lɒdʒɪkl] *adj* biologique; ~ warfare guerre *f* bactériologique.

biological clock *n* horloge *f* interne biologique.

biologist [baɪ'ɒlədʒɪst] *n* biologiste *mf.*

biology [baɪ'ɒlədʒɪ] *n* biologie *f.*

bioluminescence ['baɪəʊ,luːmɪ'nesəns] *n* bioluminescence *f.*

biomass ['baɪəʊmæs] *n* biomasse *f.*

biome ['baɪəʊm] *n* biome *m.*

biomechanics [,baɪəʊmɪ'kænɪks] *n (U)* biomécanique *f.*

biomedicine [,baɪəʊ'medɪsɪn] *n* biomédecine *f.*

biometrics [,baɪəʊ'metrɪks] *n (U)* biométrie *f.*

biometry [baɪ'ɒmɪtrɪ] *n* biométrie *f.*

bionic [baɪ'ɒnɪk] *adj* bionique.

bionics [baɪ'ɒnɪks] *n (U)* bionique *f.*

biophysicist [,baɪəʊ'fɪzɪsɪst] *n* biophysicien *m,* -enne *f.*

biophysics [,baɪəʊ'fɪzɪks] *n (U)* biophysique *f.*

biopic *inf* ['baɪəʊpɪk] *n* film *m* biographique.

biopsy ['baɪɒpsɪ] (*pl* **biopsies**) *n* biopsie *f.*

biorhythm ['baɪəʊ,rɪðm] *n* biorythme *m.*

bioscience ['baɪəʊ,saɪəns] *n* biologie *f.*

biosphere ['baɪəʊ,sfɪəʳ] *n* biosphère *f.*

biosynthesis [,baɪəʊ'sɪnθəsɪs] *n* biosynthèse *f.*

biotechnology [,baɪəʊtek'nɒlədʒɪ] *n* biotechnologie *f.*

biotic [baɪ'ɒtɪk] *adj* biotique.

biotin ['baɪətɪn] *n* biotine *f.*

biotope ['baɪətəʊp] *n* biotope *m.*

biotype ['baɪətaɪp] *n* biotype *m.*

biowarfare [,baɪəʊ'wɔːfeəʳ] *n* guerre *f* biologique.

bipartisan [,baɪpɑːtɪ'zæn] *adj* biparti, bipartite.

bipartite [,baɪ'pɑːtaɪt] *adj* BIOL & POL biparti, bipartite.

biped ['baɪped] ◇ *adj* bipède.

◇ *n* bipède *m.*

biplane ['baɪpleɪn] *n* biplan *m.*

bipod ['baɪpɒd] *n* bipied *m.*

bipolar [,baɪ'pəʊləʳ] *adj* bipolaire.

biracial [,baɪ'reɪʃl] *adj* biracial.

birch [bɜːtʃ] ◇ *n* -**1.** [tree] bouleau *m;* [wood] (bois *m* de) bouleau. -**2.** *Br* [rod for whipping] verge *f;* to give sb the ~ fouetter qqn.

◇ *vt* fouetter.

◇ *comp* [forest, furniture, wood] de bouleau; ~ plantation boulaie *f,* plantation *f* de bouleaux.

Bircher ['bɜːtʃəʳ] *n* POL *membre de la John Birch Society.*

birching ['bɜːtʃɪŋ] *n Br* correction *f;* to give sb a ~ fouetter qqn, donner une correction à qqn.

Birchism ['bɜːtʃɪzm] *n philosophie de la John Birch Society.*

bird [bɜːd] *n* -**1.** [gen] oiseau *m;* CULIN volaille *f;* she eats like a ~ elle a un appétit d'oiseau ❑ ~ of paradise [bird, flower] oiseau de paradis; ~ of passage *literal* & *fig* oiseau de passage; ~ of prey oiseau de proie, rapace *m;* a little ~ told me mon petit doigt me l'a dit; strictly for the ~s bon pour les imbéciles; the ~s and the bees *inf euph* OR *hum* les choses de la vie; the ~ has flown l'oiseau s'est envolé; to give sb the ~ *inf Br* [gen] envoyer paître qqn; THEAT siffler qqn; ~s of a feather flock together *prov* qui se ressemble s'assemble *prov;* a ~ in the hand is worth two in the bush *prov* un tiens vaut mieux que deux tu l'auras *prov;* 'The Birds' *Du Maurier, Hitchcock* 'les Oiseaux'. -**2.** *inf Br* [chap] type *m;* he's a strange ~ c'est un drôle d'oiseau. -**3.** *inf Br* [woman] nana *f.* -**4.** *Br crime sl*: to do ~ faire de la taule.

birdbath ['bɜːdbɑːθ, *pl* -bɑːðz] *n* vasque *f (pour les oiseaux)*.

bird brain *inf n pej* tête *f* de linotte, écervelé *m,* -e *f.*

bird-brained *inf* [-breɪnd] *adj* [person] écervelé, qui a une cervelle d'oiseau; [idea] insensé.

birdcage ['bɜːdkeɪdʒ] *n* [small] cage *f* à oiseaux; [large] volière *f.*

birdcall ['bɜːdkɔːl] *n* cri *m* d'oiseau.

bird dog *n* chien *m* d'arrêt *(pour le gibier à plumes)*.

bird fancier *n Br* [interested in birds] ornithologue *mf* amateur; [breeder] aviculteur *m,* -trice *f.*

birdhouse ['bɜːdhaʊs, *pl* -haʊzɪz] *n Am* volière *f.*

birdie *inf* ['bɜːdɪ] *n* -**1.** *inf* [small bird] petit oiseau *m,* oisillon *m;* watch the ~! PHOT le petit oiseau va sortir! -**2.** [in golf] birdie *m.*

birdlime ['bɜːdlaɪm] *n* glu *f.*

birdman ['bɜːdmæn] (*pl* **birdmen** [-men]) *n* [interested in birds] ornithologue *m* amateur; [breeder] aviculteur *m.*

bird-nesting *n*: to go ~ aller dénicher des oiseaux.

bird sanctuary *n* réserve *f* OR refuge *m* d'oiseaux.

birdseed ['bɜːdsiːd] *n* graine *f* pour les oiseaux.

bird's-eye ◇ *adj*: a ~ view of the coastline une vue panoramique de la côte; a ~ view of the situation *fig* une vue d'ensemble de la situation.

◇ *n* -**1.** BOT [primrose] primevère *f* farineuse; ~ speedwell véronique *f.* -**2.** [cloth] œil-de-perdrix *m.*

bird's-foot *n* BOT pied-d'oiseau *m.*

bird's-nesting = **bird-nesting**.

bird's-nest soup *n* soupe *f* aux nids d'hirondelles.

birdsong ['bɜːdsɒŋ] *n* chant *m* d'oiseau.

birdstrike ['bɜːdstraɪk] *n collision entre un avion et un oiseau.*

birdtable ['bɜːd,teɪbl] *n* mangeoire *f (pour oiseaux)*.

bird-watcher *n* ornithologue *mf* amateur.

bird-watching *n* ornithologie *f;* to go ~ aller observer les oiseaux.

bireme ['baɪriːm] *n* birème *f.*

biretta [bɪ'retə] *n* barrette *f (d'un ecclésiastique)*.

biriani [,bɪrɪ'ɑːnɪ] *n*: chicken ~ poulet *m* biriani.

Birmingham ['bɜːmɪŋəm] *pr n* Birmingham.

Biro® ['baɪərəʊ] (*pl* **biros**) *n Br* stylo *m* (à) bille, ≃ Bic® *m.*

birth [bɜːθ] *n* -**1.** [nativity] naissance *f;* deaf from ~ sourd de naissance; ~ parent parent *m* naturel; 'The Birth of Venus' *Botticelli* 'la Naissance de Vénus'. -**2.** [of child] accouchement *m,* couches *fpl;* [of animal] mise *f* bas; to give ~ [woman] accoucher; [animal] mettre bas; she gave ~ to a boy elle a accouché d'un garçon; a difficult ~ un accouchement difficile ❑ ~ pangs douleurs *fpl* de l'accouchement; the ~ pangs of democracy *fig* la naissance difficile de la démocratie. -**3.** *fig* [origin - of movement, nation] naissance *f,* origine *f;* [- of era, industry] naissance *f,* commencement *m;* [- of product, radio] apparition *f;* 'The Birth of a Nation' *Griffith* 'Naissance d'une nation'. -**4.** [ancestry, lineage] naissance *f,* ascendance *f;* he's Chinese by ~ il est chinois de naissance; of high ~ de bonne famille, bien né; of low ~ de basse extraction.

birth certificate *n* acte *m* OR extrait *m* de naissance.

birth control *n* -**1.** [contraception] contraception *f;* to practise ~ utiliser un contraceptif OR un moyen de contraception. -**2.** [family planning] contrôle *m* des naissances.

birthday ['bɜːθdeɪ] ◇ *n* anniversaire *m;* her 21st ~ ses 21 ans.

◇ *comp* [cake, card, present] d'anniversaire; they're giving him a ~ party ils organisent une fête pour son anniversaire; 'The Birthday Party' *Pinter* 'l'Anniversaire'.

Birthday Honours *npl*: the ~ *titres honorifiques et autres distinctions décernés chaque année le jour de l'anniversaire officiel du souverain britannique.*

birthday suit *inf n hum* [of man] costume *m* d'Adam; [of woman] costume *m* d'Ève.

birthmark ['bɜːθmɑːk] *n* tache *f* de vin.

birthplace ['bɜːθpleɪs] *n* [town] lieu *m* de naissance; [house] maison *f* natale; the ~ of democracy *fig* le berceau de la démocratie.

birthrate ['bɜːθreɪt] *n* (taux *m* de) natalité *f*.

birthright ['bɜːθraɪt] *n* droit *m* (acquis à la naissance); **freedom of speech is every citizen's ~** la liberté d'expression constitue un droit pour chaque citoyen.

birthstone ['bɜːθstəʊn] *n* pierre *f* porte-bonheur *(selon la date de naissance)*.

Biscay ['bɪskeɪ] *pr n* Biscaye; **the Bay of ~** le golfe de Gascogne.

biscuit ['bɪskɪt] ◇ *n* -**1.** *Br* CULIN biscuit *m*, petit gâteau *m*; **that really takes the ~!** *inf* ça, c'est vraiment le bouquet!; **you really take the ~!** *inf* vous êtes marrant, vous! *iron*. -**2.** *Am* CULIN *petit gâteau que l'on mange avec de la confiture ou avec un plat salé*, ≃ scone *m*. -**3.** [colour] beige *m*. -**4.** [ceramics] biscuit *m*.
◇ *adj* (de couleur) beige.

bisect [baɪ'sekt] *vt* [gen] couper en deux; MATH diviser en deux parties égales.

bisection [,baɪ'sekʃn] *n* [action] division *f* en deux; MATH bissection *f*.

bisector [,baɪ'sektəʳ] *n* bissectrice *f*.

bisexual [,baɪ'sekʃʊəl] ◇ *adj* -**1.** [person, tendency] bisexuel. -**2.** BIOL & ZOOL bisexué, hermaphrodite.
◇ *n* -**1.** [person] bisexuel *m*, -elle *f*. -**2.** BIOL & ZOOL hermaphrodite *m*.

bisexuality [baɪ,seksjʊ'ælɪtɪ] *n* bisexualité *f*.

bishop ['bɪʃəp] *n* -**1.** RELIG évêque *m*. -**2.** [in chess] fou *m*.

bishopric ['bɪʃəprɪk] *n* [position] épiscopat *m*; [diocese] évêché *m*.

Bismarck ['bɪzmɑːk] *pr n* Bismarck.

bismuth ['bɪzməθ] *n* bismuth *m*.

bison ['baɪsn] *n* bison *m*.

bisque [bɪsk] *n* -**1.** [colour] beige-rosé *m*. -**2.** [ceramics] biscuit *m*. -**3.** [soup] bisque *f*.

bissextile [bɪ'sekstaɪl] ◇ *adj* bissextile.
◇ *n* année *f* bissextile.

bister *Am* = **bistre**.

bistoury ['bɪstʊrɪ] (*pl* bistouries) *n* bistouri *m*.

bistre *Br*, **bister** *Am* ['bɪstəʳ] ◇ *n* bistre *m*.
◇ *adj* bistré.

bit[1] [bɪt] *n* -**1.** [piece - of cake, puzzle, wood, land, string] bout *m*; [- of book] passage *m*; [- of film] séquence *f*; **you missed out the best ~s** [of story, joke] tu as manqué le meilleur; **I liked the ~ where they were in the cave** [in book] j'aime le passage où ils sont dans la caverne; [in film] j'aime la séquence où ils sont dans la caverne; **~s and pieces of sthg** des morceaux de qqch; **she picked up her ~s and pieces** elle a ramassé ses affaires; **in ~s** en morceaux; **to take sthg to ~s** démonter qqch; **the dog tore the paper to ~s** le chien a complètement déchiré le journal; **to fall to ~s** [book, clothes] tomber en lambeaux; **the wall was falling to ~s** le mur tombait en morceaux OR en ruine ❑ **to be thrilled to ~s** être aux anges. -**2.** [unspecified (small) quantity]: **a ~ of dirt** une petite saleté; **a ~ of advice** un (petit) conseil; **a ~ of money/time** un peu d'argent/de temps; **a little ~ of tact/patience** un tout petit peu de tact/de patience; **there's been a ~ of trouble at home** il y a eu quelques problèmes à la maison; **it's a ~ of a problem** cela pose un problème; **he's a ~ of a crook** il est un peu escroc sur les bords; **I've been a ~ of a fool** j'ai été un peu bête ❑ **to do one's ~** y mettre du sien, faire un effort; **everyone did their ~** tout le monde y a mis du sien OR a fait un effort; **we did our ~ to help the children** nous avons fait ce qu'il fallait pour aider les enfants; **they ate up every ~** ils ont tout mangé jusqu'au dernier morceau; **she's every ~ as competent as he is** elle est tout aussi compétente que lui; **to have a ~ on the side** *inf* avoir un amant/une maîtresse; **this is a ~ of all right!**▽ *Br* ça c'est chouette!; **he's/she's a ~ of all right!**▽ *Br* il/elle est chouette! -**3.** *inf* [role] numéro *m*; **he's doing his perfect father ~** il nous fait son numéro du père parfait. -**4.** *inf* [small coin] pièce *f*; **a threepenny ~** une pièce de trois pence.

◆ **a bit** *adv phr* -**1.** [some time] quelque temps; **let's sit down for a ~** asseyons-nous un instant OR un peu; **we waited a good/little ~** nous avons attendu un bon/un petit moment; **he's away quite a ~** il est souvent absent; **after a ~ we left** au bout de quelque temps nous sommes partis. -**2.** [slightly] un peu; **I'm a ~ late** je suis un peu en retard; **she's a good/little ~ older than he is** elle est beaucoup/un peu plus âgée que lui; **it's a (little) ~ more expensive** c'est un (tout petit) peu plus cher ‖ [at all]: **they haven't changed a ~** ils n'ont pas du tout changé; **are we bothering you? — not a ~!** on vous dérange? – pas du tout!; **not a ~ of it!** pas le moins du monde! ❑ **it's asking a ~ much to expect her to apologize** il ne faut pas s'attendre à des excuses, c'est trop lui demander; **that's a ~ much** OR **a ~ steep** ça c'est un peu fort!

◆ **bit by bit** *adv phr* petit à petit.

bit[2] [bɪt] *pt* → **bite**.

bitch [bɪtʃ] ◇ *n* -**1.** [female canine - gen] femelle *f*; [dog] chienne *f*; [fox] renarde *f*; [wolf] louve *f*; **a collie ~** un colley femelle. -**2.** ▽ *pej* [woman] garce *f*; **she's such a ~** c'est une vraie garce; **you ~!** espèce de garce! -**3.** *inf* [thing] saloperie *f*; **it's been a ~ of a day** quelle foutue journée alors!; **a ~ of a job** une saloperie de boulot; **this problem's a real ~** c'est un vrai casse-tête! -**4.** *inf* [complaint] motif *m* de râler; **what's their latest ~?** qu'est-ce qui les fait râler maintenant?
◇ *vi* *inf* râler, rouspéter; **to ~ about sb/sthg** râler OR rouspéter contre qqn/qqch.

◆ **bitch out**▽ *vt sep* engueuler.

bitchy *inf* ['bɪtʃɪ] (*compar* bitchier, *superl* bitchiest) *adj* vache; **a ~ remark** une vacherie; **he's in a ~ mood** il est dans une sale humeur; **she was very ~ to the new girl** elle a été très vache avec la nouvelle; **don't be ~ about it!** ne sois pas vache!

bite [baɪt] (*pt* bit [bɪt], *pp* bitten ['bɪtn])
◇ *vt* -**1.** [subj: animal, person] mordre; [subj: insect, snake] piquer, mordre; **I bit a piece out of the pear** j'ai mordu dans la poire; **the dog bit him on the leg** le chien l'a mordu à la jambe; **the dog bit the rope in two** le chien a coupé la corde en deux avec ses dents; **to ~ one's nails** se ronger les ongles; **he bit his lip** il s'est mordu la lèvre; **they've been bitten by the photography bug** *fig* ils sont devenus des mordus de photographie ❑ **to ~ one's tongue** *literal* se mordre la langue; *fig* se retenir de dire qqch; **to ~ the bullet** serrer les dents; **to ~ the dust** mordre la poussière; **theirs is the latest plan to bite the dust** leur projet est le dernier à être tombé à l'eau; **to ~ the hand that feeds one** montrer de l'ingratitude envers qqn qui vous veut du bien; **once bitten, twice shy** *prov* chat échaudé craint l'eau froide *prov*. -**2.** *inf fig* [bother] agacer, contrarier; **what's biting him?** quelle mouche l'a piqué?
◇ *vi* -**1.** [animal, person] mordre; [insect, snake] piquer, mordre; [fish] mordre (à l'hameçon); **I bit into the apple** j'ai mordu dans la pomme; **does the dog ~?** il mord, votre chien?; **he bit through the cord** il coupa la ficelle avec ses dents. -**2.** [mustard, spice] piquer. -**3.** [air, wind] mordre, cingler. -**4.** [clutch, screw] mordre; [tyre] adhérer (à la route); **the acid bit into the metal** l'acide a attaqué le métal; **the rope bit into his wrists** la corde mordait dans la chair de ses poignets. -**5.** [take effet]: **the law is beginning to ~** les effets de la loi commencent à se faire sentir.
◇ *n* -**1.** [of animal, person] morsure *f*; [of insect, snake] piqûre *f*, morsure *f*; **mosquito ~s** piqûres de moustiques ❑ **to put the ~ on sb** *inf Am* taper du fric à qqn. -**2.** [piece] bouchée *f*; **chew each ~ 30 times** mâchez chaque bouchée 30 fois; **he swallowed the steak in three ~s** il a avalé le bifteck en trois bouchées; **to take a ~ of sthg** [bite into] mordre dans qqch; [taste] goûter (à) qqch; **do you want a ~?** tu veux (y) goûter? ❑ **to have** OR **to get another** OR **a second ~ at the cherry** *Br* s'y reprendre à deux fois. -**3.** *inf* [something to eat]: **we stopped for a ~ (to eat)** nous nous sommes arrêtés pour manger un morceau; **I haven't had a ~ all day** je n'ai rien mangé de la journée. -**4.** FISHING touche *f*; **did you get a ~?** ça a mordu? -**5.** [sharpness - of mustard, spice] piquant *m*; [- of speech, wit] mordant *m*; [- of air, wind] caractère *m* cinglant OR mordant. -**6.** DENT articulé *m* dentaire.

◆ **bite back** *vt sep*: **to ~ sthg back** se retenir de dire qqch.

◆ **bite off** *vt sep* arracher d'un coup de dents; **she bit off a piece of toast** elle a mordu dans la tartine ❑ **to ~ off more than one can chew** avoir les yeux plus grands OR gros que le ventre; **to ~ sb's head off** *inf* enguirlander qqn.

biter ['baɪtəʳ] *n*: **it's a case of the ~ bit** *Br* c'est l'arroseur arrosé, tel est pris qui croyait prendre *prov*.

bite-sized [-,saɪzd] *adj*: **cut the meat into ~ pieces** coupez la viande en petits dés.

biting ['baɪtɪŋ] *adj* -**1.** [insect] piqueur, vorace. -**2.** *fig* [remark, wit] mordant, cinglant; [wind] cinglant, mordant; [cold] mordant, perçant.

bitingly ['baɪtɪŋlɪ] *adj* d'un ton mordant OR cinglant; [as intensifier]: **a ~ cold wind** un vent glacial.

bit part *n* THEAT petit rôle *m*.

bitten ['bɪtn] *pp* → **bite**.

bitter ['bɪtəʳ] ◇ *adj* -**1.** [taste] amer, âpre; **~ almonds** amandes *fpl* amères ❑ **it's a ~ pill (to swallow)** c'est difficile à avaler. -**2.** [resentful - person] amer; [- look, tone] amer, plein d'amertume; [- reproach, tears] amer; **he was very ~ about the divorce** il était très amer OR plein d'amertume au sujet du divorce. -**3.** [unpleasant - disappointment, experience] amer, cruel; [- argument, struggle] violent; [- blow] dur; **the ~ truth** l'amère vérité; **we fought to the ~ end** nous avons lutté jusqu'au bout. -**4.** [extreme - enemy] acharné; [- opposition] violent, acharné; [- remorse] cuisant. -**5.** [cold - wind] cinglant, glacial; [- weather] glacial; [- winter] rude, dur.
◇ *n* [beer] *bière pression relativement amère, à forte teneur en houblon*.

◆ **bitters** *npl* bitter *m*, amer *m*; PHARM amer *m*; **whisky and ~s** *cocktail au whisky et au bitter*.

bitter aloes *n* aloès *m* (médicinal).

bitter lemon *n* Schweppes® *m* au citron.

bitterly ['bɪtəlɪ] *adv* -**1.** [speak] amèrement, avec amertume; [criticize] âprement; [weep] amèrement. -**2.** [intensely - ashamed, unhappy] profondément; [- disappointed] cruellement; **it was a ~ cold day** il faisait un froid de loup.

bittern ['bɪtən] *n* butor *m (oiseau)*.

bitterness ['bɪtənɪs] *n* -**1.** [of disappointment, person, taste] amertume *f*; [of criticism, remark] âpreté *f*. -**2.** [of opposition] violence *f*.

bitter orange *n* orange *f* amère.

bittersweet ['bɪtəswiːt] ◇ *adj* [memory, taste] aigre-doux.
◇ *n* BOT douce-amère *f*.

bitty *inf* ['bɪtɪ] (*compar* bittier, *superl* bittiest) *adj Br* décousu.

bitumen ['bɪtjʊmɪn] *n* bitume *m*.

bituminize, -ise [bɪ'tjuːmɪnaɪz] *vt* bitumer.

bituminous [bɪ'tjuːmɪnəs] *adj* bitumineux.

bivalent ['baɪ,veɪlənt] *adj* bivalent.

bivalve ['baɪvælv] ◇ *adj* bivalve.
◇ *n* bivalve *m*.

bivouac ['bɪvʊæk] (*pt* & *pp* bivouacked, *cont* bivouacking) ◇ *n* bivouac *m*.
◇ *vi* bivouaquer.

bivvy ['bɪvɪ] (*pl* bivvies) *n mil sl* bivouac *m*.

biweekly [,baɪ'wiːklɪ] (*pl* biweeklies) ◇ *adj* [every two weeks] bimensuel; [twice weekly] bihebdomadaire.
◇ *adv* [every two weeks] tous les quinze jours; [twice weekly] deux fois par semaine.
◇ *n* bimensuel *m*.

biyearly [,baɪ'jɪəlɪ] (*pl* biyearlies) ◇ *adj* [every two years] biennal; [twice yearly] semestriel.

◇ *adv* [every two years] tous les deux ans; [twice yearly] deux fois par an.
◇ *n* biennale *f*.

biz *inf* [bɪz] *n* commerce *m*.

bizarre [bɪ'zɑːʳ] *adj* bizarre.

bizarrely [bɪ'zɑːlɪ] *adv* bizarrement.

bk - **1.** *written abbr of* bank. - **2.** *written abbr of* book.

bl *written abbr of* bill of lading.

BL *n* - **1.** (*abbr of* Bachelor of Law(s)) *(titulaire d'une) licence de droit*. - **2.** (*abbr of* Bachelor of Letters) *(titulaire d'une) licence de lettres*. - **3.** *Am* (*abbr of* Bachelor of Literature) *(titulaire d'une) licence de littérature*.

blab *inf* [blæb] (*pt* & *pp* blabbed, *cont* blabbing)
◇ *vi* - **1.** [tell secret] vendre la mèche. - **2.** [prattle] jaser, babiller; she blabbed on about her holiday elle n'en finissait pas de nous raconter ses vacances.
◇ *vt* laisser échapper, divulguer.

blabber *inf* ['blæbəʳ] ◇ *vi* jaser, babiller; to ~ on about sthg parler de qqch à n'en plus finir.
◇ *n* - **1.** [person] moulin *m* à paroles. - **2.** [prattle] bavardage *m*, papotage *m*.

blabbermouth *inf* ['blæbə,maʊθ, *pl* -,maʊðz] *n* pipelette *f*; he's such a ~! c'est une vraie pipelette!

black [blæk] ◇ *adj* - **1.** [colour] noir; as ~ as ink noir comme du jais OR de l'encre; the Black Prince le Prince Noir. - **2.** [race] noir; the ~ area of New York le quartier noir de New York; he won the ~ vote il a gagné les voix de l'électorat noir ❑ ~ man Noir *m*; ~ woman Noire *f*; ~ Africa l'Afrique *f* noire; ~ American Afro-Américain *m*, -e *f*; ~ consciousness négritude *f*; Black Nationalism *mouvement nationaliste noir américain*; Black Studies UNIV *études afro-américaines*. - **3.** [coffee] noir; [tea] nature *(inv)*. - **4.** [dark] noir, sans lumière; the room was as ~ as pitch *Br* OR as ~ as tar *Am* dans la pièce il faisait noir comme dans un four. - **5.** [gloomy - future, mood, thoughts] noir; [- despair] sombre; they painted a ~ picture of our prospects ils ont peint un sombre tableau de notre avenir; the situation is not as ~ as it looks la situation n'est pas aussi désespérée qu'on pourrait le croire; the situation looks ~ les choses se présentent très mal; in a fit of ~ despair dans un moment d'extrême désespoir; it's a ~ day for the UN c'est un jour noir pour l'ONU ❑ ~ comedy comédie *f* noire; ~ humour humour *m* noir. - **6.** [angry] furieux, menaçant; he gave her a ~ look il lui a jeté OR lancé un regard noir. - **7.** [wicked] noir, mauvais; a ~ deed un crime, un forfait; he's not as ~ as he's painted il n'est pas aussi mauvais qu'on le dit ❑ the ~ art OR arts la magie noire. - **8.** [dirty] noir, sale; her hands were ~ with ink elle avait les mains pleines d'encre. - **9.** *Br* INDUST [cargo, factory, goods] boycotté; ~ economy économie *f* noire.
◇ *n* - **1.** [colour] noir *m*; to be dressed in ~ [gen] être habillé de OR en noir; [in mourning] porter le deuil; he'd swear ~ is white il refuse d'admettre l'évidence. - **2.** [darkness] obscurité *f*, noir *m*. - **3.** *phr*: to be in the ~ être créditeur.
◇ *vt* - **1.** [make black] noircir; [shoes] cirer *(avec du cirage noir)*; he ~ed his attacker's eye il a poché l'œil de son agresseur; the actors ~ed their faces les acteurs se sont noirci le visage. - **2.** *Br* INDUST boycotter.
◆ **Black** *n* [person] Noir *m*, -e *f*.
◆ **black out** ◇ *vt sep* - **1.** [extinguish lights] plonger dans l'obscurité; [in wartime] faire le black-out dans. - **2.** RADIO & TV [programme] interdire la diffusion de. - **3.** [memory] effacer (de son esprit), oublier.
◇ *vi* s'évanouir.

blackamoor ['blækə,mʊəʳ] *n arch* Noir *m*, -e *f*.

black and blue *adj* couvert de bleus; they beat him ~ ils l'ont roué de coups.

black and white ◇ *adj* - **1.** [photograph, television] noir et blanc; a black-and-white film un film en noir et blanc. - **2.** *fig* [clearcut] précis, net; there's no black-and-white solution le problème n'est pas simple; he has very black-and-white views on the war il a des idées très arrêtées sur la guerre; things aren't that ~ les choses ne sont pas si simples.
◇ *n* - **1.** [drawing, print] dessin *m* en noir et blanc; [photograph] photographie *f* en noir et blanc. - **2.** [written down]: I want the agreement in ~ je veux voir l'accord écrit noir sur blanc; to put sthg down in ~ écrire qqch noir sur blanc.

blackball ['blækbɔːl] ◇ *vt* blackbouler.
◇ *n* vote *m* contre.

black beetle *n* cafard *m*, blatte *f*.

black belt *n* ceinture *f* noire; she's a ~ in judo elle est ceinture noire de judo.

blackberry ['blækbərɪ] (*pl* blackberries)
◇ *n* mûre *f*.
◇ *vi* cueillir des mûres; to go ~ing aller ramasser OR cueillir des mûres.

blackbird ['blækbɜːd] *n* merle *m*.

blackboard ['blækbɔːd] *n* tableau *m* (noir).

black box *n* boîte *f* noire.

black cab *n* taxi *m* londonien.

blackcap ['blækkæp] *n* - **1.** ORNITH fauvette *f* à tête noire. - **2.** *Br* [of judge] bonnet *m* noir.

blackcock ['blækkɒk] *n* coq *m* de bruyère.

Black Country *pr n*: the ~ le Pays noir.

THE BLACK COUNTRY:
Le Pays noir désigne, en Grande-Bretagne, la région des West Midlands, riche en aciéries et en mines de charbon.

---

blackcurrant [,blæk'kʌrənt] *n* [bush, fruit] cassis *m*.

Black Death *n* peste *f* noire.

blacken ['blækn] ◇ *vt* - **1.** [make black - house, wall] noircir; [- shoes] cirer *(avec du cirage noir)*; he ~ed his face il s'est noirci le visage. - **2.** [make dirty] noircir, salir; fingers ~ed with ink des doigts couverts OR pleins d'encre; smoke-~ed buildings des bâtiments noircis par la fumée. - **3.** *fig* [name, reputation] noircir, ternir.
◇ *vi* [cloud, sky] s'assombrir, (se) noircir; [colour, fruit] (se) noircir, devenir noir.

black eye *n* œil *m* poché OR au beurre noir; I'll give him a ~! je vais lui faire un œil au beurre noir!

black-eyed pea *n* dolique *m*, dolic *m*, niébé *m*.

blackface ['blækfeɪs] *n* - **1.** *dated* [person] *acteur blanc maquillé pour jouer un noir*. - **2.** TYPO caractère *m* gras; in ~ en (caractères) gras.

blackfly ['blækflaɪ] (*pl inv* OR blackflies) *n* puceron *m* noir.

Blackfoot ['blækfʊt] (*pl inv* OR Blackfeet [-fiːt]) *n* Blackfoot *mf*; the ~ les Blackfoot *mpl*.

black gold *n* or *m* noir.

black grouse *n* tétras-lyre *m*, petit coq *m* de bruyère.

blackguard ['blægɑːd] *n dated* OR *hum* canaille *f*.

blackhead ['blækhed] *n* point *m* noir.

black-hearted *adj* méchant, malfaisant.

black hole *n* trou *m* noir; the Black Hole of Calcutta *célèbre prison à Calcutta au XVIIIe siècle*; it's like the Black Hole of Calcutta in there! il fait horriblement sombre et chaud là-dedans!

black ice *n* verglas *m*.

blacking ['blækɪŋ] *n* [for shoes] cirage *m* noir; [for stove] pâte *f* à noircir.

blackish ['blækɪʃ] *adj* noirâtre, tirant sur le noir.

blackjack ['blækdʒæk] ◇ *n* - **1.** [card game] vingt-et-un *m*. - **2.** *Am* [truncheon] matraque *f*.
◇ *vt Am* [beat] matraquer; [compel] contraindre (sous la menace); they ~ed him into paying ils l'ont forcé à payer.

black lead [-led] *n* graphite *m*.

blackleg ['blækleg] (*pt* & *pp* blacklegged, *cont* blacklegging) ◇ *n Br pej* jaune *m pej*, briseur *m* de grève.
◇ *vi* briser la grève.

blacklist ['blæklɪst] ◇ *n* liste *f* noire.
◇ *vt* mettre sur la liste noire.

black magic *n* magie *f* noire.

blackmail ['blækmeɪl] ◇ *vt* faire chanter; he ~ed them into meeting his demands il les a contraints par le chantage à satisfaire ses exigences.
◇ *n* chantage *m*.

blackmailer ['blækmeɪləʳ] *n* maître chanteur *m*.

Black Maria *inf* [-mə'raɪə] *n* panier *m* à salade *(fourgon)*.

black mark *n* mauvais point *m*; it's a ~ against her ça joue contre elle.

black market *n* marché *m* noir; on the ~ au marché noir.

black marketeer *n* vendeur *m*, -euse *f* au marché noir.

Black Muslim *n* Black Muslim *mf (membre d'un mouvement séparatiste noir se réclamant de l'Islam)*.

blackness ['blæknɪs] *n* - **1.** [of colour] noir *m*, couleur *f* noire; *fig* [of deed] atrocité *f*, noirceur *f*. - **2.** [of night, room] obscurité *f*, noir *m*. - **3.** [dirtiness] saleté *f*, crasse *f*.

blackout ['blækaʊt] *n* - **1.** [in wartime] black-out *m inv*; [power failure] panne *f* d'électricité. - **2.** [loss of consciousness] évanouissement *m*, étourdissement *m*; [amnesia] trou *m* de mémoire; I must have had a ~ j'ai dû m'évanouir. - **3.** RADIO & TV black-out *m inv*, censure *f*; the army imposed a news ~ on the war l'armée a fait le black-out sur la guerre.

Black Panther *n* HIST Panthère *f* noire.

black pepper *n* poivre *m* gris.

Black Power *n* POL Black Power *m (mouvement séparatiste noir né dans les années 60 aux États-Unis)*.

black pudding *n* boudin *m*.

Black Rod *n* [in Parliament] *huissier chargé par la Chambre des lords britannique de convoquer les Communes*.

Black Sea *pr n*: the ~ la mer Noire.

black sheep *n* brebis *f* galeuse.

Blackshirt ['blækʃɜːt] *n* POL Chemise *f* noire.

blacksmith ['blæksmɪθ] *n* [for horses] maréchal-ferrant *m*; [for tools] forgeron *m*.

black spot *n Br fig* & AUT point *m* noir.

blackthorn ['blækθɔːn] *n* prunelier *m*, épine *f* noire.

black tie *n nœud papillon noir porté avec une tenue de soirée*; 'black tie' [on invitation card] 'tenue de soirée exigée'.
◆ **black-tie** *adj*: black-tie dinner dîner *m* en smoking; it's black-tie il faut être en smoking.

black velvet *n* - **1.** *literal* velours *m* noir. - **2.** [cocktail] *cocktail de champagne et de stout*.

blackwater fever ['blæk,wɔːtəʳ-] *n* fièvre *f* bilieuse hémoglobinurique.

black widow *n* latrodecte *m*, veuve *f* noire.

bladder ['blædəʳ] ◇ *n* - **1.** ANAT vessie *f*. - **2.** [of leather, skin] vessie *f*. - **3.** BOT vésicule *f*.
◇ *comp*: ~ infection cystite *f*.

bladderwort ['blædəwɜːt] *n* utriculaire *f*.

bladderwrack ['blædəræk] *n* fucus *m* vésiculeux.

blade [bleɪd] *n* - **1.** [cutting edge - of knife, razor, tool] lame *f*; [- of guillotine] couperet *m*. - **2.** [of fan] pale *f*; [of propeller] pale *f*, aile *f*; [of helicopter] hélice *f*; [of turbine motor] aube *f*; [of plough] soc *m* (tranchant); [of ice skates] lame *f*; [of oar, paddle] plat *m*, pale *f*. - **3.** [of grass] brin *m*; [of wheat] pousse *f*; [of leaf] limbe *m*; wheat in the ~ blé *m* en herbe. - **4.** *lit* [sword] lame *f*. - **5.** *arch* [young man] gaillard *m*. - **6.** [of tongue] dos *m*. - **7.** [of shoulder] omoplate *f*.

-bladed [bleɪdɪd] *in cpds* - **1.** [knife, razor] à lame...; sharp~ knife couteau *m* aiguisé. - **2.** [fan, propeller] à pale...; a five~ fan un ventilateur à cinq pales. - **3.** [plant] à limbe...; broad~ leaf feuille *f* à limbe large.

blaeberry ['bleɪbərɪ] (*pl* blaeberries) *n Br* myrtille *f*.

blah *inf* [blɑː] ◇ *n* - **1.** [talk] baratin *m*, bla-bla *m inv*. - **2.** *Am* [blues]: to have the ~s avoir le cafard.

◇ *adj Am* **-1.** [uninteresting] insipide, ennuyeux. **-2.** [blue]: to feel ~ avoir le cafard.

blamable ['bleɪməbl] *adj* blâmable.

blame [bleɪm] ◇ *n* **-1.** [responsibility] responsabilité *f*, faute *f*; they laid OR put the ~ for the incident on the secretary ils ont rejeté la responsabilité de l'incident sur la secrétaire; we had to bear OR to take the ~ nous avons dû endosser la responsabilité. **-2.** [reproof] blâme *m*, réprimande *f*; her conduct has been without ~ sa conduite a été irréprochable.
◇ *vt* **-1.** [consider as responsible] rejeter la responsabilité sur; they ~ inflation on the government OR the government for inflation ils accusent le gouvernement d'être responsable de l'inflation; he is not to ~ ce n'est pas de sa faute; don't ~ me for it! ne rejetez pas la responsabilité sur moi!; you have only yourself to ~ tu ne peux t'en prendre qu'à toi-même, tu l'as voulu OR cherché. **-2.** [reproach] critiquer, reprocher; I ~ myself for having left her alone je m'en veux de l'avoir laissée seule; you have nothing to ~ yourself for tu n'as rien à te reprocher; you can't ~ her for wanting a divorce tu ne peux pas lui reprocher OR lui en vouloir de vouloir divorcer.

blamed [bleɪmd] *adj Am* damné, maudit.

blameless ['bleɪmlɪs] *adj* irréprochable, sans reproche.

blamelessly ['bleɪmlɪslɪ] *adv* d'une façon irréprochable.

blameworthy ['bleɪm,wɜːðɪ] *adj* [person] fautif, coupable; [action] répréhensible.

blanch [blɑːntʃ] ◇ *vt* [gen] décolorer, blanchir; AGR & CULIN blanchir; ~ed almonds amandes *fpl* mondées OR épluchées.
◇ *vi* blêmir.

blancmange [blə'mɒndʒ] *n entremets généralement préparé à partir d'une poudre et servi à l'occasion de goûters d'anniversaire,* ≃ flan *m* instantané.

bland [blænd] *adj* **-1.** [flavour, food] fade, insipide; [diet] fade. **-2.** [person - dull] insipide, ennuyeux; [- ingratiating] mielleux, doucereux. **-3.** [weather] doux.

blandishment ['blændɪʃmənt] *n (usu pl)* [coaxing] cajoleries *fpl*; [flattery] flatterie *f*.

blandly ['blændlɪ] *adv* [say - dully] affablement, avec affabilité; [- ingratiatingly] d'un ton mielleux.

blank [blæŋk] ◇ *adj* **-1.** [paper - with no writing] vierge, blanc; [- unruled] blanc; fill in the ~ spaces remplissez les blancs OR les (espaces) vides; leave this line ~ n'écrivez rien sur cette ligne; I need a ~ form il me faut un formulaire (vierge OR à remplir). **-2.** [empty - screen, wall] vide; [- cassette] vierge; a ~ cartridge une cartouche à blanc; to go ~ [screen] s'éteindre; [face] se vider de toute expression; my mind went ~ j'ai eu un trou. **-3.** [face, look - expressionless] vide, sans expression; [- confused] déconcerté, dérouté; she looked ~ [expressionless] elle avait le regard vide; [confused] elle avait l'air déconcerté. **-4.** [absolute - protest, refusal] absolu, net; [- dismay] absolu, profond.
◇ *n* **-1.** [empty space, void] blanc *m*, (espace *m*) vide *m*; fill in the ~s remplissez les blancs OR les (espaces) vides; she filled in the ~s of her education elle a comblé les lacunes de son éducation; the rest of his life is a ~ on ne sait rien du reste de sa vie; my mind was a total ~ j'ai eu un passage à vide complet ☐ to draw a ~ avoir un trou OR un passage à vide; she searched everywhere for him but drew a ~ elle l'a cherché partout mais sans succès. **-2.** [form] formulaire *m* (vierge OR à remplir), imprimé *m*. **-3.** [cartridge] cartouche *f* à blanc. **-4.** [in dominoes] blanc *m*.
◆ **blank out** *vt sep* [writing] rayer, effacer; [memory] oublier, effacer de son esprit.

blank cheque *n* chèque *m* en blanc; to write sb a ~ *fig* donner carte blanche à qqn.

blanket ['blæŋkɪt] ◇ *n* **-1.** [for bed] couverture *f*; to be born on the wrong side of the ~ *Br* être un enfant naturel, être (de naissance) illégitime. **-2.** *fig* [of clouds, snow] couche *f*; [of fog] manteau *m*, nappe *f*; [of smoke] voile *m*, nuage *m*; [of despair, sadness] manteau *m*.
◇ *vt* **-1.** [subj: snow] recouvrir; [subj: fog, smoke] envelopper, voiler; ~ed with snow recouvert de neige. **-2.** [noise] étouffer, assourdir.
◇ *adj* général, global; a ~ rule for all employees un règlement qui s'applique à tout le personnel; our insurance policy guarantees ~ coverage notre police d'assurance couvre tous les risques.
◆ **blanket out** *vt sep* noyer.

blanket bath *n* grande toilette *f (d'un malade alité)*.

blanket stitch *n* point *m* de feston.
◆ **blanket-stitch** *vt*: to blanket-stitch sthg border qqch au point de feston.

blankety-blank *inf* [,blæŋkətɪ-] ◇ *adj euph* fichu.
◇ *n euph* [man] sale type *m*; [woman] sale bonne femme *f*.
◇ *interj*: what the ~ are you doing here? que diable fais-tu ici?

blankly ['blæŋklɪ] *adv* **-1.** [look - without expression] avec le regard vide; [- with confusion] d'un air ahuri OR interdit. **-2.** [answer, state] carrément; [deny, refuse] tout net, sans ambages.

blank verse *n* vers *mpl* blancs OR sans rime.

blare [bleəʳ] ◇ *vi* [siren, music] beugler; [voice] brailler.
◇ *n* [gen] vacarme *m*; [of car horn, siren] bruit *m* strident; [of radio, television] beuglement *m*; [of trumpet] sonnerie *f*.
◆ **blare out** ◇ *vi insep* [radio, television] beugler, brailler; [person, voice] brailler, hurler.
◇ *vt sep* [subj: radio, television] beugler, brailler; [subj: person] brailler, hurler.

blarney *inf* ['blɑːnɪ] ◇ *n* [smooth talk] baratin *m*; [flattery] flatterie *f*.
◇ *vt* [smooth talk] baratiner; [wheedle] embobiner; [flatter] flatter.

Blarney Stone *pr n au château de Blarney, en Irlande, pierre censée donner des dons d'éloquence à ceux qui l'embrassent*; he's kissed the ~ il a la langue bien pendue.

blasé [*Br* 'blɑːzeɪ, *Am* ,blɑː'zeɪ] *adj* blasé.

blaspheme [blæs'fiːm] ◇ *vi* blasphémer; don't ~ against God ne blasphémez pas contre Dieu.
◇ *vt* blasphémer.

blasphemer [blæs'fiːməʳ] *n* blasphémateur *m*, -trice *f*.

blasphemous ['blæsfəməs] *adj* [poem, talk] blasphématoire; [person] blasphémateur.

blasphemously ['blæsfəməslɪ] *adv* de façon impie, avec impiété.

blasphemy ['blæsfəmɪ] (*pl* **blasphemies**) *n* blasphème *m*; what you're saying is ~ c'est blasphémer ce que vous dites là.

blast [blɑːst] ◇ *n* **-1.** [explosion] explosion *f*; [shock wave] souffle *m*; the house was destroyed by the ~ la maison a été soufflée par l'explosion. **-2.** [of air] bouffée *f*; [of steam] jet *m*; a ~ (of wind) un coup de vent, une rafale. **-3.** [sound - of car horn, whistle] coup *m* strident; [- of trumpet] sonnerie *f*; [- of explosion] détonation *f*; [- of rocket] rugissement *m*; a whistle ~ un coup de sifflet; he blew a couple of ~s on his whistle il a donné plusieurs coups de sifflet. **-4.** *inf Am* [fun]: we had a ~ on s'est vraiment marrés; he gets a ~ out of teasing her cela l'amuse de la taquiner; it was a ~ c'était génial. **-5.** *phr*: at full ~: she had the radio on (at) full ~ elle faisait marcher la radio à fond; the machine was going at full ~ la machine avançait à toute allure; we worked at full ~ nous travaillions comme des brutes.
◇ *vt* **-1.** [with explosives] faire sauter; they ~ed a tunnel through the mountain ils ont creusé un tunnel à travers la montagne avec des explosifs. **-2.** [with gun] tirer sur; the thieves ~ed their way through the roadblock les voleurs ont forcé le barrage routier en tirant des coups de feu. **-3.** [subj: radio, television] beugler. **-4.** BOT [blight] flétrir. **-5.** [criticize] attaquer OR critiquer violemment. **-6.** [plan] détruire; [hope] briser, anéantir.
◇ *vi* [radio, television] beugler; [music] retentir; the radio was ~ing away la radio marchait à fond.
◇ *interj inf*: ~! zut!; ~ that car! il y en a marre de cette voiture!; ~ her! ce qu'elle peut être embêtante!
◆ **blast off** *vi insep* [rocket] décoller.
◆ **blast out** ◇ *vt sep* [music] beugler.
◇ *vi insep* [radio, television] beugler; [music] retentir.

blasted ['blɑːstɪd] *adj* **-1.** [plant] flétri; a ~ oak un chêne foudroyé. **-2.** *inf* [as expletive] fichu, sacré; you ~ fool! espèce d'imbécile!; it's a ~ nuisance! c'est vraiment casse-pieds!

blastema [blæ'stiːmə] (*pl* **blastemas** OR **blastemata** [-mətə]) *n* blastème *m*.

blast furnace *n* haut-fourneau *m*.

blasting ['blɑːstɪŋ] *n* **-1.** [explosions] travail *m* aux explosifs, explosions *fpl*; TECH minage *m*; 'beware ~ in progress!' 'attention, tirs de mines!'. **-2.** *inf Br* [verbal attack] attaque *f*; he got a ~ from the boss le patron lui a passé un sacré savon.

blastoderm ['blæstəʊdɜːm] *n* blastoderme *m*.

blast-off *n* lancement *m*, mise *f* à feu *(d'une fusée spatiale)*; ten seconds to ~ dix secondes avant la mise à feu.

blastula ['blæstjʊlə] (*pl* **blastulas** OR **blastulae** [-liː]) *n* blastula *f*.

blat [blæt] (*pt & pp* **blatted**, *cont* **blatting**) *vi & vt Am* bêler.

blatancy ['bleɪtənsɪ] *n* [obviousness] évidence *f*, caractère *m* flagrant.

blatant ['bleɪtənt] *adj* [discrimination, injustice] évident, flagrant; a ~ lie un mensonge manifeste.

blatantly ['bleɪtəntlɪ] *adv* [discriminate, disregard] de façon flagrante; [cheat, lie] de façon éhontée.

blather ['blæðəʳ] *Am* ◇ *n (U)* âneries *fpl*, bêtises *fpl*.
◇ *vi* raconter des bêtises OR des âneries.

blaze [bleɪz] ◇ *n* **-1.** [flame] flamme *f*, flammes *fpl*, feu *m*; [large fire] incendie *m*; five die in ~ [in headline] un incendie a fait cinq morts. **-2.** [burst - of colour] éclat *m*, flamboiement *m*; [- of light] éclat *m*; [- of eloquence, enthusiasm] élan *m*, transport *m*; a ~ of sunlight un torrent de soleil; a ~ of gunfire des coups de feu, une fusillade; in a sudden ~ of anger sous le coup de la colère; she married in a ~ of publicity elle s'est mariée sous les feux des projecteurs; he finished in a ~ of glory il a terminé en beauté. **-3.** [of gems] éclat *m*, brillance *f*. **-4.** [mark - on tree] marque *f*, encoche *f*; [- on animal, horse] étoile *f*. **-5.** *inf Br phr*: what the ~s are you doing here? qu'est-ce que tu fabriques ici?; how the ~s would I know? comment veux-tu que je le sache?; we ran like ~s nous avons couru à toutes jambes; go to ~s! *inf* va te faire voir!
◇ *vi* **-1.** [fire] flamber; he suddenly ~d with anger/with indignation il s'est enflammé de colère/d'indignation. **-2.** [colour, light, sun] flamboyer; [gem] resplendir, briller; the fields ~d with colour les champs resplendissaient de mille couleurs. **-3.** [gun] tirer, faire feu.
◇ *vt* **-1.** [proclaim] proclamer, claironner; [publish] publier; the news was ~d across the front page la nouvelle faisait la une du journal; it's not the kind of thing you want ~d abroad ce n'est pas le genre de chose qu'on veut crier sur les toits. **-2.** *phr*: to ~ a trail frayer un chemin; they're blazing a trail in biotechnology ils font un travail de pionniers dans le domaine de la biotechnologie.
◆ **blaze away** *vi insep* **-1.** [fire] (continuer de) flamber. **-2.** *Br* [gun] faire feu; the gangsters ~d away at the police les gangsters maintenaient un feu nourri contre la police; I ~d away at the target je tirais sans cesse sur la cible.

◆ **blaze down** *vi insep* [sun] flamboyer, darder ses rayons.

◆ **blaze up** *vi insep* -**1.** [fire] prendre immédiatement OR rapidement. -**2.** [person] s'enflammer de colère, s'emporter; [anger, resentment] éclater.

blazer ['bleɪzəʳ] *n* blazer *m*.

blazing ['bleɪzɪŋ] *adj* -**1.** [building, town] en flammes, embrasé; to sit in front of a ~ fire s'installer devant une bonne flambée. -**2.** [sun] brûlant, ardent; [heat] torride; a ~ hot day une journée de chaleur torride. -**3.** [light] éclatant; [colour] très vif; [gem] brillant, étincelant; [eyes] qui jette des éclairs. -**4.** [argument] violent. -**5.** [angry] furieux.

blazon ['bleɪzn] ◇ *n* blason *m*.

◇ *vt* -**1.** [proclaim] proclamer, claironner; to ~ sthg abroad proclamer qqch, crier qqch sur les toits. -**2.** [mark] marquer; HERALD blasonner.

bleach [bliːtʃ] ◇ *n* [gen] décolorant *m*; household ~ eau *f* de Javel.

◇ *vt* -**1.** [gen] blanchir; ~ing agent produit *m* à blanchir, décolorant *m*; ~ing powder chlorure *m* de chaux. -**2.** [hair - chemically] décolorer, oxygéner; [- with sun] éclaircir; to ~ one's hair se décolorer les cheveux; a ~ed blonde une fausse blonde, une blonde décolorée.

◇ *vi* blanchir.

◆ **bleach out** *vt sep* [stain] enlever à l'aide d'un décolorant OR d'un blanchissant.

bleachers ['bliːtʃəz] *npl Am dans un stade, places les moins chères car non abritées.*

bleak [bliːk] ◇ *adj* -**1.** [place, room] froid, austère; [landscape] morne, désolé; **'Bleak House'** *Dickens* 'Bleak House'. -**2.** [weather] morne, maussade; [winter] rude, rigoureux. -**3.** [situation] sombre, morne; [life] morne, monotone; the ~ facts la vérité toute nue OR sans fard; the future looks ~ l'avenir se présente plutôt mal. -**4.** [mood, person] lugubre, morne; [smile] pâle; [tone, voice] monocorde, morne.

◇ *n* [fish] ablette *f*.

bleakly ['bliːklɪ] *adv* [speak] d'un ton morne OR monocorde; [stare] d'un air triste, lugubrement.

bleakness ['bliːknɪs] *n* -**1.** [of furnishings, room] austérité *f*; [of landscape] caractère *m* morne OR désolé. -**2.** [of weather] caractère *m* morne OR maussade; [of winter] rigueurs *fpl*. -**3.** [of situation] caractère *m* sombre OR peu prometteur; [of life] monotonie *f*. -**4.** [of mood, person] tristesse *f*; [of voice] ton *m* monocorde OR morne.

bleary ['blɪərɪ] (*compar* **blearier**, *superl* **bleariest**) *adj* -**1.** [eyes - from fatigue] trouble, voilé; [- watery] larmoyant; [vision] trouble. -**2.** [indistinct] indécis, vague.

bleary-eyed *adj* [from sleep] aux yeux troubles; [watery-eyed] aux yeux larmoyants.

bleat [bliːt] ◇ *vi* -**1.** [sheep] bêler; [goat] bêler, chevroter. -**2.** [person - speak] bêler, chevroter; [- whine] geindre, bêler.

◇ *vt* [say] dire d'un ton bêlant; [whine] geindre, bêler.

◇ *n* -**1.** [of sheep] bêlement *m*; [of goat] bêlement, chevrotement *m*. -**2.** [of person - voice] bêlement *m*; [- complaint] gémissement *m*.

bled [bled] *pt* & *pp* → **bleed**.

bleed [bliːd] (*pt* & *pp* bled [bled]) ◇ *vi* -**1.** [lose blood] saigner, perdre du sang; to ~ to death saigner à mort; my nose is ~ing je saigne du nez; my heart ~s for you! *fig* & *iron* tu me fends le cœur! -**2.** [plant] pleurer, perdre sa sève. -**3.** [cloth, colour] déteindre.

◇ *vt* -**1.** [person] saigner. -**2.** *fig* [extort money from] saigner; to ~ sb dry OR white saigner qqn à blanc. -**3.** [brake, radiator] purger.

◇ *n* TYPO fond *m* perdu, plein papier *m*.

bleeder *inf* ['bliːdəʳ] *n Br* [person - gen] type *m*; [- disagreeable] salaud *m*; the poor ~ le pauvre gars; cheeky ~ petit effronté; lucky ~ sacré veinard.

bleeding ['bliːdɪŋ] ◇ *n* -**1.** [loss of blood] saignement *m*; [haemorrhage] hémorragie *f*; [taking of blood] saignée *f*; they stopped the ~ ils ont arrêté l'hémorragie; ~ from the nose saignement de nez. -**2.** [of plant] écoulement *m* de sève.

◇ *adj* -**1.** [wound] saignant, qui saigne; [person] qui saigne. -**2.** ▽ *Br* [as intensifier] fichu, sacré; ~ idiot! espèce d'imbécile!

◇ *adv* ▽ vachement.

bleeding heart *n pej* [gen & POL] sentimental *m*.

bleed valve *n* soupape *f* de purge.

bleep [bliːp] ◇ *n* bip *m*, bip-bip *m*.

◇ *vi* émettre un bip OR un bip-bip.

◇ *vt* -**1.** [doctor] appeler (au moyen d'un bip OR d'un bip-bip). -**2.** RADIO & TV: to ~ words (out) masquer des paroles (par un bip).

bleeper ['bliːpəʳ] *n* bip *m*, bip-bip *m*.

blemish ['blemɪʃ] ◇ *n* -**1.** [flaw] défaut *m*, imperfection *f*. -**2.** [on face - pimple] bouton *m*. -**3.** [on fruit] tache *f*. -**4.** *fig* [on name, reputation] tache *f*, souillure *f lit*; her reputation is without ~ sa réputation est sans tache.

◇ *vt* -**1.** [beauty, landscape] gâter; [fruit] tacher. -**2.** *fig* [reputation] tacher, souiller *lit*.

blench [blentʃ] *vi* [recoil in fear] reculer; [turn pale] blêmir; she ~ed at the idea à cette pensée, elle pâlit OR blêmit; without ~ing sans broncher OR sourciller.

blend [blend] ◇ *vt* -**1.** [mix together - gen] mélanger, mêler; [- cultures, races] fusionner; [- feelings, qualities] joindre, unir; ~ the butter and sugar (together), ~ the sugar into the butter mélangez le beurre au OR avec le sucre; to ~ two coffees mélanger deux cafés, faire un mélange de deux cafés; to ~ old traditions with modern methods faire un mélange de traditions anciennes et de méthodes modernes; ~ed whisky blend *m (whisky obtenu par mélange de whiskies de grain industriels et de whiskies pur malt)*. -**2.** [colours - mix together] mêler, mélanger; [- put together] marier; to ~ white and black mélanger du blanc avec du noir.

◇ *vi* -**1.** [mix together - gen] se mélanger, se mêler; [- cultures, races] fusionner; [- feelings, sounds] se confondre, se mêler; [- perfumes] se marier; their voices ~ed into one leurs voix se confondaient; the new student ~ed in well le nouvel étudiant s'est bien intégré. -**2.** [colours - form one shade] se fondre; [- go well together] aller ensemble.

◇ *n* -**1.** [mixture] mélange *m*; 'house ~' 'mélange (spécial de la) maison'. -**2.** *fig* [of feelings, qualities] alliance *f*, mélange *m*; his speech was a ~ of caution and encouragement son discours était un mélange de prudence et d'encouragement.

blender ['blendəʳ] *n* CULIN mixer *m*; TECH malaxeur *m*.

bless [bles] (*pt* & *pp* blessed OR blest [blest]) *vt* -**1.** [subj: God, priest] bénir; God ~ (you)!, ~ you! *literal* que Dieu vous bénisse!; ~ you! [after sneeze] à vos/tes souhaits!; [in thanks] merci mille fois!; he remembered her birthday, ~ his heart! et il n'a pas oublié son anniversaire, le petit chéri!; ~ your heart! que tu es gentil!; ~ my soul!, ~ me! *dated* Seigneur!, mon Dieu!; ~ me if I didn't forget her name! figurez-vous que j'avais oublié son nom!; I'm ~ed if I know! *inf* que le diable m'emporte si je sais!; God ~ America *phrase traditionnellement prononcée par le président des États-Unis pour terminer une allocution*. -**2.** *(usu pass) fml* [endow, grant] douer, doter; she is ~ed with excellent health elle a le bonheur d'avoir une excellente santé; Nature has ~ed him with an extraordinary memory la nature l'a doué d'une mémoire extraordinaire.

blessed [*adj* 'blesɪd, *npl* blest] ◇ *pt* & *pp* → **bless**.

◇ *adj* -**1.** [holy] béni, sacré; the Blessed Virgin la Sainte Vierge; the Blessed Trinity la Sainte Trinité. -**2.** [favoured by God] bienheureux, heureux. -**3.** [wonderful - day, freedom, rain] béni. -**4.** *inf* [as intensifier] sacré, fichu; every ~ day chaque jour que le bon Dieu fait; the whole ~ day toute la sainte journée.

◇ *npl*: the ~ les bienheureux *mpl*.

blessing ['blesɪŋ] *n* -**1.** [God's favour] grâce *f*, faveur *f*; the ~ of the Lord be upon you que Dieu vous bénisse. -**2.** [prayer] bénédiction *f*; [before meal] bénédicité *m*; the priest said the ~ le prêtre a donné la bénédiction. -**3.** *fig* [approval] bénédiction *f*, approbation *f*; with the ~ of his parents avec la bénédiction de ses parents; does the project have the boss's ~? est-ce que le patron a donné sa bénédiction au projet? -**4.** [advantage] bienfait *m*, avantage *m*; [godsend] aubaine *f*, bénédiction *f*; it was a ~ that no one was hurt c'était une chance que personne ne soit blessé; the rain was a ~ for the farmers la pluie était un don du ciel OR une bénédiction pour les agriculteurs; what a ~! quelle chance!; it was a ~ in disguise c'était une bonne chose, en fin de compte.

blest [blest] *arch* OR *lit* = **blessed**.

blether ['bleðəʳ] ◇ *n* âneries *fpl*, bêtises *fpl*.

◇ *vi* dire des âneries OR des bêtises.

blew [bluː] *pt* → **blow**.

blight [blaɪt] ◇ *n* -**1.** BOT [of flowering plants] rouille *f*; [of fruit trees] cloque *f*; [of cereals] rouille, nielle *f*; [of potato plants] mildiou *m*. -**2.** [curse] malheur *m*, fléau *m*; the accident cast a ~ on our holiday l'accident a gâché nos vacances; her illness was a ~ on their happiness sa maladie a terni leur bonheur; air pollution is a real ~ la pollution de l'air est un vrai fléau. -**3.** [condition of decay]: inner-city ~ la dégradation des quartiers pauvres.

◇ *vt* -**1.** BOT [plants - gen] rouiller; [cereals] nieller, rouiller. -**2.** [spoil - happiness, holiday] gâcher; [- career, life] gâcher, briser; [- hopes] anéantir, détruire; [- plans] déjouer.

blighter *inf* ['blaɪtəʳ] *n Br* type *m*; you lucky ~! sacré veinard!; silly ~s! les imbéciles!

blighty *inf*, **Blighty** *inf* ['blaɪtɪ] *n Br dated* l'Angleterre *f*.

blimey *inf* ['blaɪmɪ] *interj Br*: ~! ça alors!, mon Dieu!

blimp [blɪmp] *n* [airship] dirigeable *m*.

◆ **Blimp** *inf n* vieux réac *m*.

blimpish *inf*, **Blimpish** *inf* ['blɪmpɪʃ] *adj Br* réactionnaire.

blind [blaɪnd] ◇ *adj* -**1.** [sightless] aveugle, non voyant; to go ~ devenir aveugle; his sister is ~ sa sœur est aveugle; he's ~ in one eye il est aveugle d'un œil OR borgne ❑ as ~ as a bat myope comme une taupe; ~ man's buff colin-maillard *m*; to turn a ~ eye to sthg fermer les yeux sur qqch. -**2.** [unthinking] aveugle; ~ loyalty/trust loyauté/confiance aveugle; he flew into a ~ rage il s'est mis dans une colère noire; ~ with anger aveuglé par la colère; they were ~ to the danger le danger leur échappait; she was ~ to the consequences elle ignorait les conséquences, elle ne voyait pas les conséquences; love is ~ l'amour est aveugle. -**3.** [hidden from sight - corner, turning] sans visibilité; ~ side AUT angle *m* mort; on my ~ side dans mon angle mort. -**4.** AERON [landing, take-off] aux appareils. -**5.** [as intensifier]: he was ~ drunk il était ivre mort; he didn't take a ~ bit of notice of what I said *inf* il n'a pas fait la moindre attention à ce que j'ai dit; it doesn't make a ~ bit of difference to me *inf* cela m'est complètement égal.

◇ *vt* -**1.** [deprive of sight] aveugler, rendre aveugle; [subj: flash of light] aveugler, éblouir; we were ~ed by the smoke on était aveuglé par la fumée. -**2.** [deprive of judgment, reason] aveugler; vanity ~ed him to her real motives sa vanité l'empêchait de discerner ses véritables intentions; to ~ sb with science *hum* éblouir qqn par sa science.

◇ *n* -**1.** [for window] store *m*, jalousie *f*. -**2.** *inf Br* [trick] prétexte *m*, feinte *f*; the trip was just a ~ for his smuggling activities le voyage a servi à masquer OR dissimuler ses activités de contrebande. -**3.** *Am* [hiding place] cachette *f*; HUNT affût *m*.

◇ *npl*: the ~ les aveugles *mpl*, les non-voyants *mpl*; it's a case of the ~ leading the ~ c'est l'aveugle qui conduit l'aveugle.

◇ *adv* -**1.** [drive, fly – without visibility] sans visibilité; [– using only instruments] aux instruments. -**2.** [purchase] sans avoir vu; [decide] à l'aveuglette. -**3.** [as intensifier] : **I would swear ~ he was there** j'aurais donné ma tête à couper OR j'aurais juré qu'il était là.

blind alley *n Br* impasse *f*, cul-de-sac *m*; **the government's new idea is just another ~** *fig* encore une nouvelle idée du gouvernement qui n'aboutira à rien OR ne mènera nulle part.

blind date *n* rendez-vous *m* OR rencontre *f* arrangée *(avec quelqu'un qu'on ne connaît pas)*.

blinder ['blaɪndəʳ] *n (usu pl) Am* œillère *f*.

blindfold ['blaɪndfəʊld] ◇ *n* bandeau *m*.
◇ *vt* bander les yeux à OR de.
◇ *adv* les yeux bandés; **I could do the job ~** je pourrais faire ce travail les yeux bandés OR fermés.
◇ *adj*: **~** OR **~ed prisoners** prisonniers aux yeux bandés.

blinding ['blaɪndɪŋ] ◇ *adj* [light] aveuglant, éblouissant; *fig* [speed] éblouissant.
◇ *n* -**1.** [of person, animal] aveuglement *m*. -**2.** CONSTR [on road] couche *f* de sable.

blindingly ['blaɪndɪŋlɪ] *adv* de façon aveuglante; **it was ~ obvious** ça sautait aux yeux.

blindly ['blaɪndlɪ] *adv* [unseeingly] en aveugle, à l'aveuglette; [without thinking] à l'aveuglette, aveuglément.

blindness ['blaɪndnɪs] *n* [disability] cécité *f*; **the government's ~ to social problems** l'aveuglement du gouvernement face aux problèmes sociaux.

blind side *n* AUT angle *m* mort; **on my ~** dans mon angle mort.

blind spot *n* -**1.** AUT [in mirror] angle *m* mort; [in road] endroit *m* sans visibilité. -**2.** MED point *m* aveugle. -**3.** *fig* [weak area] côté *m* faible, faiblesse *f*; **his daughter is his ~** quand il s'agit de sa fille, il refuse de voir la vérité en face; **I have a ~ about mathematics** je ne comprends rien aux mathématiques.

blindworm ['blaɪndwɜːm] *n* orvet *m*.

blink [blɪŋk] ◇ *vi* -**1.** [person] cligner OR clignoter des yeux; [eyes] cligner, clignoter; **she didn't even ~ at the news** *fig* elle n'a même pas sourcillé en apprenant la nouvelle; **they ~ at his heavy drinking** *fig* ils ferment les yeux sur le fait qu'il boit beaucoup. -**2.** [light] clignoter, vaciller.
◇ *vt* -**1. to ~ one's eyes** cligner les OR des yeux; **to ~ away** OR **to ~ back one's tears** refouler ses larmes *(en clignant des yeux)*. -**2.** *Am*: **to ~ one's lights** faire un appel de phares.
◇ *n* -**1.** [of eyelid] clignotement *m* (des yeux), battement *m* de paupières; **in the ~ of an eye** OR **eyelid** en un clin d'œil, en un rien de temps. -**2.** [glimpse] coup *m* d'œil. -**3.** [of light] lueur *f*; [of sunlight] rayon *m*. -**4.** *inf phr*: **on the ~** en panne.

blinker ['blɪŋkəʳ] ◇ *n* -**1.** [for eyes] œillère *f*; **when it comes to her family she wears ~s** elle a des œillères quand il s'agit de sa famille. -**2.** AUT: **~ (light)** [turn signal] clignotant *m*; [warning light] feu *m* de détresse.
◇ *vt* mettre des œillères à.

blinkered ['blɪŋkəd] *adj* -**1.** [horse] qui porte des œillères. -**2.** [opinion, view] borné.

blinking *inf* ['blɪnkɪŋ] ◇ *adj Br euph* sacré, fichu; **~ idiot!** espèce d'idiot!
◇ *adv* sacrément, fichtrement.

blintz(e) [blɪnts] *n* crêpe *f* fourrée.

blip [blɪp] ◇ *n* -**1.** [sound] bip *m*, bip-bip *m*; [spot of light] spot *m*; [on graph, screen etc] sommet *m*. -**2.** [temporary problem] mauvais moment *m* (à passer).
◇ *vi* faire bip OR bip-bip.

bliss [blɪs] *n* -**1.** [happiness] bonheur *m* (complet OR absolu), contentement *m*, félicité *f lit*; **what ~ to have a lie-in!** quel bonheur de pouvoir faire la grasse matinée!; **our holiday was absolute ~!** on a passé des vacances absolument merveilleuses OR divines!; **married ~** le bonheur conjugal. -**2.** RELIG béatitude *f*.

blissful ['blɪsfʊl] *adj* -**1.** [happy] bienheureux; [peaceful] serein; **three ~ years** trois années de bonheur complet; **she remained in ~ ignorance** elle était heureuse dans son ignorance. -**2.** RELIG bienheureux.

blissfully ['blɪsfʊlɪ] *adv* [agree, smile] d'un air heureux; [peaceful, quiet] merveilleusement; **they were ~ happy** ils étaient comblés de bonheur; **we were ~ unaware of the danger** nous étions dans l'ignorance la plus totale du danger.

blister ['blɪstəʳ] ◇ *n* -**1.** [on skin] ampoule *f*, cloque *f*. -**2.** [on painted surface] boursouflure *f*; [in glass] soufflure *f*, bulle *f*; [in metal] soufflure *f*.
◇ *vi* -**1.** [foot, skin] se couvrir d'ampoules. -**2.** [paint] se boursoufler; [glass] former des soufflures OR des bulles; [metal] former des soufflures.
◇ *vt* -**1.** [foot, skin] donner des ampoules à. -**2.** [paint] boursoufler; [glass] former des soufflures OR des bulles dans; [metal] former des soufflures dans. -**3.** [attack verbally] critiquer sévèrement.

blistering ['blɪstərɪŋ] *adj* -**1.** [sun] brûlant, de plomb; [heat] torride. -**2.** [attack, criticism] cinglant, virulent; [remark] caustique, cinglant.

blister pack *n Br* [for light bulb, pens] emballage *m* bulle, blister *m*; [for pills] plaquette *f*.

BLit [ˌbiːˈlɪt] *(abbr of* Bachelor of Literature) *n (titulaire d'une) licence de littérature*.

blithe [blaɪð] *adj* [cheerful] gai, joyeux; [carefree] insouciant; **~ indifference** indifférence insouciante ❑ 'Blithe Spirit' *Coward* 'l'Esprit s'amuse'.

blithely ['blaɪðlɪ] *adv* [cheerfully] gaiement, joyeusement; [carelessly] avec insouciance.

blithering *inf* ['blɪðərɪŋ] *adj* sacré; **it's a ~ nuisance!** c'est la barbe!; **he's a ~ idiot** c'est un crétin fini; **you ~ fool!** espèce d'imbécile!

BLitt [ˌbiːˈlɪt] *(abbr of* Bachelor of Letters) *n Br (titulaire d'une) licence de littérature*.

blitz [blɪts] ◇ *n* [attack] attaque *f* éclair; [bombing] bombardement *m*; **an advertising ~** une campagne publicitaire de choc; **let's have a ~ and get this work done** attaquons-nous à ce travail pour en finir.
◇ *vt* [attack] attaquer en éclair; [bomb] bombarder.
◆ **Blitz** *n* HIST: **the Blitz** le Blitz.

blizzard ['blɪzəd] *n* tempête *f* de neige, blizzard *m*.

BLM *(abbr of* Bureau of Land Management) *pr n services de l'aménagement du territoire aux États-Unis*.

bloated ['bləʊtɪd] *adj* [gen] gonflé, boursouflé; [stomach] gonflé, ballonné; **to feel ~** se sentir ballonné; **~ with self-importance** imbu de soi-même, pénétré de son importance.

bloater ['bləʊtəʳ] *n* hareng *m* saur OR fumé.

blob [blɒb] *n* [drop] goutte *f*; [stain] tache *f*; **a ~ on the horizon** une forme indistincte à l'horizon.

bloc [blɒk] *n* bloc *m*.

block [blɒk] ◇ *n* -**1.** [of ice, stone, wood] bloc *m*; [for butcher, executioner] billot *m*; **the painting was on the (auctioneer's) ~** *Am* le tableau était mis aux enchères ❑ **to put** OR **to lay one's head on the ~** prendre des risques. -**2.** [toy] : **(building) ~s** jeu *m* de construction, (jeu de) cubes *mpl*. -**3.** [of seats] groupe *m*; [of shares] tranche *f*; [of tickets] série *f*; COMPUT bloc *m*. -**4.** [area of land] pâté *m* de maisons; **we walked round the ~** nous avons fait le tour du pâté de maisons; **the school is five ~s away** *Am* l'école est cinq rues plus loin. -**5.** *esp Br* [building] immeuble *m*; [of barracks, prison] quartier *m*; [of hospital] pavillon *m*; **~ of flats** immeuble (d'habitation); **office ~** immeuble de bureaux. -**6.** [obstruction – in pipe, tube] obstruction *f*; [– in traffic] embouteillage *m*; MED & PSYCH blocage *m*; **to have a (mental) ~ about sthg** faire un blocage à propos de qqch, avoir un trou de mémoire au sujet de qqch; **I have a (mental) ~ about mathematics** j'ai la hantise des mathématiques, c'est plus fort que moi ❑ **he's suffering from writer's ~** il n'arrive pas à écrire, c'est le vide OR le blocage total. -**7.** SPORT obstruction *f*. -**8.** *inf* [head] caboche *f*; **I'll knock your ~ off!** je vais te démolir le portrait! -**9.** [of paper] bloc *m*. -**10.** TECH: **~ (and tackle)** palan *m*, moufles *mpl*.
◇ *vt* -**1.** [obstruct – pipe, tube] boucher, bloquer; [– road] bloquer, barrer; [– view] boucher, cacher; MED [– artery] obstruer; **don't ~ the door!** dégagez la porte!; **to ~ sb's way** barrer le chemin à qqn; **that building ~s the sun** ce bâtiment empêche le soleil d'entrer. -**2.** [hinder – traffic] bloquer, gêner; [– progress] gêner, enrayer; [– credit, deal, funds] bloquer; MED [pain] anesthésier; SPORT [opponent] faire obstruction à. -**3.** [hat, knitting] mettre en forme.
◇ *vi* SPORT faire de l'obstruction.
◇ *comp* [booking, vote] groupé; **~ grant** *Br* ADMIN dotation *f (aux collectivités locales)*.
◆ **block in** *vt sep* -**1.** [car] bloquer; **I've been ~ed in** ma voiture est bloquée. -**2.** [drawing, figure] colorer; *fig* [plan, scheme] ébaucher.
◆ **block off** *vt sep* [road] bloquer, barrer; [door, part of road, window] condamner; [view] boucher, cacher; [sun] cacher.
◆ **block out** *vt sep* -**1.** [light, sun] empêcher d'entrer; [view] cacher, boucher. -**2.** [ideas] empêcher; [information] interdire, censurer. -**3.** [outline] ébaucher.
◆ **block up** *vt sep* -**1.** [pipe, tube] boucher, bloquer; [sink] boucher. -**2.** [door, window] condamner.

blockade [blɒˈkeɪd] ◇ *n* -**1.** MIL blocus *m*; **to lift** OR **to raise a ~** lever un blocus; **to be under ~** être en état de blocus. -**2.** *fig* [obstacle] obstacle *m*.
◇ *vt* -**1.** MIL faire le blocus de. -**2.** *fig* [obstruct] bloquer, obstruer.

blockage ['blɒkɪdʒ] *n* [gen] obstruction *f*; [in pipe] obstruction *f*, bouchon *m*; MED [in heart] blocage *m*, obstruction *f*; [in intestine] occlusion *f*; PSYCH blocage *m*.

blockboard ['blɒkbɔːd] *n* panneau *m* latté, latté *m*.

blockbuster *inf* ['blɒkbʌstəʳ] *n* -**1.** [success – book] best-seller *m*, livre *m* à succès; [– film] superproduction *f*. -**2.** [bomb] bombe *f* de gros calibre.

blockbusting *inf* ['blɒkbʌstɪŋ] *adj* à sensation.

block capital *n* (caractère *m*) majuscule *f*; **in ~s** en majuscules.

block diagram *n* COMPUT & GEOG blocdiagramme *m*; ELECTRON schéma *m* (de principe).

blockhead *inf* ['blɒkhed] *n* imbécile *mf*, idiot *m*, -e *f*.

blockhouse ['blɒkhaʊs, *pl* -haʊzɪz] *n* blockhaus *m*, casemate *f*.

block letter *n* (caractère *m*) majuscule *f*; **in ~s** en majuscules (d'imprimerie).

block release *n Br* INDUST *système de stages de formation qui alternent avec une activité professionnelle*.

block vote *n mode de scrutin utilisé par les syndicats britanniques*.

BLOCK VOTE:
Le «block vote» donne au vote d'un délégué la valeur non pas de sa seule voix, mais de toutes les voix de la section qu'il représente.

---

bloke *inf* [bləʊk] *n Br* type *m*; **he's a good ~** c'est un brave type.

blond [blɒnd] ◇ *adj* blond.
◇ *n* blond *m*.

blonde [blɒnd] ◇ *adj* blond.
◇ *n* blond *m*, blonde *f*.

blood [blʌd] ◇ *n* -**1.** [fluid] sang *m*; **to donate** OR **to give ~** donner son sang; **to spill ~** verser OR faire couler du sang; **she bit him and drew ~** elle l'a mordu (jusqu') au sang; **the ~ rushed to his head** le sang lui est monté à la tête; **he has ~ on his hands** *fig* il a du sang sur les mains ❑ **the mafia are after his ~** *inf* la

mafia veut sa peau; **there is bad ~ between the two families** le torchon brûle entre les deux familles; **the argument made for bad ~ between them** la dispute les a brouillés; **his attitude makes my ~ boil** son attitude me met hors de moi; **it's like getting ~ out of a stone** ce n'est pas une mince affaire; **her ~ froze** OR **ran cold at the thought** rien qu'à y penser son sang s'est figé dans ses veines; **the film made my ~ run cold** le film m'a donné des frissons; **the town's ~ is up over these new taxes** la ville s'élève OR part en guerre contre les nouveaux impôts; **to do sthg in cold ~** faire qqch de sang-froid; **travelling is** OR **runs in her ~** elle a le voyage dans le sang OR dans la peau; **what we need is new** OR **fresh** OR **young ~** nous avons besoin d'un OR de sang nouveau; **they're out for ~** ils cherchent à se venger; **~ is thicker than water** *prov* la voix du sang est la plus forte; **'In Cold Blood'** *Capote* 'De sang-froid'. -**2.** [breeding, kinship]: **of noble/Italian ~** de sang noble/italien; **a prince of the ~** un prince du sang OR de sang royal. -**3.** *arch* [young man]: **a young ~** un élégant OR roué *arch*.
◇ *vt* -**1.** HUNT [hound] acharner, donner le goût du sang à; [person] donner le goût du sang à. -**2.** *fig* [beginner, soldier] donner le baptême du feu à.

blood-and-thunder *adj* [adventure] à sensation; [melodramatic] mélodramatique.

blood bank *n* banque *f* du sang.

bloodbath ['blʌdbɑːθ, *pl* -bɑːðz] *n* massacre *m*, bain *m* de sang.

blood blister *n* pinçon *m*.

blood brother *n* frère *m* de sang.

blood cell *n* cellule *f* sanguine, globule *m* (du sang).

blood count *n* numération *f* globulaire.

bloodcurdling ['blʌd,kɜːdlɪŋ] *adj* terrifiant; **a ~ scream** un cri à vous glacer OR figer le sang.

blood donor *n* donneur *m*, -euse *f* de sang.

-blooded [,blʌdɪd] *in cpds* de sang...; **blue~** de sang noble, aristocratique; **warm~** ZOOL à sang chaud.

blood feud *n* vendetta *f*.

blood group *n* groupe *m* sanguin.

blood heat *n* température *f* du sang.

bloodhound ['blʌdhaʊnd] *n* -**1.** [dog] limier *m*. -**2.** *inf* [detective] limier *m*, détective *m*.

bloodiness ['blʌdɪnɪs] *n* état *m* sanglant; **the ~ of war** les carnages de la guerre.

bloodless ['blʌdlɪs] *adj* -**1.** [without blood] exsangue. -**2.** [battle, victory] sans effusion de sang; **the Bloodless Revolution** HIST la Seconde Révolution d'Angleterre OR la Glorieuse Révolution *(1688-1689)*. -**3.** [cheeks, face] pâle.

bloodletting ['blʌd,letɪŋ] *n* -**1.** [bloodshed] carnage *m*, massacre *m*. -**2.** MED saignée *f*.

blood lust *n* soif *f* de sang.

blood money *n* prix *m* du sang.

blood orange *n* (orange *f*) sanguine *f*.

blood plasma *n* plasma *m* sanguin.

blood poisoning *n* septicémie *f*.

blood pressure *n* tension *f* (artérielle); **the doctor took my ~** le médecin m'a pris la tension; **to have high/low ~** faire de l'hypertension/de l'hypotension; **the patient's ~ is down/up** la tension du malade a baissé/monté; **her ~ goes up every time she talks politics** *fig* elle se met en colère chaque fois qu'elle parle politique; **watch your ~!** *hum* calmez-vous!

blood pudding *n* boudin *m* (noir).

blood red *adj* rouge sang *(inv)*.

blood relation *n* parent *m*, -e *f* par le sang.

blood sausage *n* boudin *m* (noir).

blood serum *n* sérum *m* sanguin.

bloodshed ['blʌdʃed] *n* carnage *m*, massacre *m*; **without ~** sans effusion *f* de sang.

bloodshot ['blʌdʃɒt] *adj* injecté (de sang); **her eyes became ~** ses yeux se sont injectés (de sang).

blood sister *n* sœur *f* de sang.

blood sport *n Br* sport *m* sanguinaire.

bloodstain ['blʌdsteɪn] *n* tache *f* de sang.

bloodstained ['blʌdsteɪnd] *adj* taché de sang.

bloodstock ['blʌdstɒk] *n* chevaux *mpl* de race OR de sang.

bloodstone ['blʌdstəʊn] *n* héliotrope *m* *(pierre)*.

bloodstream ['blʌdstriːm] *n* sang *m*, système *m* sanguin.

bloodsucker ['blʌd,sʌkə^r] *n* ZOOL OR *fig* sangsue *f*.

blood sugar *n* glycémie *f*; **to have low ~** avoir une glycémie faible; **blood-sugar level** taux *m* de glycémie.

blood test *n* analyse *f* de sang.

bloodthirsty ['blʌd,θɜːstɪ] (*compar* **bloodthirstier**, *superl* **bloodthirstiest**) *adj* [animal, person] assoiffé OR avide de sang, sanguinaire *lit*; [film] violent, sanguinaire *lit*.

blood transfusion *n* transfusion *f* sanguine OR de sang.

blood type *n* groupe *m* sanguin.

blood vessel *n* vaisseau *m* sanguin.

bloody ['blʌdɪ] (*compar* **bloodier**, *superl* **bloodiest**) ◇ *adj* -**1.** [wound] sanglant, saignant; [bandage, clothing, hand] taché OR couvert de sang; **a ~ nose** un nez en sang. -**2.** [battle, fight] sanglant, meurtrier. -**3.** [blood-coloured] rouge, rouge sang *(inv)*. -**4.** ▽ *Br* [as intensifier] foutu; **you ~ fool!** espèce *f* de crétin!; **~ hell!** et merde!; **I can't get the ~ car to start** je n'arrive pas à faire démarrer cette foutue bagnole; **it's a ~ shame she didn't come** c'est vachement dommage qu'elle n'ait pas pu venir. -**5.** *inf* [unpleasant] affreux, désagréable; **he's been perfectly ~ with me** il a été affreux avec moi.
◇ *adv* ▽ *Br* vachement; **you can ~ well do it yourself!** tu n'as qu'à te démerder (tout seul)!; **are you coming? — not ~ likely!** est-ce que tu viens? — pas question!
◇ *vt* ensanglanter, couvrir de sang; **they came out of it bloodied but unbowed** ils s'en sont sortis meurtris mais avec la tête haute.

Bloody Mary ◇ *pr n* [queen] *surnom de la reine Marie Tudor, donné par les protestants qu'elle persécuta*.
◇ *n* [cocktail] bloody mary *m inv*.

bloody-minded *inf adj Br* [person] vache; [attitude, behaviour] buté, têtu; **he's just being ~!** il le fait rien que pour emmerder le monde!

bloody-mindedness *inf* [-'maɪndɪdnɪs] *n Br* caractère *m* difficile; **his ~ didn't help things** son caractère de chien n'a pas arrangé les choses; **it's sheer ~ on your part** tu le fais uniquement pour emmerder le monde.

bloom [bluːm] ◇ *n* -**1.** [flower] fleur *f*. -**2.** [state]: **the roses are just coming into ~** les roses commencent tout juste à fleurir OR à s'épanouir; **to be in ~** [lily, rose] être éclos; [bush, garden, tree] être en floraison OR en fleurs; **to be in full ~** [lily, rose] être épanoui; [bush, garden, tree] être en pleine floraison. -**3.** [of cheeks, face] éclat *m*; **in the ~ of youth** dans la fleur de l'âge, en pleine jeunesse. -**4.** [on fruit] velouté *m*.
◇ *vi* -**1.** [flower] éclore; [bush, tree] fleurir; [garden] se couvrir de fleurs. -**2.** *fig* [person] être en pleine forme; [arts, industry] prospérer.

bloomer ['bluːmə^r] *n* -**1.** [plant] plante *f* fleurie; **a night ~** une plante qui fleurit la nuit. -**2.** *inf Br* [blunder] gaffe *f*, faux pas *m*; **I made a terrible ~** j'ai fait une gaffe terrible.

bloomers ['bluːməz] *npl*: **(a pair of) ~** une culotte bouffante.

blooming ['bluːmɪŋ] ◇ *adj* -**1.** [flower] éclos; [bush, garden, tree] en fleur, fleuri. -**2.** [glowing - with health] resplendissant, florissant; [- with happiness] épanoui, rayonnant; **~ with health** resplendissant de santé. -**3.** *inf Br* [as intensifier] sacré, fichu; **you ~ idiot!** espèce d'imbécile!; **he's a ~ nuisance** il est casse-pieds.
◇ *adv inf Br* sacrément, vachement; **you can ~ well do it yourself!** tu n'as qu'à te débrouiller tout seul!

Bloomsbury Group ['bluːmzbrɪ-] *pr n*: **the ~** *groupe d'écrivains, d'artistes et d'intellectuels anglais du début du XXe siècle.*

BLOOMSBURY GROUP:
Les membres du «Bloomsbury Group» habitaient le quartier du même nom à Londres; ce groupe comprenait notamment l'économiste John Maynard Keynes et l'écrivain Virginia Woolf.

---

blooper *inf* ['bluːpə^r] *n Am* gaffe *f*, faux pas *m*; **what a ~ he made!** la gaffe qu'il a faite!

blossom ['blɒsəm] ◇ *n* -**1.** [flower] fleur *f*. -**2.** [state]: **the cherry trees are just coming into ~** les cerisiers commencent tout juste à fleurir; **to be in ~** être en fleurs; **the chestnut trees are in full ~** les marronniers sont en pleine floraison.
◇ *vi* -**1.** [flower] éclore; [bush, tree] fleurir. -**2.** *fig* [person] s'épanouir; [arts, industry] prospérer; **she ~ed into a talented writer** elle est devenue un écrivain doué.

blot [blɒt] (*pt* & *pp* **blotted**, *cont* **blotting**) ◇ *n* -**1.** [spot - gen] tache *f*; [- of ink] tache *f*, pâté *m*. -**2.** *fig* [on character, name] tache *f*, souillure *f*; [on civilization, system] tare *f*; **it's a ~ on the landscape** ça gâche le paysage.
◇ *vt* -**1.** [dry] sécher. -**2.** [spot] tacher; [with ink] tacher, faire des pâtés sur; **to ~ one's copybook** salir sa réputation.
◆ **blot out** *vt sep* [obscure - light, sun] cacher, masquer; [- memory, thought] effacer; [- act, event] éclipser.
◆ **blot up** *vt sep* [subj: person] éponger, essuyer; [subj: blotting paper, sponge] boire.

blotch [blɒtʃ] ◇ *n* [spot - of colour, ink] tache *f*; [- on skin] tache *f*, marbrure *f*.
◇ *vi* -**1.** [skin] se couvrir de taches OR de marbrures. -**2.** [pen] faire des pâtés.
◇ *vt* -**1.** [clothing, paper] tacher, faire des taches sur. -**2.** [skin] marbrer.

blotchy ['blɒtʃɪ] (*compar* **blotchier**, *superl* **blotchiest**) *adj* [complexion, skin] marbré, couvert de taches OR de marbrures; [cloth, paper, report] couvert de taches.

blotter ['blɒtə^r] *n* -**1.** [paper] buvard *m*; [desk pad] sous-main *m inv*; **hand ~** tampon *m* buvard. -**2.** *Am* [register] registre *m (provisoire)*.

blotting pad ['blɒtɪŋ-] *n* (bloc *m*) buvard *m*.

blotting paper *n* (papier *m*) buvard *m*.

blotto *inf* ['blɒtəʊ] *adj* parti.

blouse [blaʊz] ◇ *n* [for woman] chemisier *m*, corsage *m*; [for farmer, worker] blouse *f*.
◇ *vt* faire blouser; **a ~d top** un haut blousant.

blow [bləʊ] (*pt* **blew** [bluː], *pp* **blown** [bləʊn]) ◇ *n* -**1.** [hit] coup *m*; [with fist] coup *m* de poing; **to come to ~s** en venir aux mains; **without striking a ~** sans coup férir; **to strike a ~ for freedom** *fig* rompre une lance pour la liberté. -**2.** [setback] coup *m*, malheur *m*; [shock] coup *m*, choc *m*; **her death came as a terrible ~ (to them)** sa mort a été (pour eux) un choc terrible; **to soften** OR **to cushion the ~** amortir le choc; **to deal sb/sthg a (serious) ~** porter un coup (terrible) à qqn/qqch; **it was a big ~ to her pride** son orgueil en a pris un coup. -**3.** [blast of wind] coup *m* de vent; [stronger] bourrasque *f*; **we went for a ~ on the prom** *fig* nous sommes sortis prendre l'air sur le front de mer. -**4.** [puff] souffle *m*; [through nose]: **have a good ~** mouche-toi bien. -**5.** *drugs sl Br* [marijuana] herbe *f*; *Am* [cocaine] cocaïne *f*. -**6.** [bloom] inflorescence *f*; **lilacs in full ~** des lilas en pleine floraison.
◇ *vi* -**1.** [wind] souffler; **the wind was ~ing hard** le vent soufflait fort; **the wind is ~ing from the north** le vent souffle du nord; **it's ~ing a gale out there** le vent souffle en tempête là-bas; **let's wait and see which way the wind ~s** *fig* attendons de voir de quel côté OR d'où souffle le vent. -**2.** [person] souffler; **she blew on her hands** elle a soufflé dans ses mains; **~ on your coffee** souffle sur ton café ❑ **he ~s hot and cold** il souffle le chaud et le froid. -**3.** [move with wind]: **the trees were ~ing**

in the wind le vent soufflait dans les arbres; **papers blew all over the yard** des papiers se sont envolés à travers la cour; **the window blew open/shut** un coup de vent a ouvert/fermé la fenêtre. -**4.** [wind instrument] sonner; [whistle] siffler. -**5.** [explode - tyre] éclater. -**6.** [whale] souffler; **there she ~s!** la voilà! -**7.** *inf* [leave] filer. -**8.** *Am* & *Austr* [brag] se vanter. -**9.** [bloom] fleurir; [open out] s'épanouir. -**10.** ▽ *Am* [be disgusting] : **this coffee really ~s!** il est vraiment dégueulasse, ce café!
◇ *vt* -**1.** [wind] faire bouger; [leaves] chasser, faire envoler; **the wind blew the door open/shut** un coup de vent a ouvert/fermé la porte; **a gust of wind blew the papers off the table** un coup de vent a fait s'envoler les papiers de la table; **the wind was ~ing the ship southward** le vent poussait le navire vers le sud; **the hurricane blew the ship off course** l'ouragan a fait dévier OR a dérouté le navire. -**2.** [subj: person] souffler; **~ your nose!** mouche-toi!; **he blew the dust off the book** il a soufflé sur le livre pour enlever la poussière; **to ~ sb a kiss** envoyer un baiser à qqn. -**3.** [bubbles, glass] : **to ~ bubbles/smoke rings** faire des bulles/ronds de fumée; **to ~ glass** souffler le verre. -**4.** [wind instrument] jouer de; [whistle] faire retentir; **the policeman blew his whistle** le policier a sifflé OR a donné un coup de sifflet; **the referee blew his whistle for time** l'arbitre a sifflé la fin du match ❑ **to ~ the gaff** *inf* vendre la mèche; **to ~ one's own trumpet** se vanter; **to ~ the whistle on sthg** dévoiler qqch. -**5.** [tyre] faire éclater; [fuse, safe] faire sauter; **the house was blown to pieces** la maison a été entièrement détruite par l'explosion; **the blast almost blew his hand off** l'explosion lui a presque emporté la main; **their plans were blown sky-high** *fig* leurs projets sont tombés à l'eau ❑ **he blew a fuse** OR **a gasket** *Br* **when he found out** quand il l'a appris, il a piqué une crise. -**6.** *inf* [squander - money] claquer; **he blew all his savings on a new car** il a claqué toutes ses économies pour s'acheter une nouvelle voiture. -**7.** [spoil - chance] gâcher; **I blew it!** j'ai tout gâché! -**8.** *inf* [reveal, expose] révéler; **to ~ sb's cover** griller qqn; **her article blew the whole thing wide open** son article a exposé toute l'affaire au grand jour ❑ **to ~ the lid off sthg** *inf* faire des révélations sur qqch, découvrir le pot aux roses. -**9.** *inf Am* [leave] quitter; **they blew town yesterday** ils ont fichu le camp hier. -**10.** *inf Br* [disregard] : **let's go anyway, and ~ what he thinks** allons-y quand même, je me moque de ce qu'il pense OR il peut penser ce qu'il veut; **~ the expense, we're going out to dinner** au diable l'avarice, on sort dîner ce soir. -**11.** *drugs sl Am* [drugs] prendre. -**12.** *inf phr*: **the idea blew his mind** l'idée l'a fait flipper; **oh, ~ (it)!** *Br* la barbe!, mince!; **~ it out your ear!** *Am* arrête tes conneries et fiche-moi le camp!; **to ~ one's lid** OR **stack** OR **top** exploser de rage; **our team blew them out of the water** notre équipe les a complètement écrasés; **don't ~ your cool** ne t'emballe pas; **well, I'll be ~ed!** *Br*, **~ me down!** ça par exemple!; **I'll be** OR **I'm ~ed if I'm going to apologize!** *Br* pas question que je fasse des excuses!, il peut toujours courir pour que je lui fasse des excuses!
◆ **blow away** *vt sep* -**1.** [subj: wind] chasser, disperser; **let's take a walk to ~ away the cobwebs** *Br* allons nous promener pour nous changer les idées. -**2.** *inf* [astound] sidérer; **the film just blew me away** ce film m'a complètement retourné. -**3.** *inf* [kill] abattre. -**4.** *inf Am* [defeat completely] écraser, battre à plate couture.
◆ **blow down** ◇ *vi insep* être abattu par le vent, tomber.
◇ *vt sep* [subj: wind] faire tomber, renverser; [subj: person] faire tomber OR abattre (en soufflant).
◆ **blow in** ◇ *vi insep* *inf* débarquer à l'improviste, s'amener.
◇ *vt sep* [door, window] enfoncer.
◆ **blow off** ◇ *vi insep* -**1.** [hat, roof] s'envoler. -**2.** *inf Br* [break wind] péter.
◇ *vt sep* -**1.** [subj: wind] emporter. -**2.** [release] laisser échapper, lâcher; **she needed to ~ off steam about the boss** *inf* elle avait besoin de dire tout ce qu'elle avait sur le cœur à propos de son patron.
◆ **blow out** ◇ *vt sep* -**1.** [extinguish - candle] souffler; [- fuse] faire sauter; **to ~ one's brains out** se faire sauter OR se brûler la cervelle. -**2.** [subj: storm] : **the hurricane eventually blew itself out** l'ouragan s'est finalement calmé. -**3.** [cheeks] gonfler.
◇ *vi insep* [fuse] sauter; [candle] s'éteindre; [tyre] éclater.
◆ **blow over** ◇ *vi insep* -**1.** [storm] se calmer, passer; *fig*: **the scandal soon blew over** le scandale fut vite oublié. -**2.** [tree] s'abattre, se renverser.
◇ *vt sep* [tree] abattre, renverser.
◆ **blow up** ◇ *vt sep* -**1.** [explode - bomb] faire exploser OR sauter; [- building] faire sauter. -**2.** [inflate] gonfler. -**3.** [enlarge] agrandir; [exaggerate] exagérer; **the whole issue was blown up out of all proportion** la question a été exagérée hors de (toute) proportion.
◇ *vi insep* -**1.** [explode] exploser, sauter; **the plan blew up in their faces** *fig* le projet leur a claqué dans les doigts. -**2.** [begin - wind] se lever; [- storm] se préparer; [- crisis] se déclencher. -**3.** *inf* [lose one's temper] exploser, se mettre en boule; **to ~ up at sb** engueuler qqn.

blowback ['bləʊbæk] *n* retour *m* de souffle.
blow-by-blow *adj* détaillé; **she gave me a ~ account** elle m'a tout raconté en détail.
blow-dry ◇ *vt* faire un brushing à.
◇ *n* brushing *m*.
blower ['bləʊəʳ] *n* -**1.** [device] soufflante *f*. -**2.** [grate] tablier *m* OR rideau *m* de cheminée. -**3.** MIN jet *m* de grisou. -**4.** *inf* [whale] baleine *f*. -**5.** *inf Br* [telephone] bigophone *m*.
blowfly ['bləʊflaɪ] (*pl* **blowflies**) *n* mouche *f* à viande.
blowgun ['bləʊgʌn] *n Am* sarbacane *f*.
blowhard *inf* ['bləʊhɑːd] *n Am* vantard *m*, -e *f*, fanfaron *m*, -onne *f*.
blowhole ['bləʊhəʊl] *n* -**1.** [of whale] évent *m*. -**2.** TECH bouche *f* d'aération, évent *m*.
◆ **blowholes** *npl* METALL soufflures *fpl*.
blow job▼ *n*: **to give sb a ~** tailler une pipe à qqn.
blowlamp ['bləʊlæmp] *n Br* lampe *f* à souder, chalumeau *m*.
blown [bləʊn] *pp* → **blow**.
blow-off *n* [discharge] vidange *f*; [device] bouchon *m* de vidange.
blowout ['bləʊaʊt] *n* -**1.** [of fuse] : **there's been a ~** les plombs ont sauté. -**2.** [of tyre] éclatement *m*; **I had a ~** j'ai un pneu qui a éclaté. -**3.** [of gas] éruption *f*. -**4.** *inf Br* [meal] gueuleton *m*; **let's have a ~** faisons un gueuleton OR une grande bouffe.
blowpipe ['bləʊpaɪp] *n* -**1.** *Br* [weapon] sarbacane *f*. -**2.** CHEM & INDUST [tube] chalumeau *m*; [glassmaking] canne *f* de souffleur, fêle *f*.
blowsy ['blaʊzɪ] (*compar* **blowsier**, *superl* **blowsiest**) = **blowzy**.
blowtorch ['bləʊtɔːtʃ] *n* lampe *f* à souder, chalumeau *m*.
blow-up *n* -**1.** [explosion] explosion *f*. -**2.** *inf* [argument] engueulade *f*. -**3.** PHOT agrandissement *m*.
blow wave ◇ *n* brushing *m*.
◇ *vt* faire un brushing à.
blowy ['bləʊɪ] (*compar* **blowier**, *superl* **blowiest**) *adj* venté, venteux.
blowzy ['blaʊzɪ] (*compar* **blowzier**, *superl* **blowziest**) *adj Br* -**1.** *pej* [untidy] débraillé; [sluttish] sale, de souillon. -**2.** [ruddy] rubicond.
BLS (*abbr of* **Bureau of Labor Statistics**) *pr n institut de statistiques du travail aux États-Unis*.
blub *inf* [blʌb] (*pt* & *pp* **blubbed**, *cont* **blubbing**) *vi Br* pleurer comme un veau OR une Madeleine.
blubber ['blʌbəʳ] ◇ *n* [of whale] blanc *m* de baleine; *pej* [of person] *inf* graisse *f*.
◇ *vi* pleurer comme un veau OR une madeleine.
◇ *adj* plein de graisse.
blubbery ['blʌbərɪ] *adj* plein de graisse.
bludgeon ['blʌdʒən] ◇ *n* gourdin *m*, matraque *f*.
◇ *vt* -**1.** [beat] matraquer. -**2.** [force] contraindre, forcer; **they ~ed him into selling the house** ils lui ont forcé la main pour qu'il vende la maison.
blue [bluː] (*cont* **blueing** OR **bluing**) ◇ *n* -**1.** [colour] bleu *m*, azur *m*; **dressed in ~** habillé en bleu. -**2.** **the ~** [sky] le ciel, l'azur *m lit*; **they set off into the ~** ils sont partis à l'aventure. -**3.** POL *membre du parti conservateur britannique*. -**4.** *Br* UNIV: **Oxford ~** *étudiant sélectionné dans l'équipe de l'Université d'Oxford*; **the Dark/Light Blues** l'équipe *f* universitaire d'Oxford/de Cambridge; **he got a ~ for cricket** il a représenté son université au cricket. -**5.** *inf Am* [police officer] policier *m*, flic *m*. -**6.** [for laundry] bleu *m*.
◇ *adj* -**1.** [colour] bleu; **to be ~ with cold** être bleu de froid ❑ **you can argue until you're ~ in the face but she still won't give in** vous pouvez vous tuer à discuter, elle ne s'avouera pas vaincue pour autant. -**2.** *inf* [depressed] triste, cafardeux; **to feel ~** avoir le cafard. -**3.** [obscene - language] obscène, cochon; [- book, movie] porno; **his jokes turn the air ~** *Br* ses plaisanteries sont affreusement cochonnes. -**4.** *inf phr*: **to have a ~ fit** *Br* piquer une crise; **to scream** OR **to shout ~ murder** crier comme un putois; **he talks a ~ streak** *Br* il n'arrête pas de jacasser.
◇ *vt* -**1.** *inf Br* [squander - money] claquer; **he ~d his inheritance on the horses** il a claqué son héritage en jouant aux courses. -**2.** [laundry] passer au bleu.
◆ **blues** *npl* -**1.** *inf* **the ~s** [depression] le cafard; **to get** OR **to have the ~s** avoir le cafard. -**2.** MUS: **the ~s** le blues; **to sing the ~s** chanter le blues.
◆ **Blues** *pl pr n*: **the Blues and Royals** section de la Cavalerie de la Maison du Souverain britannique.
◆ **out of the blue** *adv phr* sans prévenir; **the job offer came out of the ~** la proposition de travail est tombée du ciel.

BLUE:
Sur la scène politique britannique, la couleur bleue représente le parti conservateur. Dans le milieu des sports universitaires, le bleu foncé est porté par les joueurs d'Oxford, le bleu clair par ceux de Cambridge.

---

blue baby *n* enfant *m* bleu, enfant *f* bleue.
Bluebeard ['bluː,bɪəd] *pr n* Barbe-bleue.
bluebeat ['bluːbiːt] *n genre musical antillais des années 60, précurseur du reggae*.
bluebell ['bluːbel] *n* jacinthe *f* des bois.
blueberry ['bluːbərɪ] (*pl* **blueberries**) *n* myrtille *f*; *Can* bleuet *m*; **~ pie** tarte *f* aux myrtilles.
bluebird ['bluːbɜːd] *n* oiseau *m* bleu.
blue-black *adj* bleu tirant sur le noir, bleu-noir.
blue blood *n* sang *m* bleu OR noble.
blue-blooded *adj* aristocratique, de sang noble.
blue book *n Br* POL livre *m* bleu; *Am* UNIV cahier *m* d'examen.
bluebottle ['bluː,bɒtl] *n* -**1.** [fly] mouche *f* bleue OR de la viande. -**2.** BOT bleuet *m*. -**3.** *Br dated* [police officer] flic *m*.
blue cheese *n* (fromage *m*) bleu *m*.
blue chip *n* [stock] valeur *f* de premier ordre; [property] placement *m* de bon rapport.
◆ **blue-chip** *comp* [securities, stock] de premier ordre.
blue-collar *adj* ouvrier; **~ worker** col *m* bleu; **~ union** syndicat *m* ouvrier.
blue-eyed *adj* aux yeux bleus; **the ~ boy** *inf Br* le chouchou.
blue funk *inf n Br* sacrée frousse *f*, peur *f* bleue; **she left in a ~** elle est partie complètement terrorisée.

bluegrass ['blu:grɑ:s] *n* [grass] pâturin *m* des champs; [music] musique *f* bluegrass; the Bluegrass State *Am* le Kentucky.

blue-green algae *npl* cyanophycées *fpl spec*, algues *fpl* bleues.

blue jeans *npl Am* jean *m*.

blue laws *inf npl Am lois qui, au nom de la morale, limitent certaines activités telles que l'ouverture des commerces le dimanche, la vente d'alcool etc.*

bluenose *inf* ['blu:nəʊz] *n* -**1.** [of Nova Scotia] néo-écossais *m*, -e *f*. -**2.** *Am* [prig] prude *f*.

blue note *n tierce ou septième diminuée, très utilisée dans le blues.*

blue-pencil *vt* [edit] corriger; [censor] censurer.

blue peter *n* pavillon *m* de partance.

◆ **Blue Peter** *pr n émission télévisée britannique pour enfants, à vocation pédagogique.*

blueprint ['blu:prɪnt] ◇ *n* -**1.** [photographic] bleu *m*. -**2.** *fig* [programme] plan *m*, projet *m*; [prototype] prototype *m*; the ~ for democratic government le modèle démocratique.
◇ *vt* tirer des bleus.

blue rib(b)and, blue ribbon ◇ *n premier prix d'une compétition.*
◇ *adj* de première classe.

blue rinse *n* rinçage *m* bleu.

◆ **blue-rinse** *adj Br*: a blue-rinse lady *une dame (d'un certain âge) bien de sa personne.*

blue shark *n* requin *m* bleu.

blue-sky *comp*: ~ research recherches *fpl* sans applications immédiates; ~ law *loi américaine qui protège le public contre les titres boursiers douteux.*

bluestocking ['blu:ˌstɒkɪŋ] *n Br* bas-bleu *m*.

bluetit ['blu:tɪt] *n* mésange *f* bleue.

blue whale *n* baleine *f* bleue.

bluff [blʌf] ◇ *n* -**1.** [deception] bluff *m*. -**2.** [cliff] falaise *f*, promontoire *m*.
◇ *adj* [person] direct, franc; [landscape] escarpé, à pic.
◇ *vi* bluffer.
◇ *vt* bluffer; don't try to ~ me n'essayez pas de m'en conter; to ~ one's way through things marcher au bluff.

bluffer ['blʌfəʳ] *n* bluffeur *m*, -euse *f*.

bluish ['blu:ɪʃ] *adj* qui tire sur le bleu; *pej* bleuâtre.

blunder ['blʌndəʳ] ◇ *n* [mistake] bourde *f*; [remark] gaffe *f*, impair *m*; I made a terrible ~ j'ai fait une gaffe OR une bévue épouvantable.
◇ *vi* -**1.** [make a mistake] faire une gaffe OR un impair. -**2.** [move clumsily] avancer à l'aveuglette, tâtonner; he was ~ing about in the dark il avançait à l'aveuglette OR à tâtons dans le noir; she ~ed against OR into the bookshelf elle s'est heurtée OR cognée à la bibliothèque; he ~ed through the interview il s'embrouillait au cours de l'entretien.

blunderbuss ['blʌndəbʌs] *n* tromblon *m*.

blunderer ['blʌndərəʳ] *n* gaffeur *m*, -euse *f*.

blundering ['blʌndərɪŋ] ◇ *adj* [person] maladroit, gaffeur; [action, remark] maladroit, malavisé.
◇ *n* maladresse *f*, gaucherie *f*.

blunt [blʌnt] ◇ *adj* -**1.** [blade] peu tranchant, émoussé; [point] émoussé, épointé; [pencil] mal taillé, épointé; killed with a ~ instrument JUR assassiné avec un instrument contondant. -**2.** [frank] brusque, direct; let me be ~ permettez que je parle franchement.
◇ *vt* [blade] émousser; [pencil, point] épointer; *fig* [feelings, senses] blaser, lasser.

bluntly ['blʌntlɪ] *adv* carrément, franchement; he answered ~ il a répondu sans ménagement OR sans mâcher ses mots.

bluntness ['blʌntnɪs] *n* -**1.** [of blade] manque *m* de tranchant, état *m* émoussé. -**2.** [frankness] franchise *f*, brusquerie *f*.

blur [blɜ:ʳ] (*pt* & *pp* blurred, *cont* blurring) ◇ *n* -**1.** [vague shape] masse *f* confuse, tache *f* floue; my childhood is all a ~ to me now maintenant mon enfance n'est plus qu'un vague souvenir. -**2.** [smudge] tache *f*; [of ink] pâté *m*, bavure *f*.
◇ *vt* -**1.** [writing] estomper, effacer; [outline] estomper. -**2.** [judgment, memory, sight] troubler, brouiller; tears blurred my eyes mes yeux étaient voilés de larmes.
◇ *vi* [inscription, outline] s'estomper; [judgment, memory, sight] se troubler, se brouiller.

blurb [blɜ:b] *n* notice *f* publicitaire, argumentaire *m*; [on book] (texte *m* de) présentation *f*.

blurred [blɜ:d], **blurry** ['blɜ:rɪ] *adj* flou, indistinct.

blurt [blɜ:t] *vt* lâcher, jeter.

◆ **blurt out** *vt sep* [secret] laisser échapper; she ~ed out his name elle a laissé échapper son nom.

blush [blʌʃ] ◇ *vi* [turn red - gen] rougir, devenir rouge; [- with embarrassment] rougir; she ~ed deeply elle est devenue toute rouge; he ~ed to the roots of his hair il a rougi jusqu'aux oreilles; I ~ to think of it now maintenant quand j'y pense, j'en rougis; I ~ for her j'ai honte pour elle; the ~ing bride l'heureuse élue.
◇ *n* rougeur *f*; the ~ of a peach la couleur rosée de la pêche; "thank you", she said with a ~ «merci», dit-elle en rougissant; please, spare our ~es *hum* ne nous faites pas rougir, s'il vous plaît; the first ~ of dawn les premières rougeurs de l'aube; she was in the first ~ of youth elle était dans la prime fleur de l'âge ❑ at first ~ *Br* de prime abord, à première vue.

blusher ['blʌʃəʳ] *n* fard *m* à joues.

bluster ['blʌstəʳ] ◇ *vi* -**1.** [wind] faire rage, souffler en rafales; [storm] faire rage, se déchaîner. -**2.** [speak angrily] fulminer, tempêter. -**3.** [boast] se vanter, fanfaronner.
◇ *vt* [person] intimider; he tried to ~ his way out of doing it il a essayé de se défiler avec de grandes phrases.
◇ *n* -**1.** [boasting] fanfaronnade *f*, fanfaronnades *fpl*, vantardise *f*. -**2.** [wind] rafale *f*.

blustering ['blʌstərɪŋ] ◇ *n* fanfaronnade *f*, fanfaronnades *fpl*.
◇ *adj* fanfaron.

blustery ['blʌstərɪ] *adj* [weather] venteux, à bourrasques; [wind] qui souffle en rafales, de tempête.

Blvd (*written abbr of* boulevard) bd, boul.

BM ◇ *n* (*abbr of* Bachelor of Medicine) *(titulaire d'une) licence de médecine.*
◇ *pr n abbr of* British Museum.

BMA (*abbr of* British Medical Association) *pr n ordre britannique des médecins.*

BMJ (*abbr of* British Medical Journal) *pr n organe de la BMA.*

B-movie *n* film *m* de série B.

BMus [bi:'mʌz] (*abbr of* Bachelor of Music) *n (titulaire d'une) licence de musique.*

BMX (*abbr of* bicycle motorcross) *n* -**1.** [bicycle] VTT *m*. -**2.** SPORT cyclo-cross *m inv*.

bn *written abbr of* billion.

BO *n* -**1.** (*abbr of* body odour) *odeur corporelle*; he's got ~ il sent mauvais. -**2.** *abbr of* box office.

boa ['bəʊə] *n* -**1.** (feather) ~ boa *m*. -**2.** ~ constrictor boa constricteur *m*, constrictor *m*.

boar [bɔ:ʳ] *n* [male pig] verrat *m*; [wild pig] sanglier *m*; young (wild) ~ marcassin *m*.

board [bɔ:d] ◇ *n* -**1.** [plank] planche *f*; the ~s THEAT la scène, les planches ❑ to tread the ~s THEAT faire du théâtre; the policy applies to everybody in the company across the ~ cette politique concerne tous les employés de l'entreprise quelle que soit leur position. -**2.** [cardboard] carton *m*; [for games] tableau *m*; to sweep the ~ *Br* remporter tous les prix. -**3.** [notice board] tableau *m*. -**4.** ADMIN conseil *m*, commission *f*; ~ of directors conseil d'administration; who's on the ~? qui siège au conseil d'administration?; ~ of inquiry commission d'enquête; the ~ of health *Am* le service municipal d'hygiène; MIL le conseil de révision; medical ~ commission médicale. -**5.** SCH & UNIV: ~ of education *Am* ≃ conseil *m* d'administration *(d'un établissement scolaire)*; ~ of examiners jury *m* d'examen; ~ of governors *Br* ≃ conseil *m* d'administration *(d'un lycée ou d'un collège)*; ~ of regents *Am* ≃ conseil *m* d'université. -**6.** [meals provided] pension *f*; *arch* [table] table *f*; ~ and lodging (chambre *f* et) pension; full ~ pension complète. -**7.** AERON & NAUT bord *m*; to go on ~ monter à bord de; we're on ~ nous sommes à bord; they took provisions on ~ ils ont embarqué des provisions ❑ to go by the ~ *Br* être abandonné OR oublié; in the excitement the normal routine went by the ~ dans l'agitation la routine habituelle a été abandonnée; his principles went by the ~ il a dû abandonner ses principes; to take sthg on ~ tenir compte de qqch.
◇ *comp* [decision, meeting] du conseil d'administration.
◇ *vt* -**1.** [plane, ship] monter à bord de; [bus, train] monter dans; NAUT [in attack] monter OR prendre à l'abordage; the flight is now ~ing at gate 3 embarquement immédiat du vol porte 3. -**2.** [cover with planks] couvrir de planches. -**3.** [provide meals, lodging] prendre en pension.
◇ *vi* [lodge] être en pension; to ~ with sb être pensionnaire chez qqn.

◆ **board out** *vt sep*: she ~s the children out with us elle met les enfants en pension chez nous.

◆ **board up** *vt sep* couvrir de planches; [door, window] boucher, obturer.

boarder ['bɔ:dəʳ] *n* pensionnaire *mf*; SCH interne *mf*, pensionnaire *mf*; she takes in ~s elle prend des pensionnaires.

board game *n* jeu *m* de société.

boarding ['bɔ:dɪŋ] *n* -**1.** *(U)* [gen & fence] planches *fpl*; [floor] planchéiage *m*. -**2.** [embarking] embarquement *m*; NAUT [in attack] abordage *m*.

boarding card *n* carte *f* d'embarquement.

boarding house *n* pension *f*; SCH internat *m*.

boarding school *n* internat *m*, pensionnat *m*; to go to ~ être interne; they sent their children to ~ ils ont mis leurs enfants en internat.

Board of Trade *pr n*: the ~ *Br* le ministère du Commerce; *Am* la chambre de commerce.

boardroom ['bɔ:drʊm] ◇ *n* salle *f* de conférence; *fig* [management] administration *f*.
◇ *comp*: the decision was taken at ~ level la décision a été prise au niveau de la direction.

boardsail ['bɔ:dseɪl] *vi* faire de la planche à voile.

boardsailing ['bɔ:dseɪlɪŋ] *n* planche *f* à voile SPORT.

boardwalk ['bɔ:dwɔ:k] *n Am* passage *m* en bois; [on beach] promenade *f* (en planches).

boast [bəʊst] ◇ *n* -**1.** fanfaronnade *f*, fanfaronnades *fpl*; it's his proud ~ that he has never lost a game il se vante de n'avoir jamais perdu un jeu. -**2.** [in squash] bosse *f*.
◇ *vi* se vanter, fanfaronner; failing the exam is nothing to ~ about il n'y a pas de quoi se vanter d'avoir raté l'examen; without ~ing OR wanting to ~ sans vouloir me vanter.
◇ *vt* -**1.** [brag] se vanter de. -**2.** [possess] être fier d'avoir; the town ~s an excellent symphonic orchestra la ville se glorifie d'avoir un excellent orchestre symphonique.

boaster ['bəʊstəʳ] *n* fanfaron *m*, -onne *f*.

boastful ['bəʊstfʊl] *adj* fanfaron, vantard.

boastfully ['bəʊstfʊlɪ] *adv* en se vantant.

boasting ['bəʊstɪŋ] *n* *(U)* vantardise *f*, fanfaronnade *f*, fanfaronnades *fpl*.

boat [bəʊt] ◇ *n* [gen] bateau *m*; [for rowing] barque *f*, canot *m*; [for sailing] voilier *m*; [ship] navire *m*, paquebot *m*; we're travelling by ~ nous voyageons en bateau; I caught the ~ at Singapore j'ai embarqué OR pris le bateau à Singapour; to go by ~ prendre le bateau; they crossed the Atlantic by ~ ils ont traversé l'Atlantique en bateau; to take to the ~s monter dans les canots de sauvetage ❑ we're all in the same ~ nous sommes tous logés à la même enseigne.
◇ *vi* voyager en bateau; to go ~ing aller se

promener en bateau; he ~ed up/down the river il a remonté/descendu le fleuve en bateau.

boatbuilder ['bəʊtˌbɪldəʳ] *n* constructeur *m* naval.

boat deck *n* pont *m* des embarcations.

boater ['bəʊtəʳ] *n* canotier *m*.

boathook ['bəʊthʊk] *n* gaffe *f*.

boathouse ['bəʊthaʊs, *pl* -haʊzɪz] *n* abri *m* OR hangar *m* à bateaux.

boating ['bəʊtɪŋ] ◇ *n* canotage *m*.
◇ *comp* [accident, enthusiast, trip] de canotage.

boatload ['bəʊtləʊd] *n* [merchandise] cargaison *f*; [people] plein bateau *m*.

boatman ['bəʊtmən] (*pl* **boatmen** [-mən]) *n* [rower] passeur *m*; [renter of boats] loueur *m* de canots.

boat people *npl* boat people *mpl*.

boat race *n* ROWING course *f* d'avirons; SAILING régates *fpl*; the Boat Race *course universitaire annuelle d'avirons entre les universités d'Oxford et de Cambridge*.

boatswain ['bəʊsn] *n* maître *m* d'équipage; ~'s chair sellette *f*; ~'s mate second maître *m*.

boat train *n* *train qui assure la correspondance avec un bateau*.

boatyard ['bəʊtjɑːd] *n* chantier *m* de construction navale.

bob [bɒb] (*pt* & *pp* bobbed, *cont* bobbing, *pl sense 7 inv*) ◇ *vi* -**1.** [cork, buoy]: to ~ up and down danser sur l'eau; I could see his head bobbing up and down behind the wall je voyais par moments sa tête surgir de derrière le mur. -**2.** [curtsy] faire une petite révérence. -**3.** [move quickly]: to ~ in/out entrer/sortir rapidement. -**4.** [bobsleigh] faire du bobsleigh. -**5.** *phr*: to ~ for apples GAMES: they were bobbing for apples ils essayaient d'attraper avec les dents des pommes flottant sur l'eau.
◇ *vt* -**1.** [move up and down] faire monter et descendre; she bobbed a curtsy elle a fait une petite révérence. -**2.** [hair] couper court. -**3.** [horse's tail] écourter.
◇ *n* -**1.** [abrupt movement] petit coup *m*, petite secousse *f*; [of head] hochement *m* OR salut *m* de tête; [curtsy] petite révérence *f*. -**2.** [hairstyle] (coupe *f* au) carré *m*; she wears her hair in a short ~ elle est coiffée à la Jeanne d'Arc. -**3.** [horse's tail] queue *f* écourtée. -**4.** [fishing float] flotteur *m*, bouchon *m*; [weight] plomb *m*. -**5.** *inf phr*: all my bits and ~s toutes mes petites affaires; we'll deal with the bits and ~s later nous nous occuperons des détails plus tard. -**6.** [bobsleigh] bobsleigh *m*, bob *m*; [runner] patin *m*. -**7.** *inf Br dated* [shilling] shilling *m*.
◆ **bob down** *vi insep* se baisser subitement; [duck] baisser la tête; the children bobbed down out of sight les enfants se baissèrent subitement hors de notre vue.
◆ **bob up** *vi insep* remonter tout d'un coup.

Bob [bɒb] *pr n*: ~'s your uncle! et voilà le travail!

bobbin ['bɒbɪn] *n* [gen] bobine *f*; [for lace] fuseau *m*; ~ lace dentelle *f* aux fuseaux.

bobble ['bɒbl] ◇ *n* -**1.** [bobbing movement] secousse *f*, saccade *f*. -**2.** [pompom] pompon *m*; ~ hat chapeau *m* à pompon. -**3.** *inf Am* [mistake] boulette *f*.
◇ *vt inf Am*: he ~d the ball il n'arriva pas à bloquer la balle.
◇ *vi*: the ball ~d and the player mishit his shot il y a eu un faux rebond et le joueur a raté son tir.

bobby *inf* ['bɒbɪ] (*pl* bobbies) *n Br dated* flic *m*.

bobby-dazzler [-ˌdæzləʳ] *n Br dial*: she's a right ~! c'est un beau brin de fille!

bobby pin *n Am* pince *f* à cheveux.
◆ **bobby-pin** *vt Am* attacher *(avec une pince à cheveux)*.

bobby socks, bobby sox *npl Am* socquettes *fpl (de fille)*.

bobby-soxer *inf* [-'sɒksəʳ] *n Am* adolescente *f*, fille *f*, minette *f*.

bobcat ['bɒbkæt] *n* lynx *m*.

bobfloat ['bɒbfləʊt] *n* flotteur *m*, bouchon *m*.

bobskate ['bɒbskeɪt] *n Am* patin *m* à double lame.

bobsled ['bɒbsled], **bobsleigh** ['bɒbsleɪ]
◇ *n* bobsleigh *m*, bob *m*.
◇ *vi* faire du bobsleigh.

bobtail ['bɒbteɪl] *n* [tail] queue *f* écourtée; a ~ cat/dog un chat/chien écourté.

bobtailed ['bɒbteɪld] *adj* à (la) queue écourtée, écourté.

Boccaccio [bɒ'kɑːtʃɪəʊ] *pr n* Boccace.

Boche▽ [bɒʃ] *dated & offensive* ◇ *n* Boche *mf*.
◇ *adj* boche.

bock [bɒk] *n* -**1.** [beer] bière *f* bock. -**2.** [glass] bock *m*.

bod *inf* [bɒd] *n* -**1.** *Br* [person] type *m*; he's a bit of an odd ~ c'est plutôt un drôle d'oiseau. -**2.** [body] physique *m*, corps *m*.

bode [bəʊd] ◇ *pt* → **bide**.
◇ *vi* [presage] augurer; it ~s well for him cela est de bon augure pour lui; that ~s ill OR no good for us cela ne présage rien de bon pour nous.
◇ *vt arch* [predict] présager, annoncer.

bodge *inf* [bɒdʒ] *vt Br* -**1.** [spoil] saboter, bousiller. -**2.** [mend clumsily] rafistoler.

bodice ['bɒdɪs] *n* [of dress] corsage *m*; [corset] corset *m*.

bodice ripper *n* *hum roman grivois à trame historique*.

-bodied [ˌbɒdɪd] *in cpds*: an able~ man un homme robuste OR solide; a short~ aircraft un avion au fuselage court.

bodily ['bɒdɪlɪ] ◇ *adj* matériel; ~ functions fonctions *fpl* corporelles; to cause sb ~ harm blesser qqn.
◇ *adv* -**1.** [carry, seize] à bras-le-corps. -**2.** [entirely] entièrement; she threw herself ~ into her work elle s'est jetée à corps perdu dans son travail.

bodkin ['bɒdkɪn] *n* -**1.** [needle] grosse aiguille *f*; [for tape] passe-lacet *m*. -**2.** *arch* [dagger] poignard *m*; [hairpin] épingle *f* à cheveux.

Bodleian Library ['bɒdlɪən-] *pr n*: the ~ la bibliothèque Bodléienne *(à Oxford)*.

body ['bɒdɪ] (*pl* bodies) *n* -**1.** [human, animal] corps *m*; we belong together ~ and soul nous sommes faits l'un pour l'autre; he gave himself to her ~ and soul il s'est donné à elle corps et âme ❑ to keep ~ and soul together subsister, survivre. -**2.** [corpse] cadavre *m*, corps *m*; over my dead ~! *inf* il faudra me passer sur le corps! -**3.** [group] ensemble *m*, corps *m*; [organization] organisme *m*; the main ~ of voters le gros des électeurs; a large ~ of people une foule énorme; they came in one ~ ils sont venus en masse; taken as a ~ dans leur ensemble, pris ensemble; legislative ~ corps *m* législatif ❑ ~ corporate personne *f* morale; ~ politic corps *m* politique. -**4.** [mass] masse *f*; a ~ of water un plan d'eau; a growing ~ of evidence une accumulation de preuves; the ~ of public opinion la majorité de l'opinion publique. -**5.** [largest part - of document, speech] fond *m*, corps *m*. -**6.** [of car] carrosserie *f*; [of plane] fuselage *m*; [of ship] coque *f*; [of camera] boîtier *m*; [of dress] corsage *m*; [of building] corps *m*. -**7.** [fullness] corps *m*; a wine with (a lot of) ~ un vin qui a du corps; a shampoo that gives your hair ~ un shampooing qui donne du volume à vos cheveux. -**8.** *inf* [man] bonhomme *m*; [woman] bonne femme *f*; she's a funny little ~ c'est une drôle de petite bonne femme. -**9.** [garment] body *m*. -**10.** PHYS corps *m*.

body bag *n* sac *m* mortuaire.

body blow *n* coup *m* dur.

bodybuilder *n* [person] culturiste *mf*; [machine] extenseur *m*; [food] aliment *m* énergétique.

body building *n* culturisme *m*.

body clock *n* horloge *f* biologique.

bodyguard ['bɒdɪgɑːd] *n* garde *m* du corps.

body language *n* langage *m* du corps.

body odour *n* odeur *f* corporelle.

body paint *n* peinture *f* pour le corps.

body shop *n* -**1.** atelier *m* de carrosserie. -**2.** *inf Am* [gym] club *m* de gym.

body snatcher *n* déterreur *m*, -euse *f* de cadavres.

body stocking *n* body *m*.

body warmer [-ˌwɔːməʳ] *n* gilet *m* matelassé.

bodywork ['bɒdɪwɜːk] *n* carrosserie *f*.

Boer [bɔː] ◇ *n* Boer *mf*.
◇ *adj* boer; the ~ War HIST la guerre des Boers.

THE BOER WAR:
Conflit qui opposa, à la fin du XIXᵉ siècle, les Britanniques aux républiques sud-africaines, qui défendaient leur indépendance face aux ambitions de la «British South Africa Company» et à la suzeraineté britannique. Il s'acheva par une victoire britannique en 1902.

---

boffin *inf* ['bɒfɪn] *n Br* chercheur *m* scientifique OR technique.

bog [bɒg] (*pt* & *pp* bogged, *cont* bogging) *n* -**1.** [area] marécage *m*, marais *m*; [peat] tourbière *f*. -**2.** ▽ *Br* [lavatory] chiottes *fpl*.
◆ **bog down** *vt sep* empêcher, entraver; [vehicle] embourber, enliser; I got bogged down in paperwork *fig* je me suis laissé déborder par la paperasserie.

bogey ['bəʊgɪ] *n* -**1.** [monster] démon *m*, fantôme *m*; [pet worry] bête *f* noire. -**2.** GOLF bogey *m*, bogée *m*. -**3.** *inf* [in nose] crotte *f* de nez. -**4.** = **bogie**.

bogeyman ['bəʊgɪmæn] (*pl* bogeymen [-men]) *n* croque-mitaine *m*, père *m* fouettard; the ~ will get you le croque-mitaine va t'attraper.

boggle ['bɒgl] *vi* -**1.** [be amazed] être abasourdi; the mind ~s! ça laisse perplexe!; the mind OR imagination ~s at the thought ça laisse perplexe. -**2.** [hesitate] hésiter; she ~s at the idea of marriage elle n'est pas sûre de vouloir se marier.

boggy ['bɒgɪ] (*compar* boggier, *superl* boggiest) *adj* [swampy] marécageux; [peaty] tourbeux.

bogie ['bəʊgɪ] *n* RAIL bogie *m*; [trolley] diable *m*.

bog oak *n* chêne *m* des marais.

Bogota [ˌbɒgə'tɑː] *pr n* Bogota.

bogroll▽ ['bɒgrəʊl] *n* PQ *m*.

bogus ['bəʊgəs] *adj* faux.

bogy ['bəʊgɪ] (*pl* bogies) = **bogie**.

Bohemia [bəʊ'hiːmjə] *pr n* Bohême *f*; in ~ en Bohême.

bohemian [bəʊhiːmjən] ◇ *n* bohème *mf*.
◇ *adj* bohème.

Bohemian [bəʊ'hiːmjən] ◇ *n* [from Bohemia] Bohémien *m*, -enne *f*; [gypsy] bohémien *m*, -enne *f*.
◇ *adj* [of Bohemia] bohémien; [gypsy] bohémien.

bohunk▼ ['bəʊhʌŋk] *n Am terme injurieux désignant un travailleur migrant d'Europe centrale*.

boil [bɔɪl] ◇ *n* -**1.** [on face, body] furoncle *m*. -**2.** [boiling point]: bring the sauce to the ~ amenez la sauce à ébullition; the water was just coming to the ~ l'eau venait juste de se mettre à bouillir; the water's on the ~ *Br* l'eau bout OR est bouillante; the pan has gone off the ~ *Br* l'eau de la casserole ne bout plus; the project has gone off the ~ *Br fig* le projet a été mis en attente.
◇ *vt* -**1.** [liquid] faire bouillir, amener à ébullition. -**2.** [laundry] faire bouillir; a ~ed shirt *inf* une chemise empesée. -**3.** [food] cuire à l'eau, faire bouillir; don't ~ the kettle dry *Br* ne laissez pas s'évaporer l'eau dans la bouilloire; I can't even ~ an egg! je ne sais même pas faire cuire un œuf!
◇ *vi* -**1.** [liquid] bouillir; the kettle's ~ing l'eau bout (dans la bouilloire); don't let the soup ~ ne laisse pas bouillir la soupe; the pot ~ed dry *Br* toute l'eau de la casserole s'est évaporée. -**2.** [seethe - ocean] bouillonner; [- person] bouillir; I was ~ing with anger je bouillais de rage.
◆ **boil away** *vi insep* [continue boiling] bouillir très fort; [evaporate] s'évaporer.

◆ **boil down** *vt sep* CULIN faire réduire; *fig* réduire à l'essentiel; he ~ed the speech down to the basics il a réduit son discours à l'essentiel.

◆ **boil down to** *vt insep*: it all ~s down to money tout cela revient à une question d'argent; she didn't actually insult me, but it ~s down to the same thing elle ne m'a pas vraiment insulté mais c'est tout comme.

◆ **boil over** *vi insep* -**1.** [overflow] déborder; [milk] se sauver, déborder. -**2.** *fig* [with anger] bouillir; he ~ed over with rage il bouillait de rage; her resentment ~ed over into outright anger son ressentiment s'est transformé en véritable colère; the unrest ~ed over into violence l'agitation a débouché sur la violence.

◆ **boil up** ◇ *vi insep* [milk] monter; frustration ~ed up in her *fig* elle commençait à s'énerver sérieusement.
◇ *vt sep* [milk, water] monter.

boiled ['bɔɪld] *adj*: ~ beef [alone] bœuf *m* bouilli; [dish] pot-au-feu *m inv*; ~ egg œuf *m* à la coque; ~ ham jambon *m* cuit (à l'eau); ~ potatoes pommes de terre *fpl* à l'eau OR bouillies; ~ sweets *Br* bonbons *mpl* à sucer.

boiler ['bɔɪləʳ] *n* -**1.** [furnace] chaudière *f*; [domestic] chaudière *f*; *Br* [washing machine] lessiveuse *f*; [pot] casserole *f*. -**2.** [chicken] poule *f* à faire au pot.

boilerhouse ['bɔɪləhaʊs, *pl* -haʊzɪz] *n* bâtiment *m* des chaudières.

boilermaker ['bɔɪlə,meɪkəʳ] *n* -**1.** [workman] chaudronnier *m*. -**2.** [drink] *Br* bière *f* fortifiée; *Am* (verre *m* de) whisky *m* suivi d'une bière.

boilermaking ['bɔɪlə,meɪkɪŋ] *n* grosse chaudronnerie *f*.

boilerman ['bɔɪlə,mæn] (*pl* **boilermen** [-,men]) *n* chauffeur *m*.

boilerplate ['bɔɪləpleɪt] *n* -**1.** INDUST tôle *f* à chaudière. -**2.** [form of words] paragraphe *m* standard *(que l'on peut insérer dans un document)*.

boiler room *n* salle *f* des chaudières, chaufferie *f*; NAUT chaufferie *f*, chambre *f* de chauffe.

boiler suit *n Br* [for work] bleu *m* OR bleus *mpl* (de travail); [fashion garment] salopette *f*.

boiling ['bɔɪlɪŋ] ◇ *adj* [very hot] bouillant; the weather here is ~ il fait une chaleur infernale ici; I'm ~ *inf* je crève de chaleur.
◇ *adv*: ~ hot tout bouillant; a ~ hot cup of tea une tasse de thé bouillant; it's ~ hot today *inf* il fait une chaleur à crever aujourd'hui.
◇ *n* [action] ébullition *f*; [bubbling] bouillonnement *m*.

boiling point *n* point *m* d'ébullition; at ~ à ébullition; to reach ~ *literal* arriver à ébullition; *fig* être en ébullition.

boil-in-the-bag *adj* en sachet-cuisson.

boisterous ['bɔɪstərəs] *adj* -**1.** [exuberant] tapageur, plein d'entrain; a ~ meeting une réunion houleuse. -**2.** [sea] tumultueux, turbulent; [wind] violent, furieux.

boisterously ['bɔɪstərəslɪ] *adv* bruyamment, tumultueusement.

bold [bəʊld] ◇ *adj* -**1.** [courageous] intrépide, hardi; a ~ plan un projet audacieux OR osé; a ~ stroke un coup d'audace; he grew ~er in his efforts il s'est enhardi dans ses tentatives. -**2.** [not shy] assuré; [brazen] effronté; he was OR made so ~ as to disagree il a eu l'audace d'exprimer son désaccord; may I be so ~ as to ask your name? puis-je me permettre de vous demander qui vous êtes?; he put a ~ face on it, he put on a ~ front face à cela il a fait OR gardé bonne contenance ☐ as ~ as brass *Br* culotté. -**3.** ART & LITERAT [vigorous] puissant, hardi; with ~ strokes of the brush avec des coups de brosse vigoureux OR puissants; a ~ style of writing un style (d'écriture) hardi; in ~ relief en puissant relief. -**4.** [colours] vif, éclatant; ~ stripes des rayures éclatantes. -**5.** TYPO: in ~ en gras.
◇ *n* caractères *mpl* gras, gras *m*.

boldface ['bəʊldfeɪs] *n* caractères *mpl* gras, gras *m*; in ~ en gras.

boldfaced ['bəʊldfeɪst] *adj* impudent; a ~ lie un mensonge éhonté.

boldly ['bəʊldlɪ] *adv* -**1.** [bravely] intrépidement, audacieusement. -**2.** [impudently] avec impudence, effrontément. -**3.** [forcefully] avec vigueur, vigoureusement.

boldness ['bəʊldnɪs] *n* -**1.** [courage] intrépidité *f*, audace *f*. -**2.** [impudence] impudence *f*, effronterie *f*. -**3.** [force] vigueur *f*, hardiesse *f*.

bole [bəʊl] *n* fût *m*, tronc *m (d'arbre)*.

bolero [bə'leərəʊ] (*pl* **boleros**) *n* boléro *m*; 'Bolero' *Ravel* 'Boléro'.

boletus [bə'liːtəs] (*pl* **boletuses** OR **boleti** [-taɪ]) *n* bolet *m*.

bolide ['bəʊlaɪd] *n* bolide *m*.

Bolivia [bə'lɪvɪə] *pr n* Bolivie *f*; in ~ en Bolivie.

Bolivian [bə'lɪvɪən] ◇ *n* Bolivien *m*, -enne *f*.
◇ *adj* bolivien.

boll [bəʊl] *n* graine *f (du cotonnier, du lin)*.

bollard ['bɒlɑːd] *n* [on wharf] bollard *m*; *Br* [on road] borne *f*.

bollocking▽ ['bɒləkɪŋ] *n Br* engueulade *f*; he got/she gave him a right ~ il a reçu/elle lui a passé un sacré savon.

bollocks▼ ['bɒləks] ◇ *npl Br* [testicles] couilles *fpl*.
◇ *n (U)* [rubbish] conneries *fpl*, couillonnades *fpl*.
◇ *interj*: ~! quelles conneries!; oh, ~, I've got no money on me! quelle merde OR quelle connerie, je n'ai pas d'argent sur moi!

◆ **bollocks up**▼ *vt sep Br* semer la pagaïe dans, foutre le bordel dans.

boll weevil *n* anthonome *m (du cotonnier)*.

Bologna [bə'ləʊnjə] *pr n* Bologne.

Bolognese [,bɒlə'neɪz] (*pl inv*) ◇ *n* Bolonais *m*, -e *f*.
◇ *adj* bolonais; spaghetti ~ spaghetti (à la) bolognaise.

boloney [bə'ləʊnɪ] *n* -**1.** *Am* [sausage] *sorte de saucisson*. -**2.** = **baloney**.

Bolshevik ['bɒlʃɪvɪk] ◇ *n* bolchevik *mf*.
◇ *adj* bolchevique.

Bolshevism ['bɒlʃɪvɪzm] *n* bolchevisme *m*.

bolshie *inf*, **bolshy** *inf* ['bɒlʃɪ] ◇ *n Br* rouge *mf*.
◇ *adj* -**1.** [intractable] ronchon. -**2.** POL rouge.

bolster ['bəʊlstəʳ] ◇ *vt* -**1.** [strengthen] soutenir; he ~ed my morale il m'a remonté le moral; these laws simply ~ up the system ces lois ne font que renforcer le système. -**2.** [pad] rembourrer.
◇ *n* -**1.** [cushion] traversin *m*. -**2.** ARCHIT racinal *m*, sous-poutre *f*.

bolt [bəʊlt] ◇ *vi* -**1.** [move quickly] se précipiter; a rabbit ~ed across the lawn un lapin a traversé la pelouse à toute allure. -**2.** [escape] déguerpir; [horse] s'emballer. -**3.** [plants] monter en graine.
◇ *vt* -**1.** [lock] fermer à clé, verrouiller; did you ~ the door? avez-vous poussé OR mis les verrous? -**2.** [food] engloutir. -**3.** *Am* [break away from] abandonner, laisser tomber. -**4.** TECH [fasten] boulonner. -**5.** [sift] tamiser, passer au tamis; *fig* [examine] passer au crible OR tamis.
◇ *n* -**1.** [sliding bar to door, window] verrou *m*; [in lock] pêne *m*. -**2.** [screw] boulon *m*. -**3.** [dash]: we made a ~ for the door nous nous sommes rués sur la porte; she made a ~ for it elle s'est sauvée à toutes jambes. -**4.** [lightning] éclair *m*; the news came like a ~ from the blue *Br* la nouvelle est arrivée comme un coup de tonnerre. -**5.** [of cloth] rouleau *m*. -**6.** SPORT [of crossbow] carreau *m*; [of firearm] culasse *f* mobile; (expansion) ~ [for climbing] piton *m* (à expansion).
◇ *adv*: ~ upright droit comme un i; he was standing ~ upright il était debout, raide comme la justice OR droit comme un i.

◆ **bolt down** *vt sep* [food, meal] avaler à toute vitesse.

◆ **bolt in** *vt sep* enfermer au verrou.

◆ **bolt on** *vt sep* boulonner.

◆ **bolt out** *vi insep* sortir en coup de vent.

bolt hole *n* abri *m*, refuge *m*; he used the cottage as a ~ il s'est servi du cottage comme refuge.

bolus ['bəʊləs] (*pl* **boluses**) *n* bol *m*.

bomb [bɒm] ◇ *n* -**1.** [explosive] bombe *f*; the ~ la bombe atomique ☐ letter ~ lettre *f* piégée; parcel ~ colis *m* piégé; they're sitting on a time ~ ils dansent sur un volcan. -**2.** *inf Br* [large sum of money] fortune *f*; the repairs cost a ~ les réparations ont coûté les yeux de la tête. -**3.** *inf Am* [failure] fiasco *m*, bide *m*. -**4.** *inf phr*: like a ~: this car goes like a ~ elle fonce, cette voiture; the show went like a ~ *inf Br* le spectacle a eu un succès du tonnerre.
◇ *comp*: ~ bay soute *f* à bombes; ~ scare alerte *f* à la bombe; ~ shelter abri *m*.
◇ *vt* bombarder.
◇ *vi inf* -**1.** [go quickly] filer à toute vitesse; we ~ed down the motorway on filait à toute allure sur l'autoroute. -**2.** *Am* [fail] être un fiasco OR bide.

◆ **bomb out** ◇ *vt sep* détruire par bombardement; we were ~ed out (of our house) nous avons perdu notre maison dans le bombardement.
◇ *vi insep inf Am* [fail] foirer.

bombard [bɒm'bɑːd] *vt* bombarder; to ~ sb with questions bombarder OR assaillir qqn de questions.

bombardier [,bɒmbə'dɪəʳ] *n* [in Air Force] bombardier *m (aviateur)*; *Br* [in Royal Artillery] caporal *m* d'artillerie.

bombardment [bɒm'bɑːdmənt] *n* bombardement *m*.

bombast ['bɒmbæst] *n* grandiloquence *f*, boursouflure *f*.

bombastic [bɒm'bæstɪk] *adj* [style] ampoulé, grandiloquent; [person] grandiloquent, pompeux.

bombastically [bɒm'bæstɪklɪ] *adv* [speak] avec grandiloquence; [write] dans un style ampoulé.

Bombay [,bɒm'beɪ] *pr n* Bombay.

Bombay duck *n petit poisson séché utilisé comme accompagnement dans la cuisine indienne*.

bombazine ['bɒmbəziːn] *n* bombasin *m*.

bomb disposal *n* déminage *m*; ~ expert démineur *m*; ~ squad OR team équipe *f* de déminage.

bombed *inf* [bɒmd] *adj* [drunk] beurré; they were ~ out of their minds ils étaient complètement bourrés.

bomber ['bɒməʳ] *n* -**1.** [aircraft] bombardier *m*; ~ pilot pilote *m* de bombardier. -**2.** [terrorist] plastiqueur *m*, -euse *f*.

bomber command *n* aviation *f* de bombardement.

bomber jacket *n* blouson *m* d'aviateur.

bombing ['bɒmɪŋ] ◇ *n* [by aircraft] bombardement *m*; [by terrorist] attentat *m* à la bombe.
◇ *comp* [mission, raid] de bombardement.

bombproof ['bɒmpruːf] *adj* blindé.

bombshell ['bɒmʃel] *n* -**1.** [explosive] obus *m*. -**2.** *fig* [shock]: her death came as a real ~ sa mort nous a fait un grand choc OR nous a atterrés; their wedding announcement came as a complete ~ l'annonce de leur mariage a fait l'effet d'une bombe. -**3.** *inf* [woman]: a blonde ~ une blonde incendiaire.

bombsight ['bɒmsaɪt] *n* viseur *m* de bombardement.

bombsite ['bɒmsaɪt] *n* lieu *m* bombardé.

bona fide [,bəʊnə'faɪdɪ] *adj* [genuine] véritable, authentique; [agreement] sérieux.

bona fides [,bəʊnə'faɪdiːz] *n* JUR bonne foi *f*.

bonanza [bə'nænzə] ◇ *n* aubaine *f*, filon *m*; *Am* MIN riche filon *m*; she had a real ~ at the sales elle a fait de véritables affaires pendant les soldes.
◇ *comp* exceptionnel; 1987 was a ~ year for them ils ont connu une année exceptionnelle en 1987; the Bonanza State *Am* le Montana.

Bonaparte ['bəʊnəpɑːt] *pr n* Bonaparte.

Bonapartism ['bəʊnəpɑːtɪzm] *n* bonapartisme *m*.

bonce *inf* [bɒns] *n Br* caboche *f*.

bond [bɒnd] ◇ *n* -**1.** [link] lien *m*, liens *mpl*, attachement *m*; marriage ~s liens conjugaux. -**2.** [agreement] engagement *m*, contrat *m*; we entered into a ~ to buy the land nous nous sommes engagés à acheter la terre; my word is my ~ je n'ai qu'une parole. -**3.** JUR caution *f* financière. -**4.** FIN [certificate] bon *m*, titre *m*. -**5.** [adhesion] adhérence *f*. -**6.** [paper] papier *m* à lettres (de luxe). -**7.** CHEM liaison *f*. -**8.** CONSTR appareil *m*. -**9.** COMM: in ~ en entrepôt; he put the merchandise in ~ il a entreposé les marchandises en douane.
◇ *vt* -**1.** [hold together] lier, unir. -**2.** COMM [goods] entreposer. -**3.** JUR [place under bond] placer sous caution; [put up bond for] se porter caution pour. -**4.** FIN lier (par garantie financière). -**5.** CONSTR liaisonner.
◇ *vi* -**1.** [with adhesive]: the surfaces have ~ed les surfaces ont adhéré l'une à l'autre. -**2.** PSYCH former des liens affectifs.
◆ **bonds** *npl* [fetters] chaînes *fpl*, fers *mpl*; *fig* liens *mpl*, contraintes *fpl*.

bondage [ˈbɒndɪdʒ] *n* -**1.** *literal* esclavage *m*; *fig* esclavage *m*, servitude *f*; the serfs were in ~ to the lord HIST les serfs étaient asservis au seigneur. -**2.** [sexual] asservissement *m* sexuel.

bonded [ˈbɒndɪd] *adj* FIN titré; COMM en entrepôt; ~ warehouse entrepôt *m* des douanes.

bondholder [ˈbɒnd,həʊldəʳ] *n* porteur *m* d'obligations OR de bons.

bonding [ˈbɒndɪŋ] *n* -**1.** PSYCH liens *mpl* affectifs. -**2.** [of two objects] collage *m*. -**3.** ELEC système *m* OR circuit *m* régulateur de tension. -**4.** CONSTR liaison *f*.

bondmaid [ˈbɒndmeɪd] *n* serve *f* OR esclave *f* célibataire.

bondman [ˈbɒndmən] (*pl* bondmen [-mən]) *n* serf *m*, esclave *m*.

bondsman [ˈbɒndzmən] (*pl* bondsmen [-mən]) *n* garant *m*, caution *f*.

Bond Street [bɒnd-] *pr n grande rue commerçante de Londres.*

BOND STREET:
Cette artère commerciale de Londres est surtout célèbre pour ses magasins de mode, ses bijouteries et ses galeries de peinture.

---

bone [bəʊn] ◇ *n* -**1.** os *m*; [of fish] arête *f*; she's got good ~ structure elle a une bonne ossature; her finger was cut to the ~ elle s'est coupé le doigt jusqu'à l'os ❑ ~ marrow moelle *f*; a ~ of contention un sujet de tension; chilled OR frozen to the ~ glacé jusqu'à la moelle (des os); his comments were a bit close to OR near the ~ ses commentaires frôlaient l'indécence; I have a ~ to pick with you j'ai un compte à régler avec toi; there's trouble ahead, I can feel it in my ~s quelque chose me dit qu'il va y avoir du grabuge; to make no ~s about sthg ne pas y aller de main morte OR avec le dos de la cuillère; he'll never make old ~s il ne fera sûrement pas de vieux os; he's nothing but skin and ~ OR ~s, he's nothing but a bag of ~s il est maigre comme un clou. -**2.** [substance] os *m*; [in corset] baleine *f*. -**3.** [essential] essentiel *m*; the bare ~s of sthg l'essentiel de qqch; to cut spending down to the ~ réduire les dépenses au strict minimum.
◇ *vt* -**1.** [meat] désosser; [fish] ôter les arêtes de. -**2.** *inf Br dated* [steal] piquer, faucher.
◆ **bones** ◇ *npl* ossements *mpl*, os *mpl*; to lay sb's ~s to rest enterrer qqn.
◇ *n inf* [doctor]: the ~s le toubib.
◆ **bone up on** *inf vt insep Br*: he has to ~ up on his history il faut qu'il bûche son histoire.

bone china *n* porcelaine *f* tendre.

boned [bəʊnd] *adj* -**1.** CULIN [meat, poultry] désossé. -**2.** [corset] baleiné.

-boned *in cpds*: big~ bien charpenté; fine~ aux attaches fines.

bone-dry *adj* absolument sec.

bonehead *inf* [ˈbəʊnhed] *n* crétin *m*, -e *f*, imbécile *mf*.

boneheaded [ˈbəʊn,hedɪd] *adj* [stupid] idiot; [stubborn] têtu.

bone-idle *adj Br* paresseux comme une couleuvre.

boneless [ˈbəʊnlɪs] *adj* [meat] désossé, sans os; [fish] sans arêtes.

bone meal *n* engrais *m* (de cendres d'os).

boner [ˈbəʊnəʳ] *n Am* gaffe *f*, bourde *f*; to pull a ~ faire une gaffe.

bonesetter *inf* [ˈbəʊn,setəʳ] *n* rebouteux *m*, -euse *f*.

boneshaker [ˈbəʊn,ʃeɪkəʳ] *n* *inf* [car] tacot *m*; HIST [bicycle] vélocipède *m*.

Boney [ˈbəʊnɪ] *pr n surnom de Napoléon Bonaparte.*

bonfire [ˈbɒn,faɪəʳ] *n* (grand) feu *m*.

Bonfire Night *n Br* le 5 novembre *(commémoration de la tentative de Guy Fawkes de faire sauter le Parlement en 1605)*.

bong [bɒŋ] ◇ *n* bourdon *m*.
◇ *vi* bourdonner.

bongo [ˈbɒŋgəʊ] (*pl* bongos OR bongoes) *n* bongo *m*.

bonhomie [ˈbɒnəmiː] *n* bonhomie *f*.

Boniface [ˈbɒnɪ,feɪs] *pr n* Boniface.

bonito [bəˈniːtəʊ] (*pl* bonitos) *n* bonite *f*.

bonk▽ [bɒŋk] *hum* ◇ *vi* s'envoyer en l'air.
◇ *vt* s'envoyer en l'air avec.
◇ *n* partie *f* de jambes en l'air.

bonkers *inf* [ˈbɒŋkəz] *adj Br* fou, cinglé; to go ~ devenir fou.

Bonn [bɒn] *pr n* Bonn.

bonnet [ˈbɒnɪt] *n* -**1.** [hat - woman's] bonnet *m*, chapeau *m* à brides; [- child's] béguin *m*, bonnet *m*; *Scot* [- man's] béret *m*, bonnet *m*. -**2.** AUT *Br* capot *m*. -**3.** ARCHIT [awning] auvent *m*; [of chimney] capuchon *m*. -**4.** NAUT bonnette *f*.

Bonnie Prince Charlie [,bɒnɪprɪnsˈtʃɑːlɪ] *pr n surnom donné à Charles Édouard Stuart, le Jeune Prétendant.*

bonny [ˈbɒnɪ] (*compar* bonnier, *superl* bonniest) *adj Br dial* [pretty] joli, beau.

bonsai [ˈbɒnsaɪ] *n* bonsaï *m*.

bonus [ˈbəʊnəs] *n* -**1.** [gen & COMM] prime *f*; a Christmas ~ of £200 200 livres de prime de fin d'année; the holiday was an added ~ *fig* les vacances étaient en prime. -**2.** *Br* FIN [dividend] dividende *m* exceptionnel.

bonus issue *n Br* émission *f* d'actions gratuites.

bony [ˈbəʊnɪ] (*compar* bonier, *superl* boniest) *adj* -**1.** ANAT osseux; [knees, person] anguleux, décharné. -**2.** [fish] plein d'arêtes; [meat] plein d'os.

boo [buː] ◇ *vt* huer, siffler; the audience ~ed him off the stage il a quitté la scène sous les huées OR les sifflets du public.
◇ *vi* pousser des huées, siffler; to ~ at sb huer OR siffler qqn.
◇ *n* huée *f*.
◇ *interj* hou; he wouldn't say ~ to a goose *inf Br* c'est un grand timide.

boob *inf* [buːb] ◇ *n* -**1.** [idiot] ballot *m*. -**2.** [mistake] gaffe *f*. -**3.** [breast] sein *m*.
◇ *vi* gaffer.

boo-boo *inf* [ˈbuːbuː] (*pl* boo-boos) *n* gaffe *f*, bourde *f*.

boob tube *inf n* -**1.** *Am* [television set] télé *f*. -**2.** [strapless top] bustier *m* moulant.

booby [ˈbuːbɪ] (*pl* boobies) *n* -**1.** *inf* [idiot] nigaud *m*, -e *f*, ballot *m*. -**2.** ORNITH fou *m* (de Bassan).

booby hatch *n* -**1.** NAUT écoutillon *m*. -**2.** *inf Am* [mental hospital] asile *m* de dingues.

booby prize *n* prix *m* de consolation *(attribué par plaisanterie au dernier)*; to win OR to get the ~ gagner OR recevoir le prix de consolation.

booby trap (*pt* & *pp* booby-trapped, *cont* booby-trapping) *n* MIL objet *m* piégé; [practical joke] farce *f*.
◆ **booby-trap** *vt* piéger.

boodle *inf* [ˈbuːdl] *n* -**1.** *Am* [money] pognon *m*, fric *m*. -**2.** [bribe] pot-de-vin *m*. -**3.** *Am*: the whole ~ tout le bazar.

boogie *inf* [ˈbuːgɪ] ◇ *vi* [dance] danser; [party] faire la fête.
◇ *n* boogie *m*.

boogie-woogie [-,wuːgɪ] *n* boogie-woogie *m*.

boohoo *inf* [,buːˈhuː] ◇ *vi* pleurer à chaudes larmes, chialer.
◇ *n* pleurs *mpl*.

booing [ˈbuːɪŋ] *n* huées *fpl*.

book [bʊk] ◇ *n* -**1.** *literal* livre *m*; ~ lover bibliophile *mf*; his little black ~ *hum* son carnet d'adresses‖ *fig*: her face is an open ~ toutes ses émotions se voient sur son visage; his life is an open ~ il n'a rien à cacher; mathematics is a closed ~ to me je ne comprends rien aux mathématiques ❑ to bring sb to ~ *Br* obliger qqn à rendre des comptes; to do things OR to go by the ~ faire qqch selon les règles; the Good Book la Bible; the Book of Common Prayer *premier livre officiel de liturgie anglicane*; to be in sb's good ~s être dans les petits papiers de qqn; to be in sb's bad ~s être mal vu de qqn; in my ~ *inf* à mon avis; he can read her like a ~ pour lui elle est transparente; that's one for the ~ OR ~s! il faudra marquer ça d'une pierre blanche!; that provision is already on the ~s cette disposition figure déjà dans les textes; that law went on the ~s in 1979 cette loi est entrée en vigueur en 1979; that suits my ~ *Br* cela me va tout à fait; to throw the ~ at sb donner le maximum à qqn. -**2.** [section of work] livre *m*; [of poem] chant *m*; the ~ of Kings BIBLE le livre des Rois. -**3.** [of stamps, tickets] carnet *m*; a ~ of matches une pochette d'allumettes. -**4.** COMM: a ~ of samples, a sample ~ un jeu OR un album d'échantillons. -**5.** [betting] pari *m*; to make/to start/to keep a ~ on sthg inscrire/engager/tenir un pari sur qqch. -**6.** [script, libretto] livret *m*. -**7.** CARDS contrat *m*.
◇ *vt* -**1.** [reserve] réserver, retenir; *Br* [tickets] prendre; I've ~ed her (a seat) through to New York je lui ai réservé une place jusqu'à New York; have you already ~ed your trip? avez-vous déjà fait les réservations pour votre voyage?; the tour is fully ~ed l'excursion est complète; the performance is ~ed up OR fully ~ed on joue à bureaux OR guichets fermés; the restaurant is fully ~ed le restaurant est complet. -**2.** [engage] embaucher, engager; he's ~ed solid until next week il est complètement pris jusqu'à la semaine prochaine. -**3.** [subj: police]: he was ~ed for speeding il a attrapé une contravention pour excès de vitesse. -**4.** SPORT prendre le nom de. -**5.** COMM [order] enregistrer.
◇ *vi* réserver.
◆ **books** *npl* -**1.** COMM & FIN [accounts] livre *m* de comptes; to keep the ~s tenir les comptes OR la comptabilité; to close the ~s clore OR arrêter les comptes ❑ the ~s and records la comptabilité; to cook the ~s *inf* trafiquer les comptes. -**2.** [of club] registre *m*; she's on the association's ~s elle est membre de l'association; I had myself taken off the ~s j'ai donné ma démission.
◆ **book in** ◇ *vi insep Br* se faire enregistrer; [at hotel] prendre une chambre.
◇ *vt sep* inscrire; [at hotel] réserver une chambre pour.
◆ **book out** ◇ *vi insep* quitter une chambre, partir.
◇ *vt sep Br* [library book] emprunter.
◆ **book up** ◇ *vt sep* réserver, retenir; the restaurant is ~ed up le restaurant est complet; she's ~ed up (all) next week elle est prise (toute) la semaine prochaine.
◇ *vi insep* réserver.

THE BOOK OF COMMON PRAYER:
Édité en 1549 avec l'assentiment du Parlement, ce livre de prières introduisit une réforme du culte public, alliant la solennité des cérémonies traditionnelles à un office simplifié en anglais.

bookable ['bʊkəbl] *adj* -**1.** *Br* [seat] qui peut être réservé d'avance. -**2.** [offence] passible d'une contravention.

bookbinder ['bʊk,baɪndəʳ] *n* relieur *m*, -euse *f*.

bookbinding ['bʊk,baɪndɪŋ] *n* reliure *f*.

bookcase ['bʊkkeɪs] *n* bibliothèque *f (meuble)*.

book club *n* club *m* du livre, cercle *m* de lecture.

bookend ['bʊkend] *n* serre-livres *m inv*.

Booker Prize ['bʊkə-] *pr n*: the ~ *prix littéraire britannique*.

BOOKER PRIZE:
Le Booker Prize est accordé chaque année au meilleur roman d'expression anglaise publié pour la première fois par un éditeur britannique.

bookie *inf* ['bʊkɪ] *n* bookmaker *m*.

booking ['bʊkɪŋ] *n* -**1.** [reservation] réservation *f*; who made the ~? qui a fait la réservation? -**2.** [of actor, singer] engagement *m*.

booking office *n* bureau *m* de location.

bookish ['bʊkɪʃ] *adj* [person] qui aime la lecture, studieux; [style] livresque.

bookkeeper ['bʊk,kiːpəʳ] *n* comptable *mf*.

bookkeeping ['bʊk,kiːpɪŋ] *n* comptabilité *f*.

book-learning *n (U)* connaissances *fpl* livresques.

booklet ['bʊklɪt] *n* petit livre *m*, brochure *f*, plaquette *f*.

bookmaker ['bʊk,meɪkəʳ] *n* bookmaker *m*.

bookmark ['bʊkmɑːk] *n* signet *m*, marque *f*.

bookmobile ['bʊkməbiːl] *n Am* bibliobus *m*.

book number *n* numéro *m* ISBN, numéro *m* de dépôt légal.

bookplate ['bʊkpleɪt] *n* ex-libris *m*.

bookrest ['bʊkrest] *n* lutrin *m*, support *m* à livres.

bookseller ['bʊk,seləʳ] *n* libraire *mf*.

bookshelf ['bʊkʃelf] (*pl* **bookshelves** [-ʃelvz]) *n* étagère *f* à livres, rayon *m* (de bibliothèque).

bookshop ['bʊkʃɒp] *n Br* librairie *f*.

book society *n* club *m* du livre, cercle *m* de lecture.

bookstall ['bʊkstɔːl] *n* étalage *m* de bouquiniste; *Br* [in station] kiosque *m* à journaux.

bookstand ['bʊkstænd] *n Am* [furniture] bibliothèque *f*; [small shop] étalage *m* de bouquiniste; [in station] kiosque *m* à journaux.

bookstore ['bʊkstɔːʳ] *n Am* librairie *f*.

book token *n Br bon d'achat de livres, valable dans les librairies*.

bookworm ['bʊkwɜːm] *n* -**1.** *literal* ver *m* du papier. -**2.** *fig* rat *m* de bibliothèque.

Boolean algebra ['buːlɪən-] *n* algèbre *f* de Boole.

boom [buːm] ◇ *vi* -**1.** [resonate - gen] retentir, résonner; [- guns, thunder] tonner, gronder; [- waves] gronder, mugir; [- organ] ronfler; [- voice] tonner, tonitruer. -**2.** [prosper] prospérer, réussir; **business was ~ing** les affaires étaient en plein essor; **car sales are ~ing** les ventes de voitures connaissent une forte progression.
◇ *vt* -**1.** [say loudly] tonner; **"nonsense!", she ~ed** «quelles idioties!», dit-elle d'une voix tonitruante. -**2.** *Am* [develop] développer; [publicize] promouvoir.
◇ *n* -**1.** [sound - gen] retentissement *m*; [- of guns, thunder] grondement *m*; [- of waves] grondement *m*, mugissement *m*; [- of organ] ronflement *m*; [- of voice] rugissement *m*, grondement *m*; **sonic ~** bang *m*. -**2.** [period of expansion] (vague *f* de) prospérité *f*, boom *m*; [of trade] forte hausse *f* OR progression *f*; [of prices, sales] brusque OR très forte hausse, montée *f* en flèche; [of product] popularité *f*, vogue *f*. -**3.** NAUT [spar] gui *m*. -**4.** [for camera, microphone] perche *f*, girafe *f*; [for crane] flèche *f*. -**5.** TECH [of derrick] bras *m*. -**6.** [barrier] barrage *m* (de radeaux OR de chaînes), estacade *f*.
◆ **boom out** ◇ *vi insep* [guns, thunder] gronder, tonner; [organ] ronfler; [voice] tonner, tonitruer.
◇ *vt sep* tonner; **"of course!", he ~ed out** «bien sûr!», dit-il d'une voix tonitruante.

boom box *inf n Am* radiocassette *f*.

boomerang ['buːməræŋ] ◇ *n* boomerang *m*.
◇ *vi* faire boomerang; **his tricks will ~ on him one day** un jour ses tours lui retomberont sur le nez.

booming ['buːmɪŋ] ◇ *adj* -**1.** [sound] retentissant. -**2.** [business] prospère, en plein essor.
◇ *n* [gen] retentissement *m*; [of guns, thunder] grondement *m*; [of waves] grondement *m*, mugissement *m*; [of organ] ronflement *m*; [of voice] rugissement *m*, grondement *m*.

boom town *n* ville *f* en plein essor, ville-champignon *f*.

boon [buːn] *n* -**1.** [blessing] aubaine *f*, bénédiction *f*; **the new industrial estate is a ~ to the area** la nouvelle zone industrielle est une aubaine pour la région; **her help is a real ~ to me** son aide m'est tout à fait précieuse. -**2.** *arch* [favour] faveur *f*.

boon companion *n* bon compère *m*.

boondocks *inf* ['buːndɒks], **boonies** *inf* ['buːnɪz] *npl Am*: **the ~** le bled, la cambrousse; **in the ~** à perpète (-les-oies).

boor [bʊəʳ] *n* [rough] rustre *m*; [uncouth] goujat *m*, malotru *m*, -e *f*.

boorish ['bʊərɪʃ] *adj* grossier, rustre.

boorishly ['bʊərɪʃlɪ] *adv* grossièrement; **he behaved ~** il s'est comporté en rustre.

boorishness ['bʊərɪʃnɪs] *n* [roughness] rudesse *f*, manque *m* d'éducation OR de savoir-vivre; [uncouthness] goujaterie *f*.

boost [buːst] ◇ *vt* -**1.** [sales] faire monter, augmenter; [productivity] développer, accroître; [morale, confidence] renforcer; **a policy designed to ~ the economy** des mesures destinées à relancer l'économie. -**2.** ELEC survolter; AUT suralimenter. -**3.** [promote] faire de la réclame OR de la publicité pour.
◇ *n* -**1.** [increase] augmentation *f*, croissance *f*; [improvement] amélioration *f*; **a ~ in sales** une brusque augmentation des ventes; **the announcement gave the pound a ~ on the foreign exchanges** la nouvelle a fait grimper la livre sur le marché des changes; **the success gave her morale a much-needed ~** le succès lui a remonté le moral, ce dont elle avait bien besoin. -**2.** [promotion]: **the review gave his play a ~** la critique a fait de la publicité pour OR du battage autour de sa pièce.

booster ['buːstəʳ] *n* -**1.** AERON: ~ (rocket) fusée *f* de lancement, moteur *m* auxiliaire. -**2.** RADIO amplificateur *m*. -**3.** ELEC [device] survolteur *m*; [charge] charge *f* d'appoint. -**4.** *inf Am* [supporter] supporter *m*. -**5.** = **booster shot**.

booster shot *n* piqûre *f* de rappel.

boot [buːt] ◇ *n* -**1.** botte *f*; [ankle-length] bottillon *m*; [for babies, women] bottine *f*; [of soldier, workman] brodequin *m*; **the ~'s on the other foot** *Br* les rôles sont renversés; **to give sb the ~** *inf* flanquer qqn à la porte; **she got the ~** *inf* elle a été flanquée à la porte OR virée; **they put the ~ in** *inf Br literal* ils lui ont balancé des coups de pied; *fig* ils ont enfoncé méchamment le clou. -**2.** *Br* AUT coffre *m*, malle *f*. -**3.** *inf* [kick] coup *m* de pied; **he gave the door a ~** il flanqua un coup de pied dans la porte. -**4.** [instrument of torture] brodequin *m*.
◇ *vt* -**1.** [kick] donner des coups de pied à. -**2.** [equip with boots] botter. -**3.** COMPUT: **to ~ (up) the system** initialiser le système.
◆ **to boot** *adv phr* en plus, par-dessus le marché; **she's beautiful and intelligent to ~** elle est belle, et intelligente par-dessus le marché.
◆ **boot out** *inf vt sep* flanquer à la porte.
◆ **boot up** *vt sep* COMPUT = **boot** *vt* **3**.

bootblack ['buːtblæk] *n* cireur *m* de chaussures.

boot camp *inf n Am* MIL camp *m* d'entraînement pour nouvelles recrues; **to go into ~** ≃ faire ses classes.

booted ['buːtɪd] *adj* botté.

bootee ['buːtiː] *n* [for babies] petit chausson *m*, bottine *f*; [for women] bottine *f*, bottillon *m*.

booth [buːð] *n* -**1.** [at fair] baraque *f*, stand *m*. -**2.** [cubicle - for telephone, language laboratory] cabine *f*; [- for voting] isoloir *m*. -**3.** *Am* [in restaurant] box *m*.

bootjack ['buːtdʒæk] *n* tire-botte *m*.

bootlace ['buːtleɪs] *n* lacet *m* (de chaussure).

bootleg ['buːt,leg] (*pt* & *pp* **bootlegged**, *cont* **bootlegging**) ◇ *vi* faire de la contrebande de boissons alcoolisées.
◇ *vt* [make] fabriquer illicitement; [sell] vendre en contrebande.
◇ *n* [gen] marchandise *f* illicite; [liquor] alcool *m* fabriqué OR vendu illicitement; [record, cassette] pirate *m*.
◇ *adj* de contrebande; **~ cassette/record** cassette *f*/disque *m* pirate.

bootlegger ['buːt,legəʳ] *n* bootlegger *m*.

bootless ['buːtlɪs] *adj* -**1.** [without boots] sans bottes. -**2.** *lit* [fruitless] vain, infructueux.

bootlick *inf* ['buːtlɪk] *vi*: **he's always ~ing** c'est un vrai lèche-bottes.

bootlicker *inf* ['buːt,lɪkəʳ] *n* lèche-bottes *mf inv*.

bootmaker ['buːt,meɪkəʳ] *n* bottier *m*.

boot polish *n* cirage *m*.

boots ['buːts] (*pl inv*) *n Br garçon d'hôtel qui cire les chaussures*.

boot sale *n Br sorte de marché aux puces où des particuliers vendent des objets contenus dans le coffre de leur voiture*.

boot scraper *n* décrottoir *m*.

bootstrap ['buːtstræp] ◇ *n* -**1.** [on boot] tirant *m* de botte; **she pulled herself up by her own ~s** *fig* elle a réussi par ses propres moyens. -**2.** COMPUT programme *m* amorce, amorce *f*.
◇ *adj* autonome; **~ program** COMPUT programme *m* amorce.

booty ['buːtɪ] *n* butin *m*.

booze *inf* [buːz] ◇ *n (U)* alcool *m*, boissons *fpl* alcoolisées; **bring your own ~** apportez à boire; **to go on the ~** picoler; **he is on the ~** il picole; **she's off the ~** elle a arrêté de picoler.
◇ *vi* picoler.

boozed *inf* [buːzd] *adj* bourré.

boozer *inf* ['buːzəʳ] *n* -**1.** [drunkard] poivrot *m*, -e *f*. -**2.** *Br* [pub] bistro *m*.

booze-up *inf n Br* beuverie *f*, soûlerie *f*; **to have a ~** prendre une cuite.

boozy *inf* ['buːzɪ] (*compar* **boozier**, *superl* **booziest**) *adj* [person] soûlard; [party, evening] de soûlographie.

bop [bɒp] (*pt* & *pp* **bopped**, *cont* **bopping**)
◇ *n* -**1.** [music] bop *m*. -**2.** *inf* [dance] danse *f*; **shall we have a ~?** on danse? -**3.** *inf* [punch] coup *m* de poing.
◇ *vt inf* [hit] cogner; **he bopped me on the nose!** il m'a allongé un marron sur le nez!
◇ *vi inf* [dance] danser le bop; **we bopped (away) all night** on a dansé toute la nuit.

bo-peep [bəʊ-] *n* cache-cache *m inv*.
◆ **Bo-Peep** *pr n*: **Little Bo-Peep** la petite bergère *(comptine)*.

Bora Bora [,bɔːrə'bɔːrə] *pr n* Bora Bora; **on ~** à Bora Bora.

borage ['bɒrɪdʒ] *n* bourrache *f*.

borax ['bɔːræks] *n* borax *m*.

Bordeaux [bɔː'dəʊ] ◇ *pr n* [region] le Bordelais; **an inhabitant of ~** un Bordelais, une Bordelaise.
◇ *n* [wine] bordeaux *m*.

bordello [bɔː'deləʊ] *n* lupanar *m*.

border ['bɔːdəʳ] ◇ *n* -**1.** [boundary] frontière *f*; **on the ~ between Norway and Sweden** à la frontière entre la Norvège et la Suède; **they live near the Scottish ~** ils habitent près de la frontière écossaise; **to cross the ~** passer la

frontière; they tried to escape over the ~ ils ont tenté de s'enfuir en passant la frontière. -**2.** [outer edge - of lake] bord *m*, rive *f*; [- of field] bordure *f*, limite *f*; [- of forest] lisière *f*, limite *f*. -**3.** [edging - of dress, handkerchief] bord *m*, bordure *f*; [- of plate, notepaper] liséré *m*. -**4.** [in garden] bordure *f*, plate-bande *f*.
◇ *comp* [state, post, guard] frontière *(inv)*; [town, zone] frontière *(inv)*, frontalier; [search] à la frontière; ~ **dispute** différend *m* frontalier; ~ **incident** incident *m* de frontière; ~ **patrol** patrouille *f* frontalière; ~ **police** police *f* des frontières.
◇ *vt* -**1.** [line edges of] border; [encircle] entourer, encadrer. -**2.** [be adjacent to] toucher; **Mexico ~s Texas** le Mexique touche OR a une frontière commune avec le Texas; **their garden is ~ed on two sides by open fields** sur deux côtés, leur jardin est entouré de champs à perte de vue.
◆ **Borders** *pl pr n Br*: the Borders *région frontalière du sud-est de l'Écosse*.
◆ **border on, border upon** *vt insep* -**1.** [be adjacent to] toucher, avoisiner; **my property ~s on his** ma propriété touche la sienne; **Italy and Austria ~ on each other** l'Italie et l'Autriche ont une frontière commune OR sont limitrophes. -**2.** [verge on] frôler, approcher de; **his remark ~s on slander** sa remarque frise la calomnie; **hysteria ~ing upon madness** une crise de nerfs proche de OR qui frôle la folie.

Border collie *n* colley *m* berger.

borderer [ˈbɔːdərəʳ] *n* frontalier *m*, -ère *f*; *Br* [in Scotland] Écossais *m* frontalier, Écossaise *f* frontalière; [in England] Anglais *m* frontalier, Anglaise *f* frontalière.

borderland [ˈbɔːdəlænd] *n* [country] pays *m* frontière; *literal* & *fig* [area] région *f* limitrophe; **the ~ between fantasy and reality** la frontière entre l'imagination et la réalité.

borderline [ˈbɔːdəlaɪn] ◇ *n* limite *f*, ligne *f* de démarcation; **to be on the ~** être à la limite; **the ~ between acceptable and unacceptable behaviour** ce qui sépare un comportement acceptable d'un comportement inacceptable.
◇ *adj* limite; **a ~ case** un cas limite; **he is a ~ candidate** il est à la limite.

Border terrier *n* terrier *m*.

bore [bɔːʳ] ◇ *pt* → **bear**.
◇ *vt* -**1.** [tire] ennuyer; **housework ~s me stiff** *inf* OR **to tears** *inf* OR **to death** *inf* faire le ménage m'ennuie à mourir; **he ~s the pants off me** *inf* il me barbe profondément. -**2.** [drill - hole] percer; [- well] forer, creuser; [- tunnel] creuser.
◇ *vi* forer, sonder; **they're boring for coal** ils forent pour extraire du charbon, ils recherchent du charbon par forage; **I felt his eyes boring into me** *fig* je sentais son regard me transpercer.
◇ *n* -**1.** [person] raseur *m*, -euse *f*; [event, thing] ennui *m*, corvée *f*; **what a ~ she is!** ce qu'elle peut être lassante OR fatigante!; **visiting them is such a ~!** quelle barbe de leur rendre visite!; **homework is a real ~!** quelle corvée, les devoirs! -**2.** [from drilling] trou *m* de sonde; MECH alésage *m*. -**3.** [diameter of gun, tube] calibre *m*; **a twelve-~ shotgun** un fusil de calibre douze. -**4.** [tidal flood] mascaret *m*.

bored [bɔːd] *adj* [person] qui s'ennuie; [expression] d'ennui; **to be ~ with doing sthg** s'ennuyer à faire qqch; **I'm ~ with my job** j'en ai assez de mon travail; **to be ~ stiff** *inf* OR **to tears** *inf* OR **to death** *inf* s'ennuyer ferme OR à mourir.

boredom [ˈbɔːdəm] *n* ennui *m*; **her ~ with city life** l'ennui que lui inspirait la vie citadine.

borehole [ˈbɔːhəʊl] *n* trou *m* de sonde.

borer [ˈbɔːrəʳ] *n* -**1.** [person] foreur *m*, perceur *m*; TECH [for wood] vrille *f*, foret *m*; [for metal] alésoir *m*; [for mine, well] foret, sonde *f*. -**2.** [insect] insecte *m* térébrant.

boric [ˈbɔːrɪk] *adj* borique.

boride [ˈbɔːraɪd] *n* borure *m*.

boring [ˈbɔːrɪŋ] ◇ *adj* -**1.** [tiresome] ennuyeux; [uninteresting] sans intérêt; **the meeting was so ~** cette réunion était assommante; **the street was an endless succession of ~ shops** la rue n'était qu'une longue succession de magasins sans intérêt. -**2.** TECH [for wood]: ~ **machine** perceuse *f*; [for metal] alésoir *m*.
◇ *n* TECH [in wood] perforation *f*, forage *m*; [in metal] alésage *m*; [in ground] forage *m*, sondage *m*.

boringly [ˈbɔːrɪŋlɪ] *adv* de manière ennuyeuse.

born [bɔːn] *adj* -**1.** *literal* né; **to be ~** naître; **she was ~ blind** elle est née aveugle; **the town where I was ~** la ville où je suis né, ma ville natale; **Victor Hugo was ~ in 1802** Victor Hugo est né en 1802; **two children were ~ to her** elle a mis au monde deux enfants; **~ of an American father** né d'un père américain; **a child ~ into this world** un enfant qui vient au monde; **~ and bred** né et élevé; **she was ~ and bred in Boston** c'est une Bostonienne de souche; **they were ~ to riches** ils sont nés riches; **she was ~ Elizabeth Hughes, but writes under the name E.R. Johnson** elle est née Elisabeth Hughes mais écrit sous le nom d'E.R. Johnson ‖ *fig*: **the place where communism was ~** le lieu où est né le communisme; **anger ~ of frustration** une colère née de OR due à la frustration ❑ **in all my ~ days** *inf* de toute ma vie; **I wasn't ~ yesterday!** *inf* je ne suis pas né d'hier OR de la dernière pluie!; **she was ~ with a silver spoon in her mouth** OR **~ lucky** elle est née coiffée; **there's one ~ every minute!** *inf* il y en a toujours un qui tombe dans le panneau! -**2.** [as intensifier]: **he's a ~ musician** il est né musicien, c'est un musicien né; **you're a ~ fool** tu es un parfait idiot; **she's a ~ worrier** elle s'inquiète à tout propos; **he's a ~ loser** il est né sous une mauvaise étoile.

-born *in cpds* originaire de; **he's New York~** il est né à New York, il est originaire de New York; **she's English~** elle est d'origine anglaise.

born-again *adj* RELIG & *fig* rené; ~ **Christian** chrétien *m* rené.

borne [bɔːn] *pp* → **bear**.

-borne *in cpds* transporté par; **water~ organisms** organismes *mpl* véhiculés par l'eau.

Bornean [ˈbɔːnɪən] ◇ *n habitant de Bornéo*.
◇ *adj* de Bornéo.

Borneo [ˈbɔːnɪəʊ] *pr n* Bornéo; **in ~** à Bornéo.

Borodin [ˈbɒrədɪn] *pr n* Borodine.

boron [ˈbɔːrɒn] *n* bore *m*.

borough [ˈbʌrə] *n* -**1.** [British town] *ville représentée à la Chambre des communes par un ou plusieurs députés*. -**2.** [in London] *une des 32 subdivisions administratives de Londres*. -**3.** [in New York] *une des 5 subdivisions administratives de New York*.

borough council *n conseil municipal d'un «borough»*.

borrow [ˈbɒrəʊ] *vt* -**1.** [gen & FIN] emprunter; **to ~ sthg from sb** emprunter qqch à qqn; **she ~ed money from him** elle lui a emprunté de l'argent; **an artist who ~s his ideas from nature** un artiste qui trouve ses idées dans la nature; **we often ~ books from the library** nous empruntons souvent des livres à la bibliothèque; **a word ~ed from Russian** un mot emprunté du russe ❑ **to live on ~ed time** avoir peu de temps à vivre. -**2.** *Br* MATH [in subtraction]: **I ~ one** je retiens un.

borrower [ˈbɒrəʊəʳ] *n* emprunteur *m*, -euse *f*; **neither a ~ nor a lender be** *prov* il ne faut ni emprunter ni prêter d'argent.

borrowing [ˈbɒrəʊɪŋ] *n* FIN & LING emprunt *m*; **the ~ rate** le taux d'intérêt des emprunts.

borsch [bɔːʃ], **borscht** [bɔːʃt] *n* bortsch *m*, borchtch *m*.

borstal [ˈbɔːstl] *n Br ancien nom d'une institution pour jeunes délinquants, aujourd'hui appelée «young offenders' institution»*.

borzoi [ˈbɔːzɔɪ] *n* (lévrier *m*) barzoï *m*.

Bosch [bɒʃ] *pr n*: **Hieronymus ~** Jérôme Bosch.

bosh *inf* [bɒʃ] *n (U) Br* bêtises *fpl*, âneries *fpl*.

bosk [bɒsk] *n lit* [wooded area] bosquet *m*; [thicket] fourré *m*.

Bosnia [ˈbɒznɪə] *pr n* Bosnie *f*; **in ~** en Bosnie.

Bosnia-Herzegovina [-ˌheətsəgəˈviːnə] *pr n* Bosnie-Herzégovine *f*.

Bosnian [ˈbɒznɪən] ◇ *n* Bosnien *m*, -enne *f*, Bosniaque *mf*.
◇ *adj* bosnien, bosniaque.

bosom [ˈbʊzəm] *n* -**1.** [of person] poitrine *f*; [of woman] seins *mpl*; *fig* & *lit*: **she took the child to her ~** elle prit l'enfant sous son aile; **he harboured in his ~ feelings of deep insecurity** il nourrissait en son sein un sentiment de profonde insécurité; **a ~ friend** un ami intime. -**2.** [of dress] corsage *m*. -**3.** *fig* [centre] sein *m*, fond *m*; **in the ~ of the community** au sein de la communauté.

-bosomed [ˈbʊzəmd] *in cpds*: **big/small~** qui a des gros/petits seins.

bosomy *inf* [ˈbʊzəmɪ] *adj* [woman] qui a une forte poitrine.

Bosporus [ˈbɒspərəs], **Bosphorus** [ˈbɒsfərəs] *pr n* Bosphore *m*; **in the ~** dans le Bosphore.

bosquet [ˈbɒskɪt] *n* fourré *m*.

boss [bɒs] ◇ *n* -**1.** *inf* [person in charge] patron *m*, -onne *f*, chef *m*; **who's the ~ around here?** qui est-ce qui commande ici?; **I'll show you who's ~!** je vais te montrer qui est le chef!; **she's the ~** c'est elle qui porte la culotte; **he enjoys being his own ~** il aime être son propre patron. -**2.** *inf* [of gang] caïd *m*; *Am* [politician] manitou *m* (du parti). -**3.** [knob] bossage *m*; [on shield] ombon *m*. -**4.** ARCHIT bossage *m*. -**5.** BIOL bosse *f*. -**6.** TECH mamelon *m*, bossage *m*; [of propeller] moyeu *m*.
◇ *vt inf* [person] commander, donner des ordres à; [organization] diriger, faire marcher.
◇ *adj inf Am dated* excellent, formidable; **the party was ~!** la soirée était sensass!
◆ **boss about** *inf Br*, **boss around** *inf vt sep* mener à la baguette; **stop ~ing me around!** j'en ai assez que vous me donniez des ordres!

boss-eyed *inf adj Br* qui louche; **she is ~** elle louche.

bossily *inf* [ˈbɒsɪlɪ] *adv* d'une manière autoritaire.

bossiness *inf* [ˈbɒsɪnɪs] *n* comportement *m* autoritaire.

bossy *inf* [ˈbɒsɪ] (*compar* **bossier**, *superl* **bossiest**) *adj* autoritaire, dictatorial; **he's too ~** il veut mener tout le monde à la baguette.

Boston [ˈbɒstn] *pr n* Boston.
◆ **boston** *n* -**1.** [card game] boston *m*. -**2.** [dance]: **to do the boston (two-step)** danser le boston, bostonner.

Bostonian [bɒˈstəʊnjən] ◇ *n* Bostonien *m*, -enne *f*.
◇ *adj* bostonien.

Boston Tea Party *pr n*: **the ~** la « Boston Tea Party ».

BOSTON TEA PARTY:
Insurrection en 1773 pendant laquelle les Bostoniens jetèrent des cargaisons de thé à la mer pour protester contre les droits de douane imposés par l'Angleterre; elle marque le point de départ de la guerre d'Indépendance des États-Unis.

---

bosun [ˈbəʊsn] = **boatswain**.

Bosworth Field [ˈbɒzwɜːθ-] *pr n*: **the Battle of ~** *bataille finale de la guerre des Deux-Roses, en 1485, à l'issue de laquelle Henry Tudor devint Henry VII d'Angleterre*.

botanic(al) [bəˈtænɪk(l)] *adj* botanique; **~ garden** jardin *m* botanique.

botanist [ˈbɒtənɪst] *n* botaniste *mf*.

botanize, -ise [ˈbɒtənaɪz] *vi* herboriser.

botany [ˈbɒtənɪ] *n* botanique *f*.

botany wool *n* laine *f* mérinos.

botch *inf* [bɒtʃ] ◇ *vt* [spoil] saboter, bâcler; [repair clumsily] rafistoler; **to make a ~ed job of sthg** *Br* bousiller qqch.
◇ *n*: **those workmen made a real ~** OR **~-up of the job** ces ouvriers ont fait un travail de cochon OR ont tout salopé.

botchy *inf* [ˌbɒtʃɪ] (*compar* botchier, *superl* botchiest) *adj* bâclé.

both [bəʊθ] ◇ *predet* les deux, l'un OR l'une et l'autre; ~ **dresses are pretty** les deux robes sont jolies; **on ~ sides of the road** des deux côtés de la route; **hold it in ~ hands** tenez-le à OR des deux mains ❑ **you can't have it ~ ways!** il faut te décider!
◇ *pron* tous (les) deux *mpl*, toutes (les) deux *fpl*; ~ **(of them) are coming** ils viennent tous les deux; ~ **are to blame** c'est leur faute à tous les deux; **why not do ~?** pourquoi ne pas faire les deux?; **from ~ of us** de notre part à tous les deux; **we ~ said yes** nous avons dit oui tous les deux; **you're ~ alike** vous êtes pareils tous les deux; ~ **you and I like to travel** nous aimons tous les deux voyager; **Claire and I ~ went** Claire et moi y sommes allés tous les deux.
◆ **both... and** *conj phr*: **her job is ~ interesting and well-paid** son travail est à la fois intéressant et bien payé; **I ~ read and write Spanish** je sais lire et écrire l'espagnol; ~ **the rich and the poor voted for him** les riches et les pauvres ont voté pour lui.

bother [ˈbɒðəʳ] ◇ *vi* prendre la peine; **don't ~ to answer the phone** ce n'est pas la peine de répondre au téléphone; **please don't ~ getting up!** ne vous donnez pas la peine de vous lever!; **don't ~ about me** ne vous en faites pas OR ne vous inquiétez pas pour moi; **let's not ~ with the housework** laissons tomber le ménage.
◇ *vt* -**1.** [irritate] ennuyer, embêter; [pester] harceler; **I'm sorry to ~ you** excusez-moi de vous déranger; **would it ~ you if I opened the window?** cela vous dérange OR ennuie si j'ouvre la fenêtre?; **don't ~ him when he's resting** laisse-le tranquille quand il se repose. -**2.** [worry] tracasser; **don't ~ yourself** OR **your head about it** ne vous tracassez pas à ce sujet; **it doesn't ~ me whether they come or not** cela m'est bien égal qu'ils viennent ou pas. -**3.** [hurt] faire souffrir; **his leg is ~ing him again** sa jambe le fait de nouveau souffrir.
◇ *n* -**1.** [trouble] ennui *m*; **to be in** OR **to have a spot of ~ (with sb)** *Br* avoir des ennuis (avec qqn); **he doesn't give her any ~** il ne la dérange pas; **the trip isn't worth the ~** le voyage ne vaut pas la peine; **I didn't go to the ~ of cooking a meal** je n'ai pas pris la peine de cuisiner un repas; **thanks for babysitting – it's no ~!** merci pour le babysitting – ça ne m'ennuie pas le moins du monde! -**2.** [nuisance] ennui *m*; **homework is such a ~!** quelle corvée, les devoirs!; **sorry to be a ~** excusez-moi de vous déranger.
◇ *interj inf Br* flûte, mince; ~ **the lot of them!** qu'ils aillent au diable!, qu'ils aillent se faire pendre ailleurs!

botheration *inf* [ˌbɒðəˈreɪʃn] *interj dated* flûte, mince.

bothered [ˈbɒðəd] *adj*: **to be ~ about sb/sthg** s'inquiéter de qqn/qqch; **I can't be ~ to write letters tonight** je n'ai pas le courage d'écrire des lettres ce soir; **he can't be ~ to do his own laundry** il a la flemme de laver son linge lui-même; **are you going out tonight? – no, I can't be ~** tu sors ce soir? – non, ça ne me dit rien; **I'm not ~** ça m'est égal.

bothersome [ˈbɒðəsəm] *adj* ennuyeux, gênant.

Bothnia [ˈbɒθnɪə] *pr n* → **gulf**.

Botswana [bɒˈtswɑːnə] *pr n* Botswana *m*; **in ~** au Botswana.

bottle [ˈbɒtl] ◇ *n* -**1.** [container, contents] bouteille *f*; [of perfume] flacon *m*; [of medicine] flacon *m*, fiole *f*; [jar] bocal *m*; [made of stone] cruche *f*, cruchon *m*; **a wine ~** une bouteille à vin; **we ordered a ~ of wine** nous avons commandé une bouteille de vin; **he drank (straight) from the ~** il a bu au goulot ‖ *fig*: **he was too fond of the ~** *inf* il levait bien le coude, il aimait la bouteille; **to hit the ~** *inf* picoler dur; **to take to the ~** *inf* se mettre à picoler; **they're on the ~** *inf* ils lèvent bien le coude; **to be off the ~** *inf* s'abstenir OR s'arrêter de boire. -**2.** [for baby] biberon *m*; **her baby is on the ~** son bébé est nourri au biberon. -**3.** *inf Br* [nerve]: **he lost his ~** il s'est dégonflé; **she's got a lot of ~** elle a un sacré cran.
◇ *vt* [wine] mettre en bouteille; [fruit] mettre en bocal OR conserve, conserver.
◆ **bottle out**▽ *vi insep Br* se dégonfler.
◆ **bottle up** *vt sep* -**1.** [emotions] refouler, ravaler. -**2.** [army] embouteiller, contenir.

bottle bank *n conteneur pour la collecte du verre usagé.*

bottlebrush [ˈbɒtlbrʌʃ] *n* rince-bouteilles *m inv*, goupillon *m*.

bottled [ˈbɒtld] *adj* en bouteille OR bouteilles; ~ **beer** bière *f* en bouteille OR bouteilles; ~ **gas** gaz *m* en bouteille OR bouteilles.

bottle-fed *adj* élevé OR allaité au biberon.

bottle-feed *vt* allaiter OR nourrir au biberon.

bottle glass *n* verre *m* à bouteilles, verre *m* vert.

bottle green *n* vert *m* bouteille.
◆ **bottle-green** *adj* vert bouteille *(inv)*.

bottleneck [ˈbɒtlnek] ◇ *n* [in road] rétrécissement *m* de la chaussée, étranglement *m*; [of traffic] embouteillage *m*, bouchon *m*; [in industry] goulet *m* OR goulot *m* d'étranglement.
◇ *vt Am*: **strikes have ~ed production** les grèves ont ralenti la production.

bottle opener *n* ouvre-bouteilles *m inv*, décapsuleur *m*.

bottle party *n Br soirée où chacun des invités apporte à boire.*

bottle rack *n* casier *m* à bouteilles.

bottom [ˈbɒtəm] ◇ *n* -**1.** [lowest part – of garment, heap] bas *m*; [– of water] fond *m*; [– of hill, stairs] bas *m*, pied *m*; [– of outside of container] bas *m*; [– of inside of container] fond *m*; [– of chair] siège *m*, fond *m*; [– of ship] carène *f*; **at the ~ of the staircase** au pied OR bas de l'escalier; **at the ~ of page one** au bas de la OR en bas de page un; **the ship sunk to the ~** le navire a coulé; **the ship touched (the) ~** le navire a touché le fond ‖ *fig*: **I believe, at the ~ of my heart, that...** je crois, au fond de moi-même, que...; **he thanked them from the ~ of his heart** il les a remerciés du fond du cœur; **my reasoning knocked the ~ out of his argument** mon raisonnement a démoli son argument; **the ~ fell out of the grain market** FIN le marché des grains s'est effondré; **the ~ dropped out of her world when he died** lorsqu'il est mort, pour elle le monde s'est effondré ❑ **~s up!** *inf* cul sec! -**2.** [last place]: **he's (at the) ~ of his class** il est le dernier de sa classe; **you're at the ~ of the list** vous êtes en queue de liste; **you have to start at the ~ and work your way up** vous devez commencer au plus bas et monter dans la hiérarchie à la force du poignet. -**3.** [far end] fond *m*, bas *m*; **at the ~ of the street/garden** au bout de la rue/du jardin. -**4.** *fig* [origin, source] base *f*, origine *f*; **I'm sure she's at the ~ of all this** je suis sûr que c'est elle qui est à l'origine de cette histoire; **I intend to get to the ~ of this affair** j'entends aller au fin fond de cette affaire OR découvrir le pot aux roses. -**5.** [buttocks] derrière *m*, fesses *fpl*. -**6.** [of two-piece garment] bas *m*; **pyjama ~s** bas de pyjama; **bikini ~** bas de maillot de bain.
◇ *adj* du bas, inférieur; **the ~ half of the chart** la partie inférieure du tableau; **the ~ half of the class/list** la deuxième moitié de la classe/liste; **the ~ floor** le rez-de-chaussée; **the ~ stair** [going up] la marche du bas, la première marche; [going down] la dernière marche; **the ~ end of the table** le bas de la table; **~ gear** *Br* AUT première *f* (vitesse *f*) ❑ **~ land** OR **lands** *Am* terre *f* OR plaine *f* alluviale; **~ round** *Am* CULIN gîte *m* à la noix.
◇ *vi* [ship] toucher le fond.
◆ **at bottom** *adv phr* au fond; **at ~, their motives are purely mercenary** au fond, leurs intentions sont purement intéressées.
◆ **bottom out** *vi insep* [prices] atteindre son niveau plancher; [recession] atteindre son plus bas niveau.

bottom drawer *n Br* armoire *f* à trousseau; **she's collecting things for her ~** elle réunit des choses pour son trousseau.

bottomless [ˈbɒtəmlɪs] *adj* sans fond, insondable; [unlimited – funds, supply] inépuisable.

bottom line *n* FIN résultat *m* financier; *fig*: **the ~** l'essentiel.

bottommost [ˈbɒtəmməʊst] *adj* le plus bas.

botulism [ˈbɒtjʊlɪzm] *n* botulisme *m*.

boudoir [ˈbuːdwɑːʳ] *n* boudoir *m*.

bouffant [ˈbuːfɔːŋ] *adj* [hairstyle] gonflant; [sleeve] bouffant.

Bougainville [ˈbuːgənvɪl] *pr n* Bougainville.

bougainvill(a)ea [ˌbuːgənˈvɪlɪə] *n* bougainvillée *f*, bougainvillier *m*.

bough [baʊ] *n lit* branche *f*.

bought [bɔːt] *pt* & *pp* → **buy**.

bouillon cube [ˈbuːjɒn] *n* tablette *f* pour bouillon.

boulder [ˈbəʊldəʳ] *n* bloc *m* de roche, boulder *m spec*; [smaller] gros galet *m*.

boulder clay *n* argile *f* à blocaux.

boulevard [ˈbuːləvɑːd] *n* boulevard *m*.

bounce [baʊns] ◇ *n* -**1.** [rebound] bond *m*, rebond *m*; **he caught the ball on the ~** il a pris la balle au bond. -**2.** [spring]: **there isn't much ~ in this ball** cette balle ne rebondit pas beaucoup; **I'd like to put some ~ in my hair** je voudrais donner du volume à mes cheveux; **he's still full of ~ at seventy** *fig* à soixante-dix ans il est encore plein d'énergie. -**3.** *inf Am* [dismissal]: **to give sb the ~** virer qqn; **he got the ~** il s'est fait virer.
◇ *vi* -**1.** [object] rebondir; **the ball ~d down the steps** la balle a rebondi de marche en marche; **the knapsack ~d up and down on his back** le sac à dos tressautait sur ses épaules; **the bicycle ~d along the bumpy path** le vélo faisait des bonds sur le chemin cahoteux. -**2.** [person] bondir, sauter; **we ~d up and down on the bed** nous faisions des bonds sur le lit; **she came bouncing into/out of the room** elle est entrée dans/sortie de la pièce d'un bond. -**3.** *inf* [cheque] être refusé pour non-provision; **I hope this cheque doesn't ~** j'espère que ce chèque n'est pas sans provision.
◇ *vt* -**1.** [cause to spring] faire rebondir; **she ~d the ball against** OR **off the wall** elle fit rebondir la balle sur le mur; **he ~d the baby on his knee** il a fait sauter l'enfant sur son genou; **signals are ~d off a satellite** les signaux sont renvoyés OR retransmis par satellite; **they ~d ideas off each other** *fig* leur échange de vues créait une émulation réciproque. -**2.** *inf* [cheque]: **the bank ~d my cheque** la banque a refusé mon chèque. -**3.** *inf* [throw out] flanquer à la porte, vider.
◆ **bounce back** *vi insep* se remettre rapidement; **she ~d right back after her illness** elle s'est vite rétablie après sa maladie.

bouncer *inf* [ˈbaʊnsəʳ] *n* videur *m*.

bouncing [ˈbaʊnsɪŋ] *adj* -**1.** [healthy] qui respire la santé; **a ~ baby** un bébé en pleine santé. -**2.** [ball] qui rebondit.

bouncy [ˈbaʊnsɪ] (*compar* bouncier, *superl* bounciest) *adj* -**1.** [ball, bed] élastique; [hair] souple, qui a du volume. -**2.** [person] plein d'entrain, dynamique.

bound [baʊnd] ◇ *pt* & *pp* → **bind**.
◇ *adj* -**1.** [certain] sûr, certain; **it was ~ to happen** c'était à prévoir; **but he's ~ to say that** mais il est certain que c'est cela qu'il va dire; **he's ~ to apologize** il ne va pas manquer de s'excuser ❑ **she's up to no good, I'll be ~** je parie qu'elle ne mijote rien de bon. -**2.** [compelled] obligé; **they are ~ by the treaty to take action** l'accord les oblige à prendre des mesures; **the teacher felt ~ to report them** l'enseignant s'est cru obligé de les dénoncer ❑ **I'm ~ to say I disagree** je dois dire que je ne suis pas d'accord. -**3.** [connected]: **~ up** lié; **his frustration is ~ up with his work** sa frustration est directement liée à son travail. -**4.** [heading towards] en route pour; **to be homeward ~** être sur le chemin du retour; **I'm ~ for Chicago** je

suis en route pour Chicago; **all shipments ~ for Madrid** toutes cargaisons à destination de Madrid; **the train is ~ for Rome** le train est à destination OR en direction de Rome; **on a plane ~ for Tokyo** dans un avion à destination de OR en route pour Tokyo. -**5.** [tied] lié; LING lié; **~ hand and foot** pieds et poings liés. -**6.** [book] relié; **~ in boards** cartonné.
◇ *n* -**1.** [leap] saut *m*, bond *m*; **in a single ~** d'un seul bond OR saut. -**2.** MATH: **lower ~** minorant *m*; **upper ~** majorant *m*.
◇ *vi* [person] sauter, bondir; [animal] faire un bond OR des bonds, bondir; **the children ~ed into/out of the classroom** les enfants sont entrés dans/sortis de la salle de classe en faisant des bonds; **the dog ~ed down the hill** le chien dévala la colline en bondissant.
◇ *vt* borner, limiter; **a country ~ed on two sides by the sea** un pays limité par la mer de deux côtés.
◆ **bounds** *npl* limite *f*, borne *f*; **the situation has gone beyond the ~s of all reason** la situation est devenue complètement aberrante OR insensée; **her rage knew no ~s** sa colère était sans bornes; **within the ~s of possibility** dans la limite du possible; **to keep within ~s** *fig* rester dans la juste mesure, pratiquer la modération □ **out of ~s** [gen] dont l'accès est interdit; SPORT hors du jeu; **the castle gardens are out of ~s to visitors** les jardins du château sont interdits au public.

-bound *in cpds* -**1.** [restricted] confiné; **house~** confiné à la maison; **snow~ road** route *f* complètement enneigée; **fog~ ship** navire *m* bloqué par le brouillard. -**2.** [heading towards]: **a south~ train** un train en partance pour le Sud; **city~ traffic** circulation *f* en direction du centre-ville.

boundary ['baʊndərɪ] (*pl* **boundaries**) *n* limite *f*, frontière *f*; **~ (line)** ligne *f* frontière; SPORT limites *fpl* du terrain; [in basketball] ligne *f* de touche; **to hit** OR **to score a ~** [in cricket] envoyer la balle jusqu'aux limites du terrain.

Boundary Commission *pr n* commission *f* de délimitation des frontières *(en Grande-Bretagne)*.

boundary stone *n* borne *f*, pierre *f* de bornage.

bounden ['baʊndən] *adj fml*: **~ duty** devoir *m* impérieux.

bounder *inf* ['baʊndə^r] *n Br dated* goujat *m*, malotru *m*.

boundless ['baʊndlɪs] *adj* [energy, wealth] illimité; [ambition, gratitude] sans bornes; [space] infini.

bounteous ['baʊntɪəs], **bountiful** ['baʊntɪfʊl] *adj lit* [person] généreux, libéral; [supply] abondant; [rain] bienfaisant.

bounty ['baʊntɪ] (*pl* **bounties**) *n* -**1.** *lit* [generosity] munificence *f*. -**2.** [gift] don *m*. -**3.** [reward] prime *f*.

bounty hunter *n* chasseur *m* de primes.

bouquet [bʊ'keɪ] *n* bouquet *m*; **to throw ~s at sb** *fig* faire des compliments à qqn.

bouquet garni [-gɑː'niː] *n* bouquet *m* garni.

bourbon ['bɜːbən] *n* [whisky] bourbon *m*.

Bourbon ['bʊəbən] ◇ *adj* Bourbon.
◇ *n* Bourbon *mf*.

bourbon biscuit ['bʊəbən-] *n Br biscuit au chocolat fourré de crème au chocolat.*

bourgeois ['bɔːʒwɑː] ◇ *n* bourgeois *m*, -e *f*.
◇ *adj* bourgeois.

bourgeoisie [ˌbɔːʒwɑː'ziː] *n* bourgeoisie *f*.

bourn [bɔːn] *n Br dial* ruisseau *m*.

bout [baʊt] *n* -**1.** [period] période *f*; **a ~ of drinking** une soûlerie, une beuverie. -**2.** [of illness] attaque *f*; [of fever] accès *m*; **a ~ of rheumatism** une crise de rhumatisme; **a ~ of bronchitis** une bronchite; **a ~ of flu** une grippe; **she's prone to frequent ~s of illness** elle est souvent malade. -**3.** [boxing, wrestling] combat *m*; [fencing] assaut *m*.

boutique [buː'tiːk] *n* [shop] boutique *f*; [in department store] rayon *m*.

bouzouki [bʊ'zuːkɪ] *n* bouzouki *m*.

bovid ['bəʊvɪd] *adj* de la famille des bovidés.

bovine ['bəʊvaɪn] ◇ *adj literal* & *fig* bovin.
◇ *n* bovin *m*.

bovver *inf* ['bɒvə^r] *n (U) Br dated* [fighting] bagarre *f*.

bovver boots *inf npl Br dated* brodequins *mpl*, rangers *mpl*.

bovver boy *inf n Br dated* loubard *m*.

bow[1] [baʊ] ◇ *vi* -**1.** [in greeting] incliner la tête, saluer; **I ~ed to him** je l'ai salué de la tête □ **he refuses to ~ and scrape to anyone** il refuse de faire des courbettes OR des salamalecs à qui que ce soit. -**2.** [bend] se courber; [under load] ployer. -**3.** *fig* [yield] s'incliner; **to ~ to the inevitable** s'incliner devant l'inévitable; **the government is ~ing under** OR **to pressure from the unions** l'administration s'incline sous la pression des syndicats; **I'll ~ to your greater knowledge** je m'incline devant tant de savoir OR de science.
◇ *vt* [bend] incliner, courber; [knee] fléchir; **to ~ one's head in shame** baisser la tête de honte; **to ~ one's head in prayer** incliner la tête pour prier; **his head was ~ed in contemplation** il méditait, la tête penchée.
◇ *n* -**1.** [gen] salut *m*; **he made her a deep** OR **low ~** il l'a saluée profondément OR bien bas; **to take a ~** saluer. -**2.** [of ship] avant *m*, proue *f*; **on the port/starboard ~** par bâbord/tribord avant. -**3.** [oarsman] nageur *m* de l'avant.
◆ **bow down** ◇ *vi insep* s'incliner; **he ~ed down to her** il s'est incliné devant elle.
◇ *vt sep* faire plier; *fig* écraser, briser.
◆ **bow out** *vi insep fig* tirer sa révérence.

bow[2] [bəʊ] ◇ *n* -**1.** [curve] arc *m*. -**2.** [for arrows] arc *m*; **he drew the ~** il a tiré à l'arc. -**3.** MUS [stick] archet *m*; [stroke] coup *m* d'archet. -**4.** [in ribbon] nœud *m*, boucle *f*; **tie it in a ~** faites un nœud.
◇ *vi* MUS manier l'archet.

Bow Bells [bəʊ-] *pl pr n cloches de l'église Saint-Mary-Le-Bow à Londres.*

BOW BELLS:
Selon la tradition, un «vrai Londonien» (un Cockney) doit être né à portée du son des cloches de l'église de Saint-Mary-Le-Bow.

---

bowdlerize, -ise ['baʊdləraɪz] *vt* expurger.

bowed [baʊd] *adj* -**1.** [legs] arqué. -**2.** [back] courbé; [head] baissé.

bowel ['baʊəl] *n (usu pl)* -**1.** ANAT [human] intestin *m*, intestins *mpl*; [animal] boyau *m*, boyaux *mpl*, intestins *mpl*; **a ~ disorder** troubles *mpl* intestinaux. -**2.** *fig*: **the ~s of the earth** les entrailles *fpl* de la terre.

bowel movement *n* selles *fpl*; **to have a ~** aller à la selle.

bower ['baʊə^r] *n* -**1.** [arbour] berceau *m* de verdure, charmille *f*. -**2.** *lit* [cottage] chaumière *f*; [boudoir] boudoir *m*.

Bow Group [bəʊ-] *pr n*: **the ~** *société influente de jeunes conservateurs britanniques.*

bowie knife ['bəʊɪ-] *n* couteau *m* de chasse.

bowing[1] ['baʊɪŋ] *n (U)* [greeting] saluts *mpl*; **~ and scraping** salamalecs *mpl*, courbettes *fpl*.

bowing[2] ['bəʊɪŋ] *n* MUS technique *f* d'archet; **his ~ is perfect** il a un coup d'archet parfait.

bowl [bəʊl] ◇ *n* -**1.** [receptacle] bol *m*; [larger] bassin *m*, cuvette *f*; [shallow] jatte *f*; [made of glass] coupe *f*; [for washing-up] cuvette *f*; [of beggar] sébile *f*; **a ~ of rice** un bol de riz ‖ [contents] bolée *f*; **the cat drank a ~ of milk** le chat a bu tout un bol de lait. -**2.** [rounded part - of spoon] creux *m*; [- of pipe] fourneau *m*; [- of wine glass] coupe *f*; [- of sink, toilet] cuvette *f*. -**3.** GEOG bassin *m*, cuvette *f*. -**4.** *Am* SPORT [arena] amphithéâtre *m*; [championship] championnat *m*, coupe *f*; [trophy] coupe *f*. -**5.** [ball] boule *f*; **(game of) ~s** *Br* (jeu *m* de) boules *fpl*; **let's play (a game of) ~s!** et si on jouait aux boules!
◇ *vi* -**1.** [play bowls] jouer aux boules; [play tenpin bowling] jouer au bowling; [in cricket] lancer (la balle); **he ~s for England** [cricket] il sert pour l'Angleterre; [bowls] il joue pour l'Angleterre. -**2.** [move quickly] filer, aller bon train; **the kids came ~ing down the street** les enfants descendaient la rue à toute allure; **the bus ~ed along the country lanes** l'autocar roulait à toute vitesse sur les petites routes de campagne.
◇ *vt* -**1.** [ball, bowl] lancer, faire rouler; [hoop] faire rouler. -**2.** SPORT [score]: **I ~ed 160** j'ai marqué 160 points ‖ [in cricket]: **to ~ the ball** servir; **he ~ed (out) the batsman** il a mis le batteur hors jeu.
◆ **bowl down** *inf vt sep* renverser.
◆ **bowl out** *vt sep* [in cricket] mettre hors jeu.
◆ **bowl over** *vt sep* -**1.** [knock down] renverser, faire tomber. -**2.** *inf fig* [amaze] stupéfier, sidérer; **I was ~ed over by the news** la nouvelle m'a abasourdi; **our success really ~ed them over** notre réussite les a renversés.

bow-legged [bəʊ-] *adj* à jambes arquées.

bow legs [bəʊ-] *npl* jambes *fpl* arquées.

bowler ['bəʊlə^r] *n* SPORT [in bowls] joueur *m*, -euse *f* de boules OR pétanque, bouliste *mf*; [in tenpin bowling] joueur *m*, -euse *f* de bowling; [in cricket] lanceur *m*, -euse *f*.

bowler (hat) *n Br* (chapeau *m*) melon *m*.

bowlful ['bəʊlfʊl] *n* bolée *f*; **a ~ of water** une cuvette d'eau.

bowline ['bəʊlɪn] *n* [rope] bouline *f*; [knot] nœud *m* de chaise.

bowling ['bəʊlɪŋ] *n* [bowls] jeu *m* de boules, pétanque *f*; [tenpin] bowling *m*; [in cricket] service *m*; **to go ~** [bowls] (aller) jouer à la pétanque; [tenpin bowling] (aller) faire du bowling.

bowling alley *n* bowling *m*.

bowling green *n* terrain *m* de boules *(sur gazon)*.

bowman[1] ['bəʊmən] (*pl* **bowmen** [-mən]) *n lit* [archer] archer *m*.

bowman[2] ['baʊmən] (*pl* **bowmen** [-mən]) *n* NAUT nageur *m* de l'avant.

bowsprit ['bəʊsprɪt] *n* beaupré *m*.

bowstring ['bəʊstrɪŋ] *n* corde *f*.

bow tie [bəʊ-] *n* nœud *m* papillon.

bow window [bəʊ-] *n Br* fenêtre *f* en saillie, oriel *m*, bow-window *m*.

bow-wow [ˌbaʊ'waʊ] ◇ *n* toutou *m*.
◇ *onomat* ouâ ouâ.

box [bɒks] (*pl* **boxes**) ◇ *n* -**1.** [container, contents] boîte *f*; [with lock] coffret *m*; [crate] caisse *f*; [for money] caisse *f*; [collecting box] tronc *m*; **~ of chocolates** boîte *f* de chocolats; **how can people live in these little ~es?** *fig* comment les gens font-ils pour vivre dans ces trous de souris? □ **(cardboard) ~** (boîte en) carton *m*. -**2.** [compartment] compartiment *m*; THEAT loge *f*, baignoire *f*; JUR [for jury, reporters] banc *m*; [for witness] barre *f*; [in stable] box *m*; [of coachman] siège *m* (de cocher); **the Royal ~** *loge réservée aux membres de la famille royale.* -**3.** [designated area - on form] case *f*; [- in newspaper] encadré *m*; [- on road, sportsfield] zone *f* quadrillée. -**4.** AUT & TECH [casing] boîte *f*, carter *m*. -**5.** *inf* [television] téléviseur *m*; **what's on the ~?** qu'y a-t-il à la télé? -**6.** [postal address] boîte *f* postale. -**7.** [blow]: **a ~ on the ears** une gifle, une claque. -**8.** SPORT [protector] coquille *f*. -**9.** BOT buis *m*.
◇ *comp* [border, hedge] de OR en buis.
◇ *vi* [fight] faire de la boxe, boxer.
◇ *vt* -**1.** [fight] boxer avec, boxer. -**2.** *phr*: **to ~ sb's ears** gifler qqn; **she ~ed his ears** elle l'a giflé. -**3.** [put in box] mettre en boîte OR caisse. -**4.** NAUT: **to ~ the compass** réciter les aires du vent.
◆ **box in** *vt sep* [enclose] enfermer, confiner; [pipes] encastrer; **the car was ~ed in between two vans** la voiture était coincée entre deux camionnettes; **to feel ~ed in** se sentir à l'étroit; **don't ~ me in!** de l'air!
◆ **box off** *vt sep* compartimenter, cloisonner.
◆ **box up** *vt sep* mettre en boîte OR caisse; *fig* enfermer.

boxboard ['bɒksbɔːd] *n* carton *m* compact.

box calf *n* box *m*, box-calf *m*.

box camera *n* appareil *m* photographique rudimentaire.

boxcar ['bɒkskɑːʳ] *n Am* wagon *m* de marchandises (couvert).

boxed [bɒkst] *adj* COMM en boîte; a ~ set un coffret.

box end wrench *n Am* clef *f* polygonale.

boxer ['bɒksəʳ] *n* [fighter] boxeur *m*; [dog] boxer *m*.

boxer shorts *npl* boxer-short *m*.

box girder *n* poutre-caisson *f*.

boxing ['bɒksɪŋ] *n* boxe *f*.

Boxing Day *n Br le 26 décembre*.

boxing glove *n* gant *m* de boxe.

boxing ring *n* ring *m*.

box junction *n Br* carrefour *m (matérialisé sur la chaussée par des bandes croisées)*.

box kite *n* cerf-volant *m* cellulaire.

box number *n* [in newspaper] numéro *m* d'annonce; [at post office] numéro *m* de boîte à lettres.

box office *n* [office] bureau *m* de location; [window] guichet *m* (de location); the play was a big success at the ~ la pièce a fait recette.
◆ **box-office** *comp*: to be a box-office success être en tête du box-office.

box pleat *n* pli *m* creux.

boxroom ['bɒksrʊm] *n Br* débarras *m*, capharnaüm *m*.

box spanner *n* clef *f* OR clé *f* en douille.

box spring *n* sommier *m* à ressorts.

box stall *n Am* box *m*.

boxwood ['bɒkswʊd] *n* buis *m*.

boy [bɔɪ] ◇ *n* -**1.** [male child] garçon *m*, enfant *m*; a little ~ un petit garçon, un garçonnet; when I was a ~ quand j'étais petit OR jeune; be a good ~! sois sage!; you bad ~! vilain!; an Italian ~ un petit OR jeune Italien; the Smiths' ~ le petit Smith; sit down, my ~ assieds-toi, mon petit OR mon grand; I've known them since they were ~s je les connais depuis leur enfance OR depuis qu'ils sont petits; ~s will be ~s un garçon, c'est un garçon; he's just a ~ when it comes to women *fig* ce n'est encore qu'un gamin quand il s'agit des femmes || [son] garçon *m*, fils *m*; he's a mother's ~ c'est le petit garçon à sa maman. -**2.** *Br* SCH [student] élève *m*; day ~ externe *m*. -**3.** *inf* [term of address]: that's my ~! je te reconnais bien là!; my dear ~ mon cher ami; how are you, old ~? *Br* ça va mon vieux?; he likes to think he's one of the ~s il aime à croire qu'il fait partie de la bande; a local ~ un gars du coin; come on, ~s! allons-y les gars!; a night out with the ~s une virée entre copains ❑ the ~s in blue *inf* les flics *mpl*; the backroom ~s ceux qui restent dans les coulisses. -**4.** *offensive* [native servant] boy *m*. -**5.** [to dog, horse etc] mon beau *m*; down, ~! couché, mon beau!
◇ *interj*: (oh) ~! dis donc!

boycott ['bɔɪkɒt] ◇ *n* boycottage *m*, boycott *m*.
◇ *vt* boycotter.

boyfriend ['bɔɪfrend] *n* petit ami *m*.

boyhood ['bɔɪhʊd] *n* enfance *f*.

boyish ['bɔɪɪʃ] *adj* -**1.** [youthful] d'enfant, de garçon; [childish] enfantin, puéril. -**2.** [tomboyish - girl] garçonnier; [- behaviour] garçonnier, de garçon.

boy-meets-girl *adj*: a ~ story une histoire d'amour conventionnelle.

Boys' Brigade *pr n organisation protestante de scoutisme pour garçons*.

boy scout *n* scout *m*.

bozo *inf* ['bəʊzəʊ] *n pej* type *m*.

Bp (*written abbr of* bishop) Mgr.

bpi (*written abbr of* bits per inch) bits par pouce.

bps (*written abbr of* bits per second) bits par seconde.

Br -**1.** *written abbr of* British. -**2.** [preceding name of monk] (*written abbr of* brother) F.

BR (*abbr of* British Rail) *pr n société des chemins de fer britanniques*.

bra [brɑː] *n* soutien-gorge *m*; half-cup ~ Balconnet® *m*; underwired ~ soutien-gorge avec armature.

Brabant [brə'bænt] *pr n* Brabant *m*; in ~ dans le Brabant.

brace [breɪs] (*pl senses 1, 2, 3, 4 and 6* braces, *pl sense 5 inv*) ◇ *vt* -**1.** [strengthen] renforcer, consolider; [support] soutenir; CONSTR entretoiser; [beam] armer; to ~ a beam with sthg armer une poutre de qqch. -**2.** [steady, prepare]: he ~d his body/himself for the impact il raidit son corps/s'arc-bouta en préparation du choc; he ~d himself to try again il a rassemblé ses forces pour une nouvelle tentative; the family ~d itself for the funeral la famille s'est armée de courage pour les funérailles; ~ yourself for some bad news préparez-vous à de mauvaises nouvelles. -**3.** [subj: weather] fortifier, tonifier.
◇ *n* -**1.** [supporting or fastening device] attache *f*, agrafe *f*. -**2.** MED appareil *m* orthopédique; [for teeth] appareil *m* dentaire OR orthodontique. -**3.** CONSTR entretoise *f*. -**4.** TECH [drill]: ~ (and bit) vilebrequin *m* à main. -**5.** [of game birds, pistols] paire *f*. -**6.** MUS & TYPO [bracket] accolade *f*.
◆ **braces** *npl* -**1.** *Br* [for trousers] bretelles *fpl*. -**2.** MED [for teeth] = **brace 2**.

bracelet ['breɪslɪt] *n* bracelet *m*.
◆ **bracelets** *inf npl crime sl* [handcuffs] menottes *fpl*, bracelets *mpl arg crime*.

bracer *inf* ['breɪsəʳ] *n* remontant *m*.

brachiosaurus [,breɪkɪə'sɔːrəs] (*pl* brachiosauruses OR brachiosauri [-raɪ]) *n* brachiosaure *m*.

brachylogy [bræ'kɪlədʒɪ] (*pl* brachylogies) *n* brachylogie *f*.

bracing ['breɪsɪŋ] ◇ *adj* fortifiant, tonifiant; a ~ wind un vent vivifiant.
◇ *n* CONSTR entretoisement *m*.

bracken ['brækn] *n* fougère *f*.

bracket ['brækɪt] ◇ *n* -**1.** [L-shaped support] équerre *f*, support *m*; [for shelf] équerre *f*, tasseau *m*; [lamp fixture] fixation *f*; ARCHIT console *f*, corbeau *m*. -**2.** [category] groupe *m*, classe *f*; the 20-25 age ~ le groupe des 20-25 ans; the high/low income ~ la tranche des gros/petits revenus; my rise put me in the £20,000 a year ~ mon augmentation de salaire m'a placé dans la tranche (de revenus) des 20 000 livres annuelles. -**3.** MATH & TYPO [parenthesis] parenthèse *f*; [square] crochet *m*; in OR between ~s entre parenthèses; (brace) ~ MUS & TYPO accolade *f*.
◇ *vt* -**1.** [put in parentheses] mettre entre parenthèses; [put in square brackets] mettre entre crochets. -**2.** [link by brackets] réunir par une accolade. -**3.** *fig* [categorize] associer, mettre dans la même catégorie; he is often ~ed with the Surrealists on le range souvent parmi les surréalistes; why ~ together two such different companies? pourquoi mettre deux entreprises aussi différentes dans la même catégorie?

brackish ['brækɪʃ] *adj* saumâtre.

bract [brækt] *n* BOT bractée *f*.

brad [bræd] *n* semence *f*, clou *m* de tapissier.

bradawl ['brædɔːl] *n* poinçon *m*.

brae [breɪ] *n Scot* [hillside] colline *f*; [slope] pente *f*, côte *f*.

brag [bræg] (*pt & pp* bragged, *cont* bragging) ◇ *vi & vt* se vanter; he's always bragging about his salary il faut toujours qu'il se vante de son salaire; it's nothing to ~ about il n'y a pas là de quoi se vanter.
◇ *n* -**1.** [boasting] vantardise *f*, fanfaronnades *fpl*. -**2.** [person] = **braggart**. -**3.** [card game] *jeu de cartes qui ressemble au poker*.

braggart ['brægət] *n* vantard *m*, -e *f*, fanfaron *m*, -onne *f*.

Brahma ['brɑːmə] *pr n* Brahma.

Brahman ['brɑːmən] *n* [person] brahmane *m*.

Brahmanism ['brɑːmənɪzm] *n* brahmanisme *m*.

Brahmaputra [,brɑːmə'puːtrə] *pr n*: the ~ le Brahmapoutre.

Brahmin ['brɑːmɪn] (*pl inv* OR Brahmins) *n* -**1.** = **Brahman**. -**2.** *inf Am* intellectuel *m*, -elle *f*; she's a Boston ~ elle est d'une vieille famille bostonienne.

Brahminism ['brɑːmɪnɪzm] = **Brahmanism**.

braid [breɪd] ◇ *n* -**1.** [trimming] ganse *f*, soutache *f*; [on uniform] galon *m*. -**2.** [of hair] tresse *f*, natte *f*.
◇ *vt* -**1.** [plait] tresser, natter. -**2.** [decorate with] soutacher, galonner.

braided ['breɪdɪd] *adj* [clothing] passementé; [hair] tressé.

braille, Braille [breɪl] ◇ *adj* braille.
◇ *n* braille *m*.

brailled [breɪld] *adj* [switches, instructions] en braille.

brain [breɪn] ◇ *n* -**1.** ANAT cerveau *m*; [mind] cerveau *m*, tête *f*; CULIN cervelle. -**2.** *inf fig*: we're going to beat his ~s out on va lui casser la figure; to blow one's ~s out se faire sauter la cervelle ❑ you've got money on the ~ tu es obsédé par l'argent; she's got it on the ~ elle ne pense qu'à ça, ça la tient. -**3.** [intelligence] intelligence *f*; he's got ~s il est intelligent; you need a good ~ to solve this puzzle il faut être intelligent pour résoudre ce problème ❑ to pick sb's ~s: can I pick your ~s for a minute? j'ai besoin de tes lumières; Brain of Britain *jeu radiophonique britannique portant sur des questions de culture générale*. -**4.** *inf* [clever person] = **brains**.
◇ *comp* [damage, disease, surgery, tumour] cérébral; ~ surgeon chirurgien *m* du cerveau.
◇ *vt inf* [hit] assommer.
◆ **brains** *inf n* [clever person]: the ~s le cerveau; she's the ~s of the family c'est elle le cerveau de la famille; who's the ~s behind the scheme? [master planner] qui est le cerveau de l'affaire?

brainbox *inf* ['breɪnbɒks] *n* [skull] crâne *m*; [person] cerveau *m*.

brainchild *inf* ['breɪn,tʃaɪld] (*pl* brainchildren [-,tʃɪldrən]) *n* idée *f* personnelle; the scheme is his ~ le projet est son invention personnelle.

brain dead *adj* dans un coma dépassé he's ~ *inf pej* il n'a rien dans le cerveau.

brain death *n* mort *f* cérébrale.

brain drain *n* fuite *f* OR exode *m* des cerveaux.

brainless ['breɪnlɪs] *adj* [person] écervelé, stupide; [idea] stupide.

brainpower ['breɪn,paʊəʳ] *n* intelligence *f*.

brainstorm ['breɪnstɔːm] ◇ *n* -**1.** MED congestion *f* cérébrale. -**2.** *inf Br fig* [mental aberration] idée *f* insensée OR loufoque. -**3.** *inf Am fig* [brilliant idea] idée *f* géniale.
◇ *vi* faire du brainstorming.
◇ *vt* plancher sur.

brainstorming ['breɪn,stɔːmɪŋ] *n* brainstorming *m*, remue-méninges *m inv*.

brains trust *n Br* [panel of experts] groupe *m* d'experts.

brainteaser *inf* ['breɪn,tiːzəʳ] *n* problème *m* difficile, colle *f*.

brain trust *n Am* [advisory panel] brain-trust *m*.

brainwash ['breɪnwɒʃ] *vt* faire un lavage de cerveau à; advertisements can ~ people into believing anything la publicité peut faire croire n'importe quoi aux gens.

brainwashing ['breɪnwɒʃɪŋ] *n* lavage *m* de cerveau.

brainwave ['breɪnweɪv] *n* -**1.** MED onde *f* cérébrale. -**2.** *inf* [brilliant idea] inspiration *f*, idée *f* OR trait *m* de génie; I've had a ~! j'ai eu un éclair de génie!

brainy *inf* ['breɪnɪ] (*compar* brainier, *superl* brainiest) *adj* intelligent, futé.

braise [breɪz] *vt* braiser.

braising beef ['breɪzɪŋ-] *n* bœuf *m* à braiser.

brake [breɪk] ◇ *n* -**1.** [gen & AUT] frein *m*; to put on OR to apply the ~s freiner; release the ~ desserrez le frein || *fig*: bad weather has put a ~ on construction work le mauvais temps a mis un frein à la construction; high interest rates acted as a ~ on borrowing des taux d'intérêt élevés ont freiné les emprunts. -**2.** [carriage] break *m*. -**3.** [bracken] fougère *f*; [thicket] fourré *m*.

◇ *vi* freiner, mettre le frein.
◇ *comp* [cable, pedal] de frein.
brake block *n* sabot *m* OR patin *m* de frein.
brake drum *n* tambour *m* de frein.
brake fluid *n* liquide *m* de freins, Lockheed® *m*.
brake horsepower *n* puissance *f* au frein.
brake lever *n* frein *m* à main.
brake light *n* feu *m* de stop.
brake lining *n* garniture *f* de frein.
brakeman ['breɪkmən] (*pl* brakemen [-mən]) *n Am* RAIL garde-frein *m*.
brake parachute *n* parachute *m* de freinage.
brake shoe *n* mâchoire *f* de frein.
brakesman ['breɪksmən] (*pl* brakesmen [-mən]) *n* machiniste *m* OR mécanicien *m* d'extraction.
brake van *n Br* RAIL fourgon *m* à frein.
braking ['breɪkɪŋ] *n* freinage *m*; ~ distance distance *f* de freinage.
bramble ['bræmbl] *n* -**1.** [prickly shrub] roncier *m*, roncière *f*. -**2.** [blackberry bush] ronce *f* des haies, mûrier *m* sauvage; I fell among the ~s je suis tombé dans les ronces || [berry] mûre *f* sauvage.
brambly ['bræmblɪ] *adj* couvert de ronces.
bran [bræn] *n* son *m* (de blé), bran *m*.
branch [brɑːntʃ] ◇ *n* -**1.** [of tree] branche *f*. -**2.** [secondary part - of road] embranchement *m*; [- of river] branche *f*, bras *m*; [- of railway] bifurcation *f*, raccordement *m*; [- of pipe] branchement *m*. -**3.** [division - gen] division *f*, section *f*; [- of family] ramification *f*, branche *f*; [- of science] branche *f*; [- of police force] antenne *f*; [- of government, civil service] service *m*; LING rameau *m*. -**4.** COMM [of company] succursale *f*, filiale *f*; [of bank] agence *f*, succursale *f*; ~ manager [of bank] directeur *m*, -trice *f* d'agence. -**5.** COMPUT branchement *m*. -**6.** *Am* [stream] ruisseau *m*; ~ water *inf* eau *f* plate.
◇ *vi* -**1.** [tree] se ramifier. -**2.** [road, river] bifurquer.
◆ **branch off** *vi insep* -**1.** [road] bifurquer; a smaller path ~es off to the left un chemin plus petit bifurque vers la gauche. -**2.** [digress]: I'd like to ~ off from my main topic for a moment j'aimerais m'écarter un instant du sujet qui m'occupe.
◆ **branch out** *vi insep* étendre ses activités; they're ~ing out into the restaurant business ils étendent leurs activités à OR se lancent dans la restauration.
branch line *n* ligne *f* secondaire.
branch office *n* [of company] succursale *f*; [of bank] agence *f*, succursale *f*.
brand [brænd] ◇ *n* -**1.** COMM [trademark] marque *f* (de fabrique); he always buys the same ~ of cigars il achète toujours la même marque de cigares; he has his own ~ of humour *fig* il a un sens de l'humour particulier. -**2.** [identifying mark - on cattle] marque *f*; [- on prisoners] flétrissure *f*. -**3.** [branding iron] fer *m* à marquer. -**4.** [burning wood] tison *m*, brandon *m*; *lit* [torch] flambeau *m*.
◇ *vt* -**1.** [cattle] marquer (au fer rouge). -**2.** *fig* [label] étiqueter, stigmatiser; she was ~ed (as) a thief on lui a collé une étiquette de voleuse. -**3.** [impress indelibly]: the experience was ~ed on his memory for life l'expérience resta à jamais gravée dans sa mémoire.
branded ['brændɪd] *adj*: ~ goods produits *mpl* de marque.
Brandenburg ['brændənbɜːg] *pr n* Brandebourg; 'The ~ Concertos' *Bach* 'les Concertos brandebourgeois'.
Brandenburg Gate *pr n*: the ~ la Porte de Brandebourg.
brand image *n* image *f* de marque.
branding iron ['brændɪŋ-] *n* fer *m* à marquer.
brandish ['brændɪʃ] ◇ *vt* brandir.
◇ *n* brandissement *m*.
brand name *n* marque *f* (de fabrique).
brand-new *adj* tout OR flambant neuf.

Brand's Hatch *pr n circuit de courses automobiles en Angleterre*.
brandy ['brændɪ] (*pl* brandies) *n* [made from grapes] ≃ cognac *m*; ~ and soda brandy and soda *m* || [made of fruit] eau-de-vie *f*; cherry ~ cherry *m*.
brandy butter *n Br beurre mélangé avec du sucre et parfumé au cognac*.
brandy snap *n Br* galette *f* au gingembre.
bran loaf (*pl* loaves) *n* pain *m* au son.
bran mash *n Br* son *m* OR bran *m* mouillé.
bran tub *n Br* pêche *f* miraculeuse *(jeu)*.
brash [bræʃ] *adj* -**1.** [showy] impétueux, casse-cou *(inv)*; [impudent] effronté, impertinent. -**2.** [colour] criard.
Brasilia [brə'zɪljə] *pr n* Brasilia.
brass [brɑːs] ◇ *n* -**1.** [metal] cuivre *m* (jaune), laiton *m*; the ~ is cleaned OR done once a week les cuivres sont faits OR astiqués une fois par semaine; ~ foundry fonderie *f* de cuivre. -**2.** *Br* [memorial] plaque *f* mortuaire (en cuivre). -**3.** MUS: the ~ les cuivres *mpl*. -**4.** *inf Br* [nerve] toupet *m*, culot *m*; he had the ~ to accuse me of cheating il a eu le toupet de m'accuser de tricher. -**5.** *inf Br dial* [money] pognon *m*.
◇ *comp* [object, ornament] de OR en cuivre; I don't know how you have the ~ neck to say that! *Br* je ne sais pas comment tu peux avoir le culot de dire une chose pareille!; to get down to ~ tacks en venir au fait OR aux choses sérieuses.
brass band *n* fanfare *f*, orchestre *m* de cuivres.
brass-collar *adj Am* POL qui soutient sans faille la ligne du parti, inconditionnel.
brassed off *inf* [brɑːst-] *adj Br*: I'm ~ with waiting j'en ai marre d'attendre; I'm ~ with their complaints j'en ai plein le dos de leurs récriminations.
brasserie ['bræsərɪ] *n* brasserie *f*.
brass farthing *n Br*: it's not worth a ~ *inf* ça ne vaut pas un clou.
brass hat *inf n Br* gros bonnet *m*.
brassie ['brɑːsɪ] *n* brassie *m*.
brassiere [*Br* 'bræsɪəʳ, *Am* brə'zɪr] *n* soutien-gorge *m*.
brass knuckles *npl Am* coup-de-poing *m* américain.
brass-monkey▽ *adj Br*: it's ~ weather on se les gèle, on se les caille.
brass rubbing *n* [picture] décalque *m*; [action] décalquage *m* par frottement.
brassware ['brɑːsweəʳ] *n* [utensils] chaudronnerie *f* d'art.
brasswork ['brɑːswɜːk] *n* dinanderie *f*.
brassy ['brɑːsɪ] (*compar* brassier, *superl* brassiest, *pl* brassies) ◇ *adj* -**1.** [colour] cuivré; [sound] cuivré, claironnant. -**2.** *inf* [brazen] effronté, impertinent.
◇ *n* = **brassie**.
brat [bræt] *n pej* gosse *mf*, galopin *m*; that kid is a real ~ un vrai morveux, ce gamin; she brought her ~s elle a amené sa marmaille.
bravado [brə'vɑːdəʊ] *n* bravade *f*.
brave [breɪv] ◇ *adj* -**1.** [courageous] courageux, brave; be ~! sois courageux!, du courage!; you'll have to be ~ and tell him tu vas devoir prendre ton courage à deux mains et le lui dire; to put on a ~ face, to put a ~ face on it faire bonne contenance. -**2.** *lit* [splendid] beau, excellent; a ~ new world une utopie, un monde OR une société utopique ❑ 'Brave New World' *Huxley* 'le Meilleur des mondes'.
◇ *vt* [person] braver, défier; [danger, bad weather] braver, affronter.
◇ *npl* [people]: the ~ les courageux *mpl*; the bravest of the ~ les plus braves d'entre les braves.
◇ *n* [Indian warrior] brave *m*, guerrier *m* indien.
◆ **brave out** *vt sep* faire face à; we'll just have to ~ it out! nous devrons tout simplement faire face à la situation!
bravely ['breɪvlɪ] *adv* courageusement, bravement.
bravery ['breɪvərɪ] *n* courage *m*, vaillance *f*.

bravo [,brɑː'vəʊ] (*pl* bravos) ◇ *interj* bravo.
◇ *n* bravo *m*.
bravura [brə'vʊərə] *n* [gen & MUS] bravoure *f*.
brawl [brɔːl] ◇ *n* -**1.** [fight] bagarre *f*, rixe *f*; a drunken ~ une querelle d'ivrognes. -**2.** *inf Am* [party] java *f*.
◇ *vi* se bagarrer.
brawn [brɔːn] *n (U)* -**1.** [muscle] muscles *mpl*; [strength] muscle *m*; all ~ and no brains tout dans les bras et rien dans la tête. -**2.** *Br* CULIN fromage *m* de tête.
brawny ['brɔːnɪ] (*compar* brawnier, *superl* brawniest) *adj* [arm] musculeux; [person] musclé.
bray [breɪ] ◇ *vi* [donkey] braire; *pej* [person] brailler; [trumpet] beugler, retentir.
◇ *n* [of donkey] braiement *m*; *pej* [of person] braillement *m*; [of trumpet] beuglement *m*, bruit *m* strident.
braze [breɪz] *vt* braser, souder (au laiton).
brazen ['breɪzn] *adj* -**1.** [bold] effronté, impudent; a ~ lie un mensonge audacieux OR effronté. -**2.** [brass] de cuivre (jaune), de laiton; [sound] cuivré.
◆ **brazen out** *vt sep*: you always have to ~ it out il faut toujours que tu t'en tires par des fanfaronnades.
brazen-faced *adj* effronté, impudent.
brazenly ['breɪznlɪ] *adv* effrontément, impudemment.
brazier ['breɪzjəʳ] *n* -**1.** [for fire] brasero *m*. -**2.** [brass worker] chaudronnier *m*.
brazil [brə'zɪl] *n*: ~ (nut) noix *f* du Brézil.
Brazil [brə'zɪl] *pr n* Brésil *m*; in ~ au Brésil.
Brazilian [brə'zɪljən] ◇ *n* Brésilien *m*, -enne *f*.
◇ *adj* brésilien.
breach [briːtʃ] ◇ *n* -**1.** [gap] brèche *f*, trou *m*; our troops made a ~ in the enemy lines nos troupes ont percé les lignes ennemies; she stepped into the ~ when I fell ill *fig* elle m'a remplacé au pied levé quand je suis tombé malade. -**2.** [violation - of law] violation *f*; [- of discipline, order, rules] infraction *f*; [- of etiquette, friendship] manquement *m*; a ~ of confidence un abus de confiance; a ~ of discipline une infraction OR un manquement à la discipline; a ~ of faith [gen] un manque de foi; JUR un acte de déloyauté; ~ of privilege POL atteinte *f* aux privilèges parlementaires; ~ of professional secrecy violation du secret professionnel; ~ of contract rupture *f* de contrat; ~ of the peace JUR atteinte *f* à l'ordre public; ~ of promise [gen] manque de parole; [of marriage] violation *f* de promesse de mariage; ~ of trust abus *m* de confiance. -**3.** [rift] brouille *f*, désaccord *m*. -**4.** [of whale] saut *m*.
◇ *vt* -**1.** [make gap in] ouvrir une brèche dans, faire un trou dans; we ~ed the enemy lines nous avons percé les lignes ennemies. -**2.** [agreement] violer, rompre; [promise] manquer à.
◇ *vi* [whale] sauter hors de l'eau.
bread [bred] *n (U)* -**1.** [food] pain *m*; a loaf of ~ un pain, une miche; freshly baked ~ du pain frais; ~ and butter du pain beurré; a slice of ~ and butter une tartine (beurrée); they put the prisoner on ~ and water ils ont mis le prisonnier au pain sec et à l'eau ❑ the ~ and wine RELIG les espèces *fpl*; to earn one's daily ~ gagner sa vie OR sa croûte; translation is her ~ and butter la traduction est son gagne-pain; to take the ~ out of sb's mouth ôter le pain de la bouche à qqn; I know which side my ~ is buttered je sais où est mon intérêt. -**2.** *inf* [money] pognon *m*, fric *m*.
bread-and-butter *inf adj* -**1.** [basic]: a ~ job un travail qui assure le nécessaire; the ~ issues les questions les plus terre-à-terre. -**2.** [reliable - person] sur qui l'on peut compter. -**3.** [expressing gratitude]: a ~ letter une lettre de remerciements.
breadbasket ['bred,bɑːskɪt] *n* -**1.** [basket] corbeille *f* à pain. -**2.** GEOG région *f* céréalière. -**3.** *inf dated* [stomach] estomac *m*.
bread bin *n Br* [small] boîte *f* à pain; [larger] huche *f* à pain.

breadboard ['bredbɔːd] *n* planche *f* à pain.
bread box *Am* = **bread bin**.
breadcrumb ['bredkrʌm] *n* miette *f* de pain.
◆ **breadcrumbs** *npl* CULIN chapelure *f*, panure *f*; fish fried in ~s du poisson pané.
breaded ['bredɪd] *adj* enrobé de chapelure.
breadfruit ['bredfruːt] *n* [tree] arbre *m* à pain; [fruit] fruit *m* à pain.
breadknife ['brednaɪf] (*pl* breadknives [-naɪvz]) *n* couteau *m* à pain.
breadline ['bredlaɪn] *n* *file d'attente pour recevoir des vivres gratuits*; to live OR to be on the ~ *fig* être sans le sou OR indigent.
bread sauce *n Br* sauce *f* à la mie de pain.
breadstick ['bredstɪk] *n* gressin *m*.
breadth [bredθ] *n* -**1.** [width] largeur *f*; [of cloth] lé *m*; the stage is 60 metres in ~ la scène a 60 mètres de large. -**2.** [scope - of mind, thought] largeur *f*; [- of style] ampleur *f*; ART largeur *f* d'exécution; MUS jeu *m* large.
breadwinner ['bred,wɪnəʳ] *n* soutien *m* de famille.
break [breɪk] (*pt* broke [brəʊk], *pp* broken ['brəʊkn]) ◇ *vt* -**1.** [split into pieces - glass, furniture] casser, briser; [- branch, lace, string] casser; ~ the stick in two cassez le bâton en deux; to ~ a safe forcer un coffre-fort; to ~ bread RELIG [priest] administrer la communion; [congregation] recevoir la communion; to ~ sb's heart *fig* briser le cœur à qqn; George broke her heart Georges lui a brisé le cœur; it ~s my heart to see her unhappy ça me brise le cœur de la voir malheureuse ❑ to ~ the ice rompre OR briser la glace. -**2.** [fracture] casser, fracturer; to ~ one's leg se casser OR se fracturer la jambe; to ~ one's neck se casser OR se rompre le cou; the fall broke his back la chute lui a brisé les reins || *fig*: to ~ one's back *inf* s'échiner; they broke their backs trying to get the job done ils se sont éreintés à finir le travail; we've broken the back of the job nous avons fait le plus gros du travail; I'll ~ his neck if I catch him doing it again! *inf* je lui tords le cou si je le reprends à faire ça! ❑ ~ a leg! *inf* merde! *(pour souhaiter bonne chance)*. -**3.** [render inoperable - appliance, machine] casser; you've broken the TV tu as cassé la télé. -**4.** [cut surface of - ground] entamer; [- skin] écorcher; the seal on the coffee jar was broken le pot de café avait été ouvert; the skin isn't broken la peau n'est pas écorchée ❑ to ~ new OR fresh ground innover, faire œuvre de pionnier; scientists are ~ing new OR fresh ground in cancer research les savants font une percée dans la recherche contre le cancer. -**5.** [force a way through] enfoncer; the river broke its banks la rivière est sortie de son lit; to ~ the sound barrier franchir le mur du son; to ~ surface [diver, whale] remonter à la surface; [submarine] faire surface. -**6.** [violate - law, rule] violer, enfreindre; [- agreement, treaty] violer; [- contract] rompre; [- promise] manquer à; RELIG [- commandment] désobéir à; [- sabbath] ne pas respecter; she broke her appointment with them elle a annulé son rendez-vous avec eux; to ~ the speed limit dépasser la limitation de vitesse; he broke his word to her *lit* il a manqué à la parole qu'il lui avait donnée; to ~ parole JUR *commettre un délit qui entraîne la révocation de la mise en liberté conditionnelle*; to ~ bounds MIL violer la consigne. -**7.** [escape from, leave suddenly]: to ~ jail s'évader (de prison); to ~ camp lever le camp; to ~ cover [animal] être débusqué; [person] sortir à découvert. -**8.** [interrupt - fast, monotony, spell] rompre; we broke our journey at Brussels nous avons fait une étape à Bruxelles; a cry broke the silence un cri a déchiré OR percé le silence; the plain was broken only by an occasional small settlement la plaine n'était interrompue que par de rares petits hameaux; to ~ step rompre le pas; to ~ sb's service [in tennis] prendre le service de qqn || ELEC [circuit, current] couper. -**9.** [put an end to - strike] briser; [- uprising] mater; the new offer broke the deadlock la nouvelle proposition a permis de sortir de l'impasse; he's tried to stop smoking but he can't ~ the habit il a essayé d'arrêter de fumer mais il n'arrive pas à se débarrasser OR se défaire de l'habitude. -**10.** [wear down, destroy - enemy] détruire; [- person, will, courage, resistance] briser; [- witness] réfuter; [- health] abîmer; torture did not ~ him OR his spirit il a résisté à la torture; this scandal could ~ them ce scandale pourrait signer leur perte; the experience will either make or ~ him l'expérience lui sera ou salutaire ou fatale. -**11.** [bankrupt] ruiner; her new business will either make or ~ her sa nouvelle affaire la rendra riche ou la ruinera ❑ to ~ the bank [exhaust funds] faire sauter la banque; buying a book won't ~ the bank! *hum* acheter un livre ne nous ruinera pas! -**12.** [soften - fall] amortir, adoucir; we planted a row of trees to ~ the wind nous avons planté une rangée d'arbres pour couper le vent. -**13.** [reveal, tell] annoncer, révéler; ~ it to her gently annonce-le lui avec ménagement. -**14.** [beat, improve on] battre; to ~ a record battre un record; the golfer broke 90 le golfeur a dépassé le score de 90. -**15.** [solve - code] déchiffrer. -**16.** [divide into parts - collection] dépareiller; [- bank note] entamer; can you ~ a £10 note? pouvez-vous faire de la monnaie sur un billet de 10 livres? -**17.** [horse] dresser. -**18.** MIL [demote] casser. -**19.** NAUT [flag] déferler. -**20.** *euph*: to ~ wind lâcher un vent.
◇ *vi* -**1.** [split into pieces - glass, furniture] se casser, se briser; [- branch, stick] se casser, se rompre; [- lace, string] se casser; to ~ apart se casser OR se briser (en morceaux); the plate broke in two l'assiette s'est cassée en deux; her heart broke *fig* elle a eu le cœur brisé. -**2.** [fracture - bone, limb] se fracturer; is the bone broken? y a-t-il une fracture?; any bones broken? *hum* rien de cassé? -**3.** [become inoperable - lock, tool] casser; [- machine] tomber en panne; the dishwasher broke last week le lave-vaisselle est tombé en panne la semaine dernière. -**4.** [disperse - clouds] se disperser, se dissiper; [- troops] rompre les rangs; [- ranks] se rompre. -**5.** [escape]: to ~ free se libérer; the ship broke loose from its moorings le bateau a rompu ses amarres. -**6.** [fail - health, person, spirit] se détériorer; the witness broke under questioning le témoin a craqué au cours de l'interrogatoire; she OR her spirit did not ~ elle ne s'est pas laissée abattre; their courage finally broke leur courage a fini par les abandonner. -**7.** [take a break] faire une pause; let's ~ for coffee faisons une pause-café, arrêtons-nous pour prendre un café. -**8.** [arise suddenly - day] se lever, poindre; [- dawn] poindre; [- news] être annoncé; [- scandal, war] éclater. -**9.** [move suddenly] se précipiter, foncer. -**10.** [weather] changer; [storm] éclater. -**11.** [voice - of boy] muer; [- with emotion] se briser; she was so upset that her voice kept ~ing elle était tellement bouleversée que sa voix se brisait. -**12.** [wave] déferler. -**13.** MED: her waters have broken elle a perdu les eaux. -**14.** *phr*: to ~ even [gen] s'y retrouver; FIN rentrer dans ses frais. -**15.** *inf Am* [happen] se passer, arriver; to ~ right/badly bien/mal se passer. -**16.** LING [vowel] se diphtonguer. -**17.** [boxers] se dégager. -**18.** [ball] dévier. -**19.** [in billiards] donner l'acquit.
◇ *n* -**1.** [in china, glass] cassure *f*, brisure *f*; [in wood] cassure *f*, rupture *f*; [in bone, limb] fracture *f*; a clean ~ [in object] une cassure nette; [in bone] une fracture simple || *fig* [with friend, group] rupture *f*; [in marriage] séparation *f*; the ~ with her husband was a painful experience ça a été très pénible pour elle quand elle s'est séparée de son mari; her ~ with the party in 1968 sa rupture avec le parti en 1968; to make a clean ~ with the past rompre avec le passé. -**2.** [crack] fissure *f*, fente *f*. -**3.** [gap - in hedge, wall] trouée *f*, ouverture *f*; [- in rock] faille *f*; [- in line] interruption *f*, rupture *f*; a ~ in the clouds une éclaircie. -**4.** [interruption - in conversation] interruption *f*, pause *f*; [- in payment] interruption *f*, suspension *f*; [- in trip] arrêt *m*; a ~ in production une suspension OR rupture de production; a ~ for commercials, a (commercial) ~ RADIO un intermède de publicité; TV un écran publicitaire, une page de publicité; a ~ in transmission une interruption des programmes (due à un incident technique) || LITERAT & MUS pause *f*; [in jazz] break *m*; ELEC: a ~ in the circuit une coupure de courant. -**5.** [rest] pause *f*; [holiday] vacances *fpl*; *Br* SCH récréation *f*; let's take a ~ on fait une pause?; we worked all morning without a ~ nous avons travaillé toute la matinée sans nous arrêter; he drove for three hours without a ~ il a conduit trois heures de suite; you need a ~ [short rest] tu as besoin de faire une pause; [holiday] tu as besoin de vacances ❑ coffee ~ pause-café *f*; lunch ~ pause *f* de midi; do you get a lunch ~? tu as une pause à midi?; give me a ~! *inf* laisse-moi respirer! -**6.** [escape] évasion *f*, fuite *f*; jail ~ évasion (de prison); she made a ~ for the woods elle s'est élancée vers le bois ❑ to make a ~ for it prendre la fuite. -**7.** *inf* [opportunity] chance *f*; [luck] (coup *m* de) veine *f*; you get all the ~s! tu en as du pot!; to have a lucky ~ avoir de la veine; to have a bad ~ manquer de veine. -**8.** [change] changement *m*; a ~ in the weather un changement de temps; the decision signalled a ~ with tradition la décision marquait une rupture avec la tradition. -**9.** [carriage] break *m*. -**10.** *lit*: at ~ of day au point du jour, à l'aube. -**11.** SPORT: to have a service ~ OR a ~ (of serve) [in tennis] avoir une rupture de service *(de l'adversaire)*; he made a 70 ~ [in snooker] il a fait une série de 70.
◆ **break away** ◇ *vi insep* -**1.** [move away] se détacher; I broke away from the crowd je me suis éloigné de la foule; he broke away from her grasp il s'est dégagé de son étreinte. -**2.** [end association with] rompre; a group of MPs broke away from the party un groupe de députés a quitté le parti; as a band they have broken away from traditional jazz leur groupe a (complètement) rompu avec le jazz traditionnel. -**3.** SPORT [in racing, cycling] s'échapper, se détacher du peloton.
◇ *vt sep* détacher; they broke all the fittings away from the walls ils ont décroché toutes les appliques des murs.
◆ **break down** ◇ *vi insep* -**1.** [vehicle, machine] tomber en panne; the car has broken down la voiture est en panne. -**2.** [fail - health] se détériorer; [- authority] disparaître; [- argument, system] s'effondrer; [- negotiations, relations] échouer; radio communications broke down le contact radio a été coupé; the plan broke down due to poor organization le projet a échoué à cause d'une mauvaise organisation. -**3.** [lose one's composure] s'effondrer; to ~ down in tears fondre en larmes. -**4.** [divide] se diviser; the report ~s down into three parts le rapport comprend OR est composé de trois parties. -**5.** CHEM se décomposer; to ~ down into se décomposer en.
◇ *vt sep* -**1.** [destroy - barrier] démolir, abattre; [- door] enfoncer; *fig* [- resistance] briser; we must ~ down old prejudices il faut mettre fin aux vieux préjugés. -**2.** [analyse - idea] analyser; [- reasons] décomposer; [- accounts] analyser, détailler; COMM [- costs, figures] ventiler; CHEM [- substance] décomposer.
◆ **break forth** *vi insep lit* [light] jaillir; [storm, buds] éclater; [blossom] s'épanouir subitement.
◆ **break in** ◇ *vt sep* -**1.** [train - person] former; [- horse] dresser; a month should be enough to ~ you in to the job un mois devrait suffire pour vous faire OR vous habituer au métier. -**2.** [clothing] porter *(pour user)*; I want to ~ these shoes in je veux que ces chaussures se fassent. -**3.** [knock down - door] enfoncer.
◇ *vi insep* -**1.** [burglar] entrer; JUR entrer par effraction. -**2.** [speaker] interrompre; to ~ in on sb/sthg interrompre qqn/qqch.
◆ **break into** *vt insep* -**1.** [house, car] entrer dans; JUR entrer par effraction dans; I broke into the drawer j'ai forcé le tiroir; they broke into the safe ils ont fracturé OR forcé le coffre-fort. -**2.** [begin suddenly]: the audience broke

into applause le public s'est mis à applaudir; the horse broke into a gallop le cheval a pris le galop. -**3.** [conversation] interrompre. -**4.** [start to spend - savings] entamer; I don't want to ~ into a £20 note je ne veux pas entamer un billet de 20 livres. -**5.** COMM percer sur; the firm has broken into the Japanese market l'entreprise a percé sur le marché japonais.

◆ **break off** ◇ *vi insep* -**1.** [become separated] se détacher, se casser; a branch has broken off une branche s'est détachée (de l'arbre). -**2.** [stop abruptly] s'arrêter brusquement; he broke off in mid-sentence il s'est arrêté au milieu d'une phrase; they broke off from work [for rest] ils ont fait une pause; [for day] ils ont cessé le travail. -**3.** [end relationship] rompre; she's broken off with him elle a rompu avec lui.

◇ *vt sep* -**1.** [separate] détacher, casser; to ~ sthg off sthg casser OR détacher qqch de qqch. -**2.** [end - agreement, relationship] rompre; they've broken off their engagement ils ont rompu leurs fiançailles; Italy had broken off diplomatic relations with Libya l'Italie avait rompu ses relations diplomatiques avec la Libye.

◆ **break out** ◇ *vi insep* -**1.** [begin abruptly - argument, war, storm] éclater; [- disease] se déclarer. -**2.** [become covered]: to ~ out in spots OR in a rash avoir une éruption de boutons; to ~ out in a sweat se mettre à transpirer; she broke out in a cold sweat elle s'est mise à avoir des sueurs froides. -**3.** [escape] s'échapper; to ~ out from OR of prison s'évader (de prison); we have to ~ out of this vicious circle il faut que nous sortions de ce cercle vicieux.

◇ *vt sep* [bottle, champagne] ouvrir.

◆ **break through** ◇ *vt insep* percer; the sun broke through the clouds le soleil a percé les nuages; I broke through the crowd je me suis frayé un chemin à travers la foule; the troops broke through enemy lines les troupes ont enfoncé les lignes ennemies; she eventually broke through his reserve elle a fini par le faire sortir de sa réserve.

◇ *vi insep literal* percer; *fig* & MIL faire une percée; his hidden feelings tend to ~ through in his writing *fig* ses sentiments cachés tendent à transparaître OR percer dans ses écrits.

◆ **break up** ◇ *vt sep* -**1.** [divide up - rocks] briser, morceler; [- property] morceler; [- soil] ameublir; she broke the loaf up into four pieces elle a rompu OR partagé la miche en quatre; illustrations ~ up the text le texte est aéré par des illustrations. -**2.** [destroy - house] démolir; [- road] défoncer. -**3.** [bring to an end - fight, party] mettre fin à, arrêter; [- coalition] briser, rompre; [- organization] dissoudre; [- empire] démembrer; [- family] séparer; his drinking broke up their marriage le fait qu'il buvait a brisé OR détruit leur mariage. -**4.** [disperse - crowd] disperser; ~ it up! [people fighting or arguing] arrêtez!; [said by policeman] circulez! -**5.** *inf* [distress] bouleverser, retourner; the news really broke her up la nouvelle l'a complètement bouleversée. -**6.** *inf Am* [amuse]: her stories really ~ me up! ses histoires me font bien marrer!

◇ *vi insep* -**1.** [split into pieces - road, system] se désagréger; [- ice] craquer, se fissurer; the ship broke up on the rocks le navire s'est disloqué sur les rochers. -**2.** [come to an end - meeting, party] se terminer, prendre fin; [- partnership] cesser, prendre fin; when the meeting broke up à l'issue OR à la fin de la réunion; their marriage broke up leur mariage n'a pas marché. -**3.** [boyfriend, girlfriend] rompre; she broke up with her boyfriend elle a rompu avec son petit ami; they've broken up ils se sont séparés. -**4.** [disperse - clouds] se disperser; [- group] se disperser; [- friends] se quitter, se séparer. -**5.** *Br* SCH être en vacances; we ~ up for Christmas on the 22nd les vacances de Noël commencent le 22. -**6.** [lose one's composure] s'effondrer. -**7.** *inf Am* [laugh] se tordre de rire.

◆ **break with** *vt insep* -**1.** [end association with - person, organization] rompre avec; the defeat caused many people to ~ with the party la défaite a poussé beaucoup de gens à rompre avec le parti. -**2.** [depart from - belief, values] rompre avec; she broke with tradition by getting married away from her village elle a rompu avec la tradition en ne se mariant pas dans son village.

breakable ['breɪkəbl] *adj* fragile, cassable.

◆ **breakables** *npl*: put away all ~s rangez tout objet fragile.

breakage ['breɪkɪdʒ] *n* -**1.** [of metal] rupture *f*; [of glass] casse *f*, bris *m*. -**2.** [damages] casse *f*; the insurance pays for all ~ OR ~s l'assurance paye toute la casse.

breakaway ['breɪkəweɪ] ◇ *n* -**1.** [of people] séparation *f*; [of group] rupture *f*; SPORT [in cycling] échappée *f*; [in boxing] dégagement *m*. -**2.** CIN accessoire *m* cassable.

◇ *adj* séparatiste, dissident; a ~ group un groupe dissident.

breakdance ['breɪkdɑːns] *n* smurf *m*.

◆ **break-dance** *vi* danser le smurf.

break dancer *n* smurfer *m*.

break dancing *n* smurf *m*.

breakdown ['breɪkdaʊn] *n* -**1.** [mechanical] panne *f*; to have a ~ tomber en panne. -**2.** [of communications, negotiations] rupture *f*; [of railway system] arrêt *m* complet; [of tradition, state of affairs] détérioration *f*, dégradation *f*. -**3.** MED [nervous] dépression *f* nerveuse; to have a ~ faire une dépression (nerveuse) || [physical] effondrement *m*. -**4.** [analysis] analyse *f*; [into parts] décomposition *f*; COMM [of costs, figures] ventilation *f*; a ~ of the population by age une répartition de la population par âge; give me a ~ of the annual report faites-moi l'analyse du rapport annuel.

breakdown lorry, **breakdown truck** *n Br* dépanneuse *f*.

breaker ['breɪkəʳ] *n* -**1.** [scrap merchant]: the ship was sent to the ~'s le navire a été envoyé à la démolition. -**2.** [wave] brisant *m*. -**3.** ELECTRON = **circuit breaker**. -**4.** [machine] concasseur *m*, broyeur *m*. -**5.** [CB operator] cibiste *mf*.

break-even *adj*: ~ point seuil *m* de rentabilité, point mort *m*; ~ price prix *m* d'équilibre.

breakfast ['brekfəst] ◇ *n* petit déjeuner *m*; to have ~ prendre le petit déjeuner; what do you want for ~? que veux-tu pour ton petit déjeuner? ❑ 'Breakfast at Tiffany's' *Capote* 'Petit Déjeuner chez Tiffany'; *Edwards* 'Diamants sur canapé'.

◇ *comp* [service, set] à petit déjeuner; [tea, time] du petit déjeuner; ~ cup déjeuner *m*; ~ cereal céréales *fpl*; ~ table table *f* pour le petit déjeuner.

◇ *vi* prendre le petit déjeuner, déjeuner.

breakfast room *n* salle *f* du petit déjeuner.

breakfast television *n* télévision *f* du matin.

break-in *n* cambriolage *m*.

breaking ['breɪkɪŋ] *n* -**1.** [shattering] bris *m*; [of bone] fracture *f*; JUR [of seal] bris *m*; ~ and entering effraction *f*. -**2.** [violation - of treaty, rule, law] violation *f*; ~ of a promise manquement à une promesse; ~ of a commandment désobéissance à un commandement. -**3.** [interruption - of journey] interruption *f*; [- of silence] rupture *f*. -**4.** LING fracture *f*.

breaking point *n literal* point *m* de rupture; *fig*: I've reached ~ je suis à bout, je n'en peux plus; you're trying my patience to ~ tu pousses à bout ma patience; the situation has reached ~ la situation est devenue critique.

breakneck ['breɪknek] *adj*: at ~ speed à une allure folle, à tombeau ouvert.

breakout ['breɪkaʊt] *n* [from prison] évasion *f* (de prison).

breakpoint ['breɪkpɔɪnt] *n* -**1.** [in tennis] point *m* d'avantage. -**2.** COMPUT point *m* de rupture.

breakthrough ['breɪkθruː] *n* -**1.** [advance, discovery] découverte *f* capitale, percée *f* (technologique). -**2.** [in enemy lines] percée *f*.

breakup ['breɪkʌp] *n* -**1.** [disintegration - of association] démembrement *m*, dissolution *f*; [- of relationship] rupture *f*; before our ~ avant que nous ne rompions. -**2.** [end - of meeting, activity] fin *f*. -**3.** [of ship] dislocation *f*. -**4.** [of ice] débâcle *f*.

breakwater ['breɪk,wɔːtəʳ] *n* digue *f*, brise-lames *m inv*.

bream [briːm] (*pl inv* OR breams) *n* brème *f*.

breast [brest] ◇ *n* -**1.** [chest] poitrine *f*; [of animal] poitrine, poitrail *m*; CULIN [of chicken] blanc *m*; he held her to his ~ il la tint serrée contre sa poitrine ❑ to make a clean ~ of it *inf* tout avouer. -**2.** [bosom - of woman] sein *m*, poitrine *f*; *arch* [- of man] sein *m*; she put the baby to her ~ elle porta le bébé à son sein; a child at the ~ un enfant au sein. -**3.** MIN front *m* de taille.

◇ *vt* -**1.** [face - waves, storm] affronter, faire front à. -**2.** [reach summit of] atteindre le sommet de; the runner ~ed the tape SPORT le coureur a franchi la ligne d'arrivée (en vainqueur).

breast-beating *n* (*U*) jérémiades *fpl*.

breastbone ['brestbəʊn] *n* ANAT sternum *m*; [of bird] bréchet *m*.

breast-fed *adj* nourri au sein.

breast-feed ◇ *vt* allaiter, donner le sein à.

◇ *vi* allaiter, nourrir au sein.

breast-feeding *n* allaitement *m* au sein.

breastplate ['brestpleɪt] *n* [armour] plastron *m* (de cuirasse); [of priest] pectoral *m*.

breast pocket *n* poche *f* de poitrine.

breaststroke ['breststrəʊk] *n* brasse *f*; to swim (the) ~ nager la brasse.

breastwork ['brestwɜːk] *n* MIL parapet *m*; NAUT rambarde *f*.

breath [breθ] *n* -**1.** [of human, animal] haleine *f*, souffle *m*; to have bad ~ avoir mauvaise haleine; take a ~ respirez; he took a deep ~ il a respiré à fond; I took a deep ~ and started to explain je respirai profondément et commençai d'expliquer; let me get my ~ back laissez-moi retrouver mon souffle OR reprendre haleine; she stopped for ~ elle s'est arrêtée pour reprendre haleine; to be out of ~ être essoufflé OR à bout de souffle; to be short of ~ avoir le souffle court; he said it all in one ~ il l'a dit d'un trait; they are not to be mentioned in the same ~ on ne saurait les comparer; under one's ~ à voix basse, tout bas; she laughed under her ~ elle a ri sous cape; with her dying ~ en mourant; he drew his last ~ il a rendu l'âme OR le dernier soupir; music is the ~ of life to him la musique est toute sa vie; to hold one's ~ retenir son souffle; don't hold your ~ waiting for the money si c'est l'argent que tu attends, ne compte pas dessus OR tu perds ton temps; save your ~! inutile de gaspiller ta salive!; the sight took his ~ away la vue OR le spectacle lui a coupé le souffle; it takes my ~ away je n'en reviens pas. -**2.** [gust] souffle *m*; there isn't a ~ of air il n'y a pas un souffle d'air; we went out for a ~ of fresh air nous sommes sortis prendre l'air. -**3.** [hint] trace *f*; the first ~ of spring les premiers effluves du printemps; the faintest ~ of scandal le plus petit soupçon de scandale.

breathable ['briːðəbl] *adj* respirable.

breathalyse *Br*, **breathalyze** *Am* ['breθəlaɪz] *vt* faire passer l'Alcootest® à.

Breathalyser®, **Breathalyzer**® ['breθəlaɪzəʳ] *n* Alcootest® *m*.

breathe [briːð] ◇ *vi* -**1.** respirer; to ~ heavily OR deeply [after exertion] souffler OR respirer bruyamment; [during illness] il respirait péniblement; is he still breathing? est-il toujours en vie?, vit-il encore?; I ~d more easily OR again after the exam *fig* après l'examen j'ai enfin pu respirer; how can I work with you breathing down my neck? *fig* comment veux-tu que je travaille si tu es toujours derrière moi? -**2.** [wine] respirer.

◇ *vt* -**1.** PHYSIOL respirer; she ~d a sigh of relief elle poussa un soupir de soulagement; to ~ one's last rendre le dernier soupir OR l'âme;

she ~d new life into the project elle a insufflé de nouvelles forces au projet; she'll be breathing fire when she finds out! elle va se mettre dans une colère noire quand elle saura! -**2.** [whisper] murmurer; don't ~ a word! ne soufflez pas mot!; they didn't ~ a word about it ils n'en ont pas soufflé mot. -**3.** LING aspirer.

◆ **breathe in** *vi insep & vt sep* inspirer.

◆ **breathe out** *vi insep & vt sep* expirer.

breather *inf* ['briːðəʳ] *n* moment *m* de repos OR de répit; let's take a ~ prenons le temps de souffler un peu; I went out for a ~ je suis sorti prendre l'air ❑ heavy ~ auteur *m* de coups de fil obscènes.

breathing ['briːðɪŋ] *n* -**1.** [gen] respiration *f*, souffle *m*; [of musician] respiration *f*; heavy ~ respiration bruyante. -**2.** LING aspiration *f*; rough/smooth ~ [in ancient Greek] esprit *m* rude/doux.

breathing space *n* moment *m* de répit.

breathless ['breθlɪs] *adj* -**1.** [from exertion] essoufflé, hors d'haleine; [from illness] oppressé, qui a du mal à respirer. -**2.** [from emotion]: his kiss left her ~ son baiser lui a coupé le souffle; we waited in ~ excitement nous attendions le souffle coupé par l'émotion OR en retenant notre haleine; the film held us ~ le film nous a tenus en haleine ❑ 'Breathless' *Godard* 'À bout de souffle'. -**3.** [atmosphere] étouffant.

breathlessly ['breθlɪslɪ] *adv* [gasping] en haletant; *fig* [hurriedly] en toute hâte.

breathtaking ['breθ,teɪkɪŋ] *adj* impressionnant; a ~ view une vue à (vous) couper le souffle.

breathtakingly ['breθ,teɪkɪŋlɪ] *adv* de manière impressionnante.

breath test *n* Alcootest® *m*.

breathy ['breθɪ] (*compar* breathier, *superl* breathiest) *adj* qui respire bruyamment; MUS qui manque d'attaque; she has a ~ voice elle respire bruyamment en parlant.

Brechtian ['brektɪən] ◇ *adj* brechtien.
◇ *n* brechtien *m*, -enne *f*.

bred [bred] ◇ *pt & pp* → **breed**.
◇ *adj* élevé.

-bred *in cpds* élevé; ill/well~ mal/bien élevé.

breech [briːtʃ] ◇ *n* -**1.** [of gun] culasse *f*. -**2.** [of person] derrière *m*.
◇ *vt* [gun] munir d'une culasse.

breech birth *n* accouchement *m* par le siège *m*.

breechblock ['briːtʃblɒk] *n* bloc *m* de culasse.

breechcloth ['briːtʃklɒθ] *n Am* pagne *m*.

breech delivery = **breech birth**.

breeches ['brɪtʃɪz] *npl* pantalon *m*; [knee-length] haut-de-chausses *m*; [for riding] culotte *f*.

breeches buoy ['briːtʃɪz-] *n* bouée-culotte *f*.

breechloader ['briːtʃ,ləʊdəʳ] *n* arme *f* qui se charge par la culasse.

breech-loading *adj* qui se charge par la culasse.

breed [briːd] (*pt & pp* bred [bred]) ◇ *n* -**1.** ZOOL [race] race *f*, espèce *f*; [within race] type *m*; BOT [of plant] espèce *f*. -**2.** *fig* [kind] sorte *f*, espèce *f*; he's one of a dying ~ il fait partie d'une espèce en voie de disparition.
◇ *vt* -**1.** [raise - animals] élever, faire l'élevage de; [- plants] cultiver; [- children] *lit* OR *hum* élever; to ~ in/out a characteristic faire acquérir/éliminer une caractéristique (par la sélection); he was bred for the sea on l'a élevé pour en faire un marin plus tard. -**2.** *fig* [cause] engendrer, faire naître.
◇ *vi* se reproduire, se multiplier; to ~ like rabbits se multiplier comme des lapins.

breeder ['briːdəʳ] *n* [person] éleveur *m*, -euse *f*; [animal] reproducteur *m*, -trice *f*.

breeder reactor *n* surgénérateur *m*, surrégénérateur *m*.

breeding ['briːdɪŋ] *n* -**1.** AGR [raising - of animals] élevage *m*; [- of plants] culture *f*. -**2.** [reproduction] reproduction *f*, procréation *f*; the ~ season [for animals] la saison des amours; [for birds] la saison des nids. -**3.** [upbringing] éducation *f*; he lacks ~ il manque de savoir-vivre. -**4.** PHYS surgénération *f*, surrégénération *f*.

breeding-ground *n* -**1.** [for wild animals, birds] lieu *m* de prédilection pour l'accouplement OR la ponte. -**2.** *fig*: a ~ for terrorists une pépinière de terroristes.

breeks [briːks] *npl Scot* pantalon *m*.

breeze [briːz] ◇ *n* -**1.** [wind] brise *f*; a gentle OR light ~ une petite OR légère brise; a stiff ~ un vent frais; there's quite a ~ ça souffle ❑ to shoot the ~ *inf Am* bavarder. -**2.** *inf Am*: that's a ~ c'est l'enfance de l'art, c'est du gâteau. -**3.** [charcoal] cendres *fpl* (de charbon).
◇ *vi* -**1.** [move quickly] aller vite; the car ~d along the country lanes la voiture roulait à vive allure sur les routes de campagne. -**2.** [do easily]: I ~d through the exam *inf* j'ai passé l'examen les doigts dans le nez.

◆ **breeze in** *vi insep*: she ~d in [quickly] elle est entrée en coup de vent; [casually] elle est entrée d'un air désinvolte.

◆ **breeze out** *vi insep*: he ~d out [quickly] il est sorti en coup de vent; [casually] il est sorti d'un air désinvolte.

breezeblock ['briːzblɒk] *n Br* parpaing *m*.

breezily ['briːzɪlɪ] *adv* [casually] avec désinvolture; [cheerfully] joyeusement, jovialement.

breezy ['briːzɪ] (*compar* breezier, *superl* breeziest) *adj* -**1.** [weather, day] venteux; [place, spot] éventé. -**2.** [person - casual] désinvolte; [- cheerful] jovial, enjoué.

Bremen ['breɪmən] *pr n* Brême.

Bren gun [bren-] *n* fusil *m* mitrailleur.

brethren ['breðrən] *npl fml* [fellow members] camarades *mpl*; RELIG frères *mpl*.

Breton ['bretn] ◇ *n* -**1.** [person] Breton *m*, -onne *f*. -**2.** LING breton *m*.
◇ *adj* breton.

breve [briːv] *n* MUS & TYPO brève *f*.

breviary ['briːvjərɪ] (*pl* breviaries) *n* bréviaire *m*.

brevity ['brevɪtɪ] *n* -**1.** [shortness] brièveté *f*. -**2.** [succinctness] concision *f*; [terseness] laconisme *m*; ~ is the soul of wit *prov* la concision est le secret d'un bon mot d'esprit.

brew [bruː] ◇ *n* -**1.** [infusion] infusion *f*; [herbal] tisane *f*; a witch's ~ un brouet de sorcière. -**2.** [beer] brassage *m*; [amount made] brassin *m*.
◇ *vt* -**1.** [prepare - tea] préparer, faire infuser; [- beer] brasser. -**2.** *fig* [scheme] tramer, mijoter.
◇ *vi* -**1.** [tea] infuser; [beer] fermenter. -**2.** [make beer] brasser, faire de la bière. -**3.** *fig* [storm] couver, se préparer; [scheme] se tramer, mijoter; I could tell by her face there was a storm ~ing j'ai vu sur son visage qu'il y avait de l'orage dans l'air; there's trouble ~ing il y a de l'orage dans l'air.

◆ **brew up** *vi insep* -**1.** [storm] couver, se préparer; [trouble] se préparer, se tramer. -**2.** *inf Br* [make tea] préparer OR faire du thé.

brewer ['bruːəʳ] *n* brasseur *m*.

brewer's yeast *n* levure *f* de bière.

brewery ['brʊərɪ] (*pl* breweries) *n* brasserie *f* (*fabrique*).

brew-up *inf n Br*: we stopped work for a ~ nous avons fait une pause pour prendre un thé.

briar ['braɪəʳ] = **brier**.

briar (pipe) *n* pipe *f* de bruyère.

bribe [braɪb] ◇ *vt* soudoyer, acheter; [witness] suborner; we ~d the guard to tell us nous avons soudoyé le garde pour qu'il nous le dise; I ~d him with sweets je l'ai acheté avec des bonbons.
◇ *n* pot-de-vin *m*; to take ~s se laisser corrompre; I offered him a ~ j'ai tenté de le corrompre, je lui ai offert un pot-de-vin.

bribery ['braɪbərɪ] *n* corruption *f*; [of witness] subornation *f*; open to ~ corruptible; not open to ~ incorruptible ❑ ~ and corruption JUR corruption.

bric-à-brac ['brɪkəbræk] ◇ *n* bric-à-brac *m*.
◇ *comp*: a ~ shop/stall une boutique/un éventaire de brocanteur.

brick [brɪk] ◇ *n* -**1.** [for building] brique *f*; a house made of ~ une maison en brique ❑ to come down on sb like a ton of ~s *inf* passer un savon à qqn; you can't make ~s without straw *prov* à l'impossible nul n'est tenu *prov*. -**2.** [of ice cream] pavé *m* (de glace). -**3.** *Br* [toy] cube *m* (de construction); a box of ~s un jeu de construction. -**4.** *inf Br dated* chic type *m*, chic fille *f*; you're a ~! tu es vraiment OR super sympa!
◇ *comp* [building, wall] en brique OR briques; it's like talking to a ~ wall autant (vaut) parler à un mur OR un sourd.

◆ **brick in** = **brick up**.

◆ **brick off** *vt sep* murer.

◆ **brick up** *vt sep* murer.

brickbat ['brɪkbæt] *n* [weapon] morceau *m* de brique; *fig* [criticism] critique *f*.

brickie *inf* ['brɪkɪ] *n Br* maçon *m*, ouvrier-maçon *m*.

brick-kiln *n* four *m* à briques.

bricklayer ['brɪk,leɪəʳ] *n* maçon *m*, ouvrier-maçon *m*.

brick red *n* rouge *m* brique.

◆ **brick-red** *adj* rouge brique *(inv)*.

brickwork ['brɪkwɜːk] *n* [structure] briquetage *m*, brique *f*.

brickworks ['brɪkwɜːks] (*pl inv*), **brickyard** ['brɪkjɑːd] *n* briqueterie *f*.

bridal ['braɪdl] *adj* [gown, veil] de mariée; [chamber, procession] nuptial; [feast] de noce; the ~ suite l'appartement *m* réservé aux jeunes mariés.

bride [braɪd] *n* [before wedding] (future) mariée *f*; [after wedding] (jeune) mariée *f*; the ~ and groom les (jeunes) mariés *mpl* ❑ the ~ of Christ RELIG l'épouse *f* du Christ; 'The Bartered Bride' *Smetana* 'la Fiancée vendue'.

bridegroom ['braɪdgrʊm] *n* [before wedding] (futur) marié *m*; [after wedding] (jeune) marié *m*.

bridesmaid ['braɪdzmeɪd] *n* demoiselle *f* d'honneur.

bride-to-be *n* future mariée *f*.

bridge [brɪdʒ] ◇ *n* -**1.** [structure] pont *m*; the engineers built OR put a ~ across the river le génie a construit OR jeté un pont sur le fleuve ❑ 'The Bridge on the River Kwai' *Lean* 'le Pont de la rivière Kwaï'; 'A Bridge Too Far' *Attenborough* 'Un pont trop loin'. -**2.** *fig* [link] rapprochement *m*; building ~s between East and West efforts de rapprochement entre l'Est et l'Ouest. -**3.** [of ship] passerelle *f* (de commandement). -**4.** [of nose] arête *f*; [of glasses] arcade *f*. -**5.** [of stringed instrument] chevalet *m*. -**6.** [dentures] bridge *m*. -**7.** [card game] bridge *m*; what about a game of ~? et si on faisait un bridge?; do you play ~? jouez-vous au bridge?; they're playing ~ ils bridgent.
◇ *comp* [party, tournament] de bridge; ~ player bridgeur *m*, -euse *f*.
◇ *vt* [river] construire OR jeter un pont sur; *fig*: a composer whose work ~d two centuries un compositeur dont l'œuvre est à cheval sur deux siècles; they tried to ~ the generation gap ils ont essayé de combler le fossé entre les générations; in order to ~ the gap in our knowledge/in our resources pour combler la lacune dans notre savoir/le trou dans nos ressources.

bridgehead ['brɪdʒhed] *n* tête *f* de pont.

bridge loan *Am* = **bridging loan**.

bridgework ['brɪdʒwɜːk] *n (U)* [in dentistry]: to have ~ done se faire faire un bridge.

bridging ['brɪdʒɪŋ] *n* -**1.** [in climbing] opposition *f*. -**2.** CONSTR entretoisement *m*.

bridging loan *n Br* prêt-relais *m*.

bridle ['braɪdl] ◇ *n* [harness] bride *f*; *fig* [constraint] frein *m*, contrainte *f*.
◇ *vt* [horse] brider; *fig* [emotions] refréner; you should try to ~ your tongue tu devrais essayer de tenir ta langue.
◇ *vi* [in anger] se rebiffer, prendre la mouche; [in indignation] redresser la tête.

bridle path, **bridleway** ['braɪdlweɪ] *n* piste *f* cavalière.

brief [briːf] ◇ *adj* -**1.** [short in duration] bref, court; a ~ interval un court intervalle. -**2.** [succinct] concis, bref; to be ~, I think you're right

en bref, je crois que tu as raison; a ~ account un exposé sommaire. -**3.** [terse - person, reply] laconique; [abrupt] brusque.
◇ *vt* -**1.** [bring up to date] mettre au courant; **the boss ~ed me on the latest developments** le patron m'a mis au courant des derniers développements || [give orders to] donner des instructions à; **the soldiers were ~ed on their mission** les soldats ont reçu leurs ordres pour la mission. -**2.** JUR [lawyer] confier une cause à; [case] établir le dossier de.
◇ *n* -**1.** JUR dossier *m*, affaire *f*; **he took our ~** il a accepté de plaider notre cause ❑ **to hold a watching ~ for sb/sthg** veiller (en justice) aux intérêts de qqn/qqch; **to hold no ~ for sb/sthg** ne pas se faire l'avocat de qqn/qqch; **he holds no ~ for those who take drugs** il ne prend pas la défense de ceux qui se droguent. -**2.** [instructions] briefing *m*; **my ~ was to develop sales** la tâche OR la mission qui m'a été confiée était de développer les ventes.
◆ **briefs** *npl* [underwear] slip *m*.
◆ **in brief** *adv phr* en résumé.

briefcase ['bri:fkeɪs] *n* serviette *f*, mallette *f*.

briefing ['bri:fɪŋ] *n* MIL [meeting] briefing *m*, instructions *fpl*.

briefly ['bri:flɪ] *adv* -**1.** [for a short time] un court instant; **I visited my grandmother ~ on the way home** au retour, j'ai rendu visite à ma grand-mère en coup de vent. -**2.** [succinctly] brièvement; [tersely] laconiquement; **she told them ~ what had happened** elle leur a résumé ce qui s'était passé; **put ~, the situation is a mess** en bref, la situation est très embrouillée.

briefness ['bri:fnɪs] *n* -**1.** [of time] brièveté *f*, courte durée *f*. -**2.** [succinctness] concision *f*; [terseness] laconisme *m*; [abruptness] brusquerie *f*.

brier ['braɪəʳ] *n* -**1.** [thorny plant] ronces *fpl*; [thorn] épine *f*. -**2.** [heather] bruyère *f*; [wood] (racine *f* de) bruyère *f*.

brier rose *n* églantine *f*.

brig [brɪg] *n* -**1.** [ship] brick *m*. -**2.** *Am* [prison - on ship] prison *f (à bord d'un navire)*; **they threw him in the ~** *inf fig* ils l'ont mis au trou.

Brig. (*written abbr of* brigadier) *n*: **~ Smith** le général de brigade Smith.

brigade [brɪ'geɪd] *n* [gen & MIL] brigade *f*; **one of the old ~** *fig* un vieux de la vieille.

brigadier [,brɪgə'dɪəʳ] *n Br* général *m* de brigade.

brigadier general *n Am* [in army] général *m* de brigade; [in air force] général *m* de brigade aérienne.

brigand ['brɪgənd] *n* brigand *m*, bandit *m*.

brigantine ['brɪgənti:n] *n* brigantin *m*.

bright [braɪt] ◇ *adj* -**1.** [weather, day] clair, radieux; [sunshine] éclatant; **the weather will get ~er later** le temps s'améliorera en cours de journée; **cloudy with ~ intervals** nuageux avec des éclaircies; **the outlook for tomorrow is ~er** METEOR on prévoit une amélioration du temps pour demain; **~ and early** *fig* tôt le matin, de bon OR grand matin || [room] clair; [fire, light] vif; [colour] vif, éclatant. -**2.** [shining - diamond, star] brillant; [- metal] poli, luisant; [- eyes] brillant, vif; *fig* [- moment] agréable, bon; **it was one of the few ~ spots of our visit** ce fut l'un des rares bons moments de notre visite ❑ **she likes the ~ lights** elle aime la grande ville; **the ~ lights of London** les attractions de Londres. -**3.** [clever] intelligent; [child] éveillé, vif; **a ~ idea** une idée géniale OR lumineuse. -**4.** [cheerful] gai, joyeux; [lively] animé, vif; **you're very ~ this morning!** tu es bien gaie ce matin!; **to be ~ and breezy** avoir l'air en pleine forme. -**5.** [promising] brillant; **there are ~er days ahead** des jours meilleurs nous attendent; **to have a ~ future** avoir un brillant avenir; **the future's looking ~** l'avenir est plein de promesses OR s'annonce bien ❑ **to look on the ~ side** prendre les choses du bon côté, être optimiste.
◇ *adv lit* [burn, shine] avec éclat, brillamment.
◆ **brights** *npl Am* [headlights]: **to put the ~s on** se mettre en pleins phares.

brighten ['braɪtn] ◇ *vi* -**1.** [weather] s'améliorer. -**2.** [person] s'animer; [face] s'éclairer; [eyes] s'allumer, s'éclairer. -**3.** [prospects, situation] s'améliorer.
◇ *vt* -**1.** [decorate - place, person] égayer; [enliven - conversation] animer, égayer. -**2.** [prospects, situation] améliorer, faire paraître sous un meilleur jour. -**3.** [polish - metal] astiquer, faire reluire. -**4.** [colour] aviver.
◆ **brighten up** *vi insep* & *vt sep* = **brighten**.

bright-eyed *adj literal* aux yeux brillants; *fig* [eager] enthousiaste; **~ and bushy-tailed** *hum* frais comme la rosée.

brightly ['braɪtlɪ] *adv* -**1.** [shine] avec éclat; **the stars were shining ~** les étoiles scintillaient; **the fire burned ~** le feu flambait; **~ polished** reluisant. -**2.** [cheerfully] gaiement, joyeusement; **to smile ~** sourire d'un air radieux; **to answer ~** répondre gaiement.

brightness ['braɪtnɪs] *n* -**1.** [of sun] éclat *m*; [of light] intensité *f*; [of room] clarté *f*, luminosité *f*; [of colour] éclat *m*. -**2.** [cheerfulness] gaieté *f*, joie *f*; [liveliness] vivacité *f*; **the ~ of her smile** l'éclat de son sourire. -**3.** [cleverness] intelligence *f*.

Bright's disease [braɪts-] *n* mal *m* de Bright, néphrite *f* chronique *spec*.

bright spark *inf n Br* [clever person] lumière *f*; **you're a ~!** *iron* gros malin!

brill [brɪl] (*pl inv*) ◇ *n* [fish] barbue *f*.
◇ *adj inf Br* [terrific] super, sensass.

brilliance ['brɪljəns], **brilliancy** ['brɪljənsɪ] *n* -**1.** [of light, smile, career] éclat *m*, brillant *m*. -**2.** [cleverness] intelligence *f*; **no one doubts the ~ of her mind** il ne fait pas de doute que c'est un esprit brillant OR qu'elle est d'une intelligence supérieure.

brilliant ['brɪljənt] ◇ *adj* -**1.** [light, sunshine] éclatant, intense; [smile] éclatant, rayonnant; [colour] vif, éclatant. -**2.** [outstanding - mind, musician, writer] brillant, exceptionnel; [- film, novel, piece of work] brillant, exceptionnel; **a ~ career** une brillante carrière; **a ~ success** un succès éclatant. -**3.** *inf* [terrific] sensationnel, super. -**4.** [intelligent] brillant; **that's a ~ idea** c'est une idée lumineuse OR de génie.
◇ *n* brillant *m*.

brilliantine ['brɪljənti:n] *n* brillantine *f*.

brilliantly ['brɪljəntlɪ] *adv* -**1.** [shine] avec éclat; **~ coloured** d'une couleur vive. -**2.** [perform, talk] brillamment.

Brillo pad® ['brɪləʊ-] *n* ≃ tampon *m* Jex®.

brim [brɪm] (*pp* & *pt* **brimmed**, *cont* **brimming**)
◇ *n* [of hat] bord *m*; [of bowl, cup] bord *m*; **full to the ~** plein à ras bord.
◇ *vi* déborder; **eyes brimming with tears** des yeux pleins OR noyés de larmes; **the newcomers were brimming with ideas** *fig* les nouveaux venus avaient des idées à revendre.
◆ **brim over** *vi insep* déborder; **to be brimming over with enthusiasm** *fig* déborder d'enthousiasme.

brimful [,brɪm'fʊl] *adj Br* [cup] plein à déborder OR jusqu'au bord; *fig* débordant; **~ of confidence** très OR excessivement confiant.

brimless ['brɪmlɪs] *adj* [hat] sans bord OR bords.

brimstone ['brɪmstəʊn] *n* -**1.** [sulphur] soufre *m*. -**2.** [butterfly] citron *m*.

brindled ['brɪndld] *adj* moucheté, tavelé.

brine [braɪn] *n* -**1.** [salty water] eau *f* salée; CULIN saumure *f*. -**2.** *lit* [sea] mer *f*; [sea water] eau *f* de mer; **mussels in ~** moules saumurées.

bring [brɪŋ] (*pt* & *pp* **brought** [brɔ:t]) *vt* -**1.** [take - animal, person, vehicle] amener; **I'll ~ the books (across) tomorrow** j'apporterai les livres demain; **her father's ~ing her home today** son père la ramène à la maison aujourd'hui; **what ~s you here?** qu'est-ce qui vous amène?; **can you ~ me a beer, please?** vous pouvez m'apporter une bière, s'il vous plaît?; **that ~s the total to £350** cela fait 350 livres en tout || [fashion, idea, product] introduire, lancer; **black musicians brought jazz to Europe** les musiciens noirs ont introduit le jazz en Europe; **this programme is brought to you by the BBC** ce programme est diffusé par la BBC. -**2.** [into specified state] entraîner, amener; **to ~ sthg into play** faire jouer qqch; **to ~ sthg into question** mettre OR remettre qqch en question; **to ~ sb to his/her senses** ramener qqn à la raison; **to ~ sthg to an end** OR **a close** OR **a halt** mettre fin à qqch; **to ~ sthg to sb's attention** OR **knowledge** OR **notice** attirer l'attention de qqn sur qqch; **to ~ a child into the world** mettre un enfant au monde; **to ~ sthg to light** mettre qqch en lumière, révéler qqch. -**3.** [produce] provoquer, causer; **her performance brought wild applause** son interprétation a provoqué un tonnerre d'applaudissements; **to ~ sthg upon sb** attirer qqch sur qqn; **her foolhardiness brought misfortune upon the family** son imprudence a attiré le malheur sur la famille; **you ~ credit to the firm** vous faites honneur à la société; **they say it ~s bad/good luck** on dit que ça porte malheur/bonheur; **he brought a sense of urgency to the project** il a fait accélérer le projet; **the story brought tears to my eyes** l'histoire m'a fait venir les larmes aux yeux; **his speech brought jeers from the audience** son discours lui a valu les huées de l'assistance; **money does not always ~ happiness** l'argent ne fait pas toujours le bonheur; **the winter brought more wind and rain** l'hiver a amené encore plus de vent et de pluie; **tourism has brought prosperity to the area** le tourisme a enrichi la région; **who knows what the future will ~?** qui sait ce que l'avenir nous/lui *etc* réserve? -**4.** [force] amener; **she can't ~ herself to speak about it** elle n'arrive pas à en parler; **her performance brought the audience to its feet** les spectateurs se sont levés pour l'applaudir. -**5.** [lead] mener, amener; **the path ~s you straight (out) into the village** ce chemin vous mène (tout) droit au village; **the shock brought him to the verge of a breakdown** le choc l'a mené au bord de la dépression nerveuse; **to ~ sb into a conversation/discussion** faire participer qqn à une conversation/discussion; **that ~s us to the next question** cela nous amène à la question suivante. -**6.** JUR: **to ~ an action** OR **a suit against sb** intenter un procès à OR contre qqn; **to ~ a charge against sb** porter une accusation contre qqn; **the case was brought before the court** l'affaire a été déférée au tribunal; **he was brought before the court** il a comparu devant le tribunal; **the murderer must be brought to justice** l'assassin doit être traduit en justice; **to ~ evidence** avancer OR présenter des preuves. -**7.** [financially] rapporter; **her painting only ~s her a few thousand pounds a year** ses peintures ne lui rapportent que quelques milliers de livres par an.
◆ **bring about** *vt sep* -**1.** [cause - changes, war] provoquer, amener, entraîner; **what exactly brought about his dismissal?** pourquoi a-t-il été renvoyé exactement?, quel est le motif exact de son renvoi? -**2.** NAUT faire virer de bord.
◆ **bring along** *vt sep* [person] amener; [thing] apporter.
◆ **bring around** = **bring round**.
◆ **bring back** *vt sep* -**1.** [fetch - person] ramener; [- thing] rapporter; **no amount of crying will ~ him back** pleurer ne le ramènera pas à la vie. -**2.** [restore] restaurer; **the news brought a smile back to her face** la nouvelle lui a rendu le sourire; **they're ~ing back miniskirts** ils relancent la minijupe. -**3.** [evoke - memory] rappeler (à la mémoire); **that ~s it all back to me** ça réveille tous mes souvenirs.
◆ **bring down** *vt sep* -**1.** [fetch - person] amener; [- thing] descendre, apporter. -**2.** [reduce - prices, temperature] faire baisser; [- swelling] réduire. -**3.** [cause to land - kite] ramener (au sol); [- plane] faire atterrir. -**4.** [cause to fall - prey] descendre; [- plane, enemy, tree] abattre. -**5.** [overthrow] faire tomber, renverser. -**6.** MATH [carry] abaisser. -**7.** *inf* [depress] déprimer, don-

ner le cafard à. -**8.** *lit* [provoke - anger] attirer; to ~ **down the wrath of God on sb** attirer la colère de Dieu sur qqn.

◆ **bring forth** *vt sep fml* -**1.** [produce - fruit] produire; [- child] mettre au monde; [- animal] mettre bas. -**2.** [elicit] provoquer.

◆ **bring forward** *vt sep* -**1.** [present - person] faire avancer; [- witness] produire; [- evidence] avancer, présenter. -**2.** [move - date, meeting] avancer. -**3.** [in accounting] reporter.

◆ **bring in** *vt sep* -**1.** [fetch in - person] faire entrer; [- thing] rentrer; **they want to ~ a new person in** ils veulent prendre quelqu'un d'autre; **we will have to ~ in the police** il faudra faire intervenir la OR faire appel à la police. -**2.** [introduce - laws, system] introduire, présenter; [- fashion] lancer; **the government has brought in a new tax bill** le gouvernement a présenté OR déposé un nouveau projet de loi fiscale; **can I just ~ in a new point?** est-ce que je peux faire une autre remarque? -**3.** [yield, produce] rapporter; **to ~ in interest** rapporter des intérêts; **tourism ~s in millions of dollars each year** le tourisme rapporte des millions de dollars tous les ans; **her work doesn't ~ in much money** son travail ne lui rapporte pas grand-chose. -**4.** JUR [verdict] rendre; **they brought in a verdict of guilty** ils l'ont déclaré coupable.

◆ **bring off** *inf vt sep Br* [trick] réussir; [plan] réaliser; [deal] conclure, mener à bien; **did you manage to ~ it off?** avez-vous réussi votre coup?

◆ **bring on** *vt sep* -**1.** [induce] provoquer, causer; **the shock brought on a heart attack** le choc a provoqué une crise cardiaque. -**2.** [encourage] encourager; **the warm weather has really brought on the flowers** la chaleur a bien fait pousser les fleurs; **the idea is to ~ on new tennis players** il s'agit d'encourager de nouveaux tennismen. -**3.** THEAT [person] amener sur scène; [thing] apporter sur scène.

◆ **bring out** *vt sep* -**1.** [take out - person] faire sortir; [- thing] sortir. -**2.** [commercially - product, style] lancer; [- record] sortir; [- book] publier. -**3.** [accentuate] souligner; **that colour ~s out the green in her eyes** cette couleur met en valeur le vert de ses yeux; **her performance brought out the character's comic side** son interprétation a fait ressortir le côté comique du personnage; **to ~ out the best/worst in sb** faire apparaître qqn sous son meilleur/plus mauvais jour; **it ~s out the beast in me** *hum* cela réveille l'animal qui est en moi. -**4.** *Br* [in rash, spots]: **strawberries ~ me out in spots** les fraises me donnent des boutons. -**5.** [encourage - person] encourager; **he's very good at ~ing people out (of themselves)** il sait très bien s'y prendre pour mettre les gens à l'aise. -**6.** [workers] appeler à la grève; **they're threatening to ~ everyone out (on strike)** ils menacent d'appeler tout le monde à faire grève.

◆ **bring over** *vt sep* [take - person] amener; [- thing] apporter.

◆ **bring round** *vt sep* -**1.** [take - person] amener; [- thing] apporter; **I brought the conversation round to marriage** *fig* j'ai amené la conversation sur le mariage. -**2.** [revive] ranimer. -**3.** [persuade] convaincre, convertir; **to ~ sb round to a point of view** convertir OR amener qqn à un point de vue.

◆ **bring through** *vt sep*: **he brought the country through the depression** il a réussi à faire sortir le pays de la dépression; **the doctors brought me through my illness** grâce aux médecins, j'ai survécu à ma maladie.

◆ **bring to** *vt sep* -**1.** [revive] ranimer. -**2.** NAUT mettre en panne.

◆ **bring together** *vt sep* -**1.** [people] réunir; [facts] rassembler. -**2.** [introduce] mettre en contact, faire rencontrer; **her brother brought them together** son frère les a fait se rencontrer. -**3.** [reconcile] réconcilier; **an arbitrator is trying to ~ the two sides together** un médiateur essaie de réconcilier les deux parties.

◆ **bring up** *vt sep* -**1.** [take - person] amener; [- thing] monter. -**2.** [child] élever; **to be well/badly brought up** être bien/mal élevé. -**3.** [mention - fact, problem] signaler, mentionner; [- question] soulever; **don't ~ that up again** ne remettez pas cela sur le tapis; **we won't ~ it up again** nous n'en reparlerons plus. -**4.** [vomit] vomir, rendre. -**5.** JUR: **to ~ sb up before a judge** citer OR faire comparaître qqn devant un juge.

bring-and-buy *n Br*: ~ **(sale)** *brocante de particuliers en Grande-Bretagne.*

BRING-AND-BUY SALE:
Ces brocantes sont en général destinées à réunir des fonds pour une œuvre de charité. On y vend des articles d'occasion et des produits faits maison.

---

brink [brɪŋk] *n* bord *m*; **to be on the ~ of tears** être au bord des larmes; **the country is on the ~ of war/of a recession** le pays est au bord OR à la veille de la guerre/d'une récession; **to be on the ~ of doing sthg** être sur le point de faire qqch.

brink(s)manship ['brɪŋk(s)mənʃɪp] *n* stratégie *f* du bord de l'abîme.

briny ['braɪnɪ] (*compar* **brinier**, *superl* **briniest**)
◇ *adj* saumâtre, salé.
◇ *n lit*: **the ~** la mer.

briquet(te) [brɪ'ket] *n* [of coal] briquette *f*, aggloméré *m*; [of ice cream] pavé *m*.

brisk [brɪsk] *adj* -**1.** [person] vif, alerte; [manner] brusque. -**2.** [quick] rapide, vif; **to go for a ~ walk** se promener d'un bon pas; **to go for a ~ swim** nager vigoureusement; **at a ~ pace** à vive allure. -**3.** COMM florissant; **business is ~** les affaires marchent bien; **bidding at the auction was ~** les enchères étaient animées; **~ trading** ST. EX marché actif. -**4.** [weather] vivifiant, frais; [day, wind] frais.

brisket ['brɪskɪt] *n* [of animal] poitrine *f*; CULIN poitrine *f* de bœuf.

briskly ['brɪsklɪ] *adv* -**1.** [move] vivement; [walk] d'un bon pas; [speak] brusquement; [act] sans délai OR tarder. -**2.** COMM: **cold drinks were selling ~** les boissons fraîches se vendaient très bien OR comme des petits pains.

briskness ['brɪsknɪs] *n* -**1.** [of person] vivacité *f*; [of manner] brusquerie *f*; [of action] rapidité *f*. -**2.** COMM activité *f*. -**3.** [of weather] fraîcheur *f*.

brisling ['brɪzlɪŋ] *n* sprat *m*.

bristle ['brɪsl] ◇ *vi* -**1.** [hair] se redresser, se hérisser. -**2.** *fig* [show anger] s'irriter, se hérisser; **they ~d at any suggestion of incompetence** ils se hérissèrent lorsqu'on osa insinuer qu'ils étaient incompétents.
◇ *n* [of beard, brush] poil *m*; [of boar, pig] soie *f*; [of plant] poil *m*, soie *f*; **a brush with nylon/natural ~s** une brosse en nylon/soie.
◇ *comp* [hairbrush, paintbrush]: **a pure ~ brush** une brosse pur sanglier.

◆ **bristle with** *vt insep Br* grouiller de; **the whole subject ~s with difficulties** toute la question est hérissée de difficultés; **the town centre was bristling with police** le centre-ville grouillait de policiers.

bristling ['brɪslɪŋ] *adj* hérissé, en bataille.

bristly ['brɪslɪ] (*compar* **bristlier**, *superl* **bristliest**) *adj* [beard - in appearance] aux poils raides; [- to touch] qui pique; [chin] piquant; **his face was all ~** il avait une barbe de trois jours.

Bristol ['brɪstl] *pr n* [city] Bristol; **~ fashion** bien rangé, impeccable.

◆ **bristols**▽ *npl Br* roberts *mpl*, nichons *mpl*.

Bristol board *n* bristol *m*.

Bristol Channel *pr n*: **the ~** le canal de Bristol.

Brit [brɪt] ◇ *n inf* Britannique *mf*.
◇ *written abbr of* **British**.

Britain ['brɪtn] *pr n*: **(Great) ~** Grande-Bretagne *f*; **in ~** en Grande-Bretagne; **the Battle of ~** la bataille d'Angleterre.

THE BATTLE OF BRITAIN:
Lutte aérienne opposant, d'août à octobre 1940, la Luftwaffe à la RAF, l'objectif allemand étant de neutraliser l'espace aérien britannique en vue d'un débarquement. La résistance des forces aériennes britanniques contraignit Hitler à y renoncer.

Britannia [brɪ'tænjə] *pr n* -**1.** [figure] *femme assise portant un casque et tenant un trident, qui personnifie la Grande-Bretagne sur certaines pièces de monnaie.* -**2.** (the Royal Yacht) **~** *yacht de la famille royale britannique.*

Britannia metal *n* métal *m* anglais.

Britannia silver *n* argent *m* fin.

Britannic [brɪ'tænɪk] *adj fml*: **His** OR **Her ~ Majesty** Sa Majesté Britannique.

Britannicus [brɪ'tænɪkəs] *pr n* Britannicus.

britches ['brɪtʃɪz] *Am* = **breeches**.

briticism ['brɪtɪsɪzm] *n* anglicisme *m*.

British ['brɪtɪʃ] ◇ *adj* britannique, anglais; **~ goods** produits anglais; **~ English** anglais *m* britannique; **the ~ Embassy** l'ambassade *f* de Grande-Bretagne; **the ~ Empire** l'Empire *m* britannique; **~ Technology Group** *organisme privé britannique commercialisant des innovations technologiques élaborées par des universités ou des inventeurs.*
◇ *npl*: **the ~** les Britanniques *mpl*, les Anglais *mpl*.

British Academy *pr n*: **the ~** *organisme public d'aide à la recherche dans le domaine des lettres.*

British Antarctic Territory *pr n* territoire *m* de l'Antarctique britannique.

British Broadcasting Corporation *pr n*: **the ~** la BBC.

British Columbia *pr n* Colombie-Britannique *f*; **in ~** en Colombie-Britannique.

British Columbian ◇ *n habitant ou natif de la Colombie-Britannique.*
◇ *adj* de la Colombie-Britannique.

British Commonwealth *pr n*: **the ~** le Commonwealth.

British Council *pr n*: **the ~** *organisme culturel public.*

BRITISH COUNCIL:
Le British Council est chargé de promouvoir la langue et la culture anglaises, et de renforcer les liens culturels avec les autres pays.

British East India Company *pr n*: **the ~** la Compagnie britannique des Indes orientales.

THE BRITISH EAST INDIA COMPANY:
Fondée en 1600 pour contrôler le commerce dans les colonies, la Compagnie joua, à partir du XVIIIe siècle, un rôle de plus en plus politique en Inde, pour finalement devenir l'agent de l'impérialisme britannique; elle disparut dans les années 1870.

Britisher ['brɪtɪʃər] *n Am* Anglais *m*, -e *f*, Britannique *mf*.

British Honduras *pr n*: (former) **~** (l'ex) Honduras *m* britannique; **in ~** au Honduras britannique.

British Isles *pl pr n*: **the ~** les îles *fpl* Britanniques; **in the ~** aux îles Britanniques.

British Lions *pl pr n*: **the ~** *équipe de rugby à quinze constituée des joueurs sélectionnés dans les quatre équipes nationales (Angleterre, pays de Galles, Écosse et Irlande).*

British Museum *pr n grand musée et bibliothèque londoniens.*

British Summer Time *n heure d'été britannique.*

British Telecom [-'telɪkɒm] *pr n société britannique de télécommunications.*

BRITISH TELECOM:
Les Télécoms britanniques, qui gèrent notamment les services téléphoniques, ont été privatisés en 1984.

Briton ['brɪtn] *n* Britannique *mf*, Anglais *m*, -e *f*; HIST Breton *m*, -onne *f* (d'Angleterre).

Brittany ['brɪtənɪ] *pr n* Bretagne *f*; in ~ en Bretagne.

brittle ['brɪtl] *adj* -**1.** [breakable] cassant, fragile. -**2.** [person] froid, indifférent; [humour] mordant, caustique; a ~ reply une réponse sèche; a ~ tone of voice un ton sec OR cassant. -**3.** [sound] strident, aigu.

brittleness ['brɪtlnɪs] *n* -**1.** [fragility] fragilité *f*. -**2.** [of person] froideur *f*, insensibilité *f*; [of humour] causticité *f*, mordant *m*. -**3.** [of sound] son *m* aigu.

bro *inf* [brəʊ] (*abbr of* brother) *n*: my ~ mon frangin.

broach [brəʊtʃ] ◇ *vt* -**1.** [subject] aborder, entamer. -**2.** [barrel] percer, mettre en perce; [supplies] entamer.
◇ *vi* NAUT venir OR tomber en travers.
◇ *n* -**1.** *Am* = **brooch**. -**2.** CONSTR perçoir *m*, foret *m*. -**3.** CULIN broche *f*.

broad [brɔːd] ◇ *adj* -**1.** [wide] large; the road is 4 metres ~ la route a 4 mètres de large OR de largeur; she has a ~ back elle a une forte carrure; to be ~ in the shoulders, to have ~ shoulders être large d'épaules; a ~ grin un large OR grand sourire ❑ he has ~ shoulders, he can take it il a les reins solides, il peut encaisser; to be ~ in the beam [ship] être ventru; [person] *inf* être large des hanches; it's as ~ as it's long *Br* c'est bonnet blanc et blanc bonnet, c'est du pareil au même. -**2.** [extensive] vaste, immense; a ~ syllabus un programme très divers; we offer a ~ range of products nous offrons une large OR grande gamme de produits ❑ in ~ daylight *literal* au grand jour, en plein jour; *fig* au vu et au su de tout le monde, au grand jour. -**3.** [general] général; here is a ~ outline voilà les grandes lignes; in the ~est sense of the word au sens le plus large du mot; his books still have a very ~ appeal ses livres plaisent toujours à OR intéressent toujours un vaste public; ~ construction *Am* JUR interprétation *f* large. -**4.** [not subtle] évident; a ~ hint une allusion transparente; "surely not", she said with ~ sarcasm «pas possible», dit-elle d'un ton des plus sarcastiques; he speaks with a ~ Scots accent il a un accent écossais prononcé OR un fort accent écossais. -**5.** [liberal] libéral; ~ views idées larges; she has very ~ tastes in literature elle a des goûts littéraires très éclectiques ❑ Broad Church *groupe libéral à l'intérieur de l'Église anglicane*. -**6.** [coarse] grossier, vulgaire; ~ humour humour grivois; a ~ joke une plaisanterie osée OR leste. -**7.** PHON large.
◇ *n* -**1.** [widest part]: the ~ of the back le milieu du dos. -**2.** ▽ *Am* [woman] gonzesse *f*.

B-road *n Br* ≃ route *f* départementale OR secondaire.

broadband ['brɔːdbænd] ◇ *n* diffusion *f* en larges bandes de fréquence.
◇ *adj* à larges bandes.

broad bean *n* fève *f*.

broad-brimmed [-'brɪmd] *adj* à bords larges.

broad-brush *adj* : a ~ approach une approche grossière.

broadcast ['brɔːdkɑːst] (*pt* & *pp* broadcast OR broadcasted) ◇ *n* émission *f*; live/recorded ~ émission en direct/en différé; repeat ~ rediffusion *f*.
◇ *vt* -**1.** RADIO diffuser, radiodiffuser, émettre; TV téléviser, émettre; you don't have to ~ it! *fig* ce n'est pas la peine de le crier sur les toits OR le carillonner partout! -**2.** AGR semer à la volée.
◇ *vi* [station] émettre; [actor] participer à une émission; TV paraître à la télévision; [show host] faire une émission.
◇ *adj* RADIO radiodiffusé; TV télévisé; ~ signal/satellite signal *m*/satellite *m* de radiodiffusion.
◇ *adv* AGR à la volée.

broadcaster ['brɔːdkɑːstəʳ] *n* personnalité *f* de la radio OR de la télévision.

broadcasting ['brɔːdkɑːstɪŋ] *n* RADIO radiodiffusion *f*; TV télévision *f*; he wants to go into ~ il veut faire une carrière à la radio ou à la télévision.

Broadcasting House *pr n siège de la BBC à Londres*.

broadcloth ['brɔːdklɒθ] *n* drap *m* fin.

broaden ['brɔːdn] ◇ *vi* s'élargir; turn left where the road ~s (out) prenez à gauche, là où la route s'élargit.
◇ *vt* élargir; to ~ one's horizons OR outlook élargir son horizon.

broad jump *n Am* saut *m* en longueur.

broadleaved ['brɔːdliːvd] *adj* feuillu, latifolié *spec*.

broadloom ['brɔːdluːm] *adj* [carpet] en grande largeur.

broadly ['brɔːdlɪ] *adv* -**1.** [widely] largement; to smile ~ faire un grand sourire. -**2.** [generally] en général; ~ speaking d'une façon générale, en gros.

broadly-based *adj* composé d'éléments variés OR divers.

broad-minded *adj*: to be ~ avoir les idées larges; he has very ~ parents ses parents sont très tolérants OR larges d'esprit.

broad-mindedness [-'maɪndɪdnɪs] *n* largeur *f* d'esprit.

Broadmoor ['brɔːd,mɔː] *pr n institution britannique pour les détenus souffrant de graves troubles psychiques*.

broadness ['brɔːdnɪs] *n* -**1.** [width] largeur *f*. -**2.** [coarseness] grossièreté *f*, vulgarité *f*. -**3.** [of accent] caractère *m* prononcé.

Broads [brɔːdz] *pl pr n*: the (Norfolk) ~ *ensemble de lacs situés dans le Norfolk et le Suffolk*.

BROADS:
Les Broads sont des lacs peu profonds mais navigables, reliés entre eux par des cours d'eau; ils constituent aujourd'hui un parc national et une réserve ornithologique.

---

broadsheet ['brɔːdʃiːt] *n* -**1.** [newspaper] journal *m* plein format; the ~s *Br* PRESS les journaux *mpl* de qualité. -**2.** HIST & TYPO placard *m*.

BROADSHEET:
Les principaux journaux nationaux de qualité en Grande-Bretagne sont:
The Guardian (tendance centre gauche);
The Independent;
The Daily Telegraph (tendance conservatrice);
The Times (tendance centre droit);
The Financial Times.

---

broadside ['brɔːdsaɪd] ◇ *n* -**1.** [of ship] flanc *m*. -**2.** [volley of shots] bordée *f*; the ship fired a ~ le navire a lâché une bordée || *fig* [tirade] attaque *f* cinglante; [of insults] bordée *f* d'injures; to fire a ~ at sb/sthg s'en prendre violemment à qqn/qqch.
◇ *adv*: ~ (on) par le travers; the ship is ~ on to the wharf le navire présente le flanc OR le travers au quai; the truck hit us ~ on *Br* le camion nous a heurtés sur le côté.

broad-spectrum *adj* à large spectre.

broadsword ['brɔːdsɔːd] *n* sabre *m*.

Broadway ['brɔːdweɪ] *pr n* Broadway.

BROADWAY:
Broadway est la rue des théâtres et le centre de la vie nocturne à Manhattan.

---

brocade [brə'keɪd] ◇ *n* brocart *m*; ~ curtains rideaux *mpl* de brocart.
◇ *vt* brocher.

broccoli ['brɒkəlɪ] *n (U)* brocolis *mpl*.

brochure [*Br* 'brəʊʃəʳ, *Am* brəʊ'ʃʊr] *n* [gen] brochure *f*, dépliant *m*; SCH & UNIV prospectus *m*.

brogue [brəʊg] *n* [accent] accent *m* du terroir; [Irish] accent *m* irlandais.
◆ **brogues** *npl chaussures basses assez lourdes ornées de petits trous*.

broil [brɔɪl] *Am* ◇ *vt* griller, faire cuire sur le gril; *fig* griller.
◇ *vi* griller; ~ing sun soleil brûlant.

broiler ['brɔɪləʳ] *n* -**1.** [chicken] poulet *m* (à rôtir). -**2.** *Am* [grill] gril *m*, rôtissoire *f*; it's a ~ today *inf fig* il fait une chaleur à crever aujourd'hui.

broiler house *n* éleveuse *f* (de poulets).

broke [brəʊk] ◇ *pt* → **break**.
◇ *adj inf* fauché, à sec; to go ~ faire faillite ❑ to go for ~ risquer le tout pour le tout; to be flat OR dead OR stony *Br* ~ être fauché comme les blés, être raide comme un passe-lacet.

broken ['brəʊkn] ◇ *pp* → **break**.
◇ *adj* -**1.** [damaged - chair, toy, window] cassé, brisé; [- leg, rib] fracturé, cassé; [- biscuits] brisé; are there any ~ bones? y a-t-il des fractures?; ~ back dos brisé OR cassé || *fig*: ~ heart cœur brisé; to die of a ~ heart mourir de chagrin; she's from a ~ home elle vient d'un foyer désuni; a ~ marriage un mariage brisé, un ménage désuni. -**2.** [sleep - disturbed] interrompu; [- restless] agité. -**3.** [speech] mauvais, imparfait; he speaks ~ English il parle un mauvais anglais; in ~ French en mauvais français. -**4.** [agreement, promise] rompu, violé; [appointment] manqué. -**5.** [health] délabré; her spirit is ~ elle est abattue; he's a ~ man since his wife's death [emotionally] il a le cœur brisé OR il est très abattu depuis la mort de sa femme; the scandal left him a ~ man [financially] le scandale l'a ruiné. -**6.** [incomplete - set] incomplet; ~ lots COMM articles *mpl* dépareillés. -**7.** [uneven - ground] accidenté; [- coastline] dentelé; [- line] brisé, discontinu; ~ cloud *(U)* éclaircie *f*. -**8.** [tamed - animal] dressé, maté. -**9.** LING [vowel] diphtongué. -**10.** MATH: ~ numbers fractions *fpl*. -**11.** MUS: ~ chord arpège *m*.

broken-down *adj* -**1.** [damaged - machine] détraqué; [- car] en panne. -**2.** [worn out] fini, à bout.

brokenhearted [,brəʊkn'hɑːtɪd] *adj* au cœur brisé.

broken-winded [-'wɪndɪd] *adj* [horse] poussif.

broker ['brəʊkəʳ] *n* -**1.** COMM courtier *m*; NAUT courtier *m* maritime; ST. EX ≃ courtier *m* (en Bourse), ≃ agent *m* de change; insurance ~ courtier OR agent d'assurances. -**2.** [second-hand dealer] brocanteur *m*.

brokerage ['brəʊkərɪdʒ], **broking** ['brəʊkɪŋ] *n* courtage *m*.

brolly *inf* ['brɒlɪ] (*pl* brollies) *n Br* pépin *m (parapluie)*.

bromeliad [brəʊ'miːlɪæd] *n* broméliacée *f*.

bromide ['brəʊmaɪd] *n* -**1.** CHEM bromure *m*; [sedative] bromure *m* (de potassium). -**2.** *dated* [remark] banalité *f*, platitude *f*. -**3.** PRINT bromure *m*.

bromine ['brəʊmiːn] *n* brome *m*.

Bromo® ['brəʊməʊ] *n Am médicament contre les maux d'estomac, l'indigestion etc*.

bronchi ['brɒŋkaɪ] *pl* → **bronchus**.

bronchial ['brɒŋkjəl] *adj* des bronches, bronchique.

bronchial tubes *npl* bronches *fpl*.

bronchiole ['brɒŋkɪəʊl] *n* bronchiole *f*.

bronchitic [brɒŋ'kɪtɪk] ◇ *adj* bronchitique.
◇ *n* bronchitique *mf*.

bronchitis [brɒŋ'kaɪtɪs] *n (U)* bronchite *f*; to have (an attack of) ~ avoir OR faire une bronchite.

bronchodilator [,brɒŋkəʊdaɪ'leɪtəʳ] *n* bronchodilatateur *m*.

bronchopneumonia [,brɒŋkəʊnjuː'məʊnjə] *n* broncho-pneumonie *f*.

bronchus ['brɒŋkəs] (*pl* bronchi [-kaɪ]) *n* bronche *f*.

bronco ['brɒŋkəʊ] (*pl* broncos) *n Am* cheval *m* sauvage *(de l'Ouest)*.

broncobuster ['brɒŋkəʊ,bʌstəʳ] *n Am cowboy qui dresse les chevaux sauvages*.

brontosaurus [,brɒntə'sɔːrəs] (*pl* brontosauruses OR brontosauri [-raɪ]) *n* brontosaure *m*.

Bronx [brɒŋks] *pr n*: the ~ le Bronx *(quartier de New York)*.

Bronx cheer *inf n Am* [rude noise]: to give sb a ~ ≃ faire «prout» à qqn.

bronze [brɒnz] ◇ *n* -**1.** [alloy] bronze *m*. -**2.** [statue] bronze *m*, statue *f* de OR en bronze.
◇ *comp* -**1.** [lamp, medal, statue] de OR en bronze. -**2.** [colour, skin] (couleur *f* de) bronze *(inv)*.
◇ *vi* se bronzer, brunir.
◇ *vt* [metal] bronzer; [skin] faire bronzer, brunir.

Bronze Age *n*: the ~ l'âge *m* du bronze.

bronzed [brɒnzd] *adj* bronzé, hâlé.

bronze medal *n* médaille *f* de bronze.

bronze medallist *n*: he's a ~ il a remporté la médaille de bronze.

brooch [brəʊtʃ] (*pl* brooches) *n* broche *f (bijou)*.

brood [bruːd] ◇ *n* -**1.** [of birds] couvée *f*, nichée *f*; [of animals] nichée *f*, portée *f*; a ~ mare une (jument) poulinière. -**2.** *hum* [children] progéniture *f hum*.
◇ *vi* -**1.** [bird] couver. -**2.** [danger, storm] couver, menacer; the monument ~s over the town's main square *fig* le monument domine la grand-place de la ville. -**3.** [person] ruminer, broyer du noir; all he does is sit there ~ing il passe son temps à broyer du noir; it's no use ~ing on OR over the past cela ne sert à rien de s'appesantir sur OR remâcher le passé.

brooding ['bruːdɪŋ] ◇ *adj* menaçant, inquiétant.
◇ *n*: he's done a lot of ~ since he got home depuis son retour à la maison, il a passé beaucoup de temps à ruminer.

broody ['bruːdɪ] (*compar* broodier, *superl* broodiest) *adj* -**1.** [reflective] pensif; [gloomy] mélancolique, cafardeux. -**2.** [motherly]: a ~ hen une (poule) couveuse; to feel ~ *inf Br fig* être en mal d'enfant.

brook [brʊk] ◇ *vt (usu neg)* [tolerate] supporter, tolérer; [answer, delay] admettre, souffrir.
◇ *n* [stream] ruisseau *m*.

brookite ['brʊkaɪt] *n* brookite *m*.

brooklet ['brʊklɪt] *n* ruisselet *m*, petit ruisseau *m*.

Brooklyn ['brʊklɪn] *pr n* Brooklyn *(quartier de New York)*.

brook trout *n* saumon *m* de fontaine.

broom [bruːm] *n* -**1.** [brush] balai *m*; a new ~ sweeps clean *prov* tout nouveau tout beau *prov*. -**2.** BOT genêt *m*.

broomstick ['bruːmstɪk] *n* manche *m* à balai.

bros., Bros. [brɒs] (*abbr of* brothers) COMM Frères.

broth [brɒθ] *n* -**1.** CULIN bouillon *m (de viande et de légumes)*. -**2.** BIOL bouillon *m* de culture.

brothel ['brɒθl] *n* maison *f* close OR de passe.

brothel creeper *inf n Br chaussure de daim à semelle de crêpe pour hommes*.

brother ['brʌðər] (*pl sense 2* brethren ['breðrən]) ◇ *n* -**1.** [relative] frère *m*; older/younger ~ frère aîné/cadet ❑ the Brothers Grimm les frères Grimm; 'The Brothers Karamazov' *Dostoevski* 'les Frères Karamazov'. -**2.** [fellow member - of trade union] camarade *m*; [- of professional group] collègue *mf*; ~s in arms compagnons *mpl* OR frères *mpl* d'armes; (soul) ~ *Am* frère *m* (de race). -**3.** *inf Am* [mate]: hey, ~! [stranger] eh, camarade!; [friend] eh, mon vieux!
◇ *interj inf* dis donc, bigre.

brotherhood ['brʌðəhʊd] *n* -**1.** [relationship] fraternité *f*; *fig* [fellowship] fraternité *f*, confraternité *f*; RELIG confrérie *f*; the ~ of man la communauté humaine. -**2.** [association] confrérie *f*; the Brotherhood [in Freemasonry] la franc-maçonnerie. -**3.** *Am* [entire profession] corporation *f*.

brother-in-law (*pl* brothers-in-law) *n* beau-frère *m*.

brotherly ['brʌðəlɪ] *adj* fraternel; ~ love amour fraternel; the City of Brotherly Love *surnom donné à Philadelphie*; he felt very ~ towards her il la considérait un peu comme une sœur.

brougham ['bruːəm] *n* [carriage] voiture *f* à chevaux; [car] coupé *m* de ville.

brought [brɔːt] *pt & pp* → **bring**.

brouhaha ['bruːhɑːhɑː] *n* brouhaha *m*, vacarme *m*.

brow [braʊ] *n* -**1.** [forehead] front *m*; her troubled ~ son air inquiet. -**2.** [eyebrow] sourcil *m*. -**3.** [of hill] sommet *m*. -**4.** MIN [pithead] tour *m* d'extraction.

browband ['braʊbænd] *n* frontail *m*.

browbeat ['braʊbiːt] (*pt* browbeat, *pp* browbeaten [-biːtn]) *vt* intimider, brusquer; to ~ sb into doing sthg forcer qqn à faire qqch en usant d'intimidation.

browbeaten ['braʊbiːtn] *adj* persécuté.

brown [braʊn] ◇ *n* brun *m*, marron *m*; dressed in ~ habillée en marron.
◇ *adj* -**1.** [gen] brun, marron; [leather] marron; [hair] châtain; she has ~ hair elle est brune OR châtain; light ~ hair cheveux châtain clair; ~ eyes yeux marron; a light ~ scarf une écharpe marron clair; the leaves are turning ~ les feuilles commencent à jaunir ❑ ~ belt JUDO ceinture *f* marron; we'll do it up ~! *inf Am* nous allons fignoler ça!; in a ~ study plongé dans ses pensées, pensif. -**2.** [tanned] bronzé, bruni; as ~ as a berry tout bronzé.
◇ *vi* -**1.** CULIN dorer. -**2.** [skin] bronzer, brunir. -**3.** [plant] roussir.
◇ *vt* -**1.** CULIN faire dorer; [sauce] faire roussir. -**2.** [tan] bronzer, brunir.

brown ale *n* bière *f* brune.

brownbag *inf* ['braʊnbæg] (*pp & pt* brownbagged, *cont* brownbagging) *vt Am*: I ~ it to work j'apporte mon déjeuner tous les jours au travail.

brown bear *n* ours *m* brun.

brown bread *n (U)* pain *m* complet OR bis.

brown coal *n* lignite *m*.

browned-off *inf adj Br*: to be ~ [bored] en avoir marre; [discouraged] ne plus avoir le moral; she's ~ with her job elle en a marre OR ras le bol de son travail.

brown goods *npl* COMM *biens de consommation de taille moyenne tels que téléviseur, radio ou magnétoscope*.

brownie ['braʊnɪ] *n* -**1.** [elf] lutin *m*, farfadet *m*. -**2.** [cake] brownie *m*; chocolate ~s brownies au chocolat. -**3.** Brownie® [camera] Brownie® *m* Kodak.
◆ **Brownie (Guide)** *n* ≃ jeannette *f*; to join the Brownies s'inscrire aux jeannettes, devenir jeannette.

brownie point *inf n hum* bon point *m*; doing the ironing should earn you a few ~s tu seras dans ses petits papiers OR bien vu si tu fais le repassage.

browning ['braʊnɪŋ] *n Br* CULIN *colorant brun pour les sauces*.

Browning ['braʊnɪŋ] *n*: ~ (automatic rifle) browning *m*.

brownish ['braʊnɪʃ] *adj* qui tire sur le brun, brunâtre.

brown-nose▽ ◇ *n* lèche-bottes *mf inv*.
◇ *vt* lécher les bottes de.
◇ *vi* faire le lèche-bottes.

brownout ['braʊnaʊt] *n Am* [electric failure] baisse *f* de tension; MIL [blackout] black-out *m* partiel, camouflage *m* partiel des lumières.

brown owl *n* chat-huant *m*.

brown paper *n* papier *m* d'emballage.

brown rice *n* riz *m* complet.

Brown Shirt *n* fasciste *mf*; HIST [Nazi] chemise *f* brune.

brownstone ['braʊnstəʊn] *n Am* [stone] grès *m* brun; [house] bâtiment *m* de grès brun.

brown sugar *n* cassonade *f*, sucre *m* roux.

brown trout *n* truite *f* de rivière.

browse [braʊz] ◇ *vi* -**1.** [person] regarder, jeter un œil; she ~d through the book elle a feuilleté le livre; feel free to ~ [in shop] vous pouvez regarder si vous voulez. -**2.** [animal] brouter, paître.
◇ *n* -**1.** [look]: I popped into the shop to have a ~ around je suis passée au magasin pour jeter un coup d'œil OR regarder. -**2.** [young leaves, twigs] broutille *f*.

brucellosis [ˌbruːsɪ'ləʊsɪs] *n* brucellose *f*.

Bruges [bruːʒ] *pr n* Bruges.

bruise [bruːz] ◇ *n* [on person] bleu *m*, contusion *f*; to be covered with ~s être couvert de bleus ‖ [on fruit] meurtrissure *f*, talure *f*.
◇ *vi* [fruit] se taler, s'abîmer; to ~ easily [person] se faire facilement des bleus.
◇ *vt* -**1.** [person] faire un bleu à, contusionner; to ~ one's arm se faire un bleu au bras; to be ~d all over être couvert de bleus; he felt ~d by her harsh words *fig* ses dures paroles l'ont blessé; the only thing he ~d was his ego *fig* seul son amour-propre en a pris un coup ‖ [fruit] taler, abîmer; [lettuce] flétrir. -**2.** CULIN [crush] écraser, piler.

bruiser *inf* ['bruːzər] *n* [big man] malabar *m*; he's a bit of a ~ il fait un peu armoire à glace ‖ [fighter] cogneur *m*.

bruising ['bruːzɪŋ] ◇ *n (U)* contusion *f*, bleu *m*; he suffered ~ to his arm il a eu le bras contusionné.
◇ *adj* pénible, douloureux; it was a rather ~ experience ce fut une expérience plutôt douloureuse.

Brum *inf* [brʌm] *pr n Br nom familier de Birmingham*.

Brummie *inf* ['brʌmɪ] *Br* ◇ *n nom familier désignant un habitant de Birmingham*.
◇ *adj* de Birmingham.

Brummy ['brʌmɪ] = **Brummie**.

brunch [brʌntʃ] *n* brunch *m*.

Brunei ['bruːnaɪ] *pr n* Brunei *m*; in ~ au Brunei.

brunet [bruː'net] *Am* ◇ *n* brun *m*, brune *f*; he's a ~ il est brun.
◇ *adj* [hair] châtain.

brunette [bruː'net] ◇ *n* brune *f*, brunette *f*; she's a ~ elle est brune.
◇ *adj* [hair] châtain.

Brunswick ['brʌnzwɪk] *pr n* Brunswick.

brunt [brʌnt] *n*: the village bore the full ~ of the attack le village a essuyé le plus fort de l'attaque; she bore the ~ of his anger c'est sur elle que sa colère a éclaté.

brush [brʌʃ] (*pl* brushes) ◇ *n* -**1.** [gen] brosse *f*; [paintbrush] pinceau *m*, brosse *f*; [shaving brush] blaireau *m*; [scrubbing brush] brosse *f* dure; [broom] balai *m*; [short-handled brush] balayette *f*; hair/nail/tooth ~ brosse à cheveux/à ongles/à dents. -**2.** [sweep] coup *m* de brosse; this floor could do with a good ~ ce plancher aurait besoin d'un bon coup de balai. -**3.** [encounter, skirmish] accrochage *m*, escarmouche *f*; *fig*: to have a ~ with death frôler la mort; to have a ~ with the law avoir des démêlés avec la justice; she's had the odd ~ with the authorities elle a eu parfois maille à partir avec les autorités. -**4.** [of fox] queue *f*. -**5.** ELEC [in generator, dynamo] balai *m*; [discharge] aigrette *f*. -**6.** *(U)* [undergrowth] broussailles *fpl*; [scrubland] brousse *f*.
◇ *vt* -**1.** [clean - teeth] brosser; [tidy - hair] brosser, donner un coup de brosse; she ~ed her hair back from her face elle a brossé ses cheveux en arrière ‖ [sweep - floor] balayer. -**2.** [touch lightly] effleurer, frôler; [surface] raser. -**3.** TEX [wool] gratter.
◇ *vi* effleurer, frôler; her hair ~ed against his cheek ses cheveux ont effleuré OR frôlé sa joue.
◆ **brush aside** *vt sep* -**1.** [move aside] écarter, repousser. -**2.** [ignore] balayer OR écarter (d'un geste); you can't just ~ aside his report vous ne pouvez pas rejeter son rapport comme ça.
◆ **brush away** *vt sep* [remove - tears] essuyer; [- insect] chasser.
◆ **brush down** *vt sep* [clothing] donner un coup de brosse à; [horse] brosser.
◆ **brush off** ◇ *vt sep* -**1.** [remove] enlever *(à la brosse ou à la main)*; [insect] chasser. -**2.** [dismiss - remark] balayer OR écarter (d'un geste); [- person] écarter, repousser.
◇ *vi insep* [dirt] s'enlever.
◆ **brush past** *vt insep* frôler en passant.

◆ **brush up** *vt sep* -**1.** *inf* [revise] revoir, réviser; I have to ~ up my maths il faut que je me remette aux maths. -**2.** [sweep up - dirt] ramasser à la balayette. -**3.** TEX [wool] gratter.

◆ **brush up on** *inf vt insep* réviser.

brushed [brʌʃt] *adj* gratté; ~ cotton pilou *m*, finette *f*; ~ nylon nylon *m* gratté.

brush fire *n* -**1.** [fire] feu *m* de brousse, incendie *m* de broussailles. -**2.** [minor war] conflit *m* armé.

brush-off *inf n*: to give sb the ~ envoyer promener OR balader qqn; I got the ~ on m'a envoyé sur les roses OR bouler.

brush stroke *n* [gen] coup *m* de brosse; ART coup *m* OR trait *m* de pinceau.

brush-up *n* -**1.** *Br* [cleanup] coup *m* de brosse. -**2.** *inf* [revision] révision *f*; my German could do with a ~ j'aurais besoin de me remettre à l'allemand.

brushwood [ˈbrʌʃwʊd] *n (U)* [undergrowth] broussailles *fpl*; [cuttings] menu bois *m*, brindilles *fpl*.

brushwork [ˈbrʌʃwɜːk] *n* [gen] travail *m* au pinceau; ART facture *f*.

brusque [bruːsk] *adj* [abrupt] brusque; [curt] brusque, bourru.

brusquely [ˈbruːsklɪ] *adv* [abruptly] avec brusquerie; [curtly] avec brusquerie OR rudesse, brutalement.

brusqueness [ˈbruːsknɪs] *n* [abruptness] brusquerie *f*; [curtness] brusquerie *f*, rudesse *f*.

Brussels [ˈbrʌslz] *pr n* Bruxelles.

Brussels sprout *n* chou *m* de Bruxelles.

brutal [ˈbruːtl] *adj* [cruel - action, behaviour, person] brutal, cruel; [uncompromising - honesty] franc, brutal; [severe - climate, cold] rude, rigoureux; with ~ frankness d'une franchise brutale.

brutality [bruːˈtælətɪ] (*pl* **brutalities**) *n* -**1.** [cruelty] brutalité *f*, cruauté *f*. -**2.** [act of cruelty] brutalité *f*.

brutalize, -ise [ˈbruːtəlaɪz] *vt* -**1.** [ill-treat] brutaliser. -**2.** [make brutal] rendre brutal.

brutally [ˈbruːtəlɪ] *adv* [attack, kill, treat] brutalement, sauvagement; [say] brutalement, franchement; [cold] extrêmement; she gave a ~ honest account of events elle a raconté les événements avec une franchise brutale OR un réalisme brutal.

brute [bruːt] ◇ *n* -**1.** [animal] brute *f*, bête *f*. -**2.** [person - violent] brute *f*; [- coarse] brute *f* (épaisse), rustre *m*; a great ~ of a man une grande brute.

◇ *adj* -**1.** [animal-like] animal, bestial. -**2.** [purely physical] brutal; ~ force OR strength force *f* brutale. -**3.** [mindless] brut; an act of ~ stupidity un acte d'une bêtise sans nom.

brutish [ˈbruːtɪʃ] *adj* -**1.** [animal-like] animal, bestial. -**2.** [cruel] brutal, violent; [coarse] grossier.

Brutus [ˈbruːtəs] *pr n* Brutus.

Bryansk [brɪˈænsk] *pr n* Briansk.

bryony [ˈbraɪənɪ] (*pl* bryonies) *n* bryone *f*.

bs *written abbr of* bill of sale.

BS *n* -**1.** *Br* (*abbr of* British Standard/Standards) *indique que le chiffre qui suit renvoie au numéro de la norme fixée par l'Institut britannique de normalisation.* -**2.** *Am* UNIV (*abbr of* Bachelor of Science) *(titulaire d'une) licence de sciences.*

BSA (*abbr of* Boy Scouts of America) *pr n association américaine de scouts.*

BSc (*abbr of* Bachelor of Science) *n Br* UNIV *(titulaire d'une) licence de sciences.*

BSC (*abbr of* British Steel Corporation) *pr n entreprise sidérurgique, aujourd'hui privatisée.*

BSE (*abbr of* bovine spongiform encephalopathy) *n* EBS *f*.

BSI (*abbr of* British Standards Institution) *pr n association britannique de normalisation,* ≃ AFNOR *f*.

B-side *n* face *f* B OR 2 *(d'un disque)*; to play the ~ of a record passer la deuxième OR l'autre face d'un disque.

B Sky B (*abbr of* British Sky Broadcasting) *pr n société de diffusion de chaînes de télévision par satellites.*

BST *n abbr of* British Summer Time.

Bt. *written abbr of* baronet.

BT *pr n abbr of* British Telecom.

btu (*abbr of* British thermal unit) *n unité de chaleur (1054, 2 joules).*

bub *inf* [bʌb] *n Am*: hi, ~! [man] salut, mon vieux!; [woman] salut, ma vieille!

bubble [ˈbʌbl] ◇ *n* -**1.** [of foam] bulle *f*; soap ~s bulles de savon ‖ [in liquid] bouillon *m*; [in champagne] bulle *f*; [in glass] bulle *f*, soufflure *f*; [in paint] boursouflure *f*, cloque *f*; [in metal] soufflure *f*. -**2.** [transparent cover] cloche *f*. -**3.** *fig* [illusion]: to prick OR to burst sb's ~ réduire à néant les illusions de qqn, enlever ses illusions à qqn; the ~ finally burst finalement mes/ses *etc* illusions s'envolèrent. -**4.** COMM: ~ (scheme) affaire *f* pourrie. -**5.** [sound] glouglou *m*.

◇ *vi* -**1.** [liquid] bouillonner, faire des bulles; [champagne] pétiller; [gas] barboter; her real feelings ~d beneath the surface *fig* ses sentiments véritables bouillonnaient en elle. -**2.** [gurgle] gargouiller, glouglouter. -**3.** [brim] déborder; the children were bubbling with excitement les enfants étaient tout excités OR surexcités. -**4.** *Am* [mumble] marmonner.

◆ **bubble out** *vi insep* sortir à gros bouillons.

◆ **bubble over** *vi insep literal* & *fig* déborder; to ~ over with enthusiasm OR excitement déborder d'enthousiasme, être surexcité.

◆ **bubble up** *vi insep* [liquid] monter en bouillonnant; *fig* [feeling] monter.

bubble and squeak *n Br plat à base de pommes de terre et de choux, servi réchauffé.*

bubble bath *n* bain *m* moussant.

bubble car *n Br petite voiture à toit transparent.*

bubble gum ◇ *n* bubble-gum *m*.

◇ *adj inf*: ~ music *musique destinée aux jeunes adolescents.*

bubble head *inf n Am* imbécile *mf*.

bubblejet printer [ˈbʌbldʒet-] *n* imprimante *f* à jet d'encre.

bubble pack *n* [for toy, batteries] emballage *m* pelliculé; [for pills] plaquette *f*.

bubble store *n* mémoire *f* à bulles.

bubbly [ˈbʌblɪ] (*compar* **bubblier**, *superl* **bubbliest**) *Br* ◇ *adj* -**1.** [liquid] pétillant, plein de bulles. -**2.** [person] pétillant, plein d'entrain.

◇ *n inf* champ *m*.

bubo [ˈbjuːbəʊ] (*pl* buboes) *n* bubon *m*.

bubonic [bjuːˈbɒnɪk] *adj* bubonique; ~ plague peste *f* bubonique.

buccaneer [ˌbʌkəˈnɪəʳ] *n* -**1.** HIST boucanier *m*. -**2.** [unscrupulous person] flibustier *m*, pirate *m*.

buccaneering [ˌbʌkəˈnɪərɪŋ] *adj* entreprenant.

Bucharest [ˌbjuːkəˈrest] *pr n* Bucarest.

buck [bʌk] ◇ *n* -**1.** [male animal] mâle *m*. -**2.** *SAfr* [antelope] antilope *f*. -**3.** *inf* [young man] jeune mec *m*; *arch* [dandy] dandy *m*. -**4.** *inf Am* [dollar] dollar *m*; to be down to one's last ~ être fauché OR raide; to make a ~ gagner sa croûte; to make a fast OR quick ~ gagner du fric facilement. -**5.** *inf* [responsibility] responsabilité *f*; to pass the ~ faire porter le chapeau à qqn; the ~ stops here en dernier ressort, c'est moi le responsable. -**6.** [jump] ruade *f*. -**7.** *Am* [sawhorse] chevalet *m*, baudet *m*; [gymnastics] cheval *m*, cheval-d'arçons *m inv*.

◇ *vi* -**1.** [horse] donner une ruade; *Am* [car] cahoter, tressauter; the truck ~ed along le camion avançait en cahotant; we ~ed to a stop nous avons fait un arrêt brutal. -**2.** *Am* [charge] donner un coup de tête. -**3.** *inf Am* [resist]: to ~ against change se rebiffer contre les changements. -**4.** *inf Am* [strive] rechercher; he's ~ing for promotion il est prêt à tout pour obtenir de l'avancement.

◇ *vt* -**1.** [subj: horse]: the horse ~ed his rider (off) le cheval a désarçonné OR jeté bas son cavalier. -**2.** *inf* [resist]: to ~ the system se rebiffer contre le système; it takes courage to ~ public opinion il faut du courage pour aller à l'encontre de l'opinion publique.

◇ *comp* [goat, hare, kangaroo, rabbit] mâle; ~ deer daim *m*, chevreuil *m*.

◆ **buck up** *inf Br* ◇ *vt sep* -**1.** [cheer up] remonter le moral à. -**2.** [improve] améliorer; you'd better ~ your ideas up tu as intérêt à te remuer OR à en mettre un coup.

◇ *vi insep* -**1.** [cheer up] se secouer; ~ up!, life goes on! courage!, la vie continue! -**2.** [hurry up] se grouiller, se magner.

buckboard [ˈbʌkbɔːd] *n voiture hippomobile à quatre roues très répandue aux États-Unis à la fin du XIXᵉ siècle.*

bucked *inf* [bʌkt] *adj dated* ragaillardi.

bucket [ˈbʌkɪt] ◇ *n* -**1.** [container, contents] seau *m*; a ~ of water un seau d'eau ❑ it rained ~s *inf* il a plu à seaux; to cry OR to weep ~s *inf* pleurer comme une Madeleine OR un veau; a ~ and spade un seau et une pelle *(symbole, pour un Britannique, de vacances familiales tranquilles au bord de la mer)*. -**2.** TECH [of dredger, grain elevator] godet *m*; [of pump] piston *m*; [of wheel] auget *m*.

◇ *vt* -**1.** [put in bucket] mettre dans un seau; [carry] transporter dans un seau. -**2.** *Br* [horse] surmener; [car] conduire brutalement.

◇ *vi inf Br* -**1.** [rain] pleuvoir à seaux. -**2.** [move hurriedly] aller à fond de train; [car] rouler à fond la caisse; we were ~ing along nous roulions à fond la caisse.

◆ **bucket down** *inf vi insep Br* pleuvoir à seaux.

bucket elevator *n* élévateur *m* à godets, noria *f*.

bucketful [ˈbʌkɪtfʊl] *n* plein seau *m*; a ~ of water un seau plein d'eau; in ~s à seaux.

bucket seat *n* baquet *m*, siège-baquet *m*, siège *m* cuve.

bucket shop *n* -**1.** FIN bureau *m* OR maison *f* de contrepartie, bureau *m* de courtier marron. -**2.** *Br* [travel agency] *organisme de vente de billets d'avion à prix réduit.*

buckhorn [ˈbʌkhɔːn] ◇ *n* -**1.** [horn] corne *f* de cerf. -**2.** BOT plantain *m* lancéolé.

◇ *comp* [knife] au manche en corne de cerf.

Buck House *inf* [bʌk-] *pr n nom familier du palais de Buckingham.*

Buckingham Palace [ˈbʌkɪŋəm-] *pr n* le palais de Buckingham *(résidence officielle du souverain britannique)*.

buckle [ˈbʌkl] ◇ *n* -**1.** [clasp] boucle *f*. -**2.** [kink - in metal] gauchissement *m*, flambage *m*; [- in wheel] voilure *f*.

◇ *vi* -**1.** [fasten] se boucler, s'attacher. -**2.** [distort - metal] gauchir, se déformer; [- wheel] se voiler. -**3.** [give way - knees, legs] se dérober.

◇ *vt* -**1.** [fasten] boucler, attacher. -**2.** [distort] déformer, fausser; [metal] gauchir, fausser; [wheel] voiler.

◆ **buckle down** *inf vi insep* s'appliquer; to ~ down to work se mettre au travail; come on now, ~ down! allez, au boulot!; she'll have to ~ down if she wants to pass il faudra qu'elle en mette un coup si elle veut réussir.

◆ **buckle in** *vt sep* [person] attacher.

◆ **buckle on** *vt sep* [armour] revêtir, endosser; [gunbelt, sword] attacher, ceindre.

◆ **buckle to** *inf vi insep* s'y mettre, s'y atteler.

buckler [ˈbʌkləʳ] *n* écu *m*; [worn on arm] targe *f*.

buckram [ˈbʌkrəm] *n* bougran *m*.

Bucks *written abbr of* Buckinghamshire.

bucksaw [ˈbʌksɔː] *n* scie *f* à bûches.

buck's fizz *n Br cocktail composé de champagne et de jus d'orange.*

buckshee *inf* [ˌbʌkˈʃiː] *adj* & *adv Br* gratis, à l'œil.

buckshot [ˈbʌkʃɒt] *n* chevrotine *f*, gros plomb *m*.

buckskin [ˈbʌkskɪn] *n* peau *f* de daim.

buckthorn [ˈbʌkθɔːn] *n* nerprun *m*, bourdaine *f*.

bucktooth [bʌkˌtuːθ] (*pl* **buckteeth** [-ˌtiːθ]) *n* dent *f* proéminente OR qui avance; to have buckteeth avoir des dents de lapin.

bucktoothed [ˈbʌkˌtuːθt] *adj*: to be ~ avoir des dents de lapin.

buckwheat [ˈbʌkwiːt] *n* sarrasin *m*, blé *m* noir; ~ flour farine *f* de sarrasin.

bucolic [bjuːˈkɒlɪk] ◇ *adj* bucolique, pastoral.
◇ *n* bucolique *f*.

bud [bʌd] (*pt* & *pp* budded, *cont* budding) ◇ *n* -**1.** [shoot on plant] bourgeon *m*, œil *m*; the trees are in ~ les arbres bourgeonnent || [for grafting] écusson *m*. -**2.** [flower] bouton *m*; the roses are in ~ OR have come into ~ les roses sont en bouton. -**3.** ANAT papille *f*. -**4.** *inf Am* [term of address]: hey, ~! [to stranger] eh, vous là-bas!; [to friend] eh, mon vieux!
◇ *vi* -**1.** BOT [plant] bourgeonner; [flower] former des boutons. -**2.** [horns] (commencer à) poindre OR percer. -**3.** [talent] (commencer à) se révéler OR percer.
◇ *vt* greffer, écussonner.

Budapest [ˌbjuːdəˈpest] *pr n* Budapest.

Buddha [ˈbʊdə] *pr n* Bouddha.

Buddhism [ˈbʊdɪzm] *n* bouddhisme *m*.

Buddhist [ˈbʊdɪst] ◇ *n* Bouddhiste *mf*.
◇ *adj* [country, priest] bouddhiste; [art, philosophy] bouddhique.

budding [ˈbʌdɪŋ] *adj* -**1.** BOT [plant] bourgeonnant, couvert de bourgeons; [flower] en bouton. -**2.** *fig* [artist, genius] en herbe, prometteur; [love] naissant.

buddleia [ˈbʌdlɪə] *n* buddleia *m*.

buddy *inf* [ˈbʌdɪ] (*pl* buddies) *n* [friend] copain *m*, copine *f*; [for Aids patient] compagnon *m*, compagne *f* (d'un sidéen); say there, old ~ *Am* dis donc, mon vieux OR mon pote; since when are they such buddies OR so ~-~? depuis quand sont-ils si copains?; they're best OR big buddies ce sont les meilleurs copains du monde.

budge [bʌdʒ] ◇ *vi* -**1.** [move] bouger; it won't ~ c'est coincé, c'est bloqué. -**2.** *fig* [yield] céder, changer d'avis; she refused to ~ elle ne voulut pas en démordre; he wouldn't ~ an inch il a tenu bon.
◇ *vt* -**1.** [move] faire bouger. -**2.** [convince] convaincre, faire changer d'avis; he won't be ~d il reste inébranlable, il n'y a pas eu moyen de le faire changer d'avis.
◆ **budge over** *inf*, **budge up** *inf vi insep* se pousser.

budgerigar [ˈbʌdʒərɪgɑːʳ] *n Br* perruche *f*.

budget [ˈbʌdʒɪt] ◇ *n* -**1.** [gen & FIN] budget *m*; to be on a tight ~ disposer d'un budget serré OR modeste. -**2.** [law] budget *m*; ~ day jour *m* de la présentation du budget; ~ speech discours *m* de présentation du budget.
◇ *vt* budgétiser, inscrire au budget; to ~ one's time bien organiser son temps.
◇ *vi* dresser OR préparer un budget.
◇ *adj* -**1.** [inexpensive] économique, pour petits budgets; ~ prices prix *mpl* avantageux OR modiques. -**2.** ECON & FIN budgétaire; ~ cuts compressions *fpl* budgétaires.
◆ **budget for** *vt insep* [gen] prévoir des frais de, budgétiser; to ~ for sthg inscrire qqch au budget, prévoir des frais de qqch || ECON & FIN inscrire OR porter au budget, budgétiser.

budget account *n* [with store] compte-crédit *m*; [with bank] ≃ compte *m* permanent.

budgetary [ˈbʌdʒɪtrɪ] *adj* budgétaire.

budget plan *n Am* système *m* de crédit.

budgie *inf* [ˈbʌdʒɪ] *n Br* perruche *f*.

Buenos Aires [ˌbwenəsˈaɪrɪz] *pr n* Buenos Aires.

buff [bʌf] ◇ *n* -**1.** [colour] (couleur *f*) chamois *m*. -**2.** [leather] peau *f* de buffle; [polishing cloth] polissoir *m*. -**3.** *inf* [enthusiast] fana *mf*, mordu *m*, -e *f*; a film ~ un mordu OR un fana de cinéma. -**4.** *inf dated* & *phr*: in the ~ à poil.
◇ *vt* polir; it just needs ~ing up a bit cela a juste besoin d'être un peu astiqué.
◇ *adj* [coloured] (couleur) chamois; [leather] de OR en buffle.

buffalo [ˈbʌfələʊ] (*pl inv* OR buffaloes) ◇ *n* buffle *m*, bufflesse *f*, bufflonne *f*; *Am* bison *m*; a herd of ~ un troupeau de buffles.
◇ *vt Am inf* [intimidate] intimider; they really had him ~ed ils lui en ont mis plein la vue.

Buffalo Bill [ˈbʌfələʊˈbɪl] *pr n* Buffalo Bill.

buffalo grass *n herbe courte poussant dans les régions sèches au centre des États-Unis.*

buffer [ˈbʌfəʳ] ◇ *n* -**1.** [protection] tampon *m*; [on car] *Am* pare-chocs *m inv*; RAIL [on train] tampon *m*; [at station] butoir *m*; COMPUT mémoire *f* tampon; a ~ against inflation *fig* une mesure de protection contre l'inflation. -**2.** *Br* [fool] imbécile *mf*; old ~ vieille ganache *f*; he's a nice old ~ c'est un gentil petit pépé. -**3.** [for polishing] polissoir *m*.
◇ *vt* tamponner, amortir (le choc); to be ~ed against reality être protégé de la réalité OR des réalités (de la vie).

buffer memory *n* mémoire *f* tampon.

buffer state *n* État *m* tampon.

buffer stock *n* stock *m* tampon.

buffer zone *n* région *f* tampon.

buffet[1] [*Br* ˈbʊfeɪ, *Am* bəˈfeɪ] ◇ *n* -**1.** [refreshments] buffet *m*; cold ~ buffet froid. -**2.** [sideboard] buffet *m*. -**3.** [restaurant] buvette *f*, cafétéria *f*; [in station] buffet *m* OR café *m* de gare; [on train] wagon-restaurant *m*.
◇ *comp* [lunch, dinner] -buffet; ~ lunch déjeuner-buffet *m*.

buffet[2] [ˈbʌfɪt] ◇ *vt* -**1.** [batter]: the ship was ~ed by the waves le navire était ballotté par les vagues; the trees were ~ed by the wind les arbres étaient secoués par le vent; ~ed by misfortune *fig* & *lit* poursuivi par la malchance. -**2.** *lit* [hit - with hand] souffleter; [- with fist] donner un coup de poing à.
◇ *n lit* [blow - with hand] soufflet *m*; [- with fist] coup *m* de poing; the ~s of fate OR fortune *fig* les coups du sort.

buffet car [ˈbʊfeɪ-] *n* wagon-restaurant *m*.

buffeting [ˈbʌfɪtɪŋ] ◇ *n* -**1.** [of rain, wind] assaut *m*; the waves gave the boat a real ~ le navire a été violemment ballotté par les vagues. -**2.** *lit* [beating] bourrades *fpl*.
◇ *adj* violent.

buffing [ˈbʌfɪŋ] *n* polissage *m*.

buffoon [bəˈfuːn] *n* bouffon *m*, pitre *m*; to act OR to play the ~ faire le clown OR le pitre.

buffoonery [bəˈfuːnərɪ] *n (U)* bouffonnerie *f*, bouffonneries *fpl*.

bug [bʌg] (*pt* & *pp* bugged, *cont* bugging) ◇ *n* -**1.** *Am* [insect] insecte *m*; [bedbug] punaise *f*; *fig*: she's been bitten by the film ~ *inf* c'est une mordue de cinéma; she's been bitten by the travel ~ *inf* elle a la passion des voyages. -**2.** *inf* [germ] microbe *m*; to catch a ~ attraper un microbe; the flu ~ le virus de la grippe; I've got a stomach ~ j'ai des problèmes intestinaux; there's a ~ going round il y a un microbe dans l'air OR qui se balade. -**3.** *inf* [defect] défaut *m*, erreur *f*; there are still a few ~s to be ironed out il y a encore quelques petits trucs qui clochent || COMPUT bogue *m*. -**4.** *inf* [microphone] micro *m* (caché). -**5.** *inf Am* [car] coccinelle *f*.
◇ *vt* -**1.** *inf* [bother] taper sur les nerfs de; what's bugging him? qu'est-ce qu'il a? -**2.** [wiretap - room] poser OR installer des appareils d'écoute (clandestins) dans; [- phone] brancher sur table d'écoute.
◆ **bug out** *inf vi insep Am* -**1.** [leave hurriedly] ficher le camp. -**2.** [eyes] être globuleux OR exorbité.

bugaboo [ˈbʌgəbuː] *n* loup-garou *m*, croque-mitaine *m*.

bugbear [ˈbʌgbeəʳ] *n* [monster] épouvantail *m*, croque-mitaine *m*; *fig* [worry] bête noire *f*, cauchemar *m*.

bug-eyed *adj Am* aux yeux globuleux OR exorbités; she was ~ in amazement elle avait les yeux écarquillés d'étonnement.

bugger [ˈbʌgəʳ] ◇ *n* -**1.** ▽ [foolish person] couillon *m*; [unpleasant person] salaud *m*; silly ~! pauvre conard!; stop playing silly ~s! *Br* arrête de faire le con!; poor old ~ pauvre bougre *m*; he can be a real ~ sometimes c'est un vrai saligaud OR salopard des fois || [child] gamin *m*, -e *f*; you little ~! petite fripouille! -**2.** ▽ *Br* [job]: this job's a real ~ c'est une saloperie de boulot. -**3.** ▽ *Br* [damn]: I don't give a ~ je m'en tape. -**4.** *dated* [sodomite] pédéraste *m*.
◇ *interj* ▽ *Br* merde alors!
◇ *vt* -**1.** [sodomize] sodomiser; JUR se livrer à la pédérastie avec. -**2.** ▽ *Br* [damn]: ~ him! je l'emmerde!; well, ~ me! merde alors!; oh, ~ it! oh, merde! -**3.** ▽ *Br* [damage] bousiller.
◆ **bugger about**▽, **bugger around**▽ *Br*
◇ *vi insep* glander.
◇ *vt sep* emmerder.
◆ **bugger off**▽ *vi insep Br* foutre le camp.
◆ **bugger up**▽ *vt sep Br* saloper.

bugger all▽ *n Br* que dalle.

buggered▽ [ˈbʌgəd] *adj Br*. -**1.** [broken] foutu. -**2.** [in surprise]: well, I'll be ~! merde alors! -**3.** [in annoyance]: I'm ~ if I'll do anything to help ils peuvent toujours courir pour que je les aide; ~ if I know j'en sais foutre rien.

buggery [ˈbʌgərɪ] ◇ *n* sodomie *f*.
◇ *interj* ▽ *Br* merde!

bugging [ˈbʌgɪŋ] *n* [of room] utilisation *f* d'appareils d'écoute (clandestins); [of telephone] mise *f* sur écoute; ~ device appareil *m* d'écoute (clandestin).

buggy [ˈbʌgɪ] (*pl* buggies, *compar* buggier, *superl* buggiest) ◇ *n* -**1.** [carriage] boghei *m*; [for baby] poussette *f*, poussette-canne *f*; *Am* [pram] voiture *f* d'enfant. -**2.** *inf* [car] bagnole *f*; beach ~ buggy *m*.
◇ *adj inf Am* [crazy] cinglé.

bughouse *inf* [ˈbʌghaʊs, *pl* -haʊzɪz] *Am pej*
◇ *n* maison *f* de dingues.
◇ *adj* dingue, cinglé.

bugle [ˈbjuːgl] ◇ *n* clairon *m*; to sound the ~ faire sonner le clairon; ~ call sonnerie *f* de clairon.
◇ *vi* jouer du clairon, faire sonner le clairon.

bugler [ˈbjuːgləʳ] *n* (joueur *m* de) clairon *m*.

build [bɪld] (*pt* & *pp* built [bɪlt]) ◇ *vt* -**1.** [dwelling] bâtir, construire; [temple] bâtir, édifier; [bridge, machine, ship] construire; [nest] faire, bâtir; houses are being built des maisons sont en construction; we are planning to ~ a new garage nous avons l'intention de faire construire un nouveau garage; this bed wasn't built for two people ce lit n'a pas été conçu pour deux personnes; we're ~ing an extension on the house nous agrandissons la maison ❑ to ~ castles in the air bâtir des châteaux en Espagne. -**2.** [found] bâtir, fonder.
◇ *vi* -**1.** [construct] bâtir; developers are planning to ~ on the land les promoteurs envisagent de construire OR bâtir sur le terrain; to ~ on sand bâtir sur le sable. -**2.** [increase] augmenter, monter; excitement/tension is ~ing l'excitation/la tension augmente OR monte.
◇ *n* carrure *f*, charpente *f*; of strong ~ solidement bâti OR charpenté; of heavy ~ de forte corpulence OR taille; of medium ~ de taille OR corpulence moyenne; a man of slight ~ un homme fluet; she's about the same ~ as I am elle est à peu près de ma taille; he has the ~ of a rugby player il est bâti comme un joueur de rugby.
◆ **build in** *vt sep* CONSTR [incorporate] encastrer; *fig* [include - special features] intégrer.
◆ **build into** *vt sep* [incorporate] intégrer à.
◆ **build on** ◇ *vt sep* -**1.** CONSTR ajouter. -**2.** *fig*: his success is built on hard work sa réussite repose sur un travail acharné.
◇ *vt insep*: we need to ~ on our achievements il faut consolider nos succès.
◆ **build up** ◇ *vt sep* -**1.** [develop - business, theory] établir, développer; [- reputation] établir, bâtir; [- confidence] donner, redonner; [- strength] accroître, prendre; you need to ~ up your strength, you need ~ing up vous avez besoin de prendre des forces; he really helped to ~ up my self-confidence il m'a vraiment aidé à me donner confiance en moi. -**2.** [increase - production] accroître, augmenter; [- ex-

citement] faire monter, accroître; [- pressure] accumuler. -3. [promote] faire de la publicité pour.

◇ *vi insep* -1. [business] se développer. -2. [excitement] monter, augmenter; [pressure] s'accumuler; traffic is ~ing up il commence à y avoir beaucoup de circulation.

◆ **build upon** = **build on** *vt sep* 2.

builder ['bɪldəʳ] *n* -1. CONSTR [contractor] entrepreneur *m*; [worker] ouvrier *m* du bâtiment; [of machines, ships] constructeur *m*. -2. *fig* [founder] fondateur *m*, -trice *f*; the ~s of the empire les bâtisseurs *mpl* de l'empire.

building ['bɪldɪŋ] ◇ *n* -1. [structure] bâtiment *m*, construction *f*; [monumental] édifice *m*; [apartment, office] immeuble *m*. -2. [work] construction *f*; ~ is due to start on Monday les travaux de construction doivent commencer lundi.

◇ *comp* [land, plot] à bâtir; [materials] de construction; ~ industry OR trade (industrie *f* du) bâtiment *m*.

building block *n* [toy] cube *m*; *fig* composante *f*.

building contractor *n* entrepreneur *m* (en bâtiment OR construction).

building site *n* chantier *m* (de construction).

building society *n Br société d'investissements et de prêts immobiliers.*

BUILDING SOCIETY:

Les «building societies» fonctionnent comme des banques mais elles n'ont pas de système de compensation. Établissements consentant des prêts immobiliers aux particuliers, elles jouent un rôle important dans la vie en Grande-Bretagne.

---

buildup ['bɪldʌp] *n* -1. [increase - in pressure] intensification *f*; [- in excitement] montée *f*; traffic ~ embouteillage *m*, bouchon *m* ‖ COMM [- in production] accroissement *m*; [- in stock] accumulation *f*; MIL [- in troops] rassemblement *m*; nuclear arms ~ accumulation des armes nucléaires. -2. [publicity] campagne *f* publicitaire; they gave the product a big ~ ils ont fait beaucoup de publicité pour le produit.

built [bɪlt] ◇ *pt* & *pp* → **build**.

◇ *adj* [building] bâti, construit; [person] charpenté; brick-~ en OR de brique; to be powerfully ~ être puissamment OR solidement charpenté; to be slightly ~ être fluet.

built-in *adj* [beam, wardrobe] encastré; [device, safeguard] intégré; *fig* [feature] inné, ancré; ~ obsolescence obsolescence *f* programmée.

built-up *adj* -1. [land] bâti; a ~ area une agglomération (urbaine); the area is becoming very ~ ça s'est beaucoup construit OR on a beaucoup construit dans la région. -2. [in clothing]: ~ shoulders épaules *fpl* surhaussées; ~ shoes chaussures *fpl* à semelles compensées.

bulb [bʌlb] *n* -1. BOT bulbe *m*, oignon *m*; tulip ~ bulbe de tulipes. -2. ELEC ampoule *f*; a light ~ une ampoule. -3. [of thermometer] réservoir *m*. -4. ANAT bulbe *m*. -5. NAUT [bulbous bow] bulb *m*, bulbe *m*.

bulbous ['bʌlbəs] *adj* bulbeux; a ~ nose un gros nez, un nez bulbeux; a ~ bow NAUT un bulb, un bulbe.

Bulgaria [bʌl'geərɪə] *pr n* Bulgarie *f*; in ~ en Bulgarie.

Bulgarian [bʌl'geərɪən] ◇ *n* -1. [person] Bulgare *mf*. -2. LING bulgare *m*.

◇ *adj* bulgare.

bulge [bʌldʒ] ◇ *n* -1. [lump, swelling] renflement *m*; [on vase, jug] panse *f*, ventre *m*; *Br* MIL saillant *m*; he noticed a ~ in her pocket il remarqua quelque chose qui faisait saillie dans sa poche. -2. [increase] poussée *f*; a population ~ une explosion démographique.

◇ *vi* [swell] se gonfler, se renfler; his suitcase was bulging with gifts sa valise était bourrée de cadeaux; the town was bulging at the seams with holidaymakers *fig* la ville était pleine à craquer de vacanciers ‖ [stick out] faire saillie, saillir; he ~d (out) at the waist il était ventru, il avait du ventre; his eyes ~d il avait les yeux saillants OR globuleux.

bulging ['bʌldʒɪŋ] *adj* [eyes] saillant, globuleux; [muscles, waist] saillant; [bag, pockets] gonflé.

bulimia [bju'lɪmɪə] *n* boulimie *f*.

bulimic [bju'lɪmɪk] ◇ *adj* boulimique.

◇ *n* boulimique *mf*.

bulk [bʌlk] ◇ *n* -1. [mass] masse *f*; [stoutness] corpulence *f*; the great ~ of the cathedral loomed out of the darkness la silhouette massive de la cathédrale se dessina dans l'obscurité; a man of enormous ~ un homme très corpulent; he levered his great ~ out of the armchair il extirpa sa grosse carcasse du fauteuil. -2. [main part]: the ~ la plus grande partie, la majeure partie; the ~ of the estate was woodland la majeure partie de la propriété était boisée; she left the ~ of her fortune to charity elle légua le plus gros de sa fortune aux bonnes œuvres. -3. [in food] fibre *f* (végétale). -4. NAUT [goods] cargaison *f*.

◇ *comp* [order, supplies] en gros.

◇ *vi*: to ~ large *Br* occuper une place importante; the prospect of a further drop in prices ~ed large in their minds la perspective d'une autre baisse des prix les préoccupait vivement OR était au premier plan de leurs préoccupations.

◆ **in bulk** *adv phr* par grosses quantités; COMM en gros; NAUT en vrac.

bulk-buy *vi* & *vt* acheter en gros OR grande quantité.

bulk buying *n (U)* achat *m* par grosses quantités; COMM achat *m* en gros.

bulk carrier *n* vraquier *m*, transporteur *m* de vrac.

bulkhead ['bʌlkhed] *n* cloison *f* (d'avion, de navire).

bulkiness ['bʌlkɪnɪs] *n* [of object] grosseur *f*, caractère *m* volumineux; [of person] corpulence *f*.

bulk mail *n (U)* envois *mpl* en nombre.

bulk mailing *n* mailing *m* OR publipostage *m* à grande diffusion.

bulk rate *n* affranchissement *m* à forfait.

bulky ['bʌlkɪ] *adj* -1. [massive, large] volumineux; [cumbersome] encombrant; a ~ sweater OR jumper un gros pull; a ~ package OR parcel un paquet encombrant OR volumineux. -2. [corpulent, stout] corpulent, gros; [solidly built] massif.

bull [bʊl] ◇ *n* -1. [male cow] taureau *m*; like a ~ in a china shop comme un éléphant dans un magasin de porcelaine; to take the ~ by the horns prendre le taureau par les cornes. -2. [male of a species] mâle *m*. -3. *inf* [large, strong man] costaud *m*, malabar *m*; a great ~ of a man un homme fort comme un bœuf. -4. ST. EX haussier *m*, spéculateur *m* à la hausse. -5. [centre of target] centre *m* de la cible; to hit the ~ faire mouche, mettre dans le mille. -6. ▽ [nonsense] connerie *f*, conneries *fpl*; that's a lot OR load of ~ c'est des conneries tout ça. -7. RELIG bulle *f*.

◇ *comp* [elephant, whale] mâle *m*; ~ calf jeune taureau *m*, taurillon *m*.

◇ *vt* ST. EX [market, prices, shares] pousser à la hausse.

◆ **Bull** *n* ASTROL le Taureau.

bulldog ['bʊldɒg] *n* bouledogue *m*.

bulldog clip *n* pince *f* à dessin.

bulldoze ['bʊldəʊz] *vt* -1. [building] démolir au bulldozer; [earth, stone] passer au bulldozer; whole villages have been ~d out of existence des villages entiers ont été rasés au bulldozer. -2. *fig* [push]: to ~ sb into doing sthg forcer qqn à faire qqch, faire pression sur qqn pour lui faire faire qqch; she ~d her way to the top elle est arrivée au sommet à la force du poignet.

bulldozer ['bʊldəʊzəʳ] *n* bulldozer *m*.

bullet ['bʊlɪt] ◇ *n* -1. balle *f*; to get the ~ *inf Br* se faire virer, se faire sacquer. -2. TYPO puce *f*.

◇ *comp* [hole] de balle; [wound] par balle.

bullet-headed *adj* qui a une petite tête ronde.

bulletin ['bʊlətɪn] *n* [announcement] bulletin *m*, communiqué *m*; [newsletter] bulletin *m*.

bulletin board *n* tableau *m* d'affichage.

bulletproof ['bʊlɪtpruːf] ◇ *adj* [glass, vest] pare-balles *(inv)*; [vehicle] blindé.

◇ *vt* [door, vehicle] blinder.

bullfight ['bʊlfaɪt] *n* corrida *f*, course *f* de taureaux.

bullfighter ['bʊl,faɪtəʳ] *n* torero *m*, matador *m*.

bullfighting ['bʊl,faɪtɪŋ] *n (U)* courses *fpl* de taureaux, tauromachie *f*.

bullfinch ['bʊlfɪntʃ] *n* bouvreuil *m*.

bullfrog ['bʊlfrɒg] *n* grosse grenouille *f*.

bullhorn ['bʊlhɔːn] *n Am* mégaphone *m*, porte-voix *m inv*.

bullion ['bʊljən] *n*: gold/silver ~ or/argent *m* en lingots OR en barres.

bullish ['bʊlɪʃ] *adj* -1. ST. EX: the market is ~ les cours OR valeurs sont en hausse. -2. *inf Br* [optimistic]: to be in a ~ mood être confiant OR optimiste.

bull market *n* marché *m* à la hausse.

bull mastiff *n chien issu d'un métissage entre le bouledogue et le mastiff.*

bull-necked *adj* au cou de taureau.

bullock ['bʊlək] *n* [castrated] bœuf *m*; [young] bouvillon *m*.

bullring ['bʊlrɪŋ] *n* arène *f (pour la corrida)*.

bull session *inf n Am* causerie *f* entre hommes.

bull's eye *n* -1. [centre of target] mille *m*, centre *m* de la cible; ~! dans le mille!; to hit the ~ *literal* & *fig* faire mouche, mettre dans le mille. -2. [sweet] gros bonbon *m* à la menthe. -3. [window] œil-de-bœuf *m*, oculus *m*.

bullshit▼ ['bʊlʃɪt] ◇ *n (U)* connerie *f*, conneries *fpl*; don't give me that ~! ne raconte OR dis pas de conneries!

◇ *vt* raconter des conneries à; don't ~ me! ne me raconte pas de conneries!

◇ *vi* déconner, raconter des conneries.

bull terrier *n* bull-terrier *m*.

bullwhip ['bʊlwɪp] ◇ *n* ≃ cravache *f*.

◇ *vt* cravacher.

bully ['bʊlɪ] ◇ *n* -1. [adult] tyran *m*; [child] petite brute *f*; don't be such a ~! ne sois pas si tyrannique! -2. [in hockey] engagement *m* (du jeu).

◇ *vt* [intimidate - spouse, employee] malmener; she bullies her little sister elle est tyrannique avec sa petite sœur; to ~ sb into doing sthg: they bullied me into going on a fait pression sur moi pour que j'y aille.

◇ *interj inf*: ~ for you! chapeau!; *iron* quel exploit!, bravo!

◆ **bully off** *vi insep* [in hockey] engager le jeu, mettre la balle en jeu.

bully beef *n Br* corned-beef *m*.

bullyboy ['bʊlɪbɔɪ] *n Br* brute *f*, voyou *m*.

bullying ['bʊlɪɪŋ] ◇ *adj* [intimidating] agressif, brutal.

◇ *n (U)* brimades *fpl*.

bully-off *n* engagement *m* (du jeu).

bulrush ['bʊlrʌʃ] *n* jonc *m*, scirpe *m*.

bulwark ['bʊlwək] *n* ARCHIT rempart *m*, fortification *f*; [breakwater] digue *f*, môle *m*; *fig* [protection] rempart *m*; a ~ against the harsh realities of life un rempart OR une protection contre les dures réalités de la vie; a ~ against inflation une mesure de protection contre l'inflation.

◆ **bulwarks** *npl* NAUT bastingage *m*, pavois *m*.

bum *inf* [bʌm] (*pt* & *pp* bummed, *cont* bumming) ◇ *n* -1. *Br* [buttocks] fesses *fpl*, pétard *m*. -2. [tramp] clochard *m*, -e *f*, clodo *m*; [lazy person] fainéant *m*, -e *f*, flemmard *m*, -e *f*; [worthless person] minable *mf*, minus *m*. -3. [sports fanatic] fana *m*, mordu *m*, -e *f*; a beach ~ un fana OR mordu des plages. -4. *Am* [vagrancy]: he went on the ~ il s'est mis à dormir sous les ponts.

◇ *adj* [worthless] minable, nul; [injured, disabled] patraque, mal fichu; [untrue] faux; he got a bit of a ~ deal on a mal agi OR on s'est très

mal conduit envers lui, on lui en a fait voir de dures; he was in jail on a ~ rap *Am* il était en prison pour un délit qu'il n'avait pas commis ❑ ~ steer tuyau *m* percé.
◇ *vt* [beg, borrow]: to ~ sthg off sb emprunter qqch à qqn, taper qqn de qqch; **he's always bumming cigarettes** il est toujours à quémander OR mendier des cigarettes; **they bummed a lift to the border** ils ont gagné la frontière en faisant de l'auto-stop OR du stop.
◇ *vi Am* [be disappointed] être déprimé; [laze about] traîner.
◆ **bum about** *inf Br*, **bum around** *inf vi insep* -**1.** [drift, wander] vagabonder, se balader; **they spent three months bumming around (in) Mexico** ils ont passé trois mois à se balader au Mexique. -**2.** [loaf, idle] fainéanter, flemmarder.

bumble ['bʌmbl] *vi* -**1.** [speak incoherently] bafouiller; he ~d through his speech il a fait un discours décousu. -**2.** [move clumsily]: **he came bumbling in with a tray** il entra, l'air gauche, un plateau à la main.

bumblebee ['bʌmblbiː] *n* bourdon *m*.

bumbler ['bʌmblə^r] *n* empoté *m*, -e *f*, maladroit *m*, -e *f*.

bumbling ['bʌmblɪŋ] *adj* [person] empoté, maladroit; [behaviour] maladroit.

bumboat ['bʌmbəʊt] *n* canot *m* d'approvisionnement.

bumf *inf*, **bumph** *inf Br* [bʌmf] *n* -**1.** [documentation] doc *f*. -**2.** *pej* [useless papers] paperasse *f*. -**3.** [toilet paper] papier cul *m*.

bumfreezer *inf* ['bʌm,friːzə^r] *n Br* [jacket] blouson *m*.

bummed *inf* [bʌmd] *adj Am*: to be ~ (out) with sthg être déprimé par qqch.

bummer▽ ['bʌmə^r] *n* -**1.** [bad experience] poisse *f*; the film's a real ~ ce film est vraiment nul OR un vrai navet. -**2.** *Am* [depression]: he's on a ~ il n'a pas le moral.

bump [bʌmp] ◇ *n* -**1.** [lump] bosse *f*; **he has a big ~ on his head** il a une grosse bosse au crâne; **the car went over a ~ (in the road)** la voiture est passée sur une bosse (sur la route). -**2.** [blow, knock] choc *m*, coup *m*; **he felt a ~ as he reversed the car into the garage** il a senti un choc en reculant la voiture dans le garage ‖ [noise from blow] bruit *m* sourd, choc *m* sourd; **her head hit the shelf with a ~** il y a eu un bruit sourd quand elle s'est cognée la tête contre l'étagère. -**3.** AERON [air current] courant *m* ascendant.
◇ *vt* heurter; [elbow, head, knee] cogner.
◇ *vi* -**1.** [move with jerks] cahoter; **the old bus ~ed along the country roads** le vieil autobus cahotait le long des petites routes. -**2.** [collide] se heurter; **the boat ~ed against the pier** le bateau a buté contre l'embarcadère.
◇ *adv*: **the driver went ~ into the car in front** le conducteur est rentré en plein dans la voiture de devant.
◆ **bump into** *vt insep* [object] rentrer dedans, tamponner; [person] rencontrer par hasard, tomber sur; **he ~ed into a lamppost** il est rentré dans un réverbère; **I ~ed into an old school friend this morning** je suis tombé sur un ancien camarade d'école ce matin.
◆ **bump off** *inf vt sep* [murder] liquider, supprimer; [with a gun] descendre.
◆ **bump up** *inf vt sep* [increase] faire grimper; [prices] gonfler, faire grimper.

bumper ['bʌmpə^r] ◇ *n* -**1.** AUT pare-chocs *m inv*. -**2.** *Am* RAIL [on train] tampon *m*; [at station] butoir *m*. -**3.** [full glass] rasade *f*.
◇ *adj* [crop, harvest] exceptionnel, formidable; a ~ issue *Br* un numéro exceptionnel.

bumper car *n* auto *f* tamponneuse.

bumper sticker *n* autocollant *m (pour voiture)*.

bumper-to-bumper *adj*: ~ traffic circulation *f* difficile; **the cars are ~ on the bridge** les voitures roulent pare-chocs contre pare-chocs sur le pont.

bumpkin *inf* ['bʌmpkɪn] *n pej*: a country ~ un plouc, un péquenaud.

bump start *n démarrage d'un véhicule en le poussant.*
◆ **bump-start** *vt* démarrer en poussant.

bumptious ['bʌmpʃəs] *adj* suffisant, prétentieux.

bumpy ['bʌmpɪ] (*compar* **bumpier**, *superl* **bumpiest**) *adj* [road] cahoteux; [flight, ride] agité (de secousses); [surface, wall] bosselé; **we've got a ~ ride ahead of us** *fig* on va traverser une mauvaise passe OR une période difficile.

bun [bʌn] *n* -**1.** [bread] petit pain *m* (au lait); **she's got a ~ in the oven**▽ *Br* elle a un polichinelle dans le tiroir. -**2.** [hair] chignon *m*.

bunch [bʌntʃ] ◇ *n* -**1.** [of flowers, straw] bouquet *m*, botte *f*; [of grapes] grappe *f*; [of bananas, dates] régime *m*; [of feathers, hair] touffe *f*; [of sticks, twigs] faisceau *m*, poignée *f*; [of keys] trousseau *m*; **do you want a ~ of fives?** *inf* tu veux mon poing sur la gueule? -**2.** *inf* [of people] bande *f*; **they're a ~ of idiots** c'est une bande d'imbéciles; **her family are a strange ~** elle a une drôle de famille; **you're a fine ~!** *iron* quelle équipe vous faites!; **he's the best of a bad ~** c'est le moins mauvais de la bande ‖ [of things]: **he took out a ~ of papers from the drawer** il sortit un tas de papiers du tiroir. -**3.** CYCLING peloton *m*. -**4.** *phr*: **thanks a ~!** *iron* merci beaucoup!
◇ *vt* [straw, vegetables] mettre en bottes, botteler; [flowers] botteler, mettre en bouquets.
◆ **bunches** *npl Br* couettes *fpl*; **she wears her hair in ~es** elle porte des couettes.
◆ **bunch together** ◇ *vi insep* [people] se serrer, se presser.
◇ *vt sep* mettre ensemble; [flowers] botteler, mettre en bouquets.
◆ **bunch up** ◇ *vi insep* -**1.** [group of people] se serrer. -**2.** [clothing] se retrousser.
◇ *vt sep* mettre ensemble; [flowers] mettre en bouquets, botteler; **your dress is ~ed up at the back** le derrière de ta robe est tout retroussé.

bunco *inf* ['bʊŋkəʊ] (*pl* **buncos**) *Am* ◇ *n* arnaque *f*.
◇ *vt* arnaquer, rouler.

bundle ['bʌndl] ◇ *n* -**1.** [of clothes, linen] paquet *m*; [wrapped in a cloth] paquet *m*; [of goods] paquet *m*, ballot *m*; [of sticks, twigs] faisceau *m*, poignée *f*; [of banknotes, papers] liasse *f*; **he's a ~ of nerves** c'est un paquet de nerfs; **she's a ~ of contradictions** elle est pleine de contradictions; **a ~ of firewood** un fagot ❑ **a ~ of fun** OR **laughs** *inf* marrant, amusant; **the trip wasn't exactly a ~ of laughs** le voyage n'était pas vraiment marrant; **he's a real ~ of fun** *iron* c'est fou ce qu'on s'amuse avec lui. -**2.** *inf Am* [money]: **to make a ~** faire son beurre. -**3.** [baby] bout *m* de chou. -**4.** *Br phr*: **to go a ~ on sthg** *inf* s'emballer pour qqch; **thanks a ~!** *iron* merci beaucoup!
◇ *vt* -**1.** [clothes] mettre en paquet; [for a journey] empaqueter; [linen] mettre en paquet; [goods] mettre en paquet; [banknotes, papers] mettre en liasses; [sticks, twigs] mettre en faisceaux; [firewood] mettre en fagots; [straw] botteler, mettre en bottes. -**2.** [shove]: **she ~d the papers into the drawer** elle fourra les papiers dans le tiroir; **he was ~d into the car** on l'a poussé dans la voiture brusquement OR sans ménagement; **he quickly ~d them out of the room** il les a poussés précipitamment hors de la pièce.
◆ **bundle off** *vt sep*: **the children were ~d off to school** les enfants furent envoyés OR expédiés à l'école vite fait.
◆ **bundle up** ◇ *vt sep* -**1.** [tie up] mettre en paquet. -**2.** [dress warmly] emmitoufler; **she ~d the baby up in a warm blanket** elle emmitoufla le bébé dans une grosse couverture.
◇ *vi insep* s'emmitoufler.

bundled [bʌndld] *adj* COMPUT: ~ **software** logiciel *m* livré avec le matériel.

bun fight *inf n Br hum* [gathering] réception *f*.

bung [bʌŋ] ◇ *n* -**1.** [stopper] bondon *m*, bonde *f*. -**2.** [hole] bonde *f*.
◇ *vt* -**1.** [hole] boucher. -**2.** *inf Br* [put carelessly] balancer; **just ~ it in the rubbish bin** fiche-le à la poubelle. -**3.** *inf Br* [add] rajouter; **~ it on the bill** rajoutez-le sur la note; **we'll ~ in a few extras** on va rajouter quelques petits extras.
◆ **bung up** *inf vt sep Br* boucher; **my nose is/my eyes are ~ed up** j'ai le nez bouché/les yeux gonflés.

bungalow ['bʌŋgələʊ] *n* [one storey house] maison *f* sans étage; [in India] bungalow *m*.

bunghole ['bʌŋhəʊl] *n* bonde *f*.

bungle ['bʌŋgl] ◇ *vt* gâcher; **you ~d it** OR **the job** tu as tout gâché.
◇ *n Br*: to make a ~ of sthg gâcher qqch.

bungler ['bʌŋglə^r] *n* incapable *mf*.

bungling ['bʌŋglɪŋ] ◇ *adj* [person] incompétent, incapable; [action] maladroit, gauche.
◇ *n* incompétence *f*.

bunion ['bʌnjən] *n* oignon *m (cor)*.

bunk [bʌŋk] ◇ *n* -**1.** [berth] couchette *f*; [bed] lit *m*. -**2.** *inf Br*: **to do a ~** se tirer, se faire la malle. -**3.** *inf* [nonsense] foutaise *f*; **that's a load of ~** ce sont des foutaises.
◇ *vi inf* -**1.** [sleep] coucher. -**2.** [escape] se tailler.
◆ **bunk down** *vi insep* coucher.
◆ **bunk off** *inf vi insep Br*. -**1.** [scram] décamper, filer. -**2.** [from school] faire le mur.

bunk bed *n* lit *m* superposé.

bunker ['bʌŋkə^r] ◇ *n* -**1.** MIL blockhaus *m*, bunker *m*. -**2.** [for coal] coffre *m*; NAUT soute *f*. -**3.** GOLF bunker *m*.
◇ *vt* -**1.** NAUT [coal, oil, ship] mettre en soute. -**2.** GOLF envoyer la balle dans un bunker.

Bunker Hill *pr n*: the battle of ~ la bataille de Bunker Hill.

THE BATTLE OF BUNKER HILL:
Première grande bataille de la guerre d'Indépendance américaine, en 1775. Bien qu'ils aient dû battre en retraite, les Américains infligèrent de lourdes pertes aux Anglais, ce qui, pour les colonies, constitua un encouragement à poursuivre la lutte.

---

bunkhouse ['bʌŋkhaʊs, *pl* -haʊzɪz] *n Am* baraquement *m* (pour ouvriers).

bunko *inf* ['bʌŋkəʊ] (*pl* **bunkos**) *Am* = **bunco**.

bunkum *inf* ['bʌŋkəm] *n* [nonsense] foutaises *fpl*.

bunk-up *n Br*: **to give sb a ~** faire la courte échelle à qqn.

bunny ['bʌnɪ] *n*: ~ (rabbit) (petit) lapin *m*, Jeannot lapin *m*.

bunny girl *n* hôtesse *f* de boîte de nuit.

Bunsen burner ['bʌnsn-] *n* (bec *m*) Bunsen *m*.

bunting ['bʌntɪŋ] *n* -**1.** [fabric] étamine *f*. -**2.** *(U)* [flags] fanions *mpl*, drapeaux *mpl*; **the building was decorated with blue and white ~** le bâtiment était pavoisé de drapeaux bleus et blancs. -**3.** ORNITH bruant *m*.

buoy [*Br* bɔɪ, *Am* 'buːɪ] ◇ *n* bouée *f*, balise *f* flottante; **mooring ~** bouée *f* de corps-mort, coffre *m* d'amarrage.
◇ *vt* [waterway] baliser; [vessel, obstacle] marquer d'une bouée.
◆ **buoy up** *vt sep* -**1.** NAUT faire flotter, maintenir à flot. -**2.** *fig* [support, sustain] soutenir; [person] remonter; **her son's visit ~ed her up** OR **~ed up her spirits** la visite de son fils l'a remontée OR lui a remonté le moral.

buoyancy ['bɔɪənsɪ] *n* -**1.** [ability to float] flottabilité *f*; [of gas, liquid] poussée *f*. -**2.** *fig* [resilience] ressort *m*, force *f* morale; [cheerfulness] entrain *m*, allant *m*. -**3.** ST. EX: **the ~ of the market** la fermeté du marché.

buoyancy tank *n* réservoir *m* de flottabilité.

buoyant ['bɔɪənt] *adj* -**1.** [floatable] flottable, capable de flotter; [causing to float] qui fait flotter; **sea water is very ~** l'eau de mer porte très bien. -**2.** *fig* [cheerful] plein d'allant OR d'entrain; [mood] gai, allègre; **her spirits were ~ that morning** elle était pleine d'allant OR d'entrain ce matin-là. -**3.** FIN [economy, sector] sain, robuste; ST. EX [market] soutenu; [currency] qui se maintient, ferme.

buoyantly ['bɔɪəntlɪ] *adv* [walk] d'un pas allègre; [float, rise] légèrement; [speak] avec allant, avec entrain.

BUPA ['bu:pə] (*abbr of* British United Provident Association) *pr n association d'assurance-maladie privée*.

bur [bɜ:r] ◇ *n* BOT bardane *f*.
◇ *vt* [clothing] enlever les bardanes de.

Burberry® ['bɜ:bərɪ] *n Br* gabardine *f*, imperméable *m* Burberry®.

burble ['bɜ:bl] ◇ *vi* -**1.** [liquid] glouglouter, faire glouglou; [stream] murmurer. -**2.** *pej* [person] jacasser; **he's always burbling on about moral values** il est toujours à jacasser OR dégoiser sur les valeurs morales.
◇ *n* -**1.** [of a liquid] glouglou *m*; [of a stream] murmure *m*. -**2.** *pej* [chatter] jacasserie *f*, jacassement *m*.

burbling ['bɜ:blɪŋ] *adj* [liquid] glougloutant; [stream] murmurant; *pej* [person] qui jacasse, bavard.

burden ['bɜ:dn] ◇ *n* -**1.** *fml* [heavy weight, load] fardeau *m*, charge *f*. -**2.** *fig* [heavy responsibility, strain] fardeau *m*, charge *f*; **I don't want to be a ~ to you** je ne veux pas être un fardeau pour vous; **his guilt was a heavy ~ to bear** sa culpabilité était un lourd fardeau; **to increase/to relieve the tax ~** augmenter/alléger le fardeau OR le poids des impôts ❑ **the ~ of proof** JUR la charge de la preuve. -**3.** NAUT tonnage *m*, jauge *f*; **a ship of 500 tons ~** un navire qui jauge 500 tonneaux. -**4.** *Br* [chorus, refrain] refrain *m*; *fig* [theme, central idea] fond *m*, substance *f*; **what is the main ~ of her argument?** quel est le point essentiel de son argument?
◇ *vt* -**1.** [weigh down] charger; **to be ~ed with sthg** être chargé de qqch; **to ~ sb with taxes** *fig* accabler qqn d'impôts. -**2.** [trouble] ennuyer, importuner; **I don't want to ~ you with my problems** je ne veux pas vous ennuyer avec mes problèmes; **she was ~ed with guilt** elle était rongée par un sentiment de culpabilité.

burdensome ['bɜ:dnsəm] *adj fml* [load] pesant; [taxes] lourd.

burdock ['bɜ:dɒk] *n* bardane *f*.

bureau ['bjʊərəʊ] (*pl* **bureaus** OR **bureaux** [-rəʊz]) *n* -**1.** ADMIN service *m*, office *m*; [in private enterprise] bureau *m*. -**2.** *Br* [desk] secrétaire *m*, bureau *m*. -**3.** *Am* [chest of drawers] commode *f*.

bureaucracy [bjʊə'rɒkrəsɪ] *n* bureaucratie *f*.

bureaucrat ['bjʊərəkræt] *n* bureaucrate *mf*.

bureaucratic [,bjʊərə'krætɪk] *adj* bureaucratique.

bureaucratize, -ise [bjʊə'rɒkrətaɪz] *vt* bureaucratiser.

burette *Br*, **buret** *Am* [bjʊ'ret] *n* éprouvette *f* graduée, burette *f*.

burgeon ['bɜ:dʒən] *vi* BOT OR *lit* bourgeonner; [leaf, flower] éclore; **a ~ing industry** une industrie florissante; **a ~ing romance** un amour naissant.

burger ['bɜ:gəʳ] *n* hamburger *m*.

burgess ['bɜ:dʒɪs] *n* HIST [elected representative] député *m*, représentant *m*; *arch* [citizen] bourgeois *m*.

burgh ['bʌrə] *n Scot* ville *f*.

burgher ['bɜ:gəʳ] *n* HIST bourgeois *m*, -e *f*.

burglar ['bɜ:gləʳ] *n* cambrioleur *m*, -euse *f*.

burglar alarm *n* dispositif *m* d'alarme contre le vol, antivol *m*.

burglarize ['bɜ:gləraɪz] *vt Am* cambrioler.

burglarproof ['bɜ:gləpru:f] *adj* anti-effraction (*inv*).

burglary ['bɜ:glərɪ] (*pl* **burglaries**) *n* cambriolage *m*.

burgle ['bɜ:gl] *vt* cambrioler.

burgomaster ['bɜ:gə,mɑ:stəʳ] *n* bourgmestre *m*, maire *m*.

Burgundian [bɜ:'gʌndɪən] ◇ *n* Bourguignon *m*, - onne *f*.
◇ *adj* bourguignon.

Burgundy ['bɜ:gəndɪ] *pr n* -**1.** [region] Bourgogne *f*; in ~ en Bourgogne. -**2.** ŒNOL bourgogne *m*.

burial ['berɪəl] ◇ *n* enterrement *m*, inhumation *f*; **to give sb a Christian ~** donner à qqn une sépulture ecclésiastique.
◇ *comp* [place, service] d'inhumation.

burial ground *n* cimetière *m*.

burial mound *n* tumulus *m*.

burin ['bjʊərɪn] *n* burin *m*.

burk [bɜ:k] = **berk**.

Burke's Peerage [bɜ:ks-] *pr n annuaire de l'aristocratie britannique*.

Burkina-Faso [bɜ:,ki:nə'fæsəʊ] *pr n* Burkina *m*; in ~ au Burkina.

burlap ['bɜ:læp] *n* toile *f* à sac, gros canevas *m*.

burlesque [bɜ:'lesk] ◇ *n* -**1.** LITERAT & THEAT burlesque *m*, parodie *f*. -**2.** *Am* [bawdy comedy] revue *f* déshabillée, striptease *m*.
◇ *adj* burlesque.
◇ *vt* parodier.

burly ['bɜ:lɪ] (*compar* **burlier**, *superl* **burliest**) *adj* de forte carrure.

Burma ['bɜ:mə] *pr n* Birmanie *f*.

Burmese [,bɜ:'mi:z] ◇ *n* -**1.** [person] Birman *m*, -e *f*. -**2.** LING birman *m*.
◇ *adj* birman.

Burmese cat *n* chat *m* de Birmanie.

burn [bɜ:n] (*Br pt* & *pp* **burned** OR **burnt** [bɜ:nt], *Am pt* & *pp* **burned**) ◇ *n* -**1.** [injury] brûlure *f*. -**2.** AERON (durée *f* de) combustion *f*. -**3.** *inf* PHYSIOL: **the ~** la sensation de brûlure. -**4.** *Scot* ruisseau *m*.
◇ *vi* -**1.** *literal* brûler; **there was a lovely fire ~ing in the sitting-room** un beau feu brûlait OR flambait au salon; **I can't get the wood to ~** je n'arrive pas à faire brûler OR flamber le bois; **the toast is ~ing** le pain grillé est en train de brûler; **she could see a cigarette ~ing in the dark** elle pouvait voir une cigarette qui brûlait OR se consumait dans l'obscurité; **this material won't ~** ce tissu est ininflammable; **the church ~ed to the ground** l'église a été réduite en cendres; **a light was ~ing in the study** une lumière brûlait dans le bureau. -**2.** *fig* [face, person]: **my face was ~ing** [with embarrassment] j'avais le visage en feu, j'étais tout rouge; **the wind made her face ~** le vent lui brûlait le visage; **I'm ~ing** [from sun] je brûle; [from fever] je suis brûlant, je brûle; **she was ~ing with anger** elle bouillait de colère; **she was ~ing for adventure** elle brûlait du désir d'aventure. -**3.** *inf* [travel at speed] filer, foncer; **we ~ed down the motorway** nous foncions OR nous filions sur l'autoroute.
◇ *vt* [paper, logs, food] brûler; [car, crop, forest] brûler, incendier; **three people were burnt to death** trois personnes sont mortes carbonisées OR ont été brûlées vives; **to be burnt alive** être brûlé vif; **suspected witches were burnt at the stake** les femmes soupçonnées de sorcellerie étaient brûlées vives; **his cigarette burnt a hole in the carpet** sa cigarette a fait un trou dans la moquette; **did you ~ yourself?** est-ce que tu t'es brûlé?; **I burnt my mouth drinking hot tea** je me suis brûlé (la langue) en buvant du thé chaud; **I've burnt the potatoes** j'ai laissé brûler les pommes de terre; **the house was burnt to the ground** la maison fut réduite en cendres OR brûla entièrement ❑ **to ~ one's boats/bridges** brûler ses vaisseaux/les ponts; **to ~ one's fingers, to get one's fingers burnt** se brûler les doigts; **to have money to ~** avoir de l'argent à ne pas savoir qu'en faire; **money ~s a hole in his pocket** l'argent lui fond dans les mains OR lui file entre les doigts.

◆ **burn away** ◇ *vi insep* -**1.** [continue burning]: **the bonfire ~ed away for several hours** le feu a brûlé pendant plusieurs heures. -**2.** [be destroyed by fire] se consumer.
◇ *vt sep* brûler; [paint] brûler, décaper au chalumeau.

◆ **burn down** ◇ *vi insep* -**1.** [be destroyed by fire] brûler complètement; **the building ~ed down** le bâtiment fut complètement détruit par le feu OR brûla complètement. -**2.** [die down]: **the fire in the stove has ~ed down** le feu dans le poêle est presque éteint || [grow smaller] diminuer, baisser; **the candle has ~ed down** la bougie a diminué.
◇ *vt sep* [building] détruire par le feu, incendier.

◆ **burn off** *vt sep* [vegetation] brûler, détruire par le feu; [gas] brûler; [paint] décaper au chalumeau.

◆ **burn out** ◇ *vt sep* -**1.** [destroy by fire - building] détruire par le feu. -**2.** ELEC [wear out - bulb] griller; [- fuse] faire sauter; MECH [- engine] griller; *fig*: **if you keep working this hard you'll ~ yourself out** si tu continues à travailler aussi dur tu vas t'épuiser; **she was burnt out by thirty** elle était usée avant (l'âge de) trente ans. -**3.** [die down] diminuer, éteindre; **after twelve hours the forest fire burnt itself out** au bout de douze heures l'incendie de forêt s'est éteint.
◇ *vi insep* ELEC [bulb] griller; [fuse] sauter; MECH [brakes, engine] griller; [candle, fire] s'éteindre.

◆ **burn up** ◇ *vt sep* -**1.** [destroy by fire] brûler. -**2.** *fig* [person - consume] brûler, dévorer; **the desire for revenge was ~ing him up** il était dévoré par le désir de se venger || *Am inf* [worry]: **it really ~s me up to see you like this** ça me bouffe de te voir comme ça. -**3.** [consume]: **this car ~s up a lot of petrol** cette voiture consomme beaucoup d'essence; **to ~ up a lot of calories/energy** dépenser OR brûler beaucoup de calories/d'énergie ❑ **to ~ up the miles** aller à toute vitesse, foncer.
◇ *vi insep* -**1.** [fire] flamber. -**2.** AERON se consumer, se désintégrer.

burned-out ['bɜ:nt-] *adj* -**1.** [destroyed by fire] incendié, brûlé. -**2.** *inf* [person] lessivé, vidé.

burner ['bɜ:nəʳ] *n* [on a stove] brûleur *m*; [on a lamp] bec *m*.

burnet ['bɜ:nɪt] *n* BOT sanguisorbe *f*.

burning ['bɜ:nɪŋ] ◇ *adj* -**1.** [on fire] en flammes; [arrow, fire, torch] ardent; **the ~ bush** BIBLE le buisson ardent. -**2.** [hot] ardent, brûlant; **I have a ~ sensation in my stomach** j'ai des brûlures à l'estomac || *fig* [intense] ardent, brûlant; **he had a ~ desire to be a writer** il désirait ardemment être écrivain; **a ~ thirst** une soif brûlante; **she has a ~ interest in opera** elle s'intéresse vivement à OR se passionne pour l'opéra. -**3.** [crucial, vital] brûlant; **a ~ issue** une question brûlante.
◇ *adv*: **~ hot coals** des charbons ardents; **her forehead is ~ hot** elle a le front brûlant.
◇ *n* -**1.** [sensation, smell]: **a smell of ~ pervaded the air** une odeur de brûlé se répandit dans l'atmosphère; **he felt a ~ in his chest** il sentit une brûlure à la poitrine. -**2.** [destruction by fire]: **he witnessed the ~ of hundreds of books** il a été témoin de l'autodafé de centaines de livres. -**3.** METALL [overheating] brûlure *f*.

burnish ['bɜ:nɪʃ] ◇ *vt* -**1.** METALL brunir, polir. -**2.** *lit* lustrer.
◇ *n* -**1.** METALL brunissure *f*. -**2.** [shine] brillant *m*, lustre *m*.

burnished ['bɜ:nɪʃt] *adj* -**1.** METALL bruni, poli. -**2.** *lit* [bright, shiny] lustré.

burnous(e) [bɜ:'nu:s] *n* burnous *m*.

burnout ['bɜ:naʊt] *n* -**1.** AERON *arrêt par suite d'épuisement du combustible*. -**2.** ELEC: **what caused the ~?** qu'est-ce qui a fait griller les circuits? -**3.** [exhaustion] épuisement *m* total.

Burns' Night [bɜ:nz-] *n fête célébrée en l'honneur du poète écossais Robert Burns, le 25 janvier*.

burnt [bɜ:nt] ◇ *pt* & *pp* → **burn**.
◇ *adj* -**1.** [charred] brûlé, carbonisé. -**2.** [dark]: **~ orange/red** orange/rouge foncé.

burnt offering *n* [sacrifice] holocauste *m*; *hum* plat *m* calciné OR carbonisé.

burn-up *inf n* course *f* de vitesse.

burp *inf* [bɜ:p] ◇ *n* rot *m*; **"cheers", he said with a ~** « à ta santé », dit-il en rotant.
◇ *vi* roter.
◇ *vt*: **to ~ a baby** faire faire son rot à un bébé.

burp gun▽ *n Am* sulfateuse *f (mitraillette)*.

burr [bɜːʳ] ◇ *n* -**1.** [rough edge] barbe *f*, bavure *f*. -**2.** [tool] fraise *f*. -**3.** [on tree trunk] broussin *m*; ~ **walnut** ronce *f* de noyer. -**4.** PHON grasseyement *m*; **he speaks with a soft Devon ~** il a un léger accent du Devon. -**5.** [noise] ronflement *m*, vrombissement *m*. -**6.** = **bur**.
◇ *vt* -**1.** [file] ébarber, ébavurer. -**2.** = **bur**.
◇ *vi* -**1.** PHON grasseyer. -**2.** [make a noise] ronfler, vrombir.

burrito [bəˈriːtəʊ] *n plat mexicain constitué d'une crêpe farcie*.

burro [ˈbʊrəʊ] *n Am* baudet *m*.

burrow [ˈbʌrəʊ] ◇ *n* terrier *m*.
◇ *vt* -**1.** [subj: person] creuser; [subj: animal, insect] creuser, fouir; **he ~ed his way underneath the prison wall** il a creusé un tunnel sous le mur de la prison. -**2.** *fig* [nestle] enfouir; **the cat ~ed its head into my shoulder** le chat a blotti sa tête contre mon épaule.
◇ *vi* -**1.** [dig] creuser; **they found earthworms ~ing through the soil** ils ont trouvé des vers de terre qui creusaient des galeries dans le sol. -**2.** [search] fouiller; **I've been ~ing through the files for clues** j'ai cherché OR fouillé dans les dossiers pour trouver des indices. -**3.** [nestle] s'enfouir, s'enfoncer; **she ~ed under the sheets** elle s'est enfouie sous les draps.

bursar [ˈbɜːsəʳ] *n* -**1.** [treasurer] intendant *m*, -e *f*, économe *mf*. -**2.** *Scot* [student] boursier *m*, -ère *f*.

bursary [ˈbɜːsərɪ] (*pl* **bursaries**) *n* -**1.** [grant, scholarship] bourse *f* (d'études). -**2.** *Br* [treasury] intendance *f*.

burst [bɜːst] (*pt* & *pp* **burst**) ◇ *n* -**1.** [explosion] éclatement *m*, explosion *f*; [puncture] éclatement *m*, crevaison *f*. -**2.** [sudden eruption - of laughter] éclat *m*; [- of emotion] accès *m*, explosion *f*; [- of ideas] jaillissement *m*; [- of thunder] coup *m*; [- of flame] jet *m*, jaillissement *m*; [- of applause] salve *f*; **a ~ of gunfire** une rafale; **he had a sudden ~ of energy** il a eu un sursaut d'énergie; **to put on** OR **to have a sudden ~ of speed** faire une pointe de vitesse, accélérer soudainement; **we heard a ~ of music** on entendit quelques mesures; **a ~ of activity** une poussée d'activité; **to work in ~s** travailler par à-coups.
◇ *vi* -**1.** [break, explode - balloon] éclater; [- abscess] crever; [- tyre] crever, éclater; [- bottle] éclater, voler en éclats; **his heart felt as if it would ~ with joy/grief** *fig* il crut que son cœur allait éclater de joie/se briser de chagrin. -**2.** [enter, move suddenly]: **two policemen ~ into the house** deux policiers ont fait irruption dans la maison; **she ~ through the door** elle est entrée brusquement; **the front door ~ open** la porte d'entrée s'est ouverte brusquement; **the sun suddenly ~ through the clouds** le soleil perça OR apparut soudain à travers les nuages.
◇ *vt* [balloon, bubble] crever, faire éclater; [pipe] faire éclater; [boiler] faire éclater, faire sauter; [tyre] crever, faire éclater; [abscess] crever, percer; **the river is about to ~ its banks** le fleuve est sur le point de déborder; **to ~ a blood vessel** se faire éclater une veine, se rompre un vaisseau sanguin; **don't ~ a blood vessel to get it done** *inf Br hum* ce n'est pas la peine de te crever pour finir, ce n'est pas la peine de te tuer à la tâche.
◆ **burst forth** *vi insep lit* [liquid] jaillir; [person] sortir précipitamment, apparaître; **the children ~ forth into the playground** les enfants se précipitèrent dans la cour de récréation; **he ~ forth with a song** il se mit à chanter.
◆ **burst in** *vi insep* [enter violently] faire irruption; [interrupt] interrompre brutalement la discussion; [intrude] entrer précipitamment; **it was very rude of you to ~ in on** OR **upon us like that** c'était très mal élevé de ta part d'entrer brusquement comme ça chez nous OR de faire irruption chez nous comme ça.
◆ **burst into** *vt insep* [begin suddenly]: **to ~ into laughter** éclater de rire; **to ~ into tears** éclater en sanglots, fondre en larmes; **to ~ into song** se mettre à chanter; **to ~ into flames** prendre feu, s'enflammer.
◆ **burst out** ◇ *vi insep* [leave suddenly] sortir précipitamment; **two men suddenly ~ out of the room** deux hommes sortirent en trombe de la pièce.
◇ *vt insep* [exclaim] s'exclamer, s'écrier; **to ~ out laughing** éclater de rire; **to ~ out crying** fondre en larmes; **they all ~ out singing** ils se sont tous mis à chanter d'un coup; **"I love you", he ~ out** «je t'aime», lança-t-il.

bursting [ˈbɜːstɪŋ] *adj* -**1.** [full] plein à craquer; **to be ~ at the seams** se défaire aux coutures, se découdre; **the place was ~ at the seams (with people)** *fig* l'endroit était plein à craquer; **to be ~ with joy/pride** déborder de joie/d'orgueil; **to be ~ with health** péter la santé. -**2.** [longing, yearning]: **they were ~ to tell us the news** ils mouraient d'envie de nous apprendre la nouvelle. -**3.** *inf* [desperate to urinate]: **I'm ~** je ne peux plus attendre, ça presse.

burton *inf* [ˈbɜːtn] *n Br dated*: **gone for a ~** [broken] fichu; [lost] disparu; [dead] qui a passé l'arme à gauche; [fallen] qui a ramassé une bûche.

Burundi [bʊˈrʊndɪ] *pr n* Burundi *m*; **in ~** au Burundi.

Burundian [bʊˈrʊndjən] ◇ *n* Burundais *m*, -e *f*.
◇ *adj* burundais.

bury [ˈberɪ] (*pt* & *pp* **buried**) *vt* -**1.** [in the ground] enterrer; [in water] immerger; **to be buried alive** être enterré vivant; **to be buried at sea** être immergé en haute mer; **he's buried two wives already** *fig* il a déjà enterré deux femmes; **we agreed to ~ our differences** nous avons convenu d'oublier OR d'enterrer nos différends ❑ **to ~ the hatchet** enterrer la hache de guerre, faire la paix. -**2.** [cover completely] ensevelir, enterrer; **she buried her feet in the sand** elle a enfoncé ses pieds dans le sable ❑ **to ~ one's head in the sand** faire l'autruche. -**3.** [hide]: **where have you buried my newspaper?** où as-tu fourré mon journal?; **she buried her face in the pillow** elle enfouit OR enfonça son visage dans l'oreiller; **to ~ one's face in one's hands** enfouir son visage dans ses mains; **he always has his nose buried in a book** il a toujours le nez fourré dans un livre; **to ~ oneself in the country** *fig* s'enterrer à la campagne; **long-buried memories began to surface** des souvenirs oubliés depuis longtemps commencèrent à refaire surface; **it's buried in a drawer somewhere** c'est enfoui dans un tiroir quelque part. -**4.** [occupy]: **to ~ o.s. in (one's) work** se plonger dans son travail. -**5.** [thrust, plunge - knife] enfoncer, plonger; **he buried his hands in his pockets** il a fourré les mains dans ses poches.
◆ **bury away** *vt sep* cacher, enfouir; **the information was buried away in the small print** l'information était perdue dans la foule des détails.

burying [ˈberɪɪŋ] *adj*: **a ~ place** un cimetière.

bus [bʌs] (*pl* **buses** OR **busses**, *pt* & *pp* **bused** OR **bussed**, *cont* **busing** OR **bussing**) ◇ *n* -**1.** [vehicle] bus *m*; *Am* [coach] car *m*. -**2.** *inf Br* [old car] (vieille) bagnole, guimbarde *f*. -**3.** COMPUT bus *m*.
◇ *vi*: **we can walk or ~ home** nous pouvons rentrer à pied ou en autobus.
◇ *vt*: **the children are bussed to school** les enfants vont à l'école en autobus ‖ *Am* SCH [for purposes of racial integration] emmener à l'école en autobus *(pour favoriser l'intégration raciale)*.
◇ *comp* [route, service, strike, ticket] d'autobus, de bus.

busbar [ˈbʌsbɑː] *n* COMPUT & ELEC bus *m*.

busboy [ˈbʌsbɔɪ] *n Am* aide-serveur *m*.

busby [ˈbʌzbɪ] (*pl* **busbies**) *n Br* bonnet *m* de hussard.

bus conductor *n Br* receveur *m*, -euse *f* d'autobus.

bus driver *n* conducteur *m*, -trice *f* d'autobus.

bush [bʊʃ] *n* -**1.** [shrub] buisson *m*, arbuste *m*; **the children hid in the ~es** les enfants se cachèrent dans les fourrés; **a ~ of black hair** *fig* une tignasse de cheveux noirs. -**2.** [scrubland]: **the ~** la brousse. -**3.** MECH bague *f*.

bushbaby [ˈbʊʃˌbeɪbɪ] *n* galago *m*.

bushed *inf* [bʊʃt] *adj* [exhausted] crevé, claqué.

bushel [ˈbʊʃl] (*pt* & *pp* **busheled** OR **bushelled**, *cont* **busheling** OR **bushelling**) ◇ *vt Am* [mend] recoudre; [alter] retoucher.
◇ *n* [measure] boisseau *m*.

bushfire [ˈbʊʃˌfaɪəʳ] *n* feu *m* de brousse.

bushing [ˈbʊʃɪŋ] *n (U)* TECH bague *f*.

bush jacket *n* saharienne *f*.

bushman [ˈbʊʃmən] (*pl* **bushmen** [-mən]) *n Austr* & *NZ* broussard *m*.

Bushman [ˈbʊʃmən] (*pl inv* OR **Bushmen** [-mən]) *n* [in southern Africa] Bochiman *m*.

bushranger [ˈbʊʃˌreɪndʒəʳ] *n* [backwoodsman] broussard *m*, -e *f*.

bush telegraph *n literal* téléphone *m* de brousse; *Br fig* & *hum* [grapevine] téléphone *m* arabe.

bushwhack [ˈbʊʃwæk] ◇ *vi* -**1.** [clear a path] se frayer un passage à travers la brousse. -**2.** [live in the bush] vivre dans la brousse.
◇ *vt Am* [ambush] tendre une embuscade à.

bushwhacker [ˈbʊʃˌwækəʳ] *n* -**1.** *Am* & *Austr* [backwoodsman] broussard *m*, -e *f*. -**2.** *Am* [guerrilla] guérillero *m*.

bushy [ˈbʊʃɪ] (*compar* **bushier**, *superl* **bushiest**) *adj* -**1.** [area] broussailleux. -**2.** [tree] touffu; [beard, eyebrows, hair] touffu, fourni.

busily [ˈbɪzɪlɪ] *adv* activement; **to be ~ engaged in sthg/in doing sthg** être très occupé à qqch/à faire qqch; **she is ~ collecting material for her next book** elle est très occupée à rassembler des matériaux pour son prochain livre; **he was ~ scribbling in his notebook** il griffonnait sur son calepin d'un air affairé.

business [ˈbɪznɪs] ◇ *n* -**1.** [firm] entreprise *f*; **there has been an increase in the number of small ~es throughout the country** il y a eu une augmentation du nombre des petites entreprises à travers le pays; **he's got a mail-order ~** il a une affaire OR entreprise de vente par correspondance; **would you like to have** OR **to run your own ~?** aimeriez-vous travailler à votre compte? -**2.** *(U)* [trade] affaires *fpl*; **~ is good/bad** les affaires vont bien/mal; **how's ~?** comment vont les affaires?; **we have lost ~ to foreign competitors** nous avons perdu une partie de notre clientèle au profit de concurrents étrangers; **we can help you to increase your ~** nous pouvons vous aider à augmenter votre chiffre d'affaires; **the travel ~** les métiers OR le secteur du tourisme; **she's in the fashion ~** elle est dans la mode; **my ~ is pharmaceuticals** je travaille dans l'industrie pharmaceutique; **she knows her ~** elle connaît son métier; **he's in ~** il est dans les affaires; **this firm has been in ~ for 25 years** cette entreprise tourne depuis 25 ans; **she's in ~ for herself** elle travaille à son compte; **he wants to go into ~** il veut travailler dans les affaires; **these high interest rates will put us out of ~** ces taux d'intérêt élevés vont nous obliger à fermer; **to go out of ~** cesser une activité; **he's got no ~ sense** il n'a pas le sens des affaires; **to do ~ with** travailler OR traiter avec; **he's a man we can do ~ with** *fig* c'est un homme avec lequel nous pouvons traiter; **I've come on ~** je suis venu pour le travail OR pour affaires; **big ~ is running the country** le gros commerce gouverne le pays; **selling weapons is big ~** la vente d'armes rapporte beaucoup d'argent; **from now on I'll take my ~ elsewhere** désormais j'irai voir OR je m'adresserai ailleurs; **it's bad ~ to refuse credit** c'est mauvais en affaires de refuser le crédit; **we're not in the ~ of providing free meals** ce n'est pas notre rôle de fournir des repas gratuits ❑ **Business Expansion Scheme** ≃ plan *m* d'aide à l'investissement; **a degree in ~, a ~ degree** un diplôme de gestion; **let's get down to ~** passons aux choses sérieuses; **(now) we're in ~!** nous voilà partis! -**3.** [concern]: **it's my (own) ~ if I decide not to go** c'est mon affaire OR cela ne regarde que moi si je décide de ne pas y aller; **what ~**

is it of yours? est-ce que cela vous regarde?; it's none of your ~ cela ne vous regarde pas; tell him to mind his own ~ dis-lui de se mêler de ses affaires; I'll make it my ~ to find out je m'occuperai d'en savoir plus; people going about their ~ des gens vaquant à leurs occupations; you had no ~ reading that letter vous n'aviez pas à lire cette lettre ❑ I could see she meant ~ je voyais qu'elle ne plaisantait pas; he drank like nobody's ~ *inf* il buvait comme un trou; she worked like nobody's ~ to get it finished *inf* elle a travaillé comme un forçat pour tout terminer; I soon sent him about his ~ je l'ai vite envoyé promener. -**4.** [matter, task]: the ~ of this meeting is the training budget l'ordre du jour de cette réunion est le budget de formation; any other ~ [on agenda] points *mpl* divers; any other ~? d'autres questions à l'ordre du jour?; she had important ~ to discuss elle avait à parler d'affaires importantes; that investigation of police misconduct was a dirty ~ l'enquête sur la bavure policière a été une sale affaire; this strike ~ has gone on long enough cette histoire de grève a assez duré; I'm tired of the whole ~ je suis las de toute cette histoire. -**5.** [rigmarole]: it was a real ~ getting tickets for the concert ça a été toute une affaire pour avoir des billets pour le concert. -**6.** THEAT jeux *mpl* de scène. -**7.** *inf euph*: the dog did his ~ and ran off le chien a fait ses besoins et a détalé.

◇ *comp* [lunch, trip] d'affaires; ~ associate associé *m*, -e *f*; ~ expenses [for individual] frais *mpl* professionnels; [for firm] frais *mpl* généraux; ~ hours [of office] heures *fpl* de bureau; [of shop, public service] heures *fpl* d'ouverture; ~ studies études *fpl* commerciales OR de commerce.

business address *n* adresse *f* du lieu de travail.

business card *n* carte *f* de visite.

business centre *n* centre *m* des affaires.

business class *n* [on aeroplane] classe *f* affaires.

business college *n Br* école *f* de commerce; [for management training] école *f* (supérieure) de gestion.

business end *inf n* [of knife] partie *f* coupante; [of gun] gueule *f*.

businesslike ['bɪznɪslaɪk] *adj* -**1.** [systematic, methodical] systématique, méthodique; I was amazed at the ~ way in which she handled the funeral arrangements j'ai été étonné de voir avec quelle efficacité elle s'est occupée de l'enterrement. -**2.** [impersonal, formal]: her manner was cold and ~ son comportement était froid et direct; our conversation was courteous and ~ notre entretien a été courtois et franc.

businessman ['bɪznɪsmæn] (*pl* businessmen [-men]) *n* homme *m* d'affaires; I'm not a very good ~ je ne suis pas très doué en affaires.

business manager *n* COMM & INDUST directeur *m* commercial; SPORT manager *m*; THEAT directeur *m*.

business plan *n* projet *m* d'entreprise.

business school *Am* = **business college**.

business suit *n Am* complet-(veston) *m*.

businesswoman ['bɪznɪs,wʊmən] (*pl* businesswomen [-,wɪmɪn]) *n* femme *f* d'affaires.

busing ['bʌsɪŋ] *n Am système de ramassage scolaire aux États-Unis, qui organise la répartition des enfants noirs et des enfants blancs dans les écoles afin de lutter contre la ségrégation raciale*.

busk [bʌsk] *vi Br* jouer de la musique *(dans la rue ou le métro)*; we earned money ~ing in the street/underground nous avons gagné de l'argent en jouant dans la rue/le métro.

busker ['bʌskəʳ] *n Br* musicien *m* ambulant, musicienne *f* ambulante.

bus lane *n* voie *f* OR couloir *m* d'autobus.

busload ['bʌsləʊd] *n*: a ~ of workers arrived at the factory un autobus plein d'ouvriers arriva à l'usine; the tourists arrived by the ~ OR in ~s les touristes sont arrivés par cars entiers.

busman ['bʌsmən] (*pl* busmen [-mən]) *n Br* [driver] conducteur *m* d'autobus; [conductor] receveur *m* d'autobus; to have a ~'s holiday passer ses vacances à travailler.

bus shelter *n* Abribus® *m*.

bus station *n* gare *f* routière.

bus stop *n* arrêt *m* d'autobus OR de bus.

bust [bʌst] (*pt & pp* busted OR bust) ◇ *adj inf* -**1.** [broken] fichu. -**2.** [bankrupt]: his company went ~ after a year son entreprise a fait faillite au bout d'un an. -**3.** [broke]: I'm ~ je suis fauché. -**4.** *phr*: ... or ~! *expression indiquant la détermination à arriver quelque part*.

◇ *n* -**1.** [breasts] poitrine *f*, buste *m*; a large ~ une forte poitrine; she has a small ~ elle a peu de poitrine. -**2.** ART buste *m*. -**3.** *inf* [police raid, arrest]: there was a big drugs ~ in Chicago il y a eu un beau coup de filet chez les trafiquants de drogue de Chicago. -**4.** *inf Am* [failure] fiasco *m*.

◇ *vt inf* -**1.** [break] bousiller, abîmer; *fig*: to ~ a gut OR blood vessel se casser la nénette; I'm not going to ~ my ass for him!▽ *Am* je ne vais pas me casser le cul pour lui! -**2.** [arrest, raid]: he was ~ed on a drugs charge il s'est fait choper OR embarquer pour une affaire de drogue; the police ~ed the house at 3 a.m. la police a fait une descente dans la maison à 3 h du matin. -**3.** *Am* [tame - horse] dresser. -**4.** *Am* [demote] rétrograder. -**5.** *Am* [catch] découvrir; ~ed! je t'y prends!, je t'ai eu!

◆ **bust out** *inf vi insep* se tirer; three prisoners have ~ed out (of jail) trois prisonniers se sont fait la belle OR la paire.

◆ **bust up** *inf* ◇ *vi insep* -**1.** [boyfriend, girlfriend] rompre (après une engueulade); he's ~ up with his girlfriend il a rompu avec sa copine après une engueulade. -**2.** *Am* [laugh] éclater de rire.

◇ *vt sep* [disrupt]: demonstrators ~ed up the meeting des manifestants sont venus semer la pagaïe dans la réunion.

bustard ['bʌstəd] *n* outarde *f*.

buster *inf* ['bʌstəʳ] *n* -**1.** *Am* [pal]: thanks, ~ merci, mon (petit) gars. -**2.** *Am* [tamer, breaker] dompteur *m*, -euse *f*.

-buster *inf in cpds*: crime~s super-flics *mpl*.

bustle ['bʌsl] ◇ *vi* [hurry]: he ~d about OR around the kitchen il s'affairait dans la cuisine; the nurse came bustling in l'infirmière entra d'un air affairé.

◇ *n* -**1.** [activity] agitation *f*; I enjoy the hustle and ~ of working in a bank j'aime bien travailler dans une banque à cause de tout le va-et-vient qui y règne; the ~ of New York l'activité grouillante de New York. -**2.** [on dress] tournure *f*.

bustling ['bʌslɪŋ] ◇ *adj* [person] affairé; [place] animé; the streets were ~ with Christmas shoppers les rues grouillaient de gens faisant leurs achats de Noël.

◇ *n* [activity] agitation *f*.

bust-up *inf n* -**1.** [quarrel] engueulade *f*; Tony and Pat have had another ~ Tony et Pat se sont encore engueulés. -**2.** [brawl] bagarre *f*.

busty ['bʌstɪ] (*compar* bustier, *superl* bustiest) *adj* qui a une forte poitrine; she was a big, ~ woman c'était une femme forte, à la poitrine plantureuse.

bus way *n* couloir *m* OR voie *f* d'autobus.

busy ['bɪzɪ] (*compar* busier, *superl* busiest, *pt & pp* busied) ◇ *adj* -**1.** [person] occupé; he was too ~ to notice il était trop occupé pour s'en apercevoir; I'm ~ enough as it is! je suis déjà assez occupé!; she was ~ painting the kitchen elle était occupée à peindre la cuisine; he likes to keep ~ il aime bien s'occuper; the packing kept me ~ all afternoon j'ai été occupé à faire les valises tout l'après-midi; I'm afraid I'm ~ tomorrow malheureusement je suis pris demain; the bank manager is ~ with a customer le directeur de l'agence est occupé avec OR en rendez-vous avec un client ❑ she's as ~ as a bee, she's a ~ bee elle est très occupée. -**2.** [port, road, street] très fréquenté; [time, period] chargé, plein; I've had a ~ day j'ai eu une journée chargée; he has a ~ schedule il a un emploi du temps chargé OR bien rempli; this is our busiest period [business, shop] c'est la période où nous sommes en pleine activité; the office is very ~ at the moment nous avons beaucoup de travail au bureau en ce moment; the shops are very ~ today les magasins sont pleins (de monde) aujourd'hui. -**3.** *Am* [telephone line] occupé; I got the ~ signal ça sonnait occupé. -**4.** *pej* [excessively elaborate] chargé.

◇ *vt*: he busied himself with household chores il s'est occupé à des tâches ménagères; she busied herself by tidying the office elle s'est occupée en faisant le ménage dans le bureau.

busybody *inf* ['bɪzɪ,bɒdɪ] (*pl* busybodies) *n* fouineur *m*, -euse *f*, fouinard *m*, -e *f*.

busy lizzie [-'lɪzɪ] *n* balsamine *f*, impatiente *f*.

but [bʌt] ◇ *conj* -**1.** [to express contrast] mais; my husband smokes, ~ I don't mon mari fume, mais moi non; my husband doesn't smoke, ~ I do mon mari ne fume pas, mais moi si; I speak Spanish ~ not Italian je parle espagnol mais pas italien; she came home tired ~ happy elle est rentrée fatiguée mais heureuse. -**2.** [in exclamations] mais; ~ you can't do that! mais tu ne peux pas faire ça!; ~ that's absurd! mais c'est absurde! -**3.** [when addressing sb politely]: sorry, ~ I think that's MY umbrella pardon, mais je crois que c'est mon parapluie; excuse me, ~ there's a call for you excusez-moi, il y a un appel pour vous. -**4.** [used for emphasis]: nobody, ~ nobody, gets in without a ticket personne, absolument personne n'entre sans ticket. -**5.** [except, only] mais; it tastes like a grapefruit, ~ sweeter ça a le goût d'un pamplemousse, mais en plus sucré; I'll do it, ~ not right now je vais le faire, mais pas tout de suite. -**6.** *lit*: she never hears his name ~ she starts to weep elle ne peut entendre son nom sans verser des larmes; barely a day goes by ~ he receives another invitation il ne se passe pas un jour sans qu'il reçoive une nouvelle invitation.

◇ *adv* -**1.** [only] ne... que; I can ~ try je ne peux qu'essayer; his resignation cannot ~ confirm such suspicions *fml* sa démission ne fait que confirmer de tels soupçons; they had ~ recently become acquainted *lit* ils ne se connaissaient que depuis peu (de temps); this life is ~ transitory/~ a dream *lit* cette vie n'est qu'éphémère/qu'un rêve. -**2.** *inf Am* [used for emphasis] et; get them down here ~ fast! descends-les et vite!

◇ *prep* -**1.** [except] sauf, à part; she wouldn't see anyone ~ her lawyer elle ne voulait voir personne sauf OR à part son avocat; who ~ a fool would believe his story? il n'y a qu'un imbécile pour croire son histoire; where ~ in America could you find such a gadget? il n'y a qu'en Amérique qu'on trouve un tel gadget; nothing ~ a miracle could have saved her seul un miracle aurait pu la sauver. -**2.** *Br* [with numbers]: turn right at the next corner ~ one tournez à droite au deuxième carrefour; I was the last ~ two to finish j'étais l'avant-avant-dernier à finir.

◇ *n*: you're coming and no ~s! tu viens, et pas de mais!

◆ **but for** *prep phr* sans; ~ for her courage, many more people would have drowned sans son courage, il y aurait eu beaucoup plus de noyés.

◆ **but that** *conj phr fml*: we should have been on time, ~ that the train was delayed nous aurions été à l'heure si le train n'avait pas été retardé; I do not doubt ~ that we shall succeed je ne doute pas de notre réussite.

◆ **but then** *adv phr* enfin; ~ then, that's just the way it goes enfin, c'est comme ça.

butane ['bju:teɪn] *n* butane *m*; ~ gas gaz *m* butane, butane.

butch *inf* [bʊtʃ] ◇ *adj* [woman] hommasse; [man] macho.

◇ *n* [lesbian] *lesbienne d'apparence masculine*.

butcher ['bʊtʃəʳ] ◇ *n* **-1.** COMM boucher *m*; she's gone to the ~'s elle est partie chez le boucher; the ~'s wife la bouchère; ~'s shop boucherie *f*; ~'s boy *Br* garçon *m* boucher. **-2.** [murderer] boucher *m*; let's have a ~ (at it)! montre un peu!
◇ *vt* **-1.** [animal] abattre, tuer. **-2.** [person] massacrer. **-3.** *inf* [story, joke] massacrer.

butchery ['bʊtʃərɪ] *n* **-1.** COMM boucherie *f*; *Br* [slaughterhouse] abattoir *m*. **-2.** *fig* [massacre] boucherie *f*, massacre *m*.

butene ['bjuːtiːn] *n* butylène *m*, butène *m*.

butler ['bʌtləʳ] *n* maître *m* d'hôtel; [in large household] majordome *m*.

Butlin's ['bʌtlɪnz] *pr n chaîne britannique de villages de vacances.*

butt [bʌt] ◇ *n* **-1.** [end] bout *m*; [of rifle] crosse *f*; [of cigarette] mégot *m*; the ~ end le bout. **-2.** *inf Am* [buttocks] fesses *fpl*; why don't you get off your ~ and do something? remue-toi un peu les fesses et fais quelque chose!; you just sit around on your ~ all day! tu ne fous rien de toute la journée! **-3.** [in archery - target] but *m*; [- mound] butte *f*; the ~s MIL le champ OR la butte de tir. **-4.** [person]: she became the ~ of their teasing elle s'est trouvée en butte à leurs taquineries; he was the ~ of all the office jokes il était la cible de toutes les plaisanteries du bureau. **-5.** [barrel] tonneau *m*.
◇ *vt* **-1.** [subj: animal] donner un coup de corne à; [subj: person] donner un coup de tête à; the goat ~ed its head against the gate la chèvre donna un coup de corne à la barrière; he ~ed his way through the crowds *fig* il s'est forcé un passage dans la foule. **-2.** TECH [abut] abouter.
◆ **butt in** *vi insep* [interrupt]: excuse me for ~ing in excusez-moi de m'en mêler OR de vous interrompre; she was always ~ing in on people's conversations elle s'immisçait toujours dans les conversations des autres.

butte [bjuːt] *n Am* butte *f*, tertre *m*.

butter ['bʌtəʳ] ◇ *n* beurre *m*; ~ dish beurrier *m*; she looked as if ~ wouldn't melt in her mouth on lui aurait donné le bon Dieu sans confession.
◇ *vt* beurrer.
◆ **butter up** *inf vt sep* passer de la pommade à.

butterball *inf* ['bʌtəbɔːl] *n Am* paquet *m* de graisse.

butter bean *n sorte de haricot de Lima.*

buttercup ['bʌtəkʌp] *n* bouton *m* d'or.

butterfat ['bʌtəfæt] *n* matière *f* grasse.

butterfingered *inf* ['bʌtə,fɪŋgəd] *adj*: a ~ child un enfant aux mains malhabiles.

butterfingers *inf* ['bʌtə,fɪŋgəz] *n* maladroit *m*, -e *f (de ses mains).*

butterfly ['bʌtəflaɪ] (*pl* **butterflies**) *n* **-1.** ENTOM papillon *m*; she always has OR gets butterflies (in her stomach) before a performance elle a toujours le trac avant une représentation. **-2.** SPORT: (the) ~ la brasse papillon.

butterfly net *n* filet *m* à papillons.

butterfly nut *n* papillon *m*, écrou *m* à ailettes.

butterfly valve *n* (soupape *f* à) papillon *m*.

butter icing *n* glaçage *m* au beurre.

butter knife *n* couteau *m* à beurre.

buttermilk ['bʌtəmɪlk] *n* babeurre *m*.

butterscotch ['bʌtəskɒtʃ] *n* caramel *m* dur au beurre.

buttery ['bʌtərɪ] (*pl* **butteries**) ◇ *adj* **-1.** [smell, taste] de beurre; [fingers] couvert de beurre; [biscuits, cake] fait avec beaucoup de beurre. **-2.** *inf fig* [obsequious] mielleux.
◇ *n* **-1.** [storeroom] office *m or f*. **-2.** [snackbar] buffet *m*, buvette *f*.

butt joint *n* joint *m* abouté, soudure *f* bout à bout.

butt naked *inf adj Am* à poil.

buttock ['bʌtək] *n* fesse *f*.

button ['bʌtn] ◇ *n* **-1.** [on clothing] bouton *m*; MECH bouton *m*; FENCING bouton *m*; on the ~ *inf* exactement. **-2.** *Am* [badge] badge *m*.
◇ *vt* [gen & FENCING] se boutonner; ~ it OR your lip OR your mouth! *inf* ferme-là!, boucle-la!
◇ *vi* se boutonner; the blouse ~s at the back le chemisier se boutonne par derrière OR dans le dos.
◆ **buttons** *n Br dated* groom *m*, chasseur *m*.
◆ **button up** ◇ *vt sep* **-1.** [piece of clothing] boutonner. **-2.** *inf fig* [conclude] régler.
◇ *vi insep* **-1.** [piece of clothing] se boutonner. **-2.** *inf* [shut up]: ~ up! ferme-la!, boucle-la!

button-down *adj* **-1.** [collar] boutonné; [shirt] à col boutonné. **-2.** *Am fig* [conventional]: a ~ businessman un homme d'affaires très comme il faut.

buttonhole ['bʌtnhəʊl] ◇ *n* **-1.** [in clothing] boutonnière *f*; she gave him a carnation for his ~ elle lui donna un œillet pour mettre à sa boutonnière; ~ stitch SEW point *m* de boutonnière. **-2.** *Br* [flower]: she was wearing a pink ~ elle portait une fleur rose à la boutonnière.
◇ *vt* **-1.** [make buttonholes in] faire des boutonnières sur; [sew with buttonhole stitch] coudre au point de boutonnière. **-2.** *inf fig* [detain - person] retenir, coincer.

button mushroom *n* champignon *m* de couche OR de Paris.

button-nosed *adj* qui a un petit nez.

button-through *adj*: a ~ dress une robe-chemisier; a ~ skirt une jupe boutonnée.

buttress ['bʌtrɪs] ◇ *n* **-1.** ARCHIT contrefort *m*. **-2.** *fig* pilier *m*.
◇ *vt* **-1.** ARCHIT étayer; [cathedral] arc-bouter. **-2.** *fig* [argument, system] étayer, renforcer.

butty *inf* ['bʌtɪ] (*pl* **butties**) *n Br dial* **-1.** [sandwich] sandwich *m*, casse-croûte *m*. **-2.** [friend] copain *m*.

buxom ['bʌksəm] *adj* [plump] plantureux, bien en chair; [busty] à la poitrine plantureuse.

buy [baɪ] (*pt* & *pp* **bought** [bɔːt]) ◇ *vt* **-1.** [purchase] acheter; to ~ sthg for sb, to ~ sb sthg acheter qqch à OR pour qqn; I'll ~ it for you je te l'achète; can I ~ you a coffee? puis-je t'offrir un café?; she didn't have a pen, so he bought her one elle n'avait pas de stylo, alors il lui en a acheté un; she bought her car from her sister elle a racheté la voiture de sa sœur; I'll ~ it from you je te le rachète; they bought it for £100 ils l'ont payé 100 livres; have you bought the plane tickets? avez-vous pris les billets d'avion?; you'd better ~ the theatre tickets today tu devrais prendre OR louer les places de théâtre aujourd'hui; we're out of coffee — I'll go and ~ some more nous n'avons plus de café – je vais aller en racheter; to ~ sthg new/second-hand/on credit acheter qqch neuf/d'occasion/à crédit; she bought herself a pair of skis elle s'est acheté une paire de skis; you never ~ yourself anything! tu ne t'achètes jamais rien!; £20 won't ~ you very much these days avec 20 livres, on ne va pas très loin de nos jours. **-2.** [gain, obtain]: to ~ time gagner du temps; she bought their freedom with her life elle paya leur liberté de sa vie. **-3.** [bribe] acheter; I won't be bought on ne m'achètera pas. **-4.** *inf* [believe]: she'll never ~ that story elle n'avalera OR ne gobera jamais cette histoire; do you think he'll ~ it? tu crois qu'il va marcher?; OK, I'll ~ that! d'accord, je marche! **-5.** *phr*: to ~ it▽ [die]: he bought it in the final attack à la dernière crise, il y est resté.
◇ *n* affaire *f*; this car was a great ~ cette voiture était une très bonne affaire.
◆ **buy back** *vt sep* racheter; can I ~ my bicycle back from you? puis-je te racheter mon vélo?
◆ **buy in** ◇ *vt sep* **-1.** *Br* [stockpile] stocker; we bought in plenty of coffee before the price increase nous avons fait des provisions de café avant que les prix n'augmentent. **-2.** ST. EX acheter, acquérir. **-3.** [at auction] racheter.
◇ *vi insep* acheter.
◆ **buy into** *vt insep* FIN acheter une participation dans.
◆ **buy off** *vt sep* [bribe] acheter; they bought off the witness for £10,000 ils ont acheté le silence du témoin pour 10 000 livres.
◆ **buy out** *vt sep* **-1.** FIN racheter la part de, désintéresser; she bought out all the other shareholders elle racheta les parts de tous les autres actionnaires. **-2.** MIL racheter; he bought himself out (of the army) il a payé pour pouvoir rompre son contrat avec l'armée.
◆ **buy over** = **buy off**.
◆ **buy up** *vt sep* acheter en quantité; FIN [firm, shares, stock] racheter; the company bought up £50,000 worth of shares la société racheta des actions pour une valeur de 50 000 livres.

buyer ['baɪəʳ] *n* acheteur *m*, -euse *f*; I haven't found a ~ for my house je n'ai pas trouvé d'acheteur pour ma maison; she's a ~ at OR for Harrod's elle est responsable des achats chez Harrod's; ~s' market FIN marché *m* demandeur OR à la hausse.

buying ['baɪɪŋ] *n* achat *m*; ~ power pouvoir *m* d'achat.

buyout ['baɪaʊt] *n* rachat *m*.

buzz [bʌz] ◇ *n* **-1.** [of insect] bourdonnement *m*, vrombissement *m*; *fig*: there was a ~ of conversation in the room la pièce résonnait du brouhaha des conversations; the announcement caused a ~ of excitement l'annonce provoqua un murmure d'excitation. **-2.** [of buzzer] coup *m* de sonnette. **-3.** *inf* [telephone call] coup *m* de fil; I'll give you a ~ this evening je te passerai un coup de fil ce soir. **-4.** *inf* [gossip]: what's the ~? quoi de neuf? **-5.** [activity]: I love the ~ of London j'adore l'animation de Londres. **-6.** *inf* [strong sensation]: I get quite a ~ out of being on the stage je prends vraiment mon pied sur scène.
◇ *vi* **-1.** [insect] bourdonner, vrombir; the theatre ~ed with excitement *fig* le théâtre était tout bourdonnant d'excitation. **-2.** [ears] bourdonner, tinter; her head was ~ing elle avait des bourdonnements dans la tête; his head was ~ing with ideas les idées bourdonnaient dans sa tête. **-3.** [with buzzer]: he ~ed for his secretary il appela sa secrétaire (à l'interphone). **-4.** *inf* [be lively - person] tenir la forme; he's really ~ing tonight il tient vraiment la forme ce soir. **-5.** ▽*Am* [leave]: I wanna ~ je veux me tirer.
◇ *vt* **-1.** [with buzzer]: he ~ed the nurse il appela l'infirmière d'un coup de sonnette. **-2.** *inf Am* [telephone] passer un coup de fil à. **-3.** *inf* AERON [building, town etc] raser, frôler; [aircraft] frôler.
◆ **buzz about** *inf vi insep* s'affairer, s'agiter.
◆ **buzz off** *inf vi insep* décamper, dégager; ~ off, will you! dégage OR fiche le camp, tu veux!

buzzard ['bʌzəd] *n Br* buse *f*; *Am* urubu *m*.

buzz bomb *n* V1 *m*.

buzzer ['bʌzəʳ] *n* sonnette *f*.

buzzing ['bʌzɪŋ] ◇ *n* [of insects] bourdonnement *m*, vrombissement *m*; [in ears] bourdonnement *m*, tintement *m*.
◇ *adj* [insect] bourdonnant, vrombissant; a ~ noise OR sound un bourdonnement OR vrombissement.

buzz saw *n* scie *f* mécanique OR circulaire.

buzzword *inf* ['bʌzwɜːd] *n* mot *m* à la mode.

BVDs *npl Am* sous-vêtements *mpl (pour hommes).*

b/w (*abbr of* black and white) *adj* NB.

by [baɪ] ◇ *adv* **-1.** [past]: she drove by without stopping elle est passée (en voiture) sans s'arrêter; he managed to squeeze by il a réussi à passer (en se faufilant); if you see him, just walk on by si tu le vois, ne t'arrête pas; two hours have gone by deux heures ont passé; as time went by he became less bitter avec le temps il est devenu moins amer. **-2.** [aside, away]: she put some money by for her old age elle a mis de l'argent de côté pour ses vieux jours. **-3.** [nearby]: is there a bank close by? y a-t-il une banque près d'ici?; she sat OR stood by while they operated elle est restée là pendant qu'ils opéraient; how can you just sit OR stand by while he suffers? *fig* comment peux-tu rester là sans rien faire alors qu'il souffre?; stand by in case of an emergency ne vous éloignez pas au cas où il y aurait une urgence. -**4.** [to, at someone's home] : **I'll stop** OR **drop by this evening** je passerai ce soir; **your mother came by this morning** ta mère est passée ce matin.

◇ *prep* **A.** -**1.** [near, beside] près de, à côté de; **by a stream** au bord OR près d'un ruisseau; **by the sea** au bord de la mer; **she parked her car by the kerb** elle gara sa voiture au bord du trottoir; **come and sit by me** OR **my side** viens t'asseoir près OR auprès de moi; **don't stand by the door** ne restez pas debout près de la porte. -**2.** [past] devant; **she walked right by me** elle passa juste devant moi; **I drive by the school every day** je passe (en voiture) devant l'école tous les jours. -**3.** [through] par; **she left by the back door** elle est partie par la porte de derrière.

B. -**1.** [indicating means, method]: **to pay by cheque** payer par chèque; **by letter/phone** par courrier/téléphone; **to go by bus/car/plane/train** aller en autobus/voiture/avion/train; **send it by plane/ship** envoyez-le par avion/bateau; **it's quicker by train** ça va plus vite en train; **I know her by name/sight** je la connais de nom/vue; **he died by his own hand** il est mort de sa propre main; **you must wash it by hand** il faut le laver à la main; **was it made by hand/machine?** a-t-il été fait à la main/machine?; **by candlelight** à la lumière d'une bougie; **by moonlight** au clair de lune ☐ **I can do it by myself** je peux le faire (tout) seul; **I'm all by myself tonight** je suis tout seul ce soir. -**2.** [indicating agent or cause] par; **it was built by the Romans** il fut construit par les Romains; **the house was surrounded by the police** la police a cerné la maison; **I was shocked by his reaction** sa réaction m'a choqué; **she had two daughters by him** elle a eu deux filles de lui. -**3.** [as a result of] par; **by chance/mistake** par hasard/erreur ‖ [with present participle] en; **by working overtime he managed to pay off his debts** en faisant des heures supplémentaires il a réussi à rembourser ses dettes; **he learned to cook by watching his mother** il a appris à faire la cuisine en regardant sa mère. -**4.** [indicating authorship] de; **a book by Toni Morrison** un livre de Toni Morrison; **a quartet by Schubert** un quatuor de Schubert. -**5.** [indicating part of person, thing held] par; **carry it by the handle** prends-le par la poignée; **she took her by the hand** elle l'a prise par la main; **he seized him by the collar** il l'a saisi par le col.

C. -**1.** [not later than, before]: **she'll be here by tonight/five o'clock** elle sera ici avant ce soir/pour cinq heures; **it must be done by tomorrow** ça doit être fait pour demain; **I'll have finished by Friday** j'aurai fini pour vendredi; **by the 21st century illiteracy should be stamped out** d'ici le XXIe siècle l'analphabétisme devrait avoir disparu; **by 1960 most Americans had television sets** en 1960 la plupart des Américains avaient déjà un poste de télévision; **by the time you read this letter I'll be in California** lorsque tu liras cette lettre, je serai en Californie; **by the time the police came the thieves had left** le temps que la police arrive OR lorsque la police arriva, les voleurs étaient déjà partis; **he should be in India by now** il devrait être en Inde maintenant; **she had already married by then** à ce moment-là elle était déjà mariée. -**2.** [during] : **he works by night and sleeps by day** il travaille la nuit et dort le jour.

D. -**1.** [according to] d'après; **they're rich, even by American standards** ils sont riches même par rapport aux normes américaines; **it's 6:15 by my watch** il est 6 h 15 à OR d'après ma montre; **you can tell he's lying by the expression on his face** on voit qu'il ment à l'expression de son visage. -**2.** [in accordance with] selon, d'après; **by law** selon OR d'après la loi; **by rights you should have it** en principe, c'est vous qui devriez l'avoir; **to play by the rules** faire les choses dans les règles. -**3.** [with regard to] de; **she's Canadian by birth** elle est canadienne de naissance; **he's an actor by trade** OR **profession** il est acteur de profession; **it's all right by me** *inf* moi, je suis d'accord OR je n'ai rien contre.

E. -**1.** [indicating degree, extent] de; **she won by five points** elle a gagné de cinq points; **I missed the train by less than a minute** j'ai manqué le train de moins d'une minute; **she's older than her husband by five years** elle est plus âgée que son mari de cinq ans; **increase your income by 50%** OR **by half** augmentez vos revenus de 50 %; **his second book is better by far** son deuxième livre est nettement meilleur. -**2.** [in calculations, measurements] : **multiply/divide 12 by 6** multipliez/divisez 12 par 6; **the room is 6 metres by 3 (metres)** la pièce fait 6 mètres sur 3 (mètres). -**3.** [indicating specific amount, duration] : **to be paid by the hour/week/month** être payé à l'heure/à la semaine/au mois; **they only sell by the kilo** ils ne vendent qu'au kilo; **it sold by the thousand** ça s'est vendu par milliers; **he rents his room by the week** il loue sa chambre à la semaine. -**4.** [indicating rate or speed] : **little by little** peu à peu; **year by year** d'année en année; **two by two** deux par deux. -**5.** [used with points of the compass] quart; **north by northwest** nord quart nord-ouest.

◆ **by and by** *adv phr lit* bientôt.

◆ **by the by** ◇ *adv phr* à propos.

◇ *adj phr*: **that's by the by** ça n'a pas d'importance.

bye [baɪ] ◇ *n* CRICKET balle *f* passée.

◇ *interj* *inf* au revoir, salut.

bye-bye *inf interj* au revoir, salut; **say ~** [to child] dis au revoir.

bye-byes *inf n baby talk* dodo *m*; **go to ~ now** va faire dodo maintenant.

byelaw ['baɪlɔː] = **bylaw**.

by-election *n* élection *f* (législative) partielle *(en Grande-Bretagne)*.

Byelorussia [bɪˌeləʊ'rʌʃə] *pr n* Biélorussie *f*; **in ~** en Biélorussie.

Byelorussian [bɪˌeləʊ'rʌʃn] ◇ *n* Biélorusse *mf*.

◇ *adj* biélorusse.

bygone ['baɪgɒn] ◇ *adj lit* passé, révolu; **he displayed the gallantry of a ~ age** il faisait preuve d'une galanterie qui n'a plus cours aujourd'hui; **in ~ days** autrefois, jadis.

◇ *n* -**1.** [object] vieillerie *f*. -**2.** *phr*: **let ~s be ~s** oublions le passé.

bylaw ['baɪlɔː] *n* -**1.** *Br* ADMIN arrêté *m* municipal. -**2.** *Am* [of club, company] statut *m*.

by-line *n* signature *f (en tête d'un article)*.

BYO (*abbr of* bring your own) *n restaurant où chacun apporte sa bouteille*.

BYOB (*abbr of* bring your own bottle) *«apportez une bouteille», inscription que l'on trouve sur un carton d'invitation à une soirée*.

bypass ['baɪpɑːs] ◇ *n* -**1.** [road] rocade *f*; **the Oxford ~** la route qui contourne Oxford. -**2.** TECH [pipe] conduit *m* de dérivation, by-pass *m*. -**3.** ELEC dérivation *f*. -**4.** MED pontage *m*, by-pass *m*; **~ operation**, **~ surgery** pontage, by-pass; **he's had a heart ~** il a subi un pontage coronarien.

◇ *vt* [avoid - town] contourner, éviter; [- problem, regulation] contourner, éluder; [- superior] court-circuiter; **I ~ed the personnel officer and spoke directly to the boss** je suis allé parler directement au directeur sans passer par le chef du personnel.

byplay ['baɪpleɪ] *n* jeu *m* de scène secondaire.

by-product *n* sous-produit *m*, (produit *m*) dérivé *m*; *fig* conséquence *f* indirecte, effet *m* secondaire.

byre ['baɪə[r]] *n Br* étable *f* (à vaches).

byroad ['baɪrəʊd] = **byway**.

Byronic [baɪ'rɒnɪk] *adj* byronien.

bystander ['baɪˌstændə[r]] *n* spectateur *m*, -trice *f*.

byte [baɪt] *n* octet *m*.

byway ['baɪweɪ] *n* -**1.** [road] chemin *m* détourné OR écarté. -**2.** *fig*: **the book explores the ~s of Buddhist teaching** le livre explore les aspects peu connus OR les à-côtés de l'enseignement bouddhiste.

byword ['baɪwɜːd] *n* symbole *m*, illustration *f*; **the company has become a ~ for inefficiency** le nom de cette entreprise est devenu synonyme d'inefficacité.

by-your-leave *n lit* OR *hum* permission *f*; **without so much as a ~** sans même demander la permission.

Byzantine [*Br* bɪ'zæntaɪn, *Am* 'bɪzntiːn] ◇ *n* Byzantin *m*, -e *f*.

◇ *adj* byzantin, de Byzance.

Byzantium [bɪ'zæntɪəm] *pr n* Byzance.

c (*pl* c's OR cs), **C** (*pl* C's OR Cs) [siː] *n* [letter] c *m*, C *m*.

c -**1.** (*written abbr of* cent(s)) ct. -**2.** (*written abbr of* century) s. -**3.** (*written abbr of* circa) vers.

C ◇ *n* -**1.** MUS do *m*, ut *m*. -**2.** SCH & UNIV assez bien; I got a C in geography j'ai eu assez bien en géographie. -**3.** *inf* (*abbr of* cancer): the big C le cancer. -**4.** [Roman numeral] C *m*.
◇ (*written abbr of* Celsius, Centigrade) C.

ca. (*written abbr of* circa) vers.

c/a -**1.** *written abbr of* capital account. -**2.** *written abbr of* credit account. -**3.** *written abbr of* current account.

CA ◇ *n abbr of* Consumers' Association.
◇ -**1.** *written abbr of* chartered accountant. -**2.** *written abbr of* Central America. -**3.** *written abbr of* California.

CAA *pr n* -**1.** (*abbr of* Civil Aviation Authority) *organisme britannique de réglementation de l'aviation civile*. -**2.** *Am abbr of* Civil Aeronautics Authority.

cab [kæb] *n* -**1.** [taxi] taxi *m*; let's go by ~ allons-y en taxi; he's a ~ driver il est chauffeur de taxi. -**2.** [of lorry, train] cabine *f*. -**3.** [horse-drawn] fiacre *m*.

CAB *pr n* -**1.** *Br abbr of* Citizens' Advice Bureau. -**2.** (*abbr of* Civil Aeronautics Board) *organisme américain de réglementation de l'aviation civile*.

cabal [kəˈbæl] *n* cabale *f*.

cabala [kəˈbɑːlə] *n* cabale *f*.

cabalistic [ˌkæbəˈlɪstɪk] *adj* cabalistique.

cabana [kəˈbænə] *n Am* cabine *f (de plage)*.

cabaret [ˈkæbəreɪ] *n* [nightclub] cabaret *m*; [show] spectacle *m*; 'Cabaret' *Fosse* 'Cabaret'.

cabbage [ˈkæbɪdʒ] *n* chou *m*; I'd rather die than be a ~ for the rest of my life plutôt mourir que vivre comme un légume jusqu'à la fin de mes jours.

cabbage rose *n* rose *f* centfeuilles.

cabbage tree *n* palmiste *m*.

cabbage white *n* piéride *f* du chou.

cabbala *etc* [kəˈbɑːlə] = **cabala**.

cabby *inf*, **cabbie** *inf* [ˈkæbɪ] *n* [taxi-driver] chauffeur *m* de taxi; [coachman] cocher *m* (de fiacre).

caber [ˈkeɪbəʳ, *Scot* ˈkeɪbər] *n* SPORT tronc *m*; tossing the ~ le lancer de troncs.

cabin [ˈkæbɪn] *n* -**1.** [hut] cabane *f*, hutte *f*; log ~ cabane en rondins. -**2.** NAUT cabine *f*. -**3.** AERON: the First Class ~ le compartiment de première classe. -**4.** *Br* [signal box] cabine *f* d'aiguillage. -**5.** *Br* [of lorry, train] cabine *f*.

cabin boy *n* mousse *m*.

cabin class *n* deuxième classe *f*.

cabin crew *n* équipage *m*.

cabin cruiser *n* cruiser *m*.

cabinet [ˈkæbɪnɪt] *n* -**1.** [furniture] meuble *m* (de rangement); [for bottles] bar *m*; [radio, television] coffret *m*; [for precious objects] cabinet *m*; [with glass doors] vitrine *f*; medicine ~ (armoire *f* à) pharmacie *f*; filing ~ classeur *m*. -**2.** POL cabinet *m*; he was in Wilson's ~ il faisait partie du cabinet OR gouvernement Wilson; they took the decision in ~ ils ont pris la décision en Conseil des ministres; ~ reshuffle remaniement *m* ministériel.

cabinet-maker *n* ébéniste *m*.

cabinet-making *n* ébénisterie *f*.

cabinet minister *n* ministre *m* siégeant au cabinet; he was a ~ under Heath OR in the Heath government il était ministre sous (le gouvernement) Heath.

cabinetwork [ˈkæbɪnɪtwɜːk] *n* ébénisterie *f*.

cabin trunk *n* malle-cabine *f*.

cable [ˈkeɪbl] ◇ *n* -**1.** [rope, wire] câble *m*; electric ~ câble électrique. -**2.** [telegram] télégramme *m*; we'll send you a ~ nous t'enverrons un télégramme. -**3.** NAUT [measure] encablure *f*. -**4.** point *m* de torsade; ~ needle aiguille *f* à torsades.
◇ *vt* -**1.** [lay cables in] câbler. -**2.** [telegraph] télégraphier à; I ~d them to say I needed more money je leur ai télégraphié que j'avais encore besoin d'argent.

cable car *n* téléphérique *m*.

cablegram [ˈkeɪblgræm] *n* câblogramme *m*.

cable railway *n* funiculaire *m*.

cable release *n* déclencheur *m* souple.

cable-stayed bridge [-steɪd-] *n* pont *m* haubanné.

cable stitch *n* point *m* de torsade.
◆ **cable-stitch** *comp* [sweater] au point de torsade.

cable television, **cable TV** *n* télévision *f* par câble, câble *m*.

cableway [ˈkeɪblweɪ] *n* téléphérique *m*.

cabling [ˈkeɪblɪŋ] *n* câblage *m*.

cabman [ˈkæbmən] (*pl* **cabmen** [-mən]) *n Br* chauffeur *m* de taxi.

caboodle *inf* [kəˈbuːdl] *n*: the whole (kit and) ~ tout le bataclan OR bazar.

caboose [kəˈbuːs] *n* -**1.** *Am* RAIL fourgon *m* de queue. -**2.** NAUT coquerie *f*. -**3.** ▽ *Am* [buttocks] fesses *fpl*.

cab rank *n* station *f* de taxis.

cabriolet [ˈkæbrɪəʊleɪ] *n* cabriolet *m*.

cabstand [ˈkæbstænd] = **cab rank**.

cacao [kəˈkɑːəʊ] (*pl* cacaos) *n* [bean] cacao *m*; [tree] cacaoyer *m*, cacaotier *m*.

cache [kæʃ] ◇ *n* -**1.** [hidden supply] cache *f*; a ~ of weapons, an arms ~ une cache d'armes; ~ (memory) COMPUT antémémoire *f*, mémoire-cache *f*. -**2.** [hiding place] cachette *f*.
◇ *vt* mettre dans une cachette.

cachet [ˈkæʃeɪ] *n literal & fig* cachet *m*.

cachou [ˈkæʃuː] *n* pastille *f* rafraîchissante.

cack-handed *inf* [kæk-] *adj Br* maladroit, gauche.

cackle [ˈkækl] ◇ *vi* -**1.** [hen] caqueter. -**2.** [person - chatter] caqueter, jacasser; [- laugh] glousser.
◇ *vt*: "you're trapped", ~d the old witch «je te tiens!», gloussa la vieille sorcière.
◇ *n* -**1.** [of hen] caquet *m*. -**2.** [of person - chatter] caquetage *m*, jacasserie *f*; [- laugh] gloussement *m*; she gave a loud ~ elle gloussa bruyamment; cut the ~! *inf* assez bavardé!

cacophonous [kæˈkɒfənəs] *adj* cacophonique.

cacophony [kæˈkɒfənɪ] (*pl* cacophonies) *n* cacophonie *f*.

cactus [ˈkæktəs] (*pl* cactuses OR cacti [-taɪ]) *n* cactus *m*.

cacuminal [kæˈkjuːmɪnl] ◇ *adj* cacuminal.
◇ *n* cacuminale *f*.

cad [kæd] *n dated* goujat *m*; you ~! vous êtes ignoble OR indigne!

CAD (*abbr of* computer-aided design) *n* CAO *f*.

cadastral [kəˈdæstrəl] *adj* cadastral; ~ register (registre *m* du) cadastre *m*.

cadaver [kəˈdɑːvəʳ] *n* MED cadavre *m*.

cadaverous [kəˈdævərəs] *adj fml* OR *lit* cadavéreux, cadavérique.

caddie [ˈkædɪ] ◇ *n* -**1.** SPORT caddie *m*. -**2.** = **caddy**.
◇ *vi*: to ~ for sb être le caddie de qqn.

caddie car, **caddie cart** *n* poussette *f (pour cannes de golf)*.

caddis fly [ˈkædɪs-] *n* trichoptère *m*.

caddy [ˈkædɪ] *n* -**1.** *Br* [container - for tea] boîte *f*. -**2.** *Am* [cart] chariot *m*, Caddie® *m*.

cadence [ˈkeɪdəns] *n* cadence *f*.

cadenza [kəˈdenzə] *n* cadence *f*.

cadet [kəˈdet] ◇ *n* -**1.** MIL élève *m* officier; [police] élève *m* policier; *Br* SCH *élève qui reçoit une formation militaire*. -**2.** [younger brother, son] cadet *m*.
◇ *adj* cadet.

cadet corps *n* [for military training] peloton *m* d'instruction militaire; [for police training] corps *m* d'élèves policiers.

cadge *inf* [kædʒ] ◇ *vt* [food, money] se procurer *(en quémandant)*; he ~d a meal from OR off his aunt il s'est invité à manger chez sa tante; she ~d £10 off me elle m'a tapé de 10 livres; they ~d a lift home à force de quémander ils se sont fait ramener en voiture.
◇ *vi*: she's always cadging off her friends elle est toujours en train de taper ses amis.
◇ *n Br* -**1.** = **cadger**. -**2.** *phr*: to be on the ~ chercher à se faire payer quelque chose.

cadger *inf* [ˈkædʒəʳ] *n* pique-assiette *mf inv*, parasite *m*.

Cadiz [kəˈdɪz] *pr n* Cadix.

cadmium [ˈkædmɪəm] *n* cadmium *m*.

cadre ['kɑːdəʳ] *n* cadre *m*.
caecum *Br*, **cecum** *Am* ['siːkəm] (*Br pl* caeca [-kə], *Am pl* ceca [-kə]) *n* caecum *m*.
Caesar ['siːzəʳ] *pr n* César; Julius ~ Jules César.
Caesarean *Br*, **Cesarean** *Am* [sɪ'zeərɪən]
◇ *adj* césarien; ~ birth MED césarienne *f*.
◇ *n* = **Caesarean section**.
Caeserean section *n* césarienne *f*; to be born OR delivered by ~ naître par césarienne.
caesium *Br*, **cesium** *Am* ['siːzɪəm] *n* cæsium *m*, césium *m*.
caesura [sɪ'zjʊərə] (*pl* caesuras OR caesurae [-riː]) *n* césure *f*.
CAF (*written abbr of* cost and freight) C et F.
cafe, café ['kæfeɪ] *n* [in the UK] snack *m*; [in rest of Europe] café *m*.

CAFÉ:
En Grande-Bretagne, le mot «café» désigne une sorte de snack où l'on peut prendre un repas léger et boire du thé ou du café.

cafeteria [,kæfɪ'tɪərɪə] *n* [self-service restaurant] restaurant *m* self-service, self *m*; *Am* [canteen] cantine *f*.
caff▽ [kæf] *n* snack *m*.
caffeine ['kæfiːn] *n* caféine *f*.
caffeine-free *adj* décaféiné.
caftan ['kæftæn] *n* caftan *m*.
cage [keɪdʒ] ◇ *n* -**1.** [with bars] cage *f*. -**2.** [lift] cabine *f*; MIN cage *f* (d'extraction). -**3.** SPORT [in basketball] panier *m*; [in ice hockey] cage *f*.
◇ *vt* mettre en cage, encager.
cage bird *n* oiseau *m* d'agrément OR d'appartement.
caged [keɪdʒd] *adj* en cage; he was like a ~ animal il était comme un animal en cage.
cagey *inf* ['keɪdʒɪ] (*comp* cagier, *superl* cagiest) *adj* [cautious] mesuré, circonspect; [reticent] réticent; he was being ~ about his salary il s'est montré évasif lorsqu'il s'est agi de son salaire.
cagoule [kə'guːl] *n* veste *f* imperméable *(à capuche)*.
cagy ['keɪdʒɪ] (*compar* cagier, *superl* cagiest) = **cagey**.
cahoots *inf* [kə'huːts] *npl phr*: they discovered that the bank manager was in ~ with the gang on a découvert que le directeur de la banque était de mèche avec les voleurs.
CAI (*abbr of* computer-aided instruction) *n* EAO *m*.
Caiaphas ['kaɪəfæs] *pr n* Caïphe.
caiman ['keɪmən] = **cayman**.
Cain [keɪn] *pr n* Caïn; the mark of ~ la marque de Caïn; to raise ~ *inf* faire du foin.
cairn [keən] *n* cairn *m*.
cairngorm ['keəngɔːm] *n* [mineral] quartz *m* fumé.
◆ **Cairngorm** *pr n* GEOG: the Cairngorm Mountains, the Cairngorms les monts *mpl* Cairngorm.
cairn terrier *n* cairn *m*.
Cairo ['kaɪərəʊ] *pr n* Le Caire.
caisson ['keɪsɒn] *n* caisson *m*.
cajole [kə'dʒəʊl] *vt* enjôler; he ~d her into accepting il l'a amenée à accepter à force de cajoleries; they eventually ~d the information out of him à force de cajoleries, ils ont réussi à lui soutirer le renseignement.
cajolery [kə'dʒəʊlərɪ] *n (U)* cajoleries *fpl*.
Cajun ['keɪdʒən] ◇ *n* Cajun *mf inv*.
◇ *adj* cajun *(inv)*.
cake [keɪk] ◇ *n* -**1.** CULIN [sweet] gâteau *m*; [pastry] pâtisserie *f*; [savoury] croquette *f*; a chocolate/cherry ~ un gâteau au chocolat/aux cerises; to make OR to bake a ~ faire un gâteau ❑ birthday/Christmas ~ gâteau d'anniversaire/de Noël; it's a piece of ~ *inf* c'est du gâteau OR de la tarte; you can't have your ~ and eat it *prov* on ne peut pas avoir le beurre et l'argent du beurre *prov*. -**2.** [block - of soap, wax] pain *m*; [- of chocolate] plaquette *f*.
◇ *comp* [dish, pan, tin] à gâteau; ~ mix préparation *f* (instantanée) pour gâteau; ~ shop pâtisserie *f*; ~ stand assiette *f* montée à gâteaux; ~ stall [at fair] stand *m* à gâteaux.
◇ *vt*: his boots were ~d with mud ses bottes étaient pleines de boue; her hair was ~d with blood elle avait du sang séché dans les cheveux.
◇ *vi* durcir; the mud had ~d on his boots la boue avait séché sur ses bottes.
cakewalk ['keɪkwɔːk] *n* -**1.** [dance] cakewalk *m*. -**2.** *inf fig* [easy task]: the exam was a ~ l'examen, c'était du gâteau.
cal. (*written abbr of* calorie) cal.
CAL (*abbr of* computer-assisted learning) *n* EAO *m*.
calabash ['kæləbæʃ] *n* [fruit] calebasse *f*; [tree] calebassier *m*.
calaboose *inf* ['kæləbuːs] *n Am* taule *f*, tôle *f*.
Calabria [kə'læbrɪə] *pr n* Calabre *f*; in ~ en Calabre.
Calabrian [kə'læbrɪən] ◇ *n* Calabrais *m*, -e *f*.
◇ *adj* calabrais.
calamine ['kæləmaɪn] *n* calamine *f*; ~ lotion lotion calmante à la calamine.
calamitous [kə'læmɪtəs] *adj* calamiteux.
calamity [kə'læmətɪ] (*pl* **calamities**) *n* calamité *f*.
Calamity Jane [-dʒeɪn] *pr n* Calamity Jane.
calandria [kə'lændrɪə] *n* calandre *f*.
calcification [,kælsɪfɪ'keɪʃn] *n* calcification *f*.
calcify ['kælsɪfaɪ] (*pt* & *pp* calcified) ◇ *vt* calcifier.
◇ *vi* se calcifier.
calcination [,kælsɪ'neɪʃn] *n* calcination *f*.
calcine ['kælsaɪn] ◇ *vt* calciner.
◇ *vi* se calciner.
calcite ['kælsaɪt] *n* calcite *f*.
calcium ['kælsɪəm] *n* calcium *m*; ~ carbonate carbonate *m* de calcium.
calculate ['kælkjʊleɪt] ◇ *vt* -**1.** MATH calculer; [estimate, evaluate] calculer, évaluer; he ~d that his chances of success were reasonably good il calcula OR estima qu'il avait d'assez bonnes chances de réussir. -**2.** [design, intend]: her remark was ~d to offend the guests sa réflexion était destinée à offenser les invités; the price of the house was scarcely ~d to attract potential buyers le prix de la maison n'a guère été calculé pour attirer d'éventuels acheteurs.
◇ *vi* -**1.** MATH calculer, faire des calculs. -**2.** [count, depend]: I ~d on George lending me the money je comptais sur George pour me prêter l'argent.
calculated ['kælkjʊleɪtɪd] *adj* -**1.** [considered] calculé, mesuré; a ~ risk un risque calculé. -**2.** [deliberate, intentional] délibéré, voulu; a ~ insult une insulte délibérée.
calculating ['kælkjʊleɪtɪŋ] *adj* -**1.** *pej* [scheming] calculateur. -**2.** [cautious] prudent, mesuré. -**3.** [adding]: ~ machine machine *f* à calculer.
calculation [,kælkjʊ'leɪʃn] *n* -**1.** MATH & *fig* calcul *m*; by OR according to my ~s selon OR d'après mes calculs. -**2.** *(U) pej* [scheming]: his offer of help was free of all ~ il a offert son aide sans la moindre arrière-pensée.
calculator ['kælkjʊleɪtəʳ] *n* -**1.** [machine] calculateur *m*; [small] calculatrice *f*. -**2.** MATH [table] table *f*.
calculus ['kælkjʊləs] *n* calcul *m*.
Calcutta [kæl'kʌtə] *pr n* Calcutta.
caldron ['kɔːldrən] = **cauldron**.
Caledonia [,kælɪ'dəʊnjə] *pr n* HIST Calédonie *f*; in ~ en Calédonie.
Caledonian [,kælɪ'dəʊnjən] ◇ *n* Calédonien *m*, -enne *f*.
◇ *adj* calédonien; the ~ Canal le canal calédonien.
calendar ['kælɪndəʳ] ◇ *n* -**1.** [of dates] calendrier *m*. -**2.** [register] annuaire *m*; the university ~ l'annuaire de l'université. -**3.** *Am* [planner] agenda *m*.
◇ *comp* [day, month, year] civil, calendaire.
◇ *vt* [event] inscrire sur le calendrier; *Am* [put in planner] noter *(dans son agenda)*.
calender ['kælɪndəʳ] *n* calandre *f*, laminoir *m*.
calends ['kælɪndz] *npl* calendes *fpl*.
calf [kɑːf] (*pl* calves) *n* -**1.** [young cow, bull] veau *m*; the cow is in ~ la vache est pleine. -**2.** [skin] veau *m*, vachette *f*; a book bound in ~ un livre relié en veau. -**3.** [buffalo] bufflon *m*, buffletin *m*; [elephant] éléphanteau *m*; [giraffe] girafeau *m*, girafon *m*; [whale] baleineau *m*. -**4.** ANAT mollet *m*.
calf love *n* premier amour *m*.
calfskin ['kɑːfskɪn] *n* veau *m*, vachette *f*; ~ gloves gants *mpl* en veau OR vachette.
caliber *Am* = **calibre**.
calibrate ['kælɪbreɪt] *vt* étalonner, calibrer.
calibration [,kælɪ'breɪʃn] *n* étalonnage *m*, calibrage *m*.
calibre *Br*, **caliber** *Am* ['kælɪbəʳ] *n* -**1.** [of gun, tube] calibre *m*; a high ~ revolver un revolver de gros calibre. -**2.** [quality] qualité *f*; their work is of the highest ~ ils font un travail de grande qualité; the two applicants are not of the same ~ les deux candidats ne sont pas du même calibre OR n'ont pas la même envergure.
calico ['kælɪkəʊ] (*pl* calicoes OR calicos)
◇ *n* TEX *Br* calicot *m* blanc; *Am* calicot *m* imprimé, indienne *f*.
◇ *comp* de calicot.
California [,kælɪ'fɔːnjə] *pr n* Californie *f*; in ~ en Californie; Lower ~ la Basse-Californie.
Californian [,kælɪ'fɔːnjən] ◇ *n* Californien *m*, -enne *f*.
◇ *adj* californien.
californium [,kælɪ'fɔːnjəm] *n* californium *m*.
Caligula [kə'lɪgjʊlə] *pr n* Caligula.
caliper *Am* = **calliper**.
caliph, Caliph ['keɪlɪf] *n* calife *m*.
calisthenics [,kælɪs'θenɪks] = **callisthenics**.
calix ['keɪlɪks] (*pl* calices [-lɪsiːz]) *n* calice *m* *(récipient)*.
calk [kɔːk] ◇ *vt* -**1.** [shoe, horseshoe] munir de crampons. -**2.** = **caulk**.
◇ *n* [on shoe, horseshoe] crampon *m*.
call [kɔːl] ◇ *vi* -**1.** [with one's voice] appeler; if you need me, just ~ si tu as besoin de moi, tu n'as qu'à (m') appeler; she ~ed to her son in the crowd elle appela son fils dans la foule; duty ~s *hum* le devoir m'appelle; to ~ for help appeler à l'aide OR au secours. -**2.** [on the telephone] appeler; where are you ~ing from? d'où appelles-tu?; it's Mary ~ing c'est Mary à l'appareil; who's ~ing? qui est à l'appareil?, c'est de la part de qui? -**3.** [animal, bird] pousser un cri. -**4.** *Br* [visit] passer; did the postman ~? est-ce que le facteur est passé?; I'll ~ at the butcher's on the way home je passerai chez le boucher en revenant à la maison; do ~ again n'hésitez pas à revenir; I was out when they ~ed je n'étais pas là quand ils sont passés. -**5.** *Br* [stop] s'arrêter; does the seven fifteen ~ at Wolverhampton? est-ce que le train de 7 h 15 s'arrête à Wolverhampton?; the ship ~s at Cherbourg le navire fait escale à Cherbourg. -**6.** BRIDGE annoncer.
◇ *vt* -**1.** [with one's voice] appeler; can you ~ the children to the table? pouvez-vous appeler les enfants pour qu'ils viennent à table?; he was ~ed to the phone on l'a demandé au téléphone; to ~ the roll faire l'appel. -**2.** [telephone] appeler; ~ me tonight appelle-moi ce soir; don't ~ me at work ne m'appelle pas au bureau; we ~ed his house nous avons appelé chez lui ❑ don't ~ us, we'll ~ you on vous écrira. -**3.** [wake up] réveiller; can you ~ me at nine? pouvez-vous me réveiller à 9 h? -**4.** [name or describe as] appeler; he has a cat ~ed Felix *Br* il a un chat qui s'appelle Félix; she was ~ed "Ratty" as a child on l'appelait «Ratty» quand elle était enfant; he was ~ed Charles after his grandfather *Br* on l'a appelé Charles comme son grand-père; what's this ~ed? comment est-ce qu'on appelle ça?, comment est-ce que ça s'appelle?; she ~ed him a crook elle l'a traité d'escroc; are you ~ing me a thief? me traitez-vous de voleur?; they ~ed him all sorts of

names OR every name in the book *inf* ils l'ont traité de tous les noms. -**5.** [consider]: **Denver is where I ~ home** c'est à Denver que je me sens chez moi; **he had no home to ~ his own** il n'avait pas de chez lui; **she had no time to ~ her own** elle n'avait pas de temps à elle; **(and you) ~ yourself a Christian!** et tu te dis chrétien!; **I don't ~ that clean** ce n'est pas ce que j'appelle propre; **let's ~ it £10, shall we?** *Br* disons OR mettons dix livres, d'accord?; **let's ~ it a day** si on s'arrêtait là pour aujourd'hui? -**6.** [announce]: **to ~ an election** annoncer des élections; **to ~ a meeting** convoquer une assemblée; **to ~ a strike** appeler à la grève; **to ~ a truce** conclure une trêve. -**7.** [send for, summon] appeler, convoquer *fml*; **she was suddenly ~ed home** elle a été rappelée soudainement chez elle; **he was ~ed to his regiment** il a été rappelé à son régiment; **she was ~ed as a witness** elle a été citée comme témoin; **he ~ed me over** il m'a appelé; **to ~ sthg into being** former qqch. -**8.** FIN: **to ~ a loan** exiger le remboursement d'un prêt. -**9.** SPORT [declare, judge] juger; **he ~ed it out** il a jugé qu'elle était dehors. -**10.** BRIDGE annoncer, demander; **to ~ sb's bluff** *fig* défier qqn. -**11. to ~ heads/tails** choisir face/pile. -**12.** *phr*: **to ~ sthg to mind** rappeler qqch; **the scenery ~s to mind certain parts of Brittany** le paysage rappelle un peu certaines parties de la Bretagne; **to ~ sthg into play** faire jouer qqch; **market forces will soon be ~ed into play** on fera bientôt jouer les lois du marché; **to ~ sthg into question** remettre qqch en question; **she ~ed into question his competence as a doctor** elle a mis ses compétences de médecin en doute; **to ~ the tune** *inf Br* OR **shots** *inf* faire la loi.

◇ *n* -**1.** [cry, shout] appel *m*; [of animal, bird] cri *m*; [of bugle, drum] appel *m*; *fig*: **the ~ of the sea** l'appel du large; **a ~ for help** un appel à l'aide OR au secours. -**2.** [on the telephone] appel *m*; **can I make a ~?** puis-je téléphoner?; **to put a ~ through** passer une communication; **I've got a few ~s to make** je dois passer quelques coups de téléphone; **there's a ~ for you** on vous demande au téléphone; **I'll give you a ~ tomorrow** je t'appelle demain; **how much does a ~ to Italy cost?** combien est-ce que ça coûte d'appeler en Italie OR l'Italie? -**3.** [visit] visite *f*; **to make** OR **pay a ~ on sb** *Br* rendre visite à qqn; **she had several ~s to make in the neighbourhood** *Br* elle devait rendre quelques visites dans le voisinage; **the doctor doesn't make house ~s** le médecin ne fait pas de visites à domicile. -**4.** [stop]: **port of ~** escale *f*; **the ship made a ~ at Genoa** *Br* le navire a fait escale à Gênes. -**5.** [demand, need]: **there have been renewed ~s for a return to capital punishment** il y a des gens qui demandent à nouveau le rétablissement de la peine de mort; **there is little ~ for unskilled labour** il n'y a qu'une faible demande de travailleurs non spécialisés; **there's no ~ to shout** il n'y a aucune raison de crier; **you have first ~ on my time** je m'occuperai de vous en premier lieu. -**6.** ST. EX échéance *f*. -**7.** SPORT [decision] jugement *m*. -**8.** BRIDGE annonce *f*. -**9.** [heads or tails]: **your ~** pile ou face?

◆ **on call** *adj phr* [doctor, nurse] de garde; [police, troops] en éveil; [car] disponible; FIN [loan] remboursable sur demande.

◆ **call aside** *vt sep* prendre à part.

◆ **call away** *vt sep*: **she was ~ed away from the office** on l'a appelée et elle a dû quitter le bureau; **she's often ~ed away on business** elle doit souvent partir en déplacement OR s'absenter pour affaires.

◆ **call back** ◇ *vt sep* -**1.** [on telephone] rappeler; **I'll ~ you back later** je te rappelle plus tard. -**2.** [ask to return] rappeler; **I was already at the door when she ~ed me back** j'étais déjà près de la porte lorsqu'elle m'a rappelé.
◇ *vi insep* -**1.** [on telephone] rappeler; **can you ~ back after five?** pourriez-vous rappeler après 5 h? -**2.** [visit again] revenir, repasser; **I'll ~ back tomorrow** je reviendrai OR repasserai demain.

◆ **call down** *vt sep* -**1.** *lit* [invoke]: **he ~ed down the wrath of God on the killers** il appela la colère de Dieu sur la tête des tueurs. -**2.** *inf Am* [reprimand] engueuler.

◆ **call for** *vt insep* -**1.** *Br* [collect]: **he ~ed for her at her parents' house** il est allé la chercher chez ses parents; **whose is this parcel? — someone's ~ing for it later** à qui est ce paquet? — quelqu'un passera le prendre plus tard. -**2.** [put forward as demand] appeler, demander; [subj: agreement, treaty] prévoir; **the opposition ~ed for an official statement** l'opposition a exigé OR demandé une déclaration officielle. -**3.** [require] exiger; **the situation ~ed for quick thinking** la situation demandait OR exigeait qu'on réfléchisse vite.

◆ **call forth** *vt sep fml* provoquer, susciter *lit*; **the article ~ed forth vigorous denials** l'article suscita OR occasionna des démentis énergiques.

◆ **call in** ◇ *vt sep* -**1.** [send for] faire venir; **an accountant was ~ed in to look at the books** on a fait venir un comptable pour examiner les livres de comptes; **the army was ~ed in to assist with the evacuation** on a fait appel à l'armée pour aider à l'évacuation. -**2.** [recall - defective goods] rappeler; [- banknotes] retirer de la circulation; [- library books] faire rentrer. -**3.** FIN [debt, loan] rappeler.
◇ *vi insep* -**1.** *Br* [pay a visit] passer; **she ~ed in at her sister's to say good-bye** elle est passée chez sa sœur pour dire au revoir. -**2.** [telephone] appeler.

◆ **call off** *vt sep* -**1.** [appointment, meeting, strike] annuler. -**2.** [dog, person] rappeler.

◆ **call on** *vt insep Br* -**1.** [request, summon] faire appel à; **she ~ed on the government to take action** elle a demandé que le gouvernement agisse. -**2.** [visit] rendre visite à; **I'll ~ on her this evening** je lui rendrai visite OR je passerai chez elle ce soir.

◆ **call out** ◇ *vt sep* -**1.** [cry out]: **"over here" he ~ed out** «par ici» appela-t-il. -**2.** [summon] appeler, faire appel à; **the army was ~ed out to help** on a fait appel à l'armée pour aider; **the union ~ed out its members for 24 hours** le syndicat appela ses adhérents à une grève de 24 heures.
◇ *vi insep* [shout] appeler; **she ~ed out to a policeman** elle appela un agent de police.

◆ **call out for** *vt insep* avoir grand besoin de.

◆ **call round** *vi insep Br*: **can I ~ round this evening?** puis-je passer ce soir?; **your mother ~ed round for the parcel** votre mère est passée prendre le paquet.

◆ **call up** ◇ *vt sep* -**1.** [telephone] appeler. -**2.** MIL appeler; [reservists] rappeler; **he was ~ed up to fight in Vietnam** il a été appelé pour partir au Viêt-nam. -**3.** [evoke] évoquer, faire venir à l'esprit. -**4.** [summon] appeler, convoquer; **she was ~ed up for jury service** elle a été appelée OR convoquée pour faire partie d'un jury. -**5.** COMPUT rappeler.
◇ *vi insep* appeler.

◆ **call upon** *vt insep fml* [request, summon] faire appel à; **she may be ~ed upon to give evidence** il est possible qu'elle soit citée comme témoin; **I ~ed upon him for assistance** j'ai fait appel à son aide.

call alarm *n* alarme *f (pour personne âgée ou handicapée)*.

call box *n* -**1.** *Br* cabine *f* téléphonique. -**2.** *Am* [on roadside] borne *f* d'appel d'urgence.

callboy ['kɔːlbɔɪ] *n* -**1.** THEAT avertisseur *m*. -**2.** *Am* [bellboy] chasseur *m*, groom *m*.

caller ['kɔːləʳ] *n* -**1.** [visitor] visiteur *m*, -euse *f*. -**2.** TELEC demandeur *m*, -euse *f*. -**3.** [in bingo] ≃ animateur *m*, -trice *f*.

call girl *n* call-girl *f*.

calligraphy [kə'lɪgrəfɪ] *n* calligraphie *f*.

call-in *n* émission *f* à ligne ouverte.

calling ['kɔːlɪŋ] *n* -**1.** [vocation] appel *m* intérieur, vocation *f*. -**2.** *fml* [profession] métier *m*, profession *f*.

calling card *n Am* carte *f* de visite.

calliper *Br*, **caliper** *Am* ['kælɪpəʳ] *n* -**1.** MATH: **a pair of ~ compasses** OR **~s** un compas. -**2.** MED: **~ (splint)** attelle-étrier *f*. -**3.** TECH [for brake] étrier *m*.

callisthenics [ˌkælɪs'θenɪks] *n (U)* gymnastique *f* rythmique.

call letters *npl Am* indicatif *m* d'appel *(d'une station de radio)*.

call loan *n* prêt *m* exigible.

call money *n* argent *m* à court terme.

callosity [kæ'lɒsətɪ] (*pl* **callosities**) *n* callosité *f*.

callous ['kæləs] *adj* -**1.** [unfeeling] dur, sans cœur; [behaviour, remark] dur, impitoyable. -**2.** [skin] calleux.

calloused ['kæləst] *adj* [feet, hands] calleux, corné.

callously ['kæləslɪ] *adv* durement.

callousness ['kæləsnɪs] *n* dureté *f*.

callow ['kæləʊ] *adj* [immature] sans expérience, sans maturité; **he's a ~ youth** c'est un jeune homme sans expérience OR maturité.

call sign *n* indicatif *m* d'appel *(d'une station de radio)*.

call-up *n Br* [conscription] convocation *f* (au service militaire), ordre *m* d'incorporation; **he received his ~ papers** il reçut son ordre d'incorporation.

callus ['kæləs] *n* [on feet, hands] cal *m*, durillon *m*.

calm [kɑːm] ◇ *adj* calme; **keep ~!** du calme!, restons calmes!; **she tried to keep ~** elle essaya de garder son calme OR sang-froid; **to be ~ and collected** être maître de soi, garder son sang-froid.
◇ *n* calme *m*; **there was a strange ~ after the battle** la bataille fut suivie d'une étrange accalmie; **the ~ of the botanical gardens** le calme du jardin botanique; **when ~ descends on the town** quand le calme revient sur la ville; **the ~ before the storm** le calme qui précède la tempête.
◇ *vt* calmer; [fears] apaiser, calmer; **she tried to ~ her nerves** elle essaya de se calmer.

◆ **calm down** ◇ *vi insep* se calmer; **~ down!** calmez-vous!, ne vous énervez pas!
◇ *vt sep* calmer.

calmative ['kælmətɪv] *n* calmant *m*.

calming ['kɑːmɪŋ] *adj* calmant; **her words had a ~ effect on him** ses paroles ont réussi à le calmer.

calmly ['kɑːmlɪ] *adv* calmement; **she received the news ~** elle a reçu la nouvelle calmement OR avec calme.

calmness ['kɑːmnɪs] *n* calme *m*; **she felt a sense of ~** elle éprouvait une sensation de calme.

Calor gas® ['kæləʳ-] *n Br* butane *m*, Butagaz® *m*.

caloric [kə'lɒrɪk] *adj* calorique.

calorie ['kælərɪ] *n* calorie *f*.

calorific [ˌkælə'rɪfɪk] *adj* calorifique; **~ value** valeur *f* calorifique.

calque [kælk] *n* calque *m*.

calumniate [kə'lʌmnɪeɪt] *vt fml* calomnier.

calumny ['kæləmnɪ] (*pl* **calumnies**) *n fml* calomnie *f*.

calvary ['kælvərɪ] *n* calvaire *m*.

◆ **Calvary** *pr n* RELIG le Calvaire.

calve [kɑːv] *vi* vêler.

calves [kɑːvz] *pl* → **calf**.

Calvin ['kælvɪn] *pr n*: **John ~** Jean Calvin.

Calvinism ['kælvɪnɪzm] *n* calvinisme *m*.

Calvinist ['kælvɪnɪst] ◇ *adj* calviniste.
◇ *n* calviniste *mf*.

Calvinistic [ˌkælvɪ'nɪstɪk] *adj* calviniste.

calypso [kə'lɪpsəʊ] (*pl* **calypsos**) *n* calypso *m*.

◆ **Calypso** *pr n* MYTH Calypso.

calyx ['keɪlɪks] (*pl* **calyxes** OR **calyces** [-siːz]) *n* calice *m* BOT.

cam [kæm] *n* came *f*.

CAM (*abbr of* **computer-aided manufacturing**) *n* FAO *f*.

camaraderie [ˌkæməˈrɑːdərɪ] *n* camaraderie *f*.

camber [ˈkæmbəʳ] ◇ *n* [in road] bombement *m*; [in beam, girder] cambre *f*, cambrure *f*; [in ship's deck] tonture *f*.
◇ *vi* [road] bomber, être bombé; [beam, girder] être cambré; [ship's deck] avoir une tonture.

Cambodia [kæmˈbəʊdjə] *pr n* Cambodge *m*; in ~ au Cambodge.

Cambodian [kæmˈbəʊdjən] ◇ *n* Cambodgien *m*, -enne *f*.
◇ *adj* cambodgien.

Cambrian [ˈkæmbrɪən] ◇ *adj* cambrien; the ~ Mountains les monts *mpl* Cambriens.
◇ *n*: the ~ le cambrien.

cambric [ˈkeɪmbrɪk] *n* batiste *f*.

Cambs *written abbr of* Cambridgeshire.

came [keɪm] *pt* → **come**.

camel [ˈkæml] ◇ *n* -**1.** ZOOL chameau *m*; [with one hump] dromadaire *m*; [female] chamelle *f*. -**2.** [colour] fauve *m inv*.
◇ *comp* -**1.** [train] de chameaux; ~ **driver** chamelier *m*. -**2.** [coat, jacket - of camel hair] en poil de chameau; [- coloured] fauve *(inv)*.

camelhair [ˈkæmlheəʳ] ◇ *n* poil *m* de chameau.
◇ *comp* [coat, jacket] en poil de chameau.

camellia [kəˈmiːljə] *n* camélia *m*.

cameo [ˈkæmɪəʊ] (*pl* cameos) ◇ *n* -**1.** [piece of jewellery] camée *m*. -**2.** [piece of writing] morceau *m* bref, court texte *m*; CIN, THEAT & TV [appearance] brève apparition *f*.
◇ *comp* -**1.** [jewellery]: a ~ **brooch** un camée monté en broche. -**2.** CIN, THEAT & TV: a ~ **performance** OR **role** un petit rôle *(joué par un acteur célèbre)*.

camera [ˈkæmərə] *n* -**1.** [device - for still photos] appareil *m* (photographique), appareil photo *m*; [- for film, video] caméra *f*; **to be on** ~ être à l'écran; **off** ~ hors champ. -**2.** JUR: **in** ~ à huis clos.

cameraman [ˈkæmərəmæn] (*pl* cameramen [-men]) *n* cadreur *m*, cameraman *m*.

camera obscura [-əbˈskjʊərə] *n* chambre *f* noire.

camera-shy *adj* qui n'aime pas être photographié.

camera tube *n* tube *m* analyseur.

camerawoman [ˈkæmərəˌwʊmən] (*pl* camerawomen [-ˌwɪmɪn]) *n* cadreuse *f*.

camerawork [ˈkæmərəwɜːk] *n* prise *f* de vue.

Cameroon [ˌkæməˈruːn] *pr n* Cameroun *m*; in ~ au Cameroun.

Cameroonian [ˌkæməˈruːnɪən] ◇ *n* Camerounais *m*, -e *f*.
◇ *adj* camerounais.

camiknickers [ˌkæmɪˈnɪkəz] *npl Br* combinaison-culotte *f*.

camisole [ˈkæmɪsəʊl] *n* caraco *m*.

camomile [ˈkæməmaɪl] *n* camomille *f*; ~ **tea** infusion *f* de camomille.

camouflage [ˈkæməflɑːʒ] ◇ *n* camouflage *m*.
◇ *vt* camoufler.

camp [kæmp] ◇ *n* -**1.** [place] camp *m*; [not permanent] campement *m*; **to make** OR **to pitch** OR **to set up** ~ établir un camp; **to break** ~ lever le camp; **summer** ~ colonie *f* OR camp *m* de vacances. -**2.** [group] camp *m*, parti *m*; **the conservative** ~ le parti OR camp conservateur, les conservateurs *mpl*; **to go over to the other** ~ changer de camp; **to be in the same** ~ être du même bord ❑ **to have a foot in both** ~**s** avoir un pied dans chaque camp. -**3.** *inf* [kitsch]: **(high)** ~ kitsch *m*.
◇ *vi* camper; **are you going to** ~? allez-vous camper OR faire du camping?
◇ *adj inf* -**1.** [effeminate] efféminé. -**2.** [affected] affecté, maniéré; [theatrical - person] cabotin; [- manners] théâtral. -**3.** [in dubious taste] kitsch *(inv)*.
◆ **camp out** *vi insep* camper, faire du camping; **we ~ed out at my parents** *fig* nous avons campé chez mes parents.
◆ **camp up** *inf vt sep phr*: **to ~ it up** [overdramatize] cabotiner; [effeminate man] en rajouter dans le genre efféminé.

campaign [kæmˈpeɪn] ◇ *n* MIL, POL & *fig* campagne *f*; **to conduct** OR **to lead a ~ against drugs** mener une campagne OR faire campagne contre la drogue.
◇ *vi* mener une campagne, faire campagne; **to ~ against/for sthg** mener une campagne contre/en faveur de qqch.

campaigner [kæmˈpeɪnəʳ] *n* POL & *fig* militant *m*, -e *f*; MIL vétéran *m*; **~s in favour of/against nuclear power** des militants partisans du nucléaire/antinucléaires.

Campania [kæmˈpeɪnɪə] *pr n* Campanie *f*; in ~ en Campanie.

campanile [ˌkæmpəˈniːlɪ] *n* campanile *m*.

campanologist [ˌkæmpəˈnɒlədʒɪst] *n* carillonneur *m*.

campanology [ˌkæmpəˈnɒlədʒɪ] *n* art *m* des carillons.

campanula [kəmˈpænjʊlə] *n* campanule *f*.

camp bed *n* lit *m* de camp.

Camp David *pr n* Camp David; **the ~ agreement** les accords *mpl* de Camp David.

camper [ˈkæmpəʳ] *n* -**1.** [person] campeur *m*, -euse *f*. -**2.** [vehicle] camping-car *m*.

campfire [ˈkæmpˌfaɪəʳ] *n* feu *m* de camp.

camp follower *n* -**1.** MIL [gen] *civil qui accompagne une armée pour rendre des services*; [prostitute] prostituée *f*, fille *f* à soldats. -**2.** *fig* [supporter] sympathisant *m*, -e *f*.

campground [ˈkæmpgraʊnd] *n Am* [private] camp *m*; [commercial] terrain *m* de camping, camping *m*; [clearing] emplacement *m* de camping, endroit *m* où camper.

camphor [ˈkæmfəʳ] *n* camphre *m*.

camphorated [ˈkæmfəreɪtɪd] *adj* camphré.

camping [ˈkæmpɪŋ] ◇ *n* camping *m*; **to go ~** camper, faire du camping.
◇ *comp* [equipment] de camping; ~ **gas** butane *m*; ~ **ground** OR **grounds** OR **site** [private] camp *m*; [commercial] terrain *m* de camping, camping *m*; [clearing] emplacement *m* de camping, endroit *m* où camper; ~ **stool** pliant *m*; ~ **stove** réchaud *m* de camping, Camping-gaz® *m inv*.

campion [ˈkæmpjən] *n* BOT silène *m*, lychnis *m*.

camp meeting *n esp Am* rassemblement *m* religieux *(qui a lieu sous des tentes)*.

campsite [ˈkæmpsaɪt] *n* [commercial] terrain *m* de camping, camping *m*; [clearing] emplacement *m* de camping, endroit *m* où camper.

campus [ˈkæmpəs] (*pl* **campuses**) *n* UNIV [grounds] campus *m*; [buildings] campus *m*, complexe *m* universitaire; **to live on ~** habiter sur le campus; **to live off ~** habiter en dehors du campus ❑ **on-/off-~ housing** logements *mpl* sur le/en dehors du campus; ~ **university** université *f* regroupée sur un campus.

camshaft [ˈkæmʃɑːft] *n* arbre *m* à cames.

can[1] [*weak form* kən, *strong form* kæn] (*pt* could [*weak form* kəd, *strong form* kʊd], *negative forms* cannot [ˈkænət], *frequently shortened to* can't [kɑːnt], could not [ˈkʊdnət], *frequently shortened to* couldn't [ˈkʊdnt]) *modal vb* -**1.** [be able to] pouvoir; ~ **you come to the party?** peux-tu venir à la fête?; **I'll come if I ~** je viendrai si je (le) peux; **I'll come as soon as I ~** je viendrai aussitôt que possible OR aussitôt que je pourrai; **we'll do everything we ~ to help** nous ferons tout ce que nous pourrons OR tout notre possible pour aider; **she has everything money ~ buy** elle a tout ce qu'on peut acheter; **she ~ no longer walk** elle ne peut plus marcher; **five years ago I could run a mile in four minutes but I can't anymore** il y a cinq ans, je courais un mile en quatre minutes mais je ne peux plus maintenant; ~ **you help me?** pouvez-vous m'aider?; ~ **you tell me when the train leaves?** pouvez-vous me dire à quelle heure part le train? -**2.** [with verbs of perception or understanding]: ~ **you feel it?** tu le sens?; **we ~ hear everything our neighbours say** nous entendons tout ce que disent nos voisins; **I can't understand you when you mumble** je ne te comprends pas OR je ne comprends pas ce que tu dis quand tu marmonnes; **I ~ see his point of view** je comprends son point de vue; **there ~ be no doubt about his guilt** sa culpabilité ne fait aucun doute. -**3.** [indicating ability or skill] savoir; ~ **you drive/sew?** savez-vous conduire/coudre?; **many people can't read or write** beaucoup de gens ne savent ni lire ni écrire; **she ~ speak three languages** elle parle trois langues. -**4.** [giving or asking for permission] pouvoir; **I've already said you can't go** je t'ai déjà dit que tu ne peux pas y aller; ~ **I borrow your sweater? – yes, you ~** puis-je emprunter ton pull? – (mais oui), bien sûr; ~ **I sit with you?** puis-je m'asseoir avec vous? -**5.** [used to interrupt, intervene]: ~ **I just say something here?** est-ce que je peux dire quelque chose? -**6.** [in offers of help] pouvoir; ~ **I be of any assistance?** puis-je vous aider?; **what ~ I do for you?** que puis-je (faire) pour vous? -**7.** [indicating reluctance] pouvoir; **we can't leave the children alone** nous ne pouvons pas laisser OR il nous est impossible de laisser les enfants seuls ‖ [indicating refusal] pouvoir; **we cannot tolerate such behaviour** nous ne pouvons pas tolérer ce genre de comportement. -**8.** [expressing opinions]: **you can't let him speak to you like that!** tu ne peux pas OR tu ne devrais pas lui permettre de te parler comme ça!; **after the way he behaved you can't blame her for leaving him!** étant donné la façon dont il s'est comporté, tu ne peux pas lui reprocher de l'avoir quitté!; **you'll have to leave, it can't be helped** il faudra que tu partes, il n'y a rien à faire. -**9.** [used to urge or insist]: **can't we at least talk about it?** est-ce que nous pouvons au moins en discuter? -**10.** [indicating possibility or likelihood] pouvoir; **they ~ back out of it at any time** ils peuvent se rétracter à n'importe quel moment; **the contract ~ still be cancelled** il est toujours possible d'annuler OR on peut encore annuler le contrat; **the job can't be finished in one day** il est impossible de finir le travail OR le travail ne peut pas se faire en un jour; **the cottage ~ sleep six people** on peut loger six personnes dans ce cottage; **you ~ always try again later** tu peux toujours réessayer plus tard; **he can be very stubborn** il lui arrive d'être OR il peut être très têtu; **what ~ I have done with the keys?** qu'est-ce que j'ai bien pu faire des clés? ❑ **I'm as happy as ~ be** je suis on ne peut plus heureux; **she was as kind as ~ be** elle était on ne peut plus gentille. -**11.** [indicating disbelief or doubt]: **you can't be serious!** (ce n'est pas possible!) vous ne parlez pas sérieusement!; **he can't possibly have finished already!** ce n'est pas possible qu'il ait déjà fini!; **the house can't have been that expensive** la maison n'a pas dû coûter si cher que ça; **how ~ you say that?** comment pouvez-vous OR osez-vous dire ça?; **you can't mean it!** tu ne penses pas ce que tu dis!; **what ~ they want now?** qu'est-ce qu'ils peuvent bien vouloir maintenant?; **who on earth ~ that be?** qui diable cela peut-il bien être? -**12.** *phr*: **cannot but: his resignation cannot but confirm such suspicions** *fml* sa démission ne fait que confirmer de tels soupçons.

can[2] [kæn] (*pt* & *pp* canned, *cont* canning)
◇ *n* -**1.** [container - for liquid] bidon *m*; [- for tinned food] boîte *f* (de conserve); *Am* [- for rubbish] poubelle *f*, boîte *f* à ordures; **a ~ of tuna** une boîte de thon (en conserve); **a ~ of beer/soda** une boîte de bière/de soda ❑ **a (real) ~ of worms** un vrai casse-tête; **the film is in the ~** CIN le film est terminé; **the deal's in the ~** *inf* l'affaire est conclue. -**2.** *inf Am* [prison] taule *f*. -**3.** *inf Am* [toilet] W-C *mpl*, waters *mpl*; [buttocks] fesses *fpl*.
◇ *vt* -**1.** [food] mettre en boîte OR en conserve, conserver (en boîte). -**2.** *inf Am* [dismiss from job] virer, renvoyer. -**3.** ▽ *Am phr*: ~ **it!** ferme-la!, la ferme!

Can *written abbr of* Canada.

Cana [ˈkeɪnə] *pr n*: ~ **(of Galilee)** Cana (de Galilée).

Canada ['kænədə] *pr n* Canada *m*; in ~ au Canada.
Canada Day *n anniversaire de l'indépendance canadienne (le 1er juillet)*.
Canada goose *n* bernache *f* du Canada.
Canadian [kə'neɪdjən] ◇ *n* Canadien *m*, -enne *f*.
◇ *adj* [gen] canadien; [embassy, prime minister] canadien, du Canada; ~ **English** anglais *m* du Canada; ~ **French** français *m* canadien.
Canadianism [kə'neɪdjənɪzm] *n* [expression] canadianisme *m*.
canal [kə'næl] *n* -**1.** [waterway] canal *m*; ~ **barge** OR **boat** péniche *f*, chaland *m*. -**2.** ANAT canal *m*, conduit *m*.
canalization [,kænəlaɪ'zeɪʃn] *n* TECH & *fig* canalisation *f*.
canalize, -ise ['kænəlaɪz] *vt* TECH & *fig* canaliser.
Canal Zone *pr n*: the ~ [of Panama] la zone du canal de Panama; [of Suez] la zone du canal de Suez.
canapé ['kænəpeɪ] *n* canapé *m (petit four)*.
canard [kæ'nɑːd] *n* [false report] fausse nouvelle *f*, canard *m*.
Canaries [kə'neərɪz] *pl pr n*: the ~ les Canaries *fpl*.
canary [kə'neərɪ] (*pl* **canaries**) *n* -**1.** [bird] canari *m*, serin *m*. -**2.** [colour]: ~ **(yellow)** jaune serin *m inv*, jaune canari *m inv*; a ~ **(yellow) car** une voiture jaune serin OR jaune canari.
canary grass *n* alpiste *m*.
Canary Islands *pl pr n*: the ~ les (îles *fpl*) Canaries *fpl*; **in the** ~ aux Canaries.
canary seed *n* millet *m*.
canasta [kə'næstə] *n* canasta *f*.
Canberra ['kænbərə] *pr n* Canberra.
cancan ['kænkæn] *n* cancan *m*, french cancan *m*.
cancel ['kænsl] (*Br pt* & *pp* **cancelled**, *cont* **cancelling**, *Am pt* & *pp* **canceled**, *cont* **canceling**) *vt* -**1.** [call off - event, order, reservation] annuler; [- appointment] annuler, décommander; **the flight has been cancelled** le vol a été annulé; **they cancelled the order for three warships** ils ont annulé leur commande de trois navires de guerre. -**2.** [revoke - agreement, contract] résilier, annuler; [- cheque] faire opposition à. -**3.** [mark as no longer valid - by stamping] oblitérer; [- by punching] poinçonner. -**4.** [cross out] barrer, rayer, biffer. -**5.** MATH éliminer.
◆ **cancel out** *vt sep* -**1.** [counterbalance] neutraliser, compenser; **the factors ~ each other out** les facteurs se neutralisent OR se compensent. -**2.** MATH éliminer, annuler.
cancellation [,kænsə'leɪʃn] *n* -**1.** [calling off - of event, reservation] annulation *f*; [annulment - of agreement, contract] résiliation *f*, annulation *f*; [- of cheque] opposition *f*; **we only got a table because there had been a** ~ nous n'avons eu une table que parce que quelqu'un avait annulé sa réservation. -**2.** [act of invalidating - by punching] poinçonnage *m*; [- by stamping] oblitération *f*. -**3.** [crossing out] biffage *m*. -**4.** MATH élimination *f*.
cancer ['kænsəʳ] ◇ *n* MED & *fig* cancer *m*; **lung** ~ cancer du poumon; **to die of** ~ mourir (à la suite) d'un cancer; **cigarettes cause** ~ les cigarettes sont cancérigènes OR carcinogènes.
◇ *comp*: ~ **patient** cancéreux *m*, -euse *f*; ~ **research** oncologie *f*, cancérologie *f*; **we're collecting money for ~ research** nous recueillons des fonds pour la recherche contre le cancer; ~ **ward** [wing] service *m* oncologique; [building] pavillon *m* oncologique; **'Cancer Ward'** *Solzhenitsyn* 'le Pavillon des cancéreux'.
Cancer ['kænsəʳ] *pr n* -**1.** ASTROL & ASTRON Cancer *m*; **he's a** ~ il est (du signe du) Cancer. -**2.** GEOG: **the Tropic of** ~ le Cancer, le tropique du Cancer.
cancerous ['kænsərəs] *adj* cancéreux.
cancer stick *inf n hum* cigarette *f*.
cancroid ['kæŋkrɔɪd] *adj* MED cancroïde.
candela [kæn'diːlə] *n* PHYS candela *f*.
candelabra [,kændɪ'lɑːbrə], **candelabrum** [,kændɪ'lɑːbrəm] (*pl inv* OR **candelabras** OR **candelabrums**) *n* candélabre *m*.
candid ['kændɪd] *adj* [person] franc, sincère; [smile] franc; [account, report] qui ne cache rien; **I'd like your ~ opinion** j'aimerais que vous me disiez franchement ce que vous en pensez; **to be quite ~, I don't like it** pour parler franchement OR pour être franc, je ne l'aime pas.
candida ['kændɪdə] *n* candidose *f*.
candidacy ['kændɪdəsɪ] *n* candidature *f*.
candidate ['kændɪdət] *n* candidat *m*, -e *f*; **to be a** OR **to stand as ~ for mayor** être candidat à la mairie.
candidature ['kændɪdətʃəʳ] *n* candidature *f*.
candid camera *n* appareil *m* photo à instantanés; **Candid Camera** TV la Caméra cachée.
◆ **candid-camera** *adj*: **a candid-camera shot** un instantané.
candidly ['kændɪdlɪ] *adv* [speak] franchement; [smile] candidement, avec candeur.
candidness ['kændɪdnɪs] *n* franchise *f*.
candied ['kændɪd] *adj* [piece of fruit, peel] confit; [whole fruit] confit, glacé.
candle ['kændl] *n* -**1.** [of wax - gen] bougie *f*, chandelle *f*; [- in church] cierge *m*, chandelle *f*; **no one can hold a ~ to her when it comes to dancing** pour ce qui est de la danse, personne ne lui arrive à la cheville; **to burn the ~ at both ends** brûler la chandelle par les deux bouts. -**2.** PHYS [former unit] bougie *f*; [candela] candela *f*.
candleholder ['kændl,həʊldəʳ] *n* [single] bougeoir *m*; [branched] chandelier *m*.
candlelight ['kændllaɪt] ◇ *n* lueur *f* d'une bougie OR d'une chandelle; **they had dinner by** ~ ils ont dîné aux chandelles; **she read by** ~ elle lisait à la lueur d'une bougie.
◇ *comp* [dinner, supper] aux chandelles.
candlelit ['kændllɪt] *adj* éclairé aux bougies OR aux chandelles.
Candlemas ['kændlməs] *n* la Chandeleur.
candlepower ['kændl,paʊəʳ] *n* PHYS intensité *f* lumineuse.
candlestick ['kændlstɪk] *n* [single] bougeoir *m*; [branched] chandelier *m*.
candlewick ['kændlwɪk] ◇ *n* [yarn] chenille *f* (de coton).
◇ *comp* [bedspread] en chenille (de coton).
candour *Br*, **candor** *Am* ['kændəʳ] *n* candeur *f*, franchise *f*.
candy ['kændɪ] (*pl* **candies**, *pt* & *pp* **candied**) ◇ *n* -**1.** *Am* [piece] bonbon *m*; *(U)* [sweets in general] bonbons *mpl*, confiserie *f*; ~ **bar** barre *f* chocolatée; ~ **wrapper** papier *m* de bonbon. -**2.** CULIN [sugar] sucre *m* candi. -**3.** *drugs sl* came *f*.
◇ *vt* [ginger, pieces of fruit, orange peel] confire; [whole fruit] glacer, confire; [sugar] faire candir.
◇ *vi* se candir, se cristalliser.
candy corn *n Am bonbons que l'on mange à Halloween*.
candyfloss ['kændɪflɒs] *n Br* barbe *f* à papa.
candy store *n Am* confiserie *f*.
candy-striped *adj* à rayures multicolores.
candy striper [-,straɪpəʳ] *n Am bénévole qui travaille aux œuvres de bienfaisance dans un hôpital*.
cane [keɪn] ◇ *n* -**1.** [stem of plant] canne *f*; [in making baskets, furniture] rotin *m*, jonc *m*. -**2.** [rod - for walking] canne *f*; [- for punishment] verge *f*, baguette *f*; **to give sb the** ~ fouetter qqn; **to get the** ~ être fouetté, recevoir le fouet. -**3.** [for supporting plant] tuteur *m*.
◇ *vt* -**1.** [beat with rod] donner des coups de bâton à, fouetter. -**2.** *inf* [defeat] battre à plate couture.
◇ *comp* [furniture] en rotin; [chair - entirely in cane] en rotin; [- with cane back, seat] canné.
cane sugar *n* sucre *m* de canne.
canework ['keɪnwɜːk] *n* cannage *m*.
canine ['keɪnaɪn] ◇ *adj* -**1.** [gen] canin; ZOOL de la famille des canidés. -**2.** ANAT: ~ **tooth** canine *f*.
◇ *n* -**1.** [animal] canidé *m*. -**2.** [tooth] canine *f*.
caning ['keɪnɪŋ] *n* -**1.** [beating]: **to give sb a** ~ [gen] donner des coups de bâton OR de trique à qqn; SCH fouetter qqn. -**2.** *inf* [defeat]: **to get a** ~ être battu à plate couture.
canister ['kænɪstəʳ] *n* -**1.** [for flour, sugar] boîte *f*; **flour/sugar** ~ boîte à farine/sucre. -**2.** [for gas, shaving cream] bombe *f*; **tear gas** ~ bombe lacrymogène.
canker ['kæŋkəʳ] *n* -**1.** MED ulcère *m*, chancre *m*. -**2.** BOT & *fig* chancre *m*.
cankerous ['kæŋkərəs] *adj* [tissue] chancreux; [sore] rongeur; *fig* rongeur.
cannabis ['kænəbɪs] *n* [plant] chanvre *m* indien; [drug] cannabis *m*; ~ **resin** résine *f* de cannabis.
canned [kænd] *adj* -**1.** [food] en boîte, en conserve; ~ **goods** conserves *fpl*. -**2.** *pej* [pre-prepared, pre-recorded]: ~ **laughter** rires *mpl* préenregistrés; ~ **music** musique *f* enregistrée OR en conserve *hum* & *pej*. -**3.** *inf* [drunk] paf *(inv)*, rond; **to get** ~ se soûler.
cannelloni [,kænɪ'ləʊnɪ] *n (U)* cannelloni *mpl*.
canner ['kænəʳ] *n* conserveur *m*.
cannery ['kænərɪ] (*pl* **canneries**) *n* conserverie *f*, fabrique *f* de conserves; **'Cannery Row'** *Steinbeck* 'Rue de la sardine'.
cannibal ['kænɪbl] ◇ *adj* cannibale, anthropophage.
◇ *n* cannibale *mf*, anthropophage *mf*.
cannibalism ['kænɪbəlɪzm] *n* cannibalisme *m*, anthropophagie *f*.
cannibalize, -ise ['kænɪbəlaɪz] *vt* [car] cannibaliser, récupérer des pièces détachées de; [text] récupérer des parties de.
cannily ['kænɪlɪ] *adv* [assess] avec perspicacité; [reason] habilement, astucieusement.
canning ['kænɪŋ] ◇ *n* mise *f* en boîte OR en conserve.
◇ *comp* [process] de mise en boîte OR en conserve; ~ **factory** conserverie *f*, fabrique *f* de conserves; ~ **industry** conserverie *f*, industrie *f* de la conserve.
cannon ['kænən] (*pl inv* OR **cannons**) ◇ *n* -**1.** [weapon] canon *m*. -**2.** TECH [barrel of gun, syringe] canon *m*. -**3.** *Br* [in billiards] carambolage *m*.
◇ *vi* -**1.** [bump]: **to ~ into sthg/sb** se heurter contre qqch/qqn. -**2.** *Br* [in billiards] caramboler.
cannonade [,kænə'neɪd] ◇ *n* canonnade *f*.
◇ *vt* canonner.
cannonball ['kænənbɔːl] *n* -**1.** [ammunition] boulet *m* de canon. -**2.** SPORT: a ~ **(service)** un service en boulet de canon.
cannon fodder *n* chair *f* à canon.
cannonshot ['kænənʃɒt] *n* [firing] coup *m* de canon; [range]: **within** ~ à portée de canon.
cannot ['kænɒt] = **can not**.
cannula ['kænjʊlə] (*pl* **cannulas** OR **cannulae** [-liː]) *n* [for giving medication] canule *f*, cathéter *m*; [for draining] sonde *f*.
canny ['kænɪ] (*compar* **cannier**, *superl* **canniest**) *adj* -**1.** [astute] astucieux, habile; [shrewd] malin, rusé. -**2.** [wary] prudent, circonspect. -**3.** *Br dial* [person - thrifty] économe; [- nice] sympathique; [bargain, deal] avantageux.
canoe [kə'nuː] (*cont* **canoeing**) ◇ *n* canoë *m*; [dugout] pirogue *f*; SPORT canoë *m*, canoë-kayak *m*.
◇ *vi* [gen] faire du canoë; SPORT faire du canoë OR du canoë-kayak; **we ~d down the river** nous avons descendu le fleuve en canoë.
canoeing [kə'nuːɪŋ] *n* SPORT canoë-kayak *m*; **to go** ~ faire du canoë-kayak.
canoeist [kə'nuːɪst] *n* canoéiste *mf*.
canon ['kænən] *n* -**1.** RELIG [decree, prayer] canon *m*; [clergyman] chanoine *m*. -**2.** LITERAT œuvre *f*. -**3.** MUS canon *m*. -**4.** *fig* [rule] canon *m*, règle *f*, règles *fpl*.
canonical [kə'nɒnɪkl] *adj* -**1.** RELIG [text] canonique; [practice] conforme aux canons (de l'église); [dress, robe] sacerdotal; ~ **hours**[catholic] heures *fpl* canoniales; [C of E] *heures pendant lesquelles la célébration des mariages est autorisée (entre 8 h et 18 h)*. -**2.** MUS en canon. -**3.** *fig* [accepted] canonique, autorisé.

canonization [ˌkænənaɪˈzeɪʃn] *n* RELIG & *fig* canonisation *f.*

canonize, -ise [ˈkænənaɪz] *vt* RELIG & *fig* canoniser.

canon law *n* droit *m* canon.

canoodle *inf* [kəˈnuːdl] *vi Br* se faire des mamours.

can opener *n* ouvre-boîtes *m inv.*

canopied [ˈkænəpɪd] *adj* [bed] à baldaquin OR ciel de lit; [balcony, passageway] à auvent OR marquise; [throne] avec dais.

canopy [ˈkænəpɪ] (*pl* **canopies**) *n* **-1.** [over bed] baldaquin *m*, ciel *m* de lit; [over balcony, passageway] auvent *m*, marquise *f*; [over throne] dais *m*; ARCHIT [with columns] baldaquin *m*. **-2.** [of parachute] voilure *f*. **-3.** AERON [of cockpit] verrière *f*. **-4.** *fig* [branches, sky] voûte *f*.

cant [kænt] ◇ *n* **-1.** *(U)* [insincere talk] paroles *fpl* hypocrites; [clichés] clichés *mpl*, phrases *fpl* toutes faites. **-2.** [jargon] argot *m* de métier, jargon *m*. **-3.** [slope] pente *f*, inclinaison *f*; [oblique surface] surface *f* oblique, plan *m* incliné. **-4.** [movement] secousse *f*, cahot *m*.
◇ *vi* **-1.** [talk - insincerely] parler avec hypocrisie; [- in clichés] débiter des clichés OR des phrases toutes faites. **-2.** [use jargon] parler en argot de métier, jargonner. **-3.** [tip slightly] se pencher, s'incliner; [overturn] se renverser OR se retourner (d'un seul coup). **-4.** [slope] être incliné OR en pente.
◇ *vt* [tip slightly] pencher, incliner; [overturn] renverser OR retourner (d'un seul coup).

can't [kɑːnt] = **cannot**.

Cantab. (*written abbr of* Cantabrigiensis) *de l'université de Cambridge*.

Cantabrian Mountains [kænˈteɪbrɪən-] *pl pr n*: the ~ les monts *mpl* Cantabriques.

cantaloup(e) [ˈkæntəluːp] *n* cantaloup *m*.

cantankerous [kænˈtæŋkərəs] *adj* **-1.** [bad-tempered - habitually] acariâtre, qui a mauvais caractère, grincheux; [- temporarily] de mauvaise humeur. **-2.** [quarrelsome] querelleur.

cantata [kænˈtɑːtə] *n* cantate *f*.

canteen [kænˈtiːn] *n* **-1.** [restaurant] cantine *f*. **-2.** *Am* [flask] flasque *f*, gourde *f*. **-3.** [box for cutlery] coffret *m*; ~ of cutlery ménagère *f*. **-4.** MIL [mess tin] gamelle *f*.

canter [ˈkæntəʳ] ◇ *n* petit galop *m*; the horse set off at a ~ le cheval est parti au petit galop.
◇ *vi* aller au petit galop.
◇ *vt* faire aller au petit galop.

Canterbury [ˈkæntəbrɪ] *pr n* Cantorbéry; 'The ~ Tales' *Chaucer* 'Contes de Cantorbéry'.

Canterbury bell *n* campanule *f*.

cantharides [kænˈθærɪdiːz] *npl* cantharides *fpl*.

canticle [ˈkæntɪkl] *n* cantique *m*; the Canticle of Canticles le Cantique des cantiques.

cantilena [ˌkæntɪˈleɪnə] *n* cantilène *f*.

cantilever [ˈkæntɪliːvəʳ] ◇ *n* **-1.** [beam, girder] cantilever *m*; [projecting beam] corbeau *m*, console *f*. **-2.** AERON cantilever *m*.
◇ *vt* mettre en cantilever.
◇ *comp* [beam, girder] en cantilever, cantilever *(inv)*.

cantilever bridge *n* pont *m* cantilever.

canting [ˈkæntɪŋ] *adj* **-1.** [hypocritical] hypocrite. **-2.** [whining] pleurnichard, pleurnicheur.

canto [ˈkæntəʊ] (*pl* **cantos**) *n* chant *m (d'un poème)*.

canton [*n sense 1* ˈkæntɒn, *sense 2* ˈkæntən, *vb sense 1* kænˈtɒn, *sense 2* kænˈtuːn] ◇ *n* **-1.** ADMIN canton *m*. **-2.** HERALD canton *m*.
◇ *vt* **-1.** ADMIN [land] diviser en cantons. **-2.** MIL [soldiers] cantonner.

Canton [kænˈtɒn] *pr n* Canton.

cantonal [ˈkæntənl] *adj* cantonal.

Cantonese [ˌkæntəˈniːz] (*pl inv*) ◇ *n* **-1.** [person] Cantonais *m*, -e *f*. **-2.** LING cantonais *m*.
◇ *adj* cantonais.

cantonment [kænˈtuːnmənt] *n* cantonnement *m*.

cantor [ˈkæntɔːʳ] *n* chantre *m*.

Canuck *inf* [kəˈnʌk] *n Am* [Canadian] Canadien *m*, -enne *f*; [French Canadian] Canadien français *m*, Canadienne française *f*.

Canute [kəˈnjuːt] *pr n* Knud.

canvas [ˈkænvəs] (*pl inv* OR **canvasses**) ◇ *n* **-1.** [cloth] toile *f*; [for tapestry] canevas *m*; under ~ [in tent] sous une tente; NAUT sous voiles. **-2.** [painting] toile *f*, tableau *m*.
◇ *comp* [bag, cloth] de OR en toile.

canvass [ˈkænvəs] ◇ *vi* **-1.** [seek opinions] faire un sondage. **-2.** COMM [seek orders] visiter la clientèle, faire la place; [door to door] faire du démarchage OR du porte-à-porte. **-3.** POL [candidate, campaign worker] solliciter des voix; we're ~ing for the Greens nous sollicitons des voix pour les Verts.
◇ *vt* **-1.** [seek opinion of] sonder. **-2.** COMM [person] démarcher, solliciter des commandes de; [area] prospecter. **-3.** POL [person] solliciter la voix de; [area] faire du démarchage électoral dans. **-4.** *Am* POL [ballots] pointer.
◇ *n* **-1.** [gen & COMM] démarchage *m*; POL démarchage *m* électoral. **-2.** *Am* POL [of ballots] pointage *m*.

canvasser [ˈkænvəsəʳ] *n* **-1.** [pollster] sondeur *m*, enquêteur *m*, -euse *f*. **-2.** COMM [salesman] placier *m*; [door to door] démarcheur *m*. **-3.** POL agent *m* électoral *(qui sollicite des voix)*. **-4.** *Am* [of ballots] scrutateur *m*, -trice *f*.

canvassing [ˈkænvəsɪŋ] *n* **-1.** [gen & COMM] démarchage *m*. **-2.** POL démarchage *m* électoral.

canyon [ˈkænjən] *n* cañon *m*, canyon *m*, gorge *f*.

cap [kæp] (*pt* & *pp* **capped**, *cont* **capping**) ◇ *n* **-1.** [hat - with peak] casquette *f*; [- without peak] bonnet *m*; [- of jockey, judge] toque *f*; [- of nurse, traditional costume] coiffe *f*; [- of soldier] calot *m*; [- of officer] képi *m*; ~ and bells marotte *f* (de bouffon); ~ and gown *expression britannique évoquant le milieu universitaire*; if the ~ fits, wear it qui se sent morveux (qu'il) se mouche; to go to sb ~ in hand aller vers qqn chapeau bas; to set one's ~ at sb jeter son dévolu sur qqn. **-2.** *Br* SPORT: this is his third England ~, he has been an England ~ three times il a été sélectionné trois fois dans l'équipe d'Angleterre. **-3.** [cover, lid - of bottle, container] capsule *f*; [- of lens] cache *m*; [- of tyre valve] bouchon *m*; [- of pen] capuchon *m*; [- of mushroom] chapeau *m*; [- of tooth] couronne *f*; [- of column, pedestal] chapiteau *m*. **-4.** [for toy gun] amorce *f*. **-5.** [contraceptive device] diaphragme *m*.
◇ *vt* **-1.** [cover] couvrir, recouvrir. **-2.** [tooth] couronner, mettre une couronne à. **-3.** [outdo] surpasser; he capped that story with an even funnier one il a raconté une histoire encore plus drôle que celle-là; to ~ it all pour couronner le tout, pour comble. **-4.** [spending] limiter, restreindre. **-5.** *Br* SPORT sélectionner (dans l'équipe nationale); she was capped five times elle a joué OR elle a été sélectionnée cinq fois.

CAP (*abbr of* Common Agricultural Policy) *n* PAC *f*.

capability [ˌkeɪpəˈbɪlətɪ] (*pl* **capabilities**) *n* **-1.** [gen] aptitude *f*, capacité *f*; the work is beyond his capabilities ce travail est au-dessus de ses capacités. **-2.** MIL capacité *f*, potentiel *m*; nuclear ~ puissance *f* OR potentiel *m* nucléaire.

capable [ˈkeɪpəbl] *adj* **-1.** [able] capable; they are quite ~ of looking after themselves ils sont parfaitement capables de se débrouiller tout seuls; he's ~ of intense concentration il a une grande capacité de concentration. **-2.** [competent] capable, compétent.

capably [ˈkeɪpəblɪ] *adv* avec compétence, de façon compétente.

capacious [kəˈpeɪʃəs] *adj fml* [container] de grande capacité OR contenance.

capacitance [kəˈpæsɪtəns] *n* ELEC capacité *f*.

capacitor [kəˈpæsɪtəʳ] *n* ELEC condensateur *m*.

capacity [kəˈpæsɪtɪ] (*pl* **capacities**) ◇ *n* **-1.** [size - of container] contenance *f*, capacité *f*; [- of room] capacité *f*; the theatre has a seating ~ of 500 il y a 500 places dans le théâtre; he has an amazing ~ for beer il peut boire une quantité étonnante de bière; filled to ~ [bottle, tank] plein; [ship, theatre] plein, comble. **-2.** [aptitude] aptitude *f*, capacité *f*; ~ to learn aptitude à apprendre, capacité d'apprendre; she has a great ~ for languages elle a une grande aptitude OR capacité pour les langues, elle est douée pour les langues; the work is well within our ~ nous sommes tout à fait en mesure OR capables de faire ce travail. **-3.** [position] qualité *f*, titre *m*; JUR [legal competence] pouvoir *m* légal; she spoke in her ~ as government representative elle s'est exprimée en sa qualité de OR en tant que représentante du gouvernement; he's acting in an advisory ~ il a un rôle consultatif; they are here in an official ~ ils sont ici à titre officiel. **-4.** [of factory, industry] moyens *mpl* de production; [output] rendement *m*; the factory is (working) at full ~ l'usine produit à plein rendement; the factory has not yet reached ~ l'usine n'a pas encore atteint son rendement maximum. **-5.** [of engine] capacité *f*. **-6.** ELEC capacité *f*.
◇ *comp*: a ~ audience une salle comble; they played to a ~ crowd ils ont joué à guichets fermés.

caparison [kəˈpærɪsn] *arch* OR *lit* ◇ *n* caparaçon *m*.
◇ *vt* caparaçonner.

cape [keɪp] *n* **-1.** [cloak] cape *f*, pèlerine *f*. **-2.** GEOG [headland] cap *m*; [promontory] promontoire *m*.

CAPES:
Cape Bon cap Bon;
Cape Canaveral cap Canaveral;
Cape Cod cap Cod;
the Cape of Good Hope le cap de Bonne-Espérance;
Cape Horn le cap Horn.

Cape Coloured *n SAfr* métis sud-africain *m*, métisse sud-africaine *f*.

Cape Peninsula *pr n*: the ~ la péninsule du Cap, Le Cap.

Cape Province *pr n* province *f* du Cap.

caper [ˈkeɪpəʳ] ◇ *vi* **-1.** [jump, skip] cabrioler, gambader, faire des cabrioles OR des gambades; to ~ down/up the road descendre/monter la rue en gambadant. **-2.** [frolic] faire le fou.
◇ *n* **-1.** [jump, skip] cabriole *f*, gambade *f*. **-2.** [practical joke] farce *f*. **-3.** *inf* [nonsense]: I haven't time for all that ~ je n'ai pas de temps à perdre avec des âneries pareilles. **-4.** *inf* [illegal activity] coup *m*. **-5.** CULIN câpre *f*; [shrub] câprier *m*.
◇ *comp*: ~ sauce sauce *f* aux câpres.

capercaillie, capercailzie [ˌkæpəˈkeɪlɪ] *n* grand tétras *m*, grand coq *m* de bruyère.

Capernaum [kəˈpɜːnjəm] *pr n* Capharnaüm.

capeskin [ˈkeɪpskɪn] *n* peau *f* souple.

Capetian [kəˈpiːʃn] ◇ *adj* capétien.
◇ *n* Capétien *m*, -enne *f*.

Cape Town *pr n* Le Cap.

Cape Verde [-vɜːd] *pr n*: the ~ Islands les îles *fpl* du Cap-Vert; in ~ au Cap-Vert.

Cape Verdean [-ˈvɜːdɪən] ◇ *n* Capverdien *m*, -enne *f*.
◇ *adj* capverdien.

capful [ˈkæpfʊl] *n* [of liquid] capsule *f* (pleine).

capillarity [ˌkæpɪˈlærətɪ] *n* capillarité *f*.

capillary [kəˈpɪlərɪ] (*pl* **capillaries**) ◇ *adj* capillaire.
◇ *n* capillaire *m*.

capital [ˈkæpɪtl] ◇ *adj* **-1.** [chief, primary] capital, principal; it's of ~ importance c'est d'une importance capitale, c'est de la plus haute importance; ~ city capitale *f*. **-2.** JUR capital; ~ offence crime *m* capital. **-3.** [upper case] majuscule; ~ D D majuscule; in ~ letters en majuscules, en capitales; he's an idiot with a ~ "I" c'est un imbécile avec un grand «I» OR de premier ordre. **-4.** *inf Br dated* [wonderful] chouette, fameux.

◇ *n* -**1.** [city] capitale *f*; the financial ~ of the world la capitale financière du monde. -**2.** [letter] majuscule *f*, capitale *f*; write in ~s écrivez en (lettres) majuscules OR en capitales. -**3.** *(U)* [funds] capital *m*, capitaux *mpl*, fonds *mpl*; ECON & FIN [funds and assets] capital *m* (en espèces et en nature); to raise ~ réunir des capitaux; ~ invested, outlay of ~ mise *f* de fonds; ~ and labour capital et main-d'œuvre *f*; to try and make ~ (out) of a situation essayer de tirer profit OR parti d'une situation. -**4.** FIN [principal] capital *m*, principal *m*. -**5.** ARCHIT [of column] chapiteau *m*.
◇ *comp* de capital; ~ **allowances** amortissements *mpl* admis par le fisc; ~ **income** revenu *m* du capital; ~ **investment** mise *f* de fonds; ~ **profit** plus-value *f* sur la réalisation de biens capitaux; ~ **reserves** réserves *fpl* et provisions *fpl*; ~ **sum** capital *m*.

capital account *n* compte *m* de capitaux.

capital assets *npl* actif *m* immobilisé, immobilisations *fpl*.

capital expenditure *n (U)* dépenses *fpl* d'investissement.

capital gains *npl* gains *mpl* en capital, plus-values *fpl* (en capital).

capital gains tax *n impôt sur les plus-values.*

capital goods *npl* biens *mpl* d'équipement OR d'investissement.

capital-intensive *adj* à forte intensité de capital.

capitalism ['kæpɪtəlɪzm] *n* capitalisme *m*.

capitalist ['kæpɪtəlɪst] ◇ *adj* capitaliste.
◇ *n* capitaliste *mf*.

capitalistic [ˌkæpɪtə'lɪstɪk] *adj* capitaliste.

capitalization [ˌkæpɪtəlaɪ'zeɪʃn] *n* capitalisation *f*.

capitalize, -ise ['kæpɪtəlaɪz] ◇ *vt* -**1.** [write in upper case] mettre en majuscules. -**2.** ECON [convert into capital] capitaliser; [raise capital from through issue of stock] constituer le capital social de (par émission d'actions); [provide with capital] pourvoir de fonds OR de capital; **under-/over-~d** sous-/sur-capitalisé. -**3.** FIN [estimate value of] capitaliser; they **~d her investments at £5,000** ils ont capitalisé ses investissements à 5 000 livres.
◇ *vi*: **to ~ on sthg** [take advantage of] tirer profit OR parti de qqch; [make money on] monnayer qqch; **to ~ on a situation** tirer profit OR parti d'une situation, exploiter une situation; **he ~d on his opponent's mistakes** il a tiré profit des erreurs de son adversaire, il a tourné les erreurs de son adversaire à son avantage.

capital levy *n* impôt *m* OR prélèvement *m* sur le capital.

capitally *inf* ['kæpɪtəlɪ] *adv Br dated* fameusement *dated*, admirablement.

capital market *n* marché *m* des capitaux.

capital profit *n* plus-value *f* sur la réalisation de biens capitaux.

capital punishment *n* peine *f* capitale, peine *f* de mort.

capital stock *n* capital *m* social, fonds *mpl* propres.

capital transfer tax *n* impôt *m* sur le transfert de capitaux.

capitation [ˌkæpɪ'teɪʃn] *n* -**1.** FIN capitation *f*; ~ **(tax)** capitation. -**2.** *esp Br* SCH: ~ **(allowance** OR **expenditure)** dotation *f* forfaitaire par élève *(accordée à un établissement scolaire)*.

Capitol ['kæpɪtl] *pr n* -**1.** [in Rome]: **the ~** le Capitole. -**2.** [in US]: **the ~** [national] le Capitole *(siège du Congrès américain)*; [state] le Capitole *(siège du Congrès de l'État)*.

Capitol Hill *pr n la colline du Capitole, à Washington.*

CAPITOL HILL:
Ce nom désigne, par extension, le Congrès américain.

Capitoline Hill [kæ'pɪtəlaɪn-] *pr n*: **the ~** le mont Capitolin.

capitulate [kə'pɪtjʊleɪt] *vi* MIL & *fig* capituler.

capitulation [kəˌpɪtjʊ'leɪʃn] *n* MIL & *fig* capitulation *f*.

capo ['keɪpəʊ] *(pl* **capos)** *n* [on guitar] capo *m* (tasto).

capon ['keɪpən] *n* chapon *m*.

Cappadocia [ˌkæpə'dəʊsjə] *pr n* Cappadoce *f*; **in ~** en Cappadoce.

-capped [kæpt] *in cpds* couvert OR couronné de; **snow~ mountains** montagnes *fpl* couronnées de neige.

caprice [kə'priːs] *n* [whim] caprice *m*; [change of mood] saute *f* d'humeur.

capricious [kə'prɪʃəs] *adj* [person] capricieux, fantasque; [weather] capricieux, changeant.

capriciously [kə'prɪʃəslɪ] *adv* capricieusement.

Capricorn ['kæprɪkɔːn] *pr n* -**1.** ASTROL & ASTRON Capricorne *m*; **he's a ~** il est (du signe du) Capricorne. -**2.** GEOG: **the Tropic of ~** le tropique du Capricorne.

caps [kæps] *(abbr of* **capital letters)** cap.

cap screw *n* vis *f* à six pans creux.

capsicum ['kæpsɪkəm] *n* [fruit & plant - sweet] poivron *m*, piment *m* doux; [- hot] piment *m*.

capsize [kæp'saɪz] ◇ *vi* [gen] se renverser; [boat] chavirer.
◇ *vt* [gen] renverser; [boat] faire chavirer.

capstan ['kæpstən] *n* cabestan *m*.

capstan bar *n* barre *f* OR bras *m* de cabestan.

capstan lathe *n* tour *m* revolver.

capstone ['kæpstəʊn] *n* ARCHIT pierre *f* de faîte; *fig* sommet *m*.

capsule ['kæpsjuːl] ◇ *n* -**1.** [gen, AERON, ANAT & BOT] capsule *f*. -**2.** PHARM capsule *f*, gélule *f*.
◇ *adj* concis, bref.

capsulize, -ise ['kæpsjʊlaɪz] *vt* résumer, récapituler.

Capt. *(written abbr of* **captain)** cap.

captain ['kæptɪn] ◇ *n* -**1.** [of boat] capitaine *m*; MIL capitaine *m*. -**2.** [of group, team] chef *m*, capitaine *m*; SPORT capitaine *m* (d'équipe); **~ of industry** capitaine d'industrie. -**3.** *Am* [of police] ≃ commissaire *m* (de police) de quartier. -**4.** *Am* [head waiter] maître *m* d'hôtel; [of bell boys] responsable *m* des grooms.
◇ *vt* [gen] diriger; MIL commander; SPORT être le capitaine de.

captaincy ['kæptɪnsɪ] *n* -**1.** MIL grade *m* de capitaine; **to receive one's ~** être promu OR passer capitaine. -**2.** SPORT poste *m* de capitaine; **under the ~ of Rogers** avec Rogers comme capitaine.

caption ['kæpʃn] ◇ *n* -**1.** [under illustration] légende *f*. -**2.** [in article, chapter] sous-titre *m*. -**3.** CIN sous-titre *m*.
◇ *vt* -**1.** [illustration] mettre une légende à, légender. -**2.** CIN sous-titrer.

captious ['kæpʃəs] *adj* [person] qui trouve toujours à redire, chicanier; [attitude] chicanier.

captivate ['kæptɪveɪt] *vt* captiver, fasciner.

captivating ['kæptɪveɪtɪŋ] *adj* captivant, fascinant.

captive ['kæptɪv] ◇ *n* captif *m*, -ive *f*, prisonnier *m*, -ère *f*; **to take sb ~** faire qqn prisonnier; **to hold sb ~** garder qqn en captivité.
◇ *adj* [person] captif, prisonnier; [animal, balloon] captif; **a ~ audience** un public captif.

captivity [kæp'tɪvətɪ] *n* captivité *f*; **to hold/to raise in ~** garder/élever en captivité.

captor ['kæptəʳ] *n* [gen] personne *f* qui capture; [unlawfully] ravisseur *m*, -euse *f*.

capture ['kæptʃəʳ] ◇ *vt* -**1.** [take prisoner - animal, criminal, enemy] capturer, prendre; [- runaway] reprendre; [- city] prendre, s'emparer de; GAMES prendre. -**2.** [gain control of - market] conquérir, s'emparer de; [- attention, imagination] captiver; [- admiration, interest] gagner. -**3.** [succeed in representing] rendre, reproduire.
◇ *n* [act, person, thing] capture *f*, prise *f*.

Capua ['kæpjʊə] *pr n* Capoue.

Capuchin ['kæpjʊtʃɪn] RELIG ◇ *n*: ~ **(monk)** capucin *m*.
◇ *adj* capucin; **a monk of the ~ order** un capucin; **a nun of the ~ order** une capucine.
◆ **capuchin** *n* [cloak] cape *f* (avec capuchon).

car [kɑːʳ] ◇ *n* -**1.** [automobile] voiture *f*, automobile *f*, auto *f*; **to go by ~** aller en voiture. -**2.** *Am* [of train] wagon *m*, voiture *f*. -**3.** *Am* [tram] tramway *m*, tram *m*. -**4.** [of lift] cabine *f (d'ascenseur)*. -**5.** [of airship, balloon] nacelle *f*.
◇ *comp* [engine, tyre, wheel] de voiture, d'automobile; [journey, trip] en voiture; ~ **allowance** *Br* indemnité *f* de déplacement (en voiture); ~ **body** carrosserie *f*; ~ **bonnet** *Br* capot *m*; ~ **boot** *Br*, ~ **trunk** *Am* coffre *m*, malle *f* (arrière); ~ **boot sale** *Br marché où chacun vient avec sa voiture (dont le coffre sert de stand) pour vendre des objets de toute sorte*; ~ **chase** course-poursuite *f*; ~ **hood** *Br* capote *f*; *Am* capot *m*; ~ **industry** industrie *f* (de l') automobile; ~ **number** *Br* numéro *m* d'immatriculation; ~ **radio** autoradio *m*; ~ **worker** ouvrier *m*, -ère *f* de l'industrie automobile.

Caracas [kə'rækəs] *pr n* Caracas.

carafe [kə'ræf] *n* carafe *f*.

caramel ['kærəmel] ◇ *n* caramel *m*.
◇ *comp*: **a ~ (candy)** *Am*, **a (piece) of ~** un caramel; ~ **cream**, ~ **custard** crème *f* (au) caramel.

caramelize, -ise ['kærəməlaɪz] ◇ *vt* caraméliser.
◇ *vi* se caraméliser.

carapace ['kærəpeɪs] *n* carapace *f*.

carat *Br*, **karat** *Am* ['kærət] *n* carat *m*; **an 18 ~ gold ring** une bague en or 18 carats.

Caravaggio [ˌkærə'vædʒɪəʊ] *pr n* le Caravage; **a painting by ~** un tableau du Caravage.

caravan ['kærəvæn] *(Br pt & pp* **caravanned**, *cont* **caravanning**, *Am pt & pp* **caravaned** OR **caravaned**, *cont* **caravanning** OR **caravaning)**
◇ *n* -**1.** *Br* [vehicle] caravane *f*. -**2.** [of gipsy] roulotte *f*. -**3.** [group of travellers] caravane *f*.
◇ *vi*: **to go caravanning** faire du caravaning OR *offic* du caravanage.

caravanner *Br*, **caravaner** *Am* ['kærəvænəʳ] *n* caravanier *m*, -ère *f*.

caravanning ['kærəvænɪŋ] *n* caravaning *m*, caravanage *offic*.

caravanserai [ˌkærə'vænsəraɪ] *n* [inn] caravansérail *m*.

caravan site *n Br* [for campers] camping *m* (pour caravanes); [of gipsies] campement *m*.

caravel ['kærəvel] *n* NAUT caravelle *f*.

caraway ['kærəweɪ] *n* [plant] carvi *m*, cumin *m* des prés; ~ **seeds** (graines *fpl* de) carvi.

carbide ['kɑːbaɪd] *n* carbure *m*.

carbine ['kɑːbaɪn] *n* carabine *f*.

carbohydrate [ˌkɑːbəʊ'haɪdreɪt] *n* -**1.** CHEM hydrate *m* de carbone. -**2.** *(usu pl)* [foodstuff]: **~s** glucides *mpl*.

carbolic [kɑː'bɒlɪk] *adj* phéniqué; ~ **acid** phénol *m*.

car bomb *n* voiture *f* piégée.

carbon ['kɑːbən] *n* -**1.** CHEM carbone *m*. -**2.** [copy, paper] carbone *m*.

carbonaceous [ˌkɑːbə'neɪʃəs] *adj* carboné.

carbonate ['kɑːbənɪt] *n* carbonate *m*.

carbonated ['kɑːbəneɪtɪd] *adj* carbonaté; ~ **soft drinks** boissons *fpl* gazeuses.

carbon black *n* noir *m* de carbone.

carbon copy *n* TYPO carbone *m*; *fig* réplique *f*; **she's a ~ of her mother** c'est l'exacte réplique de sa mère.

carbon cycle *n* cycle *m* du carbone.

carbon dating *n* datation *f* au carbone 14.

carbon dioxide *n* gaz *m* carbonique, dioxyde *m* de carbone.

carbonic [kɑː'bɒnɪk] *adj* carbonique; ~ **acid** acide *m* carbonique.

carboniferous [ˌkɑːbə'nɪfərəs] *adj* carbonifère.
◆ **Carboniferous** GEOL ◇ *adj*: **the Carboniferous Period** le carbonifère.
◇ *n*: **the Carboniferous** le Carbonifère.

carbonization [ˌkɑːbənaɪ'zeɪʃn] *n* carbonisation *f*.

carbonize, -ise ['kɑːbənaɪz] *vt* carboniser.

carbon monoxide *n* monoxyde *m* de carbone.

carbon paper *n* TYPO (papier *m*) carbone *m*.

carbon steel *n* fer *m* carburé.

carbon tetrachloride *n* tétrachlorure *m* de carbone.

Carborundum® [ˌkɑːbəˈrʌndəm] *n* carborundum® *m*.

carboy [ˈkɑːˌbɔɪ] *n* bonbonne *f*, bombonne *f*.

carbuncle [ˈkɑːˌbʌŋkl] *n* **-1.** MED furoncle *m*. **-2.** [gemstone] escarboucle *f*.

carburation [ˌkɑːbjʊˈreɪʃən] *n* carburation *f*.

carburettor *Br*, **carburetor** *Am* [ˌkɑːbəˈretəʳ] *n* carburateur *m*.

carcass, carcase [ˈkɑːkəs] *n* **-1.** [of animal] carcasse *f*, cadavre *m*; [for food] carcasse *f*. **-2.** [of person - dead] cadavre *m*; **move your ~** *inf hum* pousse un peu ta viande. **-3.** [of building] carcasse *f*, charpente *f*; [of car] carcasse *f*.

carcinogen [kɑːˈsɪnədʒən] *n* (agent *m*) carcinogène *m* OR cancérogène *m*.

carcinogenic [ˌkɑːsɪnəˈdʒenɪk] *adj* carcinogène, cancérogène.

carcinoma [ˌkɑːsɪˈnəʊmə] (*pl* **carcinomas** OR **carcinomata** [-mətə]) *n* carcinome *m*.

car coat *n Br* manteau *m* trois-quarts.

card [kɑːd] ◇ *n* **-1.** GAMES carte *f*; **(playing) ~** carte (à jouer); **how about a game of ~s?** et si on jouait aux cartes?; **to play ~s** jouer aux cartes ❑ **to play one's ~s right** mener bien son jeu OR sa barque; **to play one's best** OR **strongest** OR **trump ~** jouer sa meilleure carte; **I still have a couple of ~s up my sleeve** j'ai encore quelques atouts dans mon jeu; **the management holds all the (winning) ~s** l'administration a tous les atouts (en main OR dans son jeu); **to lay** OR **to place one's ~s on the table** jouer cartes sur table; **it was on the ~s** *Br* OR **in the ~s** *Am* **that the project would fail** il était dit OR prévisible que le projet échouerait. **-2.** [with written information - gen] carte *f*; [- for business] carte *f* (de visite); [- for index] fiche *f*; [- for membership] carte *f* de membre OR d'adhérent; [- for library] carte *f* (d'abonnement); [postcard] carte *f* (postale); [programme] programme *m*; **we received a ~ inviting us to their wedding** nous avons reçu un carton OR une carte d'invitation pour leur mariage ❑ **birthday/get-well ~** carte d'anniversaire/de vœux de bon rétablissement; **identity ~** carte d'identité. **-3.** [cardboard] carton *m*. **-4.** *inf dated* [person] plaisantin *m*; **he's a ~!** c'est un marrant OR un rigolo! **-5.** TEX carde *f*.

◇ *vt* **-1.** [information] ficher, mettre sur fiche. **-2.** *Am* [ask for identity card] demander sa carte (d'identité) à. **-3.** SPORT [score] marquer. **-4.** TEX carder.

◆ **cards** *npl Br phr*: **to ask for one's ~s** quitter son travail; **to get one's ~s** être mis à la porte; **the boss gave him his ~s** le patron l'a renvoyé.

cardamom, cardamum [ˈkɑːdəməm] *n* cardamome *f*; **~ seeds** (graines *fpl* de) cardamome *f*.

cardamon [ˈkɑːdəmən] = **cardamom**.

cardboard [ˈkɑːdbɔːd] ◇ *n* carton *m*.

◇ *adj* **-1.** [container, partition] de OR en carton; **~ box** (boîte *f* en) carton *m*. **-2.** *fig* [unreal - character, leader] de carton-pâte, faux.

card-carrying *adj*: **~ member** membre *m*, adhérent *m*, -e *f*; **~ Communist** membre du parti communiste.

card catalogue *n* fichier *m* (de bibliothèque).

card file *n* fichier *m*.

card holder *n* [of club, political party] membre *m*, adhérent *m*, -e *f*; [of library] abonné *m*, -e *f*; [of credit card] titulaire *mf* d'une carte de crédit.

cardiac [ˈkɑːdɪæk] ◇ *adj* cardiaque.

◇ *n* cardiaque *mf*.

cardiac arrest *n* arrêt *m* cardiaque.

cardialgia [ˌkɑːdɪˈældʒɪə] *n* MED cardialgie *f*.

cardie *inf* [ˈkɑːdɪ] *n Br* cardigan *m*.

Cardiff [ˈkɑːdɪf] *pr n* Cardiff.

cardigan [ˈkɑːdɪgən] *n* cardigan *m*.

cardinal [ˈkɑːdɪnl] ◇ *adj* **-1.** [essential] cardinal. **-2.** [colour]: **~ (red)** rouge cardinal *(inv)*, écarlate.

◇ *n* **-1.** MATH, ORNITH & RELIG cardinal *m*. **-2.** [colour]: **~ (red)** rouge cardinal *m inv*, écarlate *f*.

cardinal number *n* MATH nombre *m* cardinal.

cardinal points *npl*: **the ~** les (quatre) points *mpl* cardinaux.

cardinal virtues *npl*: **the ~** les (quatre) vertus *fpl* cardinales.

card index *n* fichier *m*.

◆ **card-index** *vt*: **to card-index information** ficher des renseignements, mettre des renseignements sur fichier.

carding [ˈkɑːdɪŋ] *n* TEX cardage *m*.

cardiogram [ˈkɑːdɪəgræm] *n* cardiogramme *m*.

cardiograph [ˈkɑːdɪəgrɑːf] *n* cardiographe *m*.

cardiological [ˌkɑːdɪəˈlɒdʒɪkl] *adj* cardiologique.

cardiologist [ˌkɑːdɪˈɒlədʒɪst] *n* cardiologue *mf*.

cardiology [ˌkɑːdɪˈɒlədʒɪ] *n* cardiologie *f*.

cardiopulmonary [ˌkɑːdɪəʊˈpʌlmənərɪ] *adj* cardiopulmonaire.

cardiovascular [ˌkɑːdɪəʊˈvæskjʊləʳ] *adj* cardiovasculaire.

cardoon [kɑːˈduːn] *n* cardon *m*.

cardphone [ˈkɑːdfəʊn] *n Br* téléphone *m* à carte.

cardplayer [ˈkɑːdˌpleɪəʳ] *n* joueur *m*, -euse *f* de cartes.

cardpunch [ˈkɑːdpʌntʃ] *n* perforatrice *f* de cartes.

Cards *written abbr of* Cardiganshire.

cardsharp(er) [ˈkɑːdˌʃɑːpəʳ] *n* tricheur *m* (professionnel aux cartes), tricheuse *f* (professionnelle aux cartes).

card table *n* table *f* de jeu.

card trick *n* tour *m* de cartes.

card vote *n Br* vote *m* sur carte *(chaque voix représentant le nombre de voix d'adhérents représentés)*.

cardy *inf* (*pl* cardies) [ˈkɑːdɪ] = **cardie**.

care [keəʳ] ◇ *vi* **-1.** [feel concern]: **to ~ about sthg** s'intéresser à OR se soucier de qqch; **all you ~ about is your work!** il n'y a que ton travail qui t'intéresse!; **they really do ~ about the project** le projet est vraiment important pour eux; **a book for all those who ~ about the environment** un livre pour tous ceux qui s'intéressent à l'environnement OR qui se sentent concernés par les problèmes d'environnement; **she didn't seem to ~ at all** elle avait l'air de s'en moquer complètement; **I don't ~ what people think** je me moque de ce que pensent les gens; **when do you want to tell them? — I don't ~** quand veux-tu leur dire? — ça m'est égal; **I couldn't ~ less if he comes or not** ça m'est complètement égal qu'il vienne ou non; **what do I ~?** qu'est-ce que ça peut me faire?; **we could be dead for all he ~s** pour lui, nous pourrions aussi bien être morts; **they don't ~ a damn** *inf* ils s'en fichent éperdument OR comme de leur première chemise; **who ~s?** qu'est-ce que ça peut bien faire? **-2.** [feel affection]: **to ~ about** OR **for sb** aimer qqn; **do you still ~ about** OR **for her?** est-ce que tu l'aimes toujours?; **she ~s a lot about her family** elle est très attachée OR elle tient beaucoup à sa famille. **-3.** *fml* [like]: **would you ~ to join us?** voulez-vous vous joindre à nous?; **would you ~ to have a cup of coffee?** prendriez-vous OR aimeriez-vous une tasse de café?; **I was more nervous than I ~d to admit** j'étais plus intimidé que je ne voulais le dire; **the house is available whenever you ~ to use it** la maison est disponible quand vous voulez OR à n'importe quel moment; **I wouldn't ~ to go back there** cela ne me dit rien d'y retourner.

◇ *n* **-1.** [worry] ennui *m*, souci *m*; **you look as though you haven't a ~ in the world** on dirait que tu n'as pas le moindre souci; **weighed down by ~** *Br* accablé de soucis. **-2.** *(U)* [treatment - of person] soin *m*, soins *mpl*, traitement *m*; [- of machine, material] entretien *m*; **nursing ~** soins à domicile; **you should take ~ of that cough** vous devriez (faire) soigner cette toux; **she needs special ~** elle a besoin de soins spécialisés. **-3.** *(U)* [attention] attention *f*, soin *m*; **they worked with great ~** ils ont travaillé avec le plus grand soin; **'handle with ~'** [on package] 'fragile'; **take ~ not to offend her** faites attention à OR prenez soin de ne pas la vexer; **take ~ not to spill the paint** prenez garde de OR faites attention à ne pas renverser la peinture; **drive with ~** conduisez prudemment; **he was charged with driving without due ~ or attention** il a été accusé de conduite négligente; **have a ~!** *Br dated* prenez garde!, faites attention! **-4.** [protection, supervision] charge *f*, garde *f*; **I'm leaving the matter in your ~** je vous confie l'affaire, je confie l'affaire à vos soins; **the children are in the ~ of a nanny** on a laissé OR confié les enfants à une nurse OR à la garde d'une nurse; **he is under the ~ of a heart specialist** c'est un cardiologue qui le traite OR qui le soigne; **who will take ~ of your cat?** qui va s'occuper OR prendre soin de ton chat?; **I'll take ~ of the reservations** je me charge des réservations OR de faire les réservations, je vais m'occuper des réservations; **I have important business to take ~ of** j'ai une affaire importante à expédier; **take ~ (of yourself)** *expression affectueuse que l'on utilise lorsque l'on quitte quelqu'un*; **don't worry about me, I can take ~ of myself** ne vous faites pas de soucis pour moi, je peux OR je sais me débrouiller (tout seul); **the problem will take ~ of itself** le problème va s'arranger tout seul; **address the letter to me (in) ~ of Mrs Dodd** adressez-moi la lettre chez Mme Dodd. **-5.** *Br* ADMIN: **the baby was put in ~** OR **taken into ~** on a retiré aux parents la garde de leur bébé.

◆ **care for** *vt insep* **-1.** [look after - child] s'occuper de; [- invalid] soigner; **I'm glad to see you're being well ~d for** [child] je suis contente de voir qu'on s'occupe bien de toi; [invalid] je suis contente de voir qu'on te soigne bien. **-2.** [like] aimer; **he still ~s for her** [loves] il l'aime toujours; [has affection for] il est toujours attaché à elle, il tient toujours à elle; **I didn't ~ for his last book** son dernier livre ne m'a pas plu, je n'ai pas aimé son dernier livre; **she didn't ~ for the way he spoke** la façon dont il a parlé lui a déplu; **would you ~ for a cup of coffee?** *fml* aimeriez-vous OR voudriez-vous une tasse de café?

CARE [keəʳ] (*abbr of* Cooperative for American Relief Everywhere) *pr n organisation humanitaire américaine*.

care attendant *n Br* ADMIN infirmier *m*, -ère *f* à domicile.

careen [kəˈriːn] ◇ *vi* [car, train] tanguer; [ship] donner de la bande (de façon dangereuse).

◇ *vt* [car] faire tanguer; [ship] caréner.

career [kəˈrɪəʳ] ◇ *n* **-1.** [profession] carrière *f*, profession *f*; **a ~ in banking** une carrière dans la banque OR de banquier; **she made a ~ (for herself) in politics** elle a fait carrière dans la politique. **-2.** [life] vie *f*, carrière *f*; **he spent most of his ~ working as a journalist** il a travaillé presque toute sa vie comme journaliste; **her university ~** son parcours universitaire.

◇ *vi Br*: **the car ~ed wildly down the hill** la voiture a descendu la colline à toute vitesse; **to ~ along** aller à toute vitesse OR à toute allure.

◇ *comp* [diplomat, soldier] de carrière; **to be ~-minded** être ambitieux; **the job offers good ~ prospects** le poste offre de bonnes possibilités d'avancement.

◆ **careers** *comp* SCH & UNIV: **~s advisor** conseiller *m*, -ère *f* d'orientation professionnelle; **~s guidance** orientation *f* professionnelle; **~s master** conseiller *m* d'orientation professionnelle; **~s mistress** conseillère *f* d'orientation professionnelle; **~s office** centre *m* d'orientation professionnelle.

career girl *n Br* jeune fille *f* ambitieuse OR qui ne pense qu'à sa carrière.

careerism [kəˈrɪərɪzm] *n pej* carriérisme *m*.

careerist [kəˈrɪərɪst] *n pej* carriériste *mf*.

career woman *n Br* femme *f* ambitieuse OR qui ne pense qu'à sa carrière.

carefree ['keəfriː] *adj* [person] sans souci, insouciant; [look, smile] insouciant.

careful ['keəfʊl] *adj* -**1.** [cautious] prudent; be ~! (faites) attention!; be ~ of the wet floor! attention au sol mouillé!; be ~ to close the window before leaving n'oubliez pas de fermer la fenêtre avant de partir; be ~ not to OR be ~ you don't hurt her feelings faites attention à OR prenez soin de ne pas la froisser; be ~ (that) the boss doesn't find out faites attention OR prenez garde que le patron n'en sache rien; be ~ how you hold the baby fais attention à la façon dont tu prends le bébé; be ~ crossing the road fais attention en traversant OR quand tu traverses (la route); you can never be too ~ [gen] on n'est jamais assez prudent; [in double-checking sthg] deux précautions valent mieux qu'une; he was ~ not to mention her name il a pris soin de ne pas mentionner son nom; to be ~ with one's money [gen] être parcimonieux; *pej* être près de ses sous; we have to be ~ with money this month il faut que nous surveillions nos dépenses ce mois-ci. -**2.** [thorough - person, work] soigneux, consciencieux; [- consideration, examination] approfondi; they showed ~ attention to detail ils se sont montrés très attentifs aux détails.

carefully ['keəflɪ] *adv* -**1.** [cautiously] avec prudence OR précaution, prudemment; she chose her words ~ elle a pesé ses mots. -**2.** [thoroughly - work] soigneusement, avec soin; [- consider, examine] de façon approfondie, à fond; [- listen, watch] attentivement.

carefulness ['keəfʊlnɪs] *n* -**1.** [caution] prudence *f*. -**2.** [thoroughness] attention *f*, soin *m*.

careless ['keəlɪs] *adj* -**1.** [negligent - person] négligent, peu soigneux; [- work] peu soigné; a ~ mistake une faute d'inattention; he's very ~ about his appearance il ne se soucie pas du tout de son apparence; ~ of the consequences insouciant des conséquences; to be ~ with money dépenser à tort et à travers. -**2.** [thoughtless - remark] irréfléchi. -**3.** [carefree - person] sans souci, insouciant; [- look, smile] insouciant; she danced with ~ grace elle dansait avec une grâce naturelle.

carelessly ['keəlɪslɪ] *adv* -**1.** [negligently - work, write] sans soin, sans faire attention; to drive ~ conduire avec négligence. -**2.** [thoughtlessly - act, speak] sans réfléchir, à la légère; [- dress] sans soin, sans recherche. -**3.** [in carefree way] avec insouciance.

carelessness ['keəlɪsnɪs] *n* *(U)* -**1.** [negligence] négligence *f*, manque *m* de soin OR d'attention. -**2.** [thoughtlessness - of dress] négligence *f*; [- of behaviour] désinvolture *f*; [- of remark] légèreté *f*.

carer ['keərəʳ] *n terme administratif désignant toute personne qui s'occupe d'un malade ou d'un handicapé*.

caress [kə'res] ◇ *vt* caresser.
◇ *n* caresse *f*.

caret ['kærət] *n* TYPO signe *m* d'insertion.

caretaker ['keəˌteɪkəʳ] ◇ *n* -**1.** [of building] concierge *mf*, gardien *m*, -enne *f*. -**2.** *Am* [carer]: he's his grandmother's ~ il a sa grande-mère à charge.
◇ *adj* [government] intérimaire.

careworn ['keəwɔːn] *adj* accablé de soucis, rongé par les soucis.

carfare ['kɑːfeəʳ] *n Am* prix *m* du trajet.

carfax ['kɑːfæks] *n* carrefour *m*.

car ferry *n* ferry-boat *m*.

cargo ['kɑːgəʊ] (*pl* cargoes OR cargos) ◇ *n* cargaison *f*, chargement *m*.
◇ *comp*: ~ boat OR vessel cargo *m*.

car hire *n Br* location *f* de voitures.

carhop *inf* ['kɑːˌhɒp] *n Am* [serving food] serveur *m*, -euse *f (qui apporte à manger aux clients dans leur voiture)*.

Carib ['kærɪb] *n* -**1.** [person] Caraïbe *mf*. -**2.** LING caraïbe *m*.

Caribbean [*Br* kærɪ'biːən, *Am* kə'rɪbɪən] ◇ *adj* des Caraïbes; a ~ cruise une croisière aux Caraïbes; the ~ islands les Antilles *fpl*.
◇ *n*: the ~ (Sea) la mer des Caraïbes OR des Antilles; in the ~ dans les Caraïbes, aux Antilles.

caribou ['kærɪbuː] (*pl inv* OR caribous) *n* caribou *m*.

caricature ['kærɪkəˌtjʊəʳ] ◇ *n literal & fig* caricature *f*.
◇ *vt* [depict] caricaturer; [parody] caricaturer, parodier.

caricaturist ['kærɪkəˌtjʊərɪst] *n* caricaturiste *mf*.

caries ['keəriːz] (*pl inv*) *n* carie *f*.

carillon ['kærɪljən] *n* carillon *m*.

caring ['keərɪŋ] ◇ *adj* -**1.** [loving] aimant; [kindly] bienveillant; a more ~ society une société plus chaleureuse OR humaine; a ~ environment un milieu chaleureux. -**2.** [organization, profession] à vocation sociale.
◇ *n* [loving] affection *f*; [kindliness] bienveillance *f*.

Carinthia [kə'rɪnθɪə] *pr n* Carinthie *f*; in ~ en Carinthie.

cariogenic [ˌkeərɪəʊ'dʒenɪk] *adj* cariant, cariogène.

carious ['keərɪəs] *adj* carié.

carload ['kɑːˌləʊd] *n*: a ~ of boxes/people une voiture pleine de cartons/de gens.

carman ['kɑːmən] (*pl* carmen [-mən]) *n* -**1.** [driver - of car] chauffeur *m*, conducteur *m*; [- of lorry] camionneur *m*; [- of cart] charretier *m*. -**2.** [transporter] voiturier *m*. -**3.** *Am* chauffeur *m (de tram, de métro)*.

Carmel ['kɑːməl] *pr n*: Mount ~ le mont Carmel.

Carmelite ['kɑːmɪlaɪt] ◇ *adj* carmélite.
◇ *n* [nun] carmélite *f*; [friar] carme *m*.

carminative ['kɑːmɪnətɪv] ◇ *adj* carminatif.
◇ *n* carminatif *m*.

carmine ['kɑːmaɪn] ◇ *adj* carmin *(inv)*, carminé.
◇ *n* carmin *m*.

Carnaby Street ['kɑːnəbɪ-] *pr n rue de Londres*.

CARNABY STREET:
Carnaby Street était, dans les années 60, le haut lieu des milieux branchés; c'est aujourd'hui une rue spécialisée dans la fripe.

---

carnage ['kɑːnɪdʒ] *n* carnage *m*.

carnal ['kɑːnl] *adj* charnel; to have ~ knowledge of sb *fml* OR JUR avoir des rapports sexuels avec qqn.

carnally ['kɑːnəlɪ] *adv* charnellement; to know sb ~ *fml* OR JUR avoir des rapports sexuels avec qqn.

carnation [kɑː'neɪʃn] ◇ *n* œillet *m*.
◇ *adj* [pink] rose; [reddish-pink] incarnat.

Carnegie Hall [kɑː'negɪ-] *pr n grande salle de concert à New York*.

carnelian [kə'niːljən] *n* cornaline *f*.

carnet ['kɑːneɪ] *n* -**1.** [book of tickets] carnet *m*. -**2.** COMM & JUR passavant *m*.

carnival ['kɑːnɪvl] ◇ *n* -**1.** [festival] carnaval *m*. -**2.** [fun fair] fête *f* foraine.
◇ *comp* [atmosphere, parade] de carnaval.

carnivora [kɑː'nɪvərə] *npl* carnivores *mpl*.

carnivore ['kɑːnɪvɔːʳ] *n* carnivore *m*, carnassier *m*.

carnivorous [kɑː'nɪvərəs] *adj* carnivore, carnassier.

carob ['kærəb] ◇ *n* [tree] caroubier *m*; [pod] caroube *f*.
◇ *comp*: ~ bean caroube *f*; ~ cake gâteau *m* à la caroube; ~ powder farine *f* de caroube; ~ tree caroubier *m*.

carol ['kærəl] (*Br pt & pp* carolled, *cont* carolling, *Am pt & pp* caroled, *cont* caroling) ◇ *n* chant *m* (joyeux); ~ service *office religieux qui précède Noël*; ~ singer *personne qui, à l'époque de Noël, va chanter et quêter au profit des bonnes œuvres*; Christmas ~ chant de Noël, noël *m*.
◇ *vi* [person] chanter (joyeusement); [baby, bird] gazouiller; to go carolling chanter des noëls.
◇ *vt* -**1.** [sing - subj: person] chanter (joyeusement); [- subj: bird] chanter. -**2.** [praise] célébrer (par des chants).

CAROL SERVICE:
Le «Carol Service» se tient juste avant Noël et se compose surtout de chants de Noël et de lectures de la Bible.

Carolina [ˌkærə'laɪnə] *pr n* Caroline *f*; North/South ~ Caroline du Nord/du Sud.

Caroline Islands ['kærəˌlaɪn-] *pl pr n*: the ~ les îles *fpl* Carolines; in the ~ aux îles Carolines.

Carolingian [ˌkærə'lɪndʒɪən] ◇ *adj* carolingien.
◇ *n* Carolingien *m*, -enne *f*.

carom ['kærəm] *Am* ◇ *n* carambolage *m*.
◇ *vi* caramboler.

carotene ['kærəˌtiːn] *n* carotène *m*.

carotid [kə'rɒtɪd] ◇ *adj* [artery] carotide; [nerve, system] carotidien.
◇ *n* carotide *f*.

carotin ['kærətɪn] = **carotene**.

carousal [kə'raʊzl] *n lit* beuverie *f*, ribote *f arch* OR *hum*.

carouse [kə'raʊz] *vi lit* faire ribote *arch* OR *hum*.

carousel [ˌkærə'sel] *n* -**1.** PHOT [for slides] carrousel *m*. -**2.** [for luggage] carrousel *m*, tapis *m* roulant (à bagages). -**3.** *Am* [merry-go-round] manège *m* (de chevaux de bois).

carp [kɑːp] (*pl inv* OR carps) ◇ *n* [fish] carpe *f*.
◇ *vi inf* [complain] se plaindre; [find fault] critiquer; he's always ~ing on about his work il se plaint toujours de son travail.

carpal ['kɑːpəl] ANAT ◇ *n* carpe *m*.
◇ *adj* carpien.

car park *n Br* parking *m*, parc *m* de stationnement; long/short stay ~ parking longue/courte durée.

Carpathian Mountains [kɑː'peɪθɪən-], **Carpathians** [kɑː'peɪθɪənz] *pl pr n*: the ~ les Carpates *fpl*; in the ~ dans les Carpates.

carpel ['kɑːpel] *n* BOT carpelle *m*.

carpenter ['kɑːpəntəʳ] *n* [for houses, large-scale works] charpentier *m*; [for doors, furniture] menuisier *m*.

carpentry ['kɑːpəntrɪ] *n* [large-scale work] charpenterie *f*; [doors, furniture] menuiserie *f*.

carpet ['kɑːpɪt] ◇ *n* -**1.** [not fitted] tapis *m*; [fitted] moquette *f*; to be on the ~ *fig* être sur le tapis. -**2.** *fig* [of leaves, snow] tapis *m*.
◇ *vt* -**1.** [floor] recouvrir d'un tapis; [with fitted carpet] recouvrir d'une moquette, moquetter; [house, room] mettre de la moquette dans, moquetter; ~ed hallway couloir moquetté OR avec de la moquette; the road was ~ed with leaves/snow *fig* la route était tapissée de feuilles/de neige. -**2.** *inf Br* [scold] réprimander, passer un savon à.

carpetbag ['kɑːpɪtˌbæg] *n* sac *m* de voyage *(recouvert de tapisserie)*.

carpetbagger ['kɑːpɪtˌbægəʳ] *n pej* -**1.** POL candidat *m* parachuté. -**2.** *Am* HIST *nom donné aux nordistes qui s'installèrent dans le Sud des États-Unis après la guerre de Sécession pour y faire fortune*.

carpet beetle *n* anthrène *m*.

carpet-bomb *vt* bombarder, arroser de bombes.

carpeting ['kɑːpɪtɪŋ] *n* moquette *f*.

carpet slipper *n* pantoufle *f (recouverte de tapisserie)*.

carpet sweeper *n* [mechanical] balai *m* mécanique; [electric] aspirateur *m*.

carpet tile *n* carreau *m* de moquette.

carphone ['kɑːˌfəʊn] *n* téléphone *m* de voiture.

carping ['kɑːpɪŋ] ◇ *adj* [person - complaining] qui se plaint tout le temps; [- faultfinding] qui trouve toujours à redire, chicanier; [attitude] chicanier, grincheux; [criticism, voice] malveillant.

◇ *n (U)* [complaining] plaintes *fpl* (continuelles); [faultfinding] chicanerie *f*, critiques *fpl* (malveillantes).

car pool *n groupe de personnes qui s'organise pour utiliser la même voiture afin de se rendre à une destination commune.*

carport ['kɑː,pɔːt] *n* auvent *m* (pour voiture).

carrag(h)een ['kærəgiːn] *n* carragheen *m*, mousse *f* d'Irlande.

carriage ['kærɪdʒ] *n* **-1.** [vehicle - horse-drawn] calèche *f*, voiture *f* à cheval; *Br* RAIL voiture *f*, wagon *m* (de voyageurs); ~ **and four** *Br* voiture OR équipage *m* à quatre chevaux. **-2.** *Br* COMM [cost of transportation] transport *m*, fret *m*; ~ **forward** (en) port *m* dû; ~ **paid** (en) port *m* payé; ~ **free** franco de port. **-3.** [bearing, posture] port *m*, maintien *m*. **-4.** [of typewriter] chariot *m*; [of gun] affût *m*.

carriage bolt *n Am* boulon *m* à tête ronde et collet carré.

carriage clock *n Br* horloge *f* de voyage.

carriage trade *n Br* COMM clientèle *f* riche.

carriageway ['kærɪdʒweɪ] *n Br* chaussée *f*.

carrier ['kærɪə^r] *n* **-1.** [device, mechanism]: **baby** ~ porte-bébé *m inv*; **luggage** ~ porte-bagages *m inv*. **-2.** COMM [transporter - company] entreprise *f* de transport, transporteur *m*; [- aeroplane] appareil *m*, avion *m*; [- ship] navire *m*; **sent by** ~ [by road] expédié par camion OR par transporteur; [by rail] expédié par chemin de fer; [by air] expédié par avion; **common** ~ transporteur *m* (public). **-3.** MIL: **(aircraft)** ~ porte-avions *m inv*; **(personnel** OR **troop)** ~ [aeroplane] appareil *m* transporteur (de troupes); [ship] navire *m* transporteur (de troupes), transport *m* de troupes. **-4.** MED [of disease] porteur *m*, -euse *f*.

carrier bag *n Br* sac *m* en plastique.

carrier pigeon *n* pigeon *m* voyageur.

carrier wave *n* RADIO onde *f* porteuse.

carrion ['kærɪən] *n* charogne *f*.

carrion crow *n* corneille *f* noire.

carrot ['kærət] ◇ *n* **-1.** [plant & vegetable] carotte *f*. **-2.** *fig* [motivation] carotte *f*; **the boss used the promise of promotion as a** ~ le patron a promis une promotion pour nous encourager; **the** ~ **and stick approach** la méthode de la carotte et du bâton.

◇ *comp* [flavour] de carotte; ~ **coloured** (de couleur) carotte *(inv)*; ~ **cake** gâteau *m* aux carottes.

carroty ['kærətɪ] *adj* carotte *(inv)*, roux; **she has** ~ **hair** elle est rousse OR poil-de-carotte *hum*.

carrousel [,kærə'sel] = **carousel**.

carry ['kærɪ] (*pt* & *pp* **carried**) ◇ *vt* **-1.** [bear - subj: person] porter; [- heavy load] porter, transporter; **she carried her baby on her back/in her arms** elle portait son enfant sur son dos/dans ses bras; **they carried the equipment across the bridge** ils ont porté le matériel de l'autre côté du pont; **could you** ~ **the groceries into the kitchen?** pourrais-tu porter les provisions jusqu'à la cuisine?; **the porter carried the suitcases downstairs/upstairs** le porteur a descendu/monté les bagages. **-2.** [convey, transport - subj: vehicle] transporter; [- subj: river, wind] porter, emporter; [- subj: pipe] acheminer, amener; [- subj: airwaves, telephone wire] transmettre, conduire; **she ran as fast as her legs would** ~ **her** elle a couru à toutes jambes; **she carries all the facts in her head** elle a tous les faits en mémoire; **he carried the secret to his grave** il a emporté le secret dans la tombe ❑ **to** ~ **a tune** chanter juste; **to** ~ **coals to Newcastle** porter de l'eau à la rivière. **-3.** [be medium for - message, news] porter, transmettre; MED [- disease, virus] porter. **-4.** [have on one's person - identity card, papers] porter, avoir (sur soi); [- cash] avoir (sur soi); [- gun] porter. **-5.** [comprise, include] porter, comporter; **our products** ~ **a 6-month warranty** nos produits sont accompagnés d'une garantie de 6 mois || [have as consequence] entraîner; **the crime carries a long sentence** ce crime est passible d'une longue peine. **-6.** [subj: magazine, newspaper] rapporter; [subj: radio, television] transmettre; **all the newspapers carried the story** l'histoire était dans tous les journaux; **the banners carried anti-government slogans** les bannières portaient des slogans anti-gouvernementaux. **-7.** [bear, hold] porter; **to** ~ **o.s. well** [sit, stand] se tenir droit; [behave] bien se conduire OR se tenir. **-8.** [hold up, support - roof, weight] porter, supporter, soutenir; **to** ~ **a heavy load** *literal* & *fig* porter un lourd fardeau. **-9.** [win]: **she carried the audience with her** le public était avec elle; **the motion was carried** la motion a été votée ❑ **he carried all before him** ce fut un triomphe pour lui. **-10.** COMM [deal in - stock] vendre, stocker. **-11.** MATH retenir; **add nine and** ~ **one** ajoute neuf et retiens un. **-12.** [be pregnant with] attendre; **she's** ~**ing their fourth child** elle est enceinte de leur quatrième enfant. **-13.** *phr*: **to** ~ **the can** *inf Br* payer les pots cassés.

◇ *vi* [ball, sound] porter.

◆ **carry away** *vt sep* **-1.** [remove] emporter, enlever; [subj: waves, wind] emporter. **-2.** *(usu pass)* [excite]: **he was carried away by his enthusiasm/imagination** il s'est laissé emporter par son enthousiasme/imagination; **I got a bit carried away and spent all my money** je me suis emballé et j'ai dépensé tout mon argent; **don't get too carried away!** du calme!, ne t'emballe pas!

◆ **carry forward** *vt sep* FIN reporter.

◆ **carry off** *vt sep* **-1.** [remove forcibly - goods] emporter, enlever; [- person] enlever; **the thieves carried off all their jewellery** les voleurs se sont enfuis avec tous leurs bijoux. **-2.** [award, prize] remporter. **-3.** [do successfully - aim, plan] réaliser; [- deal, meeting] mener à bien; **she carried it off beautifully** elle s'en est très bien tirée. **-4.** *euph* [kill - subj: disease] emporter; **hundreds were carried off by the epidemic** des centaines de personnes ont été emportées par l'épidémie.

◆ **carry on** ◇ *vi insep* **-1.** *Br* [continue] continuer; **she carried on working** OR **with her work** elle a continué à travailler, elle a continué son travail; **they carried on to the bitter end** ils sont allés jusqu'au bout. **-2.** *inf* [make a fuss] faire une histoire OR des histoires; **the way you** ~ **on, you'd think I never did anything around the house** à t'entendre, je n'ai jamais rien fait dans cette maison. **-3.** *inf* [have affair] avoir une liaison; **he's** ~**ing on with somebody else's wife** il a une liaison avec OR il couche avec la femme d'un autre ❑ **'Carry On' films** *série de comédies britanniques, dont le titre commence toujours par «Carry On».*

◇ *vt insep* **-1.** *Br* [continue - conversation, work] continuer, poursuivre; [- tradition] entretenir, perpétuer; **we can** ~ **on this conversation later** nous pourrons poursuivre OR reprendre cette conversation plus tard. **-2.** [conduct - work] effectuer, réaliser; [- negotiations] mener; [- discussion] avoir; [- correspondence] entretenir.

◆ **carry out** *vt sep* **-1.** [take away] emporter. **-2.** [perform - programme, raid] effectuer; [- idea, plan] réaliser, mettre à exécution; [- experiment] effectuer, conduire; [- investigation, research, survey] conduire, mener; [- instruction, order] exécuter. **-3.** [fulfil - obligation] s'acquitter de; **he failed to** ~ **out his promise** il a manqué à sa parole, il n'a pas tenu OR respecté sa promesse; **to** ~ **out one's (professional) duties** s'acquitter de ses fonctions.

◆ **carry over** *vt sep* **-1.** *literal* [transport] faire traverser; *fig* [transfer] reporter, transférer. **-2.** [defer, postpone] reporter. **-3.** FIN reporter; **to** ~ **over a loss to the following year** reporter une perte sur l'année suivante. **-4.** COMM: **to** ~ **over goods from one season to another** stocker des marchandises d'une saison sur l'autre.

◆ **carry through** *vt sep* **-1.** [accomplish] réaliser, mener à bien OR à bonne fin. **-2.** [support] soutenir (dans une épreuve); **her love of life carried her through her illness** sa volonté de vivre lui a permis de vaincre sa maladie.

carryall ['kærɪɔːl] *n Am* fourre-tout *m inv (sac)*.

carrycot ['kærɪkɒt] *n Br* couffin *m*.

carrying case ['kærɪɪŋ-] *n Am* boîte *f*, étui *m*.

carrying charge *n Am* supplément *m (que l'on paye lorsqu'on achète à crédit)*.

carrying-on *inf* (*pl* **carryings-on**) *n* [fuss] histoires *fpl*; [commotion] tapage *m*, agitation *f*.

carryon ['kærɪɒn] *n Am* [suitcase] bagage *m* à main.

carry-on *inf n Br* [fuss] histoires *fpl*; [commotion] tapage *m*, agitation *f*; **what a** ~! que d'histoires!

carryout ['kærɪaʊt] *Am* & *Scot* ◇ *n* [restaurant] restaurant *m* qui fait des plats à emporter; [meal] plat *m* à emporter.

◇ *adj* [dish, food] à emporter.

carry-over *n* **-1.** [habit, influence, trace] vestige *m*. **-2.** FIN [amount] report *m*.

carsick ['kɑː,sɪk] *adj*: **to be** OR **to feel** ~ avoir le mal de la route.

car sickness *n* mal *m* de la route; **to suffer from** ~ être malade en voiture.

cart [kɑːt] ◇ *n* **-1.** [horse-drawn - for farming] charrette *f*; [- for passengers] charrette *f* (anglaise), voiture *f*; **to put the** ~ **before the horse** mettre la charrue avant les bœufs. **-2.** [handcart] charrette *f* à bras.

◇ *vt* **-1.** [transport by cart] charrier, charroyer, transporter en charrette. **-2.** *inf fig* [haul] transporter, trimballer; **I've been** ~**ing this suitcase around all day** j'ai passé la journée à trimballer cette valise.

◆ **cart away, cart off** *vt sep* [rubbish, wood] emporter; [person] *inf* emmener.

cartage ['kɑːtɪdʒ] *n* charroi *m*.

Cartagena [,kɑːtə'dʒiːnə] *pr n* Carthagène.

carte blanche [,kɑːt'blɑ̃ʃ] *n* carte *f* blanche; **to give sb** ~ **(to do sthg)** donner carte blanche à qqn (pour faire qqch).

cartel [kɑː'tel] *n* COMM & POL cartel *m*.

carter ['kɑːtə^r] *n* charretier *m*, -ère *f*.

Cartesian [kɑː'tiːzjən] ◇ *adj* cartésien.

◇ *n* cartésien *m*, -enne *f*.

Carthage ['kɑːθɪdʒ] *pr n* Carthage.

Carthaginian [,kɑːθə'dʒɪnɪən] ◇ *n* Carthaginois *m*, -e *f*.

◇ *adj* carthaginois.

carthorse ['kɑːthɔːs] *n* cheval *m* de trait.

Carthusian [kɑː'θjuːzjən] ◇ *adj* de OR des chartreux; ~ **monastery** chartreuse *f (monastère)*; ~ **monk** chartreux *m*; ~ **nun** chartreuse *f*.

◇ *n* chartreux *m*, -euse *f*.

cartilage ['kɑːtɪlɪdʒ] *n* cartilage *m*.

cartilaginous [,kɑːtɪ'lædʒɪnəs] *adj* cartilagineux.

cartload ['kɑːtləʊd] *n* charretée *f*.

cartogram ['kɑːtəgræm] *n* cartogramme *m*.

cartographer [kɑː'tɒgrəfə^r] *n* cartographe *mf*.

cartographic(al) [,kɑːtə'græfɪk(l)] *adj* cartographique.

cartography [kɑː'tɒgrəfɪ] *n* cartographie *f*.

cartomancy ['kɑːtəʊmænsɪ] *n* cartomancie *f*.

carton ['kɑːtn] *n* [cardboard box] boîte *f* (en carton), carton *m*; [of juice, milk] carton *m*, brique *f*; [of cream, yoghurt] pot *m*; [of cigarettes] cartouche *f*.

cartoon [kɑː'tuːn] *n* **-1.** [drawing] dessin *m* humoristique; [series of drawings] bande *f* dessinée. **-2.** [film] dessin *m* animé. **-3.** ART [sketch] carton *m*.

cartoonist [kɑː'tuːnɪst] *n* [of drawings] dessinateur *m*, -trice *f* humoristique; [of series of drawings] dessinateur *m*, -trice *f* de bandes dessinées; [for films] dessinateur *m*, -trice *f* de dessins animés, animateur *m*, -trice *f*.

cartridge ['kɑːtrɪdʒ] *n* **-1.** [for explosive, gun] cartouche *f*. **-2.** [for pen, tape deck, typewriter etc] cartouche *f*. **-3.** [for stylus] cellule *f*. **-4.** PHOT chargeur *m* (d'appareil photo).

cartridge belt *n* [for hunter, soldier] cartouchière *f*; [for machine gun] bande *f* (de mitrailleuse).

cartridge case *n* [for gun] douille *f*, étui *m* (de cartouche); [for cannon] douille *f*.

cartridge clip *n* chargeur *m (d'une arme à feu)*.

cartridge paper *n* papier *m* à cartouche.

cartridge pen *n* stylo *m* à cartouche.

cart track *n* chemin *m* de terre.

cartwheel ['kɑːtwiːl] ◇ *n* -**1.** [of cart] roue *f* de charrette. -**2.** [movement] roue *f*; **to do** OR **to turn a ~** faire la roue.
◇ *vi* faire la roue; **she ~ed across the floor** elle a traversé la pièce en faisant des roues.

cartwright ['kɑːtraɪt] *n* charron *m*.

caruncle ['kærəŋkl] *n* ANAT, BOT & ZOOL caroncule *f*.

carve [kɑːv] *vt* -**1.** [stone, wood] tailler; **he ~d the wood into the form of a horse, he ~d a horse from the** OR **out of the wood** il a sculpté OR taillé un cheval dans le bois; **she ~d their names on the tree trunk** elle a gravé leurs noms sur le tronc de l'arbre; **the river had ~d a channel through the rock** la rivière s'était creusé un lit dans le rocher. -**2.** CULIN découper.
◆ **carve out** *vt sep* [piece] découper, tailler; [shape] sculpter, tailler; **to ~ a figure out of marble** tailler une silhouette dans du marbre; **she ~d out a career for herself in the arts** *fig* elle a fait carrière OR elle a fait son chemin dans le monde de l'art.
◆ **carve up** *vt sep* -**1.** [cut up - meat] découper; *fig* [- country, estate] morceler, démembrer; **they ~d up the profits among them** ils se sont partagé les profits. -**2.** *inf* [person] amocher à coups de couteau; [face] balafrer, taillader. -**3.** *inf Br* AUT faire une queue de poisson à.

carver ['kɑːvə^r] *n* couteau *m* à découper; **~s** service *m* à découper.

carvery ['kɑːvərɪ] (*pl* **carveries**) *n restaurant où l'on mange de la viande découpée à table*.

carve-up *inf n* [of booty, inheritance] fractionnement *m*; [of country, estate] morcellement *m*, démembrement *m*.

carving ['kɑːvɪŋ] *n* -**1.** [sculpture] sculpture *f*; [engraving] gravure *f*. -**2.** [act] taille *f*; [skill] taille *f*, art *m* de la taille. -**3.** CULIN découpage *m*.

carving knife *n* couteau *m* à découper.

car wash *n* [place] portique *m* de lavage automatique (de voitures); [action] lavage *m* de voitures.

caryatid [kærɪ'ætɪd] *n* cariatide *f*.

Casablanca [ˌkæsə'blæŋkə] *pr n* Casablanca.

Casanova [ˌkæsə'nəʊvə] ◇ *pr n* Casanova.
◇ *n*: **he's a real ~** c'est un vrai Don Juan.

casbah ['kæzbɑː] *n* casbah *f*.

cascade [kæ'skeɪd] ◇ *n literal* cascade *f*, chute *f* d'eau; *fig* [of hair] flot *m*.
◇ *vi* [water] tomber en cascade; [hair] ruisseler.

cascara [kæ'skɑːrə] *n* cascara *f*.

case [keɪs] ◇ *n* **A.** -**1.** [container] caisse *f*, boîte *f*; [for bottles] caisse *f*; [for fruit, vegetables] cageot *m*; [chest] coffre *m*; [for jewellery] coffret *m*; [for necklace, watch] écrin *m*; [for camera, guitar] étui *m*. -**2.** [for display] vitrine *f*. -**3.** *Br* [suitcase] valise *f*. -**4.** TYPO casse *f*. -**5.** BOT & ENTOM [covering] enveloppe *f*.
B. -**1.** [instance, situation] cas *m*, exemple *m*; **it's a clear ~ of mismanagement** c'est un exemple manifeste de mauvaise gestion; **it was a ~ of having to decide on the spur of the moment** il fallait décider sur-le-champ; **we often hear of ~s where companies go bankrupt** nous entendons souvent parler de cas où des entreprises font faillite; **in the ~ of single mothers** dans le cas des mères célibataires; **in that ~** dans OR en ce cas; **in this particular ~** en l'occurrence; **in which ~** auquel cas; **in your ~** en ce qui vous concerne, dans votre cas; **in Paul's ~** dans le cas de Paul; **in many/most ~s** dans beaucoup de/la plupart des cas; **in no ~** en aucun cas; **in some ~s** dans certains cas; **in the vast majority of ~s** dans la plupart des cas; **in nine ~s out of ten** neuf fois sur dix ❑ **the current crisis is a ~ in point** la crise actuelle est un exemple typique OR un bon exemple. -**2.** [actual state of affairs] cas *m*; **can we assume that this is in fact the ~?** pouvons-nous considérer que c'est bien le cas?; **that is not the ~ in Great Britain** ce OR tel n'est pas le cas en Grande-Bretagne; **as is often/usually the ~** comme c'est souvent/ordinairement le cas; **as the ~** OR **whatever the ~ may be** selon le cas; **if such is indeed the ~** si tel est OR si c'est vraiment le cas. -**3.** [investigation] affaire *f*; **it was one of Inspector Dupont's most difficult ~s** ce fut une des affaires les plus difficiles de l'inspecteur Dupont; **a murder/fraud ~** une affaire de meurtre/fraude; **the ~ is closed** c'est une affaire classée ❑ **he's on the ~** [working on it] il s'en occupe; [alert, informed] il est très au courant; **to be on sb's ~** *inf* être sur le dos de qqn; **get off my ~!** *inf* fiche-moi la paix! -**4.** JUR affaire *f*, cause *f*, procès *m*; **a civil rights ~** une affaire de droits civils; **her ~ comes up next week** son procès a lieu la semaine prochaine; **to try a ~** juger une affaire; **he won his ~ for slander** [barrister] il a gagné le procès en diffamation; [plaintiff] il a gagné son procès OR il a eu gain de cause dans son procès en diffamation. -**5.** [argument] arguments *mpl*; **there is no ~ against him** aucune preuve n'a pu être retenue contre lui; **the ~ against/for the defendant** les arguments contre/en faveur de l'accusé; **there is a good ~ against/for establishing quotas** il y a beaucoup à dire contre/en faveur de l'établissement de quotas; **the union has a good ~** le syndicat a de bons arguments OR de bonnes raisons; **state your ~** présentez vos arguments; **there is a ~ to be answered here** il ne faut pas négliger cette question; **to make (out) a ~ for sthg** présenter des arguments pour OR en faveur de qqch. -**6.** MED [disease] cas *m*; [person] malade *mf*; **there have been several ~s of meningitis/hepatitis recently** il y a eu plusieurs cas de méningite/d'hépatite récemment; **the hospital could only take the most serious ~s** l'hôpital ne pouvait s'occuper que des cas les plus graves; **all burns ~s are treated here** tous les grands brûlés sont traités ici. -**7.** *inf* [person] cas *m*; **he's a real ~!** c'est un cas OR un phénomène!; **he's a sad ~** c'est vraiment un pauvre type. -**8.** GRAMM cas *m*.
◇ *vt* -**1.** [put in box] mettre en boîte OR caisse. -**2.** [cover] couvrir, envelopper; **~d in ice** couvert de glace. -**3.** *inf* [inspect] examiner; **the robbers had thoroughly ~d the joint** les voleurs avaient bien examiné les lieux (avant de faire leur coup).
◆ **in any case** *adv phr* -**1.** [besides] en tout cas; **in any ~ I shan't be coming** je ne viendrai pas en tout cas OR de toute façon; **in any ~, that's not the point** bref OR en tout cas, là n'est pas la question. -**2.** [at least] du moins, en tout cas; **that's what I was told, or in any ~ was led to believe** c'est ce qu'on m'a dit ou en tout cas OR ou du moins, ce qu'on m'a fait croire.
◆ **in case** ◇ *adv phr* au cas où; **I'll take my umbrella (just) in ~** je vais prendre mon parapluie au cas où.
◇ *conj phr* au cas où; **in ~ you think I'm bluffing** au cas où tu croirais que je bluffe; **I kept a place for you, in ~ you were late** je t'ai gardé une place, au cas où tu serais en retard.
◆ **in case of** *prep phr* en cas de; **in ~ of emergency/fire** en cas d'urgence/d'incendie.

casebook ['keɪsbʊk] *n* [gen] *recueil de comptes rendus de cas*; JUR recueil *m* de jurisprudence.

casebound ['keɪsbaʊnd] *adj* cartonné.

casefile ['keɪsfaɪl] *n* dossier *m*.

case grammar *n* grammaire *f* des cas.

case-harden *vt* METALL cémenter; *fig* endurcir.

case-hardened *adj* METALL cémenté; *fig* endurci.

case history *n* antécédents *mpl*.

casein ['keɪsiːn] *n* caséine *f*.

case knife *n* couteau *m* à gaine.

case law *n* jurisprudence *f*.

case load *n* (nombre *m* de) dossiers *mpl* à traiter.

casemate ['keɪsmeɪt] *n* casemate *f*.

casement ['keɪsmənt] ◇ *n* [window] fenêtre *f* à battant OR battants, croisée *f*; [window frame] châssis *m* de fenêtre (à deux battants); *lit* fenêtre *f*.
◇ *comp*: **~ window** fenêtre *f* à battant OR battants, croisée *f*.

case study *n* étude *f* de cas.

casework ['keɪswɜːk] *n travail social personnalisé*.

caseworker ['keɪsˌwɜːkə^r] *n travailleur social s'occupant de cas individuels et familiaux*.

cash [kæʃ] ◇ *n* -**1.** [coins and banknotes] espèces *fpl*, (argent *m*) liquide *m*; **I never carry much ~** je n'ai jamais beaucoup d'argent OR de liquide sur moi; **£3,000 in ~** 3 000 livres en espèces OR en liquide; **to pay (in) ~** payer en liquide OR en espèces; **hard** OR **ready ~** espèces *fpl* ❑ **to pay ~ on the nail** payer rubis sur ongle. -**2.** [money in general] argent *m*; **to be short of ~** être à court (d'argent); **I ran out of ~** je n'avais plus d'argent; **they haven't any ~** ils n'ont plus un sou. -**3.** [immediate payment]: **discount for ~** escompte *m* au comptant; **~ down** argent *m* comptant; **to pay ~ down** payer comptant ❑ **~ on delivery** paiement *m* à la livraison, (livraison *f*) contre remboursement; **~ with order** payable à la commande; **~ on shipment** comptant *m* à l'expédition.
◇ *vt* [cheque] encaisser, toucher; **could you ~ this cheque for me?** [friend] peux-tu me donner de l'argent contre ce chèque?; [bank] voudriez-vous m'encaisser ce chèque?
◇ *comp* -**1.** [problems, worries] d'argent. -**2.** [price, purchase, sale, transaction] (au) comptant; **~ bar** *Am* bar *m* payant *(à une réception)*; **~ offer** offre *f* d'achat avec paiement comptant; **she made us a ~ offer for the flat** elle nous a proposé de payer l'appartement (au) comptant; **~ payment** [immediate] paiement *m* comptant; [in cash] paiement *m* en espèces OR en liquide; **~ prize** prix *m* en espèces; **~ terms** conditions *fpl* au comptant; **~ value** valeur *f* vénale.
◆ **cash in** ◇ *vt sep* [bond, certificate] réaliser, se faire rembourser; [coupon] se faire rembourser.
◇ *vi insep inf* [take advantage]: **to ~ in on a situation** profiter OR tirer profit d'une situation; **to ~ in on one's influence/talent** monnayer son influence/talent.
◆ **cash up** *vi insep Br* COMM faire ses comptes.

cashable ['kæʃəbl] *adj* encaissable, payable.

cash and carry *n Br* libre-service *m* de gros, cash and carry *m inv*.
◆ **cash-and-carry** *Br* ◇ *adj* de libre-service de gros, de cash and carry.
◇ *adv* dans un libre-service de gros OR un cash and carry.

cashbook ['kæʃbʊk] *n* livre *m* de caisse.

cashbox ['kæʃbɒks] *n* caisse *f*.

cash card *n* carte *f* bancaire *(qui permet de retirer de l'argent dans les distributeurs automatiques)*.

cash crop *n* culture *f* de rapport OR commerciale.

cash desk *n* caisse *f*.

cash discount *n* escompte *m* au comptant.

cash dispenser *n* distributeur *m* automatique (de billets), DAB *m*.

cashew ['kæʃuː] *n* [tree] anacardier *m*; **~ (nut)** (noix *f* de) cajou *m*.

cash flow *n* marge *f* brute d'autofinancement, cash-flow *m*; **~ problems** *literal* OR *hum* problèmes *mpl* de trésorerie.

cashier [kæ'ʃɪə^r] ◇ *n* BANK & COMM caissier *m*, -ère *f*.
◇ *vt* MIL casser; *fig* renvoyer, congédier.

cashmere [kæʃ'mɪə^r] ◇ *n* cachemire *m*.
◇ *comp* [coat, sweater] de OR en cachemire.

cashpoint ['kæʃpɔɪnt] *n Br* distributeur *m* automatique (de billets), DAB *m*.

cash register *n* caisse *f* (enregistreuse).

casing ['keɪsɪŋ] *n* -**1.** [gen] revêtement *m*, enveloppe *f*; [for tyre] enveloppe *f* extérieure. -**2.** [of window] chambranle *m*, châssis *m*; [of door] encadrement *m*, chambranle *m*.

casino [kə'siːnəʊ] (*pl* casinos) *n* casino *m*.

cask [kɑːsk] *n* [barrel - gen] tonneau *m*, fût *m*; [- large] barrique *f*; [- small] baril *m*.

casket ['kɑːskɪt] *n* -**1.** [small box] coffret *m*, boîte *f*. -**2.** *Am* [coffin] cercueil *m*.

Caspian Sea ['kæspɪən-] *pr n*: the ~ la (mer) Caspienne.

Cassandra [kə'sændrə] *pr n* MYTH & *fig* Cassandre.

cassata [kə'sɑːtə] *n* cassate *f*.

cassava [kə'sɑːvə] *n* [plant] manioc *m*; [flour] farine *f* de manioc.

casserole ['kæsərəʊl] ◇ *n* -**1.** [pan] cocotte *f*. -**2.** [stew] ragoût *m*.
◇ *vt* (faire) cuire en ragoût.

cassette [kæ'set] *n* -**1.** [tape] cassette *f*. -**2.** PHOT [cartridge] chargeur *m*.

cassette deck *n* lecteur *m* de cassettes.

cassette player *n* lecteur *m* de cassettes.

cassette recorder *n* magnétophone *m* à cassettes.

Cassius ['kæsɪəs] *pr n* Cassius.

cassock ['kæsək] *n* soutane *f*.

cassowary ['kæsəweərɪ] (*pl* cassowaries) *n* casoar *m*.

cast [kɑːst] (*pt* & *pp* cast) ◇ *vt* -**1.** [throw] jeter, lancer; to ~ lots *Br* tirer au sort; to ~ a spell on sb [subj: witch] jeter un sort à qqn, ensorceler qqn; *fig* ensorceler OR envoûter qqn; to ~ one's vote for sb voter pour qqn; the number of votes ~ le nombre de voix OR de suffrages; to ~ anchor mouiller (l'ancre), jeter l'ancre; the tyrant ~ his enemies into prison *lit* le tyran a jeté ses ennemis en prison; we'll have to ~ our net wide to find the right candidate *fig* il va falloir ratisser large pour trouver le bon candidat ❑ it's (like) ~ing pearls before swine c'est donner de la confiture OR jeter des perles aux cochons. -**2.** [direct - light, shadow] projeter; [- look] jeter, diriger; the accident ~ a shadow over their lives l'accident a jeté une ombre sur leur existence; could you ~ an eye over this report? voulez-vous jeter un œil sur ce rapport?; he ~ an eye over the audience il a promené son regard sur l'auditoire; she ~ a desperate glance at her mother elle glissa à sa mère un regard désespéré, elle regarda sa mère avec désespoir; to ~ aspersions on sb's character dénigrer qqn; the report ~s doubt on the police evidence les auteurs du rapport émettent des doutes sur les preuves fournies par la police; his indecision ~ doubt on his ability to govern son irrésolution a jeté le doute sur sa capacité à gouverner; the evidence ~ suspicion on him les preuves ont jeté la suspicion sur lui. -**3.** [shed, throw off] perdre; the horse ~ a shoe le cheval a perdu un fer; ~ all fear/thought of revenge from your mind oubliez toute crainte/toute idée de revanche. -**4.** [film, play] distribuer les rôles de; [performer]: the director ~ her in the role of the mother le metteur en scène lui a attribué le rôle de la mère. -**5.** ART & TECH [form, statue] mouler; [metal] couler, fondre; [plaster] couler; civil servants are all ~ in the same mould *fig* les fonctionnaires sont tous faits sur OR sont tous coulés dans le même moule. -**6.** [horoscope] tirer.
◇ *n* -**1.** CIN & THEAT [group of actors] distribution *f*, acteurs *mpl*; the ~ is Italian tous les acteurs sont italiens; ~ list CIN & TV générique *m*; THEAT distribution *f*. -**2.** ART [colour, shade] nuance *f*, teinte *f*; white with a pinkish ~ blanc nuancé de rose. -**3.** ART & TECH [act of moulding - metal] coulage *m*, coulée *f*; [- plaster] moulage *m*; [- coin, medallion] empreinte *f*; [mould] moule *m*; [object moulded] moulage *m*; to make a bronze ~ of a statue mouler une statue en bronze. -**4.** MED [for broken limb] plâtre *m*; her arm was in a ~ elle avait un bras dans le plâtre. -**5.** MED [squint] strabisme *m*; he had a ~ in his eye il louchait d'un œil, il avait un œil qui louchait. -**6.** *fml* [type]: the delicate ~ of her features la finesse de ses traits; a peculiar ~ of mind une drôle de mentalité OR de tournure d'esprit.
◆ **cast about** *vi insep Br*: she ~ about for an idea/an excuse to leave elle essaya de trouver une idée/un prétexte pour partir.
◆ **cast aside** *vt sep lit* [book] mettre de côté; [shirt, shoes] se débarrasser de; *fig* [friend, suggestion] rejeter, écarter.
◆ **cast away** *vt sep* -**1.** [book, letter] jeter; *fig* [cares, principle] se défaire de. -**2.** NAUT: to be ~ away être naufragé.
◆ **cast back** *vt sep*: ~ your mind back to the day we met souviens-toi du OR rappelle-toi le jour de notre première rencontre; to ~ one's thoughts back se reporter en arrière.
◆ **cast down** *vt sep* -**1.** *fml* [weapon] déposer, mettre bas. -**2.** *fig* & *lit*: to be ~ down être démoralisé OR découragé.
◆ **cast off** ◇ *vt sep* -**1.** [undo] défaire; [untie] délier, dénouer; [in knitting] rabattre; NAUT [lines, rope] larguer, lâcher; [boat] larguer OR lâcher les amarres de. -**2.** *lit* [rid oneself of - clothing] enlever, se débarrasser de; *fig* [- bonds] se défaire de, se libérer de; [- cares, habit, tradition] se défaire de, abandonner.
◇ *vi insep* -**1.** NAUT larguer les amarres, appareiller. -**2.** [in knitting] rabattre les mailles.
◆ **cast on** ◇ *vi insep* monter les mailles.
◇ *vt sep* [stitches] monter.
◆ **cast out** *vt sep arch* OR *lit* [person] renvoyer, chasser; *fig* [fear, guilt] bannir.
◆ **cast up** *vt sep* [subj: sea, tide, waves] rejeter.

castanets [,kæstə'nets] *npl* castagnettes *fpl*.

castaway ['kɑːstəweɪ] NAUT ◇ *n* naufragé *m*, -e *f*; *fig* naufragé, -e, laissé-pour-compte *m*, laissée-pour-compte *f*.
◇ *adj* naufragé.

caste [kɑːst] *n* [gen] caste *f*, classe *f* sociale; [in Hindu society] caste *f*; to lose ~ *Br fig* déchoir, déroger.

castellated ['kæstəleɪtɪd] *adj* ARCHIT à tourelles; TECH [filament, nut] crénelé.

caster ['kɑːstəʳ] *n* -**1.** [sifter] saupoudroir *m*, saupoudreuse *f*. -**2.** [wheel] roulette *f*.

caster sugar *n Br* sucre *m* en poudre.

castigate ['kæstɪgeɪt] *vt fml* -**1.** [punish] corriger, punir; [scold] réprimander, tancer *fml*. -**2.** [criticize - person] critiquer sévèrement, fustiger *fml*; [- book, play] éreinter.

castigation [,kæstɪ'geɪʃn] *n fml* [punishment] correction *f*, punition *f*; [scolding] réprimande *f*; [criticism] critique *f* sévère.

Castile [kæ'stiːl] *pr n* Castille *f*.

Castilian [kæ'stɪljən] ◇ *n* -**1.** [person] Castillan *m*, -e *f*. -**2.** LING castillan *m*.
◇ *adj* castillan.

casting ['kɑːstɪŋ] *n* -**1.** ART [act & object] moulage *m*; TECH [act] coulée *f*, coulage *m*, fonte *f*; [object] pièce *f* fondue. -**2.** CIN & THEAT [selection of actors] attribution *f* des rôles, casting *m*.

casting couch *inf n*: she denied having got the part on the ~ elle a nié avoir couché avec le metteur en scène pour obtenir le rôle.

casting director *n* metteur *m* en scène (qui distribue les rôles).

casting vote *n* voix *f* prépondérante; the president has a OR the ~ le président a voix prépondérante.

cast iron *n* fonte *f*.
◆ **cast-iron** *comp* -**1.** [pot, stove] de OR en fonte. -**2.** *fig*: a cast-iron alibi un alibi inattaquable OR en béton.

castle ['kɑːsl] ◇ *n* -**1.** [building] château *m* (fort); to build ~s in the air bâtir des châteaux en Espagne; 'The Castle' *Kafka* 'le Château'. -**2.** [in chess] tour *f*.
◇ *vi* [in chess] roquer.

castling ['kɑːslɪŋ] *n* [in chess] roque *m*.

castoff ['kɑːstɒf] *n* (*usu pl*) [piece of clothing] vieux vêtement *m*; *fig* [person] laissé-pour-compte *m*, laissée-pour-compte *f*.
◆ **cast-off** *adj* dont personne ne veut; cast-off clothes vieux vêtements *mpl*.

castor ['kɑːstəʳ] *n* -**1.** = **caster**. -**2.** [secretion] castoréum *m*.
◆ **Castor** *pr n*: Castor and Pollux Castor et Pollux.

castor oil *n* huile *f* de ricin.

castor-oil plant *n* ricin *m*.

castrate [kæ'streɪt] *vt literal* châtrer, castrer; *fig* [weaken - person, political movement] émasculer.

castration [kæ'streɪʃn] *n literal* castration *f*; *fig* [of political movement] émasculation *f*.

castrato [kæ'strɑːtəʊ] (*pl* castratos OR castrati [-tiː]) *n* castrat *m*.

casual ['kæʒʊəl] ◇ *adj* -**1.** [unconcerned] désinvolte, nonchalant; [natural] simple, naturel; they're very ~ about the way they dress ils attachent très peu d'importance à leurs vêtements OR à la façon dont ils s'habillent; I tried to appear ~ when talking about it j'ai essayé d'en parler avec désinvolture. -**2.** [informal - dinner] simple, détendu; [- clothing] sport *(inv)*. -**3.** [superficial] superficiel; I took a ~ glance at the paper j'ai jeté un coup d'œil (rapide) au journal; to make ~ conversation parler de choses et d'autres, parler à bâtons rompus; it was just a ~ suggestion c'était seulement une suggestion en passant; she's just a ~ acquaintance of mine c'est quelqu'un que je connais très peu; a ~ love affair une aventure; ~ sex rapports *mpl* sexuels de rencontre. -**4.** [happening by chance - meeting] de hasard; [- onlooker] venu par hasard. -**5.** [occasional - job] intermittent; [- worker] temporaire; ~ labourer *Br* [for one day] journalier *m*, -ère *f*; [for harvest, season] (travailleur *m*) saisonnier *m*, (travailleuse *f*) saisonnière *f*; [in construction work] ouvrier *m*, -ère *f* sans travail fixe.
◇ *n* [worker - on farm for one day] journalier *m*, -ère *f*; [- on farm for harvest, season] (travailleur *m*) saisonnier *m*, (travailleuse *f*) saisonnière *f*; [- in construction work] ouvrier *m*, -ère *f* sans travail fixe.
◆ **casuals** *npl* [clothing] vêtements *mpl* sport; [shoes] chaussures *fpl* sport.

casually ['kæʒʊəlɪ] *adv* -**1.** [unconcernedly] avec désinvolture, nonchalamment. -**2.** [informally] simplement; to dress ~ s'habiller sport. -**3.** [glance, remark, suggest] en passant; they talked ~ about this and that ils ont parlé de choses et d'autres OR à bâtons rompus. -**4.** [by chance] par hasard.

casualness ['kæʒʊəlnɪs] *n* -**1.** [unconcern] désinvolture *f*, nonchalance *f*. -**2.** [informality] simplicité *f*; the ~ of their dress l'allure décontractée OR sport de leur habillement. -**3.** [haphazardness] hasard *m*, fortuité *f*.

casualty ['kæʒjʊəltɪ] (*pl* casualties) *n* -**1.** [wounded] blessé *m*, -e *f*; [dead] mort *m*, -e *f*; there were heavy casualties [gen] il y avait beaucoup de victimes OR de morts et de blessés; [dead] il y avait beaucoup de pertes; truth is often a ~ in political debates *fig* la vérité est souvent sacrifiée dans les débats politiques. -**2.** *(U)* MED [emergency ward] service *m* des urgences; [accident ward] salle *f* des accidentés.

casualty list *n* [gen] liste *f* des victimes; MIL état *m* des pertes.

casualty ward *n* [for emergencies] service *m* des urgences; [for accident victims] salle *f* des accidentés.

casuist ['kæzjʊɪst] *n* casuiste *m*.

casuistry ['kæzjʊɪstrɪ] *n* [philosophy] casuistique *f*; *(U)* [reasoning] arguments *mpl* de casuiste.

cat [kæt] *n* -**1.** ZOOL chat *m*, chatte *f*; the big ~s les grands fauves *mpl* OR félins *mpl*; to let the ~ out of the bag vendre la mèche; to be like a ~ on hot bricks *Br* OR on a hot tin roof être sur des charbons ardents; there isn't enough room to swing a ~ il n'y a pas la place de se retourner; he looked like something the ~ brought in il était dégoûtant; has the ~ got your tongue? tu as perdu ta langue?; to fight like ~ and dog se battre comme des chiffonniers; to put OR to set the ~ among the pigeons *Br* jeter un pavé dans la mare; to play (a game of) ~ and mouse with sb jouer au chat et à la souris avec qqn; to wait for the ~ to jump OR to see which way the ~ will jump *Br* attendre de voir d'où vient le vent; when the ~'s away the mice will play *prov* quand le chat n'est pas là les souris dansent *prov*; 'Cat and Mouse' *Grass* 'le Chat et la souris'; 'Cat on a Hot Tin Roof' *Williams, Brooks* 'la Chatte sur un toit brûlant'. -**2.** *pej* [woman] rosse *f*, chipie *f*. -**3.** *inf Am dated* [man] mec *m*; what a cool ~! vraiment cool, ce type! -**4.** *inf* [boat] catamaran *m*. -**5.** *inf* AUT pot *m* catalytique.

CAT (*abbr of* computer-aided teaching) *n Br* EAO *m*.

catabolism [kə'tæbəlɪzm] *n* catabolisme *m*.

catachresis [ˌkætə'kriːsɪs] *n* catachrèse *f*.

cataclysm ['kætəklɪzm] *n* cataclysme *m*.

cataclysmic [ˌkætə'klɪzmɪk] *adj* cataclysmique, cataclysmal.

catacomb ['kætəkuːm] *n* (*usu pl*) catacombe *f*.

catafalque ['kætəfælk] *n* catafalque *m*.

Catalan ['kætəˌlæn] ◇ *n* -**1.** [person] catalan *m*, -e *f*. -**2.** LING catalan *m*.

◇ *adj* catalan.

catalepsy ['kætəlepsɪ] *n* catalepsie *f*.

cataleptic [ˌkætə'leptɪk] *adj* cataleptique; to have a ~ fit tomber en catalepsie.

catalogue *Br*, **catalog** *Am* ['kætəlɒg] ◇ *n* catalogue *m*; [in library] fichier *m*; *Am* UNIV guide *m* de l'étudiant; his life story was a ~ of disasters *fig* l'histoire de sa vie a été un catalogue de malheurs.

◇ *vt* cataloguer, faire le catalogue de.

Catalonia [ˌkætə'ləʊnɪə] *pr n* Catalogne *f*; in ~ en Catalogne.

catalyse *Br*, **catalyze** *Am* ['kætəlaɪz] *vt* catalyser.

catalysis [kə'tæləsɪs] (*pl* catalyses [-siːz]) *n* catalyse *f*.

catalyst ['kætəlɪst] *n* catalyseur *m*.

catalytic [ˌkætə'lɪtɪk] *adj* catalytique.

catalytic converter *n* pot *m* catalytique.

catalyze ['kætəlaɪz] *Am* = **catalyse**.

catamaran [ˌkætəmə'ræn] *n* catamaran *m*.

Catania [kə'teɪnjə] *pr n* Catane.

cataphora [kə'tæfrə] *n* cataphore *f*.

cataplexy ['kætəpleksɪ] *n* cataplexie *f*.

catapult ['kætəpʌlt] ◇ *n* -**1.** *Br* [child's] lance-pierres *m inv*. -**2.** AERON & MIL catapulte *f*; ~ launching catapultage *m*.

◇ *vt* [gen & AERON] catapulter; she was ~ed into the leadership job *fig* elle a été catapultée à la direction.

cataract ['kætərækt] *n* -**1.** [waterfall] cataracte *f*, cascade *f*. -**2.** [downpour] déluge *m*. -**3.** MED cataracte *f*; to be operated on for a ~ être opéré de la cataracte.

catarrh [kə'tɑːʳ] *n* catarrhe *m*; to have bad ~ *Br* être très catarrheux.

catarrhal [kə'tɑːrəl] *adj* catarrheux.

catastrophe [kə'tæstrəfɪ] *n* catastrophe *f*.

catastrophic [ˌkætə'strɒfɪk] *adj* catastrophique.

catatonia [ˌkætə'təʊnɪə] *n* catatonie *f*.

catatonic [ˌkætə'tɒnɪk] *adj* catatonique.

cat burglar *n* monte-en-l'air *m inv*.

catcall ['kætkɔːl] ◇ *n* THEAT sifflet *m*; the actors were greeted with ~s les acteurs se sont fait siffler.

◇ *vi* siffler.

catch [kætʃ] (*pt* & *pp* caught [kɔːt]) ◇ *vt* -**1.** [ball, thrown object] attraper; to ~ hold of sthg attraper qqch; the dog caught the ball in its mouth le chien a attrapé la balle dans sa gueule; ~! attrape! || [take hold of]: to ~ sb's arm saisir OR prendre qqn par le bras. -**2.** [trap - fish, mouse, thief] attraper, prendre; he got caught by the police il s'est fait attraper par la police; to get caught in a traffic jam être pris dans un embouteillage; we got caught in a shower/thunderstorm nous avons été surpris par une averse/l'orage; to ~ sb doing sthg surprendre qqn à faire qqch; to ~ o.s. doing sthg se surprendre à faire qqch; I caught myself thinking about him je me suis surpris à repenser à lui; they were caught trying to escape on les a surpris en train d'essayer de s'évader; if I ~ you talking once more I'll throw you out! si je te prends OR surprends encore une fois en train de parler, je te mets à la porte!; you won't ~ me doing the washing-up! aucun danger de me surprendre en train de faire la vaisselle!; don't let me ~ you at it again! que je ne t'y reprenne pas! ❑ you'll ~ it when you get home! *inf Br* qu'est-ce que tu vas prendre en rentrant!; to ~ sb napping prendre qqn en défaut. -**3.** [disease, infection] attraper; to ~ a cold attraper un rhume; to ~ cold attraper OR prendre froid; he'll ~ his death (of cold)! *inf* il va attraper la crève! -**4.** [bus, train] attraper, prendre; I have a train to ~ at 6 o'clock j'ai un train à prendre à 6 h; to ~ the last post *Br* arriver à temps pour la dernière levée (du courrier); try and ~ the postman before you leave essayez d'attraper le facteur avant de partir; I just caught the end of the film j'ai juste vu la fin du film. -**5.** [on nail, obstacle]: he caught his finger in the door il s'est pris le doigt dans la porte; she caught her skirt in the door sa jupe s'est prise dans la porte; he caught his coat on the brambles son manteau s'est accroché aux ronces. -**6.** [hear clearly, understand] saisir, comprendre; I didn't quite ~ what you said je n'ai pas bien entendu ce que vous avez dit; I don't ~ your meaning je ne vois pas ce que vous voulez dire. -**7.** [attract]: to ~ sb's attention OR sb's eye attirer l'attention de qqn; the idea caught her imagination l'idée a enflammé son imagination; the house caught his fancy *Br* la maison lui a plu; this coat ~es fluff la poussière se voit sur ce manteau. -**8.** [in portrait, writing]: to ~ a likeness saisir une ressemblance; the author really ~es the mood of the period l'auteur saisit très bien l'ambiance de l'époque. -**9.** [hit]: to ~ sb a blow *Br* donner OR flanquer un coup à qqn; the wave caught her sideways la vague l'a frappée de côté; he fell and caught his head on the radiator il est tombé et s'est cogné la tête contre le radiateur. -**10.** [notice]: did you ~ the look on his face? vous avez remarqué l'expression de son visage? -**11.** *phr*: to ~ one's breath reprendre son souffle; he had to sit down to ~ his breath il a dû s'asseoir pour reprendre son souffle; to ~ fire prendre feu; the curtains caught fire les rideaux ont pris feu.

◇ *vi* -**1.** [ignite - fire, wood] prendre; [- engine] démarrer. -**2.** [bolt, lock] fermer; [gears] mordre. -**3.** [on nail, obstacle]: her skirt caught on a nail sa jupe s'est accrochée à un clou; his coat caught in the door son manteau s'est pris dans la porte.

◇ *n* -**1.** [act] prise *f*; good ~! SPORT bien rattrapé! -**2.** [of fish] prise *f*; a fine ~ une belle prise; he's a good ~ *hum* & *fig* [man] c'est une belle prise. -**3.** [snag] piège *m*; there must be a ~ in it somewhere il doit y avoir un truc OR un piège quelque part, ça cache quelque chose; where's OR what's the ~? qu'est-ce que ça cache?, où est le piège? -**4.** [on lock, door] loquet *m*; [on window] loqueteau *m*; [on shoe-buckle] ardillon *m*. -**5.** [in voice]: with a ~ in his voice d'une voix entrecoupée. -**6.** GAMES jeu *m* de balle; to play ~ jouer à la balle. -**7.** MUS canon *m*.

◆ **catch at** *vt insep* (essayer d') attraper.

◆ **catch on** *vi insep* -**1.** [fashion, trend, slogan] devenir populaire; this dance style caught on in the fifties cette danse a fait un tabac OR était très populaire dans les années cinquante. -**2.** *inf* [understand] piger, saisir, comprendre; I didn't quite ~ on to what he was trying to say je n'ai pas bien saisi ce qu'il essayait de dire; did you ~ on? est-ce que tu as pigé?

◆ **catch out** *vt sep Br* [by trickery] prendre en défaut; [in the act] prendre sur le fait; he tried to ~ me out with a trick question il a essayé de me coller OR prendre en défaut avec une question-piège; I won't be caught out like that again! on ne m'y prendra plus!

◆ **catch up** ◇ *vi insep* -**1.** [as verb of movement]: to ~ up with sb rattraper qqn; I had to run to ~ up with him OR to ~ him up j'ai dû courir pour le rattraper OR le rejoindre; the police caught up with him in Zurich la police l'a rattrapé à Zurich; his past will ~ up with him one day *fig* il finira par être rattrapé par son passé. -**2.** [on lost time] combler OR rattraper son retard; [on studies] rattraper son retard, se remettre au niveau; to ~ up on OR with one's work rattraper le retard qu'on a pris dans son travail; he'll have to work hard to ~ up with the rest of the class il va falloir qu'il travaille beaucoup pour rattraper le reste de la classe; I need to ~ up on some sleep j'ai du sommeil à rattraper; we had a lot of news to ~ up on nous avions beaucoup de choses à nous dire.

◇ *vt sep* -**1.** [entangle]: the material got caught up in the machinery le tissu s'est pris dans la machine. -**2.** [absorb, involve]: to get caught up in a wave of enthusiasm être gagné par une vague d'enthousiasme; he was too caught up in the film to notice what was happening il était trop absorbé par le film pour remarquer ce qui se passait; I refuse to get caught up in their private quarrel je refuse de me laisser entraîner dans leurs querelles personnelles. -**3.** [seize] ramasser vivement, s'emparer de. -**4.** [person] rattraper.

catch-all ◇ *n* fourre-tout *m inv*.

◇ *adj* fourre-tout (*inv*), qui pare à toute éventualité; ~ phrase expression *f* passe-partout.

catch-as-catch-can ◇ *n* SPORT catch *m*.

◇ *adj Am* improvisé.

catcher ['kætʃəʳ] *n* [gen & in baseball] attrapeur *m*.

catching ['kætʃɪŋ] *adj* -**1.** MED contagieux. -**2.** *fig* [enthusiasm, laughter] contagieux, communicatif; [habit] contagieux.

catchment ['kætʃmənt] *n* captage *m*.

catchment area *n* -**1.** [drainage area] bassin *m* hydrographique. -**2.** ADMIN [for hospital] circonscription *f* hospitalière; [for school] secteur *m* de recrutement scolaire.

catchment basin = **catchment area**.

catchpenny ['kætʃˌpenɪ] (*pl* catchpennies) *Br* ◇ *adj* accrocheur.

◇ *n* attrape-nigaud *m*.

catchphrase ['kætʃfreɪz] *n* [in advertising] accroche *f*; [set phrase] formule *f* toute faite; [of performer] petite phrase *f*.

catch question *n* question-piège *f*, colle *f*.

catchup ['kætʃʌp] *n Am* ketchup *m*.

catchword ['kætʃwɜːd] *n* -**1.** [slogan] slogan *m*; POL mot *m* d'ordre, slogan *m*. -**2.** [in printing - at top of page] mot-vedette *m*; [- at bottom of page] réclame *f*. -**3.** THEAT réclame *f*.

catchy ['kætʃɪ] (*compar* catchier, *superl* catchiest) *adj* [tune] qui trotte dans la tête, facile à retenir; [title] facile à retenir.

cat door = **cat flap**.

catechism ['kætəkɪzm] *n* catéchisme *m*.

catechist ['kætəkɪst] *n* catéchiste *mf*.

catechize, -ise ['kætɪkaɪz] *vt* -**1.** RELIG catéchiser. -**2.** *fig* [examine] interroger, questionner.

categoric(al) [ˌkætɪ'gɒrɪk(l)] *adj* catégorique.

categorically [ˌkætɪ'gɒrɪklɪ] *adv* catégoriquement.

categorization [ˌkætəgəraɪ'zeɪʃn] *n* catégorisation *f*.

categorize, -ise ['kætəgəraɪz] *vt* catégoriser.

category ['kætəgərɪ] (*pl* categories) *n* catégorie *f*.

cater ['keɪtəʳ] ◇ *vi* s'occuper de la nourriture, fournir des repas.

◇ *vt Am* s'occuper de la nourriture pour.

◆ **cater for** *vt insep* -**1.** [with food] s'occuper de la nourriture pour; 'coach parties ~ed for' accueil de groupes. -**2.** *fig* [needs] répondre à, pourvoir à; [tastes] satisfaire; we ~ for the needs of small companies nous répondons à la demande des petites entreprises.

◆ **cater to** *vt insep* **-1.** [accommodate]: I refuse to ~ to such outrageous demands je refuse de satisfaire des exigences aussi scandaleuses. **-2.** *Am* = **cater for**.

cater-cornered *inf Am* ◇ *adj* diagonal.
◇ *adv* diagonalement.

caterer ['keɪtərəʳ] *n* traiteur *m*.

catering ['keɪtərɪŋ] ◇ *n* restauration *f*; who did the ~ for the wedding? qui a fourni le repas pour le mariage?
◇ *comp* [industry] de la restauration; [college] hôtelier; ~ **manager** chef *m* OR responsable *m* de la restauration.

caterpillar ['kætəpɪləʳ] *n* ZOOL & TECH chenille *f*.

caterpillar track *n* chenille *f* TECH.

caterwaul ['kætəwɔːl] ◇ *vi* [cat] miauler; [person] brailler.
◇ *n* [of cat] miaulement *m*; [of person] braillement *m*.

caterwauling ['kætəwɔːlɪŋ] *n* (U) [of cat] miaulement *m*, miaulements *mpl*; [of person] braillement *m*, braillements *mpl*.

catfish ['kætfɪʃ] (*pl inv* OR **catfishes**) *n* poisson-chat *m*.

cat flap *n* chatière *f*.

catgut ['kætgʌt] *n* [for musical instrument, racket] boyau *m* (de chat); MED catgut *m*.

Cathar ['kæθəʳ] ◇ *n* cathare *mf*.
◇ *adj* cathare.

catharsis [kə'θɑːsɪs] (*pl* **catharses** [-siːz]) *n* catharsis *f*.

cathartic [kə'θɑːtɪk] ◇ *adj* cathartique.
◇ *n* MED purgatif *m*, cathartique *m*.

Cathay [kæ'θeɪ] *pr n* Cathay *m*.

cathedra [kə'θiːdrə] *n* cathèdre *f*.

cathedral [kə'θiːdrəl] *n* cathédrale *f*.

cathedral city *n* évêché *m*, ville *f* épiscopale.

Catherine ['kæθrɪn] *pr n*: Saint ~ sainte Catherine; Saint ~'s Day la Sainte-Catherine; ~ the Great Catherine la Grande; ~ **de' Medici** Catherine de Médicis; ~ **of Aragon** Catherine d'Aragon.

catherine wheel *n* [firework] soleil *m*.

catheter ['kæθɪtəʳ] *n* cathéter *m*, sonde *f* creuse.

catheterize, -ise ['kæθɪtəˌraɪz] *vt* cathétériser.

cathode ['kæθəʊd] *n* cathode *f*.

cathode ray *n* rayon *m* cathodique.

cathode ray tube *n* tube *m* cathodique.

catholic ['kæθlɪk] *adj* **-1.** [broad - tastes, sympathies] éclectique. **-2.** [liberal - views] libéral. **-3.** [universal] universel.
◆ **Catholic** ◇ *adj* RELIG catholique; the Catholic Church l'Église *f* catholique.
◇ *n* catholique *mf*.

Catholicism [kə'θɒlɪsɪzm] *n* catholicisme *m*.

cathouse▽ ['kæthaʊs, *pl* -haʊzɪz] *n Am* bordel *m*.

cation ['kætaɪən] *n* cation *m*.

catkin ['kætkɪn] *n* chaton *m* BOT.

cat lick *inf n* toilette *f* de chat, brin *m* de toilette.

catlike ['kætlaɪk] ◇ *adj* félin.
◇ *adv* comme un chat.

cat litter *n* litière *f* (pour chats).

catmint ['kætmɪnt] *n* herbe *f* aux chats.

catnap *inf* ['kætnæp] ◇ *n* (petit) somme *m*; to have a ~ faire un petit somme.
◇ *vi* sommeiller, faire un petit somme.

catnip ['kætnɪp] = **catmint**.

Cato ['keɪtəʊ] *pr n* Caton.

cat-o'-nine-tails *n* chat à neuf queues *m*, martinet *m*.

cat's cradle *n* jeu *m* de figures *(que l'on forme entre les doigts avec de la ficelle)*.

cat's eye *n Br* AUT catadioptre *m (marquant le milieu de la chaussée)*.

cat's-foot *n* pied-de-chat *m*, antennaire *f*.

cat's-paw *n* **-1.** [person] dupe *f*; to be sb's ~ tirer les marrons du feu. **-2.** [on water] (effet *m* de vague produit par une) légère brise *f*.

catsuit ['kætsuːt] *n* combinaison-pantalon *f*.

catsup ['kætsəp] *n Am* ketchup *m*.

cat's whisker *n* **-1.** RADIO chercheur *m* (de détecteur à galène). **-2.** *inf fig*: he thinks he's the ~s il se prend pour le nombril du monde.

cattery ['kætərɪ] (*pl* **catteries**) *n* pension *f* pour chats.

cattle ['kætl] *npl (U)* bétail *m*, bestiaux *mpl*, bovins *mpl*; ~ **breeder** éleveur *m* (de bétail); ~ **breeding** élevage *m* (du bétail); ~ **cake** tourteau *m* AGR; ~ **ranch** ranch *m (pour l'élevage du bétail)*; ~ **shed** étable *f*; ~ **show** concours *m* agricole; ~ **truck** fourgon *m* à bestiaux.

cattle grid *n* [sur une route] *grille destinée à empêcher le passage du bétail mais non des voitures*.

cattleman ['kætlmən] (*pl* **cattlemen** [-mən]) *n* vacher *m*, bouvier *m*.

cattle market *n* marché *m* OR foire *f* aux bestiaux; this beauty contest is just a ~ *fig* ce concours de beauté n'est qu'un marché aux bestiaux.

catty *inf* ['kætɪ] (*compar* **cattier**, *superl* **cattiest**) *adj pej* [person, gossip] méchant, vache; a ~ remark une réflexion désagréable.

Catullus [kə'tʌləs] *pr n* Catulle.

catwalk ['kætwɔːk] *n* passerelle *f*.

Caucasia [kɔː'keɪzjə] *pr n* Caucase *m*.

Caucasian [kɔː'keɪzjən], **Caucasic** [kɔː'keɪzɪk] ◇ *n* **-1.** [from Caucasia] Caucasien *m*, -enne *f*. **-2.** [race] caucasoïde *mf*. **-3.** LING caucasien *m*.
◇ *adj* **-1.** [from Caucasia] caucasien; 'The Caucasian Chalk Circle' *Brecht* 'le Cercle de craie caucasien'. **-2.** [race] caucasoïde. **-3.** LING caucasien, caucasique.

Caucasoid ['kɔːkəsɔɪd] ◇ *n* Caucasoïde *mf*.
◇ *adj* caucasoïde.

Caucasus ['kɔːkəsəs] *pr n*: the ~ le Caucase; in the ~ dans le Caucase.

caucus ['kɔːkəs] *n* **-1.** *Am* POL [committee] comité *m* électoral, caucus *m*; ~ **meeting** réunion *f* du comité électoral; the Democratic ~ le groupe OR le lobby démocrate. **-2.** *Br* POL [party organization] comité *m*; the Black ~ of the Labour Party *les personnalités noires du parti travailliste*.

CAUCUS:
Aux États-Unis, les «Caucus» sont d'immenses rassemblements politiques, au cours desquels les deux partis nationaux choisissent leurs candidats et définissent leurs objectifs.

---

caudal ['kɔːdl] *adj* caudal.

caught [kɔːt] *pt & pp* → **catch**.

caul [kɔːl] *n* coiffe *f* PHYSIOL.

cauldron ['kɔːldrən] *n* chaudron *m*.

cauliflower ['kɒlɪˌflaʊəʳ] *n* chou-fleur *m*.

cauliflower cheese *n* chou-fleur *m* au gratin.

cauliflower ear *n* oreille *f* en feuille de chou.

caulk [kɔːk] *vt* calfater.

causal ['kɔːzl] *adj* [gen] causal; GRAMM causal, causatif.

causality [kɔː'zælətɪ] *n* causalité *f*.

causally ['kɔːzəlɪ] *adv*: the two events are ~ linked les deux événements ont la même cause.

causation [kɔː'zeɪʃn] *n* [causing] causalité *f*; [cause-effect relationship] relation *f* de cause à effet.

causative ['kɔːzətɪv] ◇ *adj* [gen] causal; GRAMM causal, causatif.
◇ *n* GRAMM causatif *m*.

cause [kɔːz] ◇ *n* **-1.** [reason] cause *f*; to be the ~ of sthg être (la) cause de qqch; he was the ~ of all our trouble c'est lui qui a été la cause OR qui a été à l'origine de tous nos ennuis; the ~ of the disease is not yet known la cause de la maladie demeure inconnue; she is the ~ of his being in prison c'est à cause d'elle qu'il est en prison; the relation of ~ and effect la relation de cause à effet. **-2.** [justification] raison *f*, motif *m*; there is ~ for anxiety il y a lieu d'être inquiet, il y a de quoi s'inquiéter; there is no real ~ for concern il n'y a aucune raison valable de s'inquiéter; we mustn't give them ~ for complaint il ne faut pas leur donner de motif de se plaindre; they have ~ to be bitter ils ont lieu d'être amers, ils ont de quoi être amers; with (good) ~ à juste titre; without good ~ sans cause OR raison valable. **-3.** [principle] cause *f*; in the ~ of justice pour la cause de la justice; the ~ of equal rights la cause de l'égalité des droits; her lifelong devotion to the ~ son dévouement de toujours à la cause; to make common ~ with sb *fml* faire cause commune avec qqn; it's all in a good ~! c'est pour une bonne cause! **-4.** JUR cause *f*; ~ of action fondement *m* d'une action en justice.
◇ *vt* causer, occasionner, provoquer; it has been proved that smoking can ~ cancer on a démontré que le tabac peut provoquer des cancers; he has ~d us a lot of trouble il nous a créé beaucoup d'ennuis; it will only ~ trouble cela ne servira qu'à semer la zizanie; what ~d him to change his mind? qu'est-ce qui l'a fait changer d'avis?; this ~d me to lose my job à cause de cela, j'ai perdu mon emploi.

causeway ['kɔːzweɪ] *n* chaussée *f* GÉOG.

caustic ['kɔːstɪk] ◇ *adj* CHEM & *fig* caustique.
◇ *n* caustique *m*, substance *f* caustique.

caustic soda *n* soude *f* caustique.

cauterize, -ise ['kɔːtəraɪz] *vt* cautériser.

cautery ['kɔːtərɪ] (*pl* **cauteries**) *n* cautère *m*.

caution ['kɔːʃn] ◇ *n* **-1.** [care] circonspection *f*, prudence *f*; to proceed with ~ [gen] agir avec circonspection OR avec prudence; [in car] avancer lentement; **'caution!'** 'attention!' ❑ to throw ~ to the wind faire fi de toute prudence. **-2.** [warning] avertissement *m*; [reprimand] réprimande *f*. **-3.** JUR avertissement *m*; I got off with a ~ *Br* je m'en suis tiré avec un avertissement. **-4.** *inf Br dated* [person]: he's a ~! c'est un numéro OR un polisson!
◇ *vt* **-1.** [warn] avertir, mettre en garde; he ~ed them to be careful il leur a conseillé d'être prudents; to ~ sb against doing sthg déconseiller à qqn de faire qqch; he ~ed them against the evils of drink il les a mis en garde contre les dangers de la boisson. **-2.** JUR: to ~ a prisoner informer un prisonnier de ses droits.
◇ *vi*: to ~ against sthg déconseiller qqch.

cautionary ['kɔːʃənərɪ] *adj* qui sert d'avertissement; as a ~ measure par mesure de précaution; a ~ tale un récit édifiant.

cautious ['kɔːʃəs] *adj* circonspect, prudent; to be ~ about doing sthg faire qqch avec circonspection.

cautiously ['kɔːʃəslɪ] *adv* avec prudence, prudemment.

cavalcade [ˌkævl'keɪd] *n* cavalcade *f*.

cavalier [ˌkævə'lɪəʳ] ◇ *n* [gen & MIL] cavalier *m*.
◇ *adj* cavalier, désinvolte; he treated me in a very ~ fashion il s'est comporté envers moi d'une façon très cavalière.
◆ **Cavalier** *Br* HIST ◇ *n* Cavalier *m (partisan de Charles Ier d'Angleterre pendant la guerre civile anglaise, de 1642 à 1646)*.
◇ *adj* royaliste, Cavalier.

cavalry ['kævlrɪ] *n* cavalerie *f*.

cavalry charge *n* charge *f* de cavalerie.

cavalryman ['kævlrɪmən] (*pl* **cavalrymen** [-mən]) *n* cavalier *m (soldat)*.

cavalry officer *n* officier *m* de cavalerie.

cavalry twill *n étoffe utilisée pour faire les culottes de cheval*.

cave[1] [keɪv] ◇ *n* caverne *f*, grotte *f*; 'Fingal's Cave' *Mendelssohn* 'la Grotte de Fingal'.
◇ *vi*: to go caving faire de la spéléologie.
◆ **cave in** *vi insep* **-1.** [ceiling, floor] s'écrouler, s'effondrer, s'affaisser; [wall] s'écrouler, s'effondrer, céder. **-2.** *inf* [person] flancher, céder; eventually they ~d in and agreed ils ont finalement cédé et donné leur accord.

cave[2] ['keɪvɪ] *Br dated & school sl* ◇ *n*: to keep ~ faire le guet.
◇ *interj*: ~! pet! *dated*, vingt-deux!

caveat ['kævɪæt] *n* avertissement *m*; JUR notification *f* d'opposition.

cave dweller [keɪv-] *n* [in prehistory] homme *m* des cavernes; [troglodyte] troglodyte *m*.

cave-in [keɪv-] *n* -**1.** [of ceiling, floor] effondrement *m*, affaissement *m*. -**2.** *inf fig* effondrement *m*, dégonflage *m*.
caveman ['keɪvmæn] (*pl* cavemen [-men]) *n literal* homme *m* des cavernes; *fig* brute *f*.
cave painting [keɪv-] *n* peinture *f* rupestre.
cavern ['kævən] *n* caverne *f*.
cavernous ['kævənəs] *adj* -**1.** *fig*: a ~ building un bâtiment très vaste à l'intérieur; ~ eyes des yeux enfoncés; ~ depths des profondeurs insondables; a ~ voice une voix caverneuse. -**2.** GEOL plein de cavernes.
caviar(e) ['kævɪɑːʳ] *n* caviar *m*.
cavil ['kævl] (*Br pt* & *pp* cavilled, *cont* cavilling, *Am pt* & *pp* caviled, *cont* caviling) ◇ *vi* chicaner, ergoter; to ~ at sthg chicaner OR ergoter sur qqch.
◇ *n* chicane *f*, ergotage *m*.
caving ['keɪvɪŋ] *n* spéléologie *f*.
cavity ['kævətɪ] (*pl* cavities) *n* -**1.** [in rock, wood] cavité *f*, creux *m*. -**2.** ANAT cavité *f*; [in tooth] cavité *f*.
cavity wall ◇ *n* mur *m* creux OR à double paroi.
◇ *comp*: ~ insulation isolation *f* en murs creux.
cavort [kə'vɔːt] *vi* -**1.** *literal* cabrioler, gambader, faire des cabrioles. -**2.** *fig*: while his wife was off ~ing around Europe pendant que sa femme menait une vie de bâton de chaise en Europe.
caw [kɔː] ◇ *vi* croasser.
◇ *n* croassement *m*.
cawing ['kɔːɪŋ] *n* croassement *m*.
cay [keɪ] *n* [sandbank] banc *m* de sable; [coral reef] banc *m* OR récif *m* de corail.
Cayenne [keɪ'en] *pr n* Cayenne.
cayenne pepper *n* poivre *m* de cayenne.
cayman ['keɪmən] *n* caïman *m*.
Cayman Islands *pl pr n*: the ~ les îles *fpl* Caïmans.
CB *n* -**1.** (*abbr of* Citizens' Band) CB *f*. -**2.** (*abbr of* Companion of (the Order of) the Bath) *distinction honorifique britannique*.
CBC (*abbr of* Canadian Broadcasting Corporation) *pr n office national canadien de radiodiffusion*.
CBE (*abbr of* Companion of (the Order of) the British Empire) *n distinction honorifique britannique*.
CBI (*abbr of* Confederation of British Industry) *pr n association du patronat britannique*, ≃ CNPF *m*.
CBR (*abbr of* chemical, bacteriological and radiation) *comp* chimique, bactériologique et radioactif.
CBS (*abbr of* Columbia Broadcasting System) *pr n chaîne de télévision américaine*.
cc ◇ *n* (*abbr of* cubic centimetre) cm^3.
◇ (*written abbr of* carbon copy) pcc.
CC *written abbr of* county council.
CCA (*abbr of* Circuit Court of Appeals) *n cours d'appel du système judiciaire des États-Unis avant 1948*.
CCTV *n abbr of* closed-circuit television.
CCU *n abbr of* coronary care unit.
CD ◇ *n* -**1.** (*abbr of* compact disc) CD *m*. -**2.** *abbr of* Civil Defence.
◇ (*written abbr of* Corps Diplomatique) CD.
CDC (*abbr of* Center for Disease Control) *pr n aux États-Unis, institut fédéral de recherche sur les causes et la prévention des maladies*.
CDI (*abbr of* compact disc interactive) *n* CDI *m*.
Cdr. *written abbr of* commander.
CD-ROM [ˌsiːdiː'rɒm] (*abbr of* compact disc read only memory) *n* CD-ROM *m*, CD-Rom *m*, DOC *m offic*.
CDT *n abbr of* Central Daylight Time.
CDV (*abbr of* compact disc video) *n* CDV *m*, CD vidéo *m*.
CDW *n abbr of* collision damage waiver.
CE *n abbr of* Church of England.
cease [siːs] ◇ *vi fml* [activity, noise] cesser, s'arrêter; the rain eventually ~d il a finalement cessé de pleuvoir; to ~ and desist JUR se désister.
◇ *vt* [activity, efforts, work] cesser, arrêter; to ~ to do OR to ~ doing sthg cesser de OR arrêter de faire qqch; the firm has ~d trading l'entreprise a cessé ses activités; a county that ~d to exist in 1974 un comté qui n'existe plus depuis 1974; to ~ fire MIL cesser le feu.
◇ *n*: without ~ *fml* sans cesse.
ceasefire [ˌsiːs'faɪəʳ] *n* cessez-le-feu *m inv*; to declare a ~ déclarer un cessez-le-feu; to agree to a ~ accepter un cessez-le-feu.
ceaseless ['siːslɪs] *adj* incessant, continuel.
ceaselessly ['siːslɪslɪ] *adv* sans cesse, continuellement.
Cecilia [sɪ'siːljə] *pr n*: Saint ~ sainte Cécile.
cecum (*pl* ceca) *Am* = **caecum**.
cedar ['siːdəʳ] ◇ *n* cèdre *m*; ~ of Lebanon cèdre *m* du Liban.
◇ *comp* de OR en cèdre.
cedarwood ['siːdəwʊd] *n* (bois *m* de) cèdre *m*.
cede [siːd] *vt* céder.
cedilla [sɪ'dɪlə] *n* cédille *f*.
CEEB (*abbr of* College Entry Examination Board) *pr n commission d'admission dans l'enseignement supérieur aux États-Unis*.
Ceefax® ['siːfæks] *pr n service de télétexte de la BBC*.
ceilidh ['keɪlɪ] *n soirée de danse et de musique folklorique (en Irlande et en Écosse)*.
ceiling ['siːlɪŋ] ◇ *n* -**1.** [of room] plafond *m*. -**2.** AERON & METEOR plafond *m*; the cloud ~ le plafond de nuages. -**3.** COMM & ECON plafond *m*; prices have reached their ~ les prix ont atteint leur plafond; the government has set a 3% ~ on wage rises le gouvernement a limité à 3 % les augmentations de salaire.
◇ *comp* [charge, price] plafond *(inv)*.
celandine ['seləndaɪn] *n* chélidoine *f*.
Celebes [se'liːbɪz] *pr n* Célèbes.
Celebes Sea *pr n*: the ~ la mer de Célèbes.
celebrant ['selɪbrənt] *n* RELIG célébrant *m*, officiant *m*.
celebrate ['selɪbreɪt] ◇ *vt* -**1.** [birthday, Christmas] fêter, célébrer; [event, victory] célébrer. -**2.** [praise - person, sb's beauty] célébrer, glorifier. -**3.** RELIG: to ~ mass célébrer la messe.
◇ *vi*: let's ~! [gen] il faut fêter ça!; [with drinks] il faut arroser ça!
celebrated ['selɪbreɪtɪd] *adj* célèbre.
celebration [ˌselɪ'breɪʃn] *n* -**1.** [of birthday, Christmas] célébration *f*; [of anniversary, past event] commémoration *f*; in ~ of Christmas pour fêter OR célébrer Noël; in ~ of forty years of peace pour commémorer quarante ans de paix. -**2.** MUS & POET éloge *m*, louange *f*; he wrote the poem in ~ of her beauty il a écrit le poème pour célébrer sa beauté. -**3.** RELIG célébration *f*. -**4.** *(often pl)* [occasion - of birthday, Christmas] fête *f*, fêtes *fpl*; [- of historical event] cérémonies *fpl*, fête *f*; this calls for a ~! il faut fêter ça!, il faut arroser ça!; to join in the ~s participer à la fête OR aux festivités; birthday ~s fête d'anniversaire.
celebratory [ˌselə'breɪtərɪ] *adj* [dinner] de fête; [official ceremony] commémoratif; [atmosphere, mood] de fête, festif *fml*.
celebrity [sɪ'lebrətɪ] (*pl* celebrities) *n* -**1.** [fame] célébrité *f*. -**2.** [person] vedette *f*, célébrité *f*.
celeriac [sɪ'lerɪæk] *n* céleri-rave *m*.
celerity [sɪ'lerətɪ] *n lit* célérité *f*, rapidité *f*.
celery ['selərɪ] ◇ *n* céleri *m*.
◇ *comp* [salt, plant] de céleri.
celestial [sɪ'lestjəl] *adj literal* & *fig* céleste.
celestial equator *n* équateur *m* céleste.
celestial pole *n* pôle *m* céleste.
celibacy ['selɪbəsɪ] *n* célibat *m*.
celibate ['selɪbət] ◇ *adj* célibataire.
◇ *n* célibataire *mf*.
cell [sel] ◇ *n* -**1.** BIOL & BOT cellule *f*. -**2.** [in prison, convent] cellule *f*; he spent the night in the ~s il a passé la nuit en cellule; she was released after two days in the ~s elle a été relâchée après deux jours de cellule. -**3.** ELEC élément *m* (de pile). -**4.** POL cellule *f*.
◇ *comp* BIOL [wall] cellulaire; ~ division multiplication *f* cellulaire.
cellar ['seləʳ] *n* [for wine] cave *f*, cellier *m*; [for coal, bric-a-brac] cave *f*; [for food] cellier *m*; he keeps a good ~ il a une bonne cave.
cellist ['tʃelɪst] *n* violoncelliste *mf*.
cello ['tʃeləʊ] *n* violoncelle *m*.
Cellophane® ['seləfeɪn] *n* Cellophane® *f*.
cellular ['seljʊləʳ] *adj* -**1.** ANAT & BIOL cellulaire. -**2.** CONSTR cellulaire. -**3.** TEX [blanket] en cellular.
cellular telephone *n* téléphone *m* cellulaire.
cellulite ['seljʊlaɪt] *n* cellulite *f*.
Celluloid® ['seljʊlɔɪd] ◇ *n* Celluloïd® *m*; to capture sthg/sb on ~ *fig* filmer qqch/qqn.
◇ *adj* en Celluloïd®.
cellulose ['seljʊləʊs] ◇ *n* cellulose *f*.
◇ *adj* en OR de cellulose, cellulosique.
Celsius ['selsɪəs] *adj* Celsius; 25 degrees ~ 25 degrés Celsius.
Celt [kelt] *n* Celte *mf*.
Celtic ['keltɪk] ◇ *n* LING celtique *m*.
◇ *adj* celtique, celte; ~ cross croix *f* celtique.
cement [sɪ'ment] ◇ *n* -**1.** CONSTR & *fig* ciment *m*. -**2.** [in dentistry] amalgame *m*. -**3.** [glue] colle *f*.
◇ *vt* -**1.** CONSTR & *fig* cimenter. -**2.** [in dentistry] obturer.
cementation [ˌsiːmen'teɪʃn] *n* CONSTR & *fig* cimentation *f*.
cement mixer *n* bétonnière *f*.
cemetery ['semɪtrɪ] (*pl* cemeteries) *n* cimetière *m*.
cenotaph ['senətɑːf] *n* cénotaphe *m*; the Cenotaph *monument aux morts des deux guerres mondiales (à Londres)*.
censer ['sensəʳ] *n* encensoir *m*.
censor ['sensəʳ] ◇ *n* censeur *m* CIN & THÉÂT.
◇ *vt* censurer.
censorious [sen'sɔːrɪəs] *adj fml* [comments, criticism] sévère; [person] porté à la censure.
censorship ['sensəʃɪp] *n* -**1.** [act, practice] censure *f*. -**2.** [office of censor] censorat *m*.
censurable ['senʃərəbl] *adj fml* blâmable, qui mérite la réprobation.
censure ['senʃəʳ] ◇ *n* blâme *m*, critique *f*.
◇ *vt* blâmer, critiquer.
census ['sensəs] *n* recensement *m*; to conduct OR to take a population ~ faire le recensement de la population, recenser la population.
cent [sent] *n* [coin] cent *m*; *Am fig*: it's not worth a ~ ça ne vaut rien; I haven't got a ~ je n'ai pas un sou.
centaur ['sentɔːʳ] *n* centaure *m*.
centenarian [ˌsentɪ'neərɪən] ◇ *n* centenaire *mf*.
◇ *adj* centenaire.
centenary [sen'tiːnərɪ] (*pl* centenaries) ◇ *n* [anniversary] centenaire *m*, centième anniversaire *m*; the organization is celebrating its ~ l'organisation fête son centenaire; the ~ of Mozart's birth le centenaire de la naissance de Mozart.
◇ *adj* centenaire; ~ celebrations fêtes *fpl* du centenaire.
centennial [sen'tenjəl] ◇ *n Am* centenaire *m*, centième anniversaire *m*.
◇ *adj* -**1.** [in age] centenaire, séculaire. -**2.** [every hundred years] séculaire.
center *etc Am* = **centre**.
centerfold *Am* = **centrefold**.
centesimal [sen'tesɪml] *adj* centésimal.
centigrade ['sentɪgreɪd] *adj* centigrade; 25 degrees ~ 25 degrés centigrades.
centigram(me) ['sentɪgræm] *n* centigramme *m*.
centilitre *Br*, **centiliter** *Am* ['sentɪˌliːtəʳ] *n* centilitre *m*.
centime ['sɒntiːm] *n* centime *m*.
centimetre *Br*, **centimeter** *Am* ['sentɪˌmiːtəʳ] *n* centimètre *m*.

centipede ['sentɪpiːd] *n* mille-pattes *m inv.*

cento ['sentəʊ] (*pl* centos OR centones [sen'təʊniːz]) *n* compilation *f* littéraire.

central ['sentrəl] ◇ *adj* central; this concept is ~ to his theory ce concept est au centre de sa théorie.
◇ *n Am dated* central *m* téléphonique.

Central African ◇ *n* Centrafricain *m*, -e *f*.
◇ *adj* centrafricain.

Central African Republic *pr n*: the ~ la République centrafricaine; in the ~ en République centrafricaine.

Central America *pr n* Amérique *f* centrale; in ~ en Amérique centrale.

Central American ◇ *n* Centraméricain *m*, -e *f*.
◇ *adj* centraméricain.

Central Asia *pr n* Asie *f* centrale; in ~ en Asie centrale.

central bank *n* banque *f* centrale.

Central Daylight Time *n* heure *f* d'été du centre des États-Unis.

Central Europe *pr n* Europe *f* centrale.

Central European ◇ *n* habitant *m*, -e *f* de l'Europe centrale.
◇ *adj* d'Europe centrale.

Central European Time *n* heure *f* de l'Europe centrale.

central government *n* gouvernement *m* central.

central heating *n* chauffage *m* central.

centralism ['sentrəlɪzm] *n* centralisme *m*.

centrality [sen'trælətɪ] (*pl* centralities) *n* [of argument, idea, theme] caractère *m* central OR essentiel; [of facilities, location] situation *f* centrale.

centralization [ˌsentrəlaɪ'zeɪʃn] *n* centralisation *f*.

centralize, -ise ['sentrəlaɪz] ◇ *vt* centraliser.
◇ *vi* se centraliser.

central locking *n* AUT verrouillage *m* central.

centrally ['sentrəlɪ] *adv* [located] au centre; [organized] de façon centralisée; ~ based centralisé; ~ heated ayant le chauffage central; the house is ~ situated la maison est située de façon centrale; a ~ planned economy ECON une économie dirigée.

central nervous system *n* système *m* nerveux central.

central processing unit *n* COMPUT unité *f* centrale.

central reservation *n Br* AUT terre-plein *m* central.

Central Standard Time *n* heure *f* d'hiver du centre des États-Unis.

centre *Br*, **center** *Am* ['sentə^r] ◇ *n* -**1.** [gen & GEOM] centre *m*; in the ~ au centre ☐ ~ of gravity centre de gravité; ~ of infection MED foyer *m* d'infection. -**2.** [of town] centre *m*; urban ~ centre urbain, agglomération *f* urbaine; she lives in the city ~ elle habite dans le centre-ville. -**3.** *fig* [of unrest] foyer *m*; [of debate] cœur *m*, centre *m*; at the ~ of the debate au cœur du débat; the ~ of attention le centre d'attention. -**4.** [place, building] centre *m*; a sports/health ~ un centre sportif/médical. -**5.** POL centre *m*; to be left/right of ~ être du centre gauche/droit. -**6.** TECH: to be off ~ être décentré. -**7.** SPORT [pass] centre *m*.
◇ *comp* -**1.** [central] central; the ~ court [in tennis] le court central. -**2.** POL du centre.
◇ *vt* -**1.** [place in centre] centrer. -**2.** CIN & PHOT cadrer. -**3.** *fig* [attention] concentrer, fixer; to ~ one's hopes on sthg mettre OR fonder tous ses espoirs sur qqch. -**4.** SPORT: to ~ the ball centrer.
◆ **centre around** *vt insep* tourner autour de; the debate ~s around politics le débat tourne autour de la politique.
◆ **centre on** *vt insep* se concentrer sur; all their attention was ~d on the World Cup toute leur attention était concentrée sur la coupe du monde; the conversation ~d on politics la conversation tournait autour de la politique.
◆ **centre round** = **centre around**.

centre-back *n* arrière *m* central.

centre bit *n* TECH mèche *f* à bois.

centreboard *Br*, **centerboard** *Am* ['sentəbɔːd] *n* dérive *f* (*d'un bateau*).

-centred *Br*, **-centered** *Am* ['sentəd] *in cpds*: self~ égocentrique.

centrefold *Br*, **centerfold** *Am* ['sentəˌfəʊld] *n* grande photo *f* de pin-up (*au milieu d'un magazine*).

centre-forward *n* avant-centre *m*.

centre-half *n* demi-centre *m*.

centreline *Br*, **centerline** *Am* ['sentəlaɪn] *n* axe *m*, ligne *f* médiane.

centrepiece *Br*, **centerpiece** *Am* ['sentəpiːs] *n* [outstanding feature] joyau *m*; [on table] milieu *m* de table; [of meal] pièce *f* de résistance.

centreplate *Br*, **centerplate** *Am* ['sentəpleɪt] = **centreboard**.

centre punch *n* pointeau *m*.

centre-spread = **centrefold**.

centre three-quarter *n* trois-quarts *m* centre.

centrifugal [sen'trɪfjʊgl] *adj* centrifuge; ~ force force *f* centrifuge.

centrifuge ['sentrɪfjuːdʒ] ◇ *n* TECH centrifugeur *m*, centrifugeuse *f*.
◇ *vt* centrifuger.

centripetal [sen'trɪpɪtl] *adj* centripète; ~ force force *f* centripète.

centrism ['sentrɪzm] *n* centrisme *m*.

centrist ['sentrɪst] ◇ *adj* centriste.
◇ *n* centriste *mf*.

centuplicate [*vb* sen'tjuːplɪkeɪt, *adj* & *n* sen'tjuːplɪkət] ◇ *vt* centupler.
◇ *adj* centuple.
◇ *n* centuple *m*.

centurion [sen'tjʊərɪən] *n* centurion *m*.

century ['sentʃʊrɪ] (*pl* centuries) *n* -**1.** [time] siècle *m*; in the 20th ~ au 20e siècle; centuries old séculaire, vieux de plusieurs siècles; this house is five centuries old cette maison a OR est vieille de cinq siècles. -**2.** MIL centurie *f*.

CEO *n abbr of* chief executive officer.

cep [sep] *n* cèpe *m*.

cephalic [sə'fælɪk, ke'fælɪk] *adj* céphalique.

cephalopod ['sefələpɒd] *n* céphalopode *m*.

ceramic [sɪ'ræmɪk] ◇ *adj* [art] céramique; [vase] en céramique; a ~ hob *Br* une plaque vitrocéramique.
◇ *n* -**1.** = **ceramics**. -**2.** [object] (objet *m* en) céramique *f*.

ceramics [sɪ'ræmɪks] *n* (*U*) céramique *f*.

Cerberus ['sɜːbərəs] *pr n* Cerbère.

cereal ['sɪərɪəl] ◇ *n* -**1.** AGR [plant] céréale *f*; [grain] grain *m* (de céréale). -**2.** CULIN: baby ~ bouillie *f*; (breakfast) ~ céréales *fpl* (pour petit déjeuner).
◇ *adj* [farming] céréalier; ~ crops céréales *fpl*.

cerebellum [ˌserɪ'beləm] (*pl* cerebellums OR cerebella [-lə]) *n* cervelet *m*.

cerebral ['serɪbrəl] *adj* cérébral.

cerebral death *n* mort *f* cérébrale.

cerebral palsy *n* paralysie *f* cérébrale.

cerebration [ˌserɪ'breɪʃn] *n fml* réflexion *f*, méditation *f*; *hum* cogitation *f*.

cerebrospinal [ˌserəbrə'spaɪnl] *adj* cérébrospinal.

cerebrum ['serɪbrəm] (*pl* cerebrums OR cerebra [-brə]) *n* cerveau *m*.

ceremonial [ˌserɪ'məʊnjəl] ◇ *adj* -**1.** [rite, visit] cérémoniel; [robes] de cérémonie. -**2.** *Am* [post] honorifique.
◇ *n* cérémonial *m*; RELIG cérémonial *m*, rituel *m*.

ceremonially [ˌserɪ'məʊnjəlɪ] *adv* selon le cérémonial d'usage.

ceremonious [ˌserɪ'məʊnjəs] *adj* solennel; [mock-solemn] cérémonieux.

ceremoniously [ˌserɪ'məʊnjəslɪ] *adv* solennellement, avec cérémonie; [mock-solemnly] cérémonieusement.

ceremony [*Br* 'serɪmənɪ, *Am* 'serəməʊnɪ] (*pl* ceremonies) *n* -**1.** (*U*) [formality] cérémonie *f*, cérémonies *fpl*; with much ~ avec beaucoup de cérémonie; without ~ sans cérémonie OR cérémonies; we don't stand on ~ nous ne faisons pas de cérémonies. -**2.** [gen & RELIG] cérémonie *f*.

Ceres ['sɪəriːz] *pr n* Cérès.

cerise [sə'riːz] *adj* (de) couleur cerise, cerise (*inv*).

cerium ['sɪərɪəm] *n* cérium *m*.

cert *inf* [sɜːt] *n Br* certitude *f*; it's a dead ~ that he'll win il va gagner, ça ne fait pas un pli OR c'est couru d'avance; he's a ~ for the job il est sûr d'obtenir le poste.

cert. *written abbr of* certificate.

certain ['sɜːtn] ◇ *adj* -**1.** [sure] certain, sûr; to be ~ of sthg être sûr de qqch; I'm ~ of it! j'en suis sûr!; she was quite ~ about what she had seen elle était tout à fait sûre de ce qu'elle avait vu; he was ~ (that) she was there il était certain qu'elle était là; it's ~ that she will get the job il est sûr qu'elle aura le poste; it's still not ~ that he's going to England il n'est pas encore certain OR sûr qu'il aille en Angleterre; to be ~ to do sthg être sûr de faire qqch; he's ~ to win il est sûr qu'il va gagner; he's ~ to come il ne manquera pas de venir, il viendra sûrement; to make ~ of sthg [check] vérifier qqch, s'assurer de qqch; [be sure to have] s'assurer qqch; you ought to make ~ of the time vous devriez vérifier l'heure; he made ~ that all the doors were locked il a vérifié que toutes les portes étaient fermées; I made ~ of a good seat je me suis assuré une bonne place. -**2.** [inevitable - death, failure] certain, inévitable; the soldiers faced ~ death les soldats allaient à une mort certaine. -**3.** [definite, infallible - cure] sûr, infaillible.
◇ *det* -**1.** [particular but unspecified] certain; on a ~ day in June un certain jour de juin; in ~ places à certains endroits; he has a ~ something about him il a un certain je ne sais quoi; she has a ~ charm elle a un certain charme; if I were to ask you to meet me at a ~ time and in a ~ place... si je te demandais de me retrouver à telle heure, à tel endroit... -**2.** [not known personally] certain; a ~ Mr Roberts un certain M. Roberts. -**3.** [some] certain; there's been a ~ amount of confusion over this il y a eu une certaine confusion à ce sujet; to a ~ extent OR degree dans une certaine mesure; ~ people certaines personnes.
◇ *pron* certains *mpl*, certaines *fpl*; ~ of his colleagues certains OR quelques-uns de ses collègues; ~ of the pages certaines pages.
◆ **for certain** *adv phr* pour sûr; I don't know for ~ je n'en suis pas certain; I can't say for ~ je ne peux pas l'affirmer; you'll have it tomorrow for ~ vous l'aurez demain sans faute; that's for ~! c'est sûr et certain!, cela ne fait pas de doute!

certainly ['sɜːtnlɪ] *adv* -**1.** [without doubt] certainement, assurément, certes; he is ~ very handsome il est très beau, ça ne fait pas de doute; I will ~ come je ne manquerai pas de venir, je viendrai, c'est sûr; it will ~ be ready tomorrow cela sera prêt demain sans faute. -**2.** [of course] certainement, bien sûr; can you help me? — ~! pouvez-vous m'aider? — bien sûr OR volontiers!; ~, sir! bien sûr, monsieur!; are you angry? — I most ~ am! êtes-vous fâché? — oui, et comment!; ~ not! bien sûr que non!, certainement pas!

certainty ['sɜːtntɪ] (*pl* certainties) *n* -**1.** [conviction] certitude *f*, conviction *f*; I cannot say with any ~ when I shall arrive je ne peux pas dire exactement à quelle heure j'arriverai; we can have no ~ of success nous ne sommes pas sûrs de réussir; moral ~ certitude morale. -**2.** [fact] certitude *f*, fait *m* certain; [event] certitude *f*, événement *m* certain; for a ~ à coup sûr, sans aucun doute; I know for a ~ that he's leaving je sais à coup sûr qu'il part; their victory is now a ~ leur victoire est maintenant assurée OR ne fait aucun doute; **it's an absolute ~** c'est une chose certaine, c'est une certitude absolue.

CertEd [sɜːt'ed] (*abbr of* **Certificate in Education**) *n diplôme universitaire britannique en sciences de l'éducation*.

certifiable [ˌsɜːtɪ'faɪəbl] *adj* -**1.** [gen & JUR - fact, document] qu'on peut certifier. -**2.** [insane] bon à enfermer (à l'asile).

certificate [sə'tɪfɪkət] *n* -**1.** [gen & ADMIN] certificat *m*; **~ of airworthiness** AERON certificat de navigabilité; **~ of origin** COMM certificat d'origine; **birth ~** acte *m* OR extrait *m* de naissance; **master's ~** NAUT brevet *m* de capitaine. -**2.** [academic] diplôme *m*; [vocational - of apprenticeship] brevet *m*; **Certificate of Secondary Education** *Br* SCH → **CSE**.

certificated [sə'tɪfɪkeɪtɪd] *adj* diplômé.

certification [ˌsɜːtɪfɪ'keɪʃn] *n* -**1.** [act] certification *f*, authentification *f*. -**2.** [certificate] certificat *m*.

certified ['sɜːtɪfaɪd] *adj Am* SCH: **~ teacher** [in state school] professeur *m* diplômé; [in private school] professeur *m* habilité.

certified mail *n Am* envoi *m* recommandé; **to send sthg by ~** envoyer qqch en recommandé avec accusé de réception.

certified public accountant *n Am* ≃ expert-comptable *m*.

certify ['sɜːtɪfaɪ] (*pt* & *pp* **certified**) ◇ *vt* -**1.** [gen & ADMIN] certifier, attester; MED [death] constater; **to ~ that sthg is true** attester que qqch est vrai; **certified copy** JUR copie *f* certifiée conforme; **to ~ sb (insane)** PSYCH déclarer qqn atteint d'aliénation mentale; **he ought to be certified!** *inf fig* il est bon à enfermer! -**2.** *Am* FIN [cheque] certifier. -**3.** COMM [goods] garantir.
◇ *vi*: **to ~ to sthg** attester qqch.

certitude ['sɜːtɪtjuːd] *n fml* certitude *f*.

cerulean [sɪ'ruːljən] *adj lit* céruléen *lit*, azuré.

cerumen [sɪ'ruːmen] *n* cérumen *m*.

Cervantes [sə'væntɪz] *pr n* Cervantès.

cervical [*Br* sə'vaɪkl, *Am* 'sɜːrvɪkl] *adj* cervical.

cervical cancer *n* cancer *m* du col de l'utérus.

cervical smear *n* frottis *m* vaginal.

cervicitis [ˌsɜːvɪ'saɪtɪs] *n* (*U*) cervicite *f*.

cervix ['sɜːvɪks] (*pl* **cervixes** OR **cervices** [-siːz]) *n* col *m* de l'utérus.

Cesarean, Cesarian *Am* = **Caesarean**.

cesium *Am* = **caesium**.

cessation [se'seɪʃn] *n fml* cessation *f*, suspension *f*; **~ of hostilities** MIL cessation OR suspension des hostilités.

cession ['seʃn] *n* JUR cession *f*.

cesspit ['sespɪt] *n* fosse *f* d'aisances; *fig* cloaque *m*.

cesspool ['sespuːl] = **cesspit**.

cesura [sɪ'zjʊərə] (*pl* cesuras OR cesurae [-riː]) = **caesura**.

CET *n abbr of* **Central European Time**.

cetacean [sɪ'teɪʃjən] ◇ *adj* cétacé.
◇ *n* cétacé *m*.

cetane ['siːteɪn] *n* cétane *m*.

cetane number *n* indice *m* de cétane.

Ceylon [sɪ'lɒn] *pr n* Ceylan; **in ~** à Ceylan.

Ceylonese [ˌsɪlə'niːz] ◇ *n* -**1.** [person] Ceylanais *m*, -e *f*, Sri Lankais *m*, -e *f*. -**2.** LING cinghalais *m*.
◇ *adj* ceylanais, sri lankais.

cf. (*written abbr of* **confer**) cf.

c & f (*written abbr of* **cost and freight**) c et f.

CFC (*abbr of* **chlorofluorocarbon**) *n* CFC *m*.

cfi, CFI (*abbr of* **cost, freight and insurance**) caf, CAF.

cg (*written abbr of* **centigram**) cg.

CG *n abbr of* **coastguard**.

C & G (*abbr of* **City and Guilds**) *n diplôme britannique d'enseignement technique*.

CGT *n abbr of* **capital gains tax**.

ch (*written abbr of* **central heating**) ch. cent.

ch. (*written abbr of* **chapter**) chap.

CH *n abbr of* **Companion of Honour**.

cha-cha(-cha) ['tʃɑːtʃɑː, ˌtʃɑːtʃɑː'tʃɑː] ◇ *n* cha-cha-cha *m inv*.
◇ *vi* danser le cha-cha-cha.

Chad [tʃæd] *pr n* Tchad *m*; **in ~** au Tchad; **Lake ~** le lac Tchad.

Chadian ['tʃædɪən] ◇ *n* Tchadien *m*, -enne *f*.
◇ *adj* tchadien.

chador ['tʃɑːdɔː] *n* tchador *m*.

chafe [tʃeɪf] ◇ *vt* -**1.** [rub] frictionner, frotter. -**2.** [irritate] frotter contre, irriter; **his shirt collar ~d his neck** son col de chemise lui irritait le cou. -**3.** [wear away - collar] élimer, user (par le frottement); [paint] érafler; [rope] raguer.
◇ *vi* -**1.** [become worn - gen] s'user (par le frottement); [rope] raguer. -**2.** [skin] s'irriter; *fig* [person] s'irriter, s'impatienter; **to ~ at** OR **under sthg** s'irriter de qqch; **the media ~d under the military censorship** soumis à la censure militaire, les médias rongeaient leur frein.
◇ *n* friction *f*, usure *f*.

chaff [tʃɑːf] ◇ *n* -**1.** [of grain] balle *f*; [hay, straw] menue paille *f*. -**2.** *dated* [teasing] taquinerie *f*, raillerie *f*.
◇ *vt dated* [tease] taquiner.

chaffinch ['tʃæfɪntʃ] *n* pinson *m*.

chaffing ['tʃɑːfɪŋ] *n dated* taquinerie *f*, raillerie *f*.

chagrin ['ʃægrɪn] ◇ *n lit* (vif) dépit *m*, (vive) déception *f* OR contrariété *f*; **much to my ~** à mon grand dépit.
◇ *vt* contrarier, décevoir.

chain [tʃeɪn] ◇ *n* -**1.** [gen] chaîne *f*; **we keep the dog on a ~** notre chien est toujours attaché; **to pull the ~** tirer la chasse d'eau; **to form a human ~** former une chaîne humaine ❑ **bicycle ~** chaîne de bicyclette; **(snow) ~s** AUT chaînes (à neige). -**2.** ADMIN: **~ of office** ≃ écharpe *f* de maire. -**3.** [of mountains] chaîne *f*; [of islands] chapelet *m*. -**4.** [of events] série *f*, suite *f*; [of ideas] suite *f*. -**5.** COMM [of shops] chaîne *f*. -**6.** TECH [for surveying] chaîne *f* d'arpenteur. -**7.** [measure of length] chaînée *f (22 yards, soit environ 20 m 10)*.
◇ *vt literal* & *fig* enchaîner; [door] mettre la chaîne à; **the dog was ~ed to the post** le chien était attaché au poteau (par une chaîne); **to be ~ed to one's desk** *fig* être rivé à son bureau.
◆ **chains** *npl* [for prisoner] chaînes *fpl*, entraves *fpl*; **a prisoner in ~s** un prisonnier enchaîné.
◆ **chain down** *vt sep* enchaîner, attacher avec une chaîne.
◆ **chain up** *vt sep* [prisoner] enchaîner; [dog] mettre à l'attache, attacher.

chain armour = **chain mail**.

chain drive *n* transmission *f* par chaîne.

chain gang *n* chaîne *f* de forçats.

chain letter *n* lettre *f* faisant partie d'une chaîne.

chain lightning *n* (*U*) éclairs *mpl* en zigzag.

chain mail *n* (*U*) cotte *f* de mailles.

chain reaction *n* réaction *f* en chaîne; **to set off a ~** provoquer une réaction en chaîne.

chain saw *n* tronçonneuse *f*.

chain-smoke *vi* fumer cigarette sur cigarette.

chain smoker *n* fumeur invétéré *m*, fumeuse invétérée *f*, gros fumeur *m*, grosse fumeuse *f*.

chain stitch *n* point *m* de chaînette.
◆ **chain-stitch** *vi* & *vt* coudre au point de chaînette.

chain store *n* grand magasin *m* à succursales multiples.

chainwheel ['tʃeɪnwiːl] *n* roue *f* dentée *(de bicyclette)*, pignon *m*.

chair [tʃeə^r] ◇ *n* -**1.** [seat] chaise *f*; [armchair] fauteuil *m*; **please take a ~** asseyez-vous, je vous prie; **in the dentist's ~** dans le fauteuil du dentiste. -**2.** [chairperson] président *m*, -e *f*; **to be in the ~** présider; **to take the ~** prendre la présidence. -**3.** UNIV chaire *f*; **to hold the ~ of French** avoir OR occuper la chaire de français. -**4.** [for execution]: **to go** OR **to be sent to the ~** *inf Am* passer à la chaise électrique; **electric ~** chaise *f* électrique.
◇ *comp*: **~ back** dossier *m* de chaise; **~ leg** pied *m* de chaise.
◇ *vt* -**1.** ADMIN [meeting] présider. -**2.** *Br* [hero, victor] porter en triomphe.

chairlady ['tʃeəˌleɪdɪ] (*pl* **chairladies**) = **chairwoman**.

chair lift *n* télésiège *m*.

chairman ['tʃeəmən] (*pl* **chairmen** [-mən]) *n* -**1.** [at meeting] président *m (d'un comité)*; **to act as ~** présider la séance; **Mr Chairman** Monsieur le Président; **Madam Chairman** Madame la Présidente. -**2.** COMM président-directeur *m* général, P-D G *m*. -**3.** POL: **Chairman Mao** le président Mao.

chairmanship ['tʃeəmənʃɪp] *n* présidence *f (d'un comité etc)*; **under the ~ of Mr Black** sous la présidence de M. Black.

chairperson ['tʃeəˌpɜːsn] *n* président *m*, -e *f (d'un comité)*.

chairwoman ['tʃeəˌwʊmən] (*pl* **chairwomen** [-ˌwɪmɪn]) *n* présidente *f (d'un comité)*; **Madam Chairwoman** Madame la Présidente.

chaise [ʃeɪz] *n* cabriolet *m*.

chaise longue [-lɒŋ] *n* chaise *f* longue.

chalcedony [kæl'sedənɪ] *n* calcédoine *f*.

Chald(a)ea [kæl'diːə] *pr n* Chaldée *f*.

Chald(a)ean [kæl'diːən] ◇ *n* Chaldéen *m*, -enne *f*.
◇ *adj* chaldéen.

chalet ['ʃæleɪ] *n* chalet *m*.

chalice ['tʃælɪs] *n* -**1.** RELIG calice *m*. -**2.** [goblet] coupe *f*.

chalk [tʃɔːk] ◇ *n* -**1.** [substance] craie *f*; **a piece of ~** un morceau de craie ❑ **~ and talk** *Br méthode d'enseignement traditionnelle*; **they're as different as ~ and cheese** *Br* c'est le jour et la nuit. -**2.** [piece] craie *f*. -**3.** *phr*: **by a long ~** *Br* de beaucoup, de loin; **not by a long ~** loin de là, tant s'en faut; **the best by a long ~** le meilleur, et de loin.
◇ *vt* [write] écrire à la craie; [mark] marquer à la craie; [rub with chalk] frotter de craie; **to ~ one's name on a wall** écrire son nom sur un mur à la craie; **to ~ a billiard cue** enduire une queue de billard de craie.
◆ **chalk out** *vt sep* [draw - line, pattern] esquisser OR tracer (à la craie).
◆ **chalk up** *vt sep* -**1.** [write in chalk] écrire à la craie. -**2.** [credit]: **~ that one up to me** mettez cela sur mon compte; **to ~ sthg up to experience** *fig* mettre qqch au compte de l'expérience. -**3.** [add up - points, score] totaliser, marquer. -**4.** [attain - victory] remporter; [- profits] encaisser.

chalkboard ['tʃɔːkbɔːd] *n Am* tableau *m* (noir).

chalkface ['tʃɔːkfeɪs] *n hum* & SCH expérience *f* pratique (de l'enseignement).

chalkpit ['tʃɔːkpɪt] *n* carrière *f* de craie.

chalktalk ['tʃɔːktɔːk] *n Am* conférence *f*.

chalky ['tʃɔːkɪ] (*compar* **chalkier**, *superl* **chalkiest**) *adj* [earth, water] calcaire; [hands] couvert de craie; [complexion] crayeux, blafard; [taste] de craie.

challenge ['tʃælɪndʒ] ◇ *vt* -**1.** [gen - defy] défier; **to ~ sb** lancer un défi à qqn; **to ~ sb to do sthg** défier qqn de faire qqch; **to ~ sb to a game of tennis** inviter qqn à faire une partie de tennis; **to ~ sb to a duel** provoquer qqn en duel. -**2.** [demand effort from] mettre à l'épreuve; **she needs a job that really ~s her** elle a besoin d'un travail qui soit pour elle une gageure OR un challenge. -**3.** [contest - authority, findings, interpretation] contester, mettre en cause; **to ~ sb's right to do sthg** contester à qqn le droit de faire qqch. -**4.** MIL [subj: sentry] faire une sommation à. -**5.** JUR [juror] récuser. -**6.** *lit* [require] requérir.
◇ *n* -**1.** [in contest] défi *m*; **to issue a ~** lancer un défi; **to take up the ~** relever le défi; **Jackson's ~ for the leadership of the party** la tentative de Jackson pour s'emparer de la direction du parti; **the ~ of modern technology** *fig* le défi de la technologie moderne. -**2.** [in job, activity] défi *m*; **he needs a job that presents more of a ~** il a besoin d'un emploi plus

stimulant OR qui le mette plus à l'épreuve; the race was a great ~ to their skill la course a été un véritable défi pour eux. -**3.** [to right, authority] mise *f* en question, contestation *f*; the new law met with a ~ from the people la nouvelle loi s'est vue contestée par le peuple. -**4.** MIL [by sentry] sommation *f*; to give the ~ faire une sommation. -**5.** JUR récusation *f*.

challenged ['tʃælɪndʒd] *adj euph* handicapé; visually ~ malvoyant.

challenger ['tʃælɪndʒəʳ] *n* [gen] provocateur *m*, -trice *f*; POL & SPORT challenger *m*.

challenging ['tʃælɪndʒɪŋ] *adj* -**1.** [defiant] de défi. -**2.** [demanding - ideas, theory] provocateur, stimulant, exaltant; [- job, activity] stimulant, qui met à l'épreuve; to find o.s. in a ~ situation se trouver face à un défi.

challengingly ['tʃælɪndʒɪŋlɪ] *adv* -**1.** [defiantly] avec défiance; she stared ~ back at me elle me lança un regard lourd de défi. -**2.** [demandingly]: it's a ~ difficult task c'est une tâche difficile mais exaltante.

chamber ['tʃeɪmbəʳ] *n* -**1.** [hall, room] chambre *f*; the upper/lower Chamber *Br* POL la Chambre haute/basse. -**2.** *arch* [lodgings] logement *m*, appartement *m*. -**3.** [of a gun] chambre *f*. -**4.** ANAT [of the heart] cavité *f*; [of the eye] chambre *f*. -**5.** *inf dated* = **chamber pot**.

◆ **chambers** *npl* [of barrister, judge] cabinet *m*; [of solicitor] cabinet *m*, étude *f*; the case was heard in ~s JUR l'affaire a été jugée en référé.

chamber concert *n* concert *m* de musique de chambre.

chamberlain ['tʃeɪmbəlɪn] *n* chambellan *m*.

chambermaid ['tʃeɪmbəmeɪd] *n* femme *f* de chambre.

chamber music *n* musique *f* de chambre.

chamber of commerce *n* chambre *f* de commerce.

Chamber of Horrors *pr n*: the ~ *la Chambre des horreurs du musée de cire de Madame Tussaud (à Londres), spécialement consacrée aux meurtres et aux criminels célèbres.*

chamber of trade *n* chambre *f* des métiers.

chamber orchestra *n* orchestre *m* de chambre.

chamber pot *n* pot *m* de chambre.

chambray ['ʃæmbreɪ] *n* batiste *f*.

chameleon [kə'miːljən] *n* ZOOL & *fig* caméléon *m*.

chamfer ['tʃæmfəʳ] ◇ *n* chanfrein *m*.
◇ *vt* chanfreiner.

chammy ['ʃæmɪ] (*pl* chammies) *n* peau *f* de chamois.

chamois ['ʃæmwɑː] (*pl inv*) ◇ *n* ZOOL chamois *m*; [hide] peau *f* de chamois; (a) ~ leather (une) peau de chamois.
◇ *vt* -**1.** [leather, skin] chamoiser. -**2.** [polish] polir à la peau de chamois.

chamomile ['kæməmaɪl] = **camomile**.

champ [tʃæmp] ◇ *vt* mâchonner.
◇ *vi* -**1.** [munch] mâchonner. -**2.** [lose patience]: he was ~ing to meet his next opponent il brûlait de rencontrer son prochain adversaire ❑ to ~ at the bit: we were all ~ing at the bit to get started on rongeait tous notre frein en attendant de commencer.
◇ *n inf* crack *m*.

champagne [ʃæm'peɪn] ◇ *n* [wine] champagne *m*; a ~ glass une coupe à champagne.
◇ *adj* [colour] champagne *(inv)*; a ~-coloured sofa un canapé couleur champagne.

Champagne [ʃæm'peɪn] *pr n* Champagne *f*.

champagne cup *n* cocktail *m* au champagne.

champers *inf* ['ʃæmpəz] *n Br* champ' *m*.

champion ['tʃæmpjən] ◇ *n* -**1.** [winner] champion *m*, -onne *f*; the world chess ~ le champion du monde d'échecs; she's a ~ runner elle est championne de course. -**2.** [supporter] champion *m*, -onne *f*; he's a self-proclaimed ~ of the working man il se veut le champion des travailleurs.
◇ *vt* défendre, soutenir; she ~ed the cause of birth control elle s'est faite la championne de la régulation des naissances.

championship ['tʃæmpjənʃɪp] *n* -**1.** GAMES & SPORT championnat *m*; he plays ~ tennis il participe aux championnats de tennis. -**2.** [support] défense *f*.

chance [tʃɑːns] ◇ *n* -**1.** [possibility, likelihood]: is there any ~ of seeing you again? serait-il possible de vous revoir?; there was little ~ of him finding work il y avait peu de chances qu'il trouve du travail; we have an outside ~ of success nous avons une très faible chance de réussir; she's got a good OR strong ~ of being accepted elle a de fortes chances d'être acceptée OR reçue; there's a fifty-fifty ~ he won't turn up il y a une chance sur deux qu'il ne vienne pas; to be in with a ~: he's in with a ~ of getting the job il a une chance d'obtenir le poste. -**2.** [fortune, luck] hasard *m*; games of ~ les jeux *mpl* de hasard; there was an element of ~ in his success il y a eu une part de hasard dans sa réussite; it was pure ~ that I found it je l'ai trouvé tout à fait par hasard; to leave things to ~ laisser faire les choses; to leave nothing to ~ ne rien laisser au hasard. -**3.** [opportunity]: I haven't had a ~ to write to him je n'ai pas trouvé l'occasion de lui écrire; give her a ~ to defend herself donnez-lui l'occasion de se défendre; give peace a ~ la paix est possible, donnez-lui OR laissez-lui sa chance; it's a ~ in a million c'est une occasion unique; I'm offering you the ~ of a lifetime je vous offre la chance de votre vie; the poor man never had OR stood a ~ le pauvre homme n'avait aucune chance de s'en tirer; some children simply don't get a ~ in life pour certains enfants il n'y a tout simplement aucun avenir; this is your last ~ c'est votre dernière chance; she deserves a second ~ elle mérite une deuxième chance; he was thrown out before he had a ~ to protest il a été évincé avant même d'avoir eu l'occasion de protester. -**4.** [risk] risque *m*; I don't want to take the ~ of losing je ne veux pas prendre le risque de perdre; he took a ~ on a racehorse il a parié sur un cheval de course; take a ~ on me *fig* donne-moi une chance.
◇ *adj* de hasard; I was a ~ witness to the robbery j'ai été un témoin accidentel du vol.
◇ *vi fml* OR *lit* [happen]: I ~d to be at the same table as Sir Sydney je me suis trouvé par hasard à la même table que Sir Sydney; it ~d that no one else had heard of her il s'est trouvé que personne d'autre n'avait entendu parler d'elle.
◇ *vt* [risk] *lit* hasarder; he ~d his savings on the venture il a risqué ses économies dans l'entreprise; I can't ~ her finding out about it je ne peux pas prendre le risque qu'elle l'apprenne; she ~d going out despite the curfew elle s'est hasardée à sortir malgré le couvre-feu; let's ~ it OR our luck tentons notre chance ❑ to ~ one's arm risquer le coup.

◆ **chances** *npl* -**1.** [possibility, likelihood] chances *fpl*; ~s are (that) he'll never find out il y a de fortes OR grandes chances qu'il ne l'apprenne jamais; what are her ~s of making a full recovery? quelles sont ses chances de se rétablir complètement? -**2.** [risks] risques *mpl*; she was taking no ~s elle ne prenait pas de risques.

◆ **by chance** *adv phr* par hasard; by pure OR sheer ~ we were both staying at the same hotel il se trouvait que nous logions au même hôtel; would you by any ~ know who that man is? sauriez-vous par hasard qui est cet homme?

◆ **chance on, chance upon** *vt insep* [person] rencontrer par hasard; [thing] trouver par hasard.

chancel ['tʃɑːnsl] *n* chœur *m*.

chancellery ['tʃɑːnsələrɪ] (*pl* chancelleries) *n* chancellerie *f*.

chancellor ['tʃɑːnsələʳ] *n* -**1.** POL chancelier *m*; the Chancellor of the Exchequer POL le Chancelier de l'Échiquier, ≃ le ministre des Finances *(en Grande-Bretagne)*. -**2.** UNIV *Br* président *m*, -e *f* honoraire; *Am* président *m*, -e *f* (d'université).

chancellorship ['tʃɑːnsələʃɪp] *n* -**1.** *Br* ADMIN direction *f* des finances; the economy had done extremely well under Mr Smith's ~ l'économie avait montré d'excellents résultats avec M. Smith au ministère des Finances. -**2.** *Am* UNIV présidence *f* (d'université).

chancer *inf* ['tʃɑːnsəʳ] *n Br* filou *m*.

chancery ['tʃɑːnsərɪ] (*pl* chanceries) *n* JUR -**1.** [in UK]: the suit is in ~ l'action est en instance ❑ Chancery (Division) cour *f* de la chancellerie *(une des trois divisions de la Haute cour de justice en Angleterre)*; ward in ~ pupille *mf* de l'État. -**2.** [in US]: Court of Chancery ≃ cour *f* d'équité. -**3.** [in wrestling] clé *f*, clef *f*.

chancre ['ʃæŋkəʳ] *n* chancre *m*.

chancroid ['ʃæŋkrɔɪd] *n* chancrelle *f*, chancre *m* mou.

chancy *inf* ['tʃɑːnsɪ] (*compar* chancier, *superl* chanciest) *adj* risqué.

chandelier [ʃændə'lɪəʳ] *n* lustre *m (pour éclairer)*.

chandler ['tʃɑːndləʳ] *n* -**1.** [supplier] fournisseur *m*; ship's ~ shipchandler *m*. -**2.** [candlemaker] chandelier *m*.

change [tʃeɪndʒ] ◇ *n* -**1.** [alteration] changement *m*; we expect a ~ in the weather nous nous attendons à un changement de temps; there has been a ~ in thinking regarding nuclear power il y a eu un changement d'opinion OR une évolution de l'opinion concernant l'énergie nucléaire; a survey showed a radical ~ in public opinion un sondage a montré un revirement de l'opinion publique; the party needs a ~ of direction le parti a besoin d'un changement de direction OR d'orientation; a ~ for the better/worse un changement en mieux/mal, une amélioration/dégradation; walking to work makes a pleasant ~ from driving c'est agréable d'aller travailler à pied plutôt qu'en voiture; it'll be OR make a nice ~ for them not to have the children in the house cela les changera agréablement de ne pas avoir les enfants à la maison; she was actually early – well, that makes a ~! en fait elle était en avance – eh bien, voilà qui change!; living in the country will be a big ~ for us cela nous changera beaucoup de vivre à la campagne; there's been little ~ in his condition son état n'a guère évolué; she dislikes ~ of any kind tout changement lui déplaît; to have a ~ of heart changer d'avis; I need a ~ of scene OR scenery *fig* j'ai besoin de changer de décor OR d'air. -**2.** [fresh set or supply]: a ~ of clothes des vêtements de rechange; he had to spend a week without a ~ of clothes il a dû passer une semaine sans changer de vêtements ❑ an oil ~ une vidange. -**3.** [in journey] changement *m*, correspondance *f*; if you go by underground you'll have to make two ~s si vous y allez en métro vous serez obligé de changer deux fois; you can get there by train with a ~ at Bristol vous pouvez y aller en train avec un changement OR une correspondance à Bristol. -**4.** [money] monnaie *f*; she gave me two pounds in ~ elle m'a donné deux livres en monnaie; can you give me ~ for five pounds? pouvez-vous me faire la monnaie de cinq livres?; I don't have any loose OR small ~ je n'ai pas de petite monnaie; the machine doesn't give ~ la machine ne rend pas la monnaie ❑ you'll get no ~ out of him *inf Br* on ne peut rien en tirer. -**5.** AUT: a gear ~ un changement de vitesse. -**6.** *euph* & PHYSIOL = **change of life**. -**7.** *arch* [market] marché *m*.
◇ *vt* -**1.** [substitute, switch] changer, changer de; he's ~d his name three times il a changé de nom trois fois; she's going to ~ her name to Parker elle va prendre le nom de Parker; to ~ a fuse changer un fusible; to ~ one's clothes changer de vêtements, se changer; you'll have to ~ trains in London vous serez obligé de changer de train à Londres; they're going to ~

the guard at 11 o'clock *Br* MIL ils vont faire la relève de OR relever la garde à 11h; to ~ sides changer de côté; to ~ ends SPORT changer de camp; to ~ hands: this old desk has ~d hands many times ce vieux bureau a changé maintes fois de mains; to ~ one's mind changer d'avis; he's ~d his mind about moving to Scotland pour ce qui est de s'installer en Écosse il a changé d'avis; you'd better ~ your ways tu ferais bien de t'amender ❑ to ~ one's tune changer de ton. -**2.** [exchange] changer; when are you thinking of changing your car? quand pensez-vous changer de voiture?; if the shoes are too small we'll ~ them for you si les chaussures sont trop petites nous vous les changerons; to ~ places with sb changer de place avec qqn; I wouldn't want to ~ places with him! *fig* je n'aimerais pas être à sa place!; I'd like to ~ my pounds into dollars FIN j'aimerais changer mes livres contre des OR en dollars; does this bank ~ money? est-ce que cette banque fait le change?; can you ~ a ten pound note? [into coins] pouvez-vous me donner la monnaie d'un billet de dix livres? -**3.** [alter, modify] changer; there's no point in trying to ~ him c'est inutile d'essayer de le changer; she wants to ~ the world elle veut changer le monde; he won't ~ anything in the text il ne changera rien au texte; the illness completely ~d his personality la maladie a complètement transformé son caractère; she doesn't want to ~ her routine in any way elle ne veut rien changer à sa routine ❑ to ~ one's spots changer OR modifier totalement son caractère. -**4.** [transform] changer, transformer; the prince was ~d into a frog le prince fut changé en grenouille; to ~ water into wine BIBLE changer l'eau en vin; the liquid/her hair has ~d colour le liquide a/ses cheveux ont changé de couleur. -**5.** [baby, bed] changer; the baby needs changing le bébé a besoin d'être changé; I've ~d the sheets j'ai changé les draps. -**6.** AUT: to ~ gear changer de vitesse.

◇ *vi* -**1.** [alter, turn] changer; to ~ for the better/worse changer en mieux/pire; nothing will make him ~ rien ne le changera, il ne changera jamais; wait for the lights to ~ attendez que le feu passe au vert; winter ~d to spring le printemps a succédé à l'hiver; the wind has ~d le vent a changé OR tourné. -**2.** [become transformed] se changer, se transformer; the ogre ~d into a mouse l'ogre s'est transformé en souris. -**3.** [change clothing] se changer; she's gone upstairs to ~ elle est montée se changer; they ~d out of their uniforms ils ont enlevé leurs uniformes; he ~d into a pair of jeans il s'est changé et a mis un jean; I'm going to ~ into something warmer je vais mettre quelque chose de plus chaud. -**4.** [transportation] changer; is it a direct flight or do I have to ~? est-ce que le vol est direct ou faut-il changer?; all ~! [announcement] tout le monde descend! -**5.** *Br* AUT: she ~d into fourth gear elle a passé la quatrième. -**6.** [moon] entrer dans une nouvelle phase.

◆ **for a change** *adv phr*: it's nice to see you smiling for a ~ c'est bien de te voir sourire pour une fois.

◆ **change down** *vi insep* AUT rétrograder; he ~ed down into third il est passé en troisième.

◆ **change over** *vi insep* -**1.** *Br* [switch]: he ~d over from smoking cigarettes to smoking cigars il s'est mis à fumer des cigares à la place de cigarettes; the country has ~d over to nuclear power le pays est passé au nucléaire; one day I wash and he dries and the next day we ~ over un jour je fais la vaisselle et il l'essuie et le jour d'après on change. -**2.** SPORT [change positions] changer de côté.

◆ **change up** *vi insep* AUT passer la vitesse supérieure; he ~d up into third il a passé la troisième, il est passé en troisième.

changeability [,tʃeɪndʒə'bɪlətɪ] *n* variabilité *f*.

changeable ['tʃeɪndʒəbl] *adj* -**1.** [variable] variable; ~ weather temps variable OR instable. -**2.** [capricious, fickle] changeant, inconstant.

changed [tʃeɪndʒd] *adj* changé, différent; he's a ~ man c'est un autre homme.

changeless ['tʃeɪndʒlɪs] *adj* immuable, inaltérable.

changeling ['tʃeɪndʒlɪŋ] *n enfant substitué par les fées au véritable enfant d'un couple.*

change of life *n*: the ~ le retour d'âge.

changeover ['tʃeɪndʒəʊvəʳ] *n* -**1.** [switch] changement *m*, passage *m*; in Australia the ~ from pounds to dollars took place in 1966 en Australie le changement monétaire qui a remplacé la livre par le dollar a eu lieu en 1966; the ~ to computers went smoothly le passage à l'informatisation s'est fait en douceur. -**2.** *Br* SPORT [from one end to another] changement *m* de côté.

change purse *n Am* porte-monnaie *m inv*.

change-ringing *n manière particulière de sonner les cloches, notamment dans les églises anglicanes.*

changing ['tʃeɪndʒɪŋ] ◇ *adj* qui change; we're living in a ~ world nous vivons dans un monde en évolution.

◇ *n* changement *m*; the Changing of the Guard la relève de la garde.

changing room *n Br* SPORT vestiaire *m*; [in shop] cabine *f* d'essayage.

channel ['tʃænl] (*Br pt & pp* channelled, *cont* channelling, *Am pt & pp* channeled, *cont* channeling)

◇ *n* -**1.** [broad strait] détroit *m*, bras *m* de mer; the (English) Channel la Manche; a Channel OR cross-Channel ferry un ferry qui traverse la Manche. -**2.** [river bed] lit *m*; NAUT [navigable course] chenal *m*, passe *f*. -**3.** [passage -for gases, liquids] canal *m*, conduite *f*; [- for electrical signals] piste *f*. -**4.** [furrow, groove] sillon *m*; [on a column] cannelure *f*; [in a street] caniveau *m*; an irrigation ~ un fossé OR une rigole d'irrigation. -**5.** TV chaîne *f*; the film is on Channel 2 le film est sur la deuxième chaîne. -**6.** RADIO bande *f*. -**7.** *fig* [means] canal *m*, voie *f*; to go through (the) official ~s suivre la filière officielle; they tried to obtain his release through diplomatic ~s ils ont essayé d'obtenir sa libération par voie diplomatique; the government has suppressed all ~s of dissent le gouvernement a supprimé tout moyen d'expression de la dissidence. -**8.** COMPUT canal *m*.

◇ *vt* -**1.** [land] creuser des rigoles dans; [river] canaliser; [street] construire des caniveaux dans; [gas, water] acheminer (par des conduites); [column] canneler; the water channelled its way through the cliff l'eau a creusé une rigole dans la falaise. -**2.** *fig* [direct] canaliser, diriger; the government wants to ~ resources to those who need them most le gouvernement veut affecter les ressources en priorité à ceux qui en ont le plus besoin; she needs to ~ her energies into some useful work elle a besoin de canaliser son énergie à effectuer du travail utile.

◆ **channel off** *vt sep* canaliser.

CHANNEL FOUR:

Channel Four est une chaîne de télévision privée britannique, à vocation culturelle (documentaires, théâtre, films etc).

Channel Islander *n habitant des îles Anglo-Normandes.*

Channel Islands *pl pr n*: the ~ les îles *fpl* Anglo-Normandes ; in the ~ dans les îles Anglo-Normandes.

Channel Tunnel *n*: the ~ le tunnel sous la Manche.

chant [tʃɑːnt] ◇ *n* -**1.** MUS mélopée *f*; RELIG psalmodie *f*. -**2.** [slogan, cry] chant *m* scandé.

◇ *vi* -**1.** MUS chanter une mélopée; RELIG psalmodier. -**2.** [crowd, demonstrators] scander des slogans.

◇ *vt* -**1.** MUS chanter; RELIG psalmodier. -**2.** [slogans] scander.

chant(e)y ['ʃæntɪ] (*pl* chanties) = **shanty**.

chaos ['keɪɒs] *n* chaos *m*.

chaotic [keɪ'ɒtɪk] *adj* chaotique.

chaotically [keɪ'ɒtɪklɪ] *adv* chaotiquement.

chap [tʃæp] (*pt & pp* chapped, *cont* chapping) ◇ *n* -**1.** *inf Br* [man] type *m*; he's a nice ~ c'est un brave type; be a good ~ and tell him I'm not in sois sympa et dis-lui que je ne suis pas là; you ~s have made a big mistake messieurs, vous avez fait une grave erreur; what do you think, ~s? qu'en pensez-vous, les amis?; he's gone broke, poor ~ il a fait faillite, le pauvre; how are you, old ~? *dated* comment allez-vous, mon vieux? -**2.** [sore] gerçure *f*, crevasse *f*.

◇ *vt* gercer, crevasser; he has chapped lips il a les lèvres gercées; your hands will get chapped in this weather vous aurez les mains gercées par ce temps.

◇ *vi* (se) gercer, se crevasser.

chapel ['tʃæpl] ◇ *n* -**1.** [in church, school, residence] chapelle *f*. -**2.** *Br* [Nonconformist church] temple *m*. -**3.** *Br* [of trade unionists] *membres du syndicat dans une maison d'édition.*

◇ *adj Br* non-conformiste RELIG; are you church or ~? êtes-vous anglican ou non-conformiste?

chapel of ease *n* église *f* succursale.

chapel of rest *n chambre mortuaire dans une entreprise de pompes funèbres.*

chaperon(e) ['ʃæpərəʊn] ◇ *n* chaperon *m*; her aunt acted as her ~ sa tante lui servait de chaperon.

◇ *vt* chaperonner.

chaplain ['tʃæplɪn] *n* aumônier *m*; [in private chapel] chapelain *m*.

chaplaincy ['tʃæplɪnsɪ] *n* aumônerie *f*; ~ work le travail de l'aumônier.

chaplet ['tʃæplɪt] *n* -**1.** [wreath] guirlande *f*. -**2.** RELIG chapelet *m*.

Chappaquiddick [tʃæpə'kwɪdɪk] *pr n*: ~, the ~ incident l'affaire *f* de Chappaquiddick *(accident ayant coûté la vie à Mary-Jo Kopechne, collaboratrice du sénateur américain Edward Kennedy, dans des circonstances mal élucidées).*

chapped [tʃæpt] *adj* [hands, lips] gercé.

chappie *inf* ['tʃæpɪ] *Br dated* = **chap** *n* **1**.

chaps [tʃæps] *npl* jambières *fpl* de cuir.

chapstick® ['tʃæpstɪk] *n Am* bâton *m* de pommade pour les lèvres.

chapter ['tʃæptəʳ] *n* -**1.** [of book] chapitre *m*; it's in ~ three c'est dans le troisième chapitre ❑ she can give OR quote (you) ~ and verse on the subject elle peut citer toutes les autorités en la matière. -**2.** [era] chapitre *m*; this closed a particularly violent ~ in our history ceci marqua la fin d'un chapitre particulièrement violent de notre histoire. -**3.** [series] succession *f*, cascade *f*; a ~ of accidents une série d'accidents OR de malheurs, une série noire. -**4.** [of organization] branche *f*, section *f*. -**5.** RELIG chapitre *m*.

chapter house *n* chapitre *m*.

char [tʃɑːʳ] (*pt & pp* charred, *cont* charring) ◇ *vt* -**1.** [reduce to charcoal] carboniser, réduire en charbon. -**2.** [scorch] griller, brûler légèrement.

◇ *vi* -**1.** [scorch] brûler; [blacken] noircir. -**2.** *inf Br dated* [clean] faire des ménages; she had to go out charring to support her family elle a dû faire des ménages pour faire vivre sa famille.

◇ *n* -**1.** *inf Br dated* [cleaner] femme *f* de ménage. -**2.** *inf Br dated* thé *m*. -**3.** [fish] omble *m* chevalier.

charabanc ['ʃærəbæŋ] *n dated* autocar *m* (de tourisme).

character ['kærəktəʳ] ◇ *n* -**1.** [nature, temperament] caractère *m*; the war completely changed his ~ la guerre a complètement transformé son caractère; is there such a thing as national ~? la notion de caractère national existe-t-elle?; his remark was quite in/out of ~ cette remarque lui ressemblait tout à fait/ne lui ressemblait pas du tout. -**2.** [aspect, quality] caractère *m*; it was the vindictive ~ of the punishment she objected to c'était le caractère vindicatif du châtiment qu'elle désapprouvait. -**3.** [determination, integrity] caractère *m*; **she's a woman of great ~** c'est une femme qui a beaucoup de caractère; **he lacks ~** il manque de caractère. -**4.** [distinction, originality] caractère *m*; **the house had (great) ~** la maison avait beaucoup de caractère. -**5.** [unusual person] personnage *m*; **she seems to attract all sorts of ~s** elle semble attirer toutes sortes d'individus; **he's quite a ~** il est vraiment spécial OR très particulier. -**6.** *pej* [person] individu *m*; **there's a suspicious ~ waiting downstairs for you** il y a un individu suspect qui vous attend en bas. -**7.** CIN, LITERAT & THEAT personnage *m*; **the main ~** le personnage principal, le protagoniste; **Chaplin plays two different ~s in "The Great Dictator"** Chaplin joue deux rôles différents dans «Le Dictateur». -**8.** TYPO caractère *m*. -**9.** *lit* [handwriting] écriture *f*. -**10.** *Br dated* [written reference] références *fpl*.

◇ *comp* -**1.** CIN & THEAT: **~ part** OR **role** rôle *m* de composition. -**2.** COMPUT: **~ code** code *m* de caractère; **~ recognition** reconnaissance *f* de caractères; **~ set** jeu *m* de caractères.

character actor *n* acteur *m* de genre.

character assassination *n* diffamation *f*.

characteristic [ˌkærəktəˈrɪstɪk] ◇ *adj* caractéristique; **she refused all honours with ~ humility** elle refusa tous les honneurs avec l'humilité qui la caractérisait.

◇ *n* caractéristique *f*; **national ~s** les caractères *mpl* nationaux.

characteristically [ˌkærəktəˈrɪstɪklɪ] *adv*: **he was ~ generous with his praise** comme on pouvait s'y attendre, il fut prodigue de ses compliments OR il ne ménagea pas ses éloges; **~, she put her family first** elle fit passer sa famille en premier, ce qui était bien dans son caractère OR lui ressemblait bien.

characterization [ˌkærəktəraɪˈzeɪʃn] *n* -**1.** *fml* [description] caractérisation *f*. -**2.** LITERAT & THEAT représentation *f* OR peinture *f* des personnages; **he's very poor at ~** [writer] ses personnages ne sont pas très convaincants; [actor] il n'a aucun talent pour l'interprétation.

characterize, -ise [ˈkærəktəraɪz] *vt* caractériser; **his music is ~d by a sense of joy** sa musique se caractérise par une impression de joie; **the speaker ~d apartheid as utterly immoral** le conférencier qualifia l'apartheid de totalement immoral; **Shakespeare ~d Henry VI as a weak but pious king** Shakespeare a dépeint Henri VI comme un roi faible mais pieux.

characterless [ˈkærəktəlɪs] *adj* sans caractère.

character sketch *n* portrait *m* moral rapide.

character witness *n* témoin *m* de moralité.

charade [ʃəˈrɑːd] *n* [pretence] feinte *f*; **the trial/meeting was a complete ~!** c'était une véritable parodie de procès/de réunion!

◆ **charades** *npl* GAMES charade *f* en action; **let's play ~s** jouons aux charades.

charcoal [ˈtʃɑːkəʊl] ◇ *n* -**1.** [fuel] charbon *m* de bois. -**2.** ART fusain *m*; **he drew her in ~** il l'a dessinée au fusain.

◇ *comp* -**1.** [fuel] à charbon; **a ~ stove** un réchaud à charbon de bois. -**2.** ART au charbon, au fusain; **a ~ pencil** un (crayon) fusain; **a ~ drawing** un croquis au fusain.

charcoal burner *n* charbonnier *m*.

charcoal grey ◇ *n* gris *m* foncé.

◇ *adj* gris foncé *(inv)*, (gris) anthracite *(inv)*.

chard [tʃɑːd] *n* blette *f*, bette *f*.

charge [tʃɑːdʒ] ◇ *n* -**1.** [fee, cost] frais *mpl*; **postal/telephone ~s** frais postaux/téléphoniques; **there's a ~ of one pound for use of the locker** il faut payer une livre pour utiliser la consigne automatique; **is there any extra ~ for a single room?** est-ce qu'il faut payer un supplément pour une chambre à un lit?; **what's the ~ for delivery?** la livraison coûte combien?; **there's no ~ for children** c'est gratuit pour les enfants; **free of ~** gratuitement; **there's a small admission ~ to the museum** il y a un petit droit d'entrée au musée; **cash or ~?** *Am* comptant ou crédit? ❑ **carriage ~** OR **~s** COMM frais de port; **there's no service ~** le service est gratuit. -**2.** JUR [accusation] chef *m* d'accusation, inculpation *f*; **he was arrested on a ~ of conspiracy** il a été arrêté sous l'inculpation d'association criminelle; **you are under arrest — on what ~?** vous êtes en état d'arrestation — pour quel motif?; **to file ~s against sb** déposer une plainte contre qqn; **a ~ of drunk driving was brought against the driver** le conducteur a été mis en examen pour conduite en état d'ivresse; **the judge threw out the ~** le juge a retiré l'inculpation; **she was acquitted on both ~s** elle a été acquittée des deux chefs d'inculpation; **some of the ~s may be dropped** certains des chefs d'accusation pourraient être retirés; **he pleaded guilty to the ~ of robbery** il a plaidé coupable à l'accusation de vol; **they will have to answer** OR **face ~s of fraud** ils auront à répondre à l'accusation d'escroquerie; **she's laying herself open to ~s of malingering** elle s'expose à des accusations de simulation. -**3.** [allegation] accusation *f*; **the government rejected ~s that it was mismanaging the economy** le gouvernement a rejeté l'accusation selon laquelle il gérait mal l'économie; **~s of torture have been brought** OR **made against the regime** des accusations de torture ont été portées contre le régime. -**4.** [command, control]: **who's the person in ~ here?** qui est le responsable ici?; **who's in ~ here?** qui est-ce qui commande ici?; **she's in ~ of public relations** elle s'occupe des relations publiques; **can I leave you in ~ of the shop?** puis-je vous laisser la responsabilité du magasin?; **she was in ~ of consumer protection** elle était responsable de la protection des consommateurs; **I was put in ~ of the investigation** on m'a confié la responsabilité de l'enquête; **to take ~ of sthg** prendre en charge qqch, prendre OR assumer la direction de qqch; **she took ~ of organizing the festival** elle a pris en charge l'organisation du festival; **he took ~ of his nephew** il a pris son neveu en charge; **he had a dozen salesmen under his ~** il avait une douzaine de vendeurs sous sa responsabilité. -**5.** *fml* [burden]: **she refused to be a ~ on her family/the State** elle refusa d'être une charge pour sa famille/d'être à la charge de l'État. -**6.** *fml* [dependent] *personne confiée à la garde d'une autre*; **the governess instructed her two ~s in French and Italian** la gouvernante apprit le français et l'italien à ses deux élèves. -**7.** [duty, mission] charge *f*; **he was given the ~ of preparing the defence** on l'a chargé de préparer la défense; **the judge's ~ to the jury** JUR les recommandations du juge au jury. -**8.** [attack] charge *f*; **soldiers made several ~s against the demonstrators** les soldats ont chargé les manifestants à plusieurs reprises. -**9.** ELEC & PHYS charge *f*; **the battery needs a ~** la batterie a besoin d'être chargée; **I left it on ~ all night** je l'ai laissé charger toute la nuit. -**10.** MIL charge *f*; **the Charge of the Light Brigade** *Br* HIST la Charge de la brigade légère. -**11.** HERALD meuble *m*.

◇ *vt* -**1.** [money] faire payer; [demand payment from] demander, prendre; **the doctor ~d her $90 for a visit** le médecin lui a fait payer OR lui a pris 90 dollars pour une consultation; **how much would you ~ to take us to the airport?** combien prendriez-vous pour nous emmener à l'aéroport?; **they didn't ~ us for the coffee** ils ne nous ont pas fait payer les cafés; **you will be ~d for postage** COMM les frais postaux seront à votre charge. -**2.** [defer payment of]: **~ the bill to my account** mettez le montant de la facture sur mon compte; **I ~d all my expenses to the company** j'ai mis tous mes frais sur le compte de la société; **can I ~ this jacket?** *Am* [with a credit card] puis-je payer cette veste avec ma carte (de crédit)?; **~ it** *Am* mettez-le sur mon compte. -**3.** [accuse, allege] accuser; **the Opposition spokesman ~d that the Employment Secretary had falsified the figures** le porte-parole de l'opposition a accusé le ministre du Travail OR de l'Emploi d'avoir falsifié les chiffres; **he ~d his partner with having stolen thousands of pounds from the firm** il a accusé son associé d'avoir volé des milliers de livres à l'entreprise. -**4.** JUR inculper; **I'm charging you with the murder of X** je vous inculpe du meurtre de X; **he was ~d with assaulting a policeman** il a été inculpé de voies de fait sur un agent de police. -**5.** [attack] charger; **the police ~d the crowd** les forces de l'ordre ont chargé la foule; **the troops ~d the building** les troupes donnèrent l'assaut au bâtiment. -**6.** *fml* [command, entrust]: **I was ~d with guarding the prisoner** je fus chargé de la surveillance du prisonnier; **I ~ you to find the stolen documents** je vous confie la tâche de retrouver les documents dérobés; **she was ~d with the task of interviewing applicants** on lui confia la tâche d'interroger les candidats; **the judge ~d the jury** JUR le juge a fait ses recommandations au jury. -**7.** ELEC & MIL charger. -**8.** *fml* [fill] charger; **to ~ sb's glass** remplir le verre de qqn.

◇ *vi* -**1.** [demand in payment] demander, prendre; **how much do you ~?** combien demandez-vous OR prenez-vous?; **do you ~ for delivery?** est-ce que vous faites payer la livraison?; **he doesn't ~** il ne demande OR prend rien. -**2.** [rush] se précipiter; **the rhino suddenly ~d** tout d'un coup le rhinocéros a chargé; **suddenly two policemen ~d into the room** tout d'un coup deux policiers ont fait irruption dans la pièce; **she ~d into/out of her office** elle entra dans son/sortit de son bureau au pas de charge. -**3.** MIL [attack] charger, donner l'assaut; **~!** à l'assaut! -**4.** ELEC se charger OR recharger; **this battery won't ~** cette batterie ne veut pas se charger OR recharger.

◆ **charge up** *vt sep* -**1.** [bill]: **she ~d everything up to her account** elle a mis tous les frais sur son compte. -**2.** ELEC charger, recharger.

THE CHARGE OF THE LIGHT BRIGADE:
Célèbre poème de lord Tennyson, inspiré par un épisode de la guerre de Crimée, en 1854: une poignée de soldats britanniques se sacrifièrent pour sauver le port de Balaklava (tenu par les Anglais, les Français et les Turcs) d'une attaque par les Russes.

chargeable [ˈtʃɑːdʒəbl] *adj* -**1.** FIN: **the item is ~ with duty of £10** l'article est soumis à une taxe de 10 livres; **travelling expenses are ~ to the employer** les frais de déplacement sont à la charge de l'employeur; **~ expenses** frais déductibles. -**2.** JUR: **a ~ offence** un délit; **if they refuse to give evidence they'll be ~ with contempt of court** s'ils refusent de témoigner ils seront passibles de poursuites pour refus de comparaître.

charge account *n Am* compte *m* permanent *(dans un magasin)*.

charge card *n* carte *f* de crédit.

charged [tʃɑːdʒd] *adj* -**1.** [atmosphere] chargé; **a voice ~ with emotion** une voix pleine d'émotion; **a look ~ with suspicion** un regard lourd de soupçons. -**2.** ELEC chargé.

chargé d'affaires [ˌʃɑːʒeɪdæˈfeəʳ] (*pl* chargés d'affaires) *n* chargé *m* d'affaires.

charge hand *n Br* sous-chef *m* d'équipe.

charge nurse *n Br* infirmier *m*, -ère *f* en chef.

charger [ˈtʃɑːdʒəʳ] *n* -**1.** ELEC chargeur *m*. -**2.** *arch* OR *lit* [horse] cheval *m* de bataille.

charge sheet *n Br* procès-verbal *m*.

charily [ˈtʃeərəlɪ] *adv* -**1.** [cautiously] précautionneusement. -**2.** [sparingly] avec parcimonie.

chariot [ˈtʃærɪət] *n* char *m*; **'Chariots of Fire'** *Hudson* 'les Chariots de feu'.

charioteer [ˌtʃærɪəˈtɪəʳ] *n* aurige *m*.

charisma [kəˈrɪzmə] *n* charisme *m*.

charismatic [ˌkærɪzˈmætɪk] *adj* charismatique; **the ~ movement** RELIG le mouvement charismatique.

charitable [ˈtʃærətəbl] *adj* -**1.** [generous, kind] charitable. -**2.** [cause, institution] de bienfaisance, de charité; **~ organizations** œuvres *fpl* de bienfaisance OR de charité; **~ works** les bonnes œuvres; **a ~ donation** un don fait par charité.

charitably [ˈtʃærətəblɪ] *adv* charitablement.

charity [ˈtʃærətɪ] (*pl* charities) *n* -**1.** RELIG charité *f*; [generosity, kindness] charité; **he bought the painting out of ~** il a acheté le tableau par charité; **an act of ~** une action charitable, un acte de charité. -**2.** [help to the needy] charité *f*; **they're too proud to accept ~** ils sont trop fiers pour accepter la charité OR l'aumône; **they raised £10,000 for ~** ils ont collecté 10 000 livres pour les bonnes œuvres. -**3.** [organization] association *f* caritative, œuvre *f* de bienfaisance; **Catholic charities** les associations caritatives catholiques ❑ **~ shop** *magasin dont les employés sont des bénévoles et dont les bénéfices servent à subventionner une œuvre d'utilité publique*; **the Charity Commission** *commission gouvernementale britannique contrôlant les associations caritatives*.

charlady [ˈtʃɑːˌleɪdɪ] (*pl* charladies) *Br dated* = **char** *n* **1.**

charlatan [ˈʃɑːlətən] ◇ *n* charlatan *m*.
◇ *adj* charlatanesque.

Charlemagne [ˈʃɑːləmeɪn] *pr n* Charlemagne.

Charles [tʃɑːlz] *pr n*: **~ the Bold** Charles le Téméraire; **~ V** Charles Quint.

charleston [ˈtʃɑːlstən] *n* charleston *m*; **to do the ~** danser le charleston.

charley horse *inf* [ˈtʃɑːlɪ-] *n* (*U*) *Am* crampe *f*.

charlie *inf* [ˈtʃɑːlɪ] *n* -**1.** *Br* cloche *f*; **I felt a proper ~** je me suis senti vraiment bête; **he's a right ~** c'est une vraie cloche. -**2.** *Am mil sl* [Vietcong]: Charlie le Viêt-cong. -**3.** *drugs sl* [cocaine] coke *f*.

Charlie Chaplin [ˈtʃɑːlɪˈtʃæplɪn] *pr n* [in real life] Charlie Chaplin; [in films] Charlot.

charlotte [ˈʃɑːlət] *n* -**1.** [baked] charlotte *f*; **apple ~** charlotte aux pommes. -**2.** = **charlotte russe**.

charlotte russe [-ruːs] *n* charlotte *f* russe.

charm [tʃɑːm] ◇ *n* -**1.** [appeal, attraction] charme *m*; **he has great ~** il a beaucoup de charme; **to turn on the ~** faire du charme. -**2.** [in sorcery] charme *m*, sortilège *m*; **a lucky ~** un porte-bonheur; **to work like a ~** marcher à merveille OR à la perfection. -**3.** [piece of jewellery] breloque *f*; **a ~ bracelet** un bracelet à breloques.
◇ *vt* -**1.** [please, delight] charmer, séduire; **I was ~ed by his gentle manner** je fus charmé par ses douces manières; **she ~ed him into accepting the invitation** elle l'a si bien enjôlé qu'il a accepté l'invitation. -**2.** [subj: magician] charmer, ensorceler; [subj: snake charmer] charmer.
◆ **charms** *npl* charmes *mpl*.
◆ **charm away** *vt sep*: **he ~ed away all their fears** il a fait disparaître toutes leurs craintes comme par enchantement.

charmed [tʃɑːmd] *adj* -**1.** [delighted] enchanté; **she sang before a ~ audience** elle a chanté devant des spectateurs enchantés; **pleased to meet you — ~, I'm sure** [in introduction] heureux de faire votre connaissance — enchanté OR Monsieur, j'ai bien l'honneur. -**2.** [by magic] charmé; **to lead a ~ life** *fig* être béni des dieux.

charmer [ˈtʃɑːməʳ] *n* charmeur *m*, -euse *f*.

charming [ˈtʃɑːmɪŋ] *adj* charmant; **~!** *iron* c'est charmant!

charmingly [ˈtʃɑːmɪŋlɪ] *adv* de façon charmante; **he seemed ~ innocent** il paraissait d'une innocence charmante.

charnel house [ˈtʃɑːnl-] *n lit* charnier *m*, ossuaire *m*.

charr [tʃɑːʳ] = **char** *n* **3.**

charred [tʃɑːd] *adj* noirci (par le feu); **the ~ ruins of the building** les ruines du bâtiment noircies par le feu.

chart [tʃɑːt] ◇ *n* -**1.** NAUT carte *f* marine; ASTRON carte *f* (du ciel). -**2.** [table] tableau *m*; [graph] courbe *f*; MED courbe *f*. -**3.** ASTROL horoscope *m*.
◇ *vt* -**1.** NAUT [seas, waterway] établir la carte de, faire un levé hydrographique de; ASTRON [stars] porter sur la carte. -**2.** [record on a table, graph] faire la courbe de; **the patient's progress was carefully ~ed** MED l'évolution du malade fut soigneusement notée sur sa fiche. -**3.** *fig* [make a plan of] tracer; **the director ~ed a way out of financial collapse** le directeur a établi OR mis au point un plan pour éviter un effondrement financier.
◆ **charts** *npl* MUS hit-parade *m*; **she's (got a record) in the ~s** elle est au hit-parade.

charter [ˈtʃɑːtəʳ] ◇ *n* -**1.** [statement of rights, principles] charte *f*; [of a business, organization, university] statuts *mpl*; **the United Nations Charter** la Charte de l'Organisation des Nations unies. -**2.** [lease, licence] affrètement *m*; [charter flight] charter *m*; **we've hired three coaches on ~** *Br* nous avons affrété trois autocars.
◇ *vt* -**1.** [establish] accorder une charte à. -**2.** [hire, rent] affréter.

chartered [ˈtʃɑːtəd] *adj* -**1.** [hired, rented] affrété. -**2.** *Br* [qualified]: **a ~ accountant** un expert-comptable; **a ~ surveyor** un expert immobilier.

charter flight *n* (vol *m*) charter *m*.

charterhouse [ˈtʃɑːtəhaʊs, *pl* -haʊzɪz] *n* chartreuse *f*.

charter member *n* membre *m* fondateur.

charter party *n* NAUT charte-partie *f*.

charter plane *n* (avion *m*) charter *m*.

Chartism [ˈtʃɑːtɪzm] *n* chartisme *m*.

chartist [ˈtʃɑːtɪst] *n Am* ST. EX analyste *mf* des cours des valeurs boursières, chartiste *mf*.

Chartist [ˈtʃɑːtɪst] ◇ *n* chartiste *mf*.
◇ *adj* chartiste; **the ~ movement** le mouvement chartiste.

THE CHARTIST MOVEMENT:
Mouvement réformiste d'émancipation ouvrière fondé en Angleterre en 1838 avec l'établissement d'une «Charte du peuple» réclamant, notamment, le suffrage universel. Les chartistes présentèrent successivement trois pétitions de plus de un million de signatures au Parlement, sans succès.

---

charwoman [ˈtʃɑːˌwʊmən, *pl* -ˌwɪmɪn] *dated* = **char** *n* **1.**

chary [ˈtʃeərɪ] *adj* -**1.** [cautious] précautionneux; **he's ~ of allowing strangers into his home** il hésite à accueillir des gens qu'il ne connaît pas chez lui. -**2.** [ungenerous] parcimonieux; **he was ~ of praise** il faisait rarement des éloges, il était avare de compliments.

Charybdis [kəˈrɪbdɪs] *pr n* Charybde; **to be between Scylla and ~** tomber de Charybde en Scylla.

chase [tʃeɪs] ◇ *vt* -**1.** [pursue] poursuivre; **two police cars ~d the van** deux voitures de police ont pris la camionnette en chasse; **the dog ~d the postman down the street** le chien a poursuivi le facteur jusqu'en bas de la rue; **the reporters were ~d from OR out of the house** les journalistes furent chassés de la maison. -**2.** [amorously] courir (après); **he's always chasing young women** il est toujours à courir (après) les filles. -**3.** [metal] ciseler, repousser.
◇ *vi* [rush]: **she ~d all around London to find a wedding dress** elle a parcouru OR fait tout Londres pour trouver une robe de mariée.
◇ *n* -**1.** [pursuit] poursuite *f*; **the hounds gave ~ to the fox** la meute a pris le renard en chasse; **the prisoner climbed over the wall and the guards gave ~** le prisonnier escalada le mur et les gardiens se lancèrent à sa poursuite. -**2.** HUNT [sport, land, game] chasse *f*. -**3.** [groove] saignée. -**4.** TYPO châssis *m*.
◆ **chase after** *vt insep* courir après.
◆ **chase away, chase off** *vt sep* chasser.
◆ **chase up** *vt sep Br* -**1.** [information] rechercher. -**2.** [organization, person]: **can you ~ up the manager for me?** pouvez-vous relancer le directeur à propos de ce que je lui ai demandé?; **I had to ~ him up for the £50 he owed me** j'ai dû lui réclamer les 50 livres qu'il me devait.

chaser [ˈtʃeɪsəʳ] *n* -**1.** [drink]: **they drank scotch with beer ~s** ils ont bu du scotch suivi par de la bière; **give me a glass of vodka with an orange juice as a ~** donnez-moi un verre de vodka et un jus d'orange que je boirai après. -**2.** [pursuer] chasseur *m*. -**3.** [horse] cheval *m* de course.

chasm [ˈkæzm] *n* abîme *m*, gouffre *m*.

chassé [ˈʃæseɪ] ◇ *n* chassé *m*.
◇ *vi* chasser DANSE.

chassis [ˈʃæsɪ] (*pl inv* [-sɪz]) *n* -**1.** AUT châssis *m*; AERON train *m* d'atterrissage. -**2.** *inf* [body] châssis *m*.

chaste [tʃeɪst] *adj* chaste.

chastely [ˈtʃeɪstlɪ] *adv* chastement.

chasten [ˈtʃeɪsn] *vt fml* -**1.** [subdue, humble] corriger, maîtriser; [pride] rabaisser; **she was ~ed by her failure** elle fut abattue par son échec. -**2.** [punish, reprimand] châtier, punir.

chasteness [ˈtʃeɪstnɪs] *n* caractère *m* chaste.

chastening [ˈtʃeɪsənɪŋ] *adj*: **prison had a ~ effect on him** la prison l'a assagi; **it's a ~ thought** c'était une pensée plutôt décourageante.

chastise [tʃæˈstaɪz] *vt fml* [punish, beat] châtier, punir; [reprimand] fustiger.

chastisement [ˈtʃæstɪzmənt] *n fml* châtiment *m*.

chastity [ˈtʃæstətɪ] *n* chasteté *f*.

chastity belt *n* ceinture *f* de chasteté.

chasuble [ˈtʃæzjʊbl] *n* chasuble *f*.

chat [tʃæt] (*pt* & *pp* chatted, *cont* chatting) ◇ *vi* bavarder, causer; **we were just chatting about this and that** nous causions de choses et d'autres; **he was chatting to the man next to him** il bavardait avec l'homme qui était à côté de lui.
◇ *n*: **we had a nice ~ over lunch** nous avons eu une conversation agréable pendant le déjeuner; **she came over for a ~** elle est venue bavarder un peu; **there's too much ~ and not enough work going on here!** il y a OR on s'occupe trop de bavardage et pas assez de travail ici!
◆ **chat up** *inf vt sep Br* baratiner, draguer.

château [ˈʃætəʊ] (*pl* châteaus OR châteaux [ˈʃætəʊz]) *n* château *m*.

château-bottled *adj* mis en bouteille au château.

chat show *n Br* causerie *f* télévisée.

chattel [ˈtʃætl] *n* bien *m* meuble; **a ~ mortgage** *Am* FIN un nantissement de biens meubles.

chatter [ˈtʃætəʳ] ◇ *vi* -**1.** [person] papoter, bavarder; [bird] jaser, jacasser; [monkey] babiller; **she sat quietly while Maria ~ed away** elle restait tranquillement assise tandis que Maria palabrait ❑ **the ~ing classes** *inf* les intellos *mpl*. -**2.** [machine] cliqueter. -**3.** [teeth] claquer; **my teeth were ~ing from OR with the cold** j'avais tellement froid que je claquais des dents.
◇ *n* -**1.** [of people] bavardage *m*, papotage *m*; [of birds, monkeys] jacassement *m*. -**2.** [of machines] cliquetis *m*. -**3.** [of teeth] claquement *m*.

chatterbox *inf* [ˈtʃætəbɒks] *n* moulin *m* à paroles.

chatterer [ˈtʃætərəʳ] *n* -**1.** [talkative person] bavard *m*, -e *f*. -**2.** ORNITH cotinga *m*.

chattily [ˈtʃætɪlɪ] *adv* [speak, write] d'une façon familière.

chatty [ˈtʃætɪ] *adj* [person] bavard; [letter] plein de bavardages.

Chaucerian [tʃɔːˈsɪərɪən] *adj* de Chaucer.

chauffeur [ˈʃəʊfəʳ] ◇ *n* chauffeur *m*.
◇ *vi* travailler comme chauffeur; **he ~s for a cabinet minister** il est chauffeur de ministre.
◇ *vt* conduire.

chauffeur-driven *adj* conduit par un chauffeur.

chauvinism [ˈʃəʊvɪnɪzm] *n* [nationalism] chauvinisme *m*; [sexism] machisme *m*, phallocratie *f*.

chauvinist [ˈʃəʊvɪnɪst] *n* [nationalist] chauvin *m*, -e *f*; [sexist] phallocrate *m*, machiste *m*.

chauvinistic [ˌʃəʊvɪˈnɪstɪk] *adj* [nationalistic] chauvin; [sexist] machiste, phallocrate.

chaw [tʃɔː] *dial* ◇ *vi* & *vt* chiquer.
◇ *n* [tobacco] chique *f*.

ChE *written abbr of* chemical engineer.

cheap [tʃiːp] ◇ *adj* -**1.** [inexpensive] bon marché; labour is ~er in the Far East la main-d'œuvre est moins chère en Extrême-Orient; he bought a ~ ticket to Australia il a acheté un billet à prix OR tarif réduit pour l'Australie; it was the ~est piano in the shop c'était le piano le moins cher du magasin ❑ ~ and cheerful sans prétentions. -**2.** [poor quality] de mauvaise qualité; the furniture was ~ and nasty *Br* les meubles étaient de très mauvaise qualité. -**3.** [of little value]: human life is ~ in many countries il y a beaucoup de pays où la vie humaine a peu de valeur; that's how he gets his ~ thrills c'est ça qui l'excite. -**4.** [low, despicable]: a ~ joke une plaisanterie de mauvais goût; he made the girl feel ~ il fit en sorte que la fille eût honte; she had made herself ~ in her father's eyes elle s'était rabaissée aux yeux de son père. -**5.** *Am* [stingy] mesquin.
◇ *adv* [buy, get, sell] bon marché; I can get it for you ~er je peux vous le trouver pour moins cher; clothes of that quality don't come ~ des vêtements de cette qualité coûtent cher.
◆ **on the cheap** *adv phr*: she furnished the house on the ~ *inf* elle a meublé la maison pour pas cher; they've got immigrants working for them on the ~ *inf* ils ont des immigrés qui travaillent pour eux au rabais.

cheapen ['tʃiːpn] ◇ *vt* -**1.** [lower, debase] abaisser; I wouldn't ~ myself by accepting a bribe je ne m'abaisserais pas à accepter un pot-de-vin. -**2.** [reduce the price of] baisser le prix de.
◇ *vi* devenir moins cher.

cheap-jack *inf* ◇ *n* marchand *m* de bric-à-brac, camelot *m*.
◇ *adj* de pacotille.

cheaply ['tʃiːplɪ] *adv* à bon marché; I can do the job more ~ je peux faire le travail à meilleur marché OR pour moins cher.

cheapness ['tʃiːpnɪs] *n* -**1.** [low price] bas prix *m*. -**2.** [poor quality] mauvaise qualité *f*.

cheapo *inf* ['tʃiːpəʊ] *adj* pas cher.

cheapskate *inf* ['tʃiːpskeɪt] *n* radin *m*, -e *f*, grippe-sou *m*.

cheat [tʃiːt] ◇ *vt* -**1.** [defraud, swindle] escroquer, léser; to ~ sb out of sthg escroquer qqch à qqn; to feel ~ed se sentir lésé OR frustré. -**2.** *fig* & *lit* [deceive, trick] duper; to ~ death échapper à la mort.
◇ *vi* tricher; he always ~s at cards il triche toujours aux cartes; she was expelled from university for ~ing elle fut renvoyée de l'université pour avoir triché aux examens.
◇ *n* -**1.** [dishonest person] tricheur *m*, -euse *f*; [crook, swindler] escroc *m*, fraudeur *m*, -euse *f*. -**2.** [dishonest practice] tricherie *f*, tromperie *f*.
◆ **cheat on** *vt insep* -**1.** [falsify] tricher sur; he ~ed on his income tax il a triché sur sa déclaration d'impôts. -**2.** [be unfaithful to] tromper; he ~s on his wife il trompe sa femme.

cheating ['tʃiːtɪŋ] ◇ *n* -**1.** [at cards, games] tricherie *f*; [at exams] copiage *m*. -**2.** [fraud] fraude *f*. -**3.** *(U)* [infidelity] infidélité *f*, infidélités *fpl*.
◇ *adj* -**1.** [dishonest] malhonnête, trompeur. -**2.** [unfaithful, disloyal] infidèle.

Chechen [tʃɪ'tʃen] ◇ *n* Tchétchène *mf*.
◇ *adj* tchétchène.

check [tʃek] ◇ *vt* -**1.** [inspect, examine] contrôler, vérifier; [confirm, substantiate] vérifier; she didn't ~ her facts before writing the article elle n'a pas vérifié les faits avant d'écrire son article; the figures have to be ~ed il faut vérifier les chiffres; the doctor ~ed my blood pressure le médecin a pris ma tension; the inspector ~ed our tickets le contrôleur a contrôlé nos billets. -**2.** [contain, limit] enrayer; [emotions, troops] contenir; she almost blurted out the truth but ~ed herself in time elle a failli laisser échapper la vérité mais s'est retenue à temps; he ~ed the urge to hit him il réprima l'envie de le frapper. -**3.** *Am* [coat, hat] mettre au vestiaire; [luggage] mettre à la consigne. -**4.** *Am* [mark, tick] cocher. -**5.** [in chess] faire échec à. -**6.** *dial* [reprimand] réprimander.
◇ *vi* -**1.** [confirm] vérifier; [correspond, match] correspondre, s'accorder; I'll have to ~ with the accountant je vais devoir vérifier auprès du comptable; his description of the killer ~ed with forensic evidence sa description du tueur s'accordait avec l'expertise médico-légale. -**2.** [pause, halt] s'arrêter.
◇ *n* -**1.** [examination, inspection] contrôle *m*, vérification *f*; the airline ordered ~s on all their 747s la compagnie aérienne a ordonné que des contrôles soient faits sur tous ses 747; a routine ~ une vérification de routine. -**2.** [inquiry, investigation] enquête *f*; to do OR to run a ~ on sb se renseigner sur qqn. -**3.** [restraint] frein *m*; the House of Lords acts as a ~ upon the House of Commons la Chambre des lords met un frein au pouvoir de la Chambre des communes; (a system of) ~s and balances POL (un système d') équilibre des pouvoirs; he kept OR held his anger in ~ il a contenu OR maîtrisé sa colère; we could no longer hold OR keep the enemy in ~ MIL nous ne pouvions plus contenir l'ennemi. -**4.** [in chess] échec *m*; in ~ en échec; ~! échec au roi! -**5.** *Am* [bill] addition *f*; [receipt for coats, luggage] ticket *m*. -**6.** [square] carreau *m*; a skirt in black and white ~ une jupe à carreaux noirs et blancs. -**7.** *Am* [mark, tick] coche *f*; put a ~ next to all the verbs cochez tous les verbes. -**8.** *Am* = **cheque**.
◇ *adj* [pattern, skirt] à carreaux.
◆ **check in** ◇ *vi insep* -**1.** [at airport] se présenter à l'enregistrement. -**2.** [at hotel] se présenter à la réception.
◇ *vt sep* -**1.** [at airport] enregistrer. -**2.** [at hotel] inscrire. -**3.** [at cloakroom] mettre au vestiaire; [at left-luggage office] mettre à la consigne. -**4.** *Am* [at library]: to ~ in a book at the library rapporter un livre à la bibliothèque.
◆ **check into** *vt insep*: to ~ into a hotel descendre dans un hôtel.
◆ **check off** *vt sep Am* cocher.
◆ **check on** *vt insep* -**1.** [facts] vérifier. -**2.** [person]: the doctor ~ed on two patients before leaving the hospital le médecin est allé voir deux patients avant de quitter l'hôpital.
◆ **check out** ◇ *vi insep* -**1.** [pay hotel bill] régler sa note; [leave hotel] quitter l'hôtel. -**2.** [prove to be correct] s'avérer exact; [correspond, match] s'accorder, correspondre.
◇ *vt sep* -**1.** [library book] faire tamponner; [hotel guest] faire régler sa note à. -**2.** [investigate - person] enquêter sur, se renseigner sur; [- information, machine, place] vérifier. -**3.** *inf* [try] essayer; why don't we ~ out the restaurant that John told us about? pourquoi ne pas essayer le restaurant dont John nous a parlé?
◆ **check over** *vt sep* examiner, vérifier.
◆ **check up on** *vt insep*: to ~ up on sb enquêter OR se renseigner sur qqn; if you trusted me you wouldn't ~ up on me all the time si tu me faisais confiance tu ne serais pas toujours en train de m'espionner; to ~ up on sthg vérifier qqch; the social worker ~ed up on reports of child abuse l'assistante sociale a enquêté sur les allégations de mauvais traitements à enfant.

CHECKS AND BALANCES:
Ce système de contrôle mutuel, garanti par la Constitution, est l'un des principes fondamentaux du gouvernement américain. Il a été élaboré afin que les pouvoirs législatif, exécutif et judiciaire n'accumulent pas trop d'influence les uns par rapport aux autres.

---

checkbook *Am* = **chequebook**.

check digit *n* COMPUT chiffre *m* de contrôle OR de vérification, clé *f*.

checked [tʃekt] *adj* -**1.** [pattern, tablecloth] à carreaux. -**2.** LING [syllable] fermé, entravé.

checker ['tʃekə^r] *n Am* -**1.** [square] carreau *m*; a ~ tablecloth une nappe à carreaux. -**2.** GAMES pion *m*. -**3.** [in supermarket] caissier *m*, -ère *f*; [in left-luggage office] préposé *m*, -e *f* à la consigne; [in cloakroom] préposé *m*, -e *f* au vestiaire.

checkerboard ['tʃekəbɔːd] *n Am* [in chess] échiquier *m*; [in draughts] damier *m*.

Checker cab *n taxi américain reconnaissable au motif de damier qui en décore la carrosserie*.

checkered *Am* = **chequered**.

checkers *Am* = **chequers**.

check-in *n* enregistrement *m*.

checking account *n Am* compte *m* chèque OR chèques.

checklist ['tʃeklɪst] *n* liste *f* de vérification; AERON check-list *f*.

checkmate ['tʃekmeɪt] ◇ *n* -**1.** [in chess] échec et mat *m*. -**2.** *fig* [deadlock, standstill] impasse *f*; [defeat] échec *m* total.
◇ *vt* -**1.** [in chess] faire échec et mat à. -**2.** *fig* [frustrate, obstruct] contrecarrer; [defeat] vaincre.

checkout ['tʃekaʊt] ◇ *n* -**1.** [in supermarket] caisse *f*. -**2.** [in hotel]: ~ (time) is at 11 a.m. les chambres doivent être libérées avant 11 h.
◇ *comp*: the ~ counter la caisse, le comptoir-caisse; ~ girl caissière *f*.

checkpoint ['tʃekpɔɪnt] *n* (poste *m* de) contrôle *m*.

Checkpoint Charlie *pr n* checkpoint *m* Charlie.

checkrein ['tʃekreɪn] *n Am* fausses rênes *fpl*.

checkroom ['tʃekrʊm] *n Am* [for coats, hats] vestiaire *m*; [for luggage] consigne *f*.

checkup ['tʃekʌp] *n* MED bilan *m* de santé, check-up *m*; to give sb a ~ faire un bilan de santé à qqn; to go for OR to have a ~ faire faire un bilan de santé.

cheddar ['tʃedə^r] *n*: ~ (cheese) cheddar *m*.

cheek [tʃiːk] ◇ *n* -**1.** [of face] joue *f*; ~ to ~ joue contre joue; to be/to live ~ by jowl with sb être/vivre tout près de qqn; to turn the other ~ tendre OR présenter l'autre joue. -**2.** *inf* [buttock] fesse *f*. -**3.** *inf Br* [impudence] culot *m*, toupet *m*; he had the ~ to ask her age! il a eu le culot OR le toupet de lui demander son âge!; what (a) ~!, of all the ~! quel culot!, quel toupet!
◇ *vt inf Br* être insolent avec.

cheekbone ['tʃiːkbəʊn] *n* pommette *f*.

-cheeked [tʃiːkt] *in cpds* aux joues...; rosy~ aux joues roses OR rouges; round~ aux joues rebondies OR rondes, joufflu.

cheekily ['tʃiːkɪlɪ] *adv Br* avec effronterie OR impudence, effrontément.

cheekiness ['tʃiːkɪnɪs] *n Br* effronterie *f*, audace *f*.

cheek pouch *n* abajoue *f*.

cheeky ['tʃiːkɪ] *adj Br* [person] effronté, impudent; [attitude, behaviour] impertinent.

cheep [tʃiːp] ◇ *n* pépiement *m*.
◇ *vi* pépier.

cheer [tʃɪə^r] ◇ *n* -**1.** [cry] hourra *m*, bravo *m*; I heard a ~ go up j'ai entendu des acclamations; three ~s for the winner! un ban OR hourra pour le gagnant!; three ~s! hourra! -**2.** *lit* [good spirits] bonne humeur *f*, gaieté *f*; words of good ~ paroles *fpl* d'encouragement.
◇ *vt* -**1.** [make cheerful - person] remonter le moral à, réconforter. -**2.** [encourage by shouts] acclamer.
◇ *vi* pousser des acclamations OR des hourras.
◆ **cheer on** *vt sep* encourager (par des acclamations); his supporters ~ed him on to victory les acclamations de ses supporters l'ont encouragé jusqu'à la victoire.
◆ **cheer up** ◇ *vt sep* [person] remonter le moral à, réconforter; [house, room] égayer.
◇ *vi insep* s'égayer, se dérider; ~ up! courage!

cheerful ['tʃɪəfʊl] *adj* -**1.** [happy - person, smile] gai; [- atmosphere, mood] gai, joyeux; [- colour, wallpaper] gai, riant; [- news] réjouissant; she's always ~ elle est toujours de bonne humeur. -**2.** [enthusiastic, willing - helper, worker] de bonne volonté; [- dedication] grand.

cheerfully ['tʃɪəfʊlɪ] *adv* -**1.** [happily] joyeusement, avec entrain. -**2.** [willingly] de plein gré, avec bonne volonté; I could ~ have hit him! je l'aurais bien frappé!

cheerfulness ['tʃɪəfʊlnɪs] *n* [of person] bonne humeur *f*; [of atmosphere, colour] gaieté *f*; [of remark, smile] gaieté *f*, caractère *m* jovial.

cheerily ['tʃɪərəlɪ] *adv* joyeusement, avec entrain.

cheering ['tʃɪərɪŋ] ◇ *n (U)* acclamations *fpl*, hourras *mpl*.
◇ *adj* [remark, thought] encourageant, qui remonte le moral; [news, sight] encourageant, réconfortant; that's ~! *iron* voilà qui est réconfortant!

cheerio *inf* [,tʃɪərɪ'əʊ] *interj Br* -**1.** [goodbye] salut, tchao. -**2.** *dated* [toast] à la tienne.

cheerleader ['tʃɪə,liːdəʳ] *n majorette qui stimule l'enthousiasme des supporters des équipes sportives, surtout aux États-Unis.*

cheerless ['tʃɪəlɪs] *adj* morne, triste.

cheers *inf* [tʃɪəz] *interj Br* -**1.** [toast] à la tienne. -**2.** [goodbye] salut, tchao. -**3.** [thanks] merci.

cheery ['tʃɪərɪ] (*compar* cheerier, *superl* cheeriest) *adj* [person] gai; [smile] joyeux.

cheese [tʃiːz] ◇ *n* fromage *m*; say ~! PHOT souriez!
◇ *comp* [omelette, sandwich] au fromage; [knife] à fromage; the ~ **industry** l'industrie fromagère; ~ **biscuit** *biscuit sucré ou salé que l'on mange avec du fromage*; ~ **maker** fromager *m*, -ère *f*.
◆ **cheese off** *inf vt sep Br* embêter, barber.

cheeseboard ['tʃiːzbɔːd] *n* [board] plateau *m* à fromage OR fromages; [on menu] plateau *m* de fromages.

cheeseburger ['tʃiːz,bɜːgəʳ] *n* hamburger *m* au fromage.

cheesecake ['tʃiːzkeɪk] *n* -**1.** [dessert] gâteau *m* au fromage (blanc). -**2.** *inf (U) hum* [in photo] pin-up *f*.

cheesecloth ['tʃiːzklɒθ] *n* CULIN & TEX étamine *f*.

cheese dip *n sauce au fromage dans laquelle on trempe des légumes, des chips etc.*

cheesed off *inf* [tʃiːzd-] *adj Br*: to be ~ en avoir marre; I'm ~ **with this job** j'en ai marre de ce boulot.

cheeseparing ['tʃiːz,peərɪŋ] ◇ *n* parcimonie *f*.
◇ *adj* parcimonieux, pingre.

cheese straw *n* allumette *f* au fromage.

cheesy ['tʃiːzɪ] (*compar* cheesier, *superl* cheesiest) *adj* -**1.** [flavour] qui a un goût de fromage, qui sent le fromage; [smell] qui sent le fromage. -**2.** *inf Am* [excuse] nul.

cheetah ['tʃiːtə] *n* guépard *m*.

chef [ʃef] *n* CULIN chef *m* (de cuisine), cuisinier *m*, -ère *f*.

Chek(h)ov ['tʃekɒf] *pr n* Tchekhov.

Chelsea bun ['tʃelsɪ-] *n petit pain rond aux raisins secs.*

Chelsea Pensioner *n ancien combattant résidant au Chelsea Royal Hospital, à Londres.*

chemical ['kemɪkl] ◇ *n* produit *m* chimique.
◇ *adj* chimique; ~ **engineer** ingénieur *m* chimiste; ~ **engineering** génie *m* chimique; ~ **warfare** guerre *f* chimique; ~ **weapons** armes *fpl* chimiques.

chemically ['kemɪklɪ] *adv* chimiquement.

chemin de fer [ʃə,mændə'feəʳ] *n* GAMES chemin *m* de fer *(jeu de cartes)*.

chemise [ʃə'miːz] *n* [dress] robe-chemisier *f*; [undergarment] chemise *f (de femme)*.

chemist ['kemɪst] *n* -**1.** [scientist] chimiste *mf*. -**2.** *Br* [pharmacist] pharmacien *m*, -enne *f*; ~'s (shop) pharmacie *f*.

chemistry ['kemɪstrɪ] ◇ *n* chimie *f*; sexual ~ *fig* (bonne) entente *f* sexuelle.
◇ *comp*: ~ **set** panoplie *f* de chimiste.

chemotherapy [,kiːməʊ'θerəpɪ] *n* chimiothérapie *f*.

chemurgy ['kemɜːdʒɪ] *n* chimiurgie *f*.

Chengdu ['tʃeŋ'tuː] *pr n* Chengdu.

chenille [ʃə'niːl] *n* chenille *f (tissu)*.

Cheops ['kiːɒps] *pr n* Khéops; the **great pyramid of** ~ la grande pyramide de Khéops.

cheque *Br*, **check** *Am* [tʃek] *n* chèque *m*; a ~ for £7 OR to the amount of £7 un chèque de 7 livres; who should I make the ~ payable to? à quel nom dois-je libeller le chèque?; to pay by ~ payer par chèque; to write sb a ~ faire un chèque à qqn; a bad ~ un chèque sans provision; a **crossed/open** ~ *Br* un chèque barré/non-barré.

chequebook *Br*, **checkbook** *Am* ['tʃekbʊk] *n* carnet *m* de chèques, chéquier *m*.

chequebook journalism *n dans les milieux de la presse, pratique qui consiste à payer des sommes importantes pour le témoignage d'une personne impliquée dans une affaire.*

cheque card *n Br carte d'identité bancaire sans laquelle les chèques ne sont pas acceptés en Grande-Bretagne.*

chequered *Br*, **checkered** *Am* ['tʃekəd] *adj* -**1.** [pattern] à carreaux, à damiers. -**2.** [varied] varié; she's had a ~ **career** sa carrière a connu des hauts et des bas.

chequers *Br*, **checkers** *Am* ['tʃekəz] *n (U)* jeu *m* de dames; how about (a game of) ~? si on jouait aux dames?

Chequers ['tʃekəz] *pr n résidence secondaire officielle du Premier ministre britannique.*

cherish ['tʃerɪʃ] *vt* [person] chérir, aimer; [ambition, hope] caresser, nourrir; [experience, memory] chérir; [right, value] tenir à; one of my most ~ed memories un de mes souvenirs les plus chers.

Chernenko [tʃɜː'neŋkəʊ] *pr n* Tchernenko.

Chernobyl [tʃɜː'nəʊbl] *pr n* Tchernobyl.

Cherokee [,tʃerə'kiː] (*pl inv* OR Cherokees) ◇ *n* -**1.** [person] Cherokee *mf*. -**2.** LING cherokee *m*.
◇ *adj* cherokee; ~ **Indian** Indien *m*, -enne *f* cherokee, Cherokee *mf*.

cheroot [ʃə'ruːt] *n* petit cigare *m (à bouts coupés)*.

cherry ['tʃerɪ] (*pl* cherries) ◇ *n* -**1.** [fruit] cerise *f*; [tree] cerisier *m*. -**2.** = **cherry red**.
◇ *comp* [blossom, wood] de cerisier; [pie, tart] aux cerises; ~ **orchard** cerisaie *f*; ~ **tree** cerisier *m* ❑ 'The Cherry Orchard' *Chekhov* 'la Cerisaie'.

cherry bomb *n Am sorte de pétard rouge.*

cherry brandy *n* cherry *m*.

cherry-picking *n literal* cueillette *f* des cerises; *fig* écrémage *m*.

cherry plum *n* myrobolan *m*.

cherry red *n* cerise *f*, rouge *m* cerise.
◆ **cherry-red** *adj* (rouge) cerise *(inv)*; cherry-red lips des lèvres vermeilles.

cherry tomato *n* tomate *f* cerise.

cherub ['tʃerəb] (*pl* cherubs OR cherubim [-bɪm]) *n* ART chérubin *m*; *fig* chérubin *m*, petit ange *m*.

cherubic [tʃe'ruːbɪk] *adj* [face] de chérubin; [child, look, smile] angélique.

chervil ['tʃɜːvɪl] *n* cerfeuil *m*.

Cheshire cat ['tʃeʃə-] *n*: to grin like a ~ avoir un sourire jusqu'aux oreilles.

chess [tʃes] *n (U)* échecs *mpl*; let's play (a game of) ~ si on jouait aux échecs?; ~ **player** joueur *m*, -euse *f* d'échecs.

chessboard ['tʃesbɔːd] *n* échiquier *m*.

chessman ['tʃesmæn] (*pl* chessmen [-men]) *n* pion *m*, pièce *f (de jeu d'échecs)*.

chest [tʃest] ◇ *n* -**1.** ANAT poitrine *f*; to have a weak ~ être faible des bronches ❑ to get sthg off one's ~ dire ce qu'on a sur le cœur. -**2.** [box] coffre *m*, caisse *f*; ~ **of drawers** commode *f*; ~ **freezer** congélateur-bahut *m*.
◇ *comp* [cold, measurement, voice] de poitrine; ~ **infection** infection *f* des voies respiratoires; ~ **pain** OR **pains** douleurs *fpl* de poitrine; a ~ **X-ray** une radio des poumons ❑ ~ **expander** extenseur *m* (pour développer les pectoraux).

chesterfield ['tʃestəfiːld] *n* -**1.** [coat] pardessus *m* (de ville). -**2.** [sofa] canapé *m (dont les accoudoirs sont de la même hauteur que le dossier)*.

chestnut ['tʃesnʌt] ◇ *n* -**1.** [tree] châtaignier *m*; [fruit] châtaigne *f*. -**2.** [colour] châtain *m*. -**3.** [horse] alezan *m*, -e *f*. -**4.** *inf* [joke]: old ~ plaisanterie *f* rebattue OR éculée.
◇ *comp* -**1.** [blossom, wood] de châtaignier; [stuffing] aux marrons; ~ **tree** châtaignier *m*. -**2.** [colour, hair] châtain; [horse] alezan; ~ **brown** châtain *(inv)*.

chesty ['tʃestɪ] (*compar* chestier, *superl* chestiest) *adj* [cough] de poitrine.

cheval glass [ʃə'vælglɑːs] *n* psyché *f (glace)*.

chevron ['ʃevrən] *n* ARCHIT, HERALD & MIL chevron *m*.

chew [tʃuː] ◇ *vt* mâcher, mastiquer; to ~ **tobacco** chiquer, mâcher du tabac ❑ to ~ the cud [cow] ruminer; [person] ruminer; to ~ the fat with sb *inf* tailler une bavette avec qqn.
◇ *n* -**1.** [act] mâchement *m*, mastication *f*. -**2.** [piece of tobacco] chique *f*. -**3.** [sweet] bonbon *m*.
◆ **chew on** *vt insep* -**1.** [food] mâcher, mastiquer; [bone] ronger; [tobacco] chiquer. -**2.** *inf* [problem, question] ruminer, retourner dans sa tête.
◆ **chew out** *inf vt sep Am* engueuler, passer un savon à.
◆ **chew over** *inf vt sep* ruminer, retourner dans sa tête.
◆ **chew through** *vt insep* couper à force de ronger.
◆ **chew up** *vt sep* -**1.** [food] mâchonner, mastiquer. -**2.** [damage] abîmer à force de ronger.

chewing gum ['tʃuːɪŋ-] *n* chewing-gum *m*.

chewy ['tʃuːɪ] (*compar* chewier, *superl* chewiest) *adj* caoutchouteux.

Cheyenne [ʃaɪ'en] (*pl inv* OR Cheyennes)
◇ *n* Cheyenne *mf*.
◇ *adj* cheyenne.

Chiang Kai-shek ['tʃæŋkaɪ'ʃek] *pr n* Tchang Kaï-Chek.

chiaroscuro [kɪ,ɑːrə'skʊərəʊ] (*pl* chiaroscuros) *n* clair-obscur *m*.

chic [ʃiːk] ◇ *adj* chic, élégant.
◇ *n* chic *m*, élégance *f*.

Chicago [ʃɪ'kɑːgəʊ] *pr n* Chicago; the ~ **Board of Trade**, the ~ **Mercantile Exchange** *les deux plus importantes bourses de marchandises aux États-Unis*; the ~ **fire** l'incendie *m* de Chicago.

THE CHICAGO FIRE:
Gigantesque incendie qui détruisit une bonne partie de la ville en 1871. Selon la légende, ce serait la vache de Madame O'Leary qui, renversant une lanterne dans son étable, amorça le feu. L'incendie ravagea 20 000 habitations et fit 100 000 sans-abri.

chicane [ʃɪ'keɪn] *n* -**1.** GAMES [in bridge] partie *f* sans atout. -**2.** [barrier] chicane *f*.

chicanery [ʃɪ'keɪnərɪ] (*pl* chicaneries) *n* [trickery] ruse *f*, fourberie *f*; [legal trickery] chicane *f*.

Chicano [tʃɪ'kɑːnəʊ] (*pl* Chicanos) *n* Chicano *mf (Américain d'origine mexicaine)*.

chichi ['ʃiːʃiː] *adj* précieux.

chick [tʃɪk] *n* -**1.** [baby bird - gen] oisillon *m*; [- of chicken] poussin *m*. -**2.** *inf* [woman] poupée *f*.

chickadee ['tʃɪkədiː] *n* mésange *f (d'Amérique du Nord)*.

chicken ['tʃɪkɪn] ◇ *n* -**1.** [bird] poulet *m*; [young] poussin *m*; he's no (spring) ~ *inf* il n'est plus tout jeune; which came first, the ~ or the egg? allez savoir quelle est la cause et quel est l'effet, l'œuf ou la poule?; it's a ~-**and-egg situation** *inf* c'est le problème de l'œuf et de la poule, on ne sait pas lequel est à l'origine de l'autre. -**2.** *inf* [coward] poule *f* mouillée, froussard *m*, -e *f*.
◇ *comp* [dish, liver, stew] de poulet; [sandwich] au poulet; ~ **breast** blanc *m* (de poulet); ~ **leg** cuisse *f* (de poulet); ~ **farmer** éleveur *m* de volailles, aviculteur *m*, -trice *f*; ~ **farming** élevage *m* avicole OR de volailles, aviculture *f*.
◇ *adj inf* [cowardly] froussard.
◆ **chicken out** *inf vi insep* se dégonfler; he ~ed out of the race il s'est dégonflé et n'a pas pris part à la course.

chickenfeed ['tʃɪkɪnfiːd] *n (U)* -**1.** *literal* nourriture *f* pour volaille. -**2.** *inf fig*: he earns ~ il gagne des cacahuètes.

chicken-hearted, **chicken-livered** [-ˌlɪvəd] *adj* poltron.

chicken pox *n (U)* varicelle *f*.

chicken run *n* poulailler *m*.

chickenshit▽ [ˈtʃɪkɪnˌʃɪt] *n Am* [person] poule *f* mouillée.

chicken wire *n* grillage *m*.

chick pea *n* pois *m* chiche.

chickweed [ˈtʃɪkwiːd] *n* mouron *m* blanc OR des oiseaux.

chicly [ˈʃiːklɪ] *adv* de façon chic, élégamment.

chicory [ˈtʃɪkərɪ] (*pl* **chicories**) *n* [for salad] endive *f*; [for coffee] chicorée *f*.

chide [tʃaɪd] (*pt* **chided** OR **chid** [tʃɪd], *pp* **chid** [tʃɪd] OR **chidden** [ˈtʃɪdn]) *vt fml* gronder, réprimander.

chief [tʃiːf] ◇ *n* -**1.** [leader] chef *m*; ~ **of police** ≃ préfet *m* de police; **Chief of Staff** MIL chef *m* d'état-major; *Am* [at White House] secrétaire *m* général de la Maison Blanche; **too many ~s and not enough Indians** trop de chefs et pas assez d'hommes de troupe *(pour exécuter les ordres et faire le travail)*. -**2.** *inf* [boss] boss *m*. -**3.** HERALD chef *m*.
◇ *adj* -**1.** [most important] principal, premier; **one of the ~ conflicts** un des principaux conflits. -**2.** [head] premier, en chef; **Chief Constable** *en Grande-Bretagne, chef de la police d'un comté ou d'une région*, ≃ commissaire *m* divisionnaire; ~ **librarian** bibliothécaire *mf* en chef; **Chief Education Officer** ≃ recteur *m* d'académie; **Chief Executive** ADMIN directeur *m*, -trice *f*; *Am* POL président *m* des États-Unis, chef *m* de l'exécutif; ~ **executive officer** COMM & INDUST président-directeur général *m*; ~ **inspector** [gen] inspecteur *m* principal, inspectrice *f* principale, inspecteur *m*, -trice *f* en chef; *Br* [of police] ≃ commissaire *m* de police; *Br* SCH ≃ inspecteur général *m*, inspectrice générale *f*; ~ **justice** président *m* de la Haute Cour de justice; *Am* juge *m* à la Cour suprême; ~ **master sergeant** *Am* MIL major *m*; ~ **petty officer** NAUT ≃ maître *m*; ~ **rabbi** grand rabbin *m*; ~ **superintendent** *Br* [in police] ≃ commissaire *m* principal; ~ **technician** *Br* [in Air Force] officier *m* technicien; ~ **warrant officer** MIL adjudant *m* chef; **Chief Whip** *responsable du maintien de la discipline à l'intérieur d'un parti à la Chambre des communes*.
◆ **in chief** *adv phr* principalement, surtout.

chiefly [ˈtʃiːflɪ] *adv* principalement, surtout.

chieftain [ˈtʃiːftən] *n* chef *m (de tribu)*.

chiffon [ˈʃɪfɒn] ◇ *n* mousseline *f* de soie.
◇ *adj* -**1.** [dress, scarf] en mousseline (de soie). -**2.** CULIN à la mousse; **lemon ~ pie** ≃ tarte *f* à la mousse de citron.

chiffon(n)ier [ˌʃɪfəˈnɪəʳ] *n* chiffonnier *m*.

chigger [ˈtʃɪgəʳ] *n* -**1.** [flea] chique *f*. -**2.** *Am* [parasitic larva] aoûtat *m*.

chignon [ˈʃiːnjɒn] *n* chignon *m*.

chigoe [ˈtʃɪgəʊ] = **chigger**.

chihuahua [tʃɪˈwɑːwə] *n* chihuahua *m*.

chilblain [ˈtʃɪlbleɪn] *n* engelure *f*.

child [tʃaɪld] (*pl* **children** [ˈtʃɪldrən]) ◇ *n* -**1.** [boy or girl] enfant *mf*; **since I was a ~** depuis que je suis enfant; **while still a ~** tout enfant; **children of the 60s** des enfants des années 60; **don't be such a ~!** ne fais pas l'enfant!; **stop treating me like a ~!** arrête de me traiter comme un enfant!; **to be with ~** *arch* OR *lit* attendre un enfant, être enceinte; **to get a woman with ~** *arch* OR *lit* faire un enfant à une femme. -**2.** *lit* [result] fruit *m*.
◇ *comp* [psychiatry, psychology] de l'enfant, infantile; [psychiatrist, psychologist] pour enfants; ~ **abuse** mauvais traitements *mpl* à enfant; **she was a ~ bride** elle s'était mariée toute jeune; ~ **guidance** psycho-pédagogie *f* pour enfants caractériels; ~ **guidance centre** centre *m* psycho-pédagogique pour enfants; ~ **labour** travail *m* des enfants; **it's ~'s play for** OR **to him** *inf* c'est un jeu d'enfant pour lui; ~ **prodigy** enfant *mf* prodige; ~ **welfare** protection *f* de l'enfance.

childbearing [ˈtʃaɪldˌbeərɪŋ] ◇ *n* grossesse *f*.
◇ *adj* [complications, problems] de grossesse; **of ~ age** en âge d'avoir des enfants; **she's past ~ age** elle est trop âgée pour avoir des enfants.

childbed [ˈtʃaɪldbed] *n arch* OR *lit*: **in ~** en couches.

child benefit *n (U)* allocation *f* familiale OR allocations *fpl* familiales (pour un enfant) *(en Grande-Bretagne)*.

childbirth [ˈtʃaɪldbɜːθ] *n (U)* accouchement *m*; **in ~** en couches.

child care *n* -**1.** *Br* ADMIN protection *f* de l'enfance. -**2.** *Am* [day care]: ~ **center** crèche *f*, garderie *f*.

child-friendly *adj* [area, city] aménagé pour les enfants; [house, furniture] conçu pour les enfants.

childhood [ˈtʃaɪldhʊd] *n* enfance *f*.

childish [ˈtʃaɪldɪʃ] *adj* -**1.** [face, fears, voice] d'enfant. -**2.** [immature] enfantin, puéril; **don't be so ~** ne fais pas l'enfant.

childishly [ˈtʃaɪldɪʃlɪ] *adv* comme un enfant, en enfant.

childishness [ˈtʃaɪldɪʃnɪs] *n (U)* [of person] enfantillage *m*, puérilité *f*; [of behaviour, remark] puérilité *f*; **that's just ~!** ce sont des enfantillages!

childless [ˈtʃaɪldlɪs] *adj* sans enfants.

childlike [ˈtʃaɪldlaɪk] *adj* d'enfant.

Childline [ˈtʃaɪldˌlaɪn] *pr n numéro de téléphone mis à la disposition des enfants maltraités*, ≃ SOS enfants battus.

childminder [ˈtʃaɪldˌmaɪndəʳ] *n Br* [for very young children] nourrice *f*; [for older children] assistante *f* maternelle.

childproof [ˈtʃaɪldpruːf] *adj*: ~ **lock** serrure *f* de sécurité pour enfants.

children [ˈtʃɪldrən] *pl* → **child**.

Child Support Agency *pr n en Grande-Bretagne, organisme gouvernemental qui décide du montant des pensions alimentaires et les prélève au besoin*.

Chile [ˈtʃɪlɪ] *pr n* Chili *m*; **in ~** au Chili.

Chilean [ˈtʃɪlɪən] ◇ *n* Chilien *m*, -enne *f*.
◇ *adj* chilien; **the ~ embassy** l'ambassade *f* du Chili.

chili [ˈtʃɪlɪ] = **chilli**.

chill [tʃɪl] ◇ *vt* -**1.** [make cold – food, wine] mettre au frais; [– champagne] frapper; [– glass, person] glacer; **~ed white wine** vin blanc frais; **to be ~ed to the bone/to the marrow** être glacé jusqu'aux os/jusqu'à la moelle. -**2.** *fig* [enthusiasm] refroidir. -**3.** TECH [metal] tremper.
◇ *vi* se refroidir, rafraîchir.
◇ *n* -**1.** [coldness] fraîcheur *f*, froideur *f*; **there's a ~ in the air** il fait assez frais OR un peu froid; **to take the ~ off a room** réchauffer une pièce; **his remark cast a ~ over the meeting** *fig* son observation a jeté un froid dans l'assemblée; **I sensed a certain ~ in his welcome** *fig* j'ai senti une certaine froideur dans son accueil. -**2.** [feeling of fear] frisson *m*; **the story sent ~s down her spine** l'histoire lui a fait froid dans le dos. -**3.** [illness] coup *m* de froid, refroidissement *m*; **to catch a ~** attraper OR prendre froid.
◇ *adj* [air, weather] frais, froid; [glance, response] froid, glacial.
◆ **chill out** *inf vi insep*: **we ~ed out in the local nightclub** on a traîné dans la boîte du coin.

chiller *inf* [ˈtʃɪləʳ] *n* film *m* d'épouvante.

chilli [ˈtʃɪlɪ] ◇ *n* [spice] *sorte de piment*; [dish] chili *m*.
◇ *comp*: ~ **powder** chili *m*; ~ **sauce** sauce *f* aux tomates et piments.

chilli con carne [ˌtʃɪlɪkɒnˈkɑːnɪ] *n* chili *m* con carne.

chilliness [ˈtʃɪlɪnɪs] *n* [of air, wind] fraîcheur *f*; *fig* [of greeting, manner] froideur *f*.

chilling [ˈtʃɪlɪŋ] *adj* [wind] frais, froid; *fig* [look, smile] froid, glacial; [news, story, thought] qui donne des frissons.

chilly [ˈtʃɪlɪ] (*compar* **chillier**, *superl* **chilliest**) *adj* -**1.** [air, room] (très) frais, froid; **I feel ~** j'ai froid; **it's rather ~ this morning** il fait plutôt frais OR frisquet ce matin. -**2.** *fig* [greeting, look] froid, glacial.

Chiltern Hundreds [ˈtʃɪltən-] *pr n*: **to apply for the ~** POL & *fig* démissionner *(du Parlement britannique)*.

THE CHILTERN HUNDREDS:
Ce nom désigne une circonscription administrative du Buckinghamshire (Grande-Bretagne); il désigne aussi un titre honorifique, «Stewardship of the Chiltern Hundreds», auquel postule un parlementaire qui souhaite démissionner ou prendre sa retraite.

chime [tʃaɪm] ◇ *n* [bell] carillon *m*.
◇ *vi* -**1.** [bell, voices] carillonner; [clock] sonner. -**2.** *inf* [agree] s'accorder; **his view ~s with mine** il est d'accord avec moi.
◇ *vt* sonner; **the clock ~d 6** l'horloge a sonné 6 h.
◆ **chimes** *npl* [for door] carillon *m*, sonnette *f*.
◆ **chime in** *inf vi insep* -**1.** [say] intervenir; **all the children ~d in** tous les enfants ont fait chorus; **he ~d in with some silly remark** il est intervenu pour dire une bêtise. -**2.** [agree] s'accorder; **his explanation ~s in with the facts** son explication s'accorde avec les faits.

chimera [kaɪˈmɪərə] *n* MYTH & *fig* chimère *f*.

chimeric(al) [kaɪˈmerɪk(l)] *adj* chimérique.

chimney [ˈtʃɪmnɪ] *n* -**1.** [in building] cheminée *f*. -**2.** [of lamp] verre *m*. -**3.** GEOL cheminée *f*.

chimneybreast [ˈtʃɪmnɪbrest] *n Br* manteau *m* *(de cheminée)*.

chimney corner *n* coin *m* du feu.

chimneypiece [ˈtʃɪmnɪpiːs] *n Br* dessus *m* OR tablette *f* de cheminée.

chimneypot [ˈtʃɪmnɪpɒt] *n* tuyau *m* de cheminée.

chimneystack [ˈtʃɪmnɪstæk] *n* [of one chimney] tuyau *m* de cheminée; [group of chimneys] souche *f* de cheminée.

chimneysweep [ˈtʃɪmnɪswiːp] *n* ramoneur *m*.

chimp *inf* [tʃɪmp], **chimpanzee** [ˌtʃɪmpənˈziː] *n* chimpanzé *m*.

chin [tʃɪn] (*pt* & *pp* **chinned**, *cont* **chinning**) ◇ *n* menton *m*; **(keep your) ~ up!** courage!; **to take sthg on the ~** *inf*: **he took the news on the ~** il a encaissé la nouvelle (sans broncher).
◇ *vt*: **to ~ the bar** SPORT faire une traction à la barre fixe.

china [ˈtʃaɪnə] ◇ *n* -**1.** [material] porcelaine *f*; **a piece of ~** une porcelaine; **they treated her as if she were made of ~** ils la traitaient comme si elle était en sucre. -**2.** [porcelain objects] porcelaine *f*; [porcelain dishes] porcelaine *f*, vaisselle *f* (de porcelaine); [crockery] vaisselle *f*.
◇ *comp* [cup, plate] de OR en porcelaine; [shop] de porcelaine.

China [ˈtʃaɪnə] *pr n* Chine *f*; **in ~** en Chine; **to take a trip to ~** faire un voyage en Chine ❑ **the People's Republic of ~** la République populaire de Chine.

china cabinet *n* dressoir *m*.

china clay *n* kaolin *m*.

Chinaman [ˈtʃaɪnəmən] (*pl* **Chinamen** [-mən]) *n dated* Chinois *m*.

China rose *n* rose *f* de Chine.

China Sea *pr n*: **the ~** la mer de Chine.

China tea *n* thé *m* de Chine.

Chinatown [ˈtʃaɪnətaʊn] *n* le quartier chinois.

chinaware [ˈtʃaɪnəweəʳ] *n* [porcelain objects] porcelaine *f*; [porcelain dishes] porcelaine *f*, vaisselle *f* (en porcelaine).

chinchilla [tʃɪnˈtʃɪlə] ◇ *n* chinchilla *m*.
◇ *comp* [coat, wrap] de chinchilla.

chin-chin *inf interj Br dated*: ~! [hello, goodbye] salut!; [in toast] tchin-tchin!

chine [tʃaɪn] *n* ANAT & CULIN échine *f*.

Chinese [ˌtʃaɪˈniːz] (*pl inv*) ◇ *n* -**1.** [person] Chinois *m*, -e *f*. -**2.** LING chinois *m*. -**3.** *inf Br* [meal] repas *m* chinois.
◇ *adj* chinois; **the ~ embassy** l'ambassade de Chine.

Chinese burn *n Br* torture *f* indienne.
Chinese cabbage *n* chou *m* chinois.
Chinese chequers *n (U)* dames *fpl* chinoises.
Chinese gooseberry *n* kiwi *m (fruit)*.
Chinese lantern *n* lanterne *f* vénitienne.
Chinese leaves *npl* bettes *fpl*.
Chinese puzzle *n* casse-tête *m inv* chinois.
Chinese walls *npl murs imaginaires qui symbolisent la confidentialité indispensable dans certains milieux financiers et séparent des services qui, par ailleurs, travaillent côte à côte.*
chink [tʃɪŋk] ◇ *n* -**1.** [hole] fente *f*, fissure *f*; a ~ of light un rayon de lumière ❑ **we found a ~ in her armour** nous avons trouvé son point faible OR sensible. -**2.** [sound] tintement *m (de pièces de monnaie, de verres)*.
◇ *vi* [jingle] tinter.
◇ *vt* -**1.** [jingle] faire tinter. -**2.** *Am* [cracks] boucher les fentes dans.
Chink▼ [tʃɪnk] *n terme raciste désignant un Chinois*, ≃ Chinetoque *mf*.
chinless ['tʃɪnlɪs] *adj* [with receding chin] au menton fuyant; *fig* [cowardly] mou, sans caractère; **a ~ wonder** *inf fig Br* une chiffe molle.
chinning bar ['tʃɪnɪŋ-] *n* barre *f* fixe.
chinook [tʃɪ'nu:k] *n* [wind] chinook *m*.
Chinook [tʃɪ'nu:k] (*pl inv* OR **Chinooks**) ◇ *n* -**1.** [person] Chinook *mf*. -**2.** LING langue *f* des Chinooks, langue *f* chinook.
◇ *adj* chinook *inv*.
chinos ['tʃi:nəʊz] *npl* chinos *m*.
chinstrap ['tʃɪnstræp] *n* jugulaire *f (de casque)*.
chintz [tʃɪnts] ◇ *n* chintz *m*.
◇ *comp* [curtain] de chintz.
chintzy ['tʃɪntsɪ] (*compar* **chintzier**, *superl* **chintziest**) *adj* -**1.** *literal* [chair, sofa] recouvert de chintz. -**2.** *inf* **a ~ decor** un décor tout en tissus à fleurs. -**3.** *Am* [stingy - person] mesquin; [- measure, sum] misérable, insuffisant; [thing] de mauvaise qualité.
chin-up *n* traction *f* (à la barre fixe); **to do ~s** faire des tractions (à la barre fixe).
chinwag *inf* ['tʃɪnwæg] *n* causette *f*; **to have a ~ with sb** tailler une bavette avec qqn.
chip [tʃɪp] (*pt* & *pp* **chipped**, *cont* **chipping**) ◇ *n* -**1.** [piece] éclat *m*; [of wood] copeau *m*, éclat *m*; **she's a ~ off the old block** *inf* elle est bien la fille de son père OR de sa mère; **to have a ~ on one's shoulder** *inf* en vouloir à tout le monde. -**2.** [flaw - in dish, glass] ébréchure *f*; [- in chair, wardrobe] écornure *f*; **this glass has a ~ (in it)** ce verre est ébréché. -**3.** CULIN *Br* (pomme de terre *f*) frite *f*; *Am* chips *f inv*. -**4.** GAMES [counter] jeton *m*, fiche *f*; **to cash in one's ~s** *literal* se faire payer; *fig inf* casser sa pipe; **when the ~s are down** *inf* dans les moments difficiles; **to have had one's ~s** *inf Br* être fichu OR cuit. -**5.** COMPUT puce *f*. -**6.** [in golf] coup *m* coché.
◇ *vt* -**1.** [dish, glass] ébrécher; [furniture] écorner; [paint] écailler. -**2.** [cut into pieces] piler; **to ~ wood** faire des copeaux. -**3.** [shape by cutting] tailler. -**4.** *Br* CULIN couper en lamelles; **chipped potatoes** (pommes de terre *fpl*) frites *fpl*. -**5.** [in golf]: **to ~ the ball** cocher.
◇ *vi* [dish, glass] s'ébrécher; [furniture] s'écorner; [paint] s'écailler.
◆ **chip at** *vt insep* enlever des éclats de.
◆ **chip away at** *vt insep*: **to ~ away at sthg** décaper qqch.
◆ **chip in** *inf* ◇ *vi insep* -**1.** [contribute] contribuer; **we all chipped in with £5** nous avons tous donné 5 livres. -**2.** [speak] mettre son grain de sel; **he chipped in with a suggestion** il est intervenu pour faire une suggestion.
◇ *vt insep* -**1.** [contribute] contribuer, donner. -**2.** [say] dire.
◆ **chip off** *vt sep* enlever.
chip basket *n Br* CULIN panier *m* à frites.
chipboard ['tʃɪpbɔ:d] *n (U) Br* (panneau *m* d') aggloméré *m*, panneau *m* de particules.
chipmunk ['tʃɪpmʌŋk] *n* tamia *m*, suisse *m Can*.
chipolata [,tʃɪpə'lɑ:tə] *n* chipolata *f*.
chip pan *n* friteuse *f*.
Chippendale ['tʃɪpn,deɪl] *pr n* Chippendale *(style de mobilier britannique du XVIIIe siècle)*.
chipper *inf* ['tʃɪpəʳ] *adj* -**1.** [lively] vif, fringant; **I'm feeling very ~** j'ai la pêche. -**2.** [smartly dressed] chic, élégant.
chippie ['tʃɪpɪ] = **chippy**.
chipping ['tʃɪpɪŋ] *n* [gen] éclat *m*, fragment *m*; [of wood] copeau *m*, éclat *m*; [in roadwork] gravillon *m*; **'slow, loose ~s'** 'attention gravillons'.
chippy ['tʃɪpɪ] (*pl* **chippies**) *n* -**1.** *inf Br* [shop] *boutique où l'on vend du «fish and chips»*. -**2.** ▽ *Br* & *NZ* [carpenter] charpentier *m*. -**3.** ▽ *Am pej* [woman] femme *f* légère.
chip shop *n Br boutique où l'on vend du «fish and chips»*.
chiromancer ['kaɪərəʊmænsəʳ] *n* chiromancien *m*, -enne *f*.
chiromancy ['kaɪərəʊmænsɪ] *n* chiromancie *f*.
chiropodist [kɪ'rɒpədɪst] *n* pédicure *mf*.
chiropody [kɪ'rɒpədɪ] *n (U)* [treatment] soins *mpl* du pied; [science] podologie *f*.
chiropractic [,kaɪrə'præktɪk] *n* chiropraxie *f*, chiropractie *f*.
chiropractor ['kaɪrə,præktəʳ] *n* chiropracteur *m*, chiropracticien *m*, -enne *f*.
chirp [tʃɜ:p] ◇ *vi* [bird] pépier, gazouiller; [insect] chanter, striduler; [person] parler d'une voix flûtée.
◇ *n* [of bird] pépiement *m*, gazouillement *m*; [of insect] chant *m*, stridulation *f*.
chirpy *inf* ['tʃɜ:pɪ] (*compar* **chirpier**, *superl* **chirpiest**) *adj* [person] gai, plein d'entrain; [mood, voice] gai, enjoué.
chirrup ['tʃɪrəp] ◇ *vi* [bird] pépier, gazouiller; [insect] chanter, striduler; [person] parler d'une voix flûtée.
◇ *n* [of bird] pépiement *m*, gazouillement *m*; [of insect] chant *m*, stridulation *f*.
chisel ['tʃɪzl] (*Br pt* & *pp* **chiselled**, *cont* **chiselling**, *Am pt* & *pp* **chiseled**, *cont* **chiseling**) ◇ *n* [gen] ciseau *m*; [for engraving] burin *m*.
◇ *vt* -**1.** [carve] ciseler; **to ~ a piece out of sthg** enlever un morceau de qqch au ciseau; **to ~ sthg from** OR **in** OR **out of marble** ciseler qqch dans du marbre; **chiselled features** *fig* traits burinés. -**2.** [engrave - form, name] graver au burin; [- plate] buriner. -**3.** [cheat]: **to ~ sb out of sthg** *inf* carotter qqch à qqn.
chiseller *inf Br*, **chiseler** *inf Am* ['tʃɪzələʳ] *n* carotteur *m*, -euse *f*.
chit [tʃɪt] *n* -**1.** [memo, note] note *f*; [voucher] bon *m*; [receipt] reçu *m*, récépissé *m*. -**2.** *inf dated* & *pej* [girl] gamine *f*, chipie *f*.
chitchat ['tʃɪttʃæt] ◇ *n* bavardage *m*, papotage *m*.
◇ *vi* bavarder, papoter.
chitlings ['tʃɪtlɪŋz], **chitterlings** ['tʃɪtəlɪŋz] *npl* tripes *fpl*.
chitty ['tʃɪtɪ] (*pl* **chitties**) *n Br* note *f*.
chivalrous ['ʃɪvlrəs] *adj* -**1.** [courteous] chevaleresque, courtois; [gallant] galant. -**2.** [exploit, tournament] chevaleresque.
chivalrously ['ʃɪvlrəslɪ] *adv* [courteously] de façon chevaleresque, courtoisement; [gallantly] galamment.
chivalry ['ʃɪvlrɪ] *n* -**1.** [courtesy] conduite *f* chevaleresque, courtoisie *f*; [gallantry] galanterie *f*; **the age of ~ is not dead** *hum* la galanterie existe encore. -**2.** [knights, system] chevalerie *f*.
chives [tʃaɪvz] *npl* ciboulette *f*, civette *f*; **add some ~s** ajoutez de la ciboulette OR civette.
chiv(v)y ['tʃɪvɪ] (*pt* & *pp* **chivvied** OR **chivied**) *vt* -**1.** *inf* [nag] harceler; **to ~ sb into doing sthg** harceler qqn jusqu'à ce qu'il fasse qqch; **stop chivvying me!** laisse-moi en paix! -**2.** [hunt - game] chasser; [- criminal] pourchasser.
◆ **chivvy up** *inf vt sep* faire activer.
chloral ['klɔ:rəl] *n* chloral *m*.
chlorate ['klɔ:reɪt] *n* chlorate *m*.
chloric ['klɔ:rɪk] *adj* chlorique; **~ acid** acide *m* chlorique.
chloride ['klɔ:raɪd] *n* chlorure *m*; **sodium ~** chlorure de sodium.
chlorinate ['klɔ:rɪneɪt] *vt* [water] javelliser; CHEM chlorurer, chlorer.
chlorination [,klɔ:rɪn'eɪʃn] *n* [of water] javellisation *f*, chloration *f*; CHEM chloration *f*.
chlorine ['klɔ:ri:n] ◇ *n* CHEM chlore *m*.
◇ *comp*: **~ bleach** eau *f* de Javel.
chlorite ['klɔ:raɪt] *n* chlorite *f*.
chlorofluorocarbon ['klɔ:rəʊ'flɔ:rəʊ'kɑ:bən] *n* chlorofluorocarbone *m*.
chloroform ['klɒrəfɔ:m] ◇ *n* chloroforme *m*.
◇ *vt* chloroformer.
chlorophyll *Br*, **chlorophyl** *Am* ['klɒrəfɪl] *n* chlorophylle *f*.
chlorosis [klɔ:'rəʊsɪs] *n* chlorose *f*.
choc *inf* [tʃɒk] *n* chocolat *m*.
choc-ice *n Br* Esquimau® *m*.
chock [tʃɒk] ◇ *n* [for door, wheel] cale *f*; [for barrel] cale *f*, chantier *m*; NAUT chantier *m*, cale *f*.
◇ *vt* [barrel, door, wheel] caler; NAUT mettre sur un chantier OR sur cales.
chock-a-block *inf*, **chock-full** *inf adj* [room, theatre] plein à craquer; [container] bourré, plein à ras bord; **the town is ~ with tourists** la ville est archipleine de touristes.
chocolate ['tʃɒkələt] ◇ *n* [drink, sweet] chocolat *m*; **a piece of ~** un morceau de chocolat; **a box of ~s** une boîte de chocolats; **a cup of (hot) ~** une tasse de chocolat (chaud).
◇ *adj* chocolat *(inv)*; **~ brown** (couleur *f*) chocolat *(inv)*.
◇ *comp* [biscuit, cake] au chocolat, chocolaté; **~ chip cookie** biscuit *m* avec des perles de chocolat.
chocolate-box *inf adj*: **a ~ landscape** un paysage très carte postale.
choice [tʃɔɪs] ◇ *n* -**1.** [act of choosing] choix *m*; **you'll have to make a ~** il faudra que tu choisisses OR que tu fasses un choix; **to make one's ~** faire son choix; **to have first ~** pouvoir choisir en premier; **it's your ~** c'est à vous de choisir OR décider; **by** OR **from ~** de OR par préférence; **the profession of her ~** la profession de son choix. -**2.** [option] choix *m*, option *f*; **they were given a ~ between basketball and soccer** ils ont eu le choix entre le basket et le foot; **you have no ~** vous n'avez pas le choix; **I had no ~ but to leave** je ne pouvais que partir. -**3.** [selection] choix *m*, assortiment *m*; **a wide ~ of goods** un grand choix de marchandises. -**4.** [thing, person chosen] choix *m*; **he would be a good ~ for president** il ferait un bon président; **you made the right/wrong ~** vous avez fait le bon/mauvais choix.
◇ *adj* -**1.** [fruit, meat] de choix, de première qualité. -**2.** [well-chosen - phrase, words] bien choisi; **in a few ~ words** en quelques mots bien choisis. -**3.** [coarse - language] grossier.
choir ['kwaɪəʳ] ◇ *n* -**1.** [group of singers] chœur *m*, chorale *f*; [in church] chœur *m*, maîtrise *f*; **we sing in the ~** [gen] nous faisons partie du chœur OR de la chorale; [in church] nous faisons partie du chœur, nous chantons dans la maîtrise. -**2.** ARCHIT chœur *m*. -**3.** [group of instruments] chœur *m*.
◇ *comp*: **~ practice** répétition *f* de la chorale.
choirboy ['kwaɪəbɔɪ] *n* jeune choriste *m*.
choirmaster ['kwaɪə,mɑ:stəʳ] *n* [gen] chef *m* de chœur; [in church] maître *m* de chapelle.
choir school *n* maîtrise *f*.
choirstall ['kwaɪəstɔ:l] *n* stalle *f* du chœur.
choke [tʃəʊk] ◇ *vi* étouffer, s'étouffer, s'étrangler; **to ~ on sthg** s'étouffer OR s'étrangler en avalant qqch de travers; **to ~ to death** mourir étouffé; **to ~ with laughter** s'étouffer OR s'étrangler de rire; **to ~ with rage** s'étouffer OR s'étrangler de rage.
◇ *vt* -**1.** [asphyxiate] étrangler, étouffer; **in a voice ~d with emotion** d'une voix étranglée par l'émotion. -**2.** [strangle] étrangler; **to ~ sb to death** étrangler qqn. -**3.** [clog] boucher, obs-

truer; ~d with traffic embouteillé, bouché; ~d with weeds étouffé par les mauvaises herbes. -4. TECH [engine, fire] étouffer.

◇ *n* -1. AUT starter *m*; TECH [in pipe] buse *f*. -2. [of artichoke] foin *m*.

◆ **choke back, choke down** *vt sep* [anger] refouler, étouffer; [tears] refouler, contenir; [complaint, cry] retenir.

◆ **choke off** *vt sep* [objection, opposition] étouffer (dans l'œuf); [discussion] empêcher; [person] envoyer promener OR paître.

◆ **choke up** *vt sep* -1. [road] boucher, embouteiller. -2. *inf* [emotionally] émouvoir, toucher profondément.

choked [tʃəʊkt] *adj* -1. [cry, voice] étranglé. -2. *inf Br* [person - moved] secoué; [- sad] peiné, attristé; [- annoyed] énervé, fâché.

choker ['tʃəʊkəʳ] *n* [necklace] collier *m* (court); [neckband] tour *m* de cou.

choking ['tʃəʊkɪŋ] *n* étouffement *m*, suffocation *f*.

cholera ['kɒlərə] *n* choléra *m*.

choleric ['kɒlərɪk] *adj* colérique, coléreux.

cholesterol [kə'lestərɒl] *n* cholestérol *m*.

chomp *inf* ['tʃɒmp] ◇ *vi* & *vt* mastiquer bruyamment.

◇ *n* mastication *f* bruyante.

Chomskyan ['tʃɒmskɪən] *adj* de Chomsky.

choose [tʃuːz] (*pt* chose [tʃəʊz], *pp* chosen ['tʃəʊzn]) ◇ *vt* -1. [select] choisir, prendre; **I don't know what to ~** je ne sais pas quoi choisir; **she chose a man as her assistant** elle a pris un homme pour assistant; **~ your words carefully** pesez bien vos mots; **there's little** OR **not much to ~ between the two parties** les deux partis se valent. -2. [elect] élire. -3. [decide] décider, juger bon; **they chose to ignore his rudeness** ils ont préféré ignorer sa grossièreté; **I didn't ~ to invite her** [invited unwillingly] je l'ai invitée contre mon gré.

◇ *vi* choisir; **do as you ~** faites comme bon vous semble OR comme vous l'entendez OR comme vous voulez; **you can come if you so ~** vous pouvez venir si cela vous dit OR si vous le voulez; **she'll finish it when she so ~s** elle le terminera quand bon lui semblera; **there's not a lot to ~ from** il n'y a pas beaucoup de choix.

choos(e)y *inf* ['tʃuːzɪ] (*compar* choosier, *superl* choosiest) *adj* difficile; **she's very ~ about what she eats** elle ne mange pas n'importe quoi, elle est très difficile sur la nourriture; **you decide, I'm not ~** décide, cela m'est égal; **he can't afford to be ~** il ne peut pas se permettre de faire le difficile.

chop [tʃɒp] (*pt* & *pp* chopped, *cont* chopping) ◇ *vt* -1. [cut - gen] couper; [- wood] couper; CULIN hacher. -2. [hit] donner un coup à, frapper. -3. *inf* [reduce - budget, funding] réduire, diminuer; [- project] mettre au rancart. -4. SPORT [ball] couper.

◇ *vi* [change direction] varier; **to ~ and change** changer constamment d'avis.

◇ *n* -1. [blow - with axe] coup *m* de hache; [- with hand] coup *m*; **to get** OR **to be given the ~** *inf Br* [employee] être viré; [project] être mis au rancart; **the welfare programmes are for the ~** *inf Br* les programmes d'assistance sociale vont être supprimés; **he's for the ~** il va y passer. -2. CULIN [of meat] côtelette *f*. -3. GOLF coup *m* piqué; TENNIS volée *f* coupée OR arrêtée.

◆ **chops** *npl* [jowls - of person] joue *f*; [- of animal] bajoues *fpl*; **to lick one's ~s** se pourlécher les babines.

◆ **chop at** *vt insep* -1. [try to cut - gen] tenter de couper; [- with axe] donner des coups de hache à, tailler (à la hache). -2. [try to hit] essayer de frapper.

◆ **chop down** *vt sep* abattre.

◆ **chop off** *vt sep* trancher, couper; **they chopped off the king's head** ils ont coupé la tête au roi.

◆ **chop up** *vt sep* couper en morceaux, hacher; CULIN hacher.

chop-chop *inf* ◇ *adv* rapidement, vite; **get to work ~!** au travail et que ça saute!

◇ *interj*: **~!** allez, et que ça saute!

chophouse ['tʃɒphaʊs, *pl* -haʊzɪz] *n* restaurant *m* spécialisé dans les grillades.

chopper ['tʃɒpəʳ] *n* -1. *Br* [axe] petite hache *f*; CULIN [cleaver] couperet *m*, hachoir *m*. -2. *inf* [helicopter] hélico *m*. -3. *inf* [motorcycle] chopper *m*; [bicycle] vélo *m* (*à haut guidon*).

chopping board ['tʃɒpɪŋ-] *n* planche *f* à découper.

choppy ['tʃɒpɪ] (*compar* choppier, *superl* choppiest) *adj* -1. [lake, sea] un peu agité; [waves] clapotant. -2. [wind] variable.

chopstick ['tʃɒpstɪk] *n* baguette *f* (*pour manger*).

chopsuey [,tʃɒp'suːɪ] *n* chop suey *m*.

choral ['kɔːrəl] ◇ *adj* choral.

◇ *n* = **chorale**.

chorale [kɒ'rɑːl] *n* -1. [hymn] chœur *m*, choral *m*. -2. *Am* [choir] chœur *m*, chorale *f*.

chord [kɔːd] *n* -1. ANAT & GEOM corde *f*. -2. MUS [group of notes] accord *m*; **to strike** OR **to touch a ~** toucher la corde sensible.

chore [tʃɔːʳ] *n* [task - routine] travail *m* de routine; [- unpleasant] corvée *f*; **household ~s** travaux *mpl* ménagers; **I have to do the ~s** *Am* il faut que je fasse le ménage.

choreograph ['kɒrɪəgrɑːf] *vt* [ballet, dance] chorégraphier, faire la chorégraphie de; *fig* [meeting, party] organiser.

choreographer [,kɒrɪ'ɒgrəfəʳ] *n* chorégraphe *mf*.

choreographic [,kɒrɪə'græfɪk] *adj* chorégraphique.

choreography [,kɒrɪ'ɒgrəfɪ] *n* chorégraphie *f*.

chorister ['kɒrɪstəʳ] *n* choriste *mf*.

chortle ['tʃɔːtl] ◇ *vi* glousser; **to ~ with delight at** OR **over sthg** glousser de plaisir à propos de qqch; **he ~d to himself** il riait discrètement dans son coin.

◇ *n* gloussement *m*, petit rire *m*.

chorus ['kɔːrəs] ◇ *n* -1. [choir] chœur *m*, chorale *f*. -2. [piece of music] chœur *m*, choral *m*. -3. [refrain] refrain *m*; **we all joined in (on) the ~** nous avons tous repris le refrain (en chœur). -4. THEAT [dancers, singers] troupe *f*; [speakers] chœur *m*; **he started his career in the ~** il a débuté dans la troupe; **I'm part of the ~** je fais partie de la troupe. -5. [of complaints, groans] concert *m*.

◇ *vt* [song] chanter en chœur; [poem] réciter en chœur; [approval, discontent] dire OR exprimer en chœur.

chorus girl *n* girl *f*.

chorus line *n* troupe *f*.

chose [tʃəʊz] *pt* → **choose**.

chosen ['tʃəʊzn] ◇ *pp* → **choose**.

◇ *adj* choisi; **she told only a ~ few** elle ne s'est confiée qu'à quelques privilégiés; **a few well ~ words** quelques termes (bien) choisis; **the ~ people** les élus *mpl*.

◇ *npl*: **the ~** les élus *mpl*.

chough [tʃʌf] *n* crave *m*.

chow [tʃaʊ] *n* -1. [dog] chow-chow *m*. -2. *inf* [food] bouffe *f*.

◆ **chow down** *inf vi insep* & *vt insep Am* bouffer.

chow chow = **chow 1**.

chowder ['tʃaʊdəʳ] *n potage épais qui contient du poisson ou des fruits de mer.*

chris(o)m ['krɪzm] *n* chrême *m*.

Christ [kraɪst] ◇ *pr n* le Christ, Jésus-Christ *m*; **the ~ child** l'enfant *m* Jésus.

◇ *interj*: **~!**[▽] Bon Dieu (de Bon Dieu)!

Christchurch ['kraɪs,tʃɜːtʃ] *pr n* Christchurch.

christen ['krɪsn] *vt* -1. [gen] appeler, nommer; [nickname] baptiser, surnommer; NAUT & RELIG baptiser; **she was ~ed Victoria but is known as Vicky** son nom de baptême est Victoria mais tout le monde l'appelle Vicky; **he was ~ed after his grandfather** on lui avait donné le nom de son grand-père; **we ~ed the car "the Crate"** nous avons baptisé la voiture «le Tacot». -2. *inf* [use for first time] étrenner.

Christendom ['krɪsndəm] *n* chrétienté *f*.

christening ['krɪsnɪŋ] *n* baptême *m*.

Christian ['krɪstʃən] ◇ *n* chrétien *m*, -enne *f*; **to become a ~** se convertir au christianisme.

◇ *adj literal* chrétien; *fig* [charitable] charitable, bon.

Christianity [,krɪstɪ'ænətɪ] *n* [religion] christianisme *m*.

Christianize, -ise ['krɪstjənaɪz] *vt* christianiser.

Christian name *n* nom *m* de baptême, prénom *m*; **his ~ is Frank** il s'appelle Frank.

Christian Science *n* la Science chrétienne.

Christian Scientist *n* scientiste chrétien *m*, scientiste chrétienne *f*.

Christlike ['kraɪstlaɪk] *adj* semblable OR qui ressemble au Christ.

Christmas ['krɪsməs] ◇ *n* Noël *m*; **where are you celebrating ~?** où fêtez-vous Noël?; **I'm staying with my parents over ~** je vais passer Noël chez mes parents; **at ~** à Noël; **for ~** pour Noël; **Merry ~!** joyeux Noël!

◇ *comp* [party, present] de Noël; **~ bonus** *prime de fin d'année versée par l'État aux retraités, ou par l'employeur à ses salariés en Grande-Bretagne*; **~ dinner** déjeuner de Noël (*comprenant de la dinde rôtie et le pudding de Noël*); **~ holiday** [day] Noël *m*; [vacation] vacances *fpl* de Noël; **everyone is getting ready for the ~ holidays** tout le monde prépare les fêtes.

Christmas box *n Br* étrennes *fpl* (*offertes à Noël*).

Christmas cake *n* gâteau *m* de Noël (*cake décoré au sucre glace*).

Christmas card *n* carte *f* de Noël.

Christmas carol *n* chant *m* de Noël, noël *m*; RELIG cantique *m* de Noël; **'A Christmas Carol'** *Dickens* 'le Chant de Noël'.

Christmas club *n caisse de contributions pour les cadeaux de Noël.*

Christmas Day *n* le jour de Noël.

Christmas Eve *n* la veille de Noël.

Christmas Island *pr n* l'île *f* Christmas; **on ~** à l'île Christmas.

Christmas pudding *n Br* pudding *m*, plum-pudding *m*.

Christmas rose *n* rose *f* de Noël.

Christmas stocking *n chaussette que les enfants suspendent à la cheminée pour que le père Noël y dépose les cadeaux.*

Christmassy ['krɪsməsɪ] *adj* qui rappelle la fête de Noël; **the town looks so ~** la ville a un tel air de fête.

Christmastide ['krɪsməstaɪd] *n lit* la période de Noël OR des fêtes (de fin d'année) (*du 24 décembre au 6 janvier*).

Christmastime ['krɪsməstaɪm] *n* la période de Noël OR des fêtes (de fin d'année).

Christmas tree *n* sapin *m* OR arbre *m* de Noël.

Christopher ['krɪstəfəʳ] *pr n*: **Saint ~** saint Christophe.

chromatic [krə'mætɪk] *adj* chromatique; **~ scale** MUS gamme *f* chromatique; **~ colour** PHYS couleur *f* chromatique; **~ printing** TYPO impression *f* polychrome.

chromaticism [krə'mætɪsɪzm] *n* chromatisme *m*.

chromatography [,krəʊmə'tɒgrəfɪ] *n* chromatographie *f*.

chrome [krəʊm] ◇ *n* chrome *m*.

◇ *adj* [fittings, taps] chromé.

chrome green *n* vert *m* de chrome.

chrome red *n* rouge *m* de chrome.

chrome steel *n* acier *m* chromé, chromé *m*.

chrome yellow *n* jaune *m* de chrome.

chromium ['krəʊmɪəm] *n* chrome *m*.

chromium-plated [-'pleɪtɪd] *adj* chromé.

chromium-plating [-'pleɪtɪŋ] *n* chromage *m*.

chromolithograph [,krəʊməʊ'lɪθəgrɑːf] *n* chromolithographie *f*.

chromolithography [,krəʊməʊlɪ'θɒgrəfɪ] *n* chromolithographie *f*.

chromosome ['krəʊməsəʊm] *n* chromosome *m*.

chromosome number *n* nombre *m* chromosomique.

chronic ['krɒnɪk] *adj* -**1.** [long-lasting - illness, unemployment] chronique. -**2.** [habitual - smoker, gambler] invétéré. -**3.** [serious - problem, situation] difficile, grave. -**4.** *inf Br* [very bad] atroce, affreux.

chronically ['krɒnɪklɪ] *adv* -**1.** [habitually] chroniquement. -**2.** [severely] gravement, sérieusement.

chronicle ['krɒnɪkl] ◇ *n* chronique *f*; **their holiday was a ~ of misadventures** leurs vacances furent une succession de mésaventures.
◇ *vt* faire la chronique de, raconter.
◆ **Chronicles** *n*: the (Book of) Chronicles le livre des Chroniques.

chronicler ['krɒnɪkləʳ] *n* chroniqueur *m*, -euse *f*.

chronograph ['krɒnəgrɑːf] *n* chronographe *m*.

chronological [,krɒnə'lɒdʒɪkl] *adj* chronologique; **in ~ order** par ordre OR dans un ordre chronologique.

chronologically [,krɒnə'lɒdʒɪklɪ] *adv* chronologiquement, par ordre chronologique.

chronology [krə'nɒlədʒɪ] *n* chronologie *f*.

chronometer [krə'nɒmɪtəʳ] *n* chronomètre *m*.

chronometry [krə'nɒmɪtrɪ] *n* chronométrie *f*.

chrysalid ['krɪsəlɪd] (*pl* **chrysalides** [krɪ'sælɪdiːz]) *n* chrysalide *f*.

chrysalis ['krɪsəlɪs] (*pl* **chrysalises**) *n* chrysalide *f*.

chrysanthemum [krɪ'sænθəməm] *n* chrysanthème *m*.

chub [tʃʌb] (*pl inv* OR **chubs**) *n* chevesne *m*, chevaine *m*, chevenne *m*.

Chubb lock® [tʃʌb-] *n type de serrure réputé incrochetable*.

chubby ['tʃʌbɪ] (*compar* **chubbier**, *superl* **chubbiest**) *adj* [fingers, person] potelé; [face] joufflu; **~-cheeked** joufflu.

chuck [tʃʌk] ◇ *vt* -**1.** *inf* [toss] jeter, lancer; **she ~ed him the ball** elle lui a lancé OR envoyé le ballon; **they ~ed him off the bus** ils l'ont vidé du bus. -**2.** *inf* [give up - activity, job] laisser tomber, lâcher. -**3.** *inf* [jilt - boyfriend, girlfriend] plaquer. -**4.** [tap] tapoter; **she ~ed the child under the chin** elle a tapoté le menton l'enfant.
◇ *n Br* -**1.** [tap] petite tape *f*; **he gave her a ~ under the chin** il lui a tapoté le menton. -**2.** TECH mandrin *m*. -**3.** = **chuck steak**. -**4.** *phr*: **to give sb the ~** *inf* [employee] virer OR vider qqn; [boyfriend, girlfriend] plaquer qqn.
◆ **chuck away** *inf vt sep* [old clothing, papers] balancer; [chance, opportunity] laisser passer; [money] jeter par les fenêtres.
◆ **chuck in** *inf vt sep Br* [give up - activity, job] lâcher; [- attempt] renoncer à.
◆ **chuck out** *inf vt sep* [old clothing, papers] balancer; [person] vider, sortir; **he ~ed the troublemakers out** il a flanqué les provocateurs à la porte.
◆ **chuck up**▽ *vi insep* [vomit] vomir.

chucker-out *inf* [,tʃʌkər-] *n Br* videur *m*.

chuckle ['tʃʌkl] ◇ *vi* glousser, rire; **to ~ with delight** rire avec jubilation; **he ~d to himself** il riait tout seul.
◇ *n* gloussement *m*, petit rire *m*; **they had a good ~ over her mishap** sa mésaventure les a bien fait rire.

chucklehead *inf* ['tʃʌklhed] *n Br* balourd *m*, -e *f*.

chuck steak *n* morceau *m* de bœuf dans le paleron.

chuck wagon *n* cantine *f* ambulante *(pour les cowboys)*.

chuff [tʃʌf] *vi* souffler, haleter; **the train ~ed up the hill** le train a monté la pente en haletant.

chuffed *inf* [tʃʌft] *adj Br* vachement OR super content, ravi; **to be ~ about** OR **at sthg** être ravi de qqch.

chug [tʃʌg] ◇ *vi* -**1.** [make noise - engine, car, train] s'essouffler, haleter. -**2.** [move] avancer en soufflant OR en haletant.
◇ *n* [of engine, car, train] halètement *m*.

chukka, chukker ['tʃʌkə] *n* [in polo] période *f* de jeu *(de sept minutes et demie)*.

chukka boot, chukker boot *n* bottine *f (portée par les joueurs de polo)*.

chum *inf* [tʃʌm] *n* copain *m*, copine *f*; **the game's up, ~** c'est fichu, mon vieux.
◆ **chum up** *inf vi insep*: **to ~ up with sb** devenir copain *m*/copine *f* avec qqn.

chummy *inf* ['tʃʌmɪ] (*compar* **chummier**, *superl* **chummiest**) *adj* amical; **to be ~ with sb** être copain/copine avec qqn.

chump *inf* [tʃʌmp] *n dated* -**1.** [dolt - boy] ballot *m*; [- girl] gourde *f*. -**2.** *Br* [head] boule *f*; **you're off your ~!** tu as perdu la boule!

chump chop *n Br* côte *f (d'agneau)*.

chunder▽ ['tʃʌndəʳ] ◇ *vi* dégueuler.
◇ *n* vomi *m*.

chunk [tʃʌŋk] *n* [of meat, wood] gros morceau *m*; [of budget, time] grande partie *f*.

chunky ['tʃʌŋkɪ] (*compar* **chunkier**, *superl* **chunkiest**) *adj* -**1.** [person - stocky] trapu; [- chubby] potelé, enrobé; [food, stew] avec des morceaux. -**2.** *Br* [clothing, sweater] de grosse laine.

Chunnel *inf* ['tʃʌnl] *n Br*: **the ~** *terme familier désignant le tunnel sous la Manche*.

church [tʃɜːtʃ] ◇ *n* -**1.** [building - gen] église *f*; [- Protestant] église *f*, temple *m*. -**2.** [religious services - Protestant] office *m*; [- Catholic] messe *f*; **to be at** OR **in ~** [Protestants] être à l'office OR au temple; [Catholics] être à la messe; **to go to ~** [Protestants] aller au temple OR à l'office; [Catholics] aller à la messe OR à l'église; **do you go to ~?** êtes-vous pratiquant? -**3.** *(U)* [clergy]: **the ~** les ordres *mpl*; **to go into the ~** entrer dans les ordres.
◇ *vt Br* [gen] faire assister à la messe; [woman after childbirth] faire assister à la messe de relevailles.
◆ **Church** *n* [institution]: **the Church** l'Église *f*; **Church and State** l'Église et l'État ❑ **the Church Commissioners** *commission nommée par le gouvernement pour gérer les finances de l'Église d'Angleterre*; **Church of Christ, Scientist** Église de la Science chrétienne; **Church of England** Église anglicane; **Church of France/of Scotland** Église de France/d'Écosse; **Church of Rome** Église catholique.

THE CHURCH OF ENGLAND:
L'Église d'Angleterre (de confession anglicane) est l'Église officielle de la Grande-Bretagne; son chef laïc est le souverain, son chef spirituel l'archevêque de Cantorbéry.

---

churchgoer ['tʃɜːtʃ,gəʊəʳ] *n* pratiquant *m*, -e *f*.

church hall *n* salle *f* paroissiale.

churching ['tʃɜːtʃɪŋ] *n (U) Br* relevailles *fpl*.

churchman ['tʃɜːtʃmən] (*pl* **churchmen** [-mən]) *n* [clergyman] ecclésiastique *m*; [churchgoer] pratiquant *m*.

church school *n* ≃ catéchisme *m*.

churchwarden [,tʃɜːtʃ'wɔːdn] *n* bedeau *m*, marguillier *m*.

churchwoman ['tʃɜːtʃ,wʊmən] (*pl* **churchwomen** [-,wɪmɪn]) *n* pratiquante *f*.

churchy ['tʃɜːtʃɪ] (*compar* **churchier**, *superl* **churchiest**) *adj* -**1.** [atmosphere, song] qui rappelle l'église. -**2.** *pej* [person] bigot; **she's very ~** c'est une grenouille de bénitier *pej*.

churchyard ['tʃɜːtʃjɑːd] *n* [grounds] terrain *m* autour de l'église; [graveyard] cimetière *m (autour d'une église)*.

churl [tʃɜːl] *n dated* [ill-bred person] rustre *m*, malotru *m*; [surly person] ronchon *m*.

churlish ['tʃɜːlɪʃ] *adj* [rude] fruste, grossier; [bad-tempered - person] qui a mauvais caractère, revêche; [- attitude, behaviour] revêche, désagréable; **it would be ~ not to acknowledge the invitation** ce serait grossier OR impoli de ne pas répondre à l'invitation.

churlishly ['tʃɜːlɪʃlɪ] *adv* [rudely] grossièrement; [in bad-tempered manner] hargneusement, de façon revêche.

churlishness ['tʃɜːlɪʃnɪs] *n* [rudeness] grossièreté *f*; [bad temper - habitual] mauvais caractère *m*; [- temporary] mauvaise humeur *f*.

churn [tʃɜːn] ◇ *vt* -**1.** [cream] baratter. -**2.** [mud] remuer; [water] faire bouillonner.
◇ *vi* [sea, water] bouillonner; **the thought made my stomach ~** j'ai eu l'estomac tout retourné à cette idée.
◇ *n* -**1.** [for butter] baratte *f*. -**2.** *Br* [milk can] bidon *m*.
◆ **churn out** *inf vt sep* -**1.** [produce rapidly - gen] produire rapidement; [- novels, reports] pondre à la chaîne OR en série. -**2.** [produce mechanically] débiter.
◆ **churn up** *vt sep* [mud] remuer; [sea, water] faire bouillonner.

churning ['tʃɜːnɪŋ] *n* [act] barattage *m*.

chute [ʃuːt] *n* -**1.** [for parcels] glissière *f*. -**2.** [for sledding, in swimming pool] toboggan *m*. -**3.** [in river] rapide *m*. -**4.** *inf* [parachute] parachute *m*.

chutney ['tʃʌtnɪ] *n* chutney *m (condiment à base de fruits)*.

chutzpah *inf* ['hʊtspə] *n esp Am* culot *m*.

CI *written abbr of* Channel Islands.

CIA (*abbr of* Central Intelligence Agency) *pr n* CIA *f*.

ciborium [sɪ'bɔːrɪəm] *n* ciborium *m*.

cicada [sɪ'kɑːdə] (*pl* **cicadas** OR **cicadae** [-diː]) *n* cigale *f*.

cicatrice ['sɪkətrɪs], **cicatrix** ['sɪkətrɪks] (*pl* **cicatrices** [,sɪkə'traɪsiːz]) *n* cicatrice *f*.

Cicero ['sɪsə,rəʊ] *pr n* Cicéron.

cicerone [,tʃɪtʃə'rəʊnɪ] (*pl* **cicerones** OR **ciceroni** [-niː]) *n* cicérone *m lit*, guide *m*.

Ciceronian [,sɪsə'rəʊnɪən] *adj* cicéronien.

Cid [sɪd] *pr n*: **El ~** le Cid.

CID (*abbr of* Criminal Investigation Department) *pr n police judiciaire britannique*, ≃ PJ.

cider ['saɪdəʳ] ◇ *n* cidre *m*.
◇ *comp*: **~ press** pressoir *m* à cidre; **~ vinegar** vinaigre *m* de cidre.

cider apple *n* pomme *f* à cidre.

CIF (*abbr of* cost, insurance and freight) *adv* CAF, caf.

cig *inf* [sɪg] *n* clope *m or f*, sèche *f*.

cigar [sɪ'gɑːʳ] ◇ *n* cigare *m*.
◇ *comp* [box, case, tobacco] à cigares; [ash, smoke] de cigare; **~ holder** fume-cigare *m inv*; **~ lighter** allume-cigare *m inv*; **~-shaped** en forme de cigare.

cigaret [,sɪgə'ret] *Am* = **cigarette**.

cigarette [,sɪgə'ret] ◇ *n* cigarette *f*.
◇ *comp* [ash, smoke] de cigarette; [packet, smoke] de cigarettes; [paper, tobacco] à cigarettes; **~ case** étui *m* à cigarettes, porte-cigarettes *m inv*.

cigarette card *n image offerte autrefois avec chaque paquet de cigarettes*.

cigarette end *n* mégot *m*.

cigarette holder *n* fume-cigarette *m inv*.

cigarette lighter *n* briquet *m*.

cigarillo [,sɪgə'rɪləʊ] (*pl* **cigarillos**) *n* petit cigare *m*, cigarillo *m*.

ciggie *inf* ['sɪgɪ] *n* clope *m or f*, sèche *f*.

cilium ['sɪlɪəm] (*pl* **cilia** [-lɪə]) *n* ANAT & BIOL cil *m*.

C-in-C *written abbr of* Commander-in-Chief.

cinch [sɪntʃ] ◇ *n* -**1.** *inf* **it's a ~** [certainty] c'est du tout cuit; [easy to do] c'est du gâteau. -**2.** *Am* [girth] sous-ventrière *f*, sangle *f (de selle)*.
◇ *vt Am* [horse] sangler; [saddle] attacher par une sangle.

Cincinnati [,sɪnsɪ'nætɪ] *pr n* Cincinnati.

cinder ['sɪndəʳ] *n* cendre *f*; **~s** [in fireplace] cendres; [from furnace, volcano] scories *fpl*; **burnt to a ~** réduit en cendres.

cinder block *n Am* parpaing *m*.

Cinderella [,sɪndə'relə] ◇ *pr n* Cendrillon.
◇ *n fig* parent *m* pauvre.

cinder track *n* (piste *f*) cendrée *f*.

cineast(e) ['sɪnɪæst] *n* cinéphile *mf*.

cinecamera ['sɪnɪˌkæmərə] *n Br* caméra *f*.

cine-film ['sɪnɪ-] *n Br* film *m*.

cinema ['sɪnəmə] *n* [building] *Br* cinéma *m*; to go to the ~ aller au cinéma || [industry] (industrie *f* du) cinéma *m*.

cinemagoer ['sɪnɪməˌgəʊəʳ] *n* personne *f* qui fréquente les cinémas.

Cinemascope® ['sɪnəməskəʊp] *n* Cinémascope® *m*.

cinematic [ˌsɪnɪ'mætɪk] *adj* cinématique.

cinematograph [ˌsɪnə'mætəgrɑːf] *n Br* cinématographe *m*.

cinematography [ˌsɪnəmə'tɒgrəfɪ] *n Br* cinématographie *f*.

cine-projector ['sɪnɪ-] *n Br* projecteur *m* de cinéma.

Cinerama® [ˌsɪnə'rɑːmə] *n* Cinérama® *m*.

cineraria [ˌsɪnə'reərɪə] ◇ *pl* → **cinerarium**.
◇ *n* BOT cinéraire *f*.

cinerarium [ˌsɪnə'reərɪəm] (*pl* cineraria [-rɪə]) *n* cinéraire *m*.

cinnabar ['sɪnəbɑːʳ] *n* cinabre *m*.

cinnamon ['sɪnəmən] ◇ *n* -**1.** [spice] cannelle *f*. -**2.** [colour] cannelle *f*.
◇ *adj* cannelle *(inv)*.
◇ *comp* [flavour] à la cannelle.

Cinque Ports ['sɪŋkpɔːts] *pl pr n* Cinq ports *mpl (ancienne confédération réunissant les cinq ports de la côte sud-est de l'Angleterre)*.

cipher ['saɪfəʳ] ◇ *n* -**1.** [code] chiffre *m*, code *m* secret; written in ~ crypté, codé. -**2.** [monogram] chiffre *m*, monogramme *m*. -**3.** [Arabic numeral] chiffre *m*. -**4.** *lit* [zero] zéro *m*; they're mere ~s *fig* ce sont des moins que rien.
◇ *vt* -**1.** [encode] crypter, chiffrer, coder. -**2.** MATH chiffrer.

circa ['sɜːkə] *prep* circa, vers.

circadian [sɜː'keɪdɪən] *adj* circadien.

Circe ['sɜːsɪ] *pr n* Circé.

circle ['sɜːkl] ◇ *n* -**1.** [gen & GEOM] cercle *m*; we stood in a ~ around him nous formions (un) cercle OR nous nous tenions en cercle autour de lui; she had dark ~s under her eyes elle avait des cernes sous les yeux OR les yeux cernés; he had us going OR running round in ~s trying to find the information il nous a fait tourner en rond à chercher les renseignements; to come full ~ revenir au point de départ, boucler la boucle. -**2.** [group of people] cercle *m*, groupe *m*; she has a wide ~ of friends elle a beaucoup d'amis OR un grand cercle d'amis; his ~ of advisors son groupe de conseillers; in artistic/political ~s dans les milieux artistiques/politiques. -**3.** THEAT balcon *m*.
◇ *vt* -**1.** [draw circle round] entourer (d'un cercle), encercler. -**2.** [move round] tourner autour de; the moon ~s the earth la lune est en orbite autour OR tourne autour de la terre. -**3.** [surround] encercler, entourer.
◇ *vi* -**1.** [bird, plane] faire OR décrire des cercles; the plane ~d overhead l'avion a décrit des cercles dans le ciel. -**2.** [planet] tourner.

circlet ['sɜːklɪt] *n* [on head - crown] couronne *f*; [- for hair] bandeau *m*; [on arm] brassard *m*; [on finger] anneau *m*.

circuit ['sɜːkɪt] *n* -**1.** [series of events, places] circuit *m*; the tennis ~ le circuit des matches de tennis. -**2.** [periodical journey] tournée *f*; JUR tournée *f (d'un juge d'assises)*; to be on the western ~ faire la tournée de l'ouest. -**3.** [journey around] circuit *m*, tour *m*; we made a ~ of the grounds nous avons fait le tour des terrains; the Earth's ~ around the Sun l'orbite de la terre autour du soleil. -**4.** ELEC circuit *m*. -**5.** SPORT [track] circuit *m*, parcours *m*.

circuit breaker *n* ELEC disjoncteur *m*.

circuit judge *n juge itinérant*.

circuitous [sə'kjuːɪtəs] *adj* [route] qui fait un détour, détourné; [journey] compliqué; *fig* [reasoning, thinking] contourné, compliqué.

circuitry ['sɜːkɪtrɪ] *n* système *m* de circuits.

circuit training *n* SPORT préparation *f* OR entraînement *m (en accomplissant plusieurs sortes d'exercices)*.

circular ['sɜːkjʊləʳ] ◇ *adj* -**1.** [movement, shape, ticket] circulaire; ~ journey voyage *m* circulaire, circuit *m* ❑ ~ letter OR memo circulaire *f*; ~ saw scie *f* circulaire. -**2.** [reasoning] faux, mal fondé; ~ argument pétition *f* de principe.
◇ *n* -**1.** [letter, memo] circulaire *f*. -**2.** [advertisement] prospectus *m*.

circularity [ˌsɜːkjʊ'lærətɪ] *n* -**1.** [of movement, shape] forme *f* circulaire. -**2.** [of argument, reasoning] circularité *f*.

circularize, -ise ['sɜːkjʊləraɪz] *vt* [send letters to] envoyer des circulaires à; [send advertising to] envoyer des prospectus à.

circulate ['sɜːkjʊleɪt] ◇ *vt* [book, bottle] faire circuler; [document - from person to person] faire circuler; [- in mass mailing] diffuser; [news, rumour] propager.
◇ *vi* circuler.

circulating decimal ['sɜːkjʊleɪtɪŋ-] *n* fraction *f* périodique.

circulating library *n* bibliothèque *f* de prêt.

circulation [ˌsɜːkjʊ'leɪʃn] *n* -**1.** [gen & FIN] circulation *f*; to be in ~ [book, money] être en circulation; [person] être dans le circuit; she's out of ~ at the moment elle a disparu de la circulation pour l'instant. -**2.** [of magazine, newspaper] diffusion *f*; the Times has a ~ of 200,000 le Times tire à 200 000 exemplaires. -**3.** ANAT & BOT circulation *f*; to have good/poor ~ avoir une bonne/une mauvaise circulation. -**4.** [of traffic] circulation *f*.

circulatory [ˌsɜːkjʊ'leɪtərɪ] *adj* circulatoire.

circumcise ['sɜːkəmsaɪz] *vt* circoncire.

circumcision [ˌsɜːkəm'sɪʒn] *n* [act] circoncision *f*; [religious rite] (fête *f* de la) circoncision *f*.

circumference [sə'kʌmfərəns] *n* circonférence *f*.

circumflex ['sɜːkəmfleks] ◇ *n* accent *m* circonflexe.
◇ *adj* circonflexe.

circumlocution [ˌsɜːkəmlə'kjuːʃn] *n* circonlocution *f*.

circumlocutory [ˌsɜːkəm'lɒkjʊtərɪ] *adj* qui procède par circonlocutions.

circumlunar [ˌsɜːkəm'luːnəʳ] *adj* circumlunaire.

circumnavigate [ˌsɜːkəm'nævɪgeɪt] *vt* [iceberg, island] contourner *(en bateau)*; to ~ the world faire le tour du monde en bateau, naviguer autour du globe.

circumnavigation ['sɜːkəmˌnævɪ'geɪʃn] *n* circumnavigation *f*.

circumscribe ['sɜːkəmskraɪb] *vt* -**1.** [restrict] circonscrire, limiter. -**2.** GEOM circonscrire.

circumscription [ˌsɜːkəm'skrɪpʃn] *n* circonscription *f*.

circumsolar [ˌsɜːkəm'səʊləʳ] *adj* autour du soleil.

circumspect ['sɜːkəmspekt] *adj* circonspect.

circumspection [ˌsɜːkəm'spekʃn] *n* circonspection *f*.

circumspectly ['sɜːkəmspektlɪ] *adv* avec circonspection.

circumstance ['sɜːkəmstəns] *n* -**1.** *(U)*: force of ~ contrainte *f* OR force *f* des circonstances; I am a victim of ~ je suis victime des circonstances. -**2.** *fml (U)* [ceremony]: pomp and ~ grand apparat *m*, pompe *f fml*.
◆ **circumstances** *npl* -**1.** [conditions] circonstance *f*, situation *f*; in OR under these ~s dans les circonstances actuelles, vu la situation actuelle OR l'état actuel des choses; in OR under exceptional ~s dans des circonstances exceptionnelles; in OR under normal ~s en temps normal; under no ~s en aucun cas; under similar ~s en pareil cas. -**2.** [facts] circonstance *f*, détail *m*; the ~s of her death les circonstances de sa mort; you have to take into account the ~s il faut tenir compte des circonstances.

circumstantial [ˌsɜːkəm'stænʃl] *adj* -**1.** [incidental] accidentel, fortuit; JUR [evidence] indirect. -**2.** *fml* [description, report] circonstancié, détaillé.

circumstantiate [ˌsɜːkəm'stænʃɪeɪt] *vt* [event, report] donner des détails circonstanciés sur; JUR [evidence] confirmer en donnant des détails sur.

circumvent [ˌsɜːkəm'vent] *vt* -**1.** [law, rule] tourner, contourner. -**2.** [outwit - person] circonvenir *fml*, manipuler; [- plan] faire échouer. -**3.** [enemy] encercler, entourer.

circumvention [ˌsɜːkəm'venʃn] *n* [of law, rule] fait *m* de tourner OR contourner.

circus ['sɜːkəs] ◇ *n* -**1.** [gen & ANTIQ] cirque *m*. -**2.** *Br* [roundabout] rond-point *m*.
◇ *comp* [clown, company, tent] de cirque.

cirque [sɜːk] *n* cirque *m* GEOL.

cirrhosis [sɪ'rəʊsɪs] *n* cirrhose *f*.

cirrocumulus [ˌsɪrəʊ'kjuːmjʊləs] (*pl* cirrocumuli [-laɪ]) *n* cirrocumulus *m*.

cirrostratus [ˌsɪrəʊ'strɑːtəs] (*pl* cirrostrati [-taɪ]) *n* cirrostratus *m*.

cirrus ['sɪrəs] (*pl* cirri [-raɪ]) *n* -**1.** [cloud] cirrus *m*. -**2.** BOT vrille *f*.

CIS (*abbr of* Commonwealth of Independent States) *pr n* CEI *f*; in the ~ dans la CEI.

Cisalpine [sɪs'ælpaɪn] *adj* cisalpin; ~ Gaul Gaule *f* cisalpine.

cissy ['sɪsɪ] = **sissy**.

Cistercian [sɪ'stɜːʃn] ◇ *n* cistercien *m*, -enne *f*.
◇ *adj* cistercien; ~ monk cistercien *m*; ~ nun cistercienne *f*; the ~ Order l'ordre *m* de Cîteaux.

cistern ['sɪstən] *n* [tank] citerne *f*; [for toilet] réservoir *m* de chasse d'eau.

citadel ['sɪtədəl] *n literal* & *fig* citadelle *f*.

citation [saɪ'teɪʃn] *n* citation *f*.

cite [saɪt] *vt* -**1.** [quote] citer; he ~d it as an example il l'a cité en exemple. -**2.** [commend] citer; she was ~d for bravery elle a été citée pour sa bravoure. -**3.** JUR citer; they were ~d to appear as witnesses ils étaient cités comme témoins.

citizen ['sɪtɪzn] *n* -**1.** [of nation, state] citoyen *m*, -enne *f*; ADMIN [national] ressortissant *m*, -e *f*; to become a French ~ prendre la nationalité française. -**2.** [of town] habitant *m*, -e *f*; the ~s of Rome les habitants de Rome, les Romains. -**3.** [civilian] civil *m*, -e *f (opposé à militaire)* ❑ ~'s arrest *arrestation par un citoyen d'une personne soupçonnée d'avoir commis un délit*; 'Citizen Kane' *Welles* 'Citizen Kane'.

citizenry ['sɪtɪznrɪ] *n* [of nation] (ensemble *m* des) citoyens *mpl*; [of town] (ensemble *m* des) habitants *mpl*.

Citizens' Advice Bureau *pr n en Grande-Bretagne, bureau où les citoyens peuvent obtenir des conseils d'ordre juridique, social etc*.

Citizen's Band *n fréquence (de radio) réservée au public*; ~ radio CB *f*; ~ user cibiste *mf*.

Citizen's Charter *n programme lancé par le gouvernement britannique en 1991 et qui vise à améliorer la qualité des services publics*.

citizenship ['sɪtɪznʃɪp] *n* citoyenneté *f*, nationalité *f*; to apply for French ~ demander la citoyenneté OR nationalité française; ~ papers déclaration *f* de naturalisation.

citrate ['sɪtreɪt] *n* citrate *m*.

citric ['sɪtrɪk] *adj* citrique; ~ acid acide *m* citrique.

citron ['sɪtrən] *n* [fruit] cédrat *m*; [tree] cédratier *m*.

citronella [ˌsɪtrə'nelə] *n* citronnelle *f*.

citrus ['sɪtrəs] *adj*: ~ fruit OR fruits agrumes *mpl*.

city ['sɪtɪ] (*pl* cities) ◇ *n* [town] (grande) ville *f*, cité *f*; life in the ~ la vie en ville, la vie citadine; the whole ~ turned out toute la ville était présente, tous les habitants de la ville étaient présents.
◇ *comp* -**1.** [lights, limits, streets] de la ville; [officers, police, services] municipal; ~ life vie *f*

en ville, vie citadine ❑ ~ fathers édiles *mpl* locaux; 'City Lights' *Chaplin* 'les Lumières de la ville'. -**2.** *Br* PRESS [news, page, press] financier.
◆ **City** *pr n* [of London] *centre d'affaires de Londres*; the City la City (de Londres); he's something in the City il travaille à la City (de Londres).

THE CITY:
La City, quartier financier de la capitale, est une circonscription administrative autonome de Londres ayant sa propre police.

City and Guilds *n diplôme britannique d'enseignement technique*.
city centre *n* centre *m* de la ville, centre-ville *m*.
city desk *n* PRESS *Br* service *m* financier; *Am* service *m* des nouvelles locales.
city-dweller *n* citadin *m*, -e *f*.
city editor *n* PRESS *Br* rédacteur *m* en chef pour les nouvelles financières; *Am* rédacteur *m* en chef pour les nouvelles locales.
city hall *n* -**1.** [building] mairie *f*, hôtel *m* de ville. -**2.** *Am* [municipal government] administration *f* (municipale); you can't fight ~ on ne peut rien contre l'administration.
city manager *n Am* administrateur *m* (*payé par la municipalité pour gérer ses affaires*).
city planner *n* urbaniste *mf*.
city planning *n* urbanisme *m*.
city slicker *inf n hum* OR *pej citadin sophistiqué*.
city-state *n* cité *f* ANTIQ.
city technology college → **CTC**.
civet ['sɪvɪt] *n* [mammal, secretion] civette *f*.
civic ['sɪvɪk] *adj* [authority, building] municipal; [duty, right] civique; ~ event événement *m* officiel local; ~ university *université de ville, en Grande-Bretagne*.
civic centre *n centre administratif d'une ville, parfois complété par des équipements de loisirs*, ≃ cité administrative.
civics ['sɪvɪks] *n* (U) instruction *f* civique.
Civic Trust *pr n groupement de bénévoles animant des actions de mise en valeur du patrimoine en Grande-Bretagne*.
civies ['sɪvɪz] = **civvies**.
civil ['sɪvl] *adj* -**1.** [of community] civil; ~ disturbance émeute *f*; ~ strife conflit *m* interne OR intestin *lit*; ~ wedding OR marriage mariage *m* civil; we had a ~ wedding nous nous sommes mariés à la mairie. -**2.** [non-military] civil. -**3.** [polite] poli, courtois, civil *fml*; she was very ~ to me elle s'est montrée très aimable avec moi; keep a ~ tongue in your head! restez poli!
civil death *n* JUR mort *f* civile.
civil defence *n* protection *f* civile.
civil disobedience *n* résistance *f* passive (à la loi).
civil engineer *n* ingénieur *m* des travaux publics.
civil engineering *n* génie *m* civil.
civilian [sɪ'vɪljən] ◇ *adj* civil (*opposé à militaire*); in ~ life dans le civil.
◇ *n* civil *m*, -e *f* (*opposé à militaire*).
civility [sɪ'vɪlətɪ] (*pl* **civilities**) *n* -**1.** [quality] courtoisie *f*, civilité *f*. -**2.** [act] civilité *f*, politesse *f*.
civilization [ˌsɪvɪlaɪ'zeɪʃn] *n* civilisation *f*.
civilize, -ise ['sɪvɪlaɪz] *vt* civiliser.
civilized ['sɪvɪlaɪzd] *adj* [person, society] civilisé.
civil law *n* droit *m* civil.
civil liberty *n* liberté *f* civique.
Civil List *n* liste *f* civile (*allouée à la famille royale britannique*).
civilly ['sɪvəlɪ] *adv* poliment, courtoisement.
civil rights *npl* droits *mpl* civils OR civiques; the ~ movement la lutte pour les droits civils OR civiques.
civil servant *n* fonctionnaire *mf*.
civil service *n* fonction *f* publique, administration *f*.
civil war *n* guerre *f* civile; the American Civil War la guerre de Sécession.

THE AMERICAN CIVIL WAR:
Déclenchée par l'élection d'Abraham Lincoln, attisée par les différences sociales et économiques, la guerre civile opposa, de 1861 à 1865, le sud esclavagiste (les «Confédérés») au nord abolitionniste (les «Fédéraux»). Le conflit se termina par la victoire du camp nordiste, supérieur en hommes et en moyens.

civvy *inf* ['sɪvɪ] (*pl* **civvies**) *Br* ◇ *n* [civilian] civil *m*, -e *f* (*opposé à militaire*).
◇ *adj* civil.
◆ **civvies** *npl* [dress] vêtements *mpl* civils; in civvies (habillé) en civil.
civvy street *inf n Br* vie *f* civile; in ~ dans le civil, dans la vie civile.
cl (*written abbr of* **centilitre**) cl.
clack [klæk] ◇ *vi* [make noise] claquer; [jabber] jacasser, papoter; their friendship set tongues ~ing leur amitié a fait jaser.
◇ *vt* faire claquer.
◇ *n* -**1.** [sound] claquement *m*. -**2.** TECH [valve] clapet *m*.
clad [klæd] ◇ *pp* → **clothe**.
◇ *adj lit* habillé, vêtu; ~ in rags habillé OR vêtu de haillons.
◇ *vt* TECH revêtir.
cladding ['klædɪŋ] *n* TECH revêtement *m*, parement *m*.
claim [kleɪm] ◇ *vt* -**1.** [assert, maintain] prétendre, déclarer; it is ~ed that... on dit OR prétend que...; to ~ to be sthg se faire passer pour qqch, prétendre être qqch. -**2.** [assert one's right to] revendiquer, réclamer; [responsibility, right] revendiquer; he ~s all the credit il s'attribue tout le mérite; to ~ damages/one's due réclamer des dommages et intérêts/son dû; no one has yet ~ed responsibility for the hijacking le détournement n'a pas encore été revendiqué; workers are ~ing the right to strike les ouvriers revendiquent le droit de (faire) grève. -**3.** [apply for - money] demander; [- expenses] demander le remboursement de; to ~ financial assistance from the government demander une aide financière à l'administration. -**4.** [call for - attention] réclamer, demander; [- respect, sympathy] solliciter. -**5.** [take]: the storm ~ed five lives OR five victims l'orage a fait cinq victimes.
◇ *vi*: to ~ for OR on sthg [insurance] demander le paiement de qqch; [travel expenses] demander le remboursement de qqch.
◇ *n* -**1.** [assertion] affirmation *f*, prétention *f*; I make no ~s to understand why je ne prétends pas comprendre pourquoi. -**2.** [right] droit *m*, titre *m*; [by trade unions] demande *f* d'augmentation, revendication *f* salariale; ~ to property droit à la propriété; his only ~ to fame is that he once appeared on TV c'est à une apparition à la télévision qu'il doit d'être célèbre. -**3.** [demand] demande *f*; he has no ~s on me je ne lui suis redevable de rien; he made too many ~s on their generosity il a abusé de leur générosité; she has many ~s on her time elle est très prise; to have many ~s on one's purse avoir beaucoup de frais; to lay ~ to sthg prétendre à qqch, revendiquer son droit à qqch; we put in a ~ for better working conditions nous avons demandé de meilleures conditions de travail; pay ~ demande *f* d'augmentation (de salaire). -**4.** [in insurance] demande *f* d'indemnité, déclaration *f* de sinistre; to put in a ~ for sthg demander une indemnité pour qqch, faire une déclaration de sinistre pour qqch; the company pays 65% of all ~s la société satisfait 65 % de toutes les demandes de dédommagement. -**5.** [piece of land] concession *f*.
claimant ['kleɪmənt] *n* -**1.** ADMIN demandeur *m*, demanderesse *f*; JUR demandeur *m*, demanderesse *f*, requérant *m*, -e *f*. -**2.** [to throne] prétendant *m*, -e *f*.
clairvoyance [kleə'vɔɪəns] *n* voyance *f*, don *m* de seconde vue.
clairvoyant [kleə'vɔɪənt] ◇ *n* voyant *m*, -e *f*, extralucide *mf*.
◇ *adj* doué de seconde vue.
clam [klæm] ◇ *n* palourde *f*, clam *m*; to shut up like a ~ *inf* refuser de parler.
◇ *vi Am*: to go clamming aller ramasser des clams.
◆ **clam up** *inf vi insep* refuser de parler.
clambake ['klæmbeɪk] *n Am* -**1.** *literal repas de coquillages sur la plage*. -**2.** *fig* grande fête *f*.
clamber ['klæmbə^r] ◇ *vi* grimper (en s'aidant des mains); to ~ aboard a train se hisser à bord d'un train; we ~ed up the hill nous avons gravi la colline avec difficulté; he ~ed over the rocks il a escaladé les rochers.
◇ *n* escalade *f*.
clam chowder *n potage épais aux palourdes*.
clammy ['klæmɪ] (*compar* **clammier**, *superl* **clammiest**) *adj* [hands, skin] moite (et froid); [weather] humide, lourd; [walls] suintant, humide.
clamor *Am* = **clamour**.
clamorous ['klæmərəs] *adj* -**1.** [noisy] bruyant. -**2.** [demands] insistant.
clamour *Br*, **clamor** *Am* ['klæmə^r] ◇ *vi* vociférer, crier; to ~ for sthg demander OR réclamer qqch à grands cris OR à cor et à cri; the children ~ed to go out les enfants ont demandé à sortir à grands cris.
◇ *n* -**1.** [noise] clameur *f*, vociférations *fpl*, cri *m*, cris *mpl*. -**2.** [demand] revendication *f* bruyante.
clamp [klæmp] ◇ *n* -**1.** [fastener] pince *f*; MED clamp *m*; TECH crampon *m*; [on worktable] valet *m* (d'établi). -**2.** TECH [for joint] serre-joint *m inv*, serre-joints *m inv*. -**3.** NAUT serre-câbles *m inv*. -**4.** AGR *tas (de navets, de pommes de terre) couvert de paille*. -**5.** [of bricks] tas *m*, pile *f*.
◇ *vt* -**1.** [fasten] attacher, fixer; TECH serrer, cramponner; to ~ sthg to sthg fixer qqch sur qqch (à l'aide d'une pince). -**2.** [close tightly] serrer; to ~ one's eyes shut fermer les yeux. -**3.** [curfew, restrictions] imposer; the authorities ~ed a curfew on the town les autorités ont imposé le couvre-feu à la ville. -**4.** AGR entasser. -**5.** [vehicle] mettre un sabot à; my car has been ~ed on a mis un sabot à ma voiture.
◆ **clamp down** *vi insep* donner un coup de frein; to ~ down on [expenses, inflation] mettre un frein à; [crime, demonstrations] stopper; [information] censurer; [the press] bâillonner; [person] serrer la vis à.
clampdown ['klæmpdaʊn] *n* mesures *fpl* répressives, répression *f*; a ~ on crime un plan de lutte contre la criminalité; a ~ on demonstrations une interdiction de manifester.
clan [klæn] *n* clan *m*.
clandestine [klæn'destɪn] *adj* clandestin.
clang [klæŋ] ◇ *vi* retentir OR résonner (d'un bruit métallique); the gate ~ed shut le portail s'est fermé avec un bruit métallique.
◇ *vt* faire retentir OR résonner.
◇ *n* bruit *m* métallique.
clanger *inf* ['klæŋə^r] *n Br* gaffe *f*; to drop a ~ faire une gaffe.
clangour *Br*, **clangor** *Am* ['klæŋgə^r] *n fml* bruits *mpl* métalliques.
clank [klæŋk] ◇ *n* cliquetis *m*, bruit *m* sec et métallique.
◇ *vi* cliqueter, faire un bruit sec.
◇ *vt* faire cliqueter.
clannish ['klænɪʃ] *adj* [group] fermé, exclusif; [person] qui a l'esprit de clan OR de corps, corporatiste.
clansman ['klænzmən] (*pl* **clansmen** [-mən]) *n* membre *m* d'un clan.
clanswoman ['klænzˌwʊmən] (*pl* **clanswomen** [-ˌwɪmɪn]) *n* membre *m* d'un clan.
clap [klæp] (*pt* & *pp* **clapped**, *cont* **clapping**) ◇ *vt* -**1.** to ~ one's hands [to get attention, to mark rhythm] frapper dans ses mains, taper des mains; [to applaud] applaudir. -**2.** [pat] taper, frapper; the boss clapped her on the back la patron lui a donné une tape dans le dos. -**3.** [put] mettre, poser; she clapped her hand to her forehead elle s'est frappé le front; the judge clapped them into jail *inf* le juge les a flanqués

en prison; **he clapped his hat on his head** il a enfoncé son chapeau sur sa tête; **to ~ hold of sthg** *inf* saisir qqch; **the minute she clapped eyes on him** *inf* dès qu'elle eut posé les yeux sur lui.
◇ *vi* [in applause] applaudir; [to get attention, to mark rhythm] frapper dans ses mains.
◇ *n* -**1.** [sound - gen] claquement *m*; [- of hands] battement *m*; [- of applause] applaudissements *mpl*; **let's give them a ~!** on les applaudit (bien fort)!; **~ of thunder** coup *m* de tonnerre. -**2.** [pat] tape *f*; **she gave him a ~ on the back** elle lui a donné une tape dans le dos. -**3.** ▽ [VD] chaude-pisse *f*.

clapboard ['klæpbɔːd] *n* bardeau *m*.

Clapham ['klæpəm] *pr n*: **~ Junction** *important échangeur ferroviaire au sud de Londres*; **the man on the ~ omnibus** Monsieur Tout-le-Monde.

clapometer [klæ'pɒmɪtə^r] *n* applaudimètre *m*.

clapped-out *inf* [klæpt-] *adj Br* [machine] fichu; [person] crevé.

clapper ['klæpə^r] *n* [of bell] battant *m*.
◆ **clappers** *inf npl Br*: **to go** OR **to move like the ~s** aller à toute vitesse; **he ran like the ~s** il a couru à toutes jambes, il a pris ses jambes à son cou.

clapperboard ['klæpəbɔːd] *n* CIN claquette *f*, claquoir *m*, clap *m*.

clapping ['klæpɪŋ] *n (U)* [for attention, to music] battements *mpl* de mains; [applause] applaudissements *mpl*.

claptrap *inf* ['klæptræp] *n (U)* [nonsense] âneries *fpl*, bêtises *fpl*.

claque [klæk] *n* -**1.** THEAT [for applause] claque *f*. -**2.** [group of admirers] admirateurs *mpl*, -trices *fpl*.

claret ['klærət] ◇ *n Br* (vin *m* de) Bordeaux *m* (rouge).
◇ *adj* bordeaux *(inv)*.

Claridges ['klærɪdʒɪz] *pr n hôtel de luxe à Londres*.

clarification [,klærɪfɪ'keɪʃn] *n* -**1.** [explanation] clarification *f*, éclaircissement *m*. -**2.** [of butter] clarification *f*; [of wine] collage *m*.

clarify ['klærɪfaɪ] (*pt* & *pp* **clarified**) ◇ *vt* -**1.** [explain] clarifier, éclaircir; **to ~ sb's mind on sthg** expliquer qqch à qqn, éclaircir les idées de qqn sur qqch. -**2.** [butter] clarifier; [wine] coller.
◇ *vi* -**1.** [matter, situation] s'éclaircir. -**2.** [butter] se clarifier.

clarinet [,klærə'net] *n* clarinette *f*.

clarinet(t)ist [,klærə'netɪst] *n* clarinettiste *mf*.

clarion ['klærɪən] ◇ *n* clairon *m*.
◇ *vt lit* claironner.

clarion call *n* appel *m* de clairon; **a ~ to action** un appel à l'action.

clarity ['klærətɪ] *n* -**1.** [of explanation, of text] clarté *f*, précision *f*; **~ of mind** lucidité *f*, clarté d'esprit. -**2.** [of liquid] clarté *f*.

clash [klæʃ] ◇ *n* -**1.** [sound - gen] choc *m* métallique, fracas *m*; [- of cymbals] retentissement *m*. -**2.** [between people - fight] affrontement *m*, bagarre *f*; [- disagreement] dispute *f*, différend *m*. -**3.** [incompatibility - of ideas, opinions] incompatibilité *f*; [- of interests] conflit *m*; [- of colours] discordance *f*. -**4.** [of appointments, events] coïncidence *f* fâcheuse.
◇ *vi* -**1.** [metallic objects] s'entrechoquer, se heurter; [cymbals] résonner. -**2.** [people - fight] se battre; [- disagree] se heurter; **to ~ with sb over sthg** avoir un différend avec qqn à propos de qqch. -**3.** [be incompatible - ideas, opinions] se heurter, être incompatible OR en contradiction; [- interests] se heurter, être en conflit; [- colours] jurer, détonner; **that shirt ~es with your trousers** cette chemise jure avec ton pantalon. -**4.** [appointments, events] tomber en même temps.
◇ *vt* [metallic objects] heurter OR entrechoquer bruyamment; [cymbals] faire résonner.

clasp [klɑːsp] ◇ *vt* [hold] serrer, étreindre; [grasp] saisir; **to ~ sb/sthg in one's arms** serrer qqn/qqch dans ses bras; **to ~ sb/sthg to one's breast** serrer qqn/qqch sur son cœur; **he ~ed her hand** il lui a serré la main.
◇ *vi* s'attacher, se fermer.
◇ *n* -**1.** [fastening - of dress, necklace] fermoir *m*; [- of belt] boucle *f*. -**2.** [hold] prise *f*, étreinte *f*; **hand ~** poignée *f* de mains.

clasp knife *n* couteau *m* pliant.

class [klɑːs] ◇ *n* -**1.** [category, division] classe *f*, catégorie *f*; **what ~ are you travelling in?** en quelle classe voyagez-vous?; **~ A eggs** œufs de catégorie A; **he's just not in the same ~ as his brother** il n'arrive pas à la cheville de son frère; **to be in a ~ by oneself** OR **in a ~ of one's own** être unique, former une classe à part. -**2.** BIOL, BOT, SOCIOL & ZOOL classe *f*. -**3.** SCH & UNIV [group of students] classe *f*; [course] cours *m*, classe *f*; **he used to give a ~ in history** il donnait des cours d'histoire; **she's attending** OR **taking a psychology ~** elle suit un cours de psychologie; **the ~ of 1972** *Am* la promotion de 1972. -**4.** *Br* UNIV [grade]: **first ~ honours** licence *f* avec mention très bien. -**5.** *inf* [elegance] classe *f*; **to have ~** avoir de la classe.
◇ *vt* classer, classifier.

class action *n Am*: **~ suit** recours *m* collectif en justice.

class-conscious *adj* [person - aware] conscient des distinctions sociales; [- snobbish] snob; [attitude, manners] snob.

classic ['klæsɪk] ◇ *adj literal* & *fig* classique.
◇ *n* -**1.** [gen] classique *m*; **it's a ~ of modern cinema** c'est un classique du cinéma moderne. -**2.** [in horse racing, cycling] classique *f*. -**3.** SCH & UNIV: **the ~s** les lettres classiques *fpl*.

classical ['klæsɪkl] *adj* -**1.** [gen] classique; **~ music** musique *f* classique. -**2.** SCH & UNIV: **~ education** études *fpl* de lettres classiques; **~ scholar** humaniste *mf*.

classicalism ['klæsɪkəlɪzm] = **classicism**.

classically ['klæsɪklɪ] *adv* classiquement, de façon classique; **a ~ trained musician** un musicien de formation classique.

classicism ['klæsɪsɪzm] *n* classicisme *m*.

classicist ['klæsɪsɪst] *n* -**1.** [scholar] humaniste *mf*. -**2.** ART & LITERAT classique *m*.

classics ['klæsɪks] *n (U)* ≃ les lettres classiques *fpl*.

classifiable ['klæsɪfaɪəbl] *adj* qui peut être classifié, classable.

classification [,klæsɪfɪ'keɪʃn] *n* classification *f*.

classified ['klæsɪfaɪd] ◇ *adj* -**1.** [arranged] classifié, classé; **~ advertisement** petite annonce *f*. -**2.** [secret] (classé) secret; **~ information** renseignements *mpl* (classés) secrets.
◇ *n* petite annonce *f*; **the ~s** les petites annonces.

classifier ['klæsɪfaɪə^r] *n* classeur *m*.

classify ['klæsɪfaɪ] *vt* ranger.

classless ['klɑːslɪs] *adj* [society] sans classes; [person, accent] qui n'appartient à aucune classe (sociale).

classmate ['klɑːsmeɪt] *n* camarade *mf* de classe.

classroom ['klɑːsrʊm] *n* (salle *f* de) classe *f*.

class struggle *n* lutte *f* des classes.

class war(fare) *n* lutte *f* des classes.

classy *inf* ['klɑːsɪ] (*compar* **classier**, *superl* **classiest**) *adj* [hotel, restaurant] chic *inv*, de luxe *inv*, classe *inv*; [person] chic *inv*, qui a de la classe, classe *inv*.

clatter ['klætə^r] ◇ *n* [rattle] cliquetis *m*; [commotion] fracas *m*; **she banged her cup down with a ~** elle a posé sa tasse bruyamment; **the ~ of dishes** le bruit d'assiettes entrechoquées.
◇ *vt* heurter OR entrechoquer bruyamment.
◇ *vi* [typewriter] cliqueter; [dishes] s'entrechoquer bruyamment; [falling object] faire du bruit.

Claudius ['klɔːdɪəs] *pr n* [emperor] Claude.

clausal ['klɔːzl] *adj* -**1.** GRAMM propositionnel. -**2.** JUR relatif aux clauses.

clause [klɔːz] *n* -**1.** GRAMM proposition *f*. -**2.** JUR clause *f*, disposition *f*.

claustrophobia [,klɔːstrə'fəʊbjə] *n* claustrophobie *f*.

claustrophobic [,klɔːstrə'fəʊbɪk] *adj* [person] claustrophobe; [feeling] de claustrophobie; [place, situation] où l'on se sent claustrophobe.

clavichord ['klævɪkɔːd] *n* clavicorde *m*.

clavicle ['klævɪkl] *n* clavicule *f*.

clavier ['klævɪə^r] *n* [keyboard] clavier *m*; [instrument] instrument *m* à clavier.

claw [klɔː] ◇ *n* -**1.** [of bird, cat, dog] griffe *f*; [of bird of prey] serre *f*; [of crab, lobster] pince *f*; [hand] *inf* patte *f*; **to draw in/to show one's ~s** *literal* & *fig* rentrer/sortir ses griffes; **to get one's ~s into sb** *inf* mettre le grappin sur qqn. -**2.** TECH [of hammer] pied-de-biche *m*.
◇ *vt* [scratch] griffer; [grip] agripper OR serrer (avec ses griffes); [tear] déchirer (avec ses griffes); **he ~ed his way to the top** *fig* il a travaillé dur pour arriver en haut de l'échelle.
◆ **claw at** *vt insep* [try to scratch] essayer de griffer; [try to grab] essayer de s'agripper à.
◆ **claw back** *vt sep* récupérer.

clawback ['klɔːbæk] *n* [recovery] récupération *f*; [sum] somme *f* récupérée.

claw hammer *n* marteau *m* à pied-de-biche, marteau *m* fendu.

clay [kleɪ] ◇ *n* [gen] argile *f*, (terre *f*) glaise *f*; [for pottery] argile *f*.
◇ *comp* [brick, pot] en argile, en terre; **~ court** SPORT court *m* en terre battue.

clayey ['kleɪɪ] *adj* argileux, glaiseux.

claymore ['kleɪmɔː^r] *n* glaive *m (porté par les Écossais)*.

clay pigeon *n* -**1.** *literal* pigeon *m* d'argile OR de ball-trap; **~ shooting** ball-trap *m*. -**2.** *inf Am fig* [sitting duck] cible *f* facile.

clay pipe *n* pipe *f* en terre.

clean [kliːn] ◇ *adj* -**1.** [free from dirt - hands, shirt, room] propre, net; [- animal, person] propre; [- piece of paper] vierge, blanc; **my hands are ~** *literal* j'ai les mains propres, mes mains sont propres; *fig* j'ai la conscience nette OR tranquille; **the doctor gave him a ~ bill of health** le médecin l'a déclaré en parfait état de santé OR en parfaite santé; **he made a ~ breast of it** il a dit tout ce qu'il avait sur la conscience, il a déchargé sa conscience; **to make a ~ sweep** faire table rase. -**2.** [free from impurities - air] pur, frais; [- water] pur, clair; [- sound] net, clair. -**3.** [morally pure - conscience] net, tranquille; [- joke] qui n'a rien de choquant; **it was all good ~ fun** c'était une façon innocente de nous amuser; **keep it ~!** pas de grossièretés!; **~ living** une vie saine. -**4.** [honourable - fight] loyal; [- reputation] net, sans tache; **he's got a ~ driving licence** il n'a jamais eu de contraventions graves; **to have a ~ record** avoir un casier (judiciaire) vierge. -**5.** [smooth - curve, line] bien dessiné, net; [- shape] fin, élégant; [- cut] net, franc; **the building has ~ lines** le bâtiment a de belles lignes; **to make a ~ break** couper net; **we made a ~ break with the past** nous avons rompu avec le passé, nous avons tourné la page. -**6.** [throw] adroit, habile. -**7.** *inf* **I'm ~** [innocent] je n'ai rien à me reprocher, je n'ai rien fait; [without incriminating material] je n'ai rien sur moi; [unarmed] je n'ai pas d'arme, je ne suis pas armé. -**8.** [not radioactive] non radioactif; **a ~ bomb** une bombe propre OR sans retombées radioactives.
◇ *vt* -**1.** [room, cooker] nettoyer; [clothing] laver; **I ~ed the mud from my shoes** j'ai enlevé la boue de mes chaussures; **to ~ one's teeth** se laver OR se brosser les dents; **to ~ the windows** faire les vitres OR les carreaux. -**2.** [chicken, fish] vider.
◇ *vi* -**1.** [person] nettoyer; **she spends her day ~ing** elle passe sa journée à faire le ménage. -**2.** [carpet, paintbrush] se nettoyer; **this cooker ~s easily** ce four est facile à nettoyer OR se nettoie facilement.
◇ *adv inf* -**1.** [completely] carrément; **the handle broke ~ off** l'anse a cassé net; **the match burnt a hole ~ through the rug** l'allumette a fait un trou dans la moquette; **he cut ~ through the bone** il a coupé l'os de part en part; **the bullet went ~ through his chest** la balle lui a carrément traversé la poitrine; **the robbers got ~ away** les voleurs se sont enfuis sans laisser

de trace; we ~ forgot about the appointment nous avions complètement oublié le rendez-vous. -**2.** *phr*: to come ~ about sthg révéler qqch; the murderer finally came ~ l'assassin a fini par avouer.

◇ *n* nettoyage *m*; the carpet needs a good ~ la moquette a grand besoin d'être nettoyée; I gave my shoes a ~ j'ai nettoyé mes chaussures.

◆ **clean down** *vt sep* [wall] laver.

◆ **clean off** *vt sep* -**1.** [mud, stain] enlever. -**2.** [sofa, table] débarrasser.

◆ **clean out** *vt sep* -**1.** [tidy] nettoyer à fond; [empty] vider. -**2.** *inf* [person] nettoyer, plumer; [house] vider; we're completely ~ed out nous sommes totalement fauchés; he ~ed me out il m'a plumé.

◆ **clean up** ◇ *vt sep* -**1.** [make clean] nettoyer à fond; I ~ed the children up as best I could j'ai fait de mon mieux pour débarbouiller les enfants; ~ this mess up! nettoyez-moi ce fouillis! -**2.** [make orderly - cupboard, room] ranger; [- affairs, papers] ranger, mettre de l'ordre dans; the police intend to ~ up the city la police a l'intention d'épurer OR de nettoyer cette ville.

◇ *vi insep* -**1.** [tidy room] nettoyer; [tidy cupboard, desk] ranger; [wash oneself] faire un brin de toilette. -**2.** *inf* [make profit] gagner gros; we ~ed up on the deal nous avons touché un gros paquet sur cette affaire, cette affaire nous a rapporté gros.

clean-cut *adj* -**1.** [lines] net; [shape] bien délimité, net. -**2.** [person] propre (sur soi), soigné.

cleaner [ˈkliːnə^r] *n* -**1.** [cleaning lady] femme *f* de ménage; [man] (ouvrier *m*) nettoyeur *m*. -**2.** [product - gen] produit *m* d'entretien; [- stain remover] détachant *m*; [device] appareil *m* de nettoyage. -**3.** [dry cleaner] teinturier *m*, -ère *f*; I took the clothes to the ~'s j'ai donné les vêtements à nettoyer OR au teinturier ❑ to take sb to the ~s *inf* nettoyer OR plumer qqn.

cleaning [ˈkliːnɪŋ] *n* -**1.** [activity - gen] nettoyage *m*; [- household] ménage *m*; to do the ~ faire le ménage. -**2.** [clothes] vêtements *mpl* à faire nettoyer.

cleaning lady, cleaning woman *n* femme *f* de ménage.

clean-limbed *adj* bien proportionné OR bâti.

cleanliness [ˈklenlɪnɪs] *n* propreté *f*; ~ is next to godliness *prov* la propreté du corps s'apparente à celle de l'âme.

clean-living *adj* qui mène une vie saine.

cleanly[1] [ˈkliːnlɪ] *adv* -**1.** [smoothly] net; the handle snapped off ~ l'anse s'est cassée net; she cut it ~ in two elle l'a coupé en deux parties égales. -**2.** [fight, play] loyalement.

cleanly[2] [ˈklenlɪ] (*compar* cleanlier, *superl* cleanliest) *adj* propre.

cleanness [ˈkliːnnɪs] *n* propreté *f*.

cleanout [ˈkliːnaʊt] = **cleanup**.

cleanse [klenz] *vt* -**1.** [clean - gen] nettoyer; [- with water] laver; MED [blood] dépurer; [wound] nettoyer. -**2.** *fig* [purify] purifier; to ~ sb of their sins laver qqn de ses péchés.

cleanser [ˈklenzə^r] *n* -**1.** [detergent] détergent *m*, détersif *m*. -**2.** [for skin] (lait *m*) démaquillant *m*.

clean-shaven *adj* [face, man] rasé de près.

cleansing [ˈklenzɪŋ] ◇ *n* nettoyage *m*.

◇ *adj* [lotion] démaquillant; [power, property] de nettoyage.

cleanup [ˈkliːnʌp] *n* nettoyage *m* à fond; the house needs a good ~ la maison a besoin d'être nettoyée à fond; to give sthg a ~ nettoyer qqch à fond.

clear [klɪə^r] ◇ *adj* -**1.** [transparent - glass, plastic] transparent; [- water] clair, limpide; [- lake, river] limpide, transparent; [- air] pur; ~ honey miel liquide; ~ soup [plain stock] bouillon *m*; [with meat] consommé *m*. -**2.** [cloudless - sky] clair, dégagé; [- weather] clair, beau; on a ~ day par temps clair; the sky grew ~er le ciel se dégagea ❑ as ~ as day clair comme le jour OR comme de l'eau de roche. -**3.** [not dull - colour] vif; [- light] éclatant, radieux; [untainted - complexion, skin] clair, frais; ~ blue bleu vif. -**4.** [distinct - outline] net, clair; [- photograph] net; [- sound] clair, distinct; [- voice] clair, argentin; make sure your writing is ~ efforcez-vous d'écrire distinctement OR proprement; the lyrics are not very ~ je ne distingue pas très bien les paroles de la chanson ❑ the sound was as ~ as a bell on entendait un son aussi clair que celui d'une cloche. -**5.** [not confused - mind] pénétrant, lucide; [- thinking, argument, style] clair; [- explanation, report] clair, intelligible; [- instructions] clair, explicite; [- message] en clair; I want to keep a ~ head je veux rester lucide OR garder tous mes esprits; a ~ thinker un esprit lucide; he is quite ~ about what has to be done il sait parfaitement ce qu'il y a à faire; I've got the problem ~ in my head je comprends OR saisis le problème; now let's get this ~ — I want no nonsense comprenons-nous bien OR soyons clairs — je ne supporterai pas de sottises. -**6.** [obvious, unmistakable] évident, clair; a ~ indication of a forthcoming storm un signe certain qu'il va y avoir de l'orage; it is a ~ case of favouritism c'est manifestement du favoritisme, c'est un cas de favoritisme manifeste; it's ~ that he's lying il est évident OR clair qu'il ment; it's ~ from her letter that she's unhappy sa lettre montre clairement qu'elle est malheureuse; it becomes ~er every day cela devient plus évident chaque jour; it's far from ~ who will win the election on ne peut vraiment pas dire qui va gagner les élections; it is ~ to me that he is telling the truth pour moi, il est clair qu'il dit la vérité; he was unable to make his meaning ~ il n'arrivait pas à s'expliquer; we want to make it ~ that... nous tenons à préciser que...; she made it quite ~ to them what she wanted elle leur a bien fait comprendre ce qu'elle voulait; it is important to make ~ exactly what our aims are il est important de bien préciser quels sont nos objectifs; is that ~? est-ce que c'est clair?; do I make myself ~? est-ce que je me fais bien comprendre?, est-ce que c'est bien clair? ❑ as ~ as mud *hum* clair comme l'encre. -**7.** [free from doubt, certain] certain; she seems quite ~ about what she wants elle sait très bien ce qu'elle veut; I want to be ~ in my mind about it je veux en avoir le cœur net. -**8.** [unqualified] net, sensible; it's a ~ improvement over the other c'est nettement mieux que l'autre, il y a un net progrès par rapport à l'autre; they won by a ~ majority ils ont gagné avec une large majorité. -**9.** [unobstructed, free - floor, path] libre, dégagé; [- route] sans obstacles, sans danger; [- view] dégagé; the roads are ~ of snow les routes sont déblayées OR déneigées; ~ of obstacles sans obstacles; I left the desk ~ j'ai débarrassé le bureau; ~ space espace libre; we had a ~ view of the sea nous avions une très belle vue sur la mer; to be ~ of sthg être débarrassé de qqch; we're ~ of the traffic nous sommes sortis des encombrements; once the plane was ~ of the trees une fois que l'avion eut franchi les arbres; to be ~ of debts être libre de dettes; can you see your way ~ to lending me £5? *fig* auriez-vous la possibilité de me prêter 5 livres? -**10.** [free from guilt]: is your conscience ~? as-tu la conscience tranquille?; I can go home with a ~ conscience je peux rentrer la conscience tranquille. -**11.** [of time] libre; his schedule is ~ il n'a rien de prévu sur son emploi du temps; I have Wednesday ~ je n'ai rien de prévu pour mercredi; we have four ~ days to finish nous avons quatre jours pleins OR entiers pour finir. -**12.** [net - money, wages] net; he brings home £300 ~ il gagne 300 livres net; a ~ profit un bénéfice net; a ~ loss une perte sèche; ~ of taxes net d'impôts. -**13.** LING antérieur.

◇ *adv* -**1.** [distinctly] distinctement, nettement; reading you loud and ~ RADIO je te reçois cinq sur cinq; I can hear you as ~ as a bell je t'entends très clairement. -**2.** [out of the way]: when we got ~ of the town quand nous nous sommes éloignés de la ville; when I get ~ of my debts quand je serai débarrassé de mes dettes; we pulled him ~ of the wrecked car/of the water nous l'avons sorti de la carcasse de la voiture/de l'eau; stand ~! écartez-vous!; stand ~ of the entrance! dégagez l'entrée! -**3.** [all the way] entièrement, complètement; you can see ~ to the mountain on peut voir jusqu'à la montagne; they went ~ around the world ils ont fait le tour du monde; the thieves got ~ away les voleurs ont disparu sans laisser de trace.

◇ *n phr*: to be in the ~ [out of danger] être hors de danger; [out of trouble] être tiré d'affaire; [free of blame] être blanc comme neige; [above suspicion] être au-dessus de tout soupçon; [no longer suspected] être blanchi (de tout soupçon); SPORT être démarqué.

◇ *vt* -**1.** [remove - object] débarrasser, enlever; [- obstacle] écarter; [- weeds] arracher, enlever; ~ the papers off the desk enlevez ces papiers du bureau, débarrassez le bureau de ces papiers; she ~ed the plates from the table elle a débarrassé la table. -**2.** [remove obstruction from - gen] débarrasser; [- entrance, road] dégager, déblayer; [- forest, land] défricher; [- pipe] déboucher; it's your turn to ~ the table c'est à ton tour de débarrasser la table OR de desservir; to ~ one's throat s'éclaircir la gorge OR la voix; land that has been ~ed of trees terre qui a été déboisée; ~ the room! évacuez la salle!; the judge ~ed the court le juge a fait évacuer la salle; the police ~ed the way for the procession la police a ouvert un passage au cortège; the talks ~ed the way for a ceasefire *fig* les pourparlers ont préparé le terrain OR ont ouvert la voie pour un cessez-le-feu ❑ to ~ the ground *literal* & *fig* déblayer le terrain; to ~ the decks [prepare for action] se mettre en branle-bas de combat; [make space] faire de la place, faire le ménage. -**3.** [clarify - liquid] clarifier; [- wine] coller, clarifier; [- skin] purifier; [- complexion] éclaircir; open the windows to ~ the air ouvrez les fenêtres pour aérer; his apology ~ed the air *fig* ses excuses ont détendu l'atmosphère; I went for a walk to ~ my head [from hangover] j'ai fait un tour pour m'éclaircir les idées; [from confusion] j'ai fait un tour pour me rafraîchir les idées OR pour me remettre les idées en place. -**4.** [authorize] autoriser, approuver; the plane was ~ed for takeoff l'avion a reçu l'autorisation de décoller; the editor ~ed the article for publication le rédacteur en chef a donné son accord OR le feu vert pour publier l'article; the investigators ~ed him for top secret work après enquête, il a été autorisé à mener des activités top secret; you'll have to ~ it with the boss il faut demander l'autorisation OR l'accord OR le feu vert du patron. -**5.** [vindicate, find innocent] innocenter, disculper; to ~ sb of a charge disculper qqn d'une accusation; he was ~ed of having been drunk in charge of a ship accusé d'avoir tenu les commandes (d'un navire) en état d'ivresse, il a été disculpé; the court ~ed him of all blame la cour l'a totalement disculpé OR innocenté; give him a chance to ~ himself donnez-lui la possibilité de se justifier OR de prouver son innocence; to ~ one's name se justifier, défendre son honneur. -**6.** [avoid touching] franchir; [obstacle] éviter; the horse ~ed the fence with ease le cheval a sauté sans peine par-dessus OR a franchi sans peine la barrière; the plane barely ~ed the trees l'avion a franchi les arbres de justesse; hang the curtains so that they just ~ the floor accrochez les rideaux de façon à ce qu'ils touchent à peine le parquet. -**7.** [make a profit of]: she ~ed 10% on the deal l'affaire lui a rapporté 10 % net OR 10 % tous frais payés. -**8.** [dispatch - work] finir, terminer; COMM [stock] liquider; he ~ed the backlog of work il a rattrapé le travail en retard; we must ~ this report by Friday il faut que nous nous débarrassions de ce rapport avant vendredi. -**9.** [settle - account] liquider, solder; [- cheque] compenser; [- debt] s'acquitter de; [- dues] acquitter. -**10.** [subj: customs officer - goods] dédouaner; [- ship] expédier. -**11.** [pass through]: to ~ customs [person] passer la douane; [shipment] être dédouané; the bill ~ed the Senate le projet de loi a été voté par le Sénat. -**12.** MED [blood] dépurer, purifier; [bowels] purger, dégager. -**13.** SPORT: to ~ the ball dégager le ballon. -**14.** TECH [decode] déchiffrer.

◇ *vi* -**1.** [weather] s'éclaircir, se lever; [sky] se dégager; [fog] se lever, se dissiper; it's ~ing le temps se lève, le ciel se dégage. -**2.** [liquid] s'éclaircir; [skin] devenir plus sain; [complexion] s'éclaircir; [expression] s'éclairer; her face ~ed son visage s'est éclairé. -**3.** [cheque]: it takes three days for the cheque to ~ il y a trois jours de délai d'encaissement. -**4.** [obtain clearance] recevoir l'autorisation.

◆ **clear away** ◇ *vt sep* [remove] enlever, ôter; we ~ed away the dishes nous avons débarrassé (la table) OR desservi.

◇ *vi insep* -**1.** [tidy up] débarrasser, desservir. -**2.** [disappear - fog, mist] se dissiper.

◆ **clear off** ◇ *vi insep inf* filer; ~ off! fiche le camp!

◇ *vt sep* [get rid of - debt] s'acquitter de; COMM [- stock] liquider.

◆ **clear out** ◇ *vt sep* -**1.** [tidy] nettoyer, ranger; [empty - cupboard] vider; [- room] débarrasser. -**2.** [throw out - rubbish, old clothes] jeter; he ~ed everything out of the house il a fait le vide dans la maison; to ~ everyone out of a room faire évacuer une pièce. -**3.** *inf* [leave without money] nettoyer, plumer; that last game ~ed me out je me suis fait plumer dans cette dernière partie; I'm ~ed out je suis fauché OR à sec. -**4.** *inf* [goods, stock] épuiser.

◇ *vi insep inf* filer; he was ~ing out when I arrived il faisait ses valises quand je suis arrivé; he told us to ~ out il nous a ordonné de disparaître; ~ out (of here)! dégage!, fiche le camp!

◆ **clear up** ◇ *vt sep* -**1.** [settle - problem] résoudre; [- misunderstanding] dissiper; [- mystery] éclaircir, résoudre; can you ~ up this point? pouvez-vous éclaircir ce point?; let's ~ this matter up tirons cette affaire au clair. -**2.** [tidy up] ranger, faire du rangement dans; ~ up that mess in the garden, will you? rangemoi ce fouillis dans le jardin, d'accord?; I have a lot of work to ~ up j'ai beaucoup de travail à rattraper.

◇ *vi insep* -**1.** [weather] s'éclaircir, se lever; [fog, mist] se dissiper, se lever; it's ~ing up le temps se lève. -**2.** [illness]: his cold is ~ing up sa grippe tire à sa fin. -**3.** [tidy up] ranger, faire le ménage; I'm fed up with ~ing up after you j'en ai assez de faire le ménage derrière toi.

clearance ['klɪərəns] *n* -**1.** [removal - of buildings, litter] enlèvement *m*; [- of obstacles] déblaiement *m*; [- of people] évacuation *f*; COMM [- of merchandise] liquidation *f*; land ~ déblaiement OR dégagement *m* du terrain; slum ~ aménagement *m* des quartiers insalubres. -**2.** [space] jeu *m*, dégagement *m*; there was a 10 -centimetre ~ between the lorry and the bridge il y avait un espace de 10 centimètres entre le camion et le pont; how much ~ is there? que reste-t-il comme place? -**3.** [permission] autorisation *f*, permis *m*; [from customs] dédouanement *m*; we have to get ~ to leave il nous faut l'autorisation de OR pour partir; the plane was given ~ to land l'avion a reçu l'autorisation d'atterrir; they sent the order to headquarters for ~ ils ont envoyé la commande au siège pour contrôle. -**4.** BANK [of cheque] compensation *f*. -**5.** SPORT dégagement *m*.

clearance sale *n* liquidation *f*, soldes *mpl*.

clear-cut *adj* -**1.** [lines, shape] nettement défini, net. -**2.** [decision, situation] clair; [difference] clair, net; [opinion, plan] bien défini, précis.

clearer ['klɪərəʳ] *n Br* [bank] banque *f (appartenant à une chambre de compensation)*.

clear-eyed *adj literal* qui a de bons yeux, clairvoyant *fml*; *fig* réaliste, lucide.

clear-headed *adj* [person] lucide, perspicace; [decision] lucide, rationnel.

clear-headedness [-'hedɪdnɪs] *n* [of person] lucidité *f*, perspicacité *f*; [of decision] lucidité *f*.

clearing ['klɪərɪŋ] *n* -**1.** [in forest] clairière *f*; [in clouds] éclaircie *f*. -**2.** [of land] déblaiement *m*, défrichement *m*; [of passage] dégagement *m*, déblaiement *m*; [of pipe] débouchage *m*. -**3.** [removal - of objects] enlèvement *m*; [- of people] évacuation *f*. -**4.** [of name, reputation] réhabilitation *f*; JUR [of accused] disculpation *f*. -**5.** BANK [of cheque] compensation *f*; [of account] liquidation *f*, solde *m*. -**6.** [of debt] acquittement *m*.

clearing bank *n Br* banque *f (appartenant à une chambre de compensation)*.

clearing house *n* -**1.** BANK chambre *f* de compensation. -**2.** [for information, materials] bureau *m* central.

clearing-up *n* nettoyage *m*.

clearly ['klɪəlɪ] *adv* -**1.** [distinctly - see, understand] clairement, bien; [- hear, speak] distinctement; [- describe, explain] clairement, précisément; [- think] clairement, lucidement. -**2.** [obviously] manifestement, à l'évidence; they ~ didn't expect us il était clair OR évident qu'ils ne nous attendaient pas.

clearness ['klɪənɪs] *n* -**1.** [of air, glass] transparence *f*; [of water] limpidité *f*. -**2.** [of speech, thought] clarté *f*, précision *f*.

clearout *inf* ['klɪəraʊt] *n Br* rangement *m*; to have a ~ faire du rangement.

clear-sighted *adj fig* [person] perspicace, lucide; [decision, plan] réaliste.

clear-sightedness [-'saɪtɪdnɪs] *n fig* [of person] perspicacité *f*, lucidité *f*; [of plan] réalisme *m*.

clearway ['klɪəweɪ] *n Br* AUT route *f* à stationnement interdit.

cleat [kliːt] *n* -**1.** [on shoe] clou *m*. -**2.** [block of wood] tasseau *m*; NAUT taquet *m*.

cleavage ['kliːvɪdʒ] *n* -**1.** [of woman] décolleté *m*. -**2.** BIOL [of cell] division *f*; CHEM & GEOL clivage *m*.

cleave [kliːv] (*pt* cleaved OR clove [kləʊv] OR *arch* cleft [kleft], *pp* cleaved OR cloven ['kləʊvn] OR *arch* cleft [kleft]) *vt* -**1.** *lit* [split] fendre; *fig* diviser, séparer. -**2.** BIOL [cell] diviser; GEOL [mineral] cliver.

◆ **cleave through** *vt insep*: to ~ through the waves fendre les vagues.

◆ **cleave to** (*pt* **cleaved** OR **clove** OR *arch* **cleft**, *pp* **cleaved** OR **clove**) *vt insep* se cramponner à, s'accrocher à; they ~ to traditional values ils sont très attachés aux valeurs traditionnelles.

cleaver ['kliːvəʳ] *n* couperet *m*.

clef [klef] *n* MUS clef *f*, clé *f*.

cleft [kleft] ◇ *arch pt & pp* → **cleave**.

◇ *adj* [split - gen] fendu; [branch] fourchu; ~ stick branche *f* fourchue; to be in a ~ stick *inf Br* être OR se trouver entre le marteau et l'enclume.

◇ *n* [opening - gen] fissure *f*; [- in rock] fissure *f*, crevasse *f*.

cleft palate *n* palais *m* fendu.

clematis ['klemətɪs] *n* clématite *f*.

clemency ['klemənsɪ] *n* -**1.** [mercy] clémence *f*, magnanimité *f*. -**2.** [of weather] douceur *f*, clémence *f*.

clement ['klemənt] *adj* -**1.** [person] clément, magnanime. -**2.** [weather] doux, clément.

Clement ['klemənt] *pr n*: Saint ~ saint Clément.

clementine ['kleməntaɪn] *n* clémentine *f*.

clench [klentʃ] ◇ *vt* [fist, jaw] serrer; [grasp firmly] empoigner, agripper; [hold tightly] serrer.

◇ *n* -**1.** [grip] prise *f*, étreinte *f*. -**2.** TECH [clamp] crampon *m*.

Cleopatra [kliːə'pætrə] *pr n* Cléopâtre; ~'s Needle l'obélisque *m* de Cléopâtre.

clerestory ['klɪəstɔːrɪ] (*pl* clerestories) *n* claire-voie *f (dans une église)*.

clergy ['klɜːdʒɪ] *n (U)* (membres *mpl* du) clergé *m*.

clergyman ['klɜːdʒɪmən] (*pl* clergymen [-mən]) *n* [gen] ecclésiastique *m*; [Catholic] curé *m*, prêtre *m*; [Protestant] pasteur *m*.

clergywoman ['klɜːdʒɪˌwʊmən] (*pl* clergywomen [-ˌwɪmɪn]) *n* (femme *f*) pasteur *m*.

cleric ['klerɪk] *n* ecclésiastique *m*.

clerical ['klerɪkl] *adj* -**1.** [office - staff, work] de bureau; [- position] de commis; to do ~ work travailler dans un bureau; ~ error [in document] faute *f* de copiste; [in accounting] erreur *f* d'écriture. -**2.** RELIG clérical, du clergé; ~ collar col *m* de pasteur.

clericalism ['klerɪkəlɪzm] *n* cléricalisme *m*.

clerihew ['klerɪhjuː] *n* petit poème *m* humoristique *(qui concerne une personnalité connue)*.

clerk [*Br* klɑːk, *Am* klɜːrk] ◇ *n* -**1.** [worker - in office] employé *m*, -e *f* (de bureau), commis *m*; [- in bank] employé *m*, -e *f* de banque; ~ of works *Br* CONSTR conducteur *m* de travaux. -**2.** JUR clerc *m*; Clerk of the Court greffier *m* (du tribunal). -**3.** *Am* [sales person] vendeur *m*, -euse *f*. -**4.** *Am* [receptionist]: (desk) ~ réceptionniste *mf*. -**5.** RELIG: ~ in holy orders ecclésiastique *m*. -**6.** *arch* [scholar] savant *m*, érudit *m*, -e *f*, clerc *m lit*.

◇ *vi Am* -**1.** [as assistant]: to ~ for sb être assistant de qqn. -**2.** [as sales clerk] travailler comme vendeur.

Cleveland ['kliːvlənd] *pr n* Cleveland.

clever ['klevəʳ] *adj* -**1.** [intelligent] intelligent, astucieux; he has a ~ face il a l'air intelligent OR astucieux. -**2.** [skilful - person] adroit, habile; [- work] bien fait; to be ~ with one's hands être adroit OR habile de ses mains; to be ~ at sthg/at doing sthg être doué pour qqch/pour faire qqch; to be ~ at maths être fort en maths. -**3.** [cunning] malin, astucieux; *pej* rusé; he's too ~ by half *inf* c'est un petit malin; they were too ~ for us ils nous ont roulés. -**4.** [ingenious - book] intelligemment OR bien écrit, ingénieux; [- film] ingénieux, intelligent; [- idea, plan] ingénieux, astucieux; [- story] fin, astucieux; there's a ~ way of getting around the problem il y a une astuce pour contourner le problème.

clever-clever *inf adj Br* trop malin.

clever Dick *inf n Br* petit malin *m*.

cleverly ['klevəlɪ] *adv* [intelligently] intelligemment, astucieusement; [skilfully] adroitement, habilement; [cunningly] avec ruse; [ingeniously] ingénieusement.

cleverness ['klevənɪs] *n* [intelligence] intelligence *f*, astuce *f*; [skilfulness] habileté *f*, adresse *f*; [cunning] ruse *f*; [ingenuity] ingéniosité *f*.

clew [kluː] *n* -**1.** NAUT point *m* d'écoute. -**2.** = **clue**.

cliché [*Br* 'kliːʃeɪ, *Am* kliː'ʃeɪ] *n* -**1.** [idea] cliché *m*; [phrase] cliché *m*, lieu commun *m*, banalité *f*. -**2.** TYPO cliché *m*.

clichéd [*Br* 'kliːʃeɪd, *Am* kliː'ʃeɪd] *adj* banal; a ~ phrase un cliché, une banalité, un lieu commun.

click [klɪk] ◇ *n* -**1.** [sound] petit bruit *m* sec; [of tongue] claquement *m*; LING clic *m*, click *m*. -**2.** [of ratchet, wheel] cliquet *m*.

◇ *vt* [fingers, tongue] faire claquer; he ~ed his heels (together) il a claqué les talons.

◇ *vi* -**1.** [make sound] faire un bruit sec; the lamp ~ed on la lampe s'alluma avec un déclic; the lock ~ed into place la serrure s'est enclenchée avec un déclic. -**2.** *inf* [become clear]: it suddenly ~ed tout à coup ça a fait «tilt». -**3.** *inf* [be a success] bien marcher; [get on well]: they ~ed from the beginning ils se sont bien entendus dès le début, ça a tout de suite collé entre eux.

clickety-click [ˌklɪkətɪ-] *onomat* clic-clic *m*.

clicking ['klɪkɪŋ] *n* cliquetis *m*.

client ['klaɪənt] *n* client *m*, -e *f*.

clientele [ˌkliːɒn'tel] *n* COMM clientèle *f*; THEAT clientèle, public *m* (habituel).

cliff [klɪf] *n* escarpement *m*; [on coast] falaise *f*; [in mountaineering] à-pic *m inv*.

cliffhanger *inf* ['klɪfˌhæŋəʳ] *n* [situation in film, story] situation *f* à suspense; [moment of suspense] moment *m* d'angoisse; the election was a real ~ le résultat des élections est resté incertain jusqu'au dernier moment.

climacteric [klaɪ'mæktərɪk] ◇ *n* [gen] climatère *m spec*; [women's] ménopause *f*; [men's] andropause *f*.
◇ *adj* climatérique; *fig* crucial, critique.

climactic [klaɪ'mæktɪk] *adj* à son apogée, à son point culminant; the ~ love scene towards the end of the play la scène d'amour finale qui constitue le point culminant de la pièce.

climate ['klaɪmɪt] *n* METEOR climat *m*; *fig* climat *m*, ambiance *f*; the ~ of opinion (les courants *mpl* de) l'opinion *f*; the economic ~ la conjoncture économique.

climatic [klaɪ'mætɪk] *adj* climatique.

climatology [ˌklaɪmə'tɒlədʒɪ] *n* climatologie *f*.

climax ['klaɪmæks] ◇ *n* **-1.** [culmination] apogée *m*, point *m* culminant; the directorship was the ~ of her business career son poste d'administratrice marqua l'apogée de sa carrière dans les affaires; this brought matters to a ~ ceci a porté l'affaire à son point culminant; as the battle reached its ~ lorsque la bataille fut à son paroxysme; he worked up to the ~ of his story il amena le récit à son point culminant. **-2.** [sexual] orgasme *m*. **-3.** [in rhetoric] gradation *f*.
◇ *vi* **-1.** [film, story] atteindre le OR son point culminant; a tough election campaign ~ing in victory on polling day une campagne électorale acharnée qui a été couronnée de succès le jour du scrutin. **-2.** [sexually] atteindre l'orgasme.
◇ *vt* amener OR porter à son point culminant.

climb [klaɪm] ◇ *vi* **-1.** [road, sun] monter; [plane] monter, prendre de l'altitude; [prices] monter, augmenter; [plant] grimper. **-2.** [person] grimper; I ~ed into bed/into the boat j'ai grimpé dans mon lit/à bord du bateau; to ~ over an obstacle escalader un obstacle; he ~ed (up) out of the hole/through the opening il s'est hissé hors du trou/par l'ouverture; he ~ed into his jeans *inf* il a enfilé son jean, il a sauté dans son jean; he ~ed to power on the backs of his former colleagues *fig* il s'est servi de ses anciens collègues pour accéder au pouvoir. **-3.** SPORT faire de l'escalade; [on rocks] varapper; to go ~ing faire de l'escalade.
◇ *vt* **-1.** [ascend - stairs, steps] monter, grimper; [- hill] escalader, grimper; [- mountain] gravir, faire l'ascension de; [- cliff, wall] escalader; to ~ a ladder/tree monter sur une échelle/un arbre; she ~ed the rope elle est montée à la corde. **-2.** SPORT [rockface] escalader, grimper sur.
◇ *n* **-1.** [of hill, slope] montée *f*, côte *f*; [in mountaineering] ascension *f*, escalade *f*; it's quite a ~ ça monte dur; it was an easy ~ to the top (of the hill) ça montait en pente douce jusqu'au sommet (de la colline); there were several steep ~s along the route il y avait plusieurs bonnes côtes sur le trajet. **-2.** [of plane] montée *f*, ascension *f*.
◆ **climb down** *vi insep* **-1.** [descend] descendre; [in mountaineering] descendre, effectuer une descente. **-2.** [back down] en rabattre, céder.

climb-down *n* dérobade *f*, reculade *f*.

climber ['klaɪməʳ] *n* **-1.** [person] grimpeur *m*, -euse *f*; [mountaineer] alpiniste *mf*; [rock climber] varappeur *m*, -euse *f*; social ~ *pej* arriviste *mf*. **-2.** [plant] plante *f* grimpante. **-3.** [bird] grimpeur *m*.

climbing ['klaɪmɪŋ] ◇ *n* **-1.** [action] montée *f*, escalade *f*; the ~ of Everest l'escalade de l'Everest ❑ social ~ *pej* arrivisme *m*. **-2.** [mountaineering] alpinisme *m*; [rock climbing] varappe *f*, escalade *f*.
◇ *adj* [bird] grimpeur; [plant] grimpant; [plane, star] ascendant.

climbing frame *n Br* cage *f* à poules *(jeu)*.

climbing irons *npl* crampons *mpl*, grappins *mpl*.

climbing wall *n* mur *m* d'escalade.

clime [klaɪm] *n lit* climat *m lit*, région *f*.

clinch [klɪntʃ] ◇ *vt* **-1.** [settle - deal] conclure; [- argument] régler, résoudre; we ~ed the agreement nous avons scellé l'accord; the ~ing argument l'argument décisif; that ~es it! comme ça, c'est réglé! **-2.** TECH [nail] river; NAUT étalinguer.
◇ *vi* BOXING combattre corps à corps.
◇ *n* **-1.** TECH rivetage *m*; NAUT étalingure *f*. **-2.** BOXING corps à corps *m*; they went into a ~ ils ont lutté corps à corps. **-3.** *inf* [embrace] étreinte *f*, enlacement *m*; they were in a ~ ils étaient enlacés.

clincher *inf* ['klɪntʃəʳ] *n* argument *m* irréfutable, argument *m* massue.

cline [klaɪn] *n* cline *m*.

cling [klɪŋ] (*pt* & *pp* clung [klʌŋ]) *vi* **-1.** [hold on tightly] s'accrocher, se cramponner; they clung to one another ils se sont enlacés, ils se sont cramponnés l'un à l'autre ‖ *fig*: to ~ to a hope/a belief se raccrocher à un espoir/une croyance; we can't afford to ~ to the past il est dangereux de se raccrocher au passé; she ~s to her children even though they are now grown up elle s'accroche à ses enfants bien qu'ils soient maintenant adultes. **-2.** [stick] adhérer, coller; a dress that ~s to the body une robe très près du corps OR très ajustée. **-3.** [smell] persister.

clingfilm ['klɪŋfɪlm] *n Br* film *m* alimentaire transparent.

clinging ['klɪŋɪŋ] *adj* [clothing] collant, qui moule le corps; *pej* [person] importun; ~ vine *inf Am fig* pot *m* de colle.

clingwrap ['klɪŋræp] = **clingfilm**.

clingy ['klɪŋɪ] (*compar* clingier, *superl* clingiest) *adj* [clothing] moulant; *pej* [person] importun.

clinic ['klɪnɪk] *n* **-1.** [part of hospital] service *m*; outpatients' ~ ≃ service de consultation externe; eye ~ clinique *f* ophtalmologique. **-2.** [treatment session] consultation *f*; the doctor holds his ~ twice a week le docteur consulte deux fois par semaine. **-3.** *Br* [private hospital] clinique *f*. **-4.** [consultant's teaching session] clinique *f*. **-5.** [health centre] centre *m* médico-social OR d'hygiène sociale. **-6.** *Br* [of MP] permanence *f*.

clinical ['klɪnɪkl] *adj* **-1.** MED [lecture, tests] clinique. **-2.** *fig* [attitude] froid, aseptisé.

clinically ['klɪnɪklɪ] *adv* **-1.** MED cliniquement. **-2.** *fig* [act, speak] objectivement, froidement.

clinical psychologist *n* spécialiste *mf* en psychologie clinique.

clinical psychology *n* psychologie *f* clinique.

clinical thermometer *n* thermomètre *m* médical.

clinician [klɪ'nɪʃn] *n* clinicien *m*, -enne *f*.

clink [klɪŋk] ◇ *vt* faire tinter OR résonner; they ~ed (their) glasses (together) ils ont trinqué.
◇ *vi* tinter, résonner.
◇ *n* **-1.** [sound] tintement *m* (de verres). **-2.** [jail] *prison sl* prison *f*, taule *f*.

clinker ['klɪŋkəʳ] *n* **-1.** *(U)* [ash] mâchefer *m*, scories *fpl*. **-2.** [brick] brique *f* vitrifiée. **-3.** *inf Am* [mistake] gaffe *f*; MUS couac *m*; I pulled a real ~ j'ai fait une énorme gaffe; the orchestra hit some ~s l'orchestre a fait des canards. **-4.** *inf Am* [film, play] bide *m*.

clinker-built *adj* [boat] (bordé) à clin.

clinometer [klaɪ'nɒmɪtəʳ] *n* clinomètre *m*.

Clio ['klaɪəʊ] *pr n* Clio.

clip [klɪp] (*pt* & *pp* **clipped**, *cont* **clipping**) ◇ *vt* **-1.** [cut] couper (avec des ciseaux), rogner; [hedge] tailler; [animal] tondre; ~ the coupon out of the magazine découpez le bon dans le magazine; I clipped five seconds off my personal best j'ai amélioré mon record de cinq secondes; to ~ a bird's wings rogner les ailes d'un oiseau ❑ to ~ sb's wings laisser moins de liberté à qqn. **-2.** *Br* [ticket] poinçonner. **-3.** [attach] attacher; [papers] attacher (avec un trombone); [brooch] fixer. **-4.** *inf* [hit] frapper, cogner; to ~ sb round the ear flanquer une taloche à qqn; I clipped the gate as I drove in j'ai cogné OR heurté la barrière en rentrant la voiture. **-5.** *inf Am* [cheat] escroquer, rouler.
◇ *n* **-1.** [snip] petit coup *m* de ciseaux; to give sthg a ~ donner un coup de ciseaux à qqch. **-2.** [excerpt] CIN, RADIO & TV court extrait *m*; *Am* [from newspaper] coupure *f*. **-3.** [clasp] pince *f*; [for paper] trombone *m*, pince *f*; [for pipe] collier *m*, bague *f*. **-4.** [for bullets] chargeur *m*. **-5.** [brooch] clip *m*; [for hair] barrette *f*; [for tie] fixe-cravate *m*. **-6.** *inf* [blow] gifle *f*, taloche *f*; he got a ~ round the ear il s'est pris une taloche; at one ~ *Am fig* d'un seul coup. **-7.** *inf* [speed]: at a (good) ~ à vive allure, à toute vitesse.
◆ **clip on** ◇ *vt sep* [document] attacher (avec un trombone); [brooch, earrings] mettre.
◇ *vi* s'attacher OR se fixer avec une pince.
◆ **clip together** *vt sep* attacher.

clipboard ['klɪpbɔːd] *n* écritoire *f* à pince, clipboard *m*.

clip-clop [-klɒp] (*pt* & *pp* clip-clopped, *cont* clip-clopping) ◇ *n* & *onomat* clip-clop *m*; we heard the ~ of horses' hooves nous avons entendu les chevaux passer et le clip-clop de leurs sabots.
◇ *vi* faire clip-clop.

clip joint▽ *n boîte de nuit où l'on pratique des prix excessifs*.

clip-on *adj* amovible; ~ earrings clips *mpl (d'oreilles)*.
◆ **clip-ons** *npl* **-1.** [glasses] *verres teintés amovibles*. **-2.** [earrings] clips *mpl (d'oreilles)*.

clipped [klɪpt] *adj* **-1.** [speech, style] heurté, saccadé; a ~ manner of speech un débit heurté. **-2.** [hair] bien entretenu.

clipper ['klɪpəʳ] *n* **-1.** [ship] clipper *m*. **-2.** [horse] cheval *m* qui court vite.
◆ **clippers** *npl* [for nails] pince *f* à ongles; [for hair] tondeuse *f*; [for hedge] sécateur *m* à haie.

clippie *inf* ['klɪpɪ] *n Br* poinçonneuse *f (de bus)*.

clipping ['klɪpɪŋ] *n* [small piece] petit bout *m*, rognure *f*; [from newspaper] coupure *f* (de presse); grass ~s herbe coupée.

clique [kliːk] *n pej* clique *f*, coterie *f*.

cliquey ['kliːkɪ], **cliquish** ['kliːkɪʃ] *adj pej* exclusif, qui a l'esprit de clan.

clitic ['klɪtɪk] *adj* [enclitic] enclitique; [proclitic] proclitique.

clitoral ['klɪtərəl] *adj* clitoridien.

clitoris ['klɪtərɪs] *n* clitoris *m*.

cloak [kləʊk] ◇ *n* [cape] grande cape *f*; under the ~ of darkness *fig* sous le voile de la nuit; as a ~ for his illegal activities pour cacher OR masquer ses activités illégales.
◇ *vt* **-1.** *literal* revêtir d'un manteau. **-2.** *fig* masquer, cacher; ~ed with OR in secrecy/mystery empreint de secret/mystère.

cloak-and-dagger *adj*: a ~ story un roman d'espionnage.

cloakroom ['kləʊkrʊm] *n* **-1.** [for coats] vestiaire *m*; I left my coat in the ~ j'ai laissé mon manteau au vestiaire; ~ ticket numéro *m* de vestiaire. **-2.** *Br euph* [toilet - public] toilettes *fpl*; [- in home] cabinets *mpl*.

clobber *inf* ['klɒbəʳ] ◇ *vt* [hit] tabasser; *fig* [defeat] battre à plate couture.
◇ *n Br (U)* effets *mpl*, barda *m*.

cloche [klɒʃ] *n* cloche *f*.

clock [klɒk] ◇ *n* **-1.** [gen] horloge *f*; [small] pendule *f*; the church ~ chimed four l'horloge de l'église sonna quatre heures; it took us 15 minutes by the ~ il nous a fallu 15 minutes montre en main; to put a ~ back/forward retarder/avancer une horloge ‖ *fig*: you can't turn the ~ back ce qui est fait est fait; this law will put the ~ back a hundred years cette loi va nous ramener cent ans en arrière; they worked against OR to beat the ~ ils ont travaillé dur pour finir à temps; the jump-off was against the ~ EQUIT il y a eu un barrage contre la montre; we worked round the ~ nous avons travaillé 24 heures d'affilée; to sleep the ~ round faire le tour du cadran. **-2.** [taximeter] compteur *m*, taximètre *m*. **-3.** *inf* AUT [mileometer] ≃ compteur *m* kilométrique; a car with 30,000 miles on the ~ *inf* une voiture qui a 30 000 miles au compteur. **-4.** COMPUT horloge *f*.

◇ *vt* -**1.** [measure time] enregistrer; **winds ~ed at 50 miles per hour** des vents qui ont atteint 50 miles à l'heure || SPORT [runner] chronométrer; **she's ~ed five minutes for the mile** elle court le mile en cinq minutes. -**2.** ▽ *Br* [hit] flanquer un marron à.

◆ **clock in** *vi insep* pointer (à l'arrivée); **I ~ed in at 7 o'clock** j'ai pointé à 7 h.

◆ **clock off** *vi insep* pointer (à la sortie), dépointer.

◆ **clock on** = **clock in**.

◆ **clock out** = **clock off**.

◆ **clock up** *vt sep* [work] effectuer, accomplir; [victory] remporter; **she ~ed up 300 miles** AUT elle a fait 300 miles au compteur.

clock golf *n* jeu *m* de l'horloge.

clockmaker ['klɒk,meɪkəʳ] *n* horloger *m*, -ère *f*.

clock radio *n* radio-réveil *m*.

clock tower *n* tour *f* de l'horloge.

clock-watch *vi*: **the job is so boring that they are constantly ~ing** leur travail est tellement ennuyeux qu'ils passent leur temps à surveiller l'heure.

clock-watcher *n* tire-au-flanc *m inv*; **they're terrible ~s** ils passent leur temps à guetter l'heure (de sortie).

clockwise ['klɒkwaɪz] ◇ *adv* dans le sens des aiguilles d'une montre.

◇ *adj*: **in a ~ direction** dans le sens des aiguilles d'une montre.

clockwork ['klɒkwɜːk] ◇ *n* [of clock, watch] mouvement *m* (d'horloge); [of toy] mécanisme *m*, rouages *mpl*; **to go** OR **to run like ~** marcher comme sur des roulettes; **the office runs like ~** le travail au bureau est réglé comme du papier à musique.

◇ *adj* mécanique; **'A Clockwork Orange'** *Burgess, Kubrick* 'Orange mécanique'.

clod [klɒd] *n* -**1.** [of earth] motte *f* (de terre). -**2.** *inf* [idiot] imbécile *m*, crétin *m*.

clodhopper *inf* ['klɒd,hɒpəʳ] *n* -**1.** [clumsy person] balourd *m*, -e *f*. -**2.** *hum* [shoe] godillot *m*.

clodhopping *inf* ['klɒd,hɒpɪŋ] *adj* gauche, maladroit.

clog [klɒg] (*pt & pp* clogged, *cont* clogging) ◇ *vt* -**1.** [pipe] boucher, encrasser; [street] boucher, bloquer; [wheel] bloquer. -**2.** *fig* [hinder] entraver, gêner.

◇ *vi* se boucher.

◇ *n* [wooden] sabot *m*; [leather] sabot *m*.

◆ **clog up** ◇ *vt sep* = **clog** *vt*.

◇ *vi insep* = **clog** *vi*.

clog dance *n danse où les participants marquent le rythme avec leurs sabots*.

cloister ['klɔɪstəʳ] ◇ *n* cloître *m*.

◇ *vt* RELIG cloîtrer; *fig* éloigner OR isoler (du monde).

cloistered ['klɔɪstəd] *adj fig* [life] de reclus; **she leads a ~ life** elle mène une vie de recluse.

clone [kləʊn] ◇ *n* clone *m*.

◇ *vt* cloner.

cloning ['kləʊnɪŋ] *n* clonage *m*.

clonk [klɒŋk] ◇ *vi* faire un bruit sourd.

◇ *vt inf* cogner, frapper.

◇ *n* bruit *m* sourd.

close[1] [kləʊs] (*compar* closer, *superl* closest) ◇ *adj* -**1.** [near in space or time]: **the library is ~ to the school** la bibliothèque est près de l'école; **in ~ proximity to sthg** dans le voisinage immédiat de OR tout près de qqch; **they're very ~ in age** ils ont presque le même âge; **his death brought the war closer to home** c'est avec sa mort que nous avons vraiment pris conscience de la guerre; **too ~ for comfort** trop près; **we are ~ to an agreement** nous sommes presque arrivés à un accord; **at ~ intervals** à intervalles rapprochés; **at ~ range** à bout portant; **to be ~ at** OR **to hand** [shop, cinema etc] être tout près; [book, pencil etc] être à portée de main; **to be ~ to tears** être au bord des larmes; **I came ~ to thumping him one** *inf* j'ai bien failli lui en coller une; **he keeps things ~ to his chest** il ne fait guère de confidences; **to see sthg at ~ quarters** voir qqch de près; **to give sb a ~ shave** *literal* raser qqn de près; **that was a ~ shave** OR **thing** OR *Am* **call!** *inf* on l'a échappé belle!, on a eu chaud! -**2.** [in relationship] intime; **they're very ~ (friends)** ils sont très proches; **a ~ relative** un parent proche; **I'm very ~ to my sister** je suis très proche de ma sœur; **he has ~ ties with Israel** il a des rapports étroits avec Israël; **there's a ~ connection between the two things** il y a un rapport étroit entre les deux; **the President consulted his closest advisers** le président consulta ses conseillers les plus proches; **sources ~ to the royal family** des sources proches de la famille royale; **a subject ~ to my heart** un sujet qui me tient à cœur. -**3.** [continuous]: **they stay in ~ contact** ils restent en contact en permanence. -**4.** [in competition, race etc] serré; **it was a ~ contest** ce fut une lutte serrée. -**5.** [thorough, careful] attentif, rigoureux; **pay ~ attention to what she says** faites très attention OR prêtez une grande attention à ce qu'elle dit; **have a ~ look at these figures** examinez ces chiffres de près; **upon ~ examination** après un examen détaillé OR minutieux; **keep a ~ eye on the kids** surveillez les enfants de près; **I keep ~ control of the expenses** je contrôle étroitement les dépenses; **in ~ confinement** en détention surveillée; **under ~ arrest** aux arrêts forcés. -**6.** [roughly similar] proche; **his version of events was ~ to the truth** sa version des faits était très proche de la réalité; **he bears a ~ resemblance to his father** il ressemble beaucoup à son père; **it's the closest thing we've got to an operating theatre** c'est la pièce qui se rapproche le plus d'une salle d'opération. -**7.** [compact - handwriting, print] serré; [- grain] dense, compact; **in ~ formation** MIL en ordre serré. -**8.** *Br* [stuffy - room] mal aéré, qui manque de ventilation OR d'air; **it's very ~ in here** on manque vraiment d'air ici; **it's terribly ~ today** il fait très lourd aujourd'hui. -**9.** [secretive] renfermé, peu communicatif; **he's very ~ about his private life** il est très discret sur sa vie privée. -**10.** *inf* [stingy] avare, pingre. -**11.** LING [vowel] fermé.

◇ *adv* -**1.** [near] près; **don't come too ~** n'approche pas OR ne t'approche pas trop; **I live ~ to the river** j'habite près de la rivière; **did you win? — no, we didn't even come ~** avez-vous gagné? — non, loin de là; **they walked ~ behind us** ils nous suivaient de près; **she lives ~ by** elle habite tout près; **I looked at it ~ to** OR **up** je l'ai regardé de près; **~ together** serrés les uns contre les autres; **sit closer together!** serrez-vous! -**2.** [tight] étroitement, de près; **he held me ~** il m'a serré dans ses bras.

◇ *n* -**1.** [field] clos *m*. -**2.** *Br* [street] impasse *f*. -**3.** *Br* [of cathedral] enceinte *f*. -**4.** *Scot* allée *f*.

◆ **close on** *prep phr*: **it's ~ on 9 o'clock** il est presque 9 h; **she must be ~ on 50** elle doit friser la cinquantaine OR doit avoir près de 50 ans.

◆ **close to** *prep phr* [almost, nearly] presque; **the baby weighs ~ to 7 pounds** le bébé pèse presque 3 kilos et demi.

close[2] [kləʊz] ◇ *vt* -**1.** [shut - door, window, shop, book] fermer; **he ~d his eyes and went to sleep** il ferma les yeux et s'endormit || *fig*: **to ~ one's eyes to sthg** fermer les yeux sur qqch; **to ~ one's mind to sthg** refuser de penser à qqch; **she ~d her mind to anything new** elle s'est fermée à tout ce qui était neuf. -**2.** [opening, bottle] fermer, boucher; **we must ~ the gap between the rich and the poor** *fig* nous devons combler le fossé entre riches et pauvres. -**3.** [block - border, road] fermer; **they've ~d the airport** ils ont fermé l'aéroport. -**4.** [shut down - factory] fermer; **they plan to ~ more rural stations** ils ont l'intention de fermer d'autres petites gares de campagne. -**5.** [conclude] clore, mettre fin à; **she ~d the conference with a rallying call to the party faithful** elle termina la conférence en lançant un appel de solidarité aux fidèles du parti; **a neat way of closing the discussion** un habile moyen de clore la discussion; **the subject is now ~d** l'affaire est close. -**6.** COMM & FIN [account] arrêter, clore. -**7.** [settle - deal] conclure; **we ~d a deal with them last week** nous avons conclu un accord avec eux la semaine dernière. -**8.** [move closer together] serrer, rapprocher; **~ ranks!** MIL serrez les rangs!; **the party ~d ranks behind their leader** *fig* le parti a serré les rangs derrière le leader. -**9.** ELEC [circuit] fermer.

◇ *vi* -**1.** [shut - gate, window] fermer, se fermer; [- shop] fermer; **this window doesn't ~ properly** cette fenêtre ne ferme pas bien OR ferme mal; **the door ~d quietly behind them** la porte s'est refermée sans bruit derrière eux; **the bakery ~s on Fridays** la boulangerie ferme le vendredi; **the theatre ~s in August/at Christmas** le théâtre ferme en août/fait relâche le jour de Noël. -**2.** [wound, opening] se refermer; **the gap was closing fast** l'écart diminuait rapidement. -**3.** [cover, surround]: **the waves ~d over him** les vagues se refermèrent sur lui; **the onlookers ~d around us** un cercle de curieux se forma autour de nous; **my fingers ~d around the gun** mes doigts se resserrèrent sur le revolver. -**4.** [meeting] se terminer, prendre fin; [speaker] terminer, finir; **I ~d with a reference to Rimbaud** j'ai terminé par une référence à Rimbaud. -**5.** ST. EX: **the share index ~d two points down** l'indice (boursier) a clôturé en baisse de deux points.

◇ *n* fin *f*, conclusion *f*; **the concert came to a ~** le concert s'acheva; **the year drew to a ~** l'année s'acheva; **it's time to draw the meeting to a ~** il est temps de mettre fin à cette réunion; **at the ~ of day** à la tombée du jour; **towards the ~ of the century** vers la fin du siècle; **at ~ of play** [in cricket] à la fin du match.

◆ **close down** ◇ *vi insep* -**1.** [business, factory] fermer; **the shop had to ~ down** le magasin a dû fermer. -**2.** *Br* RADIO & TV terminer les émissions.

◇ *vt sep* [business, factory] fermer; **they had to ~ down their shop** ils ont dû fermer leur magasin.

◆ **close in** *vi insep* -**1.** [approach] approcher, se rapprocher; [encircle] cerner de près; **to ~ in on** OR **upon** se rapprocher de; **the hunters ~d in on their prey** les chasseurs se rapprochèrent de leur proie. -**2.** [evening, night] approcher, descendre; [darkness, fog] descendre; **the days are closing in** les jours raccourcissent; **darkness ~d in on us** la nuit nous enveloppa.

◆ **close off** *vt sep* isoler, fermer; **the area was ~d off to the public** le quartier était fermé au public; **some of the rooms in the house have been ~d off** certaines pièces de la maison ont été fermées.

◆ **close on** *vt insep* se rapprocher de; **we were closing on them fast** nous nous rapprochions d'eux rapidement.

◆ **close out** *vt sep Am* liquider *(avant fermeture)*.

◆ **close up** ◇ *vt sep* fermer; [opening, pipe] obturer, boucher; [wound] refermer, recoudre.

◇ *vi insep* [wound] se refermer.

◆ **close with** *vt insep* -**1.** [finalize agreement with] conclure un marché avec. -**2.** *lit* [fight with] engager la lutte OR le combat avec.

close-cropped *adj* [hair] (coupé) ras; [grass] ras.

closed [kləʊzd] *adj* -**1.** [shut - shop, museum etc] fermé; [- eyes] fermé, clos; [- opening, pipe] obturé, bouché; [- road] barré; [- economy, mind] fermé; **road ~ to traffic** route interdite à la circulation; **'~ on Tuesdays'** 'fermé le mardi'; THEAT 'relâche le mardi'; **we found the door ~** *fig* nous avons trouvé porte close ❑ **in ~ session** JUR à huis clos; **to do sthg behind ~ doors** faire qqch en cachette; **economics is a ~ book to me** *inf* je ne comprends rien à l'économie. -**2.** [restricted] exclusif; **a ~ society** un cercle fermé. -**3.** LING [syllable] couvert. -**4.** ELEC [circuit, switch] fermé.

closed circuit television *n* télévision *f* en circuit fermé.

closed-door *adj* privé; they held a ~ meeting ils ont tenu une réunion privée OR à huis clos.

closedown ['kləʊzdaʊn] *n* -**1.** [of shop] fermeture *f* (définitive). -**2.** *Br* RADIO & TV fin *f* des émissions.

closed primary *n aux États-Unis, élection primaire réservée aux membres d'un parti.*

closed set *n* ensemble *m* fermé.

closed shop *n* -**1.** [practice] monopole *m* d'embauche. -**2.** [establishment] *entreprise dans laquelle le monopole d'embauche est pratiqué.*

closefisted [,kləʊs'fɪstɪd] *adj* avare, pingre.

close-fitting [kləʊs-] *adj* ajusté, près du corps.

close-knit [kləʊs-] *adj fig* [community, family] très uni.

closely ['kləʊslɪ] *adv* -**1.** [near] de près; [tightly] en serrant fort; I held her ~ je l'ai serrée fort OR (tout) contre moi. -**2.** [carefully - watch] de près; [- study] minutieusement, de près; [- listen] attentivement. -**3.** [directly]: he's ~ related to him il est l'un de ses proches parents; ~ connected with sthg étroitement lié à qqch. -**4.** [evenly]: ~ contested elections élections très serrées OR très disputées.

closeness ['kləʊsnɪs] *n* -**1.** [nearness] proximité *f*. -**2.** [intimacy - of relationship, friendship, family] intimité *f*. -**3.** [compactness - of weave] texture *f* OR contexture *f* serrée; [- of print] resserrement *m (des caractères)*. -**4.** [similarity - of copy, translation] fidélité *f*. -**5.** [thoroughness - of examination] minutie *f*, rigueur *f*. -**6.** [of weather] lourdeur *f*; [of room] manque *m* d'air. -**7.** [stinginess] avarice *f*.

closeout ['kləʊzaʊt] *n Am* liquidation *f*.

close-range [kləʊs-] *adj* à courte portée.

close-run ['kləʊs-] = **close** *adj* **4**.

close season [kləʊs-] *n Br* HUNT fermeture *f* de la chasse; FISHING fermeture de la pêche; FTBL intersaison *f*.

close-set [kləʊs-] *adj* rapproché.

close-shaven [kləʊs-] *adj* rasé de près.

closet ['klɒzɪt] ◇ *n* -**1.** [cupboard] placard *m*, armoire *f*; [for hanging clothes] penderie *f*; *fig*: to come out of the ~ *inf* [gen] sortir de l'anonymat; [homosexual] ne plus cacher son homosexualité. -**2.** [small room] cabinet *m*. -**3.** [toilet]: (water) ~ cabinets *mpl*; [public] toilettes *fpl*.
◇ *vt* enfermer *(pour discuter)*; to be ~ed with sb être en tête à tête avec qqn.
◇ *comp* secret; she's a ~ gambler elle n'ose pas avouer qu'elle joue.

close-up [kləʊs-] ◇ *n* [photograph] gros plan *m*; [programme] portrait *m*, portrait-interview *m*; in ~ en gros plan.
◇ *adj* [shot, photograph, picture] en gros plan; a ~ lens une bonnette.

closing ['kləʊzɪŋ] ◇ *n* [of shop] fermeture *f*; [of meeting] clôture *f*; ST. EX clôture *f*.
◇ *adj* -**1.** [concluding] final, dernier; ~ remarks observations finales; ~ speech discours *m* de clôture. -**2.** [last] de fermeture; ~ date [for applications] date *f* limite de dépôt; [for project] date *f* de réalisation *(d'une opération)*. -**3.** ST. EX: ~ price cours *m* à la clôture.

closing time *n* heure *f* de fermeture; when is ~? à quelle heure fermez-vous?; ~! on ferme!

closure ['kləʊʒəʳ] *n* -**1.** [gen] fermeture *f*; [of factory, shop] fermeture *f* définitive. -**2.** [of meeting] clôture *f*; to move the ~ [in Parliament] demander la clôture; ~ rule POL *règle du Sénat américain limitant le temps de parole*. -**3.** [for container] fermeture *f*. -**4.** LING fermeture *f (d'une voyelle)*.

clot [klɒt] (*pt* & *pp* clotted, *cont* clotting)
◇ *vt* cailler, coaguler.
◇ *vi* (se) cailler, (se) coaguler.
◇ *n* -**1.** [of blood] caillot *m*; [of milk] caillot *m*, grumeau *m*; a ~ on the lung/on the brain une embolie pulmonaire/cérébrale; a blood ~, a ~ of blood un caillot de sang. -**2.** *inf Br* [fool] cruche *f*.

cloth [klɒθ] ◇ *n* -**1.** [material] tissu *m*, étoffe *f*; NAUT [sail] toile *f*, voile *f*; [for bookbinding] toile *f*; ~ of gold drap *m* d'or. -**2.** [for cleaning] chiffon *m*, linge *m*; [tablecloth] nappe *f*. -**3.** [clergy]: man of the ~ membre *m* du clergé.
◇ *comp* [clothing] de OR en tissu, de OR en étoffe.

clothbound ['klɒθbaʊnd] *adj* [book] relié toile.

cloth cap *n* casquette *f (symbole de la classe ouvrière britannique)*.

clothe [kləʊð] (*pt* & *pp* clothed OR *lit* clad [klæd]) *vt* habiller, vêtir; *fig* revêtir, couvrir; ~d in furs vêtu de fourrures; the countryside was ~d in snow *fig* la campagne était recouverte de neige.

cloth-eared *inf adj Br* dur de la feuille, sourdingue.

clothes [kləʊðz] *npl* -**1.** [garments] vêtements *mpl*, habits *mpl*; to put one's ~ on s'habiller; to take one's ~ off se déshabiller; with one's ~ on (tout) habillé; with one's ~ off déshabillé, (tout) nu; dressed in one's best ~ sur son trente et un, endimanché. -**2.** *Br* [bedclothes] draps *mpl*.

clothes basket *n* panier *m* à linge.

clothes brush *n* brosse *f* à habits.

clothes hanger *n* cintre *m*.

clotheshorse ['kləʊðzhɔːs, *pl* -hɔːsɪz] *n* -**1.** [for laundry] séchoir *m* à linge. -**2.** *fig* [model] mannequin *m*; she's such a ~ *pej* elle ne pense qu'à ses toilettes.

clothesline ['kləʊðzlaɪn] *n* corde *f* à linge.

clothes moth *n* mite *f*.

clothes peg *Br*, **clothespin** ['kləʊðzpɪn] *Am n* pince *f* à linge.

clothespole ['kləʊðzpəʊl], **clothesprop** ['kləʊðzprɒp] *n* support *m* pour corde à linge.

clothier ['kləʊðɪəʳ] *n* [cloth dealer, maker] drapier *m*; [clothes seller] marchand *m* de vêtements OR de confection.

clothing ['kləʊðɪŋ] ◇ *n (U)* -**1.** [garments] vêtements *mpl*, habits *mpl*; an article of ~ un vêtement. -**2.** [act of dressing] habillage *m*; [providing with garments] habillement *m*; RELIG [of monk, nun] prise *f* d'habit.
◇ *comp* [industry, trade] du vêtement, de l'habillement; [shop] de vêtements; ~ allowance indemnité *f* vestimentaire.

clotted cream ['klɒtɪd-] *n crème fraîche très épaisse typique du sud-ouest de l'Angleterre.*

clotting ['klɒtɪŋ] *n* caillement *m*, coagulation *f*.

cloture ['kləʊtʃəʳ] POL ◇ *n* clôture *f*; ~ rule *règle limitant le temps de parole au Sénat américain.*
◇ *vt* clôturer.

cloud [klaʊd] ◇ *n* -**1.** METEOR nuage *m*, nuée *f lit*; he resigned under a ~ [of suspicion] en butte aux soupçons, il a dû démissionner; [in disgrace] tombé en disgrâce, il a dû démissionner; to be on ~ nine être aux anges OR au septième ciel; to come down from the ~s revenir sur terre; to have one's head in the ~s être dans les nuages OR la lune; every ~ has a silver lining *prov* à quelque chose malheur est bon *prov*. -**2.** [of dust, smoke] nuage *m*; [of gas] nappe *f*; [of insects] nuée *f*. -**3.** [haze - on mirror] buée *f*; [- in liquid] nuage *m*; [- in marble] tache *f* noire.
◇ *vt* -**1.** [make hazy - mirror] embuer; [- liquid] rendre trouble; a ~ed sky un ciel couvert OR nuageux. -**2.** [confuse] obscurcir; don't ~ the issue ne brouillez pas les cartes. -**3.** [spoil - career, future] assombrir; [- reputation] ternir.
◇ *vi* -**1.** [sky] se couvrir (de nuages), s'obscurcir. -**2.** [face] s'assombrir.
◆ **cloud over** *vi insep* = **cloud** *vi*.

cloudbase ['klaʊdbeɪs] *n* plafond *m* de nuages.

cloudberry ['klaʊd,berɪ] (*pl* cloudberries) *n* [berry] (variété *f* de) framboise *f*; [bush] (variété *f* de) framboisier *m*.

cloudburst ['klaʊdbɜːst] *n* grosse averse *f*.

cloud-capped [-kæpt] *adj* couronné de nuages.

cloud-cuckoo-land *inf n Br*: they are living in ~ ils n'ont pas les pieds sur terre.

clouded ['klaʊdɪd] *adj* -**1.** = **cloudy 1**. -**2.** *fig* [expression] sombre, attristé; [reputation] terni; [judgement] altéré.

cloudiness ['klaʊdɪnɪs] *n* [of sky] nébulosité *f*; [of liquid] aspect *m* trouble; [of mirror] fait *m* d'être embué.

cloudless ['klaʊdlɪs] *adj* [sky] sans nuages; *fig* [days, future] sans nuages, serein.

cloudy ['klaʊdɪ] (*compar* cloudier, *superl* cloudiest) *adj* -**1.** METEOR nuageux, couvert; it will be ~ today le temps sera couvert aujourd'hui. -**2.** [liquid] trouble; [mirror] embué; [gem] taché, nuageux. -**3.** *fig* [confused] obscur, nébuleux; [gloomy] sombre, attristé.

clout *inf* [klaʊt] ◇ *n* -**1.** [blow] coup *m*; [with fist] coup *m* de poing. -**2.** *fig* [influence] influence *f*, poids *m*; to have OR to carry a lot of ~ avoir le bras long. -**3.** *Br dial* [cloth] chiffon *m*; [garment] vêtement *m*.
◇ *vt* frapper, cogner; [with fist] donner un coup de poing à, filer une taloche à.

clove [kləʊv] ◇ *pt* → **cleave**.
◇ *n* -**1.** [spice] clou *m* de girofle; [tree] giroflier *m*; oil of ~s essence *f* de girofle. -**2.** [of garlic] gousse *f*.

clove hitch *n* demi-clef *f*.

cloven ['kləʊvn] ◇ *pp* → **cleave**.
◇ *adj* fendu, fourchu; ~ foot OR hoof sabot *m* fendu.

cloven-footed, **cloven-hoofed** [-huːft] *adj* [animal] aux sabots fendus; [devil] aux pieds fourchus.

clover ['kləʊvəʳ] *n* trèfle *m*; to be in ~ *fig* être comme un coq en pâte.

cloverleaf ['kləʊvəliːf] (*pl* cloverleaves [-liːvz]) *n* BOT feuille *f* de trèfle; [road junction] (carrefour *m* en) trèfle *m*.

clown [klaʊn] ◇ *n* [entertainer] clown *m*; *fig* [fool] pitre *m*, imbécile *mf*; to make a ~ of oneself se rendre ridicule.
◇ *vi* [joke] faire le clown; [act foolishly] faire le pitre OR l'imbécile.
◆ **clown about**, **clown around** = **clown** *vi*.

clownery ['klaʊnərɪ], **clowning** ['klaʊnɪŋ] *n (U)* clowneries *fpl*, pitreries *fpl*.

cloy [klɔɪ] *vt literal* & *fig* écœurer.

cloying ['klɔɪɪŋ] *adj* écœurant.

club [klʌb] (*pt* & *pp* clubbed, *cont* clubbing)
◇ *n* -**1.** [association] club *m*, cercle *m*; [nightclub] boîte *f* de nuit; the ~ scene *milieux branchés fréquentant les boîtes de nuit*; a tennis ~ un club de tennis; join the ~! *hum* bienvenue au club!, vous n'êtes pas le seul!; she's in the ~ *inf Br euph* elle a un polichinelle dans le tiroir. -**2.** [weapon] matraque *f*, massue *f*. -**3.** SPORT: (golf) ~ club *m* (de golf). -**4.** CARDS trèfle *m*; ~s trèfles *mpl*; the nine of ~s le neuf de trèfle; ~s are trumps atout trèfle; to play a ~ jouer (un OR du) trèfle.
◇ *vt* matraquer, frapper avec une massue; he was clubbed to death il a été matraqué à mort.
◆ **club together** *vi insep* [share cost] se cotiser.

CLUB:
Les «clubs» britanniques sont des lieux de rencontre et de détente très fermés, traditionnellement interdits aux femmes; ils jouent un rôle important dans la vie sociale des milieux aisés en Grande-Bretagne.

clubbable ['klʌbəbl] *adj Br dated* sociable.

clubber *inf* ['klʌbəʳ] *n*: he's a real ~ il adore aller en boîte.

clubby ['klʌbɪ] (*compar* clubbier, *superl* clubbiest) *adj* [sociable] sociable; [cliquey] qui a l'esprit de club.

club class *n* classe *f* club.

clubfoot [,klʌb'fʊt] (*pl* clubfeet [-'fiːt]) *n* pied *m* bot.

clubfooted [,klʌb'fʊtɪd] *adj*: to be ~ avoir un pied bot.

clubhouse ['klʌbhaʊs, *pl* -haʊzɪz] *n* club *m*.

clubland ['klʌblænd] *n Br* [nightclubs] *quartier des boîtes de nuit*; [gentlemen's clubs] *quartier où se trouvent la plupart des clubs privés.*

clubman ['klʌbmən] (*pl* clubmen [-mən]) *n* [member of club] membre *m* d'un club; [man about town] homme *m* du monde, mondain *m*.

clubroom ['klʌbrʊm] *n* salle *f* de club OR de réunion.

clubroot ['klʌbru:t] *n* [disease of plants] hernie *f* du chou.

club sandwich *n Am* sandwich *m* mixte *(à trois étages)*.

cluck [klʌk] ◇ *vi* [hen, person] glousser; to ~ over sb *fig* être aux petits soins pour OR avec qqn; she ~ed in disapproval elle a claqué sa langue de désapprobation.
◇ *n* -**1.** [of hen] gloussement *m*; [of person - in pleasure] gloussement *m*; [- in disapproval] claquement *m* de langue. -**2.** *inf* [fool] idiot *m*, -e *f*; you dumb ~! c'est malin!

clue [klu:] *n* [gen] indice *m*, indication *f*; [in crosswords] définition *f*; give me a ~ mettez-moi sur la piste; where's John? — I haven't a ~! où est John? — je n'en ai pas la moindre idée OR je n'en ai aucune idée!; he's useless at cooking, he hasn't got a ~! il est nul en cuisine, il n'y connaît absolument rien!
◆ **clue in** *inf vt sep* [person] mettre au courant.
◆ **clue up** *inf vt sep* [person] renseigner, mettre au courant.

clued up [klu:d-] *adj* informé; to be ~ on sthg: she's really ~ on computers elle s'y connaît en informatique.

clueless *inf* ['klu:lɪs] *adj Br pej* qui ne sait rien de rien.

clump [klʌmp] ◇ *n* -**1.** [cluster - of bushes] massif *m*; [- of trees] bouquet *m*; [- of hair, grass] touffe *f*. -**2.** [mass - of earth] motte *f*. -**3.** [sound] bruit *m* sourd.
◇ *vi* [walk]: to ~ (about OR around) marcher d'un pas lourd.
◇ *vt* [gather]: to ~ (together) grouper.

clumsily ['klʌmzɪlɪ] *adv* [awkwardly] maladroitement; [tactlessly] sans tact.

clumsiness ['klʌmzɪnɪs] *n* -**1.** [lack of coordination] maladresse *f*, gaucherie *f*. -**2.** [awkwardness - of tool] caractère *m* peu pratique; [- of design] lourdeur *f*. -**3.** [tactlessness] gaucherie *f*, manque *m* de tact.

clumsy ['klʌmzɪ] *adj* -**1.** [uncoordinated - person] maladroit, gauche. -**2.** [awkward - tool] peu commode OR pratique; [- design] lourd, disgracieux; [- painting] maladroit; [- style] lourd, maladroit. -**3.** [tactless] gauche, malhabile; he made a ~ apology il s'est excusé de façon gauche.

clung [klʌŋ] *pt & pp* → **cling**.

clunk [klʌŋk] ◇ *n* [sound] bruit *m* sourd.
◇ *vi* faire un bruit sourd.

clunker *inf* ['klʌŋkə^r] *n Am* [car] tas *m* de ferraille.

cluster ['klʌstə^r] ◇ *n* -**1.** [of fruit] grappe *f*; [of dates] régime *m*; [of flowers] touffe *f*; [of trees] bouquet *m*; [of stars] amas *m*; [of diamonds] entourage *m*. -**2.** [group - of houses] groupe *m*; [- of people] rassemblement *m*, groupe *m*; [- of bees] essaim *m*. -**3.** LING groupe *m*, agglomérat *m*.
◇ *vi* -**1.** [people] se grouper; a group of children ~ed around their teacher un groupe d'enfants s'est formé autour du professeur. -**2.** [things] former un groupe; pretty cottages ~ed around the church l'église était entourée de petites maisons coquettes; to ~ together se grouper.

cluster bomb *n* bombe *f* à fragmentation.

clutch [klʌtʃ] ◇ *vt* -**1.** [hold tightly] serrer fortement, étreindre. -**2.** [seize] empoigner, se saisir de.
◇ *vi*: to ~ at sthg *literal* se cramponner à qqch, s'agripper à qqch; *fig* se cramponner à qqch, se raccrocher à qqch ❑ he's ~ing at straws il se raccroche à n'importe quoi.
◇ *n* -**1.** [grasp] étreinte *f*, prise *f*. -**2.** AUT [mechanism] embrayage *m*; [pedal] pédale *f* d'embrayage; to let in the ~ embrayer; to let out the ~ débrayer. -**3.** [cluster of eggs] couvée *f*; *fig* série *f*, ensemble *m*. -**4.** *inf Am* [crisis] crise *f*; if you're in a ~... si tu es dans le pétrin... -**5.** *Am* [bag] pochette *f (sac à main)*.
◆ **clutches** *npl fig* [control] influence *f*; to have sb in one's ~es tenir qqn en son pouvoir; to fall into sb's ~es tomber dans les griffes de qqn; he escaped the ~es of the law il a échappé aux griffes de la justice.

clutch bag *n* [handbag] pochette *f (sac à main)*.

clutter ['klʌtə^r] ◇ *n* -**1.** [mess] désordre *m*; the house is in a bit of a ~ la maison est plutôt en désordre. -**2.** [disordered objects] désordre *m*, fouillis *m*.
◇ *vt*: ~ (up) [room] mettre en désordre; a desk ~ed with papers un bureau encombré de papiers; his mind was ~ed with useless facts son esprit était encombré d'informations inutiles.

Clytemnestra [ˌklaɪtɪm'nestrə] *pr n* Clytemnestre.

cm *(written abbr of* centimetre) cm.

CNAA *(abbr of* Council for National Academic Awards) *pr n organisme non universitaire délivrant des diplômes en Grande-Bretagne*.

CND *(abbr of* Campaign for Nuclear Disarmament) *pr n en Grande-Bretagne, mouvement pour le désarmement nucléaire*.

Cnut [kə'nju:t] = **Canute**.

co- [kəʊ] *in cpds* co-; ~worker collègue *mf*; he's her ~star il partage l'affiche avec elle.

c/o *(written abbr of* care of) a/s.

Co. [kəʊ] -**1.** *(written abbr of* company) Cie. -**2.** *written abbr of* county.

CO ◇ *n* -**1.** *abbr of* commanding officer. -**2.** *abbr of* conscientious objector.
◇ *written abbr of* Colorado.

coach [kəʊtʃ] ◇ *n* -**1.** [tutor] répétiteur *m*, -trice *f*; SPORT [trainer] entraîneur *m*, -euse *f*; [ski instructor] moniteur *m*, -trice *f*. -**2.** [bus] car *m*, autocar *m*; *Br* RAIL voiture *f*, wagon *m*; [carriage] carrosse *m*; (stage) ~ diligence *f*, coche *m*.
◇ *comp* [driver] de car; [tour, trip] en car.
◇ *vt* [tutor] donner des leçons particulières à; SPORT entraîner; to ~ sb in maths/in English donner des leçons de math/d'anglais à qqn; they employed a tutor to ~ him for the exam ils ont fait appel à un professeur particulier pour le préparer à l'examen.
◇ *vi* [tutor] donner des leçons particulières; SPORT être entraîneur.

coach-and-four *n* carrosse *m* à quatre chevaux.

coach bolt *n* boulon *m* d'ancrage.

coachbuilder ['kəʊtʃˌbɪldə^r] *n* carrossier *m*.

coachbuilt ['kəʊtʃbɪlt] *adj* construit sur mesure.

coach house *n* remise *f (pour carrosse ou voiture)*.

coaching ['kəʊtʃɪŋ] *n* -**1.** SCH leçons *fpl* particulières. -**2.** SPORT entraînement *m*.

coachload ['kəʊtʃləʊd] *n*: a ~ of tourists un autocar OR car plein de touristes.

coachman ['kəʊtʃmən] *(pl* coachmen [-mən]) *n* cocher *m*.

coach park *n* emplacement *m* (de parking) réservé aux autocars.

coach party *n esp Br* excursion *f* en car.

coach station *n Br* gare *f* routière.

coachwork ['kəʊtʃwɜ:k] *n* carrosserie *f*.

coadjutant [kəʊ'ædʒʊtənt] *n* assistant *m*, -e *f*, aide *mf*.

coagulant [kəʊ'ægjʊlənt] *n* coagulant *m*.

coagulate [kəʊ'ægjʊleɪt] ◇ *vi* (se) coaguler.
◇ *vt* coaguler.

coagulation [kəʊˌægjʊ'leɪʃn] *n* coagulation *f*.

coal [kəʊl] ◇ *n* -**1.** [gen] charbon *m*; a piece OR lump of ~ un morceau de charbon ❑ he was treading on hot ~s il était sur des charbons ardents. -**2.** INDUST houille *f*; soft ~ houille grasse.
◇ *comp* [bunker, cellar, chute] à charbon; [depot, fire] de charbon; ~ industry industrie *f* houillère; ~ seam couche *f* houillère, gisement *m* houiller.
◇ *vt* [supply with coal] fournir OR ravitailler en charbon; NAUT charbonner.
◇ *vi* NAUT charbonner.

coal black ◇ *n* noir *m (couleur)*.
◇ *adj* noir comme du charbon.

coal-burning *adj* à charbon, qui marche au charbon.

coaldust ['kəʊldʌst] *n* poussier *m* OR poussière *f* de charbon.

coaler ['kəʊlə^r] *n* charbonnier *m (navire ou train)*.

coalesce [ˌkəʊə'les] *vi* s'unir (en un groupe), se fondre (ensemble).

coalescence [ˌkəʊə'lesns] *n* fusion *f*, union *f*.

coalface ['kəʊlfeɪs] *n* front *m* de taille.

coalfield ['kəʊlfi:ld] *n* bassin *m* houiller, gisement *m* de houille.

coal-fired *adj* à charbon, qui marche au charbon.

coalfish ['kəʊlfɪʃ] *(pl inv* OR coalfishes) *n* lieu *m* noir, colin *m*.

coal gas *n* gaz *m* de houille.

coalhole ['kəʊlhəʊl] *n* petite cave *f* à charbon.

coaling station ['kəʊlɪŋ-] *n* dépôt *m* de charbon.

coalition [ˌkəʊə'lɪʃn] *n* coalition *f*; ~ government gouvernement *m* de coalition.

coalman ['kəʊlmæn] *(pl* coalmen [-men]) *n* charbonnier *m*, marchand *m* de charbon.

coal merchant = **coalman**.

coalmine ['kəʊlmaɪn] *n* mine *f* de charbon, houillère *f*.

coalminer ['kəʊlˌmaɪnə^r] *n* mineur *m*.

coalmining ['kəʊlˌmaɪnɪŋ] *n* charbonnage *m*.

coal oil *n Am* kérosène *m*, pétrole *m* (lampant).

coalpit ['kəʊlpɪt] *n* mine *f* de charbon, houillère *f*.

coal scuttle *n* seau *m* à charbon.

coal tar *n* coaltar *m*, goudron *m* de houille.

coal tit *n* mésange *f* noire.

coarse [kɔ:s] *adj* -**1.** [rough in texture] gros, grossier; ~ cloth drap grossier; ~ linen grosse toile; ~ salt gros sel; ~ skin peau rude; ~ weave texture grossière; ~ hair cheveux épais. -**2.** [vulgar - person, behaviour, remark, joke] grossier, vulgaire; [- laugh] gros, gras; [- accent] commun, vulgaire. -**3.** [inferior - food, drink] ordinaire, commun; ~ red wine vin rouge ordinaire.

coarse fishing *n* pêche *f* à la ligne en eau douce.

coarse-grained *adj* à gros grain.

coarsely ['kɔ:slɪ] *adv* -**1.** [roughly] grossièrement; ~ woven de texture grossière. -**2.** [uncouthly - speak] vulgairement, grossièrement; [- laugh] grassement; [vulgarly] indécemment, crûment.

coarsen ['kɔ:sn] ◇ *vi* -**1.** [texture] devenir rude OR grossier. -**2.** [person] devenir grossier OR vulgaire; [features] s'épaissir.
◇ *vt* -**1.** [texture] rendre rude OR grossier. -**2.** [person, speech] rendre grossier OR vulgaire; [features] épaissir.

coarseness ['kɔ:snɪs] *n* -**1.** [of texture] rudesse *f*. -**2.** [uncouthness] manque *m* de savoir-vivre; [vulgarity] grossièreté *f*, vulgarité *f*.

coast [kəʊst] ◇ *n* -**1.** côte *f*; the ~ le littoral; off the ~ of Ireland au large des côtes irlandaises; broadcast from ~ to ~ diffusé dans tout le pays ❑ the ~ is clear *inf* la voie est libre. -**2.** *Am* [act of coasting] descente *f* en roue libre.
◇ *vi* [vehicle] avancer en roue libre; NAUT caboter; the car ~ed along/down the street la voiture avançait le long de la rue/descendait la rue en roue libre; he ~ed through the exam *inf fig* il a eu l'examen les doigts dans le nez.

coastal ['kəʊstl] *adj* littoral, côtier; ~ traffic navigation *f* côtière, cabotage *m*; ~ waters eaux *fpl* littorales.

coaster ['kəʊstə^r] *n* -**1.** [protective mat - for glass] dessous *m* de verre; [- for bottle] dessous *m* de bouteille; [stand, tray] présentoir *m* à bouteilles. -**2.** NAUT [ship] caboteur *m*. -**3.** *Am* = **roller coaster**.

coastguard ['kəʊstgɑ:d] *n* -**1.** [organization] ≃ gendarmerie *f* maritime. -**2.** *Br* [person] membre *m* de la gendarmerie maritime; HIST garde-côte *m*.

coastline ['kəʊstlaɪn] *n* littoral *m*.

coat [kəʊt] ◇ *n* -**1.** [overcoat] manteau *m*; [man's overcoat] manteau *m*, pardessus *m*; [jacket] veste *f*; ~ **of mail** cotte *f* de mailles || HERALD: ~ **of arms** blason *m*, armoiries *fpl*. -**2.** [of animal] pelage *m*, poil *m*; [of horse] robe *f*. -**3.** [covering -of dust, paint] couche *f*.
◇ *vt* -**1.** [cover] couvrir, revêtir; [with paint, varnish] enduire; **the shelves were ~ed with dust** les étagères étaient recouvertes de poussière; **my shoes were ~ed with mud** mes chaussures étaient couvertes de boue; **a ~ed tongue** MED une langue chargée. -**2.** CULIN: **to ~ sthg with flour/sugar** saupoudrer qqch de farine/de sucre; **to ~ sthg with chocolate** enrober qqch de chocolat; **to ~ sthg with egg** dorer qqch à l'œuf.

coatdress ['kəʊtdres] *n* robe-manteau *f*.

-coated [kəʊtɪd] *in cpds*: **sugar~ almonds** dragées *fpl*.

coat hanger *n* cintre *m*.

coating ['kəʊtɪŋ] *n* couche *f*; [on pan] revêtement *m*.

coatrack ['kəʊtræk], **coatstand** ['kəʊtstænd] *n* portemanteau *m*.

coat tails *npl* queue *f* de pie *(costume)*; **to ride on sb's ~** profiter de l'influence OR de la position de qqn; **she hangs on his ~** elle est pendue à ses basques.

coauthor [kəʊ'ɔːθəʳ] *n* coauteur *m*.

coax [kəʊks] *vt* cajoler, enjôler; **to ~ sb into doing sthg: he ~ed us into going** à force de nous cajoler, il nous a persuadés d'y aller; **I ~ed the money out of him** j'ai obtenu l'argent de lui par des cajoleries; **he ~ed the box open with a screwdriver** il est parvenu à ouvrir la boîte en faisant levier avec un tournevis.

coaxial [ˌkəʊ'æksɪəl] *adj* coaxial.

coaxing ['kəʊksɪŋ] ◇ *n (U)* cajolerie *f*, cajoleries *fpl*; **after a lot of ~, he agreed** il s'est fait prier avant d'accepter.
◇ *adj* enjôleur, cajoleur.

cob [kɒb] *n* -**1.** [horse] cob *m*. -**2.** [swan] cygne *m* mâle. -**3.** [of corn] épi *m*. -**4.** [of coal] briquette *f* de charbon; [of bread] pain *m*. -**5.** *Br* [nut] noisette *f*. -**6.** CONSTR torchis *m*, pisé *m*.

cobalt ['kəʊbɔːlt] *n* cobalt *m*; ~ **60** cobalt 60, cobalt radioactif.

cobalt blue ◇ *adj* bleu de cobalt.
◇ *n* bleu *m* de cobalt.

cobalt bomb *n* bombe *f* au cobalt.

cobber *inf* ['kɒbəʳ] *n Austr* copain *m*, pote *m*.

cobble ['kɒbl] ◇ *n* [stone] pavé *m*.
◇ *vt* paver.
◆ **cobble together** *vt sep* bricoler, concocter; **they ~d a compromise together** ils ont bricolé un compromis.

cobbled ['kɒbld] *adj* pavé.

cobbler ['kɒbləʳ] *n* -**1.** [shoemender] cordonnier *m*. -**2.** *Am* [cake] tourte *f* aux fruits; [drink] (sorte *f* de) punch *m*.
◆ **cobblers**▽ *n pl Br* couilles *fpl*; **that's a load of ~s!** *fig* c'est de la connerie!

cobblestone ['kɒblstəʊn] *n* pavé *m (rond)*.

cobnut ['kɒbnʌt] *n* noisette *f*, aveline *f*.

COBOL ['kəʊbɒl] (*abbr of* **common ordinary business oriented language**) *n* COBOL *m*.

cobra ['kəʊbrə] *n* cobra *m*.

cobweb ['kɒbweb] *n* toile *f* d'araignée; **I'm going for a walk to clear away the ~s** OR **to blow the ~s away** *fig* je vais faire un tour pour me rafraîchir les idées.

cobwebbed ['kɒbwebd] *adj* couvert de toiles d'araignée.

coca ['kəʊkə] *n* [shrub] coca *m*; [leaf substance] coca *f*.

Coca-Cola® *n* Coca® *m*, Coca-Cola® *m*.

cocaine [kəʊ'keɪn] ◇ *n* cocaïne *f*.
◇ *comp*: ~ **addict** OR **freak** *inf* cocaïnomane *mf*; ~ **addiction** cocaïnomanie *f*.

coccus ['kɒkəs] (*pl* cocci [-ksaɪ]) *n* coccidie *f*.

coccyx ['kɒksɪks] (*pl* coccyges [ˌkɒk'saɪdʒiːz]) *n* coccyx *m*.

Cochin China ['kɒˌtʃɪn-] *pr n* Cochinchine *f*; **in ~** en Cochinchine.

cochineal ['kɒtʃɪniːl] *n* [insect] cochenille *f*; [dye] cochenille *f* des teinturiers, carmin *m*.

cochlea ['kɒklɪə] (*pl* cochleae [-lɪiː] OR cochleas) *n* cochlée *f*, limaçon *m*.

cock [kɒk] ◇ *n* -**1.** [rooster] coq *m*; [male bird] (oiseau *m*) mâle *m*; **he thinks he's ~ of the walk** il se croit sorti de la cuisse de Jupiter. -**2.** [tap] robinet *m*. -**3.** [of gun] chien *m*; **at full ~** armé. -**4.** ▼ [penis] bitte *f*, bite *f*. -**5.** ▽ *Br* [nonsense] conneries *fpl*. -**6.** [tilt] inclinaison *f*, aspect *m* penché; **a ~ of the head** une inclinaison de la tête. -**7.** *inf Br* [term of address] pote *m*; **all right, ~?** ça va, mon pote? -**8.** AGR [of hay] meulon *m*.
◇ *vt* -**1.** [gun] armer. -**2.** [raise]: **the dog ~ed its ears** le chien a dressé les oreilles; **she ~ed an ear towards the door** *fig* elle a tendu une oreille du côté de la porte; **keep an eye ~ed on the kids** tenez les enfants à l'œil; **the dog ~ed its leg** le chien a levé la patte ❑ **to ~ a snook at sb** *inf Br* faire un pied de nez à qqn. -**3.** [head, hat] pencher, incliner; [thumb] tendre. -**4.** [hay] mettre en meulons.
◆ **cock up**▽ *Br* ◇ *vt sep* saloper, faire foirer.
◇ *vi insep*: **he's ~ed up again** il a encore tout fait foirer.

cockade [kɒ'keɪd] *n* cocarde *f*.

cock-a-doodle-doo [ˌkɒkəduːdl'duː] *n* & *onomat* cocorico.

cock-a-hoop *inf adj* fier comme Artaban.

cock-a-leekie *n potage de poulet et de poireaux*.

cock-and-bull story *n* histoire *f* à dormir debout.

cockatoo [ˌkɒkə'tuː] *n* cacatoès *m*.

cockchafer ['kɒkˌtʃeɪfəʳ] *n* hanneton *m*.

cockcrow ['kɒkkrəʊ] *n* aube *f*; **at ~** au chant du coq.

cocked hat *n* tricorne *m*; **to knock sthg into a ~** surpasser qqch.

cockerel ['kɒkrəl] *n* jeune coq *m*.

cocker spaniel ['kɒkəʳ-] *n* cocker *m*.

cockeyed *inf* ['kɒkaɪd] *adj* -**1.** [cross-eyed] qui louche. -**2.** [crooked] de travers. -**3.** [absurd - idea, plan] absurde; [- story] qui ne tient pas debout. -**4.** [drunk] pompette.

cockfight ['kɒkfaɪt] *n* combat *m* de coqs.

cockfighting ['kɒkˌfaɪtɪŋ] *n (U)* combats *mpl* de coqs.

cockiness ['kɒkɪnɪs] *n* impertinence *f*.

cockle ['kɒkl] ◇ *n* -**1.** [shellfish] coque *f*. -**2.** [in cloth] faux pli *m*; [in paper] froissure *f*, pliure *f*. -**3.** *fig*: **it warmed the ~s of his heart** cela lui a réchauffé le cœur.
◇ *vt* [paper] froisser; [cloth] chiffonner.
◇ *vi* [paper] se froisser; [cloth] se chiffonner.

cockleshell ['kɒklʃel] *n* [shell] coquille *f*; [boat] coque *f*.

Cockney ['kɒknɪ] ◇ *n* -**1.** [person] cockney *mf* *(Londonien né dans le «East End»)*. -**2.** LING cockney *m*.
◇ *adj* cockney.

cockpit ['kɒkpɪt] *n* -**1.** [of plane] cabine *f* de pilotage, cockpit *m*; [of racing car] poste *m* du pilote; [of yacht] cockpit *m*. -**2.** [in cockfighting] arène *f*; *fig* arènes *fpl*.

cockroach ['kɒkrəʊtʃ] *n* cafard *m*, blatte *f*.

cockscomb ['kɒkskəʊm] *n* -**1.** [of rooster] crête *f*. -**2.** BOT crête-de-coq *f*.

cock sparrow *n* moineau *m* mâle.

cocksucker▼ ['kɒkˌsʌkəʳ] *n* -**1.** *literal* suceur *m*, -euse *f*. -**2.** [despicable person] enculé *m*, -e *f*.

cocksure [ˌkɒk'ʃɔːʳ] *adj pej* suffisant.

cocktail ['kɒkteɪl] *n* [mixed drink] cocktail *m* *(boisson)*; [gen - mixture of things] mélange *m*, cocktail *m*; **fruit ~** salade *f* de fruits.

cocktail bar *n* bar *m (dans un hôtel, un aéroport)*.

cocktail dress *n* robe *f* de cocktail.

cocktail lounge *n* bar *m (dans un hôtel, un aéroport)*.

cocktail onion *n* petit oignon *m* (à apéritif).

cocktail party *n* cocktail *m (fête)*.

cocktail sausage *n* petite saucisse *f* (à apéritif).

cocktail shaker *n* shaker *m*.

cocktail stick *n* fouet *m* (à champagne).

cockteaser▼ ['kɒkˌtiːzəʳ] *n pej* allumeuse *f*.

cock-up▽ *n Br*: **it was a ~** ça a foiré; **he made a ~ of his exam** il s'est planté à l'examen.

cocky *inf* ['kɒkɪ] (*compar* cockier, *superl* cockiest) *adj* suffisant, qui a du toupet.

cocoa ['kəʊkəʊ] *n* -**1.** [powder, drink] cacao *m*. -**2.** [colour] marron *m* clair.

cocoa bean *n* graine *f* de cacao.

cocoa butter *n* beurre *m* de cacao.

coconut ['kəʊkənʌt] *n* noix *f* de coco; ~ **milk** lait *m* de coco; **desiccated ~** noix *f* de coco séchée.

coconut matting *n* tapis *m* en fibres de noix de coco.

coconut oil *n* huile *f* de coco.

coconut palm *n* cocotier *m*.

coconut shy *n* jeu *m* de massacre *pr*.

cocoon [kə'kuːn] ◇ *n* cocon *m*; *fig*: **wrapped in a ~ of blankets** emmitouflé dans des couvertures; **he felt safe in his ~ of solitude** enveloppé dans sa solitude, il se sentait à l'abri.
◇ *vt* [wrap] envelopper avec soin; [overprotect - child] couver.

cocooned [kə'kuːnd] *adj* enfermé, cloîtré.

cod [kɒd] (*pl inv* OR cods) *n* [fish] morue *f*; CULIN: **dried ~** merluche *f*, morue; **fresh ~** morue fraîche, cabillaud *m*; **the ~ war** la guerre de la morue *(série de conflits ayant opposé la Grande-Bretagne et l'Islande au sujet de zones de pêche islandaises)*.

COD (*abbr of* **cash on delivery**) *adv*: **to send sthg ~** envoyer qqch contre remboursement.

coda ['kəʊdə] *n lit* & MUS coda *f*.

coddle ['kɒdl] *vt* -**1.** [pamper - child] dorloter, choyer. -**2.** CULIN (faire) cuire à feu doux; **a ~d egg** un œuf à la coque.

code [kəʊd] ◇ *n* -**1.** [cipher] code *m*, chiffre *m*; BIOL & COMPUT code *m*; **a message in ~** un message chiffré OR codé. -**2.** [statement of rules] code *m*; ~ **of conduct/of honour** code de conduite/de l'honneur; ~ **of ethics** [gen] sens *m* des valeurs morales, moralité *f*; [professional] déontologie *f*; ~ **of practice** [gen] déontologie *f*; [rules] règlements *mpl* et usages *mpl*. -**3.** [postcode] code *m* postal. -**4.** [dialling code] code *m*, indicatif *m*.
◇ *vt* [message] coder, chiffrer.

code book *n* code *m*.

codeine ['kəʊdiːn] *n* codéine *f*.

code name *n* nom *m* de code.

code-named *adj* qui porte le nom de code de.

codeword ['kəʊdwɜːd] *n* [password] mot *m* de passe; [name] mot *m* codé.

codex ['kəʊdeks] (*pl* codices [-dɪsiːz]) *n* volume *m* de manuscrits anciens.

codfish ['kɒdfɪʃ] (*pl inv* OR codfishes) *n* morue *f*.

codger *inf* ['kɒdʒəʳ] *n* bonhomme *m*; **he's a bad-tempered old ~** c'est un vieux bonhomme bourru.

codices ['kəʊdɪsiːz] *pl* → **codex**.

codicil ['kɒdɪsɪl] *n* codicille *m*.

codification [ˌkəʊdɪfɪ'keɪʃn] *n* codification *f*.

codify ['kəʊdɪfaɪ] (*pt* & *pp* codified) *vt* codifier.

coding ['kəʊdɪŋ] *n* [of message] chiffrage *m*; COMPUT codage *m*; ~ **line** ligne *f* de programmation; ~ **sequence** séquence *f* programmée.

cod-liver oil *n* huile *f* de foie de morue.

codpiece ['kɒdpiːs] *n* braguette *f*.

codriver ['kəʊˌdraɪvəʳ] *n* [in rally, race] copilote *m*; [of bus, coach] deuxième chauffeur *m*.

codswallop *inf* ['kɒdzˌwɒləp] *n (U) Br* bêtises *fpl*, âneries *fpl*.

co-ed [-'ed] ◇ *adj abbr of* **coeducational**.
◇ *n* -**1.** *Am* [female student] *étudiante d'un établissement mixte*. -**2.** *Br* (*abbr of* **coeducational school**) école *f* mixte.

co-edit *vt* coéditer.

co-edition *n* coédition *f*.
co-editor *n* coéditeur *m*.
co-education *n* éducation *f* mixte.
co-educational *adj* mixte.
coefficient [ˌkəʊɪˈfɪʃnt] *n* coefficient *m*; ~ of expansion PHYS coefficient de dilatation.
coelacanth [ˈsiːləkænθ] *n* cœlacanthe *m*.
coeliac *Br*, **celiac** *Am* [ˈsiːlɪæk] *adj* cœliaque; ~ disease maladie *f* cœliaque.
coequal [kəʊˈiːkwəl] ◇ *adj* égal.
◇ *n* égal *m*, -e *f*.
coerce [kəʊˈɜːs] *vt* contraindre, forcer; we ~d them into confessing nous les avons contraints à avouer.
coercion [kəʊˈɜːʃn] *n (U)* coercition *f*, contrainte *f*; to act under ~ agir sous la contrainte.
coercive [kəʊˈɜːsɪv] *adj* coercitif.
coeval [kəʊˈiːvl] ◇ *adj* contemporain.
◇ *n* contemporain *m*, -e *f*.
coexist [ˌkəʊɪgˈzɪst] *vi* coexister.
coexistence [ˌkəʊɪgˈzɪstəns] *n* coexistence *f*.
coexistent [ˌkəʊɪgˈzɪstənt] *adj* coexistant.
coextensive [ˌkəʊɪkˈstensɪv] *adj*: ~ with [in space] de même étendue que; [in time] de même durée que.
C of C *n abbr of* chamber of commerce.
C of E (*abbr of* Church of England) ◇ *pr n* Église *f* anglicane.
◇ *adj* anglican; he's ~ il appartient à l'Église anglicane.
coffee [ˈkɒfɪ] ◇ *n* -**1**. [drink] café *m*; a cup of ~ une tasse de café; would you like a ~? voulez-vous un café?; we talked over ~ nous avons bavardé en prenant un café; black ~ café noir; white ~ *Br*, ~ with cream OR milk *Am* [gen] café au lait; [in café] café crème, crème *m*. -**2**. [colour] café au lait *(inv)*.
◇ *comp* [filter, service] à café; [ice cream, icing] au café; ~ cake *Br* moka *m*; *Am* gâteau *m (que l'on sert avec le café)*; ~ cream [chocolate] chocolat *m* fourré au café; ~ grounds marc *m* de café.
coffee bar *n Br* café *m*, caféteria *f*.
coffee bean *n* grain *m* de café.
coffee break *n* pause-café *f*.
coffee-coloured *adj* café au lait *(inv)*.
coffee cup *n* tasse *f* à café.
coffee grinder *n* moulin *m* à café.
coffee house *n* café *m*.
coffee klatch *inf* [-klætʃ] *n Am*: he's probably in the ~ il est sans doute en train de prendre un café et de papoter avec les autres.
coffee machine *n* [gen] cafetière *f*; [in café] percolateur *m*.
coffee mill *n* moulin *m* à café.
coffee morning *n Br rencontre amicale autour d'un café, destinée souvent à réunir de l'argent au profit d'œuvres de bienfaisance*.
coffeepot [ˈkɒfɪpɒt] *n* cafetière *f*.
coffee shop *n Am* ≃ café-restaurant *m*.
coffee spoon *n* cuillère *f* OR cuiller *f* à café, petite cuillère *f* OR cuiller *f*; [smaller] cuillère *f* OR cuiller *f* à moka.
coffee table *n* table *f* basse.
coffee-table book *n* ≃ beau livre *m (destiné à être feuilleté plutôt que véritablement lu)*.
coffee tree *n* caféier *m*.
coffer [ˈkɒfəʳ] *n* -**1**. [strongbox] coffre *m*, caisse *f*. -**2**. [watertight chamber] caisson *m*. -**3**. ARCHIT caisson *m (de plafond)*.
◆ **coffers** *npl* [funds - of nation] coffres *mpl*; [- of organization] caisses *fpl*, coffres *mpl*; the Government hasn't got much left in the ~s le gouvernement n'a plus grand-chose dans ses coffres.
cofferdam [ˈkɒfədæm] *n* batardeau *m*.
coffered [ˈkɒfəd] *adj* ARCHIT à caissons.
coffin [ˈkɒfɪn] *n* -**1**. [box] cercueil *m*, bière *f*. -**2**. [of hoof] cavité *f* du sabot.
coffin nail *inf n hum* [cigarette] cigarette *f*.
C of I (*abbr of* Church of Ireland) *pr n* Église *f* d'Irlande.
C of S (*abbr of* Church of Scotland) *pr n* Église *f* d'Écosse.
cog [kɒg] *n* [gearwheel] roue *f* dentée; [tooth] dent *f (d'engrenage)*; you're only a (small) ~ in the machine OR the wheel *fig* vous n'êtes qu'un simple rouage (dans OR de la machine).
cogency [ˈkəʊdʒənsɪ] *n* force *f*, puissance *f*.
cogent [ˈkəʊdʒənt] *adj fml* [argument, reasons - convincing] convaincant, puissant; [- pertinent] pertinent; [- compelling] irrésistible.
cogently [ˈkəʊdʒəntlɪ] *adv fml* [argue - convincingly] puissamment; [- pertinently] pertinemment, avec à-propos; [- compellingly] irrésistiblement.
cogitate [ˈkɒdʒɪteɪt] *vi fml* méditer, réfléchir; to ~ about OR on sthg méditer sur qqch, réfléchir à qqch.
cogitation [ˌkɒdʒɪˈteɪʃn] *n* réflexion *f*, méditation *f*; *hum* cogitations *fpl*.
cognac [ˈkɒnjæk] *n* cognac *m*.
cognate [ˈkɒgneɪt] ◇ *n* -**1**. LING mot *m* apparenté. -**2**. JUR [person] parent *m* proche, cognat *m* JUR.
◇ *adj* LING apparenté, de même origine; JUR parent; English is ~ with German l'anglais est apparenté à OR de même origine que l'allemand.
cognition [kɒgˈnɪʃn] *n* [gen] connaissance *f*; PHILOS cognition *f*.
cognitive [ˈkɒgnɪtɪv] *adj* cognitif.
cognizance, **-isance** [ˈkɒgnɪzəns] *n* -**1**. *fml* [knowledge] connaissance *f*; to take ~ of sthg prendre connaissance de qqch. -**2**. *fml* [range, scope] compétence *f*; the matter is outside our ~ l'affaire n'est pas de notre compétence; within the ~ of this court JUR de la compétence de ce tribunal. -**3**. HERALD [badge] emblème *m*.
cognizant, **-isant** [ˈkɒgnɪzənt] *adj* -**1**. *fml* [aware] ayant connaissance, conscient; to be ~ of a fact être instruit d'un fait. -**2**. JUR compétent.
cognomen [kɒgˈnəʊmen] (*pl* cognomens OR cognomina [-mɪnə]) *n* [surname] nom *m* de famille; [nickname] surnom *m*.
cognoscenti [ˌkɒnjəˈʃentiː] *npl* connaisseurs *mpl*.
cogwheel [ˈkɒgwiːl] *n* roue *f* dentée.
cohabit [ˌkəʊˈhæbɪt] *vi* cohabiter.
cohabitation [ˌkəʊhæbɪˈteɪʃn] *n* cohabitation *f*.
cohabitee [kəʊˌhæbɪˈtiː] *n* concubin *m*, -e *f*.
cohere [kəʊˈhɪəʳ] *vi* -**1**. [stick together] adhérer, coller. -**2**. [be logically consistent] être cohérent; [reasoning, argument] (se) tenir.
coherence [kəʊˈhɪərəns] *n* -**1**. [cohesion] adhérence *f*. -**2**. [logical consistency] cohérence *f*.
coherent [kəʊˈhɪərənt] *adj* [logical - person, structure] cohérent, logique; [- story, speech] facile à suivre OR comprendre.
coherently [kəʊˈhɪərəntlɪ] *adv* de façon cohérente.
cohesion [kəʊˈhiːʒn] *n* cohésion *f*.
cohesive [kəʊˈhiːsɪv] *adj* cohésif.
cohort [ˈkəʊhɔːt] *n* -**1**. [group, band] cohorte *f*. -**2**. MIL cohorte *f*. -**3**. [companion] comparse *mf*, compère *m*. -**4**. BIOL ordre *m*.
COHSE [ˈkəʊzɪ] (*abbr of* Confederation of Health Service Employees) *pr n ancien syndicat des employés des services de santé en Grande-Bretagne*.
COI (*abbr of* Central Office of Information) *pr n service public d'information en Grande-Bretagne*.

COI:
Le COI diffuse des informations émanant du gouvernement, publie des brochures, organise des expositions, des projections de films etc en Grande-Bretagne et à l'étranger.

---

coif [kɔɪf] *n* [headdress] coiffe *f*; [skullcap] calotte *f*.
coiffure [kwɑːˈfjʊəʳ] *n fml* coiffure *f*.
coil [kɔɪl] ◇ *n* -**1**. [spiral - of rope, wire] rouleau *m*; NAUT glène *f*; [- of hair] rouleau *m*; [in bun] chignon *m*. -**2**. [single loop - of rope, wire] tour *m*; [- of hair] boucle *f*; [- of smoke, snake] anneau *m*. -**3**. ELEC & TECH bobine *f*. -**4**. MED [for contraception] stérilet *m*.
◇ *vt* -**1**. [rope] enrouler; [hair] enrouler, torsader; the snake ~ed itself up le serpent s'est lové OR enroulé. -**2**. ELEC bobiner.
◇ *vi* -**1**. [river, smoke, procession] onduler, serpenter. -**2**. [rope] s'enrouler; [snake] se lover; the python ~ed around its prey le python s'est enroulé autour de sa proie.
◆ **coil up** *vt sep* [rope, hose] enrouler.
coiled [kɔɪld] *adj* [rope] enroulé, en spirale; [spring] en spirale; [snake] lové.
coil spring *n* ressort *m* hélicoïdal.
coin [kɔɪn] ◇ *n* -**1**. [item of metal currency] pièce *f* (de monnaie); a 5p ~ une pièce de 5 pence ❑ that's the other side of the ~ c'est le revers de la médaille. -**2**. *(U)* [metal currency] monnaie *f*; £50 in ~ 50 livres en espèces ❑ to pay sb back in his own ~ rendre à qqn la monnaie de sa pièce.
◇ *vt* -**1**. [money]: to ~ money battre monnaie ❑ she's ~ing it *inf* elle se fait du fric. -**2**. [word] fabriquer, inventer; to ~ a phrase *hum* si je puis m'exprimer ainsi.
coinage [ˈkɔɪnɪdʒ] *n* -**1**. [creation - of money] frappe *f*; *fig* [- of word] invention *f*. -**2**. [coins] monnaie *f*; [currency system] système *m* monétaire. -**3**. [invented word, phrase] invention *f*, création *f*.
coin-box *n Br* cabine *f* téléphonique (à pièces).
coincide [ˌkəʊɪnˈsaɪd] *vi* -**1**. [in space, time] coïncider. -**2**. [correspond] coïncider, s'accorder; our views ~ nous sommes d'accord, nos opinions coïncident.
coincidence [kəʊˈɪnsɪdəns] *n* -**1**. [accident] coïncidence *f*, hasard *m*. -**2**. [correspondence] coïncidence *f*.
coincidental [kəʊˌɪnsɪˈdentl] *adj* -**1**. [accidental] de coïncidence; our meeting was entirely ~ notre rencontre était une pure coïncidence. -**2**. [having same position] coïncident.
coincidentally [kəʊˌɪnsɪˈdentəlɪ] *adv* par hasard.
coin-op *inf n* laverie *f* automatique.
coin-operated [ˈɒpəˌreɪtɪd] *adj* automatique.
coinsurance [ˌkəʊɪnˈʃɔːrəns] *n* coassurance *f*.
coir [kɔɪə] *n* coir *m*.
coitus [ˈkəʊɪtəs] *n* coït *m*.
coitus interruptus [-ˌɪntəˈrʌptəs] *n* coït *m* interrompu.
coke [kəʊk] *n* -**1**. [fuel] coke *m*. -**2**. *drugs sl* [cocaine] cocaïne *f*, coke *f*.
Coke® [kəʊk] *n* [cola] Coca® *m*.
coke-fired *adj* à coke.
coke-oven *n* four *m* à coke.
col [kɒl] *n* col *m (d'une montagne)*.
Col. (*written abbr of* colonel) Col.
cola [ˈkəʊlə] *n* cola *m*.
COLA [ˈkəʊlə] *Br abbr of* cost-of-living adjustment.
colander [ˈkʌləndəʳ] *n* passoire *f*.
cold [kəʊld] ◇ *adj* -**1**. [body, object, food etc] froid; I'm ~ j'ai froid; her hands are ~ elle a les mains froides; my feet are ~ j'ai froid aux pieds; he's getting ~ il commence à avoir froid; eat it before it gets ~ mangez avant que cela refroidisse; a ~ supper un dîner froid; ~ start OR starting AUT démarrage *m* à froid; the trail was ~ *fig* toute trace avait disparu; her answer was ~ comfort to us sa réponse ne nous a pas réconfortés; is it over here? – no, you're getting ~er [in children's game] est-ce par ici? – non, tu refroidis; she poured ~ water on our plans *fig* sa réaction devant nos projets nous a refroidis ❑ ~ steel arme *f* blanche; to be as ~ as ice [thing] être froid comme de la glace; [room] être glacial; [person] être glacé jusqu'aux os; to get OR to have ~ feet avoir la trouille; ~ hands, warm heart *prov* mains froides, cœur chaud *prov*. -**2**. [weather] froid; it will be ~

today il va faire froid aujourd'hui; **it's freezing** ~ il fait un froid de loup OR de canard; **it's getting** ~**er** la température baisse. -**3.** [unfeeling] froid, indifférent; [objective] froid, objectif; [unfriendly] froid, peu aimable; **to be** ~ **towards sb** se montrer froid envers qqn; **the play left me** ~ la pièce ne m'a fait ni chaud ni froid; **to have a** ~ **heart** avoir un cœur de pierre; **in the** ~ **light of day** dans la froide lumière du jour; **in** ~ **blood** de sang-froid; **he murdered them in** ~ **blood** il les a assassinés de sang-froid. -**4.** [unconscious]: **she was out** ~ elle était sans connaissance; **he knocked him (out)** ~ il l'a mis KO. -**5.** [colour] froid.

◇ *n* -**1.** METEOR froid *m*; **in this bitter** ~ par ce froid intense; **the** ~ **doesn't bother him** il ne craint pas le froid, il n'est pas frileux; **come in out of the** ~ entrez vous mettre au chaud ❑ **to come in from the** ~ rentrer en grâce; **the newcomer was left out in the** ~ personne ne s'est occupé du nouveau venu. -**2.** MED rhume *m*; **to have a** ~ être enrhumé; **a** ~ **in the chest/in the head** un rhume de poitrine/de cerveau; **a bad** ~ un mauvais rhume.

◇ *adv* -**1.** [without preparation] à froid; **she had to play the piece** ~ elle a dû jouer le morceau sans avoir répété. -**2.** *inf Am* [absolutely]: **she turned me down** ~ elle m'a dit non carrément; **he knows his subject** ~ il connaît son sujet à fond.

cold-blooded *adj* -**1.** [animal] à sang froid. -**2.** *fig* [unfeeling] insensible; [ruthless] sans pitié; **a** ~ **murder** un meurtre commis de sang-froid; **a** ~ **murderer** un meurtrier sans pitié.

cold-bloodedly [-ˈblʌdɪdlɪ] *adv* de sang-froid.

cold chisel *n* ciseau *m* à froid.

cold cream *n* crème *f* de beauté, cold-cream *m*.

cold cuts *npl* [gen] viandes *fpl* froides; [on menu] assiette *f* anglaise.

cold fish *inf n*: **he's a** ~ *inf* c'est un pisse-froid.

cold frame *n* châssis *m* de couches *(pour plantes)*.

cold front *n* front *m* froid.

cold-hearted *adj* sans pitié, insensible.

cold-heartedly [-ˈhɑːtɪdlɪ] *adv* sans pitié.

coldly [ˈkəʊldlɪ] *adv* froidement, avec froideur.

coldness [ˈkəʊldnɪs] *n literal & fig* froideur *f*.

cold-pressed [-prest] *adj* [olive oil] pressé à froid.

cold room *n* chambre *f* froide OR frigorifique.

cold shoulder *inf n*: **to give sb the** ~ snober qqn.

◆ **cold-shoulder** *inf vt* battre froid à qqn; **we cold-shouldered them** nous leur avons battu froid OR les avons snobés.

cold snap *n* courte offensive *f* du froid.

cold sore *n* bouton *m* de fièvre.

cold storage *n* conservation *f* par le froid; **to put sthg into** ~ [food] mettre qqch en chambre froide; [furs] mettre qqch en garde; *fig* mettre qqch en attente.

cold store *n* entrepôt *m* frigorifique.

Coldstream Guards [ˈkəʊld,striːm-] *pl pr n*: **the** ~ *régiment d'infanterie de la Garde Royale britannique*.

cold sweat *n* sueur *f* froide; **to be in a** ~ **about sthg** *inf* avoir des sueurs froides au sujet de qqch; **just thinking about my exams brings me out in a** ~ *inf* rien que de penser à mes examens, j'en ai des sueurs froides.

cold turkey *n drugs sl* [drugs withdrawal] manque *m*; **to go** ~ être en manque.

cold war *n* guerre *f* froide.

cold wave *n* vague *f* de froid.

cold-weather payment *n en Grande-Bretagne, allocation complémentaire versée aux personnes âgées en période de grand froid*.

coleslaw [ˈkəʊlslɔː] *n* salade *f* de chou cru.

coley [ˈkəʊlɪ] *n* colin *m*, lieu *m* noir.

colic [ˈkɒlɪk] *n (U)* coliques *fpl*.

colicky [ˈkɒlɪkɪ] *adj* qui souffre de coliques.

Coliseum [,kɒlɪˈsɪəm] *pr n* Colisée *m*.

colitis [kɒˈlaɪtɪs] *n (U)* colite *f*.

collaborate [kəˈlæbəreɪt] *vi* collaborer; **she** ~**d with us on the project** elle a collaboré avec nous au projet; **to** ~ **with the enemy** collaborer avec l'ennemi.

collaboration [kə,læbəˈreɪʃn] *n* collaboration *f*; ~ **(with sb) on sthg** collaboration (avec qqn) à qqch; **in** ~ **with** en collaboration avec.

collaborationist [kə,læbəˈreɪʃnɪst] *n pej* collaborateur *m*, -trice *f*, collaborationniste *mf*.

collaborative [kəˈlæbərətɪv] *adj* conjugué, combiné.

collaborator [kəˈlæbəreɪtəʳ] *n* collaborateur *m*, -trice *f*.

collage [ˈkɒlɑːʒ] *n* -**1.** ART [picture, method] collage *m*. -**2.** [gen - combination of things] mélange *m*.

collagen [ˈkɒlədʒən] *n* collagène *m*.

collapse [kəˈlæps] ◇ *vi* -**1.** [building, roof] s'écrouler, s'effondrer; [beam] fléchir. -**2.** *fig* [institution] s'effondrer, s'écrouler; [government] tomber, chuter; [plan] s'écrouler; [market, defence] s'effondrer. -**3.** [person] s'écrouler, s'effondrer; [health] se délabrer, se dégrader; **he** ~**d and died** il a eu un malaise et il est mort; **he** ~**d onto the bed and slept for hours** il s'est écroulé sur son lit et a dormi pendant des heures; **to** ~ **with laughter** se tordre de rire. -**4.** [fold up] se plier; **the bicycle** ~**s so it can be stored away easily** la bicyclette se plie et peut ainsi être rangée facilement.

◇ *vt* [fold up - table, chair] plier.

◇ *n* -**1.** [of building] écroulement *m*, effondrement *m*; [of beam] rupture *f*. -**2.** *fig* [of institution, plan] effondrement *m*, écroulement *m*; [of government] chute *f*; [of market, defence] effondrement *m*. -**3.** [of person] écroulement *m*, effondrement *m*; [of health] délabrement *m*; [of lung] collapsus *m*.

collapsed [kəˈlæpst] *adj*: ~ **lung** collapsus *m* pulmonaire; **to have a** ~ **lung** avoir fait un collapsus pulmonaire.

collapsible [kəˈlæpsəbl] *adj* pliant.

collar [ˈkɒləʳ] ◇ *n* -**1.** [on clothing] col *m*; [detachable - for men] faux col *m*; [- for women] col *m*, collerette *f*; **he seized me by the** ~ il m'a attrapé par le col. -**2.** [for animal] collier *m*; [neck of animal] collier *m*; CULIN [beef] collier *m*; [mutton, veal] collet *m*. -**3.** TECH [on pipe] bague *f*.

◇ *vt* -**1.** *inf* [seize] prendre OR saisir au collet, colleter; [criminal] arrêter; [detain] intercepter, harponner. -**2.** TECH [pipe] baguer.

collarbone [ˈkɒləbəʊn] *n* clavicule *f*.

collar stud *n* bouton *m* de col.

collate [kəˈleɪt] *vt* -**1.** [information, texts] collationner. -**2.** RELIG nommer *(à un bénéfice ecclésiastique)*.

collateral [kɒˈlætərəl] ◇ *n* FIN [guarantee] nantissement *m*; **offered as** ~ remis en nantissement.

◇ *adj* -**1.** [secondary] subsidiaire, accessoire; FIN subsidiaire; ~ **loan** prêt *m* avec garantie; ~ **security** nantissement *m*. -**2.** [parallel] parallèle; [fact] concomitant; JUR & MED collatéral.

collation [kəˈleɪʃn] *n* -**1.** [of text] collation *f*. -**2.** [light meal] collation *f*.

collator [kəˈleɪtəʳ] *n* -**1.** [person] collationneur *m*, -euse *f*; [machine] collationneur *m*. -**2.** RELIG collateur *m*.

colleague [ˈkɒliːg] *n* [in office, school] collègue *mf*; [professional, doctor, lawyer] confrère *m*.

collect[1] [kəˈlekt] ◇ *vt* -**1.** [gather - objects] ramasser; [- information, documents] recueillir, rassembler; [- evidence] rassembler; [- people] réunir, rassembler; [- wealth] accumuler, amasser; **a water butt** ~**s rainwater for use in the garden** une citerne recueille l'eau de pluie pour le jardin; **to** ~ **dust** prendre la poussière; **solar panels** ~ **the heat** des panneaux solaires captent la chaleur || *fig*: **to** ~ **o.s.** [calm down] se reprendre, se calmer; [reflect] se recueillir; **to** ~ **one's thoughts**: **let me** ~ **my thoughts** laissez-moi refléchir OR me concentrer; **to** ~ **one's wits** rassembler ses esprits. -**2.** [as hobby] collectionner, faire collection de. -**3.** [money] recueillir; [taxes, fines, dues] percevoir; **she** ~**s her pension on Tuesdays** elle touche sa retraite le mardi. -**4.** *Br* [take away] ramasser; **the council** ~**s the rubbish** la commune se charge du ramassage des ordures; **when is the mail** ~**ed?** à quelle heure est la levée du courrier?; **to** ~ **an order** COMM retirer une commande. -**5.** [pick up - people] aller chercher, (passer) prendre; **he'll** ~ **us in his car** il viendra nous chercher OR passera nous prendre en voiture; **the bus** ~**s the children at 8 o'clock** le bus ramasse les enfants à 8 h.

◇ *vi* -**1.** [accumulate - people] se rassembler, se réunir; [- things] s'accumuler, s'amasser. -**2.** [raise money]: **to** ~ **for charity** faire la quête OR quêter pour une œuvre de bienfaisance.

◇ *adv Am*: **to call** ~ téléphoner en PCV.

◇ *adj Am*: **a** ~ **call** un (appel en) PCV.

◆ **collect up** *vt sep* ramasser; **they** ~**ed up their belongings and left** ils ont ramassé leurs affaires et sont partis.

collect[2] [ˈkɒlekt] *n* [prayer] collecte *f*.

collectable [kəˈlektəbl] *adj* [desirable to collectors] (très) recherché.

collect call [kəˈlekt] *n Am* appel *m* en PCV.

collected [kəˈlektɪd] *adj* -**1.** [composed] maître de soi, calme. -**2.** [complete] complet; **the** ~ **works of Whitman** les œuvres complètes de Whitman.

collecting [kəˈlektɪŋ] *n* collection *f*; **stamp** ~ philatélie *f*; ~ **tin** tronc *m*.

collection [kəˈlekʃn] *n* -**1.** *(U)* [act of collecting - objects] ramassage *m*; [- information] rassemblement *m*; [- wealth] accumulation *f*; [- rent, money] encaissement *m*; [- debts] recouvrement *m*; [- taxes] perception *f*. -**2.** [things collected] collection *f*; **a coin** ~ une collection de monnaies; **the fashion designers' winter** ~ la collection d'hiver des couturiers. -**3.** [picking up - of rubbish] ramassage *m*; *Br* [- of mail] levée *f*; **your order is ready for** ~ votre commande est prête. -**4.** [sum of money] collecte *f*, quête *f*; **to take** OR **to make a** ~ **for** faire une quête OR collecte pour ❑ ~ **box** tronc *m*; ~ **plate** [in church] corbeille *f*. -**5.** [group - of people, things] rassemblement *m*, groupe *m*; **a motley** ~ un rassemblement hétéroclite. -**6.** [anthology] recueil *m*.

collective [kəˈlektɪv] ◇ *adj* collectif; LING: ~ **noun** collectif *m*.

◇ *n* coopérative *f*.

collective bargaining *n négociations pour une convention collective*.

collective farm *n* ferme *f* collective.

collectively [kəˈlektɪvlɪ] *adv* collectivement.

collectivism [kəˈlektɪvɪzm] *n* collectivisme *m*.

collectivist [kəˈlektɪvɪst] ◇ *adj* collectiviste.

◇ *n* collectiviste *mf*.

collectivization [kə,lektɪvaɪˈzeɪʃn] *n* collectivisation *f*.

collectivize, -ise [kəˈlektɪvaɪz] *vt* collectiviser.

collector [kəˈlektəʳ] *n* -**1.** [as a hobby] collectionneur *m*, -euse *f*; ~**'s item** pièce *f* de collection; **stamp** ~ philatéliste *mf*. -**2.** [of money] encaisseur *m*; [of taxes] percepteur *m*; [of debts] receveur *m*; **ticket** ~ contrôleur *m*, -euse *f*.

colleen [ˈkɒliːn, kɒˈliːn] *n Ir* jeune fille *f*; [Irish girl] jeune Irlandaise *f*.

college [ˈkɒlɪdʒ] *n* -**1.** [institution of higher education] établissement *m* d'enseignement supérieur; [within university] collège *m (dans les universités traditionnelles, communauté indépendante d'enseignants et d'étudiants)*; **I go to** ~ ≃ je suis étudiant; **when you were at** ~ ≃ quand tu étais à l'université; **to be** ~ **bound** *Am* se destiner aux études supérieures; ~ **degree** *Am* diplôme *m* universitaire. -**2.** [for professional training] école *f* professionnelle, collège *m* technique; ~ **of agriculture** ≃ lycée *m* agricole; ~ **of art** école des beaux-arts; ~ **of music** conservatoire *m* de musique ❑ **College of Advanced Technology** *Br* ≃ institut *m* universitaire de technologie, ≃ IUT *m*; **College of Education** *Br* ≃ institut *m* de formation des maîtres; **College of Further Education** *Br* ≃ institut *m* d'éducation permanente. -**3.** [organization] société *f*, académie *f*; the College of Cardinals le Sacré Collège; the Royal College of Physicians/Surgeons l'Académie *f* de médecine/de chirurgie.

collegiate [kə'liːdʒɪət] *adj* [life] universitaire; [university] composé de diverses facultés; *Can* [school] secondaire.

collegiate church *n* collégiale *f*.

collide [kə'laɪd] *vi* -**1.** [crash] entrer en collision, se heurter; NAUT aborder; **the bus ~d with the lorry** le bus est entré en collision avec OR a heurté le camion. -**2.** *fig* [clash] entrer en conflit, se heurter; **I can see that we are going to ~ on this issue** je sens qu'on va être en désaccord sur cette question.

collie ['kɒlɪ] *n* colley *m*.

collier ['kɒlɪə'] *n Br* [miner] mineur *m*; [ship] charbonnier *m* NAUT.

colliery ['kɒljərɪ] (*pl* **collieries**) *n* houillère *f*, mine *f* (de charbon).

collimator ['kɒlɪmeɪtə'] *n* collimateur *m*; **~ viewfinder** PHOT viseur *m* à cadre lumineux.

collision [kə'lɪʒn] *n* -**1.** [crash] collision *f*, choc *m*; RAIL collision *f*, tamponnement *m*; NAUT abordage *m*; **to come into ~ with sthg** entrer en collision avec OR tamponner qqch; **the two ships came into ~** les deux navires se sont abordés ❑ **~ damage waiver** *réduction sur le prix d'une assurance accordée aux automobilistes qui acceptent de payer les dommages dont ils sont responsables*. -**2.** *fig* [clash] conflit *m*, opposition *f*; **a ~ of interests** un conflit d'intérêts.

collision course *n*: **the two planes were on a ~** les deux avions risquaient d'entrer en collision; **the government is on a ~ with the unions** le gouvernement va au-devant d'un conflit avec les syndicats.

collocate [*vb* 'kɒləkeɪt, *n* 'kɒləkət] ◇ *vi* être cooccurrent; **to ~ with sthg** être cooccurrent de qqch.
◇ *n* cooccurrent *m*.

collocation [,kɒlə'keɪʃn] *n* collocation *f*.

colloid ['kɒlɔɪd] ◇ *adj* colloïdal.
◇ *n* colloïde *m*.

colloidal [kə'lɔɪdl] *adj* colloïdal.

colloquia [kə'ləʊkwɪə] *pl* → **colloquium**.

colloquial [kə'ləʊkwɪəl] *adj* [language, expression] familier, parlé; [style] familier.

colloquialism [kə'ləʊkwɪəlɪzm] *n* expression *f* familière.

colloquially [kə'ləʊkwɪəlɪ] *adv* familièrement, dans la langue parlée.

colloquium [kə'ləʊkwɪəm] (*pl* **colloquiums** OR **colloquia** [-kwɪə]) *n* colloque *m*.

colloquy ['kɒləkwɪ] (*pl* **colloquies**) *n fml* [conversation] colloque *m*, conversation *f*; [meeting] colloque *m*.

collude [kə'luːd] *vi* être de connivence OR de mèche; **to ~ with sb (in sthg)** être de connivence avec qqn (dans OR pour qqch); **they accused the oil companies of colluding to raise prices** ils ont accusé les compagnies pétrolières de s'entendre pour augmenter les prix.

collusion [kə'luːʒn] *n* collusion *f*; **to act in ~ with sb** agir de connivence avec qqn.

collywobbles *inf* ['kɒlɪ,wɒblz] *npl Br* [stomachache] mal *m* au ventre; [nervousness] trouille *f*; **I always get the ~ before an exam** j'ai toujours la trouille avant un examen.

cologne [kə'ləʊn] *n* [perfume]: **(eau de) ~** eau *f* de Cologne.

Cologne [kə'ləʊn] *pr n* Cologne.

Colombia [kə'lɒmbɪə] *pr n* Colombie *f*; **in ~** en Colombie.

Colombian [kə'lɒmbɪən] ◇ *n* Colombien *m*, -enne *f*.
◇ *adj* colombien.

Colombo [kə'lʌmbəʊ] *pr n* Colombo.

colon ['kəʊlən] *n* -**1.** [in punctuation] deux-points *m*. -**2.** ANAT côlon *m*.

colonel ['kɜːnl] *n* colonel *m*; **Colonel Jones** le colonel Jones.

COLONEL BLIMP:
«Colonel Blimp» est un personnage de vieil officier, réfractaire à tout ce qui est nouveau, créé par le dessinateur britannique David Low; on utilise ce nom, parfois réduit à «Blimp», pour désigner une personne ayant ce même trait de caractère.

---

colonial [kə'ləʊnjəl] ◇ *adj* -**1.** [power, life] colonial; *pej* [attitude] colonialiste; **the Colonial Office** *Br* le ministère des Colonies. -**2.** *Am* [design] colonial américain *(style XVIIIe aux États-Unis)*. -**3.** BIOL [animals, insects] qui vit en colonie.
◇ *n* colonial *m*, -e *f*.

colonialism [kə'ləʊnjəlɪzm] *n* colonialisme *m*.

colonialist [kə'ləʊnjəlɪst] ◇ *adj* colonialiste.
◇ *n* colonialiste *mf*.

colonic [kə'lɒnɪk] ◇ *adj* du côlon; **~ irrigation** lavement *m*.
◇ *n* lavement *m*.

colonist ['kɒlənɪst] *n* colon *m*.

colonization [,kɒlənaɪ'zeɪʃn] *n* colonisation *f*.

colonize, -ise ['kɒlənaɪz] *vt* coloniser.

colonnade [,kɒlə'neɪd] *n* colonnade *f*.

colony ['kɒlənɪ] (*pl* **colonies**) *n* colonie *f*.

colophon ['kɒləfən] *n* -**1.** [logo] logotype *m*, colophon *m*. -**2.** [end text in book] achevé *m* d'imprimer; [end text in manuscript] colophon *m*.

color *etc Am* = **colour**.

Colorado [,kɒlə'rɑːdəʊ] *pr n* Colorado *m*; **in ~** dans le Colorado; **the ~ (River)** le Colorado.

Colorado beetle *n* doryphore *m*.

colorant ['kʌlərənt] *n* colorant *m*.

coloration [,kʌlə'reɪʃn] *n* [colouring] coloration *f*; [choice of colours] coloris *m*.

coloratura [,kɒlərə'tʊərə] *n* colorature *f*.

color line *Am* = **colour bar**.

colossal [kə'lɒsl] *adj* colossal.

Colosseum [,kɒlə'sɪəm] *n pr* Colisée *m*.

Colossian [kə'lɒʃn] *n*: **the Epistle of Paul to the ~s** l'Épître de saint Paul aux Colossiens.

colossus [kə'lɒsəs] (*pl* **colossuses** OR **colossi** [-saɪ]) *n* colosse *m*.

colostomy [kə'lɒstəmɪ] (*pl* **colostomies**) *n* colostomie *f*.

colour *Br*, **color** *Am* ['kʌlə'] ◇ *n* -**1.** [hue] couleur *f*; **what ~ are his eyes?** de quelle couleur sont ses yeux?; **the bleach took the ~ out of it** l'eau de Javel l'a décoloré; **the movie is in ~** le film est en couleur OR couleurs; **he painted the room in bright/dark ~s** il a peint la pièce de couleurs vives/sombres. -**2.** *fig*: **the political ~ of a newspaper** la couleur politique d'un journal; **under the ~ of patriotism** sous prétexte OR couleur de patriotisme ❑ **we've yet to see the ~ of his money** *inf* nous n'avons pas encore vu la couleur de son argent. -**3.** ART [shade] coloris *m*, ton *m*; [paint] peinture *f*; [dye] teinture *f*, matière *f* colorante; **a wide range of ~s** COMM un grand choix de couleurs. -**4.** [complexion] teint *m*, couleur *f (du visage)*; **her ~ isn't good** elle a mauvaise mine; **he changed ~** il a changé de couleur OR de visage; **to lose one's ~** pâlir, perdre ses couleurs; **to get one's ~ back** reprendre des couleurs; **to have a high ~** avoir le visage rouge. -**5.** [race] couleur *f*; **to discriminate against sb on grounds of ~** établir une discrimination à l'encontre de qqn à cause de la couleur de sa peau; **~ isn't an issue** ce n'est pas une question de couleur (de peau); **of ~** noir. -**6.** [interest] couleur *f*; **to add ~ to a story** colorer un récit; **a play full of ~** une pièce pleine de couleur.
◇ *vt* -**1.** [give colour to] colorer; [with paint] peindre; [with crayons] colorier; **he ~ed it blue** il l'a colorié en bleu. -**2.** *fig* [distort - judgment] fausser; [exaggerate - story, facts] exagérer.
◇ *vi* [person] rougir; [things] se colorer; [fruit] mûrir.
◇ *comp* [photography, picture, slide] en couleur, en couleurs; **~ film** [for camera] pellicule *f* (en) couleur; [movie] film *m* en couleur; **~ filter** PHOT filtre *m* coloré; **~ television** télévision *f* couleur; **~ television set** téléviseur *m* couleur.
◆ **colours** *npl* -**1.** [of team] *élément vestimentaire (écusson, cravate etc) décerné aux nouveaux membres d'une équipe sportive*; **to get** OR **to win one's ~s** être sélectionné pour faire partie d'une équipe ❑ **to show one's true ~s** se montrer sous son vrai jour. -**2.** [of school] couleurs *fpl*. -**3.** MIL [flag] couleurs *fpl*, drapeau *m*; NAUT couleurs *fpl*, pavillon *m*; **salute the ~s!** saluez le drapeau OR les couleurs!
◆ **colour in** *vt sep* colorier; **the little boy ~ed in the house in blue** le petit garçon a colorié la maison en bleu.
◆ **colour up** *vi insep* [blush] rougir.

colour bar *n Br* discrimination *f* raciale.

colour-blind *adj* daltonien.

colour blindness *n* daltonisme *m*.

colour code *n* code *m* coloré.
◆ **colour-code** *vt*: **to colour-code sthg** coder qqch avec des couleurs.

colour-coded *adj* dont la couleur correspond à un code; **the wires are ~** la couleur des fils correspond à un code.

coloured *Br*, **colored** *Am* ['kʌləd] ◇ *adj* -**1.** [having colour] coloré; [drawing] colorié; [pencils] de couleur. -**2.** [person - gen] de couleur; [- in South Africa] métis. -**3.** *fig* [distorted - judgment] faussé; [exaggerated - story] exagéré.
◇ *n* ▼: **~s** [gen] gens *mpl* de couleur; [in South Africa] métis *mpl (attention: le substantif «coloureds» est considéré comme raciste)*.

-coloured *Br*, **-colored** *Am in cpds* (de) couleur...; **rust~** couleur de rouille; **dark~** foncé; **light~** clair.

colourfast *Br*, **colorfast** *Am* ['kʌləfɑːst] *adj* grand teint, qui ne déteint pas.

colourful *Br*, **colorful** *Am* ['kʌləfʊl] *adj* -**1.** [brightly coloured] coloré, vif. -**2.** *fig* [person] original, pittoresque; [story] coloré.

colourfully *Br*, **colorfully** *Am* ['kʌləfʊlɪ] *adv*: **a ~ dressed woman** une femme vêtue de couleurs vives; **a ~ told story** *fig* une histoire très colorée.

colouring *Br*, **coloring** *Am* ['kʌlərɪŋ] ◇ *n* -**1.** [act] coloration *f*; [of drawing] coloriage *m*; **go and do some ~** [to child] va faire du coloriage. -**2.** [hue] coloration *f*, coloris *m*. -**3.** [complexion] teint *m*; **high ~** teint coloré; **fair/dark ~** teint clair/mat. -**4.** *fig* [exaggeration - of facts] travestissement *m*, dénaturation *f*. -**5.** [for food] colorant *m*.
◇ *comp*: **~ book** album *m* à colorier OR de coloriages.

colourless *Br*, **colorless** *Am* ['kʌləlɪs] *adj* -**1.** [without colour] incolore, sans couleur. -**2.** *fig* [uninteresting] sans intérêt, fade.

colour scheme *n* palette *f* OR combinaison *f* de couleurs; **to choose a ~** assortir les couleurs OR les tons.

colour sergeant *n Br* ≃ sergent-chef *m*.

colour supplement *n Br* supplément *m* illustré.

colourwash *Br*, **colorwash** *Am* ['kʌləwɒʃ]
◇ *n* badigeon *m*.
◇ *vt* badigeonner.

colourway *Br*, **colorway** *Am* ['kʌləweɪ] *n* coloris *m*.

colposcopy ['kɒlpə,skəʊpɪ] *n* MED colposcopie *f*.

colt [kəʊlt] *n* -**1.** [horse] poulain *m*. -**2.** *fig* [young person] petit jeune *m*; [inexperienced person] novice *m*.

Colt® [kəʊlt] *n* [revolver] colt *m*, pistolet *m* (automatique).

coltish ['kəʊltɪʃ] *adj* [inexperienced] jeunet, inexpérimenté; [playful] folâtre.

coltsfoot ['kəʊltsfʊt] *n* pas-d'âne *m inv*, tussilage *m*.

Columbia [kə'lʌmbɪə] *pr n* -**1.** **the District of ~** le district fédéral de Columbia. -**2.** **the ~ (River)** la Columbia.

columbine ['kɒləmbaɪn] *n* ancolie *f*.

Columbus [kə'lʌmbəs] *pr n*: Christopher ~ Christophe Colomb.

Columbus Day *n aux États-Unis, jour commémorant l'arrivée de Christophe Colomb en Amérique (deuxième lundi d'octobre)*.

column ['kɒləm] *n* -**1.** [gen & ARCHIT] colonne *f*. -**2.** PRESS [section of print] colonne *f*; [regular article] rubrique *f*; **he writes the sports ~** il tient la rubrique des sports.

column inch *n unité de mesure des espaces publicitaires équivalant à une colonne sur un pouce*.

columnist ['kɒləmnɪst] *n* chroniqueur *m*, -euse *f*, échotier *m*, -ère *f*.

colza ['kɒlzə] *n* colza *m*.

coma ['kəʊmə] *n* coma *m*; **in a ~** dans le coma.

Comanche [kə'mæntʃɪ] (*pl inv* OR **Comanches**) *n* -**1.** [person] Comanche *mf*; **the ~** les Comanches. -**2.** LING comanche *m*.

comatose ['kəʊmətəʊs] *adj* comateux; **to be ~** être dans le coma.

comb [kəʊm] ◇ *n* -**1.** [for hair] peigne *m*; [large-toothed] démêloir *m*; **to run a ~ through one's hair, to give one's hair a ~** se donner un coup de peigne, se peigner. -**2.** [for horses] étrille *f*. -**3.** TEX [for cotton, wool] peigne *m*, carde *f*; ELEC balai *m*. -**4.** [of fowl] crête *f*; [on helmet] cimier *m*. -**5.** [honeycomb] rayon *m* de miel.
◇ *vt* -**1.** [hair] peigner; **he ~ed his hair** il s'est peigné; **I ~ed the girl's hair** j'ai peigné la petite fille. -**2.** [horse] étriller. -**3.** TEX peigner, carder. -**4.** *fig* [search] fouiller, ratisser; **the police ~ed the area for clues** la police a passé le quartier au peigne fin OR a ratissé le quartier à la recherche d'indices.
◆ **comb out** *vt sep* -**1.** [hair] démêler, peigner. -**2.** *fig* [remove] éliminer.

combat ['kɒmbæt] (*pt & pp* **combated**, *cont* **combating**) ◇ *n* combat *m*; **killed/lost in ~** tué/perdu au combat.
◇ *vt* combattre, lutter contre.
◇ *vi* combattre, lutter; **the need to ~ against racism** la nécessité de lutter contre le racisme.
◇ *comp* [troops, zone] de combat; **on ~ duty** en service commandé; **~ jacket** veste *f* de treillis.

combatant ['kɒmbətənt] ◇ *n* combattant *m*, -e *f*.
◇ *adj* combattant.

combat fatigue *n* psychose *f* traumatique, syndrome *m* commotionnel.

combative ['kɒmbətɪv] *adj* combatif.

combe [kuːm] = **coomb**.

comber ['kəʊmə^r] *n* -**1.** TEX [person] peigneur *m*, -euse *f*; [machine] peigneuse *f*. -**2.** [wave] grande vague *f*.

combination [,kɒmbɪ'neɪʃn] *n* -**1.** [gen, CHEM & MATH] combinaison *f*; [of circumstances] concours *m*; **an attractive colour ~** une combinaison de couleurs attrayante. -**2.** [of lock] combinaison *f*. -**3.** [association, team] association *f*, coalition *f*; **together they formed a winning ~** ensemble ils formaient une équipe gagnante. -**4.** *Br* AUT side-car *m*.
◆ **combinations** *n pl Br* [underclothing] combinaison-culotte *f*.

combination lock *n* serrure *f* à combinaison.

combination sandwich *n Am* CULIN *très gros sandwich contenant au minimum cinq ingrédients*.

combine [*vb* kəm'baɪn, *n* 'kɒmbaɪn] ◇ *vt* [gen] combiner, joindre; CHEM combiner; **let's ~ forces** combinons OR joignons nos forces; **to ~ business and** OR **with pleasure** joindre l'utile à l'agréable; **the event was organized by all the groups ~d** la réunion a été organisée par tous les groupes réunis; **this, ~d with her other problems, made her ill** ceci, conjugué à ses autres problèmes, l'a rendue malade; **furniture combining comfort with style** meubles alliant confort et style.
◇ *vi* [unite] s'unir, s'associer; [workers] se syndiquer; POL [parties] fusionner; CHEM se combiner; **events ~d to leave her penniless** les événements ont concouru à la laisser sans le sou.
◇ *n* -**1.** [association] association *f*; FIN trust *m*, cartel *m*; JUR corporation *f*. -**2.** AGR = **combine harvester**.

combined [kəm'baɪnd] *adj* combiné, conjugué; **a ~ effort** un effort conjugué ‖ MIL: **~ forces** forces alliées; **~ operation** [by several nations] operation alliée; [by forces of one nation] opération interarmées.

combine harvester ['kɒmbaɪn-] *n* moissonneuse-batteuse *f*.

combining form [kəm'baɪnɪŋ-] *n* LING affixe *m*.

combo ['kɒmbəʊ] (*pl* **combos**) *n* -**1.** MUS combo *m*. -**2.** *inf* [combination] combinaison *f*.

combustible [kəm'bʌstəbl] *adj* combustible.

combustion [kəm'bʌstʃn] *n* combustion *f*.

combustion chamber *n* chambre *f* de combustion.

combustion engine *n* moteur *m* à combustion.

come [kʌm] (*pt* **came** [keɪm], *pp* **come** [kʌm]) ◇ *vi* -**1.** [move in direction of speaker] venir; **she won't ~ when she's called** elle ne vient pas quand on l'appelle; **it's stuck – ah, no, it's coming!** c'est coincé – ah, non, ça vient!; **coming!** j'arrive!; **~ here** venez ici; **~ to the office tomorrow** passez OR venez au bureau demain; **he came to me for advice** il est venu me demander conseil; **~ with me** [accompany] venez avec moi, accompagnez-moi; [follow] suivez-moi; **please ~ this way** par ici OR suivez-moi s'il vous plaît; **I ~ this way every week** je passe par ici toutes les semaines; **~ and look, ~ look** *Am* venez voir; **~ and get it!** *inf* à la soupe!; **he came whistling up the stairs** il a monté l'escalier en sifflant; **a car came hurtling round the corner** une voiture a pris le virage à toute vitesse ❑ **to ~ and go** [gen] aller et venir; *fig* [pains, cramps etc] être intermittent; **people are constantly coming and going** il y a un va-et-vient continuel; **fashions ~ and go** la mode change tout le temps; **after many years had ~ and gone** après bien des années; **I don't know whether I'm coming or going** *inf* je ne sais pas où j'en suis; **you have ~ a long way** *literal* vous êtes venu de loin; *fig* [made progress] vous avez fait du chemin; **the computer industry has ~ a very long way since then** l'informatique a fait énormément de progrès depuis ce temps-là; **to ~ running** *literal & fig* arriver en courant; **we could see him coming a mile off** on l'a vu venir avec ses gros sabots; **you could see it coming** *inf* on l'a vu venir de loin, c'était prévisible; **everything ~s to him who waits** *prov* tout vient à point à qui sait attendre *prov*. -**2.** [as guest, visitor] venir; **can you ~ to my party on Saturday night?** est-ce que tu peux venir à ma soirée samedi?; **I'm sorry I can't ~** (je suis) désolé, je ne peux pas venir; **would you like to ~ for lunch/dinner?** voulez-vous venir déjeuner/dîner?; **I can only ~ for an hour or so** je ne pourrai venir que pour une heure environ; **~ for a ride in the car** viens faire un tour en voiture; **she's ~ for her money** elle est venue prendre son argent; **I've got people coming** [short stay] j'ai des invités; [long stay] il y a des gens qui viennent; **Angela came and we had a chat** Angela est venue et on a bavardé; **they came for a week and stayed a month** ils sont venus pour une semaine et ils sont restés un mois; **he couldn't have ~ at a worse time** il n'aurait pas pu tomber plus mal. -**3.** [arrive] venir, arriver; **to ~ in time/late** arriver à temps/en retard; **I've just ~ from the post-office** j'arrive de la poste à l'instant; **we came to a small town** nous sommes arrivés dans une petite ville; **the time has ~ to tell the truth** le moment est venu de dire la vérité; **there will ~ a point when...** il viendra un moment où... ‖ [reach]: **her hair ~s (down) to her waist** ses cheveux lui arrivent à la taille; **the mud came (up) to our knees** la boue nous arrivait OR venait (jusqu') aux genoux. -**4.** [occupy specific place, position] venir, se trouver; **the address ~s above the date** l'adresse se met au-dessus de la date; **my birthday ~s before yours** mon anniversaire vient avant OR précède le tien; **a colonel ~s before a lieutenant** un colonel a la préséance sur un lieutenant; **Friday ~s after Thursday** vendredi vient après OR suit jeudi; **that speech ~s in Act 3/on page 10** on trouve ce discours dans l'acte 3/à la page 10. -**5.** [occur, happen] arriver, se produire; **when my turn ~s, when it ~s to my turn** quand ce sera (à) mon tour, quand mon tour viendra; **such an opportunity only ~s once in your life** une telle occasion ne se présente qu'une fois dans la vie; **he has a birthday coming** son anniversaire approche; **success was a long time coming** la réussite s'est fait attendre; **take life as it ~s** prenez la vie comme elle vient ❑ **Christmas ~s but once a year** il n'y a qu'un Noël par an; **it came to pass that...** BIBLE il advint que...; **~ what may** advienne que pourra, quoi qu'il arrive OR advienne. -**6.** [occur to the mind]: **the idea just came to me one day** l'idée m'est soudain venue un jour; **I said the first thing that came into my head** OR **that came to mind** j'ai dit la première chose qui m'est venue à l'esprit; **the answer came to her** elle a trouvé la réponse. -**7.** [be experienced in a specified way]: **writing ~s naturally** OR **natural** *inf* **to her** écrire lui est facile, elle est douée pour l'écriture; **a house doesn't ~ cheap** une maison coûte OR revient cher; **the news came as a shock to her** la nouvelle lui a fait un choc; **her visit came as a surprise** sa visite nous a beaucoup surpris; **it ~s as no surprise to learn he's gone** (le fait) qu'il soit parti n'a rien de surprenant ❑ **he's as silly as they ~** il est sot comme pas un; **they don't ~ any tougher than Big Al** on ne fait pas plus fort que Big Al; **it'll all ~ right in the end** tout cela va finir par s'arranger. -**8.** [be available] exister; **this table ~s in two sizes** cette table existe OR se fait en deux dimensions; **the dictionary ~s with a magnifying glass** le dictionnaire est livré avec une loupe. -**9.** [become] devenir; **it was a dream ~ true** c'était un rêve devenu réalité; **to ~ unhooked** se décrocher; **to ~ unravelled** se défaire; **my buttons keep coming undone** mes boutons n'arrêtent pas de s'ouvrir. -**10.** (*+ infinitive*) [indicating gradual action] en venir à, finir par; **she came to trust him** elle en est venue à OR elle a fini par lui faire confiance; **we have ~ to expect this kind of thing** nous nous attendons à ce genre de chose maintenant ‖ [indicating chance] arriver; **how did you ~ to lose your umbrella?** comment as-tu fait pour perdre ton parapluie? ❑ **(now that I) ~ to think of it** maintenant que j'y songe, réflexion faite; **it's not much money when you ~ to think of it** ce n'est pas beaucoup d'argent quand vous y réfléchissez. -**11.** [be owing, payable]: **I still have £5 coming (to me)** on me doit encore 5 livres; **there'll be money coming from her uncle's will** elle va toucher l'argent du testament de son oncle; **he got all the credit coming to him** il a eu tous les honneurs qu'il méritait ❑ **you'll get what's coming to you** *inf* tu l'auras cherché OR voulu; **he had it coming (to him)** *inf* il ne l'a pas volé. -**12.** ▽ [have orgasm] jouir. -**13.** *phr*: **how ~?** comment ça?; **~ again?** *inf* quoi?; **~ to that** à propos, au fait; **I haven't seen her in weeks, or her husband, ~ to that** ça fait des semaines que je ne l'ai pas vue, son mari non plus d'ailleurs; **if it ~s to that, I'd rather stay home** à ce moment-là OR à ce compte-là, je préfère rester à la maison; **don't ~ the fine lady with me!** ne fais pas la grande dame OR ne joue pas à la grande dame avec moi!; **don't ~ the innocent!** ne fais pas l'innocent!; **I wanted to pay you back but I can't ~ it** *Am* je voulais te rembourser mais je n'y arrive pas; **you're coming it a bit strong!** *Br* tu y vas un peu fort!; **don't ~ it with me!** *Br* [try to impress] n'essaie pas de m'en mettre plein la vue!; [lord it over] pas la peine d'être si hautain avec moi!; **to ~** prochain; **the days to ~** les prochains jours, les jours qui viennent; **the battle to ~** la bataille qui va avoir lieu; **the life to ~** RELIG l'autre vie; **in times to ~** à

l'avenir; for some time to ~ pendant quelque temps.
◇ *prep* [by]: ~ tomorrow/Tuesday you'll feel better vous vous sentirez mieux demain/mardi; I'll have been here two years ~ April ça fera deux ans en avril que je suis là; ~ the revolution you'll all be out of a job avec la révolution, vous vous retrouverez tous au chômage.
◇ *interj*: ~, ~!, ~ now! allons!, voyons!
◇ *n* ▼ foutre *m*.
◆ **come about** *vi insep* -**1.** [occur] arriver, se produire; how could such a mistake ~ about? comment une telle erreur a-t-elle pu se produire?; the discovery of penicillin came about quite by accident la pénicilline a été découverte tout à fait par hasard. -**2.** NAUT [wind] tourner, changer de direction; [ship] virer de bord.
◆ **come across** ◇ *vi insep* -**1.** [walk, travel across - field, street] traverser; as we stood talking she came across to join us pendant que nous discutions, elle est venue se joindre à nous. -**2.** [create specified impression] donner l'impression de; he came across as a total idiot il donnait l'impression d'être complètement idiot ‖ [communicate effectively]: he never ~s across as well on film as in the theatre il passe mieux au théâtre qu'à l'écran; the author's message ~s across well le message de l'auteur passe bien; her disdain for his work came across le mépris qu'elle avait pour son travail transparaissait. -**3.** ▽ [do as promised] s'exécuter, tenir parole.
◇ *vt insep* [person] rencontrer par hasard, tomber sur; [thing] trouver par hasard, tomber sur; we came across an interesting problem on a été confrontés à OR on est tombés sur un problème intéressant; she reads everything she ~s across elle lit tout ce qui lui tombe sous la main.
◆ **come across with**▽ *vt insep* [give - information] donner, fournir; [- help] offrir; [- money] raquer, se fendre de; he came across with the money he owed me il m'a filé le fric qu'il me devait; the crook came across with the names of his accomplices l'escroc a vendu ses complices.
◆ **come after** *vt insep* [pursue] poursuivre; he came after me with a stick il m'a poursuivi avec un bâton.
◆ **come along** *vi insep* -**1.** [encouraging, urging]: ~ along, drink your medicine! allez, prends OR bois ton médicament!; ~ along, we're late! dépêche-toi, nous sommes en retard! -**2.** [accompany] venir, accompagner; she asked me to ~ along (with them) elle m'a invité à aller avec eux OR à les accompagner. -**3.** [occur, happen] arriver, se présenter; an opportunity like this doesn't ~ along often une telle occasion ne se présente pas souvent; don't accept the first job that ~s along ne prenez pas le premier travail qui se présente; he married the first woman that came along il a épousé la première venue. -**4.** [progress] avancer, faire des progrès; [grow] pousser; the patient is coming along well le patient se remet bien; the work isn't coming along as expected le travail n'avance pas comme prévu; how's your computer class coming along? comment va ton cours d'informatique?
◆ **come apart** *vi insep* [object - come to pieces] se démonter; [- break] se casser; [project, policy] échouer; the book came apart in my hands le livre est tombé en morceaux quand je l'ai pris; under pressure he came apart *fig* sous la pression il a craqué.
◆ **come around** = **come round**.
◆ **come at** *vt insep* [attack] attaquer, se jeter sur; he came at me with a knife il s'est jeté sur moi avec un couteau; questions came at me from all sides *fig* j'ai été assailli de questions.
◆ **come away** *vi insep* -**1.** [leave] partir, s'en aller; ~ away from that door! écartez-vous de cette porte!; I came away with the distinct impression that all was not well je suis reparti avec la forte impression que quelque chose n'allait pas; he asked her to ~ away with him [elope] il lui a demandé de s'enfuir avec lui; *Br* [go on holiday] il lui a demandé de partir avec lui. -**2.** [separate] partir, se détacher; the page came away in my hands la page m'est restée dans les mains.
◆ **come back** *vi insep* -**1.** [return] revenir; he came back with me il est revenu avec moi; to ~ back home rentrer (à la maison) ‖ *fig*: the colour came back to her cheeks elle reprit des couleurs; we'll ~ back to that question later nous reviendrons à cette question plus tard; to ~ back to what we were saying pour en revenir à ce que nous disions. -**2.** [to memory]: it's all coming back to me tout cela me revient (à l'esprit OR à la mémoire). -**3.** [reply] répondre; *Am* [retort] rétorquer, répliquer; they came back with an argument in favour of the project ils ont répondu par un argument en faveur du projet. -**4.** [recover] remonter; he came back strongly in the second set il a bien remonté au deuxième set; they came back from 3-0 down ils ont remonté de 3 à 0 ‖ [make comeback] faire un come-back. -**5.** [become fashionable again] revenir à la mode.
◆ **come before** *vt insep* JUR [person] comparaître devant; [case] être entendu par.
◆ **come between** *vt insep* brouiller, éloigner; he came between her and her friend il l'a brouillée avec son amie, il l'a éloignée de son amie.
◆ **come by** ◇ *vi insep* [stop by] passer, venir.
◇ *vt insep* [acquire - work, money] obtenir, se procurer; [- idea] se faire; jobs are hard to ~ by il est difficile de trouver du travail; how on earth did he ~ by that idea? où est-il allé chercher cette idée?
◆ **come down** ◇ *vt insep* [descend - ladder, stairs] descendre; [- mountain] descendre, faire la descente de.
◇ *vi insep* -**1.** [descend - plane, person] descendre; ~ down from that tree! descends de cet arbre!; they came down to Paris ils sont descendus à Paris ❑ he's ~ down in the world il a déchu; to ~ down to earth: you'd better ~ down to earth tu ferais bien de revenir sur terre OR de descendre des nues. -**2.** [fall] tomber; rain was coming down in sheets il pleuvait des cordes; the ceiling came down le plafond s'est effondré. -**3.** [reach] descendre; the dress ~s down to my ankles la robe descend jusqu'à mes chevilles. -**4.** [decrease] baisser; he's ready to ~ down 10% on the price il est prêt à rabattre OR baisser le prix de 10 %. -**5.** [be passed down] être transmis (de père en fils); this custom ~s down from the Romans cette coutume nous vient des Romains. -**6.** [reach a decision] se prononcer; the majority came down in favour of/against abortion la majorité s'est prononcée en faveur de/contre l'avortement. -**7.** [be demolished] être démoli OR abattu; these shacks will soon ~ down on va bientôt démolir ces cabanes. -**8.** *Br* UNIV obtenir son diplôme. -**9.** ▽ *sl* [drugs] redescendre.
◆ **come down on** *vt insep* -**1.** [rebuke] s'en prendre à; the boss really came down on him le patron lui a passé un de ces savons. -**2.** *inf* [pressurize]: they came down on me to sell the land ils ont essayé de me faire vendre le terrain.
◆ **come down to** *vt insep* [amount] se réduire à, se résumer à; it all ~s down to what you want to do tout cela dépend de ce que vous souhaitez faire; it all ~s down to the same thing tout cela revient au même; that's what his argument ~s down to voici à quoi se réduit son raisonnement.
◆ **come down with** *vt insep* [become ill] attraper; he came down with a cold il s'est enrhumé, il a attrapé un rhume.
◆ **come forward** *vi insep* [present oneself] se présenter; more women are coming forward as candidates davantage de femmes présentent leur candidature.
◆ **come forward with** *vt insep* [offer]: the townspeople came forward with supplies les habitants de la ville ont offert des provisions; he came forward with a new proposal il a fait une nouvelle proposition; to ~ forward with evidence JUR présenter des preuves.
◆ **come from** *vt insep* venir; she ~s from China [Chinese person] elle vient OR elle est originaire de Chine; this word ~s from Latin ce mot vient du latin; this passage ~s from one of his novels ce passage est extrait OR provient d'un de ses romans; that's surprising coming from him c'est étonnant de sa part; a sob came from his throat un sanglot s'est échappé de sa gorge ❑ I'm not sure where he's coming from▽ je ne sais pas très bien ce qui le motive.
◆ **come in** *vi insep* -**1.** [enter] entrer; ~ in! entrez!; they came in through the window ils sont entrés par la fenêtre ‖ [come inside] rentrer; ~ in now, children, it's getting dark rentrez maintenant, les enfants, il commence à faire nuit. -**2.** [plane, train] arriver. -**3.** [in competition] arriver; she came in second elle est arrivée deuxième. -**4.** [be received - money, contributions] rentrer; there isn't enough money coming in to cover expenditure l'argent qui rentre ne suffit pas à couvrir les dépenses; how much do you have coming in every week? combien touchez-vous OR encaissez-vous chaque semaine? ‖ PRESS [news, report] être reçu; news is just coming in of a riot in Red Square on nous annonce à l'instant des émeutes sur la place Rouge. -**5.** RADIO & TV [begin to speak] parler; ~ in car number 1 over j'appelle voiture 1, à vous; ~ in Barry Stewart from New York à vous, Barry Stewart à New York. -**6.** [become seasonable] être de saison; when do endives ~ in? quand commence la saison des endives? ‖ [become fashionable] entrer en vogue; leather has ~ in le cuir est à la mode OR en vogue. -**7.** [prove to be]: to ~ in handy OR useful [tool, gadget] être utile OR commode; [contribution] arriver à point; these gloves ~ in handy OR useful for driving ces gants sont bien commodes OR utiles pour conduire. -**8.** [be involved] être impliqué; [participate] participer, intervenir; where do I ~ in? quel est mon rôle là-dedans?; this is where the law ~s in c'est là que la loi intervient; he should ~ in on the deal il devrait participer à l'opération; I'd like to ~ in on this [conversation] j'aimerais dire quelques mots là-dessus OR à ce sujet. -**9.** [tide] monter.
◆ **come in for** *vt insep* [be object of - criticism] être l'objet de, subir; [- blame] supporter; [- abuse, reproach] subir.
◆ **come into** *vt insep* -**1.** [inherit] hériter de; [acquire] entrer en possession de; they came into a fortune [received] ils ont reçu une fortune; [won] ils ont gagné une fortune; [inherited] ils ont hérité d'une fortune. -**2.** [play a role in] jouer un rôle; it's not simply a matter of pride, though pride does ~ into it ce n'est pas une simple question de fierté, bien que la fierté joue un certain rôle; money doesn't ~ into it! l'argent n'a rien à voir là-dedans!
◆ **come of** *vt insep* résulter de; what will ~ of it? qu'en résultera-t-il?; no good will ~ from OR of it ça ne mènera à rien de bon, il n'en résultera rien de bon; let me know what ~s of the meeting faites-moi savoir ce qui ressortira de la réunion; that's what ~s from listening to you! voilà ce qui arrive quand on vous écoute!
◆ **come off** ◇ *vt insep* -**1.** [fall off - subj: rider] tomber de; [- subj: button] se détacher de, se découdre de; [- subj: handle, label] se détacher de; [be removed - stain, mark] partir de, s'enlever de. -**2.** [stop taking - drug, medicine] arrêter de prendre; [- drink] arrêter de boire; to ~ off the pill arrêter (de prendre) la pilule. -**3.** FTBL [leave] sortir de. -**4.** *phr*: oh, ~ off it! *inf* allez, arrête ton char!
◇ *vi insep* -**1.** [rider] tomber; [handle] se détacher; [stains] partir, s'enlever; [tape, wallpaper] se détacher, se décoller; the button came off le

bouton s'est détaché OR décousu; **the handle came off in his hand** la poignée lui est restée dans la main. -**2.** FTBL [leave the field] sortir. -**3.** [fare, manage] s'en sortir, se tirer de; **you came off well in the competition** tu t'en es bien tiré au concours; **to ~ off best** gagner. -**4.** *inf* [happen] avoir lieu, se passer; **did the game ~ off all right?** le match s'est bien passé?; **my trip to China didn't ~ off** mon voyage en Chine n'a pas eu lieu || [be carried through] se réaliser; [succeed] réussir; **his plan didn't ~ off** son projet est tombé à l'eau. -**5.** CIN & THEAT [film, play] fermer. -**6.** ▽ [have orgasm] décharger.

◆ **come on** ◇ *vi insep* -**1.** [follow] suivre; **I'll ~ on after (you)** je vous suivrai. -**2.** *(in imperative)* [hurry]: **~ on!** allez!; **~ on in/up!** entre/monte donc!; **oh, ~ on, for goodness sake!** allez, arrête! -**3.** [progress] avancer, faire des progrès; [grow] pousser, venir bien; **how is your work coming on?** où en est votre travail?; **my roses are coming on nicely** mes rosiers se portent bien; **her new book is coming on quite well** son nouveau livre avance bien; **he's coming on in physics** il fait des progrès en physique. -**4.** [begin - illness] se déclarer; [- storm] survenir, éclater; [- season] arriver; **as night came on** quand la nuit a commençé à tomber; **it's coming on to rain** il va pleuvoir; **I feel a headache/cold coming on** je sens un mal de tête qui commence/que je m'enrhume. -**5.** [start functioning - electricity, gas, heater, lights, radio] s'allumer; [- motor] se mettre en marche; [- utilities at main] être mis en service; **has the water ~ on?** y a-t-il de l'eau? -**6.** [behave, act]: **don't ~ on all macho with me!** ne joue pas les machos avec moi!; **you came on a bit strong** *inf* tu y es allé un peu fort. -**7.** THEAT [actor] entrer en scène; [play] être joué OR représenté; **his new play is coming on** on va donner sa nouvelle pièce.
◇ *vt insep* = **come upon**.

◆ **come on to** *vt insep* -**1.** [proceed to consider] aborder, passer à; **I want to ~ on to the issue of epidemics** je veux passer à la question des épidémies. -**2.** ▽ *Am* [flirt with] draguer; **she was coming on to me in a big way** elle me draguait à fond.

◆ **come out** *vi insep* -**1.** [exit] sortir; **as we came out of the theatre** au moment où nous sommes sortis du théâtre ❑ **if he'd only ~ out of himself** OR **out of his shell** *fig* si seulement il sortait de sa coquille || [socially] sortir; **would you like to ~ out with me tonight?** est-ce que tu veux sortir avec moi ce soir? -**2.** [make appearance - stars, sun] paraître, se montrer; [- flowers] sortir, éclore; *fig* [- book] paraître, être publié; [- film] paraître, sortir; [- new product] sortir; **his nasty side came out** sa méchanceté s'est manifestée; **I didn't mean it the way it came out** ce n'est pas ce que je voulais dire. -**3.** [be revealed - news, secret] être divulgué OR révélé; [- facts, truth] émerger, se faire jour; **as soon as the news came out** dès qu'on a su la nouvelle, dès que la nouvelle a été annoncée. -**4.** [colour - fade] passer, se faner; [- run] déteindre; [stain] s'enlever, partir. -**5.** [declare oneself publicly] se déclarer; **the governor came out against/for abortion** le gouverneur s'est prononcé (ouvertement) contre/pour l'avortement ❑ **to ~ out (of the closet)** *inf* ne plus cacher son homosexualité. -**6.** *Br* [on strike] se mettre en OR faire grève. -**7.** [emerge, finish up] se tirer d'affaire, s'en sortir; **the government came out of the deal badly** le gouvernement s'est mal sorti de l'affaire; **everything will ~ out fine** tout va s'arranger || [in competition] se classer; **I came out top in maths** j'étais premier en maths; **to ~ out on top** gagner. -**8.** [go into society] faire ses débuts OR débuter dans le monde. -**9.** MATH [yield solution]: **this sum won't ~ out** je n'arrive pas à résoudre cette opération. -**10.** PHOT: **the pictures came out well/badly** les photos étaient très bonnes/n'ont rien donné; **the house didn't ~ out well** la maison n'est pas très bien sur les photos.

◆ **come out at** *vt insep* [amount to] s'élever à.

◆ **come out in** *vt insep*: **to ~ out in spots** OR **a rash** avoir une éruption de boutons.

◆ **come out with** *vt insep* [say] dire, sortir; **what will he ~ out with next?** qu'est-ce qu'il va nous sortir encore?; **he finally came out with it** il a fini par le sortir.

◆ **come over** ◇ *vi insep* -**1.** [move, travel in direction of speaker] venir; **at the party she came over to talk to me** pendant la soirée, elle est venue me parler; **his family came over with the early settlers** sa famille est arrivée OR venue avec les premiers pionniers; **I met him in the plane coming over** je l'ai rencontré dans l'avion en venant. -**2.** [stop by] venir, passer. -**3.** [change sides]: **they came over to our side** ils sont passés de notre côté; **he finally came over to their way of thinking** il a fini par se ranger à leur avis. -**4.** [make specified impression]: **her speech came over well** son discours a fait bon effet OR bonne impression; **he came over as honest** il a donné l'impression d'être honnête. -**5.** *inf* [feel] devenir; **he came over all funny** [felt ill] il s'est senti mal tout d'un coup, il a eu un malaise; [behaved oddly] il est devenu tout bizarre; **to ~ over dizzy** être pris de vertige; **to ~ over faint** être pris d'une faiblesse.
◇ *vt insep* affecter, envahir; **a change came over him** un changement se produisit en lui; **a feeling of fear came over him** il a été saisi de peur, la peur s'est emparée de lui; **what has ~ over him?** qu'est-ce qui lui prend?

◆ **come round** *vi insep* -**1.** [make a detour] faire le détour; **we came round by the factory** nous sommes passés par OR nous avons fait le détour par l'usine. -**2.** [stop by] passer, venir. -**3.** [occur - regular event]: **don't wait for Christmas to ~ round** n'attendez pas Noël; **when the championships/elections ~ round** au moment des championnats/élections; **the summer holidays will soon be coming round again** bientôt, ce sera de nouveau les grandes vacances. -**4.** [change mind] changer d'avis; **he finally came round to our way of thinking** il a fini par se ranger à notre avis || [change to better mood]: **don't worry, she'll soon ~ round** ne t'en fais pas, elle sera bientôt de meilleure humeur. -**5.** [recover consciousness] reprendre connaissance, revenir à soi; [get better] se remettre, se rétablir; **she's coming round after a bout of pneumonia** elle se remet d'une pneumonie. -**6.** NAUT venir au vent.

◆ **come through** ◇ *vi insep* -**1.** [be communicated]: **his sense of conviction came through** on voyait qu'il était convaincu; **her enthusiasm ~s through in her letters** son enthousiasme se lit dans ses lettres || TELEC & RADIO: **your call is coming through** je vous passe votre communication; **you're coming through loud and clear** je vous reçois cinq sur cinq; **his message came through loud and clear** *fig* son message a été reçu cinq sur cinq. -**2.** [be granted, approved] se réaliser; **did your visa ~ through?** avez-vous obtenu votre visa?; **my request for a transfer came through** ma demande de mutation a été acceptée. -**3.** [survive] survivre, s'en tirer. -**4.** *inf Am* [do what is expected]: **he came through for us** il a fait ce qu'on attendait de lui; **did he ~ through on his promise?** a-t-il tenu parole?; **they came through with the documents** ils ont fourni les documents; **he came through with the money** il a rendu l'argent comme prévu.
◇ *vt insep* -**1.** [cross] traverser; **we came through marshland** nous sommes passés par OR avons traversé des marais || *fig* [penetrate] traverser; **the rain came through my coat** la pluie a traversé mon manteau. -**2.** [survive]: **they came through the accident without a scratch** ils sont sortis de l'accident indemnes; **she came through the examination with flying colours** elle a réussi l'examen avec brio.

◆ **come to** ◇ *vi insep* -**1.** [recover consciousness] reprendre connaissance, revenir à soi. -**2.** NAUT [change course] venir au vent, lofer; [stop] s'arrêter.
◇ *vt insep* -**1.** [concern]: **when it ~s to physics, she's a genius** pour ce qui est de la physique, c'est un génie; **when it ~s to paying...** quand il faut payer... -**2.** [amount to] s'élever à, se monter à; **how much did dinner ~ to?** à combien s'élevait le dîner?; **her salary ~s to £750 a month** elle gagne 750 livres par mois. -**3.** *fig* [arrive at, reach]: **now we ~ to questions of health** nous en venons maintenant aux questions de santé; **to ~ to a conclusion** arriver à une conclusion; **to ~ to power** accéder au pouvoir ❑ **what is the world coming to?** où va le monde?; **I never thought it would ~ to this** je ne me doutais pas qu'on en arriverait là.

◆ **come together** *vi insep* -**1.** [assemble] se réunir, se rassembler; [meet] se rencontrer. -**2.** *inf* [combine successfully]: **everything came together at the final performance** tout s'est passé à merveille pour la dernière représentation.

◆ **come under** *vt insep* -**1.** [be subjected to - authority, control] dépendre de; [- influence] tomber sous, être soumis à; **the government is coming under pressure to lower taxes** le gouvernement subit des pressions visant à réduire les impôts. -**2.** [be classified under] être classé sous; **that subject ~s under 'current events'** ce sujet est classé OR se trouve sous la rubrique «actualités».

◆ **come up** *vi insep* -**1.** [move upwards] monter; [moon, sun] se lever; [travel in direction of speaker]: **I ~ up to town every Monday** je viens en ville tous les lundis; **they came up to Chicago** ils sont venus à Chicago ❑ **to ~ up for air** [diver] remonter à la surface; *fig* [take break] faire une pause; **she came up the hard way** elle a réussi à la force du poignet; **an officer who came up through the ranks** MIL un officier sorti du rang. -**2.** [approach] s'approcher; **to ~ up to sb** s'approcher de qqn, venir vers qqn; **the students came up to him with their questions** les étudiants sont venus le voir avec leurs questions; **it's coming up to 5 o'clock** il est presque 5 h; **coming up now on Channel 4, the Cosby Show** et maintenant, sur Channel 4, le Cosby Show; **one coffee, coming up!** *inf* et un café, un! -**3.** [plant] sortir, germer; **my beans are coming up nicely** mes haricots poussent bien. -**4.** [come under consideration - matter] être soulevé, être mis sur le tapis; [- question] se poser, être soulevé; **that problem has never ~ up** ce problème ne s'est jamais posé; **the question of financing always ~s up** la question du financement se pose toujours; **she ~s up for re-election this year** son mandat prend fin cette année; **my contract is coming up for review** mon contrat doit être révisé || JUR [accused] comparaître; [case] être entendu; **to ~ up before the judge** OR **the court** [accused] comparaître devant le juge; [case] être entendu par la cour; **her case ~s up next Wednesday** elle passe au tribunal mercredi prochain. -**5.** [happen unexpectedly - event] survenir, surgir; [- opportunity] se présenter; **she's ready for anything that might ~ up** elle est prête à faire face à toute éventualité; **I can't make it, something has ~ up** je ne peux pas venir, j'ai un empêchement. -**6.** [intensify - wind] se lever; [- light] s'allumer; **when the lights came up at the interval** lorsque les lumières se rallumèrent à l'entracte; [- sound] s'intensifier. -**7.** [be vomited]: **everything she eats ~s up (again)** elle vomit OR rejette tout ce qu'elle mange. -**8.** [colour, wood etc]: **the colour ~s up well when it's cleaned** la couleur revient bien au nettoyage. -**9.** *inf* [win] gagner; **did their number ~ up?** [in lottery] ont-ils gagné au loto?; *fig* est-ce qu'ils ont touché le gros lot?

◆ **come up against** *vt insep* [be confronted with] rencontrer; **they came up against some tough competition** ils se sont heurtés à des concurrents redoutables.

◆ **come up to** *vt insep* -**1.** [reach] arriver à; **the mud came up to their knees** la boue leur montait OR arrivait jusqu'aux genoux; **she ~s up to his shoulder** elle lui arrive à l'épaule.

-**2.** [equal]: **his last book doesn't ~ up to the others** son dernier livre ne vaut pas les autres; **the play didn't ~ up to our expectations** la pièce nous a déçus.

◆ **come up with** *vt insep* [offer, propose - money, loan] fournir; [think of - plan, suggestion] suggérer, proposer; **if you ~ up with the answer...** si tu trouves la réponse...; **they came up with a wonderful idea** ils ont eu une idée géniale; **what excuse did he ~ up with?** qu'est-ce qu'il a inventé OR trouvé comme excuse?; **what will she ~ up with next?** qu'est-ce qu'elle va encore inventer?

◆ **come upon** *vt insep* [find unexpectedly - person] rencontrer par hasard, tomber sur; [- object] trouver par hasard, tomber sur; **we came upon the couple just as they were kissing** nous avons surpris le couple en train de s'embrasser.

comeback *inf* ['kʌmbæk] *n* -**1.** [return] retour *m*, comeback *m*; THEAT rentrée *f*; **to make** OR **to stage a ~** faire une rentrée OR un comeback. -**2.** [retort] réplique *f*.

Comecon ['kɒmɪkɒn] (*abbr of* **Council for Mutual Economic Aid**) *pr n* Comecon *m*.

comedian [kə'miːdjən] *n* -**1.** [comic] comique *m*; *fig* [funny person] clown *m*, pitre *m*. -**2.** THEAT [comic actor] comédien *m*.

comedienne [kə,miːdɪ'en] *n* -**1.** [comic] actrice *f* comique. -**2.** THEAT [comic actress] comédienne *f*.

comedo ['kɒmɪdəʊ] (*pl* **comedones** [,kɒmɪ'dəʊniːz]) *n* MED comédon *m*.

comedown *inf* ['kʌmdaʊn] *n* déchéance *f*, dégringolade *f*; **he finds working in sales a bit of a ~** il trouve plutôt humiliant de travailler comme vendeur.

comedy ['kɒmədɪ] (*pl* **comedies**) *n* [gen] comédie *f*; THEAT genre *m* comique, comédie *f*; **~ of manners** comédie de mœurs; **'The Comedy of Errors'** *Shakespeare* 'la Comédie des erreurs'; **the whole affair has been a ~ of errors** toute cette affaire n'a été qu'une farce.

come-hither *inf adj* aguichant; **a ~ look** un regard aguichant.

comely ['kʌmlɪ] (*compar* **comelier**, *superl* **comeliest**) *adj arch* charmant, beau.

come-on *inf n* attrape-nigaud *m*; **to give sb the ~** faire les yeux doux à qqn.

comer ['kʌmə^r] *n* -**1.** [arrival] arrivant *m*, -e *f*; **the first ~s** les premiers venus; **open to all ~s** ouvert à tous OR au tout-venant. -**2.** *inf Am* [potential success]: **she's a real ~!** elle a un bel avenir devant elle!

comestible [kə'mestɪbl] *adj fml* comestible.

◆ **comestibles** *npl* comestibles *fpl*, denrées *mpl* comestibles.

comet ['kɒmɪt] *n* comète *f*.

come-uppance *inf* [,kʌm'ʌpəns] *n*: **she got her ~** elle n'a eu que ce qu'elle méritait; **you'll get your ~** tu auras ce que tu mérites.

comfort ['kʌmfət] ◇ *n* -**1.** [well-being] confort *m*, bien-être *m*; **to live in ~** vivre dans l'aisance OR à l'aise; **she's used to ~** elle a toujours eu tout le OR son confort; **the explosion was too close for ~** *fig* l'explosion a eu lieu un peu trop près à mon goût. -**2.** (*usu pl*) [amenities] aises *fpl*, commodités *fpl*; **every modern ~** tout le confort moderne; **I like my ~** OR **~s** j'aime bien mes aises. -**3.** [consolation] réconfort *m*, consolation *f*; **to take ~ in sthg** se consoler de qqch; **she took ~ from his words** elle a trouvé un réconfort dans ses paroles; **I took ~ from** OR **in the knowledge that it would soon be over** je me suis consolé en me disant que ce serait bientôt fini; **it's a ~ to know** c'est un soulagement de savoir; **if it's any ~ to you** si cela peut vous consoler; **you've been a great ~ to me** vous avez été d'un grand réconfort pour moi.

◇ *vt* -**1.** [console] consoler; [relieve] soulager. -**2.** [cheer] réconforter, encourager.

comfortable ['kʌmftəbl] *adj* -**1.** [chair, shoes, bed, room] confortable; [temperature] agréable; *fig* [lead, win] confortable. -**2.** [person] à l'aise; **are you ~?** êtes-vous bien installé?; **make yourself ~** [sit down] installez-vous confortablement; [feel at ease] mettez-vous à l'aise, faites comme chez vous; **I'm not very ~ about** OR **I don't feel ~ with the idea** l'idée m'inquiète un peu ‖ [after illness, operation, accident]: **to be ~** ne pas souffrir. -**3.** [financially secure] aisé, riche; [easy - job] tranquille; **they're very ~** ils ont une vie aisée; **~ income** revenu suffisant; **he makes a ~ living** il gagne bien sa vie. -**4.** [ample]: **that leaves us a ~ margin** ça nous laisse une marge confortable.

comfortably ['kʌmftəblɪ] *adv* -**1.** [in a relaxed position - sit, sleep] confortablement, agréablement. -**2.** [in financial comfort] à l'aise; **they live ~** ils vivent dans l'aisance OR à l'aise; **to be ~ off** être à l'aise. -**3.** [easily] facilement, à l'aise; **we can fit five people in the car ~** la voiture contient bien cinq personnes, on tient à l'aise à cinq dans la voiture; **we should manage it ~ in two hours** deux heures suffiront largement.

comforter ['kʌmfətə^r] *n* -**1.** [person] consolateur *m*, -trice *f*. -**2.** *Br* [scarf] cache-nez *m*. -**3.** [for baby] tétine *f*, sucette *f*. -**4.** *Am* [quilt] édredon *m*.

comforting ['kʌmfətɪŋ] ◇ *adj* [consoling - remark, thought] consolant, réconfortant, rassurant; [encouraging] encourageant.

◇ *n* [consolation] réconfort *m*, consolation *f*; [encouragement] encouragement *m*.

comfortless ['kʌmfətlɪs] *adj* -**1.** [room] sans confort. -**2.** [dismal - person] triste, désolé; [- thought] peu rassurant, triste.

comfort station *n Am* toilettes *fpl* publiques *(sur le bord d'une route)*.

comfy *inf* ['kʌmfɪ] (*compar* **comfier**, *superl* **comfiest**) *adj* confortable, agréable; **are you ~?** vous êtes bien installés?; **a ~ chair** un fauteuil confortable.

comic ['kɒmɪk] ◇ *adj* comique, humoristique; **~ relief** THEAT intervalle *m* comique; *fig* moment *m* de détente (comique).

◇ *n* -**1.** [entertainer] (acteur *m*) comique *m*, actrice *f* comique. -**2.** [magazine] BD *f*, bande dessinée *f*.

◆ **comics** *npl Am* [in newspaper] bandes *fpl* dessinées.

comical ['kɒmɪkl] *adj* drôle, comique.

comically ['kɒmɪklɪ] *adv* drôlement, comiquement.

comic book *n* magazine *m* de bandes dessinées.

comic opera *n* opéra *m* comique.

comic strip *n* bande *f* dessinée.

coming ['kʌmɪŋ] ◇ *adj* -**1.** [time, events] à venir, futur; [in near future] prochain; **this ~ Tuesday** mardi prochain; **the ~ storm** l'orage qui approche. -**2.** *inf* [promising - person] d'avenir, qui promet.

◇ *n* -**1.** [gen] arrivée *f*, venue *f*; **~ away** départ *m*; **~ back** retour *m*; **~ in** entrée *f*; **~ out** sortie *f* ❑ **~ and going** va-et-vient *m*; **~s and goings** allées *fpl* et venues. -**2.** RELIG avènement *m*.

coming of age *n* majorité *f*.

COMING OF AGE:

À sa majorité (18 ans) un(e) jeune Britannique acquiert le droit de voter, de faire partie d'un jury, de boire de l'alcool dans les pubs et de se marier sans le consentement de ses parents.

---

coming out *n* entrée *f* dans le monde *(d'une jeune fille)*.

Comintern ['kɒmɪntɜːn] (*abbr of* **Communist International**) *pr n* Komintern *m*.

comma ['kɒmə] *n* GRAMM & MUS virgule *f*.

command [kə'mɑːnd] ◇ *n* -**1.** [order] ordre *m*; MIL ordre *m*, commandement *m*; **the troops were withdrawn at** OR **on his ~** les troupes ont été retirées sur ses ordres; **they are at your ~** ils sont à vos ordres; **at the word of ~** au commandement. -**2.** [authority] commandement *m*; **who is in ~ here?** qui est-ce qui commande ici?; **I'm second in ~** je commande en second; **to be in ~ of sthg** avoir qqch sous ses ordres, être à la tête de qqch; **he had/took ~ of the situation** il avait/a pris la situation en main; **they are under her ~** ils sont sous ses ordres OR son commandement. -**3.** [control, mastery] maîtrise *f*; **~ of the seas** maîtrise des mers; **he's in full ~ of his faculties** il est en pleine possession de ses moyens; **she has a good ~ of two foreign languages** elle possède bien deux langues étrangères; **her ~ of Spanish** sa maîtrise de l'espagnol; **all the resources at my ~** toutes les ressources à ma disposition OR dont je dispose; **I'm at your ~** je suis à votre disposition; **~ of the market** COMM domination *f* sur le marché. -**4.** MIL [group of officers] commandement *m*; [troops] troupes *fpl*; [area] région *f* militaire. -**5.** COMPUT commande *f*.

◇ *vt* -**1.** [order] ordonner, commander; **she ~ed that we leave immediately** elle nous a ordonné OR nous a donné l'ordre de partir immédiatement; **the general ~ed his men to attack** le général a donné l'ordre à ses hommes d'attaquer. -**2.** [have control over - army] commander; [- emotions] maîtriser, dominer. -**3.** [receive as due] commander, imposer; **to ~ respect** inspirer le respect, en imposer; **to ~ the attention of one's audience** tenir son public en haleine; **the translator ~s a high fee** les services du traducteur valent cher; **this painting will ~ a high price** ce tableau se vendra à un prix élevé. -**4.** [have use of] disposer de; **all the skills and resources that the country can ~** toutes les capacités et les ressources dont le pays peut disposer. -**5.** [subj: building, statue - overlook]: **to ~ a view of** avoir vue sur, donner sur.

◇ *vi* -**1.** [order] commander, donner des ordres. -**2.** [be in control] commander; MIL commander, avoir le commandement.

commandant [,kɒmən'dænt] *n* commandant *m*.

command economy *n* économie *f* planifiée.

commandeer [,kɒmən'dɪə^r] *vt* [officially] réquisitionner; [usurp] accaparer.

commander [kə'mɑːndə^r] *n* -**1.** [person in charge] chef *m*; MIL commandant *m*; NAUT capitaine *m* de frégate. -**2.** *Br* [of police] ≃ commissaire *m* divisionnaire, ≃ divisionnaire *m*.

commander-in-chief *n* commandant *m* en chef, généralissime *m*.

commanding [kə'mɑːndɪŋ] *adj* -**1.** [in command] qui commande. -**2.** [overlooking - view] élevé; [overlooking and dominant - position] dominant, important; **to be in a ~ position** avoir une position dominante; **to have a ~ lead** avoir une solide avance. -**3.** [tone, voice] impérieux, de commandement; [look] impérieux; [air] imposant.

commanding officer *n* commandant *m*.

commandment [kə'mɑːndmənt] *n* commandement *m*; **the Ten Commandments** les dix commandements, le décalogue *fml*.

commando [kə'mɑːndəʊ] (*pl* **commandos** OR **commandoes**) ◇ *n* commando *m*.

◇ *comp* [raid, unit] de commando.

command performance *n représentation (d'un spectacle) à la requête d'un chef d'État*.

command post *n* poste *m* de commandement.

commemorate [kə'meməreɪt] *vt* commémorer.

commemoration [kə,memə'reɪʃn] *n* commémoration *f*; RELIG commémoraison *f*; **in ~ of sthg/sb** en commémoration de qqch/qqn.

commemorative [kə'memərətɪv] *adj* commémoratif.

commence [kə'mens] *fml* ◇ *vi* commencer.

◇ *vt* commencer; **the date on which you ~d employment** la date à laquelle vous avez commencé à travailler; **she ~d speaking at 2 p.m.** elle a commencé à parler à 2 h de l'après-midi; **to ~ proceedings against sb** JUR former un recours contre qqn *(devant une juridiction)*.

commencement [kə'mensmənt] *n* -**1.** *fml* [beginning] commencement *m*, début *m*; JUR [of law] date *f* d'entrée en vigueur. -**2.** *Am* UNIV remise *f* des diplômes.

Commencement Day *n jour de la remise des diplômes dans une université américaine.*

commend [kəˈmend] *vt* -**1.** [recommend] recommander, conseiller; he **~ed the proposal to the committee** il a recommandé le projet au comité; **if this policy ~s itself to the public...** si cette politique est du goût du public...; **the report has little to ~ it** il n'y a pas grand-chose d'intéressant dans ce rapport. -**2.** [praise] louer, faire l'éloge de; **to ~ sb for bravery** louer qqn pour sa bravoure; **you are to be ~ed for your hard work** on doit vous féliciter pour votre dur labeur. -**3.** [entrust] confier; **to ~ sthg to sb** confier qqch à qqn, remettre qqch aux bons soins de qqn; **we ~ our souls to God** RELIG nous recommandons notre âme à Dieu.

commendable [kəˈmendəbl] *adj* louable.

commendably [kəˈmendəblɪ] *adv* de façon louable; **his speech was ~ brief** son discours avait le mérite de la brièveté.

commendation [ˌkɒmenˈdeɪʃn] *n* -**1.** [praise] éloge *f*, louange *f*. -**2.** [recommendation] recommendation *f*. -**3.** [award for bravery] décoration *f*. -**4.** [entrusting] remise *f*.

commensurable [kəˈmenʃərəbl] *adj fml* commensurable; **to be ~ with** OR **to sthg** être commensurable avec qqch.

commensurate [kəˈmenʃərət] *adj fml* -**1.** [of equal measure] de même mesure, commensurable; **the side is ~ with the diagonal** MATH on peut mesurer le côté en fonction de la diagonale. -**2.** [proportionate] proportionné; **~ with** OR **to sthg** proportionné à qqch; **the salary will be ~ with your experience** le salaire sera en fonction de votre expérience.

comment [ˈkɒment] ◇ *n* -**1.** [remark] commentaire *m*, observation *f*; **she let it pass without ~** elle n'a pas relevé; **it's a ~ on our society** *fig* c'est une réflexion sur notre société; **no ~!** je n'ai rien à dire!; **(it's a) fair ~** c'est juste. -**2.** *(U)* [gossip, criticism]: **the decision provoked much ~** la décision a suscité de nombreux commentaires. -**3.** [note] commentaire *m*, annotation *f*; [critical] critique *f*; **teacher's ~s** SCH appréciations *fpl* du professeur.

◇ *vi* -**1.** [remark] faire une remarque OR des remarques; **she ~ed on his age** elle a fait des remarques OR commentaires sur son âge; **he ~ed that...** il a fait la remarque que... -**2.** [give opinion]: **~ on the text** commentez le texte, faites le commentaire du texte.

commentary [ˈkɒməntrɪ] (*pl* **commentaries**) *n* -**1.** [remarks] commentaire *m*, observation *f*. -**2.** RADIO & TV commentaire *m*; **with ~ by Des Lynam** commenté par Des Lynam.

commentary box *n* tribune *f* des journalistes.

commentate [ˈkɒmənteɪt] ◇ *vt* commenter.
◇ *vi* faire un reportage.

commentator [ˈkɒmənteɪtəʳ] *n* -**1.** RADIO & TV reporter *m*. -**2.** [analyst] commentateur *m*, -trice *f*.

commerce [ˈkɒmɜːs] *n* *(U)* -**1.** [trade] commerce *m*, affaires *fpl*; **Secretary/Department of Commerce** *Am* ministre *m*/ministère *m* du Commerce. -**2.** *fig & lit* [of ideas, opinions] relations *fpl*, commerce *m*.

commercial [kəˈmɜːʃl] ◇ *adj* -**1.** [economic] commercial; **~ district** quartier *m* commerçant; **~ law** droit *m* commercial; **a ~ venture** une entreprise commerciale. -**2.** [profitable] commercial, marchand; **a ~ success** un succès commercial; **~ value** valeur *f* marchande. -**3.** *pej* [profit-seeking - record, book, pop group] commercial; **their motives are purely ~** ils ont des motivations purement commerciales. -**4.** [broadcasting] commercial.
◇ *n* publicité *f*, spot *m* publicitaire.

commercial art *n* graphisme *m*.

commercial artist *n* graphiste *mf*.

commercial bank *n* banque *f* commerciale.

commercial college *n* école *f* de commerce.

commercialism [kəˈmɜːʃəlɪzm] *n* -**1.** [practice of business] (pratique *f* du) commerce *m*, (pratique des) affaires *fpl*. -**2.** *esp pej* [profit-seeking] mercantilisme *m*, esprit *m* commercial; [on large scale] affairisme *m*.

commercialization [kəˌmɜːʃəlaɪˈzeɪʃn] *n* commercialisation *f*.

commercialize, -ise [kəˈmɜːʃəlaɪz] *vt* commercialiser.

commercially [kəˈmɜːʃəlɪ] *adv* commercialement.

commercial traveller *n dated* voyageur *m* OR représentant *m* de commerce, VRP *m*.

commercial vehicle *n* véhicule *m* utilitaire, commerciale *f*.

commie *inf* [ˈkɒmɪ] *pej* ◇ *adj* coco.
◇ *n* coco *mf*.

commiserate [kəˈmɪzəreɪt] *vi*: **to ~ with sb** [feel sympathy] éprouver de la compassion pour qqn; [show sympathy] témoigner de la sympathie à qqn; **we ~d with him on his misfortune** nous avons compati à sa malchance.

commiseration [kəˌmɪzəˈreɪʃn] *n* commisération *f*.

commissar [ˈkɒmɪsɑːʳ] *n* commissaire *m* (du peuple).

commissariat [ˌkɒmɪˈseərɪət] *n* -**1.** POL commissariat *m*. -**2.** MIL [department] intendance *f*; [food supply] ravitaillement *m*.

commissary [ˈkɒmɪsərɪ] (*pl* **commissaries**) *n* -**1.** *Am* MIL [shop] intendance *f*; [officer] intendant *m*. -**2.** *Am* CIN [cafeteria] restaurant *m* (du studio). -**3.** RELIG délégué *m (d'un évêque)*.

commission [kəˈmɪʃn] ◇ *n* -**1.** [authority for special job] commission *f*, mission *f*, ordres *mpl*, instructions *fpl*; ART commande *f*; **to give a ~ to an artist** passer une commande à un artiste; **work done on ~** travail fait sur commande. -**2.** [delegation of authority] délégation *f* de pouvoir OR d'autorité, mandat *m*; [formal warrant] mandat *m*, pouvoir *m*; MIL brevet *m*; **she resigned her ~** elle a démissionné; **when he received his ~** quand il a été élevé OR promu au grade d'officier. -**3.** [committee] commission *f*, comité *m*; **~ of inquiry, fact-finding ~** commission d'enquête; **Royal Commission** *Br* POL commission extraparlementaire. -**4.** COMM [fee] commission *f*, courtage *m*; **to work on a ~ basis** travailler à la commission; **I get (a) 5% ~** je reçois une commission de 5%. -**5.** JUR [of crime] perpétration *f*. -**6.** NAUT [of ship] armement *m*; **to put a ship into ~** armer un navire.
◇ *vt* -**1.** [place order with, for] commander; **we ~ed the architect to design a new house** nous avons engagé un architecte pour faire les plans d'une nouvelle maison. -**2.** [grant authority to] donner pouvoir OR mission à, déléguer, charger; **to ~ sb to do sthg** charger qqn de faire qqch; **I was ~ed to investigate** j'ai reçu la OR pour mission d'enquêter. -**3.** MIL [make officer] nommer à un commandement; **he was ~ed general** il a été promu au grade de OR nommé général. -**4.** [make operative] mettre en service; NAUT [ship] mettre en service, armer.

◆ **in commission** *adj phr* [gen] en service; NAUT [ship] en armement, en service.

◆ **out of commission** ◇ *adj phr* [gen] hors service; [car] en panne; NAUT [not working] hors service; [in reserve] en réserve.
◇ *adv phr*: **to take a ship out of ~** désarmer un navire.

commission agent *n* commissaire *m*.

commissionaire [kəˌmɪʃəˈneəʳ] *n Br* portier *m (d'un hôtel etc)*.

commissioned officer [kəˈmɪʃənd-] *n* officier *m*.

commissioner [kəˈmɪʃnəʳ] *n* -**1.** [member of commission] membre *m* d'une commission, commissaire *m*. -**2.** [of police] *Br* ≃ préfet *m* de police, *Am* ≃ (commissaire *m*) divisionnaire *m*; [of government department] haut fonctionnaire. -**3.** *Am* SCH & UNIV: **~ of education** ≃ recteur *m*, ≃ doyen *m*. -**4.** JUR: **~ for oaths** *officier ayant qualité pour recevoir les déclarations sous serment.*

commit [kəˈmɪt] (*pt & pp* **committed**, *cont* **committing**) *vt* -**1.** [crime] commettre, perpétrer; [mistake] faire, commettre; **to ~ suicide** se suicider; **committing perjury is a crime** se parjurer OR faire un faux serment est un délit. -**2.** [entrust - thing] confier, remettre; [- person] confier; **to ~ sthg to sb's care** confier qqch aux soins de qqn OR à la garde de qqn; **he was committed to a mental hospital** il a été interné; **they committed her to prison** ils l'ont incarcérée; **I committed the poem to memory** j'ai appris le poème par cœur; **to ~ sthg to paper** coucher OR consigner qqch par écrit ❑ **committing magistrate** *Am* JUR juge *m* d'instruction. -**3.** [promise] engager; **to ~ o.s. to sthg/to do sthg** s'engager à qqch/à faire qqch; **he refused to ~ himself** il s'est tenu sur la réserve, il a refusé de prendre parti OR de s'engager; **to ~ troops (to a region)** MIL engager des troupes (dans une région). -**4.** [legislative bill] renvoyer en commission.

commitment [kəˈmɪtmənt] *n* -**1.** [promise, loyalty] engagement *m*; **to make a ~** [emotionally, intellectually] s'engager. -**2.** [obligation] obligations *fpl*, responsabilités *fpl*; **he has family ~s** il a des obligations familiales; **teaching ~s** SCH & UNIV charge *f* d'enseignement, enseignement *m* ‖ COMM & FIN engagement *m* financier; **with no ~** sans obligation d'achat. -**3.** [to prison] incarcération *f*, emprisonnement *m*; [to mental hospital] internement *m*. -**4.** [of crime] perpétration *f*. -**5.** JUR [order] mandat *m* de dépôt. -**6.** [of legislative bill] renvoi *m* en commission.

committal [kəˈmɪtl] *n* -**1.** [sending - gen] remise *f*; [- to prison] incarcération *f*, emprisonnement *m*; [- to mental hospital] internement *m*; [- to grave] mise *f* en terre. -**2.** JUR: **~ order** mandat *m* de dépôt; **~ proceedings, ~ for trial** ≃ mise *f* en accusation. -**3.** [of crime] perpétration *f*.

committed [kəˈmɪtɪd] *adj* [writer, artist] engagé; **a ~ Socialist/Christian** un socialiste/chrétien convaincu.

committee [kəˈmɪtɪ] ◇ *n* commission *f*, comité *m*; **to be** OR **to sit on a ~** faire partie d'une commission OR d'un comité ‖ [in government] commission *f*; **the House went into ~** *Br* la Chambre s'est constituée en comité; **Committee of the Whole House** *Br séance de commission étendue à la chambre entière*; **Committee of Ways and Means** commission *f* du budget.
◇ *comp* [meeting] de commission OR comité; [member] d'une commission, d'un comité.

committeeman [kəˈmɪtɪmən] (*pl* **committeemen** [-mən]) *n* membre *m* d'une commission OR d'un comité.

committeewoman [kəˈmɪtɪˌwʊmən] (*pl* **committeewomen** [-ˌwɪmɪn]) *n* membre *m (femme)* d'une commission OR d'un comité.

commode [kəˈməʊd] *n* -**1.** [chest of drawers] commode *f*. -**2.** [for chamber pot] chaise *f* percée.

commodious [kəˈməʊdjəs] *adj fml* spacieux, vaste.

commodity [kəˈmɒdətɪ] (*pl* **commodities**) *n* -**1.** [product] marchandise *f*; [consumer goods] produit *m*, article *m*; [food] denrée *f*; **a basic** OR **staple ~** un produit de base; **household commodities** articles ménagers. -**2.** ECON [raw material] produit *m* de base, matière *f* première; **the ~** OR **commodities market** le marché des matières premières; **to trade in commodities** faire le négoce de matières premières.

commodore [ˈkɒmədɔːʳ] *n* -**1.** MIL contre-amiral *m*. -**2.** NAUT [of merchant ships] commodore *m*; [of shipping line] doyen *m*; [of yacht club] président *m*.

common [ˈkɒmən] ◇ *adj* -**1.** [ordinary] commun, ordinaire; [plant] commun; **it's quite ~** c'est courant OR tout à fait banal; **it's a ~ experience** cela arrive à beaucoup de gens OR à tout le monde; **a ~ expression** une expression courante; **a ~ occurrence** une chose fréquente OR qui arrive souvent; **a ~ sight** un spectacle familier; **in ~ parlance** dans le langage courant; **the ~ horde** *Br pej* la plèbe, la populace;

the ~ man l'homme du peuple; the ~ people le peuple, les gens du commun; ~ salt sel *m* (ordinaire); a ~ soldier un simple soldat; it's only ~ courtesy to reply la politesse la plus élémentaire veut qu'on réponde ❑ to have the ~ touch *Br* savoir parler aux gens simples. -**2.** [shared, public] commun; by ~ consent d'un commun accord; the law is for the ~ good la loi vise au bien public ❑ ~ land terrain *m* communal OR banal; ~ ownership copropriété *f*; ~ ground point *m* commun, terrain *m* d'entente; there is no ~ ground between the two groups il n'y a pas de terrain d'entente entre les deux groupes; to make ~ cause with sb *Br* faire cause commune avec qqn. -**3.** [widespread] général, universel; the ~ belief la croyance universelle; in ~ use d'usage courant; it's ~ knowledge that... tout le monde sait que..., il est de notoriété publique que...; it's ~ practice to thank your host il est d'usage de remercier son hôte; it's ~ talk that... *Br* on entend souvent dire que... -**4.** *pej* [vulgar] commun, vulgaire; a ~ little man un petit homme vulgaire. -**5.** GRAMM [gender] non marqué. -**6.** MUS: ~ time OR measure mesure *f* à quatre temps.

◇ *n* -**1.** [land] terrain *m* communal; right of ~ *Br* JUR [of land] communauté *f* de jouissance; [of property] droit *m* de servitude. -**2.** *phr*: nothing out of the ~ *Br* rien d'extraordinaire.

◆ **commons** *npl arch* OR *lit*: the ~s le peuple.

◆ **Commons** *npl Br* & *Can* POL: the Commons les Communes *fpl*.

◆ **in common** *adv phr* en commun; to have sthg in ~ with sb avoir qqch en commun avec qqn; we have nothing in ~ nous n'avons rien de commun; they have certain ideas in ~ ils sont d'accord sur certaines idées.

commonalty ['kɒmənəltɪ] (*pl* commonalties) *n fml* [common people] peuple *m*.

common cold *n* rhume *m*.

common crab *n* tourteau *m*, dormeur *m*.

common denominator *n* MATH & *fig* dénominateur *m* commun.

common divisor *n* commun diviseur *m*.

Common Entrance *n examen de fin d'études primaires permettant d'entrer dans une «public school»*.

commoner ['kɒmənəʳ] *n* -**1.** [not noble] roturier *m*, -ère *f*. -**2.** *Br* JUR [with joint land rights] *personne qui a droit de vaine pâture*. -**3.** *Br* UNIV *étudiant ne bénéficiant pas de bourse (particulièrement à Oxford ou à Cambridge)*.

common factor *n* facteur *m* commun.

common fraction *n Am* fraction *f* ordinaire.

common law *n* droit *m* coutumier, common law *f*.

◆ **common-law** *adj*: common-law wife concubine *f* (reconnue juridiquement); common-law marriage mariage *m* de droit coutumier.

COMMON LAW:
Ensemble des règles de droit qui constituent la base du système juridique des pays de langue anglaise. À l'opposé des systèmes issus du droit romain, qui s'appuie sur la loi telle qu'elle est fixée dans des codes, ces règles, non écrites, sont établies par la jurisprudence.

---

common logarithm *n* logarithme *m* vulgaire OR décimal.

commonly ['kɒmənlɪ] *adv* -**1.** [usually] généralement; a species of frog ~ found in South America une espèce de grenouille que l'on trouve communément en Amérique latine; what is ~ known as... ce que l'on appelle dans le langage courant... -**2.** *pej* [vulgarly] vulgairement.

Common Market *n*: the ~ le marché commun.

common multiple *n* commun multiple *m*.

commonness ['kɒmənnɪs] *n* -**1.** [usualness] caractère *m* commun OR ordinaire. -**2.** [frequency] fréquence *f*. -**3.** [universality] généralité *f*, universalité *f*. -**4.** *pej* [vulgarness] vulgarité *f*.

common noun *n* nom *m* commun.

common-or-garden *inf adj Br*: the ~ variety le modèle standard OR ordinaire.

commonplace ['kɒmənpleɪs] ◇ *adj* banal, ordinaire; compact discs have become ~ les disques compacts sont devenus courants OR sont maintenant monnaie courante.

◇ *n* [thing] banalité *f*; [saying] lieu *m* commun, platitude *f*.

common prayer *n liturgie de l'Église anglicane*; the Book of Common Prayer *le livre liturgique anglican*.

common room *n Br* SCH & UNIV [for students] salle *f* commune; [for staff] salle *f* des professeurs.

commonsense ['kɒmən,sens], **commonsensical** [,kɒmən'sensɪkl] *adj* [attitude, approach, decision] sensé, plein de bon sens.

common sense *n* bon sens *m*, sens *m* commun.

common stock *n Am* actions *fpl* cotées en Bourse.

commonwealth ['kɒmənwelθ] *n* -**1.** [country] pays *m*; [state] État *m*; [republic] république *f*. -**2.** [body politic] corps *m* politique.

◆ **Commonwealth** ◇ *n* -**1.** the (British) Commonwealth (of Nations) le Commonwealth; Minister OR Secretary of State for Commonwealth Affairs ministre *m* du Commonwealth. -**2.** HIST: the Commonwealth *période de l'histoire britannique de 1649 (mort de Charles I) à 1660 (rétablissement de la monarchie)*.

◇ *comp* [games, nations] du Commonwealth.

Commonwealth of Independent States *pr n*: the ~ la Communauté des États Indépendants.

commotion [kə'məʊʃn] *n* -**1.** [noise] brouhaha *m*; what's all the ~ (about)? qu'est-ce que c'est que ce brouhaha OR vacarme?; who's making all this ~? qui est-ce qui fait tout ce tapage? -**2.** [disturbance] agitation *f*; what a ~! quel cirque!; to be in a (state of) ~ [person] être vivement ému; [crowd] être agité; [city] être en émoi; the news caused a real ~ la nouvelle a causé un véritable désordre. -**3.** [civil unrest] insurrection *f*, troubles *mpl*.

comms package [kɒmz-] *n* COMPUT logiciel *m* de communication.

communal ['kɒmjʊnl] *adj* -**1.** [shared] commun; a ~ room une pièce commune. -**2.** [of community] communautaire, collectif; a ~ activity une activité collective.

communalism ['kɒmjʊnəlɪzm] *n théorie confiant la plus grande partie du pouvoir aux communes*.

communally ['kɒmjʊnəlɪ] *adv* collectivement, en commun.

commune [*n* 'kɒmju:n, *vb* kə'mju:n] ◇ *n* -**1.** [group of people] communauté *f*; to live in a ~ vivre en communauté. -**2.** ADMIN [district] commune *f*.

◇ *vi* -**1.** [communicate] communier; to ~ with nature communier avec la nature. -**2.** RELIG communier.

◆ **Commune** *n* HIST: the (Paris) Commune la Commune.

communicable [kə'mju:nɪkəbl] *adj* communicable; MED [disease] contagieux, transmissible.

communicant [kə'mju:nɪkənt] ◇ *n* -**1.** RELIG communiant *m*, -e *f*. -**2.** [informant] informateur *m*, -trice *f*.

◇ *adj* -**1.** [communicating] qui communique, communicant. -**2.** RELIG pratiquant.

communicate [kə'mju:nɪkeɪt] ◇ *vi* -**1.** [be in touch] communiquer; [contact] prendre contact, se mettre en contact; they ~ with each other by phone ils communiquent par téléphone; I find it difficult to ~ (with others) j'ai du mal à entrer en relation avec les autres; they ~ well (with one another) ils s'entendent bien; she no longer ~s with him elle n'est plus en contact avec lui. -**2.** [rooms - connect] communiquer. -**3.** RELIG communier, recevoir la communion.

◇ *vt* -**1.** [impart - news] communiquer, transmettre; [- feelings] communiquer, faire partager; she ~d the news to them elle leur a fait part de la nouvelle. -**2.** [disease] transmettre.

communicating [kə'mju:nɪkeɪtɪŋ] *adj* communicant; there was a ~ door between the two bedrooms il y avait une porte de communication entre les deux chambres; a hotel suite with ~ rooms une suite avec chambres communicantes.

communication [kə,mju:nɪ'keɪʃn] *n* -**1.** [contact] communication *f*; are you in ~ with her? êtes-vous en contact OR en relation avec elle?; we broke off all ~ with him nous avons rompu tout contact avec lui; to be in radio ~ with sb communiquer avec qqn par radio, être en communication radio avec qqn ‖ [of thoughts, feelings] communication *f*; to be good at ~, to have good ~ skills avoir des talents de communication. -**2.** [message] communication *f*, message *m*.

◆ **communications** *npl* [technology] communications *fpl*; [roads, telegraph lines etc] communications *fpl*; MIL liaison *f*, communications *fpl*.

communication cord *n Br* sonnette *f* d'alarme *(dans les trains)*.

communication interface *n* interface *f* de communication.

communications satellite *n* satellite *m* de télécommunication.

communicative [kə'mju:nɪkətɪv] *adj* -**1.** [talkative] communicatif, expansif. -**2.** [ability, difficulty] de communication; ~ competence LING compétence de communication.

communicator [kə'mju:nɪkeɪtəʳ] *n personne douée pour la communication*; she's a good ~ c'est une femme de communication.

communion [kə'mju:njən] *n* -**1.** [sharing] communion *f*; a ~ of interests une communauté d'intérêts; ~ with nature communion avec la nature. -**2.** RELIG [group] communion *f*; [denomination] confession *f*; ~ cup calice *m*.

◆ **Communion** *n* RELIG [sacrament] communion *f*; to give Communion donner la communion; to take OR to receive Communion recevoir la communion; they go to Communion every Sunday ils communient tous les dimanches; she made her Communion elle a fait sa communion; to make one's Easter Communion faire ses pâques.

communiqué [kə'mju:nɪkeɪ] *n* communiqué *m*.

communism, **Communism** ['kɒmjʊnɪzm] *n* communisme *m*.

communist, **Communist** ['kɒmjʊnɪst] ◇ *n* communiste *mf*.

◇ *adj* communiste; 'The Communist Manifesto' *Marx, Engels* 'le Manifeste du parti communiste'.

community [kə'mju:nətɪ] (*pl* communities) *n* -**1.** [group of people, animals] communauté *f*, groupement *m*; RELIG communauté *f*; [locality] communauté *f*; the American ~ in Paris la communauté américaine de Paris; the business ~ le monde des affaires; the international ~ la communauté internationale; for the good of the ~ pour le bien public OR le bien de la communauté; a sense of ~ un sens communautaire OR de la solidarité ❑ ~ leader *personne qui joue un rôle actif dans la vie d'une communauté*; ~ policing ≃ îlotage *m*; ~ relations relations *fpl* publiques; ~ spirit sens *m* OR esprit *m* communautaire; ~ worker animateur *m* socioculturel, animatrice *f* socioculturelle. -**2.** [sharing] propriété *f* collective; JUR communauté *f*; ~ of goods/interests communauté de biens/d'intérêts.

◆ **Community** *n*: the (European) Community la Communauté (européenne).

community antenna *n* antenne *f* communautaire.

community association *n en Grande-Bretagne, association socioculturelle locale*.

community care *n système britannique d'assistance sociale au niveau local.*

community centre *n* foyer *m* municipal, centre *m* social.

community charge *n en Grande-Bretagne, nom officiel d'un impôt local plus connu sous le nom de «poll tax».*

community chest *n Am* fonds *m* commun *(à des fins sociales).*

community college *n Am* centre *m* universitaire (de premier cycle).

community home *n Br* -**1.** [for deprived children] assistance *f* publique. -**2.** [for young offenders] centre *m* d'éducation surveillée.

community school *n Br école servant de maison de la culture.*

community service *n* ≃ travail *m* d'intérêt général.

community singing *n* *(U)* chansons *fpl* populaires *(reprises en chœur).*

commutable [kə'mju:təbl] *adj* [exchangeable] interchangeable, permutable; JUR commuable; a death sentence ~ to life emprisonment une peine capitale commuable en emprisonnement à perpétuité.

commutation [,kɒmju:'teɪʃn] *n* -**1.** JUR [of penalty] commutation *f*; ~ of sentence commu-tation de peine. -**2.** *(U)* [exchange] échange *m*, substitution *f*. -**3.** [payment] échange *m*. -**4.** ELEC [of current] commutation *f*. -**5.** *Am* [commuting] migration *f* journalière.

commutation ticket *n Am* carte *f* d'abonnement.

commutative [kə'mju:tətɪv] *adj* [gen & MATH] commutatif.

commutator ['kɒmju:teɪtə^r] *n* commutateur *m*.

commute [kə'mju:t] ◇ *vi* faire un trajet régulier, faire la navette; I ~ from the suburbs je viens tous les jours de banlieue.
◇ *vt* -**1.** [exchange] substituer, échanger; to ~ one thing for another substituer une chose à une autre, échanger une chose pour OR contre une autre. -**2.** [convert] convertir; Midas ~d metal into gold Midas changeait le métal en or; to ~ an annuity into a lump sum FIN racheter une rente en un seul versement. -**3.** JUR [sentence] commuer; a sentence ~d to life imprisonment une peine commuée en emprisonnement à vie.

commuter [kə'mju:tə^r] ◇ *n* banlieusard *m*, -e *f* *(qui fait un trajet journalier pour se rendre au travail)*; RAIL abonné *m*, -e *f*.
◇ *comp* [line, train] de banlieue; the ~ belt *Br* la grande banlieue.

commuting [kə'mju:tɪŋ] *n* *(U)* trajets *mpl* réguliers, migrations *fpl* quotidiennes *(entre le domicile, généralement en banlieue, et le lieu de travail).*

Como ['kəʊməʊ] *pr n* Côme.

Comoran ['kɒmərən], **Comorian** [kə'mɒrjən] ◇ *n* Comorien *m*, -enne *f*.
◇ *adj* comorien.

Comoro ['kɒmərəʊ] *n*: the ~ Islands les îles Comores; the ~s les Comores; in the ~ Islands aux îles Comores; in the ~s aux Comores.

compact [*adj* & *vb* kəm'pækt, *n* 'kɒmpækt] ◇ *adj* -**1.** [small] compact, petit; [dense] dense, serré; the gadget is ~ and easy to use ce gadget ne prend pas de place et est facile à utiliser; ~ car *Am* compacte *f*, petite voiture *f*. -**2.** [concise] concis, condensé.
◇ *vt* [compress] compacter, tasser.
◇ *n* -**1.** [for powder] poudrier *m*. -**2.** *Am* (voiture *f*) compacte *f*, petite voiture *f*. -**3.** [agreement] convention *f*, contrat *m*; [informal] accord *m*, entente *f*.

compact camera [,kɒmpækt-] *n* (appareil photo *m*) compact *m*.

compact disc [,kɒmpækt-] ◇ *n* (disque *m*) compact *m*, CD *m*.
◇ *comp*: ~ player platine *f* CD.

compactly [kəm'pæktlɪ] *adv* -**1.** [made] de manière compacte; ~ designed conçu sans perte de place. -**2.** [concisely] de manière concise.

compactness [kəm'pæktnɪs] *n* -**1.** [smallness] compacité *f*; [denseness] compacité *f*, densité *f*; the ~ of the design la compacité de la conception. -**2.** [conciseness] concision *f*.

companion [kəm'pænjən] *n* -**1.** [friend] compagnon *m*, compagne *f*; [employee] dame *f* de compagnie; to be employed as a ~ to sb être employé pour tenir compagnie à qqn; a travelling ~ un compagnon de voyage; ~s in arms/distress compagnons d'armes/ d'infortune. -**2.** [one of pair] pendant *m*; to be a ~ to sthg faire pendant à qqch; the ~ volume le volume qui va de pair. -**3.** [handbook] manuel *m*. -**4.** [in titles] compagnon *m*; Companion of Honour *décoration britannique remise aux citoyens qui ont rendu des services à l'État*, ≃ chevalier *m* de la Légion d'honneur. -**5.** NAUT capot *m* (d'escalier).

companionable [kəm'pænjənəbl] *adj* [person] sociable, d'une compagnie agréable.

companionship [kəm'pænjənʃɪp] *n* *(U)* [fellowship] compagnie *f*; [friendship] amitié *f*, camaraderie *f*; she longs for ~ la compagnie OR la société (des autres) lui manque; he enjoys the ~ of the football team il aime la camaraderie qui règne au sein de l'équipe de football.

companionway [kəm'pænjənweɪ] *n* NAUT escalier *m* des cabines; [on smaller boat] montée *f*, descente *f*.

company ['kʌmpənɪ] (*pl* companies) ◇ *n* -**1.** [companionship] compagnie *f*; we enjoy one another's ~ nous aimons être ensemble; she's good ~ elle est d'agréable compagnie; to keep sb ~ tenir compagnie à qqn; in ~ with others en compagnie d'autres; we request the pleasure of your ~ at dinner nous ferez-vous le plaisir de venir dîner?; here's where we part ~ *literal* voilà où nos chemins se séparent; *fig* là, je ne suis plus d'accord avec vous; they parted ~ last year ils ont rompu l'année dernière; the handle finally parted ~ with the door *hum* la poignée a fini par fausser compagnie à la porte. -**2.** [companions] compagnie *f*, fréquentation *f*; she has got into OR she's keeping bad ~ elle a de mauvaises fréquentations; to be in good ~ être en bonne compagnie; if I'm wrong, I'm in good ~ *fig* si j'ai tort, je ne suis pas le seul; you mustn't speak like that in ~ on ne dit pas ces choses-là en société ☐ a man is known by the ~ he keeps *prov* dis-moi qui tu hantes, je te dirai qui tu es *prov*. -**3.** *(U)* [guests] invités *mpl*, compagnie *f*; are you expecting ~? attendez-vous de la visite? -**4.** [firm] société *f*, compagnie *f*; Jones & Company Jones et Compagnie. -**5.** [group of people] compagnie *f*, assemblée *f*; [of actors] troupe *f*, compagnie *f*; MIL compagnie *f*; NAUT [crew] équipage *m*.
◇ *comp* [policy] d'entreprise; he's a ~ man c'est un employé dévoué; ~ car voiture *f* de fonction.
◆ **Company** *inf pr n Am*: the Company la CIA.

company secretary *n* secrétaire *m* général, secrétaire *f* générale *(d'une entreprise).*

company sergeant-major *n* adjudant *m*.

comparability [,kɒmpərə'bɪlətɪ] *n* comparabilité *f*.

comparable ['kɒmprəbl] *adj* comparable; to be ~ to sthg être comparable à qqch; the salaries aren't at all ~ il n'y a pas de comparaison possible entre les salaires.

comparative [kəm'pærətɪv] ◇ *adj* -**1.** [relative] relatif; the ~ wealth of the two countries la fortune relative des deux pays; she's a ~ stranger to me je la connais relativement peu. -**2.** [study] comparatif; [field of study] comparé; ~ law droit *m* comparé; ~ linguistics linguistique *f* comparée. -**3.** GRAMM comparatif.
◇ *n* comparatif *m*; in the ~ au comparatif.

comparatively [kəm'pærətɪvlɪ] *adv* -**1.** [quite] relativement. -**2.** [study] comparativement.

compare [kəm'peə^r] ◇ *vt* -**1.** [contrast] comparer, mettre en comparaison; let's ~ Fitzgerald with Hemingway comparons Fitzgerald à OR avec Hemingway; ~d with OR to sthg en comparaison de OR par comparaison avec qqch; ~d with the others she's brilliant elle est brillante par rapport aux autres ☐ to ~ notes échanger ses impressions. -**2.** [liken] comparer, assimiler; his paintings have been ~d to those of Manet on a comparé ses tableaux à ceux de Manet; it's impossible to ~ the two systems il n'y a pas de comparaison possible entre les deux systèmes. -**3.** GRAMM former les degrés de comparaison de.
◇ *vi* être comparable à; to ~ favourably (with sthg) soutenir la comparaison (avec qqch); how do the two candidates ~? quelles sont les qualités respectives des deux candidats?; how do the brands ~ in (terms of) price? les marques sont-elles comparables du point de vue prix?; her cooking doesn't OR can't ~ with yours il n'y a aucune comparaison entre sa cuisine et la tienne.
◇ *n lit*: he's intelligent beyond ~ il est incomparablement intelligent; beauty beyond ~ beauté sans pareille.

comparison [kəm'pærɪsn] *n* -**1.** comparaison *f*; by ~ par comparaison; there's no ~ il n'y a aucune comparaison (possible); to draw OR to make a ~ between sthg and sthg faire la comparaison de qqch avec qqch OR entre qqch et qqch; this book stands OR bears ~ with the classics ce livre soutient la comparaison avec les classiques. -**2.** GRAMM comparaison *f*; degrees of ~ degrés *mpl* de comparaison.
◆ **in comparison with** *prep phr* en comparaison de, par rapport à.

compartment [kəm'pɑ:tmənt] *n* compartiment *m*, subdivision *f*; NAUT & RAIL compartiment *m*.

compartmentalize, -ise [,kɒmpɑ:t'mentəlaɪz] *vt* compartimenter.

compass ['kʌmpəs] ◇ *n* -**1.** [for direction] boussole *f*; NAUT compas *m*. -**2.** GEOM compas *m*. -**3.** [limits] étendue *f*; [range] portée *f*; MUS étendue *f*, portée *f*; within the narrow ~ of this book dans les limites restreintes de ce livre; that does not lie within the ~ of this committee ce n'est pas du ressort de ce comité; beyond the ~ of the human mind au-delà de la portée de l'esprit humain.
◇ *comp* [bearing, error] du compas; to take a ~ bearing prendre un relèvement au compas; a ~ course une route magnétique.
◇ *vt* [go round] faire le tour de; [surround] encercler, entourer.
◆ **compasses** *npl* GEOM: (a pair of) ~es un compas.

compass card *n* rose *f* des vents.

compassion [kəm'pæʃn] *n* compassion *f*.

compassionate [kəm'pæʃənət] *adj* compatissant; on ~ grounds pour des raisons personnelles OR familiales.

compassionate leave *n* [gen & MIL] permission *f* exceptionnelle *(pour raisons personnelles).*

compass point *n* aire *f* de vent.

compass rose *n* rose *f* des vents.

compass saw *n* scie *f* à guichet.

compass window *n* fenêtre *f* en saillie ronde.

compatibility [kəm,pætə'bɪlətɪ] *n* compatibilité *f*.

compatible [kəm'pætəbl] *adj* compatible.

compatibly [kəm'pætəblɪ] *adv* d'une manière compatible.

compatriot [kəm'pætrɪət] *n* compatriote *mf*.

compel [kəm'pel] (*pt* & *pp* compelled, *cont* compelling) *vt* -**1.** [force] contraindre, obliger; to ~ sb to do sthg contraindre OR forcer qqn à faire qqch; ill health compelled her to retire pour des raisons de santé elle a été obligée de prendre sa retraite. -**2.** [demand] imposer, forcer; the sort of woman who ~s admiration le genre de femme qu'on ne peut s'empêcher d'admirer OR qui force l'admiration; a tone of voice that ~s attention un ton de voix qui retient l'attention.

compelling [kəm'pelɪŋ] *adj* -**1.** [reason, desire] convaincant, irrésistible. -**2.** [book, story] envoûtant.

compellingly [kəm'pelɪŋlɪ] *adv* irrésistiblement, d'une façon irrésistible.

compendious [kəm'pendɪəs] *adj fml* concis.

compendium [kəm'pendɪəm] (*pl* **compendiums** OR **compendia** [-dɪə]) *n* -**1.** [summary] abrégé *m*, précis *m*. -**2.** *Br* [collection] collection *f*; a ~ **of games** une boîte de jeux.

compensate ['kɒmpenseɪt] ◇ *vt* -**1.** [make amends to - person] dédommager, indemniser; **to ~ sb for a loss** dédommager qqn d'une perte; **the firm ~d the workman for his injuries** l'entreprise a dédommagé l'ouvrier pour ses blessures. -**2.** [offset] compenser, contrebalancer; TECH compenser, neutraliser.
◇ *vi* -**1.** [make up] être une OR servir de compensation, compenser; **she ~s for her short stature by wearing high heels** elle porte des talons hauts pour compenser sa petite taille. -**2.** [with money] dédommager, indemniser.

compensation [,kɒmpen'seɪʃn] *n* -**1.** [recompense] indemnité *f*, dédommagement *m*; [payment] rémunération *f*; **working for oneself has its ~s** travailler à son compte a ses avantages; **in ~ for** en compensation de; **by way of ~ for your wasted time** pour compenser le temps perdu. -**2.** [adaptation] compensation *f*; [in weight] contrepoids *m*; TECH compensation *f*, neutralisation *f*.

compensation order *n Br* JUR *obligation de la part de l'accusé de réparer ses actions.*

compensatory [,kɒmpen'seɪtərɪ] *adj* compensateur; ~ **levy** ECON [in EEC] prélèvement *m* compensatoire.

compere ['kɒmpeə^r] *Br* ◇ *n* animateur *m*, -trice *f*, présentateur *m*, -trice *f*.
◇ *vi* & *vt* animer, présenter.

compete [kəm'piːt] *vi* -**1.** [vie] rivaliser; **to ~ with sb for sthg** rivaliser avec qqn pour qqch, disputer qqch à qqn; **seven candidates are competing for the position** sept candidats se disputent le poste; **her cooking can't ~ with yours** *fig* sa cuisine n'a rien de commun OR ne peut pas rivaliser avec la vôtre. -**2.** COMM faire concurrence; **they ~ with foreign companies for contracts** ils sont en concurrence avec des entreprises étrangères pour obtenir des contrats; **we have to ~ on an international level** nous devons être à la hauteur de la concurrence sur le plan international. -**3.** SPORT [take part] participer; [contend] concourir; **ten women are competing in the race** dix femmes participent à la course; **to ~ against sb for sthg** concourir avec qqn pour qqch; **we're competing against the Japanese** nous concourons OR sommes en compétition avec les Japonais; **there are only three teams competing** il n'y a que trois équipes sur les rangs.

competence ['kɒmpɪtəns] *n* -**1.** [ability] compétence *f*, aptitude *f*, capacité *f*; LING compétence *f*; **sb's ~ for** OR **in sthg** la compétence de qqn pour OR en qqch, l'aptitude de qqn à OR pour qqch; **to have the ~ to do sthg** avoir les moyens OR la capacité de faire qqch; **that's beyond my ~** c'est au-delà de mes moyens, ça dépasse mes compétences. -**2.** JUR compétence *f*; **to be within the ~ of the court** être de la compétence du tribunal. -**3.** *lit* [income] aisance *f*, moyens *mpl*.

competency ['kɒmpɪtənsɪ] (*pl* **competencies**) *n* -**1.** = **competence 1, 3**. -**2.** JUR [of witness] habileté *f*.

competent ['kɒmpɪtənt] *adj* -**1.** [capable] compétent, capable; [qualified] qualifié; **is she ~ to handle the accounts?** est-elle compétente OR qualifiée pour tenir la comptabilité? -**2.** [sufficient] suffisant. -**3.** JUR [witness] habile; [court] compétent; [evidence] admissible, recevable.

competently ['kɒmpɪtəntlɪ] *adv* -**1.** [capably] avec compétence. -**2.** [sufficiently] suffisamment.

competing [kəm'piːtɪŋ] *adj* en concurrence.

competition [,kɒmpɪ'tɪʃn] *n* -**1.** [rivalry] compétition *f*, rivalité *f*; ~ **for the position is fierce** il y a beaucoup de concurrence pour le poste, on se dispute âprement le poste; **we're in ~ with her** nous sommes en compétition OR concurrence avec elle ‖ COMM concurrence *f*; **unfair ~** concurrence déloyale. -**2.** [opposition] concurrence *f*; **what's the ~ doing?** que fait la concurrence?, que font nos rivaux OR concurrents? -**3.** [contest] concours *m*; SPORT compétition *f*; [race] course *f*; **beauty/fishing ~** concours de beauté/de pêche; **I'm entering the ~** je vais me présenter au concours OR me mettre sur les rangs; **the candidate will be chosen by ~** le candidat sera choisi par concours. -**4.** BIOL concurrence *f*.

competitive [kəm'petətɪv] *adj* -**1.** [involving competition] de compétition; **a ~ society/game** une société/un jeu de compétition; ~ **examination** concours *m*. -**2.** [person] qui a l'esprit de compétition. -**3.** [product, price] concurrentiel, compétitif; ~ **bidding** appel *m* d'offres; ~ **edge** (léger) avantage *m* concurrentiel.

competitively [kəm'petətɪvlɪ] *adv* avec un esprit de compétition; ~ **priced goods** COMM produits au prix compétitif.

competitiveness [kəm'petətɪvnɪs] *n* compétitivité *f*.

competitor [kəm'petɪtə^r] *n* [gen, COMM & SPORT] concurrent *m*, -e *f*; [participant] participant *m*, -e *f*.

compilation [,kɒmpɪ'leɪʃn] *n* compilation *f*.

compile [kəm'paɪl] *vt* -**1.** [gather - facts, material] compiler. -**2.** [compose - list] dresser; [- dictionary] composer *(par compilation)*; ~**d from** établi d'après. -**3.** COMPUT compiler.

compiler [kəm'paɪlə^r] *n* -**1.** [gen] compilateur *m*, -trice *f*. -**2.** [of dictionary] rédacteur *m*, -trice *f*. -**3.** COMPUT compilateur *m*.

complacence [kəm'pleɪsns], **complacency** [kəm'pleɪsnsɪ] *n* satisfaction *f* OR contentement *m* de soi, suffisance *f*.

complacent [kəm'pleɪsnt] *adj* satisfait OR content de soi, suffisant.

complacently [kəm'pleɪsntlɪ] *adv* [act] d'un air suffisant, avec suffisance; [speak] d'un ton suffisant, avec suffisance.

complain [kəm'pleɪn] ◇ *vi* -**1.** [grumble] se plaindre; **he's always ~ing** il n'arrête pas de se plaindre; **he ~ed of a headache** il s'est plaint d'un mal de tête; **how's it going? — can't ~** *inf* comment ça va? — je n'ai pas à me plaindre OR ça peut aller. -**2.** [make formal protest] formuler une plainte OR une réclamation, se plaindre; **to ~ to sb** se plaindre à OR auprès de qqn.
◇ *vt* se plaindre; **she ~ed that he was always late** elle s'est plainte qu'il était toujours en retard.

complainant [kəm'pleɪnənt] *n* demandeur *m*, demanderesse *f*.

complaint [kəm'pleɪnt] *n* -**1.** [protest] plainte *f*, récrimination *f*; **I'd like to make** OR **lodge a ~** je voudrais me plaindre ‖ COMM réclamation *f*; JUR plainte *f*; **to lodge a ~ against sb** porter plainte contre qqn. -**2.** [grievance] sujet *m* OR motif *m* de plainte, grief *m*; **I have no ~** OR **no cause for ~** je n'ai aucune raison de me plaindre. -**3.** [illness] maladie *f*, affection *f*; **she has a liver ~** elle souffre du foie; **a heart ~** une maladie du cœur.

complaisance [kəm'pleɪzəns] *n fml* complaisance *f*, obligeance *f*.

complaisant [kəm'pleɪzənt] *adj fml* complaisant, obligeant.

complement [*n* 'kɒmplɪmənt, *vb* 'kɒmplɪ,ment] ◇ *n* -**1.** [gen, MATH & MUS] complément *m*; **with a full ~** au grand complet. -**2.** GRAMM [of verb] complément *m*; [of subject] attribut *m*. -**3.** [ship's crew, staff] personnel *m*, effectif *m* (complet).
◇ *vt* compléter, être le complément de.

complementarity [,kɒmplɪmen'tærətɪ] (*pl* **complementarities**) *n* complémentarité *f*.

complementary [,kɒmplɪ'mentərɪ] *adj* [gen & MATH] complémentaire; **the two pieces are ~** les deux morceaux se complètent.

complementary colour *n* couleur *f* complémentaire.

complementary medicine *n* médecine *f* douce.

complementizer, -iser ['kɒmplɪməntaɪzə^r] *n* conjonction *f* de subordination.

complete [kəm'pliːt] ◇ *adj* -**1.** [entire] complet, total; **a ~ set of golf clubs** un jeu complet de clubs; **Christmas wouldn't be ~ without the traditional dinner** Noël ne serait pas Noël sans le repas traditionnel; **he didn't tell you the ~ story** il ne vous a pas tout dit; **the ~ works of Shakespeare** les œuvres complètes de Shakespeare. -**2.** [finished] achevé, terminé. -**3.** [as intensifier] complet, absolu; **if the job is not done to your ~ satisfaction** si vous n'êtes pas entièrement satisfait du travail effectué; **he's a ~ fool** c'est un crétin fini OR un parfait imbécile; **a ~ (and utter) failure** un échec total OR sur toute la ligne; **the project was a ~ success** le projet a pleinement réussi.
◇ *vt* -**1.** [make whole] compléter; **to ~ her happiness** pour combler son bonheur; **I just need one more card to ~ my collection** il me manque une seule carte pour compléter ma collection; **to ~ an order** COMM exécuter une commande. -**2.** [finish] achever, finir. -**3.** [form] remplir.
◆ **complete with** *prep phr* avec, doté OR pourvu de; ~ **with instructions** comprenant des instructions; **a flat ~ with furniture** un appartement meublé.

completely [kəm'pliːtlɪ] *adv* complètement.

completeness [kəm'pliːtnɪs] *n* état *m* complet.

completion [kəm'pliːʃn] *n* -**1.** [of work] achèvement *m*; JUR [of sale] exécution *f*; **the bridge is due for ~ in January** le pont doit être fini en janvier; **near ~** près d'être achevé; **the project is nearing ~** le projet est près de son terme OR s'achève; **payment on ~ of contract** paiement à l'exécution du contrat. -**2.** [of happiness, misfortune] comble *m*.

complex ['kɒmpleks] ◇ *adj* [gen, GRAMM & MATH] complexe; ~ **number** nombre *m* complexe.
◇ *n* -**1.** [system] complexe *m*, ensemble *m*; **housing ~** grand ensemble; **shopping/industrial ~** complexe commercial/industriel. -**2.** PSYCH complexe *m*; **she has a ~ about her weight** elle fait un complexe de son poids; **it gave him a ~** ça lui a donné un complexe, ça l'a complexé.

complexion [kəm'plekʃn] *n* -**1.** [of face] teint *m*. -**2.** [aspect] aspect *m*; **that puts a different ~ on things** voilà qui change la situation.

-complexioned [kəm'plekʃnd] *in cpds*: **dark~** au teint foncé; **fair~**, **light~** au teint clair.

complexity [kəm'pleksətɪ] *n* complexité *f*.

compliance [kəm'plaɪəns] *n* -**1.** [conformity] conformité *f*. -**2.** [agreement] acquiescement *m*; [submission] complaisance *f*. -**3.** TECH [flexibility] élasticité *f*.
◆ **in compliance with** *prep phr* conformément à; **in ~ with the law** conformément à la loi; **she acted in ~ with the terms of the contract** elle a agi en accord avec les stipulations du contrat.

compliant [kəm'plaɪənt] *adj* accommodant, docile.

complicate ['kɒmplɪkeɪt] *vt* compliquer, embrouiller; **don't ~ the situation any further** ne compliquez pas davantage la situation; **that ~s matters** cela complique les choses; **why ~ things?** pourquoi se compliquer la vie?; **her illness was ~d by an infection** MED sa maladie s'est compliquée d'une infection.

complicated ['kɒmplɪkeɪtɪd] *adj* [complex] compliqué, complexe; [muddled] embrouillé; **to become** OR **to get ~** se compliquer.

complication [ˌkɒmplɪˈkeɪʃn] *n* [gen & MED] complication *f*.

complicity [kəmˈplɪsətɪ] *n* complicité *f*; **his ~ in the murder** sa complicité dans le meurtre.

compliment [ˈkɒmplɪmənt] ◇ *n* [praise] compliment *m*; **to pay sb a ~** faire OR adresser un compliment à qqn; **she returned the ~** *iron* elle lui a retourné le compliment.
◇ *vt* faire des compliments à, complimenter; **she ~ed him on his calm handling of the situation** elle l'a félicité du calme avec lequel il a arrangé les choses.
◆ **compliments** *npl fml* [respects] compliments *mpl*, respects *mpl*; **we conveyed** OR **presented our ~s to her** nous lui avons présenté nos compliments OR hommages *fig*; **give him my ~s** faites-lui mes compliments; **~s of the season!** tous nos bons vœux!; **with the ~s of Mr Smith** avec les hommages OR compliments de M. Smith; **my ~s to the chef** mes compliments au chef; **to send sthg with one's ~s** COMM envoyer qqch à titre gratuit OR gracieux (avec ses compliments).

complimentary [ˌkɒmplɪˈmentərɪ] *adj* -**1.** [approving] flatteur; **~ remarks** compliments *mpl*, félicitations *fpl*. -**2.** [given free] gratuit, gracieux; **~ copy** exemplaire *m* offert à titre gracieux; **~ ticket** billet *m* de faveur.

compline, Compline [ˈkɒmplɪn] *n* (*U*) complies *fpl*.

comply [kəmˈplaɪ] (*pt* & *pp* **complied**) *vi* -**1.** [obey]: **to ~ with the law** se soumettre à la loi; **to ~ with the rules** observer OR respecter les règlements; **I will ~ with your wishes** je me conformerai à vos désirs; **he complied gracefully** il s'exécuta avec grâce; **she complied with our request** elle a accédé à notre demande; **your request has been complied with** votre demande a reçu satisfaction. -**2.** [machinery] être conforme; **cars must ~ with existing regulations** les voitures doivent être conformes aux normes en vigueur.

component [kəmˈpəʊnənt] ◇ *n* [gen] élément *m*; ELEC composant *m*; AUT & TECH pièce *f*.
◇ *adj* composant, constituant; **~ parts** parties *fpl* constituantes.

componential [ˌkɒmpəˈnenʃl] *adj* componentiel; **~ analysis** LING analyse *f* componentielle.

comport [kəmˈpɔːt] *vt fml*: **to ~ o.s.** se comporter, se conduire.

comportment [kəmˈpɔːtmənt] *n fml* comportement *m*, conduite *f*.

compose [kəmˈpəʊz] ◇ *vt* -**1.** **to be ~d of sthg** se composer OR être composé de qqch. -**2.** [create, write] composer; **to ~ a poem/a symphony** composer un poème/une symphonie; **the way the artist ~s a painting** la façon dont l'artiste compose un tableau; **I ~d a reply to his letter** j'ai formulé une réponse à sa lettre. -**3.** TYPO [set] composer. -**4.** [make calm] composer; **~ yourself!** calmez-vous!; **she ~d her features** elle a composé son visage; **I need to ~ my thoughts** j'ai besoin de mettre de l'ordre dans mes idées. -**5.** [settle - quarrel] arranger, régler.
◇ *vi* composer.

composed [kəmˈpəʊzd] *adj* calme, posé.

composer [kəmˈpəʊzəʳ] *n* TYPO & MUS compositeur *m*, -trice *f*.

composite [ˈkɒmpəzɪt] ◇ *adj* [gen, ARCHIT & PHOT] composite; BOT & MATH composé.
◇ *n* [compound] composite *m*; ARCHIT (ordre *m*) composite *m*; BOT composée *f*, composacée *f*.

composite school *n Can* école *f* polyvalente.

composition [ˌkɒmpəˈzɪʃn] *n* -**1.** [gen, ART, LITERAT & MUS] composition *f*, création *f*; **she struggled with the ~ of the letter** elle a eu du mal à rédiger la lettre; **poetry of his own ~** poésie de sa composition. -**2.** [thing created] composition *f*, œuvre *f*; SCH [essay] dissertation *f*; **one of Mozart's finest ~s** une des plus belles œuvres de Mozart. -**3.** [constitution - parts] composition *f*, constitution *f*; [- mixture] mélange *m*, composition *f*; CONSTR stuc *m*; **the chemical ~ of water** la composition chimique de l'eau. -**4.** LING [of sentence] construction *f*; [of word] composition *f*. -**5.** TYPO composition *f*. -**6.** JUR [agreement] arrangement *m* (*avec un créancier*), accommodement *m*.

compositor [kəmˈpɒzɪtəʳ] *n* compositeur *m*, -trice *f* TYPO.

compos mentis [ˌkɒmpəsˈmentɪs] *adj* sain d'esprit.

compost [*Br* ˈkɒmpɒst, *Am* ˈkɒmpəʊst] ◇ *n* compost *m*; **~ heap** tas *m* de compost.
◇ *vt* composter (*une terre*).

composure [kəmˈpəʊʒəʳ] *n* calme *m*, sang-froid *m*; **to lose one's ~** perdre son calme; **she regained her ~** elle s'est calmée OR a retrouvé son calme.

compote [ˈkɒmpɒt] *n* [dessert] compote *f*; *Am* [dish] compotier *m*.

compound [*adj* & *n* ˈkɒmpaʊnd, *vb* kəmˈpaʊnd] ◇ *adj* -**1.** [gen] composé; CHEM composé, combiné; MATH complexe; TECH [engine] compound (*inv*); **~ eye** BIOL œil *m* composé OR à facettes. -**2.** GRAMM [sentence] complexe; [tense, word] composé. -**3.** MUS composé; **~ time** mesure *f* composée.
◇ *n* -**1.** [enclosed area] enceinte *f*, enclos *m*; [for prisoners of war] camp *m*. -**2.** [mixture] composé *m*, mélange *m*; CHEM composé *m*; TECH compound *m*. -**3.** GRAMM mot *m* composé.
◇ *vt* -**1.** [combine] combiner, mélanger; [form by combining] composer. -**2.** [make worse - difficulties, mistake] aggraver. -**3.** JUR [settle] régler à l'amiable; **to ~ an offence** composer OR pactiser avec un criminel.
◇ *vi* JUR composer, transiger; **to ~ with sb for sthg** transiger avec qqn au sujet de OR pour qqch; **the neighbours ~ed for the damages** les voisins se sont arrangés au sujet des dommages.

compound fracture *n* fracture *f* compliquée.

compound interest *n* (*U*) intérêts *mpl* composés.

comprehend [ˌkɒmprɪˈhend] ◇ *vt* -**1.** [understand] comprendre, saisir. -**2.** [include] comprendre, inclure.
◇ *vi* [understand] comprendre, saisir.

comprehensible [ˌkɒmprɪˈhensəbl] *adj* compréhensible, intelligible.

comprehension [ˌkɒmprɪˈhenʃn] *n* -**1.** [understanding] compréhension *f*; **things that are beyond our ~** des choses qui nous dépassent. -**2.** SCH [exercise] exercice *m* de compréhension. -**3.** [inclusion] inclusion *f*.

comprehensive [ˌkɒmprɪˈhensɪv] ◇ *adj* -**1.** [thorough] complet, exhaustif; [detailed] détaillé, complet; **~ knowledge** connaissances vastes OR étendues; **~ measures** mesures d'ensemble; (a) **~ insurance (policy)** *Br*, **~ assurance** *Am* une assurance tous risques. -**2.** *Br* SCH polyvalent; **the schools went ~** les écoles ont abandonné les critères sélectifs d'entrée; **~ school** établissement *m* secondaire polyvalent.
◇ *n Br* [school] établissement *m* secondaire polyvalent.

comprehensively [ˌkɒmprɪˈhensɪvlɪ] *adv* [thoroughly] complètement, exhaustivement; [in detail] en détail.

compress [*vb* kəmˈpres, *n* ˈkɒmpres] ◇ *vt* [squeeze together] comprimer; *fig* [condense - ideas, facts, writing] condenser, concentrer; **three centuries are ~ed into two chapters** trois siècles sont concentrés en deux chapitres.
◇ *vi* [material] se comprimer; *fig* [be condensed] se condenser, se concentrer.
◇ *n* compresse *f*.

compressed air *n* air *m* comprimé.

compression [kəmˈpreʃn] *n* compression *f*; *fig* [condensing] réduction *f*; **the ~ stroke of a piston** TECH le temps OR la course de compression d'un piston.

compression chamber *n* chambre *f* de compression.

compression ratio *n* taux *m* de compression.

compressive [kəmˈpresɪv] *adj* qui peut être comprimé, compressible; **~ stress** MECH contrainte *f* de compression.

compressor [kəmˈpresəʳ] *n* ANAT & TECH compresseur *m*; **~ unit** groupe *m* compresseur.

comprise [kəmˈpraɪz] *vt* -**1.** [consist of] comprendre, consister en; **the group ~s** OR **is ~d of four women and two men** il y a quatre femmes et deux hommes dans le groupe, le groupe est formé de quatre femmes et deux hommes. -**2.** [constitute] constituer; **women ~ 60% of the population** les femmes représentent 60 % de la population.

compromise [ˈkɒmprəmaɪz] ◇ *n* compromis *m*; **to agree to a ~** accepter un compromis; **they eventually reached** OR **arrived at a ~** ils ont finalement abouti OR ils sont finalement parvenus à un compromis.
◇ *vi* transiger, aboutir à OR accepter un compromis; **to ~ with sb (on sthg)** transiger avec qqn OR aboutir à un compromis avec qqn (sur qqch).
◇ *vt* -**1.** [principles, reputation] compromettre; **don't say anything to ~ yourself** ne dites rien qui puisse vous compromettre; **the minister was ~d by the allegations of improper conduct** les allégations selon lesquelles il se serait conduit de façon indécente ont compromis le ministre. -**2.** [jeopardize] mettre en péril, risquer; **the party's chances of electoral success were severely ~d by the character of their leader** la personnalité du leader a sérieusement compromis les chances de victoire du parti aux élections.
◇ *comp* [decision, solution] de compromis.

compromising [ˈkɒmprəmaɪzɪŋ] *adj* compromettant.

comptroller [kənˈtrəʊləʳ] *n* ADMIN administrateur *m*, -trice *f*, intendant *m*, -e *f*; FIN contrôleur *m*, -euse *f*; **Comptroller General** *Am* ≃ Président *m* de la Cour des Comptes.

compulsion [kəmˈpʌlʃn] *n* -**1.** [force] contrainte *f*, coercition *f*; **to act under ~** agir sous la contrainte; **he is under no ~ to sell** il n'est nullement obligé de vendre, rien ne l'oblige à vendre. -**2.** PSYCH [impulse] compulsion *f*; **I felt a sudden ~ to visit my grandmother** j'ai soudain ressenti un besoin urgent de rendre visite à ma grand-mère.

compulsive [kəmˈpʌlsɪv] *adj* -**1.** PSYCH [behaviour] compulsif; **he's a ~ liar** il ne peut pas s'empêcher de mentir, mentir est un besoin chez lui. -**2.** [reason] coercitif; *fig* [absorbing] irrésistible; **this TV series is ~ viewing** quand on commence à regarder ce feuilleton de télé, on ne peut plus s'en passer.

compulsively [kəmˈpʌlsɪvlɪ] *adv* -**1.** PSYCH [drink, steal, smoke] d'une façon compulsive. -**2.** *fig* irrésistiblement.

compulsorily [kəmˈpʌlsərəlɪ] *adv* d'office, obligatoirement.

compulsory [kəmˈpʌlsərɪ] *adj* -**1.** [obligatory] obligatoire; **~ education** enseignement *m* obligatoire; **~ liquidation** FIN liquidation *f* forcée; **~ retirement** mise *f* à la retraite d'office. -**2.** [compelling] irrésistible; [law] obligatoire.

compulsory purchase *n Br* expropriation *f* pour cause d'utilité publique; **~ order** ordre *m* d'expropriation.

compunction [kəmˈpʌŋkʃn] *n* [remorse] remords *m*; [misgiving] scrupule *m*; RELIG componction *f*; **he has no ~ about stealing** il n'a aucun scrupule OR il n'hésite pas à voler; **without the slightest ~** sans le moindre scrupule.

computation [ˌkɒmpjuːˈteɪʃn] *n* -**1.** [calculation] calcul *m*. -**2.** [reckoning] estimation *f*.

computational [ˌkɒmpjuːˈteɪʃənl] *adj* quantitatif, statistique; **~ linguistics** linguistique *f* computationnelle.

compute [kəmˈpjuːt] ◇ *vt* calculer.
◇ *vi* calculer; **it doesn't ~** *inf* ça n'a pas de sens.

computer [kəm'pjuːtəʳ] ◇ *n* [electronic] ordinateur *m*; he's good at/he works in ~s il est bon en/il travaille dans l'informatique.
◇ *comp*: ~ crime *utilisation de l'informatique à des fins criminelles*; ~ model modèle *m* informatique; ~ network réseau *m* informatique; ~ printout sortie *f* papier; ~ stationery papier *m* listing.

computer-aided, computer-assisted [-ə'sɪstɪd] *adj* assisté par ordinateur.

computer dating *n rencontres sélectionnées par ordinateur*.

computer game *n* jeu *m* électronique.

computer graphics ◇ *npl* [function] graphiques *mpl* (de l'ordinateur).
◇ *n* [field] infographie *f*.

computerization [kəm,pjuːtəraɪ'zeɪʃn] *n* **-1.** [of system, of work] automatisation *f*, informatisation *f*. **-2.** [of information - inputting] saisie *f* sur ordinateur; [- processing] traitement *m* (électronique).

computerize, -ise [kəm'pjuːtəraɪz] *vt* [data - put on computer] saisir sur ordinateur; [- process by computer] traiter par ordinateur; [firm] gérer par ordinateur, informatiser.

computerized [kəm'pjuːtəraɪzd] *adj*: ~ typesetting composition *f* par ordinateur.

computer language *n* langage *m* de programmation.

computer literacy *n* compétence *f* informatique.

computer literate *adj* ayant une formation en informatique.

computernik *inf* [kəm'pjuːtənɪk] *n Am* fada *mf* d'informatique.

computer program *n* programme *m* informatique.

computer programmer *n* programmeur *m*, -euse *f*.

computer programming *n* programmation *f*.

computer science *n* informatique *f*.

computer scientist *n* informaticien *m*, -enne *f*.

computing [kəm'pjuːtɪŋ] *n* **-1.** [use of computers] informatique *f*. **-2.** [calculation] calcul *m*; [reckoning] estimation *f*.

comrade ['kɒmreɪd] *n* [gen & POL] camarade *mf*.

comrade-in-arms *n* compagnon *m* d'armes.

comradeship ['kɒmreɪdʃɪp] *n* camaraderie *f*.

con [kɒn] (*pt* & *pp* conned, *cont* conning)
◇ *vt* **-1.** *inf* [swindle] arnaquer; [trick] duper; don't try to ~ me! n'essayez pas de me faire marcher!; I've been conned! je me suis fait avoir!, on m'a eu!; he conned us into buying it il nous a persuadés de l'acheter et nous nous sommes fait avoir. **-2.** *arch* [study] étudier en détail; [learn by heart] apprendre par cœur. **-3.** NAUT [steer] gouverner, piloter.
◇ *n* **-1.** *inf* [swindle] arnaque; [trick] duperie *f*. **-2.** *inf* [convict] taulard *m*. **-3.** [disadvantage] contre *m*.

Con. *written abbr of* constable.

con artist *inf n* arnaqueur *m*.

concatenate [kɒn'kætɪneɪt] *vt* enchaîner, lier.

concatenation [kɒn,kætɪ'neɪʃn] *n* [series] série *f*, chaîne *f*; [of circumstances] enchaînement *m*; COMPUT & LING concaténation *f*.

concave [,kɒn'keɪv] *adj* concave.

concavity [kɒn'kævətɪ] *n* concavité *f*.

conceal [kən'siːl] *vt* [hide - object] cacher, dissimuler; [- emotion, truth] cacher, dissimuler; [- news] tenir secret; he ~ed the truth from her il lui a caché la vérité; in order to ~ the fact that... pour dissimuler le fait que...

concealed [kən'siːld] *adj*: ~ lighting éclairage indirect; a ~ driveway/entrance une allée/une entrée cachée.

concealment [kən'siːlmənt] *n* [act of hiding] dissimulation *f*; JUR [of criminal] recel *m*; [of facts, truth] non-divulgation *f*.

concede [kən'siːd] ◇ *vt* **-1.** [admit] concéder, admettre; to ~ a point concéder un point (important); he ~d (that) he was wrong il a admis OR reconnu qu'il avait tort; to ~ defeat s'avouer vaincu. **-2.** [give up] concéder, accorder; SPORT concéder; he refused to ~ any ground il n'a voulu céder sur rien; they ~d a free kick/a goal SPORT ils ont concédé un coup franc/un but. **-3.** [grant - privileges] concéder.
◇ *vi* céder.

conceit [kən'siːt] *n* **-1.** [vanity] vanité *f*, suffisance *f*. **-2.** LIT [witty expression] trait *m* d'esprit.

conceited [kən'siːtɪd] *adj* vaniteux, suffisant.

conceitedly [kən'siːtɪdlɪ] *adv* avec vanité OR suffisance.

conceitedness [kən'siːtɪdnɪs] *n* vanité *f*, prétention *f*, suffisance *f*.

conceivable [kən'siːvəbl] *adj* concevable, imaginable; we used every ~ means nous avons utilisé tous les moyens (possibles et) imaginables; it's quite ~ that it was an accident il est tout à fait concevable que ç'ait été un accident.

conceivably [kən'siːvəblɪ] *adv* de façon concevable; this might ~ start a war il est concevable que OR il se peut que cela déclenche une guerre; it couldn't ~ have been him il n'est pas possible que ç'ait été lui.

conceive [kən'siːv] ◇ *vt* **-1.** [idea] concevoir; I can't ~ why they did it je ne comprends vraiment pas pourquoi ils l'ont fait. **-2.** [child] concevoir; she ~d a passion for jazz *fig* elle conçut une passion pour le jazz.
◇ *vi* **-1.** [think] concevoir; can't you ~ of a better plan? ne pouvez-vous rien concevoir de mieux? **-2.** [become pregnant] concevoir.

concentrate ['kɒnsəntreɪt] ◇ *vi* **-1.** [pay attention] se concentrer, concentrer OR fixer son attention; to ~ on sthg se concentrer sur qqch; ~ on your work! appliquez-vous à votre travail!; I can't ~ with all that noise tout ce bruit m'empêche de me concentrer ‖ [focus]: the government should ~ on improving the economy le gouvernement devrait s'attacher à améliorer la situation économique; just ~ on getting the suitcases ready! occupe-toi seulement des valises!; the speaker ~d on the Luddite movement le conférencier a surtout traité le luddisme. **-2.** [gather] se concentrer, converger; the crowd ~d in the square la foule s'est rassemblée sur la place.
◇ *vt* **-1.** [focus] concentrer; to ~ one's attention on sthg concentrer son attention sur qqch; the prospect of dismissal ~s the mind wonderfully la perspective de se faire renvoyer aide énormément à se concentrer; our hopes are ~d on her success tous nos espoirs sont concentrés sur son succès. **-2.** [bring together] concentrer, rassembler; CHEM concentrer; Conservative support is ~d in the South le soutien du parti conservateur est concentré dans le Sud.
◇ *n* concentré *m*.

concentrated ['kɒnsəntreɪtɪd] *adj* **-1.** [liquid] concentré; ~ fruit juice jus de fruit concentré. **-2.** [intense] intense; a period of ~ activity une période d'activité intense.

concentration [,kɒnsən'treɪʃn] *n* [gen & CHEM] concentration *f*; to lose one's ~ perdre sa concentration.

concentration camp *n* camp *m* de concentration.

concentric [kən'sentrɪk] *adj* concentrique.

concept ['kɒnsept] *n* concept *m*.

conception [kən'sepʃn] *n* [gen & MED] conception *f*; she has no ~ of time elle n'a aucune notion du temps.

conceptual [kən'septʃʊəl] *adj* conceptuel.

conceptualism [kən'septʃʊəlɪzm] *n* conceptualisme *m*.

conceptualize, -ise [kən'septʃʊəlaɪz] *vt* concevoir, conceptualiser.

concern [kən'sɜːn] ◇ *n* **-1.** [worry] inquiétude *f*, souci *m*; there's no cause for ~ il n'y a pas de raison de s'inquiéter; she showed great ~ for their welfare elle s'est montrée très soucieuse de leur bien-être; a look of ~ un regard inquiet; this is a matter of great ~ c'est un sujet très inquiétant ‖ [source of worry] souci *m*, préoccupation *f*; my main ~ is the price ce qui m'inquiète surtout, c'est le prix. **-2.** [affair, business] affaire *f*; what ~ is it of yours? en quoi est-ce que cela vous regarde?; it's none of my ~ cela ne me regarde pas, ce n'est pas mon affaire. **-3.** COMM [firm]: a (business) ~ une affaire, une firme. **-4.** [share] intérêt *m*; we have a ~ in the restaurant nous avons des intérêts dans le restaurant. **-5.** *inf* [contrivance] truc *m*, machin *m*.
◇ *vt* **-1.** [worry] inquiéter; your health ~s me je m'inquiète OR je suis inquiet pour votre santé; they're ~ed about her ils s'inquiètent OR se font du souci à son égard; we were ~ed to learn that... nous avons appris avec inquiétude que...; I'm only ~ed with the facts je ne m'intéresse qu'aux faits. **-2.** [involve] concerner; where the budget is ~ed en ce qui concerne le budget; as far as this matter is ~ed en ce qui concerne cette question; to ~ o.s. in OR with sthg s'occuper de OR s'intéresser à qqch; there is no need for you to ~ yourself with my affairs vous n'avez pas à vous occuper de mes affaires; this doesn't ~ you cela ne vous regarde pas; as far as I'm ~ed en ce qui me concerne, quant à moi; where you are ~ed en ce qui vous concerne; to whom it may ~ à qui de droit. **-3.** [be important to] intéresser, importer; the outcome ~s us all les résultats nous importent à tous. **-4.** [subj: book, report] traiter.

concerned [kən'sɜːnd] *adj* **-1.** [worried] inquiet, soucieux; we were ~ for OR about his health nous étions inquiets pour sa santé. **-2.** [involved] intéressé; pass this request on to the department ~ transmettez cette demande au service compétent; notify the person ~ avisez qui de droit; the people ~ [in question] les personnes en question OR dont il s'agit; [involved] les intéressés.

concerning [kən'sɜːnɪŋ] *prep* en ce qui concerne, à propos de; I wrote to her ~ the lease je lui ai écrit au sujet du bail; any news ~ the accident? y a-t-il du nouveau au sujet de OR concernant l'accident?

concert [*n* & *comp* 'kɒnsət, *vb* kən'sɜːt]
◇ *n* **-1.** MUS [performance] concert *m*; Miles Davis in ~ Miles Davis en concert; to sing in ~ chanter à l'unisson OR en chœur. **-2.** *Br fig* [agreement] accord *m*, entente *f*.
◇ *vt* concerter, arranger.
◇ *comp* [hall, performer, pianist] de concert.
◆ **in concert with** *prep phr Br fml* de concert avec; we acted in ~ with the police nous avons agi de concert avec la police.

concerted [kən'sɜːtɪd] *adj* concerté; a ~ effort un effort concerté; ~ action action d'ensemble OR concertée.

concertgoer ['kɒnsət,gəʊəʳ] *n* amateur *m* de concerts.

concert grand *n* piano *m* de concert.

concertina [,kɒnsə'tiːnə] ◇ *n* concertina *m*.
◇ *vi*: the front of the car ~ed le devant de la voiture a été télescopé.

concertmaster ['kɒnsət,mɑːstəʳ] *n Am* premier violon *m*.

concerto [kən'tʃeətəʊ] (*pl* concertos OR concerti [-tiː]) *n* concerto *m*.

concert pitch *n* MUS diapason *m* (de concert); to be at ~ *fig* être en pleine forme.

concession [kən'seʃn] *n* **-1.** [gen & JUR] concession *f*; COMM [reduction] réduction *f*; to make a ~ (to sb) faire une concession (à qqn); as a ~ to sb/sthg comme concession à qqn/qqch. **-2.** MIN & PETR concession *f*; an oil ~ une concession pétrolière.

concessionaire [kən,seʃə'neəʳ] *n* concessionnaire *mf*.

concessionary [kən'seʃnərɪ] (*pl* concessionaries) ◇ *adj* [gen, FIN & JUR] concessionnaire; COMM [fare, ticket] à prix réduit.
◇ *n* concessionnaire *mf*.

concessive clause [kən'sesɪv-] *n* (proposition *f*) concessive *f*.

conch [kɒntʃ] (*pl* conches OR conchs) *n* -**1.** ZOOL [mollusc, shell] conque *f*. -**2.** ARCHIT (voûte *f* d') abside *f*.

conchie ['kɒnʃɪ] = **conchy**.

conchology [kɒŋ'kɒlədʒɪ] *n* conchyliologie *f*.

conchy *inf* ['kɒnʃɪ] (*pl* conchies) *n Br pej* & *dated* objecteur *m* de conscience.

conciliate [kən'sɪlɪeɪt] *vt* -**1.** [appease] apaiser; [win over] se concilier (l'appui de); **she managed to ~ my mother** elle a réussi à se concilier les bonnes grâces de ma mère. -**2.** [reconcile] concilier.

conciliation [kən,sɪlɪ'eɪʃn] *n* -**1.** [appeasement] apaisement *m*. -**2.** [reconciliation] conciliation *f*; INDUST médiation *f*; **a ~ service** un service de conciliation; **~ board** conseil *m* d'arbitrage.

conciliator [kən'sɪlɪeɪtə^r] *n* conciliateur *m*, -trice *f*; INDUST médiateur *m*.

conciliatory [kən'sɪlɪətrɪ] *adj* [manner, words] conciliant; [person] conciliateur, conciliant; JUR & POL [procedure] conciliatoire; **in a ~ spirit** dans un esprit de conciliation.

concise [kən'saɪs] *adj* [succinct] concis; [abridged] abrégé.

concisely [kən'saɪslɪ] *adv* avec concision.

conciseness [kən'saɪsnɪs], **concision** [kən'sɪʒn] *n* concision *f*.

conclave ['kɒŋkleɪv] *n* [private meeting] assemblée *f* OR réunion *f* à huis clos; RELIG conclave *m*; **in ~** en réunion privée.

conclude [kən'kluːd] ◇ *vt* -**1.** [finish] conclure, terminer; [meeting] clore, clôturer; **'to be ~d'** [serial in magazine] 'suite et fin au prochain numéro'; [serial on TV] 'suite et fin au prochain épisode'. -**2.** [settle - deal, treaty] conclure. -**3.** [deduce] conclure, déduire; **may I ~ from your statement that...** dois-je inférer de votre remarque que... -**4.** [decide] décider; **she ~d she would wait** elle a décidé d'attendre.
◇ *vi* -**1.** [person] conclure; **to ~, I would just like to say...** en conclusion OR pour conclure, je voudrais simplement dire... -**2.** [event] se terminer, s'achever; **the meeting ~d with the chairman's summary** la réunion s'est achevée avec la récapitulation du président.

concluding [kən'kluːdɪŋ] *adj* de conclusion, final; **he made a few ~ remarks** il a fait quelques remarques finales.

conclusion [kən'kluːʒn] *n* -**1.** [end] conclusion *f*, fin *f*; **to bring sthg to a ~** mener qqch à sa conclusion OR à terme; **she brought the matter to a successful ~** elle a mené l'affaire à (bon) terme. -**2.** [decision, judgment] conclusion *f*, décision *f*; **we've come to the ~ that...** nous avons conclu que...; **the ~ to be drawn from this matter** la conclusion à tirer de cette affaire; **it's up to you to draw your own ~s** c'est à vous d'en juger; **the facts lead me to the ~ that...** les faits m'amènent à conclure que.. -**3.** [settling - of deal, treaty] conclusion *f*. -**4.** PHILOS conclusion *f*.
◆ **in conclusion** *adv phr* en conslusion, pour conclure.

conclusive [kən'kluːsɪv] *adj* [decisive - proof, argument] concluant, décisif; [final] final.

conclusively [kən'kluːsɪvlɪ] *adv* de façon concluante OR décisive, définitivement.

concoct [kən'kɒkt] *vt* -**1.** [prepare] composer, confectionner; **to ~ a dish** mitonner OR mijoter un plat; **to ~ a meal** composer OR concocter un repas. -**2.** *fig* [invent - excuse, scheme] fabriquer, combiner, concocter.

concoction [kən'kɒkʃn] *n* -**1.** [act] confection *f*, préparation *f*. -**2.** [mixture] mélange *m*, mixture *f pej*. -**3.** *fig* [scheme] combinaison *f*.

concomitant [kən'kɒmɪtənt] *fml* ◇ *adj* concomitant; **adolescence with all its ~ anxieties** l'adolescence et les angoisses qui l'accompagnent.
◇ *n* accessoire *m*; **ill health is a common ~ of poverty** la mauvaise santé va souvent de pair avec la misère.

concomitantly [kən'kɒmɪtəntlɪ] *adv* de façon concomitante, simultanément.

concord ['kɒŋkɔːd] *n* -**1.** *fml* [harmony] concorde *f*, harmonie *f*; **to live in ~** vivre en bon accord OR en harmonie; **in complete ~** en parfaite harmonie. -**2.** [treaty] accord *m*, entente *f*. -**3.** GRAMM accord *m*; **to be in ~ with sthg** s'accorder avec qqch. -**4.** MUS accord *m*.

concordance [kən'kɔːdəns] *n* -**1.** [agreement] accord *m*; **the policy is in ~ with our declared aims** cette politique s'accorde OR est en accord avec les objectifs que nous nous sommes fixés. -**2.** [index] index *m*; [of Bible, of author's works] concordance *f*.

concordant [kən'kɔːdənt] *adj* concordant, s'accordant; **~ with** s'accordant avec.

concordat [kɒn'kɔːdæt] *n* concordat *m*.

concourse ['kɒŋkɔːs] *n* -**1.** [of people, things] multitude *f*, rassemblement *m*; [crowd] foule *f*. -**2.** [of circumstances, events] concours *m*. -**3.** [meeting place] lieu *m* de rassemblement; [in building] hall *m*; *Am* [street] boulevard *m*; [crossroads] carrefour *m*.

concrete ['kɒŋkriːt] ◇ *n* -**1.** CONSTR béton *m*. -**2.** PHILOS: **the ~** le concret.
◇ *adj* -**1.** [specific] concret, réel; **a ~ example** un exemple concret; **we need ~ proof** il nous faut des preuves concrètes OR matérielles; **he made us a ~ offer** il nous a fait une offre précise OR concrète. -**2.** GRAMM, MATH & MUS concret. -**3.** CONSTR en OR de béton; **the ~ jungle** la forêt de béton.
◇ *vt* bétonner.

concrete mixer *n* bétonnière *f*.

concrete music *n* musique *f* concrète.

concrete noun *n* nom *m* concret.

concrete poetry *n* calligramme *m*, calligrammes *mpl*.

concretion [kən'kriːʃn] *n* concrétion *f*.

concubine ['kɒŋkjʊbaɪn] *n* concubine *f*.

concupiscence [kən'kjuːpɪsəns] *n* concupiscence *f*.

concur [kən'kɜː^r] (*pt* & *pp* **concurred**, *cont* **concurring**) *vi* -**1.** [agree] être d'accord, s'entendre; **I ~ with you in your decision** je suis d'accord avec vous sur OR au sujet de cette décision; **she ~s with the proposals** elle est d'accord avec le projet; **the experts' opinions ~** les avis des experts convergent. -**2.** [occur together] coïncider, arriver en même temps; **events concurred to make it a miserable Christmas** tout a concouru à gâcher les fêtes de Noël.

concurrence [kən'kʌrəns] *n* -**1.** [agreement] accord *m*, concordance *f* de vues. -**2.** [simultaneous occurrence] coïncidence *f*, concomitance *f*, simultanéité *f*.

concurrent [kən'kʌrənt] *adj* -**1.** [simultaneous] concomitant, simultané. -**2.** [acting together] concerté. -**3.** [agreeing] concordant, d'accord. -**4.** MATH & TECH [intersecting] concourant.

concurrently [kən'kʌrəntlɪ] *adv* simultanément; **the two sentences to run ~** JUR avec confusion des deux peines.

concuss [kən'kʌs] *vt* -**1.** [injure brain] commotionner; **she was ~ed when she fell** elle était commotionnée après sa chute. -**2.** [shake] ébranler, secouer violemment.

concussion [kən'kʌʃn] *n* -**1.** *(U)* [brain injury] commotion *f* cérébrale. -**2.** [shaking] ébranlement *m*, secousse *f* violente.

condemn [kən'dem] *vt* -**1.** [gen & JUR] condamner; **~ed to death** condamné à mort; **people who are ~ed to live in poverty** *fig* les gens qui sont condamnés à vivre dans la misère. -**2.** [disapprove of] condamner, censurer. -**3.** [declare unfit] condamner, déclarer inutilisable; [building] déclarer inhabitable, condamner. -**4.** *Am* JUR [property] exproprier pour cause d'utilité publique.

condemnation [,kɒndem'neɪʃn] *n* -**1.** [gen & JUR] condamnation *f*. -**2.** [criticism] condamnation *f*, censure *f*. -**3.** [of building] condamnation *f*. -**4.** *Am* JUR [of property] expropriation *f* pour cause d'utilité publique.

condemnatory [kən'demnətrɪ] *adj* condamnatoire.

condemned [kən'demd] *adj* condamné; **the ~ man** le condamné; **~ cell** cellule *f* des condamnés.

condensation [,kɒnden'seɪʃn] *n* [gen & CHEM] condensation *f*; [on glass] buée *f*, condensation *f*.

condense [kən'dens] ◇ *vt* -**1.** [make denser] condenser, concentrer; CHEM [gas] condenser; PHYS [beam] concentrer. -**2.** [report, book] condenser, résumer.
◇ *vi* [become liquid] se condenser; [become concentrated] se concentrer.

condensed [kən'denst] *adj* condensé, concentré; **a ~ book** un livre condensé; **in ~ print** TYPO en petits caractères.

condensed milk *n* lait *m* concentré.

condenser [kən'densə^r] *n* ELEC & TECH condensateur *m*; CHEM [of gas] condenseur *m*; PHYS [of light] condensateur.

condescend [,kɒndɪ'send] *vi* -**1.** [behave patronizingly] condescendre, daigner; **to ~ to sb** se montrer condescendant envers qqn OR à l'égard de qqn. -**2.** [lower o.s.] s'abaisser; **she ~ed to speak to me** elle a condescendu à OR a daigné me parler; **he does ~ to set the table occasionally** il condescend à mettre le couvert de temps en temps.

condescending [,kɒndɪ'sendɪŋ] *adj* condescendant.

condescendingly [,kɒndɪ'sendɪŋlɪ] *adv* avec condescendance; [speak] d'un ton condescendant; **he treated me very ~** il m'a traité de haut, il m'a pris de très haut.

condescension [,kɒndɪ'senʃn] *n* condescendance *f*.

condign [kən'daɪn] *adj fml* [appropriate] adéquat, idoine; [deserved] mérité.

condiment ['kɒndɪmənt] *n* condiment *m*.

condition [kən'dɪʃn] ◇ *n* -**1.** [state] état *m*, condition *f*; **the human ~** la condition humaine; **the financial ~ of a company** l'état financier d'une entreprise; **a person's mental/physical ~** l'état mental/physique d'une personne; **you're in no ~ to drive** vous n'êtes pas en état de conduire; **books in good/poor ~** livres en bon/mauvais état; **I'm out of ~** je ne suis pas en forme; **you should get yourself into ~** vous devriez faire des exercices pour retrouver la forme; **in working ~** en état de marche. -**2.** [stipulation] condition *f*; **to make a ~ that** stipuler que; **~s of sale** COMM conditions de vente; **~s of a contract** JUR conditions OR stipulations *fpl* d'un contrat. -**3.** [illness] maladie *f*, affection *f*; **he has a heart ~** il a une maladie du cœur. -**4.** [social status] situation *f*, position *f*.
◇ *vt* -**1.** [train] conditionner; PSYCH provoquer un réflexe conditionné chez, conditionner; **her upbringing ~ed her to believe in God** son éducation l'a automatiquement portée à croire en Dieu. -**2.** [make fit - animal, person] mettre en forme; [- thing] mettre en bon état; **to ~ one's hair/skin** traiter ses cheveux/sa peau. -**3.** [determine] conditionner, déterminer; **the market is ~ed by the economic situation** le marché dépend de la conjoncture économique.
◆ **conditions** *npl* [circumstances] conditions *fpl*, circonstances *fpl*; **living/working ~s** conditions de vie/de travail; **under these ~s** dans ces conditions; **the weather ~s** les conditions météorologiques.
◆ **on condition that** *conj phr*: **I'll tell you on ~ that you keep it secret** je vais vous le dire à condition que vous gardiez le secret; **he'll do it on ~ that he's well paid** il le fera à condition d'être bien payé.

conditional [kən'dɪʃənl] ◇ *adj* -**1.** [dependent on other factors] conditionnel; **negotiations are ~ upon withdrawal of enemy forces** les négociations dépendent du retrait des troupes ennemies; **a ~ promise** une promesse conditionnelle OR sous condition. -**2.** GRAMM conditionnel.
◇ *n* conditionnel *m*; **in the ~** au conditionnel.

conditionally [kən'dɪʃnəlɪ] *adv* conditionnellement.

conditioned [kən'dɪʃnd] *adj* conditionné; ~ response réaction *f* conditionnée, réflexe *m* conditionné; ~ stimulus stimulus *m* conditionnel.

conditioner [kən'dɪʃnəʳ] *n* [for hair] baume *m* démêlant; [for skin] crème *f* traitante OR équilibrante; [for fabric] assouplisseur *m*.

conditioning [kən'dɪʃnɪŋ] ◇ *n* conditionnement *m*.
◇ *adj* traitant.

condo *inf* ['kɒndəʊ] *Am abbr of* **condominium 3**.

condole [kən'dəʊl] *vi lit* exprimer ses condoléances OR sa sympathie.

condolence [kən'dəʊləns] *n* condoléance *f*; a letter of ~ une lettre de condoléances; to offer one's ~s to sb présenter ses condoléances à qqn.

condom ['kɒndəm] *n* préservatif *m (masculin)*.

condominium [,kɒndə'mɪnɪəm] *n* -**1.** [government] condominium *m*. -**2.** [country] condominium *m*. -**3.** *Am* [ownership] copropriété *f*; [building] immeuble *m* (en copropriété); [flat] appartement *m* en copropriété.

condone [kən'dəʊn] *vt* [overlook] fermer les yeux sur; [forgive] pardonner, excuser; we cannot ~ such immoral behaviour nous ne pouvons excuser un comportement aussi immoral; to ~ adultery JUR ≃ pardonner un adultère.

condor ['kɒndɔːʳ] *n* condor *m*.

conducive [kən'djuːsɪv] *adj* favorable; this weather is not ~ to study ce temps n'incite pas à étudier.

conduct [*n* 'kɒndʌkt, *vb* kən'dʌkt] ◇ *n* -**1.** [behaviour] conduite *f*, comportement *m*; bad/good ~ mauvaise/bonne conduite; her ~ towards me son comportement envers moi OR à mon égard. -**2.** [handling - of business, negotiations] conduite *f*.
◇ *vt* -**1.** [manage, carry out] diriger; they criticized the way the campaign was being ~ed ils ont critiqué la façon dont la campagne était menée; this is not the way to ~ negotiations ce n'est pas ainsi qu'on négocie; they're ~ing an inquiry ils conduisent OR mènent une enquête; who is ~ing your case? JUR qui assure votre défense? -**2.** [guide] conduire, mener; the director ~ed us through the factory le directeur nous a fait visiter l'usine. -**3.** [behave]: to ~ o.s. se conduire, se comporter. -**4.** MUS [musicians, music] diriger; Bernstein will be ~ing (the orchestra) l'orchestre sera (placé) sous la direction de Bernstein. -**5.** ELEC & PHYS [transmit] conduire, être conducteur de; water ~s electricity l'eau est conductrice d'électricité.

conductance [kən'dʌktəns] *n* conductance *f*.

conducted tour [kən'dʌktɪd-] *n Br* [short] visite *f* guidée; [longer] voyage *m* organisé; a ~ of the museum une visite guidée du musée; he runs ~s of the region il dirige des voyages organisés OR des excursions accompagnées dans la région.

conducting [kən'dʌktɪŋ] *n* -**1.** [of business, people] conduite *f*. -**2.** MUS [of orchestra] art *m* de diriger.

conduction [kən'dʌkʃn] *n* conduction *f*.

conductive [kən'dʌktɪv] *adj* conducteur.

conductivity [,kɒndʌk'tɪvətɪ] *n* conductivité *f*.

conductor [kən'dʌktəʳ] *n* -**1.** MUS chef *m* d'orchestre. -**2.** [on bus, train] contrôleur *m*; *Am* [railway official] chef *m* de train. -**3.** ELEC & PHYS (corps *m*) conducteur *m*.

conduct report *n* rapport *m (sur la conduite d'un élève)*.

conductress [kən'dʌktrɪs] *n* contrôleuse *f*.

conduct sheet *n* feuille *f* OR certificat *m* de conduite.

conduit ['kɒndɪt] *n* [for fluid] conduit *m*, canalisation *f*; ELEC tube *m*; *fig* [for money] intermédiaire *mf*.

cone [kəʊn] *n* -**1.** [gen, MATH, OPTICS & TECH] cône *m*; a traffic ~ un cône de signalisation. -**2.** [for ice cream] cornet *m*. -**3.** BOT [of pine, fir] pomme *f*, cône *m*.
◆ **cone off** *vt sep Br* mettre des cônes de signalisation sur.

coney ['kəʊni] = **cony**.

Coney Island ['kəʊnɪ-] *pr n* Coney Island *(île située au large de New York et où se trouve un grand parc d'attractions)*.

confab *inf* ['kɒnfæb] (*pt & pp* **confabbed**, *cont* **confabbing**) *Br* ◇ *n* causette *f*.
◇ *vi* causer, bavarder.

confabulate [kən'fæbjʊleɪt] *vi* -**1.** *hum* [chat] causer, bavarder. -**2.** PSYCH fabuler.

confection [kən'fekʃn] *n* -**1.** [act] confection *f*. -**2.** CULIN [sweet] sucrerie *f*, friandise *f*; [pastry] pâtisserie *f*; [cake] gâteau *m*.

confectioner [kən'fekʃnəʳ] *n* [of sweets] confiseur *m*, -euse *f*; [of pastry] pâtissier *m*, -ère *f*; a ~'s (shop) [for sweets] une confiserie; [for pastry] une pâtisserie ❑ ~'s custard crème *f* pâtissière; ~'s sugar *Am* sucre *m* glace.

confectionery [kən'fekʃnərɪ] (*pl* **confectioneries**) *n* [sweets] confiserie *f*; [pastry] pâtisserie *f*.

confederacy [kən'fedərəsɪ] (*pl* **confederacies**) *n* -**1.** [alliance] confédération *f*. -**2.** [conspiracy] conspiration *f*.
◆ **Confederacy** *n* HIST: the Confederacy les États *mpl* confédérés *(pendant la guerre de Sécession américaine)*.

confederate [*n & adj* kən'fedərət, *vb* kən'fedəreɪt] ◇ *n* -**1.** [member of confederacy] confédéré *m*, -e *f*; HIST = **Confederate**. -**2.** [accomplice] complice *mf*.
◇ *adj* confédéré; HIST = **Confederate**.
◇ *vt* confédérer.
◇ *vi* se confédérer.
◆ **Confederate** HIST ◇ *n* sudiste *mf (pendant la guerre de Sécession américaine)*; the Confederates les Confédérés.
◇ *adj*: the Confederate States les États *mpl* confédérés *(pendant la guerre de Sécession américaine)*.

confederation [kən,fedə'reɪʃn] *n* confédération *f*.

confer [kən'fɜːʳ] (*pt & pp* **conferred**, *cont* **conferring**) ◇ *vi* conférer, s'entretenir; he conferred with her about the guest list il s'est entretenu avec elle de la liste des invités.
◇ *vt* conférer, accorder; the Queen conferred a title on him la Reine lui a conféré un titre; to ~ an award on sb remettre une récompense OR un prix à qqn; degrees were conferred on thirty students des diplômes ont été remis à trente étudiants.

conferee [,kɒnfɜː'riː] *n* -**1.** [conference member] participant *m*, -e *f*, congressiste *mf*. -**2.** [recipient - of title] anobli *m*, -e *f*; [- of scholarship] récipiendaire *mf*; [- of diploma] diplômé *m*, -e *f*, récipiendaire *mf*.

conference ['kɒnfərəns] *n* -**1.** [meeting] conférence *f*; [consultation] conférence *f*, consultation *f*; the manager is in ~ le directeur est en conférence OR en réunion. -**2.** [convention] congrès *m*, colloque *m*; POL congrès *m*, assemblée *f*; the Labour Party ~ le congrès du parti travailliste; ~ centre [building] centre de congrès; [town] *ville pouvant accueillir des congrès*. -**3.** *Am* SPORT [association] association *f*, ligue *f*.

conference call *n* téléconférence *f*.

Conference pear *n* poire *f* conférence.

conferment [kən'fɜːmənt], **conferral** [kən'fɜːrəl] *n* action *f* de conférer; [of diploma] remise *f* (de diplôme); [of favour, title] octroi *m*; the ~ of a title on sb l'anoblissement de qqn.

conferree [,kɒnfɜː'riː] = **conferee**.

confess [kən'fes] ◇ *vt* -**1.** [admit - fault, crime] avouer, confesser; to ~ one's guilt OR that one is guilty avouer sa culpabilité, s'avouer coupable; I must OR I have to ~ I was wrong je dois reconnaître OR admettre que j'avais tort. -**2.** RELIG [sins] confesser, se confesser de; [subj: priest] confesser.
◇ *vi* -**1.** [admit] faire des aveux; the thief ~ed le voleur est passé aux aveux; she ~ed to five murders elle a avoué OR confessé cinq meurtres; he ~ed to having lied il a reconnu OR avoué avoir menti; I ~ to a weakness for sweets j'avoue OR je reconnais que j'ai un faible pour les sucreries. -**2.** RELIG se confesser.

confessant [kən'fesənt] *n* pénitent *m*, -e *f*.

confessed [kən'fest] *adj* de son propre aveu; he was a ~ liar il reconnaissait lui-même être menteur.

confession [kən'feʃn] *n* -**1.** [of guilt] aveu *m*, confession *f*; to make a full ~ faire des aveux complets; on my own ~ de mon propre aveu. -**2.** RELIG confession *f*; [sect] confession *f*; do you go to ~? allez-vous vous confesser?; she made her ~ elle s'est confessée; the priest heard our ~ le prêtre nous a confessés; a ~ of faith une confession de foi.

confessional [kən'feʃənl] ◇ *n* confessionnal *m*; the secrets of the ~ les secrets du confessionnal.
◇ *adj* confessionnel.

confessor [kən'fesəʳ] *n* confesseur *m*.

confetti [kən'fetɪ] *n (U)* confettis *mpl*.

confidant [,kɒnfɪ'dænt] *n* confident *m*.

confidante [,kɒnfɪ'dænt] *n* confidente *f*.

confide [kən'faɪd] *vt* -**1.** [reveal] avouer en confidence, confier; to ~ a secret to sb confier un secret à qqn; she ~d her fear to them elle leur a avoué en confidence sa peur; I didn't ~ my thoughts to anyone je n'ai révélé mes pensées à personne. -**2.** [entrust] confier; they ~d their daughter to her ils ont confié leur fille à sa garde OR à ses soins.
◆ **confide in** *vt insep* -**1.** [talk freely to] se confier à; there's nobody I can ~ in il n'y a personne à qui je puisse me confier. -**2.** [trust] avoir confiance en, se fier à; you can ~ in me! vous pouvez me faire confiance!, fiez-vous à moi!

confidence ['kɒnfɪdəns] *n* -**1.** [faith] confiance *f*; we have ~ in her ability nous avons confiance en ses capacités; I have every ~ that you'll succeed je suis absolument certain que vous réussirez; you have to put your ~ in the system vous devez faire confiance au système; the ~ placed in me la confiance qui m'a été témoignée. -**2.** [self-assurance] confiance *f* (en soi), assurance *f*; he spoke with ~ il a parlé avec assurance; she has no ~ elle n'a aucune confiance en elle. -**3.** [certainty] confiance *f*, certitude *f*; she has every ~ that they'll win elle est certaine qu'ils vont gagner; I can say with ~ je peux dire avec confiance OR assurance. -**4.** [trust] confiance *f*; I was told in ~ on me l'a dit confidentiellement OR en confiance; she told me in the strictest ~ elle me l'a dit dans la plus stricte confidence; to take sb into one's ~ se confier à qqn, faire des confidences à qqn. -**5.** [private message] confidence *f*; to exchange ~s échanger des confidences; to repeat a ~ répéter quelque chose dit en confidence, répéter un secret.

confidence man *n* escroc *m*.

confidence trick *n* escroquerie *f*, abus *m* de confiance.

confidence trickster = **confidence man**.

confident ['kɒnfɪdənt] *adj* -**1.** [self-assured] sûr (de soi), assuré. -**2.** [certain] assuré, confiant; ~ of success sûr de réussir; in a ~ tone d'un ton assuré OR plein d'assurance; we are ~ that the plan will work nous sommes persuadés que le projet va réussir.

confidential [,kɒnfɪ'denʃl] *adj* [private] confidentiel; [on envelope] confidentiel; I would like you to treat this conversation as ~ j'aimerais que vous considériez cette conversation comme étant confidentielle; his voice became ~ il prit le ton de la confidence ❑ ~ secretary secrétaire *m* particulier, secrétaire *f* particulière.

confidentiality ['kɒnfɪ,denʃɪ'ælətɪ] *n* confidentialité *f*; 'all inquiries treated with complete ~' 'les demandes de renseignements sont traitées en toute discrétion'.

confidentially [ˌkɒnfɪˈdenʃəlɪ] *adv* confidentiellement.

confidently [ˈkɒnfɪdəntlɪ] *adv* -**1.** [with certainty] avec confiance; I can ~ predict (that)... je peux prédire avec assurance (que)... -**2.** [assuredly] avec assurance.

confiding [kənˈfaɪdɪŋ] *adj* confiant, sans méfiance.

confidingly [kənˈfaɪdɪŋlɪ] *adv* [act] d'un air confiant; [speak] en confidence.

configuration [kənˌfɪgəˈreɪʃn] *n* [gen & COMPUT] configuration *f*.

configure [kənˈfɪgə] *vt* [gen & COMPUT] configurer.

confine [kənˈfaɪn] *vt* -**1.** [restrict] limiter, borner; to ~ o.s. to sthg se borner OR s'en tenir à qqch; we ~d ourselves to (discussing) the financial arrangements nous nous en sommes tenus à discuter des dispositions financières, nous nous en sommes tenus aux dispositions financières; the report ~s itself to single women le rapport ne traite que des femmes célibataires; please ~ your remarks to the subject under consideration veuillez vous limiter au sujet en question. -**2.** [shut up] confiner, enfermer; [imprison] incarcérer, enfermer; to ~ sb to sthg enfermer qqn dans qqch; her illness ~d her to the house/to bed sa maladie l'a obligée à rester à la maison/à garder le lit; to ~ sb to barracks MIL consigner qqn.

confined [kənˈfaɪnd] *adj* -**1.** [area, atmosphere] confiné; in a ~ space dans un espace restreint OR réduit. -**2.** [shut up] renfermé; [imprisoned] emprisonné, incarcéré; to be ~ to barracks MIL être consigné. -**3.** [in childbirth]: to be ~ accoucher, être en couches.

confinement [kənˈfaɪnmənt] *n* -**1.** [detention] détention *f*, réclusion *f*; [imprisonment] emprisonnement *m*, incarcération *f*; ~ to bed alitement *m*; ~ to the house/to one's room obligation de rester à la maison/de garder la chambre; ~ to barracks MIL consigne *f* (au quartier); six months' ~ six mois de prison. -**2.** [in childbirth] couches *fpl*, accouchement *m*.

confines [ˈkɒnfaɪnz] *npl* confins *mpl*, limites *fpl*; within the ~ of reason dans les limites de la raison.

confirm [kənˈfɜːm] *vt* -**1.** [verify] confirmer, corroborer; I can ~ that story je peux confirmer cette histoire; we ~ receipt of OR that we have received your letter nous accusons réception de votre lettre. -**2.** [finalize - arrangement, booking] confirmer; ~ our reservation with the restaurant confirmez notre réservation auprès du restaurant. -**3.** [strengthen - position] assurer, consolider; [- belief, doubts, resolve] fortifier, confirmer, raffermir; that ~s her in her opinion cela la confirme dans son opinion. -**4.** [make valid - treaty] ratifier; [- election] valider; JUR entériner, homologuer. -**5.** RELIG confirmer.

confirmation [ˌkɒnfəˈmeɪʃn] *n* -**1.** [verification] confirmation *f*; the report is still awaiting ~ cette nouvelle n'a pas encore été confirmée. -**2.** [finalization - of arrangements] confirmation *f*; 'all bookings subject to ~' 'toute réservation doit être confirmée'. -**3.** [strengthening - of position] consolidation *f*, raffermissement *m*. -**4.** [validation] validation *f*; JUR entérinement *m*, homologation *f*; [of treaty] ratification *f*. -**5.** RELIG confirmation *f*.

confirmed [kənˈfɜːmd] *adj* -**1.** [long-established] invétéré; he's a ~ bachelor c'est un célibataire endurci; he's a ~ smoker c'est un fumeur invétéré. -**2.** RELIG confirmé.

confiscate [ˈkɒnfɪskeɪt] *vt* confisquer; to ~ sthg from sb confisquer qqch à qqn.

confiscation [ˌkɒnfɪˈskeɪʃn] *n* confiscation *f*.

conflagration [ˌkɒnfləˈgreɪʃn] *n fml* incendie *m*, sinistre *m fml*.

conflate [kənˈfleɪt] *vt fml* colliger.

conflict [*n* ˈkɒnflɪkt, *vb* kənˈflɪkt] ◇ *n* -**1.** [clash] conflit *m*, lutte *f*; MIL conflit *m*, guerre *f*; she often comes into ~ with her mother elle entre souvent en conflit OR se heurte souvent avec sa mère; a ~ of interests un conflit d'intérêts; armed ~ MIL conflit armé. -**2.** [disagreement] dispute *f*; JUR conflit *m*; the parties are often in ~ les partis sont souvent en désaccord; our differing beliefs brought us into ~ nos croyances divergentes nous ont opposés; the unions are in ~ with the management les syndicats sont en conflit avec la direction; there is a ~ between the two statements les deux déclarations ne concordent pas. -**3.** PSYCH [turmoil] conflit *m*.
◇ *vi* -**1.** [ideas, interests] s'opposer, se heurter; the research findings ~ with this view les résultats des recherches sont en contradiction avec OR contredisent cette idée; the policies ~ (with one another) ces politiques sont incompatibles. -**2.** [fight] être en conflit OR en lutte.

conflicting [kənˈflɪktɪŋ] *adj* [opinions] incompatible; [evidence, reports] contradictoire.

confluence [ˈkɒnfluəns] *n* -**1.** [of rivers] confluent *m*. -**2.** [gathering together] confluence *f*; *fig* [crowd] rassemblement *m*.

confluent [ˈkɒnfluənt] ◇ *adj* confluent.
◇ *n* confluent *m*.

conform [kənˈfɔːm] ◇ *vi* -**1.** [comply - person] se conformer, s'adapter; to ~ to OR with sthg se conformer OR s'adapter à qqch; you are expected to ~ tu es supposé te conformer. -**2.** [action, thing] être en conformité; all cars must ~ to OR with the regulations toute voiture doit être conforme aux normes. -**3.** [correspond] correspondre, répondre; she ~s to OR with my idea of a president elle correspond OR répond à ma conception d'un président. -**4.** RELIG être conformiste.
◇ *vt* [ideas, actions] conformer, rendre conforme.

conformable [kənˈfɔːməbl] *adj fml* -**1.** [alike] conforme. -**2.** [in agreement with] adapté, compatible; to be ~ to sthg être adapté à OR compatible avec qqch. -**3.** [obedient] accommodant.

conformation [ˌkɒnfɔːˈmeɪʃn] *n* -**1.** [configuration] conformation *f*, structure *f*. -**2.** [act of forming] conformation *f*.

conformism [kənˈfɔːmɪzm] *n* conformisme *m*.

conformist [kənˈfɔːmɪst] ◇ *adj* conformiste.
◇ *n* [gen & RELIG] conformiste *mf*.

conformity [kənˈfɔːmətɪ] (*pl* conformities) *n* -**1.** [with rules, regulations] conformité *f*. -**2.** [in behaviour, dress etc] conformisme *m*. -**3.** RELIG conformisme *m*.
◆ **in conformity with** *prep phr*: in ~ with his wishes en accord avec OR conformément à ses vœux.

confound [kənˈfaʊnd] *vt* -**1.** [perplex] déconcerter; to be ~ed être confondu. -**2.** *fml* [mix up] confondre. -**3.** *inf dated* [curse]: ~ him! qu'il aille au diable!; ~ it! quelle barbe! -**4.** *arch* [defeat - enemy] confondre.

confounded [kənˈfaʊndɪd] *adj inf dated* [wretched] maudit; it's a ~ nuisance! c'est la barbe!, quelle barbe!; that man is a ~ nuisance! ce type est une vraie plaie!; this ~ thing has broken again! ce satané truc est encore cassé!

confront [kənˈfrʌnt] *vt* -**1.** [face] affronter, faire face à; the obstacles ~ing us les obstacles auxquels nous devons faire face; the headmaster ~ed him in the corridor le directeur l'affronta dans le couloir; he had to ~ a crowd of hecklers il a dû affronter un groupe de perturbateurs; the two groups of demonstrators ~ed each other les deux groupes de manifestants se sont affrontés. -**2.** [present] confronter; she ~ed him with the facts elle l'a confronté avec les faits.

confrontation [ˌkɒnfrʌnˈteɪʃn] *n* -**1.** [conflict] conflit *m*, affrontement *m*; he hates ~ il a horreur des affrontements || MIL affrontement *m*. -**2.** [act of confronting] confrontation *f*; the ~ of the defendant with the evidence la confrontation de l'accusé aux OR avec les preuves.

confrontational [ˌkɒnfrʌnˈteɪʃənl] *adj* [situation] d'affrontement; [policy] de confrontation; [person]: to be ~ aimer les conflits.

Confucian [kənˈfjuːʃn] ◇ *adj* confucéen.
◇ *n* confucéen *m*, - enne *f*.

Confucianism [kənˈfjuːʃənɪzm] *n* confucianisme *m*.

Confucius [kənˈfjuːʃəs] *pr n* Confucius.

confusable [kənˈfjuːzəbl] *n terme qui est souvent confondu avec un autre*.

confuse [kənˈfjuːz] *vt* -**1.** [muddle - person] embrouiller; [- thoughts] embrouiller, brouiller; [- memory] brouiller; don't ~ me! ne m'embrouillez pas (les idées)! -**2.** [perplex] déconcerter, rendre perplexe; [fluster] troubler; [embarrass] embarrasser. -**3.** [mix up] confondre; you're confusing me with my brother vous me confondez avec mon frère; don't ~ the two issues ne confondez pas les deux problèmes. -**4.** [throw into disorder - plans] semer le désordre dans, bouleverser; [- opponent] confondre; to ~ the issue further pour embrouiller OR compliquer encore plus les choses.

confused [kənˈfjuːzd] *adj* -**1.** [muddled - person] désorienté; [- sounds] confus, indistinct; [- thoughts] confus, embrouillé; [- memory] confus, vague; wait a minute, I'm getting ~ attends, là, je ne suis plus; very old people often get ~ les personnes très âgées ont souvent les idées confuses. -**2.** [flustered] troublé; [embarrassed] confus. -**3.** [disordered] en désordre; [enemy] confus.

confusible [kənˈfjuːzəbl] = **confusable**.

confusing [kənˈfjuːzɪŋ] *adj* embrouillé, déroutant; the plot is ~ on se perd dans l'intrigue.

confusingly [kənˈfjuːzɪŋlɪ] *adv* de façon embrouillée.

confusion [kənˈfjuːʒn] *n* -**1.** [bewilderment] confusion *f*; [embarrassment] déconfiture *f*, trouble *m*, embarras *m*; he stared at it in ~ il le fixa d'un regard perplexe; she's in a state of ~ elle a l'esprit troublé; in my ~ I said yes dans mon embarras, j'ai dit oui. -**2.** [mixing up] confusion *f*; to avoid ~ pour éviter toute confusion; there is some ~ as to who won il y a incertitude sur le vainqueur. -**3.** [disorder] désordre *m*; [of enemy] désordre *m*, désarroi *m*; everything was in ~ tout était en désordre OR sens dessus dessous.

confute [kənˈfjuːt] *vt fml* [argument] réfuter; [person] réfuter les arguments de.

conga [ˈkɒŋgə] ◇ *n* conga *f*.
◇ *vi* danser la conga.

congeal [kənˈdʒiːl] ◇ *vi* [thicken] prendre; [oil] (se) figer; [blood] (se) coaguler; [milk] (se) cailler.
◇ *vt* [thicken] faire prendre; [oil] (faire) figer; [blood] (faire) coaguler; [milk] (faire) cailler.

congenial [kənˈdʒiːnjəl] *adj* [pleasant] sympathique, agréable; in ~ surroundings dans un cadre agréable; to spend an afternoon in ~ company passer un après-midi en agréable compagnie.

congenital [kənˈdʒenɪtl] *adj* MED congénital, de naissance; he's a ~ liar *fig* c'est un menteur né.

congenitally [kənˈdʒenɪtəlɪ] *adv* de manière congénitale, congénitalement.

conger (eel) [ˈkɒŋgəʳ-] *n* congre *m*, anguille *f* de mer.

congest [kənˈdʒest] ◇ *vt* -**1.** [crowd] encombrer. -**2.** MED [clog] congestionner.
◇ *vi* -**1.** [become crowded] s'encombrer. -**2.** MED [become clogged] se congestionner.

congested [kənˈdʒestɪd] *adj* -**1.** [area, town] surpeuplé; [road] encombré, embouteillé; [communication lines] encombré; the roads are ~ with traffic il y a des embouteillages OR des encombrements sur les routes. -**2.** MED [clogged] congestionné.

congestion [kənˈdʒestʃn] *n* -**1.** [of area] surpeuplement *m*; [of road, traffic] encombrement *m*, embouteillage *m*. -**2.** MED [blockage] congestion *f*.

conglomerate [*n* & *adj* kənˈglɒmərət, *vb* kənˈglɒməreɪt] ◇ *n* [gen, FIN & GEOL] conglomérat *m*.

◇ *adj* congloméré, aggloméré; GEOL congloméré.
◇ *vt* agglomérer, conglomérer *fml.*
◇ *vi* s'agglomérer.

conglomeration [kən,glɒmə'reɪʃn] *n* -**1.** [mass] groupement *m*, rassemblement *m*; [of buildings] agglomération *f*. -**2.** [act, state] agglomération *f*, conglomération *f fml.*

Congo ['kɒŋgəʊ] *pr n* -**1.** [country]: the ~ le Congo; in the ~ au Congo; the Belgian ~ HIST le Congo belge. -**2.** [river]: the ~ le fleuve Zaïre.

Congolese [,kɒŋgə'li:z] ◇ *n* Congolais *m*, -e *f*.
◇ *adj* congolais.

congrats *inf* [kən'græts] *interj*: ~! chapeau!

congratulate [kən'grætʃʊleɪt] *vt* féliciter, complimenter; her parents ~d her on passing her exams ses parents l'ont félicitée d'avoir réussi à ses examens; she ~d them on their engagement elle leur a présenté ses félicitations à l'occasion de leurs fiançailles; I ~d myself for having kept my temper je me suis félicité d'avoir gardé mon sang-froid.

congratulation [kən,grætʃʊ'leɪʃn] *n* félicitation *f*.
◆ **congratulations** ◇ *interj*: ~s! (toutes mes) félicitations!, je vous félicite!
◇ *npl* félicitations *fpl*; ~s on the new job/your engagement félicitations pour votre nouveau poste/vos fiançailles; I hear ~s are in order il paraît qu'il faut le féliciter; a letter of ~s une lettre de félicitations.

congratulatory [kən'grætʃʊlətrɪ] *adj* de félicitations.

congregate ['kɒŋgrɪgeɪt] *vi* se rassembler, se réunir; the demonstrators ~d in the park les manifestants se sont rassemblés dans le parc.

congregation [,kɒŋgrɪ'geɪʃn] *n* -**1.** [group] assemblée *f*, rassemblement *m*; RELIG [of worshippers] assemblée *f* (de fidèles), assistance *f*; [of priests] congrégation *f*. -**2.** *Br* UNIV assemblée *f* générale.

congregational [,kɒŋgrɪ'geɪʃənl] *adj* [gen] d'une assemblée; RELIG de l'assemblée (des fidèles); [priests] de OR d'une congrégation.
◆ **Congregational** *adj* congrégationaliste; the Congregational Church l'Église *f* congrégationaliste.

congress ['kɒŋgres] *n* -**1.** [association, meeting] congrès *m*. -**2.** *fml* [sexual intercourse] rapport *m* sexuel; to have ~ with sb avoir des rapports sexuels avec qqn.
◆ **Congress** *n* POL Congrès *m*; [session] *session du Congrès américain.*

CONGRESS:
Le Congrès, organe législatif américain, est constitué du Sénat et de la Chambre des représentants; une proposition de loi doit obligatoirement être approuvée séparément par ces deux chambres.

---

congressional [kəŋ'greʃənl] *adj* [gen] d'un congrès.
◆ **Congressional** *adj* POL du Congrès; Congressional district *circonscription d'un représentant du Congrès américain*; Congressional Record *journal officiel du Congrès américain.*

congressman ['kɒŋgresmən] (*pl* congressmen [-mən]) *n* POL ≃ député *m*, membre *m* du Congrès américain; Mr Congressman, do you believe that... Monsieur le Député, croyez-vous que... ❑ ~-at-large *représentant non attaché à une circonscription électorale.*

congresswoman ['kɒŋgres,wʊmən] (*pl* congresswomen [-,wɪmɪn]) *n* POL ≃ député *m* (femme), membre *m* (féminin) du Congrès américain; Miss/Ms/Mrs Congresswoman Madame le député.

congruence ['kɒŋgrʊəns] *n* -**1.** *fml* [similarity] conformité *f*. -**2.** *fml* [correspondence] correspondance *f*; [suitability] convenance *f*. -**3.** MATH congruence *f*.

congruent ['kɒŋgrʊənt] *adj* -**1.** *fml* [similar] conforme; ~ with OR to conforme à. -**2.** *fml* [corresponding] en harmonie; [suitable] convenable; to be ~ with sthg être en harmonie avec qqch; the sentence is ~ with the crime la peine correspond au crime. -**3.** MATH [number] congru, congruent; [triangle] congruent.

congruity [kɒŋ'gru:ətɪ] (*pl* congruities) *n fml* convenance *f*.

congruous ['kɒŋgrʊəs] *adj fml* -**1.** [corresponding] qui s'accorde; ~ with sthg qui s'accorde avec qqch. -**2.** [suitable] convenable, qui convient.

conic(al) ['kɒnɪk(l)] *adj* en forme de cône, conique.

conifer ['kɒnɪfə^r] *n* conifère *m*.

coniferous [kə'nɪfərəs] *adj* conifère; a ~ forest une forêt de conifères.

conjectural [kən'dʒektʃərəl] *adj* conjectural.

conjecture [kən'dʒektʃə^r] ◇ *n* conjecture *f*; whether he knew or not is a matter for ~ savoir s'il était au courant ou pas relève de la conjecture.
◇ *vt* conjecturer, présumer.
◇ *vi* conjecturer, faire des conjectures.

conjoin [kən'dʒɔɪn] *fml* ◇ *vt* joindre, unir.
◇ *vi* s'unir.

conjoint ['kɒndʒɔɪnt] *adj fml* conjoint, uni.

conjointly ['kɒndʒɔɪntlɪ] *adv fml* conjointement.

conjugal ['kɒndʒʊgl] *adj* conjugal.

conjugate [*vb* 'kɒndʒʊgeɪt, *adj* 'kɒndʒʊgɪt]
◇ *vt* conjuguer.
◇ *vi* se conjuguer.
◇ *adj* conjoint, uni.

conjugation [,kɒndʒʊ'geɪʃn] *n* conjugaison *f*.

conjunct [kən'dʒʌŋkt] *adj* conjoint.

conjunction [kən'dʒʌŋkʃn] *n* -**1.** [combination] conjonction *f*, union *f*. -**2.** ASTRON & GRAMM conjonction *f*.
◆ **in conjunction with** *prep phr* conjointement avec; to work in ~ with sb travailler conjointement avec qqn.

conjunctive [kən'dʒʌŋktɪv] *adj* [gen, ANAT & GRAMM] conjonctif.

conjunctivitis [kən,dʒʌŋktɪ'vaɪtɪs] *n* conjonctivite *f*; to have ~ avoir de la conjonctivite.

conjuncture [kən'dʒʌŋktʃə^r] *n fml* [combination of events] conjoncture *f*; [resulting crisis] moment *m* critique.

conjure ['kʌndʒə^r, *vt sense 2* kən'dʒʊə^r]
◇ *vt* -**1.** [produce - gen] faire apparaître, produire; [- by magic] faire apparaître *(par prestidigitation)*; to ~ a rabbit from a hat faire sortir un lapin d'un chapeau. -**2.** *arch* [appeal to] conjurer, implorer.
◇ *vi* faire des tours de passe-passe; his is a name to ~ with *Br fig* c'est quelqu'un d'important.
◆ **conjure away** *vt sep* faire disparaître.
◆ **conjure up** *vt sep* [object, rabbit] faire apparaître, produire; [gods, spirits] faire apparaître, invoquer; [memory] évoquer, rappeler; [image] évoquer.

conjurer ['kʌndʒərə^r] *n* [magician] prestidigitateur *m*, -trice *f*; [sorcerer] sorcier *m*, -ère *f*.

conjuring ['kʌndʒərɪŋ] ◇ *n* prestidigitation *f*.
◇ *adj*: ~ trick tour *m* de passe-passe OR de prestidigitation.

conjuror ['kʌndʒərə^r] = **conjurer**.

conk *inf* [kɒŋk] ◇ *vt* cogner OR frapper (sur la caboche).
◇ *n* -**1.** [blow] gnon *m*. -**2.** *Br* [head] caboche *f*. -**3.** *Br* [nose] pif *m*.
◆ **conk out** *inf vi insep* tomber en panne.

conker *inf* ['kɒŋkə^r] *n Br* marron *m*.
◆ **conkers** *n (U) jeu d'enfant très populaire en Grande-Bretagne et qui consiste à tenter de casser un marron tenu au bout d'un fil par son adversaire.*

conman *inf* ['kɒnmæn] (*pl* conmen [-men]) *n* arnaqueur *m*.

connect [kə'nekt] ◇ *vt* -**1.** [join - pipes, wires] raccorder; [- pinions, shafts, wheels] engrener, coupler; to ~ sthg to sthg joindre OR relier OR raccorder qqch à qqch. -**2.** [join to electricity, gas or water supply - machine, house, telephone] brancher, raccorder; to ~ sthg to sthg raccorder qqch à qqch, brancher qqch sur qqch; to be ~ed (up) to sthg être branché sur qqch. -**3.** TELEC mettre en communication, relier; to ~ sb to sb mettre qqn en communication avec qqn; I'm trying to ~ you j'essaie d'obtenir votre communication. -**4.** [link - subj: path, railway, road, airline] relier; the new rail link ~s Terminal 3 with OR to the train station la nouvelle liaison ferroviaire relie l'aérogare 3 à la gare. -**5.** [associate - person, place, event] associer, faire le rapprochement; to ~ sb/sthg with sb/sthg associer une personne/chose à une autre; I'd never ~ed the two things before je n'avais (encore) jamais fait le rapprochement entre les deux.
◇ *vi* -**1.** [bus, plane, train] assurer la correspondance; to ~ with assurer la correspondance avec. -**2.** [blow, fist, kick, punch] frapper; my fist ~ed with his chin *inf* je l'ai touché au menton.

connected [kə'nektɪd] *adj* -**1.** [linked - languages, subjects, species] connexe. -**2.** [coherent - speech, sentences] cohérent, suivi. -**3.** [associated]: to be ~ed with avoir un lien OR rapport avec. -**4.** [related]: to be ~ed with OR to être parent de.

Connecticut [kə'netɪkət] *pr n* le Connecticut; in ~ dans le Connecticut.

connecting [kə'nektɪŋ] *adj* [cable, wire] de connexion; ~ rod bielle *f*; ~ flight correspondance *f*; ~ door porte *f* de communication.

connection [kə'nekʃn] *n* -**1.** [link between two things] connexion *f*, lien *m*, rapport *m*; to make a ~ between OR to OR with sthg faire le lien avec qqch; does this have any ~ with what happened yesterday? ceci a-t-il un rapport quelconque avec ce qui s'est passé hier?; in this OR that ~ à ce propos, à ce sujet. -**2.** ELECTR prise *f*, raccord *m*; a loose ~ un mauvais contact. -**3.** TELEC communication *f*, ligne *f*; a bad ~ une mauvaise communication OR ligne. -**4.** [transfer - between buses, planes, trains] correspondance *f*; to miss one's ~ rater sa correspondance. -**5.** [transport] liaison *f*; the town enjoys excellent road and rail ~s la ville dispose d'excellentes liaisons routières et ferroviaires. -**6.** [relationship] rapport *m*, relation *f*; to form/to break a ~ with sb établir/rompre des relations avec qqn; he was accused of having CIA ~s on l'a accusé d'avoir des liens avec la CIA; family ~s parenté *f*. -**7.** [colleague, business contact] relation *f* (d'affaires); she has some useful ~s in the publishing world elle a des relations utiles dans le monde de l'édition.
◆ **in connection with** *prep phr* à propos de.

connective [kə'nektɪv] ◇ *adj* [word, phrase] conjonctif.
◇ *n* GRAMM conjonction *f*.

connective tissue *n* tissu *m* conjonctif.

connect-the-dots *n (U) Am jeu qui consiste à relier des points numérotés pour découvrir un dessin.*

connexion [kə'nekʃn] = **connection**.

conning tower ['kɒnɪŋ-] *n* [on submarine] kiosque *m* de timonerie; [on warship] centre *m* opérationnel.

conniption *inf* [kə'nɪpʃn] *n (often pl) Am* crise *f* d'hystérie; to be in a ~ avoir une crise d'hystérie.

connivance [kə'naɪvəns] *n pej* connivence *f*; he acted with the ~ of OR in ~ with government officials il a agi de connivence avec des membres du gouvernement.

connive [kə'naɪv] *vi pej* [plot] être de connivence; they ~d together to undermine government policy ils étaient de connivence pour déstabiliser la politique du gouvernement.
◆ **connive at** *vt insep* -**1.** [ignore] fermer les yeux sur. -**2.** [abet] être complice de.

conniving [kə'naɪvɪŋ] *adj pej* malhonnête, rusé, sournois.

connoisseur [,kɒnə'sɜ:^r] *n* connaisseur *m*, -euse *f*; a ~ of fine wine/good literature un connaisseur en vins/littérature.

connotation [,kɒnə'teɪʃn] *n* -**1.** [association] connotation *f*; for me the word has very sad

~s ce mot a pour moi des connotations très tristes; the name has ~s of quality and expertise ce nom évoque la qualité et la compétence. -2. LING connotation *f*. -3. LOGIC implication *f*.

connote [kə'nəʊt] *vt* -1. *fml* [imply - subj: word, phrase, name] évoquer. -2. LING connoter. -3. LOGIC impliquer.

connubial [kə'nju:bjəl] *adj fml* OR *hum* conjugal, matrimonial; ~ bliss bonheur *m* conjugal.

conquer ['kɒŋkəʳ] *vt* -1. [defeat - person, enemy, team] vaincre. -2. [take control of - castle, city, nation] conquérir. -3. [master - feelings, habits] surmonter; [- disease, disability] vaincre, surmonter. -4. *lit* [win over - sb's heart] conquérir; [- audience, public] conquérir, subjuguer.

conquering ['kɒŋkərɪŋ] *adj* victorieux; hail the ~ hero! *lit* vive le vainqueur!

conqueror ['kɒŋkərəʳ] *n* conquérant *m*.

conquest ['kɒŋkwest] *n* -1. [act or state of being defeated] conquête *f*; our men faced ~ by enemy forces nos hommes allaient être vaincus par les forces ennemies ❑ the Norman Conquest la conquête normande. -2. [mastery] conquête *f*; the ~ of space la conquête de l'espace. -3. [act of seduction] conquête *f*; he boasted of his ~s il se vantait de ses conquêtes ‖ [person] conquête *f*; he's her latest ~ c'est sa dernière conquête; to make a ~ faire une conquête; to make a ~ of sb faire la conquête de qqn. -4. [land] conquête *f*.

Conrail®, **ConRail**® ['kɒnreɪl] *pr n transport urbain new-yorkais*.

Cons. *written abbr of* Conservative.

consanguinity [,kɒnsæŋ'gwɪnətɪ] *n* consanguinité *f*.

conscience ['kɒnʃəns] *n* -1. [moral sense] conscience *f*; always let your ~ be your guide laissez-vous toujours guider par votre conscience; a matter of ~ un cas de conscience; to have a clear OR an easy ~ avoir la conscience tranquille; my ~ is clear j'ai la conscience tranquille; to have a bad OR guilty ~ avoir mauvaise conscience; to have sthg on one's ~ avoir qqch sur la conscience; in all ~ en toute conscience. -2. *(U)* [scruples] mauvaise conscience *f*, remords *m*, scrupule *m*; to have no ~ (about doing sthg) ne pas avoir de scrupules (à faire qqch).

conscience clause *n clause f de conscience*.

conscience money *n* argent *m* restitué *(pour soulager sa conscience)*.

conscience-stricken *adj* pris de remords; to be OR to look ~ être pris de remords, être la proie des remords; ~ faces des visages tourmentés par le remords.

conscientious [,kɒnʃɪ'enʃəs] *adj* consciencieux; she was her usual ~ self elle était consciencieuse comme toujours.

conscientiously [,kɒnʃɪ'enʃəslɪ] *adv* consciencieusement.

conscientiousness [,kɒnʃɪ'enʃəsnɪs] *n* conscience *f*.

conscientious objector *n* objecteur *m* de conscience.

conscious ['kɒnʃəs] ◇ *adj* -1. [aware] conscient; to be ~ of (doing) sthg être conscient de (faire) qqch; he's all too ~ of his shortcomings as a writer il n'est que trop conscient de ses défauts en tant qu'écrivain; to become ~ of sthg prendre conscience de qqch; politically ~ politisé. -2. [awake] conscient; to become ~ reprendre connaissance. -3. [deliberate - attempt, effort] conscient; [- cruelty, rudeness] intentionnel, délibéré. -4. [able to think - being, memory, mind] conscient.
◇ *n* PSYCH: the ~ le conscient.

-conscious *in cpds* conscient de; clothes~ qui fait attention à sa tenue; fashion~ qui suit la mode; age~ conscient de son âge.

consciously ['kɒnʃəslɪ] *adv* consciemment, délibérément; he would never ~ do such a cruel thing il ne ferait jamais une chose aussi cruelle délibérément.

consciousness ['kɒnʃəsnɪs] *n* -1. [awareness] conscience *f*; political ~ conscience politique. -2. [mentality] conscience *f*; the national ~ la conscience nationale. -3. [state of being awake] connaissance *f*; to lose ~ perdre connaissance; to regain ~ reprendre connaissance.

consciousness raising *n* sensibilisation *f*.
◆ **consciousness-raising** *comp* [group, session] de prise de conscience.

conscript [*vb* kən'skrɪpt, *n* & *adj* 'kɒnskrɪpt] ◇ *vt* [men, troops] enrôler, recruter; [workers, labourers] recruter.
◇ *n* conscrit *m*, appelé *m*.
◇ *adj* [army] de conscrits.

conscripted [kən'skrɪptɪd] *adj* [troops, labour] conscrit, enrôlé.

conscription [kən'skrɪpʃn] *n* conscription *f*.

consecrate ['kɒnsɪkreɪt] *vt* -1. [sanctify - church, building, place] consacrer; [- bread and wine] consacrer; ~d ground terre *f* sainte OR bénie. -2. [ordain - bishop] consacrer, sacrer. -3. [dedicate] consacrer, dédier; to ~ one's life to sthg consacrer sa vie à qqch. -4. [make venerable] consacrer; a custom ~d by time une coutume consacrée par l'usage.

consecration [,kɒnsɪ'kreɪʃn] *n* -1. [sanctification] consécration *f*. -2. [ordination] sacre *m*. -3. [dedication] consécration *f*. -4. [veneration] consécration *f*.

consecutive [kən'sekjʊtɪv] *adj* -1. [successive - days, weeks] consécutif; for the third ~ day pour le troisième jour consécutif; they have had five ~ home wins ils ont remporté cinq victoires consécutives sur leur terrain. -2. GRAMM [clause] consécutif.

consecutively [kən'sekjʊtɪvlɪ] *adv* consécutivement; for five years ~ pendant cinq années consécutives; the sentences to be served ~ JUR avec cumul de peines.

consensual [kən'sensjʊəl] *adj* JUR [contract, agreement] consensuel.

consensus [kən'sensəs] ◇ *n* consensus *m*; they failed to reach a ~ (of opinion) ils n'ont pas obtenu de consensus (d'opinion); what is the scientific ~ on the matter? quelle est l'opinion des scientifiques sur ce sujet?
◇ *comp* [politics] de consensus.

consent [kən'sent] ◇ *vi* consentir; to ~ to sthg consentir à qqch; to ~ to do sthg consentir à faire qqch; they ~ed to my request for compassionate leave ils ont consenti à ma demande de congé exceptionnel.
◇ *n* consentement *m*, accord *m*; we got married without my parents' ~ nous nous sommes mariés sans le consentement de mes parents; he refused his ~ to a divorce il a refusé son consentement pour le divorce; by common ~ d'un commun accord; by mutual ~ par consentement mutuel; the age of ~ l'âge *m* nubile.

consenting adult [kən'sentɪŋ-] *n Br homme ayant atteint l'âge de 21 ans et pouvant légalement avoir des rapports homosexuels*.

consequence ['kɒnsɪkwəns] *n* -1. [result] conséquence *f*, suite *f*; it all came about as a ~ of that one brief meeting tout est arrivé à la suite de cette courte réunion; she acted regardless of the ~s elle a agi sans se soucier des conséquences; the policy had terrible ~s for the poor cette mesure a eu des conséquences terribles pour les pauvres; in ~ of which par suite de quoi. -2. [importance] conséquence *f*, importance *f*; a person of no OR little ~ une personne sans importance; a man of ~ un homme important; it's of no ~ c'est sans conséquence, cela n'a pas d'importance.
◆ **in consequence** *adv phr* par conséquent.
◆ **consequences** ◇ *npl* conséquences *fpl*; to take OR to suffer the ~s accepter OR subir les conséquences; to face the ~s faire face aux conséquences.
◇ *n (U) Br* GAMES ≃ cadavres *mpl* exquis.

consequent ['kɒnsɪkwənt] *adj fml* consécutif; ~ on OR upon [resulting from] résultant de; [following] consécutif à.

consequential [,kɒnsɪ'kwenʃl] *adj fml* -1. = **consequent**. -2. [important - decision] de conséquence, conséquent.

consequently ['kɒnsɪkwəntlɪ] *adv* par conséquent, donc.

conservancy [kən'sɜ:vənsɪ] (*pl* **conservancies**) *n* -1. *Br* [commission] administration *f*. -2. = **conservation 2**.

conservation [,kɒnsə'veɪʃn] *n* -1. [of works of art] préservation *f*. -2. [of natural resources] préservation *f*; nature ~ défense *f* de l'environnement. -3. PHYS conservation *f*; the ~ of mass/energy/momentum le principe de conservation de la masse/de l'énergie/du moment.

conservation area *n* zone *f* protégée.

conservationist [,kɒnsə'veɪʃənɪst] *n* défenseur *m* de l'environnement.

conservatism [kən'sɜ:vətɪzm] *n* -1. POL = **Conservatism**. -2. [traditionalism - of policy, views] conservatisme *m*.
◆ **Conservatism** *n* [policy of Conservative Party] conservatisme *m*.

conservative [kən'sɜ:vətɪv] ◇ *n* [traditionalist] traditionaliste *mf*, conformiste *mf*.
◇ *adj* -1. [traditionalist - views, person, attitude] conformiste. -2. [conventional - suit, clothes, haircut] conventionnel. -3. [modest - estimate, guess] prudent. -4. PHYS conservateur.
◆ **Conservative** POL ◇ *n* conservateur *m*, -trice *f*.
◇ *adj* [policy, government, MP] conservateur.

conservatively [kən'sɜ:vətɪvlɪ] *adv* [dress] de façon conventionnelle.

Conservative Party *pr n*: the ~ le parti conservateur.

conservatoire [kən'sɜ:vətwɑ:ʳ] *n* conservatoire *m*.

conservator [kən'sɜ:vətəʳ] *n* gardien *m*, -enne *f*.

conservatory [kən'sɜ:vətrɪ] (*pl* **conservatories**) *n* -1. [greenhouse] jardin *m* d'hiver. -2. = **conservatoire**.

conserve [*vb* kən'sɜ:v, *n* 'kɒnsɜ:v, kən'sɜ:v] ◇ *vt* -1. [save - energy, resources, battery] économiser; to ~ one's strength ménager ses forces. -2. *lit* [preserve - privilege, freedom] protéger, préserver.
◇ *n* confiture *f*; strawberry ~ confiture de fraises.

consider [kən'sɪdəʳ] ◇ *vt* -1. [believe] considérer, estimer, penser; I've always ~ed her (to be) a good friend je l'ai toujours considérée comme une bonne amie; she ~s it wrong to say such things elle pense qu'il est mauvais de dire de telles choses; I ~ myself lucky je m'estime heureux; I would ~ it an honour je m'estimerais honoré. -2. [ponder - problem, offer, possibility] considérer, examiner; have you ever ~ed becoming an actress? avez-vous jamais songé à devenir actrice?; I'm willing to ~ your offer je suis prêt à examiner votre proposition. -3. [bear in mind - points, facts] prendre en considération; [- costs, difficulties, dangers] tenir compte de; we got off lightly, when you ~ what might have happened nous nous en sommes bien tirés, quand on pense à ce qui aurait pu arriver; all things ~ed tout bien considéré. -4. [show regard for - feelings, wishes] tenir compte de; he has a wife and family to ~ il a une femme et une famille à prendre en considération. -5. [discuss - report, case, candidate] examiner, considérer; she's being ~ed for the post of manager on pense à elle pour le poste de directeur. -6. [contemplate - face, picture, scene] examiner, observer.
◇ *vi* réfléchir; I need time to ~ j'ai besoin de temps pour réfléchir.

considerable [kən'sɪdrəbl] *adj* considérable; she showed ~ courage elle a fait preuve de beaucoup de courage; a ~ number of our members are over sixty un nombre considérable de nos membres a plus de soixante ans; to a ~ extent dans une (très) large mesure.

considerably [kən'sɪdrəblɪ] *adv* considérablement.

considerate [kən'sɪdərət] *adj* [person] prévenant, plein d'égards, aimable; **it was very ~ of you to phone first** c'est très aimable à vous d'avoir téléphoné au préalable; **he's always so ~ of** OR **towards others** il est toujours si prévenant envers les autres.

considerately [kən'sɪdərətlɪ] *adv* [behave, act] avec des égards.

consideration [kən,sɪdə'reɪʃn] *n* -**1.** [thought] considération *f*; **the matter needs careful ~** le sujet demande une attention particulière; **to take sthg into ~** prendre qqch en considération; **taking everything into ~** tout bien considéré; **after due ~** après mûre réflexion. -**2.** [factor] considération *f*, préoccupation *f*; **time is our main ~** le temps est notre principale préoccupation. -**3.** [thoughtfulness] égard *m*; **to show ~ for sb/sb's feelings** ménager qqn/la sensibilité de qqn; **have you no ~ for other people?** n'as-tu donc aucun égard pour les autres?; **she remained silent out of ~ for his family** elle se tut par égard pour sa famille. -**4.** [discussion] étude *f*; **the matter is under ~** l'affaire est à l'étude. -**5.** [importance]: **of no ~** sans importance. -**6.** *fml* [payment] rémunération *f*, finance *f*; **for a small ~** moyennant rémunération OR finance.

considered [kən'sɪdəd] *adj* -**1.** [reasoned - opinion, manner] bien pesé, mûrement réfléchi; **it's my ~ opinion that...** après mûre réflexion, je pense que... -**2.** *fml* [respected - artist, writer] considéré, respecté.

considering [kən'sɪdərɪŋ] ◇ *conj* étant donné que, vu que; **~ she'd never played the part before, she did very well** pour quelqu'un qui n'avait jamais tenu ce rôle, elle s'est très bien débrouillée.
◇ *prep* étant donné, vu; **~ how hard he tried, he did rather poorly** vu tout le mal qu'il s'est donné, c'était plutôt médiocre.
◇ *adv inf* tout compte fait, finalement; **she writes quite well, ~** elle écrit assez bien, finalement.

consign [kən'saɪn] *vt* -**1.** [send - goods] envoyer, expédier; **to ~ sthg to sb** envoyer qqch à qqn. -**2.** [relegate - thing] reléguer; **I ~ed all my clutter to the attic** j'ai relégué tout mon fourbi au grenier; **I ~ed his last letter to the rubbish bin** sa dernière lettre s'est retrouvée à la poubelle. -**3.** [entrust - person] confier; **to ~ sb to sb** confier qqn à OR aux soins de qqn; **as a child I was ~ed to the care of my grandmother** enfant, je fus confié aux soins de ma grand-mère.

consignee [,kɒnsaɪ'niː] *n* consignataire *mf*.

consigner [kən'saɪnəʳ] = **consignor**.

consignment [,kən'saɪnmənt] *n* -**1.** [despatch] envoi *m*, expédition *f*; **goods for ~** marchandise *f* à expédier; **~ note** bordereau *m* d'expédition. -**2.** [batch of goods] arrivage *m*, lot *m*; **a ~ of heavy machinery** un arrivage de machines lourdes.

consignor [kən'saɪnəʳ] *n* expéditeur *m*, -trice *f*.

consist [kən'sɪst]
◆ **consist of** *vt insep* consister en, se composer de; **the panel ~s of five senior lecturers** le jury se compose de cinq maîtres de conférence; **the book ~s largely of photos of his family** le livre est constitué surtout de photos de sa famille.
◆ **consist in** *vt insep fml*: **to ~ in (doing) sthg** consister à faire qqch OR dans qqch; **his "genius" ~s in a mere talent for mimicry** son «génie» se résume à son talent d'imitateur; **the book's success ~s largely in its simplicity** le succès du livre réside en grande partie dans sa simplicité.

consistence [kən'sɪstəns], **consistency** [kən'sɪstənsɪ] (*pl* **consistences** OR **consistencies**) *n* -**1.** [texture] consistance *f*; **keep stirring until you get the right ~** remuez jusqu'à ce que vous obteniez la consistance souhaitée; **consistencies can vary** la consistance peut changer. -**2.** [coherence - of behaviour, argument, alibi] cohérence *f*, logique *f*; **their policies lack ~** leur politique manque de cohérence.

consistent [kən'sɪstənt] *adj* -**1.** [constant - opponent, loyalty] constant. -**2.** [steady - growth, improvement] constant. -**3.** [idea, argument, account] cohérent; **his story is not ~ with the known facts** son histoire ne correspond pas aux faits.

consistently [kən'sɪstəntlɪ] *adv* régulièrement, constamment; **they have won ~ throughout the season** ils ont gagné tout au long de la saison.

consolation [,kɒnsə'leɪʃn] *n* consolation *f*, réconfort *m*; **if it's any ~, the same thing happened to me** si cela peut te consoler, il m'est arrivé la même chose; **words of ~** mots de réconfort; **she sought ~ in music** elle cherchait le réconfort dans la musique; **her children were a great ~ to her** ses enfants étaient une grande consolation pour elle.

consolation prize *n literal* & *fig* prix *m* de consolation.

consolatory [kən'sɒlətrɪ] *adj* [message, words] consolant, réconfortant.

console [*vb* kən'səʊl, *n* 'kɒnsəʊl] ◇ *vt* consoler; **to ~ sb for sthg (with** OR **by)** consoler qqn de qqch (avec OR en).
◇ *n* -**1.** [control panel] console *f*, pupitre *m*. -**2.** [cabinet] meuble *m (pour téléviseur, chaîne hi-fi)*. -**3.** MUS [on organ] console *f*. -**4.** ARCHIT console *f*.

console table *n* console *f*.

consolidate [kən'sɒlɪdeɪt] *vt* -**1.** [reinforce - forces, power] consolider; [- knowledge] consolider, renforcer; **to ~ one's position** consolider sa position. -**2.** [combine - companies, states] réunir, fusionner; [- funds, loans] consolider.

consolidated [kən'sɒlɪdeɪtɪd] *adj* [annuity, loan] consolidé; [in name of company] *désigne une société née de la fusion de deux entreprises*; **~ accounts** états *mpl* financiers consolidés.

consolidated fund *n Br* fonds *mpl* consolidés.

consolidation [kən,sɒlɪ'deɪʃn] *n* -**1.** [reinforcement - of power] consolidation *f*; [- of knowledge] consolidation *f*, renforcement *m*. -**2.** [amalgamation - of companies] fusion *f*; [- of funds, loans] consolidation *f*.

consoling [kən'səʊlɪŋ] *adj* [idea, thought] réconfortant.

consols ['kɒnsəlz] *npl Br* fonds *mpl* consolidés.

consommé [*Br* kən'sɒmeɪ, *Am* ,kɒnsə'meɪ] *n* consommé *m*.

consonance ['kɒnsənəns] *n* -**1.** *fml* [of ideas] accord *m*; **in ~ with** en accord avec. -**2.** LITERAT & MUS consonance *f*.

consonant ['kɒnsənənt] ◇ *n* consonne *f*.
◇ *adj fml* en accord; **to be ~ with** OR **to sthg** être en accord avec qqch.

consonantal [,kɒnsə'næntl] *adj* consonantique.

consonant shift *n* mutation *f* consonantique OR des consonnes.

consort [*n* 'kɒnsɔːt, *vb* kən'sɔːt] ◇ *n* -**1.** [spouse] époux *m*, épouse *f*; [of reigning monarch] consort *m*. -**2.** [ship] escorteur *m*.
◇ *vi*: **to ~ with sb** fréquenter qqn, frayer avec qqn.

consortium [kən'sɔːtjəm] (*pl* **consortiums** OR **consortia** [-tjə]) *n* consortium *m*.

conspectus [kən'spektəs] *n fml* -**1.** [overview] vue *f* d'ensemble. -**2.** [summary] résumé *m*, synopsis *m*.

conspicuous [kən'spɪkjʊəs] *adj* -**1.** [visible - behaviour, hat, person] voyant; **he felt ~ in his new hat** il avait l'impression de se faire remarquer avec son nouveau chapeau OR que son nouveau chapeau ne passait pas inaperçu; **to make o.s. ~** se faire remarquer. -**2.** [obvious - failure, lack] manifeste, évident; [- bravery, gallantry] insigne; **to be ~ by one's absence** briller par son absence.

conspicuous consumption *n* consommation *f* ostentatoire.

conspicuously [kən'spɪkjʊəslɪ] *adv* -**1.** [visibly - dressed] de façon à se faire remarquer. -**2.** [obviously - successful] de façon remarquable OR évidente.

conspiracy [kən'spɪrəsɪ] (*pl* **conspiracies**) ◇ *n* [plotting] conspiration *f*, complot *m*; [plot] complot; **he's been charged with ~** on l'a accusé de conspiration; **a ~ of silence** une conspiration du silence.
◇ *comp*: **~ theory** thèse *f* du complot.

conspirator [kən'spɪrətəʳ] *n* conspirateur *m*, -trice *f*, comploteur *m*, -euse *f*, conjuré *m*, -e *f*.

conspiratorial [kən,spɪrə'tɔːrɪəl] *adj* [smile, whisper, wink] de conspirateur; [group] de conspirateurs.

conspiratorially [kən,spɪrə'tɔːrɪəlɪ] *adv* [smile, whisper, wink] d'un air de conspiration.

conspire [kən'spaɪəʳ] *vi* -**1.** [plot] conspirer; **to ~ (with sb) to do sthg** comploter OR s'entendre (avec qqn) pour faire qqch; **to ~ against sb** conspirer contre qqn. -**2.** [combine - events, the elements] concourir, se conjurer; **to ~ to do sthg** concourir à faire qqch; **to ~ against sthg** se conjurer contre qqch.

constable ['kʌnstəbl] *n* agent *m*, gendarme *m*, sergent *m*; **excuse me, Constable** excusez-moi, monsieur l'agent; **Constable Jenkins** Sergent Jenkins; **police ~** agent *m* de police.

constabulary [kən'stæbjʊlərɪ] (*pl* **constabularies**) ◇ *n*: **the ~** la police, la gendarmerie.
◇ *adj* [duties] de policier.

constancy ['kɒnstənsɪ] *n* -**1.** [steadfastness] constance *f*; [of feelings] constance *f*, fidélité *f*. -**2.** [stability - of temperature, light] constance *f*.

constant ['kɒnstənt] ◇ *adj* -**1.** [continuous - interruptions, noise, pain] constant, continuel, perpétuel; **the entrance is in ~ use** il y a un mouvement continuel à l'entrée. -**2.** [unchanging - pressure, temperature, voltage] constant. -**3.** [faithful - affection, friend] fidèle, loyal; **he was her ~ companion** il était son fidèle compagnon.
◇ *n* [gen, MATH & PHYS] constante *f*.

Constantine ['kɒnstəntaɪn] *pr n* -**1.** [emperor] Constantin. -**2.** GEOG Constantine.

Constantinople [,kɒnstæntɪ'nəʊpl] *pr n* Constantinople.

constantly ['kɒnstəntlɪ] *adv* constamment, sans cesse.

constellation [,kɒnstə'leɪʃn] *n* -**1.** [of stars] constellation *f*. -**2.** *fig* [of celebrities] constellation *f*.

consternation [,kɒnstə'neɪʃn] *n* consternation *f*; **I watched in ~** je regardais avec OR frappé de consternation; **the meeting ended amidst general ~** la réunion s'acheva dans la consternation générale; **the prospect filled me with ~** cette perspective m'a plongé dans la consternation.

constipated ['kɒnstɪpeɪtɪd] *adj* constipé.

constipation [,kɒnstɪ'peɪʃn] *n* constipation *f*.

constituency [kən'stɪtjʊənsɪ] (*pl* **constituencies**) ◇ *n* [area] circonscription *f* électorale; [people] électeurs *mpl*.
◇ *comp* [meeting, organization] local.

constituent [kən'stɪtjʊənt] ◇ *adj* -**1.** [component - part, element] constituant, composant. -**2.** POL [assembly, power] constituant.
◇ *n* -**1.** [voter] électeur *m*, -trice *f*. -**2.** [element] élément *m* constitutif.

constitute ['kɒnstɪtjuːt] *vt* -**1.** [represent] constituer; **what exactly ~s a state of emergency?** qu'est-ce que c'est exactement qu'un état d'urgence?; **they ~ a threat to the government** ils représentent une menace pour le gouvernement. -**2.** [make up] constituer; **women ~ a large section of the workforce** les femmes constituent une grande partie de la main d'œuvre. -**3.** [set up - committee, panel] constituer. -**4.** [appoint - chairman, spokesperson] désigner.

constitution [,kɒnstɪ'tjuːʃn] *n* -**1.** POL [statute] constitution *f*; **the (United States) Constitution** *Am* POL la Constitution. -**2.** [health] constitution *f*; **to have a strong/weak ~** avoir une constitution robuste/chétive. -**3.** [structure] composition *f.*

CONSTITUTION :
La Constitution britannique, à la différence de la Constitution américaine ou française (texte écrit et définitif), n'est pas un document en soi, mais le résultat virtuel de la succession des lois dans le temps, fonctionnant sur le principe de la jurisprudence.

constitutional [ˌkɒnstɪ'tjuːʃənl] ◇ *adj* -**1.** POL constitutionnel; ~ **monarchy** monarchie constitutionnelle. -**2.** [official - head, privilege] constitutionnel. -**3.** [inherent - weakness] constitutionnel.
◇ *n dated* OR *hum*: **to go for a** ~ aller faire un petit tour.

constitutionalism [ˌkɒnstɪ'tjuːʃnəlɪzm] *n* constitutionnalisme *m.*

constitutionality ['kɒnstɪˌtjuːʃə'næləti] *n* constitutionnalité *f.*

constitutionally [ˌkɒnstɪ'tjuːʃnəlɪ] *adv* -**1.** POL [act] constitutionnellement; ~, **the government is within its rights** constitutionnellement, le gouvernement est dans ses droits. -**2.** [inherently - strong, weak] de OR par nature.

constitutive [kən'stɪtjʊtɪv] *adj* -**1.** [body, organization] constitutif. -**2.** CHEM constitutif. -**3.** = **constituent 1.**

constrain [kən'streɪn] *vt* -**1.** [force] contraindre, forcer; **to** ~ **sb to do sthg** contraindre qqn à faire qqch. -**2.** [limit - feelings, freedom] contraindre, restreindre.

constrained [kən'streɪnd] *adj* -**1.** [inhibited] contraint; **to feel** ~ **to do sthg** se sentir contraint OR obligé de faire qqch; **he felt** ~ **by his clothes** il se sentait à l'étroit dans ses vêtements. -**2.** [tense - manner, speech] contraint; [- atmosphere, smile] contraint, gêné.

constraint [kən'streɪnt] *n* -**1.** [restriction] contrainte *f*; **they are subject to the** ~**s of time and money** ils sont sujets aux contraintes du temps et de l'argent; **there are certain** ~**s on their activities** ils subissent certaines contraintes dans leurs activités; **social** ~**s** contraintes sociales; **to speak without** ~ parler librement OR sans contrainte. -**2.** [pressure] contrainte *f*; **to do sthg under** ~ agir OR faire qqch sous la contrainte.

constrict [kən'strɪkt] *vt* -**1.** [make narrower - blood vessels, throat] resserrer, serrer. -**2.** [hamper - breathing, movement] gêner.

constricted [kən'strɪktɪd] *adj* [breathing, movement] gêné, restreint; **to feel** ~ **by sthg** *literal* & *fig* se sentir limité par qqch.

constricting [kən'strɪktɪŋ] *adj* [clothes] étroit; *fig* [beliefs, ideology] limité.

constriction [kən'strɪkʃn] *n* -**1.** [feeling of tightness - in chest, throat] constriction *f.* -**2.** [restriction] restriction *f*; **social** ~**s** restrictions sociales.

constrictor [kən'strɪktə^r] → **boa.**

construct [*vb* kən'strʌkt, *n* 'kɒnstrʌkt] ◇ *vt* -**1.** [build - bridge, dam, house, road] construire; [- nest, raft] construire, bâtir; **to** ~ **sthg (out) of sthg** construire qqch à partir de qqch. -**2.** [formulate - sentence] composer; [- system, theory] bâtir; **a beautifully** ~**ed play** une pièce magnifiquement construite OR composée.
◇ *n fml* construction *f.*

construction [kən'strʌkʃn] ◇ *n* -**1.** [act of building - road, bridge, house] construction *f*; [- machine] construction *f*, réalisation *f*; [- system, theory] construction *f*, élaboration *f*; **under** ~ en construction; **to work in** ~ travailler dans le bâtiment. -**2.** [structure] construction *f*, édifice *m*, bâtiment *m*; **a building of simple/solid** ~ un bâtiment de construction simple/ solidement construit. -**3.** [interpretation] interprétation *f*; **to put a wrong** ~ **on sb's words** mal interpréter les paroles de qqn; **to put a sympathetic** ~ **on sb's words** interpréter les paroles de qqn avec indulgence. -**4.** GRAMM construction *f.* -**5.** GEOM construction *f.* -**6.** ART sculpture *f* constructiviste.
◇ *comp* [site, work] de construction; [industry, worker] du bâtiment.

constructional [kən'strʌkʃənl] *adj* de construction; [engineering, technique] mécanique.

constructive [kən'strʌktɪv] *adj* [criticism, remark] constructif.

constructive dismissal *n* démission *f* provoquée *(sous la pression de la direction).*

constructively [kən'strʌktɪvlɪ] *adv* d'une manière constructive.

constructivism [kən'strʌktɪvɪzm] *n* ART & PHILOS constructivisme *m.*

constructivist [kən'strʌktɪvɪst] *n* ART constructiviste *mf.*

constructor [kən'strʌktə^r] *n* [of building, road, bridge, machine] constructeur *m*; [of system, theory] créateur *m.*

construe [kən'struː] *vt* -**1.** [interpret, understand - attitude, response, statement] interpréter, expliquer; *dated* [Greek, Latin] expliquer. -**2.** [parse - Greek or Latin text] analyser, décomposer.

consubstantial [ˌkɒnsəb'stænʃl] *adj* consubstantiel.

consubstantiation ['kɒnsəbˌstænʃɪ'eɪʃn] *n* consubstantiation *f.*

consul ['kɒnsəl] *n* consul *m.*

consular ['kɒnsjʊlə^r] *adj* consulaire.

consulate ['kɒnsjʊlət] *n* consulat *m.*

consul general (*pl* **consuls general**) *n* consul *m* général.

consulship ['kɒnsəlʃɪp] *n* fonctions *fpl* OR charge *f* de consul.

consult [kən'sʌlt] ◇ *vt* -**1.** [ask - doctor, expert] consulter; **to** ~ **sb about sthg** consulter qqn sur OR au sujet de qqch. -**2.** [consider - person's feelings] prendre en considération. -**3.** [refer to - book, dictionary, map, notes, watch] consulter.
◇ *vi* consulter, être en consultation; **to** ~ **together over sthg** se consulter sur OR au sujet de qqch; **to** ~ **with sb** conférer avec qqn.

consultancy [kən'sʌltənsɪ] (*pl* **consultancies**) *n* -**1.** [company] cabinet *m* d'expert-conseil. -**2.** [advice] assistance *f* technique. -**3.** [hospital post] poste *m* de médecin OR chirurgien consultant.

consultant [kən'sʌltənt] ◇ *n* -**1.** [doctor - specialist] médecin *m* spécialiste, consultant *m*; [- in charge of department] consultant *m.* -**2.** [expert] expert-conseil *m*, consultant *m.*
◇ *comp* [engineer] conseil *(inv)*; [psychiatrist, physician] consultant.

consultation [ˌkɒnsəl'teɪʃn] *n* -**1.** [discussion] consultation *f*, délibération *f*; **a matter for** ~ un sujet à débattre; **the matter will be decided in** ~ **with our colleagues** la décision sera prise en consultation OR en concertation avec nos collègues; **to hold** ~**s about sthg** avoir des consultations sur qqch. -**2.** [reference] consultation *f*; **the dictionary is designed for easy** ~ le dictionnaire a été conçu pour être consulté facilement.

consultative [kən'sʌltətɪv] *adj* consultatif; **I'm here in a purely** ~ **capacity** je ne suis ici qu'à titre consultatif.

consulting [kən'sʌltɪŋ] *adj* [engineer] conseil *(inv).*

consulting room *n* cabinet *m* de consultation.

consumable [kən'sjuːməbl] *adj* [substance - by fire] consumable; [foodstuffs] consommable, de consommation.
◆ **consumables** *npl* [food] denrées *fpl* alimentaires, comestibles *mpl*; [hardware] consommables *mpl.*

consume [kən'sjuːm] *vt* -**1.** [eat or drink] consommer. -**2.** [use up - energy, fuel] consommer; [- time] dépenser. -**3.** [burn up - subj: fire, flames] consumer; **the city was** ~**d by fire** la ville a brûlé; **to be** ~**d with desire/love** *fig* brûler de désir/d'amour; **to be** ~**d with grief** *fig* être miné par le chagrin; **to be** ~**d with hatred/jealousy** *fig* être dévoré par la haine/ jalousie.

consumer [kən'sjuːmə^r] ◇ *n* -**1.** [purchaser] consommateur *m*, -trice *f.* -**2.** [user] consommateur *m*, -trice *f*; **gas/electricity** ~ abonné *m* au gaz/à l'électricité.
◇ *comp* [advice, protection, resistance] du consommateur, des consommateurs; ~ **research** étude *f* de marché; ~ **credit** crédit *m* à la consommation; ~ **durables** OR **goods** biens *mpl* de consommation durables.

consumerism [kən'sjuːmərɪzm] *n* -**1.** [consumer protection] consumérisme *m.* -**2.** *pej* [consumption] consommation *f* à outrance.

Consumers' Association *pr n association britannique des consommateurs.*

consumer society *n* société *f* de consommation.

consuming [kən'sjuːmɪŋ] *adj* [desire, interest, passion] dévorant.

consummate [*adj* kən'sʌmət, *vb* 'kɒnsəmeɪt] ◇ *adj* -**1.** [extremely skilful - artist, musician] consommé, accompli. -**2.** [utter - coward, fool, liar, snob] accompli, parfait, fini.
◇ *vt* [love, marriage] consommer.

consummation [ˌkɒnsə'meɪʃn] *n* -**1.** [of marriage] consommation *f.* -**2.** [culmination - of career, life's work] couronnement *m.* -**3.** [achievement - of ambitions, desires] achèvement *m.*

consumption [kən'sʌmpʃn] *n* -**1.** [eating, drinking] consommation *f*; **unfit for human** ~ non comestible; **his words were not intended for public** ~ *fig* ses paroles n'étaient pas destinées au public. -**2.** [purchasing] consommation *f.* -**3.** [using up - of gas, energy, oil] consommation *f*, dépense *f.* -**4.** [amount used] consommation *f*, dépense *f.* -**5.** [tuberculosis] consomption *f* (pulmonaire), phtisie *f.*

consumptive [kən'sʌmptɪv] *dated* ◇ *adj* [disease, illness] consomptif, destructif.
◇ *n* phtisique *mf*, tuberculeux *m*, -euse *f.*

cont. *written abbr of* continued.

contact ['kɒntækt] ◇ *n* -**1.** [communication] contact *m*, rapport *m*; **we don't have much** ~ **with our neighbours** nous n'avons pas beaucoup de contacts avec nos voisins; **to be in** ~ **with sb** être en contact OR en rapport avec qqn; **to come into** ~ **with sb** entrer OR se mettre en contact OR en rapport avec qqn; **to make** ~ **with sb** prendre contact avec qqn; **to lose** ~ **with sb** [lose touch] perdre contact avec qqn. -**2.** [touch] contact *m*; **always keep one foot in** ~ **with the ground** gardez toujours un pied au sol; **physical** ~ contact physique; **eye** ~ contact visuel. -**3.** [person] relation *f*; **she has some useful business** ~**s** elle a quelques bons contacts (professionnels). -**4.** ELECTR [connector] contact *m*; [connection] contact *m*; **to make (the)** ~ mettre OR établir le contact; **to break (the)** ~ couper OR rompre le contact. -**5.** MED *personne ayant approché un malade contagieux.* -**6.** = **contact print.** -**7.** *inf* = **contact lens.**
◇ *comp* -**1.** [contagious - dermatitis] par contact. -**2.** [killing on contact - herbicide, insecticide] par contact. -**3.** [involving physical contact - sport] de contact. -**4.** [maintaining contact]: ~ **number** numéro où l'on peut contacter OR joindre qqn.
◇ *vt* prendre contact avec, contacter; **we'll** ~ **you later on this week** nous vous contacterons cette semaine.

contactable [kɒn'tæktəbl] *adj* que l'on peut joindre OR contacter, joignable; **I'm** ~ **at this number** on peut me contacter OR m'appeler à ce numéro.

contact breaker *n* rupteur *m*, levier *m* de rupture.

contact flight *n* -**1.** [flight] vol *m* à basse altitude. -**2.** [navigation] navigation *f* à vue.

contact lens *n* verre *m* OR lentille *f* de contact.

contact man *n* contact *m*, agent *m* de liaison.

contact print *n* planche contact *f*, épreuve *f* par contact.

contact sport *n* sport *m* de contact.

contagion [kən'teɪdʒn] *n* -**1.** [contamination] contagion *f.* -**2.** [disease] contagion *f*, maladie *f* contagieuse. -**3.** *lit* [moral corruption] contamination *f.*

contagious [kən'teɪdʒəs] *adj literal & fig* contagieux; he's no longer ~ il n'est plus contagieux.

contain [kən'teɪn] *vt* -**1.** [hold - subj: bag, pocket, house, city] contenir. -**2.** [include - subj: pill, substance] contenir; [- subj: book, system, painting, speech] contenir, comporter; **her story does ~ some truth** il y a du vrai dans son histoire. -**3.** [restrain - feelings] contenir, cacher; **to ~ one's anger** contenir sa colère; **to ~ one's disappointment** cacher sa déception; **I could barely ~ myself** j'avais du mal à me contenir. -**4.** [curb - enemy forces, population growth, revolution, riot] contenir, maîtriser. -**5.** [hold back - fire] circonscrire; [- flood waters] contenir, endiguer. -**6.** [limit - damage] limiter. -**7.** MATH être divisible par.

container [kən'teɪnəʳ] ◇ *n* -**1.** [bottle, box, tin etc] récipient *m*, boîte *f*. -**2.** [for transporting cargo] conteneur *m*, container *m*.
◇ *comp* [port, ship, terminal] porte-conteneurs; [dock, line, transport] pour porte-conteneurs.

containerization [kən,teɪnəraɪ'zeɪʃn] *n* -**1.** [of cargo] conteneurisation *f*, transport *m* par conteneurs. -**2.** [of port] conteneurisation *f*.

containerize, -ise [kən'teɪnəraɪz] *vt* -**1.** [cargo] conteneuriser, transporter par conteneurs. -**2.** [port] conteneuriser.

containment [kən'teɪnmənt] *n* -**1.** POL endiguement *m*, freinage *m*, retenue *f*; **a policy of ~** une politique d'endiguement. -**2.** PHYS confinement *m*.

contaminate [kən'tæmɪneɪt] *vt* -**1.** [pollute - food, river, water] contaminer; *fig* [corrupt] contaminer, souiller. -**2.** [irradiate - land, person, soil] contaminer.

contaminated [kən'tæmɪneɪtɪd] *adj* -**1.** [polluted - food, river, water] contaminé; [- air] contaminé, vicié; *fig* [corrupted] contaminé, corrompu. -**2.** [irradiated - land, person, soil] contaminé.

contamination [kən,tæmɪ'neɪʃn] *n* -**1.** [pollution - of food, river, water] contamination *f*; *fig* contamination *f*, corruption *f*. -**2.** [irradiation - of land, person, soil] contamination *f*; **high levels of ~** de hauts niveaux de contamination.

contango [kən'tæŋgəʊ] (*pl* contangos, *pt* & *pp* contangoed, *cont* contangoing) ◇ *n* -**1.** [postponement of payment] report *m*. -**2.** [fee] taux *m* de report.
◇ *vt* [shares] reporter.

cont'd, contd *written abbr of* continued.

contemplate ['kɒntempleɪt] ◇ *vt* -**1.** [ponder] considérer, réfléchir sur. -**2.** [consider] considérer, envisager; **he's contemplating marriage** il envisage de OR songe à se marier; **to ~ doing sthg** envisager de OR songer à faire qqch. -**3.** [observe] contempler; **she sat contemplating the scene** elle était assise à contempler la scène.
◇ *vi* -**1.** [ponder] méditer, se recueillir. -**2.** [consider] réfléchir.

contemplation [,kɒntem'pleɪʃn] *n* -**1.** [thought] réflexion *f*; **deep in ~** en pleine réflexion; **his ~s were rudely interrupted by the doorbell** la sonnette le tira brusquement de ses réflexions. -**2.** [observation] contemplation *f*; **she returned to her ~ of the sea** elle se remit à contempler la mer. -**3.** [meditation] contemplation *f*, recueillement *m*, méditation *f*; **a period of ~** une période de recueillement.

contemplative [kən'templətɪv] ◇ *adj* [look, mood] songeur, pensif; [life] contemplatif; RELIG [order, prayer] contemplatif.
◇ *n* contemplatif *m*, -ive *f*.

contemporaneous [kən,tempə'reɪnjəs] *adj fml* contemporain; **to be ~ (with sb/sthg)** être contemporain (de qqn/qqch).

contemporaneously [kən,tempə'reɪnjəslɪ] *adv fml* [exist, live] à la même époque; **~ with** à la même époque que.

contemporary [kən'tempərərɪ] (*pl* contemporaries) ◇ *adj* -**1.** [modern - art, writer] contemporain, d'aujourd'hui; **a study of ~ Britain** une étude de la Grande-Bretagne d'aujourd'hui; **the design is very ~** la conception est très moderne. -**2.** [of the same period - account, report] contemporain; **he was ~ with Thackeray** il vivait à la même époque que OR il était contemporain de Thackeray.
◇ *n* contemporain *m*, -e *f*; **he was a ~ of mine at university** nous étions ensemble OR en même temps à l'université.

contempt [kən'tempt] *n* -**1.** [scorn] mépris *m*; **I feel nothing but ~ for him** je n'ai que du mépris pour lui; **to hold sb/sthg in ~** mépriser qqn/qqch, avoir du mépris pour qqn/qqch; **to be beneath ~** être tout ce qu'il y a de plus méprisable. -**2.** JUR outrage *m*; **to charge sb with ~ (of court)** accuser qqn d'outrage (à magistrat OR à la Cour).

contemptible [kən'temptəbl] *adj* [action, attitude, person] méprisable.

contemptuous [kən'temptʃʊəs] *adj fml* [look, manner, remark] dédaigneux, méprisant; **to be ~ of sb/sthg** dédaigner qqn/qqch, faire peu de cas de qqn/qqch.

contemptuously [kən'temptʃʊəslɪ] *adv* [laugh, reject, smile] avec mépris, avec dédain.

contend [kən'tend] ◇ *vi* -**1.** [deal]: **to ~ with sb** avoir affaire à qqn; **to ~ with sthg** être aux prises avec qqch; **this is just one of the difficulties we have to ~ with** ce n'est que l'une des difficultés auxquelles nous devons faire face; **if you do that again, you'll have me to ~ with** si tu recommences, tu auras affaire à moi. -**2.** [compete] combattre, lutter; **to ~ with sb for OR over sthg** disputer OR contester qqch à qqn.
◇ *vt fml*: **to ~ that...** soutenir que ...

contender [kən'tendəʳ] *n* [in fight] adversaire *mf*; [in race] concurrent *m*, -e *f*; [for title] prétendant *m*, -e *f*; [for political office] candidat *m*, -e *f*.

contending [kən'tendɪŋ] *adj* [parties, teams, views] opposé.

content [*n senses 1 & 2* 'kɒntent, *n sense 3, adj & vb* kən'tent] ◇ *n* -**1.** [amount contained] teneur *f*; **with a high iron ~** avec une forte teneur en fer, riche en fer. -**2.** [substance - of book, film, speech] contenu *m*; [meaning] teneur *f*, fond *m*; **his films are all style and no ~** dans ses films, il y a la forme mais pas le fond. -**3.** [satisfaction] contentement *m*, satisfaction *f*.
◇ *adj* content, satisfait; **to be ~ to do sthg** ne pas demander mieux que de faire qqch; **he seems quite ~ with his lot in life** il semble assez content de son sort.
◇ *vt*: **to ~ oneself with (doing) sthg** se contenter de OR se borner à (faire) qqch; **my reply seemed to ~ them** ils semblaient satisfaits de ma réponse.
◆ **contents** *npl* -**1.** [of bag, bottle, house etc] contenu *m*. -**2.** [of book, letter] contenu *m*; **the ~s (list), the list of ~s** la table des matières.

contented [kən'tentɪd] *adj* [person] content, satisfait; [smile] de contentement, de satisfaction; **she seems very ~ with life** elle semble très contente de son sort.

contentedly [kən'tentɪdlɪ] *adv* avec contentement.

contentedness [kən'tentɪdnɪs] *n* contentement *m*, satisfaction *f*.

contention [kən'tenʃn] *n* -**1.** *fml* [belief] affirmation *f*; **it is my ~ that...** je soutiens que ... -**2.** [disagreement] dispute *f*; **his morals are not in ~** sa moralité n'est pas ici mise en doute. -**3.** *phr*: **to be in ~ for sthg/to win sthg** être en compétition pour qqch/pour gagner qqch.

contentious [kən'tenʃəs] *adj* -**1.** [controversial - issue, subject] contesté, litigieux. -**2.** [argumentative - family, group, person] querelleur, chicanier. -**3.** JUR contentieux.

contentiousness [kən'tenʃəsnɪs] *n* -**1.** [controversial nature] nature *f* litigieuse. -**2.** [argumentativeness] humeur *f* querelleuse. -**3.** JUR contentieux *m*.

contentment [kən'tentmənt] *n* contentement *m*, satisfaction *f*; **she beamed with ~** elle rayonnait de satisfaction; **a look of ~** un regard de satisfaction.

content word ['kɒntent-] *n* LING mot *m* à contenu lexical.

conterminous [kɒn'tɜːmɪnəs] *adj fml* -**1.** [sharing the same border - country, land] limitrophe; [- estate, garden] adjacent, attenant, contigu; **to be ~ with sthg** être adjacent à qqch. -**2.** [uninterrupted] bout à bout. -**3.** [coincident - in range, scope, time] de même étendue.

contest [*n* 'kɒntest, *vb* kən'test] ◇ *n* -**1.** [competition] concours *m*; **beauty ~** concours *m* de beauté. -**2.** [struggle] combat *m*, lutte *f*; **a ~ for/between** un combat pour/entre. -**3.** SPORT rencontre *f*; [boxing] combat *m*, rencontre *f*; **a ~ with/between** un combat contre/entre.
◇ *vt* -**1.** [dispute - idea, statement] contester, discuter; **he ~ed my right to be at the meeting** il m'a contesté le droit d'assister à la réunion; **to ~ a will** contester un testament. -**2.** POL [fight for - election, seat] disputer; SPORT [- match, title] disputer; **a keenly ~ed game** une partie disputée avec acharnement.

contestant [kən'testənt] *n* concurrent *m*, -e *f*, adversaire *mf*.

contestation [,kɒntes'teɪʃn] *n* contestation *f*.

context ['kɒntekst] *n* contexte *m*; **the book places the writer in his social ~** le livre replace l'écrivain dans son contexte social; **in ~** dans son contexte; **she claimed her comments had been taken out of ~** elle a prétendu que ses commentaires avaient été retirés de leur contexte.

contextual [kɒn'tekstjʊəl] *adj* [criticism] contextuel.

contextualize, -ise [kɒn'tekstjʊəlaɪz] *vt* [events, facts] contextualiser, remettre dans son contexte.

contiguity [,kɒntɪ'gjuːətɪ] *n* contiguïté *f*.

contiguous [kən'tɪgjʊəs] *adj fml* contigu; **to be ~ to OR with sthg** être contigu à qqch.

continence ['kɒntɪnəns] *n* -**1.** MED continence *f*. -**2.** *fml* [chastity] continence *f*, chasteté *f*.

continent ['kɒntɪnənt] ◇ *n* GEOG continent *m*.
◇ *adj* -**1.** MED continent, qui n'est pas incontinent. -**2.** *fml* [chaste] continent, chaste.
◆ **Continent** *n*: **the Continent** l'Europe *f* continentale; **they're holidaying on the Continent** ils passent leurs vacances en Europe (continentale) OR outre-Manche.

continental [,kɒntɪ'nentl] ◇ *adj* -**1.** [European] d'outre-Manche, européen, d'Europe continentale. -**2.** GEOG [crust, divide] continental; **~ Latin America** l'Amérique *f* latine continentale; **~ United States** *Am désigne les 48 États des États-Unis qui forment un bloc géographique (excluant Hawaii et l'Alaska)*.
◇ *n Br* continental *m*, -e *f*, habitant *m*, -e *f* de l'Europe continentale.

continental breakfast *n* petit déjeuner *m* à la française.

CONTINENTAL BREAKFAST:
Ce terme désigne un petit déjeuner léger, par opposition au breakfast anglais, beaucoup plus copieux et comportant un plat chaud.

---

continental climate *n* climat *m* continental.

continental drift *n* dérive *f* des continents.

continental quilt *n* couette *f*, duvet *m*.

continental shelf *n* plateau *m* continental, plate-forme *f* continentale.

contingency [kən'tɪndʒənsɪ] (*pl* contingencies) ◇ *n fml* -**1.** [possibility] éventualité *f*, contingence *f*; **to provide for all contingencies** parer à toute éventualité. -**2.** [chance] événement *m* inattendu; [uncertainty] (cas *m*) imprévu *m*, éventualité *f*. -**3.** [in statistics] contingence *f*.
◇ *comp* [fund] de prévoyance; [plan] d'urgence; [table, coefficient] des imprévus.
◆ **contingencies** *npl* FIN frais *mpl* divers.

contingency fee *n* JUR *aux États-Unis, principe permettant à un avocat de recevoir une part des sommes attribuées à son client si ce dernier gagne son procès.*

contingent [kən'tɪndʒənt] ◇ *adj fml* -**1.** [dependent] contingent; to be ~ on OR upon sthg dépendre de qqch. -**2.** [accidental] accidentel, fortuit. -**3.** [uncertain] éventuel.
◇ *n* -**1.** MIL contingent *m.* -**2.** [representative group] groupe *m* représentatif.

continual [kən'tɪnjʊəl] *adj* -**1.** [continuous - pain, pleasure, struggle] continuel. -**2.** [repeated - nagging, warnings] incessant, continuel.

continually [kən'tɪnjʊəlɪ] *adv* -**1.** [continuously - change, evolve] continuellement. -**2.** [repeatedly - complain, nag, warn] sans cesse.

continuance [kən'tɪnjʊəns] *n* -**1.** [continuation] continuation *f,* persistance *f,* durée *f.* -**2.** *Am* JUR ajournement *m (d'un procès).*

continuant [kən'tɪnjʊənt] ◇ *n* LING (consonne *f*) continue *f.*
◇ *adj* continu.

continuation [kən,tɪnjʊ'eɪʃn] *n* -**1.** [sequel] continuation *f,* suite *f.* -**2.** [resumption] reprise *f.* -**3.** [prolongation] prolongement *m,* suite *f.*

continue [kən'tɪnju:] ◇ *vi* -**1.** [carry on] continuer; to ~ to do sthg OR doing sthg continuer à faire qqch; we ~d on our way nous avons poursuivi notre chemin, nous nous sommes remis en route; the path ~s on down to the river le chemin continue jusqu'à la rivière; ~ with the treatment for another week continuez le traitement encore une semaine. -**2.** [begin again] reprendre; the talks will ~ today les entretiens reprendront aujourd'hui.
◇ *vt* -**1.** [carry on - education] poursuivre, continuer; [- tradition] perpétuer, continuer; [- treatment] continuer. -**2.** [resume - conversation, performance, talks] reprendre, continuer; "furthermore", he ~d... «de plus», continua-t-il...; to be ~d à suivre; ~d on the next page suite à la page suivante.

continuity [,kɒntɪ'nju:ətɪ] (*pl* **continuities**) ◇ *n* -**1.** [cohesion] continuité *f.* -**2.** CIN & TV continuité *f.*
◇ *comp* [department, studio] pour raccords.

continuity girl *n* scripte *f.*

continuo [kən'tɪnjʊəʊ] (*pl* **continuos**) *n* continuo *m.*

continuous [kən'tɪnjʊəs] *adj* -**1.** [uninterrupted - noise, process] continu, ininterrompu; ~ assessment contrôle *m* continu; ~ performances CIN spectacle *m* permanent; ~ stationery papier *m* en continu. -**2.** [unbroken - line, surface] continu. -**3.** GRAMM [tense] continu.

continuously [kən'tɪnjʊəslɪ] *adv* continuellement, sans arrêt.

continuum [kən'tɪnjʊəm] (*pl* **continuums** OR **continua** [-njʊə]) *n* continuum *m.*

contort [kən'tɔ:t] *vt* [body, features] tordre.

contorted [kən'tɔ:tɪd] *adj* [body, features] tordu, crispé.

contortion [kən'tɔ:ʃn] *n* [of body, features] contorsion *f,* convulsion *f,* crispation *f;* mental ~s *fig* contorsions OR acrobaties *fpl* mentales.

contortionist [kən'tɔ:ʃənɪst] *n* contorsionniste *mf,* homme *m* caoutchouc; verbal ~ *fig* virtuose *mf* de la rhétorique.

contour ['kɒn,tʊə^r] ◇ *n* -**1.** [line] contour *m.* -**2.** = **contour line.** -**3.** [shape - of body, car] contour *m.*
◇ *vt* -**1.** [map] tracer les courbes de niveaux sur. -**2.** [shape - dress, car] tracer les contours de.

contour line *n* courbe *f* de niveau.

contour map *n* carte *f* topographique.

contra- ['kɒntrə] *in cpds* -**1.** [opposing] contre-, contra-. -**2.** MUS contra-.

contraband ['kɒntrəbænd] ◇ *n (U)* -**1.** [smuggling] contrebande *f.* -**2.** [smuggled goods] (marchandises *fpl* de) contrebande *f.*
◇ *adj* [activities, goods] de contrebande.

contrabassoon [,kɒntrəbə'su:n] *n* contrebasson *m.*

contraception [,kɒntrə'sepʃn] *n* contraception *f.*

contraceptive [,kɒntrə'septɪv] ◇ *n* contraceptif *m;* ~ pill pilule *f* contraceptive.
◇ *adj* [device, method] contraceptif.

contract [*n* 'kɒntrækt, *vb* kən'trækt] ◇ *n* -**1.** [agreement] contrat *m,* convention *f;* [document] contrat *m;* to be under ~ être sous contrat, avoir un contrat; to put work out to ~ sous-traiter du travail; to put out a ~ on sb *inf* mettre la tête de qqn à prix ❑ marriage ~ contrat de mariage; ~ of employment contrat de travail. -**2.** = **contract bridge.**
◇ *comp* [work] à forfait, contractuel; the police suspect it was a ~ killing la police soupçonne que c'est le travail d'un tueur à gages.
◇ *vt* -**1.** *fml* [agree]: to ~ (with sb) to do sthg s'engager par contrat à faire qqch. -**2.** *fml* [agree to - alliance, marriage] contracter. -**3.** [acquire - disease, illness, debt] contracter. -**4.** [make shorter - vowel, word] contracter. -**5.** [make tense - muscle] contracter.
◇ *vi* se contracter.
◆ **contract in** *vi insep Br* s'engager (par contrat préalable).
◆ **contract out** ◇ *vt sep* [work] sous-traiter.
◇ *vi insep Br*: to ~ out of sthg cesser de cotiser à qqch.

contract bridge *n* bridge *m* contrat.

contractile [kən'træktaɪl] *adj* contractile, de contraction.

contraction [kən'trækʃn] *n* -**1.** [shrinkage - of metal] contraction *f.* -**2.** [short form of word] contraction *f;* "haven't" is a ~ of "have not" «haven't» est une forme contractée de «have not». -**3.** [of muscle - esp in childbirth] contraction *f.*

contractor [kən'træktə^r] *n* [worker] entrepreneur *m.*

contractual [kən'træktʃʊəl] *adj* [agreement, obligation] contractuel.

contractually [kən'træktʃʊəlɪ] *adv* [binding] par contrat.

contradict [,kɒntrə'dɪkt] *vt* -**1.** [challenge - person, statement] contredire; she hates being ~ed elle déteste qu'on la contredise; don't ~ me! ne me contredisez pas! -**2.** [conflict with - subj: facts, stories] contredire.

contradiction [,kɒntrə'dɪkʃn] *n* -**1.** [inconsistency] contradiction *f;* his words are in complete ~ with his actions ses paroles sont en complet désaccord avec ses actes. -**2.** [conflicting statement] démenti *m,* contradiction *f;* a ~ in terms une contradiction dans les termes.

contradictory [,kɒntrə'dɪktərɪ] *adj* [statements, stories] contradictoire, opposé; [person] qui a l'esprit de contradiction.

contradistinction [,kɒntrədɪ'stɪŋkʃn] *n fml* opposition *f,* contraste *m;* in ~ to par opposition à, par contraste avec.

contraflow ['kɒntrəfləʊ] *Br* ◇ *n* circulation *f* à contre-courant.
◇ *comp* [system] de circulation *f* à contre-courant.

contraindication ['kɒntrə,ɪndɪ'keɪʃn] *n* contre-indication *f.*

contralto [kən'træltəʊ] (*pl* **contraltos**) ◇ *n* [voice] contralto *m;* [singer] contralto *mf.*
◇ *adj* [part, voice] de contralto.

contraposition [,kɒntrəpə'zɪʃn] *n* opposition *f,* antithèse *f.*

contraption [kən'træpʃn] *n* dispositif *m,* engin *m,* truc *m.*

contrapuntal [,kɒntrə'pʌntl] *adj* en contrepoint, contrapuntique.

contrarily [*Br sense 1* kən'treərɪlɪ, *sense 2* 'kɒntrərɪlɪ, *Am* kɒn'trerəlɪ] *adv* -**1.** [obstinately] par esprit de contradiction. -**2.** [on the other hand] contrairement.

contrariness [kən'treərɪnɪs] *n* [obstinacy] esprit *m* de contradiction.

contrariwise ['kɒntrərɪ,waɪz] *adv* -**1.** [on the other hand] d'autre part, en revanche. -**2.** [in the opposite direction] en sens opposé.

contrary ['kɒntrərɪ, *adj sense 2* kən'treərɪ] ◇ *adj* -**1.** [opposed - attitudes, ideas, opinions] contraire, en opposition; ~ to nature contre nature. -**2.** [obstinate - attitude, person] contrariant.
◇ *prep*: ~ to popular belief contrairement à ce que l'on croit généralement; ~ to what I had been told contrairement à ce qu'on m'avait dit.
◆ **on the contrary** *adv phr* au contraire.
◆ **to the contrary** *adv phr*: the meeting will be at six, unless you hear to the ~ la réunion sera à six heures, sauf contrordre OR avis contraire.

contrast [*vb* kən'trɑ:st, *n* 'kɒntrɑ:st] ◇ *vt* contraster, mettre en contraste; to ~ sb/sthg with, to ~ sb/sthg to mettre en contraste qqn/qqch avec.
◇ *vi* contraster, trancher; to ~ with sthg contraster avec qqch.
◇ *n* -**1.** [difference] contraste *m;* [person, thing] contraste *m;* there is a marked ~ between his public and his private life il y a un contraste frappant entre sa vie d'homme public et sa vie privée; life in Africa was a complete ~ to life in Europe la vie en Afrique présentait un contraste total avec la vie en Europe; her response was in stark ~ to the government's sa réponse était en contraste absolu avec celle du gouvernement. -**2.** ART & TV contraste *m.*
◆ **by contrast, in contrast** *adv phr* par contraste.
◆ **in contrast with, in contrast to** *prep phr* par opposition à, par contraste avec.

contrasting [kən'trɑ:stɪŋ], **contrastive** [kən'trɑ:stɪv] *adj* [attitudes, lifestyles, responses] qui fait contraste; [colours] opposé, contrasté.

contravene [,kɒntrə'vi:n] *vt* -**1.** [infringe - law, rule] transgresser, enfreindre, violer. -**2.** [dispute - statement] nier, opposer un démenti à.

contravention [,kɒntrə'venʃn] *n* infraction *f,* violation *f;* in ~ of the law en infraction par rapport à la loi.

contribute [kən'trɪbju:t] ◇ *vt* [give - money] donner; [- article, poem] écrire; [- ideas] apporter; the government will ~ a further two million pounds le gouvernement ajoutera deux millions de livres à sa contribution; they ~d their ideas and enthusiasm to the project ils ont apporté leurs idées et leur enthousiasme au projet.
◇ *vi* -**1.** [donate money] contribuer; we ask everyone to ~ generously nous demandons à chacun de contribuer généreusement. -**2.** [give] donner; she still has a lot to ~ to her family elle a encore beaucoup à apporter à sa famille. -**3.** [influence]: to ~ to sthg contribuer à qqch. -**4.** [journalist, author]: to ~ to écrire pour; she ~s to various literary magazines elle écrit pour divers magazines littéraires.

contribution [,kɒntrɪ'bju:ʃn] *n* -**1.** [of money, goods] contribution *f,* cotisation *f;* [of ideas, enthusiasm] apport *m;* he made a valuable ~ to the project il a apporté une collaboration précieuse au projet; we encourage the ~ of regular sums of money to charity nous encourageons les versements d'argent réguliers à des œuvres de charité ❑ national insurance ~s *Br* ≃ cotisations *fpl* à la Sécurité sociale. -**2.** [of article] article *m (écrit pour un journal).*

contributor [kən'trɪbjʊtə^r] *n* -**1.** [of money, goods] donateur *m,* -trice *f.* -**2.** [to magazine] collaborateur *m,* -trice *f.* -**3.** [factor] facteur *m.*

contributory [kən'trɪbjʊtərɪ] (*pl* **contributories**) ◇ *adj* [contributing - cause, factor, reason] contribuant, qui contribue; ~ pension scheme régime *m* de retraite *(avec participation de l'assuré).*
◇ *n* FIN *actionnaire qui doit contribuer au paiement des dettes.*

contributory negligence *n* imprudence *f,* faute *f (avant un accident).*

contrite ['kɒntraɪt] *adj* [face, look] contrit, repentant; to look/to be ~ avoir un air/être contrit.

contrition [kən'trɪʃn] *n* contrition *f,* pénitence *f.*

contrivance [kən'traɪvəns] *n* -**1.** [contraption] dispositif *m,* mécanisme *m.* -**2.** [stratagem] invention *f,* manigance *f.*

contrive [kən'traɪv] ◇ *vt* -**1.** [engineer - meeting] combiner. -**2.** [invent - device, machine] inventer, imaginer.
◇ *vi*: to ~ to do sthg trouver le moyen de faire qqch; she ~d to confuse matters still further elle a réussi à embrouiller encore plus les choses.

contrived [kən'traɪvd] *adj* -**1.** [deliberate - incident, meeting] délibéré, arrangé. -**2.** [artificial - plot, ending] forcé, peu naturel.

control [kən'trəʊl] ◇ *n* -**1.** [of country, organization] direction *f*; [of car, machine] contrôle *m*; [of one's life] maîtrise *f*; [of oneself] maîtrise *f* (de soi); SPORT [of ball] contrôle *m*; to have ~ of OR over sb avoir de l'autorité sur qqn; to have ~ of OR over sthg avoir le contrôle de qqch; the rebels have gained ~ of the capital les rebelles ont pris le contrôle de la capitale; to be in ~ of sthg être maître de qqch; to lose ~ of sthg [of car] perdre le contrôle de qqch; [of situation] ne plus être maître de qqch; under ~: the situation is under ~ nous maîtrisons la situation; everything's under ~ tout va bien, aucun problème, tout est au point; to keep sthg under ~ maîtriser qqch; dogs must be kept under ~ les chiens doivent être tenus en laisse; the fire was finally brought under ~ l'incendie fut finalement maîtrisé; public spending is under the ~ of our department le budget national relève de notre département; the country is no longer under British/government ~ le pays n'est plus sous contrôle britannique/gouvernemental; beyond OR outside one's ~ indépendant de sa volonté; out of ~: the fire was out of ~ on n'arrivait pas à maîtriser l'incendie; the crowd got out of ~ la foule s'est déchaînée; her children are completely out of ~ ses enfants sont intenables ❑ traffic ~ régulation *f* de la circulation; pest ~ lutte *f* contre les animaux/insectes nuisibles. -**2.** [check] contrôle *m*; quality ~ contrôle de qualité. -**3.** [device]: volume ~ réglage *m* du volume; ~s [on car, arcraft, machine] commandes *fpl*; the pilot was at the ~s/took over the ~s le pilote était aux commandes/a pris les commandes. -**4.** [in experiment] témoin *m*. -**5.** [checkpoint - at border] douane *f*; [- in car rally] contrôle *m*; passport and custom ~s formalités *fpl* de douane. -**6.** [restraint] contrôle *m*; price/wage ~s contrôle des prix/des salaires; immigration ~s contrôle de l'immigration.
◇ *comp* [button, knob, switch] de commande, de réglage.
◇ *vt* -**1.** [run - country, government, organization] diriger. -**2.** [regulate - machine, system] régler; [- animal] tenir, se faire obéir de; [- crowd, immigration, traffic] contrôler; this switch ~s the central heating ce commutateur règle OR commande le chauffage central. -**3.** [curb - inflation, prices, spending, fire] maîtriser; [- disease, epidemic] enrayer, juguler; [- activities, emotions, face, voice] maîtriser; try to ~ yourself essaie de te contrôler OR maîtriser; she could barely ~ her anger elle avait du mal à maîtriser sa colère. -**4.** [verify - accounts] contrôler; [- experiment] vérifier.

control account *n* compte *m* collectif.

control column *n* manche *m* à balai.

control commands *npl* commandes *fpl*.

control desk *n* bureau *m* de contrôle.

control experiment *n* cas *m* témoin.

control group *n* groupe *m* témoin.

control key *n* touche *f* «control».

controllable [kən'trəʊləbl] *adj* [animal, person, crowd] discipliné; [emotions, situation] maîtrisable; [expenditure, inflation] contrôlable.

controlled [kən'trəʊld] *adj* -**1.** [emotions, voice] contenu; she remained very ~ elle est restée très calme. -**2.** ECON: ~ economy économie *f* dirigée OR planifiée. -**3.** [directed]: ~ explosion neutralisation *f (d'un explosif)*; the bomb was let off in a ~ explosion la bombe a été neutralisée.

controller [kən'trəʊlə^r] *n* -**1.** [person in charge] responsable *m*; the new Controller of BBC1 le nouveau responsable de BBC1. -**2.** [accountant] contrôleur *m*; financial ~ contrôleur financier.

controlling [kən'trəʊlɪŋ] *adj* [factor] déterminant.

controlling interest *n* participation *f* majoritaire; they now have a ~ in the company à présent, ils ont une participation majoritaire dans cette société.

control panel *n* tableau *m* de bord.

control rod *n* NUCL barre *f* de contrôle.

control room *n* salle *f* des commandes, centre *m* de contrôle.

control tower *n* tour *f* de contrôle.

controversial [ˌkɒntrə'vɜːʃl] *adj* [book, film, issue, subject] controversé; [decision, speech] sujet à controverse; [person] controversé.

controversy ['kɒntrəvɜːsɪ, *Br* kən'trɒvəsɪ] *n* controverse *f*, polémique *f*; her speech caused a lot of ~ son discours a provoqué beaucoup de controverses; a major ~ is brewing over unemployment un grand scandale se prépare autour du chômage.

controvert ['kɒntrəvɜːt] *vt arch* controverser.

contumacious [ˌkɒntjuː'meɪʃəs] *adj lit* insubordonné.

contumacy ['kɒntjʊməsɪ] *n* -**1.** *lit* [disobedience] insubordination *f*. -**2.** JUR contumace *f*.

contumelious [ˌkɒntjuː'miːljəs] *adj lit* insolant, méprisant.

contumely ['kɒntjuːmlɪ] *n lit* [language] insolence *f*; [insult] offense *f*.

contusion [kən'tjuːʒn] *n fml* contusion *f*.

conundrum [kə'nʌndrəm] *n* -**1.** [riddle] devinette *f*, énigme *f*. -**2.** [problem] énigme *f*.

conurbation [ˌkɒnɜː'beɪʃn] *n* conurbation *f*.

convalesce [ˌkɒnvə'les] *vi* se remettre *(d'une maladie)*; she's convalescing (from a bad bout of flu) elle se remet (d'une mauvaise grippe).

convalescence [ˌkɒnvə'lesns] *n* [return to health] rétablissement *m*; [period of recovery] convalescence *f*.

convalescent [ˌkɒnvə'lesnt] ◇ *n* convalescent *m*, -e *f*.
◇ *adj*: ~ home maison *f* de convalescence OR de repos.

convection [kən'vekʃn] ◇ *n* GEOL, METEOR & PHYS convection *f*.
◇ *comp* [heater, heating] à convection; [current] de convection.

convector (heater) [kən'vektə^r-] *n* radiateur *m* à convection, convecteur *m*.

convene [kən'viːn] ◇ *vt* [conference, meeting] convoquer.
◇ *vi* [board, jury, members] se réunir.

convener [kən'viːnə^r] *n* -**1.** *Br* [trade union official] *secrétaire des délégués syndicaux*. -**2.** [of meeting] président *m*, -e *f*.

convenience [kən'viːnjəns] *n* -**1.** [ease of use] commodité *f*; [benefit] avantage *m*; I use a bicycle for ~ OR for ~'s sake j'utilise une bicyclette par commodité; our customers can now enjoy the ~ of on-site parking nous offrons désormais à notre clientèle la commodité d'un parking à proximité; please reply at your earliest ~ *fml* veuillez répondre dans les meilleurs délais; fill in the form at your ~ remplissez le formulaire quand cela vous conviendra. -**2.** [facility] commodités *fpl*, confort *m*; the house has every modern ~ la maison a tout le confort moderne. -**3.** *Br fml* & *euph* [lavatory] toilettes *fpl*; public ~s toilettes publiques.

convenience food *n* aliment *m* prêt à consommer, plat *m* cuisiné.

convenience store *n Am supérette de quartier qui reste ouverte tard le soir*.

convenient [kən'viːnjənt] *adj* -**1.** [suitable - day, time] commode; when would be ~ for you? quand cela vous arrangerait-il?; this isn't a very ~ moment to talk le moment n'est pas bien choisi pour parler. -**2.** [handy - service, tool] pratique; the house is very ~ for local shops and schools la maison est très bien située pour les magasins et les écoles; the bus stop's just round the corner – how ~! l'arrêt de bus se trouve juste au coin de la rue – c'est bien pratique! -**3.** [nearby]: I grabbed a ~ chair and sat down j'ai saisi la chaise la plus proche et me suis assis.

conveniently [kən'viːnjəntlɪ] *adv* commodément; the cottage is ~ situated for the beach le cottage est bien situé pour la plage; they very ~ forgot to enclose the cheque comme par hasard, ils ont oublié de joindre le chèque.

convening [kən'viːnɪŋ] ◇ *adj* [authority, country] habilité à convoquer, hôte.
◇ *n* convocation *f*.

convenor [kən'viːnə^r] = **convener**.

convent ['kɒnvənt] ◇ *n* -**1.** RELIG couvent *m*; to enter a ~ entrer au couvent. -**2.** [convent school] institution *f* religieuse.
◇ *comp* [education, school] religieux; she was ~-educated elle a fait ses études dans une institution religieuse.

convention [kən'venʃn] *n* -**1.** *(U)* [custom] usage *m*; to defy ~ braver les usages; according to ~ selon l'usage. -**2.** [agreement] convention *f*; to sign a ~ on sthg signer une convention sur qqch ❑ the Geneva Convention la Convention de Genève. -**3.** [meeting] convention *f*. -**4.** [accepted usage] convenances *f pl*; it's a common ~ in the nineteenth-century novel c'est une convention courante dans les romans du dix-neuvième siècle.

conventional [kən'venʃənl] *adj* -**1.** [orthodox - behaviour, ideas] conventionnel; [- person] conformiste; ~ wisdom sagesse *f* populaire; ~ wisdom has it that... d'aucuns disent que... -**2.** [traditional - medicine, methods, technique, art] classique, traditionnel. -**3.** [non-nuclear] conventionnel; ~ weapons armes *fpl* conventionnelles.

conventionally [kən'venʃnəlɪ] *adv* de façon conventionnelle.

convention centre *n* palais *m* des congrès.

converge [kən'vɜːdʒ] *vi* -**1.** [merge - paths, lines] converger; [- groups, ideas, tendencies] converger. -**2.** [gather - crowds, groups, people] se rassembler; thousands of fans ~d on the stadium des milliers de fans se sont rassemblés sur le stade. -**3.** MATH converger.

convergence [kən'vɜːdʒəns] *n* -**1.** [of paths, ideas] convergence *f*. -**2.** MATH convergence *f*.

convergent [kən'vɜːdʒənt] *adj* -**1.** [paths, tendencies] convergent. -**2.** MATH convergent.

convergent thinking *n* raisonnement *m* convergent.

converging [kən'vɜːdʒɪŋ] = **convergent**.

conversant [kən'vɜːsənt] *adj fml* qui est au courant, qui connaît; we were expected to be fully ~ with colloquial French/running an office nous étions censés avoir une connaissance parfaite du français familier/de l'administration d'un bureau.

conversation [ˌkɒnvə'seɪʃn] *n* conversation *f*; the art of ~ l'art de la conversation; we had a long ~ about fishing nous avons eu une longue conversation sur la pêche; she was deep in ~ with my sister elle était en grande conversation avec ma sœur; a telephone ~ une conversation téléphonique; to get into ~ with sb engager la conversation avec qqn; to make ~ faire la conversation; to run out of ~ n'avoir plus rien à dire ❑ that's a ~ stopper! ça jette toujours un froid dans la conversation!

conversational [ˌkɒnvə'seɪʃənl] *adj* [tone, voice] de la conversation; ~ Spanish espagnol courant.

conversationalist [ˌkɒnvə'seɪʃnəlɪst] *n* causeur *m*, -euse *f*; he's a brilliant ~ il brille dans la conversation.

conversationally [ˌkɒnvə'seɪʃnəlɪ] *adv* [mention, say] sur le ton de la conversation.

conversation piece *n* -**1.** [unusual object] curiosité *f*. -**2.** [play] *pièce au dialogue brillant*.

converse [*vb* kən'vɜːs, *n* & *adj* 'kɒnvɜːs] ◇ *vi fml* converser, s'entretenir; to ~ with sb s'entretenir avec qqn.
◇ *adj* [opinion, statement] contraire.
◇ *n* -**1.** [gen] contraire *m*, inverse *m*; I believe the ~ to be true je crois que l'inverse est vrai. -**2.** MATH & PHILOS inverse *m*. -**3.** *fml* OR *lit* conversation *f*, entretien *m*; to hold ~ with sb s'entretenir avec qqn.
conversely [kən'vɜːslɪ] *adv* inversement, réciproquement; ~, you can use the paint directly on the wood inversement, vous pouvez utiliser la peinture directement sur le bois.
conversion [kən'vɜːʃn] *n* -**1.** [process] conversion *f*, transformation *f*; the ~ of water into wine la transformation de l'eau en vin. -**2.** MATH conversion *f*. -**3.** [change of beliefs] conversion *f*. -**4.** RUGBY transformation *f*. -**5.** [converted building] *appartement aménagé dans un ancien hôtel particulier, entrepôt, atelier etc.* -**6.** JUR conversion *f*.
conversion table *n* table *f* de conversion.
convert [*vb* kən'vɜːt, *n* 'kɒnvɜːt] ◇ *vt* -**1.** [building, car, ship] aménager, convertir; [machine, system] transformer; to ~ sthg to OR into sthg transformer OR convertir qqch en qqch; the school was ~ed to house several workshops l'école a été aménagée de façon à avoir plusieurs ateliers. -**2.** MATH convertir; how do you ~ pints into litres? comment convertir des pintes en litres?; to ~ pesetas into pounds [as calculation] convertir des pesetas en livres; [by exchanging money] changer des pesetas en livres. -**3.** RELIG convertir; to ~ sb to sthg convertir qqn à qqch. -**4.** RUGBY transformer; to ~ a try transformer un essai. -**5.** JUR convertir. -**6.** FIN [bond, security] convertir.
◇ *vi* -**1.** [vehicle, machine] se convertir. -**2.** [in rugby] se transformer.
◇ *n* converti *m*, -e *f*; she's a ~ to Catholicism c'est une catholique convertie.
converted [kən'vɜːtɪd] *adj* [factory, farmhouse, school] aménagé, transformé.
converter [kən'vɜːtə^r] *n* -**1.** METALL & PHYS convertisseur *m*; RADIO modulateur *m* de fréquence; COMPUT convertisseur *m*. -**2.** = **converter reactor**.
converter reactor *n* réacteur *m* convertisseur.
convertibility [kən,vɜːtə'bɪlətɪ] *n* [of currency] convertibilité *f*; [of building, car, machine] convertibilité *f*.
convertible [kən'vɜːtəbl] ◇ *adj* [currency] convertible; [car, machine, couch] convertible.
◇ *n* AUT décapotable *f*.
convertor [kən'vɜːtə^r] = **converter**.
convex [kɒn'veks] *adj* [lens, surface] convexe.
convexity [kɒn'veksətɪ] (*pl* **convexities**) *n* convexité *f*.
convey [kən'veɪ] *vt* -**1.** *fml* [transport - cargo, people] transporter. -**2.** [communicate - information, meaning, message] transmettre; I tried to ~ to him the importance of the decision j'ai essayé de lui faire comprendre l'importance de la décision; no words can ~ my gratitude aucun mot ne peut traduire ma gratitude; please ~ my thanks (to them) veuillez leur transmettre mes remerciements. -**3.** JUR transférer.
conveyance [kən'veɪəns] *n* -**1.** [transport] transport *m*. -**2.** *dated* [vehicle] véhicule *m*. -**3.** JUR [transfer of property] cession *f*, transfert *m*; [document] acte *m* de cession.
conveyancing [kən'veɪənsɪŋ] *n Br* procédure *f* translative (de propriété).
conveyor [kən'veɪə^r] *n* -**1.** [transporter] transporteur *m*. -**2.** = **conveyor belt**.
conveyor belt *n* tapis *m* roulant.
convict [*vb* kən'vɪkt, *n* 'kɒnvɪkt] ◇ *vt* déclarer OR reconnaître coupable; she was ~ed elle a été déclarée OR reconnue coupable; to ~ sb of OR for sthg déclarer OR reconnaître qqn coupable de qqch.
◇ *n* détenu *m*, -e *f*.
◇ *vi* rendre un verdict de culpabilité; the jury is unlikely to ~ il est peu probable que le jury rende un verdict de culpabilité.
convicted [kən'vɪktɪd] *adj* [criminal, murderer] reconnu coupable.
conviction [kən'vɪkʃn] *n* -**1.** [belief] conviction *f*. -**2.** [certainty] certitude *f*, conviction *f*; he lacks ~ il manque de conviction; I suppose so, I said without much ~ je suppose, dis-je sans grande conviction. -**3.** [plausibility]: the theory carries little ~ la théorie est peu convaincante. -**4.** JUR condamnation *f*; the prosecution called for his ~ la partie plaignante a demandé sa condamnation; she has several previous ~s elle a déjà été condamnée plusieurs fois.
convince [kən'vɪns] *vt* convaincre, persuader; his arguments don't ~ me ses arguments ne me convainquent pas; to ~ sb of sthg convaincre OR persuader qqn de qqch; to ~ sb to do sthg convaincre OR persuader qqn de faire qqch.
convinced [kən'vɪnst] *adj* convaincu; to be ~ of sthg être convaincu de qqch.
convincing [kən'vɪnsɪŋ] *adj* [argument, person] convaincant; [victory, win] décisif, éclatant.
convincingly [kən'vɪnsɪŋlɪ] *adv* [argue, speak, pretend] de façon convaincante; [beat, win] de façon éclatante.
convivial [kən'vɪvɪəl] *adj* [atmosphere, gathering, lunch] convivial, joyeux; [behaviour, manner, person] joyeux, plein d'entrain.
conviviality [kən,vɪvɪ'ælətɪ] *n* convivialité *f*, gaieté *f*, jovialité *f*.
convocation [,kɒnvə'keɪʃn] *n* -**1.** [summoning] convocation *f*. -**2.** [meeting] assemblée *f*, réunion *f*; RELIG synode *m*.
convoke [kən'vəʊk] *vt* [assembly, meeting] convoquer.
convoluted ['kɒnvəluːtɪd] *adj* [shape] convoluté; [prose, reasoning, sentence] alambiqué.
convolution [,kɒnvə'luːʃn] *n fml* circonvolution *f*.
convolvulus [kən'vɒlvjʊləs] (*pl* **convolvuluses** OR **convolvuli** [-laɪ]) *n* liseron *m*.
convoy ['kɒnvɔɪ] ◇ *n* [escort of ships] convoi *m*; [ships, vehicles under escort] convoi *m*; to travel in ~ voyager en convoi.
◇ *vt* convoyer, escorter.
convulsant [kən'vʌlsənt] ◇ *adj* [drug] convulsivant.
◇ *n* convulsivant *m*.
convulse [kən'vʌls] *vi* [face, lungs, muscle] se convulser, se contracter, se crisper.
convulsed [kən'vʌlst] *adj*: he was ~ with pain il se tordait de douleur; the audience were ~ with laughter l'auditoire se tordait de rire.
convulsion [kən'vʌlʃn] *n* -**1.** MED convulsion *f*; to have ~s avoir des convulsions. -**2.** [revolution, war] bouleversement *m*; [earthquake] secousse *f*.
convulsive [kən'vʌlsɪv] *adj* [laughter, movement] convulsif.
cony ['kəʊnɪ] (*pl* **conies**) ◇ *n* [rabbit] lapin *m*; [rabbit fur] lapin *m*.
◇ *comp*: ~ skin peau *f* de lapin.
coo [kuː] (*pl* coos) ◇ *n* roucoulement *m*.
◇ *vi* [pigeon] roucouler; [baby, person] babiller, gazouiller.
◇ *vt* [endearments, sweet nothings] roucouler.
◇ *interj inf*: ~! ça alors!
cooee *inf*, **cooey** *inf* ['kuːɪ] *interj*: ~! coucou!
cooing ['kuːɪŋ] *n* [of pigeon] roucoulement *m*; [of baby, person] gazouillement *m*.
cook [kʊk] ◇ *n* cuisinier *m*, -ère *f*; she's an excellent ~ c'est une excellente cuisinière ❑ chief ~ and bottlewasher *inf* bonne *f* à tout faire; too many ~s spoil the broth *prov* trop de cuisinières gâtent la sauce.
◇ *vt* -**1.** [food, meal] cuisiner, cuire; to ~ sb's goose *inf* mettre qqn dans le pétrin. -**2.** *inf Br* [fiddle - accounts] truquer; to ~ the books truquer les comptes.
◇ *vi* [person] cuisiner; [food] cuire; he ~s well il cuisine bien; it ~s in five minutes ça cuit en cinq minutes ❑ what's ~ing? *inf* qu'est-ce qui se mijote?
◆ **cook out** *inf vi insep Am* faire un barbecue.
◆ **cook up** *inf vt sep* [plan, deal] mijoter; [excuse, story] inventer.
cookbook ['kʊk,bʊk] *n* livre *m* de cuisine.
cooked [kʊkt] *adj* [food, meat] cuit; ~ breakfast *Br* petit déjeuner *m* anglais.
cooker ['kʊkə^r] *n Br* -**1.** [stove] cuisinière *f*. -**2.** *inf* [apple] pomme *f* à cuire.
cookery ['kʊkərɪ] *n* cuisine *f*.
cookery book *n Br* livre *m* de cuisine.
cookhouse ['kʊkhaʊs, *pl* -haʊzɪz] *n* cuisine *f*.
cookie ['kʊkɪ] *n* -**1.** *Am* biscuit *m*. -**2.** *phr*: that's the way the ~ crumbles! c'est la vie!
cooking ['kʊkɪŋ] ◇ *n* [activity] cuisine *f*; [food] cuisine *f*; French/home ~ cuisine française/maison; ~ time temps *m* de cuisson.
◇ *comp* [oil, sherry] de cuisine; [apple] à cuire.
cookout ['kʊkaʊt] *n Am* barbecue *m*.
Cook Strait [kʊk-] *pr n* le détroit de Cook.
cooky ['kʊkɪ] (*pl* cookies) = **cookie**.
cool [kuːl] ◇ *adj* -**1.** [in temperature - breeze, room, weather] frais; [- drink, water] rafraîchissant, frais; [- clothes, material] léger; keep in a ~ place conservez dans un endroit frais. -**2.** [of colour - blue, green] clair. -**3.** [calm - person, manner, voice] calme; keep ~! du calme!; play it ~! *inf* ne nous énervons pas!, pas de panique!; a ~ customer *inf* une personne effrontée OR qui a du culot; to be ~ and collected être d'un calme olympien ❑ to be OR to look as ~ as a cucumber garder son sang-froid OR calme. -**4.** [unfriendly - person, greeting, welcome] froid. -**5.** *inf* [of sum of money] coquet, rondelet; she earned a ~ half million elle a gagné un petit demi-million. -**6.** *inf* [great] génial, super; that's ~! c'est génial!; I'll be there at eight — ~! je serai là à huit heures — super!
◇ *n* -**1.** [coolness] fraîcheur *f*; the ~ of evening la fraîcheur du soir. -**2.** [calm] calme *m*, sang-froid *m*; to keep/to lose one's ~ *inf* garder/perdre son calme.
◇ *vt* [air, liquid, room] rafraîchir, refroidir; [brow, feet] rafraîchir; to ~ one's heels faire le pied de grue; they left him to ~ his heels in jail ils l'ont laissé mijoter en prison; ~ it! du calme!
◇ *vi* [food, liquid] (se) refroidir; [enthusiasm, passion, temper] s'apaiser, se calmer.
◆ **cool down** ◇ *vi insep* -**1.** [engine, machine] se refroidir; *fig* [situation] se détendre. -**2.** [person] se calmer; give him time to ~ down donne-lui le temps de se calmer.
◇ *vt sep* [person] calmer; [situation] calmer, détendre.
◆ **cool off** *vi insep* [person - become calmer] se calmer.
coolant ['kuːlənt] *n* (fluide *m*) caloporteur *m*.
coolbox ['kuːlbɒks] *n* glacière *f*.
cooler ['kuːlə^r] *n* -**1.** [for food] glacière *f*. -**2.** *inf* [prison] taule *f*; in the ~ en taule. -**3.** [drink] rafraîchissement *m*.
cool-headed *adj* calme, imperturbable.
coolie ['kuːlɪ] *n* coolie *m*.
cooling ['kuːlɪŋ] *n* [in temperature] rafraîchissement *m*, refroidissement *m*; [in relationships] refroidissement *m*.
cooling-off period *n* -**1.** [in dispute] moment *m* de répit. -**2.** [after purchase] délai *m* de réflexion.
cooling system *n* système *m* de refroidissement.
cooling tower *n* refroidisseur *m*.
coolly ['kuːlɪ] *adv* -**1.** [calmly - react, respond] calmement. -**2.** [without enthusiasm - greet, welcome] froidement. -**3.** [impertinently - behave, say] avec impertinence.
coolness ['kuːlnɪs] *n* -**1.** [in temperature - of air, water, weather] fraîcheur *f*; [- of clothes] légèreté *f*. -**2.** [calmness] calme *m*, sang-froid *m*. -**3.** [lack of enthusiasm] flegme *m*. -**4.** [impertinence] culot *m*, toupet *m*.
cooly (*pl* coolies) ['kuːlɪ] = **coolie**.
coomb(e) [kuːm] *n* combe *f*.
coon [kuːn] *n* -**1.** *inf* = **raccoon**. -**2.** ▼ *terme raciste désignant un Noir*, ≃ nègre *m*, ≃ négresse *f*.

coonskin ['ku:nskɪn] *n* -**1.** [skin] peau *f* de raton laveur. -**2.** [hat] chapeau *m* en peau de raton laveur. -**3.** [coat] manteau *m* en peau de raton laveur.

coop [ku:p] *n* poulailler *m*.
◆ **coop up** *vt sep* [animal, person, prisoner] enfermer; I've been ~ed up at home all day j'ai été cloîtré chez moi toute la journée.

co-op [-,ɒp] (*abbr of* co-operative society) *n* coopérative *f*, coop *f*.
◆ **Co-op** *pr n Br*: the Co-op la Coop.

cooper ['ku:pəʳ] *n* tonnelier *m*.

cooperage ['ku:pərɪdʒ] *n* tonnellerie *f*.

cooperate [kəʊ'ɒpəreɪt] *vi* -**1.** [work together] collaborer, coopérer; to ~ with sb collaborer avec qqn. -**2.** [be willing to help] se montrer coopératif.

cooperation [kəʊ,ɒpə'reɪʃn] *n* -**1.** [collaboration] coopération *f*, concours *m*; to do sthg in ~ with OR with the ~ of sb faire qqch avec la coopération OR le concours de qqn. -**2.** [willingness to help] coopération *f*.

cooperative [kəʊ'ɒpərətɪv] ◇ *adj* -**1.** [joint - activity, enterprise, work] coopératif. -**2.** [helpful - attitude, person] coopératif; he has been most ~ il a été très coopératif.
◇ *n* coopérative *f*.

co-opt *vt* coopter, admettre; I was ~ed as a member of the committee on m'a coopté OR admis comme membre du comité; to be ~ed into OR onto sthg être coopté à qqch.

cooption [kəʊ'ɒpʃn] *n* cooptation *f*.

coordinate [*n, adj* kəʊ'ɔ:dɪnət, *vt* kəʊ'ɔ:dɪneɪt]
◇ *vt* [activity, campaign, project] coordonner; [movements] coordonner; I'm not very ~d je ne suis pas très coordonné.
◇ *n* MATH coordonnée *f*.
◇ *adj* GRAMM & MATH coordonné; ~ clause proposition *f* coordonnée; ~ geometry géométrie *f* analytique.
◆ **coordinates** *npl* coordonnés *mpl*.

coordinating [kəʊ'ɔ:dɪneɪtɪŋ] *adj* [body, officer] de coordination; ~ conjunction conjonction *f* de coordination.

coordination [kəʊ,ɔ:dɪ'neɪʃn] *n* coordination *f*; we need greater ~ between doctors and nurses il nous faut une plus grande coordination entre médecins et infirmières; she lacks ~ elle manque de coordination.

coordinator [kəʊ'ɔ:dɪneɪtəʳ] *n* coordinateur *m*, coordonnateur *m*.

coot [ku:t] *n* -**1.** [bird] foulque *f*. -**2.** *inf dated* [fool] bêta; silly old ~! gros bêta!

co-owner *n* co-propriétaire *mf*.

cop *inf* [kɒp] (*pt* & *pp* copped, *cont* copping)
◇ *n* -**1.** [policeman] flic *m*; to play ~s and robbers jouer aux gendarmes et aux voleurs. -**2.** *Br* [arrest] arrestation *f*; it's a fair ~! je suis fait! -**3.** *Br phr*: it's not much ~ ça ne vaut pas grand-chose, c'est pas terrible.
◇ *vt* attraper, empoigner; ~ hold of that rope! attrape cette corde!; you'll ~ it if he finds out! qu'est-ce que tu vas prendre s'il s'en rend compte!
◆ **cop out** *inf vi insep* se défiler, se dérober; to ~ out of sthg échapper à qqch.

copal ['kəʊpl] *n* copal *m*.

copartner [,kəʊ'pɑ:tnəʳ] *n* coassocié *m*, -e *f*.

copartnership [,kəʊ'pɑ:tnəʃɪp] *n* coassociation *f*.

cope [kəʊp] ◇ *vi* [person] se débrouiller, s'en sortir; [business, machine, system] supporter; I can't ~ anymore je n'en peux plus; she's coping very well on her own elle s'en sort très bien toute seule; to ~ with: we ~ with more than 5,000 visitors a week nous recevons plus de 5 000 visiteurs par semaine; the system can't ~ with this volume of work le système ne peut pas supporter ce volume de travail; I'll just have to ~ with the problems as they arise il faudra que je m'occupe des problèmes au fur et à mesure qu'ils se présenteront.
◇ *n* RELIG chape *f*.
◇ *vt* -**1.** [provide with coping - wall] chaperonner. -**2.** [join timbers] assembler.

Copenhagen [,kəʊpən'heɪgən] *pr n* Copenhague.

Copernican system [kə'pɜ:nɪkən-] *n* système *m* copernicien.

Copernicus [kə'pɜ:nɪkəs] *pr n* Copernic.

copestone ['kəʊpstəʊn] *n* -**1.** = **coping stone**. -**2.** = **capstone**.

copier ['kɒpɪəʳ] *n* photocopieuse *f*, copieur *m*.

co-pilot *n* copilote *mf*.

coping ['kəʊpɪŋ] *n* chaperon *m*.

coping stone *n* couronnement *m*, chaperon *m*.

copious ['kəʊpjəs] *adj* [amount, food] copieux; [sunshine] abondant; [notes] abondant; they wept ~ tears ils ont pleuré à chaudes larmes.

copiously ['kəʊpjəslɪ] *adv* [cry, produce, write] en abondance, abondamment.

cop-killer bullet *n crime sl Am balle capable de traverser un gilet pare-balles*.

copolymer [,kəʊ'pɒlɪməʳ] *n* copolymère *m*.

cop-out *inf n* dérobade *f*; what a ~! belle façon de se défiler!

copper ['kɒpəʳ] ◇ *n* -**1.** [colour, metal] cuivre *m*. -**2.** *inf* [coins] monnaie *f*. -**3.** *inf* [policeman] flic *m*. -**4.** [container] lessiveuse *f*.
◇ *comp* [coin, kettle, wire] en cuivre.
◇ *adj* [colour, hair] cuivré.

copper beech *n* hêtre *m* pourpre.

copper-bottomed [-'bɒtəmd] *adj literal* [saucepan] à fond de cuivre; *fig* [deal] en béton.

copper-coloured *adj* cuivré.

copperplate ['kɒpəpleɪt] ◇ *n* -**1.** [plate] cuivre *m*. -**2.** [print] planche *f* (de cuivre). -**3.** [handwriting] écriture *f* moulée.
◇ *comp* [handwriting] moulé.

coppersmith ['kɒpəsmɪθ] *n* chaudronnier *m*, -ère *f*.

copper sulphate *n* sulfate *m* de cuivre.

coppery ['kɒpərɪ] *adj* [colour] cuivré.

coppice ['kɒpɪs] *n* taillis *m*.

copra ['kɒprə] *n* coprah *m*.

coproduce [,kəʊprə'dju:s] *vt* [film, play] coproduire.

coproduction [,kəʊprə'dʌkʃn] *n* coproduction *f*.

copse [kɒps] *n* taillis *m*.

Copt [kɒpt] *n* Copte *mf*.

Coptic ['kɒptɪk] ◇ *adj* copte; the ~ church l'Église *f* copte.
◇ *n* copte *m*.

copula ['kɒpjʊlə] (*pl* **copulas** OR **copulae** [-li:]) *n* copule *f*.

copulate ['kɒpjʊleɪt] *vi* copuler.

copulation [,kɒpjʊ'leɪʃn] *n* copulation *f*.

copulative ['kɒpjʊlətɪv] *adj* copulatif.

copy ['kɒpɪ] (*pl* **copies**, *pt* & *pp* **copied**)
◇ *n* -**1.** [duplicate - of painting] copie *f*, reproduction *f*; [- of document, photograph] copie *f*; to make a ~ of sthg faire une copie de qqch. -**2.** [of book, magazine, record] exemplaire *m*. -**3.** *(U)* [written material] copie *f*; [in advertisement] texte *m*. -**4.** *(U)* PRESS copie *f*; his story made good ~ son histoire a fait un bon papier.
◇ *vt* -**1.** [write out - letter, notes] copier; to ~ sthg down/out noter/copier qqch. -**2.** [imitate - person, movements, gestures] copier, imiter; [- style, system] copier. -**3.** [cheat] copier. -**4.** [photocopy] photocopier.
◇ *vi* [cheat] copier, tricher; no ~ing! on ne copie pas!

copybook ['kɒpɪbʊk] ◇ *n* cahier *m*.
◇ *adj* [sentiments] commun.

copycat *inf* ['kɒpɪkæt] ◇ *n* copieur *m*, -euse *f*.
◇ *comp* [killings, murder] inspiré par un autre.

copy-edit *vt* [article, book] rédiger.

copy editor *n* secrétaire *mf* de rédaction.

copyholder ['kɒpɪ,həʊldəʳ] *n* -**1.** [reader] lecteur *m*, -trice *f*, teneur *m*, -euse *f* de copie. -**2.** [device] porte-copie *m*.

copyist ['kɒpɪɪst] *n* copiste *mf*.

copy-protected [-prə'tektɪd] *adj* COMPUT protégé contre la copie.

copyread ['kɒpɪri:d, *pp* & *pt* -red] *Am* = **subedit**.

copyreader ['kɒpɪ,ri:dəʳ] *Am* = **subeditor**.

copyright ['kɒpɪraɪt] ◇ *n* copyright *m*, droit *m* d'auteur; she has ~ on the book elle a des droits d'auteur sur le livre; ~ Lawrence Durrell copyright, Lawrence Durrell; out of ~ dans le domaine public.
◇ *vt* obtenir les droits exclusifs OR le copyright.
◇ *adj* de copyright.

copyright deposit library *n* bibliothèque *f* de dépôt légal.

copy typist *n* dactylographe *mf*.

copywriter ['kɒpɪ,raɪtəʳ] *n* rédacteur *m*, -trice *f* publicitaire.

copywriting ['kɒpɪ,raɪtɪŋ] *n* rédaction *f* publicitaire.

coquetry ['kəʊkɪtrɪ, 'kɒkɪtrɪ] (*pl* **coquetries**) *n* coquetterie *f*.

coquette [kəʊ'ket, kɒ'ket] *n* coquette *f*.

coquettish [kəʊ'ketɪʃ, kɒ'ketɪʃ] *adj* [behaviour, look, woman] coquet, provoquant.

cor *inf* [kɔ:ʳ] *interj Br*: ~! ça alors!

coracle ['kɒrəkl] *n* coracle *m*.

coral ['kɒrəl] ◇ *n* corail *m*.
◇ *adj* [pink, red, lipstick] corail; *lit* [lips] de corail.
◇ *comp* [earrings, necklace] de corail; [island] coralien.

coral-coloured *adj* (couleur) corail *(inv)*.

coral reef *n* récif *m* de corail.

Coral Sea *pr n*: the ~ la mer de Corail.

corbel ['kɔ:bəl] *n* corbeau *m*.

corbelling *Br*, **corbeling** *Am* ['kɔ:bəlɪŋ] *n* encorbellement *m*.

cord [kɔ:d] ◇ *n* -**1.** [string] cordon *m*. -**2.** [cable] câble *m*. -**3.** [corduroy] velours *m* côtelé.
◇ *comp* [skirt, trousers] en velours côtelé.
◇ *vt* corder.
◆ **cords** *inf npl*: (a pair of) ~ un pantalon *m* en velours côtelé.

cordage ['kɔ:dɪdʒ] *n* NAUT cordage *m*.

corded ['kɔ:dɪd] *adj* [material] côtelé.

cordial ['kɔ:djəl] ◇ *adj* -**1.** [warm - greeting, reception, welcome] chaleureux. -**2.** [strong - hatred] cordial; to have a ~ dislike for sb détester qqn cordialement.
◇ *n* [drink] cordial *m*.

cordiality [,kɔ:dɪ'ælətɪ] (*pl* **cordialities**) *n* cordialité *f*.

cordially ['kɔ:djəlɪ] *adv* [greet, detest etc] cordialement; ~ yours *Am* [at end of letter] salutations amicales.

cordite ['kɔ:daɪt] *n* cordite *f*.

cordless ['kɔ:dlɪs] *adj* [telephone] sans fil.

Cordoba ['kɔ:dəbə] *pr n* Cordoue.

cordon ['kɔ:dn] ◇ *n* -**1.** [barrier] cordon *m*; police ~ cordon de police; the police put a ~ round the building la police a encerclé le bâtiment. -**2.** HORT cordon *m*. -**3.** [decoration] cordon *m*.
◇ *vt* = **cordon off**.
◆ **cordon off** *vt sep* barrer, interdire l'accès à, isoler.

cordon bleu [-blɜ:] ◇ *adj* de cordon bleu; a ~ cook un cordon bleu.
◇ *n*: she's a ~ c'est un cordon bleu.

corduroy ['kɔ:dərɔɪ] ◇ *n* velours *m* côtelé; (a pair of) ~s (un) pantalon *m* de OR en velours côtelé.
◇ *adj* de velours côtelé.

corduroy road *n route pratiquée en terrain marécageux grâce à des rondins de bois*.

core [kɔ:ʳ] ◇ *n* [of apple, pear] trognon *m*, cœur *m*; [of magnet, earth, atom, group of people, organization] noyau *m*; [of electric cable] âme *f*, noyau *m*; [of nuclear reactor] cœur *m*; [of argument, philosophy] essentiel *m*, centre *m*; to be French/a socialist to the ~ *fig* être français/socialiste jusqu'à la mœlle; rotten to the ~ *fig* pourri jusqu'à l'os.
◇ *comp*: ~ curriculum SCH tronc *m* commun;

~ memory COMPUT mémoire *f* à tores (magnétiques); ~ sample GEOL carotte *f*; ~ subject SCH matière *f* principale; ~ time [in flexitime] plage *f* fixe; ~ vocabulary LING vocabulaire *m* de base.
◇ *vt* [apple, pear] enlever le trognon de.

CORE [kɔːʳ] (*abbr of* Congress On Racial Equality) *pr n ligue américaine contre le racisme*.

coreligionist [ˌkəʊrɪ'lɪdʒənɪst] *n* coreligionnaire *mf*.

corer ['kɔːrəʳ] *n*: apple ~ vide-pomme *m inv*.

co-respondent [ˌkəʊrɪ'spɒndənt] ◇ *adj* [shoes] bicolore *(style années quarante)*.
◇ *n* JUR [in divorce suit] codéfendeur *m*, -eresse *f*.

Corfu [kɔː'fuː] *pr n* Corfou; in ~ à Corfou.

corgi ['kɔːgɪ] *n* corgi *m (petit chien roux, traditionnellement l'animal de compagnie de la famille royale britannique)*.

coriander [ˌkɒrɪ'ændəʳ] *n* coriandre *f*.

Corinth ['kɒrɪnθ] *pr n* Corinthe.

Corinthian [kə'rɪnθɪən] ◇ *n* Corinthien *m*, -enne *f*; the Epistle of Paul to the ~s l'Épître de saint Paul aux Corinthiens.
◇ *adj* corinthien.

Coriolanus [ˌkɒrɪə'leɪnəs] *pr n* Coriolan.

cork [kɔːk] ◇ *n* -**1.** [substance] liège *m*. -**2.** [stopper] bouchon *m*; he took OR pulled the ~ out of the bottle il a débouché la bouteille ❑ put a ~ in it! *inf* la ferme! -**3.** FISHING [float] flotteur *m*, bouchon *m*.
◇ *comp* [tile, bathmat etc] de OR en liège.
◇ *vt* -**1.** [seal - bottle] boucher. -**2.** [blacken]: to ~ one's face se noircir le visage avec un bouchon brûlé.
◆ **cork up** *vt sep* -**1.** = **cork 1**. -**2.** [suppress - emotions, feelings] réprimer.

Cork [kɔːk] *pr n* Cork.

corkage ['kɔːkɪdʒ] *n (U) droit de débouchage sur un vin qui a été apporté par des consommateurs*.

corked [kɔːkt] *adj* [wine] qui sent le bouchon.

corker *inf* ['kɔːkəʳ] *n Br dated*: she's a real ~ [good-looking] c'est un beau brin de fille; he's a real ~ [good-looking] c'est un beau gars; that was a ~ of a joke c'était une plaisanterie à vous faire mourir de rire; it's a ~ [car, bike etc] c'est un (vrai) bijou.

corking *inf* ['kɔːkɪŋ] *adj Br dated* épatant, fameux.

cork oak *n* chêne-liège *m*.

corkscrew ['kɔːkskruː] ◇ *n* tire-bouchon *m*.
◇ *comp*: ~ curl tire-bouchon *m*.
◇ *vi* [staircase] tourner en vrille; [plane] vriller; the plane ~ed out of the sky l'avion est tombé en vrille.

cork-tipped [-tɪpt] *adj* [cigarette] (à bout) filtre.

corm [kɔːm] *n* bulbe *m*.

cormorant ['kɔːmərənt] *n* cormoran *m*.

corn [kɔːn] ◇ *n* -**1.** [cereal] *Br* blé *m*; *Am* maïs *m*; ~ on the cob épi *m* de maïs; grains of ~ grains *mpl* de maïs ❑ the Corn Laws *Br* HIST les lois *fpl* sur le blé. -**2.** *inf (U)* [banality] banalité *f*; [sentimentality] sentimentalité *f* bébête; the book/film is pure ~ le livre/film est d'une banalité finie. -**3.** [on foot] cor *m*; to tread on sb's ~s *inf Br* [upset] toucher qqn à l'endroit sensible; [trespass] marcher sur les plates-bandes de qqn.
◇ *comp*: ~ plaster pansement *m* (pour cors).

THE CORN LAWS:
Mesure protectionniste prise par le Parlement britannique en 1815 pour pallier l'effet des mauvaises récoltes et consistant à augmenter le tarif du grain importé. Très impopulaire, cette loi provoqua la naissance de la «Anti-Corn Law League», dont la liberté de commerce devint le slogan.

Corn *written abbr of* Cornwall.

cornball ['kɔːnbɔːl] *Am* ◇ *n* sentimental *m*, -e *f*.
◇ *adj* = **corny**.

corn bread *n* pain *m* à la farine de maïs.

corn bunting *n* bruant *m*.

corncob ['kɔːnkɒb] *n* épi *m* de maïs.

corncrake ['kɔːnkreɪk] *n* râle *m* des genêts.

corn dolly *n* poupée *f* de paille.

cornea ['kɔːnɪə] *n* cornée *f*.

corneal ['kɔːnɪəl] *adj* cornéen.

corned beef [kɔːnd-] *n* corned beef *m*.

cornelian [kɔː'niːlɪən] *n* cornaline *f*.

Cornelian [kɔː'niːlɪən] *adj* cornélien.

corner ['kɔːnəʳ] ◇ *n* -**1.** [of page, painting, table etc] coin *m*; to turn down the ~ of a page faire une corne à une page. -**2.** [inside room, house etc] coin *m*; to put a child in the ~ mettre un enfant au coin ❑ to fight one's ~ *Br* [argue one's case] défendre sa position; the Minister fought his ~ well and got an increase in his budget le ministre a bien défendu son point de vue et a obtenu une augmentation de son budget; to be in sb's ~ être du côté de qqn, soutenir qqn; with someone as powerful as her in your ~, you can't lose avec quelqu'un d'aussi puissant qu'elle derrière toi, tu ne peux pas perdre. -**3.** [of street] coin *m*; [bend in the road] tournant *m*, virage *m*; on OR at the ~ au coin; the house on OR at the ~ la maison qui fait l'angle; at the ~ of Regent Street and Oxford Street à l'intersection OR à l'angle de Regent Street et d'Oxford Street; he/the car took the ~ at high speed il/la voiture a pris le tournant à toute allure; to overtake on a ~ doubler dans un virage; the car takes ~s well la voiture prend bien les virages; it's just around OR *Br* round the ~ [house, shop etc] c'est à deux pas d'ici; *fig* [Christmas, economic recovery etc] c'est tout proche; it's literally just round the ~ c'est juste au coin de la rue; a cure is just round the ~ *fig* on est sur le point de découvrir un remède; you never know what's round the ~ *fig* on ne sait jamais ce qui peut arriver; to turn the ~ [car] tourner le coin, prendre le tournant; *fig* [patient] passer le moment OR stade critique; [business, economy, relationship] sortir du tunnel; to cut the ~ [in car, on bike] couper le virage, prendre le virage à la corde; [on foot] couper au plus court, prendre le plus court ❑ to cut ~s sauter des étapes. -**4.** [of eye] coin *m*; [of mouth] coin *m*, commissure *f*; with a cigarette hanging from the ~ of his mouth une cigarette au coin de la bouche; to look at sb/sthg out of the ~ of one's eye regarder qqn/qqch du coin de l'œil. -**5.** *inf* [difficulty] situation *f* difficile, mauvaise passe *f*; to drive sb into a tight ~ acculer qqn, mettre qqn dans une situation difficile. -**6.** [remote place] coin *m*; the four ~s of the earth OR world OR globe les quatre coins de la terre OR du monde OR du globe. -**7.** FTBL corner *m*. -**8.** COMM: to make OR to have a ~ in sthg avoir le monopole de qqch, accaparer qqch.
◇ *comp* [cupboard, table etc] du coin.
◇ *vt* -**1.** [animal, prey etc] coincer, acculer; she ~ed me at the party elle m'a coincé à la soirée. -**2.** COMM accaparer; to ~ the market in sthg accaparer le marché de qqch.
◇ *vi* AUT prendre un virage; the car ~s well la voiture tient bien la route dans les virages.

cornered ['kɔːnəd] *adj* [animal, prey] acculé, coincé; we've got him ~ on l'a acculé OR coincé; his opponent in the debate had him ~ son adversaire dans le débat l'avait acculé.

corner flag *n* SPORT drapeau *m* de corner.

cornering ['kɔːnərɪŋ] *n Br* -**1.** AUT [of driver] façon *f* de prendre les virages; [of car] stabilité *f* dans les virages; your ~ has improved tu prends mieux les virages. -**2.** COMM accaparement *m*.

corner kick *n* FTBL corner *m*.

corner post *n* FTBL piquet *m* de corner.

corner shop *n Br* magasin *m* du coin.

cornerstone ['kɔːnəstəʊn] *n* pierre *f* d'angle OR angulaire; *fig* pierre *f* angulaire, fondement *m*.

corner store *Am* = **corner shop**.

cornerways ['kɔːnəweɪz], **cornerwise** ['kɔːnəwaɪz] *adj* & *adv* en diagonale, en coin.

cornet ['kɔːnɪt] *n* -**1.** MUS [instrument] cornet *m* à pistons. -**2.** *Br*: (ice-cream) ~ cornet *m* (de glace).

corn exchange *n* halle *f* au blé.

corn-fed *adj* [chicken] nourri au grain.

cornfield ['kɔːnfiːld] *n Br* champ *m* de blé; *Am* champ *m* de maïs.

cornflakes ['kɔːnfleɪks] *npl* cornflakes *mpl*, pétales *mpl* OR flocons *mpl* de maïs.

cornflour ['kɔːnflaʊəʳ] *n Br* fécule *f* de maïs, Maïzena® *f*.

cornflower ['kɔːnflaʊəʳ] ◇ *n* [plant] bleuet *m*, bluet *m*, barbeau *m*; [colour] bleu *m* centaurée.
◇ *adj*: ~ (blue) bleu centaurée.

cornice ['kɔːnɪs] *n* ARCHIT corniche *f*; [snow] corniche *f*.

corniche [kɔː'niːʃ] *n* [road] corniche *f*.

Cornish ['kɔːnɪʃ] ◇ *npl* [people]: the ~ les Cornouaillais.
◇ *n* LING cornouaillais *m*.
◇ *adj* cornouaillais.

Cornishman ['kɔːnɪʃmən] (*pl* Cornishmen [-mən]) *n* Cornouaillais *m*.

Cornish pasty *n Br* CULIN *chausson à la viande et aux légumes*.

Cornishwoman ['kɔːnɪʃˌwʊmən] (*pl* Cornishwomen [-ˌwɪmɪn]) *n* Cornouaillaise *f*.

corn meal *n* farine *f* de maïs.

corn oil *n* huile *f* de maïs.

corn pone *n Am dial* pain *m* de maïs.

corn poppy *n* coquelicot *m*.

corn salad *n* mâche *f*.

cornstarch ['kɔːnstɑːtʃ] *Am* = **cornflour**.

corn syrup *n* sirop *m* de maïs.

cornucopia [ˌkɔːnjʊ'kəʊpjə] *n* MYTH & *fig* corne *f* d'abondance.

Cornwall ['kɔːnwɔːl] *pr n* Cornouailles *f*; in ~ en Cornouailles.

corn whisk(e)y *n* whisky *m* de maïs.

corny *inf* ['kɔːnɪ] (*compar* cornier, *superl* corniest) *adj* [trite - joke, film, book] bateau, banal; [sentimental - book, film] sentimental, à l'eau de rose; he's so ~ il est vraiment lourd *fig*.

corolla [kə'rɒlə] *n* BOT corolle *f*.

corollary [kə'rɒlərɪ] (*pl* corollaries) *n fml* corollaire *m*; the ~ of that is that... le corollaire de ceci, c'est que..., ceci a pour corollaire que...; as a ~ to this en corollaire à ceci.

Coromandel Coast [ˌkɒrə'mændl-] *pr n*: the ~ la côte de Coromandel.

corona [kə'rəʊnə] (*pl* coronas OR coronae [-niː]) *n* -**1.** ANAT, ASTRON, BOT & PHYS couronne *f*. -**2.** ARCHIT larmier *m*. -**3.** [cigar] corona *m*.

coronary ['kɒrənrɪ] MED ◇ *adj* coronaire; the country has a high incidence of ~ heart disease il y a de nombreux cas de maladies coronariennes dans ce pays.
◇ *n* infarctus *m* du myocarde; to have a ~ avoir un infarctus du myocarde.

coronary artery *n* MED artère *f* coronaire.

coronary bypass *n* MED pontage *m* coronaire.

coronary care unit *n* MED unité *f* de soins coronariens.

coronary thrombosis *n* MED infarctus *m* du myocarde, thrombose *f* coronarienne.

coronation [ˌkɒrə'neɪʃn] ◇ *n* [of monarch] couronnement *m*, sacre *m*.
◇ *comp* [ceremony, robes, day, oath] du couronnement, du sacre; ~ mug *Br tasse haute fabriquée spécialement à l'occasion d'un couronnement et décorée sur ce thème*; 'Coronation Street' *feuilleton télévisé britannique*.

CORONATION STREET:
Ce feuilleton à succès, le plus ancien des «soap operas» encore à l'écran, évoque la vie quotidienne de plusieurs familles ouvrières vivant dans la même rue d'une ville du nord de l'Angleterre.

coroner ['kɒrənəʳ] *n* JUR coroner *m*; ~'s inquest enquête *f* judiciaire *(menée par le coroner)*; ~'s jury jury *m* du coroner.

coronet ['kɒrənɪt] *n* [of prince, duke] couronne *f*; [for woman] diadème *m*.

Corp. -**1.** (*written abbr of* **corporation**) Cie. -**2.** *written abbr of* **corporal**.

corporal ['kɔːpərəl] ◇ *n* MIL caporal-chef *m*.
◇ *adj* corporel; ~ **punishment** châtiment *m* corporel.

corporate ['kɔːpərət] *adj* -**1.** JUR [forming a single body]: ~ **body** OR **institution** personne *f* morale. -**2.** [of a specific company] d'une société, de la société; [of companies in general] d'entreprise; [taxation] sur les sociétés; **to make one's way up the ~ ladder** faire carrière dans l'entreprise; **if we are to be regarded as a good ~ citizen** si nous voulons être considérés comme une entreprise qui assume ses responsabilités dans la société; **he's a good ~ man** il est dévoué à l'entreprise; **the restaurant is hoping for good ~ business** le restaurant espère attirer une nombreuse clientèle d'affaires; **Britain's largest ~ donors** les entreprises donatrices les plus généreuses de Grande-Bretagne; ~ **culture** culture *f* d'entreprise; **we have a number of ~ customers** certains de nos clients sont des entreprises; ~ **customers provide the bulk of our profits** la plus grande partie de nos bénéfices provient des entreprises; ~ **entertainment** divertissement *m* fourni par la société OR l'entreprise; **the company's ~ image** l'image *f* de la société; **one of our largest ~ sponsors** un de nos plus importants sponsors ❑ ~ **identity** image *f* de marque; ~ **law** droit *m* des sociétés OR des entreprises; ~ **lawyer** juriste *m* spécialisé en droit des sociétés; ~ **name** raison *f* sociale; ~ **sponsorship** sponsoring *m*, parrainage *m* d'entreprises; ~ **structure** structure *f* de l'entreprise. -**3.** [collective - decision, responsibility] collectif.

corporately ['kɔːpərətlɪ] *adv* -**1.** [as a corporation]: **I don't think we should involve ourselves ~** je ne pense pas que nous devrions nous impliquer en tant que société. -**2.** [as a group] collectivement.

corporate tax *Am* = **corporation tax**.

corporation [,kɔːpə'reɪʃn] ◇ *n* -**1.** [company] compagnie *f*, société *f*; JUR personne *f* morale. -**2.** *Br* [municipal authorities] municipalité *f*. -**3.** *inf* [paunch] bedaine *f*, brioche *f*; **to develop a ~** prendre de la bedaine OR de la brioche.
◇ *comp Br* [bus, property, worker] municipal, de la ville.

corporation tax *n Br* impôt *m* sur les sociétés.

corporatism ['kɔːpərətɪzm] *n* corporatisme *m*.

corporeal [kɔː'pɔːrɪəl] *adj* corporel, matériel.

corps [kɔːʳ] (*pl inv*) *n* -**1.** MIL corps *m*; MIL & ADMIN service *m*; **medical/intelligence ~** service de santé/de renseignements; **pay ~** service de la solde; **tank ~** blindés *mpl*. -**2.** [trained team of people] corps *m*; ~ **de ballet** corps de ballet; **diplomatic ~** corps diplomatique; **press ~** journalistes *mfpl*.

corpse [kɔːps] ◇ *n* cadavre *m*, corps *m*.
◇ *vi inf* THEAT [actor] avoir une crise de fou rire.

corpulence ['kɔːpjʊləns] *n* corpulence *f*, embonpoint *m*.

corpulent ['kɔːpjʊlənt] *adj* corpulent.

corpus ['kɔːpəs] (*pl* **corpuses** OR **corpora** [-pərə]) *n* -**1.** [collection of writings - by author] recueil *m*; [- on specific subject] corpus *m*. -**2.** [main body] corpus *m*.

Corpus Christi [,kɔːpəs'krɪstɪ] *n* la Fête-Dieu.

corpuscle ['kɔːpʌsl] *n* PHYSIOL corpuscule *m*; **red/white blood ~s** globules *mpl* rouges/blancs.

corral [kɒ'rɑːl] *Am* (*pt* & *pp* **corralled**, *cont* **corralling**) ◇ *n* corral *m*.
◇ *vt* [cattle, horses] enfermer dans un corral; *fig* encercler; **she corralled me** *inf fig* elle m'a mis le grappin dessus.

correct [kə'rekt] ◇ *adj* -**1.** [right - answer, spelling etc] correct, juste; **do you have the ~ time?** avez-vous l'heure exacte?; **that is ~** c'est exact; **to prove (to be) ~** s'avérer juste; ~ **to four decimal places** exact à quatre chiffres après la virgule; **am I ~ in thinking that...?** ai-je raison de penser que...?; **she was quite ~** elle avait tout à fait raison; **she was quite ~ in her assumptions** ses suppositions étaient parfaitement justes. -**2.** [suitable, proper - behaviour, manners etc] correct, convenable, bienséant; [- person] correct, convenable; **the ~ thing for him to do in the circumstances is to resign** dans ces circonstances la bienséance veut qu'il démissionne; **she was quite ~ to do what she did** elle a fait ce qu'il convenait de faire; **the ~ procedure** la procédure d'usage; ~ **dress must be worn** une tenue correcte est de rigueur.
◇ *vt* -**1.** [rectify - mistake, spelling etc] corriger, rectifier; [- squint, bad posture, imbalance] corriger; [- situation] rectifier. -**2.** [indicate error - to person] corriger, reprendre; [- in exam paper, homework, proofs etc] corriger; **please ~ me whenever I make a mistake** veuillez me corriger OR me reprendre si je fais des erreurs; **to ~ sb on** OR **about sthg** corriger OR reprendre qqn sur qqch; **to ~ sb's French/pronunciation** corriger le français/la prononciation de qqn, reprendre qqn sur son français/sa prononciation; **if I may ~ you** si vous permettez que je vous reprenne; ~ **me if I'm wrong, but...** corrigez-moi si je me trompe, mais...; **I stand ~ed** je reconnais mon erreur; **to ~ o.s.** se reprendre, se corriger. -**3.** *arch* [punish] punir; [physically] corriger, infliger une correction à.

correcting fluid [kə'rektɪŋ-] = **correction fluid**.

correction [kə'rekʃn] *n* -**1.** [of exam paper, homework, proofs etc] correction *f*; [of error] correction *f*, rectification *f*. -**2.** [in essay, school work, proofs etc] correction *f*; **to make ~s** faire des corrections; **to make ~s to sthg** apporter des corrections à qqch. -**3.** *arch* [punishment] correction *f*, punition *f*, châtiment *m*; **house of ~** maison *f* de correction OR de redressement.

correction fluid *n* liquide *m* correcteur.

correction tape *n* [for typewriter] ruban *m* correcteur.

corrective [kə'rektɪv] ◇ *adj* [action, measure] rectificatif, correctif; [exercises, treatment] correctif.
◇ *n* correctif *m*; MED [for teeth] appareil *m* dentaire; [for deformed limb] appareil *m* orthopédique; **a ~ to sthg** un correctif de qqch.

correctly [kə'rektlɪ] *adv* -**1.** [in the right way - answer, pronounce] correctement; **he ~ predicted that...** il a prédit avec raison que...; **the XYZ, more ~ known as...** XYZ, ou selon son appellation plus correcte... -**2.** [properly - behave, dress, speak] correctement.

correctness [kə'rektnɪs] *n* -**1.** [of answer, prediction etc] exactitude *f*, justesse *f*. -**2.** [of behaviour, dress etc] correction *f*.

Correggio [kɒ'redʒjəʊ] *pr n* le Corrège; **a painting by ~** un tableau du Corrège.

correlate ['kɒrəleɪt] ◇ *vi*: **to ~ (with sthg)** [gen] être en corrélation OR rapport (avec qqch), correspondre (à qqch); [in statistics] être en corrélation (avec qqch).
◇ *vt* [gen] mettre en corrélation OR en rapport, faire correspondre; [in statistics] corréler; **to ~ sthg with sthg** mettre qqch en corrélation OR rapport avec qqch; [in statistics] corréler qqch avec qqch; **these two trends are closely ~d** ces deux tendances sont en rapport étroit.

correlation [,kɒrə'leɪʃn] *n* corrélation *f*.

correlation coefficient *n* coefficient *m* de corrélation.

correlative [kɒ'relətɪv] ◇ *n* terme *m* corrélatif.
◇ *adj* corrélatif.

correspond [,kɒrɪ'spɒnd] *vi* -**1.** [tally - dates, statements] correspondre; **to ~ with sthg** correspondre à qqch. -**2.** [be equivalent] correspondre, équivaloir; **this animal ~s roughly with** OR **to our own domestic cat** cet animal correspond à peu près à notre OR est à peu près l'équivalent de notre chat domestique. -**3.** [exchange letters] correspondre; **we have been ~ing (with each other) for years** cela fait des années que nous correspondons; **we don't often ~** nous ne correspondons OR nous ne nous écrivons pas souvent; **we only ~ at Christmas** nous ne nous écrivons qu'à Noël.

correspondence [,kɒrɪ'spɒndəns] ◇ *n* -**1.** [relationship, similarity] correspondance *f*, rapport *m*, relation *f*. -**2.** [letter-writing] correspondance *f*; **to be in ~ with sb** être en correspondance avec qqn; **to enter into (a) ~ with sb** établir une OR entrer en correspondance avec qqn; **no ~ will be entered into** [in competition] il ne sera répondu à aucun courrier; **to keep up a ~ with sb** rester en correspondance avec qqn. -**3.** [letters] correspondance *f*, courrier *m*; **to read/to do one's ~** lire/faire son courrier OR sa correspondance; **she doesn't get much ~** elle ne reçoit pas beaucoup de courrier.
◇ *comp* [course] par correspondance; [school] d'enseignement par correspondance; ~ **column** PRESS courrier *m* des lecteurs.

correspondent [,kɒrɪ'spɒndənt] ◇ *n* -**1.** PRESS, RADIO & TV [reporter] correspondant *m*, -e *f*; **special ~** envoyé *m* spécial, envoyée *f* spéciale; **sports/foreign ~** correspondant sportif/à l'étranger; **war/environment ~** correspondant de guerre/pour les questions d'environnement; **our Moscow ~** notre correspondant à Moscou. -**2.** [letter-writer] correspondant *m*, -e *f*; **I am a very bad ~** j'écris très peu.
◇ *adj* = **corresponding**.

corresponding [,kɒrɪ'spɒndɪŋ] *adj* correspondant; **unemployment/inflation is higher than in the ~ period last year** le chômage/l'inflation a augmenté par rapport à la période correspondante de l'année dernière OR à la même période l'année dernière.

correspondingly [,kɒrɪ'spɒndɪŋlɪ] *adv* -**1.** [proportionally] proportionnellement. -**2.** [related to this, in line with this]: **the translation should be ~ informal in register** la traduction devrait être d'un niveau de familiarité correspondant; **we got a lot of negative press and our election results were ~ poor** nous avons eu beaucoup de commentaires négatifs dans la presse, ce qui nous a valu de mauvais résultats aux élections.

corridor ['kɒrɪdɔːʳ] *n* [in building] corridor *m*, couloir *m*; [in train] couloir *m*; **the ~s of power** *fig* les allées du pouvoir; [behind the scenes] les coulisses du pouvoir ❑ **air ~** couloir aérien; ~ **train** train *m* à couloir; **the Polish Corridor** HIST le corridor polonais; **'The Corridors of Power'** *Snow* 'les Couloirs du pouvoir'.

corrie ['kɒrɪ] *n Scot* GEOG cirque *m*.

corroborate [kə'rɒbəreɪt] *vt* [statement, view etc] confirmer, corroborer *lit*; **for lack of corroborating evidence** faute de preuves à l'appui.

corroboration [kə,rɒbə'reɪʃn] *n* confirmation *f*, corroboration *f lit*; **to provide ~ of sthg** confirmer OR corroborer qqch; **evidence produced in ~ of sb's testimony** des preuves fournies à l'appui du témoignage de qqn.

corroborative [kə'rɒbərətɪv] *adj* [evidence, statement] à l'appui.

corrode [kə'rəʊd] ◇ *vt* [subj: acid, rust] corroder, ronger; *fig* [happiness] entamer, miner; **it's very badly ~d** [by acid, rust] c'est très corrodé; [by rust] c'est très rouillé.
◇ *vi* [due to acid, rust] se corroder; [due to rust] se rouiller.

corrosion [kə'rəʊʒn] *n* [of metal] corrosion *f*.

corrosive [kə'rəʊsɪv] ◇ *adj* corrosif; **the ~ effects of long-term unemployment** les effets destructeurs du chômage de longue durée.
◇ *n* corrosif *m*.

corrugated ['kɒrəgeɪtɪd] *adj* [cardboard, paper] ondulé; ~ **iron** tôle *f* ondulée; **a ~ iron hut** une cabane en tôle ondulée.

corrupt [kə'rʌpt] ◇ *adj* -**1.** [dishonest - person, society] corrompu; ~ **practices** pratiques *fpl* malhonnêtes. -**2.** [depraved, immoral] dépravé, corrompu. -**3.** [containing alterations - text] altéré. -**4.** COMPUT [containing errors - disk, file] altéré.
◇ *vt* -**1.** [make dishonest] corrompre; **~ed by power** corrompu par le pouvoir. -**2.** [deprave, debase - person, society] dépraver, corrompre;

[- language] corrompre; the ~ing influence of television l'influence corruptrice de la télévision. -**3.** [alter - text] altérer, corrompre. -**4.** COMPUT altérer.

corrupter [kəˈrʌptəʳ] *n* corrupteur *m*, -trice *f*.

corruptible [kəˈrʌptəbl] *adj* corruptible.

corruption [kəˈrʌpʃn] *n* -**1.** [of official, politician etc - action, state] corruption *f*. -**2.** [depravity, debasement - action, state] dépravation *f*, corruption *f*; the ~ of minors JUR le détournement de mineurs. -**3.** [of text - action] altération *f*, corruption *f*; [- state] version *f* corrompue; [of word - action] corruption *f*; [- state] forme *f* corrompue. -**4.** COMPUT altération *f*.

corruptly [kəˈrʌptlɪ] *adv* -**1.** [dishonestly] de manière corrompue; he had ~ accepted bribes il s'est corrompu en acceptant des pots-de-vin. -**2.** [in a depraved way] d'une manière dépravée OR corrompue.

corsage [kɔːˈsɑːʒ] *n* [flowers] *petit bouquet de fleurs (à accrocher au corsage ou au poignet)*; [bodice] corsage *m*.

corsair [ˈkɔːseəʳ] *n* corsaire *m*.

corset [ˈkɔːsɪt] *n* corset *m*; surgical ~ corset orthopédique.

Corsica [ˈkɔːsɪkə] *pr n* Corse *f*; in ~ en Corse.

Corsican [ˈkɔːsɪkən] ◇ *n* -**1.** [person] Corse *mf*. -**2.** LING corse *m*.
◇ *adj* corse.

cortège [kɔːˈteɪʒ] *n* cortège *m*; funeral ~ cortège funèbre.

cortex [ˈkɔːteks] (*pl* cortices [-tɪsiːz]) *n* ANAT & BOT cortex *m*.

cortical [ˈkɔːtɪkl] *adj* cortical.

cortisone [ˈkɔːtɪzəʊn] ◇ *n* cortisone *f*.
◇ *comp*: ~ injection piqûre *f* de cortisone.

corundum [kəˈrʌndəm] *n* MINER corindon *m*.

coruscate [ˈkɒrəskeɪt] *vi fml* briller, scintiller.

coruscating [ˈkɒrəskeɪtɪŋ] *adj fml* brillant, scintillant; *fig* [wit] brillant, étincelant.

corvette [ˈkɔːvet] *n* NAUT corvette *f*.

cos[1] [kɒz] ◇ *conj inf* = **because**.
◇ *n abbr of* cosine.

cos[2] [kɒs] *n Br*: ~ (lettuce) (laitue *f*) romaine *f*.

Cosa Nostra [ˌkəʊzəˈnɒstrə] *n* Cosa Nostra *f*.

cosh [kɒʃ] ◇ *n* gourdin *m*, matraque *f*.
◇ *vt* assommer, matraquer.

cosignatory [ˌkəʊˈsɪgnətrɪ] (*pl* cosignatories) *n fml* cosignataire *mf*; cosignatories to the agreement cosignataires de l'accord.

cosily *Br*, **cozily** *Am* [ˈkəʊzɪlɪ] *adv* [furnished] confortablement; they were sitting ~ by the fire ils étaient assis confortablement près du feu.

cosine [ˈkəʊsaɪn] *n* MATH cosinus *m*.

cosiness *Br*, **coziness** *Am* [ˈkəʊzɪnɪs] *n* [of house, surroundings etc] confort *m*; there's nothing I like better than the ~ of a big comfy sofa il n'y a rien de mieux qu'un grand canapé bien confortable || *fig*: the ~ of her novels l'atmosphère douce qui règne dans ses romans; given the ~ of their relationship vu les rapports copain-copain qu'ils entretiennent.

cosmetic [kɒzˈmetɪk] ◇ *adj* [preparation] cosmétique; *fig* [superficial - change, measure] superficiel, symbolique; it's purely ~ c'est purement symbolique, c'est uniquement pour la forme; that type of dental surgery would be regarded as purely ~ ce type de chirurgie dentaire serait considéré comme purement esthétique ❑ ~ surgery chirurgie *f* esthétique; to have ~ surgery se faire faire de la chirurgie esthétique.
◇ *n* cosmétique *m*, produit *m* de beauté; the ~s industry/counter l'industrie/le rayon des cosmétiques; she's in ~s elle est dans les cosmétiques.

cosmetician [ˌkɒzməˈtɪʃn] *n* [specialist] esthéticien *m*, -enne *f*.

cosmic [ˈkɒzmɪk] *adj* cosmique; ~ dust poussières *fpl* cosmiques; ~ ray rayon *m* cosmique; of ~ proportions *fig* aux proportions gigantesques.

cosmographer [kɒzˈmɒgrəfəʳ] *n* cosmographe *mf*.

cosmography [kɒzˈmɒgrəfɪ] *n* cosmographie *f*.

cosmology [kɒzˈmɒlədʒɪ] *n* cosmologie *f*.

cosmonaut [ˈkɒzmənɔːt] *n* cosmonaute *mf*.

cosmopolitan [kɒzməˈpɒlɪtn] ◇ *adj* [city, person, restaurant etc] cosmopolite.
◇ *n* cosmopolite *mf*.

cosmos [ˈkɒzmɒs] *n* cosmos *m*; *fig* univers *m*.

co-sponsor ◇ *n entreprise ou individu contribuant à un sponsoring*; we need at least one more ~ il nous faut encore au moins un autre sponsor; I agreed to act as (a) ~ j'ai accepté d'être le deuxième sponsor OR l'un des sponsors.
◇ *vt*: the company has been approached to ~ the exhibition l'entreprise a été sollicitée pour participer au sponsoring OR pour être l'un des sponsors de l'exposition.

cosset [ˈkɒsɪt] *vt* [person] dorloter, choyer, câliner; to ~ o.s. se dorloter.

cost [kɒst] (*pp* & *pt sense 1* cost, *sense 2* costed)
◇ *vt* -**1.** coûter; how much OR what does it ~? combien ça coûte?; how much is it going to ~ me? combien est-ce que ça va me coûter?, à combien est-ce que ça va me revenir?; how much will it ~ the taxpayer? combien cela coûtera-t-il au contribuable?; it ~s £10 cela coûte 10 livres; it ~ me £200 cela m'est revenu à OR m'a coûté 200 livres; did it ~ much? est-ce que cela a coûté cher?; it ~s nothing to join l'inscription est gratuite; it's a hobby that doesn't ~ anything c'est un passe-temps qui ne coûte rien; it didn't ~ me a penny ça ne m'a rien coûté du tout, ça ne m'a pas coûté un sou; it'll ~ you! *inf* [purchase] tu vas le sentir passer!; [help, favour] ce ne sera pas gratuit!; electricity ~s money, you know! l'électricité, ce n'est pas gratuit!; it ~ her a lot of time and effort cela lui a demandé beaucoup de temps et d'efforts; the puncture ~ us a bit of time la crevaison nous a fait perdre pas mal de temps; it ~ him his job cela lui a coûté son travail, cela lui a fait perdre son travail; it ~ her her life cela lui a coûté la vie; drinking and driving ~s lives la conduite en état d'ivresse coûte des vies humaines; it doesn't ~ anything to be polite ça ne coûte rien d'être poli; it must have ~ him to say sorry cela a dû lui coûter de s'excuser; whatever it ~s [purchase] quel qu'en soit le prix; whatever it ~s, I'm not going to give up quoi qu'il m'en coûte, je n'abandonnerai pas ❑ to ~ an arm and a leg *inf*, to ~ the earth coûter les yeux de la tête OR la peau des fesses. -**2.** [work out price of - trip] évaluer le coût de; [- job, repairs] établir un devis pour; he ~ed the repairs to the car at £150 il a établi un devis de 150 livres pour les réparations de la voiture, il a évalué les réparations de la voiture à 150 livres; to ~ a product COMM établir le prix de revient d'un produit; a carefully ~ed budget un budget calculé avec soin.
◇ *n* -**1.** [amount charged or paid] coût *m*; the car was repaired at a ~ of £50 la réparation de la voiture a coûté 50 livres; the ~ of petrol has gone up le prix de l'essence a augmenté; the ~ of money le loyer de l'argent; think of the ~ (involved)! imagine un peu le prix que ça coûte!; to bear the ~ of sthg payer qqch; [with difficulty] faire face aux frais OR aux dépenses de qqch; to buy/to sell sthg at ~ [cost price] acheter/vendre qqch au prix coûtant; at no extra ~ sans frais supplémentaires; the firm cut its ~s by 30% l'entreprise a réduit ses frais de 30 % ❑ ~, insurance and freight COMM coût, assurance et fret. -**2.** *fig* prix *m*; whatever the ~ à tout prix, à n'importe quel prix; whatever the ~ to his health quoi qu'il en coûte à sa santé, quel qu'en soit le prix pour sa santé; whatever the ~ to myself quoi qu'il m'en coûte; he was always helping people, whatever the ~ to himself il était toujours à aider les autres, quoi qu'il lui en coûte; at the ~ of her job/reputation/marriage au prix de son travail/sa réputation/son mariage; he saved them at the ~ of his (own) life il les a sauvés au prix de sa vie; to find out OR to learn OR to discover to one's ~ apprendre OR découvrir à ses dépens; as I discovered to my ~ comme je l'ai appris OR découvert à mes dépens; as I know to my ~ comme j'en ai fait la dure expérience; to count the ~ of sthg faire le bilan de qqch; no-one stopped to count the ~ [in advance] personne n'a pensé au prix à payer; what will be the ~ in terms of human suffering? quel sera le prix à payer en termes de souffrances humaines?; the ~ in human life le prix en vies humaines; the ~ in human terms [of unemployment, closure] le coût humain.
◇ *comp* [analysis] de coût.
◆ **costs** *npl* JUR frais *mpl* (d'instance) et dépens *mpl*; to be awarded ~s se voir accorder des frais et dépens; to be ordered to pay ~s être condamné aux dépens.
◆ **at all costs** *adv phr* à tout prix.
◆ **at any cost** *adv phr* en aucun cas; he should not be approached at any ~ en aucun cas il ne doit être approché.
◆ **cost out** *vt sep* = **cost 2**.

Costa Brava [ˌkɒstəˈbrɑːvə] *pr n* Costa Brava *f*.

cost accountant *n* comptable *m* spécialisé en comptabilité analytique OR en comptabilité d'exploitation.

cost accounting *n* comptabilité *f* analytique OR d'exploitation.

Costa del Sol [ˌkɒstədelˈsɒl] *pr n* Costa del Sol *f*.

co-star (*pt* & *pp* co-starred, *cont* co-starring) CIN & TV ◇ *n* [of actor, actress] partenaire *mf*.
◇ *vi* [in film] être l'une des vedettes principales; to ~ with sb partager la vedette OR l'affiche avec qqn; they have co-starred in several films ils ont partagé la vedette OR l'affiche de plusieurs films; she has co-starred in three films elle a joué l'un des rôles principaux dans trois films; this is his first co-starring role c'est la première fois qu'il a un des rôles principaux.
◇ *vt*: the film ~s Joe Smith and Mary Brown le film met en scène Joe Smith et Mary Brown dans les rôles principaux OR vedettes; the film ~s Joe Smith le film met en scène Joe Smith dans l'un des rôles principaux OR vedettes; co-starring... [in credits] avec...

Costa Rica [ˌkɒstəˈriːkə] *pr n* Costa Rica *m*; in ~ au Costa Rica.

Costa Rican [ˌkɒstəˈriːkən] ◇ *n* Costaricien *m*, -enne *f*.
◇ *adj* costaricien.

cost-benefit analysis *n* analyse *f* des coûts et rendements.

cost-conscious *adj*: to be ~ contrôler ses dépenses; in these ~ days par les temps qui courent où tout le monde fait attention à OR surveille ses dépenses.

cost-cutting ◇ *n* compression *f* OR réduction *f* des coûts; further ~ may be necessary d'autres compressions OR réductions des coûts pourraient s'avérer nécessaires.
◇ *adj* de compression OR de réduction des coûts; this is only part of a larger ~ exercise ce n'est qu'un élément d'une opération plus vaste de compression OR de réduction des coûts.

cost-effective *adj* rentable.

cost-effectiveness *n* rentabilité *f*.

costermonger [ˈkɒstəˌmʌŋgəʳ] *n Br* marchand *m*, -e *f* de quatre-saisons.

costing [ˈkɒstɪŋ] *n* [of product] estimation *f* du prix de revient; [of job, repairs] établissement *m* d'un devis; based on detailed ~s basé sur des calculs détaillés.

costive [ˈkɒstɪv] *adj* MED constipé.

costiveness [ˈkɒstɪvnɪs] *n* MED constipation *f*.

costliness [ˈkɒstlɪnɪs] *n* [high price] cherté *f*; we didn't realize the ~ of our mistake *fig* nous ne nous sommes pas rendu compte combien notre erreur allait nous coûter cher.

costly [ˈkɒstlɪ] (*compar* costlier, *superl* costliest) *adj* -**1.** [expensive] coûteux, cher; this may be a ~ mistake cette erreur pourrait me/vous *etc* coûter cher; the costliest war this country has ever known in terms of human suffering la guerre la plus meurtrière et traumatisante que le pays ait jamais connue. -**2.** [of high quality] somptueux, riche.

cost of living ◇ *n* coût *m* de la vie; the ~ keeps going up le coût de la vie ne cesse d'augmenter; in order to keep up with the ~ afin de suivre le coût de la vie.
◇ *comp*: ~ allowance indemnité *f* de vie chère; ~ increase OR adjustment [in salary] augmentation *f* de salaire indexée sur le coût de la vie; ~ index indice *m* du coût de la vie.

cost-plus *adj*: on a ~ basis sur la base du prix de revient majoré.

cost price *n* prix *m* coûtant OR de revient; to buy/to sell sthg at ~ acheter/vendre qqch à prix coûtant.

costume ['kɒstjuːm] ◇ *n* -**1.** CIN, THEAT & TV costume *m (d'un acteur)*; to be (dressed) in ~ porter un costume (de scène); did you make your own ~? est-ce que vous avez fait votre costume vous-même?; I hate wearing ~ je déteste porter des costumes; ~s by... [in credits] costumes réalisés par... -**2.** [fancy dress] costume *m*, déguisement *m*; to be (dressed) in ~ être costumé OR déguisé; are you going to the party in ~? serez-vous déguisé à la soirée? -**3.** [traditional dress]: national ~ costume *m* national; to wear national ~ porter le costume national. -**4.** [for swimming]: (swimming OR bathing) ~ maillot *m* de bain. -**5.** *Br dated* [woman's suit] tailleur *m*.
◇ *comp*: ~ ball OR party bal *m* costumé; ~ designer costumier *m*, -ère *f*; ~ drama OR piece OR play pièce *f* en costumes d'époque.
◇ *vt* [film, play] réaliser les costumes pour.

costume jewellery *n (U)* bijoux *mpl* fantaisie; a piece of ~ un bijou fantaisie.

costumier [kɒ'stjuːmɪəʳ], **costumer** ['kɒstjuːməʳ] *n* costumier *m*, -ère *f*.

cosy *Br*, **cozy** *Am* ['kəʊzɪ] (*Br compar* cosier, *superl* cosiest, *Am compar* cozier, *superl* coziest) ◇ *adj* -**1.** [warm, snug - flat, room, atmosphere] douillet, confortable; it's nice and ~ in here on est bien ici; to be snug and ~ in one's bed être bien confortablement installé dans son lit; to look ~ avoir l'air bien confortable; to feel ~ se sentir bien à l'aise; she's a very ~ type of person c'est quelqu'un de très chaleureux; isn't this ~? on n'est pas bien ici? -**2.** [intimate - chat, evening etc] intime; [- novel] à l'atmosphère douce; they've got a very ~ relationship *pej* ils sont très copain-copain; a ~ deal *pej* une combine.
◇ *n* [for tea-pot] couvre-théière *m*; [for egg] couvre-œuf *m*.
◆ **cosy up to** *inf vt insep* se mettre dans les petits papiers de; he's always ~ing up to the boss il essaie tout le temps de se mettre dans les petits papiers du patron.

cot [kɒt] *n Br* [for baby] lit *m* d'enfant; *Am* [camp bed] lit *m* de camp.

cotangent [kəʊ'tændʒənt] *n* MATH cotangente *f*.

cot death *n Br* mort *f* subite du nourrisson; she lost her first child through ~ son premier enfant est mort de la mort subite du nourrisson.

cote [kəʊt] *n* [for doves] colombier *m*, pigeonnier *m*; [for sheep] abri *m*, bergerie *f*.

coterie ['kəʊtərɪ] *n* cercle *m*, cénacle *m*; *pej* coterie *f*, clique *f*.

coterminous [,kəʊ'tɜːmɪnəs] *adj fml* limitrophe, frontalier; France is ~ with Spain and Switzerland la France a des frontières communes avec l'Espagne et la Suisse.

cotill(i)on [kə'tɪljən] *n* cotillon *m*.

cottage ['kɒtɪdʒ] *n* -**1.** [in country] petite maison *f* (à la campagne), cottage *m*; thatched ~ chaumière *f*. -**2.** *Am* [holiday home] maison *f* de campagne. -**3.** ▽ *Br* toilettes *fpl* publiques *(servant aux rencontres des homosexuels)*.

cottage cheese *n* fromage *m* blanc (égoutté), cottage cheese *m*.

cottage hospital *n Br* petit hôpital *m* de campagne.

cottage industry *n* industrie *f* familiale OR artisanale.

cottage loaf *n Br miche de pain surmontée d'une miche plus petite*.

cottage pie *n Br* hachis *m* parmentier.

cottager ['kɒtɪdʒəʳ] *n Br* habitant *m*, -e *f* d'un cottage; *Am* propriétaire *mf*/locataire *mf* d'une maison de campagne.

cottaging▽ ['kɒtɪdʒɪŋ] *n (U) Br rencontres homosexuelles dans les toilettes publiques*.

cotter ['kɒtəʳ] *n* MECH [wedge] goupille *f*; ~ (pin) clavette *f*.

cotton ['kɒtn] ◇ *n* -**1.** [material, plant] coton *m*; to pick ~ cueillir le coton; put it with the rest of the ~s [garments made of cotton] mets-le avec le reste du (linge en) coton; is this dress ~? [made of cotton] cette robe est-elle en coton? ❑ absorbent ~ *Am* coton *m* hydrophile. -**2.** *Br* [thread for sewing] fil *m*.
◇ *comp* [garment] en coton; [industry, trade] du coton; [culture, field, grower, plantation] de coton; ~ picker [person] cueilleur *m*, -euse *f* de coton.
◆ **cotton on** *inf vi insep* piger; to ~ on to sthg piger qqch; one of the first companies to ~ on to the advantages of the system l'une des premières sociétés à piger les avantages du système.
◆ **cotton to** *inf vt insep Am* [like - person] être attiré par; [- idea, plan, suggestion] approuver; I didn't ~ to her at first ça n'a pas accroché avec elle au début; he didn't ~ to it much ça ne lui a pas tellement plu.

cotton batting *Am* = **cotton wool** *n*.

Cotton Belt *n* GEOG région *f* du coton aux États-Unis.

cotton candy *n Am* barbe *f* à papa.

cotton gin *n* égreneuse *f* de coton.

cotton mill *n* filature *f* de coton.

cotton-picking▽ *adj Am* sale, sacré.

cottonseed ['kɒtnsiːd] *n* graine *f* de coton; ~ oil huile *f* de coton.

cottontail ['kɒtnteɪl] *n* lapin *m* (de garenne).

cotton waste *n (U)* déchets *mpl* de coton.

cotton wool *Br* ◇ *n* coton *m* hydrophile, ouate *f*; my legs feel like ~ *inf* j'ai les jambes en coton; to wrap sb in ~ être aux petits soins pour qqn; to bring a child up in ~ élever un enfant dans du coton.
◇ *comp*: ~ balls boules *fpl* de coton; ~ pads rondelles *fpl* de coton OR d'ouate; ~ clouds *fig* nuages *mpl* cotonneux.

cotyledon [,kɒtɪ'liːdən] *n* BOT cotylédon *m*.

couch [kaʊtʃ] ◇ *n* [sofa] canapé *m*, divan *m*, sofa *m*; [in psychiatrist's office] divan *m*; to be on the ~ *inf* faire une psychanalyse, voir un psy.
◇ *vt* formuler; to be ~ed in very polite terms/in jargon [letter, document] être formulé en termes très polis/en jargon.

couchette [kuː'ʃet] *n* RAIL couchette *f*.

couch grass *n* BOT chiendent *m*.

couch potato *inf n pej*: he's a ~ il passe son temps affalé devant la télé.

cougar ['kuːgəʳ] *n* couguar *m*, cougouar *m*, puma *m*.

cough [kɒf] ◇ *n* toux *f*; her ~ doesn't seem to be getting any better sa toux n'a pas l'air de s'arranger, elle tousse toujours autant; you want to get that ~ seen to avec cette toux, tu devrais te faire examiner; I can't get rid of this ~ cette toux ne me passe pas; can you do something for this ~, doctor? pouvez-vous faire quelque chose pour soigner ma toux, docteur?; that's a nasty ~ (you've got) tu as une mauvaise toux; to have a ~ tousser; she gave a loud ~ elle a toussé fort; to give a warning ~ tousser OR toussoter en guise d'avertissement; she gave me a warning ~ that they were coming elle a toussé OR toussoté pour m'avertir qu'ils arrivaient; he cleared his throat with a loud ~ il s'est éclairci la voix en toussant bruyamment; there's a ~ in the engine *fig* le moteur tousse, le moteur a des ratés; smoker's ~ toux de fumeur; whooping ~ coqueluche *f*.
◇ *comp* [medicine, sweets] pour OR contre la toux, antitussif *spec*.
◇ *vi* tousser; the engine ~ed into life *fig* le moteur a toussé puis s'est mis en marche.
◇ *vt* [blood] cracher; the old car ~ed its way down the street *fig* la vieille voiture a descendu la rue en faisant des ratés.
◆ **cough out** *vt sep* -**1.** cracher (en toussant); you sound as if you're ~ing your insides out on dirait que tu es en train de cracher tes poumons. -**2.** [words] dire en toussant.
◆ **cough up** ◇ *vt sep* -**1.** [blood] cracher (en toussant). -**2.** *inf* [money] cracher, raquer; ~ up what you owe me crache ce que tu me dois.
◇ *vi insep inf* [pay up] banquer, raquer; come on then, ~ up! allez, banque!

cough drop *n* pastille *f* contre la toux OR antitussive.

coughing ['kɒfɪŋ] *n* toux *f*; I can't stand his ~ je ne supporte pas de l'entendre tousser; your ~ woke me up tu m'as réveillé en toussant; fit of ~, ~ fit quinte *f* de toux.

cough mixture *n* sirop *m* antitussif OR contre la toux.

cough sweet = **cough drop**.

cough syrup = **cough mixture**.

could [kʊd] *modal vb* -**1.** [be able to]: I'd come if I ~ je viendrais si je (le) pouvais; she ~ no longer walk elle ne pouvait plus marcher; they ~n't very well refuse il leur aurait été difficile de refuser; five years ago I ~ run a mile in four minutes but I ~n't anymore il y a cinq ans, je courais un mile en quatre minutes mais je ne pourrais plus maintenant; she ~ have had the job if she'd wanted it elle aurait pu obtenir cet emploi si elle l'avait voulu. -**2.** [with verbs of perception or understanding]: he ~ see her talking to her boss il la voyait qui parlait avec son patron; I ~ see his point of view je comprenais son point de vue. -**3.** [indicating ability or skill]: she ~ read and write elle savait lire et écrire; she ~ speak three languages elle parlait trois langues. -**4.** [in polite requests]: ~ I borrow your sweater? est-ce que je pourrais t'emprunter ton pull?; ~ I join you? est-ce que je pourrais me joindre à vous?; ~n't I come too? est-ce que je ne pourrais pas venir moi aussi?; ~ you help me please? pourriez-vous OR est-ce que vous pourriez m'aider, s'il vous plaît?; ~ you bring the bill, please? pourriez-vous apporter l'addition, s'il vous plaît? -**5.** [indicating supposition or speculation]: they ~ give up at any time ils pourraient abandonner n'importe quand; ~ he be lying? se pourrait-il qu'il mente?; the stock market ~ crash tomorrow le marché pourrait s'effondrer demain; you ~ well be right tu pourrais bien avoir raison; don't touch it, it ~ be dangerous n'y touchez pas, ça pourrait être dangereux; they ~ have changed their plans ils ont peut-être changé leurs plans || [indicating possibility]: you ~ have told me the truth tu aurais pu me dire la vérité; they ~ easily have got here earlier ils auraient facilement pu arriver ici plus tôt; you ~ have warned me! tu aurais pu me prévenir!; what ~ I have done with the keys? qu'est-ce que j'ai bien pu faire des clés?; I ~ kill him! je pourrais le tuer!; he ~ have jumped for joy il en aurait presque sauté de joie ❑ I'm as happy as ~ be je suis on ne peut plus heureux; she was as kind as ~ be elle était on ne peut plus gentille. -**6.** [indicating unwillingness]: I ~n't just leave him there, could I? je ne pouvais vraiment pas le laisser là; I ~n't possibly do it before tomorrow je ne pourrai vraiment pas le faire avant demain. -**7.** [in polite suggestions]: you ~ always complain to the director tu pourrais toujours te plaindre au directeur; ~n't you just apologize? tu ne pourrais pas présenter tes excuses au moins?; ~n't we at least talk about it? est-ce que nous ne pourrions pas au moins en discuter? -**8.** [introducing comments or opinions]: if I ~ just intervene here est-ce que je peux me permettre d'intervenir ici?; you ~

argue it's a waste of resources tu pourrais argumenter que c'est un gaspillage de ressources. -**9.** [indicating surprise or disbelief]: the house ~n't have been THAT expensive la maison n'a pas dû coûter si cher que ça; how ~ she have done such a thing? comment a-t-elle pu faire une chose pareille?; how ~ you say that? comment avez-vous pu dire ça OR une chose pareille?; who on earth ~ that be? qui diable cela peut-il bien être? -**10.** [inviting agreement]: he left and you ~n't blame him il est parti et on ne peut pas lui en vouloir.

couldn't ['kʊdnt] = **could not**.

couldn't-care-less *inf adj* [attitude] je-m'en-foutiste.

couldst [kʊdst] *arch 2nd pers sing* → **could**.

coulee ['kuːlɪ] *n Am* ravin *m*.

couloir ['kuːlwɑːʳ] *n* [in climbing] couloir *m*.

coulomb ['kuːlɒm] *n* coulomb *m*.

council ['kaʊnsl] ◇ *n* -**1.** [group of people] conseil *m*; the UN Security Council le Conseil de sécurité des Nations unies. -**2.** *Br* [elected local body] conseil *m*; she's standing for election to the ~ elle se présente aux élections du conseil; to be on the ~ être au conseil; the ~ are improving services le conseil est en train d'améliorer les services ❑ city OR town OR *Scot* district ~ conseil *m* municipal, municipalité *f*; county OR *Scot* regional ~ conseil *m* régional. -**3.** [meeting] conseil *m*; to hold a ~ of war tenir un conseil de guerre.

◇ *comp* -**1.** [meeting] du conseil. -**2.** *Br* [election, service, worker] municipal; [leader, meeting] du conseil municipal; ~ estate cité *f*; to live on a ~ estate habiter dans une cité; ~ flat/house ≃ habitation *f* à loyer modéré, ≃ HLM *f or m*; ~ housing ≃ habitations *fpl* à loyer modéré, ≃ HLM *fpl or mpl*; ~ tenants *locataires d'un appartement ou d'une maison appartenant à la municipalité*.

councillor *Br*, **councilor** *Am* ['kaʊnsələʳ] *n* conseiller *m*, -ère *f*; Councillor (John) Murray Monsieur le Conseiller Murray; town/county ~ conseiller municipal/régional.

councilman ['kaʊnslmæn] (*pl* councilmen [-men]) *n Am* conseiller *m*.

councilor *Am* = **councillor**.

council tax *n (U)* impôts *mpl* locaux *(en Grande-Bretagne)*.

councilwoman ['kaʊnslˌwʊmən] (*pl* councilwomen [-ˌwɪmɪn]) *n Am* conseillère *f*.

counsel ['kaʊnsəl] (*Br pt & pp* counselled, *cont* counselling, *Am pt & pp* counseled, *cont* counseling) ◇ *n* -**1.** *fml* [advice] conseil *m*; to take ~ with sb about sthg prendre conseil auprès de qqn sur qqch; to take ~ (together) tenir conseil; to keep one's own ~ garder ses opinions OR intentions pour soi. -**2.** JUR avocat *m*, -e *f*; ~ for the defence/prosecution avocat de la défense/du ministère public; to seek the advice of ~ se faire conseiller par un avocat; both parties contacted their ~ les deux parties ont contacté leurs avocats; if ~ would approach the bench si vous voulez bien vous approcher, maître ❑ King's ~, Queen's ~ *Br membre supérieur du barreau*.

◇ *vt* -**1.** *fml* conseiller; to ~ sb to do sthg conseiller à qqn de faire qqch; to ~ caution recommander la prudence. -**2.** [in therapy] conseiller.

counselling *Br*, **counseling** *Am* ['kaʊnsəlɪŋ] *n* [psychological] assistance *f*, conseils *mpl*; you need ~ tu as besoin d'assistance OR de conseils; to seek ~ se faire conseiller, prendre conseil; she does ~ at the university elle est conseillère auprès des étudiants à l'université.

counsellor *Br*, **counselor** *Am* ['kaʊnsələʳ] *n* -**1.** [in therapy] conseiller *m*, -ère *f*; marriage guidance ~ conseiller *m* conjugal, conseillère *f* conjugale. -**2.** *Am* JUR avocat *m*, -e *f*; that's enough, ~! cela suffit, maître!

count [kaʊnt] ◇ *n* -**1.** compte *m*; [of ballot papers] décompte *m*; to have a ~ faire le compte, compter; it took three/several ~s il a fallu faire trois/plusieurs fois le compte, il a fallu compter trois/plusieurs fois; to have a second ~ refaire le compte, recompter; to lose ~ perdre le compte; I've lost ~ of the number of times he's been late je ne compte plus le nombre de fois où il est arrivé en retard; to keep ~ (of sthg) tenir le compte (de qqch); I have a job keeping ~ of all your boyfriends j'ai du mal à tenir le compte de tous tes petits amis; at the last ~ [gen] la dernière fois qu'on a compté; ADMIN [of people] au dernier recensement; on the ~ of three, begin à trois, vous commencez. -**2.** [in boxing]: he took a ~ of nine il est resté à terre jusqu'à neuf; to take the ~ être mis K-O ❑ to be out for the ~ [boxer, person in brawl] être K-O; [fast asleep] dormir comme une souche. -**3.** JUR chef *m* d'accusation; guilty on three ~s of murder coupable de meurtre sur trois chefs d'accusation; the judge found him guilty on the first ~, but cleared him of the second le juge l'a déclaré coupable sur le OR quant au premier chef, mais l'a acquitté pour le second ‖ *fig*: the argument is flawed on both ~s l'argumentation est défectueuse sur les deux points; I'm annoyed with you on a number of ~s je suis fâché contre toi pour un certain nombre de raisons OR à plus d'un titre. -**4.** MED taux *m*; blood (cell) ~ numération *f* globulaire. -**5.** [nobleman] comte *m*; 'The Count of Monte Cristo' *Dumas* 'le Comte de Monte-Cristo'.

◇ *vt* -**1.** [add up - gen] compter; [- votes] compter, décompter; I ~ed ten people in the room j'ai compté dix personnes dans la pièce ❑ to ~ sheep *fig* [when sleepless] compter les moutons; to ~ the pennies faire attention à ses sous; you can ~ his good points on the fingers of one hand ses qualités se comptent sur les doigts de la main; they can be ~ed on the fingers of one hand on peut les compter sur les doigts de la main; ~ your blessings pense à tout ce que tu as pour être heureux; ~ your blessings that there was someone around tu peux t'estimer heureux qu'il y ait eu quelqu'un dans les parages; don't ~ your chickens (before they're hatched) *prov* il ne faut pas vendre la peau de l'ours (avant de l'avoir tué) *prov*. -**2.** [include] compter; have you ~ed yourself? est-ce que tu t'es compté?; ~ing Alan, there were ten of us en comptant Alan, nous étions dix; not ~ing public holidays sans compter les jours fériés. -**3.** [consider] considérer, estimer; to ~ sb among one's friends compter qqn parmi ses amis; do you ~ her as a friend? la considères-tu comme une amie?; student grants are not ~ed as taxable income les bourses d'études ne sont pas considérées comme revenu imposable; ~ yourself lucky (that...) estime-toi heureux (que...); I ~ myself as very lucky je considère OR j'estime que j'ai beaucoup de chance; I ~ myself happy je m'estime heureux; to be ~ed a success [person] être considéré comme quelqu'un qui a réussi; [project] être considéré comme un succès.

◇ *vi* -**1.** [add up] compter; to learn to ~ apprendre à compter; to ~ to twenty/fifty/a hundred compter jusqu'à vingt/cinquante/cent; to ~ on one's fingers compter sur ses doigts; ~ing from tomorrow à partir de demain. -**2.** [be considered, qualify] compter; two children ~ as one adult deux enfants comptent pour un adulte; anyone over 14 ~s as an adult toutes les personnes âgées de plus de 14 ans comptent pour des adultes; unemployment benefit ~s as taxable income les allocations (de) chômage comptent comme revenu imposable; this exam ~s towards the final mark cet examen compte dans la note finale; that/he doesn't ~ ça/il ne compte pas; she ~s among my very best friends elle compte parmi mes meilleurs amis; his reputation ~ed in his favour sa réputation a pesé en sa faveur; his record ~ed against him son casier judiciaire l'a desservi. -**3.** [be important] compter; every second/minute ~s chaque seconde/minute compte; experience ~s more than qualifications l'expérience compte davantage que les diplômes; he ~s for nothing il n'est pas important, il ne compte pas; a private education doesn't ~ for much now avoir reçu une éducation privée n'est plus un grand avantage de nos jours; what ~s around here is enthusiasm ce qui compte ici c'est l'enthousiasme; he's the one who ~s around here c'est lui qui décide ici.

◆ **count down** *vi insep* ASTRONAUT faire le compte à rebours.

◆ **count in** *vt sep* [include] compter, inclure; to ~ sb in on sthg inclure OR compter qqn dans qqch; will we ~ you in for the weekend or not? on te compte pour le week-end ou pas?; ~ me in compte sur moi, je suis partant; don't ~ me in ne compte pas sur moi.

◆ **count off** *vt sep Am* compter.

◆ **count on** *vt insep* -**1.** [rely on] compter sur; we're ~ing on you nous comptons sur toi; I wouldn't ~ on him turning up, if I were you si j'étais vous, je ne m'attendrais pas à ce qu'il vienne; you can ~ on it/me vous pouvez compter dessus/sur moi; I wouldn't ~ on it je n'y compterais pas. -**2.** [expect] compter; I wasn't ~ing on getting here so early je ne comptais pas arriver si tôt; I wasn't ~ing on my husband being here je ne comptais OR pensais pas que mon mari serait ici.

◆ **count out** *vt sep* -**1.** [money, objects] compter. -**2.** [exclude]: (you can) ~ me out ne compte surtout pas sur moi. -**3.** [in boxing]: to be ~ed out être déclaré K-O.

◆ **count up** ◇ *vt sep* compter, additionner; when you ~ it all up *fig* en fin de compte.

◇ *vi insep* compter, additionner.

◆ **count upon** *vt insep* = **count on**.

countability [ˌkaʊntə'bɪlətɪ] *n* GRAMM aspect *m* comptable.

countable ['kaʊntəbl] *adj* GRAMM [noun] comptable.

countdown ['kaʊntdaʊn] *n* ASTRONAUT compte *m* à rebours; the ~ to the wedding/Christmas has begun *fig* la date du mariage/de Noël se rapproche.

countenance ['kaʊntənəns] ◇ *n* -**1.** *fml* OR *lit* [face] visage *m*; [facial expression] expression *f*, mine *f*; to keep one's ~ faire bonne contenance; to lose ~ [subj: person] perdre contenance; [government] perdre la face. -**2.** *fml* [support, approval]: to give OR to lend ~ to sthg approuver qqch.

◇ *vt fml* [support, approve of - terrorism, violence, lying] approuver; [- idea, proposal] approuver, accepter; the government will never ~ (doing) a deal with the terrorists le gouvernement n'approuvera OR n'acceptera jamais l'idée d'un marché avec les terroristes.

counter ['kaʊntəʳ] ◇ *n* -**1.** [in shop] comptoir *m*; ask at the ~ [in bank, post office] demandez au guichet ❑ it's available over the ~ [medication] on peut l'acheter sans ordonnance; to sell sthg under the ~ *inf Br* vendre qqch en douce OR sous le manteau. -**2.** [device] compteur *m*; set the ~ to zero mettre OR remettre le compteur à zéro. -**3.** [in board game] jeton *m*; bargaining ~ *Br fig* monnaie *f* d'échange; to use sthg as a bargaining ~ in negotiations utiliser qqch comme monnaie d'échange dans des négociations.

◇ *comp*: ~ staff [in bank, post office] employés *mpl* du guichet, guichetiers *mpl*.

◇ *vt* [respond to - increase in crime, proposal] contrecarrer; [- accusation, criticism] contrer; in order to ~ the threat from the enemy tanks pour contrer la menace que constituent les tanks ennemis; he ~ed that the project... il a contré OR riposté en disant que le projet...

◇ *vi* [in boxing] contrer; then he ~ed with his left puis il a contré du gauche OR fait un contre du gauche; she ~ed with a suggestion that/by asking whether... elle a riposté en suggérant que/en demandant si...

◇ *adv*: to go OR to run ~ to sthg aller à

l'encontre de qqch; to act ~ to sb's advice/wishes agir à l'encontre des conseils/des souhaits de qqn.

counteract [,kaʊntə'rækt] *vt* [person] contrebalancer l'influence de; [influence] contrebalancer; [effects of drug, taste of sthg] neutraliser; [rising crime] lutter contre.

counterattack [ˌkaʊntərə'tæk] MIL & SPORT ◇ *n* contre-attaque *f*, contre-offensive *f*; *fig* [in business, election etc] contre-offensive *f*.
◇ *vi* contre-attaquer; *fig* riposter, contrer; the company ~ed with claims that... la compagnie a riposté OR contré en affirmant que...

counterattraction [ˌkaʊntərə'trækʃn] *n* spectacle *m* rival; TV is a ~ to live theatre la télévision fait de la concurrence au théâtre.

counterbalance [,kaʊntə'bæləns] ◇ *n* contrepoids *m*.
◇ *vt* contrebalancer, faire contrepoids à; *fig* contrebalancer, compenser.

counterblast *inf* ['kaʊntəblɑːst] *n* riposte *f*.

countercharge ['kaʊntətʃɑːdʒ] ◇ *n* JUR contre-accusation *f*.
◇ *vi* faire une contre-accusation.
◇ *vt*: to ~ that... émettre la contre-accusation que...

counterclaim ['kaʊntəkleɪm] *n* JUR demande *f* reconventionnelle.

counterclaimant ['kaʊntəkleɪmənt] *n* JUR demandeur *m* reconventionnel, demanderesse *f* reconventionnelle.

counterclockwise [,kaʊntə'klɒkwaɪz] *adj & adv Am* dans le sens inverse OR contraire des aiguilles d'une montre.

counterespionage [ˌkaʊntər'espɪənɑːʒ] *n* contre-espionnage *m*.

counterfeit ['kaʊntəfɪt] ◇ *n* [banknote, passport, document] faux *m*, contrefaçon *f*; [piece of jewellery] faux *m*.
◇ *adj* [banknote, passport, document] faux; [piece of jewellery] contrefait; *fig* [sympathy, affection] feint.
◇ *vt* [banknote, passport, document, piece of jewellery] contrefaire; *fig* [sympathy, affection] feindre.
◇ *vi*: he's been ~ing for years ça fait des années qu'il est faussaire.

counterfeiter ['kaʊntəfɪtə^r] *n* [of banknote] faux-monnayeur *m*; [of passport, document, jewellery] faussaire *m*.

counterfoil ['kaʊntəfɔɪl] *n Br* [of cheque, ticket] talon *m*.

counterinsurgency [ˌkaʊntərɪn'sɜːdʒənsɪ] ◇ *n* contre-insurrection *f*.
◇ *adj* [activities, tactics etc] de contre-insurrection.

counterintelligence [ˌkaʊntərɪn'telɪdʒəns] *n* contre-espionnage *m*; [information] renseignements *mpl* (provenant du contre-espionnage).

counterirritant [,kaʊntər'ɪrɪtənt] *n* MED révulsif *m*.

counterman ['kaʊntəmæn] (*pl* countermen [-men]) *n Am* barman *m*.

countermand [,kaʊntə'mɑːnd] *vt* [order] annuler.

countermeasure [,kaʊntə'meʒə^r] *n* contre-mesure *f*.

countermove ['kaʊntəmuːv] *n* contre-mesure *f*; in a ~ en guise de contre-mesure.

counteroffensive [,kaʊntərə'fensɪv] *n* MIL contre-offensive *f*.

counteroffer [,kaʊntər'ɒfə^r] *n* offre *f*; [higher] surenchère *f*; I'm waiting for a ~ from the other party j'attends l'offre de l'autre partie.

counterpane ['kaʊntəpeɪn] *n Br* dessus-de-lit *m inv*, couvre-lit *m*.

counterpart ['kaʊntəpɑːt] *n* homologue *mf*; [thing] équivalent *m*.

counterpoint ['kaʊntəpɔɪnt] *n* MUS contrepoint *m*.

counterpoise ['kaʊntəpɔɪz] ◇ *n* contrepoids *m*; to be in ~ *fig* être en équilibre.
◇ *vt* = **counterbalance**.

counterproductive [,kaʊntəprə'dʌktɪv] *adj* qui va à l'encontre du but recherché, qui a des effets contraires, contre-productif.

Counter-Reformation *n* HIST contre-réforme *f*.

counter-revolution *n* contre-révolution *f*.

counter-revolutionary ◇ *n* contre-révolutionnaire *mf*.
◇ *adj* contre-révolutionnaire.

countersign ['kaʊntəsaɪn] *vt* contresigner.

countersink ['kaʊntəsɪŋk] (*pt* countersank [-sæŋk], *pp* countersunk [-sʌŋk]) *vt* [screw] noyer; [hole] fraiser.

countertenor [,kaʊntə'tenə^r] *n* MUS [singer] haute-contre *m*; [voice] haute-contre *f*.

countervailing ['kaʊntəveɪlɪŋ] *adj* compensatoire, compensateur.

counterweight ['kaʊntəweɪt] *n* contrepoids *m*.

countess ['kaʊntɪs] *n* comtesse *f*.

counting ['kaʊntɪŋ] *n* calcul *m*.

counting house *n arch* salle *f* du trésor.

countless ['kaʊntlɪs] *adj* [deaths, reasons] innombrable; [difficulties, opportunities, problems] innombrable, sans nombre; ~ letters/people un nombre incalculable de lettres/personnes; I've told you ~ times not to do that je t'ai répété des centaines de fois de ne pas faire ça.

count noun *n* GRAMM nom *m* comptable.

countrified ['kʌntrɪfaɪd] *adj* -**1**. *pej* campagnard, provincial. -**2**. [rural] : it's quite ~ round here c'est vraiment la campagne ici.

country ['kʌntrɪ] (*pl* countries) ◇ *n* -**1**. [land, nation] pays *m*; [homeland] patrie *f*; the ~ is in mourning le pays est en deuil; I have the support of the ~ tout le pays me soutient; to fight/to die for one's ~ se battre/mourir pour sa patrie; to love one's ~ aimer son pays OR sa patrie; in my ~ dans mon pays, chez moi; my ~ right or wrong *expression typique du patriotisme forcené* ❑ to go to the ~ *Br* appeler le pays aux urnes. -**2**. [as opposed to the city] campagne *f*; to live in the ~ vivre à la campagne; to spend a day in the ~ passer une journée à la campagne; to travel across ~ [in car, on bike] prendre OR emprunter les petites routes (de campagne); [on foot] aller à travers champs. -**3**. [area of land, region] région *f*; the ~ around Gloucester la région autour de Gloucester; we passed through some beautiful ~ nous avons traversé de beaux paysages; this is good farming ~ c'est une bonne région agricole; Wordsworth/Constable ~ le pays de Wordsworth/Constable; this is bear ~ il y a beaucoup d'ours par ici ❑ it's not my line of ~ *Br* ce n'est pas mon domaine. -**4**. MUS = **country and western**.
◇ *comp* [house, road, town, bus] de campagne; [people] de la campagne; [life] à la campagne; ~ boy gars *m* de la campagne; 'The Country Wife' *Wycherly* 'la Provinciale'.

country and western MUS ◇ *n* musique *f* country.
◇ *comp* [band, music, singer] country; [fan] de country.

country bumpkin *inf n pej* péquenaud *m*, -e *f*, plouc *mf*; I felt like a ~ j'ai eu l'impression de débarquer de ma campagne.

country club *n club sportif ou de loisirs situé à la campagne*.

country code *n*: the ~ le code rural.

country cousin *n pej* cousin *m*, -e *f* de province.

country dance *n* danse *f* folklorique.

country dancing *n* danse *f* folklorique; to go ~ aller danser des danses folkloriques.

country-dweller *n* campagnard *m*, -e *f*, habitant *m*, -e *f* de la campagne.

country house *n grande maison de campagne, souvent historique*.

countryman ['kʌntrɪmən] (*pl* countrymen [-mən]) *n* -**1**. [who lives in the country] campagnard *m*, habitant *m* de la campagne. -**2**. [compatriot] compatriote *m*.

country seat *n* [of noble family] manoir *m*.

countryside ['kʌntrɪsaɪd] *n* campagne *f*; [scenery] paysage *m*; in the ~ à la campagne; there is some magnificent ~ around here il y a des paysages magnifiques par ici.

Countryside Commission *n*: the ~ *organisme britannique indépendant chargé de la protection du milieu rural et de la gestion des parcs nationaux*.

countrywoman ['kʌntrɪ,wʊmən] (*pl* countrywomen [-,wɪmɪn]) *n* -**1**. [who lives in the country] campagnarde *f*, habitante *f* de la campagne. -**2**. [compatriot] compatriote *f*.

county ['kaʊntɪ] (*pl* counties) ◇ *n* comté *m*.
◇ *comp* [councillor, boundary] de comté; ~ cricket *Br grands matchs de cricket disputés par les équipes du comté*.
◇ *adj Br pej*: she's very ~ elle est de la haute; the horse sale was full of ~ types le marché aux chevaux grouillait de petits hobereaux.

county council *n Br* ≃ conseil *m* général.

county court *n* [in England] tribunal *m* d'instance.

County Hall *n Br* hôtel *m* du comté, siège *m* du conseil de comté.

county seat *n* [in US] chef-lieu *m* de comté.

county town *n* [in England] chef-lieu *m* de comté.

coup [kuː] *n* -**1**. [feat] (beau) coup *m*; to pull off a ~ réussir un beau coup. -**2**. [overthrow of government] coup *m* d'État.

coupé ['kuːpeɪ] *n* AUT coupé *m*.

couple ['kʌpl] ◇ *n* -**1**. [pair] couple *m*; an engaged ~ un couple de fiancés; they make a lovely ~ ils forment un beau couple; the happy ~ les jeunes mariés; the ~s on the dance floor les couples sur la piste de danse; everyone came in ~s tout le monde est venu en couple; I'm not going if it's all ~s je n'y vais pas s'il n'y a que des couples; they go everywhere as a ~ ils vont partout ensemble OR en couple. -**2**. *phr*: a ~ [a few] quelques-uns, quelques-unes; were there many mistakes? – only a ~ est-ce qu'il y avait beaucoup de fautes? – seulement quelques-unes; a ~ of [a few] quelques; [two] deux; a ~ of drinks un verre ou deux, quelques verres; he's a ~ years older *Am* il a deux ou trois ans de plus.
◇ *vi* [animals, birds, humans] s'accoupler.
◇ *vt* -**1**. [horse] atteler; RAIL atteler, accrocher. -**2**. *fig* [studies] associer, suivre en parallèle; the name of Freud is ~d with that of Vienna le nom de Freud est associé à Vienne; she ~d her announcement with a plea for increased funding elle a profité de son annonce pour demander davantage de fonds; her name has been ~d with his [romantically] son nom a été uni au sien; ~d with [accompanied by] associé à; ~d with that,... en plus de cela,..., venant s'ajouter à cela,...

couplet ['kʌplɪt] *n* distique *m*.

coupling ['kʌplɪŋ] *n* -**1**. [mating - of animals, birds, humans] accouplement *m*. -**2**. [connecting device] accouplement *m*; RAIL attelage *m*.

coupon ['kuːpɒn] *n* [voucher, form] coupon *m*; football ~ *Br* ≃ grille *f* de Loto sportif; (money-off) ~ coupon de réduction.

courage ['kʌrɪdʒ] *n* courage *m*; to have the ~ to do sthg avoir le courage de faire qqch; he has to be told – I know, but I don't have the ~ il faut le lui dire – je (le) sais, mais je n'en ai pas le courage; a woman of great ~ une femme d'un grand courage, une femme très courageuse; people with ~ des gens courageux; to take one's ~ in both hands prendre son courage à deux mains; to take ~ from the fact that... être encouragé par le fait que...; to have the ~ of one's convictions avoir le courage de ses opinions.

courageous [kə'reɪdʒəs] *adj* courageux.

courageously [kə'reɪdʒəslɪ] *adv* courageusement.

courgette [kuː'ʒet] *n Br* courgette *f*.

courier ['kʊrɪəʳ] *n* -**1.** [messenger] courrier *m*, messager *m*; [company] messagerie *f*; **to send sthg by ~** envoyer qqch par courrier. -**2.** [on journey] accompagnateur *m*, -trice *f*.

course [kɔːs] ◇ *n* -**1.** [path, route - of ship, plane] route *f*; [- of river] cours *m*; **what is our ~?** quelle est notre route?; **to change ~** [ship, plane, company] changer de cap OR de direction; *fig* [argument, discussion] changer de direction, dévier; **to be on ~** [ship, plane] suivre le cap fixé; **to be off ~** [ship, plane] dévier de son cap; **you're a long way off ~** [walking, driving] vous n'êtes pas du tout dans la bonne direction OR sur la bonne route; [with project, workflow] vous êtes en mauvaise voie; **to be on ~** *fig* être en bonne voie; **the company is on ~ to achieve a record profit** *fig* la société est bien partie pour atteindre des bénéfices record; **to set a ~ for Marseilles** [ship, plane] mettre le cap sur Marseille. -**2.** *fig* [approach]: **~ (of action)** ligne *f* (de conduite); **what is the recommended ~ of action in such cases?** quelle est la ligne de conduite conseillée dans de tels cas?; **what other ~ is open to us?** quelle autre solution avons-nous?; **your best ~ of action is to sue** la meilleure chose que vous ayez à faire est d'intenter un procès. -**3.** [development, progress - of history, war] cours *m*; **the law must take its ~** la loi doit suivre son cours; **the illness takes** OR **runs its ~** la maladie suit son cours ☐ **in the ~ of time** finalement; **you will forget him in the ~ of time** tu finiras par l'oublier; **in the normal** OR **ordinary ~ of events** normalement, en temps normal; **a building in ~ of construction/demolition** un bâtiment en cours de construction/démolition. -**4.** SCH & UNIV enseignement *m*, cours *mpl*; **a geography/music ~** un enseignement OR des cours de géographie/musique; **it's a five-year ~** c'est un enseignement sur cinq ans; **we offer ~s in a number of subjects** nous offrons OR proposons des enseignements OR des cours dans plusieurs domaines; **I'm taking** OR **doing a computer ~** je suis des cours OR un stage d'informatique; **what are the other people on the ~ like?** comment sont les autres personnes qui suivent les cours? -**5.** MED: **a ~ of injections** une série de piqûres; **a ~ of pills** un traitement à base de comprimés; **~ of treatment** [for an illness] traitement *m*. -**6.** [in meal] plat *m*; **first ~** entrée *f*; **main ~** plat *m* de résistance; **there's a cheese ~ as well** il y a aussi du fromage. -**7.** [for golf] terrain *m*; [for horse-racing] champ *m* de courses; **to stay** OR **to stick the ~** tenir le coup. -**8.** [of bricks] assise *f*.
◇ *vi* -**1.** [flow]: **tears ~d down my cheeks** les larmes ruisselaient sur mes joues; **I could feel the blood coursing through my veins** je sentais le sang bouillonner dans mes veines. -**2.** [hunt rabbits, hares] chasser le lièvre.
◆ **in the course of** *prep phr* au cours de; **in the ~ of the next few weeks** dans le courant des semaines qui viennent.
◆ **of course** *adv phr* bien sûr; **of ~ I believe you/she loves you** bien sûr que je te crois/qu'elle t'aime; **no-one believed me, of ~** évidemment OR bien sûr, personne ne m'a cru; **I don't matter, of ~** *iron* évidemment OR naturellement, moi, je ne compte pas; **I'll keep you informed of ~** il va de soi que je vous tiendrai au courant; **may I use your phone? – of ~!** puis-je utiliser votre téléphone? – mais bien sûr!; **was there much damage? – of ~!** y a-t-il eu beaucoup de dégâts? – tu parles!; **of ~ not!** bien sûr que non!

-course *in cpds*: **a three/five~ meal** un repas comprenant trois/cinq plats; **she served a four~ dinner** elle a servi quatre plats au dîner.

'course *inf interj* = **of course**.

coursebook ['kɔːsbʊk] *n* livre *m* de classe.

coursework ['kɔːswɜːk] *n* travail *m* de l'année *(qui permet d'exercer le contrôle continu)*.

coursing ['kɔːsɪŋ] *n* chasse *f* à courre au lièvre.

court [kɔːt] ◇ *n* -**1.** JUR [institution] cour *f*, tribunal *m*; [court room, people in room] cour *f*; **the ~ rose** la cour s'est levée; **silence in ~!** silence dans la salle!; **to clear the ~** évacuer la salle; **to appear in ~** [accused, witness] comparaître au tribunal; **this is the third time you have come before this ~** c'est la troisième fois que vous comparaissez devant ce tribunal; **to take sb to ~** poursuivre qqn en justice, intenter un procès contre qqn; **to go to ~** faire appel à la justice, aller en justice; **to go to ~ over sthg** faire appel à la justice pour régler qqch; **I'll see you in ~ then!** alors nous réglerons cela au tribunal!; **to settle sthg out of ~** régler qqch à l'amiable; **it won't stand up in ~** OR **in a ~ of law** cela n'aura aucun poids au tribunal; **to put** OR **to rule sthg out of ~** *fig* exclure qqch. -**2.** [of monarch - people] cour *f*; [- building] palais *m*; **to be presented at ~** *Br* être introduit à la cour; **to hold ~** *fig* avoir une cour d'adorateurs. -**3.** SPORT [tennis, badminton] court *m*, terrain *m*; [squash] salle *f*; **they'll be coming on ~ soon** ils vont bientôt entrer sur le court OR terrain; **on ~ and off, on and off ~** sur le court et dans la vie. -**4.** [courtyard] cour *f*.
◇ *comp* -**1.** JUR: **~ reporter** chroniqueur *m* judiciaire; **~ usher** huissier *m* de justice. -**2.** [royal]: **~ jester** bouffon *m* de cour; **it is said in ~ circles that...** on dit à la cour que...
◇ *vt* -**1.** *literal* & *dated* faire la cour à, courtiser. -**2.** *fig* [voters] courtiser, chercher à séduire; **she's ~ing the director** elle essaie de gagner la faveur du metteur en scène; **to ~ popularity** chercher à se rendre populaire; **to ~ sb's approval/support** chercher à gagner l'approbation/le soutien de qqn; **to ~ danger/disaster** aller au devant du danger/désastre; **I told him he was ~ing arrest** je lui ai dit qu'il risquait de se faire arrêter.
◇ *vi dated* [one person] fréquenter; [two people] se fréquenter.

court-bouillon [ˌkɔːt'buːjɒn] *n* CULIN court-bouillon *m*.

court card *n Br* figure *f*.

court case *n* procès *m*, affaire *f*; **the whole ~ was seen on TV** le procès a été retransmis à la télévision dans son intégralité.

court circular *n rubrique d'un journal indiquant les engagements officiels de la famille royale*.

Courtelle® [kɔː'tel] *n* Courtelle® *m*.

courteous ['kɜːtjəs] *adj* [person, gesture, treatment] courtois.

courteously ['kɜːtjəslɪ] *adv* [speak, reply etc] avec courtoisie, courtoisement.

courtesan [ˌkɔːtɪ'zæn] *n* courtisane *f*.

courtesy ['kɜːtɪsɪ] (*pl* **courtesies**) ◇ *n* -**1.** [politeness] courtoisie *f*; **at least have the ~ to apologize** aie au moins la courtoisie de t'excuser; **it would only have been common ~ to apologize** la moindre des courtoisies OR politesses aurait été de s'excuser; **common ~ dictates that you should thank her** la moindre des courtoisies OR des politesses serait que tu la remercies; **do her the ~ of hearing what she has to say** aie l'obligeance d'écouter ce qu'elle a à dire. -**2.** [polite action, remark] politesse *f*; **after a brief exchange of courtesies** après un bref échange de politesses; **to show sb every ~** faire montre d'une extrême courtoisie envers qqn.
◇ *comp* [call, visit] de politesse; **to pay a ~ call on sb** faire une visite de politesse à qqn; **~ coach** OR **shuttle** [at airport] navette *f* gratuite; **~ car** voiture *f* de courtoisie *(voiture mise gracieusement à la disposition d'un client)*.
◆ **(by) courtesy of** *prep phr* avec l'aimable autorisation de; **by ~ of an agreement with the management** grâce à un accord avec la direction; **the following footage is brought to you ~ of French TV** la séquence qui suit vous est présentée avec l'aimable permission OR autorisation de la télévision française.

courtesy light *n* plafonnier *m*, éclairage *m* intérieur.

courtesy telephone *n Am téléphone mis à la disposition des usagers d'un aéroport et permettant de diffuser une annonce personnelle ou de se mettre en contact avec un appel*.

courtesy title *n Br* titre *m* de courtoisie.

courthouse ['kɔːthaʊs, *pl* -haʊzɪz] *n Am* palais *m* de justice, tribunal *m*.

courtier ['kɔːtjəʳ] *n* courtisan *m*.

courting ['kɔːtɪŋ] *dated* ◇ *n*: **this is where we did our ~** c'est ici que nous venions à l'époque où nous nous fréquentions.
◇ *adj*: **~ couple** couple *m* d'amoureux.

courtly ['kɔːtlɪ] *adj* [person, manners] plein de style et de courtoisie; **~ love** HIST amour *m* courtois.

court-martial (*pl* **courts-martial**, *Br pt* & *pp* **court-martialled**, *cont* **court-martialling**, *Am pt* & *pp* **court-martialed**, *cont* **court-martialing**) MIL ◇ *n* tribunal *m* militaire; **to be tried by ~** être jugé par un tribunal militaire; **your ~ has been postponed** la date de votre comparution devant le tribunal militaire a été reportée.
◇ *vt* faire comparaître devant un tribunal militaire; **he was court-martialled** il est passé au tribunal militaire.

Court of Appeal *pr n* cour *f* d'appel.

court of appeals *n Am* cour *f* d'appel.

court of inquiry *n Br* [body of people] commission *f* d'enquête; [investigation] enquête *f*.

court order *n* ordonnance *f* du tribunal.

courtroom ['kɔːtrʊm] *n* salle *f* d'audience.

courtship ['kɔːtʃɪp] ◇ *n* -**1.** [of couple]: **their ~ lasted six years** ils se sont fréquentés pendant six ans; **they married after a brief ~** ils se sont mariés peu de temps après avoir commencé à se fréquenter; **his ~ of new financial backers was unsuccessful** *fig* ses tentatives pour attirer de nouveaux commanditaires n'ont rien donné. -**2.** [of animals] période *f* nuptiale, période *f* des amours.
◇ *adj* [dance, display, ritual] nuptial.

court shoe *n Br* escarpin *m*.

courtyard ['kɔːtjɑːd] *n* [of building] cour *f*.

couscous ['kuːskuːs] *n* couscous *m*.

cousin ['kʌzn] *n* cousin *m*, -e *f*; **a distant ~** un cousin éloigné, une cousine éloignée; **our American ~s** [not related by blood] nos cousins américains.

couture [kuː'tʊəʳ] *n* couture *f*.

couturier [kuː'tʊərɪeɪ] *n* couturier *m*, -ère *f*.

covalent [ˌkəʊ'veɪlənt] *adj* covalent.

cove [kəʊv] *n* -**1.** [bay] crique *f*. -**2.** *Br dated* gars *m*; **a rum ~** un drôle de gars.

coven ['kʌvən] *n* ordre *m* OR réunion *f* de sorcières.

covenant ['kʌvənənt] ◇ *n* -**1.** [promise of money] convention *f*, engagement *m*; **(deed of) ~** contrat *m*. -**2.** [agreement] engagement *m*.
◇ *vt* [promise payment of] s'engager (par contrat) à payer.
◇ *vi*: **to ~ for a sum** s'engager (par contrat) à payer une somme.

Covent Garden ['kɒvənt-] *pr n* Covent Garden.

COVENT GARDEN:
«Covent Garden», jadis le marché aux fruits, légumes et fleurs du centre de Londres, est aujourd'hui une importante galerie marchande; ce nom désigne également la «Royal Opera House», située près de l'ancien marché.

Coventry ['kɒvəntrɪ] *pr n*: **to send sb to ~** *Br* mettre qqn en quarantaine *fig*.

cover ['kʌvəʳ] ◇ *n* -**1.** [material - for bed] couverture *f*; [- for cushion, typewriter] housse *f*; **loose ~** [for chair, sofa] housse. -**2.** [lid] couvercle *m*. -**3.** [of book, magazine] couverture *f*; **to read a book (from) ~ to ~** lire un livre de la première à la dernière page OR d'un bout à l'autre. -**4.** [shelter, protection] abri *m*; [for birds, animals] couvert *m*; **to take ~** se mettre à l'abri; **to take ~ from the rain** s'abriter de la pluie; **that tree will provide ~** cet arbre va nous permettre de nous abriter OR nous offrir un abri; **we'll give you ~** [by shooting] nous vous couvrirons; **we will need air ~** MIL nous aurons besoin d'une couverture aérienne; to keep sthg under ~ garder qqch à l'abri; to do sthg under ~ of darkness faire qqch à la faveur de la nuit; under ~ of the riot/noise profitant de l'émeute/du bruit; they escaped under ~ of the riot/noise ils ont profité de l'émeute/du bruit pour s'échapper; to work under ~ travailler clandestinement ❑ to break ~ [animal, person in hiding] sortir à découvert. -**5.** [in insurance] couverture *f*; to have ~ against sthg être couvert OR assuré contre qqch; I've taken out ~ for medical costs j'ai pris une assurance pour les frais médicaux. -**6.** [disguise, front - for criminal enterprise] couverture *f*; [- for spy] fausse identité *f*, identité *f* d'emprunt; your ~ has been blown *inf* vous avez été démasqué; to be a ~ for sthg servir de couverture à qqch; it's just a ~ for her shyness c'est juste pour cacher OR masquer sa timidité. -**7.** [during a person's absence] remplacement *m*; to provide ~ for sb remplacer qqn; I provide emergency ~ je fais des remplacements d'urgence. -**8.** MUS [new version of song] reprise *f*. -**9.** [in restaurant] couvert *m*. -**10.** [envelope] enveloppe *f*; under plain/separate ~ sous pli discret/séparé ❑ ~ letter *Am* lettre *f* explicative OR de couverture; first-day ~ [for philatelist] émission *f* du premier jour, enveloppe premier jour.

◇ *vt* -**1.** [in order to protect] couvrir; [in order to hide] cacher, dissimuler; [cushion, chair, settee] recouvrir; to ~ sthg with a sheet/blanket recouvrir qqch d'un drap/d'une couverture; to ~ one's eyes/ears se couvrir les yeux/les oreilles; to ~ one's face with one's hands [in shame, embarrassment] se couvrir le visage de ses mains; to ~ one's shyness/nervousness dissimuler OR masquer sa timidité/nervosité. -**2.** [coat - subj: dust, snow] recouvrir; to be ~ed in dust/snow être recouvert de poussière/neige; his face was ~ed in spots son visage était couvert de boutons; you're ~ing everything in dust/paint tu mets de la poussière/peinture partout; I was ~ed in OR with shame *fig* j'étais mort de honte; to ~ o.s. in glory *fig* se couvrir de gloire; our team did not exactly ~ itself in glory notre équipe n'est pas rentrée très glorieuse. -**3.** [extend over, occupy - subj: city, desert etc] couvrir une surface de; water ~s most of the earth's surface l'eau recouvre la plus grande partie de la surface de la terre; his interests ~ a wide field il a des intérêts très variés; does this translation ~ the figurative meaning of the word? cette traduction recouvre-t-elle bien le sens figuré du mot? -**4.** [travel over] parcourir, couvrir; we've ~ed every square inch of the park looking for it nous avons ratissé chaque centimètre carré du parc pour essayer de le retrouver. -**5.** [deal with] traiter; there's one point we haven't ~ed il y a un point que nous n'avons pas traité OR vu; is that everything ~ed? [in discussion] tout a été vu?; the law doesn't ~ that kind of situation la loi ne prévoit pas ce genre de situation. -**6.** PRESS, RADIO & TV [report on] couvrir, faire la couverture de. -**7.** [subj: salesman, representative] couvrir. -**8.** [be enough money for - damage, expenses] couvrir; [- meal] suffire à payer; £30 should ~ it 30 livres devraient suffire; to ~ one's costs [company] rentrer dans ses frais. -**9.** [insure] couvrir, garantir; to be ~ed against OR for sthg être couvert OR assuré contre qqch. -**10.** [with gun - colleague] couvrir; I've got you ~ed [to criminal] j'ai mon arme braquée sur toi. -**11.** [monitor permanently - exit, port etc] avoir sous surveillance; I want all exits ~ed immediately je veux que toutes les sorties soient mises sous surveillance immédiatement. -**12.** SPORT marquer. -**13.** MUS [song] faire une reprise de. -**14.** [subj: male animal] couvrir, s'accoupler avec.

◇ *vi*: to ~ for sb remplacer qqn.

◆ **covers** *npl* [in cricket] *partie du terrain située sur l'avant et sur la droite du batteur, à mi-distance de la limite du terrain.*

◆ **cover in** *vt sep* [hole] remplir.

◆ **cover up** ◇ *vt sep* -**1.** [hide, conceal] cacher, dissimuler; [in order to protect] recouvrir; *pej* [involvement, report etc] dissimuler, garder secret; [affair] étouffer; they ~ed up the body with a sheet ils ont recouvert le cadavre d'un drap; ~ yourself up! [for decency] couvre-toi! -**2.** [in order to keep warm] couvrir.

◇ *vi insep* [hide something]: the government is ~ing up again le gouvernement est encore en train d'étouffer une affaire; to ~ up for sb servir de couverture à qqn, couvrir qqn; stop ~ing up for him arrête de le couvrir OR de lui servir de couverture; they're ~ing up for each other ils se couvrent l'un l'autre.

coverage ['kʌvərɪdʒ] *n* -**1.** PRESS, RADIO & TV couverture *f*; his ~ of the coup la couverture qu'il a faite du coup d'État; royal weddings always get a lot of ~ les mariages de la famille royale bénéficient toujours d'une importante couverture médiatique; the author's ~ of the years 1789 to 1815 is sketchy l'auteur traite les années 1789-1815 de manière sommaire; radio/television ~ of the tournament la retransmission radiophonique/télévisée du tournoi. -**2.** [in insurance] couverture *f*.

coveralls ['kʌvərɔːlz] *npl Am* bleu *m* OR bleus *mpl* (de travail).

cover charge *n* [in restaurant] couvert *m*.

covered wagon *n* chariot *m* (à bâche).

cover girl *n* cover-girl *f*.

covering ['kʌvərɪŋ] ◇ *n* [of snow, dust] couche *f*.

◇ *adj*: ~ fire MIL tir *m* de couverture; ~ letter lettre *f* explicative OR de couverture.

coverlet ['kʌvəlɪt] *n* [for bed] dessus-de-lit *m inv*, couvre-lit *m*.

cover note *n Br* attestation *f* provisoire.

cover story *n* article *m* principal (faisant la couverture).

covert ['kʌvət] ◇ *adj* [operation, payments, contacts] secret; [threats] voilé; she had a ~ dislike of him sans le laisser paraître, elle ne pouvait pas le souffrir; he stole a ~ glance at her il lui a jeté un regard furtif.

◇ *n* [hiding place for animals] fourré *m*, couvert *m*.

covertly ['kʌvətlɪ] *adv* [sold, paid] secrètement; [threaten] de manière voilée; [signal] furtivement; he glanced at her ~ il l'a regardée à la dérobée, il lui a jeté un regard furtif.

cover-up *n*: the government has been accused of a ~ le gouvernement a été accusé d'avoir étouffé l'affaire; the government denied that there had been any ~ le gouvernement a nié avoir étouffé l'affaire; it's a ~ c'est un complot.

cover version *n* MUS [of song] reprise *f*.

covet ['kʌvɪt] *vt* [crave, long for] convoiter; [wish for] avoir très envie de; the much ~ed prix Goncourt le prix Goncourt, objet de tant de convoitise; I've always ~ed a house like this j'ai toujours eu très envie d'une maison comme celle-ci.

covetous ['kʌvɪtəs] *adj* [person] avide; [look] de convoitise; to be ~ of sthg convoiter qqch.

covetously ['kʌvɪtəslɪ] *adv* avec convoitise.

covetousness ['kʌvɪtəsnɪs] *n* convoitise *f*, avidité *f*.

covey ['kʌvɪ] *n* compagnie *f* OR vol *m* de perdrix.

cow [kaʊ] ◇ *n* -**1.** [farm animal] vache *f*; we'll be here until the ~s come home! on y sera encore dans dix ans! *fig*; I could eat chocolate ice cream until the ~s come home de la glace au chocolat, je pourrais en manger des kilos et des kilos. -**2.** [female elephant] éléphant *m* femelle, éléphante *f*; [female seal] phoque *m* femelle; [female whale] baleine *f* femelle. -**3.** ▽ *Br pej* [woman] conasse *f*; she's a real ~, that woman c'est une vraie conasse, cette bonne femme; that ~ next door la vieille bique d'à côté; you ~! espèce de conasse!; you silly ~ espèce d'abrutie.

◇ *vt* effrayer, intimider; a ~ed look un air de chien battu.

coward ['kaʊəd] *n* lâche *mf*, poltron *m*, -onne *f*; don't be such a ~ ne sois pas aussi lâche; I'm an awful ~ when it comes to physical pain j'ai très peur de OR je redoute beaucoup la douleur physique; he's a moral ~ il n'a aucune force morale.

cowardice ['kaʊədɪs] *n* lâcheté *f*; an act of ~ un acte de lâcheté; moral ~ manque *m* de force morale.

cowardliness ['kaʊədlɪnɪs] *n* lâcheté *f*.

cowardly ['kaʊədlɪ] *adj* lâche; it was ~ of him c'était lâche de sa part.

cowbell ['kaʊbel] *n* clochette *f*, sonnaille *f*.

cowboy ['kaʊbɔɪ] ◇ *n* -**1.** [in American West] cow-boy *m*; to play ~s and Indians jouer aux cow-boys et aux Indiens. -**2.** *inf pej* petit rigolo *m*; a bunch of ~s une bande de petits rigolos; some ~ builder/plumber un petit rigolo d'entrepreneur/de plombier, un soi-disant entrepreneur/plombier; there are too many ~ plumbers around here il y a trop de petits rigolos dans la plomberie.

◇ *comp* de cow-boy; ~ boots bottes *fpl* de cow-boy, santiags *fpl*; ~ film OR movie film *m* de cow-boys.

cowcatcher ['kaʊˌkætʃəʳ] *n Am* RAIL chasse-pierres *m inv*.

cower ['kaʊəʳ] *vi* [person] se recroqueviller; [animal] se tapir; I ~ed OR was ~ing in my seat j'étais recroquevillé sur ma chaise; she ~ed away from him tremblante de peur, elle s'est écartée de lui; the dog was ~ing in a corner tout tremblant, le chien était tapi dans un coin; he stood ~ing before the boss il tremblait devant le patron.

Cowes [kaʊz] *pr n*: ~ (Week) *régate et événement mondain se tenant chaque année à Cowes, sur l'île de Wight.*

cowgirl ['kaʊgɜːl] *n* vachère *f*.

cowhand ['kaʊhænd] *n* vacher *m*; [in Western] cow-boy *m*.

cowherd ['kaʊhɜːd] *n* vacher *m*, bouvier *m*.

cowhide ['kaʊhaɪd] *n* peau *f* de vache; [leather] cuir *m* OR peau *f* de vache.

cowl [kaʊl] *n* -**1.** [of chimney] capuchon *m*. -**2.** [of monk] capuchon *m*. -**3.** ~ neck OR neckline [of sweater, dress] col *m* boule. -**4.** = **cowling**.

cowlick ['kaʊˌlɪk] *n Am* mèche *f* rebelle.

cowling ['kaʊlɪŋ] *n* capot *m*.

cowman ['kaʊmən] (*pl* cowmen [-mən]) *n* vacher *m*, bouvier *m*.

co-worker *n* collègue *mf*.

cow parsley *n* cerfeuil *m* sauvage.

cowpat ['kaʊpæt] *n* bouse *f* de vache.

cowpox ['kaʊpɒks] *n* vaccine *f*.

cowpuncher *inf* ['kaʊˌpʌntʃəʳ] *n Am dated* cow-boy *m*.

cowrie, cowry ['kaʊrɪ] (*pl* cowries) *n* [shell] cauri *m*.

cowshed ['kaʊʃed] *n* étable *f*.

cowslip ['kaʊslɪp] *n* BOT primevère *f*, coucou *m*.

cox [kɒks] ◇ *n* [of rowing team] barreur *m*, -euse *f*.

◇ *vt* barrer.

◇ *vi* barrer; he has ~ed for Cambridge il a été barreur dans l'équipe de Cambridge.

coxcomb ['kɒkskəʊm] *n* -**1.** = **cockscomb**. -**2.** *arch* [fop] fat *m*, poseur *m*.

coxswain ['kɒksən] *n* [of rowing team] barreur *m*, -euse *f*; [of lifeboat] timonier *m*, homme *m* de barre.

coy [kɔɪ] *adj* -**1.** [shy - person] qui fait le/la timide; [- answer, smile] faussement timide. -**2.** [provocative, playful] coquet. -**3.** [evasive] évasif.

coyly ['kɔɪlɪ] *adv* [timidly] avec une timidité affectée OR feinte; [provocatively] coquettement.

coyness ['kɔɪnɪs] *n* [timidness] timidité *f* affectée OR feinte; [provocativeness] coquetteries *fpl*.

coyote [kɔɪ'əʊtɪ] *n* coyote *m*.

coypu ['kɔɪpuː] *n* ragondin *m*.

cozen ['kʌzn] *vt arch* duper, tromper.

cozy *etc Am* = **cosy**.

cp. (*written abbr of* compare) cf.

c/p (*written abbr of* carriage paid) pp.

CP (*abbr of* Communist Party) *pr n* PC *m*.

Cpl. *written abbr of* corporal.

c.p.s. (*written abbr of* characters per second) cps.

CPSA (*abbr of* Civil and Public Services Association) *pr n syndicat de la fonction publique*.

CPU (*abbr of* central processing unit) *n* unité *f* centrale (de traitement).

cr. -**1.** *written abbr of* credit. -**2.** *written abbr of* creditor.

crab [kræb] (*pt & pp* crabbed, *cont* crabbing) ◇ *n* -**1.** ZOOL crabe *m*. -**2.** to catch a ~ [above surface of water] donner un coup d'aviron dans le vide; [below surface of water] engager la rame trop profond. -**3.** ASTRON: the Crab le Cancer.
◇ *vi* [grumble] maugréer, rouspéter.
◆ **crabs** *npl* MED morpions *mpl*.

crab apple *n* [fruit] pomme *f* sauvage; ~ (tree) pommier *m* sauvage; ~ jelly gelée *f* de pommes sauvages.

crabbed [kræbd] *adj* -**1.** [handwriting] en pattes de mouche. -**2.** *dated* = **crabby**.

crabby *inf* ['kræbɪ] (*compar* crabbier, *superl* crabbiest) *adj* grognon, ronchon.

crab louse *n* morpion *m*.

crack [kræk] ◇ *n* -**1.** [in cup, glass, egg] fêlure *f*; [in ceiling, wall] lézarde *f*, fissure *f*; [in ground] crevasse *f*; [in varnish, enamel] craquelure *f*; [in skin] gerçure *f*, crevasse *f*; [in bone] fêlure *f*; *fig* [fault -in policy, argument etc] fissure *f*, faiblesse *f*; did you know there was a ~ in this glass? avais-tu remarqué que ce verre était fêlé?; the ~s are beginning to show in their marriage *fig* leur mariage commence à donner des signes de délabrement. -**2.** [small opening or gap]: there were some ~s in the wall le mur était fissuré. -**3.** [noise] craquement *m*; [of thunder] coup *m*. -**4.** [blow - on head, knee etc] coup *m*; that was a nasty ~ you got tu as pris un drôle de mauvais coup; I gave myself a ~ on the head je me suis cogné la tête. -**5.** *inf* [attempt]: I'll have a ~ (at it), I'll give it a ~ je vais tenter le coup, je vais essayer (un coup); do you want another ~ (at it)? tu veux réessayer?, tu veux retenter le coup?; this is her fourth ~ at (winning) the title c'est sa quatrième tentative pour gagner le titre, c'est la quatrième fois qu'elle tente de gagner le titre ❑ to give sb a fair ~ of the whip donner toutes ses chances OR sa chance à qqn. -**6.** [joke, witticism] blague *f*, plaisanterie *f*. -**7.** [drug] crack *m*. -**8.** *phr*: at the ~ of dawn au point du jour; I've been up since the ~ of dawn je suis debout OR levé depuis l'aube; we'll be here until the ~ of doom *dated & hum* on va être ici jusqu'aux calendes grecques.
◇ *adj* [regiment, team etc] d'élite; one of their ~ players un de leurs meilleurs joueurs; ~ troops soldats *mpl* d'élite; ~ shot tireur *m*, -euse *f* d'élite.
◇ *vt* -**1.** [damage - cup, glass, egg] fêler; [- ice] fendre; [- ceiling, wall] lézarder, fissurer; [- ground] crevasser; [- varnish, enamel] craqueler; [- skin] gercer, crevasser; [- bone] fêler. -**2.** [open -eggs, nuts] casser; to ~ a safe fracturer un coffre-fort; to ~ a bottle *inf* ouvrir OR déboucher une bouteille; she never ~ed a smile the entire evening *inf* elle n'a pas souri une seule fois de la soirée; I didn't ~ a book all term *Am* je n'ai pas ouvert un livre du trimestre. -**3.** [bang, hit - head, knee]: to ~ one's head/knee on sthg se cogner la tête/le genou contre qqch. -**4.** [make noise with -whip] faire claquer; [- knuckles] faire craquer; to ~ the whip faire le gendarme; he's very good at ~ing the whip il fait très bien le gendarme. -**5.** *inf phr*: to ~ a joke sortir une blague; "got a half day today?", she ~ed «tu t'es pris une demi-journée de congé?» dit-elle en blaguant OR plaisantant. -**6.** [solve]: to ~ a code déchiffrer un code; the police think they have ~ed the case la police pense qu'elle a résolu l'affaire; I think we've ~ed it je pense que nous y sommes arrivés. -**7.** CHEM craquer.
◇ *vi* -**1.** [cup, glass, ice] se fissurer, se fêler; [ceiling, wall] se lézarder, se fissurer; [ground] se crevasser; [varnish, enamel] se craqueler; [skin] se gercer, se crevasser; [bone] se fêler. -**2.** [make noise - whip] claquer; [- twigs] craquer; a rifle ~ed and he dropped to the ground un coup de fusil a retenti et il s'est effondré; the sound of submachine-guns ~ing le crépitement des mitraillettes. -**3.** [give way, collapse - through nervous exhaustion] s'effondrer, craquer; [- under questioning, surveillance] craquer; their marriage ~ed under the strain leur mariage s'est détérioré sous l'effet du stress; in a voice ~ing with emotion d'une voix cassée par l'émotion. -**4.** *inf phr*: to get ~ing [start work] s'y mettre, se mettre au boulot; [get ready, get going] se mettre en route; I'll get ~ing on dinner/cleaning the windows je vais me mettre à préparer le dîner/nettoyer les vitres; get ~ing!, let's get ~ing! au boulot!
◆ **crack down** *vi insep* sévir; to ~ down on sthg/sb sévir contre qqch/qqn.
◆ **crack open** *vt sep* [eggs, nuts] casser; [bottle] *inf* ouvrir, déboucher.
◆ **crack up** ◇ *vi insep* -**1.** [ice] se fissurer; [paint, enamel, make-up] se craqueler; [ground] se crevasser; [skin] se gercer, se crevasser. -**2.** *inf* [through nervous exhaustion] s'effondrer, craquer; I must be ~ing up [going mad] je débloque. -**3.** *inf* [with laughter] se tordre de rire.
◇ *vt sep* -**1.** [make laugh] faire se tordre de rire. -**2.** (*always pass*) [say good things about]: he's not what he's ~ed up to be il n'est pas aussi fantastique qu'on le dit OR prétend; the play is everything it's ~ed up to be la pièce a toutes les qualités qu'on lui vante.

crackbrain *inf* ['krækbreɪn] *n* fêlé *m*, -e *f*, taré *m*, -e *f*.

crackbrained *inf* ['krækbreɪnd] *adj* débile, dingue.

crackdown ['krækdaʊn] *n*: we're going to have a ~ on petty theft on va sévir contre les petits larcins; the annual Christmas ~ on drunk driving les mesures répressives prises tous les ans à Noël contre la conduite en état d'ivresse; the ~ on dissidents la répression contre les dissidents.

cracked [krækt] *adj* -**1.** [damaged - cup, glass] fêlé; [- ice] fendu; [- ceiling, wall] lézardé; [- ground] crevassé; [- varnish] craquelé; [- skin] gercé, crevassé. -**2.** *inf* [mad - person] fêlé, taré.

cracker ['krækəʳ] *n* -**1.** [savoury biscuit] biscuit *m* salé, cracker *m*. -**2.** *Br* [for pulling] *papillotte contenant un pétard et une surprise, traditionnelle au moment des fêtes*. -**3.** [firework] pétard *m*. -**4.** *inf* [good-looking person] canon *m*. -**5.** *inf* [something excellent of its kind]: that was a ~ of a goal c'était un but sensass.

CRACKER:
Les «crackers» décorent la table à Noël en Grande-Bretagne. Un «cracker» est un tube en carton enveloppé d'un papier cadeau, contenant généralement un petit jouet, une blague et un chapeau en papier. On se met à deux pour l'ouvrir, chacun tirant sur un bout du «cracker», dans lequel il y a un petit pétard.

---

cracker-barrel *adj Am* de quatre sous.

crackers *inf* ['krækəz] *adj* cinglé, fêlé, taré; to drive sb ~ faire tourner qqn en bourrique.

crackhead ['krækhed] *n drugs sl* accro *mf* au crack.

cracking ['krækɪŋ] ◇ *adj* -**1.** [excellent] génial, épatant. -**2.** [fast]: to keep up a ~ pace aller à fond de train.
◇ *adv inf Br dated*: ~ good [match, meal] de première.
◇ *n* CHEM craquage *m*; ~ plant usine *f* de craquage.

crackle ['krækl] ◇ *vi* [paper, dry leaves] craquer; [fire] crépiter, craquer; [radio] grésiller; to ~ with energy *fig* pétiller d'énergie.
◇ *vt* [glaze] craqueler.
◇ *n* [of paper, twigs] craquement *m*; [of fire] crépitement *m*, craquement *m*; [of radio] grésillement *m*; [on telephone] friture *f*; [of machine-gun fire] crépitement *m*.

crackleware ['kræklweəʳ] *n* poterie *f* craquelée.

crackling ['kræklɪŋ] *n* -**1.** CULIN couenne *f* rôtie. -**2.** [noise] = **crackle**.

crackly ['kræklɪ] (*compar* cracklier, *superl* crackliest) *adj*: the telephone is making a ~ noise il y a de la friture sur la ligne; the radio's a bit ~ la radio grésille un peu.

cracknel ['kræknl] *n* [biscuit] craquelin *m*; [filling for chocolate] nougatine *f*.

crackpot *inf* ['krækpɒt] ◇ *n* [person] tordu *m*, -e *f*, cinglé *m*, -e *f*.
◇ *adj* [idea, scheme] tordu; [person] tordu, cinglé; ~ letter lettre *f* d'un tordu OR d'un cinglé.

cracksman *inf* ['kræksmən] (*pl* cracksmen [-mən]) *n dated* casseur *m* (de coffres).

crack-up *inf n* -**1.** [of person] dépression *f* (nerveuse). -**2.** [of country, economy] effondrement *m*.

Cracow ['krækaʊ] *pr n* Cracovie.

cradle ['kreɪdl] ◇ *n* -**1.** [for baby] berceau *m*; *fig* berceau *m*; the ~ of democracy/the trade union movement le berceau de la démocratie/du mouvement syndical; from the ~ to the grave du berceau au tombeau; they've known each other since they were in their ~s ils se connaissent depuis qu'ils sont tout petits; to rob the ~ *Am hum* les prendre au berceau OR biberon. -**2.** [frame - for painter, window cleaner] pont *m* volant, échafaudage *m* volant; [- in hospital bed] arceau *m*. -**3.** TELEC support *m* (du combiné).
◇ *vt* [hold carefully - baby, kitten] tenir tendrement (dans ses bras); [- delicate object] tenir précieusement OR délicatement (dans ses bras).

cradle-snatcher *inf n Br*: I'm no ~ je ne les prends pas au berceau; ~! tu les prends au berceau!

cradle-song *n* berceuse *f*.

craft [krɑːft] (*pl sense 3 inv*) ◇ *n* -**1.** [of artist, artisan] art *m*, métier *m*; to do ~s at school faire des travaux manuels à l'école; arts and ~s artisanat *m* (d'art). -**2.** [guile, cunning] ruse *f*; to use ~ employer la ruse; to obtain sthg by ~ obtenir qqch par la ruse. -**3.** [boat, ship] bateau *m*; [aircraft] avion *m*; [spacecraft] engin *m* OR vaisseau *m* spatial; all the small ~ in the harbour tous les petits bateaux OR toutes les embarcations dans le port.
◇ *comp*: ~(s) fair foire *f* d'artisanat; ~ guild corporation *f* artisanale OR d'artisans.
◇ *vt* (*usu pass*) travailler; a hand ~ed table une table travaillée à la main; a beautifully ~ed film *fig* un film magnifiquement travaillé.

craftily ['krɑːftɪlɪ] *adv* astucieusement; to behave ~ agir astucieusement OR habilement; *pej* agir avec ruse.

craftiness ['krɑːftɪnɪs] *n* habileté *f*; *pej* ruse *f*, roublardise *f*.

craftsman ['krɑːftsmən] (*pl* craftsmen [-mən]) *n* artisan *m*, homme *m* de métier; [writer, actor] homme *m* de métier; he's not much of a ~ ce n'est pas un très bon artisan; [amateur] il n'est pas très doué de ses mains.

craftsmanship ['krɑːftsmənʃɪp] *n* connaissance *f* d'un OR du métier; a fine example of ~ un bel ouvrage, un vrai travail d'artiste; this is French ~ at its best voici l'artisanat français au sommet de sa qualité; the ~ is superb cela a été superbement travaillé; you have to pay for good ~ il faut payer si on veut du bon travail; there's no ~ these days il n'y a plus de travail bien fait de nos jours.

craftswoman ['krɑːfts,wʊmən] (*pl* craftswomen [-,wɪmɪn]) *n* artisane *f*.

craft union *n* syndicat *m* d'artisans.

crafty ['krɑːftɪ] (*compar* craftier, *superl* craftiest) *adj* [person, idea, scheme] malin, astucieux; *pej* [person] rusé, roublard; [idea, scheme] rusé; you ~ old devil! espèce de vieux renard!

crag [kræg] *n* [steep rock] rocher *m* escarpé OR à pic.

craggy ['krægɪ] (*compar* craggier, *superl* craggiest) *adj* [hill] escarpé, à pic; *fig* [features] anguleux, taillé à coups de OR à la serpe.

cram [kræm] (*pt* & *pp* crammed, *cont* cramming) ◇ *vt* -**1.** [objects] fourrer; [people] entasser; to ~ sthg into a drawer fourrer qqch dans un tiroir; there were ten of us crammed into a tiny office nous étions dix entassés dans un bureau minuscule; to ~ clothes into a suitcase bourrer des vêtements dans une valise, bourrer une valise de vêtements; you can't ~ anything else in tu ne peux plus rien y mettre, même en forçant; could you ~ one more person in? y aurait-il encore une petite place?; to ~ food into one's mouth se bourrer de nourriture, se gaver; I crammed a lot of quotations into my essay j'ai bourré ma dissertation de citations; we crammed a lot into one day on en a fait beaucoup en une seule journée; could you ~ one more visit into your schedule? pourriez-vous trouver une petite place pour ajouter une visite à votre programme chargé? -**2.** *inf* SCH [facts] apprendre à toute vitesse; [students] faire bachoter.
◇ *vi* -**1.** *inf* [study hard] bachoter. -**2.** [into small space]: people crammed into the streets to watch the parade les gens se sont entassés dans les rues pour regarder le défilé; we all crammed into his office nous nous sommes tous entassés dans son bureau.

cram-full *adj Br*: to be ~ of sthg être plein à craquer OR bourré de qqch.

crammed [kræmd] *adj* [full - bus, train, room, suitcase] bourré, bondé; to be ~ with people être bondé; to be ~ with sthg être plein à craquer OR bourré de qqch; the encyclopaedia is ~ with useful information l'encyclopédie regorge d'informations utiles.

crammer *inf* ['kræməʳ] *n Br* [teacher] répétiteur *m*, -trice *f*; [student] bachoteur *m*, -euse *f*; [school] boîte *f* à bac.

cramp [kræmp] ◇ *n* -**1.** *(U)* [muscle pain] crampe *f*; to have ~ OR *Am* a ~ avoir une crampe; I've got ~ in my leg j'ai une crampe à la jambe; she dropped out (of the race) with ~ elle a abandonné (la course) parce qu'elle avait une crampe; to have stomach ~, to have ~s *Am* avoir des crampes d'estomac ❑ writer's ~ crampe *f* des écrivains. -**2.** [in carpentry] serre-joint *m*. -**3.** = **cramp iron**.
◇ *vt* -**1.** [hamper - person] gêner; [- project] entraver, contrarier; to ~ sb's style *inf* faire perdre tous ses moyens à qqn, priver qqn de ses moyens. -**2.** [secure with a cramp] maintenir à l'aide d'un serre-joint.

cramped [kræmpt] *adj* -**1.** [room, flat] exigu; they live in very ~ conditions ils vivent très à l'étroit; we're a bit ~ for space nous sommes un peu à l'étroit. -**2.** [position] inconfortable. -**3.** [handwriting] en pattes de mouche, serré.

cramp iron *n* CONSTR crampon *m*, happe *f*, clameau *m*.

crampon ['kræmpən] *n* crampon *m* (à glace).

cranberry ['krænbərɪ] (*pl* cranberries) ◇ *n* canneberge *f*.
◇ *comp*: ~ sauce sauce *f* aux canneberges.

crane [kreɪn] ◇ *n* -**1.** ORNITH grue *f*; 'The Cranes Are Flying' *Kalatozov* 'Quand passent les cigognes'. -**2.** TECH & CIN grue *f*.
◇ *comp*: ~ driver OR operator grutier *m*.
◇ *vt*: to ~ one's neck tendre le cou.
◇ *vi*: to ~ (forward) tendre le cou.

crane fly *n* tipule *f* des prés OR des prairies.

cranesbill ['kreɪnzbɪl] *n* géranium *m*.

crania ['kreɪnjə] *pl* → **cranium**.

cranial ['kreɪnjəl] *adj* crânien.

craniology [ˌkreɪnɪ'ɒlədʒɪ] *n* craniologie *f*.

cranium ['kreɪnjəm] (*pl* crania [-njə]) *n* [skull - gen] crâne *m*; [- enclosing brain] boîte *f* crânienne.

crank [kræŋk] ◇ *n* -**1.** *inf* [eccentric] excentrique *mf*; a religious ~ un/une fanatique; she's a bit of a ~ elle est un peu excentrique, c'est un cas; what a ~! c'est vraiment un cas! -**2.** *inf Am* [bad-tempered person] grognon *m*, -onne *f*. -**3.** MECH: ~ (handle) manivelle *f*.
◇ *vt* [engine] démarrer à la manivelle; [gramophone] remonter à la manivelle; to ~ the shutters up/down remonter/baisser les volets (à la manivelle).
◆ **crank out** *inf vt sep Am* [books, plays etc] produire en quantités industrielles; this is the fourth novel he's ~ed out this year c'est le quatrième roman d'affilée qu'il sort cette année.
◆ **crank up** ◇ *vt sep* -**1.** = **crank** *vt*. -**2.** *fig* [increase] augmenter. -**3.** *phr*: to get things ~ed up mettre tout en place.
◇ *vi insep drugs sl* se shooter.

crankcase ['kræŋkkeɪs] *n* carter *m*.

crankiness *inf* ['kræŋkɪnɪs] *n* -**1.** [eccentricity] bizarrerie *f*. -**2.** *Am* [bad temper] caractère *m* de cochon; [on one occasion] mauvaise humeur *f*.

crankpin ['kræŋkpɪn] *n* maneton *m*.

crankshaft ['kræŋkʃɑːft] *n* vilebrequin *m*.

cranky *inf* ['kræŋkɪ] (*compar* crankier, *superl* crankiest) *adj* -**1.** [eccentric - person, behaviour, ideas] bizarre. -**2.** *Am* [bad-tempered] grognon. -**3.** [unreliable - machine] capricieux.

cranny ['krænɪ] (*pl* crannies) *n* fente *f*.

crap [kræp] (*pt* & *pp* crapped, *cont* crapping) ◇ *n* *(U)* -**1.** ▼ [faeces] merde *f*; to have a ~ chier. -**2.** ▽ *fig* [nonsense] conneries *fpl*; to talk ~ raconter OR dire des conneries; that's ~, I never said that! c'est des conneries, je n'ai jamais dit ça!; don't give me that ~! arrête de me raconter des conneries!; what a load of ~! quelles conneries! -**3.** ▽ *fig* [rubbish] merde *f*; get all this ~ off the table enlève tout ce bordel OR toute cette merde de la table; he writes absolute ~ ce qu'il écrit c'est de la merde; she eats ~ out of fast-food places elle bouffe la saloperie OR la merde qu'on vend dans les fast-foods; his cooking is ~ sa cuisine, c'est de la merde. -**4.** *Am* [dice game] *jeu de dés similaire au quatre-cent-vingt-et-un et où on parie sur le résultat*; ~ game partie *f* de dés.
◇ *vi* ▼ [defecate] chier.
◇ *vt* ▼: to ~ o.s. chier dans son froc.
◇ *adj* ▽ *Br* [of very poor quality] de merde, merdique; what a ~ book quel livre merdique OR de merde OR à la con; she's a ~ cook sa cuisine, c'est de la merde.
◆ **craps** *n Am*: to shoot ~ [play game] jouer aux dés, faire une partie de dés; [throw dice] lancer les dés.
◆ **crap out** *vi insep Am* -**1.** GAMES *ne pas obtenir le résultat sur lequel on a parié dans un jeu de dés*. -**2.** ▽ [back out] se dégonfler; he crapped out of asking her for a date il allait lui demander de sortir avec lui mais il s'est dégonflé.

crape [kreɪp] = **crepe**.

crappy▽ ['kræpɪ] (*compar* crappier, *superl* crappiest) *adj* [programme, book etc] de merde, merdique, à la con; [remark, action] dégueulasse.

crapshooter ['kræpˌʃuːtəʳ] *n Am* joueur *m*, -euse *f* de dés.

crash [kræʃ] ◇ *n* -**1.** [accident] accident *m*; car/plane/train ~ accident de voiture/d'avion/ferroviaire; to have a ~ avoir un accident; to be (involved) in a ~ [person] avoir un accident; the car looks as though it has been in a ~ la voiture semble avoir été accidentée. -**2.** [loud noise] fracas *m*; a ~ of thunder un coup de tonnerre; there was a loud ~ as the plate hit the ground cela a fait un bruit fracassant quand l'assiette est tombée par terre; there was a loud ~ from the kitchen un grand fracas a retenti dans la cuisine; he closed the lid with a ~ il a fermé le couvercle avec fracas; he fell to the floor with a ~ il est tombé par terre dans un grand fracas. -**3.** FIN [slump] krach *m*, débâcle *f*; the Wall Street Crash le krach de Wall Street. -**4.** COMPUT panne *f*.
◇ *comp* [diet, programme] intensif, de choc; to do a ~ tackle RUGBY plaquer violemment.
◇ *adv*: he ran ~ into a wall il est rentré en plein dans le mur; it went ~ ça a fait boum; something went ~ in the attic quelque chose est tombé dans le grenier.
◇ *interj* boum.
◇ *vi* -**1.** [car, train] avoir un accident; [plane, pilot] s'écraser, se crasher; [driver] avoir un accident; we're going to ~ [plane] on va s'écraser; [car] on va lui rentrer dedans/rentrer dans le mur etc; [train] on va avoir un accident; the car hit a patch of oil and ~ed l'accident s'est produit parce que la voiture a glissé sur une plaque d'huile; a detailed study of what actually happens when a car ~es une étude détaillée de ce qui se passe vraiment lors des accidents de voiture; the French car ~ed at the first bend la voiture française a eu un accident dans le premier virage; the cars ~ed (head on) les voitures se sont embouties OR percutées (par l'avant); to ~ into sthg percuter qqch; the car ~ed through the fence la voiture est passée à travers la clôture; to ~ into sb [subj: person] rentrer dans qqn; I ~ed into him je lui suis rentré dedans. -**2.** [make loud noise - thunder] retentir; what are you ~ing about at this hour for? pourquoi fais-tu autant de vacarme OR boucan à cette heure?; the elephants ~ed through the undergrowth les éléphants ont traversé le sous-bois dans un vacarme terrible. -**3.** [fall, hit with loud noise or violently]: the tree came ~ing down l'arbre est tombé avec fracas; her world came ~ing down (about her OR her ears) tout son monde s'est écroulé; the vase ~ed to the ground le vase s'est écrasé au sol; his fist ~ed into the other man's face son poing a percuté avec force OR violence le visage de l'autre. -**4.** ST. EX s'effondrer. -**5.** COMPUT tomber en panne. -**6.** ▽ [sleep] dormir; [fall asleep] s'endormir; can I ~ at your place? je peux dormir chez toi?; I need somewhere to ~ for the next week j'ai besoin d'un endroit où crécher la semaine prochaine.
◇ *vt* -**1.** [vehicle]: to ~ a car avoir un accident avec une voiture; [on purpose] démolir une voiture; to ~ a plane s'écraser en avion; he ~ed the car through the fence/shop-window il a traversé la clôture/la vitrine avec la voiture; she ~ed the car into a wall elle est rentrée dans OR a percuté un mur (avec la voiture). -**2.** *inf* [attend without invitation]: to ~ a party entrer dans une fête sans y être invité.
◆ **crash out**▽ *vi insep* [fall asleep] s'endormir; [spend the night, sleep] dormir; I found him ~ed out in the corner je l'ai trouvé endormi OR qui roupillait dans le coin; she's absolutely ~ed out elle dort comme une souche, elle en écrase.

crash barrier *n* glissière *f* de sécurité.

crash course *n* cours *m* intensif; a ~ in French un cours intensif de français.

crash-dive *vi* [submarine] plonger; [plane] faire un plongeon.

crash helmet *n* casque *m* (de protection).

crashing *inf* ['kræʃɪŋ] *adj Br*: he's a ~ bore c'est un raseur de première.

crashingly *inf* ['kræʃɪŋlɪ] *adv Br* [boring] incroyablement, terriblement.

crash-land ◇ *vi* [aircraft] faire un atterrissage forcé, atterrir en catastrophe.
◇ *vt* [aircraft] poser OR faire atterrir en catastrophe.

crash landing *n* atterrissage *m* forcé OR en catastrophe.

crash pad▽ *n* piaule *f* de dépannage; he let me use this place as a ~ il m'a laissé crécher chez lui pour me dépanner.

crashworthy ['kræʃˌwɜːðɪ] (*compar* crashworthier, *superl* crashworthiest) *adj* qui a une bonne résistance aux collisions.

crass [kræs] *adj* [comment, person] lourd; [behaviour, stupidity] grossier; [ignorance] grossier, crasse.

crassly ['kræslɪ] *adv* [behave, comment] lourdement.

crassness ['kræsnɪs] *n* [of comment, person] lourdeur *f*, manque *m* de finesse; the ~ of his ignorance son ignorance crasse; the ~ of his behaviour son manque de finesse.

crate [kreɪt] ◇ *n* -**1.** [for storage, transport] caisse *f*; [for fruit, vegetables] cageot *m*, cagette *f*; [for bottles] caisse *f*. -**2.** *inf Br* [old car] caisse *f*; [plane] coucou *m*.

◇ *vt* [furniture, bottles] mettre dans une caisse OR en caisses; [fruit, vegetables] mettre dans un cageot OR en cageots.

crater ['kreɪtəʳ] *n* [of volcano, moon etc] cratère *m*; **bomb ~** entonnoir *m*; **shell ~** entonnoir, trou *m* d'obus.

cravat [krə'væt] *n Br* foulard *m*.

crave [kreɪv] *vt* -**1.** [long for - cigarette, drink] avoir terriblement envie de; [- affection, love] avoir soif OR terriblement besoin de; [- stardom] avoir soif de; [- luxury, wealth] avoir soif OR être avide de; [in medical, psychological context] éprouver un besoin impérieux de. -**2.** *fml* [beg] implorer; **to ~ sb's permission to do sthg** implorer qqn pour obtenir la permission de faire qqch; **to ~ sb's pardon** implorer le pardon de qqn; **to ~ sb's indulgence** faire appel à l'indulgence de qqn; **may I ~ your attention?** puis-je me permettre de solliciter votre attention?

◆ **crave for** *vt insep* = **crave** *vt* **1**.

craven ['kreɪvn] *adj fml* [person, attitude] lâche, veule; **a ~ coward** un lâche.

craving ['kreɪvɪŋ] *n* [longing] envie *f* impérieuse OR irrésistible; [physiological need] besoin *m* impérieux; **pregnant women often get ~s** les femmes enceintes éprouvent souvent des envies irrésistibles; **to have a ~ for sthg** [chocolate, sweets, cigarette] avoir terriblement envie de qqch; [affection, love] avoir soif OR terriblement besoin de qqch; [stardom] avoir soif de qqch; [luxury, wealth] avoir soif OR être avide de qqch; [subj: alcoholic, drug addict] avoir un besoin impérieux de qqch.

craw [krɔː] *n* [of bird] jabot *m*; [of animal] estomac *m*; **it sticks in my ~** *inf* cela me reste en travers de la gorge, j'ai du mal à l'avaler.

crawfish ['krɔːfɪʃ] = **crayfish**.

crawl [krɔːl] ◇ *n* -**1.** [person]: **it involved a laborious ~ through the undergrowth** il a fallu ramper tant bien que mal à travers le sous-bois. -**2.** [vehicle] ralenti *m*; **to move at a ~** avancer au ralenti OR au pas; **the traffic/train has slowed to a ~** les voitures avancent/le train avance maintenant au pas OR au ralenti; **I had to slow to a ~** [in car] j'ai dû ralentir jusqu'à rouler au pas. -**3.** SPORT crawl *m*; **to do the ~** nager le crawl.

◇ *vi* -**1.** [move on all fours - person] ramper; [- baby] marcher à quatre pattes; **she tried to ~ away from danger** elle a essayé de s'éloigner du danger en rampant OR en se traînant sur les genoux; **he ~ed out of/into bed** il se traîna hors du/au lit; **to ~ on one's hands and knees** marcher OR se traîner à quatre pattes; **she ~ed under the desk** elle s'est mise à quatre pattes sous le bureau; **what are you ~ing about on the floor for?** qu'est-ce que tu fais à quatre pattes? -**2.** [move slowly - traffic, train] avancer au ralenti OR au pas; [- insect, snake] ramper; **the train ~ed out of the station** le train est sorti de la gare au ralenti OR au pas; **there's a caterpillar ~ing up your arm** il y a une chenille qui te grimpe sur le bras. -**3.** [be infested]: **to be ~ing with** être infesté de, grouiller de; **the kitchen was ~ing with ants** la cuisine grouillait OR était infestée de fourmis; **the streets were ~ing with police/tourists** *inf fig* les rues grouillaient de policiers/touristes. -**4.** [come out in goose pimples]: **to make sb's flesh ~** donner la chair de poule à qqn; **just the thought of it makes my skin ~** j'ai la chair de poule rien que d'y penser. -**5.** *inf* [grovel]: **I'll ~ if I have to** je me mettrai à genoux s'il le faut; **to ~ to sb** ramper OR s'aplatir devant qqn, lécher les bottes de qqn; **he got promoted by ~ing to the boss** il a été promu à force de ramper OR de s'aplatir devant le patron; **he'll come ~ing back** il reviendra te supplier à genoux. -**6.** SPORT nager le crawl.

crawler ['krɔːləʳ] *n* -**1.** *pej* [groveller] lèche-bottes *mf*. -**2.** *Br* AUT: **~ lane** file *f* OR voie *f* pour véhicules lents.

◆ **crawlers** *npl* [for baby] grenouillère *f*.

crawling ['krɔːlɪŋ] ◇ *adj* -**1.** *inf pej* [grovelling] rampant, de lèche-bottes. -**2.** [on all fours]: **she's reached the ~ stage** [baby] elle commence à marcher à quatre pattes.

◇ *n inf pej* [grovelling]: **if there's one thing I hate, it's ~ to the teacher** s'il y a bien quelque chose que je déteste, c'est qu'on lèche les bottes du prof.

crayfish ['kreɪfɪʃ] (*pl inv* OR **crayfishes**) *n* écrevisse *f*.

crayon ['kreɪɒn] ◇ *n* [coloured pencil] crayon *m* de couleur; **charcoal ~** fusain *m*; **eye/lip ~** crayon pour les yeux/à lèvres; **wax ~** crayon gras.

◇ *vt* [draw] dessiner avec des crayons de couleurs; [colour] colorier (avec des crayons).

craze [kreɪz] ◇ *n* engouement *m*, folie *f*; **it's the latest ~** c'est la dernière folie OR lubie; **the latest dance/music ~** la nouvelle danse/musique à la mode; **it's becoming a ~** ça devient une vraie folie; **a ~ for sthg** un engouement pour qqch; **this ~ for video games** cet engouement pour les jeux vidéo; **the latest ~ is wearing baggy jeans** la dernière mode, c'est de porter des jeans larges; **to have a ~ for sthg** être fou de.

◇ *vt* -**1.** [send mad] rendre fou. -**2.** [damage - ceramics] craqueler; [- windscreen, glass] étoiler.

◇ *vi* [ceramics] se craqueler; [windscreen, glass] s'étoiler.

crazed [kreɪzd] *adj* -**1.** [mad - look, expression] fou; **~ with fear/grief** fou de peur/douleur. -**2.** [ceramics] craquelé.

-crazed *in cpds* rendu fou par; **drug~** rendu fou par la drogue; **power~ dictators** des dictateurs fous de pouvoir; **he was half~ with fear** il était à moitié fou de peur.

crazily ['kreɪzɪlɪ] *adv* [behave] comme un fou.

craziness ['kreɪzɪnɪs] *n* folie *f*; **it's sheer ~** c'est de la folie.

crazy ['kreɪzɪ] (*compar* **crazier**, *superl* **craziest**) *adj* -**1.** [insane - person, dream] fou; **to have ~ eyes** avoir des yeux de fou; **that's a ~ idea!, that's ~!** c'est de la folie!; **this is ~** c'est fou; **he was ~ to do it** il a été fou de le faire; **that's the craziest thing I've ever heard** c'est la chose la plus insensée que j'aie jamais entendue; **to drive** OR **to send sb ~** rendre qqn fou; **it's enough to drive you ~** c'est à vous rendre fou; **he went ~** [insane] il est devenu fou; [angry] il est devenu fou (de colère OR de rage); **the fans went ~** *inf* les fans ne se sont plus sentis; **to be/to go ~ with fear/grief** être/devenir fou de peur/douleur; **power ~** avide de pouvoir; **you must be ~!** mais tu es fou!; **like ~** [work, drive, run, spend money] comme un fou. -**2.** *inf* [very fond]: **to be ~ about** être fou OR dingue de; **I'm not ~ about the idea** l'idée ne m'emballe pas vraiment; **he's football ~** c'est un fana OR un cinglé de foot. -**3.** [strange, fantastic] bizarre. -**4.** *Am* [very good] formidable, génial.

crazy bone *Am* = **funny bone**.

crazy paving *n Br dallage irrégulier en pierres plates*.

CRE (*abbr of* Commission for Racial Equality) *pr n*: **the ~** *commission contre la discrimination raciale*.

creak [kriːk] ◇ *vi* [chair, floorboard, person's joints] craquer; [door hinge] grincer; [new shoes] crisser; **to ~ with age** *fig* donner des signes de vieillesse; **the legal system is ~ing under the weight of untried cases** *fig* le système juridique craque sous le poids des affaires en suspens.

◇ *n* [of chair, floorboard, person's joints] craquement *m*; [of door hinge] grincement *m*; [of new shoes] crissement *m*; **to give a ~** craquer, grincer, crisser.

creaking ['kriːkɪŋ] ◇ *adj* = **creaky**.

◇ *n* [of chair, floorboard, person's joints] craquement *m*; [of door hinge] grincement *m*; [of shoes] crissement *m*.

creaky ['kriːkɪ] (*compar* **creakier**, *superl* **creakiest**) *adj* [chair, floorboard, person's joints] qui craque; [door hinge] grinçant; [shoes] qui crisse; **a ~ noise** un craquement, un grincement, un crissement.

cream [kriːm] ◇ *n* -**1.** crème *f*; **do you like ~ in your coffee?** vous prenez de la crème dans votre café?; **strawberries and ~** des fraises à la crème; **~ of tomato soup** velouté *m* de tomates ❑ **clotted ~** *Br* crème très épaisse; **single/double ~** *Br* crème fraîche liquide/épaisse; **whipping ~** crème fraîche à fouetter, crème fleurette. -**2.** [filling for biscuits, chocolates] crème *f*; **vanilla ~** [biscuit] biscuit *m* fourré à la vanille; [dessert] crème *f* à la vanille. -**3.** [mixture] mélange *m* crémeux. -**4.** *fig* [best, pick] crème *f*; **the ~ of society** la crème OR le gratin de la société; **they were the ~ of their year at university** ils formaient l'élite de leur promotion à l'université ❑ **the ~ of the crop** le dessus du panier. -**5.** [for face, shoes etc] crème *f*. -**6.** [colour] crème *m*.

◇ *comp* [cake, bun] à la crème; [jug] à crème; **~-coloured** crème; **~ sherry** sherry *m* OR xérès *m* doux.

◇ *adj* crème.

◇ *vt* -**1.** [skim - milk] écrémer. -**2.** CULIN [beat] écraser, travailler; **~ the butter and sugar** travailler le beurre et le sucre en crème; **~ed potatoes** purée *f* de pommes de terre. -**3.** [hands, face] mettre de la crème sur. -**4.** [add cream to - coffee] mettre de la crème dans. -**5.** *inf Am* [beat up] casser la figure à; [defeat] battre à plate couture, mettre la pâtée à; **we got ~ed 4-0** on s'est fait écraser 4-0. -**6.** *phr*: **to ~ one's jeans**▼ prendre son pied.

◇ *vi* -**1.** ▼ [man - ejaculate] décharger, balancer la sauce; [woman - be aroused] mouiller. -**2.** [milk] crémer.

◆ **cream off** *vt sep fig* [take for oneself] prendre pour soi; [keep for oneself] garder pour soi, se garder; [money] prélever; **to ~ off the best students** sélectionner les meilleurs étudiants; **they have ~ed off the elite** ils se sont accaparé l'élite.

cream cheese *n* fromage *m* frais.

cream cracker *n Br* biscuit *m* sec.

creamer ['kriːməʳ] *n* -**1.** [machine] écrémeuse *f*. -**2.** [for coffee] succédané *m* de crème. -**3.** *Am* [jug] pot *m* à crème.

creamery ['kriːmərɪ] *n* -**1.** INDUST laiterie *f*. -**2.** [shop] crémerie *f*.

cream of tartar *n* crème *f* de tartre.

cream puff *n* chou *m* à la crème.

cream soda *n boisson gazeuse aromatisée à la vanille*.

cream tea *n Br goûter composé de thé et de scones servis avec de la confiture et de la crème*.

creamy ['kriːmɪ] (*compar* **creamier**, *superl* **creamiest**) *adj* -**1.** [containing cream - coffee, sauce] à la crème; [- milk] qui contient de la crème; **it's too ~** il y a trop de crème. -**2.** [smooth - drink, sauce etc] crémeux; **~ complexion** teint *m* laiteux et velouté; **~ voice** voix *f* veloutée. -**3.** [colour]: **~ white** blanc cassé.

crease [kriːs] ◇ *n* -**1.** [in material, paper - made on purpose] pli *m*; [- accidental] faux pli *m*; [in skin, on face] pli *m*; **to put a ~ in a pair of trousers** faire le pli d'un pantalon; **in order to get rid of the ~s** [in shirt, blouse etc] pour le/la défroisser. -**2.** [in cricket] limite *f* du batteur.

◇ *vt* -**1.** [on purpose] faire les plis de; [accidentally] froisser, chiffonner; **this shirt is all ~d** cette chemise est toute froissée. -**2.** *inf* [amuse]: **this one'll ~ you** celle-là va te faire mourir de rire.

◇ *vi* [clothes] se froisser, se chiffonner; **his face ~d with laughter** son visage s'est plissé de rire.

◆ **crease up** *inf* ◇ *vi insep* se tordre de rire.

◇ *vt sep* faire mourir OR se tordre de rire; **you just have to look at him and he ~s you up** il suffit de le regarder pour se tordre de rire.

crease-resistant *adj* infroissable.

create [kriː'eɪt] ◇ *vt* -**1.** [employment, problem, the world] créer; [fuss, noise, impression, draught] faire; **to ~ a stir** OR **a sensation** faire sensation; **to ~ a disturbance** JUR porter atteinte à l'ordre public. -**2.** [appoint]: **he was ~d (a) baron** il a été fait baron.

◇ *vi* -**1.** [be creative] créer; **the instinct to ~ is strong in all of us** il y a un puissant instinct de création en chacun d'entre nous. -**2.** *inf Br* [cause a fuss] faire des histoires.

creation [kri:'eɪʃn] *n* -**1.** [process of creating] création *f*; **the Creation** BIBLE la Création; **the most beautiful woman in all ~** OR **the whole of ~** *fig* la plus belle femme de la terre ❑ **where in ~ did you get that hat!** *inf* où diable as-tu trouvé ce chapeau! -**2.** [something created] création *f*.

creative [kri:'eɪtɪv] *adj* [person, mind, skill] créatif; *hum & pej* (trop) libre; **the ~ instinct** l'instinct *m* de création; **to encourage sb to be ~** encourager la créativité chez qqn; **we need some ~ thinking** nous avons besoin d'idées originales ❑ **~ writing** techniques *fpl* de l'écriture.

creatively [kri:'eɪtɪvlɪ] *adv* de manière créative; **you're not thinking very ~ about your future** tu n'as pas d'idées très originales pour ton avenir.

creativeness [kri:'eɪtɪvnɪs], **creativity** [,kri:eɪ'tɪvətɪ] *n* créativité *f*.

creator [kri:'eɪtə^r] *n* créateur *m*, -trice *f*; **the Creator** le Créateur.

creature ['kri:tʃə^r] *n* -**1.** [person] créature *f*; [animal] bête *f*; **we are all God's ~s** nous sommes tous les créatures de Dieu; **~s from outer space** des créatures de l'espace; **dumb ~s** les bêtes; **poor ~!** [person, animal] le/la pauvre!; **he's a ~ of habit** il est esclave de ses habitudes. -**2.** *lit & pej* [dependent person] créature *f*.

creature comforts *npl* confort *m* matériel; **I like my ~** j'aime OR je suis attaché à mon (petit) confort.

crèche [kreʃ] *n Br* crèche *f*, garderie *f*.

credence ['kri:dns] *n* croyance *f*, foi *f*; **to give** OR **to attach ~ to sthg** ajouter foi à qqch; **to give** OR **to lend ~ to sthg** rendre qqch crédible ❑ **letters of ~** [ambassador] lettres *fpl* de créance.

credentials [krɪ'denʃlz] *npl* -**1.** [references] références *fpl*. -**2.** [identity papers] papiers *mpl* d'identité; **to ask to see sb's ~** demander ses papiers (d'identité) à qqn, demander une pièce d'identité à qqn. -**3.** [of diplomat] lettres *fpl* de créance.

credibility [,kredə'bɪlətɪ] ◇ *n* -**1.** [trustworthiness] crédibilité *f*; **the party has lost ~ with the electorate** le parti a perdu de sa crédibilité auprès de l'électorat; **there are doubts about its ~ as a deterrent** on doute de son efficacité en tant que moyen de dissuasion. -**2.** [belief]: **it's beyond ~** c'est invraisemblable, c'est difficile à croire.

◇ *comp*: **~ rating** crédibilité *f*; **he has a ~ problem** il manque de crédibilité.

credibility gap *n* manque *m* de crédibilité; **the party has a major ~** le parti souffre d'un énorme manque de crédibilité, le parti manque énormément de crédibilité; **to narrow the ~** regagner de sa crédibilité.

credible ['kredəbl] *adj* [person] crédible; [evidence, statement] crédible, plausible; **I don't find his reassurances very ~** j'ai du mal à croire ce qu'il dit pour me rassurer.

credibly ['kredəblɪ] *adv* [argue] de manière crédible.

credit ['kredɪt] ◇ *n* -**1.** FIN crédit *m*; **to be in ~** [person] avoir de l'argent sur son compte; [account] être approvisionné; **he has £50 to his ~** il a 50 livres sur son compte; **to enter** OR **to place a sum to sb's ~** créditer le compte de qqn d'une somme; **debit and ~** débit *m* et crédit ‖ [loan]: **to give sb ~, to give ~ to sb** [bank] accorder un découvert à qqn; [shop, pub] faire crédit à qqn; **'we do not give ~'** 'la maison ne fait pas crédit'; **to sell/to buy/to live on ~** vendre/acheter/vivre à crédit; **interest-free ~** crédit gratuit; **line of ~** *Am* limite *f* OR plafond *m* de crédit; **her ~ is good** elle a une bonne réputation de solvabilité; *fig* [trustworthy] elle est digne de confiance; **isn't my ~ good any more?** *fig* on ne me fait plus confiance? -**2.** [merit, honour] mérite *m*; **all the ~ should go to the team** tout le mérite doit revenir à l'équipe; **to take the ~ for sthg/doing sthg** s'attribuer le mérite de qqch/d'avoir fait qqch; **I can't take all the ~ for it** tout le mérite ne me revient pas; **to give sb the ~ for sthg/doing sthg** attribuer à qqn le mérite de qqch/d'avoir fait qqch; **management got all the ~** tout le mérite est revenu à la direction; **give her ~ for what she has achieved** reconnais ce qu'elle a accompli; **with ~** [perform] honorablement; **nobody emerged with any ~ except him** c'est le seul qui s'en soit sorti à son honneur; **it must be said to his ~ that...** il faut dire en sa faveur que...; **to her ~ she did finish the exam** il faut lui accorder qu'elle a fini l'examen; **she has five novels to her ~** elle a cinq romans à son actif; **to be a ~ to one's family/school, to do one's family/school ~** faire honneur à sa famille/son école, être l'honneur de sa famille/son école; **it does her (great) ~** c'est tout à son honneur; **it does you ~ that you gave the money back** c'est tout à votre honneur d'avoir rendu l'argent; **give me SOME ~!** je ne suis quand même pas si bête!; **~ where ~ is due** il faut reconnaître ce qui est. -**3.** [credence] croyance *f*; **to give ~ to sb/sthg** ajouter foi à qqn/qqch; **to lend ~ to sthg** accréditer qqch, rendre qqch plausible; **to lose ~** [partially] perdre de son crédit; [totally] perdre son crédit; **the theory is gaining ~** cette théorie est de plus en plus acceptée; **he's cleverer than I gave him ~ for** il est plus intelligent que je le pensais OR supposais; **I gave you ~ for more sense** je vous supposais plus de bon sens; **I gave him ~ for more sense than I perhaps should have done** j'ai peut-être surestimé son bon sens. -**4.** UNIV unité *f* de valeur, UV *f*; **how many ~s do you need?** combien d'UV faut-il que tu aies?

◇ *comp* [boom, control] du crédit; [sales] à crédit; [balance] créditeur; **~ entry** écriture *f* au crédit; **~ side** crédit *m*, avoir *m*; **on the ~ side, the proposed changes will cut costs** *fig* les changements projetés auront l'avantage de réduire les coûts; **on the ~ side, he's a good cook** *fig* il faut lui accorder qu'il cuisine bien; **to run a ~ check on sb** [enough money in account] vérifier la solvabilité de qqn, vérifier que le compte de qqn est approvisionné; [no record of bad debts] vérifier le passé bancaire de qqn ❑ **~ agency** OR *Am* **bureau** *établissement chargé de vérifier le passé bancaire de personnes ou d'entreprises sollicitant un crédit*.

◇ *vt* -**1.** FIN [account] créditer; **to ~ an account with £200, to ~ £200 to an account** créditer un compte de 200 livres. -**2.** [accord]: **to ~ sb with intelligence/tact/sense** supposer de l'intelligence/du tact/du bon sens à qqn; **I ~ed her with more sense** je lui supposais plus de bon sens; **~ me with a bit more intelligence!** tu serais gentil de ne pas sous-estimer mon intelligence!; **she is ~ed with being the first woman to attend medical school** elle est considérée comme la première femme à avoir fait des études de médecine; **he is ~ed with the discovery of DNA** on lui attribue la découverte de l'ADN. -**3.** [believe] croire; **would you ~ it!** tu te rends compte!; **you wouldn't ~ some of the things he's done** tu n'en reviendrais pas si tu savais les choses qu'il a faites; **I could hardly ~ it** j'avais du mal à le croire.

◆ **credits** *npl* CIN & TV générique *m*.

creditable ['kredɪtəbl] *adj* honorable, estimable.

creditably ['kredɪtəblɪ] *adv* honorablement.

credit account *n* -**1.** BANK compte *m* créditeur. -**2.** *Br* [with shop] compte *m* client.

credit card ◇ *n* carte *f* de crédit; **to pay by ~** payer avec une OR régler par carte de crédit.

◇ *comp*: **~ fraud** usage *m* frauduleux de cartes de crédit; **~ transactions** transactions *fpl* effectuées par carte de crédit.

credit facilities *npl* facilités *fpl* de crédit.

credit institution *n* établissement *m* de crédit.

credit limit *n* limite *f* OR plafond *m* de crédit.

credit line *n* -**1.** *Br* autorisation *f* de crédit. -**2.** *Am* = **credit limit**.

credit note *n Br* [in business] facture *f* OR note *f* d'avoir; [in shop] avoir *m*.

creditor ['kredɪtə^r] *n* créancier *m*, -ère *f*; **~ countries** nations *fpl* créancières.

credit rating *n* degré *m* de solvabilité.

credit squeeze *n* restriction *f* OR encadrement *m* du crédit; **there's a ~** le crédit est restreint OR encadré.

credit terms *npl* modalités *fpl* de crédit.

credit transfer *n* virement *m*, transfert *m* (de compte à compte).

creditworthiness ['kredɪt,wɜ:ðɪnɪs] *n* solvabilité *f*.

creditworthy ['kredɪt,wɜ:ðɪ] *adj* solvable.

credo ['kreɪdəʊ] *n* credo *m inv*.

credulity [krɪ'dju:lətɪ] *n* crédulité *f*.

credulous ['kredjʊləs] *adj* crédule, naïf.

credulously ['kredjʊləslɪ] *adv* naïvement.

creed [kri:d] *n* [religious] credo *m*, croyance *f*; [political] credo *m*; **people of every colour and ~** des gens de toutes races et de toutes croyances; **the Creed** RELIG le Credo.

creek [kri:k] *n Br* [of sea] crique *f*, anse *f*; *Am* [stream] ruisseau *m*; [river] rivière *f*; **to be up the ~** *inf* être dans de beaux draps OR dans le pétrin; **to be up shit ~ (without a paddle)**[▽] être dans la merde (jusqu'au cou).

creel [kri:l] *n* [for fish] panier *m* à poisson; [for catching lobsters] casier *m*.

creep [kri:p] (*pt & pp* **crept** [krept]) ◇ *n inf* [unpleasant person] dégoûtant OR répugnant personnage *m*, rat *m*; [weak, pathetic person] pauvre type *m*; **I can't stand that ~ she's married to** je ne peux pas voir le plouc avec qui elle est mariée.

◇ *vi* -**1.** [person, animal] se glisser; **to ~ into a room** entrer sans bruit OR se glisser dans une pièce; **I crept upstairs** je suis monté sans bruit; **to ~ into bed** se glisser dans le lit; **I was ~ing about so as not to waken you** je ne faisais pas de bruit pour ne pas te réveiller; **I can hear somebody ~ing about downstairs** j'entends quelqu'un bouger en bas; **the dog crept under the chair** le chien s'est tapi sous la chaise; **the shadows crept across the lawn** l'ombre a peu à peu envahi la pelouse; **the hours crept slowly by** les heures se sont écoulées lentement; **fear began to ~ into his heart** OR **over him** *fig* la peur a commencé à le gagner OR à s'insinuer en lui. -**2.** [plant - along the ground] ramper; [- upwards] grimper. -**3.** *phr*: **to make sb's flesh ~** donner la chair de poule à qqn, faire froid dans le dos à qqn.

◆ **creeps** *inf npl*: **he gives me the ~s** [is frightening] il me fait froid dans le dos, il me donne la chair de poule; [is unpleasant] il me dégoûte OR répugne.

◆ **creep in** *vi insep* [person] entrer sans bruit; *fig* [mistakes] se glisser; [doubts, fears] s'insinuer; **the use of the word as a verb is beginning to ~ in** l'usage de ce mot en tant que verbe commence à se répandre OR gagner du terrain.

◆ **creep out** *vi insep* sortir sans bruit.

◆ **creep up** *vi insep* -**1.** [approach] s'approcher sans bruit; **old age is ~ing up** la vieillesse s'approche doucement; **to ~ up to sthg** s'approcher sans bruit de qqch; **to ~ up behind sb** s'approcher doucement OR discrètement de qqn par derrière. -**2.** [increase - water, prices] monter lentement; [- sales] monter OR progresser lentement; **sales have crept up to the million mark** les ventes ont progressé lentement jusqu'à la barre du million.

◆ **creep up on** *vt insep* -**1.** [in order to attack, surprise] s'approcher discrètement de, s'approcher à pas de loup de; **don't ~ up on me like that!** ne t'approche pas de moi sans faire de bruit comme ça!; **darkness crept up on us** l'obscurité est arrivée sans que nous nous en rendions compte, nous avons été surpris par l'obscurité; **old age crept up on me** je suis devenu vieux sans m'en rendre compte.

-**2.** [catch up with - in competition, business etc] rattraper peu à peu; the deadline is ~ing up on us la date limite se rapproche.

creeper ['kriːpəʳ] *n* -**1.** [plant] plante *f* grimpante. -**2.** *inf Br* [shoe] chaussure *f* à semelles de crêpe.

creeping ['kriːpɪŋ] *adj* -**1.** [plant - upwards] grimpant; [- along the ground] rampant. -**2.** [insect] rampant. -**3.** *fig* [inflation] rampant; [change] graduel; ~ paralysis paralysie *f* progressive.

creepy *inf* ['kriːpɪ] (*compar* creepier, *superl* creepiest) *adj* qui donne la chair de poule, qui fait froid dans le dos; he's/it's ~ il/ça vous donne la chair de poule.

creepy-crawly *inf* [-'krɔːlɪ] (*pl* creepy-crawlies) ◇ *n Br* petite bestiole *f*.
◇ *adj*: a horrible ~ feeling une très désagréable sensation de fourmillement.

cremate [krɪ'meɪt] *vt* incinérer.

cremation [krɪ'meɪʃn] *n* incinération *f*, crémation *f*.

crematorium [ˌkremə'tɔːrɪəm] (*pl* crematoria [-rɪə] OR crematoriums) *n* [establishment] crématorium *m*; [furnace] four *m* crématoire.

crematory ['kremətrɪ] (*pl* crematories) *Am* = **crematorium**.

crème caramel [ˌkremkærə'mel] *n* crème *f* (au) caramel.

crème de la crème ['kremdəlæ'krem] *n*: the ~ le gratin, le dessus du panier.

crème de menthe ['kremdə'maːnt] *n* crème *f* de menthe.

crenellated *Br*, **crenelated** *Am* ['krenəleɪtɪd] *adj* crénelé, à créneaux.

crenellation *Br*, **crenelation** *Am* [ˌkrenə'leɪʃn] *n (usu pl)* créneau *m*.

Creole ['kriːəʊl] ◇ *n* -**1.** LING créole *m*. -**2.** [person] créole *mf*.
◇ *adj* créole.

creosote ['krɪəsəʊt] ◇ *n* créosote *f*.
◇ *vt* traiter à la créosote.

crepe [kreɪp] ◇ *n* -**1.** [fabric] crêpe *m*. -**2.** = **crepe rubber**. -**3.** = **crepe paper**. -**4.** [pancake] crêpe *f*.
◇ *comp* [skirt, blouse etc] de OR en crêpe.

crepe bandage *n* bande *f* Velpeau®.

crepe paper *n* papier *m* crépon.

crepe rubber *n* crêpe *m*.

crepe(-soled) shoes [-səʊld-] *npl* chaussures *fpl* à semelles de crêpe.

crept [krept] *pt* & *pp* → **creep**.

crepuscular [krɪ'pʌskjʊləʳ] *adj lit* crépusculaire.

crescendo [krɪ'ʃendəʊ] (*pl* crescendos OR crescendoes) ◇ *n fig* & MUS crescendo *m*.
◇ *vi* [gen] augmenter; MUS faire un crescendo.
◇ *adv* MUS crescendo, en augmentant.

crescent ['kresnt] ◇ *n* -**1.** [shape] croissant *m*; the Crescent [Islamic emblem] le Croissant; the Crescent City *surnom de La Nouvelle-Orléans*. -**2.** *Br* [street] rue *f* (en arc de cercle).
◇ *adj* [shaped] en (forme de) croissant; ~ moon croissant *m* de lune.

cress [kres] *n* cresson *m*.

Cressida ['kresɪdə] *pr n* Cressida.

crest [krest] ◇ *n* -**1.** [peak - of hill, wave] crête *f*; [- of ridge] arête *f*; [- of road] haut *m* OR sommet *m* de côte; she's (riding) on the ~ of a wave just now *fig* tout lui réussit OR elle a le vent en poupe en ce moment. -**2.** [on bird, lizard] crête *f*; [on helmet] cimier *m*. -**3.** [coat of arms] timbre *m*; [emblem] armoiries *fpl*; a family ~ des armoiries familiales.
◇ *vt* -**1.** [reach the top of] franchir la crête de. -**2.** [provide with emblem] armorier.
◇ *vi* monter en crête.

crested ['krestɪd] *adj* -**1.** [animal] orné d'une crête; [bird] huppé; ~ tit mésange *f* huppée. -**2.** [with emblem] armorié.

crestfallen ['krestˌfɔːln] *adj* découragé, déconfit; the loser looked ~ le perdant avait l'air abattu OR déconfit.

cretaceous [krɪ'teɪʃəs] *adj* crétacé; the Cretaceous (period) GEOL le crétacé.

Cretan ['kriːtn] ◇ *n* Crétois *m*, -e *f*.
◇ *adj* crétois.

Crete [kriːt] *pr n* Crète *f*; in ~ en Crète.

cretin ['kretɪn] *n* -**1.** MED crétin *m*, -e *f*. -**2.** *inf* [idiot] crétin *m*, -e *f*, imbécile *mf*.

cretinism ['kretɪnɪzm] *n* MED crétinisme *m*.

cretinous ['kretɪnəs] *adj* MED & *fig* crétin.

cretonne ['kretɒn] *n* cretonne *f*.

crevasse [krɪ'væs] *n* crevasse *f*; *Am* [in dam] crevasse *f*, fissure *f*.

crevice ['krevɪs] *n* fissure *f*, fente *f*.

crew [kruː] ◇ *Br pt* → **crow**.
◇ *n* -**1.** [gen & CIN] équipe *f*; [on plane, ship] équipage *m*. -**2.** *inf* [crowd, gang] bande *f*, équipe *f*; what a ~! (quelle) drôle d'équipe!
◇ *comp*: ~ member membre *mf* d'équipage.
◇ *vi* servir d'équipier.
◇ *vt* armer *(d'un équipage)*.

crew cut *n* coupe *f* de cheveux en brosse; ~s are in fashion again les cheveux en brosse reviennent à la mode.

crewel ['kruːəl] *n* [yarn] laine *f* à broder OR à tapisserie; ~ work tapisserie *f* sur canevas.

crew neck *n* col *m* ras le OR du cou, ras-le-cou *m*.
◆ **crew-neck** *adj*: a crew-neck sweater un pul ras le OR du cou.

crib [krɪb] (*pt* & *pp* cribbed, *cont* cribbing) ◇ *n* -**1.** *esp Am* [cot] lit *m* d'enfant. -**2.** [bin] grenier *m* (à blé); [stall] stalle *f*. -**3.** [manger] mangeoire *f*, râtelier *m*; RELIG crèche *f*. -**4.** *inf* [plagiarism] plagiat *m*; *Br* SCH [list of answers] antisèche *m* or *f*. -**5.** = **cribbage**.
◇ *vt* -**1.** *inf* [plagiarize] plagier, copier; he cribbed the answers from his friend SCH il a copié les réponses sur son ami, il a pompé sur son ami. -**2.** [line with planks] consolider avec des planches; TECH boiser.
◇ *vi* copier; the author had cribbed from Shaw l'auteur avait plagié Shaw; don't ~ off me! SCH ne copie pas sur moi!

cribbage ['krɪbɪdʒ] *n (U) jeu de cartes où les points sont marqués sur une planche de bois*.

crib death *n Am* mort *f* subite (du nourrisson).

crick [krɪk] ◇ *n* -**1.** [cramp]: to have a ~ in the neck avoir un torticolis; a ~ in one's back un tour de reins. -**2.** *inf Am dial* [stream] ruisseau *m*.
◇ *vt*: don't ~ your back! ne vous faites pas un tour de reins!; she ~ed her neck elle a attrapé un torticolis.

cricket ['krɪkɪt] ◇ *n* -**1.** [insect] grillon *m*. -**2.** [game] cricket *m*; that's not ~ *inf Br* ça ne se fait pas, ce n'est pas fair-play.
◇ *comp* [ball, bat etc] de cricket.

cricketer ['krɪkɪtəʳ] *n* joueur *m*, -euse *f* de cricket.

cried [kraɪd] *pt* & *pp* → **cry**.

crier ['kraɪəʳ] *n* crieur *m*, -euse *f*; [in court] huissier *m*.

crikey *inf* ['kraɪkɪ] *interj Br dated* mince alors.

crime [kraɪm] *n* -**1.** [gen] crime *m*; ~ is on the decline/rise il y a une baisse/une hausse de la criminalité; a life of ~ une vie de criminel; ~ doesn't pay le crime ne paie pas; a minor OR petty ~ un délit mineur; it's a ~ that she died so young *fig* c'est vraiment injuste qu'elle soit morte si jeune ❑ ~ prevention lutte *f* contre la criminalité; ~ reporter journaliste *mf* qui couvre les affaires criminelles; ~ wave vague *f* de criminalité; ~ writer auteur *m* de romans noirs; 'Crime and Punishment' *Dostoievsky* 'Crime et châtiment'. -**2.** MIL manquement *m* à la discipline, infraction *f*.

Crimea [kraɪ'mɪə] *pr n*: the ~ la Crimée; in the ~ en Crimée.

Crimean [kraɪ'mɪən] ◇ *n* Criméen *m*, -enne *f*.
◇ *adj* criméen; the ~ (War) la guerre de Crimée.

criminal ['krɪmɪnl] ◇ *n* criminel *m*, -elle *f*.
◇ *adj* criminel; to take ~ proceedings against sb JUR poursuivre qqn au pénal; it's ~ the way he treats her *fig* il ne devrait pas avoir le droit de la traiter comme ça ❑ ~ investigation enquête *f* criminelle; the Criminal Investigation Department *Br* → **CID**; the Criminal Records Office *Br* l'identité *f* judiciaire.

criminal assault *n* agression *f* criminelle, voie *f* de fait.

criminal conversation *n* JUR adultère *m*.

criminal court *n* cour *f* d'assises.

criminal damage *n délit consistant à causer volontairement des dégâts matériels*.

criminality [ˌkrɪmɪ'næləti] *n* criminalité *f*.

criminalize, -ise ['krɪmɪnəlaɪz] *vt* criminaliser.

criminal law *n* droit *m* pénal OR criminel.

criminal lawyer *n* avocat *m*, -e *f* au criminel, pénaliste *mf*.

criminally ['krɪmɪnəlɪ] *adv* criminellement; he's been ~ negligent sa négligence est criminelle.

criminal offence *n* délit *m*; drunk driving is a ~ la conduite en état d'ivresse est un crime puni par la loi.

criminal record *n* casier *m* judiciaire; she hasn't got a ~ son casier judiciaire est vierge, elle n'a pas de casier judiciaire.

criminologist [ˌkrɪmɪ'nɒlədʒɪst] *n* criminologiste *mf*.

criminology [ˌkrɪmɪ'nɒlədʒɪ] *n* criminologie *f*.

crimp [krɪmp] ◇ *vt* -**1.** [hair] crêper, friser; [pie crust] pincer; [metal] onduler. -**2.** *inf* TECH [pinch together] pincer, sertir. -**3.** *inf Am* [hinder] gêner, entraver.
◇ *n* -**1.** [wave in hair] cran *m*, ondulation *f*; [fold in metal] ondulation *f*. -**2.** *inf Am* [obstacle] obstacle *m*, entrave *f*. -**3.** TEX pli *m*.

Crimplene® ['krɪmpliːn] *n* ≃ crêpe *m* acrylique.

crimson ['krɪmzn] ◇ *adj* cramoisi; she turned ~ with OR in embarrassment elle a rougi OR est devenue cramoisie de confusion; the evening sky turned ~ le ciel nocturne est devenu pourpre OR s'est empourpré.
◇ *n* cramoisi *m*.

cringe [krɪndʒ] *vi* -**1.** [shrink back] avoir un mouvement de recul, reculer; [cower] se recroqueviller; the dog ~d in terror as the man raised his stick le chien recula de peur quand l'homme leva son bâton; to ~ with embarrassment être mort de honte; it's so sentimental, it makes me ~ un tel mélo, ça me fait fuir!; I ~ at the very thought j'ai envie de rentrer sous terre rien que d'y penser. -**2.** [be servile] ramper.

cringe-making *adj Br hum* embarrassant, gênant.

cringing ['krɪndʒɪŋ] *adj* [fearful] craintif; [servile] servile, obséquieux.

crinkle ['krɪŋkl] ◇ *vt* froisser, chiffonner.
◇ *vi* se froisser, se chiffonner.
◇ *n* -**1.** [wrinkle] fronce *f*, pli *m*; [on face] ride *f*. -**2.** [noise] froissement *m*.

crinkle-cut *adj* [crisps] de forme ondulée.

crinkly ['krɪŋklɪ] (*compar* crinklier, *superl* crinkliest) *adj* [material, paper] gaufré; [hair] crépu, crêpelé.

crinoline ['krɪnəliːn] *n* crinoline *f*.

cripes *inf* [kraɪps] *interj Br* sapristi, mince.

cripple ['krɪpl] ◇ *vt* -**1.** [person] estropier. -**2.** *fig* [damage - industry, system] paralyser; [- plane, ship] désemparer.
◇ *n* -**1.** *dated* & *offensive* [lame person] estropié *m*, -e *f*; [invalid] invalide *mf*; [maimed person] mutilé *m*, -e *f*. -**2.** *fig*: an emotional ~ un caractériel *m*, une caractérielle *f*.

crippled ['krɪpld] *adj* -**1.** [person]: to be ~ with rheumatism être perclus de rhumatismes. -**2.** *fig* [industry, country] paralysé; [plane, ship] accidenté.

crippling ['krɪplɪŋ] *adj* -**1.** [disease] invalidant. -**2.** *fig* [strikes] paralysant; [prices, taxes] écrasant.

crisis ['kraɪsɪs] (*pl* crises [-siːz]) *n* crise *f*; things have come to a ~ la situation a atteint un point critique; the government has a ~ on its hands le gouvernement se trouve face à une crise; to settle OR to resolve a ~ dénouer OR résoudre une crise; the oil ~ le choc pétrolier; a ~ of confidence une crise de confiance; an emotional ~ un passage difficile *(nerveusement)*; ~ management gestion *f* des crises; ~ point point *m* critique.

crisis centre *n* [for disasters] cellule *f* de crise; [for personal help] centre *m* d'aide; [for battered women] association *f* d'aide d'urgence.

crisp [krɪsp] ◇ *adj* -**1.** [crunchy - vegetable] croquant; [- cracker] croquant, croustillant; [- bread] croustillant; [- snow] craquant. -**2.** [fresh - clothing] pimpant; [- linen] apprêté; [- paper] craquant, raide. -**3.** [air, weather] vif, tonifiant. -**4.** [concise - style] précis, clair et net. -**5.** [brusque] tranchant, brusque; [manner] brusque; [tone] acerbe.
◇ *n*: (potato) ~s *Br* (pommes *fpl*) chips *fpl*; burnt to a ~ carbonisé.
◇ *vt* faire chauffer pour rendre croustillant.
◇ *vi* devenir croustillant.

crispbread ['krɪspbred] *n* biscuit *m* scandinave.

crisper ['krɪspəʳ] *n* bac *m* à légumes.

crisply ['krɪsplɪ] *adv* -**1.** [succinctly] avec concision. -**2.** [sharply] d'un ton acerbe OR cassant.

crispness ['krɪspnɪs] *n* -**1.** [of food, paper] craquant *m*; [of clothing, sheets, weather] fraîcheur *f*. -**2.** [of reasoning] clarté *f*, rigueur *f*. -**3.** [of style] précision *f*. -**4.** [brusqueness] tranchant *m*, brusquerie *f*.

crispy ['krɪspɪ] (*compar* crispier, *superl* crispiest) *adj* [vegetables] croquant; [biscuits] croquant, croustillant; [bacon] croustillant.

crisscross ['krɪskrɒs] ◇ *vt* entrecroiser; footpaths ~ed the hillside des chemins s'entrecroisaient sur le flanc de la colline.
◇ *vi* s'entrecroiser.
◇ *adj* [lines] entrecroisé; [in disorder] enchevêtré; in a ~ pattern en croisillons.
◇ *n* entrecroisement *m*; a ~ of paths un réseau de chemins.
◇ *adv* en réseau.

criterion [kraɪ'tɪərɪən] (*pl* criteria [-rɪə]) *n* critère *m*.

critic ['krɪtɪk] *n* [reviewer] critique *m*; [fault-finder] critique *m*, détracteur *m*, -trice *f*; it's all very well being an armchair ~ la critique est facile, l'art est difficile; film/art/theatre ~ critique *m* de cinéma/d'art/de théâtre.

critical ['krɪtɪkl] *adj* -**1.** [crucial] critique, crucial; [situation] critique; at a ~ time à un moment critique OR crucial; he's in a ~ condition OR on the ~ list il est dans un état critique; the ~ path [gen & COMPUT] le chemin critique ‖ PHYS critique; the nuclear reactor went ~ la réaction nucléaire en chaîne s'est déclenchée. -**2.** [analytical] critique; [disparaging] critique, négatif; he's very ~ of others il critique beaucoup les autres, il est très critique vis-à-vis des autres; to look at sthg with a ~ eye regarder qqch d'un œil critique; don't be so ~ ne soyez pas si négatif. -**3.** ART, LITERAT & MUS [analysis, edition] critique; [essay, study] critique, de critique; [from the critics] des critiques; the play met with ~ acclaim la pièce fut applaudie par la critique.

critical angle *n* angle *m* critique.

critically ['krɪtɪklɪ] *adj* -**1.** [analytically] d'un œil critique, en critique; [disparagingly] sévèrement. -**2.** [seriously] gravement; she is ~ ill elle est gravement malade, elle est dans un état critique.

critical mass *n* masse *f* critique.

critical temperature *n* température *f* critique.

criticism ['krɪtɪsɪzm] *n* critique *f*; to come in for ~ se faire OR se voir critiquer; this isn't meant as a ~ but... ce n'est pas une critique mais..., ce n'est pas pour critiquer mais...; literary ~ la critique littéraire.

criticize, -ise ['krɪtɪsaɪz] *vt* -**1.** [find fault with] critiquer, réprouver. -**2.** [analyse] critiquer, faire la critique de.

critique [krɪ'tiːk] ◇ *n* critique *f*; 'Critique of Pure Reason' *Kant* 'Critique de la raison pure'.
◇ *vt* faire une critique de.

critter *inf* ['krɪtəʳ] *n Am* [creature] créature *f*; [animal] bête *f*, bestiole *f*.

croak [krəʊk] ◇ *vi* -**1.** [frog] coasser; [crow] croasser. -**2.** [person] parler d'une voix rauque; [grumble] ronchonner. -**3.** *inf* [die] crever.
◇ *vt* [utter] dire d'une voix rauque OR éraillée.
◇ *n* [of frog] coassement *m*; [of crow] croassement *m*; [of person] ton *m* rauque.

croaking ['krəʊkɪŋ] *n* [of frog] coassement *m*; [of crow] croassement *m*.

croaky ['krəʊkɪ] *adj* enroué.

Croat ['krəʊæt] = **Croatian** *n*.

Croatia [krəʊ'eɪʃə] *pr n* Croatie *f*; in ~ en Croatie.

Croatian [krəʊ'eɪʃn] ◇ *n* -**1.** [person] Croate *mf*. -**2.** LING croate *m*.
◇ *adj* croate.

crochet ['krəʊʃeɪ] ◇ *n*: ~ (work) (travail *m* au) crochet *m*.
◇ *vt* faire au crochet.
◇ *vi* faire du crochet.

crochet-hook *n* crochet *m*.

crock [krɒk] *n* -**1.** [jar, pot] cruche *f*, pot *m* de terre; [broken earthenware] morceau *m* de faïence, tesson *m*; that's a ~ (of shit)!▽ *Am* tout ça, c'est de la blague! -**2.** *inf Br*: old ~ [car] tacot *m*, guimbarde *f*; [person] croulant *m*.
◆ **crocks** *npl* vaisselle *f*.

crockery ['krɒkərɪ] *n* [pottery] poterie *f*, faïence *f*; [plates, cups, bowls etc] vaisselle *f*.

crocodile ['krɒkədaɪl] *n* -**1.** [reptile] crocodile *m*. -**2.** *Br* SCH cortège *m* en rangs *(par deux)*; to walk in a ~ marcher deux par deux.

crocodile clip *n* pince *f* crocodile.

crocodile tears *npl* larmes *fpl* de crocodile.

crocus ['krəʊkəs] *n* crocus *m*.

Croesus ['kriːsəs] *pr n* Crésus; as rich as ~ riche comme Crésus.

croft [krɒft] *n Br* petite ferme *f*.

crofter ['krɒftəʳ] *n Br* [farmer] petit fermier *m*.

crofting ['krɒftɪŋ] *n* (exploitation *f* en) affermage *m*.

cromlech ['krɒmlek] *n* [circle of stones] cromlech *m*; [tomb] tombeau *m* OR tombe *f* mégalithique.

crone *inf* [krəʊn] *n* vieille bique *f*.

Cronos ['krəʊnɒs] *pr n* Cronos.

crony *inf* ['krəʊnɪ] (*pl* cronies) *n* pote *m*, copine *f*.

crook [krʊk] ◇ *n* -**1.** *inf* [thief] escroc *m*, filou *m*. -**2.** [bend - in road] courbe *f*, coude *m*; [- in river] coude *m*, détour *m*; [- in arm] coude *m*; [- in leg] flexion *f*. -**3.** [staff - of shepherd] houlette *f*; [- of bishop] crosse *f*.
◇ *vt* [finger] courber, recourber; [arm] plier.

crooked ['krʊkɪd] ◇ *adj* -**1.** [not straight, bent - stick] courbé, crochu; [- path] tortueux; [- person] courbé; a ~ smile un sourire grimaçant. -**2.** *inf* [dishonest] malhonnête.
◇ *adv* de travers.

crookedly ['krʊkɪdlɪ] *adv* -**1.** [walk, stand] de travers. -**2.** [smile] en grimaçant.

crookedness ['krʊkɪdnɪs] *n* -**1.** [curvature] courbure *f*. -**2.** *inf* [dishonesty] malhonnêteté *f*, fausseté *f*.

croon [kruːn] *vi & vt* -**1.** [sing softly] fredonner, chantonner; [professionally] chanter *(en crooner)*. -**2.** [speak softly, sentimentally] susurrer.

crooner ['kruːnəʳ] *n* crooner *m*, chanteur *m* de charme.

crop [krɒp] (*pt & pp* cropped, *cont* cropping)
◇ *n* -**1.** [produce] produit *m* agricole, culture *f*; food ~s cultures vivrières ‖ [harvest] récolte *f*; [of fruit] récolte *f*, cueillette *f*; [of grain] moisson *f*; to get in OR to harvest the ~s faire la récolte, rentrer les récoltes; we had a good wheat ~ OR ~ of wheat le blé a bien donné. -**2.** *fig* fournée *f*; what do you think of this year's ~ of students? que pensez-vous des étudiants de cette année? -**3.** [of whip] manche *m*; [riding whip] cravache *f*. -**4.** [of bird] jabot *m*. -**5.** [haircut - for man] coupe *f* rase OR courte; [- for woman] coupe courte OR à la garçonne; the barber gave me a (close) ~ le coiffeur m'a coupé les cheveux ras.
◇ *vt* -**1.** [cut - hedge] tailler, tondre; [- hair] tondre; [- tail] écourter; PHOT recadrer. -**2.** [subj: animal] brouter, paître. -**3.** [farm] cultiver; [harvest] récolter.
◇ *vi* [land, vegetables] donner OR fournir une récolte; the tomatoes are cropping well this year la récolte de tomates est bonne OR les tomates donnent bien cette année.
◆ **crop up** *inf vi insep* survenir, se présenter; his name cropped up in the conversation son nom a surgi dans la conversation; we'll deal with anything that ~s up while you're away on s'occupera de tout pendant votre absence.

crop dusting = **crop spraying**.

cropper *inf* ['krɒpəʳ] *n Br phr*: to come a ~ [fall] se casser la figure; [fail] se planter; I came a ~ in the exams je me suis ramassé OR planté aux examens.

crop rotation *n* assolement *m*, rotation *f* des cultures.

crop spraying *n* pulvérisation *f* des cultures.

croquet ['krəʊkeɪ] ◇ *n* croquet *m*.
◇ *comp* [hoop, lawn, mallet] de croquet.

croquette [krɒ'ket] *n* croquette *f*; potato ~ croquette de pomme de terre.

crosier ['krəʊʒjəʳ] *n* crosse *f (d'évêque)*.

cross [krɒs] ◇ *n* -**1.** [mark, symbol] croix *f*; he signed with a ~ il a signé d'une croix ❑ the Iron Cross la Croix de fer. -**2.** RELIG croix *f*; the Cross la Croix ‖ *fig* [burden] croix *f*; we each have our ~ to bear chacun a OR porte sa croix. -**3.** [hybrid] hybride *m*; a ~ between a horse and a donkey un croisement *m* d'un cheval et d'une ânesse; the novel is a ~ between a thriller and a comedy *fig* ce roman est un mélange de policier et de comédie. -**4.** SEW: on the ~ en biais; to cut sthg on the ~ couper qqch dans le biais; a sleeve cut on the ~ une manche coupée en biais.
◇ *vt* -**1.** [go across - road, room, sea] traverser; [- bridge, river] traverser, passer; [- fence, threshold] franchir; the bridge ~es the river at Orléans le pont franchit OR enjambe le fleuve à Orléans; she ~ed the Atlantic elle a fait la traversée de l'Atlantique; to ~ a picket line franchir un piquet de grève; a look of distaste ~ed her face une expression de dégoût passa sur son visage; it ~ed my mind that... j'ai pensé OR l'idée m'a effleuré que...; he ~ed my path again a few years later nos chemins se sont à nouveau croisés quelques années plus tard ❑ to ~ the floor (of the House) *Br* POL changer de parti politique; I'll ~ that bridge when I come to it je m'occuperai de ce problème en temps voulu. -**2.** [place one across the other] croiser; to ~ one's arms/one's legs croiser les bras/les jambes ❑ ~ your fingers OR keep your fingers ~ed for me pense à moi et croise les doigts; to ~ swords with sb croiser le fer avec qqn; we got our wires ~ed *inf* il y a un malentendu quelque part entre nous; ~ my palm (with silver)! donnez-moi une petite pièce! -**3.** [mark with cross] faire une croix; to ~ o.s. RELIG faire le signe de (la) croix, se signer; ~ your "t"s barrez OR mettez des barres à vos «t»; to ~ a cheque *Br* barrer un chèque ❑ ~ my heart and hope to die *inf* croix de bois croix de fer, si je mens je vais en enfer. -**4.** [animals, plants] croiser. -**5.** [oppose] contrarier, contrecarrer; ~ed in love malheureux en amour. -**6.** TELEC: we've got a ~ed line il y a des interférences sur la ligne.
◇ *vi* -**1.** [go across] traverser; she ~ed (over) to the door elle est allée à la porte; she ~ed (over) to the other side of the road elle a traversé la route; we ~ed from Belgium into France nous sommes passés de Belgique en France; they ~ed from Dover to Boulogne ils ont fait la traversée de Douvres à Boulogne. -**2.** [intersect - lines, paths, roads] se croiser, se rencontrer; our letters ~ed in the post nos lettres se sont croisées.
◇ *adj* -**1.** [angry] de mauvaise humeur, en colère; she's ~ with me elle est fâchée contre

moi; don't be ~ with me il ne faut pas m'en vouloir; he makes me so ~! qu'est-ce qu'il peut m'agacer!; I got ~ with them je me suis fâché contre eux; I never heard her utter a ~ word elle ne dit jamais un mot plus haut que l'autre ❑ to be as ~ as a bear *inf* être dans une colère noire. -**2.** [diagonal] diagonal; ~ member CONSTR traverse *f*, entremise *f*.

◆ **cross off** *vt sep* [item] barrer, rayer; [person] radier; to ~ sb off the list radier qqn.

◆ **cross out** *vt sep* barrer, rayer.

crossbar ['krɒsbɑːʳ] *n* [on bike] barre *f*; [on goalposts] barre *f* traversale.

crossbeam ['krɒsbiːm] *n* traverse *f*, sommier *m*.

crossbench ['krɒsbentʃ] *n (usu pl) Br* POL *banc où s'assoient les députés non inscrits à un parti*; on the ~es du côté des non-inscrits.

crossbencher [ˌkrɒs'bentʃəʳ] *n Br* POL *au Parlement britannique, membre non inscrit, assis sur les bancs transversaux*.

crossbill ['krɒsbɪl] *n* bec-croisé *m*.

crossbones ['krɒsbəʊnz] *npl* os *mpl* en croix OR de mort.

crossbow ['krɒsbəʊ] *n* arbalète *f*.

crossbred ['krɒsbred] ◇ *adj* hybride, métis.
◇ *n* hybride *m*, métis *m*, -isse *f*.

crossbreed ['krɒsbriːd] (*pt* & *pp* crossbred [-bred]) ◇ *vt* croiser.
◇ *n* [animal, plant] hybride *m*, métis *m*, -isse *f*; *pej* [person] métis *m*, -isse *f*, sang-mêlé *mf*.

cross-Channel *adj Br* [ferry, route] qui traverse la Manche.

cross-check ◇ *vt* contrôler (par contre-épreuve OR par recoupement).
◇ *vi* vérifier par recoupement.
◇ *n* contre-épreuve *f*, recoupement *m*.

cross-country ◇ *n* cross-country *m*, cross *m*.
◇ *adj*: ~ runner coureur *m*, -euse *f* de cross; ~ skiing ski *m* de fond.
◇ *adv* à travers champs.

cross-cultural *adj* interculturel.

cross-current *n* contre-courant *m*.

crosscut ['krɒskʌt] ◇ *adj* [incision] coupé en travers; [tool] qui coupe en travers; ~ chisel bédane *m*; ~ saw scie *f* passe-partout.
◇ *vt* couper en travers.

cross-dressing *n* travestisme *m*, transvestisme *m*.

crosse [krɒs] *n* crosse *f (au jeu de la crosse)*.

crossed [krɒst] *adj* croisé; ~ cheque chèque *m* barré; ~ line TELEC ligne *f* embrouillée.

cross-examination *n* contre-interrogatoire *m*.

cross-examine *vt* [gen] soumettre à un interrogatoire serré; JUR faire subir un contre-interrogatoire à.

cross-eyed *adj* qui louche; she's ~ elle louche.

cross-fertilization *n* croisement *m*; *fig* osmose *f*.

cross-fertilize, -ise *vt* croiser.

crossfire ['krɒsˌfaɪəʳ] *n* feux *mpl* croisés; to be caught in the ~ *literal* & *fig* être pris entre deux feux.

cross-grained *adj* -**1.** [wood] à fibres torses. -**2.** [person] revêche, acariâtre.

cross hairs *npl fils croisés d'une lunette qui déterminent la ligne de visée*.

cross-hatch *vt* hachurer en croisillons.

cross-hatching *n* hachures *fpl* croisées.

crosshead ['krɒshed] *n* -**1.** TYPO sous-titre *m*. -**2.** TECH [block - gen] palier *m*; [- in engine] crosse *f*. -**3.** NAUT (barre *f* de) traverse *f*.

crossheaded ['krɒshedɪd] *adj* [screwdriver] cruciforme.

cross-index ◇ *vi* renvoyer à.
◇ *vt* établir les renvois de.
◇ *n* renvoi *m*, référence *f*.

crossing ['krɒsɪŋ] *n* -**1.** [intersection] croisement *m*; [of roads] croisement *m*, carrefour *m*; pedestrian ~ passage *m* clouté. -**2.** [sea journey] traversée *f*. -**3.** [inter-breeding] croisement *m*.

cross-kick SPORT ◇ *n coup de pied qui envoie le ballon à travers le terrain*.
◇ *vi envoyer le ballon à l'autre bout du terrain*.

cross-legged ['krɒslegd] *adj* en tailleur.

crossly ['krɒslɪ] *adv* avec mauvaise humeur.

crossover ['krɒsˌəʊvəʳ] ◇ *n* -**1.** [of roads] (croisement *m* par) pont *m* routier; [for pedestrians] passage *m* clouté; RAIL voie *f* de croisement. -**2.** BIOL croisement *m*.
◇ *adj* MUS [style] hybride; a ~ record un disque hybride.

cross-party *adj* POL: ~ agreement accord *m* entre des partis.

crosspatch *inf* ['krɒspætʃ] *n* grincheux *m*, -euse *f*.

crosspiece ['krɒspiːs] *n* traverse *f*.

crossply ['krɒsplaɪ] *adj* [tyre] à carcasse diagonale.

cross-pollinate ◇ *vi* se reproduire par pollinisation croisée.
◇ *vt* féconder par pollinisation croisée.

cross-pollination *n* pollinisation *f* croisée.

cross-purposes *npl*: to be at ~ with sb [misunderstand] comprendre qqn de travers; [oppose] être en désaccord avec qqn; we were at ~ il y a eu un malentendu entre nous; they were talking at ~ leur conversation tournait autour d'un quiproquo.

cross-question = **cross-examine**.

cross-refer ◇ *vi*: to ~ to sthg renvoyer à qqch.
◇ *vt* renvoyer.

cross-reference *n* renvoi *m*, référence *f*.

crossroads ['krɒsrəʊdz] *npl* croisement *m*, carrefour *m*; her career is at a ~ sa carrière va maintenant prendre un tournant décisif.

cross-section *n* -**1.** [gen & BIOL] coupe *f* transversale. -**2.** [sample - of population] échantillon *m*.

cross-stitch ◇ *n* point *m* de croix.
◇ *vt* coudre au point de croix.

crosstalk ['krɒsˌtɔːk] *n* -**1.** RADIO & TELEC diaphonie *f*. -**2.** *Br* [witty exchange] joutes *fpl* oratoires.

crosstown ['krɒstaʊn] *Am* ◇ *adj* qui traverse la ville; ~ artery/bus voie *f*/bus *m* qui traverse la ville.
◇ *adv* à travers la ville.

crosstree ['krɒstriː] *n* traverse *f*.

crosswalk ['krɒswɔːk] *n Am* passage *m* clouté.

crosswind ['krɒswɪnd] *n* vent *m* de travers.

cross wires = **cross hairs**.

crosswise ['krɒswaɪz] *adj* & *adv* [shaped like cross] en croix; [across] en travers; [diagonally] en travers, en diagonale.

crossword (puzzle) ['krɒswɜːd-] *n* mots *mpl* croisés.

crotch [krɒtʃ] *n* [of tree] fourche *f*; [of trousers] entre-jambes *m*; she kicked him in the ~ elle lui a donné un coup de pied entre les jambes.

crotchet ['krɒtʃɪt] *n Br* noire *f*.

crotchety *inf* ['krɒtʃɪtɪ] *adj* grognon, bougon.

crouch [kraʊtʃ] ◇ *vi*: to ~ (down) [person] s'accroupir, se tapir; [animal] s'accroupir, se ramasser.
◇ *n* [posture] accroupissement *m*; [act] action *f* de se ramasser.

croup [kruːp] *n* -**1.** [of animal] croupe *f*. -**2.** MED croup *m*.

croupier ['kruːpɪəʳ] *n* croupier *m*.

crouton ['kruːtɒn] *n* croûton *m*.

crow [krəʊ] (*Br pt* crowed OR crew [kruː], *Am pt* crowed) ◇ *n* -**1.** ORNITH corbeau *m*; [smaller] corneille *f*; it's 3 miles as the ~ flies c'est à 3 miles à vol d'oiseau; he had to eat ~ *inf Am* il a dû admettre qu'il avait tort. -**2.** [sound of cock] chant *m* du coq, cocorico *m*. -**3.** [of baby] gazouillis *m*.
◇ *vi* -**1.** [cock] chanter. -**2.** [baby] gazouiller. -**3.** [boast] se vanter; it's nothing to ~ about il n'y a pas de quoi être fier; to ~ over sthg se vanter de qqch.

crowbar ['krəʊbɑːʳ] *n* (pince *f* à) levier *m*.

crowd [kraʊd] ◇ *n* -**1.** [throng] foule *f*, masse *f*; a ~ of noisy children une bande d'enfants bruyants; don't get lost in the ~ ne vous perdez pas dans la foule; a disorderly ~ une cohue; there were ~s of people in town il y avait foule en ville; there was quite a ~ at the match il y avait beaucoup de monde au match; the concert drew a good ~ le concert a attiré beaucoup de monde; she stands out in a ~ elle se distingue de la masse. -**2.** *inf* [social group] bande *f*; to be in with the wrong ~ avoir de mauvaises fréquentations; they stick to their own ~ ils font bande à part. -**3.** *fig* & *pej* [people as a whole]: the ~ la foule, la masse du peuple; she always goes with OR follows the ~ elle suit toujours le mouvement; she doesn't like to be one of the ~ elle n'aime pas faire comme tout le monde.
◇ *vi* se presser; to ~ round sb/sthg se presser autour de qqn/qqch; they ~ed round to read the poster ils se sont attroupés pour lire l'affiche; the reporters ~ed into the room les journalistes se sont entassés dans la pièce; don't all ~ together! ne vous serrez pas comme ça!; they came ~ing through the door ils se sont bousculés pour entrer; we ~ed up/down the stairs tout le monde a monté/descendu l'escalier.
◇ *vt* -**1.** [cram] serrer, entasser; people ~ed the streets/the shops des gens se pressaient dans les rues/les magasins; the tables are ~ed together les tables sont collées les unes aux autres; the park was ~ed with sunbathers le parc était plein de gens qui prenaient des bains de soleil. -**2.** *inf* [jostle] bousculer; stop ~ing me! arrêtez de me bousculer!, ne me poussez pas!; I was ~ed off the bus la foule m'a éjecté du bus. -**3.** NAUT: to ~ on sail mettre toutes les voiles dehors.

◆ **crowd in** *vi insep* -**1.** [enter] entrer en foule, affluer. -**2.** *fig* [flood in] submerger; gloomy thoughts kept ~ing in on me de sombres pensées m'assaillaient.

◆ **crowd out** ◇ *vi insep* sortir en foule.
◇ *vt sep*: we were ~ed out by a bunch of students un groupe d'étudiants nous a poussés vers la sortie; independent traders are being ~ed out by bigger stores les petits commerçants sont étouffés par les grands magasins.

crowded ['kraʊdɪd] *adj* -**1.** [busy - room, building, bus etc] bondé, plein; [- street] plein (de monde); [- town] encombré (de monde), surpeuplé; the ~ streets of Bombay les rues pleines de monde de Bombay; a room ~ with furniture/with people une pièce encombrée de meubles/pleine de monde; the shops are too ~ il y a trop de monde dans les magasins; he has a ~ schedule son emploi du temps est surchargé. -**2.** [overpopulated] surpeuplé; ~ inner-city areas les quartiers surpeuplés du centre-ville.

crowdpleaser ['kraʊdˌpliːzəʳ] *n* [person] démagogue *mf*.

crowdpuller *inf* ['kraʊdˌpʊləʳ] *n Br*: his play is a real ~ sa pièce attire les foules.

crowd scene *n* scène *f* de foule.

crowfoot ['krəʊfʊt] (*pl sense 1* crowfoots, *pl sense 2* crowfeet [-fiːt]) *n* -**1.** BOT renoncule *f*. -**2.** NAUT araignée *f*.

crown [kraʊn] ◇ *n* -**1.** [headdress] couronne *f*; to succeed to the ~ accéder au trône; she wears the ~ c'est elle qui règne; ~ of thorns couronne d'épines. -**2.** [regal power] couronne *f*, pouvoir *m* royal. -**3.** [award] prix *m*; she won the Wimbledon ~ for the second year running elle a remporté le tournoi de Wimbledon pour la seconde année consécutive. -**4.** [top - of head] sommet *m* de la tête; [- of hat] fond *m*; [- of hill, tree] sommet *m*, cime *f*; [- of roof] faîte *m*; [- of road] milieu *m*; [- of tooth] couronne *f*; ARCHIT [- of arch] clef *f*. -**5.** [coin] couronne *f*. -**6.** [outstanding achievement] couronnement *m*; it was the ~ of his career ce fut le couronnement de sa carrière. -**7.** [paper size] couronne *f*. -**8.** [of anchor] diamant *m*.
◇ *vt* -**1.** [confer a title on] couronner; she was

~ed queen/champion elle fut couronnée reine/championne; the ~ed heads of Europe les têtes couronnées de l'Europe. -2. [top] couronner; to ~ a tooth couronner une dent; her election success ~ed her career son succès aux élections a couronné sa carrière; and to ~ it all, it started to rain *fig* et pour couronner le tout, il s'est mis à pleuvoir. -3. [in draughts] damer. -4. *inf* [hit] flanquer un coup (sur la tête) à.
◆ **Crown** *n*: the Crown la Couronne, l'État *m* (monarchique); counsel for the Crown *Br* JUR conseiller *m* juridique de la Couronne; Crown witness *Br* JUR témoin *m* à charge.

Crown Agent *n fonctionnaire du ministère britannique du développement outre-mer chargé des pays étrangers et des organisations internationales.*

crown cap *n Br* capsule *f* (de bouteille).

crown colony *n Br* colonie *f* de la Couronne.

crown court *n* ≃ Cour *f* d'assises *(en Angleterre et au Pays de Galles).*

crown green *n* terrain *m* (de boules) bombé.

crown imperial *n* couronne *f* impériale.

crowning ['kraʊnɪŋ] ◇ *n* couronnement *m*.
◇ *adj fig* suprême; ~ glory [hair] *hum* chevelure *f*; the ~ glory of her career le plus grand triomphe de sa carrière.

crown jewels *npl* joyaux *mpl* de la Couronne.

crown land *n* terres *fpl* domaniales.

crown prince *n* prince *m* héritier.

crown princess *n* [heir to throne] princesse *f* héritière; [wife of crown prince] princesse *f* royale.

crown roast *n* rôti *m* en couronne.

crown wheel *n* [gen] couronne *f*; AUT grande couronne *f*; ~ and pinion couronne d'entraînement.

crow's feet *npl* [wrinkles] pattes *fpl* d'oie *(rides).*

crow's nest *n* NAUT nid *m* de pie.

crozier ['krəʊʒjəʳ] = **crosier**.

CRT (*abbr of* cathode-ray tube) *n* -1. [in TV set] tube *m* cathodique. -2. *Am* [work station] poste *m* de travail.

cruces ['kruːsiːz] *pl* → **crux**.

crucial ['kruːʃl] *adj* -1. [critical] critique, crucial; MED & PHILOS crucial. -2. ▽ [excellent] d'enfer; those jeans are ~ il est d'enfer, ce jean!

crucially ['kruːʃlɪ] *adv* fondamentalement.

crucible ['kruːsɪbl] *n* [vessel] creuset *m*; *fig* [test] (dure) épreuve *f*; 'The Crucible' *Miller* 'les Sorcières de Salem'.

crucible steel *n* acier *m* fondu au creuset.

crucifix ['kruːsɪfɪks] *n* christ *m*, crucifix *m*; (roadside) ~ calvaire *m*.

crucifixion [,kruːsɪ'fɪkʃn] *n* crucifiement *m*.
◆ **Crucifixion** *n*: the Crucifixion RELIG la crucifixion, la mise en croix.

cruciform ['kruːsɪfɔːm] *adj* cruciforme, en croix.

crucify ['kruːsɪfaɪ] (*pt* & *pp* crucified) *vt* -1. [execute] crucifier, mettre en croix. -2. *fig* [treat harshly] mettre au pilori; he was crucified in the courtroom when he tried to defend himselef il a été mis au pilori lorsqu'il a essayé de se défendre au tribunal; my mum will ~ us if she finds out! ma mère va nous étriper si elle découvre ça!

crud▽ [krʌd] *n* -1. [dirt] crasse *f*; you ~! *fig* espèce de minable! -2. [disease]: the ~ la crève.

cruddy▽ ['krʌdɪ] (*compar* cruddier, *superl* cruddiest) *adj* [dirty] crado; [lousy] dégueulasse; I feel ~ je ne me sens pas bien, je ne suis pas dans mon assiette.

crude [kruːd] ◇ *adj* -1. [vulgar - person, behaviour] vulgaire, grossier; [- manners] fruste, grossier; a ~ remark une grossièreté; ~ jokes des plaisanteries grossières. -2. [raw] brut; [sugar] non raffiné. -3. [unsophisticated - tool] grossier, rudimentaire; [- piece of work] mal fini, sommaire; [- drawing] grossier; it was a ~ attempt at self-promotion c'était une tentative grossière pour se mettre en avant. -4. [stark - colour, light] cru, vif.
◇ *n*: ~ (oil) (pétrole *m*) brut *m*.

crudely ['kruːdlɪ] *adv* -1. [vulgarly] grossièrement; [bluntly] crûment, brutalement. -2. [unsophisticatedly] grossièrement, sommairement; a ~ built hut une cabane grossière.

crudeness ['kruːdnɪs] = **crudity**.

crude oil *n* (pétrole *m*) brut *m*.

crudity ['kruːdɪtɪ] *n* -1. [vulgarity] grossièreté *f*. -2. [rawness - of material] état *m* brut. -3. [lack of sophistication - of tool] caractère *m* rudimentaire; [- of drawing, work] manque *m* de fini, caractère *m* sommaire.

cruel [krʊəl] *adj* -1. [unkind] cruel; to be ~ to sb être cruel envers qqn ❑ you've got to be ~ to be kind qui aime bien châtie bien *prov*. -2. [painful] douloureux, cruel; it was a ~ disappointment ce fut une cruelle déception; a ~ wind un vent mauvais OR cinglant.

cruelly ['krʊəlɪ] *adv* cruellement.

cruelty ['krʊəltɪ] (*pl* cruelties) *n* -1. [gen] cruauté *f*; ~ to animals la cruauté envers les animaux. -2. JUR sévices *mpl*; indicted for ~ to her children inculpée pour sévices sur ses enfants; divorce on the grounds of ~ divorce pour sévices; mental ~ cruauté *f* mentale. -3. [cruel act] cruauté *f*; he had to suffer the cruelties of his classmates il lui a fallu endurer les cruautés de ses camarades de classe.

cruet ['kruːɪt] *n* -1. [bottle - for oil, vinegar] petit flacon *m*. -2. [set of condiments] service *m* à condiments. -3. RELIG [for wine] burette *f*.

Cruft's [krʌfts] *pr n le plus important concours canin de Grande-Bretagne, qui se tient chaque année à Londres.*

cruise [kruːz] ◇ *n* -1. [sea trip] croisière *f*; they went on a ~ ils sont partis en OR ont fait une croisière; to be on a ~ être en croisière. -2. = **cruise missile**.
◇ *vi* -1. [ship] croiser; [tourists] être en croisière. -2. [car] rouler; [plane] voler; we ~d along at 70 nous roulions tranquillement à 70 km/h; I ~d through the exam j'ai trouvé l'examen très facile ‖ [police car, taxi] marauder, être en maraude; a cruising taxi un taxi en maraude; cruising speed AERON & AUT vitesse *f* OR régime *m* de croisière. -3. *inf* [for sexual partner] draguer.
◇ *vt* -1. [ocean] croiser dans. -2. *inf* [sexual partner] draguer.

cruise missile *n* missile *m* de croisière.

cruiser ['kruːzəʳ] *n* -1. [warship] croiseur *m*; [pleasure boat] yacht *m* de croisière. -2. *Am* [police patrol car] voiture *f* de police (en patrouille).

cruiserweight ['kruːzəweɪt] *n* poids *m* mi-lourd.

cruller ['krʌləʳ] *n Am* beignet *m*.

crumb [krʌm] *n* -1. [of bread] miette *f*; [inside loaf] mie *f*; *fig* [small piece] miette *f*, brin *m*; the reporters were hoping to gather a few ~s of information les journalistes espéraient récolter quelques bribes d'information; the news from the hospital didn't offer any ~s of comfort/hope les nouvelles de l'hôpital n'apportèrent pas le moindre réconfort/espoir. -2. *inf Am* [person] nul *m*, nulle *f*.

crumble ['krʌmbl] ◇ *vt* [bread, stock cube] émietter; [earth, plaster] effriter.
◇ *vi* [bread] s'émietter; [plaster] s'effriter; [building] tomber en ruines, se désagréger; [earth, stone] s'ébouler; *fig* [hopes, society] s'effondrer, s'écrouler; his world was crumbling around him *fig* tout son petit monde s'écroulait OR s'effondrait.
◇ *n* crumble *m (dessert composé d'une couche de compote de fruits recouverte de pâte sablée).*

crumbly ['krʌmblɪ] (*compar* crumblier, *superl* crumbliest) *adj* friable.

crumbs *inf* [krʌmz] *interj Br dated* mince, zut.

crummy *inf* ['krʌmɪ] (*compar* crummier, *superl* crummiest) *adj* minable, nul.

crump [krʌmp] ◇ *vi* éclater.
◇ *vt* bombarder.
◇ *n* -1. [noise] éclatement *m*. -2. *inf* MIL [shell] obus *m*.

crumpet ['krʌmpɪt] *n Br* -1. [cake] *galette épaisse qu'on mange chaude et beurrée.* -2.▽ [women] nanas *fpl*, pépées *fpl*; a nice bit of ~ une jolie nana, une belle pépée.

crumple ['krʌmpl] ◇ *vt* froisser, friper; be careful not to ~ your dress fais attention de ne pas froisser OR chiffonner ta robe; to ~ a piece of paper (up) into a ball chiffonner un papier.
◇ *vi* -1. [crease] se froisser, se chiffonner. -2. [collapse] s'effondrer, s'écrouler; his face ~d and tears came to his eyes *fig* son visage se contracta et ses yeux se remplirent de larmes.

crunch [krʌntʃ] ◇ *vi* -1. [gravel, snow] craquer, crisser; the snow ~ed beneath my feet la neige crissait sous mes pieds. -2. [chew] croquer; to ~ on sthg croquer qqch.
◇ *vt* -1. [chew] croquer; the dog was ~ing a bone le chien mordait bruyamment un os. -2. [crush underfoot] faire craquer OR crisser, écraser.
◇ *n* -1. [sound - of teeth] coup *m* de dents; [- of food] craquement *m*; [- of gravel, snow] craquement *m*, crissement *m*. -2. *inf* [critical moment] moment *m* critique; when it comes to the ~ dans une situation critique, au moment crucial; if it comes to the ~ en cas de besoin.
◇ *adj inf* critique, décisif; a ~ match un match décisif.
◆ **crunch up** *vt sep* broyer.

crunchy ['krʌntʃɪ] (*compar* crunchier, *superl* crunchiest) *adj* [food] croquant; [snow, gravel] qui craque OR crisse.

crupper ['krʌpəʳ] *n* [on saddle] croupière *f*; [of horse] croupe *f (de cheval).*

crusade [kruː'seɪd] ◇ *n fig* & HIST croisade *f*; to go on (a) ~ *fig* faire une croisade; HIST partir en croisade.
◇ *vi* HIST partir en croisade, être à la croisade; *fig* faire une croisade; to ~ for/against sthg mener une croisade pour/contre qqch.

crusader [kruː'seɪdəʳ] *n* HIST croisé *m*; *fig* champion *m*, -onne *f*, militant *m*, -e *f*; the ~s for/against nuclear power ceux qui militent pour/contre l'énergie nucléaire.

Cruse [kruːz] *pr n association de soutien aux personnes ayant perdu un proche.*

crush [krʌʃ] ◇ *vt* -1. [smash - gen] écraser, broyer; ~ed ice glace *f* pilée; his leg/arm had been ~ed in the accident sa jambe a été écrasée/son bras a été écrasé dans l'accident; they were ~ed to death by the falling rocks ils sont morts écrasés par les rochers. -2. [crease] froisser, chiffonner; ~ed velvet velours *m* frappé. -3. [defeat - enemy] écraser; [suppress - revolt] écraser, réprimer; *fig* [- hopes] écraser; she felt ~ed by the news elle a été accablée OR atterrée par la nouvelle; he ~ed any attempt at reconciliation il a fait échouer toutes les tentatives de réconciliation. -4. [squash, press] serrer; to be ~ed together être tassés OR serrés les uns contre les autres; too many things had been ~ed into the box on avait entassé trop de choses dans la boîte; we were ~ed in the race for the door nous avons été écrasés dans la ruée vers la porte.
◇ *vi* -1. [throng] se serrer, s'écraser; we all ~ed into the lift nous nous sommes tous entassés dans l'ascenseur. -2. [crease] se froisser.
◇ *n* -1. [crowd] foule *f*, cohue *f*; there was a terrible ~ il y avait un monde fou; in the ~ to enter the stadium dans la bousculade pour entrer dans le stade. -2. *inf* [infatuation] béguin *m*; he has a ~ on his teacher il a le béguin OR il en pince pour sa prof. -3. *Br* [drink] jus *m* de fruit; lemon ~ citron *m* pressé.

crush barrier *n* barrière *f* de sécurité.

crusher ['krʌʃəʳ] *n* broyeur *m*, concasseur *m*.

crushing ['krʌʃɪŋ] *adj* [defeat] écrasant; [remark] cinglant, percutant.

crush-resistant *adj* solide, résistant (au choc).

crust [krʌst] ◇ *n* -1. [of bread, pie] croûte *f*; [of snow, ice] couche *f*; a ~ of bread un croûton, une croûte; the earth's ~ GEOL la croûte OR l'écorce terrestre ❑ to earn a ~ gagner sa

croûte. -**2.** [on wound] croûte *f*, escarre *f*. -**3.** [on wine] dépôt *m*.
◇ *vt* couvrir d'une croûte.
◇ *vi* former une croûte.

crustacean [krʌ'steɪʃn] ◇ *adj* crustacé.
◇ *n* crustacé *m*.

crusty ['krʌstɪ] (*compar* crustier, *superl* crustiest) *adj* -**1.** [bread] croustillant. -**2.** [bad-tempered - person] hargneux, bourru; [- remark] brusque, sec.

crutch [krʌtʃ] *n* -**1.** [support] support *m*, soutien *m*; [for walking] béquille *f*; ARCHIT étançon *m*; NAUT support *m*; she uses ~es elle marche avec des béquilles. -**2.** *fig* soutien *m*; he uses notes as a mental ~ *fig* il se sert de ses notes comme aide-mémoire. -**3.** *Br* = **crotch**.

crux [krʌks] (*pl* cruxes OR cruces ['kruːsiːz]) *n* -**1.** [vital point] point *m* crucial OR capital; [of problem] cœur *m*; the ~ of the matter le nœud de l'affaire. -**2.** [in climbing] passage-clef *m*.

cry [kraɪ] (*pt* & *pp* cried, *pl* cries) ◇ *vi* -**1.** [weep] pleurer; she cried in OR with frustration elle pleurait d'impuissance; we laughed until we cried nous avons pleuré de rire OR avons ri aux larmes; the film made them ~ ils ont pleuré pendant le film; to ~ loudly/bitterly pleurer à chaudes larmes/amèrement ❑ it's no use ~ing over spilt milk *prov* ce qui est fait est fait. -**2.** [call out] crier, pousser un cri; to ~ (out) in pain pousser un cri de douleur; to ~ for help crier au secours; to ~ for mercy demander grâce, implorer la pitié ❑ to ~ for the moon demander la lune OR l'impossible. -**3.** [bird, animal] pousser un cri OR des cris; [hounds] donner de la voix, aboyer.
◇ *vt* -**1.** [weep] pleurer; she cried herself to sleep elle s'est endormie en pleurant; he cried tears of joy il versa des larmes de joie; he was ~ing his heart OR eyes out il pleurait toutes les larmes de son corps. -**2.** [shout] crier; "look", she cried «regardez», s'écria-t-elle; he cried quits OR mercy il s'est avoué vaincu ❑ to ~ wolf crier au loup.
◇ *n* -**1.** [exclamation] cri *m*; she gave a ~ of surprise elle a poussé un cri de surprise; he heard a ~ for help il a entendu crier au secours; there have been cries for lower taxes *fig* on a réclamé une baisse des impôts; battle ~ cri de guerre; to be in full ~ crier à tue-tête. -**2.** [of birds, animals] cri *m*; [of hounds] aboiements *mpl*, voix *f*. -**3.** [weep]: to have a good ~ pleurer un bon coup.
◆ **cry down** *vt sep* décrier.
◆ **cry off** *vi insep* [from meeting] se décommander; [from promise] se rétracter, se dédire; she's ~ing off from the project elle se retire du OR renonce au projet.
◆ **cry out** ◇ *vi insep* pousser un cri; I cried out to them je les ai appelés; to ~ out against *fig* protester contre; the country is ~ing out against high taxation tout le pays proteste contre les impôts élevés; to ~ out for sthg demander OR réclamer qqch; the system is ~ing out for revision OR to be revised *fig* le système a grand besoin d'être révisé ❑ for ~ing out loud! bon sang!
◇ *vt sep* s'écrier; "listen", she cried out «écoutez», s'écria-t-elle.
◆ **cry up** *vt sep* prôner, exalter.

crybaby *inf* ['kraɪˌbeɪbɪ] (*pl* crybabies) *n* pleurnichard *m*, -e *f*.

crying ['kraɪɪŋ] ◇ *adj* -**1.** [person] qui pleure, pleurant. -**2.** *inf* [as intensifier] criant, flagrant; there is a ~ need for more teachers on a un besoin urgent d'enseignants; it's a ~ shame c'est un scandale.
◇ *n* (*U*) -**1.** [shouting] cri *m*, cris *mpl*; we could hear the ~ of the baby on entendait les cris du bébé. -**2.** [weeping] pleurs *mpl*; stop your ~ arrête de pleurer.

cryogenic [ˌkraɪə'dʒenɪk] *adj* cryogène.

cryogenics [ˌkraɪə'dʒenɪks] *n* (*U*) [science] cryologie *f*; [production] cryogénie *f*.

crypt [krɪpt] *n* crypte *f*.

cryptanalysis [ˌkrɪptə'næləsɪs] *n* cryptographie *f*.

cryptic ['krɪptɪk] *adj* [secret] secret; [obscure] énigmatique, sibyllin; ~ crossword *mot-croisé dont les définitions sont des énigmes qu'il faut résoudre*.

cryptically ['krɪptɪklɪ] *adv* [secretly] secrètement; [obscurely] énigmatiquement.

crypto- ['krɪptəʊ] *in cpds* crypto-; ~fascist cryptofasciste *mf*.

cryptogram ['krɪptəʊgræm] *n* cryptogramme *m*.

cryptographer [krɪp'tɒgrəfəʳ] *n* cryptographe *mf*.

cryptographic(al) [ˌkrɪptə'græfɪk(l)] *adj* cryptographique.

cryptography [krɪp'tɒgrəfɪ], **cryptology** [krɪp'tɒlədʒɪ] *n* cryptographie *f*.

crystal ['krɪstl] ◇ *n* -**1.** [gen & MINER] cristal *m*. -**2.** [chip] cristal *m*; salt/snow ~s cristaux de sel/de neige. -**3.** *Am* [of watch] verre *m* (de montre). -**4.** ELECTRON galène *f*.
◇ *adj* [vase, glass, water] de cristal; ~ factory cristallerie *f*.

crystal ball *n* boule *f* de cristal.

crystal clear *adj* clair comme le jour OR comme de l'eau de roche; [voice] cristalline.

crystal-gazer *n* voyant *m*, -e *f (qui lit dans une boule de cristal)*.

crystal-gazing *n* (*U*) [in ball] (art *m* de la) voyance *f*; *fig* prédictions *fpl*, prophéties *fpl*.

crystalline ['krɪstəlaɪn] *n* cristallin.

crystalline lens *n* cristallin *m*.

crystallization [ˌkrɪstəlaɪ'zeɪʃn] *n* [gen & SCI] cristallisation *f*.

crystallize, -ise ['krɪstəlaɪz] ◇ *vi literal* & *fig* se cristalliser.
◇ *vt* cristalliser; [sugar] (faire) candir; ~d fruit fruits *mpl* confits.

crystallography [ˌkrɪstə'lɒgrəfɪ] *n* cristallographie *f*.

crystalloid ['krɪstəlɔɪd] ◇ *adj* cristalloïde.
◇ *n* cristalloïde *m*.

crystal set *n* poste *m* à galène.

CSA *pr n abbr of* Confederate States of America

CSC (*abbr of* Civil Service Commission) *pr n commission de recrutement des fonctionnaires*.

CSE (*abbr of* Certificate of Secondary Education) *n ancien brevet de l'enseignement secondaire en Grande-Bretagne, aujourd'hui remplacé par le GCSE*.

CSEU (*abbr of* Confederation of Shipbuilding and Engineering Unions) *pr n confédération britannique des syndicats de la construction navale et de la mécanique*.

CS gas *n Br* gaz *m* CS OR lacrymogène.

CSM *n abbr of* Company Sergeant-Major.

CST *n abbr of* Central Standard Time.

CSU (*abbr of* Civil Service Union) *pr n syndicat de la fonction publique*.

ct *written abbr of* carat.

CT *written abbr of* Connecticut.

CTC (*abbr of* city technology college) *n collège technique britannique, généralement établi dans des quartiers défavorisés*.

cu. *written abbr of* cubic.

cub [kʌb] *n* -**1.** [animal] petit *m*, -e *f*. -**2.** *inf* [youngster]: young ~ jeune blanc-bec *m*. -**3.** [scout]: ~ (scout) louveteau *m (scout)*.

Cuba ['kjuːbə] *pr n* Cuba; in ~ à Cuba.

Cuba libre [ˌkjuːbə'liːbrə] *n Am cocktail contenant du Coca, du rhum et du jus de citron vert*.

Cuban ['kjuːbən] ◇ *n* Cubain *m*, -e *f*.
◇ *adj* cubain; ~ heel talon *m* cubain; the ~ missile crisis la crise de Cuba *(conflit américano-soviétique dû à la présence de missiles soviétiques à Cuba (1962))*.

cubbyhole ['kʌbɪhəʊl] *n* -**1.** [cupboard] débarras *m*, remise *f*; [small room] cagibi *m*, réduit *m*. -**2.** [in desk] case *f*; AUT vide-poches *m*.

cube [kjuːb] ◇ *n* [gen & MATH] cube *m*; sugar ~ morceau *m* de sucre.
◇ *vt* -**1.** [cut into cubes] couper en cubes OR en dés. -**2.** MATH cuber; TECH [measure] cuber.

cube root *n* racine *f* cubique.

cubic ['kjuːbɪk] *adj* [shape, volume] cubique; [measurement] cube; ~ capacity volume *m*; ~ content capacité *f* cubique; ~ equation MATH équation *f* du troisième degré; ~ measure mesure *f* de volume; ~ metre mètre *m* cube.

cubicle ['kjuːbɪkl] *n* [in dormitory, hospital ward] alcôve *f*, box *m*; [in swimming baths, public toilets] cabine *f*.

cubism, **Cubism** ['kjuːbɪzm] *n* cubisme *m*.

cubist, **Cubist** ['kjuːbɪst] ◇ *adj* cubiste.
◇ *n* cubiste *mf*.

cubit ['kjuːbɪt] *n* [measurement] coudée *f (unité de mesure)*.

cub master *n* chef *m (des scouts)*.

cub mistress *n* cheftaine *f (des scouts)*.

cub reporter *n* jeune journaliste *mf*.

cub scout, **Cub Scout** *n* louveteau *m (scout)*.

cuckold ['kʌkəʊld] ◇ *n* (mari *m*) cocu *m*.
◇ *vt* faire cocu, cocufier.

cuckoo ['kʊkuː] (*pl* cuckoos) ◇ *n* -**1.** ORNITH [bird, sound] coucou *m*; 'One Flew Over the Cuckoo's Nest' *Kesey, Forman* 'Vol au-dessus d'un nid de coucou'. -**2.** *inf* [mad person] imbécile *mf*, idiot *m*, -e *f*.
◇ *adj inf* [mad] loufoque, toqué; to go ~ perdre la boule.

cuckoo clock *n* coucou *m (pendule)*.

cuckoopint ['kʊkuːpɪnt] *n* pied-de-veau *m*.

cuckoo spit *n* crachat *m* de coucou.

cucumber ['kjuːkʌmbəʳ] *n* concombre *m*; ~ sandwich *petit sandwich au pain de mie et au concombre (l'expression est parfois utilisée pour évoquer certains milieux bourgeois)*.

cud [kʌd] *n* bol *m* alimentaire *(d'un ruminant)*.

cuddle ['kʌdl] ◇ *vi* se faire un câlin, se câliner; they were cuddling on the sofa ils se faisaient un câlin sur le divan.
◇ *vt* câliner, caresser; [child] bercer *(dans ses bras)*.
◇ *n* câlin *m*, caresse *f*, caresses *fpl*; they were having a ~ ils se faisaient un câlin; she gave the child a ~ elle a fait un câlin à l'enfant.
◆ **cuddle up** *vi insep* se blottir, se pelotonner; she ~d up close to him elle se blottit contre lui.

cuddly ['kʌdlɪ] (*compar* cuddlier, *superl* cuddliest) *adj* [child, animal] câlin; ~ toy peluche *f*.

cudgel ['kʌdʒəl] (*Br pt* & *pp* cudgelled, *cont* cudgelling, *Am pt* & *pp* cudgeled, *cont* cudgeling) ◇ *n* gourdin *m*, trique *f*; to take up OR to carry the ~s for sthg/sb prendre fait et cause pour qqch/qqn.
◇ *vt* battre à coups de gourdin; to ~ sb to death tuer qqn à coups de gourdin; he cudgelled his brains *inf fig* il s'est creusé la tête OR le cerveau.

cue [kjuː] ◇ *n* -**1.** CIN & THEAT [verbal] réplique *f*; [action] signal *m*; MUS signal *m* d'entrée; to give sb their ~ donner la réplique à qqn; he took his ~ il a entamé sa réplique; her cough was my ~ to enter elle devait tousser pour me signaler que je pouvais entrer; her yawn was our ~ to leave nous avons compris qu'il fallait partir quand elle s'est mise à bâiller. -**2.** *fig* [signal] signal *m*; I took my ~ from Mother j'ai pris exemple sur ma mère; right on ~, the door opened la porte s'est ouverte juste au bon moment OR à point nommé. -**3.** [for snooker, pool] queue *f (de billard)*; ~ rade porte-queue *m*. -**4.** [of hair] queue *f (de cheval)*.
◇ *vi* [in snooker, pool] queuter.
◇ *vt* [prompt] donner le signal à; THEAT donner la réplique à.
◆ **cue in** *vt sep* [gen, RADIO & TV] donner le signal à; THEAT donner la réplique à.

cue ball *n* bille *f* de joueur.

cue bid *n* CARDS *annonce qui montre un as ou un vide*.

cuff [kʌf] ◇ *n* -**1.** [of sleeve] poignet *m*, manchette *f*; [of glove] poignet *m*; [of coat] parement *m*; *Am* [of trousers] revers *m*; off the ~ à l'improviste; she was speaking off the ~ elle improvisait son discours, elle faisait un discours

improvisé; he bought it on the ~ *Am* il l'a acheté à crédit. -**2.** [blow] gifle *f*, claque *f*; I got a ~ round the ear j'ai reçu une claque OR une gifle.
◇ *vt* -**1.** [hit] gifler, donner une gifle OR une claque à. -**2.** *inf* [handcuff] mettre OR passer les menottes à. -**3.** *Am* [trousers] faire un revers à.
◆ **cuffs** *inf npl* [handcuffs] menottes *fpl*.

cuff link *n* bouton *m* de manchette.

cu.in. *written abbr of* cubic inch(es).

cuisine [kwɪ'ziːn] *n* cuisine *f*.

cul-de-sac ['kʌldəsæk] *n* cul-de-sac *m*, impasse *f*; 'cul-de-sac' 'voie sans issue'.

culinary ['kʌlɪnərɪ] *adj* culinaire.

cull [kʌl] ◇ *vt* -**1.** [sample] sélectionner. -**2.** [remove from herd] éliminer, supprimer; [slaughter - seals] abattre, massacrer. -**3.** [gather - flowers, fruit] cueillir.
◇ *n* -**1.** [slaughter] massacre *m*. -**2.** [animal] animal *m* à éliminer.

Culloden Moor [kə'lɒdn'mɔːʳ] *pr n bataille à l'issue de laquelle, en 1746, les partisans écossais de Charles-Édouard Stuart furent vaincus par l'armée anglaise.*

culminate ['kʌlmɪneɪt] *vi* ASTRON culminer.
◆ **culminate in** *vt insep*: the demonstration ~d in a riot la manifestation s'est terminée en émeute; the disagreement ~d in the end of their friendship le différend a mis fin à leur amitié.

culminating ['kʌlmɪneɪtɪŋ] *adj* culminant.

culmination [,kʌlmɪ'neɪʃn] *n* -**1.** [climax - of career] apogée *m*; [- of efforts] maximum *m*; [- of disagreement] point *m* culminant. -**2.** ASTRON culmination *f*.

culottes [kjuː'lɒts] *npl* jupe-culotte *f*.

culpability [,kʌlpə'bɪlətɪ] *n* culpabilité *f*.

culpable ['kʌlpəbl] *adj fml* coupable; JUR: ~ homicide homicide *m* volontaire; ~ negligence négligence *f* coupable.

culprit ['kʌlprɪt] *n* coupable *mf*.

cult [kʌlt] ◇ *n fig* OU RELIG culte *m*; personality ~ culte *m* de la personnalité.
◇ *comp* [book, film] culte; ~ figure idole *f*; the film has a ~ following c'est un film culte.

cultivar ['kʌltɪ,vɑː] *n* cultivar *m*.

cultivate ['kʌltɪveɪt] *vt* -**1.** [land] cultiver, exploiter; [crop] cultiver. -**2.** *fig* [idea, person] cultiver; reading is the best way to ~ the mind la lecture est le meilleur moyen de se cultiver (l'esprit).

cultivated ['kʌltɪveɪtɪd] *adj* [land] cultivé, exploité; [person] cultivé; [voice] distingué.

cultivation [,kʌltɪ'veɪʃn] *n* -**1.** [of land, crops] culture *f*; fields under ~ cultures *fpl*. -**2.** *fig* [of taste] éducation *f*; [of relations] entretien *m*.

cultivator ['kʌltɪveɪtəʳ] *n* [person] cultivateur *m*, -trice *f*; [tool] cultivateur *m*; [power-driven] motoculteur *m*.

cultural ['kʌltʃərəl] *adj* -**1.** [events, background] culturel; the ~ environment le milieu culturel; ~ integration acculturation *f*; a ~ desert *fig* un désert culturel. -**2.** AGR de culture, cultural.

culturally ['kʌltʃərəlɪ] *adv* culturellement.

Cultural Revolution *n*: the ~ la Révolution culturelle.

culture ['kʌltʃəʳ] ◇ *n* -**1.** [civilization, learning] culture *f*; a man of ~ un homme cultivé OR qui a de la culture; to have no ~ être inculte; physical ~ culture physique. -**2.** AGR [of land, crops] culture *f*; [of animals] élevage *m*; [of fowl] aviculture *f*. -**3.** BIOL culture *f*.
◇ *vt* [plants] cultiver; [animals] élever; [bacteria] faire une culture de.

cultured ['kʌltʃəd] *adj* -**1.** [refined - person] cultivé, lettré; the fullback has a ~ left foot *fig* l'arrière a un très bon pied gauche. -**2.** [grown artificially] cultivé; ~ pearls perles *fpl* de culture.

culture gap *n* fossé *m* culturel.

culture medium *n* milieu *m* de culture.

culture shock *n* choc *m* culturel.

culture vulture *inf n hum* fana *mf* de culture, culturophage *mf*.

culvert ['kʌlvət] *n* [for water] caniveau *m*; [for cable] conduit *m*.

cum [kʌm] ◇ *prep* avec; a kitchen-~-dining area une cuisine *f* avec coin-repas; he's a teacher-~-philosopher il est philosophe aussi bien qu'enseignant.
◇ *n* ▼ [semen] foutre *m*.

cumbersome ['kʌmbəsəm] *adj* [bulky] encombrant, embarrassant; *fig* [process, system, style] lourd, pesant.

cumin ['kʌmɪn] *n* cumin *m*.

cum laude [kʌm'lɔːdɪ] *adv* UNIV avec distinction.

cummerbund ['kʌməbʌnd] *n* large ceinture *f (de smoking)*.

cumulative ['kjuːmjʊlətɪv] *adj* cumulatif; ~ evidence JUR preuve *f* par accumulation de témoignages; ~ interest FIN intérêts *mpl* cumulatifs; ~ voting POL vote *m* plural.

cumuli ['kjuːmjʊlaɪ] *pl* → **cumulus**.

cumulonimbus [,kjuːmjʊləʊ'nɪmbəs] (*pl* cumulonimbi [-baɪ] OR **cumulonimbuses**) *n* cumulo-nimbus *m*.

cumulus ['kjuːmjʊləs] (*pl* **cumuli** [-laɪ]) *n* cumulus *m*.

cuneiform ['kjuːnɪɪfɔːm] ◇ *adj* cunéiforme.
◇ *n* écriture *f* cunéiforme.

cunnilingus [,kʌnɪ'lɪŋgəs] *n* cunnilingus *m*.

cunning ['kʌnɪŋ] ◇ *adj* -**1.** [shrewd] astucieux, malin; *pej* rusé, fourbe; he's as ~ as a fox il est rusé comme un renard. -**2.** [skilful] habile, astucieux. -**3.** *Am* [cute] mignon, charmant.
◇ *n* -**1.** [guile] finesse *f*, astuce *f*; *pej* ruse *f*, fourberie *f*. -**2.** [skill] habileté *f*, adresse *f*.

cunningly ['kʌnɪŋlɪ] *adv* -**1.** [shrewdly] astucieusement, finement; *pej* avec ruse OR fourberie. -**2.** [skilfully] habilement, astucieusement.

cunt▼ [kʌnt] *n* -**1.** [vagina] con *m*, chatte *f*. -**2.** [man] enculé *m*; [woman] salope *f*.

cup [kʌp] (*pt* & *pp* cupped, *cont* cupping)
◇ *n* -**1.** [for drinking, cupful] tasse *f*; RELIG calice *m*; a ~ of coffee une tasse de café; would you like another ~? en voulez-vous encore une tasse?; add two ~s of sugar CULIN ajoutez deux tasses de sucre ☐ that's just her ~ of tea c'est exactement ce qu'il lui faut; my ~ runneth over *lit* mon bonheur est complet OR parfait; he drained the ~ of sorrow *lit* il a bu la coupe jusqu'à la lie; he's not (really) my ~ of tea *inf* il n'est pas (tout à fait) mon genre; jazz isn't everyone's ~ of tea *inf* tout le monde n'aime pas le jazz; he was in his ~s *inf dated* il avait du vent dans les voiles. -**2.** SPORT [trophy, competition] coupe *f*. -**3.** [shape - of plant] corolle *f*; [- of bone] cavité *f* articulaire, glène *f*; [- of bra] bonnet *m*. -**4.** [punch] boisson *f* alcoolisée; champagne ~ punch *m* au champagne; fruit ~ cocktail *m* aux fruits *(pouvant contenir de l'alcool)*. -**5.** TECH godet *m*, cuvette *f*. -**6.** *Am* [in golf] trou *m*.
◇ *vt* -**1.** [hands] mettre en coupe; [hold]: to ~ one's hands around sthg mettre ses mains autour de qqch; he cupped a hand to his ear il mit sa main derrière son oreille; she cupped her hands around her mouth and shouted elle mit ses mains en porte-voix et cria; he sat with his chin cupped in his hand il était assis, le menton dans le creux de sa main. -**2.** MED [with cupping glass] appliquer des ventouses sur. -**3.** *Am* [in golf]: to ~ the ball faire un divot.
◇ *comp* -**1.** SPORT [winners, holders, match] de coupe. -**2.** [handle] de tasse; [rack] pour tasses.

cup-and-ball *adj* MECH: ~ joint joint *m* à rotule.

cupbearer ['kʌp,beərəʳ] *n* échanson *m*.

cupboard ['kʌbəd] *n* [on wall] placard *m*; [free-standing - for dishes, pans] buffet *m*, placard *m*; [- for clothes, linen] placard *m*, armoire *f*; the ~ is bare *fig* il n'y a rien à se mettre sous la dent.

cupboard love *n Br* amour *m* intéressé.

cup cake *n* petit gâteau *m*.

cup final *n* finale *f* de la coupe; the Cup Final *Br* la finale de la Coupe de Football.

cupful ['kʌpfʊl] *n* tasse *f*; a ~ of sugar une tasse de sucre.

Cupid ['kjuːpɪd] *pr n* MYTH Cupidon *m*; ~'s dart OR arrow les flèches *fpl* de Cupidon; to play ~ *fig* jouer les entremetteurs *mpl*, -euses *fpl*.
◆ **cupid** *n* ART [cherub] chérubin *m*, amour *m*.

cupidity [kjuː'pɪdɪtɪ] *n* cupidité *f*.

Cupid's bow *n* bouche *f* en forme de cœur.

cupola ['kjuːpələ] *n* -**1.** ARCHIT [ceiling, roof] coupole *f*, dôme *m*; [tower] belvédère *m*. -**2.** NAUT coupole *f*. -**3.** METALL [furnace] cubilot *m*.

cuppa *inf* ['kʌpə] *n Br* tasse *f* de thé.

cupping glass ['kʌpɪŋ-] *n* ventouse *f*.

cupric ['kjuːprɪk] *adj* cuprique; ~ oxide oxyde *m* de cuivre.

cupro-nickel [,kjuːprəʊ-] *n* cupronickel *m*.

cup tie *n* match *m* de coupe.

cup-tied *adj* [player] disqualifié pour un match de coupe.

cur [kɜːʳ] *n* -**1.** [dog] (chien *m*) bâtard *m*, sale chien *m*. -**2.** [person] malotru *m*, -e *f*, roquet *m*.

curable ['kjʊərəbl] *adj* guérissable, curable.

curacy ['kjʊərəsɪ] (*pl* **curacies**) *n* vicariat *m*.

curare, curari [kjʊ'rɑːrɪ] *n* curare *m*.

curate ['kjʊərət] *n* vicaire *m (de l'Église anglicane)*.

curate's egg *n Br*: it's like the ~ il y a du bon et du mauvais.

curative ['kjʊərətɪv] *adj* curatif.

curator [,kjʊə'reɪtəʳ] *n* -**1.** [of museum] conservateur *m*, -trice *f*. -**2.** *Scot* [guardian] curateur *m*, -trice *f*.

curatorship [kjʊə'reɪtəʃɪp] *n* -**1.** [of museum] fonction *f* de conservateur. -**2.** *Scot* [of child] fonction *f* de curateur.

curb [kɜːb] ◇ *n* -**1.** [restraint] frein *m*; a ~ on trade une restriction au commerce; she put a ~ on her anger elle a refréné sa colère. -**2.** [on harness]: ~ (bit) mors *m*; ~ (chain) gourmette *f*; ~ reins rênes *fpl* de filet. -**3.** [of well] margelle *f*. -**4.** *Am* = **kerb**.
◇ *vt* -**1.** [restrain - emotion] refréner, maîtriser; [- expenses] restreindre, mettre un frein à; [- child] modérer, freiner; ~ your tongue! mesure tes paroles! -**2.** [horse] mettre un mors à. -**3.** *Am*: '~ your dog' votre chien doit faire ses besoins dans le caniveau.

curb roof *n* comble *m* brisé.

curb(-side) service *n Am* service *m* au volant *(dans un restaurant drive-in)*.

curbstone ['kɜːbstəʊn] *Am* = **kerbstone**.

curd [kɜːd] *n (usu pl)* [of milk] caillot *m*, grumeau *m*; ~s lait *m* caillé, caillebotte *f*; ~s and whey lait caillé sucré.

curd cheese *n* fromage *m* blanc battu.

curdle ['kɜːdl] ◇ *vi* [milk] cailler; [sauce] tourner; [mayonnaise] tomber; his screams made my blood ~ *fig* ses cris m'ont glacé le sang.
◇ *vt* [milk] cailler; [sauce] faire tourner; [mayonnaise] faire tomber; the thought's enough to ~ one's blood *fig* c'est une idée à vous glacer le sang.

cure [kjʊəʳ] ◇ *vt* -**1.** [disease, person] guérir; *fig* [problem] éliminer, remédier à; he was ~d of cancer il a été guéri du cancer; the nap seems to have ~d my headache on dirait que la sieste m'a fait passer mon mal de tête; he ~d himself of nailbiting il a réussi à arrêter de se ronger les ongles; his experiences in politics ~d him of all his illusions *fig* son expérience de la politique lui a fait perdre toutes ses illusions ☐ what can't be ~d must be endured *prov* il faut faire avec. -**2.** [tobacco, meat, fish - gen] traiter; [- with salt] saler; [- by smoking] fumer; [- by drying] sécher.
◇ *n* -**1.** [remedy] remède *m*, cure *f*; a ~ for the common cold un remède contre le rhume de cerveau; there's no known ~ on ne connaît pas de remède; to take OR to follow a ~ faire une cure; a ~ for all ills *fig* la panacée. -**2.** [recovery] guérison *f*; to be beyond OR past

~ [person] être incurable; *fig* [problem, situation] être irrémédiable. -**3.** RELIG: the ~ of souls charge *f* d'âmes.

cure-all *n* panacée *f*.

curettage [ˌkjʊərɪˈtɑːʒ, kjʊəˈretɪdʒ] *n* curetage *m*.

curfew [ˈkɜːfjuː] *n* couvre-feu *m*; **the authorities imposed a/lifted the ~** les autorités ont imposé/levé le couvre-feu.

curie [ˈkjʊərɪ] *n* curie *m*.

curing [ˈkjʊərɪŋ] *n* -**1.** [of disease, patient] guérison *f*. -**2.** [of meat, tobacco, fish - gen] traitement *m*; [- by salting] salaison *f*; [- by smoking] fumaison *f*; [- by drying] séchage *m*.

curio [ˈkjʊərɪəʊ] (*pl* **curios**) *n* curiosité *f*, bibelot *m*.

curiosity [ˌkjʊərɪˈɒsətɪ] (*pl* **curiosities**) *n* -**1.** [interest] curiosité *f*; **out of ~** par curiosité ❑ **~ killed the cat** *prov* la curiosité est un vilain défaut *prov*. -**2.** [novelty] curiosité *f*; **they considered me to be something of a ~** on me regardait un peu comme une bête curieuse.

curious [ˈkjʊərɪəs] *adj* -**1.** [inquisitive] curieux; **I'm ~ to see/know** je suis curieux de voir/savoir; **I'm ~ as to what happened next** je serais curieux de savoir ce qui s'est passé après. -**2.** [strange] curieux, singulier; **the ~ thing (about it) is...** ce qui est curieux là-dedans OR dans tout ça, c'est...

curiously [ˈkjʊərɪəslɪ] *adv* -**1.** [inquisitively] avec curiosité. -**2.** [strangely] curieusement, singulièrement; **~ enough** chose bizarre OR curieuse.

curl [kɜːl] ◇ *vi* -**1.** [hair] friser; [loosely] boucler; **the thought's enough to make your hair ~** *inf fig* l'idée suffit à vous faire dresser les cheveux sur la tête. -**2.** [paper, leaf] se recroqueviller, se racornir; [lip] se retrousser; **her lip ~ed in contempt** elle fit une moue de mépris. -**3.** [road] serpenter; [smoke] monter en spirale. -**4.** SPORT jouer au curling.

◇ *vt* -**1.** [hair] friser; [loosely] (faire) boucler. -**2.** [paper] enrouler; [ribbon] faire boucler; [lip] retrousser; **he ~ed his lip in scorn** il a fait une moue de mépris.

◇ *n* -**1.** [of hair] boucle *f* (de cheveux); **her hair hung over her shoulders in ~s** ses cheveux lui tombaient en boucles sur les épaules. -**2.** [spiral] courbe *f*; [of smoke] spirale *f*; [of wave] ondulation *f*; **with a scornful ~ of the lip** *fig* avec une moue méprisante.

◆ **curl up** ◇ *vi insep* -**1.** [leaf, paper] s'enrouler, se recroqueviller; [bread] se racornir. -**2.** [person] se pelotonner; [cat] se mettre en boule, se pelotonner; [dog] se coucher en rond; **the cat was sleeping ~ed up in a ball** le chat dormait roulé en boule; **she ~ed up in front of the fire with a book** elle s'est pelotonnée devant le feu avec un livre; **to ~ up with laughter** se tordre de rire; **I just wanted to ~ up and die** *fig* [in shame] j'aurais voulu rentrer sous terre.

◇ *vt sep* enrouler; **to ~ o.s. up** [person] se pelotonner; [cat] se mettre en boule, se pelotonner; [dog] se coucher en rond.

curler [ˈkɜːləʳ] *n* -**1.** [for hair] bigoudi *m*, rouleau *m*. -**2.** SPORT joueur *m*, -euse *f* de curling.

curlew [ˈkɜːljuː] *n* courlis *m*.

curlicue [ˈkɜːlɪkjuː] *n* [in design, handwriting] enjolivure *f*; [in skating] figure *f* (compliquée).

curling [ˈkɜːlɪŋ] *n* SPORT curling *m*; **~ stone** pierre *f* de curling.

curling iron *n*, **curling tongs** *npl* fer *m* à friser.

curlpaper [ˈkɜːlˌpeɪpəʳ] *n* papillote *f*.

curly [ˈkɜːlɪ] (*compar* **curlier**, *superl* **curliest**) *adj* [hair - tight] frisé; [- loose] bouclé; **~ eyelashes** des cils recourbés; **~ lettuce** (laitue *f*) frisée *f*.

curly kale *n* chou *m* frisé.

curmudgeon [kɜːˈmʌdʒən] *n* [grouch] rouspéteur *m*, -euse *f*; [miser] avare *mf*, grippe-sou *m*.

currant [ˈkʌrənt] *n* -**1.** BOT [fruit] groseille *f*; **~ bush** groseillier *m*. -**2.** [dried grape] raisin *m* de Corinthe.

currant bun *n* petit pain *m* aux raisins.

currency [ˈkʌrənsɪ] (*pl* **currencies**) *n* -**1.** ECON & FIN monnaie *f*, devise *f*; **foreign ~** devise, monnaie étrangère; **he has no Spanish ~** il n'a pas d'argent espagnol; **this coin is no longer legal ~** cette pièce n'a plus cours (légal) OR n'est plus en circulation; **~ unit** unité *f* monétaire. -**2.** *fig* [prevalence] cours *m*, circulation *f*; **the theory has gained ~** cette théorie s'est répandue; **I give no ~ to that idea** je n'accrédite pas cette idée; **ideas which had ~ in the 1960s** des idées qui avaient cours dans les années 60.

currency note *n* billet *m* de banque.

current [ˈkʌrənt] ◇ *n* [gen & ELEC] courant *m*; *fig* [trend] cours *m*, tendance *f*; **the boat drifts with the ~** le courant fait dériver le bateau; **the ~s of opinion** les tendances de l'opinion; **to go against the ~** *literal* remonter le courant; *fig* aller à contre-courant; **to go with the ~** *literal* & *fig* suivre le courant.

◇ *adj* -**1.** [widespread] courant, commun; **the ~ theory** la théorie actuelle; **to be ~** être courant, avoir cours; **it's in ~ use** c'est d'usage courant; **words that are in ~ use** des mots courants OR qui s'emploient couramment; **as ~ rumour has it, she...** on dit qu'elle..., si l'on en croit les rumeurs, elle... -**2.** [most recent - fashion, trend] actuel; [- price] courant; **~ events** les événements *mpl* actuels, l'actualité *f*; **the ~ issue of this magazine** le dernier numéro de cette revue; **the ~ month** le mois courant OR en cours; **the ~ week** la semaine en cours; **the ~ projects** les projets en cours; **the ~ exhibition at the Louvre** l'exposition qui a lieu en ce moment au Louvre; **his ~ girlfriend** la fille avec qui il est en ce moment, sa copine du moment; **the ~ rate of exchange** FIN le cours actuel du change.

current account *n Br* compte *m* courant.

current affairs ◇ *npl* l'actualité *f*, les questions *fpl* d'actualité.

◇ *comp* [programme, magazine] d'actualités.

current assets *npl* actif *m* de roulement.

current expenses *npl* dépenses *fpl* de fonctionnement OR d'exploitation.

current liabilities *npl* passif *m* exigible.

currently [ˈkʌrəntlɪ] *adv* actuellement, à présent.

curriculum [kəˈrɪkjələm] (*pl* **curricula** [-lə] OR **curriculums**) *n* programme *m* d'enseignement; **the maths ~** le programme de maths; **the National Curriculum** *Br programme introduit en 1988 définissant au niveau national (Angleterre et pays de Galles) le contenu de l'enseignement primaire et secondaire*.

curriculum vitae [-ˈviːtaɪ] (*pl* **curricula vitae**) *n Br* curriculum *m* (vitae).

curried [ˈkʌrɪd] *adj* au curry OR cari; **~ eggs** des œufs au curry OR à l'indienne.

curry [ˈkʌrɪ] (*pl* **curries**, *pt* & *pp* **curried**) ◇ *n* CULIN curry *m*, cari *m*; **chicken ~** curry de poulet.

◇ *vt* -**1.** CULIN accommoder au curry. -**2.** [horse] étriller; [leather] corroyer; **he's trying to ~ favour with the boss** il cherche à se faire bien voir du patron.

currycomb [ˈkʌrɪkəʊm] *n* étrille *f*.

curry powder *n* curry *m*, cari *m*.

curry sauce *n* sauce *f* au curry OR cari.

curse [kɜːs] ◇ *n* -**1.** [evil spell] malédiction *f*; **to call down OR to put a ~ on sb** maudire qqn; **a ~ on the day I met you!** maudit soit le jour où je vous ai connu!; **the town is under a ~** la ville est sous le coup d'une malédiction. -**2.** [swearword] juron *m*, imprécation *f*; **~s!** *inf* zut!, mince alors! -**3.** *fig* [bane] fléau *m*, calamité *f*; **the ~ of loneliness** le fléau de la solitude. -**4.** *inf euph* [menstruation]: **the ~** les règles *fpl*; **she's got the ~** *inf* elle a ses règles.

◇ *vt* -**1.** [damn] maudire; **~ him!** maudit soit-il! -**2.** [swear at] injurier. -**3.** [afflict] affliger; **he's ~d with a bad temper** il est affligé d'un mauvais caractère.

◇ *vi* [swear] jurer, blasphémer.

cursed [ˈkɜːsɪd] *adj* maudit.

cursive [ˈkɜːsɪv] ◇ *adj* cursif.

◇ *n* (écriture *f*) cursive *f*.

cursor [ˈkɜːsəʳ] *n* curseur *m*.

cursorily [ˈkɜːsərəlɪ] *adv* [superficially] superficiellement; [hastily] hâtivement, à la hâte.

cursory [ˈkɜːsərɪ] *adj* [superficial] superficiel; [hasty] hâtif; **she gave the painting only a ~ glance** elle n'a jeté qu'un bref coup d'œil au tableau; **after a ~ examination of the document** après avoir lu le document en diagonale.

curt [kɜːt] *adj* [blunt - person, reply, manner] brusque, sec; **in a ~ tone** d'un ton cassant OR sec; **with a ~ nod** avec un bref signe de tête.

curtail [kɜːˈteɪl] *vt* -**1.** [cut short - story, visit, studies] écourter. -**2.** [reduce - expenses] réduire, rogner; [- power, freedom] limiter, réduire.

curtailment [kɜːˈteɪlmənt] *n* -**1.** [of studies, visit] raccourcissement *m*. -**2.** [of expenses] réduction *f*; [of power, freedom] limitation *f*, réduction *f*.

curtain [ˈkɜːtn] ◇ *n* -**1.** [gen & THEAT] rideau *m*; *fig* rideau *m*, voile *m*; **draw the ~s** tirez les rideaux; **a ~ of smoke** *fig* un rideau de fumée ❑ **if she finds out, it's ~s for us** *inf* si elle apprend ça, on est fichus. -**2.** THEAT [for actor] rappel *m*; **the singer took four ~s** le chanteur a été rappelé quatre fois.

◇ *vt* garnir de rideaux.

◆ **curtain off** *vt sep* séparer par un rideau.

curtain call *n* rappel *m*; **she took four ~s** elle a été rappelée quatre fois.

curtained [ˈkɜːtnd] *adj* [window, door] garni d'un rideau OR de rideaux.

curtain hook *n* crochet *m* de rideau.

curtain rail *n* tringle *f* à rideau OR à rideaux.

curtain raiser *n* THEAT lever *m* de rideau; *fig* événement *m* avant-coureur, prélude *m*.

curtain ring *n* anneau *m* de rideau.

curtain rod = **curtain rail**.

curtly [ˈkɜːtlɪ] *adv* [bluntly - say, reply] avec brusquerie, sèchement, sans ménagement.

curtness [ˈkɜːtnɪs] *n* [bluntness - of tone, reply, manner, person] brusquerie *f*, sécheresse *f*.

curtsey, curtsy [ˈkɜːtsɪ] (*pl* **curtseys** OR **curtsies**, *pt* & *pp* **curtseyed** OR **curtsied**) ◇ *n* révérence *f*; **she made OR gave a ~** elle a fait une révérence.

◇ *vi* faire une révérence.

curvaceous [kɜːˈveɪʃəs] *adj hum* bien fait.

curvature [ˈkɜːvətjəʳ] *n* [gen] courbure *f*; **the ~ of space** la courbure de l'espace || MED déviation *f*; **~ of the spine** [abnormal] déviation de la colonne vertébrale, scoliose *f*.

curve [kɜːv] ◇ *n* -**1.** [gen] courbe *f*; [in road] tournant *m*, virage *m*; ARCHIT [of arch] voussure *f*; [of beam] cambrure *f*; **the ~ of the bay** la courbe de la baie; **a woman's ~s** les rondeurs *fpl* d'une femme. -**2.** MATH courbe *f*.

◇ *vi* [gen] se courber; [road] être en courbe, faire une courbe; **the road ~s up the mountainside** la route monte en lacets le long de la montagne; **the path ~d round to the left** le chemin tournait vers la gauche; **the river ~s through the valley** la rivière serpente dans la vallée.

◇ *vt* [gen] courber; TECH cintrer.

curveball [ˈkɜːvbɔːl] *n Am* balle *f* coupée.

curved [kɜːvd] *adj* [gen] courbe; [edge] arrondi; [road] en courbe; [convex] convexe; TECH cintré.

curvet [kɜːˈvet] (*Br pt* & *pp* **curvetted**, *cont* **curvetting**, *Am pt* & *pp* **curveted**, *cont* **curveting**)

◇ *n* courbette *f*.

◇ *vi* faire une courbette OR des courbettes.

curvilinear [ˌkɜːvɪˈlɪnɪəʳ] *adj* curviligne.

curvy [ˈkɜːvɪ] (*compar* **curvier**, *superl* **curviest**) *adj* -**1.** [road, line] sinueux. -**2.** *inf* [woman] bien fait.

cushion [ˈkʊʃn] ◇ *n* -**1.** [pillow] coussin *m*; *fig* tampon *m*; **the hovercraft floats on a ~ of air** *fig* l'hovercraft flotte sur un coussin d'air. -**2.** [in snooker, billiards etc] bande *f*; **to play off the ~** jouer par la bande; **stroke off the ~** doublé *m*.

◇ *vt* -**1.** [sofa] mettre des coussins à; [seat] rembourrer; TECH matelasser. -**2.** *fig* [shock, blow] amortir; to ~ a fall amortir une chute; he chose his words to ~ her against disappointment il choisit ses mots afin d'atténuer sa déception; tax cuts that ~ price rises des réductions d'impôts qui amortissent la hausse des prix.

cushioning ['kʊʃnɪŋ] *n* matelassage *m*.

cushy *inf* ['kʊʃɪ] (*compar* cushier, *superl* cushiest) *adj* peinard, pépère; a ~ job une bonne planque; he has a ~ life il a une petite vie peinarde.

cusp [kʌsp] *n* ANAT & BOT cuspide *f*; ASTRON [of moon] cuspide *f*; ASTROL corne *f*.

cuspidor ['kʌspɪdɔːr] *n Am* crachoir *m*.

cuss *inf* [kʌs] ◇ *vi* jurer, blasphémer.
◇ *vt* injurier.
◇ *n* -**1.** [oath] juron *m*. -**2.** [person] type *m pej*.
◆ **cuss out** *inf vt sep Am*: to ~ sb out traiter qqn de tous les noms.

cussed *inf* ['kʌsɪd] *adj* -**1.** [obstinate] têtu, entêté. -**2.** [cursed] sacré.

cussedness *inf* ['kʌsɪdnɪs] *n* esprit *m* de contradiction; out of sheer ~ rien que pour embêter le monde.

custard ['kʌstəd] -**1.** [sauce] *crème sucrée épaisse servie chaude ou froide*, ≃ crème *f* anglaise. -**2.** [dessert] crème *f* renversée, flan *m*.

custard apple *n* anone *f*.

custard cream (biscuit) *n* biscuit *m* fourré.

custard pie *n* tarte *f* à la crème.

custard powder *n* crème *f* instantanée *(en poudre)*.

custard tart = **custard pie**.

Custer ['kʌstər] *pr n* Custer; ~'s Last Stand *expression désignant la bataille de Little Bighorn*.

custodial [kʌ'stəʊdjəl] *adj* -**1.** JUR de prison; ~ sentence peine *f* de prison. -**2.** [guarding]: ~ staff personnel *m* de surveillance.

custodian [kʌ'stəʊdjən] *n* -**1.** [of building] gardien *m*, -enne *f*; [of museum] conservateur *m*, -trice *f*; [of prisoner] gardien *m*, -enne *f*, surveillant *m*, -e *f*. -**2.** *fig* [of morals, tradition] gardien *m*, -enne *f*, protecteur *m*, -trice *f*.

custodianship [kʌ'stəʊdjənʃɪp] *n* -**1.** [guarding] surveillance *f*. -**2.** *Br* JUR *garde d'un enfant à long terme sans obligation d'adoption*.

custody ['kʌstədɪ] (*pl* custodies) *n* -**1.** [care] garde *f*; the son is in the ~ of his mother le fils est sous la garde de sa mère; to be given OR awarded ~ of a child JUR obtenir la garde d'un enfant; in safe ~ sous bonne garde. -**2.** [detention] garde *f* à vue; [imprisonment] emprisonnement *m*; [before trial] détention *f* préventive; the police held her in ~ la police l'a mise en garde à vue; he was taken into (police) ~ il a été mis en état d'arrestation.

custom ['kʌstəm] *n* -**1.** [tradition] coutume *f*, usage *m*; it is the ~ to eat fish on Friday l'usage veut qu'on mange du poisson le vendredi; as ~ has it selon la coutume OR les us et coutumes; it's her ~ to read before going to sleep elle a l'habitude de lire avant de s'endormir. -**2.** COMM [trade] clientèle *f*; they have a lot of foreign ~ ils ont beaucoup de clients étrangers; he has lost all his ~ il a perdu toute sa clientèle; I'll take my ~ elsewhere je vais me fournir ailleurs. -**3.** JUR coutume *f*, droit *m* coutumier.

customary ['kʌstəmrɪ] *adj fml* -**1.** [traditional] coutumier, habituel; [usual] habituel; as is ~ comme le veut l'usage; it is ~ to tip taxi drivers l'usage OR la coutume veut que l'on donne un pourboire aux chauffeurs de taxi; at the ~ time à l'heure habituelle. -**2.** JUR coutumier; ~ tenant tenancier *m* censitaire.

custom-built *adj* (fait) sur commande.

customer ['kʌstəmər] *n* -**1.** [client] client *m*, -e *f*. -**2.** *inf* [character] type *m pej*; she's a cool ~ elle en prend à son aise; he's an awkward ~ il n'est pas commode; a queer ~ un drôle de type.

customize, -ise ['kʌstəmaɪz] *vt* [make to order] faire OR fabriquer OR construire sur commande; [personalize] personnaliser; ~d software COMPUT logiciel *m* sur mesure.

custom-made *adj* [clothing] (fait) sur mesure; [other articles] (fait) sur commande.

customs ['kʌstəmz] *npl* -**1.** [authorities, checkpoint] douane *f*; to go through ~ passer la douane; at ~ à la douane ❑ Customs and Excise *Br* ≃ la Régie. -**2.** [duty] droits *mpl* de douane.

customs duty *n* droit *m* OR droits *mpl* de douane.

customs house *n* (poste *m* OR bureau *m* de) douane *f*.

customs officer *n* douanier *m*, -ère *f*.

customs union *n* union *f* douanière.

cut [kʌt] (*pt* & *pp* cut, *cont* cutting) ◇ *vt* -**1.** [incise, slash, sever] couper; ~ the box open with the knife ouvrez la boîte avec le couteau; he fell and ~ his knee (open) il s'est ouvert le genou en tombant; she ~ her hand elle s'est coupé la main OR à la main; he ~ his wrists il s'est ouvert OR taillé les veines; they ~ his throat ils lui ont coupé la gorge, ils l'ont égorgé; they ~ the prisoners free OR loose ils ont détaché les prisonniers; they ~ our supply line ils nous ont coupé notre approvisionnement ‖ *fig*: the fog is so thick you could ~ it with a knife il y a un brouillard à couper au couteau; the atmosphere was so tense, you could ~ it with a knife l'atmosphère était extrêmement tendue; you're cutting your own throat c'est du suicide. -**2.** [divide into parts] couper, découper; [meat] découper; [slice] découper en tranches; she ~ articles from the paper elle découpait des articles dans le journal; ~ the cake in half/in three pieces coupez le gâteau en deux/en trois; to ~ sthg to shreds OR to ribbons mettre qqch en pièces; the enemy ~ the army to pieces *fig* l'ennemi a taillé l'armée en pièces; the critics ~ the play to pieces *fig* les critiques ont esquinté la pièce. -**3.** [trim - grass, lawn] tondre; [- bush, tree] tailler; [reap - crop] couper, faucher; I'll have to ~ the grass this weekend il faudra que je tonde la pelouse ce week-end; I ~ my nails/my hair je me suis coupé les ongles/les cheveux; you've had your hair ~ vous vous êtes fait couper les cheveux. -**4.** [shape - dress, suit] couper; [- diamond, glass, key] tailler; [- screw] fileter; [dig - channel, tunnel] creuser, percer; [engrave] graver; [sculpt] sculpter; steps had been ~ in the rock on avait taillé des marches dans le rocher; we ~ our way through the crowd nous nous sommes frayé OR ouvert un chemin à travers la foule; the advance ~ a swath through the enemy's defences l'avance des troupes ouvrit une brèche dans la défense ennemie ❑ you must ~ your coat according to your cloth il ne faut pas vivre au-dessus de ses moyens. -**5.** [cross, traverse] couper, croiser; MATH couper; where the path ~s the road à l'endroit où le chemin coupe la route. -**6.** [interrupt] interrompre, couper; to ~ sb short couper la parole à qqn; we had to ~ our visit short nous avons dû écourter notre visite; his career was tragically ~ short by illness sa carrière a été tragiquement interrompue par la maladie ❑ to ~ a long story short, I left bref OR en deux mots, je suis parti. -**7.** [stop] arrêter, cesser; he ~ working weekends il a arrêté de travailler le weekend; ~ the crap![▽] arrête tes conneries! -**8.** [switch off] couper; ~ the lights! coupez la lumière!, éteignez!; he ~ the engine il a coupé OR arrêté le moteur. -**9.** [reduce] réduire, diminuer; we ~ our costs by half nous avons réduit nos frais de moitié; they ~ taxes in the run-up to the election ils ont réduit les impôts juste avant les élections; to ~ prices casser les prix; the athlete ~ 5 seconds off the world record OR ~ the world record by 5 seconds l'athlète a amélioré le record mondial de 5 secondes. -**10.** [edit out] faire des coupures dans, réduire; the censors ~ all scenes of violence la censure a coupé OR supprimé toutes les scènes de violence. -**11.** [hurt feelings of] blesser profondément; her remark ~ me deeply sa remarque m'a profondément blessé. -**12.** *inf* [ignore, snub] faire semblant de ne pas voir; they ~ me (dead) in the street dans la rue ils ont fait comme s'ils ne me voyaient pas; he ~ me dead for days after our argument il m'a battu froid pendant des jours après notre dispute. -**13.** *inf* [absent oneself from - meeting, appointment etc] manquer (volontairement), sauter; I had to ~ lunch in order to get there on time j'ai dû me passer de déjeuner pour arriver à l'heure; the students ~ class les étudiants ont séché le cours; to ~ school sécher les cours. -**14.** [tooth] percer; the baby is cutting his first tooth le bébé perce sa première dent; a pianist who ~ her teeth on Bach *inf fig* une pianiste qui s'est fait la main sur du Bach. -**15.** [dilute] couper. -**16.** [record, track] graver, faire. -**17.** [pack of cards] couper. -**18.** CIN [film] monter. -**19.** MED [incise] inciser; VETER [castrate] châtrer. -**20.** SPORT [ball] couper. -**21.** *phr*: to ~ the ground from under sb's feet couper l'herbe sous le pied de qqn; her promotion ~ the ground from under his feet sa promotion lui a coupé l'herbe sous le pied; he couldn't ~ the mustard *Am* il n'était pas à la hauteur; to ~ sthg fine compter un peu juste, ne pas se laisser de marge; you're cutting it a bit fine vous comptez un peu juste; an hour is cutting it too fine une heure, ce n'est pas suffisant; that argument ~s no ice with me *inf* cet argument ne m'impressionne pas; to ~ a dash faire de l'effet; her evening dress ~ quite a dash sa robe de soirée a fait de l'effet; to ~ a fine figure avoir beaucoup d'allure; he ~ a sorry figure il faisait piètre figure; to ~ one's losses sauver les meubles; we decided to ~ our losses nous avons décidé de sauver les meubles; to ~ a caper OR capers [skip] faire des cabrioles, gambader; [fool around] faire l'idiot; to ~ a corner AUT prendre un virage à la corde, couper un virage; she doesn't believe in cutting corners *fig* elle fait toujours les choses à fond; they ~ corners to finish on time *fig* ils ont brûlé les étapes pour finir à l'heure.
◇ *vi* -**1.** [incise, slash] couper, trancher; this knife doesn't ~ ce couteau ne coupe pas bien; ~ around the edge découpez OR coupez en suivant le bord; she ~ into the bread elle a entamé le pain; the rope ~ into my wrists la corde m'a coupé OR cisaillé les poignets; he ~ through all the red tape *fig* il s'est dispensé de toutes les formalités administratives; the whip ~ through the air *fig* le fouet fendit l'air; the yacht ~ through the waves *fig* le yacht fendait les vagues; the boat ~ loose NAUT le bateau a rompu les amarres; to ~ loose *fig* se libérer ❑ to ~ and run se sauver, filer; that argument ~s both OR two ways c'est un argument à double tranchant. -**2.** [cloth, paper] se couper; this meat ~s easily cette viande se coupe facilement; the cake will ~ into six pieces ce gâteau peut se couper en six. -**3.** [hurtfully] faire mal. -**4.** [take shorter route] couper, passer; ~ through the back way and you'll get there first coupez par derrière et vous arriverez (là-bas) les premiers; we ~ across the fields nous avons coupé par les champs. -**5.** [cross] traverser, couper; MATH [lines] se couper; this path ~s across OR through the swamp ce sentier traverse OR coupe à travers le marécage. -**6.** [in cards] couper; they ~ for the deal ils ont coupé avant de donner. -**7.** CIN & TV [stop filming] couper; [change scenes]: the film ~s straight from the love scene to the funeral l'image passe directement de la scène d'amour à l'enterrement; ~! coupez!
◇ *n* -**1.** [slit] coupure *f*; [deeper] entaille *f*; [wound] balafre *f*; MED incision *f*; a ~ on the arm une coupure OR une entaille au bras; she had a nasty ~ on her leg from the fall elle s'était fait une vilaine entaille à la jambe en tombant ❑ to be a ~ above the rest être nettement mieux que les autres OR le reste; that film is a ~ above the others ce film est nettement mieux que les autres. -**2.** [act of cutting] coupure *f*, entaille *f*; to make a ~ in sthg [with knife, scissors etc] faire une entaille dans qqch. -**3.** [blow, stroke] coup *m*; a knife/sword ~ un coup de couteau/d'épée; a saw ~ un trait de scie; his treachery was the unkind-

est ~ of all *fig* sa trahison était le coup le plus perfide ❑ the ~ and thrust of parliamentary debate les joutes oratoires des débats parlementaires. -**4.** [meat - piece] morceau *m*; [- slice] tranche *f*; a ~ off the joint CULIN un morceau de rôti; prime ~ morceau de premier choix. -**5.** [reduction - in price, taxes] réduction *f*, diminution *f*; [- in staff] compression *f*; a ~ in government spending une réduction OR diminution des dépenses publiques; the ~s in the Health Service la réduction OR diminution du budget de la Sécurité sociale; she took a ~ in pay elle a subi une diminution OR réduction de salaire; the ~s FIN les compressions *fpl* budgétaires. -**6.** [deletion] coupure *f*; they made several ~s in the film ils ont fait plusieurs coupures dans le film. -**7.** [gibe, nasty remark] trait *m*, coup *m*. -**8.** [shape, style - of clothes, hair] coupe *f*; [- of jewel] taille *f*; the ~ of a suit la coupe d'un costume ❑ I don't like the ~ of his jib *inf* je n'aime pas son allure. -**9.** *inf* [portion, share] part *f*; what's his ~ (of the profits)? à combien s'élève sa part? -**10.** *inf Am* [absence] absence *f*. -**11.** [in cards] coupe *f*. -**12.** *inf* [on record] plage *f*. -**13.** CIN & TV coupe *f*; the ~ from the love scene to the funeral le changement de séquence de la scène d'amour à l'enterrement. -**14.** SPORT [backspin] effet *m*. -**15.** TYPO *Am* [block] cliché *m*.

◇ *adj* -**1.** [hand, flowers] coupé; [tobacco] découpé. -**2.** [reduced] réduit; to sell sthg at ~ prices vendre qqch au rabais. -**3.** [shaped - clothing] coupé; [faceted - gem] taillé; a well-~ suit un costume bien coupé OR de bonne coupe. -**4.** *inf Br* [drunk] soûl, plein.

◆ **cut across** *vt insep* -**1.** [cross, traverse] traverser, couper à travers; it's quicker if you ~ across the fields c'est plus rapide si tu coupes à travers (les) champs; they ~ across country ils ont coupé à travers champs. -**2.** [go beyond] surpasser, transcender; the issue ~s across party lines la question déborde le clivage des partis. -**3.** [contradict] contredire, aller à l'encontre de; it ~s across all my principles ça va à l'encontre de tous mes principes.

◆ **cut along** *inf vi insep Br* filer.

◆ **cut away** *vt sep* [remove] enlever OR ôter (en coupant); [branch] élaguer, émonder.

◆ **cut back** ◇ *vi insep* -**1.** [return] rebrousser chemin, revenir sur ses pas; we ~ back to the car nous sommes revenus à la voiture. -**2.** CIN revenir en arrière.

◇ *vt sep* -**1.** [reduce] réduire, diminuer. -**2.** [prune, trim] tailler; [shrub, tree] élaguer, tailler.

◆ **cut back on** *vt insep* réduire; the factory ~ back on production la fabrique a réduit la production.

◆ **cut down** *vt sep* -**1.** [tree] couper, abattre; [person - in battle] abattre; he was ~ down by malaria *fig* [killed] il est mort de la malaria; [incapacitated] il était terrassé par la malaria. -**2.** [make smaller - article, speech] couper, tronquer; [- clothing] rendre plus petit; she ~s down her dresses for her daughter elle ajuste ses robes pour sa fille ❑ to ~ sb down to size remettre qqn à sa place. -**3.** [curtail] réduire, diminuer; [expenses] réduire, rogner; he ~ his smoking down to 10 a day il ne fume plus que 10 cigarettes par jour.

◆ **cut down on** *vt insep* réduire; I'm going to ~ down on drinking/smoking je vais boire/fumer moins; they have ~ down on eating out in restaurants ils vont moins souvent au restaurant.

◆ **cut in** *inf* ◇ *vi insep* -**1.** [interrupt] interrompre; she ~ in on their conversation elle est intervenue dans leur conversation; he ~ in on me to ask a question il m'a coupé la parole pour poser une question; the new store is cutting in on our business *fig* le nouveau magasin nous fait perdre de la clientèle. -**2.** AUT faire une queue de poisson; the taxi ~ in on them le taxi leur a fait une queue de poisson.

◇ *vt sep* [include]: we should ~ him in on the deal nous devrions l'intéresser à l'affaire.

◆ **cut off** *vt sep* -**1.** [hair, piece of meat, bread] couper; [arm, leg] amputer, couper; they ~ off the king's head ils ont décapité le roi ❑ he was ~ off in his prime il a été emporté à la fleur de l'âge; she ~ off her nose to spite her face elle l'a fait par esprit de contradiction. -**2.** [interrupt - speaker] interrompre, couper; he was ~ off in mid sentence il a été interrompu au milieu de sa phrase. -**3.** [disconnect, discontinue] couper; they ~ off the electricity OR power ils ont coupé le courant; they ~ off his allowance ils lui ont coupé les vivres; her family ~ her off without a penny sa famille l'a déshéritée; I was ~ off TELEC j'ai été coupé. -**4.** [separate, isolate] isoler; the house was ~ off by snow drifts la maison était isolée par des congères; he ~ himself off from his family/from his former life il a rompu avec sa famille/avec son passé; housewives often feel ~ off les femmes au foyer se sentent souvent isolées. -**5.** [bar passage of] couper la route à; the police ~ off the thief la police a barré le passage au voleur; the battalion ~ off the enemy's retreat le bataillon a coupé la retraite à l'ennemi.

◆ **cut out** ◇ *vt sep* -**1.** [make by cutting - coat, dress] couper, tailler; [- statue] sculpter, tailler; a valley ~ out by the river une vallée creusée par le fleuve ❑ I'm not ~ out for living abroad je ne suis pas fait pour vivre à l'étranger; he's not ~ out to be a politician il n'a pas l'étoffe d'un homme politique; you have your work ~ out for you vous avez du pain sur la planche OR de quoi vous occuper; she has her work ~ out to prepare the report on time elle aura du mal à préparer le rapport à l'heure. -**2.** [remove by cutting - article, picture] découper; advertisements ~ out from OR of the paper des annonces découpées dans le journal. -**3.** [eliminate] supprimer; [stop] arrêter; unnecessary expense must be ~ out il faut éliminer OR supprimer les frais superflus; they ~ out all references to the president ils ont supprimé toute référence au président; try and ~ out all unnecessary details essayez de supprimer tous les détails superflus; he ~ out smoking il a arrêté de fumer; ~ out the screaming! arrête de crier!, assez crié! ❑ ~ it out! *inf* ça suffit!, ça va comme ça! -**4.** *inf* [rival] supplanter. -**5.** [deprive] priver; his father ~ him out of his will son père l'a rayé de son testament; they ~ him out of his share ils lui ont escroqué sa part. -**6.** PHOT & TYPO détourer.

◇ *vi insep* [machine - stop operating] caler; [- switch off] s'éteindre.

◆ **cut up** ◇ *vt sep* -**1.** [food, wood] couper; [meat - carve] découper; [- chop up] hacher. -**2.** *inf (usu pass)* [affect deeply]: she's really ~ up about her dog's death la mort de son chien a été un coup pour elle.

◇ *vi insep* *inf* -**1.** *Br phr*: to ~ up rough se mettre en rogne OR en boule. -**2.** *Am* [fool around] faire le pitre.

cut-and-dried *inf adj*: a ~ formula une formule toute faite; it's all ~ [prearranged] tout est déjà décidé; [inevitable] il n'y a rien à (y) faire.

cut-and-paste *vt & vi* couper-coller.

cutaneous [kju'teɪnjəs] *adj* cutané.

cutaway ['kʌtəweɪ] *n* -**1.** [coat] jaquette *f (d'homme)*. -**2.** [drawing, model] écorché *m*. -**3.** CIN changement *m* de plan.

cutback ['kʌtbæk] *n* -**1.** [reduction - in costs] réduction *f*, diminution *f*; [- in staff] compression *f*; a ~ in production une réduction de production. -**2.** *Am* CIN retour *m* en arrière, flash-back *m*.

cute *inf* [kjuːt] *adj* -**1.** [pretty] mignon; *Am pej* affecté. -**2.** [clever] malin; don't get ~ with me *pej* ne fais pas le malin avec moi.

cut glass *n* cristal *m* taillé.

◆ **cut-glass** *adj*: a cut-glass vase un vase *m* en cristal taillé; a cut-glass accent *Br fig* un accent distingué.

cuticle ['kjuːtɪkl] *n* -**1.** [skin] épiderme *m*; [on nails] petites peaux *fpl*, envie *f*. -**2.** BOT cuticule *f*.

cuticle remover *n* repousse-peaux *m*.

cutie *inf* ['kjuːtɪ] *n* -**1.** [child, baby] mignon *m*, -onne *f*; [term of endearment] mon chou. -**2.** [shrewd person] malin *m*, maligne *f*.

cutie-pie *inf n* mon chou, mon lapin.

cutlass ['kʌtləs] *n* coutelas *m*.

cutler ['kʌtlə^r] *n* coutelier *m*.

cutlery ['kʌtlərɪ] *n (U)* -**1.** [eating utensils] couverts *mpl*. -**2.** [knives, trade] coutellerie *f*.

cutlet ['kʌtlɪt] *n* -**1.** [gen] côtelette *f*; [of veal] escalope *f*. -**2.** *Br* [croquette] croquette *f*; vegetable ~s croquettes de légumes.

cutoff ['kʌtɒf] *n* -**1.** [stopping point] arrêt *m*; $100 is our ~ (point) nous nous arrêtons à 100 dollars; ~ device TECH système *m* d'arrêt; ~ switch TECH interrupteur *m*. -**2.** *Am* [shortcut] raccourci *m*.

◆ **cutoffs** *npl*: (a pair of) ~s *un jean coupé pour en faire un short*.

cutout ['kʌtaʊt] *n* -**1.** [figure] découpage *m*; a ~ book un livre de découpages; cardboard ~s découpages *mpl* en carton. -**2.** ELEC disjoncteur *m*, coupe-circuit *m*; AUT échappement *m* libre; ~ point AERON [of rocket] point *m* de largage.

cut-price ◇ *adj* [articles] à prix réduit, au rabais; [shop] à prix réduits; [manufacturer] qui vend à prix réduits.

◇ *adv* à prix réduit.

cutter ['kʌtə^r] *n* -**1.** [person - of clothes] coupeur *m*, -euse *f*; [- of jewels] tailleur *m*; [- of film] monteur *m*, -euse *f*. -**2.** [tool] coupoir *m*; wire ~s cisailles *fpl*, pince *f* coupante. -**3.** [sailing boat] cotre *m*, cutter *m*; [motorboat] vedette *f*; [of coastguard] garde-côte *m*; [warship] canot *m*.

cutthroat ['kʌtθrəʊt] ◇ *n* -**1.** [murderer] assassin *m*. -**2.** [razor]: ~ (razor) rasoir *m* à main.

◇ *adj* féroce; [competition] acharné; [prices] très compétitif; lexicography is a ~ business le milieu de la lexicographie est un panier de crabes; ~ game [in cards] partie *f* à trois.

cutting ['kʌtɪŋ] ◇ *n* -**1.** [act] coupe *f*; [of jewel, stone] taille *f*; [of film] montage *m*; [of trees] coupe *f*, abattage *m*. -**2.** [piece - of cloth] coupon *m*; [- from newspaper] coupure *f*; AGR [of shrub, vine] marcotte *f*; HORT [of plant] bouture *f*. -**3.** [for railway, road] tranchée *f*.

◇ *adj* -**1.** [tool] tranchant, coupant; ~ pliers pinces *fpl* coupantes; ~ edge *literal* tranchant *m*; to be at the ~ edge of technological progress *fig* être à la pointe du progrès en technologie. -**2.** [wind] glacial, cinglant; [rain] cinglant. -**3.** [hurtful - remark] mordant, tranchant; [- word] cinglant, blessant.

cuttingly ['kʌtɪŋlɪ] *adv* méchamment.

cuttlebone ['kʌtlbəʊn] *n* os *m* de seiche.

cuttlefish ['kʌtlfɪʃ] *(pl inv) n* seiche *f*.

cutup *inf* ['kʌtʌp] *n Am* farceur *m*, rigolo *m*, -ote *f*.

CV *(abbr of* curriculum vitae) *n Br* CV *m*.

CVS *(abbr of* chorionic villus sampling) *n* prélèvement *m* des villosités choriales.

CW ◇ *npl (abbr of* continuous waves) RADIO ondes *fpl* entretenues.

◇ *n* [Morse code] morse *m*.

C & W *n abbr of* country and western (music).

cwm [kuːm] *n* GEOL cirque *m* (glaciaire); [in Wales] vallée *f*.

c.w.o., CWO *(written abbr of* cash with order) payable à la commande.

cwt. *written abbr of* hundredweight.

cyan ['saɪən] ◇ *adj* cyan.

◇ *n* cyan *m*.

cyanide ['saɪənaɪd] *n* cyanure *m*.

cyanosis [,saɪə'nəʊsɪs] *n (U)* cyanose *f*.

Cybele ['sɪbəlɪ] *pr n* Cybèle.

cybernetics [,saɪbə'netɪks] *n (U)* cybernétique *f*.

Cyclades ['sɪklədiːz] *pl pr n*: the ~ les Cyclades *fpl*; in the ~ dans les Cyclades.

Cycladic [sɪ'klædɪk] *adj* cycladique.

cyclamate ['saɪkləmeɪt] *n* cyclamate *m*.

cyclamen ['sɪkləmən] *(pl inv) n* cyclamen *m*.

cycle ['saɪkl] ◇ *n* -**1.** [gen, COMPUT, ELEC & LITERAT] cycle *m*; the life ~ of the butterfly le cycle de vie du papillon. -**2.** [bicycle] bicyclette *f*, vélo *m*; [tricycle] tricycle *m*; [motorcycle] motocyclette *f*, moto *f*.
◇ *comp* [path, track] cyclable; [race] cycliste; [chain, lamp, wheel] de bicyclette; ~ **bell** sonnette *f* OR timbre *m* de bicyclette; ~ **clips** pinces *fpl* à vélo; ~ **pump** pompe *f* à vélo; ~ **racing track** vélodrome *m*; ~ **rack** [on pavement] râtelier *m* à bicyclettes; [on car] porte-vélos *m*.
◇ *vi* faire de la bicyclette OR du vélo; she ~**d into town everyday** elle allait en ville à bicyclette OR à vélo chaque jour.

cycler ['saɪkləʳ] *Am* = **cyclist**.

cyclic(al) ['saɪklɪk(l)] *adj* cyclique.

cycling ['saɪklɪŋ] ◇ *n* cyclisme *m*; I go ~ **every weekend** [gen] je fais du vélo tous les week-ends; SPORT tous les week-ends, je fais du cyclisme.
◇ *comp* [magazine, shoes, shorts] de cyclisme; ~ **clothes** tenue *f* cycliste; a ~ **tour** un circuit à bicyclette OR à vélo; **we went on a** ~ **holiday** nous avons fait du cyclotourisme.

cyclist ['saɪklɪst] *n* cycliste *mf*.

cyclo-cross ['saɪkləʊkrɒs] *n* cyclo-cross *m*.

cyclone ['saɪkləʊn] *n* cyclone *m*.

cyclone cellar *n* abri *m* anticyclone.

cyclonic [saɪ'klɒnɪk] *adj* cyclonique, cyclonal.

cyclops ['saɪklɒps] *n* cyclope *m*.
◆ **Cyclops** *n*: (the) ~ le Cyclope.

cyclorama [ˌsaɪklə'rɑːmə] *n* cyclorama *m*.

cyclostyle ['saɪkləʊstaɪl] ◇ *n* machine *f* à polycopier.
◇ *vt* polycopier.

cyclotron ['saɪklətrɒn] *n* cyclotron *m*.

cygnet ['sɪgnɪt] *n* jeune cygne *m*.

cylinder ['sɪlɪndəʳ] *n* -**1.** AUT, MATH & TECH cylindre *m*; **four** ~ **engine** moteur *m* à quatre cylindres; **six** ~ **car** six-cylindres *f*; **oxygen** ~ bouteille *f* d'oxygène. -**2.** [of typewriter] rouleau *m*; [of gun] barillet *m*.

cylinder block *n* bloc-cylindres *m*.

cylinder head *n* culasse *f (d'un moteur)*.

cylinder press *n* presse *f* à cylindres.

cylinder seal *n* cylindre-sceau *m*.

cylindrical [sɪ'lɪndrɪkl] *adj* cylindrique.

cymbal ['sɪmbl] *n* cymbale *f*.

cynic ['sɪnɪk] ◇ *adj* [gen & PHILOS] cynique.
◇ *n* cynique *mf*.

cynical ['sɪnɪkl] *adj* [gen & PHILOS] cynique.

cynically ['sɪnɪklɪ] *adv* cyniquement, avec cynisme.

cynicism ['sɪnɪsɪzm] *n* [gen & PHILOS] cynisme *m*; ~**s** remarques *fpl* cyniques.

cynosure ['sɪnəˌzjʊəʳ] *n* centre *m* d'attraction, point *m* de mire.

CYO (*abbr of* Catholic Youth Organization) *pr n association de jeunes catholiques aux États-Unis*.

cypher ['saɪfəʳ] = **cipher**.

cypress ['saɪprəs] *n* cyprès *m*.

Cypriot ['sɪprɪət] ◇ *n* Chypriote *mf*, Cypriote *mf*; **Greek** ~ Chypriote grec *m*, Chypriote grecque *f*; **Turkish** ~ Chypriote turc *m*, Chypriote turque *f*.
◇ *adj* chypriote, cypriote.

Cyprus ['saɪprəs] *pr n* Chypre; in ~ à Chypre.

Cyrillic [sɪ'rɪlɪk] ◇ *adj* cyrillique.
◇ *n* alphabet *m* cyrillique.

cyst [sɪst] *n* -**1.** MED kyste *m*. -**2.** BIOL sac *m* (membraneux).

cystic fibrosis ['sɪstɪk-] *n* mucoviscidose *f*.

cystitis [sɪs'taɪtɪs] *n* cystite *f*.

cytology [saɪ'tɒlədʒɪ] *n* cytologie *f*.

cytoplasm ['saɪtəʊˌplæzm] *n* cytoplasme *m*.

CZ *pr n abbr of* Canal Zone.

czar [zɑːʳ] *n* tsar *m*.

czarevitch ['zɑːrəvɪtʃ] *n* tsarévitch *m*.

czarina [zɑː'riːnə] *n* tsarine *f*.

czarism ['zɑːrɪzm] *n* tsarisme *m*.

czarist ['zɑːrɪst] ◇ *adj* tsariste.
◇ *n* tsariste *mf*.

Czech [tʃek] ◇ *n* -**1.** [person] Tchèque *mf*. -**2.** LING tchèque *m*.
◇ *adj* tchèque.

Czechoslovak [ˌtʃekə'sləʊvæk] = **Czechoslovakian**.

Czechoslovakia [ˌtʃekəslə'vækɪə] *pr n* Tchécoslovaquie *f*; in ~ en Tchécoslovaquie.

Czechoslovakian [ˌtʃekəslə'vækɪən] ◇ *n* Tchécoslovaque *mf*.
◇ *adj* tchécoslovaque.

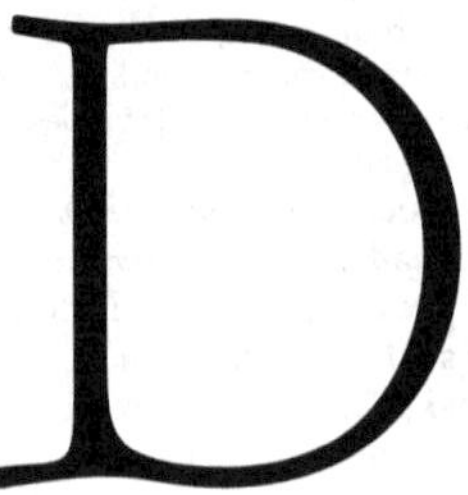

d (*pl* d's OR ds), **D** (*pl* D's OR Ds) [diː] *n* [letter] d *m*, D *m*; D for dog OR David ≃ D comme Désirée; in 3-D en trois dimensions, en 3-D.

d -**1.** (*written abbr of* penny) *symbole du penny anglais jusqu'en 1971.* -**2.** (*written abbr of* died): d 1913 mort en 1913.

D ◇ *n* -**1.** MUS ré *m*. -**2.** SCH & UNIV [grade] *note inférieure à la moyenne (7 sur 20).*
◇ *Am written abbr of* democrat(ic).

DA (*abbr of* District Attorney) *n* -**1.** *Am* ≃ Procureur *m* de la République. -**2.** (*abbr of* duck's arse) ≃ banane *f (coiffure).*

dab [dæb] (*pt* & *pp* dabbed, *cont* dabbing)
◇ *n* -**1.** [small amount]: a ~ un petit peu; a ~ of rouge une goutte de rouge. -**2.** [fish] limande *f*.
◇ *vt* -**1.** [touch lightly] tamponner; she dabbed her eyes elle s'est tamponné OR essuyé les yeux; she dabbed the graze with cotton wool elle tamponna l'écorchure avec du coton. -**2.** [daub]: he dabbed the canvas with paint il posait la peinture sur la toile par petites touches.
◆ **dabs**▽ *npl Br* [fingerprints] empreintes *fpl* digitales.
◆ **dab at** *vt insep* = **dab** *vt* **1**.
◆ **dab on** *vt sep* appliquer par petites touches.

dabble ['dæbl] ◇ *vt* mouiller; they ~d their feet in the water ils trempaient les pieds dans l'eau.
◇ *vi fig*: he ~s at painting il fait un peu de peinture; she ~s in politics elle fait un peu de politique; to ~ on the Stock Market boursicoter.

dabbler ['dæbləʳ] *n* dilettante *mf*.

dabbling ['dæblɪŋ] *n* dilettantisme *m*.

dabchick ['dæbtʃɪk] *n* petit grèbe *m*.

dab hand *inf n Br*: to be a ~ at sthg être doué en OR pour qqch; to be a ~ at doing sthg être doué pour faire qqch.

Dacca ['dækə] *pr n* Dacca.

dace [deɪs] *n* dard *m*, vandoise *f*.

dachshund ['dækshʊnd] *n* teckel *m*.

Dacron® ['dækrɒn] *n* Dacron® *m*, ≃ Tergal® *m*.

dactyl ['dæktɪl] *n* dactyle *m*.

dactylography [ˌdæktɪ'lɒgrəfɪ] *n Am* dactyloscopie *f*.

dad *inf* [dæd] *n* [father] papa *m*; [old man] pépé *m*.

Dada ['dɑːdɑː] ◇ *n* dada *m*.
◇ *adj* dada, dadaïste.

Dadaism ['dɑːdɑːɪzm] *n* dadaïsme *m*.

Dadaist ['dɑːdɑːɪst] ◇ *adj* dadaïste.
◇ *n* dadaïste *mf*.

daddy *inf* ['dædɪ] (*pl* daddies) *n* papa *m*; the ~ of them all *inf Am* le meilleur de tous.

daddy longlegs [-'lɒŋlegz] *n Br* [cranefly] tipule *f*; *Am* [harvestman] faucheur *m*, faucheux *m*.

dado ['deɪdəʊ] (*pl* dadoes) *n* [of wall] lambris *m* d'appui; ARCHIT [of pedestal] dé *m*.

Daedalus ['daɪdələs] *pr n* MYTH Dédale.

daemon ['diːmən] *n* -**1.** [demigod] demi-dieu *m*. -**2.** = **demon**.

daff *inf* [dæf] = **daffodil**.

daffodil ['dæfədɪl] *n* jonquille *f*; ~ yellow jaune *m* d'or.

DAFFODIL:
La jonquille est le symbole du pays de Galles; le jour de la Saint David, les Galloises en portent une épinglée à la boutonnière.

---

daffy *inf* ['dæfɪ] (*compar* daffier, *superl* daffiest) *adj* loufoque, timbré.

daft *inf* [dɑːft] ◇ *adj Br* [foolish - idea, person] idiot, bête; **don't be** ~! (ne) fais pas l'idiot!; he's ~ about her il est fou d'elle.
◇ *adv*: **don't talk** ~ ne dites pas de bêtises.

dagger ['dægəʳ] *n* -**1.** [weapon] poignard *m*; [smaller] dague *f*; to be at ~s drawn with sb être à couteaux tirés avec qqn; to look OR to shoot *Am* ~s at sb foudroyer qqn du regard. -**2.** TYPO croix *f*.

dago▼ ['deɪgəʊ] (*pl* dagos OR dagoes) *n terme injurieux désignant une personne d'origine espagnole, italienne ou portugaise.*

daguerreotype [də'gerətaɪp] *n* daguerréotype *m*.

dahlia ['deɪljə] *n* dahlia *m*.

Dail [daɪl] *n chambre des députés de la république d'Irlande.*

daily ['deɪlɪ] (*pl* dailies) ◇ *adj* -**1.** [routine, task] quotidien, de tous les jours; [output, wage] journalier; a ~ **paper** un quotidien; to be paid on a ~ basis être payé à la journée; (to earn) one's ~ bread (gagner) son pain quotidien; the ~ round la tournée quotidienne; the ~ routine OR grind *inf* le train-train quotidien ❑ ~ dozen *inf Br* gym *f* quotidienne; she has a ~ help *inf Br* elle a une femme de ménage. -**2.** PRESS: the Daily Express *quotidien britannique populaire conservateur*; the Daily Mail *quotidien britannique populaire du centre droit*; the Daily Mirror *quotidien britannique populaire du centre gauche*; the Daily Sport *quotidien britannique à sensation de droite*; the Daily Star *quotidien britannique à sensation de droite*; the Daily Telegraph *quotidien britannique de qualité, de tendance conservatrice.*
◇ *adv* tous les jours, quotidiennement; twice ~ deux fois par jour.
◇ *n* -**1.** [newspaper] quotidien *m*. -**2.** *inf Br* [cleaner] femme *f* de ménage.

daimon ['diːmən] = **daemon**.

daintily ['deɪntɪlɪ] *adv* -**1.** [eat, hold] délicatement; [walk] avec grâce. -**2.** [dress] coquettement.

daintiness ['deɪntɪnɪs] *n* -**1.** [of manner] délicatesse *f*, raffinement *m*. -**2.** [of dress] coquetterie *f*.

dainty ['deɪntɪ] (*compar* daintier, *superl* daintiest, *pl* dainties) ◇ *adj* -**1.** [small] menu, petit; [delicate] délicat; to walk with ~ steps marcher à petits pas délicats. -**2.** [food] de choix, délicat; ~ **morsels** mets *mpl* de choix. -**3.** [fussy]: she's a ~ eater elle est difficile pour OR sur la nourriture.
◇ *n* [food] mets *m* délicat; [sweet] friandise *f*.

daiquiri ['daɪkɪrɪ] *n* daiquiri *m*.

dairy ['deərɪ] (*pl* dairies) ◇ *n* AGR [building on farm] laiterie *f*; [shop] crémerie *f*, laiterie *f*.
◇ *comp* [cow, farm, products] laitier; [butter, cream] fermier; ~ **cattle** vaches *fpl* laitières; ~ **farmer** producteur *m* de lait OR laitier; ~ **farming** industrie *f* laitière.

dairying ['deərɪɪŋ] *n* industrie *f* laitière.

dairymaid ['deərɪmeɪd] *n* fille *f* de laiterie.

dairyman ['deərɪmən] (*pl* dairymen [-mən]) *n* [on farm] employé *m* de laiterie; [in shop] crémier *m*, laitier *m*.

dais ['deɪɪs] *n* estrade *f*.

daisied ['deɪzɪd] *adj lit* émaillé de pâquerettes.

daisy ['deɪzɪ] (*pl* daisies) *n* marguerite *f*; [smaller] pâquerette *f*.

daisy chain *n* guirlande *f* de pâquerettes.

daisy wheel *n* marguerite *f*; ~ **printer** imprimante *f* à marguerite.

Dakar ['dækɑː] *pr n* Dakar.

Dakota [də'kəʊtə] *pr n* Dakota *m*; in ~ dans le Dakota.

dal [dɑːl] *n* légume *m* sec.

Dalai Lama [ˌdælaɪ'lɑːmə] *pr n* dalaï-lama *m*.

dale [deɪl] *n* vallée *f*, vallon *m*.

Dalek ['dɑːlek] *n créature de science-fiction au comportement agressif et impitoyable.*

Dallas ['dæləs] *pr n* Dallas; the ~ shooting *l'assassinat de J.F. Kennedy.*

dalliance ['dælɪəns] *n* -**1.** [dawdling] perte *f* de temps. -**2.** *arch* [flirtation] badinage *m* amoureux.

dally ['dælɪ] (*pt* & *pp* dallied) *vi* -**1.** [dawdle] lanterner; to ~ over sthg lanterner sur OR dans qqch. -**2.** [toy] badiner; to ~ with an idea caresser une idée; he dallied with her affections il a joué avec ses sentiments. -**3.** *arch* [flirt] flirter.

Dalmatia [dæl'meɪʃə] *pr n* Dalmatie *f*; in ~ en Dalmatie.

Dalmatian [dæl'meɪʃn] ◇ *n* -**1.** [dog] dalmatien *m*, -enne *f*. -**2.** [person] habitant *m*, -e *f* de la Dalmatie.
◇ *adj* dalmate.

dalmatic [dæl'mætɪk] *n* dalmatique *f*.

dalton ['dɔːltən] *n* dalton *m*.

daltonism ['dɔːltəˌnɪzm] *n* daltonisme *m*.

dam [dæm] (*pt* & *pp* **dammed**, *cont* **damming**) ◇ *n* -**1.** [barrier - on river, lake] barrage *m* (de retenue). -**2.** [reservoir] réservoir *m*. -**3.** [animal] mère *f*.
◇ *vt* construire un barrage sur; plans to ~ the Seine projet de construction d'un barrage pour contenir les eaux de la Seine.
◆ **dam up** *vt sep* -**1.** *literal* construire un barrage sur. -**2.** *fig* [feelings] refouler, ravaler; [words] endiguer.

damage ['dæmɪdʒ] ◇ *n* -**1.** *(U)* [harm] dommage *m*, dommages *mpl*; [visible effects] dégâts *mpl*, dommages *mpl*; [to ship, shipment] avarie *f*, avaries *fpl*; ~ to property dégâts *mpl* matériels; the storm did a lot of ~ l'orage a causé des dégâts importants; he said he would make good the ~ il a dit qu'il allait réparer les dégâts; ~ limitation effort *m* pour limiter les dégâts. -**2.** *fig* tort *m*, préjudice *m*; the scandal has done the government serious ~ le scandale a fait énormément de tort OR a énormément porté préjudice au gouvernement; the ~ is done le mal est fait; what's the ~? *inf hum* c'est combien la soustraction?
◇ *vt* [harm - crop, object] endommager, causer des dégâts à; [- food] abîmer, gâter; [- eyes, health] abîmer; [- ship, shipment] avarier; [- reputation] porter atteinte à, nuire à; [- cause] faire du tort à, porter préjudice à.
◆ **damages** *npl* JUR dommages *mpl* et intérêts *mpl*; to award ~s to sb for sthg accorder des dommages et intérêts à qqn pour qqch; liable for ~s civilement responsable; war ~s dommages *mpl* OR indemnités *fpl* de guerre.

damaging ['dæmɪdʒɪŋ] *adj* dommageable, nuisible; JUR préjudiciable; psychologically ~ dommageable sur le plan psychologique.

Damascus [də'mæskəs] *pr n* Damas.

damask ['dæməsk] ◇ *n* -**1.** [silk] damas *m*, soie *f* damassée; [linen] damassé *m*. -**2.** [steel] (acier *m*) damasquiné *m*. -**3.** [colour] vieux rose *m*.
◇ *adj* [cloth] damassé.

damask rose *n* rose *f* de Damas.

Dam Busters ['dæmbʌstəz] *npl aviateurs de la RAF ayant bombardé des barrages dans la région de la Ruhr en 1943*.

dame [deɪm] *n* -**1.** *arch* OR *lit* [noble] dame *f*; Dame Fortune Dame Fortune; (pantomime) ~ *Br* THEAT *rôle travesti outré et ridicule dans la pantomime anglaise*. -**2.** *Br* [title]: Dame *titre donné à une femme ayant reçu certaines distinctions honorifiques*. -**3.** ▽ *Am dated* pépée *f*.

dame school *n* HIST *école dirigée par une vieille dame, souvent dans sa propre maison*.

dammit *inf* ['dæmɪt] *interj* mince; as near as ~ *Br* à un cheveu près.

damn [dæm] ◇ *interj inf*: ~! mince!
◇ *n inf*: I don't give a ~ about the money je me fiche pas mal de l'argent; it's not worth a ~ ça ne vaut pas un pet de lapin OR un clou.
◇ *vt* -**1.** RELIG damner. -**2.** [condemn] condamner; they ~ed him with faint praise ils l'ont éreinté sous couleur d'éloge. -**3.** *inf phr*: ~ you! va te faire voir!; he found out, ~ him! il a trouvé, le salaud!; well I'll be ~ed! ça, c'est le comble!; I'll be ~ed if I'll apologize! m'excuser? plutôt mourir!
◇ *adj inf* fichu, sacré; you ~ fool! espèce d'idiot!; he's a ~ nuisance il est vraiment casse-pied; it's a ~ nuisance! ce que c'est casse-pied!, quelle barbe!; it's one ~ thing after another quand ce n'est pas une chose c'est l'autre.
◇ *adv inf* -**1.** [as intensifier] très; he knows ~ well what I mean il sait exactement OR très bien ce que je veux dire. -**2.** *Br phr*: ~ all que dalle; she did ~ all elle n'a rien fichu; he knows ~ all about it il n'en sait fichtre rien.

damnable ['dæmnəbl] *adj* -**1.** RELIG damnable. -**2.** *inf dated* [awful] exécrable, odieux.

damnably *inf* ['dæmnəblɪ] *adv dated* rudement.

damnation [dæm'neɪʃn] ◇ *n* damnation *f*.
◇ *interj inf*: ~! enfer et damnation! *hum*.

damned [dæmd] ◇ *adj* -**1.** RELIG damné, maudit. -**2.** *inf* = **damn**.
◇ *adv inf* rudement, vachement; do what you ~ well like! fais ce que tu veux, je m'en fiche.
◇ *npl* RELIG OR *lit*: the ~ les damnés *mpl*.

damnedest *inf* ['dæmdəst] ◇ *n* [utmost]: to do one's ~: he did his ~ to ruin the party il a vraiment fait tout ce qu'il pouvait pour gâcher la soirée.
◇ *adj Am* incroyable; it was the ~ thing! il fallait voir ça!

damn-fool *inf adj* crétin, idiot.

damning ['dæmɪŋ] *adj* [evidence, statement] accablant.

Damocles ['dæməˌkliːz] *pr n* Damoclès; the sword of ~ l'épée *f* de Damoclès.

damp [dæmp] ◇ *adj* [air, clothes, heat] humide; [skin] moite.
◇ *n* -**1.** [moisture] humidité *f*. -**2.** MIN [air] mofette *f*; [gas] grisou *m*.
◇ *vt* -**1.** [wet] humecter. -**2.** [stifle - sounds] amortir, étouffer; MUS étouffer; *fig* [spirits] décourager, refroidir. -**3.** [fire] couvrir. -**4.** TECH amortir.
◆ **damp down** *vt sep* [fire] couvrir; *fig* [enthusiasm] refroidir; [crisis] atténuer, rendre moins violent.

damp course *n* couche *f* isolante.

dampen ['dæmpən] *vt* -**1.** [wet] humecter. -**2.** [ardour, courage] refroidir; don't ~ their spirits ne les découragez pas.

dampener ['dæmpənəʳ], **damper** ['dæmpəʳ] *n* -**1.** [in furnace] registre *m*. -**2.** *fig* douche *f* froide; the news put a ~ on the party/his enthusiasm la nouvelle a jeté un froid sur la fête/a refroidi son enthousiasme. -**3.** AUT, ELEC & TECH amortisseur *m*; MUS étouffoir *m*. -**4.** [for linen, stamps] mouilleur *m*.

damping ['dæmpɪŋ] *n* -**1.** [wetting] mouillage *m*. -**2.** AUT, ELEC & TECH amortissement *m*.

dampish ['dæmpɪʃ] *adj* un peu humide.

dampness ['dæmpnɪs] *n* humidité *f*; [of skin] moiteur *f*.

damp-proof *adj* protégé contre l'humidité, hydrofuge; ~ course CONSTR couche *f* d'étanchéité.

damp squib *inf n Br* déception *f*.

damsel ['dæmzl] *n arch* OR *lit* damoiselle *f*; a ~ in distress *hum* une demoiselle en détresse.

damselfish ['dæmzlfɪʃ] *n* poisson-ange *m*.

damselfly ['dæmzlflaɪ] (*pl* **damselflies**) *n* demoiselle *f*, libellule *f*.

damson ['dæmzn] ◇ *n* [tree] prunier *m* de Damas; [fruit] prune *f* de Damas.
◇ *comp* [jam, jelly, wine] de prunes (de Damas).

dan [dæn] *n* [in judo] dan *m*.

dance [dɑːns] ◇ *n* -**1.** danse *f*; may I have the next ~? voulez-vous m'accorder la prochaine danse?; shall we have one more ~? dansons-nous encore une fois?; to do a ~ [in exultation] sauter de joie ❑ ~ of death danse macabre; to lead sb a (merry OR pretty) ~ [exasperate] donner du fil à retordre à qqn; [deceive] faire marcher qqn; [in romantic context] mener qqn en bateau; 'Dance of Death' *Strindberg* 'la Danse de mort'. -**2.** [piece of music] morceau *m* (de musique). -**3.** [art] danse *f*; the world of ~ le milieu de la danse. -**4.** [social occasion] soirée *f* dansante; [larger] bal *m*; to hold a ~ donner une soirée dansante OR un bal.
◇ *comp* [class, school, step, studio] de danse; ~ band orchestre *m* de bal; ~ card carnet *m* de bal; ~ floor piste *f* de danse; ~ hall salle *f* de bal; ~ music musique *f* dansante.
◇ *vi* [person] danser; *fig* [leaves, light, words] danser; [eyes] scintiller; do you want to ~? tu veux danser?; to ~ with sb danser avec qqn; to ask sb to ~ inviter qqn à danser; it's not the type of music you can ~ to ce n'est pas le genre de musique sur lequel on peut danser; to ~ for joy sauter de joie; she ~d along the street elle descendit la rue d'un pas joyeux ❑ to ~ to sb's tune obéir à qqn au doigt et à l'œil.
◇ *vt* [waltz, polka] danser; to ~ a step faire OR exécuter un pas de danse; we ~d every ~ nous n'avons pas arrêté de danser; they ~d every ~ together ils n'ont pas arrêté de danser ensemble; to ~ a baby on one's knee faire sauter un bébé sur ses genoux; to ~ attendance on sb *Br* s'empresser auprès de qqn.

dancer ['dɑːnsəʳ] *n* danseur *m*, -euse *f*.

dancing ['dɑːnsɪŋ] ◇ *n* danse *f*; to go ~ aller danser; a book on ~ un livre sur la danse.
◇ *comp* [class, teacher] de danse; ~ dervish derviche *m* tourneur; ~ partner cavalier *m*, -ère *f*.
◇ *adj* [eyes] scintillant.

dancing girl *n* danseuse *f*.

dancing shoe *n* [for dance] chaussure *f* de bal; [for ballet] chausson *m* de danse.

D and C (*abbr of* **dilation and curettage**) *n* MED (dilation *f* et) curetage *m*.

dandelion ['dændɪlaɪən] *n* pissenlit *m*, dent-de-lion *f*.

dandelion clock *n* aigrettes *fpl* de pissenlits; to play ~s *Br* [children's game] *souffler sur les aigrettes de pissenlits pour savoir l'heure*.

dander *inf* ['dændəʳ] *n*: to get one's/sb's ~ up se mettre/mettre qqn en rogne.

dandified ['dændɪfaɪd] *adj* [person] à l'allure de dandy; [appearance] de dandy.

dandle ['dændl] *vt Br* [small child - on knee] faire sauter; [- in arms] bercer.

dandruff ['dændrʌf] *n (U)* pellicules *fpl*; to have ~ avoir des pellicules; ~ shampoo shampooing *m* antipelliculaire.

dandy ['dændɪ] (*pl* **dandies**) ◇ *n* dandy *m*.
◇ *adj Am* extra, épatant; everything's fine and ~ tout va très bien; that's just ~! *iron* c'est vraiment génial!

Dane [deɪn] *n* Danois *m*, -e *f*.

dang▽ *Am* [dæŋ] = **damn** *interj* & *adv*.

danger ['deɪndʒəʳ] ◇ *n* danger *m*; is there any ~ of fire/explosion y a-t-il un danger OR risque d'incendie/d'explosion?; the ~s of smoking/making rash judgements les dangers du tabac/des jugements hâtifs; '~, keep out!' 'danger, entrée interdite!'; fraught with ~ extrêmement dangereux; to be out of/in ~ être hors de/en danger; to put sb/sthg in ~ mettre qqn/qqch en danger; he was in no ~ il n'était pas en danger, il ne courait aucun danger; she was in little ~ elle ne courait pas un grand danger; her life is in ~ sa vie est en danger, elle est en danger de mort; to be in ~ of doing sthg courir le risque OR risquer de faire qqch; to be a ~ to sb/sthg être un danger pour qqn/qqch; it's a ~ to my health c'est dangereux pour ma santé; there is some ~ of that il y a un certain risque que cela se produise; there is no ~ of that happening il n'y a pas de danger OR de risque que cela se produise; that's the ~ in this case voilà le danger OR le risque qui menace ici; no ~ *inf* pas de danger; there's no ~ of him doing that! il n'y a pas de danger OR de risque qu'il le fasse!; there's no ~ of that! il n'y a pas de danger!
◇ *comp*: ~ area OR zone zone *f* dangereuse; to be on the ~ list MED être dans un état critique; to be off the ~ list être hors de danger; ~ money prime *f* de risque; ~ point cote *f* d'alerte; ~ signal RAIL signal *m* d'arrêt; *fig* signal *m* d'alerte OR d'alarme.

dangerous ['deɪndʒərəs] *adj* [job, sport, criminal, animal] dangereux; MED [illness] dangereux, grave; [operation] délicat, périlleux; [assumption] risqué; to be on ~ ground *fig* être sur un terrain glissant ❑ ~ driving conduite *f* dangereuse.

dangerously ['deɪndʒərəslɪ] *adv* dangereusement; [ill] gravement; to live ~ vivre dangereusement; the car was ~ near the edge of the cliff la voiture était dangereusement près du bord de la falaise; you're coming ~ close to being fired/spanked continue comme ça et tu es viré/tu as une fessée; this firm is ~ close to collapse/bankruptcy cette entreprise est au bord de l'effondrement/la faillite.

dangle ['dæŋgl] ◇ *vt* [legs, arms, hands] laisser pendre; [object on chain, string] balancer; to ~ sthg in front of sb balancer qqch devant qqn; *fig* faire miroiter qqch aux yeux de qqn; they ~d promotion in front of her ils lui ont fait miroiter un avancement.
◇ *vi* [legs, arms, hands] pendre; [keys, earrings] se balancer; with his legs/arms dangling les jambes/bras pendant dans le vide; the climber was dangling at the end of the rope l'alpiniste se balançait OR était suspendu au bout de la corde; to keep sb dangling *fig* laisser qqn dans le vague.

dangling participle *n en anglais, participe qui, de par sa position dans la phrase, vient qualifier un élément autre que celui auquel il se rapporte: 'having prepared the meal, an idea came into Mary's mind'.*

Daniel ['dænjəl] *pr n* Daniel.

Danish ['deɪnɪʃ] ◇ *n* -**1.** LING danois *m*. -**2.** [pastry] = **danish pastry**.
◇ *adj* [person, Parliament, food, countryside] danois; [king] du Danemark; [ambassador, embassy, representative] danois, du Danemark; [dictionary, teacher] de danois; the ~ people les Danois *mpl*.

Danish blue *n* [cheese] bleu *m* du Danemark.

Danish pastry *n* CULIN *sorte de pâtisserie fourrée.*

dank [dæŋk] *adj* humide et froid.

Dante ['dæntɪ] *pr n* Dante.

Dantean ['dæntɪən], **Dantesque** [dæn'tesk] *adj* dantesque.

Danube ['dænju:b] *pr n*: the ~ le Danube; 'The Blue ~' *Strauss* 'le Beau Danube bleu'.

daphne ['dæfnɪ] *n* BOT daphné *m*.

Daphne ['dæfnɪ] *pr n* MYTH Daphné.

dapper ['dæpəʳ] *adj* propre sur soi, soigné.

dapple ['dæpl] *vt* tacheter; sunlight ~d the wall/water le soleil faisait des taches sur le mur/l'eau.

dappled ['dæpld] *adj* [animal] tacheté; ~ shade ombre *f* mouchetée de lumière.

dapple-grey ◇ *adj* gris pommelé.
◇ *n* [colour] gris *m* pommelé; [horse] cheval *m*, jument *f* gris pommelé.

Darby and Joan [,dɑ:bɪən'dʒəʊn] *n* Roméo et Juliette du troisième âge; ~ club club *m* du troisième âge *(en Grande-Bretagne)*.

Dardanelles [,dɑ:də'nelz] *pl pr n*: the ~ les Dardanelles *fpl*.

dare [deəʳ] ◇ *modal vb* [venture] oser; to ~ (to) do sthg oser faire qqch; I daren't think OR don't ~ (to) think about it je n'ose (pas) y penser; nobody would ~ (to) contradict her personne n'oserait la contredire; she didn't ~ (to) OR ~d not say a word elle n'a pas osé dire un mot; I lay there hardly daring to breathe j'étais couché là, osant à peine respirer; let them try it if they ~! qu'ils essaient s'ils osent!; ~ I interrupt? puis-je me permettre de vous interrompre?; don't you ~ tell me what to do! ne t'avise surtout pas de me dire ce que j'ai à faire!; don't you ~! je te le déconseille!; how ~ you speak to me in that tone of voice! comment oses-tu me parler sur ce ton! ❑ ~ I say it si j'ose m'exprimer ainsi; I ~ say you're hungry after your journey je suppose que vous êtes affamés après ce voyage; I ~ say she's right elle a probablement raison; he was most apologetic – I ~ say! il s'est confondu en excuses – j'imagine!
◇ *vt* -**1.** [challenge] défier; to ~ sb to do sthg défier qqn de faire qqch; I ~ you! chiche! -**2.** *lit* [death, dishonour] braver, défier; [displeasure] braver.
◇ *n* [challenge] défi *m*; to do sthg for a ~ faire qqch par défi.

daredevil ['deə,devl] ◇ *n* casse-cou *m inv*.
◇ *adj* casse-cou.

daresay [,deə'seɪ] *vi Br*: I ~ [probably, I suppose] j'imagine, je suppose; she's telling the truth – I ~ (she is) elle dit la vérité – je veux bien le croire.

Dar es-Salaam [,dɑ:ressə'lɑ:m] *pr n* Dar es-Salaam.

daring ['deərɪŋ] ◇ *n* [of person] audace *f*, hardiesse *f*; [of feat] hardiesse *f*; of great ~ très audacieux.
◇ *adj* [audacious] audacieux, hardi; [provocative] audacieux, provocant.

daringly ['deərɪŋlɪ] *adv* audacieusement, hardiment; a ~ low neckline un décolleté audacieux OR provocant; to be ~ different afficher sa différence avec audace.

dark [dɑ:k] ◇ *n* noir *m*; to see in the ~ voir dans le noir; before/after ~ avant/après la tombée de la nuit ❑ in the ~: I can't work in the ~! je ne peux pas travailler sans savoir où je vais!; to keep sb in the ~ about sthg maintenir qqn dans l'ignorance à propos de qqch; to be in the ~ about sthg être dans l'ignorance à propos de qqch; she left us in the ~ elle nous a laissés dans l'ignorance.
◇ *adj* -**1.** [without light – night, room, street] sombre; *fig* [thoughts] sombre; [ideas] noir; it's very ~ in here il fait très sombre ici; it's too ~ to see what I'm doing il fait OR c'est trop sombre pour que je voie ce que je suis en train de faire; it's getting ~ il commence à faire nuit, la nuit tombe; it's getting ~er il fait de plus en plus nuit; it gets ~ early il fait nuit de bonne heure; to get ~ [sky] s'assombrir; it won't be ~ for another hour yet il ne fera pas nuit avant une heure; it's still ~ (outside) il fait encore nuit; the ~ days of the war la sombre période de la guerre; to look on the ~ side voir tout en noir ❑ ~ satanic mills *citation d'un hymne religieux utilisée pour évoquer le paysage industriel du nord de l'Angleterre.* -**2.** [colour] foncé; [dress, suit] sombre; she always wears ~ colours elle porte toujours des couleurs sombres; ~ chocolate chocolat *m* noir. -**3.** [hair, eyes] foncé; [skin, complexion] foncé, brun; a ~ man un brun; a ~ woman une brune; to be ~ être brun; to have ~ hair avoir les cheveux bruns, être brun; to get ~er [hair] foncer; his ~ good looks sa beauté de brun. -**4.** [hidden, mysterious] mystérieux, secret; [secret] bien gardé; [hint] mystérieux, énigmatique; the ~ side of the moon la face cachée de la lune; to keep sthg ~ tenir qqch secret; keep it ~! garde-le pour toi!; you kept it very ~! tu nous avais caché ça! -**5.** [sinister] noir; to give sb a ~ look lancer un regard noir à qqn; there's a ~ side to her elle a un côté désagréable; a ~ chapter in the country's history un chapitre peu glorieux de l'histoire du pays.

Dark Ages *npl* HIST Haut Moyen Âge *m*; he's still in the ~ *fig* il est resté au Moyen Âge.

Dark Continent *n dated* Afrique *f*.

darken ['dɑ:kn] ◇ *vt* [sky] assombrir; [colour] foncer; to ~ a room [make look darker] assombrir OR obscurcir une pièce; [plunge into darkness] faire l'obscurité dans une pièce; a ~ed building un immeuble sans lumières; a ~ed room une pièce sombre ❑ never ~ my door again! ne viens plus jamais frapper à ma porte!
◇ *vi* [sky, room] s'assombrir, s'obscurcir; [hair, wood] foncer; [face] s'assombrir; [painting] s'obscurcir.

dark-eyed *adj* aux yeux sombres OR foncés.

dark glasses *npl* lunettes *fpl* noires.

dark horse *n* -**1.** [secretive person]: to be a ~ être très secret; you're a ~! tu nous en caches des choses! -**2.** [competitor, horse] participant *m* inconnu; *Am* POL candidat *m* surprise.

darkish ['dɑ:kɪʃ] *adj* [colour, sky, wood] plutôt OR assez sombre; [hair, skin] plutôt brun OR foncé; [person] plutôt brun.

darkly ['dɑ:klɪ] *adv* [hint] énigmatiquement; [say] sur un ton sinistre.

darkness ['dɑ:knɪs] *n* -**1.** [of night, room, street] obscurité *f*; to be in ~ être plongé dans l'obscurité ❑ 'Darkness at Noon' *Koestler* 'le Zéro et l'infini'. -**2.** [of hair, skin] couleur *f* foncée.

darkroom ['dɑ:krʊm] *n* PHOT chambre *f* noire.

dark-skinned *adj* à la peau foncée.

darky▼ ['dɑ:kɪ] (*pl* darkies) *n terme raciste et vieilli désignant un Noir*, ≃ moricaud *m*, -e *f*.

darling ['dɑ:lɪŋ] ◇ *n* -**1.** [term of affection] chéri *m*, -e *f*; yes ~? oui (mon) chéri?; Jenny ~ Jenny chérie; she's a ~ c'est un amour; you ~! tu es un amour!; he was an absolute ~ about it il a été absolument charmant; be a ~ and… sois gentil OR un amour et… -**2.** [favourite – of teacher, parents] favori *m*, -ite *f*, chouchou *m*, -oute *f*; [– of media] coqueluche *f*.
◇ *adj* [beloved] chéri; [delightful] charmant, adorable; you ~ man! tu es un amour!, tu es adorable!

darn [dɑ:n] ◇ *n* -**1.** SEW reprise *f*; there was a ~ in the elbow of his sweater son pull était reprisé au coude. -**2.** *inf phr*: I couldn't OR I don't give a ~ je m'en fiche.
◇ *vt* -**1.** SEW repriser, raccommoder. -**2.** *inf* [damn]: ~ it! bon sang!; ~ that cat/man! encore ce chat/bonhomme de malheur!; I'll be ~ed! ça alors!, oh, la vache!
◇ *interj inf* bon sang.
◇ *adj inf* de malheur.
◇ *adv inf* vachement; it's ~ late il est vachement tard; it's too ~ late bon sang, il est trop tard; don't be so ~ stupid! ce que tu peux être bête!; that's just too ~ bad tant pis; to have a ~ good try faire un sacré effort.

darned *inf* [dɑ:nd] *Am* = **darn** *adj* & *adv*.

darning ['dɑ:nɪŋ] *adj* [action] reprise *f*, raccommodage *m*; [items to be darned] linge *m* à repriser OR raccommoder.

darning needle *n* aiguille *f* à repriser.

dart [dɑ:t] ◇ *n* -**1.** SPORT fléchette *f*; [weapon] flèche *f*; to play ~s jouer aux fléchettes; ~s champion champion *m*, -onne *f* de fléchettes; ~s match match *m* de fléchettes. -**2.** SEW pince *f*. -**3.** [sudden movement]: to make a ~ for the door/telephone se précipiter vers la porte/sur le téléphone; to make a ~ at sb/sthg se précipiter sur qqn/qqch.
◇ *vt* [glance, look – quickly] lancer, jeter; [– angrily] darder; [rays] lancer; [stronger] darder.
◇ *vi*: to ~ away OR off partir en OR comme une flèche; to ~ for the door/telephone se précipiter vers la porte/sur le téléphone; to ~ at sthg/sb se précipiter sur qqch/qqn; to ~ in/out entrer/sortir comme une flèche.

dartboard ['dɑ:tbɔ:d] *n* cible *f* (de jeu de fléchettes).

Darwinian [dɑ:'wɪnɪən] *adj* [of Darwin – theory] darwinien; [in favour of Darwinism – thinker] darwiniste.

Darwinism ['dɑ:wɪnɪzm] *n* darwinisme *m*.

Darwinist ['dɑ:wɪnɪst] *n* darwiniste *mf*.

dash [dæʃ] ◇ *n* -**1.** [quick movement] mouvement *m* précipité; to make a ~ for freedom s'enfuir vers la liberté; to make a ~ for it [rush] se précipiter; [escape] s'enfuir, s'échapper; it was a headlong ~ to the station ça n'a été qu'une course effrénée jusqu'à la gare. -**2.** *Am* SPORT sprint *m*. -**3.** [small amount – of water, soda] goutte *f*, trait *m*; [– of cream, milk] nuage *m*; [– of lemon juice, vinegar] filet *m*; [– of salt, pepper] soupçon *m*; [– of colour, humour] pointe *f*. -**4.** [punctuation mark] tiret *m*; [in Morse code] trait *m*. -**5.** [style] panache *m*; to cut a ~ faire de l'effet. -**6.** = **dashboard**.
◇ *vt* -**1.** [throw] jeter (avec violence); to ~ sthg to the ground jeter qqch par terre avec violence; several boats were ~ed against the cliffs plusieurs bateaux ont été projetés OR précipités contre les falaises; to ~ sb's hopes *fig* réduire les espoirs de qqn à néant; to ~ sb's spirits *fig* démoraliser OR abattre qqn. -**2.** [damn]: ~ it! bon sang!; I'll be ~ed! ça alors!, oh, la vache!
◇ *vi* -**1.** [rush] se précipiter; I must ~ *esp Br* je dois filer; he ~ed back to his room il est retourné à sa chambre en vitesse, il s'est dépêché de retourner à sa chambre; I'll just ~ out to the shops *Br* je vais faire quelques courses en vitesse; I'll just ~ out to the post-office/library *Br* je vais juste faire un saut à la poste/bibliothèque; ~ upstairs and fetch it, will you? *Br* monte vite le chercher, s'il te plaît;

the dog ~ed across the road in front of us le chien a traversé la route à toute vitesse devant nous. -**2.** [waves] se jeter.
◇ *interj Br*: ~! bon sang!
◆ **dash off** ◇ *vi insep* partir en flèche.
◇ *vt sep* [letter, memo] écrire en vitesse; [drawing] faire en vitesse.
dashboard ['dæʃbɔːd] *n* AUT tableau *m* de bord.
dashed [dæʃt] *Br dated* ◇ *adj* de malheur.
◇ *adv* vachement.
dashing ['dæʃɪŋ] *adj* pimpant, fringant.
dashingly ['dæʃɪŋlɪ] *adv* [behave] avec allant; [be dressed] dans un style fringuant.
dastardly ['dæstədlɪ] *adj lit* [act, person] odieux, infâme.
DAT [dæt] (*abbr of* digital audio tape) *n* DAT *m*.
data ['deɪtə] (*pl of datum usu with sing vb*) ◇ *n* informations *fpl*, données *fpl*; COMPUT données *fpl*; a piece of ~ une information, une donnée; COMPUT une donnée.
◇ *comp* COMPUT [retrieval, security, input] de données.
data bank *n* COMPUT banque *f* de données.
database ['deɪtəbeɪs] ◇ *n* COMPUT base *f* de données; ~ management gestion *f* de base de données.
◇ *vt* mettre sous forme de base de données.
data capture *n* COMPUT saisie *f* de données.
data carrier *n* support *m* de données.
Datapost® ['deɪtəpəʊst] *n service postal britannique pour paquets urgents*.
data processing ◇ *n* traitement *m* de l'information.
◇ *comp* [department, service] de traitement des données OR de l'information, informatique.
data processor *n* [machine] ordinateur *m*; [person] informaticien *m*, -enne *f*.
data protection *n* protection *f* de l'information.
Data Protection Act *n* loi *f* sur la protection de l'information (*en Grande-Bretagne*).
data switch *n* commutateur *m* de données.
data transmission *n* transmission *f* de données.
date [deɪt] ◇ *n* -**1.** [of letter, day of the week] date *f*; what's the ~ today?, what's today's ~? quelle est la date aujourd'hui?, le combien sommes-nous aujourd'hui?; today's ~ is the 20th January nous sommes le 20 janvier; what's the ~ of the coin/building? de quelle année est cette pièce/ce bâtiment?; would you be free on that ~? est-ce que vous seriez libre ce jour-là OR à cette date?; at a later OR some future ~ plus tard; *fml* ultérieurement; of an earlier/a later ~ plus ancien/récent; to set a ~ fixer une date; [engaged couple] fixer la date de son mariage; to put a ~ to sthg [remember when it happened] se souvenir de la date de qqch; [estimate when built, established etc] attribuer une date à qqch, dater qqch ❑ ~ of birth date de naissance. -**2.** [meeting] rendez-vous *m*; let's make a ~ for lunch prenons rendez-vous pour déjeuner ensemble; to have a ~ avoir rendez-vous; I already have a ~ on Saturday night j'ai déjà un rendez-vous samedi soir; to go out on a ~ sortir en compagnie de quelqu'un; her parents don't let her go out on ~s ses parents ne la laissent pas sortir avec des garçons; I went out on a ~ with him once je suis sortie avec lui une fois; on our first ~ la première fois que nous sommes sortis ensemble. -**3.** [person] ami *m*, -e *f*; who's your ~ tonight? avec qui sors-tu ce soir?; do you have a ~ for the dance? as-tu un cavalier pour le bal?; can I bring a ~? puis-je amener un ami? -**4.** [fruit] datte *f*.
◇ *vt* -**1.** [write date on - cheque, letter, memo] dater; a fax ~d May 6th un fax daté du 6 mai. -**2.** [attribute date to - building, settlement etc] dater; to ~ sb [show age of] donner une idée de l'âge de qqn; gosh, that ~s him! eh bien, ça montre qu'il n'est plus tout jeune OR ça ne lerajeunit pas! -**3.** *Am* [go out with] sortir avec.
◇ *vi* -**1.** [clothes, style] se démoder; [novel] vieillir. -**2.** *Am* [go out on dates] sortir avec des garçons/filles; how long have you two been dating? ça fait combien de temps que vous sortez ensemble OR que vous vous voyez?
◆ **out of date** *adj phr*: to be out of ~ [dress, style, concept, slang] être démodé OR dépassé; [magazine, newspaper] être vieux; [dictionary] ne pas être à jour OR à la page; [passport, season ticket etc] être périmé; it's the kind of dress that will never go out of ~ c'est le genre de robe indémodable OR qui ne se démodera jamais.
◆ **to date** *adv phr* à ce jour.
◆ **up to date** *adj phr*: to be up to ~ [dress, style, person] être à la mode OR à la page; [newspaper, magazine] être du jour/de la semaine etc; [dictionary] être à la page OR à jour; [passport] être valide OR valable; [list] être à jour; I'm not up to ~ on what's been happening je ne suis pas au courant de ce qui s'est passé dernièrement; to keep up to ~ with the news/scientific developments se tenir au courant de l'actualité/des progrès de la science; to keep sb up to ~ on sthg tenir qqn au courant de qqch; to bring sb up to ~ on sthg mettre qqn au courant de qqch.
◆ **date back to, date from** *vt insep* dater de.

DATE:
En anglais américain, on n'utilise pas l'article dans les dates. On aura donc: December ninth Am ou the ninth Br. D'autre part, les Américains, lorsqu'ils donnent une date en chiffres, la présentent dans l'ordre suivant: mois, jour, année. Les Britanniques, eux, indiquent le jour puis le mois.

---

dated ['deɪtɪd] *adj* [clothes, style] démodé; [novel, term, expression, concept] vieilli.
dateless ['deɪtlɪs] *adj* [timeless] indémodable.
dateline ['deɪt,laɪn] *n* -**1.** PRESS date *f* de rédaction. -**2.** = **international date-line**.
date palm *n* palmier *m* dattier.
date rape *n viol commis par une connaissance, un ami etc*; ~ frequently goes unreported peu de femmes violées par une connaissance OR un ami portent plainte.
datestamp ['deɪtstæmp] ◇ *n* tampon *m* dateur; [used for cancelling] oblitérateur *m*, timbre *m* à date; [postmark] cachet *m* de la poste.
◇ *vt* [book] tamponner, mettre le cachet de la date sur; [letter] oblitérer.
dating ['deɪtɪŋ] *n* [of a building, settlement etc] datation *f*.
dative ['deɪtɪv] ◇ *n* datif *m*; in the ~ au datif.
◇ *adj* datif.
datum ['deɪtəm] (*pl* data) *n fml* donnée *f*.
daub [dɔːb] ◇ *n* -**1.** [of paint] tache *f*, barbouillage *m*; [done on purpose] barbouillage *m*. -**2.** *pej* [painting] croûte *f*. -**3.** [for walls] enduit *m*.
◇ *vt* enduire; [with mud] couvrir; a wall ~ed with slogans un mur couvert de slogans.
◇ *vi pej* [paint badly] peinturlurer, barbouiller.
dauber ['dɔːbəʳ] *n pej* barbouilleur *m*, -euse *f*.
daughter ['dɔːtəʳ] *n* fille *f*; 'Ryan's Daughter' *Lean* 'la Fille de Ryan'.
daughter board *n* COMPUT carte *f* fille.
daughter-in-law *n* bru *f*, belle-fille *f*.
daughterly ['dɔːtəlɪ] *adj* filial.
Daughters of the American Revolution *pr n organisme regroupant des femmes descendant des patriotes de la guerre d'Indépendance aux États-Unis*.
daunt [dɔːnt] *vt* intimider; nothing ~ed *lit* nullement découragé.
daunting ['dɔːntɪŋ] *adj* [task, question] intimidant.
dauntless ['dɔːntlɪs] *adj* déterminé.
dauntlessly ['dɔːntlɪslɪ] *adv* sans se décourager.
dauphin ['dɔːfɪn] *n* HIST dauphin *m*.
dauphine ['dɔːfiːn] *n* HIST dauphine *f*.
davenport ['dævnpɔːt] *n* -**1.** *Br* [desk] secrétaire *m*. -**2.** *Am* [sofa] canapé *m*.
David ['deɪvɪd] *pr n* David; 'David Copperfield' *Dickens* 'David Copperfield'.
davit ['dævɪt] *n* NAUT bossoir *m*, portemanteau *m*.
Davy Jones ['deɪvɪ,dʒəʊnz] *n*: in ~'s locker [person, ship] au fond de la mer.
Davy lamp *n* lampe *f* de sécurité de mineur.
dawdle ['dɔːdl] *vi pej* traîner, lambiner, traînasser; to ~ over breakfast traînasser OR traîner en prenant son petit déjeuner.
◆ **dawdle about** *vi insep* = **dawdle**.
◆ **dawdle away** *vt sep*: to ~ away the entire morning passer toute la matinée à traîner OR traînasser.
dawdler ['dɔːdləʳ] *n* lambin *m*, -e *f*, traînard *m*, -e *f*.
dawdling ['dɔːdlɪŋ] ◇ *n*: stop all this ~! arrête de traînasser!
◇ *adj* traînard.
dawn [dɔːn] ◇ *n* -**1.** *literal* aube *f*; at ~ à l'aube; from ~ till dusk du matin au soir; at the crack of ~ au point du jour; (just) as ~ was breaking alors que l'aube pointait; to watch the ~ regarder le jour se lever. -**2.** *fig* [of civilization, era] aube *f*; [of hope] naissance *f*, éclosion *f*; since the ~ of time depuis la nuit des temps.
◇ *vi* -**1.** [day] se lever. -**2.** *fig* [new era, hope] naître; the truth ~ed on OR upon him la vérité lui apparut; it suddenly ~ed on her that... il lui est soudain apparu que...; that's just ~ed on you, has it? voilà seulement OR c'est seulement maintenant que tu t'en rends compte?
dawn chorus *n* chant *m* des oiseaux à l'aube.
dawning ['dɔːnɪŋ] ◇ *adj* naissant.
◇ *n* = **dawn 2**.
dawn raid *n* descente *f* à l'aube; [by police] descente *f* OR rafle *f* à l'aube; ST. EX attaque *f* à l'ouverture.
day [deɪ] ◇ *n* -**1.** [period of twenty-four hours] jour *m*, journée *f*; it's a nice OR fine ~ c'est une belle journée, il fait beau aujourd'hui; on a clear ~ par temps clair; a summer's/winter's ~ un jour d'été/d'hiver; to have a ~ out aller passer une journée quelque part; a ~ at the seaside/the races une journée au bord de la mer/aux courses; we went to the country for the ~ nous sommes allés passer la journée à la campagne; to have a lazy ~ passer une journée à paresser; when ~ is done *lit* quand le jour s'achève; what ~ is it (today)? quel jour sommes-nous (aujourd'hui)?; what ~ is she arriving (on)? quel jour arrive-t-elle?; (on) that ~ ce jour-là; (on) the ~ (that OR when) she was born le jour où elle est née; on the first/last ~ of the holidays le premier/dernier jour des vacances; on a ~ like this/today un jour comme celui-là/aujourd'hui; the ~ after, (on) the next OR following ~ le lendemain, le jour suivant; the ~ after the party le lendemain de OR le jour d'après la fête; two ~s after the party le surlendemain de OR deux jours après la fête; the ~ after tomorrow après-demain; the ~ before, (on) the previous ~ la veille, le jour d'avant; I had first met him two ~s before je l'avais rencontré l'avant-veille pour la première fois; the ~ before yesterday avant-hier; four ~s before/later quatre jours plus tôt/tard; in four ~s, in four ~s' time dans quatre jours; it took me four ~s to do it ça m'a pris quatre jours pour le faire; once/twice a ~ une fois/deux fois par jour || [in greetings]: good ~! bonjour!; have a nice ~! bonne journée! ❑ Day of Judgment RELIG (jour du) jugement dernier; ~ of reckoning jour de vérité; any ~ now d'un jour à l'autre; ~ after ~, ~ in ~ out jour après jour; for ~s on end OR at a time pendant des jours et des jours; from ~ to ~ de jour en jour; to live from ~ to ~ vivre au jour le jour; from one ~ to the next d'un jour à l'autre; from that ~ on OR onwards à partir de ce jour-là; from that ~ to this depuis ce jour-là; from this ~ forth *lit* à partir OR à compter d'aujourd'hui; to the ~ I die OR my dying ~ jusqu'à mon dernier jour; I'd rather work in Madrid any ~ (of the week) je préférerais largement OR de loin travailler à Madrid; dish of the ~ plat *m* du jour; you've done enough mischief for one ~ tu as fait

assez de bêtises pour une seule journée; **from Day One** depuis le premier jour; **she's seventy if she's a ~** elle a au moins soixante-dix ans; **it's a bit late in the ~ for that** il est un peu tard pour ça; **it's been one of those ~s!** tu parles d'une journée!; **let's make a ~ of it** passons-y la journée; **to make sb's ~: you've made my ~!** rien ne saurait me faire plus plaisir!; **it's not my (lucky) ~** ce n'est pas mon jour (de chance); **that'll be the ~!** *inf* [it's highly unlikely] il n'y a pas de danger que ça arrive de sitôt! **-2.** [hours of daylight] jour *m*, journée *f*; **in the cold light of ~** à la froide lumière du jour; **all ~ (long)** toute la journée; **we haven't got all ~** nous n'avons pas que ça à faire; **to travel during the** OR **by ~** voyager pendant la journée OR de jour; **to sleep during the** OR **by ~** dormir le jour; **~ and night, night and ~** jour et nuit, nuit et jour. **-3.** [working hours] journée *f*; **paid by the ~** payé à la journée; **to work a seven-hour ~** travailler sept heures par jour, faire des journées de sept heures; **how was your ~?, what kind of ~ have you had?** comment s'est passée ta journée?; **did you have a good ~?** tu as passé une bonne journée?; **it's been a hard/long ~** la journée a été dure/longue ❑ **~ off** jour *m* de congé; **~ of rest** jour *m* de repos; **let's call it a ~** [stop work] arrêtons-nous pour aujourd'hui; [end relationship] finissons-en; **it's all in a ~'s work!** ça fait partie du travail! **-4.** *(often pl)* [lifetime, era] époque *f*; **in Caesar's ~** du temps de César; **in the ~s of King Arthur, in King Arthur's ~** du temps du Roi Arthur; **in ~s to come** à l'avenir; **in ~s gone by** par le passé; **in ~s of old** OR **yore** *lit* OR *hum* il y a fort longtemps; **in the good old ~s** dans le temps; **in my/our ~** de mon/notre temps; **he was well-known in his ~** il était connu de son temps OR à son époque; **in his working/married ~s** du temps où il travaillait/était marié; **in his younger ~s** dans son jeune temps, dans sa jeunesse; **the happiest/worst ~s of my life** les plus beaux/les pires jours de ma vie; **during the early ~s of the strike/my childhood** au tout début de la grève/de mon enfance ❑ **her ~ will come** son heure viendra; **he's had his ~** il a eu son heure; **it's had its ~** ça a fait son temps; **to end one's ~s in hospital/poverty** finir ses jours à l'hôpital/dans la pauvreté; **he's/this chair has seen better ~s** il/cette chaise a connu des jours meilleurs; **those were the ~s** c'était le bon temps. **-5.** [battle, game]: **to win** OR **to carry the ~** l'emporter; **to lose the ~** perdre la partie.
◇ *comp*: **~ labourer** journalier *m*, -ère *f*; **~ pass** [for skiing] forfait *m* journalier; **~ work** travail *m* de jour.
◆ **days** *adv*: **to work ~** travailler de jour.
◆ **in this day and age** *adv phr* de nos jours, aujourd'hui.
◆ **in those days** *adv phr* à l'époque.
◆ **one day** *adv phr* un jour.
◆ **one of these days** *adv phr* un de ces jours.
◆ **some day** *adv phr* un jour.
◆ **the other day** *adv phr* l'autre jour.
◆ **these days** *adv phr*: **what are you up to these ~s?** qu'est-ce que tu fais de beau ces temps-ci?; **honestly, teenagers these ~s!** vraiment, les adolescents d'aujourd'hui!
◆ **this day week** *adv phr* dans huit jours aujourd'hui.
◆ **to the day** *adv phr* jour pour jour; **it's a year ago to the ~** il y a un an jour pour jour OR aujourd'hui.
◆ **to this day** *adv phr* jusqu'à aujourd'hui, aujourd'hui encore.

day bed *n* lit *m* de repos.

daybook ['deɪbʊk] *n* main *f* courante, journal *m*.

dayboy ['deɪbɔɪ] *n Br* SCH demi-pensionnaire *m*.

daybreak ['deɪbreɪk] *n* point *m* du jour; **at ~** au point du jour.

day care *n* [for the elderly] service *m* d'accueil de jour; [for children] service *m* de garderie.
◆ **day-care** *adj* [facilities - for elderly] d'accueil de jour; [- for children] de garderie; **~ centre** *centre d'animation et d'aide sociale*; *Am* [for children] crèche *f*.

daydream ['deɪdriːm] ◇ *n* rêverie *f*; *pej* rêvasserie *f*; **to have a ~** rêver, rêvasser; **to be in the middle of a ~** être en pleine rêverie.
◇ *vi* rêver; *pej* rêvasser; **to ~ about sthg** rêver OR rêvasser à qqch; **~ing again?** encore en train de rêvasser OR de rêver tout éveillé?

daydreamer ['deɪdriːmə^r] *n* rêveur *m*, -euse *f*.

daydreaming ['deɪdriːmɪŋ] *n (U)* rêveries *fpl*, rêvasseries *fpl*.

daygirl ['deɪgɜːl] *n Br* SCH demi-pensionnaire *f*.

Day-Glo® ['deɪgləʊ] ◇ *n* tissu *m* fluorescent; **~ cycling shorts** collant *m* de cycliste fluorescent.
◇ *adj* fluorescent.

daylight ['deɪlaɪt] *n* **-1.** [dawn] = **daybreak**. **-2.** [light of day] jour *m*, lumière *f* du jour; **it was still ~** il faisait encore jour; **in ~** de jour; **in broad ~** en plein jour; **to begin to see ~** *fig* [approach end of task] commencer à voir le bout (du tunnel); [begin to understand] commencer à voir clair ❑ **to beat** OR **to thrash** OR **to knock the living ~s out of sb** *inf* tabasser qqn; **to scare** OR **to frighten the living ~s out of sb** *inf* flanquer une trouille bleue à qqn.

daylight robbery *inf n*: **it's ~** c'est du vol pur et simple.

daylight-saving (time) *n* heure *f* d'été.

daylong ['deɪlɒŋ] *adj* [meeting, journey] d'une journée.

day nursery *n* garderie *f*.

day-old *adj* [chick, baby] d'un jour.

day pupil *n* SCH (élève *mf*) externe *mf*.

day release *n Br* formation *f* continue en alternance.

day return *n Br* RAIL aller-retour *m* valable pour la journée.

day school *n* externat *m*.

day shift *n* [period worked] service *m* de jour; [workers] équipe *f* de jour; **to work the ~** travailler de jour, être (dans l'équipe) de jour; **when do you go on ~?** quand est-ce que tu prends le service de jour?

daytime ['deɪtaɪm] ◇ *n* journée *f*; **in the ~** le jour, pendant la journée.
◇ *adj* de jour.

day-to-day *adj* [life, running of business] quotidien; [chores, tasks] journalier, quotidien; **to lead a ~ existence** vivre au jour le jour; [with difficulty] vivre péniblement jour après jour.

day trip *n* excursion *f*.

day tripper *n* excursionniste *mf*.

daze [deɪz] ◇ *n* [caused by blow] étourdissement *m*; [caused by emotional shock, surprise] ahurissement *m*; [caused by medication] abrutissement *m*; **to be in a ~** [because of blow] être étourdi; [because of emotional shock, surprise] être abasourdi OR ahuri; [because of medication] être abruti.
◇ *vt* [subj: blow] étourdir; [subj: emotional shock, surprise] abasourdir, ahurir; [subj: medication] abrutir.

dazed [deɪzd] *adj* [by blow] étourdi; [by emotional shock, surprise] abasourdi, ahuri; [by medication] abruti.

dazzle ['dæzl] *vt literal & fig* éblouir.

dazzling ['dæzlɪŋ] *adj* éblouissant.

dazzlingly ['dæzlɪŋlɪ] *adv*: **a ~ bright day** une journée d'une clarté éblouissante; **he is ~ successful** il réussit brillamment dans la vie; **~ beautiful** d'une beauté éblouissante.

DBE (*abbr of* **Dame Commander of the Order of the British Empire**) *n distinction honorifique britannique pour les femmes*.

DBMS (*abbr of* **database management system**) *n* SGBD *m*.

DBS (*abbr of* **direct broadcasting by satellite**) *n* télédiffusion *f* directe par satellite.

DC *n* **-1.** *abbr of* **direct current**. **-2.** *abbr of* **District of Columbia**.

dd. *written abbr of* **delivered**.

DD (*abbr of* **Doctor of Divinity**) *n (titulaire d'un) doctorat en théologie*.

D/D *written abbr of* **direct debit**.

D-day *n* le jour J.

DDS (*abbr of* **Doctor of Dental Science**) *n (titulaire d'un) doctorat en dentisterie*.

DDT (*abbr of* **dichlorodiphenyltrichloroethane**) *n* DDT *m*.

DE *written abbr of* **Delaware**.

DEA (*abbr of* **Drug Enforcement Administration**) *pr n agence américaine de lutte contre la drogue*.

deacon ['diːkn] *n* RELIG diacre *m*.

deaconess [,diːkə'nes] *n* RELIG diaconesse *f*.

deactivate [diː'æktɪ,veɪt] *vt* désamorcer.

dead [ded] ◇ *adj* **-1.** [not alive - person, animal, plant] mort; [- flower] fané; **~ man** mort *m*; **~ woman** morte *f*; **the ~ woman's husband** le mari de la défunte; **he has been ~ for five years** il est mort OR décédé il y a cinq ans, cela fait cinq ans qu'il est mort; **to be ~ on arrival** être mort OR décédé à l'arrivée à l'hôpital; **~ or alive** mort ou vif; **more ~ than alive** plus mort que vif; **half ~ with hunger/exhaustion/fear** à demi mort de faim/d'épuisement/de peur; **~ and buried** *literal & fig* mort et enterré; **stone ~** raide mort; **to drop (down)** OR **to fall down ~** tomber mort; **to shoot sb ~** tuer qqn (avec une arme à feu), abattre qqn, descendre qqn; **to leave sb for ~** laisser qqn pour mort; **you're ~ if he finds out** *inf fig* c'en est fini de toi s'il l'apprend ❑ **drop ~!** *inf* va te faire voir!; **~ as a doornail** OR **a dodo** on ne peut plus mort; **to step into ~ men's shoes** prendre une place qui vient d'être libérée; **to be waiting for ~ men's shoes** attendre qu'une place se libère; **over my ~ body** je ne permettrai pas cela de mon vivant, moi vivant, c'est hors de question; **you'll marry him over my ~ body** je ne permettrai jamais que tu l'épouses, moi vivant, tu ne l'épouseras pas; **I wouldn't be seen ~ in that restaurant** je ne mettrai jamais les pieds dans ce restaurant; **I wouldn't be seen ~ wearing something like that** jamais de la vie je ne mettrai quelque chose comme ça; **I wouldn't be seen ~ with him** plutôt mourir que de me montrer en sa compagnie; **~ men tell no tales** *prov* les morts ne parlent pas. **-2.** [lacking in sensation - fingers, toes etc] engourdi; **to go ~** s'engourdir; **he is ~ to reason** il ne veut pas entendre raison ❑ **she's ~ from the neck up** *inf* elle n'a rien dans la tête; **to be ~ to the world** *inf* dormir d'un sommeil de plomb. **-3.** [not alight - fire] mort, éteint; [- coals] éteint; [- match] usé. **-4.** [lacking activity - town] mort; [- business, market] très calme. **-5.** [language] mort. **-6.** SPORT [out of play - ball] hors jeu *(inv)*. **-7.** ELEC [battery] mort, à plat; TELEC [phone, line] coupé; **the line went ~** la ligne a été coupée. **-8.** [dull - colour] terne, fade; [- sound] sourd. **-9.** *inf* [tired out] mort, crevé. **-10.** [finished with -cigar] entièrement fumé; **~ copy** TYPO vieille épreuve *f*; **are these (glasses) ~?** *inf* est-ce que vous avez fini avec ces verres? **-11.** *inf* [no longer working - TV, fridge etc] foutu. **-12.** [complete, exact]: **~ stop** arrêt *m* brutal; **to come to a ~ stop** s'arrêter net; **~ calm** NAUT calme *m* plat; **~ silence** silence *m* complet OR de mort; **on a ~ level with sthg** exactement au même niveau que qqch; **in ~ earnest** [be] très sérieux; [speak] très sérieusement; **~ cert** *inf Br* [in race, competition] valeur *f* sûre; **it's a ~ cert that he'll be there** il sera là à coup sûr; **he's the ~ spit of his father** *inf* c'est son père tout craché; **she fell to the floor in a ~ faint** elle tomba à terre, inconsciente; **~ loss** *Br* COMM perte *f* sèche; **to be a ~ loss** *inf Br* [person, thing] être complètement nul.
◇ *adv* **-1.** [precisely]: **~ ahead** tout droit; **~ in the middle** juste au milieu, au beau milieu; **to be ~ level (with sthg)** *Br* être exactement au même niveau (que qqch); **~ on time** *Br* juste à l'heure; **to arrive ~ on the hour** *Br* arriver à l'heure pile OR juste à l'heure; **~ on target** *Br*

[hit sthg] en plein dans le mille; you're ~ right *inf Br* tu as entièrement raison; you're ~ on *inf Br* c'est exactement ça. -**2.** *inf* [very] super; ~ broke complètement fauché; ~ drunk ivre mort; ~ easy super facile, fastoche; ~ good *Br* super bon; it was ~ lucky *Br* c'était un super coup de bol OR de pot; ~ tired mort, crevé. -**3.** [completely]: the sea was ~ calm la mer était parfaitement calme; to be ~ against sthg/sb être absolument contre qqch/qqn. -**4.** ~ slow AUT au pas. -**5.** *phr*: to play ~ faire le mort; to stop ~ s'arrêter net; to stop sb ~ arrêter qqn net.

◇ *npl*: the ~ les morts; to rise from the ~ RELIG ressusciter d'entre les morts.

◇ *n* [depth]: in the ~ of winter au cœur de l'hiver; at ~ of night, in the ~ of night au milieu OR au plus profond de la nuit.

dead-and-alive *adj Br*: it's a ~ sort of place c'est un vrai trou.

dead-ball line *n* RUGBY ligne *f* de ballon mort.

deadbeat *inf* ['dedbiːt] *n* bon à rien *m*, bonne à rien *f*; [tramp] épave *f*, loque *f*.

dead beat *inf adj* crevé, mort.

dead centre *n* TECH point *m* mort.

dead duck *inf n* [plan, proposal - which will fail] désastre *m* assuré, plan *m* foireux; [- which has failed] désastre *m*, fiasco *m*; he's a ~ c'en est fini de lui.

deaden ['dedn] *vt* [sound] assourdir; [sense, nerve, hunger pangs] calmer; [pain] endormir, calmer; [blow] amortir; the ~ing effects of alcohol les effets insensibilisants OR anesthésiants de l'alcool.

dead end *n* cul *m* de sac, voie *f* sans issue, impasse *f*; it's a ~ [job] il n'y a aucune perspective d'avenir; [line of investigation, research] cela ne mènera OR conduira à rien; to come to a ~ [street] se terminer en cul de sac; to come to OR to reach a ~ *fig* aboutir à une impasse.

◆ **dead-end** *adj* [street] sans issue; a dead-end job *fig* un travail qui n'offre aucune perspective d'avenir.

deadening ['dednɪŋ] *adj* [boredom, task] abrutissant.

dead hand *n* -**1.** [influence] mainmise *f*, emprise *f*. -**2.** JUR mainmorte *f*.

deadhead ['dedhed] ◇ *n* -**1.** [dull person] nullité *f*. -**2.** [person using free ticket - in theatre] spectateur *m*, -trice *f* ayant un billet de faveur; [- on train] voyageur *m*, -euse *f* muni(e) d'un billet gratuit. -**3.** *Am* [empty train, plane, lorry etc] *train, avion, camion etc circulant à vide*.

◇ *vt* [flowers] enlever les fleurs fanées de.

◇ *vi Am* [train] circuler à vide.

dead heat *n course dont les vainqueurs sont déclarés ex aequo*; [horse race] dead-heat *m*; it was a ~ [athletics race] les coureurs sont arrivés ex aequo.

dead letter *n* -**1.** [letter that cannot be delivered] lettre *f* non distribuée, (lettre *f* passée au) rebut *m*. -**2.** [law, rule] loi *f* OR règle *f* caduque OR tombée en désuétude; it's a ~ *fig* c'est mort et enterré.

dead-letter box, dead-letter drop *n* cachette *f*.

deadline ['dedlaɪn] *n* [day] date *f* limite; [hour] heure *f* limite; Monday is the absolute ~ c'est pour lundi dernier délai OR dernière limite; to meet/to miss a ~ respecter/laisser passer une date limite; I'm working to a ~ j'ai un délai à respecter; must be able to work to ~s [in job advert] doit être capable de travailler en fonction de délais précis.

deadliness ['dedlɪnɪs] *n* [of poison, snake] caractère *m* mortel; [of weapon] caractère *m* meurtrier.

deadlock ['dedlɒk] ◇ *n* impasse *f*; to reach (a) ~ arriver à une impasse; to break the ~ [negotiators] sortir de l'impasse; [concession] apporter une solution à l'impasse.

◇ *vt* mettre dans une impasse; to be ~ed être dans une impasse.

deadly ['dedlɪ] (*compar* deadlier, *superl* deadliest) ◇ *adj* -**1.** [lethal - poison, blow] mortel; [- snake] au venin mortel; [- weapon] meurtrier; *fig* [hatred] mortel; [silence, pallor] de mort, mortel; they are ~ enemies *fig* ce sont des ennemis mortels ☐ the seven ~ sins les sept péchés capitaux. -**2.** [precise]: his aim is ~ il a un tir excellent; with ~ accuracy avec une extrême précision. -**3.** [extreme]: in ~ earnest [say] avec le plus grand sérieux; I am ~ earnest je suis on ne peut plus sérieux. -**4.** *inf* [boring] mortel, barbant.

◇ *adv* extrêmement, terriblement; ~ pale pâle comme la mort, d'une pâleur de mort OR mortelle; it was ~ boring c'était mortellement ennuyeux.

deadly nightshade *n* BOT belladone *f*.

deadman ['dedmæn] (*pl* deadmen [-men]) *n* CIV ENG ancrage *m*; [in mountaineering] piton *m* à neige.

dead man's handle *n* RAIL manette *f* d'homme-mort.

dead march *n* marche *f* funèbre.

deadness ['dednɪs] *n* -**1.** [of limbs] engourdissement *m*. -**2.** [of sound] caractère *m* sourd. -**3.** [of colour] caractère *m* terne. -**4.** [of place] caractère *m* ennuyeux OR mortel.

dead-nettle *n* ortie *f* blanche.

deadpan ['dedpæn] ◇ *adj* [face, expression] impassible; [humour] pince-sans-rire *(inv)*.

◇ *adv* d'un air impassible.

dead reckoning *n* NAUT estime *f*; to navigate by ~ naviguer à l'estime.

dead ringer *inf n* sosie *m*; to be a ~ for sb être le sosie de qqn.

Dead Sea *pr n*: the ~ la mer Morte.

dead set ◇ *adj*: to be ~ on doing sthg être fermement décidé à faire qqch; to be ~ on sthg tenir absolument OR à tout prix à qqch; to be ~ against sthg/sb être résolument opposé à qqch/qqn.

◇ *n*: to make a ~ at sb *Br dated* [romantically] jeter son dévolu sur qqn.

dead stock *n* AGR machines *fpl* agricoles.

dead weight *n literal* & *fig* poids *m* mort.

dead wood *Br*, **deadwood** *Am* ['dedwʊd] *n* [dead trees, branches] bois *m* mort; *fig* [useless people] personnel *m* inutile.

deaf [def] ◇ *adj* sourd; ~ in one ear sourd d'une oreille; ~ people les sourds *mpl*; are you ~? tu es sourd?; to turn a ~ ear to sthg/sb *fig* faire la sourde oreille à qqch/qqn; our complaints fell on ~ ears *fig* nos protestations n'ont pas été entendues ☐ (as) ~ as a post sourd comme un pot; there are none so ~ as those who will not hear *prov* il n'est pire sourd que celui qui ne veut entendre *prov*.

◇ *npl*: the ~ les sourds *mpl*.

deaf-aid *n* appareil *m* acoustique.

deaf-and-dumb ◇ *adj* sourd-muet *(attention: le terme 'deaf-and-dumb' est considéré comme injurieux)*.

◇ *n* sourd-muet *m*, sourde-muette *f*.

deafen ['defn] *vt literal* rendre sourd; *fig* casser les oreilles à.

deafening ['defnɪŋ] *adj* [music, noise, roar] assourdissant; [applause] retentissant; the silence was ~ *hum* il y avait un grand silence OR un silence impressionnant.

deafeningly ['defnɪŋlɪ] *adv*: ~ loud assourdissant.

deaf-mute = **deaf-and-dumb**.

deafness ['defnɪs] *n* surdité *f*.

deal [diːl] (*pt* & *pp* dealt [delt]) ◇ *n* -**1.** [agreement] affaire *f*, marché *m*; ST. EX opération *f*, transaction *f*; business ~ affaire, marché, transaction; to do OR to make a ~ with sb conclure une affaire OR un marché avec qqn; I'll make a ~ with you je te propose un marché; the ~ is off l'affaire est annulée, le marché est rompu; the government does not do ~s with terrorists le gouvernement ne traite pas avec les terroristes; no ~s! pas de marchandage!; no ~! je ne marche pas!; it's a ~! marché conclu!; you've got (yourself) a ~! *inf* ça marche!; that wasn't the ~ ce n'est pas ce qui était convenu; a good/bad ~ une bonne/mauvaise affaire; to get a good ~ faire une bonne affaire; what's the ~? *inf Am* qu'est-ce qui se passe? -**2.** [treatment]: to give sb a fair ~ traiter loyalement avec qqn; the government promised (to give) teachers a better ~ le gouvernement a promis d'améliorer la condition des enseignants; to get a rotten ~ out of life ne pas être gâté par la vie ☐ the New Deal le New Deal, la Nouvelle Donne. -**3.** CARDS donne *f*, distribution *f*; it's my ~ c'est à moi de donner. -**4.** [quantity]: a (good) ~ of, a great ~ of [money, time etc] beaucoup de; he thinks a good/great ~ of her il l'estime beaucoup/énormément; I didn't enjoy it a great ~ je n'ai pas trop OR pas tellement aimé; there's a good OR great ~ of truth in what you say il y a beaucoup de vrai dans ce que vous dites; I didn't do a great ~ last night je n'ai pas fait grand-chose hier soir; a good/great ~ faster beaucoup plus vite; big ~! *inf iron* tu parles d'un coup!, la belle affaire!; he made a big ~ out of it *inf* il en a fait tout un plat OR tout un cinéma; what's the big ~? *inf* et alors?, et puis quoi?; that's not such a big ~ *inf* ça ne vaut pas la peine qu'on en fasse tout un plat OR tout un cinéma. -**5.** [timber] planche *f*; a ~ table une table en bois.

◇ *vt* -**1.** CARDS donner, distribuer. -**2.** [strike]: to ~ sb a blow assener un coup à qqn; to ~ sthg a blow, to ~ a blow to sthg *fig* porter un coup à qqch. -**3.** [drugs] revendre.

◇ *vi* -**1.** CARDS distribuer les cartes; it's your turn OR it's you to ~ c'est à toi de distribuer OR de donner. -**2.** COMM négocier, traiter; the firm has been ~ing for over 50 years cette société est en activité depuis plus de 50 ans; to ~ on the Stock Exchange faire des opérations OR des transactions en bourse; to ~ in drugs revendre de la drogue; to ~ in death/human misery *fig* être un marchand de mort/de misère humaine. -**3.** *inf* [in drugs] revendre de la drogue.

◆ **deal in** *vt sep* CARDS [player] donner OR distribuer des cartes à, servir; ~ me in *fig* tu peux compter sur moi.

◆ **deal out** *vt sep* [cards, gifts] donner, distribuer; [justice] rendre; [punishment] distribuer; ~ me out *fig* ne compte pas sur moi.

◆ **deal with** *vt insep* -**1.** [handle - problem, situation, query, complaint] traiter; [- customer, member of the public] traiter avec; [- difficult situation] s'occuper de; a difficult child to ~ with un enfant difficile; a job that involves ~ing with the public un travail qui implique un contact avec le public; the author ~s with the question very sensitively l'auteur traite OR aborde ce sujet avec beaucoup de délicatesse; I'll ~ with it [problem, situation etc] je m'en occupe, je m'en charge; I'll ~ with you later [to naughty child] je vais m'occuper de toi OR de ton cas plus tard; I can't ~ with all the work I've got je ne me sors pas de tout le travail que j'ai; the management dealt with the situation promptly la direction a réagi immédiatement; the culprits were dealt with severely les coupables ont été sévèrement punis; the switchboard ~s with over 1,000 calls a day le standard traite OR reçoit plus de 1 000 appels par jour; that's that dealt with voilà qui est fait. -**2.** [do business with] traiter OR négocier avec; she's not an easy woman to ~ with ce n'est pas facile de traiter OR négocier avec elle. -**3.** [be concerned with] traiter de; in my lecture, I shall ~ with... dans mon cours, je traiterai de...

dealer ['diːləʳ] *n* -**1.** COMM marchand *m*, -e *f*, négociant *m*, -e *f*; ST. EX marchand *m*, -e *f* de titres; AUT concessionnaire *mf*. -**2.** [in drugs] dealer *m*. -**3.** CARDS donneur *m*, -euse *f*.

dealership ['diːləʃɪp] *n* AUT & COMM concession *f*.

dealing ['diːlɪŋ] *n* -**1.** *(U)* ST. EX opérations *fpl*, transactions *fpl*; [trading] commerce *m*. -**2.** *(U)* [of cards] donne *f*, distribution *f*. -**3.** ~s [business] affaires *fpl*, transactions *fpl*; [personal] relations *fpl*; to have ~s with sb [in business] traiter avec qqn, avoir affaire à qqn; [personal] avoir affaire à qqn. **-4.** [in drugs] trafic *m* de drogue.

dealt [delt] *pt* & *pp* → **deal**.

dean [di:n] *n* UNIV & RELIG doyen *m*, -enne *f*.

deanery ['di:nərɪ] *n* RELIG doyenné *m*; UNIV résidence *f* du doyen.

dear [dɪəʳ] ◇ *adj* **-1.** [loved] cher; [precious] cher, précieux; [appealing] adorable, charmant; **he is a ~ friend of mine** c'est un ami très cher; **she's such a ~ girl** elle est tellement gentille; **Margaret ~** est ma chère Margaret; **he/the memory is very ~ to me** il/ce souvenir m'est très cher; **to hold sb/sthg ~** *lit* chérir qqn/qqch; **all that I hold ~ (in life)** tout ce qui m'est cher; **to run for ~ life** courir à toute vitesse; **to hang on for ~ life** s'accrocher désespérément; MED s'accrocher à la vie; **my ~ fellow** mon cher ami; **my ~ girl** ma chère; **my ~ Mrs Stevens** chère madame Stevens; **what a ~ little child/cottage/frock!** quel enfant/quel cottage/quelle robe adorable! **-2.** [in letter]: **Dear Sir** Monsieur; **Dear Madam** Madame; **Dear Sir or Madam** Madame, Monsieur; **Dear Sirs** Messieurs; **Dear Mrs Baker/Mr McLeod** Madame/Monsieur; [less formal] Chère Madame/Cher Monsieur; [informal] Chère Madame Baker/Cher Monsieur McLeod; **Dear Henry** Cher Henry; **Dear Mum and Dad** Chers Maman et Papa; **My ~ Clare** Ma chère Clare; **Dearest Richard** Très cher Richard. **-3.** [expensive - item, shop] cher; [- price] haut, élevé; **things are getting ~er** *esp Br* la vie augmente.
◇ *interj*: **~!, ~! ~!, ~ me!, oh ~!** [surprise] oh mon Dieu!; [regret] oh là là!; **oh ~!** [worry] mon Dieu!
◇ *n*: **my ~** [to child, spouse, lover] mon chéri, ma chérie; [to friend] mon cher, ma chère; **my ~** est mon chéri, ma chérie; **she's such a ~** elle est tellement gentille; **I gave the old ~ my seat** *inf Br* j'ai laissé ma place à la vieille dame; **poor ~** pauvre chéri, pauvre chérie; **be a ~ and answer the phone, answer the phone, there's a ~** sois gentil OR un amour, réponds au téléphone.
◇ *adv* [sell, pay, cost] cher *(adv)*.

dear Abby [-'æbɪ] *n Am la rubrique courrier du cœur.*

dearie *inf* ['dɪərɪ] ◇ *n* chéri *m*, -e *f*.
◇ *interj*: **(oh) ~ me!** oh mon Dieu!

Dear John (letter) *inf n* lettre *f* de rupture.

dearly ['dɪəlɪ] *adv* **-1.** [very much] beaucoup, énormément; **I would ~ love to live in the country** j'aimerais beaucoup OR j'adorerais vivre à la campagne; **~ beloved son of...** [on gravestone] fils bien-aimé de...; **~ beloved, we are gathered here today...** mes biens chers frères, nous sommes aujourd'hui rassemblés... **-2.** [at high cost]: **to pay ~ for sthg** payer cher qqch.

dearness ['dɪənɪs] *n* **-1.** [costliness] cherté *f*. **-2.** [of loved one]: **her ~ to him grew with every day that passed** l'affection qu'il avait pour elle croissait de jour en jour.

dearth [dɜ:θ] *n* pénurie *f*.

deary *inf* ['dɪərɪ] = **dearie** *n*.

death [deθ] *n* mort *f*; JUR décès *m*; **his ~ came as a shock to me** sa mort a été un choc pour moi; **I was with him at the time of his ~** j'étais auprès de lui quand il est mort; **how many ~s were there?** combien y a-t-il eu de morts?; **their ~s were caused by smoke inhalation** leur mort a été causée OR provoquée par l'inhalation de fumée; **a ~ in the family** un décès dans la famille; **to fall/to jump to one's ~** se tuer en tombant/se jetant dans le vide; **to freeze/to starve to ~** mourir de froid/de faim; **to be beaten to ~** être battu à mort; **to be burnt to ~** mourir brûlé; **to bleed to ~** perdre tout son sang; **to fight to the ~** se battre à mort; **to meet one's ~** trouver la mort; **to meet an early ~** mourir jeune; **condemned to OR under sentence of ~** condamné à mort; **to sentence/to put sb to ~** condamner/mettre qqn à mort; **to smoke/to drink o.s. to ~** se tuer à force de fumer/boire; **~ to the Czar!** mort au Tsar!; **till ~ do us part** jusqu'à ce que la mort nous sépare; **this means the ~ of the steel industry** cela sonne le glas de la sidérurgie; **it's been done to ~** *fig* [play, subject for novel etc] ça a été fait et refait; **to discuss sthg to ~** *fig* discuter de qqch jusqu'à l'épuisement du sujet; **to look like ~ (warmed up)** *inf* avoir une mine de déterré; **to feel like ~ (warmed up)** *inf* être en piteux état; **to catch one's ~ (of cold)** *inf* attraper la mort OR la crève; **to be in at the ~** *fig* être présent à la fin; **to die a horrible ~** avoir une mort atroce; **to be sick OR tired to ~ of** *inf* en avoir ras le bol de; **to be bored to ~** *inf* s'ennuyer à mourir; **to be worried/scared to ~** *inf* être mort d'inquiétude/de frousse; **you'll be the ~ of me** *inf* [with amusement] tu me feras mourir (de rire); [with irritation] tu es tuant; **that job will be the ~ of her** ce travail la tuera □ **to be at ~'s door** [patient] être à l'article de la mort; **to die a thousand ~s** [worry about somebody] mourir d'inquiétude; [worry about oneself] être mort de peur; [be embarrassed] mourir de honte; **to die the ~** *inf* [actor, film] faire un bide; [joke] tomber à plat; [idea, plan, hope] tomber à l'eau; **~ by misadventure** mort accidentelle; **to hang OR to hold OR to cling on like grim ~** s'accrocher désespérément; **'Death in the Afternoon'** *Hemingway* 'Mort dans l'après-midi'; **'Death of a Salesman'** *Miller* 'Mort d'un commis voyageur'; **'Death in Venice'** *Mann, Visconti* 'Mort à Venise'.

deathbed ['deθbed] ◇ *n* lit *m* de mort; **on one's ~** sur son lit de mort.
◇ *adj* [confession] fait à l'article de la mort; [repentance] exprimé à l'article de la mort; **the ~ scene** THEAT la scène du lit de mort.

deathblow ['deθbləʊ] *n fig* coup *m* fatal OR mortel; **to be the ~ for sthg** porter un coup fatal OR mortel à qqch.

death camp *n* camp *m* de la mort.

death cap *n* BOT amanite *f* phalloïde.

death cell *n* cellule *f* de condamné à mort.

death certificate *n* acte *m* OR certificat *m* de décès.

death-dealing *adj* mortel, fatal.

death duty *n* droits *mpl* de succession.

death knell *n* glas *m*; **to sound the ~ for OR of sthg** *fig* sonner le glas de qqch.

deathless ['deθlɪs] *adj* immortel; *hum* inimitable.

deathlike ['deθlaɪk] *adj* de mort, mortel.

deathly ['deθlɪ] ◇ *adj* [silence, pallor] de mort, mortel.
◇ *adv*: **~ pale** pâle comme la mort; **~ cold** glacial; **the house was ~ quiet** [silent] la maison était plongée dans un profond silence; [sinister] la maison était plongée dans un silence de mort.

death march = **dead march**.

death mask *n* masque *m* mortuaire.

death penalty *n* peine *f* de mort, peine *f* capitale.

death rate *n* taux *m* de mortalité.

death rattle *n* râle *m* d'agonie.

death row *n* quartier *m* des condamnés à mort; **he's been on ~ for ten years** cela fait dix ans qu'il est au quartier des condamnés à mort.

death seat *inf n Am* & *Austr* [in a vehicle] place *f* du mort.

death sentence *n* condamnation *f* à mort.

death's-head *n* tête *f* de mort.

death's-head moth *n* sphinx *m* tête-de-mort.

death squad *n* escadron *m* de la mort.

death tax *Am* = **death duty**.

death throes *npl* agonie *f*; [painful] affres *fpl* de la mort; *fig* agonie *f*; **to be in one's ~** agoniser, être agonisant; [suffering] connaître les affres de la mort; **to be in its ~** *fig* [project, business etc] agoniser, être agonisant.

death toll *n* nombre *m* de morts; **the ~ stands at 567** il y a 567 morts, le bilan est de 567 morts.

death trap *n véhicule ou endroit extrêmement dangereux*; **the building is a ~** l'édifice est extrêmement dangereux.

Death Valley *pr n* la Vallée de la Mort.

death warrant *n* ordre *m* d'exécution; **to sign one's own ~** *fig* signer son propre arrêt de mort.

deathwatch ['deθwɒtʃ] *n* veillée *f* mortuaire.

deathwatch beetle *n* grande OR grosse vrillette *f*, horloger *m* de la mort.

death wish *n* PSYCH désir *m* de mort; **the government seems to have a ~** *fig* le gouvernement semble avoir un instinct suicidaire.

deb *inf* [deb] = **debutante**.

debacle [de'bɑ:kl] *n* débâcle *f*.

debag *inf* [,di:'bæg] (*pt* & *pp* debagged, *cont* debagging) *vt* déculotter de force.

debar [di:'bɑ:ʳ] (*pt* & *pp* debarred, *cont* debarring) *vt* interdire à; **to ~ sb from sthg/doing sthg** interdire qqch à qqn/à qqn de faire qqch.

debark *etc* [dɪ'bɑ:k] = **disembark**.

debarment [dɪ'bɑ:mənt] *n* interdiction *f*.

debase [dɪ'beɪs] *vt* [degrade - person, sport] avilir, abaisser; [- quality of object] dégrader, altérer; **to ~ the coinage** altérer la monnaie; *fig* dévaloriser la monnaie.

debasement [dɪ'beɪsmənt] *n* [of person, sport] avilissement *m*, abaissement *m*; [of quality of object] dégradation *f*, altération *f*; [of currency] altération *f*; *fig* dévalorisation *f*.

debatable [dɪ'beɪtəbl] *adj* discutable, contestable; **it is ~ whether...** on peut se demander si..., on peut se poser la question de savoir si...

debate [dɪ'beɪt] ◇ *vt* débattre, discuter; **to ~ what to do** [two or more people] discuter de OR débattre de ce qu'on va faire; [one person] se demander ce qu'on va faire; **a much ~d question** une question très débattue.
◇ *vi* discuter; **to ~ (with o.s.) whether to do sthg or not** se demander si on doit faire qqch.
◇ *n* [gen] discussion *f*; [organized] débat *m*; **to have OR to hold a ~ about OR on sthg** tenir un débat OR avoir une discussion sur OR à propos de qqch; **there's been a lot of ~ about it** cela a été très OR longuement débattu; **the subject under ~** le sujet des débats; **open to ~** discutable, contestable; **after much OR lengthy ~** [between two or more people] après de longs débats; [with oneself] après de longs débats intérieurs; **to be the subject of ~** faire le thème de débats.

debater [dɪ'beɪtəʳ] *n* débatteur *m*; **to be a skilled ~** exceller dans les débats.

debating [dɪ'beɪtɪŋ] ◇ *n* art *m* du débat.
◇ *comp*: **~ society** société *f* de débats contradictoires.

debauch [dɪ'bɔ:tʃ] ◇ *vt* débaucher; *arch* OR *lit* [woman] séduire.
◇ *n arch* OR *lit* partie *f* de débauche.

debauched [dɪ'bɔ:tʃt] *adj* débauché.

debauchee [dɪbɔ:'tʃi:] *n* débauché *m*, -e *f*.

debauchery [dɪ'bɔ:tʃərɪ] *n* débauche *f*.

debenture [dɪ'bentʃəʳ] FIN ◇ *n* obligation *f*.
◇ *comp*: **~ bond** titre *m* d'obligation; **~ holder** obligataire *mf*, détenteur *m*, -trice *f* d'obligations; **~ stock** obligation *f* sans garantie.

debilitate [dɪ'bɪlɪteɪt] *vt* débiliter.

debilitating [dɪ'bɪlɪteɪtɪŋ] *adj* [illness] débilitant; [climate] anémiant.

debility [dɪ'bɪlətɪ] *n* débilité *f*.

debit ['debɪt] FIN ◇ *n* débit *m*; **your account is in ~** *Br* votre compte est déficitaire OR débiteur.
◇ *comp* [balance, account] débiteur; **~ card** *carte de paiement à débit immédiat*; **~ entry** écriture *f* au débit; **~ side** débit *m*; **on the ~ side, he is not very presentable** *fig* ce qui le dessert, c'est qu'il n'est pas très présentable; **on the ~ side, it means we won't see her** *fig* l'inconvénient, c'est que nous ne la verrons pas.
◇ *vt* [account] débiter; [person] porter au débit de qqn; **to ~ £50 from sb's account, to ~ sb's account with £50** débiter 50 livres du compte de qqn, débiter le compte de qqn de 50 livres.

DEBIT CARD:
La «debit card» permet de régler des achats et des services en débitant directement le compte bancaire de l'utilisateur; elle se distingue par là de la carte de crédit (qui débite le compte une fois par mois). Elle permet également de retirer de l'argent.

debonair [ˌdebəˈneəʳ] *adj* d'une élégance nonchalante.

Deborah [ˈdebərə] *pr n* Déborah.

debouch [dɪˈbaʊtʃ] *vi* GEOG & MIL déboucher.

Debrett [dəˈbret] (*abbr of* Debrett's Peerage) *n annuaire de l'aristocratie britannique.*

debrief [ˌdiːˈbriːf] *vt* faire faire un compte rendu verbal de mission à, débriefer; pilots are ~ed after every flight on fait faire un compte rendu verbal de mission aux pilotes OR on débriefe les pilotes après chaque vol.

debriefing [ˌdiːˈbriːfɪŋ] ◇ *n* compte rendu *m* verbal de mission.
◇ *comp*: ~ officer officier *m* chargé de recevoir le compte rendu verbal des pilotes; ~ room salle *f* de compte rendu de mission.

debris [ˈdeɪbriː] *n (U)* débris *mpl*.

debt [det] ◇ *n* [gen] dette *f*; ADMIN créance *f*; to be in ~, to have ~s avoir des dettes, être endetté; to be out of ~ s'être acquitté de ses dettes; to get OR to run into ~ s'endetter; to get out of ~ s'acquitter de ses dettes; to pay one's ~s régler ses dettes; he has paid his ~ to society il s'est acquitté de sa dette envers la société; to be in ~ to sb être endetté auprès de qqn; *fig* avoir une dette envers qqn, être redevable à qqn ❑ bad ~ mauvaise créance; ~ of honour dette d'honneur; outstanding ~ dette OR créance à recouvrer.
◇ *comp* [rescheduling, servicing] de la dette; ~ collector agent *m* de recouvrement; ~ collection agency bureau *m* de recouvrement OR récupération des créances.

debtor [ˈdetəʳ] *n* débiteur *m*, -trice *f*; ~ nations pays *mpl* débiteurs.

debt-ridden *adj* criblé de dettes.

debug [ˌdiːˈbʌg] (*pt & pp* debugged, *cont* debugging) *vt* -**1.** COMPUT [program] déboguer; [machine] mettre au point. -**2.** [remove hidden microphones from] débarrasser des micros (cachés). -**3.** [remove insects from] débarrasser des insectes, désinsectiser.

debugging [ˌdiːˈbʌgɪŋ] ◇ *n* -**1.** COMPUT [of program] débogage *m*; [of machine] mise *f* au point. -**2.** [removal of microphones] élimination *f* des micros (cachés). -**3.** [removal of insects] désinsectisation *f*.
◇ *comp* -**1.** COMPUT de débogage. -**2.** [to remove microphones - operation] d'élimination des micros (cachés); [- team] chargé d'éliminer les micros (cachés); [- expert] dans l'élimination de micros (cachés). -**3.** [to remove insects] de désinsectisation.

debunk *inf* [ˌdiːˈbʌŋk] *vt* [ridicule] tourner en ridicule; [show to be false] discréditer.

debut [ˈdeɪbjuː] (*pt & pp* debut'd) ◇ *n* début *m*; to make one's ~ faire ses débuts.
◇ *vi* débuter; to ~ as débuter dans le rôle de.

debutante [ˈdebjʊtɑːnt] *n* débutante *f*.

Dec. (*written abbr of* December) déc.

decade [ˈdekeɪd] *n* -**1.** [ten years] décennie *f*; before the end of the ~ avant la fin de cette décennie; over a ~ ago il y a plus de dix ans. -**2.** RELIG dizaine *f*.

decadence [ˈdekədəns] *n* décadence *f*.

decadent [ˈdekədənt] ◇ *adj* décadent.
◇ *n* -**1.** personne *f* décadente. -**2.** ART décadent *m*, -e *f*.

decadently [ˈdekədəntlɪ] *adv* de manière décadente.

decaf *inf* [ˈdiːkæf] *n* [coffee] déca *m*.

decaffeinated [dɪˈkæfɪneɪtɪd] *adj* décaféiné.

decagon [ˈdekəgən] *n* décagone *m*.

decagramme *Br*, **decagram** *Am* [ˈdekəgræm] *n* décagramme *m*.

decal *inf* [ˈdiːkæl] *n Am* décalcomanie *f*.

decalcification [ˈdiːˌkælsɪfɪˈkeɪʃn] *n* décalcification *f*.

decalcify [ˌdiːˈkælsɪfaɪ] *vt* décalcifier.

decalcomania [dɪˌkælkəˈmeɪnjə] *n* décalcomanie *f*.

decalitre *Br*, **decaliter** *Am* [ˈdekəˌliːtəʳ] *n* décalitre *m*.

Decalogue [ˈdekəlɒg] *pr n* BIBLE décalogue *m*.

decametre *Br*, **decameter** *Am* [ˈdekəˌmiːtəʳ] *n* décamètre *m*.

decamp [dɪˈkæmp] *vi* -**1.** MIL lever le camp. -**2.** *inf* [abscond] décamper, ficher le camp.

decant [dɪˈkænt] *vt* décanter.

decanter [dɪˈkæntəʳ] *n* carafe *f*.

decapitate [dɪˈkæpɪteɪt] *vt* décapiter.

decapitation [dɪˌkæpɪˈteɪʃn] *n* décapitation *f*.

decapod [ˈdekəpɒd] *n* décapode *m*.

decarbonization [diːˌkɑːbənaɪˈzeɪʃn] *n* décarbonisation *f*; AUT décalaminage *m*; METALL décarburation *f*.

decarbonize [ˌdiːˈkɑːbənaɪz] *vt* décarboniser; AUT décalaminer; METALL décarburer.

decathlete [dɪˈkæθliːt] *n* décathlonien *m*, -enne *f*.

decathlon [dɪˈkæθlɒn] *n* décathlon *m*.

decay [dɪˈkeɪ] ◇ *vi* -**1.** [rot - food, wood, flowers] pourrir; [- meat] s'avarier, pourrir; [- corpse] se décomposer; [- tooth] se carier; [- building] se délabrer; [- stone] s'effriter, se désagréger; *fig* [- beauty, civilization, faculties] décliner. -**2.** PHYS dépérir, se dégrader, se désintégrer.
◇ *vt* [wood] pourrir; [stone] désagréger; [tooth] carier.
◇ *n* -**1.** [of food, wood, flowers] pourrissement *m*; [of corpse] décomposition *f*; [of building] délabrement *m*; [of stone] effritement *m*, désagrégation *f*; *fig* [of beauty, faculties] délabrement *m*; [of civilization] déclin *m*; area of ~ [in tooth] zone *f* cariée; to fall into ~ *literal & fig* se délabrer; in an advanced state of ~ dans un état de délabrement avancé; moral ~ déchéance *f* morale ❑ senile ~ dégénérescence *f* sénile; tooth ~ carie *f*. -**2.** PHYS désintégration *f*, dégradation *f*.

decayed [dɪˈkeɪd] *adj* [food, wood, flowers] pourri; [meat] avarié, pourri; [corpse] décomposé; [tooth] carié; [building] délabré, en ruines; [stone] effrité, désagrégé; *fig* [beauty] fané; [civilization] délabré, en ruines.

decaying [dɪˈkeɪɪŋ] *adj* [food, wood, flowers] pourrissant; [meat] en train de s'avarier; [corpse] en décomposition; [tooth] en train de se carier; [building] qui se délabre; [stone] en désagrégation; *fig* [beauty] qui se fane; [civilization] sur le déclin.

Deccan [ˈdekən] *pr n* Deccan *m*.

decease [dɪˈsiːs] ◇ *n* décès *m*.
◇ *vi* décéder.

deceased [dɪˈsiːst] (*pl inv*) ◇ *adj* décédé, défunt.
◇ *n*: the ~ le défunt, la défunte.

deceit [dɪˈsiːt] *n* -**1.** [quality] duplicité *f*. -**2.** [trick] supercherie *f*, tromperie *f*. -**3.** JUR fraude *f*; by ~ frauduleusement.

deceitful [dɪˈsiːtfʊl] *adj* trompeur; [behaviour] trompeur, sournois.

deceitfully [dɪˈsiːtfʊlɪ] *adv* trompeusement, avec duplicité.

deceitfulness [dɪˈsiːtfʊlnɪs] *n* tromperie *f*, duplicité *f*.

deceive [dɪˈsiːv] *vt* tromper; to ~ sb into doing sthg amener qqn à faire qqch par la tromperie; she ~d me into believing that... elle m'a fait croire que...; to ~ o.s. se mentir à soi-même; unless my eyes ~ me à moins que mes yeux ne me jouent des tours OR que ma vue ne me joue des tours.

deceiver [dɪˈsiːvəʳ] *n* trompeur *m*, -euse *f*.

decelerate [ˌdiːˈseləreɪt] *vi & vt* ralentir.

deceleration [diːˌseləˈreɪʃn] *n* ralentissement *m*.

December [dɪˈsembəʳ] *n* décembre.

decency [ˈdiːsnsɪ] (*pl* decencies) *n* décence *f*; for ~'s sake pour respecter les convenances; for ~'s sake! un peu de décence!; an offence against public ~ *Br* un outrage à la pudeur; to have the (common) ~ to do sthg avoir la décence de faire qqch; to observe the decencies observer les convenances.

decent [ˈdiːsnt] *adj* -**1.** [proper, morally correct] décent, convenable; ~, church-going folk des gens comme il faut, qui vont à l'église; after a ~ length of time après une période de temps convenable; to do the ~ thing se comporter OR agir dans les règles; [marry woman one has made pregnant] faire son devoir, réparer; are you ~? [dressed] es-tu visible? -**2.** [satisfactory, reasonable - housing, wage] décent, convenable; [- price] convenable, raisonnable; a ~ meal un bon repas; a ~ night's sleep une bonne nuit de sommeil; the rooms are a ~ size les pièces sont de bonne taille; to speak ~ French parler assez bien OR parler convenablement le français. -**3.** *inf* [kind, good] bien, sympa; he's a ~ sort (of chap) *Br* c'est un type bien; that's very ~ of you c'est très sympa de ta part.

decently [ˈdiːsntlɪ] *adv* -**1.** [properly] décemment, convenablement; you can't ~ ask her to do that tu ne peux pas décemment lui demander de faire cela. -**2.** [reasonably]: the job pays ~ le travail paie raisonnablement bien. -**3.** *inf* [kindly] de manière sympa.

decentralization [diːˌsentrəlaɪˈzeɪʃn] *n* décentralisation *f*.

decentralize [ˌdiːˈsentrəlaɪz] *vt* décentraliser.

deception [dɪˈsepʃn] *n* -**1.** [act of deceiving] tromperie *f*, duperie *f*; by ~ en usant de tromperie. -**2.** [trick] subterfuge *m*, tromperie *f*. -**3.** [state of being deceived] duperie *f*.

deceptive [dɪˈseptɪv] *adj* trompeur; appearances can be ~ il ne faut pas se fier aux apparences, les apparences sont trompeuses.

deceptively [dɪˈseptɪvlɪ] *adv*: it looks ~ easy/near cela donne l'illusion d'être facile/tout près, on a l'impression que c'est facile/tout près; he has a ~ calm exterior il a une apparence calme qui n'est qu'illusoire.

deceptiveness [dɪˈseptɪvnɪs] *n* caractère *m* trompeur.

decibel [ˈdesɪbel] *n* décibel *m*; to measure the ~ level of a concert mesurer le niveau en décibels d'un concert; the ~ level was quite overpowering le bruit était assourdissant.

decide [dɪˈsaɪd] ◇ *vt* -**1.** [resolve] décider; to ~ to do sthg décider de faire qqch; it was ~d to alter our strategy il a été décidé que nous devions modifier notre stratégie; nothing has been ~d rien n'a été décidé; what have you ~d? qu'avez-vous décidé?; the weather hasn't ~d what it's doing yet le temps n'arrive pas à se décider. -**2.** [determine - outcome, sb's fate, career] décider de, déterminer; [- person] décider; that was what ~d me to leave him c'est ce qui m'a décidé à le quitter. -**3.** [settle - debate, war] décider de l'issue de.
◇ *vi* -**1.** [make up one's mind] décider, se décider; I can't ~ je n'arrive pas à me décider; you ~ c'est toi qui décides; I haven't ~d yet je n'ai pas encore décidé; he'll need time to ~ il lui faudra du temps pour décider; you'll have to ~ for yourself c'est toi qui devras décider; to ~ against/in favour of doing sthg décider de ne pas/de faire qqch; to ~ in favour of sb/sthg JUR décider en faveur de qqn/qqch; to ~ against sb/sthg JUR décider contre qqn/qqch. -**2.** [determine]: but circumstances ~d otherwise mais les circonstances en ont décidé autrement.
◆ **decide on** *vt insep* décider de, se décider pour; what plan of action have you ~d on? pour quel plan d'action vous êtes-vous décidé?, quel plan d'action avez-vous décidé de suivre?; to ~ on a day for the wedding/a name for the baby décider du jour du mariage/du nom du bébé.

decided [dɪˈsaɪdɪd] *adj* -**1.** [distinct - improvement, difference] net, incontestable; [- success] éclatant. -**2.** [resolute - person, look] décidé, résolu; [- opinion, stance] ferme; [- effort] résolu; [- refusal] ferme, catégorique; I'm quite ~ about leaving je suis fermement décidé à partir.

decidedly [dɪ'saɪdɪdlɪ] *adv* -**1.** [distinctly - better, different] décidément; I feel ~ unwell today je ne me sens vraiment pas bien aujourd'hui, décidément, je ne me sens pas bien aujourd'hui; so she's better? – yes, ~ so alors, elle va mieux? – beaucoup OR nettement mieux, oui; was the weather unpleasant? – yes, ~ so avez-vous eu du mauvais temps? – extrêmement mauvais, oui. -**2.** [resolutely] résolument, fermement.

decider [dɪ'saɪdəʳ] *n* [goal] but *m* décisif; [point] point *m* décisif; [match] match *m* décisif, rencontre *f* décisive; [factor] facteur *m* décisif.

deciding [dɪ'saɪdɪŋ] *adj* décisif, déterminant; the chairperson has the ~ vote la voix du président est prépondérante.

deciduous [dɪ'sɪdjʊəs] *adj* [tree] à feuilles caduques; [leaves, antlers] caduc.

decilitre *Br*, **deciliter** *Am* ['desɪˌliːtəʳ] *n* décilitre *m*.

decimal ['desɪml] ◇ *adj* décimal; to go ~ adopter le système décimal.
◇ *n* chiffre *m* décimal; we haven't done ~s yet on n'a pas encore vu les chiffres décimaux.

decimal fraction = **decimal** *n*.

decimalization [ˌdesɪməlaɪ'zeɪʃn] *n* décimalisation *f*.

decimalize ['desɪməlaɪz] ◇ *vt* décimaliser.
◇ *vi* adopter le système décimal.

decimal place *n* décimale *f*; correct to four ~s exact jusqu'à la quatrième décimale OR jusqu'au quatrième chiffre après la virgule OR au dix millième près.

decimal point *n* virgule *f*.

decimal system *n* système *m* décimal.

decimate ['desɪmeɪt] *vt* décimer.

decimation [ˌdesɪ'meɪʃn] *n* décimation *f*.

decimetre *Br*, **decimeter** *Am* ['desɪˌmiːtəʳ] *n* décimètre *m*.

decipher [dɪ'saɪfəʳ] *vt* [code, handwriting] déchiffrer.

decipherable [dɪ'saɪfərəbl] *adj* déchiffrable.

decision [dɪ'sɪʒn] ◇ *n* -**1.** décision *f*; to make OR to take a ~ prendre une décision, se décider; JUR & ADMIN prendre une décision; to come to OR to arrive at OR to reach a ~ parvenir à une décision; to make the right/wrong ~ faire le bon/mauvais choix; it's your ~ c'est toi qui décides; is that your ~? ta décision est prise?; the referee's ~ is final la décision de l'arbitre est irrévocable OR sans appel. -**2.** *fml* [decisiveness] décision *f*, résolution *f*, fermeté *f*. -**3.** [decision-making]: it's a matter for personal ~ c'est une affaire de choix personnel.
◇ *comp* COMPUT: ~ table table *f* de décision.

decision-maker *n* [person responsible for decisions] décideur *m*, -euse *f*, décisionnaire *mf*; he's not a ~ [he's no good at making decisions] il n'aime pas prendre des décisions.

decision-making *n* prise *f* de décision; the ~ process le processus de (prise de) décision; he's no good at ~ il ne sait pas prendre des décisions; a job which calls for a lot of ~ un travail qui demande qu'on prenne beaucoup de décisions.

decisive [dɪ'saɪsɪv] *adj* -**1.** [manner, person] décidé, résolu; be ~! montre-toi décidé OR résolu! -**2.** [factor, argument] décisif, déterminant.

decisively [dɪ'saɪsɪvlɪ] *adv* -**1.** [resolutely] résolument, sans hésitation. -**2.** [conclusively] de manière décisive.

decisiveness [dɪ'saɪsɪvnɪs] *n* -**1.** [of person] décision *f*; to say sthg with ~ dire qqch d'un air décidé OR résolu. -**2.** [of battle] caractère *m* décisif OR déterminant.

deck [dek] ◇ *n* -**1.** NAUT pont *m*; upper/lower ~ pont supérieur/inférieur; on ~ sur le pont; to go (up) on ~ monter sur le pont; below ~ OR ~s sous le pont; to clear the ~s *fig* mettre de l'ordre avant de passer à l'action. -**2.** [of plane, bus] étage *m*; top OR upper ~ [of bus] impériale *f*. -**3.** CARDS jeu *m* de cartes; to shuffle the ~ battre les cartes; there are only 51 cards in this ~ il n'y a que 51 cartes dans ce jeu. -**4.** [in hi-fi system] platine *f*. -**5.** *Am* [of house] ponton *m*.
◇ *comp* NAUT [officer, cabin, crane] de pont; ~ cargo pontée *f*.
◇ *vt* -**1.** = **deck out**. -**2.** *inf* [knock to the ground] envoyer au tapis.
◆ **deck out** *vt sep* parer, orner; to ~ o.s. out in one's best clothes se mettre sur son trente et un.

deck chair *n* chaise *f* longue, transat *m*.

deckel ['dekl] = **deckle**.

-decker ['dekəʳ] *in cpds*: double~ bus bus *m* à impériale; double~ sandwich sandwich *m* double.

deckhand ['dekhænd] *n* matelot *m*.

deckhouse ['dekhaʊs, *pl* -haʊzɪz] *n* rouf *m*.

deckle ['dekl] *n* cadre *m* volant *(utilisé dans la fabrication artisanale du papier)*.

deckle edge *n* [on paper] bord *m* frangeux, barbes *fpl*.

deckle-edged *adj* [paper] à bord frangeux, à barbes.

deck tennis *n sorte de tennis joué sur le pont d'un navire*.

declaim [dɪ'kleɪm] ◇ *vi* déclamer; to ~ against sthg récriminer OR se récrier contre qqch.
◇ *vt* déclamer.

declamation [ˌdeklə'meɪʃn] *n* déclamation *f*.

declamatory [dɪ'klæmətrɪ] *adj* [style] déclamatoire.

declarant [dɪ'kleərənt] *n* JUR déclarant *m*, -e *f*.

declaration [ˌdeklə'reɪʃn] *n* -**1.** [gen] déclaration *f*; to make a ~ that... déclarer que...; ~ of love/war/independence déclaration d'amour/de guerre/d'indépendance; customs ~ déclaration en douane. -**2.** CARDS annonce *f*.

Declaration of Independence *n*: the ~ *Am* HIST la Déclaration d'indépendance (américaine).

THE DECLARATION OF INDEPENDENCE:
Document rédigé par Thomas Jefferson, proclamant, le 4 juillet 1776, l'indépendance des 13 colonies composant la Nouvelle-Angleterre et considéré comme l'acte de naissance des États-Unis d'Amérique.

---

declarative [dɪ'klærətɪv] *adj* déclaratif.

declaratory [dɪ'klærətrɪ] *adj* JUR déclaratoire; ~ judgement jugement *m* déclaratoire.

declare [dɪ'kleəʳ] ◇ *vt* -**1.** [proclaim - independence, war etc] déclarer; have you anything to ~? [at customs] avez-vous quelque chose à déclarer?; I ~ this meeting officially open je déclare la séance ouverte. -**2.** [announce] déclarer; to ~ o.s. [proclaim one's love] se déclarer; POL se présenter, présenter sa candidature; to ~ o.s. for/against se déclarer pour/contre. -**3.** CARDS: to ~ one's hand annoncer son jeu.
◇ *vi* -**1.** to ~ for/against faire une déclaration en faveur de/contre; well, I (do) ~! eh bien ça alors! -**2.** CARDS faire l'annonce, annoncer; [in cricket] déclarer la tournée terminée *(avant sa fin normale)*.

declared [dɪ'kleəd] *adj* [intention, opponent] déclaré, ouvert.

declarer [dɪ'kleərəʳ] *n* CARDS demandeur *m*.

declassification [diːˌklæsɪfɪ'keɪʃn] *n* [of information] déclassement *m*.

declassified [ˌdiː'klæsɪfaɪd] *adj* [information] déclassé.

declassify [ˌdiː'klæsɪfaɪ] (*pt* & *pp* **declassified**) *vt* [information] déclasser.

declension [dɪ'klenʃn] *n* GRAMM déclinaison *f*.

declination [ˌdeklɪ'neɪʃn] *n* ASTRON déclinaison *f*.

decline [dɪ'klaɪn] ◇ *n* [decrease - in prices, standards, crime, profits] baisse *f*; *fig* [of civilization] déclin *m*; there has been a ~ in child mortality il y a eu une baisse de la mortalité infantile; to be in ~ être en déclin; to be on the ~ [prices, sales] être en baisse; [civilization, influence] être sur le déclin; to fall into ~ *fig* dépérir; to fall into a ~ *dated* [person] dépérir ❑ 'Decline and Fall' *Waugh* 'Grandeur et décadence'; 'The Decline and Fall of the Roman Empire' *Gibbon* 'Histoire du déclin et de la chute de l'empire romain'; 'The Decline of the West' *Spengler* 'Déclin de l'Occident'.
◇ *vt* -**1.** [refuse - invitation, honour, offer of help] décliner, refuser; [- food, drink] refuser; [- responsibility] décliner; to ~ to do sthg refuser de faire qqch. -**2.** GRAMM décliner.
◇ *vi* -**1.** [decrease, diminish - empire, health] décliner; [- prices, sales, population] baisser, être en baisse, diminuer; [- influence, enthusiasm, fame] baisser, diminuer; to ~ in importance/value/significance perdre de son importance/de sa valeur/de sa signification. -**2.** [refuse] refuser; she ~d with thanks elle a refusé avec ses remerciements. -**3.** [slope downwards] être en pente, descendre. -**4.** GRAMM se décliner.

declining [dɪ'klaɪnɪŋ] *adj* [health, industry, market] sur le déclin; he is in ~ health sa santé décline OR faiblit; she was in her ~ years elle était au déclin de sa vie; he wants to spend his ~ years in Britain il veut passer les dernières années de sa vie en Grande-Bretagne.

declivity [dɪ'klɪvətɪ] *n* déclivité *f*.

declutch [dɪ'klʌtʃ] *vi* AUT débrayer.

decoct [dɪ'kɒkt] *vt* obtenir par décoction.

decoction [dɪ'kɒkʃn] *n* décoction *f*.

decode [ˌdiː'kəʊd] *vt* décoder, déchiffrer; COMPUT & TV décoder.

decoder [ˌdiː'kəʊdəʳ] *n* décodeur *m*.

decoding [ˌdiː'kəʊdɪŋ] *n* décodage *m*.

decoke [ˌdiː'kəʊk] *Br* AUT ◇ *vt* décalaminer.
◇ *n* décalaminage *m*.

décolletage [ˌdeɪkɒl'tɑːʒ] = **décolleté** *n*.

décolleté [deɪ'kɒlteɪ] ◇ *adj* décolleté.
◇ *n* décolleté *m*.

decolonization [diːˌkɒlənaɪ'zeɪʃn] *n* décolonisation *f*.

decolonize [diː'kɒlənaɪz] *vt* décoloniser.

decommission [ˌdiːkə'mɪʃn] *vt* -**1.** [shut down - nuclear power station] déclasser. -**2.** MIL [remove from active service - warship, aircraft] mettre hors service.

decommissioning [ˌdiːkə'mɪʃənɪŋ] *n* -**1.** [of nuclear power station] déclassement *m*. -**2.** MIL [of warship, aircraft] mise *f* hors service.

decompartmentalize [ˌdiːkɒmpɑːt'mentəlaɪz] *vt* SOCIOL décompartementaliser.

decompose [ˌdiːkəm'pəʊz] ◇ *vi* se décomposer.
◇ *vt* CHEM & PHYS décomposer.

decomposition [ˌdiːkɒmpə'zɪʃn] *n* [gen, CHEM & PHYS] décomposition *f*.

decompress [ˌdiːkəm'pres] *vt* [gas, air] décomprimer; [diver] faire passer en chambre de décompression.

decompression [ˌdiːkəm'preʃn] *n* décompression *f*.

decompression chamber *n* chambre *f* de décompression.

decompression sickness *n* maladie *f* des caissons.

decondition [ˌdiːkən'dɪʃn] *vt* PSYCH déconditionner.

decongestant [ˌdiːkən'dʒestənt] MED ◇ *n* décongestif *m*.
◇ *adj* décongestif.

deconsecrate [ˌdiː'kɒnsɪkreɪt] *vt* RELIG désaffecter.

deconstruct [ˌdiːkən'strʌkt] *vt* déconstruire.

deconstruction [ˌdiːkən'strʌkʃn] *n* déconstruction *f*.

decontaminate [ˌdiːkən'tæmɪneɪt] *vt* décontaminer.

decontamination ['diːkənˌtæmɪ'neɪʃn] ◇ *n* décontamination *f*.
◇ *comp* [equipment, team] de décontamination; [expert] en décontamination.

decontrol [ˌdiːkən'trəʊl] ◇ *vt* lever le contrôle gouvernemental sur; to ~ prices libérer les prix.
◇ *n* [of prices] libération *f*.

decontrolled road [ˌdiːkənˈtrəʊld-] *n* route *f* sans limitation de vitesse.

decor [ˈdeɪkɔːʳ] *n* décor *m*.

decorate [ˈdekəreɪt] ◇ *vt* **-1.** [house, room - paint] peindre; [- wallpaper] tapisser, décorer. **-2.** [dress, hat] garnir, orner; [cake, tree, street] décorer. **-3.** [give medal to] décorer, médailler; to be ~d for bravery être décoré pour son courage.
◇ *vi* [paint] peindre; [wallpaper] tapisser.

decorating [ˈdekəreɪtɪŋ] *n* **-1.** [of house, room] décoration *f*; painting and ~ *Br* peinture *f* et décoration. **-2.** [of dress, hat] garnissage *m*, ornementation *f*; [of cake, tree, street] décoration *f*.

decoration [ˌdekəˈreɪʃn] *n* **-1.** [action - of house, street, cake, tree] décoration *f*; [- of dress, hat] ornementation *f*; interior ~ [action] décoration intérieure. **-2.** [ornament - for house, street, cake, tree] décoration *f*; [- for dress, hat] garniture *f*, ornements *mpl*; Christmas ~s décorations de Noël. **-3.** [medal] décoration *f*, médaille *f*.

Decoration Day *n fête nationale américaine en souvenir des soldats morts à la guerre; appelée aussi 'Memorial Day' (dernier lundi de mai)*.

decorative [ˈdekərətɪv] *adj* décoratif, ornemental.

decorator [ˈdekəreɪtəʳ] *n* décorateur *m*, -trice *f*; interior ~ décorateur *m*, -trice *f* d'intérieur; painter and ~ *Br* peintre-décorateur *m*, -trice *f*.

decorous [ˈdekərəs] *adj fml* [behaviour] bienséant, séant, convenable; [person] convenable, comme il faut.

decorously [ˈdekərəslɪ] *adv fml* [dressed] convenablement, comme il faut; to behave ~ se conduire convenablement OR comme il faut, respecter les convenances.

decorum [dɪˈkɔːrəm] *n* bienséance *f*, décorum *m*; to behave with ~ se comporter comme il faut OR avec bienséance; to have a sense of ~ avoir le sens des convenances; his sense of ~ was offended il a été choqué dans son sens des convenances.

decoy [*n* ˈdiːkɔɪ, *vb* dɪˈkɔɪ] ◇ *n* **-1.** [for catching birds - live bird] appeau *m*, chanterelle *f*; [- artificial device] leurre *m*. **-2.** *fig* [person] appât *m*; [message, tactic] piège *m*; we want you to act as a ~ nous voulons que vous serviez d'appât.
◇ *comp*: ~ duck [live] appeau *m*, chanterelle *f*; [wooden] leurre *m*.
◇ *vt* [bird - using live bird] attirer à l'appeau OR à la chanterelle; [- using artificial means] attirer au leurre; [person] appâter, attirer; they ~ed him into leaving his house ils l'ont appâté OR attiré hors de chez lui.

decrease [*vb* dɪˈkriːs, *n* ˈdiːkriːs] ◇ *vi* [number, enthusiasm, population, speed] décroître, diminuer; [value, price] diminuer, baisser; [in knitting] diminuer, faire des diminutions.
◇ *vt* réduire, diminuer; '~ speed now' 'ralentir'.
◇ *n* [in size] réduction *f*, diminution *f*; [in popularity] baisse *f*; ~ in price réduction OR baisse du prix; a ~ in numbers une baisse des effectifs; to be on the ~ être en diminution OR en baisse.

decreasing [diːˈkriːsɪŋ] *adj* [amount, energy, population] décroissant; [price, value, popularity] en baisse; in ~ order of importance par ordre d'importance décroissant; a ~ number of students are going into industry de moins en moins d'étudiants se dirigent vers l'industrie.

decreasingly [diːˈkriːsɪŋlɪ] *adv* de moins en moins.

decree [dɪˈkriː] ◇ *n* POL décret *m*, arrêté *m*; RELIG décret *m*; JUR jugement *m*, arrêt *m*; by royal ~ par décret du roi/de la reine; by presidential ~ par décret présidentiel; we have received a ~ from management that... *hum* la direction a décrété que...
◇ *vt* décréter; POL décréter, arrêter; RELIG décréter; JUR ordonner (par jugement).

decree absolute *n* JUR jugement *m* définitif (de divorce).

decree nisi [-ˈnaɪsaɪ] *n* JUR jugement *m* provisoire (de divorce).

decrepit [dɪˈkrepɪt] *adj* [building, furniture] délabré; [person, animal] décrépit.

decrepitude [dɪˈkrepɪtjuːd] *n* décrépitude *f*.

decriminalization [diːˌkrɪmɪnəlaɪˈzeɪʃn] *n* dépénalisation *f*.

decriminalize [diːˈkrɪmɪnəˌlaɪz] *vt* dépénaliser.

decry [dɪˈkraɪ] (*pt* & *pp* decried) *vt* décrier, dénigrer.

decrypt [diːˈkrɪpt] *vt* décrypter.

dedicate [ˈdedɪkeɪt] *vt* **-1.** [devote] consacrer; to ~ o.s. to sb/sthg se consacrer à qqn/qqch. **-2.** [book, record etc] dédier; to ~ sthg to sb dédier qqch à qqn. **-3.** [consecrate - church, shrine] consacrer.

dedicated [ˈdedɪkeɪtɪd] *adj* **-1.** [devoted] dévoué; to be ~ to one's work être dévoué à son travail; she is ~ to her family/to helping the poor elle se dévoue pour sa famille/pour aider les pauvres; she is a ~ teacher/doctor c'est un professeur/médecin dévoué à son travail; you've got to be ~ (to do this job) il faut pouvoir tout donner (pour faire ce travail); he is ~ il se donne à fond. **-2.** COMPUT dédié; ~ terminal terminal *m* dédié; ~ word processor machine *f* exclusivement destinée au traitement de texte.

dedication [ˌdedɪˈkeɪʃn] *n* **-1.** [devotion] dévouement *m*; his ~ to his job son dévouement à son travail; ~ is what is needed il est essentiel de pouvoir tout donner. **-2.** [in book, on photograph etc] dédicace *f*; I asked the author for a ~ j'ai demandé à l'auteur qu'il me dédicace mon livre, j'ai demandé une dédicace à l'auteur; I've got a few ~s to play [records] j'ai quelques dédicaces à passer. **-3.** [of church, shrine] consécration *f*.

deduce [dɪˈdjuːs] *vt* déduire; to ~ sthg from sthg déduire qqch de qqch; what do you ~ from that? qu'en déduisez-vous?; I ~d that she was lying j'en ai déduit qu'elle mentait.

deducible [dɪˈdjuːsəbl] *adj* qui peut se déduire.

deduct [dɪˈdʌkt] *vt* déduire, retrancher; [tax] prélever; to ~ £10 from the price déduire OR retrancher 10 livres du prix; to ~ 25% from a salary prélever 25 % d'un salaire; to be ~ed at source [tax] être prélevé à la source; after ~ing expenses après déduction des frais.

deductible [dɪˈdʌktəbl] *adj* déductible.

deduction [dɪˈdʌkʃn] *n* **-1.** [inference] déduction *f*; your ~ is correct vous avez fait une bonne déduction; by (a process of) ~ par déduction. **-2.** [subtraction] déduction *f*; how much is that after ~s? combien reste-t-il après déductions? ❑ tax ~s prélèvements *mpl* fiscaux.

deductive [dɪˈdʌktɪv] *adj* déductif.

deed [diːd] ◇ *n* **-1.** [action] action *f*; in word and ~ en parole et en fait OR action; brave ~ acte *m* de bravoure; to do one's good ~ for the day faire sa bonne action OR sa BA de la journée; we want ~s not words nous voulons du concret OR des actions, pas des discours. **-2.** JUR acte *m* notarié; ~ of covenant contrat *m*; mortgage ~ contrat *m* d'hypothèque; title ~ titre *m* de propriété.
◇ *vt Am* JUR transférer par acte notarié; the house was ~ed to his daughter la maison a été transférée à sa fille par acte notarié.

deed box *n* classeur *m* à documents.

deed poll *n* JUR contrat *m* unilatéral; to change one's name by ~ changer de nom par contrat unilatéral JUR, changer de nom officiellement.

deejay *inf* [ˈdiːdʒeɪ] *n* DJ *mf*.

deem [diːm] *vt fml* juger, considérer, estimer; it was ~ed necessary/advisable to call an enquiry on a jugé qu'il était nécessaire/opportun d'ordonner une enquête; if you ~ it necessary si vous le jugez nécessaire; he ~ed it a great honour il considéra cela comme un grand honneur, il estima que c'était un grand honneur; she was ~ed (to be) the rightful owner elle était considérée comme la propriétaire de droit.

de-emphasize [diːˈemfəsaɪz] *vt* [need, claim, feature] moins insister sur, se montrer moins insistant sur.

deep [diːp] ◇ *adj* **-1.** [going far down - water, hole, wound etc] profond; ~ snow lay round about une épaisse couche de neige recouvrait les alentours; the water/hole is 5 metres ~ l'eau/le trou a 5 mètres de profondeur; the road was a foot ~ in snow la route était sous OR recouverte de trente centimètres de neige; a hole ten feet ~ un trou de trois mètres de profondeur; the ~ blue sea le vaste océan; to be in a ~ sleep être profondément endormi; ~ in thought/study plongé dans ses pensées/l'étude; ~ in debt criblé de dettes; to get ~er and ~er into debt s'endetter de plus en plus; a ~ breath une inspiration profonde; take a ~ breath and just do it *fig* respire un bon coup et vas-y; ~ breathing [action, noise] respiration *f* profonde; [exercices] exercices *mpl* respiratoires; we're in ~ trouble nous sommes dans de sales draps; the ~ end [of swimming pool] le grand bain ❑ to plunge OR to jump in at the ~ end y aller carrément; to be in ~ water être dans le pétrin, avoir des problèmes; you're getting into ~ water tu vas te mettre dans le pétrin, tu vas avoir des problèmes; to go off the ~ end *inf* [lose one's temper] piquer une crise OR une colère; [panic] perdre tous ses moyens, paniquer à mort; to be thrown in at the ~ end *fig* être mis dans le bain tout de suite. **-2.** [going far back - forest, cupboard etc] profond; ~ in the forest au (fin) fond de la forêt; the crowd stood fifteen ~ la foule se tenait sur quinze rangées; a very ~ serve [in tennis] un service très profond; ~ in Buckinghamshire, in ~est Buckinghamshire *hum* dans le Buckinghamshire profond ❑ the Deep South [of the USA] le Sud profond; ~ space profondeurs *fpl* de l'espace. **-3.** [strong - feelings] profond; with ~est sympathy avec mes plus sincères condoléances. **-4.** [profound - thinker] profond. **-5.** [mysterious, difficult to understand - book] profond; a ~ mystery un mystère profond OR épais; a ~ dark secret un sinistre secret; he's a ~ one on ne peut jamais savoir ce qu'il pense. **-6.** [dark - colour] profond; ~ blue eyes des yeux d'un bleu profond; to be in ~ mourning être en grand deuil. **-7.** [low - sound, note] grave; [- voice] grave, profond.
◇ *adv* profondément; they went ~ into the forest ils se sont enfoncés dans la forêt; the snow lay ~ on the ground il y avait une épaisse couche de neige sur le sol; he dug (down) ~ into the ground il a creusé profond OR profondément dans la terre; he looked ~ into her eyes [romantically] il a plongé ses yeux dans les siens; [probingly] il l'a regardée intensément dans les yeux; the goalkeeper kicked the ball ~ into the opposition's half le gardien de but a shooté loin dans le camp adverse; to go OR to run ~ [emotions] être profond; ~ down she knew she was right au fond OR dans son for intérieur elle savait qu'elle avait raison; he thrust his hands ~ into his pockets il plongea les mains au fond de ses poches; ~ into the night tard dans la nuit; don't go in too ~ [in water] n'allez pas où c'est profond, n'allez pas trop loin; don't get in too ~ [involved] ne t'implique pas trop; she's in it pretty ~ *inf* elle est dedans jusqu'au cou.
◇ *n lit* **-1.** [ocean]: the ~ l'océan *m*. **-2.** [depth]: in the ~ of winter au plus profond OR au cœur de l'hiver.

-deep *in cpds*: she was knee/waist~ in water elle avait de l'eau jusqu'aux genoux/jusqu'à la taille; the water is only ankle~ l'eau ne monte OR n'arrive qu'aux chevilles; a ten-foot~ hole un trou de trois mètres de profondeur.

deepen [ˈdiːpn] ◇ *vt* [hole, river bed, knowledge] approfondir; [mystery] épaissir; [love, friendship] faire grandir, intensifier; [sound, voice] rendre

plus grave; [colour] rendre plus profond, intensifier.
◇ *vi* [sea, river] devenir plus profond; [silence, mystery] s'épaissir; [crisis] s'aggraver, s'intensifier; [knowledge] s'approfondir; [love, friendship] s'intensifier, grandir; [colour] devenir plus profond, s'intensifier; [sound] devenir plus grave.

deepening ['di:pnɪŋ] ◇ *adj* [silence, shadows, emotion] de plus en plus profond; [crisis] qui s'aggrave OR s'intensifie; [love, friendship] de plus en plus profond.
◇ *n* [of hole, channel] approfondissement *m*; [of silence, love] intensification *f*.

deep-fat fryer *n* friteuse *f*.

deep freeze *n* [in home, shop] congélateur *m*; [industrial] surgélateur *m*.
◆ **deep-freeze** *vt* [at home] congeler; [industrially] surgeler.

deep-fried *adj* frit.

deep-frozen *adj* [at home] congelé; [industrially] surgelé.

deep-fry *vt* faire frire.

deep-fryer = **deep-fat fryer**.

deep-heat treatment *n* MED thermothérapie *f*.

deep-laid *adj* [plan, scheme] secret, machiné dans le secret.

deeply ['di:plɪ] *adv* -**1.** [dig, breathe, sleep, admire, regret, think] profondément; [drink] à grands traits; **to fall ~ in love with sb** tomber profondément amoureux de qqn; **to go ~ into sthg** approfondir qqch. -**2.** [offended, relieved, grateful, religious] profondément, extrêmement; **his forehead was ~ lined** son front était creusé de rides profondes.

deepness ['di:pnɪs] *n* [of ocean, voice, writer, remark] profondeur *f*; [of note, sound] gravité *f*.

deep-rooted *adj* [tree] dont les racines sont profondes; *fig* [ideas, belief, prejudice] profondément ancré OR enraciné; [feeling] profond.

deep-sea *adj* [creatures, exploration] des grands fonds; **~ diver** plongeur *m* sous-marin, plongeuse *f* sous-marine; **~ diving** plongée *f* sous-marine; **~ fisherman** pêcheur *m* hauturier OR en haute mer; **~ fishing** pêche *f* hauturière OR en haute mer.

deep-seated [-'si:tɪd] *adj* [sorrow, dislike] profond; [idea, belief, complex, prejudice] profondément ancré OR enraciné.

deep-set *adj* enfoncé.

deep structure *n* LING structure *f* profonde.

deep-throated [-'θrəʊtɪd] *adj* [cough, laugh] caverneux.

deer [dɪəʳ] (*pl inv*) ◇ *n* cerf *m*, biche *f*; **a herd of ~** un troupeau OR une harde de cerfs ❑ **fallow ~** daim *m*; **red ~** cerf; **roe ~** chevreuil *m*.
◇ *comp* [hunter, park] de cerf OR cerfs; 'The Deer Hunter' *Cimino* 'Voyage au bout de l'enfer'.

deerhound ['dɪəhaʊnd] *n* limier *m*.

deerskin ['dɪəskɪn] *n* peau *f* de daim; **~ coat** manteau *m* en daim.

deerstalker ['dɪə,stɔ:kəʳ] *n* -**1.** [hunter] chasseur *m*, -euse *f* de cerf. -**2.** [hat] chapeau *m* à la Sherlock Holmes.

deerstalking ['dɪə,stɔ:kɪŋ] *n* chasse *f* au cerf.

de-escalate [,di:'eskəleɪt] ◇ *vt* [crisis] désamorcer; [tension] faire baisser.
◇ *vi* [crisis] se désamorcer; [tension] baisser.

de-escalation [,di:eskə'leɪʃn] *n* [of crisis] désescalade *f*, désamorçage *m*; [of tension] baisse *f*.

deface [dɪ'feɪs] *vt* [statue, painting - with paint, aerosol spray] barbouiller; [- by writing slogans] dégrader par des inscriptions; [book] abîmer OR endommager par des gribouillages OR des inscriptions.

de facto [deɪ'fæktəʊ] *adv* & *adj* de facto, de fait.

defalcation [,di:fæl'keɪʃn] *n* détournement *m* de fonds.

defamation [,defə'meɪʃn] *n* diffamation *f*; **to sue sb for ~ of character** poursuivre qqn en justice pour diffamation.

defamatory [dɪ'fæmətrɪ] *adj* diffamatoire.

defame [dɪ'feɪm] *vt* diffamer, calomnier.

default [dɪ'fɔ:lt] ◇ *n* -**1.** JUR [non-appearance - in civil court] défaut *m*, non-comparution *f*; [- in criminal court] contumace *f*; **judgement by ~** jugement *m* par défaut OR contumace. -**2.** *fml* [absence]: **in ~ of** à défaut de. -**3.** COMPUT sélection *f* par défaut; **drive C is the ~** C est l'unité de disque par défaut. -**4.** FIN défaut *m* de paiement, manquement *m* à payer.
◇ *comp* COMPUT [drive, font, setting] par défaut.
◇ *vi* -**1.** JUR manquer à comparaître, faire défaut. -**2.** FIN manquer OR faillir à ses engagements; **to ~ on a payment** ne pas honorer un paiement. -**3.** SPORT déclarer forfait. -**4.** COMPUT prendre une sélection par défaut; **the computer automatically ~s to drive C** l'ordinateur sélectionne l'unité de disque C par défaut.
◆ **by default** *adv phr* -**1.** [lack of action]: **you are responsible by ~** tu es responsable pour n'avoir rien fait. -**2.** SPORT par forfait; **to win/to lose by ~** gagner/perdre par forfait. -**3.** COMPUT par défaut.

defaulter [dɪ'fɔ:ltəʳ] *n* -**1.** JUR inculpé *m*, -e *f* contumace OR défaillant(e) OR par défaut, témoin *m* défaillant. -**2.** FIN & ST. EX débiteur *m* défaillant, débitrice *f* défaillante. -**3.** *Br* MIL & NAUT soldat *m* OR marin *m* qui a transgressé la discipline.

defaulting [dɪ'fɔ:ltɪŋ] *adj* JUR contumace, défaillant; FIN & ST. EX défaillant.

defeat [dɪ'fi:t] ◇ *n* [of army, opposition] défaite *f*; [of project, bill] échec *m*; **to suffer a ~** connaître une défaite, échouer; **to admit ~** s'avouer vaincu.
◇ *vt* [army, adversary] vaincre; [team, government] battre; [attempts, project, bill] faire échouer; **they were ~ed by one goal to nil** ils ont été battus par un but à zéro; **we were ~ed by the weather** nous avons échoué à cause du temps; **that ~s the object** ça n'avance à rien.

defeatism [dɪ'fi:tɪzm] *n* défaitisme *m*.

defeatist [dɪ'fi:tɪst] ◇ *adj* défaitiste.
◇ *n* défaitiste *mf*.

defecate ['defəkeɪt] *vi* déféquer.

defecation [,defə'keɪʃn] *n* défécation *f*.

defect [*n* 'di:fekt, *vb* dɪ'fekt] ◇ *n* défaut *m*; **physical ~** malformation *f*; **hearing/speech ~** défaut de l'ouïe/de prononciation.
◇ *vi* POL [to another country] quitter son pays pour un autre; [to another party] quitter son parti pour un autre; **to ~ to the West** passer à l'Ouest; **to ~ to the enemy** passer à l'ennemi; **yet another dissident has ~ed** un nouveau dissident est passé à l'étranger; **he ~ed from his native Poland** il s'est enfui de sa Pologne natale.

defection [dɪ'fekʃn] *n* [to another country] passage *m* à un pays ennemi; [to another party] passage *m* à un parti adverse; **there were many successful ~s by East Germans** beaucoup d'Allemands de l'Est ont réussi à passer à l'Ouest; **the country was shocked by his ~** le pays a été choqué quand il est passé à l'étranger; **after his ~ from his native Poland** après qu'il se fut enfui de sa Pologne natale.

defective [dɪ'fektɪv] ◇ *adj* -**1.** [machine, reasoning] défectueux; [hearing, sight, organ] déficient; **to be mentally ~** souffrir de débilité mentale. -**2.** GRAMM défectif.
◇ *n*: **mental ~** débile *m* mental, débile *f* mentale.

defector [dɪ'fektəʳ] *n* POL & *fig* transfuge *mf*.

defence *Br*, **defense** *Am* [dɪ'fens] ◇ *n* -**1.** [protection] défense *f*; **how much is spent on ~?** combien dépense-t-on pour la défense?; **to carry a weapon for ~** porter une arme pour se défendre; **to come to sb's ~** venir à la défense de qqn; **to act/to speak in ~ of sthg** [following attack] agir/parler en défense de qqch; [in support of] agir/parler en faveur de qqch; **to speak in ~ of sb, to speak in sb's ~** [following attack] parler en défense de qqn; [in support of] parler en faveur de qqn; **the best form of ~ is attack** la meilleure forme de défense, c'est l'attaque ❑ **Ministry of Defence** *Br*, **Department of Defense** *Am* ≃ ministère *m* de la Défense; **Secretary of State for Defence** *Br*, **Secretary of Defense** *Am* ≃ ministre *m* de la Défense. -**2.** [thing providing protection] protection *f*, défense *f*; [argument] défense *f*; **~s** [weapons] moyens *mpl* de défense; [fortifications] défenses, fortifications *fpl*; **to use sthg as a ~ against sthg** se servir de qqch comme défense OR protection contre qqch, se servir de qqch pour se défendre OR se protéger de qqch; **the body's natural ~s against infection** les défenses naturelles de l'organisme contre l'infection; **to put up a stubborn ~** se défendre avec entêtement; **to catch sb when his/her ~s are down** prendre qqn quand il/elle n'est pas en position de se défendre OR de faire face; **to draw up a ~ of sthg** préparer la défense de qqch. -**3.** JUR défense *f*; **the ~** [lawyers] la défense; **who have we got for the ~?** qui assurera la défense?; **counsel for the ~** avocat *m* de la défense; **witness for the ~** témoin *m* à décharge, témoin de la défense; **to appear for the ~** comparaître pour la défense; **the case for the ~** la défense; **what is our ~ going to be?** quelle ligne de défense allons-nous adopter?; **to conduct one's own ~** assurer sa propre défense; **do you have anything to say in your ~?** avez-vous quelque chose à dire pour votre défense?; **it must be said in her ~ that...** il faut dire à sa décharge OR pour sa défense que... -**4.** SPORT défense *f*; **the ~** [players] la défense; **to turn ~ into attack** faire OR lancer une contre-attaque.
◇ *comp* -**1.** MIL [forces] de défense; [cuts, minister, spending] de la défense. -**2.** JUR [lawyer] de la défense; [witness] à décharge.

defenceless *Br*, **defenseless** *Am* [dɪ'fenslɪs] *adj* sans défense, vulnérable.

defencelessness *Br*, **defenselessness** *Am* [dɪ'fenslɪsnɪs] *n* vulnérabilité *f*.

defence mechanism *n* mécanisme *m* de défense.

defend [dɪ'fend] *vt* -**1.** [protect] défendre; [justify] justifier; **to ~ sthg/sb from** OR **against attack** défendre qqch/qqn contre une attaque; **to ~ o.s.** se défendre. -**2.** SPORT [goalmouth, title] défendre. -**3.** JUR défendre.

defendant [dɪ'fendənt] *n* JUR [in civil court] défendeur *m*, -eresse *f*; [in criminal court] inculpé *m*, -e *f*; [accused of serious crimes] accusé *m*, -e *f*.

defender [dɪ'fendəʳ] *n* -**1.** [of a cause, rights etc] défenseur *m*, avocat *m*, -e *f*; **Defender of the Faith** Défenseur de la foi. -**2.** SPORT [player] défenseur *m*; [of title, record] détenteur *m*, -trice *f*. -**3.** *Am* JUR: **public ~** avocat *m* commis d'office.

defending [dɪ'fendɪŋ] *adj* -**1.** SPORT [champion] en titre. -**2.** JUR de la défense.

defenestration [,di:fenɪ'streɪʃn] *n* défenestration *f*.

defense *etc Am* = **defence**.

defensible [dɪ'fensəbl] *adj* [idea, opinion etc] défendable.

defensive [dɪ'fensɪv] ◇ *adj* [strategy, weapon etc] défensif; **they're playing a very ~ game** SPORT ils ont un jeu très défensif; **to get ~** se mettre sur la défensive; **she's very ~ about it** elle est très susceptible quand on parle de cela; **why be so ~ about it?** pourquoi te mets-tu ainsi sur la défensive?
◇ *n* MIL & *fig* défensive *f*; **to be on the ~** être OR se tenir sur la défensive; **to go on the ~** se mettre sur la défensive.

defensively [dɪ'fensɪvlɪ] *adv*: **they played very ~** SPORT ils ont eu un jeu très défensif; **used ~** MIL utilisé pour la défense; **"it's not my fault", she said, ~** «ce n'est pas de ma faute», dit-elle, sur la défensive.

defensiveness [dɪ'fensɪvnɪs] *n*: **I get really tired of his ~** j'en ai vraiment assez qu'il soit toujours sur la défensive.

defer [dɪ'fɜ:ʳ] (*pt* & *pp* deferred, *cont* deferring)
◇ *vt* [decision, meeting] remettre, reporter; [payment, business, judgment] différer, retarder; **to ~ sentencing** JUR suspendre le prononcé du juge-

ment; to ~ sb on medical grounds MIL réformer qqn temporairement pour raisons médicales.

◇ *vi* [give way]: to ~ to sb s'en remettre à qqn; to ~ to sb's judgment/knowledge s'en remettre au jugement/aux connaissances de qqn; to ~ to sb's wishes agir conformément aux souhaits de qqn, se soumettre à la volonté de qqn.

deference ['defərəns] *n* déférence *f*, égard *m*, considération *f*; out of OR in ~ to sb/sb's wishes par égard OR considération pour qqn/les souhaits de qqn; to treat sb with ~, to pay OR to show ~ to sb traiter qqn avec déférence OR égards.

deferential [,defə'renʃl] *adj* déférent, révérencieux; to be ~ to sb faire montre de déférence OR d'égards envers qqn.

deferentially [,defə'renʃəlɪ] *adv* avec déférence.

deferment [dɪ'fɜːmənt], **deferral** [dɪ'fɜːrəl] *n* [of decision, meeting, payment, sentence] report *m*, ajournement *m*; to apply for ~ MIL demander à être réformé.

deferred [dɪ'fɜːd] *adj* [gen] ajourné, retardé; [payment, shares] différé; [annuity] à paiement différé, à jouissance différée; ~ sentence JUR jugement *m* dont le prononcé est suspendu, jugement ajourné; ~ pay rappel *m* de traitement.

defiance [dɪ'faɪəns] *n* défi *m*; I will not tolerate any further ~ je ne tolérerai plus qu'on me défie ainsi; your ~ of my orders meant that people's lives were put at risk en défiant mes ordres vous avez mis la vie d'autrui en danger; gesture/act of ~ geste *m*/acte *m* de défi.

◆ **in defiance of** *prep phr*: in ~ of sb/sthg au mépris de qqn/qqch.

defiant [dɪ'faɪənt] *adj* [gesture, remark, look] de défi; [person, reply] provocateur.

defiantly [dɪ'faɪəntlɪ] *adv* [act] avec une attitude de défi; [reply, look at] d'un air de défi.

defibrillation [diː,faɪbrɪ'leɪʃn] *n* MED défibrillation *f*.

defibrillator [,diː'faɪbrɪleɪtəʳ] *n* MED défibrillateur *m*.

deficiency [dɪ'fɪʃnsɪ] (*pl* deficiencies) *n* -**1.** MED [shortage] carence *f*; a ~ in OR of calcium, a calcium ~ une carence en calcium; mental ~ déficience *f* mentale. -**2.** [flaw - in character, system] défaut *m*.

deficiency disease *n* maladie *f* de carence.

deficient [dɪ'fɪʃnt] *adj* -**1.** [insufficient] insuffisant; to be ~ in sthg manquer de qqch. -**2.** [defective] défectueux; to be mentally ~ avoir une déficience mentale.

deficit ['defɪsɪt] *n* FIN & COMM déficit *m*; to be in ~ être en déficit, être déficitaire; budget ~ déficit budgétaire; the balance of payments shows a ~ of £800 million la balance des paiements indique un déficit de 800 millions de livres.

defile [*vb* dɪ'faɪl, *n* 'diːfaɪl] ◇ *vt* [grave, memory] profaner.

◇ *vi* MIL défiler.

◇ *n* [valley, passage] défilé *m*.

defilement [dɪ'faɪlmənt] *n* [of grave, memory] profanation *f*.

definable [dɪ'faɪnəbl] *adj* définissable.

define [dɪ'faɪn] *vt* -**1.** [term, word] définir; [boundary, role, subject] définir, délimiter; [concept, idea, feeling] définir, préciser; he ~s politics as being the art of the possible il définit la politique comme l'art du possible. -**2.** [object, shape] définir; the figures in the painting are not clearly ~d les formes humaines du tableau ne sont pas bien définies.

defining [dɪ'faɪnɪŋ] *adj* restrictif.

definite ['defɪnɪt] *adj* -**1.** [precise, clear] précis; [advantage, answer, opinion] net; [orders, proof] formel; [price] fixe; there's been a ~ improvement in his work il y a eu une très nette amélioration dans son travail; their plans to marry are still not ~ leurs projets de mariage sont encore vagues; the boss was very ~ about the need for punctuality le patron a été très ferme en ce qui concerne la ponctualité. -**2.** [certain] certain, sûr; is it ~ that the Pope is coming to England? est-il certain OR sûr que le pape vienne en Angleterre?; I've heard rumours of a merger, but nothing ~ j'ai entendu dire qu'il allait y avoir une fusion, mais rien de sûr pour l'instant. -**3.** MATH: ~ integral intégrale *f* définie.

definite article *n* article *m* défini.

definitely ['defɪnɪtlɪ] *adv* certainement, sans aucun doute; he has ~ decided to resign il ne fait aucun doute qu'il a décidé de démissionner; she's ~ leaving, but I don't know when je sais qu'elle part, mais je ne sais pas quand; are you ~ giving up your flat? allez-vous vraiment quitter votre appartement?; that's ~ not the man I saw je suis sûr que ce n'est pas l'homme que j'ai vu; are you going to the show? — ~! est-ce que tu vas au spectacle? — absolument!

definition [defɪ'nɪʃn] *n* -**1.** [of term, word] définition *f*; [of duties, territory] définition, délimitation *f*; by ~ par définition. -**2.** [of photograph, sound] netteté *f*; TV définition *f*.

definitive [dɪ'fɪnɪtɪv] *adj* -**1.** [conclusive] définitif; [battle, victory] définitif, décisif; [result] définitif, qui fait autorité. -**2.** [authoritative]: the ~ book on the subject le livre qui fait autorité OR décisif en la matière. -**3.** ZOOL [fully developed] définitif.

definitively [dɪ'fɪnɪtɪvlɪ] *adv* définitivement.

deflate [dɪ'fleɪt] ◇ *vt* -**1.** [balloon, tyre] dégonfler; *fig* [person] démonter. -**2.** ECON [prices] faire baisser, faire tomber; the measure is intended to ~ the economy cette mesure est destinée à faire de la déflation.

◇ *vi* [balloon, tyre] se dégonfler.

deflation [dɪ'fleɪʃn] *n* -**1.** [of balloon, tyre] dégonflement *m*. -**2.** ECON & GEOG déflation *f*. -**3.** [anticlimax] abattement *m*.

deflationary [dɪ'fleɪʃnərɪ] *adj* déflationniste.

deflect [dɪ'flekt] ◇ *vt* faire dévier; *fig* [attention, criticism] détourner; he would not be ~ed from his purpose rien ne l'aurait détourné de son but.

◇ *vi* dévier; [magnetic needle] décliner.

deflection [dɪ'flekʃn] *n* déviation *f*; [of magnetic needle] déclinaison *f*; PHYS déflexion *f*.

deflector [dɪ'flektəʳ] *n* déflecteur *m*.

defloration [,diːflɔː'reɪʃn] *n* défloration *f*.

deflower [,diː'flaʊəʳ] *vt* -**1.** *lit* [woman] déflorer. -**2.** BOT défleurir.

defoliant [,diː'fəʊlɪənt] *n* défoliant *m*.

defoliate [,diː'fəʊlɪeɪt] *vt* défolier.

defoliation [,diːfəʊlɪ'eɪʃn] *n* défoliation *f*.

deforest [,diː'fɒrɪst] *vt* déboiser.

deforestation [diː,fɒrɪ'steɪʃn] *n* déboisement *m*, déforestation *f*.

deform [diː'fɔːm] *vt* déformer; *fig* [distort, ruin] défigurer.

deformation [,diːfɔː'meɪʃn] *n* déformation *f*.

deformed [dɪ'fɔːmd] *adj* difforme.

deformity [dɪ'fɔːmətɪ] *n* difformité *f*.

defraud [dɪ'frɔːd] *vt* [the state] frauder; [company, person] escroquer, frustrer *spec*; he ~ed the government of £15,000 in unemployment benefits il a frauduleusement perçu 15 000 livres d'allocations chômage.

defrauder [dɪ'frɔːdəʳ] *n* fraudeur *m*, -euse *f*.

defray [dɪ'freɪ] *vt fml* rembourser, prendre en charge; all charges to be ~ed by the purchaser COMM tous les frais sont à la charge de l'acheteur; we will ~ the cost of your air fare nous vous rembourserons le prix de votre billet d'avion.

defrock [,diː'frɒk] *vt* défroquer.

defrost [,diː'frɒst] ◇ *vt* -**1.** [food] décongeler; [refrigerator] dégivrer. -**2.** *Am* [demist] désembuer; [de-ice] dégivrer.

◇ *vi* [food] se décongeler; [refrigerator] se dégivrer.

defroster [,diː'frɒstəʳ] *n* dégivreur *m*.

deft [deft] *adj* adroit, habile; [fingers] habile.

deftly ['deftlɪ] *adv* adroitement, habilement.

deftness ['deftnɪs] *n* adresse *f*, habileté *f*.

defunct [dɪ'fʌŋkt] *adj* défunt.

defuse [,diː'fjuːz] *vt literal* & *fig* désamorcer.

defy [dɪ'faɪ] (*pt* & *pp* defied) *vt* -**1.** [disobey] s'opposer à; [law, rule] braver; the union defied the court order le syndicat n'a pas tenu compte de la décision judiciaire. -**2.** [challenge, dare] défier; she defied him to justify his claims elle l'a défié OR mis au défi de justifier ses revendications; a death-~ing feat un exploit téméraire. -**3.** *fig* [make impossible] défier; his behaviour defies explanation son comportement défie toute explication.

degas [,diː'gæs] (*pt* & *pp* degassed OR degased, *cont* degassing OR degasing) *vt* dégazer.

degeneracy [dɪ'dʒenərəsɪ] *n* [process] dégénérescence *f*; [state] décadence *f*, corruption *f*.

degenerate [*vb* dɪ'dʒenəreɪt, *adj* & *n* dɪ'dʒenərət] ◇ *vi* dégénérer; the discussion ~d into an argument *fig* la discussion dégénéra en dispute.

◇ *adj lit* dégénéré; [person] dépravé.

◇ *n lit* [person] dépravé *m*, -e *f*.

degeneration [dɪ,dʒenə'reɪʃn] *n* [process, state] dégénérescence *f*.

degenerative [dɪ'dʒenərətɪv] *adj* dégénératif.

degradable [dɪ'greɪdəbl] *adj* dégradable.

degradation [,degrə'deɪʃn] *n* -**1.** [deterioration] dégradation *f*; ECOL dégradation *f*. -**2.** [corruption, debasement] avilissement *m*, dégradation *f*; [poverty] misère *f* abjecte.

degrade [dɪ'greɪd] *vt* -**1.** [deteriorate] dégrader. -**2.** [debase] avilir, dégrader; I refuse to ~ myself (by) playing these silly games je refuse de m'abaisser à ces jeux idiots.

degrading [dɪ'greɪdɪŋ] *adj* avilissant, dégradant.

degrease [,diː'griːs] *vt* dégraisser.

degree [dɪ'griː] *n* -**1.** [unit of measurement] degré *m*; the temperature is 28 ~s in New York la température est de 28 degrés à New York; he had to work in 32 ~s of heat il a dû travailler par une chaleur de 32 degrés; it's three ~s outside il fait trois degrés dehors; Paris is about two ~s east of Greenwich GEOG Paris est environ à deux degrés de longitude est de Greenwich; a 90 ~ angle GEOM un angle de 90 degrés. -**2.** [extent, amount]: there was a certain ~ of mistrust between them il y avait un certain degré de méfiance entre eux; the Prime Minister does accept criticism to a ~ le Premier ministre accepte les critiques, mais jusqu'à un certain point; there are varying ~s of opposition to the new law il y a une opposition plus ou moins forte à la nouvelle loi; his allergy affected him to such a ~ that he had to stop working son allergie était un tel handicap pour lui qu'il a dû s'arrêter de travailler. -**3.** [stage, step] degré *m*; an honour of the highest ~ un honneur du plus haut degré; his calculations have reached a ~ of precision never before thought possible ses calculs ont atteint un niveau de précision jusqu'à présent considéré comme inaccessible. -**4.** [academic qualification] diplôme *m* universitaire; she has a ~ in economics elle est diplômée en sciences économiques; he's taking OR doing a ~ in biology il fait une licence de biologie; it took me five years to get my ~ j'ai mis cinq ans pour avoir mon diplôme. -**5.** GRAMM & MUS degré *m*. -**6.** *arch* OR *lit* [rank, status] rang *m*; a man of high ~ un homme de haut rang. -**7.** *Am* JUR: murder in the first ~ ≃ meurtre *m* commis avec préméditation.

◆ **by degrees** *adv phr* par degrés, au fur et à mesure; he realized, by ~s, that his wife no longer loved him petit à petit il s'est rendu compte que sa femme ne l'aimait plus.

-degree *in cpds*: first/second/third~ burns brûlures *fpl* au premier/deuxième/troisième degré; first~ murder *Am* JUR ≃ meurtre *m* commis avec préméditation.

degression [dɪ'greʃn] *n* dégression *f*.

degressive [dɪ'gresɪv] *adj* dégressif.

dehumanization [diːˌhjuːmənaɪ'zeɪʃn] *n* déshumanisation *f.*

dehumanize, -ise [diː'hjuːmənaɪz] *vt* déshumaniser.

dehumidifier [ˌdiːhjuː'mɪdɪfaɪəʳ] *n* déshumidificateur *m.*

dehumidify [ˌdiːhjuː'mɪdɪfaɪ] *vt* déshumidifier.

dehydrate [ˌdiːhaɪ'dreɪt] *vt* déshydrater.

dehydration [ˌdiːhaɪ'dreɪʃn] *n* déshydratation *f.*

de-ice [diː'aɪs] *vt* dégivrer.

de-icer [diː'aɪsəʳ] *n* dégivreur *m.*

de-icing [diː'aɪsɪŋ] *n* dégivrage *m.*

deictic ['daɪktɪk] *adj* déictique.

deification [ˌdiːɪfɪ'keɪʃn] *n* déification *f.*

deify ['diːɪfaɪ] *vt* déifier.

deign [deɪn] *vt* daigner; **he didn't ~ to reply** *fml* OR *hum* il n'a pas daigné répondre.

deindex [ˌdiː'ɪndeks] *vt*: **to ~ wages** supprimer l'indexation des salaires.

deindustrialization, -isation [ˈdiːɪnˌdʌstrɪəlaɪ'zeɪʃn] *n* désindustrialisation *f.*

deionizer, -iser [ˌdiːaɪən'aɪzəʳ] *n* dispositif *m* de désionisation.

deism ['diːɪzm] *n* déisme *m.*

deist ['diːɪst] *n* déiste *mf.*

deity ['diːɪtɪ] (*pl* **deities**) *n* **-1.** MYTH dieu *m*, déesse *f*, divinité *f.* **-2.** RELIG: **the Deity** Dieu *m*, la Divinité.

deixis ['daɪksɪs] *n* déixis *f.*

déjà vu [ˌdeʒɑː'vjuː] *n* déjà-vu *m inv*; **to have a feeling of ~** avoir une impression de déjà-vu.

dejected [dɪ'dʒektɪd] *adj* abattu, découragé; **he looked sad and ~** il avait l'air triste et abattu; **the ~ loser left the court** le perdant quitta le court d'un air abattu.

dejectedly [dɪ'dʒektɪdlɪ] *adv* [speak] d'un ton abattu; [look] d'un air abattu.

dejection [dɪ'dʒekʃn] *n* abattement *m*, découragement *m.*

de jure [deɪ'dʒʊəreɪ] *adv* de jure, en droit.

dekko▽ ['dekəʊ] (*pl* **dekkos**) *n Br*: **to have** OR **to take a ~ at sthg** jeter un coup d' œil OR un œil à qqch.

Del (*written abbr of* **delete**) [on keyboard] Suppr.

Del. *written abbr of* **Delaware.**

Delaware ['deləweəʳ] *pr n* Delaware *m*; **in ~** dans le Delaware.

delay [dɪ'leɪ] ◇ *vt* **-1.** [cause to be late] retarder; [person] retarder, retenir; **the flight was ~ed (for) three hours** le vol a été retardé de trois heures. **-2.** [postpone, defer] reporter, remettre; **she ~ed handing in her resignation** elle a tardé à donner sa démission; **the publication of the book has been ~ed** la publication du livre a été différée OR reportée; **the poison had a ~ed effect** le poison a agi avec retard; **he had a ~ed reaction to the news of his mother's death** il a mis un certain temps à réagir à la nouvelle de la mort de sa mère.

◇ *vi* tarder; **don't ~, write off today for your free sample** demandez aujourd'hui même votre échantillon gratuit.

◇ *n* **-1.** [lateness] retard *m*; **there are long ~s on the M25** *Br* la circulation est très ralentie OR est très perturbée sur la M25; **there's a 3 to 4 hour ~ on all international flights** il y a 3 à 4 heures de retard sur tous les vols internationaux. **-2.** [waiting period] : **without ~** sans tarder OR délai; **the defence lawyer requested a ~ in the hearing** l'avocat de la défense demanda un report de (la) séance; **there's no time for ~** il n'y a pas de temps à perdre.

delayed-action [dɪ'leɪd-] *adj* [fuse, shutter] à retardement.

delaying [dɪ'leɪɪŋ] *adj* dilatoire; **~ tactics** OR **action** manœuvres *fpl* dilatoires.

delectable [dɪ'lektəbl] *adj* délectable.

delectation [ˌdiːlek'teɪʃn] *n lit* OR *hum* délectation *f*; **for your ~** pour votre plus grand plaisir.

delegate [*n* 'delɪgət, *vb* 'delɪgeɪt] ◇ *n* délégué *m*, -e *f.*

◇ *vt* déléguer; **the parents ~d Mrs Parker to represent them at the meeting** les parents déléguèrent OR designèrent Mme Parker pour les représenter à la réunion.

◇ *vi* déléguer.

delegation [ˌdelɪ'geɪʃn] *n* **-1.** [group of delegates] délégation *f.* **-2.** [of duties, power] délégation *f.*

delete [dɪ'liːt] *vt* supprimer; [erase] effacer; [cross out] barrer, biffer.

deleterious [ˌdelɪ'tɪərɪəs] *adj fml* [effect] nuisible; [influence, substance] nuisible, délétère.

deletion [dɪ'liːʃn] *n* suppression *f*; **the editor circled certain words for ~** l'éditeur a entouré certains mots à supprimer; **I made a lot of ~s in the text** j'ai supprimé beaucoup de choses OR j'ai fait beaucoup de coupes dans le texte.

delft [delft] *n* faïence *f* (de Delft).

Delhi ['delɪ] *pr n* Delhi.

deli *inf* ['delɪ] *n abbr of* **delicatessen.**

deliberate [*adj* dɪ'lɪbərət, *vb* dɪ'lɪbəreɪt] ◇ *adj* **-1.** [intentional] délibéré, volontaire, voulu; **the reporter's question was a ~ attempt to embarrass the minister** la question du journaliste visait délibérément à embarrasser le ministre. **-2.** [unhurried, careful] mesuré, posé; **her speech was slow and ~** elle parlait lentement et posément.

◇ *vi* délibérer; **the committee will ~ on** OR **upon the appointment** le comité va délibérer sur la nomination; **they ~d whether or not to expel him** ils ont délibéré pour savoir s'ils allaient l'expulser.

◇ *vt* délibérer sur.

deliberately [dɪ'lɪbərətlɪ] *adv* **-1.** [intentionally] volontairement; **I didn't hurt him ~** je n'ai pas fait exprès de le blesser; **you have ~ lied to the court** vous avez menti délibérément OR sciemment à la cour. **-2.** [carefully] de façon mesurée, avec mesure; [walk] d'un pas ferme.

deliberation [dɪˌlɪbə'reɪʃn] *n* **-1.** [consideration, reflection] délibération *f*, réflexion *f*; **after much ~ we have decided to accept your application** après délibération OR mûre réflexion, nous avons décidé d'accepter votre demande. **-2.** [care, caution] attention *f*, soin *m.*

◆ **deliberations** *npl* délibérations *fpl.*

deliberative [dɪ'lɪbərətɪv] *adj* **-1.** [group, body] délibérant; **a ~ assembly** une assemblée délibérante. **-2.** [conclusion] mûrement réfléchi.

delicacy ['delɪkəsɪ] (*pl* **delicacies**) *n* **-1.** [refinement] délicatesse *f*, finesse *f*; [fragility, frailty] délicatesse *f*, fragilité *f*; [difficulty] délicatesse *f*; [tact] délicatesse *f*; **it's a matter of great ~** c'est une affaire très délicate; **the question must be handled with ~** la question doit être traitée avec délicatesse. **-2.** [fine food] mets *m* délicat; **it's considered a great ~ in China** c'est considéré comme un mets très délicat OR fin en Chine.

delicate ['delɪkət] *adj* **-1.** [fingers, lace, china] délicat, fin. **-2.** [child, health] délicat, fragile. **-3.** [situation, question] délicat, difficile; **a ~ international situation** une situation internationale délicate. **-4.** [smell, colour] délicat. **-5.** [instrument] délicat, sensible.

delicately ['delɪkətlɪ] *adv* délicatement, avec délicatesse.

delicatessen [ˌdelɪkə'tesn] *n* **-1.** *Br* [fine foods shop] épicerie fine *f.* **-2.** *Am* [food shop] ≃ traiteur *m*; [restaurant] ≃ restaurant *m.*

delicious [dɪ'lɪʃəs] *adj* délicieux.

deliciously [dɪ'lɪʃəslɪ] *adv* délicieusement.

delict ['diːlɪkt] *n* JUR délit *m.*

delight [dɪ'laɪt] ◇ *vi*: **he ~s in publicity** il adore faire parler de lui; **she ~s in irritating people** elle prend plaisir OR se complaît à énerver les gens; **she ~s in her grandchildren** elle adore ses petits-enfants.

◇ *vt* ravir, réjouir; **her show has ~ed audiences everywhere** son spectacle a partout conquis OR ravi le public.

◇ *n* [pleasure] joie *f*, (grand) plaisir *m*; **she listened with ~** elle écoutait avec délectation; **to the ~ of the audience she joined in the singing** à la plus grande joie OR pour le plus grand plaisir de l'auditoire elle se joignit à ceux qui chantaient; **her brother took (great) ~ in teasing her** son frère prenait (un malin) plaisir à la taquiner; **the ~s of gardening** les charmes *mpl* OR délices *fpl* du jardinage; **the child was a ~ to teach** c'était un plaisir d'enseigner à cet enfant; **the film was sheer ~** le film était une pure merveille.

delighted [dɪ'laɪtɪd] *adj* ravi; **I'm ~ to see you again** je suis ravi de vous revoir; **we are ~ that you were able to accept our invitation** nous sommes ravis que vous ayez pu accepter notre invitation; **a ~ smile** un sourire ravi; **I was ~ at the news** la nouvelle m'a fait très plaisir; **they're ~ with their new home** ils sont ravis de leur nouvelle maison; **could you come to dinner on Saturday? – I'd be ~** pourriez-vous venir dîner samedi? – avec (grand) plaisir.

delightedly [dɪ'laɪtɪdlɪ] *adv* avec joie, joyeusement.

delightful [dɪ'laɪtfʊl] *adj* [person, place] charmant; [book, experience, film] merveilleux; **the garden was simply ~** le jardin était tout simplement merveilleux; **this rose has a ~ perfume** cette rose a un parfum délicieux; **she looked ~ in her new dress** sa nouvelle robe lui allait à ravir.

delightfully [dɪ'laɪtfʊlɪ] *adv* [dance, perform, sing] merveilleusement, à ravir; **the evenings were ~ cool** les soirées étaient merveilleusement fraîches; **he was ~ unpretentious** il était merveilleusement simple.

Delilah [dɪ'laɪlə] *pr n* Dalila.

delimit [diː'lɪmɪt] *vt fml* délimiter.

delimitation [diːˌlɪmɪ'teɪʃn] *n* délimitation *f.*

delineate [dɪ'lɪnɪeɪt] *vt fml* **-1.** [outline, sketch] tracer. **-2.** *fig* [define, describe] définir, décrire.

delineation [dɪˌlɪnɪ'eɪʃn] *n* **-1.** [sketch] tracé *m.* **-2.** [definition] définition *f*, description *f.*

delinquency [dɪ'lɪŋkwənsɪ] (*pl* **delinquencies**) *n* **-1.** [criminal behaviour] délinquance *f.* **-2.** [negligence] faute *f.*

delinquent [dɪ'lɪŋkwənt] ◇ *adj* **-1.** [lawbreaking] délinquant; [negligent] fautif. **-2.** FIN [overdue] impayé.

◇ *n* **-1.** [law-breaker] délinquant *m*, -e *f.* **-2.** [bad debtor] mauvais payeur *m.*

deliquescence [ˌdelɪ'kwesəns] *n* déliquescence *f.*

deliquescent [ˌdelɪ'kwesənt] *adj* déliquescent.

delirious [dɪ'lɪrɪəs] *adj* **-1.** MED en délire; **the fever made him ~** la fièvre l'a fait délirer; **the patient became ~** le patient s'est mis à délirer OR a été pris de délire. **-2.** *fig* [excited, wild] délirant, en délire; **he was ~ with joy** il était délirant de joie.

deliriously [dɪ'lɪrɪəslɪ] *adv* de façon délirante, frénétiquement; **they were ~ happy together** ils étaient follement heureux ensemble.

delirium [dɪ'lɪrɪəm] *n* **-1.** MED délire *m.* **-2.** *fig* [state of excitement] délire *m.*

delirium tremens [-'triːmenz] *n* delirium tremens *m.*

delish *inf* [dɪ'lɪʃ] (*abbr of* **delicious**) *adj* extra *inv.*

deliver [dɪ'lɪvəʳ] ◇ *vt* **-1.** [carry, transport] remettre; COMM livrer; **what time is the post** OR **mail ~ed?** le courrier est distribué à quelle heure?; **I ~ed the books to the library** j'ai remis les livres à la bibliothèque; **the train ~ed us safely home** nous sommes rentrés en train sans problème ❑ **can he ~ the goods?** *inf* est-ce qu'il peut tenir parole? **-2.** *fml* OR *lit* [save, rescue] délivrer; **~ us from evil** BIBLE délivre-nous du mal. **-3.** MED: **to ~ a baby** faire un accouchement; **she was ~ed of a daughter** *fml* OR *lit* elle accoucha d'une fille; **he ~ed the mare of her foal** il aida la jument à mettre bas. **-4.** [pronounce, utter] : **to ~ a sermon/speech** prononcer un sermon/discours; **to ~ o.s. of an opinion** *fml* faire part de OR émettre son opinion; **the jury ~ed a verdict of not guilty** JUR le jury a rendu un verdict de non-culpabilité. **-5.** *Am* POL: **can he ~ the Black vote?** est-ce

qu'il peut nous assurer les voix des Noirs? -**6.** [strike]: to ~ a blow (to the head/stomach) porter OR *lit* asséner un coup (à la tête/à l'estomac).
◇ *vi* -**1.** [make delivery] livrer. -**2.** *inf* [do as promised] tenir parole, tenir bon.
◆ **deliver over** *vt sep* remettre; he ~ed himself over to the police il s'est livré OR rendu à la police.
◆ **deliver up** *vt sep* [fugitive, town] livrer.

deliverance [dɪ'lɪvərəns] *n* -**1.** *fml* OR *lit* [release, rescue] délivrance *f*. -**2.** [pronouncement] déclaration *f*; JUR prononcé *m*.

deliverer [dɪ'lɪvərəʳ] *n* -**1.** *fml* OR *lit* [saviour] sauveur *m*. -**2.** COMM livreur *m*.

delivery [dɪ'lɪvərɪ] (*pl* **deliveries**) ◇ *n* -**1.** COMM livraison *f*; post OR mail deliveries are rather irregular la distribution du courrier est assez irrégulière; to take ~ of sthg prendre livraison de qqch; 'allow two weeks for ~' 'délai de livraison: deux semaines'; payment on ~ règlement *m* OR paiement *m* à la livraison. -**2.** [transfer, handing over] remise *f*; I was entrusted with (the) ~ of the documents on m'a confié la remise des documents. -**3.** MED accouchement *m*. -**4.** [manner of speaking] débit *m*, élocution *f*. -**5.** *fml* OR *lit* [release, rescue] délivrance *f*.
◇ *comp* -**1.** COMM [note, truck, van] de livraison. -**2.** MED: the ~ room la salle de travail OR d'accouchement.

deliveryman [dɪ'lɪvərɪmæn] (*pl* **deliverymen** [-men]) *n* livreur *m*.

dell [del] *n* vallon *m*.

Delos ['di:lɒs] *pr n* Délos; in ~ à Délos.

delouse [,di:'laʊs] *vt* [animal, person] épouiller; [clothing, furniture] enlever les poux de.

Delphi ['delfaɪ] *pr n* Delphes; at ~ à Delphes.

Delphic ['delfɪk] *adj* delphique, de Delphes; *fig* [obscure] obscur.

delphinium [del'fɪnɪəm] (*pl* **delphiniums** OR **delphinia** [-nɪə]) *n* delphinium *m*.

delta ['deltə] ◇ *n* delta *m*.
◇ *comp* en delta.

delta ray *n* rayon *m* delta.

delta wing *n* aile *f* (en) delta.

deltoid ['deltɔɪd] ◇ *n* deltoïde *m*.
◇ *adj* deltoïde.

delude [dɪ'lu:d] *vt* tromper, duper; he ~d investors into thinking that the company was doing well il a fait croire aux investisseurs que la société se portait bien; he's deluding himself if he thinks his wife will forgive him il se fait des illusions OR il se leurre s'il pense que sa femme va lui pardonner; let's not ~ ourselves about his motives ne nous leurrons pas sur ses motivations.

deluded [dɪ'lu:dɪd] *adj* -**1.** [mistaken, foolish]: a poor ~ young man un pauvre jeune homme qu'on a trompé OR induit en erreur. -**2.** PSYCH sujet à des délires.

deluge ['delju:dʒ] ◇ *n literal* & *fig* déluge *m*.
◇ *vt* inonder; we have been ~d with letters nous avons été submergés OR inondés de lettres.

delusion [dɪ'lu:ʒn] *n* -**1.** [illusion, mistaken idea] illusion *f*; she's under the ~ that her illness isn't serious elle s'imagine à tort que sa maladie n'est pas grave. -**2.** PSYCH délire *m*; he has ~s of grandeur *fig* il est sujet au délire de grandeur.

delusive [dɪ'lu:sɪv] *adj* trompeur, illusoire.

delusiveness [dɪ'lu:sɪvnɪs] *n* caractère *m* trompeur OR illusoire.

delusory [dɪ'lu:sərɪ] = **delusive**.

deluxe [də'lʌks] *adj* de luxe.

delve [delv] *vi* -**1.** [investigate] fouiller; she preferred not to ~ too deeply into the past elle préférait ne pas fouiller trop profondément (dans) le passé. -**2.** [search]: he ~d into the bag il a fouillé dans le sac. -**3.** [dig, burrow] creuser; [animal] fouiller.

Dem. *written abbr of* Democrat(ic).

demagnetize, -ise [,di:'mægnɪtaɪz] *vt* démagnétiser.

demagog ['deməgɒg] *Am* = **demagogue**.

demagogic [,demə'gɒgɪk] *adj* démagogique.

demagogue ['deməgɒg] *n* démagogue *mf*.

demagoguery [,demə'gɒgərɪ] *n* démagogie *f*.

demagogy ['deməgɒgɪ] *n* démagogie *f*.

de-man [,di:'mæn] (*pt* & *pp* de-manned, *cont* de-manning) *vt Br* INDUST réduire les effectifs de.

demand [dɪ'mɑ:nd] ◇ *vt* -**1.** [ask forcefully] exiger; [money] réclamer; I ~ to see the manager appelez-moi le gérant; the terrorists ~ed to be flown to Tehran les terroristes exigeaient d'être emmenés en avion à Téhéran; pressure groups are ~ing that fuller information be released les groupes de pression exigent la publication de plus amples informations; to ~ one's rights revendiquer ses droits; she ~ed nothing of OR from her children elle n'exigeait rien de ses enfants; he ~ed to know/to be told the truth il exigeait de connaître/qu'on lui dise la vérité. -**2.** [require, necessitate] exiger, réclamer; he doesn't have the imagination ~ed of a good writer il n'a pas l'imagination que l'on attend d'un bon écrivain.
◇ *n* -**1.** [obligation, requirement] exigence *f*; the ~s of motherhood les exigences de la maternité; to make ~s on sb exiger beaucoup de qqn; his work makes great ~s on his time son travail lui prend beaucoup de temps; he makes a lot of emotional ~s il a une très grande demande affective; there are many ~s on her at work elle est très prise au travail. -**2.** [firm request]: wage ~s revendications *fpl* salariales; there have been many ~s for the minister's resignation beaucoup de voix se sont élevées pour exiger la démission du ministre. -**3.** ECON & COMM demande *f*; due to public ~ à la demande du public; there is not much ~ for books on the subject les livres sur ce sujet ne sont pas très demandés; qualified maths teachers are in increasing ~ les professeurs de mathématiques diplômés sont de plus en plus demandés; American jeans were in great ~ in Eastern Europe les jeans américains étaient très demandés OR recherchés dans les pays de l'Est.
◆ **on demand** *adv phr* sur demande; she's in favour of abortion on ~ elle est pour l'avortement libre.

demand bill *n* bon *m* à vue.

demand deposit *n Br* épargne *f* disponible sur demande.

demanding [dɪ'mɑ:ndɪŋ] *adj* [person] exigeant; [job, profession] difficile, astreignant; the work is not physically ~ ce travail ne demande pas beaucoup de force physique.

demand management *n* contrôle *m* de la demande.

demand note *n* bon *m* à vue.

demarcate ['di:mɑ:keɪt] *vt fml* délimiter.

demarcation [,di:mɑ:'keɪʃn] *n* -**1.** [boundary, border] démarcation *f*; a line of ~, a ~ line une ligne de démarcation. -**2.** INDUST attributions *fpl*; ~ dispute conflit *m* d'attributions.

demean [dɪ'mi:n] *vt fml* avilir, rabaisser; she wouldn't ~ herself by marrying him elle refusait de se rabaisser en l'épousant; your behaviour ~s the office you hold votre comportement déshonore la charge que vous occupez.

demeaning [dɪ'mi:nɪŋ] *adj* avilissant, déshonorant.

demeanour *Br*, **demeanor** *Am* [dɪ'mi:nəʳ] *n fml* [behaviour] comportement *m*; [manner] allure *f*, maintien *m*; he had the ~ of a gentleman il avait des allures d'homme raffiné OR de gentleman.

demented [dɪ'mentɪd] *adj* MED dément; *fig* fou.

dementedly [dɪ'mentɪdlɪ] *adv* comme un fou.

dementia [dɪ'menʃə] *n* démence *f*.

dementia praecox [-'pri:kɒks] *n dated* démence *f* précoce.

demerara [,demə'reərə] *n*: ~ sugar cassonade *f*.

demerger [,di:'mɜ:dʒəʳ] *n* scission *f*.

demerit [di:'merɪt] *n* -**1.** *fml* [flaw] démérite *m*, faute *f*. -**2.** *Am* SCH & MIL blâme *m*.

demesne [dɪ'meɪn] *n* -**1.** [land] domaine *m*. -**2.** JUR: land held in ~ terrain possédé en toute propriété.

Demetrius [dɪ'mi:trɪəs] *pr n* Démétrios.

demigod ['demɪgɒd] *n* demi-dieu *m*.

demijohn ['demɪdʒɒn] *n* dame-jeanne *f*, bonbonne *f*.

demilitarization ['di:,mɪlɪtəraɪ'zeɪʃn] *n* démilitarisation *f*.

demilitarize, -ise [,di:'mɪlɪtəraɪz] *vt* démilitariser; a ~d zone une zone démilitarisée.

demimonde [,demɪ'mɒnd] *n* demi-monde *m*.

demineralize, -ise [,di:'mɪnərəlaɪz] *vt* déminéraliser.

demise [dɪ'maɪz] ◇ *n* -**1.** *arch* OR *lit* [death] mort *f*, disparition *f*; [end] fin *f*, mort *f*. -**2.** JUR [transfer] cession *f*. -**3.** HIST: the ~ of the Crown la transmission de la Couronne.
◇ *vt* -**1.** JUR [lease] louer à bail; [bequeath] léguer. -**2.** HIST [transfer] transmettre.

demisemiquaver ['demɪsemɪ,kweɪvəʳ] *n Br* triple croche *f*.

demist [,di:'mɪst] *vt Br* désembuer.

demister [,di:'mɪstəʳ] *n Br* dispositif *m* antibuée.

demitasse ['demɪtæs] *n* [cup] tasse *f* à café; [coffee] café *m* serré, express *m inv*.

demiurge ['demɪɜ:dʒ] *n* démiurge *m*.

demo *inf* ['deməʊ] (*pl* **demos**) (*abbr of* demonstration) *n* manif *f*.

demob *inf* [,di:'mɒb] (*pt* & *pp* **demobbed**, *cont* **demobbing**) *Br* ◇ *vt* démobiliser.
◇ *n* -**1.** [demobilization] démobilisation *f*. -**2.** [soldier] soldat *m* démobilisé.
◇ *comp*: ~ suit ≃ tenue *f* civile, ≃ vêtements *mpl* civils.

demobilization [di:,məʊbɪlaɪ'zeɪʃn] *n* démobilisation *f*.

demobilize, -ise [,di:'məʊbɪlaɪz] *vt* démobiliser.

democracy [dɪ'mɒkrəsɪ] (*pl* **democracies**) *n* démocratie *f*.

democrat ['deməkræt] *n* démocrate *mf*.
◆ **Democrat** *n* -**1.** [in US] démocrate *mf*. -**2.** [in UK] *membre des «Liberal Democrats»*.

democratic [,demə'krætɪk] *adj* [country, organization, principle] démocratique; [person] démocrate; the Democratic Party le parti démocrate (américain); the Democratic Convention la convention démocrate.

democratically [,demə'krætɪklɪ] *adv* démocratiquement.

democratize, -ise [dɪ'mɒkrətaɪz] ◇ *vt* démocratiser.
◇ *vi* se démocratiser.

Democritus [dɪ'mɒkrɪtəs] *pr n* Démocrite.

demodulate [,di:'mɒdjʊleɪt] *vt* démoduler.

demodulation ['di:,mɒdjʊ'leɪʃn] *n* démodulation *f*.

demographer [dɪ'mɒgrəfəʳ] *n* démographe *mf*.

demographic [,demə'græfɪk] *adj* démographique.

demographics [,demə'græfɪks] ◇ *n* (U) [science] (étude *f* de la) démographie *f*.
◇ *npl* [statistics] statistiques *fpl* démographiques.

demography [dɪ'mɒgrəfɪ] *n* démographie *f*.

demolish [dɪ'mɒlɪʃ] *vt* -**1.** *literal* & *fig* [destroy] démolir. -**2.** *inf* [devour] dévorer.

demolisher [dɪ'mɒlɪʃəʳ] *n literal* & *fig* démolisseur *m*.

demolition [,demə'lɪʃn] *n literal* & *fig* [destruction] démolition *f*.
◆ **demolitions** *npl* MIL explosifs *mpl*; a ~s expert *Br* un expert en explosifs.

demon ['di:mən] *n* -**1.** [devil, evil spirit] démon *m*. -**2.** *fig* diable *m*; she works like a ~ c'est un bourreau de travail; he's a ~ tennis player il joue au tennis comme un dieu.

demonetarize, -ise [,di:'mʌnətəraɪz], **demonetize, -ise** [di:'mʌnɪtaɪz] *vt* démonétiser.

demoniac [dɪ'məʊnɪæk] ◇ *adj* démoniaque.
◇ *n* démoniaque *mf*.
demoniacal [diːmə'naɪəkl] *adj* démoniaque.
demonic [diː'mɒnɪk] *adj* diabolique.
demonology [ˌdiːmə'nɒlədʒɪ] *n* démonologie *f*.
demonstrable [dɪ'mɒnstrəbl] *adj* démontrable.
demonstrably [dɪ'mɒnstrəblɪ] *adv* manifestement.
demonstrate ['demənstreɪt] ◇ *vt* -**1.** [prove, establish] démontrer. -**2.** [appliance, machine] faire une démonstration de; he **~d how to use a sewing machine** il a montré comment se servir d'une machine à coudre. -**3.** [ability, quality] faire preuve de; she **~d great musical ability** elle a fait preuve de grandes prédispositions pour la musique.
◇ *vi* POL manifester; **the students are demonstrating against higher fees** les étudiants manifestent contre l'augmentation des frais de scolarité.
demonstration [ˌdemən'streɪʃn] ◇ *n* -**1.** [proof] démonstration *f*. -**2.** COMM & INDUST démonstration *f*; **the salesman gave a ~ of the word processor** le vendeur a fait une démonstration de la machine de traitement de texte. -**3.** POL [protest] manifestation *f*; **to hold a ~** faire une manifestation. -**4.** [of emotion] démonstration *f*, manifestation *f*. -**5.** MIL démonstration *f*.
◇ *comp* [car, lesson, model] de démonstration.
demonstrative [dɪ'mɒnstrətɪv] ◇ *adj* démonstratif; **~ pronoun** pronom *m* démonstratif.
◇ *n* démonstratif *m*.
demonstrator ['demənstreɪtəʳ] *n* -**1.** COMM & INDUST [person] démonstrateur *m*, -trice *f*. -**2.** POL [protester] manifestant *m*, -e *f*. -**3.** *Br* UNIV ≃ préparateur *m*, -trice *f*. -**4.** *Am* COMM [appliance, machine] modèle *m* de démonstration.
demoralization [dɪˌmɒrəlaɪ'zeɪʃn] *n* démoralisation *f*.
demoralize, -ise [dɪ'mɒrəlaɪz] *vt* démoraliser; **after losing the election he became completely ~d** après avoir perdu aux élections, il a complètement perdu courage OR le moral.
demoralizing [dɪ'mɒrəlaɪzɪŋ] *adj* démoralisant.
demoralizingly [dɪ'mɒrəlaɪzɪŋlɪ] *adv*: **our results were ~ poor** nos résultats étaient si médiocres que c'en était démoralisant.
demos ['diːmɒs] *n fml* peuple *m*.
Demosthenes [dɪ'mɒsθəniːz] *pr n* Démosthène.
demote [ˌdiː'məʊt] *vt* rétrograder.
demotic [dɪ'mɒtɪk] ◇ *adj* -**1.** [of the common people] populaire. -**2.** LING démotique.
◇ *n* [ancient Egyptian] démotique *m*.
◆ **Demotic** *n* grec *m* démotique.
demotion [ˌdiː'məʊʃn] *n* rétrogradation *f*.
demotivate [ˌdiː'məʊtɪveɪt] *vt* démotiver.
demount [ˌdiː'maʊnt] *vt* démonter.
demulcent [dɪ'mʌlsənt] ◇ *adj* lénifiant.
◇ *n* onguent *m*.
demur [dɪ'mɜːʳ] (*pt* & *pp* **demurred**, *cont* **demurring**) ◇ *vi* -**1.** *fml* soulever une objection; **he demurred at the idea of accepting a reward** il s'est opposé à l'idée de recevoir une récompense; **I suggested she join us but she demurred** j'ai proposé qu'elle se joigne à nous mais elle s'y est opposée. -**2.** JUR opposer une exception.
◇ *n* objection *f*; **without ~** sans sourciller OR faire d'objection.
demure [dɪ'mjʊəʳ] *adj* -**1.** [modest] modeste, pudique; [well-behaved] sage; [reserved] retenu. -**2.** *pej* [coy] d'une modestie affectée.
demurely [dɪ'mjʊəlɪ] *adv* -**1.** [modestly] modestement; [reservedly] avec retenue; **she sipped her tea ~** elle buvait son thé à petites gorgées OR avec délicatesse. -**2.** *pej* [coyly] avec une modestie affectée.
demureness [dɪ'mjʊənɪs] *n* modestie *f*, pudeur *f*.
demystification [ˌdiːˌmɪstɪfɪ'keɪʃn] *n* démystification *f*.
demystify [ˌdiː'mɪstɪfaɪ] (*pt* & *pp* **demystified**) *vt* démystifier.
demythologization ['diːmɪˌθɒlədʒaɪ'zeɪʃn] *n* démythification *f*.
demythologize, -ise [ˌdiːmɪ'θɒlədʒaɪz] *vt* démythifier.
den [den] *n* -**1.** ZOOL repaire *m*, tanière *f*; *fig* [hideout] repaire *m*, nid *m*; **a ~ of thieves** un nid de brigands; **a ~ of iniquity** un lieu de perdition. -**2.** [room, study] ≃ bureau *m*, ≃ cabinet *m* de travail.
denary ['diːnərɪ] *adj* décimal.
denationalization [ˌdiːˌnæʃnəlaɪ'zeɪʃn] *n* dénationalisation *f*.
denationalize, -ise [ˌdiː'næʃnəlaɪz] *vt* dénationaliser.
denaturalize, -ise [ˌdiː'nætʃrəlaɪz] *vt* -**1.** [deprive of nationality] dénaturaliser. -**2.** [make unnatural] dénaturer.
denature [ˌdiː'neɪtʃəʳ] *vt* dénaturer.
dendrology [den'drɒlədʒɪ] *n* dendrologie *f*.
dene [diːn] *n Br* [valley] val *m*, vallée *f*.
dengue ['deŋgɪ] *n* dengue *f*.
deniable [dɪ'naɪəbl] *adj* niable.
denial [dɪ'naɪəl] *n* -**1.** [of story, rumour] démenti *m*; [of wrongdoing] dénégation *f*; [of request, right] refus *m*; **~ of justice** JUR déni *m* de justice; **the minister's ~ of responsibility was greeted with outrage** c'est avec indignation qu'on a appris que le ministre rejetait toute responsabilité. -**2.** [disavowal, repudiation] reniement *m*; **Peter's ~ of Christ** BIBLE le reniement du Christ par Pierre. -**3.** [abstinence] abnégation *f*; **the monks led a life of ~** les moines menaient une vie d'abnégation. -**4.** PSYCH dénégation *f*.
denier ['denɪəʳ, də'nɪəʳ] *n* -**1.** *Br* [measure] denier *m*; **15 ~ stockings** bas *m* de 15 deniers. -**2.** [coin] denier *m*.
denigrate ['denɪgreɪt] *vt* dénigrer.
denigration [ˌdenɪ'greɪʃn] *n* dénigrement *m*.
denigrator ['denɪgreɪtəʳ] *n* dénigreur *m*, -euse *f*.
denim ['denɪm] ◇ *n* TEX (toile *f* de) jean *m*, denim *m*.
◇ *comp* [jacket] en jean.
◆ **denims** *npl* blue-jean *m*, jean *m*; **all the students were wearing ~s** tous les étudiants portaient des jeans.
denitrification [ˌdiːˌnaɪtrɪfɪ'keɪʃn] *n* dénitrification *f*.
denitrify [ˌdiː'naɪtrɪfaɪ] (*pt* & *pp* **denitrified**) *vt* dénitrifier.
denizen ['denɪzn] *n* -**1.** *lit* OR *hum* [inhabitant] habitant *m*, -e *f*, hôte *mf lit*; [regular visitor] habitué *m*, -e *f*. -**2.** *Br* [permanent resident] ≃ résident *m*, -e *f*. -**3.** [non-native plant] plante *f* allogène; [non-native animal] animal *m* allogène.
Denmark ['denmɑːk] *pr n* Danemark *m*; **in ~** au Danemark.
denominate [dɪ'nɒmɪneɪt] *vt* dénommer.
denomination [dɪˌnɒmɪ'neɪʃn] *n* -**1.** FIN valeur *f*; **small/large ~ notes** petites/grosses coupures; **coins of different ~s** des pièces de différentes valeurs. -**2.** RELIG confession *f*, culte *m*. -**3.** *fml* [designation, specification] dénomination *f*.
denominational [dɪˌnɒmɪ'neɪʃənl] *adj*: **a ~ school** une école confessionnelle.
denominationalism [dɪˌnɒmɪ'neɪʃnəlɪzm] *n* appartenance *f* à une confession.
denominative [dɪ'nɒmɪnətɪv] ◇ *adj* dénominatif.
◇ *n* dénominatif *m*.
denominator [dɪ'nɒmɪneɪtəʳ] *n* dénominateur *m*.
denotation [ˌdiːnəʊ'teɪʃn] *n* (*U*) [indication] dénotation *f*; [representation, symbol] signes *mpl*, symboles *mpl*; [specific meaning] signification *f*.
denotative [dɪ'nəʊtətɪv] *adj* dénotatif.
denote [dɪ'nəʊt] *vt* [indicate] dénoter; [represent] signifier.
denounce [dɪ'naʊns] *vt* dénoncer; **his wife ~d him as a traitor** sa femme l'a dénoncé comme traître; **to ~ an agreement/a treaty** dénoncer un accord/un traité; **the union's president ~d the practice as unjust** le président du syndicat a dénoncé cette pratique comme étant injuste.
denouncement [dɪ'naʊnsmənt] *n* dénonciation *f*.
denouncer [dɪ'naʊnsəʳ] *n* dénonciateur *m*, -trice *f*.
dense [dens] *adj* -**1.** [thick] dense; [fog, smoke] épais; [undergrowth, vegetation] dense, dru *lit*; PHOT opaque. -**2.** [prose] dense, ramassé. -**3.** *inf* [stupid] bouché, obtus.
densely ['denslɪ] *adv*: **a ~ populated area** une région très peuplée OR à forte densité de population; **the book is very ~ written** le livre est écrit d'une manière dense OR ramassée; **a ~ wooded valley** une vallée très boisée.
denseness ['densnɪs] *n* -**1.** [thickness] densité *f*. -**2.** *inf* [stupidity] stupidité *f*.
densitometer [ˌdensɪ'tɒmɪtəʳ] *n* densitomètre *m*.
density ['densətɪ] *n* densité *f*.
dent [dent] ◇ *n* -**1.** [in metal] bosse *f*; [in bed, pillow] creux *m*; **he made a ~ in his car** il a cabossé sa voiture; **the car has a ~ in the bumper** la voiture a le pare-chocs cabossé. -**2.** *fig* [reduction]: **to make a ~ in one's savings** faire un trou dans ses économies.
◇ *vt* [metal] cabosser, bosseler; *fig* [pride] froisser; [confidence] entamer.
dental ['dentl] ◇ *adj* -**1.** MED dentaire. -**2.** LING dental.
◇ *n* dentale *f*.
dental floss *n* fil *m* dentaire.
dental hygienist *n* ≃ assistant *m*, -e *f* dentaire *(qui s'occupe du détartrage etc)*.
dental mechanic *n* mécanicien-dentiste *m*.
dental plate *n* dentier *m*.
dental surgeon *n Br* chirurgien-dentiste *m*.
dental surgery *n* -**1.** [activity] chirurgie *f* dentaire. -**2.** *Br* [office] cabinet *m* dentaire.
dental technician *n* prothésiste *mf* (dentaire).
dentate ['denteɪt] *adj* denté, dentelé.
dentifrice ['dentɪfrɪs] *n* [paste] pâte *f* dentifrice; [powder] poudre *f* dentifrice.
dentine ['dentiːn], **dentin** ['dentɪn] *Am* *n* dentine *f*.
dentist ['dentɪst] *n* dentiste *mf*; **the ~'s surgery** *Br* OR **office** *Am* le cabinet dentaire; **to go to the ~'s** aller chez le dentiste.
dentistry ['dentɪstrɪ] *n* dentisterie *f*.
dentition [den'tɪʃn] *n* dentition *f*.
denture ['dentʃəʳ] *n* [artificial tooth] prothèse *f* dentaire.
◆ **dentures** *npl* dentier *m*.
denuclearization ['diːˌnjuːklɪəraɪ'zeɪʃn] *n* dénucléarisation *f*.
denuclearize, -ise [ˌdiː'njuːklɪəraɪz] *vt* dénucléariser.
denude [dɪ'njuːd] *vt* dénuder.
denumerable [dɪ'njuːmərəbl] *adj* dénombrable.
denunciation [dɪˌnʌnsɪ'eɪʃn] *n* dénonciation *f*.
denunciator [dɪ'nʌnsɪeɪtəʳ] *n* dénonciateur *m*, -trice *f*.
deny [dɪ'naɪ] (*pt* & *pp* **denied**) *vt* -**1.** [declare untrue] nier; [report, rumour] démentir; **the prisoner denied having conspired** OR **conspiring against the government** le prisonnier nia avoir conspiré contre le gouvernement; **he denied that he had been involved** il nia avoir été impliqué; **there's no ~ing that we have a problem** il est indéniable que nous avons un problème; **he denied all knowledge of the incident** il a nié être au courant de l'incident. -**2.** [refuse] refuser, dénier *lit*; **in many countries people are denied even basic human rights** dans beaucoup de pays les gens sont privés des droits les plus fondamentaux. -**3.** [deprive] priver; **she thought that by ~ing herself she could help others** elle pensait qu'en se privant

elle pourrait aider les autres. -**4.** *arch* OR *lit* [disavow, repudiate] renier; **before the cock crow, thou shalt ~ me thrice** BIBLE avant que le coq chante, tu m'auras renié trois fois.

deodorant [diːˈəʊdərənt] *n* déodorant *m.*

deodorize, -ise [diːˈəʊdəraɪz] *vt* désodoriser.

deontological [dɪˌɒntəˈlɒdʒɪkl] *adj* déontologique.

deontology [ˌdiːɒnˈtɒlədʒɪ] *n* déontologie *f.*

deoxidize, -ise [diːˈɒksɪdaɪz] *vt* désoxyder.

deoxygenate [ˌdiːˈɒksɪdʒəneɪt] *vt* désoxygéner.

deoxyribonucleic [ˈdiːɒksɪˌraɪbəʊnjuːˈkliːɪk] *adj*: **~ acid** acide *m* désoxyribonucléique.

depart [dɪˈpɑːt] ◇ *vi fml* -**1.** [leave] partir; **the train now ~ing from platform two is the express to Liverpool** le train en partance au quai numéro deux est l'express de Liverpool. -**2.** [deviate, vary] s'écarter; **to ~ from tradition** s'écarter de la tradition.
◇ *vt* quitter; **to ~ this life** *euph* quitter ce monde, partir pour l'autre monde.

departed [dɪˈpɑːtɪd] *euph* & *fml* ◇ *adj* [dead] défunt, disparu.
◇ *n*: **the ~** le défunt, la défunte, le disparu, la disparue.

department [dɪˈpɑːtmənt] *n* -**1.** ADMIN [division] département *m*; [ministery] ministère *m*; **she works in the housing ~** elle travaille au ministère du Logement ❑ **the Department of State** *Am* le Département d'État, ≃ le ministère des Affaires étrangères; **the Department of Trade and Industry** *Br* ≃ le ministère de l'Industrie et du Commerce; **the Department for** *Br* OR **of** *Am* **Education** ≃ (le ministère de) l'Éducation nationale. -**2.** INDUST service *m*; **the sales/personnel ~** le service commercial/du personnel; **the complaints ~** le service des réclamations. -**3.** [field, responsibility] domaine *m*; **recruiting staff is not my ~** le recrutement du personnel n'est pas mon domaine OR de mon ressort; **cooking's not really my ~** *fig* la cuisine n'est pas vraiment mon domaine OR ma spécialité. -**4.** COMM rayon *m*; **he works in the toy ~** il travaille au rayon des jouets. -**5.** SCH & UNIV département *m.* -**6.** GEOG département *m.*

departmental [ˌdiːpɑːtˈmentl] *adj* -**1.** ADMIN du département; INDUST du service; COMM du rayon. -**2.** GEOG du département, départemental.

department store *n* grand magasin *m.*

departure [dɪˈpɑːtʃəʳ] ◇ *n* -**1.** [leaving] départ *m*; **the crew were preparing for ~** l'équipage se préparait au départ; **our ~ was delayed for three hours** notre départ a été retardé de trois heures. -**2.** [variation, deviation] modification *f*; **the introduction of bonuses was a ~ from standard company policy** l'introduction de primes représentait une entorse à la politique habituelle de l'entreprise. -**3.** [orientation] orientation *f*; **farming was an entirely new ~ for him** l'agriculture était une voie OR orientation tout à fait nouvelle pour lui. -**4.** *arch* [death] disparition *f*, trépas *m lit.*
◇ *comp* [gate, time] de départ; **~ lounge** salle *f* d'embarquement.

depend [dɪˈpend]
◆ **depend on** *vt insep* -**1.** [be determined by] dépendre de; **the outcome of the war will ~ on** OR **upon a number of factors** l'issue de la guerre dépendra d'un certain nombre de facteurs; **his job ~s on his** OR **him getting the contract** il ne gardera son emploi que s'il obtient le contrat; **survival ~ed on their finding enough water** pour survivre, il leur fallait trouver suffisamment d'eau; **her future may ~ on it** son avenir en dépend peut-être; **are we going out? – it (all) ~s** est-ce qu'on sort? – ça dépend. -**2.** [rely on] dépendre de; **the firm ~s heavily on orders from abroad** l'entreprise dépend beaucoup des commandes de l'étranger; **she ~s on the money her children give her** l'argent qu'elle reçoit de ses enfants est sa seule ressource. -**3.** [trust, be sure of]: **he's a friend you can ~ on** c'est un ami sur qui vous pouvez compter; **I'm ~ing on you to help me** je compte sur vous pour m'aider; **you can ~ on it!** vous pouvez en être sûr OR compter là-dessus!
◆ **depending on** *prep phr* selon; **a degree takes two or three years of study, ~ing on the subject chosen** un diplôme demande deux ou trois ans d'études, selon la matière choisie.

dependability [dɪˌpendəˈbɪlətɪ] *n* fiabilité *f.*

dependable [dɪˈpendəbl] *adj* [machine] fiable; [person] fiable, sérieux; [organization, shop] sérieux.

dependably [dɪˈpendəblɪ] *adv* d'une manière sûre.

dependant [dɪˈpendənt] *n* ADMIN personne *f* à charge; **do you have any ~s?** avez-vous des personnes à charge?

dependence [dɪˈpendəns] *n* dépendance *f*; **the government hopes to reduce our ~ on oil** le gouvernement espère diminuer notre dépendance vis-à-vis du pétrole; **her ~ on her children increased with the years** elle devenait de plus en plus dépendante de ses enfants au fil des années.

dependency [dɪˈpendənsɪ] (*pl* **dependencies**) *n* dépendance *f.*

dependent [dɪˈpendənt] ◇ *adj* -**1.** [person] dépendant; **he became increasingly ~ on his children** il devenait de plus en plus dépendant de ses enfants; **she's financially ~ on her parents** elle dépend financièrement OR elle est à la charge de ses parents; **he has two ~ children** ADMIN il a deux enfants à charge; **she's heavily ~ on sleeping pills** elle ne peut se passer de somnifères. -**2.** [contingent]: **their economy is highly ~ on foreign investment** leur économie dépend énormément des investissements étrangers; **the prosperity of his business was ~ on the continuation of the war** la prospérité de son entreprise dépendait OR était tributaire de la poursuite de la guerre; **her father's consent to the wedding was ~ on the young man's success** son père a donné son assentiment au mariage à condition que le jeune homme réussisse. -**3.** GRAMM [clause] subordonné. -**4.** MATH [variable] dépendant.
◇ *n* GRAMM subordonnée *f.*

depersonalization [diːˌpɜːsnəlaɪˈzeɪʃn] *n* dépersonnalisation *f.*

depersonalize, -ise [ˌdiːˈpɜːsnəlaɪz] *vt* dépersonnaliser.

depict [dɪˈpɪkt] *vt* -**1.** [describe] dépeindre; **Shakespeare ~s Richard III as cruel and calculating** Shakespeare dépeint Richard III comme un homme cruel et calculateur. -**2.** [paint, draw] représenter.

depiction [dɪˈpɪkʃn] *n* -**1.** [description] description *f.* -**2.** [picture] représentation *f.*

depilate [ˈdepɪleɪt] *vt* épiler.

depilatory [dɪˈpɪlətrɪ] (*pl* **depilatories**) ◇ *adj* épilatoire, dépilatoire; **~ cream** crème *f* dépilatoire.
◇ *n* épilatoire *m*, dépilatoire *m.*

deplane [ˌdiːˈpleɪn] *vi* descendre d'avion.

deplete [dɪˈpliːt] *vt* -**1.** [reduce] diminuer, réduire; **the illness ~d her strength** la maladie amoindrissait ses forces; **our stocks have become ~d** nos stocks ont beaucoup diminué. -**2.** [impoverish, exhaust] épuiser; **overproduction has ~d the soil** la surproduction a épuisé OR appauvri la terre; **the stream is ~d of fish** la rivière est beaucoup moins poissonneuse qu'avant.

depletion [dɪˈpliːʃn] *n* -**1.** [decrease, reduction] diminution *f*, réduction *f.* -**2.** [exhaustion, elimination] épuisement *m*; [of soil] appauvrissement *m.*

deplorable [dɪˈplɔːrəbl] *adj* déplorable, lamentable.

deplorably [dɪˈplɔːrəblɪ] *adv* d'une manière déplorable, lamentablement.

deplore [dɪˈplɔːʳ] *vt* -**1.** [regret] déplorer, regretter; **we all ~d the loss of life** nous avons tous déploré la perte de vies humaines. -**2.** [condemn, disapprove of] désapprouver, condamner; **the President ~d the use of force against unarmed civilians** le Président a condamné l'usage de la force envers des civils non armés.

deploy [dɪˈplɔɪ] ◇ *vt* déployer.
◇ *vi* se déployer.

deployment [dɪˈplɔɪmənt] *n* déploiement *m.*

depolarization [diːˌpəʊləraɪˈzeɪʃn] *n* dépolarisation *f.*

depolarize, -ise [ˌdiːˈpəʊləraɪz] *vt* dépolariser.

depoliticize, -ise [ˌdiːpəˈlɪtɪsaɪz] *vt* dépolitiser.

deponent [dɪˈpəʊnənt] ◇ *n* -**1.** GRAMM déponent *m.* -**2.** JUR déposant *m*, -e *f.*
◇ *adj* déponent.

depopulate [ˌdiːˈpɒpjʊleɪt] *vt* dépeupler.

depopulation [diːˌpɒpjʊˈleɪʃn] *n* dépeuplement *m.*

deport [dɪˈpɔːt] *vt* -**1.** [expel] expulser; HIST [to colonies, camp] déporter; **fifty illegal immigrants were ~ed to Mexico** cinquante immigrants clandestins furent expulsés vers le Mexique. -**2.** *fml* [behave]: **to ~ o.s.** se comporter, se conduire.

deportation [ˌdiːpɔːˈteɪʃn] *n* expulsion *f*; HIST [to colonies, camp] déportation *f*; **~ order** arrêt *m* d'expulsion; **many refugees were threatened with ~** beaucoup de réfugiés furent menacés d'expulsion; **resistance fighters risked ~ or death** les combattants de la résistance risquaient la déportation ou la mort.

deportee [ˌdiːpɔːˈtiː] *n* expulsé *m*, -e *f*; HIST [prisoner] déporté *m*, -e *f.*

deportment [dɪˈpɔːtmənt] *n fml* OR *dated* [behaviour] comportement *m*; [carriage, posture] maintien *m.*

depose [dɪˈpəʊz] ◇ *vt* -**1.** [remove] destituer; [sovereign] déposer, destituer. -**2.** JUR déposer.
◇ *vi* faire une déposition.

deposit [dɪˈpɒzɪt] ◇ *vt* -**1.** [leave, place] déposer; **she ~ed her belongings in a locker at Victoria Station** elle déposa OR laissa ses affaires dans une consigne à la gare Victoria; **the bus ~ed me in front of my house** le bus m'a déposé devant ma maison. -**2.** [subj: liquid, river] déposer; **the river had ~ed silt along its banks** le fleuve avait laissé un dépôt de vase le long de ses rives. -**3.** BANK déposer, remettre; **I'd like to ~ £500** j'aimerais faire un versement de 500 livres; **to ~ a cheque** déposer OR remettre un chèque (à la banque). -**4.** [pay] verser; **you must ~ 10% of the value of the house** vous devez faire un premier versement correspondant à 10 % de la valeur de la maison. -**5.** *Am* [insert] mettre; **please ~ one dollar for your call** veuillez introduire un dollar pour votre appel.
◇ *vi* GEOL se déposer.
◇ *n* -**1.** BANK dépôt *m*; **to make a ~ of £200** faire un versement de 200 livres; **on ~** en dépôt. -**2.** FIN & COMM [down payment] acompte *m*, arrhes *fpl*; **she put down a ~ on a house** elle a versé un acompte OR a fait un premier versement pour une maison; **he left a £50 ~ on a TV set** il a laissé 50 livres d'acompte OR d'arrhes pour réserver un téléviseur. -**3.** [guarantee against loss or damage] caution *f*; [on a bottle] consigne *f*; **is there a ~ on the bottle?** est-ce que la bouteille est consignée?; **the landlord asked for two months' ~** le propriétaire a demandé une caution de deux mois. -**4.** *Br* POL cautionnement *m*; **to lose one's ~** perdre son cautionnement. -**5.** MINER gisement *m*; **oil ~s** gisements de pétrole. -**6.** [sediment, silt] dépôt *m*; [in wine] dépôt *m.*

deposit account *n Br* compte *m* sur livret.

depositary [dɪˈpɒzɪtrɪ] (*pl* **depositaries**) *n* dépositaire *mf.*

deposition [ˌdepəˈzɪʃn] *n* -**1.** JUR déposition *f.* -**2.** MINER dépôt *m.* -**3.** [removal of leader] déposition *f.*

depositor [dəˈpɒzɪtəʳ] *n* déposant *m*, -e *f.*

depository [dəˈpɒzɪtrɪ] (*pl* **depositories**) *n* dépôt *m.*

deposit slip *n* bulletin *m* de versement.

depot [*sense 1 & 2* ˈdepəʊ, *sense 3* ˈdiːpəʊ] *n* -**1.** [warehouse] dépôt *m*; *Br* [garage] dépôt *m*, garage *m*. -**2.** *Br* MIL ≃ caserne *f*. -**3.** *Am* [station] gare *f*; bus ~ gare routière.

depravation [ˌdeprəˈveɪʃn] *n* dépravation *f*.

deprave [dɪˈpreɪv] *vt* dépraver.

depraved [dɪˈpreɪvd] *adj* dépravé, perverti.

depravity [dɪˈprævətɪ] (*pl* **depravities**) *n* dépravation *f*, corruption *f*.

deprecate [ˈdeprɪkeɪt] *vt* -**1.** *fml* [disapprove of, deplore] désapprouver; any renunciation of sovereignty over the territory is to be ~d il faut condamner toute renonciation de souveraineté sur le territoire. -**2.** [denigrate, disparage] dénigrer.

deprecating [ˈdeprɪkeɪtɪŋ] = **deprecatory**.

deprecatingly [ˈdeprɪkeɪtɪŋlɪ] *adv* -**1.** [disapprovingly - say, speak] d'un ton désapprobateur; [- look] avec désapprobation. -**2.** [apologetically] avec remords.

deprecatory [ˈdeprɪkətrɪ] *adj* -**1.** [disapproving] désapprobateur; [derogatory] dénigrant. -**2.** [apologetic] navré.

depreciable [dɪˈpriːʃəbl] *adj* -**1.** *Am* FIN amortissable. -**2.** [liable to depreciation] dépréciable.

depreciate [dɪˈpriːʃɪeɪt] ◇ *vt* -**1.** FIN [devalue] déprécier, dévaloriser. -**2.** [denigrate] dénigrer, déprécier.
◇ *vi* se déprécier, se dévaloriser.

depreciation [dɪˌpriːʃɪˈeɪʃn] *n* -**1.** FIN dépréciation *f*, dévalorisation *f*. -**2.** [disparagement] dénigrement *m*, dépréciation *f*.

depredation [ˌdeprɪˈdeɪʃn] *n* déprédation *f*.

depress [dɪˈpres] *vt* -**1.** [deject, sadden] déprimer; it ~ed her to talk about her father le fait de parler de son père la déprimait OR lui donnait le cafard. -**2.** ECON [reduce] (faire) baisser. -**3.** *fml* [press, push down on] appuyer sur.

depressant [dɪˈpresənt] MED ◇ *adj* dépresseur.
◇ *n* dépresseur *m*.

depressed [dɪˈprest] *adj* -**1.** [melancholy] déprimé, abattu; MED déprimé; you mustn't get ~ about your exam results tu ne dois pas te laisser abattre OR perdre le moral à cause de tes résultats d'examen; it's nothing to get ~ about il n'y a pas de quoi se laisser abattre; visiting her grandparents made her feel ~ le fait de rendre visite à ses grands-parents la déprimait OR lui donnait le cafard. -**2.** ECON [area, industry] en déclin, touché par la crise; [prices, profits, wages] en baisse; the market is ~ ST. EX les cours sont en baisse. -**3.** [sunken, hollow] creux.

depressing [dɪˈpresɪŋ] *adj* déprimant; [idea, place] triste, sinistre; what a ~ thought! quelle triste idée!; the failure of the talks was ~ news l'échec des pourparlers fut une nouvelle déprimante OR décourageante.

depressingly [dɪˈpresɪŋlɪ] *adv* [say, speak] d'un ton abattu; unemployment is ~ high le taux de chômage est déprimant; his meaning was ~ clear la signification de ses paroles était d'une clarté déprimante.

depression [dɪˈpreʃn] *n* -**1.** [melancholy] dépression *f*; MED dépression *f* (nerveuse); she suffers from ~ elle fait de la dépression; he's in a state of ~ il est dans un état dépressif. -**2.** ECON [slump] dépression *f*, crise *f* économique; the country's economy is in a state of ~ l'économie du pays est en crise ❑ the Great Depression *Am* HIST la grande dépression. -**3.** [hollow, indentation] creux *m*; GEOG dépression *f*. -**4.** METEOR dépression *f*.

THE GREAT DEPRESSION:
La plus profonde crise économique qu'aient connue les États-Unis et qui, de 1929 (date du krach de Wall Street) au début des années 40, plongea de nombreux Américains dans le chômage et la misère.

---

depressive [dɪˈpresɪv] ◇ *adj* dépressif.
◇ *n* dépressif *m*, -ive *f*.

depressor [dɪˈpresəʳ] *n* abaisseur *m*; a tongue ~ un abaisse-langue.

depressurization [diːˌpreʃəraɪˈzeɪʃn] *n* dépressurisation *f*.

depressurize, -ise [ˌdiːˈpreʃəraɪz] *vt* dépressuriser.

deprivation [ˌdeprɪˈveɪʃn] *n* (*U*) privation *f*; a life of ~ and misery une vie de souffrances et de privations.

deprive [dɪˈpraɪv] *vt* priver; to ~ sb of sthg priver qqn de qqch; the prisoners were ~d of letters for a month les prisonniers furent privés de lettres pendant un mois; he was ~d of his rank il fut déchu de son grade; she ~s herself of nothing elle ne se prive de rien; the legitimate heir was ~d of his inheritance l'héritier légitime fut frustré OR dépossédé de son héritage.

deprived [dɪˈpraɪvd] *adj* [area, child] défavorisé; the boy is emotionally ~ le garçon souffre d'une carence affective; many of these young offenders come from ~ backgrounds beaucoup de ces jeunes délinquants viennent de milieux défavorisés.

dept. *written abbr of* department.

depth [depθ] *n* -**1.** [distance downwards] profondeur *f*; the wreck was located at a ~ of 200 metres l'épave a été repérée à 200 mètres de profondeur OR par 200 mètres de fond; the canal is about 12 metres in ~ le canal a environ 12 mètres de profondeur; this submarine could dive to a ~ of 500 feet ce sous-marin pouvait descendre jusqu'à une profondeur de 500 pieds. -**2.** [in deep water]: the child was warned not to go out of his ~ l'enfant a été averti de ne pas aller où il n'avait pas pied; she swam too far and got out of her ~ elle a nagé trop loin et a perdu pied ❑ to be out of one's ~ *literal* ne plus avoir pied; *fig* perdre pied. -**3.** PHOT: ~ of field/focus profondeur *f* de champ/foyer. -**4.** [of a voice, sound] registre *m* grave. -**5.** [extent, intensity] profondeur *f*; [of colour] intensité *f*; the ~ of his knowledge of the subject was impressive sa connaissance approfondie du sujet était impressionnante; he had not realized her ~ of feeling on the matter il ne s'était pas rendu compte à quel point ce sujet lui tenait à cœur; we must study the proposal in ~ nous devons étudier à fond OR en profondeur cette proposition.
◆ **depths** *npl*: the ocean ~s les grands fonds *mpl*; the ~s of the earth les profondeurs *fpl* OR entrailles *fpl* de la terre; in the ~s of the forest au (fin) fond de la forêt || *fig*: in the ~s of his soul au plus profond de son âme; she's in the ~s of despair elle touche le fond du désespoir; in the ~s of winter au cœur de l'hiver.

depth charge *n* grenade *f* sous-marine.

depth finder = **depth recorder**.

depth psychology *n* psychologie *f* des profondeurs.

depth recorder *n* sondeur *m*.

deputation [ˌdepjʊˈteɪʃn] *n* députation *f*, délégation *f*.

depute [dɪˈpjuːt] *vt fml* [person] députer; [authority, power] déléguer; she ~d the running of the business to her eldest son elle délégua la gestion de l'entreprise à son fils aîné.

deputize, -ise [ˈdepjʊtaɪz] ◇ *vt* députer.
◇ *vi*: the First Secretary ~d for the Ambassador at the reception le premier secrétaire représentait l'ambassadeur à la réception.

deputy [ˈdepjʊtɪ] (*pl* **deputies**) ◇ *n* -**1.** [assistant] adjoint *m*, -e *f*. -**2.** [substitute] remplaçant *m*, -e *f*; to act as ~ remplacer qqn, agir en tant qu'adjoint. -**3.** POL [elected representative] député *m*. -**4.** *Am* [law enforcement agent] shérif *m* adjoint.
◇ *comp*: ~ chairman vice-président *m*; ~ head teacher, ~ head *inf* directeur *m* adjoint, directrice *f* adjointe; ~ manager directeur *m* adjoint; ~ sheriff shérif *m* adjoint.

derail [dɪˈreɪl] ◇ *vt* faire dérailler.
◇ *vi* dérailler.

derailleur [dɪˈreɪljəʳ] *n Br* dérailleur *m*.

derailment [dɪˈreɪlmənt] *n* déraillement *m*.

derange [dɪˈreɪndʒ] *vt* -**1.** [disarrange, disorder] déranger. -**2.** [drive insane] rendre fou.

deranged [dɪˈreɪndʒd] *adj* dérangé, détraqué; the killer must have been ~ le tueur devait être fou OR déséquilibré; the old woman seemed slightly ~ la vieille femme semblait un peu dérangée OR avoir l'esprit un peu dérangé; it's the work of a ~ mind c'est l'œuvre d'un esprit dérangé OR détraqué.

derangement [dɪˈreɪndʒmənt] *n* -**1.** [disorder, disarray] désordre *m*. -**2.** [mental illness] démence *f*.

derate [ˌdiːˈreɪt] *vt Br* [property] dégrever.

deration [ˌdiːˈræʃn] *vt* cesser le rationnement de.

derby [*Br* ˈdɑːbɪ, *Am* ˈdɜːbɪ] *n* -**1.** [match]: a local ~ un derby. -**2.** *Am* [race] derby *m*. -**3.** *Am* [hat] chapeau *m* melon.
◆ **Derby** *pr n*: the Derby *grande course annuelle de chevaux à Epsom, en Grande-Bretagne*.

deregister [ˌdiːˈredʒɪstəʳ] *vt* enlever du registre.

deregulate [ˌdiːˈregjʊleɪt] *vt* -**1.** ECON [prices, wages] libérer, déréguler. -**2.** [relax restrictions on] assouplir les règlements de, déréglementer; some members of the EC are in favour of deregulating air travel certains membres de la CEE sont favorables à la déréglementation du trafic aérien.

deregulation [ˌdiːregjʊˈleɪʃn] *n* -**1.** ECON [of prices, wages] libération *f*, dérégulation *f*. -**2.** [relaxation of restrictions] assouplissement *m* des règlements, déréglementation *f*.

derelict [ˈderəlɪkt] ◇ *adj* -**1.** [abandoned] abandonné, délaissé; a ~ old building un vieux bâtiment à l'abandon. -**2.** [negligent, neglectful] négligent.
◇ *n* -**1.** [vagrant] clochard *m*, -e *f*, vagabond *m*, -e *f*. -**2.** NAUT navire *m* abandonné.

dereliction [ˌderəˈlɪkʃn] *n* -**1.** [abandonment] abandon *m*. -**2.** *Br* [negligence] négligence *f*; ~ of duty manquement *m* au devoir.

derestrict [ˌdiːrɪˈstrɪkt] *vt Br*: to ~ a road supprimer une limitation de vitesse sur une route; a ~ed road une route sans limitation de vitesse.

derestriction [ˌdiːrɪˈstrɪkʃn] *n* exemption *f*.

deride [dɪˈraɪd] *vt* tourner en dérision, railler.

derision [dɪˈrɪʒn] *n* dérision *f*.

derisive [dɪˈraɪsɪv] *adj* moqueur.

derisively [dɪˈraɪsɪvlɪ] *adv* avec dérision; [say, speak] d'un ton moqueur.

derisory [dəˈraɪzərɪ] *adj* -**1.** [ridiculous] dérisoire. -**2.** [mocking, scornful] moqueur.

derivation [ˌderɪˈveɪʃn] *n* dérivation *f*.

derivative [dɪˈrɪvətɪv] ◇ *adj* -**1.** [gen] dérivé. -**2.** *lit & pej* [unoriginal] peu original, banal.
◇ *n* [gen] dérivé *m*; MATH dérivée *f*.

derive [dɪˈraɪv] ◇ *vt* -**1.** [gain, obtain]: she ~s great pleasure from her garden elle tire beaucoup de plaisir de son jardin; the young man ~d little benefit from his expensive education le jeune homme n'a guère tiré profit de ses études coûteuses; to ~ courage/strength from trouver du courage/des forces dans. -**2.** [deduce] dériver de.
◇ *vi*: to ~ from provenir de; the word "coward" ~s originally from French LING le mot «coward» vient du français.

derived unit *n* unité *f* dérivée.

dermal [ˈdɜːml] *adj* dermique.

dermatitis [ˌdɜːməˈtaɪtɪs] *n* dermite *f*, dermatite *f*.

dermatologist [ˌdɜːməˈtɒlədʒɪst] *n* dermatologiste *mf*, dermatologue *mf*.

dermatology [ˌdɜːməˈtɒlədʒɪ] *n* dermatologie *f*.

dermatoplasty [ˌdɜːmətəʊˈplæstɪ] *n* dermatoplastie *f*.

dermatosis [ˌdɜːməˈtəʊsɪs] (*pl* **dermatoses** [-siːz]) *n* dermatose *f*.

dermis [ˈdɜːmɪs] *n* derme *m*.

derogate [ˈderəgeɪt] ◇ *vt fml* [disparage] dénigrer, déprécier.

◇ *vi*: to ~ from porter atteinte à; the claims in no way ~ from her reputation as an artist ces affirmations n'ont en aucune manière altéré sa réputation d'artiste.

derogation [ˌderəˈgeɪʃn] *n* dépréciation *f*.

derogatorily [dɪˈrɒgətrəlɪ] *adv* de façon péjorative.

derogatory [dɪˈrɒgətrɪ] *adj* [comment, remark] désobligeant, critique; [word] péjoratif.

derrick [ˈderɪk] *n Br* [crane] mât *m* de charge; PETR derrick *m*.

derrière [ˌderɪˈeəʳ] *n euph* derrière *m*.

derring-do [ˌderɪŋˈduː] *n lit* OR *hum* bravoure *f*; deeds of ~ prouesses *fpl*.

derringer [ˈderɪndʒəʳ] *n Am* pistolet *m* (à gros calibre).

derv [dɜːv] *n Br* gas-oil *m*.

dervish [ˈdɜːvɪʃ] *n* derviche *m*; a whirling ~ un derviche tourneur.

DES (*abbr of* Department of Education and Science) *pr n ancien ministère britannique de l'Éducation et de la Recherche scientifique*.

desalinate [ˌdiːˈsælɪneɪt] *vt* dessaler.

desalination [diːˌsælɪˈneɪʃn] ◇ *n* dessalement *m*.
◇ *comp* [plant] de dessalement.

desalinize, **-ise** [ˌdiːˈsælɪnaɪz] = **desalinate**.

desalt [ˌdiːˈsɔːlt] = **desalinate**.

desaturate [ˌdiːˈsætʃəreɪt] *vt* désaturer.

descale [ˌdiːˈskeɪl] *vt* détartrer.

descant [ˈdeskænt] ◇ *n* déchant *m*.
◇ *comp*: ~ recorder flûte *f* à bec soprano.
◇ *vi* -**1.** MUS déchanter. -**2.** *lit* & *pej* [comment, ramble] discourir, pérorer *pej*; to ~ on OR upon sthg pérorer au sujet de qqch.

Descartes [deɪˈkɑːt] *pr n* Descartes.

descend [dɪˈsend] *vi* -**1.** *fml* [go, move down] descendre; she ~ed from the train elle est descendue du train; the path ~s to the sea le sentier descend jusqu'à la mer. -**2.** [fall] tomber, s'abattre; a thick blanket of fog ~ed on the valley une couche épaisse de brouillard tomba sur la vallée; despair ~ed upon the families of the missing men *fig* le désespoir gagna OR envahit les familles des disparus. -**3.** [pass on by ancestry] descendre; [pass on by inheritance] revenir; dogs and wolves probably ~ from a common ancestor les chiens et les loups descendent probablement d'un ancêtre commun; Lord Grey's title ~ed to his grandson le titre de Lord Grey est revenu à son petit-fils. -**4.** [attack, invade] s'abattre; Henry's army ~ed on the French coast l'armée de Henri s'abattit sur la côte française; my in-laws ~ed on us last weekend *hum* ma belle-famille a débarqué chez nous le week-end dernier. -**5.** [sink, stoop] s'abaisser, descendre; I never thought she would ~ to malicious gossip je n'aurais jamais pensé qu'elle s'abaisserait à cancaner; you don't want to ~ to their level tu ne vas quand même pas te rabaisser à leur niveau.

descendant [dɪˈsendənt] *n* descendant *m*, -e *f*.

descended [dɪˈsendɪd] *adj*: she is ~ from the Russian aristocracy elle descend OR est issue de l'aristocratie russe; man is ~ from the apes l'homme descend du singe.

descender [dɪˈsendəʳ] *n* jambage *m*.

descending [dɪˈsendɪŋ] *adj* descendant; in ~ order of importance par ordre décroissant d'importance.

descent [dɪˈsent] *n* -**1.** [move downward] descente *f*; the aircraft made a sudden ~ l'avion a fait une descente subite; the stream makes a gentle ~ le lit du ruisseau est en pente douce. -**2.** *fig* & *lit* [decline] chute *f*; a ~ into hell une descente aux enfers. -**3.** [origin] origine *f*; John Kennedy was of Irish ~ John Kennedy était d'origine irlandaise; I've traced my ~ back to a sixteenth-century noble family j'ai retrouvé la trace de mes ascendants dans une famille noble du seizième siècle. -**4.** [succession, transmission] transmission *f*. -**5.** [invasion] descente *f*; we're braced for the ~ on the town of thousands of football fans nous sommes prêts pour la venue des milliers de fans de football qui vont s'abattre sur la ville.

descramble [ˌdiːˈskræmbl] *vt* débrouiller.

describe [dɪˈskraɪb] *vt* -**1.** [recount, represent] décrire; how would you ~ yourself? comment vous décririez-vous?; witnesses ~d the man as tall and dark-haired des témoins ont décrit l'homme comme étant grand et brun; she ~d her attacker to the police elle a fait une description OR un portrait de son agresseur à la police; he ~d her to them in great detail il la leur a décrite de façon très détaillée. -**2.** [characterize] définir, qualifier; the general ~d himself as a simple man le général s'est défini comme un homme simple; the Chancellor's methods have been ~ed as unorthodox on a qualifié les méthodes du Chancelier de pas très orthodoxes; our relations with them could best be ~d as strained nos relations avec eux pourraient être qualifiées de OR sont pour le moins tendues. -**3.** [outline, draw] décrire.

description [dɪˈskrɪpʃn] *n* -**1.** [account, representation] description *f*; [physical] portrait *m*; ADMIN signalement *m*; the brochure gives a detailed ~ of the hotel la brochure donne une description détaillée de l'hôtel; can you give us a ~ of the man? pouvez-vous nous faire un portrait de l'homme?; a man answering the police ~ un homme correspondant au signalement donné par la police; the food at the reception was beyond OR past ~ le repas servi à la réception était indescriptible; her father was angry beyond ~ son père était dans une colère indescriptible. -**2.** [kind] sorte *f*, genre *m*; the police seized weapons of every ~ la police a saisi toutes sortes d'armes; we were unable to find a vehicle of any ~ nous étions incapables de trouver un quelconque véhicule.

descriptive [dɪˈskrɪptɪv] *adj* descriptif.

descriptive geometry *n* géométrie *f* descriptive.

descriptive linguistics *n* linguistique *f* descriptive.

descriptively [dɪˈskrɪptɪvlɪ] *adv* de façon descriptive; he gave a ~ accurate account of events il nous a fait une description très fidèle des faits.

descriptivism [dɪˈskrɪptɪvɪzm] *n* descriptivisme *m*.

descriptor [dɪˈskrɪptəʳ] *n* descripteur *m*.

descry [dɪˈskraɪ] (*pt* & *pp* descried) *vt lit* apercevoir, distinguer.

desecrate [ˈdesɪkreɪt] *vt* profaner.

desecration [ˌdesɪˈkreɪʃn] *n* profanation *f*.

desegregate [ˌdiːˈsegrɪgeɪt] *vt* abolir la ségrégation raciale dans; ~d schools écoles qui ne sont plus soumises à la ségrégation raciale.

desegregation [ˌdiːsegrɪˈgeɪʃn] *n* déségrégation *f*.

deselect [ˌdiːsɪˈlekt] *vt Br* POL ne pas réinvestir *(un candidat)*.

desensitize, **-ise** [ˌdiːˈsensɪtaɪz] *vt* désensibiliser.

desert[1] [ˈdezət] ◇ *n* [wilderness] désert *m*; 'The Desert Song' *del Ruth* 'le Chant du désert'.
◇ *comp* [area, plant, sand] désertique.

desert[2] [dɪˈzɜːt] ◇ *vt* [person] abandonner, délaisser *lit*; [place] abandonner, déserter; [organization, principle] déserter; the soldier ~ed his post MIL le soldat déserta son poste; the streets were ~ed les rues étaient désertes; his wits ~ed him *fig* il a perdu son sang-froid.
◇ *vi* MIL déserter; one of the officers ~ed to the enemy un des officiers est passé à l'ennemi.

desert boots *npl chaussures en daim à lacets*.

deserter [dɪˈzɜːtəʳ] *n* déserteur *m*.

desertification [dɪˌzɜːtɪfɪˈkeɪʃn] *n* désertification *f*.

desertion [dɪˈzɜːʃn] *n* MIL désertion *f*; JUR [of spouse] abandon *m* (du domicile conjugal); [of cause, organization] défection *f*, désertion *f*.

desert island *n* île *f* déserte.

Desert Island Discs *pr n émission de radio hebdomadaire britannique*.

DESERT ISLAND DISCS:
«Desert Island Discs» est une émission radiophonique au cours de laquelle les personnalités invitées doivent choisir les disques, livres etc qu'ils emporteraient avec eux sur une île déserte.

---

desert rat *n* -**1.** ZOOL gerboise *f*. -**2.** *Br* MIL *soldat britannique combattant en Afrique du Nord (pendant la Seconde Guerre mondiale)*.

deserts [dɪˈzɜːts] *npl* [reward]: to get one's just ~ avoir ce que l'on mérite.

deserve [dɪˈzɜːv] ◇ *vt* mériter; the book, though controversial, didn't ~ to be banned le livre, bien que controversé, ne méritait pas d'être interdit OR qu'on l'interdise; he ~s to die il mérite la mort; she ~s wider recognition elle mérite d'être plus largement reconnue; she's taking a much ~d holiday elle prend des vacances bien méritées; I think he got what he ~d je pense qu'il a eu ce qu'il méritait; frankly, they ~ each other franchement ils se valent l'un l'autre OR ils sont dignes l'un de l'autre.
◇ *vi* mériter; to ~ well of sthg *fml* bien mériter de qqch.

deservedly [dɪˈzɜːvɪdlɪ] *adv* à juste titre, à bon droit; Mozart has been described as a genius, and ~ so on a décrit Mozart comme un génie, à juste titre.

deserving [dɪˈzɜːvɪŋ] *adj* [person] méritant; [cause, organization] méritoire; a musician ~ of greater recognition *fml* un musicien qui mérite d'être davantage reconnu du public.

desex [ˌdiːˈseks] *vt* désexualiser.

deshabille [ˈdezæbiːl] *n*: in ~ en déshabillé, en négligé.

desiccant [ˈdesɪkənt] *n* dessiccatif *m*.

desiccate [ˈdesɪkeɪt] *vt* dessécher, sécher.

desiccated [ˈdesɪkeɪtɪd] *adj* -**1.** [dehydrated]: ~ coconut noix *f* de coco séchée. -**2.** [dull - style] aride; [- person] desséché.

desiccation [ˌdesɪˈkeɪʃn] *n* dessication *f*.

desiccator [ˈdesɪkeɪtəʳ] *n* dessicateur *m*.

desideratum [dɪˌzɪdəˈrɑːtəm] (*pl* desiderata [-tə]) *n (usu pl)* desideratum *m*.

design [dɪˈzaɪn] ◇ *n* -**1.** [drawing, sketch] dessin *m*; INDUST dessin *m*, plan *m*; ARCHIT plan *m*, projet *m*; TEX modèle *m*; [of book] maquette *f*; the ~ for the new museum has been severely criticized les projets OR plans du nouveau musée ont été sévèrement critiqués. -**2.** INDUST [composition, structure - of car, computer etc] conception *f*; the problems were all due to poor ~ tous les problèmes viennent de ce que la conception est mauvaise. -**3.** [subject for study] design *m*; book ~ conception *f* graphique; fashion ~ stylisme *m*; industrial ~ dessin *m* industriel. -**4.** [pattern] motif *m*; a geometric ~ un motif géométrique. -**5.** [purpose, intent] dessein *m*; to do sthg by ~ faire qqch à dessein OR exprès; to have ~s on sb/sthg avoir des vues sur qqn/qqch.
◇ *vt* [plan] concevoir; [on paper] dessiner; ARCHIT faire les plans de; TEX concevoir, créer; the system is ~ed to favour the landowners le système est conçu pour OR vise à favoriser les propriétaires terriens; it's specially ~ed for very low temperatures c'est spécialement conçu pour les très basses températures; she ~s jewellery elle dessine des bijoux.
◇ *comp* [course] de dessin; ~ award prix *m* du meilleur design; ~ department bureau *m* d'études; ~ engineer ingénieur *m* d'études; ~ studio cabinet *m* de design.

designate [*vb* ˈdezɪgneɪt, *adj* ˈdezɪgnət] ◇ *vt fml* -**1.** [appoint, name] désigner, nommer; the Ambassador to the United States has been ~d as the new Foreign Minister l'ambassadeur aux États-Unis a été désigné pour être le nouveau ministre des Affaires étrangères; a special prosecutor was ~d to investigate the charges un procureur spécial fut désigné pour enquêter sur les accusations; the theatre should rightfully

be ~d a national monument il serait légitime que le théâtre soit classé monument historique; the school was ~d as a civil defence training centre l'école fut choisie comme centre de défense civile. -2. [indicate, signify] indiquer, montrer; the flags on the map ~ enemy positions les drapeaux sur la carte indiquent OR signalent les positions ennemies.
◇ *adj* désigné.

designation [ˌdezɪgˈneɪʃn] *n* désignation *f*.

designedly [dɪˈzaɪnɪdlɪ] *adv* à dessein.

designer [dɪˈzaɪnəʳ] ◇ *n* ART & INDUST dessinateur *m*, -trice *f*; TEX modéliste *mf*, styliste *mf*; CIN & THEAT décorateur *m*, -trice *f*; [of high fashion clothes] couturier *m*, -ère *f*; [of books, magazines] maquettiste *mf*; [of furniture] designer *m*; she's a jewellery ~ elle est dessinatrice en bijouterie.
◇ *comp* [jeans] haute couture; [glasses, handbag] de marque; [furniture] design; ~ stubble *hum* barbe *f* de deux jours.

designing [dɪˈzaɪnɪŋ] ◇ *adj* [cunning] rusé; [scheming] intrigant.
◇ *n* [design work] conception *f*, dessin *m*, design *m*.

desinence [ˈdesɪnəns] *n* désinence *f*.

desirability [dɪˌzaɪərəˈbɪlətɪ] *n* *(U)* -1. [benefits] intérêt *m*, avantage *m*, opportunité *f*; no one questions the ~ of lowering interest rates personne ne conteste les avantages d'une baisse des taux d'intérêts. -2. [attractiveness] charmes *mpl*, attraits *mpl*.

desirable [dɪˈzaɪərəbl] *adj* -1. [advisable] souhaitable, désirable *fml*; some knowledge of languages is ~ *fml* des connaissances en langues étrangères sont souhaitables. -2. [attractive] à désirer, tentant; a ~ residence une belle propriété. -3. [sexually appealing] désirable, séduisant.

desire [dɪˈzaɪəʳ] ◇ *n* -1. [wish] désir *m*, envie *f*; she had no ~ to go back elle n'avait aucune envie d'y retourner; he had not the least OR slightest ~ to find a job il n'avait nullement OR pas la moindre envie de trouver un emploi; my one ~ is that you should be happy mon seul désir OR tout ce que je souhaite, c'est que vous soyez heureux; it is your father's ~ that you should become an officer c'est le désir de votre père que vous deveniez officier. -2. [sexual attraction] désir *m*; to feel ~ for sb désirer OR avoir envie de qqn.
◇ *vt* -1. [want, wish] désirer; you may spend the night here, if you so ~ vous pouvez passer la nuit ici, si vous le désirez; your presence is ~d at the palace *fml* votre présence est requise au palais; the Prince ~s that you should be his guest tonight *fml* le Prince désire que vous soyez son invité ce soir; the agreement left much OR a great deal OR a lot to be ~d l'accord laissait beaucoup à désirer; his words had the ~d effect ses paroles eurent l'effet désiré OR escompté. -2. [want sexually] désirer; she no longer ~d him elle ne le désirait plus, elle n'avait plus envie de lui.

desirous [dɪˈzaɪərəs] *adj fml* désireux; he was ~ of re-establishing friendly relations il était désireux de rétablir des relations amicales.

desist [dɪˈzɪst] *vi fml* cesser; he was asked to ~ from his political activities on lui a demandé de cesser ses activités politiques.

desk [desk] ◇ *n* -1. [in home, office] bureau *m*; [with folding top] secrétaire *m*; SCH [for pupil] pupitre *m*; [for teacher] bureau *m*. -2. [reception counter] réception *f*; [cashier] caisse *f*. -3. PRESS [section] service *m*; the sports ~ le service des informations sportives.
◇ *comp* [diary, job, lamp] de bureau; ~ blotter *Br* sous-main *m inv*.

deskbound [ˈdeskbaʊnd] *adj* sédentaire; she hates being ~ elle déteste faire un travail sédentaire.

desk clerk *n Am* réceptionniste *mf*.

desk editor *n* rédacteur *m*, -trice *f*.

deskill [ˌdiːˈskɪl] *vt* déqualifier.

desktop [ˈdesktɒp] *adj* [computer, model] de bureau; ~ publishing publication *f* assistée par ordinateur.

desolate [*adj* ˈdesələt, *vb* ˈdesəleɪt] ◇ *adj* -1. [area, place - empty] désert; [- barren, lifeless] désolé; *fig* [gloomy, bleak] morne, sombre. -2. [person - sorrowful] consterné, abattu; [- friendless] délaissé.
◇ *vt* -1. [area, place - devastate] dévaster, saccager; [- depopulate] dépeupler. -2. [person] désoler, navrer; he was ~d at OR by the loss of his job il était désolé OR navré d'avoir perdu son emploi.

desolation [ˌdesəˈleɪʃn] *n* -1. [barrenness, emptiness] caractère *m* désert, désolation *f*; [devastation, ruin] dévastation *f*, ravages *mpl*. -2. [despair, sorrow] désolation *f*, consternation *f*; [loneliness] solitude *f*.

despair [dɪˈspeəʳ] ◇ *n* -1. [hopelessness] désespoir *m*; in ~, she took her own life de désespoir elle a mis fin à ses jours; his ~ at ever finding a job made him turn to crime parce qu'il désespérait de trouver un emploi, il est tombé dans la délinquance; the people are in ~ at OR over the prospect of war les gens sont désespérés à cause des perspectives de guerre; their son drove them to ~ leur fils les désespérait OR les réduisait au désespoir. -2. [cause of distress] désespoir *m*; William was the ~ of his teachers William faisait OR était le désespoir de tous ses professeurs.
◇ *vi* désespérer; she began to ~ of ever finding her brother alive elle commençait à désespérer de retrouver un jour son frère vivant; he ~ed at the thought of all the work he had to do il était désespéré à l'idée de tout le travail qu'il avait à faire; don't ~, help is on the way ne désespérez pas, les secours arrivent.

despairing [dɪˈspeərɪŋ] *adj* [cry, look] de désespoir, désespéré; [person] abattu, consterné.

despairingly [dɪˈspeərɪŋlɪ] *adv* [look, speak] avec désespoir.

despatch [dɪˈspætʃ] = **dispatch**.

desperado [ˌdespəˈrɑːdəʊ] (*pl* desperadoes OR desperados) *n lit* OR *hum* desperado *m*, hors-la-loi *m inv*.

desperate [ˈdesprət] *adj* -1. [hopeless, serious] désespéré; we were in a ~ state nous étions dans une situation désespérée; the refugees are in ~ need of help les réfugiés ont désespérément besoin d'assistance. -2. [reckless] désespéré; he died in a ~ attempt to escape il est mort en essayant désespérément de s'évader; we heard ~ screams nous avons entendu des cris désespérés OR de désespoir; I'm afraid she'll do something ~ j'ai bien peur qu'elle ne tente un acte désespéré; a ~ criminal/man un criminel/homme prêt à tout. -3. [intent, eager]: to be ~ for money avoir un besoin urgent d'argent; she was ~ to leave home elle voulait à tout prix partir de chez elle; I'm ~ to go to the loo *inf*, I'm ~ *inf hum* je ne tiens plus, ça urge.

desperately [ˈdesprətlɪ] *adv* -1. [hopelessly, seriously] désespérément; their country is ~ poor leur pays est d'une pauvreté désespérante; he was ~ ill with malaria il était gravement atteint par le paludisme; they're ~ in love ils s'aiment éperdument. -2. [recklessly] désespérément; the soldiers fought ~ les soldats se battaient désespérément OR avec acharnement. -3. [as intensifier] terriblement; he ~ wanted to become an actor il voulait à tout prix devenir acteur; we're ~ busy at the moment nous sommes terriblement occupés en ce moment; he's ~ sorry il est affreusement désolé; do you want to go – not ~ tu veux y aller? – pas vraiment.

desperation [ˌdespəˈreɪʃn] *n* désespoir *m*; he agreed in ~ en désespoir de cause, il a accepté.

despicable [dɪˈspɪkəbl] *adj* [person] méprisable, détestable; [action, behaviour] méprisable, ignoble; it was a ~ thing to do c'était un acte indigne.

despicably [dɪˈspɪkəblɪ] *adv* [behave] bassement, d'une façon indigne.

despise [dɪˈspaɪz] *vt* [feel contempt for] mépriser; he ~d himself for his cowardice il se méprisait d'avoir été lâche.

despite [dɪˈspaɪt] ◇ *prep* malgré, en dépit de; ~ leaving early, I still missed the train bien que je sois parti de bonne heure, j'ai manqué mon train; ~ having a degree she's still unemployed bien que diplômée OR malgré son diplôme, elle est toujours au chômage; he laughed ~ himself il n'a pas pu s'empêcher de rire.
◇ *n arch* [malice, spite] dépit *m*.

despoil [dɪˈspɔɪl] *vt fml* OR *lit* [person] spolier, dépouiller; [land, town] piller.

despoiler [dɪˈspɔɪləʳ] *n* spoliateur *m*, -trice *f*.

despoiling [dɪˈspɔɪlɪŋ] *n* spoliation *f*.

despondence [dɪˈspɒndəns], **despondency** [dɪˈspɒndənsɪ] *n* abattement *m*, consternation *f*.

despondent [dɪˈspɒndənt] *adj* abattu, consterné.

despondently [dɪˈspɒndəntlɪ] *adv* d'un air consterné; [say, speak] d'un ton consterné; he wrote ~ of his failure to find work il écrivit une lettre découragée où il disait qu'il ne trouvait pas de travail.

despot [ˈdespɒt] *n* despote *m*.

despotic [deˈspɒtɪk] *adj* despotique.

despotically [deˈspɒtɪklɪ] *adv* despotiquement; to govern/to rule ~ gouverner/régner en despote.

despotism [ˈdespətɪzm] *n* despotisme *m*.

dessert [dɪˈzɜːt] ◇ *n* dessert *m*; what's for ~? qu'est-ce qu'il y a comme dessert?; we had ice cream for ~ nous avons eu de la glace en dessert.
◇ *comp* [dish, plate] à dessert; a ~ apple une pomme à couteau; a ~ wine un vin de dessert.

dessertspoon [dɪˈzɜːtspuːn] *n* cuiller *f* à dessert.

dessertspoonful [dɪˈzɜːtspuːnˌfʊl] *n* cuillerée *f* à dessert.

destabilization [diːˌsteɪbɪlaɪˈzeɪʃn] *n* déstabilisation *f*.

destabilize, -ise [ˌdiːˈsteɪbɪlaɪz] *vt* déstabiliser.

de-Stalinization [ˈdiːˌstɑːlɪnaɪˈzeɪʃn] *n* déstalinisation *f*.

de-Stalinize, -ise [ˌdiːˈstɑːlɪnaɪz] *vt* déstaliniser.

destination [ˌdestɪˈneɪʃn] *n* destination *f*.

destined [ˈdestɪnd] *adj* -1. [intended]: she felt she was ~ for an acting career elle sentait qu'elle était destinée à une carrière d'actrice; she was ~ for greater things elle était promise à un plus grand avenir; their plan was ~ to fail OR for failure leur projet était voué à l'échec; she was ~ never to have children le destin a voulu qu'elle n'ait jamais d'enfant; De Gaulle felt he was ~ to lead France De Gaulle sentait que son destin était de diriger la France. -2. [bound]: the flight was ~ for Sydney le vol était à destination de Sydney.

destiny [ˈdestɪnɪ] *n* [fate] destin *m*; [personal fate] destinée *f*, destin *m*; she felt it was her ~ to become a writer elle avait le sentiment que c'était son destin de devenir écrivain.

destitute [ˈdestɪtjuːt] ◇ *adj* -1. [extremely poor] dans la misère, sans ressources; the drought has left many farmers ~ la sécheresse a réduit beaucoup d'agriculteurs à la misère. -2. *fml* [lacking]: ~ of dépourvu de; ~ of talent *fig* dépourvu OR démuni de talent.
◇ *npl*: the ~ les indigents *mpl* OR démunis *mpl*.

destitution [ˌdestɪˈtjuːʃn] *n* misère *f*, indigence *f*; the old woman lived in utter ~ la vieille femme vivait dans une misère noire.

destroy [dɪˈstrɔɪ] *vt* -1. [demolish, wreck] détruire; an explosion has completely ~ed the railway station une explosion a dévasté OR complètement détruit la gare; they threaten to ~ our democratic way of life ils menacent d'anéantir OR de détruire nos institutions démocratiques. -2. [ruin, spoil - efforts, hope, love] anéantir, briser; [- career, friendship, marriage] briser; [- health] ruiner; his wartime experiences ~ed his faith in humanity ses expériences de guerre ont brisé sa foi en l'humanité; to ~ sb's life briser la vie de qqn. -3. [kill - farm animal] abattre; [- pet] supprimer, (faire) piquer; we had to have the dog ~ed nous avons dû faire piquer le chien.

destroyer [dɪ'strɔɪəʳ] *n* -1. MIL destroyer *m*, contre-torpilleur *m*. -2. [person] destructeur *m*, -trice *f*.

destroyer escort *n* escorteur *m*.

destruct [dɪ'strʌkt] ◇ *vt* détruire.
◇ *vi* se détruire.
◇ *n* destruction *f*.
◇ *comp* [button, mechanism] de destruction.

destructible [dɪ'strʌktəbl] *adj* destructible.

destruction [dɪ'strʌkʃn] *n* -1. [demolition, devastation] destruction *f*; the earthquake brought about the ~ of whole villages le tremblement de terre a entraîné la disparition de villages entiers; a nuclear war would result in total ~ une guerre nucléaire mènerait à une destruction totale. -2. [elimination - of evidence] suppression *f*; [- of life, hope] anéantissement *m*. -3. *fig* [ruin] ruine *f*; drink and drugs proved to be his ~ l'alcool et la drogue l'ont détruit OR mené à sa perte.

destructive [dɪ'strʌktɪv] *adj* destructeur; the ~ power of a bomb le pouvoir destructif d'une bombe; she's a ~ child c'est une enfant qui aime casser; ~ criticism une critique destructrice OR accablante.

destructively [dɪ'strʌktɪvlɪ] *adv* de façon destructrice.

destructiveness [dɪ'strʌktɪvnɪs] *n* [of bomb, weapon] capacité *f* destructrice; [of criticism] caractère *m* destructeur; [of person] penchant *m* destructeur.

destructor [dɪ'strʌktəʳ] *n Br* [incinerator] incinérateur *m*; AERON bouton *m* explosif.

desuetude [dɪ'sju:ɪtju:d] *n lit* désuétude *f*.

desultory ['desəltrɪ] *adj fml* [conversation] décousu, sans suite; [attempt] peu suivi, peu soutenu, sans suite; he made only a ~ attempt to learn Italian il n'a pas vraiment fait d'efforts pour apprendre l'italien.

Det. *written abbr of* detective.

detach [dɪ'tætʃ] *vt* -1. [handle, hood] détacher. -2. [person]: to ~ o.s. se détacher, prendre du recul; he can't ~ himself sufficiently from the conflict il n'a pas assez de recul par rapport au conflit. -3. MIL [troops] envoyer en détachement.

detachable [dɪ'tætʃəbl] *adj* détachable; [collar, lining] amovible.

detached [dɪ'tætʃt] *adj* -1. [separate] détaché, séparé; ~ house *Br* maison *f* individuelle, pavillon *m*. -2. [objective] objectif; [unemotional] détaché.

detachment [dɪ'tætʃmənt] *n* -1. [separation] séparation *f*. -2. [indifference] détachement *m*; [objectivity] objectivité *f*. -3. MIL détachement *m*.

detail [*Br* 'di:teɪl, *Am* dɪ'teɪl] ◇ *n* -1. [item, element] détail *m*; there's no need to go into ~ OR ~s ça ne sert à rien d'entrer dans les détails; the author recounts his childhood in great ~ l'auteur raconte son enfance dans les moindres détails; attention to ~ is important il faut être minutieux OR méticuleux; that's a mere ~! ce n'est qu'un point de détail! -2. MIL détachement *m*.
◇ *vt* -1. [enumerate, specify] raconter en détail, détailler, énumérer; operating instructions are fully ~ed in the booklet le mode d'emploi détaillé se trouve dans le livret. -2. MIL détacher, affecter.
◆ **details** *npl* [particulars] renseignements *mpl*, précisions *fpl*; [name, address etc] coordonnées *fpl*.

detail drawing *n* épure *f*.

detailed [*Br* 'di:teɪld, *Am* dɪ'teɪld] *adj* détaillé; a ~ account un compte rendu détaillé OR très précis.

detain [dɪ'teɪn] *vt* -1. *fml* [delay] retenir; I won't ~ you any longer than is necessary je ne vous retiendrai pas plus longtemps que nécessaire OR qu'il n'est nécessaire. -2. JUR [keep in custody] retenir, garder à vue; to ~ sb for questioning mettre OR placer qqn en garde à vue.

detainee [,di:teɪ'ni:] *n* détenu *m*, -e *f*.

detect [dɪ'tekt] *vt* déceler, discerner, distinguer, découvrir; MIL & MIN détecter; MED dépister; the aircraft cannot be ~ed by radar l'avion ne peut pas être détecté OR repéré par radar; do I ~ a certain lack of enthusiasm on your part? je crois déceler un certain manque d'enthousiasme de ta part.

detectable [dɪ'tektəbl] *adj* MIL & MIN détectable; [illness] que l'on peut dépister; the poison is not ~ in the bloodstream on ne peut pas déceler la présence du poison dans le sang.

detection [dɪ'tekʃn] ◇ *n* -1. [discovery] découverte *f*; MIL & MIN détection *f*; MED dépistage *m*; athletes who have used banned drugs have so far escaped ~ on n'a pas encore repéré les athlètes qui se sont dopés avec des substances interdites; the thieves managed to enter the building without ~ les cambrioleurs ont pénétré dans le bâtiment sans éveiller l'attention OR sans qu'on s'en aperçoive. -2. [investigation] recherche *f*; crime ~ la recherche des criminels; the killer escaped ~ le tueur échappa aux recherches.
◇ *adj* [device] de détection; MED de dépistage.

detective [dɪ'tektɪv] ◇ *n* [on a police force] ≃ inspecteur *m*, -trice *f* de police; [private] détective *m*; 'Emil and the Detectives' *Kästner* 'Émile et les détectives'.
◇ *comp* [film, novel, story] policier.

detective constable *n Br* ≃ inspecteur *m*, -trice *f* de police.

detective inspector *n Br* ≃ inspecteur de police principal *m*, inspectrice de police principale *f*.

detective sergeant *n Br* ≃ inspecteur *m*, -trice *f* de police.

detector [dɪ'tektəʳ] *n* détecteur *m*.

detector van *n Br voiture-radar utilisée pour la détection des postes de télévision non déclarés.*

detention [dɪ'tenʃn] *n* -1. [captivity] détention *f*; in ~ [gen] en détention; MIL aux arrêts. -2. SCH retenue *f*, consigne *f*; the entire class was given an hour's ~ toute la classe a eu une heure de retenue; to put sb in ~ consigner qqn, mettre qqn en retenue.

detention centre *n jusqu'en 1988, centre de détention pour jeunes délinquants (aujourd'hui: 'young offenders' institution').*

deter [dɪ'tɜ:ʳ] (*pt* & *pp* deterred, *cont* deterring) *vt* -1. [discourage - person] dissuader; to ~ sb from doing sthg dissuader qqn de faire qqch; he was not to be deterred from his purpose il n'allait pas se laisser détourner de son but. -2. [prevent - attack] prévenir.

detergent [dɪ'tɜ:dʒənt] ◇ *n* détergent *m*, détersif *m*; *Am* [washing powder] lessive *f*.
◇ *adj* détersif, détergent.

deteriorate [dɪ'tɪərɪəreɪt] *vi* se détériorer; her health has ~d rapidly over the past few months sa santé s'est détériorée OR dégradée rapidement au cours des derniers mois.

deterioration [dɪ,tɪərɪə'reɪʃn] *n* détérioration *f*; [in health, relations] dégradation *f*, détérioration *f*; there has been a ~ in the weather le temps s'est dégradé OR gâté.

determinant [dɪ'tɜ:mɪnənt] ◇ *n* déterminant *m*.
◇ *adj* déterminant.

determination [dɪ,tɜ:mɪ'neɪʃn] *n* -1. [resolve] détermination *f*, résolution *f*; she showed a dogged ~ to find her natural mother elle était plus que déterminée OR résolue à retrouver sa vraie mère; he set off with an air of ~ il se mit en route d'un air résolu OR décidé. -2. [establishment, fixing - of prices, wages etc] détermination *f*, fixation *f*; [- of boundaries] délimitation *f*, établissement *m*.

determinative [dɪ'tɜ:mɪnətɪv] ◇ *adj* déterminant; GRAMM déterminatif.
◇ *n* élément *m* déterminant; GRAMM déterminant *m*, déterminatif *m*.

determine [dɪ'tɜ:mɪn] *vt* -1. [control, govern] déterminer, décider de; the commanding officer ~d the fate of the prisoners le commandant décida du sort des prisonniers. -2. [establish, find out] déterminer, établir; the police were unable to ~ the cause of death la police n'a pas pu déterminer OR établir la cause du décès. -3. [fix, settle - date, price, wage] déterminer, fixer; [- boundary] délimiter, établir. -4. *lit* [resolve]: she ~d to prove her innocence elle a décidé de OR s'est résolue à prouver son innocence.

determined [dɪ'tɜ:mɪnd] *adj* -1. [decided, resolved] déterminé, décidé; to be ~ to do sthg être déterminé OR résolu à faire qqch; she was ~ (that) her son would go to university elle était bien décidée OR déterminée à ce que son fils fasse des études supérieures; he's a very ~ young man c'est un jeune homme très décidé OR qui a de la suite dans les idées. -2. [resolute]: they made ~ efforts to find all survivors ils ont fait tout ce qu'ils ont pu pour retrouver tous les survivants.

determinedly [dɪ'tɜ:mɪndlɪ] *adv* avec détermination.

determiner [dɪ'tɜ:mɪnəʳ] *n* déterminant *m*.

determining [dɪ'tɜ:mɪnɪŋ] *adj* déterminant.

determinism [dɪ'tɜ:mɪnɪzm] *n* déterminisme *m*.

determinist [dɪ'tɜ:mɪnɪst] ◇ *adj* déterministe.
◇ *n* déterministe *mf*.

deterministic [dɪ,tɜ:mɪ'nɪstɪk] = **determinist** *adj*.

deterrence [dɪ'terəns] *n* [gen] dissuasion *f*; MIL force *f* de dissuasion.

deterrent [dɪ'terənt] ◇ *n* -1. [gen] agent *m* de dissuasion; fear acted as a strong ~ la peur a eu un très grand effet de dissuasion. -2. MIL arme *f* de dissuasion.
◇ *adj* dissuasif, de dissuasion.

detest [dɪ'test] *vt* détester; I ~ housework j'ai horreur de OR je déteste faire le ménage; she ~s having to make small talk elle a horreur de OR elle déteste papoter.

detestable [dɪ'testəbl] *adj* détestable, exécrable.

detestation [,di:te'steɪʃn] *n* haine *f*, horreur *f*.

dethrone [dɪ'θrəʊn] *vt* détrôner, déposer.

dethronement [dɪ'θrəʊnmənt] *n* déposition *f (d'un souverain)*.

detonate ['detəneɪt] ◇ *vt* faire détoner OR exploser.
◇ *vi* détoner, exploser.

detonation [,detə'neɪʃn] *n* détonation *f*, explosion *f*.

detonator ['detəneɪtəʳ] *n* détonateur *m*, amorce *f*; RAIL pétard *m*.

detour ['di:,tʊəʳ] ◇ *n* [in road, stream] détour *m*; [for traffic] déviation *f*.
◇ *vi* faire un détour.
◇ *vt* (faire) dévier.

detoxicate [,di:'tɒksɪkeɪt] *vt* -1. [person] désintoxiquer. -2. [poison] détoxiquer.

detoxication ['di:,tɒksɪ'keɪʃn] *n* -1. [of person] désintoxication *f*. -2. [of poison] détoxication *f*.

detoxification [di:,tɒksɪfɪ'keɪʃn] *n* [of person] désintoxication *f*.

detoxify [,di:'tɒksɪfaɪ] (*pt* & *pp* detoxified) *vt* [person] désintoxiquer.

detract [dɪ'trækt] *vi*: to ~ from sthg diminuer qqch; the bad weather did not in the least ~ from our enjoyment of the holiday le mauvais temps ne nous a pas le moins du monde empêchés d'apprécier nos vacances; the criticism in no way ~s from her achievements la critique ne réduit en rien la portée de OR n'enlève rien à ce qu'elle a accompli.

detraction [dɪ'trækʃn] *n* critique *f*, dénigrement *m*.

detractor [dɪ'træktəʳ] *n* détracteur *m*, -trice *f*.

detrain [ˌdiːˈtreɪn] *fml* ◇ *vi* descendre *(d'un train)*.
◇ *vt* débarquer *(d'un train)*.

detriment [ˈdetrɪmənt] *n*: to his ~ à son détriment OR préjudice; to the ~ of his work aux dépens de son travail; without ~ to the truth sans porter atteinte OR sans nuire à la vérité.

detrimental [ˌdetrɪˈmentl] *adj*: ~ to [health, reputation] nuisible à, préjudiciable à; ~ to [interests] qui nuit à, qui cause un préjudice à; pollution has a ~ effect on OR is ~ to plant life la pollution nuit à la flore.

detritus [dɪˈtraɪtəs] *n (U) fml* [debris] détritus *m*; GEOL roches *fpl* détritiques, pierrailles *fpl*.

Detroit [dɪˈtrɔɪt] *pr n* Detroit.

detumescence [ˌdiːtjuːˈmesəns] *n* détumescence *f*.

detumescent [ˌdiːtjuːˈmesənt] *adj* détumescent.

deuce [djuːs] *n* -**1.** [on card, dice] deux *m*. -**2.** TENNIS égalité *f*. -**3.** *inf dated* [as expletive]: where the ~ is it? où diable peut-il bien être?; how the ~ should I know? comment voulez-vous que je sache?; we're in a ~ of a mess nous sommes dans un sacré OR satané pétrin.

deuced *inf* [djuːst] ◇ *adj dated* sacré, satané, fichu.
◇ *adv* diablement, bigrement.

deus ex machina [ˌdeɪəseksˈmækɪnə] *n* deus ex machina *m*.

deuterium [djuːˈtɪərɪəm] *n* deutérium *m*.

deuterium oxide *n* eau *f* lourde.

Deuteronomy [ˌdjuːtəˈrɒnəmɪ] *pr n* Deutéronome.

Deutsche Mark, Deutschmark [ˈdɔɪtʃˌmɑːk] *n* (Deutsche) Mark *m*.

devaluation [ˌdiːvæljʊˈeɪʃn] *n* dévaluation *f*.

devalue [ˌdiːˈvæljuː] *vt* dévaluer.

devastate [ˈdevəsteɪt] *vt* -**1.** [country, town] dévaster, ravager; [enemy] anéantir. -**2.** [overwhelm] foudroyer, accabler, anéantir; he was ~d by his mother's death la mort de sa mère l'a complètement anéanti.

devastating [ˈdevəsteɪtɪŋ] *adj* -**1.** [disastrous - passion, storm] dévastateur, ravageur; [- news] accablant; [- argument, effect] accablant, écrasant. -**2.** [highly effective - person, charm] irrésistible; he has a ~ wit son (sens de l') humour est irrésistible.

devastatingly [ˈdevəsteɪtɪŋlɪ] *adv* de manière dévastatrice; [as intensifier]: ~ beautiful d'une beauté irrésistible; ~ funny d'une drôlerie irrésistible.

devastation [ˌdevəˈsteɪʃn] *n* [disaster] dévastation *f*; scenes of ~ des scènes de dévastation.

develop [dɪˈveləp] ◇ *vi* -**1.** [evolve - country, person] se développer, évoluer; [- feeling] se former, grandir; [- plot] se développer, se dérouler; to ~ into sthg devenir qqch; let's see how things ~ attendons de voir comment les choses évoluent OR tournent. -**2.** [become apparent - disease] se manifester, se déclarer; [- talent, trend] se manifester; [- event] se produire; it later ~ed that they had never actually met il s'est avéré OR il est devenu évident par la suite qu'ils ne s'étaient en fait jamais rencontrés. -**3.** PHOT se développer.
◇ *vt* -**1.** [form - body, mind] développer, former; [- story] développer; [- feeling] former. -**2.** [expand - business, market] développer; [- idea, argument] développer, expliquer (en détail), exposer (en détail). -**3.** [improve - skill] développer, travailler; [- machine, process] mettre au point. -**4.** [acquire - disease] contracter; [- cold, tic] attraper; [- symptoms] présenter; she ~ed a habit of biting her nails elle a pris l'habitude de se ronger les ongles; I've ~ed a taste for jazz je me suis mis à aimer le jazz; she's ~ed a tendency to stutter elle s'est plus ou moins mise à bégayer. -**5.** [land, resources] exploiter, mettre en valeur, aménager; the site is to be ~ed on va construire sur ce terrain, on va aménager le site. -**6.** MATH, MUS & PHOT développer.

developed [dɪˈveləpt] *adj* [film] développé; [land] mis en valeur, aménagé; [country] développé.

developer [dɪˈveləpəʳ] *n* -**1.** [of land] promoteur *m* (de construction). -**2.** [person]: to be a late ~ se développer sur le tard. -**3.** PHOT révélateur *m*, développateur *m*.

developing [dɪˈveləpɪŋ] ◇ *adj* [crisis, storm] qui se prépare, qui s'annonce; [industry] en expansion.
◇ *n* PHOT développement *m*; '~ and printing' travaux photographiques, développement et tirage ❑ ~ bath (bain *m*) révélateur *m*; ~ tank cuve *f* à développement.

developing country, developing nation *n* pays *m* OR nation *f* en voie de développement.

development [dɪˈveləpmənt] *n* -**1.** [of body, person, mind] développement *m*, formation *f*; [of ideas, language] développement *m*, évolution *f*; [of argument, theme] développement *m*, exposé *m*; [of plot, situation] déroulement *m*, développement *m*; [of business] développement *m*, expansion *f*; [of invention, process] mise *f* au point; [of region] mise *f* en valeur, exploitation *f*; they propose the ~ of this land as a residential area ils suggèrent d'aménager ce terrain en zone résidentielle ❑ ~ grant subvention *f* pour le développement. -**2.** [incident] fait *m* nouveau; we're awaiting further ~s nous attendons la suite des événements OR les derniers développements; a surprise ~ un rebondissement; there has been an unexpected ~ l'affaire a pris une tournure inattendue; there are no new ~s il n'y a rien de nouveau. -**3.** [tract of land]: housing ~ cité *f* (ouvrière); industrial ~ zone *f* industrielle. -**4.** MATH, MUS & PHOT développement *m*.

developmental [dɪˌveləpˈmentl] *adj* de développement.

development area *n zone économiquement sinistrée bénéficiant d'aides publiques en vue de sa reconversion*.

development system *n système informatique conçu pour le développement de logiciels*.

deviance [ˈdiːvjəns], **deviancy** [ˈdiːvjənsɪ] *n* [gen & PSYCH] déviance *f*; ~ from the norm écart *m* par rapport à la norme.

deviant [ˈdiːvjənt] ◇ *adj* -**1.** [behaviour] déviant, qui s'écarte de la norme; [growth] anormal; sexually ~ perverti. -**2.** LING déviant.
◇ *n* déviant *m*, -e *f*; sexual ~ pervers *m*, -e *f*.

deviate [ˈdiːvɪeɪt] *vi* -**1.** [differ] dévier, s'écarter; those who ~ from the norm ceux qui s'écartent de la norme. -**2.** [plane, ship] dévier, dériver; [missile] dévier.

deviation [ˌdiːvɪˈeɪʃn] *n* -**1.** [from custom, principle] déviation *f*; [from social norm] déviance *f*; there must be no ~ from the party line on ne doit en aucun cas s'écarter de la ligne du parti. -**2.** [in statistics] écart *m*. -**3.** [of plane, ship] déviation *f*, dérive *f*; [of missile] déviation *f*, dérivation *f*. -**4.** MATH, MED & PHILOS déviation *f*.

deviationism [ˌdiːvɪˈeɪʃənɪzm] *n* déviationnisme *m*.

deviationist [ˌdiːvɪˈeɪʃənɪst] ◇ *adj* déviationniste.
◇ *n* déviationniste *mf*.

device [dɪˈvaɪs] *n* -**1.** [gadget] appareil *m*, engin *m*, mécanisme *m*; a clever ~ un gadget astucieux ❑ safety ~ dispositif *m* de sécurité; nuclear ~ engin nucléaire. -**2.** [scheme] ruse *f*, stratagème *m*; it was just a ~ to get attention ce n'était qu'une ruse pour OR c'était juste un moyen de se faire remarquer ❑ to leave sb to their own ~s laisser qqn se débrouiller (tout seul). -**3.** *lit* [figure of speech] formule *f*. -**4.** HERALD devis *m*, emblème *m*.

devil [ˈdevl] (*Br pt & pp* devilled, *cont* devilling, *Am pt & pp* deviled, *cont* deviling) ◇ *n* -**1.** [demon] diable *m*, démon *m*; the Devil RELIG le Diable, Satan *m*; the ~ take him! *dated* qu'il aille au diable!, que le diable l'emporte!; go to the ~! *inf dated* va te faire voir!, va au diable! ❑ to play ~'s advocate se faire l'avocat du diable; 'The Devil's Disciple' *Shaw* 'le Disciple du Diable'. -**2.** *inf fig* [person]: you little ~! petit monstre!; you lucky ~! veinard!; poor ~! pauvre diable! ❑ go on, be a ~! *hum* allez, laisse-toi faire OR tenter! -**3.** *inf* [as intensifier]: what the ~ are you doing? mais enfin, qu'est-ce que tu fabriques?; where the ~ is it? où diable peut-il bien être?, mais où est-ce que ça pourrait bien être?; how the ~ should I know? comment voulez-vous que je sache?; who the ~ are you? qui diable êtes-vous?, et d'où est-ce que vous sortez, vous?; this house is the very ~ to keep clean c'est vraiment la galère de nettoyer cette maison; they worked/ran like the ~ ils ont travaillé/couru comme des fous OR des malades; he has a ~ of a temper il a un fichu caractère, il a un caractère de cochon; I had a ~ of a time getting here j'ai eu un mal fou OR un mal de chien à arriver jusqu'ici; there'll be the ~ to pay when your father finds out ça va barder quand ton père apprendra ça; we had the ~ of a job OR the ~'s own job finding the house on a eu un mal fou à trouver la maison ❑ between the ~ and the deep blue sea entre l'enclume et le marteau; to give the ~ his due... en toute honnêteté, il faut dire que..., rendons OR rendons-lui justice...; he has the luck of the ~ OR the ~'s own luck il a une veine de pendu OR de cocu; speak OR talk of the ~ (and he appears)! quand on parle du loup (on en voit la queue)!; better the ~ you know than the ~ you don't *prov* on sait ce qu'on perd, on ne sait pas ce qu'on trouve; the ~ finds OR makes work for idle hands *prov* l'oisiveté est (la) mère de tous les vices *prov*; let the ~ take the hindmost *prov* chacun pour soi et Dieu pour tous *prov*. -**4.** [brazier] brasero *m*. -**5.** [ghostwriter] nègre *m (d'un écrivain)*; JUR [assistant] avocat *m* stagiaire; printer's ~ TYPO apprenti *m* imprimeur.
◇ *vt* -**1.** CULIN accommoder à la moutarde et au poivre; devilled egg œuf *m* à la diable. -**2.** *inf Am* [harass] harceler.
◇ *vi Br*: to ~ for sb [author] servir de nègre à qqn; [lawyer] être avocat stagiaire auprès de qqn; [printer] être apprenti imprimeur chez qqn.

devilfish [ˈdevlfɪʃ] *n* mante *f*.

devilish [ˈdevlɪʃ] ◇ *adj* -**1.** [fiendish] diabolique, infernal; [mischievous] espiègle. -**2.** *inf dated* [extreme] sacré, satané.
◇ *adv inf dated* sacrément, rudement; this work is ~ hard ce travail est sacrément OR rudement dur.

devilishly [ˈdevlɪʃlɪ] *adv* -**1.** [fiendishly] diaboliquement; [mischievously] par espièglerie. -**2.** *inf dated* [as intensifier] rudement, sacrément.

devil-may-care *adj* [careless] insouciant; [reckless] casse-cou.

devilment [ˈdevlmənt] *n* [mischief] espièglerie *f*; [malice] méchanceté *f*, malice *f*; a piece of ~ une espièglerie, une diablerie; out of sheer ~ par pure méchanceté.

devilry [ˈdevlrɪ] *n (U)* -**1.** [mischief] espièglerie *f*; [recklessness] témérité *f*. -**2.** [black magic] magie *f* noire, maléfices *mpl*.

devil's food cake *n* gâteau *m* au chocolat noir.

devils-on-horseback *npl* CULIN *pruneaux enveloppés de lard fumé et grillés*.

devious [ˈdiːvjəs] *adj* -**1.** [cunning - person] retors, sournois; [- means, method] détourné; [- mind] tortueux; she can be very ~ elle fait parfois les choses en dessous OR en sous-main. -**2.** [winding - route] sinueux.

deviously [ˈdiːvjəslɪ] *adv* sournoisement.

deviousness [ˈdiːvjəsnɪs] *n* [of person] sournoiserie *f*; [of plan] complexité *f*.

devise [dɪˈvaɪz] ◇ *vt* -**1.** [plan] imaginer, inventer, concevoir, élaborer; [plot] combiner, manigancer; a scheme of my own devising un plan de mon invention. -**2.** JUR [property] léguer.
◇ *n* legs *m* (de biens immobiliers).

deviser [dɪ'vaɪzəʳ] *n* [of plan] inventeur *m*, -trice *f*; [of scheme] auteur *m*.
devitalize, -ise [ˌdiː'vaɪtəlaɪz] *vt* affaiblir.
devitrify [ˌdiː'vɪtrɪfaɪ] (*pt* & *pp* **devitrified**) ◇ *vt* dévitrifier.
◇ *vi* se dévitrifier.
devocalize, -ise [ˌdiː'vəʊkəlaɪz] *vt* assourdir.
devoice [diː'vɔɪs] *vt* assourdir.
devoid [dɪ'vɔɪd] *adj*: ~ **of** dépourvu de; ~ **of interest** dépourvu d'intérêt, sans intérêt; **he appears to be ~ of all moral sense** il semble être dénué de tout sens moral.
devolution [ˌdiːvə'luːʃn] *n* -**1.** [of duty, power] délégation *f*; JUR [of property] transmission *f*, dévolution *f*. -**2.** POL décentralisation *f*. -**3.** BIOL dégénérescence *f*.
devolutionist [ˌdiːvə'luːʃnɪst] ◇ *adj* décentralisateur.
◇ *n* partisan *m* de la décentralisation.
devolve [dɪ'vɒlv] ◇ *vi* -**1.** [duty, job] incomber; [by chance] incomber, échoir; **it ~s on** OR **upon me to decide** c'est à moi (qu'il incombe) de décider; **the responsibility ~s on** OR **upon him** la responsabilité lui incombe OR lui échoit. -**2.** JUR [estate] passer; **the property ~s on** OR **upon the son** les biens passent OR sont transmis au fils.
◇ *vt* déléguer; **to ~ sthg on** OR **upon** OR **to sb** déléguer qqch à qqn, charger qqn de qqch.
Devonian [de'vəʊnjən] GEOL ◇ *adj* dévonien.
◇ *n* dévonien *m*.
Devonshire cream ['devənʃəʳ-] *n* crème *f* caillée.
devote [dɪ'vəʊt] *vt* consacrer; **to ~ o.s. to** [study, work] se consacrer OR s'adonner à; [a cause] se vouer OR se consacrer à; [pleasure] se livrer à; **she ~s all her energies to writing** elle se consacre entièrement à l'écriture; **all funds are ~d entirely to research** tous les crédits sont entièrement consacrés OR affectés à la recherche.
devoted [dɪ'vəʊtɪd] *adj* [friend, servant, service] dévoué, fidèle; [admirer] fervent; **I'm ~ to my children** je ferais tout pour mes enfants.
devotedly [dɪ'vəʊtɪdlɪ] *adv* avec dévouement.
devotee [ˌdevə'tiː] *n* [of opera, sport etc] passionné *m*, -e *f*; [of doctrine] adepte *mf*, partisan *m*, -e *f*; [of religion] adepte *mf*.
devotion [dɪ'vəʊʃn] *n* -**1.** [to person] dévouement *m*, attachement *m*; [to cause] dévouement *m*; **no one doubts her ~ to her work** personne ne met en doute OR ne doute de son dévouement professionnel; **he showed great ~ to duty** il a prouvé son sens du devoir. -**2.** RELIG dévotion *f*, piété *f*.
◆ **devotions** *npl* dévotions *fpl*, prières *fpl*.
devotional [dɪ'vəʊʃənl] ◇ *adj* [book, work] de dévotion OR piété; [attitude] de prière, pieux.
◇ *n* service *m* (religieux).
devour [dɪ'vaʊəʳ] *vt* -**1.** [food] dévorer, engloutir; *fig* [book] dévorer; **he ~ed her with his eyes** il l'a dévorée des yeux. -**2.** [subj: fire] dévorer, consumer; **~ed by hatred** *fig* dévoré de haine.
devouring [dɪ'vaʊərɪŋ] *adj* [hunger, jealousy] dévorant; [interest] ardent; [need] urgent.
devout [dɪ'vaʊt] *adj* [person] pieux, dévot; [hope, prayer] fervent.
devoutly [dɪ'vaʊtlɪ] *adv* -**1.** [pray] avec dévotion, dévotement. -**2.** *fml* [earnestly] sincèrement; **I ~ hope that some good comes of this war** j'espère vivement OR profondément que cette guerre servira à quelque chose.
dew [djuː] *n* rosée *f*.
dewclaw ['djuːklɔː] *n* ergot *m*.
dewdrop ['djuːdrɒp] *n* goutte *f* de rosée; **to have a ~** [on end of nose] avoir la goutte au nez.
Dewey Decimal System ['djuːɪ-] *n* classification *f* décimale de Dewey.
dewfall ['djuːfɔːl] *n* formation *f* de la rosée, serein *m lit*; *poet* [evening] tombée *f* de la nuit.
dewlap ['djuːlæp] *n* fanon *m*.
deworm [ˌdiː'wɜːm] *vt* administrer un vermifuge à.
dew point *n* point *m* de rosée.
dewpond ['djuːpɒnd] *n Br* mare *f* artificielle *(alimentée par les eaux de condensation)*.
dewy ['djuːɪ] (*compar* **dewier**, *superl* **dewiest**) *adj* couvert OR humide de rosée; ~ **complexion** *fig* teint frais.
dewy-eyed *adj* [innocent] innocent; [trusting] naïf, ingénu; **she looked at him ~** elle l'a regardé d'un air ingénu.
Dexedrine® ['deksɪdriːn] *n* Dexédrine® *f*.
dexterity [dek'sterətɪ] *n* adresse *f*, dextérité *f*; **manual ~** habileté *f* manuelle; **the job requires great ~** ce travail nécessite beaucoup d'adresse.
dexterous ['dekstrəs] *adj* [person] adroit, habile; [movement] adroit, habile, agile.
dexterously ['dekstrəslɪ] *adv* adroitement, habilement.
dextrin ['dekstrɪn] *n* dextrine *f*.
dextrose ['dekstrəʊs] *n* dextrose *m*.
dextrous *etc* ['dekstrəs] = **dexterous**.
DF *n abbr of* Direction Finder.
DFC (*abbr of* Distinguished Flying Cross) *n distinction honorifique des armées de l'air américaine et britannique*.
DFE *pr n abbr of* Department for Education.
DFM (*abbr of* Distinguished Flying Medal) *n médaille des armées de l'air américaine et britannique*.
DG *n abbr of* director-general.
dhal [dɑːl] *n sorte de légumineuse*; CULIN *plat à base de lentilles et d'épices*.
DHSS *pr n* -**1.** *Br* (*abbr of* Department of Health and Social Security) *ancien nom du ministère britannique de la santé et de la Sécurité sociale*. -**2.** *Am* (*abbr of* Department of Health and Social Services) ≃ ministère *m* de la Santé.
diabetes [ˌdaɪə'biːtiːz] *n* diabète *m*.
diabetic [ˌdaɪə'betɪk] ◇ *adj* diabétique.
◇ *n* diabétique *mf*.
diabolic [ˌdaɪə'bɒlɪk] *adj* [action, plan] diabolique, infernal; [look, smile] diabolique, satanique.
diabolical [ˌdaɪə'bɒlɪkl] *adj* -**1.** = **diabolic**. -**2.** *inf* [terrible] atroce, épouvantable, infernal; **the food was ~** la nourriture était infecte; **she speaks ~ French** elle parle français comme une vache espagnole; **I think it's a ~ liberty** il faut un toupet monstre OR un sacré culot pour faire une chose pareille.
diabolically [ˌdaɪə'bɒlɪklɪ] *adv* -**1.** [fiendishly] diaboliquement, de manière diabolique. -**2.** *inf Br* [as intensifier] vachement, rudement, sacrément.
diachronic [ˌdaɪə'krɒnɪk] *adj* diachronique.
diacid [daɪ'æsɪd] ◇ *adj* biacide, diacide.
◇ *n* biacide *m*, diacide *m*.
diaconal [daɪ'ækənl] *adj* diaconal.
diaconate [daɪ'ækəneɪt] *n* diaconat *m*.
diacritic [ˌdaɪə'krɪtɪk] ◇ *adj* diacritique.
◇ *n* signe *m* diacritique.
diacritical [ˌdaɪə'krɪtɪkl] *adj* diacritique.
diactinic [ˌdaɪæk'tɪnɪk] *adj* capable de transmettre des rayons actiniques.
diadem ['daɪədem] *n* diadème *m*.
diaeresis [daɪ'erɪsɪs] (*pl* **diaereses** [-siːz]) = **dieresis**.
diagnosable [ˌdaɪəg'nəʊzəbl] *adj* susceptible d'être diagnostiqué, décelable.
diagnose ['daɪəgnəʊz] *vt* [illness] diagnostiquer; **they ~d her illness as cancer** ils ont diagnostiqué un cancer ‖ *fig* [fault, problem] déceler, discerner.
diagnosis [ˌdaɪəg'nəʊsɪs] (*pl* **diagnoses** [-siːz]) *n* MED & *fig* diagnostic *m*; BIOL & BOT diagnose *f*.
diagnostic [ˌdaɪəg'nɒstɪk] *adj* diagnostique.
diagnostician [ˌdaɪəgnɒs'tɪʃn] *n* diagnostiqueur *m*.
diagnostics [ˌdaɪəg'nɒstɪks] *n (U)* COMPUT & MED diagnostic *m*.
diagonal [daɪ'ægənl] ◇ *adj* diagonal.
◇ *n* diagonale *f*.
diagonally [daɪ'ægənəlɪ] *adv* en diagonale, diagonalement, obliquement; **we cut ~ across the field** nous avons traversé le champ en diagonale OR en biais; **his desk is ~ across from mine** son bureau est diagonalement opposé au mien; **a ribbon worn ~ across the chest** un ruban porté en écharpe sur la poitrine.
diagram ['daɪəgræm] (*Br pt* & *pp* **diagrammed**, *cont* **diagramming**, *Am pt* & *pp* **diagramed** OR **diagrammed**, *cont* **diagraming** OR **diagramming**) ◇ *n* [gen] diagramme *m*, schéma *m*; MATH diagramme *m*, figure *f*.
◇ *vt* donner une représentation graphique de.
diagrammatic [ˌdaɪəgrə'mætɪk] *adj* schématique.
dial ['daɪəl] (*Br pt* & *pp* **dialled**, *cont* **dialling**, *Am pt* & *pp* **dialed**, *cont* **dialing**) ◇ *n* -**1.** [of clock, telephone] cadran *m*; [of radio, TV] bouton *m* (de réglage); **tune in to 98 on the FM ~** réglez vos postes sur 98 sur la bande FM. -**2.** *inf Br dated* [face] tronche *f*.
◇ *vt* faire, composer; **to ~ a wrong number** faire OR composer un mauvais OR faux numéro; **to ~ Spain direct** appeler l'Espagne par l'automatique; **~ the operator** appelez l'opératrice ❑ **~-a-joke/disc** la plaisanterie/le disque du jour par téléphone.

DIAL-A-...:
Ce préfixe introduit le nom de certains services téléphoniques, surtout aux États-Unis: «dial-a-wake-up» (réveil); «dial-a-date» (rencontres); «dial-a-prayer» (prières préenregistrées) etc.

---

dial. *written abbr of* dialect.
dialect ['daɪəlekt] *n* [regional] dialecte *m*, parler *m*; [local, rural] patois *m*.
dialectal [ˌdaɪə'lektl] *adj* dialectal, de dialecte.
dialectic [ˌdaɪə'lektɪk] ◇ *adj* dialectique.
◇ *n* dialectique *f*.
dialectical [ˌdaɪə'lektɪkl] *adj* dialectique.
dialectical materialism *n* matérialisme *m* dialectique.
dialectician [ˌdaɪəlek'tɪʃn] *n* dialecticien *m*, -enne *f*.
dialectics [ˌdaɪə'lektɪks] *n (U)* dialectique *f*.
dialectologist [ˌdaɪəlek'tɒlədʒɪst] *n* dialectologue *mf*.
dialectology [ˌdaɪəlek'tɒlədʒɪ] *n* dialectologie *f*.
dialling code ['daɪəlɪŋ-] *n Br* indicatif *m*.
dialling tone *Br*, **dial tone** *Am n* tonalité *f*.
dialogue, dialog *Am* ['daɪəlɒg] *n* dialogue *m*.
dial tone *Am* = **dialling tone**.
dial-up service *n* service *m* de télétraitement.
dialyse *Br*, **dialyze** *Am* ['daɪəlaɪz] *vt* dialyser.
dialysis [daɪ'ælɪsɪs] (*pl* **dialyses** [-siːz]) *n* dialyse *f*; ~ **machine** rein *m* artificiel.
diamanté [dɪə'mɒnteɪ] *n* tissu *m* diamanté.
diamantine [ˌdaɪə'mæntaɪn] *adj* diamantin.
diameter [daɪ'æmɪtəʳ] *n* -**1.** [gen & GEOM] diamètre *m*; **the tree is two metres in ~** l'arbre fait deux mètres de diamètre. -**2.** [of microscope] unité *f* de grossissement.
diametric(al) [ˌdaɪə'metrɪk(l)] *adj* GEOM & *fig* diamétral.
diametrically [ˌdaɪə'metrɪklɪ] *adv* GEOM & *fig* diamétralement; ~ **opposed** diamétralement opposé.
diamond ['daɪəmənd] ◇ *n* -**1.** [gem] diamant *m*; **he's a ~ in the rough** *esp Am* il a un cœur d'or sous ses dehors frustes. -**2.** [shape] losange *m*. -**3.** CARDS carreau *m*; **the ace/jack of ~s** l'as/le valet de carreau; **do you have any ~s?** avez-vous du carreau?; **~s are trumps** atout carreau. -**4.** [in baseball] terrain *m* (de baseball).
◇ *comp* -**1.** [brooch, ring etc] de diamant OR diamants; ~ **necklace** collier *m* OR rivière *f* de diamants. -**2.** [mine] de diamant OR diamants; ~ **drill** foreuse *f* à pointe de diamant; ~ **merchant** diamantaire *m*.
diamondback ['daɪəməndbæk] *n* [snake] *sorte de crotale*; [turtle] *sorte de tortue d'eau douce*.

diamond jubilee *n* (célébration *f* du) soixantième anniversaire *m*.
diamond-shaped *adj* en forme de losange.
diamond wedding *n* noces *fpl* de diamant.
Diana [daɪ'ænə] *pr n* MYTH Diane.
diapason [ˌdaɪə'peɪsn] *n* MUS diapason *m*; [of organ]: open/stopped ~ diapason large/étroit.
diaper ['daɪəpəʳ] *n* -**1.** *Am* [nappy] couche *f* (de bébé). -**2.** [fabric] damassé *m*.
diaphanous [daɪ'æfənəs] *adj* diaphane.
diaphone ['daɪəfəʊn] *n* -**1.** LING *série complète des phonèmes d'une langue*. -**2.** [foghorn] sirène *f* de brume à deux tons.
diaphony [daɪ'æfənɪ] *n* MUS & TECH diaphonie *f*.
diaphragm ['daɪəfræm] *n* diaphragme *m*.
diarist ['daɪərɪst] *n* [private] auteur *m* d'un journal intime; [of public affairs] chroniqueur *m*.
diarrhoea *Br*, **diarrhea** *Am* [ˌdaɪə'rɪə] *n* diarrhée *f*; to have ~ avoir la diarrhée.
diary ['daɪərɪ] (*pl* diaries) *n* -**1.** [personal record] journal *m* (intime); to keep a ~ tenir un journal. -**2.** *Br* [for business] agenda *m*; I've written it down in my ~ je l'ai noté dans mon agenda.
diascope ['daɪəskəʊp] *n* diascope *m*.
diaspora [daɪ'æspərə] *n* HIST & *fig* diaspora *f*.
diastole [daɪ'æstəlɪ] *n* diastole *f*.
diathermy ['daɪəθɜːmɪ] *n* diathermie *f*.
diatomic [ˌdaɪə'tɒmɪk] *adj* diatomique.
diatonic [ˌdaɪə'tɒnɪk] *adj* diatonique.
diatribe ['daɪətraɪb] *n* diatribe *f*.
diazepam [daɪ'æzɪpæm] *n* diazépam *m*.
dib [dɪb] (*pt* & *pp* dibbed, *cont* dibbing) *vi* pêcher à la ligne flottante.
dibasic [daɪ'beɪsɪk] *adj* dibasique.
dibber ['dɪbəʳ] *Br* = **dibble** *n*.
dibble ['dɪbl] ◇ *n* plantoir *m*.
◇ *vt* -**1.** [plant] repiquer au plantoir. -**2.** [dabble]: they ~d their feet in the water ils ont trempé les pieds dans l'eau.
dibs [dɪbz] *npl* -**1.** [jacks] osselets *mpl*. -**2.** *inf* [claim]: to have ~ on sthg avoir des droits sur qqch. -**3.** ▽ *Br* [money] fric *m*, pognon *m*.
dice [daɪs] (*pl inv*) ◇ *n* -**1.** [game] dé *m*; to play ~ jouer aux dés ❑ no ~! *inf Am* des clous! -**2.** CULIN dé *m*, cube *m*.
◇ *vt* CULIN couper en dés OR en cubes.
◇ *vi* jouer aux dés; to ~ with death jouer avec sa vie.
dicey *inf* ['daɪsɪ] (*compar* dicier, *superl* diciest) *adj* risqué, dangereux, délicat.
dichotomy [daɪ'kɒtəmɪ] (*pl* dichotomies) *n* dichotomie *f*.
dick [dɪk] *n* -**1.** ▼ [penis] queue *f*. -**2.** *inf Am* [detective] privé *m*. -**3.** ▽ *Br* [idiot] con *m*.
dickens *inf* ['dɪkɪnz] *n*: what the ~ are you doing? mais qu'est-ce que tu fabriques?; a ~ of a noise un bruit d'enfer; we had a ~ of a job getting a babysitter ça a été la galère OR la croix et la bannière pour trouver une baby-sitter.
Dickensian [dɪ'kenzɪən] *adj* à la Dickens.
dicker ['dɪkəʳ] *vi* marchander; to ~ with sb (for sthg) marchander avec qqn (pour obtenir qqch).
dickey ['dɪkɪ] *n* -**1.** [shirt] faux plastron *m* (de chemise). -**2.** *Br* [in carriage] siège *m* du cocher; AUT spider *m*, strapontin *m*. -**3.** *inf Br* [bow tie]: ~ (bow) nœud *m* pap. -**4.** *inf Br* [donkey] âne *m*.
dickhead▽ ['dɪkhed] *n* con *m*.
Dick Whittington [dɪk'wɪtɪŋtən] *pr n personnage de conte de fées et de pantomime, toujours accompagné d'un chat*.
dicky ['dɪkɪ] (*pl* dickies, *compar* dickier, *superl* dickiest) ◇ *n* = **dickey**.
◇ *adj inf Br* [ladder] peu solide, branlant; [heart] qui flanche; [situation] peu sûr.
dickybird *inf* ['dɪkɪbɜːd] *n* petit oiseau *m*.
dicta ['dɪktə] *pl* → **dictum**.
Dictaphone® ['dɪktəfəʊn] *n* Dictaphone® *m*, machine *f* à dicter.
dictate [*vb* dɪk'teɪt, *n* 'dɪkteɪt] ◇ *vt* -**1.** [letter] dicter; to ~ sthg to sb dicter qqch à qqn. -**2.** [order] dicter, imposer; her behaviour was ~d by the situation elle s'est comportée comme le lui a dicté la situation.
◇ *vi* -**1.** [give dictation] dicter. -**2.** [impose one's will]: to ~ to donner des ordres à; I won't be ~d to! je n'ai pas d'ordres à recevoir!
◇ *n* -**1.** [order] ordre *m*. -**2.** (*usu pl*) [principle] précepte *m*; the ~s of conscience/reason la voix de la conscience/raison.
dictation [dɪk'teɪʃn] *n* [of letter, story] dictée *f*; to take ~ écrire sous la dictée; at ~ speed à la vitesse d'une dictée; French ~ dictée de français.
dictator [dɪk'teɪtəʳ] *n* dictateur *m*.
dictatorial [ˌdɪktə'tɔːrɪəl] *adj* dictatorial.
dictatorially [ˌdɪktə'tɔːrɪəlɪ] *adv* dictatorialement, en dictateur.
dictatorship [dɪk'teɪtəʃɪp] *n* dictature *f*.
diction ['dɪkʃn] *n* -**1.** [pronunciation] diction *f*, élocution *f*. -**2.** [phrasing] style *m*, langage *m*.
dictionary ['dɪkʃənrɪ] (*pl* dictionaries) *n* dictionnaire *m*; a French-English ~ un dictionnaire français-anglais; look it up in the ~ cherchez dans le dictionnaire; she's a walking ~ *fig* c'est un dictionnaire ambulant.
Dictograph® ['dɪktəgrɑːf] *n* appareil *m* enregistreur (pour écoutes téléphoniques).
dictum ['dɪktəm] (*pl* dicta [-tə] OR dictums) *n fml* -**1.** [statement] affirmation *f*; JUR remarque *f* superfétatoire. -**2.** [maxim] dicton *m*, maxime *f*.
did [dɪd] *pt* → **do**.
didactic [dɪ'dæktɪk] *adj* didactique.
didactically [dɪ'dæktɪklɪ] *adv* didactiquement.
diddle *inf* ['dɪdl] *vt Br* duper, rouler; to ~ sb out of sthg carotter qqch à qqn; I've been ~d je me suis fait avoir.
diddums *inf* ['dɪdəmz] *n* pauvre petit.
didn't ['dɪdnt] = **did not**.
Dido ['daɪdəʊ] *pr n* Didon; '~ and Aeneas' *Purcell* 'Didon et Énée'.
didst [dɪdst] *arch 2nd pers sing* → **did**.
die [daɪ] (*pl sense 1* dice [daɪs], *pl sense 2* dies) ◇ *vi* -**1.** [person] mourir, décéder; she's dying elle est mourante OR à l'agonie; she ~d of cancer elle est morte du OR d'un cancer; thousands are dying of hunger des milliers de gens meurent de faim; she ~d by her own hand *lit* elle s'est suicidée OR donné la mort, elle a mis fin à ses jours; to ~ a hero mourir en héros; he left us to ~ il nous a abandonnés à la mort; to ~ in one's bed mourir dans son lit || *fig*: to ~ laughing *inf* mourir de rire; I nearly ~d *inf*, I could have ~d *inf* [from fear] j'étais mort de trouille; [from embarrassment] j'aurais voulu rentrer sous terre, je ne savais plus où me mettre; he'll do it or ~ in the attempt il y arrivera coûte que coûte ❑ to ~ with one's boots on OR in harness mourir debout OR en pleine activité; never say ~! il ne faut jamais désespérer! -**2.** [animal, plant] mourir. -**3.** [engine] caler, s'arrêter. -**4.** [fire, love, memory] s'éteindre, mourir; [tradition] s'éteindre, disparaître, mourir; [smile] disparaître, s'évanouir; old habits ~ hard les mauvaises habitudes ne se perdent pas facilement; her secret ~d with her elle a emporté son secret dans la tombe. -**5.** *inf* [want very much]: to be dying for sthg avoir une envie folle de qqch; I'm dying for a drink j'ai une envie folle de boire qqch; to be dying to do sthg mourir d'envie de faire qqch; she's dying to see him elle meurt d'envie de le voir.
◇ *vt*: to ~ a natural/violent death mourir de sa belle mort/de mort violente ❑ to ~ the death *fig* & *hum* faire un bide; to ~ a thousand deaths *lit* être au supplice.
◇ *n* -**1.** GAMES dé *m* (à jouer); the ~ is cast *fig* les dés sont jetés. -**2.** ARCHIT [dado] dé *m (d'un piédestal)*; TECH [stamp] matrice *f*; [in minting] coin *m*; stamping ~ étampe *f*; as straight as a ~ franc comme l'or.
◆ **die away** *vi insep* s'affaiblir, s'éteindre, mourir.
◆ **die back** *vi insep* [plant] dépérir.
◆ **die down** *vi insep* -**1.** [wind] tomber, se calmer; [fire - in chimney] baisser; [- in building, forest] s'apaiser, diminuer; [noise] diminuer; [anger, protest] se calmer, s'apaiser. -**2.** [plant] se flétrir, perdre ses feuilles et sa tige.
◆ **die off** *vi insep* mourir les uns après les autres.
◆ **die out** *vi insep* [family, tribe, tradition] disparaître, s'éteindre; [fire] s'éteindre; the panda is in danger of dying out le panda est menacé d'extinction.
dieback ['daɪbæk] *n maladie des plantes se traduisant par un dépérissement des pousses*.
die-cast ◇ *vt* mouler sous pression OR en matrice.
◇ *adj* moulé sous pression OR en matrice.
die-casting *n* moulage *m* en matrice.
dieffenbachia [ˌdiːfn'bækɪə] *n* dieffenbachia *f*.
diehard ['daɪhɑːd] ◇ *n* conservateur *m*, -trice *f*, réactionnaire *mf*; the party ~s les durs du parti.
◇ *adj* intransigeant; POL réactionnaire; a ~ liberal un libéral pur et dur.
dielectric [ˌdaɪɪ'lektrɪk] ◇ *adj* diélectrique.
◇ *n* diélectrique *m*.
Dien Bien Phu [ˌdjenbjen'fuː] *pr n* Diên Biên Phu.
dieresis [daɪ'erɪsɪs] (*pl* diereses [-siːz]) *n* [sound] diérèse *f*; [sign] tréma *m*.
diesel ['diːzl] *n* [vehicle] diesel *m*; [fuel] gas-oil *m*, gazole *m*.
diesel-electric ◇ *adj* diesel-électrique.
◇ *n* diesel-électrique *m*.
diesel engine *n* AUT moteur *m* diesel; RAIL motrice *f*.
diesel fuel, diesel oil *n* gas-oil *m*, gazole *m*.
diesel train *n* autorail *m*.
dieses ['daɪɪsiːz] *pl* → **diesis**.
diesinker ['daɪˌsɪŋkəʳ] *n personne ou machine qui fabrique des matrices industrielles*.
diesis ['daɪɪsɪs] (*pl* dieses [-siːz]) *n* MUS dièse *m*; TYPO double croix *f*.
diestock ['daɪstɒk] *n* porte-filière *m*.
diet ['daɪət] ◇ *n* -**1.** [regular food] alimentation *f*, nourriture *f*; they live on a ~ of rice and fish ils se nourrissent de riz et de poisson; a balanced ~ un régime équilibré; a poor ~ un régime mal équilibré, une alimentation mal équilibrée. -**2.** [restricted or special food] régime *m*; to be on a ~ être au régime; to go on a ~ faire OR suivre un régime; to put sb on a ~ mettre qqn au régime; to be put on a starvation ~ être mis à la diète; a low-fat ~ un régime à faible teneur en matières grasses. -**3.** [assembly] diète *f*.
◇ *vi* suivre un régime.
◇ *comp* [drink, food] de régime, basses calories.
dietary ['daɪətrɪ] (*pl* dietaries) ◇ *adj* [supplement] alimentaire; [of special food] de régime, diététique; ~ laws règles *fpl* diététiques; ~ fibre cellulose *f* végétale.
◇ *n* régime *m* alimentaire *(d'un malade, d'une prison)*.
dietetic [ˌdaɪə'tetɪk] *adj* diététique.
dietetics [ˌdaɪə'tetɪks] *n (U)* diététique *f*.
dietician [ˌdaɪə'tɪʃn] *n* diététicien *m*, -enne *f*.
differ ['dɪfəʳ] *vi* -**1.** [vary] différer, être différent; in what way does this text ~ from the first? en quoi ce texte diffère-t-il du premier?; the two approaches ~ quite considerably les deux approches n'ont pas grand-chose à voir l'une avec l'autre; the houses ~ in size and design les maisons diffèrent par leurs dimensions et leur conception. -**2.** [disagree] être en désaccord, ne pas être d'accord; the authorities ~ on the dates les experts ne sont pas d'accord sur les dates; he ~s with me about the best solution to apply il n'est pas d'accord avec moi OR il ne partage pas mon avis sur la meilleure solution à adopter.
difference ['dɪfrəns] *n* -**1.** [dissimilarity] différence *f*; [in age, size, weight] écart *m*, différence *f*; there's a big ~ between living with someone

and marrying them il y a une grande différence entre vivre ensemble et être mariés; there are many ~s between the two cultures les deux cultures sont très différentes l'une de l'autre; I can't tell the ~ between the two je ne vois pas la différence entre les deux; there's a ~ in height of about six inches il y a une différence de hauteur de quinze centimètres; she says the age ~ doesn't matter elle dit que la différence d'âge n'a pas d'importance; it makes no ~, it doesn't make the slightest ~ ça n'a aucune importance, ça revient au même, ça ne change absolument rien; it makes no ~ to me (one way or the other) (d'une manière ou d'une autre), cela m'est (parfaitement) égal; it made a big ~ to him cela a beaucoup compté OR a tout changé pour lui; does it make any ~ whether he comes or not? est-ce que ça change quelque chose qu'il vienne ou pas?; that makes all the ~ voilà qui change tout; a lick of paint makes all the ~ un petit coup de peinture et ça n'a plus du tout la même allure; a house with a ~ une maison pas comme les autres. -**2.** [disagreement] différend *m*; we have our ~s nous ne sommes pas toujours d'accord; a ~ of opinion une différence OR divergence d'opinion. -**3.** [in numbers, quantity] différence *f*; I'll pay the ~ je paierai la différence OR le reste.

different ['dɪfrənt] *adj* -**1.** [not identical] différent, autre; ~ from OR to OR *esp Am* than différent de; this book is very ~ from her first ce livre est très différent de OR n'a rien à voir avec son premier; it's very ~ from any other city I've visited ça ne ressemble en rien aux autres villes que j'ai visitées; he reads a ~ paper every day il lit chaque jour un journal différent; you look ~ today tu n'es pas comme d'habitude aujourd'hui; he put on a ~ shirt il a mis une autre chemise; she's a ~ person since their wedding elle a beaucoup changé depuis leur mariage; I feel like a ~ person since my holiday j'ai l'impression d'avoir fait peau neuve depuis mes vacances; what's ~ about it? qu'est-ce qu'il y a de différent OR de changé?; let's do something ~ faisons quelque chose de nouveau OR de différent; I now see things in a ~ light je vois désormais les choses sous un autre jour OR angle; that's quite a ~ matter ça, c'est une autre affaire OR histoire. -**2.** [various] divers, différents, plusieurs; she visited ~ schools elle a visité diverses OR différentes écoles. -**3.** [unusual] singulier; I'm looking for something ~ je cherche quelque chose d'original OR qui sorte de l'ordinaire; she always has to be ~ elle veut toujours se singulariser, elle ne peut jamais faire comme tout le monde; I've been out with a lot of men before, but he's ~ je suis sortie avec beaucoup d'hommes, mais celui-là n'est pas comme les autres.

differential [,dɪfə'renʃl] ◇ *adj* -**1.** MATH différentiel; ~ operator opérateur *m* différentiel. -**2.** AUT différentiel *m*; ~ housing boîtier *m* de différentiel.

◇ *n* -**1.** [in salary] écart *m* salarial. -**2.** MATH différentielle *f*. -**3.** = **differential gear**.

differential calculus *n* calcul *m* différentiel.

differential coefficient *n* dérivé *m*.

differential equation *n* différentielle *f*.

differential gear *n* différentiel *m*.

differentiate [,dɪfə'renʃɪeɪt] ◇ *vt* -**1.** [distinguish] différencier, distinguer; what ~s this product from its competitors? qu'est-ce qui différencie OR distingue ce produit de ses concurrents? -**2.** MATH différencier, calculer la différentielle de.

◇ *vi* faire la différence OR distinction; I'm unable to ~ between the two je ne vois pas de différence entre les deux; she ~s between morality and religion elle fait une distinction entre moralité et religion.

differentiation [,dɪfərenʃɪ'eɪʃn] *n* [gen] différenciation *f*; MATH différentiation *f*.

differently ['dɪfrəntlɪ] *adv* différemment, autrement; I do it ~ from OR *esp Am* than you je le fais différemment de OR autrement que vous, je ne fais pas ça comme vous; she acts ~ from OR *esp Am* than the others elle n'a pas le même comportement que OR elle ne se comporte pas comme les autres.

difficult ['dɪfɪkəlt] *adj* -**1.** [problem, task] difficile, dur, ardu; [book, question] difficile; it was a ~ decision to make ce n'était pas une décision facile à prendre; he's had a ~ life il a eu une vie difficile; that's not so ~ ce n'est pas si difficile que ça; I find it ~ to believe she's gone j'ai du mal à OR il m'est difficile de croire qu'elle est partie; the most ~ part is over le plus difficile OR le plus dur est fait. -**2.** [awkward] difficile, peu commode; don't be so ~! ne fais pas le difficile!, ne fais pas la fine bouche!; he's ~ to get along with il n'est pas commode, il a un caractère difficile; we could make life/things very ~ for you on pourrait sérieusement vous compliquer la vie/les choses.

difficulty ['dɪfɪkəltɪ] (*pl* **difficulties**) *n* -**1.** *(U)* [trouble] difficulté *f*, difficultés *fpl*; to have ~ (in) doing sthg avoir du mal à faire qqch; I had ~ (in) climbing the stairs j'ai eu du mal OR de la peine OR des difficultés à monter l'escalier; she experienced ~ breathing elle avait du mal OR de la peine OR des difficultés à respirer, elle respirait difficilement; with ~ avec difficulté OR peine; without ~ sans difficulté OR peine; it can be done, but with ~ cela peut se faire, mais difficilement. -**2.** [obstacle, problem] difficulté *f*, problème *m*; the main ~ is getting the staff le plus difficile, c'est de trouver le personnel; I don't foresee any difficulties je ne prévois aucun problème OR aucune difficulté ‖ [predicament] difficulté *f*, embarras *m*; to get into difficulties être OR se trouver en difficulté; to be in financial difficulties avoir des ennuis d'argent, être dans l'embarras; he's always getting into all kinds of ~ il se crée OR s'attire toujours toutes sortes d'ennuis.

diffidence ['dɪfɪdəns] *n* manque *m* d'assurance OR de confiance en soi, timidité *f*.

diffident ['dɪfɪdənt] *adj* [person] qui manque de confiance en soi OR d'assurance; [remark, smile] timide; [tone] hésitant; he was ~ about speaking out il hésitait à parler (par timidité).

diffidently ['dɪfɪdəntlɪ] *adv* avec timidité OR embarras, de façon embarrassée.

diffract [dɪ'frækt] *vt* diffracter.

diffraction [dɪ'frækʃn] *n* diffraction *f*; ~ grating réseau *m* de diffraction.

diffractometer [,dɪfræk'tɒmɪtəʳ] *n* diffractomètre *m*.

diffuse [*vb* dɪ'fju:z, *adj* dɪ'fju:s] ◇ *vt* diffuser, répandre.

◇ *vi* se diffuser, se répandre.

◇ *adj* -**1.** [light] diffus; [thought] diffus, vague. -**2.** [wordy] diffus, prolixe.

diffused [dɪ'fju:zd] *adj* diffus; ~ lighting éclairage *m* diffus OR indirect.

diffuser [dɪ'fju:zəʳ] *n* [gen & ELEC] diffuseur *m*.

diffusion [dɪ'fju:ʒn] *n* -**1.** [of light, news] diffusion *f*. -**2.** [of style] prolixité *f*.

diffusor [dɪ'fju:zəʳ] = **diffuser**.

dig [dɪg] (*pt* & *pp* **dug** [dʌg], *cont* **digging**) ◇ *vt* -**1.** [in ground - hole] creuser; [- tunnel] creuser, percer; [with spade] bêcher; he dug his way under the fence il s'est creusé un passage sous la clôture; he's been out digging the garden il a bêché le jardin; to ~ potatoes arracher des pommes de terre ❑ to ~ one's own grave creuser sa propre tombe. -**2.** [jab] enfoncer; she dug me in the ribs (with her elbow) elle m'a donné un coup de coude dans les côtes. -**3.** ▽ *dated* [understand] piger; [appreciate, like] aimer; [look at] viser; ~ that music! écoute-moi (un peu) cette musique!

◇ *vi* -**1.** [person] creuser; [animal] fouiller, fouir; to ~ for gold creuser pour trouver de l'or; he spends hours digging about in old junk shops *fig* il passe des heures à fouiller dans les magasins de brocante. -**2.** ▽ *dated* [understand] piger.

◇ *n* -**1.** [in ground] coup *m* de bêche. -**2.** ARCHEOL fouilles *fpl*; to go on a ~ faire des fouilles. -**3.** [jab] coup *m*; to give sb a ~ in the ribs donner un coup de coude dans les côtes de qqn. -**4.** *inf* [snide remark] coup *m* de patte; he made a nasty ~ at the government il a lancé une pique au gouvernement; that was a ~ at you c'était une pierre dans votre jardin.

◆ **dig in** ◇ *vi insep* -**1.** MIL [dig trenches] se retrancher; *fig* tenir bon. -**2.** *inf* [eat] commencer à manger; ~ in! allez-y, mangez!, attaquez!

◇ *vt sep* -**1.** [mix with ground] enterrer. -**2.** [jab] enfoncer; he dug in his spurs il a éperonné son cheval ❑ to ~ in one's heels se braquer, se buter; to ~ o.s. in *literal* se retrancher; *fig* camper sur ses positions; he's really dug himself in il s'est encroûté.

◆ **dig into** *vt insep* -**1.** [delve into] fouiller dans; don't ~ into your savings *fig* n'entame pas tes économies, ne pioche pas dans tes économies. -**2.** [jab]: your elbow is digging into me ton coude me rentre dans les côtes.

◆ **dig out** *vt sep* -**1.** [remove] extraire; [from ground] déterrer; they had to ~ the car out of the snow il a fallu qu'ils dégagent la voiture de la neige (à la pelle). -**2.** *inf* [find] dénicher.

◆ **dig up** *vt sep* -**1.** [ground - gen] retourner; [- with spade] bêcher. -**2.** [plant] arracher. -**3.** [unearth] déterrer; *fig* [find] *inf*dénicher; where did you ~ him up? où est-ce que tu l'as pêché OR dégoté?

digest [*vb* dɪ'dʒest, *n* 'daɪdʒest] ◇ *vt* -**1.** [food] digérer; I find cheese difficult to ~ je digère mal le fromage. -**2.** [idea] assimiler, digérer. -**3.** [classify] classer; [sum up] résumer.

◇ *vi* digérer.

◇ *n* -**1.** [of book, facts] résumé *m*; in ~ form en abrégé. -**2.** JUR digeste *m*. -**3.** [magazine] digest *m*.

digestible [dɪ'dʒestəbl] *adj literal* & *fig* digeste, facile à digérer.

digestion [dɪ'dʒestʃn] *n* digestion *f*.

digestive [dɪ'dʒestɪv] ◇ *adj* digestif; ~ troubles troubles *mpl* de la digestion ❑ ~ biscuit *Br sorte de sablé*; ~ system/tract système *m*/appareil *m* digestif.

◇ *n* [drink] digestif *m*; *Br* [biscuit] *sorte de sablé*.

digger ['dɪgəʳ] *n* -**1.** [miner] mineur *m*; *Br inf* CONSTR terrassier *m*. -**2.** [machine] excavatrice *f*, pelleteuse *f*. -**3.** *inf* [Australian] Australien *m*, -enne *f*; [New Zealander] Néo-Zélandais *m*, -e *f*.

diggings ['dɪgɪŋz] *npl* -**1.** ARCHEOL fouilles *fpl*. -**2.** MIN [dirt] terrassement *m*; [pit] creusement *m*, excavation *f*; [of gold] placer *m*. -**3.** *inf Br dated* = **digs**.

digit ['dɪdʒɪt] *n* -**1.** [number] chiffre *m*; three-~ number nombre à trois chiffres. -**2.** [finger] doigt *m*; [toe] orteil *m*. -**3.** ASTRON doigt *m*.

digital ['dɪdʒɪtl] *adj* -**1.** ANAT digital. -**2.** [clock, watch] à affichage numérique; [display] numérique; COMPUT numérique.

digital audio tape = **DAT**.

digital computer *n* calculateur *m* numérique.

digitalin [,dɪdʒɪ'teɪlɪn] *n* digitaline *f*.

digitalis [,dɪdʒɪ'teɪlɪs] *n* BOT digitale *f*; PHARM digitaline *f*.

digital recording *n* enregistrement *m* numérique.

digitization [,dɪdʒɪtaɪ'zeɪʃn] *n* numérisation *f*.

digitize, -ise ['dɪdʒɪtaɪz] *vt* numériser.

digitizer ['dɪdʒɪtaɪzəʳ] *n* convertisseur *m* numérique OR analogique-numérique.

diglossia [daɪ'glɒsɪə] *n* diglossie *f*.

dignified ['dɪgnɪfaɪd] *adj* [person] plein de dignité, digne; [silence] digne; he behaved in a very ~ manner il s'est comporté avec beaucoup de dignité; she wasn't very ~ elle manquait de dignité OR de tenue.

dignify ['dɪgnɪfaɪ] (*pt* & *pp* **dignified**) *vt* donner de la dignité à; I refuse to even ~ that question with an answer cette question n'est même pas digne de réponse OR ne mérite même pas une réponse.

dignitary ['dɪgnɪtrɪ] (*pl* **dignitaries**) *n* dignitaire *m*.

dignity ['dɪgnətɪ] (*pl* dignities) *n* -**1.** [importance, poise] dignité *f*; it would be beneath my ~ to accept accepter serait indigne de moi OR serait m'abaisser; she considered it beneath her ~ elle s'estimait au-dessus de ça; to stand on one's ~ se draper dans sa dignité. -**2.** [rank] dignité *f*, haut rang *m*; [title] titre *m*, dignité *f*.

digraph ['daɪgrɑːf] *n* digramme *m*.

digress [daɪ'gres] *vi* s'éloigner, s'écarter; you're ~ing from the subject vous vous éloignez du sujet; but I ~ mais je m'égare, revenons à nos moutons.

digression [daɪ'greʃn] *n* digression *f*.

digressive [daɪ'gresɪv] *adj* qui s'écarte OR s'éloigne du sujet.

digs *inf* [dɪgz] *npl Br* piaule *f*; to live in ~ avoir une piaule; I'm in ~ in Wimbledon je crèche OR j'ai une piaule à Wimbledon.

dihedral [daɪ'hiːdrəl] ◇ *adj* dièdre.
◇ *n* dièdre *m*.

dike [daɪk] = **dyke**.

diktat ['dɪktæt] *n* -**1.** POL [decree] diktat *m*. -**2.** [statement] affirmation *f* catégorique.

dilapidated [dɪ'læpɪdeɪtɪd] *adj* [house] délabré; [car] déglingué; in a ~ state dans un état de délabrement OR de dégradation avancé.

dilapidation [dɪ,læpɪ'deɪʃn] *n* -**1.** [of building] délabrement *m*, dégradation *f*; in a state of ~ dans un état de délabrement OR de dégradation avancé. -**2.** (*usu pl*) JUR détérioration *f* (*causée par un locataire*).

dilate [daɪ'leɪt] ◇ *vi* -**1.** [physically] se dilater. -**2.** *fml* [talk]: to ~ on OR upon a topic s'étendre sur un sujet.
◇ *vt* dilater.

dilation [daɪ'leɪʃn] *n* -**1.** [gen & MED] dilatation *f*; ~ and curettage (dilatation et) curetage *m*. -**2.** *fml* [talk] exposition *f* en détail.

dilator [daɪ'leɪtə^r] *n* [instrument] dilatateur *m*; [muscle] muscle *m* dilatateur.

dilatoriness ['dɪlətrɪnɪs] *n fml* lenteur *f*.

dilatory ['dɪlətrɪ] *adj fml* [action, method] dilatoire; [person] lent; forgive me for being so ~ in coming to a decision veuillez m'excuser pour avoir mis tant de temps à me décider.

dildo ['dɪldəʊ] (*pl* dildos) *n* godemiché *m*.

dilemma [dɪ'lemə] *n* dilemme *m*; to be in a ~ être pris dans un dilemme; her decision leaves me in something of a ~ sa décision me pose un cruel dilemme.

dilettante [,dɪlɪ'tæntɪ] (*pl* dilettantes OR dilettanti [-tɪ]) ◇ *n* dilettante *mf*.
◇ *adj* dilettante.

dilettantism [,dɪlɪ'tæntɪzm] *n* dilettantisme *m*.

diligence ['dɪlɪdʒəns] *n* -**1.** [effort] assiduité *f*, application *f*, zèle *m*; she shows great ~ in her work elle fait preuve de beaucoup de zèle OR d'assiduité dans son travail. -**2.** [carriage] diligence *f*.

diligent ['dɪlɪdʒənt] *adj* [person] assidu, appliqué; [work] appliqué, diligent; he is very ~ in his work OR carrying out his work il fait son travail avec beaucoup d'assiduité OR beaucoup de zèle.

diligently ['dɪlɪdʒəntlɪ] *adv* avec assiduité OR soin OR application, assidûment.

dill [dɪl] *n* aneth *m*.

dill pickle *n* cornichon *m* à l'aneth.

dilly *inf* ['dɪlɪ] (*pl* dillies) *n Am dated*: she's a real ~! elle est formidable OR sensationnelle!; a ~ of a joke une blague vachement marrante; a ~ of a storm un sacré orage.

dilly-dally *inf* ['dɪlɪdælɪ] (*pt & pp* dilly-dallied) *vi* [dawdle] lanterner, lambiner; [hesitate] hésiter, tergiverser.

dilly-dallying *inf* ['dɪlɪdælɪŋ] *n* (*U*) [dawdling] flânerie *f*; [hesitation] hésitation *f*, hésitations *fpl*, tergiversation *f*, tergiversations *fpl*.

dilute [daɪ'luːt] ◇ *vt* -**1.** [liquid] diluer, étendre; [milk, wine] mouiller, couper d'eau; [sauce] délayer, allonger; [colour] délayer; '~ to taste' diluer selon votre goût. -**2.** PHARM diluer. -**3.** *fig* [weaken] diluer, édulcorer; ~d socialism socialisme affadi OR édulcoré.
◇ *adj* [liquid] dilué, coupé OR étendu (d'eau); [colour] délayé, adouci; *fig* dilué, édulcoré.

dilution [daɪ'luːʃn] *n* [act, product] dilution *f*; [of milk, wine] coupage *m*, mouillage *m*; *fig* édulcoration *f*.

dim [dɪm] (*pt & pp* dimmed, *cont* dimming) ◇ *adj* -**1.** [light] faible, pâle; [lamp] faible; [room] sombre; [colour] terne, sans éclat; to grow ~ [light] baisser; [room] devenir sombre; [colour] devenir terne; her eyes grew ~ with tears ses yeux se voilèrent de larmes. -**2.** [indistinct - shape] vague, imprécis; [- sight] faible, trouble; [- sound] vague, indistinct; she has only a ~ memory of it elle n'en a qu'un vague souvenir; in the ~ and distant past *hum* au temps jadis; to grow ~ [shape, memory] s'estomper, s'effacer; [sight] baisser, se troubler; [sound] s'affaiblir. -**3.** [gloomy] sombre, morne; to take a ~ view of sthg *inf* ne pas beaucoup apprécier qqch, voir qqch d'un mauvais œil; she takes a pretty ~ view of him going out with other women elle n'apprécie guère qu'il sorte avec d'autres femmes. -**4.** *inf* [stupid] gourde.
◇ *vt* -**1.** [light] baisser; I'll ~ the lamp je vais mettre la lampe en veilleuse; ~ your headlights *Am* AUT mettez-vous en codes. -**2.** [beauty, colour, hope, metal] ternir; [memory] estomper, effacer; [mind, senses] affaiblir, troubler; [sound] affaiblir; [sight] baisser, troubler; his eyes were dimmed with tears ses yeux étaient voilés de larmes.
◇ *vi* [light] baisser, s'affaiblir; [beauty, glory, hope] se ternir; [colour] devenir terne OR mat; [memory] s'estomper, s'effacer; [sound] s'affaiblir; [sight] baisser, se troubler.
◆ **dim out** *vt sep Am* plonger dans un black-out partiel.

dime [daɪm] *n Am* pièce *f* de dix cents; ~ bag *inf* [drugs] *sachet de drogue*; guys like that are a ~ a dozen *inf* des types comme lui, on en trouve à la pelle; it's not worth a ~ OR one thin ~ *inf* ça ne vaut pas un clou.

dime novel *n Am* roman *m* à quatre sous.

dimension [dɪ'menʃn] *n* -**1.** [measurement, size] dimension *f*; ARCHIT & GEOM dimension *f*, cote *f*; MATH & PHYS dimension *f*. -**2.** *fig* [scope] étendue *f*; [aspect] dimension *f*; the book opens up a whole new ~ of thought ce livre ouvre un nouveau champ de réflexion.

-dimensional [dɪ'menʃənl] *in cpds*: two/four~ à deux/quatre dimensions.

dime store *n Am* supérette *f* de quartier.

dimeter ['dɪmɪtə^r] *n* dimètre *m*.

diminish [dɪ'mɪnɪʃ] ◇ *vt* -**1.** [number] diminuer, réduire; [effect, power] diminuer, amoindrir; [value] réduire. -**2.** [person] déprécier, rabaisser. -**3.** ARCHIT [column] amincir, diminuer; MUS diminuer.
◇ *vi* diminuer, se réduire; their profits have ~ed leurs bénéfices ont diminué; the number of homeless has ~ed le nombre des sans-abri a diminué.

diminished [dɪ'mɪnɪʃt] *adj* -**1.** [number, power, speed] diminué, amoindri; [reputation] diminué, terni; [value] réduit; ~ responsibility JUR responsabilité *f* atténuée. -**2.** MUS diminué.

diminishing [dɪ'mɪnɪʃɪŋ] ◇ *adj* [influence, number, speed] décroissant, qui va en diminuant; [price, quality] qui baisse, en baisse; the law of ~ returns la loi des rendements décroissants.
◇ *n* diminution *f*, baisse *f*.

diminuendo [dɪ,mɪnjʊ'endəʊ] (*pl* diminuendos) ◇ *n* diminuendo *m*.
◇ *adv* diminuendo.

diminution [,dɪmɪ'njuːʃn] *n* -**1.** [in number, value] diminution *f*, baisse *f*; [in speed] réduction *f*; [in intensity, importance, strength] diminution *f*, affaiblissement *m*; [in temperature] baisse *f*, abaissement *m*; [in authority, price] baisse *f*; there has been no ~ in OR of our enthusiasm notre enthousiasme n'a en rien faibli. -**2.** MUS diminution *f*.

diminutive [dɪ'mɪnjʊtɪv] ◇ *adj* [tiny] minuscule, tout petit; LING diminutif.
◇ *n* diminutif *m*.

dimity ['dɪmɪtɪ] *n* futaine *f* croisée.

dimly ['dɪmlɪ] *adv* [shine] faiblement, sans éclat; [see] indistinctement, à peine; [remember] vaguement, à peine; the room was ~ lit la pièce était mal OR faiblement éclairée.

dimmer ['dɪmə^r] *n* -**1.** [on lamp] rhéostat *m* OR variateur *m* (de lumière). -**2.** *Am* AUT [switch] basculeur *m* (de phares); ~s [headlights] phares *mpl* code; [parking lights] feux *mpl* de position.

dimmer switch *n* variateur *m* (de lumière).

dimming ['dɪmɪŋ] *n* [of light] affaiblissement *m*, obscurcissement *m*; [of colour, metal, reputation] ternissement *m*; [of memory] affaiblissement *m*; *Am* AUT [of headlights] mise *f* en codes.

dimness ['dɪmnɪs] *n* -**1.** [of light, sight] affaiblissement *m*; [of room] obscurité *f*; [of colour, metal] aspect *m* terne; [of memory, shape] imprécision *f*. -**2.** *inf* [stupidity] sottise *f*.

dimout ['dɪmaʊt] *n Am* black-out *m* partiel.

dimple ['dɪmpl] ◇ *n* [in cheek, chin] fossette *f*; [in surface of ground, water] ride *f*, ondulation *f*.
◇ *vi* [cheek] former OR creuser des fossettes; [surface of ground] onduler, former des rides; [surface of water] onduler, se rider.

dimpled ['dɪmpld] *adj* [cheek, chin] à fossettes; [arm, knee] potelé; [surface] ridé, ondulé.

dimwit *inf* ['dɪmwɪt] *n* crétin *m*, -e *f*.

dim-witted *inf adj* crétin, gourde; my ~ brother mon crétin de frère.

din [dɪn] (*pt & pp* dinned, *cont* dinning) ◇ *n* [of people] tapage *m*, tumulte *m*; [in classroom] chahut *m*; [of industry, traffic] vacarme *m*; they were making OR kicking up *inf* a real ~ ils faisaient un boucan d'enfer OR monstre.
◇ *vt*: to ~ sthg into sb *inf* faire (bien) comprendre qqch à qqn, faire entrer qqch dans la tête à qqn.

DIN [dɪn] *n* -**1.** (*abbr of* Deutsche Industrie Norm) (indice *m*) DIN *f*. -**2.** PHOT DIN *f*.

dinar ['diːnɑː^r] *n* dinar *m*.

dindins *inf* ['dɪndɪnz] *n* dîner *m*.

dine [daɪn] ◇ *vi* dîner; she ~d off OR on trout and fresh strawberries elle a dîné d'une truite et de fraises fraîches; we're dining in tonight nous dînons à la maison ce soir.
◇ *vt* offrir à dîner à.
◆ **dine out** *vi insep* dîner dehors OR en ville; I ~d out on that story for weeks *fig* ça m'a fait une bonne histoire à raconter pendant des semaines.

diner ['daɪnə^r] *n* -**1.** [person] dîneur *m*, -euse *f*. -**2.** RAIL wagon-restaurant *m*; *Am* petit restaurant *m* sans façon.

dinette [daɪ'net] *n* coin-repas *m*.

ding [dɪŋ] ◇ *vi* tinter.
◇ *vt* = **din**.
◇ *n* tintement *m*.

ding-a-ling ['dɪŋə,lɪŋ] *n* -**1.** [ring] dring dring *m*, tintement *m*. -**2.** *inf Am* [fool] cloche *f*, imbécile *mf*.

dingbat *inf* ['dɪŋbæt] *n* -**1.** *Am* [thing] truc *m*, machin *m*. -**2.** [fool] crétin *m*, -e *f*, gourde *f*.

dingdong [,dɪŋ'dɒŋ] ◇ *n* -**1.** [sound] ding dong *m*. -**2.** *inf Br* [quarrel] dispute *f*; [fight] bagarre *f*.
◇ *adj inf* [argument, fight] acharné; [race] très disputé.

dinge [dɪndʒ] = **dinginess**.

dinger *inf* ['dɪŋə^r] *n Am* [person] imbécile *mf*.

dinghy ['dɪŋgɪ] (*pl* dinghies) *n* [rowing boat] petit canot *m*, youyou *m*; [sailboat] dériveur *m*; [rubber] canot *m* pneumatique, dinghy *m*.

dinginess ['dɪndʒɪnɪs] *n* [shabbiness] aspect *m* miteux OR douteux; [drabness] couleur *f* terne.

dingle ['dɪŋgl] *n* vallon *m* boisé.

dingo ['dɪŋgəʊ] (*pl* dingoes) *n* dingo *m*.

dingus *inf* ['dɪŋʌs] *n Am* truc *m*, machin *m*.

dingy ['dɪndʒɪ] (*compar* dingier, *superl* dingiest) *adj* [shabby] miteux; [dirty] douteux; [colour] terne.
dining car ['daɪnɪŋ-] *n* wagon-restaurant *m*.
dining hall *n* réfectoire *m*, salle *f* à manger.
dining room ◇ *n* salle *f* à manger.
◇ *comp* [curtains, furniture] de (la) salle à manger; ~ suite salle *f* à manger *(meubles)*.
dining table *n* table *f* de salle à manger.
dink [dɪŋk] *n* -**1.** *inf* [person] imbécile *mf*. -**2.** ▽ [penis] queue *f*.
dinkie ['dɪŋkɪ] (*abbr of* double income no kids) *n personne mariée aisée et sans enfants*.
dinky *inf* ['dɪŋkɪ] (*compar* dinkier, *superl* dinkiest) *adj* -**1.** *Br* [small, neat] mignon, coquet. -**2.** *Am pej* [insignificant] de rien du tout.
dinner ['dɪnəʳ] ◇ *n* [evening meal] dîner *m*; [- very late] souper *m*; *dial* [lunch] déjeuner *m*; to be at ~ être en train de dîner; they were just getting up from ~ ils sortaient à peine de table; ask her round for ~ next week invite-la à venir dîner la semaine prochaine; she's having guests to ~ elle a des invités à dîner; they went out to ~ [in restaurant] ils ont dîné au restaurant OR en ville; [at friends] ils ont dîné chez des amis; ~'s on the table OR ready! le dîner est prêt!, c'est prêt!, à table!; did you have a good ~? avez-vous bien mangé OR dîné?; did you give the cat its ~? avez-vous donné à manger au chat?; a formal ~ un grand dîner OR dîner officiel ❑ I've played more cup matches in my time than you've had hot ~s *inf Br* j'ai joué plus de matchs de coupe dans ma vie que tu n'en joueras jamais.
◇ *comp* [fork, knife] de table; she rang the ~ bell elle a sonné pour annoncer le dîner; ~ duty SCH service *m* de réfectoire; ~ hour [at work] heure *f* du déjeuner; [at school] pause *f* de midi; ~ plate (grande) assiette *f*; ~ roll petit pain *m*.
dinner dance *n* dîner *m* dansant.
dinner jacket *n* smoking *m*.
dinner lady *n Br employée d'une cantine scolaire*.
dinner party *n* dîner *m (sur invitation)*; we're having OR giving a ~ nous avons du monde à dîner, nous donnons un dîner.
dinner service *n* service *m* de table.
dinner table *n* table *f* de salle à manger; at OR over the ~ pendant le dîner, au dîner.
dinnertime ['dɪnətaɪm] *n* heure *f* du dîner.
dinnerware ['dɪnəweəʳ] *n Am* vaisselle *f*.
dinosaur ['daɪnəsɔːʳ] *n* dinosaure *m*; the institute's become a bit of a ~ *fig* l'institut est le survivant d'une époque révolue OR a fait son temps.
dint [dɪnt] *vt* = **dent**.
◆ **by dint of** *prep phr* à force de; she succeeded by ~ of sheer hard work elle a réussi à force de travailler dur.
diocesan [daɪ'ɒsɪsn] ◇ *adj* diocésain.
◇ *n* (évêque *m*) diocésain *m*.
diocese ['daɪəsɪs] *n* diocèse *m*.
diode ['daɪəʊd] *n* diode *f*.
Diogenes [daɪ'ɒdʒɪniːz] *pr n* Diogène.
Dionysiac [,daɪə'nɪzɪæk], **Dionysian** [,daɪə'nɪzɪən] *adj* dionysiaque.
Dionysus [,daɪə'naɪsəs] *pr n* Dionysos.
diopter *Am* = **dioptre**.
dioptometer [,daɪɒp'tɒmɪtəʳ] *n* instrument *m* de mesure dioptrique.
dioptre *Br*, **diopter** *Am* [daɪ'ɒptəʳ] *n* dioptrie *f*.
diorama [,daɪə'rɑːmə] *n* diorama *m*.
dioxide [daɪ'ɒksaɪd] *n* dioxyde *m*.
dioxin [daɪ'ɒksɪn] *n* dioxine *f*.
dip [dɪp] (*pt* & *pp* dipped, *cont* dipping) ◇ *vi* -**1.** [incline - ground] descendre, s'incliner; [- road] descendre, plonger; [- head] pencher, s'incliner. -**2.** [drop - sun] baisser, descendre à l'horizon; [- price] diminuer, baisser; [- temperature] baisser; [- plane] piquer; [- boat] tanguer, piquer.
◇ *vt* -**1.** [immerse] tremper, plonger; TECH tremper; [clean] décaper; [dye] teindre; [sheep] laver. -**2.** [plunge] plonger; to ~ one's hand in one's pocket *fig* mettre la main à la poche. -**3.** *Br* AUT: to ~ one's headlights se mettre en codes; dipped headlights codes *mpl*, feux *mpl* de croisement; to drive on OR with dipped headlights rouler en codes.
◇ *n* -**1.** *inf* [swim] baignade *f*, bain *m (en mer, en piscine)*; to go for a ~ aller se baigner, aller faire trempette; a brief ~ into Homer *fig* un survol rapide d'Homère. -**2.** [liquid] bain *m*; [for sheep] bain *m* parasiticide. -**3.** [slope - in ground] déclivité *f*; [- in road] descente *f*; GEOL pendage *m*; angle of ~ PHYS inclinaison *f* magnétique. -**4.** [bob] inclinaison *f*; [of head] hochement *m*. -**5.** [drop - in temperature] baisse *f*; [- in price] fléchissement *m*, baisse *f*. -**6.** CULIN *pâte ou mousse (à tartiner) servie avec du pain ou des biscuits salés*; avocado ~ mousse *f* à l'avocat; cheese ~ [cold] hors d'œuvre *m* au fromage; [hot] fondue *f* savoyarde OR au fromage. -**7.** ▽ *Am* [idiot] con *m*, conne *f*.
◆ **dip into** *vt insep* -**1.** [dabble]: I've only really dipped into Shakespeare j'ai seulement survolé OR feuilleté Shakespeare. -**2.** [draw upon] puiser dans; we've had to ~ into our savings nous avons dû puiser dans nos économies.
Dip. *written abbr of* diploma.
DipEd [dɪp'ed] (*abbr of* Diploma in Education) *n Br* ≃ CAPES *m*.
diphase ['daɪfeɪz] *adj* diphasé.
diphosgene [daɪ'fɒsdʒiːn] *n composé toxique de la phosgène et du méthanol*.
diphtheria [dɪf'θɪərɪə] *n* diphtérie *f*; ~ vaccine vaccin *m* antidiphtérique.
diphthong ['dɪfθɒŋ] *n* diphtongue *f*.
diphthongize, -ise ['dɪfθɒŋgaɪz] ◇ *vt* diphtonguer.
◇ *vi* se diphtonguer.
diplex ['daɪpleks] *adj* duplex.
diploid ['dɪplɔɪd] *adj* diploïde.
diploma [dɪ'pləʊmə] *n* diplôme *m*; she has a ~ in business studies elle est diplômée de OR en commerce; teaching ~ diplôme d'enseignement.
diplomacy [dɪ'pləʊməsɪ] *n* POL & *fig* diplomatie *f*; you have to use a bit of ~ vous devez user d'un peu de diplomatie, il faut être un peu diplomate.
diplomat ['dɪpləmæt] *n* POL & *fig* diplomate *mf*.
diplomate ['dɪpləmeɪt] *n* [gen] diplômé *m*, -e *f*; MED diplômé spécialiste *m*, diplômée spécialiste *f*.
diplomatic [,dɪplə'mætɪk] *adj* -**1.** POL diplomatique. -**2.** *fig* [person] diplomate; [action, remark] diplomatique; you have to be ~ when dealing with these people il faut faire preuve de tact OR user de diplomatie pour traiter avec ces gens-là; that wasn't very ~ ça manquait un peu de tact OR de diplomatie.
diplomatically [,dɪplə'mætɪklɪ] *adv* POL diplomatiquement; *fig* avec diplomatie, diplomatiquement.
diplomatic bag *Br*, **diplomatic pouch** *Am* *n* valise *f* diplomatique.
diplomatic corps *n* corps *m* diplomatique.
diplomatic immunity *n* immunité *f* diplomatique; to claim ~ faire valoir l'immunité diplomatique.
Diplomatic Service *n*: the ~ la diplomatie, le service diplomatique; to enter the ~ entrer dans la diplomatie.
diplomatist [dɪ'pləʊmətɪst] = **diplomat**.
diplopia [dɪ'pləʊpɪə] *n* diplopie *f*.
dip needle *n* aiguille *f* aimantée *(de boussole)*.
dipole ['daɪpəʊl] *n* dipôle *m*.
dipper ['dɪpəʳ] *n* -**1.** [ladle] louche *f*. -**2.** [of machine] godet *m* (de pelleteuse); [for lake, river] benne *f* (de drague), hotte *f* à draguer. -**3.** *Br* AUT basculeur *m* (de phares). -**4.** ORNITH cincle *m* (plongeur).
dippy *inf* ['dɪpɪ] (*compar* dippier, *superl* dippiest) *adj* écervelé.
diprod ['dɪprɒd] *n Am* jauge *f* (de niveau d'huile).
dipshit▼ ['dɪpʃɪt] *n Am* con *m*, conne *f*.
dipso▽ ['dɪpsəʊ] *n* alcoolo *mf*.
dipsomania [,dɪpsə'meɪnjə] *n* dipsomanie *f*.
dipsomaniac [,dɪpsə'meɪnɪæk] ◇ *adj* dipsomane.
◇ *n* dipsomane *mf*.
dipstick ['dɪpstɪk] *n Br* jauge *f* (de niveau d'huile).
dipswitch ['dɪpswɪtʃ] *n Br* basculeur *m* (des phares).
diptera ['dɪptərə] *npl* diptères *mpl*.
dipterous ['dɪptərəs] *adj* diptère.
diptych ['dɪptɪk] *n* diptyque *m*.
dire ['daɪəʳ] *adj* -**1.** [fearful] affreux, terrible; [ominous] sinistre; ~ warnings avertissements sinistres. -**2.** [very bad]: the film was pretty ~ le film était vraiment mauvais. -**3.** [extreme] extrême; he's in ~ need of sleep il a absolument besoin de sommeil; ~ poverty misère noire ❑ to be in ~ straits être dans une mauvaise passe OR aux abois.
direct [dɪ'rekt] ◇ *vt* -**1.** [supervise - business] diriger, gérer, mener; [- office, work] diriger; [- movements] guider; [- traffic] régler. -**2.** CIN, RADIO & TV [film, programme] réaliser; [actors] diriger; THEAT [play] mettre en scène. -**3.** [address] adresser; please ~ your remarks to the chairperson veuillez adresser vos observations au président; the accusation was ~ed at him l'accusation le visait; he ~ed my attention to the map il a attiré mon attention sur la carte; we should ~ all our efforts towards improving our education service nous devrions consacrer tous nos efforts à améliorer notre système scolaire. -**4.** [point] diriger; I ~ed my steps homewards je me suis dirigé vers la maison; can you ~ me to the train station? pourriez-vous m'indiquer le chemin de la gare? -**5.** [instruct] ordonner; he ~ed them to leave at once il leur a donné l'ordre de partir immédiatement; she ~ed him to take control of the project elle l'a chargé de prendre en main le projet; I did as I was ~ed j'ai fait comme on m'avait dit OR comme on m'en avait donné l'ordre; 'take as ~ed' 'se conformer à la prescription du médecin'. -**6.** JUR: to ~ the jury instruire le jury; the judge ~ed the jury to bring in a verdict of guilty le juge incita le jury à rendre un verdict de culpabilité ❑ ~ed verdict *Am verdict rendu par le jury sur la recommandation du juge*. -**7.** *Am* MUS diriger.
◇ *vi* -**1.** [command] diriger, commander. -**2.** *Am* MUS diriger; THEAT mettre en scène; it's her first chance to ~ c'est la première fois qu'elle peut faire une mise en scène.
◇ *adj* -**1.** [straight] direct; ~ flight/route vol *m*/chemin *m* direct; ~ heating/lighting chauffage *m*/éclairage *m* direct ❑ ~ memory access COMPUT accès *m* direct à la mémoire. -**2.** MIL: ~ hit coup *m* au but; the missile made a ~ hit le missile a atteint son objectif. -**3.** [immediate - cause, effect] direct, immédiat; she has ~ control over the finances les questions financières relèvent directement de sa responsabilité; he's a ~ descendant of the King il descend du roi en ligne directe; 'keep out of ~ sunlight' évitez l'exposition directe au soleil; you're not in ~ danger of catching the disease vous ne courez pas de risque immédiat d'attraper cette maladie ❑ ~ advertising publicité *f* directe. -**4.** [frank] franc, direct; [denial, refusal] catégorique, absolu; he was always very ~ with us il nous a toujours parlé très franchement; she asked some very ~ questions elle a posé des questions parfois très directes. -**5.** [exact] exact, précis; ~ quotation citation exacte; it's the ~ opposite of what I said c'est exactement le contraire de ce que j'ai dit. -**6.** ASTRON, GRAMM & LOGIC direct; ~ question GRAMM question *f* au style direct.
◇ *adv* directement.
direct access *n* accès *m* direct.
direct action *n* action *f* directe.
direct current *n* courant *m* continu.
direct debit *n* prélèvement *m* automatique.

direct discourse *Am* = **direct speech.**

direct-grant school *n Br établissement scolaire privé subventionné par l'État si l'établissement accepte un certain nombre d'élèves qui ne paient pas.*

direction [dɪ'rekʃn] *n* -**1.** [way] direction *f*, sens *m*; in every ~ dans toutes les directions, en tous sens, dans tous les sens; in the opposite ~ dans la direction opposée, en sens inverse; in the right/wrong ~ dans le bon/mauvais sens, dans la bonne/mauvaise direction; in the ~ of Chicago dans la OR en direction de Chicago; which ~ are you going (in)? vers où allez-vous?, quelle direction prenez-vous?; a step in the right ~ *fig* un pas dans la bonne voie OR direction; she lacks ~ *fig* elle ne sait pas très bien où elle va. -**2.** [control] direction *f*; the investigation was carried out under the ~ of an independent body l'enquête a été menée sous la direction OR conduite d'un organisme indépendant. -**3.** CIN, RADIO & TV réalisation *f*; THEAT mise *f* en scène; under the ~ of... CIN, RADIO & TV réalisation de..., réalisé par...; THEAT mise en scène de...
◆ **directions** *npl* indications *fpl*, instructions *fpl*, mode *m* d'emploi; read the ~s lisez le mode d'emploi; I asked for ~s to the station j'ai demandé le chemin de la gare ❑ stage ~s THEAT indications scéniques.

directional [dɪ'rekʃənl] *adj* [gen & ELECTRON] directionnel.

direction finder *n* radiogoniomètre *m*.

direction indicator *n* clignotant *m*.

directive [dɪ'rektɪv] ◇ *n* directive *f*, instruction *f*.
◇ *adj* directeur.

directly [dɪ'rektlɪ] ◇ *adv* -**1.** [straight] directement; go ~ to the police station allez directement OR tout droit au poste de police; to be ~ descended from sb descendre en droite ligne OR en ligne directe de qqn; the affair concerns me ~ cette affaire me concerne directement. -**2.** [promptly] immédiatement; ~ after lunch tout de suite après le déjeuner; ~ before the film juste avant le film; I'll be there ~ j'arrive tout de suite. -**3.** [frankly] franchement. -**4.** [exactly] exactement; ~ opposite the station juste en face de la gare.
◇ *conj Br* aussitôt que, dès que; we'll leave ~ the money arrives nous partirons dès que l'argent sera arrivé.

directness [dɪ'rektnɪs] *n* -**1.** [of person, reply] franchise *f*; [of remark] absence *f* d'ambiguïté. -**2.** [of attack] caractère *m* direct.

direct object *n* complément *m* (d'objet) direct.

director [dɪ'rektəʳ] *n* -**1.** [person - of business] directeur *m*, -trice *f*, chef *m*; [- of organization] directeur *m*, -trice *f*; Director of Education *Br* ≃ recteur *m* d'académie; Director of Public Prosecutions *Br* JUR ≃ procureur *m* de la République; ~ of studies UNIV directeur *m*, -trice *f* d'études OR de travaux. -**2.** *Am* MUS chef *m* d'orchestre. -**3.** CIN, RADIO & TV réalisateur *m*, -trice *f*; THEAT metteur *m* en scène. -**4.** [device] guide *m*.

directorate [dɪ'rektərət] *n* -**1.** [board] conseil *m* d'administration. -**2.** [position] direction *f*, poste *m* de directeur.

director-general *n* directeur *m* général.

directorial [,daɪrek'tɔːrɪəl] *adj* de mise en scène.

director's chair *n* régisseur *m*.

directorship [dɪ'rektəʃɪp] *n* direction *f*, poste *m* OR fonctions *fpl* de directeur.

directory [dɪ'rektərɪ] (*pl* directories) ◇ *n* -**1.** [of addresses] répertoire *m* (d'adresses); TELEC annuaire *m* (des téléphones), bottin *m*; COMPUT répertoire *m*; street ~ répertoire des rues; commercial ~ annuaire du commerce. -**2.** [of instructions] mode *m* d'emploi; RELIG directoire *m*.
◇ *adj* directeur.
◆ **Directory** *n* HIST: the Directory le Directoire.

directory enquiries *Br*, **directory assistance** *Am n* (service *m* des) renseignements *mpl* téléphoniques.

directrix [dɪ'rektrɪks] *n* [gen & GEOM] directrice *f*.

direct rule *n contrôle direct du maintien de l'ordre par le gouvernement britannique en Irlande du Nord, depuis 1972.*

direct speech *n Br* discours *m* OR style *m* direct.

direct tax *n* impôt *m* direct.

dirge [dɜːdʒ] *n* hymne *m* OR chant *m* funèbre; *fig* chant *m* lugubre.

dirham ['dɪəræm] *n* dirham *m*, dirhem *m*.

dirigible ['dɪrɪdʒəbl] ◇ *adj* dirigeable.
◇ *n* dirigeable *m*.

dirigisme ['dɪrɪʒɪzm] *n* dirigisme *m*.

dirk [dɜːk] *n Scot* dague *f*, poignard *m*.

dirndl ['dɜːndl] *n large jupe froncée.*

dirt [dɜːt] *n* -**1.** [grime] saleté *f*, crasse *f*; [mud] boue *f*; [excrement] crotte *f*, ordure *f*; don't tread ~ into the carpet ne ramène pas de boue sur la moquette; she was covered in ~ elle était toute sale OR couverte de crasse; this dress really shows the ~ cette robe fait vite sale OR est très salissante. -**2.** [soil] terre *f*; stop scrabbling in the ~ arrête de gratter la terre ❑ to be as common as ~ être tout à fait banal; to treat sb like ~ traiter qqn comme un chien. -**3.** [obscenity] obscénité *f*. -**4.** *inf (U)* [scandal] ragots *mpl*, cancans *mpl*; to dig up some ~ on sb répandre des calomnies sur qqn. -**5.** INDUST [in material, solution] impuretés *fpl*, corps *mpl* étrangers; [in machine] encrassement *m*; the wheel is full of ~ la roue est encrassée.

dirt-cheap *inf adv* pour rien; I bought it ~ je l'ai payé trois fois rien.

dirt farmer *n* petit fermier *m*.

dirt road *n* chemin *m* de terre OR non goudronné.

dirt track *n* [gen] piste *f*; SPORT (piste) cendrée *f*; ~ racing courses *fpl* sur cendrée.

dirty ['dɜːtɪ] (*compar* dirtier, *superl* dirtiest, *pt & pp* dirtied) ◇ *adj* -**1.** [not clean - clothes, hands, person] sale, malpropre, crasseux; [- machine] encrassé; [- wound] infecté; [muddy] plein de boue, crotté; don't get ~! ne vous salissez pas!; he got his shirt ~ il a sali sa chemise; this rug gets ~ easily ce tapis est salissant. -**2.** [colour] sale. -**3.** [nasty] sale; no ~ cracks! *inf* pas de vacheries!; it was a ~ business c'était une sale histoire; politics is a ~ business il est difficile de garder les mains propres quand on fait de la politique; a ~ campaign une campagne sordide; that's a ~ lie ce n'est absolument pas vrai; ~ money argent sale OR mal acquis; he's a ~ fighter il se bat en traître ❑ to give sb a ~ look regarder qqn de travers OR d'un sale œil; that's ~ pool! *Am* c'est un tour de cochon!; you ~ rat! *inf* espèce de salaud! -**4.** [weather] sale, vilain. -**5.** [obscene] grossier, obscène; to have a ~ mind avoir l'esprit mal tourné; to have a ~ mouth être mal embouché ❑ ~ magazines revues *fpl* pornographiques; a ~ old man *inf* un vieux cochon OR vicelard; a ~ joke/story une blague/histoire cochonne; a ~ word une grossièreté, un gros mot; "middle class" is a ~ word around here *inf* le terme «classe moyenne» est une insulte par ici. -**6.** *inf* [sexy]: a ~ weekend un week-end coquin.
◇ *adv inf* -**1.** [fight, play] déloyalement; [talk] grossièrement. -**2.** *Br* [as intensifier] vachement; a ~ great skyscraper un gratte-ciel énorme.
◇ *vt* [soil] salir; [machine] encrasser; to ~ one's hands *literal & fig* se salir les mains.
◇ *n Br*: to do the ~ on sb *inf* jouer un sale tour OR faire une vacherie à qqn.

dirty-minded *adj* qui a l'esprit mal tourné.

dirty trick *n* [malicious act] sale tour *m*; to play a ~ on sb jouer un sale tour OR un tour de cochon à qqn.
◆ **dirty tricks** *npl*: they've been up to their ~s again ils ont encore fait des leurs; ~ campaign POL *manœuvre visant à discréditer un parti politique.*

dirty work *n* -**1.** [unpleasant work] travail *m* salissant; I always get the ~ c'est toujours moi qui fais le sale travail; he wants someone else to do his ~ il veut que quelqu'un d'autre se salisse les mains à sa place. -**2.** *inf* [dishonest work] magouille *f*.

disability [,dɪsə'bɪlətɪ] (*pl* **disabilities**) *n* -**1.** [state - physical] incapacité *f*, invalidité *f*; partial/total ~ incapacité partielle/totale. -**2.** [handicap] infirmité *f*, handicap *m* ADMIN; her ~ makes her eligible for a pension son infirmité lui donne droit à une pension. -**3.** JUR: ~ to do sthg incapacité *f* OR inhabilité *f* à faire qqch.

disability clause *n clause d'une police d'assurance-vie permettant à l'assuré de cesser tout paiement et de recevoir une pension en cas d'invalidité.*

disability pension *n* pension *f* d'invalidité.

disable [dɪs'eɪbl] *vt* -**1.** [accident, illness] rendre infirme; [maim] mutiler, estropier; a disabling disease une maladie invalidante; to ~ sb from doing sthg *fig* mettre qqn hors d'état de faire qqch. -**2.** [machine] mettre hors service; [ship] faire subir une avarie à, désemparer; [gun, tank] mettre hors d'action; [army, battalion] mettre hors de combat. -**3.** JUR: to ~ sb from doing sthg rendre qqn inhabile à faire qqch; [pronounce] prononcer qqn inhabile à faire qqch.

disabled [dɪs'eɪbld] ◇ *adj* -**1.** [handicapped] infirme, handicapé ADMIN; [maimed] mutilé, estropié; ~ ex-servicemen invalides *mpl* OR mutilés *mpl* de guerre. -**2.** MIL mis hors de combat. -**3.** [machine] hors service; [ship] avarié, désemparé; [propeller] immobilisé. -**4.** JUR: to be ~ from doing sthg être incapable de OR inhabile à faire qqch.
◇ *npl*: the ~ [handicapped] les handicapés *mpl*; [maimed] les mutilés *mpl* OR estropiés *mpl*; the war ~ les mutilés OR invalides *mpl* de guerre.

disablement [dɪs'eɪblmənt] *n* invalidité *f*, infirmité *f*; ~ benefit allocation *f* d'invalidité; ~ insurance assurance *f* invalidité; ~ pension pension *f* d'invalidité.

disabuse [,dɪsə'bjuːz] *vt* détromper, ôter ses illusions à; to ~ sb of sthg détromper qqn de qqch.

disadvantage [,dɪsəd'vɑːntɪdʒ] ◇ *n* -**1.** [condition] désavantage *m*, inconvénient *m*; to be at a ~ être désavantagé OR dans une position désavantageuse; she's at a big ~ being the youngest le fait qu'elle soit la plus jeune la désavantage nettement; to put sb at a ~ désavantager OR défavoriser qqn; the situation works OR is to her ~ la situation est un handicap OR un désavantage pour elle; it would be to his ~ to sue cela lui porterait préjudice OR lui ferait du tort d'intenter un procès. -**2.** COMM [loss] perte *f*.
◇ *vt* désavantager, défavoriser.

disadvantaged [,dɪsəd'vɑːntɪdʒd] ◇ *adj* [gen] défavorisé; [economically] déshérité; socially ~ défavorisé sur le plan social.
◇ *npl*: the ~ les défavorisés *mpl*.

disadvantageous [,dɪsædvɑːn'teɪdʒəs] *adj* désavantageux, défavorable; to be ~ to sb être désavantageux OR défavorable à qqn.

disadvantageously [,dɪsædvɑːn'teɪdʒəslɪ] *adv* d'une manière désavantageuse, désavantageusement.

disaffected [,dɪsə'fektɪd] *adj* [discontented] hostile, mécontent; [disloyal] rebelle; ~ youth jeunesse révoltée.

disaffection [,dɪsə'fekʃn] *n* désaffection *f*, détachement *m*.

disagree [,dɪsə'griː] *vi* -**1.** [person, people] ne pas être d'accord, être en désaccord; she ~s elle n'est pas d'accord, elle n'est pas de cet avis; to ~ with sb about OR on sthg ne pas être d'accord avec OR ne pas être du même avis que qqn sur qqch; I ~ with everything they've done je suis contre OR je désapprouve tout ce qu'ils ont fait; we ~ on everything [differ] nous ne sommes jamais d'accord. -**2.** [figures, records] ne pas concorder; the two men's accounts of events ~ les récits des deux hommes sur ce qui s'est passé ne concordent pas. -**3.** [food, weather] ne pas convenir; spicy food ~s with him les plats épicés ne lui réussissent pas, il digère mal les plats épicés; I must have eaten something that ~d with me j'ai dû manger quelque chose qui n'est pas bien passé.

disagreeable [ˌdɪsəˈgrɪəbl] *adj* [person, remark] désagréable, désobligeant; [experience, job] désagréable, pénible; [smell] désagréable, déplaisant; don't be so ~! vous êtes vraiment pénibles!

disagreeably [ˌdɪsəˈgrɪəblɪ] *adv* désagréablement, d'une façon désagréable OR désobligeante; he behaved so ~! il a été tellement insupportable!

disagreement [ˌdɪsəˈgriːmənt] *n* -**1.** [of opinions, records] désaccord *m*, conflit *m*; I'm in complete ~ with you about OR on this je ne partage pas du tout votre avis là-dessus; they are in ~ about OR on what action to take ils ne sont pas d'accord sur les mesures à prendre. -**2.** [quarrel] différend *m*, querelle *f*; they've had a ~ over OR about money ils se sont disputés à propos d'argent, ils ont eu une querelle d'argent.

disallow [ˌdɪsəˈlaʊ] *vt* [argument, opinion] rejeter; SPORT refuser; JUR débouter, rejeter.

disambiguate [ˌdɪsæmˈbɪgjʊeɪt] *vt* désambiguïser.

disambiguation [ˈdɪsæmˌbɪgjʊˈeɪʃn] *n* désambiguïsation *f*.

disappear [ˌdɪsəˈpɪəʳ] *vi* -**1.** [vanish - person, snow] disparaître; [- object] disparaître, s'égarer; LING s'amuïr; she ~ed from sight on l'a perdue de vue; he ~ed into the crowd il s'est perdu dans la foule; to ~ over the horizon disparaître à l'horizon; to make sthg ~ [gen] faire disparaître qqch; [magician] escamoter qqch; they ~ed into thin air ils ont disparu sans laisser de trace, ils se sont volatilisés; he did his usual ~ing act *inf* il a encore joué la fille de l'air. -**2.** [cease to exist - pain, tribe] disparaître; [- problem] disparaître, s'aplanir; [- memory] s'effacer, s'estomper; [- tradition] disparaître, tomber en désuétude; as a species, the turtle is fast ~ing les tortues sont une espèce en voie de disparition.

disappearance [ˌdɪsəˈpɪərəns] *n* [gen] disparition *f*; LING amuïssement *m*.

disappoint [ˌdɪsəˈpɔɪnt] *vt* -**1.** [person] décevoir, désappointer; you promised to come, so don't ~ him vous avez promis de venir, alors ne lui faites pas faux bond. -**2.** [hope] décevoir; [plan] contrarier, contrecarrer.

disappointed [ˌdɪsəˈpɔɪntɪd] *adj* -**1.** [person] déçu, désappointé; I'm very ~ in him il m'a beaucoup déçu; I was ~ to hear you won't be coming j'ai été déçu d'apprendre que vous ne viendrez pas; are you ~ at OR with the results? les résultats vous ont-ils déçu?, avez-vous été déçu par les résultats?; to be ~ in love être malheureux en amour. -**2.** [ambition, hope] déçu; [plan] contrarié, contrecarré.

disappointing [ˌdɪsəˈpɔɪntɪŋ] *adj* décevant; how ~! quelle déception!, comme c'est décevant!; I found the film very ~ j'ai trouvé le film vraiment décevant, j'ai été vraiment déçu par le film.

disappointingly [ˌdɪsəˈpɔɪntɪŋlɪ] *adv*: ~ low grades des notes d'une faiblesse décourageante OR décevante; he did ~ badly in the exam ses résultats à l'examen ont été très décevants.

disappointment [ˌdɪsəˈpɔɪntmənt] *n* -**1.** [state] déception *f*, désappointement *m*, déconvenue *f*; to her great ~ she failed à sa grande déception OR déconvenue, elle a échoué. -**2.** [letdown] déception *f*, désillusion *f*; she has suffered many ~s elle a essuyé bien des déboires; he has been a great ~ to me il m'a beaucoup déçu.

disapprobation [ˌdɪsæprəˈbeɪʃn] *n fml* désapprobation *f*; [strong] réprobation *f*; a murmur of ~ un murmure désapprobateur OR de désapprobation.

disapproval [ˌdɪsəˈpruːvl] *n* désapprobation *f*; [strong] réprobation *f*; a look of ~ un regard désapprobateur OR de désapprobation; to shake one's head in ~ faire un signe désapprobateur de la tête; she showed/expressed her ~ of his decision elle a montré/exprimé sa désapprobation à l'égard de sa décision; much to my ~ she decided to get married elle a décidé de se marier, ce que je désapprouve entièrement.

disapprove [ˌdɪsəˈpruːv] ◇ *vi* désapprouver; to ~ of sthg désapprouver qqch; she ~s of smoking elle désapprouve OR elle est contre le tabac; your mother ~s of your going votre mère n'est pas d'accord pour que vous y alliez; he ~s of everything I do il trouve à redire à tout ce que je fais; her father ~s of me son père ne me trouve pas à son goût.
◇ *vt* désapprouver.

disapproving [ˌdɪsəˈpruːvɪŋ] *adj* désapprobateur, de désapprobation; don't look so ~ ne prends pas cet air désapprobateur.

disapprovingly [ˌdɪsəˈpruːvɪŋlɪ] *adv* [look] d'un air désapprobateur; [speak] d'un ton désapprobateur, avec désapprobation.

disarm [dɪsˈɑːm] ◇ *vt* -**1.** [country, enemy, critic] désarmer. -**2.** [charm] désarmer, toucher.
◇ *vi* désarmer.

disarmament [dɪsˈɑːməmənt] ◇ *n* désarmement *m*.
◇ *comp* [conference, negotiations, talks] sur le désarmement.

disarming [dɪsˈɑːmɪŋ] ◇ *adj* désarmant, touchant.
◇ *n* désarmement *m*.

disarmingly [dɪsˈɑːmɪŋlɪ] *adv* de façon désarmante; ~ honest/friendly d'une honnêteté/amabilité désarmante.

disarrange [ˌdɪsəˈreɪndʒ] *vt* [order, room] déranger, mettre en désordre; [plans] déranger, bouleverser; [hair] défaire.

disarray [ˌdɪsəˈreɪ] *n* [of person] confusion *f*, désordre *m*; [of clothing] désordre *m*; the group was thrown into ~ la confusion OR le désordre régnait dans le groupe; the enemy was in ~ l'ennemi était en déroute; the party is in complete ~ le parti est en plein désarroi; her thoughts were in ~ ses pensées étaient très confuses.

disassemble [ˌdɪsəˈsembl] *vt* démonter, désassembler.

disassembly [ˌdɪsəˈsemblɪ] *n* démontage *m*, désassemblage *m*.

disassociate *etc* [ˌdɪsəˈsəʊʃɪeɪt] = **dissociate**.

disaster [dɪˈzɑːstəʳ] ◇ *n* -**1.** [misfortune] désastre *m*, catastrophe *f*; [natural] catastrophe *f*, sinistre *m*; air ~ catastrophe aérienne; financial ~ désastre financier; a series of ~s une suite de désastres OR de malheurs; at the scene of the ~ sur les lieux de la catastrophe OR du sinistre; the town has suffered one ~ after another la ville a subi désastre après désastre; the project is heading for ~ le projet est voué à l'échec OR à la catastrophe; she's heading for OR courting ~ elle court à sa perte OR à la catastrophe; we were going along quite happily then ~ struck nous suivions notre petit bonhomme de chemin, quand soudain, catastrophe! -**2.** *fig*: as a manager, he's a ~! en tant que directeur, ce n'est pas une réussite!; my hair's a ~ this morning! mes cheveux sont dans un état épouvantable ce matin!
◇ *comp* [fund] d'aide aux sinistrés; [area] sinistré.

disaster area *n* région *f* sinistrée.

disastrous [dɪˈzɑːstrəs] *adj* désastreux, catastrophique.

disastrously [dɪˈzɑːstrəslɪ] *adv* désastreusement.

disavow [ˌdɪsəˈvaʊ] *vt fml* [child, opinion] désavouer; [responsibility, faith] renier.

disavowal [ˌdɪsəˈvaʊəl] *n fml* [of child, opinion] désaveu *m*; [of responsibility, faith] reniement *m*.

disband [dɪsˈbænd] ◇ *vt* [army, club] disperser; [organization] disperser, dissoudre.
◇ *vi* [army] se disperser; [organization] se dissoudre.

disbandment [dɪsˈbændmənt] *n* [of army, club] dispersion *f*; [of organization] dissolution *f*.

disbar [dɪsˈbɑːʳ] (*pt* & *pp* disbarred, *cont* disbarring) *vt* JUR rayer du barreau OR du tableau de l'ordre *(des avocats)*; he was disbarred for malpractice il s'est fait rayer du barreau pour faute professionnelle.

disbarment [dɪsˈbɑːmənt] *n* JUR radiation *f* (du barreau).

disbelief [ˌdɪsbɪˈliːf] *n* incrédulité *f*; she looked at him in ~ elle l'a regardé avec incrédulité.

disbelieve [ˌdɪsbɪˈliːv] ◇ *vt* [person] ne pas croire; [news, story] ne pas croire à; I see no reason to ~ his story je ne vois pas pourquoi on ne croirait pas à ce qu'il dit.
◇ *vi* RELIG ne pas croire.

disbeliever [ˌdɪsbɪˈliːvəʳ] *n* [gen] incrédule *mf*; RELIG incroyant *m*, -e *f*, incrédule *mf*.

disbelieving [ˌdɪsbɪˈliːvɪŋ] *adj* incrédule.

disburse [dɪsˈbɜːs] *vt* débourser.

disbursement [dɪsˈbɜːsmənt] *n* -**1.** [payment] débours *m*, dépense *f*. -**2.** [action] déboursement *m*.

disc [dɪsk] *n* -**1.** [flat circular object] disque *m*; the ~ of the moon le disque de la lune. -**2.** [record] disque *m*. -**3.** ANAT disque *m* (invertébral). -**4.** [identity tag] plaque *f* d'identité; parking ~ AUT disque *m* de stationnement.

disc. *written abbr of* discount.

discard [*n* ˈdɪskɑːd, *vb* dɪˈskɑːd] ◇ *vt* -**1.** [get rid of] se débarrasser de, mettre au rebut; [idea, system] renoncer, abandonner. -**2.** CARDS se défausser de, défausser; [in cribbage] écarter.
◇ *vi* CARDS se défausser; [in cribbage] écarter.
◇ *n* -**1.** COMM & INDUST [reject] pièce *f* de rebut. -**2.** CARDS défausse *f*; [in cribbage] écart *m*.

disc brake *n* frein *m* à disque.

discern [dɪˈsɜːn] *vt* [see] discerner, distinguer; [understand] discerner.

discernible [dɪˈsɜːnəbl] *adj* [visible] visible; [detectable] discernable, perceptible; he left for no ~ reason il est parti sans raison apparente.

discernibly [dɪˈsɜːnəblɪ] *adv* [visibly] visiblement; [perceptibly] perceptiblement, sensiblement.

discerning [dɪˈsɜːnɪŋ] *adj* [person] judicieux, sagace; [taste] fin, délicat; [look] perspicace.

discernment [dɪˈsɜːnmənt] *n* discernement *m*, perspicacité *f*.

discharge [*vb* dɪsˈtʃɑːdʒ, *n* ˈdɪstʃɑːdʒ] ◇ *vt* -**1.** [release - patient] laisser sortir, libérer; [- prisoner] libérer, mettre en liberté; he was ~d yesterday il est sorti hier; the patient ~d herself la malade a signé une décharge et est partie. -**2.** [dismiss - employee] renvoyer, congédier; [- official] destituer; JUR [jury] dessaisir; [accused] acquitter, relaxer; MIL [from service] renvoyer à la vie civile; [from active duty] démobiliser; [for lack of fitness] réformer; ~d bankrupt failli *m* réhabilité. -**3.** [unload - cargo] décharger; [- passengers] débarquer. -**4.** [emit - liquid] dégorger, déverser; [- gas] dégager, émettre; ELEC décharger; the wound was discharging pus MED la blessure suppurait. -**5.** [perform - duty] remplir, s'acquitter de; [- function] remplir. -**6.** [debt] acquitter, régler. -**7.** [gun] décharger, tirer; [arrow] décocher.
◇ *vi* -**1.** [ship] décharger. -**2.** [wound] suinter. -**3.** ELEC être en décharge.
◇ *n* -**1.** [release - of patient] sortie *f*; [of prisoner] libération *f*, mise *f* en liberté. -**2.** [dismissal - of employee] renvoi *m*; [- of soldier] libération *f*; [after active duty] démobilisation *f*; JUR [acquittal] acquittement *m*. -**3.** [of cargo] déchargement *m*. -**4.** [emission] émission *f*; [of liquid] écoulement *m*; MED [of wound] suintement *m*; [vaginal] pertes *fpl* (blanches); [of pus] suppuration *f*; ELEC décharge *f*. -**5.** [of duty] exécution *f*, accomplissement *m*. -**6.** [of debt] acquittement *m*. -**7.** [of gun] décharge *f*.

disc harrow *n* pulvériseur *m*.

disciple [dɪ'saɪpl] *n* [gen & RELIG] disciple *m*.

disciplinarian [,dɪsɪplɪ'neərɪən] ◇ *n* partisan *m* de la manière forte.
◇ *adj* disciplinaire.

disciplinary ['dɪsɪplɪnərɪ] *adj* -**1.** [corrective - measure] disciplinaire; [committee] de discipline; ~ action mesures *fpl* disciplinaires. -**2.** [relating to field] relatif à une discipline.

discipline ['dɪsɪplɪn] ◇ *n* -**1.** [training, control] discipline *f*; to keep OR to enforce ~ in the classroom maintenir la discipline dans la classe; with iron ~ avec une discipline de fer. -**2.** [area of study] discipline *f*, matière *f*.
◇ *vt* -**1.** [train - person] discipliner; [- mind] discipliner, former. -**2.** [punish] punir.

disciplined ['dɪsɪplɪnd] *adj* discipliné.

disc jockey *n* animateur *m*, -trice *f (de radio ou de discothèque)*, disc-jockey *m*.

disclaim [dɪs'kleɪm] *vt* -**1.** [deny - responsibility] rejeter, décliner; [- knowledge] nier; [- news, remark] démentir; [- paternity] désavouer. -**2.** JUR se désister de, renoncer à.

disclaimer [dɪs'kleɪmə^r] *n* -**1.** [denial] démenti *m*, désaveu *m*; the president issued a ~ denying all knowledge of affair le président a démenti officiellement être au courant de cette affaire. -**2.** JUR désistement *m*, renonciation *f*.

disclose [dɪs'kləʊz] *vt* -**1.** [reveal - secret] divulguer, dévoiler; [- news] divulguer; [- feelings] révéler. -**2.** [uncover] exposer, montrer.

disclosure [dɪs'kləʊʒə^r] *n* -**1.** [revelation] divulgation *f*, révélation *f*. -**2.** [fact revealed] révélation *f*.

disco ['dɪskəʊ] (*pl* discos) ◇ *n* discothèque *f*, boîte *f*.
◇ *comp* [dancing, music] disco.

discography [dɪs'kɒgrəfɪ] *n* discographie *f*.

discoid ['dɪskɔɪd] *adj* discoïde, discoïdal.

discolor *Am* = **discolour**.

discoloration [dɪs,kʌlə'reɪʃn] *n* [fading] décoloration *f*; [yellowing] jaunissement *m*; [dulling] ternissement *m*.

discolour *Br*, **discolor** *Am* [dɪs'kʌlə^r] ◇ *vt* [change colour of, fade] décolorer; [turn yellow] jaunir.
◇ *vi* [change colour, fade] se décolorer; [turn yellow] jaunir.

discombobulate *inf* [,dɪskəm'bɒbjʊleɪt] *vt Am* chambarder.

discomfit [dɪs'kʌmfɪt] *vt fml* -**1.** [confuse, embarrass] déconcerter, gêner. -**2.** [thwart - plan, project] contrecarrer, contrarier.

discomfiture [dɪs'kʌmfɪtʃə^r] *n fml* [embarrassment] embarras *m*, gêne *f*.

discomfort [dɪs'kʌmfət] ◇ *n* -**1.** [pain] malaise *m*; [unease] gêne *f*; she's in some ~ elle a assez mal; you may experience some ~ il se peut que vous ressentiez une gêne; her letter caused him some ~ sa lettre l'a mis un peu mal à l'aise. -**2.** [cause of pain, unease] incommodité *f*, inconfort *m*.
◇ *vt* incommoder, gêner.

discommode [,dɪskə'məʊd] *vt fml* importuner.

discompose [,dɪskəm'pəʊz] *vt fml* déconcerter, décontenancer.

discomposure [,dɪskəm'pəʊʒə^r] *n fml* embarras *m*, gêne *f*.

disconcert [,dɪskən'sɜːt] *vt* -**1.** [fluster] déconcerter, dérouter. -**2.** [upset] troubler, gêner.

disconcerting [,dɪskən'sɜːtɪŋ] *adj* -**1.** [unnerving] déconcertant, déroutant. -**2.** [upsetting] gênant.

disconcertingly [,dɪskən'sɜːtɪŋlɪ] *adv* de façon déconcertante OR déroutante.

disconnect [,dɪskə'nekt] *vt* -**1.** [detach] détacher, séparer; [plug, pipe, radio, TV] débrancher; RAIL [carriages] décrocher. -**2.** [gas, electricity, telephone, water] couper; the operator ~ed us TELEC la standardiste nous a coupés OR a interrompu la communication; we must have been ~ed nous avons dû être coupés; their phone has been ~ed on leur a coupé le téléphone.

disconnected [,dɪskə'nektɪd] *adj* -**1.** [remarks, thoughts] décousu, sans suite; [facts] sans rapport. -**2.** [detached - wire, plug etc] détaché; [- telephone] déconnecté.

disconsolate [dɪs'kɒnsələt] *adj* triste, inconsolable.

disconsolately [dɪs'kɒnsələtlɪ] *adv* tristement, inconsolablement.

discontent [,dɪskən'tent] ◇ *n* -**1.** [dissatisfaction] mécontentement *m*; general OR public ~ malaise *m*; a cause of ~ grief *m*. -**2.** [person] mécontent *m*, -e *f*.
◇ *adj* mécontent.
◇ *vt* mécontenter.

discontented [,dɪskən'tentɪd] *adj* mécontent.

discontinue [,dɪskən'tɪnjuː] *vt* -**1.** [gen] cesser, interrompre; I've ~d my subscription j'ai arrêté mon abonnement || COMM & INDUST [production] abandonner; [product] interrompre; [publication] interrompre la publication de; this item/model has been ~d cet article/ce modèle ne se fait plus; ~d line fin *f* de série. -**2.** JUR [action, suit] abandonner.

discontinuity [,dɪskɒntɪ'njuːətɪ] (*pl* discontinuities) *n* -**1.** [gen & MATH] discontinuité *f*. -**2.** GEOL zone *f* de discontinuité.

discontinuous [,dɪskən'tɪnjʊəs] *adj* [gen, LING & MATH] discontinu.

discord ['dɪskɔːd] *n* -**1.** *(U)* [conflict] désaccord *m*, discorde *f*; civil ~ dissensions *fpl* sociales. -**2.** MUS dissonance *f*.

discordant [dɪ'skɔːdənt] *adj* -**1.** [opinions] incompatible, opposé; [colours, sounds] discordant. -**2.** MUS dissonant.

discotheque ['dɪskəʊtek] *n* discothèque *f (pour danser)*.

discount [*n* 'dɪskaʊnt, *vb* 'dɪskaʊnt, dɪs'kaʊnt]
◇ *n* -**1.** COMM [price reduction] remise *f*, rabais *m*; I bought it at a ~ je l'ai acheté au rabais; she got a ~ on lui a fait une remise; the store is currently offering a 5% ~ on radios le magasin fait (une réduction de) 5% sur les radios en ce moment. -**2.** FIN [deduction] escompte *m*; '~ for cash' escompte au comptant; shares offered at a ~ des actions offertes en dessous du pair.
◇ *vt* -**1.** [disregard] ne pas tenir compte de; you have to ~ half of what she says il ne faut pas croire la moitié de ce qu'elle raconte; they did not ~ the possibility ils n'ont pas écarté cette possibilité. -**2.** COMM [article] faire une remise OR un rabais sur. -**3.** FIN [sum of money] faire une remise de, escompter; [bill, banknote] prendre à l'escompte, escompter.

discount house *n* -**1.** *Br* FIN [bank] banque *f* d'escompte; [organization] *organisme qui escompte des traites ou des effets*. -**2.** *Am* [shop] solderie *f*, magasin *m* de vente au rabais.

discount rate *n* taux *m* d'escompte.

discount store *n* solderie *f*.

discourage [dɪ'skʌrɪdʒ] *vt* -**1.** [dishearten] décourager; to become ~d se laisser décourager; the art school ~d his ideas l'école des beaux-arts a tenté de le faire changer d'idées. -**2.** [dissuade] décourager, dissuader; to ~ sb from doing sthg dissuader qqn de faire qqch; we are trying to ~ smoking nous essayons de dissuader les gens de fumer; in order to ~ burglars pour décourager les voleurs; a type of diet which should be ~d un type de régime qui devrait être déconseillé.

discouraged [dɪs'kʌrɪdʒd] *adj* découragé; don't be ~ ne te laisse pas abattre OR décourager.

discouragement [dɪ'skʌrɪdʒmənt] *n* -**1.** [attempt to discourage]: I met with ~ on all sides tout le monde a essayé de me décourager; my plans met with ~ on a essayé de me dissuader de poursuivre mes projets. -**2.** [deterrent]: the metal shutters act as a ~ to vandals les rideaux métalliques servent à décourager les vandales; at least it will act as a ~ au moins cela aura un effet dissuasif.

discouraging [dɪ'skʌrɪdʒɪŋ] *adj* décourageant.

discouragingly [dɪ'skʌrɪdʒɪŋlɪ] *adv* [speak] d'une manière décourageante; ~, the government has refused to finance the research ce qui est décourageant, c'est que le gouvernement a refusé de financer la recherche.

discourse [*n* 'dɪskɔːs, *vb* dɪ'skɔːs] ◇ *n* -**1.** *fml* [sermon] discours *m*; [dissertation] discours *m*, traité *m*; 'Discourse on Method' *Descartes* 'Discours de la méthode'. -**2.** LING discours *m*. -**3.** *(U) lit* [conversation] conversation *f*, débat *m*; to be engaged in ~ with sb s'entretenir avec qqn.
◇ *vi* -**1.** *fml* [speak]: to ~ on OR upon sthg traiter de OR parler de qqch; to ~ at great length on sthg discourir longuement sur qqch. -**2.** *lit* [converse] s'entretenir; to ~ with sb s'entretenir avec qqn.

discourse analysis *n* LING analyse *f* du discours.

discourteous [dɪs'kɜːtjəs] *adj* discourtois, impoli; to be ~ to OR towards sb être discourtois OR impoli avec OR envers qqn.

discourteously [dɪs'kɜːtjəslɪ] *adv* d'une façon discourtoise OR impolie; to behave ~ towards sb manquer de politesse envers qqn, se montrer impoli OR discourtois avec qqn.

discourtesy [dɪs'kɜːtɪsɪ] (*pl* discourtesies) *n* manque *m* de courtoisie, impolitesse *f*; to behave with great ~ se comporter de façon très discourtoise; to treat sb with ~ manquer de courtoisie envers qqn; I meant no ~ je ne voulais pas me montrer discourtois.

discover [dɪ'skʌvə^r] *vt* -**1.** [country, answer, reason] découvrir; the police ~ed who the guilty party was la police a découvert qui était coupable; I finally ~ed my glasses in my desk j'ai fini par trouver mes lunettes dans mon bureau. -**2.** [realize] se rendre compte; when did you ~ that your wallet had been stolen? quand vous êtes-vous rendu compte qu'on vous avait volé votre portefeuille?; to be ~ed [singer, actor etc] être découvert. -**3.** [actor, singer etc] découvrir.

discoverer [dɪ'skʌvərə^r] *n* découvreur *m*; Christopher Columbus was the ~ of America Christophe Colomb a découvert l'Amérique; the ~ of penicillin la personne qui a découvert la pénicilline.

discovery [dɪ'skʌvərɪ] (*pl* discoveries) *n* -**1.** [act, event] découverte *f*. -**2.** [actor, singer, place, thing] découverte *f*. -**3.** JUR [of documents] divulgation *f*.

discredit [dɪs'kredɪt] ◇ *vt* -**1.** [person] discréditer. -**2.** [report, theory - cast doubt on] discréditer, mettre en doute; [- show to be false] montrer l'inexactitude de; this theory is now considered ~ed by most linguists cette théorie est maintenant en discrédit auprès de la majorité des linguistes.
◇ *n* [loss of good reputation] discrédit *m*; to bring ~ on OR upon jeter le discrédit sur; it is very much to his ~ ce n'est pas du tout à son honneur; to his great ~, he told a lie à sa grand honte, il a menti; to be a ~ to one's family/school déshonorer sa famille/son école.

discreditable [dɪs'kredɪtəbl] *adj* peu honorable, indigne.

discreet [dɪ'skriːt] *adj* discret; to follow sb at a ~ distance suivre qqn à une distance respectueuse.

discreetly [dɪ'skriːtlɪ] *adv* discrètement, de manière discrète.

discrepancy [dɪ'skrepənsɪ] (*pl* discrepancies) *n* [in figures] contradiction *f*; [in statements] contradiction *f*, désaccord *m*, divergence *f*; there's a ~ between these reports ces rapports se contredisent OR divergent (sur un point).

discrete [dɪ'skriːt] *adj* [gen, TECH & MATH] discret.

discretion [dɪ'skreʃn] *n* -**1.** [tact, prudence] discrétion *f*; to be the soul of ~ être la discrétion même; ~ is the better part of valour *prov* prudence est mère de sûreté *prov*. -**2.** [judgment, taste] jugement *m*; I'll leave it to your ~ je laisse cela à votre discrétion OR jugement; use your own ~ jugez par vous-même; a woman of ~ une femme de raison; you have reached the age of ~ tu as atteint l'âge de raison; at the manager's ~ à la discrétion du directeur; the committee has ~ to award more than one prize à la discrétion du comité, plus d'un prix peut être accordé.

discretionary [dɪ'skreʃnərɪ] *adj* discrétionnaire.

discriminate [dɪ'skrɪmɪneɪt] ◇ *vi* -**1.** [on grounds of race, sex etc]: to ~ in favour of favoriser; she was ~d against elle faisait l'objet OR était victime de discriminations; there are many people being sexually/racially ~d against nombreux sont ceux qui sont victimes de discrimination sexuelle/raciale. -**2.** [distinguish] établir OR faire une distinction, faire une différence; to ~ between right and wrong distinguer le bien du mal.
◇ *vt* distinguer; to ~ right from wrong distinguer le bien du mal.

discriminating [dɪ'skrɪmɪneɪtɪŋ] *adj* -**1.** [showing discernment] judicieux; [in matters of taste] qui a un goût sûr; he is not very ~ in his choice of friends il n'est pas très difficile dans le choix de ses amis; the company was very ~ in its choice of employees l'entreprise était très sélective dans le choix de ses employés; a car for the ~ motorist une voiture pour l'automobiliste averti. -**2.** [tax, tariff] différentiel.

discrimination [dɪˌskrɪmɪ'neɪʃn] *n* -**1.** [on grounds of race, sex etc] discrimination *f*; sexual/racial ~ discrimination sexuelle/raciale. -**2.** [good judgment] discernement *m*; [in matters of taste] goût *m*; he shows no ~ in his choice of clothes/friends il ne fait preuve d'aucun discernement dans le choix de ses vêtements/amis; he is a man of great ~ c'est un homme qui a énormément de goût. -**3.** [ability to make distinctions]: powers of ~ capacités *fpl* de distinction, discernement *m*.

discriminatory [dɪ'skrɪmɪnətrɪ] *adj* [treatment, proposals] discriminatoire; the company is being ~ la société pratique la discrimination.

discursive [dɪ'skɜːsɪv] *adj fml* [essay, report, person etc] discursif.

discus ['dɪskəs] (*pl* discuses OR disci [-kaɪ]) *n* SPORT disque *m*; ~ thrower lanceur *m*, -euse *f* de disque; to come first in the ~ être premier au lancer du disque ‖ [in antiquity] discobole *m*.

discuss [dɪ'skʌs] *vt* [talk about - problem, price, subject etc] discuter de, parler de; [- person] parler de; [debate] discuter de; [examine - subj: author, book, report etc] examiner, parler de, traiter de; I'll ~ it with you later nous en parlerons OR discuterons plus tard; I'll ~ it with him j'en parlerai OR discuterai avec lui; it is being ~ed c'est en cours de discussion; I don't want to ~ it je ne veux pas en parler; I refuse to ~ rumours je refuse de commenter des rumeurs.

discussion [dɪ'skʌʃn] *n* [talk] discussion *f*; [debate] débat *m*; [examination - by author in report] traitement *m*; [- of report] examen *m*; the report contained a ~ of the recent findings le rapport parlait OR traitait des découvertes récentes; there's been a lot of ~ about it on en a beaucoup parlé; [in parliament, on board etc] cela a été beaucoup débattu; [in press, in media] cela a été largement traité; an ideal subject for ~ un sujet de discussion idéal; to come up for ~ [report, proposal etc] être discuté; the subject under ~ was highly controversial le sujet dont il était question prêtait à controverse; it is still under ~ c'est encore en cours de discussion.

disdain [dɪs'deɪn] ◇ *vt fml* dédaigner; he ~ed to reply to her letter/remark il n'a pas daigné répondre à sa lettre/remarque.
◇ *n* dédain *m*, mépris *m*; she was an object of ~ to him il la dédaignait OR la méprisait; with OR in ~ avec dédain, dédaigneusement; a look of ~ un regard dédaigneux.

disdainful [dɪs'deɪnfʊl] *adj* dédaigneux; to be ~ of sb/sthg se montrer dédaigneux envers qqn/qqch, dédaigner qqn/qqch.

disdainfully [dɪs'deɪnfʊlɪ] *adv* avec dédain, dédaigneusement.

disease [dɪ'ziːz] *n* -**1.** BOT, MED & VETER maladie *f*; he's suffering from a kidney ~ MED il a une maladie des reins, il est malade des reins; the elimination of ~ l'élimination OR l'éradication des maladies; to combat ~ combattre la maladie ❑ heart ~ maladie cardiaque OR du cœur; Hodgkin's ~ MED maladie de Hodgkin. -**2.** *fig* mal *m*, maladie *f*; boredom is a ~ of the rich l'ennui est une maladie OR un mal de riches.

diseased [dɪ'ziːzd] *adj* BOT, MED & VETER malade; *fig* [mind] malade, dérangé; [imagination] malade.

diseconomy [dɪsɪ'kɒnəmɪ] *n* ECON déséconomie *f*.

disembark [ˌdɪsɪm'bɑːk] ◇ *vi* débarquer; to ~ from the ferry débarquer du ferry.
◇ *vt* [passengers, cargo] débarquer.

disembarkation [ˌdɪsembɑː'keɪʃn], **disembarkment** [ˌdɪsɪm'bɑːkmənt] *n* [of passengers, cargo] débarquement *m*.

disembodied [ˌdɪsɪm'bɒdɪd] *adj* [voice, spirit] désincarné.

disembowel [ˌdɪsɪm'baʊəl] *vt* éviscérer, éventrer.

disenchanted [ˌdɪsɪn'tʃɑːntɪd] *adj* désillusionné; to be ~ with sb/sthg avoir perdu ses illusions sur qqn/qqch, être désillusionné par qqn/qqch; to become ~ with sb/sthg perdre ses illusions sur qqn/qqch.

disenchantment [ˌdɪsɪn'tʃɑːntmənt] *n* désillusion *f*; ~ with the government has been growing de plus en plus de gens sont déçus par le gouvernement.

disenfranchise [ˌdɪsɪn'fræntʃaɪz] *vt* priver du droit de vote.

disengage [ˌdɪsɪn'geɪdʒ] ◇ *vt* -**1.** MECH désenclencher; [lever, catch] dégager; AUT [handbrake] desserrer; to ~ the clutch AUT débrayer. -**2.** [release] dégager; I tried to ~ my hand from his j'ai essayé de dégager ma main de la sienne. -**3.** MIL: the order came through to ~ the troops l'ordre arriva de cesser le combat.
◇ *vi* -**1.** MIL cesser le combat. -**2.** MECH se désenclencher.

disengagement [ˌdɪsɪn'geɪdʒmənt] *n* -**1.** [from political grouping, organization] désengagement *m*. -**2.** MIL cessez-le-feu *m inv*.

disentangle [ˌdɪsɪn'tæŋgl] *vt* [string, plot, mystery] démêler; I tried to ~ myself from the net j'ai essayé de me dépêtrer du filet; to ~ o.s. from a difficult situation se sortir à grand-peine d'une situation difficile.

disequilibrium [ˌdɪsekwɪ'lɪbrɪəm] *n fml* déséquilibre *m*.

disestablish [ˌdɪsɪ'stæblɪʃ] *vt* séparer; to ~ the Church séparer l'Église de l'État.

disestablishment [ˌdɪsɪ'stæblɪʃmənt] *n* séparation *f*.

disfavour *Br*, **disfavor** *Am* [dɪs'feɪvəʳ] *n* désapprobation *f*, défaveur *f*; to regard sthg/sb with ~ considérer qqch/qqn avec désapprobation, voir qqch/qqn d'un mauvais œil; to fall into ~ with sb tomber en défaveur auprès de qqn.

disfigure [dɪs'fɪgəʳ] *vt* défigurer.

disfigured [dɪs'fɪgəd] *adj* défiguré.

disfigurement [dɪs'fɪgəmənt] *n* défigurement *m*.

disfranchise [ˌdɪs'fræntʃaɪz] = **disenfranchise**.

disgorge [dɪs'gɔːdʒ] ◇ *vt* -**1.** [food] régurgiter, rendre; *fig* [contents, passengers, pollutants] déverser; chimneys disgorging smoke des cheminées crachant de la fumée. -**2.** [give unwillingly - information] donner avec répugnance OR à contrecœur.
◇ *vi* [river] se jeter, se dégorger.

disgrace [dɪs'greɪs] ◇ *n* -**1.** [dishonour] disgrâce *f*; it will bring ~ on OR to the family cela fera tomber la famille dans la disgrâce, cela déshonorera la famille; there's no ~ in not knowing il n'y a pas de honte à ne pas savoir; it's no ~ to be poor il n'y a pas de honte à être pauvre. -**2.** [disapproval]: to be in ~ (with sb) être en disgrâce (auprès de qqn). -**3.** [shameful example or thing] honte *f*; it's a ~ c'est une honte, c'est honteux; it's a ~ that they weren't allowed into the country il est honteux OR c'est une honte qu'on leur ait interdit l'entrée dans le pays; these streets are a ~ ces rues sont une honte; look at you, you're a ~! regarde-toi, tu fais honte (à voir)!; that jacket is a ~! [very shabby] cette veste est une vraie guenille!; look at you, your hair's a ~ regarde-toi, tu es coiffé n'importe comment; he's a ~ to this profession il déshonore sa profession; you're a ~ to your family tu déshonores ta famille, tu es la honte de ta famille.
◇ *vt* -**1.** [bring shame on] faire honte à, couvrir de honte, déshonorer; to ~ o.s. se couvrir de honte. -**2.** *(usu pass)* [discredit] disgracier.

disgraceful [dɪs'greɪsfʊl] *adj* [behaviour] honteux, scandaleux; [hat, jacket etc] *inf* miteux; look at you, you're ~! regarde-toi, tu fais honte (à voir)!; it's ~ c'est honteux; it's ~ that he wasn't there il est honteux qu'il ne soit pas venu.

disgracefully [dɪs'greɪsfʊlɪ] *adv* honteusement; a ~ untidy room une pièce honteusement mal rangée.

disgruntled [dɪs'grʌntld] *adj* mécontent; to be ~ at OR about (doing) sthg être mécontent de (faire) qqch.

disguise [dɪs'gaɪz] ◇ *n* déguisement *m*; in ~ déguisé; to put on a ~ se déguiser; it was all a ~ *fig* ce n'était qu'un masque; to be a master of ~ être un roi du déguisement.
◇ *vt* -**1.** [voice, handwriting, person] déguiser; to be ~d as sb/sthg être déguisé en qqn/qqch. -**2.** [feelings, disappointment etc] dissimuler, masquer; [truth, facts] dissimuler; [unsightly feature] cacher; [bad taste of food, cough mixture etc] couvrir; there's no disguising the fact that business is bad on ne peut pas cacher le fait que les affaires vont mal; there's no disguising the fact that I'm in love with you je dois avouer que je vous aime.

disgust [dɪs'gʌst] ◇ *n* [sick feeling] dégoût *m*, aversion *f*, répugnance *f*; [displeasure] écœurement *m*, dégoût *m*; to be filled with ~ by sthg être écœuré par qqch; in order to express our ~ with the decision pour montrer que nous sommes écœurés par cette décision; I resigned in ~ dégoûté OR écœuré, j'ai démissionné.
◇ *vt* [sicken] dégoûter; [displease] écœurer; I am ~ed with him/this government/his behaviour il/ce gouvernement/son comportement m'écœure; I was ~ed by the accounts of torture [sickened] les récits de torture m'ont écœuré OR m'ont donné la nausée; to be ~ed with o.s. [displeased] s'en vouloir; I am ~ed with OR at my own stupidity [displeased] je m'en veux d'être aussi stupide.

disgusted [dɪs'gʌstɪd] *adj* [displeased] écœuré; [sick] écœuré, dégoûté; Disgusted, Tunbridge Wells *Br surnom et adresse fictifs correspondant au stéréotype du réactionnaire borné qui écrit à la rédaction des journaux pour protester*.

disgustedly [dɪs'gʌstɪdlɪ] *adv* d'un air écœuré.

disgusting [dɪs'gʌstɪŋ] *adj* [sickening - person, behaviour, smell] écœurant, dégoûtant; [- habit, language] dégoûtant; [very bad] écœurant, déplorable; how ~! c'est écœurant!, c'est dégoûtant!; you ~ little boy! espèce de petit dégoûtant!

disgustingly [dɪs'gʌstɪŋlɪ] *adv*: a ~ bad meal un repas épouvantable; to be ~ rich *inf* être scandaleusement riche; she is ~ clever/successful *inf* elle est intelligente/elle réussit au point que c'en est écœurant.

dish [dɪʃ] ◇ *n* -**1.** [plate] assiette *f*; the ~es la vaisselle; to wash OR to do the ~es faire la vaisselle; to wash ~es [in restaurant] faire la plonge. -**2.** [food] plat *m*. -**3.** [amount of food] plat *m*. -**4.** *inf* [good looking man or woman] canon *m*. -**5.** [of telescope] miroir *m* concave *(de télescope)*.

◇ *vt inf* -**1.** *Br* [chances, hopes] ruiner. -**2.** *Am* [criticize]: to ~ sb critiquer qqn. -**3.** *phr*: to ~ the dirt [gossip] faire des commérages.

◆ **dish out** ◇ *vt sep* -**1.** [food] servir. -**2.** *inf fig* [money, leaflets etc] distribuer; [advice] prodiguer; you can ~ it out but you can't take it [criticism] tu es bon pour critiquer mais pour ce qui est d'accepter la critique, c'est un autre problème!; you're going to have to take whatever they ~ out [punishment, discipline] il va te falloir accepter ce qu'ils te réservent; he's really ~ing it out [boxer] il frappe vraiment à coups redoublés.

◇ *vi insep* [serve food] faire le service.

◆ **dish up** ◇ *vt sep* [food] servir OR verser OR mettre dans un plat; [arguments, excuses etc] *inf* ressortir.

◇ *vi insep* [serve food] servir.

dish aerial *n Br* TV antenne *f* parabolique.

disharmonious [ˌdɪshɑːˈməʊnjəs] *adj* qui manque d'harmonie.

disharmony [ˌdɪsˈhɑːmənɪ] *n* manque *m* d'harmonie.

dishcloth [ˈdɪʃklɒθ] *n* torchon *m* (à vaisselle).

dishearten [dɪsˈhɑːtn] *vt* décourager, abattre, démoraliser; don't get ~ed ne te décourage pas, ne te laisse pas abattre.

disheartening [dɪsˈhɑːtnɪŋ] *adj* décourageant.

dished [dɪʃt] *adj* [angled] non parallèle; [convex] lenticulaire.

dishevelled *Br*, **disheveled** *Am* [dɪˈʃevld] *adj* [hair] ébouriffé, dépeigné; [clothes] débraillé, en désordre; [person, appearance] débraillé.

dishful [ˈdɪʃfʊl] *n* [of food] plat *m*.

dish mop *n* lavette *f*.

dishonest [dɪsˈɒnɪst] *adj* malhonnête; you're being ~ not telling him how you feel c'est malhonnête de ne pas lui dire ce que tu ressens.

dishonestly [dɪsˈɒnɪstlɪ] *adv* de manière malhonnête, malhonnêtement.

dishonesty [dɪsˈɒnɪstɪ] *n* malhonnêteté *f*.

dishonour *Br*, **dishonor** *Am* [dɪsˈɒnəʳ] ◇ *n* déshonneur *m*; to bring ~ on sb/one's country déshonorer qqn/son pays; death before ~! plutôt mourir qu'être déshonoré!

◇ *vt* -**1.** [family, country, profession etc] déshonorer. -**2.** FIN [cheque] refuser d'honorer.

dishonourable *Br*, **dishonorable** *Am* [dɪsˈɒnrəbl] *adj* [conduct] déshonorant; he was given a ~ discharge MIL il a été renvoyé pour manquement à l'honneur.

dishonourably *Br*, **dishonorably** *Am* [dɪsˈɒnrəblɪ] *adv* [behave] de façon OR manière déshonorante.

dishpan [ˈdɪʃpæn] *n Am* bassine *f*; to have ~ hands avoir les mains abîmées par la vaisselle.

dish rack *n* égouttoir *m* (à vaisselle).

dishrag [ˈdɪʃræg] = **dishcloth**.

dishtowel [ˈdɪʃtaʊəl] *Am* = **tea towel**.

dishwasher [ˈdɪʃˌwɒʃəʳ] *n* [machine] lave-vaisselle *m*; [person] plongeur *m*, -euse *f*.

dishwater [ˈdɪʃˌwɔːtəʳ] *n* eau *f* de vaisselle; this coffee is like ~! c'est du jus de chaussettes, ce café!

dishy *inf* [ˈdɪʃɪ] (*compar* dishier, *superl* dishiest) *adj Br* séduisant, sexy.

disillusion [ˌdɪsɪˈluːʒn] ◇ *vt* faire perdre ses illusions à, désillusionner; I hate to ~ you but he's really after your money je suis désolé de devoir t'ôter tes illusions mais c'est après ton argent qu'il en a; he has been ~ed by his experiences ses expériences lui ont fait perdre ses illusions OR l'ont désillusionné.

◇ *n* = **disillusionment**.

disillusioned [ˌdɪsɪˈluːʒnd] *adj* désillusionné, désabusé; to be ~ with sb/sthg avoir perdu ses illusions sur qqn/qqch.

disillusionment [ˌdɪsɪˈluːʒnmənt] *n* désillusion *f*, désabusement *m*; the fans' increasing ~ with club management la désillusion grandissante des fans envers la direction du club; ~ was not long in coming il ne m'a/lui a pas fallu beaucoup de temps pour perdre mes/ses illusions; her ~ was complete elle était complètement désillusionnée OR désabusée.

disincentive [ˌdɪsɪnˈsentɪv] *n*: taxes are a ~ to expansion les impôts découragent l'expansion; this will act as a ~ ceci aura un effet dissuasif OR de dissuasion; are social security payments a ~ to work? est-ce que les prestations sociales dissuadent les gens de travailler?

disinclination [ˌdɪsɪnklɪˈneɪʃn] *n* [of person] peu *m* d'inclination; her ~ to believe him sa tendance à ne pas le croire; the West's ~ to go on lending le peu d'enthousiasme dont fait preuve l'Occident pour continuer à prêter de l'argent; he showed a marked ~ to take part il a mis une mauvaise volonté évidente à participer; to show a ~ for work montrer OR manifester peu d'inclination au travail.

disinclined [ˌdɪsɪnˈklaɪnd] *adj*: to be ~ to do sthg être peu disposé OR enclin à faire qqch; because I feel ~ to do so parce que je ne me sens pas disposé à le faire.

disinfect [ˌdɪsɪnˈfekt] *vt* désinfecter.

disinfectant [ˌdɪsɪnˈfektənt] *n* désinfectant *m*.

disinfection [ˌdɪsɪnˈfekʃn] *n* désinfection *f*.

disinflation [ˌdɪsɪnˈfleɪʃn] *n* ECON désinflation *f*.

disinformation [ˌdɪsɪnfəˈmeɪʃn] *n* désinformation *f*.

disingenuous [ˌdɪsɪnˈdʒenjʊəs] *adj* peu sincère.

disingenuously [ˌdɪsɪnˈdʒenjʊəslɪ] *adv* avec peu de sincérité.

disingenuousness [ˌdɪsɪnˈdʒenjʊəsnɪs] *n* manque *m* de sincérité.

disinherit [ˌdɪsɪnˈherɪt] *vt* déshériter.

disinherited [ˌdɪsɪnˈherɪtɪd] ◇ *adj* déshérité.

◇ *npl*: the ~ of the earth *fig* les déshérités *mpl* de la terre.

disintegrate [dɪsˈɪntɪgreɪt] *vi* [stone, wet paper] se désagréger; [plane, rocket] se désintégrer; *fig* [coalition, the family] se désagréger.

disintegration [dɪsˌɪntɪˈgreɪʃn] *n* [of stone, wet paper] désagrégation *f*; [of plane, rocket] désintégration *f*; *fig* [of coalition, the family] désagrégation *f*.

disinter [ˌdɪsɪnˈtɜːʳ] (*pt* & *pp* disinterred, *cont* disinterring) *vt* [body] déterrer, exhumer.

disinterest [dɪsˈɪntərest] *n* -**1.** [objectivity]: his ~ was the reason we chose him on l'a choisi parce qu'il n'avait aucun intérêt dans l'affaire. -**2.** [lack of interest] manque *m* d'intérêt.

disinterested [dɪsˈɪntrəstɪd] *adj* -**1.** [objective] désintéressé. -**2.** *inf* [uninterested] indifférent.

disinterestedness [dɪsˈɪntrəstɪdnɪs] = **disinterest**.

disinterment [ˌdɪsɪnˈtɜːmənt] *n* déterrement *m*, exhumation *f*.

disinvest [ˌdɪsɪnˈvest] *vi* désinvestir.

disinvestment [ˌdɪsɪnˈvestmənt] *n* désinvestissement *m*.

disjointed [dɪsˈdʒɔɪntɪd] *adj* [conversation, film, speech] décousu, incohérent.

disjointedly [dɪsˈdʒɔɪntɪdlɪ] *adv* de manière décousue OR incohérente.

disjunctive [dɪsˈdʒʌŋktɪv] *adj* GRAMM disjonctif.

disk [dɪsk] *n* -**1.** COMPUT [hard] disque *m*; [soft] disquette *f*; on ~ sur disque, sur disquette; to write sthg to ~ sauvegarder qqch sur disque OR disquette. -**2.** *Am* = **disc**.

disk crash *n* COMPUT crash *m* de tête.

disk drive *n* COMPUT lecteur *m* de disquettes.

diskette [dɪsˈket] *n* COMPUT disquette *f*.

diskette drive *Am* = **disk drive**.

disk operating system *n* COMPUT système *m* d'exploitation de disques.

dislikable [dɪsˈlaɪkəbl] *adj* antipathique.

dislike [dɪsˈlaɪk] ◇ *vt* ne pas aimer; I ~ flying je n'aime pas prendre l'avion; why do you ~ me so much? pourquoi me détestes-tu autant?; he is much ~d il est loin d'être apprécié; I don't ~ him je n'ai rien contre lui.

◇ *n* [for sb] aversion *f*, antipathie *f*; [for sthg] aversion *f*; to have a ~ for OR of détester; mutual ~ antipathie mutuelle; to take a ~ to sb/sthg prendre qqn/qqch en grippe; we all have our likes and ~s on est tous pareils, il y a des choses qu'on aime et des choses qu'on n'aime pas.

dislocate [ˈdɪsləkeɪt] *vt* -**1.** [shoulder, knee etc - subj: person] se démettre, se déboîter, se luxer; [- subj: accident, fall] démettre, déboîter, luxer; he has ~d his shoulder il s'est démis OR déboîté OR luxé l'épaule; a ~d shoulder une épaule démise OR déboîtée OR luxée. -**2.** [disrupt - plans] désorganiser, perturber.

dislocation [ˌdɪsləˈkeɪʃn] *n* -**1.** [of shoulder, knee etc] luxation *f*, déboîtement *m*. -**2.** [disruption - of plans] perturbation *f*.

dislodge [dɪsˈlɒdʒ] *vt* [fish bone, piece of apple etc] dégager; [large rock] déplacer; *fig* [enemy, prey] déloger; [leader, title holder] prendre la place de.

disloyal [ˌdɪsˈlɔɪəl] *adj* déloyal; to be ~ to sb/sthg être déloyal envers qqn/qqch.

disloyally [ˌdɪsˈlɔɪəlɪ] *adv* déloyalement.

disloyalty [ˌdɪsˈlɔɪəltɪ] *n* déloyauté *f*; your ~ to the company votre déloyauté envers la compagnie; an act of ~ un acte déloyal.

dismal [ˈdɪzml] *adj* [day, weather] horrible; [streets, countryside] lugubre; [song] mélancolique, triste; *fig* [result, performance] lamentable; [future, prospect] sombre; what are you looking so ~ about? pourquoi as-tu l'air aussi lugubre?; to be a ~ failure [person] être un zéro sur toute la ligne; [film, project] échouer lamentablement.

dismally [ˈdɪzməlɪ] *adv* lugubrement; [fail] lamentablement.

dismantle [dɪsˈmæntl] ◇ *vt* [object, scenery, exhibition] démonter; *fig* [system, arrangement] démanteler.

◇ *vi* se démonter.

dismantling [dɪsˈmæntlɪŋ] *n* [of object, scenery, exhibition] démontage *m*; *fig* [of system, reforms] démantèlement *m*.

dismast [ˌdɪsˈmɑːst] *vt* [ship] démâter.

dismay [dɪsˈmeɪ] ◇ *n* consternation *f*; [stronger] désarroi *m*; there was a look of ~ on his face la consternation OR le désarroi se lisait sur son visage; in OR with ~ avec consternation OR désarroi; in her ~ at the news dans la consternation OR le désarroi où l'avaient mise les nouvelles; to be filled with ~ by sthg être consterné par OR rempli de désarroi à cause de qqch; (much) to my ~ à ma grande consternation, à mon grand désarroi.

◇ *vt* consterner; [stronger] emplir de désarroi, effondrer; we were ~ed by the news nous avons été effondrés par la nouvelle, la nouvelle nous a remplis de désarroi.

dismayed [dɪsˈmeɪd] *adj* consterné, effondré; don't look so ~ n'aie pas l'air si consterné OR effondré.

dismember [dɪsˈmembəʳ] *vt* démembrer.

dismemberment [dɪsˈmembəmənt] *n* démembrement *m*.

dismiss [dɪsˈmɪs] ◇ *vt* -**1.** [from job - employee] licencier, congédier, renvoyer; [- magistrate, official] destituer, révoquer, relever de ses fonctions. -**2.** [not take seriously - proposal] rejeter; [- objection, warning] ne pas tenir compte de, ne pas prendre au sérieux; [- problem] écarter, refuser de considérer; you cannot go on ~ing the threats/evidence vous ne pouvez pas continuer à ignorer ces menaces/preuves; he ~ed him as a crank il a déclaré que c'était un excentrique à ne pas prendre au sérieux; he was long ~ed as a crank on l'a longtemps pris pour un excentrique; it has been ~ed as a rumour on a rejeté cette information en n'y voyant qu'une simple rumeur; police ~ed the warning as a hoax la police n'a pas tenu compte de l'avertissement et l'a pris pour une mauvaise plaisanterie. -**3.** [send away] congédier; *fig* [thought, possibility] écarter; [memory] effacer; [suggestion, idea] rejeter; SCH [class] laisser partir; ~ him from your thoughts chasse-le de tes pensées; you can ~ that idea from your thoughts! tu peux t'ôter cette idée de la tête!; class ~ed! vous pouvez sortir!; ~ed! MIL rompez! -4. JUR [hung jury] dissoudre; to ~ a charge [judge] rendre une ordonnance de non-lieu; all charges against her have been ~ed toutes les accusations qui pesaient sur elle ont été levées; to ~ a case classer une affaire; the judge ~ed the case le juge a rendu une fin de non-recevoir; case ~ed! affaire classée! -5. [in cricket - batsman, team] éliminer; England were ~ed for 127 l'équipe d'Angleterre a été éliminée avec 127 points.

◇ vi: class ~! vous pouvez sortir!; ~! MIL rompez (les rangs)!

dismissal [dɪs'mɪsl] n -1. [from work - of employee] licenciement m, renvoi m; [- of magistrate, official] destitution f, révocation f; he's claiming unfair ~ il prétend avoir été injustement licencié OR fait l'objet d'un licenciement abusif. -2. [of proposal] rejet m; the police's ~ of the telephone call le fait que la police n'ait pas pris le coup de téléphone au sérieux. -3. JUR: the judge's ~ of the case met with widespread approval la fin de non-recevoir rendue par le juge a été accueillie avec satisfaction; ~ of the charge non-lieu m; the ~ of the charges against you le non-lieu qui a été prononcé en votre faveur.

dismissive [dɪs'mɪsɪv] adj [tone of voice, gesture] dédaigneux; to be ~ of sb ne faire aucun cas de qqn; to be ~ of sthg rejeter qqch, ne faire aucun cas de qqch; you're always so ~ of my efforts tu fais toujours si peu de cas de mes efforts.

dismissively [dɪs'mɪsɪvlɪ] adv [offhandedly] d'un ton dédaigneux; [in final tone of voice] d'un ton sans appel.

dismount [,dɪs'maʊnt] ◇ vi descendre; she ~ed from her horse/bike elle est descendue de son cheval/vélo.

◇ vt -1. [cause to fall - from horse] désarçonner, démonter; [- from bicycle, motorcycle] faire tomber. -2. [gun, device] démonter.

disobedience [,dɪsə'bi:djəns] n désobéissance f; she was punished for (her) ~ elle a été punie pour avoir désobéi; an act of ~ un acte de désobéissance.

disobedient [,dɪsə'bi:djənt] adj désobéissant; don't be ~ to your father! ne désobéis pas à ton père!

disobediently [,dɪsə'bi:djəntlɪ] adv de manière désobéissante.

disobey [,dɪsə'beɪ] vt désobéir à.

disobliging [,dɪsə'blaɪdʒɪŋ] adj fml -1. [unhelpful]: I'm sorry to be ~ je suis désolé de ne pouvoir vous rendre service. -2. [unpleasant] désobligeant.

disobligingly [,dɪsə'blaɪdʒɪŋlɪ] adv [unpleasantly] avec désobligeance.

disorder [dɪs'ɔ:də'] ◇ n -1. [untidiness - of house, room, desk] désordre m; to be in (a state of) ~ être en désordre; his financial affairs were in total ~ le désordre le plus total régnait dans ses finances; the meeting broke up in ~ la réunion s'est achevée dans le désordre OR la confusion; the army is retreating in ~ l'armée se retire en désordre. -2. [unrest] trouble m; public ~ atteinte f à OR trouble m de l'ordre public. -3. MED trouble m, troubles mpl; nervous/blood ~ troubles nerveux/de la circulation.

◇ vt [make untidy - files, papers] mettre en désordre.

disordered [dɪs'ɔ:dəd] adj [room] en désordre; to lead a ~ life mener une vie désordonnée; to be mentally ~ Br souffrir de troubles mentaux.

disorderly [dɪs'ɔ:dəlɪ] adj -1. [untidy - room, house] en désordre, désordonné. -2. [unruly - crowd, mob] désordonné, agité; [- conduct] désordonné; [- meeting, demonstration] désordonné, confus; to keep a ~ house JUR tenir une maison close.

disorganization [dɪs,ɔ:gənaɪ'zeɪʃn] n désorganisation f; in a state of ~ désorganisé.

disorganize, -ise [dɪs'ɔ:gənaɪz] vt [disrupt - plans, schedule] déranger.

disorganized [dɪs'ɔ:gənaɪzd] adj désorganisé.

disorient [dɪs'ɔ:rɪənt], **disorientate** [dɪs'ɔ:rɪənteɪt] Br vt désorienter; to be ~ed être désorienté; it's easy to become ~ed c'est facile de perdre son sens de l'orientation; fig on a vite fait d'être désorienté.

disorientation [dɪs,ɔ:rɪən'teɪʃn] n désorientation f.

disown [dɪs'əʊn] vt [child, opinion, statement] renier, désavouer; [country] renier.

disparage [dɪ'spærɪdʒ] vt dénigrer, décrier.

disparagement [dɪ'spærɪdʒmənt] n dénigrement m.

disparaging [dɪ'spærɪdʒɪŋ] adj [person - about person] désobligeant; [- about proposals, ideas] critique; [newspaper report - about person] malveillant, désobligeant; [- about proposals] dénigrant; to make ~ remarks about sb faire des remarques désobligeantes à propos de OR sur qqn; she made ~ remarks about his project elle a fait des remarques qui dénigraient son projet; why are you so ~ about him? pourquoi est-ce que tu es si désobligeant à son égard?; the critics were very ~ about his latest play les critiques ont beaucoup dénigré sa dernière pièce.

disparagingly [dɪ'spærɪdʒɪŋlɪ] adv [say, look at] d'un air désobligeant; you have written very ~ about him in the past vous avez écrit des propos fort désobligeants à son égard dans le passé.

disparate ['dɪspərət] adj fml disparate.

disparity [dɪ'spærətɪ] (pl disparities) n [in ages] disparité f; [in report, statement] contradiction f.

dispassionate [dɪ'spæʃnət] adj [objective - person, report, analysis etc] impartial, objectif; to be ~ [unemotional] ne pas exprimer ses sentiments; [objective] rester objectif OR impartial.

dispassionately [dɪ'spæʃnətlɪ] adv [unemotionally] calmement, sans émotion; [objectively] objectivement, impartialement.

dispatch [dɪ'spætʃ] ◇ vt -1. [send - letter, merchandise, telegram] envoyer, expédier; [- messenger] envoyer, dépêcher; [- troops, envoy] envoyer. -2. [complete - task, work] expédier, en finir avec. -3. euph [kill - person] tuer. -4. inf [food] s'envoyer.

◇ n -1. [of letter, merchandise, telegram] envoi m, expédition f; [of messenger, troops, envoy] envoi m. -2. MIL & PRESS [report] dépêche f; to be mentioned in ~es MIL être cité à l'ordre du jour. -3. [swiftness] promptitude f; with ~ avec promptitude, rapidement.

◇ comp: ~ clerk expéditionnaire mf; ~ note bordereau m d'expédition.

dispatch box n -1. [for documents] boîte f à documents. -2. Br POL: the ~ *tribune d'où parlent les membres du gouvernement et leurs homologues du cabinet fantôme*.

dispatch case n serviette f, porte-documents m inv.

dispatcher [dɪ'spætʃə'] n expéditeur m, -trice f.

dispatch rider n estafette f.

dispel [dɪ'spel] (pt & pp dispelled, cont dispelling) vt [clouds, mist - subj: sun] dissiper; [- subj: wind] chasser; [doubts, fears, anxiety] dissiper.

dispensable [dɪ'spensəbl] adj dont on peut se passer, superflu; the rest of the employees were ~ les autres employés n'étaient pas indispensables; the rest is ~ le reste est superflu; do you think this is ~? penses-tu qu'on puisse se débarrasser de cela?

dispensary [dɪ'spensərɪ] (pl dispensaries) n pharmacie f; [for free distribution of medicine] dispensaire m.

dispensation [,dɪspen'seɪʃn] n -1. [handing out] distribution f. -2. [administration - of charity, justice] exercice m. -3. ADMIN, JUR & RELIG [exemption] dispense f; he received ~ from military service il a été exempté du service militaire; she was granted ~ from the exam elle a été dispensée de l'examen; as a special ~ the prisoner was allowed to attend the funeral le prisonnier a reçu une permission exceptionnelle pour assister à l'enterrement. -4. POL & RELIG [system] régime m.

dispense [dɪ'spens] vt -1. [subj: person, machine] distribuer. -2. [administer - justice, charity] exercer. -3. PHARM préparer. -4. fml [exempt] dispenser; to ~ sb from (doing) sthg dispenser qqn de (faire) qqch.

◆ **dispense with** vt insep [do without] se passer de; [get rid of] se débarrasser de; to ~ with the formalities couper court aux OR se dispenser des formalités; let's ~ with that idea for a start commençons par éliminer cette idée; to ~ with the need for sthg rendre qqch superflu; credit cards ~ with the need for cash avec les cartes de crédit, on n'a plus besoin d'avoir de l'argent liquide.

dispenser [dɪ'spensə'] n -1. PHARM pharmacien m, -enne f. -2. [machine] distributeur m; soap/coffee ~ distributeur de savon/café; cash ~ distributeur automatique de billets.

dispensing [dɪ'spensɪŋ] adj Br: ~ chemist [person] préparateur m, -trice f en pharmacie; [establishment] pharmacie f; ~ optician opticien m; ~ machine distributeur m.

dispersal [dɪ'spɜ:sl] n [of crowd, seeds] dispersion f; [of gas - disappearance] dissipation f; [- spread] dispersion f; [of light - by prism] dispersion f, décomposition f.

dispersant [dɪ'spɜ:sənt] n CHEM dispersant m.

disperse [dɪ'spɜ:s] ◇ vt -1. [crowd, seeds] disperser; [clouds, mist - subj: sun] dissiper; [- subj: wind] chasser; [gas, chemical - cause to spread] propager; [- cause to vanish] disperser; a prism ~s light un prisme disperse OR décompose la lumière. -2. [place at intervals] répartir; policemen were ~d along the length of the road des agents de police étaient répartis OR disséminés le long de la route.

◇ vi [crowds, seeds] se disperser; [clouds, mist, smoke - with sun] se dissiper; [- with wind] être chassé; [gas, chemicals - spread] se propager; [- vanish] se dissiper; [light - with prism] se décomposer.

dispersion [dɪ'spɜ:ʃn] n -1. = **dispersal**. -2. RELIG: the Dispersion la Diaspora.

dispirited [dɪ'spɪrɪtɪd] adj abattu.

displace [dɪs'pleɪs] vt -1. [refugees, population] déplacer; to ~ a bone se déplacer un os. -2. [supplant] supplanter, remplacer. -3. CHEM & PHYS [water, air etc] déplacer.

displaced [dɪs'pleɪst] adj: ~ person ADMIN & POL personne f déplacée.

displacement [dɪs'pleɪsmənt] n -1. [of people, bone] déplacement m. -2. [supplanting] remplacement m. -3. NAUT déplacement m; a ship of 10,000 tons ~ un bateau de 10 000 tonnes de déplacement. -4. PSYCH déplacement m.

displacement activity n PSYCH déplacement m.

displacement ton n NAUT tonne f.

display [dɪ'spleɪ] ◇ vt -1. [gifts, medals, ornaments etc] exposer; pej exhiber; [items in exhibition] exposer, mettre en exposition; COMM [goods for sale] mettre en étalage, exposer. -2. [notice, poster, exam results] afficher. -3. [courage, determination, skill] faire preuve de, montrer; [anger, affection, friendship, interest] manifester; the country ~ed its military might le pays a montré sa puissance militaire; to ~ one's ignorance/talent faire la preuve de son ignorance/talent. -4. PRESS & TYPO mettre en vedette. -5. COMPUT [subj: screen] afficher; [subj: user] visualiser.

◇ vi [birds, fish etc] faire la parade.

◇ n -1. [of gifts, medals, ornaments, items in exhibition] exposition f; COMM [of goods, merchandise] mise f en étalage; [goods, merchandise] étalage m, exposition f; to be on ~ être exposé; to put sthg on ~ exposer qqch; it's the first time the painting has been on public ~ c'est la première fois que le tableau est exposé au public; 'for ~ (only)' [on book] 'exemplaire de démonstration'. -2. [of poster, notice etc] affi-

chage *m*; the exam results were on ~ les résultats des examens étaient affichés. -**3.** [of affection, friendship, interest, anger] manifestation *f*; [of courage, determination, ignorance etc] démonstration *f*; an air ~ un meeting aérien; a military ~ une parade militaire; a fireworks ~ un feu d'artifice; a ~ of force une démonstration de force; he gave us a ~ of his juggling skills il nous a fait une démonstration de ses talents de jongleur; I have never seen such a ~ of incompetence je n'ai jamais vu un tel déploiement OR étalage d'incompétence; to make a great ~ of sthg faire parade de qqch; he made a great ~ of being injured il a joué les grands blessés. -**4.** PRESS & TYPO: to give top ~ to sthg mettre qqch en vedette. -**5.** COMPUT [screen, device] écran *m*; [visual information] affichage *m*, visualisation *f*; [of calculator] viseur *m*. -**6.** [by birds, fish] parade *f*.
◇ *comp*: ~ advertising publicité *f* par affichage; ~ cabinet OR case [in shop] étalage *m*, vitrine *f*; [in home] vitrine *f*; ~ copy [of book] exemplaire *m* de démonstration; ~ lighting éclairage *m* de l'étalage OR de la vitrine; ~ panel tableau *m* OR panneau *m* d'affichage; ~ rack OR unit présentoir *m*; ~ unit COMPUT unité *f* de visualisation OR d'affichage; ~ window [of calculator] viseur *m*.

displease [dɪs'pliːz] *vt* mécontenter.

displeased [dɪs'pliːzd] *adj* mécontent; to be ~ with OR at être mécontent de.

displeasure [dɪs'pleʒəʳ] *n* mécontentement *m*; to incur sb's ~ encourir OR s'attirer le mécontentement de qqn.

disport [dɪ'spɔːt] *vt fml*: to ~ o.s. s'ébattre, folâtrer.

disposable [dɪ'spəʊzəbl] ◇ *adj* -**1.** [throwaway - lighter, nappy, cup, plate] jetable; [- bottle] non consigné; [- wrapping] perdu. -**2.** [available - money, time] disponible; ~ assets FIN fonds *mpl* disponibles; ~ income FIN revenus *mpl* disponibles (après impôts); people with high ~ incomes personnes disposant de hauts revenus.
◇ *n* -**1.** [nappy] couche *f* jetable. -**2.** [lighter] briquet *m* jetable.
◆ **disposables** COMM = **disposable goods**.

disposable goods *npl* biens *mpl* de consommation non durables.

disposal [dɪ'spəʊzl] *n* -**1.** [taking away] enlèvement *m*; [of rubbish, by authority] enlèvement *m*, ramassage *m*; [sale] vente *f*; JUR [of property] cession *f*; she left no instructions for the ~ of her property elle n'a laissé aucune instruction quant à ce qui devait être fait de ses biens; an ingenious method for the ~ of the body une idée ingénieuse pour se débarrasser du corps ❑ waste OR refuse ~ traitement *m* des ordures; (waste) ~ unit broyeur *m* d'ordures *(dans un évier)*. -**2.** [resolution - of problem, question] résolution *f*; [- of business] exécution *f*, expédition *f*. -**3.** *Am* [disposal unit] broyeur *m* d'ordures *(dans un évier)*. -**4.** [availability]: to be at sb's ~ être à la disposition de qqn; to have sthg at one's ~ avoir qqch à sa disposition; to put sthg/sb at sb's ~ mettre qqch/qqn à la disposition de qqn; in the time at your ~ dans le temps dont tu disposes. -**5.** *fml* [arrangement] disposition *f*, arrangement *m*; [of troops] déploiement *m*.

dispose [dɪ'spəʊz] ◇ *vt* -**1.** *fml* [arrange - ornaments, books] disposer, arranger; [- troops, forces] déployer. -**2.** [make willing] disposer.
◇ *vi*: man proposes, God ~s *prov* l'homme propose, Dieu dispose *prov*.
◆ **dispose of** *vt insep* -**1.** [get rid of - nuclear waste, rubbish, problem] se débarrasser de; [by removing, taking away - refuse] enlever, ramasser; [by selling] vendre; [by throwing away] jeter; [workers] congédier, renvoyer; I'll ~ of it as I like j'en ferai ce que je voudrai; I can ~ of this old table for you je peux te débarrasser de cette vieille table. -**2.** [deal with - problem, question] résoudre, régler; [- task, matter under discussion] expédier, régler; [- food] s'envoyer; to ~ of an argument détruire un argument. -**3.** [have at one's disposal] disposer de, avoir à sa disposition. -**4.** *inf* [kill - person, animal] liquider; *fig* [team, competitor] se débarrasser de.

disposed [dɪ'spəʊzd] *adj*: to ~ sb to do sthg disposer qqn à faire qqch; to be ~d to do sthg être disposé à faire qqch; I am ~d to be lenient je suis disposé à me montrer indulgent; to be well/ill ~d towards sb être bien/mal disposé envers qqn.

disposition [,dɪspə'zɪʃn] *n* -**1.** [temperament, nature] naturel *m*; to have OR to be of a cheerful ~ être d'un naturel enjoué. -**2.** *fml* [arrangement - of troops, buildings] disposition *f*; [- of ornaments] disposition *f*, arrangement *m*. -**3.** [inclination, tendency] disposition *f*.

dispossess [,dɪspə'zes] *vt* déposséder; JUR exproprier; to ~ sb of sthg déposséder qqn de qqch.

dispossessed [,dɪspə'zest] ◇ *npl*: the ~ les dépossédés *mpl*.
◇ *adj* dépossédé.

dispossession [,dɪspə'zeʃn] *n* dépossession *f*; JUR expropriation *f*.

disproportion [,dɪsprə'pɔːʃn] *n* disproportion *f*.

disproportionate [,dɪsprə'pɔːʃnət] *adj* [excessive] disproportionné; to be ~ to sthg être disproportionné à OR avec qqch; we spent a ~ amount of time on it [more than expected] on a passé un temps incroyable dessus; [unwarranted] on a passé plus de temps dessus que cela ne le méritait.

disproportionately [,dɪsprə'pɔːʃnətlɪ] *adv* d'une façon disproportionnée; a ~ large sum une somme disproportionnée.

disprove [,dɪs'pruːv] (*pp* disproved OR disproven [-'pruːvn]) *vt* prouver la fausseté de; you can't ~ it tu ne peux pas prouver que ce n'est pas vrai.

disputable [dɪ'spjuːtəbl] *adj* discutable, contestable.

disputation [,dɪspjuː'teɪʃn] *n fml* [argument] débat *m*, controverse *f*.

disputatious [,dɪspjuː'teɪʃəs] *adj fml* raisonneur.

dispute [dɪ'spjuːt] ◇ *vt* -**1.** [question - claim, theory, statement etc] contester, mettre en doute; JUR [will] contester; I'm not disputing that je ne conteste pas cela, je ne mets pas cela en doute; I would ~ that je ne suis pas d'accord. -**2.** [debate - subject, motion] discuter, débattre. -**3.** [fight for - territory, championship, title] disputer.
◇ *vi* [argue] se disputer; [debate] discuter, débattre; to ~ over OR about sthg débattre qqch OR de qqch.
◇ *n* -**1.** [debate] discussion *f*, débat *m*; there's some ~ about the veracity of his statement la véracité de sa déclaration fait l'objet de discussions OR est sujette à controverse; your honesty is not in ~ votre honnêteté n'est pas mise en doute OR contestée; the matter is beyond (all) ~ la question est tout à fait incontestable; he is beyond (all) ~ OR without ~ the best player the team has got c'est incontestablement OR indiscutablement le meilleur joueur de l'équipe; open to ~ contestable. -**2.** [argument - between individuals] dispute *f*, différend *m*; [- between management and workers] conflit *m*; JUR litige *m*; these are the main areas of ~ ce sont là les questions les plus conflictuelles OR litigieuses; there has been much ~ over the new proposals les nouvelles propositions ont fait l'objet d'un conflit; in ~ is the right of employees to strike l'enjeu des discussions est le droit des employés à faire grève; to be in ~ with sb over sthg être en conflit avec qqn sur qqch; to be in ~ [proposals, territory, ownership] faire l'objet d'un conflit; a border ~ un litige portant sur une question de frontière.

disputed [dɪ'spjuːtɪd] *adj* -**1.** [decision, fact, claim, ownership] contesté. -**2.** [fought over]: this is a much ~ territory ce territoire fait l'objet de beaucoup de conflits.

disqualification [dɪs,kwɒlɪfɪ'keɪʃn] *n* [from standing for election] exclusion *f*; [from sporting event] disqualification *f*; [from exam] exclusion *f*; JUR [of witness] inhabilité *f*, incapacité *f*; [of testimony] exclusion *f*; it's not necessarily a ~ cela ne vous exclut pas forcément; reasons for the ~ of jurors include the following voici quelques-uns des motifs donnant lieu à une exclusion du jury; your ~ from driving will last for four years vous aurez un retrait de permis (de conduire) de quatre ans.

disqualify [dɪs'kwɒlɪfaɪ] (*pt* & *pp* disqualified) *vt* exclure; SPORT disqualifier; SCH exclure; JUR [witness] rendre inhabile OR incapable; [testimony] exclure; [juror] empêcher de faire partie du jury; to ~ sb from driving retirer son permis (de conduire) OR infliger un retrait de permis (de conduire) à qqn; he's been disqualified for speeding AUT on lui a retiré son permis OR il a eu un retrait de permis pour excès de vitesse.

disquiet [dɪs'kwaɪət] *fml* ◇ *n* inquiétude *f*.
◇ *vt* inquiéter, troubler; to be ~ed by sthg être inquiet OR s'inquiéter de qqch.

disquieting [dɪs'kwaɪətɪŋ] *adj fml* inquiétant, troublant.

disquisition [,dɪskwɪ'zɪʃn] *n fml* [in writing] dissertation *f*, étude *f*; [in speech] discours *m*.

disregard [,dɪsrɪ'gɑːd] ◇ *vt* [person, order, law, rules] ne tenir aucun compte de; [sb's feelings, instructions, remark, warning] ne tenir aucun compte de, négliger; [danger] ne tenir aucun compte de, ignorer; I'll ~ what you just said je ne tiendrai pas compte de ce que tu viens de dire.
◇ *n* [for person, feelings] manque *m* de considération; [of order, warning, danger etc] mépris *m*; he showed a flagrant ~ for the rules il a fait preuve d'un mépris flagrant pour le règlement; with complete ~ for her own safety au mépris total de sa vie.

disremember *inf* [,dɪsrɪ'membəʳ] *vt Am* ne pas se rappeler, ne pas se souvenir de.

disrepair [,dɪsrɪ'peəʳ] *n* [of building] mauvais état *m*, délabrement *m*; [of road] mauvais état *m*; in (a state of) ~ en mauvais état; to fall into ~ [building] se délabrer; [road] se dégrader, s'abîmer.

disreputable [dɪs'repjʊtəbl] *adj* [dishonourable - behaviour] honteux, déshonorant; [not respectable - person] de mauvaise réputation, louche; [- area, club] mal famé, de mauvaise réputation; *hum* [- clothing] miteux, mangé aux mites.

disreputably [dɪs'repjʊtəblɪ] *adv* [behave] d'une manière déshonorante OR honteuse; he was dressed rather ~ il avait l'air d'un vrai loqueteux.

disrepute [,dɪsrɪ'pjuːt] *n* discrédit *m*; to bring sthg into ~ discréditer qqch; to fall into ~ [acquire bad reputation] tomber en discrédit; [become unpopular] tomber en défaveur.

disrespect [,dɪsrɪ'spekt] *n* irrespect *m*, irrévérence *f*; she has a healthy ~ for authority elle porte un irrespect OR une irrévérence salutaire à toute forme d'autorité; I meant no ~ (to your family) je ne voulais pas me montrer irrespectueux OR irrévérencieux (envers votre famille); to show ~ towards sb/sthg manquer de respect à qqn/qqch; to treat sb/sthg with ~ traiter qqn/qqch irrespectueusement.

disrespectful [,dɪsrɪ'spektfʊl] *adj* irrespectueux, irrévérencieux; to be ~ to sb manquer de respect à qqn; it would be ~ not to go to the funeral ce serait manquer de respect que de ne pas assister à l'enterrement.

disrespectfully [,dɪsrɪ'spektfʊlɪ] *adv* irrespectueusement.

disrobe [dɪs'rəʊb] *fml* ◇ *vi* [judge, priest] enlever sa robe; [undress] se déshabiller.
◇ *vt* [judge, priest] aider à enlever sa robe; [undress] déshabiller.

disrupt [dɪs'rʌpt] *vt* [lesson, meeting, train service] perturber; [conversation] interrompre; [plans] déranger, perturber.

disruption [dɪsˈrʌpʃn] *n* [of lesson, meeting, train service, plans] perturbation *f*; [of conversation] interruption *f*.

disruptive [dɪsˈrʌptɪv] *adj* [factor, behaviour] perturbateur; he is OR has a ~ **influence** il a une influence perturbatrice; the ~ **element** l'élément perturbateur; **your presence would be** ~ votre présence aurait un effet perturbateur.

dissatisfaction [ˈdɪs,sætɪsˈfækʃn] *n* mécontentement *m*; **there is growing** ~ **with his policies** le mécontentement grandit à l'égard de sa politique.

dissatisfied [,dɪsˈsætɪsfaɪd] *adj* mécontent; **to be** ~ **with sb/sthg** être mécontent de qqn/qqch.

dissatisfy [,dɪsˈsætɪsfaɪ] (*pt* & *pp* **dissatisfied**) *vt* mécontenter.

dissect [dɪˈsekt] *vt* [animal, plant] disséquer; *fig* [argument, theory] disséquer; [book, report] éplucher.

dissected [dɪˈsektɪd] *adj* [body] disséqué; BOT [leaf] découpé.

dissecting [dɪˈsektɪŋ] *adj*: ~ **knife** scalpel *m*.

dissection [dɪˈsekʃn] *n* [of body] dissection *f*; *fig* [of argument, theory] dissection *f*; [of book, report] épluchage *m*.

dissemble [dɪˈsembl] *lit* ◇ *vi* dissimuler.
◇ *vt* [feelings, motives] dissimuler.

disseminate [dɪˈsemɪneɪt] *vt* [knowledge, ideas] disséminer, propager; [information, news] diffuser, propager.

disseminated [dɪˈsemɪneɪtɪd] *adj* MED: ~ **sclerosis** sclérose *f* en plaques.

dissemination [dɪ,semɪˈneɪʃn] *n* [of knowledge, of ideas] propagation *f*, dissémination *f*; [of information] diffusion *f*, propagation *f*.

dissension [dɪˈsenʃn] *n* dissension *f*, discorde *f*; **there is** ~ **in the ranks** il y a de la dissension OR discorde dans les rangs.

dissent [dɪˈsent] ◇ *vi* -**1.** [gen] avoir une opinion différente; **to** ~ **from an opinion** être en désaccord avec une opinion; **two members of the enquiry** ~**ed from the findings** deux membres de l'enquête ont exprimé une opinion divergente sur les conclusions. -**2.** RELIG être dissident OR en dissidence.
◇ *n* -**1.** [gen] opinion *f* OR avis *m* contraire; **to voice** OR **to express one's** ~ exprimer son désaccord; **he has been booked for** ~ FTBL l'arbitre a pris son nom après qu'il eut refusé d'obtempérer. -**2.** RELIG dissidence *f*. -**3.** *Am* JUR avis *m* contraire *(d'un juge)*.

dissenter [dɪˈsentəʳ] *n* -**1.** [gen] dissident *m*, -e *f*. -**2.** RELIG: **Dissenter** *dissident de l'Église anglicane*.

dissenting [dɪˈsentɪŋ] *adj* [opinion] divergent; **mine was the only** ~ **voice** j'étais le seul à ne pas être d'accord.

dissertation [,dɪsəˈteɪʃn] *n* -**1.** UNIV *Br* mémoire *m*; *Am* thèse *f*. -**2.** *fml* [long essay] dissertation *f*; [long speech] exposé *m*.

disservice [,dɪsˈsɜːvɪs] *n* mauvais service *m*; **to do sb a** ~ faire du tort à qqn, rendre un mauvais service à qqn; **to do o.s. a** ~ se faire du tort.

dissidence [ˈdɪsɪdəns] *n* [disagreement] désaccord *m*; POL dissidence *f*.

dissident [ˈdɪsɪdənt] ◇ *n* dissident *m*, -e *f*.
◇ *adj* dissident.

dissimilar [,dɪˈsɪmɪləʳ] *adj* différent; **they are not** ~ ils se ressemblent; **the situation now is not** ~ **to what was going on 20 years ago** la situation actuelle n'est pas sans rappeler ce qui s'est passé il y a 20 ans.

dissimilarity [,dɪsɪmɪˈlærətɪ] (*pl* **dissimilarities**) *n* différence *f*.

dissimulate [dɪˈsɪmjʊleɪt] *fml* ◇ *vt* dissimuler, cacher.
◇ *vi* dissimuler.

dissimulation [dɪ,sɪmjʊˈleɪʃn] *n fml* dissimulation *f*.

dissipate [ˈdɪsɪpeɪt] ◇ *vt* [disperse - cloud, fears, suspicions] dissiper; [waste - fortune] dilapider, gaspiller; [- energies] disperser, gaspiller; PHYS [heat, energy] dissiper.
◇ *vi* [cloud, mist, crowd] se disperser; [fears, suspicions, hopes] s'évanouir; PHYS [energy] se dissiper.

dissipated [ˈdɪsɪpeɪtɪd] *adj* [person] débauché; [habit] de débauche; [society] décadent; **to lead** OR **to live a** ~ **life** mener une vie de débauche.

dissipation [,dɪsɪˈpeɪʃn] *n* -**1.** [of cloud, fears, hopes etc] dissipation *f*; [of fortune] dilapidation *f*; [of energies] dispersion *f*, gaspillage *m*; PHYS [of energy, heat] dissipation *f*. -**2.** [debauchery] débauche *f*; **to lead** OR **to live a life of** ~ mener une vie de débauche.

dissociate [dɪˈsəʊʃɪeɪt] ◇ *vt* -**1.** [gen] dissocier, séparer; **to** ~ **o.s. from sthg** se dissocier OR désolidariser de qqch. -**2.** CHEM dissocier.
◇ *vi* CHEM [subj: chemist] opérer une dissociation; [subj: molecules] se dissocier.

dissociation [dɪ,səʊsɪˈeɪʃn] *n* dissociation *f*.

dissoluble [dɪˈsɒljʊbl] *adj* soluble.

dissolute [ˈdɪsəluːt] *adj* [person] débauché; [life] de débauche, dissolu *lit*.

dissoluteness [ˈdɪsəluːtnɪs] *n* débauche *f*.

dissolution [,dɪsəˈluːʃn] *n* -**1.** [gen] dissolution *f*. -**2.** *Am* JUR [divorce] divorce *m*.

dissolvable [dɪˈzɒlvəbl] *adj* soluble.

dissolve [dɪˈzɒlv] ◇ *vt* -**1.** [salt, sugar] dissoudre. -**2.** [empire, marriage, Parliament] dissoudre.
◇ *vi* -**1.** [salt, sugar] se dissoudre; *fig* [fear, hopes] s'évanouir, s'envoler; [apparition] s'évanouir; [crowd] se disperser; [clouds] disparaître; **to** ~ **into tears** fondre en larmes; **to** ~ **into laughter** être pris de rire. -**2.** [marriage, Parliament] être dissout; [empire] se dissoudre. -**3.** CIN & TV faire un fondu enchaîné.
◇ *n* CIN & TV fondu enchaîné *m*.

dissonance [ˈdɪsənəns] *n* MUS dissonance *f*; *fig* discordance *f*.

dissonant [ˈdɪsənənt] *adj* MUS dissonant; *fig* [colours, opinions] discordant.

dissuade [dɪˈsweɪd] *vt* [person] dissuader; **to** ~ **sb from doing sthg** dissuader qqn de faire qqch; **to** ~ **sb from sthg** détourner qqn de qqch.

dissuasion [dɪˈsweɪʒn] *n* dissuasion *f*.

dissuasive [dɪˈsweɪsɪv] *adj* [person, effect] dissuasif; **it had a** ~ **effect on them** cela les a dissuadés.

distaff [ˈdɪstɑːf] *n* [for spinning] quenouille *f*; **on the** ~ **side** *fig* du côté maternel.

distance [ˈdɪstəns] ◇ *n* -**1.** [between two places] distance *f*; ~ **is measured in miles/kilometres** on mesure la distance en miles/kilomètres; **modern technology makes** ~ **irrelevant** avec la technologie moderne, les distances ne veulent plus rien dire; **at a** ~ **of 50 metres** à (une distance de) 50 mètres; **within walking/cycling** ~ **from the station** à quelques minutes de marche/en vélo de la gare; **is it within walking** ~? peut-on y aller à pied?; **the house is some** ~ **from the village** la maison est assez loin du village; **it's some** OR **quite a** OR **a good** ~ **from here** c'est assez loin d'ici; **a short** ~ **away** tout près; **it's no** ~ **(at all)** c'est tout près OR à deux pas; **we covered the** ~ **in ten hours** nous avons fait le trajet en dix heures; **to cover great** ~**s on foot** couvrir de grandes distances à pied; ~ **(is) no object** [in advertisement] toutes distances couvertes, toutes destinations; **to keep at a safe** ~ **(from)** se tenir à une distance prudente (de) ‖ *fig*: **to keep sb at a** ~ tenir qqn à distance (respectueuse); **to keep one's** ~ **(from sb)** garder ses distances (par rapport à qqn); **we keep our** ~ **from each other** nous gardons nos distances (l'un par rapport à l'autre) ❑ **braking/stopping** ~ AUT distance de freinage/d'arrêt; **to go the** ~ [boxer, political campaigner] tenir la distance; **the fight went the** ~ le combat est allé jusqu'à la limite. -**2.** [distant point, place]: **to see/to hear sthg in the** ~ voir/entendre qqch au loin; **in the middle** ~ au second plan; **to see sthg from a** ~ voir qqch de loin; **you can't see it from** OR **at this** ~ on ne peut pas le voir à cette distance; **to admire sb from** OR **at a** ~ admirer qqn de loin. -**3.** [separation in time]: **at a** ~ **of 200 years, it's very difficult to know** 200 ans plus tard, il est très difficile de savoir; **it's very hard for me to remember at this** ~ **in time** c'est très difficile de m'en souvenir après tout ce temps. -**4.** *fig* [gap]: **there's a great** ~ **between us** il y a un grand fossé entre nous. -**5.** *fig* [aloofness, reserve] froideur *f*.
◇ *comp*: ~ **learning** OR **teaching** enseignement *m* à distance; ~ **race** SPORT épreuve *f* de fond; ~ **runner** SPORT coureur *m*, -euse *f* de fond.
◇ *vt*: **she is distancing herself from the other runners** elle est en train de distancer les autres coureurs OR de se détacher des autres coureurs; **to** ~ **o.s. (from sb/sthg)** *fig* prendre ses distances (par rapport à qqn/qqch).

distant [ˈdɪstənt] ◇ *adj* -**1.** [faraway - country, galaxy, place] lointain, éloigné; **in the most** ~ **corner of the universe** dans le coin le plus éloigné OR reculé de l'univers; **we had a** ~ **view of the sea from the hotel** on pouvait voir la mer au loin depuis l'hôtel; **the** ~ **sound of the sea** le bruit de la mer au loin. -**2.** [in past - times] lointain, reculé; [- memory] lointain; **in the (dim and)** ~ **past** il y a bien OR très longtemps, dans le temps. -**3.** [in future - prospect] lointain; **in the** ~ **future** dans un avenir lointain; **in the not too** ~ **future** dans un avenir proche, prochainement. -**4.** [relation] éloigné; [resemblance] vague. -**5.** [remote - person, look] distant; [aloof] froid; **to have a** ~ **manner** être distant OR froid.
◇ *adv*: **three miles** ~ **from here** à trois miles d'ici; **not far** ~ pas très loin.

distantly [ˈdɪstəntlɪ] *adv* -**1.** [in the distance] au loin. -**2.** [resemble] vaguement; **to be** ~ **related** [people] avoir un lien de parenté éloigné; [ideas, concepts etc] avoir un rapport éloigné. -**3.** [speak, behave, look] froidement, d'un air distant OR froid.

distaste [dɪsˈteɪst] *n* dégoût *m*, répugnance *f*; **to feel** ~ **for sthg** ne pas aimer qqch; [stronger] éprouver du dégoût OR de la répugnance pour qqch.

distasteful [dɪsˈteɪstfʊl] *adj* [unpleasant - task] désagréable; [in bad taste - joke, remark etc] de mauvais goût; **to be** ~ **to sb** déplaire à qqn; **I find it extremely** ~ je trouve ça tout à fait déplaisant.

distastefully [dɪsˈteɪstfʊlɪ] *adv* [with repugnance - look] d'un air dégoûté; [with bad taste - presented, portrayed] avec mauvais goût.

Dist. Atty *written abbr of* **district attorney**.

distemper [dɪˈstempəʳ] ◇ *n* -**1.** [paint] détrempe *f*. -**2.** VETER maladie *f* de Carré.
◇ *vt* peindre à la OR en détrempe.

distend [dɪˈstend] ◇ *vt* gonfler; ~**ed stomach** ventre *m* gonflé.
◇ *vi* [stomach] se ballonner, se gonfler; [sails] se gonfler.

distension [dɪˈstenʃn] *n* dilatation *f*, distension *f*.

distil *Br*, **distill** *Am* [dɪˈstɪl] (*pt* & *pp* **distilled**, *cont* **distilling**) ◇ *vt literal* & *fig* distiller; **distilled water** eau *f* distillée.
◇ *vi* se distiller.

distillate [ˈdɪstɪlət] *n* CHEM distillat *m*.

distillation [,dɪstɪˈleɪʃn] *n literal* & *fig* distillation *f*; **fractional** ~ distillation fractionnée.

distiller [dɪˈstɪləʳ] *n* distillateur *m*.

distillery [dɪˈstɪlərɪ] (*pl* **distilleries**) *n* distillerie *f*; **whisky** ~ distillerie de whisky.

distinct [dɪˈstɪŋkt] *adj* -**1.** [different] distinct; **to be** ~ **from** se distinguer de; **the two poems are quite** ~ **from each other** les deux poèmes sont tout à fait distincts, les deux poèmes sont tout à fait différents l'un de l'autre. -**2.** [clear - memory] clair, net; [- voice, announcement] distinct. -**3.** [decided, evident - accent] prononcé; [- preference] marqué; [- lack of respect, interest] évident; [- likeness] clair, net, prononcé; [- advantage, improvement] net; **to make** ~ **progress** progresser nettement; **she had a** ~ **feeling that something would go wrong** elle avait le sen-

timent très net que quelque chose allait mal tourner; I have the ~ impression you're trying to avoid me j'ai la nette impression que tu essaies de m'éviter; there's a ~ smell of smoke in here cela sent vraiment la fumée ici; a ~ possibility une forte possibilité; there is a ~ possibility of rain tomorrow il est fort possible qu'il pleuve demain; it is a ~ possibility [in answer to question] c'est fort possible.
◆ **as distinct from** *prep phr* par opposition à.

distinction [dɪ'stɪŋkʃn] *n* -**1.** [difference] distinction *f*; her ~ between the two things la distinction qu'elle fait entre les deux choses; to make OR to draw a ~ between two things faire OR établir une distinction entre deux choses. -**2.** [excellence] distinction *f*; a writer/artist of great ~ un écrivain/artiste très réputé; to win OR to gain ~ (as) se distinguer (en tant que); she has the ~ of being the only woman to become Prime Minister elle se distingue pour être la seule femme à avoir été nommée Premier ministre. -**3.** SCH & UNIV [mark] mention *f*; he got a ~ in maths il a été reçu en maths avec mention; to pass with ~ réussir un examen avec mention. -**4.** [honour, award] honneur *m*.

distinctive [dɪ'stɪŋktɪv] *adj* [colour, appearance, feature] distinctif; her car is quite ~ sa voiture se remarque facilement.

distinctively [dɪ'stɪŋktɪvlɪ] *adv* [coloured] de manière distinctive.

distinctly [dɪ'stɪŋktlɪ] *adv* -**1.** [clearly - speak, hear] distinctement, clairement; [remember] clairement; I ~ told you not to do that je t'ai bien dit de ne pas faire cela, je t'ai formellement défendu de faire cela. -**2.** [very] vraiment, franchement; he was ~ rude to the old lady il a été vraiment grossier avec la vieille dame.

distinguish [dɪ'stɪŋgwɪʃ] ◇ *vt* -**1.** [set apart] distinguer; to ~ o.s. se distinguer; to ~ sthg from sthg distinguer qqch de qqch. -**2.** [tell apart] distinguer. -**3.** [discern] distinguer.
◇ *vi* faire OR établir une distinction; to ~ between two things/people faire la distinction entre deux choses/personnes.

distinguishable [dɪ'stɪŋgwɪʃəbl] *adj* -**1.** [visible] visible; the horizon was hardly ~ on distinguait à peine l'horizon. -**2.** [recognizable] reconnaissable; to be easily ~ from se distinguer facilement de, être facile à distinguer de; the male is ~ by his red legs le mâle est reconnaissable à OR se distingue par ses pattes rouges.

distinguished [dɪ'stɪŋgwɪʃt] *adj* -**1.** [eminent] distingué. -**2.** [refined - manners, voice] distingué; ~-looking distingué; ~-sounding [voice] distingué; [person] à la voix distinguée.

distinguishing [dɪ'stɪŋgwɪʃɪŋ] *adj* [feature, mark, characteristic etc] distinctif; ~ features [on passport] signes *mpl* particuliers.

distort [dɪ'stɔːt] ◇ *vt* -**1.** [face, image, structure etc] déformer; *fig* [facts, truth] déformer, dénaturer; [judgment] fausser; his upbringing ~ed his view of life son éducation a déformé OR faussé son image de la vie. -**2.** ELECTRON, RADIO & TV déformer.
◇ *vi* [face, structure, sound] se déformer.

distorted [dɪ'stɔːtɪd] *adj* [face, limbs] déformé; *fig* [facts, truth, account] déformé, dénaturé; [view of life] déformé, faussé; [judgment] faussé.

distortion [dɪ'stɔːʃn] *n* -**1.** *literal* & *fig* déformation *f*. -**2.** ELECTRON & RADIO distorsion *f*; TV déformation *f*.

distract [dɪ'strækt] *vt* -**1.** [break concentration of] distraire; [disturb] déranger; to ~ sb from his/her work distraire qqn de son travail; to ~ sb from his/her objective détourner qqn de son but; to ~ sb's attention [accidentally] distraire l'attention de qqn; [on purpose] détourner l'attention de qqn; ~ her for a couple of minutes détourne son attention pendant quelques minutes. -**2.** [amuse] distraire.

distracted [dɪ'stræktɪd] *adj* -**1.** [with thoughts elsewhere] distrait. -**2.** [upset] affolé, bouleversé; ~ with worry/with grief fou d'inquiétude/de chagrin.

distractedly [dɪ'stræktɪdlɪ] *adv* -**1.** [with thoughts elsewhere] distraitement. -**2.** [anxiously] d'un air affolé OR bouleversé; she was sobbing ~ elle sanglotait, éperdue de douleur.

distracting [dɪ'stræktɪŋ] *adj* -**1.** [disruptive]: I find it ~ ça m'empêche de me concentrer; it's very ~ having so many people in the office c'est très difficile de se concentrer (sur son travail) avec autant de gens dans le bureau. -**2.** [amusing] distrayant.

distraction [dɪ'strækʃn] *n* -**1.** [diversion - of attention] distraction *f*; taking on another job now would just be an unwelcome ~ for us entreprendre un nouveau travail maintenant nous détournerait de notre objet. -**2.** [amusement] distraction *f*; to do sthg for ~ faire qqch pour se distraire. -**3.** [anxiety] affolement *m*; [absent-mindedness] distraction *f*. -**4.** [madness] affolement *m*; to drive sb to ~ rendre qqn fou; I'm being driven to ~ je deviens fou; to love sb to ~ aimer qqn éperdument OR à la folie.

distrain [dɪ'streɪn] *vi* JUR: to ~ on sb's goods saisir les biens de qqn; ~ing order ordre *m* de saisie.

distraint [dɪ'streɪnt] *n* JUR saisie *f*.

distraught [dɪ'strɔːt] *adj* [with worry] angoissé, fou d'angoisse; [after death] fou OR éperdu de douleur, désespéré; the ~ mother made a plea to the kidnappers folle d'angoisse, la mère a imploré les kidnappeurs; he sounds ~ il a l'air affolé; to be ~ with grief être fou de douleur; to be ~ over sthg être angoissé à cause de OR désespéré par qqch.

distress [dɪ'stres] ◇ *n* [suffering - mental] angoisse *f*; [- physical] souffrance *f*; [hardship] détresse *f*; to cause sb ~ causer du tourment à qqn; to be in ~ [horse, athlete] souffrir; [mentally] être angoissé; [ship] être en détresse OR perdition; [aircraft] être en détresse; to be in financial ~ avoir de sérieux problèmes financiers.
◇ *comp*: ~ merchandise *Am* COMM *marchandises écoulées à bas prix parce qu'elles sont endommagées ou pour permettre de régler des dettes importantes.*
◇ *vt* -**1.** [upset] faire de la peine à, tourmenter; he was ~ed by the animal's suffering les souffrances de la bête lui faisaient de la peine. -**2.** [furniture] vieillir.

distressed [dɪ'strest] *adj* -**1.** [mentally] tourmenté; [very sorry] affligé; [physically] souffrant; [financially] dans le besoin; there's no need to get ~ ce n'est pas la peine de vous tourmenter; we were ~ to hear of his death nous avons été affligés d'apprendre sa mort; to be ~ by OR about sthg être affligé par qqch; they are in ~ circumstances ils sont dans le besoin; ~ area zone *f* sinistrée. -**2.** [furniture, leather, clothing] vieilli.

distressing [dɪ'stresɪŋ] *adj* pénible.

distressingly [dɪ'stresɪŋlɪ] *adv* désespérément.

distress signal *n* signal *m* de détresse; to send out a ~ [ship, aircraft] envoyer un signal de détresse; to send out ~s *fig* envoyer des signaux de détresse.

distribute [dɪ'strɪbjuːt] *vt* -**1.** [hand out - money, leaflets, gifts etc] distribuer. -**2.** [share out, allocate - wealth, weight] répartir; [- paint] répandre. -**3.** CIN & COMM [supply] distribuer.

distribution [ˌdɪstrɪ'bjuːʃn] ◇ *n* -**1.** [of leaflets, money etc] distribution *f*. -**2.** CIN & COMM [delivery, supply] distribution *f*; to have a wide ~ COMM être largement distribué ‖ [of books] diffusion *f*. -**3.** [of wealth] répartition *f*, distribution *f*; [of load] répartition *f*.
◇ *comp* COMM [channel, network] de distribution; ~ rights CIN droits *mpl* de distribution.

distributive [dɪ'strɪbjʊtɪv] ◇ *adj* -**1.** COMM: the ~ trades le secteur de la distribution. -**2.** GRAMM distributif.
◇ *n* GRAMM [pronoun] pronom *m* distributif; [adjective] adjectif *m* distributif.

distributor [dɪ'strɪbjʊtə^r] *n* -**1.** CIN & COMM distributeur *m*. -**2.** AUT distributeur *m*; ~ cap tête *f* de Delco® OR d'allumeur.

district ['dɪstrɪkt] ◇ *n* [of country] région *f*; [of town] quartier *m*; [administrative area - of country] district *m*; [- of city] arrondissement *m*; [surrounding area] région *f*; postal ~ secteur *m* postal.
◇ *comp*: ~ manager COMM directeur *m* régional, directrice *f* régionale.

district attorney *n* [in US] procureur *m* de la République.

district council *n* [in UK] conseil *m* municipal.

district court *n* [in US] ≃ tribunal *m* d'instance (fédéral).

district nurse *n Br* infirmière *f* visiteuse.

District of Columbia *pr n* district *m* de Columbia; in the ~ dans le district de Columbia.

distrust [dɪs'trʌst] ◇ *vt* se méfier de.
◇ *n* méfiance *f*; my ~ of her la méfiance que j'éprouve pour elle OR à son égard; to have a deep ~ of sb/sthg éprouver une profonde méfiance à l'égard de qqn/qqch.

distrustful [dɪs'trʌstfʊl] *adj* méfiant; to be deeply ~ of éprouver une extrême méfiance pour OR à l'égard de.

distrustfully [dɪs'trʌstfʊlɪ] *adv* avec méfiance.

disturb [dɪ'stɜːb] *vt* -**1.** [interrupt - person] déranger; [- silence, sleep] troubler; '(please) do not ~' '(prière de) ne pas déranger'; to ~ the peace JUR troubler l'ordre public. -**2.** [distress, upset] troubler, perturber; [alarm] inquiéter. -**3.** [alter condition of - water] troubler; [- mud, sediment] agiter, remuer; [- papers] déranger.

disturbance [dɪ'stɜːbəns] *n* -**1.** [interruption, disruption] dérangement *m*. -**2.** POL: ~s [unrest] troubles *mpl*, émeute *f*. -**3.** [noise] bruit *m*, vacarme *m*; to cause a ~ JUR troubler l'ordre public; you're creating a ~ vous dérangez tout le monde; they create such a ~ when they leave the disco ils font tant de chahut OR de tapage lorsqu'ils sortent de la discothèque; police were called to a ~ in the early hours of the morning la police a été appelée au petit matin pour mettre fin à un tapage nocturne. -**4.** [distress, alarm] trouble *m*, perturbation *f*.

disturbed [dɪ'stɜːbd] *adj* -**1.** [distressed, upset] troublé, perturbé; [alarmed] inquiet; to be ~ at OR by sthg être troublé par OR perturbé par OR inquiet de qqch; I am ~ by it cela me dérange OR perturbe, cela m'inquiète; mentally ~ mentalement dérangé; emotionally ~ children enfants souffrant de troubles émotionnels OR affectifs. -**2.** [interrupted - sleep] troublé; we had a ~ night notre sommeil a été troublé.

disturbing [dɪ'stɜːbɪŋ] *adj* [news, development - alarming] inquiétant; [- distressing, upsetting] troublant, perturbant; some viewers may find the programme ~ cette émission pourrait troubler OR perturber certains spectateurs.

disturbingly [dɪ'stɜːbɪŋlɪ] *adv*: the level of pollution is ~ high la pollution a atteint un niveau inquiétant; it is ~ evident that the cease-fire will not hold il est inquiétant de voir que le cessez-le-feu n'a aucune chance d'être respecté.

disunite [ˌdɪsjuː'naɪt] *vt* désunir.

disunited [ˌdɪsjuː'naɪtɪd] *adj* désuni.

disunity [ˌdɪs'juːnətɪ] *n* désunion *f*.

disuse [ˌdɪs'juːs] *n*: the machine has rusted from ~ la machine a rouillé à force de ne pas être utilisée; to be in ~ [building, mine etc] être abandonné OR désaffecté; to fall into ~ [word, custom, law] tomber en désuétude.

disused [ˌdɪs'juːzd] *adj* [building, mine] abandonné, désaffecté.

disyllabic [ˌdɪsɪ'læbɪk] *adj* dissyllabe, dissyllabique.

ditch [dɪtʃ] ◇ *n* -**1.** [by roadside] fossé *m*; [for irrigation, drainage] rigole *f*; he drove the car into the ~ il est tombé dans le fossé avec la voiture. -**2.** *inf* AERON: the ~ la baille, la flotte.
◇ *vt inf* -**1.** [abandon - car] abandonner; [- plan, idea] abandonner, laisser tomber; [- boyfriend, girlfriend] plaquer, laisser tomber; [throw out] se débarrasser de; the lorry driver ~ed us le chauffeur du camion nous a laissés en rade. -**2.** AERON: to ~ a plane faire un amerrissage forcé.

◇ *vi* -**1.** AERON faire un amerrissage forcé. -**2.** AGR creuser un fossé.

ditching ['dɪtʃɪŋ] *n* -**1.** AGR creusement *m* de fossés. -**2.** *inf* [dumping - of car, plan, etc] abandon *m*. -**3.** AERON amerrissage *m* forcé.

ditchwater ['dɪtʃ,wɔːtəʳ] *n phr*: to be as dull as ~ *inf* être ennuyeux comme la pluie.

dither *inf* ['dɪðəʳ] ◇ *vi* [be indecisive] hésiter, se tâter; to ~ about whether to do sthg hésiter à OR se tâter pour faire qqch; stop ~ing (about) [decide] décide-toi; [make a start] arrête de tourner en rond.

◇ *n*: to be in a ~ hésiter, se tâter; I'm in a ~ about what to do je n'arrive pas à me décider sur ce que je dois faire; he was in OR all of a ~ about his exams il était dans tous ses états à cause de ses examens.

ditherer *inf* ['dɪðərəʳ] *n*: he's such a terrible ~ il est toujours à hésiter sur tout.

dithery *inf* ['dɪðərɪ] *adj* -**1.** [indecisive] hésitant, indécis. -**2.** [agitated] nerveux, agité.

ditransitive [dɪ'trænsɪtɪv] *adj* à deux compléments d'objet.

ditsy *inf* ['dɪtsɪ] (*compar* ditsier, *superl* ditsiest) *adj Am* écervelé.

ditto ['dɪtəʊ] ◇ *adv inf*: I feel like a drink – ~ j'ai bien envie de prendre un verre – idem; I don't like her – ~ je ne l'aime pas – moi non plus.

◇ *comp*: ~ mark guillemets *mpl* itératifs, signes *mpl* d'itération.

ditty ['dɪtɪ] (*pl* ditties) *n hum* chanson *f*.

diuresis [,daɪjʊ'riːsɪs] *n* MED diurèse *f*.

diuretic [,daɪjʊ'retɪk] MED ◇ *adj* diurétique.

◇ *n* diurétique *m*.

diurnal [daɪ'ɜːnl] *adj lit* diurne.

diva ['diːvə] *n* diva *f*.

divan [dɪ'væn] *n* divan *m*; ~ (bed) divan-lit *m*.

dive [daɪv] (*Br pt & pp* dived, *Am pt* dove [dəʊv] OR dived, *pp* dived) ◇ *vi* -**1.** [person, bird, submarine] plonger; [aircraft] plonger, piquer, descendre en piqué; to ~ for clams/pearls pêcher la palourde/des perles *(en plongée)*; the bird ~d on its prey l'oiseau a plongé OR fondu sur sa proie; she ~d off the side of the boat elle a plongé depuis le bord du bateau; to ~ for the ball [goalkeeper] plonger sur le ballon. -**2.** [as sport] faire de la plongée. -**3.** *inf* [rush]: they ~d for the exit ils se sont précipités OR ils ont foncé vers la sortie; he ~d for his camera il s'est rué sur son appareil photo; the soldiers ~d into the doorway les soldats se sont engouffrés dans l'entrée; the rabbit ~d down its hole le lapin s'est enfoui OR a plongé dans son trou; he ~d into the car il s'engouffra dans la voiture; he ~d into his pocket/the bag il a plongé la main dans sa poche/le sac; she always ~s headlong into a task *fig* elle fonce toujours tête baissée pour faire quelque chose; she ~d out of sight elle s'est cachée précipitamment; to ~ under the table plonger OR se jeter sous la table; he ~d under the covers and shut his eyes il s'est enfoui OR il a plongé sous les couvertures et a fermé les yeux.

◇ *n* -**1.** [of swimmer, bird, submarine] plongeon *m*; [by aircraft] piqué *m*; to go into a ~ [aircraft] plonger, piquer, descendre en piqué; to pull out of a ~ [aircraft] se redresser d'un piqué; to make a ~ for the ball plonger sur le ballon; to take a ~ *inf* [in boxing] feindre le K-O; he took a ~ in the box FTBL il a feint de s'effondrer dans la surface de réparation. -**2.** *inf* [sudden movement]: to make a ~ for the exit se précipiter vers la sortie; to make a ~ for shelter se précipiter pour se mettre à l'abri; I made a ~ for the vase [to stop it breaking] je me suis précipité vers le vase. -**3.** *inf pej* [bar, café etc] bouge *m*.

◆ **dive in** *vi insep* -**1.** [swimmer] plonger. -**2.** *inf* ~ in! [eat] attaquez!; we're just going to have to ~ in [set to work] il va falloir qu'on s'y mette; we can't just ~ in without any preparation nous ne pouvons pas nous lancer comme ça sans aucune préparation.

dive-bomb *vt* [subj: plane] bombarder OR attaquer en piqué; [subj: bird] attaquer en piqué.

dive-bomber *n* chasseur *m* bombardier.

dive-bombing *n* [by plane] bombardement *m* en piqué.

diver ['daɪvəʳ] *n* -**1.** [from diving board, underwater] plongeur *m*, -euse *f*; [deep-sea] scaphandrier *m*; pearl/clam ~ pêcheur *m*, -euse *f* de perles/de palourdes *(en plongée)*. -**2.** [bird] plongeur *m*.

diverge [daɪ'vɜːdʒ] *vi* [paths] se séparer, diverger; *fig* [opinions] diverger; to ~ from the truth s'écarter de la vérité.

divergence [daɪ'vɜːdʒəns] *n* [of paths] séparation *f*, divergence *f*; *fig* [of opinions] divergence *f*; this ~ in our opinions cette divergence d'opinion entre nous.

divergent [daɪ'vɜːdʒənt] *adj* [opinions] divergent.

divers ['daɪvəz] *adj arch* OR *lit* [several] divers, plusieurs.

diverse [daɪ'vɜːs] *adj* divers.

diversification [daɪ,vɜːsɪfɪ'keɪʃn] *n* diversification *f*; the company's recent ~ into cosmetics la diversification qu'a récemment entreprise la société en pénétrant le marché des cosmétiques.

diversify [daɪ'vɜːsɪfaɪ] (*pt & pp* diversified) ◇ *vi* [company] se diversifier; to ~ into a new market se diversifier en pénétrant un nouveau marché; to ~ into a new product [make new product] se diversifier en fabriquant un nouveau produit.

◇ *vt* diversifier.

diversion [daɪ'vɜːʃn] *n* -**1.** [of traffic] déviation *f*; [of river] dérivation *f*, détournement *m*. -**2.** [distraction] diversion *f*; it was a welcome ~ cela a été une diversion agréable; to create a ~ [distract attention] faire (une) diversion; MIL opérer une diversion. -**3.** [amusement] distraction *f*.

diversionary [daɪ'vɜːʃnrɪ] *adj* [remark, proposal] destiné à faire diversion; ~ tactics tactique *f* de diversion.

diversity [daɪ'vɜːsətɪ] *n* diversité *f*.

divert [daɪ'vɜːt] *vt* -**1.** [reroute - traffic] dévier; [- train, plane, ship] dévier (la route de); [- river, attention, conversation, blow] détourner; the train was ~ed via Birmingham le train a été dévié par Birmingham; the plane was ~ed to London l'avion a été dévié OR détourné sur Londres; to ~ water from a river détourner de l'eau d'une rivière. -**2.** [money] transférer; [illegally] détourner. -**3.** [amuse] distraire.

diverticulitis [,daɪvə,tɪkjʊ'laɪtɪs] *n (U)* diverticulite *f*.

diverting [daɪ'vɜːtɪŋ] *adj* divertissant.

divest [daɪ'vest] *vt fml* -**1.** [take away from] priver; to ~ sb of sthg priver qqn de qqch. -**2.** [rid]: to ~ o.s. of [opinion, belief] se défaire de; [coat] enlever; [luggage] se débarrasser de.

divestiture [daɪ'vestɪtʃəʳ] *n Am* désinvestissement *m*.

divestment [daɪ'vestmənt] *n Am* désinvestissement *m*.

divide [dɪ'vaɪd] ◇ *vt* -**1.** [split up - territory, property, work] diviser; [share out] partager, répartir; to ~ sthg in OR into two couper OR diviser qqch en deux; she ~d the cake into six equal portions elle a partagé OR coupé le gâteau en six parts égales; she ~d the cake equally among the children elle a partagé le gâteau en parts égales entre les enfants; they ~d the work between them ils se sont partagé OR réparti le travail; he ~s his time between the office and home il partage son temps entre le bureau et la maison. -**2.** [separate] séparer; to ~ sthg from sthg séparer qqch de qqch; the Berlin Wall used to ~ East and West le mur de Berlin séparait l'Est de l'Ouest. -**3.** MATH diviser; to ~ 10 by 2 diviser 10 par 2; 40 ~d by 5 equals 8 40 divisé par 5 égale 8. -**4.** [disunite - family, party] diviser. -**5.** *Br* POL: to ~ the House faire voter la Chambre.

◇ *vi* -**1.** [cells, group of people, novel] se diviser; a policy of ~ and rule POL une politique consistant à diviser pour régner; the class ~d into groups la classe s'est divisée OR répartie en groupes. -**2.** [river, road, train] se séparer. -**3.** MATH diviser; we're learning to ~ nous apprenons à faire des divisions; 10 ~s by 2 10 est divisible par 2, 10 est un multiple de 2. -**4.** *Br* POL: the House ~d on the question la Chambre a voté sur la question.

◇ *n* -**1.** [gap] fossé *m*; the North-South ~ la division Nord-Sud. -**2.** *Am* GEOG [watershed] ligne *f* de partage des eaux; the Great OR Continental Divide ligne de partage des eaux des Rocheuses; to cross the Great Divide [die] passer de vie à trépas.

◆ **divide off** *vt sep* séparer; to ~ sthg off from sthg séparer qqch de qqch.

◆ **divide out** *vt sep* partager, répartir; to ~ sthg out between OR among people partager qqch entre des gens.

◆ **divide up** ◇ *vi insep* = **divide** *vi* **1**.

◇ *vt sep* = **divide** *vt* **1**.

divided [dɪ'vaɪdɪd] *adj* -**1.** [property, territory] divisé; BOT découpé; ~ highway *Am* route *f* à quatre voies; ~ skirt jupe-culotte *f*. -**2.** [disunited - family, party] divisé; the party is ~ on the issue le parti est divisé sur ce problème; opinion is ~ on the matter les avis sont partagés sur ce problème; I feel ~ (in my mind) OR my mind is ~ on the issue je suis partagé sur la question; to have ~ loyalties être déchiré; my loyalties are ~ je suis déchiré.

dividend ['dɪvɪdend] *n* FIN & MATH dividende *m*; to pay a ~ FIN [company] verser un dividende; [shares] rapporter un dividende; to pay ~s *fig* porter ses fruits.

divider [dɪ'vaɪdəʳ] *n* [in room] meuble *m* de séparation.

◆ **dividers** *npl* MATH: (a pair of) ~s un compas à pointes sèches.

dividing [dɪ'vaɪdɪŋ] *adj* [fence, wall] de séparation; ~ line *literal* limite *f*; *fig* distinction *f*; it's a very thin ~ line *fig* c'est une distinction très subtile.

divination [,dɪvɪ'neɪʃn] *n* divination *f*.

divine [dɪ'vaɪn] ◇ *adj* -**1.** RELIG divin; to attend ~ service *fml* aller à l'église; the ~ right of kings HIST la monarchie de droit divin; it was ~ retribution c'était le châtiment de Dieu; 'The Divine Comedy' *Dante* 'la Divine Comédie'. -**2.** *inf* [delightful] divin; you look simply ~! tu es absolument divine!

◇ *n* [priest] théologien *m*.

◇ *vt* -**1.** *lit* [foretell - the future] présager, prédire. -**2.** *lit* [conjecture, guess] deviner. -**3.** *lit* [perceive by intuition] pressentir. -**4.** [locate - water, metal] détecter OR découvrir par la radiesthésie.

◇ *vi*: to ~ for water détecter OR découvrir de l'eau par la radiesthésie.

divinely [dɪ'vaɪnlɪ] *adv* divinement.

diviner [dɪ'vaɪnəʳ] *n* [of future] devin *m*, devineresse *f*; [for water] sourcier *m*, radiesthésiste *mf*.

diving ['daɪvɪŋ] *n* [underwater] plongée *f* sous-marine; [from board] plongeon *m*; she doesn't like ~ [from board] elle n'aime pas plonger *(d'un plongeoir)*; [underwater] elle n'aime pas la plongée sous-marine.

diving bell *n* cloche *f* à plongeur OR de plongée.

diving board *n* plongeoir *m*.

diving suit *n* scaphandre *m*.

divining rod [dɪ'vaɪnɪŋ-] *n* baguette *f* de sourcier.

divinity [dɪ'vɪnətɪ] (*pl* divinities) ◇ *n* -**1.** [quality, state] divinité *f*. -**2.** [god, goddess] divinité *f*; the Divinity la Divinité. -**3.** [theology] théologie *f*; SCOL instruction *f* religieuse; Faculty/Doctor of Divinity faculté *f* de/docteur *m* en théologie.

◇ *comp*: ~ student étudiant *m*, -e *f* en théologie.

divisible [dɪ'vɪzəbl] *adj* divisible.

division [dɪ'vɪʒn] *n* -**1.** [act, state] division *f*; [sharing out] partage *m*; the ~ of labour la division du travail; the ~ of responsibility le partage des responsabilités. -**2.** [section - of company, organization] division *f*; [- of scale, thermometer] graduation *f*; [compartment - in box, bag] compartiment *m*. -**3.** BIOL, MIL & SPORT division *f*. -**4.** MATH division *f*. -**5.** [that which separates] division *f*; [dividing line] division *f*, scission *f*; [in room] cloison *f*; **class ~s** divisions entre les classes, divisions sociales; **the motorway forms a ~ between the two halves of the city** l'autoroute sépare la ville en deux. -**6.** [dissension] division *f*. -**7.** *Br* POL *vote officiel à la Chambre des communes (pour lequel les députés se répartissent dans les deux «division lobbies»)*; **a ~ will be necessary** il faudra procéder à un vote; **the bill was passed without ~** le projet de loi a été adopté sans qu'on ait procédé à un vote; **to carry a ~** avoir OR remporter la majorité des voix; **to come to a ~** procéder à un vote; **to call a ~** annoncer un vote; **to call for a ~ on sthg** demander que qqch soit soumis à un vote.

divisional [dɪ'vɪʒənl] *adj* de la division, de division; **the ~ manager** le directeur de la division; **there were six ~ managers there** il y avait six directeurs de division.

division bell *n Br* POL *sonnerie à la Chambre des communes prévenant les députés qu'il faut venir voter.*

division lobby *n Br* POL *nom des deux salles dans lesquelles les députés britanniques se répartissent pour voter.*

division sign *n* MATH symbole *m* de division.

divisive [dɪ'vaɪsɪv] *adj* [policy, issue] qui crée des divisions.

divisiveness [dɪ'vaɪsɪvnɪs] *n*: **the ~ of this policy is evident to everyone** il apparaît clairement à tout le monde que cette politique crée des OR est source de divisions.

divisor [dɪ'vaɪzəʳ] *n* MATH diviseur *m*.

divorce [dɪ'vɔːs] ◇ *n* -**1.** JUR divorce *m*; **I want a ~** je veux divorcer, je veux le divorce; **he asked his wife for a ~** il a demandé à sa femme de divorcer, il a demandé le divorce à sa femme; **a lawyer who specializes in ~** un avocat spécialisé dans les affaires OR cas de divorce; **her first marriage ended in ~** son premier mariage s'est soldé par un divorce; **to file** OR **to sue for (a) ~** demander le divorce; **to get** OR **to obtain a ~** obtenir le divorce; **Mary's getting a ~ from John** Mary divorce d'avec John; **they're getting a ~** ils divorcent; **why don't you get a ~?** pourquoi ne divorces-tu pas?; **grounds for ~** motifs *mpl* de divorce; **that's grounds for ~!** *hum* ça, c'est un motif de divorce! ❑ **'Divorce Italian Style'** *Germi* 'Divorce à l'italienne'. -**2.** *fig* séparation *f*, divorce *m*.
◇ *comp* [case, proceedings] de divorce; **~ court** *chambre spécialisée dans les affaires familiales au tribunal de grande instance*; **~ lawyer** avocat *m* spécialisé dans les affaires OR cas de divorce.
◇ *vt* -**1.** JUR [subj: husband, wife] divorcer d'avec; [subj: judge] prononcer le divorce de; **you should ~ him** tu devrais divorcer (d'avec lui); **they got ~d a few years ago** ils ont divorcé il y a quelques années. -**2.** *fig* séparer; **to ~ sthg from sthg** séparer qqch de qqch.
◇ *vi* divorcer.

divorcé [dɪ'vɔːseɪ] *n* divorcé *m*.

divorced [dɪ'vɔːst] *adj* -**1.** JUR divorcé; **a ~ woman** une (femme) divorcée. -**2.** *fig*: **to be ~ from reality** [person] être coupé de la réalité, ne pas avoir les pieds sur terre; [suggestion, plan] être irréaliste.

divorcée [dɪvɔː'siː] *n* divorcée *f*.

divot ['dɪvət] *n* motte *f* de terre.

divulge [daɪ'vʌldʒ] *vt* divulguer, révéler.

divvy *inf* ['dɪvɪ] (*pl* divvies, *pt* & *pp* divvied, *cont* divvying) *n Br abbr of* **dividend**.
◆ **divvy up** *inf* ◇ *vt sep* partager; **they divvied up the money between them** ils se sont partagé l'argent.
◇ *vi insep* faire le partage.

dixie ['dɪksɪ] *n Br mil sl* gamelle *f*.

Dixie *inf* ['dɪksɪ] *pr n Am* le Sud *(terme désignant le sud-est des États-Unis, particulièrement les anciens États esclavagistes)*.

Dixieland ['dɪksɪlænd] MUS ◇ *n* jazz *m* dixieland.
◇ *adj*: **~ jazz** le (jazz) dixieland.

DIY *n* & *comp abbr of* **do-it-yourself**.

dizzily ['dɪzɪlɪ] *adv* -**1.** [walk] avec une sensation de vertige. -**2.** [behave] étourdiment.

dizziness ['dɪzɪnɪs] *n (U)* vertiges *mpl*.

dizzy ['dɪzɪ] (*compar* dizzier, *superl* dizziest) *adj* -**1.** [giddy]: **to feel ~** avoir le vertige, avoir la tête qui tourne; **you'll make yourself ~** tu vas avoir la tête qui tourne; **it makes me (feel) ~** cela me donne le vertige; **~ spell** OR **turn** éblouissement *m*. -**2.** [height, speed] vertigineux; **the ~ heights of fame** les sommets grisants de la célébrité OR gloire. -**3.** *inf* [scatterbrained] étourdi; **a ~ blonde** une blonde évaporée.

DJ (*abbr of* **disc jockey**) *n* DJ *m*.

Djakarta [dʒə'kɑːtə] = **Jakarta**.

Djerba ['dʒɜːbə] *pr n* Djerba; **in ~** à Djerba.

DJIA *pr n Am abbr of* **Dow Jones Industrial Average**.

Djibouti [dʒɪ'buːtɪ] *pr n* (République *f* de) Djibouti; **in ~** à Djibouti.

Djibouti City *pr n* Djibouti; **in ~** à Djibouti.

djinn [dʒɪn] *n* djinn *m*.

dl (*written abbr of* **decilitre**) dl.

DLit(t) [,diː'lɪt] *n* -**1.** (*abbr of* **Doctor of Literature**) docteur *m* ès lettres. -**2.** (*abbr of* **Doctor of Letters**) docteur *m* ès lettres.

DLO *n abbr of* **dead-letter office**.

dm (*written abbr of* **decimetre**) dm.

DM (*written abbr of* **Deutsche Mark**) DM.

DMA *n abbr of* **direct memory access**.

DMus [,diː'mjuːz] (*abbr of* **Doctor of Music**) *n* docteur *m* en musique.

DMZ *n abbr of* **demilitarized zone**.

DNA (*abbr of* **deoxyribonucleic acid**) *n* ADN *m*.

Dnieper ['dniːpəʳ] *pr n*: **the (River) ~** le Dniepr.

D-notice *n consigne donnée par le gouvernement britannique à la presse pour empêcher la diffusion d'informations touchant à la sécurité du pays.*

do[1] [duː] (*pres 3rd sing* does [dʌz], *pt* did [dɪd], *pp* done [dʌn], *negative forms* do not, does not, did not *frequently shortened to* don't [dəʊnt], doesn't [dʌznt], didn't [dɪdnt], *cont* doing ['duːɪŋ]) ◇ *aux vb* -**1.** [in questions]: **do you know her?** est-ce que tu la connais?, la connais-tu?; **don't/didn't you know?** vous ne le savez/saviez pas?; **did I understand you correctly?** vous ai-je bien compris?, est-ce que je vous ai bien compris?; **why don't you tell her?** pourquoi est-ce que tu ne (le) lui dis pas?, pourquoi ne (le) lui dis-tu pas? || [in exclamations]: **do I know London!** si je connais Londres?; **boy, do I hate paperwork!** nom d'un chien, qu'est-ce que je peux avoir horreur des paperasses! -**2.** [in tag questions]: **he takes you out a lot, doesn't he?** il te sort souvent, n'est-ce pas OR hein?; **he doesn't take you out very often, does he?** il ne te sort pas souvent, n'est-ce pas OR hein?; **so you want to be an actress, do you?** alors tu veux devenir actrice?; **you didn't sign it, did you?** [disbelief, horror] tu ne l'as pas signé, quand même?; **you surely don't want any more, do you?** tu ne veux quand même pas en reprendre, si?; **look, we don't want any trouble, do we?** [encouraging, threatening] écoute, nous ne voulons pas d'histoires, hein? -**3.** [with the negative]: **I don't believe you** je ne te crois pas; **please don't tell her** s'il te plaît, ne (le) lui dis pas; **don't let's go out** *Br* ne sortons pas. -**4.** [for emphasis]: **I DO believe you** sincèrement, je vous crois; **do you mind if I smoke? — yes I DO mind** cela vous dérange-t-il que je fume? — justement, oui, ça me dérange; **he DOES know where it is** il sait bien où c'est; **we DO like it here** [refuting accusation] mais si, nous nous plaisons ici, bien sûr que nous nous plaisons ici; [like it very much] nous nous plaisons vraiment ici; **I DID tell you** [refuting sb's denial] mais si, je te l'ai dit, bien sûr que je te l'ai dit; [emphasizing earlier warning] je te l'avais bien dit; **if you DO decide to buy it** si tu décides finalement de l'acheter; **let me know when you DO decide** dis-moi quand tu auras décidé; **DO sit down** asseyez-vous donc; **DO let us know how your mother is** surtout dites-nous comment va votre mère; **DO stop crying** mais arrête de pleurer, enfin. -**5.** [elliptically]: **you know as much as/more than I do** tu en sais autant que/plus que moi; **so do I/does she** moi/elle aussi; **neither do I/does she** moi/elle non plus; **he didn't know and neither did I** il ne savait pas et moi non plus; **do you smoke? — I do/don't** est-ce que vous fumez? — oui/non; **may I sit down? — please do** puis-je m'asseoir? — je vous en prie; **I'll talk to her about it — please do/don't!** je lui en parlerai — oh, oui/non s'il vous plaît!; **will you tell her? — I may do** (le) lui diras-tu? — peut-être; **I may come to Paris next month — let me know if you do** il se peut que je vienne à Paris le mois prochain — préviens-moi si tu viens; **you said eight o'clock — oh, so I did** tu as dit huit heures — oh, c'est vrai; **I liked her — you didn't!** [surprised] elle m'a plu — non! vraiment?; **I wear a toupee — you do?** [astonished] je porte une perruque — vraiment? OR non! OR pas possible!; **it belongs/it doesn't belong to me — does/doesn't it?** cela m'appartient/ne m'appartient pas — vraiment? || [asserting opposites]: **yes you do — no I don't** mais si — mais non; **yes it does — no it doesn't** mais si — mais non; **you know her, I don't** tu la connais, moi pas; **you don't know her — I do!** tu ne la connais pas — si (, je la connais)! ❑ **I do** [marriage service] ≃ oui. -**6.** [in sentences beginning with adverbial phrase]: **not only did you lie...** non seulement tu as menti...; **little did I realize...** j'étais bien loin de m'imaginer...
◇ *vt* -**1.** [be busy or occupied with] faire; **what are you doing?** qu'est-ce que tu fais?, que fais-tu?, qu'es-tu en train de faire?; **are you doing anything next Saturday?** est-ce que tu fais quelque chose samedi prochain?; **what do you do for a living?** qu'est-ce que vous faites dans la vie?; **what are these files doing here?** qu'est-ce que ces dossiers font ici?; **somebody DO something!** que quelqu'un fasse quelque chose!; **there's nothing more to be done** il n'y a plus rien à faire; **he does nothing but sleep, all he does is sleep** il ne fait que dormir || [carry out - task, work] faire; **you'll have to do it again** il va falloir que tu le refasses; **he did a good job** il a fait du bon travail; **what do I do to start the machine?** comment est-ce que je fais pour mettre la machine en marche?; **what do I have to do to make you understand?** mais qu'est-ce que je dois faire pour que tu comprennes?; **have I done the right thing?** ai-je fait ce qu'il fallait?; **to do sthg about sthg/sb**: **what are you going to do about the noise?** qu'est-ce que tu vas faire au sujet du bruit?; **to do sthg for sb/sthg**: **what can I do for you?** que puis-je (faire) pour vous?; **the doctors can't do anything more for him** la médecine ne peut plus rien pour lui; **that dress really does something/nothing for you** cette robe te va vraiment très bien/ne te va vraiment pas du tout; **the new wallpaper does a lot for the room** le nouveau papier peint transforme la pièce; **what do you do for entertainment?** quelles sont vos distractions?, comment est-ce que vous vous distrayez?; **what shall we do for water to wash in?** où est-ce qu'on va trouver de l'eau pour se laver?; **to do sthg to sb/sthg**: **who did this to you?** qui est-ce qui t'a fait ça?; **what have you done to your hair?** qu'est-ce que tu as fait à tes cheveux?; **I hate what your job is doing to you** je n'aime pas du tout l'effet que ton travail a sur toi; **it does something to me** ça me fait quelque chose ❑ **don't do anything I wouldn't do** *hum* ne fais pas de bêtises; **that does it!** cette fois c'en est trop!; **that's done it, the battery's flat** et voilà, la batterie est à plat. -**2.** [produce, provide - copy, report] faire; **I don't do portraits** je ne fais pas les portraits; **the pub does a good lunch** *Br* on sert un bon déjeuner dans ce pub; **could you do me a quick translation of this?** pourriez-vous me traduire ceci

rapidement?; do you do day trips to France? [to travel agent] est-ce que vous avez des excursions d'une journée en France? -**3.** [work on, attend to] s'occuper de; he's doing your car now il est en train de s'occuper de votre voiture; can you do Mrs Baker first? [in hairdresser's] peux-tu t'occuper de Mme Baker d'abord?; to do the garden: I'm the one who does the garden c'est moi qui m'occupe du jardin; he's doing the garden il est en train de jardiner ❑ they do you very well in this hotel on est très bien dans cet hôtel; this old car has done me well over the years cette voiture m'a bien servi au cours des années. -**4.** [clean, tidy - room, cupboard] faire; [decorate - room] faire la décoration de; to do one's teeth se brosser les dents || [arrange - flowers] arranger; to have one's hair done aller chez le coiffeur. -**5.** SCH & UNIV [subject] étudier; *Br* [course] suivre; to do medicine/law étudier la médecine/le droit, faire sa médecine/son droit; we're doing Tartuffe nous étudions Tartuffe. -**6.** [solve - sums, crossword, equation] faire. -**7.** AUT & TRANSP [speed, distance] faire; the car will do over 100 la voiture peut faire du 160; it does thirty-five miles to the gallon elle fait sept litres aux cents (kilomètres); we did the trip in under two hours nous avons fait le voyage en moins de deux heures. -**8.** CIN, THEAT & TV [produce - play, film] faire; [appear in] être dans; [play part of] faire; MUS [perform] jouer. -**9.** CULIN [cook] faire; [prepare - vegetables, salad] préparer; to do sthg in the oven faire (cuire) qqch au four; how would you like your steak done? comment voulez-vous votre steak? -**10.** *inf* [spend time - working, in prison] faire; she's doing three years for robbery elle fait trois ans pour vol. -**11.** [be enough or suitable for] suffire; will £10 do you? 10 livres, ça te suffira?; those shoes will have to do the children for another year les enfants devront encore faire un an avec ces chaussures. -**12.** [finish]: well that's that done, thank goodness bon, voilà qui est fait, dieu merci; once I've done what I'm doing dès que j'aurai fini ce que je suis en train de faire; have you done eating/crying? tu as fini de manger/pleurer?; it will never be done in time ce ne sera jamais fini à temps; done! [in bargain] marché conclu! -**13.** [imitate] imiter, faire; he does you very well il t'imite très bien. -**14.** *inf Br* [arrest]: she was done for speeding elle s'est fait pincer pour excès de vitesse; we could do you for dangerous driving nous pourrions vous arrêter pour conduite dangereuse. -**15.** *inf* [rob, burgle - bank, shop] cambrioler, se faire. -**16.** *inf* [cheat] rouler, avoir; you've been done tu t'es fait rouler OR avoir. -**17.** *inf* [visit] faire; to do the sights faire le tour des sites touristiques. -**18.** ▽ [take]: to do drugs se camer. -**19.** *inf Br* [beat up] s'occuper de qqn, en mettre une à qqn; I'll do you! je vais m'occuper de toi, moi!

◇ *vi* -**1.** [perform - in exam, competition etc] s'en tirer, s'en sortir; you did very well tu t'en es très bien tiré OR sorti; his team didn't do well in the match son équipe ne s'en est pas très bien tirée pendant le match; the company's not doing too badly l'entreprise ne se débrouille pas trop mal; how are you doing in the new job/at school? comment te débrouilles-tu dans ton nouveau travail/à l'école?; try to do better in future essaie de mieux faire à l'avenir; how are we doing with the corrections? [checking progress] où en sommes-nous avec les corrections?; well done! bien joué!, bravo! -**2.** [referring to health]: how is she doing, doctor? comment va-t-elle, docteur?; he's not doing too well il ne va pas trop bien; mother and baby are both doing well la maman et le bébé se portent tous les deux à merveille; how is your eldest boy doing? comment va votre aîné? ❑ how do you do? [greeting] comment allez-vous?; [on being introduced] ≃ enchanté, ravi. -**3.** [act, behave] faire; do as you please fais ce qui te plaît, fais ce que tu veux; do as you're told! fais ce qu'on te dit! ❑ you would do well to listen to your mother tu ferais bien d'écouter ta mère; to do well by sb bien traiter qqn; to be/to feel hard done by *Br* être/se sentir lésé; do as you would be done by *prov* traite les autres comme tu voudrais être traité. -**4.** [be enough] suffire; will £20 do? 20 livres, ça ira OR suffira?; that will do! [stop it] ça suffit comme ça! -**5.** [be suitable] aller; that will do (nicely) ça ira OR conviendra parfaitement, cela fera très bien l'affaire; this won't do ça ne peut pas continuer comme ça; it wouldn't do to be late ce ne serait pas bien d'arriver en retard; will that do? [as alternative] est-ce que ça ira?; will Sunday do instead? et dimanche, ça irait? -**6.** *(always in continuous form)* [happen]: is there anything doing at the club tonight? est-ce qu'il y a quelque chose au club ce soir?; there's nothing doing here at weekends il n'y a rien à faire ici le week-end ❑ nothing doing *inf* [rejection, refusal] rien à faire. -**7.** *(always in perfect tense)* [finish]: have you done? tu as fini? -**8.** [be connected with]: it has to do with your missing car c'est au sujet de votre voiture volée; that's got nothing to do with it! [is irrelevant] cela n'a rien à voir!; I want nothing to do with it/you je ne veux rien avoir à faire là-dedans/avec toi; I had nothing at all to do with it je n'avais rien à voir là-dedans, je n'y étais pour rien; it's nothing to do with me je n'y suis pour rien; we don't have much to do with the people next door nous n'avons pas beaucoup de contacts avec les gens d'à côté; what I said to him has got nothing to do with you [it's none of your business] ce que je lui ai dit ne te regarde pas; [it's not about you] ce que je lui ai dit n'a rien à voir avec toi; that has a lot to do with it cela joue un rôle très important; he is OR has something to do with printing il est dans l'imprimerie. -**9.** *inf Br* [work as cleaner] faire le ménage; to do for sb faire le ménage chez qqn.

◇ *n* -**1.** [tip]: the do's and don'ts of car maintenance les choses à faire et à ne pas faire dans l'entretien des voitures. -**2.** *inf* [party, celebration] fête *f*; he's having a do to celebrate his promotion il donne une fête pour célébrer sa promotion.

◆ **do away with** *vt insep* -**1.** [abolish - institution, rule, restriction] abolir; [get rid of - object] se débarrasser de. -**2.** [kill] se débarrasser de, faire disparaître; to do away with o.s. mettre fin à ses jours.

◆ **do down** *inf vt sep Br* -**1.** [criticize, disparage] rabaisser, médire sur, dire du mal de; to do o.s. down se rabaisser. -**2.** [cheat] avoir, rouler.

◆ **do for**▽ *vt insep* -**1.** *Br* [murder] zigouiller; [cause death of] tuer. -**2.** [ruin - object, engine] bousiller; [cause failure of - plan] ruiner; [- company] couler; I'm done for je suis cuit; the project is done for le projet est tombé à l'eau OR foutu; the industry is done for l'industrie est fichue. -**3.** *Br* [exhaust] tuer, crever; shopping always does for me je suis toujours crevé après les courses; I'm done for je suis mort OR crevé.

◆ **do in**▽ *vt sep* -**1.** [murder, kill] zigouiller, buter, butter. -**2.** [exhaust] = **do for 3**. -**3.** [injure]: to do one's back/one's knee in se bousiller le dos/le genou; you'll do your lungs in tu vas te bousiller les poumons ❑ it's doing my head in▽ ça me bousille.

◆ **do out** *inf vt sep Br* [clean thoroughly] nettoyer à fond; [decorate] refaire.

◆ **do out of** *inf vt sep* [money, job] faire perdre.

◆ **do over** *vt sep* -**1.** [room] refaire; the whole house needs doing over toute la maison a besoin d'être refaite. -**2.** *Am* [do again] refaire. -**3.** *inf* [beat up] casser la gueule OR la tête à. -**4.** *inf* [burgle, rob - house, bank etc] cambrioler.

◆ **do up** ◇ *vt sep* -**1.** [fasten - dress, jacket] fermer; [- zip] fermer, remonter; [- buttons] boutonner; [- shoelaces] attacher; do me up will you? tu peux fermer ma robe? -**2.** [wrap, bundle up] emballer; envelopes done up in bundles of 20 des enveloppes en paquets de 20; a parcel done up in brown paper un paquet emballé dans du papier kraft. -**3.** *inf* [renovate - house, cottage etc] refaire, retaper; [-old dress, hat] arranger; the house needs a bit of doing up la maison a besoin d'être un peu refaite OR retapée || [make more glamorous]: to do o.s. up se faire beau/belle; I didn't recognize you all done up like that je ne t'ai pas reconnu tout beau comme ça.

◇ *vi insep* [skirt, dress] se fermer; [zip] se fermer, se remonter; [buttons] se fermer, se boutonner; it does up at the side cela se ferme sur le côté.

◆ **do with** *vt insep* -**1.** *inf Br (after 'could')* [need, want] avoir besoin de; I could have done with some help j'aurais eu bien besoin d'aide; I could do with a drink je prendrais bien un verre, j'ai bien envie de prendre un verre. -**2.** *inf Br (after 'can't')* [tolerate] supporter; I can't do OR be doing with all this noise je ne supporte pas ce vacarme. -**3.** *(after 'what')* [act with regard to] faire de; they don't know what to do with themselves ils ne savent pas comment s'occuper; what are we going to do with your father for two whole weeks! qu'allons-nous faire de ton père pendant deux semaines entières?; what do you want me to do with this? que veux-tu que je fasse de ça?; what have you done with the hammer? qu'as-tu fait du marteau? -**4.** *(always with pp)* [finish with] finir avec; I'm done with men for ever j'en ai fini pour toujours avec les hommes; I'm done with trying to be nice to her je n'essaierai plus jamais d'être gentil avec elle; can I borrow the ashtray if you've done with it? puis-je emprunter le cendrier si tu n'en as plus besoin?

◆ **do without** ◇ *vi insep* faire sans; he'll have to do without il devra s'en passer OR faire sans.

◇ *vt insep* se passer de; I could have done without this long wait j'aurais bien pu me passer de cette longue attente.

do[2] [dəʊ] *n* MUS do *m*.

do. *Br* (*written abbr of* ditto) do.

DOA *adj Br abbr of* dead on arrival.

Doberman (pinscher) ['dəʊbəmən('pɪnʃəʳ)] *n* doberman *m*.

doc *inf* [dɒk] [doctor] toubib *m*; morning, ~ bonjour docteur.

docile [*Br* 'dəʊsaɪl, *Am* 'dɒsəl] *adj* [person, animal] docile.

docilely [*Br* 'dəʊsaɪllɪ, *Am* 'dɒsəllɪ] *adv* docilement.

docility [də'sɪlətɪ] *n* docilité *f*.

dock [dɒk] ◇ *vi* [ship] se mettre à quai; [spacecraft] s'amarrer.

◇ *vt* -**1.** [ship] mettre à quai; [spacecraft] amarrer. -**2.** [money]: to ~ sb's pay/pocket money faire une retenue sur la paye/réduire l'argent de poche de qqn; you'll be ~ed £20 on retiendra 20 livres sur votre salaire; they ~ed me for being late ils ont fait une retenue sur mon salaire à cause de mon retard. -**3.** [animal's tail] couper.

◇ *n* -**1.** NAUT dock *m*, docks *mpl*; the ~s les docks; to be in dry ~ [ship] être en cale sèche; to be in ~ *fig* être en réparation. -**2.** JUR banc *m* des accusés; the prisoner in the ~ l'accusé; prisoner in the ~, have you anything to say in your defence? accusé, avez-vous quelque chose à dire pour votre défense?; to be in the ~ *fig* être sur la sellette. -**3.** BOT patience *f*.

◇ *comp* [manager] des docks; ~ worker *Br* docker *m*; ~ strike grève *f* des dockers.

docker ['dɒkəʳ] *n Br* docker *m*.

docket ['dɒkɪt] ◇ *n* -**1.** *Br* [on file, package] fiche *f* (de renseignements). -**2.** JUR *Am* liste *f* des affaires en instance; *Br* compte-rendu *m* des jugements.

◇ *vt* -**1.** [package, file] mettre une fiche (indiquant le contenu) sur; the parcel has been ~ed le colis porte une fiche indiquant son contenu. -**2.** JUR [make summary of] résumer; [register] enregistrer.

docking ['dɒkɪŋ] *n* [of ship] mise *f* à quai; [of spacecraft] amarrage *m*; ~ manoeuvre accostage *m*.

dockland ['dɒklənd] *n* quartier *m* des docks.

◆ **Docklands** *pr n quartier d'affaires très moderne à Londres sur les bords de la Tamise.*

dockside ['dɒksaɪd] *n*: on the ~ sur le quai.

dockyard ['dɒkjɑːd] *n* chantier *m* naval OR de constructions navales; naval ~ arsenal *m* maritime OR de la marine.

Doc Martens® [-'mɑːtənz] *npl* Doc Martens® *fpl.*

doctor ['dɒktəʳ] ◇ *n* -**1.** MED docteur *m*, médecin *m*; good morning, ~ bonjour docteur; dear Doctor Cameron [in letter] docteur; I've an appointment with Doctor Cameron j'ai rendez-vous avec le docteur Cameron; he/she is a ~ il/elle est docteur OR médecin; to go to the ~ OR ~'s aller chez le docteur OR médecin; you should see a ~ tu devrais consulter un docteur OR médecin; to be under the ~ *inf* être sous traitement médical; woman ~ *Br*, female ~ *Am* femme *f* médecin; army ~ médecin militaire ❑ ~'s line OR note certificat *m* médical; that's just what the ~ ordered! *inf* c'est exactement ce qu'il me faut OR fallait!; Doctor Who *série télévisée britannique de science-fiction, dont le héros dispose d'une machine à voyager dans le temps*; 'The Doctor's Dilemma' *Shaw* 'le Dilemme du docteur'; 'Doctor Strangelove' *Kubrick* 'Docteur Folamour'; 'Doctor Zhivago' *Pasternak, Lean* 'le Docteur Jivago'; 'Doctor Faustus' *Mann* 'le Docteur Faustus'; *Marlowe* 'la Tragique Histoire du docteur Faustus'. -**2.** UNIV docteur *m*; Doctor of Science docteur ès OR en sciences; to do a OR to take one's ~'s degree faire un doctorat.
◇ *vt* -**1.** [tamper with - results, figures] falsifier, trafiquer; [- wine] frelater; we'll need to ~ the figures a little il va falloir un peu arranger ces chiffres. -**2.** [drug - drink, food] mettre de la drogue dans; [- racehorse] doper. -**3.** *Br* [castrate, sterilize - cat, dog] châtrer. -**4.** [treat] soigner.

doctoral ['dɒktərəl] *adj* [thesis, degree] de doctorat.

doctorate ['dɒktərət] *n* doctorat *m*; to have/to do a ~ in sthg avoir/faire un doctorat en qqch.

doctrinaire [,dɒktrɪ'neəʳ] *adj* doctrinaire.

doctrinal [dɒk'traɪnl] *adj* doctrinal.

doctrine ['dɒktrɪn] *n* doctrine *f.*

docudrama [,dɒkjʊ'drɑːmə] *n* TV docudrame *m.*

document [*n* 'dɒkjʊmənt, *vb* 'dɒkjʊment] ◇ *n* document *m*; JUR acte *m*; to draw up a ~ rédiger un document; may I have a look at your travel ~s, sir? pourrais-je voir votre titre de transport, monsieur?; the ~s in the case JUR le dossier de l'affaire.
◇ *vt* -**1.** [write about in detail] décrire (de façon détaillée); [record on film - subj: film] montrer (en détail), présenter (de façon détaillée); [- subj: photographer] faire un reportage sur; the book ~s life in the 1920s le livre décrit la vie dans les années 20; it is well ~ed c'est bien documenté; the first ~ed case of smallpox le premier cas de variole qu'on ait enregistré. -**2.** [support - with evidence or proof] fournir des preuves à l'appui de, attester; [- with citations, references] documenter.

documentary [,dɒkjʊ'mentərɪ] (*pl* documentaries) ◇ *adj* -**1.** JUR [consisting of documents]: ~ evidence preuve *f* littérale; ~ credit crédit *m* documentaire. -**2.** [factual - film, programme] documentaire.
◇ *n* CIN & TV documentaire *m.*

documentation [,dɒkjʊmen'teɪʃn] *n* documentation *f.*

document case *n* porte-documents *m inv.*

DOD *pr n Am abbr of* Department of Defense.

dodder ['dɒdəʳ] *vi* [walk] marcher d'un pas hésitant.

dodderer *inf* ['dɒdərəʳ] *n pej* croulant *m*, -e *f*, gâteux *m*, -euse *f.*

doddering *inf* ['dɒdərɪŋ] *adj* [walk] hésitant, chancelant; *pej* [elderly person] gâteux; a ~ old fool un vieux gâteux.

doddery *inf* ['dɒdərɪ] *adj* [walk] hésitant; I still feel a bit ~ [after illness] je me sens encore un peu faible OR flagada.

doddle *inf* ['dɒdl] *n Br*: it's a ~ c'est simple comme bonjour, c'est du gâteau.

dodecagon [dəʊ'dekəgən] *n* dodécagone *m.*

dodecahedron [,dəʊdekə'hiːdrən] *n* dodécaèdre *m.*

Dodecanese [,dəʊdɪkə'niːz] *pl pr n*: the ~ le Dodécanèse; in the ~ dans le Dodécanèse.

dodge [dɒdʒ] ◇ *n* -**1.** [evasive movement] écart *m*; [by footballer, boxer] esquive *f*; to make a ~ faire un écart OR une esquive. -**2.** *inf Br* [trick] truc *m*, combine *f*; to be up to all the ~s connaître toutes les combines.
◇ *vi* [make evasive movement] s'écarter vivement; [footballer, boxer] faire une esquive; he ~d into the doorway il s'est esquivé OR il a disparu dans l'entrée; she ~d to the side elle a fait un bond de côté; to ~ in and out of the crowd faire du slalom dans la foule; to ~ out of the way s'écarter vivement; to ~ out of doing sthg *fig* se défiler pour ne pas faire qqch.
◇ *vt* [blow] esquiver; [falling rock, ball] éviter; [bullets] passer entre, éviter; [pursuer, police] échapper à; [creditor, landlord etc] éviter; [question] éluder; he has ~d the taxman OR paying tax all his life il a échappé au fisc toute sa vie; to ~ military service échapper au service militaire; to ~ the issue éluder OR esquiver le problème; you ~d doing the dishes last night! tu t'es défilé pour la vaisselle hier soir!; to ~ school sécher l'école.

Dodgem® ['dɒdʒəm] *n Br* auto *f* tamponneuse; to have a ride on the ~s faire un tour d'autos tamponneuses.

dodger *inf* ['dɒdʒəʳ] *n* [workshy] tire-au-flanc *m inv*; [dishonest] combinard *m*, -e *f*, roublard *m*, -e *f*; draft ~ *Am* MIL réfractaire *m*; fare ~ resquilleur *m*, -euse *f.*

dodgy *inf* ['dɒdʒɪ] (*compar* dodgier, *superl* dodgiest) *adj Br* -**1.** [risky, dangerous - plan, idea] risqué; the brakes are really ~ les freins sont très douteux; the engine sounds a bit ~ le moteur fait un bruit suspect; the weather looks pretty ~ [unreliable] le temps a l'air plutôt douteux OR menaçant. -**2.** [dishonest - person] roublard, combinard; [- scheme] douteux, suspect.

dodo ['dəʊdəʊ] (*pl* dodos OR dodoes) *n* -**1.** [extinct bird] dronte *m*, dodo *m*; as dead as a ~ *inf* mort et enterré. -**2.** *inf* [fool] andouille *f*; what a ~ you are! quelle andouille tu fais!

doe [dəʊ] *n* [deer] biche *f*; [rabbit] lapine *f*; [hare] hase *f*; [rat] rate *f*, ratte *f.*

DoE (*abbr of* Department of the Environment) *pr n ministère britannique de l'Environnement.*

DOE (*abbr of* Department of Energy) *pr n ministère américain de l'Énergie.*

doe-eyed *adj* [person] aux yeux de biche; her ~ gaze son regard de biche.

doer ['duːəʳ] *n*: she is more (of) a ~ than a talker elle préfère l'action à la parole.

does [*weak form* dəz, *strong form* dʌz] → **do** *vb.*

doeskin ['dəʊskɪn] ◇ *n* peau *f* de daim; made of ~ en daim.
◇ *comp* [gloves, shoes etc] en daim.

doesn't ['dʌznt] = **does not.**

doff [dɒf] *vt* [cap, hat] ôter; to ~ one's cap to sb *literal* ôter son chapeau OR se découvrir devant qqn; *fig* faire preuve de respect envers qqn.

dog [dɒg] (*pt* & *pp* dogged, *cont* dogging) ◇ *n* -**1.** chien *m*; 'beware of the ~' 'attention, chien méchant'; to treat sb like a ~ traiter qqn comme un chien; to follow sb about like a ~ suivre qqn comme un petit chien ❑ sheep/guide/guard/police ~ chien de berger/d'aveugle/de garde/policier; this is a real ~'s dinner OR breakfast [mess] *Br* c'est un vrai torchon OR gâchis; you've made a real ~'s dinner OR breakfast of this *Br* ton travail est un vrai torchon; to be dressed OR done up like a ~'s dinner *inf Br* [gaudy, showy] être habillé de façon extravagante; to lead sb a ~'s life mener la vie dure à qqn; it's a ~'s life being a traffic warden c'est une vie de chien que d'être contractuel; he doesn't have OR stand a ~'s chance *inf Br* il n'a pas la moindre chance, il n'a aucune chance; a ~ in the manger un empêcheur de danser OR tourner en rond; I'm going to see a man about a ~ *inf façon humoristique d'éviter de dire où l'on va*; it's (a case of) ~ eat ~ c'est la loi de la jungle; to put on the ~ *inf Am* se donner de grands airs; every ~ has its OR his day *prov* tout le monde a son heure de gloire; give a ~ a bad name (and hang him) *prov* qui veut noyer son chien l'accuse de la rage *prov*; let sleeping ~s lie *prov* n'éveillez pas le chat qui dort *prov*; you can't teach an old ~ new tricks *prov* les vieilles habitudes ont la vie dure; 'The Dog Years' *Grass* 'les Années de chien'; the ~s *inf Br* SPORT les courses de lévriers; to go to the ~s aller aux courses de lévriers; he's gone to the ~s *inf* il a mal tourné; this country's going to the ~s *inf* le pays va à sa ruine. -**2.** [male fox, wolf etc] mâle *m*. -**3.** *inf* [person]: an old sea ~ un vieux loup de mer; you lucky ~! sacré veinard!; dirty ~ sale type *m*; sly ~ (vieux) malin *m*; gay ~ *dated* joyeux luron *m*; he's (the) top ~ c'est lui le chef; there's life in the old ~ yet! je ne suis/ce n'est pas encore un vieux croulant! -**4.** ▽ *pej* [ugly woman] cageot *m*, boudin *m*. -**5.** *inf Am* [hopeless - product, company] catastrophe *f*; [- thing]: it's a ~ c'est nul. -**6.** ▽ *Br*: ~s [feet] panards *mpl.* -**7.** [firedog] chenet *m*. -**8.** TECH [pawl] cliquet *m*; [cramp] crampon *m*. -**9.** *Am* [hot dog] hot dog *m*; a chili ~ *un hot dog avec une garniture de chili con carne.*
◇ *comp* [breeder, breeding] de chiens; [bowl, basket, food] pour chien; the ~ family la famille des chiens; ~ fox renard *m* mâle; ~ racing courses *fpl* de lévriers; ~ show exposition *f* canine; ~ team attelage *m* de chiens; ~ track cynodrome *m.*
◇ *vt* -**1.** [follow closely] suivre de près; to ~ sb's footsteps ne pas lâcher qqn d'une semelle. -**2.** [plague]: to be dogged by bad health/problems ne pas arrêter d'avoir des ennuis de santé/des problèmes; the team has been dogged by injury l'équipe n'a pas arrêté d'avoir des blessés; she is dogged by misfortune OR bad luck elle est poursuivie par la malchance. -**3.** *inf Am* [get rid of] se débarrasser de.

dog biscuit *n* biscuit *m* pour chien.

dogcart ['dɒgkɑːt] *n* dog-cart *m.*

dog-catcher *n* employé *m*, -e *f* de la fourrière.

dog collar *n* [for dog] collier *m* pour OR de chien; *hum* [of clergyman] col *m* d'ecclésiastique.

dog days *npl* canicule *f.*

doge [dəʊdʒ] *n* doge *m.*

dog-ear ◇ *n* corne *f.*
◇ *vt* [page] corner.

dog-eared *adj* [page] corné; [book] aux pages cornées.

dog-eat-dog *adj* [business] impitoyable, sans pitié; it's a ~ world c'est un monde impitoyable OR sans pitié, c'est un monde où les loups se mangent entre eux.

dog-end *inf n* [of cigarette] mégot *m.*

dogfight ['dɒgfaɪt] *n* [between dogs] combat *m* de chiens; MIL [between aircraft] combat *m* rapproché.

dogfish ['dɒgfɪʃ] *n* roussette *f*, chien *m* de mer.

dogged ['dɒgɪd] *adj* [courage, perseverance] tenace; [person, character] tenace, déterminé, persévérant; [refusal] obstiné.

doggedly ['dɒgɪdlɪ] *adv* [fight, persist] avec ténacité OR persévérance; [refuse] obstinément.

doggedness ['dɒgɪdnɪs] *n* [of person] ténacité *f*, persévérance *f*; [of courage] ténacité *f*; the ~ of his refusal l'obstination avec laquelle il a refusé.

doggerel ['dɒgərəl] ◇ *n* poésie *f* burlesque.
◇ *adj* [rhyme, verse] burlesque.

doggie ['dɒgɪ] = **doggy.**

doggo *inf* ['dɒgəʊ] *adv Br*: to lie ~ se tenir coi.

doggone *inf* ['dɒgɒn] *Am* ◇ *interj*: ~ (it)! zut!, nom d'une pipe!
◇ *adj* = **doggoned.**

doggoned *inf* ['dɒgɒnd] *adj Am* fichu; well, I'll be ~! ça, c'est trop fort!; it's a ~ shame! c'est vraiment honteux!

doggy *inf* [ˈdɒgɪ] (*pl* doggies) ◇ *n baby talk* toutou *m*; **~-fashion**▽ en levrette.
◇ *adj* [smell] de chien; **he's a ~ person** il adore les chiens.

doggy bag *n sachet (ou boîte) que l'on propose aux clients dans les restaurants pour qu'ils emportent ce qu'ils n'ont pas consommé.*

doggy paddle ◇ *n* nage *f* du petit chien.
◇ *vi* faire la nage du petit chien.

dog handler *n* maître-chien *m*.

doghouse [ˈdɒghaʊs, *pl* -haʊzɪz] *n* -**1.** *Am* [kennel] chenil *m*, niche *f*. -**2.** *inf phr*: **to be in the ~ (with sb)** ne pas être en odeur de sainteté OR être en disgrâce (auprès de qqn); **am I in the ~ again?** est-ce que je suis de nouveau en disgrâce?

dogie [ˈdəʊgɪ] *n Am* veau *m* sans mère.

dog iron *n* chenet *m*.

dog Latin *n* latin *m* de cuisine.

dogleg [ˈdɒgleg] ◇ *n* [in pipe, road] coude *m*.
◇ *vi* [pipe, road] faire un coude.
◇ *adj* [pipe, road] qui fait un coude.

dog licence *n Br permis de posséder un chien.*

doglike [ˈdɒglaɪk] *adj*: **~ devotion** *fig* dévotion *f* aveugle.

dogma [ˈdɒgmə] *n* dogme *m*.

dogmatic [dɒgˈmætɪk] *adj* dogmatique; **to be ~ about sthg** être dogmatique au sujet de qqch.

dogmatically [dɒgˈmætɪklɪ] *adv* dogmatiquement.

dogmatism [ˈdɒgmətɪzm] *n* dogmatisme *m*.

dogmatist [ˈdɒgmətɪst] *n* personne *f* dogmatique.

do-gooder *inf* [-ˈgʊdəʳ] *n pej* âme *f* charitable, bonne âme *f*.

dog paddle = **doggy paddle**.

dog rose *n* églantine *f*.

dogsbody *inf* [ˈdɒgz,bɒdɪ] (*pl* dogsbodies) *n Br* bonne *f* à tout faire; **I'm not your ~** je ne suis pas ton chien OR ta bonne.

dog show *n* exposition *f* canine.

dogsled [ˈdɒgsled] *n* luge *f* tirée par des chiens.

Dog Star *pr n* Sirius.

dog's-tooth check *n Br* pied-de-poule *m*.

dog tag *n Am* MIL plaque *f* d'identification.

dog-tired *inf adj* épuisé.

dogtrot [ˈdɒgtrɒt] *n* petit trot *m*; **at a ~** au petit trot.

dogwatch [ˈdɒgwɒtʃ] *n* NAUT petit quart *m*.

dogwood [ˈdɒgwʊd] *n* [bush] cornouiller *m*.

dogy [ˈdəʊgɪ] (*pl* dogies [-giːz]) *Am* = **dogie**.

doh [dəʊ] *n* MUS do *m*.

Doha [ˈdəʊə] *pr n* (al-) Dawha, (al-) Doha.

doily [ˈdɔɪlɪ] (*pl* doilies) *n* napperon *m*.

doing [ˈduːɪŋ] *n* -**1.** [work, activity]: **it's all your ~** tout cela, c'est de ta faute; **is this your ~?** [have you done this?] c'est toi qui as fait cela?; [are you behind this?] c'est toi qui es derrière cela?; **it's none of my ~** je n'y suis pour rien; **that'll take some ~** cela ne va pas être facile; **it will take some ~ to persuade him** cela ne va pas être facile de le persuader; **a job like this is going to take a lot of ~** un tel travail ne se fera pas en un tour de main OR en un tournemain; **he told them all about his ~s on holiday** il leur a raconté tout ce qu'il avait fait en vacances. -**2.** *inf* [beating]: **to give sb a ~ (over)** passer qqn à tabac, tabasser qqn.

doings *inf* [ˈduːɪŋz] *n Br* [thing] machin *m*, truc *m*.

do-it-yourself ◇ *n* bricolage *m*.
◇ *comp* [manual, shop] de bricolage; **a ~ enthusiast** un bricoleur; **the ~ craze** l'engouement pour le bricolage; **a ~ kit** des éléments en kit.

do-it-yourselfer *inf* [-jəˈselfəʳ] *n* bricoleur *m*, -euse *f*.

Dolby® [ˈdɒlbɪ] *n* Dolby® *m*; **in ~ stereo** en Dolby stéréo.

doldrums [ˈdɒldrəmz] *npl* -**1.** GEOG [zone] zones *fpl* des calmes équatoriaux, pot au noir *m*; [weather] calme *m* équatorial. -**2.** *phr*: **to be in the ~** [person] avoir le cafard, broyer du noir; [activity, trade] être en plein marasme.

dole *inf* [dəʊl] *n (U) Br*: **~ (money)** (indemnités *fpl* de) chômage *m*; **how much is the ~?** combien est-ce qu'on touche au chômage?; **there was no ~ in those days** on ne touchait pas de chômage à cette époque; **to be/to go on the ~** être/s'inscrire au chômage; **the ~ queues are getting longer** de plus en plus de gens pointent au chômage.
◆ **dole out** *vt sep* [distribute] distribuer; [in small amounts] distribuer au compte-gouttes.

doleful [ˈdəʊlfʊl] *adj* [mournful - look, voice] malheureux; [- person, song] triste.

dolefully [ˈdəʊlfʊlɪ] *adv* d'un air malheureux.

dolefulness [ˈdəʊlfʊlnɪs] *n* tristesse *f*.

doll [dɒl] *n* -**1.** [for child] poupée *f*; [for ventriloquist] marionnette *f* de ventriloque; **to play with ~s** jouer à la poupée; **~'s pram** poussette *f* de poupée ❑ **~'s house** *Br*, **~ house** *Am literal* & *fig* maison *f* de poupée; 'A Doll's House' *Ibsen* 'Maison de poupée'. -**2.** *inf* [girl] nana *f*, souris *f*; [attractive girl] poupée *f*; **hi ~!** *Am* salut poupée! -**3.** *inf* [love, dear] amour *m*; **you're a ~** tu es un amour. -**4.** *inf Am* [nice person]: **he's a real ~** il est vraiment adorable.
◆ **doll up** *vt sep*: **to get ~ed up, to ~ o.s. up** se faire beau/belle, se pomponner; **she was all ~ed up** elle s'était faite toute belle, elle était toute pomponnée; **to ~ sb up** pomponner qqn.

dollar [ˈdɒləʳ] ◇ *n* -**1.** [currency] dollar *m*; **you can bet your bottom ~** OR **~s to doughnuts that he'll be there** tu peux être sûr qu'il sera là; **I feel like a million ~s** je me sens merveilleusement bien; **you look like a million ~s in that dress** *inf* tu es magnifique avec cette robe; **that's the sixty-four thousand ~ question** c'est la question à mille francs. -**2.** *inf Br dated cinq shillings.*
◇ *comp*: **~ area** zone *f* dollar; **~ bill** billet *m* d'un dollar; **~ diplomacy** diplomatie *f* du dollar; **~ rate** cours *m* du dollar; **~ sign** (signe *m* du) dollar *m*.

dollop *inf* [ˈdɒləp] ◇ *n* [of mashed potatoes, cream etc] (bonne) cuillerée *f*; [of mud, plaster, clay] (petit) tas *m*; [of butter, margarine] (gros OR bon) morceau *m*.
◇ *vt*: **to ~ food out onto plates** balancer de la nourriture dans des assiettes.

dolly [ˈdɒlɪ] (*pt* & *pp* dollied, *pl* dollies) ◇ *n* -**1.** *inf* [for child] = **doll 1**. -**2.** CIN & TV [for camera] chariot *m*. -**3.** *inf* = **dolly bird**. -**4.** [in cricket] prise *f* au vol facile; [in tennis] coup *m* facile.
◇ *vt* CIN & TV: **to ~ a camera in /out** faire un travelling avant/arrière.
◇ *vi*: **to ~ in/out** CIN & TV faire un travelling avant/arrière.

dolly bird *inf n Br dated* poupée *f*.

dolly mixtures *npl Br* [sweets] petits bonbons *mpl* assortis.

dolman sleeve [ˈdɒlmən-] *n* manche *f* chauve-souris.

dolmen [ˈdɒlmən] *n* ARCHEOL dolmen *m*.

dolomite [ˈdɒləmaɪt] *n* dolomie *f*, dolomite *f*.

Dolomites [ˈdɒləmaɪts] *pl pr n*: **the ~** les Dolomites *fpl*, les Alpes *fpl* dolomitiques.

dolphin [ˈdɒlfɪn] *n* dauphin *m*; **~-friendly** [tuna] *pêché sans dommages pour les dauphins.*

dolphinarium [,dɒlfɪˈneərɪəm] *n* aquarium *m* à dauphins.

dolt [dəʊlt] *n* [stupid person] lourdaud *m*, gourde *f*.

doltish [ˈdəʊltɪʃ] *adj* [person] lourdaud; [behaviour] idiot.

domain [dəˈmeɪn] *n* -**1.** [territory, sphere of interest] domaine *m*; **that's your ~** *fig* c'est ton domaine; **to be in the public ~** [information] être dans le domaine public. -**2.** MATH & SCI domaine *m*.

dome [dəʊm] *n* -**1.** ARCHIT dôme *m*, coupole *f*. -**2.** [of head] calotte *f*; [of hill] dôme *m*; [of heavens, sky] voûte *f*; **the ~ of his bald head** le sommet de son crâne chauve.

domed [dəʊmd] *adj* [building] à coupole, à dôme; [roof] en forme de dôme OR de coupole; [forehead] bombé.

dome fastener *n Am* bouton-pression *m*, pression *f*.

Domesday Book [ˈduːmzdeɪ-] *pr n*: **the ~** *recueil cadastral établi à la fin du XI*ᵉ *siècle à l'initiative de Guillaume le Conquérant afin de permettre l'évaluation des droits fiscaux sur les terres d'Angleterre.*

domestic [dəˈmestɪk] ◇ *adj* -**1.** [household - duty, chore] ménager; **a ~ servant** un domestique; **to be in ~ service** être employé de maison; **~ staff** employés *mpl* de maison, domestiques *mpl*; **a ~ help** une aide ménagère; **'for ~ use only'** 'réservé à l'usage domestique'; **~ appliance/product** appareil *m*/produit *m* ménager; **~ refuse** ordures *fpl* ménagères ❑ **~ science** *Br* SCH & *dated* enseignement *m* ménager. -**2.** [of the family - duties, problems] familial; [- life] familial, de famille; **they lived in ~ bliss for many years** ça a été un ménage très heureux pendant de nombreuses années; **a minor ~ crisis** un petit problème à la maison; **to be a ~ sort of person** [woman] être une femme d'intérieur; [man] être un homme d'intérieur; **this is all very ~** tout ceci donne une ambiance très familiale. -**3.** [not foreign - affairs, flight, trade, policy, problem] intérieur; [- currency, economy, news, produce] national. -**4.** [not wild - animal] domestique.
◇ *n fml Br* domestique *mf*; *Am* femme *f* de ménage.

domestically [dəˈmestɪklɪ] *adv* -**1.** **to be ~ inclined** être une personne d'intérieur. -**2.** ECON & POL: **to be produced ~** être produit à l'intérieur du pays OR au niveau national.

domesticate [dəˈmestɪkeɪt] *vt* [animal] domestiquer, apprivoiser; *hum* [person] habituer aux tâches ménagères.

domesticated [dəˈmestɪkeɪtɪd] *adj* [animal] domestiqué, apprivoisé; **she's very ~** c'est une vraie femme d'intérieur; **her husband is quite ~** son mari est un vrai petit homme d'intérieur.

domestication [də,mestɪˈkeɪʃn] *n* [of animal] domestication *f*, apprivoisement *m*.

domesticity [,dəʊmeˈstɪsətɪ] *n* [home life] vie *f* de famille.

domicile [ˈdɒmɪsaɪl] ADMIN, FIN & JUR
◇ *n* domicile *m*.
◇ *vt* domicilier; **~d at** domicilié à.

domiciliary [,dɒmɪˈsɪljərɪ] *adj* ADMIN [visit] domiciliaire; [care, services] à domicile.

dominance [ˈdɒmɪnəns] *n* -**1.** [ascendancy - of race, person, football team etc] prédominance *f*; [- of animal, gene] dominance *f*. -**2.** [importance] importance *f*.

dominant [ˈdɒmɪnənt] ◇ *adj* -**1.** dominant; [nation, political party, team etc] prédominant; [person, personality] dominateur; [building, geographical feature - most elevated] dominant; [- most striking] le plus frappant; **the ~ male** le mâle dominant; **the ~ female** la femelle dominante. -**2.** MUS de dominante.
◇ *n* MUS dominante *f*; SCI dominance *f*.

dominate [ˈdɒmɪneɪt] ◇ *vt* dominer; **to be ~d by sb** être dominé par qqn.
◇ *vi* dominer.

dominating [ˈdɒmɪneɪtɪŋ] *adj* dominateur.

domination [,dɒmɪˈneɪʃn] *n* domination *f*; [of organization] contrôle *m*; [of conversation] monopolisation *f*; **Spain was under Roman ~ at the time** à cette époque, l'Espagne était sous la domination romaine.

domineer [,dɒmɪˈnɪəʳ] *vi* se montrer autoritaire; **to ~ over sb** se montrer autoritaire avec qqn.

domineering [,dɒmɪˈnɪərɪŋ] *adj* autoritaire.

Dominic [ˈdɒmɪnɪk] *pr n*: **Saint ~** saint Dominique.

Dominica [dəˈmɪnɪkə] *pr n* Dominique *f*; **in ~** à la Dominique.

Dominican [dəˈmɪnɪkən] ◇ *n* -**1.** [person from the Dominican Republic] Dominicain *m*, -e *f*.

-**2.** [person from Dominica] Dominiquais *m*, -e *f*. -**3.** RELIG dominicain *m*, -e *f*.
◇ *adj* -**1.** [from the Dominican Republic] dominicain. -**2.** [from Dominica] dominiquais. -**3.** RELIG dominicain.

Dominican Republic *pr n*: the ~ la République Dominicaine; in the ~ en République Dominicaine.

dominion [dəˈmɪnjən] *n* -**1.** [rule] domination *f*, empire *m*; **to have ~ over a country** avoir un pays sous sa domination; **under foreign ~** sous domination étrangère. -**2.** [territory] territoire *m*; [in British Commonwealth] dominion *m*.

domino [ˈdɒmɪnəʊ] (*pl* dominoes) ◇ *n* -**1.** domino *m*; **to play ~es** jouer aux dominos. -**2.** [cloak, mask] domino *m*.
◇ *comp*: **~ effect** effet *m* d'entraînement; **~ theory** théorie *f* des dominos.

don [dɒn] (*pt* & *pp* donned, *cont* donning)
◇ *vt fml* [put on] mettre.
◇ *n* -**1.** *Br* UNIV *professeur d'université (en particulier à Oxford et Cambridge)*. -**2.** [Spanish title] don *m*. -**3.** *Am* chef *m* de la Mafia.

Don [dɒn] *pr n*: **the (River) ~** le Don.

Donald Duck [ˈdɒnld-] *pr n* Donald.

donate [dəˈneɪt] ◇ *vt* [money, goods] faire un don de; [specific amount] faire (un) don de; **to ~ blood** donner son OR du sang; **the strips were ~d to the team by a local sports shop** les tenues ont été données à l'équipe par un magasin de sport local; **would you care to ~ something?** voudriez-vous faire un don OR donner quelque chose?
◇ *vi* [give money, goods] faire un don, faire des dons; **I've been donating for ten years** [blood] je donne mon sang depuis dix ans.

donation [dəˈneɪʃn] *n* [action] don *m*, donation *f*; [money, goods or blood given] don *m*; **would you care to make a ~?** voudriez-vous faire un don OR faire une donation OR donner quelque chose?; **to make a ~ to a charity** faire un don OR une donation à une œuvre (de charité).

done [dʌn] ◇ *pp* → **do**.
◇ *adj* -**1.** [finished] fini; **are you ~ yet?** tu as enfin fini?; **aren't you ~ yet?** tu n'as pas encore fini?; **to get sthg ~** [completed] finir qqch. -**2.** [cooked - food] cuit. -**3.** *inf* [exhausted] crevé, claqué. -**4.** *inf* [used up]: **that's the milk ~** il n'y a plus de lait; **when the ammunition was ~** quand ils ont été à court de munitions. -**5.** [fitting]: **it's not the ~ thing, it's not ~** ça ne se fait pas; **speaking with your mouth full is not ~** OR **the ~ thing** ça ne se fait pas de parler la bouche pleine; **it used to be the ~ thing to send your hostess flowers** ça se faisait d'envoyer des fleurs à son hôtesse.

dong [dɒŋ] *n* -**1.** [noise of bell] ding-dong *m*. -**2.** ▼ [penis] queue *f*, bite *f*.

dongle [ˈdɒŋgl] *n* COMPUT boîtier *m* de sécurité, clé *f* gigogne.

Don Juan [-ˈdʒuːən] *n literal* & *fig* don Juan *m*; **he's a bit of a ~** il est un peu du genre don Juan ❑ 'Don Juan' *Byron* 'Don Juan'; *Molière* 'Dom Juan'.

donkey [ˈdɒŋkɪ] *n* âne *m*, ânesse *f*; **I haven't seen her for ~'s years** *inf* je ne l'ai pas vue depuis une éternité; **he's worked in the same place for ~'s years** ça fait une éternité qu'il travaille au même endroit.

donkey engine *n* moteur *m* auxiliaire.

donkey jacket *n Br veste longue en tissu épais, généralement bleu foncé*.

donkey ride *n* promenade *f* à dos d'âne.

donkeywork *inf* [ˈdɒŋkɪwɜːk] *n (U)* [drudgery] travail *m* de bête de somme, travail *m* pénible; [basis] gros *m* du travail; **to do all the ~** se taper tout le travail pénible, faire le gros du travail.

donnish [ˈdɒnɪʃ] *adj Br* [person] érudit, savant; [look, speech] d'érudit, cultivé; *pej* pédant.

donnishly [ˈdɒnɪʃlɪ] *adv Br* de façon érudite OR savante, savamment; *pej* doctoralement, doctement.

donor [ˈdəʊnəʳ] *n* -**1.** [gen & JUR] donateur *m*, -trice *f*. -**2.** MED [of blood, organ] donneur *m*, -euse *f*.

donor card *n* carte *f* de don d'organe.

Don Quixote [-ˈkwɪksət] *pr n* Don Quichotte.

don't [dəʊnt] ◇ *vb* = **do not**.
◇ *n (usu pl)* chose *f* à ne pas faire.

dontcha▽, **dontcher**▽ *Br* [ˈdəʊntʃə] = **don't you**.

don't know *n* [on survey] sans opinion *mf inv*; [voter] indécis *m*, -e *f*.

donut [ˈdəʊnʌt] *Am* = **doughnut**.

doodah *inf* [ˈduːdɑː] *n* truc *m*, bidule *m*.

doodle [ˈduːdl] ◇ *vi* & *vt* gribouiller, griffonner.
◇ *n* gribouillage *m*, griffonnage *m*.

doodlebug [ˈduːdlbʌg] *n* -**1.** *inf* [bomb] V1 *m*, bombe *f* volante. -**2.** *Am* [insect] larve *f* de cicindèle.

doohickey *inf* [ˈduːˌhɪkɪ] *n Am* truc *m*, machin *m*.

doolally *inf* [ˌduːˈlælɪ] *adj* timbré.

doom [duːm] ◇ *n (U)* [terrible fate] destin *m* (malheureux), sort *m* (tragique); [ruin] perte *f*, ruine *f*; [death] mort *f*; **to meet one's ~** trouver la mort; **thousands were sent to their ~** on envoya des milliers de gens à la mort.
◇ *vt* condamner; **to be ~ed (to failure)** être voué à l'échec; **she is ~ed to a life of poverty** elle est destinée à une vie de misère; **the ~ed ship set sail that day** le navire condamné à sombrer prit la mer ce jour-là.

doom-laden *adj* de mauvais augure, sinistre.

Doomsday [ˈduːmzdeɪ] *n* jour *m* du Jugement dernier; **till ~** *inf* jusqu'à la fin du monde OR des temps.

Doomsday Book = **Domesday Book**.

doomster *inf* [ˈduːmstəʳ] *n Br* prophète *m* de malheur.

doomwatch [ˈduːmwɒtʃ] *n* [of environment] surveillance *f* de l'environnement.

door [dɔːʳ] *n* -**1.** [of building, room] porte *f*; **she walked through the ~** elle franchit la porte; **they shut the ~ in my face** ils m'ont fermé la porte au nez; **he lives two ~s down** il habite deux portes plus loin; **I found the ~ closed** j'ai trouvé porte close; **out of ~s** dehors, en plein air; **to go from ~ to ~** aller de porte en porte; **can someone answer the ~?** est-ce que quelqu'un peut aller ouvrir?; **I'll see you to the ~** je vous reconduis jusqu'à la porte; **the bank closes its ~s at 3:30** la banque ferme à 15 h 30; **the business finally closes its ~s tomorrow** l'entreprise ferme définitivement demain; **'tickets available at the ~'** THEAT 'billets en vente à l'entrée'; **the agreement leaves the ~ open for further discussion** l'accord laisse la porte ouverte à des discussions ultérieures; **the discovery opens the ~ to medical advances** la découverte ouvre la voie à des progrès médicaux; **to get in by the back ~** entrer par la petite porte; **having a famous name certainly helps to open ~s** avoir un nom célèbre permet sans aucun doute de voir s'ouvrir des portes; **to lay sthg at sb's ~** imputer qqch à qqn, reprocher qqch à qqn; **she closed** OR **shut the ~ on any further negotiations** elle a rendu toute nouvelle négociation impossible; **to show someone the ~** *literal* & *fig* montrer la porte à qqn. -**2.** [of car] porte *f*, portière *f*; [of train] portière *f*.

doorbell [ˈdɔːbel] *n* sonnette *f*; **the ~ rang** on sonna à la porte.

door chain *n* chaînette *f* de sûreté.

do-or-die *adj* [chance, effort] désespéré, ultime; [attitude, person] jusqu'au-boutiste.

doorframe [ˈdɔːfreɪm] *n* chambranle *m*, châssis *m* de porte.

door-handle *n* poignée *f* de porte; AUT poignée *f* de portière.

doorjamb [ˈdɔːdʒæm] *n* montant *m* de porte, jambage *m*.

doorkeeper [ˈdɔːˌkiːpəʳ] *n* [at hotel] portier *m*; [at apartment building] concierge *mf*.

doorknob [ˈdɔːnɒb] *n* poignée *f* de porte.

doorknocker [ˈdɔːˌnɒkəʳ] *n* heurtoir *m*, marteau *m (de porte)*.

doorman [ˈdɔːmən] (*pl* doormen [-mən]) *n* [at hotel] portier *m*; [at apartment building] concierge *m*.

doormat [ˈdɔːmæt] *n literal* paillasson *m*, essuie-pieds *m inv*; *fig* [person] chiffe *f* molle; **to treat sb like a ~** traiter qqn comme un moins que rien.

doornail [ˈdɔːneɪl] *n* clou *m* de porte.

doorpost [ˈdɔːpəʊst] *n* montant *m* de porte, jambage *m*.

doorsill [ˈdɔːsɪl] *n* seuil *m* de porte.

doorstep [ˈdɔːstep] ◇ *n* -**1.** [step] pas *m* de la porte, seuil *m* de porte; **leave the milk on the ~** laissez le lait devant la porte; **don't leave him standing on the ~, ask him to come in!** ne le laisse pas à la porte, fais-le entrer!; **they're building a huge factory practically on my ~** ils construisent une immense usine presque à ma porte. -**2.** *Br hum* [piece of bread] grosse tranche *f* de pain.
◇ *adj Br*: **~ salesman** vendeur *m* à domicile, démarcheur *m*; **~ selling** vente *f* à domicile, porte-à-porte *m inv*, démarchage *m*.

doorstepping [ˈdɔːstepɪŋ] *Br* ◇ *n* [by politician] démarchage *m* électoral; [by journalists] *pratique journalistique qui consiste à harceler les gens jusque chez eux*.
◇ *adj* [politician] *qui fait du démarchage électoral*; [journalist] *qui harcèle les gens jusque chez eux*.

doorstop [ˈdɔːstɒp] *n* butoir *m* de porte.

door-to-door ◇ *adj*: **~ salesman** vendeur *m* à domicile, démarcheur *m*; **he's a ~ salesman** il fait du porte-à-porte; **~ selling** vente *f* à domicile, porte-à-porte *m inv*; **~ service** service *m* à domicile.
◇ *adv*: **a 2-hour trip ~** un trajet de 2 heures de porte à porte.

doorway [ˈdɔːweɪ] *n* porte *f*; **standing in the ~** debout dans l'embrasure de la porte.

dopamine [ˈdəʊpəmɪn] *n* dopamine *f*.

dope [dəʊp] ◇ *n* -**1.** *inf (U)* [illegal drug] drogue *f*, dope *f*. -**2.** [for athlete, horse] dopant *m*. -**3.** *inf* [idiot] crétin *m*, -e *f*, andouille *f*. -**4.** *inf (U) dated* [news] tuyau *m*, renseignement *m*; **have you got any ~ on the murder/murderer?** avez-vous des tuyaux OR renseignements sur le meurtre/meurtrier? -**5.** [varnish] enduit *m*; AUT, CHEM & TECH dopant *m*. -**6.** [for dynamite] absorbant *m*.
◇ *comp inf* [drugs]: **~ addict** toxicomane *mf*, drogué *m*, -e *f*; **~ dealer** OR **pusher** revendeur *m*, -euse *f* de drogue, dealer *m*; **~ test** test *m* antidoping.
◇ *vt* -**1.** [drug - horse, person] doper; [- drink, food] mettre une drogue OR un dopant dans; **she was all ~d up** *inf* elle planait complètement. -**2.** AUT, CHEM & TECH doper.
◆ **dope out** *inf vt sep Am* [devise] combiner, bidouiller; [solve] deviner, piger.

dope sheet▽ *n Br journal des courses*.

dopey [ˈdəʊpɪ] (*compar* dopier, *superl* dopiest) = **dopy**.

doppelgänger [ˈdɒplˌgæŋəʳ] *n* double *m (d'une personne vivante)*, sosie *m*.

Doppler effect [ˈdɒpləʳ-] *n* effet *m* Doppler.

dopy [ˈdəʊpɪ] (*compar* dopier, *superl* dopiest) *adj* -**1.** [drugged] drogué, dopé; [sleepy] (à moitié) endormi. -**2.** *inf* [silly] idiot, abruti.

Dorchester [ˈdɔːtʃɪstəʳ] *pr n*: **the ~** *hôtel de luxe à Londres*.

Dorian [ˈdɔːrɪən] ◇ *n* Dorien *m*, -enne *f*.
◇ *adj* LING & MUS dorien.

Doric [ˈdɒrɪk] ◇ *adj* dorique.
◇ *n* dorique *m*.

dorm *inf* [dɔːm] *n abbr of* **dormitory**.

dormancy [ˈdɔːmənsɪ] *n fml* [of animal] état *m* endormi; [of plant] dormance *f*; [of volcano] état *m* inactif.

dormant [ˈdɔːmənt] *adj* -**1.** [idea, passion] qui sommeille; [energy, reserves] inexploité; [disease] à l'état latent; [law] inappliqué; **to lie ~** sommeiller. -**2.** [animal] endormi; [plant] dormant. -**3.** [volcano] en repos, en sommeil. -**4.** HERALD dormant.

dormer ['dɔːməʳ] *n*: ~ (window) lucarne *f*.

dormice ['dɔːmaɪs] *pl* → **dormouse**.

dormie ['dɔːmɪ] *adj* GOLF dormie.

dormitory ['dɔːmətrɪ] (*pl* **dormitories**) ◇ *n* [room] dortoir *m*; *Am* UNIV résidence *f* universitaire.
◇ *comp Br*: ~ town ville-dortoir *f*.

dorm mother *inf n Am* surveillante *f*.

Dormobile® ['dɔːmə,biːl] *n Br* camping-car *m*.

dormouse ['dɔːmaʊs] (*pl* dormice [-maɪs]) *n* loir *m*.

Dors *written abbr of* Dorset.

dorsal ['dɔːsl] ◇ *adj* ANAT, LING & ZOOL dorsal.
◇ *n* dorsale *f*.

dorsal fin *n* nageoire *f* dorsale.

dory ['dɔːrɪ] (*pl* dories) *n* -**1.** [salt water fish] saint-pierre *m inv*, dorée *f*; [fresh water fish] dorée *f*. -**2.** *Am* [boat] doris *m*.

DOS [dɒs] (*abbr of* disk operating system) *n* DOS *m*.

dosage ['dəʊsɪdʒ] *n* [giving of dose] dosage *m*; [amount] dose *f*; [directions on bottle] posologie *f*.

dose [dəʊs] ◇ *n* -**1.** [amount] dose *f*; she took her daily ~ of medicine elle a pris son médicament quotidien; in small/large ~s à faible/haute dose; I can only take him in small ~s je ne peux le supporter qu'à petites doses; with a strong ~ of humour avec beaucoup d'humour. -**2.** [of illness] attaque *f*; a bad ~ of flu une mauvaise grippe. -**3.** ▽ [venereal disease] bléno *f*.
◇ *vt* -**1.** [subj: pharmacist] doser. -**2.** [person] administrer un médicament à; she ~d herself (up) with pills elle s'est bourrée de médicaments.

dosh▽ [dɒʃ] *n Br* fric *m*.

do-si-do [,dəʊsɪ'dəʊ] *n figure de quadrille où les danseurs sont dos à dos*.

doss▽ [dɒs] *Br* ◇ *n* -**1.** [bed] lit *m*, pieu *m*. -**2.** [nap] somme *m*, roupillon *m*. -**3.** [easy thing]: it was a real ~ c'était fastoche.
◇ *vi* coucher, roupiller.
◆ **doss around**▽ *vi insep* glander.
◆ **doss down**▽ *vi insep* coucher, crécher.

dosser▽ ['dɒsəʳ] *n Br* [person] sans-abri *mf inv*, clochard *m*, -e *f*; [house] foyer *m* de sans-abri.

dosshouse *inf* ['dɒshaʊs, *pl* -haʊzɪz] *n Br* foyer *m* de sans-abri.

dossier ['dɒsɪeɪ] *n* dossier *m*, documents *mpl*.

Dostoievsky [,dɒstɔɪ'efskɪ] *pr n* Dostoïevski.

dot [dɒt] (*pt* & *pp* dotted, *cont* dotting) ◇ *n* [gen & MUS] point *m*; [on material] pois *m*; ~, ~, ~ [in punctuation] points de suspension; ~s and dashes [Morse code] points et traits *mpl*
❑ since the year ~ *inf Br* de temps immémorial.
◇ *vt* -**1.** [mark] marquer avec des points, pointiller; [an "i"] mettre un point sur; to ~ one's i's and cross one's t's *fig* mettre les points sur les i. -**2.** [spot] parsemer; the lake was dotted with boats des bateaux étaient dispersés sur le lac; ~ the surface with butter CULIN mettez des morceaux de beurre sur le dessus.
◆ **on the dot** *adv phr*: at 3 o'clock on the ~ à 3 h pile OR tapantes; he always pays right on the ~ il paye toujours recta.

DOT (*abbr of* Department of Transportation) *pr n ministère américain des transports*.

dotage ['dəʊtɪdʒ] *n* gâtisme *m*; to be in one's ~ être gâteux, être retombé en enfance.

dotard ['dəʊtəd] *n* gâteux *m*, -euse *f*.

dote [dəʊt] *vi*: to ~ on sb être fou de qqn, aimer qqn à la folie.

doth [*weak form* dəθ, *strong form* dʌθ] *arch 3rd pers sing* → **do** *vb*.

doting ['dəʊtɪŋ] *adj*: he has a ~ mother sa mère l'aime à la folie.

dot-matrix printer *n* imprimante *f* matricielle.

dotted ['dɒtɪd] *adj* -**1.** [shirt, tie] à pois. -**2.** ~ line ligne *f* en pointillés ‖ AUT ligne *f* discontinue; tear along the ~ line détachez suivant le pointillé. -**3.** MUS: ~ note note *f* pointée; ~ rhythm notes *fpl* pointées.

dottel ['dɒtl] = **dottle**.

dotterel ['dɒtrəl] *n* ORNITH pluvier *m* (guignard); *dial* [person] gourde *f*.

dottle ['dɒtl] *n* culot *m (dans une pipe)*.

dotty *inf* ['dɒtɪ] (*compar* dottier, *superl* dottiest) *adj Br* [crazy] fou, dingue; she's slightly ~ elle travaille du chapeau, elle est toquée; he's absolutely ~ about her il est fou d'elle; he's ~ about steam trains c'est un fana OR un mordu des trains à vapeur.

Douay Bible ['daʊeɪ-] *n* Bible *f* de Douai.

double ['dʌbl] ◇ *adj* -**1.** [twice as large - quantity, portion] double; a ~ whisky un double whisky. -**2.** BOT double. -**3.** [line, row] double; ~ doors, a ~ door une porte à deux battants; an egg with a ~ yolk un œuf à deux jaunes ‖ [with figures, letters] deux fois; ~ five two one [figure] deux fois cinq deux un; [phone number] cinquante-cinq, vingt et un; 'letter' is spelt with a ~ 't' «lettre» s'écrit avec deux «t»; to throw a ~ six/three faire un double six/trois; to be into ~ figures dépasser la dizaine. -**4.** [folded in two] en double, replié; ~ thickness double épaisseur. -**5.** [for two people] pour OR à deux personnes. -**6.** [dual - purpose, advantage] double; [ambiguous] double, ambigu; a word with a ~ meaning un mot à double sens; to lead a ~ life mener une double vie.
◇ *predet* [twice] deux fois plus; she earns ~ my salary elle gagne deux fois plus que moi OR le double de moi; we ordered ~ the usual quantity nous avons commandé le double de la quantité habituelle; food here costs nearly ~ what it does at home la nourriture ici coûte presque le double de chez moi.
◇ *n* -**1.** [twice the amount] double *m*; [of alcohol] double *m*; he charged us ~ il nous a fait payer le double; they pay him ~ if he works nights on le paye (au tarif) double s'il travaille la nuit
❑ at OR on the ~ au pas de course; on the ~! *literal* & *fig* magnez-vous!; ~ or quits quitte ou double. -**2.** [duplicate] double *m*, réplique *f*; [of person] double *m*, sosie *m*; CIN & TV [stand-in] doublure *f*; THEAT [actor with two parts] acteur *m*, -trice *f* qui tient deux rôles. -**3.** [turn] demi-tour *m*. -**4.** [in horse-racing] pari *m* couplé; [in cards games] contre *m*; [in darts] double *m*.
◇ *adv* [in two] en deux; to fold sthg ~ plier qqch en deux; I was bent ~ with pain j'étais plié en deux de douleur ‖ [two of the same]: to see ~ voir double.
◇ *vt* -**1.** [increase] doubler; he ~d my salary il a doublé mon salaire; to ~ the stakes doubler la mise. -**2.** [fold] plier en deux, replier. -**3.** CIN & TV doubler. -**4.** CARDS [bid, opponent] contrer.
◇ *vi* -**1.** [increase] doubler. -**2.** [turn] tourner, faire un crochet. -**3.** CARDS contrer; ~! BRIDGE contre! -**4.** [serve two purposes]: the dining room ~s as a study la salle à manger sert également de bureau; he ~s as the priest and the servant THEAT il joue les rôles du prêtre et du domestique.
◆ **double back** ◇ *vi insep* [animal, person, road] tourner brusquement; he ~d back down a side road il a rebroussé chemin par une petite route; the path ~s back on itself le sentier te ramène sur tes pas.
◇ *vt sep* [sheet, blanket] mettre en double.
◆ **double for** *vt insep* CIN & THEAT doubler.
◆ **double over** = **double up 1**.
◆ **double up** ◇ *vi insep* -**1.** [bend over] se plier, se courber; he ~d up in pain il se plia en deux de douleur; to ~ up with laughter se tordre de rire. -**2.** [share] partager; there weren't enough rooms so we ~d up il n'y avait pas assez de place, alors nous nous sommes mis à deux par chambre.
◇ *vt sep* plier en deux, replier.

double-acting *adj* à double effet.

double agent *n* agent *m* double.

double bar *n* double barre *f*.

double-barrelled *Br*, **double-barreled** *Am* [-'bærəld] *adj* -**1.** [gun] à deux coups; *fig* [question, remark] équivoque. -**2.** *Br* [name] ≃ à particule.

double bass *n* contrebasse *f*.

double bassoon *n* contrebasson *m*.

double bed *n* grand lit *m*, lit *m* à deux places.

double bill *n* double programme *m*.

double bind *n* PSYCH double contrainte *f*; to be caught in a ~ se trouver dans une situation insoluble, être dans une impasse.

double-blind *adj* [experiment, test] en double aveugle; [method] à double insu, à double anonymat.

double boiler *n Am* casserole *f* à double fond; to heat sthg in a ~ faire chauffer qqch au bain-marie.

double-breasted [-'brestɪd] *adj* croisé.

double-check *vi* & *vt* revérifier.
◆ **double check** *n* revérification *f*.

double chin *n* double menton *m*.

double cream *n Br* crème *f* fraîche épaisse.

double-cross *vt* trahir, doubler; he ~ed them il les a doublés.
◆ **double cross** *n* trahison *f*, traîtrise *f*.

double-crosser [-'krɒsəʳ] *n* traître *m*, -esse *f*, faux jeton *m*.

double dagger *n* TYPO diésis *m*.

double date *n* sortie *f* à quatre *(deux couples)*.
◆ **double-date** *vi Am* sortir à quatre *(deux couples)*.

double-dealer *n* fourbe *m*.

double-dealing ◇ *n* fourberie *f*, double jeu *m*.
◇ *adj* fourbe, faux comme un jeton.

double-decker *n* -**1.** *Br* [bus] autobus *m* à impériale. -**2.** *Am* [aircraft] deux-ponts *m*. -**3.** *inf* [sandwich] club sandwich *m*.

double-declutch *vi Br* faire un double débrayage.

double-density *adj* [disk] double densité.

double-digit *adj* à deux chiffres.

double-dutch *inf n Br* charabia *m*, baragouin *m*; it's all ~ to me! c'est de l'hébreu pour moi!

double-dyed *adj lit* invétéré; a ~ villain *fig* une crapule de la pire espèce.

double-edged *adj* [blade, knife, sword] à double tranchant, à deux tranchants; *fig* [compliment, remark] à double tranchant.

double entendre [,duːblɑ̃'tɑ̃dr] *n* mot *m* OR expression *f* à double sens.

double entry *n* comptabilité *f* en partie double; ~ bookkeeping digraphie *f*, comptabilité en partie double.

double exposure *n* surimpression *f*.

double-faced *adj* réversible, à double face.

double fault *n* double faute *f*.
◆ **double-fault** *vi* faire une double faute.

double feature *n séance de cinéma où sont projetés deux longs métrages*.

double first *n Br* ≃ mention *f* très bien *(dans deux disciplines à la fois)*.

double flat *n* double bémol *m*.

double-glaze *vt Br* isoler *(par système de double vitrage)*; to ~ a window poser un double vitrage.

double-glazing *Br* ◇ *n* (*U*) double vitrage *m*; to put in OR to install ~ installer un double vitrage.
◇ *comp* [salesman] de double vitrage.

double helix *n* double hélice *f*.

double indemnity *n Am* indemnité *f* double.

double-jointed *adj* désarticulé.

double knit ◇ *n* tricot *m* double face.
◇ *adj* double face.

double knitting *n laine assez épaisse utilisée en tricot*.

double knot *n* double nœud *m*.

double-lock *vt* fermer à double tour.

double negative *n* double négation *f*.

double-park ◇ *vi* stationner en double file.
◇ *vt* garer en double file.

double parking *n* stationnement *m* en double file.

double pneumonia *n* pneumonie *f* double.

double precision *n* COMPUT *utilisation de deux mots (informatiques) pour représenter un chiffre afin d'obtenir un calcul plus précis.*

double-quick *adj* très rapide; **in ~ time** [move] au pas de course OR de gymnastique; [finish, work] en vitesse, en moins de rien.

double room *n* chambre *f* pour deux personnes.

doubles ['dʌblz] (*pl inv*) *n* double *m*; **to play ~** jouer un double; **a ~ player** un joueur de double; **mixed ~** double mixte; **ladies'/men's ~** double dames/messieurs.

double saucepan *n Br* casserole *f* à double fond; **to cook in a ~** faire cuire au bain-marie.

double sharp *n* double dièse *m*.

double-sided *adj* [disk] double face.

double-space *vt* taper à double interligne; **the text is ~d** le texte est à double interligne.

double spacing *n* double interligne *m*; **in ~** à double interligne.

double standard *n*: **to have ~s** faire deux poids, deux mesures.

double star *n* étoile *f* double.

double stopping *n* double-corde *f*.

doublet ['dʌblɪt] *n* -**1.** [jacket] pourpoint *m*, justaucorps *m*. -**2.** [of words] doublet *m*. -**3.** TYPO doublon *m*. -**4.** [of dice] doublet *m*.

double take *inf n*: **to do a ~** marquer un temps d'arrêt *(par surprise)*; **he did a ~ when I told him** lorsque je le lui ai dit, il a marqué un temps d'arrêt.

double talk *inf n (U)* [ambiguous] *propos ambigus et contournés*; [gibberish] charabia *m*.

doublethink ['dʌbl,θɪŋk] *n raisonnement de mauvaise foi qui contient des contradictions flagrantes.*

double time *n* -**1.** [pay] salaire *m* double; **I get ~ on Sundays** je suis payé le double le dimanche. -**2.** MIL pas *m* redoublé; **to march in ~** marcher à pas redoublés. -**3.** MUS mesure *f* double; **in ~** en mesure double.

doubleton ['dʌbltən] *n* doublette *f*.

double-tongue *vi* MUS faire des doubles coups de langue *(sur un instrument à vent)*.

double vision *n* double vision *f*.

double whammy *inf* [-'wæmɪ] *n* double malédiction *f*.

doubling ['dʌblɪŋ] *n* [of letter, number] redoublement *m*, doublement *m*.

doubloon [dʌ'blu:n] *n* doublon *m*.

doubly ['dʌblɪ] *adv* [twice as much] doublement, deux fois plus; [in two ways] doublement; **she's ~ careful now** elle redouble de prudence maintenant.

doubt [daʊt] ◇ *n* -**1.** [uncertainty - about fact] doute *m*, incertitude *f*; **there is now considerable ~ about the convictions** on a maintenant de sérieux doutes au sujet des condamnations; **beyond all reasonable ~** à n'en pas douter, sans le moindre doute; **to cast ~ on sthg** mettre en doute OR jeter le doute sur qqch; **her honesty is in ~** OR **open to ~** [generally] on a des doutes sur son honnêteté, son honnêteté est sujette à caution; [this time] son honnêteté est mise en doute; **we are in no ~ as to his competence** nous n'avons aucun doute sur ses compétences; **the future of the company is in some ~** l'avenir de l'entreprise est incertain; **if** OR **when in ~** s'il y a un doute, en cas de doute; **when in ~, do nothing** dans le doute, abstiens-toi *prov*; **there is some ~ as to whether they paid** on n'est pas certain qu'ils aient payé; **there is no ~ about it** cela ne fait pas de doute; **there's no ~ (but) that it will be a difficult journey** il n'y a pas de doute que le voyage sera pénible; **no ~** sans doute; **he'll no ~ be late** il sera sûrement en retard; **there is room for ~** il est permis de douter; **without (any) ~** sans aucun OR le moindre doute. -**2.** [feeling of distrust] doute *m*; **I have my ~s about him** j'ai des doutes sur lui OR à son sujet; **she has her ~s (about) whether it's true** elle doute que cela soit vrai; **I have no ~** OR **~s about it** je n'en doute pas.
◇ *vt* -**1.** [consider unlikely]: **I ~ (whether) she'll be there** je doute qu'elle soit là; **she'll be there – I don't ~ it** elle sera là – je n'en doute pas OR j'en suis certain; **I ~ it** j'en doute; **I never once ~ed that they would succeed** je n'ai pas douté une seule fois qu'ils réussiraient; **I ~ if it makes him happy** je doute que cela le rende heureux. -**2.** [distrust] douter de; **there was no ~ing their sincerity** on ne pouvait pas mettre en doute leur sincérité; **she began to ~ the evidence of her own eyes** elle n'en croyait pas ses yeux.
◇ *vi* douter, avoir des doutes.

doubter ['daʊtəʳ] *n* incrédule *mf*, sceptique *mf*.

doubtful ['daʊtfʊl] *adj* -**1.** [unlikely] improbable, douteux. -**2.** [uncertain - person] incertain, indécis; **I'm ~ about his chances** je doute de OR j'ai des doutes sur ses chances; **we're ~ about accepting** nous hésitons à accepter; **it's ~ whether they're really serious** il est douteux qu'ils soient vraiment sérieux, on ne sait pas s'ils sont vraiment sérieux; **she looked ~** elle avait l'air peu convaincu. -**3.** [questionable - answer, results] douteux, discutable. -**4.** [dubious - person] louche, suspect; [- affair] douteux, louche; **a joke in ~ taste** une plaisanterie d'un goût douteux.

doubtfully ['daʊtfʊlɪ] *adv* [uncertainly] avec doute, d'un air de doute; [indecisively] avec hésitation, de façon indécise.

doubtfulness ['daʊtfʊlnɪs] *n* -**1.** [uncertainty] incertitude *f*; [hesitation] indécision *f*. -**2.** [dubiousness] caractère *m* équivoque OR douteux.

doubting ['daʊtɪŋ] *adj* sceptique, incrédule.

doubting Thomas *n* Thomas *m* l'incrédule; **don't be such a ~** ne fais pas l'incrédule, ne fais pas comme saint Thomas.

doubtless ['daʊtlɪs] *adv* [certainly] sans aucun OR le moindre doute; [probably] (très) probablement.

douche [du:ʃ] ◇ *n* MED lavage *m* interne, douche *f*; [instrument] poire *f* à injections.
◇ *vt* doucher.

dough [dəʊ] *n* -**1.** CULIN pâte *f*; **bread ~** pâte à pain. -**2.** *inf* [money] blé *m*.

doughboy ['dəʊ,bɔɪ] *n* -**1.** CULIN boulette *f* (de pâte). -**2.** *inf Am* MIL sammy *m*.

doughnut ['dəʊnʌt] *n* beignet *m*.

doughty ['daʊtɪ] (*compar* **doughtier**, *superl* **doughtiest**) *adj lit* vaillant.

doughy ['dəʊɪ] (*compar* **doughier**, *superl* **doughiest**) *adj* -**1.** [consistency] pâteux; [bread] mal cuit. -**2.** [complexion] terreux.

dour [dʊəʳ] *adj* [sullen] renfrogné; [stern] austère, dur; [stubborn] buté.

dourly ['dʊəlɪ] *adv* [look] d'un air dur OR renfrogné; [say] d'un ton dur OR maussade.

douse [daʊs] *vt* -**1.** [fire] éteindre. -**2.** [drench] tremper, inonder.

dove[1] [dʌv] *n* ORNITH & POL colombe *f*.

dove[2] [dəʊv] *Am pt* → **dive**.

dovecot(e) ['dʌvkɒt] *n* colombier *m*, pigeonnier *m*.

dove-grey *adj* gris perle *(inv)*.

Dover ['dəʊvəʳ] *pr n* Douvres.

Dover sole *n* sole *f* ZOOL.

dovetail ['dʌvteɪl] ◇ *vt* TECH assembler à queue d'aronde; [fit] faire concorder, raccorder; **he managed to ~ his plans with hers** il s'est débrouillé pour accorder OR faire concorder ses projets avec les siens.
◇ *vi* -**1.** TECH se raccorder; **to ~ into** se raccorder à. -**2.** [combine] bien cadrer, concorder; **the two projects ~ nicely** les deux projets se rejoignent parfaitement.
◇ *n* TECH queue-d'aronde *f*; **a ~ joint** un assemblage à queue-d'aronde.

dowager ['daʊədʒəʳ] *n* douairière *f*; **the ~ duchess** la duchesse douairière.

dowdily ['daʊdɪlɪ] *adv* de façon démodée.

dowdiness ['daʊdɪnɪs] *n* manque *m* d'élégance OR de distinction.

dowdy ['daʊdɪ] (*compar* **dowdier**, *superl* **dowdiest**, *pl* **dowdies**) ◇ *adj* [person] sans chic, inélégant; [dress] peu flatteur, sans chic.
◇ *n dated* femme *f* sans chic.

dowel ['daʊəl] ◇ *n*: **~ (pin)** cheville *f* en bois, goujon *m*.
◇ *vt* assembler avec des goujons, goujonner.

dowel(l)ing ['daʊəlɪŋ] *n* -**1.** [act] assemblage *m* à goujons, goujonnage *m*. -**2.** [wood] tourillon *m*.

dower house ['daʊəʳ-] *n Br* petit manoir *m* (de douairière).

Dow-Jones [,daʊ'dʒəʊnz] *pr n*: **the ~ (average** OR **index)** l'indice *m* Dow Jones.

down[1] [daʊn] ◇ *prep* -**1.** [towards lower level of]: **a line ~ the middle of the page** une ligne verticale au milieu de la page; **to go ~ the steps/the escalator/the mountain** descendre l'escalier/l'escalier mécanique/la montagne; **she fell ~ the stairs** elle est tombée dans l'escalier; **tears ran ~ her face** des larmes coulaient le long de son visage; **her hair hung ~ her back** les cheveux lui tombaient dans le dos || [into]: **to go ~ the plughole** passer par le trou (de l'évier/de la baignoire *etc*); **the rabbit disappeared back ~ its hole** le lapin a redisparu dans son trou. -**2.** [at lower level of] en bas de; **it's ~ the stairs** c'est en bas de l'escalier; **to work ~ a mine** travailler au fond d'une mine; **they live ~ the street** ils habitent plus loin OR plus bas dans la rue. -**3.** [along] le long de; **he walked ~ the street** il a descendu la rue; **look ~ the corridor** regardez le long du couloir. -**4.** [through] à travers; **~ (through) the ages** à travers les âges. -**5.** *inf Br* [to] à; **they went ~ the shops** ils sont partis faire des courses.
◇ *adv* -**1.** [downwards] vers le bas, en bas; **~!** [to dog] couché!, bas les pattes!; **~ and ~** de plus en plus bas; **to come** OR **go ~** descendre; **my trousers keep slipping ~** mon pantalon n'arrête pas de descendre OR tomber. -**2.** [on lower level] en bas; **~ at the bottom of the hill/page** en bas de la colline/de la page; **~ there** là-bas; **I'm ~ here** je suis ici en bas; **she lives three floors ~** elle habite trois étages plus bas; **his office is three doors ~ on the left** [along passage] son bureau est trois portes plus loin sur la gauche; **the blinds are ~** les stores sont baissés || [downstairs]: **I'll be ~ in a minute** je descends dans un instant; **they aren't ~ yet** ils ne sont pas encore descendus || [on the ground or floor] à terre; **he was ~ for a count of eight** il est resté à terre le temps de compter jusqu'à huit ❑ **to hit a man when he's ~** frapper un homme à terre. -**3.** [facing downwards] vers le bas, dessous; **smooth side ~** le côté lisse dessous. -**4.** [reduced, lower]: **prices are ~** les prix ont baissé; **the pound is ~ two cents against the dollar** FIN la livre a baissé de deux cents par rapport au dollar || [below expected, desired level]: **the tyres are ~** [underinflated] les pneus sont dégonflés; [flat] les pneus sont à plat; **the cashier is £10 ~** il manque 10 livres au caissier; **we were two goals ~ at half-time** FTBL nous perdions par deux buts à la mi-temps. -**5.** [on paper]: **get it ~ in writing** OR **on paper** mettez-le par écrit; **it's ~ in my diary/on the calendar** c'est dans mon agenda/sur le calendrier; **he's ~ to speak at the conference** il est inscrit en tant qu'intervenant à la conférence. -**6.** [from city, the north]: **she came ~ from Berlin** elle est arrivée de Berlin; **we're going ~ south** nous descendons vers le sud; **they're going ~ to the coast** ils descendent sur la côte; **to go ~ East** *Am* aller au nord-est de la Nouvelle-Angleterre || *Br* UNIV: **she came ~ from Oxford** [on vacation] elle est descendue d'Oxford; [graduated] elle est sortie d'Oxford. -**7.** [out of action - machine, computer] en panne; **the wires are ~** les lignes sont coupées; **the computer has gone ~** l'ordinateur est tombé en panne. -**8.** [paid]: **he paid** OR **put £5 ~** [whole amount] il a payé 5 livres comptant; [as deposit] il a versé (un acompte de) 5 livres ❑ **5 ~ and**

3 to go ça fait 5, il en reste 3. -**9.** [ill]: **he's (gone) ~ with flu** il est au lit avec la grippe. -**10.** *phr*: **to be ~ on sb** *inf* être monté contre qqn; **she's ~ on her luck** elle n'a pas de chance OR de veine en ce moment; **~ with...!** à bas...!; **~ with the system!** à bas le système!
◇ *adj* -**1.** [depressed] déprimé, malheureux; **to feel ~** avoir le cafard. -**2.** *Br* [train] *en provenance d'une grande ville*. -**3.** [elevator] qui descend.
◇ *vt* -**1.** [knock down - opponent] mettre à terre; [- object, target] faire tomber; **the pilot ~ed two enemy aircraft** le pilote a descendu deux avions ennemis. -**2.** [drink, eat]: **he ~ed three beers** il a descendu trois bières.
◇ *n* -**1.** [setback] revers *m*, bas *m*. -**2.** *phr*: **to have a ~ on sb** *inf* avoir une dent contre qqn.
◆ **down for** *prep phr*: **she's ~ for physics** elle est inscrite au cours de physique; **they've got me ~ for the 200 m hurdles** ils m'ont inscrit au 200 m haies; **the meeting is ~ for today** la réunion est prévue pour aujourd'hui.
◆ **down to** *prep phr* -**1.** [through to and including] jusqu'à; **~ to the smallest details** jusqu'aux moindres détails; **she sold everything right ~ to the house** elle a tout vendu, y compris la maison; **from the richest ~ to the poorest** du plus riche (jusqu') au plus pauvre; **from the boss ~ to the office boy** depuis le patron jusqu'au garçon de bureau; **from the Middle Ages ~ to the present** du OR depuis le Moyen Âge jusqu'à nos jours. -**2.** [reduced to]: **I'm ~ to my last pound** il ne me reste qu'une livre; **the team was ~ to 10 men** l'équipe était réduite à 10 hommes. -**3.** [indicating responsibility]: **it's ~ to you now** c'est à toi de jouer maintenant *fig*; **any breakages will be ~ to you** si vous cassez quelque chose, c'est vous qui paierez les dégâts.

down[2] [daʊn] *n* -**1.** [on bird, person, plant, fruit] duvet *m*. -**2.** [hill] colline *f* dénudée; [sand dune] dune *f*.

down-and-out ◇ *adj* indigent, sans ressources; **'Down and Out in Paris and London'** *Orwell* 'Dans la dèche à Paris et à Londres'.
◇ *n* clochard *m*, -e *f*; **the ~** OR **~s** les sans-abri *mpl*.

down-at-heel *adj* [shabby] miteux; [shoe] éculé.

downbeat ['daʊnbiːt] ◇ *n* MUS temps *m* frappé.
◇ *adj inf* -**1.** [gloomy - person] abattu, triste; [- story] pessimiste. -**2.** [relaxed - person] décontracté, flegmatique; [- situation] décontracté.

downcast ['daʊnkɑːst] ◇ *adj* -**1.** [dejected] abattu, démoralisé. -**2.** [eyes, look] baissé.
◇ *n* MIN puits *m* d'aérage.

downdraught ['daʊndrɑːft] *n Br* vent *m* qui descend des montagnes.

downer ['daʊnəʳ] *n* -**1.** *inf* [experience] expérience *f* déprimante; **to be on a ~** faire de la déprime, être déprimé; **that film's a real ~** ce film est à vous donner le cafard. -**2.** ▽ [drug] tranquillisant *m*, sédatif *m*.

downfall ['daʊnfɔːl] *n* -**1.** [of person, institution] chute *f*, ruine *f*; [of dream, hopes] effondrement *m*; **drink was his ~** la boisson l'a perdu. -**2.** [of rain, snow] chute *f*.

downgrade ['daʊngreɪd] ◇ *vt* -**1.** [job] dévaloriser, déclasser; [person] rétrograder; [hotel] déclasser. -**2.** [belittle] rabaisser.
◇ *n* descente *f*.

downhearted [,daʊn'hɑːtɪd] *adj* abattu, découragé.

downhill [,daʊn'hɪl] ◇ *adv*: **to go ~** [car, road] descendre, aller en descendant; [business] péricliter ‖ *fig*: **television is going rapidly ~** la télévision baisse OR se dégrade de plus en plus; **he let himself go ~ after he lost his job** il a dégringolé OR il s'est laissé aller après avoir perdu son travail; **her health went rapidly ~** sa santé déclina OR baissa rapidement.
◇ *adj* -**1.** [road] en pente, incliné; [walk] en descente; *fig*: **when you get to 40, it's ~ all the way** passé la quarantaine, vous ne faites plus que décliner; **it should all be ~ from now on** maintenant ça devrait aller comme sur des roulettes. -**2.** [in skiing]: **~ skiing** ski *m* alpin; **~ race** descente *f*; **~ racer** OR **skier** descendeur *m*, -euse *f*.
◇ *n* [of road] descente *f*; [in skiing] descente *f*.

down-home *inf adj Am* (des États) du Sud; *pej* plouc.

Downing Street ['daʊnɪŋ-] *pr n* Downing Street.

DOWNING STREET:
C'est à Downing Street à Londres que se trouvent les résidences officielles du Premier ministre, au nº 10, et du ministre des Finances, au nº 11. Le terme «Downing Street» est souvent employé pour désigner le gouvernement.

---

down-in-the-mouth *adj*: **to be ~** être abattu; **she looks ~** elle a l'air plutôt abattue.

downland ['daʊnlænd] *n (U)* collines *fpl* herbeuses.

download [,daʊn'ləʊd] *vt* COMPUT télécharger.

downloadable [,daʊn'ləʊdəbl] *adj* COMPUT téléchargeable.

downloading [,daʊn'ləʊdɪŋ] *n* COMPUT téléchargement *m*.

down-market *adj* [product] bas de gamme; [book] grande diffusion *(inv)*; **it's a rather ~ area** ce n'est pas un quartier très chic.

down payment *n* acompte *m*; **to make a ~ on sthg** verser un acompte pour qqch.

downpipe ['daʊnpaɪp] *n Br* (tuyau *m* de) descente *f*.

downplay ['daʊnpleɪ] *vt* [event, person] minimiser l'importance de; [situation] dédramatiser.

downpour ['daʊnpɔːʳ] *n* averse *f*, déluge *m*.

downright ['daʊnraɪt] ◇ *adj* -**1.** [lie] effronté, flagrant; [refusal] catégorique; **~ stupidity** bêtise crasse; **a ~ fool** un crétin achevé. -**2.** [of person, speech] franc, direct.
◇ *adv* [as intensifier] franchement, carrément; **the sales assistant was ~ rude** la vendeuse a été franchement grossière.

downriver [,daʊn'rɪvəʳ] ◇ *adj* en aval.
◇ *adv* vers l'aval, en aval.

downs [daʊnz] *n pl Br*: **the ~** les Downs *fpl*; **the South/North Downs** les Downs du Sud/du Nord.

downshift [,daʊn'ʃɪft] *vi Am* rétrograder.

downside ['daʊnsaɪd] *n* -**1.** [underside] dessous *m*; **~ up** *Am* sens dessous dessus. -**2.** [trend]: **prices have tended to be on the ~** la tendance des prix est plutôt à la baisse. -**3.** [disadvantage] inconvénient *m*.

downsize ['daʊnsaɪz] *vt* [company] réduire les effectifs de.

downspout ['daʊnspaʊt] *n Am* (tuyau *m* de) descente *f*.

Down's syndrome [daʊnz-] *n* trisomie 21 *f*; **~ baby** bébé *m* trisomique.

downstage [,daʊn'steɪdʒ] ◇ *adj* du devant de la scène.
◇ *adv* vers le devant de la scène; **~ from her** vers le devant de la scène par rapport à elle.
◇ *n* avant-scène *f*.

downstairs [,daʊn'steəz] ◇ *adv* -**1.** [gen] en bas (de l'escalier); **to come** OR **to go ~** descendre (les escaliers); **she ran ~** elle a descendu l'escalier OR elle est descendue en courant; **he fell ~** il a dégringolé l'escalier. -**2.** [on lower floor] à l'étage en dessous OR inférieur; [on ground floor] au rez-de-chaussée; **the family ~** la famille du dessous.
◇ *adj* -**1.** [gen] en bas; **I'm using the ~ phone** j'utilise le téléphone d'en bas. -**2.** [of lower floor] de l'étage au-dessous OR inférieur; [of ground floor] du rez-de-chaussée.
◇ *n* rez-de-chaussée *m inv*.

downstate ['daʊnsteɪt] *Am* ◇ *adj* [in the country] de la campagne; [in the south] du sud de l'État.
◇ *adv* [go] vers le sud; [be] dans le sud.
◇ *n* campagne *f*, sud *m* de l'État.

downstream [,daʊn'striːm] ◇ *adv* en aval, vers l'aval; **the boat drifted ~** le bateau était poussé par le courant.
◇ *adj* en aval.

downstroke ['daʊnstrəʊk] *n* [of piston] course *f* descendante; [in handwriting] plein *m*.

downswept ['daʊnswept] *adj* surbaissé.

downswing ['daʊnswɪŋ] *n* -**1.** [trend] tendance *f* à la baisse, baisse *f*. -**2.** GOLF mouvement *m* descendant.

downtime ['daʊntaɪm] *n (U)* période *f* de non-fonctionnement *(d'une machine, d'une usine)*.

down-to-earth *adj* terre à terre *(inv)*, réaliste; **she's very ~** elle a les pieds sur terre.

downtown [,daʊn'taʊn] *Am* ◇ *n* centre-ville *m*.
◇ *adj*: **~ New York** le centre OR centre-ville de New York.
◇ *adv* en ville.

downtrend ['daʊntrend] *n* baisse *f*.

downtrodden ['daʊn,trɒdn] *adj* -**1.** [person] opprimé. -**2.** [grass] piétiné.

downturn ['daʊntɜːn] *n* baisse *f*.

down under *inf Br adv*: **to go/to live ~** [to Australia] aller/vivre en Australie; [to New Zealand] aller/vivre en Nouvelle-Zélande; [gen] aller/vivre aux antipodes.

downward ['daʊnwəd] ◇ *adj* [movement] vers le bas; *fig*: **a ~ trend** une tendance à la baisse; **the economy is on a ~ path** l'économie est sur une mauvaise pente.
◇ *adv* = **downwards**.

downwards ['daʊnwədz] *adv* vers le bas, de haut en bas; **she put the letter face ~** elle a posé la lettre à l'envers; **the garden slopes ~ away from the house** le jardin descend en pente depuis la maison; **the road drops sharply ~** la route descend brusquement ‖ *fig*: **everyone from the president ~** tout le monde depuis le président jusqu'en bas de la hiérarchie; **from the Middle Ages ~** depuis le Moyen Âge; **we will have to revise our estimates ~** il faudra que nous revoyions nos estimations à la baisse; **prices started to spiral ~** les prix commencèrent à dégringoler.

downwash ['daʊnwɒʃ] *n* déflexion *f* vers le bas.

downwind [,daʊn'wɪnd] *adj* & *adv* sous le vent; **to be ~ of sthg** être sous le vent de qqch.

downy ['daʊnɪ] (*compar* **downier**, *superl* **downiest**) *adj* -**1.** [leaf, skin] couvert de duvet, duveté; [fruit] duveté, velouté. -**2.** [fluffy] duveteux. -**3.** [filled with down] garni de duvet.

dowry ['daʊərɪ] (*pl* **dowries**) *n* dot *f*.

dowse [daʊz] ◇ *vi* [for water, for minerals] faire de la radiesthésie, prospecter à la baguette.
◇ *vt* = **douse**.

dowser ['daʊzəʳ] *n* [for water] sourcier *m*, radiesthésiste *mf*; [for minerals] radiesthésiste *mf*.

dowsing ['daʊzɪŋ] *n* radiesthésie *f*.

dowsing rod *n* baguette *f* (de sourcier).

doxology [dɒk'sɒlədʒɪ] *n* doxologie *f*.

doxy ['dɒksɪ] (*pl* **doxies**) *n* -**1.** [doctrine] doctrine *f*. -**2.** ▽ *arch* [prostitute] catin *f*; [mistress] maîtresse *f*.

doyen ['dɔɪən] *n* doyen *m* (d'âge).

doyenne ['dɔɪen] *n* doyenne *f* (d'âge).

doyly ['dɔɪlɪ] (*pl* **doylies**) = **doily**.

doz. (*written abbr of* **dozen**) douz.

doze [dəʊz] ◇ *vi* sommeiller.
◇ *n* somme *m*; **I had a little ~** j'ai fait un petit somme.
◆ **doze off** *vi insep* s'assoupir.

dozen [dʌzn] *n* douzaine *f*; **a ~ eggs** une douzaine d'œufs; **30 pence a ~** 30 pence la douzaine; **half a ~** une demi-douzaine; **have some more, there are ~s of them** reprenez-en, il y en a beaucoup OR des tas; **I've told you a ~ times** je te l'ai dit vingt fois; **there are ~s of men like him** des hommes comme lui, on en trouve à la douzaine.

dozer *inf* ['dəʊzəʳ] *n Br* bulldozer *m*, bouteur *m* *offic*.

dozy ['dəʊzɪ] (*compar* dozier, *superl* doziest) *adj* -**1.** [drowsy] à moitié endormi, assoupi. -**2.** *inf* [stupid] lent, engourdi.

DP *n* -**1.** *abbr of* data processing. -**2.** *abbr of* disabled person.

DPh *written abbr of* Doctor of Philosophy.

DPH (*abbr of* Diploma in Public Health) *n* diplôme *m* de santé publique.

DPhil [ˌdiː'fɪl] = **DPh**.

DPP *pr n abbr of* Director of Public Prosecutions.

DPT (*abbr of* diphtheria, pertussis, tetanus) *n* DCT.

DPW (*abbr of* Department of Public Works) *pr n* ≃ ministère *m* de l'Équipement.

dr *written abbr of* debtor.

Dr -**1.** (*written abbr of* Doctor): ~ Jones [on envelope] Dr Jones; Dear ~ Jones [in letter] Monsieur, Madame; [less formal] Cher Monsieur, Chère Madame; [if acquainted] Cher Docteur. -**2.** *written abbr of* drive.

drab [dræb] (*compar* drabber, *superl* drabbest)
◇ *adj* -**1.** [colour] terne, fade; [surroundings] morne, triste. -**2.** [shabby] miteux.
◇ *n* -**1.** [colour] gris-vert *m*, gris-beige *m*. -**2.** [cloth] grosse toile *f* bise. -**3.** *arch* [woman] souillon *f*.

drabble ['dræbl] ◇ *vt* salir, crotter.
◇ *vi* devenir sale, se salir, se crotter.

drabness ['dræbnɪs] *n* [of colour] caractère *m* OR aspect *m* terne, fadeur *f*; [of surroundings] caractère *m* OR aspect *m* morne, tristesse *f*, grisaille *f*.

drachm [dræm] *n* -**1.** [gen & PHARM] drachme *m*. -**2.** [currency] drachme *f*.

drachma ['drækmə] (*pl* drachmas OR drachmae [-miː]) *n* -**1.** [currency] drachme *f*. -**2.** [gen & PHARM] drachme *m*.

draconian [drə'kəʊnjən] *adj* draconien.

Dracula ['drækjʊlə] *pr n* Dracula.

draft [drɑːft] ◇ *n* -**1.** [of letter] brouillon *m*; [of novel, speech] premier jet *m*, ébauche *f*; [of plan] avant-projet *m*; **this is only the first ~** ceci n'est qu'une ébauche; **~ quality** COMPUT qualité *f* brouillon. -**2.** COMM & FIN traite *f*, effet *m*; **a ~ on my bank in England for £500** une traite de 500 livres sur ma banque en Angleterre. -**3.** MIL [detachment] détachement *m*. -**4.** *Am* MIL conscription *f*; **he left in order to avoid the ~** il est parti pour éviter de faire son service. -**5.** *Am* = **draught**.
◇ *vt* -**1.** [draw up - first version] faire le brouillon de, rédiger; [- diagram] dresser; [- plan] esquisser, dresser; JUR [contract, will] rédiger, dresser; **to ~ a bill** préparer un projet de loi. -**2.** [gen & MIL] détacher, désigner; **to ~ sb to sthg/to do sthg** détacher qqn à qqch/pour faire qqch. -**3.** *Am* MIL [enlist] appeler (sous les drapeaux), incorporer; **he was ~ed into the army** il fut appelé sous les drapeaux.
◇ *comp* [version] préliminaire; **~ letter** [gen] brouillon *m* de lettre; [formal] projet *m* de lettre; **~ treaty** projet *m* de convention.

draft board *n Am* conseil *m* de révision.

draft card *n Am* ordre *m* d'incorporation.

draft dodger *n Am* réfractaire *m*.

draftee [ˌdrɑːf'tiː] *n Am* recrue *f*.

draft resister *n Am* réfractaire *m* MIL.

draftsman (*pl* draftsmen) *etc Am* = **draughtsman**.

drafty (*compar* draftier, *superl* draftiest) *etc Am* = **draughty**.

drag [dræg] (*pt* & *pp* dragged, *cont* dragging)
◇ *vt* -**1.** [pull] traîner, tirer; **to ~ sthg on** OR **along the ground** traîner qqch par terre; **he dragged me to a concert** il m'a traîné OR entraîné à un concert; **stop dragging your feet!** arrête de traîner les pieds!; **don't ~ me into this!** ne me mêlez pas à vos histoires!; **I had to ~ the truth out of her** il m'a fallu lui arracher la vérité; **to ~ anchor** NAUT chasser sur ses ancres ❑ **the government has been accused of dragging its feet** OR **heels over the issue** on a accusé le gouvernement de montrer peu d'empressement à s'occuper de la question; **to ~ sb's name through the mud** traîner qqn dans la boue. -**2.** [search] draguer; **they dragged the lake for the body** ils ont dragué le lac à la recherche du corps.
◇ *vi* -**1.** [trail] traîner (par terre); [anchor] chasser. -**2.** [hang behind] traîner, rester à l'arrière. -**3.** [search] draguer. -**4.** [go on and on] traîner, s'éterniser. -**5.** AUT [brakes] frotter, gripper, se gripper.
◇ *n* -**1.** [pull] tirage *m*; AERON, AUT & NAUT résistance *f*, traînée *f*. -**2.** [dredge] drague *f*; [sledge] traîneau *m*; AGR [harrow] herse *f*; NAUT araignée *f*. -**3.** [brake] sabot *m* OR patin *m* de frein. -**4.** [handicap] entrave *f*, frein *m*; **unemployment is a ~ on the economy** le chômage est un frein pour l'économie. -**5.** [trail of fox] piste *f*. -**6.** *inf* [bore]: **don't invite him, he's a real ~!** ne l'invite pas, c'est un casse-pieds fini!; **the exams are a real ~** quelle barbe ces examens!; **what a ~** quelle barbe!, c'est la barbe! -**7.** *inf* [puff on cigarette] bouffée *f*, taffe *f*; **I had a ~ on** OR **of his cigarette** j'ai tiré une bouffée de sa cigarette. -**8.** *inf* [women's clothing]: **in ~** en travesti. -**9.** *inf Am* [street]: **the main ~** la rue principale. -**10.** ▽ *Am* [influence] piston *m*; **she has a lot of ~** elle a le bras long; **use your ~** usez de votre influence.
◇ *comp inf* [disco, show] de travestis; **~ artist** artiste *m* de spectacles de travestis.

◆ **drag along** *vt sep* -**1.** [chair, toy] tirer, traîner; [person] traîner, entraîner. -**2. to ~ o.s. along** se traîner.

◆ **drag apart** *vt sep* séparer de force.

◆ **drag away** *vt sep* emmener de force; **I couldn't ~ him away from his work** je ne pouvais pas l'arracher à son travail.

◆ **drag down** *vt sep* -**1.** [lower] entraîner (en bas); **being rude only ~s you down to his level** être grossier ne fait que vous rabaisser à son niveau. -**2.** [weaken] affaiblir; [depress] déprimer, décourager.

◆ **drag in** *vt sep* apporter (de force); **he insisted on dragging in the issue of housing** il voulait à tout prix mettre la question du logement sur le tapis.

◆ **drag on** ◇ *vi insep* se prolonger, s'éterniser; **don't let the matter ~ on** ne laissez pas traîner l'affaire; **the day dragged on** la journée s'éternisait OR n'en finissait pas.
◇ *vt insep*: **to ~ on a cigarette** tirer sur une cigarette.

◆ **drag out** *vt sep* [prolong] faire traîner; **to ~ out talks** faire traîner des négociations.

◆ **drag up** *vt sep* -**1.** [affair, story] remettre sur le tapis, ressortir. -**2.** *inf Br* [child] élever à la diable OR tant bien que mal; **where were you dragged up?** *hum* où donc as-tu été élevé?

drag factor *n* AERON & AUT coefficient *m* de traînée.

draggy *inf* ['drægɪ] (*compar* draggier, *superl* draggiest) *adj Br* [boring] ennuyeux, assommant; [listless] mou, avachi.

drag hunt *n* drag *m*.

dragnet ['drægnet] *n* -**1.** [for fish] seine *f*, drège *f*; [for game] tirasse *f*. -**2.** [for criminals] rafle *f*.

dragoman ['drægəʊmən] (*pl* dragomen [-mən]) *n* drogman *m*.

dragon ['drægən] *n* MYTH, ZOOL & *fig* dragon *m*.

dragonfly ['drægənflaɪ] (*pl* dragonflies) *n* libellule *f*.

dragoon [drə'guːn] ◇ *n* dragon *m*.
◇ *vt* [force] contraindre, forcer; **he ~ed us into going** il nous a contraints à y aller.

drag queen *inf n* travelo *m*.

drag race *n* course *f* de dragsters.

drag racer *n participant à des courses de dragsters*.

dragrope ['drægrəʊp] *n* AERON guiderope *m*.

dragster ['drægstəʳ] *n* voiture *f* à moteur gonflé, dragster *m*.

dragsville *inf* ['drægzvɪl] *n Am dated*: **it was ~** c'était casse-pieds OR la barbe.

drain [dreɪn] ◇ *n* -**1.** [in house] canalisation *f* OR tuyau *m* d'évacuation; [of dishwasher] tuyau *m* de vidange; [outside house] puisard *m*; [sewer] égout *m*; [grid in street] bouche *f* d'égout; **to go down the ~**: **the family business went down the ~** l'entreprise familiale a fait faillite; **all our plans went down the ~** tous nos projets sont tombés à l'eau; **to laugh like a ~** rire comme une baleine. -**2.** AGR & MED drain *m*. -**3.** [depletion] perte *f*, épuisement *m*; **a ~ on resources** une ponction sur les ressources; **all that travelling was a terrible ~ on him** tous ces voyages l'ont terriblement épuisé.
◇ *vt* -**1.** [dry - dishes, vegetables] égoutter; [- land] drainer, assécher; [- reservoir] vider, mettre à sec; [- mine] drainer; [- oil tank] vider, vidanger; AGR & MED drainer; **well ~ed soil** sol *m* bien drainé; **she ~ed her glass** elle a vidé son verre OR a tout bu jusqu'à la dernière goutte; **~ed weight** COMM poids *m* net égoutté. -**2.** [deplete] épuiser; **to ~ sb of his/her strength** épuiser qqn; **the war ~ed the country of its resources** la guerre a saigné le pays.
◇ *vi* -**1.** [colour] disparaître; [blood] s'écouler; **the colour ~ed from her face** son visage a blêmi. -**2.** [dishes, vegetables] s'égoutter; **leave the dishes to ~** laisse égoutter la vaisselle.

◆ **drain away** ◇ *vi insep* [liquid] s'écouler; [hope, strength] s'épuiser.
◇ *vt sep* faire écouler.

◆ **drain off** ◇ *vt sep* -**1.** [liquid] faire écouler; [dishes, vegetables] égoutter. -**2.** AGR & MED drainer.
◇ *vi insep* s'écouler.

drainage ['dreɪnɪdʒ] *n* (*U*) -**1.** [process] drainage *m*, assèchement *m*. -**2.** [system - in house] système *m* d'évacuation des eaux; [- in town] système *m* d'égouts; [- of land] système *m* de drainage; GEOL système *m* hydrographique. -**3.** [sewage] eaux *fpl* usées, vidanges *fpl*.

drainage area, **drainage basin** *n* bassin *m* hydrographique.

drainboard ['dreɪnbɔːrd] *Am* = **drainer**.

drained [dreɪnd] *adj* épuisé, éreinté; **he looked tired and ~** il avait l'air fatigué et à bout de forces; **the incident left me emotionally ~** l'incident m'a épuisé nerveusement.

drainer ['dreɪnəʳ], **draining board** *n* égouttoir *m*.

draining ['dreɪnɪŋ] *adj* [person, task] épuisant.

drainpipe ['dreɪnpaɪp] *n* [from roof] (tuyau *m* de) descente *f*; [from sink] tuyau *m* d'écoulement; AGR [on land] drain *m*.

drainpipe trousers *npl Br* pantalon-cigarette *m*.

drake [dreɪk] *n* canard *m* (mâle).

Dralon® ['dreɪlɒn] *n* Dralon® *m*.

dram [dræm] *n* -**1.** [gen & PHARM] drachme *m*. -**2.** *inf* [drop] goutte *f*; **a ~ (of whisky)** un petit verre (de whisky).

drama ['drɑːmə] *n* -**1.** [theatre] théâtre *m*; **she teaches ~** elle enseigne l'art dramatique; **Spanish ~** le théâtre espagnol; **~ critic** critique *m* de théâtre; **~ school** école *f* de théâtre. -**2.** [play] pièce *f* (de théâtre), drame *m*. -**3.** [situation] drame *m*. -**4.** [excitement] drame *m*.

dramatic [drə'mætɪk] *adj* -**1.** LITERAT, MUS & THEAT dramatique; **the ~ works of Racine** le théâtre de Racine. -**2.** [effect, entry] théâtral, dramatique; [change] remarquable, spectaculaire; **the story took a ~ turn** l'histoire prit un tour dramatique.

dramatically [drə'mætɪklɪ] *adv* -**1.** LITERAT, MUS & THEAT du point de vue théâtral. -**2.** [act, speak] de manière dramatique, dramatiquement; [change] de manière remarquable OR spectaculaire.

dramatic irony *n* ironie *f* dramatique.

dramatics [drə'mætɪks] ◇ *n* (*U*) THEAT art *m* dramatique, dramaturgie *f*.
◇ *npl fig* [behaviour] comédie *f*, cirque *m*.

dramatis personae [ˌdrɑːmətɪspɜː'səʊnaɪ] *npl* personnages *mpl* (*d'une pièce ou d'un roman*).

dramatist ['dræmətɪst] *n* auteur *m* dramatique, dramaturge *m*.

dramatization [ˌdræmətaɪ'zeɪʃn] *n* -**1.** [for theatre] adaptation *f* pour la scène; [for film] adaptation *f* pour l'écran; [for television] adaptation *f* pour la télévision. -**2.** [exaggeration] dramatisation *f*.

dramatize, -ise ['dræmətaɪz] ◇ *vt* -**1.** [for theatre] adapter pour la scène; [for film] adapter pour l'écran; [for television] adapter pour la télévision. -**2.** [exaggerate] faire un drame de, dramatiser; [make dramatic] rendre dramatique.
◇ *vi* dramatiser.

dramaturgy ['dræmətɜːdʒɪ] *n* dramaturgie *f*.

Drambuie® [dræm'bjuːɪ] *n* Drambuie® *m*.

drank [dræŋk] *pt* → **drink**.

drape [dreɪp] ◇ *n* [way something hangs] drapé *m*.
◇ *vt* -**1.** [adorn - person, window] draper; [- altar, room] tendre; **the stage was ~d with** OR **in black** la scène était tendue de noir. -**2.** [hang] étendre; **she ~d a leg over the chair arm** elle a étendu sa jambe sur l'accoudoir; **he ~d himself over the sofa** il s'est étalé sur le canapé.
◆ **drapes** *npl Br* [drapery] tentures *fpl*; *Am* [curtains] rideaux *mpl*.

draper ['dreɪpəʳ] *n Br* marchand *m*, -e *f* de tissus.

drapery ['dreɪpərɪ] (*pl* **draperies**) *n* -**1.** *(U)* [material] étoffes *fpl*; [arrangement of material] draperie *f*. -**2.** *(usu pl)* [hangings] tentures *fpl*; [curtains] rideaux *mpl*. -**3.** *Br* [shop] magasin *m* de tissus.

drastic ['dræstɪk] *adj* [measures] sévère, draconien; [change, effect] radical; [remedy] énergique; **~ cutbacks** ECON coupes *fpl* sombres; **~ reductions** COMM réductions *fpl* massives; **to take ~ steps** trancher dans le vif, prendre des mesures draconiennes OR énergiques.

drastically ['dræstɪklɪ] *adv* radicalement; [cut, reduce] radicalement, sévèrement; **prices rose ~** les prix ont augmenté considérablement.

drat *inf* [dræt] *interj*: **~!** diable!, bon sang!; **oh, ~!** bon sang!, nom de nom!

dratted *inf* ['drætɪd] *adj* sacré; **that ~ car** cette maudite voiture.

draught *Br*, **draft** *Am* [drɑːft] ◇ *n* -**1.** [breeze] courant *m* d'air; **I can feel a ~** je suis dans un courant d'air; **there's a terrific ~ in here** il y a un courant d'air terrible ici. -**2.** [in fireplace] tirage *m*. -**3.** [drink - swallow] trait *m*, gorgée *f*; **a ~ of water** une gorgée d'eau; **in one ~** d'un seul trait OR coup. -**4.** [medicine] potion *f*, breuvage *m*. -**5.** **on ~** [beer] à la pression. -**6.** GAMES dame *f*. -**7.** [pulling] traction *f*, tirage *m*; NAUT [of ship] tirant *m* (d'eau).
◇ *adj* [horse] de trait.

draught beer *n* bière *f* pression.

draughtboard ['drɑːftbɔːd] *n Br* GAMES damier *m*.

draught excluder [-ɪk'skluːdəʳ] *n Br* bourrelet *m* (de porte).

draughtiness *Br*, **draftiness** *Am* ['drɑːftɪnɪs] *n* courants *mpl* d'air.

draught-proof ◇ *vt* calfeutrer.
◇ *adj* calfeutré.

draught-proofing [-ˌpruːfɪŋ] *n* calfeutrage *m*.

draughts [drɑːfts] *n Br* GAMES (jeu *m* de) dames *fpl*; **a game of ~** un jeu de dames.

draughtsman *Br*, **draftsman** *Am* ['drɑːftsmən] (*Br pl* **draughtsmen** [-mən], *Am pl* **draftsmen** [-mən]) *n* [artist] dessinateur *m*, -trice *f*; ARCHIT & INDUST dessinateur *m* industriel, dessinatrice *f* industrielle.

draughtsmanship *Br*, **draftsmanship** *Am* ['drɑːftsmənʃɪp] *n* [of artist] talent *m* de dessinateur, coup *m* de crayon; [of work] art *m* du dessin.

draughty *Br*, **drafty** *Am* ['drɑːftɪ] (*Br compar* **draughtier**, *superl* **draughtiest**, *Am compar* **draftier**, *superl* **draftiest**) *adj* [house, room] plein de courants d'air; [street, corner] exposé à tous les vents OR aux quatre vents.

Dravidian [drə'vɪdɪən] ◇ *adj* dravidien.
◇ *n* dravidien *m*.

draw [drɔː] (*pt* **drew** [druː], *pp* **drawn** [drɔːn])
◇ *vt* -**1.** [pull] tirer; **to ~ the curtains** [open] tirer OR ouvrir les rideaux; [shut] tirer OR fermer les rideaux; **he drew the blankets round him** il a tiré les couvertures autour de lui; **I drew my coat closer around me** je me suis enveloppé dans mon manteau; **he drew his hand wearily across his forehead** il se passa la main sur le front avec lassitude; **to ~ a bow** [in archery] tirer à l'arc. -**2.** [haul, pull behind - car] tirer, traîner, remorquer; [- trailer] remorquer; **a carriage drawn by two horses** un équipage attelé à OR tiré par deux chevaux. -**3.** [take out] tirer, retirer; [remove] retirer, enlever; [tooth] arracher, extraire; **he drew his knife from** OR **out of his pocket** il a tiré son couteau de sa poche; **the thief drew a gun on us** le voleur a sorti un pistolet et l'a braqué sur nous; **to ~ a sword** dégainer une épée. -**4.** [lead] conduire, entraîner; **she drew me towards the door** elle m'a entraîné vers la porte ‖ *fig*: **I was drawn into the controversy** j'ai été mêlé à OR entraîné dans la dispute; **the senator refused to be drawn** [refused to answer] le sénateur refusa de répondre; [refused to be provoked] le sénateur refusa de réagir; **to ~ a meeting to a close** mettre fin à une réunion. -**5.** [attract, elicit] attirer; **to be drawn to sb** être attiré par qqn; **his remarks drew a lot of criticism** ses observations lui ont attiré de nombreuses critiques; **to ~ sb's attention to sthg** faire remarquer qqch à qqn; **to ~ the enemy's fire** *fig* attirer le feu de l'ennemi sur soi. -**6.** [take from source] tirer, puiser; **to ~ water from a well** puiser de l'eau dans un puits; **to ~ (out) money from the bank** retirer de l'argent à la banque; **the university ~s its students from all social backgrounds** l'université recrute ses étudiants dans toutes les couches sociales; **to ~ blood**: **the dog bit her and drew blood** le chien l'a mordue jusqu'au sang; **his last question drew blood** *fig* sa dernière question a fait mouche; **her performance drew an ovation from the audience** son interprétation lui a valu l'ovation du public; **his confession drew tears from his mother** son aveu a arraché des larmes à sa mère; **I ~ comfort from the fact that he didn't suffer** je me console en me disant qu'il n'a pas souffert; **Cézanne drew inspiration from the French countryside** Cézanne s'est inspiré de OR a tiré inspiration de la campagne française; **to ~ trumps** CARDS faire tomber les atouts. -**7.** [breathe in]: **we barely had time to ~ (a) breath** nous avons à peine eu le temps de souffler. -**8.** [choose at random] tirer; **he drew the winning number** il a tiré le numéro gagnant; **to ~ lots** tirer au sort ▫ **to ~ a blank** faire chou blanc, échouer. -**9.** [earn - amount, salary] gagner, toucher; [- pension] toucher; FIN [- interest] rapporter. -**10.** [sketch] dessiner; [line, triangle] tracer; **to ~ a picture of sb** faire le portrait de qqn; **he drew us a map of the village** il nous a fait un plan du village; **do you want me to ~ you a map?** *hum* tu veux que je te fasse un dessin?; **she drew a vivid picture of village life** *fig* elle (nous) a fait une description vivante de la vie de village; **the author has drawn his characters well** *fig* l'auteur a bien dépeint ses personnages ▫ **to ~ the line at sthg** ne pas admettre qqch, se refuser à qqch; **you have to ~ the line somewhere** il faut fixer des limites, il y a des limites. -**11.** [formulate - comparison, parallel, distinction] établir, faire; **to ~ a conclusion** tirer une conclusion; **she drew a direct comparison between our situation and her own** elle a établi une comparaison explicite entre notre situation et la sienne. -**12.** FIN: **to ~ a cheque on one's account** tirer un chèque sur son compte. -**13.** [disembowel] vider. -**14.** SPORT [tie]: **the game was drawn** SPORT ils ont fait match nul; CARDS ils ont fait partie nulle. -**15.** HUNT [game] débusquer; [covert] battre. -**16.** MED [abscess] crever, percer. -**17.** NAUT: **the ocean liner ~s 8 metres** le paquebot a un tirant d'eau de 8 mètres. -**18.** TECH [metal] étirer; [wire] tréfiler.
◇ *vi* -**1.** [move]: **the crowd drew to one side** la foule s'est rangée sur le côté OR s'est écartée; **the bus drew into the coach station** l'autocar est arrivé OR entré dans la gare routière; **to ~ ahead of sb** prendre de l'avance sur qqn; **one cyclist drew ahead of the others** un cycliste s'est détaché du peloton; **to ~ to a halt** s'arrêter; **they drew level with** OR **alongside the window** ils sont arrivés à la hauteur de la fenêtre; **they drew nearer to us** ils se sont approchés un peu plus de nous; **night ~s near** la nuit approche; **to ~ to an end** OR **to a close** tirer OR toucher à sa fin. -**2.** [pull out gun] tirer; **the policeman drew and fired** le policier a dégainé OR sorti son pistolet et a tiré. -**3.** [choose at random] tirer au hasard; **they drew for partners** ils ont tiré au sort leurs partenaires. -**4.** [sketch] dessiner; **she ~s well** elle dessine bien. -**5.** [fireplace, pipe] tirer; [pump, vacuum cleaner] aspirer. -**6.** [tea] infuser. -**7.** [be equal - two competitors] être ex aequo *(inv)*; [- two teams] faire match nul; **Italy drew against Spain** l'Italie et l'Espagne ont fait match nul; **the two contestants drew for third prize** les deux concurrents ont remporté le troisième prix ex aequo OR sont arrivés troisièmes ex aequo.
◇ *n* -**1.** [act of pulling]: **to be quick on the ~** *literal* dégainer vite, avoir la détente rapide; *fig* avoir de la repartie; **to beat sb to the ~** *literal* dégainer plus vite que qqn; *fig* devancer qqn. -**2.** [card] carte *f* tirée; **it's your ~** c'est à vous de tirer une carte. -**3.** [raffle, lottery] loterie *f*, tombola *f*; **the ~ will take place tonight** le tirage aura lieu ce soir. -**4.** [attraction] attraction *f*; **the polar bears are the main ~ at the zoo** les ours polaires sont la grande attraction du zoo; **the show proved to be a big ~** le spectacle s'est révélé être un grand succès. -**5.** GAMES partie *f* nulle; SPORT match *m* nul; **the chess tournament ended in a ~** le tournoi d'échecs s'est terminé par une partie nulle; **two wins and three ~s** deux matches gagnés et trois matches nuls. -**6.** *Am* [gully] ravine *f*; [drain] rigole *f*. -**7.** *Am* [sum of money] avance *f*.
◆ **draw along** *vt sep* [cart, caravan] tirer, traîner; [person] entraîner.
◆ **draw apart** ◇ *vi insep* se séparer; **they drew apart when I entered the room** ils se sont éloignés OR écartés l'un de l'autre quand je suis entré dans la pièce.
◇ *vt sep* prendre à l'écart.
◆ **draw aside** ◇ *vi insep* s'écarter, se ranger; **I drew aside to let them pass** je me suis écarté (du chemin) OR je me suis rangé pour les laisser passer.
◇ *vt sep* [person] prendre OR tirer à l'écart; [thing] écarter.
◆ **draw away** *vi insep* -**1.** [move away - person] s'éloigner, s'écarter; [- vehicle] s'éloigner, démarrer; **she drew away from the crowd** elle s'est éloignée OR écartée de la foule. -**2.** [move ahead] prendre de l'avance; **the leading runner drew away from the others** le coureur de tête a pris de l'avance sur les OR s'est détaché des autres.
◆ **draw back** ◇ *vi insep* -**1.** [move backwards] reculer, se reculer, avoir un mouvement de recul; **the child drew back in fear** l'enfant a reculé de peur. -**2.** [avoid commitment] se retirer.
◇ *vt sep* [person] faire reculer; [one's hand, thing] retirer.
◆ **draw down** *vt sep* -**1.** [lower - blinds] baisser, descendre. -**2.** [provoke] attirer; **their policy drew down a storm of protest** leur politique a soulevé une vague de protestations.
◆ **draw in** ◇ *vi insep* -**1.** [move]: **the train drew in** le train est entré en gare; **the bus drew in to the kerb** [pulled over] le bus s'est rapproché du trottoir; [stopped] le bus s'est arrêté le long du trottoir. -**2.** [day, evening] diminuer, raccourcir; **the nights are ~ing in** les nuits raccourcissent OR diminuent.

◇ *vt sep* -**1.** [pull in] rentrer; to ~ in the reins tirer sur les rênes, serrer la bride; the cat drew in its claws le chat fit patte de velours OR rentra ses griffes ❑ to ~ in one's horns *Br* [spend less money] restreindre son train de vie; [back down] en rabattre. -**2.** [involve] impliquer, mêler; he drew me into the conversation il m'a mêlé à la conversation; I got drawn into the project je me suis laissé impliquer dans le projet; he listened to the debate but refused to be drawn in il a écouté le débat mais a refusé d'y participer OR de s'y joindre. -**3.** [attract] attirer; the film is ~ing in huge crowds le film fait de grosses recettes. -**4.** [sketch] ébaucher. -**5.** [air] aspirer, respirer; to ~ in a deep breath respirer profondément.

◆ **draw off** *vt sep* -**1.** *Br* [remove - clothing] enlever, ôter; [- gloves] retirer, ôter. -**2.** [liquid] tirer; he drew off some wine from the cask il a tiré du vin du fût.

◆ **draw on** ◇ *vt sep Br* -**1.** [put on - gloves, trousers, socks] enfiler. -**2.** [entice, encourage] encourager, entraîner; the thought of success drew him on la perspective de la réussite l'encourageait à continuer.

◇ *vt insep* -**1.** [as source] faire appel à; the campaigners drew on the community's support les militants ont fait appel au soutien de la communauté locale; I drew on my own experiences for the novel je me suis inspiré OR servi de mes propres expériences pour mon roman; I had to ~ on my savings j'ai dû prendre OR tirer sur mes économies. -**2.** [suck] tirer; to ~ on a pipe tirer sur une pipe.

◇ *vi insep* [time - come near] approcher; [- get late] avancer; the winter drew on l'hiver approchait.

◆ **draw out** ◇ *vt sep* -**1.** [remove] sortir, retirer, tirer; she drew some papers out of her pocket elle a sorti des papiers de sa poche; how much money did you ~ out (of the bank)? combien d'argent as-tu retiré (de la banque)? -**2.** [extend - sound, visit] prolonger; [- meeting, speech] prolonger, faire traîner; TECH [- metal] étirer; [- wire] tréfiler. -**3.** [cause to speak freely] faire parler; she has a way of ~ing people out elle sait faire parler les gens, elle sait faire sortir les gens de leur coquille. -**4.** [information, secret] soutirer; the police managed to ~ the names out of him la police est arrivée à lui soutirer les noms.

◇ *vi insep* [vehicle] sortir, s'éloigner; the train drew out (of the station) le train est sorti de la gare.

◆ **draw up** ◇ *vt sep* -**1.** *Br* [pull up] tirer; I drew the covers up around my neck j'ai ramené les couvertures autour de mon cou; to ~ a boat up (on the beach) tirer un bateau à sec; she drew herself up (to her full height) elle s'est redressée (de toute sa hauteur). -**2.** *Br* [move closer - chair] approcher; MIL [- troops] aligner, ranger; ~ your chair up to the table approche ta chaise de la table. -**3.** [formulate - document] dresser, rédiger; [- bill, list] dresser, établir; [- plan] préparer, établir.

◇ *vi insep Br* -**1.** [move] se diriger; the other boat drew up alongside us l'autre bateau est arrivé à notre hauteur OR à côté de nous. -**2.** [stop - vehicle] s'arrêter, stopper; [- person] s'arrêter.

◆ **draw upon** *vt insep*: they had to ~ upon their emergency funds ils ont dû tirer sur OR prendre sur leur caisse de réserve; you have to ~ upon your previous experience il faut faire appel à votre expérience antérieure.

drawback ['drɔːbæk] *n* inconvénient *m*, désavantage *m*; there are ~s to the scheme ce projet présente des inconvénients; the main ~ to the plan is its cost le principal inconvénient du projet est son coût.

drawbridge ['drɔːbrɪdʒ] *n* pont-levis *m*, pont *m* basculant OR à bascule.

drawee [drɔː'iː] *n* tiré *m*.

drawer [*sense 1* drɔːʳ, *sense 2* 'drɔːəʳ] *n* -**1.** [in chest, desk] tiroir *m*. -**2.** [of cheque] tireur *m*.

drawers [drɔːz] *npl dated* OR *hum* [for men] caleçon *m*; [for women] culotte *f*.

drawing ['drɔːɪŋ] ◇ *n* -**1.** ART dessin *m*; to study ~ étudier le dessin; a pen ~ un dessin à la plume. -**2.** METALL [shaping, tapering] étirage *m*.

◇ *comp* [paper, table] à dessin; [lesson, teacher] de dessin; ~ pen tire-ligne *m*.

drawing account *n Am* compte *m* courant *(pour frais professionnels)*.

drawing board *n* planche *f* à dessin; it's back to the ~ il faudra tout recommencer.

drawing pin *n Br* punaise *f (à papier)*.

drawing room *n* -**1.** [living room] salon *m*; [reception room] salle *f* OR salon *m* de réception. -**2.** *Am* RAIL compartiment *m* privé.

drawl [drɔːl] ◇ *n* débit *m* traînant, voix *f* traînante; a Southern ~ un accent du Sud; "sure I do", he said with a ~ «bien sûr», dit-il d'une voix traînante.

◇ *vi* parler d'une voix traînante.

◇ *vt* dire d'une voix traînante.

drawn [drɔːn] ◇ *pp* → **draw**.

◇ *adj* -**1.** [blind, curtain] fermé, tiré. -**2.** [face, features] tiré; he looked tired and ~ il avait l'air fatigué et avait les traits tirés. -**3.** [game] nul. -**4.** CULIN: ~ butter beurre fondu.

drawn-out *adj* prolongé, qui traîne; a long ~ dispute un conflit qui traîne en longueur OR qui n'en finit pas.

drawn (thread) work *n* ouvrage *m* à jours.

drawsheet ['drɔːʃiːt] *n* alaise *f*.

drawstring ['drɔːstrɪŋ] *n* cordon *m*.

dray [dreɪ] *n* [for barrels] haquet *m*; [for stones, wood] binard *m*, fardier *m*.

dread [dred] ◇ *n* terreur *f*, effroi *m*; she lives in ~ of her ex-husband elle vit dans la crainte de son ex-mari.

◇ *vt* craindre, redouter; she's ~ing the journey elle redoute OR elle appréhende le voyage; I ~ to think of what might happen je n'ose pas imaginer ce qui pourrait arriver.

◇ *adj* redoutable, effrayant.

dreaded ['dredɪd] *adj* redoutable, terrible *aussi hum*.

dreadful ['dredfʊl] *adj* -**1.** [terrible - crime, pain] affreux, épouvantable; [- enemy, weapon] redoutable; how ~! quelle horreur! -**2.** [unpleasant] atroce, affreux; what a ~ child! cet enfant est insupportable!; they said some ~ things about her ils ont raconté des horreurs sur son compte; I feel ~ [ill] je ne me sens pas du tout bien; [embarrassed] je suis vraiment gêné. -**3.** [as intensifier]: he's a ~ bore! c'est un casse-pieds insupportable!, c'est un horrible casse-pieds!; what a ~ waste! quel affreux gaspillage!

dreadfully ['dredfʊlɪ] *adv* -**1.** [very] terriblement; he was ~ afraid il avait horriblement peur OR une peur atroce; I'm ~ sorry je regrette infiniment OR énormément; his handwriting is ~ untidy son écriture est terriblement mauvaise, il écrit horriblement mal. -**2.** [badly] affreusement; the children behaved ~ les enfants se sont affreusement mal comportés.

dreadlocks ['dredlɒks] *npl coiffure des rastas*; he's got ~ il a les cheveux à la rasta.

dreadnought ['drednɔːt] *n* cuirassé *m*.

dream [driːm] (*pt* & *pp* dreamt [dremt] OR dreamed) ◇ *vi* -**1.** [in sleep] rêver; to ~ about sb rêver de qqn; it can't be true, I must be ~ing ce n'est pas vrai, je rêve. -**2.** [daydream] rêvasser, rêver; he's always ~ing il est toujours dans la lune; stop ~ing and get on with your work! arrête de rêver OR de rêvasser et remets-toi au travail!; for years she'd dreamt of having a cottage in the country elle a, durant des années, rêvé d'avoir un cottage à la campagne; I know it'll never happen but there's nothing to stop me ~ing! je sais que ça n'arrivera jamais, mais je ne peux pas m'empêcher de rêver!; ~ on! *inf* on peut toujours rêver! -**3.** [imagine]: to ~ of doing sthg songer à faire qqch; nobody dreamt of suspecting her personne n'a songé à OR il n'est venu à l'idée de personne de la soupçonner; don't tell anyone — I wouldn't ~ of it! ne le dis à personne — jamais je ne songerais à faire une chose pareille!; she'd never ~ of complaining jamais elle ne songerait à se plaindre.

◇ *vt* -**1.** [in sleep] rêver; he dreamt a ~ il a fait un rêve; she dreamt we were in Spain elle a rêvé que nous étions en Espagne; you must have dreamt it vous avez dû le rêver. -**2.** [daydream] rêvasser; to ~ idle ~s se nourrir d'illusions, rêver creux. -**3.** [imagine] songer, imaginer; I never dreamt that he would actually accept the offer! j'étais à mille lieues de supposer qu'il accepterait effectivement la proposition!

◇ *n* -**1.** [during sleep] rêve *m*; I had a ~ about my mother last night j'ai rêvé de ma mère la nuit dernière; to see sthg in a ~ voir qqch en rêve; the child had a bad ~ l'enfant a fait un mauvais rêve OR un cauchemar; the meeting was like a bad ~ la réunion était un cauchemar; sweet ~s! faites de beaux rêves!; life is but a ~ *lit* la vie n'est qu'un songe ❑ 'The Dream of Gerontius' *Newman, Elgar* 'le Songe de Gerontius'. -**2.** [wish, fantasy] rêve *m*, désir *m*; the woman of his ~s la femme de ses rêves; her ~ was to become a pilot elle rêvait de devenir pilote; a job beyond my wildest ~s un travail comme je n'ai jamais osé imaginer OR qui dépasse tous mes rêves; even in her wildest ~s she never thought she'd win first prize même dans ses rêves les plus fous, elle n'avait jamais pensé remporter le premier prix; the American ~ le rêve américain; may all your ~s come true que tous vos rêves se réalisent; the holiday was like a ~ come true les vacances étaient comme un rêve devenu réalité; this boat is a sailor's ~ come true ce bateau est la matérialisation du rêve d'un marin. -**3.** [marvel] merveille *f*; my interview went like a ~ mon entretien s'est passé à merveille; this car goes like a ~ cette voiture marche à merveille; a ~ of a house *inf* une maison de rêve; she's a real ~ *inf* c'est un amour, elle est vraiment adorable. -**4.** [daydream] rêverie *f*, rêve *m*; he's always in a ~ il est toujours dans les nuages OR en train de rêver.

◇ *comp* [car, person, house] de rêve; a ~ world [ideal] un monde utopique; [imaginary] un monde imaginaire; she lives in a ~ world elle vit dans les nuages; the ~ ticket POL [policies] le programme utopique OR à faire rêver; [candidates] le couple idéal; ~ sequence CIN séquence *f* onirique.

◆ **dream away** *vt sep* passer OR perdre en rêveries; she would ~ away the hours watching the clouds float by elle passait des heures à rêver en regardant passer les nuages.

◆ **dream up** *vt sep* imaginer, inventer; some wonderful new scheme that the government has dreamt up encore un de ces merveilleux projets concotés par le gouvernement; where did you ~ that up? où es-tu allé pêcher ça?

«I HAVE A DREAM»:
Célèbre discours de Martin Luther King Jr. prononcé à Washington le 28 août 1963 à l'occasion d'un immense rassemblement de partisans des droits civiques aux États-Unis. Il y dépeint son espoir de connaître un jour un pays où toutes les communautés vivraient en harmonie.

dreamboat *inf* ['driːmbəʊt] *n dated* homme *m*, femme *f* de rêve.

dreamer ['driːməʳ] *n literal* rêveur *m*, -euse *f*; [idealist] rêveur *m*, -euse *f*, utopiste *mf*; *pej* songe-creux *m inv*.

dreamily ['driːmɪlɪ] *adv* [act] d'un air rêveur OR songeur; [speak] d'un ton rêveur OR songeur; [absent-mindedly] d'un air absent.

dreamland ['driːmlænd] *n* pays *m* imaginaire OR des rêves OR des songes; she's in ~ elle est au pays des rêves.

dreamless ['driːmlɪs] *adj* sans rêves.

dreamlike ['driːmlaɪk] *adj* irréel, onirique; the music/the play has a ~ quality la musique/la pièce a quelque chose d'irréel.

dreamt [dremt] *pt* & *pp* → **dream**.

dreamy ['driːmɪ] (*compar* dreamier, *superl* dreamiest) *adj* -**1.** [vague - person] rêveur, songeur; [- expression] rêveur; [absent-minded] rêveur, distrait. -**2.** [impractical - person] utopique, rêveur; [- idea] chimérique, utopique. -**3.** [music, voice] langoureux. -**4.** *inf* [wonderful] magnifique, ravissant.

drearily ['drɪərəlɪ] *adv* tristement; ~ dressed tristement vêtu; ~ furnished tristement meublé.

dreariness ['drɪərɪnɪs] *n* [of surroundings] aspect *m* morne OR terne, monotonie *f*; [of life] monotonie *f*, tristesse *f*.

dreary ['drɪərɪ] (*compar* drearier, *superl* dreariest) *adj* [surroundings] morne, triste; [life] morne, monotone; [work, job] monotone, ennuyeux; [person] ennuyeux (comme la pluie); [weather] maussade, morne.

dreck▽ [drek] *n (U) Am* [rubbish] ordures *fpl*; [excrement] merde *f*.

drecky▽ ['drekɪ] (*compar* dreckier, *superl* dreckiest) *adj Am* merdique.

dredge [dredʒ] ◇ *vt* -**1.** [river] draguer; they ~d the river for the body ils ont dragué le fleuve à la recherche du corps. -**2.** CULIN [with flour, sugar] saupoudrer; [with breadcrumbs] paner.
◇ *n* NAUT drague *f*.
◆ **dredge up** *vt sep literal* draguer; *fig* [scandal, unpleasant news] déterrer, ressortir.

dredger ['dredʒəʳ] *n* -**1.** NAUT [ship] dragueur *m*; [machine] drague *f*. -**2.** CULIN saupoudreuse *f*, saupoudroir *m*.

dregs [dregz] *npl literal* & *fig* lie *f*; she drank the tea down to the ~ elle a bu le thé jusqu'à la dernière goutte; the ~ of society la lie OR les bas-fonds de la société.

drench [drentʃ] ◇ *vt* -**1.** [soak] tremper, mouiller; by the time we got home we were absolutely ~ed le temps d'arriver à la maison, nous étions complètement trempés; she had ~ed herself with perfume *fig* elle s'était aspergée de parfum. -**2.** VETER donner OR faire avaler un médicament à.
◇ *n* VETER (dose *f* de) médicament *m*.

drenching ['drentʃɪŋ] ◇ *n* trempage *m*.
◇ *adj*: ~ rain pluie *f* battante OR diluvienne.

Dresden ['drezdən] ◇ *pr n* [city] Dresde.
◇ *n* [china] porcelaine *f* de Saxe, saxe *m*; a piece of ~ china un saxe.

dress [dres] ◇ *n* -**1.** [frock] robe *f*; a cotton/summer ~ une robe de coton/d'été. -**2.** [clothing] habillement *m*, tenue *f*. -**3.** [style of dress] tenue *f*, toilette *f*; formal/informal ~ tenue de cérémonie/de ville; in Indian ~ en tenue indienne.
◇ *vt* -**1.** [clothe] habiller; she ~ed herself OR got ~ed elle s'est habillée. -**2.** [arrange] orner, parer; [groom - horse] panser; [- hair] coiffer; [- shop window] faire la vitrine de; [- ship] pavoiser. -**3.** [wound] panser; he ~ed my wound il a fait mon pansement. -**4.** CULIN [salad] assaisonner, garnir; [meat, fish] parer; ~ed chicken poulet *m* prêt à cuire; ~ed crab crabe *m* tout préparé pour la table. -**5.** [treat - cloth, skins] préparer, apprêter; [- leather] corroyer; [- stone] tailler, dresser; [- metal] polir; [- timber] dégrossir. -**6.** [bush, tree] tailler; [woods] dégrossir. -**7.** AGR [field] façonner. -**8.** MIL [troops] aligner; to ~ ranks se mettre en rangs. -**9.** [neuter - animal] dresser.
◇ *vi* -**1.** [get dressed, wear clothes] s'habiller; she always ~es very smartly elle s'habille toujours avec beaucoup d'élégance; to ~ for dinner [gen] se mettre en tenue de soirée; [men] se mettre en smoking; [women] se mettre en robe du soir; do we have to ~ for dinner? est-ce qu'il faut s'habiller pour le dîner? -**2.** MIL [soldiers] s'aligner.
◆ **dress down** *Br* ◇ *vi insep* s'habiller simplement.
◇ *vt sep inf* [scold] passer un savon à.
◆ **dress up** ◇ *vi insep* -**1.** [put on best clothes] s'habiller, se mettre sur son trente et un; he was all ~ed up il était tout endimanché. -**2.** [put on disguise] se déguiser, se costumer; she ~ed up as a clown elle s'est déguisée en clown.
◇ *vt sep* -**1.** [put on best clothes] habiller. -**2.** [disguise] déguiser; his mother had ~ed him up as a soldier sa mère l'avait déguisé en soldat. -**3.** [smarten] rendre plus habillé. -**4.** [embellish] orner; you could ~ up the outfit with a nice scarf tu pourrais rendre la tenue plus habillée avec un joli foulard || *fig*: it's basically the same old machine ~ed up in a smart new case c'est pratiquement le même appareil mais l'emballage a changé; they accused the government of ~ing up old ideas in a new format ils ont accusé le gouvernement de reprendre de vieilles idées et de les présenter autrement.

dressage ['dresɑːʒ] *n* dressage *m* ÉQUIT.

dress circle *n* premier balcon *m*, corbeille *f*.

dress coat *n* habit *m*, queue-de-pie *f*.

dress designer *n* modéliste *mf*, dessinateur *m*, -trice *f* de mode; [famous] couturier *m*.

dressed ['drest] *adj* habillé; a well-~/smartly-~ man un homme bien habillé/élégant; ~ in blue chiffon vêtu de mousseline de soie bleue; I'm not ~ yet je ne suis pas encore habillé; she was not appropriately ~ for the country/for gardening elle n'avait pas la tenue appropriée OR qui convenait pour la campagne/pour jardiner; she was ~ as a man elle était habillée en homme ❑ she was ~ to kill *inf* elle avait un look d'enfer.

dresser ['dresəʳ] *n* -**1.** [person]: he's a smart/sloppy ~ il s'habille avec beaucoup de goût/avec négligence. -**2.** THEAT habilleur *m*, -euse *f*. -**3.** [tool - for wood] raboteuse *f*; [- for stone] rabotin *m*. -**4.** [for dishes] buffet *m*, dressoir *m*. -**5.** *Am* [for clothing] commode *f*.

dressing ['dresɪŋ] *n* -**1.** [act of getting dressed] habillement *m*, habillage *m*. -**2.** CULIN [sauce] sauce *f*, assaisonnement *m*; *Am* [stuffing] farce *f*; an oil and vinegar ~ une vinaigrette. -**3.** [for wound] pansement *m*. -**4.** AGR [fertilizer] engrais *m*. -**5.** [for cloth, leather] apprêt *m*.
◆ **dressings** *npl* CONSTR moulures *fpl*, parement *m*.

dressing case *n dated* trousse *f* de toilette, nécessaire *m* de toilette.

dressing-down *inf n Br* réprimande *f*, semonce *f*; to give sb a ~ passer un savon à qqn; his boss gave him a real OR severe ~ son patron lui a passé un sacré OR sérieux savon; he got a ~ il s'est fait passer un savon.

dressing gown *n* robe *f* de chambre, peignoir *m*.

dressing room *n* [at home] dressing-room *m*, dressing *m*, vestiaire *m*; [at gymnasium, sports ground] vestiaire *m*; THEAT loge *f* (d'acteur); *Am* [in shop] cabine *f* d'essayage.

dressing station *n* poste *m* de secours.

dressing table *n* coiffeuse *f*, (table *f* de) toilette *f*.

dressing-table set *n* accessoires *mpl* pour coiffeuse.

dressing-up *n* [children's game] déguisement *m*.

dressmaker ['dres,meɪkəʳ] *n* couturière *f*; [famous] couturier *m*.

dressmaking ['dres,meɪkɪŋ] *n* couture *f*, confection *f* des robes.

dress rehearsal *n* THEAT (répétition *f*) générale *f*; *fig* [practice] répétition *f* générale.

dress shield *n* dessous-de-bras *m inv*.

dress shirt *n* chemise *f* de soirée.

dress suit *n* habit *m*, tenue *f* de soirée.

dress uniform *n* tenue *f* de cérémonie.

dressy ['dresɪ] (*compar* dressier, *superl* dressiest) *adj* [clothes] (qui fait) habillé, élégant; [person] élégant, chic; the charity ball is always a very ~ occasion le bal de charité est toujours un événement très habillé.

drew [druː] *pt* → **draw**.

drib [drɪb] *n phr*: in ~s and drabs petit à petit.

dribble ['drɪbl] ◇ *vi* -**1.** [trickle] couler lentement, tomber goutte à goutte; the strikers slowly ~d back to work *fig* les grévistes reprenaient le travail par petits groupes. -**2.** [baby] baver. -**3.** SPORT dribbler.
◇ *vt* -**1.** [trickle] laisser couler OR tomber lentement; he was dribbling milk from his mouth du lait dégoulinait de sa bouche; you're dribbling water everywhere! tu fais dégouliner de l'eau partout! -**2.** SPORT [ball, puck] dribbler.
◇ *n* -**1.** [trickle] filet *m*. -**2.** *fig* [small amount]: a ~ of un petit peu de. -**3.** SPORT dribble *m*.

dried [draɪd] *adj* [fruit] sec; [meat] séché; [milk, eggs] déshydraté.

dried-up *adj* [apple, person] ratatiné, desséché; [talent, well] tari; [beauty, love] fané.

drier ['draɪəʳ] ◇ *compar* → **dry**.
◇ *n* [for clothes] séchoir *m* (à linge); [for hair - hand-held] séchoir *m* (à cheveux), sèche-cheveux *m inv*; [- helmet] casque *m* (sèche-cheveux); under the ~ sous le casque.

driest ['draɪɪst] *superl* → **dry**.

drift [drɪft] ◇ *vi* -**1.** [float - on water] aller à la dérive, dériver; [- in current, wind] être emporté; AERON dériver; the boat ~ed downstream le bateau descendait le fleuve à la dérive OR à vau-l'eau; the clouds ~ed les nuages étaient poussés par le vent. -**2.** [sand, snow] s'amonceler, s'entasser. -**3.** [move aimlessly] marcher nonchalamment; people began to ~ away/in/out les gens commençaient à s'en aller/entrer/sortir d'un pas nonchalant || *fig*: the conversation ~ed from one topic to another la conversation passait d'un sujet à un autre; he just ~s along il flâne simplement; to ~ apart [friends] se perdre de vue; [couple] se séparer petit à petit; he ~ed into a life of crime il s'est laissé entraîner dans la criminalité. -**4.** ELECTRON se décaler.
◇ *vt* -**1.** [subj: current] entraîner, charrier; [subj: wind] emporter, pousser. -**2.** [sand, snow] amonceler, entasser.
◇ *n* -**1.** [flow] mouvement *m*, force *f*; [of air, water] poussée *f*; the ~ of the current took us southwards le courant nous a emportés vers le sud; the ~ of the tide [speed] la vitesse de la marée; [direction] le sens de la marée; the population ~ towards the city *fig* l'exode *m* rural, la migration vers la ville ❑ the North Atlantic Drift GEOG le courant nord-atlantique. -**2.** [of leaves, sand] amoncellement *m*, entassement *m*; [of fallen snow] amoncellement *m*, congère *f*; [of falling snow] rafale *f*, bourrasque *f*; [of clouds] traînée *f*; [of dust, mist] nuage *m*; GEOL [deposits] apports *mpl*. -**3.** [of plane, ship] dérivation *f*; [of missile] déviation *f*; [deviation from course] dérive *f*; continental ~ dérive des continents. -**4.** ELECTRON déviation *f*. -**5.** [trend] tendance *f*; the ~ back towards the classics le retour aux classiques. -**6.** [meaning] sens *m*, portée *f*; do you get my ~? voyez-vous où je veux en venir?; I caught his ~ j'ai compris ce qu'il voulait dire. -**7.** LING évolution *f (d'une langue)*. -**8.** MIN galerie *f* chassante.
◆ **drift off** *vi insep* [fall asleep] s'assoupir; I ~ed off for a while je me suis assoupi quelques instants.

drift anchor *n* ancre *f* flottante.

drifter ['drɪftəʳ] *n* -**1.** [person] *personne qui n'a pas de but dans la vie*; he's a bit of a ~ il n'arrive pas à se fixer, il ne sait pas ce qu'il veut. -**2.** [boat] drifter *m*, dériveur *m*.

drift ice *n (U)* glaces *fpl* flottantes OR en dérive.

drift net *n* filet *m* dérivant.

driftwood ['drɪftwʊd] *n (U)* bois *mpl* flottants.

drill [drɪl] ◇ *n* -**1.** [manual] porte-foret *m*; [electric] perceuse *f*; [of dentist] fraise *f (de dentiste)*, roulette *f*; [for oil well] trépan *m*; [pneumatic] marteau *m* piqueur; MIN perforatrice *f*. -**2.** [bit]: ~ (bit) foret *m*, mèche *f*. -**3.** [exercise] exer-

cice *m*; MIL manœuvre *f*, drill *m*; I know the ~ *inf Br fig* je sais ce qu'il faut faire, je connais la marche à suivre. -**4.** TEX treillis *m*, coutil *m*. -**5.** AGR [machine] semoir *m*; [furrow] sillon *m*.
◇ *vt* -**1.** [metal, wood] forer, percer; [hole] percer; [dentist] fraiser; to ~ an oil well forer un puits de pétrole. -**2.** *inf* SPORT [ball]: he ~ed the ball into the back of the net il envoya la balle droit au fond du filet. -**3.** [train] faire faire des exercices à; I ~ed him as to what to say je lui ai fait la leçon sur ce qu'il fallait dire || MIL faire faire l'exercice à; the troops are well ~ed les troupes sont bien entraînées. -**4.** [seeds] semer en sillon; [field] tracer des sillons dans.
◇ *vi* -**1.** [bore] forer; they are ~ing for oil ils forent OR effectuent des forages pour trouver du pétrole. -**2.** [train] faire de l'exercice, s'entraîner; MIL être à l'exercice, manœuvrer.
◆ **drill into** *vt sep* faire comprendre, enfoncer dans la tête; it was ~ed into them from an early age not to accept lifts from strangers depuis leur plus jeune âge, on leur avait enfoncé dans la tête qu'il ne fallait pas accepter de monter en voiture avec des inconnus.

drilling ['drɪlɪŋ] *n (U)* [in metal, wood] forage *m*, perçage *m*; [by dentist] fraisage *m*; ~ for oil forage pétrolier.

drilling platform *n* plate-forme *f* (de forage).

drilling rig *n* -**1.** [on land] derrick *m*. -**2.** [at sea] = **drilling platform**.

drilling ship *n* navire *m* de forage.

drill sergeant *n* sergent *m* instructeur.

drily ['draɪlɪ] *adv* [wryly] d'un air pince-sans-rire; [coldly] sèchement, d'un ton sec.

drink [drɪŋk] (*pt* drank [dræŋk], *pp* drunk [drʌŋk]) ◇ *vt* boire, prendre; would you like something to ~? voulez-vous boire quelque chose?; I never ~ coffee je ne prends jamais de café; what are you ~ing tonight? que voulez-vous boire ce soir?; the water is not fit to ~ l'eau n'est pas potable; this coffee isn't fit to ~ ce café est imbuvable; red Burgundy is best drunk at room temperature le bourgogne rouge est meilleur bu chambré; ~ your soup mange ta soupe; to ~ one's fill boire à sa soif; to ~ sb's health, to ~ a toast to sb boire à la santé de qqn; he drank himself into a stupor il s'est soûlé jusqu'à l'hébétude; I could ~ the well dry je boirais la mer et ses poissons; he's ~ing himself to death l'alcool le tue peu à peu ❑ to ~ sb under the table faire rouler qqn sous la table.
◇ *vi* boire; I don't ~ je ne bois pas; she drank out of OR from the bottle elle a bu à la bouteille; I only ~ socially je ne bois jamais seul; 'don't ~ and drive' 'boire ou conduire, il faut choisir' ❑ he ~s like a fish il boit comme un trou.
◇ *n* -**1.** [nonalcoholic] boisson *f*; may I have a ~? puis-je boire quelque chose?; a ~ of water un verre d'eau; give the children a ~ donnez à boire aux enfants; there's plenty of food and ~ il y a tout ce qu'on veut à boire et à manger; you can get ~s from the machine vous pouvez prendre des boissons à la machine; hot ~s boissons chaudes. -**2.** [alcoholic] verre *m*; [before dinner] apéritif *m*; [after dinner] digestif *m*; we invited them in for a ~ nous les avons invités à prendre un verre; fancy a ~? *inf* que diriez-vous d'un verre?; I need a ~! vite, donnez-moi à boire!; he likes OR enjoys a ~ il aime bien boire un verre; to buy OR to stand a round of ~s payer une tournée; ~s are on the house! la maison offre à boire!; he'd had one ~ too many il avait bu un verre de trop, il avait un verre dans le nez. -**3.** [mouthful] gorgée *f*; have another little ~ prends encore une petite gorgée. -**4.** [alcohol] la boisson, l'alcool *m*; she's taken to ~ elle s'adonne à la boisson, elle boit; to be the worse for ~ être en état d'ébriété; to drive under the influence of ~ conduire en état d'ivresse OR d'ébriété; to smell of ~ sentir l'alcool. -**5.** *inf Br* [sea] flotte *f*; to be in the ~ être dans la flotte OR à la baille.
◇ *comp*: he has a ~ problem il boit trop, il s'adonne à la boisson.
◆ **drink away** *vt sep*: he's trying to ~ his troubles away il essaie de noyer ses ennuis dans l'alcool; to ~ away one's fortune boire sa fortune.
◆ **drink down** *vt sep* avaler OR boire d'un trait.
◆ **drink in** *vt sep* -**1.** [water] absorber, boire. -**2.** *fig* [story, words] boire; [atmosphere, surroundings] s'imprégner de; we drank in every word pas un seul mot ne nous a échappé, nous avons bu ses paroles.
◆ **drink to** *vt insep* boire à, porter un toast à; I'll ~ to that! je suis pour!; we drank to their success nous avons bu OR porté un toast à leur succès.
◆ **drink up** ◇ *vt sep* boire (jusqu'à la dernière goutte), finir.
◇ *vi insep* vider son verre; ~ up! finissez vos verres!

drinkable ['drɪŋkəbl] *adj* [safe to drink] potable; [tasty] buvable; this wine's very ~ c'est un vin qui se laisse boire.

drink-driving *n* conduite *f* en état d'ivresse.

drinker ['drɪŋkə^r] *n* buveur *m*, -euse *f*; I'm not a coffee ~ je ne suis pas un buveur de café; he's a hard OR heavy ~ il boit sec OR beaucoup; we're not really ~s nous ne sommes pas des grands buveurs.

drinking ['drɪŋkɪŋ] ◇ *n* fait *m* de boire; eating and ~ manger et boire; heavy ~ ivrognerie *f*; I'm not used to ~ je n'ai pas l'habitude de boire; his ~ is becoming a problem le fait qu'il boive devient un problème.
◇ *comp* [man] qui boit; [habits] de buveur; [bout, companion, session] de beuverie.

drinking chocolate *n* chocolat *m* à boire; [powder] chocolat *m* en poudre; [hot drink] chocolat *m* chaud.

drinking fountain *n* [in street] fontaine *f* publique; [in corridor, public conveniences] jet *m* d'eau potable.

drinking song *n* chanson *f* à boire.

drinking trough *n* abreuvoir *m*.

drinking-up time *n Br période où les clients doivent finir leur verre avant la fermeture du bar.*

drinking water *n* eau *f* potable.

drip [drɪp] (*pt* & *pp* dripped, *cont* dripping) ◇ *vi* -**1.** [liquid] tomber goutte à goutte, dégoutter; the rain is dripping down my neck la pluie me dégouline dans le cou; sweat dripped from his brow son front ruisselait de sueur; I was dripping with sweat j'étais en nage; her hands dripped with blood du sang dégoulinait de ses mains; dripping with sentimentality *fig* dégoulinant de sentimentalité. -**2.** [tap] fuir, goutter; [nose] couler; [washing] s'égoutter; [walls] suinter; [hair, trees] dégoutter, ruisseler.
◇ *vt* laisser tomber goutte à goutte; you're dripping coffee everywhere tu mets du café partout.
◇ *n* -**1.** [falling drops - from tap, gutter, ceiling] égouttement *m*, dégoulinement *m*. -**2.** [sound - from trees, roofs] bruit *m* de l'eau qui goutte; [- from tap] bruit d'un robinet qui fuit OR goutte. -**3.** [drop] goutte *f*. -**4.** *inf pej* [person] nouille *f*, lavette *f*. -**5.** MED [device] goutte-à-goutte *m inv*; [solution] perfusion *f*; she's on a ~ elle est sous perfusion. -**6.** ARCHIT larmier *m*.

drip-dry ◇ *adj* qui ne nécessite aucun repassage.
◇ *vi* s'égoutter.
◇ *vt* (faire) égoutter.

drip-feed ◇ *n* [device] goutte-à-goutte *m inv*; [solution] perfusion *f*.
◇ *vt* alimenter par perfusion.

drip mat *n* dessous-de-verre *m inv*.

drip pan *n* lèchefrite *f*.

dripping ['drɪpɪŋ] ◇ *n* -**1.** CULIN [of meat] graisse *f (de rôti)*; bread and ~ tartine *f* à la graisse. -**2.** [of liquid] égouttement *m*, égouttage *m*.
◇ *adj* -**1.** [tap] qui fuit OR goutte; ~ with blood/with sweat ruisselant de sang/de sueur. -**2.** [very wet] trempé.
◇ *adv*: his clothes were ~ wet ses vêtements étaient trempés OR étaient à tordre.

drip-proof *adj* [paint, varnish] qui ne coule pas.

drippy ['drɪpɪ] (*compar* drippier, *superl* drippiest) *adj* -**1.** *inf pej* [person] mou. -**2.** [tap] qui fuit OR goutte.

drip tray = **drip pan**.

drivability [ˌdraɪvə'bɪlətɪ] = **driveability**.

drive [draɪv] (*pt* drove [drəʊv], *pp* driven ['drɪvn]) ◇ *vt* -**1.** [bus, car, train] conduire; [racing car] piloter; can you ~ a minibus? savez-vous conduire un minibus?; I ~ a Volvo j'ai une Volvo; he ~s a taxi/lorry il est chauffeur de taxi/camionneur; she ~s racing cars elle est pilote de course; he drove her into town il l'a conduite OR emmenée en voiture en ville; could you ~ me home? pourriez-vous me reconduire chez moi?; she drove the car into a tree elle a heurté un arbre avec la voiture. -**2.** [chase] chasser, pousser; to ~ sb out of the house/of the country chasser qqn de la maison/du pays; we drove the cattle back into the shed nous avons fait rentrer le bétail dans l'étable; the wind drove the snow up against the wall le vent chassait la neige contre le mur; the waves drove the ship against the rocks les vagues ont jeté le navire contre les rochers; the strong winds had driven the ship off course les vents forts avaient dévié le navire de sa route || *fig*: her words drove all worries from his mind ses paroles lui ont fait complètement oublier ses soucis; they have driven us into a corner ils nous ont mis au pied du mur. -**3.** [work]: it doesn't pay to ~ your workers too hard on ne gagne rien à surmener ses employés; he ~s himself too hard il exige trop de lui-même. -**4.** [force] pousser, inciter; he was driven to it on lui a forcé la main; driven by jealousy, he killed her il l'a tuée sous l'emprise de la jalousie; it's enough to ~ you to drink! cela vous pousserait un honnête homme à boire!; it's driving him to drink cela le pousse à boire OR à la boisson; the situation is driving me to despair/distraction la situation me pousse au désespoir/me rend fou; to ~ sb crazy OR mad OR up the wall *inf* rendre qqn fou; his performance drove the audience wild *inf* son spectacle a mis le public en délire. -**5.** [hammer - nail] enfoncer; [- rivet] poser; [- stake] enfoncer, ficher; to ~ a nail home enfoncer un clou || *fig*: to ~ a point home faire admettre son point de vue; I can't ~ it into his thick head that... je n'arrive pas à faire comprendre à cet idiot que...; to ~ a hard bargain avoir toujours le dernier mot en affaires, être dur en affaires. -**6.** [bore - hole] percer; [- tunnel] percer, creuser. -**7.** [operate - machine] faire fonctionner; MECH entraîner; driven by electricity marchant à l'électricité; the pinion is driven in rotation le pignon est actionné par rotation. -**8.** SPORT: to ~ a ball exécuter un drive; [in golf] driver. -**9.** HUNT [game] rabattre; [area] battre.
◇ *vi* -**1.** [operate a vehicle] conduire; [travel in vehicle] aller en voiture; do you OR can you ~? savez-vous conduire?; I was driving at 100 mph je roulais à 160 km/h; we drove home/down to the coast nous sommes rentrés/descendus sur la côte en voiture; they drove all night ils ont roulé toute la nuit; are you walking or driving? êtes-vous à pied ou en voiture?; ~ on the right roulez à droite, tenez votre droite; to ~ while intoxicated OR under the influence of alcohol conduire en état d'ivresse OR d'ébriété. -**2.** [car] rouler; this car ~s like a dream *inf* c'est un plaisir de conduire cette voiture. -**3.** [dash] se ruer; rain was driving against the window la pluie fouettait les vitres.
◇ *n* -**1.** AUT [trip] promenade *f* OR trajet *m* (en voiture); we went for a ~ nous avons fait une promenade OR un tour en voiture; it's an hour's ~ from here c'est à une heure d'ici en voiture. -**2.** [road - public] avenue *f*, rue *f*; [- private] voie *f* privée *(menant à une habitation)*; [in street names] allée *f*. -**3.** [energy] dynamisme *m*, énergie *f*; we need someone with ~ il nous faut quelqu'un de dynamique OR d'entreprenant; to have

plenty of ~ avoir de l'énergie OR du dynamisme; he lacks ~ il manque d'allant OR de dynamisme. -4. [urge] besoin *m*, instinct *m*. -5. [campaign] campagne *f*; the company is having a sales ~ la compagnie fait une campagne de vente. -6. *Br* [for bridge, whist] tournoi *m*. -7. SPORT [in cricket, tennis] coup *m* droit; [in golf] drive *m*; [in football] tir *m*, shoot *m*. -8. [of animals] rassemblement *m*; [in hunting] battue *f*; cattle ~ rassemblement du bétail. -9. TECH [power transmission] transmission *f*, commande *f*; AUT: four-wheel ~ quatre roues motrices *f inv*, quatre-quatre *m inv ou f inv*; front-wheel ~ traction *f* avant; left-hand ~ conduite *f* à gauche; rear-wheel ~ traction *f* OR propulsion *f* arrière. -10. COMPUT [for disk] unité *f* OR lecteur *m* de disquettes; [for tape] dérouleur *m*. -11. MIL poussée *f*, offensive *f*.

◇ *comp* TECH [mechanism, device] d'entraînement, d'actionnement, de transmission.

◆ **drive along** ◇ *vi insep* [car] rouler, circuler; [person] rouler, conduire.

◇ *vt sep* [subj: river, wind] pousser, chasser.

◆ **drive at** *vt insep* vouloir dire; **she didn't understand what he was driving at** elle ne comprenait pas où il voulait en venir; **I see what you're driving at** je vous vois venir.

◆ **drive away** ◇ *vi insep* [person] s'en aller OR partir (en voiture); [car] démarrer.

◇ *vt sep* [car] démarrer; [person] *literal* emmener en voiture; *fig* repousser, écarter; [animal] chasser, éloigner.

◆ **drive back** ◇ *vi insep* [person] rentrer en voiture; [car] retourner.

◇ *vt sep* -1. [person] ramener OR reconduire en voiture; [car] reculer. -2. [repel] repousser, refouler; **the soldiers were driven back by heavy machine-gun fire** les soldats furent repoussés par un puissant tir de mitrailleuse; **fear drove them back** la peur leur a fait rebrousser chemin.

◆ **drive in** ◇ *vi insep* [person] entrer (en voiture); [car] entrer.

◇ *vt sep* [nail, stake] enfoncer; [screw] visser.

◆ **drive off** ◇ *vi insep* -1. [leave - person] s'en aller OR s'éloigner en voiture; [- car] démarrer. -2. GOLF driver.

◇ *vt sep* [frighten away] éloigner, chasser.

◆ **drive on** ◇ *vi insep* [continue trip] poursuivre sa route; [after stopping] reprendre la route.

◇ *vt sep* [push] pousser, inciter; **she drove him on to work even harder** elle l'a poussé à travailler encore plus.

◆ **drive out** ◇ *vi insep* [person] sortir (en voiture); [car] sortir.

◇ *vt sep* [person] chasser, faire sortir; [thought] chasser; **to ~ out evil spirits** [from a place] chasser les mauvais esprits; [from a person] chasser le mauvais œil.

◆ **drive over** ◇ *vi insep* venir OR aller en voiture; **we drove over to visit some friends** nous sommes allés en voiture rendre visite à des amis.

◇ *vt insep* [crush] écraser.

◇ *vt sep* conduire OR emmener en voiture.

◆ **drive up** *vi insep* [person] arriver (en voiture); [car] arriver.

driveability [ˌdraɪvəˈbɪlətɪ] *n* maniabilité *f*, manœuvrabilité *m inv*.

drive-in ◇ *n* [cinema] drive-in *m inv*, ciné-parc *m offic*; [restaurant, bank etc] *désigne tout commerce où l'on est servi dans sa voiture*.

◇ *adj* où l'on reste dans sa voiture.

drivel [ˈdrɪvl] (*Br pt & pp* **drivelled**, *cont* **drivelling**, *Am pt & pp* **driveled**, *cont* **driveling**) ◇ *n* (*U*) -1. [nonsense] bêtises *fpl*, radotage *m*; **you're talking ~!** tu racontes n'importe quoi! -2. [saliva] bave *f*.

◇ *vi* -1. [speak foolishly] dire des bêtises, radoter; **what's he drivelling on about?** qu'est-ce qu'il radote? -2. [dribble] baver.

driven [ˈdrɪvn] ◇ *pp* → **drive**.

◇ *adj* TECH: a ~ shaft un arbre mené OR récepteur.

-driven *in cpds* -1. MECH (fonctionnant) à; **electricity/steam~ engine** machine électrique/à vapeur. -2. *fig* déterminé par; **market/consumer~** déterminé par les contraintes du marché/les exigences du consommateur. -3. COMPUT contrôlé par; **menu~** contrôlé par menu.

driver [ˈdraɪvəʳ] *n* -1. [of car] conducteur *m*, -trice *f*; [of bus, taxi, lorry] chauffeur *m*, conducteur *m*, -trice *f*; [of racing car] pilote *m*; [of train] mécanicien *m*, conducteur *m*, -trice *f*; [of cart] charretier *m*, -ère *f*; SPORT [of horse-drawn vehicle] driver *m*; **she's a good ~** elle conduit bien; **car ~s** automobilistes *mpl*; **the ~'s seat** la place du conducteur. -2. [of animals] conducteur *m*, -trice *f*. -3. [golf club] driver *m*.

driver's licence *n Am* permis *m* de conduire.

drive shaft *n* arbre *m* de transmission.

drive-through ◇ *adj* où l'on reste dans sa voiture.

◇ *n* drive-in *m inv*, ciné-parc *m offic*.

driveway [ˈdraɪvweɪ] *n* voie *f* privée *(menant à une habitation)*.

driving [ˈdraɪvɪŋ] ◇ *adj* -1. [rain] battant. -2. [powerful] fort; **she has a ~ ambition to be a pop star** elle a la ferme ambition de devenir une pop star.

◇ *n* conduite *f*; **her ~ is good** elle conduit bien; **I like ~** j'aime conduire; **bad ~** conduite imprudente; **dangerous ~** JUR conduite dangereuse; **reckless ~** JUR conduite imprudente.

driving force *n* MECH force *f* motrice; **she's the ~ force behind the project** *fig* c'est elle le moteur du projet.

driving instructor *n* moniteur *m*, -trice *f* de conduite OR d'auto-école.

driving lesson *n* leçon *f* de conduite.

driving licence *n Br* permis *m* de conduire.

driving mirror *n* rétroviseur *m*.

driving school *n* auto-école *f*.

driving seat *n* place *f* du conducteur; **she's in the ~** *fig* c'est elle qui mène l'affaire OR qui tient les rênes.

driving shaft *n* arbre *m* moteur.

driving test *n* examen *m* du permis de conduire; **I passed my ~ today/in 1972** j'ai eu mon permis aujourd'hui/en 1972; **he failed his ~** il a raté son permis.

driving wheel *n* roue *f* motrice.

drizzle [ˈdrɪzl] ◇ *n* bruine *f*, crachin *m*.

◇ *vi* bruiner, crachiner.

drizzly [ˈdrɪzlɪ] *adj* de bruine OR crachin, bruineux.

drogue [drəʊg] *n* -1. AERON [parachute] parachute *m* antivrille; [windsock] manche *f* à air. -2. NAUT ancre *f* flottante.

droll [drəʊl] *adj* [comical] drôle, comique; [odd] curieux, drôle.

drollery [ˈdrəʊlərɪ] (*pl* **drolleries**) *n* -1. [of situation] caractère *m* drôle, comique *m*; [of person] humour *m*. -2. [act, story, remark] drôlerie *f*, bouffonnerie *f*, farce *f*.

dromedary [ˈdrɒmədərɪ] (*pl* **dromedaries**) *n* dromadaire *m*.

drone [drəʊn] ◇ *n* -1. [sound - of bee] bourdonnement *m*; [- of engine] ronronnement *m*; [louder] vrombissement *m*; **the ~ of his voice** *fig* le ronronnement de sa voix. -2. [male bee] abeille *f* mâle, faux-bourdon *m*; *pej* [person] fainéant *m*, -e *f*. -3. MUS bourdon *m*. -4. [plane] avion *m* téléguidé, drone *m*.

◇ *vi* [bee] bourdonner; [engine] ronronner; [loudly] vrombir; **to ~ on** [person] parler d'un ton monotone; **he ~d on for hours (about...)** il radotait pendant des heures de sa voix monotone (sur...).

drongo [ˈdrɒŋgəʊ] (*pl* **drongos**) *n* -1. ORNITH drongo *m*. -2. ▽ [idiot] abruti *m*, -e *f*.

drool [druːl] *vi* baver; **he was ~ing over the sports cars in the showroom** *fig* il s'extasiait OR bavait d'admiration devant les voitures de sport exposées.

droop [druːp] ◇ *vi* [head] pencher; [eyelids] s'abaisser; [body] s'affaisser; [shoulders] tomber; [flowers] commencer à baisser la tête OR à se faner; **her spirits ~ed** elle s'est démoralisée.

◇ *n* [of eyelids] abaissement *m*; [of head] attitude *f* penchée; [of body, shoulders] affaissement *m*; [of spirits] langueur *f*, abattement *m*.

drooping [ˈdruːpɪŋ] *adj* [eyelids] abaissé; [flowers] qui commence à se faner.

droopy [ˈdruːpɪ] (*compar* **droopier**, *superl* **droopiest**) *adj* [moustache, shoulders] qui tombe; [flowers] qui commence à se faner.

drop [drɒp] (*pt & pp* **dropped**, *cont* **dropping**) ◇ *vt* -1. [let fall - accidentally] laisser tomber; [- liquid] laisser tomber goutte à goutte; [- trousers] laisser tomber; [release] lâcher; **be careful not to ~ it** fais attention à ne pas le laisser tomber; **~ it!** [to dog] lâche ça!; **they dropped soldiers/supplies by parachute** ils ont parachuté des soldats/du ravitaillement; **when the planes dropped their bombs** lorsque les avions ont lancé OR lâché leurs bombes; **to ~ a curtsy** faire une révérence; **to ~ a stitch** sauter OR laisser tomber une maille; **to ~ anchor** NAUT mouiller, jeter l'ancre ‖ SPORT: **to ~ a goal** [in rugby] marquer un drop; **she dropped the ball over the net** [in tennis] elle a placé un amorti juste derrière le filet ❑ **to ~ a brick** *inf* OR **a clanger** *inf Br* faire une gaffe. -2. [lower] baisser; **he dropped his voice** il a baissé la voix; **the car driver dropped his speed when he saw the police car** le conducteur a réduit sa vitesse en voyant la voiture de police; **to ~ a hem** ressortir un ourlet. -3. [deliver] déposer; **could you ~ me at the corner please?** pouvez-vous me déposer au coin s'il vous plaît?; **we dropped the parcel at John's on the way home** nous avons déposé le paquet chez John en rentrant. -4. [abandon - friend] laisser tomber!, lâcher; [- discussion, work] abandonner, laisser tomber; **I've dropped the idea of going** j'ai renoncé à y aller; **he dropped what he was doing and came round to help us** il a abandonné ce qu'il était en train de faire pour venir nous aider; **let's ~ the subject** ne parlons plus de cela, parlons d'autre chose; **she dropped me to go out with the captain of the rugby team** elle m'a laissé tomber pour sortir avec le capitaine de l'équipe de rugby; **just ~ it!** laissez tomber!, assez! -5. [utter - remark] laisser échapper; **to ~ a hint about sthg** faire allusion à qqch; **he dropped me a hint that she wanted to come** il m'a fait comprendre qu'elle voulait venir; **she let (it) ~ that she had been there** [accidentally] elle a laissé échapper qu'elle y était allée; [deliberately] elle a fait comprendre qu'elle y était allée. -6. [send - letter, note] écrire, envoyer; **I'll ~ you a line next week** je t'enverrai un petit mot la semaine prochaine; **I'll ~ it in the post** OR **mail** je la mettrai à la poste. -7. [omit - when speaking] ne pas prononcer; [- when writing] omettre; [- intentionally] supprimer; **we dropped the love scene** nous avons supprimé la scène d'amour; **he ~s his h's** il n'aspire pas les h; **let's ~ the formalities, shall we?** oublions les formalités, d'accord?; **to ~ a player from a team** SPORT écarter un joueur d'une équipe. -8. *Br* [lose] perdre; **he dropped $50 gambling** il a laissé OR perdu 50 dollars au jeu; **they dropped one game** SPORT ils ont perdu un match. -9. *inf* [knock down - with punch] sonner; [- with shot] descendre. -10. *drugs sl*: **to ~ acid** prendre OR avaler de l'acide.

◇ *vi* -1. [fall - object] tomber, retomber; [- liquid] tomber goutte à goutte; [- ground] s'abaisser; **the road ~s into the valley** la route plonge vers la vallée; **it all dropped into place** *fig* tout s'est mis en place; **the curtain dropped** THEAT le rideau tomba ❑ **you could have heard a pin ~** on aurait entendu voler une mouche. -2. [sink down - person] se laisser tomber, tomber; [collapse] s'écrouler, s'affaisser; **she dropped to her knees** elle est tombée à genoux; **I dropped exhausted into a chair** je me suis écroulé exténué sur une chaise; **I'm ready to ~** [from fatigue] je tombe de fatigue, je ne tiens plus sur mes jambes; [from sleepiness] je tombe de sommeil; **he'll work until he ~s** il va travailler jusqu'à épuisement; **she dropped dead** elle est tombée raide morte; **~ dead!** *inf* va te faire voir!; **I find that I ~ back into the local dialect when I go home** je réalise que je retombe dans le dialecte quand je rentre chez moi; **the team dropped to third place** l'équipe est descendue à la troisième position. -**3.** [decrease - price, speed] baisser, diminuer; [- temperature] baisser; [- wind] se calmer, tomber; [- voice] baisser. -**4.** [end] cesser; **there the matter dropped** l'affaire en est restée là. -**5.** [give birth - subj: animals] mettre bas.

◇ *n* -**1.** [of liquid] goutte *f*; **the rain fell in huge ~s** la pluie tombait à grosses gouttes; **~ by ~** goutte à goutte; **there hasn't been a ~ of rain for weeks** il n'y a pas eu une goutte de pluie depuis des semaines; **would you like a ~ of wine?** que diriez-vous d'une goutte OR d'une larme de vin?; **there's a ~ left in the bottle** il reste une goutte dans la bouteille; **he's had a ~ too much (to drink)** *inf* il a bu un verre de trop ❑ **it's just a ~ in the ocean** ce n'est qu'une goutte d'eau dans la mer. -**2.** [decrease - in price] baisse *f*, chute *f*; [- in temperature] baisse *f*; **a ~ in prices** une baisse OR une chute des prix; **a ~ in voltage** ELEC une chute de tension. -**3.** [fall] chute *f*; [in parachuting] saut *m* (en parachute); **it was a long ~ from the top of the wall** ça faisait haut depuis le haut du mur ❑ **at the ~ of a hat** sans hésiter, à tout moment; **she'll offer to sing at the ~ of a hat** elle propose de chanter pour un oui ou pour un non. -**4.** [vertical distance] hauteur *f* de chute; [slope] descente *f* brusque; [abyss] à-pic *m inv*, précipice *m*; [in climbing] vide *m*; **a sudden ~ in the ground level** une soudaine dénivellation; **it's a 50 m ~ from the cliff to the sea** il y a (un dénivelé de OR une hauteur de) 50 m entre le haut de la falaise et la mer ❑ **to have the ~ on sb** *Am* avoir l'avantage sur qqn. -**5.** [earring] pendant *m*, pendeloque *f*; [on necklace] pendentif *m*; [on chandelier] pendeloque *f*. -**6.** [sweet] bonbon *m*, pastille *f*; **lemon ~s** bonbons au citron; **cough ~s** pastilles pour la toux. -**7.** [delivery] livraison *f*; [from plane] parachutage *m*, droppage *m*; **to make a ~** déposer un colis. -**8.** [hiding place] cachette *f*, dépôt *m* (clandestin). -**9.** [place to leave sthg] lieu *m* de dépôt; **a mail ~** *un lieu de dépôt pour le courrier*.

◆ **drops** *npl* MED gouttes *fpl*.

◆ **drop away** *vi insep* -**1.** [interest, support] diminuer, baisser. -**2.** [land] s'abaisser.

◆ **drop back** *vi insep* retourner en arrière, se laisser devancer OR distancer.

◆ **drop by** *vi insep* passer.

◆ **drop down** *vi insep* [person] tomber (par terre); [table leaf] se rabattre.

◆ **drop in** ◇ *vi insep* passer; **I just dropped in for a chat** je suis seulement passé bavarder un moment; **to ~ in on sb** passer voir qqn; **he dropped in on his friend** il a rendu visite à son ami.

◇ *vt sep* [deliver] déposer; **I'll ~ it in on my way to work** je le déposerai demain en allant au travail.

◆ **drop off** ◇ *vt sep* [person] déposer; [package, thing] déposer, laisser.

◇ *vi insep* -**1.** [fall asleep] s'endormir; [have a nap] faire un (petit) somme. -**2.** [decrease] diminuer, baisser. -**3.** [fall off] tomber; **all the flowers dropped off when I moved the plant** toutes les fleurs sont tombées lorsque j'ai déplacé la plante.

◆ **drop out** *vi insep* -**1.** [fall out] tomber; **my purse must have dropped out of my bag** mon porte-monnaie a dû tomber de mon sac. -**2.** [withdraw] renoncer; **she dropped out of the race** elle s'est retirée de la course; **he dropped out of school** il a abandonné ses études; **words that have dropped out of current usage** des mots qui ont disparu de l'usage courant ‖ [from society] vivre en marge de la société.

◆ **drop round** *Br* ◇ *vi insep* = **drop in**.

◇ *vt sep* [deliver] déposer; **I'll ~ that book round for you tomorrow** je déposerai ce livre chez toi demain.

drop curtain *n* rideau *m* (à la française).

drop forge ◇ *n* marteau-pilon *m*.

◇ *vt* forger au marteau-pilon.

drop front *adj* [bureau] à abattant.

drop goal *n* drop-goal *m*, drop *m*.

drop hammer *n* marteau-pilon *m*.

drop handlebars *npl* guidon *m* renversé.

drophead coupé ['drɒphed-] *n Br* coupé *m* décapotable.

drop-in centre *n Br* centre *m* d'assistance sociale *(où l'on peut aller sans rendez-vous)*.

dropkick ['drɒpkɪk] *n* coup *m* de pied tombé.

◆ **drop-kick** ◇ *vt*: **to drop-kick the ball** donner un coup de pied tombé (au ballon); **to drop-kick a goal** marquer un point par un coup de pied tombé.

◇ *vi* donner un coup de pied tombé.

drop-leaf *adj*: **a ~ table** une table à abattants OR à volets.

droplet ['drɒplɪt] *n* gouttelette *f*.

drop-off *n* -**1.** [decrease] baisse *f*, diminution *f*; **a ~ in sales** une baisse des ventes. -**2.** *Am* [descent] à-pic *m inv*; **there's a sharp ~ in the road** la rue descend en pente très raide.

drop-off charge *n Am* [for hired car] *supplément compté lorsque l'on rend un véhicule de location dans une autre ville que celle où on l'a loué*.

dropout *inf* ['drɒpaʊt] *n* [from society] marginal *m*, -e *f*; [from studies] étudiant *m*, -e *f* qui abandonne ses études; **he's a high school ~** *Am* il a quitté le lycée avant le bac.

drop-out *n* RUGBY renvoi *m* aux 22 mètres.

dropper ['drɒpəʳ] *n* compte-gouttes *m inv*.

droppings ['drɒpɪŋz] *npl* [of animal] crottes *fpl*; [of bird] fiente *f*.

drop scone *n Br sorte de crêpe épaisse*.

drop shipment *n envoi commercial facturé à un grossiste mais expédié directement au détaillant*.

drop shot *n* amorti *m*.

dropsy *n* ['drɒpsɪ] *n* hydropisie *f*.

drop zone *n* zone *f* de droppage.

drosophila [drɒ'sɒfɪlə] (*pl* **drosophilas** OR **drosophilae** [-liː]) *n* drosophile *f*.

dross [drɒs] *n* *(U)* -**1.** METALL scories *fpl*, crasse *f*; INDUST [of minerals] schlamm *m*. -**2.** [waste] déchets *mpl*, impuretés *fpl*; **they chose all the nice things and we were left with the ~** *fig* ils ont choisi tout ce qu'il y avait de joli et nous ont laissé le rebut.

drought [draʊt] *n* -**1.** [no rain] sécheresse *f*. -**2.** [shortage] disette *f*, manque *m*.

drove [drəʊv] ◇ *pt* → **drive**.

◇ *n* -**1.** [of animals] troupeau *m* en marche; [of people] foule *f*, multitude *f*; **~s of students** des foules d'étudiants; **every summer the tourists come in ~s** chaque été les touristes arrivent en foule. -**2.** [chisel] boucharde *f*.

◇ *vt* -**1.** [animals] chasser, conduire. -**2.** [stone] boucharder.

drover ['drəʊvəʳ] *n* toucheur *m* de bestiaux.

drown [draʊn] ◇ *vt* -**1.** [person, animal] noyer; **to be ~ed** se noyer; [in battle, disaster etc] mourir noyé; **to ~ o.s.** se noyer. -**2.** [field, village] noyer; **don't ~ it!** [my drink] ne mets pas trop d'eau!; **the pie was absolutely ~ed in cream** le gâteau baignait dans la crème ❑ **to ~ one's sorrows** noyer son chagrin (dans la boisson). -**3.** [make inaudible] noyer, couvrir; **his voice was ~ed (out) by the music** sa voix était couverte par la musique.

◇ *vi* se noyer; [in battle, disaster etc] mourir noyé.

◆ **drown out** *vt sep* = **drown 3**.

drowned [draʊnd] *adj* noyé; **a ~ man** un noyé ❑ **you look like a ~ rat!** tu es trempé comme une soupe!

drowning ['draʊnɪŋ] ◇ *adj*: **a ~ man** un homme en train de se noyer; **the ~ woman was saved just in time** la noyée a été sauvée de justesse ❑ **a ~ man will clutch at a straw** *prov* dans une situation désespérée on se raccroche à un rien.

◇ *n* noyade *f*; **four ~s** OR **cases of ~** quatre noyades; **to save sb from ~** sauver qqn de la noyade; **he died of ~** il est mort noyé.

drowse [draʊz] *vi* somnoler.

◆ **drowse off** *vi insep* s'assoupir.

drowsily ['draʊzɪlɪ] *adv* d'un air somnolent.

drowsiness ['draʊzɪnɪs] *n (U)* somnolence *f*; **'may cause ~'** 'peut provoquer des somnolences'.

drowsy ['draʊzɪ] (*compar* **drowsier**, *superl* **drowsiest**) *adj* [person, voice] somnolent, engourdi; [place] endormi; **to feel ~** être tout endormi; **to make sb feel ~** [atmosphere] engourdir qqn; [drug] endormir qqn, provoquer des somnolences chez qqn.

drub [drʌb] (*pt* & *pp* **drubbed**, *cont* **drubbing**) *vt* -**1.** [defeat thoroughly] anéantir, battre à plate couture. -**2.** *arch* [beat with stick] battre, rosser. -**3.** [instil forcefully]: **to ~ sthg into sb** faire entrer qqch dans la tête de qqn.

drubbing ['drʌbɪŋ] *n* [thorough defeat] volée *f* de coups; **to give sb a real ~** donner une correction à qqn; **to get a good ~** se faire battre à plate couture.

drudge [drʌdʒ] ◇ *n* -**1.** [person] bête *f* de somme. -**2.** [work] besogne *f*.

◇ *vi* besogner, peiner.

drudgery ['drʌdʒərɪ] *n (U)* travail *m* de bête de somme; **the sheer ~ of it!** quelle corvée!

drug [drʌg] (*pt* & *pp* **drugged**, *cont* **drugging**) ◇ *n* -**1.** [medication] médicament *m*; **to be on ~s** prendre des médicaments; **to be put on ~s by the doctor** se voir prescrire des médicaments par le médecin. -**2.** [illegal substance] drogue *f*; JUR stupéfiant *m*; **to be on ~s** se droguer; **to take ~s** se droguer; [athlete] se doper; **to do** *inf* OR **to use ~s** se droguer; **I don't do ~s** je ne touche pas à la drogue; **music is (like) a ~ for him** la musique est (comme) une drogue pour lui ❑ **a ~ on the market** un produit qui ne se vend pas.

◇ *comp* [abuse, dealing, trafficking] de drogue; **~-related** [crime, offence] lié à la drogue; **~ baron** gros bonnet *m* de la drogue; **to be arrested on ~s charges** [possession] être arrêté pour détention de drogue OR de stupéfiants; [trafficking] être arrêté pour trafic de drogue; **~ courier** passeur *m*, -euse *f* de drogue; **~ money** argent *m* de la drogue; **~ offence** infraction *f* liée à la drogue; **Drug Squad** [police] Brigade *f* des stupéfiants; **~ taker** [addict] drogué *m*, -e *f*; [athlete] consommateur *m*, -trice *f* de produits dopants; **~ taking** dopage *m*; **~s test** [of athlete, horse] contrôle *m* antidopage; **~ traffic** trafic *m* de drogue OR stupéfiants; **~ user** drogué *m*, -e *f*.

◇ *vt* droguer; [athlete, horse] doper; **to ~ sb's drink** mettre de la drogue dans le verre de qqn; **to be drugged with sleep** *fig* être engourdi de sommeil.

drug addict *n* drogué *m*, -e *f*, toxicomane *mf*.

drug addiction *n* toxicomanie *f*.

drugget ['drʌgɪt] *n sorte de tapis en toile de jute*.

druggie *inf* ['drʌgɪ] *n* camé *m*, -e *f*.

druggist ['drʌgɪst] *n Am* [person] pharmacien *m*, -enne *f*; [shop]: **~, ~'s** pharmacie *f*.

druggy *inf* ['drʌgɪ] (*pl* **druggies**) = **druggie**.

drugstore ['drʌgstɔːʳ] *n Am* drugstore *m*.

druid ['druːɪd] *n* druide *m*, -esse *f*.

drum [drʌm] (*pt* & *pp* **drummed**, *cont* **drumming**) ◇ *n* -**1.** [instrument - gen] tambour *m*; [- African] tam-tam *m*; **to play (the) ~s** jouer de la batterie; **Keith Wilson on ~s** Keith Wilson à la batterie; **to beat** OR **to bang a ~** taper OR frapper sur un tambour ❑ **to beat the ~ for sb/sthg** faire de la publicité pour qqn/qqch. -**2.** [for fuel] fût *m*, bidon *m*; [for wire, rope] cylindre *m*; COMPUT [cylinder] tambour *m*; **(concrete) mixing ~** tambour *m* mélangeur

(de béton). -**3.** ANAT [eardrum] tympan *m*. -**4.** [noise - of rain, fingers] tambourinement *m*.
◇ *vi* -**1.** MUS [on drum kit] jouer de la batterie; [on one drum] jouer du tambour. -**2.** [rain, fingers] tambouriner.
◇ *vt* [on instrument] tambouriner, jouer sur un tambour; to ~ one's fingers on the table tambouriner de ses doigts sur la table.
◆ **drum in** *vt sep* insister lourdement sur.
◆ **drum into** *vt sep*: to ~ sthg into sb enfoncer qqch dans la tête de qqn; we had it drummed into us that... on nous a enfoncé dans la tête que...; ~ it into her that... mets-lui bien dans la tête que...
◆ **drum out** *vt sep* expulser; to ~ sb out of a club/of the army expulser qqn d'un club/de l'armée.
◆ **drum up** *vt insep* [customers, support] attirer, rechercher; [supporters] battre le rappel de; [enthusiasm] chercher à susciter; to ~ up business rechercher des clients.

drumbeat ['drʌmbiːt] *n* battement *m* de tambour.

drum brake *n* AUT frein *m* à tambour.

drumfire ['drʌmfaɪəʳ] *n* MIL tir *m* de barrage, feu *m* roulant.

drumhead ['drʌmhed] *n* MUS peau *f* de tambour; ~ court-martial MIL conseil *m* de guerre.

drum kit *n* batterie *f*.

drum machine *n* boîte *f* à rythmes.

drum major *n* MIL tambour-major *m*.

drum majorette *n esp Am* chef-majorette *f*.

drummer ['drʌməʳ] *n* [in band] batteur *m*; [in native tribe] joueur *m* de tambour; MIL tambour *m*.

drumming ['drʌmɪŋ] *n* *(U)* [sound - of one drum] son *m* du tambour; [- of set of drums] son *m* de la batterie; [- of fingers, rain, in the ears] tambourinement *m*, tambourinage *m*; [- of woodpecker] tambourinement *m*, tambourinage *m*; I really like his ~ j'aime beaucoup sa façon de jouer de la batterie; some really great ~ un jeu de batterie superbe.

drum printer *n* COMPUT imprimante *f* à tambour.

drum roll *n* roulement *m* de tambour.

drumstick ['drʌmstɪk] *n* -**1.** MUS baguette *f*. -**2.** CULIN pilon *m*.

drunk [drʌŋk] ◇ *pp* → **drink**.
◇ *adj* -**1.** *literal* soûl, saoul, ivre; to get ~ (on beer/on wine) se soûler (à la bière/au vin); to get sb ~ soûler qqn; he gets ~ on very little, it doesn't take much to make him ~ il lui en faut très peu pour être soûl; ~ and disorderly JUR en état d'ivresse publique; he was arrested for being ~ and disorderly il s'est fait arrêter pour ivresse publique; dead OR blind ~ *inf* ivre mort □ as ~ as a lord soûl comme une grive; ~ and incapable en état d'ivresse manifeste. -**2.** *fig*: ~ with power/success ivre de pouvoir/succès.
◇ *n* [habitual] ivrogne *mf*; [on one occasion] homme *m* soûl OR ivre, femme *f* soûle OR ivre.

drunkard ['drʌŋkəd] *n* [habitual] ivrogne *mf*.

drunk driving = **drink driving**.

drunken ['drʌŋkn] *adj* [person] ivre; [laughter, sleep] d'ivrogne; [evening, party] très arrosé; ~ brawl querelle *f* d'ivrognes; ~ orgy beuverie *f*, soûlerie *f*.

drunkenly ['drʌŋkənlɪ] *adv* [speak, sing, shout etc] comme un ivrogne; he slumped ~ into an armchair complètement soûl, il s'affala dans un fauteuil; he staggered ~ down the street/the stairs il a descendu la rue/l'escalier en titubant.

drunkenness ['drʌŋkənnɪs] *n* [state] ivresse *f*; [habit] ivrognerie *f*.

drunkometer [drʌŋ'kɒmɪtəʳ] *n Am* Alcootest® *m*.

drupe [druːp] *n* drupe *f*.

Drury Lane ['drʊərɪ-] *pr n nom courant du Théâtre Royal de Londres.*

DRURY LANE:
«Drury Lane» est le plus ancien théâtre de Londres encore en activité; fondé en 1663, il est connu pour ses comédies musicales. Il doit son nom à la rue située derrière le bâtiment.

Druse [druːz] *n* Druze *mf*; the ~ les Druzes.

Drusean ['druːzɪən] *adj* druze.

dry [draɪ] (*compar* drier, *superl* driest, *pt* & *pp* dried) ◇ *adj* -**1.** [climate, season, clothing, skin] sec; ~ spell période *f* sèche; to go OR to run ~ [well, river] s'assécher, se tarir; to be ~ [be thirsty] mourir de soif *fig*, avoir soif; [cow] être tarie OR sèche; to pump a well ~ épuiser un puits; to keep sthg ~ garder qqch au sec; 'to be kept ~' 'conserver à l'abri de l'humidité'; her mouth had gone OR turned ~ with fear elle avait la bouche sèche de peur □ to be (as) ~ as a bone, to be bone ~ [washing, earth etc] être très sec; to be (as) ~ as a bone [very thirsty] mourir de soif *fig*; there wasn't a ~ eye in the house tout le monde pleurait. -**2.** [vermouth, wine] sec; [champagne] brut; medium ~ [wine] demi-sec. -**3.** [where alcohol is banned] où l'alcool est prohibé; [where alcohol is not sold] où on ne vend pas d'alcool; we've run ~ [at party] il n'y a plus rien à boire; ~ state *Am État ayant adopté les lois de la prohibition*. -**4.** [boring - book, lecture] aride; ~ as dust ennuyeux comme la pluie. -**5.** [sarcasm, wit, sense of humour] caustique, mordant. -**6.** *inf Br* POL [hardline] *en faveur de la politique extrémiste du parti conservateur*.
◇ *n* -**1.** *inf Br* POL [hardliner] *conservateur en faveur de la politique extrémiste du parti*. -**2.** *inf Austr* [dry season] saison *f* sèche. -**3.** [dry place]: come into the ~ viens te mettre au sec. -**4.** [with towel, cloth] to give sthg a ~ essuyer qqch; give your hair a ~ sèche tes cheveux.
◇ *vt* [hair, clothes, fruit, leaves] (faire) sécher; [dishes] essuyer; to ~ one's eyes se sécher les yeux, sécher ses yeux; to ~ one's tears sécher ses larmes; to ~ o.s. se sécher, s'essuyer.
◇ *vi* -**1.** [clothes, hair, fruit, leaves] sécher; you wash, I'll ~ tu laves et moi j'essuie. -**2.** [cow] se tarir.
◆ **dry off** ◇ *vi insep* [clothes, person] = **dry out 1**.
◇ *vt sep* sécher; to ~ o.s. off se sécher.
◆ **dry out** ◇ *vi insep* -**1.** [clothes] sécher; [person] se sécher. -**2.** [alcoholic] se désintoxiquer.
◇ *vt sep* [alcoholic] désintoxiquer.
◆ **dry up** *vi insep* -**1.** [well, river] s'assécher, se tarir; [puddle, street] sécher; [inspiration] se tarir; [cow] se tarir. -**2.** [dry the dishes] essuyer la vaisselle. -**3.** *inf* [be quiet] la fermer, la boucler; ~ up, will you? ferme-la OR boucle-la, tu veux? -**4.** *inf* [actor, speaker] avoir un trou (de mémoire).

dryad ['draɪəd] (*pl* dryads OR dryades [-diːz]) *n* MYTH dryade *f*.

dry battery = **dry cell**.

dry-bulb thermometer *n* thermomètre *m* (à réservoir) sec.

dry cell *n* pile *f* sèche.

dry-clean *vt* nettoyer à sec; to have sthg ~ed faire nettoyer qqch (à sec); to take sthg to be ~ed emmener qqch au nettoyage (à sec) OR chez le teinturier OR à la teinturerie; '~ only' 'nettoyage à sec uniquement'.

dry-cleaner *n* [person] teinturier *m*, -ère *f*; ~'s [shop] teinturerie *f*; to be in OR at the ~'s être chez le teinturier OR à la teinturerie; to take sthg to the ~'s porter qqch chez le teinturier OR à la teinturerie.

dry-cleaning *n* *(U)* -**1.** [action] nettoyage *m* à sec. -**2.** [clothes - being cleaned] vêtements *mpl* laissés au nettoyage (à sec) OR chez le teinturier OR à la teinturerie; [- to be cleaned] vêtements à emmener au nettoyage (à sec) OR chez le teinturier OR à la teinturerie.

dry dock *n* cale *f* sèche; in ~ en cale sèche.

dryer ['draɪəʳ] = **drier**.

dry-eyed *adj* à l'œil sec.

dry farming *n* AGR culture *f* sèche, dry-farming *m*.

dry-fly fishing pêche *f* à la mouche sèche OR artificielle.

dry goods *npl Am* tissus et articles de bonneterie *mpl*.

dry ice *n* neige *f* carbonique.

drying ['draɪɪŋ] ◇ *n* [of clothes, hair] séchage *m*; [of skin, flowers, wood] dessèchement *m*; [with a cloth] essuyage *m*.
◇ *adj* [wind] desséchant.

drying cupboard *n* armoire *f* sèche-linge.

drying room *n* séchoir *m*.

drying up *n Br* [of dishes]: to do the ~ essuyer la vaisselle.

drying-up cloth *n* torchon *m* (à vaisselle), essuie-verres *m inv*.

dry land *n* terre *f* ferme.

dryly ['draɪlɪ] = **drily**.

dry martini *n* martini dry *m*.

dry measure *n unité de mesure des matières sèches*.

dryness ['draɪnɪs] *n* -**1.** [of region, weather, skin] sécheresse *f*. -**2.** [of wit, humour] mordant *m*, causticité *f*.

dry nurse *n* nourrice *f* sèche.

dry riser *n* colonne *f* sèche.

dry-roasted *adj* [peanuts] grillé à sec.

dry rot *n* *(U)* [in wood] moisissure *f* sèche; [in potatoes] pourriture *f* sèche.

dry run *n* -**1.** [trial, practice] coup *m* d'essai, test *m*; to give sthg a ~ tester qqch; to have a ~ faire un essai. -**2.** MIL entraînement *m* avec tir à blanc.

drysalter ['draɪˌsɔːltəʳ] *n arch* marchand *m*, -e *f* de salaisons et de couleurs.

dry-shod *adj lit* à pied sec.

dry ski slope *n* piste *f* de ski artificielle.

dry-stone *adj* [wall] en pierres sèches.

DSc (*abbr of* Doctor of Science) *n (titulaire d'un) doctorat en sciences*.

DSS (*abbr of* Department of Social Security) *pr n ministère britannique de la Sécurité sociale*.

DST *n abbr of* daylight saving time.

DT *n abbr of* data transmission.

DTI (*abbr of* Department of Trade and Industry) *pr n ministère britannique du Commerce et de l'Industrie*.

DTp (*abbr of* Department of Transports) *pr n Br* ≃ ministère *m* des Transports.

DTP (*abbr of* desktop publishing) *n* PAO *f*.

DT's *inf* [ˌdiː'tiːz] (*abbr of* delirium tremens) *n*: to have the ~ avoir une crise de delirium tremens.

dual ['djuːəl] *adj* [purpose, role, nationality] double; to have a ~ purpose OR function avoir une double fonction; with the ~ aim of reducing inflation and stimulating demand dans le but à la fois de réduire l'inflation et de stimuler la demande □ to have a ~ personality souffrir d'un dédoublement de la personnalité; ~ controls AERON & AUT double commande *f*; ~ personality PSYCH dédoublement *m* de la personnalité.

dual carriageway *n Br* AUT route *f* à quatre voies.

dual-control *adj* [car, plane] à double commande.

dualism ['djuːəlɪzm] *n* PHILOS & RELIG dualisme *m*.

dualist ['djuːəlɪst] *adj* PHILOS & RELIG dualiste.

duality [djuː'ælətɪ] *n* dualité *f*.

dual-purpose *adj* à double fonction.

dub [dʌb] (*pt* & *pp* dubbed, *cont* dubbing) *vt* -**1.** [nickname] surnommer. -**2.** CIN & TV [add soundtrack, voice] sonoriser; [in foreign language] doubler; the film has been dubbed into French le film a été doublé en français. -**3.** *lit* OR *arch* armer chevalier.

Dubai [ˌduː'baɪ] *pr n* Dubayy; in ~ à Dubayy.

dubbin ['dʌbɪn] ◇ *n* graisse *f* à chaussures, dégras *m*.
◇ *vt* graisser.

dubbing ['dʌbɪŋ] *n* CIN & TV [addition of soundtrack] sonorisation *f*; [in a foreign language] doublage *m*.

dubiety [djuː'baɪətɪ] *fml* = **dubiousness 1**.

dubious ['djuːbjəs] *adj* **-1.** [unsure - reply, voice] dubitatif; [- expression] dubitatif, d'incertitude; [- outcome, value] incertain; to look ~ [person] avoir l'air dubitatif; I'm rather ~ about the whole thing j'ai des doutes sur toute cette affaire; I'm a bit ~ about whether it will work je ne suis pas très sûr que ça marche; to be ~ (about) whether to do sthg hésiter à faire qqch. **-2.** [suspect - person, nature, reputation, decision] douteux; of ~ character douteux; he's a ~ character c'est un type douteux; a ~ distinction OR honour un triste honneur.

dubiously ['djuːbjəslɪ] *adv* **-1.** [unsurely] d'un air de doute. **-2.** [in suspect manner] d'une manière douteuse.

dubiousness ['djuːbjəsnɪs] *n* **-1.** [uncertainty - in voice, of expression, reply] incertitude *f*; [- of outcome] nature *f* incertaine. **-2.** [suspect nature - of decision, proposal, reputation] nature *f* douteuse.

Dublin ['dʌblɪn] *pr n* Dublin.

Dublin Bay prawn *n* grosse crevette *f*.

Dubliner ['dʌblɪnəʳ] *n* Dublinois *m*, -e *f*; 'Dubliners' *Joyce* 'Gens de Dublin'.

ducal ['djuːkl] *adj* ducal.

ducat ['dʌkət] *n* ducat *m*.

duchess ['dʌtʃɪs] *n* duchesse *f*; 'The Duchess of Malfi' *Webster* 'la Duchesse de Malfi'.

duchesse ['djʊʃes] *n* CULIN: ~ potatoes pommes *fpl* (de terre) duchesse.

duchy ['dʌtʃɪ] (*pl* **duchies**) *n* duché *m*.

duck [dʌk] ◇ *n* **-1.** [bird] canard *m*; to take to sthg like a ~ to water [become good at very quickly] se mettre à qqch très rapidement; [develop a liking for] mordre à qqch; it's like water off a ~'s back [criticism, insult] ça glisse comme sur les plumes d'un canard. **-2.** [in cricket] score *m* nul; to be out for a ~ ne marquer aucun point, faire un score nul; to break one's ~ marquer son premier point. **-3.** MIL véhicule *m* amphibie. **-4.** [material] coutil *m*.
◇ *vt* **-1.** [dodge - blow] esquiver; to ~ one's head (out of the way) baisser vivement la tête. **-2.** [submerge in water] faire boire la tasse à. **-3.** [evade - question, responsibility] se dérober à, esquiver.
◇ *vi* **-1.** [move down quickly] se baisser vivement; [in boxing] esquiver un coup; ~! baissetoi!; to ~ under the water plonger sous l'eau; to ~ behind a hedge se cacher derrière une haie. **-2.** [move quickly]: to ~ out of a room s'esquiver d'une pièce. **-3.** *inf* [avoid] se défiler; to ~ out of doing sthg se défiler pour ne pas faire qqch.

duckbilled platypus [ˌdʌkbɪld'plætɪpəs] *n* ornithorynque *m*.

duckboards ['dʌkbɔːdz] *npl* caillebotis *m*.

duck-egg blue ◇ *n* bleu-vert *m* pâle.
◇ *adj* bleu-vert pâle.

duckie *inf* ['dʌkɪ] = **ducky**.

ducking ['dʌkɪŋ] *n*: he got a ~ on lui a fait boire la tasse.

duckling ['dʌklɪŋ] *n* caneton *m*; [female] canette *f*; [older] canardeau *m*.

duckpond ['dʌkpɒnd] *n* mare *f* aux canards.

ducks [dʌks] ◇ *n inf Br* = **ducky** *n*.
◇ *npl* [trousers] pantalon *m* de coutil.

ducks and drakes *n Br* [game]: to play ~ *literal* faire des ricochets; to play ~ with sthg gaspiller qqch; to play ~ with one's money jeter l'argent par les fenêtres, gaspiller son argent.

duck soup *inf n Am* [something easily done]: it's ~ c'est du gâteau.

duckweed ['dʌkwiːd] *n* lentille *f* d'eau.

ducky *inf* ['dʌkɪ] ◇ *n Br* [term of endearment] mon canard; [in shop]: what can I get you, ~? [to woman] qu'est-ce qu'elle voulait la petite dame OR demoiselle?; [to man] qu'est-ce qu'il voulait le petit monsieur?
◇ *adj Am* **-1.** [perfect] impec; that's just ~ c'est impec. **-2.** [cute] joli.

duct [dʌkt] *n* [for gas, liquid, electricity] conduite *f*; ANAT conduit *m*; BOT vaisseau *m*; tear/hepatic ~ canal *m* lacrymal/hépatique.

ductile ['dʌktaɪl] *adj* [metal, plastic] ductile; *fig* [person] malléable, influençable.

ductless ['dʌktlɪs] *adj* ANAT: ~ gland glande *f* endocrine.

dud *inf* [dʌd] ◇ *adj* [false - coin, note] faux; [useless - drill, video] qui ne marche pas; [- shell, bomb] qui a raté; [- idea] débile; ~ cheque chèque *m* en bois.
◇ *n* [person] nullité *f*, tache *f*; [cheque] chèque *m* en bois; [coin] fausse pièce *f* de monnaie; [note] faux billet *m*; [shell] obus *m* qui a raté OR qui n'a pas explosé; it's a ~ [firework] ça a raté, c'est pas parti; to be a ~ at maths/sport être nul en maths/sport.

dude *inf* [djuːd] *n Am* **-1.** [man] type *m*, mec *m*; hi, ~! salut mon vieux! **-2.** [city dweller] citadin *m*, -e *f*.

dude ranch *n Am ranch qui propose des activités touristiques*.

dudgeon ['dʌdʒən] *n*: in high ~ *fml* très en colère, fort indigné.

due [djuː] ◇ *n* [what one deserves]: but then, to give him his ~... mais pour lui rendre justice...
◇ *adj* **-1.** [owed, payable - amount, balance, money] dû; when's the next instalment ~? quand le prochain versement doit-il être fait?; ~ and payable now [bill] payable dès maintenant; he's ~ some money from me je lui dois de l'argent; I'm ~ some money next week on doit me verser de l'argent la semaine prochaine; repayment ~ on December 1st remboursement à effectuer le 1er décembre; to fall ~ [bill] arriver à échéance; ~ date [of bill, payment] échéance *f*; to be ~ an apology avoir droit à des excuses; to be ~ a bit of luck/some good weather mériter un peu de chance/du beau temps; I'm ~ (for) a rise [I will receive one] je vais être augmenté, je vais recevoir une augmentation; [I deserve one] je suis en droit d'attendre une augmentation; (to give) credit where credit's ~ pour dire ce qui est, pour être juste. **-2.** [expected]: we're ~ round there at 7:30 on nous attend à 7 h 30, nous devons y être à 7 h 30; to be ~ to do sthg devoir faire qqch; we were ~ to meet at 10 p.m. nous devions nous retrouver à 22 h; the train is ~ (in OR to arrive) now le train devrait arriver d'un instant à l'autre; when is he/the train ~? quand doit-il/quand le train doit-il arriver?; she's ~ back next week elle doit rentrer la semaine prochaine; the next issue is ~ out next week le prochain numéro doit sortir la semaine prochaine; her baby is OR she's ~ any day now elle doit accoucher d'un jour à l'autre. **-3.** [proper - care, respect] dû; to give sthg ~ consideration accorder mûre réflexion à qqch; after ~ consideration après mûre réflexion; to fail to exercise ~ care and attention ne pas prêter l'attention nécessaire; to give sb ~ warning prévenir qqn suffisamment tôt; ~ process of law garantie suffisante du droit ❑ in ~ course [at the proper time] en temps voulu; [in the natural course of events] à un certain moment; [at a later stage, eventually] plus tard; to treat sb with ~ respect traiter qqn avec le respect qui lui est dû; with (all) ~ respect... avec tout le respect que je vous dois..., sauf votre respect...; with (all) ~ respect to the Prime Minister avec tout le respect qui est dû au Premier ministre.
◇ *adv* [east, west etc] plein.
◆ **due to** *prep phr* **-1.** [owing to] à cause de, en raison de; ~ to bad weather they arrived late ils sont arrivés en retard à cause du mauvais temps. **-2.** [because of] grâce à; it's all ~ to you c'est grâce à toi; her success was ~ in (large) part to hard work elle doit sa réussite en grande partie à son travail acharné; our late arrival was ~ to the bad weather notre retard était dû au mauvais temps.

duel ['djuːəl] (*Br pt & pp* **duelled**, *cont* **duelling**, *Am pt & pp* **dueled**, *cont* **dueling**) ◇ *n* duel *m*; to fight a ~ se battre en duel; to challenge sb to a ~ provoquer qqn en duel ❑ 'Duel in the Sun' *Vidor* 'Duel au soleil'.
◇ *vi* se battre en duel.

duelling *Br*, **dueling** *Am* ['djuːəlɪŋ] *adj*: ~ pistols pistolets *mpl* de duel.

duellist *Br*, **duelist** *Am* ['djuːəlɪst] *n* duelliste *mf*.

dues [djuːz] *npl* droits *mpl*.

duet [djuː'et] *n* duo *m*; to sing/to play a ~ chanter/jouer en duo; piano/violin ~ duo de piano/de violon.

duettist [djuː'etɪst] *n* duettiste *mf*.

duff [dʌf] ◇ *adj inf Br* [useless] qui ne marche pas; [idea] débile; to be ~ at sthg être nul en qqch.
◇ *n* CULIN *variante du plum-pudding*.
◆ **duff up** *inf vt sep Br* [give a beating to] tabasser, démolir.

duffel ['dʌfl] *n* [fabric] tissu *m* de laine.

duffel bag *n* sac *m* marin.

duffel coat *n* duffel-coat *m*, duffle-coat *m*.

duffer *inf* ['dʌfəʳ] *n Br* **-1.** [useless person] gourde *f*; SCH nullité *f*, cancre *m*; to be a ~ at sthg être nul en qqch. **-2.** [old man] vieux bonhomme *m*.

duffle ['dʌfl] = **duffel**.

dug [dʌg] ◇ *pt & pp* → **dig**.
◇ *n* mamelle *f*; [of cow, goat] pis *m*.

dugong ['duːgɒŋ] *n* dugon *m*, dugong *m*.

dugout ['dʌgaʊt] *n* **-1.** MIL tranchée-abri *f*; SPORT banc *m* abri de touche. **-2.** [canoe] canoë *m* creusé dans un tronc.

duke [djuːk] *n* duc *m*.

dukedom ['djuːkdəm] *n* [territory] duché *m*; [title] titre *m* de duc.

Duke of Edinburgh's Award Scheme *pr n*: the ~ ≃ la bourse du duc d'Édimbourg.

> **DUKE OF EDINBURGH'S AWARD SCHEME:**
> Cette bourse récompense, par des médailles de bronze, d'argent et d'or, les projets d'intérêt collectif ou personnel réalisés par des jeunes de 14 à 23 ans.

dukes *inf* [djuːks] *npl* [fists] poings *mpl*; to put up one's ~ se mettre en garde.

dulcet ['dʌlsɪt] *adj lit* doux, suave; her ~ tones ses intonations douces; *hum* sa douce voix.

dulcimer ['dʌlsɪməʳ] *n* MUS dulcimer *m*, tympanon *m*.

dull [dʌl] ◇ *adj* **-1.** [slow-witted - person] peu intelligent; [- reflexes] ralenti; she's very ~ when it comes to maths elle est très médiocre en maths; to grow ~ [intellectual capacities] s'affaiblir, décliner. **-2.** [boring - book, person, lecture] ennuyeux, assommant; there's never a ~ moment with him around on ne s'ennuie jamais avec lui; deadly ~ mortel, ennuyeux à mourir ❑ (as) ~ as ditchwater ennuyeux comme la pluie. **-3.** [not bright - colour] terne, fade; [- light, eyes] terne; [- weather, sky] sombre, maussade. **-4.** [not sharp - blade] émoussé; [- pain] sourd; [- sound] sourd, étouffé; the knife is ~ le couteau ne coupe plus bien. **-5.** [listless - person] abattu.
◇ *vt* [sound] assourdir; [colour, metal] ternir; [blade, pleasure, senses, impression] émousser; [grief] endormir.
◇ *vi* [colour] se ternir, perdre son éclat; [pleasure] s'émousser; [pain] s'atténuer; [eyes] s'assombrir, perdre son éclat; [mind] s'affaiblir, décliner.

dullard ['dʌləd] *n lit* benêt *m*.

dullness ['dʌlnɪs] *n* **-1.** [slow-wittedness] lenteur *f* OR lourdeur *f* d'esprit. **-2.** [tedium - of book, speech] caractère *m* ennuyeux. **-3.** [dimness - of light] faiblesse *f*; [- of weather] caractère *m* maussade. **-4.** [of sound, pain] caractère *m* sourd; [of blade] manque *m* de tranchant. **-5.** [listlessness] apathie *f*.

dullsville *inf* ['dʌlzvɪl] *n* [boring place] trou *m*; it's ~ round here c'est un vrai trou ici.

dully ['dʌlɪ] *adv* **-1.** [listlessly] d'un air déprimé. **-2.** [tediously] de manière ennuyeuse. **-3.** [dimly] faiblement. **-4.** [not sharply] sourdement.

duly ['dju:lɪ] *adv* **-1.** [properly] comme il convient; [in accordance with the rules] dans les règles, dûment. **-2.** [as expected - arrive, call] comme prévu; I was ~ surprised comme de bien entendu, j'ai été surpris; and he ~ did what he had promised et il a bien fait ce qu'il avait promis.

dumb [dʌm] *adj* **-1.** [unable or unwilling to speak] muet; to be struck ~ (with fear/surprise) rester muet (de peur/surprise); have you been struck ~? tu es devenu muet?; ~ animal bête *f*, animal *m*; ~ insolence silence *m* OR mutisme *m* insolent. **-2.** *inf* [stupid] bête; that was a ~ thing to do c'est bête OR idiot d'avoir fait ça; he's really ~ il est complètement abruti; don't act ~ with me ne joue pas les imbéciles avec moi; ~ blonde *pej* blonde *f* évaporée.

dumbbell ['dʌmbel] *n* **-1.** SPORT haltère *m*. **-2.** *inf Am* [fool] abruti *m*, -e *f*.

dumbfound [dʌm'faʊnd] *vt* abasourdir, interloquer.

dumbfounded [dʌm'faʊndɪd] *adj* [person] muet de stupeur, abasourdi, interloqué; [silence] stupéfait; to be ~ at OR by sthg être abasourdi OR interloqué par qqch.

dumbly ['dʌmlɪ] *adv* silencieusement, sans prononcer un mot.

dumbness ['dʌmnɪs] *n* **-1.** [inability to speak] mutité *f*; [unwillingness to speak] mutisme *m*. **-2.** *inf* [stupidity] bêtise *f*, stupidité *f*, imbécillité *f*.

dumbo *inf* ['dʌmbəʊ] *n* [fool] abruti *m*, -e *f*.

dumb show *n pantomime faisant partie d'une pièce de théâtre*; she told us to go in ~ *fig* elle nous a fait signe de partir.

dumbstruck ['dʌmstrʌk], **dumbstricken** ['dʌmstrɪkn] = **dumbfounded**.

dumb waiter *n Br* [lift] monte-plats *m inv*; [trolley] table *f* roulante; [revolving tray] plateau *m* tournant.

dumdum ['dʌmdʌm] *n* **-1.** MIL [bullet] balle *f* dum-dum. **-2.** *inf* [fool] imbécile *mf*.

dummy ['dʌmɪ] (*pl* dummies) ◇ *n* **-1.** [human figure - in shop window, for dressmaking] mannequin *m*; [- of ventriloquist] marionnette *f*; FIN [representative] prête-nom *m*, homme *m* de paille; [fake object] objet *m* factice; [book, model for display] maquette *f*; all the bottles are dummies toutes les bouteilles sont factices. **-2.** *Br* [for baby] tétine *f*. **-3.** [in bridge - cards] main *f* du mort; [- player] mort *m*; he is ~ c'est lui le mort. **-4.** *pej* [mute] muet *m*, -ette *f*. **-5.** *inf* [fool] imbécile *mf*. **-6.** SPORT feinte *f*; to sell sb a ~ feinter qqn.

◇ *adj* [fake] factice; ~ buyer FIN acheteur *m* prête-nom; this is just a ~ version ce n'est qu'un modèle factice.

◇ *vi* & *vt* SPORT feinter.

dummy run *n* [trial] essai *m*; AERON & MIL attaque *f* simulée OR d'entraînement; to give sthg a ~ faire l'essai de qqch.

dump [dʌmp] ◇ *vt* **-1.** [rubbish, waste] déverser, déposer; [sand, gravel] déverser; [car, corpse] abandonner; [oil - subj: ship] vidanger; to ~ waste at sea rejeter OR immerger des déchets dans la mer; he just ~ed me off at the motorway exit il m'a déposé à la sortie de l'autoroute; to ~ sb *inf* [boyfriend, girlfriend] plaquer qqn; [member of government, board] se débarrasser de qqn; to ~ sb/sthg on sb *inf* laisser qqn/qqch sur les bras de qqn. **-2.** [set down - bags, shopping, suitcase] poser. **-3.** COMM vendre en dumping. **-4.** COMPUT [memory] vider.

◇ *n* **-1.** [rubbish heap] tas *m* d'ordures; [place] décharge *f*, dépôt *m* d'ordures. **-2.** MIL dépôt *m*. **-3.** *inf pej* [town, village] trou *m*; [messy room, flat] dépotoir *m*; it's a real ~ here [town] c'est vraiment mortel ici; this ~ of a school cette école à la manque. **-4.** COMPUT [of memory] vidage *m*.

dumper ['dʌmpə^r] *n* **-1.** [vehicle] = **dump truck**. **-2.** [of waste - person] personne *f* qui déverse des ordures; [- company] entreprise *f* déposant des déchets (toxiques). **-3.** COMM [of goods] entreprise *f* pratiquant le dumping.

dumper truck = **dump truck**.

dumping ['dʌmpɪŋ] *n* **-1.** [of rubbish, waste] dépôt *m* OR décharge *f* d'ordures OR de déchets; [of toxic or nuclear waste - at sea] déversement *m* OR immersion *f* de déchets; [- underground] entreposage *m* sous terre de déchets; [of oil from ship] vidange *f*; 'no ~' 'dépôt d'ordures interdit', 'décharge interdite'. **-2.** COMM dumping *m*. **-3.** COMPUT [of memory] vidage *m*.

dumping ground *n* [for rubbish] décharge *f*, dépôt *m* d'ordures; *fig* [for inferior goods] dépotoir *m*.

dumpling ['dʌmplɪŋ] *n* **-1.** CULIN [savoury] boulette *f* de pâte, knödel *m*; *Scot* [sweet] *variante du plum-pudding*; apple ~ pomme *f* en chausson. **-2.** *inf fig* [plump person] boulot *m*, -otte *f*.

dumps *inf* [dʌmps] *npl*: to be down in the ~ avoir le cafard OR bourdon.

Dumpster® ['dʌmpstə^r] *n Am* benne *f* à ordures.

dump truck *n* dumper *m*, tombereau *m*.

dumpy *inf* ['dʌmpɪ] *adj* [person] courtaud; [bottle] pansu.

dun [dʌn] (*pt* & *pp* dunned, *cont* dunning) ◇ *adj* brun gris *(inv)*.

◇ *n* [colour] brun *m* gris; [horse] cheval *m* louvet; [mare] jument *f* louvette.

◇ *vt* COMM presser, harceler; to ~ sb for money OR payment presser OR harceler qqn pour qu'il paye.

dunce [dʌns] *n* âne *m*, cancre *m*; to be a ~ at sthg être nul en qqch.

dunce cap, **dunce's cap** *n* bonnet *m* d'âne.

Dundee cake [dʌn'di:-] *n cake épicé aux fruits secs, décoré avec des amandes*.

dunderhead ['dʌndəhed] *n* âne *m*; ~! espèce d'âne!

dune [dju:n] *n* dune *f*.

dune buggy *n* buggy *m*.

dung [dʌŋ] *n (U)* crotte *f*; [of cow] bouse *f*; [of horse] crottin *m*; [of wild animal] fumées *fpl*; [manure] fumier *m*.

dungarees [,dʌŋgə'ri:z] *npl Br* salopette *f*; *Am* [overalls] bleu *m* de travail; a pair of ~ *Br* une salopette; *Am* un bleu de travail.

dung beetle, **dung chafer** *n* bousier *m*.

dungeon ['dʌndʒən] *n* [in castle] cachot *m* souterrain; [tower] donjon *m*.

dungheap ['dʌŋhi:p] *n* tas *m* de fumier.

dunghill ['dʌŋhɪl] *n* gros tas *m* de fumier.

dunk [dʌŋk] *vt* tremper; to ~ one's bread tremper son pain.

Dunkirk, **Dunkerque** [dʌn'kɜ:k] *pr n* **-1.** GEOG Dunkerque. **-2.** HIST *l'évacuation des troupes alliées de Dunkerque, en mai-juin 1940*.

dunlin ['dʌnlɪn] *n* bécasseau *m* variable, alouette *f* de mer.

dunno *inf* [də'nəʊ] = **I don't know**.

dunnock ['dʌnək] *n* accenteur *m* mouchet.

duo ['dju:əʊ] *n* MUS & THEAT duo *m*; [couple] couple *m*.

duodecimal [,dju:əʊ'desɪml] *adj* duodécimal.

duodenal [,dju:əʊ'di:nl] *adj* duodénal.

duodenum [,dju:əʊ'di:nəm] (*pl* duodenums OR duodena [-nə]) *n* duodénum *m*.

duopoly [djʊ'ɒpəlɪ] (*pl* duopolies) *n* duopole *m*.

dupe [dju:p] ◇ *vt* duper, leurrer; to ~ sb into doing sthg duper OR leurrer qqn pour qu'il/elle fasse qqch.

◇ *n* dupe *f*.

duple ['dju:pl] *adj* **-1.** *fml* [double] double. **-2.** MUS binaire, à deux temps; ~ time rythme *m* binaire OR à deux temps.

duplex ['dju:pleks] ◇ *adj* **-1.** [double, twofold] double; ~ (apartment) (appartement *m* en) duplex *m*. **-2.** ELEC & TELEC duplex; *Am* [house] *maison convertie en deux appartements*.

◇ *n* [apartment] (appartement *m* en) duplex *m*.

duplicate [*vb* 'dju:plɪkeɪt, *n* & *adj* 'dju:plɪkət] ◇ *vt* **-1.** [document] dupliquer, faire un double OR des doubles de; [key] faire un double OR des doubles de. **-2.** [repeat - work] refaire; [- feat] reproduire; this bill merely ~s my proposal ce projet de loi ne fait que reprendre ma proposition.

◇ *n* [of document, key] double *m*; ADMIN & JUR duplicata *m*, copie *f* conforme; in ~ en double, en deux exemplaires.

◇ *adj* [key, document] en double; [receipt, certificate] en duplicata; ~ copy [of key] double *m*; [of receipt, certificate] duplicata *m*.

duplicating machine ['dju:plɪkeɪtɪŋ-] *n* duplicateur *m*.

duplication [,dju:plɪ'keɪʃn] *n* **-1.** [on machine] reproduction *f*; [result] double *m*. **-2.** [repetition - of work, efforts] répétition *f*; that would just be a ~ of what we've already done ce ne serait que répéter OR refaire ce que nous avons déjà fait.

duplicator ['dju:plɪkeɪtə^r] *n* duplicateur *m*.

duplicity [dju:'plɪsətɪ] *n* fausseté *f*, duplicité *f*.

Dur *Br written abbr of* Durham.

durability [,djʊərə'bɪlətɪ] *n* [of construction, relationship, peace] caractère *m* durable, durabilité *f*; [of fabric] résistance *f*; [of politician, athlete] longévité *f*.

durable ['djʊərəbl] *adj* [construction, friendship, peace] durable; [fabric, metal] résistant; [politician, athlete] qui jouit d'une grande longévité; COMM: ~ goods biens *mpl* durables OR non périssables.

◆ **durables** *npl* biens *mpl* durables OR non périssables.

Duralumin® [djʊə'ræljʊmɪn] *n* Duralumin® *m*.

duration [djʊ'reɪʃn] *n* durée *f*; of short ~ de courte durée; to be of long ~ durer longtemps; for the ~ of the summer holiday pendant toute la durée des grandes vacances; for the ~ *hum* pour l'instant.

duress [djʊ'res] *n* contrainte *f*; under ~ sous la contrainte.

Durex® ['djʊəreks] *n* **-1.** *Br* [condom] préservatif *m*. **-2.** *Austr* Scotch® *m (ruban adhésif)*.

durian ['djʊərɪən] *n* durion *m*.

during ['djʊərɪŋ] *prep* pendant; they met ~ the war ils se sont rencontrés pendant la guerre ‖ [in the course of] au cours de; ~ the investigation it emerged that... au cours de l'enquête, il est apparu que...

durst [dɜ:st] *arch* OR *lit pt* → **dare**.

durum (wheat) ['djʊərəm-] *n* blé *m* dur.

dusk [dʌsk] *n* crépuscule *m*; at ~ au crépuscule.

duskiness ['dʌskɪnɪs] *n* [of complexion] matité *f*.

dusky ['dʌskɪ] (*compar* duskier, *superl* duskiest) *adj* **-1.** [light] crépusculaire; [colour] sombre, foncé; [room] sombre. **-2.** [skin] mat; ~ maiden *lit* jeune fille au teint bistre.

dust [dʌst] ◇ *n* **-1.** *(U)* [on furniture, of gold, coal] poussière *f*; a speck of ~ une poussière, un grain de poussière; thick ~ covered the furniture une poussière épaisse couvrait les meubles; to shake the ~ off one's feet secouer la poussière de ses souliers; to gather ~ [ornaments] amasser la poussière; [plans, proposals] rester en plan; to lay OR to settle the ~ mouiller la poussière ❑ to allow the ~ to OR let the ~ settle *fig* attendre que les choses se calment; once the ~ has settled *fig* quand les choses se seront calmées; to trample sb in the ~ *fig* fouler qqn aux pieds; to kick up OR to raise a ~ *inf* faire tout un cinéma OR foin; to throw ~ in sb's eyes tromper qqn; we won't see him for

~ [he'll leave] il partira en moins de temps qu'il n'en faut pour le dire. -**2.** [action]: to give sthg a ~ épousseter qqch. -**3.** [earthly remains] poussière *f*.

◇ *vt* -**1.** [furniture, room] épousseter. -**2.** [with powder, flour] saupoudrer; to ~ a field with insecticide répandre de l'insecticide sur un champ.

◆ **dust down** *vt sep* [with brush] brosser; [with hand] épousseter.

◆ **dust off** *vt sep* [dust, crumbs, dandruff] nettoyer, enlever; *fig* [skill] se remettre à; [speech, lecture notes] ressortir.

dust bag *n* [for vacuum cleaner] sac *m* à poussière.

dust-bath *n*: to take a ~ [bird] prendre un bain de poussière.

dustbin ['dʌstbɪn] *n Br* poubelle *f*.

dustbin man *Br* = **dustman**.

dust bowl *n* GEOG zone *f* semi-désertique; [in US]: the Dust Bowl le Dust Bowl.

THE DUST BOWL:
Nom donné à une région des Grandes Plaines aux États-Unis où sévissaient, dans les années 30, de redoutables tempêtes de poussière provoquées par la sécheresse et l'érosion. Ce phénomène fut la cause de la migration de milliers de paysans vers la Californie, thème du roman «les Raisins de la colère» de J. Steinbeck.

dustcart ['dʌstkɑːt] *n Br* camion *m* des éboueurs.

dustcloth ['dʌstklɒθ] *Am* = **duster 1**.

dustcloud ['dʌstklaʊd] *n* nuage *m* de poussière.

dust coat *n* cache-poussière *m inv*.

dust cover *n* -**1.** = **dust jacket**. -**2.** [for machine] housse *f* de rangement; [for furniture] housse *f* de protection.

dust devil *n* tourbillon *m* de poussière.

duster ['dʌstəʳ] *n* -**1.** [cloth] chiffon *m* (à poussière); [for blackboard] tampon *m* effaceur. -**2.** *Am* [garment - for doing housework] blouse *f*, tablier *m*; [- for driving] cache-poussière *m inv*. -**3.** [lightweight coat] manteau *m* léger. -**4.** AGR poudreuse *f*; [aircraft] *avion servant à répandre de l'insecticide sur les champs*.

dust-free *adj* [environment] protégé de la poussière.

dustheap ['dʌsthiːp] *n Am* [rubbish heap] tas *m* d'ordures; to be consigned to the ~ *fig* être mis au rebut.

dustiness ['dʌstɪnɪs] *n* état *m* poussiéreux.

dusting ['dʌstɪŋ] *n* -**1.** [of room, furniture] époussetage *m*, dépoussiérage *m*; to do the ~ épousseter, enlever OR faire la poussière. -**2.** [with sugar, insecticide] saupoudrage *m*; give the cake a ~ of icing sugar saupoudrez le gâteau de sucre glace.

dusting powder *n* talc *m*.

dust jacket *n* [for book] jaquette *f*.

dustman ['dʌstmən] (*pl* dustmen [-mən]) *n Br* éboueur *m*.

dustpan ['dʌstpæn] *n* pelle *f* à poussière.

dustproof ['dʌstpruːf] *adj* imperméable OR étanche à la poussière.

dust sheet *n Br* housse *f* de protection.

dust storm *n* tempête *f* de poussière.

dust trap *n* nid *m* à poussière.

dust-up *inf n* accrochage *m*, prise *f* de bec; to have a bit of a ~ with sb avoir une prise de bec avec qqn; to have a ~ over OR about sthg avoir une prise de bec à propos de qqch.

dust wrapper = **dust jacket**.

dusty ['dʌstɪ] (*compar* dustier, *superl* dustiest) *adj* -**1.** [room, furniture, road] poussiéreux; to get ~ s'empoussiérer, se couvrir de poussière; not so ~ *inf dated* pas si mal. -**2.** [colour] cendré. -**3.** *inf phr dated*: to get a ~ answer se faire envoyer balader OR paître, se faire recevoir.

dutch▽ [dʌtʃ] *n Br*: the old ~ [wife] la patronne.

Dutch [dʌtʃ] ◇ *npl*: the ~ les Hollandais *mpl*, les Néerlandais *mpl*.

◇ *n* LING néerlandais *m*.

◇ *adj* [bulbs, city] hollandais; [cheese] de Hollande; [embassy, government etc] néerlandais; [dictionary, teacher] de néerlandais.

◇ *adv*: to go ~ (with sb) *inf* [share cost equally] partager les frais (avec qqn).

Dutch auction *n* vente *f* à la baisse.

Dutch barn *n Br* hangar *m* à armature métallique.

Dutch cap *n* diaphragme *m (contraceptif)*.

Dutch courage *inf n courage trouvé dans la boisson*; I need some ~ il faut que je boive un verre pour me donner du courage.

Dutch door *n Am* porte *f* à deux vantaux.

Dutch elm disease *n (U)* maladie *f* des ormes.

Dutchman ['dʌtʃmən] (*pl* Dutchmen [-mən]) *n* Hollandais *m*, Néerlandais *m*; (then) I'm a ~! *fig* je mange mon chapeau!

Dutch oven *n* [casserole] marmite *f*, fait-tout *m inv*.

Dutch treat *inf n sortie où chacun paye son écot*; to go on a ~ partager les frais.

Dutch uncle *n* moralisateur *m*; to talk (to sb) like a ~ faire la morale (à qqn).

Dutchwoman ['dʌtʃ,wʊmən] (*pl* Dutchwomen [-,wɪmɪn]) *n* Hollandaise *f*, Néerlandaise *f*.

dutiable ['djuːtjəbl] *adj* taxable.

dutiful ['djuːtɪfʊl] *adj* [child] obéissant, respectueux; [husband, wife] qui remplit ses devoirs conjugaux; [worker, employee] consciencieux.

dutifully ['djuːtɪflɪ] *adv* consciencieusement.

duty ['djuːtɪ] *n* -**1.** [moral or legal obligation] devoir *m*; to do one's ~ (by sb) faire son devoir (envers qqn); to fail in one's ~ manquer à son devoir; it is my ~ to say that... il est de mon devoir de dire que...; it is my painful ~ to inform you that... j'ai la douloureuse tâche de vous informer que...; to make it one's ~ to do sthg se faire un devoir de faire qqch; ~ calls le devoir m'appelle; to do sthg out of a sense of ~ faire qqch par sens du devoir. -**2.** (*usu pl*) [responsibility] fonction *f*; to take up one's duties entrer en fonction; to hand over one's duties (to sb) transmettre ses fonctions (à qqn); in the course of one's duties dans l'exercice de ses fonctions; public duties responsabilités *fpl* publiques OR envers la communauté. -**3.** *phr*: on ~ [soldier, doctor] de garde; [policeman] de service; to go on/off ~ [soldier] prendre/laisser la garde; [doctor] prendre la/cesser d'être de garde; [policeman] prendre/quitter son service; to do ~ for sb remplacer qqn; to do ~ for sthg *fig* faire office de qqch ☐ active ~ *Am* MIL service *m* actif; tour of ~ MIL service *m*. -**4.** [tax] taxe *f*, droit *m*.

duty-bound *adj* tenu (par son devoir).

duty call *n* visite *f* de politesse.

duty doctor *n* médecin *m* de garde.

duty-free ◇ *adj* [goods] hors taxe, en franchise; [shop] hors taxe; my ~ allowance les marchandises hors taxe auxquelles j'ai droit.

◇ *adv* hors taxe, en franchise; how much can I bring back ~? combien de marchandises puis-je rapporter hors taxe OR en franchise?

◇ *n* marchandises *fpl* hors taxe OR en franchise.

duty officer *n* officier *m* de service.

duty roster, duty rota *n* tableau *m* de service.

duvet ['duːveɪ] *n* couette *f*; ~ cover housse *f* de couette.

dux [dʌks] *n Scot* SCH premier *m* de la classe OR de l'école.

DV (*written abbr of* Deo volente) si Dieu le veut.

DVLC (*abbr of* Driver and Vehicle Licensing Centre) *pr n service des immatriculations et des permis de conduire en Grande-Bretagne*.

DVM (*abbr of* Doctor of Veterinary Medicine) *n docteur vétérinaire*.

dwarf [dwɔːf] (*pl inv* OR dwarves [dwɔːvz]) ◇ *n* -**1.** [person] nain *m*, -e *f*. -**2.** [tree] arbre *m* nain. -**3.** MYTH nain *m*, -e *f*.

◇ *adj* [plant, animal] nain.

◇ *vt* -**1.** *fig* [in size] écraser; [in ability] éclipser. -**2.** [make small - tree] rabougrir.

dwarfish ['dwɔːfɪʃ] *adj* [hands, feet] de nain; [person] de taille très petite.

dwarfism ['dwɔːfɪzm] *n* nanisme *m*.

dwarf star *n* ASTRON étoile *f* naine, naine *f*.

dwell [dwel] (*pt* & *pp* dwelt [dwelt] OR dwelled) *vi lit* résider, demeurer; to ~ in sb's mind [image, thought] rester dans l'esprit de qqn.

◆ **dwell on, dwell upon** *vt insep* [the past - think about] penser sans cesse à; [- talk about] parler sans cesse de; [problem, fact, detail] s'attarder sur; don't ~ on it [in thought] n'y pense pas trop; to ~ on sthg at some length [in speech] s'étendre assez longuement sur qqch.

-dweller ['dweləʳ] *in cpds* habitant *m*, -e *f*; city~ citadin *m*, -e *f*; cave~ troglodyte *mf*.

dwelling ['dwelɪŋ] *n hum* OR *lit* résidence *f*.

dwelling house *n* JUR maison *f* d'habitation.

dwelt [dwelt] *pt* & *pp* → **dwell**.

dwindle ['dwɪndl] *vi* [hopes, savings, population] se réduire, diminuer; the island's population has ~d to 120 la population de l'île est descendue à 120 habitants; to ~ (away) to nothing [hopes, savings] se réduire à rien; [population] se réduire à presque rien.

dwindling ['dwɪndlɪŋ] ◇ *n* [of savings, hopes] diminution *f*; [of population, membership] baisse *f*, diminution *f*.

◇ *adj* [population, audience] en baisse, décroissant; [savings, hopes] décroissant.

dye [daɪ] ◇ *n* [substance] teinture *f*; [colour] teinte *f*, couleur *f*; the ~ will run in the wash la couleur partira au lavage; it's the ~ from my shoes ce sont mes chaussures qui déteignent; it isn't taking the ~ la teinture ne prend pas; ~ powder poudre *f* de teinture.

◇ *vt* [fabric, hair] teindre; to ~ sthg yellow/green teindre qqch en jaune/en vert; to ~ one's hair se teindre les cheveux; ~d blond hair les cheveux teints en blond.

◇ *vi* [fabric] se teindre; nylon doesn't ~ well le nylon est difficile à teindre OR se teint difficilement.

dyed-in-the-wool [daɪd-] *adj* [uncompromising] bon teint *(inv)*.

dyeing ['daɪɪŋ] *n* [action] teinture *f*.

dyer ['daɪəʳ] *n* teinturier *m*, -ère *f*.

dyestuff ['daɪstʌf] *n* teinture *f*, colorant *m*.

dyeworks ['daɪwɜːks] (*pl inv*) *n* teinturerie *f*.

dying ['daɪɪŋ] ◇ *adj* [person, animal] mourant; *lit* agonisant; [tree, forest] mourant; [species] en voie de disparition; *fig* [art, craft] en train de disparaître; [industry] agonisant, en train de disparaître; the ~ man le mourant; her ~ words les mots qu'elle a prononcés en mourant, ses derniers mots; it was her ~ wish that... sa dernière volonté était que...; to OR till my ~ day jusqu'à ma mort, jusqu'à mon dernier jour; men like him are a ~ breed des hommes comme lui, on n'en fait plus.

◇ *n* [death] mort *f*.

◇ *npl*: the ~ les mourants *mpl*, les agonisants *mpl*.

dyke [daɪk] *n* -**1.** [against flooding] digue *f*; [for carrying water away] fossé *m*; *Scot* [wall] mur *m*. -**2.** ▽ [lesbian] gouine *f*.

dynamic [daɪ'næmɪk] ◇ *adj* -**1.** [person, company] dynamique. -**2.** TECH dynamique; ~ RAM COMPUT mémoire *f* RAM dynamique.

◇ *n* dynamique *f*.

dynamically [daɪ'næmɪklɪ] *adv* dynamiquement.

dynamics [daɪ'næmɪks] ◇ *npl* [of a situation, group] dynamique *f*.

◇ *n (U)* TECH dynamique *f*.

dynamism ['daɪnəmɪzm] *n* [of person, company] dynamisme *m*.

dynamite ['daɪnəmaɪt] ◇ *n* [explosive] dynamite *f*; a stick of ~ un bâton de dynamite; this story is ~! *fig* cette histoire, c'est de la dynamite!; this band is ~! *fig* ce groupe est génial! ◇ *vt* [blow up] dynamiter.

dynamo ['daɪnəməʊ] *n* TECH dynamo *f*; a human ~ *fig* une boule d'énergie.

dynastic [dɪ'næstɪk] *adj* dynastique.

dynasty [*Br* 'dɪnəstɪ, *Am* 'daɪnəstɪ] *n* dynastie *f*; the Romanov/Bourbon ~ la dynastie des Romanov/des Bourbon.

dyne [daɪn] *n* PHYS dyne *f*.

dysenteric [ˌdɪsn'terɪk] *adj* MED dysentérique.

dysentery ['dɪsntrɪ] *n (U)* MED dysenterie *f*.

dysfunction [dɪs'fʌŋkʃn] *n* MED dysfonction *f*, dysfonctionnement *m*.

dysfunctional [dɪs'fʌŋkʃənl] *adj* dysfonctionnel.

dyslexia [dɪs'leksɪə] *n* [word blindness] dyslexie *f*.

dyslexic [dɪs'leksɪk] ◇ *adj* dyslexique. ◇ *n* dyslexique *mf*.

dysmenorrhoea *Br*, **dysmenorrhea** *Am* [ˌdɪsmenə'rɪə] *n (U)* MED dysménorrhée *f*; to have ~ souffrir de dysménorrhée.

dyspepsia [dɪs'pepsɪə] *n (U)* MED dyspepsie *f*; to have ~ souffrir de dyspepsie.

dyspeptic [dɪs'peptɪk] ◇ *adj* -**1.** MED dyspeptique, dyspepsique. -**2.** *fig* [irritable] irritable. ◇ *n* MED dyspeptique *mf*, dyspepsique *mf*.

dysphasia [dɪs'feɪzjə] *n* dysphasie *f*.

dystrophy ['dɪstrəfɪ] *n* MED dystrophie *f*.

E

e (*pl* e's OR es), **E** (*pl* E's OR Es) [iː] *n* [letter] e *m*, E *m*.

E ◇ *n* -**1.** MUS mi *m*; in E flat en mi bémol. -**2.** *drugs sl* (*abbr of* ecstasy) [drug] ecstasy *m*; [pill] comprimé *m* d'ecstasy.
◇ (*written abbr of* East) E.

ea. (*written abbr of* each): £3.00 ~ 3 livres pièce.

EA *n abbr of* educational age.

each [iːtʃ] ◇ *det* chaque; ~ child has a different name chaque enfant a un nom différent; ~ day chaque jour, tous les jours; ~ (and every) one of us/you/them chacun/chacune d'entre nous/vous/eux (sans exception); you're mad, ~ and every one of you! vous êtes fous, tous autant que vous êtes!
◇ *pron* [every one] chacun, chacune; ~ of his six children chacun de ses six enfants; a number of suggestions, ~ more crazy than the last un certain nombre de suggestions toutes plus folles les unes que les autres; or would you like some of ~? ou bien voudriez-vous un peu de chaque? ❑ to ~ his own à chacun ses goûts.
◇ *adv* [apiece]: we have a book/a room ~ nous avons chacun un livre/une pièce; the tickets cost £20 ~ les billets coûtent 20 livres chacun.
◆ **each other** *pron phr*: to hate ~ other se détester (l'un l'autre); [more than two people] se détester (les uns les autres); do you two know ~ other? est-ce que vous vous connaissez?; the children took ~ other's hand les enfants se sont pris par la main; the two sisters wear ~ other's clothes les deux sœurs échangent leurs vêtements; they walked towards ~ other ils ont marché l'un vers l'autre; we get on ~ other's nerves nous nous portons mutuellement sur les nerfs; we get on very well with ~ other's parents nous nous entendons très bien avec les parents l'un de l'autre.

each way ◇ *adj*: ~ bet pari sur un cheval gagnant, premier ou placé.
◇ *adv* [in betting] placé; to put money ~ on a horse jouer un cheval placé; French Silk, £50 ~ French Silk, 50 livres placé.

eager [ˈiːgəʳ] *adj* [impatient, keen] impatient; [learner, helper] enthousiaste, fervent; [crowd, face, look] passionné, enfiévré; to be ~ to do sthg [impatient] avoir hâte de faire qqch; [very willing] faire preuve d'enthousiasme OR de ferveur pour faire qqch; I am ~ to help in any way I can je tiens absolument à apporter mon aide; to be ~ to please avoir envie de faire plaisir; to be ~ for affection/for success être avide d'affection/de succès; to be ~ for acceptance tenir beaucoup à être accepté; he's ~ for me to see his work il a très envie que je voie son travail; don't be too ~ ne te montre pas trop empressé.

eager beaver *inf n* travailleur *m* acharné, travailleuse *f* acharnée, mordu *m*, -e *f* du travail.

eagerly [ˈiːgəlɪ] *adv* [wait] impatiemment; [help] avec empressement; [say, look at] avec passion OR enthousiasme.

eagerness [ˈiːgənɪs] *n* [to know, see, find out] impatience *f*; [to help, please] empressement *m*; [in eyes, voice] excitation *f*, enthousiasme *m*; ~ to learn soif *f* de savoir.

eagle [ˈiːgl] *n* -**1.** [bird] aigle *m*; to have an ~ avoir un œil d'aigle. -**2.** [standard, seal] aigle *f*. -**3.** [lectern] aigle *m*. -**4.** GOLF eagle *m*.

eagle-eyed ◇ *adj* aux yeux d'aigle.
◇ *adv* [watch] avec une grande attention.

eagle owl *n* grand-duc *m*.

eaglet [ˈiːglɪt] *n* aiglon *m*, -onne *f*.

Ealing comedy [ˈiːlɪŋ-] *n genre de film comique britannique produit dans les studios d'Ealing (Londres) vers 1950.*

E and OE (*written abbr of* errors and omissions excepted) *Br* s e & o.

ear [ɪəʳ] *n* -**1.** [of person, animal] oreille *f*; to have a good ~ avoir de l'oreille; to have an ~ for music avoir l'oreille musicale; to have an ~ for poetry être sensible à la poésie; to keep an ~ OR one's ~s open ouvrir les oreilles, tendre l'oreille; keep an ~ open for the baby ouvre l'oreille au cas où le bébé pleurerait; to reach sb's ~s [news] arriver aux oreilles de qqn; it has reached my ~s that... j'ai entendu dire que...; to shut OR to close one's ~s faire la sourde oreille; he closed his ~s to her request for help elle lui a demandé de l'aide mais il a fait la sourde oreille; I've heard that until it's coming out of my ~s *inf* je l'ai tellement entendu que ça me sort par les oreilles; to have the ~ of sb [have influence with] avoir l'oreille de qqn; to be grinning from ~ to ~ sourire jusqu'aux oreilles ❑ ~ infection otite *f*; to be all ~s être tout oreilles OR tout ouïe; to be out on one's ~ *inf* [from job, school] être viré; he's out on his ~ [been dismissed] il s'est fait virer; [from family home] il s'est fait flanquer dehors; to chuck sb out on his/her ~ *inf* [from job, school] virer qqn; [from family home] flanquer qqn dehors; to be up to one's ~s in work OR in it *inf* être débordé (de travail); his ~s are flapping [he's listening closely] ses oreilles sont grandes ouvertes; it just goes in one ~ and out the other ça entre par une oreille et ça ressort par l'autre; to keep one's ~ to the ground ouvrir l'oreille, être à l'écoute; my ~s are burning j'ai les oreilles qui (me) sifflent; to play by ~ MUS jouer à l'oreille; to play it by ~ improviser. -**2.** [of grain] épi *m*.

earache [ˈɪəreɪk] *n* mal *m* d'oreille; to have ~ *Br* OR an ~ *Am* avoir mal aux oreilles.

eardrops [ˈɪədrɒps] *npl* gouttes *fpl* pour les oreilles.

eardrum [ˈɪədrʌm] *n* tympan *m*.

-eared [ɪəd] *in cpds*: long/short~ à oreilles *fpl* longues/courtes; pointy~ *inf* aux oreilles en pointe.

ear flap *n* [on cap] oreillette *f*.

earful [ˈɪəfʊl] *n*: to get an ~ of water prendre de l'eau plein l'oreille ❑ to get an ~ *inf* [be told off] se faire passer un savon; to give sb an ~ *inf* [tell off] passer un savon à qqn; to give sb an ~ about sthg *Am* [say a lot to] raconter qqch à qqn en long, en large et en travers.

earhole *inf* [ˈɪəhəʊl] *n Br* [ear] esgourde *f*.

earl [ɜːl] *n* comte *m*.

earldom [ˈɜːldəm] *n* [title] titre *m* de comte; [estates, land] comté *m*.

earlobe [ˈɪələʊb] *n* lobe *m* de l'oreille.

Earls Court [ɜːlz-] *pr n grand centre d'exposition à Londres.*

early [ˈɜːlɪ] (*compar* earlier, *superl* earliest)
◇ *adj* -**1.** [in the morning - hour, person] matinal; I had an ~ breakfast j'ai déjeuné de bonne heure; to get off to an ~ start partir de bonne heure; the ~ shuttle to London le premier avion pour Londres; it's too ~ to get up il est trop tôt pour se lever; it's earlier than I thought il est plus tôt que je ne pensais; to be an ~ riser être matinal OR un lève-tôt. -**2.** [of the beginning of a period of time - machine, film, poem] premier; [- Edwardian, Victorian etc] du début de l'époque; in the ~ afternoon/spring/fifties au début de l'après-midi/du printemps/des années cinquante; the earlier applicants were better than the later ones les premiers candidats étaient meilleurs que les derniers; let's have an ~ lunch déjeunons de bonne heure; when was that? — ~ September quand était-ce? — début septembre; the ~ Roman Empire l'Empire romain naissant; an ~ 18th-century form of democracy une forme de démocratie propre au début du XVIIIe siècle; the ~ American settlers les premiers pionniers américains; ~ music [baroque] musique *f* ancienne; from the earliest days of the century depuis le tout début du siècle; ~ reports from the front indicate that... les premières nouvelles du front semblent indiquer que...; it's ~ days yet *Br* [difficult to be definite] il est trop tôt pour se prononcer; [might yet be worse, better] il est encore tôt; from the earliest times depuis le début des temps; I need an ~ night je dois me coucher de bonne heure; a couple of ~ nights wouldn't do you any harm cela ne te ferait pas de mal de te coucher de bonne heure pendant quelques jours; it's too ~ il est trop tôt; the earliest human artefacts les premiers objets fabriqués par l'homme; an ~ Picasso une des premières œuvres de Picasso; he's in his ~ twenties il a une vingtaine d'années; in his ~ youth quand il était très jeune; a man in ~ middle age un homme d'une quarantaine d'années; from an ~ age dès l'enfance; at an ~ age

de bonne heure, très jeune; ~ vegetables légumes *mpl* précoces, primeurs *fpl*; ~ fruit fruits *mpl* précoces, primeurs *fpl*. -**3.** [ahead of time]: to be ~ [person, train, flight, winter] être en avance; you're too ~ vous arrivez trop tôt, vous êtes en avance; Easter is ~ this year Pâques est de bonne heure cette année. -**4.** [relating to the future - reply] prochain; at an ~ date de bonne heure; at an earlier date plus tôt; we need an ~ meeting il faut que nous nous réunissions bientôt; at your earliest convenience COMM dans les meilleurs délais; what is your earliest possible delivery date? quelle est votre première possibilité de livraison?; give us the earliest possible notice avertissez-nous le plus tôt possible.
◇ *adv* -**1.** [in the morning - rise, leave] tôt, de bonne heure; let's set off as ~ as we can mettons-nous en route le plus tôt possible; how ~ should I get there? à quelle heure dois-je y être? -**2.** [relating to the beginning of a period of time]: ~ in the evening/in the afternoon tôt le soir/(dans) l'après-midi; ~ in the year/winter au début de l'année/de l'hiver; I can't make it earlier than 2:30 je ne peux pas avant 14 h 30; what's the earliest you can make it? [be here] quand pouvez-vous être ici? ❑ ~ on au début; ~ on in June au début du mois de juin; earlier on plus tôt. -**3.** [ahead of schedule] en avance; [earlier than usual] de bonne heure; I want to leave ~ tonight [from work] je veux partir de bonne heure ce soir; shop/post ~ for Christmas faites vos achats/postez votre courrier à l'avance pour Noël. -**4.** [relating to the future]: at the earliest au plus tôt; we can't deliver earlier than Friday nous ne pouvons pas livrer avant vendredi.

early bird *n*: to be an ~ *inf* être matinal ❑ it's the ~ that catches the worm *prov* [it's good to get up early] le monde appartient à ceux qui se lèvent tôt *prov*; [it's good to arrive early] les premiers arrivés sont les mieux servis.

early call *n* [in hotel]: could you give me an ~ at 6:30? pouvez-vous me réveiller à 6 h 30?

early closing *n Br* COMM *jour où l'on ferme tôt*; it's ~ today [for all shops] les magasins ferment de bonne heure aujourd'hui; [for this shop] on ferme de bonne heure aujourd'hui.

early-warning *adj*: ~ system système *m* de préalerte.

earmark ['ɪəmɑːk] ◇ *vt* réserver; [money] affecter, assigner; this money has been ~ed for research cet argent a été affecté à la recherche; I'll just ~ that for myself je me le réserve; this land is ~ed for development ce terrain est réservé OR assigné à l'aménagement.
◇ *n* marque *f* à l'oreille.

earmuffs ['ɪəmʌfs] *npl* protège-oreille *m*.

earn [ɜːn] ◇ *vt* -**1.** [money] gagner; [interest] rapporter; to ~ a living gagner sa vie; I certainly do ~ my living [I work hard] je peux vraiment dire que je mérite mon salaire ❑ ~ed income revenu *m* salarial, revenus *mpl* salariaux. -**2.** [respect, reputation, punishment - subj: activities] valoir; [- subj: person] mériter; it ~ed him ten years in prison cela lui a valu dix ans de prison; you're going to have to ~ your fame tu vas devoir travailler à ta gloire; you've ~ed it! tu l'as mérité!
◇ *vi* [person] gagner de l'argent; [investment] rapporter; ~ing capacity [of person] potentiel *m* de revenu; [of firm] rentabilité *f*.

earner ['ɜːnəʳ] *n* -**1.** [person] salarié *m*, -e *f*; one of the biggest ~s in the company un des plus gros salaires de l'entreprise; she's the main ~ in the family c'est elle qui fait vivre la famille. -**2.** *inf Br* [source of income]: it's a nice little ~ [business, shop etc] c'est une bonne petite affaire; interested in a little ~, mate? ça te dirait de te faire un peu d'argent, mec?

earnest ['ɜːnɪst] ◇ *adj* -**1.** [person, expression, tone] sérieux. -**2.** [hope, request] ardent, fervent; [endeavour] fervent; [desire] profond.
◇ *n arch* OR *fml* [guarantee, deposit] gage *m*, garantie *f*.

◆ **in earnest** ◇ *adv phr* [seriously] sérieusement, sincèrement; [in a determined way] sérieusement; it's raining in ~ now il pleut pour de bon cette fois.
◇ *adj phr*: to be in ~ être sérieux.

earnestly ['ɜːnɪstlɪ] *adv* [behave] sérieusement; [study, work] sérieusement, avec ardeur; [speak, nod, look at] gravement; we ~ hope that... nous espérons sincèrement que...

earnestness ['ɜːnɪstnɪs] *n* [of person, tone] sérieux *m*, gravité *f*.

earnings ['ɜːnɪŋz] *npl* [of person, business] revenus *mpl*; do you have ~ from any other sources? avez-vous d'autres sources de revenus?; to live off immoral ~ gagner sa vie par des procédés immoraux.

earnings-related *adj* proportionnel au revenu.

ear, nose and throat *comp* [department, hospital] d'oto-rhino-laryngologie; ~ doctor oto-rhino *mf*, oto-rhino-laryngologiste *mf*.

earphones ['ɪəfəʊnz] *npl* écouteurs *mpl*, casque *m*.

earpiece ['ɪəpiːs] *n* [of telephone receiver, personal stereo] écouteur *m*.

ear piercing *n* (*U*): 'ear piercing' 'ici, on perce les oreilles'.
◆ **ear-piercing** *adj* [noise] perçant, strident.

earplug ['ɪəplʌg] *n* [for sleeping] boule *f* Quiès®; [for protection against water, noise] protège-tympan *m*.

earring ['ɪərɪŋ] *n* boucle *f* d'oreille.

ear shell *n* ZOOL ormeau *m*.

earshot ['ɪəʃɒt] *n*: out of/within ~ hors de/à portée de voix.

ear-splitting *adj* [noise] assourdissant.

earth [ɜːθ] ◇ *n* -**1.** [the world, the planet] terre *f*; the planet Earth la planète Terre; on ~ sur terre; here on ~ [not in heaven] ici-bas ❑ why/how/who on ~? pourquoi/comment/qui diable?; where on ~ did you find that? où diable as-tu trouvé cela?, où as-tu bien pu trouver cela?; what on ~ do you think you're doing? non mais, où tu te crois?; there's nowhere else on ~ I'd rather be c'est le seul endroit sur terre où j'ai envie d'être; there's nothing on ~ I'd like better il n'y a rien au monde dont j'aie plus envie; to cost the ~ *inf* coûter les yeux de la tête OR la peau des fesses; to promise the ~ promettre la lune, promettre monts et merveilles. -**2.** [ground] terre *f*; to fall to ~ tomber par terre ❑ to bring sb down to ~ (with a bump) ramener qqn sur terre (brutalement); to come back down to ~ again revenir OR redescendre sur terre; did the ~ move for you too, darling? *inf hum* est-ce que tu es montée au septième ciel aussi, chérie? -**3.** [soil] terre *f*. -**4.** *Br* ELEC [connection, terminal] terre *f*; ~ lead conducteur *m* de terre. -**5.** [of fox] terrier *m*, tanière *f*; to run a fox to ~ chasser un renard jusqu'à son terrier OR sa tanière; to run sb/sthg to ~ [find] dénicher qqn/qqch; to go to ~ *literal* & *fig* aller se terrer.
◇ *comp*: ~ floor sol *m* en terre battue.
◇ *vt Br* ELEC mettre à la terre.
◆ **earth up** *vt sep* [plant] chausser, enchausser, butter.

earthborn ['ɜːθbɔːn] *adj lit* humain, mortel.

earthbound ['ɜːθbaʊnd] *adj* -**1.** [insects] non volant. -**2.** [spaceship] progressant en direction de la terre; [journey] en direction de la terre. -**3.** [unimaginative] terre à terre.

earth closet *n* fosse *f* d'aisance.

earthen ['ɜːθn] *adj* [dish] en OR de terre (cuite); [floor] en terre.

earthenware ['ɜːθnweəʳ] ◇ *n* [pottery] poterie *f*; [glazed] faïence *f*.
◇ *adj* en OR de terre (cuite), en OR de faïence.

earthiness ['ɜːθɪnɪs] *n* -**1.** [of humour] truculence *f*; [of person, character] nature *f* directe. -**2.** [of food] goût *m* de terre.

earthling ['ɜːθlɪŋ] *n* terrien *m*, -enne *f*.

earthly ['ɜːθlɪ] ◇ *adj* -**1.** [worldly] terrestre; ~ possessions biens *mpl* matériels. -**2.** *inf* [possible]: there's no ~ reason why I should believe you je n'ai absolument aucune raison de te croire; she hasn't an ~ chance of succeeding elle n'a pas la moindre chance OR la plus petite chance de réussir.
◇ *n inf Br* -**1.** [chance]: he doesn't have an ~ of passing the exam il n'a aucune chance de réussir à l'examen. -**2.** [idea]: I haven't an ~ where he is je ne sais vraiment pas où il se trouve.

earthman ['ɜːθmən] (*pl* earthmen [-mən]) *n* terrien *m*.

earth mother *n* -**1.** MYTH déesse *f* de la terre. -**2.** *inf fig* mère *f* nourricière.

earthmover ['ɜːθ,muːvəʳ] *n* bouteur *m offic*, bulldozer *m*.

earthmoving ['ɜːθ,muːvɪŋ] *adj*: ~ equipment engin *m* de terrassement.

earthquake ['ɜːθkweɪk] *n* tremblement *m* de terre.

earth sciences *npl* sciences *fpl* de la terre.

earth-shaking *inf* [-ʃeɪkɪŋ], **earth-shattering** *inf adj* [event, news, importance] capital; [discovery] révolutionnaire.

earth tremor *n* secousse *f* sismique.

earthward ['ɜːθwəd] ◇ *adj* [journey] en direction de la Terre; in an ~ direction [travel] en direction de la Terre, (avec) cap sur la Terre.
◇ *adv* en direction de la Terre.

earthwards ['ɜːθwədz] *adv* en direction de la Terre.

earth woman *n* terrienne *f*.

earthwork(s) ['ɜːθwɜːk(s)] *n* CONSTR terrassement *m*; ARCHEOL & MIL fortification *f* en terre.

earthworm ['ɜːθwɜːm] *n* ver *m* de terre, lombric *m*.

earthy ['ɜːθɪ] *adj* -**1.** [taste, smell] de terre. -**2.** [humour] truculent; [person, character] direct.

ear trumpet *n* cornet *m* acoustique.

ear wax *n* cire *f* (*sécrétée par les oreilles*), cérumen *m*.

earwig ['ɪəwɪg] *n* perce-oreille *m*.

ease [iːz] ◇ *n* -**1.** [comfort] aise *f*; to be OR to feel at ~ être OR se sentir à l'aise; to be OR to feel ill at ~ être OR se sentir mal à l'aise; we're at ~ with each other now maintenant nous nous sentons à l'aise ensemble; I feel at ~ about the new proposals les nouvelles propositions me conviennent tout à fait; to set sb's mind at ~ tranquilliser qqn; now that your mind's at ~ maintenant que tu es tranquillisé; to put sb at (his OR her) ~ mettre qqn à l'aise; (stand) at ~! MIL repos!; to take one's ~ *dated* prendre ses aises, se mettre à l'aise. -**2.** [facility] facilité *f*; [of movements] aisance *f*; to do sthg with ~ faire qqch facilement OR aisément; to speak with ~ parler avec aisance; ~ of access facilité d'accès. -**3.** [affluence]: to live a life of ~ avoir la belle vie, mener une vie facile.
◇ *vt* -**1.** [alleviate - anxiety, worry] calmer; [- pain] calmer, soulager; [- pressure, tension] relâcher; [- traffic flow] rendre plus fluide; [- sb's workload] alléger; to ~ sb's mind rassurer qqn; to ~ sb of a burden décharger qqn d'un fardeau, retirer un fardeau des épaules de qqn; to ~ sb of their anxiety/pain calmer l'inquiétude/la douleur de qqn. -**2.** [move gently]: to ~ o.s. into a chair s'installer délicatement dans un fauteuil; to ~ in the clutch AUT embrayer en douceur; she ~d the rucksack from her back elle fit glisser le sac à dos de ses épaules; they ~d him out of the car ils l'ont aidé à sortir de la voiture; to ~ sthg out faire sortir qqch délicatement; to ~ sb out [from position, job] pousser qqn vers la sortie *fig*; they ~d him out ils se sont débarrassés de lui en douceur; he ~d himself through the gap in the hedge il s'est glissé OR faufilé à travers le trou dans la haie.
◇ *vi* [pain] se calmer, s'adoucir; [situation, tension, rain] se calmer; the awkwardness between them ~d le malaise qu'il y avait entre eux s'est dissipé.
◆ **ease back** *vt sep* [throttle, lever] tirer doucement.
◆ **ease off** ◇ *vt sep* [lid, bandage] enlever délicatement.

◇ *vi insep* [rain] se calmer; [business] ralentir; [traffic] diminuer; [tension] se relâcher; work has ~d off il y a moins de travail.

◆ **ease up** *vi insep* [slow down - in car] ralentir; [rain] se calmer; [business, work] ralentir; [traffic] diminuer; to ~ up on sb/sthg y aller doucement avec qqn/qqch.

easel ['iːzl] *n* chevalet *m*.

easily ['iːzɪlɪ] *adv* -**1.** [without difficulty] facilement; that's ~ said/done c'est facile à dire/faire; she is ~ pleased elle n'est pas difficile. -**2.** [undoubtedly] sans aucun doute; she's ~ the best c'est de loin la meilleure; it's ~ two hours from here c'est facilement à deux heures d'ici. -**3.** [very possibly]: he could ~ change his mind il pourrait bien changer d'avis. -**4.** [in a relaxed manner - talk] de manière décontractée; [- smile, answer] d'un air décontracté.

easiness ['iːzɪnɪs] *n* -**1.** [lack of difficulty] facilité *f*. -**2.** [relaxed nature] décontraction *f*.

easing ['iːzɪŋ] *n* [of discomfort] soulagement *m*; the ~ of tension in the area le relâchement de la tension dans la région.

east [iːst] ◇ *n* est *m*; the East [the Orient] l'Orient *m*; [Eastern Europe] l'Est *m*; [in US] l'Est *m (États situés à l'est du Mississippi)*; East-West relations relations *fpl* Est-Ouest; room facing (the) ~ pièce donnant OR exposée à l'est; on the ~ of the island à l'est de l'île; to the ~ of the mainland à l'est OR au large de la côte est du continent; the wind is (coming) from the ~ le vent vient de l'est.

◇ *adj* [coast, shore, face of mountain] est, oriental; [wind] d'est; to live in ~ London habiter dans l'est de Londres.

◇ *adv* [go, look, travel] en direction de l'est, vers l'est; [sail] cap sur l'est; further ~ plus à l'est; ~ of à l'est de; ~ by north/south est quart nord/sud; back ~ *Am inf* dans l'est *(des États-Unis)*.

East Africa *pr n* Afrique *f* orientale.

East African ◇ *adj* d'Afrique orientale.

◇ *n* Africain *m*, -e *f* de l'est.

East Berlin *pr n* Berlin-Est.

East Berliner *n* Berlinois *m*, -e *f* de l'Est.

eastbound ['iːstbaʊnd] *adj* [traffic, train] en direction de l'est; there's a jam on the ~ carriageway il y a un bouchon en direction de l'est.

East End *n* [of city] quartiers *mpl* est; to live in the ~ of Glasgow habiter dans l'est de Glasgow; the ~ *quartier industriel de Londres, connu pour ses docks et, autrefois, pour sa pauvreté*.

East Ender [-'endəʳ] *n* habitant *m*, -e *f* de l'est de Londres.

Easter ['iːstəʳ] ◇ *n* Pâques *fpl*; Happy ~! joyeuses Pâques!; last/next ~ à Pâques l'année dernière/l'année prochaine.

◇ *comp* [holiday, Monday, weekend] de Pâques; [week] de Pâques, pascal; [celebrations] pascal; ~ Day (jour *m* de) Pâques; ~ Sunday dimanche *m* de Pâques.

Easter egg *n* œuf *m* de Pâques.

Easter Island *pr n* l'île *f* de Pâques; in OR on ~ à l'île de Pâques.

easterly ['iːstəlɪ] ◇ *adj* [in the east] situé à l'est; [from the east] d'est; [to the east] vers l'est, en direction de l'est.

◇ *n* vent *m* d'est.

eastern ['iːstən] *adj* [Europe] de l'Est; [France, Spain, Scotland etc] de l'Est; [region, seaboard] est, oriental; [culture, philosophy] oriental; ~ hemisphere hémisphère *m* oriental; the Eastern Church l'Église d'Orient; the Eastern Bloc le bloc de l'Est; the Eastern Townships [of Canada] les Cantons *mpl* de l'Est.

Eastern Daylight Time *n* heure *f* d'été de New York.

Easterner ['iːstənəʳ] *n* -**1.** [in US] *personne qui vient de l'est des États-Unis*. -**2.** [oriental] Oriental *m*, -e *f*.

Eastern European Time *n* heure *f* d'Europe orientale.

easternmost ['iːstənməʊst] *adj* situé le plus à l'est.

Eastern Standard Time *n* heure *f* d'hiver de New York.

Eastertide ['iːstətaɪd] *n lit* (saison *f* de) Pâques *fpl*.

east-facing *adj* exposé OR donnant à l'est.

East German ◇ *adj* est-allemand, d'Allemagne de l'Est.

◇ *n* Allemand *m*, -e *f* de l'Est.

East Germany *pr n*: (former) ~ (l'ex-) Allemagne *f* de l'Est; in ~ en Allemagne de l'Est.

East Indian HIST ◇ *adj* des Indes orientales.

◇ *n* natif *m*, -ive *f* des Indes orientales.

East Indies *pl pr n* HIST: the ~ les Indes orientales.

east-northeast ◇ *n* est-nord-est *m*.

◇ *adj* [direction] est-nord-est; [wind] d'est-nord-est.

◇ *adv* en direction de l'est-nord-est; [blow] d'est-nord-est.

East Side *pr n*: the ~ l'East Side *m (quartier situé à l'est de Manhattan)*.

east-southeast ◇ *n* est-sud-est *m*.

◇ *adj* [direction] est-sud-est; [wind] d'est-sud-est.

◇ *adv* en direction de l'est-sud-est; [blow] d'est-sud-est.

eastward ['iːstwəd] ◇ *adj* est.

◇ *adv* = **eastwards**.

eastwardly ['iːstwədlɪ] *adj* [direction] est.

eastwards ['iːstwədz] *adv* en direction de l'est, vers l'est; facing ~ [building] exposé OR donnant à l'est; to sail ~ naviguer cap sur l'est.

easy ['iːzɪ] (*compar* **easier**, *superl* **easiest**) ◇ *adj* -**1.** [not difficult] facile; it's ~ to see why/that... on voit bien pourquoi/que...; it's ~ to say that... c'est facile de dire que...; it's ~ for her to say that... c'est facile pour elle de dire que...; this should make the job easier (to do) cela devrait faciliter le travail; she is (an) ~ (person) to please c'est facile de lui faire plaisir; it's an ~ mistake to make c'est une erreur qui est facile à faire; it's not ~ being the eldest child ce n'est pas facile d'être l'aîné; it's far from ~, it's none too ~ c'est loin d'être facile, ce n'est pas facile du tout; in ~ stages [travel] par petites étapes; [learn] sans peine; learn Japanese in ten ~ stages! apprenez le japonais en dix petites leçons!; within ~ reach of près de; the shop is within ~ walking distance of here d'ici, on peut facilement aller au magasin à pied; the ~ way out OR option la solution facile OR de facilité; ~ to get on with facile à vivre; to have an ~ time (of it) [a good life] avoir la belle vie OR la vie facile; she had an ~ time of it [in exams] ç'a été facile pour elle; she hadn't had an ~ time of it elle n'avait pas eu une vie facile; it's ~ money *inf* c'est de l'argent gagné facilement OR sans se fatiguer; to come in an ~ first [in a race] gagner haut la main; an ~ prey OR victim une proie facile ❑ ~ game OR meat *inf* bonne poire *f*; as ~ as pie OR ABC *inf* simple comme bonjour OR tout; to be on ~ street *inf* rouler sur l'or. -**2.** [at peace]: to feel ~ in one's mind être tranquille, avoir l'esprit tranquille. -**3.** [easy-going - person, atmosphere] décontracté; [- disposition, nature] facile; [- manner] décontracté, naturel; [- style] coulant, facile; I'm ~ *inf* [I don't mind] ça m'est égal; to be on ~ terms with sb avoir des rapports plutôt amicaux avec qqn; on ~ terms COMM avec facilités de paiement; to go at an ~ pace aller tranquillement; to be an ~ fit [clothes] être confortable. -**4.** [sexually]: a woman of ~ virtue *lit* une femme de petite vertu OR aux mœurs légères; she's an ~ lay▽ *pej* elle couche avec tout le monde, c'est une Marie-couche-toi-là. -**5.** [pleasant]: to be ~ on the eye [film, painting] être agréable à regarder; [person] être un plaisir pour les yeux; to be ~ on the ear [music] être agréable à écouter. -**6.** ST. EX [market] calme.

◇ *adv* [in a relaxed or sparing way] doucement; to go ~ y aller doucement; to go ~ on OR with sb y aller doucement avec qqn; to go ~ on OR with sthg y aller doucement avec OR sur qqch; go ~ on the cream vas-y doucement avec la crème; he's got it ~ *inf* [has an easy life] il se la coule douce, il a la belle vie; take it ~! doucement!; to take things OR it OR life ~ [relax] se reposer; ~ now! *inf*, ~ does it! *inf* doucement!; to sleep ~ in one's bed dormir sur ses deux oreilles; stand ~! MIL repos!; easier said than done plus facile à dire qu'à faire; it's ~ come ~ go l'argent, ça va ça vient.

easy-care *adj* d'entretien facile.

easy chair *n* fauteuil *m*.

easy-clean *adj* [garment, surface] facile à nettoyer, d'entretien facile.

easy-going *adj* [person] décontracté, facile à vivre; [lifestyle] décontracté.

eat [iːt] (*pt* ate [et, eɪt], *pp* eaten ['iːtn]) ◇ *vt* manger; to ~ (one's) breakfast/lunch/dinner prendre son petit déjeuner/déjeuner/dîner; to ~ one's fill manger tout son soûl OR content; there's nothing to ~ il n'y a rien à manger; to ~ one's way through a whole cake manger un gâteau en entier; it looks good enough to ~! on en mangerait!; he/she looks good enough to ~ il est beau/elle est belle à croquer; go on, she's not going to ~ you allez, elle ne va pas te manger ❑ I could ~ a horse j'ai une faim de loup; I'll ~ my hat if he gets elected s'il est élu, je mange mon chapeau; he ~s people like you for breakfast il ne fait qu'une bouchée des gens comme toi; to ~ one's words ravaler ses mots; they ate us out of house and home ils ont dévalisé notre frigo; what's ~ing you? *inf* qu'est-ce que tu as?

◇ *vi* manger; I haven't eaten at all today je n'ai pas mangé de toute la journée; have you eaten yet? as-tu déjà mangé?; let's ~ à table; to ~ for two [pregnant woman] manger pour deux ❑ to ~ like a horse/a bird manger comme un ogre/un oiseau; to have sb ~ing out of one's hand faire ce qu'on veut de qqn.

◆ **eat away** ◇ *vt sep* [subj: waves] ronger; [subj: mice] ronger; [subj: acid, rust] ronger, corroder; *fig* [confidence] miner; [support, capital, resources] entamer.

◇ *vi insep* [person] manger.

◆ **eat away at** *vt insep* = **eat away** *vt sep*.

◆ **eat in** *vi insep* manger chez soi OR à la maison.

◆ **eat into** *vt insep* -**1.** [destroy] attaquer. -**2.** [use up - savings] entamer; [- time] empiéter sur.

◆ **eat out** ◇ *vi insep* sortir déjeuner OR dîner, aller au restaurant.

◇ *vt sep*: to ~ one's heart out se morfondre; ~ your heart out! dommage pour toi!

◆ **eat up** ◇ *vi insep* manger.

◇ *vt sep* [food] terminer, finir; *fig* [electricity, gas, petrol] consommer beaucoup de; to ~ up the miles dévorer OR avaler les kilomètres; eaten up with [jealousy, hate, ambition] rongé OR dévoré par.

eatable ['iːtəbl] *adj* [fit to eat] mangeable; [edible] comestible.

eatables ['iːtəblz] *npl hum* vivres *mpl*, victuailles *fpl*.

eaten ['iːtn] *pp* → **eat**.

eater ['iːtəʳ] *n* -**1.** [person] mangeur *m*, -euse *f*; big/small ~ gros/petit mangeur; to be a messy ~ manger salement; to be a fussy ~ être difficile (sur la nourriture). -**2.** *inf Br* [apple] pomme *f* à couteau.

eatery *inf* ['iːtərɪ] (*pl* **eateries**) *n* café-restaurant *m*.

eating ['iːtɪŋ] ◇ *n*: ~ is one of his favourite pastimes manger constitue un de ses passe-temps favoris; to make good ~ [be good to eat] être bon.

◇ *adj* -**1.** [for eating]: ~ apple/pear pomme *f*/poire *f* à couteau; ~ place OR house restaurant *m*. -**2.** [of eating]: ~ habits habitudes *fpl* alimentaires; ~ disorder trouble *m* du comportement alimentaire.

eats *inf* ['iːts] *npl* bouffe *f*; what's for ~? qu'est-ce qu'il y a à becqueter?

eau de Cologne [ˌəʊdəkəˈləʊn] *n* eau *f* de Cologne.
eaves [ˈiːvz] *npl* avant-toit *m*, corniche *f*.
eavesdrop [ˈiːvzdrɒp] (*pt* & *pp* eavesdropped, *cont* eavesdropping) *vi* écouter de manière indiscrète, espionner; try and ~ on them essaie d'espionner leur conversation; to ~ on sb's conversation espionner la conversation de qqn.
eavesdropper [ˈiːvzˌdrɒpəʳ] *n* indiscret *m*, -ète *f*, personne *f* qui écoute aux portes.
ebb [eb] ◇ *n* [of tide] reflux *m*; [of public opinion] variations *fpl*; ~ and flow flux *m* et reflux; to be on the ~ descendre; to be at a low ~ *fig* [person] ne pas avoir le moral; [patient, enthusiasm, spirits] être bien bas; [business] aller mal, être OR tourner au ralenti; [finances, relations] aller mal; to be at one's lowest ~ [person] avoir le moral à zéro; [patient] être au plus mal OR bas; to be at its lowest ~ [enthusiasm, spirits] être au plus bas; [business, finances, relations] aller au plus mal.
◇ *vi* -**1.** [tide] baisser, descendre; to ~ and flow monter et baisser OR descendre. -**2.** *fig* = **ebb away**.
◆ **ebb away** *vi insep* [confidence, enthusiasm, strength etc] baisser peu à peu; [completely] disparaître.
ebb tide *n* marée *f* descendante.
ebonite [ˈebənaɪt] *n* ébonite *f*.
ebony [ˈebənɪ] ◇ *n* [tree] ébénier *m*; [wood] ébène *m*.
◇ *adj* [chair, table etc] en ébène; *fig* [eyes, hair] d'ébène.
EBRD (*abbr of* European Bank of Reconstruction and Development) *pr n* BERD *f*.
ebullience [ɪˈbʊljəns] *n* exubérance *f*.
ebullient [ɪˈbʊljənt] *adj* exubérant.
EC (*abbr of* European Community) *pr n* CE *f*.
eccentric [ɪkˈsentrɪk] ◇ *adj* -**1.** [person, clothes, behaviour] excentrique. -**2.** ASTRON, MATH & TECH excentrique, excentré.
◇ *n* -**1.** [person] excentrique *mf*. -**2.** TECH excentrique *m*.
eccentrically [ɪkˈsentrɪklɪ] *adv* -**1.** [dress, talk] de manière excentrique. -**2.** ASTRON, MATH & TECH excentriquement.
eccentricity [ˌeksenˈtrɪsətɪ] (*pl* eccentricities) *n* excentricité *f*.
Eccles cake [ˈeklz-] *n petit gâteau rond en pâte feuilletée fourré de fruits secs.*
Ecclesiastes [ɪˌkliːzɪˈæstiːz] *pr n* BIBLE: (the book of) ~ l'Ecclésiaste *m*.
ecclesiastic [ɪˌkliːzɪˈæstɪk] ◇ *adj* = **ecclesiastical**.
◇ *n* ecclésiastique *m*.
ecclesiastical [ɪˌkliːzɪˈæstɪkl] *adj* [robes, traditions, calendar] ecclésiastique; [history] de l'Église; [music] d'église.
ECG *n* -**1.** (*abbr of* electrocardiogram) ECG *m*. -**2.** (*abbr of* electrocardiograph) ECG *m*.
ECGD (*abbr of* Export Credits Guarantee Department) *pr n organisme d'assurance pour le commerce extérieur*, ≃ COFACE *f*.
ECH *written abbr of* electric central heating.
echelon [ˈeʃəlɒn] *n* -**1.** [level] échelon *m*. -**2.** MIL échelon *m*.
echinoderm [ɪˈkaɪnəʊdɜːm] *n* échinoderme *m*.
echo [ˈekəʊ] (*pl* echoes) ◇ *n* écho *m*; ~es of Kafka *fig* des éléments qui rappellent OR évoquent Kafka.
◇ *vt* [sound] répéter; *fig* [colour, theme] reprendre, rappeler; [architecture, style] rappeler, évoquer; to ~ sb's opinions [person] se faire l'écho des opinions de qqn; [editorial] reprendre les opinions de qqn.
◇ *vi* [noise, voice, music] résonner; [place] faire écho, résonner; the corridor ~ed with shouts/footsteps des cris/bruits de pas résonnèrent dans le couloir, le couloir résonna de cris/bruits de pas.
◆ **Echo** *pr n* Écho.
echo chamber *n* chambre *f* de réverbération.
echo sounder *n* échosondeur *m*, sondeur *m* par ultrasons.
éclair [eɪˈkleəʳ] *n* CULIN éclair *m*.
eclampsia [ɪˈklæmpsɪə] *n* MED éclampsie *f*.
éclat [eɪˈklɑː] *n* éclat *m*.
eclectic [ɪˈklektɪk] ◇ *n* éclectique *mf*.
◇ *adj* éclectique.
eclecticism [ɪˈklektɪsɪzm] *n* éclectisme *m*.
eclipse [ɪˈklɪps] ASTRON & *fig* ◇ *n* éclipse *f*; an ~ of the sun/moon une éclipse de soleil/lune; to be in ~ être éclipsé; to go into ~ [sun, moon] s'éclipser; his career went into ~ *fig* il a connu une traversée du désert.
◇ *vt* éclipser.
ecliptic [ɪˈklɪptɪk] ASTRON ◇ *n* écliptique *m*.
◇ *adj* écliptique.
ecocide [ˈiːkəʊsaɪd] *n* écocide *m*.
eco-friendly [ˌiːkəʊ-] *adj* qui respecte l'environnement.
ecological [ˌiːkəˈlɒdʒɪkl] *adj* écologique.
ecologically [ˌiːkəˈlɒdʒɪklɪ] *adv* écologiquement; ~ (speaking) du point de vue de l'écologie; ~ harmful/sound qui est nuisible à/qui respecte l'environnement; to be ~ conscious OR aware se préoccuper OR se soucier de l'environnement.
ecologist [ɪˈkɒlədʒɪst] *n* écologiste *mf*.
ecology [ɪˈkɒlədʒɪ] *n* écologie *f*.
econometric [ɪˌkɒnəˈmetrɪk] *adj* économétrique.
econometrician [ɪˌkɒnəmeˈtrɪʃn] *n* économétricien *m*, -enne *f*.
econometrics [ɪˌkɒnəˈmetrɪks] *n (U)* économétrie *f*.
economic [ˌiːkəˈnɒmɪk] *adj* -**1.** ECON [growth, system, indicator] économique; ~ performance [of a country] résultats *mpl* économiques. -**2.** [profitable] rentable; ~ rate of return taux de rentabilité économique; ~ rent loyer rentable; it isn't ~, it doesn't make ~ sense ce n'est pas économique OR avantageux.
economical [ˌiːkəˈnɒmɪkl] *adj* [person] économe; [machine, method, approach] économique; it's more ~ to buy in bulk c'est plus économique OR avantageux d'acheter par grandes quantités; to be ~ to run [car, heating] être économique; to be ~ with sthg économiser qqch; to be ~ with the truth *euph* dire la vérité avec parcimonie; ~ use of language emploi sobre du langage.
economically [ˌiːkəˈnɒmɪklɪ] *adv* -**1.** ECON économiquement. -**2.** [live] de manière économe; [write] avec sobriété; [use] de manière économe, avec parcimonie.
economics [ˌiːkəˈnɒmɪks] ◇ *n (U)* [science] économie *f* (politique), sciences *fpl* économiques.
◇ *npl* [financial aspects] aspect *m* économique.
economist [ɪˈkɒnəmɪst] *n* économiste *mf*; the Economist PRESS *hebdomadaire britannique politique, économique et financier*.
economize [ɪˈkɒnəmaɪz] *vi* économiser, faire des économies; to ~ on sthg économiser sur qqch.
economy [ɪˈkɒnəmɪ] (*pl* economies) ◇ *n* -**1.** [system] économie *f*; planned ~ économie planifiée. -**2.** [saving] économie *f*; to practise ~ économiser, épargner; with ~ of effort sans effort inutile; ~ of language sobriété *f* de langage ❑ economies of scale économies d'échelle; false ~ fausse économie.
◇ *comp* [pack, size] économique; ~ car *aux États-Unis, voiture de taille moyenne, consommant peu par rapport aux «grosses américaines»*; ~ class classe *f* touriste; ~ drive politique *f* de réduction des dépenses.
◇ *adv* [fly, travel] en classe touriste.
ecosphere [ˈiːkəʊˌsfɪə] *n* écosphère *f*.
ecosystem [ˈiːkəʊˌsɪstəm] *n* écosystème *m*.
ecotype [ˈiːkəʊtaɪp] *n* écotype *m*.
ecru [ˈeɪkruː] ◇ *n* écru *m*.
◇ *adj* écru.
ECSC (*abbr of* European Coal & Steel Community) *pr n* CECA *f*.
ecstasy [ˈekstəsɪ] (*pl* ecstasies) *n* -**1.** extase *f*, ravissement *m*; to be in an ~ of delight être transporté de joie; to be in/to go into ecstasies être/tomber en extase. -**2.** [drug] ecstasy *f*.
ecstatic [ekˈstætɪk] *adj* ravi; to be ~ about sthg/sb [in admiration] être en extase devant qqch/qqn; [with joy] être ravi de qqch/qqn; I'm not ~ about it cela ne m'enchante pas.
ecstatically [ekˈstætɪklɪ] *adv* avec extase; to be ~ happy être dans un bonheur extatique.
ECT *n abbr of* electroconvulsive therapy.
ectomorph [ˈektəʊmɔːf] *n* ectomorphe *mf*.
ectomorphic [ˌektəʊˈmɔːfɪk] *adj* ectomorphe.
ectopic [ekˈtɒpɪk] *adj*: ~ pregnancy grossesse *f* extra-utérine OR ectopique.
ectoplasm [ˈektəplæzm] *n* ectoplasme *m*.
ECU [ˈekjuː] (*abbr of* European Currency Unit) *n* ECU *m*, écu *m*.
Ecuador [ˈekwədɔːʳ] *pr n* Équateur *m*; in ~ en Équateur.
Ecuadoran [ˌekwəˈdɔːrən], **Ecuadorian** [ˌekwəˈdɔːrɪən] ◇ *n* Équatorien *m*, -enne *f*.
◇ *adj* équatorien.
ecumenical [iːkjʊˈmenɪkl] *adj* œcuménique.
ecumenism [iːˈkjuːmənɪm], **ecumenicism** [ˌiːkjʊˈmenɪkɪzəm] *n* œcuménisme *m*.
eczema [ˈeksɪmə] *n* MED eczéma *m*; to have ~ avoir de l'eczéma.
ed. ◇ -**1.** (*written abbr of* edited) sous la dir. de, coll. -**2.** (*written abbr of* edition) éd., édit. -**3.** (*written abbr of* education) éduc.
◇ *n* (*abbr of* editor) éd., édit.
ED *pr n abbr of* Employment Department.
Edam [ˈiːdæm] *n* édam *m*.
eddy [ˈedɪ] (*pl* eddies) ◇ *n* tourbillon *m*.
◇ *vi* tourbillonner.
eddy currents *npl* ELEC courants *mpl* de Foucault.
edelweiss [ˈeɪdlvaɪs] *n* edelweiss *m*, immortelle *f* des neiges.
edema *Am* = **œdema**.
Eden [ˈiːdn] *pr n* BIBLE Éden *m*; *fig* éden *m*; 'East of ~' *Steinbeck, Kazan* 'À l'est d'Éden'.
edentate [iːˈdenteɪt] ◇ *n* édenté *m*.
◇ *adj* édenté.
edge [edʒ] ◇ *n* -**1.** [of blade] fil *m*, tranchant *m*; knife with a sharp OR keen ~ couteau à la lame aiguisée OR affilée; to put an ~ on [knife, blade] aiguiser, affiler, affûter; to take the ~ off [blade] émousser; seeing that accident has taken the ~ off my appetite ça m'a coupé l'appétit de voir cet accident; the sandwich took the ~ off my hunger ce sandwich a calmé ma faim; the walk gave an ~ to his appetite la promenade lui a ouvert l'appétit; to have the ~ on [be better] avoir légèrement le dessus OR l'avantage sur; [be at an advantage] avoir l'avantage sur; to give sb/sthg that extra ~ donner un plus à qqn/qqch; the performance lacked ~ le spectacle manquait de ressort OR d'énergie; I've lost my ~ [athlete] j'ai perdu mon brio; [writer] j'ai perdu mon mordant; with an ~ in one's voice d'un ton forcé. -**2.** [outer limit - of table, cliff, road] bord *m*; [- of page] bord *m*, marge *f*; [- of forest] lisière *f*, orée *f*; [- of cube, brick] arête *f*; [- of coin, book] tranche *f*; [- of ski] carre *f*; at OR by the water's ~ au bord de l'eau; to stand sthg on its ~ [coin, book] mettre qqch sur la tranche; [brick, stone] poser OR mettre qqch de OR sur chant; to be on the ~ of [war, disaster, madness] être au bord de; I was on the ~ of my seat *fig* [waiting for news] j'étais sur des charbons ardents; this film will have you on the ~ of your seat *fig* ce film est d'un suspense à vous faire frémir; to be close to the ~ *literal* être près du bord; *fig* être au bord du précipice; to push sb over the ~ *fig* faire craquer qqn.
◇ *vt* -**1.** [give a border to] border; to ~ sthg with sthg border qqch de qqch. -**2.** [sharpen] aiguiser, affiler, affûter. -**3.** [in skiing]: to ~ one's skis planter ses carres. -**4.** [move gradually]: to ~ one's way avancer OR progresser lentement; to ~ one's way along a ledge avancer OR

progresser lentement le long d'une corniche; to ~ one's chair nearer sb/sthg approcher peu à peu sa chaise de qqn/qqch.
◇ *vi* avancer OR progresser lentement; to ~ through the crowd se frayer un chemin à travers la foule; to ~ past sb/sthg se faufiler à côté de qqn/qqch; to ~ into a room se faufiler dans une pièce; to ~ away (from sb/sthg) s'éloigner doucement OR discrètement (de qqn/qqch); the car ~d forward/backward la voiture avança/recula doucement.
◆ **edge out** ◇ *vt sep*: to ~ sb out of a job pousser qqn vers la sortie en douceur.
◇ *vi insep* sortir lentement; to ~ out of a room se glisser hors d'une pièce.
◆ **edge up** ◇ *vt sep*: to ~ prices up faire monter les prix doucement.
◇ *vi insep* -**1.** [prices] monter doucement. -**2.** [approach slowly]: to ~ up to sb/sthg s'avancer lentement vers qqn/qqch.
◆ **on edge** *adj* & *adv phr*: to be on ~ être énervé OR sur les nerfs; to set sb's teeth on ~ faire grincer les dents à qqn; to set sb's nerves on ~ mettre les nerfs de qqn à fleur de peau.

-edged [edʒd] *in cpds*: double~ à double tranchant; sharp~ bien affilé OR aiguisé.

edge tool *n* outil *m* tranchant.

edgewise ['edʒwaɪz], **edgeways** ['edʒweɪz] *adv* de côté; I couldn't get a word in ~ je n'ai pas pu placer un mot.

edginess ['edʒɪnɪs] *n* nervosité *f*; there was an ~ about him il était assez nerveux.

edging ['edʒɪŋ] *n* [border - on dress, of flowers etc] bordure *f*; ~ shears cisailles *fpl* à gazon.

edgy ['edʒɪ] (*compar* edgier, *superl* edgiest) *adj* nerveux, sur les nerfs.

edible ['edɪbl] *adj* [mushroom, berry] comestible; ~ crab tourteau *m*; is it ~? c'est bon à manger?; this is very ~! c'est délicieux!
◆ **edibles** *npl* comestibles *mpl*.

edict ['iːdɪkt] *n* POL décret *m*; *fig* ordre *m*; the Edict of Nantes HIST l'édit *m* de Nantes.

edification [ˌedɪfɪ'keɪʃn] *n fml* édification *f*, instruction *f*.

edifice ['edɪfɪs] *n literal* & *fig* édifice *m*.

edify ['edɪfaɪ] (*pt* & *pp* edified) *vt fml* édifier.

edifying ['edɪfaɪɪŋ] *adj fml* édifiant; it was hardly an ~ spectacle/experience *hum* le spectacle/l'expérience était loin d'être édifiant/édifiante.

Edinburgh ['edɪnbrə] *pr n* Édimbourg; the ~ Festival le Festival d'Édimbourg.

EDINBURGH FESTIVAL:
Le Festival international d'Édimbourg, créé en 1947, est aujourd'hui un des plus grands festivals de théâtre et de musique au monde; il se tient chaque année en août et en septembre. Le festival «off» (Fringe) est une grande rencontre du théâtre expérimental.

---

edit ['edɪt] ◇ *n* [of text] révision *f*, correction *f*.
◇ *vt* -**1.** [correct - article, book] corriger, réviser; COMPUT [- file] éditer; [prepare for release - book, article] éditer, préparer à la publication; [- film, TV programme, tape] monter; the footnotes were ~ed from the book les notes ont été coupées dans le OR retranchées du livre. -**2.** [be in charge of - review, newspaper] diriger la rédaction de.
◆ **edit down** *vt sep* raccourcir.
◆ **edit out** *vt sep* couper, supprimer.

editing ['edɪtɪŋ] *n* [of newspaper, magazine] rédaction *f*; [initial corrections] révision *f*, correction *f*; [in preparation for publication] édition *f*, préparation *f* à la publication; [of film, tape] montage *m*; COMPUT [of file] édition *f*.

edition [ɪ'dɪʃn] *n* [of book, newspaper] édition *f*; first ~ première édition; revised/limited ~ édition revue et corrigée/à tirage limité.

editor ['edɪtəʳ] *n* -**1.** [of newspaper, review] rédacteur *m*, -trice *f* en chef; [of author] éditeur *m*, -trice *f*; [of dictionary] rédacteur *m*, -trice *f*; [of book, article - who makes corrections] correcteur *m*, -trice *f*; [- who writes] rédacteur *m*, -trice *f*; [of film] monteur *m*, -euse *f*; political ~ PRESS rédacteur *m*, -trice *f* politique; sports ~ PRESS rédacteur *m* sportif, rédactrice *f* sportive; ~'s note PRESS note *f* de la rédaction. -**2.** COMPUT éditeur *m*.

editorial [ˌedɪ'tɔːrɪəl] ◇ *adj* PRESS [decision, comment] de la rédaction; [job, problems, skills] de rédaction, rédactionnel; the ~ staff le personnel de rédaction; from an ~ point of view du point de vue de la rédaction; ~ freedom [in publishing] liberté *f* de publier; [of columnist] liberté *f* d'expression; ~ changes corrections *fpl*.
◇ *n* PRESS éditorial *m*.

editorialist [ˌedɪ'tɔːrɪəlɪst] *n* éditorialiste *mf*.

editorially [ˌedɪ'tɔːrɪəlɪ] *adv* du point de vue de la rédaction.

editor-in-chief *n* rédacteur *m*, -trice *f* en chef.

editorship ['edɪtəʃɪp] *n* rédaction *f*; during her ~ quand elle dirigeait la rédaction.

EDP *n abbr of* electronic data processing.

EDT *n abbr of* Eastern Daylight Time.

educable ['edʒʊkəbl] *adj fml* éducable.

educate ['edʒʊkeɪt] *vt* [pupil] instruire, donner une éducation à; [mind, tastes, palate] éduquer, former; [customers, public] éduquer; she was ~d in Edinburgh/at Birmingham University elle a fait sa scolarité à Édimbourg/ses études à l'université de Birmingham.

educated ['edʒʊkeɪtɪd] *adj* [person] instruit; [voice] distingué; to make an ~ guess faire une supposition bien informée.

education [ˌedʒʊ'keɪʃn] ◇ *n* éducation *f*; [teaching] enseignement *m*; a classical/scientific ~ une formation classique/scientifique; the ~ of poor countries in modern farming techniques la formation des pays pauvres aux techniques agricoles modernes; to have OR to receive a good ~ recevoir une bonne éducation OR formation; she completed her ~ in Italy elle a terminé ses études en Italie; standards of ~ niveau *m* scolaire; to have gaps in one's ~ avoir des lacunes dans son éducation; it was an ~ cela m'a beaucoup appris; *hum* c'était très édifiant ❑ adult OR continuing ~ éducation *f* pour adultes, formation *f* continue; Department of Education and Science *Br dated* ≃ ministère *m* de l'Éducation nationale; further ~ *enseignement postscolaire, mais non universitaire*; higher OR university ~ enseignement *m* supérieur OR universitaire; Minister of OR Secretary of State for Education *Br* ministre *m* de l'Éducation; physical ~ éducation *f* physique; primary/secondary ~ (enseignement *m*) primaire *m*/secondaire *m*; tertiary ~ enseignement *m* supérieur.
◇ *comp* [costs, budget] de l'éducation; Education Act ≃ réforme *f* (de l'Éducation); ~ correspondent PRESS correspondant chargé, correspondante chargée des problèmes d'enseignement; the ~ system le système éducatif; (local) ~ authority *Br* ≃ académie *f* régionale.

educational [ˌedʒʊ'keɪʃənl] *adj* [programme, system] éducatif; [establishment] d'éducation, d'enseignement; [books, publisher] scolaire; [method, film, visit, TV] éducatif, pédagogique; they talked about rising/falling ~ standards ils ont évoqué la hausse/baisse du niveau scolaire; ~ qualifications qualifications *fpl*, diplômes *mpl*; it was very ~ c'était très instructif; *hum* c'était très édifiant ❑ ~ age niveau *m* scolaire; ~ psychologist psychopédagogue *mf*.

educationalist [ˌedʒʊ'keɪʃnəlɪst] *n* pédagogue *mf*.

educationally [ˌedʒʊ'keɪʃnəlɪ] *adv* d'un point de vue éducatif; ~ deprived child *enfant qui n'a pas suivi une scolarité normale*; ~ subnormal *dated* en retard sur le plan scolaire.

educationist [ˌedʒʊ'keɪʃnɪst] = **educationalist**.

educative ['edʒʊkətɪv] *adj* éducatif.

educator ['edʒʊkeɪtəʳ] *n esp Am* éducateur *m*, -trice *f*.

educe [ɪ'djuːs] *vt fml* dégager, tirer.

Edward ['edwəd] *pr n*: ~ the Confessor Édouard le Confesseur; Prince ~ le prince Edward.

Edwardian [ed'wɔːdɪən] ◇ *adj* [architecture, design] édouardien, de style Édouard VII, (des années) 1900; [society, gentleman] de l'époque d'Édouard VII, des années 1900; ~ style style *m* Édouard VII; the ~ era ≃ la Belle Époque.
◇ *n Britannique qui vivait sous le règne d'Édouard VII*.

EE *n abbr of* electrical engineer.

EEC (*abbr of* European Economic Community) *pr n* CEE *f*.

EEG *n* -**1.** (*abbr of* electroencephalogram) EEG *m*. -**2.** (*abbr of* electroencephalograph) EEG *m*.

eek *inf* [iːk] *interj* hi.

eel [iːl] *n* anguille *f*; jellied ~s anguille en gelée; to be as slippery as an ~ glisser comme une anguille.

eelworm ['iːlwɔːm] *n* anguillule *f*.

e'en [iːn] *lit* = **even** *adv*.

EEOC (*abbr of* Equal Employment Opportunity Commission) *pr n Commission pour l'égalité des chances d'emploi aux États-Unis*.

e'er [eəʳ] *lit* = **ever** *adv*.

eerie ['ɪərɪ] (*compar* eerier, *superl* eeriest) *adj* [house, silence, sound] inquiétant, sinistre; it gave me an ~ feeling ça m'a fait froid dans le dos.

eerily ['ɪərəlɪ] *adv* sinistrement, d'une manière sinistre; it was ~ quiet in the house un calme inquiétant régnait dans la maison; to fall ~ silent tomber dans un silence étrange.

eeriness ['ɪərɪnɪs] *n* caractère *m* étrange OR sinistre.

eery ['ɪərɪ] (*compar* eerier, *superl* eeriest) = **eerie**.

EET *n abbr of* Eastern European Time.

eff▽ [ef] *vi Br euph*: to ~ and blind jurer à tout va.
◆ **eff off**▽ *vi insep Br*: ~ off! va te faire voir!; I told him to ~ off je lui ai dit d'aller se faire voir.

efface [ɪ'feɪs] *vt literal* & *fig* effacer; to ~ o.s. s'effacer.

effect [ɪ'fekt] ◇ *n* -**1.** [of action, law] effet *m*; [of chemical, drug, weather] effet *m*, action *f*; to have an ~ on avoir OR produire un effet sur; feeling the ~s, are you? *inf* [of over-indulgence] alors, on se ressent de ses excès?; the ~ of the law will be to... la loi aura pour effet de...; the ~ of all this is that... tout cela a pour résultat que...; with ~ from January 1st *Br* à partir OR à compter du 1er janvier; with immediate ~ à compter d'aujourd'hui; to no OR little ~ en vain; to use OR to put sthg to good ~ [technique, talent] utiliser qqch avec succès; [money, inheritance] faire bon usage de qqch; to such good ~ that... tellement bien que...; to put OR to bring OR to carry into ~ [law] mettre en pratique; to come into OR to take ~ [law] entrer en vigueur; to take ~ [drug] (commencer à) faire effet. -**2.** [meaning] sens *m*; to this OR that ~ dans ce sens; letters to the same ~ des lettres allant dans le même sens; a rumour to the ~ that... une rumeur selon laquelle...; a telegram/an announcement to the ~ that... un télégramme/une annonce disant que...; or words to that ~ ou quelque chose dans le genre. -**3.** [impression] effet *m*; (just) for ~ (juste) pour faire de l'effet. -**4.** THEAT: stage ~s effets *mpl* de scène. -**5.** *fml*: household ~s articles *mpl* ménagers; personal ~s effets *mpl* personnels.
◇ *vt fml* [reform] effectuer; [sale, purchase] réaliser, effectuer; [improvement] produire, apporter; [cure, rescue, reconciliation] mener à bien; to ~ one's escape s'échapper; to ~ entry JUR entrer; to ~ a saving in OR of sthg faire OR réaliser une économie de qqch.
◆ **in effect** ◇ *adj phr* [law, system] en vigueur.
◇ *adv phr* [in fact] en fait, en réalité.

effective [ɪ'fektɪv] *adj* -**1.** [which works well - measure, treatment, advertising etc] efficace; [- ar-

gument] qui porte; [- service, system] qui fonctionne bien; [- disguise] réussi; an ~ way of doing sthg un moyen efficace de faire qqch. -**2.** ADMIN & FIN: ~ date date *f* d'entrée en vigueur; ~ as from January 1st [law] en vigueur OR applicable à compter du 1er janvier; ~ January 1st à compter du 1er janvier; to cease to be ~ [policy, law] cesser d'être applicable; to become ~ entrer en vigueur. -**3.** [actual] véritable; to assume ~ command of a team assumer la direction réelle d'une équipe; ~ income revenu *m* réel. -**4.** [creating effect - colour, illustration] qui fait de l'effet.
◆ **effectives** *npl* effectifs *mpl*.

effectively [ɪ'fektɪvlɪ] *adv* -**1.** [efficiently - work, run, manage] efficacement. -**2.** [successfully] avec succès. -**3.** [in fact] en réalité, en fait. -**4.** [impressively] d'une manière impressionnante.

effectiveness [ɪ'fektɪvnɪs] *n* -**1.** [efficiency - of treatment, advertising] efficacité *f*; [- of undertaking, attempt] succès *m*. -**2.** [effect - of entrance, gesture, colour] effet *m*; to improve the ~ of your disguise pour rendre votre déguisement plus réussi.

effector [ɪ'fektə^r] PHYSIOL ◇ *n* effecteur *m*.
◇ *adj* effecteur.

effectual [ɪ'fektʃʊəl] *adj fml* [action, plan, law] efficace.

effectuate [ɪ'fektjʊeɪt] *vt fml* effectuer, réaliser.

effeminacy [ɪ'femɪnəsɪ] *n* [of man] caractère *m* efféminé; the ~ of his voice sa voix efféminée.

effeminate [ɪ'femɪnət] *adj* [man, voice] efféminé.

effeminately [ɪ'femɪnətlɪ] *adv* [dress, behave] de manière efféminée; [speak] d'une voix efféminée.

effervesce [,efə'ves] *vi* [liquid] être en effervescence; [wine] pétiller; [gas] s'échapper (d'un liquide) par effervescence; *fig* [person] déborder de vie; when the mixture ~s quand le mélange entre en effervescence.

effervescence [,efə'vesəns] *n* [of liquid] effervescence *f*; [of wine] pétillement *m*; *fig* [of person] vitalité *f*, pétulance *f*; [of personality] pétulance *f*.

effervescent [,efə'vesənt] *adj* [liquid] effervescent; [wine] pétillant; *fig* [person] débordant de vie, pétulant; [personality] pétulant.

effete [ɪ'fi:t] *adj fml* [weak - person] mou; [- civilization, society] affaibli; [decadent] décadent.

effeteness [ɪ'fi:tnɪs] *n fml* [weakness - of person] mollesse *f*; [- of civilization, society] affaiblissement *m*; [decadence] décadence *f*.

efficacious [efɪ'keɪʃəs] *adj fml* efficace.

efficacy ['efɪkəsɪ] *n fml* efficacité *f*.

efficiency [ɪ'fɪʃənsɪ] *n* -**1.** [of person, company, method] efficacité *f*; [of machine - in operation] fonctionnement *m*; [- in output] rendement *m*. -**2.** *Am* = **efficiency apartment**.

efficiency apartment *n Am* studio *m*.

efficiency expert *n* expert *m* en organisation.

efficient [ɪ'fɪʃənt] *adj* [person, staff, method, company] efficace; [piece of work] bien fait; [machine - in operation] qui fonctionne bien; [- in output] qui a un bon rendement; the machine is now at its most ~ [functions well] la machine a maintenant un fonctionnement optimal; [has high output] la machine a maintenant un rendement optimal; to make more ~ use of sthg utiliser qqch de manière plus efficace; the cast was ~ if not inspired sans être brillants, les acteurs ont fait preuve de professionnalisme.

efficiently [ɪ'fɪʃəntlɪ] *adv* [work - person] efficacement; the machine works ~ [functions well] la machine fonctionne bien; [has high output] la machine a un bon rendement.

effigy ['efɪdʒɪ] (*pl* **effigies**) *n* effigie *f*; to burn sb in ~ brûler qqn en effigie.

effing▽ ['efɪŋ] *Br* ◇ *adj* de merde; you ~ idiot! espèce de connard!
◇ *adv* foutrement; don't be so ~ stupid! qu'est-ce que tu peux être con!
◇ *n*: there was a lot of ~ and blinding on a eu droit à un chapelet de jurons.

efflorescence [eflɔ:'resəns] *n lit* [flowering] floraison *f*; *fig* efflorescence *f*.

effluent ['eflʊənt] *n* -**1.** [waste] effluent *m*. -**2.** [stream] effluent *m*.

effluvium [ɪ'flu:vjəm] (*pl* **effluviums** OR **effluvia** [-vjə]) *n fml* émanation *f* pestilentielle.

effort ['efət] *n* -**1.** [physical or mental exertion] effort *m*; it will be a bit of an ~ ce sera un peu difficile; without much ~ sans trop d'effort OR de peine; with an ~ en faisant un effort; your ~s on our behalf les efforts que vous avez faits pour nous; it was an ~ for me to stay awake j'avais du mal à rester éveillé; [stronger] rester éveillé me coûtait; put some ~ into it! fais un effort!; I put a lot of ~ into that project je me suis donné beaucoup de mal OR de peine pour ce projet; well, make some ~ to help allons, fais un petit effort pour nous aider; in an ~ to do sthg dans le but de faire qqch; not to make the slightest ~ to do sthg ne pas faire le moindre effort pour faire qqch, ne pas s'efforcer le moins du monde de faire qqch; to make no ~ to do sthg ne pas essayer de faire qqch; to make every ~ to do sthg faire tout son possible pour faire qqch; it's not worth the ~ ça ne vaut pas la peine de se fatiguer. -**2.** [attempt] essai *m*; it's only my first ~ ce n'est que la première fois que j'essaie; it was a good ~ pour un essai, c'était bien.

effortless ['efətlɪs] *adj* [win] facile; [style, movement] aisé; it seems so ~ cela a l'air si facile.

effortlessly ['efətlɪslɪ] *adv* facilement, sans effort OR peine.

effrontery [ɪ'frʌntərɪ] *n* effronterie *f*.

effulgence [ɪ'fʌldʒəns] *n lit* rayonnement *m*.

effulgent [ɪ'fʌldʒənt] *adj lit* rayonnant.

effusion [ɪ'fju:ʒn] *n lit* -**1.** [of words] effusion *f*. -**2.** [of liquid] écoulement *m*; [of blood] hémorragie *f*.

effusive [ɪ'fju:sɪv] *adj* [person] expansif; [welcome, thanks] chaleureux; *pej* exagéré.

effusively [ɪ'fju:sɪvlɪ] *adv* avec effusion; *pej* avec une effusion exagérée.

EFL (*abbr of* English as a foreign language) *n anglais langue étrangère*.

eft [eft] *n* triton *m*.

EFT [eft] (*abbr of* electronic funds transfer) *n transfert électronique de fonds*.

EFTA ['eftə] (*abbr of* European Free Trade Association) *pr n* AELE *f*, AEL-E *f*.

EFTPOS ['eftpɒs] (*abbr of* electronic funds transfer at point of sale) *n transfert électronique de fonds au point de vente*.

EFTS [efts] (*abbr of* electronic funds transfer system) *n système électronique de transfert de fonds*.

e.g. (*abbr of* exempli gratia) *adv* par exemple.

egad [i:'gæd] *interj arch* sacredieu.

egalitarian [ɪ,gælɪ'teərɪən] ◇ *n* égalitariste *mf*.
◇ *adj* égalitaire.

egalitarianism [ɪ,gælɪ'teərɪənɪzm] *n* égalitarisme *m*.

egg [eg] *n* -**1.** CULIN œuf *m*; ~s and bacon œufs au bacon; fried ~ œuf sur le plat; hard-boiled ~ œuf dur; soft-boiled ~ œuf à la coque; ~ white/yolk blanc *m*/jaune *m* d'œuf; to be left with OR to get ~ on one's face avoir l'air ridicule; that's how you get ~ on your face c'est comme ça qu'on se couvre de ridicule. -**2.** [of bird, insect, fish] œuf *m*; [of woman] ovule *m*; to lay an ~ [bird] pondre un œuf; *Am*▽[person, performer] être nul; *Am*▽[play, film etc] faire un bide; to put all one's ~s in one basket mettre tous ses œufs dans le même panier. -**3.** *Br dated* [person]: he's a good ~ ce n'est pas un mauvais bougre, c'est un bon diable; a bad ~ un sale individu.
◆ **egg on** *vt sep* encourager, inciter; to ~ sb on to do sthg encourager OR inciter qqn à faire qqch.

egg-and-spoon race *n jeu consistant à courir en tenant un œuf dans une cuillère*.

eggbeater ['eg,bi:tə^r] *n* -**1.** = **egg whisk**. -**2.** *inf Am* [helicopter] hélico *m*.

eggcup ['egkʌp] *n* coquetier *m*.

egg custard *n* CULIN ≃ crème *f* anglaise.

egg flip = **eggnog**.

egghead *inf* ['eghed] *n* intello *mf*.

eggnog [eg'nɒg] *n boisson composée d'œufs, de lait, de sucre, d'épices, de brandy, de rhum etc*.

eggplant ['egplɑ:nt] *n Am* aubergine *f*.

egg roll *n Am* CULIN pâté *m* impérial.

egg-shaped *adj* en forme d'œuf, ovoïde.

eggshell ['egʃel] ◇ *n* -**1.** coquille *f* d'œuf. -**2.** [colour] coquille *f* d'œuf.
◇ *adj* [finish, paint] coquille d'œuf (*inv*).

eggshell china, **eggshell porcelain** *n* coquille *f* d'œuf.

egg spoon *n* cuillère *f* à œufs (à la coque).

egg timer *n* sablier *m*.

egg tooth *n* [of chicken, snake] dent *f* d'éclosion.

egg whisk *n* fouet *m* CULIN.

eglantine ['egləntaɪn] *n* BOT [bush] églantier *m*; [flower] églantine *f*.

ego ['i:gəʊ] *n* [self-esteem] amour-propre *m*; PSYCH ego *m inv*, moi *m inv*; to have an enormous ~ être imbu de soi-même; it's just your ~ that's hurt tu es seulement blessé dans ton amour-propre.

egocentric [,i:gəʊ'sentrɪk] *adj* égocentrique.

egocentricity [,i:gəʊsen'trɪsətɪ], **egocentrism** [,i:gəʊ'sentrɪzm] *n* égocentrisme *m*.

egoism ['i:gəʊɪzm] *n* [selfishness] égoïsme *m*.

egoist ['i:gəʊɪst] *n* égoïste *mf*.

egoistic(al) [,i:gəʊ'ɪstɪk(l)] *adj* égoïste.

egoistically [,i:gəʊ'ɪstɪklɪ] *adv* égoïstement.

egomania [,i:gəʊ'meɪnjə] *n* égocentrisme *m* extrême.

egomaniac [,i:gəʊ'meɪnɪæk] *n* égocentrique *mf*.

egotism ['i:gətɪzm] *n* égocentrisme *m*, égotisme *m*.

egotist ['i:gətɪst] *n* égocentrique *mf*, égotiste *mf*.

egotistic(al) [,i:gə'tɪstɪk(l)] *adj* égocentrique, égotiste.

egotistically [,i:gə'tɪstɪklɪ] *adv* de manière égocentrique OR égotiste.

ego trip *inf n*: she's just on an ~ c'est par vanité qu'elle le fait.
◆ **ego-trip** *inf vi*: you're just ego-tripping tu fais ça par vanité.

egregious [ɪ'gri:dʒəs] *adj fml* [blatant - error, mistake] monumental, énorme; [- lie] énorme; [- cowardice, incompetence] extrême.

egress ['i:gres] *n fml* [way out, exit] sortie *f*, issue *f*; [action of going out] sortie *f*; means of ~ issue.

egret ['i:grɪt] *n* [bird] aigrette *f*.

Egypt ['i:dʒɪpt] *pr n* Égypte *f*; in ~ en Égypte; Lower ~ Basse-Égypte *f*; Upper ~ Haute-Égypte *f*.

Egyptian [ɪ'dʒɪpʃn] ◇ *n* -**1.** [person] Égyptien *m*, -enne *f*. -**2.** LING égyptien *m*.
◇ *adj* égyptien.

Egyptologist [,i:dʒɪp'tɒlədʒɪst] *n* égyptologue *mf*.

Egyptology [,i:dʒɪp'tɒlədʒɪ] *n* égyptologie *f*.

eh [eɪ] *interj* -**1.** [what did you say?] hein? -**2.** [seeking agreement] hein? -**3.** [in astonishment] quoi? -**4.** [in doubt, hesitation] heu.

eider ['aɪdə^r] *n* [bird] eider *m*.

eiderdown ['aɪdədaʊn] *n* -**1.** [feathers] duvet *m* d'eider. -**2.** [for bed] édredon *m*.

eider duck = **eider**.

eidetic [aɪ'detɪk] *adj* PSYCH eidétique.

Eiffel ['aɪfl] *pr n*: the ~ Tower la tour Eiffel.

eight [eɪt] ◇ *n* -**1.** [number, numeral] huit *m*; to live at number ~ habiter au huit ❑ to have had one over the ~ *Br* avoir bu plus que son compte; 'Butterfield 8' *O'Hara* 'Gloria'; 'Eight and a Half' *Fellini* 'Huit et demi'. -**2.** [in rowing] huit *m*.

◇ *adj* huit; to work an ~-hour day travailler huit heures par jour, faire des journées de huit heures.
◇ *pron* huit; I need ~ j'en ai besoin de huit.
eight ball *n Am* [ball] bille *f* numéro huit; [game] *variante du billard*; to be right behind the ~ *inf fig* être en mauvaise posture.
eighteen [ˌeɪ'tiːn] ◇ *pron* dix-huit.
◇ *adj* dix-huit.
◇ *n* dix-huit *m*; ~ is not enough dix-huit, ce n'est pas assez.
eighteenth [ˌeɪ'tiːnθ] ◇ *adj* dix-huitième.
◇ *n* [in series] dix-huitième *mf*; [fraction] dix-huitième *m*.
eighth [eɪtθ] ◇ *adj* huitième.
◇ *n* [in series] huitième *mf*; [fraction] huitième *m*.
eighth note *n Am* MUS croche *f*.
eightieth ['eɪtɪɪθ] ◇ *adj* quatre-vingtième.
◇ *n* [in series] quatre-vingtième *mf*; [fraction] quatre-vingtième *m*.
eightsome (reel) ['eɪtsəm-] *n danse folklorique écossaise pour huit danseurs*.
Eights Week [eɪts-] *n semaine de la course d'avirons aux universités de Cambridge et d'Oxford*.
eighty ['eɪtɪ] ◇ *pron* quatre-vingt.
◇ *adj* quatre-vingts; ~ one quatre-vingt-un; ~ two quatre-vingt-deux; ~ first quatre-vingt-unième; ~ second quatre-vingt-deuxième; page ~ page quatre-vingt; ~ million quatre-vingts millions.
◇ *n* quatre-vingt *m*.
Eilat [eɪ'lɑːt] *pr n* Eilat.
einsteinium [aɪn'staɪnɪəm] *n* einsteinium *m*.
Eire ['eərə] *pr n* Eire *f*.
EIS (*abbr of* Educational Institute of Scotland) *pr n syndicat écossais d'enseignants*.
eisteddfod [aɪ'stedfɒd] *n festival annuel de musique, littérature et théâtre au pays de Galles*.
either [*esp Br* 'aɪðəʳ, *esp Am* 'iːðəʳ] ◇ *det* -**1.** [one or the other] l'un ou l'autre, l'une ou l'autre; if you don't agree with ~ suggestion... si vous n'approuvez ni l'une ni l'autre OR aucune de ces suggestions...; you can take ~ route tu peux prendre l'un ou l'autre de ces chemins; ~ bus will get you there les deux bus y vont; he can write with ~ hand il peut écrire avec la main droite ou avec la main gauche ❑ ~ way d'une façon comme de l'autre. -**2.** [each] chaque; there were candles at ~ end of the table il y avait des bougies aux deux bouts OR à chaque bout de la table; there were people standing on ~ side of the road il y avait des gens de chaque côté OR de part et d'autre de la route.
◇ *pron* [one or the other] l'un ou l'autre, l'une ou l'autre; you can take ~ [bus, train etc] vous pouvez prendre l'un ou l'autre OR n'importe lequel (des deux); I don't like ~ of them je ne les aime ni l'un ni l'autre; if ~ of you two makes the slightest noise si l'un de vous deux fait le moindre bruit; which would you like? – ~ lequel voudriez-vous? – n'importe lequel.
◇ *adv* non plus; we can't hear anything ~ nous n'entendons rien non plus || [emphatic use]: and don't take too long about it ~! et ne traîne pas, surtout!; he had a suggestion to make and not such a silly one ~ il avait une suggestion à faire et qui n'était pas bête en plus.
◆ **either... or** *conj phr* ou... ou, soit... soit; [with negative] ni... ni; ~ you stop complaining or I go home! ou tu arrêtes de te plaindre, ou je rentre chez moi; they're ~ very rich or very stupid ils sont soit très riches soit très bêtes; she usually goes out with ~ Ian or Simon d'habitude elle sort (ou) avec Ian ou avec Simon OR soit avec Ian soit avec Simon; ~ come in or go out! entre ou sors!; ~ pay up or be taken to court! tu payes ou sinon c'est le tribunal!; I've not met ~ him or his brother je n'ai rencontré ni lui ni son frère.
either-or *adj*: it's an ~ situation il n'y a que deux solutions possibles.
ejaculate [ɪ'dʒækjʊleɪt] ◇ *vi* -**1.** PHYSIOL éjaculer. -**2.** *fml* [call out] s'écrier, s'exclamer.
◇ *vt* -**1.** PHYSIOL éjaculer. -**2.** *fml* [utter] lancer, pousser.
ejaculatory [ɪ'dʒækjʊlətrɪ] *adj* PHYSIOL éjaculateur.
eject [ɪ'dʒekt] ◇ *vt* -**1.** [troublemaker] expulser. -**2.** [cartridge, pilot] éjecter; [lava] projeter.
◇ *vi* [pilot] s'éjecter.
ejection [ɪ'dʒekʃn] *n* -**1.** [of troublemaker] expulsion *f*. -**2.** [of cartridge, pilot] éjection *f*; [of lava] projection *f*.
ejection seat = **ejector seat**.
ejector [ɪ'dʒektəʳ] *n* [on gun] éjecteur *m*.
ejector seat *n* siège *m* éjectable.
eke [iːk]
◆ **eke out** *vt sep* -**1.** [make last] faire durer. -**2.** [scrape]: to ~ out a living gagner tout juste sa vie. -**3.** [by adding something] augmenter.
EKG (*abbr of* electrocardiogram) *n Am* ECG *m*.
el *inf* [el] (*abbr of* elevated railroad) *n Am* métro *m* aérien.
elaborate [*adj* ɪ'læbrət, *vb* ɪ'læbəreɪt] ◇ *adj* [system, preparations] élaboré; [style, costume] recherché, travaillé; [pattern] compliqué; [details] minutieux; [map, plans] détaillé; in ~ detail de manière très détaillée; the whole thing was an ~ joke c'était une vaste plaisanterie.
◇ *vt* [work out in detail – plan, scheme etc] élaborer; [describe in detail] décrire en détail.
◇ *vi* [go into detail] donner des détails; there's no need to ~ further inutile de donner plus de détails.
◆ **elaborate on** *vt insep* [idea, statement] développer.
elaborately [ɪ'læbərətlɪ] *adv* [decorated, designed etc] minutieusement, avec recherche; [planned] minutieusement; [packaged] de manière élaborée.
elaborateness [ɪ'læbərətnɪs] *n* [of system, preparations] caractère *m* élaboré, complexité *f*; [of costume] caractère *m* élaboré; [of details, decoration] minutie *f*; [of map] caractère *m* détaillé.
elaboration [ɪˌlæbə'reɪʃn] *n* [working out – of scheme, plan] élaboration *f*; [details] exposé *m* minutieux.
élan [eɪ'læn] *n* vigueur *f*, énergie *f*.
eland ['iːlənd] *n* éland *m*.
elapse [ɪ'læps] *vi* s'écouler, passer.
elastic [ɪ'læstɪk] ◇ *adj* -**1.** [material] élastique; ~ stockings bas *mpl* anti-varices. -**2.** *fig* [timetable, arrangements, concept] souple; [word, moral principles] élastique, souple; [working hours] élastique. -**3.** *lit* [step] élastique.
◇ *n* -**1.** [material] élastique *m*. -**2.** *Am* [rubber band] élastique *m*, caoutchouc *m*.
elasticated [ɪ'læstɪkeɪtɪd] *adj* [stockings, waist] élastique.
elastic band *n Br* élastique *m*.
elasticity [ˌelæ'stɪsətɪ] *n* élasticité *f*.
elastomer [ɪ'læstəməʳ] *n* élastomère *m*.
Elastoplast® [ɪ'læstəplɑːst] *n Br* pansement *m* adhésif.
elate [ɪ'leɪt] *vt* remplir de joie, rendre euphorique.
elated [ɪ'leɪtɪd] *adj* fou de joie, exultant, euphorique; in an ~ mood d'une humeur exultante, dans un état euphorique; to feel ~ être fou de joie, exulter.
elation [ɪ'leɪʃn] *n* allégresse *f*, exultation *f*, euphorie *f*.
Elba ['elbə] *pr n* l'île *f* d'Elbe; on ~ sur l'île d'Elbe.
Elbe [elb] *pr n*: the (River) ~ l'Elbe *m*.
elbow ['elbəʊ] ◇ *n* [of arm, jacket, pipe, river] coude *m*; out at the ~s [jacket] troué aux coudes; with his ~s on the bar les coudes sur le bar, accoudé au bar; to have sthg at one's ~ [close by] avoir qqch sous la OR à portée de main ❑ to give sb the ~ *inf Br* [employee] virer qqn; [boyfriend, girlfriend] larguer OR jeter qqn; [tenant] mettre qqn à la porte; to get the ~ *inf Br* [employee] se faire virer; [boyfriend, girlfriend] se faire larguer OR jeter; [tenant] se faire mettre à la porte; to lift the ~ *inf Br* picoler, lever le coude.
◇ *vt* [hit] donner un coup de coude à; [push] pousser du coude; he ~ed his way up to the bar il s'est approché du bar en jouant des coudes; he just ~ed me aside il m'a écarté du coude.
◆ **elbow out** *vt sep* [from job] se débarrasser de.
elbow grease *inf n* huile *f* de coude.
elbowroom ['elbəʊrʊm] *n*: I don't have enough ~ je n'ai pas assez de place (pour me retourner); *fig* je n'ai pas suffisamment de liberté d'action.
elder ['eldəʳ] ◇ *adj* [brother, sister] aîné; Pitt the Elder le Premier Pitt; Brueghel the Elder Brueghel l'ancien.
◇ *n* -**1.** [of two children] aîné *m*, -e *f*. -**2.** [of tribe, the Church] ancien *m*. -**3.** [senior]: you should respect your ~s (and betters) vous devez le respect à vos aînés. -**4.** BOT sureau *m*.
elderberry ['eldəˌberɪ] *n* baie *f* de sureau; ~ wine vin *m* de sureau.
elderly ['eldəlɪ] ◇ *adj* âgé; my ~ uncle mon vieil oncle; she's getting rather ~ elle se fait bien vieille.
◇ *npl*: the ~ les personnes *fpl* âgées.
elder statesman *n* [gen] vétéran *m*; [politician] vétéran *m* de la politique.
eldest ['eldɪst] ◇ *adj* aîné.
◇ *n* aîné *m*, -e *f*.
Eldorado, El Dorado [ˌeldɒ'rɑːdəʊ] *pr n* l'Eldorado *m*.
Eleanor ['elɪnəʳ] *pr n*: ~ of Aquitaine Aliénor OR Éléonore d'Aquitaine.
elect [ɪ'lekt] ◇ *vt* -**1.** [by voting] élire; to ~ sb President élire qqn président; to ~ sb to office élire qqn; as an ~ed official of the society en tant que représentant élu de la société. -**2.** *fml* [choose] choisir; to ~ to do sthg choisir de faire qqch.
◇ *adj*: the President ~ le président élu.
◇ *npl* RELIG: the ~ les élus *mpl*.
election [ɪ'lekʃn] ◇ *n* élection *f*; to stand for ~ se présenter aux élections; the ~s les élections.
◇ *comp* [day, results] des élections; [campaign, speech] électoral.
electioneer [ɪlekʃə'nɪəʳ] *vi* participer à la campagne électorale; *pej* faire de la propagande électorale.
electioneering [ɪˌlekʃə'nɪərɪŋ] ◇ *n* campagne *f* électorale; *pej* propagande *f* électorale.
◇ *adj* [speech, campaign] électoral; *pej* propagandiste.
elective [ɪ'lektɪv] ◇ *adj* -**1.** [with power to elect – assembly] électoral. -**2.** [chosen – official, post] électif. -**3.** [optional – course, subject] optionnel, facultatif; ~ surgery chirurgie *f* de confort.
◇ *n Am* SCH & UNIV [subject] cours *m* optionnel OR facultatif.
elector [ɪ'lektəʳ] *n* -**1.** électeur *m*, -trice *f*. -**2.** HIST: the Elector l'Électeur.
electoral [ɪ'lektərəl] *adj* électoral; ~ college collège *m* électoral *(qui élit le président des États-Unis)*; on the ~ roll OR register sur la liste électorale.
electorate [ɪ'lektərət] *n* électorat *m*.
Electra [ɪ'lektrə] *pr n* Électre.
Electra complex *n* PSYCH complexe *m* d'Électre.
electric [ɪ'lektrɪk] ◇ *adj* [cooker, cable, current, musical instrument] électrique; *fig* [atmosphere] chargé d'électricité; [effect] électrisant; ~ blanket couverture *f* chauffante; ~ chair chaise *f* électrique; to go to the ~ chair être envoyé à la chaise électrique; ~ eel ZOOL anguille *f* électrique; ~ eye œil *m* électrique; ~ fence clôture *f* électrique; ~ field champ *m* électrique; ~ fire OR heater appareil *m* de chauffage électrique; ~ light [individual appliance] lumière *f* électrique; [lighting] éclairage *m* OR lumière *f* électrique; ~ motor moteur *m* électrique; ~

ray torpille *f*; ~ storm orage *m*; ~ underblanket protège-matelas *m* chauffant.
◇ *n inf Br* électricité *f*.
◆ **electrics** *npl Br* installation *f* électrique.

electrical [ɪ'lektrɪkl] *adj* [appliance] électrique; [failure, fault] au niveau de l'installation électrique; ~ engineer ingénieur *m* électricien; ~ engineering électrotechnique *f*.

electrically [ɪ'lektrɪklɪ] *adv* électriquement; ~ operated [machine] fonctionnant à l'électricité; [windows] à commande électrique; ~ charged chargé d'électricité.

electrical shock *Am* = **electric shock**.

electric blue ◇ *n* bleu *m* électrique.
◇ *adj* bleu électrique.

electrician [ˌɪlek'trɪʃn] *n* électricien *m*, -enne *f*.

electricity [ˌɪlek'trɪsətɪ] ◇ *n* électricité *f*; to turn OR to switch the ~ off couper le courant; to turn OR to switch the ~ on mettre le courant; to connect the ~ up to a house installer OR poser l'électricité dans une maison; to be without ~ [because of power cut] être privé d'électricité; [not installed] ne pas avoir l'électricité; there was ~ in the air *fig* il y avait de l'électricité dans l'air.
◇ *comp*: ~ bill note *f* d'électricité; ~ board *Br* agence *f* régionale de distribution de l'électricité; ~ supply alimentation *f* en électricité.

electric shock *n* décharge *f* électrique; to get an ~ prendre une décharge (électrique), prendre le courant ❑ ~ treatment traitement *m* par électrochocs.

electrification [ɪˌlektrɪfɪ'keɪʃn] *n* électrification *f*.

electrify [ɪ'lektrɪfaɪ] *vt* [railway line] électrifier; *fig* [audience] électriser.

electrifying [ɪ'lektrɪfaɪɪŋ] *adj fig* électrisant.

electrocardiogram [ɪˌlektrəʊ'kɑːdɪəgræm] *n* électrocardiogramme *m*.

electrocardiograph [ɪˌlektrəʊ'kɑːdɪəgrɑːf] *n* électrocardiographe *m*.

electroconvulsive [ɪˌlektrəʊkən'vʌlsɪv] *adj*: ~ therapy thérapie *f* par électrochocs.

electrocute [ɪ'lektrəkjuːt] *vt* électrocuter; you'll ~ yourself [give yourself a shock] tu vas prendre une décharge.

electrocution [ɪˌlektrə'kjuːʃn] *n* électrocution *f*.

electrode [ɪ'lektrəʊd] *n* électrode *f*.

electrodialysis [ɪˌlektrəʊdaɪ'ælɪsɪs] *n* électrodialyse *f*.

electroencephalogram [ɪˌlektrəʊen'sefələgræm] *n* électroencéphalogramme *m*.

electroencephalograph [ɪˌlektrəʊen'sefələgrɑːf] *n* électroencéphalographe *m*.

electrolysis [ˌɪlek'trɒləsɪs] *n* électrolyse *f*.

electrolyte [ɪ'lektrəʊlaɪt] *n* électrolyte *m*.

electrolytic [ɪˌlektrəʊ'lɪtɪk] *adj* électrolytique.

electromagnet [ɪˌlektrəʊ'mægnɪt] *n* électroaimant *m*.

electromagnetic [ɪˌlektrəʊmæg'netɪk] *adj* électromagnétique.

electromagnetism [ɪˌlektrəʊ'mægnɪtɪzm] *n* électromagnétisme *m*.

electromechanical [ɪˌlektrəʊmɪ'kænɪkl] *adj* électromécanique.

electrometer [ˌɪlek'trɒmɪtə^r] *n* électromètre *m*.

electromotive [ɪˌlektrəʊ'məʊtɪv] *adj* électromoteur.

electron [ɪ'lektrɒn] *n* électron *m*.

electron camera *n* caméra *f* électronique.

electron gun *n* canon *m* électronique OR à électrons.

electronic [ˌɪlek'trɒnɪk] *adj* électronique; ~ banking opérations *fpl* bancaires électroniques; ~ brain cerveau *m* électronique; ~ data processing traitement *m* électronique de l'information; ~ flash PHOT flash *m* électronique; ~ transfer of funds transfert *m* de fonds électronique; ~ ignition allumage *m* électronique; ~ mail courrier *m* électronique; ~ monetary systems monétique *f*; ~ music musique *f* électronique; ~ office bureau *m* informatisé; ~ organ orgue *m* électronique; ~ publishing édition *f* électronique; ~ surveillance surveillance *f* électronique.
◆ **electronics** ◇ *n (U)* électronique *f*.
◇ *npl* composants *mpl* électroniques.
◇ *comp*: ~s company société *f* d'électronique; ~s engineer ingénieur *m* électronicien, électronicien *m*, -enne *f*; ~s industry industrie *f* électronique.

electronically [ˌɪlek'trɒnɪklɪ] *adv* électroniquement; [operated] par voie électronique.

electron microscope *n* microscope *m* électronique.

electron telescope *n* télescope *m* électronique.

electron tube *n* tube *m* électronique.

electrophoresis [ɪˌlektrəʊfə'riːsɪs] *n* électrophorèse *f*.

electroplate [ɪ'lektrəʊpleɪt] ◇ *vt* plaquer par galvanoplastie; [with gold] dorer par galvanoplastie; [with silver] argenter par galvanoplastie.
◇ *n (U)* articles *mpl* plaqués (par galvanoplastie); [with silver] articles *mpl* argentés.

electroshock [ɪ'lektrəʊʃɒk] *n* électrochoc *m*; ~ therapy thérapie *f* par électrochocs.

electrostatic [ɪˌlektrəʊ'stætɪk] *adj* électrostatique.

electrostatics [ɪˌlektrəʊ'stætɪks] *n (U)* électrostatique *f*.

electrotherapy [ɪˌlektrəʊ'θerəpɪ] *n* électrothérapie *f*.

elegance ['elɪgəns] *n* élégance *f*.

elegant ['elɪgənt] *adj* [person, style, solution] élégant; [building, furniture] aux lignes élégantes.

elegantly ['elɪgəntlɪ] *adv* élégamment.

elegiac [elɪ'dʒaɪək] ◇ *adj* élégiaque.
◇ *n* élégie *f*.

elegy ['elɪdʒɪ] (*pl* elegies) *n* élégie *f*; 'Elegy (Written) in a Country Churchyard' *Gray* 'Élégie écrite dans un cimetière campagnard'.

element ['elɪmənt] *n* -**1.** [water, air etc] élément *m*; the four ~s les quatre éléments; to be exposed to/to brave the ~s être exposé aux/affronter les éléments; to be in/out of one's ~ *fig* être/ne pas être dans son élément. -**2.** [in kettle, electric heater] résistance *f*. -**3.** [small amount - of danger, truth, the unknown] part *f*; the ~ of chance le facteur chance; the ~ of surprise l'élément de OR le facteur surprise. -**4.** (*usu pl*) [rudiment] rudiment *m*; the ~s of computing les rudiments de l'informatique. -**5.** [in society, group] élément *m*; the hooligan ~ l'élément hooligan de la société; a disruptive ~ [in class] un élément perturbateur.

elemental [ˌelɪ'mentl] ◇ *adj* -**1.** [basic] fondamental, de base; the ~ needs of man les besoins fondamentaux de l'homme. -**2.** [relating to the elements] propre aux éléments; the ~ force of the storm la force des éléments déchaînés dans la tempête. -**3.** CHEM élémentaire.
◇ *n lit* esprit *m*.

elementary [ˌelɪ'mentərɪ] *adj* élémentaire; I only speak ~ Russian mon russe est rudimentaire; ~, my dear Watson! élémentaire, mon cher Watson! ❑ ~ school/education école *f*/enseignement *m* primaire; ~ particle particule *f* élémentaire.

elephant ['elɪfənt] *n* éléphant *m*; ~ calf éléphanteau *m*; African/Indian ~ éléphant d'Afrique/d'Asie.

elephantiasis [ˌelɪfən'taɪəsɪs] *n* éléphantiasis *m*.

elephantine [ˌelɪ'fæntaɪn] *adj* [proportions, size] éléphantesque; [gait] lourd, pesant; [movement] gauche, maladroit.

elephant seal *n* éléphant *m* de mer.

elevate ['elɪveɪt] *vt* [raise - in height, rank etc] élever; to ~ the Host RELIG élever l'hostie; to ~ sb to the rank of general élever qqn au rang de général.

elevated ['elɪveɪtɪd] *adj* -**1.** [height, position, rank] haut, élevé; [thoughts] noble, élevé; [style] élevé, soutenu. -**2.** [raised - road] surélevé; ~ railway OR railroad *Am* métro *m* aérien.

elevation [ˌelɪ'veɪʃn] *n* -**1.** [of roof, in rank] élévation *f*; RELIG [of host] élévation *f*; [of style, language] caractère *m* élevé OR soutenu. -**2.** [height]: ~ above sea-level élévation *f* par rapport au niveau de la mer. -**3.** [hill] élévation *f*, hauteur *f*. -**4.** [of cannon] hausse *f*; angle of ~ angle *m* de hausse OR d'élévation. -**5.** ARCHIT élévation *f*; angle of ~ angle *m* d'élévation.

elevator ['elɪveɪtə^r] *n* -**1.** *Am* [lift] ascenseur *m*. -**2.** [for grain] élévateur *m*.

elevator shoes *npl* chaussures *fpl* à semelles compensées.

eleven [ɪ'levn] ◇ *pron* onze.
◇ *adj* onze.
◇ *n* onze *m*; SPORT équipe *f*; FTBL onze *m*, équipe *f*; the English ~ SPORT l'équipe de football OR le onze d'Angleterre.

eleven-plus *n Br* SCH *examen de sélection pour l'entrée dans le secondaire en Grande-Bretagne*.

elevenses *inf* [ɪ'levnzɪz] *n Br boisson ou en-cas pour la pause de onze heures*.

eleventh [ɪ'levnθ] ◇ *adj* onzième.
◇ *n* [in series] onze *mf*; [fraction] onzième *m*.

eleventh hour *n*: at the ~ à la dernière minute.
◆ **eleventh-hour** *adj* de dernière minute; eleventh-hour talks discussions *fpl* de dernière minute.

elf [elf] (*pl* elves [elvz]) *n* elfe *m*.

elfin ['elfɪn] *adj fig* [face, features] délicat.

elfish ['elfɪʃ] = **elfin**.

Elgin Marbles ['elgɪn-] *npl*: the ~ les marbres d'Elgin *(sculptures du Parthénon, exposées au British Museum)*.

El Gîzah [el'giːzə] = **Gîza**.

elicit [ɪ'lɪsɪt] *vt* [information, explanation, response] obtenir; [facts, truth] découvrir, mettre au jour; to ~ sthg from sb tirer qqch de qqn; to ~ a smile from sb tirer un sourire de qqn, arracher un sourire à qqn.

elide [ɪ'laɪd] *vt* élider.

eligibility [ˌelɪdʒə'bɪlətɪ] *n* [to vote] éligibilité *f*; [for a job] admissibilité *f*; there was no doubt as to his ~ [for marriage] c'était sans aucun doute un bon parti; to determine sb's ~ for promotion décider si qqn présente les conditions requises pour bénéficier d'une promotion.

eligible ['elɪdʒəbl] *adj* [to vote] éligible; [for a job] admissible; [for promotion] pouvant bénéficier d'une promotion; [for marriage] mariable; to be ~ for a pension/a tax rebate avoir droit à une retraite/un dégrèvement fiscal; to be ~ [as possible husband or boyfriend] être un bon OR beau parti; an ~ bachelor un bon OR beau parti; there were lots of ~ men at the party il y avait beaucoup de bons OR beaux partis à la fête.

Elijah [ɪ'laɪdʒə] *pr n* Élie.

eliminate [ɪ'lɪmɪneɪt] *vt* [competitor, alternative] éliminer; [stain, mark] enlever, faire disparaître; [item from diet] supprimer, éliminer; [possibility] écarter, éliminer; [kill] éliminer, supprimer; MATHS & PHYSIOL éliminer; to ~ hunger and poverty from the world éliminer OR supprimer la faim et la pauvreté dans le monde.

elimination [ɪˌlɪmɪ'neɪʃn] *n* élimination *f*; by (a process of) ~ par élimination.

eliminatory [ɪ'lɪmɪnətrɪ] *adj* éliminatoire.

Elisha [ɪ'laɪʃə] *pr n* Élisée.

elision [ɪ'lɪʒn] *n* élision *f*.

elite [ɪ'liːt], **élite** [eɪ'liːt] ◇ *n* élite *f*; the ~ of society l'élite de la société; to be one of the ~ faire partie de l'élite.
◇ *adj* d'élite.

elitism [ɪ'liːtɪzm] *n* élitisme *m*.

elitist [ɪ'liːtɪst] ◇ *n* élitiste *mf*.
◇ *adj* élitiste.

elixir [ɪ'lɪksə^r] *n* élixir *m*; ~ of life élixir *m* de vie.

Elizabeth [ɪ'lɪzəbəθ] *pr n*: Saint ~ sainte Élisabeth; Queen ~ la reine Élisabeth.

Elizabethan [ɪˌlɪzə'biːθn] ◇ *adj* élisabéthain.
◇ *n* Élisabéthain *m*, -e *f*.

elk [elk] *n* élan *m*; American ~ wapiti *m*.
El Khalil [ˌelkæ'liːl] *pr n* al-Khalil.
ell [el] *n arch* aune *f*.
ellipse [ɪ'lɪps] *n* MATH ellipse *f*.
ellipsis [ɪ'lɪpsɪs] (*pl* **ellipses** [-siːz]) *n* ellipse *f* GRAMM.
ellipsoid [ɪ'lɪpsɔɪd] MATH ◇ *adj* ellipsoïde.
◇ *n* ellipsoïde *m*.
elliptic(al) [ɪ'lɪptɪk(l)] *adj* elliptique.
elliptically [ɪ'lɪptɪklɪ] *adv* de manière elliptique, par ellipse.
Ellis Island ['elɪs-] *pr n* Ellis Island *(dans la première moitié du XXe siècle, lieu de débarquement des immigrés, situé au large de New York)*.
elm [elm] *n* orme *m*; ~ **grove** ormaie *f*.
elocution [ˌelə'kjuːʃn] *n* élocution *f*, diction *f*; ~ **lessons** cours *mpl* d'élocution OR de diction.
elocutionist [ˌelə'kjuːʃənɪst] *n* professeur *m* d'élocution OR de diction.
elongate ['iːlɒŋgeɪt] ◇ *vt* allonger; [line] prolonger.
◇ *vi* s'allonger, s'étendre.
elongated ['iːlɒŋgeɪtɪd] *adj* [in space] allongé; [in time] prolongé.
elongation [ˌiːlɒŋ'geɪʃn] *n* allongement *m*; [of line] prolongement *m*.
elope [ɪ'ləʊp] *vi* s'enfuir pour se marier; **to ~ with sb** s'enfuir avec qqn pour l'épouser.
elopement [ɪ'ləʊpmənt] *n* fugue *f* amoureuse *(en vue d'un mariage)*.
eloquence ['eləkwəns] *n* éloquence *f*.
eloquent ['eləkwənt] *adj* éloquent.
eloquently ['eləkwəntlɪ] *adv* éloquemment, avec éloquence.
El Salvador [el'sælvədɔːʳ] *pr n* Salvador *m*; **in ~** au Salvador.
Elsan® ['elsæn] *n W-C chimique portable*.
else [els] *adv* **-1.** [after indefinite pronoun] d'autre; **anybody** OR **anyone ~** [at all] n'importe qui d'autre; [in addition] quelqu'un d'autre; **anyone ~ would have phoned the police** n'importe qui d'autre aurait appelé la police; **is there anybody ~?** y a-t-il quelqu'un d'autre?; **he's no cleverer than anybody ~** il n'est pas plus intelligent qu'un autre; **anything ~** [at all] n'importe quoi d'autre; [in addition] quelque chose d'autre; **would you like** OR **will there be anything ~?** [in shop] vous fallait-il autre chose?; [in restaurant] désirez-vous autre chose?; **I couldn't do anything ~ but** OR **except apologize** je ne pouvais (rien faire d'autre) que m'excuser; **anywhere ~** ailleurs; **I haven't got anywhere ~** OR **I've got nowhere ~ to go** je n'ai nulle part ailleurs où aller; **everybody ~** tous les autres; **everything ~** tout le reste; **everywhere ~** partout ailleurs; **there is little ~ we can do** nous ne pouvons pas faire grand-chose d'autre; **and much ~ (besides)** et beaucoup de choses encore; **nobody** OR **no one ~** personne d'autre; **nothing ~** rien d'autre; **we're alive, nothing ~ matters** nous sommes vivants, c'est tout ce qui compte; **there's nothing ~ for it** il n'y a rien d'autre à faire; **nowhere ~** nulle part ailleurs; **there's nowhere ~ I'd rather be but here** c'est ici et nulle part ailleurs que je veux être; **somebody** OR **someone ~** quelqu'un d'autre; **this is somebody ~'s** c'est à quelqu'un d'autre; **something ~** autre chose, quelque chose d'autre; **somewhere** OR *Am* **someplace ~** ailleurs, autre part ❑ **if all ~ fails** en dernier recours; **it'll teach him a lesson, if nothing ~** au moins, ça lui servira de leçon; **he's/she's/it's something ~!** *inf* il est/elle est/c'est incroyable!; **the price of petrol is something ~!** *inf* bonjour le prix de l'essence! **-2.** *(after interrogative pronoun)* [in addition] d'autre; **what/who ~?** quoi/qui d'autre?; **what ~ can I do?** que puis-je faire d'autre?; **who ~ but Frank?** qui d'autre que Frank?; [otherwise] autrement; **how/why ~ would I do it?** comment/pourquoi le ferais-je sinon?; **where ~ would he be?** où peut-il être à part là?; **so we're all meeting at Henry's – where ~?** alors, on se retrouve tous chez Henry – où d'autre?
elsewhere [els'weəʳ] *adv* ailleurs; **to go ~** aller ailleurs; **~ in France the tradition has died out** ailleurs en France, la tradition n'existe plus.
ELT (*abbr of* **English language teaching**) *n enseignement de l'anglais*.
elucidate [ɪ'luːsɪdeɪt] ◇ *vt* [point, question] élucider, expliciter; [reasons] expliquer.
◇ *vi* expliquer, être plus clair; **could you ~?** pourrais-tu être plus clair?
elucidation [ɪˌluːsɪ'deɪʃn] *n* [of point, question] élucidation *f*, éclaircissement *m*; [of reasons] explication *f*.
elude [ɪ'luːd] *vt* [enemy, pursuers] échapper à; [question] éluder; [blow] esquiver; [sb's gaze] éviter, fuir; [obligation, responsibility] se dérober à, se soustraire à; [justice] se soustraire à; **his name/that word ~s me** son nom/ce mot m'échappe; **to ~ sb's grasp** échapper à (l'emprise de) qqn; **happiness/success has always ~d her** le bonheur/la réussite lui a toujours échappé.
elusive [ɪ'luːsɪv] *adj* [enemy, prey, happiness, thought] insaisissable; [word, concept] difficile à définir; [answer] élusif, évasif; **she's being rather ~** [difficult to find] elle se fait plutôt discrète ces derniers temps; [vague] elle se montre assez évasive.
elusively [ɪ'luːsɪvlɪ] *adv* [answer] de manière élusive; [move] de manière insaisissable.
elusiveness [ɪ'luːsɪvnɪs] *n* [of answer] caractère *m* élusif OR évasif; [of thoughts, happiness] caractère *m* insaisissable.
elver ['elvəʳ] *n* civelle *f*, pibale *f*.
elves [elvz] *pl* → **elf**.
Elysium [ɪ'lɪzɪəm] *n* MYTH Élysée *m*.
em [em] *n* TYPO cadratin *m*.
'em *inf* [em] = **them**.
emaciated [ɪ'meɪʃɪeɪtɪd] *adj* émacié, décharné; **to become ~** s'émacier, se décharner.
emaciation [ɪˌmeɪsɪ'eɪʃn] *n* émaciation *f*; **in a state of ~** émacié, décharné.
email, e-mail ['iːmeɪl] (*abbr of* **electronic mail**) ◇ *n* courrier *m* électronique.
◇ *vt* envoyer par courrier électronique.
emanate ['eməneɪt] ◇ *vi*: **to ~ from** émaner de.
◇ *vt* [love, affection] exsuder, rayonner de; [concern] respirer.
emanation [ˌemə'neɪʃn] *n* émanation *f*.
emancipate [ɪ'mænsɪpeɪt] *vt* [women] émanciper; [slaves] affranchir.
emancipated [ɪ'mænsɪpeɪtɪd] *adj* émancipé.
emancipation [ɪˌmænsɪ'peɪʃn] *n* émancipation *f*; **the Emancipation Proclamation** *Am* HIST la proclamation d'émancipation.

THE EMANCIPATION PROCLAMATION:
Allocution prononcée par le président américain Abraham Lincoln en 1863 et proclamant les esclaves de la Confédération (États sudistes) «libres à jamais». Bien qu'elle n'ait eu aucun effet concret (ces États échappaient au contrôle fédéral), c'est à cette proclamation que les Américains font référence en parlant de l'émancipation des esclaves par Lincoln.

---

emasculate [ɪ'mæskjʊleɪt] *vt* [castrate] émasculer; *fig* émasculer, affaiblir.
emasculation [ɪˌmæskjʊ'leɪʃn] *n* [castration] émasculation *f*; *fig* émasculation *f*, affaiblissement *m*.
embalm [ɪm'bɑːm] *vt* embaumer.
embalmer [ɪm'bɑːməʳ] *n* embaumeur *m*, thanatopracteur *m*.
embalming [ɪm'bɑːmɪŋ] *n* embaumement *m*; ~ **fluid** fluide *m* de thanatopraxie.
embankment [ɪm'bæŋkmənt] *n* [of concrete] quai *m*; [of earth] berge *f*; [to contain river] digue *f*; [along railway, road] talus *m*.
◆ **Embankment** *pr n*: **the Embankment** *nom abrégé du «Victoria Embankment», rue de la rive nord de la Tamise à Londres*.
embargo [em'bɑːgəʊ] (*pl* **embargoes**) ◇ *n* **-1.** COMM & POL embargo *m*; **to put** OR **to place** OR **to lay an ~ on sthg** mettre l'embargo sur qqch; **to lift/to break an ~** lever/enfreindre un embargo; **there is still an ~ on arms, arms are still under an ~** les armes sont encore sous embargo; **oil/arms ~** embargo pétrolier/sur les armes; **trade ~** embargo commercial. **-2.** *fig* [on spending] interdiction *f*; **to put an ~ on sthg** interdire OR bannir qqch.
◇ *vt* COMM & POL mettre l'embargo sur; *fig* interdire.
embark [ɪm'bɑːk] ◇ *vt* [passengers, cargo] embarquer.
◇ *vi* embarquer, monter à bord.
◆ **embark on, embark upon** *vt insep* [journey, career] commencer, entreprendre; [explanation, venture] se lancer dans; [risky operations] s'embarquer dans.
embarkation [ˌembɑː'keɪʃn], **embarkment** [ɪm'bɑːkmənt] *n* [of passengers, cargo] embarquement *m*; ~ **papers** OR **card** carte *f* d'embarquement.
embarrass [ɪm'bærəs] *vt* embarrasser, gêner; **to ~ the government/one's family** mettre le gouvernement/sa famille dans l'embarras; **to feel ~ed (about sthg)** être embarrassé OR se sentir gêné (à propos de qqch); **to look ~ed** avoir l'air embarrassé OR gêné; **to be (financially) ~ed** être gêné, avoir des problèmes d'argent.
embarrassing [ɪm'bærəsɪŋ] *adj* [experience, person] embarrassant, gênant; [situation] embarrassant, délicat; **how ~!** comme c'est gênant OR embarrassant!; **how ~ for you!** comme cela a dû être gênant OR embarrassant pour toi!; **this is rather ~ but...** cela me gêne beaucoup mais...
embarrassingly [ɪm'bærəsɪŋlɪ] *adv* de manière embarrassante; **it was ~ obvious** c'était évident au point d'en être embarrassant; **he gave an ~ bad performance** sa prestation était tellement mauvaise qu'on en était gêné pour lui; **to be ~ candid** être d'une franchise embarrassante.
embarrassment [ɪm'bærəsmənt] *n* embarras *m*, gêne *f*; **(much) to my ~** à mon grand embarras; **to cringe with ~** vouloir rentrer sous terre; **to cause sb ~** mettre qqn dans l'embarras; **to be in a state of financial ~** avoir des problèmes OR embarras financiers; **to be an ~** OR **a source of ~ to sb** être une source d'embarras pour qqn, faire honte à qqn.
embassy ['embəsɪ] (*pl* **embassies**) *n* ambassade *f*; **the British/French Embassy** l'ambassade de Grande-Bretagne/France.
embattled [ɪm'bætld] *adj* [army] engagé dans la bataille; [town] ravagé par les combats; *fig* en difficulté, aux prises avec des difficultés.
embed [ɪm'bed] (*pt* & *pp* **embedded**, *cont* **embedding**) *vt* [in wood] enfoncer; [in rock] sceller; [in cement] sceller, noyer; [jewels] enchâsser, incruster; **embedded in my memory** gravé dans ma mémoire; **the event has become embedded in my memory** l'événement s'est gravé dans ma mémoire ❑ **embedded command** COMPUT commande *f* intégrée; **embedded clause** GRAMM proposition *f* enchâssée.
embedding [ɪm'bedɪŋ] *n* [in wood] enfoncement *m*; [in rock, cement] scellement *m*; GRAMM enchâssement *m*.
embellish [ɪm'belɪʃ] *vt* [garment, building] embellir, décorer, orner; [account, story etc] enjoliver, embellir.
embellishment [ɪm'belɪʃmənt] *n* [of building] embellissement *m*; [of garment] décoration *f*; [of account, story etc] enjolivement *m*, embellissement *m*; [in handwriting] fioritures *fpl*.
ember ['embəʳ] *n* charbon *m* ardent, morceau *m* de braise; **~s** braise *f*.
embezzle [ɪm'bezl] ◇ *vt* [money] détourner, escroquer; **to ~ money from sb** escroquer de l'argent à qqn.
◇ *vi*: **to ~ from a company** détourner les fonds d'une société.

embezzlement [ɪm'bezlmənt] *n* [of funds] détournement *m*; to be convicted of ~ être reconnu coupable de détournement de fonds.
embezzler [ɪm'bezləʳ] *n* escroc *m*, fraudeur *m*, -euse *f*.
embitter [ɪm'bɪtəʳ] *vt* [person] remplir d'amertume, aigrir; [relations] altérer, détériorer.
embittered [ɪm'bɪtəd] *adj* aigri.
embitterment [ɪm'bɪtəmənt] *n* [of person] amertume *f*, aigreur *f*; [of relations] détérioration *f*, altération *f*.
emblazon [ɪm'bleɪzn] *vt* blasonner; the shield is ~ed with dragons le bouclier porte des dragons.
emblem ['embləm] *n* emblème *m*.
emblematic [,emblə'mætɪk] *adj* emblématique.
embodiment [ɪm'bɒdɪmənt] *n* -**1.** [epitome] incarnation *f*, personnification *f*; to be the ~ of goodness/evil [person] être la bonté même/le mal incarné; the new building is the ~ of modernity ce nouveau bâtiment est la modernité même. -**2.** [inclusion] intégration *f*, incorporation *f*.
embody [ɪm'bɒdɪ] (*pt* & *pp* embodied) *vt* -**1.** [epitomize - subj: person] incarner; [- subj: action] exprimer. -**2.** [include] inclure, intégrer.
embolden [ɪm'bəʊldən] *vt* *fml* enhardir, donner du courage à; to ~ sb to do sthg enhardir qqn à faire qqch, donner à qqn le courage de faire qqch; to feel ~ed to do sthg se sentir le courage de faire qqch.
embolism ['embəlɪzm] *n* MED embolie *f*; to suffer OR to have an ~ faire OR avoir une embolie.
embolus ['embələs] (*pl* emboli [-laɪ]) *n* MED embole *m*, embolus *m*.
emboss [ɪm'bɒs] *vt* [metal] repousser, estamper; [leather] estamper, gaufrer; [cloth, paper] gaufrer.
embossed [ɪm'bɒst] *adj* [metal] repoussé; [leather] gaufré; [cloth, wallpaper] gaufré, à motifs en relief.
embouchure [,ɑːmbuː'ʃʊəʳ] *n* MUS embouchure *f*.
embrace [ɪm'breɪs] ◇ *vt* -**1.** [friend, child] étreindre; [lover] étreindre, enlacer; [official, visitor, statesman] donner l'accolade à. -**2.** [include] regrouper, comprendre, embrasser. -**3.** [adopt - religion, cause] embrasser; [- opportunity] saisir.
◇ *vi* [friends] s'étreindre; [lovers] s'étreindre, s'enlacer; [statesmen] se donner l'accolade.
◇ *n* [of friend, child] étreinte *f*; [of lover] étreinte *f*, enlacement *m*; [of official visitor, statesman] accolade *f*; to hold OR to clasp sb in an ~ étreindre qqn; to greet sb with an ~ accueillir qqn dans une étreinte.
embrasure [ɪm'breɪʒəʳ] *n* embrasure *f*.
embrocation [,embrə'keɪʃn] *n* embrocation *f*.
embroider [ɪm'brɔɪdəʳ] ◇ *vt* [garment, cloth] broder; *fig* [story, truth] embellir, enjoliver.
◇ *vi* [with needle] broder; *fig* [embellish] broder, enjoliver.
embroidery [ɪm'brɔɪdərɪ] (*pl* embroideries) *n* [on garment, cloth] broderie *f*; *fig* [of story, truth] enjolivement *m*, embellissement *m*.
embroil [ɪm'brɔɪl] *vt* mêler, impliquer; to ~ sb in sthg mêler qqn à qqch, impliquer qqn dans qqch; to get ~ed in sthg se retrouver mêlé à qqch; to get ~ed with sb [romantically] avoir une liaison avec qqn.
embroilment [ɪm'brɔɪlmənt] *n* *fml* [in matter, situation] implication *f*; [with lover] liaison *f*.
embryo ['embrɪəʊ] (*pl* embryos) *n* BIOL & *fig* embryon *m*; I have the ~ of an idea j'ai un embryon d'idée; in ~ [foetus, idea] à l'état embryonnaire.
embryological [,embrɪə'lɒdʒɪkl] *adj* embryonnaire.
embryologist [,embrɪ'ɒlədʒɪst] *n* embryologiste *mf*.
embryology [,embrɪ'ɒlədʒɪ] *n* embryologie *f*.
embryonic [,embrɪ'ɒnɪk] *adj* BIOL embryonnaire; *fig* à l'état embryonnaire.
embus [ɪm'bʌs] MIL ◇ *vt* faire monter à bord d'un autocar.
◇ *vi* monter à bord d'un autocar.
emcee *inf* [,em'siː] ◇ *n* *abbr of* master of ceremonies.
◇ *vt* animer.
emend [iː'mend] *vt* corriger.
emendation [,iːmen'deɪʃn] *n* *fml* correction *f*.
emerald ['emərəld] ◇ *n* -**1.** [gem stone] émeraude *f*. -**2.** ~ (green) [colour] (vert *m*) émeraude *m*.
◇ *comp* [brooch, ring] en émeraude; ~ necklace collier d'émeraudes.
Emerald Isle *pr n* *lit* Île *f* d'Émeraude.
emerge [ɪ'mɜːdʒ] *vi* [person, animal] sortir; [sun] sortir, émerger; [truth, difficulty] émerger, apparaître; to ~ from the water [diver, submarine, island] émerger; to ~ from hiding sortir de sa cachette; new playwrights have ~d on the scene de nouveaux dramaturges ont fait leur apparition; to ~ as favourite apparaître comme le favori; it ~s that... il apparaît OR ressort que...; it later ~d that... il est apparu par la suite que...; to ~ victorious OR the winner sortir vainqueur; to ~ unscathed sortir indemne.
emergence [ɪ'mɜːdʒəns] *n* émergence *f*.
emergency [ɪ'mɜːdʒənsɪ] (*pl* emergencies) ◇ *n* -**1.** (cas *m* d') urgence *f*; this is an ~! c'est une urgence!; in case of ~, in an ~ en cas d'urgence; to provide for emergencies parer à l'imprévu; to be prepared for any ~ être prêt à toutes les éventualités ❑ national ~, state of ~ état *m* d'urgence; to declare a state of ~ déclarer l'état d'urgence. -**2.** MED [department] (service *m* des) urgences *fpl*.
◇ *comp* [measures, procedure, meeting] d'urgence; ~ brake frein *m* de secours; ~ case MED urgence *f*; ~ exit sortie *f* de secours; ~ food aid aide *f* alimentaire d'urgence; ~ landing AERON atterrissage *m* forcé; ~ operation MED opération *f* à chaud; ~ patient urgence *f*; ~ powers pouvoirs *mpl* extraordinaires; ~ rations vivres *mpl* de secours OR de réserve; ~ repairs réparations *fpl* d'urgence; ~ service AUT service *m* de dépannage; MED service *m* des urgences; ~ services services *mpl* d'urgence; ~ stop AUT arrêt *m* d'urgence; ~ supply réserve *f*; ~ tank AERON réservoir *m* auxiliaire; 'for ~ use only' 'à n'utiliser qu'en cas d'urgence'; ~ ward *Br*, ~ room *Am* MED salle *f* des urgences.
emergent [ɪ'mɜːdʒənt] *adj* [theory, nation] naissant.
emeritus [ɪ'merɪtəs] *adj* UNIV honoraire.
emery ['emərɪ] *n* émeri *m*.
emery board *n* lime *f* à ongles.
emery cloth *n* toile *f* (d') émeri.
emery paper *n* papier *m* (d') émeri.
emetic [ɪ'metɪk] ◇ *adj* émétique.
◇ *n* émétique *m*, vomitif *m*.
emigrant ['emɪgrənt] ◇ *n* émigrant *m*, -e *f*; [when established abroad] émigré *m*, -e *f*.
◇ *comp* [worker, population] émigré.
emigrate ['emɪgreɪt] *vi* émigrer.
emigration [,emɪ'greɪʃn] *n* émigration *f*.
émigré ['emɪgreɪ] *n* émigré *m*.
eminence ['emɪnəns] *n* -**1.** [prominence] rang *m* éminent; to occupy a position of ~ avoir un rang éminent; to achieve ~ in one's profession atteindre un rang éminent dans sa profession. -**2.** [high ground] éminence *f*, hauteur *f*.
◆ **Eminence** *n* RELIG [title] Éminence *f*; Your/His Eminence Votre/Son Éminence.
Eminency ['emɪnənsɪ] = **Eminence**.
eminent ['emɪnənt] *adj* [distinguished] éminent; [conspicuous] éminent, remarquable, insigne.
eminently ['emɪnəntlɪ] *adv* éminemment; to be ~ successful réussir brillamment; ~ suitable qui convient parfaitement; it is ~ desirable that... il est fort à souhaiter que..., il est éminemment souhaitable que...
emir [e'mɪəʳ] *n* émir *m*.
emirate ['emərət] *n* émirat *m*.
emissary ['emɪsərɪ] (*pl* emissaries) *n* émissaire *m*.
emission [ɪ'mɪʃn] *n* émission *f*.
emit [ɪ'mɪt] (*pt* & *pp* emitted, *cont* emitting) *vt* [sound, radiation, light] émettre; [heat] dégager, émettre; [gas] dégager; [sparks, cry] lancer.
emitter [ɪ'mɪtəʳ] *n* NUCL, PHYS & ELECTRON émetteur *m*.
Emmental, Emmenthal ['emən,tɑːl] *n* Emmental *m*.
Emmentaler, Emmenthaler ['emən,tɑːləʳ] = **Emmental**.
Emmy ['emɪ] *n*: ~ (award) *distinction récompensant les meilleures émissions télévisées américaines de l'année*.
emollient [ɪ'mɒlɪənt] ◇ *adj* émollient; *fig* adoucissant, calmant.
◇ *n* émollient *m*.
emolument [ɪ'mɒljʊmənt] *n* *fml (usu pl)*: ~s émoluments *mpl*, rémunération *f*.
emote [ɪ'məʊt] *vi* [on stage] faire dans le genre tragique; [in life] avoir un comportement théâtral.
emotion [ɪ'məʊʃn] *n* [particular feeling] sentiment *m*; [faculty] émotion *f*; to be in control of one's ~s contrôler OR maîtriser ses émotions; to show no ~ ne laisser paraître aucune émotion; to shake with ~ [person, voice] trembler d'émotion; to appeal to the ~s faire appel aux sentiments; to express one's ~s exprimer ses sentiments; don't let your ~s get in the way ne te laisse pas influencer par tes sentiments.
emotional [ɪ'məʊʃənl] *adj* -**1.** [stress] émotionnel; [life, problems] affectif. -**2.** [person - easily moved] sensible, qui s'émeut facilement; [- stronger] émotif; [appealing to the emotions - plea, speech, music] émouvant; [charged with emotion - issue] passionné, brûlant; [- reunion, scene] chargé d'émotion; [governed by emotions - person] passionné, ardent; [- reaction, state] émotionnel; he got very ~ at the funeral il était très ému à l'enterrement; why do you always have to get so ~? pourquoi faut-il toujours que tu te mettes dans de tels états?; you shouldn't be so ~ tu es vraiment trop sensible; ~ blackmail chantage *m* affectif.
emotionalism [ɪ'məʊʃnəlɪzm] *n* *pej* sensiblerie *f*.
emotionally [ɪ'məʊʃnəlɪ] *adv* [react, speak] avec émotion; to feel ~ exhausted OR drained se sentir vidé (sur le plan émotionnel); to be ~ disturbed souffrir de troubles affectifs; an ~ charged atmosphere une atmosphère chargée d'émotion; ~, he's not strong enough for the job sur le plan émotionnel,il n'est pas assez solide pour ce travail; to be ~ immature manquer de maturité sur le plan affectif; to be ~ involved with sb avoir des liens affectifs avec qqn; I don't want to get ~ involved je ne veux pas m'attacher.
emotionless [ɪ'məʊʃnlɪs] *adj* [face, eyes] qui n'exprime aucune émotion, impassible; [person] impassible; [style] froid.
emotive [ɪ'məʊtɪv] *adj* [issue] sensible; [word, phrase] à forte teneur émotionnelle.
empanel [ɪm'pænl] (*Br pt* & *pp* empanelled, *cont* empanelling, *Am pt* & *pp* empaneled, *cont* empaneling) *vt* [jury] constituer; [juror] mettre sur la liste OR le tableau du jury.
empathetic [,empə'θetɪk] *adj* empathique.
empathize ['empəθaɪz] *vi*: to ~ with sb s'identifier à qqn; in his case I find it difficult to ~ j'ai du mal à m'identifier à lui.
empathy ['empəθɪ] *n* [affinity - gen] affinité *f*, affinités *fpl*, sympathie *f*; PHILOS & PSYCH empathie *f*; [power, ability] capacité *f* à s'identifier à autrui; the part calls for a good deal of ~ le rôle exige une grande capacité à s'identifier au personnage; the ~ between them les affinités qui existent entre eux; our ~ with her pain notre sympathie à sa douleur.

emperor ['empərəʳ] *n* empereur *m*; 'The Emperor's New Clothes' *Andersen* 'les Nouveaux Habits de l'empereur'.

emperor moth *n* saturnie *f*, paon de nuit *m*.

emperor penguin *n* manchot *m* empereur.

emphasis ['emfəsɪs] (*pl* **emphases** [-siːz]) *n* **-1.** [importance] accent *m*; to place OR to lay OR to put ~ on sthg mettre l'accent sur qqch; there is too much ~ on materialism in our society on accorde trop d'importance aux choses matérielles dans notre société; this year the ~ is on bright colours/steady growth cette année, l'accent est mis sur les couleurs vives/sur une croissance régulière; a change of ~ un changement de priorités; the ~ now is on winning votes ce qui est important maintenant c'est de gagner des voix. **-2.** LING [stress] accent *m*; the ~ comes on the last syllable l'accent est placé OR tombe sur la dernière syllabe; to say sthg with ~ dire qqch avec emphase OR emphatiquement.

emphasize ['emfəsaɪz] *vt* **-1.** [detail, need, importance] insister sur; I can't ~ this strongly enough je n'insisterai jamais assez sur cela. **-2.** [physical feature] accentuer; to ~ the waist [dress] marquer OR accentuer la taille. **-3.** LING [syllable] accentuer; [word] accentuer, appuyer sur.

emphatic [ɪm'fætɪk] *adj* [gesture, refusal] emphatique; [speaker, manner] énergique, vigoureux; LING emphatique; to be ~ insister; to be ~ in one's denials nier avec emphase.

emphatically [ɪm'fætɪklɪ] *adv* **-1.** [forcefully] emphatiquement, avec emphase; [deny] avec emphase. **-2.** [definitely] clairement; I most ~ do not agree with you je ne suis absolument pas d'accord avec vous.

emphysema [,emfɪ'siːmə] *n* emphysème *m*.

empire ['empaɪəʳ] *n* empire *m*; the Holy Roman Empire HIST le Saint-Empire romain; 'The Empire Strikes Back' *Kershner* 'l'Empire contre-attaque'.
◆ **Empire** *comp* [costume, furniture, style] Empire.

empire-build *vi*: he's ~ing again il est encore à jouer les bâtisseurs d'empires.

empire-builder *n fig* bâtisseur *m* d'empires.

empire-building ◇ *adj* de bâtisseur d'empires.
◇ *n*: there's too much ~ going on on joue trop les bâtisseurs d'empires.

empiric [ɪm'pɪrɪk] ◇ *adj* empirique.
◇ *n* empiriste *mf*.

empirical [ɪm'pɪrɪkl] *adj* empirique.

empirically [ɪm'pɪrɪklɪ] *adv* empiriquement.

empiricism [ɪm'pɪrɪsɪzm] *n* empirisme *m*.

empiricist [ɪm'pɪrɪsɪst] *n* empiriste *mf*.

emplacement [ɪm'pleɪsmənt] *n* MIL [of canon] emplacement *m*.

emplane [ɪm'pleɪn] ◇ *vt* embarquer (à bord d'un avion).
◇ *vi* embarquer (à bord d'un avion).

employ [ɪm'plɔɪ] ◇ *vt* **-1.** [give work to] employer; they ~ 245 staff ils ont 245 employés; to ~ sb as a receptionist employer qqn comme réceptionniste; he has been ~ed with the firm for twenty years il travaille pour cette entreprise depuis vingt ans. **-2.** [use - means, method, word] employer, utiliser; [- skill, diplomacy] faire usage de, employer; [- force] employer, avoir recours à. **-3.** [occupy]: to ~ oneself/to be ~ed in doing sthg s'occuper/être occupé à faire qqch; you'd be better ~ed doing your homework tu ferais mieux de faire tes devoirs; have you no better way of ~ing your time? tu n'as rien de mieux à faire?
◇ *n fml* service *m*; to be in sb's ~ travailler pour qqn, être au service de qqn; to have sb in one's ~ employer qqn, avoir qqn à son service.

employable [ɪm'plɔɪəbl] *adj* [person] susceptible d'être employé; [method] utilisable; a good education makes you more ~ une bonne formation donne plus de chances de trouver du travail.

employed [ɪm'plɔɪd] ◇ *adj* employé; I am not ~ at the moment je n'ai pas de travail en ce moment; to be gainfully ~ avoir un emploi rémunéré.
◇ *npl* personnes *fpl* qui ont un emploi; employers and ~ patronat *m* et salariat *m*.

employee [ɪm'plɔɪiː] ◇ *n* employé *m*, -e *f*, salarié *m*, -e *f*; she is an ~ of Company X, she is a Company X ~ c'est une employée de la Société X; management and ~s la direction et les employés OR le personnel; [in negociations] les partenaires *mpl* sociaux; ~'s contribution OR share [to benefits] cotisation *f* ouvrière.
◇ *comp*: ~ benefits avantages *mpl* accordés aux employés.

employer [ɪm'plɔɪəʳ] *n* employeur *m*, patron *m*; ADMIN employeur *m*; they are good ~s ce sont de bons employeurs OR patrons; who is your ~? pour qui travaillez-vous?; ~s [as a body] patronat *m*; ~'s contribution OR share [to employee benefits] cotisation *f* patronale.

employment [ɪm'plɔɪmənt] *n* **-1.** [work] emploi *m*; to be without ~ être sans emploi OR travail; to be in ~ avoir un emploi OR du travail; full ~ plein emploi; gainful ~ emploi *m* rémunéré; conditions of ~ conditions *fpl* de travail; to look for OR to seek ~ chercher du travail OR un emploi, être demandeur d'emploi; to give OR to provide ~ donner OR fournir du travail; ~ figures are up les chiffres de l'emploi ont progressé ❑ Department of Employment *Am* OR *dated Br*, Employment Department ≃ ministère *m* du Travail; Secretary (of State) for OR Minister of Employment *Br*, Secretary for Employment *Am* ≃ ministre *m* du Travail. **-2.** [recruitment] embauche *f*; [providing work] emploi *m*. **-3.** [use - of method, word] emploi *m*; [- of force, skill] usage *m*, emploi *m*.

employment agency, **employment bureau** *n* agence *f* OR bureau *m* de placement.

employment exchange, **employment office** *n Br dated* ≃ ANPE *f*.

emporium [em'pɔːrɪəm] (*pl* **emporiums** OR **emporia** [-rɪə]) *n* grand magasin *m*.

empower [ɪm'paʊəʳ] *vt fml* habiliter, autoriser; to ~ sb to do sthg habiliter OR autoriser qqn à faire qqch.

empress ['emprɪs] *n* impératrice *f*.

emptiness ['emptɪnɪs] *n* vide *m*; a feeling of ~ un sentiment de vide; the ~ of my life/days le vide de mon existence/mes journées.

empty ['emptɪ] (*pl* **empties**, *compar* **emptier**, *superl* **emptiest**) ◇ *adj* [glass, room, box etc] vide; [city, street] désert; [cinema] désert, vide; [job, post] vacant, à pourvoir; *fig* [words, talk] creux; [promise] en l'air, vain; [gesture] dénué de sens; [threat] en l'air; ~ of meaning vide OR dénué de sens; the house was ~ of people la maison était vide; my stomach is ~ [I'm hungry] j'ai un creux (à l'estomac); to do sthg on an ~ stomach faire qqch à jeun; to be taken on an ~ stomach MED à prendre à jeun; to feel ~ [drained of emotion] se sentir vidé (sur le plan émotionnel); the fuel gauge was at OR showing ~ le niveau du réservoir était à zéro ❑ ~ vessels make most noise *prov* moins on en sait, plus on parle.
◇ *n inf* [bottle] bouteille *f* vide; [glass] verre *m* vide.
◇ *vt* [glass, pocket, room] vider; [car, lorry] décharger.
◇ *vi* [building, street, container] se vider; [water] s'écouler; to ~ into the sea [river] se jeter dans la mer.
◆ **empty out** ◇ *vt sep* vider.
◇ *vi insep* [tank, container] se vider; [water, liquid] s'écouler.

empty-handed *adj* les mains vides; to return ~ rentrer bredouille OR les mains vides.

empty-headed *adj* écervelé, sans cervelle.

empyrean [,empaɪ'riːən] *n lit* empyrée *m*.

EMS (*abbr of* European Monetary System) *pr n* SME *m*.

EMT (*abbr of* emergency medical technician) *n technicien médical des services d'urgence*.

emu ['iːmjuː] *n* émeu *m*.

emulate ['emjʊleɪt] *vt* [person, action] imiter; COMPUT émuler.

emulation [,emjʊ'leɪʃn] *n* [gen & COMPUT] émulation *f*.

emulator ['emjʊleɪtəʳ] *n* COMPUT émulateur *m*.

emulsifier [ɪ'mʌlsɪfaɪəʳ] *n* émulsifiant *m*.

emulsify [ɪ'mʌlsɪfaɪ] *vt* émulsionner, émulsifier.

emulsion [ɪ'mʌlʃn] ◇ *n* **-1.** CHEM & PHOT émulsion *f*. **-2.** [paint] (peinture *f*) émulsion *f*.
◇ *vt* appliquer de la peinture émulsion sur.

emulsion paint = **emulsion** *n* **2**.

en [en] *n* TYPO demi-cadratin *m*.

EN (*abbr of* enrolled nurse) *n Br infirmière diplômée*.

enable [ɪ'neɪbl] *vt*: to ~ sb to do sthg permettre à qqn de faire qqch; JUR habiliter OR autoriser qqn à faire qqch.

enabling [ɪ'neɪblɪŋ] *adj* JUR habilitant.

enact [ɪ'nækt] *vt* **-1.** JUR [bill, law] promulguer. **-2.** [scene, play] jouer; to be ~ed *fig* se dérouler.

enactment [ɪ'næktmənt] *n* **-1.** JUR [of bill, law etc] promulgation *f*. **-2.** [of play] représentation *f*.

enamel [ɪ'næml] (*Br pt & pp* **enamelled**, *cont* **enamelling**, *Am pt & pp* **enameled**, *cont* **enameling**) ◇ *n* **-1.** ART [on clay, glass etc] émail *m*. **-2.** [paint] peinture *f* laquée OR vernie. **-3.** [on teeth] émail *m*.
◇ *comp* [mug, saucepan] en émail, émaillé; ~ paint peinture *f* laquée OR vernie; ~ painting peinture *f* sur émail.
◇ *vt* émailler.

enamelled *Br*, **enameled** *Am* [ɪ'næmld] *adj* [mug, saucepan] émaillé, en émail.

enamelling *Br*, **enameling** *Am* [ɪ'næməlɪŋ] *n* émaillage *m*.

enamelware [ɪ'næmlweəʳ] *n* ustensiles *mpl* en émail.

enamoured *Br*, **enamored** *Am* [ɪ'næməd] *adj*: to be ~ of *lit* [person] être amoureux OR épris de; [job, flat] être enchanté OR ravi de; he wasn't exactly ~ of our proposal notre proposition ne l'enchantait guère.

enc. **-1.** *written abbr of* enclosure. **-2.** *written abbr of* enclosed.

encamp [ɪn'kæmp] ◇ *vi* camper.
◇ *vt* faire camper; to be ~ed camper.

encampment [ɪn'kæmpmənt] *n* campement *m*.

encapsulate [ɪn'kæpsjʊleɪt] *vt* PHARM mettre en capsule; *fig* résumer.

encase [ɪn'keɪs] *vt* recouvrir, entourer.

encash [ɪn'kæʃ] *vt Br* encaisser.

encashment [ɪn'kæʃmənt] *n Br* encaissement *m*.

encaustic [en'kɔːstɪk] ◇ *adj* [brick, tile] émaillé; [painting] encaustique.
◇ *n* peinture *f* à l'encaustique.

encephalic [,enkə'fælɪk] *adj* encéphalique.

encephalitis [,enkefə'laɪtɪs] *n* encéphalite *f*.

encephalogram [en'sefələgræm] *n* encéphalogramme *m*.

enchain [ɪn'tʃeɪn] *vt* enchaîner.

enchant [ɪn'tʃɑːnt] *vt* **-1.** [delight] enchanter, ravir. **-2.** [put spell on] enchanter, ensorceler.

enchanted [ɪn'tʃɑːntɪd] *adj* enchanté; the ~ed wood le bois enchanté.

enchanter [ɪn'tʃɑːntəʳ] *n* enchanteur *m*.

enchanting [ɪn'tʃɑːntɪŋ] *adj* charmant.

enchantingly [ɪn'tʃɑːntɪŋlɪ] *adv* avec charme.

enchantment [ɪn'tʃɑːntmənt] *n* **-1.** [delight] enchantement *m*, ravissement *m*; to fill sb with ~ enchanter OR ravir qqn. **-2.** [casting of spell] enchantement *m*, ensorcellement *m*.

enchantress [ɪn'tʃɑːntrɪs] *n* enchanteresse *f*.

enchilada [,entʃɪ'lɑːdə] *n plat mexicain consistant en une galette de maïs frite, farcie à la viande et servie avec une sauce piquante*.

encircle [ɪn'sɜːkl] *vt* entourer; MIL & HUNT encercler, cerner.

encirclement [ɪn'sɜːklmənt] *n* encerclement *m*.

encircling [ɪn'sɜːklɪŋ] ◇ *n* encerclement *m*.
◇ *adj* MIL: ~ movement manœuvre *f* d'encerclement.

enclave ['enkleɪv] *n* enclave *f*.

enclose [ɪn'kləʊz] *vt* -**1.** [surround - with wall] entourer, ceinturer; [- with fence] clôturer; an ~d space un espace clos. -**2.** [in letter] joindre; to ~ sthg with a letter joindre qqch à une lettre; please find ~d my CV veuillez trouver ci-joint OR ci-inclus mon CV; I ~ a cheque for £20 je joins un chèque de 20 livres; the ~d cheque le chèque ci-joint OR ci-inclus.

enclosed order [ɪn'kləʊzd-] *n* RELIG ordre *m* claustral.

enclosure [ɪn'kləʊʒəʳ] *n* -**1.** [enclosed area] enclos *m*, enceinte *f*; public ~ [at sports ground, racecourse] pelouse *f*; royal ~ enceinte *f* de la famille royale. -**2.** [with letter] pièce *f* jointe OR annexée OR incluse. -**3.** [action] action *f* de clôturer. -**4.** *Br* HIST enclosure *f*.

ENCLOSURE:
«Clôture des champs», dont l'apparition, vers la fin du XVᵉ siècle en Angleterre, a accéléré le passage d'une forme communautaire à une forme individualiste d'économie agraire, provoquant une importante crise sociale.

---

encode [en'kəʊd] *vt* coder, chiffrer; COMPUT encoder.

encoder [en'kəʊdəʳ] *n* [gen & COMPUT] encodeur *m*.

encoding [en'kəʊdɪŋ] *n* codage *m*; COMPUT encodage *m*.

encomium [en'kəʊmjəm] (*pl* **encomiums** OR encomia [-mjə]) *n fml* panégyrique *m*.

encompass [ɪn'kʌmpəs] *vt* -**1.** [include] englober, comprendre, regrouper. -**2.** *fml* [surround] entourer, encercler.

encore ['ɒŋkɔːʳ] ◇ *interj*: ~!, ~! bis!, bis!
◇ *n* bis *m*; to call for an ~ bisser; to give an ~ [performer] donner un bis; to give an ~ of a song rechanter OR rejouer une chanson en bis; how many ~s were there? combien de rappels y a-t-il eu?
◇ *vt* [singer, performer] rappeler, bisser; [song] bisser.

encounter [ɪn'kaʊntəʳ] ◇ *vt* [person, enemy] rencontrer; [difficulty, resistance, danger] rencontrer, se heurter à.
◇ *n* [gen & MIL] rencontre *f*; 'Brief Encounter' *Lean* 'Brève rencontre'; 'Close Encounters of the Third Kind' *Spielberg* 'Rencontres du troisième type'.

encounter group *n séance de psychothérapie de groupe*.

encourage [ɪn'kʌrɪdʒ] *vt* [person] encourager, inciter; [project, research, attitude] encourager; to ~ sb to do sthg encourager OR inciter qqn à faire qqch; don't ~ him! [in bad behaviour] ne l'encourage pas!; to ~ sb in his/her belief that... renforcer qqn dans sa conviction que..., conforter qqn dans son idée que...

encouragement [ɪn'kʌrɪdʒmənt] *n* encouragement *m*; to give sb ~, to give ~ to sb donner des encouragements à OR encourager qqn; to get OR to receive ~ from sb recevoir des encouragements de la part de qqn; all he needs is a bit of ~ tout ce qu'il lui faut c'est un peu d'encouragement; without your ~ sans vos encouragements; shouts/words of ~ cris/mots d'encouragement.

encouraging [ɪn'kʌrɪdʒɪŋ] *adj* encourageant; [smile, words] d'encouragement.

encouragingly [ɪn'kʌrɪdʒɪŋlɪ] *adv* de manière encourageante; ~, a working party has been set up fait encourageant, un groupe de travail a été mis en place.

encroach [ɪn'krəʊtʃ]
◆ **encroach on, encroach upon** *vi insep*: the sea is gradually ~ing on the land la mer gagne progressivement du terrain; the new buildings are ~ing on the countryside les nouveaux bâtiments envahissent la campagne; to ~ on sb's territory *fig* marcher OR empiéter sur les plates-bandes de qqn.

encroachment [ɪn'krəʊtʃmənt] *n* [on freedom, property, time] empiétement *m*; [by sea, river] envahissement *m*, ingression *f spec*; [buildings] envahissement.

encrust [ɪn'krʌst] *vt* [with jewels] incruster; [with mud, snow, ice] couvrir; to be ~ed with sthg être incrusté OR couvert OR recouvert de qqch.

encrustation [ˌɪnkrʌs'teɪʃn] *n* incrustation *f*.

encrypt [en'krɪpt] *vt* coder, chiffrer; COMPUT encoder.

encumber [ɪn'kʌmbəʳ] *vt fml* [person, room] encombrer, embarrasser; ~ed with too many clothes empêtré dans ses vêtements; ~ed estate JUR [with debts] propriété *f* grevée de dettes; [with mortgage] propriété *f* grevée d'hypothèques.

encumbrance [ɪn'kʌmbrəns] *n fml* [burden] charge *f*, fardeau *m*; JUR charge *f* grevant une propriété.

encyclical [ɪn'sɪklɪkl] RELIG ◇ *adj* encyclique.
◇ *n* encyclique *f*.

encyclopaedia *etc* [ɪnˌsaɪklə'piːdjə] = **encyclopedia**.

encyclopedia [ɪnˌsaɪklə'piːdjə] *n* encyclopédie *f*; she's a walking ~ c'est une encyclopédie ambulante OR vivante ❑ the Encyclopaedia Britannica l'Encyclopaedia Britannica.

encyclopedic [ɪnˌsaɪkləʊ'piːdɪk] *adj* encyclopédique.

encyclopedist [ɪnˌsaɪklə'piːdɪst] *n* encyclopédiste *mf*.

end [end] ◇ *n* -**1.** [furthermost part, tip, edge] bout *m*; at the ~ of the garden au bout OR fond du jardin; the rope is frayed at this ~/at that ~/at one ~ la corde est effilochée à ce bout-ci/à ce bout-là/au bout; at either ~ of the political spectrum/of the social scale aux deux extrémités de l'éventail politique/de l'échelle sociale; at the other ~ of the line TELEC au bout de la ligne; from one ~ of the country/of the town to the other d'un bout à l'autre du pays/de la ville; third from the ~ troisième en partant de la fin; the deep/shallow ~ le grand/petit bain; to change ~s SPORT changer de côté ‖ [area, aspect] côté *m*; how are things (at) your ~? comment ça va de ton côté OR pour toi?; the marketing/manufacturing ~ of the operation le côté marketing/fabrication de l'opération, tout ce qui est marketing/fabrication ❑ to be at the ~ of one's tether être au bout du rouleau; this is the ~ of the road OR line c'est fini; to get OR have one's ~ away▽ *Br* tirer un OR son coup; to go to the ~s of the earth aller jusqu'au bout du monde; to keep one's ~ of the bargain tenir parole; to keep one's ~ up tenir bon; he doesn't know OR can't tell one ~ of an ice axe/a word processor from the other il ne sait même pas à quoi ressemble un piolet/un traitement de texte; to make (both) ~s meet [financially] joindre les deux bouts. -**2.** [conclusion, finish] fin *f*; at the ~ of July/of spring/of the year à la fin du mois de juillet/du printemps/de l'année; from beginning to ~ du début à la fin, de bout en bout; to read to the ~ of a book, to read a book to the ~ lire un livre jusqu'au bout OR jusqu'à la fin; I waited until the ~ of the meeting j'ai attendu la fin de la réunion; to be at an ~ être terminé OR fini; my patience is at OR has come to an ~ ma patience est à bout; to be at the ~ of one's resources/one's strength avoir épuisé ses ressources/ses forces; to bring sthg to an ~ [meeting] clore qqch; [situation] mettre fin à qqch; [speech] achever qqch; to come to an ~ s'achever, prendre fin; to draw to an ~ arriver OR toucher à sa fin; to put an ~ to sthg mettre fin à qqch; we want an ~ to the war nous voulons que cette guerre cesse OR prenne fin; the ~ of the world/of time la fin du monde/des temps; the ~ is nigh la fin est proche; and that was the ~ of that et ça s'est terminé comme ça ❑ he's/you're the ~! *inf* [impossible] il est/tu es incroyable!; [extremely funny] il est/tu es trop (drôle)!; to come to a bad ~ mal finir; ~ of story! *inf* [stop arguing] plus de discussions!; [I don't want to talk about it] un point, c'est tout!; it's not the ~ of the world *inf* ce n'est pas la fin du monde; we'll never hear the ~ of it on n'a pas fini d'en entendre parler; is there no ~ to his talents? a-t-il donc tous les talents?, n'y a-t-il pas de limite à ses talents? -**3.** [aim] but *m*, fin *f*; to achieve OR to attain one's ~ atteindre son but; with this ~ in view OR mind, to this ~ dans ce but, à cette fin; to what ~? *fml* dans quel but?, à quelle fin?; for political ~s à des fins politiques ❑ an ~ in itself une fin en soi; the ~ justifies the means la fin justifie les moyens. -**4.** [remnant - of cloth, rope] bout *m*; [- of loaf] croûton *m*. -**5.** *euph* OR *lit* [death] mort *f*; to meet one's ~ trouver la mort; to be nearing one's ~ être à l'article de la mort; I was with him at the ~ j'étais auprès de lui dans ses derniers moments.
◇ *vt* [speech, novel] terminer, conclure; [meeting, discussion] clore; [day] terminer, finir; [war, speculation, relationship] mettre fin OR un terme à; [work] terminer, finir, achever; she ~ed the letter with a promise to write again soon elle a terminé la lettre en promettant de récrire bientôt; the war to ~ all wars la dernière de toutes les guerres; the joke to ~ all jokes la meilleure blague qu'on ait jamais entendue ❑ he decided to ~ it all [life, relationship] il décida d'en finir; she ~ed her days in a retirement home elle a fini ses jours dans une maison de retraite.
◇ *vi* [story, film] finir, se terminer, s'achever; [path, road etc] se terminer, s'arrêter; [season, holiday] se terminer, toucher à sa fin; how OR where will it all ~? comment tout cela finira-t-il OR se terminera-t-il?; where does society ~ and the individual begin? où s'arrête la société et où commence l'individu?; to ~ in a point se terminer en pointe; the discussion ~ed in an argument la discussion s'est terminée en dispute; to ~ in failure/divorce se solder par un échec/un divorce; the word ~s in -ed le mot se termine par OR en -ed; the book ~s with a quotation le livre se termine par une citation ❑ it'll ~ in tears ça va mal finir; all's well that ~s well *prov* tout est bien qui finit bien *prov*.
◇ *comp* [house, seat, table] du bout.
◆ **at the end of the day** *adv phr literal* à la fin de la journée; *fig* au bout du compte, en fin de compte.
◆ **end on** *adv phr* par le bout.
◆ **end to end** *adv phr* -**1.** [with ends adjacent] bout à bout. -**2.** = **from end to end**.
◆ **from end to end** *adv phr* d'un bout à l'autre.
◆ **in the end** *adv phr* finalement; we got there in the ~ finalement nous y sommes arrivés, nous avons fini par y arriver.
◆ **no end** *inf adv phr*: it upset her/cheered her up no ~ ça l'a bouleversée/ravie à un point (inimaginable) ❑ to think no ~ of sb porter qqn aux nues.
◆ **no end of** *inf det phr*: it'll do you no ~ of good cela vous fera un bien fou; to have no ~ of trouble doing sthg avoir énormément de mal OR un mal fou OR un mal de chien à faire qqch; we met no ~ of interesting people on a rencontré des tas de gens intéressants.
◆ **on end** *adv phr* -**1.** [upright] debout; to stand sthg on ~ mettre qqch debout; her hair was standing on ~ elle avait les cheveux dressés sur la tête. -**2.** [in succession] entier; for hours/days on ~ pendant des heures entières/des jours entiers; for four hours on ~ pendant quatre heures de suite OR d'affilée.
◆ **end off** *vt sep* terminer; they ~ed off the evening with a dance ils ont terminé la soirée par une danse.
◆ **end up** *vi insep* finir; they took a wrong turning and ~ed up in Manchester/back at the station ils ont pris la mauvaise bifurcation

et se sont retrouvés à Manchester/à la gare; to ~ up in hospital/in prison finir à l'hôpital/en prison; if you keep driving like that, you're going to ~ up killing yourself si tu continues à conduire comme ça, tu finiras par te tuer; to ~ up doing sthg finir par faire qqch; to ~ up (as) the boss/on the dole finir patron/chômeur; I wonder what he'll ~ up as/how he'll ~ up je me demande ce qu'il deviendra/comment il finira.

end-all → **be-all**.

endanger [ɪn'deɪndʒəʳ] *vt* [life, country] mettre en danger; [health, reputation, future, chances] compromettre; an ~ed species une espèce en danger OR menacée (de disparition).

endear [ɪn'dɪəʳ] *vt* faire aimer; what ~s him to me ce qui le rend cher à mes yeux; to ~ o.s. to sb se faire aimer de qqn; the Chancellor's decision did not ~ him to the voters la décision du Chancelier ne lui a pas gagné la faveur des électeurs.

endearing [ɪn'dɪərɪŋ] *adj* [personality, person] attachant; [smile] engageant; it's a very ~ characteristic of his c'est un trait de caractère qui le rend très attachant.

endearingly [ɪn'dɪərɪŋlɪ] *adv* de manière attachante; [smile] de manière engageante.

endearment [ɪn'dɪəmənt] *n*: ~s, words of ~ mots *mpl* tendres; term of ~ terme *m* affectueux.

endeavour *Br*, **endeavor** *Am* [ɪn'devəʳ] *fml*
◇ *n* effort *m*; to make every ~ to obtain sthg faire tout son possible pour obtenir qqch; in an ~ to stop the strike en tentant de mettre fin à la grève; despite her best ~s malgré tous ses efforts; to use one's best ~s to do sthg employer tous ses efforts à faire qqch; a new field of human ~ une nouvelle perspective pour l'homme; one of the greatest achievements of human ~ une des plus belles victoires OR conquêtes de l'homme.
◇ *vi*: to ~ to do sthg s'efforcer OR essayer de faire qqch.

endemic [en'demɪk] MED ◇ *adj* endémique.
◇ *n* endémie *f*.

endgame ['endgeɪm] *n* CHESS fin *f* de partie; 'Endgame' *Beckett* 'Fin de partie'.

ending ['endɪŋ] *n* **-1.** [of story, book] fin *f*; a story with a happy/sad ~ une histoire qui finit bien/mal. **-2.** LING terminaison *f*.

endive ['endaɪv] *n* **-1.** [curly-leaved] (chicorée *f*) frisée *f*. **-2.** *esp Am* [chicory] endive *f*.

endless ['endlɪs] *adj* [speech, road, job] interminable, sans fin; [patience] sans bornes, infini; [resources] inépuisable, infini; [desert] infini; the possibilities are ~ les possibilités sont innombrables; to ask ~ questions poser des questions à n'en plus finir; ~ belt TECH courroie *f* sans fin.

endlessly ['endlɪslɪ] *adv* [speak] continuellement, sans cesse; [extend] à perte de vue, interminablement; to be ~ patient/generous être d'une patience/générosité sans bornes.

endmost ['endməʊst] *adj* du bout.

endocarditis [,endəʊkɑː'daɪtɪs] *n* MED endocardite *f*.

endocardium [,endəʊ'kɑːdɪəm] *n* ANAT endocarde *m*.

endocarp ['endəʊkɑːp] *n* endocarpe *m*.

endocrine ['endəʊkraɪn] *adj* PHYSIOL [disorders, system] endocrinien; ~ gland glande *f* endocrine.

endocrinologist [,endəʊkraɪ'nɒlədʒɪst] *n* MED endocrinologue *mf*, endocrinologiste *mf*.

endocrinology [,endəʊkraɪ'nɒlədʒɪ] *n* MED endocrinologie *f*.

endogamy [en'dɒgəmɪ] *n* ANTHR endogamie *f*.

endogenous [en'dɒdʒɪnəs] *adj* BIOL endogène.

endomorph ['endəʊmɔːf] *n* endomorphe *m*.

endomorphic [,endəʊ'mɔːfɪk] *adj* endomorphique.

endorphin [en'dɔːfɪn] *n* MED endorphine *f*.

endorse [ɪn'dɔːs] *vt* **-1.** [cheque] endosser; [document - sign] apposer sa signature sur; [- annotate] apposer une remarque sur. **-2.** *Br* JUR: to ~ a driving licence faire état d'une infraction sur un permis de conduire. **-3.** [approve - action, decision] approuver; [- opinion] soutenir, adhérer à; [- appeal, candidature] appuyer; sportswear ~d by top athletes vêtements de sport adoptés par les athlètes de haut niveau; should footballers be seen to ~ alcoholic drinks? est-il acceptable que les footballeurs fassent de la publicité pour les boissons alcoolisées?

endorsement [ɪn'dɔːsmənt] *n* **-1.** [of cheque] endossement *m*; [of document - signature] signature *f*; [- annotation] remarque *f*. **-2.** *Br* JUR [on driving licence] *infraction dont il est fait état sur le permis de conduire*. **-3.** [approval - of action, decision] approbation *f*; [- of claim, candidature] appui *m*; their ~ of this opinion leur adhésion à cette opinion.

endoscope ['endəʊskəʊp] *n* MED endoscope *m*.

endoscopy [en'dɒskəpɪ] *n* MED endoscopie *f*.

endoskeleton [,endəʊ'skelɪtn] *n* endosquelette *m*.

endothermic [,endəʊ'θɜːmɪk] *adj* endothermique.

endow [ɪn'daʊ] *vt* **-1.** [institution] doter; [university chair, hospital ward] fonder; to ~ a hospice with £1 million doter un hospice d'un million de livres. **-2.** *(usu pass)*: to be ~ed with sthg être doté de qqch; well ~ed *inf* [man] bien monté; she's well ~ed il y a du monde au balcon.

endowment [ɪn'daʊmənt] *n* **-1.** [action, money] dotation *f*. **-2.** *(usu pl) fml* [talent, gift] don *m*, talent *m*.

endowment assurance, **endowment insurance** *n* assurance *f* à dotation fixe.

endowment mortgage *n* emprunt-logement *m* garanti par une assurance-vie.

endowment policy *n* assurance *f* mixte.

endpaper ['end,peɪpə] *n* garde *f*, page *f* de garde.

end product *n* INDUST & COMM produit *m* final; *fig* résultat *m*.

end result *n* résultat *m* final.

endue [ɪn'djuː] *vt lit* doter.

endurable [ɪn'djʊərəbl] *adj* supportable, endurable.

endurance [ɪn'djʊərəns] ◇ *n* endurance *f*; powers of ~ endurance; it is beyond ~ c'est insupportable; she was tried beyond ~ elle a été éprouvée au-delà des limites du supportable.
◇ *comp*: ~ race SPORT course *f* d'endurance; ~ test épreuve *f* d'endurance.

endure [ɪn'djʊəʳ] ◇ *vt* [bear - hardship] endurer, subir; [- pain] endurer; [- person, stupidity, laziness] supporter, souffrir; she can't ~ being kept waiting elle ne supporte OR ne souffre pas qu'on la fasse attendre; he can't ~ seeing OR to see children mistreated il ne supporte pas qu'on maltraite des enfants.
◇ *vi fml* [relationship, ceasefire, fame] durer; [memory] rester; he won't be able to ~ for long in this weather il ne résistera OR ne tiendra pas longtemps avec un temps pareil.

enduring [ɪn'djʊərɪŋ] *adj* [friendship, fame, peace] durable; [democracy, dictatorship] qui dure; [epidemic, suffering] tenace; [actor, politician] qui jouit d'une grande longévité *(en tant qu'acteur, homme politique etc)*.

enduringly [ɪn'djʊərɪŋlɪ] *adv* de manière durable.

end user *n* [gen & COMPUT] utilisateur *m* final.

endways ['endweɪz] *adv*: put it ~ on mets-le en long; put them ~ on mets-les bout à bout.

endwise ['endwaɪz] *Am* = **endways**.

enema ['enɪmə] *n* [act] lavement *m*; [liquid] produit *m* à lavement; to give sb an ~ administrer un lavement à qqn.

enemy ['enɪmɪ] (*pl* enemies) ◇ *n* **-1.** ennemi *m*, -e *f*; to make enemies se faire des ennemis; I made an ~ of her je m'en suis fait une ennemie; to be one's own worst ~ se nuire à soi-même; deadly enemies ennemis mortels OR jurés ❑ 'An Enemy of the People' *Ibsen* 'Un ennemi du peuple'. **-2.** MIL: the ~ l'ennemi *m*; the ~ was OR were advancing l'ennemi avançait; boredom is the ~ l'ennui, voilà l'ennemi.
◇ *comp* [forces, missile, country] ennemi; [advance, strategy] de l'ennemi; ~ alien ressortissant *m*, -e *f* d'un pays ennemi; ~ attack attaque *f* ennemie; ~ fire feu *m* de l'ennemi; ~-occupied territory territoire *m* occupé par l'ennemi.

energetic [,enə'dʒetɪk] *adj* [person, measures] énergique; [music] vif, rapide; [activity] qui consomme de l'énergie; [campaigner, supporter] enthousiaste; to feel ~ se sentir plein d'énergie; after a very ~ day après une journée très chargée; do you feel ~ enough for it? t'en sens-tu l'énergie?; I don't want to do anything too ~ je ne veux rien faire qui demande trop d'énergie.

energetically [,enə'dʒetɪklɪ] *adv* énergiquement.

energize ['enədʒaɪz] *vt* [person] donner de l'énergie à, stimuler; ELEC exciter, envoyer de l'électricité dans.

energizing ['enədʒaɪzɪŋ] *adj* [food, effect] énergisant.

energy ['enədʒɪ] (*pl* energies) ◇ *n* **-1.** [vitality] énergie *f*; to be/to feel full of ~ être/se sentir plein d'énergie; to have no ~ se sentir sans énergie; to conserve one's ~ économiser son énergie; she didn't have the ~ for an argument elle n'avait pas assez d'énergie pour se disputer; glucose is full of ~ le glucose est très énergétique. **-2.** [effort] énergie *f*; to devote OR to apply (all) one's energies to sthg consacrer toute son énergie OR toutes ses énergies à qqch. **-3.** PHYS énergie *f*; kinetic/potential ~ énergie cinétique/potentielle; atomic ~ énergie nucléaire OR atomique. **-4.** [power] énergie *f*; to save OR to conserve ~ faire des économies d'énergie; to consume ~ consommer de l'énergie; a source of ~ une source d'énergie ❑ Minister of OR Secretary (of State) for Energy ministre *m* de l'Énergie.
◇ *comp* [conservation, consumption] d'énergie; [supplies, programme, level] énergétique; ~ crisis crise *f* énergétique OR de l'énergie; ~-giving énergétique; ~-intensive [appliance, industry] grand consommateur d'énergie; ~-saving [device] d'économie d'énergie.

enervate ['enəveɪt] *vt* amollir, débiliter.

enervating ['enəveɪtɪŋ] *adj* amollissant, débilitant.

enfeeble [ɪn'fiːbl] *vt* affaiblir.

enfeeblement [ɪn'fiːblmənt] *n* affaiblissement *m*.

enfilade [,enfɪ'leɪd] MIL ◇ *n* enfilade *f*.
◇ *vt* prendre en enfilade.

enfold [ɪn'fəʊld] *vt* [embrace] étreindre; to ~ sb in one's arms étreindre qqn, entourer qqn de ses bras.

enforce [ɪn'fɔːs] *vt* [policy, decision] mettre en œuvre, appliquer; [law] mettre en vigueur; [subj: police] faire exécuter; [one's rights] faire valoir; [one's will, discipline] faire respecter; [contract] faire exécuter; to ~ obedience se faire obéir.

enforceable [ɪn'fɔːsəbl] *adj* exécutoire.

enforced [ɪn'fɔːst] *adj* forcé.

enforcement [ɪn'fɔːsmənt] *n* [of law] application *f*; [of contract] exécution *f*.

enfranchise [ɪn'fræntʃaɪz] *vt* [give vote to - women, workers] accorder le droit de vote à; [emancipate - slaves] affranchir.

enfranchisement [ɪn'fræntʃɪzmənt] *n* [of women, workers] octroi *m* du droit de vote; [of slaves] affranchissement *m*.

engage [ɪn'geɪdʒ] ◇ *vt* **-1.** [occupy, involve]: to ~ sb in conversation [talk to] discuter avec qqn; [begin talking to] engager la conversation avec qqn; while we were ~d in conversation pendant que nous discutions. **-2.** *fml* [employ - staff] engager; [- lawyer] engager les services de; to ~ the services of sb employer les services de qqn. **-3.** *fml* [attract, draw - interest, attention]

attirer; [- sympathy] susciter. -**4.** AUT & TECH engager; to ~ the clutch embrayer; to ~ a gear engager une vitesse. -**5.** MIL: to ~ the enemy engager (le combat avec) l'ennemi.
◇ *vi* -**1.** [take part]: to ~ in prendre part à; to ~ in conversation discuter. -**2.** MIL: to ~ in battle with the enemy engager le combat avec l'ennemi. -**3.** AUT & TECH s'engager; [cogs] s'engrener; [machine part] s'enclencher. -**4.** *fml* [promise]: to ~ to do sthg s'engager à faire qqch.

engaged [ɪn'geɪdʒd] *adj* -**1.** [of couple] fiancé; to be ~ to be married être fiancé; to get ~ se fiancer; the ~ couple les fiancés *mpl*. -**2.** [busy, occupied] occupé; I'm otherwise ~ je suis déjà pris; to be ~ in discussions with sb être engagé dans des discussions avec qqn; to be ~ in a conversation être en pleine discussion. -**3.** *Br* [telephone] occupé; the line OR number is ~ la ligne est occupée; I got the ~ tone ça sonnait occupé. -**4.** [toilet] occupé.

engagement [ɪn'geɪdʒmənt] *n* -**1.** [betrothal] fiançailles *fpl*; they announced their ~ ils ont annoncé leurs fiançailles. -**2.** [appointment] rendez-vous *m*; dinner ~ rendez-vous pour dîner; he couldn't come, owing to a prior OR previous ~ il n'a pas pu venir car il était déjà pris. -**3.** MIL engagement *m*. -**4.** AUT & TECH engagement *m*. -**5.** [recruitment] engagement *m*, embauche *f*. -**6.** *fml* [promise] obligation *f*, engagement *m*. -**7.** [for actor, performer] engagement *m*, contrat *m*.

engagement diary *n* agenda *m*.

engagement ring *n* bague *f* de fiançailles.

engaging [ɪn'geɪdʒɪŋ] *adj* [smile, manner, tone] engageant; [person, personality] aimable, attachant.

engagingly [ɪn'geɪdʒɪŋlɪ] *adv* de manière engageante.

engender [ɪn'dʒendəʳ] *vt* engendrer, créer; to ~ sthg in sb engendrer qqch chez qqn.

engine ['endʒɪn] ◇ *n* [in car, plane] moteur *m*; [in ship] machine *f*; (railway) ~ *Br* locomotive *f*; to sit with one's back to the ~ être assis dans le sens opposé à OR inverse de la marche; to sit facing the ~ être assis dans le sens de la marche.
◇ *comp* [failure, trouble] de moteur OR machine; ~ block AUT bloc-moteur *m*; ~ oil AUT huile *f* à OR de moteur.

-engined ['endʒɪnd] *in cpds*: twin~ bimoteur.

engine driver *n Br* RAIL mécanicien *m*, conducteur *m*.

engineer [,endʒɪ'nɪəʳ] ◇ *n* -**1.** [for roads, machines, bridges] ingénieur *m*; [repairer] dépanneur *m*, réparateur *m*; MIL soldat *m* du génie; NAUT mécanicien *m*; aircraft ~ AERON mécanicien *m* de piste OR d'avion; flight ~ AERON ingénieur de vol, mécanicien *m* naviguant; the Royal Engineers MIL le génie *(britannique)*. -**2.** *Am* RAIL = **engine driver**. -**3.** *fig* [of plot, scheme etc] instigateur *m*, -trice *f*, artisan *m*.
◇ *vt* -**1.** [road, bridge, car] concevoir. -**2.** *pej* [bring about - event, situation] manigancer. -**3.** [work - goal, victory] amener.

engineering [,endʒɪ'nɪərɪŋ] ◇ *n* ingénierie *f*, engineering *m*; to study ~ faire des études d'ingénieur; an incredible feat of ~ une merveille de la technique; an intricate piece of ~ une mécanique très complexe.
◇ *comp*: ~ consultancy [firm] compagnie *f* d'ingénieurs-conseils; ~ consultant ingénieur-conseil *m*; ~ department service *m* technique; ~ and design department bureau *m* d'études; ~ firm entreprise *f* de construction mécanique; ~ work [on railway line] travail *m* d'ingénierie.

engineman ['endʒɪnmæn] (*pl* enginemen [-men]) *Am* = **engine driver**.

engine room *n* NAUT salle *f* des machines.

engine shed *n* RAIL dépôt *m*.

England ['ɪŋglənd] *pr n* Angleterre *f*; to live in ~ habiter l'Angleterre OR en Angleterre; to go to ~ aller en Angleterre; the ~ team SPORT l'équipe d'Angleterre; an ~ player un joueur anglais; an ~ victory une victoire de OR pour l'Angleterre.

English ['ɪŋglɪʃ] ◇ *adj* anglais; [history, embassy] d'Angleterre; [dictionary, teacher] d'anglais; the ~ disease *terme faisant référence à la fréquence des grèves avant les lois anti-syndicales en Grande-Bretagne*.
◇ *n* LING anglais *m*; do OR can you speak ~? parlez-vous (l')anglais?; to study ~ étudier OR apprendre l'anglais; she speaks excellent ~ elle parle très bien (l')anglais; we spoke (in) ~ to each other nous nous sommes parlé en anglais; that's not good ~ ce n'est pas du bon anglais; in plain OR simple ~ clairement; so what you mean, in plain OR simple ~, is that... autrement dit OR en d'autres termes, ce que vous voulez dire, c'est que...; can you put that in plain OR simple ~? pouvez-vous vous exprimer plus clairement?; why can't lawyers talk in plain OR simple ~? pourquoi les hommes de loi ne parlent-ils pas comme vous et moi? ❑ ~ as a Foreign Language anglais langue étrangère; the King's OR Queen's ~ l'anglais correct; ~ as a Second Language anglais deuxième langue.
◇ *npl*: the ~ les Anglais *mpl*.

English breakfast *n* petit déjeuner *m* anglais OR à l'anglaise, breakfast *m*.

ENGLISH BREAKFAST:
Le petit déjeuner traditionnel anglais se compose d'un plat chaud (des œufs au bacon, par exemple), de céréales ou de porridge, et de toasts à la marmelade d'oranges, le tout accompagné de café ou de thé; aujourd'hui il est généralement remplacé par une collation plus légère.

English Channel *pr n*: the ~ la Manche.

English Heritage *pr n organisme britannique de protection du patrimoine historique*.

English horn *n Am* cor *m* anglais.

Englishman ['ɪŋglɪʃmən] (*pl* Englishmen [-mən]) *n* Anglais *m*; an ~'s home is his castle *prov* charbonnier est maître dans sa maison *prov*.

English muffin *n Am sorte de gaufre*.

English rose *n* femme *f* au charme anglais, beauté *f* britannique.

English setter *n* setter *m* anglais.

English speaker *n* [as native speaker] anglophone *mf*; [as non-native speaker] personne *f* parlant anglais.

English-speaking *adj* [as native language] anglophone; [as learned language] parlant anglais.

Englishwoman ['ɪŋglɪʃ,wʊmən] (*pl* Englishwomen [-,wɪmɪn]) *n* Anglaise *f*.

engrave [ɪn'greɪv] *vt* graver; ~d on her memory gravé dans sa mémoire.

engraver [ɪn'greɪvəʳ] *n* graveur *m*.

engraving [ɪn'greɪvɪŋ] *n* gravure *f*.

engross [ɪn'grəʊs] *vt* -**1.** *(usu pass)* [absorb] absorber; to be ~ed in a book être absorbé OR plongé dans un livre; I was so ~ed in what I was doing j'étais tellement absorbé par ce que je faisais. -**2.** JUR [make clear copy of - manuscript, document] grossoyer.

engrossing [ɪn'grəʊsɪŋ] *adj* absorbant.

engulf [ɪn'gʌlf] *vt* engloutir; to be ~ed by the sea/in flames être englouti par la mer/les flammes; the little man was ~ed in OR by his overcoat le petit bonhomme disparaissait sous son pardessus; ~ed in silence plongé dans le silence.

enhance [ɪn'hɑːns] *vt* [quality, reputation, performance] améliorer; [value, chances, prestige] augmenter, accroître; [taste, beauty] rehausser, mettre en valeur.

enhanced [ɪn'hɑːnst] *adj* [quality, reputation, performance] amélioré, meilleur; [value, chances, prestige] augmenté, accru; [taste, beauty] rehaussé, mis en valeur.

-enhanced *in cpds*: computer~ [graphics] optimisé par ordinateur; protein~ enrichi en protéines.

enhancement [ɪn'hɑːnsmənt] *n* [of quality, reputation, performance] amélioration *f*; [of value, chances, prestige] augmentation *f*, accroissement *m*; [of taste, beauty] rehaussement *m*, mise *f* en valeur.

enigma [ɪ'nɪgmə] *n* énigme *f*; he remains an ~ to us il est encore une énigme pour nous.

enigmatic [,enɪg'mætɪk] *adj* énigmatique.

enigmatically [,enɪg'mætɪklɪ] *adv* [smile, speak] d'un air énigmatique; [worded] énigmatiquement, d'une manière énigmatique.

enjoin [ɪn'dʒɔɪn] *vt fml* -**1.** [urge strongly] exhorter, recommander fortement OR vivement à; [order, command] enjoindre, ordonner à; to ~ sb to do sthg [urge] exhorter qqn à faire qqch, recommander fortement OR vivement à qqn de faire qqch; [command] enjoindre OR ordonner à qqn de faire qqch; to ~ silence on OR upon sb [urge] exhorter qqn au silence; [command] enjoindre OR ordonner le silence à qqn. -**2.** *Am* [forbid] interdire à.

enjoy [ɪn'dʒɔɪ] ◇ *vt* -**1.** [like - in general] aimer; [- on particular occasion] apprécier; to ~ sthg/doing sthg aimer qqch/faire qqch; to ~ a hot bath aimer prendre des bains chauds; to ~ a glass of wine with one's meal aimer boire un verre de vin avec son repas; to ~ life aimer la vie; he ~s swimming/going to the cinema il aime la natation/aller au cinéma; I don't ~ being made fun of je n'aime pas qu'on se moque de moi; ~ your meal! bon appétit!; did you ~ your meal, sir? avez-vous bien mangé, monsieur?; I ~ed that [book, film] cela m'a plu; [meal] je me suis régalé; I thoroughly ~ed the weekend/party j'ai passé un excellent week-end/une excellente soirée; I ~ the various advantages the job has to offer j'apprécie les divers avantages qu'offre ce poste; I'm really ~ing this fine weather quel plaisir, ce beau temps; did you ~ it? cela t'a plu?; what did you ~ most? qu'avez-vous préféré?, qu'est-ce qui vous a le plus plu?; to ~ o.s. s'amuser; ~ yourselves! amusez-vous bien!; did you ~ yourself? alors, c'était bien?; the Duke and Duchess, ~ing a joke with their daughter le Duc et la Duchesse, riant avec leur fille d'une plaisanterie. -**2.** [possess - rights, respect, privilege, income, good health] jouir de; [profits] bénéficier de.
◇ *vi*: ~! *Am* [enjoy yourself] amusez-vous bien!; [in restaurant] bon appétit!

enjoyable [ɪn'dʒɔɪəbl] *adj* [book, film, day] agréable; [match, contest] beau; [meal] excellent.

enjoyably [ɪn'dʒɔɪəblɪ] *adv* de manière agréable.

enjoyment [ɪn'dʒɔɪmənt] *n* -**1.** [pleasure] plaisir *m*; to get ~ from sthg/doing sthg tirer du plaisir de qqch/à faire qqch; she doesn't get much ~ elle n'a pas beaucoup de distractions; to get ~ out of life jouir de la vie; nothing could spoil his ~ of the meal rien ne pouvait gâcher le plaisir que lui procurait ce repas; I don't do this for ~ je ne fais pas cela pour le OR mon plaisir. -**2.** [of privileges, rights etc] jouissance *f*.

enlarge [ɪn'lɑːdʒ] ◇ *vt* -**1.** [expand - territory, house, business] agrandir; [- field of knowledge, group of friends] étendre, élargir; [- hole] agrandir, élargir; [- pores] dilater; MED [- organ] hypertrophier; ~d edition édition *f* augmentée. -**2.** PHOT agrandir.
◇ *vi* -**1.** [pores] se dilater; MED [organ] s'hypertrophier. -**2.** PHOT: the photo won't ~ well la photo ne donnera pas un bon agrandissement OR ne rendra pas bien en agrandissement.
◆ **enlarge on, enlarge upon** *vt insep* [elaborate on] s'étendre sur, donner des détails sur.

enlargement [ɪn'lɑːdʒmənt] *n* [of territory, house, business] agrandissement *m*; [of group of friends, field of knowledge] élargissement *m*; [of hole] agrandissement, élargissement; [of pore] dilatation *f*; MED [of organ] hypertrophie *f*; PHOT agrandissement *m*.

enlarger [ɪn'lɑːdʒəʳ] *n* PHOT agrandisseur *m*.

enlighten [ɪn'laɪtn] *vt* éclairer; to ~ sb on

sthg/as to why... éclairer qqn sur qqch/sur la raison pour laquelle...

enlightened [ɪn'laɪtnd] *adj* [person, view, policy] éclairé; ~ self-interest magnanimité *f* intéressée; ~ despot HIST despote *m* éclairé.

enlightening [ɪn'laɪtnɪŋ] *adj* [book, experience] instructif; the film was very ~ about the subject le film en apprenait beaucoup sur le sujet; that's not very ~! ça ne m'apprend OR ne me dit pas grand-chose!

enlightenment [ɪn'laɪtnmənt] *n* [explanation, information] éclaircissements *mpl*; [state] édification *f*, instruction *f*; for your ~ pour votre édification OR instruction.

◆ **Enlightenment** *n* HIST: the (Age of) Enlightenment le Siècle des lumières.

enlist [ɪn'lɪst] *vt* -1. MIL enrôler. -2. [help, support etc] mobiliser, faire appel à.

enlisted [ɪn'lɪstɪd] *adj Am*: ~ man (simple) soldat *m*.

enlistment [ɪn'lɪstmənt] *n* MIL enrôlement *m*, engagement *m*.

enliven [ɪn'laɪvn] *vt* [conversation, party] animer.

enmesh [ɪn'meʃ] *vt literal* prendre dans un filet; *fig* mêler; he got ~ed in the plot il s'est trouvé mêlé au complot.

enmity ['enmətɪ] (*pl* enmities) *n fml* inimitié *f*, hostilité *f*; ~ for/towards sb inimitié pour/envers qqn; ~ among OR between people inimitié entre personnes.

ennoble [ɪ'nəʊbl] *vt* [confer title upon] anoblir; *fig* [exalt, dignify] ennoblir, grandir.

enology *etc* [iː'nɒlədʒɪ] *Am* = **oenology**.

enormity [ɪ'nɔːmətɪ] (*pl* enormities) *n* -1. [of action, crime] énormité *f*. -2. *fml* [atrocity] atrocité *f*; [crime] crime *m* très grave. -3. [great size] énormité *f*; they were aware of the ~ of the task ahead of them ils se rendaient compte de l'énormité de la tâche qui les attendait.

enormous [ɪ'nɔːməs] *adj* -1. [very large - thing] énorme; [- amount, number] énorme, colossal; they've got an ~ dog ils ont un chien énorme; ~ amounts of food une quantité énorme OR énormément de vivres; an ~ crowd had gathered un monde fou s'était rassemblé; he made one last ~ effort il fit un dernier effort démesuré; there's an ~ difference between the two estimates il y a une énorme différence entre les deux estimations; an ~ number of cars une énorme quantité de voitures. -2. [as intensifier] énorme, grand; the operation was an ~ success l'opération a été un très grand succès; it has given me ~ pleasure cela m'a fait énormément plaisir.

enormously [ɪ'nɔːməslɪ] *adv* énormément, extrêmement; demand has increased ~ la demande a énormément augmenté; an ~ big house une maison terriblement grande; it was ~ successful ce fut extrêmement réussi.

enough [ɪ'nʌf] ◇ *det* assez de; ~ money assez OR suffisamment d'argent; do you have ~ money to pay? avez-vous de quoi payer?; are there ~ copies for all the children? y a-t-il assez OR suffisamment d'exemplaires pour tous les enfants?; you've had more than ~ wine tu as bu plus qu'assez de vin; the report is proof ~ le rapport est une preuve suffisante; she's not fool ~ to believe that! elle n'est pas assez bête pour le croire!

◇ *pron*: do you need some money? — I've got ~ avez-vous besoin d'argent? — j'en ai assez OR suffisamment; we earn ~ to live on nous gagnons de quoi vivre; there's ~ for everybody il y en a assez pour tout le monde; ~/not ~ is known for us to be able to make a prediction on en sait assez/on n'en sait pas assez pour faire une prévision; not ~ of us are here to take a vote on n'est pas assez nombreux pour voter; he's had ~ to eat il a assez mangé; more than ~ plus qu'il n'en faut ☐ ~ is ~! ça suffit comme ça!, trop c'est trop!; ~ is as good as a feast mieux vaut assez que trop; ~ said! *inf* je vois!; that's ~! ça suffit!; it's ~ to drive you mad c'est à vous rendre fou; I can't get ~ of his films je ne me lasse jamais de ses films; to have had ~ (of sthg) en avoir assez de qqch; she's had ~ of working late elle en a assez de travailler tard le soir.

◇ *adv* -1. [sufficiently] assez, suffisamment; he's old ~ to understand il est assez grand pour comprendre; it's a good ~ reason c'est une raison suffisante; you know well ~ what I mean vous savez très bien ce que je veux dire. -2. [fairly] assez; to do sthg well ~ faire qqch passablement bien; she's honest ~ elle est assez honnête; it's good ~ in its own way ce n'est pas mal dans le genre. -3. [with adverb]: oddly OR strangely ~, nobody knows her chose curieuse, personne ne la connaît.

en passant [ɑ̃'pæsɑ̃] *adv* en passant.

enplane [ɪn'pleɪn] = **emplane**.

enquire *etc* [ɪn'kwaɪəʳ] = **inquire**.

enrage [ɪn'reɪdʒ] *vt* rendre furieux, mettre en rage; he was ~d to discover that... il enrageait de découvrir que...; ~d, I left furieux, je suis parti.

enrapture [ɪn'ræptʃəʳ] *vt* enchanter, ravir; we were ~d by the beauty of the island nous étions en extase devant la beauté de l'île.

enrich [ɪn'rɪtʃ] *vt* [mind, person, life] enrichir; [soil] fertiliser, amender; PHYS enrichir; breakfast cereals ~ed with vitamins céréales *fpl* enrichies en vitamines.

enriching [ɪn'rɪtʃɪŋ] *adj* enrichissant.

enrichment [ɪn'rɪtʃmənt] *n* [of mind, person, life] enrichissement *m*; [of soil] fertilisation *f*, amendement *m*; PHYS enrichissement *m*.

enrol *Br*, **enroll** *Am* [ɪn'rəʊl] (*pt* & *pp* enrolled, *cont* enrolling) ◇ *vt* -1. [student] inscrire, immatriculer; [member] inscrire; MIL [recruit] enrôler, recruter. -2. *Am* POL [prepare] dresser, rédiger; [register] enregistrer; ~ed bill projet *m* de loi enregistré.

◇ *vi* [student] s'inscrire; MIL s'engager, s'enrôler; to ~ on OR for a course s'inscrire à un cours; to ~ as a student s'inscrire à la faculté.

enrolment *Br*, **enrollment** *Am* [ɪn'rəʊlmənt] *n* [registration - of members] inscription *f*; [- of students] inscription *f*, immatriculation *f*; [- of workers] embauche *f*; MIL enrôlement *m*, recrutement *m*; the club has an ~ of 500 members le club compte 500 membres; a school with an ~ of 300 students une école avec un effectif de 300 élèves.

ensconce [ɪn'skɒns] *vt fml* OR *hum* installer; she ~d herself/was ~d in the armchair elle se cala/était bien calée dans le fauteuil.

ensemble [ɒn'sɒmbl] *n* [gen & MUS] ensemble *m*.

enshrine [ɪn'ʃraɪn] *vt literal* enchâsser; *fig* [cherish] conserver pieusement OR religieusement; our fundamental rights are ~d in the constitution nos droits fondamentaux font partie intégrante de la constitution.

enshroud [ɪn'ʃraʊd] *vt fml* ensevelir; the countryside was ~ed in mist le paysage était enseveli sous la brume; ~ed in mystery enveloppé de mystère.

ensign ['ensaɪn] *n* -1. [flag] drapeau *m*, enseigne *f*; NAUT pavillon *m*; the red ~ *Br* ≃ le pavillon marchand; the white ~ *Br le pavillon de la marine britannique et du Royal Yacht Squadron*. -2. [symbol] insigne *m*, emblème *m*. -3. *Br* MIL (officier *m*) porte-étendard *m*. -4. *Am* NAUT enseigne *m* de vaisseau de deuxième classe.

enslave [ɪn'sleɪv] *vt literal* réduire en esclavage, asservir; *fig* asservir, captiver; he was ~d by his conscience il était l'esclave de sa conscience.

enslavement [ɪn'sleɪvmənt] *n literal* asservissement *m*, assujettissement *m*; *fig* sujétion *f*, asservissement *m*, assujettissement *m*.

ensnare [ɪn'sneəʳ] *vt literal* & *fig* prendre au piège; ~d by her charms séduit par ses charmes.

ensue [ɪn'sjuː] *vi* s'ensuivre, résulter; the problems that have ~d from government cutbacks les problèmes qui ont résulté des restrictions gouvernementales.

ensuing [ɪn'sjuːɪŋ] *adj* [action, event] qui s'ensuit; [month, year] suivant.

en suite [,ɒn'swiːt] *adj* & *adv*: with ~ bathroom, with bathroom ~ avec salle de bain particulière.

ensure [ɪn'ʃɔːʳ] *vt* -1. [guarantee] assurer, garantir; I did everything I could to ~ that he would succeed OR to ~ his success j'ai fait tout ce que j'ai pu pour m'assurer qu'il réussirait OR pour assurer son succès. -2. [protect] protéger, assurer.

ENT (*abbr of* ear, nose & throat) ◇ *n* ORL *f*. ◇ *adj* ORL.

entail [ɪn'teɪl] *vt* -1. [imply - consequence, expense] entraîner; [- difficulty, risk] comporter; [- delay, expense] occasionner; LOGIC entraîner; starting a new job often ~s a lot of work prendre un nouveau poste exige souvent OR nécessite souvent beaucoup de travail. -2. JUR: to ~ an estate substituer un héritage; an ~ed estate un bien grevé.

entailment [ɪn'teɪlmənt] *n* -1. [of consequences] entraînement *m*; LOGIC enchaînement *m*. -2. JUR substitution *f*.

entangle [ɪn'tæŋgl] *vt* -1. [ensnare] empêtrer, enchevêtrer; the bird was ~d in the net l'oiseau était empêtré dans le filet. -2. [snarl - hair] emmêler; [- threads] emmêler, embrouiller. -3. *fig* [involve] entraîner, impliquer; she got ~d in the dispute elle s'est retrouvée impliquée dans la dispute; he became ~d with a group of drug dealers il s'est retrouvé mêlé à un groupe de dealers.

entanglement [ɪn'tæŋglmənt] *n* -1. [in net, undergrowth] enchevêtrement *m*. -2. [of hair, thread] emmêlement *m*. -3. *fig* [involvement] implication *f*; emotional ~s complications *fpl* sentimentales; his ~ with Marie/with the police son histoire avec Marie/avec la police.

entente [ɒn'tɒnt] *n* entente *f*.

enter ['entəʳ] ◇ *vt* -1. [go into - room] entrer dans; [- building] entrer dans, pénétrer dans; as I ~ed the building comme j'entrais dans le bâtiment; the ship ~ed the harbour le navire est entré au OR dans le port; where the bullet ~ed the body l'endroit où la balle a pénétré le corps; as we ~ a new decade alors que nous entrons dans une nouvelle décennie; the war ~ed a new phase la guerre est entrée dans une phase nouvelle; a note of sadness ~ed her voice une note de tristesse s'est glissée dans sa voix; the thought never ~ed my head l'idée ne m'est jamais venue à l'esprit. -2. [join - university] s'inscrire à, se faire inscrire à; [- profession] entrer dans; [- army] s'engager OR entrer dans; [- politics] se lancer dans; to ~ the church entrer dans les ordres. -3. [register] inscrire; the school ~ed the pupils for the exam/in the competition l'école a présenté les élèves à l'examen/au concours; to ~ a horse for a race engager OR inscrire un cheval dans une course. -4. [record - on list] inscrire; [- in book] noter; COMPUT [data] entrer, introduire; he ~ed the figures in the ledger il a porté les chiffres sur le livre de comptes. -5. [submit] présenter; to ~ a proposal présenter une proposition; to ~ a protest protester officiellement; to ~ an appeal JUR interjeter appel.

◇ *vi* -1. [come in] entrer; ~ Juliet THEAT entre Juliette. -2. [register] s'inscrire; she ~ed for the race/for the exam elle s'est inscrite pour la course/à l'examen.

◆ **enter into** *vt insep* -1. [begin - explanation] se lancer dans; [- conversation, relations] entrer en; [- negotiations] entamer; I won't ~ into detail at this stage je ne vais pas entrer dans les détails à ce stade. -2. [become involved in]: to ~ into an agreement with sb conclure un accord avec qqn; I ~ed into the spirit of the game *fig* je suis entré dans le jeu. -3. [affect] entrer dans; an element of chance ~s into every business venture un facteur hasard entre en jeu dans toute entreprise commerciale; my feelings don't ~ into my decision mes sentiments n'ont rien à voir avec OR ne sont pour rien dans ma décision.

◆ **enter up** *vt sep* [amount] inscrire, porter

◆ **enter upon** *vt insep* -**1.** [career] débuter OR entrer dans; [negotiations] entamer; [policy] commencer. -**2.** JUR [inheritance] prendre possession de.

enteric [en'terɪk] *adj* entérique; ~ **fever** (fièvre *f*) typhoïde *f*.

enteritis [ˌentə'raɪtɪs] *n (U)* entérite *f*.

enterobacterium [ˌentərəʊbæk'tɪərɪəm] (*pl* enterobacteria [-rɪə]) *n* entérobactérie *f*.

enterovirus [ˌentərəʊ'vaɪrəs] *n* entérovirus *m*.

enterprise ['entəpraɪz] *n* -**1.** [business, project] entreprise *f*. -**2.** [initiative] initiative *f*, esprit *m* entreprenant OR d'initiative; **men of** ~ des hommes entreprenants; **she showed great** ~ elle a fait preuve d'un esprit entreprenant.

enterprise zone *n Br zone d'encouragement à l'implantation d'entreprises dans les régions économiquement défavorisées.*

enterprising ['entəpraɪzɪŋ] *adj* [person] entreprenant, plein d'initiative; [project] audacieux, hardi; **she's very** ~ elle fait preuve d'initiative.

enterprisingly ['entəpraɪzɪŋlɪ] *adv* [boldly] audacieusement, hardiment; [independently] de sa propre initiative.

entertain [ˌentə'teɪn] ◇ *vt* -**1.** [amuse] amuser, divertir; **I** ~**ed them with a story** je leur ai raconté une histoire pour les distraire OR amuser. -**2.** [show hospitality towards] recevoir; **he** ~**ed them to dinner** [at restaurant] il leur a offert le dîner; [at home] il les a reçus à dîner. -**3.** [idea] considérer, penser à; **she had never** ~**ed hopes of becoming rich** elle n'avait jamais nourri OR caressé l'espoir de devenir riche; **he** ~**s grave doubts about it** il entretient de sérieux doutes à ce propos; **I refused to** ~ **such a suggestion** j'ai refusé d'admettre pareille suggestion.
◇ *vi* recevoir; **we** ~ **quite often** nous recevons (du monde) assez souvent.

entertainer [ˌentə'teɪnəʳ] *n* [comedian] comique *m*, amuseur *m*, -euse *f*; [in music hall] artiste *mf* (de music-hall), fantaisiste *mf*; **a well-known television** ~ un artiste de télévision bien connu.

entertaining [ˌentə'teɪnɪŋ] ◇ *n*: **she enjoys** ~ elle aime bien recevoir; **they do a lot of business** ~ ils donnent pas mal de réceptions d'affaires.
◇ *adj* amusant, divertissant.

entertainingly [ˌentə'teɪnɪŋlɪ] *adv* de façon amusante OR divertissante.

entertainment [ˌentə'teɪnmənt] *n* -**1.** [amusement] amusement *m*, divertissement *m*; **for your** ~, **we have organized...** pour vous distraire OR amuser, nous avons organisé...; **much to the** ~ **of the crowd** au grand amusement de la foule; **this film is** OR **provides good family** ~ ce film est un bon divertissement familial; **her favourite** ~ **is reading** la lecture est sa distraction préférée. -**2.** [performance] spectacle *m*, attraction *f*; **musical** ~**s will be provided** des attractions musicales sont prévues.

enthral *Br*, **enthrall** *Am* [ɪn'θrɔːl] (*pt* & *pp* enthralled, *cont* enthralling) *vt* -**1.** [fascinate] captiver, passionner; **she was** ~**ed by the idea** elle était séduite par l'idée. -**2.** *arch* [enslave] asservir.

enthralling [ɪn'θrɔːlɪŋ] *adj* [book, film] captivant, passionnant; [beauty, charm] séduisant.

enthrone [ɪn'θrəʊn] *vt* -**1.** [monarch] mettre sur le trône, introniser; [bishop] introniser. -**2.** *lit* [idea] révérer.

enthronement [ɪn'θrəʊnmənt] *n* intronisation *f*.

enthuse [ɪn'θjuːz] ◇ *vi* s'enthousiasmer; **she** ~**d over the plan** elle parlait du projet avec beaucoup d'enthousiasme.
◇ *vt* enthousiasmer, emballer; **you don't seem very** ~**d about it** tu n'as pas l'air emballé par l'idée.

enthusiasm [ɪn'θjuːzɪæzm] *n* -**1.** [interest] enthousiasme *m*; **she hasn't much** ~ **for the project** elle n'a pas beaucoup d'enthousiasme pour le projet; **the discovery has aroused** OR **stirred up considerable** ~ **among historians** la découverte a suscité un grand enthousiasme chez les historiens. -**2.** [hobby] passion *f*.

enthusiast [ɪn'θjuːzɪæst] *n* enthousiaste *mf*, fervent *m*, -e *f*; **she's a jazz** ~ elle est passionnée de OR elle se passionne pour le jazz; **football** ~**s** passionnés *mpl* de football.

enthusiastic [ɪnˌθjuːzɪ'æstɪk] *adj* [person, response] enthousiaste; [shout, applause] enthousiaste, d'enthousiasme; **they gave me an** ~ **welcome** ils m'ont accueilli chaleureusement; **he's an** ~ **football player** c'est un footballeur passionné; **she's very** ~ **about the project** elle est très enthousiaste à l'idée de ce projet; **to be** ~ **about a suggestion** accueillir une proposition avec enthousiasme; **we're not very** ~ **about moving** déménager ne nous dit pas grand-chose, nous ne sommes pas enchantés de déménager.

enthusiastically [ɪnˌθjuːzɪ'æstɪklɪ] *adv* [receive] avec enthousiasme; [speak, support] avec enthousiasme OR ferveur; [work] avec zèle.

entice [ɪn'taɪs] *vt* attirer, séduire; **to** ~ **sb away from sthg** éloigner qqn de qqch; **I managed to** ~ **him away from the television** j'ai réussi à l'arracher à la télévision; **they** ~**d him into a card game** ils l'ont attiré dans une partie de cartes; ~**d by their offer** alléché OR attiré par leur proposition.

enticement [ɪn'taɪsmənt] *n* -**1.** [attraction] attrait *m*, appât *m*. -**2.** [act] séduction *f*.

enticing [ɪn'taɪsɪŋ] *adj* [offer] attrayant, séduisant; [person] séduisant; [food] alléchant, appétissant.

enticingly [ɪn'taɪsɪŋlɪ] *adv* de façon séduisante; **delicious smells wafted** ~ **from the kitchen** de délicieuses odeurs de cuisine mettaient l'eau à la bouche.

entire [ɪn'taɪəʳ] *adj* -**1.** [whole] entier, tout; **my** ~ **life** toute ma vie, ma vie entière; **the** ~ **world** le monde entier. -**2.** [total] entier, complet; [absolute] total, absolu; **she has my** ~ **support** elle peut compter sur mon soutien sans réserve. -**3.** [intact] entier, intact.

entirely [ɪn'taɪəlɪ] *adv* entièrement, totalement; **I agree with you** ~ je suis entièrement d'accord avec vous; **that's** ~ **unnecessary** c'est absolument inutile; **I'm not** ~ **satisfied** je ne suis pas complètement satisfait; **they lived their lives** ~ **in the jungle** ils passèrent toute leur vie dans la jungle; **it's** ~ **my fault** c'est entièrement ma faute.

entirety [ɪn'taɪətɪ] (*pl* entireties) *n* -**1.** [completeness] intégralité *f*; **in its** ~ en (son) entier, intégralement; **the book tells the story in its** ~ le livre raconte l'histoire dans son entier. -**2.** [total] totalité *f*; **the** ~ **of his estate** la totalité de ses biens.

entitle [ɪn'taɪtl] *vt* -**1.** [give right to] autoriser; **the results** ~ **them to believe that...** les résultats les autorisent à croire que...; **his disability** ~**s him to a pension** son infirmité lui donne droit à une pension; **this ticket** ~**s the bearer to free admission** ce billet donne au porteur le droit à une entrée gratuite; **to be** ~**d to do sthg** [by status] avoir qualité pour OR être habilité à faire qqch; [by rules] avoir le droit OR être en droit de faire qqch; **you're** ~**d to your own opinion but...** vous avez le droit d'avoir votre avis mais...; **we're** ~**d to some fun!** nous avons bien le droit de nous amuser un peu!; **you're quite** ~**d to say that...** vous pouvez dire à juste titre que...; **to be** ~**d to vote** avoir le droit de vote ‖ JUR habiliter; **to be** ~**d to act** être habilité à agir. -**2.** [film, painting etc] intituler; **the book is** ~**d...** le livre s'intitule... -**3.** [bestow title on] donner un titre à.

entitlement [ɪn'taɪtlmənt] *n* droit *m*; ~ **to social security** droit à la sécurité sociale.

entity ['entətɪ] (*pl* entities) *n* entité *f*; **legal** ~ personne *f* morale.

entomb [ɪn'tuːm] *vt literal* mettre au tombeau, ensevelir; *fig* ensevelir.

entombment [ɪn'tuːmmənt] *n literal* mise *f* au tombeau, ensevelissement *m*; *fig* ensevelissement *m*.

entomological [ˌentəmə'lɒdʒɪkl] *adj* entomologique.

entomologist [ˌentə'mɒlədʒɪst] *n* entomologiste *mf*.

entomology [ˌentə'mɒlədʒɪ] *n* entomologie *f*.

entopic [en'tɒpɪk] *adj* entopique.

entourage [ˌɒntʊ'rɑːʒ] *n* entourage *m*.

entr'acte ['ɒntrækt] *n* entracte *m*.

entrails ['entreɪlz] *npl literal* & *fig* entrailles *fpl*.

entrain [ɪn'treɪn] ◇ *vi fml* monter dans un train.
◇ *vt* -**1.** *fml* [person] embarquer dans un train. -**2.** [subj: liquid, gas] entraîner.

entrance[1] ['entrəns] ◇ *n* -**1.** [means of entry] entrée *f*; [large] portail *m*; [foyer] entrée *f*, vestibule *m*; **the** ~ **to the store** l'entrée du magasin; **I'll meet you at the** ~ je te retrouverai à l'entrée. -**2.** [arrival] entrée *f*; **to make an** ~ [gen] faire une entrée; THEAT entrer en scène. -**3.** [admission] admission *f*; **'the management reserves the right to refuse** ~**'** 'la direction se réserve le droit de refuser l'entrée'; **passing this exam does not guarantee you** ~ **to the school** la réussite à cet examen ne te garantit pas l'admission à l'école; **he gained** ~ **to the university/profession** il a été admis à l'université/dans la profession. -**4.** [access] accès *m*, admission *f*; **the police gained** ~ **to the building from the back** la police a accédé au bâtiment par derrière.
◇ *comp* [card, ticket] d'entrée, d'admission; ~ **examination** [for school] examen *m* d'entrée; [for job] concours *m* de recrutement; ~ **requirements** qualifications *fpl* exigées à l'entrée.

entrance[2] [ɪn'trɑːns] *vt* -**1.** [hypnotize] hypnotiser, faire entrer en transe. -**2.** *fig* [delight] ravir, enchanter; **she was** ~**d by the beauty of the place** elle était en extase devant la beauté de l'endroit.

entrance fee ['entrəns-] *n* droit *m* OR frais *mpl* d'inscription.

entrance hall ['entrəns-] *n* [in house] vestibule *m*; [in hotel] hall *m*.

entrance ramp ['entrəns-] *n Am* bretelle *f* d'accès.

entrancing [ɪn'trɑːnsɪŋ] *adj* enchanteur, ravissant.

entrancingly [ɪn'trɑːnsɪŋlɪ] *adv* [smile] de façon ravissante OR séduisante; [dance, sing] à ravir; ~ **beautiful** beau à ravir.

entrant ['entrənt] *n* -**1.** [in exam] candidat *m*, -e *f*; [in race] concurrent *m*, -e *f*, participant *m*, -e *f*; **all** ~**s for the exam/competition** tous les candidats à l'examen/participants à la compétition. -**2.** [to profession, society] débutant *m*, -e *f*; **a training course for (new)** ~**s to the profession** un cours de formation pour ceux qui débutent dans la profession.

entrap [ɪn'træp] (*pt* & *pp* entrapped, *cont* entrapping) *vt fml* prendre au piège; **she had been entrapped into helping the thieves** elle avait été insidieusement amenée à aider les voleurs.

entrapment [ɪn'træpmənt] *n incitation au délit par un policier afin de justifier une arrestation.*

entreat [ɪn'triːt] *vt fml* implorer, supplier; **I** ~ **you to help me** je vous supplie de m'aider; **spare his life, I** ~ **you** épargnez sa vie, je vous en conjure; **I** ~**ed her not to be cross with him** je l'ai priée instamment de ne pas se fâcher contre lui.

entreating [ɪn'triːtɪŋ] *fml* ◇ *adj* suppliant, implorant.
◇ *n (U)* supplications *fpl*.

entreatingly [ɪn'triːtɪŋlɪ] *adv fml* [look] d'un air suppliant; [ask] d'un ton suppliant, d'une voix suppliante.

entreaty [ɪn'triːtɪ] (*pl* entreaties) *n fml* supplication *f*, prière *f*; **a look of** ~ un regard suppliant; **no one responded to her urgent entreaties** personne ne répondit à ses prières insistantes.

entrée ['ɒntreɪ] *n* -**1.** [right of entry] entrée *f*. -**2.** CULIN [course preceding main dish] entrée *f*; *Am* [main dish] plat *m* principal OR de résistance.

entrench [ɪn'trentʃ] *vt* MIL retrancher.

entrenched [ɪn'trentʃt] *adj* -**1.** MIL retranché. -**2.** *fig* [person] inflexible, inébranlable; [idea] arrêté; [power, tradition] implanté; the two neighbours became ~ in a long-running feud les deux voisins se retrouvèrent engagés dans une longue querelle; attitudes that are firmly ~ in our society des attitudes qui sont fermement ancrées dans notre société.

entrenchment [ɪn'trentʃmənt] *n* MIL OR *fig* retranchement *m*.

entrepreneur [,ɒntrəprə'nɜːʳ] *n* entrepreneur *m (homme d'affaires)*.

entrepreneurial [,ɒntrəprə'nɜːrɪəl] *adj* [spirit, attitude] d'entrepreneur; [society, person] qui a l'esprit d'entreprise; [skills] d'entrepreneur.

entropy ['entrəpɪ] *n* entropie *f*.

entrust [ɪn'trʌst] *vt* confier; to ~ sthg to sb confier qqch à qqn; she ~ed her children to them elle leur a confié ses enfants, elle a confié ses enfants à leur garde; to ~ sb with a job charger qqn d'une tâche, confier une tâche à qqn; she ~ed him with the responsibility of selling it elle l'a chargé de le vendre, elle lui a confié le soin de le vendre.

entry ['entrɪ] (*pl* entries) ◇ *n* -**1.** [way in] entrée *f*; [larger] portail *m*. -**2.** [act] entrée *f*; to make an ~ [gen] faire une entrée; THEAT entrer en scène; Spain's ~ into the EEC l'entrée de l'Espagne dans la CEE. -**3.** [admission] entrée *f*, accès *m*; this ticket gives you free ~ to the exhibition ce billet te donne le droit d'entrer gratuitement à l'exposition; she was refused ~ to the country on lui a refusé l'entrée dans le pays; 'no ~' [on door] 'défense d'entrer', 'entrée interdite'; [in street] 'sens interdit'. -**4.** [in dictionary] entrée *f*; [in diary] notation *f*; [in encyclopedia] article *m*; [on list] inscription *f*; COMPUT [of data] entrée (des données); [in account book, ledger] écriture *f*; an ~ in the log NAUT un élément du journal de bord; single/double ~ bookkeeping comptabilité *f* en partie simple/double. -**5.** [competitor] inscription *f*; [item submitted for competition] participant *m*, -e *f*, concurrent *m*, -e *f*; a late ~ SPORT un participant de dernière minute. -**6.** *(U)* [number of entrants] taux *m* de participation; the ~ is down this year [in competition] le taux de participation est en baisse cette année; [in exam] les candidats sont moins nombreux cette année; [at school, university] le nombre d'inscriptions a baissé cette année.
◇ *comp* [fee, form] d'inscription.

entryism ['entrɪɪzm] *n* POL entrisme *m*, noyautage *m*.

entryist ['entrɪɪst] POL ◇ *adj* d'entrisme, de noyautage.
◇ *n* personne *f* qui pratique l'entrisme OR le noyautage.

Entryphone® ['entrɪ,fəʊn] *n* Interphone® *m (à l'entrée d'un immeuble ou de bureaux)*.

entryway ['entrɪ,weɪ] *n Am* entrée *f*; [larger] portail *m*; [foyer] foyer *m*, vestibule *m*.

entwine [ɪn'twaɪn] *vt* entrelacer; the ivy had become ~d OR had ~d itself around the trellis le lierre s'était entortillé autour du treillis.

E number *inf n Br* additif *m* code E; there are a lot of ~s in this jam il y a beaucoup d'additifs dans cette confiture.

enumerable [ɪ'njuːmərəbl] *adj* dénombrable.

enumerate [ɪ'njuːməreɪt] *vt* énumérer, dénombrer.

enumeration [ɪ,njuːmə'reɪʃn] *n* énumération *f*, dénombrement *m*.

enumerator [ɪ'njuːməreɪtəʳ] *n* ADMIN recenseur *m*, -euse *f (qui passe à domicile remplir le formulaire)*.

enunciate [ɪ'nʌnsɪeɪt] ◇ *vt* -**1.** [articulate] articuler, prononcer. -**2.** *fml* [formulate - idea, theory, policy] énoncer, exprimer.
◇ *vi* articuler.

enunciation [ɪ,nʌnsɪ'eɪʃn] *n* -**1.** [of sound, word] articulation *f*, prononciation *f*. -**2.** *fml* [of theory] énonciation *f*, exposition *f*; [of problem] énoncé *m*.

enuresis [,enjʊə'riːsɪs] *n* énurésie *f*.

enuretic [,enjʊ'retɪk] ◇ *adj* énurétique.
◇ *n* énurétique *mf*.

envelop [ɪn'veləp] *vt* envelopper; ~ed in a blanket enveloppé dans une couverture; ~ed in mystery entouré OR voilé de mystère; the tops of the hills were ~ed in mist le haut des collines était voilé de brume.

envelope ['envələʊp] *n* -**1.** [for letter] enveloppe *f*; put the letter in an ~ mettez la lettre sous enveloppe; in a sealed ~ sous pli cacheté; they came in the same ~ ils sont arrivés dans le même pli. -**2.** BIOL enveloppe *f*, tunique *f*; MATH enveloppe *f*; ELECTRON enveloppe *f*. -**3.** [of balloon] enveloppe *f*.

envenom [ɪn'venəm] *vt literal* & *fig* envenimer.

enviable ['envɪəbl] *adj* enviable.

envious ['envɪəs] *adj* [person] envieux, jaloux; [look, tone] envieux, d'envie; she's ~ of their new house elle est envieuse de leur nouvelle maison; I am very ~ of you! comme je t'envie!; her success only made people ~ son succès n'a fait que des envieux OR jaloux.

enviously ['envɪəslɪ] *adv* avec envie.

environment [ɪn'vaɪərənmənt] *n* -**1.** ECOL & POL [nature] environnement *m*; the Secretary of State for the Environment ≃ le ministre de l'Équipement. -**2.** [surroundings - physical] cadre *m*, milieu *m*; [- social] milieu *m*, environnement *m*; [- psychological] milieu *m*, ambiance *f*; BIOL, BOT & GEOG milieu *m*; LING & COMPUT environnement *m*; an animal in its natural ~ un animal dans son milieu naturel; a hostile ~ un climat d'hostilité, une ambiance hostile; the novel examines the effect of ~ on character le roman étudie les effets du milieu ambiant sur le caractère; a pleasant working ~ des conditions de travail agréables.

environmental [ɪn,vaɪərən'mentl] *adj* -**1.** ECOL & POL écologique; ~ impact impact *m* de l'environnement; ~ pressure groups des groupes de pression pour la défense de l'environnement ❑ Environmental Protection Agency *Am* Agence *f* pour la protection de l'environnement; ~ science/studies science *f*/ études *fpl* de l'environnement. -**2.** [of surroundings] du milieu; ~ stimuli stimuli *mpl* provenant du milieu ambiant.

environmentalism [ɪn,vaɪərən'mentəlɪzm] *n* -**1.** ECOL étude *f* de l'environnement. -**2.** PSYCH environnementalisme *m*.

environmentalist [ɪn,vaɪərən'mentəlɪst] *n* -**1.** ECOL écologiste *mf*. -**2.** PSYCH environnementaliste *mf*.

environmentally [ɪn,vaɪərən'mentəlɪ] *adv* ECOL écologiquement.

environment-friendly, **environmentally friendly** *adj* [policy] respectueux de l'environnement; [product] non polluant.

environs [ɪn'vaɪərənz] *npl fml* environs *mpl*, alentours *mpl*; Paris and its ~ Paris et ses environs.

envisage [ɪn'vɪzɪdʒ] *vt* [imagine] envisager; [predict] prévoir; I don't ~ (that there will be) any difficulty je n'envisage pas (qu'il puisse y avoir) la moindre difficulté.

envision [ɪn'vɪʒn] *Am* = **envisage**.

envoy ['envɔɪ] *n* -**1.** [emissary] envoyé *m*, -e *f*, représentant *m*, -e *f*; ~ (extraordinary) POL ministre *m* plénipotentiaire. -**2.** LITERAT envoi *m*.

envy ['envɪ] (*pl* envies, *pt* & *pp* envied) ◇ *n* -**1.** [jealousy] envie *f*, jalousie *f*; out of ~ par envie OR jalousie; filled with ~ dévoré de jalousie. -**2.** [object of jealousy] objet *m* d'envie; she was the ~ of all her friends elle excitait OR faisait l'envie de tous ses amis.
◇ *vt* envier; I do ~ her je l'envie vraiment; I don't ~ you! je ne t'envie pas!; I can't say I ~ you je ne peux pas dire que je t'envie; I ~ him his success je lui envie son succès.

enzyme ['enzaɪm] *n* enzyme *f*.

EOC *pr n abbr of* Equal Opportunities Commission.

Eocene ['iːəʊsiːn] ◇ *adj* éocène.
◇ *n* éocène *m*.

Eolian [iː'əʊlɪən] *Am* = **Aeolian**.

eolith ['iːəʊlɪθ] *n* éolithe *m*.

Eolithic [,iːəʊ'lɪθɪk] *adj* éolithique.

eon ['iːən] *Am* = **aeon**.

eosin(e) ['iːəʊsɪn] *n* éosine *f*.

Eozoic [,iːəʊ'zəʊɪk] *adj* précambrien.

EP (*abbr of* extended play) *n* -**1.** super 45 tours *m*, EP *m*. -**2.** *abbr of* European Plan.

EPA *pr n abbr of* Environmental Protection Agency.

epaulette *Br*, **epaulet** *Am* [,epə'let] *n* [gen & MIL] épaulette *f*.

epeirogeny [,epaɪ'rɒdʒənɪ] *n* mouvement *m* épeirogénique.

ephedrin(e) [*Br* 'efɪdriːn, *Am* ɪ'fedrən] *n* éphédrine *f*.

ephemera [ɪ'femərə] (*pl* ephemeras OR ephemerae [-riː]) *n* -**1.** ZOOL éphémère *m*. -**2.** [short-lived thing] chose *f* éphémère.

ephemeral [ɪ'femərəl] *adj* [short-lived] éphémère, fugitif; ZOOL éphémère.

ephemerid [ɪ'femərɪd] *n* éphémère *m*.

ephemeris [ɪ'femərɪs] (*pl* ephemerides [,efɪ'merɪ,diːz]) *n* éphéméride *f*.

Ephesian [ɪ'fiːʒn] ◇ *n* [person] Éphésien *m*, -enne *f*; the Epistle of Paul to the ~s l'Épître de saint Paul aux Éphésiens.
◇ *adj* éphésien.
◆ **Ephesians** *npl (U)* BIBLE Éphésiens *mpl*.

Ephesus ['efəsəs] *pr n* Éphèse.

Ephraim ['iːfreɪɪm] *pr n* Éphraïm.

epic ['epɪk] ◇ *adj* -**1.** [impressive] héroïque, épique; *hum* épique, homérique. -**2.** LITERAT épique.
◇ *n* -**1.** LITERAT épopée *f*, poème *m* OR récit *m* épique. -**2.** [film] film *m* à grand spectacle.

epicarp ['epɪ,kɑːp] *n* épicarpe *m*.

epicene ['epɪsiːn] *adj* -**1.** [hermaphrodite] hermaphrodite; [sexless] asexué. -**2.** [effeminate] efféminé. -**3.** GRAMM épicène.

epicentre *Br*, **epicenter** *Am* ['epɪsentəʳ] *n* épicentre *m*.

epicure ['epɪ,kjʊəʳ] *n lit* gourmet *m*, gastronome *mf*.

epicurean [,epɪkjʊə'riːən] ◇ *adj* [gen] épicurien.
◇ *n* -**1.** [gen] épicurien *m*, -enne *f*. -**2.** [gourmet] gourmet *m*, gastronome *mf*.
◆ **Epicurean** PHILOS ◇ *adj* épicurien.
◇ *n* épicurien *m*, -enne *f*.

Epicureanism [,epɪkjʊə'riːənɪzm] *n* épicurisme *m*.

Epicurus [,epɪ'kjʊərəs] *pr n* Épicure.

epicyclic [,epɪ'saɪklɪk] *adj* épicycloïdal; ~ train OR gear train *m* épicycloïdal.

Epidaurus [,epɪ'dɔːrəs] *pr n* Épidaure.

epidemic [,epɪ'demɪk] *literal* & *fig* ◇ *n* épidémie *f*.
◇ *adj* épidémique; of ~ proportions qui prend les proportions d'une épidémie.

epidemiologist ['epɪ,diːmɪ'ɒlədʒɪst] *n* épidémiologiste *mf*.

epidemiology ['epɪ,diːmɪ'ɒlədʒɪ] *n* épidémiologie *f*.

epidermis [,epɪ'dɜːmɪs] *n* épiderme *m*.

epidiascope [,epɪ'daɪəskəʊp] *n* épidiascope *m*.

epidural [,epɪ'djʊərəl] ◇ *adj* épidural.
◇ *n* anesthésie *f* épidurale, péridurale *f*.

epifocal [,epɪ'fəʊkl] *adj* épicentral.

epigenesis [,epɪ'dʒenɪsɪs] *n* BIOL épigenèse *f*; GEOL épigénie *f*.

epiglottis [,epɪ'glɒtɪs] (*pl* epiglottises OR epiglotides [-tɪ,diːz]) *n* épiglotte *f*.

epigram ['epɪgræm] *n* épigramme *f*.

epigrammatic(al) [,epɪgrə'mætɪk(l)] *adj* épigrammatique.

epigraph ['epɪgrɑːf] *n* épigraphe *f*.

epilepsy ['epɪlepsɪ] *n* épilepsie *f*.
epileptic [,epɪ'leptɪk] ◇ *adj* épileptique; an ~ fit une crise d'épilepsie.
◇ *n* épileptique *mf*.
epilogue ['epɪlɒg], **epilog** [e'pɪlɒg] *Am n* épilogue *m*.
epinephrine [,epɪ'nefrɪn] *n Am* adrénaline *f*.
Epiphany [ɪ'pɪfənɪ] *n* Épiphanie *f*, fête *f* des rois.
epiphenomenon [,epɪfɪ'nɒmɪnən] (*pl* epiphenomena [-nə]) *n* épiphénomène *m*.
epiphyte ['epɪ,faɪt] *n* épiphyte *m*.
epiphytic [,epɪ'fɪtɪk] *adj* épiphyte.
Epirus [e'paɪərəs] *pr n* Épire.
episcopacy [ɪ'pɪskəpəsɪ] (*pl* episcopacies) *n* -**1.** [church government] gouvernement *m* d'une Église par les évêques. -**2.** = **episcopate**.
episcopal [ɪ'pɪskəpl] *adj* épiscopal.
Episcopal Church *n*: the ~ l'Église *f* épiscopale.
episcopalian [ɪ,pɪskəʊ'peɪljən] ◇ *adj* épiscopal, épiscopalien.
◇ *n* épiscopalien *m*, -enne *f*; the Episcopalians les épiscopaux *mpl*, les épiscopaliens *mpl*.
episcopate [ɪ'pɪskəpət] *n* épiscopat *m*.
episcope ['epɪskəʊp] *n Br* épiscope *m*.
episiotomy [ɪ,pɪzɪ'ɒtəmɪ] (*pl* episiotomies) *n* épisiotomie *f*.
episode ['epɪsəʊd] *n* [period, event] épisode *m*; [part of story] épisode *m*; an unhappy ~ in my life un épisode malheureux de ma vie; the first ~ will be broadcast on Sunday le premier épisode sera diffusé dimanche.
episodic [,epɪ'sɒdɪk] *adj* épisodique.
episodically [,epɪ'sɒdɪklɪ] *adv* épisodiquement.
epistemic [,epɪ'stiːmɪk] *adj* épistémique.
epistemological [e,pɪstɪmə'lɒdʒɪkl] *adj* épistémologique.
epistemology [e,pɪstiː'mɒlədʒɪ] *n* épistémologie *f*.
epistle [ɪ'pɪsl] *n* -**1.** *fml* OR *hum* [letter] lettre *f*, épître *f hum*; ADMIN courrier *m*. -**2.** LITERAT épître *f*.
◆ **Epistle** *n* BIBLE: the Epistle to the Romans l'Épître *f* aux Romains.
epistolary [ɪ'pɪstələrɪ] *adj fml* épistolaire.
epitaph ['epɪtɑːf] *n* épitaphe *f*.
epitaxial [,epɪ'tæksɪəl] *adj* épitaxial.
epithelium [,epɪ'θiːljəm] (*pl* epitheliums OR epithelia [-ljə]) *n* épithélium *m*.
epithet ['epɪθet] *n* épithète *f*.
epitome [ɪ'pɪtəmɪ] *n* -**1.** [typical example] modèle *m*, type *m* OR exemple *m* même; she's the ~ of generosity elle est l'exemple même de la générosité OR la générosité même; the house is the ~ of Baroque architecture la maison est l'exemple même de l'architecture baroque. -**2.** [of book] abrégé *m*, résumé *m*.
epitomize, -ise [ɪ'pɪtəmaɪz] *vt* -**1.** [typify] personnifier, incarner; this latest announcement ~s the government's attitude towards education cette dernière déclaration est caractéristique de l'attitude du gouvernement concernant l'éducation. -**2.** [book] abréger, résumer.
epizoic [,epɪ'zəʊɪk] *adj* épizoïque.
EPNS (*abbr of* electroplated nickel silver) *n* ruolz *m*.
epoch ['iːpɒk] *n* époque *f*; the discovery marked a new ~ in the history of science cette découverte a fait date dans l'histoire de la science.
epoch-making *adj* qui fait époque, qui fait date.
eponym ['epəʊnɪm] *n* éponyme *m*.
eponymous [ɪ'pɒnɪməs] *adj* du même nom, éponyme.
EPOS ['iːpɒs] (*abbr of* electronic point of sale) *n point de vente électronique*.
epoxy [ɪ'pɒksɪ] (*pl* epoxies) ◇ *adj* CHEM [function, group] époxy *inv*.
◇ *n* époxyde *m*.
epoxy resin *n* résine *f* époxyde OR époxy.
EPROM ['iːprɒm] (*abbr of* erasable programmable read only memory) *n* mémoire *f* morte effaçable.
Epsom ['epsəm] *pr n célèbre terrain de courses de chevaux en Angleterre*.
Epsom salts *npl* sel *m* d'Epsom, epsomite *f*.
equable ['ekwəbl] *adj* [character, person] égal, placide; [climate] égal, constant.
equably ['ekwəblɪ] *adv* tranquillement, placidement.
equal ['iːkwəl] (*Br pt* & *pp* equalled, *cont* equalling, *Am pt* & *pp* equaled, *cont* equaling) ◇ *adj* -**1.** [of same size, amount, degree, type] égal; ~ in number égal en nombre; ~ in size to an orange d'une taille égale à une orange; to be ~ to sthg égaler qqch; mix ~ parts of sand and cement mélangez du sable et du ciment en parts égales; an ~ amount of money une même somme d'argent; she speaks French and German with ~ ease elle parle français et allemand avec la même facilité; to be on an ~ footing with sb être sur un pied d'égalité avec qqn; to meet/to talk to sb on ~ terms rencontrer qqn/parler à qqn d'égal à égal; other OR all things being ~ toutes choses égales par ailleurs ❑ ~ opportunities, ~ op's *inf* chances *fpl* égales, égalité *f* des chances; ~ opportunity employer *entreprise s'engageant à respecter la législation sur la non-discrimination dans l'emploi*; ~ pay for ~ work à travail égal salaire égal; ~ rights égalité des droits; Equal Rights Amendment → **ERA**; ~ time RADIO & TV droit *m* de réponse. -**2.** [adequate]: ~ to: he proved ~ to the task il s'est montré à la hauteur de la tâche; the machine is not ~ to such heavy work la machine n'est pas faite pour fournir un si grand effort; to feel ~ to doing sthg se sentir le courage de faire qqch; I don't feel ~ to discussing it today je ne me sens pas le courage d'en parler aujourd'hui.
◇ *n* égal *m*, -e *f*, pair *m*; a woman who is your intellectual ~ une femme qui est votre égale intellectuellement; to talk to sb as an ~ parler à qqn d'égal à égal; we worked together as ~s nous avons travaillé ensemble sur un pied d'égalité; he has no ~ il est hors pair, il n'a pas son pareil.
◇ *vt* -**1.** [gen & MATH] égaler; 2 and 2 ~s 4 2 et 2 égalent OR font 4; let x ~ y si x égale y. -**2.** [match] égaler; no one in parliament could ~ his eloquence personne au parlement ne pouvait égaler son éloquence; there is nothing to ~ it il n'y a rien de comparable OR de tel; his arrogance is only equalled by his vulgarity son arrogance n'a d'égale que sa vulgarité.
equality [iː'kwɒlətɪ] (*pl* equalities) *n* égalité *f*; ~ of opportunity égalité des chances; ~ in the eyes of the law égalité devant la loi; women are still fighting for ~ les femmes se battent encore pour l'égalité.
equalization [,iːkwəlaɪ'zeɪʃn] *n* [gen] égalisation *f*; ELECTRON régularisation *f*; FIN péréquation *f*.
equalize, -ise ['iːkwəlaɪz] ◇ *vt* [chances] égaliser; [taxes, wealth] faire la péréquation de.
◇ *vi* SPORT égaliser.
equalizer ['iːkwəlaɪzə^r] *n* -**1.** SPORT but *m* OR point *m* égalisateur. -**2.** ELECTRON égaliseur *m*.
equally ['iːkwəlɪ] *adv* -**1.** [evenly] également; divided ~ divisé en parts OR parties égales; ~ spaced également espacé. -**2.** [to same degree] également, aussi; they were ~ responsible ils étaient également responsables OR responsables au même degré; I was ~ surprised j'ai été tout aussi surpris; ~ well tout aussi bien; ~ talented students élèves également OR pareillement doués. -**3.** [by the same token]: efficiency is important, but ~ we must consider the welfare of the workforce l'efficacité, c'est important, mais nous devons tout autant considérer le bien-être du personnel.
Equal Opportunities Commission *pr n* commission *f* pour l'égalité des chances *(en Grande-Bretagne)*.
equal sign, equals sign *n* signe *m* d'égalité OR d'équivalence.
equanimity [,ekwə'nɪmətɪ] *n fml* sérénité *f*, équanimité *f lit*; to recover one's ~ se ressaisir; with ~ avec sérénité.
equatable [ɪ'kweɪtəbl] *adj* comparable, assimilable.
equate [ɪ'kweɪt] *vt* -**1.** [regard as equivalent] assimiler, mettre sur le même pied; some people wrongly ~ culture with elitism certaines personnes assimilent à tort culture et élitisme; you can't ~ Joyce with Homer on ne peut pas mettre Homère et Joyce sur le même pied. -**2.** [make equal] égaler, égaliser; our aim is to ~ exports and imports notre but est d'amener au même niveau les exportations et les importations; to ~ sthg to sthg MATH mettre qqch en équation avec qqch.
equation [ɪ'kweɪʒn] *n* -**1.** *fml* [association] assimilation *f*. -**2.** *fml* [equalization] égalisation *f*. -**3.** CHEM & MATH équation *f*; ~ of time ASTRON équation du temps.
equator [ɪ'kweɪtə^r] *n* équateur *m*; at OR on the ~ sous OR à l'équateur.
equatorial [,ekwə'tɔːrɪəl] *adj* équatorial.
Equatorial Guinea *pr n* Guinée-Équatoriale *f*; in ~ en Guinée-Équatoriale.
equerry ['ekwərɪ] (*pl* equerries) *n Br* [of household] intendant *m*, -e *f (de la maison du roi, de la reine)*; [of stable] écuyer *m*, -ère *f*.
equestrian [ɪ'kwestrɪən] ◇ *adj* [event] hippique; [skills] équestre; [statue] équestre; [equipment, clothing] d'équitation.
◇ *n* [rider] cavalier *m*, -ère *f*; [in circus & MIL] écuyer *m*, -ère *f*.
equestrianism [ɪ'kwestrɪənɪzm] *n* équitation *f*, hippisme *m*.
equidistant [,iːkwɪ'dɪstənt] *adj* équidistant, à distance égale.
equilateral [,iːkwɪ'lætərəl] *adj* équilatéral; ~ triangle triangle *m* équilatéral.
equilibrium [,iːkwɪ'lɪbrɪəm] *n* équilibre *m*; in ~ en équilibre; how does the spinning top maintain its ~? comment la toupie garde-t-elle l'équilibre?; she lost her ~ elle a perdu l'équilibre.
equine ['ekwaɪn] *adj* [disease, family] équin; [profile] chevalin.
equinoctial [,iːkwɪ'nɒkʃl] *adj* [flower, line, point] équinoxial; [storm, tide] d'équinoxe.
equinox ['iːkwɪnɒks] *n* équinoxe *m*; autumnal ~ équinoxe d'automne; spring OR vernal ~ équinoxe de printemps, point *m* vernal.
equip [ɪ'kwɪp] (*pt* & *pp* equipped, *cont* equipping) *vt* -**1.** [fit out - factory] équiper, outiller; [- laboratory, kitchen] installer, équiper; [- army, ship] équiper; the hospital is not equipped to perform heart surgery l'hôpital n'est pas équipé pour pratiquer la chirurgie du cœur. -**2.** *fig* [prepare]: to be well-equipped to do sthg avoir tout ce qu'il faut pour faire qqch; it won't ~ her for life's hardships cela ne la préparera pas à affronter les épreuves de la vie; he is ill-equipped to handle the situation il est mal armé pour faire face à la situation. -**3.** [supply - person] équiper, pourvoir; [- army, machine, factory] équiper, munir; the fighter plane is equipped with the latest technology l'avion de combat est doté des équipements les plus modernes; she equipped herself for the hike with a tent and a sleeping bag elle s'est munie pour la randonnée d'une tente et d'un sac de couchage; if your computer is equipped with a hard disk si votre ordinateur est pourvu d'un disque dur.
equipage ['ekwɪpɪdʒ] *n* [carriage & MIL] équipage *m*.
equipment [ɪ'kwɪpmənt] *n* *(U)* -**1.** [gen] équipement *m*; [in laboratory, office, school] matériel *m*; MIL & SPORT équipement *m*, matériel *m*; camping ~ matériel de camping; electrical ~ appareillage *m* électrique; factory ~ outillage *m*; kitchen ~ ustensiles *mpl* de cuisine; lifesaving ~ matériel de sauvetage. -**2.** [act] équipement *m*.

equipoise ['ekwɪpɔɪz] *fml* ◇ *n* [equilibrium] équilibre *m*; [counterbalance] contrepoids *m*.
◇ *vt* contrebalancer, faire contrepoids à.

equitable ['ekwɪtəbl] *adj* équitable, juste.

equitably ['ekwɪtəblɪ] *adv* équitablement, avec justice.

equitation [,ekwɪ'teɪʃn] *n fml* équitation *f*.

equity ['ekwətɪ] (*pl* equities) *n* -**1.** [fairness] équité *f*. -**2.** JUR [system] équité *f*; [right] droit *m* équitable. -**3.** FIN [market value] fonds *mpl* OR capitaux *mpl* propres; [share] action *f* ordinaire; **the equities market** le marché des actions ordinaires.
◆ **Equity** *pr n principal syndicat britannique des gens du spectacle*.

equivalence [ɪ'kwɪvələns] *n* équivalence *f*.

equivalent [ɪ'kwɪvələnt] ◇ *adj* équivalent; **to be ~ to sthg** être équivalent à qqch, équivaloir à qqch; **is there an ~ organization in France?** y a-t-il une organisation équivalente en France?
◇ *n* équivalent *m*; **the French ~ for "pound"** l'équivalent français du mot « pound »; **it costs the ~ of £5 per week** cela coûte l'équivalent de 5 livres par semaine.

equivocal [ɪ'kwɪvəkl] *adj* -**1.** [ambiguous - words, attitude] ambigu, équivoque. -**2.** [dubious - behaviour, person] suspect, douteux; [- outcome] incertain, douteux.

equivocally [ɪ'kwɪvəklɪ] *adv* -**1.** [ambiguously] de manière équivoque OR ambiguë. -**2.** [dubiously] de manière douteuse.

equivocate [ɪ'kwɪvəkeɪt] *vi fml* user d'équivoques OR de faux-fuyants, équivoquer *lit*.

equivocation [ɪ,kwɪvə'keɪʃn] *n (U) fml* [words] paroles *fpl* équivoques; [prevarication] tergiversation *f*.

er [ɜːʳ] *interj* heu.

ER (*written abbr of* Elizabeth Regina) *emblème de la reine Élisabeth*.

era ['ɪərə] *n* [gen] époque *f*; GEOL & HIST ère *f*; **her election marked a new ~ in politics** son élection a marqué un tournant dans la vie politique; **the ~ of horse travel** l'époque OR le temps des voyages à cheval.

ERA ['ɪərə] (*abbr of* Equal Rights Amendment) *n projet de loi américain rejeté en 1982 qui posait comme principe l'égalité des individus quels que soient leur sexe, leur religion ou leur race*.

eradicate [ɪ'rædɪkeɪt] *vt* [disease] éradiquer, faire disparaître; [poverty, problem] faire disparaître, supprimer; [abuse, crime] extirper, supprimer; [practice] bannir, mettre fin à; [weeds] détruire, déraciner.

eradication [ɪ,rædɪ'keɪʃn] *n* [of disease] éradication *f*; [of poverty, problem] suppression *f*; [of abuse, crime] extirpation *f*, suppression *f*; [of practice] fin *f*; [of weeds] destruction *f*, déracinement *m*.

erase [ɪ'reɪz] ◇ *vt* [writing] effacer, gratter; [with rubber] gommer; *fig* & COMPUT effacer.
◇ *vi* s'effacer.

erase head *n* tête *f* d'effacement.

eraser [ɪ'reɪzəʳ] *n* gomme *f*.

erasing [ɪ'reɪzɪŋ] *n* effacement *m*.

Erasmus [ɪ'ræzməs] *pr n* Érasme.

erasure [ɪ'reɪʒəʳ] *n* -**1.** [act] effacement *m*, grattage *m*. -**2.** [mark] rature *f*, grattage *m*.

erbium ['ɜːbɪəm] *n* erbium *m*.

ere [eəʳ] ◇ *prep lit* avant; **~ long** sous peu; **~ now, ~ this** déjà, auparavant; **~ then** d'ici là.
◇ *conj arch* OR *lit* avant que; **~ I leave** avant que je ne parte.

erect [ɪ'rekt] ◇ *adj* -**1.** [upright] droit; [standing] debout; **man walks ~** l'homme marche debout; **she holds herself very ~** elle se tient bien droite; **with head ~** la tête haute; **the dog sat with ears ~** le chien était assis les oreilles dressées. -**2.** PHYSIOL [penis, nipples] dur.
◇ *vt* -**1.** [build - building, wall] bâtir, construire; [- statue, temple] ériger, élever; [- equipment] installer; [- roadblock, tent] dresser. -**2.** *fig* [system] édifier; [obstacle] élever.

erectile [ɪ'rektaɪl] *adj* érectile.

erection [ɪ'rekʃn] *n* -**1.** [of building, wall] construction *f*; [of statue, temple] érection *f*; [of equipment] installation *f*; [of roadblock, tent] dressage *m*; *fig* [of system, obstacle] édification *f*. -**2.** [building] bâtiment *m*, construction *f*. -**3.** PHYSIOL érection *f*; **to have** OR **to get an ~** avoir une érection.

erector [ɪ'rektəʳ] *n* -**1.** [muscle] érecteur *m*. -**2.** [builder] constructeur *m*, -trice *f*; **~ set** *Am* jeu *m* de construction.

erg [ɜːg] *n* PHYS & GEOG erg *m*.

ergative ['ɜːgətɪv] ◇ *adj* ergatif.
◇ *n* ergatif *m*.

ergo ['ɜːgəʊ] *adv fml* OR *hum* donc, par conséquent.

ergonomic [,ɜːgəʊ'nɒmɪk] *adj* ergonomique.

ergonomically [,ɜːgəʊ'nɒmɪkəlɪ] *adv* du point de vue ergonomique.

ergonomics [,ɜːgə'nɒmɪks] *n (U)* ergonomie *f*.

ergot ['ɜːgət] *n* AGR ergot *m*; PHARM ergot *m* de seigle.

ergotism ['ɜːgətɪzm] *n* ergotisme *m*.

Erie ['ɪərɪ] *pr n*: **Lake ~** le lac Érié; **the ~ Canal** le canal de l'Érié.

Erin ['ɪərɪn] *pr n arch* OR *lit* Irlande *f*.

ERISA [ə'riːsə] (*abbr of* Employee Retirement Income Security Act) *n loi américaine sur les pensions de retraite*.

Eritrea [,erɪ'treɪə] *pr n* Erythrée *f*; **in ~** en Erythrée.

Eritrean [,erɪ'treɪən] ◇ *n* Erythréen *m*, -enne *f*.
◇ *adj* érythréen.

ERM (*abbr of* exchange rate mechanism) *n* mécanisme *m* de change (du SME).

ermine ['ɜːmɪn] *n* [fur, robe, stoat] hermine *f*.

Ernie ['ɜːnɪ] (*abbr of* Electronic Random Number Indicator Equipment) *n en Grande-Bretagne, ordinateur qui sert au tirage des numéros gagnants des bons à lots*.

erode [ɪ'rəʊd] ◇ *vt* [subj: water, wind] éroder, ronger; [subj: acid, rust] ronger, corroder; *fig* [courage, power] ronger, miner; **the rock face had been ~d away** la paroi du rocher avait été érodée.
◇ *vi* [rock, soil] s'éroder; **the cliff is slowly eroding (away)** la falaise est lentement en train de s'éroder.

erogenous [ɪ'rɒdʒɪnəs] *adj* érogène; **~ zone** zone *f* érogène.

Eros ['ɪərɒs] *pr n* -**1.** MYTH Éros. -**2.** *Br surnom donné au monument en l'honneur du comte de Shaftesbury, à Piccadilly Circus*.

erosion [ɪ'rəʊʒn] *n* [of soil, rock] érosion *f*; [of metal] corrosion *f*; *fig* [of courage, power] érosion *f*, corrosion *f*.

erosive [ɪ'rəʊsɪv] *adj* érosif; [corrosive] corrosif.

erotic [ɪ'rɒtɪk] *adj* érotique.

erotica [ɪ'rɒtɪkə] *npl* ART art *m* érotique; LITERAT littérature *f* érotique.

erotically [ɪ'rɒtɪklɪ] *adv* érotiquement.

eroticism [ɪ'rɒtɪsɪzm] *n* érotisme *m*.

erotomania [ɪ,rɒtəʊ'meɪnjə] *n* érotomanie *f*.

err [ɜːʳ] *vi fml* -**1.** [make mistake] se tromper; **I ~ed on the side of caution** j'ai péché par excès de prudence ☐ **to ~ is human (to forgive divine)** *prov* l'erreur est humaine (le pardon divin). -**2.** [sin] pécher, commettre une faute.

errand ['erənd] *n* commission *f*, course *f*; **to go on** OR **to do** OR **to run an ~ (for sb)** faire une course (pour qqn); **I did** OR **ran all the ~s** j'ai fait toutes les commissions OR les courses; **I've come on an ~ of mercy** je suis venu en mission de charité; **she sent me on a fool's errand** elle m'y a envoyé pour rien.

errand boy *n* garçon *m* de courses.

errant ['erənt] *adj* -**1.** [wayward] dévoyé. -**2.** [roaming] errant.

errata [e'rɑːtə] ◇ *pl* → **erratum**.
◇ *npl* [list] errata *m inv*.

erratic [ɪ'rætɪk] ◇ *adj* -**1.** [irregular - results] irrégulier; [- performance] irrégulier, inégal; [- person] fantasque, excentrique; [- mood] changeant; [- movement, course] mal assuré; **he is a bit ~** on ne sait jamais comment il va réagir; **~ driving** conduite *f* déconcertante. -**2.** GEOL & MED erratique.
◇ *n* GEOL bloc *m* OR roche *f* erratique.

erratically [ɪ'rætɪklɪ] *adv* [act, behave] de manière fantasque OR capricieuse; [move, work] irrégulièrement, par à-coups; **he drives ~** il conduit de façon mal assurée OR déconcertante.

erratum [e'rɑːtəm] (*pl* errata [-tə]) *n* erratum *m*.

erroneous [ɪ'rəʊnjəs] *adj* erroné, inexact.

erroneously [ɪ'rəʊnjəslɪ] *adv* erronément, à tort.

error ['erəʳ] *n* -**1.** [mistake] erreur *f*, faute *f*; **to make** OR **to commit an ~** faire (une) erreur; **an ~ of judgment** une erreur de jugement; **it would be an ~ to assume that...** ce serait une erreur OR on aurait tort de supposer que...; **~s and omissions excepted** COMM sauf erreur ou omission. -**2.** MATH [mistake] faute *f*; [deviation] écart *m*. -**3.** [mistakenness] erreur *f*; **it was done in ~** cela a été fait par erreur OR méprise; **he was in ~ over** OR **on this point of law** il était dans l'erreur OR il avait tort sur ce point de loi; **I've seen the ~ of my ways** je suis revenu de mes erreurs; **to be in/to fall into ~** RELIG être/tomber dans l'erreur.

error correction *n* correction *f* d'erreur.

error message *n* message *m* d'erreur.

ersatz ['eəzæts] ◇ *adj*: **this is ~ coffee** c'est de l'ersatz OR du succédané de café; **this sugar is ~** ce sucre est un ersatz OR un succédané.
◇ *n* ersatz *m*, succédané *m*.

Erse [ɜːs] ◇ *adj* gaélique, erse.
◇ *n* gaélique *m*.

erstwhile ['ɜːstwaɪl] *lit* OR *hum* ◇ *adj* d'autrefois.
◇ *adv* autrefois, jadis.

eructation [,iːrʌk'teɪʃn] *n* éructation *f*.

erudite ['eruːdaɪt] *adj* [book, person] érudit, savant; [word] savant.

eruditely ['eruːdaɪtlɪ] *adv* de manière savante avec érudition.

erudition [,eruː'dɪʃn] *n* érudition *f*.

erupt [ɪ'rʌpt] *vi* -**1.** [volcano - start] entrer en éruption; [- continue] faire éruption; **an ~ing volcano** un volcan en éruption. -**2.** [pimples] sortir, apparaître; [tooth] percer; **her face ~ed in spots** elle a eu une éruption de boutons sur le visage. -**3.** *fig* [fire, laughter, war] éclater; [anger] exploser; **the city ~ed into violence** il y eut une explosion de violence dans la ville.

eruption [ɪ'rʌpʃn] *n* -**1.** [of volcano] éruption *f* -**2.** [of pimples] éruption *f*, poussée *f*; [of teeth] percée *f*. -**3.** *fig* [of laughter] éclat *m*, éruption *f* [of anger] accès *m*, éruption *f*; [of violence] explosion *f*, accès *m*.

erysipelas [,erɪ'sɪpɪləs] *n* érysipèle *m*, érésipèle *m*.

erythema [,erɪ'θiːmə] *n* érythème *m*.

erythrocyte [ɪ'rɪθrəʊ,saɪt] *n* érythrocyte *m*.

ESA (*abbr of* European Space Agency) *pr n* ESA *f*, ASE *f*.

Esau ['iːsɔː] *pr n* Ésaü.

escalate ['eskəleɪt] ◇ *vi* [fighting, war] s'intensifier; [prices] monter en flèche.
◇ *vt* [fighting] intensifier; [problem] aggraver [prices] faire grimper.

escalation [,eskə'leɪʃn] *n* [of fighting, war] escalade *f*, intensification *f*; [of prices] escalade *f* montée *f* en flèche.

escalator ['eskəleɪtəʳ] *n* escalier *m* roulant OR mécanique, escalator *m*.

escalator clause *n* clause *f* d'indexation OR de révision.

escalope ['eskəlɒp] *n* escalope *f*.

escapade [,eskə'peɪd] *n* [adventure] équipée *f*; [scrape] fredaine *f*, escapade *f*; [prank] frasque *f*.

escape [ɪ'skeɪp] ◇ *vi* -**1.** [get away - person, animal] échapper, s'échapper; [- prisoner] s'évader; **they ~d from the enemy/from the hands of their kidnappers** ils ont échappé à l'ennemi, des mains de leurs ravisseurs; **the thieves ~d after a police chase** les voleurs ont pris la fuite après avoir été poursuivis par la police; **she ~d from the camp** elle s'est échappée du camp; **to ~ from the crowd** *fig* fuir la foule; **he ~d to Italy** il s'est enfui en Italie. -**2.** [gas, liquid, steam] s'échapper, fuir. -**3.** [survive, avoid injury] s'en tirer, en réchapper; **she ~d uninjured** elle s'en est tirée sans aucun mal; **they ~d with just a few cuts and bruises** ils en ont été quittes pour quelques coupures et des bleus; **he ~d with a reprimand** il en a été quitte pour une réprimande.

◇ *vt* -**1.** [avoid] échapper à; **to ~ doing sthg** éviter de faire qqch; **I narrowly ~d being killed** j'ai failli OR manqué me faire tuer; **he ~d detection** il ne s'est pas fait repérer; **she narrowly ~d death** elle a échappé de justesse à la mort; **there's no escaping the fact that...** il n'y a pas moyen d'échapper au fait que... -**2.** [elude notice, memory of] échapper à; **her name ~s me** son nom m'échappe; **nothing ~s them** rien ne leur échappe; **her blunder ~d notice** sa gaffe est passée inaperçue.

◇ *n* -**1.** [of person] fuite *f*, évasion *f*; [of prisoner] évasion *f*; [of animal] fuite *f*; **I made my ~** je me suis échappé OR évadé; **they planned their ~** ils ont combiné leur plan d'évasion; **he had a narrow ~** *fig* [from danger] il l'a échappé belle, il a eu chaud; [from illness] il revient de loin. -**2.** [diversion] évasion *f*; **an ~ from reality** une évasion hors de la réalité. -**3.** [of gas, liquid] fuite *f*; [of exhaust fumes, steam] échappement *m*.

◇ *comp* [plot, route] d'évasion; [device] de sortie, de secours; **~ routine** COMPUT procédure *f* d'échappement.

escape clause *n* clause *f* échappatoire.

escaped [ɪ'skeɪpt] *adj* échappé; **an ~ prisoner** un évadé.

escapee [ˌɪskeɪ'piː] *n* évadé *m*, -e *f*.

escape hatch *n* trappe *f* de secours.

escape mechanism *n* *literal* mécanisme *m* de secours; PSYCH fuite *f* (devant la réalité).

escapement [ɪ'skeɪpmənt] *n* [of clock, piano] échappement *m*; MECH échappement *m*.

escape pipe *n* tuyau *m* d'échappement OR de refoulement, tuyère *f*.

escape road *n* talus *m* de protection.

escape valve *n* soupape *f* d'échappement.

escape velocity *n* vitesse *f* de libération.

escape wheel *n* roue *f* d'échappement.

escapism [ɪ'skeɪpɪzm] *n* évasion *f* hors de la réalité, fuite *f* devant la réalité.

escapist [ɪ'skeɪpɪst] ◇ *n* personne *f* cherchant à s'évader du réel.

◇ *adj* d'évasion.

escapologist [ˌeskeɪ'pɒlədʒɪst] *n* *virtuose de l'évasion dans les spectacles de magie*.

escapology [ˌeskeɪ'pɒlədʒɪ] *n* *art de l'évasion dans les spectacles de magie*.

escarpment [ɪ'skɑːpmənt] *n* escarpement *m*.

eschatological [ˌeskətə'lɒdʒɪkl] *adj* eschatologique.

eschatology [ˌeskə'tɒlədʒɪ] *n* eschatologie *f*.

escheat [ɪs'tʃiːt] *n* JUR dévolution *f* des biens à l'État *(en l'absence des héritiers)*.

eschew [ɪs'tʃuː] *vt* *fml* [duty, work] éviter; [alcohol] s'abstenir de boire; [publicity, temptation, involvement] fuir; [activity, action] éviter.

escort [*n* & *comp* 'eskɔːt, *vb* ɪ'skɔːt] ◇ *n* -**1.** [guard] escorte *f*, cortège *m*; MIL & NAUT escorte *f*; **under the ~ of** sous l'escorte de; **under police ~** sous escorte policière; **they were given a police ~** on leur a donné une escorte de police. -**2.** [consort - male] cavalier *m*; [- female] hôtesse *f*.

◇ *comp* d'escorte; **an ~ vessel** un bâtiment d'escorte, un (vaisseau) escorteur.

◇ *vt* *fml* accompagner, escorter; **may I ~ you home?** permettez-moi de vous raccompagner; **kindly ~ these gentlemen to the door** veuillez raccompagner ces messieurs jusqu'à la porte ‖ [police & MIL] escorter; **they ~ed him in/out** ils l'ont fait entrer/sortir sous escorte.

escort agency *n* service *m* OR bureau *m* d'hôtesses.

escrow ['eskrəʊ] *n* JUR dépôt *m* fiduciaire OR conditionnel; **in ~** en dépôt fiduciaire, en main tierce.

escutcheon [ɪ'skʌtʃn] *n* -**1.** [shield] écu *m*, écusson *m*. -**2.** [on door, handle, light switch] écusson *m*.

ESE *written abbr of* east-southeast.

esker ['eskəʳ] *n* os *m* GEOL.

Eskimo ['eskɪməʊ] (*pl inv* OR **Eskimos**) ◇ *n* -**1.** [person] Esquimau *m*, Esquimaude *f*. -**2.** LING esquimau *m*.

◇ *adj* esquimau; **~ dog** chien *m* esquimau.

ESL (*abbr of* **English as a Second Language**) *n anglais langue seconde*.

ESN *adj abbr of* educationally subnormal.

esophagus [iː'sɒfəgəs] (*pl* **esophagi** [-gaɪ]) *Am* = **oesophagus**.

esoteric [ˌesə'terɪk] *adj* [obscure] ésotérique; [private] secret.

esp. *written abbr of* especially.

ESP *n* -**1.** (*abbr of* **extrasensory perception**) perception *f* extrasensorielle. -**2.** (*abbr of* **English for special purposes**) *anglais spécialisé*.

espadrille [ˌespə'drɪl] *n* espadrille *f*.

espalier [ɪ'spæljəʳ] ◇ *n* [tree] arbre *m* en espalier; [trellis] espalier *m*; [method] culture *f* en espalier.

◇ *vt* cultiver en espalier.

esparto [e'spɑːtəʊ] (*pl* **espartos**) *n*: **~ (grass)** alfa *m*.

especial [ɪ'speʃl] *adj fml* [notable] particulier, exceptionnel; [specific] particulier.

especially [ɪ'speʃəlɪ] *adv* -**1.** [to a particular degree] particulièrement, spécialement; [particularly] en particulier, surtout; **the condition usually affects women, ~ women over fifty** cette maladie touche généralement les femmes, et particulièrement celles de plus de 50 ans; **I can't mention it, ~ since** OR **as I'm not supposed to know anything about it** je ne peux pas en parler d'autant que OR surtout que je ne suis pas censé savoir quoi que ce soit à ce sujet; **you ~ ought to know better!** vous devriez le savoir mieux que personne!; **the food at this restaurant is ~ good** la cuisine de ce restaurant est particulièrement bonne; **be ~ careful with this one** faites particulièrement attention à celui-ci. -**2.** [for a particular purpose] exprès; **he went ~ to meet her** il est allé exprès pour la rencontrer.

Esperantist [ˌespə'ræntɪst] ◇ *adj* espérantiste.

◇ *n* espérantiste *mf*.

Esperanto [ˌespə'ræntəʊ] ◇ *n* espéranto *m*.

◇ *adj* en espéranto.

espionage ['espɪəˌnɑːʒ] *n* espionnage *m*.

esplanade [ˌesplə'neɪd] *n* esplanade *f*.

espousal [ɪ'spaʊzl] *n* -**1.** *fml* [of belief, cause] adoption *f*. -**2.** *arch* [marriage] mariage *m*.

espouse [ɪ'spaʊz] *vt* -**1.** *fml* [belief, cause] épouser, adopter. -**2.** *arch* [marry] épouser.

espresso [e'spresəʊ] (*pl* **espressos**) *n* (café *m*) express *m*; **~ machine** machine *f* à express.

espy [ɪ'spaɪ] (*pt* & *pp* **espied**) *vt lit* apercevoir, distinguer.

Esq. (*written abbr of* esquire): **James Roberts, ~** M. James Roberts.

esquire [ɪ'skwaɪəʳ] *n Br* -**1.** = **Esq.** -**2.** HIST écuyer *m*.

essay [*n* 'eseɪ, *vb* e'seɪ] ◇ *n* -**1.** LITERAT essai *m*; SCH composition *f*, dissertation *f*; UNIV dissertation *f*; **'Essay Concerning Human Understanding'** *Locke* 'Essai sur l'entendement humain'; **'An Essay on Man'** *Pope* 'Essai sur l'homme'. -**2.** *fml* [attempt] essai *m*, tentative *f*.

◇ *vt fml* -**1.** [try] essayer, tenter. -**2.** [test] mettre à l'épreuve.

essayist ['eseɪɪst] *n* essayiste *mf*.

essence ['esns] *n* -**1.** [gen] essence *f*, essentiel *m*; **the ~ of her speech was that...** l'essentiel de son discours tenait en ceci que...; **time is of the ~** il est essentiel de faire vite, la vitesse s'impose; **she's the ~ of generosity** elle est la générosité même. -**2.** PHILOS essence *f*, nature *f*; RELIG essence *f*. -**3.** CHEM essence *f*; **~ of rosemary** essence de romarin. -**4.** CULIN extrait *m*; **vanilla ~** extrait de vanille.

◆ **in essence** *adv phr* essentiellement, surtout; **it is in ~ a question of...** c'est essentiellement OR surtout une question de...

essential [ɪ'senʃl] ◇ *adj* -**1.** [vital - action, equipment, services] essentiel, indispensable; [- point, role] essentiel, capital; [- question] essentiel, fondamental; **a well-trained workforce is ~ to the success of your business** un personnel qualifié est essentiel au succès de votre entreprise; **it is ~ to know whether...** il est essentiel OR il importe de savoir si...; **the ~ thing is to relax** l'essentiel est de rester calme; **a balanced diet is ~ for good health** un régime équilibré est essentiel pour être en bonne santé; **~ goods** biens *m* de première nécessité. -**2.** [basic] essentiel, fondamental; **the ~ goodness of man** la bonté essentielle de l'homme; **~ oils** huiles *fpl* essentielles.

◇ *n* objet *m* indispensable; **the ~s** l'essentiel; **we can only afford to buy the ~s** nous n'avons les moyens d'acheter que l'essentiel; **a dishwasher is an ~ of a modern kitchen** un lave-vaisselle est un élément indispensable dans une cuisine moderne; **the ~s of astronomy** les rudiments *mpl* de l'astronomie; **in (all) ~s** essentiellement.

essentially [ɪ'senʃəlɪ] *adv* [fundamentally] essentiellement, fondamentalement; [mainly] essentiellement, principalement; **it's ~ a question of taste** c'est avant tout une question de goût.

est [est] *n* (*abbr of* **Erhard Seminars Training**) *méthode de formation psychologique créée par Werner Erhard*.

est. -**1.** *written abbr of* established. -**2.** *written abbr of* estimated.

EST *n abbr of* Eastern Standard Time.

establish [ɪ'stæblɪʃ] *vt* -**1.** [create, set up - business] fonder, créer; [- government] constituer, établir; [- society, system] constituer; [- factory] établir, monter; [- contact] établir; [- relations] établir, nouer; [- custom, law] instaurer; [- precedent] créer; [- order, peace] faire régner. -**2.** [confirm - authority, power] affermir; [- reputation] établir; **she has already ~ed her reputation as a physicist/as an artist** elle s'est déjà fait une réputation de physicienne/comme artiste; **he ~ed himself as a computer consultant** il s'est établi conseiller en informatique. -**3.** [prove - fact, identity, truth] établir; [- cause, nature] déterminer, établir; [- guilt, need] établir, prouver; [- innocence] établir, démontrer; **it has been ~ed that there is no case against the defendant** il a été démontré qu'il n'y a pas lieu de poursuivre l'accusé.

established [ɪ'stæblɪʃt] *adj* -**1.** [existing, solid - order, system] établi; [- government] établi, au pouvoir; [- business] établi, solide; [- law] établi, en vigueur; [- tradition] établi, enraciné; [- reputation] établi, bien assis; **~ in 1890** COMM maison fondée en 1890; **the ~ Church** l'Église *f* officielle. -**2.** [proven - fact] acquis, reconnu; [- truth] établi, démontré.

establishment [ɪ'stæblɪʃmənt] *n* -**1.** [of business] fondation *f*, création *f*; [of government] constitution *f*; [of society, system] constitution *f*, création *f*; [of law] instauration *f*. -**2.** [institution] établissement *m*; **a business ~** un établissement commercial, une firme; **a research ~** un établissement de recherche. -**3.** [staff] personnel *m*; MIL & NAUT effectif *m*.

◆ **Establishment** *n* [ruling powers]: **the Establishment** les pouvoirs *mpl* établis, l'ordre *m* établi, l'establishment *m*; **the financial Establishment** ceux qui comptent dans le monde financier; **he's such an Establishment figure** il fait vraiment partie de l'establishment.

estate [ɪ'steɪt] *n* -**1.** [land] propriété *f*, domaine *m*; **her country ~** ses terres *fpl*. -**2.** *Br* [development - housing] lotissement *m*, cité *f*; [- trading] zone *f* commerciale. -**3.** JUR [property] biens *mpl*, fortune *f*; [of deceased] succession *f*; **she left a large ~** elle a laissé une grosse fortune (en héritage). **-4.** *fml* [state, position] état *m*, rang *m*; men of low/high ~ les hommes d'humble condition/de haut rang; the ~ of matrimony la condition du mariage; the three ~s les trois états.

estate agency *n Br* agence *f* immobilière.

estate agent *n Br* **-1.** [salesperson] agent *m* immobilier. **-2.** [manager] intendant *m*, régisseur *m*.

estate car *n Br* break *m*.

estate duty *n Br* droits *mpl* de succession.

estd., est'd. *written abbr of* established.

esteem [ɪ'stiːm] ◇ *vt* **-1.** [respect - person] avoir de l'estime pour, estimer; [- quality] estimer, apprécier. **-2.** *fml* [consider] estimer, considérer; I ~ it a great honour je m'estime très honoré. ◇ *n* estime *f*, considération *f*; to hold sb/sthg in high ~ tenir qqn/qqch en haute estime.

esteemed [ɪ'stiːmd] *adj fml* estimé; our ~ president notre (très) estimé président.

ester ['estəʳ] *n* ester *m*.

Esther ['estəʳ] *pr n* Esther.

esthete *etc* ['iːsθiːt] *Am* = **aesthete**.

Esthonia *etc* [e'stəʊnjə] = **Estonia**.

estimate [*n* 'estɪmət, *vb* 'estɪmeɪt] ◇ *n* **-1.** [evaluation] évaluation *f*, estimation *f*; give me an ~ of how much you think it will cost donnez-moi une idée du prix que cela coûtera, à votre avis; his ~ of 500 tonnes is way off the mark *inf* son estimation de 500 tonnes est très éloignée de la réalité; at a rough ~ approximativement; these figures are only a rough ~ ces chiffres ne sont que très approximatifs; at the lowest ~ it will take five years il faudra cinq ans au bas mot; at an optimistic ~ dans le meilleur des cas. **-2.** COMM [quote] devis *m*; get several ~s before deciding who to employ faites faire plusieurs devis avant de décider quelle entreprise choisir; ask the garage to give you an ~ for the repairs demandez au garage de vous établir un devis pour les réparations. ◇ *vt* **-1.** [calculate - cost, number] estimer, évaluer; [- distance, speed] estimer, apprécier; the cost was ~d at £2,000 le coût était évalué à 2 000 livres; an ~d 50,000 people attended the demonstration environ 50 000 personnes auraient manifesté; I ~ (that) it will take at least five years à mon avis cela prendra au moins cinq ans, j'estime que cela prendra au moins cinq ans ❑ ~d time of arrival/of departure heure probable d'arrivée/de départ. **-2.** [judge] estimer, juger; I don't ~ him very highly je n'ai guère d'estime pour lui.

estimation [,estɪ'meɪʃn] *n* **-1.** [calculation] estimation *f*, évaluation *f*. **-2.** [judgment] jugement *m*, opinion *f*; in my ~ à mon avis, selon moi. **-3.** [esteem] estime *f*, considération *f*; he went down/up in my ~ il a baissé/monté dans mon estime.

estivate *etc* ['iːstɪ,veɪt] *Am* = **aestivate**.

Estonia [e'stəʊnjə] *pr n* Estonie *f*; in ~ en Estonie.

Estonian [e'stəʊnjən] ◇ *n* **-1.** [person] Estonien *m*, -enne *f*. **-2.** LING estonien *m*. ◇ *adj* estonien.

estrange [ɪ'streɪndʒ] *vt* aliéner, éloigner; to become ~d from sb se brouiller avec OR se détacher de qqn; he is ~d from his wife il est séparé de sa femme; her ~d husband son mari, dont elle est séparée.

estrangement [ɪ'streɪndʒmənt] *n* éloignement *m*; [from spouse] séparation *f*.

estrogen *Am* = **oestrogen**.

estrus *Am* = **oestrus**.

estuary ['estjʊərɪ] (*pl* estuaries) *n* estuaire *m*.

ET (*abbr of* Employment Training) *n programme gouvernemental en faveur des chômeurs de longue durée en Grande-Bretagne*.

ETA (*abbr of* estimated time of arrival) *n* HPA.

et al. [,et'æl] (*abbr of* et alii) et coll., et al.

etc. (*written abbr of* et catera) etc.

et cetera [ɪt'setərə] ◇ *adv* et cetera, et cætera. ◇ *n*: the ~s les et cætera *mpl*.

etch [etʃ] *vi* & *vt* graver; ART & TYPO graver à l'eau-forte; ~ed on my memory *fig* gravé dans ma mémoire.

etching ['etʃɪŋ] *n* **-1.** [print] (gravure *f* à l') eau-forte *f*. **-2.** [technique] gravure *f* à l'eau-forte.

ETD (*abbr of* estimated time of departure) *n* HPD *f*.

eternal [ɪ'tɜːnl] ◇ *adj* **-1.** [gen, PHILOS & RELIG] éternel. **-2.** [perpetual] continuel, perpétuel; [arguments, problems] éternel; [discussion, wrangling] continuel, sempiternel *pej*; ~ complaints perpétuelles récriminations *fpl*; he's an ~ student c'est l'étudiant éternel; to my ~ shame à ma grande honte. ◇ *n*: the Eternal l'Éternel *m*.

eternally [ɪ'tɜːnəlɪ] *adv* **-1.** [forever] éternellement; I shall be ~ grateful je serai infiniment reconnaissant. **-2.** *pej* [perpetually] perpétuellement, continuellement.

eternal triangle *n*: the ~ l'éternel trio *m (femme, mari, amant)*.

eternity [ɪ'tɜːnətɪ] (*pl* eternities) *n literal* & *fig* éternité *f*; it seemed like an ~ on aurait dit une éternité; he kept me waiting for an ~ il m'a fait attendre une éternité OR des éternités ❑ 'From Here to Eternity' *Jones, Zinnemann* 'Tant qu'il y aura des hommes'.

eternity ring *n* bague *f* de fidélité.

ethane ['iːθeɪn] *n* éthane *m*.

ethanol ['eθənɒl] *n* alcool *m* éthylique, éthanol *m*.

ether ['iːθəʳ] *n* **-1.** CHEM & PHYS éther *m*. **-2.** *lit* & MYTH [sky]: the ~ l'éther *m*, la voûte céleste; over OR through the ~ RADIO sur les ondes.

ethereal [ɪ'θɪərɪəl] *adj* [fragile] éthéré, délicat; [spiritual] éthéré, noble.

ethic ['eθɪk] ◇ *n* éthique *f*, morale *f*. ◇ *adj* = **ethical**.

ethical ['eθɪkl] *adj* moral, éthique *fml*; it is not ~ c'est contraire à la morale; an ~ code un code déontologique.

ethically ['eθɪklɪ] *adv* d'un point de vue éthique.

ethics ['eθɪks] ◇ *n (U)* [study] éthique *f*, morale *f*. ◇ *npl* [principles] morale *f*; [morality] moralité *f*; dubious ~ morale douteuse ❑ medical ~ code *m* déontologique OR de déontologie.

Ethiopia [,iːθɪ'əʊpjə] *pr n* Éthiopie *f*; in ~ en Éthiopie.

Ethiopian [,iːθɪ'əʊpjən] ◇ *n* **-1.** [person] Éthiopien *m*, -enne *f*. **-2.** LING éthiopien *m*. ◇ *adj* éthiopien.

ethnic ['eθnɪk] ◇ *adj* **-1.** [of race] ethnique; ~ cleansing purification *f* ethnique. **-2.** [traditional] folklorique, traditionnel. ◇ *n Am* membre *m* d'une minorité ethnique.

ethnically ['eθnɪklɪ] *adv* du point de vue ethnique, ethniquement.

ethnicity [eθ'nɪsɪtɪ] *n* appartenance *f* ethnique.

ethnic minority *n* minorité *f* ethnique.

ethnocentric [,eθnəʊ'sentrɪk] *adj* ethnocentrique.

ethnocentrism [,eθnəʊ'sentrɪzm] *n* ethnocentrisme *m*.

ethnographer [eθ'nɒgrəfəʳ] *n* ethnographe *mf*.

ethnography [eθ'nɒgrəfɪ] *n* ethnographie *f*.

ethnolinguistics [,eθnəʊlɪŋ'gwɪstɪks] *n (U)* ethnolinguistique *f*.

ethnologist [eθ'nɒlədʒɪst] *n* ethnologue *mf*.

ethnology [eθ'nɒlədʒɪ] *n* ethnologie *f*.

ethology [ɪ'θɒlədʒɪ] *n* éthologie *f*, éthographie *f*.

ethos ['iːθɒs] *n* éthos *m*.

ethyl ['eθɪl, 'iːθaɪl] *n* éthyle *m*; ~ acetate acétate *m* d'éthyle.

ethyl alcohol *n* alcool *m* éthylique, éthanol *m*.

ethylene ['eθɪliːn] *n* éthylène *m*.

etiolate ['iːtɪəʊleɪt] ◇ *vt* étioler. ◇ *vi* s'étioler.

etiology [,iːtɪ'ɒlədʒɪ] *Am* = **aetiology**.

etiquette ['etɪket] *n (U)* [code of practice] étiquette *f*; [customs] bon usage *m*, convenance *fpl*; according to ~ selon l'usage; courtroom ~ cérémonial *m* de cour; medical ~ déontologie *f* médicale; that's not professional ~ c'est contraire à la déontologie OR aux usages de la profession.

Etna ['etnə] *pr n*: (Mount) ~ l'Etna *m*.

Eton ['iːtn] *pr n*: ~ (College) l'école d'Eton.

> **ETON:**
> Eton, l'une des plus anciennes et des plus célèbres «public schools», est fréquentée essentiellement par les enfants de la grande bourgeoisie et de l'aristocratie. Plusieurs anciens premiers ministres britanniques y ont fait leurs études.

Etonian [iː'təʊnjən] *n* élève *m* de l'école d'Eton.

Etruria [ɪ'trʊərɪə] *pr n* Étrurie *f*.

Etruscan [ɪ'trʌskən] ◇ *n* **-1.** [person] Étrusque *mf*. **-2.** LING étrusque *m*. ◇ *adj* étrusque.

ETU (*abbr of* Electrical Trades Union) *pr n syndicat britannique d'électriciens*.

ETV (*abbr of* Educational Television) *n Am* chaîne *f* de télévision éducative et culturelle.

etymological [,etɪmə'lɒdʒɪkl] *adj* étymologique.

etymologically [,etɪmə'lɒdʒɪklɪ] *adv* étymologiquement.

etymologist [,etɪ'mɒlədʒɪst] *n* étymologiste *mf*.

etymology [,etɪ'mɒlədʒɪ] *n* étymologie *f*.

etymon ['etɪmɒn] (*pl* etymons OR etyma [-mə]) *n* étymon *m*.

eucalyptus [,juːkə'lɪptəs] (*pl* eucalyptuses OR eucalypti [-taɪ]) *n* eucalyptus *m*.

eucalyptus oil *n* essence *f* d'eucalyptus.

Eucharist ['juːkərɪst] *n* Eucharistie *f*.

euchre ['juːkəʳ] *Am* ◇ *n* euchre *m (jeu de cartes)*. ◇ *vt* **-1.** CARDS empêcher de faire trois levées. **-2.** *inf fig* [cheat] carotter; he ~d them out of $10 il leur a carotté 10 dollars.

Euclid ['juːklɪd] *pr n* Euclide.

Euclidian [juː'klɪdɪən] *adj* euclidien; ~ geometry la géométrie euclidienne.

eugenic [juː'dʒenɪk] *adj* eugénique.

◆ **eugenics** *n (U)* eugénique *f*, eugénisme *m*.

eulogistic [,juːlə'dʒɪstɪk] *adj* très élogieux, louangeur.

eulogize, -ise ['juːlədʒaɪz] *vt* faire l'éloge OR le panégyrique de.

eulogy ['juːlədʒɪ] (*pl* eulogies) *n* panégyrique *m*.

Eumenides [juː'menɪ,diːz] *npl*: the ~ les Euménides.

eunuch ['juːnək] *n* eunuque *m*.

eupepsia [juː'pepsɪə] *n* eupepsie *f*.

euphemism ['juːfəmɪzm] *n* euphémisme *m*.

euphemistic [,juːfə'mɪstɪk] *adj* euphémique.

euphemistically [,juːfə'mɪstɪklɪ] *adv* par euphémisme, euphémiquement *fml*.

euphonic [juː'fɒnɪk] *adj* euphonique.

euphonium [juː'fəʊnjəm] *n* euphonium *m*.

euphony ['juːfənɪ] *n* euphonie *f*.

euphorbia [juː'fɔːbɪə] *n* euphorbe *f*.

euphoria [juː'fɔːrɪə] *n* euphorie *f*.

euphoric [juː'fɒrɪk] *adj* euphorique.

Euphrates [juː'freɪtiːz] *pr n*: the (River) ~ l'Euphrate *m*.

euphuism ['juːfjuːɪzm] *n* euphuisme *m*, préciosité *f*.

Eurasia [jʊə'reɪʒjə] *pr n* Eurasie *f*.

Eurasian [jʊə'reɪʒjən] ◇ *n* Eurasien *m*, -enne *f*. ◇ *adj* [person] eurasien; [continent] eurasiatique.

Euratom [jʊər'ætəm] (*abbr of* European Atomic Energy Community) *pr n* CEEA *f*.

eureka [jʊə'riːkə] *interj*: ~! eurêka!

eurhythmics [juː'rɪðmɪks] *n (U)* gymnastique rythmique.

Euripedes [jʊəˈrɪpɪˌdiːz] *pr n* Euripide.
Eurobank [ˈjʊərəʊˌbæŋk] *n* eurobanque *f.*
Eurobond [ˈjʊərəʊˌbɒnd] *n* euro-obligation *f.*
Eurocentric [ˈjʊərəʊˌsentrɪk] *adj* européocentrique.
Eurocheque [ˈjʊərəʊˌtʃek] *n* eurochèque *m.*
Eurocommunism [ˌjʊərəʊˈkɒmjʊˌnɪzm] *n* eurocommunisme *m.*
Eurocommunist [ˌjʊərəʊˈkɒmjʊnɪst] ◇ *adj* eurocommuniste.
◇ *n* eurocommuniste *mf.*
Eurocrat [ˈjʊərəʊˌkræt] *n* eurocrate *mf.*
Eurocurrency [ˈjʊərəʊˌkʌrənsɪ] *n* eurodevise *f*, euromonnaie *f.*
Eurodollar [ˈjʊərəʊˌdɒlə[r]] *n* eurodollar *m.*
Euro-MP (*abbr of* European Member of Parliament) [ˈjʊərəʊ-] *n* député *m* OR parlementaire *m* européen.
Europa [jʊˈrəʊpə] *pr n* MYTH Europe.
Europe [ˈjʊərəp] *pr n* Europe *f*; in ~ en Europe.
European [ˌjʊərəˈpiːən] ◇ *n* [inhabitant of Europe] Européen *m*, -enne *f*; [pro-Europe] partisan *m* de l'Europe unie, Européen *m*, -enne *f.*
◇ *adj* européen; the Single ~ Market le marché unique (européen); we must adopt a more ~ outlook nous devons adopter un point de vue plus européen OR plus ouvert sur l'Europe ❑ ~ Bank of reconstruction and development Banque *f* européenne de reconstruction et de développement; ~ plan *Am* [in hotel] chambre *f* sans pension.
European Economic Community *pr n* Communauté *f* économique européenne.
European Free Trade Association *pr n* Association *f* européenne de libre-échange.
Europeanize, -ise [ˌjʊərəˈpiːənaɪz] *vt* européaniser.
European Parliament *pr n* Parlement *m* européen.
Europhile [ˈjʊərəʊˌfaɪl] *n* partisan *m* de l'Europe unie.
europium [jʊˈrəʊpɪəm] *n* europium *m.*
Eurosceptic [ˈjʊərəʊˌskeptɪk] *n* eurosceptique *mf.*
Euroscepticism [ˈjʊərəʊˌskeptɪsɪzm] *n* euroscepticisme *m.*
Eurosterling [ˈjʊərəʊˌstɜːlɪŋ] *n* eurosterling *m.*
Eurovision® [ˈjʊərəʊˌvɪʒn] *n* Eurovision® *f*; the ~ Song Contest le concours Eurovision de la chanson.
Eurydice [jʊˈrɪdɪsɪ] *pr n* Eurydice.
eurythmics [juːˈrɪðmɪks] *Am* = **eurhythmics**.
Eustachian tube [juːˈsteɪʃən-] *n* trompe *f* d'Eustache.
eustatic [juːˈstætɪk] *adj* eustatique.
euthanasia [ˌjuːθəˈneɪzjə] *n* euthanasie *f.*
EVA (*abbr of* extravehicular activity) *n activité qui a lieu en dehors d'un engin spatial.*
evacuate [ɪˈvækjʊeɪt] *vt* [gen & PHYSIOL] évacuer.
evacuation [ɪˌvækjʊˈeɪʃn] *n* [gen & PHYSIOL] évacuation *f.*
evacuee [ɪˌvækjuːˈiː] *n* évacué *m*, -e *f.*
evade [ɪˈveɪd] *vt* -**1.** [escape from - pursuers] échapper à; [- punishment] échapper à, se soustraire à. -**2.** [avoid - responsibility] éviter, esquiver; [- question] esquiver, éluder; [- eyes, glance] éviter; to ~ the issue éluder le problème; people who try to ~ paying taxes risk imprisonment ceux qui essaient de frauder le fisc risquent l'emprisonnement; to ~ military service se dérober à ses obligations militaires.
evaluate [ɪˈvæljʊeɪt] *vt* -**1.** [value] évaluer, déterminer le montant de. -**2.** [assess - situation, success, work] évaluer, former un jugement sur la valeur de; [- evidence, reasons] peser, évaluer.
evaluation [ɪˌvæljʊˈeɪʃn] *n* -**1.** [of damages, worth] évaluation *f.* -**2.** [of situation, work] évaluation *f*, jugement *m*; [of evidence, reasons] évaluation *f.*
evanescent [ˌiːvəˈnesnt] *adj* évanescent, fugitif.
evangelical [ˌiːvænˈdʒelɪkl] ◇ *adj* évangélique.
◇ *n* évangélique *m.*
evangelicalism [ˌiːvænˈdʒelɪkəlɪzm] *n* évangélisme *m.*
evangelism [ɪˈvændʒəlɪzm] *n* évangélisme *m.*
evangelist [ɪˈvændʒəlɪst] *n* -**1.** BIBLE: Evangelist évangéliste *m.* -**2.** [preacher] évangélisateur *m*, -trice *f.* -**3.** *fig* [zealous advocate] prêcheur *m*, -euse *f.*
evangelize, -ise [ɪˈvændʒəlaɪz] ◇ *vt* évangéliser, prêcher l'Évangile à.
◇ *vi* -**1.** RELIG prêcher l'Évangile. -**2.** *fig* [advocate] prêcher.
evaporate [ɪˈvæpəreɪt] ◇ *vi* [liquid] s'évaporer; *fig* [hopes, doubts] s'envoler, se volatiliser.
◇ *vt* faire évaporer.
evaporated milk [ɪˈvæpəreɪtɪd-] *n* lait *m* condensé.
evaporation [ɪˌvæpəˈreɪʃn] *n* évaporation *f.*
evasion [ɪˈveɪʒn] *n* -**1.** [avoidance] fuite *f*, évasion *f*; [of duty] dérobade *f*; ~ of a responsibility dérobade devant une responsabilité. -**2.** [deception, trickery] détour *m*, subterfuge *m*, échappatoire *f*; to answer without ~ répondre sans détours OR sans biaiser.
evasive [ɪˈveɪsɪv] *adj* évasif; an ~ answer une réponse évasive OR de Normand; to take ~ action [gen] louvoyer; MIL effectuer une manœuvre dilatoire.
evasively [ɪˈveɪsɪvlɪ] *adv* évasivement; he replied ~ il a répondu en termes évasifs.
eve [iːv] *n* veille *f*; RELIG vigile *f*; on the ~ of the election à la veille des élections.
Eve [iːv] *pr n* Ève; 'All About ~' *Mankiewicz* 'Ève'.
even[1] [ˈiːvn] ◇ *adj* -**1.** [level] plat, plan; [smooth] uni; to make sthg ~ égaliser OR aplanir qqch; it's ~ with the desk c'est au même niveau que le bureau. -**2.** [steady - breathing, temperature] égal; [- rate, rhythm] régulier. -**3.** [equal - distribution, spread] égal; the score is OR the scores are ~ ils sont à égalité; it's an ~ game la partie est égale; now we're ~ nous voilà quittes, nous sommes quittes maintenant; there's an ~ chance he'll lose il y a une chance sur deux qu'il perde; the odds OR chances are about ~ les chances sont à peu près égales ❑ to bet ~ money [gen] donner chances égales; [in betting] parier le même enjeu; to get ~ with sb se venger de qqn; I'll get ~ with you for that! je vous revaudrai ça! -**4.** [calm - temper] égal; [- voice] égal, calme. -**5.** [number] pair.
◇ *adv* -**1.** [indicating surprise] même; he ~ works on Sundays il travaille même le dimanche; ~ the teacher laughed même le professeur a ri, le professeur lui-même a ri; she's ~ forgotten his name elle a oublié jusqu'à son nom; he ~ said so il a été jusqu'à le dire, il l'a même dit; without ~ apologizing sans même OR sans seulement s'excuser; he can't ~ walk il ne peut même pas marcher; not ~ même pas. -**2.** (*with comparative*) [still] encore; ~ better encore mieux; ~ more tired encore plus fatigué; you know ~ less than I do vous en savez encore moins que moi. -**3.** [qualifying]: he seemed indifferent, ~ hostile il avait l'air indifférent, hostile même.
◇ *vt* égaliser, aplanir.
◇ *vi* s'égaliser, s'aplanir.
◆ **even as** *conj phr* -**1.** *fml* [at the very moment that] au moment même où; ~ as we speak au moment même où nous parlons. -**2.** *lit* OR *arch* [just as] comme; it came to pass ~ as he had foretold tout arriva comme il l'avait prédit.
◆ **even if** *conj phr* même si; ~ if I say so myself sans fausse modestie; ~ if he did say that, what does it matter? et même s'il a dit ça, quelle importance est-ce que ça a?
◆ **even now** *adv phr* -**1.** [despite what happened before] même maintenant. -**2.** *lit* [at this very moment] en ce moment même.
◆ **even so** *adv phr* [nevertheless] quand même, pourtant; yes, but ~ so oui, mais quand même.
◆ **even then** *adv phr* -**1.** [in that case also] quand même; but ~ then we wouldn't be able to afford it mais nous ne pourrions quand même pas nous le permettre. -**2.** [at that time also] même à ce moment-là; things were difficult enough ~ then les choses étaient assez difficiles même à ce moment-là.
◆ **even though** *conj phr*: ~ though he tries malgré ses efforts; ~ though she explained it in detail bien qu'elle l'ait expliqué en détail.
◆ **even with** *prep phr* même avec, malgré.
◆ **even out** ◇ *vt sep* [surface] égaliser, aplanir; [prices] égaliser; [supply] répartir OR distribuer plus également.
◇ *vi insep* [road] s'égaliser, s'aplanir; [prices] s'égaliser; [supply] être réparti plus également.
◆ **even up** *vt sep* égaliser; to ~ things up rétablir l'équilibre.
even[2] [ˈiːvn] *n arch* & *lit* [evening] soir *m.*
even-handed *adj* équitable, impartial.
even-handedly [-ˈhændɪdlɪ] *adv* équitablement, impartialement.
evening [ˈiːvnɪŋ] ◇ *n* -**1.** [part of day] soir *m*; (good) ~! bonsoir!; in the ~ le soir; we went out in the ~ nous sommes sortis le soir; it is 8 o'clock in the ~ il est 8 h du soir; I'm hardly ever at home ~s *Am* OR in the ~ *Br* je suis rarement chez moi le soir; this ~ ce soir; that ~ ce soir-là; tomorrow ~ demain soir; on the ~ of the next day, on the following ~ le lendemain soir, le soir suivant; on the ~ of the fifteenth le quinze au soir; on the ~ of her departure le soir de son départ; one fine spring ~ (par) un beau soir de printemps; every ~ tous les soirs, chaque soir; every Friday ~ tous les vendredis soir OR soirs; the long winter ~s les longues soirées OR veillées d'hiver; I work ~s je travaille le soir; we've had several ~s out this week nous sommes sortis plusieurs soirs cette semaine; in the ~ of her life *fig* au soir OR au déclin de sa vie. -**2.** [length of time] soirée *f*; all ~ toute la soirée; we spent the ~ playing cards nous avons passé la soirée à jouer aux cartes. -**3.** [entertainment] soirée *f*; a musical ~ une soirée musicale.
◇ *comp* [newspaper, train] du soir; the ~ performance starts at 7.30 en soirée la représentation débute à 19 h 30; she's going to an ~ performance of the ballet elle va voir le ballet en soirée; ~ prayers/service RELIG office *m*/service *m* du soir; an ~ match SPORT une nocturne ❑ the Evening Standard PRESS *quotidien populaire londonien de tendance conservatrice.*
evening class *n* cours *m* du soir.
evening dress *n* [for men] tenue *f* de soirée, habit *m*; [for women] robe *f* du soir; in ~ [man] en tenue de soirée; [woman] en robe du soir, en toilette de soirée.
evening primrose *n* onagre *f*, herbe *f* aux ânes; ~ oil huile *f* d'onagre.
evening star *n* étoile *f* du berger.
evening wear *n* (*U*) = **evening dress**.
evenly [ˈiːvnlɪ] *adv* -**1.** [breathe, move] régulièrement; [talk] calmement, posément. -**2.** [equally - divide] également, de façon égale; [- spread] de façon égale, régulièrement; they are ~ matched ils sont de force égale.
evenness [ˈiːvnnɪs] *n* -**1.** [of surface] égalité *f*, caractère *m* lisse. -**2.** [of competition, movement] régularité *f.*
evens *Br* [ˈiːvənz], **even odds** *Am* ◇ *npl*: to lay ~ donner à égalité.
◇ *comp*: ~ favorite favori *m*, -ite *f* à égalité.
evensong [ˈiːvnsɒŋ] *n* [Anglican] office *m* du soir; [Roman Catholic] vêpres *fpl.*
event [ɪˈvent] *n* -**1.** [happening] événement *m*; a historical ~ un événement historique; the course of ~s la suite des événements, le déroulement des faits; in the course of ~s par la suite, au cours des événements; in the normal course of ~s normalement; I realized after the ~ j'ai réalisé après coup; the party was quite an ~ la soirée était un véritable événement. -**2.** [organized activity] manifestation *f*; the society organizes a number of social ~s l'association organise un certain nombre de soirées OR de rencontres. -**3.** SPORT [meeting] manifestation *f*; [competition] épreuve *f*; [in

horseracing] course *f*; field ~s épreuves d'athlétisme; track ~s épreuves sur piste; the sponsoring of sports ~s la sponsorisation des manifestations sportives.
◆ **at all events, in any event** *adv phr* en tout cas, de toute façon.
◆ **in either event** *adv phr* dans l'un ou l'autre cas.
◆ **in the event** *adv phr* en fait, en l'occurence; a result that in the ~ was most satisfying un résultat qui était en fait très satisfaisant.
◆ **in the event of** *prep phr*: in the ~ of rain en cas de pluie; in the ~ of her refusing au cas où OR dans le cas où elle refuserait.
◆ **in the event that** *conj phr* au cas où; in the unlikely ~ that he comes au cas OR dans le cas fort improbable où il viendrait.

even-tempered *adj* d'humeur égale.

eventful [ɪ'ventfʊl] *adj* -**1.** [busy - day, holiday, life] mouvementé, fertile en événements. -**2.** [important] mémorable, très important.

eventide ['iːvntaɪd] *n lit* soir *m*, tombée *f* du jour; ~ home *euph* résidence *f* de retraite.

eventing [ɪ'ventɪŋ] *n participation à toutes les épreuves d'un concours hippique*.

eventual [ɪ'ventʃʊəl] *adj* [final] final, ultime; [resulting] qui s'ensuit; bad management led to the ~ collapse of the company une mauvaise gestion a finalement provoqué la faillite de l'entreprise; the disease causes deterioration of the muscles and ~ paralysis la maladie entraîne la dégénérescence des muscles et la paralysie qui en résulte OR qui s'ensuit.

eventuality [ɪ,ventʃʊ'ælətɪ] (*pl* eventualities) *n* éventualité *f*.

eventually [ɪ'ventʃʊəlɪ] *adv* finalement, en fin de compte; I'll get around to it ~ je le ferai un jour ou l'autre; she ~ became a lawyer elle a fini par devenir avocat; the people who will ~ benefit from these changes les personnes qui, en fin de compte OR en définitive, bénéficieront de ces changements; our arguments ~ persuaded him nos arguments ont fini par le convaincre OR l'ont finalement convaincu; ~, I decided to give up pour finir OR en fin de compte, j'ai décidé d'abandonner, j'ai finalement décidé d'abandonner.

eventuate [ɪ'ventʃʊeɪt] *vi fml* arriver, se produire; his illness ~d in death sa maladie a fini par l'emporter.

ever ['evəʳ] *adv* -**1.** [always] toujours; ~ more important de plus en plus important; ~-increasing influence influence toujours croissante OR qui croît de jour en jour; an ~-present fear une peur constante; ~ hopeful/the pessimist, he... toujours plein d'espoir/pessimiste, il...; yours ~, ~ yours [in letter] amicalement vôtre. -**2.** [at any time] jamais; have you ~ met him? l'avez-vous jamais rencontré?; do you ~ meet him? est-ce qu'il vous arrive (jamais) de le rencontrer?; nothing ~ happens il n'arrive OR ne se passe jamais rien; all they ~ do is work ils ne font que travailler; he hardly OR scarcely ~ smokes il ne fume presque jamais; don't ~ come in here again! ne mettez plus jamais les pieds ici! || *(with comparatives)*: lovelier/more slowly than ~ plus joli/plus lentement que jamais; he's as sarcastic as ~ il est toujours aussi sarcastique || *(with superlatives)*: the first/biggest ~ le tout premier/plus grand qu'on ait jamais vu; she's my best friend ~ c'est la meilleure amie que j'aie jamais eue; the worst earthquake ~ le pire tremblement de terre qu'on ait jamais connu; the best vacation we've ~ had les meilleures vacances qu'on ait jamais eues. -**3.** *inf* [in exclamations]: is it ~ big! *Am* comme c'est grand!; was he ~ angry! *Am* qu'est-ce qu'il était furax!; do you enjoy dancing? – do I ~! *Am* aimez-vous danser? – et comment! ❑ well, did you ~! ça, par exemple! -**4.** [as intensifier]: as quickly as ~ you can aussi vite que vous pourrez; as soon as ~ she comes aussitôt OR dès qu'elle sera là; before ~ they OR before they ~ set out avant même qu'ils partent || [in questions]: how ~ did you manage that? comment donc y êtes-vous parvenu?; what ~ is the matter with you? mais qu'est-ce que vous avez donc?; when will they ~ stop? quand donc arrêteront-ils?; where ~ can it be? où diable peut-il être?; who ~ can it be? qui est-ce que ça peut bien être?; why ~ not? mais enfin, pourquoi pas?
◆ **ever after** *adv phr* pour toujours; they lived happily ~ after ils vécurent heureux jusqu'à la fin de leurs jours.
◆ **ever since** ◇ *conj phr* depuis que.
◇ *prep phr* depuis.
◇ *adv phr* depuis lors, depuis ce moment-là; I've been afraid of driving ~ since depuis lors OR depuis ce moment-là, j'ai peur de conduire.
◆ **ever so** *adv phr* -**1.** *inf* [extremely] vraiment; she's ~ so clever elle est vraiment intelligente; it's ~ so kind of you c'est vraiment aimable à vous; ~ so slightly off-centre un tout petit peu décentré; thanks ~ so (much) merci vraiment. -**2.** *fml* [however]: no teacher, be he ~ so patient... aucun enseignant, aussi patient soit-il...
◆ **ever such** *inf det phr* vraiment; they've got ~ such pretty curtains in the shop ils ont vraiment de jolis rideaux dans ce magasin; it's ~ such a shame c'est vraiment dommage.

Everest ['evərɪst] *pr n*: (Mount) ~ le mont Everest, l'Everest *m*; it was his ~ [goal] c'était son but ultime; [achievement] c'était sa plus grande réussite.

Everglades ['evəgleɪdz] *pl pr n*: the ~ les Everglades *mpl*; the ~ National Park le Parc national des Everglades.

evergreen ['evəgriːn] ◇ *n* -**1.** [tree] arbre *m* à feuilles persistantes; [conifer] conifère *m*; [bush] arbuste *m* à feuilles persistantes. -**2.** *fig* [song, story] chanson *f* OR histoire *f* qui ne vieillit jamais.
◇ *adj* -**1.** [bush, tree] à feuilles persistantes; the Evergreen State *Am* le Washington. -**2.** *fig* [song, story] qui ne vieillit pas.

everlasting [,evə'lɑːstɪŋ] *adj* -**1.** [eternal - hope, mercy] éternel, infini; [- fame] éternel, immortel; [- God, life] éternel. -**2.** [incessant] perpétuel, éternel; a life of ~ misery une vie de misère.

everlastingly [,evə'lɑːstɪŋlɪ] *adv* -**1.** [eternally] éternellement. -**2.** [incessantly] sans cesse, perpétuellement.

evermore [,evə'mɔːʳ] *adv* toujours; for ~ pour toujours, à jamais.

every ['evrɪ] *det* -**1.** [each] tout, chaque; ~ room has a view of the sea les chambres ont toutes vue OR toutes les chambres ont vue sur la mer; not ~ room is as big as this toutes les chambres ne sont pas aussi grandes que celle-ci; ~ word he says tout ce qu'il dit; he drank ~ drop il a bu jusqu'à la dernière goutte; ~ one of these apples chacune de OR toutes ces pommes; I've read ~ one je les ai lus tous; ~ one of them arrived late ils sont tous arrivés en retard; ~ (single) one of us was there nous étions tous là (au grand complet); ~ (single) one of these pencils is broken tous ces crayons (sans exception) sont cassés; ~ (single) person in the room tous ceux qui étaient dans la pièce (sans exception); ~ day tous les jours, chaque jour; she's feeling a little better ~ day elle se sent un peu mieux chaque jour; ~ time I go out chaque fois que je sors; that's what fools them ~ time c'est ce qui les trompe à tous les coups OR à chaque fois; of ~ age/~ sort/~ colour de tout âge/toute sorte/toutes les couleurs; in ~ way [by any means] par tous les moyens; [from any viewpoint] à tous (les) égards, sous tous les rapports ❑ ~ little helps *prov* les petits ruisseaux font les grandes rivières *prov*. -**2.** [with units of time, measurement etc] tout; ~ two days, ~ second day, ~ other day tous les deux jours, un jour sur deux; ~ quarter of an hour tous les quarts d'heure; ~ few days tous les deux ou trois jours; ~ few minutes toutes les cinq minutes; once ~ month une fois par mois; ~ 10 miles tous les 10 miles; ~ third man un homme sur trois; three women out of OR in ~ ten, three out of ~ ten women trois femmes sur dix ❑ ~ other Sunday un dimanche sur deux; write on ~ other lin[e] écrivez en sautant une ligne sur deux. -**3.** [indicating confidence, optimism] tout; I have ~ confidence that... je ne doute pas un instan[t] que...; there's ~ chance that we'll succee[d] nous avons toutes les chances de réussir; yo[u] have ~ reason to be happy vous avez toute[s] les raisons OR tout lieu d'être heureux; we wis[h] you ~ success nous vous souhaitons trè[s] bonne chance. -**4.** [with possessive adj] chacun[,] moindre; his ~ action bears witness to [his...] chacun de ses gestes OR tout ce qu'il fait e[n] témoigne; her ~ wish son moindre désir, tou[s] ses désirs.
◆ **every now and again, every once in** [**a**] **while, every so often** *adv phr* de temps e[n] temps, de temps à autre.
◆ **every which way** *adv phr Am* [everywhere] partout; [from all sides] de toutes parts; he cam[e] home with his hair ~ which way il est rentr[é] les cheveux en bataille.

everybody ['evrɪ,bɒdɪ] = **everyone**.

everyday ['evrɪdeɪ] *adj* -**1.** [daily] de tous le[s] jours, quotidien; my ~ routine mon train-trai[n] quotidien; ~ life la vie de tous les jour[s]. -**2.** [ordinary] banal, ordinaire; an ~ expressio[n] une expression courante; in ~ use d'usag[e] courant; it's not an ~ experience on ne vit pa[s] ça tous les jours.

Everyman ['evrɪmæn] *n* l'homme *m* de la ru[e].

everyone ['evrɪwʌn] *pron* tout le monde, ch[a]cun; as ~ knows comme chacun OR tout l[e] monde le sait; ~ knows that! tout le monde c[onnaît ça] n'importe qui sait cela!; ~ here/in this roo[m] tout le monde ici/dans cette pièce; ~ else tou[s] les autres; in a small town where ~ knows ~ (else) dans une petite ville où tout le monde s[e] connaît ❑ ~ who was anyone was there tou[s] les gens qui comptent étaient là.

everyplace ['evrɪ,pleɪs] *adv Am* = **everywher[e]**.

everything ['evrɪθɪŋ] *pron* -**1.** [all things] tou[t]; ~ he says tout ce qu'il dit; they sell ~ i[ls] vendent de tout; she means ~ to me elle e[st] tout pour moi, je ne vis que pour elle; you ca[n] have ~ you ever wanted tu peux avoir tout c[e] que tu as toujours voulu ❑ a party wit[h] clowns, cakes and ~ *inf* une fête avec de[s] clowns, des gâteaux et tout. -**2.** [the most important thing] l'essentiel *m*; winning is ~ l'e[s]sentiel, c'est de gagner; beauty/money isn't ~ il n'y a pas que la beauté/l'argent qui compt[e].

everywhere ['evrɪweəʳ] ◇ *adv* partout; [I] looked for it ~ je l'ai cherché partout; ~ sh[e] went partout où elle allait; cash dispensers a[re] ~ these days on trouve des distributeurs (d[e] billets) partout de nos jours; he's been ~ il e[st] allé partout ❑ the card indexes were ~ *inf* [in] complete disorder] les cartes étaient rangé[es] n'importe comment.
◇ *pron inf* tout; ~'s in such a mess tout e[st] sens dessus dessous.

evict [ɪ'vɪkt] *vt* -**1.** [person] expulser, chasse[r]. -**2.** [property] récupérer par moyens juridique[s].

eviction [ɪ'vɪkʃn] *n* expulsion *f*; an ~ notice u[n] mandat d'expulsion.

evidence ['evɪdəns] ◇ *n* -**1.** [proof] évidence[,] preuve *f*; [testimony] témoignage *m*; we ha[ve] clear ~ that... on a la preuve manifeste que... on the ~ of eye witnesses à en croire l[es] témoins. -**2.** JUR [proof] preuve *f*; [testimon[y]] témoignage *m*; to give ~ against/for sb témo[i]gner contre/en faveur de qqn; her statement being held in ~ sa déposition fait partie d[es] témoignages; the ~ is against him les preuv[es] pèsent contre lui ❑ to turn King's OR Queen['s] ~ *Br*, to turn State's ~ *Am* témoigner cont[re] ses complices. -**3.** [indication] signe *m*, marque[;] the building bears ~ of recent habitation [il] apparaît clairement que l'immeuble était e[n]core occupé récemment; her face showed n[o] ~ of her anger son visage ne témoignait pas [de] OR ne trahissait pas sa colère; to be in ~ [pe]rson]: his daughter was not in ~ sa fille n'ét[ait] pas là OR n'était pas présente; a politician ve much in ~ these days un politicien très en vue ces temps-ci.

◇ *vt* manifester, montrer.

evident ['evɪdənt] *adj* évident, manifeste; **with ~ pleasure** avec un plaisir manifeste; **it is ~ from the way she talks** cela se voit à sa manière de parler; **it is quite ~ that he's not interested** on voit bien qu'il ne s'y intéresse pas, il ne s'y intéresse pas, c'est évident; **he's lying, that's ~** il ment, c'est évident.

evidently ['evɪdəntlɪ] *adv* **-1.** [apparently] apparemment; **did he refuse? — ~** not a-t-il refusé? — non apparemment OR à ce qu'il paraît; **unemployment is ~ rising again** de toute évidence le chômage est à nouveau en hausse. **-2.** [clearly] évidemment, manifestement; **he was ~ in pain** il était évident OR clair qu'il souffrait.

evil ['iːvl] (*Br compar* **eviller**, *superl* **evillest**, *Am compar* **eviler**, *superl* **evilest**) ◇ *adj* **-1.** [wicked - person] malveillant, méchant; [- deed, plan, reputation] mauvais; [- influence] néfaste; [- doctrine, spell, spirit] malfaisant; **he's in an ~ mood** il est d'une humeur massacrante; **she has an ~ temper** elle a un sale caractère OR un caractère de chien ❑ **the Evil One** le Malin. **-2.** [smell, taste] infect, infâme.

◇ *n* mal *m*; **to speak ~ of sb** dire du mal de qqn; **I wish her no ~** je ne lui veux pas de mal; **social ~s** plaies sociales, maux sociaux; **the ~s of drink** les conséquences *fpl* funestes de la boisson; **a necessary ~** un mal nécessaire; **pollution is one of the ~s of our era** la pollution est un fléau de notre époque; **it's the lesser ~ OR of two ~s** c'est le moindre mal.

evildoer [,iːvl'duːəʳ] *n* méchant *m*, -e *f*, scélérat *m*, -e *f*.

evil eye *n*: **the ~** le mauvais œil; **to give sb the ~** jeter le mauvais œil à qqn; **to ward off the ~** se protéger du mauvais œil.

evil-looking *adj* [person] qui a l'air mauvais; [weapon] menaçant.

evilly ['iːvəlɪ] *adv* avec malveillance.

evil-minded *adj* malveillant, mal intentionné.

evil-smelling *adj* nauséabond.

evince [ɪ'vɪns] *vt fml* [show - interest, surprise] manifester, montrer; [- quality] faire preuve de, manifester.

eviscerate [ɪ'vɪsəreɪt] *vt* éventrer, étriper; MED éviscérer.

evocation [,evəʊ'keɪʃn] *n* évocation *f*.

evocative [ɪ'vɒkətɪv] *adj* **-1.** [picture, scent] évocateur. **-2.** [magic] évocatoire.

evoke [ɪ'vəʊk] *vt* **-1.** [summon up - memory, spirit] évoquer. **-2.** [elicit - admiration] susciter; [- response, smile] susciter, provoquer.

evolution [,iːvə'luːʃn] *n* **-1.** [of language, situation] évolution *f*; [of art, society, technology] développement *m*, évolution *f*; [of events] développement *m*, déroulement *m*. **-2.** BIOL, BOT & ZOOL évolution *f*. **-3.** [of dancers, troops] évolution *f*. **-4.** MATH extraction *f* (de la racine).

evolutionary [,iːvə'luːʃnərɪ] *adj* évolutionniste.

evolutionism [,iːvə'luːʃənɪzm] *n* évolutionnisme *m*.

evolutionist [,iːvə'luːʃənɪst] ◇ *adj* évolutionniste.

◇ *n* évolutionniste *mf*.

evolve [ɪ'vɒlv] ◇ *vi* évoluer, se développer; BIOL, BOT & ZOOL évoluer; **to ~ from sthg** se développer à partir de qqch; **the theory has ~d over the years** la théorie a évolué au fil des années.

◇ *vt* [system, theory] développer, élaborer.

ewe [juː] *n* brebis *f*; **a ~ lamb** une agnelle.

ewer ['juːəʳ] *n* aiguière *f*.

ex [eks] ◇ *prep* **-1.** COMM départ, sortie; **price ~ works** prix *m* départ OR sortie usine. **-2.** FIN sans; **~ interest** sans OR exonéré d'intérêts.

◇ *n* [gen] ex *mf*; [husband] ex-mari *m*; [wife] ex-femme *f*; **my ~** [girlfriend] mon ancienne petite amie; [boyfriend] mon ancien petit ami.

ex- *in cpds* ex-, ancien; **his ~wife** son ex-femme; **he's an ~teacher** c'est un ancien enseignant; **the ~president** l'ancien président, l'ex-président.

exacerbate [ɪg'zæsəbeɪt] *vt fml* **-1.** [make worse] exacerber, aggraver. **-2.** [annoy] énerver, exaspérer.

exact [ɪg'zækt] ◇ *adj* **-1.** [accurate, correct] exact, juste; **it's an ~ copy** [picture] c'est fidèle à l'original; [document] c'est une copie conforme OR textuelle; **she told me the ~ opposite** elle m'a dit exactement le contraire; **that's the ~ problem** c'est précisément le problème; **those were her ~ words** ce furent ses propres paroles, voilà ce qu'elle a dit textuellement. **-2.** [precise - amount, idea, value] exact, précis; [- directions, place, time] précis; **is it 5 o'clock? — 5:03 to be ~** est-il 5 h? — 5 h 03 plus exactement OR précisément; **I'm 35 and 2 days to be ~** j'ai exactement 35 ans et 2 jours; **she likes music, or to be ~, classical music** elle aime la musique, ou plus précisément la musique classique; **can you be more ~?** pouvez-vous préciser?; **we need ~ details** il nous faut des précisions. **-3.** [meticulous - work] rigoureux, précis; [- mind] rigoureux; [- science] exact; [- instrument] de précision.

◇ *vt* **-1.** [demand - money] extorquer. **-2.** [insist upon] exiger.

exacting [ɪg'zæktɪŋ] *adj* [person] exigeant; [activity, job] astreignant, exigeant.

exaction [ɪg'zækʃn] *n* **-1.** [act] exaction *f*, extorsion *f*. **-2.** [money] paiement *m*. **-3.** [demand] extorsion *f*, exigence *f*.

exactitude [ɪg'zæktɪtjuːd] *n* exactitude *f*.

exactly [ɪg'zæktlɪ] *adv* **-1.** [accurately] précisément, avec précision; **I followed her instructions ~** j'ai suivi ses instructions à la lettre OR avec précision; **the computer can reproduce this sound ~** l'ordinateur peut reproduire exactement ce son. **-2.** [entirely, precisely] exactement, justement; **I don't remember ~** je ne me rappelle pas au juste; **that's not ~ what I meant** ce n'est pas exactement ce que je voulais dire; **he did ~ the opposite of what I told him** il a fait exactement le contraire de ce que je lui ai dit; **it's ~ the same thing** c'est exactement la même chose; **it's ~ 5 o'clock** il est 5 h juste; **it's been six months ~** cela fait six mois jour pour jour; **the journey took ~ three hours** le voyage a duré très exactement trois heures; **are you ill? — not ~** êtes-vous malade? — pas exactement OR pas vraiment; **he's not ~ poor** il n'est pas exactement (ce que l'on appelle) pauvre; **~!** exactement!, parfaitement!

exactness [ɪg'zæktnɪs] *n* exactitude *f*, soin *m*.

exaggerate [ɪg'zædʒəreɪt] ◇ *vi* exagérer; **don't ~!** n'exagère pas!; **she always ~s** elle exagère toujours.

◇ *vt* **-1.** [overstate - quality, situation, size] exagérer; [- facts] amplifier; [- importance] s'exagérer; **he is exaggerating the seriousness of the problem** il s'exagère la gravité du problème. **-2.** [emphasize] accentuer; **she ~s her weakness to gain sympathy** elle se prétend plus faible qu'elle ne l'est réellement pour s'attirer la compassion; **tight trousers will ~ your thinness** des pantalons serrés accentueront ta minceur OR te feront paraître encore plus mince.

exaggerated [ɪg'zædʒəreɪtɪd] *adj* **-1.** [number, story] exagéré; [fashion, style] outré; **to have an ~ opinion of o.s. OR of one's own worth** avoir une trop haute opinion de soi-même. **-2.** MED exagéré.

exaggeratedly [ɪg'zædʒəreɪtɪdlɪ] *adv* d'une manière exagérée, exagérément.

exaggeration [ɪg,zædʒə'reɪʃn] *n* exagération *f*.

exalt [ɪg'zɔːlt] *vt* **-1.** [praise highly] exalter, chanter les louanges de. **-2.** [in rank] élever (à un rang plus important).

exaltation [,egzɔːl'teɪʃn] *n* (*U*) **-1.** [praise] louange *f*, louanges *fpl*, exaltation *f*. **-2.** [elation] exultation *f*, exaltation *f*.

exalted [ɪg'zɔːltɪd] *adj* **-1.** [prominent - person] de haut rang, haut placé; [- position, rank] élevé. **-2.** [elated] exalté, passionné.

exam [ɪg'zæm] (*abbr of* examination) ◇ *n*: **to sit OR to take an ~** passer un examen; **to pass/to fail an ~** réussir à/échouer à un examen; **~ board** commission *f* d'examen.

◇ *comp* d'examen; **~ nerves** trac *m* des examens; **when do the ~ results come out?** quand les résultats de l'examen seront-ils connus?; **~ paper** [set of questions] sujet *m* d'examen; [written answer] copie *f* (d'examen).

examination [ɪg,zæmɪ'neɪʃn] ◇ *n* **-1.** [of records, proposal etc] examen *m*; [of building - by official] inspection *f*; [- by potential buyer] visite *f*; **it doesn't stand up to ~** [argument, theory] cela ne résiste pas à l'examen; [alibi] cela ne tient pas; **to carry out OR to make an ~ of sthg** procéder à l'examen de qqch; **her latest novel is an ~ of the generation gap** son dernier roman est une analyse du fossé entre les générations; **the device was removed for ~** on a enlevé le mécanisme afin de l'examiner; **on ~** après examen; **the proposal is still under ~** la proposition est encore à l'étude. **-2.** MED examen *m* médical; [at school, work] visite *f* médicale; [regular] bilan *m* de santé; **I'm just going in for an ~** j'y vais juste pour passer un examen médical. **-3.** *fml*, SCH & UNIV examen *m*. **-4.** JUR [of witness] audition *f*; [of suspect] interrogatoire *m*.

◇ *comp* [question, results] d'examen.

examine [ɪg'zæmɪn] *vt* **-1.** [records, proposal etc] examiner, étudier; [building] inspecter; **the weapon is being ~d for fingerprints** on est en train d'examiner l'arme pour voir si elle porte des empreintes digitales. **-2.** MED examiner. **-3.** SCH & UNIV faire passer un examen à; **you'll be ~d in French/in all six subjects/on your knowledge of the subject** vous aurez à passer un examen de français/dans ces six matières/pour évaluer vos connaissances sur le sujet. **-4.** JUR [witness] entendre; [suspect] interroger.

examinee [ɪg,zæmɪ'niː] *n* candidat *m*, -e *f* (*à un examen*).

examiner [ɪg'zæmɪnəʳ] *n* [in school, driving test] examinateur *m*, -trice *f*; **the ~s** SCH & UNIV les examinateurs, le jury.

examining body [ɪg'zæmɪnɪŋ-] *n* jury *m* d'examen.

examining magistrate *n Br* JUR juge *m* d'instruction.

example [ɪg'zɑːmpl] *n* **-1.** [illustration] exemple *m*; **can you give us an ~?** pouvez-vous nous donner un exemple?; **to mention just a few ~s** pour ne citer que quelques exemples; **this is an excellent ~ of what I meant** ceci illustre parfaitement ce que je voulais dire; **it's a classic ~ of 1960's architecture** c'est un exemple classique de l'architecture des années 60. **-2.** [person or action to be imitated] exemple *m*, modèle *m*; **you're an ~ to us all** vous êtes un modèle pour nous tous; **to follow sb's ~** suivre l'exemple de qqn; **I followed your ~ and complained about the poor service** j'ai fait comme vous et me suis plaint de la médiocrité du service; **following France's ~, Britain has introduced sanctions** à l'exemple OR à l'instar de la France, la Grande-Bretagne a pris des sanctions; **to set an ~** montrer l'exemple; **she sets us all an ~** elle nous montre l'exemple à tous; **to set a good/bad ~** montrer le bon/mauvais exemple; **you're setting your little brother a bad ~** tu montres le mauvais exemple à ton petit frère; **my mother's always holding my cousin up as an ~** ma mère cite tout le temps mon cousin en exemple. **-3.** [sample, specimen] exemple *m*, spécimen *m*; [of work] échantillon *m*. **-4.** [warning] exemple *m*; **let this be an ~ to you** que ça te serve d'exemple; **to make an ~ of sb** faire un exemple du cas de qqn.

◆ **for example** *adv phr* par exemple.

exarch ['eksɑːk] *n* RELIG exarque *m*.

exasperate [ɪg'zæspəreɪt] *vt* [irritate] exaspérer; **her father was so ~d with her that he lost his temper** elle a tellement exaspéré son père que celui-ci s'est mis en colère.

exasperating [ɪg'zæspəreɪtɪŋ] *adj* [person, situation] exaspérant; **it's been an ~ day** j'ai passé une journée exaspérante.

exasperatingly [ɪg'zæspəreɪtɪŋlɪ] *adv*: **the service is ~ slow in this restaurant** le service est d'une lenteur exaspérante OR désespérante dans ce restaurant; **he's ~ arrogant** son arrogance est exaspérante.

exasperation [ɪg,zæspə'reɪʃn] *n* [irritation, frustration] exaspération *f*; **to look at sb in ~** regarder qqn avec exaspération OR un air exaspéré; **she was nearly weeping with** OR **from ~** elle pleurait presque d'exaspération; **I did it out of sheer ~** j'ai fait cela parce que j'étais exaspéré OR je n'en pouvais plus.

ex cathedra [ekskə'θiːdrə] *adj & adv* ex cathedra.

excavate ['ekskəveɪt] *vt* -**1.** [hole, trench] creuser, excaver. -**2.** ARCHEOL [temple, building] mettre au jour; **to ~ a site** faire des fouilles sur un site.

excavation [,ekskə'veɪʃn] *n* -**1.** [of hole, trench] excavation *f*, creusement *m*. -**2.** ARCHEOL [of temple, building] mise *f* au jour; **the ~s at Knossos** les fouilles *fpl* de Knossos.

excavator ['ekskəveɪtə[r]] *n* -**1.** [machine] excavateur *m*, excavatrice *f*. -**2.** [archaeologist] personne qui conduit des fouilles.

exceed [ɪk'siːd] *vt* -**1.** [be more than] dépasser, excéder; **her salary ~s mine by £5,000 a year** son salaire annuel dépasse le mien de 5 000 livres. -**2.** [go beyond - expectations, fears] dépasser; [- budget] excéder, déborder; **to ~ one's authority** outrepasser ses pouvoirs; **to ~ the speed limit** dépasser la limite de vitesse, faire un excès de vitesse; **to be fined for ~ing the speed limit** avoir une amende pour excès de vitesse.

exceeding [ɪk'siːdɪŋ] *arch* = **exceedingly**.

exceedingly [ɪk'siːdɪŋlɪ] *adv* [extremely] extrêmement.

excel [ɪk'sel] (*pt & pp* **excelled**) ◇ *vi* exceller; **this is a field where Scots ~** c'est un domaine où les Écossais excellent; **to ~ at** OR **in music** exceller en musique; **I've never excelled at games** je n'ai jamais été très fort en sport; **the company ~s in the export field** la société excelle dans l'exportation; **the company doesn't exactly ~ at after-sales service** *hum* le service après-vente n'est pas vraiment le point fort de la société.

◇ *vt* surpasser; **to ~ o.s.** *literal* OR *iron* se surpasser; **you've really excelled yourself this time!** tu t'es vraiment surpassé cette fois-ci!

excellence ['eksələns] *n* [high quality] qualité *f* excellente; [commercially] excellence *f*; **a prize for general ~** SCH un prix d'excellence; **to strive for ~** s'efforcer d'atteindre une qualité excellente; **~ is our hallmark** l'excellence est notre signe distinctif; **awards for ~** prix d'excellence ❑ **centre of ~** centre *m* d'excellence.

Excellency ['eksələnsɪ] (*pl* **Excellencies**) *n* Excellence *f*; **Your/His ~** Votre/Son Excellence.

excellent ['eksələnt] *adj* excellent; [weather] magnifique; **~!** formidable!, parfait!

excellently ['eksələntlɪ] *adv* de façon excellente, superbement; **it was ~ done** cela a été fait de main de maître.

Excelsior® [ek'selsɪɔː[r]] *n* (*U*) *Am* copeaux *mpl* de bois.

except [ɪk'sept] ◇ *prep* [apart from] à part, excepté, sauf; **everybody was there ~ him, everybody ~ him was there** tout le monde était là à part OR excepté OR sauf lui; **~ weekends** à part OR excepté OR sauf le week-end; **any day ~ Saturday and anywhere ~ here** n'importe quel jour sauf le samedi et n'importe où sauf ici; **I know nothing about it ~ what he told me** je ne sais rien d'autre que ce qu'il m'a raconté; **I remember nothing ~ that I was scared** je ne me souviens de rien sauf que OR excepté que j'avais peur.

◇ *conj* -**1.** [apart from]: **I'll do anything ~ sell the car** je ferai tout sauf vendre la voiture; **~ if** sauf OR à part si; **~ when** sauf OR à part quand. -**2.** [only] seulement, mais; **I would tell her ~ she wouldn't believe me** je le lui dirais bien, mais OR seulement elle ne me croirait pas; **we would stay longer ~ (that) we have no more money** nous resterions bien plus longtemps, mais OR seulement nous n'avons plus d'argent. -**3.** *arch* OR BIBLE [unless] à moins que.

◇ *vt* [exclude] excepter, exclure; **all countries, France ~ed** tous les pays, la France exceptée OR à l'exception de la France; **present company ~ed** à l'exception des personnes présentes, les personnes présentes exceptées.

◆ **except for** *prep phr* sauf, à part; **the typing's finished ~ for the last page** il ne reste plus que la dernière page à taper; **the office will be empty over Christmas ~ for the boss and me** il n'y aura que le patron et moi au bureau au moment de Noël; **he would have got away with it ~ for that one mistake** sans cette erreur il s'en serait tiré.

excepting [ɪk'septɪŋ] ◇ *prep* à part, excepté, sauf; **not ~ ...** y compris; **always ~ really outstanding candidates** à l'exception OR en dehors des candidats vraiment brillants.

◇ *conj arch* = **unless**.

exception [ɪk'sepʃn] *n* -**1.** [deviation, exemption] exception *f*; **the ~ proves the rule** l'exception confirme la règle; **I'll make an ~ this time/in your case** je ferai une exception cette fois/dans votre cas; **without ~** sans exception; **but she's an ~** mais elle n'est pas comme les autres; **the only ~ being Britain, Britain being the only ~** la seule exception étant la Grande-Bretagne; **with the ~ of Daniel** à l'exception de Daniel; **and you're no ~** et cela te concerne aussi; **all Western countries are feeling the effects of the oil crisis, and Britain is no ~** tous les pays occidentaux ressentent les effets de la crise pétrolière, et la Grande-Bretagne n'est pas épargnée. -**2.** *phr*: **to take ~ to sthg** s'offenser OR s'offusquer de qqch, être outré par qqch; **I take ~ to that remark** je suis outré par cette remarque; **he takes ~ to being kept waiting** il n'aime pas du tout qu'on le fasse attendre.

exceptionable [ɪk'sepʃnəbl] *adj* [objectionable] offensant, outrageant.

exceptional [ɪk'sepʃənl] *adj* exceptionnel; **in ~ circumstances** dans des circonstances exceptionnelles; **these are ~ times we live in** nous vivons une époque exceptionnelle.

exceptionally [ɪk'sepʃnəlɪ] *adv* exceptionnellement; **that's ~ kind of you** c'est extrêmement gentil de votre part; **~, some companies prefer to recruit people over 40** il y a des cas exceptionnels de sociétés qui préfèrent recruter des gens de plus de 40 ans; **she's an ~ bright child** c'est une enfant d'une intelligence exceptionnelle.

excerpt ['eksɜːpt] *n* [extract] extrait *m*; **an ~ from sthg** un extrait de qqch.

excess [*n* ɪk'ses, *adj* 'ekses] ◇ *n* -**1.** [unreasonable amount] excès *m*; **an ~ of salt/fat in the diet** un excès de sel/de graisses dans l'alimentation. -**2.** [difference between two amounts] supplément *m*, surplus *m*; [in insurance] franchise *f*. -**3.** [over-indulgence] excès *m*; **a life of ~** une vie d'excès. -**4.** (*usu pl*) [unacceptable action] excès *m*, abus *m*; **the ~es of the occupying troops** les excès OR abus commis par les soldats pendant l'occupation; **he is famous for his ~es** il est réputé pour ses excès.

◇ *adj* [extra] en trop, excédentaire; **you're carrying a lot of ~ weight** tu as beaucoup de kilos en trop OR à perdre.

◆ **in excess of** *prep phr* [a stated percentage, weight] au-dessus de; **she earns in ~ of £25,000 a year** elle gagne plus de 25 000 livres par an.

◆ **to excess** *adv phr*: **to carry sthg to ~** pousser qqch trop loin; **he does** OR **carries it to ~** il exagère, il dépasse les bornes; **to eat/to drink to ~** manger/boire à l'excès.

excess baggage ['ekses-] *n* (*U*) [on plane] excédent *m* de bagages; **I had 10 kilos of ~** j'avais 10 kilos d'excédent de bagages.

excess fare ['ekses-] *n* *Br* supplément *m* de pri

excessive [ɪk'sesɪv] *adj* [unreasonable] excessi [demand] excessif, démesuré; **that's a bit ~** c'est un peu excessif; **to show ~ interest i sb/sthg** faire preuve d'un intérêt excessif pou qqn/qqch; **in ~ detail** avec trop de détails.

excessively [ɪk'sesɪvlɪ] *adv* excessivement.

exchange [ɪks'tʃeɪndʒ] ◇ *vt* -**1.** [give and receive gifts, letters, blows] échanger; **we didn't ~ mor than a couple of words all evening** nou n'avons pas échangé plus de quelques mots d toute la soirée; **shots were ~d** il y a eu u échange de coups de feu; **to ~ sthg with s** échanger qqch avec qqn; **to ~ places with s** changer de place avec qqn; **we ~d place (with each other)** nous avons échangé no places; **would you like to ~ places?** voulez vous changer de place avec moi?; **we ~ addresses** nous avons échangé nos adresses; **~d addresses with Nadine** Nadine et mo avons échangé nos adresses. -**2.** [give in return fo sthg else] échanger; **to ~ sthg for sthg** échange qqch contre qqch; **I would not ~ my happ ness for anything** je n'échangerais OR ne don nerais mon bonheur contre rien au monde.

◇ *n* -**1.** [of prisoners, ideas] échange *m*; **his ol car for my new one didn't seem a fair ~** échanger sa vieille voiture contre ma neuve n me semblait pas équitable ❑ **~ of contract** échange *m* de contrats à la signature; **fair ~ i no robbery** *Br prov* donnant donnant; **Ex change and Mart** *hebdomadaire britannique d petites annonces*. -**2.** [discussion] échange *m*; **heated ~** un échange enflammé. -**3.** [cultura educational] échange *m*; **as part of an ~** dans l cadre d'un échange; **he took part in an ~ wit a school in France** il a participé à un échang avec une école française; **she took up smokin on the French ~** elle a commencé à fumer lor de l'échange avec la France ❑ **~ studen** *étudiant qui prend part à un échange avec l'étranger* **the Spanish students are here on an ~ visit** le étudiants espagnols sont en visite ici dans l cadre d'un échange. -**4.** TELEC central *m* télépho nique. -**5.** COMM bourse *f*.

◆ **in exchange** *adv phr* en échange.

◆ **in exchange for** *prep phr* en échange de; **i ~ for helping with the housework she wa given food and lodging** elle aidait aux travau ménagers et en échange OR en contrepartie ell était nourrie et logée.

exchangeable [ɪks'tʃeɪndʒəbl] *adj* échan geable, qui peut être échangé; **goods are ~ only when accompanied by a valid receipt** le articles ne peuvent être échangés que s'ils son accompagnés du ticket de caisse.

exchange rate *n* taux *m* de change.

Exchange Rate Mechanism *pr n* méca nisme *m* (des taux) de change (du SME).

exchequer [ɪks'tʃekə[r]] *n* [finances] finances *fp*

◆ **Exchequer** *n* POL [department]: **the ~** ministère des Finances *(en Grande-Bretagne)*.

excipient [ɪk'sɪpɪənt] *n* PHARM excipient *m*.

excisable [ɪk'saɪzəbl] *adj* [taxable] taxable, im posable.

excise[1] ['eksaɪz] *n* -**1.** [tax] taxe *f*, contribution indirecte. -**2.** *Br* [government office] régie *f*, se vice *m* des contributions indirectes; **men fron the ~** [customs officers] officiers *mpl* des doua nes; [VAT inspectors] inspecteurs *mpl* de la TVA

excise[2] [ek'saɪz] *vt* -**1.** *fml* [remove from a text retrancher. -**2.** MED exciser.

excise duty ['eksaɪz-] *n* [taxation] contribution indirecte; **~ on sthg** contribution indirecte su qqch.

exciseman ['eksaɪzmæn] (*pl* **exciseme [-men]**) *n* *Br* employé *m* de la régie OR de contributions indirectes.

excise tax ['eksaɪz-] = **excise duty**.

excision [ek'sɪʒn] *n* -**1.** *fml* [of a piece of tex coupure *f*, retranchement *m*. -**2.** MED excision

excitability [ɪk,saɪtə'bɪlətɪ] *n* nervosité *f*, ém tivité *f*.

excitable [ɪk'saɪtəbl] *adj* excitable, nerveux.

excitation [ˌeksɪ'teɪʃn] *n* -**1.** [process, state] excitation *f*. -**2.** TECH excitation *f*; ~ current courant *m* d'excitation.

excite [ɪk'saɪt] *vt* -**1.** [agitate] exciter, énerver; **the doctor said you weren't to ~ yourself** le docteur a dit qu'il ne te fallait pas d'excitation OR qu'il ne fallait pas que tu t'énerves; **the sight of the rabbit had ~d the dogs** la vue du lapin avait excité les chiens; **~d by the gunfire, the horses bolted** excités OR énervés par les coups de feu, les chevaux se sont emballés. -**2.** [fill with enthusiasm] enthousiasmer; **it takes a lot to ~ her** il en faut beaucoup pour l'enthousiasmer; **I'm very ~d by this latest development** ce fait nouveau me remplit d'enthousiasme. -**3.** [sexually] exciter. -**4.** [arouse - interest, curiosity] exciter, soulever, éveiller. -**5.** PHYSIOL exciter.

excited [ɪk'saɪtɪd] *adj* -**1.** [enthusiastic, eager] excité; **to be ~ about OR at sthg** être excité par qqch; **the children were ~ at the prospect of going to the seaside** les enfants étaient tout excités à l'idée d'aller au bord de la mer; **you must be very ~ at being chosen to play for your country** vous devez être fou de joie d'avoir été choisi pour jouer pour votre pays; **don't get too ~** ne t'excite OR t'emballe pas trop; **well, don't sound too ~!** *iron* eh bien, quel enthousiasme!; **you don't seem very ~** ça n'a pas l'air de t'emballer. -**2.** [agitated]: **don't go getting ~, don't get ~** ne va pas t'énerver; **it doesn't do him any good getting ~ at his age** cela ne lui vaut rien de s'énerver OR s'agiter à son âge. -**3.** [sexually] excité. -**4.** PHYS excité.

excitedly [ɪk'saɪtɪdlɪ] *adv* [behave, watch] avec agitation; [say] sur un ton animé; [wait] fébrilement.

excitement [ɪk'saɪtmənt] *n* -**1.** [enthusiasm] excitation *f*, animation *f*, enthousiasme *m*; **in her ~ at the news she knocked over a vase** les nouvelles l'ont mise dans un tel état d'excitation OR d'enthousiasme qu'elle a renversé un vase; **her ~ at the news was obvious** elle était de toute évidence très excitée OR enthousiasmée par les nouvelles; **there was a look of ~ on the child's face** l'excitation OR l'enthousiasme se lisait sur le visage de l'enfant; **an atmosphere of intense ~** une grande effervescence OR animation; **when the ~ had died down** quand l'agitation OR l'effervescence fut retombée. -**2.** [agitation] excitation *f*, agitation *f*; **the doctor advised her to avoid ~** le médecin lui a déconseillé toute agitation OR toute surexcitation OR tout énervement; **I don't think I could stand the ~** *hum* je ne crois pas que je supporterais des sensations OR émotions aussi fortes; **the ~ would kill her** une telle émotion lui serait fatale; **I've had quite enough ~ for one day** j'ai eu assez de sensations fortes pour une seule journée. -**3.** [sexual] excitation *f*. -**4.** [exciting events] animation *f*; **there should be plenty of ~ in today's match** le match d'aujourd'hui devrait être très animé; **we don't get much ~ round here** il n'y a pas beaucoup d'animation par ici; **all the ~ seemed to have gone out of their marriage** leur mariage semblait maintenant totalement dénué de passion; **what's all the ~ about?** mais que se passe-t-il?; **you shouldn't have had yesterday off, you missed all the ~** c'est dommage que tu n'aies pas travaillé hier, il y a eu beaucoup d'animation OR c'était très animé; **I don't want to miss the ~** je ne veux pas rater ça.

exciting [ɪk'saɪtɪŋ] *adj* -**1.** [day, life, events, match] passionnant, palpitant; [prospect] palpitant; [person, novel, restaurant] formidable; [news] sensationnel; **we've had an ~ time (of it) recently** ces derniers temps ont été mouvementés; **nothing ~ ever happens around here** il ne se passe jamais rien d'excitant OR de palpitant par ici; **it was ~ to think that we'd soon be in New York** c'était excitant de penser que nous serions bientôt à New York; **it was an ~ place to live** c'était passionnant de vivre là-bas. -**2.** [sexually] excitant.

excl. (*written abbr of* excluding): **~ taxes** HT.

exclaim [ɪk'skleɪm] ◇ *vi* s'exclamer.
◇ *vt*: **"but why?", he ~ed** «mais pourquoi?», s'exclama-t-il.

exclamation [ˌekskləˈmeɪʃn] *n* exclamation *f*.

exclamation mark *Br*, **exclamation point** *Am n* point *m* d'exclamation.

exclamatory [ɪk'sklæmətrɪ] *adj* exclamatif.

exclude [ɪk'skluːd] *vt* -**1.** [bar] exclure; **to ~ sb from sthg** exclure qqn de qqch; **I felt that I was being ~d from the conversation** je sentais qu'on m'excluait de la conversation; **his disability ~d him from many leisure pursuits** son infirmité l'empêchait de pratiquer de nombreux loisirs. -**2.** [not take into consideration] exclure; **to ~ sthg/sb from sthg** exclure qqch/qqn de qqch; **submarine-launched missiles were ~d from the arms talks** les missiles sous-marins n'entraient pas dans le cadre des négociations sur les armements.

excluding [ɪk'skluːdɪŋ] *prep* à l'exclusion OR l'exception de, sauf, à part; **not ~...** ... y compris.

exclusion [ɪk'skluːʒn] *n* -**1.** [barring] exclusion *f*; **the ~ of sb from a society/conversation** l'exclusion de qqn d'une société/conversation. -**2.** [omission] exclusion *f*; **the ~ of sthg/sb from sthg** l'exclusion de qqch/qqn de qqch; **to the ~ of everything OR all else** à l'exclusion de toute autre chose.

exclusionist [ɪk'skluːʒənɪst] POL ◇ *adj* [action, measure] relevant d'une politique d'exclusion; [person] partisan d'une politique d'exclusion.
◇ *n* partisan *m*, -e *f* d'une politique d'exclusion.

exclusive [ɪk'skluːsɪv] ◇ *adj* -**1.** [select - restaurant, neighbourhood] chic; [- club] fermé; **they live at a very ~ address** ils vivent dans un quartier très chic. -**2.** [deal] exclusif; **to have an ~ contract with a company** avoir un contrat exclusif avec une société; **~ economic zone** zone *f* économique exclusive; **~ to** réservé (exclusivement) à. -**3.** [excluding taxes, charges etc]: **~ of VAT** TVA non comprise; **a single room is £30 a night, ~** une chambre pour une personne coûte 30 livres la nuit, hors taxe; **the rent is £100 a week ~** le loyer est de 100 livres par semaine sans les charges. -**4.** [excluding time]: **from the 14th to the 19th October, ~** du 14 au 19 octobre exclu. -**5.** [incompatible] exclusif; **the two propositions are/are not mutually ~** les deux propositions sont/ne sont pas incompatibles; **they are mutually ~** [propositions] l'une exclut l'autre, elles sont incompatibles. -**6.** [sole] unique; **their ~ concern** leur seul souci; **the ~ use of gold** l'emploi exclusif d'or.
◇ *n* PRESS exclusivité *f*; [interview] interview *f* exclusive; **a Tribune ~** une exclusivité de la Tribune.

exclusively [ɪk'skluːsɪvlɪ] *adv* [only] exclusivement; **published ~ in the Times** publié en exclusivité dans le Times.

exclusiveness [ɪk'skluːsɪvnɪs] *n* -**1.** [of restaurant, address, district] chic *m*. -**2.** [of contract] nature *f* exclusive.

exclusivity [ˌeksklu:'sɪvətɪ] = **exclusiveness**.

excommunicate [ˌekskə'mjuːnɪkeɪt] *vt* RELIG excommunier.

excommunication ['ekskəˌmjuːnɪ'keɪʃn] *n* RELIG excommunication *f*.

excoriate [eks'kɔːrɪeɪt] *vt fml* [censure, reprimand] condamner.

excrement ['ekskrɪmənt] *n* (*U*) *fml* excréments *mpl*.

excrescence [ɪk'skresəns] *n* [growth] excroissance *f*.

excreta [ɪk'skriːtə] *npl fml* excréments *mpl*.

excrete [ɪk'skriːt] *vt* excréter.

excretion [ɪk'skriːʃn] *n* -**1.** [action] excrétion *f*. -**2.** [substance] sécrétion *f*.

excretory [ɪk'skriːtərɪ] *adj* excréteur.

excruciating [ɪk'skruːʃɪeɪtɪŋ] *adj* -**1.** [extremely painful] extrêmement douloureux, atroce; **the pain was ~** la douleur était atroce. -**2.** *inf* [extremely bad] atroce, abominable; **it was ~** [embarrassing] c'était affreux; [boring] c'était atroce.

excruciatingly [ɪk'skruːʃɪeɪtɪŋlɪ] *adv* [painful, boring] atrocement, affreusement; **it was ~ funny** c'était à mourir de rire.

exculpate ['ekskʌlpeɪt] *vt fml* disculper; **to ~ sb from sthg** disculper qqn de qqch.

exculpation [ˌekskʌl'peɪʃn] *n fml* disculpation *f*.

excursion [ɪk'skɜːʃn] *n* -**1.** [organized trip] excursion *f*. -**2.** [short local journey] expédition *f*. -**3.** [into a different field] incursion *f*; **after a brief ~ into politics** après une brève incursion dans la politique.

excursion ticket *n Br* RAIL billet *m* circulaire *(bénéficiant de tarifs réduits)*.

excusable [ɪk'skjuːzəbl] *adj* excusable, pardonnable.

excusably [ɪk'skjuːzəblɪ] *adv*: **~ perhaps, she refused to speak to them** elle a refusé de leur parler, ce qui est peut-être excusable OR pardonnable.

excuse [*n* ɪk'skjuːs, *vb* ɪk'skjuːz] ◇ *n* -**1.** [explanation, justification] excuse *f*; **her ~ for not coming** son excuse pour n'être pas venue; **to give sthg as one's ~** donner qqch comme excuse; **that's no ~** ce n'est pas une excuse OR une raison; **that's no ~ for being rude** ce n'est pas une raison OR une excuse pour être grossier; **there's no ~ for that kind of behaviour** ce genre de comportement est sans excuse OR inexcusable; **there's no ~ for it** c'est sans excuse, c'est inexcusable; **he has no ~ for not finishing the job on time** il n'a pas d'excuse pour ne pas avoir terminé le travail à temps; **I don't want (to hear) any ~s!** je ne veux pas d'excuse!; **well, what's your ~ this time?** alors, quelle excuse as-tu trouvé cette fois?; **you'd better have a good ~!** tu as intérêt à avoir une bonne excuse!; **~s, ~s!** des excuses, toujours des excuses!; **he's always finding ~s for them/for their behaviour** il est tout le temps en train de leur trouver des excuses/d'excuser leur comportement; **I'm not making ~s for them** je ne les excuse pas; **to make one's ~s** s'excuser, présenter ses excuses; **make my ~s to them** présente-leur mes excuses; **ignorance is no ~** l'ignorance n'excuse pas tout; **by way of (an) ~** en guise d'excuse. -**2.** [example]: **a poor ~ for a father** un père lamentable; **this is a poor ~ for a bus service** ce service d'autobus est lamentable. -**3.** [pretext] excuse *f*, prétexte *m*; **an ~ to do OR for doing sthg** une excuse OR un prétexte pour faire qqch; **any ~ will do** n'importe quelle excuse OR n'importe quel prétexte fera l'affaire; **the government keeps finding ~s for not introducing reforms** le gouvernement n'arrête pas de trouver des excuses pour retarder l'introduction de réformes; **you know them, any ~ for a drink!** tu les connais, toutes les excuses sont bonnes pour boire un verre!
◇ *vt* -**1.** [justify - bad behaviour] excuser; **he tried to ~ himself by saying that...** il a essayé de se justifier en disant que... -**2.** [forgive - bad behaviour, person] excuser, pardonner; **you can ~ that in someone of his age** c'est pardonnable chez quelqu'un de son âge; **I'll ~ your lateness (just) this once** je te pardonne ton retard pour cette fois; **now, if you will ~ me** maintenant, si vous voulez bien m'excuser; **one could be ~d for thinking that he was much younger** on dirait OR croirait qu'il est beaucoup plus jeune; **~ my interrupting, but...** excusez-moi OR pardon de vous interrompre, mais...; **~ me** [to get past] pardon; [as interruption, to attract sb's attention] pardon, excusez-moi; *Am* [as apology] pardon, excusez-moi; **~ me, (but) aren't you...?** excusez-moi, vous ne seriez pas...?; **~ me for asking!** oh, ça va, je ne faisais que demander!, ce n'était qu'une question!; **well, ~ me for mentioning it!** oh, ça va, je n'en parlerai plus!; **to ~ o.s.** s'excuser. -**3.** [exempt] dispenser; **to ~ sb from sthg** dispenser qqn de qqch; **to ~ sb from doing sthg** dispenser qqn de faire qqch; **he is ~d gym** il est dispensé de gymnastique. -**4.** [allow to go] excuser; **please**

may I be ~d? [to go to lavatory] puis-je sortir, s'il vous plaît?; [from the table] puis-je sortir de table, s'il vous plaît?

excuse-me [ɪk'skjuːz-] *n danse pendant laquelle on peut prendre le ou la partenaire de quelqu'un d'autre.*

ex-directory *Br* ◇ *adj* sur la liste rouge; an ~ number un numéro ne figurant pas dans l'annuaire OR figurant sur la liste rouge.
◇ *adv*: to go ~ se mettre sur la liste rouge.

ex dividend *adj* ST. EX ex-dividende.

exeat ['eksɪæt] *n Br* UNIV *fml* permission *f* de sortie.

exec. [ɪg'zek] *abbr of* executive.

execrable ['eksɪkrəbl] *adj fml* exécrable.

execrably ['eksɪkrəblɪ] *adv fml* exécrablement.

execrate ['eksɪkreɪt] *vt fml* -**1.** [loathe] exécrer. -**2.** [denounce] condamner, s'élever contre.

execration [,eksɪ'kreɪʃn] *n fml* -**1.** [loathing] exécration *f*. -**2.** [denunciation] condamnation *f*, accusation *f*.

executant [ɪg'zekjʊtənt] *n* -**1.** *fml* [of an order] exécutant *m*, -e *f*. -**2.** MUS exécutant *m*, -e *f*.

execute ['eksɪkjuːt] *vt* -**1.** [put to death] exécuter; ~d for murder/treason exécuté pour meurtre/trahison. -**2.** *fml* [carry out] exécuter; a superbly ~d carving une sculpture superbement exécutée. -**3.** JUR [will, sentence, law] exécuter. -**4.** COMPUT exécuter.

execution [,eksɪ'kjuːʃn] *n* -**1.** [of person] exécution *f*. -**2.** *fml* [of order, plan, drawing] exécution *f*; in the ~ of one's duty dans l'exercice de ses fonctions; to put sthg into ~ mettre qqch à exécution. -**3.** JUR [of will, sentence, law] exécution *f*. -**4.** COMPUT exécution *f*.

executioner [,eksɪ'kjuːʃnəʳ] *n* bourreau *m*.

executive [ɪg'zekjʊtɪv] ◇ *n* -**1.** [person] cadre *m*; a business ~ un cadre commercial; she looked the ~ type elle avait l'allure d'un cadre. -**2.** [body] corps *m* exécutif; POL [branch of government] exécutif *m*.
◇ *adj* -**1.** [dining room, washroom etc] des cadres, de la direction; [suite, chair] de cadre, spécial cadre; ~ model OR version [of car] modèle *m* grand luxe ❑ ~ briefcase attaché-case *m*; ~ toys gadgets *mpl* pour cadres. -**2.** [function, role] exécutif; an ~ officer in the civil service un cadre de l'administration; he's not good at making ~ decisions il n'est pas doué pour prendre des décisions importantes; we need an ~ decision il faut trancher; you'll have to make an ~ decision *hum* il va falloir que tu prennes une décision capitale OR déterminante; ~ producer producteur *m* délégué.

executor [ɪg'zekjʊtəʳ] *n* JUR [of will] exécuteur *m*, -trice *f* testamentaire; to make sb one's ~ désigner qqn comme son exécuteur testamentaire.

executrix [ɪg'zekjʊtrɪks] *n* JUR [of will] exécutrice *f* testamentaire.

exegesis [,eksɪ'dʒiːsɪs] *n* exégèse *f*.

exemplary [ɪg'zemplərɪ] *adj* -**1.** [very good - behaviour, pupil] exemplaire. -**2.** [serving as a warning] exemplaire; ~ punishment châtiment exemplaire; ~ damages JUR dommages-intérêts *mpl* exemplaires OR à titre exemplaire.

exemplification [ɪg,zemplɪfɪ'keɪʃn] *n* illustration *f*, illustrations *fpl*, exemplification *f*; a few case studies serving as an ~ of the thesis quelques études de cas servant d'illustration OR d'exemplification à la thèse; this chapter could do with more ~ ce chapitre aurait besoin d'un peu plus d'illustrations OR d'une illustration plus riche.

exemplify [ɪg'zemplɪfaɪ] *vt* -**1.** [give example of] illustrer, exemplifier. -**2.** [be example of] illustrer.

exempt [ɪg'zempt] ◇ *adj* exempt; to be ~ from sthg être exempt de qqch.
◇ *vt* [gen] exempter; [from tax] exonérer; to ~ sb/sthg from sthg exempter qqn/qqch de qqch.

exemption [ɪg'zempʃn] *n* [action, state] exemption *f*; tax ~ exonération *f* fiscale.

exercise ['eksəsaɪz] ◇ *n* -**1.** [physical] exercice *m*; ~ is good for you l'exercice est bon pour la santé; it's good ~ c'est un bon exercice; I don't get much ~ these days je ne fais pas beaucoup d'exercice ces temps-ci; I'll walk, I need the ~ j'y vais à pied, j'ai besoin d'exercice; the doctor has told him to take more ~ le docteur lui a dit de faire plus d'exercice; this is a good ~ for the calf muscles c'est un bon exercice pour les muscles des mollets. -**2.** [mental, in education] exercice *m*; piano ~s exercices de piano. -**3.** [use] exercice *m*; in the ~ of one's duties dans l'exercice de ses fonctions; by the ~ of a little imagination en usant d'un peu d'imagination, avec un peu d'imagination. -**4.** MIL exercice *m*; they're on ~s ils sont à l'exercice. -**5.** [activity, operation]: a fact-finding ~ une mission d'enquête; it was an interesting ~ cela a été une expérience intéressante; this is more than just a PR ~ ce n'est pas seulement de la poudre aux yeux; it was a pointless ~ cela n'a servi absolument à rien. -**6.** *Am* [ceremony] cérémonie *f*; graduation ~s cérémonie de remise des diplômes.
◇ *vt* -**1.** [body, muscle] exercer, faire travailler; [dog, horse] donner de l'exercice à; if you were to ~ your brain on the problem si tu faisais travailler tes méninges pour régler ce problème; I'm not saying this just to ~ my voice! je ne dis pas ça simplement pour le plaisir! -**2.** [troops] entraîner. -**3.** [use, put into practice - right, option, authority] exercer. -**4.** *fml* [preoccupy] préoccuper.
◇ *vi* -**1.** [take exercise] faire de l'exercice. -**2.** [train] s'exercer, s'entraîner; he was exercising on the rings il s'exerçait OR s'entraînait aux anneaux.

exercise bike *n* vélo *m* d'appartement.

exercise book *n* -**1.** [for writing in] cahier *m* d'exercices. -**2.** [containing exercises] livre *m* d'exercices.

exerciser ['eksəsaɪzəʳ] *n* -**1.** [piece of equipment] appareil *m* de gymnastique; [bike] vélo *m* d'appartement. -**2.** [person] personne *f* qui fait de l'exercice.

exercise yard *n* [in prison] cour *f*, préau *m*.

exert [ɪg'zɜːt] *vt* -**1.** [pressure, force] exercer; they were willing to ~ their influence on behalf of our campaign ils étaient d'accord pour mettre leur influence au service de notre campagne. -**2.** to ~ o.s. [make effort] se donner de la peine OR du mal; don't ~ yourself! *iron* ne te donne pas trop de mal, surtout!

exertion [ɪg'zɜːʃn] *n* -**1.** [of force] exercice *m*; the ~ of pressure on sb/sthg la pression exercée sur qqn/qqch; the ~ of influence on political figures by powerful industrialists la manière dont certains puissants industriels utilisent leur influence sur les personnalités politiques. -**2.** [effort] effort *m*; after the day's ~s après les efforts de la journée; by one's own ~s par ses propres moyens.

exeunt ['eksɪʌnt] *vi* THEAT [in stage directions]: ~ the witches les sorcières sortent.

exfoliate [eks'fəʊlɪeɪt] ◇ *vi* s'exfolier.
◇ *vt* exfolier.

ex gratia [eks'greɪʃə] *adj*: ~ payment paiement *m* à titre gracieux.

exhalation [,eksə'leɪʃn] *n* -**1.** [breathing out - of air] expiration *f*; [- of smoke, fumes] exhalation *f*. -**2.** [air breathed out] air *m* expiré, souffle *m*, exhalaison *f*.

exhale [eks'heɪl] ◇ *vt* [air] expirer; [gas, fumes] exhaler.
◇ *vi* [breathe out] expirer.

exhaust [ɪg'zɔːst] ◇ *n* -**1.** [on vehicle - system] échappement *m*; [- pipe] pot *m* OR tuyau *m* d'échappement. -**2.** *(U)* [fumes] gaz *mpl* d'échappement.
◇ *vt* -**1.** [use up - supplies, possibilities] épuiser; you're ~ing my patience tu mets ma patience à bout. -**2.** [tire out] épuiser, exténuer.

exhausted [ɪg'zɔːstɪd] *adj* -**1.** [person, smile] épuisé, exténué. -**2.** [used up - mine, land] épuisé; my patience is ~ je suis à bout de patience.

exhaustedly [ɪg'zɔːstɪdlɪ] *adv* [move, smile, sigh] d'un air épuisé OR exténué.

exhaust fumes *npl* gaz *mpl* d'échappement.

exhausting [ɪg'zɔːstɪŋ] *adj* [job, climb, climate] épuisant, exténuant, éreintant; [person] fatigant, excédant.

exhaustion [ɪg'zɔːstʃn] *n* -**1.** [tiredness] épuisement *m*, éreintement *m*, grande fatigue *f*; to be suffering from ~ être dans un état d'épuisement; to be in a state of total ~ être dans un état d'épuisement total OR complet; they worked to the point of ~ ils ont travaillé jusqu'à épuisement. -**2.** [of supplies, topic] épuisement *m*.

exhaustive [ɪg'zɔːstɪv] *adj* [analysis, treatment] exhaustif; [investigation, enquiry] approfondi, poussé; the list is not ~ cette liste n'est pas exhaustive.

exhaustively [ɪg'zɔːstɪvlɪ] *adv* exhaustivement.

exhaustiveness [ɪg'zɔːstɪvnɪs] *n* [of analysis, treatment] caractère *m* exhaustif, exhaustivité *f*; [of investigation, enquiry] caractère *m* approfondi OR poussé.

exhaust manifold *n* MECH collecteur *m* d'échappement.

exhaust pipe *n Br* pot *m* OR tuyau *m* d'échappement.

exhaust stroke *n* MECH [in internal combustion engine] temps *m* d'échappement.

exhaust system *n* AUT échappement *m*.

exhibit [ɪg'zɪbɪt] ◇ *vt* -**1.** [subj: artist] exposer; [subj: companies] présenter. -**2.** [show, display - ID card, passport] montrer; this permit must be clearly ~ed in the windscreen ce permis doit être disposé bien en vue derrière le pare-brise. -**3.** [manifest - courage, self-control] montrer, manifester.
◇ *vi* [painter, company] exposer.
◇ *n* -**1.** [in an exhibition] objet *m* (exposé); one of the most interesting ~s at the fair l'une des pièces les plus intéressantes en exposition à la foire. -**2.** JUR pièce *f* à conviction. -**3.** *Am* [exhibition] exposition *f*.

exhibition [,eksɪ'bɪʃn] *n* -**1.** [of paintings, products] exposition *f*; [of film] présentation *f*; he's having an ~ at the new gallery il expose à la nouvelle galerie; the Klee ~ l'exposition Klee; trade ~ exposition commerciale ❑ ~ centre centre *m* d'exposition. -**2.** [of bad manners, ingenuity] démonstration *f*; to give sb an ~ of sthg faire une démonstration de qqch à qqn; did you see the way she behaved? what an ~! avez-vous vu la manière dont elle s'est comportée? quel spectacle!; to make an ~ of o.s. se donner en spectacle. -**3.** *Br* UNIV bourse *f* d'études.

exhibitioner [,eksɪ'bɪʃnəʳ] *n Br* UNIV boursier *m*, -ère *f*.

exhibitionism [,eksɪ'bɪʃnɪzm] *n* -**1.** [gen] besoin *m* OR volonté *f* de se faire remarquer. -**2.** PSYCH exhibitionnisme *m*.

exhibitionist [,eksɪ'bɪʃnɪst] *n* -**1.** [gen] *personne qui cherche toujours à se faire remarquer*; he's a terrible ~ il faut toujours qu'il cherche à se faire remarquer. -**2.** PSYCH exhibitionniste *mf*.

exhibitionistic [,eksɪ,bɪʃə'nɪstɪk] *adj* [behaviour, person] démonstratif, exubérant.

exhibition match *n* match-exhibition *m*.

exhibitor [ɪg'zɪbɪtəʳ] *n* [at gallery, trade fair] exposant *m*.

exhilarate [ɪg'zɪləreɪt] *vt* exalter, griser.

exhilarated [ɪg'zɪləreɪtɪd] *adj* [mood, laugh] exalté; to feel ~ se sentir exalté.

exhilarating [ɪg'zɪləreɪtɪŋ] *adj* exaltant, grisant.

exhilaration [ɪg,zɪlə'reɪʃn] *n* exaltation *f*, griserie *f*.

exhort [ɪg'zɔːt] *vt fml* exhorter; to ~ sb to do sthg exhorter qqn à faire qqch.

exhortation [,egzɔː'teɪʃn] *n fml* [act, words] exhortation *f*.

exhumation [,ekshjuː'meɪʃn] *n fml* exhumation *f*; ~ order ordre *m* d'exhumer.

exhume [eks'hjuːm] *vt fml* exhumer.

ex-husband *n* ex-mari *m*.

exigency ['eksɪdʒənsɪ] (*pl* exigencies), **exigence** ['eksɪdʒəns] *n fml* -**1.** *(usu pl)* [demand] exigence *f*; the exigencies of the situation les exigences de la situation. **-2.** [urgent situation] situation *f* urgente. **-3.** [urgency] urgence *f*; a matter of some ~ une affaire assez urgente OR pressante.

exigent ['eksɪdʒənt] *adj fml* **-1.** [urgent] urgent, pressant. **-2.** [demanding, exacting] exigeant.

exiguity [eksɪ'gju:ətɪ] (*pl* exiguities) *n fml* exiguïté *f*.

exiguous [eg'zɪgjʊəs] *adj fml* [means, income, quarters] exigu.

exile ['eksaɪl] ◇ *n* **-1.** [banishment] exil *m*; his self-imposed ~ son exil volontaire; to live in ~ vivre en exil; to send sb into ~ envoyer qqn en exil; to go into ~ partir en exil; they formed a government in ~ ils ont formé un gouvernement en exil; to return from ~ rentrer d'exil. **-2.** [person] exilé *m*, -e *f*; tax ~ *personne qui s'expatrie pour échapper au fisc*.
◇ *vt* exiler, expatrier; he was ~d from his native Poland il a été exilé OR expatrié de sa Pologne natale.

exiled ['eksaɪld] *adj* exilé; the ~ government le gouvernement en exil.

exist [ɪg'zɪst] *vi* exister; do ghosts ~? les fantômes existent-ils?; the half-litre pack doesn't ~ any more le carton d'un demi-litre n'existe OR ne se fait plus; they ~ in three sizes elles existent en trois tailles; the species now only ~s in zoos cette espèce n'existe que dans les zoos; there ~s an ancient tradition which... il existe une tradition ancienne qui...; she treats me as if I don't ~ elle fait comme si je n'existais pas; that's not living, that's just ~ing! je n'appelle pas ça vivre, j'appelle ça subsister OR survivre; can life ~ under these conditions? la vie est-elle possible dans ces conditions?; he earns enough to ~ on il gagne suffisamment pour vivre; the conditions that are necessary for life to ~ les conditions qui sont nécessaires à la vie; we can't ~ without oxygen nous ne pouvons pas vivre sans oxygène.

existence [ɪg'zɪstəns] *n* **-1.** [being] existence *f*; ever since the ~ of man depuis que l'homme existe; the continued ~ of life on this planet/of these old-fashioned procedures la survivance de la vie sur la planète/de ces procédures arriérées; to come into ~ [species] apparaître; [the earth] se former; [law, institution] naître, être créé; it didn't come into ~ until quite recently cela n'existait pas il y a encore peu de temps; to be in ~ exister; the oldest steam engine still in ~ la plus vieille machine à vapeur encore existante; the only whale left in ~ la dernière baleine encore en vie; to go out of ~ cesser d'exister. **-2.** [life] existence *f*; to lead a pleasant/wretched ~ mener une existence agréable/misérable.

existent [ɪg'zɪstənt] *adj* existant.

existential [,egzɪ'stenʃl] *adj* existentiel.

existentialism [,egzɪ'stenʃəlɪzm] *n* existentialisme *m*.

existentialist [,egzɪ'stenʃəlɪst] ◇ *n* existentialiste *mf*.
◇ *adj* existentialiste.

existing [ɪg'zɪstɪŋ] *adj* actuel; under the ~ circumstances dans les circonstances actuelles OR présentes.

exit ['eksɪt] ◇ *n* **-1.** [way out - from room, motorway] sortie *f*; let's turn off at the next ~ prenons la prochaine sortie; '~ only' 'réservé à la sortie'. **-2.** THEAT sortie *f*, exit *m inv*; [act of going out - from a room] sortie *f*; this was to be his final ~ from my life il sortait alors définitivement de ma vie; the bullet made its ~ through the shoulder la balle est ressortie par l'épaule; to make one's ~ THEAT OR *fig* faire sa sortie. **-3.** COMPUT sortie *f*.
◇ *vi* **-1.** THEAT sortir; he then ~s stage left puis il sort côté jardin; ~ Anne [as stage direction] exit Anne, Anne sort. **-2.** [go out, leave] sortir; [bullet] ressortir; he ~ed through the rear door il est sorti OR parti par la porte de derrière. **-3.** COMPUT sortir.
◇ *vt* COMPUT sortir de; [leave] quitter, sortir de.

exit permit *n Br* permis *m* de sortie.

exit poll *n Br sondage réalisé auprès des votants à la sortie du bureau de vote*.

exit visa *n* visa *m* de sortie.

ex libris [eks'li:brɪs] *n* [bookplate] ex-libris *m inv*.

exocrine ['eksəʊkraɪn] *adj* PHYSIOL exocrine.

exodus ['eksədəs] *n* exode *m*; the ~ of capital abroad l'exode des capitaux à l'étranger; there was a general ~ to the bar il y a eu un mouvement de masse en direction du bar.
◆ **Exodus** *n* **-1.** [book]: (the Book of) Exodus (l') Exode; as it says in Exodus comme il est dit dans l'Exode. **-2.** [journey] exode *m*.

ex officio [eksə'fɪʃɪəʊ] ◇ *adj* [member] de droit.
◇ *adv* [act, decide etc] de droit.

exogamy [ek'sɒgəmɪ] *n* SOCIOL exogamie *f*.

exogenous [ek'sɒdʒənəs] *adj* [gen & BIOL] exogène.

exonerate [ɪg'zɒnəreɪt] *vt* disculper, innocenter; to ~ o.s. se disculper.

exoneration [ɪg,zɒnə'reɪʃn] *n* disculpation *f*.

exorbitance [ɪg'zɔ:bɪtəns] *n* [of price, demands] énormité *f*, démesure *f*.

exorbitant [ɪg'zɔ:bɪtənt] *adj* [price, demands, claims] exorbitant, démesuré, excessif; £85 for that? that's ~! 85 livres pour ça? c'est exorbitant!

exorbitantly [ɪg'zɔ:bɪtəntlɪ] *adv* [priced] excessivement, démesurément; it's so ~ expensive c'est excessivement OR démesurément cher.

exorcism ['eksɔ:sɪzm] *n* exorcisme *m*; to carry out OR to perform an ~ pratiquer un exorcisme.

exorcist ['eksɔ:sɪst] *n* exorciste *mf*.

exorcize, -ise ['eksɔ:saɪz] *vt* [evil spirits, place] exorciser.

exoskeleton ['eksəʊ,skelɪtn] *n* ZOOL exosquelette *m*, cuticule *f*.

exosphere ['eksəʊ,sfɪə^r] *n* exosphère *f*.

exoteric [,eksəʊ'terɪk] *adj fml* exotérique.

exothermic [,eksəʊ'θɜ:mɪk] *adj* CHEM exothermique.

exotic [ɪg'zɒtɪk] ◇ *adj* exotique; an ~-sounding name un nom à consonance exotique; ~-looking exotique.
◇ *n* [plant] plante *f* exotique.

exotica [ɪg'zɒtɪkə] *npl* objets *mpl* exotiques; a collection of literary ~ une collection de pièces littéraires rares.

exotically [ɪg'zɒtɪklɪ] *adv* [dressed, decorated] avec exotisme; ~ perfumed [flower] aux senteurs exotiques; [person] au parfum exotique.

exoticism [ɪg'zɒtɪsɪzm] *n* exotisme *m*.

expand [ɪk'spænd] ◇ *vt* **-1.** [empire, army, staff] agrandir; [company, business] agrandir, développer; [chest, muscles, ideas] développer; [knowledge, influence] élargir, étendre; COMPUT [memory] étendre; [gas, metal] dilater; to ~ ideas into a theory développer des idées pour en faire une théorie; this idea could do with a little ~ing cette idée gagnerait à être un peu développée; to ~ a company into a multinational agrandir une société pour en faire une multinationale. **-2.** MATH [equation] développer.
◇ *vi* **-1.** [empire, army, staff] s'agrandir; [company, business] s'agrandir, se développer; [chest, muscles, market] se développer; [knowledge, influence] s'étendre, s'élargir; [gas, metal] se dilater; [volume of traffic] augmenter; [in business] se développer, s'agrandir; we are looking to ~ into the cosmetics industry nous envisageons de nous diversifier en nous lançant dans l'industrie des cosmétiques. **-2.** [on an idea] s'étendre.
◆ **expand on** *vt insep* développer; in the next chapter I shall ~ further on these ideas je développerai ces idées OR je m'étendrai davantage sur ces idées au chapitre suivant.

expandable [ɪk'spændɪbl] *adj* [gas, material] expansible; [idea, theory] qui peut être développé; [basic set] qui peut être complété; COMPUT [memory] extensible.

expanded [ɪk'spændɪd] *adj* [metal, gas] expansé; ~ polystyrene polystyrène expansé.

expanding [ɪk'spændɪŋ] *adj* **-1.** [company, empire, gas, metal] en expansion; [influence] grandissant; [industry, market] en expansion, qui se développe; the ~ universe l'univers en expansion; the ~ universe theory la théorie de l'expansion de l'univers. **-2.** [extendable]: ~ watch strap bracelet de montre extensible; ~ suitcase/briefcase valise/serviette extensible.

expanse [ɪk'spæns] *n* étendue *f*; the vast ~ of the plain l'immensité de la plaine; the huge ~ of his stomach l'énormité de son ventre; she was showing a large ~ of thigh on lui voyait une bonne partie des cuisses.

expansion [ɪk'spænʃn] *n* [of empire] expansion *f*, élargissement *m*; [of army, staff] augmentation *f*, accroissement *m*; [of chest, muscles, ideas] développement *m*; [of knowledge, influence] élargissement *m*; [of gas, metal] expansion *f*, dilatation *f*; COMPUT [of memory] extension *f*; [of business] développement *m*, agrandissement *m*, extension *f*.

expansion bolt *n* CONSTR boulon *m* de scellement OR d'expansion; [in rock-climbing] boulon *m* d'expansion.

expansion bottle *n* [for car radiator] vase *m* d'expansion.

expansion card *n* COMPUT carte *f* d'extension.

expansionism [ɪk'spænʃənɪzm] *n* expansionnisme *m*.

expansionist [ɪk'spænʃənɪst] ◇ *adj* expansionniste.
◇ *n* expansionniste *mf*.

expansion joint *n* MECH joint *m* de dilatation.

expansion slot *n* COMPUT emplacement *m* OR logement *m* pour carte d'extension.

expansive [ɪk'spænsɪv] *adj* **-1.** [person, mood, gesture] expansif. **-2.** PHYS [gas] expansible, dilatable.

expansively [ɪk'spænsɪvlɪ] *adv* [talk, gesture] de manière expansive.

expansiveness [ɪk'spænsɪvnɪs] *n* [of person, mood] expansivité *f*.

expat *inf* [,eks'pæt] (*abbr of* **expatriate**)
◇ *n* expatrié *m*, -e *f*.
◇ *adj* [Briton, American] expatrié; [bar, community] des expatriés.

expatiate [eks'peɪʃɪeɪt] *vi fml* s'étendre, discourir; to ~ on sthg s'étendre OR discourir sur qqch.

expatriate [*n* & *adj* eks'pætrɪət, *vb* eks'pætrɪeɪt]
◇ *n* expatrié *m*, -e *f*.
◇ *adj* [Briton, American etc] expatrié; [bar, community] des expatriés.
◇ *vt* expatrier, exiler.

expatriation [eks,pætrɪ'eɪʃn] *n* expatriation *f*.

expect [ɪk'spekt] ◇ *vt* **-1.** [anticipate] s'attendre à; they are ~ing an increase in prices ils s'attendent à une hausse des prix; we ~ rain/bad weather nous nous attendons à de la pluie/du mauvais temps; we ~ed that it would be much bigger nous nous attendions à ce qu'il soit beaucoup plus gros, nous pensions qu'il allait être beaucoup plus gros; we ~ed you to bring your own nous pensions que vous alliez apporter le vôtre; to ~ sb to do sthg s'attendre à ce que qqn fasse qqch; she knew more Russian than I ~ed her to elle était meilleure en russe que je ne m'y attendais; I hadn't ~ed them to be French je ne m'attendais pas à ce qu'ils soient français; to ~ the worst s'attendre au pire; I ~ed as much! je m'en doutais!, c'est bien ce que je pensais!; it was better/worse than I ~ed c'était mieux/pire que je ne m'y attendais; she is as well as can be ~ed elle va aussi bien que sa condition le permet; I had ~ed better of OR from you je n'aurais pas cru ça de vous; what can you ~? que voulez-vous?; what can you ~ from a government like that? que voulez-vous, avec un gouvernement pareil!; as might have been ~ed, as was to be ~ed comme on pouvait s'y attendre; I never know what to ~ with you je ne sais jamais à quoi m'attendre OR m'en tenir avec vous. **-2.** [count on]: we're ~ing you to help us nous comptons sur votre aide; don't ~

me to be there! ne t'attends pas à ce que j'y sois! -**3.** [demand]: to ~ sb to do sthg demander à qqn de faire qqch; I ~ complete obedience je demande une obéissance totale; you ~ too much of him tu lui en demandes trop; it's no less than I would have ~ed from my own family je ne me serais pas attendu à moins de la part de ma propre famille; I'm ~ed to write all his speeches je suis censé OR supposé rédiger tous ses discours. -**4.** [suppose, imagine] imaginer, penser, supposer; I ~ so je pense, j'imagine; I don't ~ so je ne pense pas, j'imagine que non; I ~ you're right tu dois avoir raison; I ~ it's where you left it il doit être là où tu l'as laissé; I ~ you'll be wanting something to drink vous boirez bien quelque chose; [grudgingly] j'imagine que vous voulez quelque chose à boire. -**5.** [baby] attendre. -**6.** [await] attendre; I'm ~ing friends for dinner j'attends des amis à dîner; (at) what time should we ~ you then? à quelle heure devons-nous vous attendre alors?; I'll ~ you when I see you then *inf Br* bon, alors je verrai bien quand tu arrives; you'll just have to ~ me when you see me *inf Br* tu verras bien quand j'arriverai; we're ~ing them back any minute now nous attendons leur retour d'une minute à l'autre.
◇ *vi*: to be ~ing [be pregnant] être enceinte, attendre un enfant.

expectancy [ɪk'spektənsɪ], **expectance** [ɪk'spektəns] *n* [anticipation]: the look of ~ on his face l'attente qui se lisait sur son visage; in a tone of eager ~ sur un ton plein d'espérance OR d'espoir.

expectant [ɪk'spektənt] *adj* -**1.** [anticipating]: with an ~ look in his eye avec dans son regard l'air d'attendre quelque chose; in an ~ tone of voice la voix chargée d'espoir. -**2.** [pregnant]: ~ mother future maman *f*.

expectantly [ɪk'spektəntlɪ] *adv* [enquire, glance] avec l'air d'attendre quelque chose; [wait] impatiemment.

expectation [,ekspek'teɪʃn] *n* -**1.** *(U)* [anticipation]: can there be any ~ that some of the miners will still be alive? y a-t-il un espoir que certains mineurs soient encore en vie?; with eager ~ avec l'air d'espérer quelque chose; in a tone of gloomy ~ avec appréhension; in ~ of dans l'attente de; in the sure ~ of life everlasting RELIG dans la certitude d'une vie éternelle; we live in ~ nous vivons dans l'attente OR l'expectative. -**2.** *(usu pl)* [sthg expected] attente *f*; my ~s for its success were not that high je n'espérais pas vraiment que ça réussirait; their ~s that he would fail were not fulfilled ils s'attendaient à ce qu'il échoue, mais finalement ils se sont trompés; performance did not confirm City ~s les résultats n'ont pas répondu à l'attente de la City; these unrealistically high profit ~s ces prévisions de bénéfices totalement fantaisistes; this merely confirms our worst ~s cela ne fait que confirmer nos prévisions les plus noires; contrary to ~s contrairement à OR contre toute attente; to exceed sb's ~s dépasser l'attente OR les espérances de qqn; (not) to come up to ~s (ne pas) être à la hauteur des espérances; to have high ~s of sb/sthg attendre beaucoup de qqn/qqch; we have certain ~s of our employees [requirements] nous avons certaines exigences envers nos employés; to have great ~s [prospects] avoir de grandes espérances; what are your ~s? [for salary, job prospects] quelles sont vos conditions OR exigences? ❑ 'Great Expectations' *Dickens* 'les Grandes Espérances'.

expected [ɪk'spektɪd] *adj* attendu.

expectorant [ɪk'spektərənt] *n* expectorant *m*.

expectorate [ɪk'spektəreɪt] MED & *fml* ◇ *vi* rejeter des expectorations.
◇ *vt* expectorer.

expediency [ɪk'spiːdjənsɪ] (*pl* expediencies), **expedience** [ɪk'spiːdjəns] *n* [advisability - of measure, policy etc] opportunité *f*; [self-interest] opportunisme *m*.

expedient [ɪk'spiːdjənt] ◇ *adj* [advisable] indiqué, convenable, opportun; [involving self-interest] commode.
◇ *n* expédient *m*.

expedite ['ekspɪdaɪt] *vt fml* [work, legal process] hâter, activer, accélérer; [completion of contract, deal, conclusion of arrangement] hâter; to ~ matters accélérer OR activer les choses.

expedition [,ekspɪ'dɪʃn] *n* -**1.** [scientific, of explorers, to shops etc] expédition *f*; one (member) of the ~ un des membres de l'expédition; to go on an ~ aller OR partir en expédition, aller faire une expédition; ~ leader chef *m* d'expédition. -**2.** *arch* OR *lit* [speed] diligence *f*; with all possible ~ avec la plus grande diligence.

expeditionary [,ekspɪ'dɪʃnərɪ] *adj* MIL: ~ mission mission *f* d'expédition; ~ force force *f* expéditionnaire.

expeditious [,ekspɪ'dɪʃəs] *adj fml* diligent.

expeditiously [,ekspɪ'dɪʃəslɪ] *adv fml* diligemment.

expel [ɪk'spel] *vt* -**1.** [from school] renvoyer; [from country, club] expulser. -**2.** [gas, liquid] expulser.

expend [ɪk'spend] *vt* -**1.** [time, energy] consacrer; [resources] utiliser, employer; to ~ time/energy on sthg consacrer du temps/de l'énergie à qqch. -**2.** [use up] épuiser.

expendability [ɪk,spendə'bɪlətɪ] *n* [of people, workforce, equipment] superfluité *f*; [of troops, spies] caractère *m* sacrifiable.

expendable [ɪk'spendəbl] *adj* [person, workforce, object] superflu; [troops, spies] qui peut être sacrifié; they decided I'm ~ ils ont décidé qu'ils pouvaient se passer de moi; none of them was ~ toutes étaient indispensables; he thinks people are ~ il pense qu'il peut se débarrasser des gens comme bon lui semble.

expenditure [ɪk'spendɪtʃə^r] *n* -**1.** [act of spending] dépense *f*. -**2.** *(U)* [money spent] dépenses *fpl*; ~ on sthg dépenses en qqch; arms/defence ~ dépenses en armes/liées à la défense; this will involve us in fairly heavy ~ cela va nous entraîner dans des dépenses assez considérables.

expense [ɪk'spens] *n* -**1.** [cost] coût *m*; anything we can do to offset the ~ tout ce que nous pouvons faire pour compenser le coût OR les coûts OR les frais; it's not so much the ~ I'm worried about ce n'est pas tant le coût que cela représente qui m'inquiète; that's an ~ I hadn't reckoned with c'est une dépense que je n'avais pas prévue; if it can really be done with such little ~ si cela peut vraiment se faire à si peu de frais; the huge ~ of moving house le coût énorme qu'entraîne un déménagement; to go to considerable ~ to do sthg faire beaucoup de frais pour faire qqch; don't go to any ~ over it ne vous mettez pas en frais pour cela; they had gone to the ~ of hiring a firm of caterers ils s'étaient mis en frais et avaient engagé des traiteurs; no ~ was spared on n'a pas regardé à la dépense; I'll do it regardless of ~ je le ferai quel qu'en soit le prix OR sans regarder à la dépense; without any thought for the ~ sans penser au coût que cela représentait; to do sthg at great personal ~ faire qqch à grands frais personnels; I'll do it at my own ~ je le ferai à mes frais; she had the book published at her own ~ elle a publié le livre à ses frais OR à compte d'auteur. -**2.** [expensiveness] cherté *f*, coût *m* élevé. -**3.** *fig*: a joke at somebody else's ~ une plaisanterie aux dépens de quelqu'un d'autre; at the ~ of sthg aux dépens de qqch; to succeed at other people's ~ réussir aux dépens des autres; not at my ~, you won't pas à mes dépens, il n'en est pas question. -**4.** COMM: no, that's my ~ non, c'est sur mon compte.
◆ **expenses** *npl* frais *mpl*; it's on ~s c'est l'entreprise qui paie, cela passe dans les notes de frais; to live on ~s vivre sur ses notes de frais, vivre aux frais de son entreprise; to put sthg on ~s mettre qqch dans les notes de frais; to get ~s [be paid expenses] être indemnisé de ses frais; travelling ~s frais de déplacement; accommodation ~s frais d'hôtel OR de séjour; entertainment ~s frais de représentation; incidental ~s faux frais; all ~s paid tous frais payés.

expense account ◇ *n* indemnité *f* OR allocation *f* pour frais professionnels; the firm gives him an ~ for basic entertaining l'entreprise lui attribue une allocation pour ses frais de représentation; to put sthg on the ~ mettre qqch dans les (notes de) frais.
◇ *comp*: an ~ dinner un dîner passé dans les notes de frais; after years of ~ living après des années passées à vivre sur ses notes de frais OR aux frais de son entreprise.

expenses-paid *adj* [trip, holiday] tous frais payés.

expensive [ɪk'spensɪv] *adj* cher; it's an ~ hobby c'est un passe-temps coûteux OR qui coûte cher; the central heating became too ~ to run le chauffage central a commencé à revenir trop cher; to have ~ tastes avoir des goûts de luxe; it's an ~ place to live la vie y est chère; exactly how ~ was it? combien cela a-t-il coûté exactement?; that could be an ~ mistake *literal* & *fig* c'est une erreur qui pourrait coûter cher.

expensively [ɪk'pensɪvlɪ] *adv* à grands frais; they entertain very ~ ils reçoivent à grands frais; if we could all try to live less ~ si nous essayions tous de vivre à moindres frais.

expensiveness [ɪk'spensɪvnɪs] *n* cherté *f*; [of mistake] coût *m*; she was famous for the ~ of her tastes elle était réputée pour ses goûts de luxe; if the quality of their service only matched the ~ of their prices si au moins la qualité de leur service était à la hauteur de leurs prix.

experience [ɪk'spɪərɪəns] ◇ *n* -**1.** [in life, in a subject] expérience *f*; he has lots of ~ il a beaucoup d'expérience OR une grande expérience; I had no previous ~ je n'avais aucune expérience préalable; do you have any ~ of working with animals? avez-vous déjà travaillé avec des animaux?; she has considerable management ~ elle a une expérience considérable de OR dans la gestion; to lack ~ manquer d'expérience OR de pratique; ~ shows OR proves that... l'expérience démontre OR montre OR prouve que...; I know from ~ that he's not to be trusted je sais par expérience qu'il ne faut pas lui faire confiance; to know from bitter ~ savoir pour en avoir fait la cruelle expérience; to speak from ~ parler en connaissance de cause; in OR from my (own) ~, (speaking) from personal ~ d'après mon expérience personnelle; my ~ has been OR it has been my ~ that... d'après mon expérience...; has that been your ~? [do you agree?] avez-vous remarqué la même chose?; to put sthg down to ~ tirer un enseignement OR une leçon de qqch; let's just put it down to ~ prenons-en notre parti; it's all good ~ [as consolation] à quelque chose malheur est bon; ~ is the best teacher l'expérience est le meilleur des enseignements. -**2.** [event] expérience *f*; I had so many exciting ~s j'ai fait tellement d'expériences passionnantes; how did you enjoy the American ~? comment as-tu trouvé l'Amérique?; my first ~ of French cooking/of a real Scottish New Year la première fois que j'ai goûté à la cuisine française/que j'ai assisté à un vrai réveillon écossais; the crossing promises to be quite an ~ la traversée promet d'être une expérience mémorable; I hope it wasn't a nasty ~ for you j'espère que cela n'a pas été trop désagréable pour toi.
◇ *vt* -**1.** [undergo - hunger, hardship, recession] connaître; to ~ military combat faire l'expérience du combat militaire; he ~d great difficulty in opening the door il a eu beaucoup de mal à ouvrir la porte. -**2.** [feel - thrill, emotion,

despair] sentir, ressentir; she ~d a certain feeling of fear elle a ressenti une certaine frayeur; he is experiencing a great deal of anxiety at the moment il est très angoissé en ce moment. -**3.** [have personal knowledge of]: come and ~ Manhattan venez découvrir Manhattan; if you've never ~d French cooking si vous n'avez jamais goûté à la cuisine française; to ~ a real Scottish New Year assister à un vrai réveillon écossais.

experienced [ɪk'spɪərɪənst] *adj* expérimenté; we're looking for someone a bit more ~ nous recherchons quelqu'un qui ait un peu plus d'expérience; to be ~ in sthg avoir l'expérience de qqch; to be ~ at doing sthg avoir l'habitude de faire qqch.

experiential [ɪkspɪərɪ'enʃəl] *adj fml* & PHILOS empirique, expérientiel.

experiment [ɪk'sperɪmənt] ◇ *n literal* & *fig* expérience *f*; to carry out OR to conduct an ~ réaliser OR effectuer une expérience; an ~ in sthg une expérience de qqch; ~s on animals des expériences sur les animaux; as an OR by way of ~ à titre d'expérience; it's a bit of an ~ actually [as modest apology] je vous préviens, c'est une innovation.
◇ *vi* faire une expérience OR des expériences; to ~ with a new technique expérimenter une nouvelle technique; to ~ with drugs essayer la drogue; to ~ on animals faire des expériences sur les animaux.

experimental [ɪk,sperɪ'mentl] *adj* expérimental.

experimentally [ɪk,sperɪ'mentəlɪ] *adv* [by experimenting] expérimentalement; [as an experiment] à titre expérimental.

experimentation [ɪk,sperɪmen'teɪʃn] *n* expérimentation *f*.

experimenter [ɪk'sperɪmentə^r] *n* expérimentateur *m*, -trice *f*; I've always been a bit of an ~ j'ai toujours aimé faire des expériences.

expert ['ekspɜːt] ◇ *n* expert *m*, spécialiste *mf*; to be an ~ on one's subject/in one's field être un expert dans sa matière/dans son domaine; he's an ~ at archery c'est un expert au tir à l'arc; to look at sthg with the eye of an ~ regarder qqch avec l'œil d'un expert; I'm no ~, but... je ne suis pas expert OR spécialiste en la matière, mais...; do it yourself, you're the ~! fais-le toi-même, c'est toi l'expert!
◇ *adj* [person] expert; [advice, opinion] autorisé, d'expert; to be ~ at doing sthg être expert à faire qqch; to be ~ at sthg être expert en qqch; to run OR to cast an ~ eye over sthg jeter un œil expert sur qqch; ~ testimony JUR témoignage *m* d'expert; ~ panel commission *f* d'experts.

expertise [,ekspɜː'tiːz] *n* compétence *f* d'expert, expertise *f*; to do sthg with great ~ faire qqch avec beaucoup de compétence.

expertly ['ekspɜːtlɪ] *adv* d'une manière experte, expertement.

expertness ['ekspɜːtnɪs] = **expertise**.

expert system *n* COMPUT système *m* expert.

expert witness *n* JUR expert *m (appelé comme témoin)*; to appear OR to be called as an ~ paraître OR être appelé à la cour comme expert.

expiate ['ekspɪeɪt] *vt fml* expier.

expiation [,ekspɪ'eɪʃn] *n fml* expiation *f*; in ~ of one's sins en expiation de ses péchés.

expiatory ['ekspɪətərɪ] *adj fml* expiatoire.

expiration [,ekspɪ'reɪʃn] *n* -**1.** *fml* [expiry] expiration *f*. -**2.** *fml* [exhalation] expiration *f*. -**3.** *arch* OR *lit* [death] mort *f*.

expire [ɪk'spaɪə^r] *vi* -**1.** [contract, lease, visa etc] expirer, arriver à terme. -**2.** [exhale] expirer. -**3.** *arch* OR *lit* [die] expirer.

expiry [ɪk'spaɪərɪ] *n* [of contract, lease, visa etc] expiration *f*, échéance *f*.

expiry date *n* [of contract, lease, visa etc] date *f* d'expiration OR d'échéance.

explain [ɪk'spleɪn] ◇ *vt* -**1.** [clarify] expliquer; he ~ed to us how the machine worked il nous a expliqué comment la machine marchait; to ~ sthg in full expliquer qqch en détail; she ~ed that she was a tourist in the city elle a expliqué qu'elle était dans la ville en touriste; that is easily ~ed, that is easy to ~ c'est facile à expliquer, cela s'explique facilement; that ~s everything cela explique tout. -**2.** [account for] expliquer; she's got a cold which ~s OR will ~ why she's off work today elle a un rhume, ce qui explique pourquoi elle ne travaille pas aujourd'hui; to ~ o.s. s'expliquer; I think you'd better ~ yourself je crois que tu ferais mieux de t'expliquer.
◇ *vi* [clarify] expliquer; I don't understand, you'll need to ~ je ne comprends pas, il va falloir que tu m'expliques; you've got a bit of OR a little OR some ~ing to do il va falloir que tu t'expliques.
◆ **explain away** *vt sep* [justify, excuse] justifier; ~ that away if you can! essayez donc de justifier cela!

explainable [ɪk'spleɪnəbl] *adj* [explicable]: it's easily ~ cela s'explique facilement, c'est facilement explicable.

explanation [,eksplə'neɪʃn] *n* -**1.** [clarification] explication *f*; the instructions for this new video need a bit of ~ les instructions de ce nouveau magnétoscope nécessitent des explications; to give OR to offer an ~ for sthg donner une explication à qqch; to find an ~ for sthg trouver une explication à qqch; the lecturer gave an ~ of the term le professeur a donné une explication de ce terme. -**2.** [justification] explication *f*; I want an ~! je veux une explication!; you'd better have a good ~! j'espère que tu as une bonne excuse OR une explication valable!

explanatory [ɪk'splænətrɪ] *adj* explicatif.

explant [eks'plɑːnt] ◇ *vt* explanter *(prélever en vue d'une culture in vitro)*.
◇ *n* explant *m*.

expletive [ɪk'spliːtɪv] ◇ *n* -**1.** [swearword] juron *m*; a string of ~s un chapelet de jurons. -**2.** GRAMM explétif *m*.
◇ *adj* GRAMM explétif.

explicable [ɪk'splɪkəbl] *adj* explicable.

explicate ['eksplɪkeɪt] *vt fml* éclaircir, clarifier.

explicit [ɪk'splɪsɪt] *adj* [denial, meaning, support] explicite; ~ sex and violence on the television le sexe et la violence montrés ouvertement à la télévision; sexually ~ cru.

explicitly [ɪk'splɪsɪtlɪ] *adv* explicitement.

explode [ɪk'spləʊd] ◇ *vt* [detonate] faire exploser OR sauter; *fig* [theory, myth etc] détruire, anéantir.
◇ *vi* [bomb, mine etc] exploser, sauter; *fig*: to ~ with laughter éclater de rire; to ~ into fits of giggles partir dans des fous rires; to ~ with anger exploser de colère; the game ~d into life le match s'est animé d'un seul coup; the boxer ~d into action le boxeur est entré en action d'une manière fulgurante; the population ~d with the advent of the industrial revolution l'avènement de la révolution industrielle a provoqué une explosion démographique.

exploded [ɪk'spləʊdɪd] *adj* -**1.** [bomb, mine etc] qu'on a fait exploser; *fig* [theory, myth etc] détruit, anéanti. -**2.** [view, diagram] éclaté.

exploit [*n* 'eksplɔɪt, *vb* ɪk'splɔɪt] ◇ *n* exploit *m*.
◇ *vt* -**1.** [workers] exploiter. -**2.** [natural resources] exploiter.

exploitable [ɪk'splɔɪtəbl] *adj* [resource] exploitable.

exploitation [,eksplɔɪ'teɪʃn] *n* [of workers, of natural resources] exploitation *f*.

exploitative [ɪk'splɔɪtətɪv] *adj* [practices] relevant de l'exploitation; the company's ~ attitude towards the workforce la manière dont l'entreprise exploite la main-d'œuvre.

exploiter [ɪk'splɔɪtə^r] *n* -**1.** [of workers] exploiteur *m*, -euse *f*. -**2.** [of natural resources] exploitant *m*, -e *f*.

exploration [,eksplə'reɪʃn] *n* -**1.** [of place, problem] exploration *f*; to set off on an ~ of the world partir explorer le monde, se lancer à la découverte du monde; voyage of ~ voyage *m* d'exploration. -**2.** MED exploration *f*.

exploratory [ɪk'splɒrətrɪ] *adj* [journey] d'exploration; [talks, discussions] exploratoire; ~ drilling forage *m* d'exploration; ~ surgery chirurgie *f* exploratrice.

explore [ɪk'splɔː^r] ◇ *vt* -**1.** [country] explorer; [town] découvrir; she ~d her new filling with the tip of her tongue elle a tâté son nouveau plombage du bout de la langue. -**2.** [issue, possibility, problem] explorer, examiner; to ~ every avenue *fig* explorer toutes les voies OR solutions possibles; to ~ the ground *fig* tâter le terrain. -**3.** MED explorer, sonder.
◇ *vi* faire une exploration; let's go exploring [in the woods, countryside etc] partons en exploration; [in a city] allons découvrir la ville.

explorer [ɪk'splɔːrə^r] *n* -**1.** [person] explorateur *m*, -trice *f*. -**2.** [instrument] sonde *f*.

explosion [ɪk'spləʊʒn] *n* -**1.** [of bomb, gas] explosion *f*; an ~ ripped through the building une explosion a ébranlé le bâtiment || *fig*: an ~ of anger une explosion de colère; there was an ~ of laughter from the dining room une explosion OR une tempête de rires est arrivée de la salle à manger. -**2.** [act of exploding] explosion *f*; to carry out a carefully controlled ~ conduire une explosion soigneusement contrôlée.

explosive [ɪk'spləʊsɪv] ◇ *adj* -**1.** explosif; [gas] explosible; ~ device dispositif *m* explosif; ~ situation *fig* situation *f* explosive. -**2.** LING explosif.
◇ *n* -**1.** [in bomb] explosif *m*; high ~ explosif puissant. -**2.** LING explosive *f*.

expo ['ekspəʊ] (*pl* expos) *n* [exhibition] expo *f*.

exponent [ɪk'spəʊnənt] *n* -**1.** [of idea, theory] apôtre *m*, avocat *m*, -e *f*; [of skill] représentant *m*, -e *f*; he is a leading ~ of this theory il est l'un des plus fervents apôtres de cette théorie. -**2.** MATH exposant *m*.

exponential [,ekspə'nenʃl] *adj* exponentiel.

exponentially [,ekspə'nenʃəlɪ] *adv* de manière exponentielle.

export [*n* 'ekspɔːt, *vb* ɪk'spɔːt] ◇ *n* -**1.** [action] exportation *f*; for ~ only réservé à l'exportation. -**2.** [product] exportation *f*; visible/invisible ~s exportations visibles/invisibles.
◇ *comp* [duty, licence, trade] d'exportation; ~ drive campagne *f* visant à stimuler l'exportation; ~-driven [expansion, recovery] basé OR centré sur les exportations; ~ earnings revenus *mpl* OR recettes *fpl* de l'exportation; ~-intensive [country] fortement exportateur; ~ reject produit *m* impropre à l'exportation.
◇ *vt* -**1.** *literal* & *fig* exporter; to ~ goods to other countries exporter des marchandises vers d'autres pays. -**2.** COMPUT exporter.
◇ *vi* exporter; the firm ~s all over the world l'entreprise exporte dans le monde entier; ~ing company société exportatrice.

exportable [ɪk'spɔːtəbl] *adj* exportable.

exportation [,ekspɔː'teɪʃn] *n fml* exportation *f*.

exporter [ek'spɔːtə^r] *n* exportateur *m*, -trice *f*.

expose [ɪk'spəʊz] *vt* -**1.** [uncover] découvrir; PHOT exposer; her low-cut dress leaves her shoulders ~d sa robe décolletée découvre OR laisse voir ses épaules; to ~ sb/sthg to sthg exposer qqn/qqch à qqch; to be ~d to attack être exposé aux attaques; he was ~d to German from the age of five il a été au contact de l'allemand depuis l'âge de cinq ans; to ~ sthg to view exposer qqch à la vue; to ~ o.s. [exhibitionist] s'exhiber; to ~ oneself is an offence l'exhibitionnisme est un délit; to ~ o.s. to sthg [to criticism, ridicule, risk] s'exposer à qqch. -**2.** [reveal, unmask - plot] découvrir; [- spy] découvrir, démasquer.

exposé [eks'pəʊzeɪ] *n* PRESS révélations *fpl*; the newspaper's ~ of the MP's activities les révélations du journal sur les activités du parlementaire.

exposed [ɪk'spəʊzd] *adj* [location, house, position etc] exposé; TECH [parts, gears] apparent, à découvert; ARCHIT [beam] apparent; the troops are in an ~ position les soldats sont à découvert; the Chancellor is left in an ~ position after today's revelation *fig* la révélation d'aujourd'hui a mis le Chancelier dans une position précaire.

exposition [,ekspə'zɪʃn] *n* **-1.** [explanation] exposition *f.* **-2.** [exhibition] exposition *f.*

expostulate [ɪk'spɒstjʊleɪt] *vi fml* récriminer; to ~ with sb about sthg récriminer contre qqn à propos de qqch.

expostulation [ɪk,spɒstjʊ'leɪʃn] *n fml* récrimination *f.*

exposure [ɪk'spəʊʒəʳ] *n* **-1.** [to harm, radiation] exposition *f*; ~ to danger is something he encounters daily il est quotidiennement exposé au danger. **-2.** [to cold]: to suffer from the effects of ~ souffrir des effets d'une exposition au froid; to die of ~ mourir de froid. **-3.** [unmasking, revealing - of crime, scandal] révélation *f*, divulgation *f.* **-4.** PHOT pose *f*; a film with 24 ~s une pellicule de 24 poses ❑ time ~ pose; ~ time temps *m* de pose; ~ counter compteur *m* de prises de vue. **-5.** [position of house] exposition *f*; the building has a southern ~ le bâtiment est exposé au sud. **-6.** [media coverage] couverture *f*; to receive a lot of ~ [book, person] faire l'objet d'une couverture médiatique importante; pop stars suffer from too much media ~ les stars de la musique pop sont l'objet d'une attention excessive des média.

exposure meter *n* exposimètre *m*, posemètre *m.*

expound [ɪk'spaʊnd] *vt* exposer.

express [ɪk'spres] ◇ *n* **-1.** [train] express *m*; to travel by ~ voyager en express. **-2.** [system of delivery] exprès *m*; the Express PRESS *nom abrégé du Daily Express*.
◇ *adj* **-1.** [clear - instructions, purpose] clair; with the ~ intention of... avec la claire intention de... **-2.** [fast - delivery, messenger] express; ~ company entreprise *f* de livraison exprès; ~ train train *m* express, express *m.*
◇ *adv* [send] en exprès.
◇ *vt* **-1.** [voice, convey] exprimer; to ~ an interest in (doing) sthg manifester de l'intérêt pour (faire) qqch; she ~es her feelings by painting elle exprime ses sentiments par OR à travers la peinture; the two men ~ed optimism that a peaceful solution would be found les deux hommes se sont montrés optimistes quant à un règlement pacifique; to ~ o.s. s'exprimer; to ~ o.s. through sthg s'exprimer par OR à travers qqch. **-2.** [render in a different form] exprimer; it's difficult to ~ this idea in Russian cette idée est difficile à exprimer en russe; to ~ sthg as a fraction MATH exprimer qqch sous la forme d'une fraction. **-3.** *fml* [juice] extraire, exprimer; [milk] tirer. **-4.** [send] envoyer en exprès.

expression [ɪk'spreʃn] *n* **-1.** [of feelings, thoughts, friendship] expression *f*; as an ~ of our thanks, we took her out for a meal pour lui exprimer nos remerciements, nous l'avons emmenée dîner au restaurant; we'd like you to have it as an ~ of our gratitude nous vous l'offrons en témoignage de notre reconnaissance; to give ~ to sthg exprimer qqch; her feelings found ~ in music ses sentiments trouvèrent leur expression dans la musique; freedom of ~ liberté *f* d'expression. **-2.** [feeling - in art, music] expression *f*; to play/to paint with ~ jouer/peindre avec expression; he puts a lot of ~ into what he plays il met beaucoup d'expression dans ce qu'il joue. **-3.** [phrase] expression *f*; set OR fixed ~ LING expression OR locution *f* figée OR toute faite; algebraic ~ MATH expression algébrique. **-4.** [facial] expression *f*; I could tell by her ~ je voyais bien à son expression.

expressionism [ɪk'spreʃənɪzm] *n* ART expressionnisme *m.*

expressionist [ɪk'spreʃənɪst] ART ◇ *adj* expressionniste.
◇ *n* expressionniste *mf.*

expressionistic [ɪk,spreʃə'nɪstɪk] *adj* ART expressionniste.

expressionless [ɪk'spreʃənlɪs] *adj* [face, person] inexpressif, sans expression; [voice] inexpressif, éteint, terne; the accused sat ~ in the dock l'inculpé était assis sans expression au banc des accusés.

expressive [ɪk'spresɪv] *adj* [face, gesture, smile] expressif; to be ~ of sthg être indicatif de qqch.

expressively [ɪk'spresɪvlɪ] *adv* [gesture, smile] avec expression.

expressiveness [ɪk'spresɪvnɪs] *n* [of face, gesture, smile] expressivité *f.*

expressly [ɪk'spreslɪ] *adv* expressément.

expressman [ɪk'spresmæn] (*pl* expressmen [-men]) *n Am* messager *m* d'une compagnie de livraison exprès.

expressway [ɪk'spresweɪ] *n Am* autoroute *f.*

expropriate [eks'prəʊprɪeɪt] *vt* exproprier.

expropriation [eks,prəʊprɪ'eɪʃn] *n* expropriation *f.*

expulsion [ɪk'spʌlʃn] *n* **-1.** [from party, country] expulsion *f*; [from school] renvoi *m.* **-2.** [of breath] expulsion *f.*

expunge [ɪk'spʌndʒ] *vt fml* [delete] supprimer, effacer; [from memory] effacer.

expurgate ['ekspəgeɪt] *vt* [book, play] expurger; ~d edition édition *f* expurgée.

exquisite [ɪk'skwɪzɪt] *adj* **-1.** [food, beauty, manners] exquis; [jewellery, craftsmanship] raffiné; a face of ~ beauty un visage d'une beauté exquise. **-2.** [intense - pleasure, pain, thrill] intense.

exquisitely [ɪk'skwɪzɪtlɪ] *adv* **-1.** [superbly] de façon exquise, exquisément *lit*; ~ polite d'une exquise courtoisie; an ~ timed interjection une interjection exquisément opportune. **-2.** [intensely] intensément.

ex-service *adj Br* retraité de l'armée.

ex-serviceman (*pl* ex-servicemen) *n* retraité *m* de l'armée.

ex-servicewoman (*pl* ex-servicewomen) *n* retraitée *f* de l'armée.

ext. (*written abbr of* extension): ~ 4174 p. 4174.

extant [ek'stænt] *adj fml* encore existant.

extemporaneous [ɪk,stempə'reɪnjəs], **extemporary** [ɪk'stemprərɪ] *adj* improvisé, impromptu.

extempore [ɪk'stempərɪ] ◇ *adj* improvisé, impromptu.
◇ *adv* [speak] impromptu.

extemporize [ɪk'stempəraɪz] ◇ *vt* [speech, piece of music] improviser.
◇ *vi* [speaker, musician] improviser.

extend [ɪk'stend] ◇ *vt* **-1.** [stretch out - arm, leg] étendre, allonger; [- wings] ouvrir, déployer; [- aerial] déplier, déployer; to ~ one's hand to sb tendre la main à qqn. **-2.** [in length, duration - guarantee, visa, news programme] prolonger; [- road, runway] prolonger, allonger; they ~ed his visa by six months on a prolongé son visa de six mois. **-3.** [make larger, widen - frontiers, law, enquiry, search] étendre; [- building] agrandir; [- vocabulary] enrichir, élargir; the company decided to ~ its activities into the export market la société a décidé d'étendre ses activités au marché de l'exportation. **-4.** [offer - friendship, hospitality] offrir; [- thanks, condolences, congratulations] présenter; [- credit] accorder; to ~ an invitation to sb faire une invitation à qqn; to ~ a welcome to sb souhaiter la bienvenue à qqn. **-5.** [stretch - horse, person] pousser au bout de ses capacités OR à son maximum; to ~ o.s. in a race se donner à fond dans une course.
◇ *vi* **-1.** [protrude - wall, cliff] avancer, former une avancée. **-2.** [stretch - country, forest, hills etc] s'étendre; the queue ~ed all the way down the street il y avait la queue jusqu'au bout de la rue ‖ *fig*: the parliamentary recess ~s into October les vacances parlementaires se prolongent jusqu'en octobre; the laughter ~ed to the others in the room le rire a gagné le reste de la salle; the legislation does not ~ to single mothers la législation ne concerne pas les mères célibataires.

extendable [ɪk'stendəbl] *adj* **-1.** [in space]: ~ aerial antenne *f* télescopique; ~ ladder échelle *f* à coulisse. **-2.** [in time - contract, visa] renouvelable; tenancy ~ by one year contrat de location pouvant être prolongé d'un an.

extended [ɪk'stendɪd] *adj* **-1.** [in time - contract, visit] prolongé; the firm gave him an ~ contract la société a reconduit son contrat; to be on ~ leave être en arrêt prolongé; owing to the ~ news bulletin en raison de la prolongation du bulletin d'informations ❑ ~ coverage [on radio, TV] *informations détaillées sur un événement.* **-2.** [larger, wider - frontiers, enquiry, search] étendu; the ~ family la famille élargie; ~ coverage [in insurance] couverture *f* multirisque; the bank granted him ~ credit la banque lui a accordé un crédit à long terme. **-3.** [in space] étendu, allongé; [building] agrandi.

extended-play *adj* [record] double.

extendible [ɪk'stendəbl] = **extendable.**

extending [ɪk'stendɪŋ] ◇ *adj* [table] à rallonge OR rallonges; [ladder] à coulisse.
◇ *n* **-1.** [of arm, leg, freedom] extension *f.* **-2.** [of contract, visa, road] prolongation *f.*

extensible [ɪk'stensəbl] = **extendable 1.**

extension [ɪk'stenʃn] *n* **-1.** [of arm, legislation, frontiers] extension *f.* **-2.** [of house, building]: to build an ~ onto agrandir; do you like the new ~? [to the house] la nouvelle partie de la maison vous plaît-elle?; [of library, museum etc] la nouvelle aile vous plaît-elle? **-3.** [of contract, visa, time period] prolongation *f*; to ask for/to get an ~ [to pay, hand in work] demander/obtenir un délai; the bar's been granted an ~ le bar a obtenu une prolongation de ses heures d'ouverture. **-4.** [telephone - in office building] poste *m*; [- in house] poste *m* supplémentaire; can I have ~ 946? pouvez-vous me passer le poste 946? **-5.** ELEC prolongateur *m*, rallonge *f.*
◆ **by extension** *adv phr* par extension.

extension college *n* collège *m* d'éducation permanente.

extension course *n* cours *m* d'éducation permanente.

extension ladder *n* échelle *f* à coulisse.

extension lead *n Br* prolongateur *m*, rallonge *f.*

extensive [ɪk'stensɪv] *adj* [desert, rash, powers, knowledge] étendu; [damage] important, considérable; [tests, research, investigation] approfondi; AGR extensif; the area is remarkable for its ~ tree cover cette région se distingue par l'étendue considérable de ses bois; the issue has been given ~ coverage in the media ce problème a été largement traité dans les médias; to make ~ use of sthg beaucoup utiliser qqch, faire un usage considérable de qqch.

extensively [ɪk'stensɪvlɪ] *adv* [damaged, altered, revised] considérablement; [quote] abondamment; [travel, read] beaucoup; [discuss] en profondeur; the car has been ~ tested la voiture a subi des tests approfondis OR poussés; to research sthg ~ faire des recherches approfondies sur qqch; to use sthg ~ beaucoup utiliser qqch, faire un usage considérable de qqch.

extensor [ɪk'stensəʳ] *n* ANAT extenseur *m.*

extent [ɪk'stent] *n* **-1.** [size, range - of ground, damage, knowledge] étendue *f*; [- of debts] importance *f*; trees ran along the entire ~ of the boulevard des arbres longeaient le boulevard sur toute sa longueur; debts to the ~ of £1,000 dettes d'une valeur OR d'un montant de 1 000 livres. **-2.** [degree] mesure *f*, degré *m*; these figures show the ~ to which tourism has been affected ces chiffres montrent à quel point le tourisme a été affecté; to what ~? dans quelle mesure ?; to that ~ sur ce point, à cet égard; to the ~ that..., to such an ~ that... à tel point que...

◆ **to a large extent, to a great extent** *adv phr* dans une grande mesure, à un haut point OR degré.

◆ **to an extent, to some extent, to a certain extent** *adv phr* dans une certaine mesure, jusqu'à un certain point OR degré.

extenuate [ɪk'stenjʊeɪt] *vt* atténuer.

extenuating [ɪk'stenjʊeɪtɪŋ] *adj*: ~ circumstances circonstances *fpl* atténuantes.

extenuation [ɪk,stenjʊ'eɪʃn] *n* atténuation *f*.

exterior [ɪk'stɪərɪə^r] ◇ *adj* extérieur; ~ angle MATH angle externe; ~ to extérieur à.

◇ *n* [of house, building] extérieur *m*; [of person] apparence *f*, dehors *m*; our house has a whitewashed ~ notre maison a une façade blanchie à la chaux.

exterminate [ɪk'stɜːmɪneɪt] *vt* [pests] exterminer; [race, people] exterminer, anéantir.

extermination [ɪk,stɜːmɪ'neɪʃn] *n* [of pests] extermination *f*; [of race, people] extermination *f*, anéantissement *m*.

exterminator [ɪk'stɜːmɪneɪtə^r] *n* [person - gen] exterminateur *m*, -trice *f*; [- of rats, mice] dératiseur *m*; [poison] mort-aux-rats *f inv*.

extern ['ekstɜːn] *n Am* MED externe *mf*.

external [ɪk'stɜːnl] ◇ *adj* [events, relations, trade, wall] extérieur; ~ ear oreille *f* externe; 'for ~ use only' PHARM 'à usage externe uniquement'; ~ pressure [on person] pression *f* de l'extérieur; [on device] pression *f* extérieure OR du dehors; ~ examiner UNIV examinateur *m*, -trice *f* venant de l'extérieur; ~ device COMPUT unité *f* extérieure OR non-intégrée; ~ financing FIN financement *m* externe.

◇ *n (usu pl)*: he judges people by ~s il juge les gens sur leur apparence.

externalize, -ise [ɪk'stɜːnəlaɪz] *vt* extérioriser.

externally [ɪk'stɜːnəlɪ] *adv* à l'extérieur; 'to be used ~' PHARM 'à usage externe'.

externe ['ekstɜːn] = **extern**.

extinct [ɪk'stɪŋkt] *adj* [species, animal, race] disparu; ~ volcano volcan *m* éteint; the horse and plough are nearly ~ le cheval et la charrue sont en voie d'extinction; to become ~ [species, tradition] s'éteindre, disparaître; [method] disparaître.

extinction [ɪk'stɪŋkʃn] *n* [of race, species] extinction *f*, disparition *f*; [of fire] extinction *f*; to be threatened with ~ être menacé d'extinction; to threaten sthg with ~ menacer qqch d'extinction; to hunt an animal to ~ chasser un animal jusqu'à extinction de l'espèce.

extinguish [ɪk'stɪŋgwɪʃ] *vt* [fire, candle etc] éteindre; *fig* [memory] effacer.

extinguisher [ɪk'stɪŋgwɪʃə^r] *n* extincteur *m*.

extirpate ['ekstəpeɪt] *vt fml* extirper.

extirpation [,ekstə'peɪʃn] *n fml* extirpation *f*.

extn. = **ext.**

extol, extoll *Am* [ɪk'stəʊl] (*pt & pp* **extolled**, *cont* **extolling**) *vt fml* [person] chanter les louanges de; [system, virtues, merits] vanter.

extort [ɪk'stɔːt] *vt* [money] extorquer, soutirer; [confession, promise] extorquer, arracher; to ~ money from sb extorquer OR soutirer de l'argent à qqn.

extortion [ɪk'stɔːʃn] *n* [of money, promise, confession] extorsion *f*; that's sheer ~! [very expensive] c'est du vol pur et simple!

extortionate [ɪk'stɔːʃnət] *adj* [price, demand] exorbitant, démesuré; that's ~! [very expensive] c'est exorbitant OR du vol!

extortionately [ɪk'stɔːʃnətlɪ] *adv* démesurément, excessivement.

extortioner [ɪk'stɔːʃnə^r], **extortionist** [ɪk'stɔːʃnɪst] *n* extorqueur *m*, -euse *f*.

extra ['ekstrə] ◇ *adj* -**1.** [additional] supplémentaire; there are some ~ questions overleaf il y a des questions supplémentaires au dos; I put an ~ jumper on j'ai mis un pull en plus; ~ revision classes des cours de révision supplémentaires OR en plus; he made an ~ effort to get there on time il a redoublé d'efforts pour y arriver à l'heure; as an ~ precaution pour plus de précaution; an ~ helping of cake une autre part de gâteau; no ~ charge/cost aucun supplément de prix/frais supplémentaire; service/VAT is ~ le service/la TVA est en supplément; ~ pay supplément de salaire; she asked for an ~ £2 elle a demandé 2 livres de plus; at no ~ charge sans supplément de prix ❑ ~ time [to pay, finish etc] délai *m*; SPORT prolongations *fpl*; the game has gone into ~ time les joueurs sont en train de jouer les prolongations. -**2.** [spare] en plus; an ~ sheet of paper une feuille en plus.

◇ *adv* -**1.** [extremely - polite, kind] extrêmement; [- strong, white] super-; to work ~ hard travailler d'arrache-pied; ~ dry [wine] très sec; [champagne, vermouth] extra-dry *(inv)*; ~ fine [flour, sugar] extrafin, surfin; ~ smart [dress, outfit] superchic, ultrachic; for an ~ white wash pour un linge extra-blanc. -**2.** [in addition] plus, davantage; to pay ~ for a double room payer plus OR un supplément pour une chambre double.

◇ *n* -**1.** [addition] supplément *m*; the paper comes with a business ~ le journal est vendu avec un supplément affaires; a car with many ~s une voiture avec de nombreux accessoires en option. -**2.** [in film] figurant *m*, *-e f*. -**3.** [additional charge] supplément *m*. -**4.** [luxury]: little ~s petits extras *mpl* OR luxes *mpl*.

extra- *in cpds* extra-; ~large grande taille; ~special ultra-spécial; you'll have to take ~special care over it il faudra que tu y fasses super attention.

extract [*vb* ɪk'strækt, *n* 'ekstrækt] ◇ *vt* -**1.** [take out - juice, oil, bullet] extraire; [- tooth] arracher, extraire; [- cork] ôter, enlever; he ~ed a comb from his pocket il tira un peigne de sa poche; to ~ a quotation from a passage extraire OR tirer une citation d'un passage. -**2.** [obtain - information] soutirer, arracher; [- money] soutirer; to ~ a confession from sb soutirer OR arracher un aveu à qqn.

◇ *n* -**1.** [from book, piece of music] extrait *m*. -**2.** [substance] extrait *m*; PHARM extrait *m*, essence *f*; beef/malt/vegetable ~ extrait de bœuf/de malt/de légumes.

extraction [ɪk'strækʃn] *n* -**1.** [removal - of juice, oil, bullet] extraction *f*; [- of tooth] extraction *f*, arrachage *m*. -**2.** [descent] extraction *f*; of noble/humble ~ de noble/modeste extraction; he is of Scottish ~ il est d'origine écossaise.

extractor [ɪk'stræktə^r] *n* [machine, tool] extracteur *m*; [fan] ventilateur *m*, aérateur *m*; juice ~ *Br* presse-fruits *m inv*.

extractor fan *n* ventilateur *m*, aérateur *m*.

extractor hood *n* [on stove] hotte *f* aspirante.

extracurricular [,ekstrəkə'rɪkjʊlə^r] *adj* SCH hors programme, extrascolaire; UNIV hors programme; ~ activities activités *fpl* extrascolaires.

extraditable ['ekstrədaɪtəbl] *adj* passible d'extradition.

extradite ['ekstrədaɪt] *vt* [send back] extrader; [procure extradition of] obtenir l'extradition de.

extradition [,ekstrə'dɪʃn] *n* extradition *f*; to request/to obtain the ~ of sb demander/obtenir l'extradition de qqn ❑ ~ order ordre *m* d'extrader OR d'extradition; ~ treaty traité *m* d'extradition.

extragalactic [,ekstrəgə'læktɪk] *adj* extragalactique.

extrajudicial [,ekstrədʒuː'dɪʃl] *adj* extrajudiciaire.

extramarital [,ekstrə'mærɪtl] *adj* extraconjugal; ~ relations relations *fpl* extraconjugales; ~ sex rapports *mpl* extraconjugaux.

extramural [,ekstrə'mjʊərəl] *adj* -**1.** UNIV [course, studies, activities]: Department of Extramural Studies ≃ Institut *m* d'éducation permanente. -**2.** [district] extra-muros.

extraneous [ɪk'streɪnjəs] *adj* -**1.** [irrelevant - idea, point, consideration, issue] étranger, extérieur; to be ~ to sthg [idea, point, issue] être étranger à qqch; [detail] être sans rapport avec qqch. -**2.** [from outside - noise, force] extérieur.

extraordinarily [ɪk'strɔːdnrəlɪ] *adv* -**1.** [as intensifier] extraordinairement, incroyablement; what an ~ well taken goal! quel tir extraordinaire!; that play was ~ badly acted cette pièce était incroyablement mal jouée; it took an ~ long time to get there nous avons mis un temps incroyable pour arriver. -**2.** [unusually] extraordinairement, d'une manière inhabituelle.

extraordinary [ɪk'strɔːdnrɪ] *adj* -**1.** [remarkable] extraordinaire; quite ~! absolument extraordinaire!; (why,) that's OR how ~! c'est extraordinaire OR incroyable! -**2.** [additional] extraordinaire; to call an ~ session of Parliament convoquer une session extraordinaire du Parlement.

extrapolate [ɪk'stræpəleɪt] ◇ *vt* [infer from facts] déduire par extrapolation; MATH établir par extrapolation; if we ~ these figures [use them as a basis] si nous extrapolons à partir de ces chiffres; [arrive at by extrapolation] si nous déduisons ces chiffres par extrapolation; to ~ a curve on a graph tracer une courbe par extrapolation.

◇ *vi* extrapoler; to ~ from sthg extrapoler à partir de qqch.

extrapolation [ɪk,stræpə'leɪʃn] *n* extrapolation *f*.

extrasensory [,ekstrə'sensərɪ] *adj* extrasensoriel; ~ perception perception *f* extrasensorielle.

extraterrestrial [,ekstrətə'restrɪəl] ◇ *adj* extraterrestre.

◇ *n* extraterrestre *mf*.

extraterritorial ['ekstrə,terɪ'tɔːrɪəl] *adj* [possessions] situé hors du territoire national; [rights] d'exterritorialité, d'extra-territorialité.

extraterritoriality ['ekstrəterɪ,tɔːrɪ'ælətɪ] *n* exterritorialité *f*, extraterritorialité *f*.

extrauterine [,ekstrə'juːtəraɪn] *adj* extra-utérin.

extravagance [ɪk'strævəgəns] *n* -**1.** [wasteful spending] dépenses *fpl* extravagantes; a piece of ~ une folie. -**2.** [extravagant purchase] folie *f*; to allow o.s. little ~s se permettre des petites folies.

extravagant [ɪk'strævəgənt] *adj* -**1.** [wasteful, profligate - person] dépensier, prodigue; [- tastes] coûteux, dispendieux; that was much too ~ of you tu as fait des folies; I think you're being a bit ~, having the central heating on all the time je trouve que c'est du gaspillage de laisser le chauffage central allumé en permanence comme tu le fais; to be ~ with one's money être gaspilleur OR dépensier, gaspiller son argent. -**2.** [exaggerated - idea, notion, opinion] extravagant; [- claim, behaviour, prices] extravagant, excessif; to make ~ claims avoir des prétentions exagérées OR excessives; his ~ prose style le style excessif de sa prose.

extravagantly [ɪk'strævəgəntlɪ] *adv* -**1.** [wastefully]: to spend money ~ jeter l'argent par les fenêtres; to live ~ vivre sur un grand pied; to entertain ~ recevoir sans regarder à la dépense; an ~ furnished room une pièce meublée à grands frais OR luxueusement meublée; ~ overpriced goods marchandises à des prix excessifs. -**2.** [exaggeratedly - behave, act, talk] de manière extravagante; [- praise] avec excès; "I'm so hungry I could eat a horse", he claimed ~ «j'ai si faim que je pourrais manger un cheval», exagéra-t-il; ~ worded claims des affirmations exagérées OR excessives.

extravaganza [ɪk,strævə'gænzə] *n* [lavish performance] œuvre *f* à grand spectacle.

extravehicular [,ekstrəvɪ'hɪkjʊlə^r] *adj* ASTRONAUT extravéhiculaire.

extravert ['ekstrəvɜːt] = **extrovert**.

extreme [ɪk'striːm] ◇ *adj* -**1.** [heat, pain, views, measures] extrême; they live in ~ poverty ils vivent dans une misère extrême; to be in ~

pain souffrir terriblement OR atrocement; to be ~ in one's beliefs être extrême dans ses convictions; the ~ left wing of the party l'aile d'extrême gauche du parti; ~ old age grand âge *m*. -**2.** [furthest away] extrême; at the ~ end of the platform à l'extrémité du quai; on the ~ right of the screen à l'extrême droite de l'écran; they are ~ opposites of the political spectrum ils sont aux deux extrémités de l'éventail politique.

◇ *n* extrême *m*; ~s of temperature extrêmes de température; to go to ~s exagérer; to take OR to carry sthg to ~s, to go to ~s with sthg pousser qqch à l'extrême; to be driven to ~s être poussé à bout; to go from one ~ to the other aller OR passer d'un extrême à l'autre; don't go to the opposite ~ ne tombe pas dans l'extrême inverse.

◆ **in the extreme** *adv phr* à l'extrême; polite/careful in the ~ poli/soigneux à l'extrême.

extremely [ɪk'striːmlɪ] *adv* [as intensifier] extrêmement.

extreme unction *n* RELIG extrême-onction *f*.

extremis [ɪk'striːmɪs]

◆ **in extremis** *adv phr* [in an extremity] en dernier recours, au pire; we'll use him in ~ nous ne ferons appel à lui qu'en dernier recours.

extremism [ɪk'striːmɪzm] *n* POL extrémisme *m*.

extremist [ɪk'striːmɪst] ◇ *adj* extrémiste.

◇ *n* extrémiste *mf*.

extremity [ɪk'stremətɪ] (*pl* **extremities**) *n* -**1.** [furthermost tip] extrémité *f*; at the southernmost ~ of the peninsula à l'extrémité sud de la péninsule. -**2.** (*usu pl*) [hand, foot]: the extremities les extrémités *fpl*. -**3.** [extreme nature - of belief, view etc] extrémité *f*. -**4.** [adversity, danger] extrémité *f*; she was reduced to the ~ of selling the family house elle s'est vue réduite à vendre la maison familiale; to help sb in their ~ aider qqn dans son malheur. -**5.** (*usu pl*) [extreme measure] extrémité *f*; to resort to extremities en venir à des extrêmes; to drive sb to extremities pousser OR conduire qqn à des extrêmes.

extricate ['ekstrɪkeɪt] *vt* [thing] extirper, dégager; [person] dégager; to ~ o.s. from a tricky situation se sortir OR se tirer d'une situation délicate; to ~ o.s. from a boring conversation s'échapper d'une conversation ennuyeuse.

extrinsic [ek'strɪnsɪk] *adj* extrinsèque.

extrinsically [ek'strɪnsɪklɪ] *adv* extrinsèquement.

extroversion [,ekstrə'vɜːʃn] *n* PSYCH extraversion *f*, extroversion *f*.

extrovert ['ekstrəvɜːt] PSYCH ◇ *adj* extraverti, extroverti.

◇ *n* extraverti *m*, -e *f*, extroverti *m*, -e *f*; he's an ~ c'est un extraverti.

extrude [ɪk'struːd] ◇ *vt* -**1.** TECH [metals, plastics] extruder. -**2.** *fml* [force out - lava] extruder.

◇ *vi* [protrude] déborder, s'avancer.

extrusion [ɪk'struːʒn] *n* -**1.** TECH [of metal, plastic] extrusion *f*. -**2.** *fml* [action] extraction *f*. -**3.** [protrusion] extrusion *f*.

extrusive [ɪk'struːsɪv] *adj* [rock] effusif.

exuberance [ɪg'zjuːbərəns] *n* -**1.** [of person, writing] exubérance *f*; to be full of ~ être plein d'exubérance; youthful/natural ~ exubérance juvénile/naturelle. -**2.** [of vegetation] exubérance *f*.

exuberant [ɪg'zjuːbərənt] *adj* -**1.** [person, mood, style] exubérant. -**2.** [vegetation] exubérant.

exuberantly [ɪg'zjuːbərəntlɪ] *adv* avec exubérance.

exude [ɪg'zjuːd] ◇ *vi* [liquid, sap, blood etc] exsuder.

◇ *vt* [blood, sap] exsuder; *fig* [confidence, love] déborder de.

exult [ɪg'zʌlt] *vi* [rejoice] exulter, jubiler; [triumph] exulter; to ~ at OR in one's success [rejoice] se réjouir de son succès; to ~ over defeated opponents [triumph] exulter de la défaite de ses adversaires.

exultant [ɪg'zʌltənt] *adj* [feeling, shout, look] d'exultation; [mood, crowd] jubilant; to look ~ avoir l'air d'exulter; to be OR to feel ~ exulter.

exultantly [ɪg'zʌltəntlɪ] *adv* avec exultation.

exultation [,egzʌl'teɪʃn] *n* exultation *f*.

exurbia [eks'ɜːbɪə] *n Am* grande banlieue *f* résidentielle.

ex-voto [eks'vəʊtəʊ] RELIG ◇ *adj*: an ~ offering un ex-voto.

◇ *n* ex-voto *m inv*.

ex-wife *n* ex-femme *f*.

eye [aɪ] (*cont* eyeing OR eying) ◇ *n* -**1.** [organ] œil *m*; to have green ~s avoir les yeux verts; a girl with green ~s une fille aux yeux verts; before your very ~s! sous vos yeux!; look me in the ~ and say that regarde-moi bien dans les yeux et dis-le moi; I saw it with my own ~s je l'ai vu de mes yeux vu OR de mes propres yeux; with one's ~s closed/open les yeux fermés/ouverts; she can't keep her ~s open *fig* elle dort debout ☐ I could do it with my ~s closed je pourrais le faire les yeux fermés; he went into it with his ~s open il s'y est lancé en toute connaissance de cause. -**2.** [gaze] regard *m*; her ~s fell on the letter son regard est tombé sur la lettre; under the watchful ~ of his teacher sous l'œil vigilant de son professeur; the film looks at the world through the ~s of a child dans ce film, on voit le monde à travers les yeux d'un enfant; with a critical/an anxious ~ d'un œil critique/inquiet; I couldn't believe my ~s je n'en croyais pas mes yeux; he couldn't take his ~s off her il ne pouvait pas la quitter des yeux. -**3.** MIL: ~s left/right! tête à gauche/à droite!; ~s front! fixe! -**4.** SEW [of needle] chas *m*, œil *m*; [eyelet] œillet *m*. -**5.** [of potato, twig] œil *m*. -**6.** [of storm] œil *m*, centre *m*. -**7.** [photocell] œil *m* électrique. -**8.** *phr*: we can't close OR shut our ~s to the problem on ne peut pas fermer les yeux sur ce problème; to close one's ~s to the evidence se refuser à l'évidence; they can't close their ~s to the fact that the company's at fault ils sont bien obligés d'admettre que la société est en faute; the incident opened his ~s to the truth about her l'incident lui ouvrit les yeux sur ce qu'elle était vraiment; for your ~s only ultra-confidentiel; she has a good ~ for detail elle a l'œil pour ce qui est des détails; to get one's ~ in *Br* prendre ses repères; he only has ~s for her il n'a d'yeux que pour elle; the boss has his ~ on Smith for the job le patron a Smith en vue pour le poste; she has her ~ on the mayor's position elle vise la mairie; he always has an ~ for OR to the main chance il ne perd jamais de vue ses propres intérêts; in my/her ~s à mes/ses yeux; in the ~s of the law aux yeux OR au regard de la loi; to run OR to cast one's ~ over sthg jeter un coup d'œil à qqch; she ran an ~ over the contract elle a parcouru le contrat; to try to catch sb's ~ essayer d'attirer le regard de qqn; keep your ~ on the ball fixez OR regardez bien la balle; could you keep your ~ on the children/the house? pourriez-vous surveiller les enfants/la maison?; I have to keep an ~ on him il faut que je l'aie à l'œil; she keeps an ~ on things elle a l'œil à tout; to keep a close ~ on sthg surveiller qqch de près; keep an ~ on the situation suivez de près la situation; to keep one's ~ open for sthg être attentif à qqch; keep your ~s open OR an ~ out for a filling station essayez de repérer une station service; the children were all ~s les enfants n'en perdaient pas une miette; an ~ for an ~ (and a tooth for a tooth) œil pour œil, dent pour dent; his ~s are too big for his stomach il a les yeux plus grands que le ventre; to give sb the ~ *inf* [flirt] faire de l'œil à qqn; [give signal] faire signe à qqn (d'un clin d'œil); he has ~s in the back of his head il a des yeux derrière la tête; I've never set OR laid OR clapped *inf* ~s on her je ne l'ai jamais vue de ma vie; keep your ~s skinned *inf* OR peeled *inf* for trouble restez vigilant; to make ~s at sb faire de l'œil à qqn; my ~! *inf* mon œil!; she and I don't see ~ to ~ [disagree] elle ne voit pas les choses du même œil que moi, elle n'est pas de mon avis; [dislike one another] elle et moi, nous ne nous entendons pas; that's one in the ~ for him! *inf* ça lui fera les pieds!; there's more to this than meets the ~ [suspicious] on ne connaît pas les dessous de l'affaire; [difficult] c'est moins simple que cela n'en a l'air; we're up to our ~s in it! [overworked] on a du travail jusque là!; [in deep trouble] on est dans les ennuis jusqu'au cou!

◇ *comp* [hospital, specialist] des yeux; ~ bank banque *f* des yeux.

◇ *vt* regarder, mesurer du regard; the child ~d the man warily l'enfant dévisagea l'homme avec circonspection; she stood eyeing the sweets counter elle restait là à lorgner les bonbons; to ~ sthg hungrily dévorer qqch du regard.

◆ **with an eye to** *prep phr*: with an ~ to sthg/to doing sthg en vue de qqch/de faire qqch; with an ~ to the future en vue OR en prévision de l'avenir.

◆ **eye up**▽ *vt sep* reluquer.

eyeball ['aɪbɔːl] ◇ *n* globe *m* oculaire; drugged (up) to the ~s *fig* drogué à mort; ~ to ~ (with) nez à nez (avec).

◇ *vt inf* regarder fixement, reluquer.

eyeball-to-eyeball *inf adj* nez à nez; an ~ confrontation une confrontation entre quatre yeux OR quat'z'yeux, un face-à-face *(inv)*.

eyebath ['aɪbɑːθ] *n Br* œillère *f* MÉD.

eyebrow ['aɪbraʊ] *n* sourcil *m*; to raise one's ~s lever les sourcils; her behaviour raised a few ~s *fig* son comportement en a fait tiquer quelques-uns; to be up to one's ~s in sthg être dans qqch jusqu'au cou.

eyebrow pencil *n* crayon *m* à sourcils.

eye-catching *adj* [colour, dress] qui attire l'œil; [poster, title] accrocheur, tapageur.

eye contact *n* croisement *m* des regards; to establish ~ (with sb) croiser le regard (de qqn); to maintain ~ (with sb) regarder (qqn) dans les yeux.

eyecup ['aɪkʌp] *Am* = **eyebath**.

-eyed [aɪd] *in cpds* aux yeux...; blue~ aux yeux bleus; she stared at him, wide~ elle le regardait, les yeux écarquillés; one~ borgne, qui n'a qu'un œil.

eye drops *npl* gouttes *fpl* (pour les yeux).

eyeful ['aɪfʊl] *n* -**1.** [of dirt, dust]: I got an ~ of sand j'ai reçu du sable plein les yeux. -**2.** *inf* [look] regard *m*; get an ~ of that! visez un peu ça! -**3.** *inf* [woman] belle fille *f*.

eyeglass ['aɪglɑːs] *n* [monocle] monocle *m*.

◆ **eyeglasses** *npl Am* [spectacles] lunettes *fpl*.

eyehole ['aɪhəʊl] *n* -**1.** [peephole - in mask] trou *m* pour les yeux; [- in door, wall] judas *m*. -**2.** [eyelet] œillet *m*. -**3.** *inf* [eye socket] orbite *f*.

eyelash ['aɪlæʃ] *n* cil *m*.

eyeless ['aɪlɪs] *adj* [without eyes] sans yeux; [blind] aveugle; 'Eyeless in Gaza' *Huxley* 'la Paix des profondeurs'.

eyelet ['aɪlɪt] *n* -**1.** [gen & SEW] œillet *m*. -**2.** [peephole - in mask] trou *m* pour les yeux; [- in door, wall] judas *m*.

eye level ◇ *n*: at ~ au niveau des yeux.

◇ *adj* qui est au niveau des yeux; ~ grill gril *m* surélevé.

eyelid ['aɪlɪd] *n* paupière *f*.

eyeliner ['aɪ,laɪnəʳ] *n* eye-liner *m*.

eye-opener *inf n* -**1.** [surprise] révélation *f*, surprise *f*; her behaviour was a real ~ for him son comportement lui a ouvert les yeux; the experience proved a bit of an ~! l'expérience a été assez révélatrice! -**2.** *Am* [drink] *petit verre pris au réveil*.

eyepatch ['aɪpætʃ] *n* [after operation] cache *m*, pansement *m (sur l'œil)*; [permanent] bandeau *m*.

eyepiece ['aɪpiːs] *n* oculaire *m*.
eye rhyme *n* rime *f* pour l'œil.
eyeshade ['aɪʃeɪd] *n* visière *f*.
eye shadow *n* fard *m* à paupières.
eyesight ['aɪsaɪt] *n* vue *f*; do you have good ~? avez-vous une bonne vue OR de bons yeux?; his ~ is failing sa vue baisse; to lose one's ~ perdre la vue.
eye socket *n* orbite *f*.
eyesore ['aɪsɔːʳ] *n* abomination *f*, horreur *f*.
eyestrain ['aɪstreɪn] *n* fatigue *f* des yeux; computer screens can cause ~ les ordinateurs fatiguent les yeux; to suffer from ~ avoir la vue fatiguée.
Eyetie▼ ['aɪtaɪ] *n Br terme injurieux désignant un Italien*, ≃ Rital *m*.
eyetooth ['aɪtuːθ] (*pl* eyeteeth [-tiːθ]) *n* canine *f* supérieure; I'd give my eyeteeth for a bike like that/to beinvited *inf* je donnerais n'importe quoi pour avoir un vélo comme ça/pour être invité.
eyewash ['aɪwɒʃ] *n* MED collyre *m*; that's a load of ~! *inf Br fig* [nonsense] c'est de la foutaise!; [boasting] ce n'est que de la frime!
eyewitness [ˌaɪ'wɪtnɪs] ◇ *n* témoin *m* oculaire. ◇ *comp* [account, description] d'un témoin oculaire.
eyot [eɪt] *n Br arch* îlot *m*.
eyrie ['ɪərɪ] *n* aire *f (d'aigle)*.
Ezekiel [ɪ'ziːkjəl] *pr n* Ézéchiel.
Ezra ['ezrə] *pr n* Ezra.

f (*pl* f's OR fs), **F** (*pl* F's OR Fs) [ef] ◇ *n* [letter] f *m*, F *m*; **is that spelt with an f?** est-ce que ça s'écrit avec un f?; **how many fs are there in "buffoon"?** il y a combien d'f dans «buffoon»?; **f for Freddie** ≃ F comme François; **the F word** *Br euph le mot «fuck»*, ≃ le mot de Cambronne.
◇ -**1.** *written abbr of* **fathom**. -**2.** *written abbr of* **female**. -**3.** (*written abbr of* **feminine**) f, fém.

f -**1.** (*written abbr of* **function of**) MATH f de. -**2.** (*written abbr of* **forte**) MUS f.

F ◇ *n* -**1.** MUS fa *m*; **a concerto in F** un concerto en fa. -**2.** SCH [grade]: **to get an F** échouer.
◇ -**1.** (*written abbr of* **Fahrenheit**) F. -**2.** (*written abbr of* **franc**) F. -**3.** (*written abbr of* **fluorine**) CHEM F. -**4.** (*written abbr of* **farad**) PHYS F. -**5.** (*written abbr of* **force**) PHYS F. -**6.** (*written abbr of* **frequency**) PHYS F. -**7.** *written abbr of* **false**.

fa [fɑː] = **fah**.

f.a., FA *inf* (*abbr of* **fanny adams**) *n Br*: **sweet ~** que dalle.

FA (*abbr of* **Football Association**) *pr n*: **the ~** la Fédération britannique de football; **the ~ cup** *championnat de football dont la finale se joue à Wembley*.

FAA (*abbr of* **Federal Aviation Administration**) *pr n direction fédérale de l'aviation civile américaine*.

fab *inf* [fæb] *adj Br dated* sensass.

Fabian [ˈfeɪbjən] ◇ *adj* temporisateur.
◇ *n* Fabien *m*, -enne *f*.

Fabianism [ˈfeɪbjənɪzm] *n* fabianisme *m*.

Fabian Society *pr n*: **the ~** *groupe socialiste de la fin du XIX*e *siècle en Grande-Bretagne*.

THE FABIAN SOCIETY:
Association fondée en 1883 dans le cadre de l'émergence du socialisme en Grande-Bretagne. Composée en grande partie d'intellectuels, elle avait pour but de parvenir à un «changement graduel et pacifique» de la société capitaliste. Son influence se fit sentir jusque dans les années 30.

---

fable [ˈfeɪbl] *n* -**1.** [legend] fable *f*, légende *f*; LITERAT fable. -**2.** [false account] fable *f*.

fabled [ˈfeɪbld] *adj* [famous] légendaire, célèbre; [fictitious] légendaire, fabuleux.

fabric [ˈfæbrɪk] *n* -**1.** [cloth] tissu *m*, étoffe *f*. -**2.** [framework, structure] structure *f*, tissu *m*; **the ~ of society** *fig* la structure de la société.

fabricate [ˈfæbrɪkeɪt] *vt* -**1.** [make] fabriquer. -**2.** [story] inventer, fabriquer; [document] faire un faux, contrefaire.

fabrication [ˌfæbrɪˈkeɪʃn] *n* -**1.** [manufacture] fabrication *f*, production *f*. -**2.** [falsehood] fabrication *f*; **it's pure ~** c'est de la pure invention.

fabric softener *n* assouplissant *m* (textile).

fabulist [ˈfæbjʊlɪst] *n lit* [storyteller] fabuliste *mf*; [liar] fabulateur *m*, -trice *f*, menteur *m*, -euse *f*.

fabulous [ˈfæbjʊləs] *adj* -**1.** [astounding] fabuleux, incroyable; **~ wealth** une fortune fabuleuse OR incroyable. -**2.** *inf* [good] génial; **we had a ~ time** on s'est amusés comme des fous; **it's ~!** c'est super! -**3.** [fictitious] fabuleux, légendaire.

fabulously [ˈfæbjʊləslɪ] *adv* fabuleusement; **a ~ successful actor** un acteur qui a un succès fabuleux OR fou; **~ rich** fabuleusement riche.

facade, façade [fəˈsɑːd] *n* ARCHIT & *fig* façade *f*.

face [feɪs] ◇ *n* -**1.** ANAT visage *m*, figure *f*; **a handsome ~** un beau visage; **injuries to the ~** MED blessures *fpl* à la face OR au visage; **I know that ~** je connais cette tête-là, cette tête me dit quelque chose; **I have a good memory for ~s** j'ai une bonne mémoire des visages; **to fall flat on one's ~** tomber à plat ventre OR face contre terre; **she was lying ~ down** OR **downwards** elle était étendue à plat ventre OR face contre terre; **she was lying ~ up** OR **upwards** elle était étendue sur le dos; **he told her to her ~ what he thought of her** il lui a dit en face OR sans ambages ce qu'il pensait d'elle; **to look sb in the ~** *literal* regarder qqn en face OR dans les yeux; **I'll never be able to look him in the ~ again** *fig* je n'oserai plus jamais le regarder en face ❑ **to put on one's ~** *inf* [woman] se maquiller. -**2.** [expression] mine *f*, expression *f*; **to make** OR **to pull a ~ at sb** faire une grimace à qqn; **to pull a funny ~** faire des simagrées, faire le singe; **what a grumpy ~!** quel air renfrogné! ❑ **she put on a brave** OR **bold ~** elle a fait bon visage OR bonne contenance; **put a good** OR **brave ~ on it** vous n'avez qu'à faire contre mauvaise fortune bon cœur. -**3.** [appearance] apparence *f*, aspect *m*; **it changed the ~ of the town** cela a changé la physionomie de la ville; **this is the ugly ~ of capitalism** voici l'autre visage OR le mauvais côté du capitalisme. -**4.** [front - of building] façade *f*, devant *m*; [- of cliff] paroi *f*; [of mountain] face *f*. -**5.** [of clock] cadran *m*; [of coin] face *f*; [of page] recto *m*; [of playing card] face *f*, dessous *m*; [of the earth] surface *f*; **it fell ~ down/up** [gen] c'est tombé du mauvais/bon côté; [card, coin] c'est tombé face en dessous/en dessus; **she has vanished off the ~ of the earth** *fig* elle a complètement disparu de la circulation. -**6.** *inf Br* [impudence] culot *m*, toupet *m*. -**7.** MIN front *m* de taille. -**8.** TYPO [typeface] œil *m*; [fount] fonte *f*. -**9.** *phr*: **she laughed/shut the door in his ~** elle lui a ri/fermé la porte au nez; **to lose/to save ~** perdre/sauver la face; **to suffer a loss of ~** subir une humiliation; **he set his ~ against our marriage** il s'est élevé contre notre mariage; **he won't show his ~ here again!** il ne risque pas de remettre les pieds ici!; **her plans blew up in her ~** tous ses projets se sont retournés contre elle.
◇ *comp* [cream] pour le visage.
◇ *vt* -**1.** [turn towards] faire face à; **I turned and ~d him** je me retournai et lui fis face; **~ the wall** tournez-vous vers le mur. -**2.** [be turned towards] faire face à, être en face de; **he ~d the blackboard** il était face au OR faisait face au tableau; **she was facing him** elle était en face de lui; **facing one another** l'un en face de l'autre, en vis-à-vis; **we were facing one another** nous étions face à face, nous nous faisions face; **a room facing the courtyard** une chambre sur cour OR donnant sur la cour; **the house ~s south** la maison est orientée OR exposée au sud; **my chair ~d the window** ma chaise était OR faisait face à la fenêtre; **two rows of seats facing one another** deux rangées de sièges en vis-à-vis; **facing page 9** en regard OR en face de la page 9. -**3.** [confront] faire face OR front à, affronter; **to be ~d with sthg** être obligé de faire face à OR être confronté à qqch; **I was ~d with having to pay for the damage** j'ai été obligé OR dans l'obligation de payer les dégâts; **he was ~d with a difficult choice** il était confronté à un choix difficile; **~d with the evidence** devant l'évidence, confronté à l'évidence ❑ **we'll just have to ~ the music** *inf* il va falloir affronter la tempête OR faire front. -**4.** [deal with] faire face à; **to ~ a problem** faire face OR s'attaquer à un problème; **I can't ~ telling her** je n'ai pas le courage de le lui dire; **we must ~ facts** il faut voir les choses comme elles sont; **they won't ~ the fact that it's too late** ils ne veulent pas se rendre à l'évidence et admettre qu'il est trop tard; **let's ~ it, we're lost** admettons-le, nous sommes perdus. -**5.** [risk - disaster] être menacé de; [- defeat, fine, prison] encourir, risquer; **she ~s the possibility of having to move** elle risque d'être obligée de déménager; **~d with eviction, he paid his rent** face à OR devant la perspective d'une expulsion, il a payé son loyer; **thousands ~ unemployment** des milliers de personnes sont menacés de chômage. -**6.** [subj: problem, situation] se présenter à; **the problem facing us** le problème qui se pose (à nous) OR devant lequel on se trouve; **the difficulties facing the EC** les difficultés que rencontre la CEE OR auxquelles la CEE doit faire face. -**7.** [cover] revêtir de.
◇ *vi* -**1.** [turn] se tourner; [be turned] être tourné; **she was facing towards the camera** elle était tournée vers OR elle faisait face à l'appareil photo ‖ MIL: **right ~!** *Am* à droite, droite!; **about ~!** *Am* demi-tour! -**2.** [house, window] être orienté; [look over] faire face à, donner sur; **the terrace ~s towards the mountain** la terrasse donne sur la montagne; **facing forwards** [in bus, train] dans le sens de la marche; **facing backwards** dans le mauvais sens.

◆ **in the face of** *prep phr*: she succeeded in the ~ of fierce opposition elle a réussi malgré une opposition farouche; in the ~ of adversity face à l'adversité.
◆ **on the face of it** *adv phr* à première vue.
◆ **face down** *vt sep Am* tenir tête (à).
◆ **face out** *vt sep Br* surmonter.
◆ **face up to** *vt insep* faire face à, affronter; he won't ~ up to the fact that he's getting older il ne veut pas admettre qu'il vieillit.

face-ache *n* -**1.** *literal* névralgie *f* faciale. -**2.** *inf fig* face *f* de rat.

face card *n Am* figure *f (de jeu de cartes)*.

facecloth ['feɪsklɒθ] *n Br* = gant *m* de toilette.

-faced [feɪst] *in cpds* au visage...; round~ au visage rond; white~ blême.

face flannel *n Br* gant *m* de toilette.

faceguard ['feɪsgɑːd] *n* visière *f* de protection.

faceless ['feɪslɪs] *adj* anonyme.

face-lift *n* -**1.** [surgery] lifting *m*; to have a ~ se faire faire un lifting. -**2.** *inf* [renovation] restauration *f*; the house could do with a ~ la maison a besoin d'être ravalée OR retapée; the school has had a ~ l'école a fait peau neuve.

face mask *n* [cosmetic] masque *m* de beauté; SPORT masque *m*.

face-off *n* SPORT remise *f* en jeu; *fig* confrontation *f*.

face pack *n* masque *m* de beauté.

faceplate ['feɪspleɪt] *n* [on lathe] plateau *m* de tour.

face powder *n* poudre *f* de riz.

facer ['feɪsəʳ] *n* -**1.** [tool] planeuse *f*. -**2.** *inf Br* [problem] os *m*, tuile *f*.

face-saver *n* quelque chose qui sauve la face; the new legislation is just a ~ le gouvernement passe ces nouvelles lois simplement pour sauver la face.

face-saving *adj* qui sauve la face; a ~ measure une mesure qui sauve la face.

facet ['fæsɪt] *n* -**1.** [gen, ANAT, ARCHIT & ENTOM] facette *f*. -**2.** [aspect] aspect *m*, facette *f*.

faceted ['fæsɪtɪd] *adj* à facettes.

facetious [fə'siːʃəs] *adj* [person] facétieux, moqueur; [remark] facétieux, comique.

facetiously [fə'siːʃəslɪ] *adv* de manière facétieuse, facétieusement.

facetiousness [fə'siːʃəsnɪs] *n* caractère *m* facétieux OR comique.

face to face *adv* face à face; she brought him ~ with her father elle l'a confronté avec son père; it brought us ~ with the problem cela nous a mis directement devant le problème.
◆ **face-to-face** *adj* [discussion, confrontation] face à face; a face-to-face meeting un face-à-face.

face towel *n* serviette *f* de toilette.

face value *n* FIN valeur *f* nominale; I took her remark at ~ *fig* j'ai pris sa remarque au pied de la lettre OR pour argent comptant; don't take him at ~ ne le jugez pas sur les apparences.

facia ['feɪʃə] = **fascia**.

facial ['feɪʃl] ◇ *adj* facial; ~ hair poils *mpl* du visage; to remove ~ hair enlever les poils disgracieux (du visage); ~ scrub lotion *f* exfoliante pour le visage.
◇ *n* soin *m* du visage; to have a ~ se faire faire un soin du visage.

facially ['feɪʃəlɪ] *adv* de visage.

facies ['feɪʃɪiːz] (*pl inv*) *n* faciès *m*.

facile [*Br* 'fæsaɪl, *Am* 'fæsl] *adj* [solution, victory] facile; [remark, reasoning] facile, creux; [style] facile, coulant; [person] superficiel, complaisant.

facilitate [fə'sɪlɪteɪt] *vt* faciliter.

facilitator [fə'sɪlɪteɪtəʳ] *n* SOCIOL animateur *m*, -trice *f* de groupe.

facility [fə'sɪlətɪ] (*pl* facilities) *n* -**1.** [ease] facilité *f*; with great ~ avec beaucoup de facilité. -**2.** [skill] facilité *f*, aptitude *f*; to have a ~ for OR with languages avoir des facilités OR des aptitudes pour les langues. -**3.** (*usu pl*) [equipment] équipement *m*; [means] moyen *m*; feel free to use the facilities n'hésitez pas à utiliser toutes les installations; there are facilities for cooking il y a la possibilité de OR il y a ce qu'il faut pour faire la cuisine; books and other facilities for study des livres et autres instruments de travail; we don't have the facilities to hold a conference here nous ne sommes pas équipés pour organiser une conférence ici; washing facilities installations sanitaires; sports facilities équipements sportifs; transport facilities moyens de transport; the facilities *euph* les toilettes *fpl*. -**4.** [building] installation *f*. -**5.** [device] mécanisme *m*; COMPUT fonction *f*; the clock also has a radio ~ ce réveil fait aussi radio; an automatic timing ~ un minuteur automatique. -**6.** [service] service *m*; we offer easy credit facilities nous offrons des facilités de paiement OR crédit; an overdraft ~ *Br* une autorisation de découvert.

facing ['feɪsɪŋ] *n* CONSTR revêtement *m*; SEW revers *m*.

-facing *in cpds* orienté vers...; north~ orienté OR exposé au nord.

facsimile [fæk'sɪmɪlɪ] *n* fac-similé *m*; in ~ en fac-similé.

facsimile machine *n* télécopieur *m*.

facsimile transmission *n* télécopie *f*.

fact [fækt] *n* -**1.** [true item of data] fait *m*; it's a (well-known) ~ that... tout le monde sait (bien) que...; just stick to the ~s tenez-vous en aux faits; let's get the ~s straight mettons les choses au clair; ten ~s about whales dix choses à savoir sur les baleines; I'll give you all the ~s and figures je vous donnerai tous les détails voulus ‖ [known circumstance]: the ~ that he left is in itself incriminating le fait qu'il soit parti est compromettant en soi; he broke his promise, there's no getting away from the ~ disons les choses comme elles sont, il n'a pas tenu sa promesse; I'm her friend, a ~ you seem to have overlooked vous semblez ne pas tenir compte du fait que je suis son ami ❑ I know for a ~ that they're friends je sais pertinemment qu'ils sont amis; I know it for a ~ je le sais de source sûre, c'est un fait certain; to teach sb the ~s of life [sex] apprendre à qqn comment les enfants viennent au monde; [hard reality] apprendre à qqn la réalité des choses, mettre qqn devant la réalité de la vie; there's something strange going on, (and) that's a ~ il se passe quelque chose de bizarre, c'est sûr; is that a ~? c'est pas vrai? -**2.** *(U)* [reality] faits *mpl*, réalité *f*; based on ~ [argument] basé sur des faits; [book, film] basé sur des faits réels; ~ and fiction le réel et l'imaginaire ❑ the ~ (of the matter) is that I forgot all about it la vérité, c'est que j'ai complètement oublié; the ~ remains he's my brother il n'en est pas moins mon frère. -**3.** JUR [act] fait *m*, action *f*.
◆ **in fact** *adv phr* -**1.** [giving extra information]: he asked us, in ~ ordered us, to be quiet il nous a demandé, ou plutôt ordonné, de nous taire. -**2.** [correcting, contradicting] en fait; he claims to be a writer, but in (actual) ~ he's a journalist il prétend être écrivain mais en fait c'est un journaliste. -**3.** [emphasizing, reinforcing]: did she in ~ say when she was going to arrive? est-ce qu'elle a dit quand elle arriverait en fait?; he said it'd take two days and he was in ~ correct il a dit que cela mettrait deux jours et en fait, il avait raison.

fact-finding *adj* d'information; a ~ mission une mission d'information; he's on a ~ tour of the disaster area il enquête sur la région sinistrée.

faction ['fækʃn] *n* -**1.** [group] faction *f*. -**2.** [strife] dissension *f*, discorde *f*. -**3.** [book, programme] docudrame *m*.

factional ['fækʃənl] *adj* de faction; ~ strife luttes *fpl* intestines.

factious ['fækʃəs] *adj* factieux.

factitious [fæk'tɪʃəs] *adj lit* factice, artificiel.

factitive ['fæktɪtɪv] *adj* factitif.

factor ['fæktəʳ] *n* -**1.** [element] facteur *m*, élément *m*; age is an important ~ l'âge joue un rôle important; a determining ~ un facteur décisif OR déterminant; the human ~ le facteur humain; the safety ~ le facteur de sécurité; the chill ~ le coefficient de froid; ~ 6 [in suntan cream] indice *m* 6. -**2.** BIOL & MATH facteur *m*. -**3.** [agent] agent *m*. -**4.** *Scot* [manager] syndic *m*.

factorage ['fæktərɪdʒ] *n* courtage *m*, commission *f*.

factor analysis *n* analyse *f* factorielle.

factorial [fæk'tɔːrɪəl] ◇ *adj* factoriel.
◇ *n* factorielle *f*.

factoring ['fæktərɪŋ] *n* affacturage *m*.

factorization [ˌfæktəraɪ'zeɪʃn] *n* mise *f* en facteurs.

factorize, **-ise** ['fæktəraɪz] *vt* mettre en facteurs.

factory ['fæktərɪ] (*pl* factories) ◇ *n* usine *f*; [smaller] fabrique *f*; a car ~ une usine d'automobiles; an arms ~ une fabrique d'armes; a porcelain ~ une manufacture de porcelaine.
◇ *comp* [chimney, worker] d'usine; ~ work travail *m* en usine OR d'usine; on the ~ floor dans les ateliers, parmi les ouvriers; prices at the ~ gate prix *mpl* départ usine.

factory act *n Br* législation *f* industrielle.

factory farm *n* ferme *f* industrielle.

factory farming *n* élevage *m* industriel.

factory inspector *n* inspecteur *m*, -trice *f* du travail.

factory ship *n* navire-usine *m*.

factotum [fæk'təʊtəm] *n* factotum *m*.

fact sheet *n* prospectus *m*, brochure *f*.

factual ['fæktʃʊəl] *adj* [account, speech] factuel, basé sur les OR des faits; [event] réel.

factually ['fæktʃʊəlɪ] *adv* en se tenant aux faits; ~ inaccurate inexact dans les faits.

facultative ['fækltətɪv] *adj* -**1.** [optional] facultatif. -**2.** PHILOS casuel, contingent.

faculty ['fækltɪ] (*pl* faculties) ◇ *n* -**1.** [of reason, sight] faculté *f*; she's in full command of her faculties elle a toutes ses facultés; his critical faculties son sens critique. -**2.** UNIV [section] faculté *f*; [staff] corps *m* enseignant; the Faculty of Arts/of Medicine la faculté de lettres/de médecine.
◇ *comp* [member, staff] de faculté.

fad *inf* [fæd] *n* [craze] mode *f*, vogue *f*; [personal] lubie *f*, (petite) manie *f*; it's just a (passing) ~ ce n'est qu'une lubie.

faddish *inf* ['fædɪʃ] *adj* [idea, taste] capricieux; [person] maniaque, capricieux.

faddy *inf* ['fædɪ] (*compar* faddier, *superl* faddiest) *adj Br* [idea, taste] capricieux; [person] maniaque, capricieux.

fade [feɪd] ◇ *vi* -**1.** [colour] pâlir, passer; [material] se décolorer, passer; [light] baisser, diminuer; the light ~d from the sky le jour baissa peu à peu; guaranteed not to ~ TEX garanti bon teint. -**2.** [wither - flower] se faner, se flétrir; *fig* [- beauty] se faner. -**3.** [disappear - figure] disparaître; [- memory, sight] baisser; [- thing remembered, writing] s'effacer; [- sound] baisser, s'éteindre; [- anger, interest] diminuer; [- hope, smile] s'éteindre; to ~ from sight disparaître aux regards; the sound keeps fading RADIO & TV il y a du fading, le son s'en va. -**4.** *lit* [die] dépérir, s'éteindre; he's fading fast il dépérit à vue d'œil.
◇ *vt* -**1.** [discolour - material] décolorer; [- colour] faner. -**2.** [reduce] baisser; CIN & TV faire disparaître en fondu.
◇ *n* disparition *f*; CIN & TV disparition *f* en fondu.
◆ **fade away** *vi insep* [gen] disparaître; [memory, sight] baisser; [thing remembered, writing] s'effacer; [sound] s'éteindre; [anger, interest] diminuer; [hope, smile] s'éteindre; he ~d away il a peu à peu dépéri.
◆ **fade in** ◇ *vt sep* CIN & TV faire apparaître en fondu; RADIO monter.
◇ *vi insep* CIN & TV apparaître en fondu.
◆ **fade out** ◇ *vi insep* -**1.** [sound] disparaître, s'éteindre; *fig* [interest] diminuer, tomber; [fashion] passer. -**2.** CIN & TV disparaître en fondu; RADIO être coupé par un fondu sonore.

◇ *vt sep* CIN & TV faire disparaître en fondu; RADIO couper par un fondu sonore.

fade-away *n* CIN fondu *m* en fermeture; TV disparition *f* graduelle; RADIO évanouissement *m*, fading *m*.

faded ['feɪdɪd] *adj* [material] décoloré, déteint; [jeans] délavé; [flower] fané, flétri; [beauty] défraîchi, fané.

fade-in *n* CIN fondu *m* en ouverture; TV apparition *f* graduelle; RADIO fondu *m* sonore.

fade-out *n* CIN fondu *m* en fermeture; TV disparition *f* graduelle; RADIO fondu sonore.

fading ['feɪdɪŋ] *n* RADIO fading *m*, atténuation *f* (du son).

faecal *Br*, **fecal** *Am* ['fi:kl] *adj* fécal.

faeces *Br*, **feces** *Am* ['fi:si:z] *npl* fèces *fpl*.

Faeroe ['feərəʊ] *pr n*: the ~ Islands, the ~s les îles Féroé *fpl*; in the ~ Islands aux îles Féroé.

Faeroese [,feərəʊ'i:z] (*pl inv*) ◇ *n* -**1.** [person] Féroïen *m*, -enne *f*, Féringien *m*, -enne *f*. -**2.** LING féroïen *m*, féringien *m*.
◇ *adj* féroïen, féringien.

faff *inf* [fæf] *Br* ◇ *vi* faire la mouche du coche; stop ~ing (about OR around)! arrêtez de tourner en rond!
◇ *n* [panic] panique *f*; [effort]: I can't be bothered, it's too much of a ~ je renonce, c'est trop compliqué.

fag [fæg] (*pt* & *pp* fagged, *cont* fagging) ◇ *n* -**1.** *Br* [at school] *jeune élève d'une «public school» assujetti à un «ancien»*. -**2.** *inf Br* [task] corvée *f*, barbe *f*. -**3.** *inf Br* [cigarette] clope *m or f*. -**4.** ▽ *Am pej* [homosexual] pédé *m*.
◇ *vi Br* [at school]: to ~ for sb faire les corvées de qqn.
◇ *vt* ▽ crever.

fag end *inf n Br* [remainder] reste *m*; [of cloth] bout *m*; [of conversation] dernières bribes *fpl*; [cigarette] mégot *m*.

fagged *inf* [fægd] *adj Br* -**1.** [exhausted] crevé, claqué; we all ended up completely ~ (out) nous étions tous complètement crevés OR claqués à la fin. -**2.** [bothered]: I'm supposed to finish it today but I can't be ~ je suis censé terminer ça aujourd'hui mais j'ai trop la flemme.

fagging ['fægɪŋ] *n Br sujétion d'un jeune élève à un «ancien» dans une «public school»*.

FAGGING:
Cette pratique, jadis assez répandue dans les «public schools» en Grande-Bretagne, est maintenant interdite. Les «grands» avaient le droit de donner des ordres aux «petits», qui devaient porter leurs affaires, leur faire à manger etc.

faggot ['fægət] *n* -**1.** *Br* [of sticks] fagot *m*. -**2.** *Br* CULIN boulette *f* de viande. -**3.** ▽ *Am pej* [homosexual] pédé *m*, tapette *f*.

fagot ['fægət] *Am* = **faggot 1**.

fah [fɑ:] *n* fa *m*.

Fahrenheit ['færənhaɪt] *adj* Fahrenheit *(inv)*; the ~ scale l'échelle *f* Fahrenheit; it's 6° Centigrade — what's that in ~? il fait 6° Centigrade — ça fait combien en Fahrenheit?

fail [feɪl] ◇ *vi* -**1.** [not succeed - attempt, plan] échouer, ne pas réussir; [- negotiations] échouer, ne pas aboutir; [- person] échouer; he ~ed (in his efforts) to convince us il n'a pas réussi OR il n'est pas arrivé à nous convaincre; her attempt was bound to ~ sa tentative était vouée à l'échec; to ~ by three votes/five minutes échouer à trois voix près/cinq minutes près; it never ~s ça ne rate jamais; if all else ~s en désespoir de cause. -**2.** SCH & UNIV échouer, être recalé; I ~ed in maths j'ai été collé OR recalé en maths. -**3.** [stop working] tomber en panne, céder; [brakes] lâcher; his heart ~ed son cœur s'est arrêté; the power ~ed il y a eu une panne d'électricité. -**4.** [grow weak - eyesight, health, memory] baisser, faiblir; [- person, voice] s'affaiblir; [- light] baisser. -**5.** [be insufficient] manquer, faire défaut; their crops ~ed because of the drought ils ont perdu les récoltes à cause de la sécheresse; she ~ed in her duty elle a manqué OR failli à son devoir. -**6.** [go bankrupt] faire faillite.
◇ *vt* -**1.** [not succeed in] échouer à, ne pas réussir à; he ~ed his driving test il n'a pas eu son permis || SCH & UNIV [exam] échouer à, être recalé à; [candidate] refuser, recaler; he ~ed the exam/history il a échoué à l'examen/en histoire; she ~ed ten students elle a refusé OR recalé dix étudiants. -**2.** [let down] décevoir, laisser tomber; I won't ~ you je ne vous laisserai pas tomber, vous pouvez compter sur moi; his heart ~ed him le cœur lui a manqué; my memory ~s me la mémoire me fait défaut, ma mémoire me trahit; her courage ~ed her le courage lui a fait défaut OR lui a manqué; words ~ed me je ne sais pas quoi dire. -**3.** [neglect] manquer, négliger; he ~ed to mention he was married il a omis de signaler qu'il était marié; they never ~ to call ils ne manquent jamais d'appeler; he ~ed to keep his word il a manqué à sa parole; she ~ed to answer his letter elle n'a pas répondu à sa lettre; I ~ to see how I can help je ne vois pas comment je peux aider; I ~ to understand why she came je n'arrive pas à comprendre pourquoi elle est venue; such success never ~s to arouse jealousy une telle réussite ne va jamais sans provoquer des jalousies; to ~ to appear JUR faire défaut.
◇ *n* SCH & UNIV échec *m*; he only had one ~ and that was in maths il n'a échoué OR été recalé qu'en maths; out of a class of 25, I had 23 passes and 2 ~s sur une classe de 25, 23 ont été reçus et 2 ont été recalés.
◆ **without fail** *adv phr* [for certain] sans faute, à coup sûr; [always] inévitablement, immanquablement.

failed [feɪld] *adj* qui n'a pas réussi, raté; she's a ~ artist c'est une artiste manquée; a ~ marriage un mariage manqué OR raté.

failing ['feɪlɪŋ] ◇ *n* défaut *m*.
◇ *prep* à défaut de; ~ this à défaut; ~ which faute OR à défaut de quoi; ~ any advice/evidence to the contrary sauf avis contraire, sauf preuve du contraire.
◇ *adj* [health] défaillant; [business] qui fait faillite; [marriage] qui va à la dérive; *Am* [student] faible, mauvais.

fail-safe ◇ *adj* [device, machine] à sûreté intégrée; [plan] infaillible.
◇ *n* dispositif *m* de sécurité OR de sûreté (intégrée).

failure ['feɪljə^r] *n* -**1.** [lack of success] échec *m*, insuccès *m*; to end in ~ se terminer par un échec; doomed to ~ voué à l'échec OR l'insuccès. -**2.** SCH & UNIV échec *m*; ~ in an exam/in maths échec à un examen/en maths. -**3.** [fiasco] échec *m*, fiasco *m*; [of plan] échec *m*, avortement *m*; the party was a total ~ la soirée a été un fiasco complet; their plan was a complete ~ leur projet a été un échec total OR a échoué sur toute la ligne; the play was a dismal ~ la pièce a été OR a fait un four noir. -**4.** [person] raté *m*, -e *f*; he's a ~ as a father il fait un mauvais père, il n'est pas doué pour la paternité; I feel a complete ~ je me sens vraiment nulle, j'ai l'impression d'être complètement nulle; I'm a complete ~ at maths je suis totalement nul en maths. -**5.** [breakdown] panne *f*; a power ~ une panne d'électricité. -**6.** [lack] manque *m*; a ~ of nerve un manque de courage; crop ~ perte *f* des récoltes. -**7.** [non-performance] manquement *m*, défaut *m*; ~ to keep one's word manquement à sa parole; his ~ to arrive on time le fait qu'il soit arrivé en retard; his ~ to appear meant I had to take charge du fait qu'il ne s'est pas montré, j'ai dû me charger de tout; the press criticized the government's ~ to act la presse a critiqué l'immobilité du gouvernement; ~ to observe the rules will result in a fine le manquement au règlement est passible d'une amende; ~ to appear JUR défaut *m* de comparution. -**8.** [bankruptcy] faillite *f*.

fain [feɪn] *adv arch* volontiers.

faint [feɪnt] ◇ *adj* -**1.** [slight - breeze, feeling, sound, smell] faible, léger; [- idea] flou, vague [- breathing, light] faible; [- voice] faible, éteint there was a ~ glow on the horizon il y avait une faible lueur à l'horizon; he hasn't the ~est chance of winning il n'a pas la moindre chance de gagner; I haven't the ~est idea je n'en ai pas la moindre idée; her cries grew ~er ses cris s'estompaient OR diminuaient. -**2.** [colour] pâle, délavé. -**3.** [half-hearted] faible, sans conviction; a ~ smile [feeble] un vague sourire; [sad] un pauvre OR triste sourire; ~ praise éloges *mpl* tièdes. -**4.** [dizzy] prêt à s'évanouir, défaillant; to feel ~ se sentir mal, être pris d'un malaise; he was ~ with exhaustion la tête lui tournait de fatigue. -**5.** *phr*: ~ heart never won fair lady *Br prov* la pusillanimité n'a jamais conquis de cœur féminin.
◇ *vi* s'évanouir; he ~ed from the pain il s'est évanoui de douleur; a ~ing fit un évanouissement; to be ~ing from OR with hunger défaillir de faim; I almost ~ed when they told me I'd got the job *fig* j'ai failli m'évanouir quand on m'a dit que j'avais le poste.
◇ *n* évanouissement *m*, syncope *f*; she fell to the floor in a (dead) ~ elle s'est évanouie OR est tombée en syncope.

faint-hearted ◇ *adj* [person] timoré, pusillanime; [attempt] timide, sans conviction.
◇ *npl*: not for the ~ à déconseiller aux peureux.

faintly ['feɪntlɪ] *adv* -**1.** [breathe, shine] faiblement; [mark, write] légèrement; [say, speak] d'une voix éteinte, faiblement. -**2.** [slightly] légèrement, vaguement; she smiled ~ elle esquissa un sourire; the taste is ~ reminiscent of cinnamon cela rappelle vaguement la cannelle; ~ absurd/ridiculous quelque peu absurde/ridicule.

faintness ['feɪntnɪs] *n* -**1.** [of light, sound, voice] faiblesse *f*; [of breeze] légèreté *f*; [of image, writing] manque *m* de clarté. -**2.** [dizziness] malaise *m*, défaillance *f*.

fair [feə^r] ◇ *adj* -**1.** [just - person, decision] juste, équitable; [- contest, match, player] loyal, correct; [- deal, exchange] équitable, honnête; [- price] correct, convenable; [- criticism, profit] justifié, mérité; it's not ~ ce n'est pas juste; it's not ~ to the others ce n'est pas juste OR honnête vis-à-vis des autres; that's a ~ point c'est une remarque pertinente; she's strict but ~ elle est sévère mais juste OR impartiale; to be ~ (to them), they did contribute their time rendons-leur cette justice, ils ont donné de leur temps; it's only ~ to let him speak ce n'est que justice de le laisser parler; as is only ~ ce n'est que justice, comme de juste; I gave him ~ warning je l'ai prévenu à temps; a ~ sample un échantillon représentatif; he got his ~ share of the property il a eu tous les biens qui lui revenaient (de droit); she's had more than her ~ share of problems elle a largement eu sa part de problèmes ❑ ~ competition codes règles *fpl* de concurrence loyale *(établies aux États-Unis pendant le New Deal -en 1933- entre les patrons et les salariés)*; to have a ~ crack of the whip *Br* ne pas être désavantagé par rapport aux autres; the boss gave her a ~ deal OR a ~ go *inf Am* OR a ~ shake (of the dice) *inf* le patron l'a traitée équitablement OR a été fair-play *(inv)* avec elle; it's all ~ and above board, it's all ~ and square tout est régulier OR correct; all's ~ in love and war tous les moyens sont bons; by ~ means or foul par tous les moyens, d'une manière ou d'une autre; ~ do's for all! *Br* à chacun son dû!; ~ enough! très bien!, d'accord!; that's ~ enough but don't you think that... très bien OR d'accord, mais est-ce que vous ne pensez pas que...; ~ exchange (is) no robbery *Br* échange n'est pas vol; ~'s ~, it's her turn now il faut être juste, c'est son tour maintenant. -**2.** [light - hair] blond; [- skin] clair, blanc; he's very ~ il est très blond. -**3.** *lit* [lovely] beau; his ~ lady sa belle. -**4.** [weather] beau; [tide, wind] favorable, propice; the wind's set

~ for France le temps est au beau fixe sur la France. -**5.** [adequate] passable, assez bon; **in ~ condition** en assez bon état; **you have a ~ chance of winning** vous avez des chances de gagner; **he has achieved a ~ standard** il est arrivé à un assez bon niveau ❑ **~ to middling** passable, pas mal; **how are you? – ~ to middling** comment allez-vous? – comme çi comme ça. -**6.** [substantial] considérable; **he makes a ~ amount of money** il gagne pas mal d'argent; **she reads a ~ amount** elle lit pas mal; **I have a ~ idea (of) why** je crois bien savoir pourquoi; **a ~ number** un nombre respectable; **at a ~ pace** à une bonne allure. -**7.** *inf Br* [real] véritable; **I had a ~ old time getting here** j'ai eu pas mal de difficultés à arriver jusqu'ici.
◇ *adv* -**1.** [act] équitablement, loyalement; **to play ~** jouer franc jeu ❑ **he told us ~ and square** il nous l'a dit sans détours OR carrément. -**2.** *inf Br dial* [completely] tout à fait, vraiment; **you ~ scared me to death** tu m'as vraiment fait une peur atroce. -**3.** *phr*: **the play bids ~ to being a success** cette pièce a de grandes chances d'être OR sera probablement un succès.
◇ *n* -**1.** [entertainment] foire *f*, fête *f* foraine; [for charity] kermesse *f*, fête *f*. -**2.** COMM foire *f*; **the Book Fair** la Foire du livre; [in Paris] le Salon du livre.

fair copy *n Br* copie *f* au propre OR au net; **I made a ~ of the report** j'ai recopié le rapport au propre.

fair game *n* proie *f* idéale; **after such behaviour he was ~ for an attack** *fig* après s'être comporté de cette façon, il méritait bien qu'on s'en prenne à lui.

fairground ['feəgraʊnd] *n* champ *m* de foire.

fair-haired *adj* [blond] blond, aux cheveux blonds; **the ~ girl** la blonde ❑ **the boss's ~ boy** *inf Am* le favori OR le chouchou du patron.

fairing ['feərɪŋ] *n* [on vehicle] carénage *m*.

fairish ['feərɪʃ] *adj* -**1.** [chances, salary, weather] assez bon; [number] respectable; **there's a ~ amount of work still to do** il y a encore pas mal de travail. -**2.** [blondish] plutôt blond.

Fair Isle, Fairisle ['feəraɪl] ◇ *adj* tricoté avec des motifs de couleurs vives.
◇ *pr n* GEOG Fair Isle *(dans les îles Shetland)*.
◇ *n* [sweater] *pull avec des motifs de couleurs vives*.

fairly ['feəlɪ] *adv* -**1.** [justly - treat] équitablement, avec justice; [- compare, judge] impartialement, avec impartialité. -**2.** [honestly] honnêtement, loyalement; **to fight/to play ~** se battre/jouer loyalement; **~ priced goods** articles à un prix honnête OR raisonnable. -**3.** [moderately] assez, passablement; **a ~ good book** un assez bon livre; **I'm ~ certain** je suis à peu près certain; **she sings ~ well** elle chante passablement bien; **he works ~ hard** il travaille plutôt dur. -**4.** *Br* [positively] absolument, vraiment; **he was ~ beside himself with worry** il était dans tous ses états.

fair-minded *adj* équitable, impartial.

fairness ['feənɪs] *n* -**1.** [justice] justice *f*, honnêteté *f*; **the report questions the ~ of the decision** le rapport met en cause l'honnêteté OR l'impartialité de cette décision; **in all ~** en toute justice; **in ~ OR out of ~ to you** pour être juste envers OR avec vous. -**2.** [of hair] blondeur *f*, blond *m*; [of skin] blancheur *f*.

fair play *n* fair-play *m inv*, franc-jeu *m offic*.

fair rent *n Br loyer fixé après un examen officiel du logement par l'administration*.

fair sex *n*: **the ~** le beau sexe.

fair-sized *adj* assez grand.

fair-skinned *adj* blanc de peau.

fair-spoken *adj lit* qui parle courtoisement.

fairway ['feəweɪ] *n* -**1.** [in golf] fairway *m*. -**2.** NAUT chenal *m*, passe *f*.

fair-weather *adj* [clothing, vessel] qui convient seulement au beau temps; **a ~ friend** un ami des beaux OR bons jours.

fairy ['feərɪ] (*pl* fairies) ◇ *n* -**1.** [sprite] fée *f*; **the bad ~** la fée Carabosse. -**2.** ▽ *pej* [homosexual] pédé *m*, tapette *f*.
◇ *adj* [enchanted] magique; [fairylike] féerique, de fée; **~ voices** des voix de fées; **~ footsteps** des pas légers.

fairy cycle *n Br* bicyclette *f* d'enfant.

fairy godmother *n* LITERAT & *fig* bonne fée *f*.

fairyland ['feərɪlænd] *n* LITERAT royaume *m* des fées, féerie *f*; *fig* féerie *f*.

fairy lights *npl* guirlande *f* électrique.

fairy queen *n* reine *f* des fées.

fairy ring *n* cercle *m* OR rond *m* des sorcières.

fairy story *n* LITERAT conte *m* de fées; [untruth] histoire *f* à dormir debout.

fairy tale *n* LITERAT conte *m* de fées; [untruth] histoire *f* invraisemblable OR à dormir debout.
◆ **fairy-tale** *adj*: **a fairy-tale ending** une fin digne d'un conte de fées; **a fairy-tale romance** une histoire d'amour digne d'un conte de fée.

fait accompli [ˌfeɪtə'kɒmplɪ] *n* fait *m* accompli.

faith [feɪθ] *n* -**1.** [trust] confiance *f*; **I have ~ in him** je lui fais confiance; **she has lost (all) ~ in the doctors** elle n'a plus aucune confiance dans les médecins; **he's lost ~ in their promises** il ne croit plus à leurs promesses; **they put their ~ in British justice** ils ont mis tous leurs espoirs dans la justice britannique. -**2.** RELIG [belief] foi *f*; **~ in God** foi en Dieu; **Faith, Hope and Charity** la foi, l'espérance et la charité. -**3.** [particular religion] foi *f*, religion *f*; **the Buddhist ~** la religion bouddhiste. -**4.** [honesty]: **he did it in good ~** il l'a fait en toute bonne foi; **he acted in bad ~** il a agi de mauvaise foi. -**5.** [loyalty] fidélité *f*; **you must keep ~ with the movement** il faut tenir vos engagements envers le mouvement; **keep the ~!** *inf* bon courage!; **to break ~ with sb** manquer à sa parole envers qqn.

faithful ['feɪθfʊl] ◇ *adj* -**1.** [believer, friend, lover] fidèle; **~ to sb/sthg** fidèle à qqn/qqch. -**2.** [reliable] sûr, solide; **he's a ~ employee** c'est quelqu'un de sérieux OR sur qui on peut compter. -**3.** [accurate - account, translation] fidèle, exact; [- copy] conforme.
◇ *npl*: **the ~** [supporters] les fidèles *mpl*; RELIG les fidèles OR croyants *mpl*.

faithfully ['feɪθfʊlɪ] *adv* -**1.** [loyally] fidèlement, loyalement; **she promised ~ to come** elle a donné sa parole qu'elle viendrait; **yours ~** [in letter] veuillez agréer mes salutations distinguées. -**2.** [accurately] exactement, fidèlement.

faithfulness ['feɪθfʊlnɪs] *n* -**1.** [loyalty] fidélité *f*, loyauté *f*; **~ to the cause** fidélité à OR loyauté envers la cause. -**2.** [of report, translation] fidélité *f*, exactitude *f*; [of copy] conformité *f*.

faith healer *n* guérisseur *m*, -euse *f*.

faith healing *n* guérison *f* par la foi.

faithless ['feɪθlɪs] *adj* -**1.** [dishonest, unreliable] déloyal, perfide. -**2.** RELIG infidèle, non-croyant.

faithlessness ['feɪθlɪsnɪs] *n* -**1.** [dishonesty] déloyauté *f*, perfidie *f*. -**2.** RELIG manque *m* de foi.

fajitas [fɑː'hiːtəz] *npl plat mexicain constitué d'une crêpe fine fourrée*.

fake [feɪk] ◇ *vt* -**1.** [make - document, painting] faire un faux de, contrefaire; [- style, furniture] imiter. -**2.** [alter - document] falsifier, maquiller; [- account] falsifier; [- election, interview, photograph] truquer. -**3.** [simulate] feindre; **he ~d a headache/sadness** il a fait semblant d'avoir mal à la tête/d'être triste; **to ~ a pass** SPORT feinter la passe. -**4.** [ad-lib] improviser.
◇ *vi* faire semblant; SPORT feinter.
◇ *n* -**1.** [thing] article *m* OR objet *m* truqué; [antique, painting] faux *m*. -**2.** [person] imposteur *m*; **she's a ~** elle n'est pas ce qu'elle prétend être.
◇ *adj* [antique, painting] faux; [account, document] falsifié, faux; [elections, interview, photograph] truqué; **the pearls are ~** les perles sont fausses.

fakir ['feɪˌkɪəʳ] *n* fakir *m*.

Falangist [fæ'lændʒɪst] ◇ *adj* phalangiste.
◇ *n* phalangiste *mf*.

falcon ['fɔːlkən] *n* faucon *m*.

falconer ['fɔːlkənəʳ] *n* fauconnier *m*.

falconry ['fɔːlkənrɪ] *n* fauconnerie *f*.

falderol ['fældɪˌrɒl] = **folderol**.

Falkland ['fɔːklənd] *pr n*: **the ~ Islands, the ~s** les (îles *fpl*) Falkland *fpl*, les (îles *fpl*) Malouines *fpl*; **in the ~ Islands** aux îles Falkland, aux Malouines; **the Falklands War** la guerre des Malouines.

THE FALKLANDS WAR:
Guerre qui opposa, en 1982, l'Argentine au Royaume-Uni. Elle fut provoquée par l'attaque des îles Malouines par la junte militaire argentine, qui se rendit deux mois après le début du conflit. Cette victoire, très populaire en Angleterre, renforça de manière significative la cote de popularité de son Premier ministre, Margaret Thatcher.

Falklander ['fɔːkləndəʳ] *n* habitant *m*, -e *f* des îles Malouines OR îles Falkland.

fall [fɔːl] (*pt* fell [fel], *pp* fallen ['fɔːln])
◇ *vi* -**1.** [barrier, cup, napkin, person] tomber; **the napkin fell to the floor** la serviette est tombée par terre; **I slipped and fell on the ice** j'ai dérapé sur la glace et je suis tombé; **the child fell into the pond** l'enfant est tombé dans la mare; **she fell off the stool/out of the window** elle est tombée du tabouret/par la fenêtre; **he fell over the pile of books** il est tombé en butant contre le tas de livres; **just let your arms ~ to your sides** laissez simplement vos bras pendre OR tomber sur les côtés; **he fell in a heap on the floor** il s'est affaissé OR il est tombé comme une masse; **he fell full length** il est tombé de tout son long; **the crowd fell on OR to their knees** la foule est tombée à genoux; **he fell at her feet to ask forgiveness** il est tombé à genoux devant elle pour lui demander pardon; **she did let ~ a few hints** elle a fait effectivement quelques allusions; **the book fell open at page 20** le livre s'est ouvert à la page 20 ❑ **to ~ on one's feet** *literal* & *fig* retomber sur ses pieds; **a cat always ~s on its feet** un chat retombe toujours sur ses pattes; **I fell flat on my face** *literal* je suis tombé à plat ventre OR face contre terre; *fig inf* je me suis planté; **he fell flat on his ass**▽ *Am literal* & *fig* il s'est cassé la gueule; **his only joke fell flat** la seule plaisanterie qu'il a faite est tombée à plat; **despite all their efforts, the party fell flat** en dépit de leurs efforts, la soirée a fait un flop; **to ~ to bits OR to pieces** tomber en morceaux; **all her good intentions fell by the wayside** toutes ses bonnes intentions sont tombées à l'eau; **the job fell short of her expectations** le poste ne répondait pas à ses attentes. -**2.** [move deliberately] se laisser tomber; **I fell into the armchair** je me suis laissé tomber dans le fauteuil; **the two lovers fell into one another's arms** les deux amants sont tombés dans les bras l'un de l'autre. -**3.** [bridge, building] s'écrouler, s'effondrer. -**4.** [err, go astray] s'écarter du droit chemin; RELIG [sin] pécher; **to ~ from grace** RELIG perdre la grâce; *fig* tomber en disgrâce. -**5.** [ground] descendre, aller en pente. -**6.** [government] tomber, être renversé; [city, country] tomber; **after a long siege the city fell** après un long siège, la ville a capitulé; **Constantinople fell to the Turks** Constantinople est tombée aux mains des Turcs. -**7.** [darkness, light, night, rain, snow] tomber; **as night fell** à la tombée de la nuit; **the tree's shadow fell across the lawn** l'arbre projetait son ombre sur la pelouse. -**8.** [land, eyes, blow, weapon] tomber; **my eyes fell on the letter** mon regard est tombé sur la lettre. -**9.** [face, spirits] s'assombrir; **at the sight of her, his face fell** quand il l'a vue, son visage s'est assombri OR s'est allongé; **my spirits fell** tout d'un coup, j'ai perdu le moral. -**10.** [hang down] tomber, descendre; **the curtains ~ right to the floor** les rideaux tombent OR descendent jusqu'au sol; **the fabric ~s in gentle folds** ce tissu retombe en faisant de jolis plis. -**11.** [decrease in level, value - price, temperature] baisser, tomber; **their voices fell to a whisper** ils se sont mis à chuchoter; **the boss fell in our esteem** le patron a baissé dans notre estime. -**12.** [issue forth] tomber, s'échapper; **curses fell from her lips**

elle laissa échapper des jurons; **the tears started to ~** elle laissa échapper ses larmes. -**13.** [occur] tomber; **May Day ~s on a Tuesday this year** le Premier Mai tombe un mardi cette année; **the accent ~s on the third syllable** l'accent tombe sur la troisième syllabe. -**14.** [descend]: **a great sadness fell over the town** une grande tristesse s'abattit sur la ville; **a hush fell among** OR **over the crowd** tout d'un coup, la foule s'est tue. -**15.** [become]: **to ~ asleep** s'endormir; **the child fell fast asleep** l'enfant est tombé dans un profond sommeil; **the bill ~s due on the 6th** la facture arrive à échéance le 6; **he will ~ heir to a vast fortune** il va hériter d'une grande fortune; **to ~ ill** OR **sick** tomber malade; **to ~ pregnant** tomber enceinte; **to ~ in love with sb** tomber amoureux de qqn; **they fell in love** ils sont tombés amoureux l'un de l'autre; **to ~ silent** se taire; **it ~s vacant in February** [job] il se trouvera vacant au mois de février; [apartment] il se trouvera libre OR il se libérera au mois de février; **to ~ victim to sthg** être victime de qqch; **she fell victim to depression** elle a fait une dépression. -**16.** [die] mourir; **the young men who fell in battle** MIL les jeunes tombés au champ d'honneur. -**17.** [be classified]: **the athletes ~ into two categories** les sportifs se divisent en deux catégories; **that ~s outside my area of responsibility** cela ne relève pas de ma responsabilité; **that does not ~ within the scope of our agreement** ceci n'entre pas dans le cadre de OR ne fait pas partie de notre accord. -**18.** [inheritance]: **the fortune fell to his niece** c'est sa nièce qui a hérité de sa fortune. -**19.** SPORT [in cricket]: **two English wickets fell on the first day** deux batteurs anglais ont été éliminés le premier jour.

◇ *n* -**1.** [tumble] chute *f*; **have you had a ~?** êtes-vous tombé?, avez-vous fait une chute?; **a ~ from a horse** une chute de cheval; **a forty-metre ~** une chute de quarante mètres ☐ **the ~ of night** *lit* la tombée de la nuit; **the Fall (of Man)** RELIG la chute (de l'homme); **to be heading** OR **riding for a ~** courir à l'échec; **the government is riding for a ~** le gouvernement va au-devant de la défaite. -**2.** [of rain, snow] chute *f*; **there was a heavy ~ of snow overnight** il est tombé beaucoup de neige OR il y a eu de fortes chutes de neige dans la nuit. -**3.** [collapse - of building, wall] chute *f*, effondrement *m*; [- of dirt, rock] éboulement *m*, chute *f*; [- of city, country] chute *f*, capitulation *f*; [- of regime] chute *f*, renversement *m*; **the ~ of the Roman Empire** la chute de l'Empire romain ☐ **'The Fall of the House of Usher'** *Poe* 'la Chute de la maison Usher'. -**4.** [decrease - in price, temperature] baisse *f*; [- in currency] dépréciation *f*, baisse *f*; [more marked] chute *f*. -**5.** [drape]: **the ~ of her gown** le drapé de sa robe, la façon dont tombe sa robe. -**6.** [slope] pente *f*, inclinaison *f*. -**7.** *Am* [autumn] automne *m*; **in the ~** en automne. -**8.** SPORT [in judo] chute *f*; [in wrestling] chute *f*.

◇ *adj Am* [colours] automnal.

◆ **falls** *npl* [waterfall] cascade *f*, chute *f* d'eau; **Niagara Falls** les chutes du Niagara.

◆ **fall about** *inf vi insep Br* se tordre de rire; **they fell about (laughing)** ils se tordaient de rire.

◆ **fall apart** *vi insep* -**1.** [book, furniture] tomber en morceaux; *fig* [nation] se désagréger; [conference] échouer; [system] s'écrouler, s'effondrer; **her plans fell apart at the seams** ses projets sont tombés à l'eau; **her life was ~ing apart** toute sa vie s'écroulait; **their marriage is ~ing apart** leur mariage est en train de se briser OR va à vau-l'eau. -**2.** [person] s'effondrer; **he more or less fell apart after his wife's death** il a plus ou moins craqué après la mort de sa femme.

◆ **fall away** *vi insep* -**1.** [paint, plaster] s'écailler. -**2.** [diminish in size - attendance, figures] diminuer; [- fears] se dissiper, fondre. -**3.** [defect] déserter; **support for his policies is beginning to ~ away** dans la politique qu'il mène il commence à perdre ses appuis. -**4.** [land, slope] s'affaisser.

◆ **fall back** *vi insep* -**1.** [retreat, recede] reculer, se retirer; MIL se replier, battre en retraite. -**2.** [lag, trail] se laisser distancer, être à la traîne.

◆ **fall back on** *vt insep*: **to ~ back on sthg** avoir recours à qqch; **it's good to have sthg to ~ back on** [skill] c'est bien de pouvoir se raccrocher à qqch; [money] il vaut mieux avoir d'autres ressources.

◆ **fall behind** ◇ *vi insep* se laisser distancer, être à la traîne; SPORT se laisser distancer; [in cycling] décrocher; **she fell behind in** OR **with her work** elle a pris du retard dans son travail; **they've fallen behind with their reading** ils ont pris du retard dans leurs lectures; **we can't ~ behind in** OR **with the rent** nous ne pouvons pas être en retard pour le loyer.

◇ *vt insep* prendre du retard sur; **he's fallen behind the rest of the class** il a pris du retard sur le reste de la classe.

◆ **fall down** *vi insep* [book, person, picture] tomber (par terre); [bridge, building] s'effondrer, s'écrouler; [argument, comparison] s'écrouler, s'effondrer; **that house looks as if it's about to ~ down** on dirait que cette maison va s'écrouler.

◆ **fall down on** *vt insep*: **to ~ down on sthg** échouer à qqch; **he's been ~ing down on the job lately** il n'était pas OR ne s'est pas montré à la hauteur dernièrement.

◆ **fall for** *inf vt insep* -**1.** [become infatuated with] tomber amoureux de; **they fell for each other** ils sont tombés amoureux l'un de l'autre; **they really fell for Spain in a big way** ils ont vraiment été emballés par l'Espagne. -**2.** [be deceived by] se laisser prendre par; **they really fell for it!** ils ont vraiment mordu!, ils se sont vraiment fait avoir!; **don't ~ for that hard luck story of his** ne te fais pas avoir quand il te raconte qu'il a la poisse.

◆ **fall in** *vi insep* -**1.** [tumble] tomber; **you'll ~ in!** tu vas tomber dedans!; **he leant too far over the side of the boat and fell in** il s'est trop penché hors du bateau et il est tombé. -**2.** [roof] s'effondrer, s'écrouler; **then the roof fell in** *fig* puis tout s'est écroulé. -**3.** [line up] se mettre en rang, s'aligner; MIL [troops] former les rangs; [one soldier] rentrer dans les rangs; **~ in!** à vos rangs!

◆ **fall in with** *vt insep* -**1.** [frequent]: **to ~ in with sb** se mettre à fréquenter qqn; **she fell in with a bad crowd** elle s'est mise à fréquenter des gens louches. -**2.** [agree with]: **I'll ~ in with whatever you decide to do** *Br* je me rangerai à ce que tu décideras.

◆ **fall into** *vt insep* -**1.** [tumble into] tomber dans; **they fell into the trap** ils sont tombés dans le piège; **to ~ into sb's clutches** OR **sb's hands** tomber dans les griffes de qqn, tomber entre les mains de qqn; **the pieces began to ~ into place** *fig* les éléments ont commencé à se mettre en place. -**2.** [begin]: **she fell into conversation with the stranger** elle est entrée en conversation avec l'étranger; **to ~ into line with** se ranger à, se conformer à; **to ~ into step with sb** *literal* se mettre au pas de qqn; *fig* se ranger à l'avis de qqn.

◆ **fall off** *vi insep* -**1.** [drop off] tomber; [in mountain climbing] dévisser; **the leaves of this plant are ~ing off** les feuilles de cette plante tombent, cette plante perd ses feuilles; **she fell off the bicycle/horse** elle est tombée du vélo/de cheval. -**2.** [diminish - attendance, exports, numbers, sales] diminuer, baisser; [- enthusiasm, production] baisser, tomber; [- population, rate] baisser, décroître; [- interest, zeal] se relâcher.

◆ **fall on** *vt insep* -**1.** [drop on] tomber sur; **something fell on my head** j'ai reçu quelque chose sur la tête ☐ **to ~ on deaf ears** ne provoquer aucune réaction. -**2.** [attack] attaquer, se jeter sur; **the starving children fell on the food** les enfants, affamés, se sont jetés sur la nourriture; **the guerrillas fell on the unsuspecting troops** MIL les guérilleros ont fondu sur OR attaqué les troupes sans qu'elles s'y attendent. -**3.** [meet with] tomber sur, trouver; **they fell on hard times** ils sont tombés dans la misère, ils ont subi des revers de fortune. -**4.** [responsibility] revenir à, incomber à; **responsibility for looking after them ~s on me** c'est à moi qu'il incombe de prendre soin d'eux.

◆ **fall out** *vi insep* -**1.** [drop out] tomber; **the keys must have fallen out of my pocket** les clés ont dû tomber de ma poche; **his hair is ~ing out** ses cheveux tombent, il perd ses cheveux. -**2.** [quarrel] se brouiller, se disputer; **she's fallen out with her boyfriend** elle est OR s'est brouillée avec son petit ami. -**3.** [happen] se passer, advenir. -**4.** MIL rompre les rangs; **~ out!** rompez!

◆ **fall over** *vi insep* -**1.** [lose balance] tomber (par terre). -**2.** *inf phr*: **she was ~ing over herself to make us feel welcome** elle se mettait en quatre pour nous faire bon accueil; **the men were ~ing over each other to help her** les hommes ne savaient pas quoi inventer pour l'aider.

◆ **fall through** *vi insep* échouer; **the deal fell through** l'affaire n'a pas abouti; **all our plans fell through at the last minute** tous nos projets sont tombés à l'eau au dernier moment.

◆ **fall to** ◇ *vt insep* -**1.** *Br* [begin] se mettre à; **we fell to work** nous nous sommes mis à l'œuvre; **we all fell to talking about the past** nous nous sommes tous mis à parler du passé. -**2.** [devolve upon] appartenir à, incomber à; **the task that ~s to us is not an easy one** la tâche qui nous incombe OR revient n'est pas facile; **it fell to her to break the news to him** ce fut à elle de lui annoncer la nouvelle.

◇ *vi insep* [eat]: **he brought in the food and they fell to** il a apporté à manger et ils se sont jetés dessus; **she fell to as if she hadn't eaten for a week** elle a attaqué comme si elle n'avait rien mangé depuis huit jours.

◆ **fall upon** *vt insep* -**1.** [attack] attaquer, se jeter sur; **the army fell upon the enemy** MIL l'armée s'est abattue OR a fondu sur l'ennemi; **they fell upon the food** ils se sont jetés sur la nourriture. -**2.** [meet with] tomber sur, trouver; **the family fell upon hard times** la famille a subi des revers de fortune.

fallacious [fəˈleɪʃəs] *adj* [statement] fallacieux, faux; [hope] faux, illusoire.

fallaciousness [fəˈleɪʃəsnɪs] *n* caractère *m* fallacieux, fausseté *f*.

fallacy [ˈfæləsɪ] (*pl* **fallacies**) *n* [misconception] erreur *f*, idée *f* fausse; [false reasoning] mauvais raisonnement *m*, sophisme *m*; LOGIC sophisme *m*.

fallback [ˈfɔːlbæk] *n* -**1.** [retreat] retraite *f*, recul *m*. -**2.** [reserve] réserve *f*; **what's our ~ position?** sur quoi est-ce qu'on peut se rabattre?

fallen [ˈfɔːln] ◇ *pp* → **fall**.

◇ *adj* -**1.** [gen] tombé; [hero, soldier] tombé, mort; [leaf] mort. -**2.** [immoral] perdu; [angel, woman] déchu.

◇ *npl*: **the ~** ceux qui sont morts à la guerre.

fallen arches *npl* MED affaissement *m* de la voûte plantaire.

fall guy *inf n* [dupe] pigeon *m*; [scapegoat] bouc *m* émissaire.

fallibility [ˌfæləˈbɪlətɪ] *n* faillibilité *f*.

fallible [ˈfæləbl] *adj* faillible; **everyone is ~** tout le monde peut se tromper.

falling [ˈfɔːlɪŋ] *adj* [gen] qui tombe; [population] décroissant; [prices, value] en baisse.

falling-off *n* réduction *f*, diminution *f*; **a ~ in production** une baisse de production; **a gradual ~ of interest/of support** une baisse progressive d'intérêt/de soutien.

falling star *n* étoile *f* filante.

falloff [ˈfɔːlɒf] = **falling-off**.

Fallopian tube [fəˈləʊpɪən-] *n* trompe *f* utérine OR de Fallope.

fallout [ˈfɔːlaʊt] *n (U)* [radioactive] retombées *fpl* (radioactives); *fig inf* [consequences] retombées *fpl*, répercussions *fpl*; **~ shelter** abri *m* antiatomique.

fallow [ˈfæləʊ] ◇ *adj* -**1.** AGR [field, land] en jachère, en friche; **to lie ~** être en jachère; **a ~**

period in the composer's life *fig* une période non productive OR de repos dans la vie du compositeur. -**2.** [colour] fauve.
◇ *n* jachère *f*, friche *f*.

fallow deer *n* daim *m*.

false [fɔːls] ◇ *adj* -**1.** [wrong] faux; [untrue] erroné, inexact; a ~ idea une idée fausse OR erronée; a ~ statement une fausse déclaration; she put a ~ interpretation on his invitation elle a mal interprété son invitation; her lies lulled him into a ~ sense of security ses mensonges l'ont entretenu dans l'illusion de la sécurité; in a ~ position dans une position fausse; to strike a ~ note faire une fausse note ❑ ~ dawn lueurs annonciatrices de l'aube; don't make any ~ moves ne faites pas de faux pas; ~ pride vanité *f*; ~ start faux départ *m*. -**2.** [fake] faux; [artificial] artificiel; a ~ bottom un double fond; a suitcase with a ~ bottom une valise à double fond; ~ eyelashes faux cils *mpl*. -**3.** [deceptive] faux, mensonger; ~ promises promesses mensongères, fausses promesses; a ~ report OR rumour une fausse rumeur || JUR: under ~ pretences par des moyens frauduleux; you've got me here under ~ pretences *fig* tu m'as bien piégé; to bear ~ witness porter un faux témoignage. -**4.** [insincere] perfide, fourbe; [disloyal] déloyal; a ~ friend un ami déloyal ❑ ~ modesty fausse modestie *f*.
◇ *adv* faux; her story rings ~ son histoire sonne faux; to play sb ~ trahir qqn.

false alarm *n* fausse alerte *f*.

falsehood ['fɔːlshʊd] *n fml* -**1.** [lie] mensonge *m*; to tell OR to utter a ~ mentir, dire des mensonges. -**2.** [lying] faux *m*; truth and ~ le vrai et le faux. -**3.** [falseness] fausseté *f*.

falsely ['fɔːlslɪ] *adv* [claim, state] faussement; [accuse, judge] à tort, injustement; [interpret] mal; [act] déloyalement; she sounded ~ cheerful on the telephone sa gaieté sonnait faux au téléphone.

falseness ['fɔːlsnɪs] *n* -**1.** [of belief, statement] fausseté *f*. -**2.** [of friend, lover] infidélité *f*. -**3.** [insincerity] fausseté *f*, manque *m* de sincérité.

false ribs *npl* fausses côtes *fpl*.

false teeth *npl* dentier *m*.

falsetto [fɔːl'setəʊ] (*pl* falsettos) ◇ *n* fausset *m*.
◇ *adj* de fausset, de tête.

falsies *inf* ['fɔːlsɪz] *npl* soutien-gorge *m* rembourré.

falsification [,fɔːlsɪfɪ'keɪʃn] *n* falsification *f*.

falsify ['fɔːlsɪfaɪ] (*pt* & *pp* falsified) *vt* -**1.** [document] falsifier; [evidence] maquiller; [accounts, figures] truquer. -**2.** [misrepresent] déformer, dénaturer. -**3.** [disprove] réfuter.

falsity ['fɔːlsətɪ] (*pl* falsities) *n* -**1.** [falseness] fausseté *f*, erreur *f*. -**2.** [lie] mensonge *m*.

falter ['fɔːltə^r] ◇ *vi* -**1.** [waver] vaciller, chanceler; [courage, memory] faiblir; demand for luxury goods has begun to ~ la demande de produits de luxe a commencé à baisser. -**2.** [stumble] chanceler, tituber. -**3.** [in speech] hésiter, parler d'une voix mal assurée.
◇ *vt* balbutier, bredouiller; "I'm not sure, I don't... I can't... ", he ~ed «je ne suis pas sûr, je... non... non...», bredouilla-t-il OR balbutia-t-il.

faltering ['fɔːltərɪŋ] *adj* [attempt] timide, hésitant; [voice] hésitant; [steps] chancelant, mal assuré; [courage, memory] défaillant.

falteringly ['fɔːltərɪŋlɪ] *adv* avec hésitation; [move] d'un pas chancelant OR mal assuré; [speak] d'une voix hésitante OR mal assurée.

fame [feɪm] *n* célébrité *f*, renommée *f*; the television series brought her instant ~ la série télévisée l'a rendue immédiatement célèbre OR a fait immédiatement sa renommée; his thirst for ~ and fortune sa soif de gloire et d'argent; to rise to ~ se faire un nom; Mick Jagger of Rolling Stones ~ Mick Jagger, le chanteur du célèbre groupe The Rolling Stones.

famed [feɪmd] *adj* célèbre, renommé; ~ for his generosity connu OR célèbre pour sa générosité.

familial [fə'mɪlɪəl] *adj* familial.

familiar [fə'mɪljə^r] ◇ *adj* -**1.** [well-known] familier; a ~ face un visage familier OR connu; his name is ~ j'ai déjà entendu son nom (quelque part), son nom me dit quelque chose; she's a ~ sight about town tout le monde la connaît de vue en ville; there's something ~ about the place il me semble connaître cet endroit; a ~ feeling un sentiment bien connu; it's a ~ story c'est toujours la même histoire; we're on ~ territory *fig* nous voilà en terrain de connaissance. -**2.** [acquainted]: to be ~ with sthg bien connaître qqch; she's ~ with the situation elle est au courant OR au fait de la situation; to become ~ with sthg se familiariser avec qqch. -**3.** [informal] familier, intime; to be on ~ terms with sb entretenir des rapports amicaux avec qqn; ~ language/tone langage *m*/ton *m* familier. -**4.** *pej* [presumptuous] trop entreprenant; don't let him get too ~ (with you) empêchez-le de se permettre des familiarités OR de se montrer familier avec vous.
◇ *n* -**1.** [friend] familier *m*, ami *m*, -e *f*. -**2.** [spirit] démon *m* familier.

familiarity [fə,mɪlɪ'ærətɪ] (*pl* familiarities) *n* -**1.** [of face, place] caractère *m* familier. -**2.** [with book, rules, language] connaissance *f*; her ~ with his work sa connaissance de ses œuvres ❑ ~ breeds contempt *prov* la familiarité engendre le mépris. -**3.** [intimacy] familiarité *f*, intimité *f*. -**4.** (*usu pl*) *pej* [undue intimacy] familiarité *f*, privauté *f*.

familiarization [fə,mɪljəraɪ'zeɪʃn] *n* familiarisation *f*.

familiarize, -ise [fə'mɪljəraɪz] *vt* -**1.** [inform] familiariser; to ~ o.s. with sthg se familiariser avec qqch; she ~d him with the rules elle l'a familiarisé avec les OR l'a initié aux règles. -**2.** [make widely known] répandre, vulgariser.

familiarly [fə'mɪljəlɪ] *adv* familièrement.

family ['fæmlɪ] (*pl* families) ◇ *n* [gen, BIOL, BOT & LING] famille *f*; have you any ~? [relatives] avez-vous de la famille?; [children] avez-vous des enfants?; to raise a ~ élever des enfants; a large ~ une famille nombreuse; all the children in the ~ are redheads tous les enfants de la famille sont roux; to start a ~ avoir un (premier) enfant; she's (just like) one of the ~ elle fait (tout à fait) partie OR elle est (tout à fait) de la famille; his musical talent runs in the ~ il tient son talent musical de la famille; of good ~ de bonne famille.
◇ *comp* [life] familial, de famille; [car, friend] de la famille; [dinner, likeness, quarrel] de famille; a ~ audience un public OR auditoire familial; a ~ business une affaire familiale; a ~ hotel une pension de famille; a ~ programme une émission familiale; ~ room [in hotel] chambre *f* familiale; a ~-size OR ~-sized jar of jam un pot de confiture familial ❑ ~ Bible Bible *f* familiale OR de famille; ~ butcher boucher *m* habituel; ~ circle cercle *m* de (la) famille; ~ doctor docteur *m* de famille; ~ law droit *m* de la famille; ~ practice *Am* médecine *f* générale; ~ practitioner *Am* médecin *m* de famille, (médecin) généraliste *m*; Family Restaurants *chaîne américaine de restaurants bon marché*; to be in the ~ way *inf euph* être enceinte, attendre un enfant.

family allowance *n Br* allocations *fpl* familiales *(aujourd'hui «child benefit»)*.

family court *n Am tribunal pour toute affaire concernant des enfants*.

family credit *n prestation complémentaire pour familles à faibles revenus ayant au moins un enfant*.

Family Division *n Br* JUR *division du «High Court» s'occupant des affaires matrimoniales*.

family income supplement *n* ≃ complément *m* familial *(aujourd'hui «family credit»)*.

family man *n* père *m* de famille; he's a ~ il aime la vie de famille, c'est un bon père de famille.

family name *n* nom *m* de famille.

family planning *n* planning *m* familial; a ~ clinic un centre de planning familial.

family tree *n* arbre *m* généalogique.

famine ['fæmɪn] *n* famine *f*.

famished ['fæmɪʃt] *adj* affamé; I'm ~! *inf* je meurs de faim!, j'ai une faim de loup!

famous ['feɪməs] *adj* -**1.** [renowned] célèbre, renommé; the stately home is ~ for its gardens le château est connu OR célèbre pour ses jardins; a ~ victory une victoire célèbre; so much for her ~ cooking! voilà ce que vaut OR on sait maintenant ce que vaut sa fameuse cuisine! ❑ ~ last words! c'est ce que tu crois! -**2.** *dated* [first-rate] fameux, formidable.

famously *inf* ['feɪməslɪ] *adv* fameusement, rudement bien; they get on ~ ils s'entendent à merveille OR comme larrons en foire; the project is coming along ~ l'opération marche comme sur des roulettes.

fan [fæn] (*pt* & *pp* fanned, *cont* fanning)
◇ *n* -**1.** [supporter] enthousiaste *mf*, passionné *m*, -e *f*; [of celebrity] fan *mf*; SPORT supporteur *m*, -trice *f*; she's a chess/jazz ~ elle se passionne pour les échecs/le jazz; a crowd of football ~s une foule de supporters de football; he's a ~ of Thai cooking c'est un amateur de cuisine thaïlandaise; I'm not one of her ~s, I'm not a great ~ of hers je suis loin d'être un de ses admirateurs; movie ~s des cinéphiles *mpl*. -**2.** [ventilator - mechanical] ventilateur *m*; [- hand-held] éventail *m*; shaped like a ~ en éventail. -**3.** AGR [machine] tarare *m*; [basket] van *m*.
◇ *vt* -**1.** [face, person] éventer; to ~ o.s. s'éventer. -**2.** [fire] attiser, souffler sur; things are bad enough already, don't ~ the flames *fig* ça suffit déjà OR ça va déjà assez mal comme ça, ne jetez pas de l'huile sur le feu; huge price increases fanned public hostility to the regime la hausse considérable des prix a attisé l'hostilité du peuple contre le régime. -**3.** = **fan out**.
◇ *vi* s'étaler (en éventail).
◆ **fan out** ◇ *vi insep* [spread out] s'étaler (en éventail); [army, search party] se déployer.
◇ *vt sep* étaler (en éventail).

fanatic [fə'nætɪk] ◇ *adj* fanatique.
◇ *n* fanatique *mf*.

fanatical [fə'nætɪkl] *adj* fanatique.

fanatically [fə'nætɪkəlɪ] *adv* fanatiquement.

fanaticism [fə'nætɪsɪzm] *n* fanatisme *m*.

fan belt *n* courroie *f* de ventilateur.

fanciable *inf* ['fænsɪəbl] *adj Br* plutôt bien, pas mal du tout.

fancied ['fænsɪd] *adj* -**1.** [imagined] imaginaire. -**2.** SPORT [favoured] coté, en vogue.

fancier ['fænsɪə^r] *n* -**1.** [fan] amateur *m*, -trice *f*. -**2.** [breeder] éleveur *m*, -euse *f*; he's a pigeon ~ c'est un colombophile.

fanciful ['fænsɪfʊl] *adj* -**1.** [imaginary] imaginaire. -**2.** [imaginative] imaginatif, plein d'imagination. -**3.** [whimsical - person] capricieux, fantaisiste; [- notion] fantasque, excentrique; [- clothing] extravagant.

fancifully ['fænsɪfʊlɪ] *adv* -**1.** [draw, write] avec imagination. -**2.** [act] capricieusement; [dress] d'une façon extravagante OR fantaisiste.

fancily ['fænsɪlɪ] *adv* d'une façon recherchée OR raffinée; they were very ~ dressed ils étaient habillés avec soin, ils étaient endimanchés; ~ decorated décoré d'une manière compliquée OR avec recherche.

fanciness ['fænsɪnɪs] *n* caractère *m* raffiné.

fan club *n* cercle *m* OR club *m* de fans; her ~ is here *fig* ses admirateurs sont là.

fancy ['fænsɪ] (*compar* fancier, *superl* fanciest, *pl* fancies, *pt* & *pp* fancied) ◇ *adj* -**1.** [elaborate - clothes] recherché, raffiné; [- style] recherché, travaillé; [- excuse] recherché, compliqué; ~ cakes pâtisseries *fpl*; a ~ dog un chien de luxe. -**2.** [high-quality] de qualité supérieure, de luxe; ~ food denrées alimentaires de qualité supérieure. -**3.** *pej* [overrated - price] exorbitant; [- talk, words] extravagant; with all her ~ ways avec ses grands airs.
◇ *n* -**1.** [whim] caprice *m*, fantaisie *f*; as the ~ takes him comme ça lui chante; it's just a passing ~ ce n'est qu'une lubie. -**2.** *Br* [liking]

goût *m*, penchant *m*; **I've taken a ~ to avocado pears lately** je me suis mis depuis quelque temps à aimer les avocats; **to take a ~ to sb** se prendre d'affection pour qqn; **the dress took** OR **caught her ~** la robe lui a fait envie OR lui a tapé dans l'œil ❑ **the idea tickled my ~** *inf* l'idée m'a séduit. -**3.** [imagination] imagination *f*, fantaisie *f*; **a flight of ~** un élan d'imagination; **the realm of ~** *lit* le domaine de l'imaginaire, le royaume des chimères. -**4.** [notion] idée *f* fantasque, fantasme *m*; **I have a ~ that...** j'ai idée que...; **one of my fancies as a child was to join the circus** enfant, je rêvais de faire partie d'un cirque.

◇ *vt* -**1.** *inf Br* [want] avoir envie de; [like] aimer; **do you ~ a cup of tea?** voulez-vous une tasse de thé?; **I don't ~ travelling** je n'ai pas envie OR cela ne me dit rien de voyager; **I've never fancied science fiction** je n'ai jamais été attiré par la science-fiction; **I don't ~ your chances of getting that job** j'imagine mal que vous obteniez ce travail; **to fancy sb** s'enticher de qqn; **she really fancies herself** *inf* elle ne se prend vraiment pas pour rien; **which horse do you ~?** SPORT à votre avis, quel sera le cheval gagnant?, quel cheval donnez-vous gagnant? -**2.** *inf* [imagine] imaginer, s'imaginer; **she fancies herself as an intellectual** elle se prend pour une intellectuelle; **~ meeting you here!** tiens! je ne m'attendais pas à vous voir ici!; **~ anyone wanting to do that!** qu'est-ce que les gens vont chercher!; **~ her coming!** qui aurait cru qu'elle allait venir! ❑ **~ that!** tiens! voyez-vous cela! -**3.** *lit* [believe] croire, se figurer; **he fancies he knows everything** il se figure tout savoir; **she fancied she heard the baby crying** elle a cru entendre pleurer le bébé; **I ~ we've met before** j'ai l'impression que nous nous sommes déjà rencontrés.

fancy dress *n Br* déguisement *m*, costume *m*; **in ~** déguisé; **a ~ ball** un bal masqué OR costumé; **~ party** fête *f* déguisée.

fancy-free *adj* sans souci.

fancy goods *npl* nouveautés *fpl*, articles *mpl* de fantaisie.

fancy man *inf n pej* jules *m*; **he's her new ~** c'est son nouveau jules OR mec.

fancy woman *inf n pej* maîtresse *f*, petite amie *f*.

fancywork ['fænsɪwɜːk] *n (U)* ouvrages *mpl* d'agrément.

fan dance *n* danse *f* des éventails.

fandangle *inf* [fæn'dæŋgl] *n* -**1.** [ornament] ornement *m* clinquant. -**2.** *(U)* [nonsense] sottises *fpl*.

fandango [fæn'dæŋgəʊ] (*pl* **fandangos**) *n* fandango *m*.

fanfare ['fænfeəʳ] *n* MUS fanfare *f*; *fig* [ostentation]: **with much ~** avec des roulements de tambour, avec éclat.

fang [fæŋ] *n* [of snake] crochet *m*; [of wolf, vampire] croc *m*, canine *f*.

fan heater *n* radiateur *m* soufflant.

fan-jet *n* [engine] turboréacteur *m*; [plane] avion *m* à turboréacteurs.

fan letter *n* lettre *f* d'un admirateur.

fanlight ['fænlaɪt] *n* imposte *f* (semi-circulaire).

fan mail *n* courrier *m* des admirateurs.

fanny ['fænɪ] (*pl* **fannies**) *n* -**1.** ▼ *Br* [female genitals] chatte *f*. -**2.** *inf Am* [buttocks] fesses *fpl*.

fanny adams *inf n Br*: **(sweet) ~** que dalle.

fanny pack *n Am* banane *f (sac)*.

fantabulous *inf* [fæn'tæbjʊləs] *adj* chic, chouette.

fantail (pigeon) ['fænteɪl-] *n* pigeon *m* paon.

fantasia [fæn'teɪzjə] *n* LITERAT & MUS fantaisie *f*.

fantasize, -ise ['fæntəsaɪz] *vi* fantasmer, se livrer à des fantasmes; **she ~d about becoming rich and famous** elle rêvait de devenir riche et célèbre.

fantastic [fæn'tæstɪk] *adj* -**1.** *inf* [wonderful] fantastique, sensationnel; **what a ~ goal!** quel but fantastique OR superbe! -**2.** *inf* [very large - success] inouï, fabuleux; [- amount, rate] phénoménal, faramineux. -**3.** [preposterous, strange - idea, plan, story] fantastique, bizarre.

fantastically [fæn'tæstɪklɪ] *adv* fantastiquement, extraordinairement; **it's ~ expensive** c'est incroyablement OR terriblement cher.

fantasy ['fæntəsɪ] (*pl* **fantasies**) *n* -**1.** [dream] fantasme *m*; PSYCH fantasme *m*; [notion] idée *f* fantasque; **to indulge in ~** se livrer à des fantasmes OR rêveries. -**2.** [imagination] imagination *f*, fantaisie *f*; **~ and reality** l'imaginaire *m* et la réalité; **to live in a ~ world** vivre dans un monde à soi. -**3.** LITERAT & MUS fantaisie *f*.

fan vaulting *n (U)* voûte *f* OR voûtes *fpl* en éventail.

fanzine ['fænziːn] *n* revue *f* spécialisée, fanzine *m*.

fao (*written abbr of* **attention of**) à l'attention de.

FAO (*abbr of* **Food and Agriculture Organization**) *pr n* FAO *f*.

FAQ (*abbr of* **free alongside quay**) *adv Br* FLQ.

far [fɑːʳ] (*compar* **farther** ['fɑːðəʳ] OR **further** ['fɜːðəʳ], *superl* **farthest** ['fɑːðɪst] OR **furthest** ['fɜːðɪst]) ◇ *adv* -**1.** [distant in space] loin; **is it ~?** est-ce (que c'est) loin?; **how ~ is it to town?** combien y a-t-il jusqu'à la ville?; **how ~ is he going?** jusqu'où va-t-il?; **have you come ~?** êtes-vous venu de loin?; **the police are looking for them, they won't get very ~** la police est à leur recherche, ils n'iront pas très loin; **he went as ~ north as Alaska** il est allé au nord jusqu'en Alaska; **~ away** OR **off in the distance** au loin, dans le lointain; **he doesn't live ~ away** OR **off** il n'habite pas loin; **~ above/below** loin au-dessus/au-dessous; **~ beyond** bien au-delà; **~ out at sea** en pleine mer ‖ *fig*: **his thoughts are ~ away** son esprit est ailleurs; **his work is ~ above the others'** son travail est de loin supérieur à celui des autres; **that's ~ beyond me** [physically] c'est bien au-dessus de mes forces; [intellectually] ça me dépasse; **how ~ can you trust him?** jusqu'à quel point peut-on lui faire confiance?; **how ~ (on) are you in the book?** où en es-tu dans le livre?; **how ~ have you got with the translation?** où en es-tu de la traduction? ❑ **~ and wide** de tous côtés; **they came from ~ and wide** ils sont venus de partout; **he travels ~ and wide** il court le monde; **~ be it from me to interfere!** loin de moi l'idée d'intervenir!; **to be ~ out** *Br*, **to be ~ off** *Am* [person] se tromper complètement; [report, survey] être complètement erroné; [guess] être loin du compte; **he's not ~ off** OR **wrong** il n'a pas tout à fait tort; **she's not ~ off being finished** elle n'est pas loin d'avoir fini; **to carry** OR **to take sthg too ~** pousser qqch trop loin; **have you got ~ to go?** *literal* avez-vous encore beaucoup de chemin à faire?; *fig* êtes-vous loin du but?; **you won't get ~ with that attitude** vous n'irez pas loin avec ce genre de comportement; **sincerity won't get you very ~** la sincérité ne vous mènera pas loin. -**2.** [distant in time] loin; **as ~ back as 1800** déjà en 1800, dès 1800; **as ~ back as I can remember** aussi loin que je m'en souvienne; **I can't look ~ beyond August** je ne sais pas ce qui se passera après le mois d'août; **she worked ~ into the night** elle a travaillé très avant OR jusque tard dans la nuit; **don't look so ~ into the future** ne vous préoccupez pas de ce qui se passera dans un avenir aussi lointain; **the holidays aren't ~ off** les vacances ne sont plus loin OR approchent; **he's not ~ off sixty** il n'a pas loin de la soixantaine. -**3.** *(with comparatives)* [much] beaucoup, bien; **this is ~ better** c'est beaucoup OR bien mieux; **a ~ greater problem** un problème bien OR autrement OR beaucoup plus grave; **she is ~ more intelligent than I am** elle est bien OR beaucoup plus intelligente que moi. -**4.** *phr*: **to go ~** [person, idea] aller loin, faire son chemin; **this has gone ~ enough** trop, c'est trop; **his policy doesn't go ~ enough** sa politique ne va pas assez loin; **I would even go so ~ as to say...** j'irais même jusqu'à dire..., je dirais même...; **he went so ~ as to claim that...** il est allé jusqu'à prétendre que...; **to go too ~** [exaggerate] dépasser les bornes, exagérer; **you're going too ~!** vous exagérez! ‖ [make progress]: **she's gone too ~ to back out** elle s'est trop engagée pour reculer; **this goes quite ~ towards solving the problem** on approche d'une solution ‖ [money]: **£5 doesn't go ~ nowadays** on ne va pas loin avec 5 livres de nos jours.

◇ *adj* -**1.** [distant] lointain, éloigné; [remote] éloigné; **it's a ~ cry from what she expected** ce n'est pas du tout OR c'est loin de ce qu'elle attendait. -**2.** [more distant] autre, plus éloigné; **on the ~ side** de l'autre côté; **the ~ end of** l'autre bout de, l'extrémité de; **at the ~ end of the room** au fond de la salle. -**3.** [extreme] extrême; **the ~ north** l'extrême nord *m*; **the ~ left/right** POL l'extrême gauche *f*/droite *f*.

◆ **as far as** ◇ *prep phr* jusqu'à; **I'll walk with you as ~ as the end of the lane** je vais vous accompagner jusqu'au bout du chemin.

◇ *conj phr* -**1.** [distance]: **as ~ as the eye can see** à perte de vue ❑ **that's fine as ~ as it goes** c'est très bien, jusqu'à un certain point. -**2.** [to the extent that] autant que; **as ~ as possible** autant que possible, dans la mesure du possible; **as ~ as I can** dans la mesure de mon possible; **as ~ as I can judge** (pour) autant que je puisse (en) juger; **as ~ as I know** (pour) autant que je sache; **as ~ as she's/I'm concerned** en ce qui la/me concerne, pour sa/ma part; **as ~ as money goes** OR **is concerned** pour ce qui est de l'argent.

◆ **by far** *adv phr* de loin, de beaucoup; **she's by ~ the cleverest** OR **the cleverest by ~** c'est de loin OR de beaucoup la plus intelligente.

◆ **far and away** *adv phr* de loin.

◆ **far from** ◇ *adv phr* [not at all] loin de; **~ from clean** loin d'être propre; **the report was ~ from complimentary** le rapport était loin d'être flatteur; **I'm ~ from approving all he does** je suis loin d'approuver tout ce qu'il fait ❑ **he's not rich, ~ from it** il n'est pas riche, loin de là OR tant s'en faut.

◇ *prep phr* [rather than] loin de; **~ from being generous, he is rather stingy** loin d'être généreux, il est plutôt radin; **~ from improving, the situation got worse** loin de s'améliorer, les choses ont empiré.

◆ **in so far as** *conj phr* dans la mesure où.

◆ **so far** *adv phr* jusqu'ici, jusqu'à présent; **so ~ this month** depuis le début du mois ❑ **so ~ so good** jusqu'ici ça va.

◆ **so far as** *conj phr* = **as far as 2**.

farad ['færəd] *n* farad *m*.

faraday ['færədeɪ] *n* faraday *m*.

faraway ['fɑːrəweɪ] *adj* [distant] lointain, éloigné; [isolated] éloigné; [sound, voice] lointain; [look] absent; **her eyes had a ~ look** son regard était perdu dans le vague.

farce [fɑːs] *n* -**1.** THEAT & *fig* farce *f*; **this law is a ~** cette loi est grotesque OR dérisoire. -**2.** CULIN farce *f*.

farcical ['fɑːsɪkl] *adj* risible, ridicule; **the election was completely ~** l'élection était grotesque OR était une pure comédie.

fare [feəʳ] ◇ *n* -**1.** [charge - for bus, underground] prix *m* du billet OR ticket; [- for boat, plane, train] prix *m* du billet; [- in taxi] prix *m* de la course; **what is the ~?** [gen] combien coûte le billet?; [in taxi] combien je vous dois?; **~s are going up** les tarifs des transports augmentent; **have you got the ~?** avez-vous de quoi payer le billet?; **(any more) ~s, please!** [in bus, train] qui n'a pas son ticket? -**2.** [passenger] voyageur *m*, -euse *f*; [in taxi] client *m*, -e *f*. -**3.** [food] nourriture *f*, chère *f*; **hospital ~** régime *m* d'hôpital.

◇ *comp*: **~ dodger** resquilleur *m*, -euse *f*.

◇ *vi*: **how did you ~ at the booking office?** comment ça s'est passé au bureau de réservation?

Far East *pr n*: **the ~** l'Extrême-Orient *m*.

Far Eastern *adj* extrême-oriental.

fare stage *n Br* [of bus] section *f*.

fare-thee-well *inf n Am*: **to a ~** à la perfection.

farewell [,feə'wel] ◇ *n* adieu *m*; ~! adieu!; to bid sb ~ dire adieu à qqn; we said our ~s and left nous avons fait nos adieux et nous sommes partis; you can say ~ to your chances of winning! tu peux dire adieu à tes chances de victoire!, tu n'as plus aucune chance de gagner! ❑ 'A Farewell to Arms' *Hemingway* 'l'Adieu aux armes'.
◇ *comp* [dinner, party] d'adieu.

far-fetched [-'fetʃt] *adj* bizarre, farfelu; a ~ alibi un alibi tiré par les cheveux; a ~ story une histoire à dormir debout.

far-flung *adj* [widespread] étendu, vaste; [far] lointain.

farinaceous [,færɪ'neɪʃəs] *adj* farinacé.

farm [fɑːm] ◇ *n* ferme *f*, exploitation *f* (agricole); to work on a ~ travailler dans une ferme.
◇ *comp* [equipment, worker] agricole; ~ produce produits *mpl* agricoles OR de ferme; ~ shop *magasin qui vend des produits de la ferme*.
◇ *vt* [land] cultiver, exploiter; [animals] élever.
◇ *vi* être fermier, être cultivateur.
◆ **farm out** *vt sep* -**1.** [shop] mettre en gérance; [work] donner OR confier à un sous-traitant; she ~s some work out to local people elle cède du travail à des sous-traitants locaux. -**2.** [child] confier; she ~s her children out on an aunt elle confie (la garde de) ses enfants à une tante.

farmer ['fɑːmə^r] *n* [of land] fermier *m*, -ère *f*, agriculteur *m*, -trice *f*; [of animals] éleveur *m*, -euse *f*.

farmhand ['fɑːmhænd] *n* ouvrier *m*, -ère *f* agricole.

farmhouse ['fɑːmhaʊs, *pl* -haʊzɪz] *n* (maison *f* de) ferme *f*.

farming ['fɑːmɪŋ] ◇ *n* agriculture *f*; fish/mink ~ élevage *m* de poisson/vison; fruit/vegetable ~ culture *f* fruitière/maraîchère.
◇ *comp* [methods] de culture, cultural; [equipment, machines] agricole; [community, region] rural.

farmland ['fɑːmlænd] *n* (U) terre *f* arable, terres *fpl* arables.

farmstead ['fɑːmsted] *n* ferme *f (et ses dépendances)*.

farmyard ['fɑːmjɑːd] *n* cour *f* de ferme.

Far North *pr n*: the ~ le Grand Nord.

faro ['feərəʊ] *n jeu de cartes où l'on joue contre le donneur*.

Faroe *etc* ['feərəʊ] = **Faeroe**.

far-off *adj* [place, time] lointain, éloigné.

far-out *inf adj* -**1.** [odd] bizarre, farfelu; [avant-garde] d'avant-garde. -**2.** [excellent] génial, super.

farrago [fə'rɑːgəʊ] (*pl* farragoes) *n* amas *m*; a ~ of lies un fatras de mensonges.

far-reaching [-'riːtʃɪŋ] *adj* d'une grande portée; to have ~ consequences avoir des conséquences considérables OR d'une portée considérable.

farrier ['færɪə^r] *n Br* [blacksmith] maréchal-ferrant *m*; [vet] vétérinaire *mf*.

farrow ['færəʊ] ◇ *vi* & *vt* mettre bas.
◇ *n* portée *f* (de cochons).

farseeing [,fɑː'siːɪŋ] *adj* [person] prévoyant, perspicace; [action] prévoyant; [décision] pris avec clairvoyance.

Farsi [,fɑː'siː] *n* farsi *m*.

farsighted [,fɑː'saɪtɪd] *adj* -**1.** [shrewd - person] prévoyant, perspicace; [- action] prévoyant; [decision] pris avec clairvoyance. -**2.** *Am* MED hypermétrope.

farsightedness [,fɑː'saɪtɪdnɪs] *n* -**1.** [of person] prévoyance *f*, perspicacité *f*; [of act, decision] clairvoyance *f*. -**2.** *Am* MED hypermétropie *f*, presbytie *f*.

fart▽ [fɑːt] ◇ *n* -**1.** [gas] pet *m*. -**2.** [person] birbe *m*; he's a boring old ~ il est rasoir, c'est un raseur.
◇ *vi* péter.
◆ **fart about**▽, **fart around**▽ *vi insep* gaspiller OR perdre son temps, glander.

farther ['fɑːðə^r] (*compar of* far) ◇ *adv* -**1.** [more distant] plus loin; ~ north plus (loin) au nord; how much ~ is it? c'est encore à combien?; have we much ~ to go? avons-nous encore beaucoup de chemin à faire?; ~ than the shop plus loin que le magasin; ~ ahead loin devant; ~ along the corridor plus loin dans le couloir; ~ away, ~ off plus éloigné, plus loin; to move ~ and ~ away s'éloigner de plus en plus; ~ back plus (loin) en arrière; move ~ back reculez (-vous); ~ back than 1900 avant 1900; ~ down/up plus bas/haut; ~ on OR forward plus loin. -**2.** [in addition] en plus, de plus.
◇ *adj* plus éloigné, plus lointain; on the ~ side of the room de l'autre côté OR au fond de la salle; the ~ end of the tunnel l'autre bout du tunnel.

farthermost ['fɑːðə,məʊst] *adj* plus lointain, plus éloigné; to the ~ ends of the earth jusqu'aux confins de la terre.

farthest ['fɑːðɪst] (*superl of* far) ◇ *adj* le plus lointain, le plus éloigné; in the ~ depths of Africa au fin fond de l'Afrique.
◇ *adv* le plus loin; it's 3 km at the ~ il y a 3 km au plus OR au maximum; the ~ removed le plus éloigné.

farthing ['fɑːðɪŋ] *n pièce de monnaie qui valait le quart d'un ancien penny*; we haven't a ~ nous n'avons pas le sou.

FAS (*abbr of* free alongside ship) *adv Br* FLB.

fascia [*sense 1* & *2* 'feɪʃə, *sense 3* 'fæʃɪə] (*pl* fasciae [-ʃiiː]) *n* -**1.** [on building] panneau *m*. -**2.** *Br* [dashboard] tableau *m* de bord. -**3.** ANAT fascia *m*.

fascicle ['fæsɪkl] *n* -**1.** [gen, ANAT & BOT] faisceau *m*. -**2.** PRINT = **fascicule**.

fascicule ['fæsɪkjuːl] *n* fascicule *m*.

fascinate ['fæsɪneɪt] *vt* -**1.** [delight] fasciner, captiver; she was ~d by OR with his story elle était fascinée par son histoire. -**2.** [prey] fasciner.

fascinating ['fæsɪneɪtɪŋ] *adj* [country, idea, person] fascinant, captivant; [book, speaker, speech] fascinant, passionnant.

fascinatingly ['fæsɪneɪtɪŋlɪ] *adv* d'une façon fascinante OR passionnante.

fascination [,fæsɪ'neɪʃn] *n* fascination *f*, attrait *m*; her ~ for the Orient la fascination qu'exerce sur elle l'Orient.

fascism ['fæʃɪzm] *n* fascisme *m*.

fascist ['fæʃɪst] ◇ *adj* fasciste.
◇ *n* fasciste *mf*.

fascistic [fə'ʃɪstɪk] *adj* fasciste.

fashion ['fæʃn] ◇ *n* -**1.** [current style] mode *f*; in ~ à la mode, en vogue; miniskirts are coming back into ~ les minijupes reviennent à la mode; big weddings are no longer in ~ ça ne se fait plus, les grands mariages; she dresses in the latest ~ elle s'habille à la dernière mode; the Paris ~s les collections (de mode) parisiennes; hats are the ~ again les chapeaux reviennent à la mode; to set the ~ donner le ton, lancer la mode; it is the ~ to take a year out before university il est bien vu OR de bon ton de prendre une année avant d'entrer à l'université; out of ~ démodé, passé de mode; to go out of ~ se démoder. -**2.** [manner] façon *f*, manière *f*; in an orderly ~ d'une façon méthodique, méthodiquement; after the ~ of Shakespeare à la manière de Shakespeare; after the French ~ à la française; after a ~ tant bien que mal; he can paint after a ~ il peint à sa manière.
◇ *comp* [editor, magazine] de mode; [industry] de la mode; ~ designer modéliste *mf*; the great ~ designers les grands couturiers; ~ house maison *f* de (haute) couture; ~ model mannequin *m*; ~ show présentation *f* des modèles OR des collections, défilé *m* de mode.
◇ *vt* [gen] fabriquer, modeler; [carving, sculpture] façonner; [dress] confectionner; *fig* [character, person] former, façonner; to ~ sthg out of clay façonner qqch en argile.

-fashion *in cpds*: he wore his scarf pirate~ il portait son foulard comme les pirates.

fashionable ['fæʃnəbl] *adj* [clothing] à la mode; [café, neighbourhood] chic, à la mode; [subject, writer] à la mode, en vogue; black is ~ this year le noir se porte beaucoup cette année; a café ~ with writers un café fréquenté par des écrivains; it is ~ to say il est de bon ton OR bien vu de dire; it is no longer ~ to eat red meat cela ne se fait plus de manger de la viande rouge; ~ society les gens à la mode.

fashionably ['fæʃnəblɪ] *adv* élégamment, à la mode; her hair is ~ short elle a les cheveux coupés court selon la mode.

fashion-conscious *adj* qui suit la mode.

fashion plate *n literal* gravure *f* de mode; *fig* élégant *m*, -e *f*.

fashion victim *n hum* victime *f* de la mode.

fast [fɑːst] ◇ *adj* -**1.** [quick] rapide; a ~ film une pellicule rapide; she's a ~ runner elle court vite; at a ~ pace d'un pas vif OR rapide; a grass court is ~er than a hard one [in tennis] le jeu est plus rapide sur gazon que sur un court en dur ❑ ~ bowler [in cricket] lanceur *m* rapide; ~ train rapide *m*; to make a ~ buck *inf* se remplir les poches, se faire plein de fric; to pull a ~ one on sb *inf* jouer un mauvais tour à qqn; he's a ~ worker *literal* il va vite en besogne; *fig* il ne perd pas de temps. -**2.** [clock] en avance; my watch is (three minutes) ~ ma montre avance (de trois minutes). -**3.** [secure - knot, rope] solide; [- door, window] bien fermé; [- grip] ferme, solide; [- friend] sûr, fidèle; to make a boat ~ amarrer un bateau. -**4.** [colour] bon teint *(inv)*, grand teint *(inv)*; the colour is not ~ la couleur déteint OR s'en va. -**5.** [wild] libertin; ~ life, ~ living vie dissolue OR de dissipation; he's in with a ~ set *inf* il fréquente une bande de viveurs OR de fêtards.
◇ *adv* -**1.** [quickly] vite, rapidement; how ~ is the car going? à quelle vitesse roule la voiture?; he needs help ~ il lui faut de l'aide de toute urgence; she ran off as ~ as her legs would carry her elle s'est sauvée à toutes jambes, elle a pris ses jambes à son cou; the insults came ~ and furious les insultes volaient OR pleuvaient dru; as ~ as I ate he gave me more il me resservait à mesure que je mangeais; he'll do it ~ enough if you pay well il ne se fera pas prier si vous payez bien; not so ~! doucement!, pas si vite!; not so ~, I haven't finished une minute, je n'ai pas fini. -**2.** [ahead of correct time] en avance; my watch is running ~ ma montre avance. -**3.** [securely] ferme, solidement; shut ~ bien fermé; to hold ~ (on) to sthg tenir fermement qqch; they held ~ despite the threats *fig* ils ont tenu bon malgré les menaces. -**4.** [soundly] profondément; to be ~ asleep dormir à poings fermés OR profondément. -**5.** *arch* [near] tout près; ~ by the school qui jouxte l'école, attenant à l'école.
◇ *n* jeûne *m*; to break one's ~ rompre le jeûne; a ~ day RELIG un jour maigre OR de jeûne.
◇ *vi* [gen] jeûner, rester à jeun; RELIG jeûner, faire maigre.

fastback ['fɑːstbæk] *n* voiture *f* deux-volumes, voiture *f* à hayon arrière.

fast breeder reactor *n* surgénérateur *m*, surgénérateur *m*.

fasten ['fɑːsn] ◇ *vt* -**1.** [attach] attacher; [close] fermer; to ~ sthg with glue/nails/string to sthg coller/clouer/lier qqch à qqch; ~ your seatbelts attachez votre ceinture; he ~ed the two ends together il a attaché les deux bouts ensemble OR l'un à l'autre. -**2.** [attention, eyes] fixer; he ~ed his eyes on the door il a fixé la porte des yeux OR a fixé son regard sur la porte. -**3.** [ascribe - guilt, responsibility] attribuer; [- crime] imputer; to ~ sthg on sb attribuer qqch à qqn; they ~ed the blame on him ils ont rejeté la faute sur lui; to ~ one's attention on sthg fixer son attention sur qqch.
◇ *vi* [bra, dress] s'attacher; [bag, door, window] se fermer.
◆ **fasten down** *vt sep* [flap, shutter] fermer; [envelope, sticker] coller.
◆ **fasten on** *vt sep* [belt, holster] fixer.
◆ **fasten onto** *vt insep* -**1.** [seize upon] saisir; to ~ onto an idea se mettre une idée en tête.

-**2.** [grip] se cramponner à, s'accrocher à; he ~ed onto our group *fig* il s'est attaché à notre groupe.

◆ **fasten up** *vt sep* fermer, attacher.

◆ **fasten upon** *vt insep* -**1.** [gaze at] fixer; her eyes ~ed upon the letter elle fixait la lettre du regard OR des yeux. -**2.** [seize upon] saisir; to ~ upon an excuse saisir un prétexte; she ~ed upon the idea of escaping elle s'est mis en tête de s'échapper OR de s'évader.

fastener ['fɑːsnə^r], **fastening** ['fɑːsnɪŋ] *n* [gen] attache *f*; [on box, door] fermeture *f*; [on bag, necklace] fermoir *m*; [on clothing] fermeture *f*; [button] bouton *m*; [hook] agrafe *f*; [press stud] pression *f*, bouton-pression *m*; [zip] fermeture *f* Éclair®; what kind of ~ is it? comment cela se ferme-t-il OR s'attache-t-il?

fast food *n* fast-food *m*, prêt-à-manger *m offic.*

◆ **fast-food** *comp* [place, restaurant] de restauration rapide, de fast-food; fast-food restaurants des fast-foods *mpl.*

fast-forward ◇ *vi* se dérouler en avance rapide.

◇ *vt*: to ~ a tape faire avancer OR défiler une cassette.

◇ *comp*: ~ button touche *f* d'avance rapide.

fastidious [fə'stɪdɪəs] *adj* -**1.** [fussy about details] tatillon, pointilleux; [meticulous - person] méticuleux, minutieux; [- work] minutieux; he is ~ about the way he dresses il est d'une coquetterie méticuleuse; the manager is really ~ le patron est vraiment exigeant OR pointilleux; she is ~ about protocol elle est pointilleuse OR à cheval sur le protocole. -**2.** [fussy about cleanliness] méticuleux, tatillon.

fastidiously [fə'stɪdɪəslɪ] *adv* -**1.** [meticulously] méticuleusement, minutieusement; [fussily] d'une façon pointilleuse. -**2.** [fussily about cleanliness] d'une façon tatillonne OR méticuleuse.

fastidiousness [fə'stɪdɪəsnɪs] *n* -**1.** [meticulousness] minutie *f*, méticulosité *f lit*; [fussiness about detail] caractère *m* pointilleux OR tatillon. -**2.** [fussiness about cleanliness] méticulosité *f*.

fastigiate [fæ'stɪdʒɪət] *adj* fastigié.

fast lane *n* [in the UK] voie *f* de droite; [on the continent, in the US etc] voie *f* de gauche; life in the ~ *fig* vie *f* excitante.

fast-moving *adj* [film] plein d'action; ~ events des évènements rapides.

fastness ['fɑːstnɪs] *n* -**1.** [secureness] solidité *f*. -**2.** [of colour] solidité *f*, résistance *f*. -**3.** [stronghold] place *f* forte, repaire *m*.

fast talk *inf n* baratin *m*.

◆ **fast-talk** *inf vt* baratiner; he fast-talked me into it il m'a persuadé grâce à son baratin.

fast-track *adj*: ~ executives *des cadres qui gravissent rapidement les échelons*.

fat [fæt] (*compar* fatter, *superl* fattest, *pt* & *pp* fatted, *cont* fatting) ◇ *adj* -**1.** [heavy, overweight - person] gros, gras; [- cheeks, limb] gros; [- face] joufflu; to get OR to grow ~ grossir, engraisser; she's getting ~ elle prend de l'embonpoint; they had grown ~ on their investments *fig* ils s'étaient enrichis OR engraissés grâce à leurs investissements ❑ he's a ~ cat *inf* [rich] c'est un richard; [important] c'est une huile; as ~ as a pig gras comme un cochon OR un moine. -**2.** [meat] gras. -**3.** [thick, hefty] gros; a ~ book un gros livre, un livre épais; he made a ~ profit *inf* il a fait de gros bénéfices; a ~ wallet un portefeuille bien garni. -**4.** [productive - year] gras, prospère; [- land, soil] fertile, riche; to be in ~ city *inf Am* être plein aux as. -**5.** *inf phr*: get this into your ~ head mets-toi ça dans la tête une fois pour toutes; I reckon you'll get it back — ~ chance! je pense qu'on te le rendra – tu parles!; ~ chance you have of winning! comme si tu avais la moindre chance de gagner!; a ~ lot of good it did him! ça l'a bien avancé!, le voilà bien avancé!; a ~ lot he cares! il s'en fout pas mal!; a ~ lot you know about it! comme si tu en savais quelque chose!

◇ *n* -**1.** [gen & ANAT] graisse *f*; rolls of ~ des bourrelets *mpl* de graisse. -**2.** CULIN [on raw meat] graisse *f*, gras *m*; [on cooked meat] gras *m*; [as cooking medium] matière *f* grasse; [as part of controlled diet] lipide *m*; we are trying to eat less ~ nous nous efforçons de manger moins de matières grasses OR corps gras; margarine low in ~ margarine pauvre en matières grasses OR allégée; beef/mutton ~ graisse de bœuf/de mouton; pork ~ saindoux *m*; fry in deep ~ faites frire; fry in shallow ~ faites revenir; ~ content (teneur *f* en) matières *fpl* grasses ❑ the ~ is in the fire *inf* ça va chauffer; to live off the ~ of the land vivre comme un coq en pâte.

◇ *vt* engraisser; to kill the fatted calf *fig* tuer le veau gras.

fatal ['feɪtl] *adj* -**1.** [deadly - disease, injury] mortel; [- blow] fatal, mortel; [- result] fatal. -**2.** [ruinous - action, consequences] désastreux, catastrophique; [- influence] néfaste, pernicieux; [- mistake] fatal, grave; such a decision would be ~ to our plans une décision de ce type porterait un coup fatal OR le coup de grâce à nos projets. -**3.** [crucial] fatal, fatidique.

fatalism ['feɪtəlɪzm] *n* fatalisme *m*.

fatalist ['feɪtəlɪst] ◇ *adj* fataliste.

◇ *n* fataliste *mf*.

fatalistic [,feɪtə'lɪstɪk] *adj* fataliste.

fatality [fə'tælətɪ] (*pl* fatalities) *n* -**1.** [accident] accident *m* mortel; [person killed] mort *m*, -e *f*; bathing fatalities noyades *fpl*; road fatalities morts sur la route; a child was one of the fatalities il y avait un enfant parmi les victimes. -**2.** *fml* [destiny] fatalité *f*.

fatally ['feɪtəlɪ] *adv* -**1.** [mortally] mortellement; ~ ill condamné, perdu. -**2.** [inevitably] fatalement; the plan was ~ flawed le projet était fatalement OR forcément imparfait.

fatback ['fætbæk] *n* lard *m* salé.

fate [feɪt] *n* -**1.** [destiny] destin *m*, sort *m*; what does ~ have in store for them? qu'est-ce que le destin OR le sort leur réserve? -**2.** [of person, thing] sort *m*; I left her to her ~ je l'ai abandonnée à son sort; to meet one's ~ trouver la mort; the new project met with a similar ~ le nouveau projet a connu un destin semblable; a ~ worse than death *fig* un sort pire que la mort.

◆ **Fates** *pl pr n*: the ~ les Parques *fpl*.

fated ['feɪtɪd] *adj* -**1.** [destined] destiné; they seem ~ to be unhappy ils semblent destinés OR condamnés à être malheureux; he was ~ never to return il devait ne plus jamais revenir. -**2.** [doomed] voué au malheur.

fateful ['feɪtfʊl] *adj* -**1.** [decisive - day, decision] fatal, décisif; [disastrous] désastreux, catastrophique. -**2.** [prophetic] fatidique.

fat farm *inf n Am* centre *m* d'amaigrissement.

fat-free *adj* sans matières grasses, sans corps gras.

fathead *inf* ['fæthed] *n* imbécile *mf*.

fat-headed *inf adj* idiot, imbécile.

father ['fɑːðə^r] ◇ *n* -**1.** [male parent] père *m*; he's a good ~ c'est un bon père; he's like a ~ to me il est comme un père pour moi; from ~ to son de père en fils; on my ~'s side du côté de mon père; yes, Father oui, père, oui, papa; she's her ~'s daughter c'est bien la fille de son père ❑ like ~, like son *prov* tel père, tel fils *prov*, bon chien chasse de race *prov*; 'Fathers and Sons' *Turgenev* 'Pères et fils'. -**2.** (*usu pl*) [ancestor] ancêtre *m*, père *m*. -**3.** [founder, leader] père *m*, fondateur *m*; one of the founding ~s of the Society l'un des pères fondateurs de la société.

◇ *vt* -**1.** [child] engendrer; *fig* [idea, science] concevoir, inventer. -**2.** [impose] attribuer; to ~ sthg on sb attribuer qqch à qqn; they ~ed the blame on her ils lui ont fait porter le blâme.

◆ **Father** *n* RELIG -**1.** [priest] père *m*; Father Brown le (révérend) père Brown; yes, Father oui, mon père. -**2.** [God]: the Father, the Son and the Holy Ghost le Père, le Fils et le Saint Esprit; Our Father who art in Heaven Notre Père qui êtes aux cieux; to say the Our Father dire le Notre Père. -**3.** POL: the Father of the House *titre traditionnel donné au doyen (par l'ancienneté) des parlementaires britanniques*.

Father Christmas *pr n Br* le Père Noël.

father confessor *n* directeur *m* de conscience, père *m* spirituel.

father figure *n* personne *f* qui joue le rôle du père; he was a ~ for all the employees le personnel le considérait un peu comme un père.

fatherhood ['fɑːðəhʊd] *n* paternité *f*.

father-in-law *n* beau-père *m*.

fatherland ['fɑːðəlænd] *n* patrie *f*, mère *f* patrie.

fatherless ['fɑːðəlɪs] *adj* sans père.

fatherly ['fɑːðəlɪ] *adj* paternel.

Father's Day *n* fête *f* des pères.

Father Time *n*: (Old) ~ le Temps.

fathom ['fæðəm] (*pl inv* OR fathoms) ◇ *n* brasse *f (mesure)*; the ship lies 50 ~s down le navire repose par 91 mètres de fond.

◇ *vt* -**1.** [measure depth of] sonder. -**2.** *inf* [understand] sonder, pénétrer; I just can't ~ it je n'y comprends rien.

fathomless ['fæðəmlɪs] *adj* -**1.** [unmeasurable] insondable. -**2.** [impenetrable] insondable, impénétrable.

fatigue [fə'tiːg] ◇ *n* -**1.** [exhaustion] fatigue *f*, épuisement *m*. -**2.** TECH [in material] fatigue *f*; metal ~ fatigue du métal. -**3.** MIL [chore] corvée *f*; I'm on ~s je suis de corvée.

◇ *comp* -**1.** MIL [shirt, trousers] de corvée; ~ dress OR uniform treillis *m* OR tenue *f* de corvée; ~ duty corvée *f*; a ~ party une corvée. -**2.** TECH [limit] de fatigue.

◇ *vt* -**1.** *fml* [person] fatiguer, épuiser; he felt ~d after a long day in the office il se sentait las après une longue journée de bureau. -**2.** TECH [material] fatiguer.

◆ **fatigues** *npl* MIL [clothing] treillis *m*, tenue *f* de corvée.

fatiguing [fə'tiːgɪŋ] *adj* fatigant, épuisant.

fatless ['fætlɪs] *adj* sans matières grasses.

fatling ['fætlɪŋ] *n* jeune bête *f* à l'engrais.

fatness ['fætnɪs] *n* -**1.** [of person] embonpoint *m*, corpulence *f*. -**2.** [of meat] teneur *f* en graisse.

fatso *inf* ['fætsəʊ] (*pl* fatsoes) *n pej* gros lard *m*.

fat-soluble *adj* liposoluble.

fatstock ['fætstɒk] *n (U)* animaux *mpl* de boucherie.

fatten ['fætn] ◇ *vt* [animal, person] engraisser; [ducks, geese] gaver.

◇ *vi* [animals] engraisser; [person] engraisser, prendre de l'embonpoint.

◆ **fatten up** *vt sep* [person] engraisser, faire grossir; AGR [animal] mettre à l'engrais.

fattening ['fætnɪŋ] ◇ *adj* qui fait grossir.

◇ *n* [of animals] engraissement *m*; [of ducks, geese] gavage *m*.

fatty ['fætɪ] (*compar* fattier, *superl* fattiest, *pl* fatties) ◇ *adj* -**1.** [food] gras; avoid ~ food évitez les matières grasses OR les aliments gras. -**2.** [tissue] adipeux; ~ degeneration MED dégénérescence *f* graisseuse.

◇ *n inf pej* gros *m* (bonhomme *m*), grosse *f* (bonne femme *f*).

fatty acid *n* acide *m* gras.

fatuity [fə'tjuːətɪ] (*pl* fatuities) *n* sottise *f*, niaiserie *f*.

fatuous ['fætjʊəs] *adj* [person, remark] sot, niais; [look, smile] niais, béat.

fatuously ['fætjʊəslɪ] *adv* [say] sottement, niaisement; [smile] niaisement, béatement.

fatuousness ['fætjʊəsnɪs] *n* sottise *f*, niaiserie *f*.

faucet ['fɔːsɪt] *n Am* robinet *m*.

faugh [fɔː] *interj*: ~! pouah!

fault ['fɔːlt] ◇ *n* -**1.** *(U)* [blame, responsibility] faute *f*; it's not my ~ ce n'est pas de ma faute; whose ~ is it? à qui la faute?, qui est fautif?; whose ~ is it if you're unhappy? et à qui la faute si vous êtes malheureux?; it's nobody's ~ but your own vous n'avez à vous en prendre qu'à vous-même; it's through no ~ of mine ce

n'est absolument pas de ma faute; to be at ~ être fautif OR coupable; he's at ~ this time c'est lui le fautif OR il est fautif cette fois; she's at ~ for not having taken action elle est coupable de ne pas avoir agi OR de ne pas être intervenue; the judge found him to be at ~ le juge lui a donné tort. -2. [mistake] erreur *f*; a ~ in the addition une erreur d'addition. -3. [flaw - in person] défaut *m*; [- in machine] défaut *m*, anomalie *f*; an electrical ~ un défaut électrique; a ~ in the air supply un défaut dans l'arrivée d'air; for all her ~s, in spite of her ~s malgré tous ses défauts ❑ honest to a ~ honnête à l'excès; to find ~ with sthg trouver à redire à qqch, critiquer qqch; to find ~ with sb critiquer qqn; she finds ~ with everything elle trouve toujours à redire. -4. GEOL faille *f*. -5. TENNIS faute *f*.
◇ *vt* critiquer; to ~ sthg/sb trouver des défauts à qqch/chez qqn; you can't ~ her on her work il n'y a rien à redire à son travail, vous ne pouvez pas prendre son travail en défaut; you can't ~ her for effort vous ne pouvez pas critiquer ses efforts; I can't ~ her logic je ne trouve aucune faille à sa logique.
◇ *vi* [make mistake] commettre une faute.

faultfinder ['fɔːlt,faɪndəʳ] *n pej* mécontent *m*, -e *f*, chicaneur *m*, -euse *f*.

faultfinding ['fɔːlt,faɪndɪŋ] *pej* ◇ *n (U)* critiques *fpl*.
◇ *adj* chicanier, grincheux.

faultless ['fɔːltlɪs] *adj* [performance, work] impeccable, irréprochable; [behaviour, person] irréprochable; [logic, reasoning] sans faille.

faultlessly ['fɔːltlɪslɪ] *adv* impeccablement, parfaitement.

fault line *n* GEOL ligne *f* de faille.

faulty ['fɔːltɪ] (*compar* faultier, *superl* faultiest) *adj* [machine] défectueux; [work] défectueux, mal fait; [reasoning] défectueux, erroné; the wiring is ~ il y a un défaut dans l'installation électrique.

faun [fɔːn] *n* faune *m*.

fauna ['fɔːnə] (*pl* faunas OR faunae [-niː]) *n* faune *f*.

Faunus ['fɔːnəs] *pr n* Faune.

Faustian ['faʊstɪən] *adj* faustien.

Fauvism ['fəʊvɪzm] *n* fauvisme *m*.

Fauvist ['fəʊvɪst] ◇ *adj* fauve.
◇ *n* fauve *m*.

faux pas [,fəʊ'pɑː] (*pl inv* [,fəʊ'pɑːz]) *n* bévue *f*, gaffe *f*.

favor *etc Am* = **favour**.

favorite *etc Am* = **favourite**.

favour *Br*, **favor** *Am* ['feɪvəʳ] ◇ *n* -1. [approval] faveur *f*, approbation *f*; to be in ~ [person] être bien en cour, être bien vu; [artist, fashion] être à la mode OR en vogue; to be out of ~ [person] être mal en cour, ne pas être bien vu; [artist, book] ne pas être à la mode OR en vogue; [fashion] être démodé OR dépassé; she's in ~ with the boss elle est bien vue du patron; he speaks in their ~ il parle en leur faveur; to fall out of ~ with sb perdre les bonnes grâces de qqn; to find ~ with sb trouver grâce aux yeux de qqn, gagner l'approbation de qqn; he is prepared to look with ~ upon the suggestion il est prêt à approuver OR à examiner favorablement la proposition; he looks with ~ upon us il est bien disposé à notre égard; to be in ~ of sthg être partisan de qqch, être pour qqch; to be in ~ of doing sthg être d'avis de OR être pour faire qqch. -2. [act of goodwill] service *m*, faveur *f*; will you do me a ~ OR do a ~ for me? voulez-vous me rendre (un) service?; may I ask a ~ of you OR ask you a ~? puis-je vous demander un service OR solliciter une faveur de votre part?; I did it as a ~ to her je l'ai fait pour lui rendre service; I ask you as a ~ not to say anything je vous serais très reconnaissant de ne rien dire; do me a ~ and play somewhere else soyez gentil, allez jouer ailleurs ❑ are you going to buy it? — do me a ~! *inf* tu vas l'acheter? — je t'en prie! -3. [advantage]: everything is in our ~ tout joue en notre faveur, nous avons tout pour nous; the odds are in his ~ il est (donné) favori; a point in her ~ un bon point pour elle, un point en sa faveur; the magistrates decided in his ~ les juges lui ont donné raison OR gain de cause; he dropped the idea in ~ of our suggestion il a laissé tomber l'idée au profit de notre suggestion; a will in ~ of the children un testament en faveur des enfants; a cheque in ~ of un chèque payable à; 'credit in your ~' 'à votre crédit'. -4. [partiality] faveur *f*, partialité *f*. -5. HIST faveur *f*; a woman's ~s *lit* les faveurs d'une femme. -6. [gift] petit cadeau *m (offert aux invités lors d'une fête)*. -7. *Br arch* & COMM [letter] communication *f*.
◇ *vt* -1. [prefer] préférer; [show preference for] montrer une préférence pour. -2. [support - suggestion, team] être partisan de, être pour; [- candidate, project] favoriser, appuyer; [- theory] soutenir. -3. [benefit] favoriser, faciliter; the ground is quite firm, which ~s this horse le terrain est très ferme, ce qui est favorable à ce cheval OR ce qui avantage ce cheval; circumstances that would ~ a June election des circonstances (qui seraient) favorables à une élection en juin. -4. [honour] favoriser, gratifier; she ~ed him with a smile elle l'a gratifié d'un sourire; he ~ed us with his company il nous a fait l'honneur de se joindre à nous; ~ed with talent talentueux, doué; ~ed with good looks avantagé par la nature. -5. [resemble] ressembler à; he ~s his mother il ressemble à OR tient de sa mère.

favourable *Br*, **favorable** *Am* ['feɪvrəbl] *adj* [answer, comparison, impression] favorable; [time, terms] bon, avantageux; [weather, wind] propice; in a ~ light sous un jour favorable; to be ~ to an idea approuver une idée; the election will be held at the time most ~ to the government les élections auront lieu au moment (qui sera) le plus favorable au gouvernement.

favourably *Br*, **favorably** *Am* ['feɪvrəblɪ] *adv* [compare, react] favorablement; [consider] d'un bon œil; to be ~ disposed to OR towards sthg voir qqch d'un bon œil; to be ~ disposed to OR towards sb être bien disposé envers qqn; she speaks very ~ of you elle parle de vous en très bons termes.

favoured *Br*, **favored** *Am* ['feɪvəd] *adj* favorisé; the ~ few les privilégiés *mpl*; most ~ nation clause/status clause *f*/statut *m* de la nation la plus favorisée.

favourite *Br*, **favorite** *Am* ['feɪvrɪt] ◇ *adj* favori, préféré; he's not one of my ~ people je ne le porte pas dans mon cœur.
◇ *n* -1. [gen] favori *m*, -ite *f*, préféré *m*, -e *f*; he's the teacher's ~ c'est le chouchou du professeur; she's everyone's ~ tout le monde l'adore; that book is one of my ~s c'est un de mes livres préférés; let's listen to some old ~s écoutons de vieilles chansons à succès. -2. SPORT favori *m*.

favouritism *Br*, **favoritism** *Am* ['feɪvrɪtɪzm] *n* favoritisme *m*.

fawn [fɔːn] ◇ *n* -1. [animal] faon *m*. -2. [colour] fauve *m*.
◇ *adj* (de couleur) fauve.
◇ *vi*: to ~ on sb [person] ramper devant qqn, passer de la pommade à qqn; [dog] faire la fête à qqn; he ~s on the boss il courbe l'échine OR il rampe devant le patron.

fawning ['fɔːnɪŋ] *adj* [attitude, person] flagorneur, servile; [dog] trop affectueux OR démonstratif.

fax [fæks] ◇ *n* [machine] fax *m*, télécopieur *m offic*; [document] fax *m*, télécopie *f offic*; by ~ par télécopie; ~ message fax.
◇ *vt* envoyer par télécopie OR par télécopieur; ~ me (through) the information faxez-moi l'information.

fay [feɪ] *n lit* [fairy] fée *f*.

faze *inf* [feɪz] *vt* déconcerter, dérouter.

FBI (*abbr of* Federal Bureau of Investigation) *pr n*: the ~ le FBI.

FC *n written abbr of* Football Club.

FCC (*abbr of* Federal Communications Commission) *pr n conseil fédéral de l'audiovisuel aux États-Unis*, ≃ CSA *m*.

FCO *pr n abbr of* Foreign and Commonwealth Office.

FD ◇ *Br* (*written abbr of* Fidei Defensor) *Défenseur de la foi*.
◇ *n Am abbr of* Fire Department.

FDA *pr n abbr of* Food and Drug Administration.

fealty ['fiːəltɪ] (*pl* fealties) *n* fidélité *f*, allégeance *f*.

fear [fɪəʳ] ◇ *n* -1. [dread] crainte *f*, peur *f*; many people have an irrational ~ of snakes beaucoup de personnes ont une peur irrationnelle des serpents; have no ~ ne craignez rien, soyez sans crainte; he expressed his ~s about their future il a exprimé son inquiétude en ce qui concerne leur avenir; there are ~s that he has escaped on craint fort qu'il ne se soit échappé; to be OR to go in ~ for one's life craindre pour sa vie; she lives in a state of constant ~ elle vit dans la peur; ~ drove him to desperate action sous l'effet de la peur, il a commis un acte désespéré; for ~ of what people would think par peur du qu'en-dira-t-on; for ~ that she might find out de peur qu'elle ne l'apprenne ❑ without ~ or favour impartialement; overcome with ~ paralysé OR transi de peur; (a) ~ of heights (le) vertige. -2. [awe] crainte *f*, respect *m*; the ~ of God la crainte OR le respect de Dieu; I put the ~ of God into him *inf* [scared] je lui ai fait une peur bleue; [scolded] je lui ai passé un savon. -3. [risk] risque *m*, danger *m*; there is no ~ of her leaving elle ne risque pas de partir, il est peu probable qu'elle parte; there's no ~ of that ça ne risque pas d'arriver ❑ will you tell him? — no ~! *inf* lui direz-vous? — pas de danger OR pas question!
◇ *vt* -1. [be afraid of] craindre, avoir peur de; she ~s nothing/no one elle n'a peur de rien/de personne; he ~ed asking again il a eu peur de redemander OR de poser à nouveau la question; to ~ the worst craindre le pire; he is a man to be ~ed c'est un homme redoutable; I ~ he's in danger je crains OR j'ai peur qu'il ne soit en danger; it is to be ~ed that... *fml* il est à craindre que...; never ~, ~ not *fml* OR *dated* ne craignez rien, soyez tranquille. -2. *fml* [be sorry] regretter; I ~ it's too late je crois bien qu'il est trop tard. -3. [revere - God] révérer, craindre.
◇ *vi*: I ~ for my children je crains OR je tremble pour mes enfants; he ~s for his life il craint pour sa vie; they ~ for the future ils craignent OR sont inquiets pour l'avenir.

fearful ['fɪəfʊl] *adj* -1. [very bad] épouvantable, affreux; he has a ~ temper il a un caractère épouvantable. -2. *inf dated* [as intensifier] affreux; he's a ~ bore! c'est un raseur de première!; they were making a ~ din ils faisaient un bruit épouvantable OR un boucan infernal. -3. [afraid] peureux, craintif; she is ~ of angering him elle craint de le mettre en colère.

fearfully ['fɪəfʊlɪ] *adv* -1. [look, say] peureusement, craintivement. -2. *inf dated* [as intensifier] affreusement, horriblement; he's ~ mean il est méchant à faire peur.

fearfulness ['fɪəfʊlnɪs] *n* [fear] crainte *f*, peur *f*; [shyness] extrême timidité *f*.

fearless ['fɪəlɪs] *adj* intrépide, sans peur; they set off, ~ of the danger ils se mirent en route sans crainte du danger OR bravant le danger.

fearlessly ['fɪəlɪslɪ] *adv* avec intrépidité.

fearlessness ['fɪəlɪsnɪs] *n* audace *f*, absence *f* de peur.

fearsome ['fɪəsəm] *adj* -1. [frightening] redoutable, effroyable. -2. *lit* [afraid] peureux, craintif; [timid] extrêmement timide.

fearsomely ['fɪəsəmlɪ] *adv* redoutablement, effroyablement.

feasibility [,fiːzə'bɪlətɪ] *n*: to show the ~ of a plan démontrer qu'un plan est réalisable OR faisable; the ~ of doing sthg la possibilité de faire qqch.

feasibility study *n* étude *f* de faisabilité.
feasible ['fiːzəbl] *adj* [plan, suggestion] faisable, réalisable.
feast [fiːst] ◇ *n* **-1.** [large meal] festin *m*; **midnight ~** festin *m* nocturne; **a ~ for the eyes** *fig* un régal OR une fête pour les yeux; **a ~ of entertainment** *fig* une multitude de divertissements; **a ~ of music/poetry** *fig* une véritable fête de la musique/poésie. **-2.** RELIG fête *f*; **movable/immovable ~** fête mobile/fixe.
◇ *comp*: **~ day** (jour *m* de) fête *f*.
◇ *vi* festoyer; **to ~ on** OR **off sthg** se régaler de qqch.
◇ *vt* **-1.** *fig*: **to ~ o.s. on sthg** se régaler de qqch; **to ~ one's eyes on sthg** repaître ses yeux de qqch *lit*, se délecter à la vue de qqch. **-2.** [give feast to] donner un banquet en l'honneur de.
feasting ['fiːstɪŋ] *n* festin *m*.
feat [fiːt] *n* exploit *m*, prouesse *f*; **it was quite a ~ getting the boss to agree to the idea** ça a été un véritable exploit OR une véritable prouesse que de faire accepter cette idée au chef; **that was some ~!** quel exploit!, quelle prouesse!; **a ~ of courage** un acte courageux; **~ of arms** fait *m* d'armes; **~ of strength/of skill** tour *m* de force/d'adresse; **a ~ of engineering** une (véritable) prouesse technique, un chef-d'œuvre de la technique.
feather ['feðəʳ] ◇ *n* [of bird] plume *f*; [on tail, wing] penne *f*; [of arrow] penne *f*; **as light as a ~** léger comme une plume; **in fine ~** en pleine forme; **to show the white ~** manquer de courage; **that's a ~ in his cap** il peut en être fier; **that's another ~ in her cap** encore une chose dont elle peut être fière OR se vanter; **to make the ~s fly** mettre le feu aux poudres; **you could have knocked me down with a ~** les bras m'en sont tombés.
◇ *comp* [mattress] de plume; [headdress] de plumes.
◇ *vt* **-1.** [put feathers on - arrow] empenner; **to ~ one's (own) nest** *pej* faire son beurre. **-2.** AERON [propeller] mettre en drapeau.
◇ *vi* [in rowing] plumer.
featherbed ['feðəbed] (*pt* & *pp* **featherbedded**, *cont* **featherbedding**) *vt pej* [industry, business] protéger (excessivement).
feather bed *n* lit *m* de plumes.
featherbedding ['feðəbedɪŋ] *n pej* protection *f* excessive.
feather boa *n* boa *m* de plumes.
featherbrained *inf* ['feðəbreɪnd] *adj* étourdi, tête en l'air.
feather duster *n* plumeau *m*.
feathered ['feðəd] *adj* [headdress] de plumes; **our ~ friends** *hum* nos amis les oiseaux.
featherweight ['feðəweɪt] ◇ *n* **-1.** [boxer, category] poids plume *m inv*; **he started at ~** il a commencé (dans les) poids plume. **-2.** *fig* [person of little importance] poids plume *m inv*; **he's a (political/literary) ~** il n'a pas beaucoup de poids (sur le plan politique/littéraire).
◇ *adj* [contest, championship] poids plume; [champion] de la catégorie OR des poids plume.
feathery ['feðərɪ] *adj* **-1.** [bird] à plumes. **-2.** *fig* [light and soft - snowflake] doux et léger comme la plume; **~ strokes** [with pencil] traits *mpl* légers.
feature ['fiːtʃəʳ] ◇ *n* **-1.** [facial] trait *m*; **a woman with delicate ~s** une femme aux traits fins. **-2.** [characteristic - of style, landscape, play etc] caractéristique *f*, particularité *f*; [- of personality] trait *m*, caractéristique *f*; [- of car, machine, house, room] caractéristique *f*; **safety ~s** dispositifs *mpl* de sécurité; **this is a ~ of the novel** c'est un élément caractéristique du roman; **the most interesting ~ of the exhibition** l'élément OR l'aspect le plus intéressant de l'exposition; **seafood is a special ~ of the menu** les fruits de mer sont l'un des points forts du menu; **to make a ~ of sthg** mettre qqch en valeur; **the novel has just one redeeming ~** le roman est sauvé par un seul élément. **-3.** RADIO & TV reportage *m*; PRESS [special] article *m* de fond; [regular] chronique *f*. **-4.** CIN film *m*, long métrage *m*; **full-length ~** long métrage; **double-~ (programme)** programme *m* proposant deux films.
◇ *vt* **-1.** CIN [star - actor, actress] avoir pour vedette; **also featuring Mark Williams** avec Mark Williams. **-2.** PRESS [display prominently]: **the story/the picture is ~d on the front page** le récit/la photo est en première page; **all the papers ~ the disaster on the front page** tous les journaux présentent la catastrophe en première page. **-3.** COMM [promote] promouvoir, mettre en promotion. **-4.** [subj: car, appliance] comporter, être équipé OR doté de; [subj: house, room] comporter.
◇ *vi* **-1.** CIN figurer, jouer. **-2.** [appear, figure] figurer; **meat does not ~ on the menu** la viande ne figure pas au menu; **the millionaire ~d prominently in the scandal** le millionnaire était très impliqué dans le scandale; **do I ~ in your plans?** est-ce que je figure dans tes projets?
feature article *n* PRESS article *m* de fond.
feature film *n* CIN long métrage *m*.
feature-length *adj* CIN: **a ~ film** un long métrage; **a ~ cartoon** un film d'animation.
featureless ['fiːtʃəlɪs] *adj* [desert, city etc] sans traits distinctifs OR marquants.
features editor *n journaliste responsable d'une rubrique*.
feature story = **feature article**.
feature writer *n* PRESS journaliste *mf*.
Feb. (*written abbr of* February) févr.
febrile ['fiːbraɪl] *adj lit* fébrile, fiévreux.
February ['februərɪ] ◇ *n* février *m*; **I don't like ~** je n'aime pas le mois de février; **this has been the wettest ~ on record** cela a été le mois de février le plus pluvieux qu'on ait jamais vu; **~ was a difficult month** le mois de février a été difficile; **in ~** en février, au mois de février; **in the month of ~** au mois de février; **the first/ninth of ~, ~ the first/ninth, ~ first/ninth** *Am* le premier/neuf février; **during (the month of) ~** pendant le mois de février; **last/next ~** en février dernier/prochain; **at the beginning/end of ~** au début/à la fin février; **in the middle of ~** au milieu du mois de février, à la mi-février; **early/late in ~, in early/late ~** au début/à la fin du mois de février; **every** OR **each ~** tous les ans en février.
◇ *comp* [weather] de février, du mois de février.
fecal *Am* = **faecal**.
feces *Am* = **faeces**.
feckless ['feklɪs] *adj* [ineffectual] incapable, qui manque d'efficacité; [irresponsible] irresponsable.
fecklessness ['feklɪsnɪs] *n* [ineffectuality] manque *m* d'efficacité; [irresponsibility] irresponsabilité *f*.
fecund ['fiːkənd] *adj lit*. **-1.** *literal* [woman, female animal] fécond. **-2.** *fig* [author] fécond; [imagination] fécond, fertile.
fecundity [fɪ'kʌndətɪ] *n lit*. **-1.** *literal* [of woman, female animal] fécondité *f*. **-2.** *fig* [of author] fécondité *f*; [of imagination] fécondité *f*, fertilité *f*.
fed [fed] ◇ *pt* & *pp* → **feed**.
◇ *n inf Am* agent *m* (du bureau) fédéral OR du FBI.
Fed [fed] ◇ *pr n* **-1.** *abbr of* Federal Reserve Board. **-2.** *abbr of* Federal Reserve System.
◇ **-1.** *written abbr of* federal. **-2.** *written abbr of* federation.
federal ['fedrəl] ◇ *adj* **-1.** [republic, system] fédéral; **there's no need to make a ~ case out of it** *Am fig* il n'y a pas de quoi en faire une affaire d'État ❑ **the Federal Republic of Germany** la République fédérale d'Allemagne; **the Federal Reserve Board** *organe de contrôle de la banque centrale américaine*; **the Federal Reserve System** *système bancaire fédéral américain*; **the Federal Trade Commission** *l'une des deux autorités fédérales chargées du respect de la loi antitrust aux États-Unis*. **-2.** [responsibility, funding] du gouvernement fédéral; [taxes] fédéral.
◇ *n Am* HIST nordiste *m*, fédéral *m*.
federalism ['fedrəlɪzm] *n* fédéralisme *m*.
federalist ['fedrəlɪst] ◇ *adj* fédéraliste.
◇ *n* fédéraliste *mf*.
federalize ['fedrəlaɪz] ◇ *vt* fédéraliser.
◇ *vi* se fédéraliser.
federally ['fedrəlɪ] *adv*: **to be ~ funded** être financé par le gouvernement fédéral.
federate [*vb* 'fedəreɪt, *adj* & *n* 'fedərət]
◇ *vt* fédérer.
◇ *vi* se fédérer.
◇ *adj* fédéré.
federation [ˌfedə'reɪʃn] *n* fédération *f*.
fedora [fɪ'dɔːrə] *n* [hat] chapeau *m* mou.
fed up *inf adj*: **to be ~** en avoir marre, en avoir ras le bol; **she's ~ with him** elle en a marre de lui; **she's ~ with it** elle en a marre; **to be ~ (to the back teeth) with sb/with sthg/with doing sthg** en avoir (vraiment) marre OR ras le bol de qqn/de qqch/de faire qqch; **I'm ~ with the way you don't pay any attention to me** j'en ai marre OR ras le bol que tu ne fasses pas attention à moi; **what are you looking so ~ about?** pourquoi as-tu l'air aussi écœuré?; **you sound ~** tu as l'air d'en avoir marre OR ras le bol.
fee [fiː] *n* **-1.** [for doctor, lawyer] honoraires *mpl*. **-2.** [for speaker, performer] cachet *m*; [retainer - for company director] jetons *mpl* de présence *(d'un administrateur)*; [for private tutor] appointements *mpl*; [for translator] tarif *m*; [for agency] commission *f*; **school ~s** frais *mpl* de scolarité; **registration ~** droits *mpl* d'inscription; **membership ~** cotisation *f*; **entrance ~** droit *m* d'entrée; **for a small ~** contre une somme modique; **could you post that letter for me? – OK, for a small ~** *hum* tu peux poster cette lettre pour moi? – d'accord, ça sera 100 balles. **-3.** JUR: **property held in ~ simple** propriété inconditionnelle.
feeble ['fiːbəl] *adj* **-1.** [lacking strength] faible; **don't be so ~!** ne sois pas une telle mauviette! **-2.** [lacking conviction, force - attempt, excuse] piètre; [- argument] léger; [- smile] timide; **that's a pretty ~ excuse** c'est une bien piètre excuse, c'est un peu léger comme excuse. **-3.** [silly - joke] qui manque de finesse, bête.
feeble-minded *adj* faible d'esprit.
feebly ['fiːblɪ] *adv* [say, shine] faiblement; [smile] timidement; [suggest] sans (grande) conviction.
feed [fiːd] (*pt* & *pp* **fed** [fed]) ◇ *vt* **-1.** [provide food for - person, family] nourrir; [- country] approvisionner; [- army] ravitailler; **she insisted on ~ing us** elle a tenu à nous faire manger; **there are ten mouths to ~** il y a dix bouches à nourrir; **there's enough here to ~ an army** *hum* il y a de quoi nourrir toute une armée; **the country is no longer able to ~ itself** le pays n'est plus capable de subvenir à ses besoins alimentaires; **he earns just enough money to ~ himself** il gagne juste de quoi se nourrir; **they were well fed at the restaurant** ils ont bien mangé au restaurant. **-2.** [give food to - person, animal] donner à manger à; [subj: bird] donner la becquée à; [breastfeed] allaiter; [bottlefeed] donner le biberon à; [fertilize - plant, soil, lawn etc] nourrir; **to ~ sthg to sb, to ~ sb sthg** donner qqch à manger à qqn; **she is so ill she isn't even able to ~ herself** elle est si malade qu'elle n'est pas capable de se nourrir OR de manger toute seule; **our little son has just learnt to ~ himself** notre petit garçon commence juste à manger tout seul; **'please do not ~ the animals'** 'prière de ne pas donner à manger aux animaux'; **how much do you ~ your cats?** quelle quantité de nourriture donnez-vous à vos chats?; **the chimps are fed a diet of nuts and bananas** on donne des noix et des bananes à manger aux chimpanzés. **-3.** *fig* [supply - fire, furnace] alimenter; [- lake, river] se jeter dans; [- imagination, hope, rumour] alimenter, nourrir; **to ~ a parking meter** mettre des pièces dans un parcmètre. **-4.** [transmit]: **the results are fed to the departments concerned** les résultats sont transmis aux services concernés; **to ~ information to sb, to ~ sb information** donner des informations à qqn; [in

order to mislead] donner de fausses informations à qqn *(afin de le tromper)* ❑ to ~ sb a line *inf* faire avaler une histoire à qqn. -**5.** TECH [introduce - liquid] faire passer; [- solid] faire avancer; [insert - paper, wire etc] introduire; to ~ **data into a computer** entrer des données dans un ordinateur. -**6.** THEAT [give cue to] donner la réplique à. -**7.** SPORT passer la balle à, servir.

◇ *vi* [person, animal] manger; [baby - gen] manger; [- breastfeed] téter; to ~ **on demand** [nursing mother] donner la tétée chaque fois que le bébé le réclame OR à la demande; **to put the cattle out to** ~ mettre le bétail en OR au pâturage.

◇ *n* -**1.** [foodstuff for animal] nourriture *f*; [hay, oats etc] fourrage *m*. -**2.** [meal for baby - breast milk] tétée *f*; [- bottled milk] biberon *m*; **the baby gets its last ~ at midnight** le bébé boit sa dernière tétée OR son dernier biberon à minuit ‖ [meal for animal]: **the dog gets two ~s a day** le chien a à manger deux fois par jour. -**3.** *inf* [meal] repas *m*; **that was the best ~ I've ever had!** je n'ai jamais aussi bien bouffé! -**4.** TECH [introduction - of liquid] alimentation *f*; [- of solid] avancement *m*; [device] dispositif *m* d'alimentation OR d'avancement; **petrol** ~ alimentation en essence; ~ **pump** pompe *f* d'alimentation OR de circulation ‖ COMPUT: **sheet** ~ dispositif d'alimentation feuille à feuille; **line** ~ changement *m* de ligne. -**5.** *inf* THEAT [cue] réplique *f*; [comedian's partner] faire-valoir *m*.

◆ **feed back** *vt sep* [information, results] renvoyer.

◆ **feed in** *vt sep* [paper, wire] introduire; COMPUT [data] entrer.

◆ **feed on** *vt insep* se nourrir de; *fig* se repaître de.

◆ **feed up** *vt sep* [animal] engraisser; [goose] gaver; **he needs ~ing up** [person] il a besoin d'engraisser un peu.

feedback ['fi:dbæk] *n* -**1.** ELECTRON rétroaction *f*; [in microphone] effet *m* Larsen; COMPUT réaction *f*, rétroaction *f*, retour *m* OR remontée *f* de l'information; **positive/negative** ~ ELECTRON réactions positives/négatives. -**2.** *(U)* [information] réactions *fpl*, échos *mpl*; **we haven't had much ~ from them** nous n'avons pas eu beaucoup de réactions OR d'échos de leur part; **we welcome ~ from customers** nous sommes toujours heureux d'avoir les impressions OR les réactions de nos clients; **we need more** ~ nous avons besoin de plus d'information OR d'informations en retour; **this will provide us with much-needed ~ on public opinion** ceci nous fournira des informations dont nous avons grand besoin sur l'opinion publique.

feedbag ['fi:dbæg] *n* -**1.** [container] sac *m* à nourriture; [containing food] sac *m* de nourriture. -**2.** *Am* [for horse] = **nosebag**.

feeder ['fi:dəʳ] ◇ *n* -**1.** [person] mangeur *m*; **to be a heavy** ~ [person, animal] manger beaucoup; **the plant is a heavy** ~ cette plante a besoin de beaucoup de nourriture. -**2.** [child's bottle] biberon *m*. -**3.** [feeding device - for cattle] nourrisseur *m*, mangeoire *f* automatique; [- for poultry] mangeoire *f* automatique; [- for machine] chargeur *m*. -**4.** [river] affluent *m*; [road] voie *f* OR bretelle *f* de raccordement; [air route] ligne *f* régionale de rabattement *(regroupant les passagers vers un aéroport principal)*. -**5.** ELEC câble *m* OR ligne *f* d'alimentation.

◇ *comp*: ~ **primary school** *école primaire fournissant des élèves à un collège*; **Broughton has five ~ primary schools** les élèves de Broughton viennent de cinq écoles primaires différentes; ~ **road** voie *f* OR bretelle *f* de raccordement; ~ **route** [in air transport] ligne *f* régionale de rabattement *(regroupant les passagers vers un aéroport principal)*.

feeding ['fi:dɪŋ] ◇ *n* [of person, baby, animal, machine] alimentation *f*.

◇ *comp*: ~ **bottle** biberon *m*; ~ **cup** MED canard *m*; **to be in a ~ frenzy** [sharks] être rendu fou OR frénétique par la présence de nourriture; ~ **ground** OR **grounds** *lieux où viennent se nourrir des animaux*; ~ **mechanism** INDUST mécanisme *m* d'avance OR d'avancement; [for sthg liquid] mécanisme *m* d'alimentation; ~ **stuff** nourriture *f* OR aliments *mpl* pour animaux; ~ **time** [for child, animal] heure *f* des repas; **it must be (his) ~ time** ce doit être l'heure de son repas; **it's like ~ time at the zoo** *hum* on dirait le moment du repas dans un zoo.

feed pipe *n* tuyau *m* d'alimentation.

feedstock ['fi:dstɒk] *n* matière *f* première.

feedstuff ['fi:dstʌf] *n* nourriture *f* OR aliments *mpl* pour animaux.

feel [fi:l] (*pt* & *pp* **felt** [felt]) ◇ *vi (with complement)* -**1.** [physically]: **to ~ hot/cold/hungry/thirsty** avoir chaud/froid/faim/soif; **my hands/feet ~ cold** j'ai froid aux mains/pieds; **my leg ~s numb** j'ai la jambe engourdie, ma jambe est engourdie; **to ~ good/old/full of energy** se sentir bien/vieux/plein d'énergie; **how do you ~** OR **are you ~ing today?** comment te sens-tu aujourd'hui?; **are you ~ing all right?** [physically] est-ce que tu te sens bien? *also hum*; **she's ~ing a lot better** elle se sent beaucoup mieux; **I felt really bad about it** j'étais dans mes petits souliers; **to ~ as though** OR **as if** OR **like** *inf* croire que, avoir l'impression que; **I ~** OR **it ~s as if I've been hit on the head with a hammer** j'ai l'impression qu'on m'a donné un coup de marteau sur la tête ❑ **he's not ~ing himself today** il n'est pas en forme aujourd'hui; **you'll soon be ~ing (more) yourself** OR **your old self again** tu iras bientôt mieux, tu seras bientôt remis; **you're as old as you ~** on a l'âge que l'on veut bien avoir. -**2.** [emotionally]: **to ~ glad/sad/undecided** être heureux/triste/indécis; **to ~ (like) a fool** se sentir bête; **to ~ (like) a failure** avoir l'impression d'être un raté; **I felt like a criminal** j'ai eu l'impression d'être un criminel; **I know how you ~** je sais ce que tu ressens; **if that's how you ~...** si c'est comme ça que tu vois les choses...; **how do you think it makes ME ~?** qu'est-ce que tu crois que je ressens, moi?; **how would you ~ if it happened to you?** comment te sentirais-tu OR qu'est-ce que ça te ferait si ça t'arrivait à toi?; **how do you ~ about him/the plan?** qu'est-ce que tu penses de lui/ce projet?, comment le trouves-tu/trouves-tu ce projet?; **she ~s very strongly about it** elle a une position très arrêtée là-dessus; **how do you ~ about him coming to stay with us for a few months?** qu'est-ce que ça te ferait s'il venait habiter chez nous pendant quelques mois? -**3.** [in impersonal constructions]: **it ~s good to be alive/home** c'est bon d'être en vie/chez soi; **it ~s strange to be back** ça fait drôle d'être de retour; **does that ~ better?** est-ce que c'est mieux comme ça?; **it ~s all wrong for me to be doing this** ça me gêne de faire ça; **it ~s like rain/snow** on dirait qu'il va pleuvoir/neiger; **it ~s like spring** ça sent le printemps; **what does it ~ like** OR **how does it ~ to be Prime Minister?** quelle impression ça fait d'être Premier ministre? -**4.** [give specified sensation]: **to ~ hard/soft/smooth/rough** être dur/doux/lisse/rêche (au toucher); **the room felt hot/stuffy** il faisait chaud/l'atmosphère était étouffante dans la pièce; **your forehead ~s hot** ton front est brûlant; **your neck ~s swollen** on dirait que ton cou est enflé. -**5.** [be capable of sensation] sentir. -**6.** [grope] = **feel about**. -**7.** *phr*: **to ~ like** [want, have wish for] avoir envie de; **I ~ like a cup of coffee/something to eat** j'ai envie d'une tasse de café/de manger quelque chose; **do you ~ like going out tonight?** ça te dit de sortir ce soir?; **don't do it if you don't ~ like it** ne le fais pas si tu n'en as pas envie OR si ça ne te dit rien.

◇ *vt* -**1.** [touch] toucher; [explore] tâter, palper; ~ **it, it's so smooth** touche-le, c'est tellement doux; ~ **the quality of this cloth** apprécie la qualité de ce tissu; **I felt the lump on my arm** j'ai tâté OR palpé la grosseur sur mon bras; **he felt his pockets** il tâta ses poches ❑ **to ~ one's way** avancer à tâtons; [in new job, difficult situation etc] avancer avec précaution; **to ~ one's way into/out of/up** entrer/sortir/monter à tâtons; **I'm still ~ing my way** je suis en train de m'habituer tout doucement. -**2.** [be aware of - wind, sunshine, atmosphere, tension] sentir; [- pain] sentir, ressentir; [be sensitive to - cold, beauty] être sensible à; **I can't ~ anything in my foot** je ne sens plus rien dans mon pied; **I could ~ her foot touching mine** je sentais son pied contre le mien; **I could ~ myself blushing** je me sentais rougir; ~ **the weight of it!** soupèse-moi ça!; **he felt the full force of the blow** il a reçu le coup de plein fouet; **I bet he felt that!** il a dû le sentir passer!; **I can ~ a cold coming on** je sens que je suis en train de m'enrhumer; **I could ~ somebody else in the room** je sentais qu'il y avait quelqu'un d'autre dans la pièce ❑ **I can ~ it in my bones** j'en ai le pressentiment. -**3.** [experience - sadness, happiness, joy, relief] ressentir, éprouver; [to be affected by - sb's absence, death] être affecté par; **to ~ fear/regret** avoir peur/des regrets; **he ~s things very deeply** il ressent les choses très profondément; **to ~ the effects of sthg** ressentir les effets de qqch. -**4.** [think] penser, estimer; **I ~ it is my duty to tell you** j'estime qu'il est de mon devoir de te le dire; **she ~s very strongly that...** elle est tout à fait convaincue que...; **I can't help ~ing that...** je ne peux pas m'empêcher de penser que...; **I ~ that things have changed between us** j'ai l'impression que les choses ont changé entre nous; **you mustn't ~ you have to do it** il ne faut pas que tu te sentes obligé de le faire.

◇ *n* -**1.** [tactile quality, sensation]: **I could tell by the ~ of it** je m'en étais rendu compte rien qu'au toucher; **this garment has a really nice ~ to it** ce vêtement est vraiment agréable au toucher; **I like the ~ of cotton next to** OR **against my skin** j'aime bien le contact du coton sur ma peau. -**2.** [act of feeling, touching]: **to have a ~ of sthg** toucher qqch; **can I have a ~?** je peux toucher?; **he's always having a quick ~** ▽ [sexually] il a la main baladeuse. -**3.** [knack]: **to get the ~ of sthg** s'habituer à qqch; **to have a real ~ for translation/music** avoir la traduction/la musique dans la peau. -**4.** [atmosphere] atmosphère *f*; **the room has a nice homely ~ (to it)** on se sent vraiment bien dans cette pièce; **his music has a really Latin ~ (to it)** il y a vraiment une influence latine dans sa musique.

◆ **feel about** *vi insep* [in drawer, pocket] fouiller; **to ~ about in one's pocket for the key** fouiller dans sa poche pour trouver sa clé; **to ~ about in the dark for sthg** chercher qqch à tâtons dans le noir, tâtonner dans le noir pour trouver qqch.

◆ **feel for** *vt insep* -**1.** [sympathize with]: **I ~ for you** je compatis; *hum* comme je te plains!; **that poor woman, I ~ for her** la pauvre, ça me fait de la peine pour elle. -**2.** [in drawer, handbag, pocket] chercher.

◆ **feel up** *inf vt sep* [sexually] peloter, tripoter.

◆ **feel up to** *vt insep*: **to ~ up to (doing) sthg** [feel like] se sentir le courage de faire qqch; [feel physically strong enough] se sentir la force de faire qqch; [feel qualified, competent] se sentir capable OR à même de faire qqch; **I don't really ~ up to it** [feel like] je ne m'en sens pas le courage; [feel strong enough] je ne m'en sens pas la force; [feel competent enough] je ne me sens pas à la hauteur; **if you ~ up to it, how about a weekend in London?** si tu t'en sens le courage, que dirais-tu d'un week-end à Londres?

feeler ['fi:ləʳ] *n* [of insect] antenne *f*; [of snail] corne *f*; [of octopus] tentacule *m*; **to put out ~s** *fig* tâter le terrain.

feeler gauge *n* jauge *f* d'épaisseur.

feelgood *inf* ['fi:lgʊd] *adj*: **it's a real ~ film** c'est un film qui donne la pêche.

feeling ['fi:lɪŋ] ◇ *n* -**1.** [sensation] sensation *f*; **she gets a tingling ~ in her fingers** elle a une sensation de fourmillement dans les doigts; **I don't have any ~ in my left foot** je n'ai plus aucune sensation dans le pied gauche; **there's a ~ of spring in the air** ça sent le printemps; **a ~ of unease came over her** elle a commencé à se sentir mal à l'aise. -**2.** [opinion] avis *m*, opinion *f*; she has very strong ~s about it elle a des opinions très arrêtées là-dessus; what is your ~ about...? que pensez-vous de...?; the ~ I have is that... à mon avis...; the general ~ is that..., there is a general ~ that... l'opinion générale est que... -**3.** [awareness - relating to the future] pressentiment *m*; [- caused by external factors] impression *f*; I had a ~ he would write j'avais le pressentiment qu'il allait écrire; I had a ~ you'd say that j'étais sûr que tu allais dire ça; I have a nasty ~ that... j'ai le mauvais pressentiment que...; it's just a ~ c'est un pressentiment, ce n'est qu'une impression; I have a ~ that somebody's watching us j'ai l'impression que quelqu'un nous observe; I have the ~ you're trying to avoid me j'ai l'impression que tu essaies de m'éviter. -**4.** [sensitivity, understanding] émotion *f*, sensibilité *f*; a writer/a person of great ~ un écrivain/une personne d'une grande sensibilité; to play the piano/to sing with ~ jouer du piano/chanter avec cœur OR sentiment; to have a ~ for poetry/music être sensible à OR apprécier la poésie/la musique; she has a tremendous ~ for Latin-American rhythm elle a vraiment le rythme de la musique latino-américaine dans la peau; to show ~ for sb faire preuve de sympathie pour qqn; you have no ~ for other people les autres te sont indifférents. -**5.** *(often pl)* [emotion] sentiment *m*; to have mixed ~s about sb/sthg avoir des sentiments mitigés à l'égard de q qn/qqch; ~s are running high les passions sont déchaînées; ~s are running high about the new road la nouvelle route déchaîne les passions; to hurt sb's ~s blesser qqn; bad OR ill ~ hostilité *f*; it has caused a lot of bad ~ cela a provoqué une grande hostilité; I know the ~ je sais ce que c'est; the ~ is mutual c'est réciproque; he spoke on the subject of poverty with great ~ il a parlé de la pauvreté avec énormément d'émotion; to say sthg with ~ dire qqch avec émotion ❑ no hard ~s? sans rancune?

◇ *adj* [person, look] sympathique.

feelingly ['fi:lɪŋlɪ] *adv* avec émotion.

fee-paying *adj* [school] privé; ~ students *étudiants qui paient tous les droits d'inscription*.

feet [fi:t] *pl* → **foot**.

feign [feɪn] *vt* [surprise, innocence] feindre; [madness, death] simuler; to ~ sleep faire semblant OR mine de dormir; to ~ illness/interest faire semblant OR mine d'être malade/intéressé; with ~ed surprise/innocence avec une surprise/innocence feinte.

feint [feɪnt] MIL & SPORT ◇ *n* feinte *f*.

◇ *vi* faire une feinte.

feint-ruled *adj* [paper] à réglure légère.

feistiness *inf* ['faɪstɪnɪs] *n* [liveliness] entrain *m*; [combativeness] cran *m*.

feisty *inf* ['faɪstɪ] (*compar* feistier, *superl* feistiest) *adj* [lively] plein d'entrain; [combative] qui a du cran.

feldspar ['feldspɑ:ʳ] *n* MINER feldspath *m*.

felicitous [fɪ'lɪsɪtəs] *adj fml* -**1.** [happy] heureux. -**2.** [word] bien trouvé, heureux; [colour combination] heureux.

felicity [fɪ'lɪsətɪ] *n fml* -**1.** [happiness] félicité *f*. -**2.** [aptness - of word, term] à-propos *m*, justesse *f*.

feline ['fi:laɪn] ◇ *adj* [grace] félin; [characteristic] du chat.

◇ *n* félin *m*.

fell [fel] ◇ *pt* → **fall**.

◇ *vt* [tree] abattre, couper; *fig* [opponent] abattre, terrasser.

◇ *n* -**1.** *Br* GEOG montagne *f*, colline *f*; the ~s [high moorland] les landes *fpl* des plateaux. -**2.** [hide, pelt] fourrure *f*, peau *f*.

◇ *comp*: ~ walking randonnée *f* en basse montagne; ~ walker randonneur *m*, -euse *f* de basse montagne; ~ running course *f* en basse montagne; ~ runner coureur *m*, -euse *f* en basse montagne.

◇ *adj* -**1.** *arch* OR *lit* [fierce - person] féroce, cruel; [deadly - disease] cruel. -**2.** *phr*: in OR at one ~ swoop d'un seul coup.

fella *inf* ['felə] *n* [man] mec *m*, type *m*.

fellah ['felə] *n* -**1.** [Arab peasant] fellah *m*. -**2.** *inf* = **fellow 1**.

fellatio [fe'leɪʃɪəʊ] *n* fellation *f*.

feller *inf* ['feləʳ] *Br* = **fellow** *n* **1**.

felling ['felɪŋ] *n* [of tree] abattage *m*.

fellow ['feləʊ] ◇ *n* -**1.** *inf dated* [man] gars *m*, type *m*; a good ~ un type OR gars bien; an old ~ un vieux bonhomme; poor old ~ pauvre vieux; the poor ~'s just lost his job le pauvre vient juste de perdre son travail; the poor little ~ [animal] la pauvre bête; hello, old ~ salut, mon vieux; my dear ~ mon cher ami; give a ~ a chance! donne-moi une chance! -**2.** *lit* [comrade] ami *m*, -e *f*, camarade *mf*; [other human being] semblable *mf*; [person in same profession] confrère *m*, consœur *f*; ~s in misfortune compagnons *mpl* d'infortune; school ~ camarade d'école. -**3.** UNIV [professor] professeur *m (faisant également partie du conseil d'administration)*; [postgraduate student] étudiant *m*, -e *f* de troisième cycle *(souvent chargé de cours)*; research ~ chercheur *m*, -euse *f* dans une université. -**4.** [of society] membre *m*. -**5.** [one of a pair]: where is the ~ to this sock/glove? où est la chaussette/le gant qui va avec celle-là/celui-là?

◇ *adj*: ~ prisoner/student camarade *mf* de prison/d'études; ~ passenger/sufferer/soldier compagnon *m* de voyage/d'infortune/d'armes; ~ being OR creature semblable *mf*, pareil *m*, -eille *f*; one's ~ man son semblable; ~ worker [in office] collègue *mf* (de travail); [in factory] camarade *mf* (de travail), compagnon *m* de travail; ~ citizen concitoyen *m*, -enne *f*; ~ countryman/countrywoman compatriote *mf*; ~ traveller [companion on journey] compagnon *m* de voyage OR de route; *fig* compagnon *m* de route; POL communisant *m*, -e *f*; it's rare to meet a ~ hang-glider c'est rare de rencontrer un autre adepte du deltaplane; an opportunity to meet your ~ translators une occasion de rencontrer vos confrères traducteurs.

fellow feeling *n* sympathie *f*.

fellowship ['feləʊʃɪp] *n* -**1.** [friendship] camaraderie *f*; [company] compagnie *f*. -**2.** [organization] association *f*, société *f*; RELIG confrérie *f*. -**3.** UNIV [scholarship] bourse *f* d'études de l'enseignement supérieur; [position] poste *m* de chercheur.

felon ['felən] *n* JUR criminel *m*, -elle *f*.

felonious [fɪ'ləʊnjəs] *adj* JUR criminel.

felony ['felənɪ] *n* JUR crime *m*.

felspar ['felspɑ:ʳ] = **feldspar**.

felt [felt] ◇ *pt* & *pp* → **feel**.

◇ *n* TEX feutre *m*; roofing ~ feutre *m* bitumé.

◇ *comp* de OR en feutre; a ~ hat un (chapeau de OR en) feutre; ~ pen feutre *m*.

felt-tip (pen) *n* (stylo *m*) feutre *m*.

fem [fem] *abbr of* feminine.

female ['fi:meɪl] ◇ *adj* -**1.** [animal, plant, egg] femelle; [sex, quality, voice, employee] féminin; [vote] des femmes; [equality] de la femme, des femmes; a traditionally ~ job un travail traditionnellement réservé aux femmes; the young ~ giraffe la jeune girafe femelle; ~ slave femme esclave; a study of the ~ character une étude du caractère de la femme; ~ company la compagnie féminine OR des femmes; the ~ sex organs les organes sexuels féminins OR de la femme; more ~ students than male study languages il y a plus d'étudiantes que d'étudiants en langues; male and ~ clients des clients et des clientes; there are not enough ~ politicians il n'y a pas assez de femmes sur la scène politique; that's typical ~ thinking! c'est un raisonnement typiquement féminin! -**2.** TECH femelle.

◇ *n* [animal, plant] femelle *f*; the ~ of the species la femelle || *offensive* gonzesse *f*.

female impersonator *n* travesti *m (dans un spectacle)*.

feminine ['femɪnɪn] ◇ *adj* -**1.** [dress, woman, hands etc] féminin; the bedroom is very ~ c'est une vraie chambre de femme; this flat needs the ~ touch cet appartement a besoin de la présence d'une femme. -**2.** GRAMM [ending, form] féminin.

◇ *n* GRAMM féminin *m*; in the ~ au féminin.

femininity [,femɪ'nɪnətɪ] *n* féminité *f*.

feminism ['femɪnɪzm] *n* féminisme *m*; I really admire her ~ j'admire vraiment la façon dont elle soutient la cause de la femme OR des femmes.

feminist ['femɪnɪst] ◇ *adj* féministe; what will be the ~ reaction? comment les féministes réagiront-elles?

◇ *n* féministe *mf*.

femoral ['femərəl] *adj* ANAT fémoral.

femur ['fi:məʳ] *n* ANAT fémur *m*.

fen [fen] *n* marais *m*, marécage *m*; the Fens *région de plaines anciennement marécageuses dans le sud de l'Angleterre*.

fence [fens] ◇ *n* -**1.** [gen] barrière *f*; [completely enclosing] barrière *f*, clôture *f*; [high and wooden] palissade *f*; electric/barbed-wire ~ clôture électrique/en fil barbelé ❑ to come down on the right/wrong side of the ~ choisir le bon/mauvais parti; to be on the other side of the ~ être de l'opinion contraire; to mend one's ~s [with fans, electorate] se refaire une réputation; [with friends, colleagues] se regagner des faveurs; to mend one's ~s with sb [fans, electorate] se refaire une réputation auprès OR regagner les faveurs de qqn; [friends, colleagues] se réconcilier avec qqn; to sit on the ~ ne pas se prononcer, rester neutre; stop sitting on OR come down off the ~ prononce-toi. -**2.** [in show-jumping] obstacle *m*; to rush one's ~s [horse] arriver trop vite sur l'obstacle; *fig* aller trop vite en besogne. -**3.** ▽ [of stolen goods] receleur *m*, -euse *f*. -**4.** TECH protection *f*.

◇ *comp*: ~ post piquet *m* de clôture.

◇ *vt* -**1.** [land] clôturer. -**2.** ▽ [stolen goods] receler.

◇ *vi* -**1.** SPORT faire de l'escrime. -**2.** [evade question] se dérober; [joust verbally] s'affronter verbalement. -**3.** ▽ [handle stolen goods] faire du recel.

◆ **fence in** *vt sep* -**1.** [garden] clôturer. -**2.** *fig* [restrict - person] enfermer, étouffer; he feels pretty ~d in il se sent enfermé, il étouffe; to feel ~d in by sthg étouffer sous le poids de qqch.

◆ **fence off** *vt sep* séparer à l'aide d'une clôture.

fencer ['fensəʳ] *n* SPORT escrimeur *m*, -euse *f*.

fencing ['fensɪŋ] ◇ *n* -**1.** SPORT escrime *f*. -**2.** [fences] clôture *f*, barrière *f*; [material] matériaux *mpl* pour clôture. -**3.** ▽ [handling stolen goods] recel *m*.

◇ *comp* [lesson, match] d'escrime.

fend [fend] *vi*: to ~ for o.s. se débrouiller tout seul; [financially] s'assumer, subvenir à ses besoins.

◆ **fend off** *vt sep* [blow] parer; [attack, attacker] repousser; *fig* [question] éluder, se dérober à; [person at door, on telephone] éconduire.

fender ['fendəʳ] *n* -**1.** [for fireplace] garde-feu *m inv*. -**2.** NAUT défense *f*. -**3.** *Am* [on car] aile *f*; [on bicycle] garde-boue *m inv*; [on train, tram - shock absorber] pare-chocs *m inv*; [- for clearing track] chasse-pierres *m inv*.

fender-bender *inf n Am* AUT [minor accident] petit accrochage *m*.

fenestration [fenɪ'streɪʃn] *n* -**1.** ARCHIT fenêtrage *m*. -**2.** MED fenestration *f*.

fennel ['fenl] *n* fenouil *m*.

fenugreek ['fenjʊgri:k] *n* fenugrec *m*.

feral ['fɪərəl] *adj* [cat, goat, sheep] devenu sauvage.

ferment [*vb* fə'ment, *n* 'fɜ:ment] ◇ *vt* faire fermenter; to ~ trouble *fig* fomenter des troubles.

◇ *vi* fermenter.

◇ *n* -**1.** [agent] ferment *m*; [fermentation] fermentation *f*. -**2.** *fig* [unrest] agitation *f*; to be in (a state of) ~ être en effervescence.

fermentation [ˌfɜːmən'teɪʃn] *n* fermentation *f*.

fern [fɜːn] *n* fougère *f*.

ferocious [fə'rəʊʃəs] *adj* [animal, appetite, criticism, fighting] féroce; [weapon] meurtrier; [competition] acharné; [heat] terrible, intense; [climate] rude; a ~ war une guerre sanguinaire.

ferociously [fə'rəʊʃəslɪ] *adv* [bark, criticize, attack] avec férocité, férocement; [look at sb] d'un œil féroce; this business is ~ competitive ce secteur est caractérisé par une concurrence acharnée.

ferociousness [fə'rəʊʃəsnɪs], **ferocity** [fə'rɒsətɪ] *n* [of person, animal, attack, criticism] férocité *f*; [of climate] rudesse *f*; [of heat] intensité *f*, caractère *m* torride; the ~ of the competition for a place at university la concurrence acharnée pour les places à l'université.

Ferrara [fə'rɑːrə] *pr n* Ferrare.

ferret ['ferɪt] ◇ *n* furet *m*.

◇ *vi* -**1.** [hunt with ferrets] chasser au furet; to go ~ing aller à la chasse au furet. -**2.** *fig* = **ferret about, ferret around**.

◆ **ferret about, ferret around** *vi insep* [in pocket, drawer] fouiller; [in room] fouiller, fureter; to ~ about for information fureter dans le but de trouver des renseignements; to ~ about in sb's past fureter dans le passé de qqn; he's been ~ing about il a fureté un peu partout.

◆ **ferret out** *vt sep* [information, truth] dénicher.

ferreting ['ferɪtɪŋ] *n* chasse *f* au furet.

ferric ['ferɪk] *adj* ferrique.

Ferris wheel ['ferɪs-] *n* grande roue *f*.

ferroconcrete [ˌferəʊ'kɒŋkriːt] *n* béton *m* armé.

ferrous ['ferəs] *adj* ferreux.

ferrule ['feruːl] *n* [of umbrella, walking stick] virole *f*.

ferry ['ferɪ] (*pl* **ferries**, *pt* & *pp* **ferried**) ◇ *n* [large] ferry *m*; [small] bac *m*; to take the ~ prendre le ferry OR le bac; we took the ~ to France nous sommes allés en France en ferry; a ~ crossing une traversée en ferry OR bac; ~ service ligne *f* de ferry; passenger ~ ferry *m* pour passagers piétons; car ~ car-ferry *m*.

◇ *vt* -**1.** [by large boat - subj: company] transporter en ferry; [by small boat - subj: company] faire traverser en bac; [- subj: boat] transporter; Donald will ~ you across in his rowing boat Donald vous fera traverser dans sa barque. -**2.** *fig* [by vehicle - goods] transporter; [- people] conduire; he spends most of his time ~ing the kids around il passe la majeure partie de son temps à conduire les enfants à droite et à gauche.

ferryboat ['ferɪbəʊt] *n* ferry *m*.

ferryman ['ferɪmən] (*pl* **ferrymen** [-mən]) *n* passeur *m*.

fertile ['fɜːtaɪl] *adj* [land, soil] fertile; [person, couple, animal] fécond; *fig* [imagination] fertile, fécond; a ~ egg un œuf fécondé; to fall on ~ ground *fig* trouver un terrain propice.

fertility [fɜː'tɪlətɪ] ◇ *n* [of land, soil] fertilité *f*; [of person, animal] fécondité *f*; *fig* [of imagination] fertilité *f*, fécondité *f*.

◇ *comp* [rate] de fécondité; [rite, symbol] de fertilité; ~ clinic centre *m* de traitement de la stérilité; ~ drug médicament *m* pour le traitement de la stérilité.

fertilization [ˌfɜːtɪlaɪ'zeɪʃn] *n* -**1.** BIOL [of egg] fécondation *f*. -**2.** AGR [of soil] fertilisation *f*.

fertilize, -ise ['fɜːtɪlaɪz] *vt* -**1.** BIOL [animal, plant, egg] féconder. -**2.** AGR [land, soil] fertiliser.

fertilizer ['fɜːtɪlaɪzəʳ] *n* AGR engrais *m*.

ferule ['feruːl] = **ferrule**.

fervent ['fɜːvənt] *adj* [desire, supporter etc] fervent, ardent; he is a ~ believer in reincarnation il croit ardemment à la réincarnation.

fervently ['fɜːvəntlɪ] *adv* [beg, desire, speak etc] avec ferveur; [believe] ardemment.

fervid *etc* ['fɜːvɪd] *fml* = **fervent**.

fervour *Br*, **fervor** *Am* ['fɜːvəʳ] *n* ferveur *f*.

fester ['festəʳ] *vi* -**1.** [wound] suppurer; *fig* [memory, resentment] s'aigrir. -**2.** *inf Br* [do nothing] buller.

festering ['festrɪŋ] *adj* [wound] suppurant.

festival ['festəvl] *n* [of music, film etc] festival *m*; RELIG fête *f*; street ~ festival de rue; the Cannes Film Festival le Festival de Cannes.

festive ['festɪv] *adj* [atmosphere] de fête; their golden wedding celebration was a very ~ occasion ils ont fait une grande fête pour célébrer leurs noces d'or; there was a really ~ atmosphere l'atmosphère était vraiment à la fête; the ~ season la période des fêtes; to be in ~ mood [person] se sentir d'une humeur de fête; the village is in ~ mood une ambiance de fête règne dans le village; to look ~ [place] être décoré comme pour une fête.

festivity [fes'tɪvətɪ] (*pl* **festivities**) *n* [merriness] fête *f*.

◆ **festivities** *npl* festivités *fpl*; the Christmas festivities les fêtes *fpl* de Noël; come and join the festivities viens te joindre à la fête, viens faire la fête avec nous.

festoon [fe'stuːn] ◇ *n* feston *m*, guirlande *f*.

◇ *vt* orner de festons, festonner; to be ~ed in sthg *fig* [draped with] être couvert de qqch.

feta ['fetə] *n*: ~ (cheese) feta *f*.

fetal *Am* = **foetal**.

fetch [fetʃ] ◇ *vt* -**1.** [go to get] aller chercher; [come to get] venir chercher; to ~ sb back aller chercher qqn; to ~ sb from the station/from school aller chercher qqn à la gare/à l'école; go/run and ~ him va/va vite le chercher; to ~ sb in faire rentrer qqn; to ~ sthg in rentrer qqch; she ~ed him down from upstairs elle est montée le chercher. -**2.** [generate]: the speech ~ed a round of applause le discours a été reçu par des applaudissements; the joke ~ed a laugh la plaisanterie a suscité des rires; it ~ed no response cela n'a suscité OR soulevé aucune réaction. -**3.** [be sold for - money] rapporter; [- price] atteindre; it should ~ you £8,000 cela devrait vous rapporter 8 000 livres, vous devriez en tirer 8 000 livres; the painting ~ed £8,000 le tableau a atteint la somme de 8 000 livres. -**4.** *fml* [utter - sigh, groan] pousser. -**5.** *inf* [deal - blow]: he ~ed him one with his right fist il lui a flanqué OR envoyé un droit; move or I'll ~ you one! dégage ou je t'en mets une!

◇ *vi* aller chercher; ~! [to dog] va chercher!; to ~ and carry for sb faire le grouillot pour qqn, être le grouillot de qqn.

◆ **fetch up** *inf* ◇ *vi insep* -**1.** [end up] se retrouver; to ~ up in hospital/in a ditch se retrouver à l'hôpital/dans un fossé. -**2.** [vomit] rendre.

◇ *vt sep* [vomit] rendre.

fetching ['fetʃɪŋ] *adj* [smile, person, look] séduisant; [hat, dress] seyant.

fetchingly ['fetʃɪŋlɪ] *adv* [smile] d'un air séduisant; with his hat balanced ~ on his head avec son chapeau élégamment posé sur la tête.

fête [feɪt] ◇ *n* fête *f*, kermesse *f*; village ~ fête du village.

◇ *vt* fêter.

FÊTE:

En Grande-Bretagne, les «village fêtes» sont des manifestations en plein air où l'on vend des produits faits maison et où l'on organise des manifestations sportives et des jeux pour enfants; elles sont généralement destinées à réunir des fonds pour une œuvre de charité.

---

fetid ['fetɪd] *adj* fétide.

fetish ['fetɪʃ] *n* PSYCH & RELIG fétiche *m*; to have a ~ for sthg PSYCH être un fétichiste de qqch; to have a ~ for OR to make a ~ of sthg être obsédé par qqch, être un maniaque de qqch; there's no need to make a ~ of it il ne faut pas que cela devienne une obsession.

fetishism ['fetɪʃɪzm] *n* PSYCH & RELIG fétichisme *m*; food ~ obsession *f* pour la nourriture; foot ~ fétichisme du pied.

fetishist ['fetɪʃɪst] *n* PSYCH & RELIG fétichiste *mf*; food ~ personne *f* obsédée par la nourriture; foot ~ fétichiste du pied.

fetishistic [ˌfetɪ'ʃɪstɪk] *adj* PSYCH fétichiste; that borders on the ~ cela confine au fétichisme.

fetlock ['fetlɒk] *n* [of horse - part of leg] partie *f* postérieure du pied; [- joint] boulet *m*; [- hair] fanon *m*.

fetter ['fetəʳ] *vt* [slave, prisoner] enchaîner; [horse] entraver; *fig* entraver.

◆ **fetters** *npl* [of prisoner] fers *mpl*, chaînes *fpl*; [of horse] entraves *fpl*; *fig* [of marriage, job] chaînes *fpl*, sujétions *fpl*; in ~s [prisoner] enchaîné; *fig* entravé; to put sb in ~s mettre qqn aux fers; *fig* entraver qqn.

fettle *inf* ['fetl] *n*: to be in fine OR good ~ aller bien.

fetus *Am* = **foetus**.

feu [fjuː] *n Scot* JUR bail *m* perpétuel; ~ duty loyer *m* (de la terre).

feud [fjuːd] ◇ *n* [between people, families] querelle *f*; [more aggressive - between families] vendetta *f*; a bloody ~ une vendetta; to have a ~ with sb être à couteaux tirés avec qqn.

◇ *vi* se quereller, se disputer; to ~ with sb (over sthg) se quereller OR se disputer avec qqn (pour qqch); they were ~ing with each other over who owned the property ils se disputaient la possession de la propriété.

feudal ['fjuːdl] *adj* [society, system] féodal; *pej* [extremely old-fashioned] moyenâgeux.

feudalism ['fjuːdəlɪzm] *n* féodalisme *m*.

feuding ['fjuːdɪŋ] *n (U)* querelle *f*, querelles *fpl*; [more aggressive] vendetta *f*.

fever ['fiːvəʳ] *n* -**1.** MED [illness] fièvre *f*; a bout of ~ un accès OR une poussée de fièvre; to have a ~ [high temperature] avoir de la température OR de la fièvre; to have a high ~ avoir beaucoup de température OR de fièvre. -**2.** *fig* excitation *f* fébrile; a ~ of anticipation une attente fiévreuse OR fébrile; football/election/gold ~ fièvre *f* du football/des élections/de l'or; gambling ~ démon *m* du jeu; the entire hall went into a ~ of excitement la salle entière s'enfiévra; to be in a ~ about sthg [nervous, excited] être tout excité à cause de qqch.

fevered ['fiːvəd] *adj* [brow] fiévreux; *fig* [imagination] enfiévré.

feverish ['fiːvərɪʃ] *adj* MED fiévreux; *fig* [activity, atmosphere] fébrile.

feverishness ['fiːvərɪʃnɪs] *n* MED état *m* fébrile, fébrilité *f*.

fever pitch *n fig*: things are at ~ here l'excitation ici est à son comble; excitement is rising to ~ l'excitation est de plus en plus fébrile.

few [fjuː] ◇ *det* -**1.** [not many] peu de; ~ people have done that peu de gens ont fait cela; there are very ~ suitable candidates for the post très peu de candidats ont le profil requis; so/too ~ books to read si/trop peu de livres à lire; there are four books too ~ il manque quatre livres; we are ~ (in number) nous sommes peu nombreux; with ~ exceptions à peu d'exceptions près, sauf de rares exceptions || *(with def art, poss adj etc)*: on the ~ occasions that I have met him les rares fois où je l'ai rencontré; her ~ remaining possessions le peu de biens qui lui restaient; these ~ precious souvenirs ces quelques précieux souvenirs; it is one of the ~ surviving examples of... c'est un des rares exemples qui restent de...; she is one of the ~ women to have held the post c'est une des rares femmes à avoir assumé ces fonctions ❑ visitors are ~ and far between les visiteurs sont rares; grants will be ~ and far between in future les bourses se feront rares à l'avenir. -**2.** [indicating an unspecified or approximate number]: every ~ minutes toutes les deux ou trois minutes; the first ~ copies les deux ou trois premiers exemplaires; in the past/next ~ days pendant les deux ou trois derniers/

prochains jours; **he's been living in London for the past ~ years** ça fait quelques années qu'il habite à Londres; **these past ~ weeks have been wonderful** ces dernières semaines ont été merveilleuses.
◇ *pron* [not many]: **how many of them are there? – very ~** combien sont-ils? – très peu nombreux; **I didn't realize how ~ there were** je ne m'étais pas rendu compte qu'ils étaient aussi peu nombreux; **~ could have predicted the outcome** peu de personnes OR rares sont ceux qui auraient pu prévoir le résultat; **the ~ who knew her** les quelques personnes qui la connaissaient ❑ **the chosen ~** les heureux élus; **the Few** *Br* HIST *les aviateurs britanniques qui ont défendu leur pays pendant la bataille d'Angleterre*; **many are called but ~ are chosen** BIBLE il y a beaucoup d'appelés mais peu d'élus.
◆ **a few** ◇ *det phr* quelques; **I have a ~ ideas** j'ai quelques idées; **he has a ~ more friends than I have** il a un peu plus d'amis que moi; **a ~ more days/months/years** quelques jours/mois/années de plus; **a ~ more days should see the job done** encore quelques jours et le travail devrait être fini.
◇ *pron phr* quelques-uns, quelques-unes; **do you have many friends? – I have a ~** est-ce que tu as beaucoup d'amis? – (j'en ai) quelques-uns; **we need a ~ more/less** il nous en faut un peu plus/moins; **a ~ of you** quelques-uns d'entre vous; **there are only a ~ of us who attend regularly** seuls quelques-uns parmi nous y vont régulièrement ❑ **he's had a ~** *inf* [drinks] il a bu un coup; **he's had a ~ too many** il a bu un coup de trop; **to name but a ~** pour n'en citer que quelques-uns; **not a ~** pas peu.
◆ **a good few, quite a few** ◇ *det phr* un assez grand nombre de; **there were a good ~ OR quite a ~ mistakes in it** il y avait un assez grand nombre de OR pas mal de fautes dedans.
◇ *pron phr* un assez grand nombre; **quite a ~ agreed with me** ils étaient assez nombreux à être d'accord avec moi; **quite a ~ of us/of the books** un assez grand nombre d'entre nous/de livres; **I hadn't seen all her films, but I'd seen a good ~** je n'avais pas vu tous ses films, mais j'en avais vu un assez grand nombre.

fewer ['fju:ə^r] (*compar of* few) ◇ *det* moins de; **more applicants are competing for ~ jobs** il y a plus de candidats et moins de postes; **there have been ~ accidents than last year** il y a eu moins d'accidents que l'an dernier; **~ and ~ people** de moins en moins de gens; **the ~ people turn up the better** moins il y aura de monde et mieux ce sera ❑ **no ~ than** pas moins de.
◇ *pron* moins; **there are ~ of you than I thought** vous êtes moins nombreux que je ne le pensais; **I've got even/a lot ~ than you** j'en ai encore/beaucoup moins que toi; **the ~ the better** moins il y en a mieux c'est; **how many days are you going to spend there? – the ~ the better** combien de jours vas-tu passer là-bas? – le moins possible.

fewest ['fju:ɪst] (*superl of* few) ◇ *adj* le moins de; **the ~ mistakes possible** le moins d'erreurs possible; **this is the part where the ~ people live** c'est la région la moins peuplée.
◇ *pron*: **I had the ~** c'est moi qui en ai eu le moins; **who's got the ~?** qui en a le moins?

fey [feɪ] *adj* -**1.** [whimsical - person, behaviour] bizarre. -**2.** *Scot* [clairvoyant] extralucide. -**3.** *Scot* [having feeling of impending death] qui a des pressentiments de mort.

fez [fez] *n* fez *m*.

Fez [fez] *pr n* Fès.

FFA (*abbr of* Future Farmers of America) *pr n* *aux États-Unis, organisation nationale d'étudiants en agriculture*.

FH *Br written abbr of* fire hydrant.

FHA (*abbr of* Federal Housing Administration) *pr n* *organisme de gestion des logements sociaux aux États-Unis*.

fiancé [fɪ'ɒnseɪ] *n* fiancé *m*.

fiancée [fɪ'ɒnseɪ] *n* fiancée *f*.

fiasco [fɪ'æskəʊ] (*pl* fiascos OR fiascoes) *n* fiasco *m*; **it was a ~** ça a été un véritable fiasco; **to end in ~** se terminer par un fiasco.

fiat ['faɪæt] *n* [decree] décret *m*.

fib *inf* [fɪb] ◇ *n* petit mensonge *m*; **to tell ~s** raconter des histoires; **what a ~!** c'est des histoires!
◇ *vi* raconter des histoires.

fibber *inf* ['fɪbə^r] *n* menteur *m*, -euse *f*.

fibre *Br*, **fiber** *Am* ['faɪbə^r] *n* -**1.** [of cloth, wood] fibre *f*; **artificial/natural ~s** fibres artificielles/naturelles; **moral ~** *fig* force *f* morale; **to love sb/sthg with every ~ of one's being** *fig* aimer qqn/qqch de tout son être. -**2.** *(U)* [in diet] fibres *fpl*; **to be high in ~** [foodstuff] être riche en fibres; **high-~ diet** régime *m* OR alimentation *f* riche en fibres.

fibreboard *Br*, **fiberboard** *Am* ['faɪbəbɔ:d] *n* panneau *m* de fibres.

fibreglass *Br*, **fiberglass** *Am* ['faɪbəglɑ:s] ◇ *n* fibre *f* de verre; **it's (made of) ~** c'est en OR de la fibre de verre.
◇ *comp* [boat, hull etc] en fibre de verre.

fibre optic ◇ *n*: **~s** fibre *f* optique, fibres *fpl* optiques.
◇ *adj* [cable] en fibres optiques.

fibre-tip pen *n* feutre *m* pointe fibre.

fibrillation [,faɪbrɪ'leɪʃn] *n* fibrillation *f*.

fibroid ['faɪbrɔɪd] ◇ *adj* [tissue] fibreux; **~ tumour** fibrome *m*.
◇ *n* [tumour] fibrome *m*.

fibrosis [faɪ'brəʊsɪs] *n (U)* fibrose *f*.

fibrositis [,faɪbrə'saɪtɪs] *n (U)* fibrosite *f*.

fibrous ['faɪbrəs] *adj* fibreux.

fibula ['fɪbjʊlə] (*pl* fibulas OR fibulae [-li:]) *n* ANAT péroné *m*.

FICA (*abbr of* Federal Insurance Contributions Act) *pr n* *loi américaine régissant les cotisations sociales*.

fickle ['fɪkl] *adj* [friend, fan] inconstant; [weather] changeant, incertain; [lover] inconstant, volage.

fickleness ['fɪklnɪs] *n* [of friend, fan, public, lover] inconstance *f*; [of weather] instabilité *f*.

fiction ['fɪkʃn] ◇ *n* -**1.** *(U)* LITERAT ouvrages *mpl* OR œuvres *fpl* de fiction; **first prize for ~** premier prix de fiction; **a work OR piece of ~** un ouvrage OR une œuvre de fiction. -**2.** [invention] fiction *f*; **she has difficulty separating fact from ~** elle a du mal à distinguer la réalité de la fiction; **it's pure ~** c'est de la pure fiction; **we'll have to keep up the ~ a little longer** il nous faudra continuer encore un peu à faire semblant.
◇ *comp*: **~ writer** auteur *m* d'ouvrages de fiction.

fictional ['fɪkʃənl] *adj* fictif; **a well-known ~ character** un célèbre personnage de la littérature; **the ~ treatment of women** le thème de la femme dans les ouvrages de fiction.

fictionalize ['fɪkʃənəlaɪz] *vt* romancer.

fictitious [fɪk'tɪʃəs] *adj* [imaginary, invented] fictif.

fiddle ['fɪdl] ◇ *n* -**1.** MUS [instrument] violon *m*; **to be as fit as a ~** être en pleine forme, être frais comme un gardon; **her face was as long as a ~** elle faisait une tête d'enterrement; **to play second ~ to sb** jouer les seconds violons OR rôles auprès de qqn. -**2.** *inf* [swindle] truc *m*, combine *f*; **to work a ~** *Br* combiner quelque chose; **it's a ~** c'est un attrape-nigaud; **to be on the ~** traficoter; **tax ~** fraude *f* fiscale.
◇ *vi* -**1.** [be restless]: **stop fiddling!** tiens-toi tranquille!, arrête de remuer!; **to ~ with sthg** [aimlessly, nervously] jouer avec qqch; [interfere with] jouer avec OR tripoter qqch. -**2.** [tinker] bricoler; **he ~d with the knobs on the television** il a tourné les boutons de la télé dans tous les sens. -**3.** MUS jouer du violon; **to ~ while Rome burns** s'occuper de futilités alors qu'il est urgent d'agir. -**4.** *inf* [cheat] trafiquer.
◇ *vt* -**1.** *inf* [falsify - results, financial accounts] truquer, falsifier; [- election] truquer; **to ~ one's income tax** falsifier sa déclaration d'impôts; **he ~d it so that he got the results he wanted** il a trafiqué pour obtenir les résultats qu'il voulait. -**2.** *inf* [gain dishonestly - money, time off] carotter. -**3.** *inf* [swindle - person]: **he ~d me out of £20** il m'a refait de 20 livres; **I've been ~d!** je me suis fait escroquer! -**4.** [play - tune] jouer au violon.
◆ **fiddle about** *Br*, **fiddle around** *vi insep* -**1.** [fidget] jouer. -**2.** *inf* [mess about] bricoler; [loaf about, waste time] traînasser.

fiddlededee *inf* [,fɪdldi:'di:], **fiddle-faddle** *inf* [-,fædl] = **fiddlesticks**.

fiddler *inf* ['fɪdlə^r] *n* -**1.** MUS joueur *m*, -euse *f* de violon, violoniste *mf*. -**2.** [swindler] arnaqueur *m*, -euse *f*.

fiddlesticks *inf* ['fɪdlstɪks] *interj dated* [in disagreement] balivernes *fpl*, sornettes *fpl*; [in annoyance] bon sang de bonsoir.

fiddling ['fɪdlɪŋ] ◇ *adj* [trivial - job] futile, insignifiant.
◇ *n* -**1.** [fidgeting]: **stop your ~!** arrête de gigoter! -**2.** *inf* [swindling] trafic *m*, falsification *f*; **his ~ of the books** sa falsification des livres de comptes; **in spite of all his ~** malgré toutes ses combines.

fiddly *inf* ['fɪdlɪ] *adj* [awkward - job, task] délicat, minutieux; [- small object] difficile à manier, difficile à tenir entre les doigts; **it's a bit ~** ça demande de la minutie.

fidelity [fɪ'deləti] *n* -**1.** [of people] fidélité *f*; **they vowed ~ to one another** ils se sont juré fidélité. -**2.** [of translation] fidélité *f*. -**3.** ELECTRON fidélité *f*; **high ~** haute fidélité.

fidget *inf* ['fɪdʒɪt] ◇ *vi* [be restless] avoir la bougeotte, gigoter; **stop ~ing!** arrête de gigoter!; **to ~ with sthg** jouer avec qqch, tripoter qqch.
◇ *n* -**1.** [restless person]: **she's a little ~** elle ne tient pas en place, elle gigote tout le temps; **what a ~ you are today!** tu ne tiens pas en place OR tu as la bougeotte aujourd'hui!; **don't be such a ~!** arrête de gigoter! -**2.** *phr*: **to have OR to get the ~s** [be restless, nervous] ne pas tenir en place.

fidgety *inf* ['fɪdʒɪtɪ] *adj* qui ne tient pas en place; **I feel ~** je ne tiens plus en place.

fiduciary [fɪ'du:ʃjərɪ] JUR & FIN ◇ *adj* fiduciaire.
◇ *n* fiduciaire *m*.

fie [faɪ] *interj arch* OR *hum*: **~ on you!** vous devriez avoir honte!

fief [fi:f] *n* HIST & *fig* fief *m*.

fiefdom ['fi:fdəm] *n* HIST & *fig* fief *m*.

field [fi:ld] ◇ *n* -**1.** AGR champ *m*; **to work in the ~s** travailler dans les OR aux champs. -**2.** SPORT [pitch] terrain *m*; **the ~** [in baseball] les défenseurs *mpl*; **Smith is way ahead of the (rest of the) ~** Smith est loin devant OR devance largement les autres; **there's a very strong ~ for the 100 metres** il y a une très belle brochette de concurrents OR participants au départ du 100 mètres ❑ **football ~** terrain de football; **sports OR games ~** terrain de sport; **to take the ~** entrer sur le terrain; **to lead the ~** [in race] mener la course, être en tête; *fig* [in sales, area of study] être en tête; [subj: theory] faire autorité; **to play the ~** *inf* [romantically] jouer sur plusieurs tableaux. -**3.** [of oil, minerals etc] gisement *m*; **oil/coal/gas ~** gisement de pétrole/de charbon/de gaz; **to work in the oil ~s** travailler sur les lieux de forage pétrolier; **ice ~** surface *f* glacée; **snow ~** champ *m* de neige. -**4.** MIL: **~ (of battle)** champ *m* de bataille; **bravery in the ~** bravoure sur le champ de bataille; **to die on the ~ of honour** mourir OR tomber au champ d'honneur; **to hold the ~** ne pas lâcher de terrain, tenir; **the French now held the ~** les Français étaient maintenant maîtres du champ de bataille. -**5.** [sphere of activity, knowledge] domaine *m*; **experts from every ~** des experts provenant de tous les domaines; **to be an expert in one's ~** être expert dans son domaine; **in the political ~, in the ~ of politics** dans le domaine politique; **to contribute to the ~ of human knowledge** contribuer à la connaissance humaine; **what's your ~?, what ~ are you in?** quel est ton domaine?; **that's not my**

~ ce n'est pas de mon domaine OR dans mes compétences. -**6.** [practice rather than theory] terrain *m*; to work/to study in the ~ travailler/étudier sur le terrain; to go out into the ~ aller sur le terrain. -**7.** PHYS & OPTICS champ *m*; ~ of vision champ visuel OR de vision; magnetic ~ champ magnétique || MIL: ~ of fire champ *m* de tir. -**8.** COMPUT champ *m*. -**9.** HERALD [on coat of arms, coin] champ *m*; [on flag] fond *m*.

◇ *vt* -**1.** [team] présenter; [player] faire jouer; MIL [men, hardware] réunir; POL [candidate] présenter. -**2.** [in cricket, baseball - ball] arrêter (et renvoyer); to ~ a question *fig* savoir répondre à une question; well ~ed *fig* bien répondu.

◇ *vi* [in cricket, baseball] être en défense, tenir le champ.

field ambulance *n* MIL ambulance *f*.

field artillery *n* MIL artillerie *f* de campagne.

fieldcraft ['fi:ldkrɑ:ft] *n* *(U)* connaissances *fpl* de la nature.

field day *n* SCH journée *f* en plein air; MIL jour *m* des grandes manœuvres; to have a ~ *inf fig* s'en donner à cœur joie; [do good business] faire recette; what a ~ they had! ils s'en sont vraiment donné à cœur joie!

fielder ['fi:ldəʳ] *n* [in cricket, baseball] joueur *m* de l'équipe défendante OR champ.

field event *n* SPORT compétition *f* d'athlétisme *(autre que course)*; ~s concours *mpl*.

fieldfare ['fi:ldfeəʳ] *n* ORNITH litorne *f*.

field glasses *npl* jumelles *fpl*.

field gun *n* MIL canon *m*.

field hockey *n* *Am* hockey *m* (sur gazon).

field hospital *n* MIL antenne *f* chirurgicale, hôpital *m* de campagne.

fielding ['fi:ldɪŋ] *n* [in cricket, baseball] défense *f*.

field kitchen *n* MIL cuisine *f* roulante.

field marshal *n* MIL maréchal *m*.

fieldmouse ['fi:ldmaʊs] (*pl* **fieldmice** [-maɪs]) *n* mulot *m*.

field officer *n* MIL officier *m* supérieur.

fieldsman ['fi:ldzmən] (*pl* **fieldsmen** [-mən]) = **fielder**.

field sports *npl la chasse et la pêche*.

field study *n* étude *f* sur le terrain.

field test *n* essai *m* sur le terrain.

◆ **field-test** *vt* [machine] soumettre à des essais sur le terrain.

field trials *npl* [for machine] essais *mpl* sur le terrain.

field trip *n* SCH & UNIV voyage *m* d'études; [of one afternoon, one day] sortie *f* d'études; geography ~ excursion *f* d'études de géographie.

fieldwork ['fi:ldwɜ:k] *n* *(U)* travaux *mpl* sur le terrain; [research] recherches *fpl* sur le terrain.

field worker *n* [social worker] travailleur *m* social, travailleuse *f* sociale; [researcher] chercheur *m*, -euse *f* de terrain.

fiend [fi:nd] *n* -**1.** [demon] démon *m*, diable *m*; [evil person] monstre *m*. -**2.** *inf* [fanatic, freak] mordu *m*, -e *f*, fana *mf*; tennis ~ fana OR mordu de tennis; a health ~ un maniaque de la santé; dope OR drug ~ toxico *mf*; sex ~ satyre *m*; [in newspaper headline] maniaque *m* sexuel.

fiendish ['fi:ndɪʃ] *adj* -**1.** [fierce - cruelty, look] diabolique, démoniaque. -**2.** *inf* [plan, cunning] diabolique; [very difficult - problem] abominable, atroce; a trick of ~ difficulty un tour extrêmement difficile; to take a ~ delight OR pleasure in doing sthg prendre un plaisir diabolique à faire qqch.

fiendishly ['fi:ndɪʃlɪ] *adv* -**1.** [cruelly] diaboliquement. -**2.** *inf* [extremely]: ~ clever d'une intelligence diabolique; ~ difficult abominablement OR atrocement difficile.

fierce [fɪəs] *adj* -**1.** [animal, person, look, words] féroce. -**2.** [heat, sun] torride; [competition, fighting, loyalty, resistance] acharné; [battle, criticism, desire, hatred, temper] féroce.

fiercely ['fɪəslɪ] *adv* -**1.** *literal* férocement; to look ~ at sb regarder qqn d'un air féroce. -**2.** *fig* [argue, attack, criticize, fight] violemment; [independent] farouchement; to resist ~ résister avec acharnement; to compete ~ se livrer à une concurrence acharnée; it is a ~ competitive business c'est un secteur où la concurrence est acharnée; to be ~ loyal to sb faire preuve d'une loyauté à toute épreuve OR farouche envers qqn.

fierceness ['fɪəsnɪs] *n* -**1.** [of animal, look, person] férocité *f*. -**2.** [of desire] violence *f*; [of sun] ardeur *f*; [of resistance] acharnement *m*; [of criticism] férocité *f*.

fiery ['faɪərɪ] *adj* [heat, sun, coals] ardent; [speech] violent, fougueux; [sky, sunset] embrasé; a ~ red colour une couleur rouge feu; ~ red hair cheveux d'un roux flamboyant; ~ liquor alcool très fort; a ~ curry un curry très épicé OR qui emporte la bouche; to have a ~ temper avoir un tempérament OR caractère fougueux ❑ the ~ cross *Am* la croix en flammes *(symbole du Ku Klux Klan)*.

fiesta [fɪ'estə] *n* fiesta *f*.

FIFA ['fi:fə] (*abbr of* **Fédération Internationale de Football Association**) *pr n* FIFA *f*.

fife [faɪf] *n* MUS fifre *m*.

fifteen [fɪf'ti:n] ◇ *adj* quinze; ~ people quinze personnes; about ~ people une quinzaine de personnes; to be ~ avoir quinze ans.

◇ *n* -**1.** [numeral] quinze *m inv*; about ~ une quinzaine. -**2.** [in rugby] quinze *m*; the opposing ~ l'équipe rivale; the school/Scottish ~ le quinze de l'école/d'Écosse.

◇ *pron* quinze; ~ is not enough quinze, ce n'est pas assez; I need ~ il m'en faut quinze.

fifteenth [fɪf'ti:nθ] ◇ *adj* quinzième; on the ~ day of the month le quinze du mois; Louis the Fifteenth Louis Quinze.

◇ *n* [fraction] quinzième *m*; [in series] quinzième *mf*.

fifth [fɪfθ] ◇ *adj* cinquième; a ~ part un cinquième; the ~ day of the month le cinq du mois; in ~ place à la cinquième place; she came OR was ~ [in race, exam etc] elle est arrivée cinquième; ~ from the end/right cinquième en partant de la fin/droite; on the ~ floor *Br* au cinquième étage; *Am* au quatrième étage; ~ gear AUT cinquième vitesse; ~ form *Br* SCH ≃ classe de seconde ❑ to feel like a ~ wheel *Am* avoir l'impression d'être la cinquième roue du carrosse; Fifth Amendment Cinquième Amendement *m (de la Constitution des États-Unis, permettant à un accusé de ne pas répondre à une question risquant de jouer en sa défaveur)*; I plead the Fifth (Amendment) *hum* ≃ je ne parlerai qu'en présence de mon avocat; Fifth Avenue la cinquième avenue; she's very Fifth Avenue elle est très cinquième avenue *(fait référence à l'élite sociale new-yorkaise)*; the Fifth Republic la Cinquième OR Vᵉ République; George the Fifth Georges Cinq.

◇ *n* -**1.** [day of month] cinq *m inv*; the ~, on the ~ le cinq; the ~ of July, July the ~, July ~ *Am* le cinq juillet; today is the ~ nous sommes le cinq aujourd'hui ❑ the ~ of November *jour anniversaire de la conspiration des poudres aussi appelé Guy Fawkes' Day* || [fraction] cinquième *m*; [in series] cinquième *mf*. -**2.** MUS quinte *f*. -**3.** *Am* [Fifth Amendment]: I'll take the Fifth *Am expression utilisée par une personne appréhendée pour invoquer le Cinquième Amendement*.

fifth column *n* cinquième colonne *f*.

fifth columnist *n* membre *m* de la cinquième colonne.

fifth-generation *adj* COMPUT de cinquième génération.

fifthly ['fɪfθlɪ] *adv* cinquièmement.

fiftieth ['fɪftɪəθ] ◇ *adj* cinquantième.

◇ *n* [fraction] cinquantième *m*; [in series] cinquantième *mf*.

fifty ['fɪftɪ] ◇ *adj* cinquante; ~ people cinquante personnes; about ~ people une cinquantaine de personnes.

◇ *n* -**1.** [numeral] cinquante *m inv*; there are ~ of them il y en a cinquante; he works a ~ hour week il travaille cinquante heures par semaine; about ~ une cinquantaine; to be ~ avoir cinquante ans; the fifties les années cinquante; in the early/late fifties au début/à la fin des années cinquante; the temperature will be in the high fifties la température sera environ de quinze degrés; she is in her fifties elle a dans les cinquante ans; to be in one's early/late fifties avoir une petite cinquantaine/la cinquantaine bien sonnée; to do ~ AUT ≃ faire du quatre-vingts. -**2.** *Am* [money] billet *m* de cinquante (dollars).

◇ *pron* cinquante; ~ is not enough cinquante, ce n'est pas assez; I need ~ il m'en faut cinquante.

◇ *comp*: ~-one cinquante et un; ~-two/-three cinquante-deux/-trois; ~-first cinquante et unième; ~-second cinquante-deuxième; there were ~-odd people at the party il y avait une cinquantaine de personnes à la soirée.

fifty-fifty ◇ *adj*: on a ~ basis moitié-moitié, fifty-fifty; his chances of winning/surviving are ~ il a une chance sur deux de gagner/de s'en tirer; the animal's chances of survival are no more than ~ les chances de survie de l'animal ne dépassent pas cinquante pour cent.

◇ *adv* moitié-moitié, fifty-fifty; let's go ~ partageons moitié-moitié OR fifty-fifty; to go ~ (on sthg with sb) se mettre de moitié (dans qqch avec qqn); I went ~ with my brother on it je me suis mis de moitié avec mon frère.

fig [fɪg] *n* [fruit] figue *f*; ~ (tree) figuier *m*; it's not worth a ~ *inf dated* ça ne vaut pas un radis; I don't give OR care a ~ *inf dated* je m'en moque comme de ma première chemise; I don't give OR care a ~ what she thinks je me contrefiche de ce qu'elle pense.

fight [faɪt] (*pt* & *pp* **fought** [fɔ:t]) ◇ *n* -**1.** [physical] bagarre *f*; [verbal] dispute *f*; [of army, boxer] combat *m*, affrontement *m*; [against disease, poverty etc] lutte *f*, combat *m*; do you want a ~? tu veux te battre?; he enjoys a good ~ [physical] il aime la bagarre OR les bagarres; [verbal] il aime les disputes; [boxing match] il aime les bons combats de boxe; to have OR to get into a ~ with sb [physical] se battre avec qqn; [verbal] se disputer avec qqn; they are always having ~s ils sont toujours en train de se bagarrer OR se disputer; you've been in a ~ again tu t'es encore battu OR bagarré; to pick a ~ (with sb) chercher la bagarre (avec qqn); are you trying to pick a ~ (with me)? tu me provoques?, tu cherches la bagarre?; a ~ to the death une lutte à mort; are you going to the ~? [boxing match] est-ce que tu vas voir le combat?; to put up a (good) ~ (bien) se défendre; the boxer put up a great ~ le boxeur s'est défendu avec acharnement; to make a ~ of it se défendre avec acharnement; to give in without (putting up) a ~ capituler sans (opposer de) résistance; he realized he would have a ~ on his hands il s'est rendu compte qu'il allait devoir lutter. -**2.** [fighting spirit] combativité *f*; there's not much ~ left in him il a perdu beaucoup de sa combativité; the news of the defeat took all the ~ out of us la nouvelle de la défaite nous a fait perdre tout cœur à nous battre OR nous a enlevé le courage de nous battre; to show ~ montrer de la combativité, ne pas se laisser faire.

◇ *vi* [physically - person, soldier] se battre; [- boxer] combattre; [- two boxers] s'affronter; [verbally] se disputer; [against disease, injustice etc] lutter; to ~ to the death/the last se battre à mort/jusqu'à la fin; he fought in the war il a fait la guerre; they were ~ing with each other ils étaient en train de se battre OR se disputer; they were always ~ing over OR about money ils se disputaient toujours pour des problèmes d'argent; the children were ~ing over the last biscuit les enfants se disputaient pour avoir le dernier biscuit; to ~ for one's rights/to clear one's name lutter pour ses droits/pour prouver son innocence; they fought for the leadership of the party ils se sont disputé la direction du parti; he fought for breath il se débattait OR il luttait pour respirer ❑ to ~ for one's life [ill person] lutter contre la mort; *fig* [in race, competition] se battre avec la dernière énergie, se démener ❑ to go down ~ing se battre jusqu'au bout; to ~ shy of doing sthg tout faire pour éviter de faire qqch; to ~ shy of sb éviter qqn.

◇ *vt* [person, animal] se battre contre; [boxer] combattre (contre), se battre contre; [disease, terrorism etc] lutter contre, combattre; to ~ a **duel** se battre en duel; to ~ **a battle** livrer (une) bataille; **I'm not going to ~ your battles for you** *fig* c'est à toi de te débrouiller; to ~ **a fire** lutter contre un incendie; to ~ **a court case** [subj: lawyer] défendre une cause; [subj: plaintiff, defendant] être en procès; to ~ **an election** [politician] se présenter à une élection; to ~ **an election campaign** *Br* mener une campagne électorale; **John Brown is ~ing Smithtown for the Tories** *Br* John Brown se présente à Smithtown pour les conservateurs; **I'll ~ you for it** on réglera ça par une bagarre; to ~ **a losing battle (against sthg)** livrer une bataille perdue d'avance (contre qqch); **she fought the urge to laugh** elle essayait de réprimer une forte envie de rire; **don't ~ it** [pain, emotion] n'essaie pas de lutter; **you've got to ~ it** il faut que tu te battes; to ~ **sb/a newspaper in court** emmener qqn/un journal devant les tribunaux, faire un procès à qqn/à un journal; to ~ **one's way through the crowd/the undergrowth** se frayer un passage à travers la foule/les broussailles; to ~ **one's way to the top of one's profession** se battre pour atteindre le sommet de sa profession; **he fought his way back to power** c'est en luttant qu'il est revenu au pouvoir.

◆ **fight back** ◇ *vi insep* [in physical or verbal dispute] se défendre, riposter; [in boxing, football match] se reprendre; [in race] revenir.

◇ *vt sep* [tears] refouler; [despair, fear, laughter] réprimer.

◆ **fight off** *vt sep* [attack, enemy, advances] repousser; [sleep] combattre; [disease] résister à; **she has to ~ men off** [has a lot of admirers] elle a des admirateurs à la pelle OR à ne plus savoir qu'en faire.

◆ **fight on** *vi insep* continuer le combat.

◆ **fight out** *vt sep*: **just leave them to ~ it out** laisse-les se bagarrer et régler cela entre eux.

fightback ['faɪtbæk] *n* reprise *f*.

fighter ['faɪtəʳ] ◇ *n* -**1.** [person who fights] combattant *m*, -e *f*; [boxer] boxeur *m*; **he's a ~** *fig* c'est un battant. -**2.** [plane] avion *m* de chasse, chasseur *m*.

◇ *comp* [pilot] de chasseur, d'avion de chasse; [squadron] de chasseurs, d'avions de chasse; [plane] de chasse.

fighter-bomber *n* MIL chasseur *m* bombardier.

fighting ['faɪtɪŋ] ◇ *n (U)* [physical] bagarre *f*, bagarres *fpl*; [verbal] dispute *f*, disputes *fpl*, bagarre *f*, bagarres *fpl*; MIL combat *m*, combats *mpl*; ~ **broke out between police and fans** une bagarre s'est déclenchée entre la police et les fans; **the ~ is now at its height** on est au plus fort du combat; **there has been fierce ~ in all parts of the country** des combats acharnés ont eu lieu dans l'ensemble du pays; ~ **is not allowed in the playground** il est interdit de se bagarrer dans la cour.

◇ *comp* [forces, unit] de combat; ~ **cock** coq *m* de combat; ~ **men** MIL combattants *mpl*; **to be in with** OR **to have a ~ chance** avoir de bonnes chances; to be ~ **fit** être dans une forme éblouissante, avoir la forme olympique; ~ **spirit** esprit *m* combatif; **that's ~ talk!** c'est un langage offensif!

fig leaf *n* BOT feuille *f* de figuier; [on statue, in painting] feuille *f* de vigne; *fig* camouflage *m*.

figment ['fɪgmənt] *n*: **a ~ of the imagination** un produit OR une création de l'imagination.

figurative ['fɪgərətɪv] *adj* -**1.** [language, meaning] figuré. -**2.** ART figuratif.

figuratively ['fɪgərətɪvlɪ] *adv* au (sens) figuré.

figure [*Br* 'fɪgəʳ, *Am* 'fɪgjər] ◇ *n* -**1.** [number, symbol] chiffre *m*; [amount] somme *f*; **unemployment ~s** chiffres du chômage; **trade ~s** résultats *mpl* financiers; **four-/five-/six-~ number** nombre de quatre/cinq/six chiffres; **his salary is in** OR **runs to six ~s** ≃ il gagne plus d'un million de francs; **in round ~s** en chiffres ronds; **to be in double ~s** [inflation, unemployment] dépasser la barre OR le seuil des 10 %; **he refused to put a ~ on his proposals** [give cost] il a refusé d'évaluer le coût de OR de chiffrer ses propositions; **I couldn't put a ~ on the number of people there** je ne pourrais pas dire combien de personnes il y avait; **she's good at ~s** elle est bonne en calcul; **he has no head for ~s** il n'est pas doué en calcul; **have you done your ~s?** as-tu fait tes calculs?; **name your ~** [to purchaser, seller] quel est votre prix?; **the boss told him to name his ~** [for pay rise] le patron lui a demandé combien il voulait. -**2.** [human shape] ligne *f*; **she is always worrying about her ~** elle s'inquiète constamment pour sa ligne; **she has a good ~** elle a une jolie silhouette, elle est bien faite; **to look after one's ~** faire attention à sa ligne; **think of your ~!** pense à ta ligne!; **to keep/to lose one's ~** garder/perdre la ligne ❑ **a fine ~ of a woman/man** une femme/un homme qui a de l'allure; **to cut a fine/poor ~** faire bonne/mauvaise impression; **he was a sorry ~ standing there on the doorstep** [wet, dirty etc] il faisait piètre figure, debout sur les marches. -**3.** [human outline] silhouette *f*; **a ~ appeared on the horizon** une silhouette est apparue à l'horizon. -**4.** [character in novel, film etc] personnage *m*; **the group of ~s on the left** le groupe de personnes à gauche ❑ **public/key ~** personnage public/central; ~ **of fun** objet *m* de risée OR ridicule. -**5.** [in geometry, skating, dancing] figure *f*; ~ **of eight** *Br*, ~ **eight** *Am* huit *m*. -**6.** [illustration, diagram] figure *f*. -**7.** [rhetorical]: ~ **of speech** figure *f* de rhétorique; **it was just a ~ of speech** ce n'était qu'une façon de parler. -**8.** [statuette] figurine *f*.

◇ *vi* -**1.** [appear] figurer, apparaître; **does he ~ in your plans?** est-ce qu'il figure dans tes projets?; **where do I ~ in all this?** quelle est ma place dans tout cela?; **guilt ~s quite a lot in his novels** la culpabilité a OR tient une place relativement importante dans ses romans; **she ~d prominently in the scandal** elle a été très impliquée dans le scandale. -**2.** *inf Am* [make sense] sembler logique OR normal; **it just doesn't ~** ça n'a pas de sens; **it ~s that he'd do that** ça paraît logique OR normal qu'il ait fait ça; **that ~s!** c'était fatal!, ça devait arriver! ❑ **go ~!** qui aurait imaginé ça?

◇ *vt* -**1.** *inf* [reckon] penser; **we ~d something like that must have happened** nous pensions OR nous nous doutions bien que quelque chose de ce genre était arrivé. -**2.** *inf Am* = **figure out 1**. -**3.** [decorate - silk] brocher; **~d velvet** *Br* velours *m* figuré. -**4.** MUS chiffrer.

◆ **figure on** *inf vt insep* [plan on] compter; **when are you figuring on leaving?** quand comptes-tu OR penses-tu partir?; **you didn't ~ on that (happening), did you?** tu ne comptais OR pensais pas que ça arriverait, hein?, tu ne comptais pas là-dessus, hein?

◆ **figure out** *vt sep* -**1.** [understand - person] arriver à comprendre; **we couldn't ~ it out** nous n'arrivions pas à comprendre OR saisir. -**2.** [work out - sum, cost etc] calculer; ~ **it out for yourself** réfléchis donc un peu; **she still hasn't ~d out how to do it** elle n'a toujours pas trouvé comment faire.

figurehead ['fɪgəhed] *n* NAUT figure *f* de proue; *fig* [of organization, society] représentant *m* nominal, représentante *f* nominale; *pej* homme *m* de paille.

figure-hugging [-,hʌgɪŋ] *adj* [dress] moulant.

figure-skate *vi* faire des figures en patinage, faire du patinage artistique.

figure-skater *n* patineur *m*, -euse *f* artistique.

figure-skating ◇ *n* patinage *m* artistique.

◇ *comp* [champion, championship] de patinage artistique.

figurine [*Br* 'fɪgəriːn, *Am* ,fɪgjə'riːn] *n* figurine *f*.

Fiji ['fiːdʒiː] *pr n* Fidji; **in ~** à Fidji; **the ~ Islands** les îles *fpl* Fidji; **in the ~ Islands** aux îles Fidji.

Fijian [,fiː'dʒiːən] ◇ *n* -**1.** [person] Fidjien *m*, -enne *f*. -**2.** LING fidjien *m*.

◇ *adj* fidjien.

filament ['fɪləmənt] *n* BOT & ELEC filament *m*.

filbert ['fɪlbət] *n* [nut] *espèce de grosse noisette*.

filch *inf* [fɪltʃ] *vt* [steal] piquer.

filching *inf* ['fɪltʃɪŋ] *n* [theft] fauche *f*; **there's a lot of ~ from hotels** les gens piquent beaucoup dans les hôtels.

file [faɪl] ◇ *n* -**1.** [folder] chemise *f*; [box] classeur *m*; **accordeon ~** classeur accordéon. -**2.** [dossier, documents] dossier *m*; [series or system of files] fichier *m*; **this ~ belongs in the customer ~** ce dossier va dans le fichier clients; **to have/to keep sthg on ~** avoir/garder qqch dans ses dossiers; **it's on ~** c'est dans les dossiers, c'est classé; **we have placed your CV on ~** OR **in our ~s** nous avons classé votre CV dans nos dossiers; **these papers are for the ~** ces papiers sont à mettre dans les dossiers OR sont à classer; **to have/to keep a ~ on** avoir/garder un dossier sur; **to open/to close a ~ on** ouvrir/fermer un dossier sur; **the police have closed their ~ on the case** la police a classé l'affaire; **he's been on our ~** OR **~s for a long time** cela fait longtemps qu'il est dans nos dossiers. -**3.** COMPUT fichier *m*; **data on ~** données *fpl* sur fichier; **data ~** fichier de données. -**4.** [row, line] file *f*; **in single** OR **Indian ~** en OR à la file indienne. -**5.** [for metal, fingernails] lime *f*.

◇ *comp*: ~ **copy** copie *f* à classer; ~ **name** COMPUT nom *m* de fichier.

◇ *vt* -**1.** [documents, information] classer; **to be ~d under a letter/subject** être classé sous une lettre/dans une catégorie. -**2.** JUR: **to ~ a suit against sb** intenter un procès à qqn; **to ~ a complaint (with the police/the manager)** déposer une plainte (au commissariat/auprès du directeur); **to ~ a claim** déposer une demande; **to ~ a claim for damages** intenter un procès en dommages-intérêts; **to ~ a petition in bankruptcy** déposer son bilan. -**3.** [metal] limer; **to ~ one's fingernails** se limer les ongles; **to ~ through sthg** limer qqch.

◇ *vi* -**1.** [classify documents, information] faire du classement. -**2.** [walk one behind the other]: **they ~d up the hill** ils ont monté la colline en file (indienne) OR les uns derrière les autres; **the troops ~d under the bridge** les soldats sont passés sous le pont en file indienne OR à la file; **the troops ~d past the general** les troupes ont défilé devant le général; **the crowd ~d slowly past the coffin** la foule a défilé lentement devant le cercueil; **to ~ into a room** entrer dans une pièce à la OR en file; **to ~ out of a room** sortir d'une pièce à la OR en file; **they all ~d in/out** ils sont tous entrés/sortis à la file.

◆ **file away** *vt sep* -**1.** [documents] classer. -**2.** [rough edges] polir à la lime; [excess material] enlever à la lime.

◆ **file down** *vt sep* [metal, fingernails, rough surface] polir à la lime.

◆ **file for** *vt insep*: **to ~ for divorce** demander le divorce.

file cabinet *n Am* classeur *m*.

file card *n* fiche *f* (de classeur).

file clerk *n Am* documentaliste *mf*.

file management *n* COMPUT gestion *f* de fichiers.

file server *n* COMPUT serveur *m* de fichiers.

filet *Am* = **fillet**.

filial ['fɪljəl] *adj* [devotion, respect] filial.

filibuster ['fɪlɪbʌstəʳ] POL ◇ *n* obstruction *f* (parlementaire).

◇ *vi* faire de l'obstruction; **~ing tactics** tactiques obstructionnistes.

◇ *vt* [legislation] faire obstruction à.

filibusterer ['fɪlɪbʌstərəʳ] *n* POL obstructionniste *mf*.

filibustering ['fɪlɪbʌstərɪŋ] *n* POL obstructionnisme *m*.

filigree ['fɪlɪgriː] ◇ *n* filigrane *m*.
◇ *adj* en OR de filigrane.

filing ['faɪlɪŋ] *n* **-1.** [of documents] classement *m*; I do the ~ je m'occupe du classement; I still have a lot of ~ to do j'ai encore beaucoup de choses à classer. **-2.** JUR [of complaint, claim] dépôt *m*.

filing cabinet *n* classeur *m*.

filing clerk *n* documentaliste *mf*.

filings ['faɪlɪŋz] *npl* [of metal] limaille *f*.

Filipino [ˌfɪlɪ'piːnəʊ] (*pl* **Filipinos**) ◇ *n* **-1.** [person] Philippin *m*. **-2.** LING = **Tagalog**.
◇ *adj* philippin.

fill [fɪl] ◇ *n*: to eat one's ~ manger à sa faim, se rassasier; to drink one's ~ boire tout son soûl; when they had eaten their ~ quand ils eurent mangé tout leur content; a ~ of tobacco [for pipe] une pipe de tabac ❑ I've had my ~ of it/her *inf* j'en ai assez/assez d'elle.
◇ *vt* **-1.** [cup, glass, bottle] remplir; [room, streets - subj: people, smoke, laughter] envahir; [chocolates] fourrer; [cake, pie] garnir; [vegetables] farcir; [pipe] bourrer; *fig*: to ~ a page with writing remplir une page d'écriture; wind ~ed the sails le vent a gonflé les voiles; she ~ed his head with nonsense elle lui a bourré le crâne de bêtises; to be ~ed with people [room, street] être plein OR rempli de gens; to be ~ed with horror/admiration être rempli d'horreur/d'admiration; she was ~ed with horror at the news cette nouvelle l'a remplie d'horreur; it ~ed me with sorrow cela m'a profondément peiné; such were the thoughts that ~ed his mind telles étaient les pensées qui occupaient son esprit. **-2.** [plug - hole] boucher; [- tooth] plomber; to have a tooth ~ed se faire plomber une dent; the product ~ed a gap in the market le produit a comblé un vide sur le marché ❑ ...or I'll ~ you full of lead! [shoot]...ou je te farcis le crâne de plomb!; that's ~ed a hole! *inf* [satisfied hunger] ça cale! **-3.** [position, vacancy - subj: employee] occuper; [- subj: employer] pourvoir; to ~ the office of president remplir les fonctions de président; the post has been ~ed le poste a été pris OR pourvu. **-4.** [occupy - time] occuper. **-5.** [meet - requirement] répondre à; to ~ the bill *inf* faire l'affaire. **-6.** [supply]: to ~ an order [in bar, restaurant] apporter ce qui a été commandé; [for stationery, equipment etc] livrer une commande; to ~ a prescription préparer une ordonnance.
◇ *vi* [room, bath, bus] se remplir; [sail] se gonfler; her eyes ~ed with tears ses yeux se sont remplis de larmes.

◆ **fill in** ◇ *vi insep* faire un remplacement; I'm often asked to ~ in on me demande souvent de faire des remplacements; to ~ in for sb remplacer qqn; I'll ~ in for you if necessary je te remplacerai si besoin est.
◇ *vt sep* **-1.** [hole, window, door] boucher; he ~ed it in in green [outline] il l'a colorié OR rempli en vert; to ~ in the gaps in one's knowledge combler ses lacunes. **-2.** [complete - form, questionnaire] compléter, remplir; [insert - name, missing word] insérer. **-3.** [bring up to date] mettre au courant; to ~ sb in on sthg mettre qqn au courant de qqch. **-4.** [use - time] occuper; he's just ~ing in time il fait ça pour s'occuper OR pour occuper son temps; I've got a couple of months to ~ in je dois occuper mon temps pendant environ deux mois.

◆ **fill out** ◇ *vi insep* **-1.** [cheeks] se remplir; [person] s'étoffer. **-2.** [sails] se gonfler.
◇ *vt sep* **-1.** [complete - form] remplir. **-2.** [pad out - essay, speech] étoffer.

◆ **fill up** ◇ *vi insep* se remplir; to ~ up with petrol faire le plein d'essence; don't ~ up on biscuits, you two! ne vous gavez pas de biscuits, vous deux!
◇ *vt sep* **-1.** [make full] remplir; [person with food] rassasier; he ~ed the car up il a fait le plein (d'essence); ~ her OR it up, please AUT le plein, s'il vous plaît. **-2.** [use - day, time] occuper. **-3.** = **fill out** *vt sep* **1**.

filler ['fɪlə^r] *n* **-1.** [for holes, cracks] mastic *m*; [for cavity, open space] matière *f* de remplissage. **-2.** [funnel] entonnoir *m*. **-3.** [in quilt, bean bag etc] matière *f* de rembourrage; [in cigar] tripe *f*. **-4.** PRESS & TV bouche-trou *m*. **-5.** LING: ~ (word) mot *m* de remplissage.

filler cap *n* bouchon *m* du réservoir d'essence.

fillet ['fɪlɪt] ◇ *n* CULIN filet *m*; two pieces of ~ steak deux biftecks dans le filet; ~ steak is expensive le filet de bœuf est cher.
◇ *vt* [meat, fish - prepare] préparer; [cut into fillets - fish] faire des filets dans, lever les filets de; [- meat] faire des steaks dans; ~ed sole filets *mpl* de sole.

fill-in *inf n* [person] remplaçant *m*, -e *f*.

filling ['fɪlɪŋ] ◇ *adj* [foodstuff] qui rassasie, nourrissant; it was very ~ cela m'a rassasié.
◇ *n* **-1.** [in tooth] plombage *m*; I had to have a ~ il a fallu qu'on me fasse un plombage. **-2.** CULIN [for cake, pie - sweet] garniture *f*; [for vegetables, poultry - savoury] farce *f*; they all have different ~s [chocolates] ils sont tous fourrés différemment.

filling station *n* station-service *f*, station *f* d'essence.

fillip ['fɪlɪp] *n* coup *m* de fouet; to give sb/sthg a ~ donner un coup de fouet à qqn/qqch.

filly ['fɪlɪ] (*pl* **fillies**) *n* **-1.** [horse] pouliche *f*. **-2.** *inf dated* OR *hum* [girl] fille *f*; she's a fine young ~, isn't she? c'est un beau brin de fille, non?

film [fɪlm] ◇ *n* **-1.** [thin layer - of oil, mist, dust] film *m*, pellicule *f*; plastic ~ film plastique. **-2.** PHOT pellicule *f*; I left a ~ to be developed j'ai laissé une pellicule à développer; a roll of ~ une pellicule. **-3.** CIN film *m*; the ~ of the book le film tiré du livre; full-length/short-length ~ (film) long/court métrage *m*; to shoot OR to make a ~ (about sthg) tourner OR faire un film (sur qqch); the ~'s on at the local cinema le film passe au cinéma du coin; to be in ~s faire du cinéma.
◇ *comp* [critic, studio, producer] de cinéma; [clip, premiere, sequence] d'un film; [archives, award] cinématographique; ~ buff *inf* cinéphile *mf*, fana *mf* de cinéma; the ~ crew les techniciens du film; a ~ crew une équipe de cinéma; ~ director metteur *m* en scène; the ~ industry l'industrie *f* cinématographique OR du cinéma; ~ library cinémathèque *f*; ~ maker cinéaste *mf*; ~ rights droits *mpl* d'adaptation cinématographique; ~ script scénario *m*; ~ set plateau *m* de tournage; ~ speed PHOT sensibilité *f* d'une pellicule; ~ star star *f* OR vedette *f* de cinéma; ~ strip bande *f* (de film) fixe.
◇ *vt* [event, people] filmer; CIN [scene] filmer, tourner.
◇ *vi* **-1.** [record] filmer; CIN tourner; they started ~ing at 7a.m. ils ont commencé à tourner OR le tournage a commencé à 7 h; to ~ well [be photogenic] bien passer à l'écran. **-2.** = **film over**.

◆ **film over** *vi insep* s'embuer, se voiler; to ~ over with tears s'embuer de larmes.

filmgoer ['fɪlmˌgəʊə^r] *n* amateur *m* de cinéma, cinéphile *mf*; she is a regular ~ elle va régulièrement au cinéma.

filmic ['fɪlmɪk] *adj* cinématographique.

filming ['fɪlmɪŋ] *n* CIN tournage *m*.

filmography [fɪl'mɒgrəfɪ] *n* filmographie *f*.

filmset ['fɪlmset] *vt Br* photocomposer.

filmsetter ['fɪlmˌsetə^r] *n Br* [machine] photocomposeuse *f*; [person] photocompositeur *m*.

filmsetting ['fɪlmˌsetɪŋ] *n Br* photocomposition *f*.

filmy ['fɪlmɪ] *adj* [material] léger, vaporeux, aérien.

filo ['fiːləʊ] *n* CULIN: ~ (pastry) *pâte feuilletée très fine utilisée dans les pâtisseries moyen-orientales*.

Filofax® ['faɪləʊfæks] *n* agenda *m* classeur.

filter ['fɪltə^r] ◇ *n* **-1.** CHEM, MECH & PHOT filtre *m*; coffee ~ filtre à café. **-2.** *Br* AUT flèche *f* lumineuse *(autorisant le dégagement des voitures à droite ou à gauche)*.
◇ *comp*: ~ coffee café *m* filtre; ~ lane *Br* AUT voie *f* de dégagement.
◇ *vt* [coffee, oil, water etc] filtrer.
◇ *vi* **-1.** [liquid, light] filtrer. **-2.** *Br* AUT suivre la voie de dégagement; the cars ~ed to the left les voitures ont suivi la voie de dégagement vers la gauche.

◆ **filter in** *vi insep* [light, sound, information, news] filtrer; [people] entrer petit à petit.

◆ **filter out** ◇ *vt sep* [sediment, impurities] éliminer par filtrage OR filtration.
◇ *vi insep* [people] sortir petit à petit.

◆ **filter through** *vi insep literal* & *fig* filtrer.

filter bed *n* couche *f* de filtration.

filter paper *n* papier *m* filtre.

filter tip *n* [tip] (bout *m*) filtre *m*; [cigarette] cigarette *f* (bout) filtre.

filter-tipped *adj* [cigarette] (bout) filtre.

filth [fɪlθ] *n* *(U)* **-1.** [on skin, clothes] crasse *f*; [in street] saleté *f*. **-2.** [obscene books, films etc] ordures *fpl*, obscénités *fpl*; [obscene words, jokes] grossièretés *fpl*, obscénités *fpl*; it's sheer ~ [film, book] c'est un recueil d'ordures OR d'obscénités. **-3.** ▽ *Br*: the ~ [police] les flics *mpl*.

filthy ['fɪlθɪ] (*compar* **filthier**, *superl* **filthiest**)
◇ *adj* **-1.** [dirty] dégoûtant, crasseux; you ~ pig! espèce de gros dégoûtant! **-2.** [obscene, smutty - language, talk, jokes] grossier, obscène, ordurier; [- person] grossier, dégoûtant; [- film, book, photograph] obscène, dégoûtant; [- habit] dégoûtant; to have a ~ mind avoir l'esprit mal tourné; you ~ pig! espèce de gros dégoûtant! **-3.** *inf* [nasty - temper, day] atroce, abominable; [- trick] vicieux, méchant; [- look] méchant; what ~ weather! quel sale temps!; he's in a ~ mood il est de sale humeur, il est d'une humeur massacrante.
◇ *adv*: to be ~ rich *inf* être plein aux as.

filtrate ['fɪltreɪt] *n* filtrat *m*.

filtration [fɪl'treɪʃn] *n* filtrage *m*, filtration *f*.

fin [fɪn] *n* **-1.** [of fish] nageoire *f*; [of shark] aileron *m*; [of boat] dérive *f*. **-2.** [of aircraft, spacecraft] empennage *m*; [of rocket, bomb] ailette *f*. **-3.** AUT [of radiator] ailette *f*. **-4.** [for swimming]: ~s palmes *fpl*.

final ['faɪnl] ◇ *adj* **-1.** [last] dernier; the ~ instalment [of hire purchase agreement] le dernier versement, le versement libératoire; to put the ~ touches to sthg mettre la dernière main OR touche à qqch, mettre la touche finale à qqch; ~ demand dernier rappel *m*; ~ date date *f* limite; the ~ irony le comble de l'ironie; ~ examinations UNIV examens *mpl* de dernière année; a ~-year student UNIV un étudiant en OR de dernière année. **-2.** [definitive] définitif; [score] final; that's my ~ offer c'est ma dernière offre; I'm not moving, and that's ~! je ne bouge pas, un point c'est tout!; the referee's decision is ~ la décision de l'arbitre est sans appel; is that your ~ answer? c'est ta réponse définitive?; nothing's ~ yet il n'y a encore rien de définitif, rien n'est encore arrêté. **-3.** PHILOS [cause] final; GRAMM [clause] de but, final.
◇ *n* **-1.** SPORT finale *f*; to get to the ~ arriver en finale; are they in the ~ OR ~s? est-ce qu'ils sont en finale?; how far did they get in the ~s? jusqu'où sont-ils arrivés en finale OR dans les épreuves de finale? **-2.** PRESS dernière édition *f*; late ~ dernière édition du soir.

◆ **finals** *npl* UNIV examens *mpl* de dernière année; to sit one's ~s passer ses examens de dernière année; how did you do in your ~s? comment ça a marché à tes examens?

finale [fɪ'nɑːlɪ] *n* MUS finale *m*; *fig* final *m*, finale *m*; grand ~ apothéose *f*.

finalist ['faɪnəlɪst] *n* [in competition] finaliste *mf*; cup ~ finaliste de la coupe.

finality [faɪ'nælətɪ] *n* [of decision, death] irrévocabilité *f*, caractère *m* définitif; there was a note of ~ in his voice il y avait quelque chose d'irrévocable dans sa voix.

finalization [ˌfaɪnəlaɪ'zeɪʃn] *n* [of details, plans, arrangements] mise *f* au point; [of deal, agreement] conclusion *f*; work involved in the ~ of preparations le travail nécessaire pour mettre la dernière main OR la dernière touche OR la touche finale aux préparatifs.

finalize, -ise ['faɪnəlaɪz] *vt* [details, plans] mettre au point; [deal, decision, agreement] mener à bonne fin; [preparations] mettre la dernière main OR touche à, mettre la touche finale à; [date] arrêter; **that hasn't been ~d yet** cela n'a pas encore été décidé OR arrêté; **nothing has been ~d yet** rien n'a encore été décidé OR arrêté.

finally ['faɪnəlɪ] *adv* **-1.** [eventually] finalement, enfin; **when he ~ arrived** finalement, quand il est arrivé; **she ~ agreed to come** elle a fini par accepter de venir; **~!** enfin! **-2.** [lastly] enfin; **and, ~, I would like to say...** et pour finir je voudrais dire que...; **we are, ~, only human** nous ne sommes, en fin de compte, que des hommes. **-3.** [irrevocably] définitivement; **no, she said ~** non, dit-elle fermement.

finance [*n* 'faɪnæns, *vb* faɪ'næns] ◇ *n (U)* [money management] finance *f*; [financing] financement *m*; **in the world of French ~** dans le monde français de la finance; **it's a problem of ~** c'est un problème de financement; **through lack of ~** à cause d'un manque de financement ❑ **high ~** la haute finance; **Minister/Ministry of Finance** ministre *m*/ministère *m* des Finances.

◇ *vt* financer; [project, enterprise] financer, trouver les fonds pour.

◆ **finances** *npl* finances *fpl*; **my ~s are a bit low just now** je ne suis pas très en fonds en ce moment.

finance bill *n* POL projet *m* de loi de finances.

finance company *n* établissement *m* de crédit.

finance director *n* directeur *m* financier.

finance house *n société britannique de financement pour les achats à crédit.*

financial [fɪ'nænʃl] *adj* financier; **but does it make ~ sense?** mais est-ce que c'est avantageux OR intéressant du point de vue financier?; **~ adviser** conseiller *m* financier; **~ backer** bailleur *m* de fonds; **~ director** directeur *m* financier.

financially [fɪ'nænʃəlɪ] *adv* financièrement; **are they ~ sound?** est-ce qu'ils ont une bonne assise financière?; **he's ~ naive** il est naïf sur les questions d'argent.

Financial Times *pr n*: **the ~** *quotidien britannique d'information financière.*

FINANCIAL TIMES:
Le «Financial Times» est un quotidien britannique de qualité spécialisé dans l'actualité financière et économique; il est reconnaissable à la couleur rose de son papier. Il existe une édition internationale, diffusée notamment en Allemagne et en France.

---

financial year *n*: **the ~** [in business] l'exercice *m* financier; [in politics] l'année *f* budgétaire.

FINANCIAL YEAR:
Pour les impôts sur le revenu en Grande-Bretagne, l'année fiscale commence le 5 avril.

---

financier [fɪ'nænsɪəʳ] *n* financier *m*.

finch [fɪntʃ] *n* fringillidé *m spec*; [goldfinch] chardonneret *m*; [chaffinch] pinson *m*; [bullfinch] bouvreuil *m*.

find [faɪnd] (*pt* & *pp* found [faʊnd]) ◇ *vt* **-1.** [by searching] trouver; [lost thing, person] retrouver; **I can't ~ it anywhere** je ne le trouve nulle part; **did you ~ what you were looking for?** as-tu trouvé ce que tu cherchais?; **she couldn't ~ anything to say** elle ne trouvait rien à dire; **the police could ~ no reason** OR **explanation for his disappearance** la police n'arrivait pas à expliquer sa disparition; **I never did ~ those earrings** je n'ai jamais pu trouver ces boucles d'oreilles; **the missing airmen were found alive** les aviateurs disparus ont été retrouvés sains et saufs; **I can't ~ my place** [in book] je ne sais plus où j'en suis; **my wallet/he was nowhere to be found** mon portefeuille/il était introuvable || [look for, fetch] chercher; **~ and replace** COMPUT chercher OR rechercher et remplacer; **he went to ~ help/a doctor** il est allé chercher de l'aide/un médecin; **go and ~ me a pair of scissors** va me chercher une paire de ciseaux; **could you ~ me a cloth?** tu peux me trouver un chiffon?; **he said he'd try to ~ me a job** il a dit qu'il essaierait de me trouver un travail; **to ~ the time/money to do sthg** trouver le temps de/l'argent nécessaire pour faire qqch; **to ~ the courage/strength to do sthg** trouver le courage/la force de faire qqch ❑ **to ~ one's feet** [in new job, situation] prendre ses repères; **I'm still ~ing my feet** je ne suis pas encore complètement dans le bain; **she couldn't ~ it in her heart** OR **herself to say no** elle n'a pas eu le cœur de dire non; **the bullet found its mark** la balle a atteint son but; **to ~ one's way** trouver son chemin; **I'll ~ my own way out** je trouverai la sortie tout seul; **she found her way back home** elle a réussi à rentrer chez elle; **somehow, the book had found its way into my room** sans que je sache comment, le livre s'était retrouvé dans ma chambre. **-2.** [come across by chance - answer, solution, error] trouver; [- place, restaurant] trouver; **we left everything as we found it** nous avons tout laissé dans l'état où nous l'avions trouvé; **we found this wonderful little bistro on our last visit** nous avons découvert un adorable petit bistro lors de notre dernière visite; **you won't ~ a better bargain anywhere** nulle part, vous ne trouverez meilleur prix; **this bird is found all over Britain** on trouve cet oiseau dans toute la Grande-Bretagne; **the complete list is to be found on page 18** la liste complète se trouve page 18; **I found him at home** je l'ai trouvé chez lui; **I found her waiting outside** je l'ai trouvée qui attendait dehors; **you'll ~ someone else** tu trouveras quelqu'un d'autre; **to ~ happiness/peace** trouver le bonheur/la paix ❑ **I take people as I ~ them** je prends les gens comme ils sont; **I hope this letter ~s you in good health** j'espère que vous allez bien. **-3.** [expressing an opinion, personal view] trouver; **I don't ~ that funny at all** je ne trouve pas ça drôle du tout; **I ~ her very pretty** je la trouve très jolie; **she ~s it very difficult/impossible to talk about it** il lui est très difficile/impossible d'en parler; **he ~s it very hard/impossible to make friends** il a beaucoup de mal à/il n'arrive pas à se faire des amis; **I ~ it hot/cold in here** je trouve qu'il fait chaud/froid ici; **how did you ~ your new boss/your steak?** comment avez-vous trouvé votre nouveau patron/votre steak? ❑ **Rovers have been found wanting** OR **lacking in defence** les Rovers ont fait preuve de faiblesse au niveau de la défense. **-4.** [discover, learn] constater; **I found (that) the car wouldn't start** j'ai constaté que la voiture ne voulait pas démarrer; **they came back to ~ the house had been burgled** à leur retour, ils ont constaté que la maison avait été cambriolée; **I ~ I have time on my hands now that I am no longer working** je m'aperçois que j'ai du temps à moi maintenant que je ne travaille plus; **I think you'll ~ I'm right** je pense que tu t'apercevras que j'ai raison. **-5.** JUR: **to ~ sb guilty/innocent** déclarer qqn coupable/non coupable; **how do you ~ the accused?** déclarez-vous l'accusé coupable ou non coupable?; **the court found that the evidence was inconclusive** le tribunal a déclaré que les preuves n'étaient pas suffisantes. **-6.** *dated* OR *fml* [provide - one's own tools, uniform] fournir; **£65 a week all found** 65 livres par semaine nourri et logé. **-7.** [reflexive use]: **to ~ o.s.**: **I woke up to ~ myself on a ship** je me suis réveillé sur un bateau; **he found himself out of a job** il s'est retrouvé sans emploi; **I ~/found myself in an impossible situation** je me trouve/me suis retrouvé dans une situation impossible; **I ~ myself unable to agree to your request** *fml* je me vois dans l'impossibilité d'accéder à votre demande; **she found herself forced to retaliate** elle s'est trouvée dans l'obligation de riposter.

◇ *vi* JUR: **to ~ for/against the plaintiff** prononcer en faveur de l'accusation/de la défense.

◇ *n* [object] trouvaille *f*; [person] merveille *f*.

◆ **find out** ◇ *vi insep* **-1.** [investigate, make enquiries] se renseigner; **to ~ out about sthg** se renseigner sur qqch. **-2.** [learn, discover]: **his wife/his boss found out** sa femme/son chef a tout découvert; **his wife found out about his affair** sa femme a découvert qu'il avait une liaison; **what if the police ~ out?** et si la police l'apprend?; **I didn't ~ out about the party in time** on ne m'a pas mis au courant de la fête à temps; **I didn't ~ out about it in time** je ne l'ai pas su à temps.

◇ *vt sep* **-1.** [learn, discover - truth, real identity] découvrir; [- answer, phone number] trouver; [- by making enquiries, reading instructions] se renseigner sur; **what have you found out about him/it?** qu'est-ce que tu as découvert sur lui/là-dessus?; **can you ~ out the date of the meeting for me?** est-ce que tu peux te renseigner sur la date de la réunion?; **when I found out the date of the meeting** quand j'ai appris la date de la réunion; **to ~ out how to do sthg/what sb is really like** découvrir comment faire qqch/la véritable nature de qqn; **I found out where he'd put it** j'ai trouvé où il l'avait mis. **-2.** [catch being dishonest] prendre; [show to be a fraud] prendre en défaut; **make sure you don't get found out** veille à ne pas te faire prendre; **you've been found out** tu as été découvert.

finder ['faɪndəʳ] *n* **-1.** [of lost object]: **it becomes the property of the ~** celui/celle qui l'a trouvé en devient propriétaire ❑ **~s keepers (, losers weepers)** celui qui le trouve le garde. **-2.** [of camera] viseur *m*.

finding ['faɪndɪŋ] *n* **-1.** [discovery, conclusion]: **~s** conclusions *fpl*, résultats *mpl*. **-2.** JUR verdict *m*.

fine [faɪn] (*compar* finer, *superl* finest) ◇ *adj* **-1.** [of high quality - meal, speech, view] excellent; [beautiful and elegant - clothes, house] beau; [- fabric] précieux; **this is very ~ workmanship** c'est un travail d'une grande qualité; **she is a very ~ athlete** c'est une excellente athlète; **this is a very ~ wine** c'est un vin vraiment excellent; **a ~ chap** *Br* un bon gars; **she is a ~ lady** [admirable character] c'est une femme admirable; [elegant] c'est une femme élégante; **to appeal to sb's finer feelings** faire appel aux nobles sentiments de qqn; **to play at being the ~ lady** jouer les grandes dames; **that was a ~ effort by Webb** superbe effort de la part de Webb; **a ~ example** un bel exemple; **of the finest quality** de première qualité; **made from the finest barley** fabriqué à base d'orge de la meilleure qualité; **her finest hour was winning the gold** elle a eu son heure de gloire quand elle a remporté la médaille d'or. **-2.** [very thin - hair, nib, thread] fin; **in this case there is a ~ line between fact and fiction** dans le cas présent la frontière est très mince entre la réalité et la fiction; **it's a ~ line** la différence OR la distinction est infime OR très subtile. **-3.** [not coarse - powder, grain, drizzle] fin; [- features, skin] fin, délicat; **to chop** OR **to cut sthg (up) ~** hacher qqch menu ❑ **to cut it ~** calculer juste; **that's cutting it a bit ~** tu calcules un peu juste. **-4.** [good, OK]: **how is everyone? — oh, they're all ~** comment va tout le monde? — tout le monde va bien; **I'm just ~, thanks** ça va très bien, merci; **how are you? — ~, thanks** comment ça va? — bien, merci; **more coffee? — no thanks, I'm ~** encore du café? — non, ça va, merci; **the tent's ~ for two, but too small for three** la tente convient pour deux personnes, mais elle est trop petite pour trois; **I'll be back in about an hour or so — ~** je serai de retour d'ici environ une heure — d'accord OR entendu OR très bien; **I was a bit worried about the new job, but it turned out ~ in the end** j'étais un peu inquiet à propos de mon nouveau travail mais ça s'est finalement bien passé; **that's ~ by** OR **with me** ça me va; **that's all very ~, but what about me?** tout ça c'est bien joli, mais moi qu'est-ce que je deviens dans l'affaire?; **this is ~ for those who can afford it** c'est très bien pour ceux qui peuvent se le permettre. **-5.** [well]:

that looks ~ to me cela m'a l'air d'aller; he looks ~ now [in health] il a l'air de bien aller maintenant; you look just ~, it's a very nice dress tu es très bien, c'est une très jolie robe; that sounds ~ [suggestion, idea] très bien, parfait; [way of playing music] cela rend très bien. -**6.** *Br* [weather] beau; a ~ day une belle journée; there will be ~ weather OR it will be ~ in all parts of the country il fera beau OR il y aura du beau temps dans tout le pays; it's turned out ~ again il fait encore beau; it was a bit cloudy in the morning, but it turned out ~ in the end le temps était un peu nuageux le matin, mais finalement ça a été une belle journée; I hope it keeps ~ for the barbecue pourvu que le beau temps continue pour le barbecue; I hope it keeps ~ for you j'espère que tu auras du beau temps; one of these ~ days un de ces jours; one ~ day un beau jour. -**7.** [subtle - distinction, language] subtil; [precise - calculations] minutieux, précis; ~ detail petit détail *m*; to make some ~ adjustments to sthg [to text, plan] peaufiner qqch; [to engine] faire des petits réglages sur qqch; there are still a few ~ adjustments to be made il reste quelques petits détails à régler ❑ not to put too ~ a point on it pour parler carrément. -**8.** *inf iron* [awful, terrible]: that's a ~ thing to say! c'est charmant de dire ça!; she was in a ~ state elle était dans un état épouvantable; look at you, you're in a ~ state! non mais tu t'es vu, ah tu es dans un bel état!; you picked a ~ time to leave me/tell me! tu as bien choisi ton moment pour me quitter/me le dire!; this is a ~ time to start that again! c'est bien le moment de remettre ça sur le tapis!; you're a ~ one to talk! ça te va bien de dire ça!; here's another ~ mess you've got me into! tu m'as encore mis dans un beau pétrin!; a ~ friend you are! eh bien, tu fais un bon copain/une bonne copine!; this is a ~ time to come in/get up! c'est à cette heure-ci que tu rentres/te lèves?

◇ *adv* [well] bien; yes, that suits me ~ oui, cela me va très bien; the baby is doing ~ le bébé va très bien; we get along ~ together on s'entend très bien.

◇ *n* [punishment] amende *f*, contravention *f*; to impose a ~ on sb infliger une amende à qqn; a parking ~ une contravention OR amende pour stationnement illégal; she was made to pay a ~ elle a dû payer une amende; a £25 ~ une amende de 25 livres.

◇ *vt* [order to pay] condamner à une amende, donner une contravention à; she was ~d heavily elle a été condamnée à une lourde amende OR contravention; she was ~d for speeding elle a reçu une contravention pour excès de vitesse; they ~d her £25 for illegal parking ils lui ont donné OR elle a eu une amende OR contravention de 25 livres pour stationnement illégal.

◆ **fine down** *vt sep* [smooth - wood] polir, poncer; *fig* [hone - theory, text] affiner.

fine art *n (U)* beaux-arts *mpl*; to study ~ étudier les beaux-arts ❑ he's got it down to a ~ *inf* il est expert en la matière.

fine-cut *adj* [tobacco] haché fin.

fine-drawn *adj fig* [distinction] subtil; [features] fin.

fine-grain *adj* PHOT [image] à grain fin; [developer] pour grain fin.

fine-grained *adj* [wood] à fibres fines, à fil fin; ~ leather cuir *m* à grain peu apparent.

finely [ˈfaɪnlɪ] *adv* -**1.** [grated, ground, sliced] finement; ~ chopped haché menu, finement haché; ~ powdered en poudre fine. -**2.** [delicately, subtly - tuned] avec précision; the situation is very ~ balanced la situation est caractérisée par un équilibre précaire. -**3.** [carved, sewn etc] délicatement.

fineness [ˈfaɪnnɪs] *n* -**1.** [of clothes, manners] raffinement *m*; [of work of art, features, handwriting] finesse *f*. -**2.** [of sand, sugar etc] finesse *f*. -**3.** [purity - of metal] pureté *f*. -**4.** [thinness - of thread, hair, nib] finesse *f*; *fig* [of detail, distinction] subtilité *f*.

finery [ˈfaɪnərɪ] *n (U)* parure *f*; the princess in all her ~ la princesse dans OR parée de ses plus beaux atours; to be dressed in all one's ~ porter sa tenue d'apparat.

finespun [ˌfaɪnˈspʌn] *adj* [yarn, wool] (filé) fin; *fig* [argument, logic] subtil.

finesse [fɪˈnes] ◇ *n* -**1.** [skill] finesse *f*. -**2.** CARDS impasse *f*.

◇ *vi* CARDS: to ~ against a card faire l'impasse à une carte.

◇ *vt* CARDS: to ~ a card faire l'impasse en jouant une carte.

fine-tooth(ed) comb *n* peigne *m* fin; to go through sthg with a ~ *fig* passer qqch au peigne fin.

fine-tune *vt* [machine, engine, radio] régler avec précision; *fig* [plan] peaufiner; [economy] *régler grâce à des mesures fiscales et monétaires*.

fine-tuning [-ˈtjuːnɪŋ] *n* [of machine, engine, radio] réglage *m* fin; *fig* [of plan] peaufinage *m*; [of economy] *réglage obtenu par des mesures fiscales et monétaires*.

finger [ˈfɪŋgəʳ] ◇ *n* -**1.** ANAT doigt *m*; to wear a ring on one's ~ porter une bague au doigt; she ran her ~s through her hair elle s'est passé les doigts OR la main dans les cheveux; she ran her ~s through his hair elle a passé ses doigts OR sa main dans ses cheveux; to lick one's ~s se lécher les doigts; to hold sthg between ~ and thumb tenir qqch entre le pouce et l'index; to type with two ~s taper (à la machine) avec deux doigts; a ~'s breadth un doigt; to point a ~ at sb/sthg montrer qqn/qqch du doigt ❑ index ~ index *m*; middle ~ majeur *m*; ring ~ annulaire *m*; little ~ auriculaire *m*, petit doigt *m*; to twist sb round one's little ~ faire ce qu'on veut de qqn; I can twist him round my little ~ j'en fais ce que je veux; to be all ~s and thumbs avoir des mains de beurre, avoir deux mains gauches; get OR pull your ~ out!▽ *Br* remue-toi!; to have a ~ in every pie jouer sur tous les tableaux; he has a ~ in the pie il a des intérêts dans l'affaire; if you lay a ~ on her si tu touches à un seul de ses cheveux; to keep one's ~s crossed croiser les doigts *(pour souhaiter bonne chance)*; I'll keep my ~s crossed for you je croiserai les doigts pour toi; to point the ~ (of suspicion) at sb diriger les soupçons sur qqn; the ~ of suspicion points at the accountant les soupçons pèsent sur le comptable; who are you to point the ~? qui es-tu pour accuser les autres?; to put the ~ on sb *inf* [inform against] balancer OR donner qqn; to put one's ~ on sthg [identify] mettre le doigt sur qqch; something has changed but I can't put my ~ on it il y a quelque chose de changé mais je n'arrive pas à dire ce que c'est; to have one's ~ on the pulse [person] être très au fait de ce qui se passe; [magazine, TV programme] être à la pointe de l'actualité; to put two ~s up at sb *inf Br*, to give sb the ~ *inf Am* ≃ faire un bras d'honneur à qqn; success/happiness/the suspect slipped through his ~s le succès/le bonheur/le suspect lui a glissé entre les doigts; to work one's ~s to the bone s'épuiser à la tâche; you never lift OR raise a ~ to help tu ne lèves jamais le petit doigt pour aider. -**2.** [of glove] doigt *m*. -**3.** [of alcohol] doigt *m*; [of land] bande *f*; to cut a cake into ~s couper un gâteau en petits morceaux rectangulaires.

◇ *comp*: ~ exercises MUS exercices *mpl* de doigté; ~ food *petits fours, petits sandwiches et légumes crus, servis à un buffet et que l'on mange avec les doigts*; ~ puppet marionnette *f* à doigt.◇

◇ *vt* -**1.** [feel] tâter du doigt; *pej* tripoter. -**2.** MUS doigter, indiquer le doigté de. -**3.** ▽ [inform on] balancer, donner.

fingerboard [ˈfɪŋgəbɔːd] *n* MUS touche *f*.

finger bowl *n* rince-doigts *m inv*.

finger buffet *n buffet où sont servis des petits sandwiches, des petits fours et des légumes crus*.

fingered [ˈfɪŋgəd] *adj* -**1.** [dirty, soiled] qui a été tripoté. -**2.** MUS doigté.

finger hole *n* MUS trou *m*.

fingering [ˈfɪŋgərɪŋ] *n* -**1.** MUS [technique, numerals] doigté *m*. -**2.** *pej* [touching] tripotage *m*. -**3.** [knitting wool] laine *f* fine à tricoter.

fingerless [ˈfɪŋgələs] *adj*: ~ glove mitaine *f*.

fingermark [ˈfɪŋgəmɑːk] *n* trace *f* OR marque *f* de doigt.

fingernail [ˈfɪŋgəneɪl] *n* ongle *m* (de la main); to hang on by one's ~s *literal* se retenir du bout des doigts; *fig* se raccrocher comme on peut.

finger paint *n* peinture *f* pour peindre avec les doigts.

finger painting *n* peinture *f* avec les doigts; children love ~ les enfants adorent peindre avec leurs doigts.

fingerplate [ˈfɪŋgəpleɪt] *n* plaque *f* de propreté *(pour protéger une porte des marques de doigts)*.

fingerprint [ˈfɪŋgəprɪnt] ◇ *n* empreinte *f* digitale; five different sets of ~s cinq empreintes digitales différentes; his ~s are all over it *literal* c'est couvert de ses empreintes digitales; *fig* tout indique que c'est lui; to take sb's ~s prendre les empreintes digitales de qqn ❑ genetic ~ empreinte OR code *m* génétique.

◇ *comp*: ~ expert spécialiste *mf* en empreintes digitales OR en dactyloscopie.

◇ *vt* [person] prendre les empreintes digitales de; [object, weapon] relever les empreintes digitales sur; to ~ sb genetically identifier l'empreinte OR le code génétique de qqn.

fingerprinting [ˈfɪŋgəˌprɪntɪŋ] *n (U)* [of person] prise *f* d'empreintes digitales; [of object] relevé *m* d'empreintes digitales; genetic ~ identification *f* de l'empreinte OR du code génétique.

fingerstall [ˈfɪŋgəstɔːl] *n* doigtier *m*.

fingertip [ˈfɪŋgətɪp] ◇ *n* bout *m* du doigt; he rolled a cigarette between his ~s il s'est roulé une cigarette entre les doigts ❑ to be Irish to one's ~s être irlandais jusqu'au bout des ongles; to have information at one's ~s [be conversant with] connaître des informations sur le bout des doigts; [readily available] avoir des informations à portée de main.

◇ *comp*: ~ controls commandes *fpl* à touches.

finicky [ˈfɪnɪkɪ] *adj* -**1.** [person] pointilleux, tatillon *pej*; [habit] tatillon; to be ~ about sthg être pointilleux OR *pej* tatillon sur qqch; to be a ~ eater être difficile sur la nourriture. -**2.** [job, task] minutieux.

finish [ˈfɪnɪʃ] ◇ *n* -**1.** [end, closing stage - of life, game etc] fin *f*; [- of race] arrivée *f*; a close ~ [in race] une arrivée serrée OR dans un mouchoir; from start to ~ du début à la fin ❑ to fight to the ~ se battre jusqu'au bout; it was a fight to the ~ la partie fut serrée; to be in at the ~ voir la fin. -**2.** [created with paint, varnish, veneer] finitions *fpl*; stained with a walnut ~ teinté imitation noyer. -**3.** [quality of workmanship, presentation etc] finition *f*; his prose/acting lacks ~ sa prose/son jeu manque de poli. -**4.** SPORT [of athlete] finish *m*. -**5.** [shot at goal] but *m*; a superb ~ un but magnifique.

◇ *vt* -**1.** [end, complete - work, meal, school] finir, terminer, achever; [- race] finir, terminer; [consume - supplies, food, drink] finir, terminer; to ~ doing sthg finir OR terminer de faire qqch; when do you ~ work? [time] à quelle heure est-ce que tu finis?; [date] quand OR à quelle date finis-tu?; to be in a hurry to get sthg ~ed être pressé de finir OR terminer qqch; ~ your drinks finissez OR videz vos verres. -**2.** [ruin - sb's career] mettre un terme à; [- sb's chances] détruire, anéantir. -**3.** [exhaust] achever, tuer. -**4.** [put finish on - wood, garment] finir, mettre les finitions à.

◇ *vi* [come to an end - concert, film etc] (se) finir, se terminer, s'achever; [complete activity - person] finir, terminer; to ~ by doing sthg finir OR terminer en faisant qqch; when does the concert ~? à quelle heure le concert (se) finit-il OR se termine-t-il OR s'achève-t-il?; please let me ~ [speaking] s'il te plaît, laisse-moi finir OR terminer; to ~ first/third [in race] arriver premier/troisième; where did he ~? [in race]

en quelle position est-il arrivé OR a-t-il fini?; **the runner ~ed strongly/well** [in race] le coureur a fini fort/a bien fini.

◆ **finish off** ◇ *vi insep* [in speech, meal] finir, terminer; **they ~ed off with a coffee/by singing the national anthem** ils ont terminé par un café/en chantant l'hymne national.

◇ *vt sep* -**1.** [complete - work, letter] finir, terminer, achever; [- passing move in sport] terminer, finir, conclure. -**2.** [consume - drink] finir, terminer. -**3.** [kill - person, wounded animal] achever; *fig* [exhaust - person] achever, tuer; **fierce competition ~ed the industry off** *fig* une concurrence féroce a eu raison de cette industrie.

◆ **finish up** ◇ *vi insep* [end up] finir; **to ~ up in jail/hospital** finir en prison/à l'hôpital; **they ~ed up arguing** ils ont fini par se disputer; **she ~ed up a nervous wreck** à la fin c'était une vraie boule de nerfs, elle a fini à bout de nerfs; **you might ~ up dead** tu risques de te faire tuer.

◇ *vt sep* [meal, food, drink] finir, terminer; **~ up your drink** finissez OR terminez OR videz votre verre.

◆ **finish with** *vt insep* -**1.** [have no further use for] ne plus avoir besoin de; **have you ~ed with the paper/milk?** tu n'as plus besoin du journal/du lait?, tu as fini avec le journal/le lait?; **I haven't ~ed with it yet** j'en ai encore besoin. -**2.** [want no more contact with] en finir avec; **I've ~ed with journalism for good** j'en ai fini à jamais avec le journalisme, moi et le journalisme, c'est fini. -**3.** [end relationship] rompre avec; **she ~ed with her boyfriend** elle a rompu avec son petit ami. -**4.** [stop punishing] régler son compte à; **just wait till I ~ with him** attends que je lui règle son compte, attends que j'en aie fini avec lui; **I haven't ~ed with you yet** je n'en ai pas encore fini avec toi.

finished ['fɪnɪʃt] *adj* -**1.** fini; *fig* [performance] parfaitement exécuté; [appearance] raffiné; **machine-~** fini à la machine, finitions machine; **it's beautifully ~** les finitions sont magnifiques, c'est magnifiquement fini. -**2.** *inf* [exhausted] mort, crevé. -**3.** [ruined - career] fini, terminé; **he's ~ as a politician** sa carrière d'homme politique est terminée OR finie, il est fini en tant qu'homme politique; **you're ~** c'est fini OR terminé pour vous; **you're ~ in this company** tu es fini dans cette société. -**4.** [completed - work, job] fini, terminé, achevé; [consumed - wine, cake] fini; **the butter is ~** il n'y a plus de beurre; **the plumber was ~ by 4 p.m.** le plombier avait terminé OR fini à 16 h ❑ **~ product** OR **article** produit *m* fini. -**5.** [over] fini; **you and I are ~** toi et moi, c'est fini; **I'm ~ with him/my boyfriend** lui/mon petit ami et moi, c'est fini; **I'm ~ with politics/journalism** la politique/le journalisme et moi, c'est fini, j'en ai fini avec la politique/le journalisme; **the headmaster was not ~ with him yet** le principal n'en avait pas encore fini avec lui.

finisher ['fɪnɪʃəʳ] *n* -**1.** SPORT finisseur *m*, -euse *f*; FTBL marqueur *m*; **he's a fast ~** [athlete] il finit vite, il est rapide au finish. -**2.** [thorough person]: **he's not a ~** il ne finit jamais complètement son travail. -**3.** INDUST finisseur *m*, -euse *f*.

finishing line ['fɪnɪʃɪŋ-] *Br*, **finish line** *Am* *n* SPORT ligne *f* d'arrivée.

finishing school *n école privée de jeunes filles surtout axée sur l'enseignement des bonnes manières.*

finishing touch *n*: **to put the ~es to sthg** mettre la dernière touche OR la dernière main à qqch.

finite ['faɪnaɪt] *adj* limité; PHILOS & MATH [number, universe] fini; GRAMM [verb] à aspect fini.

fink *inf* [fɪŋk] *Am* ◇ *n* [strikebreaker] jaune *m*; [informer] mouchard *m*, -e *f*; [to police] indic *m*, balance *f*; [nasty person] salaud *m*, salope *f*.

◇ *vi*: **to ~ on sb** [to police] donner OR balancer qqn; [to teacher, parent] moucharder qqn.

◆ **fink out** *inf vi insep Am* [withdraw - from undertaking] laisser tomber, se dégonfler; [- from promise] ne pas tenir parole; **to ~ out of doing sthg** laisser tomber OR se dégonfler et ne pas faire qqch.

Finland ['fɪnlənd] *pr n* Finlande *f*; **in ~** en Finlande.

Finlander ['fɪnləndəʳ] *n* Finlandais *m*, -e *f*.

Finn [fɪn] *n* -**1.** [inhabitant of Finland] Finlandais *m*, -e *f*. -**2.** HIST Finnois *m*, -e *f*.

Finnish ['fɪnɪʃ] ◇ *n* LING finnois *m*.

◇ *adj* -**1.** [gen] finlandais. -**2.** HIST finnois.

fiord [fjɔːd] *n* fjord *m*.

fir [fɜːʳ] ◇ *n* [tree, wood] sapin *m*.

◇ *comp*: **~ cone** *Br* pomme *f* de pin; **~ tree** sapin *m*.

fire ['faɪəʳ] ◇ *n* -**1.** [destructive] incendie *m*; **~!** au feu!; **to catch ~** prendre feu; **to set ~ to sthg, to set sthg on ~** mettre le feu à qqch; **be careful or you'll set ~ to yourself** fais attention ou tu vas mettre le feu à tes vêtements; **to cause** OR **to start a ~** [person, faulty wiring] provoquer un incendie; **I'm always worried about ~s** j'ai toujours peur d'un incendie; **that's how ~s start** c'est comme ça qu'on met le feu; **on ~** en feu; **the building/village was set on ~** le bâtiment/village a été incendié; **my throat's on ~** *fig* j'ai la gorge en feu; **his forehead/he is on ~** *fig* [because of fever] son front/il est brûlant ❑ **forest ~** incendie OR feu *m* de forêt; **to play with ~** jouer avec le feu; **fight ~ with ~** combattre le mal par le mal; **he would go through ~ and water for her** il se jetterait au feu pour elle; **this novel is not going to set the world** OR *Br* **the Thames on ~** *inf* ce roman ne casse pas des briques; **he'll never set the world** OR *Br* **the Thames on ~** il n'a jamais cassé trois pattes à un canard; **the Great Fire of London** le grand incendie de Londres *(qui, en 1666, détruisit les trois quarts de la ville, et notamment la cathédrale Saint-Paul)*. -**2.** [in hearth, campsite] feu *m*; **a roaring ~** une belle flambée; **to lay a ~** préparer un feu; **to light** OR **to make a ~** allumer un feu, faire du feu ❑ **camp/open ~** feu de camp/de cheminée; **wood/coal ~** feu de bois/de charbon. -**3.** [element] feu *m*; **before man discovered ~** avant que l'homme ait découvert le feu; **to be afraid of ~** avoir peur du feu. -**4.** MIL feu *m*; **open ~!** ouvrez le feu!; **to open/to cease ~** ouvrir/cesser le feu; **to open ~ on sb** ouvrir le feu OR tirer sur qqn; **to draw the enemy's ~** faire diversion en attirant le feu de l'ennemi; **to return (sb's) ~** riposter (au tir de qqn); **hold your ~** [don't shoot] ne tirez pas; [stop shooting] cessez le feu ❑ **to be in the line of ~** être dans la ligne de tir; **to come under ~** *literal* essuyer le feu de l'ennemi; *fig* être vivement critiqué OR attaqué; **between two ~s** entre deux feux. -**5.** *Br* [heater] appareil *m* de chauffage; **to turn the ~ on/off** allumer/éteindre le chauffage. -**6.** [passion, ardour] flamme *f*; **the ~ of youth** la fougue de la jeunesse.

◇ *comp*: **~ appliance** *Br* camion *m* de pompiers; **~ prevention** mesures *fpl* de sécurité contre l'incendie; **~ prevention officer** personne *f* chargée des mesures de sécurité contre l'incendie; **~ regulations** consignes *fpl* en cas d'incendie; **~ sign** ASTROL signe *m* de feu; **~ worship** culte *m* du feu.

◇ *vt* -**1.** [shot, bullet] tirer; [gun, cannon, torpedo] décharger; [arrow] décocher; **only three bullets had been ~d from the gun** seulement trois balles avaient été tirées avec le pistolet; **without a shot being ~d** sans un seul coup de feu; **to ~ a twenty one-gun salute** tirer vingt et un coups de canon; **to ~ questions at sb** *fig* bombarder qqn de questions. -**2.** [inspire - person, an audience, supporters, the imagination] enflammer; **to ~ sb with enthusiasm/desire** remplir qqn d'enthousiasme/de désir. -**3.** [in kiln] cuire. -**4.** [power, fuel - furnace] chauffer. -**5.** *inf* [dismiss] virer; **you're ~d!** vous êtes viré!

◇ *vi* -**1.** [shoot - person] tirer, faire feu; **the rifle failed to ~** le coup n'est pas parti; **~!** MIL feu!; **~ at will!** MIL feu à volonté!; **to ~ at** OR **on sb** tirer sur qqn. -**2.** [engine] tourner; [spark plug] s'allumer; [pin on print head] se déclencher; **the engine is only firing on two cylinders** le moteur ne tourne que sur deux cylindres ❑ **to ~ on all cylinders** *literal* & *fig* marcher à pleins tubes.

◆ **fire away** *inf vi insep* [go ahead]: **~ away!** allez-y!

◆ **fire off** *vt sep* [round of ammunition] tirer; *fig* [facts, figures] balancer; **to ~ off questions at sb** bombarder qqn de questions.

fire alarm *n* alarme *f* d'incendie.

fire-and-brimstone *adj* [preacher, sermon] menaçant des feux de l'enfer.

firearm ['faɪərɑːm] *n* arme *f* à feu; **~s training** entraînement *m* à l'utilisation des armes à feu; **~s offence** JUR délit *m* lié à la détention d'armes à feu.

fireball ['faɪəbɔːl] *n* boule *f* de feu.

fireboat ['faɪəbəʊt] *n* bateau-pompe *m*.

firebomb ['faɪəbɒm] ◇ *n* bombe *f* incendiaire.

◇ *vt* [building] attaquer à la bombe incendiaire.

firebrand ['faɪəbrænd] *n fig* exalté *m*, -e *f*.

firebreak ['faɪəbreɪk] *n* [in forest] coupe-feu *m inv*.

firebrick ['faɪəbrɪk] *n* brique *f* réfractaire.

fire brigade *n* brigade *f* des pompiers OR sapeurs-pompiers; **have you called the ~?** as-tu appelé les pompiers?

firebug *inf* ['faɪəbʌg] *n* incendiaire *mf*, pyromane *mf*.

fire chief *n Am* capitaine *m* des pompiers OR sapeurs-pompiers.

fire clay *n* argile *f* réfractaire.

firecracker ['faɪəˌkrækəʳ] *n* pétard *m*.

fire curtain *n* THEAT rideau *m* de fer.

-fired ['faɪəd] *in cpds* chauffé à; **oil~/gas~ central heating** chauffage central au mazout/gaz.

firedamp ['faɪədæmp] *n* MIN grisou *m*; **~ explosion** coup *m* de grisou.

fire department *Am* = **fire brigade**.

firedog ['faɪədɒg] *n* chenet *m*.

fire door *n* porte *f* coupe-feu.

fire drill *n* exercice *m* de sécurité *(en cas d'incendie)*.

fire-eater *n* [in circus] cracheur *m* de feu; *fig* personne *f* belliqueuse, bagarreur *m*, -euse *f*.

fire engine *n* voiture *f* de pompiers.

fire escape *n* escalier *m* de secours OR d'incendie.

fire exit *n* sortie *f* de secours.

fire extinguisher *n* extincteur *m*.

fire fighter *n* pompier *m*, sapeur-pompier *m* (volontaire).

fire-fighting ◇ *n* lutte *f* contre les incendies.

◇ *comp* [equipment, techniques] de lutte contre les incendies.

firefly ['faɪəflaɪ] (*pl* **fireflies**) *n* luciole *f*.

fireguard ['faɪəgɑːd] *n* [for open fire] garde-feu *m*.

fire hazard *n*: **all those empty boxes are a ~** toutes ces boîtes vides constituent OR représentent un risque d'incendie; **smoking is forbidden since it is a ~** il est interdit de fumer car cela pourrait provoquer un incendie.

fire hose *n* tuyau *m* de pompe à incendie.

fire hydrant *n* bouche *f* d'incendie.

fire insurance *n (U)* assurance-incendie *f*.

fire irons *npl* accessoires *mpl* de cheminée.

firelight ['faɪəlaɪt] *n* lueur *f* OR lumière *f* du feu; **in the ~** à la lueur OR lumière du feu.

firelighter ['faɪəlaɪtəʳ] *n* allume-feu *m*.

fireman ['faɪəmən] (*pl* **firemen** [-mən]) *n* -**1.** pompier *m*, sapeur-pompier *m*. -**2.** RAIL chauffeur *m* de locomotive.

fire marshal *Am* = **fire chief**.

fireplace ['faɪəpleɪs] *n* cheminée *f*.

fire-plug *n Am* -**1.** [fire hydrant] bouche *f* d'incendie. -**2.** *inf* [person] *personne petite et grosse*

fire power *n* puissance *f* de feu.

fireproof ['faɪəpru:f] ◇ *adj* [door, safe] à l'épreuve du feu; [clothing, toys] ininflammable; [dish] allant au feu.
◇ *vt* ignifuger, rendre ininflammable.
fireproofing ['faɪəpru:fɪŋ] *adj* [spray, material] ignifuge, ignifugeant.
fire-raiser *n* pyromane *mf*, incendiaire *mf*.
fire-raising [-'reɪzɪŋ] *n* pyromanie *f*.
fire risk = **fire hazard**.
fire sale *n* *vente au rabais de marchandises ayant subi de légers dégâts à la suite d'un incendie*.
fire screen *n* écran *m* de cheminée.
fire service = **fire brigade**.
fireside ['faɪəsaɪd] *n* coin *m* du feu; **sitting by the ~** assis au coin du feu; **~ chat** [by politician] causerie *f* au coin du feu.
fire station *n* caserne *f* de pompiers.
firestone ['faɪəstəun] *n* pierre *f* réfractaire.
firetrap ['faɪətræp] *n*: **there are too many of these ~s** il y a trop de bâtiments qui sont de véritables pièges en cas d'incendie.
fire truck *n* *Am* voiture *f* de pompiers.
fire walker *n* *personne en transe qui marche sur des braises*.
fire walking *n*: **the ritual of ~** le rituel consistant à marcher sur des braises.
fire wall *n* cloison *f* pare-feu.
fire warden *n* [in forest] guetteur *m* d'incendie.
firewater *inf* ['faɪə,wɔ:tər] *n* gnôle *f*.
firewood ['faɪəwʊd] *n* bois *m* à brûler; [for use in home] bois *m* de chauffage.
firework ['faɪəwɜ:k] *n* pièce *f* d'artifice; **~** OR **~s display** feu *m* d'artifice; **there were ~s at the meeting** *inf fig* il y a eu des étincelles à la réunion.
firing ['faɪərɪŋ] ◇ *n* -**1.** *(U)* MIL tir *m*; **~ has been heavy** de nombreux coups de feu ont été tirés; **burst of ~** fusillade *f*. -**2.** [of piece of pottery] cuisson *f*, cuite *f*. -**3.** *inf* [dismissal] renvoi *m*. -**4.** AUT [of engine, sparkplug] allumage *m*.
◇ *comp*: **~ order** OR **sequence** AUT [of engine] ordre *m* d'allumage; **~ pin** percuteur *m*; **~ practice** exercice *m* de tir; **~ range** champ *m* de tir.
firing line *n* MIL ligne *f* de tir; **to be in the ~** *fig* être dans la ligne de tir.
firing squad *n* peloton *m* d'exécution; **to be executed by ~** passer devant le peloton d'exécution.
firm [fɜ:m] ◇ *n* [company] entreprise *f*; [of solicitors] étude *f*; [of lawyers, barristers, consultants] cabinet *m*; **it's a good ~ to work for** cette entreprise est un bon employeur.
◇ *adj* -**1.** [solid, hard - flesh, fruit, mattress etc] ferme; **on ~ ground** *literal* sur la terre ferme; *fig* sur un terrain solide. -**2.** [stable, secure - basis] solide; [- foundations] stable; COMM & FIN [currency, market etc] stable. -**3.** [strong - handshake, grip, leadership] ferme; **to have a ~ hold** OR **grasp** OR **grip of sthg** tenir qqch fermement; **to rule with a ~ hand** diriger avec de la poigne. -**4.** [unshakeable, definite - belief, evidence, friendship] solide; [- view, opinion] déterminé, arrêté; [- intention, voice, agreement, offer] ferme; [- date] définitif; **they are ~ friends** ce sont de bons amis; **he was very ~ about this** il a été très ferme à ce propos; **she gave a ~ denial** elle a nié fermement; **I am a ~ believer in women's equality** je crois fermement à l'égalité de la femme; **to be ~ with a child/dog** être ferme avec un enfant/chien; **he was polite but ~** il a été poli mais ferme.
◇ *adv*: **to stand ~ on sthg** ne pas céder sur qqch; **he stands ~ on this issue** il a une position bien arrêtée sur le sujet.
◇ *vt*: **to ~ the soil** tasser le sol.
◇ *vi* = **firm up** *vi insep*.
◆ **firm up** ◇ *vt sep* [make firm - muscles, prices] raffermir; **to ~ up an agreement** régler les derniers détails d'un accord.
◇ *vi insep* [muscles, prices] se raffermir.
firmament ['fɜ:məmənt] *n arch* OR *lit* [sky] firmament *m*.
firmly ['fɜ:mlɪ] *adv* -**1.** [securely - hold, grasp sthg] fermement; [- closed, secured] bien; **to keep one's feet ~ on the ground** *fig* bien garder les pieds sur terre, rester fermement ancré dans la réalité. -**2.** [say, deny, refuse, deal with] fermement, avec fermeté.
firmness ['fɜ:mnɪs] *n* -**1.** [hardness - of flesh, fruit, mattress] fermeté *f*. -**2.** [stability - of basis] solidité *f*; [- of foundations] stabilité *f*; COMM & FIN [of currency, market, prices] stabilité *f*. -**3.** [strength -of grip, character, belief] fermeté *f*. -**4.** [of voice, denial, refusal] fermeté *f*.
firmware ['fɜ:mweər] *n* COMPUT microprogramme *m*.
first [fɜ:st] ◇ *adj num* -**1.** [in series] premier; **the ~ few days** les deux ou trois premiers jours; **the ~ six months** les six premiers mois; **Louis the First** Louis Premier OR Ier; **to be ~ in the queue** être le premier de la queue; **I'm ~** je suis OR c'est moi le premier; **she was ~ in English Literature** elle était première en littérature anglaise; **she's in ~ place** [in race] elle est en tête; **to win ~ prize** gagner le premier prix; **this is the ~ time I've been to New York** c'est la première fois que je viens à New York ❑ **~ floor** *Br* premier étage *m*; *Am* rez-de-chaussée *m*; **~ gear** AUT première *f* (vitesse *f*); **put the car into ~ gear** passe la première (vitesse); **~ year** *Br* UNIV première année *f*; SCH sixième *f*; **a ~-year university student** *Br* UNIV un étudiant de première année à l'université; **I learnt of it at ~ hand** je l'ai appris de la bouche de l'intéressé/l'intéressée, c'est lui-même/elle-même qui me l'a appris; **I learned of her resignation at ~ hand** c'est elle-même qui m'a appris sa démission; **I haven't (got) the ~ idea** je n'en ai pas la moindre idée; **I'll pick you up ~ thing (in the morning)** je passerai te chercher demain matin à la première heure; **I'm not at my best ~ thing in the morning** je ne suis pas au mieux de ma forme très tôt le matin; **there's a ~ time for everything** il y a un début à tout. -**2.** [immediately] tout de suite; **~ thing after lunch** tout de suite après le déjeuner; **I don't know the ~ thing about cars** je n'y connais absolument rien en voitures; **she's past her ~ youth** *lit* elle n'est plus de la première jeunesse. -**3.** [most important - duty, concern] premier; **the ~ priority** la priorité des priorités ❑ **to put ~ things ~** commencer par le commencement; **~ things ~!** prenons les choses dans l'ordre!
◇ *adv* -**1.** [before the others - arrive, leave, speak] le premier, la première, en premier; **I saw it ~!** c'est moi qui l'ai vu le premier OR en premier!; **you go ~** vas-y en premier; **ladies ~** les dames d'abord; **women and children ~** les femmes et les enfants d'abord; **~ in, ~ out** COMPUT premier entré premier sorti; **last in, ~ out** ADMIN dernier entré premier sorti ❑ **to come ~** [in race] arriver premier; [in exam] avoir la première place, être premier; **her career comes ~** sa carrière passe d'abord OR avant tout; **I've never come ~ with you, have I?** tu ne m'as jamais fait passer avant le reste, n'est-ce pas?; **~ come ~ served** *prov* les premiers arrivés sont les premiers servis; **to put one's family ~** faire passer sa famille d'abord OR avant tout. -**2.** [firstly, before anything else] d'abord; **~, I want to say thank you** tout d'abord, je voudrais vous remercier, je voudrais d'abord vous remercier; **~ prepare the meat** préparez d'abord la viande; **I need to go to the lavatory ~** il faut d'abord que j'aille aux toilettes; **what should I do ~?** qu'est-ce que je dois faire en premier?; **~ hear the arguments, then make up your mind** écoutez d'abord les arguments, ensuite vous vous déciderez; **she says ~ one thing then another** elle dit d'abord une chose, et puis une autre; **I'm a mother ~ and a wife second** je suis une mère avant d'être une épouse. -**3.** [for the first time] pour la première fois; **we ~ met in London** nous nous sommes rencontrés à Londres ‖ [initially] au début; **when I ~ knew him** quand je l'ai connu. -**4.** [sooner, rather]: **I'd die ~** plutôt mourir; **I'll see him damned ~** OR **in hell ~** *inf* j'aimerais bien voir ça.
◇ *n* -**1.** [before all others]: **the ~** le premier, la première; **he was among the ~ to realise** il a été parmi les premiers à s'en rendre compte; **she was the ~ in our family to go to university** c'était la première de la famille à aller à l'université; **he came in an easy ~** [in race] il est arrivé premier haut la main. -**2.** [achievement] première *f*; **that's a notable ~ for France** c'est une grande première pour la France. -**3.** [first time]: **the ~ we heard/knew of it was when...** nous en avons entendu parler pour la première fois/l'avons appris quand...; **it's the ~ I've heard of it!** première nouvelle! -**4.** *Br* UNIV: **he got a ~ in economics** ≃ il a eu mention très bien en économie; **she got a double ~ in French and Russian** ≃ elle a eu mention très bien en français et en russe. -**5.** AUT première *f*.
◆ **at first** *adv phr* au début.
◆ **first and foremost** *adv phr* d'abord et surtout.
◆ **first and last** *adv phr* avant tout.
◆ **first of all** *adv phr* tout d'abord, pour commencer.
◆ **first off** *inf adv phr* pour commencer.
◆ **from first to last** *adv phr* du début à la fin.
◆ **from the (very) first** *adv phr* dès le début.
◆ **in the first instance** *adv phr* d'abord; **apply in the ~ instance to the personnel department** adressez d'abord votre demande au service du personnel.
◆ **in the first place** *adv phr* -**1.** [referring to a past action] d'abord; **why did you do it in the ~ place?** et puis d'abord, pourquoi as-tu fait cela?; **I don't understand why he married her in the ~ place** d'abord, je ne comprends pas ce qui a bien pu le pousser à se marier avec elle. -**2.** [introducing an argument] d'abord; **in the ~ place... and in the second place** d'abord... et ensuite.
first aid ◇ *n (U)* [technique] secourisme *m*; [attention] premiers soins *mpl*; **does anyone know any ~?** quelqu'un s'y connaît-il en secourisme?; **to give/to receive ~** donner/recevoir les premiers soins.
◇ *comp* [class, manual] de secourisme; **~ kit** OR **box** trousse *f* à pharmacie; **~ post** OR **station** *Br* poste *m* de secours.
first-aider [-'eɪdər] *n* secouriste *mf*.
First Amendment *n* *Am*: **the ~** le Premier Amendement *(garantissant les libertés individuelles du citoyen américain, notamment la liberté d'expression)*.
first-born ◇ *adj* premier-né.
◇ *n* premier-né *m*, première-née *f*.
first class *n* -**1.** [on train, plane] première classe *f*. -**2.** [for letter, parcel] tarif *m* normal.
◆ **first-class** ◇ *adj* -**1.** [seat] en première classe; [compartment, ticket] de première classe. -**2.** [letter, stamp] au tarif normal; **to send a letter by first-class mail** envoyer une lettre au tarif normal. -**3.** *Br* UNIV: **she got a first-class honours degree (in French)** elle a eu mention très bien (en français); **to graduate with first-class honours** obtenir son diplôme avec mention très bien. -**4.** [excellent] = **first-rate**.
◇ *adv* [travel] en première classe; [send letter] au tarif normal.
first cousin *n* cousin *m* germain, cousine *f* germaine.
first-day cover *n* [for stamp collector] émission *f* premier jour.
first-degree *adj* -**1.** MED [burn] au premier degré. -**2.** JUR [in US]: **~ murder** homicide *m* volontaire.
first-ever *inf n* tout premier *m*, toute première *f*.
first floor *n* *Br* premier étage *m*; *Am* rez-de-chaussée *m*; **on the ~** *Br* au premier étage; *Am* au rez-de-chaussée.
first-foot *vt* *Scot*: **to ~ sb** *être le premier à rendre visite à qqn pour lui souhaiter la bonne année la nuit de la Saint-Sylvestre*.
first-footer *n* *Scot* *premier visiteur venant souhaiter la bonne année, la nuit de la Saint-Sylvestre*.

first form *n Br* SCH sixième *f*.

first-former *n Br* SCH élève *mf* de sixième.

first fruits *npl literal* & *fig* premiers fruits *mpl*.

first-generation *adj* de première génération.

first-hand ◇ *adj* [knowledge, information, news] de première main; I know from ~ experience what it is like to be poor je sais d'expérience ce que c'est que d'être pauvre.
◇ *adv* [hear of sthg] de première main.

first lady *n* [in US] *femme du président des États-Unis*; the ~ of rock/of the detective novel *fig* la grande dame du rock/du roman policier.

first language *n* langue *f* maternelle.

first lieutenant *n* NAUT lieutenant *m* de vaisseau; *Am* MIL & AERON lieutenant *m*.

firstly ['fɜːstlɪ] *adv* premièrement.

first mate *n* NAUT second *m*.

first name *n* prénom *m*; to be on ~ terms with sb appeler qqn par son prénom; we're on ~ terms ≃ on se tutoie.

first night THEAT ◇ *n* première *f*.
◇ *comp*: ~ nerves trac *m (du soir de la première)*.

first-nighter [-'naɪtəʳ] *n* THEAT spectateur *m*, -trice *f* assistant OR ayant assisté à la première.

first offender *n* délinquant *m*, -e *f* primaire.

first officer = **first mate**.

first-past-the-post *adj Br* POL [system] majoritaire à un tour; the ~ electoral system le scrutin majoritaire à un tour.

first person *n* GRAMM première personne *f*; in the ~ à la première personne.
◆ **first-person** *adj* GRAMM [pronoun] de la première personne; a first-person narrative un récit à la première personne.

first principle *n* principe *m* fondamental OR de base.

first-rate *adj* [excellent - wine, meal, restaurant] de première qualité, excellent; [- idea, performance, student] excellent; of ~ quality d'excellente OR de première qualité; he's a ~ badminton/chess player il est excellent au badminton/aux échecs; that's absolutely ~! *Br* [idea, news etc] c'est formidable!

first reading *n* POL [of bill] première lecture *f*.

first refusal *n* préférence *f*; to give sb ~ on sthg donner la préférence à qqn pour qqch; I promised Nadine ~ j'ai promis à Nadine que je lui donnerais la préférence.

first-strike *adj* MIL [missile] de première frappe; a ~ capability une force de frappe importante (permettant d'attaquer en premier).

first string *n* SPORT meilleur joueur *m*, meilleure joueuse *f (d'une équipe)*.
◆ **first-string** *adj* SPORT: first-string player [regular] joueur *m* régulier, joueuse *f* régulière *(d'une équipe)*; [best] meilleur joueur *m*, meilleure joueuse *f (d'une équipe)*.

first-time *adj*: ~ (house) buyer personne *f* devenant propriétaire pour la première fois; ~ visitors to the country les personnes visitant le pays pour la première fois.

first violin *n* MUS [person, instrument] premier violon *m*.

First World *n*: the ~ les pays industrialisés.

firth [fɜːθ] *n Scot* estuaire *m*.

FIS *n abbr of* Family Income Supplement.

fiscal ['fɪskl] ◇ *adj* [measures, policy etc] fiscal; ~ year *Am* [of company] exercice *m* (financier); ADMIN année *f* budgétaire.
◇ *n Scot* JUR: procurator ~ ≃ procureur *m* de la République.

fish [fɪʃ] (*pl inv* OR fishes) ◇ *n* poisson *m*; to catch a ~ pêcher un poisson; he caught three ~ il a attrapé OR pris trois poissons; I eat a lot of ~ je mange beaucoup de poisson ❑ ~ and chips poisson frit avec des frites; he's a queer ~ *inf* c'est un drôle de type; a cold ~ [unemotional] un cœur de pierre; to feel like a ~ out of water ne pas se sentir dans son élément; to drink like a ~ *inf* boire comme un trou; there are plenty more ~ in the sea un de perdu, dix de retrouvés; to have other ~ to fry avoir d'autres chats à fouetter; to be a big ~ in a little pond être le premier dans son village; to be a little ~ in a big pond être perdu dans la masse; neither ~ nor fowl (nor good red herring) ni chair ni poisson.
◇ *comp* [course, restaurant] de poisson.
◇ *vi* -**1.** SPORT pêcher; to ~ with a line/a rod pêcher à la ligne/avec une canne; to go ~ing aller à la pêche; to go trout ~ing OR ~ing for trout aller à la pêche à la truite, aller pêcher la truite; to ~ in troubled waters *fig* pêcher en eau trouble. -**2.** [search, seek]: he ~ed around for his pen under the papers il a fouillé sous ses papiers pour trouver son crayon; to ~ for information essayer de soutirer des informations; to ~ for compliments rechercher les compliments.
◇ *vt* [river, lake etc] pêcher dans.
◆ **fish out** *vt sep* [from water] repêcher; he ~ed out his wallet *fig* il a sorti son portefeuille; [with difficulty] il a extrait son portefeuille; she ~ed her keys out of her bag elle a fouillé dans son sac et en a extrait ses clés.
◆ **fish up** *vt sep* [from water] repêcher; to ~ up sthg from one's memory ressortir qqch de sa mémoire; where did you ~ that up from? *inf* [object] où est-ce que tu as été dénicher ça?; [idea] où est-ce que tu as été pêcher ça?

fish-and-chip shop *n Br magasin vendant du poisson frit et des frites*.

fishbone ['fɪʃbəʊn] *n* arête *f* de poisson.

fishbowl ['fɪʃbəʊl] *n* bocal *m* à poissons.

fishcake ['fɪʃkeɪk] *n* CULIN croquette *f* de poisson.

fish eagle *n* ORNITH balbuzard *m*.

fisher ['fɪʃəʳ] *n* -**1.** *arch* [fisherman] pêcheur *m*; ~s of men BIBLE pêcheurs d'hommes. -**2.** [bird, animal] pêcheur *m*.

fisherman ['fɪʃəmən] (*pl* fishermen [-mən]) *n* pêcheur *m*.

fishery ['fɪʃərɪ] (*pl* fisheries) *n* [fishing ground] pêcherie *f*; [fishing industry] industrie *f* de la pêche; ~ protection vessel vedette *f* garde-pêche.

fish-eye-lens *n* PHOT fish-eye *m*.

fish farm *n* établissement *m* piscicole.

fish farmer *n* pisciculteur *m*, -trice *f*.

fish farming *n* pisciculture *f*.

fish finger *n* CULIN bâtonnet *m* de poisson pané.

fish glue *n* colle *f* de poisson.

fish hawk = **fish eagle**.

fish-hook *n* hameçon *m*.

fishing ['fɪʃɪŋ] ◇ *n* pêche *f*; trout/salmon ~ pêche à la truite/au saumon; there is some good ~ to be had along this river il y a de bons coins de pêche dans cette rivière; we can do some ~ nous pourrons aller à la pêche; 'no ~' 'pêche interdite'.
◇ *comp* [vessel, permit, port, trip] de pêche; [season] de la pêche; [village, party] de pêcheurs.

fishing boat *n* bateau *m* de pêche.

fishing ground *n* zone *f* de pêche.

fishing line *n* ligne *f* de pêche.

fishing net *n* filet *m* de pêche.

fishing rod *n* canne *f* à pêche, gaule *f*.

fishing tackle *n* matériel *m* de pêche.

fish kettle *n* poissonnière *f*.

fish ladder *n* échelle *f* à poissons.

fish market *n* marché *m* au poisson.

fish meal *n* farine *f* de poisson.

fishmonger ['fɪʃˌmʌŋgəʳ] *n Br* poissonnier *m*, -ère *f*; ~'s [shop] poissonnerie *f*; to go to the ~'s aller à la poissonnerie OR chez le poissonnier.

fishnet ['fɪʃnet] ◇ *n Am* [for catching fish] filet *m* (de pêche).
◇ *adj*: ~ stockings/tights bas *mpl*/collants *mpl* résille.

fish paste *n* pâte *f* de poisson.

fishplate ['fɪʃpleɪt] *n* RAIL éclisse *f*.

fishpond ['fɪʃpɒnd] *n* étang *m* (à poissons).

fish shop *n* poissonnerie *f*.

fish slice *n* pelle *f* à poisson.

fish stick *Am* = **fish finger**.

fish tank *n* [in house] aquarium *m*; [in restaurant, on fish farm] vivier *m*.

fishway ['fɪʃweɪ] *Am* = **fish ladder**.

fishwife ['fɪʃwaɪf] (*pl* fishwives [-waɪvz]) *n* poissonnière *f*, marchande *f* de poisson; she's a real ~ *fig* elle a un langage de charretier, elle parle comme un charretier.

fishy ['fɪʃɪ] (*compar* fishier, *superl* fishiest) *adj* -**1.** [smell] de poisson. -**2.** *inf* [suspicious] louche; there's something ~ going on il se passe quelque chose de louche; there's something ~ about her alibi il y a quelque chose qui ne colle pas dans son alibi.

fissile ['fɪsaɪl] *adj* fissible.

fission ['fɪʃn] *n* PHYS fission *f*; BIOL scissiparité *f*; nuclear ~ fission nucléaire.

fissionable ['fɪʃnəbl] *adj* PHYS fissible.

fission bomb *n* bombe *f* atomique.

fission reactor *n* pile *f* atomique.

fissure ['fɪʃəʳ] ◇ *n* [crevice, crack] fissure *f*; *fig* fissure *f*, brèche *f*.
◇ *vi* se fissurer, se fendre.

fissured ['fɪʃəd] *adj* fissuré.

fist [fɪst] *n* poing *m*; to clench one's ~s serrer les poings; he shook his ~ at me il m'a menacé du poing; to put one's ~s up se mettre en garde; make a ~ serrez le poing.

fistfight ['fɪstfaɪt] *n* bagarre *f* aux poings; to have a ~ with sb se battre aux poings contre qqn.

fistful ['fɪstfʊl] *n* poignée *f*; 'A Fistful of Dollars' *Leone* 'Pour une poignée de dollars'.

fisticuffs ['fɪstɪkʌfs] *n (U) hum* bagarre *f*.

fistula ['fɪstjʊlə] *n* fistule *f*.

fit [fɪt] (*compar* fitter, *superl* fittest, *Br pt* & *pp* fitted, *Am pt* & *pp* fit, *cont* fitting) ◇ *adj* -**1.** [suitable] convenable; that dress isn't ~ to wear cette robe n'est pas mettable; a country ~ for heroes to live in un pays digne d'accueillir ses héros; ~ to eat [edible] mangeable; [not poisonous] comestible; ~ to drink [water] potable; this coffee is not ~ to drink ce café est imbuvable; a meal ~ for a king un repas digne d'un roi; she's not ~ to look after children elle ne devrait pas avoir le droit de s'occuper d'enfants; she's not a ~ mother c'est une mère indigne; my grandmother is no longer ~ to drive ma grand-mère n'est plus capable de conduire; I'm not ~ to be seen je ne suis pas présentable; these programmes aren't ~ for children ce ne sont pas des programmes pour les enfants; throw it in the bin, that's all it's ~ for jette-le à la poubelle, c'est tout ce que ça mérite; that's all he's ~ for c'est tout ce qu'il mérite; to think OR to see ~ to do sthg trouver OR juger bon de faire qqch; do as you see OR think ~ fais comme tu penses OR juges bon. -**2.** *inf* [ready]: to be ~ to drop être mort de fatigue; I feel ~ to burst je me sens prêt à éclater; to laugh ~ to burst être plié en deux de rire ❑ I was ~ to be tied *Am* [extremely angry] j'étais furieux. -**3.** [healthy] en forme; to get ~ *Br* retrouver la forme; I've never felt fitter in my life *Br* je ne me suis jamais senti en meilleure forme; to keep OR to stay ~ entretenir sa forme; the patient is not ~ enough to be discharged le patient n'est pas en état de quitter l'hôpital; she is not a ~ woman [well] elle n'est pas en bonne santé; the fittest member of the team la personne la plus en forme de l'équipe; it's a case of the survival of the fittest ce sont les plus forts qui survivent ❑ to be as ~ as a fiddle se porter comme un charme.
◇ *n* -**1.** [size]: it's a perfect ~ [item of clothing] cela me/vous *etc* va à merveille; [fridge, stove, piece of furniture] cela s'adapte parfaitement; [two interlocking pieces] cela s'emboîte bien; it's not a very good ~ [too large] c'est trop grand; [too tight] c'est trop juste; tight/loose/comfortable ~ [item of clothing] coupe *f* ajustée/ample/confortable; these trousers are a bit of a tight ~ ce pantalon est un peu juste; it was a bit of a tight ~ [in room, car] on était un peu à l'étroit; [parking car] il n'y avait pas beaucoup

de place. -**2.** MED [of apoplexy, epilepsy, hysterics] crise *f*; ~ **of coughing, coughing** ~ quinte *f* de toux; ~ **of crying** crise de larmes ❑ **to have a** ~ MED avoir une crise; **she'll have a** ~ **when she finds out** *fig* elle va faire une crise quand elle le saura; **to throw a** ~ *inf* piquer une crise. -**3.** [outburst - of anger] mouvement *m*, accès *m*, moment *m*; [- of depression] crise *f*; [- of pique, generosity] moment *m*; **he did it in a** ~ **of rage** il a fait cela dans un mouvement de rage; **to be in** ~**s (of laughter)** avoir le fou rire; **he had us all in** ~**s** il nous a fait hurler OR mourir de rire; **to get a** ~ **of the giggles** être pris d'un OR piquer un fou rire; **in a sudden** ~ **of energy** dans un sursaut d'énergie ❑ **to work by** OR **in** ~**s and starts** travailler par à-coups.

◇ *vt* -**1.** [be of the correct size for]: **those trousers** ~ **you better than the other ones** ce pantalon te va mieux que l'autre; **none of the keys fitted the lock** aucune des clés n'entrait dans la serrure; **the nut doesn't** ~ **the bolt** l'écrou n'est pas de la même taille que le boulon; **doesn't the lid** ~ **the box/jar?** le couvercle ne va-t-il pas sur la boîte/le bocal?; **the lid doesn't** ~ **the pot very well** ce couvercle n'est pas très bien adapté à la casserole. -**2.** [correspond to, match - description] correspondre à; **to make the punishment** ~ **the crime** adapter le châtiment au crime; **the music fitted the occasion** la musique était de circonstance ❑ **to** ~ **the bill** faire l'affaire. -**3.** [make suitable for]: **what do you think** ~**s you for the job?** en quoi estimez-vous correspondre au profil de l'emploi? -**4.** [install - lock, door, window etc] installer; **to have double-glazing fitted** *Br* se faire installer OR mettre le double vitrage; **to** ~ **a carpet** *Br* poser une moquette; **to** ~ **a kitchen** *Br* installer une cuisine; **to** ~ **a key in a lock** engager OR mettre une clé dans une serrure; **I've got special tyres fitted** *Br* je me suis fait mettre des pneus spéciaux. -**5.** [attach, fix on] fixer; **then you** ~ **the parts together** puis vous assemblez les différentes pièces. -**6.** [equip] équiper; **to** ~ **sthg with sthg** équiper qqch de qqch; **fitted with electronic security devices** équipé de dispositifs de sécurité électroniques; **she has been fitted with a new hip replacement** elle s'est fait mettre une nouvelle hanche artificielle. -**7.** [take measurements of - person]: **to be fitted for a new suit** faire un essayage pour un nouveau costume; **the next time you come back to be fitted** lors de votre prochain essayage. -**8.** [adjust - idea, theory] adapter; **I'll** ~ **the dress on you** j'essaierai la robe sur vous.

◇ *vi* -**1.** [be of the correct size]: **the dress doesn't** ~ la robe ne lui/me *etc* va pas; **this lid/key doesn't** ~ ce couvercle/cette clé n'est pas le bon/la bonne; **the key won't** ~ **in the lock** la clé n'entre pas dans la serrure; **do these pieces** ~ **together?** est-ce que ces morceaux vont ensemble?; **it won't** ~ cela n'ira pas; **this lid doesn't** ~ **very well** ce couvercle n'est pas très bien adapté; **we won't all** ~ **round one table** nous ne tiendrons pas tous autour d'une table; **cut the pieces to** ~ couper les morceaux aux mesures adéquates. -**2.** [correspond, match - description] correspondre; **it all** ~**s** tout concorde; **to** ~ **with sthg** correspondre à qqch ❑ **my face didn't** ~ *inf* je n'avais pas le profil de l'emploi.

◆ **fit in** ◇ *vi insep* -**1.** [go in space available] tenir; **we won't all** ~ **in** nous ne tiendrons pas tous; **that piece** ~**s in here** [jigsaw] ce morceau va là. -**2.** [in company, group etc] s'intégrer; **you don't** ~ **in here** tu n'es pas à ta place ici; **I feel that I don't** ~ **in** j'ai l'impression de ne pas être à ma place; **I've tried to** ~ **in** j'ai essayé de m'intégrer; **to** ~ **in with** [statement] correspondre à; [plans, arrangements] cadrer avec; [colour scheme] s'accorder avec; **she doesn't** ~ **in easily with other people** elle a du mal à s'entendre avec les autres; **I think you should** ~ **in with what I want to do** je pense que tu devrais t'adapter à ce que je veux faire.

◇ *vt sep* -**1.** [install] installer. -**2.** [find room for - clothes in suitcase] faire entrer; **can you** ~ **one more in?** [in car] peux-tu prendre une personne de plus?; **how on earth are you going to** ~ **everyone in?** [in room, car etc] comment diable vas-tu réussir à faire tenir tout le monde? -**3.** [find time for - patient] prendre; [- friend] trouver du temps pour; **could you** ~ **in this translation by the end of the week?** est-ce que vous pourriez faire cette traduction d'ici la fin de la semaine?; **could you** ~ **in lunch this week?** [with me] est-ce que tu seras libre pour déjeuner avec moi cette semaine?; **I hope we've got time to** ~ **in a visit to the Louvre** j'espère que nous aurons le temps de visiter le Louvre; **I don't know how he** ~**s it all in** je me demande comment il trouve le temps de tout faire.

◆ **fit into** ◇ *vt insep* [furniture into room, clothes into suitcase etc] entrer dans, tenir dans; [people into room, car] tenir dans; [piece into another] s'emboîter dans.

◇ *vt sep*: **to** ~ **sthg into sthg** faire entrer OR tenir qqch dans qqch; **he** ~**s a lot into one day** il en fait beaucoup en une journée.

◆ **fit on** ◇ *vi insep*: **this lid won't** ~ **on** ce couvercle ne va pas; **where does this part** ~ **on?** où va cette pièce?

◇ *vt sep* [attach] mettre.

◆ **fit out** *vt sep* [ship] armer; [person - with equipment] équiper; **to** ~ **a child out with new clothes** renouveler la garde-robe d'un enfant.

◆ **fit up** *vt sep* -**1.** [equip - house, car] équiper; [- person] munir; **to** ~ **sb/sthg up with sthg** munir qqn/équiper qqch de qqch. -**2.** *Br crime sl* monter un coup contre; **I've been fitted up** c'est un coup monté.

fitful ['fɪtfʊl] *adj* [sleep] intermittent; **attendance has been** ~ les gens ne sont pas venus régulièrement.

fitfully ['fɪtfʊlɪ] *adv* [work] par à-coups; [attend] irrégulièrement; [sleep] de manière intermittente.

fitment ['fɪtmənt] *n Br* [in bathroom, kitchen etc] élément *m* démontable.

fitness ['fɪtnɪs] ◇ *n* -**1.** [health] forme *f* physique. -**2.** [suitability - of person for job] aptitude *f*; **your** ~ **as a mother is not in question** vos compétences de mère ne sont pas en cause.

◇ *comp*: ~ **centre** *Br* club *m* de mise en forme; ~ **freak** *inf* fana *mf* d'exercice physique; ~ **room** salle *f* de mise en forme; ~ **training** entraînement *m* physique.

fitted ['fɪtəd] *adj* -**1.** [jacket] ajusté. -**2.** *Br* [made to measure]: **the house has** ~ **carpets in every room** toutes les pièces de la maison sont moquettées, il y a de la moquette dans toutes les pièces de la maison; **to lay a** ~ **carpet in a room** moquetter OR poser une moquette dans une pièce; ~ **sheet** drap-housse *m*. -**3.** *Br* [built-in - cupboard] encastré; ~ **kitchen** cuisine *f* encastrée. -**4.** [suited]: **to be** ~ **for sthg/doing sthg** être apte à qqch/à faire qqch.

fitter ['fɪtə^r] *n* -**1.** [of machine] monteur *m*, -euse *f*; [of carpet] poseur *m*, -euse *f*. -**2.** [of clothes] essayeur *m*, -euse *f*.

fitting ['fɪtɪŋ] ◇ *adj* [suitable - conclusion, remark] approprié; [- tribute] adéquat; [socially correct] convenable.

◇ *n* -**1.** [trying on - of clothes] essayage *m*. -**2.** *Br* [of shoe]: **have you got it in a wider/narrower** ~? l'avez-vous en plus large/plus étroit?

◇ *comp*: ~ **room** salon *m* OR salle *f* d'essayage; [cubicle] cabine *f* d'essayage.

◆ **fittings** *npl Br*: **bathroom** ~**s** éléments *mpl* de salle de bains; **office** ~**s** équipement *m* de bureau; **electrical** ~**s** appareillage *m* électrique.

-fitting *in cpds*: **close**~, **tight**~ [item of clothing] moulant; [screwtop lid] qui ferme bien; [lid of saucepan] adapté; **loose**~ [item of clothing] ample.

fittingly ['fɪtɪŋlɪ] *adv* [dressed] convenablement; ~, **the government has agreed to ratify the treaty** comme il le fallait, le gouvernement a accepté de ratifier le traité.

fit-up *n Br crime sl* coup *m* monté.

five [faɪv] ◇ *n* [number, numeral, playing card] cinq *m*; ~ **times table** table *f* des cinq; **I'm waiting for a number** ~ **(bus)** j'attends le (bus numéro) cinq; **it's** ~ **o'clock** il est cinq heures; **it's** ~ **to/past** il est cinq heures moins cinq/cinq heures cinq; **to get** ~ **out of ten** avoir cinq sur dix; **a table for** ~ une table pour cinq (personnes).

◇ *adj* cinq; ~ **people** cinq personnes; **trains leave at** ~ **minutes to the hour** le train part toutes les heures à moins cinq; **to be** ~ **(years old)** avoir cinq ans ❑ **'Five Easy Pieces'** *Rafelson* 'Cinq pièces faciles'.

◇ *pron* cinq; ~ **is not enough** cinq, ce n'est pas assez; **I need** ~ il m'en faut cinq; **there are** ~ **of them** [people] ils sont cinq; [objects] il y en a cinq; **give me** ~**!**▽ tope là! *(pour conclure un marché, dire bonjour ou manifester son approbation)*.

◆ **fives** *n sorte de squash où l'on utilise ses mains ou des battes en guise de raquettes.*

five and dime *n* bazar *m*, supérette *f*.

five-a-side *Br* SPORT ◇ *n* football *m* à dix.

◇ *comp*: ~ **football** football *m* à dix; ~ **tournament** tournoi *m* de football à dix.

five-finger *adj* MUS: ~ **exercises** exercices *mpl* de doigté.

fivefold ['faɪvfəʊld] ◇ *adj* [increase] au quintuple.

◇ *adv* par cinq, au quintuple; **to increase** ~ être multiplié par cinq, augmenter au quintuple, quintupler.

five-o'clock shadow *n* barbe *f* d'un jour, barbe *f* naissante; **he's always got** ~ il a toujours l'air mal rasé.

fiver *inf* ['faɪvə^r] *n* [five pounds] billet *m* de cinq livres; [five dollars] billet *m* de cinq dollars.

five spot *inf n Am* billet *m* de cinq dollars.

five-star *adj* [hotel] cinq étoiles.

five-year *adj* [plan] quinquennal.

five-yearly *adj* [election] quinquennal; [festival, event] qui a lieu tous les cinq ans.

fix [fɪks] ◇ *vt* -**1.** [fasten in position - mirror, sign] fixer; [attention, gaze] fixer; [sthg in mind] inscrire, graver; **to** ~ **a post in the ground** enfoncer un poteau dans le sol; ~ **bayonets!** MIL baïonnettes aux canons!; **to** ~ **the blame on sb** attribuer OR imputer la faute à qqn; **to** ~ **one's hopes on sthg/sb** mettre tous ses espoirs en qqch/qqn. -**2.** [set - date, price, rate, limit] fixer; [- meeting place] convenir de; **nothing has been** ~**ed yet** rien n'a encore été fixé; **have you (got) anything** ~**ed for Friday?** as-tu quelque chose de prévu pour vendredi? -**3.** [arrange, sort out] s'occuper de; **I'll** ~ **it** je vais m'en occuper; **try to** ~ **it so we don't have to stay overnight** essaye de t'arranger pour que nous ne soyons pas obligés de passer la nuit là-bas; **I'll** ~ **it with your teacher** j'arrangerai cela avec ton professeur; **I've** ~**ed it for them to come tomorrow** je me suis arrangé pour qu'ils viennent demain. -**4.** *inf* [settle a score with] s'occuper de, régler son compte à; **I'll** ~ **him** je vais m'occuper de lui, je vais lui régler son compte; **that'll** ~ **him** ça devrait lui régler son compte. -**5.** *inf Am* [prepare - meal, drink] préparer; **can I** ~ **you a drink?** puis-je te servir un verre? -**6.** *inf* [adjust - make-up, tie] arranger; **to** ~ **one's hair** se coiffer; [redo] se recoiffer. -**7.** [mend, repair - car, puncture etc] réparer; **I've been meaning to get that** ~**ed for ages** ça fait une éternité que j'ai l'intention de faire réparer ça. -**8.** *inf* [race, fight, election, result] truquer; [interview] arranger; [jury, official, security guard etc - bribe] acheter. -**9.** *inf Am* [intend, plan] prévoir de; [be determined] être résolu à; **he's** ~**ing to go on holiday** [planning] il a prévu de partir en vacances; [determined] il est résolu à partir en vacances. -**10.** AERON & NAUT [position] déterminer. -**11.** CHEM [nitrogen] fixer. -**12.** ART & PHOT [drawing, photo] fixer.

◇ *n* -**1.** *inf* [tight spot, predicament] pétrin *m*; **to be in a** ~ être dans une mauvaise passe; **to get into/out of a** ~ se mettre dans une/sortir d'une mauvaise passe; **you've put me in a bit** of a ~ tu me mets dans l'embarras. -**2.** *drugs sl* dose *f*, fix *m*; **to give o.s. a ~** prendre un fix, se piquer; **to get one's ~ of coffee/news** *hum* avoir sa dose de café/d'informations. -**3.** AERON & NAUT: **to get a ~ on** [ship] déterminer la position de; *fig* [get clear idea of] se faire une idée de. -**4.** *inf* [unfair arrangement]: **the result/race was a ~** le résultat/la course avait été truqué/truquée.

◆ **fix on** ◇ *vt sep* [attach] fixer.
◇ *vt insep* [decide on - date, candidate] choisir.

◆ **fix up** ◇ *vt sep* -**1.** [install, erect] mettre en place, installer. -**2.** *inf* [arrange - date, meeting] fixer; [- deal, holiday] organiser, mettre au point; **~ me up with an appointment with the dentist** prends-moi un rendez-vous chez le dentiste; **he'll try to ~ something up for us** il va essayer de nous arranger quelque chose; **have you got anything ~ed up for this evening?** as-tu quelque chose de prévu pour ce soir?; **have you got ~ed up for your holidays?** est-ce que tu t'es organisé pour tes vacances?; **I've managed to ~ him up with some work** j'ai réussi à lui trouver du travail; **they ~ed me up in a hotel** ils m'ont pris une chambre dans un hôtel; **you can stay here until you get ~ed up (with a place to stay)** tu peux loger ici jusqu'à ce que tu trouves un endroit où habiter; **to ~ sb up with a date** trouver un partenaire/une partenaire à qqn. -**3.** [room] refaire; [flat, house] refaire, retaper; **we could always ~ the smallest bedroom up as a study** on pourrait toujours transformer la plus petite chambre en bureau.
◇ *vi insep* s'arranger pour que; **I've ~ed up for us to see the flat tomorrow** je me suis arrangé pour que nous visitions l'appartement demain.

fixated [fɪk'seɪtɪd] *adj* fixé; **to be ~ on sthg** être fixé sur qqch.

fixation [fɪk'seɪʃn] *n* -**1.** PSYCH fixation *f*; **to have a ~ about sthg** faire une fixation sur qqch; **you've got a ~!** c'est une idée fixe chez toi! -**2.** CHEM fixation *f*.

fixative ['fɪksətɪv] *n* PHOT fixateur *m*; ART fixatif *m*.

fixed [fɪkst] *adj* -**1.** [immovable - glare] fixe; [- idea] arrêté; [- smile] figé; **the seats are ~ to the floor** les sièges sont fixés au sol. -**2.** [set, unchangeable - price, rate, plans] fixe; **people on ~ incomes** des gens disposant de revenus fixes; **of no ~ abode** JUR sans domicile fixe; **~ assets** FIN immobilisations *fpl*; **~ capital** FIN capitaux *mpl* immobilisés; **~ costs** FIN coûts *mpl* fixes; **~ disk** COMPUT disque *m* non amovible; **~ property** FIN immeubles *mpl*; **~ star** ASTRON étoile *f* fixe. -**3.** *inf* [placed]: **how are you ~ for time/money?** [how much] combien de temps/d'argent as-tu?; [is it sufficient] as-tu suffisamment de temps/d'argent?

fixedly ['fɪksɪdlɪ] *adv* [stare] fixement.

fixer ['fɪksə^r] *n* -**1.** *inf* [person] combinard *m*, -e *f*. -**2.** PHOT fixateur *m*. -**3.** [adhesive] adhésif *m*.

fixing bath *n* [container] cuvette *f* de fixage; [solution] bain *m* de fixage.

fixings ['fɪksɪŋz] *npl Am* CULIN accompagnement *m*.

fixing solution *n* solution *f* de fixage.

fixity ['fɪksətɪ] *n* [of gaze] fixité *f*; **~ of purpose** détermination *f*.

fixture ['fɪkstʃə^r] ◇ *n* -**1.** [in building] installation *f* fixe; **she's become a ~ here** *fig* elle fait partie des meubles à présent; **the Christmas party is a ~ in most offices** *fig* faire une fête à Noël est une tradition dans la plupart des bureaux ❑ **bathroom ~s** installations *fpl* sanitaires; **'~s and fittings £2000'** 'reprise 2 000 livres'. -**2.** SPORT rencontre *f*.
◇ *comp*: **~ list** SPORT calendrier *m*.

fizz [fɪz] ◇ *vi* [drink] pétiller; [firework] crépiter; **to be ~ing** *inf fig* [extremely angry] bouillir (de rage).
◇ *n* -**1.** [of drink] pétillement *m*; **the champagne has lost its ~** le champagne est éventé; **their marriage has lost its ~** leur mariage a perdu de son piment. -**2.** [sound] sifflement *m*. -**3.** *inf* [soft drink] boisson *f* gazeuse; *Br* [champagne] champagne *m*.

◆ **fizz up** *vi insep* [drink] mousser, faire de la mousse.

fizziness ['fɪzɪnɪs] *n* [of drink] pétillement *m*; **the champagne has lost its ~** le champagne est éventé.

fizzle ['fɪzl] *vi* [drink] pétiller; [fire, firework] crépiter.

◆ **fizzle out** *vi insep fig* [interest, enthusiasm] tomber; [plan, project] tomber à l'eau; [book, film, party, strike etc] tourner OR partir en eau de boudin; [career] tourner court.

fizzy ['fɪzɪ] (*compar* **fizzier**, *superl* **fizziest**) *adj* [soft drink] gazeux; [wine] pétillant, mousseux.

fjord [fjɔːd] = **fiord**.

FL *written abbr of* Florida.

flab *inf* [flæb] *n* [of person] graisse *f*, lard *m*; [in text] délayage *m*, verbiage *m*; **to fight the ~** essayer de perdre sa graisse.

flabbergast *inf* ['flæbəgæst] *vt* sidérer; **I was ~ed at** OR **by the news** j'ai été sidéré par la nouvelle, la nouvelle m'a sidéré; **I was ~ed by how much he had improved** j'ai été sidéré OR époustouflé par ses progrès.

flabby *inf* ['flæbɪ] (*compar* **flabbier**, *superl* **flabbiest**) *adj* [arms, stomach] flasque, mou; [person] empâté; *fig* [argument, speech] qui manque de concision.

flaccid ['flæsɪd] *adj* flasque.

flag [flæg] (*pt* & *pp* **flagged**, *cont* **flagging**) ◇ *n* -**1.** [emblem of country, signal] drapeau *m*; [for celebration] banderole *f*, fanion *m*; NAUT pavillon *m*; **all the ~s are out in the city** la ville est pavoisée ❑ **black ~** [of pirate ship] drapeau noir; **~ of convenience** NAUT pavillon de complaisance; **red ~** POL drapeau rouge; **The Red Flag** *hymne du parti travailliste*; **yellow ~** NAUT pavillon de quarantaine; **to fly the ~** défendre les couleurs de son pays; **to go down with all ~s flying** NAUT couler pavillon haut; *fig* échouer la tête haute; **to keep the ~ flying** faire front; **to put out the ~s for sb** organiser une fête en l'honneur de qqn; **to show the ~** NAUT battre pavillon; *fig* faire acte de présence. -**2.** [for charity] *badge ou autocollant que l'on obtient lorsque l'on verse de l'argent à une œuvre de charité*. -**3.** [in taxi]: **the ~ was down/up** le taxi était pris/libre; **the driver put the ~ down** le chauffeur a éteint son signal lumineux pour indiquer qu'il n'était plus libre. -**4.** COMPUT drapeau *m*, fanion *m*. -**5.** [on floor] dalle *f*. -**6.** BOT iris *m*.
◇ *vt* -**1.** [put marker on - page of book] marquer; **to ~ an error** COMPUT indiquer OR signaler une erreur par un drapeau OR un fanion. -**2.** [floor] daller.
◇ *vi* [strength] faiblir; [energy, enthusiasm, interest, spirits] faiblir, tomber; [efforts] se relâcher; [conversation] tomber, s'épuiser; **I'm flagging** [becoming physically or mentally tired] je fatigue; [unable to eat any more] je commence à être rassasié, je cale.

◆ **flag down** *vt sep* [taxi, bus, motorist etc] faire signe de s'arrêter à.

◆ **flag up** *vt sep* [identify] marquer.

flag day *n* -**1.** [in UK] *jour de quête d'une œuvre de charité*. -**2.** [in US]: Flag Day le 14 juin *(fête nationale des États-Unis)*.

FLAG DAY:
Les «flag days» britanniques, durant lesquels on sollicite des donations auprès des passants, ont généralement lieu le samedi. Les donateurs reçoivent un papillon en papier qu'ils portent tout au long de la journée.

---

flagellant ['flædʒələnt] *n* RELIG flagellant *m*; [sexual] adepte *mf* de la flagellation.

flagellate ['flædʒəleɪt] ◇ *vt fml* flageller; *fig* fustiger.
◇ *adj* BIOL & BOT flagellé.
◇ *n* BIOL & BOT flagellé *m*.

flagellation [ˌflædʒɪ'leɪʃn] *n* flagellation *f*.

flagellum [flə'dʒeləm] *n* BIOL & BOT flagelle *m*.

flagged [flægd] *adj* dallé.

flagging ['flægɪŋ] ◇ *n* [on floor] dallage *m*.
◇ *adj* [enthusiasm, spirits] qui baisse; [conversation] qui tombe OR s'épuise.

flag officer *n* NAUT contre-amiral *m*.

flagon ['flægən] *n* [jug] cruche *f*; [bottle] bouteille *f*.

flagpole ['flægpəʊl] *n* mât *m*; **let's run it up the ~** *inf* soumettons-le et voyons les réactions.

flagrant ['fleɪgrənt] *adj* [injustice, lie, abuse] flagrant; **a ~ disregard for the safety of others** un mépris flagrant OR évident pour la sécurité d'autrui.

flagrante delicto [flə'græntɪdɪ'lɪktəʊ] *adv phr*: **to be caught in ~** être surpris en flagrant délit.

flagrantly ['fleɪgrəntlɪ] *adv* [abuse, disregard, defy etc] d'une manière flagrante.

flagship ['flægʃɪp] ◇ *n* NAUT vaisseau *m* OR bâtiment *m* amiral; *fig* [product] tête *f* de gamme.
◇ *comp*: **~ restaurant/store** restaurant *m*/magasin *m* principal; **~ model/product** modèle *m*/produit *m* vedette, tête *f* de gamme.

flagstaff ['flægstɑːf] = **flagpole**.

flagstone ['flægstəʊn] = **flag** *n* **5**.

flag-waving *inf n (U) fig* discours *mpl* cocardiers.

flail [fleɪl] ◇ *n* AGR fléau *m*.
◇ *vt* AGR battre au fléau; [arms] agiter.
◇ *vi* [person, limbs] s'agiter violemment.

◆ **flail about** ◇ *vi insep* [person, limbs] s'agiter dans tous les sens.
◇ *vt sep* [arms, legs] battre.

flair [fleə^r] *n* -**1.** [stylishness] style *m*. -**2.** [gift] don *m*; **to have a ~ for sthg** avoir un don pour qqch.

flak [flæk] ◇ *n* -**1.** [gunfire] tir *m* antiaérien OR de DCA. -**2.** *inf (U) fig* [criticism] critiques *fpl*; **I took a lot of ~ over it** on m'a beaucoup critiqué pour cela; **to come in for a lot of ~** se heurter à beaucoup de critiques.
◇ *comp*: **~ jacket** gilet *m* pare-balles.

flake [fleɪk] ◇ *n* -**1.** [of snow] flocon *m*; [of metal] paillette *f*; [of skin] peau *f* morte; [of paint] écaille *f*; **~s of dandruff** pellicules *fpl* ❑ **soap ~s** paillettes *fpl* de savon. -**2.** *inf Am* [person] barjo *mf*.
◇ *vi* [plaster] s'effriter, s'écailler; [paint] s'écailler; [skin] peler; [fish] s'émietter.
◇ *vt* CULIN [fish] émietter; **~d almonds** amandes *fpl* effilées.

◆ **flake off** *vi insep* = **flake** *vi*.

◆ **flake out** *inf vi insep* s'écrouler; [fall asleep] s'endormir; **she was ~d out on the couch** elle roupillait sur le canapé.

flakiness *inf* ['flækɪnəs] *n Am (U)* [of person] bizarreries *fpl*.

flaky ['fleɪkɪ] (*compar* **flakier**, *superl* **flakiest**) *adj* -**1.** [paint, rock] effrité; **~ pastry** CULIN pâte *f* feuilletée. -**2.** *inf Am* [person] barjo; [idea] loufoque.

flamboyance [flæm'bɔɪəns] *n* [of style, dress, behaviour etc] extravagance *f*.

flamboyant [flæm'bɔɪənt] *adj* [behaviour, lifestyle, personality] extravagant; [colour] éclatant; [clothes] aux couleurs éclatantes; *pej* voyant; ARCHIT flamboyant.

flamboyantly [flæm'bɔɪəntlɪ] *adv* de manière extravagante.

flame [fleɪm] ◇ *n* -**1.** [of fire, candle] flamme *f*; **to be in ~s** [building, car] être en flammes; **to burst into ~s** prendre feu, s'enflammer; **to go up in ~s** s'embraser; **~ red** rouge feu ❑ **to be shot down in ~s** *literal* & *fig* être descendu en flammes. -**2.** *lit* [of passion, desire] flamme *f*.
◇ *vi fig* [face, cheeks] s'empourprer; [passion, anger] brûler.
◇ *vt* CULIN flamber.

◆ **flame up** *vi insep* [fire] s'embraser; *fig* [person] s'enflammer.

flamenco [flə'meŋkəʊ] ◇ *n* [dance, music] flamenco *m*.
◇ *comp* [dancer] de flamenco; ~ **music** flamenco *m*.

flameproof ['fleɪmpru:f] *adj* [clothing] ininflammable, à l'épreuve des flammes.

flame retardant ◇ *n* retardateur *m* de flamme, ignifuge *m*.
◇ *comp* [upholstery, sofa etc] ignifugé.

flamethrower ['fleɪmθrəʊəʳ] *n* lance-flammes *m inv*.

flaming ['fleɪmɪŋ] ◇ *adj* -**1.** [sun, sky] embrasé; [fire] flamboyant. -**2.** *inf Br* [extremely angry] : **to be in a ~ temper** être d'une humeur massacrante, être furax; **we had a ~ row about it** nous avons eu une belle engueulade là-dessus. -**3.** *inf* [as intensifier] fichu; **you ~ idiot!** espèce d'abruti!; **you're a ~ pain in the neck!** tu es un sacré enquiquineur!; **where are my ~ keys!** où sont mes fichues clés!
◇ *adv Br* [as intensifier] fichtrement; **don't be so ~ stupid!** ne sois donc pas aussi bête!; **you know ~ well what I mean** tu sais fichtrement bien ce que je veux dire.

flamingo [flə'mɪŋgəʊ] *n* flamant *m* rose.

flammable ['flæməbl] *adj* [material, substance] inflammable.

flan [flæn] CULIN ◇ *n* tarte *f*; [savoury] quiche *f*.
◇ *comp*: ~ **case** fond *m* de tarte.

Flanders ['flɑ:ndəz] *pr n* Flandre *f*, Flandres *fpl*; **in ~** dans les Flandres, en Flandre.

flange [flændʒ] ◇ *n* [on pipe] bride *f*, collerette *f*; RAIL [on rail] patin *m*.
◇ *comp*: ~ **girder** poutre *f* en I.

flanged [flændʒd] *adj* [with flanges] à brides; [attached by flanges] fixé par brides.

flank [flæŋk] ◇ *n* flanc *m*; **to protect one's ~s** MIL protéger ses flancs □ ~ **of beef** CULIN flanchet *m*.
◇ *vt* -**1.** [be on either side of] encadrer; **~ed by his wife and daughter** entouré de sa femme et de sa fille. -**2.** MIL flanquer.

flanker ['flæŋkəʳ] *n* RUGBY avant-aile *m*, flanqueur *m*.

flannel ['flænl] (*Br pt & pp* **flannelled**, *cont* **flannelling**, *Am pt & pp* **flanneled**, *cont* **flanneling**) ◇ *n* -**1.** TEX flanelle *f*; **~s** [trousers] pantalon *m* en OR de flanelle. -**2.** *Br* [for washing] gant *m* de toilette. -**3.** *inf (U) Br* [empty words] baratin *m*, blabla *m*, blablabla *m*; **to talk a lot of ~** faire beaucoup de baratin OR de blabla.
◇ *comp* TEX [nightgown, sheet, trousers, suit] en OR de flanelle.
◇ *vi inf Br* [use empty words] faire du baratin OR du blabla OR du blablabla; **stop flannelling!** arrête ton baratin OR ton blablabla!

flannelette [flænə'let] TEX ◇ *n* pilou *m*.
◇ *comp* [nightgown, sheet] en OR de pilou.

flap [flæp] (*pt & pp* **flapped**, *cont* **flapping**) ◇ *n* -**1.** [of sails] claquement *m*; [of wings] battement *m*; **the bird gave a ~ of its wings** l'oiseau a battu des ailes. -**2.** [of counter, desk - hinged] abattant *m*; [- sliding] rallonge *f*; [of pocket, cap, tent, envelope] rabat *m*; [in floor, door] trappe *f*; [of aircraft] volet *m* (hypersustentateur); **a ~ of skin** un morceau de peau décollée. -**3.** *inf* [panic] panique *f*; **to be in a ~** être dans tous ses états, être paniqué; **to get into a ~** se mettre dans tous ses états, paniquer; **there's a ~ on at the office** c'est la panique au bureau.
◇ *vi* -**1.** [wings] battre; [sails, shutters, washing, curtains] claquer; **the seagull flapped away** la mouette est partie dans un battement d'ailes. -**2.** *inf* [panic] paniquer, s'affoler.
◇ *vt*: **the bird flapped its wings** l'oiseau a battu des ailes; **he was flapping his arms about to keep warm** il agitait ses bras pour se tenir chaud.

flapjack ['flæpdʒæk] *n* CULIN [in UK] biscuit *m* à l'avoine; [in US] *petite crêpe épaisse*.

flapper ['flæpəʳ] *n jeune fille dans le vent (dans les années 20)*.

flare [fleəʳ] ◇ *n* -**1.** [bright flame - of gas fire, match] flamboiement *m*. -**2.** [signal] signal *m* lumineux; [rocket] fusée *f* éclairante. -**3.** [in clothes] évasement *m*; **a skirt with a ~ in it** une jupe à godets; **trousers with a ~** un pantalon à pattes d'éléphant.
◇ *vi* -**1.** [flame, match] flamboyer. -**2.** [tempers] s'échauffer; **tempers ~d** les esprits se sont échauffés. -**3.** [nostrils] frémir. -**4.** [dress, trousers] s'évaser.
◇ *vt* [dress, trousers] évaser.
◆ **flares** *npl*: (a pair of) **~s** un pantalon à pattes d'éléphant.
◆ **flare up** *vi insep* [fire] s'embraser; *fig* [dispute, quarrel, violence] éclater; [disease, epidemic, crisis] apparaître, se déclarer; [person] s'emporter; **he ~d up at me** il s'est emporté contre moi.

flared [fleəd] *adj* [trousers] à pattes d'éléphant; [dress] évasé; [skirt] évasé, à godets.

flare gun *n* pistolet *m* de détresse, lance-fusées *m inv*.

flare path *n* piste *f* à balises lumineuses.

flare-up *n* [of fire, light] flamboiement *m*; *fig* [of anger, violence] explosion *f*; [of tension] montée *f*; [of disease, epidemic] apparition *f*; [quarrel] dispute *f*; **renewed ~** [of anger, violence] reprise *f*, nouvelle explosion; [of tension] remontée *f*; [of disease, epidemic] réapparition *f*.

flash [flæʃ] ◇ *n* -**1.** [of light, diamond] éclat *m*; [of metal] reflet *m*, éclat *m*; **we saw a ~ of light in the distance** nous avons vu l'éclat d'une lumière au loin; **give three ~es of the torch** allume la torche trois fois; **~ of wit/humour** pointe *f* d'esprit/d'humour; **~ of inspiration** éclair *m* de génie; **in a ~** [very quickly] en un éclair, en un clin d'œil; **it came to me in a ~** cela m'est venu d'un seul coup □ ~ **of lightning** éclair *m*; **a ~ in the pan** un feu de paille; **(as) quick as a ~** aussi rapide que l'éclair, rapide comme l'éclair. -**2.** [of news] flash *m* (d'information). -**3.** MIL [on uniform] écusson *m*. -**4.** [of colour] tache *f*. -**5.** PHOT flash *m*; **are you going to use a ~ for this one?** est-ce que tu vas la prendre au flash, celle-ci? -**6.** *inf Am* [flashlight] torche *f*.
◇ *vi* -**1.** [light, torch, sign] clignoter; [diamond] briller, lancer des éclats; **lightning ~ed directly overhead** il y a eu des éclairs juste au-dessus; **her eyes ~ed** ses yeux ont lancé des éclairs; **to ~ at sb** AUT faire un appel de phares à qqn. -**2.** [move fast] filer comme l'éclair, aller à la vitesse de l'éclair; **to ~ in/out/past** [person, car] entrer/sortir/passer comme un éclair; **to ~ past** OR **by** [time] passer à toute vitesse; **the day/the days seemed to ~ by** la journée a semblé passer/les jours ont semblé défiler à toute vitesse; **the thought ~ed through** OR **across her mind that...** la pensée que... lui a traversé l'esprit; **a smile ~ed across his face** un sourire éclaira soudain son visage; **information ~ed onto** OR **up on the screen** des informations sont apparues sur l'écran; **my life ~ed before me** ma vie a défilé devant mes yeux. -**3.** *inf Br* [expose o.s.] s'exhiber.
◇ *vt* -**1.** [torch - turn on and off] faire clignoter; **to ~ a light in sb's face** OR **eyes** diriger une lumière dans les yeux de qqn; **to ~ (one's headlights at) sb** AUT faire un appel de phares à qqn; **to ~ a smile at sb** *fig* lancer OR adresser un sourire à qqn; **she ~ed me a look of contempt** *fig* elle m'a décoché un regard méprisant. -**2.** [give brief glimpse of - passport, photograph etc] montrer rapidement; **to ~ one's money around** [to impress] dépenser son argent avec ostentation; [be indiscreet] montrer son argent. -**3.** [news, information] diffuser; **to ~ a message up on the screen** faire apparaître un message sur l'écran.
◇ *adj inf* = **flashy**.
◆ **flash back** ◇ *vi insep* [in novel, film etc] : **to ~ back to sthg** revenir en arrière sur qqch, faire un flash-back sur qqch; **my mind ~ed back to 1942** l'année 1942 m'est soudain revenue à l'esprit.
◇ *vt sep* [news] envoyer OR transmettre rapidement.

flashback ['flæʃbæk] *n* [in novel, film, etc] flash-back *m inv*, retour *m* en arrière; **a ~ to the war** un flash-back sur la guerre; **I had a ~ to when I was a child** mon enfance m'est revenue à l'esprit.

flashbulb ['flæʃbʌlb] *n* PHOT ampoule *f* de flash.

flash burn *n* brûlure *f (causée par un éclat très violent et brûlant, comme celui d'une bombe)*.

flash card *n* SCH *carte portant un mot, une image etc utilisée dans l'enseignement comme aide à l'apprentissage*.

flashcube ['flæʃkju:b] *n* PHOT cube *m* de flash.

flasher ['flæʃəʳ] *n* -**1.** AUT [indicator] clignotant *m*. -**2.** *inf* [person] exhibitionniste *mf*.

flash flood *n* crue *f* subite.

flash freezing *n* surgélation *f*.

flash-fry *vt* saisir.

flash gun *n* PHOT flash *m*.

flash Harry *inf* [-'hærɪ] *n Br personne qui se comporte et s'habille tapageusement*.

flashily *inf* ['flæʃɪlɪ] *adv pej* d'une manière tapageuse OR tape-à-l'œil, tapageusement.

flashing ['flæʃɪŋ] ◇ *adj* [indicator, light, torch] clignotant; **with ~ eyes, she stormed out** elle sortit brutalement, les yeux ardents (de colère) □ ~ **emergency lights** AUT feux *mpl* de détresse; ~ **light** [on police car] gyrophare *m*.
◇ *n* -**1.** *inf* [indecent exposure] exhibitionnisme *m*. -**2.** [on roof] revêtement *m* de protection; [of lead] noue *f*.

flashlight ['flæʃlaɪt] *n* -**1.** PHOT ampoule *f* de flash. -**2.** *esp Am* [torch] torche *f* électrique, lampe *f* électrique OR de poche. -**3.** [flashing signal] fanal *m*.

flash photography *n* photographie *f* au flash.

flash point *n* -**1.** CHEM point *m* d'éclair. -**2.** *fig* [trouble spot] poudrière *f*; **the situation has reached ~** *fig* la situation est explosive OR sur le point d'exploser.

flashy *inf* ['flæʃɪ] *adj* [person, car, clothes, taste] tapageur, tape-à-l'œil *(inv)*; [colour] voyant, criard.

flask [flɑ:sk] *n* PHARM fiole *f*; CHEM ballon *m*; [for water, wine] gourde *f*; **vacuum** OR **Thermos® ~** (bouteille *f*) Thermos® *f*.

flat [flæt] ◇ *adj* -**1.** [countryside, feet, stomach] plat; [surface] plan; [roof] plat, en terrasse; [nose] épaté, camus; [tyre - deflated] à plat, dégonflé; [- punctured] crevé; [ball, balloon] dégonflé; ~ **calm** NAUT calme *m* plat; **to stretch out ~** [person] s'allonger à plat; **to stand ~ against the wall** [person] se plaquer contre le mur; [item of furniture] être adossé contre le mur; **it folds up ~** c'est pliable; **to lie ~ on one's back** être allongé à plat sur le dos; **to be ~ on one's back** *fig* [with illness] être alité; **lay the book ~ on the desk** pose le livre à plat sur le bureau; **the blow laid him ~** le coup l'a assommé; **to fall ~ on one's back** tomber sur le dos; **to fall ~** [joke] tomber à plat □ **to fall ~ on one's face** *literal* tomber la tête la première; *fig* se casser le nez. -**2.** [soft drink, beer, champagne] éventé; *fig* [monotonous - style, voice] monotone, terne; [without emotion - voice] éteint; [stock market, business] au point mort; [social life] peu animé; **to feel ~** *fig* se sentir vidé OR à plat; **to go ~** [beer, soft drink] s'éventer, perdre ses bulles. -**3.** [battery] à plat. -**4.** MUS en dessous du ton; **to be ~** [singer] chanter en dessous du ton; [instrumentalist] jouer en dessous du ton; **E ~** mi bémol. -**5.** [categorical - refusal, denial] catégorique; **to give a ~ refusal** refuser catégoriquement; **you're not going, and that's ~!** tu n'iras pas, un point c'est tout! -**6.** COMM [rate, fare, fee] fixe. -**7.** *phr*: **to be in a ~ spin** *inf* être dans tous ses états.
◇ *adv* -**1.** [categorically] catégoriquement; **she turned me down ~** elle m'a opposé un refus catégorique. -**2.** [exactly] : **in thirty seconds ~** en trente secondes pile. -**3.** MUS en dessous du ton. -**4.** *inf phr*: ~ **broke** complètement fauché.
◇ *n* -**1.** *Br* appartement *m*; **(block of) ~s** immeuble *m* (d'habitation). -**2.** [of hand, blade] plat *m*. -**3.** [in horse racing] : **the ~** [races] le plat; [season] la saison des courses de plat; **on the ~** sur le plat. -**4.** MUS bémol *m*. -**5.** *inf* [puncture]

crevaison *f*; [punctured tyre] pneu *m* crevé; [deflated tyre] pneu *m* à plat; we got a ~ [puncture] nous avons crevé. -**6.** THEAT ferme *f*.
◆ **flats** *npl* GEOG: mud ~s bancs *mpl* de boue; salt ~s marais *mpl* salants.
◆ **flat out** *adv phr*: to work ~ out travailler d'arrache-pied; to be ~ out [exhausted] être à plat, être vidé; [drunk] être fin saoul; [knocked out] être K-O; to be going ~ out [car] être à sa vitesse maximum; [driver, runner, horse] être au maximum OR à fond; the car does 100 mph ~ out la vitesse maximale OR de pointe de la voiture est de 160 km/h; she's going ~ out to win the chairmanship elle met tout en jeu pour obtenir la présidence.
flat-bed lorry *n* semi-remorque *m* à plateau.
flat-bottomed boat [-'bɒtəmd-] *n* bateau *m* à fond plat.
flat cap *n* casquette *f* *(traditionnellement perçue comme typique de l'ouvrier en Grande-Bretagne)*.
flat-chested [-'tʃestɪd] *adj*: to be ~ ne pas avoir de poitrine; *pej* être plat comme une planche à pain OR une limande.
flat-dweller *n Br* personne *f* vivant en appartement.
flatfish ['flætfɪʃ] *n* poisson *m* plat.
flat-footed *adj* -**1.** MED aux pieds plats. -**2.** *inf* [clumsy] empoté; [tactless] maladroit, lourdaud. -**3.** *inf* [off guard]: to catch sb ~ prendre qqn par surprise.
flat-hunt *vi (usu in progressive) Br* chercher un appartement; I've spent the whole day ~ing j'ai passé toute la journée à chercher un appartement.
flat-hunting *n Br* recherche *f* d'appartement; ~ takes up all my free time la recherche d'un appartement occupe tout mon temps libre.
flatiron ['flætaɪən] *n* fer *m* à repasser *(non électrique)*.
flatland ['flætlænd] *n* plaine *f*.
flatlet ['flætlɪt] *n Br* studio *m*.
flatly ['flætlɪ] *adv* -**1.** [categorically - deny, refuse] catégoriquement. -**2.** [without emotion - say, speak] d'une voix éteinte; [monotonously] avec monotonie.
flatmate ['flætmeɪt] *n Br personne avec qui on partage un appartement*; she and I were ~s in London elle et moi partagions un appartement à Londres.
flat race *n* [in horse racing] course *f* de plat.
flat racing *n* [in horse racing - races] plat *m*; [- season] saison *f* des courses de plat.
flat-screen *adj* TV & COMPUT à écran plat.
flat season *n* [in horse racing] saison *f* des courses de plat.
flatten ['flætn] ◇ *vt* -**1.** [path, road, ground] aplanir; [dough, metal] aplatir; [animal, person - subj: vehicle] écraser; [house, village - subj: bulldozer, earthquake] raser; [crop - subj: wind, storm] écraser, aplatir; [piece of paper] étaler; to ~ o.s. against a wall se plaquer OR se coller contre un mur. -**2.** *inf* [defeat thoroughly] écraser, battre à plate couture. -**3.** *inf* [knock to the ground] démolir. -**4.** *inf* [subdue - person] clouer le bec à; that'll ~ her ça lui clouera le bec, ça la remettra à sa place. -**5.** MUS [note] baisser d'un demi-ton, bémoliser.
◇ *vi* = **flatten out**.
◆ **flatten out** ◇ *vi insep* -**1.** [countryside, hills] s'aplanir. -**2.** AERON [plane] se redresser; [pilot] redresser l'appareil.
◇ *vt sep* [piece of paper] étaler à plat; [bump, path, road] aplanir.
flatter ['flætəʳ] ◇ *vt* [subj: person] flatter; [subj: dress, photo, colour] avantager; I'm ~ed to have been chosen je suis flatté d'avoir été choisi OR que l'on m'ait choisi; don't ~ yourself!, you ~ yourself! non mais tu rêves!; we ~ ourselves on offering a more efficient service nous nous flattons d'offrir un service plus efficace; he ~s himself (that) he's a good singer il a la prétention d'être un bon chanteur.
◇ *vi* flatter.
flatterer ['flætərəʳ] *n* flatteur *m*, -euse *f*.
flattering ['flætərɪŋ] *adj* [remark, person, offer] flatteur; [picture, portrait, colour] avantageux, flatteur; [dress] seyant; how ~! comme c'est flatteur!
flatteringly ['flætərɪŋlɪ] *adv* [speak of, describe] en termes flatteurs, flatteusement.
flattery ['flætərɪ] (*pl* **flatteries**) *n* flatterie *f*; to use ~ employer la flatterie OR des flatteries; ~ will get you nowhere la flatterie ne vous mènera nulle part, vous n'obtiendrez rien par la flatterie.
flattie ['flætɪ] *n* chaussure *f* plate.
flat top *n* -**1.** [haircut] brosse *f*. -**2.** *inf Am* NAUT porte-avions *m inv*.
flatulence ['flætjʊləns] *n* flatulence *f*.
flatulent ['flætjʊlənt] *adj* flatulent.
flatware ['flætweəʳ] *n (U) Am* [cutlery] couverts *mpl*; [serving dishes] plats *mpl*; [plates] assiettes *fpl*.
flatways ['flætweɪz], **flatwise** ['flætwaɪz] *adv Am* à plat.
flatworm ['flæt,wɜːm] *n* plathelminthe *m*, ver *m* plat.
flaunt [flɔːnt] *vt* [wealth, beauty] étaler, faire étalage de; [car, jewellery] faire parade de, exhiber; to ~ o.s. s'afficher; if you've got it, ~ it si tu as ce qu'il faut, ne t'en cache pas.
flautist ['flɔːtɪst] *n Br* MUS flûtiste *mf*.
Flavius ['fleɪvjəs] *pr n*: ~ Josephus Flavius Josèphe.
flavor *etc Am* = **flavour**.
flavour *Br*, **flavor** *Am* ['fleɪvəʳ] ◇ *n* [of food, drink] goût *m*; [of ice-cream, tea] parfum *m*; chocolate/coffee ~ ice-cream glace au chocolat/au café; this coffee keeps its ~ well ce café garde bien sa saveur; it doesn't have much ~ cela n'a pas beaucoup de goût; it's got quite a spicy ~ c'est assez épicé; it gives the film a South American ~ *fig* cela donne une note sud-américaine au film ❑ to be ~ of the month [in vogue] être au goût du jour; you're not exactly ~ of the month at the moment *inf* tu n'es pas comme qui dirait en odeur de sainteté en ce moment, tu n'as pas vraiment la cote en ce moment.
◇ *comp*: ~ enhancers agents *mpl* de sapidité.
◇ *vt* [with spices, herbs etc] assaisonner; [with fruit, alcohol] parfumer; chocolate-~ed au chocolat; vanilla-~ed à la vanille.
flavouring *Br*, **flavoring** *Am* ['fleɪvərɪŋ] *n* CULIN [savoury] assaisonnement *m*; [sweet] parfum *m*, arôme *m*; 'no artificial ~s' [on tin, package] 'sans arômes artificiels'.
flavourless *Br*, **flavorless** *Am* ['fleɪvəlɪs] *adj* sans goût, insipide.
flaw [flɔː] ◇ *n* [in material, plan, character] défaut *m*; JUR vice *m* de forme.
◇ *vt* [object] endommager; [sb's character, beauty] altérer.
flawed [flɔːd] *adj* imparfait; the argument is, however, ~ cette argumentation a cependant un défaut OR des défauts.
flawless ['flɔːlɪs] *adj* parfait.
flawlessly ['flɔːlɪslɪ] *adv* parfaitement.
flax [flæks] *n* lin *m*.
flaxen ['flæksn] *adj* [hair] blond pâle OR filasse.
flaxen-haired *adj* aux cheveux blond pâle OR filasse.
flay [fleɪ] *vt* [animal] dépouiller, écorcher; [person] fouetter; *fig* [criticize] éreinter; to ~ sb alive faire la peau à qqn.
flea [fliː] ◇ *n* puce *f*; to have ~s avoir des puces ❑ to send sb off with a ~ in his/her ear *inf* [dismiss] envoyer balader qqn; [scold] passer un savon à qqn.
◇ *comp*: ~ circus cirque *m* de puces savantes.
fleabag *inf* ['fliːbæg] *n* -**1.** *Br* [animal, person] sac *m* à puces. -**2.** *Am* [cheap hotel] hôtel *m* miteux.
fleabite ['fliːbaɪt] *n* piqûre *f* OR morsure *f* de puce; *fig* [trifle] broutille *f*.
flea-bitten *adj* couvert de puces; *fig* [shabby] miteux.
flea collar *n* collier *m* anti-puces.
flea market *n* marché *m* aux puces.
fleapit *inf* ['fliːpɪt] *n* cinéma *m* OR théâtre *m* miteux; the local ~ *hum* le cinéma du coin.
fleck [flek] ◇ *n* [of colour] moucheture *f*, tacheture *f*; [of sunlight] moucheture *f*; [of dust] particule *f*.
◇ *vt* [with colour] moucheter, tacheter; [with sunlight] moucheter; hair ~ed with grey cheveux *mpl* grisonnants; white ~ed with brown blanc moucheté OR tacheté de marron.
fled [fled] *pt & pp* → **flee**.
fledged [fledʒd] *adj* [bird] emplumé.
fledg(e)ling ['fledʒlɪŋ] ◇ *n* -**1.** [young bird] oisillon *m*. -**2.** *fig* novice *mf*, débutant *m*, -e *f*.
◇ *comp* [company, industry, political party etc] naissant; a ~ doctor/lawyer un docteur/avocat débutant.
flee [fliː] (*pt & pp* **fled** [fled]) ◇ *vi* s'enfuir, fuir; to ~ from sb/sthg fuir qqn/qqch; to ~ from a house/country s'enfuir d'une maison/d'un pays; to ~ from temptation fuir la tentation.
◇ *vt* [person, danger, temptation] fuir; [country, town] s'enfuir de.
fleece [fliːs] ◇ *n* -**1.** [of sheep] toison *f*; the Golden Fleece MYTH la Toison d'or. -**2.** TEX peau *f* de mouton.
◇ *comp* [lining] en peau de mouton; ~ lined [coat, jacket, gloves] doublé en peau de mouton.
◇ *vt* -**1.** *inf* [cheat] escroquer; I've been ~d je me suis fait escroquer. -**2.** [shear - sheep] tondre.
fleecy ['fliːsɪ] *adj* [material] laineux; [clouds] cotonneux.
fleet [fliːt] ◇ *n* -**1.** NAUT flotte *f*; [smaller] flottille *f*. -**2.** [of buses, taxis] parc *m*; a ~ of ambulances took the injured to hospital plusieurs ambulances ont transporté les blessés à l'hôpital.
◇ *adj lit* rapide; ~ of foot aux pieds ailés.
fleet admiral *n* NAUT ≃ amiral *m* de France.
Fleet Air Arm *pr n*: the ~ *l'aéronavale britannique*.
fleeting ['fliːtɪŋ] *adj* [memory] fugace; [beauty, pleasure] passager; for a ~ moment l'espace d'un instant; to catch a ~ glimpse of sthg/sb apercevoir OR entrevoir qqch/qqn; to pay sb a ~ visit rendre visite à qqn en coup de vent.
fleetingly ['fliːtɪŋlɪ] *adv* [glimpse] rapidement.
Fleet Street [fliːt-] *pr n rue de Londres, dont le nom sert à désigner les grands journaux britanniques.*

FLEET STREET:
Cette rue de la City est traditionnellement celle des journaux. Aujourd'hui, beaucoup de journaux ont établi leur siège dans d'autres quartiers, notamment les Docklands. Cependant, le terme «Fleet Street» est encore employé pour désigner la presse et le monde du journalisme.

Fleming ['flemɪŋ] *n* Flamand *m*, -e *f*.
Flemish ['flemɪʃ] ◇ *n* LING flamand *m*.
◇ *npl*: the ~ les Flamands *mpl*.
◇ *adj* flamand.
flesh [fleʃ] *n* -**1.** [of person, animal, fruit] chair *f*; there's not much ~ on her elle n'est pas très grasse; to put on ~ [person] forcir; [animal] engraisser; it needs a bit more ~ *fig* [proposal, essay etc] il a besoin d'être un peu étoffé; she looks better on TV than she does in the ~ elle est plus jolie à la télé qu'en chair et en os ❑ creatures of ~ and blood êtres *mpl* de chair et de sang; I'm only ~ and blood, you know je suis comme tout le monde, tu sais; it's more than ~ and blood can bear OR stand c'est plus que ce que la nature humaine peut endurer; she's my own ~ and blood c'est ma chair et mon sang; he wants his pound of ~ il veut ce qui lui est dû; to press the ~ *inf* [politicians, royalty etc] serrer des mains. -**2.** RELIG chair *f*; pleasures/sins of the ~ plaisirs de la/péchés de chair; the spirit is willing but the ~ is weak l'esprit est prompt mais la chair est faible; to go the way of all ~ retourner à la OR redevenir poussière. -**3.** [colour] couleur *f* chair.

◆ **flesh out** ◇ *vt sep* [essay, report etc] étoffer.
◇ *vi insep* [person] s'étoffer, prendre de la carrure.

flesh-coloured *adj* [tights] couleur chair.

fleshpots ['fleʃpɒts] *npl hum* OR *pej* lieux *mpl* de plaisir.

flesh wound *n* blessure *f* superficielle OR légère.

fleshy ['fleʃɪ] (*compar* **fleshier**, *superl* **fleshiest**) *adj* [person] bien en chair; [part of the body, fruit, leaf] charnu.

fleur-de-lis, fleur-de-lys [,flɜːdə'liː] *n* HERALD fleur *f* de lis OR lys.

flew [fluː] *pt* → **fly**.

flex [fleks] ◇ *vt* [one's arms, knees] fléchir; to ~ one's muscles *literal* bander OR faire jouer ses muscles; *fig* faire étalage de sa force.
◇ *n* [wire] fil *m*; [heavy duty] câble *m*.

flexibility [,fleksə'bɪlətɪ] *n* [of object] flexibilité *f*, souplesse *f*; *fig* [of plan, approach] flexibilité *f*; [of person's character] souplesse *f*; **he has always shown a lot of ~** [in timing, arrangements] il s'est toujours montré très disponible OR arrangeant; **what I like about this software is its ~** ce qui me plaît dans ce logiciel, c'est sa flexibilité OR souplesse d'emploi.

flexible ['fleksəbl] *adj* flexible, souple; *fig* [approach, plans, timetable etc] flexible; [person's character] souple; [as regards timing, arrangements] arrangeant; **~ working hours** horaires *mpl* (de travail) à la carte OR flexibles; **my working hours are very ~** j'ai des horaires de travail très libres OR souples; **~ response** MIL riposte *f* graduée.

flexion ['flekʃn] *n* GRAM flexion *f*.

flexitime ['fleksɪtaɪm] *n* (*U*) horaires *m* à la carte OR flexibles; **to be on** OR **to work ~** avoir des horaires à la carte OR flexibles.

flexor ['fleksəʳ] ANAT ◇ *adj* [muscle] fléchisseur.
◇ *n* fléchisseur *m*.

flextime ['flekstaɪm] = **flexitime**.

flibbertigibbet [,flɪbətɪ'dʒɪbɪt] *n* écervelé *m*, -e *f*, tête *f* de linotte.

flick [flɪk] ◇ *n* [with finger] chiquenaude *f*; [with wrist] petit OR léger mouvement *m*; [with tail, whip, duster] petit OR léger coup *m*; **with a ~ of his finger** d'une chiquenaude; **give the table a quick ~ with a duster** donne un petit coup de chiffon à OR sur la table; **at the ~ of a switch** en appuyant simplement sur un interrupteur.
◇ *vt* [switch] appuyer sur; **he ~ed the horse with his whip** il a donné un petit coup de fouet au cheval; **don't ~ your ash on the floor** ne mets pas tes cendres par terre; **she ~ed the ash off the table** [with duster] d'un coup de chiffon, elle a enlevé la cendre de la table; [with finger] d'une chiquenaude, elle a enlevé la cendre de la table.

◆ **flicks** *inf npl dated*: **the ~s** le ciné, le cinoche.

◆ **flick off** *vt sep* [with finger - ash, paper etc] envoyer promener OR enlever d'une chiquenaude; [light, computer] éteindre.

◆ **flick on** *vt sep* [light, computer] allumer.

◆ **flick over** *vt sep* [pages of book, newspaper etc] tourner rapidement.

◆ **flick through** *vt insep* [book, newspaper] feuilleter; **to ~ through the channels** TV passer rapidement d'une chaîne à une autre.

flicker ['flɪkəʳ] ◇ *vi* [flame, light] vaciller, trembler; [eyelids, TV screen, snake's tongue] trembler; **the candle was ~ing** la flamme de la bougie vacillait.
◇ *n* [of flame, light] vacillement *m*, tremblement *m*; [of eyelids, TV screen] tremblement *m*.

flickering ['flɪkərɪŋ] ◇ *adj* [light] vacillant; [image] tremblotant.
◇ *n* -**1.** [of light, flame] vacillement *m*. -**2.** [of image] tremblement *m*.

flick-knife *n* (couteau *m* à) cran *m* d'arrêt.

flier ['flaɪəʳ] *n* -**1.** AERON [pilot] aviateur *m*, -trice *f*; [passenger]: **she's a good/bad ~** [likes/dislikes flying] elle supporte bien/ne supporte pas l'avion; **she's a frequent ~** elle prend souvent l'avion. -**2.** ORNITH: **the heron is a rather ungainly ~** le héron a un vol peu élégant. -**3.** *inf* SPORT [start to race] départ *m* lancé; [false start] faux départ *m*; **to get a ~** [good start] partir comme un boulet de canon. -**4.** *inf* [fall] vol *m* plané; **to take a ~** faire un vol plané. -**5.** *inf Am* [speculative venture] entreprise *f* à risques; **it's a bit of a ~, don't you think?** c'est un peu risqué, tu ne crois pas? -**6.** [leaflet] prospectus *m*.

flies [flaɪz] *npl* -**1.** = **fly 2.** -**2.** THEAT dessus *mpl*, cintres *mpl*.

flight [flaɪt] *n* -**1.** [flying] vol *m*; **capable of ~** capable de voler; **to be in ~** être en vol. -**2.** [journey - of bird, spacecraft, plane, missile] vol *m*; **manned ~** [of spacecraft] vol habité; **a ~ of 500 miles is nothing to a swallow** les hirondelles peuvent facilement effectuer des vols de 800 kilomètres. -**3.** AERON [journey in plane - by passenger] voyage *m*; [- by pilot] vol *m*; [plane itself] vol *m*; **how was your ~?** as-tu fait bon voyage?; **this is my first transatlantic ~** [passenger] c'est la première fois que je traverse l'Atlantique en avion; [pilot] c'est mon premier vol OR ma première traversée transatlantique; **~ BA 314 to New York is now boarding at gate 4** l'embarquement du vol BA 314 à destination de New York vient de commencer porte numéro quatre; **when is the next ~ to Newcastle?** à quelle heure part le prochain vol pour OR à destination de Newcastle?; **all ~s out of Charles de Gaulle** tous les vols en provenance de Charles-de-Gaulle. -**4.** [group of birds] vol *m*, volée *f*; [group of aircraft] flotte *f* aérienne. -**5.** [fleeing] fuite *f*; **to be in full ~** être en pleine retraite; **to take (to) ~** prendre la fuite; **to put sb/the enemy to ~** mettre qqn/l'ennemi en fuite; **the ~ of capital overseas** *fig* la fuite des capitaux à l'étranger ❑ **the Flight into Egypt** la fuite en Égypte. -**6.** [of stairs]: **~ (of stairs** OR **steps)** escalier *m*; **I had to walk up all ten ~s** j'ai dû monter les dix étages à pied; **it's another three ~s up** c'est trois étages plus haut; **I'm not carrying this wardrobe up all those ~s of stairs** je refuse de monter cette penderie tout là-haut; **a short ~ of steps** quelques marches. -**7.** *fig*: **a ~ of the imagination** une envolée de l'imagination; **it was just a ~ of fancy** ce n'était qu'une idée folle. -**8.** [on arrow, dart] penne *f*, empennage *m*. -**9.** *phr*: **to be in the first** OR **top ~** faire partie de l'élite.

flight attendant *n* [male] steward *m*; [female] hôtesse *f* de l'air; **one of our ~s** un des membres de l'équipage.

flight control *n* [place] contrôle *m* aérien; [people] contrôleurs *mpl* aériens.

flight crew *n* équipage *m (d'un avion)*.

flight deck *n* [of aircraft] poste *m* OR cabine *f* de pilotage, habitacle *m*; [of aircraft carrier] pont *m* d'envol.

flight engineer *n* mécanicien *m* navigant *(d'avion)*, ingénieur *m* de vol.

flightiness ['flaɪtɪnɪs] *n* inconstance *f*.

flightless ['flaɪtlɪs] *adj* [bird] coureur.

flight lieutenant *n capitaine de l'armée de l'air britannique*.

flight number *n* numéro *m* de vol.

flight path *n* trajectoire *f* de vol.

flight plan *n* plan *m* de vol.

flight recorder *n* enregistreur *m* de vol.

flight sergeant *n sergent-chef de l'armée de l'air britannique*.

flight simulator *n* simulateur *m* de vol.

flighty ['flaɪtɪ] (*compar* **flightier**, *superl* **flightiest**) *adj* inconstant; [in romantic relationships] volage, inconstant.

flimflam *inf* ['flɪmflæm] *n* (*U*) [deceitful talk] baratin *m*, blabla *m*, blablabla *m*.

flimsily ['flɪmzɪlɪ] *adv* [built, constructed] d'une manière peu solide, peu solidement.

flimsy ['flɪmzɪ] (*compar* **flimsier**, *superl* **flimsiest**) ◇ *adj* -**1.** [material] fin, léger; [clothes, shoes] léger; [sthg built] peu solide; [paper] peu résistant, fragile; [toys, books] fragile. -**2.** [argument, case, excuse etc] léger.
◇ *n* [paper] papier *m* pelure; [with typing on it] double *m* sur pelure.

flinch [flɪntʃ] *vi* -**1.** [wince, with pain] tressaillir; **without ~ing** sans broncher. -**2.** [shy away]: **to ~ from one's duty/obligations** reculer devant son devoir/ses obligations; **she didn't ~ from doing her duty** elle n'a pas reculé devant son devoir; **she ~ed at the thought** l'idée l'a fait reculer.

fling [flɪŋ] (*pt* & *pp* **flung** [flʌŋ]) ◇ *vt* lancer, jeter; **don't just ~ it, aim when you throw** ne le lance pas n'importe où, vise d'abord; **to ~ one's arms around sb's neck** jeter ses bras autour du cou de qqn; **~ it in the dustbin** jette-le à la poubelle; **he flung himself into an armchair** il s'est jeté dans un fauteuil; **to ~ oneself into a task** se lancer dans une tâche; **I flung a few things into a suitcase** j'ai fourré quelques affaires dans une valise; **you shouldn't just ~ yourself into these jobs/relationships** tu ne devrais pas te lancer sans réfléchir dans ce type de travail/relation; **to ~ sb into jail** jeter qqn en prison; **don't just ~ yourself at him** ne te jette pas dans ses bras; **he flung himself off the top of the cliff** il s'est jeté du haut de la falaise; **with his coat casually flung over his shoulders** avec son manteau négligemment jeté sur ses épaules; **she flung the windows wide open** elle ouvrit les fenêtres en grand; **just ~ in a bit of wine to give it taste** *inf* ajoute juste un peu de vin pour donner du goût; **she was ~ing insults left right and centre** elle lançait des insultes de toutes parts; **to ~ sthg in sb's face** *fig* envoyer qqch à la figure de qqn.
◇ *n* -**1.** *inf* [attempt, try]: **to have a ~ at sthg** essayer de faire qqch; **let's give it a ~** essayons un coup. -**2.** [wild behaviour]: **youth must have its ~** il faut que jeunesse se passe; **I enjoy a little ~** j'aime bien me payer du bon temps; **to have a ~ with sb** *inf* [affair] avoir une aventure avec qqn; **the two of them are having a ~** ils ont une aventure; [buying things] faire des folies. -**3.** [dance] *danse traditionnelle écossaise qui se danse en solo*.

◆ **fling about** *vt sep* [objects, ball] lancer; **the luggage got flung about a bit during the flight** les bagages ont été un peu secoués pendant le vol; **he flung his arms about wildly** [fighting] il se démenait violemment; [gesticulating] il gesticulait violemment.

◆ **fling away** *vt sep* [discard] jeter (de côté); **that's just ~ing your money away** c'est jeter ton argent par les fenêtres.

◆ **fling back** *vt sep* [ball] renvoyer; [curtains] ouvrir brusquement; **she flung back her head** elle a rejeté sa tête en arrière.

◆ **fling down** *vt sep* [object] jeter par terre; **don't just ~ the books down anywhere** ne jette pas les livres n'importe où; **to ~ down a challenge** lancer OR jeter un défi.

◆ **fling off** *vt sep* -**1.** [coat, dress] jeter. -**2.** [attacker] repousser violemment. -**3.** [casual remarks] dire avec désinvolture; [poems, article] écrire d'un trait.

◆ **fling out** *vt sep* [object] jeter, balancer; [person] mettre à la porte, jeter dehors.

◆ **fling up** *vt sep* [throw - in air] jeter en l'air; [- to sb in higher position] lancer, envoyer; **he flung up his hands in horror** horrifié, il leva les bras au ciel.

flint [flɪnt] ◇ *n* [substance] silex *m*; [for cigarette lighter] pierre *f* à briquet.
◇ *comp* [tools, axe] en silex.

flintlock ['flɪntlɒk] *n* [rifle] mousquet *m*; [pistol] pistolet *m* à fusil.

flinty ['flɪntɪ] (*compar* **flintier**, *superl* **flintiest**) *adj* [rocks, soil] siliceux; *fig* [heart] de pierre.

flip [flɪp] (*pt* & *pp* **flipped**, *cont* **flipping**) ◇ *n* -**1.** [little push, flick] petit coup *m*; **to give sthg a ~** donner un petit coup à qqch. -**2.** [turning movement] demi-tour *m (sur soi-même)*; [somersault - in diving] saut *m* périlleux; [- in gymnastics] flip-flap *m*. -**3. to have a (quick) ~ through a magazine** feuilleter un magazine. -**4.** [drink] *boisson alcoolisée à l'œuf*.

◇ *vt* -**1.** [move with a flick] donner un petit coup sec à; he flipped the packet shut d'un petit coup sec il a refermé le paquet. -**2.** [throw] envoyer, balancer; **he casually flipped her back onto the trapeze** sans effort apparent, il l'a renvoyée sur le trapèze; to ~ **a coin (for sthg)** décider (qqch) à pile ou face. -**3.** *phr*: **to ~ one's lid** *inf* = **flip** *vi* **2**.
◇ *vi inf* -**1.** [become ecstatic] être emballé, flasher; to ~ **over sthg** être emballé par qqch, flasher sur qqch. -**2.** [get angry] exploser, piquer une crise; [go mad] devenir dingue, perdre la boule; [under effects of stress] craquer.
◇ *adj inf* [flippant, too casual] désinvolte.
◇ *interj inf* mince, zut.
◆ **flip off** *vt sep* [flick off - dirt, dust etc] faire tomber; to ~ **sthg off sthg** faire tomber qqch de qqch.
◆ **flip out** *vi insep* -**1.** *inf* [get angry] exploser, piquer une crise; [become ecstatic] être emballé, flasher. -**2.** [trailer of vehicle, racing car] faire un écart.
◆ **flip over** ◇ *vt sep* [turn over - stone, person] retourner; [- page] tourner.
◇ *vi insep* [turn over - plane, boat, fish] se retourner; [- page] tourner tout seul.
◆ **flip through** *vt insep* [magazine] feuilleter.

flip chart *n* tableau *m* à feuilles.

flip-flop ◇ *n* -**1.** [sandal] tong *f*. -**2.** ELECTRON bascule *f*. -**3.** *inf Am* [in attitude, policy] volte-face *f inv*, revirement *m*; to do a ~ faire volte-face, retourner sa veste.
◇ *vi inf Am* faire volte-face, retourner sa veste.

flippancy ['flɪpənsɪ] *n* [of person, attitude] légèreté *f*, désinvolture *f*; [of remark] désinvolture *f*.

flippant ['flɪpənt] *adj* désinvolte; **he was just being ~** il ne parlait pas sérieusement.

flippantly ['flɪpəntlɪ] *adv* avec désinvolture.

flipper ['flɪpəʳ] *n* -**1.** [for swimming] palme *f*. -**2.** [of seal, penguin] nageoire *f*.

flipping *inf* ['flɪpɪŋ] *Br* ◇ *adj* [as intensifier] fichu; **you've got a ~ nerve!** tu as un fichu OR sacré culot!; **you ~ idiot!** espèce d'idiot!; **he's a ~ genius** c'est un super génie.
◇ *adv* [as intensifier] fichtrement; **it's ~ hot/cold in here** il fait fichtrement chaud/froid là-dedans; **it's too ~ late now** il est bien trop tard maintenant; **not ~ likely!** il n'y a pas de risque!; **isn't it just ~ marvellous!** *iron* c'est pas formidable!; **you can ~ well do it yourself!** tu n'as qu'à le faire toi-même si c'est comme ça!

flip side *inf n* [of record] face *f* B.

flip top *n* [of packet] couvercle *m* à rabat; **in the new flip-top pack** avec le nouveau couvercle à rabat.

flirt [flɜːt] ◇ *vi* flirter; **he ~s with everybody** il flirte avec tout le monde; **to ~ with danger/death** frayer avec le danger/la mort; **to ~ with an idea** jouer avec une idée.
◇ *n* -**1.** [person] personne *f* qui aime à badiner amoureusement OR à faire du charme, charmeur *m*, -euse *f*; **he's just a ~** il fait du charme à tout le monde, c'est un charmeur. -**2.** [act] badinage *m* amoureux.

flirtation [flɜː'teɪʃn] *n* badinage *m* amoureux; **his ~ with danger/the idea ended in disaster** il a frayé avec le danger/joué avec cette idée et cela a tourné au désastre.

flirtatious [flɜː'teɪʃəs] *adj* charmeur.

flirtatiously [flɜː'teɪʃəslɪ] *adv* d'un air charmeur.

flit [flɪt] (*pt* & *pp* **flitted**, *cont* **flitting**) ◇ *vi* -**1.** [bird, bat etc] voleter; **bats were flitting about** des chauves-souris voletaient de-ci de-là ‖ [person]: **people were constantly flitting in and out of his office** les gens n'arrêtaient pas d'entrer et de sortir de son bureau; **an idea flitted into my mind** une idée me vint soudain à l'esprit; **to ~ from one subject to another** sauter d'un sujet à un autre, passer du coq à l'âne; **to ~ from woman to woman/job to job** passer continuellement d'une femme à une autre/d'un emploi à un autre. -**2.** *inf Br* [move house without informing landlord etc] déménager à la cloche de bois. -**3.** *inf Br dial* [move house] déménager.
◇ *n Br*: **to do a (moonlight) ~** [move house secretly] déménager à la cloche de bois; [leave discreetly] partir en douce, filer à l'anglaise.

flitch [flɪtʃ] *n* [of pork] flèche *f*.

flitting *inf* ['flɪtɪŋ] *n Br dial* déménagement *m*.

float [fləʊt] ◇ *n* -**1.** [for fishing line] bouchon *m*, flotteur *m*; [on raft, seaplane, fishing net, in carburettor, toilet cistern] flotteur *m*; [for swimming] planche *f*. -**2.** [vehicle - in parade, carnival] char *m*; [- for milk delivery] voiture *f* du livreur de lait. -**3.** [cash advance] avance *f*; [business loan] prêt *m* de lancement; [money in cash register] encaisse *f*. -**4.** [drink] *soda avec une boule de glace*.
◇ *vi* -**1.** [on water] flotter; [be afloat - boat] flotter, être à flot; **the raft/log ~ed down the river** le radeau/le tronc d'arbre a descendu la rivière au fil de l'eau; **the bottle ~ed out to sea** la bouteille a été emportée vers le large; **the diver ~ed slowly up to the surface** le plongeur est remonté lentement à la surface; **we ~ed downstream** [in boat] le courant nous a portés. -**2.** [in the air - balloon, piece of paper] voltiger; [- mist, clouds] flotter; [- ghost, apparition] flotter, planer; **music/the sound of laughter ~ed in through the open window** de la musique est entrée/des bruits de rires sont entrés par la fenêtre ouverte. -**3.** [currency] flotter.
◇ *vt* -**1.** [put on water - ship, raft, platform] mettre à flot; **the timber is then ~ed downstream to the mill** le bois descend ensuite jusqu'à l'usine au fil de l'eau, le bois est ensuite flotté jusqu'à l'usine située en aval. -**2.** [launch - company] lancer, créer; FIN [bonds, share issue] émettre. -**3.** FIN [currency] faire flotter. -**4.** *fig* [idea] lancer, proposer; [plan] proposer.
◆ **float about** *inf*, **float around** *inf vi insep* [rumours] courir; [person - do nothing in particular] traîner; **she's/it's ~ing about somewhere** elle/il traîne dans les parages.
◆ **float off** ◇ *vt sep* [free - boat] remettre à flot.
◇ *vi insep* -**1.** [be carried away - log, ship etc] partir OR être emporté au fil de l'eau; [in the air - balloon, piece of paper] s'envoler. -**2.** *fig* [person] s'envoler, disparaître.

floatation [fləʊ'teɪʃn] = **flotation**.

float chamber *n* [in carburettor] cuve *f*.

floater ['fləʊtəʳ] *n Am* [floating voter] (électeur *m*) indécis *m*, électrice *f* indécise.
◆ **floaters** *npl* MED [in eye] mouches *fpl* volantes, corps *mpl* flottants.

floating ['fləʊtɪŋ] ◇ *adj* -**1.** [on water] flottant; **~ crane** ponton-grue *m*; **~ dock** dock *m* flottant. -**2.** [not fixed]: **he has led a sort of ~ existence** il a mené une vie assez vagabonde ❑ **~ population** [within country] population *f* migrante; **there's a fairly large ~ vote** les indécis sont assez nombreux; **the ~ vote will determine the outcome** les voix des indécis détermineront le résultat; **~ voter** (électeur *m*) indécis *m*, électrice *f* indécise. -**3.** FIN [currency, exchange rate] flottant; [capital] disponible. -**4.** COMPUT [accent] flottant; **~ point** virgule *f* flottante. -**5.** MED: **~ bodies** [in eye] mouches *fpl* volantes, corps *mpl* flottants; **~ kidney** rein *m* flottant.
◇ *n* -**1.** [putting on the water] mise *f* à flot; [getting afloat again] remise *f* à flot. -**2.** [of new company] lancement *m*, création *f*. -**3.** [of currency] flottement *m*. -**4.** [of new idea, plan] proposition *f*.

floating-point *adj* COMPUT à OR en virgule flottante.

flock [flɒk] ◇ *n* [of sheep] troupeau *m*; [of birds] vol *m*, volée *f*; [of people] *inf* foule *f*; RELIG ouailles *fpl*; **they came in ~s** ils sont venus en foule OR en masse ‖ TEX bourre *f* ❑ **~ wallpaper** papier *m* tontisse.
◇ *vi* aller OR venir en foule OR en masse, affluer; **people are ~ing to see it** les gens vont le voir en foule OR en masse, les gens affluent pour le voir; **audiences are ~ing in** les spectateurs viennent en foule OR en masse, les spectateurs affluent; **the people ~ed around him** les gens se sont massés OR attroupés autour de lui.
◆ **flock together** *vi insep* [sheep] se regrouper, s'attrouper.

floe [fləʊ] = **ice floe**.

flog [flɒg] (*pt* & *pp* **flogged**, *cont* **flogging**) *vt* -**1.** [beat] fouetter; **we're just flogging a dead horse** *inf* nous nous dépensons en pure perte, nous nous acharnons inutilement; **to ~ an idea/a joke to death** *inf* accommoder une idée/blague à toutes les sauces. -**2.** *inf Br* [sell] vendre.
◆ **flog off** *inf vt sep Br* [sell off] bazarder; **they're flogging them off cheap** ils les bazardent pour pas cher.

flogging ['flɒgɪŋ] *n* [beating] flagellation *f*; JUR supplice *m* du fouet OR de la flagellation.

flood [flʌd] ◇ *n* -**1.** *literal* inondation *f*; **the Flood** le déluge; **to be in ~** [river] être en crue; **you've caused a ~ in the bathroom** tu as inondé la salle de bains. -**2.** *fig* [of applications, letters, offers] déluge *m*; [of light] flot *m*; **~s of tears** un déluge OR torrent de larmes; **to be in ~s of tears** pleurer à chaudes larmes. -**3.** = **flood tide**. -**4.** = **floodlight**.
◇ *vt* -**1.** [unintentionally] inonder; [deliberately] inonder, noyer; **you've ~ed the bathroom** tu as inondé la salle de bains. -**2.** AUT [carburettor] noyer. -**3.** [river - subj: rain] faire déborder. -**4.** *fig* (*usu pass*) [person - with letters, replies] inonder, submerger; **to be ~ed with applications/letters** être submergé de demandes/lettres; **to be ~ed in light** [room, valley] être inondé de lumière. -**5.** COMM: **to ~ the market** inonder le marché.
◇ *vi* -**1.** [river] être en crue, déborder. -**2.** [land, area] être inondé. -**3.** *fig* [move in large quantities]: **to ~ into the streets** envahir les rues; **refugees are still ~ing across the border** les réfugiés continuent à passer la frontière en foule OR en masse; **the light was ~ing through the window** la lumière entrait à flots par la fenêtre; **new energy was ~ing through his veins** une énergie nouvelle coulait dans ses veines.
◆ **flood back** *vi insep* [people] revenir en foule OR en masse; [strength, energy, memories] revenir à flots, affluer; **suddenly it all came ~ing back to me** soudain tous mes souvenirs ont reflué en masse.
◆ **flood in** *vi insep* [people] entrer en foule OR en masse, affluer; [applications, letters] affluer; [light, sunshine] entrer à flots.
◆ **flood out** ◇ *vt sep* inonder; **hundreds of families have been ~ed out** [from homes] l'inondation a forcé des centaines de familles à quitter leurs maisons.
◇ *vi insep* [people] sortir en foule OR en masse; [words] sortir à flots; [ideas] se bousculer, affluer.

flood barrier *n* digue *f* de retenue.

flood control *n* contrôle *m* des crues.

flood-damaged *adj* abîmé OR endommagé par les eaux.

flooded ['flʌdɪd] *adj* [land, house] inondé; [engine] noyé.

floodgate ['flʌdgeɪt] *n* vanne *f*, porte *f* d'écluse; **to open the ~s** *fig*: **the new law will open the ~s to all kinds of fraudulent practices** cette nouvelle loi est la porte ouverte à toutes sortes de pratiques frauduleuses.

flooding ['flʌdɪŋ] *n* (*U*) inondation *f*; [of submarine's tanks] remplissage *m*; **~ is a major problem** les inondations sont un grand problème.

floodlight ['flʌdlaɪt] (*pt* & *pp* **floodlit** [-lɪt] OR **floodlighted**) ◇ *n* [lamp] projecteur *m*; [light] lumière *f* des projecteurs; **to play under ~s** jouer à la lumière des projecteurs.
◇ *vt* [football pitch, stage] éclairer (aux projecteurs); [building] illuminer *f*.

floodlighting ['flʌdlaɪtɪŋ] *n* (*U*) [of pitch, stage] éclairage *m* (aux projecteurs); [of building] illumination *f*.

floodlit ['flʌdlɪt] *adj* [match, stage] éclairé (aux projecteurs); [building] illuminé.

floodplain ['flʌdpleɪn] *n* lit *m* majeur.
flood tide *n* marée *f* montante.
floor [flɔːʳ] ◇ *n* -**1.** [ground - gen] sol *m*; [- wooden] plancher *m*, parquet *m*; [- tiled] carrelage *m*; earthen ~ sol en terre battue; to put sthg/to sit on the ~ poser qqch/s'asseoir par terre; the forest ~ le sol de la forêt, la couverture *spec* ❑ to wipe the ~ with sb *inf* [in match, fight] battre qqn à plate couture, réduire qqn en miettes; [in argument] descendre qqn. -**2.** [bottom part - of lift, cage] plancher *m*; [- of sea, ocean] fond *m*. -**3.** [storey] étage *m*; we live ten ~s up nous habitons au dixième étage; on the same ~ au même étage; on the ~ below à l'étage en-dessous; on the second ~ *Br* au deuxième étage; *Am* au premier étage. -**4.** [for dancing] piste *f* (de danse); to take the ~ aller sur la piste (de danse); shall we take the ~? voulez-vous m'accorder cette danse? -**5.** [in parliament, assembly etc] ≃ arène *f*; [of stock exchange] parquet *m*; the ~ of the House l'arène; to have/to take the ~ [speaker] avoir/prendre la parole; he had the ~ for twenty minutes il a parlé OR a gardé la parole pendant vingt minutes; to give sb the ~ accorder OR donner la parole à qqn; questions from the ~ questions du public ❑ to cross the ~ [in parliament] changer de parti.
◇ *vt* -**1.** [building, house] faire le sol de; [with linoleum] poser le revêtement de sol dans; [with parquet] poser le parquet OR plancher dans, parqueter; [with tiles] poser le carrelage dans, carreler. -**2.** *inf* [opponent] terrasser. -**3.** *inf* [puzzle, baffle] dérouter; [surprise, amaze] abasourdir.
floor area *n* [of room, office] surface *f*.
floorboard ['flɔːbɔːd] *n* latte *f* OR planche *f* (de plancher); to take the ~s up enlever les lattes du plancher.
floorcloth ['flɔːklɒθ] *n* serpillière *f*; [old rag] chiffon *m*.
floor covering *n* [linoleum, fitted carpet] revêtement *m* de sol; [rug] tapis *m*.
floor exercise *n* [in gymnastics] exercice *m* au sol.
flooring ['flɔːrɪŋ] *n* *(U)* -**1.** [act]: the ~ has still to be done il reste encore le plancher à faire. -**2.** [material] revêtement *m* de sol; ~ tiles carreaux *mpl*.
floor lamp *n* *Am* lampadaire *m*.
floor leader *n* POL *chef de file d'un parti siégeant au Sénat ou à la Chambre des représentants aux États-Unis*.
floor manager *n* -**1.** [in department store] chef *m* de rayon. -**2.** TV régisseur *m*, -euse *f* de plateau.
floor-mounted [-'maʊntɪd] *adj* [gear lever] au plancher.
floor plan *n* plan *m*.
floor polish *n* encaustique *f*, cire *f*.
floor polisher *n* [machine] cireuse *f*.
floor show *n* spectacle *m* de cabaret.
floorspace ['flɔːspeɪs] *n* espace *m*.
floor tile *n* carreau *m*.
floorwalker ['flɔːˌwɔːkəʳ] *n* *Am* ≃ chef *m* de rayon.
floor wax *n* cire *f*, encaustique *f*.
floozie *inf*, **floozy** *inf* ['fluːzɪ] (*pl* floozies) *n* traînée *f*.
flop [flɒp] (*pt* & *pp* flopped, *cont* flopping) ◇ *vi* -**1.** [fall slackly - head, arm etc] tomber; [- person] s'affaler, s'effondrer. -**2.** *inf* [attempt, idea, recipe] louper; [fail - play, film] faire un four OR un bide; [- actor] faire un bide.
◇ *n* *inf* [failure] fiasco *m*, bide *m*; this cake is a ~ ce gâteau est complètement loupé; he was a ~ as Othello il était complètement nul dans le rôle d'Othello OR en Othello.
◇ *adv* *inf*: it went ~ into the water ça a fait plouf OR floc en tombant dans l'eau.
◆ **flop about** *vi insep*: the fish flopped about on the deck les poissons frétillaient sur le pont; he flopped about all day in his slippers il traînait toute la journée en chaussons.
◆ **flop down** *vi insep* se laisser tomber lourdement.
◆ **flop over** *vi insep* se renverser.

flophouse *inf* ['flɒphaʊs, *pl* -haʊzɪz] *n* *Am* asile *m* de nuit.
floppy ['flɒpɪ] (*compar* floppier, *superl* floppiest) ◇ *adj* [ears, tail, plant] pendant; [brim of hat] mou; [trousers, sweater] flottant, large; [collar] mou; the jumper went all ~ when I washed it le pull s'est complètement déformé au lavage; this heat makes you feel all ~ *Br* cette chaleur vous rend tout mou.
◇ *n* COMPUT disquette *f*.
floppy disk *n* COMPUT disquette *f*.
flora ['flɔːrə] *npl* flore *f*.
◆ **Flora** *pr n* MYTH Flore.
floral ['flɔːrəl] *adj* [arrangement, display] floral; [pattern, fabric, dress] à fleurs, fleuri; ~ tribute bouquet *m* OR gerbe *f* de fleurs; [funeral wreath] couronne *f* de fleurs.
Florence ['flɒrəns] *pr n* Florence.
Florentine ['flɒrəntaɪn] ◇ *adj* florentin.
◇ *n* -**1.** [person] Florentin *m*, -e *f*. -**2.** CULIN florentin *m*.
floret ['flɔːrɪt] *n* fleuron *m*.
florid ['flɒrɪd] *adj* -**1.** [complexion] coloré. -**2.** [style, architecture] chargé; [music] qui comporte trop de fioritures.
Florida ['flɒrɪdə] *pr n* Floride *f*; in ~ en Floride.
florin ['flɒrɪn] *n* [British, Dutch] florin *m*.
florist ['flɒrɪst] *n* fleuriste *mf*; ~'s (shop) fleuriste *m*.
floss [flɒs] ◇ *n* -**1.** [for embroidery] fil *m* de schappe OR de bourrette. -**2.** [for teeth] fil *m* OR soie *f* dentaire.
◇ *vt* [teeth] nettoyer au fil OR à la soie dentaire.
flotation [fləʊ'teɪʃn] *n* -**1.** [of ship - putting into water] mise *f* à flot; [- off sandbank] remise *f* à flot; [of logs] flottage *m*; ~ rings flotteurs *mpl*; ~ tank caisson *m* étanche. -**2.** [of new company] lancement *m*, création *f*; FIN [of loan by means of share issues] émission *f* d'actions *(permettant de financer la création d'une entreprise)*.
flotilla [flə'tɪlə] *n* flottille *f*.
flotsam ['flɒtsəm] *n* *(U)* morceaux *mpl* d'épave; ~ and jetsam morceaux d'épave et détritus *mpl*; the ~ and jetsam of society *fig* les laissés-pour-compte *mpl* de la société.
flounce [flaʊns] ◇ *n* [in garment] volant *m*.
◇ *vi*: to ~ into/out of a room entrer dans une/sortir d'une pièce de façon très théâtrale; she's been flouncing around all morning elle s'est agitée toute la matinée.
flounced [flaʊnst] *adj* [skirt] à volants.
flounder ['flaʊndəʳ] ◇ *vi* -**1.** [in water, mud] patauger péniblement; the dolphin was ~ing about in a few inches of water le dauphin se débattait dans quelques centimètres d'eau. -**2.** [in speech, lecture etc] perdre pied, s'empêtrer; I knew I had put my foot in it, but ~ed on regardless je savais que j'avais gaffé mais j'ai continué à m'enfoncer lamentablement; somehow he ~ed through his speech il est allé tant bien que mal jusqu'à la fin de son discours; the economy is still ~ing l'économie est encore instable.
◇ *n* [fish] flet *m*.
flour ['flaʊəʳ] ◇ *n* farine *f*.
◇ *vt* saupoudrer de farine, fariner.
flour bin *n* boîte *f* à farine.
flour dredger = **flour shaker**.
flourish ['flʌrɪʃ] ◇ *vi* [business, economy, plant] prospérer; [arts, literature etc] fleurir, s'épanouir; [in health] être en pleine forme OR santé.
◇ *vt* [wave, brandish - sword, diploma] brandir.
◇ *n* -**1.** [in lettering, design] ornement *m*, fioriture *f*; [in signature] paraphe *m*, parafe *m*. -**2.** [wave] grand geste *m* de la main; with an elaborate ~ of his hat avec un grand mouvement de chapeau; with a ~ of his sword en faisant un moulinet avec son épée. -**3.** [in musical or written style] fioriture *f*; a ~ of trumpets MUS une fanfare; a little literary ~ un petit effet de style.

flourishing ['flʌrɪʃɪŋ] *adj* [business, trade] florissant, prospère; [trader] prospère; [in health] en pleine forme OR santé; [plant] qui prospère.
flourmill ['flaʊəmɪl] *n* minoterie *f*.
flour shaker *n* saupoudreuse *f* à farine.
floury ['flaʊərɪ] *adj* -**1.** [covered in flour - hands] enfariné; [- clothes] couvert de farine. -**2.** [potatoes] farineux.
flout [flaʊt] *vt* [orders, instructions] passer outre à; [tradition, convention] se moquer de; [laws of physics] défier.
flow [fləʊ] ◇ *vi* -**1.** [liquid] couler; [electric current, air] circuler; the river ~s into the sea la rivière se jette dans la mer; I let the waves ~ over me j'ai laissé les vagues glisser sur moi; blood was still ~ing from the wound le sang continuait à couler OR s'écouler de la blessure; a lot of blood will ~ before peace is established beaucoup de sang sera versé avant que la paix ne soit rétablie; I could feel a new vital force ~ing through my veins je sentais un regain de force vitale m'envahir; I let the sound of the music just ~ over me *fig* j'ai laissé la musique m'envahir. -**2.** [traffic, crowd] circuler, s'écouler; new measures designed to enable the traffic to ~ more freely de nouvelles mesures destinées à rendre la circulation plus fluide; the traffic isn't ~ing as it should la circulation n'est pas aussi fluide qu'elle devrait l'être. -**3.** [hair, dress] flotter. -**4.** [prose, style, novel] couler; [work, project] avancer, progresser; this essay doesn't ~ very well cette dissertation n'est pas très fluide; play it this way, it ~s better MUS joue-le comme ça, ça coule mieux; in order to keep the conversation ~ing pour entretenir la conversation. -**5.** [appear in abundance]: the whisky ~ed freely le whisky a coulé à flots; ideas ~ed fast and furious les idées fusaient de tous côtés; a land ~ing with milk and honey une terre d'abondance. -**6.** [tide] monter. -**7.** [emanate] provenir; decisions ~ing from head office les décisions qui proviennent OR émanent du siège social.
◇ *n* -**1.** [of liquid] circulation *f*; [of river] écoulement *m*; [of lava] coulée *f*; [of tears] ruissellement *m*; the decreasing ~ of oil from the North Sea la quantité décroissante de pétrole en provenance de la mer du Nord. -**2.** [amount - of traffic, people, information, work] flux *m*; [movement from one person to another - of work] acheminement *m*; [- of information] circulation *f*; there is normally a very heavy ~ of traffic here il y a généralement beaucoup de circulation OR une circulation intense par ici. -**3.** [of dress, cape] drapé *m*. -**4.** [of prose, novel, piece of music] flot *m*; to be in full ~ [orator] être en plein discours; there's no stopping him once he's in full ~ il n'y a pas moyen de l'arrêter quand il est lancé. -**5.** [of the tide] flux *m*.
◆ **flow in** *vi insep* [water, liquid] entrer, s'écouler; [contributions, messages of sympathy, people] affluer.
◆ **flow out** *vi insep* [water, liquid] sortir, s'écouler; [people, crowds] s'écouler; the sewage then ~s out of the pipe into the lake les égouts se déversent ensuite du conduit dans le lac.
flowchart ['fləʊtʃɑːt] *n* organigramme *m*, graphique *m* d'évolution.
flow diagram = **flowchart**.
flower ['flaʊəʳ] ◇ *n* -**1.** BOT fleur *f*; to be in ~ être en fleur OR fleurs; to come into ~ fleurir; the tree is coming into ~ l'arbre commence à fleurir; no ~s please [at funeral] ni fleurs ni couronnes; to do the ~s [arrange] s'occuper des compositions florales. -**2.** *fig*: the ~ of the youth of Athens/of the army *lit* la fine fleur de la jeunesse athénienne/de l'armée; in the full ~ of youth dans la fleur de la jeunesse. -**3.** CHEM: ~s of sulphur fleur *f* de soufre.
◇ *vi* -**1.** [plant, tree] fleurir. -**2.** *lit* [artistic movement, genre] fleurir, s'épanouir.
flower arrangement *n* art *m* floral; [actual arrangement] composition *f* florale.

flower arranging [-ə'reɪndʒɪŋ] *n (U)* art *m* floral; the ~ took no time at all la composition florale a été réalisée en un rien de temps.
flowerbed ['flaʊəbed] *n* parterre *m* de fleurs.
flower child *n* hippy *mf*, hippie *mf (surtout des années soixante)*.
flowered ['flaʊəd] *adj* [dress, pattern] fleuri, à fleurs.
flower garden *n* jardin *m* d'agrément.
flower girl *n* -**1.** [selling flowers] marchande *f* de fleurs. -**2.** *Am & Scot* [at wedding] *petite fille qui porte des fleurs dans un mariage*, ≃ demoiselle *f* d'honneur.
flower head *n* capitule *m*.
flowering ['flaʊərɪŋ] ◇ *n* -**1.** [of plant, tree] floraison *f*. -**2.** [of artistic movement, talents] épanouissement *m*.
◇ *adj* [plant, tree - which flowers] à fleurs; [- which is in flower] en fleurs; ~ cherry cerisier *m* à fleurs.
flower people *n* hippies *mpl (surtout des années soixante)*.
flowerpot ['flaʊəpɒt] *n* pot *m* de fleurs.
flower power *n pacifisme prôné par les hippies, surtout dans les années soixante*.
flower-seller *n* vendeur *m*, -euse *f* de fleurs.
flower shop *n*: the ~ on the corner le fleuriste du coin; she owns two ~s elle est propriétaire de deux boutiques de fleurs.
flower show *n* exposition *f* de fleurs; [outdoors, on a large scale] floralies *fpl*.
flowery ['flaʊərɪ] *adj* -**1.** [fields, perfume] fleuri; [smell] de fleurs; [pattern, dress, carpet] à fleurs. -**2.** [language, compliments] fleuri.
flowing ['fləʊɪŋ] *adj* [style, prose] fluide; [beard, hair, robes] flottant; [movement] fluide, coulant.
flown [fləʊn] *pp* → **fly**.
fl. oz. *written abbr of* fluid ounce.
flu [fluː] *n* grippe *f*; to have ~ *Br*, to have the ~ avoir la grippe, être grippé.
fluctuate ['flʌktʃʊeɪt] *vi* [rate, temperature, results etc] fluctuer; [interest, enthusiasm, support] être fluctuant OR variable; [person - in enthusiasm, opinions etc] être fluctuant OR changeant; our production ~s from week to week notre production est fluctuante OR varie d'une semaine sur l'autre.
fluctuating ['flʌktʃʊeɪtɪŋ] *adj* [rate, figures, results etc] fluctuant; [enthusiasm, support etc] fluctuant, variable; [attitude, opinions etc] fluctuant, changeant.
fluctuation [ˌflʌktʃʊ'eɪʃn] *n* fluctuation *f*.
flue [fluː] *n* [chimney] conduit *m*; [for stove, boiler] tuyau *m*; MUS [of organ] tuyau *m*.
flue brush *n* hérisson *m*.
fluency ['fluːənsɪ] *n* -**1.** [in speaking, writing] facilité *f*, aisance *f*. -**2.** [in a foreign language]: ~ in French is desirable la connaissance du français parlé est souhaitable; we can identify various levels of ~ on peut distinguer différents niveaux de maîtrise de la langue; the course aims at ~ rather than at explicit knowledge of grammar le cours met l'accent sur l'expression plutôt que sur une connaissance formelle de la grammaire; I doubt whether I'll ever achieve complete ~ je doute d'arriver un jour à parler couramment. -**3.** SPORT [of play, strokes] facilité *f*, aisance *f*.
fluent ['fluːənt] *adj* -**1.** [prose, style] fluide; he's a ~ speaker il s'exprime aisément OR avec facilité. -**2.** [in a foreign language]: to be ~ in French, to speak ~ French parler couramment (le) français; he replied in ~ Urdu il a répondu dans un ourdou aisé OR coulant; I'll never be ~ je ne parlerai jamais couramment. -**3.** SPORT [play, strokes] facile, aisé.
fluently ['fluːəntlɪ] *adv* -**1.** [speak, write] avec facilité OR aisance. -**2.** [speak a foreign language] couramment. -**3.** SPORT [play] avec facilité OR aisance.
flue pipe *n* MUS [of organ] tuyau *m*.
fluff [flʌf] ◇ *n* -**1.** *(U)* [on baby animal, baby's head] duvet *m*; [from pillow, material etc] peluches *fpl*; [collected dust] moutons *mpl*; a bit of ~ des peluches; *inf Br* [pretty girl] une minette, une nana. -**2.** *inf Br* [mistake] raté *m*; he made a complete ~ of the line il a complètement raté sa réplique.
◇ *vt inf Br* [lines, entrance] rater, louper; to ~ it se planter.
◆ **fluff out** *vt sep* [feathers] hérisser, ébouriffer; [hair] faire bouffer; [pillows, cushions] secouer.
◆ **fluff up** *vt sep* [feathers] hérisser, ébouriffer; [pillows, cushions] secouer.
fluffy ['flʌfɪ] *(compar* fluffier, *superl* fluffiest) *adj* -**1.** [material, sweater] pelucheux; [chick, kitten, beard, hair] duveteux; [cake, sponge] léger; [clouds] cotonneux; ~ toy *Br* (jouet *m* en) peluche *f*. -**2.** [covered in fluff, dust] couvert de moutons.
flugelhorn ['fluːgəlhɔːn] *n* bugle *m*.
fluid ['fluːɪd] ◇ *adj* -**1.** [substance] fluide, liquide. -**2.** [flowing - style, play, match] fluide. -**3.** [liable to change - situation] indécis, indéterminé; [- plans] indéterminé.
◇ *n* fluide *m*, liquide *m*; body ~s sécrétions *fpl* corporelles; to be on ~s [patient] ne prendre que des liquides.
fluidity [fluː'ɪdətɪ] *n* -**1.** [of substance] fluidité *f*. -**2.** [of style, play] fluidité *f*. -**3.** [liability to change - of situation, plans] indétermination *f*.
fluid mechanics *n (U)* mécanique *f* des fluides.
fluid ounce *n Br* ≃ 0,028 litre; *Am* ≃ 0,03 litre.
fluke [fluːk] ◇ *n* -**1.** *inf* [piece of good luck] coup *m* de bol OR pot; [coincidence] hasard *m*; by (a) sheer ~ [coincidence] par un pur hasard. -**2.** [on anchor] patte *f*, bras *m*; [on whale's tail] lobe *m* de la nageoire caudale. -**3.** [flounder] flet *m*; [flatworm] douve *f*.
◇ *comp* [shot, discovery] heureux; it was a ~ discovery cela a été découvert par hasard.
fluky *inf* ['fluːkɪ] *adj* [lucky - shot, guess] heureux; [- person] chanceux; what a ~ goal! quel coup de bol, ce but!
flume [fluːm] *n* -**1.** [channel] buse *f*. -**2.** [at swimming pool] *sorte de toboggan dans lequel coule de l'eau*.
flummery ['flʌmərɪ] *n* -**1.** *Br* [dessert] *dessert à base de flocons d'avoine*. -**2.** *inf (U)* [flattering nonsense] baratin *m*.
flummox ['flʌməks] *vt* déconcerter, dérouter; to get ~ed perdre tous ses moyens.
flung [flʌŋ] *pt & pp* → **fling**.
flunk *inf* [flʌŋk] ◇ *vi* [in exam, course] se planter.
◇ *vt* [subj: student - French, maths] se planter en; [- exam] se planter à; he ~ed his test il s'est planté à son examen; the professor ~ed her paper in geography le prof ne lui a pas mis la moyenne à sa dissert' de géo.
◆ **flunk out** *inf Am* ◇ *vi insep* [from college, university] se faire virer *(à cause de la médiocrité de ses résultats)*.
◇ *n* raté *m*, -e *f*; he's a complete ~ c'est un vrai raté.
flunk(e)y ['flʌŋkɪ] *(pl* flunkies OR flunkeys) *n* [manservant] laquais *m*; *pej* [assistant] larbin *m*.
fluorescence [flʊə'resəns] *n* fluorescence *f*.
fluorescent [flʊə'resənt] *adj* [lighting, paint] fluorescent; ~ tube tube *m* fluorescent.
fluoridate ['flʊərɪdeɪt] *vt* [water] enrichir en fluor.
fluoridation [ˌflʊərɪ'deɪʃn] *n* fluoration *f*, fluoruration *f*.
fluoride ['flʊəraɪd] *n* fluorure *m*; ~ toothpaste dentifrice *m* au fluor.
fluorine ['flʊəriːn] *n* fluor *m*.
fluorocarbon [ˌflʊərəʊ'kaːbən] *n* hydrocarbone *m* fluoré, fluorocarbone *m*.
flurried ['flʌrɪd] *adj* paniqué; to get ~ perdre la tête, paniquer.
flurry ['flʌrɪ] *(pl* flurries, *pt & pp* flurried, *cont* flurrying) ◇ *n* -**1.** [of snow, wind] rafale *f*. -**2.** *fig*: a ~ of activity un branle-bas de combat; to be in a ~ of excitement être tout excité.
◇ *vt (usu pass)* [make excited and nervous] agiter, troubler.
flush [flʌʃ] ◇ *n* -**1.** [facial redness] rougeur *f*; to bring a ~ to sb's cheeks [compliment, crude joke] faire rougir qqn; [wine] mettre le feu aux joues à qqn ❑ hot ~es MED bouffées *fpl* de chaleur. -**2.** [of beauty, youth] éclat *m*; in the full ~ of youth dans tout l'éclat de la jeunesse; in the first ~ of victory/success dans l'ivresse de la victoire/du succès. -**3.** [on toilet - device] chasse *f* (d'eau); with a single ~ en tirant la chasse (d'eau) une seule fois; to give sthg a (good) ~ (out) [drains, pipes etc] nettoyer qqch à grande eau. -**4.** [in card games] flush *m*.
◇ *vi* -**1.** [face, person] rougir; his face ~ed scarlet il est devenu écarlate; to ~ with embarrassment rougir d'embarras; I can't drink punch, it makes me ~ je ne peux pas boire de punch, ça me met le feu aux joues. -**2.** [toilet]: it's not ~ing properly la chasse d'eau ne marche pas bien; a public toilet which ~es automatically des toilettes publiques avec chasse d'eau automatique; the toilet keeps on ~ing la chasse d'eau n'arrête pas de couler.
◇ *vt* -**1.** [cheeks, face] empourprer. -**2.** [with water]: to ~ the toilet tirer la chasse (d'eau); you ~ it by pushing this button/pulling this chain pour actionner la chasse d'eau, appuyez sur le bouton/tirez sur la chaîne; to ~ sthg down the toilet/sink jeter qqch dans les toilettes/l'évier. -**3.** HUNT lever, faire sortir.
◇ *adj* -**1.** [level] au même niveau; ~ with the side of the cupboard dans l'alignement du placard; ~ with the ground au niveau du sol, à ras de terre. -**2.** *inf* [with money] en fonds; feeling ~ today, are you? tu es en fonds aujourd'hui? -**3.** TYPO justifié.
◇ *adv* -**1.** [fit, be positioned]: this piece has to fit ~ into the frame ce morceau doit être de niveau avec la charpente. -**2.** TYPO: set ~ left/right justifié à gauche/droite.
◆ **flush away** *vt sep* [in toilet] jeter dans les toilettes; [in sink] jeter dans l'évier.
◆ **flush out** *vt sep* -**1.** [clean out - container, sink etc] nettoyer à grande eau; [- dirt, waste] faire partir. -**2.** HUNT [animals] faire sortir, lever; *fig* [gang of thieves, person from meeting] faire sortir; [undercover agents] forcer à se trahir; [the truth] faire éclater.
flushed [flʌʃt] *adj* -**1.** [person] rouge; [cheeks] rouge, en feu; he was looking rather ~ il était plutôt rouge. -**2.** *fig*: ~ with success enivré OR grisé par le succès.
fluster ['flʌstə'] ◇ *vt* [make agitated, nervous] troubler, rendre nerveux; you're looking a bit ~ed tu as l'air un peu agité; to get ~ed se troubler, devenir nerveux.
◇ *n*: to be in a ~ être troublé OR nerveux; to get into a ~ se troubler, devenir nerveux.
flute [fluːt] *n* -**1.** MUS flûte *f*. -**2.** ARCHIT [groove on column] cannelure *f*. -**3.** [glass] flûte *f*.
fluted ['fluːtɪd] *adj* ARCHIT cannelé.
fluting ['fluːtɪŋ] *n* ARCHIT cannelures *fpl*.
flutist ['fluːtɪst] *Am* = **flautist**.
flutter ['flʌtə'] ◇ *vi* -**1.** [wings] battre; [flag] flotter; [washing] flotter, voler; [heart] palpiter; [pulse] battre irrégulièrement; sometimes I feel my heart ~ MED j'ai parfois des palpitations. -**2.** [butterfly, bat, bird] voleter, voltiger; [leaf, piece of paper] voltiger; a butterfly ~ed in through the window un papillon est entré par la fenêtre en voletant OR voltigeant; to ~ away [bird, butterfly] s'envoler en voletant OR voltigeant; what is she ~ing about for? pourquoi est-ce qu'elle s'agite dans tous les sens comme ça?; her mother kept ~ing in and out of the room sa mère entrait et sortait de la pièce sans arrêt.
◇ *vt* [fan, piece of paper] agiter; [wings] battre; to ~ one's legs [swimmer] battre des jambes; to ~ one's eyelashes at sb aguicher qqn en battant des cils.
◇ *n* -**1.** [of heart] battement *m* irrégulier, pulsation *f* irrégulière; [of pulse] battement *m* irrégulier; MED palpitation *f*; [of wings] battement *m*; with a ~ of her eyelashes avec un battement de cils aguichant. -**2.** *inf* [nervous state]: to be all in OR of a ~ être dans tous ses

états. -3. AERON oscillation *f*. -4. *Br inf* [gamble] pari *m*; I have the odd little ~ from time to time [on horse] je fais un petit pari OR je parie de petites sommes de temps en temps; to have a ~ on the Stock Exchange tenter sa chance à la Bourse.

flutterboard ['flʌtəbɔːd] *n Am* planche *f (de natation)*.

flutter kick *n* [in swimming] battement *m* des jambes.

fluvial ['fluːvjəl] *adj fml* fluvial.

flux [flʌks] *n (U)* -1. [constant change]: to be in a state of constant ~ [universe] être en perpétuel devenir; [government, private life etc] être en proie à des changements permanents; all is ~ tout est devenir. -2. MED flux *m*. -3. METALL fondant *m*.

fly [flaɪ] (*pl* flies, *pt* flew [fluː], *pp* flown [fləʊn])
◇ *n* -1. ENTOM & FISHING mouche *f*; they're dropping like flies *inf* [dying, fainting] ils tombent comme des mouches; this illness is killing them off like flies *inf* cette maladie les fait tomber comme des mouches; the recession is killing companies off like flies *inf* la récession fait une véritable hécatombe parmi les entreprises; the ~ in the ointment *inf* [person] l'empêcheur *m* de tourner en rond; [problem] l'os *m*; there's a ~ in the ointment *inf* il y a un os; there are no flies on him *inf* il n'est pas fou; he wouldn't hurt a ~ il ne ferait pas de mal à une mouche; I wouldn't mind being a ~ on the wall *inf* j'aimerais bien être une petite souris; to catch flies *inf* [yawn, have mouth open] gober les mouches; to live on the ~ *inf Am* vivre à cent à l'heure. -2. *(often pl)* [on trousers] braguette *f*. -3. [entrance to tent] rabat *m*. -4. = **flysheet**. -5. = **flywheel**. -6. [in aeroplane]: to go for a ~ faire un tour en avion. -7. *inf Br phr*: to do sthg on the ~ [craftily, secretively] faire qqch en douce.
◇ *vi* -1. [bird, insect, plane, pilot] voler; [passenger] prendre l'avion; [arrow, bullet, missile] voler, filer; the first plane to ~ faster than the speed of sound le premier avion à dépasser la vitesse du son; it flies well [plane] il se pilote bien; I'm ~ing to Berlin tomorrow [passenger] je prends l'avion pour Berlin demain; [pilot] je vole à Berlin demain; he flies to Paris about twice a month [passenger] il va à Paris en avion environ deux fois par mois; soon we'll be ~ing over Manchester nous allons bientôt survoler Manchester; those who have flown in *Br* OR with *Am* Concorde ceux qui ont voyagé en Concorde, ceux qui ont pris le Concorde; he flies for an American airline il est pilote dans une compagnie aérienne américaine; which airline did you ~ with? avec quelle compagnie aérienne as-tu voyagé?; the trapeze artist flew through the air le trapéziste a voltigé ❑ the bird had already flown *inf* l'oiseau s'était envolé. -2. [move quickly - person] filer; [- time] passer à toute vitesse; [shoot into the air - sparks, dust, shavings] voler; I really must ~! il faut vraiment que je file OR que je me sauve!; she flew out of the room elle est sortie de la pièce comme un bolide; he came ~ing round the corner il a débouché du coin comme un bolide; he flew to her rescue il a volé à son secours; the time seems to have flown le temps est passé à une vitesse!; the past two years have just flown les deux dernières années ont passé à toute vitesse OR se sont envolées; time flies!, doesn't time ~! comme le temps passe!; the door flew open and there stood... la porte s'est ouverte brusquement sur...; to ~ into a rage OR temper s'emporter, sortir de ses gonds; to knock OR to send sb ~ing envoyer qqn rouler à terre; to knock OR to send sthg ~ing envoyer qqch voler; his hat went ~ing across the room son chapeau a volé OR voltigé à travers la pièce. -3. [kite] voler; [flag] être déployé; with the new flag ~ing proudly over the... avec le nouveau drapeau flottant fièrement au-dessus de...; with his coat ~ing in the breeze behind him avec son manteau flottant au vent derrière lui. -4. *phr*: to let ~ [physically] envoyer OR décocher un coup; [verbally] s'emporter; he let ~ with a powerful left hook il a décoché OR envoyé un puissant crochet du gauche; she then let ~ with a string of accusations elle a alors lancé un flot d'accusations; to (let) ~ at sb [physically] sauter OR se jeter sur qqn; [verbally] s'en prendre violemment à qqn; to ~ in the face of sthg [reason, evidence, logic] défier qqch; this flies in the face of our agreement cela contrecarre notre accord.
◇ *vt* -1. [plane, helicopter - subj: pilot] piloter; to ~ Concorde [pilot] piloter le Concorde; [passenger] prendre le Concorde, voyager en Concorde. -2. [passengers, people, goods] transporter en avion; [route - subj: pilot, passenger] emprunter; [airline] voyager avec; [distance - subj: passenger, pilot, plane] parcourir; [combat mission] effectuer; to ~ the Atlantic [pilot, passenger] traverser l'Atlantique en avion; [plane] traverser l'Atlantique. -3. [flag - subj: ship] arborer; [kite] faire voler; a flag is flown on public buildings when... tous les bâtiments publics arborent un drapeau quand... -4. [flee from - the country] fuir; to ~ the coop *inf* se faire la malle; to ~ the nest [baby bird] quitter le nid; *fig* quitter le foyer familial.
◇ *adj inf Br dated* [sharp] malin, rusé; a ~ guy un malin, un rusé.
◆ **fly about** *vi insep* [bird, insect] voleter, voltiger; [plane, helicopter, pilot] voler dans les parages, survoler les parages.
◆ **fly away** *vi insep* [bird, insect, plane] s'envoler.
◆ **fly back** ◇ *vi insep* [bird, insect] revenir; [plane] revenir; [passenger] rentrer en avion.
◇ *vt sep* [person, passengers - to an area] emmener en avion; [- from an area] ramener en avion; [- to own country] rapatrier en avion.
◆ **fly by** *vi insep* [time] passer à toute vitesse.
◆ **fly in** ◇ *vi insep* -1. [person] arriver en avion; [plane] arriver. -2. [bird, insect] entrer.
◇ *vt sep* [troops, reinforcements, food] envoyer en avion; [subj: pilot - to an area] emmener; [- from an area] amener.
◆ **fly off** ◇ *vi insep* -1. [bird, insect] s'envoler; [plane] décoller; [person] partir en avion; when do you ~ off to Paris? quand prenez-vous l'avion pour Paris?; she's always ~ing off somewhere elle est toujours entre deux avions. -2. [hat, lid] s'envoler; [button] sauter.
◇ *vt sep* -1. [from oil rig, island etc] évacuer en avion OR hélicoptère. -2. [transport by plane - to an area] emmener en avion; [- from an area] amener en avion.
◆ **fly out** ◇ *vi insep* -1. [person] partir (en avion), prendre l'avion; [plane] s'envoler; planes ~ out of the airport at a rate of 20 an hour les avions décollent de l'aéroport au rythme de 20 par heure; which airport did you ~ out of? de quel aéroport es-tu parti?; I'll ~ out to join you next Monday je prendrai l'avion pour te rejoindre lundi prochain; we flew out but we're going back by boat nous avons fait l'aller en avion mais nous rentrons en bateau. -2. [come out suddenly - from box, pocket] s'échapper.
◇ *vt sep* [person, troops, supplies - to an area] envoyer par avion; [- from an area] évacuer par avion; they flew the President out [to a place] ils ont emmené le président en avion; [from a place] ils ont ramené le président en avion.
◆ **fly past** *vi insep* -1. [plane, bird] passer; [plane - as part of display, ceremony] défiler. -2. [time, days] passer à toute vitesse.
◆ **fly up** *vi insep* -1. [plane, bird] s'envoler; the plane flew up to 10,000 metres l'avion est monté à 10 000 mètres. -2. [end of plank, lid] se soulever; glass flew up into the air des éclats de verre ont été projetés en l'air.

fly agaric *n* amanite *f* tue-mouches.

flyaway ['flaɪə,weɪ] *adj* -1. [hair] fin, difficile. -2. [person] frivole, étourdi; [idea] frivole.

flyblown ['flaɪbləʊn] *adj literal* couvert OR plein de chiures de mouches; *fig* très défraîchi; ~ meat viande *f* avariée.

flyby ['flaɪ,baɪ] (*pl* flybys) *n* -1. *passage d'un avion ou d'un engin spatial à proximité d'un objectif*. -2. *Am* = **flypast**.

fly-by-night *inf* ◇ *adj* -1. [unreliable] peu fiable, sur qui on ne peut pas compter; [firm, operation] véreux, louche. -2. [passing] éphémère.
◇ *n* -1. [person - irresponsible] écervelé *m*, -e *f*; [- in debt] débiteur *m*, -trice *f* qui décampe en douce. -2. [nightclubber] fêtard *m*, -e *f*, couche-tard *mf*.

fly-by-wire *n* commandes *fpl* informatisées.

flycatcher ['flaɪ,kætʃəʳ] *n* gobe-mouches *m inv*.

fly-drive *adj*: a ~ holiday package une formule avion plus voiture.

flyer ['flaɪəʳ] = **flier**.

fly-fish *vi* pêcher à la mouche; to go ~ing aller à la pêche à la mouche.

fly-fishing *n* pêche *f* à la mouche.

fly half *n* RUGBY demi *m* d'ouverture; to play ~ jouer (en) demi d'ouverture.

flying ['flaɪɪŋ] ◇ *n* [piloting plane] pilotage *m*; [travelling by plane] voyage *m* en avion; I love ~ [as traveller] j'adore prendre l'avion; to be afraid of ~ avoir peur de prendre l'avion; he goes ~ at the weekends le week-end, il fait de l'aviation.
◇ *adj* -1. [animal, insect] volant; ~ machine machine *f* volante. -2. [school] d'aviation; [staff] navigant; ~ club aéro-club *m*; ~ lessons leçons *fpl* de pilotage (aérien); ~ time heures *fpl* OR temps *m* de vol. -3. [fast] rapide; a ~ jump OR leap un saut avec élan; she took a ~ leap over the fence elle a sauté par-dessus la barrière.

flying boat *n* hydravion *m*.

flying bomb *n* bombe *f* volante.

flying buttress *n* arc-boutant *m*.

flying circus *n* [exhibition] voltige *f* aérienne; [group] groupe *m* de voltige aérienne.

flying colours *npl*: to pass with ~ réussir brillamment.

flying doctor *n* médecin *m* volant.

Flying Dutchman *n*: the ~ [legend] le Hollandais volant; 'The Flying Dutchman' *Wagner* 'le Vaisseau fantôme'.

flying fish *n* poisson *m* volant, exocet *m*.

flying fortress *n* forteresse *f* volante.

flying fox *n* roussette *f*.

flying officer *n* lieutenant *m* de l'armée de l'air.

flying picket *n* piquet *m* de grève volant.

flying saucer *n* soucoupe *f* volante.

Flying Squad *pr n*: the ~ *brigade de détectives britanniques spécialisés dans la grande criminalité*.

flying start *n* SPORT départ *m* lancé; the runner got off to a ~ le coureur est parti comme une flèche || *fig*: she got off to a ~ in the competition lors de la compétition, elle est partie comme une flèche OR elle a pris un départ foudroyant; the campaign got off to a ~ la campagne a démarré sur les chapeaux de roues; his experience gives him a ~ over the others son expérience lui donne un très net avantage sur les autres.

flying visit *n* visite *f* éclair.

fly kick *n* coup *m* de pied à suivre.

flyleaf ['flaɪliːf] (*pl* flyleaves [-liːvz]) *n* page *f* de garde.

flyover ['flaɪ,əʊvəʳ] *n* -1. *Br* AUT pont *m* routier. -2. *Am* = **flypast**.

flypaper ['flaɪ,peɪpəʳ] *n* papier *m* tue-mouches.

flypast ['flaɪ,pɑːst] *n Br* défilé *m* aérien.

flyposting ['flaɪ,pəʊstɪŋ] *n* affichage *m* illégal.

fly rod *n* canne *f* à mouche.

flyscreen ['flaɪskriːn] *n* moustiquaire *f*.

flysheet ['flaɪʃiːt] *n* -1. [on tent] auvent *m*. -2. [circular] feuille *f* volante; [instructions] mode *m* d'emploi.

flyspeck ['flaɪspek] *n* [of fly] chiure *f* de mouche; [gen] tache *f*.

flyspecked ['flaɪspekt] *adj* sali par les mouches.

fly spray *n* bombe *f* insecticide.

flyswat ['flaɪswɒt], **flyswatter** ['flaɪ,swɒtəʳ] *n* tapette *f (pour tuer les mouches)*.

fly-tipping *n* dépôt *m* d'ordures illégal.

flytrap ['flaɪtræp] *n* [plant] dionée *f*, tue-mouches *m inv*; [device] attrape-mouches *m inv*.

flyweight ['flaɪweɪt] ◇ *n* poids *m* mouche.
◇ *adj* de poids mouche.

flywheel ['flaɪwiːl] *n* volant *m* TECH.

flywhisk ['flaɪwɪsk] *n* chasse-mouches *m inv*.

FM *n* -**1.** (*abbr of* Frequency Modulation) FM *f*; ~ radio (radio *f*) FM; broadcast on ~ only diffusion en FM seulement. -**2.** *abbr of* Field Marshal.

FMB (*abbr of* Federal Maritime Board) *pr n Conseil supérieur de la Marine marchande aux États-Unis*.

FMCS (*abbr of* Federal Mediation and Conciliation Services) *pr n organisme américain de conciliation des conflits du travail*.

FO *n* -**1.** *abbr of* Field Officer. -**2.** *Br* MIL *abbr of* Flying Officer. -**3.** *Br abbr of* Foreign Office.

foal [fəʊl] ◇ *n* [of horse] poulain *m*; [of donkey] ânon *m*; the mare is in ~ la jument est pleine.
◇ *vi* mettre bas, pouliner.

foam [fəʊm] ◇ *n* [gen] mousse *f*; [of mouth, sea] écume *f*; [in fire-fighting] mousse *f* (carbonique); ~ bath bain *m* moussant.
◇ *vi* [soapy water] mousser, faire de la mousse; [sea] écumer, moutonner; to ~ at the mouth [animal] baver, écumer; [person] baver, avoir l'écume aux lèvres; she was practically ~ing at the mouth *inf fig* elle écumait de rage.

foam-backed *adj* avec envers de mousse.

foaming ['fəʊmɪŋ] = **foamy**.

foam rubber *n* caoutchouc *m* Mousse®.

foamy ['fəʊmɪ] (*compar* foamier, *superl* foamiest) *adj* [liquid] mousseux; [sea] écumeux.

fob[1] [fɒb] (*pt* & *pp* fobbed, *cont* fobbing) *n* [pocket] gousset *m*; [chain] chaîne *f* (de gousset); [ornament] breloque *f*.
◆ **fob off** *vt sep* se débarrasser de; he fobbed her off with promises il s'est débarrassé d'elle avec de belles promesses; don't try to ~ that rubbish off on me! n'essayez pas de me refiler cette camelote!

fob[2], **FOB** (*abbr of* free on board) *adj* FOB.

fob watch *n* montre *f* de gousset.

focal ['fəʊkl] *adj* focal.

focal distance = **focal length**.

focal length *n* distance *f* focale, focale *f*.

focal plane *n* -**1.** OPT plan *m* focal. -**2.** PHOT: ~ shutter obturateur *m* focal OR à rideau.

focal point *n* OPT foyer *m*; *fig* [of room] point *m* de convergence; the ~ of the debate le point central du débat.

focal ratio *n* diaphragme *m*.

foci ['fəʊsaɪ] *pl* → **focus**.

fo'c'sle ['fəʊksl] = **forecastle**.

focus ['fəʊkəs] (*pl* focuses OR foci [-saɪ], *pt* & *pp* focussed, *cont* focussing) ◇ *n* -**1.** OPT foyer *m*; the picture is in/out of ~ l'image est nette/floue, l'image est/n'est pas au point; bring the image into ~ fais la mise au point, mets l'image au point. -**2.** [centre - of interest] point *m* central; [- of trouble] foyer *m*, siège *m*; taxes are currently the ~ of attention en ce moment, les impôts sont au centre des préoccupations; the government is trying to shift the ~ of the debate le gouvernement tente de déplacer le débat; let's try and bring the problem into ~ essayons de préciser le problème; the ~ of the conference is on human rights le point central de la conférence, ce sont les droits de l'homme. -**3.** MED siège *m*, foyer *m*.
◇ *vt* -**1.** OPT mettre au point; to ~ a camera (on sthg) faire la mise au point d'un appareil photo (sur qqch). -**2.** [eyes] fixer; he couldn't ~ his eyes il voyait trouble; all eyes were focussed on him tous les regards étaient rivés sur lui. -**3.** [direct - heat, light] faire converger; [- beam, ray] diriger; *fig* [attention] concentrer.
◇ *vi* -**1.** OPT mettre au point. -**2.** [eyes] se fixer, accommoder *spec*; to ~ on sthg [eyes] se fixer sur qqch; [person] fixer le regard sur qqch; I can't ~ properly je vois trouble, je n'arrive pas à accommoder. -**3.** [converge - light, rays] converger; *fig* [- attention] se concentrer; the debate focussed on unemployment le débat était centré sur le problème du chômage; his speech focussed on the role of the media son discours a porté principalement sur le rôle des médias.

focussed ['fəʊkəst] *adj*: she's very ~ elle sait où elle va.

fodder ['fɒdə^r] *n* (*U*) [feed] fourrage *m*; *fig* & *pej* [material] substance *f*, matière *f*.

foe [fəʊ] *n lit* OR *fml* ennemi *m*, -e *f*, adversaire *mf*.

FOE *pr n* -**1.** (*abbr of* Friends of the Earth) AT *mpl*. -**2.** (*abbr of* Fraternal Order of Eagles) *organisation caritative américaine*.

foetal *Br*, **fetal** *Am* ['fiːtl] *adj* fœtal; in the ~ position en position fœtale, dans la position du fœtus; ~ heartbeat rythme *m* cardiaque du fœtus; ~ distress souffrance *f* fœtale.

foetid ['fiːtɪd] = **fetid**.

foetus *Br*, **fetus** *Am* ['fiːtəs] *n* fœtus *m*.

fog [fɒg] (*pt* & *pp* fogged, *cont* fogging) ◇ *n* -**1.** [mist] brouillard *m*, brume *f*. -**2.** *fig* [mental] brouillard *m*, confusion *f*; my mind is in a ~ today je suis dans le brouillard OR je ne sais plus où j'en suis aujourd'hui. -**3.** PHOT voile *f*.
◇ *vt* -**1.** [glass, mirror] embuer; PHOT [film] voiler. -**2.** [confuse] embrouiller; studying for too long just ~s the mind quand on travaille trop longtemps, ça embrouille les idées.
◇ *vi*: to ~ (over OR up) [glass, mirror] s'embuer; PHOT [film] se voiler.

fog bank *n* banc *m* de brume.

fogbound ['fɒgbaʊnd] *adj* pris dans le brouillard OR la brume.

fogey *inf* ['fəʊgɪ] *n* schnock *m*; he's an old ~ c'est un vieux schnock; she's a bit of an old ~ elle est un peu vieux jeu.

fogged [fɒgd] *adj* PHOT voilé.

foggy ['fɒgɪ] (*compar* foggier, *superl* foggiest) *adj* -**1.** [misty] brumeux; it's ~ il y a du brouillard OR de la brume; it's getting ~ le brouillard commence à tomber; on a ~ day par un jour de brouillard. -**2.** [confused] confus; I haven't the foggiest idea OR notion je n'ai aucune idée, je n'en ai pas la moindre idée. -**3.** PHOT [film] voilé.

Foggy Bottom *pr n surnom donné au ministère américain des Affaires étrangères*.

foghorn ['fɒghɔːn] *n* corne *f* OR sirène *f* de brume; a voice like a ~ une voix tonitruante OR de stentor.

fog lamp *Br*, **foglight** ['fɒglaɪt] *Am n* feu *m* de brouillard.

fogy ['fəʊgɪ] (*pl* fogies) = **fogey**.

FOI *abbr of* freedom of information.

foible ['fɔɪbl] *n* [quirk] marotte *f*, manie *f*; [weakness] faiblesse *f*.

foil [fɔɪl] ◇ *n* -**1.** [metal sheet] feuille *f* OR lame *f* de métal; (silver) ~ CULIN (papier *m*) aluminium *m*, papier *m* alu; cooked in ~ en papillote CULIN. -**2.** [complement] repoussoir *m*; [person] faire-valoir *m inv*; he's the perfect ~ to his wife il sert de faire-valoir à sa femme; it acts as a ~ to her beauty cela met en valeur sa beauté. -**3.** [sword] fleuret *m*.
◇ *vt* [thwart - attempt] déjouer; [- plan, plot] contrecarrer.

foist [fɔɪst]
◆ **foist on** *vt sep* -**1.** [pass on]: you're not ~ing (off) your old rubbish on OR onto me il n'est pas question que j'hérite de ta vieille camelote. -**2.** [impose on]: she ~ed her ideas on us elle nous a imposé ses idées; they ~ed themselves on us for the weekend ils se sont imposés OR invités pour le week-end.

fold [fəʊld] ◇ *vt* [bend] plier; ~ the blanket in two pliez la couverture en deux; she sat with her legs ~ed under her elle s'assit les jambes repliées sous elle; he ~ed his arms il s'est croisé les bras; she sat with her hands ~ed in her lap elle était assise, les mains jointes sur les genoux; the bird ~ed its wings l'oiseau replia ses ailes; he ~ed her in his arms il l'a serrée dans ses bras, il l'a enlacée.
◇ *vi* -**1.** [bed, chair] se plier, se replier. -**2.** *inf* [fail - business] faire faillite, fermer (ses portes); [- newspaper] disparaître, cesser de paraître; [- play] être retiré de l'affiche; the bakery ~ed last year le boulanger a mis la clef sous la porte l'année dernière.
◇ *n* -**1.** [crease] pli *m*; the soft ~s of her dress les plis soyeux de sa robe. -**2.** [enclosure] parc *m* à moutons; [flock] troupeau *m*. -**3.** *fig* [group] sein *m*; the ~ of the Party/the Church le sein du Parti/de l'Église; to return to the ~ rentrer au bercail. -**4.** GEOL pli *m*.
◆ **folds** *npl* GEOL plissement *m*.
◆ **fold away** ◇ *vt sep* plier et ranger.
◇ *vi insep* se plier, se replier.
◆ **fold back** ◇ *vt sep* [sheet, sleeve] replier, rabattre; [door, shutter] rabattre.
◇ *vi insep* se rabattre, se replier.
◆ **fold down** ◇ *vt sep* [sheet] replier, rabattre; [chair, table] plier; he ~ed down a corner of the page il a corné la page.
◇ *vi insep* se rabattre, se replier.
◆ **fold in** *vt sep* CULIN incorporer; ~ in the sugar incorporez le sucre.
◆ **fold over** ◇ *vt sep* [newspaper] plier, replier; [sheet] replier, rabattre.
◇ *vi insep* se rabattre, se replier.
◆ **fold up** ◇ *vt sep* plier, replier.
◇ *vi insep* -**1.** [chair, table] se plier, se replier. -**2.** = **fold** *vi* **2**.

-fold *in cpds*: a ten~ increase une multiplication par dix; your investment should multiply six~ votre investissement devrait vous rapporter six fois plus.

foldaway ['fəʊldəˌweɪ] *adj* pliant.

folder ['fəʊldə^r] *n* -**1.** [cover] chemise *f*; [binder] classeur *m*; [for drawings] carton *m*; where's the ~ on the new project? où est le dossier sur le nouveau projet? -**2.** [circular] dépliant *m*, brochure *f*. -**3.** TYPO [machine] plieuse *f*.

folderol ['fɒldərɒl] *n lit* -**1.** (*U*) [nonsense] absurdités *fpl*, sottises *fpl*. -**2.** [trifle] bibelot *m*, babiole *f*.

folding ['fəʊldɪŋ] *adj* pliant; ~ chair [without arms] chaise *f* pliante; [with arms] fauteuil *m* pliant; ~ door porte *f* (en) accordéon; ~ seat OR stool [gen] pliant *m*; AUT & THEAT strapontin *m*.

folding money *inf n* billets *mpl* de banque.

foldout ['fəʊldaʊt] *n* encart *m*.

foliage ['fəʊlɪɪdʒ] *n* feuillage *m*; ~ plant plante *f* verte.

foliate ['fəʊlɪeɪt] ◇ *vt* -**1.** [book] folioter. -**2.** [metal] battre; [mirror] étamer. -**3.** [decorate] orner de rinceaux.
◇ *vi* -**1.** BOT se garnir de feuilles, feuiller *spec*. -**2.** [split] se fendre.

foliation [ˌfəʊlɪ'eɪʃn] *n* -**1.** [of book] foliotage *m*. -**2.** [of metal] battage *m*; [of mirror] étamage *m*. -**3.** BOT foliation *f*, feuillaison *f*; GEOL foliation *f*. -**4.** [decoration] rinceaux *mpl*.

folic acid ['fəʊlɪk-] *n* acide *m* folique.

folio ['fəʊlɪəʊ] (*pl* folios) *n* -**1.** [of paper] folio *m*, feuillet *m*. -**2.** [book] (livre *m*) in-folio *m inv*.

folk [fəʊk] ◇ *npl* -**1.** [people] gens *mpl*; they're good ~ ce sont de braves OR de bonnes gens; most ~ just want a quiet life la plupart des gens veulent avoir une vie tranquille; what will ~ think? qu'est-ce que les gens vont penser?, qu'est-ce qu'on va penser?; the old ~ les vieux *mpl*; the young ~ les jeunes *mpl* ❑ city ~ les gens *mpl* de la ville; country ~ les gens *mpl* de la campagne. -**2.** [race, tribe] race *f*, peuple *m*.
◇ *n* MUS [traditional] musique *f* folklorique; [contemporary] musique *f* folk, folk *m*.
◇ *adj*: ~ dance OR dancing danse *f* folklorique; ~ wisdom la sagesse populaire.
◆ **folks** *npl* -**1.** *esp Am* [family] famille *f*, parents *mpl*; my ~s are from Chicago ma famille vient OR est de Chicago. -**2.** *inf* [people]: the old ~s les vieux *mpl*; the young ~s les jeunes *mpl*; hi ~s! bonjour tout le monde!

folk etymology *n* étymologie *f* populaire.

folklore ['fəʊklɔːʳ] *n* folklore *m*.
folk medicine *n (U)* remèdes *mpl* de bonne femme.
folk memory *n* tradition *f* populaire.
folk music *n* [traditional] musique *f* folklorique; [contemporary] musique *f* folk, folk *m*.
folk rock *n* folk-rock *m*.
folk singer *n* [traditional] chanteur *m*, -euse *f* de chansons folkloriques; [contemporary] chanteur *m*, -euse *f* folk.
folk song *n* [traditional] chanson *f* OR chant *m* folklorique; [contemporary] chanson *f* folk.
folksy *inf* ['fəʊksɪ] (*compar* folksier, *superl* folksiest) *adj* -**1.** *Am* [friendly] sympa. -**2.** [casual - person] sans façon; [- speech] populaire. -**3.** [dress, manners, town] typique; [story] populaire.
follicle ['fɒlɪkl] *n* follicule *m*.
follicle-stimulating hormone *n* hormone *f* folliculo-stimulante.
follow ['fɒləʊ] ◇ *vt* -**1.** [come after] suivre; [in procession] aller OR venir à la suite de, suivre; ~ me suivez-moi; he left, ~ed by his brother il est parti, suivi de son frère; the dog ~s her (about) everywhere le chien la suit partout OR est toujours sur ses talons; to ~ sb in/out entrer/sortir à la suite de qqn; he ~ed me into the house il m'a suivi dans la maison; his eyes ~ed her everywhere il la suivait partout du regard OR des yeux; she always ~s the crowd elle suit toujours la foule OR le mouvement; his talk will be ~ed by a discussion son exposé sera suivi d'une discussion; she ~ed this remark with a rather feeble joke elle agrémenta cette remarque d'une plaisanterie un peu facile; in the days that ~ed the accident dans les jours qui suivirent l'accident; he ~ed his father into politics il est entré en politique sur les traces de son père; she'll be a hard person OR hard act *inf* to ~ il sera difficile de lui succéder; to ~ suit [in cards] fournir; she sat down and I ~ed suit *fig* elle s'est assise, et j'en ai fait autant OR j'ai fait de même ☐ just ~ your nose [walk] continuez tout droit; [act] suivez votre instinct. -**2.** [pursue] suivre, poursuivre; [suspect] filer; he ~ed them to Rome il les a suivis OR il a suivi leurs traces jusqu'à Rome; she had her husband ~ed elle a fait filer son mari; ~ that car! suivez cette voiture!; I'm being ~ed on me suit; we're continuing to ~ this line of enquiry nous continuons l'enquête dans la même direction. -**3.** [go along] suivre, longer; ~ the path suivez le chemin; ~ the arrows suivez les flèches; the border ~s the river la frontière suit OR longe le fleuve; the streets ~ an irregular pattern les rues suivent un schéma irrégulier. -**4.** [conform to - diet, instructions, rules] suivre; [- orders] exécuter; [- fashion] suivre, se conformer à; I ~ed his advice/example j'ai suivi son conseil/exemple. -**5.** [understand] suivre, comprendre; do you ~ me? vous me suivez?; I don't quite ~ you je ne vous suis pas vraiment. -**6.** [watch] suivre OR regarder attentivement; [listen] suivre OR écouter attentivement; to ~ a score suivre une partition. -**7.** [take an interest in] suivre, se tenir au courant de; she ~ed the murder case in the papers elle a suivi l'affaire de meurtre dans les journaux; have you been ~ing that nature series on TV? avez-vous suivi ces émissions sur la nature à la télé? -**8.** [accept - ideas] suivre; [- leader] appuyer, être partisan de; [- cause, party] être partisan de, être pour. -**9.** [practice - profession] exercer, suivre; [- career] poursuivre; [- religion] pratiquer; [- method] employer, suivre.
◇ *vi* -**1.** [come after] suivre; in the years that ~ed dans les années qui suivirent; he answered as ~s il a répondu comme suit; my theory is as ~s ma théorie est la suivante; his sister ~ed hard on his heels *fig* sa sœur le suivait de près OR était sur ses talons; revolution ~ed hard on the heels of the elections la révolution suivit de très près OR immédiatement les élections; to ~ in sb's footsteps *literal* & *fig* suivre les traces de qqn; ~ing in her father's footsteps, she became a writer elle a suivi les traces de son père et est devenue écrivain. -**2.** [ensue] s'ensuivre, résulter; it doesn't necessarily ~ that he'll die cela ne veut pas forcément dire qu'il va mourir; from what he says, it ~s that he'll be standing for Parliament de ce qu'il a dit, il ressort qu'il sera candidat au Parlement; that doesn't ~ ce n'est pas forcément OR nécessairement vrai; a disturbing conclusion ~s (from this) une conclusion inquiétante en découle. -**3.** [understand] suivre, comprendre. -**4.** [imitate] suivre, faire de même; Paris sets the trend and the world ~s Paris donne le ton et le reste du monde suit.
◆ **follow on** *vi insep* -**1.** [come after] suivre. -**2.** [in cricket] *reprendre la garde du guichet au début de la seconde partie faute d'avoir marqué le nombre de points requis.*
◆ **follow through** ◇ *vt sep* [idea, plan] poursuivre jusqu'au bout OR jusqu'à sa conclusion; he didn't ~ our proposal through il n'a pas donné suite à notre proposition.
◇ *vi insep* [in ball games] accompagner son coup OR sa balle; [in billiards] faire OR jouer un coulé.
◆ **follow up** ◇ *vt sep* -**1.** [pursue - advantage, success] exploiter, tirer parti de; [- offer] donner suite à. -**2.** [maintain contact] suivre; [subj: doctor] suivre, surveiller. -**3.** [continue, supplement] faire suivre, compléter; ~ up your initial phone call with a letter confirmez votre coup de téléphone par écrit; I ~ed up your suggestion for a research project j'ai repris votre suggestion pour un projet de recherche.
◇ *vi insep* exploiter un avantage, tirer parti d'un avantage.
follower ['fɒləʊəʳ] *n* -**1.** [disciple] disciple *m*, partisan *m*, -e *f*; a ~ of fashion quelqu'un qui suit la mode. -**2.** SPORT [supporter] partisan *m*, fan *mf*; a ~ of tennis quelqu'un qui s'intéresse au tennis. -**3.** [attendant] domestique *mf*; the king and his ~s le roi et sa suite. -**4.** *arch* [male admirer] amoureux *m*.
following ['fɒləʊɪŋ] ◇ *adj* -**1.** [next] suivant; the ~ day le jour suivant, le lendemain; the ~ names les noms suivants, les noms que voici; the ~ methods of payment are acceptable sont acceptés les modes de paiement suivants. -**2.** [wind] arrière *(inv)*.
◇ *prep* après, suite à; ~ his accident, he walked with a limp après OR suite à son accident, il est resté boiteux; ~ our conversation suite à notre entretien; ~ your letter COMM suite à OR en réponse à votre lettre.
◇ *n* -**1.** [supporters] partisans *mpl*, disciples *mpl*; [entourage] suite *f*; she has a large ~ elle a de nombreux partisans OR fidèles. -**2.** [about to be mentioned]: he said the ~ il a dit ceci; her reasons are the ~ ses raisons sont les suivantes; the ~ have been selected from among the candidates les personnes suivantes ont été choisies parmi les candidats.
follow-my-leader *n Br jeu où tout le monde doit imiter tous les mouvements d'un joueur désigné.*
follow-on *n* [in cricket] *reprise de la garde du guichet par une équipe au début de la deuxième partie faute d'avoir marqué assez de points.*
follow-the-leader *Am* = **follow my-leader**.
follow-through *n* -**1.** [to plan] suite *f*, continuation *f*. -**2.** [in ball games] accompagnement *m (d'un coup)*; [in billiards] coulé *m*.
follow-up ◇ *n* -**1.** [to event, programme] suite *f*; [on case, file] suivi *m*; MED [appointment] visite *f* OR examen *m* de contrôle; this meeting is a ~ to that held in May cette réunion est la suite de celle tenue en mai. -**2.** [bill, letter] rappel *m*.
◇ *adj* [action, survey, work] complémentaire; ~ visit visite *f* de contrôle; a ~ letter/phone call une lettre/un coup de téléphone de rappel OR de relance; ~ care MED soins *mpl* post-hospitaliers.
folly ['fɒlɪ] (*pl* follies) *n* -**1.** *(U) fml* [foolishness] folie *f*, sottise *f*; it would be ~ to continue ce serait folie de continuer. -**2.** [building] folie *f* ARCHIT.
◆ **follies** *npl* THEAT folies *fpl*.
foment [fəʊ'ment] *vt* MED & *fig* fomenter.
fomentation [,fəʊmen'teɪʃn] *n* MED & *fig* fomentation *f*.
fond [fɒnd] *adj* -**1.** [loving - friend, wife] affectueux, tendre; [- parent] indulgent, bon; [- look] tendre; to be ~ of sb aimer beaucoup OR avoir de l'affection pour qqn; to be ~ of sthg aimer beaucoup OR être amateur de qqch; I'm very ~ of sweet things je suis très friande de sucreries, j'aime beaucoup les sucreries; I'm rather ~ of her je l'aime bien; he's ~ of reading il aime lire. -**2.** [hope] fervent; [ambition, wish] cher; my ~est dream mon rêve le plus cher. -**3.** *lit* [foolish] naïf.
fondant ['fɒndənt] *n* fondant *m*.
fondle ['fɒndl] *vt* caresser.
fondly ['fɒndlɪ] *adv* -**1.** [lovingly] tendrement, affectueusement. -**2.** [foolishly] naïvement; he ~ believed she would accept il avait la naïveté de croire OR il croyait naïvement qu'elle accepterait.
fondness ['fɒndnɪs] *n* [for person] affection *f*, tendresse *f*; [for things] prédilection *f*, penchant *m*; ~ for sb affection pour OR envers qqn; to have a ~ for drink avoir un penchant pour la boisson.
fondue ['fɒndjuː] *n* fondue *f*; ~ set service *m* à fondue.
font [fɒnt] *n* -**1.** RELIG fonts *mpl* baptismaux. -**2.** TYPO fonte *f*.
fontanelle *Br*, **fontanel** *Am* [,fɒntə'nel] *n* fontanelle *f*.
food [fuːd] ◇ *n* -**1.** *(U)* [nourishment] nourriture *f*, vivres *mpl*; is there any ~ in the house? y a-t-il de quoi manger à la maison?; do you have enough ~ for everyone? avez-vous assez à manger OR assez de nourriture pour tout le monde?; they like spicy ~ ils aiment la cuisine épicée; we need to buy some ~ il faut qu'on achète à manger OR qu'on fasse des provisions; we gave them ~ nous leur avons donné à manger; the ~ here is especially good dans ce restaurant la cuisine est particulièrement bonne; he's off his ~ il n'a pas d'appétit, il a perdu l'appétit; the cost of ~ le prix de la nourriture OR des denrées (alimentaires); ~ for babies/for pets aliments *mpl* pour bébés/pour animaux; ~s recommended for diabetics aliments conseillés aux diabétiques; cans of cat/dog/pet ~ des boîtes *fpl* de pâtée pour chats/chiens/animaux. -**2.** *fig* [material] matière *f*; the accident gave her much ~ for thought l'accident l'a fait beaucoup réfléchir; the book provides the reader with ~ for reflection ce livre donne au lecteur matière à réflexion. -**3.** HORT engrais *m*.
◇ *comp* [industry, product] alimentaire; [crop, grain] vivrier; ~ hall [in shop] rayon *m* d'alimentation; ~ processing [preparation] traitement *m* industriel des aliments; [industry] industrie *f* alimentaire; ~ stamp *Am* bon *m* alimentaire *(accordé aux personnes sans ressources)*; ~ value valeur *f* nutritive; Food and Agriculture Organization Organisation *f* des Nations Unies pour l'alimentation et l'agriculture; Food and Drug Administration *Am organisme officiel chargé de contrôler la qualité des aliments et de délivrer les autorisations de mise sur le marché pour les produits pharmaceutiques.*
food chain *n* chaîne *f* alimentaire.
foodie *inf* ['fuːdɪ] *n* fin gourmet *m*.
food mixer *n* mixeur *m*.
food parcel *n* colis *m* de vivres.
food poisoning *n* intoxication *f* alimentaire.
food processor *n* robot *m* ménager OR de cuisine.
foodstuff ['fuːdstʌf] *n* aliment *m*.
foody *inf* ['fuːdɪ] (*pl* foodies) = **foodie**.
fool [fuːl] ◇ *n* -**1.** [idiot] idiot *m*, -e *f*, imbécile *mf*; you stupid ~! espèce d'imbécile OR d'abruti!; what a ~ I am! suis-je idiot OR bête!; don't be a ~! ne fais pas l'idiot!; she was a ~ to go elle a été idiote d'y aller; I felt such a ~ je me suis senti bête; he was ~ enough to

agree il a été assez bête pour accepter, il a fait la bêtise d'accepter; he's more of a ~ than I thought il est encore plus idiot que je ne pensais; he's no ~ OR nobody's ~ il n'est pas bête, il n'est pas né d'hier; some ~ of a politician un imbécile OR un abruti de politicien; any ~ can do it n'importe quel imbécile peut le faire; to make a ~ of sb [ridicule] ridiculiser qqn, se payer la tête de qqn; [trick] duper qqn; she doesn't want to make a ~ of herself elle ne veut pas passer pour une imbécile OR se ridiculiser ❑ more ~ you! tu n'as qu'à t'en prendre à toi-même!; there's no ~ like an old ~ il n'y a pire imbécile qu'un vieil imbécile; a ~ and his money are soon parted *prov* aux idiots l'argent brûle les doigts *prov.* -**2.** [jester] bouffon *m*, fou *m.* -**3.** CULIN *sorte de mousse aux fruits*; raspberry ~ mousse *f* aux framboises.

◇ *vt* [deceive] duper, berner; (I) ~ed you! je t'ai eu!; don't try to ~ me n'essayez pas de me faire marcher; your excuses don't ~ me vos excuses ne prennent pas avec moi; he ~ed me into believing it il a réussi à me le faire croire.

◇ *vi* -**1.** [joke] faire l'imbécile OR le pitre; I'm only ~ing je ne fais que plaisanter, c'est pour rire; stop ~ing! arrête de faire l'imbécile! -**2.** [trifle] traiter à la légère; you'd better not ~ with him on ne plaisante pas avec lui.

◇ *adj Am* idiot, sot; that's just the kind of ~ thing he'd do c'est tout à fait le genre de bêtise OR d'ânerie qu'il ferait; that ~ son of yours *inf* ton imbécile de fils; what's all this (damn) ~ nonsense about getting married? *inf* se marier? qu'est-ce que c'est que ces foutaises?

◆ **fool about** *Br*, **fool around** *vi insep* -**1.** [joke] faire l'imbécile OR le pitre; I'm only ~ing around je ne fais que plaisanter, c'est pour rire. -**2.** [waste time] perdre du temps; stop ~ing around and get up! arrête de traîner et lève-toi! -**3.** [trifle] traiter à la légère; stop ~ing around with that computer! arrête de jouer avec cet ordinateur!; he's been ~ing around with a married woman il batifole avec une femme mariée. -**4.** *inf Am* [have sex] avoir OR se payer des aventures.

foolery ['fuːlərɪ] (*pl* fooleries) *n* [behaviour] bouffonnerie *f*, pitrerie *f*, pitreries *fpl*; [act, remark] bêtise *f*, sottise *f*; [joke] farce *f*, tour *m*.

foolhardy ['fuːl,hɑːdɪ] *adj* [act, person] téméraire, imprudent; [remark] imprudent.

foolish ['fuːlɪʃ] *adj* -**1.** [unwise] insensé, imprudent; it would be ~ to leave now ce serait de la folie de partir maintenant; that was very ~ of her ce n'était pas très malin de sa part; I was ~ enough to believe her j'ai été assez bête pour la croire; don't do anything ~ ne faites pas de bêtises. -**2.** [ridiculous] ridicule, bête; I felt rather ~ je me sentais plutôt idiot OR ridicule; I feel really ~ in this costume je me sens vraiment ridicule dans ce costume; the question made him look ~ la question l'a ridiculisé.

foolishly ['fuːlɪʃlɪ] *adv* [stupidly] bêtement, sottement; [unwisely] imprudemment; ~, I believed him comme un imbécile OR un idiot, je l'ai cru.

foolishness ['fuːlɪʃnɪs] *n* bêtise *f*, sottise *f*.

foolproof ['fuːlpruːf] ◇ *adj* [machine] indéréglable; [plan] infaillible, à toute épreuve.

◇ *vt* [machine] rendre indéréglable, protéger contre les fausses manœuvres; [idea, plan] rendre infaillible.

foolscap ['fuːlzkæp] ◇ *n* ≃ papier *m* ministre.

◇ *comp* [paper, size] ministre *(inv)*; ~ envelope enveloppe *f* longue; ~ pad bloc *m* de papier ministre.

foot [fʊt] (*pl* feet [fiːt]) ◇ *n* -**1.** [of person, cow, horse, pig] pied *m*; [of bird, cat, dog] patte *f*; I came on ~ je suis venu à pied; to be on one's feet [standing] être OR se tenir debout; [after illness] être sur pied OR rétabli OR remis; she's on her feet all day elle est debout toute la journée; on your feet! debout!; the speech brought the audience to its feet l'auditoire s'est levé pour applaudir le discours; to get OR to rise to one's feet se mettre debout, se lever; put your feet up reposez-vous un peu; to put OR to set sb on their feet again [cure] remettre qqn d'aplomb; [in business] remettre qqn en selle; to set ~ on land poser le pied sur la terre ferme; I've never set ~ in her house je n'ai jamais mis les pieds dans sa maison; never set ~ in this house again! ne remettez plus les pieds dans cette maison!; we got the project back on its feet *fig* on a relancé le projet; it's slippery under ~ c'est glissant par terre; the children are always under my feet les enfants sont toujours dans mes jambes ❑ ~ passenger piéton *m (passager sans véhicule)*. -**2.** *phr*: feet first *inf* les pieds devant; the only way I'll leave this house is feet first je ne quitterai cette maison que les pieds devant; to run OR to rush sb off their feet accabler qqn de travail, ne pas laisser à qqn le temps de souffler; I've been rushed off my feet all day je n'ai pas arrêté de toute la journée; he claims he's divorced – divorced, my ~! *inf* il prétend être divorcé – divorcé, mon œil!; to fall OR to land on one's feet retomber sur ses pieds; to find one's feet s'adapter; to get a ~ in the door poser des jalons, établir le contact; to have a ~ in the door être dans la place; well at least it's a ~ in the door au moins, c'est un premier pas OR contact; to have a ~ in both camps avoir un pied dans chaque camp; to have one ~ in the grave *inf* [person] avoir un pied dans la tombe; [business] être moribond; to have one's OR both feet (firmly) on the ground avoir les pieds sur terre; to have two left feet *inf* être pataud OR empoté; to have feet of clay avoir un point faible OR vulnérable, avoir une faiblesse de caractère; to put one's best ~ forward [hurry] se dépêcher, presser le pas; [do one's best] faire de son mieux; right, best ~ forward now [hurry] bon, dépêchons-nous; [do one's best] bon, faisons de notre mieux; to put one's ~ down faire acte d'autorité; AUT accélérer; to put one's ~ in it *inf Br* OR in one's mouth *inf Am* mettre les pieds dans le plat; she didn't put a ~ wrong *Br* elle n'a pas commis la moindre erreur; I never seem able to put a ~ right *Br* j'ai l'impression que je ne peux jamais rien faire comme il faut; to get OR to start off on the right/wrong ~ être bien/mal parti; the boot *Br* OR shoe *Am* is on the other ~ les rôles sont inversés. -**3.** [of chair, glass, lamp] pied *m*. -**4.** [lower end - of bed, stocking] pied *m*; [- of table] bout *m*; [- of cliff, mountain, hill] pied *m*; [- of page, stairs] bas *m*; at the ~ of the page au bas OR en bas de la page; at the ~ of the stairs en bas de l'escalier. -**5.** [measurement] pied *m* (anglais); a 40-~ fall, a fall of 40 feet une chute de 40 pieds ❑ to feel ten feet tall *inf* être aux anges OR au septième ciel. -**6.** LITERAT pied *m*. -**7.** *Br* MIL infanterie *f*.

◇ *vt* -**1.** [walk]: he decided to ~ it home *inf* il a décidé de rentrer à pied. -**2.** [pay]: to ~ the bill *inf* payer (l'addition); who's going to ~ the bill? qui va régler la douloureuse?

footage ['fʊtɪdʒ] *n* -**1.** [length] longueur *f* en pieds. -**2.** CIN [length] métrage *m*; [material filmed] séquences *fpl*; the film contains previously unseen ~ on OR about the war le film contient des séquences inédites sur la guerre.

foot-and-mouth disease *n* fièvre *f* aphteuse.

football ['fʊtbɔːl] ◇ *n* -**1.** *Br* football *m*; *Am* football américain. -**2.** [ball] ballon *m* (de football), balle *f*; the abortion issue has become a political ~ *fig* les partis politiques n'arrêtent pas de se renvoyer la balle au sujet (du problème) de l'avortement.

◇ *comp* [match, team] de football; [season] du football; ~ ground terrain *m* de football; ~ hooligans hooligans *mpl*; ~ hooliganism vandalisme *m*, hooliganisme *m*; ~ fan fan *mf* de foot; league ~ *Br* championnat *m* de football; the Football League *association réunissant la majorité des clubs de football professionnels en Angleterre*.

football coupon *n Br* grille *f* de loto sportif.

footballer ['fʊtbɔːləʳ] *n* joueur *m*, -euse *f* de football, footballeur *m*, -euse *f*.

football pools *npl Br* pronostics *mpl (sur les matchs de football)*; to do the ~ parier sur les matchs de football; he won £20 on the ~ il a gagné 20 livres en pariant sur les matchs de football.

footbath ['fʊtbɑːθ, *pl* -bɑːðz] *n* bain *m* de pieds.

footboard ['fʊtbɔːd] *n* [lever] pédale *f*; [on bed] panneau *m* de pied.

foot brake *n* frein *m* à pied.

footbridge ['fʊtbrɪdʒ] *n* passerelle *f*.

-footed [,fʊtɪd] *in cpds* au pied...; swift~ au pied léger OR rapide.

footer *inf* ['fʊtəʳ] *n Br* foot *m*.

-footer *in cpds*: the boat is a 15~ le bateau mesure 15 pieds OR environ 4,50 mètres.

footfall ['fʊtfɔːl] *n* bruit *m* de pas.

foot fault *n* faute *f* de pied TENNIS.

footgear ['fʊt,gɪəʳ] *n (U)* chaussures *fpl*.

foothill ['fʊthɪl] *n (usu pl)* contrefort *m*.

foothold ['fʊthəʊld] *n literal* prise *f* de pied; *fig* position *f* avantageuse; to gain OR to get a ~ *literal & fig* prendre pied; he gained a ~ in the jazz world il a su s'imposer dans le monde du jazz; to get OR to secure a ~ in a market COMM prendre pied sur un marché.

footing ['fʊtɪŋ] *n* -**1.** [balance] prise *f* de pied; to get one's ~ prendre pied; to keep/to lose one's ~ garder/perdre l'équilibre. -**2.** [position]: to be on an equal ~ être sur un pied d'égalité; let's try to keep things on a friendly ~ essayons de rester en bons termes; on a war ~ sur le pied de guerre; the business is now on a firm ~ l'affaire est maintenant en bonne voie.

footle *inf* ['fuːtl]

◆ **footle about** *Br*, **footle around** *vi insep dated* -**1.** [potter] passer son temps à des futilités. -**2.** [talk nonsense] dire des bêtises, radoter.

footless ['fʊtlɪs] *adj* -**1.** [tights] sans pieds. -**2.** *Am fig* [stupid] idiot, stupide.

footlights ['fʊtlaɪts] *npl literal* rampe; *fig* [the stage] le théâtre, les planches *fpl*.

footling *inf* ['fuːtlɪŋ] *adj dated* [trivial] insignifiant, futile.

footloose ['fʊtluːs] *adj*: ~ and fancy-free libre comme l'air.

footman ['fʊtmən] (*pl* footmen [-mən]) *n* valet *m* de pied.

footmark ['fʊtmɑːk] *n Br* empreinte *f* (de pied).

footmen ['fʊtmən] *pl* → **footman**.

footnote ['fʊtnəʊt] ◇ *n* [on page] note *f* en bas de page; [in speech] remarque *f* supplémentaire; as a ~ I should just mention... en dernière remarque, je signalerai que...; he was doomed to become just a ~ in the history of events *fig* il était destiné à rester en marge de l'histoire des événements OR à ne jouer qu'un rôle secondaire dans l'histoire des événements.

◇ *vt* annoter, mettre des notes de bas de page.

footpad ['fʊtpæd] *n* -**1.** *arch* [thief] voleur *m*. -**2.** TECH [of spacecraft] semelle *f*.

footpath ['fʊtpɑːθ, *pl* -pɑːðz] *n* [path] sentier *m*; [paved] trottoir *m*.

footplate ['fʊtpleɪt] *n Br* plate-forme *f (d'une locomotive)*.

footplateman ['fʊtpleɪtmən] (*pl* footplatemen [-mən]) *n Br* agent *m* de conduite.

footprint ['fʊtprɪnt] *n* -**1.** [of foot] empreinte *f* (de pied). -**2.** [of satellite] empreinte *f*. -**3.** COMPUT encombrement *m*.

footrest ['fʊtrest] *n* [gen] repose-pieds *m*; [stool] tabouret *m*.

foot rot *n* BOT & VETER piétin *m*.

footrule ['fʊtruːl] *n* règle *f* (d'un pied de long).

footsie *inf* ['fʊtsɪ] *n*: to play ~ with sb *Br* faire du pied à qqn; *Am* être le complice de qqn.

Footsie *inf* ['fʊtsɪ] *pr n nom familier de l'indice boursier du Financial Times*.

footslog *inf* ['fʊtslɒg] (*pt & pp* footslogged, *cont* footslogging) *vi Br* marcher (d'un pas lourd).

footslogging [ˈfʊtˌslɒgɪŋ] *n* marche *f*; **this job involves a lot of ~** dans ce travail, il faut marcher beaucoup.

foot soldier *n* fantassin *m*.

footsore [ˈfʊtsɔːʳ] *adj* aux pieds endoloris OR meurtris; **I was tired and ~** j'étais fatigué et j'avais mal aux pieds.

footstep [ˈfʊtstep] *n* [action] pas *m*; [sound] bruit *m* de pas.

footstool [ˈfʊtstuːl] *n* tabouret *m*.

foot-up *n* faute *f* de pied.

footway [ˈfʊtweɪ] *n Br* [path] sentier *m*; [paved] passerelle *f*.

footwear [ˈfʊtweəʳ] *n (U)* chaussures *fpl*; **he's in ~** COMM il est dans la chaussure.

footwork [ˈfʊtwɜːk] *n* -**1.** SPORT jeu *m* de jambes; **good ~** bon jeu de jambes; **it took some fancy ~ to avoid legal action** *fig* il a fallu manœuvrer adroitement pour éviter un procès. -**2.** [walking] marche *f*; **the job entails a lot of ~** le travail oblige à beaucoup marcher.

fop [fɒp] *n* dandy *m*.

foppish [ˈfɒpɪʃ] *adj* [man] dandy; [dress] de dandy; [manner] de dandy.

for [fɔːʳ] ◇ *prep* **A.** -**1.** [expressing purpose or function] pour; **we were in Vienna ~ a holiday/~ work** nous étions à Vienne en vacances/pour le travail; **what ~?** pourquoi?; **I don't know what she said that ~** je ne sais pas pourquoi elle a dit ça; **what's this knob ~?** à quoi sert ce bouton?; **it's ~ adjusting the volume** ça sert à régler le volume; **what's this medicine ~?** à quoi sert ce médicament?; **an instrument ~ measuring temperature** un instrument pour mesurer la température; **clothes ~ tall men** vêtements pour hommes grands; **'not suitable ~ freezing'** 'ne pas congeler'. -**2.** [in order to obtain] pour; **write ~ a free catalogue** demandez votre catalogue gratuit *(par écrit)*; **~ further information write to...** pour de plus amples renseignements, écrivez à...; **they play ~ money** ils jouent pour de l'argent. -**3.** [indicating recipient or beneficiary] pour, à l'intention de; **these flowers are ~ her** ces fleurs sont pour elle; **there's a phone call ~ you** il y a un appel pour vous; **I've got some news ~ you** j'ai une nouvelle à vous annoncer; **he left a note ~ them** il leur a laissé un mot, il a laissé un mot à leur intention; **opera is not ~ me** l'opéra, ça n'est pas pour moi; **equal pay ~ women** un salaire égal pour les femmes; **'parking ~ customers only'** 'parking réservé à la clientèle'; **what can I do ~ you?** que puis-je faire pour vous?; **he's doing everything he can ~ us** il fait tout son possible pour nous; **a collection ~ the poor** une quête pour les OR en faveur des pauvres; **it's ~ your own good** c'est pour ton bien; **he often cooks ~ himself** il se fait souvent la cuisine; **see ~ yourself!** voyez par vous-même!; **she writes ~ a sports magazine** elle écrit des articles pour un magazine de sport; **I work ~ an advertising agency** je travaille pour une agence de publicité. -**4.** [indicating direction, destination] pour, dans la direction de; **they left ~ Spain** ils sont partis pour l'Espagne; **before leaving ~ the office** avant de partir au bureau; **she ran ~ the door** elle s'est précipitée vers la porte en courant; **he made ~ home** il a pris la direction de la maison; **the ship made ~ port** le navire a mis le cap sur le port; **trains ~ the suburbs** les trains pour la banlieue; **change trains here ~ Beaune** changez de train ici pour Beaune; **flight 402 bound ~ Chicago is now boarding** les passagers du vol 402 à destination de Chicago sont invités à se présenter à l'embarquement. -**5.** [available for] à; **'~ rent'** 'à louer'; **'~ sale'** 'à vendre'; **these books are ~ reference only** ces livres sont à consulter sur place.

B. -**1.** [indicating span of time - past, future] pour, pendant; [- action uncompleted] depuis; **they're going away ~ the weekend** ils partent pour le week-end; **they will be gone ~ some time** ils seront absents (pendant OR pour) quelque temps; **they were in Spain ~ two weeks** ils étaient en Espagne pour deux semaines; **I lived there ~ one month** j'y ai vécu pendant un mois; **I've lived here ~ two years** j'habite ici depuis deux ans; **I'd only lived there ~ a week when the heating went wrong** je n'habitais là que depuis une semaine quand la chaudière est tombée en panne; **my mother has been here ~ two weeks** ma mère est ici depuis deux semaines; **you haven't been here ~ a long time** il y a OR voilà OR ça fait longtemps que vous n'êtes pas venu; **we've known them ~ years** nous les connaissons depuis des années, il y a des années que nous les connaissons; **she won't be able to go out ~ another day or two** elle devra rester sans sortir pendant encore un jour ou deux; **can you stay ~ a while?** pouvez-vous rester un moment?; **it's the worst accident ~ years** c'est le pire accident qui soit arrivé depuis des années. -**2.** [indicating a specific occasion or time] pour; **I went home ~ Christmas** je suis rentré chez moi pour Noël; **he took me out to dinner ~ my birthday** il m'a emmené dîner au restaurant pour mon anniversaire; **we made an appointment ~ the 6th** nous avons pris rendez-vous pour le 6; **the meeting was set ~ five o'clock** la réunion était fixée pour cinq heures; **it's time ~ bed** c'est l'heure de se coucher OR d'aller au lit; **~ the last/third time** pour la dernière/troisième fois. -**3.** [indicating distance] pendant; **you could see ~ miles around** on voyait à des kilomètres à la ronde; **we walked ~ several miles** nous avons marché pendant plusieurs kilomètres; **they drove ~ miles without seeing another car** ils ont roulé (pendant) des kilomètres sans croiser une seule voiture. -**4.** [indicating amount]: **they paid him £100 ~ his services** ils lui ont donné 100 livres pour ses services; **it's £2 ~ a ticket** c'est 2 livres le billet; **he's selling it ~ £200** il le vend 200 livres; **I wrote a cheque ~ £15** j'ai fait un chèque de 15 livres.

C. -**1.** [indicating exchange, equivalence]: **do you have change ~ a pound?** vous avez la monnaie d'une livre?; **he exchanged the bike ~ another model** il a échangé le vélo contre OR pour un autre modèle; **what will you give me in exchange ~ this book?** que me donnerez-vous en échange de ce livre?; **he gave blow ~ blow** il a rendu coup pour coup; **"salvia" is the Latin term ~ "sage"** «salvia» veut dire «sauge» en latin; **what's the Spanish ~ "good"?** comment dit-on «bon» en espagnol?; **F ~ François** F comme François; **what's the M ~?** qu'est-ce que le M veut dire?; **red ~ danger** rouge veut dire danger; **he has cereal ~ breakfast** il prend des céréales au petit déjeuner; **I know it ~ a fact** je sais que c'est vrai; **I ~ one don't care** pour ma part, je m'en fiche; **do you take me ~ a fool?** me prenez-vous pour un imbécile? -**2.** [indicating ratio] pour; **there's one woman applicant ~ every five men** sur six postulants il y a une femme et cinq hommes; **~ every honest politician there are a hundred dishonest ones** pour un homme politique honnête, il y en a cent qui sont malhonnêtes. -**3.** [on behalf of] pour; **I'm speaking ~ all parents** je parle pour OR au nom de tous les parents; **the lawyer was acting ~ his client** l'avocat agissait au nom de OR pour le compte de son client; **I'll go to the meeting ~ you** j'irai à la réunion à votre place; **the representative ~ the union** le représentant du syndicat. -**4.** [in favour of] pour; **~ or against** pour ou contre; **vote ~ Smith!** votez (pour) Smith!; **they voted ~ the proposal** ils ont voté en faveur de la proposition; **he's ~ the ecologists** il est pour les écologistes; **I'm ~ shortening the hunting season** je suis pour une saison de chasse plus courte; **who's ~ a drink?** qui veut boire un verre?; **I'm ~ bed** je vais me coucher. -**5.** [because of] pour, en raison de; **candidates were selected ~ their ability** les candidats ont été retenus en raison de leurs compétences; **she couldn't sleep ~ the pain** la douleur l'empêchait de dormir; **he's known ~ his wit** il est connu pour son esprit; **the region is famous ~ its wine** la région est célèbre pour son vin; **she's in prison ~ treason** elle est en prison pour trahison; **he couldn't speak ~ laughing** il ne pouvait pas parler tellement il riait; **you'll feel better ~ a rest** vous vous sentirez mieux quand vous vous serez reposé; **if it weren't ~ you, I'd leave** sans vous, je partirais; **~ this reason** pour cette raison; **~ fear of waking him** de crainte de le réveiller; **do it ~ my sake** faites-le pour moi; **~ old time's sake** en souvenir du passé. -**6.** [indicating cause, reason] de; **the reason ~ his leaving** la raison de son départ; **there are no grounds ~ believing it's true** il n'y a pas de raison de croire que c'est vrai; **she apologized ~ being late** elle s'est excusée d'être en retard; **I thanked him ~ his kindness** je l'ai remercié de OR pour sa gentillesse. -**7.** [concerning, as regards] pour; **so much ~ that** voilà qui est classé; **it may be true ~ all I know** c'est peut-être vrai, je n'en sais rien; **~ my part, I refuse to go** pour ma part OR quant à moi, je refuse d'y aller; **I'm very happy ~ her** je suis très heureux pour elle; **what are her feelings ~ him?** quels sont ses sentiments pour lui? -**8.** [given normal expectations] pour; **it's warm ~ March** il fait bon pour un mois de mars; **that's a good score ~ him** c'est un bon score pour lui; **she looks very young ~ her age** elle fait très jeune pour son âge. -**9.** [in phrase with infinitive verbs]: **it's not ~ him to decide** il ne lui appartient pas OR ce n'est pas à lui de décider; **it's not ~ her to tell me what to do** ce n'est pas à elle de me dire ce que je dois faire; **it was difficult ~ her to apologize** il lui était difficile de s'excuser; **this job is too complicated ~ us to finish today** ce travail est trop compliqué pour que nous le finissions aujourd'hui; **there is still time ~ her to finish** elle a encore le temps de finir; **~ us to arrive on time we'd better leave now** si nous voulons être à l'heure, il vaut mieux partir maintenant; **the easiest thing would be ~ you to lead the way** le plus facile serait que vous nous montriez le chemin; **there's no need ~ you to worry** il n'y a pas de raison de vous inquiéter.

D. *phr*: **oh ~ a holiday!** ah, si je pouvais être en vacances!; **you'll be (in) ~ it if your mother sees you!** ça va être ta fête si ta mère te voit!; **now we're (in) ~ it!** qu'est-ce qu'on va prendre!; **there's nothing ~ it but to pay him** il n'y a qu'à OR il ne nous reste qu'à le payer; **that's the postal service ~ you!** ça c'est bien la poste!

◇ *conj fml* car, parce que; **I was surprised when he arrived punctually, ~ he was usually late** je fus surpris de le voir arriver à l'heure, car il était souvent en retard.

◆ **for all** ◇ *prep phr* malgré; **~ all their efforts** malgré tous leurs efforts; **~ all his success, he's very insecure** malgré sa réussite, il manque vraiment de confiance en soi.

◇ *conj phr*: **~ all she may say** quoi qu'elle en dise ‖ [as far as]: **~ all I know** autant que je sache.

◆ **for all that** ◇ *adv phr* pour autant, malgré tout.

◇ *conj phr* [whatever]: **~ all the good it does** pour tout l'effet que ça fait.

◆ **for ever** *adv phr* [last, continue] pour toujours; [leave] pour toujours, sans retour; **it'll take ~ ever** ça va prendre une éternité ❑ **~ ever and a day** jusqu'à la fin des temps; **~ ever and ever** à tout jamais, éternellement; **~ ever and ever, amen** pour les siècles des siècles, amen.

FOR *adv abbr of* free on rail.

fora [ˈfɔːrə] *pl* → **forum**.

forage [ˈfɒrɪdʒ] ◇ *n* -**1.** [search] fouille *f*; [food] fourrage *m*. -**2.** MIL [raid] raid *m*, incursion *f*.

◇ *vi* -**1.** [search] fourrager, fouiller; **to ~ for sthg** fouiller pour trouver qqch. -**2.** MIL [raid] faire un raid OR une incursion.

◇ *vt* -**1.** [obtain] trouver en fourrageant. -**2.** [feed] donner du fourrage à, donner à manger à.

forage cap *n* calot *m*.

forasmuch as [fərəz'mʌtʃ-] *conj arch* OR *lit* vu que.

foray ['fɒreɪ] ◇ *n* MIL [raid] raid *m*, incursion *f*; [excursion] incursion *f*; **he made a ~ into politics** il a fait une incursion dans la politique.
◇ *vi* faire un raid OR une incursion.

forbad(e) [fə'bæd] *pt* → **forbid**.

forbear [fɔː'beəʳ] (*pt* forbore [-'bɔːʳ], *pp* forborne [-'bɔːn]) *fml* ◇ *vi* [abstain] s'abstenir; **to ~ from doing** OR **to do sthg** se garder OR s'abstenir de faire qqch; **she forbore to make any comment** elle s'abstint de tout commentaire.
◇ *vt* renoncer à, se priver de.
◇ *n* = **forebear**.

forbearance [fɔː'beərəns] *n* -**1.** [patience] patience *f*, tolérance *f*. -**2.** [restraint] abstention *f*.

forbearing [fɔː'beərɪŋ] *adj* patient.

forbid [fə'bɪd] (*pt* forbad OR forbade [-'bæd], *pp* forbidden [-'bɪdn]) *vt* -**1.** [not allow] interdire, défendre; **to ~ sb alcohol** interdire l'alcool à qqn; **to ~ sb to do sthg** défendre OR interdire à qqn de faire qqch; **students are forbidden to talk during exams** les étudiants n'ont pas le droit de parler pendant les examens; **it is strictly forbidden to smoke** il est formellement interdit de fumer. -**2.** [prevent] empêcher; **if she were to die, Heaven** OR **God ~, I don't know what I'd do** si elle venait à mourir, Dieu (m'en) préserve, je ne sais pas ce que je ferais; **Heaven ~ (that) all her family should come** à Dieu ne plaise que toute sa famille vienne.

forbidden [fə'bɪdn] ◇ *pp* → **forbid**.
◇ *adj* interdit, défendu.

forbidden fruit *n* fruit *m* défendu.

forbidding [fə'bɪdɪŋ] *adj* [building, look, sky] menaçant; [person] sévère, menaçant.

forbore [fɔː'bɔːʳ] *pt* → **forbear**.

forborne [fɔː'bɔːn] *pp* → **forbear**.

force [fɔːs] ◇ *vt* -**1.** [compel] forcer, obliger; **to ~ sb to do sthg** contraindre OR forcer qqn à faire qqch; **I ~d myself to be nice to them** je me suis forcé à être aimable avec eux; **don't ~ yourself!** *hum* ne te force surtout pas!; **they were ~d to admit I was right** ils ont été obligés de reconnaître que j'avais raison; **he was ~d to retire** il a été mis à la retraite d'office ❑ **to ~ sb's hand** forcer la main à qqn. -**2.** [wrest] arracher, extorquer; **I ~d a confession from** OR **out of him** je lui ai arraché une confession. -**3.** [impose] imposer; **to ~ sthg on** OR **upon sb** imposer qqch à qqn; **to ~ o.s. on sb** imposer sa présence à qqn; **he ~d himself** OR **his attentions on her** il l'a poursuivie de ses assiduités. -**4.** [push] pousser; **to ~ one's way into a building** entrer OR pénétrer de force dans un immeuble; **I ~d my way through the crowd** je me suis frayé un chemin OR passage à travers la foule; **don't ~ it** ne force pas; **the car ~d us off the road** la voiture nous a forcés à quitter la route; **to ~ a bill through Parliament** forcer la Chambre à voter une loi ❑ **to ~ sb into a corner** *literal* pousser qqn dans un coin; *fig* mettre qqn au pied du mur. -**5.** [break open] forcer; **to ~ open a door/lock** forcer une porte/une serrure. -**6.** [answer, smile] forcer; **she managed to ~ a smile** elle eut un sourire forcé. -**7.** [hurry] forcer, hâter; **to ~ flowers/plants** forcer des fleurs/des plantes; **we ~d the pace** nous avons forcé l'allure OR le pas; **I felt I had to ~ the issue** j'ai senti qu'il fallait que je force la décision. -**8.** [strain - metaphor, voice] forcer; [- word] forcer le sens de.
◇ *n* -**1.** [power] force *f*; **~s of evil/nature** forces du mal/de la nature; **Europe is becoming a powerful economic ~** l'Europe devient une grande puissance économique; **television could be a ~ for good** la télévision pourrait avoir une bonne influence; **France is a ~ to be reckoned with** la France est une puissance OR force avec laquelle il faut compter; **there are several ~s at work** il y a plusieurs forces en jeu. -**2.** [strength] force *f*; [violence] force *f*, violence *f*; **I'm against the use of ~** je suis contre le recours à la force; **the ~ of the blow laid him out** la violence du coup l'a mis K-O; **they used ~ to control the crowd** ils ont employé la force pour contrôler la foule; **I hit it with as much ~ as I could muster** je l'ai frappé aussi fort que j'ai pu. -**3.** [of argument, word] force *f*, poids *m*; **I don't see the ~ of her argument** je ne perçois pas la force de son argument. -**4.** *phr*: **~ of circumstances** force *f* des choses; **by** OR **from ~ of habit** par la force de l'habitude; **by sheer ~** de vive force; **she managed it through sheer ~ of will** elle y est arrivée uniquement à force de volonté; **the law comes into ~ this year** la loi entre en vigueur cette année. -**5.** PHYS force *f*; **centrifugal/coercive ~** force centrifuge/coercitive; **the ~ of gravity** la pesanteur. -**6.** [of people] force *f*; **our sales ~** COMM notre force de vente; **the allied ~s** les armées *fpl* alliées, les alliés *mpl*; **the (armed) ~s** les forces armées; **the (police) ~** les forces de police.

◆ **in force** ◇ *adj phr* en application, en vigueur; **the rules now in ~** le règlement en vigueur.
◇ *adv phr* en force; **the demonstrators arrived in ~** les manifestants sont arrivés en force; **the students were there in ~** les étudiants étaient là en force OR en grand nombre; **in full ~** au grand complet.

◆ **force back** *vt sep* -**1.** [push back] repousser, refouler; MIL faire reculer, obliger à reculer. -**2.** [repress] réprimer; **she ~d back the urge to laugh** elle réprima une envie de rire; **I ~d back my tears** j'ai refoulé mes larmes.

◆ **force down** *vt sep* -**1.** [push down] faire descendre (de force); **he ~d down the lid of the box** il a fermé la boîte en forçant; **to ~ down prices** faire baisser les prix. -**2.** [plane] forcer à atterrir. -**3.** [food] se forcer à manger OR à avaler; **more cake? — I expect I could ~ down another slice** *hum* encore un peu de gâteau? — ma foi, je suis sûr que j'ai encore un peu de place pour un autre petit morceau.

◆ **force out** *vt sep* -**1.** [push out] faire sortir (de force); **hunger eventually ~d them out** la faim les a finalement obligés à sortir; **the opposition ~d him out** *fig* l'opposition l'a poussé dehors. -**2.** [remark]: **he ~d out an apology** il s'est excusé du bout des lèvres.

◆ **force up** *vt sep* faire monter (de force); **to ~ prices up** faire monter les prix.

forced [fɔːst] *adj* -**1.** [compulsory] forcé; **~ labour** travail *m* forcé; **a ~ landing** un atterrissage forcé; **~ march** MIL marche *f* forcée. -**2.** [smile] forcé, artificiel; **he gave a ~ laugh** il a ri du bout des lèvres. -**3.** [plant] forcé.

force-feed *vt* nourrir de force; [livestock] gaver.

forceful ['fɔːsfʊl] *adj* [person] énergique, fort; [argument, style] puissant; [impression] puissant; **he's not very ~** il n'est pas très énergique.

forcefully ['fɔːsfʊlɪ] *adv* avec force, avec vigueur.

forcemeat ['fɔːsmiːt] *n* farce *f*.

forceps ['fɔːseps] *npl*: **(a pair of) ~** un forceps; **~ delivery** accouchement *m* au forceps.

forcible ['fɔːsəbl] *adj* -**1.** [by force] de OR par force; **~ entry** JUR effraction *f*. -**2.** [powerful - argument, style] puissant; [- personality] puissant, fort; [- speaker] puissant. -**3.** [emphatic - opinion] catégorique; [- wish] vif.

forcibly ['fɔːsəblɪ] *adv* -**1.** [by force] de force, par la force; **they were ~ removed from the house** on les a fait sortir de force de la maison. -**2.** [argue, speak] énergiquement, avec vigueur OR force. -**3.** [recommend, remind] fortement.

forcing bid ['fɔːsɪŋ-] *n* annonce forcée OR de forcing.

forcing house *n* forcerie *f*, serre *f* chaude.

ford [fɔːd] ◇ *n* gué *m*.
◇ *vt* passer OR traverser à gué.

fordable ['fɔːdəbl] *adj* guéable.

fore [fɔːʳ] ◇ *adj* -**1.** [front] à l'avant, antérieur; **the ~ and hind legs** les pattes de devant et de derrière. -**2.** NAUT à l'avant.
◇ *n* NAUT avant *m*, devant *m*; *fig*: **to come to the ~** percer, commencer à être connu; **her courage came to the ~** son courage s'est manifesté OR révélé; **the revolt brought these issues to the ~** la révolte a mis ces problèmes en évidence, la révolte a attiré l'attention sur ces problèmes.
◇ *adv* NAUT à l'avant; **~ and aft** de l'avant à l'arrière.
◇ *interj* [in golf]: **~!** attention!, gare!

fore-and-aft *adj* NAUT aurique; **~ rig** gréement *m* aurique; **~ sail** voile *f* aurique.

forearm [*n* 'fɔːrˌɑːm, *vb* fɔːr'ɑːm] ◇ *n* avant-bras *m*.
◇ *vt* prémunir.

forebear ['fɔːbeəʳ] *n* ancêtre *m*; **our ~s** nos aïeux *mpl*.

forebode [fɔː'bəʊd] *vt fml* augurer.

foreboding [fɔː'bəʊdɪŋ] *n* [feeling] pressentiment *m*, prémonition *f*; [omen] présage *m*, augure *m*; **she had a ~ that things would go seriously wrong** elle a eu le pressentiment que les choses allaient très mal tourner; **her laughter filled me with ~** ses rires m'ont rendu très appréhensif.

forebrain ['fɔːbreɪn] *n* prosencéphale *m*.

forecast ['fɔːkɑːst] (*pt* & *pp* forecast OR forecasted) ◇ *vt* [gen & METEOR] prévoir; [in betting] pronostiquer.
◇ *n* -**1.** [gen & METEOR] prévision *f*; **the ~ is not good** [gen] les prévisions ne sont pas bonnes; [weather] la météo n'est pas bonne; **sales ~s** COMM prévisions de ventes; **economic ~** prévisions économiques; **the weather ~** le bulletin météorologique, la météo. -**2.** [in betting] pronostic *m*.

forecaster ['fɔːkɑːstəʳ] *n* pronostiqueur *m*, -euse *f*; **weather ~** météorologiste *mf*, météorologue *mf*.

forecastle ['fəʊksl] *n* NAUT gaillard *m* d'avant; [in merchant navy] poste *m* d'équipage.

foreclose [fɔː'kləʊz] ◇ *vt* saisir; **to ~ a mortgage** saisir un bien hypothéqué.
◇ *vi* saisir le bien hypothéqué; **to ~ on sb** saisir les biens de qqn; **to ~ on a mortgage** saisir un bien hypothéqué.

foreclosure [fɔː'kləʊʒəʳ] *n* forclusion *f*.

forecourt ['fɔːkɔːt] *n* avant-cour *f*, cour *f* de devant; [of petrol station] devant *m*; **~ prices** prix à la pompe.

foredoomed [fɔː'duːmd] *adj lit* voué à l'échec.

forefather ['fɔːˌfɑːðəʳ] *n* ancêtre *m*; **our ~s** nos aïeux *mpl*.

forefinger ['fɔːˌfɪŋgəʳ] *n* index *m*.

forefoot ['fɔːfʊt] (*pl* forefeet [-fiːt]) *n* [of cow, horse] pied *m* de devant OR antérieur; [of cat, dog] patte *f* de devant OR antérieure.

forefront ['fɔːfrʌnt] *n* premier rang *m*; **she's in** OR **at the ~ of her field of research** c'est une sommité dans son domaine de recherche.

foregather [fɔː'gæðəʳ] = **forgather**.

forego [fɔː'gəʊ] (*pt* forewent [-'went], *pp* foregone [-'gɒn]) = **forgo**.

foregoing [fɔː'gəʊɪŋ] ◇ *adj* précédent, susdit; **the ~ study** la susdite étude.
◇ *n* précédent *m*, -e *f*; **if we are to believe the ~** si nous devons croire ce qui précède.

foregone [fɔː'gɒn] *pp* → **forego**.

foregone conclusion ['fɔːgɒn-] *n* issue *f* certaine OR prévisible; **it was a ~** c'était gagné d'avance.

foreground ['fɔːgraʊnd] ◇ *n* [gen, ART & PHOT] premier plan; **in the ~** au premier plan; **the Mayor is in the ~** *fig* le maire est bien en évidence.
◇ *vt* privilégier.

forehand ['fɔːhænd] ◇ *n* -**1.** SPORT coup *m* droit. -**2.** [of horse] avant-main *m*.
◇ *adj*: **~ drive** coup *m* droit; **~ volley** volée *f* de face.

forehead ['fɔːhed] *n* front *m*.

foreign ['fɒrən] *adj* -**1.** [country, language, person] étranger; [aid, visit - to country] à l'étranger; [- from country] de l'étranger; [products] de l'étranger; [trade] extérieur; **students from ~ countries** des étudiants venant de l'étranger;

relations with ~ countries les relations avec l'étranger; a ~-owned company une firme sous contrôle étranger; ~ relations relations *fpl* avec l'étranger; ~ travel voyages *mpl* à l'étranger ❑ ~ affairs affaires *fpl* étrangères; ~ agent [spy] agent *m* étranger; COMM représentant *m*, -e *f* à l'étranger; ~ correspondent correspondant *m*, -e *f* à l'étranger; ~ currency OR exchange devises *fpl* étrangères; ~ exchange market marché *m* des changes; ~ policy politique *f* étrangère OR extérieure. -**2.** [alien] étranger; such thinking is ~ to them un tel raisonnement leur est étranger; a ~ body, ~ matter un corps étranger.

foreigner ['fɒrənəʳ] *n* étranger *m*, -ère *f*.

Foreign Legion *n*: the ~ la Légion (étrangère).

Foreign Office *n*: the Foreign (and Commonwealth) Office *le ministère britannique des Affaires étrangères*.

Foreign Secretary, Foreign and Commonwealth Secretary *n*: the ~ *le ministre britannique des Affaires étrangères*.

foreign service *n Am* service *m* diplomatique.

foreknowledge [,fɔː'nɒlɪdʒ] *n fml* connaissance *f* anticipée, prescience *f*; I had no ~ of her plans je ne savais pas à l'avance quels étaient ses projets.

foreland ['fɔːlənd] *n* promontoire *m*, cap *m*.

foreleg ['fɔːleg] *n* [of horse] jambe *f* de devant OR antérieure; [of dog, cat] patte *f* de devant OR antérieure.

forelock ['fɔːlɒk] *n* [of person] mèche *f*, toupet *m*; [of horse] toupet *m*; to touch OR to tug one's ~ saluer en portant la main au front.

foreman ['fɔːmən] (*pl* **foremen** [-mən]) *n* INDUST contremaître *m*, chef *m* d'équipe; JUR [of jury] président *m*, -e *f*.

foremast ['fɔːmɑːst] *n* mât *m* de misaine.

foremost ['fɔːməʊst] ◇ *adj* [first - in position] le plus en avant; [- in importance] principal, le plus important.
◇ *adv* en avant.

forename ['fɔːneɪm] *n Br* prénom *m*.

forenamed ['fɔːneɪmd] *adj* susdit, précité.

forenoon ['fɔːnuːn] *n arch, lit* OR *dial* matinée *f*.

forensic [fə'rensɪk] *adj* -**1.** [chemistry] légal; [expert] légiste; ~ department département de médecine légale; ~ evidence expertise médico-légale; ~ medicine OR science médecine *f* légale; ~ scientist médecin *m* légiste; ~ tests showed him to be the killer les tests médico-légaux ont prouvé qu'il était l'assassin. -**2.** [skill, term] du barreau.

forensics [fə'rensɪks] *n (U)* art *m* de la discussion OR du débat.

foreordain [,fɔːrɔː'deɪn] *vt fml* prédestiner.

forepart ['fɔːpɑːt] *n fml* [gen] devant *m*, avant *m*; [of century, day] début *m*.

forepaw ['fɔːpɔː] *n* patte de devant OR antérieure.

foreplay ['fɔːpleɪ] *n (U)* préliminaires *mpl*.

forequarters ['fɔː,kwɔːtəz] *npl* [of animal] avant-train *m*; [of carcass] quartiers *mpl* de devant.

forerunner ['fɔː,rʌnəʳ] *n* [precursor] précurseur *m*; [omen] présage *m*, signe *m* avant-coureur.

foresail ['fɔːseɪl] *n* (voile *f* de) misaine *f*.

foresee [fɔː'siː] (*pt* **foresaw** [-'sɔː], *pp* **foreseen** [-'siːn]) *vt* prévoir, présager.

foreseeable [fɔː'siːəbl] *adj* prévisible; in the ~ future dans un avenir prévisible.

foreseen [fɔː'siːn] *pp* → **foresee**.

foreshadow [fɔː'ʃædəʊ] *vt* présager, annoncer; her first novel ~ed this masterpiece son premier roman a laissé prévoir ce chef-d'œuvre.

foreshore ['fɔːʃɔːʳ] *n* [beach] plage *f*; GEOG laisse *f* de mer.

foreshorten [fɔː'ʃɔːtn] *vt* -**1.** ART faire un raccourci de; PHOT [horizontally] réduire; [vertically] écraser. -**2.** [reduce] réduire; [story] résumer.

foreshortening [fɔː'ʃɔːtnɪŋ] *n* -**1.** ART raccourci *m*; PHOT [horizontal] réduction *f*; [vertical] écrasement *m*. -**2.** [reduction] réduction *f*; [of story] résumé *m*.

foresight ['fɔːsaɪt] *n* prévoyance *f*; lack of ~ imprévoyance *f*.

foreskin ['fɔːskɪn] *n* prépuce *m*.

forest ['fɒrɪst] *n* forêt *f*; a ~ of hands *fig* une multitude de mains.

forestall [fɔː'stɔːl] *vt* -**1.** [prevent] empêcher, retenir; she wanted to leave but he ~ed her elle voulut partir mais il l'en empêcha. -**2.** [anticipate - desire, possibility] anticiper, prévenir; [- person] devancer, prendre les devants sur.

forestation [,fɒrɪ'steɪʃn] *n* boisement *m*.

forester ['fɒrɪstəʳ] *n* forestier *m*, -ère *f*.

forest ranger *n Am* garde *m* forestier.

forestry ['fɒrɪstrɪ] *n* sylviculture *f*; the Forestry Commission *organisme britannique de gestion des forêts domaniales*, ≃ les eaux et forêts *fpl*.

foretaste ['fɔːteɪst] *n* avant-goût *m*.

foretell [fɔː'tel] (*pt & pp* **foretold** [-'təʊld]) *vt* prédire.

forethought ['fɔːθɔːt] *n* [premeditation] préméditation *f*; [foresight] prévoyance *f*.

foretold [fɔː'təʊld] *pt & pp* → **foretell**.

forever [fə'revəʳ] *adv* -**1.** [eternally] (pour) toujours, éternellement; it won't last ~ ça ne durera pas toujours; I'll love you ~ je t'aimerai toujours; Europe ~! vive l'Europe! -**2.** [incessantly] toujours, sans cesse; he's ~ finding fault il trouve toujours à redire. -**3.** [for good] pour toujours; dinosaurs have vanished ~ les dinosaures ont disparu pour toujours. -**4.** *inf* [a long time] très longtemps; it'll take ~ ça va prendre des heures; he took ~ to get ready il a mis des heures à se préparer; we can't wait ~ nous ne pouvons pas attendre jusqu'à la saint-glinglin.

forewarn [fɔː'wɔːn] *vt* prévenir, avertir; he ~ed them that life there would be difficult il les a prévenus que là-bas la vie serait difficile ❑ ~ed is forearmed *prov* un homme averti en vaut deux *prov*.

forewent [fɔː'went] *pt* → **forego**.

foreword ['fɔːwɜːd] *n* avant-propos *m*, préface *f*.

forfeit ['fɔːfɪt] ◇ *vt* -**1.** [lose] perdre; [give up] renoncer à, abandonner; to ~ one's rights perdre OR être déchu de ses droits. -**2.** JUR [lose] perdre (par confiscation); [confiscate] confisquer.
◇ *n* -**1.** [penalty] prix *m*, peine *f*; COMM [sum] amende *f*, dédit *m*. -**2.** JUR [loss] perte *f* (par confiscation). -**3.** [game]: to play ~s jouer aux gages; to pay a ~ avoir un gage.
◇ *adj fml* [subject to confiscation] susceptible d'être confisqué; [confiscated] confisqué; her life could be ~ *fig* elle pourrait le payer de sa vie.

forfeiture ['fɔːfɪtʃəʳ] *n* -**1.** JUR [loss] perte *f* par confiscation; *fig* [surrender] renonciation *f*; ~ of rights renonciation aux droits. -**2.** [penalty] prix *m*, peine *f*; COMM [sum] amende *f*, dédit *m*.

forgather [fɔː'gæðəʳ] *vi fml* se réunir, s'assembler.

forgave [fə'geɪv] *pt* → **forgive**.

forge [fɔːdʒ] ◇ *vt* -**1.** [metal, sword] forger; to ~ an alliance/a friendship *fig* sceller une alliance/une amitié. -**2.** [counterfeit - money, signature] contrefaire; [- picture] faire un faux de, contrefaire; [- document] faire un faux de; a ~d passport un faux passeport; a ~d £20 note un faux billet de 20 livres.
◇ *vi* [go forward] avancer; we ~d on, hoping to reach the village by nightfall nous avons continué à toute allure dans l'espoir d'arriver au village avant la tombée de la nuit; to ~ into the lead prendre la tête.
◇ *n* [machine, place] forge *f*.
◆ **forge ahead** *vi insep* prendre de l'avance; *fig* faire son chemin, réussir, prospérer.

forger ['fɔːdʒəʳ] *n* [gen] faussaire *mf*; [of money] faux-monnayeur *m*, faussaire *mf*.

forgery ['fɔːdʒərɪ] (*pl* **forgeries**) *n* -**1.** [of money, picture, signature] contrefaçon *f*; [of document] falsification *f*; to prosecute sb for ~ poursuivre qqn pour faux (et usage de faux). -**2.** [object] faux *m*.

forget [fə'get] (*pt* **forgot** [-'gɒt], *pp* **forgotten** [-'gɒtn]) ◇ *vt* -**1.** [be unable to recall] oublier; he'll never ~ her il ne l'oubliera jamais; have you forgotten all your Latin? avez-vous oublié tout votre latin?; I'll never ~ seeing him play Lear je ne l'oublierai jamais OR je le reverrai toujours dans le rôle de Lear; I forgot (that) you had a sister j'avais oublié que tu avais une sœur; she's forgotten how to swim elle ne sait plus (comment) nager; I forgot which house is his je ne sais plus OR j'ai oublié quelle maison est la sienne; I never ~ a face j'ai la mémoire des visages; she'll never let him ~ his mistake elle n'est pas près de lui pardonner son erreur || [not think about] oublier; I forgot the time j'ai oublié l'heure; to ~ one's manners oublier ses manières; to ~ o.s. s'oublier; he was so overwhelmed by emotion that he quite forgot himself il était tellement ému qu'il perdit toute retenue; it's my idea and don't you ~ it! c'est moi qui ai eu cette idée, tâchez de ne pas l'oublier!; such things are best forgotten il vaut mieux ne pas penser à de telles choses; that never-to-be-forgotten day ce jour inoubliable OR mémorable. -**2.** [neglect, overlook] oublier, omettre; she forgot to mention that she was married elle a oublié OR a omis de dire qu'elle était mariée; he seems to have forgotten his old friends il semble avoir oublié ses anciens amis; don't ~ the poor at Christmas n'oubliez pas les pauvres à Noël; rent and food, not forgetting clothing, come to £200 le loyer et la nourriture, sans oublier les vêtements, font 200 livres; let's ~ our differences oublions nos différends; ~ it! *inf* [in reply to thanks] il n'y a pas de quoi!; [in reply to apology] ce n'est pas grave!, ne vous en faites pas!; [in irritation] laissez tomber!; what were we talking about? – oh, ~ it! de quoi parlions-nous? – oh, cela n'a aucune importance OR peu importe! -**3.** [leave behind] oublier, laisser; don't ~ your umbrella! n'oublie pas ton parapluie! -**4.** [give up - idea, plan] abandonner, renoncer à; if we don't get financial backing, we'll just have to ~ the whole thing si nous n'obtenons pas de soutien financier il nous faudra renoncer au projet.
◇ *vi*: to ~ about sb/sthg oublier qqn/qqch; sorry, I completely forgot about it désolé, j'avais complètement oublié; he agreed to ~ about the outburst il a accepté de fermer les yeux sur l'incartade.

forgetful [fə'getful] *adj* [absent-minded] distrait; [careless] négligent, étourdi; she's so ~ elle oublie tout, elle est tellement distraite; to be ~ of sthg être oublieux de qqch.

forgetfulness [fə'getfulnɪs] *n* [absent-mindedness] manque *m* de mémoire; [carelessness] négligence *f*, étourderie *f*; in a moment of ~ dans un moment d'étourderie.

forget-me-not *n* myosotis *m*.

forgettable [fə'getəbl] *adj* qui ne présente pas d'intérêt.

forgivable [fə'gɪvəbl] *adj* pardonnable.

forgivably [fə'gɪvəblɪ] *adv*: she was, quite ~, rather annoyed with him! elle était plutôt en colère contre lui, et on la comprend!

forgive [fə'gɪv] (*pt* **forgave** [-'geɪv], *pp* **forgiven** [-'gɪvn]) *vt* -**1.** [pardon] pardonner; to ~ sb (for) sthg pardonner qqch à qqn; he asked me to ~ him il m'a demandé pardon; ~ my ignorance, but who exactly was Galsworthy? pardonnez mon ignorance, mais qui était Galsworthy exactement?; can you ever ~ me? pourras-tu jamais me pardonner?; ~ me, but haven't we met before? pardonnez-moi OR excusez-moi, mais est-ce qu'on ne s'est pas déjà rencontrés?; one might be forgiven for thinking that... on pourrait penser que...; ~ and forget pardonner et oublier. -**2.** [debt, payment]: to ~ (sb) a debt faire grâce (à qqn) d'une dette.

forgiveable [fə'gɪvəbl] = **forgivable**.

forgiveness [fəˈgɪvnɪs] *n* -**1.** [pardon] pardon *m*; **to ask sb's ~** demander pardon à qqn. -**2.** [tolerance] indulgence *f*, clémence *f*.

forgiving [fəˈgɪvɪŋ] *adj* indulgent, clément.

forgo [fɔːˈgəʊ] (*pt* **forwent** [-ˈwent], *pp* **forgone** [-ˈgɒn]) *vt* renoncer à, se priver de.

forgot [fəˈgɒt] *pt* → **forget**.

forgotten [fəˈgɒtn] *pp* → **forget**.

fork [fɔːk] ◇ *n* -**1.** [for eating] fourchette *f*. -**2.** AGR fourche *f*. -**3.** [junction - in road, railway] bifurcation *f*, embranchement *m*; **take the right ~** tournez OR prenez à droite à l'embranchement. -**4.** [on bicycle, motorbike] fourche *f*.
◇ *vt* -**1.** AGR fourcher. -**2.** [food] prendre avec une fourchette; **she was ~ing food into her mouth** elle enfournait la nourriture avec sa fourchette.
◇ *vi* -**1.** [river, road] bifurquer, fourcher; **the road ~s at Newton** la route fait une fourche à Newton. -**2.** [car, person] bifurquer, tourner; **he ~ed left** il a pris OR a tourné à gauche; **~ right for the airport** prenez à droite pour l'aéroport.
◆ **fork out** *inf* ◇ *vt sep* allonger, cracher.
◇ *vi insep* casquer.
◆ **fork over** *vt sep* -**1.** AGR fourcher. -**2.** *inf* [money] allonger, cracher.
◆ **fork up** *inf* = **fork out**.

forked [fɔːkt] *adj* [tongue] fourchu; [river, road] à bifurcation.

forked lightning *n* éclair *m* en zigzags.

forklift [ˈfɔːklɪft] *n*: **~ (truck)** chariot *m* élévateur.

forlorn [fəˈlɔːn] *adj* -**1.** [wretched] triste, malheureux; **a ~ cry** un cri de désespoir. -**2.** [lonely - person] abandonné, délaissé; [- place] désolé, désert; **the empty house had a ~ look about it** la maison vide avait l'air abandonné. -**3.** [desperate] désespéré; **I went there in the ~ hope that she'd see me** j'y suis allé en espérant contre tout espoir OR sans trop y croire qu'elle accepterait de me voir; **they made one last ~ attempt to contact her** ils ont fait un dernier effort désespéré pour la contacter.

form [fɔːm] ◇ *n* -**1.** [shape] forme *f*; **in the ~ of a heart** en forme de cœur; **her plan began to take ~** son projet a commencé à prendre tournure OR forme. -**2.** [body, figure] forme *f*, silhouette *f*; **a slender ~ appeared at the door** une silhouette élancée apparut à la porte; **the human ~** la forme humaine. -**3.** [aspect, mode] forme *f*; **it's written in the ~ of a letter** c'est écrit sous forme de lettre; **the Devil appeared in the ~ of a goat** le diable apparut sous la forme d'une chèvre; **the same product in a new ~** le même produit présenté différemment; **what ~ should my questions take?** comment devrais-je formuler mes questions?; **the interview took the ~ of an informal chat** l'entrevue prit la forme d'une discussion informelle; **her anxiety showed itself in the ~ of anger** son inquiétude se manifesta par de la colère. -**4.** [kind, type] forme *f*, sorte *f*; **one ~ of cancer** une forme de cancer; **we studied three different ~s of government** nous avons examiné trois systèmes de gouvernement OR trois régimes différents; **all ~s of sugar** le sucre sous toutes ses formes; **she sent some flowers as a ~ of thanks** elle a envoyé des fleurs en guise de remerciements. -**5.** [document] formulaire *m*; [for bank, telegram] formule *f*; **to fill in** OR **out a ~** remplir un formulaire ▫ **order ~** bon *m* de commande; **printed ~** imprimé *m*; **tax ~** feuille *f* d'impôts. -**6.** [condition] forme *f*, condition *f*; **in good ~** en pleine forme, en excellente condition; **on ~** *Br*, **in ~** *Am* en forme; **John was on** *Br* OR **in** *Am* **good ~ at lunch** John était en forme OR plein d'entrain pendant le déjeuner; **he's off ~** *Br* OR **out of ~** *Am* il n'est pas en forme; **I'm on** *Br* OR **in** *Am* **top ~** je suis en pleine forme; **on** *Br* OR **in** *Am* **their current ~ they're unlikely to win** étant donné leur forme actuelle ils ont peu de chances de gagner; **to study ~** [in horse racing] examiner le tableau des performances des chevaux. -**7.** [gen, ART, LITERAT & MUS] forme *f*; **~ and content** la forme et le fond; **his writing lacks ~** ce qu'il écrit n'est pas clair; **her ideas lack ~** ses idées sont confuses. -**8.** [standard practice] forme *f*, règle *f*; **to do sthg for ~'s sake** OR **as a matter of ~** faire qqch pour la forme; **what's the usual ~ in these cases?** que fait-on d'habitude OR quelle est la marche à suivre dans ces cas-là?; **in due ~** JUR en bonne et due forme. -**9.** *dated* [etiquette] forme *f*, formalité *f*; **it's bad ~** cela ne se fait pas; **it's good ~** c'est de bon ton, cela se fait. -**10.** [formula] forme *f*, formule *f*; **~ of address** formule de politesse; **the correct ~ of address for a senator** la manière correcte de s'adresser à un sénateur; **it's only a ~ of speech** ce n'est qu'une façon de parler; **the ~ of the marriage service** les rites *mpl* du mariage. -**11.** [mould] forme *f*, moule *m*. -**12.** GRAMM & LING forme *f*; **the masculine ~** la forme du masculin, le masculin. -**13.** PHILOS [structure] forme *f*; [essence] essence *f*. -**14.** *Br* SCH [class] classe *f*; **she's in the first ~** ≃ elle est en sixième. -**15.** *Br* [bench] banc *m*. -**16.** *Br crime sl* [criminal record] casier *m* (judiciaire).
◇ *comp Br* SCH: **~ master**, **~ mistress**, **~ teacher** professeur *m* principal.
◇ *vt* -**1.** [shape] former, construire; [character, mind] former, façonner; **he ~ed the model out of** OR **from clay** il a sculpté OR façonné le modèle dans l'argile; **~ the dough into a ball** pétrissez la pâte en forme de boule; **she has trouble ~ing certain words** elle a du mal à prononcer certains mots; **to ~ a sentence** construire une phrase; **it was certainly a character-~ing experience** c'est sans aucun doute une expérience qui forme OR façonne le caractère. -**2.** [take the shape of] former, faire; **the coastline ~s a series of curves** la côte forme une série de courbes; **the children ~ed a circle** les enfants formèrent un cercle; **~ a line please** faites la queue s'il vous plaît; **the applicants ~ed a queue** les candidats firent la queue. -**3.** [develop - opinion] se former, se faire; [- plan] concevoir, élaborer; [- habit] contracter; **he's wary of ~ing friendships** il hésite à nouer des amitiés; **to ~ an impression** avoir une impression. -**4.** [organize - association, club] créer, fonder; [- committee, government] former; COMM [- company] fonder, créer. -**5.** [constitute] composer, former; **to ~ the basis of sthg** constituer la base de OR servir de base à qqch; **to ~ a part of sthg** faire partie de qqch; **the countries ~ing the alliance** les pays qui constituent l'alliance. -**6.** GRAMM former; **how to ~ the past tense** comment former le passé composé.
◇ *vi* -**1.** [materialize] se former, prendre forme; **doubts began to ~ in his mind** des doutes commencèrent à prendre forme dans son esprit, il commença à avoir des doutes. -**2.** [take shape] se former; **~ into a line!** alignez-vous!; **we ~ed into groups** nous nous sommes mis en groupes, nous avons formé des groupes.
◆ **form up** *vi insep Br* se mettre en ligne, s'aligner.

formal [ˈfɔːml] ◇ *adj* -**1.** [conventional - function] officiel, solennel; [- greeting] solennel, cérémonieux; **a ~ dance** un grand bal; **a ~ dinner** un dîner officiel; **~ dress** [for ceremony] tenue *f* de cérémonie; [for evening] tenue *f* de soirée. -**2.** [official - announcement, approval] officiel; [- order] formel, explicite; **~ agreement/contract** accord *m*/contrat *m* en bonne et due forme; **a ~ denial** un démenti formel OR catégorique; **she had no ~ education** elle n'a jamais fait d'études; **no ~ training is required** aucune formation spécifique n'est exigée; **we gave him a ~ warning** nous l'avons averti officiellement OR dans les règles. -**3.** [correct - person] solennel; [- behaviour, style] soigné, solennel, guindé *pej*; **she's very ~** elle est très à cheval sur les conventions; **don't be so ~** ne sois pas si sérieux, sois un peu plus détendu; **in ~ language** dans un style soigné OR soutenu; **"vous" is the ~ form** «vous» est la formule de politesse. -**4.** [ordered] formaliste, méthodique; **~ garden** jardin *m* à la française. -**5.** [nominal] de forme; **~ agreement** accord *m* de forme; **she is the ~ head of State** c'est elle le chef d'État officiel. -**6.** GRAMM & LING formaliste, formel. -**7.** PHILOS formel.
◇ *n Am* -**1.** [dance] bal *m*. -**2.** [suit] habit *m* de soirée.

formaldehyde [fɔːˈmældɪhaɪd] *n* formaldéhyde *m*.

formalin(e) [ˈfɔːməlɪn] *n* formol *m*.

formalism [ˈfɔːməlɪzm] *n* formalisme *m*.

formalist [ˈfɔːməlɪst] ◇ *adj* formaliste.
◇ *n* formaliste *mf*.

formality [fɔːˈmælətɪ] (*pl* **formalities**) *n* -**1.** [ceremoniousness] cérémonie *f*; [solemnity] solennité *f*, gravité *f*; [stiffness] froideur *f*, raideur *f*; [convention] formalité *f*, étiquette *f*. -**2.** [procedure] formalité *f*; **it's a mere ~** c'est une simple formalité; **let's forget the formalities** dispensons-nous des formalités.

formalize, **-ise** [ˈfɔːməlaɪz] *vt* formaliser.

formally [ˈfɔːməlɪ] *adv* -**1.** [conventionally] solennellement, cérémonieusement; **~ dressed** [for ceremony] en tenue de cérémonie; [for evening] en tenue de soirée. -**2.** [officially] officiellement, dans les règles; **an agreement was ~ drawn up** un accord a été rédigé en bonne et due forme. -**3.** [speak] de façon soignée; [behave] de façon solennelle OR guindée *pej*. -**4.** [study, research] de façon méthodique; [arrange] de façon régulière. -**5.** [nominally] pour la forme; **he did consult his father before proceeding, if only ~** il a demandé conseil à son père avant d'agir, ne serait-ce que pour la forme.

formant [ˈfɔːmənt] *n* formant *m*.

format [ˈfɔːmæt] (*cont* **formatting**, *pt* & *pp* **formatted**) ◇ *n* -**1.** [size] format *m*. -**2.** [layout] présentation *f*; **the news on TV now has a new ~** le journal télévisé a adopté une nouvelle présentation. -**3.** COMPUT format *m*.
◇ *vt* -**1.** [layout] composer la présentation de. -**2.** COMPUT formater.

formation [fɔːˈmeɪʃn] *n* -**1.** [establishment - of club] création *f*, fondation *f*; [- of committee, company] formation *f*, fondation *f*; [- of government] formation *f*. -**2.** [development - of character, person] formation *f*; [- of idea] développement *m*, élaboration *f*; [- of plan] élaboration *f*, mise *f* en place. -**3.** BOT, GEOL & MED formation *f*. -**4.** [arrangement] formation *f*, disposition *f*; MIL [unit] formation *f*, dispositif *m*; **battle ~** formation de combat; **in close ~** en ordre serré.

formation dancing *n* danse *f* en formation.

formation flying *n* vol *m* en formation.

formative [ˈfɔːmətɪv] ◇ *adj* formateur; **the ~ years** les années *fpl* formatrices.
◇ *n* formant *m*, élément *m* formateur.

formatting [ˈfɔːmætɪŋ] *n* COMPUT formatage *m*.

form class *n* catégorie *f* grammaticale.

forme *Br*, **form** *Am* [fɔːm] *n* PRINT forme *f*.

-formed [fɔːmd] *in cpds* formé; **badly/well~ letters** lettres mal/bien formées.

former [ˈfɔːmə^r] ◇ *adj* -**1.** [time] passé; **in ~ times** OR **days** autrefois, dans le passé. -**2.** [earlier, previous] ancien, précédent; **my ~ boss** mon ancien patron; **I'm a ~ student of his** je suis un de ses anciens élèves; **my ~ wife** mon ex-femme; **in a ~ life** dans une vie antérieure; **he's only a shadow of his ~ self** il n'est plus que l'ombre de lui-même. -**3.** [first] premier; **I prefer the ~ idea to the latter** je préfère la première idée à la dernière.
◇ *n* -**1.** [first] premier *m*, -ère *f*, celui-là *m*, celle-là *f*; **of the two methods I prefer the ~** des deux méthodes je préfère la première. -**2.** TECH gabarit *m*.

-former *in cpds Br* élève de; **first~** ≃ élève *mf* de sixième.

formerly [ˈfɔːməlɪ] *adv* autrefois, jadis.

form feed *n* COMPUT avancement *m* du papier.

formic [ˈfɔːmɪk] *adj* formique.

Formica® [fɔːˈmaɪkə] *n* Formica® *m*, plastique *m* laminé.

formidable ['fɔːmɪdəbl] *adj* **-1.** [inspiring fear] redoutable, terrible; [inspiring respect] remarquable; she's a ~ athlete c'est une athlète remarquable; his book reveals a ~ intellect son livre révèle un esprit brillant. **-2.** [difficult] redoutable, ardu; a ~ problem un problème difficile.

formidably ['fɔːmɪdəblɪ] *adv* redoutablement, terriblement.

formless ['fɔːmlɪs] *adj* [shape] informe; [fear, idea] vague.

form letter *n* lettre *f* circulaire.

Formosa [fɔː'məʊsə] *pr n* Formose; in ~ à Formose.

formula ['fɔːmjʊlə] (*pl sense 1* **formulas** OR **formulae** [-liː], *pl senses 2 and 4* **formulas**) *n* **-1.** [gen, CHEM & MATH] formule *f*; a ~ acceptable to both sides une formule OR solution qui soit acceptable pour les deux parties; a ~ for happiness une recette qui assure le bonheur. **-2.** [expression] formule *f*. **-3.** AUT formule *f*; ~ 1 (racing) la formule 1; a ~ 1 car une voiture de formule 1. **-4.** *Am* [for baby] ≃ bouillie *f (pour bébé)*.

formulaic [,fɔːmjʊ'leɪɪk] *adj*: ~ expression formule *f*.

formulate ['fɔːmjʊleɪt] *vt* **-1.** [express] formuler. **-2.** [plan] élaborer.

formulation [,fɔːmjʊ'leɪʃn] *n* **-1.** [of idea] formulation *f*, expression *f*. **-2.** [of plan] élaboration *f*.

fornicate ['fɔːnɪkeɪt] *vi fml* forniquer.

fornication [,fɔːnɪ'keɪʃn] *n fml* fornication *f*.

forsake [fə'seɪk] (*pt* **forsook** [-'sʊk], *pp* **forsaken** [-'seɪkn]) *vt fml* **-1.** [abandon - family, spouse] abandonner; [- friend] délaisser; [- place] quitter; her customary patience forsook her sa patience habituelle lui fit défaut. **-2.** [give up] renoncer à.

forsaken [fə'seɪkn] ◇ *pp* → **forsake**.
◇ *adj lit* [person] abandonné; [place] abandonné, désert; ~ by all abandonné de tous.

forsook [fə'sʊk] *pt* → **forsake**.

forsooth [fə'suːθ] *arch* ◇ *adv* à vrai dire, en vérité.
◇ *interj* ma foi, par exemple.

forswear [fɔː'sweəʳ] (*pt* **forswore** [-'swɔːʳ], *pp* **forsworn** [-'swɔːn]) *fml* ◇ *vt* **-1.** [renounce] abjurer. **-2.** [deny] désavouer; to ~ o.s. se parjurer.
◇ *vi* se parjurer, commettre un parjure.

forsythia [fɔː'saɪθjə] *n* forsythia *m*.

fort [fɔːt] *n* fort *m*; [smaller] fortin *m*; to hold the ~ *Br*, to hold down the ~ *Am* assurer la permanence.

forte[1] ['fɔːteɪ] *n* [strong point] fort *m*; patience is hardly his ~ la patience n'est pas vraiment son (point) fort.

forte[2] ['fɔːtɪ] ◇ *adj* & *adv* MUS forte.
◇ *n* forte *m*.

fortepiano [,fɔːtɪpɪ'ænəʊ] *n* pianoforte *m*.

forth [fɔːθ] *adv lit* **-1.** [out, forward] en avant; to go OR to set ~ se mettre en route; to bring ~ produire; to send ~ envoyer. **-2.** [forwards in time]: from this moment ~ dorénavant, désormais; from this day ~ à partir d'aujourd'hui OR de ce jour.

forthright ['fɔːθraɪt] *adj* [person] direct, franc; [remark, opposition] franc, direct; she's very ~ elle ne mâche pas ses mots; he has always been a ~ critic of the government il a toujours critiqué le gouvernement ouvertement.

forthwith [,fɔːθ'wɪθ] *adv fml* incontinent *lit*, sur-le-champ.

fortieth ['fɔːtɪɪθ] ◇ *n* **-1.** [ordinal] quarantième *m*. **-2.** [fraction] quarantième *m*.
◇ *adj* quarantième.

fortification [,fɔːtɪfɪ'keɪʃn] *n* fortification *f*.

fortified ['fɔːtɪfaɪd] *adj* fortifié.

fortified wine *n Br* vin *m* de liqueur, vin *m* doux naturel.

fortify ['fɔːtɪfaɪ] (*pt* & *pp* **fortified**) *vt* **-1.** [place] fortifier, armer; *fig* [person] réconforter, remonter; have a drink to ~ yourself prenez un verre pour vous remonter. **-2.** [wine] augmenter la teneur en alcool, alcooliser; [food] renforcer en vitamines.

fortitude ['fɔːtɪtjuːd] *n* courage *m*, force *f* morale.

fortnight ['fɔːtnaɪt] *n Br* quinzaine *f*, quinze jours *mpl*; for a ~ pour quinze jours; a ~ ago il y a quinze jours; a ~ tomorrow demain en quinze; a ~'s holiday quinze jours de vacances; it's been postponed for a ~ cela a été remis à quinzaine.

fortnightly ['fɔːt,naɪtlɪ] (*pl* **fortnightlies**) *Br*
◇ *adj* bimensuel.
◇ *adv* tous les quinze jours.
◇ *n* bimensuel *m*.

Fortran, FORTRAN ['fɔːtræn] *n* fortran *m*.

fortress ['fɔːtrɪs] *n* [fort] fort *m*; [prison] forteresse *f*; [castle] château *m* fort; [place, town] place *f* forte.

fortuitous [fɔː'tjuːɪtəs] *adj* fortuit, imprévu.

fortuitously [fɔː'tjuːɪtəslɪ] *adv* fortuitement, par hasard.

Fortuna [fɔː'tjuːnə] *pr n* Fortune.

fortunate ['fɔːtʃnət] ◇ *adj* [person] heureux, chanceux; [choice, meeting] heureux, propice; you are ~ vous avez de la chance; I was ~ enough to get the job j'ai eu la chance d'obtenir le travail; he is ~ in his friends il a de bons amis; how ~! quelle chance!
◇ *npl*: we're collecting money for the less ~ nous faisons une collecte pour les déshérités.

fortunately ['fɔːtʃnətlɪ] *adv* heureusement, par bonheur.

fortune ['fɔːtʃuːn] *n* **-1.** [wealth] fortune *f*; he came to London to make his ~ il est venu à Londres pour faire fortune; she makes a ~ elle gagne beaucoup d'argent; he made a ~ on the house il a gagné beaucoup d'argent en vendant la maison; to come into a ~ hériter d'une fortune, faire un gros héritage; a man of ~ un homme fortuné; to cost/to pay/to spend a (small) ~ coûter/payer/dépenser une (petite) fortune. **-2.** [future] destin *m*; to tell sb's ~ dire la bonne aventure à qqn; she tells ~s elle dit la bonne aventure. **-3.** [chance, fate] sort *m*, fortune *f*; ~ smiled upon him OR has been kind to him la chance lui a souri; the novel traces its hero's changing ~s le roman retrace les tribulations de son héros; the ~s of war les hasards de la guerre. **-4.** [luck] fortune *f*, chance *f*; he had the good ~ to win il a eu la chance de gagner; by good ~ par chance, par bonheur; to try one's ~ tenter sa chance.

fortune cookie *n Am biscuit chinois dans lequel est caché un horoscope*.

Fortune Five Hundred *npl les 500 plus grosses entreprises américaines (dont la liste est établie, chaque année, par le magazine Fortune)*.

fortune-hunter *n pej* [man] coureur *m* de dot; [woman] aventurière *f*, femme *f* intéressée.

fortune-teller *n* [gen] diseur *m*, -euse *f* de bonne aventure, voyant *m*, -e *f*; [with cards] tireur *m*, -euse *f* de cartes, cartomancien *m*, -enne *f*.

fortune-telling *n* [gen] *fait de dire la bonne aventure*; [with cards] cartomancie *f*.

forty ['fɔːtɪ] (*pl* **forties**) ◇ *adj* quarante *(inv)*; about ~ children une quarantaine d'enfants, environ quarante enfants.
◇ *n* quarante *m*; about ~ environ quarante, une quarantaine; the lower ~-eight *Am* les quarante-huit États américains *(à part l'Alaska et Hawaï)*.

forty-five *n* **-1.** [record] quarante-cinq tours *m*. **-2.** *Am* [pistol] quarante-cinq *m*.

forty-niner [-'naɪnəʳ] *n Am*: the ~s *chercheurs d'or partis en Californie en 1849*.

forty winks *inf npl* petit somme *m*; to have ~ faire un petit somme.

forum ['fɔːrəm] (*pl* **forums** OR **fora** [-rə]) *n* [gen & *fig*] forum *m*, tribune *f*; HIST forum *m*.

forward ['fɔːwəd] ◇ *adj* **-1.** [towards front - movement] en avant, vers l'avant; [- position] avant; the seat is too far ~ le siège est trop avancé OR en avant; ~ line SPORT ligne *f* des avants. **-2.** [advanced]: the project is no further ~ le projet n'a pas avancé; ~ planning planification *f* à long terme. **-3.** [brash] effronté, impertinent. **-4.** [buying, delivery] à terme.
◇ *adv* **-1.** [in space] en avant; NAUT à l'avant; to move ~ avancer; keep going straight ~ continuez tout droit; he reached ~ il a tendu le bras en avant; three witnesses came ~ *fig* trois témoins se sont présentés; ~, march! MIL en avant, marche!; clocks go ~ one hour at midnight il faut avancer les pendules d'une heure à minuit. **-2.** *fml* [in time]: from this moment ~ à partir de maintenant; from this day ~ désormais, dorénavant.
◇ *vt* **-1.** [send on] faire suivre; COMM expédier, envoyer; I've arranged to have my mail ~ed j'ai fait le nécessaire pour qu'on fasse suivre mon courrier; 'please ~' 'faire suivre SVP', 'prière de faire suivre'. **-2.** [advance, promote] avancer, favoriser.
◇ *n* avant *m*.

forwarding ['fɔːwədɪŋ] *n* **-1.** [sending] expédition *f*, envoi *m*. **-2.** TYPO collage *m* et endossage *m*.

forwarding address *n* adresse *f* pour faire suivre le courrier; COMM adresse *f* pour l'expédition; he left no ~ il est parti sans laisser d'adresse.

forwarding agent *n* transitaire *m*.

forward-looking *adj* [person] tourné vers OR ouvert sur l'avenir; [plans] tourné vers l'avenir OR le progrès; [company, policy] qui va de l'avant, dynamique, entreprenant.

forward market *n* marché *m* à terme.

forwardness ['fɔːwədnɪs] *n* **-1.** [presumption] effronterie *f*, impertinence *f*; [eagerness] empressement *m*. **-2.** *Br* [of child, season] précocité *f*; [of project] état *m* avancé.

forward pass *n* en-avant *m inv*, passe *f* en avant.

forward roll *n* cabriole *f*, culbute *f*.

forwards ['fɔːwədz] *adv* = **forward**.

forwent [fɔː'went] *pt* → **forgo**.

Fosbury flop ['fɒzbərɪ-] *n* rouleau *m* dorsal.

fossa ['fɒsə] (*pl* **fossae** [-siː]) *n* ANAT fosse *f*.

fossil ['fɒsl] ◇ *n* fossile *m*; he's an old ~! *inf fig* c'est un vieux fossile!
◇ *adj* fossilisé.

fossil fuel *n* combustible *m* fossile.

fossilize, -ise ['fɒsɪlaɪz] ◇ *vt* fossiliser.
◇ *vi* se fossiliser.

fossilized ['fɒsɪlaɪzd] *adj* **-1.** *literal* fossilisé. **-2.** *fig* fossilisé, figé; LING figé.

foster ['fɒstəʳ] ◇ *vt* **-1.** *Br* JUR [subj: family, person] accueillir; [subj: authorities, court] placer; the children were ~ed (out) at an early age les enfants ont été placés dans une famille tout jeunes. **-2.** [idea, hope] nourrir, entretenir. **-3.** [promote] favoriser, encourager.
◇ *adj*: ~ child enfant *m* placé dans une famille d'accueil; ~ home OR parents famille *f* d'accueil; ~ mother/father mère *f*/père *m* de la famille d'accueil.

fostering ['fɒstərɪŋ] *n* JUR accueil *m (d'un enfant)*.

fought [fɔːt] *pt* & *pp* → **fight**.

foul [faʊl] ◇ *adj* **-1.** [food, taste] infect; [smell] infect, fétide; [breath] fétide; to smell ~ puer; to taste ~ avoir un goût infect. **-2.** [filthy - linen] sale, souillé; [- place] immonde, crasseux; [- air] vicié, pollué; [- water] croupi. **-3.** *inf* [horrible - weather] pourri; [- person] infect, ignoble; I've had a ~ day j'ai eu une sale journée; she's in a ~ mood elle est d'une humeur massacrante; he has a ~ temper il a un sale caractère OR un caractère de chien; ~ weather [gen] sale temps, temps de chien; NAUT gros temps; he's being really ~ to me il est absolument odieux OR ignoble avec moi. **-4.** [language] grossier, ordurier; he has a ~ mouth il est très grossier. **-5.** *lit* [vile] vil; [unfair] déloyal. **-6.** [clogged] obstrué, encrassé. **-7.** *phr*: to fall OR to run ~ of sb se brouiller avec qqn; he fell ~ of the boss il s'est mis le patron à dos; they fell ~ of the law ils ont eu des démêlés avec la justice; to fall ~ of a reef/ship entrer en collision avec un récif/un navire.

◇ *n* SPORT [in boxing] coup *m* bas; [in football, baseball] faute *f*; [in basketball]: **personal/technical ~** faute personnelle/technique.

◇ *vt* -**1.** [dirty] salir; [air, water] polluer, infecter; **it is an offence to allow a dog to ~ the pavement** *Br* il est contraire à la loi de laisser son chien souiller le trottoir. -**2.** [clog] obstruer, encrasser; [entangle] embrouiller, emmêler; [nets] se prendre dans. -**3.** [collide with] entrer en collision avec. -**4.** SPORT commettre une faute contre. -**5.** *fig* [reputation] salir.

◇ *vi* -**1.** [tangle] s'emmêler, s'embrouiller. -**2.** SPORT commettre une faute.

◆ **foul out** *vi insep* être exclu *(pour excès de fautes)*.

◆ **foul up** *vt sep* -**1.** [contaminate] polluer; [clog] obstruer, encrasser. -**2.** *inf* [bungle] ficher en l'air, flanquer par terre.

foul line *n* [in baseball] ligne *f* de jeu; [in basketball] ligne *f* de lancer franc; [in bowling] ligne *f* de faute.

foul-mouthed *adj* au langage grossier.

foul play *n* SPORT jeu *m* irrégulier OR déloyal; [in cards, games] tricherie *f*; **the police suspect ~** *fig* la police croit qu'il y a eu meurtre OR croit au meurtre.

foul-smelling [-'smelɪŋ] *adj* puant, fétide.

foul-up *inf n* [mix-up] cafouillage *m*; [mechanical difficulty] problème *m* OR difficulté *f* mécanique.

found [faʊnd] ◇ *pt & pp* → **find**.

◇ *adj dated* -**1.** [furnished] équipé; **the flat is well ~** l'appartement est bien équipé. -**2.** *phr*: **all ~** *Br* tout compris; **£30 a week all ~** 30 livres la semaine tout compris.

◇ *vt* -**1.** [establish - organization, town] fonder, créer; [- business] fonder, établir. -**2.** [base] fonder, baser; **our society is ~ed on the idea of equality** notre société est fondée sur la notion d'égalité. -**3.** [cast] fondre.

foundation [faʊn'deɪʃn] *n* -**1.** [of business, organization, town] fondation *f*, création *f*. -**2.** [institution] fondation *f*, institution *f* dotée; [endowment] dotation *f*, fondation *f*. -**3.** [basis] base *f*, fondement *m*; **the ~ OR ~s of our society** les fondements de notre société; **his work laid the ~ OR ~s of modern science** son œuvre a jeté les bases de la science moderne; **the rumour is entirely without ~** la rumeur est dénuée de tout fondement. -**4.** [make-up] fond *m* de teint. -**5.** *Am* [of building] fondations *fpl*.

◆ **foundations** *npl* CONSTR fondations *fpl*; **to lay the ~s** poser les fondations.

foundation course *n* cours *m* introductif.

foundation cream *n* fond *m* de teint.

foundation garment *n* [girdle] gaine *f*, combiné *m*; [bra] soutien-gorge *m*.

foundation stone *n* pierre *f* commémorative; **to lay the ~** poser la première pierre.

founder ['faʊndəʳ] ◇ *n* fondateur *m*, -trice *f*; **~ member** *Br* membre *m* fondateur.

◇ *vi* -**1.** [ship] sombrer, chavirer. -**2.** *fig* [fail] s'effondrer, s'écrouler; **the project ~ed for lack of financial support** le projet s'est effondré faute de soutien financier. -**3.** [horse - in mud] s'embourber; [- go lame] se mettre à boîter.

founding ['faʊndɪŋ] ◇ *n* [of business, organization, town] fondation *f*, création *f*.

◇ *adj* fondateur.

founding father *n* père *m* fondateur.

Founding Fathers *pl pr n*: **the ~** *les «pères fondateurs» des États-Unis (qui ont rédigé la Constitution de 1787: Washington, Jefferson, Franklin)*.

foundling ['faʊndlɪŋ] *n fml* enfant *mf* trouvé; **~ hospital** hospice *m* pour enfants trouvés.

foundry ['faʊndrɪ] (*pl* **foundries**) *n* [place] fonderie *f*; [of articles] fonderie *f*, fonte *f*; [articles] fonte *f*.

fount [faʊnt] *n* -**1.** *Br* TYPO fonte *f*. -**2.** *lit* [spring] source *f*; **a ~ of knowledge** un puits de science.

fountain ['faʊntɪn] *n* -**1.** [natural] fontaine *f*, source *f*; [man-made] fontaine *f*, jet *m* d'eau; **drinking ~** [in street] fontaine publique; [in building] fontaine d'eau potable. -**2.** *fig* [source] source *f*; **the ~ of youth** la source de la jeunesse.

fountainhead ['faʊntɪnhed] *n* [spring] source *f*; *fig* [source] source *f*, origine *f*.

fountain pen *n* stylo *m* à encre.

four [fɔːʳ] ◇ *n* -**1.** [number] quatre *m*; **on all ~s** à quatre pattes. -**2.** [in rowing] quatre *m*.

◇ *adj* quatre; **the ~ corners of the earth** les quatre coins du monde; **open to the ~ winds** ouvert à tous les vents OR aux quatre vents ❑ **the Four Horsemen of the Apocalypse** les quatre cavaliers de l'Apocalypse.

four-ball *n partie de golf se jouant avec deux équipes de deux joueurs, chacun ayant sa propre balle*.

four-colour *adj* quadrichrome; **~ printing process** TYPO quadrichromie *f*.

four-door *adj* à quatre portes.

four-engined *adj* à quatre moteurs.

four-eyes *inf n* binoclard *m*, -e *f*.

four-flusher *inf* [-'flʌʃəʳ] *n Am* bluffeur *m*, -euse *f*.

fourfold ['fɔːˌfəʊld] ◇ *adv* au quadruple.

◇ *adj* quadruple.

four-four *n* quatre-quatre *m*; **in ~ (time)** à quatre-quatre.

Four H (club) *pr n association éducative pour jeunes ruraux*.

four-handed *adj* à quatre mains.

four hundred, **Four Hundred** *npl Am*: **the ~** l'élite *f* sociale.

Fourierism ['fʊrɪərɪzm] *n* fouriérisme *m*.

four-in-hand *n* -**1.** [carriage] attelage *m* à quatre. -**2.** [tie] cravate *f*.

four-leaf clover, **four-leaved clover** *n* trèfle *m* à quatre feuilles.

four-legged *adj* quadrupède, à quatre pattes; **our ~ friends** *hum* nos compagnons à quatre pattes.

four-letter word *n* gros mot *m*, obscénité *f*.

fourpence ['fɔːpəns] *n* -**1.** [sum of money] quatre pence. -**2.** [coin] *ancienne pièce de monnaie anglaise qui valait quatre pence*.

four-ply *adj* [wool] à quatre fils; [wood] contreplaqué *(à quatre plis)*.

four-poster (bed) *n* lit *m* à baldaquin OR à colonnes.

fourscore [ˌfɔː'skɔːʳ] *arch* ◇ *adj* quatre-vingts; **~ years and ten** quatre-vingt-dix ans.

◇ *n* quatre-vingts *m*.

four-seater *n* voiture *f* à quatre places.

foursome ['fɔːsəm] *n* -**1.** [people] groupe *m* de quatre personnes; [two couples] deux couples *mpl*; **we went as a ~** nous y sommes allés à quatre. -**2.** [game] partie *f* à quatre; **will you make up a ~ for bridge?** voulez-vous faire le quatrième au bridge?

foursquare [ˌfɔː'skweəʳ] ◇ *adj* -**1.** [square] carré. -**2.** [position, style] solide; [approach, decision] ferme, inébranlable. -**3.** [forthright] franc.

◇ *adv* [solidly] fermement, solidement; [resolutely] résolument, fermement.

four-star *adj* [gen & MIL] à quatre étoiles; **~ hotel** hôtel *m* quatre étoiles OR de première catégorie; **~ petrol** *Br* super *m*, supercarburant *m*.

four-stroke ◇ *adj* à quatre temps.

◇ *n* moteur *m* à quatre temps.

fourteen [ˌfɔː'tiːn] ◇ *adj* quatorze.

◇ *n* quatorze *m*.

fourteenth [ˌfɔː'tiːnθ] ◇ *n* -**1.** [ordinal] quatorzième *mf*; **the Fourteenth of July** le quatorze juillet *(fête nationale française)*. -**2.** [fraction] quatorzième *m*.

◇ *adj* quatorzième; **Louis the Fourteenth** Louis Quatorze.

◇ *adv* quatorzièmement; **he came ~ in the marathon** il est arrivé en quatorzième position OR quatorzième dans le marathon.

fourth [fɔːθ] ◇ *n* -**1.** [ordinal] quatrième *mf*; **the Fourth of July** le quatre juillet *(fête nationale de l'Indépendance aux États-Unis)*. -**2.** [fraction] quart *m*. -**3.** MUS quarte *f*.

◇ *adj* quatrième; **~-class mail** *Am* paquet-poste *m* ordinaire; **the ~ finger** l'annulaire *m*; **to go OR to change into ~ (gear)** AUT passer en quatrième.

◇ *adv* quatrièmement; **she finished ~ in the race** elle a fini la course à la quatrième place.

fourth dimension *n*: **the ~** la quatrième dimension.

fourth estate *n*: **the ~** le quatrième pouvoir, la presse.

fourthly ['fɔːθlɪ] *adv* quatrièmement, en quatrième lieu.

Fourth World *pr n*: **the ~** le quart-monde.

four-way stop *n Am* carrefour *m* à quatre stops.

four-wheel *vi Am* faire du quatre-quatre.

four-wheel drive *n* propulsion *f* à quatre roues motrices; **with ~** à quatre roues motrices.

four-wheeler *n* véhicule *m* à quatre roues.

fowl [faʊl] (*pl inv* OR **fowls**) ◇ *n* -**1.** [for eating - collectively] volaille *f*; [- one bird] volaille *f*, volatile *m*. -**2.** *arch* OR *lit* [bird] oiseau *m*; **all the ~s of the air** tous les oiseaux.

◇ *vi* chasser le gibier à plumes.

fowling piece ['faʊlɪŋ-] *n* carabine *f*, fusil *m* de chasse léger.

fowl pest *n* peste *f* aviaire.

fox [fɒks] (*pl inv* OR **foxes**) ◇ *n* -**1.** [animal, fur] renard *m*; **he's a sly old ~** *fig* c'est un vieux renard; **~ cub** renardeau *m*; **as sly as a ~** rusé comme un renard; **it's like setting the ~ to mind the chickens** c'est faire entrer le loup dans la bergerie. -**2.** *inf Am dated* [woman] canon *m*.

◇ *vt* -**1.** [outwit] duper, berner. -**2.** *inf* [baffle] souffler. -**3.** [paper] marquer OR tacher de rousseurs.

foxed [fɒkst] *adj* [paper] marqué OR taché de rousseurs.

foxglove ['fɒksglʌv] *n* digitale *f* (pourprée).

foxhole ['fɒkshəʊl] *n* -**1.** [of fox] terrier *m* de renard, renardière *f*. -**2.** MIL gourbi *m*.

foxhound ['fɒkshaʊnd] *n* fox-hound *m*, chien *m* courant.

foxhunt ['fɒkshʌnt] *n* chasse *f* au renard.

foxhunter ['fɒksˌhʌntəʳ] *n* chasseur *m*, -euse *f* de renard.

foxhunting ['fɒksˌhʌntɪŋ] *n* chasse *f* au renard; **to go ~** aller chasser le renard OR à la chasse au renard.

foxtail ['fɒksteɪl] *n* BOT [grass] vulpin *m*; [flower] queue-de-renard *f*.

fox terrier *n* fox *m inv*, fox-terrier *m*.

foxtrot ['fɒkstrɒt] ◇ *n* fox-trot *m*.

◇ *vi* danser le fox-trot.

foxy ['fɒksɪ] (*compar* **foxier**, *superl* **foxiest**) *adj* -**1.** [wily] rusé, malin. -**2.** [colour] roux. -**3.** [paper] marqué OR taché de rousseurs. -**4.** *inf Am dated* [sexy] sexy *(inv)*.

foyer ['fɔɪeɪ] *n* -**1.** [of cinema, hotel] hall *m*, vestibule *m*; [of theatre] foyer *m*. -**2.** *Am* [of house] entrée *f*, vestibule *m*.

FP *n* -**1.** *abbr of* **former pupil**. -**2.** *Am abbr of* **fire-plug**.

FPA (*abbr of* **Family Planning Association**) *pr n association pour le planning familial*.

Fr. -**1.** (*written abbr of* **father**) P. -**2.** (*written abbr of* **friar**) F.

fracas [*Br* 'frækɑː, *Am* 'freɪkæs] (*Br pl inv* [-kɑːz], *Am pl* **fracases** [-kəsɪz]) *n* [brawl] rixe *f*, bagarre *f*; [noise] fracas *m*.

fraction ['frækʃn] *n* -**1.** MATH fraction *f*. -**2.** *fig* [bit] fraction *f*, petite partie *f*; **at a ~ of the cost** pour une fraction du prix; **for a ~ of a second** pendant une fraction de seconde; **move back just a ~** reculez un tout petit peu.

fractional ['frækʃənl] *adj* -**1.** MATH fractionnaire. -**2.** *fig* [tiny] tout petit, infime; **~ part** fraction *f*; **a ~ difference** une différence minime.

fractional currency *n* petite monnaie *f*.

fractional distillation *n* distillation *f* fractionnée.

fractionally ['frækʃnəlɪ] *adv* -**1.** [slightly] un tout petit peu. -**2.** CHEM par fractionnement.

fractious ['frækʃəs] *adj fml* -**1.** [unruly] indiscipliné, turbulent. -**2.** [irritable - child] grognon, pleurnicheur; [- adult] irascible, revêche.

fracture ['fræktʃəʳ] ◇ *n* fracture *f*.
◇ *vt* [break] fracturer; **he ~d his arm** il s'est fracturé le bras; **their withdrawal ~d the alliance** *fig* leur retrait brisa l'alliance.
◇ *vi* [break] se fracturer.

frag▽ [fræg] (*pt* & *pp* **fragged**, *cont* **fragging**) *Am mil sl* ◇ *n* grenade *f* offensive.
◇ *vt tuer ou blesser intentionnellement un officier ou un compagnon d'armes avec une grenade*.

fragile [*Br* 'frædʒaɪl, *Am* 'frædʒl] *adj* -**1.** [china, glass] fragile; *fig*: **a ~ peace/happiness** une paix/un bonheur précaire OR fragile; **a ~ relationship** des relations fragiles OR précaires; **a ~ link with the past** un lien fragile avec le passé. -**2.** [person] fragile, frêle; **I'm feeling a bit ~ today** *hum* je ne suis pas dans mon assiette OR je ne me sens pas très bien ce matin.

fragility [frə'dʒɪlətɪ] *n* fragilité *f*.

fragment [*n* 'frægmənt, *vb* fræg'ment] ◇ *n* [of china, text] fragment *m*, morceau *m*; [of bomb] éclat *m*; **I overheard only ~s of their conversation** je n'ai entendu que des bribes de leur conversation; **the report contains not a ~ of truth** le rapport ne contient pas un atome OR une once de vérité.
◇ *vt* [break] fragmenter, briser; [divide] fragmenter, morceler.
◇ *vi* se fragmenter.

fragmental [fræg'mentl] *adj* fragmentaire; GEOL clastique, détritique.

fragmentary ['frægməntrɪ] *adj* fragmentaire.

fragmentation [,frægmen'teɪʃn] *n* [breaking] fragmentation *f*; [division] fragmentation *f*, morcellement *m*; **~ bomb** bombe *f* à fragmentation; **~ grenade** grenade *f* offensive.

fragmented [fræg'mentɪd] *adj* fragmentaire, morcelé.

fragrance ['freɪgrəns] *n* parfum *m*; **our new ~** COMM notre nouveau parfum.

fragrant ['freɪgrənt] *adj* parfumé; **a garden ~ with flowers** *lit* un jardin où embaument les fleurs.

frail [freɪl] *adj* -**1.** [object] fragile; [person] fragile, frêle; [health] délicat, fragile; **she's rather ~** elle a une petite santé. -**2.** [happiness, hope] fragile, éphémère; **human nature is very ~** *fig* la nature humaine est très fragile.

frailty ['freɪltɪ] (*pl* **frailties**) *n* [of health, hope, person] fragilité *f*; [of character] faiblesse *f*.

frame [freɪm] ◇ *n* -**1.** [border - gen] cadre *m*; [- of canvas, picture etc] cadre *m*, encadrement *m*; [- of window] cadre *m*, châssis *m*; [- of door] encadrement *m*; [- for spectacles] monture *f*; **glasses with red ~s** des lunettes avec une monture rouge. -**2.** [support, structure - gén] cadre *m*; CONSTR charpente *f*; [- of bicycle] cadre *m*; [- of car] châssis *m*; [- of lampshade, racket, tent] armature *f*; [- of machine] bâti *m*; TEX métier *m*; [- for walking] déambulateur *m*; **the bed has a wooden ~** le lit est muni d'un cadre en bois. -**3.** [body] charpente *f*; **the wrestler heaved his massive ~ up from the floor** le lutteur releva sa masse imposante; **his slender ~ was shaken by sobs** son corps menu OR fluet était secoué par des sanglots. -**4.** [setting, background] cadre *m*; [area, scope] cadre *m*. -**5.** PHOT image *f*; CIN image *f*, photogramme *m*; TV trame *f*.
◇ *vt* -**1.** [enclose, encase] encadrer; **she's had all her diplomas ~d** elle a fait encadrer tous ses diplômes; **her face was ~d by a white silk scarf** *fig* un foulard de soie blanc encadrait son visage. -**2.** *fml* [design, draft] élaborer; [formulate, express] formuler; **to ~ a plan/system** élaborer un projet/système; **the contract was ~d in legal jargon** le contrat était formulé en jargon juridique. -**3.** *inf* [incriminate falsely]: **to ~ sb** monter un (mauvais) coup contre qqn; **I've been ~d** j'ai été victime d'un coup monté.

frame house *n* maison *f* en bois.

frame of mind *n* état *m* d'esprit; **I'm not in the right ~ for celebrating** je ne suis pas d'humeur à faire la fête.

frame of reference *n* système *m* de référence.

framer ['freɪməʳ] *n* encadreur *m*.

frame rucksack *Br*, **frame backpack** *Am* *n* sac *m* à dos à armature.

frame-up *inf n* coup *m* monté.

framework ['freɪmwɜːk] *n* -**1.** [structure] cadre *m*, structure *f*; CONSTR charpente *f*; TECH bâti *m*. -**2.** *fig*: **the bill seeks to provide a legal ~ for divorce** le projet de loi vise à instaurer un cadre juridique pour les procédures de divorce.

framing ['freɪmɪŋ] *n* encadrement *m*.

franc [fræŋk] *n* franc *m*.

France [frɑːns] *pr n* France *f*; **in ~** en France.

franchise ['fræntʃaɪz] ◇ *n* -**1.** POL suffrage *m*, droit *m* de vote. -**2.** COMM & JUR franchise *f*.
◇ *vt* accorder une franchise à.

franchisee [,fræntʃaɪ'ziː] *n* COMM franchisé *m*.

franchiser ['fræntʃaɪzəʳ] *n* COMM franchiseur *m*.

franchising ['fræntʃaɪzɪŋ] *n* franchisage *m*.

Francis ['frɑːnsɪs] *pr n*: **Saint ~ (of Assisi)** saint François (d'Assise).

Franciscan [fræn'sɪskən] ◇ *adj* franciscain.
◇ *n* franciscain *m*, -e *f*.

francium ['frænsɪəm] *n* francium *m*.

Franco- ['fræŋkəʊ] *in cpds* franco-.

Francophile ['fræŋkəfaɪl] ◇ *adj* francophile.
◇ *n* francophile *mf*.

Francophobe ['fræŋkəfəʊb] ◇ *adj* francophobe.
◇ *n* francophobe *mf*.

Francophone ['fræŋkəfəʊn] ◇ *adj* francophone.
◇ *n* francophone *mf*.

frangipane ['frændʒɪpeɪn] *n* frangipane *f*.

frangipani [,frændʒɪ'pɑːnɪ] *n* frangipanier *m*.

Franglais ['frɒŋgleɪ] *n* franglais *m*.

frank [fræŋk] ◇ *adj* franc; **I'll be ~ with you** je vais vous parler franchement OR être franc avec vous; **to be (perfectly) ~, I think you're wrong** franchement OR sincèrement, je crois que vous avez tort.
◇ *vt Br* affranchir.
◇ *n Br* -**1.** [on letter] affranchissement *m*. -**2.** *inf Am* [sausage] saucisse *f* (de Francfort); [hot dog] hot-dog *m*.

Frank [fræŋk] *n* HIST Franc *m*, Franque *f*.

Frankenstein ['fræŋkənstaɪn] *pr n* Frankenstein.

Frankfurt ['fræŋkfət] *pr n*: **~ (am Main)** Francfort (-sur-le-Main).

frankfurter ['fræŋkfɜːtəʳ] *n* saucisse *f* de Francfort.

frankincense ['fræŋkɪnsens] *n* encens *m*.

franking machine ['fræŋkɪŋ-] *n* machine *f* à affranchir.

Frankish ['fræŋkɪʃ] ◇ *adj* franc.
◇ *n* francique *m*.

frankly ['fræŋklɪ] *adv* franchement; **can I speak ~?** puis-je parler franchement OR en toute franchise?; **(quite) ~, I think he's wrong** franchement OR sincèrement, je crois qu'il a tort.

frankness ['fræŋknɪs] *n* franchise *f*; **I admire his ~** j'admire sa franchise OR son franc-parler.

frantic ['fræntɪk] *adj* -**1.** [distraught, wild] éperdu, affolé; **she was ~ with worry** elle était folle d'inquiétude; **~ screams** des cris éperdus OR d'affolement. -**2.** [very busy]: **a scene of ~ activity** une scène d'activité frénétique; **things are pretty ~ at the office just now** *inf* il y a un travail fou au bureau en ce moment.

frantically ['fræntɪklɪ] *adv* désespérément; **she worked ~ to finish the dress** elle travailla comme une forcenée pour terminer la robe; **the shop is ~ busy just before Christmas** il y a un monde fou au magasin juste avant Noël.

frappe [*Br* 'fræpeɪ, *Am* fræ'peɪ] *n* [drink] milk-shake *m (épais)*.

fraternal [frə'tɜːnl] *adj* fraternel; **~ twins** des faux jumeaux.

fraternally [frə'tɜːnəlɪ] *adv* fraternellement.

fraternity [frə'tɜːnətɪ] (*pl* **fraternities**) *n* -**1.** [friendship] fraternité *f*. -**2.** [association] confrérie *f*; **the medical ~** la confrérie des médecins. -**3.** *Am* UNIV ≃ club *m* d'étudiants.

fraternity pin *n Am* UNIV insigne *m* de confrérie.

fraternization [,frætənaɪ'zeɪʃn] *n* fraternisation *f*.

fraternize, -ise ['frætənaɪz] *vi* fraterniser.

fratricidal [,frætrɪ'saɪdl] *adj* fratricide.

fratricide ['frætrɪsaɪd] *n* fratricide *mf*.

fraud [frɔːd] *n* -**1.** JUR fraude *f*; FIN escroquerie *f*; **she's been charged with ~** elle a été inculpée de fraude; **tax ~** fraude fiscale; **he obtained the painting by ~** il a eu le tableau en fraude. -**2.** [dishonest person] imposteur *m*. -**3.** [product, work] supercherie *f*.

Fraud Squad *n Br*: **the ~** *section de la police britannique spécialisée dans les fraudes des entreprises*.

fraudulence ['frɔːdjʊləns] *n* caractère *m* frauduleux.

fraudulent ['frɔːdjʊlənt] *adj* frauduleux; JUR fraudatoire.

fraudulently ['frɔːdjʊləntlɪ] *adv* frauduleusement.

fraught [frɔːt] *adj* -**1.** [filled] chargé, lourd; **~ with danger** rempli de dangers. -**2.** *inf Br* [tense] tendu; **I'm feeling a bit ~** je me sens un peu angoissé OR tendu; **things got rather ~ at work today** l'atmosphère était plutôt tendue au bureau aujourd'hui; **I've had a particularly ~ week** j'ai eu une semaine particulièrement stressante.

fray [freɪ] ◇ *vt* (*usu pass*) -**1.** [clothing, fabric, rope] effilocher. -**2.** [nerves] mettre à vif; **her nerves were ~ed** elle avait les nerfs à vif.
◇ *vi* -**1.** [clothing, fabric, rope] s'effilocher; **her dress is ~ing at the hem** l'ourlet de sa robe s'effiloche. -**2.** *fig*: **tempers began to ~** les gens commençaient à s'énerver OR perdre patience.
◇ *n*: **the ~** la mêlée; **to enter** OR **to join the ~** se jeter dans la mêlée.

frayed [freɪd] *adj* -**1.** [garment] élimé; **her jacket was ~ at the cuffs** sa veste était élimée aux poignets. -**2.** *fig*: **tempers were increasingly ~** les gens étaient de plus en plus irritables.

frazzle *inf* ['fræzl] ◇ *vt* [exhaust] tuer, crever.
◇ *n*: **worn to a ~** crevé; **burnt to a ~** carbonisé, calciné.

frazzled *inf* ['fræzld] *adj* [exhausted] crevé.

FRCO (*abbr of* **Fellow of the Royal College of Organists**) *n membre du RCO*.

FRCP (*abbr of* **Fellow of the Royal College of Physicians**) *n membre du RCP*.

FRCS (*abbr of* **Fellow of the Royal College of Surgeons**) *n membre du RCS*.

freak [friːk] ◇ *n* -**1.** [abnormal event] caprice *m* de la nature; [abnormal person] phénomène *m* de foire; [eccentric person] phénomène *m*, farfelu *m*, -e *f*; **by a ~ of nature** par un caprice de la nature; **by some ~ (of chance)** par un hasard inouï; **just because I choose not to eat meat, that doesn't make me a ~** ce n'est pas parce que je ne mange pas de viande que je suis anormal ❑ **~ show** exhibition *f* de monstres *(à la foire)*. -**2.** *inf* [fanatic] fana *mf*; **a health ~** un fana de la forme. -**3.** ▽ [hippie] hippie *mf*. -**4.** *lit* [caprice, whim] foucade *f*.
◇ *adj* [accident, result, storm] insolite, anormal; **~ weather conditions** des conditions atmosphériques anormales.
◇ *vi* ▽ = **freak out** *vi insep*.
◆ **freak out**▽ ◇ *vi insep* -**1.** [on drugs] flipper. -**2.** [lose control of one's emotions] perdre les pédales.

◇ *vt sep* -**1.** [cause to hallucinate] faire flipper. -**2.** [upset emotionally] déboussoler.

freakish ['fri:kɪʃ] *adj* -**1.** [abnormal, strange] étrange, insolite; a ~**-looking man** un homme d'aspect bizarre OR insolite. -**2.** *lit* [capricious, changeable] changeant.

freaky *inf* ['fri:kɪ] *adj* bizarre, insolite.

freckle ['frekl] ◇ *n* tache *f* de rousseur OR son.
◇ *vt* marquer de taches de rousseur.
◇ *vi* se couvrir de taches de rousseur.

freckled ['frekld] *adj* taché de son, marqué de taches de rousseur; a ~ **face/nose** un visage/nez couvert de taches de rousseur.

Frederick ['fredrɪk] *pr n*: ~ **the Great** Frédéric le Grand.

free [fri:] ◇ *adj* -**1.** [unconfined, unrestricted - person, animal, passage, way] libre; **the hostage managed to get** ~ l'otage a réussi à se libérer; **to cut sb** ~ délivrer qqn en coupant ses liens; **to let sb go** ~ relâcher qqn, remettre qqn en liberté; **to set** ~ [prisoner, animal] remettre en liberté; [slave] affranchir; [hostage] libérer; **you are** ~ **to leave** vous êtes libre de partir; **you are** ~ **to refuse** libre à vous de refuser; **they gave us** ~ **access to their files** ils nous ont donné libre accès à leurs dossiers; **feel** ~ **to visit us any time** ne vous gênez pas pour nous rendre visite quand vous voulez; **can I use the phone? – yes, feel** ~ puis-je téléphoner? – mais certainement ❑ ~ **pardon** JUR grâce *f*. -**2.** [unattached] libre, sans attaches; **grab the** ~ **end of the rope** attrape le bout libre de la corde. -**3.** [democratic] libre; **it's a** ~ **country!** on est en république!; **a** ~ **press** une presse libre ❑ **the Free World** POL le monde libre. -**4.** [at no cost] gratuit; ~ **admission** entrée *f* gratuite OR libre ❑ ~ **gift** COMM cadeau *m*; ~ **sample** COMM échantillon *m* gratuit; **there's no such thing as a** ~ **lunch** les gens sont tous intéressés. -**5.** [not in use, unoccupied] libre; **is that seat** ~? est-ce que ce siège est libre?; **she doesn't have a** ~ **moment** elle n'a pas un moment de libre; **are you** ~ **for lunch today?** êtes-vous libre pour déjeuner aujourd'hui?; **could you let us know when you're** ~? pourriez-vous nous faire savoir quand vous êtes libre OR disponible?; **what do you do in your** ~ **time?** que faites-vous pendant vos loisirs?; **she has very little** ~ **time** elle a peu de temps libre. -**6.** [unhampered]: **the jury was not entirely** ~ **of** OR **from prejudice** les jurés n'étaient pas entièrement sans préjugés OR parti pris; **to be** ~ **from care** être sans souci; **to be** ~ **from pain** ne pas souffrir; **I just want to be** ~ **of him!** je veux être débarrassé de lui!; **they're trying to keep Antarctica** ~ **from pollution** ils essaient de préserver l'Antarctique de la pollution ❑ ~ **and easy** désinvolte, décontracté; **she has a very** ~ **and easy attitude to life** elle prend la vie de façon très décontractée; ~ **love union** *f* libre. -**7.** [generous]: **she's very** ~ **with her criticism** elle ne ménage pas ses critiques. -**8.** [disrespectful] trop familier; **he's a bit** ~ **in his manners for my liking** il est un peu trop sans gêne à mon goût. -**9.** CHEM libre, non combiné; ~ **nitrogen** azote *m* à l'état libre.
◇ *adv* -**1.** [at no cost] gratuitement; **they will deliver** ~ **of charge** ils livreront gratuitement; **children under twelve travel (for)** ~ les enfants de moins de douze ans voyagent gratuitement. -**2.** [without restraint] librement; **wolves roamed** ~ **through the forests** les loups rôdaient librement à travers les forêts; **to make** ~ **with sthg** se servir de qqch sans se gêner; **he made very** ~ **with his wife's money** il ne se gênait pas pour dépenser l'argent de sa femme.
◇ *vt* -**1.** [release - gen] libérer; [- prisoner] libérer, relâcher; [- tied-up animal] détacher; [- caged animal] libérer; [- serf, slave] affranchir; **giving up work has** ~**d me to get on with my painting** arrêter de travailler m'a permis de continuer à peindre ‖ COMM [prices, trade] libérer; **the government has undertaken to** ~ **more funds for the arts** le gouvernement a promis de débloquer d'autres crédits pour les arts. -**2.** [disengage, disentangle] dégager; **it took two hours to** ~ **the driver from the wreckage** il a fallu deux heures pour dégager le conducteur de sa voiture; **she tried to** ~ **herself from his grasp** elle essaya de se libérer OR dégager de son étreinte; **he cannot** ~ **himself of guilt** *fig* il ne peut pas se débarrasser d'un sentiment de culpabilité. -**3.** [unblock - pipe] déboucher; [- passage] libérer.

-free *in cpds*: **additive**~ sans additifs; **salt**~ sans sel; **trouble**~ sans ennuis OR problèmes.

free agent *n* personne *f* libre OR indépendante; **she's a** ~ **now** elle est libre d'agir comme bon lui semble OR libre de ses mouvements maintenant.

free association *n* association *f* libre.

freebase ['fri:beɪs] *vi drugs sl* [purify cocaine] purifier de la cocaïne.

freebie *inf*, **freebee** *inf* ['fri:bɪ] ◇ *n* fleur *f*.
◇ *adj* gratis *(inv)*.

freeboard ['fri:bɔ:d] *n* franc-bord *m*.

freebooter ['fri:,bu:tə^r] *n* flibustier *m*.

freeborn ['fri:bɔ:n] *adj* né libre.

freedom ['fri:dəm] *n* liberté *f*; **the students were ready to die for** ~ les étudiants étaient prêts à mourir pour la liberté; **the journalists were given complete** ~ **to talk to dissidents** les journalistes ont pu parler aux dissidents en toute liberté; ~ **of speech/association** liberté d'expression/de réunion; ~ **of information** liberté d'information; ~ **of worship** liberté du culte; ~ **from hunger** le droit de manger à sa faim; ~ **from persecution** le droit de vivre sans persécution; ~ **from responsibility** le fait d'être dégagé de toute responsabilité; **she had the** ~ **of the whole house** elle avait la maison à son entière disposition ❑ **to be given** OR **granted the** ~ **of the city** être nommé citoyen d'honneur de la ville; ~ **of the seas** liberté de la haute mer.

freedom fighter *n* combattant *m*, -e *f* de la liberté.

free enterprise *n* libre entreprise *f*.

free-fall *n* chute *f* libre.

free-floating *adj* en mouvement libre.

Freefone® ['fri:fəʊn] *n Br appel gratuit*, ≃ numéro *m* vert; **call** ~ **800** appelez le numéro vert 800.

free-for-all *inf n* mêlée *f* générale.

free hand *n* liberté *f* d'action; **to give sb a** ~ **to do sthg** donner carte blanche à qqn pour faire qqch; **they gave me a completely** ~ ils m'ont donné toute liberté d'action.
◆ **freehand** *adj & adv* à main levée.

freehanded [,fri:'hændɪd] *adj* libéral, large.

freehearted [,fri:'hɑ:tɪd] *adj* [frank] franc; [generous] large.

freehold ['fri:həʊld] ◇ *n* ≃ propriété *f* foncière inaliénable.
◇ *adv*: **to buy/to sell sthg** ~ acheter/vendre qqch en propriété inaliénable.
◇ *adj*: ~ **property** propriété *f* inaliénable.

freeholder ['fri:həʊldə^r] *n* ≃ propriétaire *m* foncier, ≃ propriétaire *f* foncière *(à perpétuité)*.

free house *n Br pub libre de ses approvisionnements (et non lié à une brasserie particulière)*.

freeing ['fri:ɪŋ] *n* [of prisoner] libération *f*, délivrance *f*; [of slave] affranchissement *m*.

free kick *n* coup *m* franc.

freelance ['fri:lɑ:ns] ◇ *n* travailleur *m* indépendant, travailleuse *f* indépendante, freelance *mf inv*; [journalist, writer] pigiste *mf*.
◇ *adj* indépendant, free-lance.
◇ *adv* en free-lance, en indépendant.
◇ *vi* travailler en free-lance OR indépendant.

freelancer ['fri:lɑ:nsə^r] *n* travailleur *m* indépendant, travailleuse *f* indépendante, freelance *mf inv*.

freeload *inf* ['fri:ləʊd] *vi* vivre aux crochets des autres.

freeloader *inf* ['fri:ləʊdə^r] *n* pique-assiette *mf*, parasite *mf*.

freeloading *inf* ['fri:ləʊdɪŋ] *adj* parasite.

freely ['fri:lɪ] *adv* -**1.** [without constraint] librement; **can I speak** ~? puis-je parler librement?; **she made her confession** ~ elle a avoué de son plein gré; **traffic is moving** ~ **again** la circulation est redevenue fluide; **the book is now** ~ **available** on peut se procurer le livre facilement maintenant. -**2.** [liberally, lavishly - spend] largement; [- perspire, weep] abondamment; **the plant grows** ~ **in hot countries** cette plante pousse en abondance dans les pays chauds.

freeman ['fri:mən] (*pl* **freemen** [-mən]) *n* HIST homme *m* libre; [citizen] citoyen *m*; **he's a** ~ **of the city** il est citoyen d'honneur de la ville.

free-market *adj*: ~ **economy** économie *f* de marché.

freemason, Freemason ['fri:,meɪsn] *n* franc-maçon *m*.

freemasonry, Freemasonry ['fri:,meɪsnrɪ] *n* franc-maçonnerie *f*.

free on board *adv* franco à bord.

free on rail *adv* franco wagon.

free port *n* port *m* franc.

Freepost® ['fri:pəʊst] *n Br* port *m* payé.

free-range *adj* fermier; ~ **eggs** œufs *mpl* de poules élevées en plein air.

freesia ['fri:zjə] *n* freesia *m*.

free speech *n* liberté *f* de parole OR d'expression.

free spirit *n* non-conformiste *mf*.

free-spoken *adj* franc.

free-standing *adj* isolé; GRAMM indépendant.

freestone ['fri:stəʊn] *n* pierre *f* de taille.

freestyle ['fri:staɪl] *n* [in swimming] nage *f* libre.

freethinker [,fri:'θɪŋkə^r] *n* libre-penseur *m*.

Freetown ['fri:taʊn] *pr n* Freetown.

free trade *n* libre-échange *m*.

free verse *n* vers *m* libre.

free vote *n* vote *m* libre.

freeway ['fri:weɪ] *n Am* autoroute *f*.

freewheel [,fri:'wi:l] ◇ *n* [on bicycle] roue libre.
◇ *vi* -**1.** [cyclist] être en roue libre; **to** ~ **down a slope** descendre une pente en roue libre. -**2.** [motorist] rouler au point mort.

freewheeling *inf* [,fri:'wi:lɪŋ] *adj* désinvolte, sans-gêne *(inv)*.

free will *n* libre arbitre *m*; **to do sthg of one's own** ~ faire qqch de son plein gré.

freeze [fri:z] (*pt* **froze** [frəʊz], *pp* **frozen** ['frəʊzn]) ◇ *vi* -**1.** [earth, pipes, water] geler; [food] se congeler; **to** ~ **to death** mourir de froid; **we'll** ~ **if you open the window!** nous allons geler si vous ouvrez la fenêtre! -**2.** *fig* [stop moving]: **(everybody)** ~! que personne ne bouge!; **she froze (in her tracks)** elle est restée figée sur place; **her blood froze** son sang se figea OR se glaça dans ses veines.
◇ *vt* -**1.** [water] geler, congeler; [food] congeler; [at very low temperatures] surgeler; MED [blood, human tissue] congeler. -**2.** ECON & FIN [assets] geler; [prices, wages] bloquer. -**3.** CIN: ~ **it** arrêtez l'image!
◇ *n* METEOR gel *m*; ECON & FIN gel *m*, blocage *m*; **we're in for another big** ~ METEOR il va y avoir une période de très grand froid; ECON il va y avoir une crise économique; **they called for a** ~ **in the production of nuclear weapons** ils ont appelé à un gel de la production d'armes nucléaires ❑ **pay** ~ gel OR blocage des salaires.
◆ **freeze out** *inf vt sep Br* [eliminate] se débarrasser de.
◆ **freeze over** *vi insep* geler.
◆ **freeze up** *vi insep* -**1.** [turn to ice] geler. -**2.** *inf* [become immobilized] rester pétrifié.

freeze-dry *vt* lyophiliser.

freeze-frame *n* arrêt *m* sur image.

freezer ['fri:zə^r] *n* congélateur *m*; [in refrigerator] freezer *m*; ~ **compartment** compartiment *m* congélateur *(d'un réfrigérateur)*; **in the** ~ **section of your supermarket** au rayon surgelés de votre supermarché.

freeze-up *inf n* gel *m*.
freezing ['fri:zɪŋ] ◇ *adj* METEOR glacial; [person] gelé, glacé; I'm ~ je suis gelé; ~ rain neige *f* fondue; a ~ wind was blowing un vent glacial soufflait; it's ~ in this room! on gèle dans cette pièce!; your hands are ~ vous avez les mains gelées OR glacées.
◇ *n*: it's two degrees above/below ~ il fait deux degrés au-dessus/au-dessous de zéro.
◇ *adv*: a ~ cold day une journée glaciale; it's ~ cold outside il fait un froid glacial dehors.
freezing point *n* point *m* de congélation.
freight [freɪt] ◇ *n* -**1.** [goods] fret *m*. -**2.** [transport]: to send goods by ~ envoyer des marchandises en régime ordinaire; air ~ fret *m* par avion.
◇ *vt* transporter.
◇ *comp* [aircraft, transport] de fret; ~ charges frais *mpl* de port; ~ note bordereau *m* d'expédition.
freightage ['freɪtɪdʒ] *n* fret *m*.
freight car *n Am* wagon *m* de marchandises, fourgon *m*.
freighter ['freɪtəʳ] *n* NAUT navire *m* de charge; AERON avion-cargo *m*, avion *m* de fret.
Freightliner® ['freɪt,laɪnəʳ] *n* train *m* de transport de conteneurs.
freight train *n Am* train *m* de marchandises.
French [frentʃ] ◇ *npl* [people]: the ~ les Français.
◇ *n* LING français *m*; pardon my ~ *hum* excusez la grossièreté de mon langage.
◇ *adj* [person, cooking, customs] français; [ambassador, embassy, king] de France; 'The French Lieutenant's Woman' *Fowles* 'Sarah et le lieutenant français'.
French bean *n* haricot *m* vert.
French bread *n* baguette *f*.
French Canadian ◇ *adj* canadien français.
◇ *n* -**1.** [person] Canadien *m* français, Canadienne *f* française. -**2.** LING français *m* canadien.
French chalk *n* craie *f* de tailleur.
French cricket *n version simplifiée du cricket surtout pratiquée par les enfants*.
French curve *n* pistolet *m* (de dessinateur).
French door *Am* = **French window**.
French dressing *n* [in UK] vinaigrette *f*; [in US] *sauce de salade à base de mayonnaise et de ketchup*.
French fried potatoes *npl* pommes *fpl* frites.
French fries *npl* frites *fpl*.
French horn *n* cor *m* d'harmonie.
Frenchie *inf* ['frentʃɪ] ◇ *adj* français.
◇ *n* Français *m*, -e *f*.
frenchify *inf* (*pt* & *pp* frenchified), **Frenchify** *inf* (*pt* & *pp* Frenchified) ['frentʃɪfaɪ] *vt* franciser.
French kiss ◇ *n* baiser *m* profond.
◇ *vt* embrasser sur la bouche *(avec la langue)*.
◇ *vi* s'embrasser sur la bouche *(avec la langue)*.
French knickers *npl* ≃ caleçon *m (culotte pour femme)*.
French leave *n*: to take ~ *inf Br* filer à l'anglaise.
French letter *inf n Br* [condom] capote *f* anglaise.
French loaf *n* baguette *f*.
Frenchman ['frentʃmən] (*pl* Frenchmen [-mən]) *n* Français *m*.
French marigold *n* œillet *m* d'Inde.
French polish *n Br* vernis *m* (à l'alcool).
◆ **French-polish** *vt Br* vernir (à l'alcool).
French Riviera *pr n*: the ~ la Côte d'Azur.
French seam *n* couture *f* anglaise.
French-speaking *adj* francophone.
French stick *n Br* baguette *f*.
French toast *n* [in UK] *pain grillé d'un seul côté*; [in US] pain *m* perdu.
French Triangle *pr n*: the ~ *région du sud des États-Unis comprise entre La Nouvelle-Orléans, Alexandria et Cameron*.
French window *n Br* porte-fenêtre *f*.
Frenchwoman ['frentʃ,wʊmən] (*pl* Frenchwomen [-,wɪmɪn]) *n* Française *f*.
Frenchy *inf* ['frentʃɪ] (*pl* Frenchies) = **Frenchie**.
frenetic [frə'netɪk] *adj* frénétique.
frenetically [frə'netɪklɪ] *adv* frénétiquement.
frenzied ['frenzɪd] *adj* [activity] frénétique, forcené; [crowd] déchaîné; [person] forcené, déchaîné.
frenzy ['frenzɪ] *n* -**1.** [fury, passion] frénésie *f*; to work o.s. (up) into a ~ (over sthg) se mettre dans une colère noire. -**2.** [fit, outburst] accès *m*, crise *f*; in a ~ of anger dans un accès OR une crise de colère.
frequency ['fri:kwənsɪ] *n* fréquence *f*.
frequency distribution *n* distribution *f* des fréquences.
frequency modulation *n* modulation *f* de fréquence.
frequent [*adj* 'fri:kwənt, *vb* frɪ'kwent]
◇ *adj* fréquent; a ~ visitor un habitué.
◇ *vt lit* fréquenter.
frequentative [frɪ'kwentətɪv] *adj* LING fréquentatif.
frequently ['fri:kwəntlɪ] *adv* fréquemment, souvent.
fresco ['freskəʊ] (*pl* frescoes OR frescos) *n* fresque *f*; ~ painter fresquiste *mf*.
fresh [freʃ] ◇ *adj* -**1.** [recently made or produced] frais; ~ bread/butter pain *m*/beurre *m* frais; there's some ~ coffee in the pot il y a du café (tout) frais dans la cafetière; ~ flowers fleurs *fpl* fraîches; the vegetables are ~ from the garden les légumes viennent directement du jardin; there were ~ tracks in the snow il y avait des traces toutes fraîches dans la neige; young graduates ~ from OR out of university de jeunes licenciés (tout) frais émoulus de l'université. -**2.** [new - idea, problem] nouveau, original; [- news, paint, supplies] frais; [vivid - impression] frais; I need some ~ air j'ai besoin de prendre l'air; a ~ approach une approche nouvelle; management and unions have agreed to ~ talks la direction et les syndicats ont accepté de reprendre leurs négociations; to make a ~ start prendre un nouveau départ; he put on a ~ shirt il mit une chemise propre; start on a ~ page prenez une nouvelle page; the incident was still ~ in his mind le souvenir de l'incident était encore tout frais dans sa mémoire; the memory of her loss was still ~ le souvenir de sa mort était encore tout frais. -**3.** [not salt - water] doux. -**4.** [rested] frais; she looked ~ and relaxed elle avait l'air fraîche et reposée ☐ as ~ as a daisy frais comme une rose. -**5.** [clean] frais, pur; a ~ complexion un teint frais; the ~ scent of lemons le parfum frais des citrons. -**6.** [bright]: ~ colours des couleurs fraîches. -**7.** METEOR [gen] frais; [on Beaufort scale]: ~ breeze bonne brise *f*; ~ gale coup *m* de vent. -**8.** [refreshing - taste] rafraîchissant. -**9.** *inf Am* [impudent] insolent; [child] mal élevé; don't you get ~ with me, young man! pas d'insolence avec moi, jeune homme! -**10.** *inf Am* [sexually forward] effronté; he started to get ~ so she hit him il commença à prendre des libertés avec elle alors elle le frappa.
◇ *adv* fraîchement; ~ cut flowers des fleurs fraîchement cueillies; to be ~ out of sthg *inf* être à court de OR manquer de qqch.
freshen ['freʃn] ◇ *vt* rafraîchir.
◇ *vi* NAUT [wind] fraîchir.
◆ **freshen up** ◇ *vi insep* faire un brin de toilette.
◇ *vt sep* -**1.** [person] faire un brin de toilette à. -**2.** [house, room] donner un petit coup de peinture à. -**3.** [drink]: let me ~ up your drink laisse-moi te resservir à boire.
fresher *inf* ['freʃəʳ] *n* UNIV bizut *m*, bizuth *m*, étudiant *m*, -e *f* de première année.
freshet ['freʃɪt] *n* -**1.** *lit* [stream] ruisseau *m*, ruisselet *m*. -**2.** [rise in water level] crue *f*; [flood] inondation *f*.
freshly ['freʃlɪ] *adv* récemment; ~ made coffee du café qui vient d'être fait; ~ squeezed orange juice jus *m* d'oranges pressées; the grave had been ~ dug la fosse avait été fraîchement creusée.
freshman ['freʃmən] (*pl* freshmen [-mən]) *Am* = **fresher**.
freshness ['freʃnɪs] *n* fraîcheur *f*.
freshwater ['freʃ,wɔ:təʳ] *adj*: ~ fish poisson *m* d'eau douce.
fret [fret] (*pt* & *pp* fretted, *cont* fretting)
◇ *vi* [worry] tracasser; she's always fretting about OR over her children elle se fait toujours du souci pour ses enfants; don't ~, I'll be alright ne te tracasse pas pour moi, tout ira bien; the small boy was fretting for his mother le petit garçon réclamait sa mère en pleurant; the dog fretted for its owner le chien s'agitait parce que son maître n'était pas là.
◇ *vt* -**1.** [worry]: to ~ one's life away passer sa vie à se tourmenter OR à se faire du mauvais sang. -**2.** [erode, wear down] ronger; a fretted rope une corde effilochée. -**3.** [decorate - metal, wood] chantourner.
◇ *n* -**1.** *inf* [state]: to get in a ~ about sthg se faire du mauvais sang OR se ronger les sangs à propos de qqch. -**2.** [on a guitar] touchette *f*, frette *f*.
fretful ['fretfʊl] *adj* [anxious] soucieux; [irritable, complaining] grincheux, maussade; a ~ child un enfant grognon; the baby's ~ crying les pleurs du bébé.
fretfully ['fretfʊlɪ] *adv* -**1.** [anxiously - ask, say] avec inquiétude; the dog waited ~ by the door le chien attendait impatiemment à la porte. -**2.** [irritably] d'une manière maussade; [ask, say] d'un ton grincheux OR maussade.
fretsaw ['fretsɔ:] *n* scie *f* à chantourner.
fretwork ['fretwɜ:k] *n* chantournement *m*.
Freudian ['frɔɪdɪən] ◇ *adj* freudien.
◇ *n* disciple *mf* de Freud.
Freudian slip *n* lapsus *m*.
FRG (*abbr of* Federal Republic of Germany) *pr n* RFA *f*.
Fri. (*written abbr of* Friday) ven.
friable ['fraɪəbl] *adj* friable.
friar ['fraɪəʳ] *n* frère *m*, moine *m*.
friar's balsam *n* benjoin *m*.
friary ['fraɪərɪ] (*pl* friaries) *n* monastère *m*.
fricassee ['frɪkəsi:] ◇ *n* fricassée *f*.
◇ *vt* fricasser.
fricative ['frɪkətɪv] ◇ *adj* constrictif, fricatif.
◇ *n* constrictive *f*, fricative *f*.
friction ['frɪkʃn] *n* -**1.** PHYS friction *f*. -**2.** [discord] friction *f*, conflit *m*; it's an issue that often causes ~ between neighbours c'est un problème qui est souvent cause de frictions entre voisins.
friction clutch *n* embrayage *m* à friction.
friction drive *n* entraînement *m* par friction.
frictionless ['frɪkʃənlɪs] *adj* sans friction.
friction tape *n Am* chatterton *m*.
Friday ['fraɪdɪ] *n* vendredi *m*; it's ~ today nous sommes OR on est vendredi aujourd'hui; I'll see you (on) ~ je te verrai vendredi; he leaves on ~, he leaves ~ *Am* il part vendredi; the cleaning woman comes on ~s la femme de ménage vient le vendredi; I work ~s je travaille le vendredi; there's a market each ~ OR every ~ il y a un marché tous les vendredis OR chaque vendredi; every other ~, every second ~ un vendredi sur deux; the first/last ~ of every month le premier/dernier vendredi de chaque mois; we arrive on the ~ and leave on the Sunday nous arrivons le vendredi et repartons le dimanche; the programme's usually shown on a ~ généralement cette émission passe le vendredi; the following ~ le vendredi suivant; she saw the doctor last ~ elle a vu le médecin vendredi dernier; I have an appointment next ~ j'ai un rendez-vous vendredi prochain; the ~ after next vendredi en huit; the ~ before last l'autre vendredi; a week from ~, a week on ~ *Br*, ~ week *Br* vendredi en huit; a fortnight on ~, ~ fortnight *Br* vendredi en quinze; a week/fortnight ago ~ il y a eu huit/quinze jours vendredi; ~ morning vendredi matin; ~ afternoon vendredi après-midi; ~ evening vendredi soir; we're going out (on)

~ night nous sortons vendredi soir; she spent ~ night at her friend's house elle a passé la nuit de vendredi chez son amie; we caught the ~ morning boat nous avons pris le bateau du vendredi matin; ~ 26 February vendredi 26 février; they were married on ~ June 12th ils se sont mariés le vendredi 12 juin; ~ the thirteenth vendredi treize.

fridge [frɪdʒ] *n* frigidaire *m*.

fridge-freezer *n* réfrigérateur-congélateur *m*.

fried [fraɪd] *adj* frit; ~ eggs œufs *mpl* poêlés OR sur le plat; ~ food friture *f*; ~ potatoes pommes *fpl* frites; (special) ~ rice riz *m* cantonais.

friend [frend] *n* -**1.** [gen] ami *m*, -e *f*; his school ~s ses camarades d'école; Bill's a good ~ of mine Bill est un grand ami à moi; we're just good ~s nous sommes bons amis sans plus; my best ~ mon meilleur ami, ma meilleure amie; he's a ~ of the family c'est un ami de la famille; she's someone I used to be ~s with nous avons été amies; to make ~s se faire des amis; he tried to make ~s with her brother il essaya d'être ami avec son frère; shall we be ~s? on est amis?; [after a quarrel] on fait la paix?; she's no ~ of mine elle ne fait pas partie de mes amis; I tell you this as a ~ je vous dis ça en ami; she doesn't realize what a good ~ you are elle n'apprécie pas votre amitié à sa juste valeur; they wanted to part ~s ils voulaient se quitter en amis; you're among ~s here tu es entre amis ici; I've always been a good ~ to her j'ai toujours été un bon ami pour elle ❑ she has ~s in high places elle a des amis en haut lieu OR bien placés; Friends of the Earth les Amis de la Terre; the (Society of) Friends RELIG la Société des Amis, les Quakers; a ~ in need is a ~ indeed *prov* c'est dans le besoin qu'on reconnaît ses vrais amis. -**2.** [colleague] collègue *mf*; ~s, we are gathered here tonight... chers amis OR collègues, nous sommes réunis ici ce soir... -**3.** [patron] mécène *m*, ami *m*, -e *f*; the Friends of the Tate Gallery les Amis de la Tate Gallery.

friendless ['frendlɪs] *adj* sans amis.

friendliness ['frendlɪnɪs] *n* [kindness, warmth] gentillesse *f*; an atmosphere of warmth and ~ une ambiance chaleureuse et sympathique.

friendly ['frendlɪ] (*compar* friendlier, *superl* friendliest) ◇ *adj* -**1.** [kind, pleasant - person] aimable, gentil; [- animal] gentil; [amicable - advice, game, smile] amical; to be ~ to OR towards sb être gentil OR aimable avec qqn; a ~ welcome OR reception un accueil chaleureux; that wasn't very ~ of him! ce n'était pas très gentil de sa part! -**2.** [close, intimate] ami; [allied] ami; they've become very ~ lately elles sont devenues très amies dernièrement; Anne is still on ~ terms with her brother Anne est toujours en bons termes avec son frère; a ~ nation un pays ami; don't let him get too ~ *inf* garde tes distances avec lui.
◇ *n* [match] match *m* amical.

friendly society *n Br* société *f* mutuelle OR de secours mutuels.

friendship ['frendʃɪp] *n* amitié *f*; I would never jeopardize my ~ with him pour rien au monde je ne compromettrais notre amitié; to form a ~ with sb se lier d'amitié avec qqn, nouer une amitié avec qqn; to strike up a ~ with sb lier amitié avec qqn; he did it out of ~ for her il l'a fait par amitié pour elle; to live in peace and ~ vivre en paix et bonne intelligence; the aim is to promote ~ between nations le but est de promouvoir l'amitié entre les nations.

frier ['fraɪə^r] = **fryer**.

Friesian ['fri:zjən] *n* frisonne *f*.

frieze [fri:z] *n* -**1.** ARCHIT frise *f*. -**2.** TEX ratine *f*.

frig^∇ [frɪg] (*pt* & *pp* frigged, *cont* frigging) *vi Br*: to ~ about OR around déconner, faire l'imbécile; stop frigging about and get in the car arrête de déconner OR de faire l'imbécile et monte dans la voiture.

frigate ['frɪgət] *n* frégate *f*.

frigging^∇ ['frɪgɪŋ] *adj*: move your ~ car! enlève-moi cette foutue bagnole!

fright [fraɪt] *n* -**1.** [sudden fear] frayeur *f*, peur *f*; his face was pale with ~ il était vert de peur; to take ~ at sthg avoir peur de qqch; to give sb a ~ faire une frayeur à qqn; you gave me a terrible ~! vous m'avez fait une de ces frayeurs!; I got the ~ of my life when he said that j'ai eu la peur de ma vie quand il a dit ça. -**2.** *inf* [mess]: you look an absolute ~ tu fais vraiment peur à voir.

frighten ['fraɪtn] *vt* effrayer, faire peur à; stop it, you're ~ing me! arrête, tu me fais peur!; to ~ sb out of doing sthg dissuader qqn de faire qqch en lui faisant peur; to ~ sb into doing sthg obliger qqn à faire qqch en lui faisant peur; to ~ sb to death OR out of their wits, to ~ the life out of sb faire une peur bleue à qqn.
◆ **frighten away** *vt sep* faire fuir (par la peur); [animal] effaroucher; the burglars were ~ed away by the police siren effrayés par la sirène de police, les cambrioleurs ont pris la fuite.
◆ **frighten off** *vt sep* -**1.** [cause to flee] faire fuir; [animal] effaroucher. -**2.** [intimidate, scare] chasser, faire peur à; rising inflation has ~ed off potential investors l'inflation croissante a fait fuir les investisseurs potentiels.

frightened ['fraɪtnd] *adj* effrayé; to be ~ of sthg avoir peur de qqch; I was too ~ to speak je n'arrivais pas à parler tellement j'avais peur; there's nothing to be ~ of il n'y a rien à craindre; he looked ~ il avait l'air d'avoir peur; ~ faces/children des visages/des enfants apeurés.

frightener ['fraɪtnə^r] *n phr*: to put the ~s on sb^∇ filer la trouille à qqn.

frightening ['fraɪtnɪŋ] *adj* effrayant; the consequences are too ~ to think of on n'ose pas imaginer les conséquences; it's ~ to think what might have happened ça fait peur de penser à ce qui aurait pu arriver.

frighteningly ['fraɪtnɪŋlɪ] *adv* à faire peur; the story was ~ true to life l'histoire était d'un réalisme effrayant.

frightful ['fraɪtfʊl] *adj* -**1.** [horrible] affreux, horrible; the soldier had ~ wounds le soldat avait d'affreuses blessures. -**2.** *inf Br* [unpleasant]: we had a ~ time parking the car on a eu un mal fou à garer la voiture; he's a ~ bore [as intensifier] il est horriblement OR affreusement casse-pieds.

frightfully *inf* ['fraɪtfʊlɪ] *adv Br*: he's a ~ good dancer il danse remarquablement bien; it was ~ generous of you to buy me lunch c'était vraiment très généreux à vous de m'inviter à déjeuner; I'm ~ sorry about missing the meeting je suis absolument désolé d'avoir manqué la réunion.

frigid ['frɪdʒɪd] *adj* -**1.** [very cold] glacial, glacé; GEOG & METEOR glacial. -**2.** [sexually] frigide.

frigidity [frɪ'dʒɪdətɪ] *n* -**1.** [coldness] froideur *f*. -**2.** PSYCH frigidité *f*.

Frigid Zone *pr n* régions *fpl* polaires.

frijoles [frɪ'həʊlɪz] *npl purée de haricots rouges frits.*

frill [frɪl] *n* TEX ruche *f*, volant *m*; CULIN papillote *f*; ORNITH collerette *f*.
◆ **frills** *npl* [ornamentation, luxuries]: without ~s sans façon; a cheap, basic package holiday with no ~s des vacances organisées simples et pas chères.

frilly ['frɪlɪ] *adj* -**1.** TEX orné de fanfreluches. -**2.** [style] affecté, apprêté.

fringe ['frɪndʒ] ◇ *n* -**1.** [decorative edge] frange *f*; a ~ of trees une bordure d'arbres. -**2.** [of hair] frange *f*. -**3.** [periphery] périphérie *f*, frange *f*; the gamekeeper lives in a cottage on the ~ OR ~s of the estate le garde-chasse vit dans une maisonnette en bordure de la propriété ; to live on the ~s of society *fig* vivre en marge de la société; she's on the ~ OR ~s of the party *fig* elle est en marge du parti ❑ ~ area zone *f* limitrophe; ~ group frange *f*; she belongs to a ~ group of the Labour Party elle fait partie d'une frange du parti travailliste -**4.** THEAT: the Fringe (festival) *Br* le festival off.
◇ *vt* franger; the path was ~d with rose bushes le sentier était bordé de rosiers, palm-~d beaches des plages bordées de palmiers.

fringe benefit *n* avantage *m* annexe OR en nature.

fringe theatre *n Br* théâtre *m* d'avant-garde OR expérimental.

fringing reef ['frɪndʒɪŋ-] *n* récif *m* frangeant.

frippery ['frɪpərɪ] (*pl* fripperies) *n* -**1.** [showy objects] colifichets *mpl*, babioles *fpl*; [on clothing] fanfreluches *fpl*. -**2.** [ostentation] mignardises *fpl*, chichi *m*.

Frisbee® ['frɪzbɪ] *n* Frisbee® *m*.

Frisco *inf* ['frɪskəʊ] *pr n* San Francisco.

Frisian ['fri:ʒən] ◇ *n* -**1.** [person] Frison *m* -onne *f*. -**2.** LING frison *m*.
◇ *adj* frison.

Frisian Islands *pl pr n*: the ~ l'archipel *m* frison.

frisk [frɪsk] ◇ *vi* [play] gambader; the two kittens ~ed about in the garden les deux chatons gambadaient dans le jardin.
◇ *vt* [search] fouiller.
◇ *n* [search] fouille *f*.

frisky ['frɪskɪ] (*compar* friskier, *superl* friskiest) *adj* [animal] fringant; [person] gaillard.

fritillary [frɪ'tɪlərɪ] *n* fritillaire *f*.

fritter ['frɪtə^r] ◇ *n* CULIN beignet *m*; banana ~s beignets *mpl* de banane.
◇ *vt* = **fritter away**.
◆ **fritter away** *vt sep* gaspiller.

frivolity [frɪ'vɒlətɪ] (*pl* frivolities) *n* frivolité *f*.

frivolous ['frɪvələs] *adj* frivole.

frizz [frɪz] ◇ *n*: she had a ~ of blond hair elle avait des cheveux blonds tout frisés.
◇ *vt* faire friser.
◇ *vi* friser.

frizzle ['frɪzl] ◇ *vt* -**1.** CULIN [overcook] griller [burn] calciner, carboniser. -**2.** [curl] faire friser
◇ *vi* -**1.** [cook noisily] grésiller. -**2.** [curl] friser

frizzly ['frɪzlɪ] (*compar* frizzlier, *superl* frizzliest) **frizzy** ['frɪzɪ] (*compar* frizzier, *superl* frizziest) *adj* crépu.

fro [frəʊ] → **to and fro**.

frock [frɒk] *n* [dress] robe *f*; RELIG froc *m*.

frock coat *n* redingote *f*.

frog [frɒg] *n* -**1.** ZOOL grenouille *f*; ~'s legs CULIN cuisses *fpl* de grenouille; to have a ~ in one's throat *inf* avoir un chat dans la gorge -**2.** [on uniform] brandebourg *m*; [on women's clothing] soutache *f*.
◆ **Frog**^∇ *n Br* [French person] *terme injurieux désignant un Français.*

frogged [frɒgd] *adj* à brandebourgs.

frogging ['frɒgɪŋ] *n* (*U*) soutaches *fpl*.

Froggy^∇ ['frɒgɪ] *n Br terme injurieux désignant un Français.*

frogman ['frɒgmən] (*pl* frogmen [-mən]) *n* homme-grenouille *m*.

frogmarch ['frɒgmɑ:tʃ] *vt Br porter par les bras et les jambes, le visage vers le sol*; the protesters were ~ed to a police van les manifestants furent entraînés jusqu'au fourgon de police; they ~ed us out of the building [moved forcibly] ils nous ont délogés du bâtiment sans ménagement.

frogspawn ['frɒgspɔ:n] *n* frai *m* de grenouilles

frog spit, frog spittle *n* crachat *m* de coucou

fro-ing ['frəʊɪŋ] → **to-ing and fro-ing**.

frolic ['frɒlɪk] (*pt* & *pp* frolicked, *cont* frolicking ◇ *vi* s'ébattre, gambader; the children frolicked about on the grass les enfants gambadaient sur la pelouse.
◇ *n* [run] gambades *fpl*, ébats *mpl*; [game] jeu *m*; we let the dogs have a ~ in the park on a laissé les chiens s'ébattre dans le parc.

frolicsome ['frɒlɪksəm] *adj* enjoué, badin.

from [*weak form* frəm, *strong form* frɒm] *prep* **-1.** [indicating starting point - in space] de; [- in time] de, à partir de, depuis; [- in price, quantity] à partir de; **Einstein came to this country ~ Germany** Einstein a quitté l'Allemagne pour s'établir ici; **her parents came ~ Russia** ses parents venaient de Russie; **where's your friend ~?** d'où est OR vient votre ami?; **I've just come back ~ there** j'en reviens; **there are no direct flights ~ Hobart** il n'y a pas de vol direct à partir d'Hobart; **the 11:10 ~ Cambridge** le train de 11 h 10 en provenance de Cambridge; **the airport is about 15 kilometres ~ the city centre** l'aéroport se trouve à 15 kilomètres environ du centre-ville; **it rained all the way ~ Calais to Paris** il a plu pendant tout le trajet de Calais à Paris; **it takes 15 minutes ~ here to my house** il faut 15 minutes pour aller d'ici à chez moi; **~ now on** désormais, dorénavant; **~ the age of four** à partir de quatre ans; **she was unhappy ~ her first day at boarding school** elle a été malheureuse dès son premier jour à l'internat; **~ the start** dès OR depuis le début; **a week ~ today** dans huit jours; **where will we be a year ~ now?** où serons-nous dans un an?; **we've got food left over ~ last night** nous avons des restes d'hier soir; **potatoes ~ 50 pence a kilo** des pommes de terre à partir de 50 pence le kilo; **knives ~ £2 each** des couteaux à partir de 2 livres la pièce; **6 ~ 14 is 8** 6 ôté de 14 donne 8; **we went ~ 3 employees to 15 in a year** nous sommes passés de 3 à 15 employés en un an. **-2.** [indicating origin, source] de; **who's the letter ~?** de qui est la lettre?; **don't tell her that the flowers are ~ me** ne lui dites pas que les fleurs viennent de moi; **I got a phone call ~ her yesterday** j'ai reçu un coup de fil d'elle hier; **he got the idea ~ a book he read** il a trouvé l'idée dans un livre qu'il a lu; **where did you get the ring ~?** où avez-vous eu la bague?; **you can get a money order ~ the post office** vous pouvez avoir un mandat à la poste; **I bought my piano ~ a neighbour** j'ai acheté mon piano à un voisin; **you mustn't borrow money ~ them** vous ne devez pas leur emprunter de l'argent; **she stole some documents ~ the ministry** elle a volé des documents au ministère; **who stole the key ~ her?** qui lui a volé la clef?; **I heard about it ~ the landlady** c'est la propriétaire qui m'en a parlé; **a scene ~ a play** une scène d'une pièce; **he translates ~ English into French** il traduit d'anglais en français; **she still has injuries resulting ~ the crash** elle a encore des blessures qui datent de l'accident; **she's been away ~ work for a week** ça fait une semaine qu'elle n'est pas allée au travail; **they returned ~ their holidays yesterday** ils sont rentrés de vacances hier; **the man ~ the Inland Revenue** le monsieur du fisc. **-3.** [off, out of]: **she took a book ~ the shelf** elle a pris un livre sur l'étagère; **he drank straight ~ the bottle** il a bu à même la bouteille; **she drew a gun ~ her pocket** elle sortit un revolver de sa poche; **he took a beer ~ the fridge** il a pris une bière dans le frigo; **'guaranteed to remove stains ~ all surfaces'** 'enlève les taches sur toutes les surfaces'. **-4.** [indicating position, location] de; **~ the top you can see the whole city** du haut on voit toute la ville; **you get a great view ~ the bridge** on a une très belle vue du pont; **the rock juts out ~ the cliff** le rocher dépasse de la falaise. **-5.** [indicating cause, reason]: **you can get sick ~ drinking the water** vous pouvez tomber malade en buvant l'eau; **his back hurt ~ lifting heavy boxes** il avait mal au dos après avoir soulevé des gros cartons; **I guessed she was Australian ~ the way she spoke** j'ai deviné qu'elle était australienne à sa façon de parler; **he died ~ grief** il est mort de chagrin. **-6.** [using]: **they are made ~ flour** ils sont faits à base de farine; **Calvados is made ~ apples** le calvados est fait avec des pommes; **she played the piece ~ memory** elle joua le morceau de mémoire; **I speak ~ personal experience** je sais de quoi je parle. **-7.** [judging by] d'après; **~ the way she talks you'd think she was the boss** à l'entendre, on croirait que c'est elle le patron; **~ the way she sings you'd think she were a professional** à l'entendre chanter on dirait que c'est son métier; **~ what I gather...** d'après ce que j'ai cru comprendre... **-8.** [in comparisons] de; **it's no different ~ riding a bike** c'est comme faire du vélo; **how do you tell one ~ the other?** comment les reconnais-tu l'un de l'autre? **-9.** [indicating prevention, protection] de; **she saved me ~ drowning** elle m'a sauvé de la noyade; **we sheltered ~ the rain in a cave** nous nous sommes abrités de la pluie dans une caverne; **they were hidden ~ view** on ne les voyait pas.

frond [frɒnd] *n* fronde *f*; [on palm tree] feuille *f*.

front [frʌnt] ◇ *n* **-1.** [forward part] devant *m*; [of vehicle] avant *m*; **I'll be at the ~ of the train** je serai en tête de OR à l'avant du train; **he sat up ~ near the driver** il s'est assis à l'avant près du conducteur; **our seats were at the ~ of the theatre** nous avions des places aux premiers rangs (du théâtre); **come to the ~ of the class** venez devant; **she went to the ~ of the queue** elle alla se mettre au début de la queue; **the actors stood at the ~ of the stage** les comédiens étaient debout sur le devant de la scène; **the ~ of the house has been repainted** la façade de la maison a été repeinte; **the Times's theatre critic is out ~ tonight** le critique dramatique du Times est dans la salle ce soir; **she wrote her name on the ~ of the envelope** elle écrivit son nom sur le devant de l'enveloppe; **he got wine down his ~** OR **the ~ of his shirt** du vin a été renversé sur le devant de sa chemise; **his portrait was in the ~ of every schoolbook** son portrait figurait sur la couverture de tous les livres de classe. **-2.** [seashore] bord *m* de mer, front *m* de mer; **the hotel is on the ~** l'hôtel est au bord de la OR sur le front de mer; **a walk along** OR **on the ~** une promenade au bord de la mer. **-3.** MIL front *m*; **on the Eastern/Western ~** sur le front Est/Ouest; **he fought at the ~** il a combattu au front || *fig*: **the Prime Minister is being attacked on all ~s** on s'en prend au Premier ministre de tous côtés; **little had been achieved on the domestic** OR **home ~** on avait accompli peu de choses sur le plan intérieur ❑ **'All Quiet on the Western Front'** *Remarque* 'À l'Ouest, rien de nouveau'. **-4.** [joint effort] front *m*; **to present a united ~ (on sthg)** faire front commun (devant qqch). **-5.** [appearance] façade *f*; **his apparent optimism was only a ~** son optimisme apparent n'était qu'une façade; **to put on a bold** OR **brave ~** faire preuve de courage. **-6.** [cover] façade *f*, couverture *f*; **the shop is just a ~ for a drugs ring** le magasin n'est qu'une couverture pour des trafiquants de drogue. **-7.** METEOR front *m*; **cold/warm ~** front *m* froid/chaud. **-8.** ARCHIT façade *f*; **the north/south ~** la façade nord/sud. **-9.** *phr*: **up ~** *inf* d'avance; **they want £5,000 up ~** ils veulent 5 000 livres d'avance.

◇ *adj* **-1.** [in a forward position] de devant; **~ seat/wheel** AUT siège *m*/roue *f* avant; **she was sitting in the ~ row** elle était assise au premier rang; **the ~ page** PRESS la première page; **his picture is on the ~ page** sa photo est en première page; **he came in through a ~ window** il est entré par une fenêtre de devant; **I'll be in the ~ end of the train** je serai en tête de OR à l'avant du train; **his name is on the ~ cover** son nom est en couverture; **a ~ view** une vue de face. **-2.** [bogus, fake] de façade. **-3.** LING: **a ~ vowel** une voyelle avant OR antérieure.

◇ *adv* par devant; **eyes ~!** MIL fixe!

◇ *vi* **-1.** *Br* [face]: **the hotel ~s onto the beach** l'hôtel donne sur la plage. **-2.** [cover]: **the newspaper ~ed for a terrorist organization** le journal servait de façade à une organisation terroriste.

◇ *vt* **-1.** [stand before]: **lush gardens ~ed the building** il y avait des jardins luxuriants devant le bâtiment. **-2.** CONSTR: **the house was ~ed with stone** la maison avait une façade en pierre. **-3.** [lead] être à la tête de, diriger; TV [present] présenter.

◆ **in front** *adv phr* [in theatre, vehicle] à l'avant; [ahead, leading] en avant; **there was a very tall man in the row in ~** il y avait un très grand homme assis devant moi; **the women walked in ~ and the children behind** les femmes marchaient devant et les enfants derrière; **to be in ~** SPORT être en tête OR premier.

◆ **in front of** *prep phr* devant; **she was sitting in ~ of the TV** elle était assise devant la télé; **he was right in ~ of me** il était juste devant moi; **not in ~ of the children!** pas devant les enfants!

frontage ['frʌntɪdʒ] *n* **-1.** [wall] façade *f*; [shopfront] devanture *f*. **-2.** [land] terrain *m* en bordure.

frontage road *n Am* contre-allée *f*.

frontal ['frʌntl] ◇ *adj* MIL [assault, attack] de front; ANAT & MED frontal; **~ system** METEOR système *m* de fronts.

◇ *n* RELIG parement *m*.

frontbench [,frʌnt'bentʃ] *n Br* POL [members of the government] ministres *mpl*; [members of the Opposition] ministres *mpl* du cabinet fantôme; **he's never been on the ~** [Government] il n'a jamais été ministre; [Opposition] il n'a jamais été membre du cabinet fantôme; **the ~es** [in Parliament] *à la Chambre des communes, bancs situés à droite et à gauche du Président et occupés respectivement par les ministres du gouvernement en exercice et ceux du gouvernement fantôme.*

frontbencher [,frʌnt'bentʃə^r] *n Br* POL [member of the Government] ministre *m*; [member of the Opposition] membre *m* du cabinet fantôme.

front door *n* [of house] porte *f* d'entrée; [of vehicle] portière *f* avant.

front-end processor *n* processeur *m* frontal.

frontier [*Br* 'frʌn,tɪə^r, *Am* frʌn'tɪər] ◇ *n* **-1.** *literal* & *fig* [border] frontière *f*; **the ~s of science** les frontières OR limites de la science. **-2.** *Am*: **the ~** la Frontière *(nom donné à la limite des terres habitées par les colons pendant la colonisation de l'Amérique du Nord).*

◇ *comp* **-1.** [dispute] de frontière; [post] frontière. **-2.** *Am* [spirit] de pionnier; **a ~ town** *une bourgade d'une région limitrophe du pays.*

frontiersman [*Br* 'frʌntɪəzmən, *Am* frʌn'tɪrzmən] (*pl* **frontiersmen** [-mən]) *n* pionnier *m*.

frontispiece ['frʌntɪspiːs] *n* frontispice *m*.

front line *n*: **the ~** MIL la première ligne; **she is in the ~ in the fight against drug abuse** *fig* elle joue un rôle important dans la lutte contre la toxicomanie.

◆ **front-line** *adj* **-1.** MIL [soldiers, troops] en première ligne; [ambulance] de zone de combat. **-2.** POL: **the ~ states** les États *mpl* limitrophes. **-3.** *Am* SPORT: **~ player** avant *m*.

front-loading *adj* [washing machine] à chargement frontal.

front man *n* **-1.** [representative, spokesman] porte-parole *m inv*, représentant *m*. **-2.** *pej* [figurehead] prête-nom *m*. **-3.** TV [presenter] présentateur *m*.

front matter *n pages préliminaires (avant le texte) d'un livre.*

front of house *n* THEAT *partie d'un théâtre où peuvent circuler les spectateurs.*

front-page *adj* [article, story] de première page; **it wasn't exactly ~ news** ça n'a pas fait la une des journaux.

front room *n* [at front of house] *pièce qui donne sur le devant de la maison*; [sitting room] salon *m*.

front-runner *n* favori *m*, -ite *f*.

frontwards ['frʌntwədz] *adv* en avant, vers l'avant.

front-wheel drive *n* traction *f* avant.

frost [frɒst] ◇ *n* **-1.** [freezing weather] gel *m*, gelée *f*; **there was a ~ last night** il a gelé hier soir; **a late ~** des gelées tardives; **eight degrees of ~** huit degrés au-dessous de zéro. **-2.** [frozen dew] givre *m*, gelée *f* blanche; the grass was covered in ~ le gazon était couvert de givre. -**3.** *inf* [cold manner] froideur *f*. -**4.** *inf Am* [fiasco] four *m*, fiasco *m*.

◇ *vt* -**1.** [freeze] geler; [cover with frost] givrer; the rim of the glass was ~ed with sugar le bord du verre avait été givré avec du sucre. -**2.** *Am* [cake] glacer. -**3.** TECH [glass pane] dépolir.

◇ *vi* [freeze] geler; [become covered with frost] se givrer.

◆ **frost over, frost up** ◇ *vi insep* se givrer.

◇ *vt sep* givrer.

frostbite ['frɒstbaɪt] *n (U)* gelure *f*; he got ~ in his toes il a eu les orteils gelés; the climber died of ~ l'alpiniste est mort gelé.

frostbitten ['frɒst,bɪtn] *adj* [hands, nose] gelé; [plant] gelé, grillé par le gel.

frosted ['frɒstɪd] *adj* -**1.** [frozen] gelé; [covered with frost] givré. -**2.** [pane of glass] dépoli. -**3.** *Am* [cake] glacé. -**4.** [lipstick, nail varnish] nacré. -**5.** [hair] grisonnant; his hair was ~ with white ses cheveux grisonnaient.

frostily ['frɒstɪlɪ] *adv* de manière glaciale, froidement.

frosting ['frɒstɪŋ] *n Am* glaçage *m*, glace *f*.

frosty ['frɒstɪ] (*compar* frostier, *superl* frostiest) *adj* -**1.** [weather, air] glacial; we had several ~ nights il a gelé plusieurs nuits. -**2.** [ground, window] couvert de givre. -**3.** [answer, manner] glacial, froid.

froth [frɒθ] ◇ *n (U)* -**1.** [foam] écume *f*, mousse *f*; [on beer] mousse *f*; [on lips] écume *f*. -**2.** [trivialities, empty talk] futilités *fpl*.

◇ *vi* [liquid] écumer, mousser; [beer, soap] mousser; the detergent ~ed out of the washing machine la mousse a débordé de la machine à laver; to ~ at the mouth écumer, baver; he was so angry he was practically ~ing at the mouth *hum* il écumait de rage.

◇ *vt* faire mousser.

frothy ['frɒθɪ] (*compar* frothier, *superl* frothiest) *adj* -**1.** [liquid] mousseux, écumeux; [beer] mousseux; [sea] écumeux. -**2.** [entertainment, literature] creux. -**3.** [dress, lace] léger, vaporeux.

frown [fraʊn] ◇ *vi* froncer les sourcils, se renfrogner; she ~ed at my remark mon observation lui a fait froncer les sourcils; to ~ at sb regarder qqn de travers, faire les gros yeux à qqn.

◇ *n* froncement *m* de sourcils; she looked up with a disapproving/worried ~ elle leva les yeux avec un froncement de sourcils désapprobateur/inquiet; he gave a ~ il fronça les sourcils.

◇ *comp*: ~ lines rides *fpl* intersourcilières.

◆ **frown on, frown upon** *vt insep* désapprouver; her parents ~ upon their friendship ses parents voient leur amitié d'un mauvais œil; such behaviour is rather ~ed upon ce type de comportement n'est pas vu d'un très bon œil.

frowsty ['fraʊstɪ] (*compar* frowstier, *superl* frowstiest) *adj* qui sent le renfermé.

frowsy ['fraʊzɪ] (*compar* frowsier, *superl* frowsiest) *adj Br* -**1.** [shabby - person] négligé; [- clothing] élimé, rapé. -**2.** = **frowsty**.

frowzy ['fraʊzɪ] (*compar* frowzier, *superl* frowziest) = **frowsy**.

froze [frəʊz] *pt* → **freeze**.

frozen ['frəʊzn] ◇ *pp* → **freeze**.

◇ *adj* -**1.** [ground, lake, pipes] gelé; [person] gelé, glacé; the lake is ~ solid le lac est complètement gelé; my hands are ~ j'ai les mains gelées OR glacées; I'm ~ stiff je suis gelé jusqu'à la moelle (des os); ~ with terror *fig* mort de peur ❑ ~ food [in refrigerator] aliments *mpl* congelés; [industrially frozen] surgelés *mpl*; ~ food compartment congélateur *m*. -**2.** [prices, salaries] bloqué; FIN [assets, credit] gelé, bloqué. -**3.** MED: ~ shoulder épaule *f* ankylosée.

FRS ◇ *n* (*abbr of* Fellow of the Royal Society) ≃ membre *m* de l'Académie des sciences.

◇ *pr n* *abbr of* Federal Reserve System.

fructification [,frʌktɪfɪ'keɪʃn] *n fml* fructification *f*.

fructify ['frʌktɪfaɪ] (*pt* & *pp* fructified) *fml*

◇ *vi* fructifier.

◇ *vt* faire fructifier.

fructose ['frʌktəʊs] *n* fructose *m*.

frugal ['fru:gl] *adj* -**1.** [person] économe, frugal; she's very ~ with her money elle est près de ses sous; a ~ life une vie frugale OR simple. -**2.** [meal] frugal.

frugality [fru:'gælətɪ] *n* -**1.** [of person] parcimonie *f*, frugalité *f*; [of life] frugalité *f*, simplicité *f*. -**2.** [of meal] frugalité *f*.

frugally ['fru:gəlɪ] *adv* [live] simplement, frugalement; [distribute, give] parcimonieusement; we dined ~ on bread and cheese nous avons dîné simplement de pain et de fromage.

fruit [fru:t] (*pl sense 1 inv* OR fruits) ◇ *n* -**1.** *literal* fruit *m*; to eat ~ manger des fruits; a piece of ~ un fruit; would you like ~ or cheese? voulez-vous un fruit ou du fromage?; we eat a lot of ~ nous mangeons beaucoup de fruits; a tree in ~ un arbre qui porte des fruits; the ~ OR ~s of the earth les fruits de la terre ‖ *fig*: the ~ of her womb le fruit de ses entrailles; their plans have never borne fruit leurs projets ne se sont jamais réalisés; his book is the ~ of much research son livre est le fruit de longues recherches. -**2.** *inf Br dated* [term of address]: old ~ mon vieux. -**3.** ▽*Am pej* [homosexual] pédé *m*, tante *f*.

◇ *comp* [basket, bowl, knife] à fruits; [diet, farm, stall] fruitier; ~ dish [individual] coupe *f*, coupelle *f*; [large] coupe *f* à fruits, compotier *m*; ~ farmer arboriculteur *m* (fruitier); ~ farming arboriculture *f* (fruitière); ~ juice/salad jus *m*/salade *f* de fruits; ~ tree arbre *m* fruitier.

◇ *vi* BOT donner.

fruit bat *n* chauve-souris *f* frugivore.

fruit cake *n* -**1.** [cake] cake *m*. -**2.** *inf* [lunatic] cinglé *m*, -e *f*.

fruit cocktail *n* macédoine *f* de fruits.

fruit cup *n* [dessert] coupe *f* de fruits; [drink] boisson *f* aux fruits *(parfois alcoolisée)*.

fruit drop *n* bonbon *m* aux fruits.

fruiterer ['fru:tərə^r] *n Br* marchand *m*, -e *f* de fruits, fruitier *m*, -ère *f*.

fruit fly *n* mouche *f* du vinaigre, drosophile *f*.

fruitful ['fru:tfʊl] *adj* -**1.** [discussion, suggestion] fructueux, utile; [attempt, collaboration] fructueux. -**2.** [soil] fertile, fécond; [plant, tree] fécond, productif.

fruitfully ['fru:tfʊlɪ] *adv* fructueusement.

fruit gum *n Br* boule *f* de gomme.

fruition [fru:'ɪʃn] *n fml* réalisation *f*; to come to ~ se réaliser; to bring sthg to ~ réaliser qqch, concrétiser qqch.

fruitless ['fru:tlɪs] *adj* -**1.** [discussion, effort] vain, sans résultat. -**2.** [plant, tree] stérile, infécond; [soil] stérile.

fruitlessly ['fru:tlɪslɪ] *adv* en vain, vainement.

fruit machine *n Br* machine *f* à sous.

fruit salts *npl* sels *mpl* purgatifs.

fruit sugar *n* fructose *m*.

fruity ['fru:tɪ] (*compar* fruitier, *superl* fruitiest) *adj* -**1.** [flavour, sauce] fruité, de fruit; [perfume, wine] fruité; the wine has a ~ taste le vin a un goût fruité; it has a ~ smell ça a une odeur fruitée. -**2.** [voice] étoffé, timbré. -**3.** *inf* [joke, story] corsé, salé.

frump [frʌmp] *n* femme *f* mal habillée; she looks a bit of a ~ these days elle s'habille vraiment mal ces temps-ci.

frumpish ['frʌmpɪʃ], **frumpy** ['frʌmpɪ] *adj* mal habillé; she wears rather ~ clothes elle s'habille plutôt mal; she was dressed in a ~ skirt and jumper elle portait une jupe et un pull sans aucune allure.

frustrate [frʌ'streɪt] *vt* [person] frustrer, agacer; [efforts, plans] contrecarrer, faire échouer; [plot] déjouer, faire échouer; the rain ~d our plans la pluie a contrarié nos projets; the prisoner was ~d in his attempt to escape le prisonnier a raté sa tentative d'évasion.

frustrated [frʌ'streɪtɪd] *adj* -**1.** [annoyed] frustré, agacé; [disappointed] frustré, déçu; [sexually] frustré; a ~ poet un poète manqué. -**2.** [attempt, effort] vain; all our efforts to contact her were ~ tous nos efforts pour la contacter ont été vains OR ont échoué.

frustrating [frʌ'streɪtɪŋ] *adj* agaçant, frustrant; it's very ~ having to wait c'est vraiment pénible de devoir attendre; a ~ person une personne agaçante OR pénible.

frustration [frʌ'streɪʃn] *n* [gen & PSYCH] frustration *f*; it's one of the ~s of the job c'est un des aspects frustrants du travail.

fry [fraɪ] (*pt* & *pp* fried, *pl* fries) ◇ *vt* CULIN faire frire, frire; he fried himself an egg il s'est fait un œuf sur le plat ❑ go ~ an egg! *inf Am* va te faire cuire un œuf!

◇ *vi* -**1.** [food] frire; *fig* [person] griller. -**2.** ▽*Am* [be electrocuted] être exécuté sur la chaise électrique.

◇ *n* -**1.** *(U)* ZOOL [fish] fretin *m*; [frogs] têtards *mpl*. -**2.** *Am sorte de pique-nique où on mange de la friture*.

◆ **fries** *npl Am* = **french fries**.

◆ **fry up** *vt sep* faire frire, frire.

fryer ['fraɪə^r] *n* -**1.** [pan] poêle *f* (à frire); [for deep-fat frying] friteuse *f*. -**2.** [chicken] poulet *m* à frire.

frying ['fraɪɪŋ] *n* friture *f*.

frying pan *Br*, **fry pan** *Am n* poêle *f* (à frire); to jump out of the ~ into the fire tomber de Charybde en Scylla, changer un cheval borgne pour un cheval aveugle.

fry-up *inf n Br plat constitué de plusieurs aliments frits ensemble*.

FSH *n* *abbr of* follicle-stimulating hormone.

f-stop *n* ouverture *f* (du diaphragme); ~ scale échelle *f* des diaphragmes.

ft -**1.** *written abbr of* foot. -**2.** *written abbr of* fort.

FT *pr n* *abbr of* Financial Times.

FTC *pr n* *abbr of* Federal Trade Commission.

FT Index (*abbr of* Financial Times Industrial Ordinary Share Index) *n Br* indice *m* du «Financial Times» *(moyenne quotidienne des principales valeurs boursières britanniques)*.

fuchsia ['fju:ʃə] *n* [colour] fuchsia *m*; BOT fuchsia *m*.

fuchsine ['fu:ksi:n] *n* fuchsine *f*.

fuck▽ [fʌk] ◇ *vt* baiser; ~ you! va te faire enculer OR foutre!; ~ it! putain de merde!; ~ me! putain!

◇ *vi* baiser; don't ~ with me! *fig* essaie pas de te foutre de ma gueule!

◇ *n* -**1.** [act] baise *f*. -**2.** [sexual partner]: he's a good ~ il baise bien. -**3.** *Am* [idiot]: you stupid ~! espèce de connard! -**4.** *phr*: I don't give a ~ j'en ai rien à branler. -**5.** [as intensifier]: what the ~ do you want me to do about it? mais qu'est-ce que tu veux que j'y fasse, putain de merde?

◇ *interj* putain de merde!

◆ **fuck about**▽ *Br*, **fuck around**▽ ◇ *vi insep* déconner; stop ~ing about with the radio! mais laisse donc cette putain de radio tranquille!

◇ *vt* faire chier.

◆ **fuck off**▽ *vi insep* foutre le camp; ~ off! va te faire enculer OR foutre!

◆ **fuck up**▽ ◇ *vt sep* [plan, project] foutre la merde dans; [person] foutre dans la merde; he's really ~ed up emotionally il est complètement paumé.

◇ *vi insep* merder.

fuck all▽ *n* que dalle; it's got ~ to do with you! occupe-toi donc de tes fesses!

fucker▽ ['fʌkə^r] *n*: you stupid ~! mais qu'est-ce que tu peux être con!

fucking▽ ['fʌkɪŋ] ◇ *adj*: I'm fed up with this ~ car! j'en ai plein le cul de cette putain de bagnole!; you ~ idiot! pauvre con!; ~ hell! putain de merde!

◇ *adv*: he's ~ stupid! tu parles d'un con!; it was a ~ awful day! tu parles d'une putain de journée!

fuck-up▼ *n* -**1.** [situation] merde *f.* -**2.** [bungler] bousilleur *m*, -euse *f*; **he's a real ~** il fout sa merde partout.

fuddle ['fʌdl] *vt* [confuse - ideas, person] embrouiller; [intoxicate] griser.

fuddled ['fʌdld] *adj* [ideas, mind] embrouillé, confus; [person - confused] confus; [- tipsy] gris, éméché.

fuddy-duddy *inf* ['fʌdɪˌdʌdɪ] (*pl* **fuddy-duddies**) *n*: **she's a bit of a ~** c'est un drôle d'oiseau.

fudge [fʌdʒ] ◇ *n* -**1.** *(U)* [sweet] caramel *m*; **a piece of ~** un caramel; **I made some ~** j'ai fait des caramels. -**2.** *(U)* [nonsense] balivernes *fpl*, âneries *fpl*. -**3.** *(U)* [dodging] faux-fuyant *m*, échappatoire *f*. -**4.** TYPO [stop press box] emplacement *m* de la dernière heure; [stop press news] (insertion *f* de) dernière heure *f*, dernières nouvelles *fpl*.
◇ *vi* [evade, hedge] esquiver le problème; **the President ~d on the budget issue** le président a esquivé les questions sur le budget.
◇ *vt* -**1.** [make up - excuse] inventer; [- story] monter; [- figures, results] truquer. -**2.** [avoid, dodge] esquiver.
◇ *interj dated*: **~!** balivernes!

fuel [fjʊəl] (*Br pt & pp* **fuelled**, *cont* **fuelling**, *Am pt & pp* **fueled**, *cont* **fueling**) ◇ *n* -**1.** [gen & AERON] combustible *m*; [coal] charbon *m*; [oil] mazout *m*, fuel *m*, fioul *m*; [wood] bois *m*; AUT carburant *m*; **what ~ do you use?** quel combustible utilisez-vous?; **coal is not a very efficient ~** le charbon n'est pas une source d'énergie très efficace ❑ **nuclear ~** combustible *m* nucléaire. -**2.** *fig*: **to add ~ to the flames** jeter de l'huile sur le feu; **his words were merely ~ to her anger** ses paroles n'ont fait qu'attiser OR qu'aviver sa colère.
◇ *comp* [bill, costs] de chauffage; **~ injector** injecteur *m* de carburant; **~ pump** pompe *f* d'alimentation; **~ tank** [in home] cuve *f* à mazout; [in car] réservoir *m* de carburant OR d'essence; [in ship] soute *f* à mazout OR à fuel.
◇ *vt* -**1.** [furnace] alimenter (en combustible); [car, plane, ship] approvisionner en carburant. -**2.** *fig* [controversy] aviver; **his words only fuelled their anger/their suspicions** ses paroles n'ont servi qu'à aviver leur colère/leurs soupçons.
◆ **fuel up** *vi insep* s'approvisionner OR se ravitailler en carburant OR combustible.

fuel cell *n* élément *m* de conversion.

fuel-efficient *adj* économique, qui ne consomme pas beaucoup.

fuel element *n* élément *m* combustible.

fuel injection *n* injection *f* (de carburant).

fuel oil *n* mazout *m*, fuel *m*, fioul *m*.

fug [fʌg] *n Br* renfermé *m*; **there's a terrible ~ in here** ça sent vraiment le renfermé ici.

fuggy ['fʌgɪ] (*compar* **fuggier**, *superl* **fuggiest**) *adj Br* [house, room] qui sent le renfermé; [space] confiné.

fugitive ['fjuːdʒətɪv] ◇ *n* [escapee] fugitif *m*, -ive *f*, évadé *m*, -e *f*; [refugee] refugié *m*, -e *f*; **she's a ~ from justice** elle fuit la justice, elle est recherchée par la justice.
◇ *adj* -**1.** [debtor, slave] fugitif; **~ slave law** *loi qui obligeait tout citoyen à livrer les esclaves fugitifs à leur propriétaire, avant l'abolition de l'esclavage aux États-Unis.* -**2.** *lit* [beauty, happiness] éphémère, passager; [impression, thought, vision] fugitif, passager.

fugue [fjuːg] *n* MUS & PSYCH fugue *f*.

Fuji ['fuːdʒɪ] *pr n*: **Mount ~** le Fuji-Yama.

Fula(h) ['fuːlə] (*pl inv* OR **Fulahs** OR **Fulas**), **Fulani** [fuː'lɑːnɪ] (*pl inv* OR **Fulanis**) *n* -**1.** [person] Peul *m*, -e *f*. -**2.** LING peul *m*, foulani *m*.

fulcrum ['fʊlkrəm] (*pl* **fulcrums** OR **fulcra** [-krə]) *n* [pivot] pivot *m*, point *m* d'appui; *fig* [prop, support] point *m* d'appui.

fulfil *Br*, **fulfill** *Am* [fʊl'fɪl] (*pt & pp* **fulfilled**, *cont* **fulfilling**) *vt* -**1.** [carry out - ambition, dream, plan] réaliser; [- prophecy, task] accomplir, réaliser; [- promise] tenir; [- duty, obligation] remplir, s'acquitter de. -**2.** [satisfy - condition] remplir; [- norm, regulation] répondre à, obéir à; [- desire, need] satisfaire, répondre à; [- prayer, wish] exaucer; **to ~ o.s.** se réaliser; **she fulfilled herself both as an artist and as a mother** elle s'est épanouie à la fois comme artiste et comme mère; **it's important to feel fulfilled** il est important de se réaliser (dans la vie). -**3.** [complete, finish - prison sentence] achever, terminer. -**4.** COMM [order] exécuter; [contract] remplir, respecter.

fulfilled [fʊl'fɪld] *adj* [life] épanoui, heureux; [person] épanoui, comblé.

fulfilling [fʊl'fɪlɪŋ] *adj* extrêmement satisfaisant.

fulfilment *Br*, **fulfillment** *Am* [fʊl'fɪlmənt] *n* -**1.** [of ambition, dream, wish] réalisation *f*; [of desire] satisfaction *f*; [of plan, condition, contract] exécution *f*; [of duty, prophecy] accomplissement *m*; [of prayer] exaucement *m*. -**2.** [satisfaction] (sentiment *m* de) contentement *m* OR satisfaction *f*; **she gets a sense** OR **feeling of ~ from her work** son travail la comble. -**3.** [of prison sentence] achèvement *m*, fin *f*. -**4.** COMM [of order] exécution *f*.

fulgent ['fʌldʒənt] *adj lit* fulgurant.

full [fʊl] ◇ *adj* -**1.** [completely filled] plein, rempli; **the cup was ~ to the brim** OR **~ to overflowing with coffee** la tasse était pleine à ras bord de café; **this box is only half ~** cette boîte n'est remplie qu'à moitié OR n'est qu'à moitié pleine; **will you open the door for me, my hands are ~** vous voulez bien m'ouvrir la porte, j'ai les mains occupées; **don't talk with your mouth ~** ne parle pas la bouche pleine; **you shouldn't go swimming on a ~ stomach** tu ne devrais pas nager après avoir mangé; **I've got a ~ week ahead of me** j'ai une semaine chargée devant moi. -**2.** *fig*: (to be) **~ of** [filled with] (être) plein de; **her arms were ~ of flowers** elle portait des brassées de fleurs, elle avait des fleurs plein les bras; **her eyes were ~ of tears** elle avait les yeux pleins de larmes; **a look ~ of gratitude** un regard plein OR chargé de reconnaissance; **his look was ~ of admiration** son regard était plein d'admiration; **the children were ~ of excitement** les enfants étaient très excités; **her parents were ~ of hope** ses parents étaient remplis d'espoir; **she's ~ of good ideas** elle est pleine de bonnes idées; **the day was ~ of surprises** la journée a été pleine de surprises; **her letters are ~ of spelling mistakes** ses lettres sont truffées de fautes d'orthographe; **~ of energy** OR **of life** plein de vie; **to be ~ of o.s.** être plein de soi-même OR imbu de sa personne; **he's ~ of his own importance** il est pénétré de sa propre importance; **they/the papers were ~ of news about China** ils/les journaux ne parlaient que de la Chine ❑ **to be ~ of shit**▼ OR **~ of it** *inf* brasser du vent. -**3.** [crowded - room, theatre] comble, plein; [- hotel, restaurant, train] complet; **the hotel was ~ (up)** l'hôtel était complet; **'house ~'** THEAT 'complet'. -**4.** [satiated] rassasié, repu; **I'm ~ (up)!** *Br* je n'en peux plus! -**5.** [complete, whole] tout, complet; **she listened to him for three ~ hours** elle l'a écouté pendant trois heures entières; **the house is a ~ 10 miles from town** la maison est à 15 bons kilomètres OR est au moins à 15 kilomètres de la ville; **in ~ sunlight** en plein soleil; **~ fare** [for adult] plein tarif; [for child] une place entière; **he rose to his ~ height** il s'est dressé de toute sa hauteur; **to fall ~ length** tomber de tout son long; **he leads a very ~ life** il a une vie bien remplie; **I don't want a ~ meal** je ne veux pas un repas entier; **~ member** membre *m* à part entière; **give him your ~ name and address** donnez-lui vos nom, prénom et adresse; **in ~ uniform** en grande tenue; **in ~ view of the cameras/of the teacher** devant les caméras/le professeur ❑ **~ marks**: **to get ~ marks** avoir vingt sur vingt; **I got ~ marks in my maths test** j'ai eu vingt sur vingt à mon examen de maths; **~ marks!** *fig* bravo!; **~ marks for observation!** bravo, vous êtes très observateur! -**6.** [maximum] plein; **make ~ use of this opportunity** mettez bien cette occasion à profit, tirez bien profit de cette occasion; **they had the music on ~ volume** ils avaient mis la musique à fond; **peonies in ~ bloom** des pivoines épanouies; **the trees are in ~ bloom** les arbres sont en fleurs; **it was going ~ blast** [heating] ça chauffait au maximum; [radio, TV] ça marchait à pleins tubes; [car] ça roulait à toute allure; **the orchestra was at ~ strength** l'orchestre était au grand complet; **~ employment** ECON plein emploi *m*; **she caught the ~ force of the blow** elle a reçu le coup de plein fouet. -**7.** [detailed] détaillé; **I didn't get the ~ story** je n'ai pas entendu tous les détails de l'histoire; **he gave us a ~ report** il nous a donné un rapport détaillé; **I asked for ~ information** j'ai demandé des renseignements complets. -**8.** [plump - face] plein, rond; [- figure] rondelet, replet; [- lips] charnu; **dresses designed to flatter the ~er figure** des robes qui mettent en valeur les silhouettes épanouies. -**9.** [ample, wide - clothes] large, ample; **a ~ skirt** une jupe ample OR large. -**10.** [sound] timbré; [voice] étoffé, timbré. -**11.** [flavour] parfumé; [wine] robuste, qui a du corps. -**12.** [brother, sister] germain. -**13.** *Br* MIL: **~ colonel** colonel *m*; **~ general** ≃ général *m* à cinq étoiles.
◇ *adv* -**1.** [entirely, completely] complètement, entièrement; **I turned the heat ~ on** *Br* OR **on ~** *Am* j'ai mis le chauffage à fond; **he put the radio ~ on** *Br* il a mis la radio à fond. -**2.** [directly, exactly] carrément; **the blow caught her ~ in the face** elle a reçu le coup en pleine figure. -**3.** *phr*: **you know ~ well I'm right** tu sais très bien OR parfaitement que j'ai raison; **~ out** *Br* à toute vitesse, à pleins gaz; **to ride ~ out** filer à toute vitesse, foncer.
◆ **in full** *adv phr* intégralement; **she paid in ~** elle a tout payé; **we paid the bill in ~** nous avons payé la facture dans son intégralité; **they refunded my money in ~** ils m'ont entièrement remboursé; **write out your name in ~** écrivez votre nom en toutes lettres; **they published the book in ~** ils ont publié le texte intégral OR dans son intégralité.
◆ **to the full** *adv phr* au plus haut degré, au plus haut point; **enjoy life to the ~** *Br* profitez de la vie au maximum.

fullback ['fʊlbæk] *n* arrière *m*.

full-blooded *adj* -**1.** [hearty - person] vigoureux, robuste; [- effort] vigoureux, puissant; [- argument] violent; **you have our ~ support** vous avez notre soutien inconditionnel. -**2.** [purebred] de pure race, pur sang; **a ~ Socialist** *fig* un socialiste pur et dur.

full-blown *adj* -**1.** [flower] épanoui. -**2.** *fig* [complete] à part entière; **a ~ doctor** *Br* un médecin diplômé; **~ war** la guerre totale; **the discussion developed into a ~ argument** la discussion a dégénéré en véritable dispute. -**3.** MED: **~ AIDS** *Br* sida *m* avéré.

full board *n* pension *f* complète.

full-bodied *adj* [wine] qui a du corps, corsé.

full dress *n* [evening clothes] tenue *f* de soirée; [uniform] grande tenue *f*.
◆ **full-dress** *adj*: **full-dress uniform** tenue *f* de cérémonie, grande tenue *f*; **full-dress rehearsal** THEAT répétition *f* générale.

fuller's earth ['fʊləz-] *n* terre *f* à foulon.

full-face(d) *adj* -**1.** [person] au visage rond. -**2.** [photograph] de face. -**3.** TYPO gras.

full-fashioned *Am* = **fully-fashioned**.

full-fledged *Am* = **fully-fledged**.

full frontal *n photographie montrant une personne nue de face.*
◆ **full-frontal** *adj*: **full-frontal photograph** nu *m* de face *(photographie)*; **full-frontal nudity** [in show] nu *m* intégral.

full-grown *adj* adulte.

full house *n* -**1.** CARDS full *m*. -**2.** THEAT salle *f* comble; **to play to a ~** jouer à guichets fermés.

full-length ◇ *adj* [mirror, portrait] en pied; [curtain, dress] long; a ~ **film** un long métrage.
◇ *adv*: he stretched out ~ on the floor il s'est couché de tout son long par terre.

full moon *n* pleine lune *f*; at ~ à la pleine lune.

fullness ['fʊlnɪs] *n* -**1.** [state] état *m* plein, plénitude *f*; MED [of stomach] plénitude *f*; in the ~ of time avec le temps. -**2.** [of details, information] abondance *f*. -**3.** [of face, figure] rondeur *f*; the ~ of his lips ses lèvres charnues. -**4.** [of skirt, sound, voice] ampleur *f*.

full-page *adj* pleine page; ~ advertisement annonce *f* pleine page.

full professor *n Am* professeur *m* d'université *(titulaire d'une chaire)*.

full sail *adv* toutes voiles dehors; in ~ *fig* toutes voiles dehors, à toute vapeur.

full-scale *adj* -**1.** [model, plan] grandeur nature *(inv)*. -**2.** [all-out - strike, war] total; [- attack, investigation] de grande envergure; the factory starts ~ production this week l'usine commence a tourner à plein rendement cette semaine; ~ fighting MIL bataille *f* rangée.

full score *n* grande partition *f*.

full-size(d) *adj* [animal, plant] adulte; [drawing, model] grandeur nature *(inv)*; ~ car *Am* grosse voiture *f*.

full stop *n Br* -**1.** [pause] arrêt *m* complet; the parade came to a ~ le défilé s'est arrêté; the whole airport came to a ~ toute activité a cessé dans l'aéroport. -**2.** GRAMM point *m*; I won't do it, ~! je ne le ferai pas, un point c'est tout!

full-term ◇ *adj* né à terme.
◇ *adv* à terme.

full-throated [-'θrəʊtɪd] *adj* à pleine gorge.

full time *n* [of working week] temps *m* complet; SPORT fin *f* de match.
◆ **full-time** ◇ *adj* -**1.** [job] à plein temps; she's a full-time translator elle est traductrice à plein temps; it's a full-time job taking care of a baby! ça prend beaucoup de temps de s'occuper d'un bébé! -**2.** SPORT: full-time score score *m* final.
◇ *adv* à plein temps, à temps plein.

full-timer *n personne qui travaille à plein temps*.

fully ['fʊlɪ] *adv* -**1.** [totally - automatic, dressed, satisfied, trained] complètement, entièrement; I ~ understand je comprends très bien OR parfaitement; I ~ agree je suis tout à fait d'accord. -**2.** [thoroughly - answer, examine, explain] à fond, dans le détail. -**3.** [at least] au moins, bien; it was ~ two hours before he arrived au moins deux heures ont passé avant qu'il n'arrive; ~ half of the planes were faulty la moitié des avions au moins OR une bonne moitié des avions étaient défectueux.

fully-fashioned *adj Br* moulant.

fully-fledged *adj* -**1.** [bird] qui a toutes ses plumes. -**2.** *fig* à part entière; a ~ doctor un médecin diplômé; a ~ member un membre à part entière; a ~ atheist un athée pur et dur.

fulmar ['fʊlmə^r] *n* fulmar *m*.

fulminate ['fʌlmɪneɪt] ◇ *vi fml* fulminer, pester; he ~d against OR at his students il fulminait OR pestait contre ses étudiants; the preacher ~d against the abuse of drugs le pasteur fulminait contre l'abus de stupéfiants.
◇ *n* fulminate *m*; ~ of mercury fulminate *m* de mercure.

fulness ['fʊlnɪs] = **fullness**.

fulsome ['fʊlsəm] *adj* [apology, thanks] excessif, exagéré; [welcome] plein d'effusions; [compliments, praise] dithyrambique.

fumarole ['fjuːmərəʊl] *n* fumerolle *f*.

fumble ['fʌmbl] ◇ *vi* [grope - in the dark] tâtonner; [- in pocket, purse] fouiller; he ~d (about OR around) in the dark for the light switch il a cherché l'interrupteur à tâtons dans l'obscurité; she ~d in her bag for a pen elle a fouillé dans son sac pour trouver un stylo; to ~ for words *fig* chercher ses mots.
◇ *vt* -**1.** [handle awkwardly] manier gauchement OR maladroitement; she ~d her way down the dark corridor elle chercha son chemin à tâtons le long du couloir sombre; he ~d his lines il récita son texte en bafouillant. -**2.** SPORT [miss - catch] attraper OR arrêter maladroitement.
◇ *n* -**1.** [grope] tâtonnements *mpl*. -**2.** SPORT [bad catch] prise *f* de balle maladroite.

fume [fjuːm] ◇ *n (usu pl)*: ~s [gen] exhalaisons *fpl*, émanations *fpl*; [of gas, liquid] vapeurs *fpl*; factory ~s fumées *fpl* d'usine; tobacco ~s fumée *f* (de cigarette).
◇ *vi* -**1.** [gas] émettre OR exhaler des vapeurs; [liquid] fumer. -**2.** [person] rager; I'm fuming because I haven't been invited je suis furieux de ne pas avoir été invité; the boss is fuming le patron est furieux.
◇ *vt* -**1.** [treat with fumes] fumer, fumiger. -**2.** [rage]: "this is your fault", she ~d «c'est de ta faute», dit-elle d'un ton rageur.

fume cupboard *n* sorbonne *f* (de laboratoire).

fumigate ['fjuːmɪgeɪt] *vi* & *vt* désinfecter par fumigation, fumiger *fml*.

fun [fʌn] (*pt* & *pp* funned, *cont* funning) ◇ *n* -**1.** [amusement] amusement *m*; [pleasure] plaisir *m*; to have ~ s'amuser; we had ~ at the party nous nous sommes bien amusés à la soirée; have ~! amusez-vous bien!; what ~! ce que c'est drôle OR amusant!; I don't see the ~ in kicking a ball round a field je ne trouve pas ça drôle de faire le tour d'un terrain en donnant des coups de pied dans un ballon; skiing is good OR great ~ c'est très amusant de faire du ski; it's ~ to go cycling c'est marrant de faire du vélo; she's tremendous ~ elle est drôlement marrante; her brother is a lot of ~ son frère est très drôle; the children got a lot of ~ out of the bicycle les enfants se sont bien amusés avec le vélo; I'm learning Chinese for ~ OR for the ~ of it j'apprends le chinois pour mon plaisir; he only went for the ~ of it il n'y est allé que pour s'amuser; just for the ~ of it he pretended to be the boss histoire de rire, il a fait semblant d'être le patron; are you reading Marx for ~? c'est par plaisir que tu lis Marx?; his sister spoiled the ~ sa sœur a joué les trouble-fête OR les rabat-joie; I don't want to spoil your ~, but could you keep the noise down? je ne veux pas jouer les trouble-fête, mais est-ce que vous pourriez faire un peu moins de bruit?; having to wear a crash helmet takes all the ~ out of motorcycling devoir porter un casque gâche tout le plaisir qu'on a à faire de la moto; her boyfriend walked in and that's when the ~ began *iron* son copain est entré et c'est là qu'on a commencé à rire; the president has become a figure of ~ le président est devenu la risée de tous; to make ~ of OR to poke ~ at sb se moquer de qqn; ~ and games: we'll have a children's party with lots of ~ and games on va organiser une fête pour les enfants avec des tas de jeux OR divertissements; I've had enough of your ~ and games [foolish behaviour] j'en ai assez de tes blagues OR farces; there'll be some ~ and games if his wife finds out ça va mal aller si sa femme l'apprend. -**2.** [playfulness] enjouement *m*, gaieté *f*; to be full of ~ être plein d'entrain OR très gai; he said it in ~ il l'a dit pour rire OR en plaisantant.
◇ *adj inf* rigolo, marrant; he's a ~ guy OR person il est rigolo OR marrant.
◇ *vi inf Am* plaisanter, badiner; I was just funning! c'était pour rire!

funambulist [fjuː'næmbjʊlɪst] *n* funambule *mf*.

Funchal [fʊn'ʃɑːl] *pr n* Funchal.

function ['fʌŋkʃn] ◇ *vi* fonctionner, marcher; this room ~s as a study cette pièce sert de bureau OR fait fonction de bureau.
◇ *n* -**1.** [role - of machine, organ] fonction *f*; [- of person] fonction *f*, charge *f*; vital ~s MED fonctions vitales; it is the ~ of a lawyer to provide sound legal advice l'avocat a pour fonction OR tâche de donner de bons conseils juridiques. -**2.** [working] fonctionnement *m*; they tested the heart ~ ils ont examiné le fonctionnement du cœur. -**3.** [ceremony] cérémonie *f*; [reception] réception *f*; [meeting] réunion *f*. -**4.** [gen, LING & MATH] fonction *f*; x is a ~ of y x est une fonction de y. -**5.** COMPUT fonction *f*.

functional ['fʌŋkʃənl] *adj* -**1.** [gen, MATH & PSYCH] fonctionnel; ~ illiterate *personne qui, sans être tout à fait analphabète, est incapable de faire face à la vie de tous les jours dans une société industrialisée*. -**2.** [in working order]: the machine is no longer ~ la machine ne marche plus OR ne fonctionne plus.

functionalism ['fʌŋkʃnəlɪzm] *n* fonctionnalisme *m*.

functionalist ['fʌŋkʃnəlɪst] ◇ *adj* fonctionnaliste.
◇ *n* fonctionnaliste *mf*.

functionary ['fʌŋkʃnərɪ] (*pl* **functionaries**) *n* [employee] employé *m*, -e *f (dans une administration)*; [civil servant] fonctionnaire *mf*.

function key *n* touche *f* de fonction.

function room *n* salle *f* de réception.

function word *n* mot *m* fonctionnel.

fund [fʌnd] ◇ *n* -**1.** [reserve of money] fonds *m*, caisse *f*; they've set up a ~ for the earthquake victims ils ont ouvert une souscription en faveur des victimes du séisme. -**2.** *fig* fond *m*, réserve *f*; she has a large ~ of amusing anecdotes elle a tout un répertoire d'anecdotes amusantes; a ~ of knowledge un trésor de connaissances.
◇ *vt* -**1.** [provide money for] financer. -**2.** FIN [debt] consolider.
◆ **funds** *npl* [cash resources] fonds *mpl*; public ~s fonds public; secret ~s une caisse noire; we spent all of our scarce ~s on housing nous avons dépensé le peu de capitaux dont nous disposions pour le logement; to be in/out of ~s être/ne pas être en fonds; I'm a bit short of ~s je n'ai pas beaucoup d'argent; insufficient ~s [in banking] défaut *m* de provision.

fundament ['fʌndəmənt] *n* -**1.** [of building] fondation *f*. -**2.** *lit* [principle] principe *m* de base, fondement *m*. -**3.** *hum* [buttocks] fondement *m*.

fundamental [,fʌndə'mentl] ◇ *adj* -**1.** [basic - concept, principle, rule] fondamental, de base; [- difference, quality] fondamental, essentiel; [- change, mistake] fondamental; a knowledge of economics is ~ to a proper understanding of this problem il est essentiel OR fondamental d'avoir des connaissances en économie pour bien comprendre ce problème; ~ research recherche *f* fondamentale. -**2.** [central] fondamental, principal; it's of ~ importance c'est d'une importance capitale. -**3.** MUS fondamental.
◇ *n* -**1.** *(usu pl)*: the ~s of chemistry les principes *mpl* de base de la chimie; when it comes to the ~s quand on en vient à l'essentiel. -**2.** MUS fondamentale *f*.

fundamentalism [,fʌndə'mentəlɪzm] *n* [gen & RELIG] fondamentalisme *m*; [Muslim] intégrisme *m*.

fundamentalist [,fʌndə'mentəlɪst] ◇ *adj* [gen & RELIG] fondamentaliste; [Muslim] intégriste.
◇ *n* [gen & RELIG] fondamentaliste *mf*; [Muslim] intégriste *mf*.

fundamentally [,fʌndə'mentəlɪ] *adv* -**1.** [at bottom] fondamentalement, essentiellement; she seems hard but ~ she's good-hearted elle a l'air dure, mais au fond elle a bon cœur. -**2.** [completely]: I disagree ~ with his policies je suis radicalement OR fondamentalement opposé à sa politique.

fundamental particle *n* particule *f* élémentaire.

fundholder ['fʌndhəʊldə^r] *n cabinet médical ayant obtenu le droit de gérer son propre budget auprès du système de sécurité sociale britannique*.

funding ['fʌndɪŋ] *n (U)* fonds *mpl*, financement *m*.

fundraiser ['fʌnd,reɪzə^r] *n* [person] collecteur *m*, -trice *f* de fonds; [event] *projet organisé pour collecter des fonds*.

fund-raising ◇ *n* collecte *f* de fonds.
◇ *adj* [dinner, project, sale] organisé pour collecter des fonds.
funeral ['fjuːnərəl] ◇ *n* -**1.** [service] enterrement *m*, obsèques *fpl*; [more formal] funérailles *fpl*; [in announcement] obsèques *fpl*; [burial] enterrement *m* ☐ it's OR that's your ~! *inf* débrouille-toi!, c'est ton affaire! -**2.** [procession - on foot] cortège *m* funèbre; [- in cars] convoi *m* mortuaire.
◇ *adj* funèbre.
funeral director *n* entrepreneur *m* de pompes funèbres.
funeral home *Am* = **funeral parlour**.
funeral march *n* marche *f* funèbre.
funeral parlour *n* entreprise *f* de pompes funèbres.
funeral procession *n* [on foot] cortège *m* funèbre; [in cars] convoi *m* mortuaire.
funeral pyre *n* bûcher *m* (funéraire).
funeral service *n* service *m* OR office *m* funèbre.
funerary ['fjuːnərərɪ] *adj fml* funéraire.
funereal [fjuː'nɪərɪəl] *adj* [atmosphere, expression] funèbre, lugubre; [voice] sépulcral, lugubre; [pace] lent, mesuré.
funfair ['fʌnfeəʳ] *n* fête *f* foraine.
fun fur *n* similifourrure *f*.
fungal ['fʌŋgl] *adj* fongique.
fungi ['fʌŋgaɪ] *pl* → **fungus**.
fungicide ['fʌndʒɪsaɪd] *n* fongicide *m*.
fungoid ['fʌŋgɔɪd] *adj* fongique.
fungus ['fʌŋgəs] (*pl* **fungi** [-gaɪ]) ◇ *n* BOT champignon *m*; [mould] moisissure *f*; MED fongus *m*.
◇ *comp*: ~ infection fongus *m*.
funicular [fjuː'nɪkjʊləʳ] ◇ *adj* funiculaire; ~ railway funiculaire *m*.
◇ *n* funiculaire *m*.
funk [fʌŋk] ◇ *n* -**1.** MUS musique *f* funk, funk *m inv*. -**2.** *inf dated* [fear] trouille *f*, frousse *f*; [depression] découragement *m*; to be in a ~ [afraid] avoir la trouille; [depressed] avoir le cafard; to be in a blue ~ avoir une peur bleue. -**3.** *dated* [coward] froussard *m*, -e *f*. -**4.** *inf Am* [stink] puanteur *f*, odeur *f* infecte; what a ~! ce que ça pue!
◇ *vt* -**1.** [be afraid of] ne pas avoir le courage de; she had her chance and she ~ed it elle a eu sa chance mais elle s'est dégonflée; I ~ed telling him je n'ai pas eu le courage de lui dire. -**2.** *(usu pass)* [make afraid] ficher la frousse à.
◇ *adj* funky *(inv)*.
funky *inf* ['fʌŋkɪ] (*compar* **funkier**, *superl* **funkiest**) *adj* -**1.** *esp Am* [excellent] génial, super; [fashionable] branché, dans le vent. -**2.** MUS funky *(inv)*; ~ jazz jazz *m* funky. -**3.** *Am* [foul] qui pue.
fun-loving *adj* qui aime s'amuser OR rire.
funnel ['fʌnl] (*Br pt & pp* **funnelled**, *cont* **funnelling**, *Am pt & pp* **funneled**, *cont* **funneling**)
◇ *n* -**1.** [utensil] entonnoir *m*. -**2.** [smokestack] cheminée *f*.
◇ *vt* [liquid] (faire) passer dans un entonnoir; [crowd, funds] canaliser.
◇ *vi*: the crowd funnelled out of the gates la foule s'est écoulée par les grilles.
funnies ['fʌnɪz] *npl*: the ~ les bandes *fpl* dessinées *(dans un journal)*.
funnily ['fʌnɪlɪ] *adv* -**1.** [oddly] curieusement, bizarrement; ~ enough, I was just thinking of you c'est drôle OR chose curieuse, je pensais justement à toi. -**2.** [in a funny manner] drôlement, comiquement.
funny ['fʌnɪ] ◇ *adj* -**1.** [amusing] amusant, drôle, comique; I don't think that's ~ je ne trouve pas ça drôle; it's not ~ ce n'est pas drôle; you looked so ~ in that hat tu étais si drôle OR amusant avec ce chapeau; she didn't see the ~ side of it elle n'a pas vu le côté comique de la situation; he's trying to be ~ il cherche à faire de l'esprit; stop trying to be ~! ce n'est pas le moment de plaisanter!; was it ~ ha-ha or ~ peculiar? *inf* c'était drôle-rigolo ou drôle-bizarre? -**2.** [odd] bizarre, curieux, drôle; she has some ~ ideas about work elle a de drôles d'idées sur le travail; the wine tastes ~ le vin a un drôle de goût; I think it's ~ that he should turn up now je trouve (ça) bizarre qu'il arrive maintenant; the ~ thing (about it) is that she claimed she was away ce qu'il y a de bizarre OR de curieux c'est qu'elle ait prétendu ne pas être là; the ~ thing is I just phoned you c'est drôle, je viens juste de t'appeler; she's ~ that way *inf* elle est comme ça; that's ~, I thought I heard the phone ring c'est curieux OR drôle, j'ai cru entendre le téléphone; the whole conversation left me with a ~ feeling la conversation m'a fait un drôle d'effet; I've got a ~ feeling that's not the last we've seen of her j'ai comme l'impression qu'on va la revoir; I feel a bit ~ *inf* [odd] je me sens tout drôle OR tout chose; [ill] je ne suis pas dans mon assiette, je suis un peu patraque; he went all ~ when he heard the news *inf* la nouvelle l'a rendu tout chose; the computer went all ~ *inf* l'ordinateur s'est détraqué. -**3.** [dubious, suspicious] louche; none of your ~ business! *inf*, don't try anything ~! ne fais pas le malin!; there's something ~ OR there's some ~ business *inf* going on il se passe quelque chose de louche OR de pas très catholique; there's something ~ about her wanting to see him ça me paraît louche qu'elle veuille le voir; there's something ~ about that man cet homme n'a pas l'air très catholique. -**4.** *inf Br* [mad] fou; he went ~ in the head il a perdu la tête.
◇ *n inf* [joke] blague *f*; to pull a ~ on sb *Am* jouer un tour à qqn, faire une farce à qqn.
funny bone *inf n* ANAT petit juif *m*.
funny farm *inf n euph* maison *f* de fous.
fun run *n* course *f* à pied pour amateurs *(pour collecter des fonds)*.
fur [fɜːʳ] (*pt & pp* **furred**, *cont* **furring**) ◇ *n* -**1.** [on animal] poil *m*, pelage *m*, fourrure *f*; her remark made the ~ fly OR set the ~ flying ça a fait du grabuge quand elle a dit ça; the ~ really flew! ça a bardé! -**2.** [coat, pelt] fourrure *f*; she was dressed in expensive ~s elle portait des fourrures de prix. -**3.** [in kettle, pipe] incrustation *f*, (dépôt *m* de) tartre *m*. -**4.** MED [on tongue] enduit *m*.
◇ *vt* -**1.** [person] habiller de fourrures. -**2.** [kettle, pipe] entartrer, incruster. -**3.** MED [tongue] empâter.
◇ *vi*: to ~ (up) [kettle, pipe] s'entartrer, s'incruster.
furbelow ['fɜːbɪləʊ] *n* falbala *m pej*; frills and ~s des falbalas, des fanfreluches *fpl pej*.
furbish ['fɜːbɪʃ] *vt* [polish] fourbir, astiquer; [renovate] remettre à neuf.
furious ['fjʊərɪəs] *adj* -**1.** [angry] furieux; she was ~ with me for being late elle m'en voulait de mon retard; he was ~ when he saw the car il s'est mis en colère quand il a vu la voiture; a ~ look un regard furibond. -**2.** [raging, violent - sea, storm] déchaîné; [- effort, struggle] acharné; [- pace, speed] fou.
furiously ['fjʊərɪəslɪ] *adv* -**1.** [answer, look] furieusement. -**2.** [fight, work] avec acharnement; [drive, run] à une allure folle.
furl [fɜːl] *vt* [flag, umbrella] rouler; NAUT [sail] ferler, serrer.
furlong ['fɜːlɒŋ] *n* furlong *m (= 201,17 mètres)*.
furlough ['fɜːləʊ] ◇ *n Am* -**1.** MIL [leave of absence] permission *f*, congé *m*; to be on ~ être en permission. -**2.** [laying off] mise *f* à pied provisoire.
◇ *vt* -**1.** MIL [grant leave of absence] accorder une permission à. -**2.** *Am* [lay off] mettre à pied provisoirement.
furnace ['fɜːnɪs] *n* [for central heating] chaudière *f*; INDUST fourneau *m*, four *m*; the office was like a ~ *fig* le bureau était une vraie fournaise.
furnish ['fɜːnɪʃ] *vt* -**1.** [supply - food, provisions] fournir; [- information, reason] fournir, donner; they ~ed us with the translation il nous ont donné la traduction; they ~ed the ship with provisions ils ont ravitaillé le navire. -**2.** [house, room] meubler; she ~ed her house with antiques elle a meublé sa maison avec des antiquités; a comfortably ~ed house une maison confortablement aménagée.
furnished ['fɜːnɪʃt] *adj* [room, apartment] meublé.
furnishing fabric *n* tissu *m* d'ameublement.
furnishings ['fɜːnɪʃɪŋz] *npl* -**1.** [furniture] meubles *mpl*, mobilier *m*, ameublement *m*. -**2.** *Am* [clothing] habits *mpl*, vêtements *mpl*; [accessories] accessoires *fpl*.
furniture ['fɜːnɪtʃəʳ] ◇ *n (U)* -**1.** [for house] meubles *mpl*, mobilier *m*, ameublement *m*; a piece of ~ un meuble; antique ~ des meubles anciens, du mobilier ancien; living room ~ un salon, des meubles OR du mobilier de salon; the room has little ~ il n'y a pas beaucoup de meubles dans la chambre; Louis XV ~ du mobilier OR des meubles Louis XV; she feels as though she's just part of the ~ *inf* elle a l'impression de faire partie des meubles; he treats me like I was part of the ~ *inf* pour lui, je fais partie des meubles. -**2.** NAUT & TYPO garniture *f*. -**3.** [accessories]: street ~ mobilier *m* urbain; door ~ *éléments décoratifs pour portes d'entrée*.
◇ *comp* [shop, store] d'ameublement, de meubles; ~ van camion *m* de déménagement; ~ polish encaustique *f*, cire *f*.
furniture beetle *n* vrillette *f*.
furore [fjʊ'rɔːrɪ] *Br*, **furor** ['fjʊrər] *Am* *n* scandale *m*, tumulte *m*; to cause OR to create a ~ faire un scandale.
furred [fɜːd] *adj* -**1.** [animal] à poils. -**2.** [kettle, pipe] entartré; [tongue] pâteux, chargé.
furrier ['fʌrɪəʳ] *n* fourreur *m*.
furrow ['fʌrəʊ] ◇ *n* [in field] sillon *m*; [in garden] rayon *m*, sillon *m*; [on forehead] ride *f*, sillon *m*; [on sea] sillage *m*.
◇ *vt* -**1.** [soil, surface] sillonner. -**2.** [brow] rider.
◇ *vi* se plisser; her brow ~ed son front se plissa.
furrowed ['fʌrəʊd] *adj* ridé, sillonné de rides; he looked up with ~ed brow il a levé les yeux en plissant le front.
furry ['fɜːrɪ] (*compar* **furrier**, *superl* **furriest**) *adj* -**1.** [animal] à poils; [fabric] qui ressemble à de la fourrure; [toy] en peluche. -**2.** [kettle, pipe] entartré; [tongue] pâteux, chargé.
fur seal *n* loutre *f*.
further ['fɜːðəʳ] ◇ *adv* -**1.** [at a greater distance in space, time] plus loin; I walked ~ than I intended to je suis allé plus loin que je n'en avais l'intention; ~ to the south plus au sud; she's never been ~ north than Leicester elle n'est jamais allée plus au nord que Leicester; ~ along the beach plus loin sur la plage; how much ~ is it? c'est encore loin?; have you much ~ to go? vous allez encore loin?; he got ~ and ~ away from the shore il a continué à s'éloigner de la rive; she moved ~ back elle a reculé encore plus; ~ back than 1960 avant 1960; ~ forward, ~ on plus en avant, plus loin; she's ~ on than the rest of the students *fig* elle est en avance sur les autres étudiants; I've got no ~ with finding a nanny mes recherches pour trouver une nourrice n'ont pas beaucoup avancé; nothing could be ~ from the truth rien n'est moins vrai; nothing could be ~ from my mind j'étais bien loin de penser à ça. -**2.** [more] plus, davantage; I have nothing ~ to say je n'ai rien à ajouter, je n'ai rien d'autre OR rien de plus à dire; don't try my patience any ~ ne pousse pas ma patience à bout, n'abuse pas de ma patience; the police want to question him ~ la police veut encore l'interroger; she heard nothing ~ from her sister elle n'a pas eu d'autres nouvelles de sa sœur; I want nothing ~ to do with him je ne veux plus avoir affaire à lui; until you hear ~ jusqu'à nouvel avis; unless you hear ~ sauf avis contraire. -**3.** [to a greater degree]: her

arrival only complicated things ~ son arrivée n'a fait que compliquer les choses; play was ~ interrupted by rain le jeu fut à nouveau interrompu par la pluie. -4. *fml* [moreover] de plus, en outre; and ~ I think it best we don't see each other again et de plus OR et en outre je crois qu'il vaut mieux que nous ne nous voyions plus. -5. *phr*: I would go even ~ and say he's a genius j'irais même jusqu'à dire que c'est un génie; we need to go ~ into the matter il faut approfondir davantage la question; I'll go no ~ [move] je n'irai pas plus loin; [say nothing more] je vais en rester là; this information must go no ~ cette information doit rester entre nous OR ne doit pas être divulguée.

◇ *adj* -1. [more distant] plus éloigné, plus lointain; she walked to the ~ end of the room elle est allée à l'autre bout de la pièce. -2. [additional - comments, negotiations] additionnel, autre; [- information, news] supplémentaire, complémentaire; do you have any ~ questions? avez-vous d'autres questions à poser?; I need a ~ nine hundred pounds j'ai encore besoin de neuf cents livres; upon ~ consideration à la réflexion, après plus ample réflexion; I have no ~ use for it je ne m'en sers plus, je n'en ai plus besoin OR l'usage; she needs one or two ~ details elle a besoin d'un ou deux autres petits renseignements; I would like ~ details of the programme j'aimerais avoir quelques précisions OR indications supplémentaires sur le programme; for ~ information, phone this number pour tout renseignement complémentaire, appelez ce numéro; please send me ~ information concerning the project veuillez m'envoyer de plus amples renseignements sur OR concernant le projet; without ~ delay sans autre délai, sans plus attendre; until ~ notice jusqu'à nouvel ordre ❑ without ~ ado sans plus de cérémonie.

◇ *vt* [cause, one's interests] avancer, servir, favoriser; [career] servir, favoriser; to ~ one's chances augmenter ses chances.

◆ **further to** *prep phr fml* suite à; ~ to your letter of July 12 suite à votre lettre du 12 juillet; ~ to our discussion/conversation suite à notre discussion/conversation.

furtherance ['fɜːðərəns] *n fml*: in ~ of their policy pour servir leur politique.

further education ◇ *n Br* enseignement *m* postscolaire.

◇ *comp* [class, college] d'éducation permanente.

furthermore [ˌfɜːðə'mɔːʳ] *adv* en outre, par ailleurs.

furthermost ['fɜːðəməʊst] *adj lit* le plus éloigné, le plus lointain.

furthest ['fɜːðɪst] ◇ *adv* le plus loin; her house is the ~ away sa maison est la plus éloignée.

◇ *adj* le plus lointain, le plus éloigné; it's 10 miles at the ~ il y a 16 kilomètres au plus OR au maximum.

furtive ['fɜːtɪv] *adj* [behaviour, look] furtif; [person] sournois.

furtively ['fɜːtɪvlɪ] *adv* furtivement, en douce.

fury ['fjʊərɪ] (*pl* furies) *n* -1. [anger] fureur *f*, furie *f*; to be in a ~ être dans une colère noire OR en furie; he was beside himself with ~ il était hors de lui. -2. [violence - of storm, wind] violence *f*; [- of fight, struggle] acharnement *m*; to work like ~ *Br* travailler d'arrache-pied OR avec acharnement; to run like ~ *Br* courir ventre à terre; it's raining like ~ *Br* il pleut des cordes. -3. [frenzy] frénésie *f*; a ~ of activity une période d'activité débordante.

◆ **Furies** *npl* MYTH: the Furies les Furies *fpl*, les Érynies *fpl*.

furze [fɜːz] *n (U)* ajoncs *mpl*.

fuse [fjuːz] ◇ *vi* -1. [melt] fondre; [melt together] fusionner; the two metals ~d (together) les deux métaux ont fusionné. -2. [join] s'unifier, fusionner; at some point the aims of the parties ~d à un moment donné les objectifs des partis se sont rejoints OR confondus. -3. *Br* ELEC: the lights OR the appliance ~d les plombs ont sauté.

◇ *vt* -1. [melt] fondre; [melt together] fondre, mettre en fusion. -2. [unite] fusionner, unifier, amalgamer; an attempt to ~ traditional and modern methods une tentative pour associer les méthodes modernes et traditionnelles. -3. *Br* ELEC: to ~ the lights faire sauter les plombs. -4. [explosive] amorcer.

◇ *n* -1. ELEC plomb *m*, fusible *m*; to blow a ~ faire sauter un plomb OR un fusible; the ~ keeps blowing les plombs n'arrêtent pas de sauter; there's a ~ blown un des fusibles a sauté || *fig*: to blow a ~ se mettre dans une colère noire; she nearly blew a ~ when we broke the window elle a failli exploser quand on a cassé le carreau. -2. [of explosive] amorce *f*, détonateur *m*; MIN cordeau *m*; to have a short ~ *inf* être soupe au lait, se mettre facilement en rogne.

fuse box *n* boite *f* à fusibles, coupe-circuit *m inv*; AUT porte-fusible *m*.

fused [fjuːzd] *adj* [kettle, plug] avec fusible incorporé.

fuselage ['fjuːzəlɑːʒ] *n* fuselage *m*.

fusel oil [ˌfjʊːzl-] *n* fusel *m*, huile *f* de fusel.

fuse wire *n* fusible *m*.

fusible ['fjuːzəbl] *adj* fusible; ~ alloy OR metal alliage *m* fusible.

fusilier [ˌfjuːzə'lɪəʳ] *n* fusilier *m*.

fusillade [ˌfjuːzə'leɪd] *n* fusillade *f*.

fusion ['fjuːʒn] *n* METALL fonte *f*, fusion *f*; PHYS fusion *f*; *fig* [of ideas, parties] fusion *f*, fusionnement *m*.

fusion bomb *n* bombe *f* thermonucléaire OR à hydrogène.

fusion reactor *n* réacteur *m* nucléaire.

fuss [fʌs] ◇ *n* -1. *(U)* [bother] histoires *fpl*; what a lot of ~ about nothing! que d'histoires pour rien!; all that ~ over a game of football! tout ça pour un match de foot!; after a great deal of ~ she accepted après avoir fait toutes sortes de manières, elle a accepté. -2. [state of agitation] panique *f*; don't get into a ~ over it! ne t'affole pas pour ça! -3. *phr*: to make OR to kick up *inf* a ~ about OR over sthg faire des histoires OR tout un plat au sujet de qqch; he kicked up quite a ~ about the bill il a fait toute une histoire pour la facture; people are making a ~ about the new road les gens protestent contre la nouvelle route; you should have made a ~ about it tu n'aurais pas dû laisser passer ça; to make a ~ of OR over sb être aux petits soins pour qqn; they made quite a ~ over her when she went to visit them ils ont été aux petits soins pour elle quand elle est allée les voir; he likes to be made a ~ over il aime bien qu'on fasse grand cas de lui.

◇ *vi* -1. [become agitated] s'agiter; [worry] s'inquiéter, se tracasser; [rush around] s'affairer; she kept ~ing with her hair elle n'arrêtait pas de tripoter ses cheveux; to ~ over sb être aux petits soins pour qqn; he ~ed over his grandchildren il était aux petits soins pour ses petits-enfants; stop ~ing over me! laisse-moi tranquille!; don't ~, we'll be on time ne t'en fais pas, on sera à l'heure. -2. *inf Br phr*: do you want meat or fish? – I'm not ~ed veux-tu de la viande ou du poisson? – ça m'est égal; I don't think he's particularly ~ed whether we go or not je crois que cela lui est égal qu'on y aille ou pas.

◇ *vt esp Am* agacer, embêter.

◆ **fuss about** *Br*, **fuss around** *vi insep* [rush around] s'affairer.

fussbudget ['fʌsˌbʌdʒət] *Am* = **fusspot**.

fussily ['fʌsɪlɪ] *adv* -1. [fastidiously] de façon méticuleuse OR tatillonne; [nervously] avec anxiété. -2. [over-ornate] de façon tarabiscotée.

fussiness ['fʌsɪnɪs] *n* -1. [fastidiousness] côté *m* tatillon. -2. [ornateness - of decoration] tarabiscotage *m*.

fusspot *inf* ['fʌspɒt] *n* -1. [worrier] anxieux *m*, -euse *f*; don't be such a ~ arrête de te faire du mauvais sang. -2. [fastidious person] tatillon *m*, -onne *f*; she's such a ~! qu'est-ce qu'elle peut être difficile!

fussy ['fʌsɪ] (*compar* fussier, *superl* fussiest) *adj* -1. [fastidious] tatillon, pointilleux; her daughter is very ~ about what she eats sa fille est très difficile sur la nourriture; he's ~ about his food/about what he wears il fait très attention à ce qu'il mange/à ce qu'il porte; where shall we go? – I'm not ~ où est-ce qu'on va? – ça m'est égal. -2. [over-ornate - decoration] trop chargé, tarabiscoté; [- style] ampoulé, qui manque de simplicité.

fustian ['fʌstɪən] *n* [fabric] futaine *f*; *fig* & *lit* [bombast] grandiloquence *f*.

fusty ['fʌstɪ] (*compar* fustier, *superl* fustiest) *adj* [room] qui sent le renfermé; [smell] de renfermé, de moisi; *fig* [idea, outlook] vieux jeu.

futile [*Br* 'fjuːtaɪl, *Am* 'fuːtl] *adj* [action, effort] vain; [remark, question] futile, vain; [idea] futile, creux; it's ~ trying to reason with him il est inutile d'essayer de lui faire entendre raison; all our attemps were ~ toutes nos tentatives ont été inutiles OR vaines.

futility [fjuː'tɪlətɪ] (*pl* futilities) *n* [of action, effort] futilité *f*, inutilité *f*; [of remark, question] inanité *f*; [of gesture] futilité *f*.

futon ['fuːtɒn] *n* futon *m*.

future ['fjuːtʃəʳ] ◇ *n* -1. [time ahead] avenir *m*; in (the) ~ à l'avenir; sometime in the near ~ OR in the not so distant ~ [gen] bientôt; [more formal] dans un avenir proche; in the distant ~ dans un avenir lointain; the ~ is still uncertain l'avenir est encore incertain; young people today don't have much of a ~ les jeunes d'aujourd'hui n'ont pas beaucoup d'avenir; he has a great ~ ahead of him as an actor c'est un comédien plein d'avenir; she wants to assure her son's ~ elle veut assurer un bon avenir à son fils; there is a ~ ahead for bilingual people in publishing le monde de l'édition offre des possibilités d'avenir pour les personnes bilingues; there's no ~ in farming l'agriculture n'est pas un métier d'avenir; I'll have to see what the ~ holds OR has in store on verra ce que l'avenir me réserve; you have to think of the ~ il faut songer à l'avenir -2. GRAMM futur *m*; the ~ of the verb "to be" le futur du verbe «être».

◇ *adj* -1. futur; ~ generations les générations futures OR à venir; my ~ wife ma future épouse OR femme; current and ~ needs les besoins actuels et futurs; at a ~ date à une date ultérieure; I kept it for ~ reference je l'ai conservé comme document; the ~ tense GRAMM le futur. -2. COMM [delivery, estate] à terme.

◆ **in future** *adv phr* à l'avenir; I shan't offer my advice in ~! je ne donnerai plus de conseils désormais!; in ~, please ask before taking anything à l'avenir, je vous prie de demander la permission avant de prendre quoi que ce soit.

futureless ['fjuːtʃəlɪs] *adj* sans avenir.

future perfect *n* futur *m* antérieur.

futures ['fjuːtʃəz] *npl* ST. EX marchandises *fpl* achetées à terme; the ~ market le marché à terme; sugar ~ sucre *m* (acheté) à terme.

futurism ['fjuːtʃərɪzm] *n* futurisme *m*.

futurist ['fjuːtʃərɪst] ◇ *adj* futuriste.

◇ *n* futuriste *mf*.

futuristic [ˌfjuːtʃə'rɪstɪk] *adj* futuriste.

futurity [fjuː'tjʊərətɪ] (*pl* futurities) *n fml* -1. [future time] avenir *m*, futur *m*. -2. [event] événement *m* futur OR à venir.

futurologist [ˌfjuːtʃə'rɒlədʒɪst] *n* futurologue *mf*.

futurology [ˌfjuːtʃə'rɒlədʒɪ] *n* futurologie *f* prospective *f*.

fuze [fjuːz] *Am* = **fuse** *n*.

fuzz [fʌz] ◇ *n* *(U)* -1. [down - on peach] duvet *m* [- on body] duvet *m*, poils *mpl* fins; [- on head]

duvet *m*, cheveux *mpl* fins. -**2.** [frizzy hair] cheveux *mpl* crépus OR frisottants. -**3.** [on blanket, sweater] peluches *fpl*. -**4.** ▽ [police]: the ~ les flics *mpl*. -**5.** *Am* [lint] peluches *fpl*.
◇ *vt* -**1.** [hair] frisotter. -**2.** [image, sight] rendre flou.
◇ *vi* -**1.** [hair] frisotter. -**2.** [image, sight] devenir flou. -**3.** [blanket, sweater] pelucher.

fuzzball ['fʌzbɔːl] *n* [on garment] peluche *f*; [on floor] mouton *m*.

fuzzy ['fʌzɪ] (*compar* fuzzier, *superl* fuzziest) *adj* -**1.** [cloth, garment] peluché, pelucheux. -**2.** [image, picture] flou. -**3.** [confused - ideas] confus; **my head feels a bit ~ today** j'ai un peu la tête qui tourne aujourd'hui. -**4.** [hair] crépu, frisottant.

fuzzy-wuzzy▼ ['fʌzɪˌwʌzɪ] *n Br terme raciste et vieilli désignant un Noir.*

fwd. *written abbr of* forward.

fwy *written abbr of* freeway.

FY *n abbr of* fiscal year.

FYI (*written abbr of* for your information) à titre indicatif.

g (*pl* g's OR gs), **G** (*pl* G's OR Gs) [dʒiː] *n* [letter] g *m*, G *m*.

g -**1.** (*written abbr of* gram) g. -**2.** (*written abbr of* gravity) g.

G ◇ *n* -**1.** MUS [note] sol *m*. -**2.** *inf Am* (*abbr of* grand) *mille dollars*.
◇ -**1.** (*written abbr of* good) B. -**2.** *Am* (*written abbr of* general (audience)) *tous publics*.

GA *written abbr of* Georgia.

gab *inf* [gæb] (*pt* & *pp* gabbed, *cont* gabbing)
◇ *n (U)* [chatter] parlotte *f*, parlote *f*.
◇ *vi* papoter.

gabardine [ˌgæbəˈdiːn] = **gaberdine**.

gabble [ˈgæbl] ◇ *vi* -**1.** [idly] faire la parlote, papoter; they ~ (away) for hours ils papotent pendant des heures. -**2.** [inarticulately] bredouiller, balbutier.
◇ *vt* bredouiller, bafouiller; she ~d (out) her story elle a raconté son histoire en bredouillant.
◇ *n* baragouin *m*, flot *m* de paroles; a ~ of voices un bruit confus de conversations; to talk at a ~ parler vite OR avec volubilité, jacasser.

gabbler [ˈgæbləʳ] *n* bavard *m*, -e *f*.

gabbling [ˈgæblɪŋ] *n* caquetage *m*, jacasserie *f*; stop your ~! arrêtez de jacasser!

gabbro [ˈgæbrəʊ] *n* GEOL gabbro *m*.

gabby *inf* [ˈgæbɪ] (*compar* gabbier, *superl* gabbiest) *adj* bavard.

gaberdine [ˌgæbəˈdiːn] ◇ *n* gabardine *f*.
◇ *comp*: ~ raincoat gabardine *f*.

gabfest *inf* [ˈgæbfest] *n Am* réunion *f (où l'on parle beaucoup)*.

gable [ˈgeɪbl] *n* [wall] pignon *m*; [over arch, door etc] gâble *m*, gable *m*.

gabled [ˈgeɪbld] *adj* [house] à pignon OR pignons; [wall] en pignon; [roof] sur pignon OR pignons; [arch] à gâble.

gable-end *n* pignon *m*.

gable window *n* fenêtre *f* sur pignon.

Gabon [gæˈbɒn] *pr n* Gabon *m*; in ~ au Gabon.

Gabonese [gæbɒˈniːz] ◇ *n* Gabonais *m*, -e *f*.
◇ *npl*: the ~ les Gabonais.
◇ *adj* gabonais.

Gabriel [ˈgeɪbrɪəl] *pr n* Gabriel.

gad [gæd] (*pt* & *pp* gadded, *cont* gadding)
◇ *vi*: to ~ about OR around se balader; she goes gadding all over the world elle court le monde.
◇ *vt* MIN casser au coin OR au picot.
◇ *n* -**1.** MIN [chisel] coin *m*; [pick] picot *m*. -**2.** [goad] aiguillon *m*. -**3.** *Am* [spur] éperon *m*.

Gad [gæd] *interj arch* OR *hum*: (by) ~! sapristi!, sacrebleu!

gadabout *inf* [ˈgædəbaʊt] *n Br* vadrouilleur *m*, -euse *f*.

Gadarene swine [gædəˈriːn-] *npl* BIBLE: the ~ les moutons de Panurge.

gadfly [ˈgædflaɪ] (*pl* gadflies) *n* -**1.** [insect] taon *m*. -**2.** [annoying person] enquiquineur *m*, -euse *f*, casse-pieds *mf inv*.

gadget [ˈgædʒɪt] *n* gadget *m*; a kitchen with all the latest ~s une cuisine avec tous les derniers gadgets.

gadgetry [ˈgædʒɪtrɪ] *n (U)* gadgets *mpl*.

gadid [ˈgeɪdɪd] *n* ZOOL gadidé *m*, gade *m*.

gadolinium [ˌgædəˈlɪnɪəm] *n* gadolinium *m*.

gadzooks *inf* [gædˈzuːks] *arch* OR *hum* = **Gad**.

Gael [geɪl] *n*: the ~s les Gaëls *mpl*.

Gaelic [ˈgeɪlɪk] ◇ *adj* gaélique.
◇ *n* LING gaélique *m*.

Gaelic coffee *n* Irish coffee *m*.

Gaelic football *n* football *m* gaélique.

Gaeltacht [ˈgeɪltæxt] *n*: the ~ *les régions d'Irlande où l'on parle le gaélique*.

gaff [gæf] ◇ *n* -**1.** [fishhook] gaffe *f*. -**2.** NAUT [spar] corne *f*. -**3.** *inf Br (U)* [nonsense] foutaise *f*, foutaises *fpl*. -**4.** *phr*: to blow the ~ *inf* vendre la mèche; to blow the ~ on sb vendre qqn.
◇ *vt* [fish] gaffer.

gaffe [gæf] *n* [blunder] bévue *f*; to commit OR to make a ~ commettre une bévue; a social ~ un faux pas, un impair.

gaffer *inf* [ˈgæfəʳ] *n* -**1.** *Br* [boss]: the ~ le patron, le chef. -**2.** [old man] vieux *m*.

gaff-rigged *adj* à gréement aurique.

gaff-sail *n* voile *f* aurique OR à corne.

gag [gæg] (*pt* & *pp* gagged, *cont* gagging)
◇ *n* -**1.** [over mouth] bâillon *m*; they want to put a ~ on the press *fig* ils veulent bâillonner la presse. -**2.** *inf* [joke] gag *m*; the funniest ~ in the film le gag le plus drôle du film. -**3.** MED ouvre-bouche *m*.
◇ *vt* [silence] bâillonner; *fig* bâillonner, museler.
◇ *vi* -**1.** [retch] avoir un haut-le-cœur; he gagged on a fishbone il a failli s'étrangler avec une arête de poisson. -**2.** *inf* [joke] blaguer, rigoler. -**3.** THEAT faire des improvisations comiques.

gaga *inf* [ˈgɑːgɑː] *adj* [senile, crazy] gaga; he's absolutely ~ about her il est complètement fou d'elle.

Gagarin [gəˈgɑːrɪn] *pr n*: Yuri ~ Iouri Gagarine.

gag-bit *n* mors *m* de force.

gage [geɪdʒ] ◇ *n* -**1.** *Am* = **gauge**. -**2.** [pledge] gage *m*. -**3.** [challenge] défi *m*. -**4.** *arch* [glove] gant *m*.
◇ *vt arch* [pledge, wager] gager.

gaggle [ˈgægl] ◇ *n literal* & *fig* troupeau *m*.
◇ *vi* cacarder.

gag resolution, **gag rule** *n Am* règle *f* du bâillon *(procédure parlementaire permettant de limiter le temps de parole et d'éviter l'obstruction systématique)*.

gaiety [ˈgeɪətɪ] (*pl* gaieties) *n* gaieté *f*; it broug[ht] a bit of ~ into their lives ça a apporté un pe[u] de gaieté dans leur vie.
◆ **gaieties** *npl lit* [merry-making] réjouissa[n]ces *fpl*.

gaily [ˈgeɪlɪ] *adv* -**1.** [brightly] gaiement; [~] coloured clothes des vêtements aux couleu[rs] vives. -**2.** [casually] tranquillement.

gain [geɪn] ◇ *n* -**1.** [profit] gain *m*, profit [*m*,] bénéfice *m*; *fig* avantage *m*, gain *m*; to do st[h] for personal ~ faire qqch par intérêt; their lo[ss] is our ~ ce n'est pas perdu pour tout le mond[e]. -**2.** [acquisition] gain *m*; there were large Co[n]servative ~s le parti conservateur a gagné [de] nombreux sièges. -**3.** [increase] augmentation [*f*]; a ~ in speed/weight une augmentation [de] vitesse/poids. -**4.** ELECTRON gain *m*.
◇ *vt* -**1.** [earn, win, obtain] gagner; what woul[d] we (have to) ~ by joining? quel intér[êt] avons-nous à adhérer?; to ~ friends (by doi[ng] sthg) se faire des amis (en faisant qqch); they'[re] trying to ~ our sympathy ils essaient [de] gagner notre sympathie; they managed to [~] entry to the building ils ont réussi à s'intr[o]duire dans le bâtiment; he managed to ~ [a] hearing il a réussi à se faire écouter. -**2.** [increase] gagner; the share index has ~ed two poin[ts] l'indice des actions a gagné deux points. -**3.** [ob]tain more] gagner, obtenir; to ~ weight/spe[ed] prendre du poids/de la vitesse; to ~ expe[ri]ence acquérir de l'expérience; to ~ groun[d] gagner du terrain; to ~ time gagner du temp[s]. -**4.** [subj: clock, watch] avancer de; my watch [~s] ten minutes a day ma montre avance de d[ix] minutes par jour. -**5.** *lit* [reach] atteindre, g[a]gner; we finally ~ed the shore nous avons fi[ni] par atteindre la rive.
◇ *vi* -**1.** [profit] profiter, gagner; who stands [to] ~ by this deal? qui y gagne dans cette affaire[?] -**2.** [clock] avancer.
◆ **gain on**, **gain upon** *vt insep* [catch up] ra[t]traper; his pursuers are ~ing on him s[es] poursuivants sont en train de le rattraper.

gain control *n* réglage *m* du gain.

gainer [ˈgeɪnəʳ] *n* gagnant *m*, -e *f*.

gainful [ˈgeɪnfʊl] *adj* -**1.** [profitable] profitabl[e,] rémunérateur. -**2.** [paid] rémunéré; ~ emplo[y]ment un emploi rémunéré.

gainfully [ˈgeɪnfʊlɪ] *adv* de façon profitabl[e,] avantageusement; to be ~ employed avoir u[n] emploi rémunéré.

gainsay [ˌgeɪnˈseɪ] (*pt* & *pp* gainsaid [-ˈsed]) *vt fml* [deny] nier; [contradict] contredire; yo[u] can't ~ the facts tu ne peux pas nier l'évidenc[e;] there's no ~ing her skill as an artist on ne pe[ut] pas nier son talent artistique.

gainsayer [geɪnˈseɪəʳ] *n* [contradictor] contr[a]dicteur *m*; [opponent] opposant *m*, -e *f*.

gainst [geɪnst], **'gainst** [genst] *lit* = **again[st]** *prep*.

gait [geɪt] *n* démarche *f*, allure *f*; to walk with an unsteady ~ marcher d'un pas chancelant.
gaiter ['geɪtəʳ] *n* guêtre *f*.
Gaius ['gaɪəs] *pr n* Gaius.
gal [gæl] *n* **-1.** *inf* [girl] fille *f*. **-2.** PHYS [unit of acceleration] gal *m*.
gal. *written abbr of* gallon.
gala ['gɑːlə] ◇ *n* **-1.** [festivity] gala *m*. **-2.** *Br* SPORT réunion *f* sportive; swimming ~ concours *m* de natation.
◇ *comp* [dress, day, evening] de gala; a ~ occasion une grande occasion.
galactic [gə'læktɪk] *adj* galactique; ~ plane plan *m* galactique; ~ poles pôles *mpl* galactiques.
galactometer [,gælək'tɒmɪtəʳ] *n* galactomètre *m*, pèse-lait *m inv*.
galactopoiesis [gə,læktəupɔɪ'iːsɪs] *n* galactopoïèse *f*.
galactose [gə'læktəus] *n* galactose *m*.
galago [gə'lɑːgəu] (*pl* galagos) *n* galago *m*.
Galahad ['gæləhæd] ◇ *pr n*: Sir ~ Galaad.
◇ *n*: he's a real Sir ~ *inf Br* c'est un vrai gentleman.
galantine ['gæləntiːn] *n* CULIN galantine *f*.
Galapagos Islands [gə'læpəgəs-] *pl pr n*: the ~ les (îles *fpl*) Galapagos *fpl*; in the ~ aux (îles) Galapagos.
Galatian [gə'leɪʃjən] *n*: the Epistle of Paul to the ~s l'Épître de saint Paul aux Galates.
galaxy ['gæləksɪ] (*pl* galaxies) *n* **-1.** ASTRON galaxie *f*; the Galaxy la Voie lactée. **-2.** [gathering] constellation *f*, pléiade *f*; a ~ of film stars une pléiade de vedettes de cinéma.
gale [geɪl] *n* **-1.** [wind] coup *m* de vent, grand vent *m*; a force 9 ~ un vent de force 9; it's blowing a ~ outside! quel vent! ❑ ~ warning avis *m* de coup de vent. **-2.** [outburst] éclat *m*; ~s of laughter des éclats de rire.
gale force *n* force *f* 8 à 9; gale-force winds coups *mpl* de vent.
galena [gə'liːnə] *n* galène *f*.
galenical [gə'lenɪkl] PHARM ◇ *adj* galénique.
◇ *n* médicament *m*.
galenite [gə'liːnaɪt] = **galena**.
Galicia [gə'lɪʃɪə] *pr n* **-1.** [Central Europe] Galicie *f*; in ~ en Galicie. **-2.** [Spain] Galice *f*; in ~ en Galice.
Galician [gə'lɪʃɪən] ◇ *adj* galicien.
◇ *n* **-1.** [person] Galicien *m*, -enne *f*. **-2.** LING galicien *m*.
Galilean [,gælɪ'liːən] ◇ *adj* galiléen.
◇ *n* Galiléen *m*, -enne *f*.
Galilee ['gælɪliː] Galilée *f*; in ~ en Galilée; the Sea of ~ le lac de Tibériade, la mer de Galilée.
Galileo [,gælɪ'leɪəu] *pr n* Galilée.
galingale ['gælɪŋgeɪl] *n* souchet *m*.
gall [gɔːl] ◇ *n* **-1.** ANAT [human] bile *f*; [animal] fiel *m*. **-2.** [bitterness] fiel *m*, amertume *f*. **-3.** [nerve] culot *m*; he had the ~ to say it was my fault! il a eu le culot de dire que c'était de ma faute! **-4.** BOT galle *f*. **-5.** MED & VETER écorchure *f*, excoriation *f*.
◇ *vt* **-1.** [annoy] énerver; it ~ed him to have to admit he was wrong ça l'a énervé de devoir reconnaître qu'il avait tort. **-2.** MED & VETER excorier.
◇ *comp*: ~ duct ANAT voie *f* biliaire.
gall. *written abbr of* gallon.
gallant [*adj sense 1* & *3* 'gælənt, *adj sense 2* gə'lænt, 'gælənt, *n* 'gælənt] ◇ *adj* **-1.** [brave] courageux, vaillant; ~ deeds des actions d'éclat, des prouesses. **-2.** [chivalrous] galant. **-3.** *lit* [noble] noble; [splendid] superbe, splendide.
◇ *n lit* galant *m*.
gallantly ['gæləntlɪ] *adv* **-1.** [bravely] courageusement, vaillamment. **-2.** [chivalrously] galamment.
gallantry ['gæləntrɪ] (*pl* gallantries) *n* **-1.** [bravery] courage *m*, vaillance *f*. **-2.** [brave deed] prouesse *f*, action *f* d'éclat. **-3.** [chivalry, amorousness] galanterie *f*.

gall bladder *n* vésicule *f* biliaire.
galleon ['gælɪən] *n* galion *m*.
galleria [gælə'rɪə] *n* puits *m (aménagé dans un grand magasin à plusieurs étages)*.
galleried ['gælərɪd] *adj* ARCHIT à galerie OR galeries.
gallery ['gælərɪ] (*pl* galleries) ◇ *n* **-1.** [of art] musée *m* (des beaux-arts); private ~ galerie *f*. **-2.** [balcony] galerie *f*; [for spectators] tribune *f*; the press ~ la tribune de la presse. **-3.** [covered passageway] galerie *f*. **-4.** THEAT [upper balcony] dernier balcon *m*; [audience] galerie *f*; to play to the ~ *fig* poser pour la galerie. **-5.** [tunnel] galerie *f*. **-6.** GOLF [spectators] public *m*.
◇ *comp*: ~ forest forêt-galerie *f*, galerie *f* forestière.
galley ['gælɪ] ◇ *n* **-1.** [ship] galère *f*; [ship's kitchen] cambuse *f*; [aircraft kitchen] office *m or f*. **-2.** TYPO [container] galée *f*; [proof] placard *m*.
◇ *comp*: ~ kitchen kitchenette *f*, cuisinette *f offic*.
galley proof *n* TYPO placard *m*.
galley slave *n* galérien *m*.
galley-west *inf* ['gælɪwest] *adv Am*: to knock sb ~ [knock out] mettre qqn K-O; [stupefy] renverser qqn; I was knocked ~! j'en suis resté baba!; to knock sthg ~ [send flying] envoyer valser qqch; [mess up] chambouler qqch, mettre qqch sens dessus dessous.
gallic ['gælɪk] *adj* CHEM gallique.
Gallic ['gælɪk] *adj* **-1.** [French] français; ~ charm charme *m* latin. **-2.** [of Gaul] gaulois; the ~ Wars la guerre des Gaules.
gallic acid *n* acide *m* gallique.
gallicism ['gælɪsɪzm] *n* gallicisme *m*.
gallicize, -ise ['gælɪsaɪz] *vt* franciser.
gallimaufry [,gælɪ'mɔːfrɪ] (*pl* gallimaufries) *n lit* fatras *m*, fouillis *m*.
gallinaceous [,gælɪ'neɪʃəs] *adj* ZOOL gallinacé.
galling ['gɔːlɪŋ] *adj* [annoying] irritant; [humiliating] humiliant, vexant.
gallingly ['gɔːlɪŋlɪ] *adv* de façon irritante.
gallinule ['gælɪnjuːl] *n* ZOOL poule *f* d'eau.
gallium ['gælɪəm] *n* gallium *m*.
gallivant [,gælɪ'vænt] *vi hum*: to ~ about OR around se balader; he's off ~ing around Europe il se balade quelque part en Europe.
gallon ['gælən] *n* gallon *m*.
gallonage ['gælənɪdʒ] *n* TECH capacité *f* (en gallons).
galloon [gə'luːn] *n* SEW galon *m*.
gallop ['gæləp] ◇ *vi* galoper; we ~ed across the fields nous avons galopé à travers les champs; to ~ away OR off partir au galop; he came ~ing down the stairs *fig* il a descendu l'escalier au galop.
◇ *vt* faire galoper; to ~ a horse faire galoper un cheval.
◇ *n* galop *m*; the pony broke into a ~ le poney a pris le galop; we decided to go for a ~ in the woods nous décidâmes d'aller faire un galop dans les bois; to do sthg at a ~ *fig* faire qqch à toute vitesse.
◆ **gallop through** *vt insep* faire à toute vitesse; she ~ed through her homework elle a expédié ses devoirs; I positively ~ed through the book j'ai vraiment lu ce livre à toute allure.
galloping ['gæləpɪŋ] *adj* [horse] au galop; *fig* galopant; ~ inflation inflation *f* galopante.
Gallo-Roman [,gæləu'rəumən] ◇ *adj* [dialects] gallo-roman; [civilization, remains] gallo-romain.
◇ *n* LING gallo-roman *m*.
gallows ['gæləuz] (*pl inv*) *n* potence *f*, gibet *m*.
gallows humour *n Br* humour *m* noir.
gallows tree = **gallows**.
gallstone ['gɔːlstəun] *n* calcul *m* biliaire.
Gallup Poll ['gæləp-] *n* sondage *m* (d'opinion) *(réalisé par l'institut Gallup)*.
galore [gə'lɔːʳ] *adv* en abondance; we've got food ~ nous avons de la nourriture en abondance.
galoshes [gə'lɒʃɪz] *npl* caoutchoucs *mpl (pour protéger les chaussures)*.

galumph *inf* [gə'lʌmf] *vi* courir lourdement OR comme un pachyderme; he came ~ing down the stairs il a descendu l'escalier avec la légèreté d'un éléphant OR d'un hippopotame.
galvanic [gæl'vænɪk] *adj* **-1.** ELEC galvanique. **-2.** [convulsive] convulsif. **-3.** [stimulating] galvanisant.
galvanism ['gælvənɪzm] *n* galvanisme *m*.
galvanize, -ise ['gælvənaɪz] *vt* MED, METALL & *fig* galvaniser; it ~d the workers into action ça a poussé les travailleurs à agir.
galvanometer [,gælvə'nɒmɪtəʳ] *n* galvanomètre *m*.
galvanoscope [gæl'vænəuskəup] *n* galvanoscope *m*.
galvanotropism [,gælvə'nɒtrəpɪzm] *n* galvanotropisme *m*.
Gambia ['gæmbɪə] *pr n*: (the) ~ (la) Gambie; in (the) ~ en Gambie.
Gambian ['gæmbɪən] ◇ *n* Gambien *m*, -enne *f*.
◇ *adj* gambien.
gambit ['gæmbɪt] *n* [chess] gambit *m*; king's/queen's ~ gambit du roi/de la reine ❑ opening ~ *literal* gambit *m*; *fig* manœuvre *f*, ruse *f*.
gamble ['gæmbl] ◇ *vi* jouer; to ~ on the stock exchange jouer à la Bourse, boursicoter.
◇ *vt* parier, miser.
◇ *n* **-1.** [wager] pari *m*; I like an occasional ~ on the horses j'aime bien jouer aux courses de temps en temps. **-2.** [risk] coup *m* de poker; his ~ paid off son coup de poker a payé; it's a ~ we have to take c'est un risque qu'il faut prendre; it's a bit of a ~ whether it'll work or not nous n'avons aucun moyen de savoir si ça marchera.
◆ **gamble away** *vt sep* perdre au jeu.
◆ **gamble on** *vt insep* miser OR tabler OR compter sur; we'd ~d on having fine weather on avait misé sur le beau temps; I wouldn't ~ on the plan succeeding je ne tablerais pas sur la réussite du projet.
gambler ['gæmbləʳ] *n* joueur *m*, -euse *f*.
gambling ['gæmblɪŋ] ◇ *n (U)* jeu *m*, jeux *mpl* d'argent; ~ debts dettes *fpl* de jeu; 'no ~' 'les jeux d'argent sont interdits'.
◇ *adj* joueur; I'm not a ~ man but I would guess that they will accept the offer je ne suis pas homme à parier mais je crois qu'il vont accepter la proposition.
gambling den *n pej* maison *f* de jeu, tripot *m*.
gambling house *n* maison *f* de jeu.
gamboge [gæm'buːʒ] ◇ *n* gomme-gutte *f*.
◇ *adj* [light] jaune.
gambol ['gæmbl] (*Br pt* & *pp* gambolled, *cont* gambolling, *Am pt* & *pp* gamboled, *cont* gamboling) ◇ *vi* gambader, cabrioler.
◇ *n* gambade *f*, cabriole *f*.
game [geɪm] ◇ *n* **-1.** [gen] jeu *m*; card/party ~s jeux de cartes/de société; a ~ of chance/of skill un jeu de hasard/d'adresse; ball ~s are forbidden il est interdit de jouer au ballon; the rules of the ~ la règle du jeu; she plays a good ~ of chess c'est une bonne joueuse d'échecs, elle joue bien aux échecs; it's only a ~! ce n'est qu'un jeu!; I'm off my ~ today je joue mal aujourd'hui; it put me right off my ~ ça m'a complètement déconcentré; to play sb's ~ entrer dans le jeu de qqn; you're not playing the ~! tu ne joues pas le jeu!; politics is just a ~ to him pour lui, la politique n'est qu'un jeu ❑ the ~ is not worth the candle *Br* le jeu n'en vaut pas la chandelle. **-2.** [contest] partie *f*; [esp professional] match *m*; do you fancy a ~ of chess? ça te dit de faire une partie d'échecs?; tonight's big ~ le grand match de ce soir. **-3.** [division of match – in tennis, bridge] jeu *m*; ~, set and match jeu, set et match; (one) ~ all un jeu partout. **-4.** [playing equipment, set] jeu *m*. **-5.** *inf* [scheme, trick] ruse *f*, stratagème *m*; what's your (little) ~? qu'est-ce que tu manigances?, à quel jeu joues-tu? ❑ to play a double ~ jouer un double jeu; to beat sb at his/her own game battre qqn sur son propre terrain; the ~'s up! tout est perdu!; two can

play at that ~, you know! moi aussi je peux jouer à ce petit jeu-là, tu sais!; **don't come that ~ with me!** tu ne m'auras pas à ce petit jeu-là!; **to give the ~ away** vendre la mèche; **that gave the ~ away** c'est comme ça qu'on a découvert le pot aux roses. -**6.** *inf* [undertaking, operation]: **at this stage in the ~** à ce stade des opérations □ **to be ahead of the ~** mener le jeu *fig*. -**7.** [activity] travail *m*; **I'm new to this ~** je suis novice en la matière; **when you've been in this ~ as long as I have, you'll understand** quand tu auras fait ça aussi longtemps que moi, tu comprendras. -**8.** CULIN & HUNT gibier *m*. -**9.** *phr*: **to be on the ~**▽ *Br* faire le tapin.

◇ *adj* -**1.** [plucky] courageux, brave. -**2.** [willing] prêt, partant; **they're ~ for anything** ils sont toujours partants; **I'm ~ if you are!** si tu es partant, moi aussi! -**3.** *Br* [lame] estropié; **he's got a ~ leg** il a une jambe estropiée.

◇ *comp* de chasse; **~ bag** gibecière *f*; **~ laws** réglementation *f* de la chasse.

◇ *vi fml* [gamble] jouer (de l'argent).

◆ **games** *npl* [international] jeux *mpl*; *Br* SCH sport *m*; **they have ~s on Wednesdays** le mercredi ils ont sport □ **the Olympic Games** les jeux Olympiques.

game bird *n*: **the partridge is a ~** on chasse la perdrix; **~s** gibier *m* à plumes.

gamecock ['geɪmkɒk] *n Br* coq *m* de combat.

game fish *n* poisson *m* noble *(saumon, brochet)*.

game-fishing *n* pêche *f (au saumon, à la truite, au brochet)*.

game fowl = **game bird**.

gamekeeper ['geɪm,kiːpəʳ] *n* garde-chasse *m*.

game laws *npl* réglementation *f* de la chasse.

gamely ['geɪmlɪ] *adv* courageusement, vaillamment.

game park *n* [in Africa] réserve *f*.

game pie *n* tourte *f* au gibier, ≃ pâté *m* en croûte.

game plan *n* stratégie *f*, plan *m* d'attaque.

game point *n* balle *f* de jeu.

game reserve *n* réserve *f (pour animaux sauvages)*.

gamesmanship ['geɪmzmənʃɪp] *n art de gagner (aux jeux) en déconcertant son adversaire*.

gamester ['geɪmstəʳ] *n* [game-player, gambler] joueur *m*, -euse *f*.

gamete ['gæmiːt] *n* gamète *m*.

game theory *n* théorie *f* des jeux.

gametic [gə'metɪk] *adj* gamétique.

gametocyte [gə'miːtəʊsaɪt] *n* gamétocyte *m*.

gametogenesis [,gæmɪtəʊ'dʒenɪsɪs] *n* gamétogenèse *f*.

gametophyte [gə'miːtəʊfaɪt] *n* gamétophyte *m*.

game warden *n* -**1.** [gamekeeper] garde-chasse *m*. -**2.** [in safari park] garde *m* (d'une réserve).

gamey ['geɪmɪ] (*compar* **gamier**, *superl* **gamiest**) = **gamy**.

gamine ['gæmiːn] *Br* ◇ *n* [impish girl] jeune fille *f* espiègle; [tomboy] garçon *m* manqué.

◇ *adj* gamin; **a ~ haircut** une coupe à la garçonne.

gaming ['geɪmɪŋ] *fml* = **gambling** *n*.

gaming laws *npl lois réglementant les jeux de hasard*.

gaming table *n* table *f* de jeu.

gamma ['gæmə] *n* gamma *m*.

gamma globulin *n* gammaglobuline *f*.

gamma radiation *n (U)* rayons *mpl* gamma.

gamma ray *n* rayon *m* gamma.

gammon ['gæmən] ◇ *n* -**1.** *Br* [cut] jambon *m*; [meat] jambon *m* fumé. -**2.** [in backgammon] *victoire avant que l'adversaire ne puisse retirer aucune de ses pièces*.

◇ *vt* battre en réalisant un «gammon».

gammon steak *n Br* (épaisse) tranche *f* de jambon fumé.

gammy *inf* ['gæmɪ] (*compar* **gammier**, *superl* **gammiest**) *adj Br* estropié; **to have a ~ leg** avoir une jambe estropiée, avoir une patte folle.

gamogenesis [,gæməʊ'dʒenɪsɪs] *n* gamogénèse *f*.

gamp *inf* [gæmp] *n Br arch* pébroque *m*.

gamut ['gæmət] *n* MUS & *fig* gamme *f*; **to run the (whole) ~ of sthg** passer par toute la gamme de qqch.

gamy ['geɪmɪ] (*compar* **gamier**, *superl* **gamiest**) *adj* [meat] faisandé.

gander ['gændəʳ] *n* -**1.** [goose] jars *m*. -**2.** *inf Br* [simpleton] nigaud *m*, -e *f*, andouille *f*. -**3.** *inf Br* [look]: **to have** OR **to take a ~ at sthg** jeter un coup d'œil sur qqch; **have a ~ at this!** jette un coup là-dessus!

gang [gæŋ] ◇ *n* -**1.** [gen] bande *f*; [of criminals] gang *m*; **a ~ of young thugs** une bande de jeunes voyous; **she went out with a ~ of friends** elle est sortie avec une bande de copains; **he's one of the ~ now** il fait partie de la bande maintenant. -**2.** [of workmen] équipe *f*; [of convicts] convoi *m*. -**3.** TECH [of tools] série *f*.

◇ *vt* TECH [tools, instruments] coupler.

◆ **gang together** *vi insep* se réunir (en bande), se mettre à plusieurs.

◆ **gang up** *vi insep* se mettre à plusieurs; **to ~ up against** OR **on sb** se liguer contre qqn.

gang-bang▼ *n* viol *m* collectif.

ganger ['gæŋəʳ] *n Br* [foreman] contremaître *m*, chef *m* d'équipe.

Ganges ['gændʒiːz] *pr n*: **the (River) ~** le Gange.

gangland ['gæŋlænd] ◇ *n* le milieu.

◇ *comp*: **a ~ killing** un règlement de comptes *(dans le milieu)*.

ganglia ['gæŋglɪə] *pl* → **ganglion**.

gangling ['gæŋglɪŋ] *adj* dégingandé; **a tall, ~ young lad** un grand jeune homme dégingandé.

ganglion ['gæŋglɪən] (*pl* **ganglia** [-glɪə]) *n* -**1.** ANAT ganglion *m*. -**2.** [centre, focus] centre *m*, foyer *m*.

gangly ['gæŋlɪ] = **gangling**.

gangplank ['gæŋplæŋk] *n* passerelle *f*; **to walk the ~** être soumis au supplice de la planche *(par des pirates)*.

gangrene ['gæŋgriːn] ◇ *n* MED & *fig* gangrène *f*.

◇ *vi* se gangrener.

gangrenous ['gæŋgrɪnəs] *adj* gangreneux; **the wound went ~** la blessure s'est gangrenée.

gang saw *n* scie *f* multiple.

gang show *n spectacle de variétés organisé par les scouts*.

gangster ['gæŋstəʳ] ◇ *n* gangster *m*.

◇ *comp* [film, story] de gangsters.

gangue [gæŋ] *n* MINER gangue *f*.

gangway ['gæŋweɪ] ◇ *n* -**1.** NAUT = **gangplank**. -**2.** [passage] passage *m*; *Br* [in theatre] allée *f*.

◇ *interj*: **~!** dégagez le passage!

gannet ['gænɪt] *n* -**1.** ORNITH fou *m* de Bassan. -**2.** *inf Br* [greedy person] glouton *m*, -onne *f*.

gantry ['gæntrɪ] (*pl* **gantries**) *n* [for crane] portique *m*; **(launching) ~** ASTRON portique (de lancement); **(signal) ~** RAIL portique (à signaux).

gantry crane *n* grue *f* (à) portique.

Ganymede ['gænɪmiːd] *pr n* Ganymède.

GAO (*abbr of* **General Accounting Office**) *pr n Cour des comptes américaine*.

gaol *etc* [dʒeɪl] *Br* = **jail**.

gap [gæp] *n* -**1.** [hole, breach] trou *m*, brèche *f*; **a ~ in the wall** un trou dans le mur; **the sun shone through a ~ in the clouds** le soleil perça à travers les nuages. -**2.** [space between objects] espace *m*; [narrower] interstice *m*, jour *m*; **there was a ~ of a few metres between each car** il y avait une distance de quelques mètres entre chaque voiture; **he has a ~ between his front teeth** il a les dents de devant écartées; **I could see through a ~ in the curtains** je voyais par la fente entre les rideaux. -**3.** [blank] blanc *m*; **fill in the ~s with the missing letters** remplissez les blancs avec les lettres manquantes. -**4.** [in time] intervalle *m*; **there's a perceptible ~ between stimulus and response** il y a un intervalle sensible entre le stimulus et la réponse; **she returned to work after a ~ of six years** elle s'est remise à travailler après une interruption de six ans. -**5.** [lack] vide *m*; **to bridge** OR **to fill a ~** combler un vide; **his death left a ~ in our lives** sa mort a laissé un vide dans notre vie; **a ~ in the market** un créneau sur le marché. -**6.** [omission] lacune *f*; **there are several ~s in his story** il y a plusieurs lacunes dans son histoire. -**7.** [silence] pause *f*, silence *m*. -**8.** [disparity] écart *m*, inégalité *f*; **we need to reduce the ~ between theory and practice** il nous faut réduire l'écart entre la théorie et la pratique; **there's a technology ~ between our two countries** il y a un écart technologique entre nos deux pays. -**9.** [mountain pass] col *m*.

gape [geɪp] ◇ *vi* -**1.** [stare] regarder bouche bée; **he ~d at me** il m'a regardé bouche bée; **what are you gaping at?** qu'est-ce que tu regardes avec cet air bête? -**2.** [open one's mouth wide] ouvrir la bouche toute grande. -**3.** [be open] être béant, béer *lit*; **a chasm ~d at our feet** un gouffre béant s'ouvrait à nos pieds.

◇ *n* [stare] regard *m* ébahi.

gaper ['geɪpəʳ] *n* -**1.** [starer] badaud *m*, -e *f*. -**2.** [clam] mye *f*.

gaping ['geɪpɪŋ] *adj* -**1.** [staring] bouche bée *(inv)*. -**2.** [wide open] béant; **a ~ wound** une blessure béante.

gappy ['gæpɪ] (*compar* **gappier**, *superl* **gappiest**) *adj* -**1.** [account, knowledge] plein de lacunes. -**2.** **~ teeth** des dents écartées.

gap-toothed *adj* [with spaces between teeth] aux dents écartées; [with missing teeth] à qui il manque des dents.

garage [*n Br* 'gærɑːʒ, 'gærɪdʒ, *Am* gə'rɑːʒ, *vb Br* 'gærɑːʒ, *Am* gə'rɑːʒ] ◇ *n* garage *m*.

◇ *vt* mettre au garage.

garage hand *n* mécanicien *m*, -enne *f*.

garage man *n* [mechanic] mécanicien *m*, -enne *f*; [owner] garagiste *mf*.

garage sale *n vente d'occasion chez un particulier*.

garb [gɑːb] *lit* ◇ *n* costume *m*, mise *f*; **she was in gipsy ~** elle était en costume de gitane, elle était déguisée en gitane; **a man dressed in very strange ~** un homme bizarrement accoutré.

◇ *vt* vêtir.

garbage ['gɑːbɪdʒ] *n (U)* -**1.** *Am* [waste matter] ordures *fpl*, détritus *mpl*; **throw it in the ~** jette-le à la poubelle. -**2.** *inf* [nonsense] bêtises *fpl*, âneries *fpl*; **you're talking ~!** tu racontes des bêtises!; **this newspaper is ~!** ce journal est nul! -**3.** COMPUT données *fpl* erronées; **~ in, ~ out** la qualité des résultats est fonction de la qualité des données à l'entrée.

garbage can *n Am* poubelle *f*.

garbage chute *n Am* vide-ordures *m inv*.

garbage collector *n Am* éboueur *m*.

garbage disposal unit *n Am* broyeur *m* d'ordures.

garbage dump *n Am* décharge *f*.

garbage man *Am* = **garbage collector**.

garbage truck *n Am* camion *m* des éboueurs.

garbanzo [gɑː'bɑːnzəʊ] (*pl* **garbanzos**) *n Am* pois *m* chiche.

garble ['gɑːbl] *vt* [involuntarily - story, message] embrouiller; [- quotation] déformer; [deliberately - facts] dénaturer, déformer.

garbled ['gɑːbld] *adj* [story, message, explanation - involuntarily] embrouillé, confus; [- deliberately] dénaturé, déformé.

garda ['gɑːdə] (*pl* **gardai** [-diː]) *n* policier *m (en République d'Irlande)*.

garden ['gɑːdn] ◇ *n* -**1.** [with flowers] jardin *m*; [with vegetables] (jardin *m*) potager *m*; **to do the ~** jardiner, faire du jardinage □ **the Garden of Eden** le jardin *m* d'Éden, l'Éden *m*; **everything in the ~ is rosy** OR **lovely** tout va bien. -**2.** [fertile region] jardin *m*; **the Garden of England** *surnom du comté de Kent, célèbre pour ses vergers et ses champs de houblon*.

◇ *comp* de jardinage, de jardin; **~ path** allée *(dans un jardin)*; **he ran down the ~ path** il a

descendu l'allée du jardin en courant; ~ **produce** produits *mpl* maraîchers; ~ **seat** banc *m* de jardin; ~ **shears** cisaille *f* OR cisailles *fpl* de jardin; ~ **shed** resserre *f*; ~ **tools** outils *mpl* de jardinage; ~ **wall** mur *m* du jardin.
◇ *vi* jardiner, faire du jardinage.
◆ **gardens** *npl* [park] jardin *m* public.

garden centre *n* jardinerie *f*.

garden city *n* cité-jardin *f*.

gardener ['gɑːdnəʳ] *n* jardinier *m*, -ère *f*.

garden flat *n* rez-de-jardin *m inv*.

garden gnome *n* gnome *m* (décoratif).

gardenia [gɑː'diːnjə] *n* gardénia *m*.

gardening ['gɑːdnɪŋ] ◇ *n* jardinage *m*; **he's fond of** ~ il aime jardiner.
◇ *comp* [book, programme] de OR sur le jardinage; [gloves] de jardinage.

garden party *n Br* garden-party *f*.

garden suburb *n* banlieue *f* verte.

garden-variety *adj Am* ordinaire.

garfish ['gɑːfɪʃ] *n* orphie *f*, aiguille *f* de mer.

gargantuan [gɑː'gæntjʊən] *adj* gargantuesque.

gargle ['gɑːgl] ◇ *vi* se gargariser, faire des gargarismes.
◇ *n* gargarisme *m*.

gargoyle ['gɑːgɔɪl] *n* gargouille *f*.

garibaldi [ˌgærɪ'bɔːldɪ] *n Br biscuit aux raisins secs*.

garish ['geərɪʃ] *adj* [colour] voyant, criard; [clothes] voyant, tapageur; [light] cru, aveuglant.

garishly ['geərɪʃlɪ] *adv*: ~ **dressed** vêtu de manière tapageuse; ~ **made-up** outrageusement fardé OR maquillé.

garishness ['geərɪʃnɪs] *n* [of appearance] tape-à-l'œil *m inv*; [of colour] crudité *f*, violence *f*.

garland ['gɑːlənd] ◇ *n* -**1.** [on head] couronne *f* de fleurs; [round neck] guirlande *f* OR collier *m* de fleurs; [hung on wall] guirlande *f*. -**2.** LITERAT [of poems] guirlande *f*, florilège *m*.
◇ *vt* [decorate] décorer avec des guirlandes, enguirlander; [crown] couronner de fleurs.

garlic ['gɑːlɪk] *n* ail *m*; **clove of** ~ gousse *f* d'ail; ~ **bread** *pain beurré frotté d'ail et servi chaud*; ~ **butter** beurre *m* d'ail; ~ **salt** sel *m* d'ail; ~ **sausage** saucisson *m* à l'ail.

garlicky ['gɑːlɪkɪ] *adj* [taste] d'ail; [breath] qui sent l'ail; **it smells** ~ ça sent l'ail.

garlic mustard *n* alliaire *f*.

garlic press *n* presse-ail *m inv*.

garment ['gɑːmənt] *n* vêtement *m*; **the** ~ **industry** la confection.

garner ['gɑːnəʳ] ◇ *n lit* grenier *m* (à grain), grange *f*.
◇ *vt* [grain] rentrer, engranger; *fig* [information] glaner, grappiller; [compliments] recueillir.
◆ **garner in, garner up** *vt sep* engranger.

garnet ['gɑːnɪt] ◇ *n* [stone, colour] grenat *m*.
◇ *adj* -**1.** [in colour] grenat *(inv)*. -**2.** [jewellery] de OR en grenat.

garnish ['gɑːnɪʃ] ◇ *vt* CULIN garnir; [decorate] embellir; ~**ed with slices of lemon and tomato** garni de rondelles de citron et de tomate.
◇ *n* garniture *f*.

garnishing ['gɑːnɪʃɪŋ] *n* CULIN garniture *f*; *fig* embellissement *m*.

garnishment ['gɑːnɪʃmənt] *n* -**1.** JUR saisie-arrêt *f*. -**2.** CULIN garniture *f*.

garotte [gə'rɒt] = **garrot(t)e**.

garret ['gærət] *n* [room] mansarde *f*; **to live in a** ~ habiter une chambre sous les combles.

garrison ['gærɪsn] ◇ *n* garnison *f*.
◇ *vt* -**1.** [troops] mettre en garnison; **they were** ~**ed in Scotland** ils étaient en garnison en Écosse. -**2.** [town] placer une garnison dans.

garrison town *n* ville *f* de garnison.

garrison troops *npl* (troupes *fpl* de) garnison *f*.

garrot(t)e [gə'rɒt] ◇ *n* -**1.** [execution] (supplice *m* du) garrot *m*. -**2.** [collar] garrot *m*.
◇ *vt* garrotter.

garrulous ['gærələs] *adj* -**1.** [person] loquace, bavard. -**2.** [style] prolixe, verbeux.

garrulously ['gærələslɪ] *adv* verbeusement.

garryowen [ˌgærɪ'əʊɪn] *n Br* SPORT [in rugby] (coup *m* de pied en) chandelle *f*.

garter ['gɑːtəʳ] *n* -**1.** *Br* [for stockings] jarretière *f*; [for socks] fixe-chaussette *m*; **Order of the Garter** ordre *m* de la Jarretière; **Knight of the Garter** chevalier *m* de l'ordre de la Jarretière. -**2.** *Am* [suspender] jarretelle *f*.

garter belt *n Am* porte-jarretelles *m inv*.

garter snake *n* couleuvre *f (d'Amérique du Nord)*.

garter stitch *n* point *m* mousse.

gas [gæs] (*pl* gasses) ◇ *n* -**1.** [domestic] gaz *m*; **to turn on/off the** ~ allumer/éteindre le gaz; **to use** ~ **for cooking** faire la cuisine OR cuisiner au gaz; **a street lit by** ~ une rue éclairée au gaz ❑ ~ **bracket** applique *f* à gaz; ~ **industry** industrie *f* du gaz. -**2.** CHEM gaz *m*. -**3.** MIN grisou *m*. -**4.** MED gaz *m* anesthésique OR anesthésiant; **to have** ~ subir une anesthésie gazeuse OR par inhalation; **the dentist gave me** ~ le dentiste m'a endormi au gaz. -**5.** *Am* AUT essence *f*; ~ **gauge** jauge *f* d'essence; ~ **pedal** accélérateur *m*; **step on the** ~! *inf literal* appuie sur le champignon!; *fig* grouille!, grouille-toi! -**6.** *inf Am* [amusement]: **the party was a real** ~ on s'est bien marrés OR on a bien rigolé à la soirée. -**7.** *inf Br* [chatter] bavardage *m*; **they had a good** ~ **on the phone** ils ont taillé une bonne bavette au téléphone. -**8.** *(U) Am* [in stomach] gaz *mpl*.
◇ *vt* -**1.** [poison] asphyxier OR intoxiquer au gaz; **to** ~ **o.s.** [poison] s'asphyxier au gaz; [suicide] se suicider au gaz. -**2.** MIL gazer.
◇ *vi* -**1.** *inf* [chatter] bavarder, jacasser. -**2.** CHEM dégager des gaz.
◆ **gas up** *Am* ◇ *vt sep*: **to** ~ **the automobile up** faire le plein d'essence.
◇ *vi insep* faire le plein d'essence.

gasbag *inf* ['gæsbæg] *n Br pej* OR *hum* moulin *m* à paroles, pie *f*.

gas burner *n* brûleur *m*.

gas chamber *n* chambre *f* à gaz.

gas chromatography *n* chromatographie *f* en phase gazeuse.

Gascon ['gæskən] ◇ -**1.** [person] Gascon *m*, -onne *f*. -**2.** LING gascon *m*.
◇ *adj* gascon.

Gascony ['gæskənɪ] *pr n* Gascogne *f*; **in** ~ en Gascogne.

gas cooker *n Br* cuisinière *f* à gaz, gazinière *f*.

gas-cooled reactor *n* réacteur *m* graphite-gaz.

gaseous ['gæsjəs] *adj* PHYS gazeux.

gas fire *n Br* (appareil *m* de) chauffage *m* au gaz.

gas-fired *adj Br*: ~ **central heating** chauffage *m* central au gaz.

gas fitter *n* installateur *m* d'appareils à gaz.

gas gangrene *n (U)* gangrène *f* gazeuse.

gas guzzler *inf n Am* AUT voiture *f* qui consomme beaucoup.

gash [gæʃ] ◇ *vt* -**1.** [knee, hand] entailler; [face] balafrer, taillader; **she fell and** ~**ed her knee** elle est tombée et s'est entaillé OR ouvert le genou. -**2.** [material] déchirer, lacérer.
◇ *n* -**1.** [on knee, hand] entaille *f*; [on face] balafre *f*, estafilade *f*; **there was a great** ~ **in the side of the ship** il y avait une profonde entaille OR une large brèche dans le flanc du navire. -**2.** [in material] (grande) déchirure *f*, déchiqueture *f*.
◇ *adj* ▽ [surplus] superflu, en trop.

gas heater *n* [radiator] radiateur *m* à gaz; [for water] chauffe-eau *m inv* à gaz.

gasholder ['gæsˌhəʊldəʳ] *n* gazomètre *m*.

gasify ['gæsɪfaɪ] (*pt & pp* gasified) *vt* gazéifier.

gas jet *n* brûleur *m*.

gasket ['gæskɪt] *n* -**1.** MECH joint *m* (d'étanchéité); **(cylinder) head** ~ AUT joint *m* de culasse. -**2.** NAUT raban *m* de ferlage.

gaslight ['gæslaɪt] *n* -**1.** [lamp] lampe *f* à gaz, appareil *m* d'éclairage à gaz; [in street] bec *m* de gaz. -**2.** [light produced] lumière *f* produite par du gaz; **by** ~ à la lumière d'une lampe à gaz.

gas lighter *n* [for cooker] allume-gaz *m*; [for cigarettes] briquet *m* à gaz.

gaslit ['gæslɪt] *adj* éclairé au gaz.

gas main *n* conduite *f* de gaz.

gasman ['gæsmæn] (*pl* gasmen [-men]) *n* employé *m* du gaz, gazier *m vieilli*.

gas mantle *n* manchon *m* à incandescence.

gas mask *n* masque *m* à gaz.

gas meter *n* compteur *m* à gaz.

gas oil *n* gas-oil *m*, gazole *m*.

gasoline, gasolene ['gæsəliːn] *n Am* AUT essence *f*.

gasometer [gæ'sɒmɪtəʳ] *n* gazomètre *m*.

gas oven *n* [domestic] four *m* à gaz; [cremation chamber] four *m* crématoire.

gasp [gɑːsp] ◇ *vi* -**1.** [be short of breath] haleter, souffler; **to** ~ **for breath** OR **for air** haleter, suffoquer. -**2.** [in shock, surprise] avoir le souffle coupé; **to** ~ **in** OR **with amazement** avoir le souffle coupé par la surprise. -**3.** *inf Br fig*: **I'm** ~**ing for a cigarette** je meurs d'envie de fumer une cigarette; **I'm** ~**ing for a drink** je meurs de soif.
◇ *vt*: **what? he** ~**ed** quoi? dit-il d'une voix pantelante; **she** ~**ed out an explanation** elle s'est expliquée d'une voix haletante.
◇ *n* halètement *m*; **she gave** OR **she let out a** ~ **of surprise** elle a eu un hoquet de surprise; **to give a** ~ **of horror** avoir le souffle coupé par l'horreur; **he was at his last** ~ [dying] il allait rendre son dernier souffle OR soupir; [exhausted] il était à bout de souffle; **to the last** ~ jusqu'au dernier souffle.

gasper *inf* ['gɑːspəʳ] *n Br dated* sèche *f*, clope *m or f*.

gas pipe *n* tuyau *m* à gaz.

gas pipeline *n* gazoduc *m*.

gas range *n* fourneau *m* à gaz.

gas ring *n* [part of cooker] brûleur *m*; [small cooker] réchaud *m* à gaz.

gas station *n Am* poste *m* d'essence, station-service *f*.

gas stove *n Br* [in kitchen] cuisinière *f* à gaz, gazinière *f*; [for camping] réchaud *m* à gaz.

gassy ['gæsɪ] (*compar* gassier, *superl* gassiest) *adj* -**1.** CHEM gazeux. -**2.** [drink] gazeux. -**3.** *inf* [person] bavard. -**4.** MIN grisouteux.

gas tank *n* -**1.** [domestic] cuve *f* à gaz. -**2.** *Am* AUT réservoir *m* à essence.

gas tap *n* [on cooker] bouton *m* de cuisinière à gaz; [at mains] robinet *m* de gaz.

gasteropod ['gæstrəpɒd] = **gastropod**.

gastrectomy [gæs'trektəmɪ] (*pl* gastrectomies) *n* gastrectomie *f*.

gastric ['gæstrɪk] *adj* gastrique.

gastric flu *n (U)* grippe *f* intestinale OR gastro-intestinale.

gastric juice *n* suc *m* gastrique.

gastric ulcer *n* ulcère *m* de l'estomac, gastrite *f* ulcéreuse.

gastritis [gæs'traɪtɪs] *n* gastrite *f*.

gastroenteritis ['gæstrəʊˌentə'raɪtɪs] *n (U)* gastro-entérite *f*; **to have** ~ avoir une gastro-entérite.

gastronome ['gæstrənəʊm] *n* gastronome *mf*.

gastronomic(al) [ˌgæstrə'nɒmɪk(l)] *adj* gastronomique.

gastronomist [gæs'trɒnəmɪst] = **gastronome**.

gastronomy [gæs'trɒnəmɪ] *n* gastronomie *f*.

gastropod ['gæstrəpɒd] ◇ *n* gastéropode *m*, gastropode *m*.
◇ *adj* de gastéropode.

gas turbine *n* turbine *f* à gaz.

gasworks ['gæswɜːks] (*pl inv*) *n* usine *f* à gaz.

gat [gæt] ◇ *arch pt* → **get**.
◇ *n* ▽ *Am* flingue *m*, pétard *m*.

gate [geɪt] ◇ *n* -**1.** [into garden] porte *f*; [into driveway, field] barrière *f*; [bigger - of mansion] portail *m*; [- into courtyard] porte *f* cochère; [low] portillon *m*; [wrought iron] grille *f*; **the main** ~ la porte OR l'entrée principale; **the** ~**s of heaven/hell** les portes du paradis/de l'enfer;

to pay at the ~ [for match] payer à l'entrée ❑ to give sb the ~ *inf Am* flanquer qqn à la porte; 'The Gates of Hell' *Rodin* 'la Porte de l'enfer'. -**2.** [at airport] porte *f*; **proceed to ~ 22** embarquement porte 22; **departure ~** porte d'embarquement. -**3.** [on ski slope] porte *f*. -**4.** [on canal]: **lock ~s** écluse *f*, portes *fpl* d'écluse. -**5.** SPORT [spectators] nombre *m* de spectateurs (admis); [money] recette *f*, entrées *fpl*; **there was a good/poor ~** il y a eu beaucoup/peu de spectateurs; **the match needed a ~ of 50,000 to break even** il fallait 50 000 spectateurs au match pour que le club rentre dans ses frais. -**6.** ELECTRON gâchette *f*. -**7.** PHOT fenêtre *f*. -**8.** [in horse racing] starting-gate *f*.
◇ *vt Br* SCH consigner, mettre en retenue.

gateau ['gætəʊ] (*pl* **gateaux** [-təʊz]) *n* gros gâteau *m (décoré et fourré à la crème)*.

gate-crash *inf* ◇ *vi* [at party] s'inviter, jouer les pique-assiette; [at paying event] resquiller.
◇ *vt*: **to ~ a party** aller à une fête sans invitation; **to ~ a concert** aller à un concert sans payer.

gate-crasher *inf* [-'kræʃəʳ] *n* [at party] pique-assiette *mf*; [at paying event] resquilleur *m*, -euse *f*.

gatefold ['geɪtfəʊld] *n* encart *m* dépliant *(dans un magazine)*.

gatehouse [-'geɪthaʊs, *pl* -haʊzɪz] *n* [of estate] loge *f* du portier; [of castle] corps *m* de garde.

gatekeeper ['geɪt,kiːpəʳ] *n* portier *m*, -ère *f*; RAIL garde-barrière *mf*.

gate-leg table, gate-legged table *n* table *f* pliante.

gate money *n* recette *f*, montant *m* des entrées.

gatepost ['geɪtpəʊst] *n* montant *m* de barrière OR de porte; **between you, me and the ~** *inf Br* soit dit entre nous.

gateway ['geɪtweɪ] *n* porte *f*, entrée *f*; **Istanbul, ~ to the East** Istanbul, la porte de l'Orient; **the ~ to success/happiness** la porte du succès/du bonheur.

gather ['gæðəʳ] ◇ *vt* -**1.** [pick, collect - mushrooms, wood] ramasser; [- flowers, fruit] cueillir. -**2.** [bring together - information] recueillir; [- taxes] percevoir, recouvrer; **to ~ a crowd** attirer une foule de gens; **~ your things, we're leaving now** ramasse tes affaires, on s'en va. -**3.** [gain] prendre; **to ~ strength** prendre des forces; **to ~ speed** prendre de la vitesse. -**4.** [prepare]: **to ~ one's thoughts** se concentrer; **to ~ one's wits** rassembler ses esprits. -**5.** [embrace] serrer; **he ~ed the children to him** il serra les enfants dans ses bras OR sur son cœur. -**6.** [clothes] ramasser; **she ~ed her skirts about her** elle ramassa ses jupes. -**7.** [deduce] déduire, comprendre; **from what she told me, I ~ there will be an enquiry** à l'en croire, il y aura une enquête; **I ~ he isn't coming** j'en déduis qu'il ne vient pas, donc il ne vient pas; **as far as I can ~** d'après ce que j'ai cru comprendre. -**8.** SEW froncer; **the dress is ~ed at the waist** la robe est froncée à la taille. -**9.** TYPO [signatures] assembler. -**10.** *phr*: **to ~ dust** ramasser la poussière; **these books are just ~ing dust** ces livres ne servent qu'à ramasser OR prendre la poussière.
◇ *vi* -**1.** [people] se regrouper, se rassembler; [crowd] se former; [troops] se masser; **they all ~ed round the fire** ils se sont rassemblés autour du feu. -**2.** [clouds] s'amonceler; [darkness] s'épaissir; [storm] menacer, se préparer. -**3.** MED [abscess] mûrir; [pus] se former.
◆ **gathers** *npl* SEW fronces *fpl*.
◆ **gather in** *vt sep* -**1.** [harvest] rentrer; [wheat] récolter; [money, taxes] recouvrer; [books, exam papers] ramasser. -**2.** SEW: **~ed in at the waist** froncé à la taille.
◆ **gather round** *vi insep* se regrouper, se rassembler; **~ round and listen** approchez (-vous) et écoutez.
◆ **gather together** ◇ *vi insep* se regrouper, se rassembler.
◇ *vt sep* [people] rassembler, réunir; [books, belongings] rassembler, ramasser.
◆ **gather up** *vt sep* -**1.** [objects, belongings] ramasser; **he ~ed up the toys and put them away** il ramassa les jouets et les mit de côté. -**2.** [skirts] ramasser, retrousser; [hair] ramasser, relever; **her hair was ~ed up into a bun** ses cheveux étaient ramassés OR relevés en chignon.

gatherer ['gæðərəʳ] *n* ramasseur *m*, -euse *f*.

gathering ['gæðərɪŋ] ◇ *n* -**1.** [group] assemblée *f*, réunion *f*; **a ~ of top scientists** une réunion de scientifiques de haut niveau. -**2.** [accumulation] accumulation *f*; [of clouds] amoncellement *m*. -**3.** [bringing together - of people] rassemblement *m*; [- of objects] accumulation *f*, amoncellement *m*. -**4.** [harvesting] récolte *f*; [picking] cueillette *f*. -**5.** [increase - in speed, force] accroissement *m*. -**6.** *(U)* SEW froncis *m*, fronces *fpl*. -**7.** *(U)* MED [abscess] abcès *m*.
◇ *adj lit*: **the ~ darkness** l'obscurité grandissante; **the ~ storm** l'orage qui se prépare OR qui menace.

GATT [gæt] (*abbr of* **General Agreement on Tariffs and Trade**) *pr n* GATT *m*.

gauche [gəʊʃ] *adj* gauche, maladroit.

gaucherie ['gəʊʃərɪ] *n* gaucherie *f*, maladresse *f*.

gaucho ['gaʊtʃəʊ] (*pl* **gauchos**) *n* gaucho *m*.

gaudily ['gɔːdɪlɪ] *adv* [dress] de manière voyante, tapageusement; [decorate] de couleurs criardes.

gaudiness ['gɔːdɪnɪs] *n* [of colours] violence *f*; [of clothes, décor] style *m* voyant, mauvais goût *m*.

gaudy ['gɔːdɪ] (*compar* **gaudier**, *superl* **gaudiest**) ◇ *adj* [dress] voyant; [colour] voyant, criard, tape-à-l'œil *(inv)*; [display] tapageur.
◇ *n Br* UNIV fête *f* annuelle *(des étudiants)*.

gauge *Br*, **gage** *Am* [geɪdʒ] ◇ *n* -**1.** [instrument] jauge *f*, indicateur *m*; **petrol** OR **fuel ~** jauge à essence; **pressure ~** manomètre *m*; **temperature ~** indicateur de température. -**2.** [standard measurement] calibre *m*, gabarit *m*; [diameter - of wire, cylinder, gun] calibre *m*. -**3.** RAIL [of track] écartement *m*; AUT [of wheels] écartement *m*. -**4.** TECH [of steel] jauge *f*. -**5.** CIN [of film] pas *m*. -**6.** *fig*: **the survey provides an accurate ~ of current trends** le sondage permet d'évaluer avec précision les tendances actuelles.
◇ *vt* -**1.** [measure, calculate] mesurer, jauger; **to ~ the wind** mesurer la vitesse du vent; **to ~ the temperature of the political situation** jauger la situation politique; **she tried to ~ how much it would cost her** elle a essayé d'évaluer combien ça lui coûterait. -**2.** [predict] prévoir; **he tried to ~ what her reaction would be** il essaya de prévoir sa réaction. -**3.** [standardize] normaliser.

Gaul [gɔːl] ◇ *pr n* GEOG Gaule *f*.
◇ *n* [person] Gaulois *m*, -e *f*.

Gaullism ['gəʊlɪzm] *n* POL Gaullisme *m*.

Gaullist ['gəʊlɪst] POL ◇ *adj* Gaulliste.
◇ *n* Gaulliste *mf*.

gaunt [gɔːnt] *adj* -**1.** [emaciated - face] creux, émacié; [- body] décharné, émacié. -**2.** [desolate - landscape] morne, lugubre, désolé; [- building] lugubre, désert.

gauntlet ['gɔːntlɪt] *n* [medieval glove] gantelet *m*; [for motorcyclist, fencer] gant *m* (à crispin OR à manchette); **to throw down/to take up the ~** jeter/relever le gant; **to run the ~** *literal* passer par les baguettes; *fig* se faire fustiger; **to run the ~ of an angry mob** se forcer OR se frayer un passage à travers une foule hostile; **she had to run the ~ of their anger** elle a dû affronter leur colère.

gauntness ['gɔːntnɪs] *n* -**1.** [of face, body] maigreur *f*; **the ~ of his face** la maigreur de son visage. -**2.** [of landscape] aspect *m* morne OR lugubre, désolation *f*; [of house] aspect *m* lugubre.

gauss [gaʊs] *n* gauss *m*.

gauze [gɔːz] *n* gaze *f*.

gave [geɪv] *pt* → **give**.

gavel ['gævl] *n* marteau *m (de magistrat etc)*.

gavotte [gə'vɒt] *n* gavotte *f*.

Gawd *inf* [gɔːd] *interj Br* mon Dieu!

gawk *inf* [gɔːk] ◇ *vi* être OR rester bouche bée; **to ~ at sb** regarder qqn bouche bée.
◇ *n* [person] godiche *f*, grand dadais *m*.

gawkish ['gɔːkɪʃ] *adj* gauche, emprunté.

gawky *inf* ['gɔːkɪ] (*compar* **gawkier**, *superl* **gawkiest**) *adj* gauche, emprunté.

gawp *inf* [gɔːp] *vi Br* rester bouche bée; **don't just stand there ~ing!** ne reste pas là à bayer aux corneilles OR à rêvasser!

gay [geɪ] ◇ *adj* -**1.** [cheerful, lively - appearance, temperament, party, atmosphere] gai, joyeux; [- laughter] enjoué, joyeux; [- music, rhythm] gai, entraînant, allègre; **she led a ~ life** elle a mené joyeuse vie; **to have a ~ time** prendre du bon temps; **with ~ abandon** avec une totale OR parfaite désinvolture. -**2.** [bright - colours, lights] gai, vif, éclatant; **the streets were ~ with coloured flags/flowers** les rues étaient égayées de drapeaux/de fleurs aux couleurs vives. -**3.** [homosexual] gay, homosexuel.
◇ *n* homosexuel *m*, -elle *f*, gay *m*; **we support ~ rights** nous défendons les droits des homosexuels; **the Gay Liberation Movement** le mouvement de libération des homosexuels.

Gay Gordons [-'gɔːdnz] *n*: **the ~** *quadrille écossais*.

Gay Lib *n abbr of* **Gay Liberation movement**.

gayness ['geɪnɪs] *n* -**1.** [of appearance, mood] gaieté *f*; [of colours] gaieté *f*, éclat *m*. -**2.** [homosexuality] homosexualité *f*.

Gaza ['gɑːzə] *pr n* Gaza.

Gaza Strip *pr n*: **the ~** la bande de Gaza.

gaze [geɪz] ◇ *vi*: **to ~ at sthg** regarder qqch fixement OR longuement; **he was gazing at the ceiling** il regardait fixement le plafond, il fixait le plafond du regard; **she ~d at the landscape dreamily** elle regarda le paysage d'un air rêveur; **to ~ into space** avoir le regard perdu dans le vague, regarder dans le vide.
◇ *n* regard *m* fixe.
◆ **gaze about** *Br*, **gaze around** *vi insep* regarder autour de soi.

gazebo [gə'ziːbəʊ] (*pl* **gazebos**) *n* belvédère *m*.

gazelle [gə'zel] *n* gazelle *f*.

gazette [gə'zet] ◇ *n* [newspaper] journal *m*; [official publication] journal *m* officiel.
◇ *vt Br* publier OR faire paraître au journal officiel.

gazetteer [,gæzɪ'tɪəʳ] *n* index *m* OR nomenclature *f* géographique.

gazpacho [gə'spɑːtʃəʊ] *n* gaspacho *m*.

gazump *inf* [gə'zʌmp] *Br* ◇ *vt augmenter le prix d'une maison après une promesse de vente orale*; **we've been ~ed** la maison nous est passée sous le nez.
◇ *vi rompre une promesse de vente (d'une maison) à la suite d'une surenchère*.

GB (*abbr of* **Great Britain**) *pr n* G-B *f*.

GBH *n abbr of* **grievous bodily harm**.

GC (*abbr of* **George Cross**) *n distinction honorifique britannique*.

GCE (*abbr of* **General Certificate of Education**) *n certificat de fin d'études secondaires en deux étapes (0 level et A level) dont la première est aujourd'hui remplacée par le GCSE*.

GCH *Br written abbr of* **gas central heating**.

GCHQ (*abbr of* **Government Communications Headquarters**) *pr n centre d'interception des télécommunications étrangères en Grande-Bretagne*.

GCSE (*abbr of* **General Certificate of Secondary Education**) *n premier examen de fin de scolarité en Grande-Bretagne*.

> **GCSE:**
> Cet examen a remplacé le GCE 0 level et le CSE. On le passe après cinq ans de scolarité dans l'enseignement secondaire. Chaque élève choisit les matières dans lesquelles il veut se présenter (généralement entre 5 et 10) selon un système d'unités de valeur. Le nombre d'unités et les notes obtenues déterminent le passage dans la classe supérieure.

Gdansk [gə'dænsk] *pr n* Gdansk.

Gdns. *written abbr of* Gardens.
GDP (*abbr of* gross domestic product) *n Br* PNB *m*.
GDR (*abbr of* German Democratic Republic) *pr n* RDA *f*.
gear [gɪəʳ] ◇ *n* -**1.** *(U)* [accessories, equipment - for photography, camping, fishing] equipement *m*, matériel *m*; [- for manual work] outils *mpl*, matériel *m*; [- for household, kitchen] ustensiles *mpl*; **he brought along all his skiing ~** il a apporté tout son équipement OR toutes ses affaires de ski; **gardening ~** matériel de jardinage. -**2.** *(U)* [personal belongings] effets *mpl* personnels, affaires *fpl*; [luggage] bagages *mpl*. -**3.** *(U)* [clothes] vêtements *mpl*, tenue *f*; **she was in her jogging/swimming ~** elle était en (tenue de) jogging/en maillot de bain. -**4.** *inf (U) Br* [fashionable clothes] fringues *fpl*; **I like the ~** j'aime bien les fringues. -**5.** *(U)* [apparatus] mécanisme *m*, dispositif *m*. -**6.** [in car, on bicycle] vitesse *f*; **to change ~** changer de vitesse; **put the car in ~** passez une vitesse; **to be in first/second ~** être en première/seconde; **'use** OR **engage low ~'** utiliser le frein moteur, rétrograder; **I'm back in ~ again now** *fig* c'est reparti pour moi maintenant. -**7.** MECH [cogwheel] roue *f* dentée, pignon *m*; [system of cogs] engrenage *m*.
◇ *vt* -**1.** [adapt] adapter; **the army was not ~ed for modern warfare** l'armée n'était pas prête pour la guerre moderne; **her work schedule is ~ed to fit in with her holiday plans** son programme de travail concorde avec ses projets de vacances; **the government's policies were not ~ed to cope with an economic recession** la politique mise en place par le gouvernement n'était pas prévue pour faire face à une récession économique; **the city's hospitals were not ~ed to cater for such an emergency** les hôpitaux de la ville n'étaient pas équipés pour répondre à une telle situation d'urgence. -**2.** AUT & TECH engrener.
◆ **gear down** *vt sep* -**1.** [reduce] réduire. -**2.** MECH démultiplier.
◆ **gear up** *vt sep* [prepare]: **to be ~ed up** être paré OR fin prêt; **the sprinters were all ~ed up and ready to go** les sprinters étaient fin prêts à partir; **she'd ~ed herself up to meet them** elle s'était mise en condition pour les rencontrer.
gearbox ['gɪəbɒks] *n* boîte *f* de vitesses.
gear change *n* changement *m* de vitesse.
gearing ['gɪərɪŋ] *n* -**1.** MECH engrenage *m*. -**2.** *Br* FIN effet *m* de levier.
gear lever *Br*, **gear shift** *Am* *n* levier *m* de vitesse.
gear shift *Am* = **gear lever**.
gear stick *n* levier *m* de changement de vitesse.
gear wheel *n* roue *f* dentée, pignon *m*.
gecko ['gekəʊ] *n* gecko *m*.
GED (*abbr of* general equivalency diploma) *n aux États-Unis, diplôme d'études secondaires pour adultes souvent obtenu par correspondance*.
gee *inf* [dʒiː] *interj Am* ça alors!; **~ whiz!** super!, génial!
gee-gee ['dʒiːdʒiː] *n Br baby talk* dada *m*.
geese [giːs] *pl* → **goose**.
gee up ◇ *interj* hue!
◇ *vt sep inf Br* faire avancer.
geezer *inf* ['giːzəʳ] *n Br* bonhomme *m*, coco *m*.
Geiger counter ['gaɪgəʳ-] *n* compteur *m* Geiger.
geisha (girl) ['geɪʃə-] *n* geisha *f*.
gel[1] [dʒel] (*pt & pp* **gelled**, *cont* **gelling**)
◇ *n* -**1.** [CHEM & gen] gel *m*. -**2.** THEAT filtre *m* coloré.
◇ *vi* -**1.** [idea, plan - take shape] prendre forme OR tournure, se cristalliser. -**2.** [jellify] se gélifier.
gel[2] [gel] *Br hum* = **girl**.
gelatin ['dʒelətɪn], **gelatine** [,dʒelə'tiːn] *n* -**1.** [substance] gélatine *f*. -**2.** THEAT filtre *m* coloré.
gelatinous [dʒə'lætɪnəs] *adj* gélatineux.
gelation [dʒɪ'leɪʃn] *n* -**1.** [forming a gel] gélification *f*. -**2.** [freezing] gélation *f*.
geld [geld] *vt* [bull] châtrer; [horse] hongrer.
gelding ['geldɪŋ] *n* (cheval *m*) hongre *m*.
gelid ['dʒelɪd] *adj lit* glacial.
gelignite ['dʒelɪgnaɪt] *n* gélignite *f*.
gem [dʒem] ◇ *n* -**1.** [precious stone] gemme *f*, pierre *f* précieuse; [semiprecious stone] gemme *f*, pierre *f* fine. -**2.** [masterpiece] joyau *m*, bijou *m*, merveille *f*; **the Petit Trianon is an architectural ~** le Petit Trianon est un joyau architectural; **that antique table is a real ~** cette table d'époque est une vraie merveille; **the ~ of the collection** le joyau de la collection. -**3.** [person]: **you're a ~!** tu es un ange!; **our baby-sitter is a real ~** notre baby-sitter est une perle. -**4.** [in printing] diamant *m*.
◇ *vt* orner, parer.
geminate ['dʒemɪneɪt] ◇ *adj* géminé.
◇ *vt* géminer.
gemination [,dʒemɪ'neɪʃn] *n* gémination *f*.
Gemini ['dʒemɪnaɪ] *pr n* ASTROL & ASTRON Gémeaux *mpl*; **he's a ~** il est Gémeaux.
Gemini Program *pr n*: **the ~** *le programme spatial américain Gemini*.
gemma ['dʒemmə] (*pl* **gemmae** [-miː]) *n* BOT gemme *f*.
gemmology [dʒem'ɒlədʒɪ] *n* gemmologie *f*.
gemstone ['dʒemstəʊn] *n* [precious] gemme *f*, pierre *f* précieuse; [semiprecious] gemme *f*, pierre *f* fine.
gen *inf* [dʒen] (*pt & pp* **genned**, *cont* **genning**) *n (U) Br* tuyaux *mpl*, renseignements *mpl*; **she gave me the latest ~ on our new assignment** elle m'a donné les derniers renseignements concernant notre nouvelle mission; **what's the ~ on the new neighbours?** qu'est-ce qu'on raconte sur les nouveaux voisins?
◆ **gen up** *inf Br* ◇ *vi insep* se rencarder; **I'm genning up on computers** je me rencarde sur les ordinateurs.
◇ *vt sep* rencarder, mettre au parfum; **she genned me up on the latest developments** elle m'a renseigné sur les OR elle m'a mis au parfum des derniers événements.
gen. (*written abbr of* general, generally) gén.
Gen. (*written abbr of* general) Gal.
gender ['dʒendəʳ] *n* -**1.** GRAMM genre *m*; **common ~** genre commun. -**2.** [sex] sexe *m*; **~ studies** *à l'université, matière issue des mouvements féministes et qui formule une critique des rôles de l'homme et de la femme tels qu'ils sont établis par la société*.
gender-bender▽ *n* travelo *m*.
gene [dʒiːn] *n* gène *m*; **dominant/recessive ~** gène dominant/récessif.
genealogical [,dʒiːnjə'lɒdʒɪkl] *adj* généalogique.
genealogical tree *n* arbre *m* généalogique.
genealogist [,dʒiːnɪ'ælədʒɪst] *n* généalogiste *mf*.
genealogy [,dʒiːnɪ'ælədʒɪ] *n* généalogie *f*.
gene flow *n* flux *m* génétique.
gene frequency *n* fréquence *f* génétique.
gene pool *n* patrimoine *m* OR bagage *m* héréditaire.
genera ['dʒenərə] *pl* → **genus**.
general ['dʒenərəl] ◇ *adj* -**1.** [common] général; **as a ~ rule** en règle générale, en général; **in ~ terms** en termes généraux; **in the ~ interest** dans l'intérêt de tous; **the ~ feeling was that he should have won** le sentiment général était qu'il aurait dû gagner; **there was a ~ movement to leave the room** la plupart des gens se sont levés pour sortir. -**2.** [approximate] général; **a ~ resemblance** une vague ressemblance. -**3.** [widespread] général, répandu; **a ~ opinion** une opinion générale OR répandue; **to be in ~ use** être d'usage courant OR répandu; **this word is no longer in ~ use** ce mot est tombé en désuétude; **there is ~ agreement on the matter** il y a consensus sur la question; **this kind of attitude is fairly ~ in Europe** ce genre d'attitude est assez répandu en Europe. -**4.** [overall - direction]: **to go in the ~ direction of sthg** se diriger plus ou moins vers qqch; **their house is over in that ~ direction** leur maison se trouve vers là-bas. -**5.** [outline, plan, view] d'ensemble; **the ~ effect is quite pleasing** le résultat général est assez agréable; **to have a ~ impression of sthg** avoir une impression globale OR d'ensemble de qqch; **I get the ~ idea** je vois en gros; **he gave her a ~ idea** OR **outline of his work** il lui a décrit son travail dans les grandes lignes. -**6.** [ordinary]: **this book is for the ~ reader** ce livre est destiné au lecteur moyen; **the ~ public** le grand public *m*. -**7.** ADMIN [after title]: **secretary ~** secrétaire *m* général.
◇ *n* -**1.** [in reasoning]: **in ~** en général; **to go from the ~ to the particular** aller du général au particulier. -**2.** MIL général *m*. -**3.** [domestic servant] bonne *f* à tout faire.
general anaesthetic *n* anesthésie *f* générale.
general assembly *n* assemblée *f* générale.
general dealer *Am* = **general store**.
general degree *n* UNIV licence *f* comportant plusieurs matières.
general delivery *n Am* poste *f* restante.
general election *n* élections *fpl* législatives.
general headquarters *n* (grand) quartier *m* général.
general hospital *n* centre *m* hospitalier.
generalissimo [,dʒenərə'lɪsɪməʊ] (*pl* **generalissimos**) *n* généralissime *m*.
generalist ['dʒenərəlɪst] *n* non-spécialiste *mf*, généraliste *mf*.
generality [,dʒenə'rælətɪ] (*pl* **generalities**) *n* -**1.** [generalization] généralité *f*; **the Minister's speech was full of generalities** lors de son discours le Ministre n'a évoqué que des généralités; **a principle of great ~** un principe très général; **in the ~** en règle générale. -**2.** *fml* [majority] plupart *f*; **the ~ of people is** OR **are against euthanasia** la plupart des gens sont hostiles à l'euthanasie.
generalization [,dʒenərəlaɪ'zeɪʃn] *n* -**1.** [general comment] généralisation *f*. -**2.** [spread] généralisation *f*.
generalize, -ise ['dʒenərəlaɪz] ◇ *vt* généraliser.
◇ *vi* -**1.** [speak in generalities] généraliser. -**2.** MED [disease] se généraliser.
generalized ['dʒenərəlaɪzd] *adj* -**1.** [involving many] généralisé. -**2.** [non-specific] général.
general knowledge *n* culture *f* générale.
generally ['dʒenərəlɪ] *adv* -**1.** [usually] en général, d'habitude; **he ~ comes in the afternoon** d'habitude, il vient l'après-midi. -**2.** [in a general way] en général, de façon générale; **~ speaking** en général, en règle générale. -**3.** [by most] dans l'ensemble; **it is ~ agreed that it cannot be done** on s'accorde en général à penser que c'est infaisable.
general manager *n* directeur *m* général, directrice *f* générale.
general meeting *n* assemblée *f* générale.
general officer *n* général *m* en chef.
General Post Office = **GPO**.
general practice *n* médecine *f* générale.
general practitioner *n* médecin *m* généraliste, omnipraticien *m*, -enne *f*.
general purpose *adj* polyvalent.
generalship ['dʒenərəlʃɪp] *n* *(U)* -**1.** MIL [skill, duties] tactique *f*. -**2.** ADMIN capacités *fpl* administratives.
general staff *n* état-major *m*.
general store *n* bazar *m*.
general strike *n* grève *f* générale; **the General Strike** *la grève de mai 1926 en Grande-Bretagne, lancée par les syndicats par solidarité avec les mineurs*.
General Studies *n* SCH ≃ cours *m* de culture générale.
General Synod *pr n le Synode général de l'Église d'Angleterre*.
generate ['dʒenəreɪt] *vt* [produce - electricity, power] produire, générer; [- emotion] susciter, donner naissance à; [- offspring] engendrer; LING générer.
generating station *n* centrale *f* électrique.
generating unit *n* groupe *m* électrogène.

generation [ˌdʒenəˈreɪʃn] *n* -**1.** [age group] génération *f*; the present ~ is OR are anxious about the future la génération actuelle est inquiète face à l'avenir; the 1960s saw the appearance of the hippie ~ la génération hippie est apparue au cours des années 60; the rising ~ la jeune OR nouvelle génération; a new ~ of writers une nouvelle génération d'écrivains; from ~ to ~ de génération en génération, de père en fils. -**2.** [by birth]: she is second ~ Irish elle est née de parents irlandais; third ~ black Britons still face racial prejudice les noirs britanniques de la troisième génération sont encore confrontés au racisme. -**3.** [period of time] génération *f*; the house has been in the family for three ~s la maison est dans la famille depuis trois générations; traditions that have been practised for ~s des traditions en vigueur depuis des générations. -**4.** [model - of machine] génération *f*; a third-~ micro processor un microprocesseur de la troisième génération. -**5.** *(U)* [of electricity] génération *f*, production *f*; LING génération *f*.

generation gap *n* écart *m* entre les générations; [conflict] conflit *m* des générations.

generative [ˈdʒenərətɪv] *adj* génératif; ~ cell cellule *f* générative.

generative grammar *n* grammaire *f* générative.

generative semantics *n* sémantique *f* générative.

generator [ˈdʒenəreɪtəʳ] *n* -**1.** [electric] générateur *m*, groupe *m* électrogène; [of steam] générateur *m*, chaudière *f* (à vapeur); [of gas] gazogène *m*. -**2.** [person] générateur *m*, -trice *f*.

generatrix [ˈdʒenəreɪtrɪks] (*pl* generatrices [-trɪsiːz]) *n* génératrice *f*.

generic [dʒɪˈnerɪk] *adj* générique.

generically [dʒɪˈnerɪklɪ] *adv* génériquement.

generosity [ˌdʒenəˈrɒsətɪ] *n* générosité *f*.

generous [ˈdʒenərəs] *adj* -**1.** [unsparing, liberal]: he's a very ~ person c'est quelqu'un de très généreux; she's always ~ with her time elle n'est pas avare de son temps; he was very ~ in his praise il ne tarissait pas d'éloges; she has a ~ nature elle est d'une nature généreuse. -**2.** [in value - gift] généreux; [in quantity - sum, salary] généreux, élevé. -**3.** [copious] copieux, abondant; [large] bon, abondant; a ~ portion une part copieuse OR généreuse; food and drink were in ~ supply il y avait à boire et à manger; she cut him a ~ slice of cake elle lui a servi une bonne tranche de gâteau; they serve ~ helpings of cream ils ne lésinent pas sur la crème; a ~ harvest une récolte abondante. -**4.** *Br* [strong - wine] généreux. -**5.** [physically - size] généreux, ample; to have ~ curves *euph* avoir des formes généreuses.

generously [ˈdʒenərəslɪ] *adv* -**1.** [unsparingly] généreusement, avec générosité. -**2.** [with magnanimity - agree, offer] généreusement; [- forgive] généreusement, avec magnanimité. -**3.** [copiously]: a plate of fish and chips ~ sprinkled with salt and vinegar une assiette de «fish and chips» généreusement salée et vinaigrée; the soup was rather ~ salted [oversalted] la soupe était très généreusement salée. -**4.** [in size] amplement; to be ~ built *euph* avoir des formes généreuses.

genesis [ˈdʒenəsɪs] (*pl* geneses [-siːz]) *n* genèse *f*, origine *f*.

◆ **Genesis** *n* BIBLE la Genèse.

genet [ˈdʒenɪt] *n* genette *f*.

genetic [dʒɪˈnetɪk] *adj* génétique; ~ map/marker carte *f*/marqueur *m* génétique.

genetical [dʒɪˈnetɪkl] = **genetic**.

genetically [dʒɪˈnetɪklɪ] *adv* génétiquement.

genetic code *n* code *m* génétique.

genetic engineer *n* généticien *m*, -enne *f*.

genetic engineering *n* génie *m* génétique.

geneticist [dʒɪˈnetɪsɪst] *n* généticien *m*, -enne *f*.

genetics [dʒɪˈnetɪks] *n (U)* génétique *f*.

Geneva [dʒɪˈniːvə] *pr n* Genève; Lake ~ le lac Léman.

Geneva Convention *pr n*: the ~ la Convention de Genève.

Genevan [dʒɪˈniːvn], **Genevese** [ˌdʒenɪˈviːz] (*pl inv*) ◇ *n* Genevois *m*, -e *f*.

◇ *adj* genevois.

Genghis Khan [ˌgeŋgɪsˈkɑːn] *pr n* Gengis Khan.

genial [ˈdʒiːnjəl] *adj* -**1.** [friendly - person] aimable, affable; [- expression, voice] cordial, chaleureux. -**2.** *lit* [clement - weather] clément.

geniality [ˌdʒiːnɪˈælətɪ] *n* -**1.** [of person, expression] cordialité *f*, amabilité *f*. -**2.** *lit* [of weather] clémence *f*.

genially [ˈdʒiːnjəlɪ] *adv* affablement, cordialement, chaleureusement.

genie [ˈdʒiːnɪ] (*pl* genii [-nɪaɪ]) *n* génie *m*, djinn *m*.

genii [ˈdʒiːnɪaɪ] *pl* → **genie, genius**.

genital [ˈdʒenɪtl] *adj* génital; the ~ organs les organes *mpl* génitaux.

◆ **genitals** *npl* organes *mpl* génitaux.

genitalia [ˌdʒenɪˈteɪlɪə] *npl* organes *mpl* génitaux, parties *fpl* génitales.

genitival [ˌdʒenɪˈtaɪvl] *adj* du génitif.

genitive [ˈdʒenɪtɪv] ◇ *n* génitif *m*; in the ~ au génitif.

◇ *adj* du génitif; the ~ case le génitif.

genito-urinary [ˌdʒenɪtəʊˈjʊərɪnərɪ] *adj* génito-urinaire; the ~ tract l'appareil *m* génito-urinaire.

genius [ˈdʒiːnjəs] (*pl senses 1, 2 & 3* geniuses, *pl sense 4* genii [-nɪaɪ]) *n* -**1.** [person] génie *m*; she's a ~ at music c'est un génie en musique. -**2.** [special ability] génie *m*; a work/writer of ~ une œuvre/un écrivain de génie; he has a ~ for public relations il a le génie des relations publiques; some people have great natural ~ il y a des gens très doués de naissance; her ~ lies in her power to evoke atmosphere son génie, c'est de savoir recréer une atmosphère; she has a ~ for remembering people's faces elle a le génie OR le don de se souvenir des visages. -**3.** [special character - of system, idea] génie *m* (particulier), esprit *m*. -**4.** [spirit, demon] génie *m*; good/evil ~ bon/mauvais génie.

genoa [ˈdʒenəʊə] *n* NAUT génois *m*.

Genoa [ˈdʒenəʊə] *pr n* Gênes.

genocidal [ˌdʒenəˈsaɪdl] *adj* génocide.

genocide [ˈdʒenəsaɪd] *n* génocide *m*.

Genoese [ˌdʒenəʊˈiːz] (*pl inv*), **Genovese** [ˌdʒenəˈviːz] (*pl inv*) ◇ *n* Génois *m*, -e *f*.

◇ *adj* génois.

genotype [ˈdʒenəʊtaɪp] *n* génotype *m*.

genre [ˈʒɑ̃rə] ◇ *n* genre *m*.

◇ *comp*: ~ painting peinture *f* de genre.

gent *inf* [dʒent] (*abbr of* gentleman) *n esp Br* monsieur *m*; to behave like a (real) ~ agir en gentleman; ~s' outfitters magasin *m* de confection OR d'habillement pour hommes.

◆ **gents** *inf n*: the ~s les toilettes *fpl* (pour hommes); where's the ~s? où sont les toilettes?

genteel [dʒenˈtiːl] *adj* -**1.** [refined] comme il faut, distingué; to live in ~ poverty vivre dans une misère respectable OR une misère qui s'efforce de sauver les apparences. -**2.** [affected - speech] maniéré, affecté; [- manner] affecté; [- language] précieux.

gentian [ˈdʒenʃɪən] *n* gentiane *f*.

gentian blue *n* bleu *m* gentiane.

gentian violet *n* violet *m* gentiane.

Gentile [ˈdʒentaɪl] ◇ *n* gentil *m*.

◇ *adj* des gentils.

gentility [dʒenˈtɪlətɪ] *n (U)* -**1.** [good breeding] distinction *f*. -**2.** [gentry] petite noblesse *f*. -**3.** [affected politeness] manières *fpl* affectées.

gentle [ˈdʒentl] ◇ *adj* -**1.** [mild - person, smile, voice] doux; [- landscape] agréable; he is of a ~ disposition il est facile à vivre; a ~ soul une bonne âme, une âme charitable; ~ reader *lit* aimable lecteur; to use ~ methods employer la douceur ❑ the ~ sex le sexe *m* faible; as ~ as a lamb doux comme un agneau. -**2.** [light - knock, push, breeze] léger; [- rain] fin, léger [- exercise] modéré. -**3.** [discreet - rebuke, reminder] discret; to try ~ persuasion on s[omeone] essayer de convaincre qqn par la douceur; we gave him a ~ hint nous l'avons discrètemen[t] mis sur la voie. -**4.** [gradual - slope, climb] doux a ~ transition une transition progressive O[R] sans heurts; to come to a ~ halt s'arrêter san[s] à-coup. -**5.** *arch* [noble] noble, de bonne nais[sance]; of ~ birth de bonne famille. -**6.** *iron*: th[e] ~ art of persuasion l'art subtil de l[a] persuasion.

◇ *vt* [animal] apaiser, calmer.

◇ *n* [maggot] asticot *m*.

gentlefolk [ˈdʒentlfəʊk] *npl arch* personnes *fp[l]* de bonne famille OR de la petite noblesse.

gentleman [ˈdʒentlmən] (*pl* gentlemen [-mən]) *n* -**1.** [man] monsieur *m*; show the ~ in faite[s] entrer monsieur; come in, gentlemen! entrez, messieurs! -**2.** [well-bred man] homme *m* du monde, gentleman *m*; he's a real ~ c'est un vrai gentleman; to act like a ~ agir en gentle[-] man; that's not how a ~ would behave c'es[t] (une conduite) indigne d'un gentleman; a born ~ un gentleman né; the word of a ~ la parole (d'honneur) d'un gentleman ❑ 'Gentlemen Prefer Blondes' *Hawks* 'les Hommes préfèrent les blondes'. -**3.** [man of substance] rentier *m*; [at court] gentilhomme *m*.

gentleman-at-arms *n Br* gentilhomme *m* à la garde.

gentleman farmer *n* gentleman-farmer *m*.

gentleman-in-waiting *n Br* gentilhomme *m* (au service du roi).

gentlemanly [ˈdʒentlmənlɪ] *adj* [person] bien élevé; [appearance, behaviour] distingué; [status] noble; to behave in a ~ way agir en gentleman.

gentleman's agreement *n* gentleman's agreement *m*, accord *m* reposant sur l'honneur.

gentleman's gentleman *n Br domestique personnel d'un gentleman*.

gentlemen [ˈdʒentlmən] *pl* → **gentleman**.

gentlemen's club *n* club *m* de gentlemen.

gentleness [ˈdʒentlnɪs] *n (U)* douceur *f*, légèreté *f*.

gentlewoman [ˈdʒentlˌwʊmən] (*pl* gentlewomen [-ˌwɪmɪn]) *n* -**1.** [of noble birth] dame *f*. -**2.** [refined] femme *f* du monde. -**3.** [lady-in-waiting] dame *f* d'honneur OR de compagnie.

gently [ˈdʒentlɪ] *adv* -**1.** [mildly - speak, smile] avec douceur; [discreetly - remind, reprimand, suggest] discrètement; [kindly]: he broke the news to her as ~ as possible il fit de son mieux pour lui annoncer la nouvelle avec tact OR ménagement. -**2.** [lightly]: a light breeze blew the curtains ~ to and fro une légère brise faisait onduler les rideaux; the rain was falling ~ la pluie tombait doucement. -**3.** [gradually] doucement, progressivement; the hill slopes ~ down to the sea la colline descend doucement OR en pente douce vers la mer; ~ rolling hills des collines qui ondoient (doucement). -**4.** [slowly - move, heat] doucement; a ~ flowing river une rivière qui coule paisiblement; ~ does it! doucement!

gentrification [ˌdʒentrɪfɪˈkeɪʃn] *n* embourgeoisement *m*.

gentrify [ˈdʒentrɪfaɪ] (*pt & pp* gentrified) *vt* [suburb] embourgeoiser, rendre chic OR élégant; the area has been gentrified le quartier est devenu chic.

gentry [ˈdʒentrɪ] (*pl* gentries) *n* petite noblesse *f*; the landed ~ la noblesse terrienne.

genuflect [ˈdʒenjuːflekt] *vi* faire une génuflexion.

genuflection, genuflexion [ˌdʒenjuːˈflekʃn] *n* génuflexion *f*.

genuine [ˈdʒenjʊɪn] *adj* -**1.** [authentic - antique] authentique; [- gold, mahogany] véritable, vrai; a ~ Van Gogh un Van Gogh authentique; it's a ~ article c'est une pièce authentique; he's the ~ article *fig* c'est un vrai de vrai. -**2.** [sincere - person] naturel, franc; [- emotion] sincère, vrai;

[- smile, laugh] vrai, franc; **it is my ~ belief that he is innocent** je suis intimement persuadé de son innocence; **her regret seemed ~** elle semblait sincèrement désolée. -**3.** [real - mistake] fait de bonne foi. -**4.** [not impersonated - repairman, official] vrai, véritable. -**5.** [serious - buyer] sérieux; **'~ enquiries only'** [in advert] 'pas sérieux s'abstenir'.

genuinely ['dʒenjʊɪnlɪ] *adv* [truly] authentiquement; [sincerely] sincèrement, véritablement.

genus ['dʒiːnəs] (*pl* genera ['dʒenərə]) *n* BIOL genre *m*.

geocentric [,dʒiːəʊ'sentrɪk] *adj* géocentrique.

geochemistry [,dʒiːəʊ'kemɪstrɪ] *n* géochimie *f*.

geode ['dʒiːəʊd] *n* géode *f*.

geodesic [,dʒiːəʊ'desɪk] *adj* géodésique; **~ line** (ligne *f*) géodésique *f*.

geodesic dome *n* dôme *m* géodésique.

geodesy [dʒiː'ɒdɪsɪ] *n* géodésie *f*.

geodetic [,dʒiːəʊ'detɪk] = **geodesic**.

geographer [dʒɪ'ɒgrəfə'] *n* géographe *mf*.

geographic(al) [dʒɪə'græfɪk(l)] *adj* géographique.

geographically [dʒɪə'græfɪklɪ] *adv* géographiquement.

geographical mile *n* mille *m* marin.

geography [dʒɪ'ɒgrəfɪ] (*pl* **geographies**) *n* -**1.** [science] géographie *f*; **physical/social ~** géographie physique/humaine. -**2.** [lay-out]: **I don't know the ~ of the building** je ne connais pas le plan du bâtiment.

geological [,dʒɪə'lɒdʒɪkl] *adj* géologique; **~ time** temps *m* géologique.

geologically [,dʒɪə'lɒdʒɪklɪ] *adv* du point de vue géologique.

geologist [dʒɪ'ɒlədʒɪst] *n* géologue *mf*.

geology [dʒɪ'ɒlədʒɪ] *n* géologie *f*.

geomagnetic [,dʒiːəʊmæg'netɪk] *adj* géomagnétique; **a ~ storm** un orage magnétique.

geomagnetism [,dʒiːəʊ'mægnɪtɪzm] *n* géomagnétisme *m*, magnétisme *m* terrestre.

geometer [dʒɪ'ɒmɪtə'] *n* géomètre *mf*.

geometric [,dʒɪə'metrɪk] *adj* géométrique; **~ distribution** distribution *f* géométrique.

geometrical [,dʒɪə'metrɪkl] *adj* géométrique.

geometrically [,dʒɪə'metrɪklɪ] *adv* géométriquement.

geometrician [,dʒɪəʊmə'trɪʃn] *n* géomètre *mf*.

geometric mean *n* moyenne *f* géométrique.

geometric progression *n* progression *f* géométrique.

geometric series *n* série *f* géométrique.

geometry [dʒɪ'ɒmətrɪ] *n* géométrie *f*.

geomorphic [,dʒiːəʊ'mɔːfɪk] *adj* géomorphologique.

geomorphology [,dʒiːəʊmɔː'fɒlədʒɪ] *n* géomorphologie *f*.

geophysical [,dʒiːəʊ'fɪzɪkl] *adj* géophysique.

geophysicist [,dʒiːəʊ'fɪzɪsɪst] *n* géophysicien *m*, -enne *f*.

geophysics [,dʒiːəʊ'fɪzɪks] *n (U)* géophysique *f*.

geopolitical [,dʒiːəʊpə'lɪtɪkl] *adj* géopolitique.

geopolitics [,dʒiːəʊ'pɒlətɪks] *n (U)* géopolitique *f*.

Geordie *inf* ['dʒɔːdɪ] *Br* ◇ *n* -**1.** [person] *surnom des habitants de Tyneside, dans le Nord-Est de l'Angleterre*. -**2.** [dialect] *dialecte parlé par les habitants de Tyneside*.
◇ *adj caractéristique du Tyneside*.

George [dʒɔːdʒ] *pr n* -**1.** Saint **~** saint Georges; **King ~ V** le roi George V; **by ~!** *inf dated* sapristi! *dated*, mon Dieu! -**2.** *inf Br* AERON *le pilote automatique*.

georgette [dʒɔː'dʒet] *n* crêpe *m* georgette.

Georgia ['dʒɔːdʒjə] *pr n* [in US, CIS] Géorgie *f*; **in ~** en Géorgie.

Georgian ['dʒɔːdʒjən] ◇ *n* -**1.** [inhabitant of Georgia] Géorgien *m*, -enne *f*. -**2.** LING géorgien *m*.
◇ *adj* -**1.** [of Georgia] géorgien. -**2.** HIST géorgien (*du règne des rois George I-IV (1714-1830)*; **~ architecture** architecture *f* de style géorgien. -**3.** LITERAT: **~ poetry** poésie *f* géorgienne (*poésie britannique des années 1912-1922*).

geoscience [,dʒiːəʊ'saɪəns] *n* -**1.** [particular] science *f* de la terre. -**2.** *(U)* [collectively] sciences *fpl* de la terre.

geostationary [,dʒiːəʊ'steɪʃnərɪ] *adj* géostationnaire; **in ~ orbit** en orbite géostationnaire.

geosyncline [,dʒiːəʊ'sɪŋklaɪn] *n* géosynclinal *m*.

geotectonic [,dʒiːəʊtek'tɒnɪk] *adj* géotectonique.

geothermal [,dʒiːəʊ'θɜːml], **geothermic** [,dʒiːəʊ'θɜːmɪk] *adj* géothermique.

geotropism [dʒɪ'ɒtrə,pɪzm] *n* géotropisme *m*.

geranium [dʒɪ'reɪnjəm] ◇ *n* géranium *m*.
◇ *adj* rouge géranium *(inv)*, incarnat.

gerbil(le) ['dʒɜːbɪl] *n* gerbille *f*.

geriatric [,dʒerɪ'ætrɪk] ◇ *adj* MED gériatrique; **~ hospital** hospice *m*; **~ medicine** gériatrie *f*; **~ nurse** infirmier *m* (spécialisé), infirmière *f* (spécialisée) en gériatrie; **~ ward** service *m* de gériatrie.
◇ *n* -**1.** [patient] malade *mf* en gériatrie. -**2.** *pej* vieux *m*, vieille *f*.

geriatrician [,dʒerɪə'trɪʃn] *n* gériatre *mf*.

geriatrics [,dʒerɪ'ætrɪks] *n (U)* gériatrie *f*.

germ [dʒɜːm] *n* -**1.** [microbe] microbe *m*, germe *m*. -**2.** BIOL germe *m*. -**3.** *fig* germe *m*, ferment *m*; **the ~ of an idea** le germe d'une idée.

german ['dʒɜːmən] ◇ *adj fml* -**1.** [cousin, brother] germain. -**2.** = **germane**.
◇ *n Am* [dance] allemande *f*.

German ['dʒɜːmən] ◇ *n* -**1.** [person] Allemand *m*, -e *f*. -**2.** LING allemand *m*.
◇ *adj* allemand.

German Democratic Republic *pr n*: **the ~** la République démocratique allemande, la RDA.

germane [dʒɜː'meɪn] *adj fml* pertinent; **~ to** en rapport avec; **it is not ~ to my argument** cela n'a aucun rapport avec mon argument.

Germanic [dʒɜː'mænɪk] ◇ *adj* germanique.
◇ *n* LING germanique *m*.

germanium [dʒɜː'meɪnɪəm] *n* germanium *m*.

germanize, -ise ['dʒɜːmənaɪz] *vt* germaniser.

German measles *n (U)* rubéole *f*.

Germanophile [dʒɜː'mænəfaɪl] *n* germanophile *mf*.

Germanophobe [dʒɜː'mænəfəʊb] *n* germanophobe *mf*.

German shepherd (dog) *n* berger *m* allemand.

Germany ['dʒɜːmənɪ] *pr n* Allemagne *f*; **in ~** en Allemagne; **East ~** Allemagne de l'Est; **West ~** Allemagne fédérale OR de l'Ouest.

germ cell *n* cellule *f* germinale OR reproductrice.

germfree [,dʒɜːm'friː] *adj* stérilisé, aseptisé.

germicidal [,dʒɜːmɪ'saɪdl] *adj* germicide, bactéricide.

germicide ['dʒɜːmɪsaɪd] *n* bactéricide *m*.

germinal ['dʒɜːmɪnl] *adj* -**1.** BIOL germinal. -**2.** *fig* & *fml* embryonnaire.

germinate ['dʒɜːmɪneɪt] ◇ *vi* -**1.** BIOL germer. -**2.** *fig* [originate] germer, prendre naissance.
◇ *vt* -**1.** BIOL faire germer. -**2.** *fig* faire germer, donner naissance à.

germination [,dʒɜːmɪ'neɪʃn] *n* germination *f*.

germ killer *n* germicide *m*, microbicide *m*.

germ warfare *n (U)* guerre *f* bactériologique.

Gerona [dʒə'rəʊnə] *pr n* Gérone.

gerontocracy [,dʒerɒn'tɒkrəsɪ] (*pl* **gerontocracies**) *n* gérontocratie *f*.

gerontologist [,dʒerɒn'tɒlədʒɪst] *n* gérontologue *mf*.

gerontology [,dʒerɒn'tɒlədʒɪ] *n* gérontologie *f*.

gerrymander ['dʒerɪmændə'] *pej* ◇ *vi* faire du charcutage électoral, redécouper des circonscriptions.
◇ *vt* redécouper (à des fins électorales).
◇ *n* charcutage *m* électoral.

gerrymandering ['dʒerɪmændərɪŋ] *n pej* charcutage *m* électoral.

gerund ['dʒerənd] *n* gérondif *m*.

gerundive [dʒɪ'rʌndɪv] ◇ *n* adjectif *m* verbal.
◇ *adj* du gérondif.

gesso ['dʒesəʊ] *n* [for painting] enduit *m* (au plâtre); [for sculpture] plâtre *m* (de Paris).

gestalt [gə'ʃtælt] *n* gestalt *f*.

gestalt psychology *n* gestaltisme *m*, théorie *f* de la forme.

Gestapo [ge'stɑːpəʊ] *pr n* Gestapo *f*.

gestate [dʒe'steɪt] ◇ *vi* être en gestation; *fig* mûrir; **my ideas need time to ~** mes idées ont besoin de mûrir.
◇ *vt* -**1.** BIOL [young] porter. -**2.** *fig* [idea, plan] laisser mûrir.

gestation [dʒe'steɪʃn] *n* gestation *f*; **~ period** période *f* de gestation.

gesticulate [dʒe'stɪkjʊleɪt] ◇ *vi* gesticuler.
◇ *vt* [answer, meaning] mimer.

gesticulation [dʒe,stɪkjʊ'leɪʃn] *n* gesticulation *f*.

gesture ['dʒestʃə'] ◇ *n* -**1.** [expressive movement] geste *m*; **to make a ~** faire un geste; **a ~ of acknowledgement** un signe de reconnaissance; **he made a ~ of dismissal** il les a congédiés d'un geste. -**2.** [sign, token] geste *m*; **as a ~ of friendship** en signe OR témoignage d'amitié; **they offered him a salary rise as a ~ of goodwill** ils lui ont offert une augmentation en gage de leur bonne volonté.
◇ *vi*: **to ~ with one's hands/head** faire un signe de la main/de la tête; **he ~d to me to stand up** il m'a fait signe de me lever; **he ~d to his wife** il fit signe à sa femme; **she ~d towards the pile of books** elle désigna OR montra la pile de livres d'un geste.
◇ *vt* mimer.

get [get] (*Br pt & pp* **got** [gɒt], *cont* **getting** [getɪŋ], *Am pt* **got** [gɒt], *pp* **gotten** [gɒtn], *cont* **getting** [getɪŋ]) ◇ *vt* **A.** -**1.** [receive - gift, letter, phone call] recevoir, avoir; [- benefits, pension] recevoir, toucher; MED [- treatment] suivre; **I got a bike for my birthday** on m'a donné OR j'ai eu OR reçu un vélo pour mon anniversaire; **I ~ "The Times" at home** je reçois le «Times» à la maison; **this part of the country doesn't ~ much rain** cette région ne reçoit pas beaucoup de pluie, il ne pleut pas beaucoup dans cette région; **the living room ~s a lot of sun** le salon est très ensoleillé; **I rang and rang but I got no answer** [at door] j'ai sonné et resonné mais je n'ai pas obtenu OR eu de réponse; [on phone] j'ai appelé je ne sais combien de fois sans obtenir de réponse; **many students ~ grants** beaucoup d'étudiants ont une bourse; **he got 5 years for smuggling** il a écopé de OR il a pris 5 ans (de prison) pour contrebande ❑ **you're really going to ~ it!** *inf* qu'est-ce que tu vas prendre OR écoper!; **I'll see that you ~ yours!** *inf* je vais te régler ton compte! -**2.** [obtain - gen] avoir, trouver, obtenir; [- through effort] se procurer, obtenir; [- licence, loan, permission] obtenir; [- diploma, grades] avoir, obtenir; **where did you ~ that book?** où avez-vous trouvé ce livre?; **they got him a job** ils lui ont trouvé du travail; **I got the job!** ils m'ont embauché!; **can you ~ them the report?** pouvez-vous leur procurer le rapport?; **I got a glimpse of her face** j'ai pu apercevoir son visage; **the town ~s its water from the reservoir** la ville reçoit son eau du réservoir; **we ~ our wine directly from the vineyard** en vin OR pour le vin, nous nous fournissons directement chez le producteur; **they stopped in town to ~ some lunch** [had lunch there] ils se sont arrêtés en ville pour déjeuner; [bought sthg to eat] ils se sont arrêtés en ville pour acheter de quoi déjeuner; **I'm going out to ~ a breath of fresh air** je sors prendre l'air; **I'm going to ~ something to drink/eat** [fetch] je vais chercher quelque chose à boire/manger; [eat] je vais boire/manger quelque chose; can I ~ a coffee? *Am* je pourrais avoir un café, s'il vous plaît?; ~ yourself a good lawyer trouvez-vous un bon avocat; ~ advice from your doctor demandez conseil à votre médecin; to ~ (o.s.) a wife/husband se trouver une femme/un mari; to ~ sb to o.s. avoir qqn pour soi tout seul; to ~ a divorce obtenir le divorce; ~ plenty of exercise faites plein d'exercice; ~ plenty of sleep dormez beaucoup; try and ~ a few days off work essayez de prendre quelques jours de congé; I got a lot from OR out of my trip to China mon voyage en Chine m'a beaucoup apporté; he didn't ~ a chance to introduce himself il n'a pas eu l'occasion de se présenter. -**3.** [inherit - characteristic] tenir; she ~s her shyness from her father elle tient sa timidité de son père. -**4.** [obtain in exchange] recevoir; they got a lot of money for their flat la vente de leur appartement leur a rapporté beaucoup d'argent; they got a good price for the painting le tableau s'est vendu à un bon prix; he got nothing for his trouble il s'est donné de la peine pour rien; you don't ~ something for nothing on n'a rien pour rien. -**5.** [offer as gift] offrir, donner; what did she ~ him for Christmas? qu'est-ce qu'elle lui a offert OR donné pour Noël?; I don't know what to ~ Jill for her birthday je ne sais pas quoi acheter à Jill pour son anniversaire. -**6.** [buy] acheter, prendre; ~ your father a magazine when you go out achète une revue à ton père quand tu sortiras; ~ the paper too prends OR achète le journal aussi; we got the house cheap on a eu la maison (à) bon marché. -**7.** [learn - information, news] recevoir, apprendre; we turned on the radio to ~ the news nous avons allumé la radio pour écouter les informations; she just got news OR word of the accident elle vient juste d'apprendre la nouvelle de l'accident; he broke down when he got the news en apprenant la nouvelle il a fondu en larmes. -**8.** [reach by calculation or experimentation - answer, solution] trouver; [- result] obtenir; multiply 5 by 2 and you ~ 10 multipliez 5 par 2 et vous obtenez 10. -**9.** [earn, win - salary] recevoir, gagner, toucher; [- prize] gagner; [- reputation] se faire; plumbers ~ £20 an hour un plombier gagne OR touche 20 livres de l'heure; he got a good name OR a reputation as an architect il s'est fait une réputation dans le milieu de l'architecture; someone's trying to ~ your attention [calling] quelqu'un vous appelle; [waving] quelqu'un vous fait signe. -**10.** [bring, fetch] (aller) chercher; ~ me my coat va me chercher OR apporte-moi mon manteau; we had to ~ a doctor nous avons dû faire venir un médecin; he went to ~ a taxi il est parti chercher un taxi; what can I ~ you to drink? qu'est-ce que je vous sers à boire?; they sent him to ~ help ils l'ont envoyé chercher de l'aide. -**11.** [catch - ball] attraper; [- bus, train] prendre, attraper; did you ~ your train? est-ce que tu as eu ton train? -**12.** [capture] attraper, prendre; [seize] prendre, saisir; the Mounties always ~ their man les Mounties attrapent toujours ceux qu'ils cherchent; he got me by the arm il m'a attrapé par le bras; the dog got him by the leg le chien l'a attrapé à la jambe; (I've) got you! je te tiens! -**13.** [book, reserve] réserver, retenir; we're trying to ~ a flight to Budapest nous essayons de réserver un vol pour Budapest. -**14.** [answer - door, telephone] répondre; the doorbell's ringing – I'll ~ it! quelqu'un sonne à la porte – j'y vais!; will you ~ the phone? peux-tu répondre au téléphone?

B. -**1.** [become ill with] attraper; he got a chill il a pris OR attrapé froid; I ~ a headache when I drink red wine le vin rouge me donne mal à la tête ❑ to ~ it bad for sb *inf* avoir quelqu'un dans la peau. -**2.** [experience, feel - shock] recevoir, ressentir, avoir; [- fun, pain, surprise] avoir; I got the feeling something horrible would happen j'ai eu l'impression OR le pressentiment que quelque chose d'horrible allait arriver; I ~ the impression he doesn't like me j'ai l'impression que je ne lui plais pas; to ~ a thrill out of (doing) sthg prendre plaisir à (faire) qqch; to ~ religion *inf* devenir croyant. -**3.** [encounter]: you ~ some odd people on these tours il y a de drôles de gens dans ces voyages organisés.

C. -**1.** *(with adj or past participle)* [cause to be]: she managed to ~ the window closed/open elle a réussi à fermer/ouvrir la fenêtre; I got the car started j'ai démarré la voiture; don't ~ your feet wet! ne te mouille pas les pieds!; ~ the suitcases ready préparez les bagages; the children are getting themselves ready for school les enfants se préparent pour (aller à) l'école; we managed to ~ him in a good mood nous avons réussi à le mettre de bonne humeur; let me ~ this clear que ce soit bien clair; to ~ things under control prendre les choses en main; he likes his bath as hot as he can ~ it il aime que son bain soit aussi chaud que possible; the flat is as clean as I'm going to ~ it j'ai nettoyé l'appartement le mieux que j'ai pu; he got himself nominated president il s'est fait nommer président; don't ~ yourself all worked up ne t'en fais pas. -**2.** *(with infinitive)* [cause to do or carry out]: we couldn't ~ her to leave on n'a pas pu la faire partir; ~ him to move the car demande-lui de déplacer la voiture; I got it to work OR working j'ai réussi à le faire marcher; we have to ~ the government to tighten up on pollution control il faut que l'on obtienne du gouvernement qu'il renforce les lois contre la pollution; he got the other members to agree il a réussi à obtenir l'accord des autres membres; I can always ~ someone else to do it je peux toujours le faire faire par quelqu'un d'autre; I got her to talk about life in China je lui ai demandé de parler de la vie en Chine; they can't ~ the landlord to fix the roof ils n'arrivent pas à obtenir du propriétaire qu'il fasse réparer le toit; how do you ~ jasmine to grow indoors? comment peut-on faire pousser du jasmin à l'intérieur? -**3.** *(with past participle)* [cause to be done or carried out]: to ~ sthg done/repaired faire faire/réparer qqch; to ~ one's hair cut se faire couper les cheveux; I didn't ~ anything done today je n'ai rien fait aujourd'hui; it's impossible to ~ anything done around here [by oneself] il est impossible de faire quoi que ce soit ici; [by someone else] il est impossible d'obtenir quoi que ce soit ici. -**4.** [cause to come, go, move]: how are you going to ~ this package to them? comment allez-vous leur faire parvenir ce paquet?; they eventually got all the boxes downstairs/upstairs ils ont fini par descendre/monter toutes leurs boîtes; I managed to ~ the old man downstairs/upstairs j'ai réussi à faire descendre/monter le vieil homme; I managed to ~ him away from the others j'ai réussi à l'éloigner des autres; ~ him away from me débarrassez-moi de lui; can you ~ me home? pouvez-vous me raccompagner?; his friends managed to ~ him home ses amis ont réussi à le ramener (à la maison); how are we going to ~ the bike home? comment est-ce qu'on va ramener le vélo à la maison?; he can't ~ the kids to bed il n'arrive pas à mettre les enfants au lit; I can't ~ my boots off/on je n'arrive pas à enlever/mettre mes bottes; we couldn't ~ the bed through the door nous n'avons pas pu faire passer le lit par la porte; that won't ~ you very far! ça ne te servira pas à grand-chose!, tu ne seras pas beaucoup plus avancé!

D. -**1.** [prepare] préparer; he's in the kitchen getting dinner il est à la cuisine en train de préparer le dîner; who's going to ~ the children breakfast? qui va préparer le petit déjeuner pour les enfants? -**2.** [hear correctly] entendre, saisir; I didn't ~ his name je n'ai pas saisi son nom. -**3.** [establish telephone contact with]: I got her father on the phone j'ai parlé à son père OR j'ai eu son père au téléphone; did you ~ the number you wanted? avez-vous obtenu le numéro que vous vouliez?; ~ me extension 3500 passez-moi OR donnez-moi le poste 3500. -**4.** *inf* [understand] comprendre, saisir; I don't ~ it, I don't ~ the point je ne comprends OR ne saisis pas, je n'y suis pas du tout; I don't ~ you OR your meaning je ne comprends pas ce que vous voulez dire; don't ~ me wrong comprenez-moi bien; I think he's got the message now je crois qu'il a compris maintenant; I don't ~ the joke je ne vois pas ce qui est (si) drôle; ~ it?, ~ me?, ~ my drift? tu saisis?, tu piges?; (I've) got it! ça y est!, j'y suis! -**5.** [take note of] remarquer; did you ~ his address? lui avez-vous demandé son adresse? -**6.** ▽ [look at] viser; ~ him! who does he think he is? vise un peu ce mec, mais pour qui il se prend?; ~ (a load of) that! vise-ça un peu!

E. -**1.** *inf* [hit] atteindre; [hit and kill] tuer; she got him in the face with a pie elle lui a jeté une tarte à la crème à la figure; the bullet got him in the back il a pris la balle OR la balle l'a atteint dans le dos; a car got him il a été tué par une voiture. -**2.** *inf* [harm, punish]: everyone's out to ~ me tout le monde est après moi. -**3.** *inf* [take vengeance on] se venger de; we'll ~ you for this! on te revaudra ça!; I'll ~ him for that! je lui revaudrai ça! -**4.** *inf* [affect - physically]: the pain ~s me in the back j'ai des douleurs dans le dos; [- emotionally] émouvoir; that song really ~s me cette chanson me fait vraiment quelque chose. -**5.** *inf* [baffle, puzzle]: you've got me there alors là, aucune idée. -**6.** *inf* [irritate] énerver, agacer; it really ~s me when you're late qu'est-ce que ça peut m'énerver quand tu es en retard! -**7.** *Am* [learn] apprendre; to ~ sthg by heart apprendre qqch par cœur. -**8.** *arch* [beget] engendrer; to ~ sb with child faire un enfant à qqn. -**9.** RADIO & TV [signal, station] capter, recevoir. -**10.** *phr*: he got his in Vietnam *inf* il est mort au Viêt-nam.

◇ *vi* **A.** -**1.** [become] devenir; I'm getting hungry/thirsty je commence à avoir faim/soif; ~ dressed! habille-toi!; to ~ fat grossir; to ~ married se marier; to ~ divorced divorcer; don't ~ lost! ne vous perdez pas!; how did that vase ~ broken? comment se fait-il que ce vase soit cassé?; to ~ old vieillir; it's getting late il se fait tard; this is getting boring ça devient ennuyeux; to ~ used to (doing) sthg s'habituer à (faire) qqch; will you ~ with it! *Am* mais réveille-toi un peu! -**2.** [used to form passive]: to ~ elected se faire élire, être élu; suppose he ~s killed et s'il se fait tuer?; we got paid last week on a été payés la semaine dernière; I'm always getting invited to parties on m'invite toujours à des soirées. -**3.** *(with present participle)* [start] commencer à, se mettre à; let's ~ going OR moving! [let's leave] allons-y!; [let's hurry] dépêchons (-nous)!, grouillons-nous!; [let's start to work] au travail!; I'll ~ going on that right away je m'y mets tout de suite; I can't seem to ~ going today je n'arrive pas à m'activer aujourd'hui; she got talking to the neighbours elle s'est mise à discuter avec les voisins; we got talking about racism nous en sommes venus à parler de racisme; he got to thinking about it il s'est mis à réfléchir à la question.

B. -**1.** [go] aller, se rendre; [arrive] arriver; when did you ~ home? quand es-tu rentré?; it's nice to ~ home ça fait du bien de rentrer chez soi; how do you ~ to the museum? comment est-ce qu'on fait pour aller au musée?; how did you ~ in here? comment êtes-vous entré?; they should ~ here today ils devraient arriver ici aujourd'hui; how did you ~ here? comment es-tu venu?; how did that bicycle ~ here? comment se fait-il que ce vélo se trouve ici?; I took the train from Madrid to ~ there j'ai pris le train de Madrid pour y aller; she's successful now but it took her a while to ~ there elle a une bonne situation maintenant, mais ça ne s'est pas fait du jour au lendemain; he got as far as buying the tickets il est allé jusqu'à acheter les billets; I'd hoped things wouldn't ~ this far j'avais espéré qu'on n'en arriverait pas là; are you getting anywhere with that report? il avance, ce rapport?; now you're getting somewhere! enfin tu avances!;

I'm not getting anywhere OR I'm getting nowhere (fast *inf*) with this project je fais du sur place avec ce projet; **we're not getting anywhere with this meeting** cette réunion est une perte de temps; **she won't ~ anywhere** OR **she'll ~ nowhere if she's rude to people** elle n'arrivera à rien en étant grossière avec les gens; **where's your sister got to?** où est passée ta sœur?; **where did my keys ~ to?** où sont passées mes clés? **-2.** [move in specified direction]: **he got along the ledge as best he could** il a avancé le long du rebord du mieux qu'il pouvait; **to ~ into bed** se coucher; **~ in** OR **into the car!** monte dans la voiture!; **~ over here!** viens ici!; **we couldn't ~ past the truck** nous ne pouvions pas passer le camion. **-3.** *(with infinitive)* [start] commencer à, se mettre à; **each city is getting to look like another** toutes les grandes villes commencent à se ressembler; **to ~ to know sb** apprendre à connaître qqn; **we got to like her husband** nous nous sommes mis à apprécier OR à aimer son mari; **you'll ~ to like it in the end** ça finira par te plaire; **his father got to hear of the rumours** son père a fini par entendre les rumeurs; **he's getting to be known** il commence à être connu, il se fait connaître; **they got to talking about the past** ils en sont venus OR ils se sont mis à parler du passé. **-4.** [become] devenir; **it's getting to be impossible to find a flat** ça devient impossible de trouver un appartement; **she may ~ to be president one day** elle pourrait devenir OR être président un jour. **-5.** [manage] réussir à; **we never got to see that film** nous n'avons jamais réussi à OR nous ne sommes jamais arrivés à voir ce film. **-6.** *inf* [be allowed to]: **he never ~s to stay up late** on ne le laisse jamais se coucher tard; **I never ~ to drive** on ne me laisse jamais conduire. **-7.** *inf Am* [leave] se tirer; **~!** fous le camp!, tire-toi!

◆ **get about** *vi insep* **-1.** [be up and about, move around] se déplacer; **how do you ~ about town?** comment vous déplacez-vous en ville?; **she ~s about on crutches/in a wheelchair** elle se déplace avec des béquilles/en chaise roulante; **I don't ~ about much these days** je ne me déplace pas beaucoup ces temps-ci. **-2.** [travel] voyager; **I ~ about quite a bit in my job** je suis assez souvent en déplacement pour mon travail. **-3.** [be socially active]: **she certainly ~s about** elle connaît beaucoup de monde. **-4.** [story, rumour] se répandre, circuler; **the news got about that they were splitting up** la nouvelle de leur séparation s'est répandue.

◆ **get across** ◇ *vi insep* pénétrer, passer; **the river was flooded but we managed to ~ across** la rivière était en crue mais nous avons réussi à traverser.

◇ *vt sep* communiquer; **I can't seem to ~ the idea across to them** je n'arrive pas à leur faire comprendre ça; **he managed to ~ his point across** il a réussi à faire passer son message.

◆ **get after** *vt insep* poursuivre.

◆ **get ahead** *vi insep* [succeed] réussir, arriver; **to ~ ahead in life** OR **in the world** réussir dans la vie; **if you want to ~ ahead at the office, you have to work** si tu veux de l'avancement au bureau, il faut que tu travailles.

◆ **get along** *vi insep* **-1.** [fare, manage] aller; **how are you getting along?** comment vas-tu?, comment ça va?; **she's getting along well in her new job** elle se débrouille bien dans son nouveau travail; **we can ~ along without him** nous pouvons nous passer de lui OR nous débrouiller sans lui. **-2.** [advance, progress] avancer, progresser; **the patient is getting along nicely** le patient est en bonne voie OR fait des progrès. **-3.** [be on good terms] s'entendre; **we ~ along fine** nous nous entendons très bien, nous faisons bon ménage; **she doesn't ~ along with my mother** elle ne s'entend pas avec ma mère; **she's easy to ~ along with** elle est facile à vivre. **-4.** [move away] s'en aller, partir; [go] aller, se rendre; **I must be getting along to the office** il faut que j'aille au bureau ❑ **~ along with you now!** ne restez pas là!; **~ along with you!** *Br* [leave] va-t-en!, fiche le camp!; [I don't believe you] *inf* à d'autres!

◆ **get around** ◇ *vt insep* [obstacle, problem] contourner; [law, rule] tourner.

◇ *vi insep* = **get about**.

◆ **get around to** *vt insep*: **she won't ~ around to reading it before tomorrow** elle n'arrivera pas à (trouver le temps de) le lire avant demain; **he finally got around to fixing the radiator** il a fini par OR il est finalement arrivé à réparer le radiateur; **it was some time before I got around to writing to her** j'ai mis pas mal de temps avant de lui écrire.

◆ **get at** *vt insep* **-1.** [reach - object, shelf] atteindre; [- place] parvenir à, atteindre; **I've put the pills where the children can't ~ at them** j'ai mis les pilules là où les enfants ne peuvent pas les prendre. **-2.** [discover, find] trouver; **to ~ at the truth** connaître la vérité. **-3.** [mean, intend] entendre; **I see what you're getting at** je vois où vous voulez en venir; **just what are you getting at?** qu'est-ce que vous entendez par là?, où voulez-vous en venir?; **what I'm getting at is why did she leave now?** ce que je veux dire, c'est pourquoi est-elle partie maintenant? **-4.** *inf* [criticize, nag] s'en prendre à, s'attaquer à; **you're always getting at me** tu t'en prends toujours à moi. **-5.** *inf* [bribe, influence] acheter, suborner; **the witnesses had been got at** les témoins avaient été achetés.

◆ **get away** *vi insep* **-1.** [leave] s'en aller, partir; **she has to ~ away from home/her parents** il faut qu'elle parte de chez elle/s'éloigne de ses parents; **I was in a meeting and couldn't ~ away** j'étais en réunion et je ne pouvais pas m'échapper OR m'en aller; **will you be able to ~ away at Christmas?** allez-vous pouvoir partir (en vacances) à Noël?; **to ~ away from the daily grind** échapper au train-train quotidien; **~ away from it all, come to Florida!** quittez tout, venez en Floride!; **she's gone off for a couple of weeks to ~ away from it all** elle est partie quelques semaines loin de tout. **-2.** [move away] s'éloigner; **~ away from that door!** éloignez-vous OR écartez-vous de cette porte!; **~ away from me!** fichez-moi le camp! **-3.** [escape] s'échapper, se sauver; **the murderer got away** l'assassin s'est échappé; **the thief got away with all the jewels** le voleur est parti OR s'est sauvé avec tous les bijoux ❑ **there's no getting away from** OR **you can't ~ away from the fact that the other solution would have been cheaper** on ne peut pas nier (le fait) que l'autre solution aurait coûté moins cher; **you can't ~ away from it, there's no getting away from it** c'est comme ça, on n'y peut rien. **-4.** *Br phr*: **~ away (with you)!** *inf* à d'autres!

◆ **get away with** *vt insep*: **he got away with cheating on his taxes** [escaped notice] personne ne s'est aperçu qu'il avait fraudé le fisc; **I can't believe you got away with it!** je n'arrive pas à croire que personne ne t'ait rien dit! ❑ **he lets his son ~ away with murder** *fig* il passe tout à son fils; **with his charm, he can ~ away with murder** il a un tel charme qu'on lui pardonne tout.

◆ **get back** ◇ *vi insep* **-1.** [move backwards] reculer; **~ back!** éloignez-vous!, reculez! **-2.** [return] revenir, retourner; **I can't wait to ~ back home** je suis impatient de rentrer (à la maison); **~ back in bed!** va te recoucher!, retourne au lit!; **I got back in the car/on the bus** je suis remonté dans la voiture/dans le bus; **to ~ back to sleep** se rendormir; **to ~ back to work** [after break] se remettre au travail; [after holiday, illness] reprendre le travail; **things eventually got back to normal** les choses ont peu à peu repris leur cours (normal); **getting** OR **to ~ back to the point** pour en revenir au sujet qui nous préoccupe; **let's ~ back to your basic reasons for leaving** revenons aux raisons pour lesquelles vous voulez partir; **I'll ~ back to you on that** [call back] je vous rappelle pour vous dire ce qu'il en est; [discuss again] nous reparlerons de cela plus tard. **-3.** [return to political power] revenir; **do you think the Democrats will ~ back in?** croyez-vous que le parti démocrate reviendra au pouvoir?

◇ *vt sep* **-1.** [recover - something lost or lent] récupérer; [- force, strength] reprendre, récupérer; [- health, motivation] retrouver; **he got his job back** il a été repris; **I got back nearly all the money I invested** j'ai récupéré presque tout l'argent que j'avais investi; **you'll have to ~ your money back from the shop** il faut que vous vous fassiez rembourser par le magasin. **-2.** [return] rendre; **we have to ~ this book back to her** il faut que nous lui rendions ce livre. **-3.** [return to original place] remettre, replacer; **I can't ~ it back in the box** je n'arrive pas à le remettre OR le faire rentrer dans le carton; **I want to ~ these suitcases back down to the cellar** je veux redescendre ces valises à la cave; **he managed to ~ the children back to bed** il a réussi à remettre les enfants au lit. **-4.** *phr*: **to ~ one's own back (on sb)** *inf* se venger (de qqn).

◆ **get back at** *vt insep* se venger de; **he only said it to ~ back at him** il n'a dit ça que pour se venger de lui.

◆ **get behind** *vi insep* [gen] rester à l'arrière, se laisser distancer; SPORT se laisser distancer; *fig*: **he got behind with his work** il a pris du retard dans son travail; **we mustn't ~ behind with the rent** il ne faut pas qu'on soit en retard pour le loyer.

◆ **get by** *vi insep* **-1.** [pass] passer; **let me ~ by** laissez-moi passer. **-2.** [be acceptable] passer, être acceptable; **their work just about ~s by** leur travail est tout juste passable OR acceptable. **-3.** [manage, survive] se débrouiller, s'en sortir; **how do you ~ by on that salary?** comment tu te débrouilles OR tu t'en sors avec un salaire comme ça?; **they ~ by as best they can** ils se débrouillent OR s'en sortent tant bien que mal; **we can ~ by without him** nous pouvons nous passer de lui OR nous débrouiller sans lui.

◆ **get down** ◇ *vi insep* descendre; **~ down off that chair!** descends de cette chaise!; **may I ~ down (from the table)?** [leave the table] puis-je sortir de table?; **they got down on their knees** ils se sont mis à genoux; **~ down!** [hide] couchez-vous!; [to dog] bas les pattes!

◇ *vt sep* **-1.** [write down] noter; **I didn't manage to ~ down what she said** je n'ai pas réussi à noter ce qu'elle a dit. **-2.** [depress] déprimer, démoraliser; **work is really getting me down at the moment** le travail me déprime vraiment en ce moment; **this rainy weather ~s him down** cette pluie lui fiche le cafard; **don't let it ~ you down** ne te laisse pas abattre. **-3.** [swallow] avaler, faire descendre.

◆ **get down to** *vt insep* se mettre à; **I have to ~ down to balancing the books** il faut que je me mette à faire les comptes; **it's not so difficult once you ~ down to it** ce n'est pas si difficile une fois qu'on s'y met; **he got down to working on it this morning** il s'y est mis OR s'y est attelé ce matin; **it's hard getting down to work after the weekend** c'est difficile de reprendre le travail après le week-end.

◆ **get in** ◇ *vi insep* **-1.** [into building] entrer; **the thief got in through the window** le cambrioleur est entré par la fenêtre || [into vehicule]: **a car pulled up and she got in** une voiture s'est arrêtée et elle est montée dedans. **-2.** [return home] rentrer; **we got in about 4 a.m.** nous sommes rentrés vers 4 h du matin. **-3.** [arrive] arriver; **what time does your plane ~ in?** à quelle heure ton avion arrive-t-il? **-4.** [be admitted - to club] se faire admettre; [- to school, university] entrer, être admis OR reçu; **he applied to Oxford but he didn't ~ in** il voulait entrer à Oxford mais il n'a pas pu. **-5.** [be elected - person] être élu; [- party] accéder au pouvoir. **-6.** *inf* [become involved] participer; **she got in at the beginning** elle est arrivée au début. **-7.** [interject] glisser; **"what about me?" she managed to ~ in** «et moi?», réussit-elle à glisser.

◇ *vt sep* **-1.** [fit in]: **I hope to ~ in a bit of reading on holiday** j'espère pouvoir lire OR que je trouverai le temps de lire pendant mes vacances. -**2.** [collect, gather - crops] rentrer, engranger; [- debts] recouvrer; [- taxes] percevoir. -**3.** [lay in]: **I must ~ in some more coal** je dois faire une provision de charbon; **to ~ in supplies** s'approvisionner. -**4.** [call in - doctor, plumber] faire venir. -**5.** [hand in, submit] rendre, remettre; **did you ~ your application in on time?** as-tu remis ton dossier de candidature à temps? -**6.** [cause to be admitted - to club, university] faire admettre OR accepter; [cause to be elected] faire élire. -**7.** [plant - seeds] planter, semer; [- bulbs, plants] planter. -**8.** *inf Br* [pay for, stand] payer, offrir; **he got the next round in** il a payé la tournée suivante.

◇ *vt insep* [building] entrer dans; [vehicle] monter dans; **he had just got in the door when the phone rang** il venait juste d'arriver OR d'entrer quand le téléphone a sonné.

◆ **get in on** ◇ *vt insep*: **to ~ in on a deal** prendre part à un marché; **to ~ in on the fun** se mettre de la partie.

◇ *vt sep* faire participer; **he got me in on the deal** il m'a intéressé à l'affaire.

◆ **get into** ◇ *vt insep* -**1.** [arrive in] arriver à; **we ~ into Madrid at 3 o'clock** nous arrivons à Madrid à 3 h; **the train got into the station** le train est entré en gare. -**2.** [put on - dress, shirt, shoes] mettre; [- trousers, stockings] enfiler, mettre; [- coat] endosser; **she got into her clothes** elle a mis ses vêtements OR s'est habillée; **can you still ~ into your jeans?** est-ce que tu rentres encore dans ton jean? -**3.** [be admitted to - club] entrer dans; [- school, university] entrer dans; **he'd like to ~ into the club** il voudrait devenir membre du club; **her daughter got into medical school** sa fille a été admise dans OR est entrée dans une école de médecine; **to ~ into office** être élu. -**4.** [become involved in]: **he wants to ~ into politics** il veut se lancer dans la politique; **they got into a conversation about South Africa** ils se sont mis à parler de l'Afrique du Sud; **we got into a fight over who had to do the dishes** nous nous sommes disputés pour savoir qui devait faire la vaisselle; **this is not the moment to ~ into that** ce n'est pas le moment de parler de ça. -**5.** *inf* [take up] s'intéresser à; **he got into Eastern religions** il a commencé à s'intéresser aux religions orientales. -**6.** [become accustomed to]: **he soon got into her way of doing things** il s'est vite fait OR s'est vite mis à sa façon de faire les choses. -**7.** [experience a specified condition or state]: **to ~ into debt** s'endetter; **he got into a real mess** il s'est mis dans un vrai pétrin; **the children were always getting into mischief** les enfants passaient leur temps à faire des bêtises; **I got into a real state about the test** j'étais dans tous mes états à cause du test; **she got into trouble with the teacher** elle a eu des ennuis avec le professeur. -**8.** [cause to act strangely] prendre; **what's got into you?** qu'est-ce qui te prend?, quelle mouche te pique?; **I wonder what got into him to make him act like that** je me demande ce qui l'a poussé à réagir comme ça.

◇ *vt sep* -**1.** [cause to be admitted to - club] faire entrer à; [- school, university] faire entrer dans; **he got his friend into the club** il a permis à son ami de devenir membre du club; **the president got his son into Harvard** le président a fait entrer OR accepter OR admettre son fils à Harvard. -**2.** [cause to be in a specified condition or state] mettre; **she got herself into a terrible state** elle s'est mis dans tous ses états; **he got them into a lot of trouble** il leur a attiré de gros ennuis. -**3.** [involve in] impliquer dans, entraîner dans; **you're the one who got us into this** c'est toi qui nous as embarqués dans cette histoire. -**4.** *inf* [make interested in] faire découvrir; [accustom to] habituer à, faire prendre l'habitude de; **he got me into jazz** il m'a initié au jazz.

◆ **get in with** *vt insep* s'insinuer dans les bonnes grâces de, se faire bien voir de; **they tried to ~ in with the new director** ils ont essayé de se faire bien voir du nouveau directeur.

◆ **get off** ◇ *vi insep* -**1.** [leave bus, train etc] descendre; **~ off at the next stop** descendez au prochain arrêt ❑ **I told him where to ~ off!** *inf* je l'ai envoyé sur les roses!, je l'ai envoyé promener!; **where do you ~ off telling me what to do?** *inf Am* qu'est-ce qui te prend de me dicter ce que je dois faire? -**2.** [depart - person] s'en aller, partir; [- car] démarrer; [- plane] décoller; [- letter, parcel] partir; **I have to be getting off to work** il faut que j'aille au travail; **the project got off to a bad/good start** *fig* le projet a pris un mauvais/bon départ. -**3.** [leave work] finir, s'en aller; [take time off] se libérer; **what time do you ~ off?** à quelle heure finissez-vous?; **can you ~ off early tomorrow?** peux-tu quitter le travail de bonne heure demain? -**4.** [escape punishment] s'en sortir, s'en tirer, en être quitte; **she didn't think she'd ~ off so lightly** elle n'espérait pas s'en tirer à si bon compte; **the students got off with a fine/warning** les étudiants en ont été quittes pour une amende/un avertissement. -**5.** [go to sleep] s'endormir.

◇ *vt insep* -**1.** [leave - bus, train etc] descendre de; **she got off the bicycle/train/plane** elle est descendue du vélo/du train/de l'avion; **he got off his horse** il est descendu de cheval ❑ **if only the boss would ~ off my back** si seulement le patron me fichait la paix. -**2.** [depart from] partir de, décamper de; **~ off my property** fichez le camp de chez moi; **we got off the road to let the ambulance pass** nous sommes sortis de la route pour laisser passer l'ambulance. -**3.** [escape from] se libérer de; [avoid] échapper à; **she managed to ~ off work** elle a réussi à se libérer; **how did you ~ off doing the housework?** comment as-tu fait pour échapper au ménage?

◇ *vt sep* -**1.** [cause to leave, climb down] faire descendre; **~ the cat off the table** fais descendre le chat de (sur) la table; **the conductor got the passengers off the train** le conducteur a fait descendre les passagers du train; **try to ~ her mind off her troubles** *fig* essaie de lui changer les idées. -**2.** [send] envoyer, faire partir; **I want to ~ this letter off** je veux expédier cette lettre OR mettre cette lettre à la poste; **she got the boys off to school** elle a expédié OR envoyé les garçons à l'école; **we got him off on the morning train** nous l'avons mis au train du matin. -**3.** [remove - clothing, lid] enlever, ôter; [- stains] faire partir OR disparaître, enlever; **I can't ~ this ink off my hands** je n'arrive pas à faire partir cette encre de mes mains; **~ your hands off that cake!** ne touche pas à ce gâteau!; **~ your hands off me!** ne me touche pas!; **he'd like to ~ that house off his hands** *fig* il aimerait bien se débarrasser de cette maison. -**4.** [free from punishment] tirer d'affaire; [in court] faire acquitter; **he'll need a good lawyer to ~ him off** il lui faudra un bon avocat pour se tirer d'affaire. -**5.** [put to sleep] endormir; **I've just managed to ~ the baby off (to sleep)** je viens de réussir à endormir le bébé.

◆ **get off on** *vt insep* -**1.** *inf* [sexually]: **he ~s off on pornographic films** il prend son pied en regardant des films porno; **is that what you ~ off on?** c'est comme ça que tu prends ton pied? || *fig*: **he ~s off on teasing people** il adore taquiner les gens; **I really ~ off on jazz!** j'adore le jazz! -**2.** *drugs sl*: **he ~s off on heroin** il se défonce à l'héroïne.

◆ **get off with** *inf vt insep Br* sortir avec; **did you ~ off with anyone last night?** est-ce que tu as fait des rencontres hier soir?

◆ **get on** ◇ *vi insep* -**1.** [bus, plane, train] monter; [ship] monter à bord. -**2.** [fare, manage]: **how's your husband getting on?** comment va votre mari?; **how did he ~ on at the interview?** comment s'est passé son entretien?, comment ça a marché pour son entretien?; **you'll ~ on far better if you think about it first** tout ira mieux si tu réfléchis avant. -**3.** [make progress] avancer, progresser; **John is getting on very well in maths** John se débrouille très bien en maths; **how's your work getting on?** ça avance, ton travail? -**4.** [succeed] réussir, arriver; **to ~ on in life** OR **in the world** faire son chemin OR réussir dans la vie; **some say that in order to ~ on, you often have to compromise** il y a des gens qui disent que pour réussir (dans la vie), il faut souvent faire des compromis. -**5.** [continue] continuer; **we must be getting on** il faut que nous partions; **do you think we can ~ on with the meeting now?** croyez-vous que nous puissions poursuivre notre réunion maintenant?; **~ on with your work!** allez! au travail!; **they got on with the job** ils se sont remis au travail. -**6.** [be on good terms] s'entendre; **my mother and I ~ on well** je m'entends bien avec ma mère; **they don't ~ on** ils ne s'entendent pas; **she's never got on with him** elle ne s'est jamais entendue avec lui; **to be difficult/easy to ~ on with** être difficile/facile à vivre. -**7.** [grow late - time]: **time's getting on** il se fait tard; **it was getting on in the evening, the evening was getting on** la soirée tirait à sa fin. -**8.** [grow old - person] se faire vieux; **she's getting on (in years)** elle commence à se faire vieille. -**9.** *phr*: **~ on with it!** [continue speaking] continuez!; [continue working] allez! au travail! [hurry up] mais dépêchez-vous enfin!; **~ on with you!** [I don't believe you] à d'autres!

◇ *vt insep* [bus, train] monter dans; [plane] monter dans, monter à bord de; [ship] monter à bord de; [bed, horse, table] monter sur; **he got on his bike** il est monté sur OR il a enfourché son vélo; **~ on your feet** levez-vous, mettez-vous debout; **it took the patient a while to ~ (back) on his feet** *fig* le patient a mis longtemps à se remettre sur pied.

◇ *vt sep* -**1.** [help onto - bus, train] faire monter dans; [- bed, bike, horse, table] faire monter sur; **they got him on his feet** ils l'ont mis debout; **the doctor got her on her feet** *fig* le médecin l'a remise sur pied. -**2.** [coat, gloves, shoes] mettre, enfiler; [lid] mettre.

◆ **get on for** *vt insep*: **the president is getting on for sixty** le président approche la soixantaine OR a presque soixante ans; **it's getting on for midnight** il est presque minuit, il n'est pas loin de minuit; **it's getting on for three weeks since we saw her** ça va faire bientôt trois semaines que nous ne l'avons pas vue; **there were getting on for ten thousand demonstrators** il n'y avait pas loin OR il y avait près de dix mille manifestants.

◆ **get onto** ◇ *vt insep* -**1.** = **get on** *vt insep*. -**2.** [turn attention to]: **to ~ onto a subject** OR **onto a topic** aborder un sujet; **how did we ~ onto reincarnation?** comment est-ce qu'on en est venus à parler de réincarnation?; **I'll ~ right onto it!** je vais m'y mettre tout de suite! -**3.** *inf* [contact] prendre contact avec, se mettre en rapport avec; [speak to] parler à; [call] téléphoner à, donner un coup de fil à. -**4.** *inf* [become aware of] découvrir; **the plan worked well until the police got onto it** le plan marchait bien jusqu'à ce que la police tombe dessus. -**5.** [nag, rebuke] harceler; **his father is always getting onto him to find a job** son père est toujours à le harceler pour qu'il trouve du travail. -**6.** [be elected to]: **he got onto the school board** il a été élu au conseil d'administration de l'école.

◇ *vt sep* -**1.** = **get on** *vt sep* **1.** -**2.** [cause to talk about] faire parler de, amener à parler de; **we got him onto (the subject of) his activities in the Resistance** nous l'avons amené à parler de ses activités dans la Résistance.

◆ **get out** ◇ *vi insep* -**1.** [of building, room] sortir; [of car, train] descendre; [of organization, town] quitter; **he got out of the car** il est sorti de la voiture; **to ~ out of bed** se lever, sortir de son lit; **you'd better ~ out of here** tu ferais bien de partir OR sortir; **~ out!** sortez! ❑ **~ out of here!** [leave] sortez d'ici!; *Am* [I don't believe it] *inf* mon œil!; **to ~ out while the going is good** partir au bon moment. -**2.** [go out] sortir; **they don't ~ out much** ils ne sortent pas beaucoup. -**3.** [information, news] se répandre, s'ébruiter; **the secret got out** le secret a été éventé. -**4.** [escape] s'échapper; **the prisoner got out of his cell** le prisonnier s'est échappé de sa cellule; **he was lucky to ~ out alive** il a eu de la chance de s'en sortir vivant.

◇ *vt sep* -**1.** [champagne, furniture] sortir; [person] (faire) sortir. -**2.** [produce, publish - book] publier, sortir; [- list] établir, dresser. -**3.** [speak with difficulty] prononcer, sortir; **I could barely ~ a word out** c'est à peine si je pouvais dire OR prononcer OR sortir un mot ❑ **to ~ out from under** *inf* s'en sortir, s'en tirer.

◆ **get out of** ◇ *vt insep* -**1.** [avoid] éviter, échapper à; **how did you ~ out of doing the dishes?** comment as-tu pu échapper à la vaisselle?; **he tried to ~ out of helping me** il a essayé de se débrouiller pour ne pas devoir m'aider; **to ~ out of an obligation** se dérober OR se soustraire à une obligation; **we have to go, there's no getting out of it** il faut qu'on y aille, il n'y a rien à faire OR il n'y a pas moyen d'y échapper; **there's no getting out of it, you were the better candidate** il faut le reconnaître OR il n'y a pas à dire, vous étiez le meilleur candidat. -**2.** [escape from]: **to ~ out of trouble** se tirer d'affaire; **they managed to ~ out of the clutches of the mafia** ils ont réussi à se tirer des griffes de la mafia; **how can I ~ out of this mess?** comment puis-je me tirer de ce pétrin?

◇ *vt sep* -**1.** [take out of]: **~ the baby out of the house every now and then** sors le bébé de temps en temps; **she got a handkerchief out of her handbag** elle a sorti un mouchoir de son sac à main; **how many books did you ~ out of the library?** combien de livres as-tu emprunté à OR sorti de la bibliothèque? -**2.** [help to avoid]: **the lawyer got his client out of jail** l'avocat a fait sortir son client de prison; **the phone call got her out of having to talk to me** *fig* le coup de fil lui a évité d'avoir à me parler; **he'll never ~ himself out of this one!** il ne s'en sortira jamais!; **my confession got him out of trouble** ma confession l'a tiré d'affaire. -**3.** [extract - cork] sortir de; [- nail, splinter] enlever de; [- stain] faire partir de, enlever de; **I can't ~ the cork out of the bottle** je n'arrive pas à déboucher la bouteille; **the police got a confession/the truth out of him** la police lui a arraché une confession/la vérité; **we got the money out of him** nous avons réussi à obtenir l'argent de lui; **I can't ~ anything out of him** je ne peux rien tirer de lui. -**4.** [gain from] gagner, retirer; **to ~ a lot out of sthg** tirer (un) grand profit de qqch; **I didn't ~ much out of that class** ce cours ne m'a pas apporté grand-chose, je n'ai pas retiré grand-chose de ce cours; **the job was difficult but she got something out of it** la tâche était difficile, mais elle y a trouvé son compte OR en a tiré profit.

◆ **get over** ◇ *vt insep* -**1.** [cross - river, street] traverser, franchir; [- fence, wall] franchir, passer par-dessus. -**2.** [recover from - illness] se remettre de, guérir de; [- accident] se remettre de; [- loss] se remettre de, se consoler de; **I'll never ~ over her** je ne l'oublierai jamais; **he can't ~ over her death** il n'arrive pas à se remettre de sa mort OR disparition; **we couldn't ~ over our surprise** nous n'arrivions pas à nous remettre de notre surprise; **I can't ~ over how much he's grown!** qu'est-ce qu'il a grandi, je n'en reviens pas!; **I can't ~ over it!** je n'en reviens pas!; **he couldn't ~ over the fact that she had come back** il n'en revenait pas qu'elle soit revenue; **I can't ~ over your having refused** je n'en reviens pas que vous ayez refusé; **he'll ~ over it!** il n'en mourra pas! -**3.** [master, overcome - obstacle] surmonter; [- difficulty] surmonter, venir à bout de; **they soon got over their shyness** ils ont vite oublié OR surmonté leur timidité.

◇ *vt sep* -**1.** [cause to cross] faire traverser, faire passer. -**2.** [communicate - idea, message] faire passer.

◇ *vi insep* -**1.** [cross] traverser. -**2.** [idea, message] passer.

◆ **get over with** *vt insep* [finish with] en finir avec; **let's ~ it over (with)** finissons-en; **I expect you'll be glad to ~ it over (with)** j'imagine que vous serez soulagé quand ce sera terminé.

◆ **get round** ◇ *vt insep* = **get around**.

◇ *vt sep* = **get around**.

◇ *vi insep* = **get about**.

◆ **get round to** = **get around to**.

◆ **get through** ◇ *vi insep* -**1.** [reach destination] parvenir; **they managed to ~ through to the wounded** ils ont réussi à parvenir jusqu'aux blessés; **the letter got through to her** la lettre lui est parvenue; **the message didn't ~ through** le message n'est pas arrivé; **despite the crowds, I managed to ~ through** malgré la foule, j'ai réussi à passer. -**2.** [candidate, student - succeed] réussir; [- in exam] être reçu, réussir; **the team got through to the final** l'équipe s'est classée pour la finale. -**3.** [bill, motion] passer, être adopté OR voté. -**4.** [make oneself understood] se faire comprendre; **I can't seem to ~ through to her** elle et moi ne sommes pas sur la même longueur d'onde. -**5.** [contact] contacter; TELEC obtenir la communication; **I can't ~ through to his office** je n'arrive pas à avoir son bureau. -**6.** *Am* [finish] finir, terminer; **call me when you ~ through** appelez-moi quand vous aurez OR avez fini.

◇ *vt insep* -**1.** [come through - hole, window] passer par; [- crowd] se frayer un chemin à travers OR dans; [- military lines] percer, franchir. -**2.** [survive - storm, winter] survivre à; [- difficulty] se sortir de, se tirer de; **he got through it alive** il s'en est sorti (vivant). -**3.** [complete, finish - book] finir, terminer; [- job, project] achever, venir à bout de; **I got through an enormous amount of work** j'ai abattu beaucoup de travail; **it took us one week to ~ through the entire play** il nous a fallu une semaine pour venir à bout de la pièce. -**4.** [consume, use up] consommer; **we ~ through a litre of olive oil a week** nous utilisons un litre d'huile d'olive par semaine; **they got through their monthly salary in one week** en une semaine ils avaient dépensé tout leur salaire du mois. -**5.** [endure, pass - time] faire passer; **how will I ~ through this without you?** comment pourrai-je vivre cette épreuve sans toi? -**6.** [exam] réussir, être reçu à. -**7.** [subj: bill, motion] passer; **the bill got through both Houses** le projet de loi a été adopté par les deux Chambres.

◇ *vt sep* -**1.** [transmit - message] faire passer, transmettre, faire parvenir; **can you ~ this letter through to my family?** pouvez-vous transmettre OR faire parvenir cette lettre à ma famille? -**2.** [make understood] faire comprendre; **when will you ~ it through your thick head that I don't want to go?** *inf* quand est-ce que tu vas enfin comprendre que je ne veux pas y aller? -**3.** [bill, motion] faire adopter, faire passer; **the party got the bill through the Senate** le parti a fait voter OR adopter le projet de loi par le Sénat.

◆ **get together** ◇ *vi insep* -**1.** [meet] se réunir, se rassembler; **can we ~ together after the meeting?** on peut se retrouver après la réunion? -**2.** [reach an agreement] se mettre d'accord; **the committee got together on the date** les membres du comité se sont entendus OR se sont mis d'accord sur la date; **you'd better ~ together with him on the proposal** vous feriez bien de vous entendre avec lui au sujet de la proposition.

◇ *vt sep* [people] réunir, rassembler; [things] rassembler, ramasser; **let me ~ my thoughts together** laissez-moi rassembler mes idées; **to ~ one's act together** *inf* se secouer.

◆ **get to** *vt insep* -**1.** [reach] arriver à; **where have you got to in the book?** où en es-tu dans le livre?; **it got to the point where he couldn't walk another step** il en est arrivé au point de ne plus pouvoir faire un pas. -**2.** [deal with] s'occuper de; **I'll ~ to you in a minute** je suis à toi OR je m'occupe de toi dans quelques secondes; **he'll ~ to it tomorrow** il va s'en occuper demain. -**3.** *inf* [have an effect on]: **that music really ~s to me** [moves me] cette musique me touche vraiment; [annoys me] cette musique me tape sur le système; **don't let it ~ to you!** ne t'énerve pas pour ça! -**4.** *inf Am*: **they got to the witness** [bribed] ils ont acheté le témoin; [killed] ils ont descendu le témoin.

◆ **get up** ◇ *vi insep* -**1.** [arise from bed] se lever; **it was 6 o'clock when we got up** il était 6 h quand nous nous sommes levés; **I like to ~ up late on Sundays** j'aime faire la grasse matinée le dimanche; **~ up!** sors du lit!, debout!, lève-toi! -**2.** [rise to one's feet] se lever, se mettre debout; **she had to ~ up from her chair** elle a été obligée de se lever de sa chaise; **to ~ up from the table** se lever OR sortir de table; **~ up off the floor!** relève-toi!; **please don't bother getting up** restez assis, je vous prie. -**3.** [climb up] monter; **they got up on the roof** ils sont montés sur le toit; **she got up behind him on the motorcycle** elle est montée derrière lui sur la moto. -**4.** [subj: wind] se lever. -**5.** [to horse]: **~ up!** allez!

◇ *vt insep* [stairs] monter; [ladder, tree] monter à; [hill] gravir.

◇ *vt sep* -**1.** [cause to rise to feet] faire lever; [awaken] réveiller. -**2.** [generate, work up]: **to ~ up speed** gagner de la vitesse; **to ~ one's courage up** rassembler son courage; **I can't ~ up any enthusiasm for the job** je n'arrive pas à éprouver aucun enthousiasme pour ce travail. -**3.** *inf* [organize - entertainment, party] organiser, monter; [- petition] organiser; [- play] monter; [- excuse, story] fabriquer, forger. -**4.** [dress up] habiller; [in costume] déguiser; **their children are always so nicely got up** leurs enfants sont toujours si bien habillés; **to ~ o.s. up** se mettre sur son trente et un. -**5.** *inf* [study - subject] travailler, bûcher; [- notes, speech] préparer. -**6.** ▽ *phr*: **to ~ it up** bander.

◆ **get up to** *vt insep* faire; **he ~s up to all kinds of mischief** il fait des tas de bêtises; **what have you been getting up to lately?** qu'est-ce que tu fais de beau ces derniers temps?

getatable *inf* [get'ætəbl] *adj* [place, shelf] accessible, d'accès facile; [person] accessible.

getaway ['getəweɪ] ◇ *n* -**1.** [escape] fuite *f*; **to make one's ~** s'enfuir, filer; **they made a quick ~** ils ont vite filé. -**2.** AUT [start] démarrage *m*; [in racing] départ *m*.

◇ *adj*: **a ~ car/vehicle** une voiture/un véhicule de fuyard.

Gethsemane [geθ'semənɪ] *pr n* Gethsémani.

get-rich-quick *inf adj*: **a ~ scheme** un projet pour faire fortune rapidement.

get-together *n* [meeting] (petite) réunion *f*; [party] (petite) fête *f*.

Gettysburg Address ['getɪzbɜːg-] *pr n*: **the ~** *discours prononcé par Abraham Lincoln pendant la guerre de Sécession.*

THE GETTYSBURG ADDRESS:
Ce fameux discours, prononcé sur le site de la bataille du même nom, appelle à la volonté de construire une nation libre, dirigée «par le peuple, pour le peuple» («a government of the people, by the people, for the people»); cette formule est souvent utilisée comme définition de la démocratie.

---

getup *inf* ['getʌp] *n* -**1.** [outfit] toilette *f*, tenue *f*; [disguise] déguisement *m*; **you're not going out in that ~!** tu ne vas pas sortir (habillé) comme ça OR dans cet accoutrement! -**2.** [of book, product] présentation *f*.

get-up-and-go *inf n* allant *m*, dynamisme *m*; **to have plenty of ~** avoir beaucoup d'allant, être très dynamique; **my ~ has got up and gone** *hum* je suis vanné.

get-well card *n carte de vœux pour un bon rétablissement.*

geum ['dʒiːəm] *n* benoîte *f*.

gewgaw ['gjuːgɔː] *n Br* bibelot *m*, babiole *f*, colifichet *m*.

geyser [*Br* 'giːzəʳ, *Am* 'gaɪzər] *n* -**1.** GEOL geyser *m*. -**2.** *Br* [domestic] chauffe-eau *m inv* (à gaz).

Ghana ['gɑːnə] *pr n* Ghana *m*; **in ~** au Ghana.

Ghanaian [gɑː'neɪən], **Ghanian** ['gɑːnɪən]
◇ *n* Ghanéen *m*, -enne *f*.
◇ *adj* ghanéen.

ghastliness ['gɑːstlɪnɪs] *n* -**1.** [of crime] horreur *f*, atrocité *f*. -**2.** [of place, building, sight] aspect *m* sinistre OR épouvantable; [of experience, situation] caractère *m* horrible OR affreux.

ghastly ['gɑːstlɪ] (*compar* ghastlier, *superl* ghastliest) *adj* -**1.** [awful - crime, news] affreux, épouvantable, atroce; it was a ~ experience c'était une expérience horrible; she wore the most ~ outfit! elle était accoutrée d'une façon indescriptible!; we went to a really ~ party nous sommes allés à une soirée vraiment épouvantable; the interview was ~ l'interview s'est très mal passée. -**2.** [pale, ill] blême, blafard, livide; ~ pale OR white d'une pâleur mortelle; you look ~! – I feel ~! vous avez l'air d'un déterré! – je me sens effectivement très mal! -**3.** [frightening, unnatural] horrible, effrayant; a ~ silence un silence effrayant. -**4.** [serious] sérieux, grave; there's been a ~ mistake une terrible erreur a été commise.

Ghent [gent] *pr n* Gand.

gherkin ['gɜːkɪn] *n* cornichon *m*.

ghetto ['getəʊ] (*pl* ghettos OR ghettoes) *n* ghetto *m*.

ghetto-blaster *inf* [-ˌblɑːstəʳ] *n* grand radiocassette *m* portatif.

ghettoization [getəʊaɪ'zeɪʃn] *n* ghettoïsation *f*.

ghost [gəʊst] ◇ *n* -**1.** [phantom] revenant *m*, fantôme *m*, spectre *m*; to believe in ~s croire aux fantômes; you look as if you've just seen a ~! on dirait que vous venez de voir un fantôme! -**2.** [shadow] ombre *f*; the ~ of a smile l'ombre d'un sourire, un vague sourire; you don't have the ~ of a chance vous n'avez pas la moindre chance OR l'ombre d'une chance. -**3.** TV image *f* secondaire OR résiduelle. -**4.** *phr*: to give up the ~ *literal* rendre l'âme; this typewriter has given up the ~ *fig* & *hum* cette machine à écrire a rendu l'âme. -**5.** [writer] nègre *m*.
◇ *vt*: to ~ a book for an author servir de nègre à l'auteur d'un livre.
◇ *adj* [story, film] de revenants, de fantômes; a ~ ship/train un vaisseau/un train fantôme.

ghostly ['gəʊstlɪ] (*compar* ghostlier, *superl* ghostliest) *adj* spectral, fantomatique; a ~ figure une véritable apparition; a ~ silence un silence de mort.

ghost town *n* ville *f* fantôme.

ghostwrite ['gəʊstraɪt] (*pt* ghostwrote [-rəʊt], *pp* ghostwritten [-ˌrɪtn]) ◇ *vt* écrire OR rédiger (comme nègre); I'm sure his books are ghostwritten je suis sûr qu'il n'a écrit aucun des livres publiés sous son nom.
◇ *vi*: to ~ for sb servir de nègre à qqn.

ghostwriter ['gəʊstˌraɪtəʳ] *n* nègre *m*.

ghostwritten ['gəʊstˌrɪtn] *pp* → **ghostwrite**.

ghostwrote ['gəʊstrəʊt] *pt* → **ghostwrite**.

ghoul [guːl] *n* -**1.** [evil spirit] goule *f*. -**2.** [macabre person] amateur *mf* de macabre; don't be such a ~! tu es vraiment morbide!

ghoulish ['guːlɪʃ] *adj* -**1.** [ghostly] de goule, vampirique. -**2.** [person, humour] morbide, macabre.

GHQ (*abbr of* general headquarters) *n* GQG *m*.

GI (*abbr of* Government Issue) ◇ *n* [soldier]: ~ (Joe) GI *m*, soldat *m* américain.
◇ *comp*: ~ bride épouse *f* (étrangère) d'un GI.

giant ['dʒaɪənt] ◇ *n* géant *m*, -e *f*; a literary ~ un géant de la littérature; an industrial ~ un magnat de l'industrie.
◇ *adj* géant, gigantesque; with ~ footsteps à pas de géant; ~-size pack COMM paquet *m* géant.

giantess ['dʒaɪəntes] *n* géante *f*.

giantism ['dʒaɪəntɪzm] *n* MED gigantisme *m*.

giantkiller ['dʒaɪəntˌkɪləʳ] *n* SPORT *petite équipe victorieuse d'une équipe plus forte*.

giant panda *n* panda *m* géant.

Giant's Causeway *pr n*: the ~ la Chaussée des Géants.

giant sequoia *n* séquoia *m* géant.

giant star *n* étoile *f* géante.

gibber ['dʒɪbəʳ] *vi* [person] bredouiller, bafouiller; to ~ with fear bafouiller de peur; stop ~ing and tell me exactly what happened! arrête de bafouiller et explique-toi clairement!

gibbering ['dʒɪbərɪŋ] *adj*: I was a ~ wreck! j'étais dans un de ces états!; he's a ~ idiot *inf* c'est un sacré imbécile.

gibberish ['dʒɪbərɪʃ] *n* (*U*) baragouin *m*, charabia *m*; it's complete ~ to me je ne comprends absolument rien; this instruction leaflet is a load of ~ *inf* ce mode d'emploi, c'est du vrai charabia; the man's talking ~ ce que dit cet homme est totalement incompréhensible OR n'a ni queue ni tête.

gibbet ['dʒɪbɪt] ◇ *n* potence *f*, gibet *m*.
◇ *vt* [execute] pendre.

gibbon ['gɪbən] *n* gibbon *m*.

gibbous ['gɪbəs] *adj* -**1.** ASTRON gibbeux. -**2.** [humpbacked] bossu.

gibe [dʒaɪb] ◇ *vt* [taunt] railler, se moquer de.
◇ *vi*: to ~ at sb railler qqn, se moquer de qqn.
◇ *n* [remark] raillerie *f*, moquerie *f*.

giblets ['dʒɪblɪts] *npl* abats *mpl* de volaille.

Gibraltar [dʒɪ'brɔːltəʳ] *pr n* Gibraltar; in ~ à Gibraltar; the Rock of ~ le rocher de Gibraltar.

giddily ['gɪdɪlɪ] *adv* -**1.** [dizzily] vertigineusement. -**2.** [frivolously] à la légère, avec insouciance.

giddiness ['gɪdɪnɪs] *n* (*U*) -**1.** [dizziness] vertiges *mpl*, étourdissements *mpl*. -**2.** [frivolousness] légèreté *f*, étourderie *f*.

giddy ['gɪdɪ] (*compar* giddier, *superl* giddiest) *adj* -**1.** [dizzy - person]: to be OR to feel ~ [afraid of height] avoir le vertige, être pris de vertige; [unwell] avoir un étourdissement; I feel ~ just watching them j'ai la tête qui tourne OR le vertige rien que de les regarder. -**2.** [lofty] vertigineux, qui donne le vertige; the ~ heights of success les hautes cimes de la réussite. -**3.** [frivolous - person, behaviour] frivole, écervelé; she behaves just like a ~ schoolgirl elle se comporte vraiment comme une jeune idiote OR écervelée; a ~ round of parties and social events un tourbillon de soirées et de sorties mondaines; my ~ aunt! *inf Br* oh la la!

giddy up *interj* [to horse]: ~! hue!

Gideon ['gɪdɪən] *pr n* Gédéon.

Gideon('s) Bible *n bible placée dans les chambres d'hôtel*.

gift [gɪft] ◇ *n* -**1.** [present - personal] cadeau *m*; [- official] don *m*; to make sb a ~ of sthg offrir qqch à qqn, faire cadeau de qqch à qqn; is it a ~? c'est pour offrir?; I wouldn't have it as a ~! je n'en voudrais pas même si on m'en faisait cadeau!; he thinks he's God's ~ to mankind *inf*/to women *inf* il se prend pour le Messie/pour Don Juan; he's God's ~ to advertising c'est le roi de la pub; her offer of help came like a ~ from the gods l'aide qu'elle nous offrait OR sa proposition d'aide était un cadeau tombé du ciel; the ~ of friendship/of tears *lit* le don de l'amitié/des larmes; free ~ COMM cadeau. -**2.** [talent] don *m*; he has a great ~ for telling jokes il n'a pas son pareil pour raconter des plaisanteries; she has a ~ for music elle a un don OR elle est douée pour la musique ❑ to have the ~ of the gab *inf* avoir la langue bien pendue, avoir du bagou(t). -**3.** *inf* [bargain] affaire *f*; at £5, it's a ~ 5 livres, c'est donné. -**4.** *inf* [easy thing]: that exam question was a ~ ce sujet d'examen, c'était du gâteau. -**5.** [donation] don *m*, donation *f*; as a ~ JUR à titre d'avantage OR gracieux; the posts abroad are in the ~ of the French department l'attribution des postes à l'étranger relève du département de français. -**6.** RELIG: the ~ of faith la grâce de la foi; the ~ of tongues le don des langues.
◇ *vt Am fml* donner, faire don de; '~ed by Mr Evans' [on plaque] 'don de M. Evans'.

GIFT [gɪft] (*abbr of* gamete in fallopian transfer) *n* FIVETE *f*.

gift coupon *n* bon *m* de réduction, point-cadeau *m*.

gifted ['gɪftɪd] *adj* [person] doué; [performance] talentueux; highly ~ children des enfants surdoués; she's ~ with a fantastic memory elle a une mémoire fantastique.

gift horse *n*: don't OR never look a ~ in the mouth *prov* à cheval donné on ne regarde pas la bouche *prov*.

gift shop *n* boutique *f* de cadeaux.

gift token *n* bon *m* d'achat.

gift voucher *Br* -**1.** = **gift token**. -**2.** = **gift coupon**.

gift-wrap *vt* faire un paquet cadeau de; do you want it gift-wrapped? je vous fais un paquet cadeau?

gift wrapping *n* papier-cadeau *m*.

gig [gɪg] *n* -**1.** [carriage] cabriolet *m*. -**2.** [boat] yole *f*, guigue *f*. -**3.** *inf* [concert] concert *m* (*de rock, de jazz*).

gigabyte ['gɪgəbaɪt] *n* gigaoctet *m*.

gigahertz ['gɪgəhɜːts] *n* gigahertz *m*.

gigantic [dʒaɪ'gæntɪk] *adj* géant, gigantesque.

gigantism [dʒaɪ'gæntɪzm] *n* gigantisme *m*.

giggle ['gɪgl] ◇ *vi* [stupidly] rire bêtement, ricaner; [nervously] rire nerveusement; they couldn't stop giggling ils ne pouvaient pas se retenir de glousser OR de pouffer.
◇ *n* [uncontrollable] fou rire *m*; [nervous] petit rire *m* nerveux; [stupid] ricanement *m*; to have a fit of the ~s avoir le fou rire; to do sthg for a ~ *inf Br* faire qqch pour rigoler.

giggling ['gɪglɪŋ] ◇ *adj* = **giggly**.
◇ *n* (*U*) fou rire *m*.

giggly ['gɪglɪ] *adj* qui rit bêtement; they're like ~ schoolgirls elles n'arrêtent pas de rire comme des gamines.

GIGO ['gaɪgəʊ] *n abbr of* garbage in, garbage out.

gigolo ['ʒɪgələʊ] (*pl* gigolos) *n* gigolo *m*.

GI Joe *n surnom collectif des soldats américains, notamment pendant la Deuxième Guerre mondiale*.

Gilbert and Sullivan ['gɪlbətən'sʌlɪvn] *pr n*: ~ opera *opérettes satiriques dues au compositeur Sullivan et au librettiste Gilbert (fin du XIXe siècle)*.

gild [gɪld] (*pt* gilded, *pp* gilded OR gilt [gɪlt])
◇ *n* = **guild**.
◇ *vt* dorer; ~ed youth jeunesse *f* dorée ❑ it would be ~ing the lily ce serait du peaufinage.

gilding ['gɪldɪŋ] *n* dorure *f*.

gill[1] [dʒɪl] *n* [measure] quart *m* de pinte.

gill[2] [gɪl] *n* -**1.** [of mushroom] lamelle *f*. -**2.** *Br dial* [ravine] ravin *m*; [stream] ruisseau *m* (*de montagne*).
◆ **gills** *npl* [of fish] ouïes *fpl*, branchies *fpl*; to be/to go green around the ~s [from shock] être/devenir vert (de peur); [from illness] avoir mauvaise mine.

gillie ['gɪlɪ] *n Scot* [for hunting] guide *m*, accompagnateur *m*; [for fishing] accompagnateur *m*.

gillion ['dʒɪljən] *n Br* milliard *m*.

gill slit *n* fente *f* branchiale.

gillyflower ['dʒɪlɪˌflaʊəʳ] *n* giroflée *f*.

gilt [gɪlt] ◇ *pp* → **gild**.
◇ *adj* doré.
◇ *n* -**1.** [gilding] dorure *f*; to take the ~ off the gingerbread *Br* gâcher le plaisir. -**2.** [security] valeur *f* de tout repos.

gilt-edged *adj* -**1.** ST. EX [securities] de père de famille, sans risque. -**2.** [page] doré sur tranche.

gimbal ring ['dʒɪmbl-] *n*, **gimbals** ['dʒɪmbəlz] *npl* AERON & NAUT cardan *m*.

gimcrack ['dʒɪmkræk] *adj* [jewellery] en toc; [ornament, car] de pacotille; [theory, idea] bidon.

gimlet ['gɪmlɪt] *n* vrille *f*; to have eyes like ~s avoir des yeux perçants; his ~ eyes stared at her il la fixa de ses yeux perçants.

gimlet-eyed *adj* à l'œil perçant, aux yeux perçants.

gimme *inf* ['gɪmɪ] = **give me**.

gimmick *inf* ['gɪmɪk] *n* -**1.** [sales trick] truc *m*, astuce *f*; [in politics] astuce *f*, gadget *m*; advertising ~ trouvaille *f* publicitaire; it's just a sales ~ c'est un truc pour faire vendre; the voters aren't fooled by election ~s les électeurs ne sont pas dupes des gadgets électoralistes. -**2.** [gadget, device] gadget *m*. -**3.** [personal trick] truc *m*; **he does a tapdance in the middle of the show purely as a ~** il fait un numéro de claquettes au milieu du spectacle simplement pour l'effet.

gimmickry *inf* ['gɪmɪkrɪ] *n (U)* truquage *m*, astuces *fpl*, gadgets *mpl*; **I'm sick of all this commercial ~** j'en ai assez de tout ce tape-à-l'œil commercial.

gimmicky *inf* ['gɪmɪkɪ] *adj* qui relève du procédé; **the show was too ~** le spectacle relevait trop du procédé.

gimp *inf* [gɪmp] *n Am* -**1.** *pej* [person] gogol *mf*. -**2.** [object] scoubidou *m*.

gin [dʒɪn] (*pt* & *pp* **ginned**, *cont* **ginning**) ◇ *n* -**1.** [drink] gin *m*; **~ and tonic** gin-tonic *m*; **~ and it** *Br* martini-gin *m*. -**2.** [trap] piège *m*. -**3.** INDUST [machine] égreneuse *f* (de coton).
◇ *vt* attraper, piéger.

ginger ['dʒɪndʒəʳ] ◇ *n* -**1.** [spice] gingembre *m*; **crystallized ~** gingembre confit; **ground ~** gingembre en poudre; **root** OR **fresh ~** gingembre en racine OR frais. -**2.** *inf fig* entrain *m*, allant *m*, dynamisme *m*. -**3.** [colour] brun roux *m*. -**4.** *inf* [nickname]: **Ginger** Poil de Carotte.
◇ *adj* [hair] roux, rouquin; [cat] roux.
◆ **ginger up** *vt sep* [activity, group, meeting] animer; [speech, story] relever, pimenter, égayer.

ginger ale *n boisson gazeuse aux extraits de gingembre*.

ginger beer *n boisson légèrement alcoolisée obtenue par la fermentation de gingembre*.

gingerbread ['dʒɪndʒəbred] ◇ *n* pain *m* d'épices; **~ man** sujet *m* en pain d'épices.
◇ *adj* [ornament, style] tarabiscoté.

ginger group *n dans une organisation politique ou autre, faction dynamique cherchant à faire bouger les choses en incitant à l'action*.

gingerly ['dʒɪndʒəlɪ] ◇ *adv* [cautiously] avec circonspection, précautionneusement; [delicately] délicatement.
◇ *adj* [cautious] circonspect, prudent; [delicate] délicat; **to do sthg in a ~ fashion** faire qqch avec beaucoup de précaution.

ginger nut *n* biscuit *m* au gingembre.

ginger pop = **ginger ale**.

ginger snap = **ginger nut**.

ginger wine *n boisson alcoolisée à base de gingembre*.

gingery ['dʒɪndʒərɪ] *adj* -**1.** [taste] de gingembre; [colour] roux. -**2.** *fig* [full of vigour] animé; [biting] acerbe.

gingham ['gɪŋəm] *n* (toile *f* de) vichy *m*.

gingival [dʒɪn'dʒaɪvl] *adj* gingival.

gingivitis [,dʒɪndʒɪ'vaɪtɪs] *n (U)* MED gingivite *f*.

gink▽ [gɪŋk] *n Br* type *m*, bonhomme *m*.

ginormous *inf* [,dʒaɪ'nɔːməs] *adj* gigantesque.

gin palace *Br*, **gin mill** *Am n* tripot *m*.

gin rummy *n* gin-rummy *m*, gin-rami *m*.

ginseng ['dʒɪnseŋ] *n* ginseng *m*.

gin sling *n* gin-fizz *m inv*.

gippo▼ ['dʒɪpəʊ] (*pl* **gippoes**) *n Br terme injurieux désignant un gitan*.

gippy *inf* ['dʒɪpɪ] *adj Br*: **to have a ~ tummy** avoir la courante.

gipsy ['dʒɪpsɪ] (*pl* **gipsies**) ◇ *n* gitan *m*, -e *f*, bohémien *m*, -enne *f*; *fig* [wanderer] vagabond *m*, -e *f*; **she's a ~ at heart** c'est une bohème dans l'âme.
◇ *adj* [camp] de gitans; [dance, music] gitan; **~ caravan** roulotte *f*.

gipsy moth *n* zigzag *m*, bombyx *m* disparate.

giraffe [dʒɪ'rɑːf] *n* girafe *f*; **a young** OR **baby ~** un girafeau, un girafon.

gird [gɜːd] (*pt* & *pp* **girded** OR **girt** [gɜːt]) *vt lit* -**1.** [waist] ceindre; **a sea-girt country** *fig* un pays encerclé par la mer; **to ~ (up) one's loins** se préparer à l'action. -**2.** [clothe]: **to ~ with ceremonial robes** revêtir d'une robe de cérémonie.
◆ **gird on** *vt sep arch* OR *lit*: **to ~ on one's sword** ceindre l'épée.

girder ['gɜːdəʳ] *n* poutre *f* (métallique), fer *m* profilé; [light] poutrelle *f*.

girdle ['gɜːdl] ◇ *n* -**1.** [corset] gaine *f*. -**2.** *lit* [belt] ceinture *f*. -**3.** [in tree] incision *f* annulaire.
◇ *vt* -**1.** *lit*: **to ~ sthg with sthg** ceindre qqch de qqch. -**2.** [tree] baguer.

girdle cake, girdle scone *n Br sorte de petite galette*.

girl [gɜːl] *n* -**1.** [child] (petite) fille *f*; **a little ~** une fillette, une petite fille; **a ~s' school** une école de filles; **I knew her when she was a ~** je l'ai connue toute petite; **poor little ~!** pauvre petite! -**2.** [daughter] fille *f*; **the Murphy ~** la fille des Murphy. -**3.** [young woman] (jeune) fille *f*; **the other ~s at the office** les autres filles du bureau; **come in, ~s!** entrez, mesdemoiselles!; **she's having an evening with the ~s** elle passe la soirée dehors avec les filles; **he married a French ~** il a épousé une Française; **my dear ~** ma chère. -**4.** *inf* [girlfriend] (petite) amie *f*, copine *f*. -**5.** SCH [pupil] élève *f*. -**6.** [employee] (jeune) employée *f*; [maid] bonne *f*; [in shop] vendeuse *f*; [in factory] ouvrière *f*.

girl Friday *n employée de bureau affectée à des tâches diverses*.

girlfriend ['gɜːlfrend] *n* [of boy] copine *f*, (petite) amie *f*; *Am* [of girl] copine *f*, amie *f*.

Girl Guide *Br*, **Girl Scout** *Am n* éclaireuse *f*.

girlhood ['gɜːlhʊd] *n* [as child] enfance *f*; [as adolescent] adolescence *f*.

girlie *inf* ['gɜːlɪ] *adj*: **~ magazine** magazine *m* masculin, revue *f* érotique.

girlish ['gɜːlɪʃ] *adj* [appearance, smile, voice] de fillette, de petite fille; *pej* [boy] efféminé.

girlishly ['gɜːlɪʃlɪ] *adv* comme une petite fille.

Girl Scout *Am* = **Girl Guide**.

giro ['dʒaɪrəʊ] *n* -**1.** [system] *système de virement interbancaire introduit par la Poste britannique*; **~ account** compte *m* chèque postal; **(bank) ~** virement *m* bancaire; **to pay by bank ~** payer par virement bancaire; **~ cheque** chèque *m* postal; **National Giro** ≃ Comptes Chèques Postaux. -**2.** *inf* [for unemployed] chèque *m* d'allocation de chômage.

girt [gɜːt] *pt* & *pp* → **gird**.

girth [gɜːθ] ◇ *n* -**1.** [circumference] circonférence *f*, tour *m*. -**2.** [stoutness] corpulence *f*, embonpoint *m*. -**3.** [of saddle] sangle *f*.
◇ *vt* [horse] sangler.

gist [dʒɪst] *n* essentiel *m*; **I get the ~ of your argument** je comprends OR saisis l'essentiel de ton argument; **give me the ~ of the discussion** expliquez-moi les grandes lignes du débat.

git▽ [gɪt] *n Br* connard *m*, connasse *f*.

give [gɪv] (*pt* **gave** [geɪv], *pp* **given** ['gɪvn]) ◇ *vt* **A.** -**1.** [hand over] donner; [as gift] donner, offrir; **I gave him the book, I gave the book to him** je lui ai donné le livre; **we gave our host a gift** nous avons offert un cadeau à notre hôte; **the family gave the paintings to the museum** la famille a fait don des tableaux au musée; **he gave his daughter in marriage** il a donné sa fille en mariage; **she gave him her hand** [to hold] elle lui a donné OR tendu la main; [in marriage] elle lui a accordé sa main; **to ~ o.s. to sb** *lit* se donner à qqn; **I ~ you the newlyweds!** [in toast] je lève mon verre au bonheur des nouveaux mariés!; **I gave him my coat to hold** je lui ai confié mon manteau; **she gave them her trust** elle leur a fait confiance, elle leur a donné sa confiance; **in any relationship you have to learn to ~ and take** dans toutes les relations, il faut apprendre à prendre et à donner ❑ **to ~ as good as one gets** *inf* rendre coup pour coup; **~ it all you've got!** *inf* mets-y le paquet!; **I'll ~ you something to cry about!** *inf* je vais te donner une bonne raison de pleurer, moi! -**2.** [grant - right, permission, importance etc] donner; **~ the matter your full attention** prêtez une attention toute particulière à cette affaire; **he gave your suggestion careful consideration** il a considéré votre suggestion avec beaucoup d'attention; **the court gave her custody of the child** JUR la cour lui a accordé la garde de l'enfant; **she hasn't given her approval yet** elle n'a pas encore donné son consentement. -**3.** [provide with - drink, food] donner, offrir; [- lessons, classes] donner; [- help] prêter; **~ our guests something to eat/drink** donnez à manger/à boire à nos invités; **we gave them lunch** nous les avons invités OR nous leur avons fait à déjeuner; **I think I'll ~ them beef for lunch** je crois que je vais leur faire du bœuf au déjeuner; **let me ~ you some advice** laissez-moi vous donner un conseil; **I gave her the biggest bedroom** je lui ai donné la plus grande chambre; **they're giving us a pay rise** ils nous donnent une augmentation de salaire; **the children can wash up, it will ~ them something to do** les enfants peuvent faire la vaisselle, ça les occupera; **she gave him two lovely daughters** elle lui a donné deux adorables filles; **to ~ sb/sthg one's support** soutenir qqn/qqch; **do you ~ a discount?** faites-vous des tarifs préférentiels?; **~ me time to think** donnez-moi OR laissez-moi le temps de réfléchir; **she didn't ~ him time to say no** elle ne lui a pas laissé le temps de dire non; **just ~ me time!** sois patient!; **such talent is not given to us all** nous n'avons pas tous un tel talent ❑ **~ me jazz any day!** *inf* à mon avis rien ne vaut le jazz!
B. -**1.** [confer - award] conférer; **they gave her an honorary degree** ils lui ont conféré un diplôme honorifique. -**2.** [dedicate] donner, consacrer; **she gave all she had to the cause** elle s'est entièrement consacrée à cette cause; **can you ~ me a few minutes?** pouvez-vous m'accorder OR me consacrer quelques instants?; **he gave his life to save the child** il est mort OR il a donné sa vie pour sauver l'enfant. -**3.** [in exchange] donner; [pay] payer; **I gave him my sweater in exchange for his gloves** je lui ai échangé mon pull contre ses gants; **I'll ~ you a good price for the table** je vous donnerai OR payerai un bon prix pour la table; **how much will you ~ me for it?** combien m'en donneras-tu? -**4.** [transmit] donner, passer; **I hope I don't ~ you my cold** j'espère que je ne vais pas te passer mon rhume.
C. -**1.** [cause] donner, causer; [headache] donner; [pleasure, surprise] faire; **the walk gave him an appetite** la promenade l'a mis en appétit OR lui a ouvert l'appétit; **the news gave me a shock** la nouvelle m'a fait un choc. -**2.** [impose - task] imposer; [- punishment] infliger; **the teacher gave us three tests this week** le professeur nous a donné trois interrogations cette semaine; **to ~ sb a black mark** infliger un blâme à qqn; **he was given (a sentence of) 15 years** JUR il a été condamné à 15 ans de prison. -**3.** [announce - verdict, judgment]: **the court ~s its decision today** la cour prononce OR rend l'arrêt aujourd'hui; **the court gave the case against/for the management** la cour a décidé contre/en faveur de la direction; **given this third day of March** délivré le trois mars; **given under my hand and seal** reçu par-devant moi et sous mon sceau; **the umpire gave the batsman out** l'arbitre a déclaré le joueur hors jeu. -**4.** [communicate - impression, order, signal] donner; [- address, information] donner, fournir; [- news] annoncer; **to ~ sb a message** communiquer un message à qqn; **she gave her age as 45** elle a déclaré avoir 45 ans; **he is to ~ his decision tomorrow** il devra faire connaître OR annoncer sa décision demain; **I gave a description of the suspect** j'ai donné OR fourni une description du suspect; **you gave me to believe he was trustworthy** vous m'avez laissé entendre qu'on pouvait lui faire confiance; **I was given to understand she was ill** on m'a donné à croire qu'elle était malade; **she gave no sign of life** elle n'a donné aucun signe de vie. -**5.** [suggest, propose - explanation, reason] donner, avancer; [- hint] donner; **that's given me an idea** ça me donne une idée; **~ us a clue** donne-nous un indice; **let me ~ you an**

example laissez-moi vous donner un exemple; **don't ~ me any nonsense about missing your train!** ne me raconte pas que tu as raté ton train!; **don't ~ me that (rubbish)!** *inf* ne me raconte pas d'histoires! -**6.** [admit, concede] reconnaître, accorder; **she's certainly intelligent, I'll ~ you that** elle est très intelligente, ça, je te l'accorde; **he gave me the game** SPORT il m'a concédé la partie.

D. -**1.** [utter - sound] rendre, émettre; [- answer] donner, faire; [- cry, sigh] pousser; **he gave a laugh** il a laissé échapper un rire; **he gave a loud laugh** il a éclaté de rire; **~ us a song** chantez-nous quelque chose. -**2.** [make - action, gesture] faire; **she gave them an odd look** elle leur a jeté OR lancé un regard curieux; **he gave her hand a squeeze** il lui a pressé la main; **~ me a kiss** [gen] fais-moi la bise; [lover] embrasse-moi; **I gave the boy a push** j'ai poussé le garçon; **the train gave a lurch** le train a cahoté; **she gave him a slap** elle lui a donné une claque; **she gave him a flirtatious smile** elle lui a adressé OR fait un sourire séducteur; **he gave an embarrassed smile** il a eu un sourire gêné. -**3.** [perform in public - concert] donner; [- lecture, speech] faire; [- interview] accorder; **that evening, she gave the performance of a lifetime** ce soir-là, elle était au sommet de son art . -**4.** [hold - lunch, party, supper] donner, organiser; **they gave a dinner for the professor** ils ont donné un dîner en l'honneur du professeur. -**5.** [estimate the duration of] donner, estimer; **I ~ him one week at most** je lui donne une semaine (au) maximum; **I'd ~ their marriage about a year if that** je donne un an maximum à leur mariage. -**6.** [care]: **the manager doesn't ~ a damn about the workers' problems** *inf* le directeur se fiche des problèmes des ouvriers; **I don't ~ a hoot about what he thinks** *inf* je n'ai rien à faire OR je me fiche de ce qu'il pense. -**7.** MATH [produce] donner, faire; **17 minus 4 ~s 13** 17 moins 4 font OR égalent 13; **that ~s a total of 26** ça donne un total de 26. -**8.** *phr*: **to ~ way** [ground] s'affaisser; [bridge, building, ceiling] s'effondrer, s'affaisser; [ladder, rope] céder, (se) casser; **the ground gave way beneath** OR **under our feet** le terrain s'est affaissé sous nos pieds; **her legs gave way (beneath her)** ses jambes se sont dérobées sous elle; **his health finally gave way** sa santé a fini par se détériorer OR se gâter; **their strength gave way** leurs forces leur ont manqué; **it's easier to ~ way to his demands than to argue** il est plus commode de céder à ses exigences que de lui résister; **don't ~ way if he cries** ne cède pas s'il pleure; **I gave way to tears/to anger** je me suis laissé aller à pleurer/ emporter par la colère; **he gave way to despair** il s'est abandonné au désespoir; **the fields gave way to factories** les champs ont fait place aux usines; **his joy gave way to sorrow** sa joie a fait place à la peine; **'~ way to vehicles on your right'** 'priorité aux véhicules qui viennent de droite'; **'~ way to pedestrians'** 'priorité aux piétons'; **'~ way'** 'cédez le passage'.

◇ *vi* -**1.** [contribute] donner; **please ~ generously** nous nous en remettons à votre générosité. -**2.** [collapse, yield - ground, wall] s'affaisser; **the fence gave beneath** OR **under my weight** la barrière a cédé OR s'est affaissée sous mon poids; **something's got to ~** quelque chose va lâcher; [- cloth, elastic] se relâcher; [- person] céder. -**3.** *inf Am* [talk] : **now ~!** accouche!, vide ton sac! -**4.** *inf Am*: **what ~s?** qu'est-ce qui se passe?

◇ *n* [of metal, wood] élasticité *f*, souplesse *f*; **there's not enough ~ in this sweater** ce pull n'est pas assez ample.

◆ **give or take** *prep phr* à... près; **~ or take a few days** à quelques jours près.

◆ **give away** *vt sep* -**1.** [hand over] donner; [as gift] donner, faire cadeau de; **to ~ prizes away** distribuer des prix; **it's so cheap they're practically giving it away** c'est tellement bon marché, c'est comme s'ils en faisaient cadeau. -**2.** [bride] conduire à l'autel. -**3.** [throw away - chance, opportunity] gâcher, gaspiller. -**4.** [reveal - information] révéler; [- secret] révéler, trahir; **he didn't ~ anything away** il n'a rien dit. -**5.** [betray] trahir; **her accent gave her away** son accent l'a trahie; **no prisoner would ~ another prisoner away** aucun prisonnier n'en trahirait un autre.

◆ **give back** *vt sep* -**1.** [return] rendre; [property, stolen object] restituer; **~ the book back to her** rendez-lui le livre; **the store gave him his money back** le magasin l'a remboursé. -**2.** [reflect - image, light] refléter, renvoyer; [sound] renvoyer.

◆ **give in** ◇ *vi insep* [relent, yield] céder; **to ~ in to sthg/sb** céder à qqch/qqn; **the country refused to ~ in to terrorist threats** le pays a refusé de céder aux menaces des terroristes.

◇ *vt sep* [hand in - book, exam paper] rendre; [- found object, parcel] remettre; [- application, name] donner.

◆ **give off** *vt sep* -**1.** [emit, produce - gas, smell] émettre. -**2.** BOT [shoots] former.

◆ **give onto** *vt insep* donner sur.

◆ **give out** ◇ *vt sep* -**1.** [hand out] distribuer. -**2.** [emit] émettre, faire entendre. -**3.** [make known] annoncer, faire savoir; **the hospital gave out information on her condition to them** l'hôpital les a renseignés sur son état de santé; **it was given out that he was leaving** on a dit OR annoncé qu'il partait.

◇ *vi insep* -**1.** [break down - machine] tomber en panne; [- brakes] lâcher; [- heart] flancher; **the old car finally gave out** la vieille voiture a fini par rendre l'âme *hum*. -**2.** [run out] s'épuiser, manquer; **her strength was giving out** elle était à bout de forces, elle n'en pouvait plus; **his mother's patience gave out** sa mère a perdu patience; **my luck gave out** la chance m'a abandonné.

◆ **give over** ◇ *vt sep* -**1.** [entrust] donner, confier; **he gave the children over to his mother** il a confié les enfants à sa mère. -**2.** [set aside for] donner, consacrer; ADMIN affecter; **the land was given over to agriculture** la terre a été consacrée à l'agriculture; **she gave herself over to helping the poor** elle s'est consacrée à l'aide aux pauvres.

◇ *vt insep inf Br* cesser de, arrêter de; **~ over crying!** cesse de pleurer!

◇ *vi insep inf Br* cesser, arrêter; **~ over!** assez!, arrête!

◆ **give up** ◇ *vt sep* -**1.** [renounce - habit] renoncer à, abandonner; [- friend] abandonner, délaisser; [- chair, place] céder; [- activity] cesser; **she'll never ~ him up** elle ne renoncera jamais à lui; **he's given up smoking** il a arrêté de fumer, il a renoncé au tabac; **I haven't given up the idea of going to China** je n'ai pas renoncé à l'idée d'aller en Chine; **he gave up his seat to the old woman** il a cédé sa place à la vieille dame; **don't ~ up hope** ne perdez pas espoir; **he was ready to ~ up his life for his country** il était prêt à mourir pour la patrie; **they gave up the game** OR **the struggle** ils ont abandonné la partie; **we gave her brother up for dead** nous avons conclu que son frère était mort; **they gave the cause up for lost** ils ont considéré que c'était une cause perdue; **to ~ up the throne** renoncer au trône. -**2.** [resign from - job] quitter; [- position] démissionner de; **they gave up the restaurant business** ils se sont retirés de la restauration. -**3.** [hand over - keys] rendre, remettre; [- prisoner] livrer; [- responsibility] se démettre de; **the murderer gave himself up (to the police)** le meurtrier s'est rendu OR livré (à la police); **he gave his accomplices up to the police** il a dénoncé OR livré ses complices à la police.

◇ *vi insep*: **I ~ up** [in game, project] je renonce; [in guessing game] je donne ma langue au chat; **we can't ~ up now!** on ne va pas laisser tomber maintenant!

◆ **give up on** *vt insep*: **to ~ up on sb** [stop waiting for] renoncer à attendre qqn; [stop expecting sthg from] ne plus rien attendre de qqn; **I ~ up on him, he won't even try** j'abandonne, il ne fait pas le moindre effort.

◆ **give up to** *vt sep*: **to ~ o.s. up to sthg** se livrer à qqch; **they gave themselves up to a life of pleasure** ils se sont livrés à une vie de plaisir; **he gave his life up to caring for the elderly** il a consacré sa vie à soigner les personnes âgées.

give-and-take *n* -**1.** [compromise] concessions *fpl* (mutuelles); **in a relationship there has to be some ~** pour fonder une relation, il faut que chacun fasse des concessions OR que chacun y mette du sien. -**2.** [in conversation] échange; **to encourage the ~ of ideas and opinions** favoriser l'échange d'idées.

giveaway ['gɪvə,weɪ] ◇ *n* -**1.** [free gift] cadeau *m*; COMM prime *f*, cadeau *m* publicitaire. -**2.** *Am* RADIO & TV jeu *m* (doté de prix). -**3.** *inf* [revelation] révélation *f* (involontaire); **her guilty expression was a dead ~** son air coupable l'a trahie; **the fact that he knew her address was a ~** le fait qu'il sache son adresse était révélateur OR en disait long.

◇ *adj* -**1.** [free] gratuit; [price] dérisoire. -**2.** *Am*: **~ program** RADIO jeu *m* radiophonique; TV jeu *m* télévisé. -**3.** *inf* [revealing] révélateur.

given ['gɪvn] ◇ *pp* → **give**.

◇ *adj* -**1.** [specified] donné; [precise] déterminé; **at a ~ moment** à un moment donné. -**2.** [prone] : **to be ~ to sthg** avoir une tendance à qqch; **to be ~ to doing sthg** être enclin à faire qqch; **he's ~ to attacks of depression** il a des tendances dépressives; **I'm not ~ to telling lies** je n'ai pas l'habitude de mentir ‖ [on official statement] : **~ in Melbourne on the sixth day of March** fait à Melbourne le six mars.

◇ *prep* -**1.** [considering] étant donné; **~ the circumstances** étant donné les circonstances, les circonstances étant ce qu'elles sont; **~ the rectangle ABCD** MATH soit le rectangle ABCD. -**2.** *phr*: **~ the chance** OR **opportunity** si l'occasion se présentait; **she could be a good teacher, ~ the opportunity** elle ferait un bon professeur si l'occasion se présentait; **~ the chance, I'd emigrate to Canada** si l'occasion se présentait, j'émigrerais au Canada.

◆ **given that** *conj phr* étant donné que.

given name *n Am* prénom *m*.

giver ['gɪvə^r] *n* donateur *m*, -trice *f*.

Gîza ['giːzə] *pr n*: (El) ~ Gizeh, Guizèh.

gizmo *inf* ['gɪzməʊ] (*pl* **gizmos**) *n Am* gadget *m*, truc *m*.

gizzard ['gɪzəd] *n* gésier *m*; **it sticks in my ~** *fig* ça me reste en travers de la gorge.

glacé ['glæseɪ] *adj* -**1.** [cherries] glacé, confit; **~ icing** glaçage *m (d'un gâteau)*. -**2.** [leather, silk] glacé. -**3.** *Am* [frozen] glacé, gelé.

glacial ['gleɪsjəl] *adj* -**1.** [weather, wind] glacial. -**2.** [politeness, atmosphere] glacial. -**3.** GEOL glaciaire. -**4.** CHEM cristallisé, en cristaux.

glacially ['gleɪsjəlɪ] *adv* glacialement.

glaciation [,gleɪsɪ'eɪʃn] *n* glaciation *f*.

glacier ['glæsjə^r] *n* glacier *m*.

glaciology [,glæsɪ'ɒlədʒɪ] *n* glaciologie *f*.

glacis ['glæsɪs] (*pl inv* [-sɪz] OR **glacises** ['glæsiːz]) *n* glacis *m*.

glad [glæd] ◇ *adj* -**1.** [person] heureux, content; **(I'm) ~ you came** (je suis) heureux OR bien content que tu sois venu; **I'm feeling a lot better today — oh, I am ~!** je me sens beaucoup mieux aujourd'hui – j'en suis ravi!; **he's decided not to go — I'm ~ about that** il a décidé de ne pas partir – tant mieux; **I was ~ to hear the news** j'étais ravi d'apprendre la nouvelle; **he was only too ~ to be asked** il n'attendait qu'une chose, c'est qu'on le lui demande; **I'd be only too ~ to help** je ne demanderais pas mieux que d'aider; **could you do me a favour? — I'd be ~ to** pourriez-vous me rendre service? – avec plaisir OR volontiers; **(I'm) ~ to meet you!** enchanté!; **they were ~ of the money** cet argent tombait à point nommé OR à pic; **we were ~ of the opportunity to meet her** nous avons été heureux de pouvoir faire sa connaissance; **I was ~ of your help** votre aide a été la bienvenue. -**2.** *lit* [news, occasion] joyeux, heureux; [laughter] de bonheur; [shout] joyeux; **it's a ~ day for all of us**

c'est un jour de fête pour nous tous. -**3.** *phr*: to give sb the ~ eye faire les yeux doux à qqn, faire de l'œil à qqn.

◇ *n inf* = **gladiolus**.

gladden ['glædn] *vt* rendre heureux, réjouir; it ~s my heart to think of it c'est une pensée qui me réjouit le cœur.

glade [gleɪd] *n lit* clairière *f*.

glad hand *inf n*: to give sb the ~ accueillir qqn chaleureusement OR à bras ouverts.

◆ **glad-hand** *inf vt*: to ~ sb serrer la main de qqn avec de grands sourires.

gladiator ['glædɪeɪtə^r] *n* gladiateur *m*.

gladiatorial [ˌglædɪə'tɔːrɪəl] *adj* de gladiateurs.

gladiolus [ˌglædɪ'əʊləs] (*pl* **gladioli** [-laɪ] OR **gladioluses**) *n* glaïeul *m*.

gladly ['glædlɪ] *adv* avec plaisir, avec joie, de bon cœur.

gladness ['glædnɪs] *n* contentement *m*, joie *f*.

glad rags *inf npl* vêtements *mpl* chic; to put on one's ~ se mettre sur son trente et un, se saper.

gladsome ['glædsəm] *adj arch* OR *lit* joyeux, gai.

Gladstone bag ['glædstən-] *n sacoche de voyage en cuir*.

glair(e) [gleə^r] *n* glaire *f*.

glam *inf* [glæm] (*pt* & *pp* **glammed**, *cont* **glamming**) *Br* ◇ *adj* = **glamorous**.

◇ *n* = **glamour**.

◆ **glam up** *inf vt sep* -**1.** [person]: to get glammed up [with clothes] mettre ses belles fringues, se saper; [with make-up] se faire une beauté, se faire toute belle. -**2.** [building] retaper; [town] embellir.

glamor *Am* = **glamour**.

glamorization [ˌglæməraɪ'zeɪʃn] *n* idéalisation *f*.

glamorize, -ise ['glæməraɪz] *vt* idéaliser, montrer OR présenter sous un jour séduisant; the film ~s peasant life le film idéalise la vie des paysans.

glamorous ['glæmərəs] *adj* -**1.** [alluring - person, appearance] séduisant, fascinant, éblouissant; a ~ actress une actrice éblouissante OR resplendissante; ~ dresses robes éblouissantes OR d'un chic inouï. -**2.** [exciting - lifestyle] brillant; [- career] brillant, prestigieux; [- show] splendide; the ~ parts of the French Riviera les endroits chics de la Côte d'Azur.

glamorously ['glæmərəslɪ] *adv* brillamment, de manière éblouissante.

glamour *Br*, **glamor** *Am* ['glæmə^r] ◇ *n* -**1.** [allure - of person] charme *m*, fascination *f*; [- of appearance, dress] élégance *f*, chic *m*. -**2.** [excitement - of lifestyle, show, career] éclat *m*, prestige *m*; the novel captures all the ~ of London in the 1920s le roman dépeint tout l'éclat du Londres des années vingt; there isn't much ~ in my job mon travail n'a rien de bien excitant OR passionnant.

◇ *comp* de charme; ~ boy *inf* beau gosse *m*; ~ girl *inf* pin-up *f inv*; [model] mannequin *m*.

glamourize, -ise ['glæməraɪz] = **glamorize**.

glamourless ['glæməlɪs] *adj* [person] sans charme, sans élégance, fade; [life] sans éclat, terne; [job] terne, peu intéressant.

glamourous ['glæmərəs] = **glamorous**.

glance [glɑːns] ◇ *vi* -**1.** [look]: to ~ at sthg jeter un coup d'œil (rapide) sur qqch; to ~ at sb jeter un coup d'œil à qqn; he ~d at his watch il jeta un coup d'œil sur sa montre; he ~d at her quickly il lui jeta un rapide coup d'œil. -**2.** [read quickly]: she ~d through OR over the letter elle parcourut rapidement la lettre; to ~ through a book feuilleter un livre; to ~ through a newspaper lire un journal en diagonale, feuilleter un journal. -**3.** [look in given direction]: he ~d back OR behind il a jeté un coup d'œil en arrière; she opened the door and ~d round the room elle ouvrit la porte et jeta un coup d'œil autour de la pièce; they ~d towards the door leurs regards se sont tournés vers la porte. -**4.** [gleam] étinceler.

◇ *n* -**1.** [look] coup *m* d'œil, regard *m*; to have OR to take a ~ at jeter un coup d'œil sur; at first ~ au premier coup d'œil, à première vue; I could tell OR see at a ~ je m'en suis aperçu tout de suite; one ~ was enough il m'a suffi d'un regard; I didn't give it a second ~ je n'y ai guère prêté attention; she walked away without a backward ~ elle est partie sans se retourner; to give sb a sidelong ~ lancer un regard oblique à qqn; he cast an affectionate/anxious ~ in her direction il jeta un regard affectueux/inquiet dans sa direction. -**2.** [gleam] lueur *f*, éclat *m*; [in water] reflet *m*.

◆ **glance away** *vi insep* détourner les yeux.

◆ **glance off** ◇ *vi insep* [arrow, bullet] ricocher, faire ricochet; [sword, spear] être dévié, ricocher; the arrow hit a tree and ~d off la flèche a ricoché sur un arbre.

◇ *vt insep*: to ~ off sthg [subj: arrow, bullet] ricocher sur qqch; [subj: sword, spear] dévier sur qqch.

◆ **glance up** *vi insep* -**1.** [look upwards] regarder en l'air OR vers le haut. -**2.** [from book, newspaper] lever les yeux; he ~d up from (reading) his book il leva les yeux de son livre.

glancing ['glɑːnsɪŋ] *adj* -**1.** [blow]: he struck me a ~ blow il m'asséna un coup oblique. -**2.** [gleaming - sunlight] étincelant. -**3.** [indirect - allusion] indirect, fortuit.

gland [glænd] *n* -**1.** PHYSIOL glande *f*. -**2.** MECH presse-étoupe *m inv*.

glanders ['glændəz] *n (U)* VETER morve *f*.

glandes ['glændiːz] *pl* → **glans**.

glandular ['glændjʊlə^r] *adj* glandulaire, glanduleux.

glandular fever *n (U)* mononucléose *f* (infectieuse).

glans [glæns] (*pl* **glandes** ['glændiːz]) *n* ANAT gland *m*.

glare [gleə^r] ◇ *vi* -**1.** [sun, light] briller d'un éclat éblouissant; the sun ~d down from the cloudless sky il faisait un soleil éclatant OR éblouissant dans un ciel sans nuage; the sun ~d down on them un soleil de plomb les aveuglait. -**2.** [person]: to ~ at sb regarder qqn avec colère; they ~d at each other ils échangèrent un regard menaçant; he ~d angrily at me il m'a lancé un regard furieux.

◇ *vt*: to ~ hatred/defiance at sb lancer un regard plein de haine/de défi à qqn.

◇ *n* -**1.** [light] lumière *f* éblouissante OR aveuglante; [of sun] éclat *m*; he stood in the ~ of the headlights il était pris dans la lumière (aveuglante) des phares. -**2.** [of publicity] feux *mpl*; politicians lead their lives in the (full) ~ of publicity la vie des hommes politiques est toujours sous les feux des projecteurs. -**3.** [angry stare] regard *m* furieux; she looked at him with a ~ of contempt elle lui a lancé un regard méprisant. -**4.** *Am* [sheet of ice] plaque *f* de verglas.

glare ice *n Am* verglas *m*.

glaring ['gleərɪŋ] *adj* -**1.** [dazzling - light] éblouissant, éclatant; [- car headlights] éblouissant; [- sun] aveuglant. -**2.** [bright - colour] vif; *pej* criard, voyant. -**3.** [angry] furieux. -**4.** [obvious - error] qui saute aux yeux, qui crève les yeux, patent; [- injustice, lie] flagrant, criant; a ~ abuse of public funds un détournement manifeste des fonds publics.

glaringly ['gleərɪŋlɪ] *adv*: it's ~ obvious ça crève les yeux.

Glasgow ['glɑːzgəʊ] *pr n* Glasgow.

glass [glɑːs] ◇ *n* -**1.** [substance] verre *m*; made of ~ en verre; a pane of ~ un carreau, une vitre; these plants are grown under ~ ces plantes sont cultivées en serre. -**2.** [vessel, contents] verre *m*; a ~ of water/beer un verre d'eau/de bière; a ~ of champagne une coupe de champagne; to raise one's ~ to sb [in toast] lever son verre à qqn; beer ~ verre à bière, bock *m*. -**3.** [in shop, museum] vitrine *f*; displayed under ~ exposé en vitrine. -**4.** [glassware] verrerie *f*. -**5.** [mirror]: (looking) ~ glace *f*, miroir *m*. -**6.** [telescope] longue-vue *f*. -**7.** [barometer] baromètre *m*; the ~ is falling le baromètre baisse.

◇ *comp* [ornament, bottle] en verre; [door] vitré; [industry] du verre; 'The Glass Menagerie' *Williams* 'la Ménagerie de verre'.

◇ *vt* [bookcase, porch] vitrer; [photograph] mettre sous verre.

◆ **glasses** *npl* -**1.** [spectacles] lunettes *fpl*; to wear ~es porter des lunettes; ~ case étui *m* à lunettes. -**2.** [binoculars] jumelles *fpl*.

◆ **glass in** *vt sep* = **glass** *vt*.

glassblower ['glɑːsˌbləʊə^r] *n* souffleur *m (de verre)*.

glassblowing ['glɑːsˌbləʊɪŋ] *n* soufflage *m (du verre)*.

glass case *n* [for display] vitrine *f*.

glass cloth *n* essuie-verres *m inv*.

glasscutter ['glɑːsˌkʌtə^r] *n* -**1.** [person] vitrier *m*. -**2.** [implement] coupe-verre *m inv*, diamant *m*.

glass eye *n* œil *m* de verre.

glass factory *n* verrerie *f (usine)*.

glass fibre ◇ *n* fibre *m* de verre.

◇ *adj* en fibre de verre.

glassful ['glɑːsfʊl] *n* (plein) verre *m*.

glasshouse ['glɑːshaʊs, *pl* -haʊzɪz] *n* -**1.** *Br* [greenhouse] serre *f*. -**2.** *Am* [factory] verrerie *f (usine)*. -**3.** *Br mil sl* [prison] prison *f* militaire, trou *m*.

glassily ['glɑːsɪlɪ] *adv* d'un œil vitreux OR terne.

glassine [glæ'siːn] *n* papier *m* cristal.

glass jaw *inf n* [in boxing]: to have a ~ avoir la mâchoire fragile.

glasspaper ['glɑːsˌpeɪpə^r] ◇ *n* papier *m* de verre.

◇ *vt* poncer au papier de verre.

glass slipper *n* pantoufle *f* de verre.

glass snake *n* serpent *m* de verre.

glassware ['glɑːsweə^r] *n* [glass objects] verrerie *f*; [tumblers] verrerie *f*, gobeleterie *f*.

glass wool *n* laine *f* de verre.

glasswork ['glɑːswɜːk] *n* vitrerie *f*.

glassworks ['glɑːswɜːks] (*pl inv*) *n* verrerie *f (usine)*.

glasswort ['glɑːswɜːt] *n* [marsh samphire] salicorne *f*; [saltwort] kali *m*.

glassy ['glɑːsɪ] (*compar* **glassier**, *superl* **glassiest**) *adj* -**1.** [eye, expression] vitreux, terne. -**2.** [smooth - surface] uni, lisse; a ~ sea une mer d'huile.

glassy-eyed *adj* à l'œil terne OR vitreux; to be ~ avoir le regard vitreux OR terne; he looked at me ~ il me fixa d'un œil vitreux.

Glaswegian [glæz'wiːdʒjən] ◇ *n* [inhabitant] habitant *m*, -e *f* de Glasgow; [by birth] natif *m*, -ive *f* de Glasgow; [dialect] dialecte *m* de Glasgow.

◇ *adj* de Glasgow.

glaucoma [glɔː'kəʊmə] *n (U)* glaucome *m*.

glaucous ['glɔːkəs] *adj lit* glauque.

glaze [gleɪz] ◇ *vt* -**1.** [floor, tiles] vitrifier; [pottery, china] vernisser; [leather, silk] glacer. -**2.** [photo, painting] glacer. -**3.** CULIN glacer. -**4.** [window] vitrer.

◇ *n* -**1.** [on pottery] vernis *m*; [on floor, tiles] vernis *m*, enduit *m* vitrifié; [on cotton, silk] glacé *m*. -**2.** [on painting, on paper, photo] glacé *m*, glacis *m*. -**3.** CULIN glace *f*. -**4.** *Am* [ice] verglas *m*.

◆ **glaze over** *vi insep*: his eyes ~d over ses yeux sont devenus vitreux.

glazed [gleɪzd] *adj* -**1.** [floor, tiles] vitrifié; [pottery] vernissé, émaillé; [leather, silk] glacé. -**2.** [photo, painting] glacé. -**3.** CULIN glacé. -**4.** [window] vitré; [picture] sous verre. -**5.** [eyes] vitreux, terne; there was a ~ look in her eyes elle avait le regard vitreux OR absent.

glaze ice *n Br* verglas *m*.

glazier ['gleɪzjə^r] *n* vitrier *m*.

glazing ['gleɪzɪŋ] *n* -**1.** [of pottery] vernissage *m*; [of floor, tiles] vitrification *f*; [of leather, silk] glaçage *m*. -**2.** CULIN [process] glaçage *m*; [substance] glace *f*.

GLC (*abbr of* **Greater London Council**) *pr n ancien organe administratif du grand Londres*.

gleam [gliːm] ◇ *vi* -**1.** [metal, polished surface] luire, reluire; [stronger] briller; [cat's eyes] luire;

[water] miroiter. -**2.** *fig*: her eyes **~ed with anticipation/mischief** ses yeux brillaient d'espoir/de malice.

◇ *n* -**1.** [on surface] lueur *f*, miroitement *m*. -**2.** *fig*: a **~ of hope** une lueur d'espoir; **she had a strange ~ in her eye** il y avait une lueur étrange dans son regard.

gleaming ['gli:mɪŋ] *adj* [metal] luisant, brillant; [furniture] reluisant; [kitchen] étincelant.

glean [gli:n] *vt* -**1.** [collect - information, news] glaner, grappiller. -**2.** AGR glaner.

gleaner ['gli:nər] *n* glaneur *m*, -euse *f*.

gleanings ['gli:nɪŋz] *npl* -**1.** [information] bribes *fpl* de renseignements (glanées çà et là). -**2.** AGR glanure *f*, glanures *fpl*.

glebe [gli:b] *n* -**1.** *poet* glèbe *f*, terre *f*. -**2.** *Br* RELIG *terres faisant partie d'un bénéfice ecclésiastique*.

glee [gli:] *n* -**1.** [joy] joie *f*, allégresse *f*; **to jump up and down/to rub one's hands with ~** sauter/se frotter les mains de joie; **with great ~** avec allégresse. -**2.** MUS chant *m* a capella *(à plusieurs voix)*.

glee club *n Am* chorale *f*.

gleeful ['gli:fʊl] *adj* joyeux, radieux.

gleefully ['gli:fʊlɪ] *adv* joyeusement, avec allégresse OR joie.

glen [glen] *n* vallon *m*, vallée *f* étroite et encaissée *(en Écosse ou en Irlande)*.

glib [glɪb] *adj* [answer, excuse] (trop) facile, désinvolte; [lie] éhonté, désinvolte; **he's rather too ~** il parle trop facilement, il est trop volubile; **a ~ talker** [as salesman] un beau parleur; **he has a ~ tongue** il a la langue bien pendue.

glibly ['glɪblɪ] *adv* [talk, argue, reply] avec aisance, facilement; [lie] avec désinvolture, sans sourciller.

glibness ['glɪbnɪs] *n* -**1.** [of person] facilité *f* de parole. -**2.** [of argument, excuse] facilité *f*, désinvolture *f*.

glide [glaɪd] ◇ *vi* -**1.** [gen] glisser; [person]: **to ~ in/out/past** [noiselessly] entrer/sortir/passer sans bruit; [gracefully] entrer/sortir/passer avec grâce; [stealthily] entrer/sortir/passer furtivement; **the swans ~d across the lake** les cygnes traversaient le lac avec grâce OR glissaient sur le lac; **the clouds ~d across the sky** les nuages passaient dans le ciel; **the boat ~d silently down the river** le bateau glissait sans bruit sur la rivière OR descendait la rivière sans bruit; **the actress ~d majestically into the room** la comédienne entra dans la salle d'un pas majestueux; **the motorcade ~d past** le cortège de voitures passa sans bruit. -**2.** *fig* [time, weeks]: **to ~ by** s'écouler. -**3.** AERON planer; **to go gliding** faire du vol à voile. -**4.** [in skating, skiing] glisser.

◇ *vt* (faire) glisser.

◇ *n* -**1.** [gen] glissement *m*. -**2.** DANCE glissade *f*. -**3.** MUS port *m* de voix. -**4.** AERON vol *m* plané. -**5.** LING [in diphthong] glissement *m*; [between two vowels] semi-voyelle *f* de transition.

glide path *n* AERON ligne *f* d'approche.

glider ['glaɪdər] *n* -**1.** AERON planeur *m*. -**2.** *Am* [swing] balançoire *f*.

glide slope = **glide path**.

gliding ['glaɪdɪŋ] *n* AERON vol *m* à voile.

glimmer ['glɪmər] ◇ *vi* [moonlight, candle] jeter une faible lueur, luire faiblement.

◇ *n* -**1.** [of light] (faible) lueur *f*. -**2.** *fig*: **a ~ of hope/interest** une (faible) lueur d'espoir/d'intérêt; **he showed not the faintest ~ of intelligence** il n'y avait pas la moindre étincelle d'intelligence chez lui OR dans son regard.

glimmering ['glɪmərɪŋ] *adj* [light] qui luit faiblement.

glimpse [glɪmps] ◇ *vt* entrevoir, entrapercevoir.

◇ *n*: **to catch a ~ of sthg** entrevoir OR entrapercevoir qqch.

glint [glɪnt] ◇ *vi* -**1.** [knife] étinceler, miroiter; [water] miroiter. -**2.** *fig* [eyes] étinceler.

◇ *n* -**1.** [of light] reflet *m*, miroitement *m*. -**2.** *fig*: **there was a strange ~ in his eye** il y avait une lueur étrange dans son regard; **"perhaps not" he said, with a ~ in his eye** «peut-être que non» dit-il, une lueur dans le regard; **a ~ of humour/anger** une lueur d'humour/de colère.

glissade [glɪ'sɑ:d] ◇ *vi* -**1.** [in climbing] glisser, descendre en ramasse. -**2.** DANCE faire une glissade.

◇ *n* glissade *f*.

glissando [glɪ'sændəʊ] (*pl* **glissandos** OR **glissandi** [-di:]) *n* glissando *m*.

glisten ['glɪsn] *vi* [wet or damp surface] luire, miroiter; **his eyes ~ed with tears** des larmes brillaient dans ses yeux; **dewdrops ~ed in the grass** des gouttes de rosée luisaient dans l'herbe.

glistening ['glɪsnɪŋ] *adj* luisant.

glister ['glɪstər] *arch* OR *lit* = **glisten**.

glitch *inf* [glɪtʃ] *n* [in plan] pépin *m*; [in machine] *signal indiquant une baisse de tension du courant*.

glitter ['glɪtər] ◇ *vi* -**1.** [bright object] étinceler, scintiller, miroiter; [jewel] chatoyer, étinceler; [metal] reluire; **her fingers ~ed with jewels** ses doigts brillaient de l'éclat des bijoux ❑ **all that ~s is not gold** *prov* tout ce qui brille n'est pas or *prov*. -**2.** [eyes] briller.

◇ *n* -**1.** [of bright object] scintillement *m*. -**2.** [of glamour] éclat *m*, splendeur *f*. -**3.** [decoration, make-up] paillettes *fpl*.

glitterati *inf* [,glɪtə'rɑ:ti:] *n*: **the ~** *hum* le beau monde *m inv*.

glittering ['glɪtərɪŋ] *adj* -**1.** [jewels] scintillant, étincelant, brillant. -**2.** [glamorous] éclatant, resplendissant.

glittery ['glɪtərɪ] *adj* -**1.** [light] scintillant, brillant. -**2.** *pej* [jewellery] clinquant; [make-up, décor] voyant, tape-à-l'œil.

glitz *inf* [glɪts] *n* tape-à-l'œil *m*, clinquant *m*; **Hollywood ~** le clinquant d'Hollywood.

glitzy *inf* ['glɪtsɪ] (*compar* **glitzier**, *superl* **glitziest**) *adj* tape-à-l'œil *(inv)*; **the premiere was one of the year's glitziest occasions** la première fut l'un des événements les plus tape-à-l'œil de l'année.

gloaming ['gləʊmɪŋ] *n Scot* OR *lit* crépuscule *m*.

gloat [gləʊt] ◇ *vi* exulter, se délecter, jubiler; **to ~ over sthg** se réjouir de qqch; **they ~ed over their treasures** ils dévoraient leurs trésors des yeux; **he ~ed over his success** son succès l'enivrait OR le faisait jubiler; **she ~ed over the downfall of her enemy** elle se réjouissait de la chute de son ennemi.

◇ *n* exultation *f*, jubilation *f*; **to have a ~** exulter.

gloating ['gləʊtɪŋ] *adj* [smile, look] triomphant.

gloatingly ['gləʊtɪŋlɪ] *adv* avec exultation, avec jubilation; [over defeated enemy] triomphalement.

glob [glɒb] *n* globule *m*, (petite) boule *f*; **a ~ of spittle** un crachat.

global ['gləʊbl] *adj* -**1.** [world-wide] mondial, planétaire; **~ warming** réchauffement *m* de la planète. -**2.** [overall - system, view] global.

globalize, -ise ['gləʊbəlaɪz] *vt* -**1.** [make world-wide] rendre mondial; **a ~d conflict** un conflit mondial. -**2.** [generalize] globaliser.

globally ['gləʊbəlɪ] *adv* -**1.** [world-wide] mondialement, à l'échelle planétaire. -**2.** [generally] globalement.

globe [gləʊb] *n* -**1.** GEOG globe *m* (terrestre), terre *f*; **all over the ~** [surface] sur toute la surface du globe; [in all parts] dans le monde entier. -**2.** [model] globe *m*, mappemonde *f*. -**3.** [spherical object] globe *m*, sphère *f*; [as lampshade] globe; [as goldfish bowl] bocal *m*; [of eye] globe. -**4.** *Austr* & *NZ* [bulb] ampoule *f (électrique)*.

globe artichoke *n* artichaut *m*.

globetrotter ['gləʊb,trɒtər] *n* globe-trotter *m*.

globetrotting ['gləʊb,trɒtɪŋ] *n (U)* voyages *mpl* aux quatre coins du monde.

globular ['glɒbjʊlər] *adj* globulaire, globuleux.

globule ['glɒbju:l] *n* globule *m*.

globulin ['glɒbjʊlɪn] *n* globuline *f*.

glockenspiel ['glɒkənʃpi:l] *n* glockenspiel *m*.

gloom [glu:m] ◇ *n (U)* -**1.** [darkness] obscurité *f*, ténèbres *fpl*. -**2.** [despondency] tristesse *f*, mélancolie *f*; **the news filled me with ~** la nouvelle me plongea dans la consternation; **the announcement cast ~ over the meeting** l'annonce jeta un froid sur la réunion; **~ fell over the household** un voile de tristesse s'abattit sur la maison; **the news is all ~ and doom these days** les nouvelles sont des plus sombres ces temps-ci.

◇ *vi* [person] être mélancolique, broyer du noir.

gloomily ['glu:mɪlɪ] *adv* sombrement, mélancoliquement, tristement; **he looked around him ~** il regarda autour de lui d'un air sombre OR morose.

gloominess ['glu:mɪnɪs] = **gloom** *n*.

gloomy ['glu:mɪ] (*compar* **gloomier**, *superl* **gloomiest**) *adj* -**1.** [person - depressed] triste, mélancolique; [- morose] sombre, lugubre; **to feel ~** broyer du noir, avoir le cafard; **don't look so ~** ne prends pas cet air malheureux. -**2.** [pessimistic - outlook] sombre; [- news] triste; **she always takes a ~ view of things** elle voit toujours tout en noir; **the future looks ~** l'avenir se présente sous des couleurs sombres; **he paints a ~ view of life** sa vision de la vie est assez noire. -**3.** [sky] obscur, sombre; [weather] morne, triste; **to become ~** s'assombrir. -**4.** [place, landscape] morne, lugubre.

glop *inf* [glɒp] *n Am* -**1.** [gooey matter] matière *f* visqueuse, mixture *f*; [sentimentality] mièvrerie *f*. -**2.** = **glob**.

glorification [,glɔ:rɪfɪ'keɪʃn] *n* glorification *f*.

glorified ['glɔ:rɪfaɪd] *adj*: **he's called an engineer but he's really just a ~ mechanic** on a beau l'appeler ingénieur, il n'est que mécanicien, il n'a d'ingénieur que le nom, en réalité c'est un mécanicien; **they call it a health club but it's just a ~ swimming pool** en fait de centre de remise en forme, il ne s'agit que d'une vulgaire piscine.

glorify ['glɔ:rɪfaɪ] (*pt* & *pp* **glorified**) *vt* -**1.** RELIG glorifier, rendre gloire à. -**2.** [praise - hero, writer] exalter; **the film glorifies war** le film fait l'apologie de OR magnifie la guerre.

glorious ['glɔ:rɪəs] *adj* -**1.** [illustrious - reign, saint, victory] glorieux; [- hero] glorieux, illustre; [- deed] glorieux, éclatant; **the Glorious Twelfth** [in Ireland] *célébration de la victoire des Protestants sur les Catholiques (le 12 juillet 1690) en Irlande*; [in UK] *date d'ouverture de la chasse à la grouse (le 12 août)*. -**2.** [wonderful - sunset, view, place] merveilleux, splendide; [- weather, day] splendide, superbe, magnifique; [- colours] superbe; [- holiday, party] merveilleux, sensationnel; **everything was in a ~ mess!** tout était dans le plus beau désordre!

gloriously ['glɔ:rɪəslɪ] *adv* glorieusement.

Glorious Revolution *pr n*: **the ~** *Br* HIST la glorieuse Révolution.

THE GLORIOUS REVOLUTION:
Face à la politique religieuse menée par le roi catholique Jacques II, ses adversaires protestants firent appel à Guillaume d'Orange pour le renverser, en 1688. Jacques II ayant fui en France, le Parlement proclama son abdication et couronna sa fille Mary conjointement à Guillaume en 1689.

glory ['glɔ:rɪ] (*pl* **glories**, *pt* & *pp* **gloried**) *n* -**1.** [honour, fame] gloire *f*; [magnificence] magnificence *f*, éclat *m*; **to be covered in ~** être couvert de gloire; **a garden at the height of its ~** un jardin au plus beau moment; **to have one's hour of ~** avoir son heure de gloire. -**2.** [splendour] gloire *f*, splendeur *f*; **the ~ of a midsummer's day** la splendeur d'un jour au cœur de l'été; **in all her ~** dans toute sa splendeur OR gloire; **Hollywood in all its ~** Hollywood dans toute sa splendeur. -**3.** [masterpiece] gloire *f*, joyau *m*; **the palace is one of the greatest glories of the age** le palais est un des joyaux OR des chefs-d'œuvre de cette époque. -**4.** RELIG: **to give ~ to God** rendre gloire à Dieu; **Christ in ~** le Christ en majesté OR en gloire; **to the greater ~ of God** pour la plus grande gloire de Dieu; ~ be! *inf* mon Dieu! -**5.** *euph* [death]: to go to ~ passer de vie à trépas; to send sb to ~ expédier qqn ad patres. -**6.** *Am*: Old Glory *le drapeau américain*.

◆ **glory in** *vt insep*: to ~ in (doing) sthg se glorifier de OR s'enorgueillir de (faire) qqch; **he glories in it** il s'en glorifie, il en est très fier; **she was ~ing in her new-found freedom** elle jouissait de OR elle savourait sa nouvelle liberté; **he glories in the title of King of Hollywood** il se donne le titre ronflant de roi d'Hollywood.

glory box *n Austr & NZ* trousseau *m (pour le mariage)*.

glory hole *n* -**1.** *inf Br* [cupboard] débarras *m*; [untidy place] capharnaüm *m*. -**2.** NAUT [locker] petit placard *m*; [storeroom] soute *f*.

Glos *written abbr of* Gloucestershire.

gloss [glɒs] ◇ *n* -**1.** [sheen] lustre *m*, brillant *m*, éclat *m*; [on paper, photo] glacé *m*, brillant *m*; [on furniture] vernis *m*. -**2.** [appearance] apparence *f*, vernis *m*; a ~ **of politeness/respectability** un vernis de politesse/de respectabilité. -**3.** [charm] charme *m*, attrait *m*; **to take the ~ off sthg** gâcher OR gâter qqch. -**4.** [annotation, paraphrase] glose *f*, commentaire *m*. -**5.** = **gloss paint**.
◇ *vt* -**1.** [paper] satiner, glacer; [metal] faire briller, lustrer. -**2.** [explain, paraphrase] gloser.

◆ **gloss over** *vt insep* -**1.** [minimize - failure, fault, mistake] glisser sur, passer sur, atténuer. -**2.** [hide - truth, facts] dissimuler, passer sous silence.

glossary ['glɒsərɪ] (*pl* glossaries) *n* glossaire *m*.

glossematics [,glɒsɪ'mætɪks] *n (U)* glossématique *f*.

glosseme ['glɒsiːm] *n* glossème *m*.

gloss finish *n* -**1.** [painted] brillant *m*. -**2.** PHOT glaçage *m*.

glossiness ['glɒsɪnɪs] *n* lustre *m*, brillant *m*, éclat *m*.

glossolalia [,glɒsə'leɪlɪə] *n* glossolalie *f*.

gloss paint *n* peinture *f* brillante.

glossy ['glɒsɪ] (*compar* glossier, *superl* glossiest, *pl* glossies) ◇ *adj* -**1.** [shiny - fur] lustré, luisant; [- hair] brillant; [- leather, satin] lustré, luisant, glacé; [- leaves] luisant; [surface - polished] brillant, poli; [- painted] brillant, laqué. -**2.** *fig* [display, presentation, spectacle] brillant, scintillant, clinquant *pej*. -**3.** [photo] glacé, sur papier glacé; [paper] glacé.
◇ *n inf* = **glossy magazine**.

glossy magazine *n* magazine *m (sur papier glacé)*.

glottal ['glɒtl] *adj* -**1.** ANAT glottique. -**2.** LING glottal; ~ **stop** coup *m* de glotte.

glottis ['glɒtɪs] *n* glotte *f*.

glove [glʌv] ◇ *n* gant *m*; **I take size 7 in ~s** je prends du 7 pour les gants, je gante du 7 ▫ **it fits like a ~** ça me/te/lui *etc* va comme un gant; **the ~s are off** plus la peine de prendre des gants; **once the campaign started the ~s were off!** une fois la campagne partie, plus question de prendre des gants OR tous les coups étaient permis!
◇ *comp* à gants, de gants; ~ **factory** ganterie *f (usine)*; ~ **maker** gantier *m*, -ère *f*; ~ **shop** ganterie *f (magasin)*.

glove box *n* AUT & NUCL boîte *f* à gants.

glove compartment *n* AUT boîte *f* à gants.

gloved [glʌvd] *adj* ganté.

glove puppet *n* marionnette *f (à gaine)*.

glover ['glʌvəʳ] *n* gantier *m*, -ère *f*.

glow [gləʊ] ◇ *vi* -**1.** [embers, heated metal] rougeoyer; [sky, sunset] s'embraser, flamboyer; [jewel] briller, rutiler. -**2.** [person] rayonner; [eyes] briller, flamboyer; to ~ **with health** éclater OR rayonner de santé; **her face ~ed in the cold wind** le vent froid lui avait fouetté le visage; to ~ **with pleasure/happiness** rayonner de plaisir/de bonheur; **his words made her ~ with pride** ses mots la firent rayonner de fierté.
◇ *n* -**1.** [of fire, embers] rougeoiement *m*; [of heated metal] lueur *f*; [of sky, sunset] embrasement *m*, flamboiement *m*; [of sun] feux *mpl*; [of colours, jewel] éclat *m*; **it gives off a blue ~** cela émet une lumière bleue. -**2.** [of health, beauty] éclat *m*; **the compliments brought a ~ to her cheeks** les compliments la faisaient rougir de plaisir. -**3.** [pleasure] plaisir *m*; **he gets a ~ out of helping others** il prend plaisir à aider les autres.

glower ['glaʊəʳ] *vi* avoir l'air furieux, lancer des regards furieux; to ~ **at sb** [angrily] lancer à qqn un regard noir; [threateningly] jeter à qqn un regard menaçant; **she sat ~ing in a corner** elle restait assise dans un coin, l'air furieux.

glowering ['glaʊərɪŋ] *adj* [expression] mauvais, méchant, hostile; [person] à l'air mauvais OR méchant.

glowing ['gləʊɪŋ] *adj* -**1.** [fire, embers] rougeoyant; [heated metal] incandescent; [sky, sunset] radieux, flamboyant; [jewel] brillant. -**2.** [complexion] éclatant; [eyes] brillant, flamboyant; ~ **with health** rayonnant OR florissant (de santé); ~ **with happiness** rayonnant de joie. -**3.** [laudatory] élogieux, dithyrambique; **I had read ~ reports of the play** j'avais lu des critiques dithyrambiques de la pièce; **he spoke of you in ~ terms** il a chanté tes louanges; **to paint sthg in ~ colours** présenter qqch sous un jour favorable.

glowingly ['gləʊɪŋlɪ] *adv*: to speak ~ of sb/sthg parler de qqn/qqch en termes enthousiastes OR chaleureux.

glow-worm *n* ver *m* luisant.

glucose ['gluːkəʊs] *n* glucose *m*.

glucoside ['gluːkəsaɪd] *n* glucoside *m*.

glue [gluː] ◇ *vt* -**1.** [stick] coller; to ~ **sthg to/onto sthg** coller qqch à/sur qqch; **you'll have to ~ it (back) together again** il faudra le recoller; **can't you ~ it down?** vous ne pouvez pas le faire tenir avec de la colle? -**2.** *fig* coller; **to be ~d to the spot** être OR rester cloué sur place; **he kept his eyes ~d on the ball** il garda les yeux rivés sur la balle; **they're always ~d to the TV screen** ils sont en permanence plantés devant la télé; **he's always ~d to her side** il ne la quitte pas d'un pas OR d'une semelle.
◇ *n* colle *f*.

glue-sniffer [-,snɪfəʳ] *n*: **to be a ~** inhaler OR sniffer (de la colle).

glue-sniffing [-,snɪfɪŋ] *n* inhalation *f* de colle.

gluey ['gluːɪ] *adj* collant, gluant.

glum [glʌm] *adj* triste, morose; **to be OR to feel ~** avoir le cafard, broyer du noir; **to look ~** avoir l'air triste OR sombre; **don't look so ~!** ne fais pas cette tête-là!, ne sois pas si triste!

glumly ['glʌmlɪ] *adv* tristement, avec morosité; **he watched them ~** il les regarda d'un œil triste OR morose.

glumness ['glʌmnɪs] *n* tristesse *f*, morosité *f*.

gluon ['gluːɒn] *n* gluon *m*.

glut [glʌt] (*pt & pp* glutted, *cont* glutting)
◇ *vt* -**1.** [with food]: **to ~ o.s. with OR on sthg** se gorger OR se gaver de qqch; **to be glutted with television** *fig* être saturé de télévision. -**2.** [saturate - market] saturer, inonder, surcharger; **the growers glutted the market with tomatoes** les producteurs de tomates ont saturé le marché; **the market is glutted with luxury goods** il y a surabondance d'objets de luxe sur le marché.
◇ *n* excès *m*, surabondance *f*, surplus *m*; **there's a ~ of fruit on the market** il y a surabondance de fruits sur le marché; **there's a ~ of apples this year** il y a surproduction de pommes cette année.

glutamate ['gluːtəmeɪt] *n* glutamate *m*.

glutamic [gluː'tæmɪk] *adj* glutamique; ~ **acid** acide *m* glutamique.

glutamine ['gluːtəmiːn] *n* glutamine *f*.

gluten ['gluːtən] *n* gluten *m*; ~ **bread** pain *m* au gluten.

gluten-free *adj* sans gluten.

glutinous ['gluːtɪnəs] *adj* glutineux.

glutton ['glʌtn] *n* glouton *m*, -onne *f*, goulu *m*, -e *f*; **to be a ~ for punishment** *fig* être un peu masochiste; **he's a ~ for work** c'est un bourreau OR un forcené de travail.

gluttonous ['glʌtənəs] *adj* glouton, goulu.

gluttonously ['glʌtənəslɪ] *adv* gloutonnement, goulûment.

gluttony ['glʌtənɪ] *n* gloutonnerie *f*, goinfrerie *f*.

glyceric [glɪ'serɪk] *adj* glycérique; ~ **acid** acide *m* glycérique.

glycerin ['glɪsərɪn], **glycerine** ['glɪsəriːn] *n* glycérine *f*.

glycerol ['glɪsərɒl] *n* glycérol *m*.

glycine ['glaɪsiːn] *n* glycine *f*, glycocolle *m*.

glycogen ['glaɪkəʊdʒən] *n* glycogène *m*.

glycol ['glaɪkɒl] *n* glycol *m*.

glycolic [glaɪ'kɒlɪk] *adj* glycolique; ~ **acid** acide *m* glycolique.

glycolysis [glaɪ'kɒlɪsɪs] *n* glycolyse *f*.

glycosuria [,glaɪkəʊ'sjʊərɪə] *n* glycosurie *f*.

Glyndebourne ['glaɪnd,bɔːn] *pr n lieu d'un festival annuel d'opéra dans le Sussex*.

glyph [glɪf] *n* glyphe *m*.

gm (*written abbr of* gram) g.

G-man *inf n Am* agent *m* du FBI.

GMAT (*abbr of* Graduate Management Admissions Test) *n test d'admission dans le 2e cycle de l'enseignement supérieur aux États-Unis*.

GMB (*abbr of* General, Municipal, Boilermakers and Allied Trades Union) *pr n important syndicat britannique*.

GMT (*abbr of* Greenwich Mean Time) *n* GMT *m*.

GMWU (*abbr of* General and Municipal Workers' Union) *pr n syndicat britannique des employés des collectivités locales*.

gnarl [nɑːl] *n* BOT nœud *m*.

gnarled [nɑːld] *adj* -**1.** [tree, fingers] noueux. -**2.** [character] grincheux, hargneux.

gnash [næʃ] ◇ *vt*: **to ~ one's teeth** grincer des dents; **there was much wailing and ~ing of teeth** il y a eu des pleurs et des grincements de dents.
◇ *n* grincement *m* (de dents).

gnat [næt] *n* moustique *m*.

gnaw [nɔː] ◇ *vt* [bone] ronger; **to ~ one's fingernails** se ronger les ongles; **the rats have ~ed their way into the cupboard** les rats ont fini par percer un trou dans le placard.
◇ *vi*: **to ~ (away) at sthg** ronger qqch; **to ~ through sthg** ronger qqch jusqu'à le percer; **guilt and sorrow ~ed at his heart** *fig* la culpabilité et le chagrin lui rongeaient le cœur; **hunger ~ed at him** *fig* il était tenaillé par la faim.

◆ **gnaw away** *vt sep* -**1.** [animal] ronger. -**2.** [erode] ronger, miner.

◆ **gnaw off** *vt sep*: **to ~ sthg off** ronger qqch jusqu'à le détacher.

gnawing ['nɔːɪŋ] *adj* -**1.** [pain] lancinant, tenaillant; [hunger] tenaillant; **the ~ pains of hunger** les affres OR les tiraillements de la faim. -**2.** [anxiety, doubt] tenaillant, torturant.

gneiss [naɪs] *n* gneiss *m*.

gnocchi ['nɒkɪ] *npl* gnocchi *mpl*, gnocchis *mpl*.

gnome [nəʊm] *n* -**1.** MYTH gnome *m*; **the ~s of Zurich** *pej* les grands banquiers OR financiers suisses. -**2.** [aphorism] aphorisme *m*.

gnomic ['nəʊmɪk] *adj* gnomique.

gnomish ['nəʊmɪʃ] *adj* de gnome.

gnostic, Gnostic ['nɒstɪk] ◇ *adj* gnostique.
◇ *n* gnostique *mf*.

gnosticism, Gnosticism ['nɒstɪsɪzm] *n* gnosticisme *m*.

GNP (*abbr of* gross national product) *n* PNB *m*.

gnu [nuː] *n* gnou *m*.

go[1] [gəʊ] *n* [game] go *m*.

go[2] [gəʊ] (*3rd pres sing* goes [gəʊz], *pt* went [went], *pp* gone [gɒn], *pl* goes [gəʊz])
◇ *vi* **A.** -**1.** [move, travel - person] aller; [- vehicle] aller, rouler; **we're going to Paris/Japan/Spain** nous allons à Paris/au Japon/en Espagne; **he went to the office/a friend's house** il est allé au

bureau/chez un ami; **I want to go home** je veux rentrer; **the salesman went from house to house** le vendeur est allé de maison en maison; **we went by car/on foot** nous y sommes allés en voiture/à pied; **there goes the train!** voilà le train (qui passe)!; **the bus goes by way of** OR **through Dover** le bus passe par Douvres; **does this train go to Glasgow?** ce train va-t-il à Glasgow?; **the truck was going at 150 kilometres an hour** le camion roulait à OR faisait 150 kilomètres par heure; **go behind those bushes** va derrière ces arbustes; **where do we go from here?** *literal* où va-t-on maintenant?; *fig* qu'est-ce qu'on fait maintenant?; **to go to the doctor** aller voir OR aller chez le médecin; **he went straight to the director** il est allé directement voir OR trouver le directeur; **to go to sb for advice** aller demander conseil à qqn; **they discussed it as they went (along)** ils en ont parlé chemin faisant OR en chemin; **let the children go first** laissez les enfants passer devant, laissez passer les enfants d'abord; **I'll go next** c'est à moi après; **who goes next?** [in game] c'est à qui (le tour)?; **who goes there?** MIL qui va là?, qui vive?; **here we go again!** ça y est! ça recommence!; **there he goes!** le voilà!; **there he goes again!** [there he is again] le revoilà!; [he's doing it again] ça y est, il est reparti! -**2.** [engage in a specified activity] aller; **to go shopping** aller faire des courses; **to go fishing/hunting** aller à la pêche/à la chasse; **to go riding** aller faire du cheval; **let's go for a walk/bike ride/swim** allons nous promener/faire un tour à vélo/nous baigner; **they went on a trip** ils sont partis en voyage; **go and buy the paper** *Br*, **go buy the paper** *Am* va acheter le journal; **I'll go to see her** OR *Am* **go see her tomorrow** j'irai la voir demain; **don't go and tell him!, don't go telling him!** ne va pas le lui dire!, ne le lui dis pas!; **don't go bothering your sister** ne va pas embêter ta sœur; **you had to go and tell him!** il a fallu que tu le lui dises!; **he's gone and locked us out!** il nous a enfermés dehors! -**3.** [proceed to specified limit] aller; **he'll go as high as £300** il ira jusqu'à 300 livres; **the temperature went as high as 36° C** la température est montée jusqu'à 36° C; **he went so far as to say it was her fault** il est allé jusqu'à dire que c'était de sa faute à elle; **now you've gone too far!** là tu as dépassé les bornes!; **I'll go further and say he should resign** j'irai plus loin et je dirai qu'il OR j'irai jusqu'à dire qu'il devrait démissionner; **the temperature sometimes goes below zero** la température descend OR tombe parfois au-dessous de zéro; **her attitude went beyond mere impertinence** son comportement était plus qu'impertinent. -**4.** [depart, leave] s'en aller, partir; **I must be going** il faut que je m'en aille OR que je parte; **they went early** ils sont partis tôt; **you may go** vous pouvez partir; **what time does the train go?** à quelle heure part le train?; **get going!** *inf* vas-y!, file!; **be gone!** *arch* allez-vous-en!; **either he goes or I go** l'un de nous deux doit partir. -**5.** [indicating regular attendance] aller, assister; **to go to church/school** aller à l'église/l'école; **to go to a meeting** aller OR assister à une réunion; **to go to work** [to one's place of work] aller au travail. -**6.** [indicating direction or route] aller, mener; **that road goes to the market square** cette route va OR mène à la place du marché.
B. -**1.** [be or remain in specified state] être; **to go barefoot/naked** se promener pieds nus/tout nu; **to go armed** porter une arme; **her family goes in rags** sa famille est en haillons; **the job went unfilled** le poste est resté vacant; **to go unnoticed** passer inaperçu; **such crimes must not go unpunished** de tels crimes ne doivent pas rester impunis. -**2.** [become] devenir; **my father is going grey** mon père grisonne; **she went white with rage** elle a blêmi de colère; **my hands went clammy** mes mains sont devenues moites; **have you gone mad?** tu es devenu fou?; **to go bankrupt** faire faillite; **the country has gone Republican** le pays est maintenant républicain. -**3.** [stop working – engine] tomber en panne; [– fuse] sauter; [– bulb, lamp] sauter, griller; **the battery's going** la pile commence à être usée. -**4.** [wear out] s'user; [split] craquer; **his trousers are going at the knees** ses pantalons s'usent aux genoux; **the jacket went at the seams** la veste a craqué aux coutures. -**5.** [deteriorate, fail – health] se détériorer; [– hearing, sight] baisser; **all his strength went and he fell to the floor** il a perdu toutes ses forces et il est tombé par terre; **his voice is going** il devient aphone; **his voice is gone** il est aphone, il a une extinction de voix; **her mind has started to go** elle n'a plus toute sa tête OR toutes ses facultés.
C. -**1.** [begin an activity] commencer; **what are we waiting for? let's go!** qu'est-ce qu'on attend? allons-y!; **here we go!, here goes!** *inf* allez! on y va!; **go!** partez!; **you'd better get going on** OR **with that report!** tu ferais bien de te mettre à OR de t'attaquer à ce rapport!; **it won't be so hard once you get going** ça ne sera pas si difficile une fois que tu seras lancé; **go to it!** *inf* [get to work] au boulot!; [in encouragement] allez-y! -**2.** [expressing intention]: **to be going to do sthg** [be about to] aller faire qqch, être sur le point de faire qqch; [intend to] avoir l'intention de faire qqch; **you were just going to tell me about it** vous étiez sur le point de OR vous alliez m'en parler; **I was going to visit her yesterday but her mother arrived** j'avais l'intention de OR j'allais lui rendre visite hier mais sa mère est arrivée. -**3.** [expressing immediate future]: **are you going to be at home tonight?** est-ce que vous serez chez vous ce soir?; **we're going to do exactly as we please** nous ferons ce que nous voulons; **she's going to be a doctor** elle va être médecin; **there's going to be a storm** il va faire un orage; **he's going to have to work really hard** il va falloir qu'il travaille très dur. -**4.** [function – clock, machine] marcher, fonctionner; [start functioning] démarrer; **is the fan going?** est-ce que le ventilateur est en marche OR marche?; **the car won't go** la voiture ne veut pas démarrer; **he had the television and the radio going** il avait mis la télévision et la radio en marche; **the washing machine is still going** la machine à laver tourne encore, la lessive n'est pas terminée; **to get sthg going** [car, machine] mettre qqch en marche; [business, project] lancer qqch; **her daughter kept the business going** sa fille a continué à faire marcher l'affaire; **to keep a conversation/fire going** entretenir une conversation/un feu. -**5.** [sound – alarm clock, bell] sonner; [– alarm, siren] retentir. -**6.** [make movement]: **she went like this with her eyebrows** elle a fait comme ça avec ses sourcils. -**7.** [appear]: **to go on radio/television** passer à la radio/à la télévision.
D. -**1.** [disappear] disparaître; **the snow has gone** la neige a fondu OR disparu; **all the sugar's gone** il n'y a plus de sucre; **my coat has gone** mon manteau n'est plus là OR a disparu; **all our money has gone** [spent] nous avons dépensé tout notre argent; [lost] nous avons perdu tout notre argent; [stolen] on a volé tout notre argent; **I don't know where the money goes these days** l'argent disparaît à une vitesse incroyable ces temps-ci; **gone are the days when he took her dancing** elle est bien loin, l'époque où il l'emmenait danser. -**2.** [be eliminated]: **the last paragraph must go** il faut supprimer le dernier paragraphe; **I've decided that car has to go** j'ai décidé de me débarrasser de cette voiture; **that new secretary has got to go** il va falloir se débarrasser de la nouvelle secrétaire. -**3.** *euph* [die] disparaître, s'éteindre; **he is (dead and) gone** il nous a quittés; **after I go...** quand je ne serai plus là...
E. -**1.** [extend, reach] aller, s'étendre; **our property goes as far as the forest** notre propriété va OR s'étend jusqu'au bois; **the path goes right down to the beach** le chemin descend jusqu'à la mer || *fig*: **her thinking didn't go that far** elle n'a pas poussé le raisonnement aussi loin; **my salary doesn't go very far** je ne vais pas loin avec mon salaire; **money doesn't go very far these days** l'argent part vite à notre époque; **their difference of opinion goes deeper than I thought** leur différend est plus profond que je ne pensais. -**2.** [belong] aller, se mettre, se ranger; **the dictionaries go on that shelf** les dictionnaires se rangent OR vont sur cette étagère; **where do the towels go?** où est-ce qu'on met les serviettes?; **that painting goes here** ce tableau se met OR va là. -**3.** [be contained in, fit] aller; **this last sweater won't go in the suitcase** ce dernier pull n'ira pas OR n'entrera pas dans la valise; **the piano barely goes through the door** le piano entre OR passe de justesse par la porte; **this belt just goes round my waist** cette ceinture est juste assez longue pour faire le tour de ma taille; **the lid goes on easily enough** le couvercle se met assez facilement. -**4.** [develop, turn out] se passer; **how did your interview go?** comment s'est passé ton entretien?; **I'll see how things go** je vais voir comment ça se passe; **we can't tell how things will go** on ne sait pas comment ça se passera; **everything went well** tout s'est bien passé; **the meeting went badly/well** la réunion s'est mal/bien passée; **the negotiations are going well** les négociations sont en bonne voie; **the vote went against them/in their favour** le vote leur a été défavorable/favorable; **there's no doubt as to which way the decision will go** on sait ce qui sera décidé; **everything was going fine until she showed up** tout allait OR se passait très bien jusqu'à ce qu'elle arrive; **everything went wrong** ça a mal tourné; **how's it going?** *inf*, **how are things going?** (comment) ça va? ❑ **the way things are going, we might both be out of a job soon** au train où vont OR vu comment vont les choses, nous allons bientôt nous retrouver tous les deux au chômage. -**5.** [time – elapse] s'écouler, passer; [– last] durer; **the journey went quickly** je n'ai pas vu le temps passer pendant le voyage; **time goes so slowly when you're not here** le temps me paraît tellement long quand tu n'es pas là; **how's the time going?** combien de temps reste-t-il?
F. -**1.** [be accepted]: **what your mother says goes!** fais ce que dit ta mère!; **whatever the boss says goes** c'est le patron qui fait la loi. -**2.** [be valid, hold true] s'appliquer; **that rule goes for everyone** cette règle s'applique à tout le monde; **that goes for us too** [that applies to us] ça s'applique à nous aussi; [we agree with that] nous sommes aussi de cet avis. -**3.** [be expressed, run – report, story]: **the story** OR **rumour goes that she left him** le bruit court qu'elle l'a quitté; **so the story goes** du moins c'est ce que l'on dit OR d'après les on-dit; **how does the story go?** comment c'est cette histoire?; **I forget how the poem goes now** j'ai oublié le poème maintenant; **the tune goes like this** l'air c'est ça; **her theory goes something like this** sa théorie est plus ou moins la suivante. -**4.** [be identified as]: **to go by** OR **under the name of** répondre au nom de; **he now goes by** OR **under another name** il se fait appeler autrement maintenant. -**5.** [be sold] se vendre; **flats are going cheap at the moment** les appartements ne se vendent pas très cher en ce moment; **the necklace went for £350** le collier s'est vendu 350 livres; **going, going, gone!** une fois, deux fois, adjugé!
G. -**1.** [be given – award, prize] aller, être donné; [– inheritance, property] passer; **the contract is to go to a private firm** le contrat ira à une entreprise privée; **credit should go to the teachers** le mérite en revient aux enseignants; **every penny will go to charity** tout l'argent va OR est destiné à une œuvre de bienfaisance. -**2.** [be spent]: **a small portion of the budget went on education** une petite part du budget a été consacrée OR est allée à l'éducation; **all his money goes on drink** tout son argent part dans la boisson. -**3.** [contribute] contribuer, servir; **all that just goes to prove my point** tout ça confirme bien ce que j'ai dit; **it has all the qualities that go to make a good film** ça a toutes les qualités d'un bon film. -**4.** [have recourse] avoir recours, recourir; **to go to arbitration** recourir à l'arbitrage.

H. -**1.** [be compatible - colours, flavours] aller ensemble; **orange and mauve don't really go** l'orange et le mauve ne vont pas vraiment ensemble. -**2.** [be available] : **let me know if you hear of any jobs going** faites-moi savoir si vous entendez parler d'un emploi; **are there any flats going for rent in this building?** y a-t-il des appartements à louer dans cet immeuble?; **any whisky going?** *inf* tu as un whisky à m'offrir? -**3.** [endure] supporter, tenir le coup; **we can't go much longer without water** nous ne pourrons pas tenir beaucoup plus longtemps si nous n'avons pas d'eau. -**4.** *euph* [go to the toilet] : **we'll only stop if you're really desperate to go** on ne s'arrête que si vraiment tu ne tiens plus. -**5.** MATH : **5 into 60 goes 12** 60 divisé par 5 égale 12; **6 into 5 won't go** 5 n'est pas divisible par 6. -**6.** *phr*: **she isn't bad, as teachers go** elle n'est pas mal comme enseignante; **as houses go, it's pretty cheap** ce n'est pas cher pour une maison; **there goes my chance of winning a prize** je peux abandonner tout espoir de gagner un prix; **there you go again, always blaming other people** ça y est, toujours à rejeter la responsabilité sur les autres!; **there you go!** [here you are] tiens!; [I told you so] voilà!; **there you go, two hamburgers and a coke** et voici, deux hamburgers et un coca; **there you go, what did I tell you?** voilà OR tiens, qu'est-ce que je t'avais dit!

◇ *vt* -**1.** [follow, proceed along] aller, suivre; **if we go this way, we'll get there much more quickly** si nous passons par là, nous arriverons bien plus vite. -**2.** [travel] faire, voyager; **we've only gone 5 kilometres** nous n'avons fait que 5 kilomètres; **she went the whole length of the street before coming back** elle a descendu toute la rue avant de revenir. -**3.** [say] faire; [make specified noise] faire; **the ducks go "quack"** les canards font «coin-coin»; **the clock goes "tick tock"** l'horloge fait «tic tac»; **the gun went bang** et pan! le coup est parti; **then he goes "hand it over"** *inf* puis il fait «donne-le-moi». -**4.** *phr*: **to go it** *dated* [go fast] filer; [behave wildly] se défoncer; **how goes it?** *inf* ça marche?

◇ *n* -**1.** *Br* [attempt, try] coup *m*, essai *m*; **to have a go at sthg/doing sthg** essayer qqch/de faire qqch; **he had another go** il a fait une nouvelle tentative, il a essayé; **let's have a go!** essayons!; **have another go!** encore un coup!; **she passed her exams at first go** elle a eu ses examens du premier coup; **he knocked down all the skittles at one go** il a renversé toutes les quilles d'un coup. -**2.** *Br* GAMES [turn] tour *m*; **it's your go** c'est ton tour OR c'est à toi (de jouer); **whose go is it?** à qui de jouer?, à qui le tour? -**3.** *inf* [energy, vitality] dynamisme *m*, entrain *m*; **to be full of go** avoir plein d'énergie, être très dynamique; **she's got plenty of go** elle est pleine d'entrain; **the new man has no go in him** le nouveau manque d'entrain. -**4.** *inf* [success] succès *m*, réussite *f*; **he's made a go of the business** il a réussi à faire marcher l'affaire; **to make a go of a marriage** réussir un mariage ☐ **I tried to persuade her but it was no go** j'ai essayé de la convaincre mais il n'y avait rien à faire. -**5.** [fashion] mode *f*; **short hair is all the go** les cheveux courts sont le dernier cri OR font fureur. -**6.** *inf phr*: **to have a go at sb** [physically] rentrer dans qqn; [verbally] passer un savon à qqn; **they had a real go at one another!** qu'est-ce qu'ils se sont mis!; **she had a go at her boyfriend** elle a passé un de ces savons à son copain. -**7.** *inf Br phr*: **to have a go** [tackle a criminal] : **police have warned the public not to have a go, the fugitive may be armed** la police a prévenu la population de ne pas s'en prendre au fugitif car il pourrait être armé. -**8.** *inf phr*: **it's all go** ça n'arrête pas!; **all systems go!** c'est parti!; **the shuttle is go for landing** la navette est bonne OR est parée OR a le feu vert pour l'atterrissage.

◆ **going on** *adv phr*: **he must be going on fifty** il doit approcher la OR aller sur la cinquantaine; **it was going on (for) midnight by the time we finished** il était près de minuit quand on a terminé.

◆ **on the go** *inf adj phr* -**1.** [busy] : **I've been on the go all day** je n'ai pas arrêté de toute la journée. -**2.** [in hand] : **I have several projects on the go at present** j'ai plusieurs projets en route en ce moment.

◆ **to go** ◇ *adv phr* à faire; **there are only three weeks/five miles to go** il ne reste plus que trois semaines/cinq miles; **five done, three to go** cinq de faits, trois à faire.

◇ *adj phr esp Am*: **two hamburgers to go** deux hamburgers à emporter!

◆ **go about** ◇ *vi insep* -**1.** [socially] : **her son goes about with an older crowd** son fils fréquente des gens plus âgés que lui; **he's going about with Mary these days** il sort avec Mary en ce moment. -**2.** NAUT [change tack] virer de bord.

◇ *vt insep* -**1.** [get on with] s'occuper de; **to go about one's business** vaquer à ses occupations. -**2.** [set about] se mettre à; **she showed me how to go about it** elle m'a montré comment faire OR comment m'y prendre; **how do you go about applying for the job?** comment doit-on s'y prendre OR faire pour postuler l'emploi?

◆ **go across** ◇ *vt insep* traverser.

◇ *vi insep* traverser; **your brother has just gone across to the shop** ton frère est allé faire un saut au magasin d'en face.

◆ **go after** *vt insep* -**1.** [follow] suivre. -**2.** [pursue, seek - criminal] poursuivre; [- prey] chasser; [- job, prize] essayer d'obtenir; **he goes after all the women** il court après toutes les femmes; **I'm going after that job** je vais essayer d'obtenir cet emploi.

◆ **go against** *vt insep* -**1.** [disregard] aller contre, aller à l'encontre de; **she went against my advice** elle n'a pas suivi mon conseil; **I went against my mother's wishes** je suis allé contre OR j'ai contrarié les désirs de ma mère. -**2.** [conflict with] contredire; **that goes against what he told me** c'est en contradiction avec OR ça contredit ce qu'il m'a dit; **the decision went against public opinion** la décision est allée à l'encontre de OR a heurté l'opinion publique; **it goes against my principles** c'est contre mes principes. -**3.** [be unfavourable to - subj: luck, situation] être contraire à; [- subj: opinion] être défavorable à; [- subj: behaviour, evidence] nuire à, être préjudiciable à; **the verdict went against the defendant** le verdict a été défavorable à l'accusé OR a été prononcé contre l'accusé; **if luck should go against him** si la chance lui était contraire; **her divorce may go against her winning the election** son divorce pourrait nuire à ses chances de gagner les élections.

◆ **go ahead** *vi insep* -**1.** [precede] passer devant; **Mary went (on) ahead of us** Mary est partie avant nous; **I let him go ahead of me in the queue** je l'ai fait passer devant moi dans la queue. -**2.** [proceed] aller de l'avant, mettre à exécution; **go ahead! tell me!** vas-y! dis-le-moi!; **the mayor allowed the demonstrations to go ahead** le maire a permis aux manifestations d'avoir lieu; **the move had gone ahead as planned** le déménagement s'était déroulé comme prévu . -**3.** [advance, progress] progresser, faire des progrès.

◆ **go along** *vi insep* -**1.** [move from one place to another] aller, avancer; **go along and ask your mother** va demander à ta mère; **she went along with them to the fair** elle les a accompagnés OR elle est allée avec eux à la foire; **we can talk it over as we go along** nous pouvons en discuter en chemin OR en cours de route ☐ **I just make it up as I go along** j'invente au fur et à mesure. -**2.** [progress] se dérouler, se passer; **things were going along nicely** tout allait OR se passait bien.

◆ **go along with** *vt insep* [decision, order] accepter, s'incliner devant; [rule] observer, respecter; **that's what they decided and I went along with it** c'est la décision qu'ils ont prise et je l'ai acceptée; **I go along with the committee on that point** je suis d'accord avec OR je soutiens le comité sur ce point; **I can't go along with you on that** je ne suis pas d'accord avec vous là-dessus; **he went along with his father's wishes** il s'est conformé aux OR a respecté les désirs de son père.

◆ **go around** *vi insep* -**1.** [habitually] passer son temps à; **he goes around mumbling to himself** il passe son temps à radoter; **she just goes around annoying everyone** elle passe son temps à énerver tout le monde; **he goes around in black leather** il se promène toujours en OR il est toujours habillé en cuir noir. -**2.** [document, illness] circuler; [gossip, rumour] courir, circuler. -**3.** [be long enough for] : **will that belt go around your waist?** est-ce que cette ceinture sera assez grande pour toi?

◆ **go around with** *vt insep* sortir avec, fréquenter; **her son goes around with some very odd people** son fils sort avec OR fréquente des gens bizarres; **he goes around with my sister** il sort avec ma sœur.

◆ **go at** *inf vt insep literal & fig* [attack - food] attaquer, se jeter sur; [- job, task] s'attaquer à; **they were still going at it the next day** ils y étaient encore le lendemain; **she went at the cleaning with a will** elle s'est attaquée au nettoyage avec ardeur.

◆ **go away** *vi insep* partir, s'en aller; **go away!** va-t-en!; **I'm going away for a few days** je pars pour quelques jours; **she's gone away to think about it** elle est partie réfléchir.

◆ **go back** *vi insep* -**1.** [return] revenir, retourner; **she went back to bed** elle est retournée au lit, elle s'est recouchée; **to go back to sleep** se rendormir; **they went back home** ils sont rentrés (chez eux OR à la maison); **I went back downstairs/upstairs** je suis redescendu/remonté; **to go back to work** [continue interrupted task] se remettre au travail; [return to place of work] retourner travailler; [return to employment] reprendre le travail; **to go back on one's steps** rebrousser chemin, revenir sur ses pas; **let's go back to chapter two** revenons OR retournons au deuxième chapitre; **we went back to the beginning** nous avons recommencé; **let's go back to why you said that** revenons à la question de savoir pourquoi vous avez dit ça; **the clocks go back one hour today** on retarde les pendules d'une heure aujourd'hui. -**2.** [retreat] reculer; **go back!** recule! -**3.** [revert] revenir; **we went back to the old system** nous sommes revenus à l'ancien système; **he went back to his old habits** il a repris ses anciennes habitudes; **the conversation kept going back to the same subject** la conversation revenait sans cesse sur le même sujet; **men are going back to wearing their hair long** les hommes reviennent aux cheveux longs OR se laissent à nouveau pousser les cheveux. -**4.** [in time] remonter; **our records go back to 1850** nos archives remontent à 1850; **this building goes back to the Revolution** ce bâtiment date de OR remonte à la Révolution; **we go back a long way, Sam and me** *inf* ça remonte à loin, Sam et moi. -**5.** [extend, reach] s'étendre; **the garden goes back 150 metres** le jardin s'étend sur 150 mètres.

◆ **go back on** *vt insep* [fail to keep - agreement] rompre, violer; [- promise] manquer à, revenir sur; **they went back on their decision** ils sont revenus sur leur décision; **he won't go back on his word** il ne manquera pas à sa parole.

◆ **go before** ◇ *vi insep* [precede] passer devant; [happen before] précéder; **that question has nothing to do with what went before** cette question n'a rien à voir avec ce qui précède OR avec ce qui a été dit avant; **the election was like nothing that had gone before** gol'élection ne ressemblait en rien aux précédentes.

◇ *vt insep* -**1.** [precede] précéder; **we are indebted to those who have gone before us** nous devons beaucoup à ceux qui nous ont précédés. -**2.** [appear before] : **your suggestion will go before the committee** votre suggestion sera soumise au comité; **to go before a judge/jury** passer devant un juge/un jury; **the matter went before the court** l'affaire est allée devant les tribunaux.

◆ **go below** *vi insep* NAUT descendre dans l'entrepont.

◆ **go by** ◇ *vi insep* [pass - car, person] passer; [- time] passer, s'écouler; **as the years go by** avec les années, à mesure que les années passent; **in days** OR **in times** OR **in years gone by** autrefois, jadis.

◇ *vt insep* -**1.** [act in accordance with, be guided by] suivre, se baser sur; **don't go by the map** ne vous fiez pas à la carte; **I'll go by what the boss says** je me baserai sur ce que dit le patron; **he goes by the rules** il suit le règlement. -**2.** [judge by] juger d'après; **going by her accent, I'd say she's from New York** si j'en juge d'après son accent, je dirais qu'elle vient de New York; **you can't go by appearances** on ne peut pas juger d'après OR sur les apparences.

◆ **go down** ◇ *vi insep* -**1.** [descend, move to lower level] descendre; [from a vertical position]: **he went down on all fours** OR **on his hands and knees** il s'est mis à quatre pattes. -**2.** [proceed, travel] aller; **we're going down to Tours/the country/the shop** nous allons à Tours/à la campagne/au magasin. -**3.** [set - moon, sun] se coucher, tomber. -**4.** [sink - ship] couler, sombrer; [- person] couler, disparaître (sous l'eau). -**5.** [decrease, decline - level, price, quality] baisser; [- amount, numbers] diminuer; [- rate, temperature] baisser, s'abaisser; [- fever] baisser, tomber; [- tide] descendre; **the dollar is going down in value** le dollar perd de sa valeur, le dollar baisse; **eggs are going down (in price)** le prix des œufs baisse; **he's gone down in my estimation** il a baissé dans mon estime; **the neighbourhood's really gone down since then** le quartier ne s'est vraiment pas arrangé depuis. -**6.** [become less swollen - swelling] désenfler, dégonfler; [- balloon, tyre] se dégonfler. -**7.** [food, medicine] descendre; **this wine goes down very smoothly** ce vin se laisse boire (comme du petit lait). -**8.** [produce specified reaction] être reçu; **a cup of coffee would go down nicely** une tasse de café serait la bienvenue; **his speech went down badly/well** son discours a été mal/bien reçu; **how will the proposal go down with the students?** comment les étudiants vont-ils prendre la proposition?; **that kind of talk doesn't go down well with me** je n'apprécie pas du tout ce genre de propos. -**9.** [lose] être battu; **Mexico went down to Germany** le Mexique s'est incliné devant l'Allemagne; **Madrid went down to Milan by three points** Milan a battu Madrid de trois points. -**10.** [be relegated] descendre; **our team has gone down to the second division** notre équipe est descendue en deuxième division. -**11.** [be noted, recorded] être noté; [in writing] être pris OR couché par écrit; **this day will go down in history** ce jour restera une date historique; **she will go down in history as a woman of great courage** elle entrera dans l'histoire grâce à son grand courage. -**12.** [reach as far as] descendre, s'étendre; **this path goes down to the beach** ce sentier va OR descend à la plage. -**13.** [continue as far as] aller, continuer; **go down to the end of the street** allez OR continuez jusqu'en bas de la rue. -**14.** *Br* UNIV entrer dans la période des vacances. -**15.** [in bridge] chuter. -**16.** COMPUT tomber en panne; **the computer's gone down** l'ordinateur est en panne. -**17.** MUS [lower pitch] descendre. -**18.** ▽ *Br* [be sent to prison]: **how long do you think he'll go down for?** il écopera de combien, à ton avis?; **he went down for three years** il a écopé de trois ans. -**19.** *inf* [happen] se passer.

◇ *vt insep* descendre de; **my food went down the wrong way** j'ai avalé de travers; **the pianist went down an octave** MUS le pianiste a joué une octave plus bas OR a descendu d'une octave; **to go down a class** *Br* SCH descendre d'une classe.

◆ **go down on**▼ *vt insep* sucer.

◆ **go down with** *vt insep* tomber malade de; **he went down with pneumonia** il a attrapé une pneumonie.

◆ **go for** *vt insep* -**1.** [fetch] aller chercher; **he went for a doctor** il est allé OR parti chercher un médecin. -**2.** [try to obtain] essayer d'obtenir, viser; **she's going for his job** elle va essayer d'obtenir son poste; **go for it!** *inf* vas-y!; **I'd go for it if I were you!** à ta place, je n'hésiterais pas! -**3.** [attack - physically] tomber sur, s'élancer sur; [- verbally] s'en prendre à; **dogs usually go for the throat** en général, les chiens attaquent à la gorge; **they went for each other** [physically] ils se sont jetés l'un sur l'autre; [verbally] ils s'en sont pris l'un à l'autre; **the newspapers really went for the senator** les journaux s'en sont pris au sénateur sans retenue; **go for him!** [to dog] attaque! -**4.** *inf* [like] aimer, adorer; **I don't really go for that idea** l'idée ne me dit pas grand-chose; **he really goes for her in a big way** il est vraiment fou d'elle. -**5.** [choose, prefer] choisir, préférer. -**6.** [apply to, concern] concerner, s'appliquer à; **what I said goes for both of you** ce que j'ai dit vaut pour OR s'applique à vous deux; **pollution is a real problem in Paris — that goes for Rome too** la pollution pose un énorme problème à Paris — c'est la même chose à Rome; **and the same goes for me** et moi aussi. -**7.** [have as result] servir à; **his twenty years of service went for nothing** ses vingt ans de service n'ont servi à rien. -**8.** [be to the advantage of]: **she has a lot going for her** elle a beaucoup d'atouts; **that idea hasn't got much going for it, frankly** cette idée n'est franchement pas très convaincante.

◆ **go forth** *vi insep arch* OR *lit* -**1.** [leave] sortir; **the army went forth into battle** l'armée s'est mise en route pour la bataille; **go forth and multiply** BIBLE croissez et multipliez-vous. -**2.** [be pronounced] être prononcé; [be published] paraître; **the command went forth that...** il fut décrété que...

◆ **go in** *vi insep* -**1.** [enter] entrer, rentrer; **it's cold — let's go in** il fait froid — entrons. -**2.** [disappear - moon, sun] se cacher.

◆ **go in for** *vt insep* -**1.** [engage in - activity, hobby, sport] pratiquer, faire; [- occupation] se consacrer à; [- politics] s'occuper de, faire; **she went in for company law** elle s'est lancée dans le droit commercial; **he thought about going in for teaching** il a pensé devenir enseignant. -**2.** *inf* [be interested in] s'intéresser à; [like] aimer; **I don't go in much for opera** je n'aime pas trop l'opéra, l'opéra ne me dit rien; **he goes in for special effects in a big way** il est très effets spéciaux; **we don't go in for that kind of film** nous n'aimons pas ce genre de film. -**3.** [take part in - competition, race] prendre part à; [- examination] se présenter à. -**4.** [apply for - job, position] poser sa candidature à, postuler.

◆ **go into** *vt insep* -**1.** [enter - building, house] entrer dans; [- activity, profession] entrer à OR dans; **to go into politics** se lancer dans la politique; **to go into the army** [as profession] devenir militaire de carrière; [as conscript] partir au service; **to go into business** se lancer dans les affaires; **he went into medicine** il a choisi la médecine. -**2.** [be invested, expended - subj: effort, money, time]: **a lot of care had gone into making her feel at home** on s'était donné beaucoup de peine pour la mettre à l'aise; **two months of research went into our report** nous avons mis OR investi deux mois de recherche dans notre rapport. -**3.** [embark on - action] commencer à; [- explanation, speech] se lancer OR s'embarquer dans, (se mettre à) donner; **I'll go into the problem of your taxes later** j'aborderai le problème de vos impôts plus tard; **the car went into a skid** la voiture a commencé à déraper; **to go into hysterics** avoir une crise de nerfs. -**4.** [examine, investigate] examiner, étudier; **you need to go into the question more deeply** vous devez examiner le problème de plus près; **the matter is being gone into** l'affaire est à l'étude. -**5.** [explain in depth] entrer dans; **the essay goes into the moral aspects of the question** l'essai aborde les aspects moraux de la question; **I won't go into details** je ne vais pas entrer dans les détails; **let's not go into that** ne parlons pas de ça. -**6.** [begin to wear] se mettre à porter; **to go into mourning** prendre le deuil. -**7.** [hit, run into] entrer dans; **a car went into him** une voiture lui est rentrée dedans.

◆ **go off** ◇ *vi insep* -**1.** [leave] partir, s'en aller; **she went off to work** elle est partie travailler; **her husband has gone off and left her** son mari l'a quittée; **the actors went off** THEAT les acteurs ont quitté la scène. -**2.** [stop operating - light, radio] s'éteindre; [- heating] s'éteindre, s'arrêter; [- pain] partir, s'arrêter; **the electricity went off** l'électricité a été coupée. -**3.** [become activated - bomb] exploser; [- gun] partir; [- alarm] sonner; **the grenade went off in her hand** la grenade a explosé dans sa main; **the gun didn't go off** le coup n'est pas parti; **to go off into fits of laughter** *fig* être pris d'un fou rire. -**4.** [have specified outcome] se passer; **the interview went off badly/well** l'entretien s'est mal/bien passé; **her speech went off well** son discours a été bien reçu. -**5.** [fall asleep] s'endormir. -**6.** *Br* [deteriorate - food] s'avarier, se gâter; [- milk] tourner; [- butter] rancir; **the play goes off in the second half** la pièce se gâte pendant la seconde partie.

◇ *vt insep inf Br* [stop liking] perdre le goût de; **he's gone off jazz/smoking** il n'aime plus le jazz/fumer, le jazz/fumer ne l'intéresse plus; **she's gone off her boyfriend** son copain ne l'intéresse plus.

◆ **go off with** *vt insep* -**1.** [leave with] partir avec; **they went off with my sister** ils sont partis avec ma sœur. -**2.** [make off with] partir avec; **someone has gone off with his keys** quelqu'un est parti avec ses clés; **he went off with the jewels** il s'est enfui avec les bijoux.

◆ **go on** ◇ *vi insep* -**1.** [move, proceed] aller; [without stopping] poursuivre son chemin; [after stopping] repartir, se remettre en route; **you go on, I'll catch up** allez-y, je vous rattraperai (en chemin); **they went on without us** ils sont partis sans nous; **after dinner they went on to Susan's house** après le dîner, ils sont allés chez Susan; **we went on home** nous sommes rentrés. -**2.** [continue action] continuer; **she went on (with her) reading** elle a continué à OR de lire; **the chairman went on speaking** le président a continué son discours; **you can't go on being a student for ever!** tu ne peux pas être étudiant toute ta vie!; **go on looking!** cherchez encore!; **go on, ask her** vas-y, demande-lui; **go on, be a devil** *inf* vas-y, laisse-toi tenter!; **go on, I'm listening** continuez, je vous écoute; **I can't go on like this!** je ne peux plus continuer comme ça!; **if he goes on like this, he'll get the sack** s'il continue comme ça, il va se faire renvoyer; **their affair has been going on for years** leur liaison dure depuis des années; **the party went on into the small hours** la soirée s'est prolongée jusqu'à très tôt le matin; **life goes on** la vie continue OR va son train ❑ **go on (with you)!** *inf Br* allons, arrête de me faire marcher!; **they have enough (work) to be going on with** ils ont du pain sur la planche OR de quoi faire pour le moment; **here's £25 to be going on with** voilà 25 livres pour te dépanner. -**3.** [proceed to another action]: **he went on to explain why** il a ensuite expliqué pourquoi; **she went on to become a doctor** elle est ensuite devenue médecin. -**4.** [be placed, fit] aller; **the lid goes on this way** le couvercle se met comme ça; **I can't get the lid to go on** je n'arrive pas à mettre le couvercle; **the cap goes on the other end** le bouchon se met OR va sur l'autre bout. -**5.** [happen, take place] se passer; **what's going on here?** qu'est-ce qui se passe ici?; **there was a fight going on** il y avait une bagarre; **a lot of cheating goes on during the exams** on triche beaucoup pendant les examens; **several conversations were going on at once** il y avait plusieurs conversations à la fois; **while the war was going on** pendant la guerre. -**6.** [elapse] passer, s'écouler; **as the week went on** au fur et à mesure que la semaine passait; **as time goes on** avec le temps, à mesure que le temps passe. -**7.** *inf* [chatter, talk] parler, jacasser; **she does go on!** elle n'arrête pas de parler!, c'est un vrai moulin à paroles!; **to go on about sthg**: **he goes on and on about politics** il parle politique sans cesse; **don't go on about it!** ça va, on a compris! -**8.** [act, behave] se conduire, se comporter; **what a way to go on!** en voilà des manières! -**9.** [start operating - light, radio, television] s'allumer; [- heating, motor, power] s'allumer, se mettre en marche. -**10.** SPORT [player] prendre sa place, entrer en jeu. -**11.** THEAT [actor] entrer en scène.

◇ *vt insep* -**1.** [be guided by] se laisser guider par, se fonder OR se baser sur; **the detective didn't have much to go on** le détective n'avait pas grand-chose sur quoi s'appuyer OR qui puisse le guider; **she goes a lot on instinct** elle se fie beaucoup à OR se fonde beaucoup sur son instinct. -**2.** *inf Br (usu neg)* [appreciate, like] aimer; **I don't go much on abstract art** l'art abstrait ne me dit pas grand-chose.

◆ **go on at** *inf vt insep* [criticize] critiquer; [nag] s'en prendre à; **the boss went on and on at her at the meeting** le patron n'a pas cessé de s'en prendre à elle pendant la réunion; **he's always going on at his wife about money** il est toujours sur le dos de sa femme avec les questions d'argent; **I went on at my mother to go and see the doctor** j'ai embêté ma mère pour qu'elle aille voir le médecin; **don't go on at me!** laisse-moi tranquille!

◆ **go out** *vi insep* -**1.** [leave] sortir; **my parents made us go out of the room** mes parents nous ont fait sortir de la pièce OR quitter la pièce; **to go out to dinner** sortir dîner; **to go out for a walk** aller se promener, aller faire une promenade; **they went out to the country** ils sont allés OR ils ont fait une sortie à la campagne; **she goes out to work** elle travaille en dehors de la maison OR hors de chez elle; **he went out of her life** il est sorti de sa vie. -**2.** [travel] partir; [emigrate] émigrer; **they went out to Africa** [travelled] ils sont partis en Afrique; [emigrated] ils sont partis vivre OR ils ont émigré en Afrique. -**3.** [date] sortir; **to go out with sb** sortir avec qqn; **we've been going out together for a month** ça fait un mois que nous sortons ensemble. -**4.** [fire, light] s'éteindre. -**5.** [disappear] disparaître; **the joy went out of her eyes** la joie a disparu de son regard; **the spring went out of his step** il a perdu sa démarche légère; **all the heart went out of her** elle a perdu courage. -**6.** [cease to be fashionable] passer de mode, se démoder; **to go out of style/fashion** ne plus être le bon style/à la mode; **that hair style went out with the ark** *inf* cette coiffure remonte au déluge. -**7.** [tide] descendre, se retirer; **the tide has gone out** la marée est descendue, la mer s'est retirée; **the tide goes out 6 kilometres** la mer se retire sur 6 kilomètres. -**8.** *fig* [set out]: **I went out to see for myself** j'ai décidé de voir par moi-même; **we have to go out and do something about this** il faut que nous prenions des mesures OR que nous fassions quelque chose. -**9.** [be published - brochure, pamphlet] être distribué; [be broadcast - radio or television programme] être diffusé. -**10.** [feelings, sympathies] aller; **our thoughts go out to all those who suffer** nos pensées vont vers tous ceux qui souffrent; **my heart goes out to her** je suis de tout cœur avec elle dans son chagrin. -**11.** CARDS terminer. -**12.** *phr*: **to go all out** *inf* mettre le paquet; **she went all out to help us** elle a fait tout son possible pour nous aider.

◆ **go over** ◇ *vi insep* -**1.** [move overhead] passer; **I just saw a plane go over** je viens de voir passer un avion. -**2.** [move in particular direction] aller; [cross] traverser; **I went over to see her** je suis allé la voir; **they went over to talk to her** ils sont allés lui parler; **to go over to Europe** aller en Europe || [capsize - boat] chavirer, capoter. -**3.** [change, switch] changer; **I've gone over to another brand of washing powder** je viens de changer de marque de lessive; **when will we go over to the metric system?** quand est-ce qu'on va passer au système métrique? -**4.** [change allegiance] passer, se joindre; **he's gone over to the Socialists** il est passé dans le camp des socialistes; **she went over to the enemy** elle est passée à l'ennemi. -**5.** [be received] passer; **the speech went over badly/well** le discours a mal/bien passé.

◇ *vt insep* -**1.** [move, travel over] passer par-dessus; **the horse went over the fence** le cheval a sauté (par-dessus) la barrière; **we went over a bump** on a pris une bosse. -**2.** [examine - argument, problem] examiner, considérer; [- accounts, report] examiner, vérifier; **would you go over my report?** voulez-vous regarder mon rapport? -**3.** [repeat] répéter; [review - notes, speech] réviser, revoir; [- facts] récapituler, revoir; SCH réviser; **she went over the interview in her mind** elle a repassé l'entretien dans son esprit; **I kept going over everything leading up to the accident** je continuais de repenser à tous les détails qui avaient conduit à l'accident; **let's go over it again** reprenons, récapitulons; **he goes over and over the same stories** il rabâche les mêmes histoires. -**4.** TV & RADIO: **let's go over now to our Birmingham studios** passons l'antenne à notre studio de Birmingham; **we're going over live now to Paris** nous allons maintenant à Paris où nous sommes en direct.

◆ **go past** *vt insep* [move in front of] passer devant; [move beyond] dépasser.

◆ **go round** *vi insep* -**1.** [be enough]: **is there enough cake to go round?** est-ce qu'il y a assez de gâteau pour tout le monde? -**2.** [visit] aller; **we went round to his house** nous sommes allés chez lui; **I'm going round there later on** j'y vais plus tard. -**3.** [be continuously present - idea, tune]: **that song keeps going round in my head** j'ai cette chanson dans la tête. -**4.** [spin - wheel] tourner; **my head's going round** *fig* j'ai la tête qui tourne.

◆ **go through** ◇ *vt insep* -**1.** [crowd, tunnel] traverser; **a shiver went through her** *fig* un frisson l'a parcourue OR traversée. -**2.** [endure, experience] subir, souffrir; **he's going through hell** c'est l'enfer pour lui; **we all have to go through it sometime** on doit tous y passer un jour ou l'autre; **I can't face going through all that again** je ne supporterais pas de passer par là une deuxième fois; **after everything she's gone through** après tout ce qu'elle a subi OR enduré; **we've gone through a lot together** nous avons vécu beaucoup de choses ensemble. -**3.** [consume, use up - supplies] épuiser; [- money] dépenser; [wear out] user; **he goes through a pair of socks a week** il use une paire de chaussettes par semaine; **I've gone through the toes of my socks** j'ai usé OR troué mes chaussettes au bout; **how many assistants has he gone through now?** *hum* combien d'assistants a-t-il déjà eus?; **his novel has gone through six editions** il y a déjà eu six éditions de son roman. -**4.** [examine - accounts, document] examiner, vérifier; [- list, proposal] éplucher; [- mail] dépouiller; [- drawer, pockets] fouiller dans; [- files] chercher dans; [sort] trier; **we went through the contract together** nous avons regardé OR examiné le contrat ensemble; **did customs go through your suitcase?** est-ce qu'ils ont fouillé votre valise à la douane?; **he went through her pockets** il a fouillé ses poches. -**5.** [subj: bill, law] être voté; **the bill went through Parliament last week** le projet de loi a été voté la semaine dernière au Parlement. -**6.** [carry out, perform - movement, work] faire; [- formalities] remplir, accomplir; **let's go through the introduction again** MUS reprenons l'introduction; **we had to go through the whole business of applying for a visa** nous avons dû nous farcir toutes les démarches pour obtenir un visa. -**7.** [participate in - course of study] étudier; [- ceremony] participer à. -**8.** [practise - lesson, poem] réciter; THEAT [- role, scene] répéter; **let's go through it again from the beginning** reprenons dès le début.

◇ *vi insep* [offer, proposal] être accepté; [business deal] être conclu, se faire; [bill, law] passer, être voté; **the adoption finally went through** l'adoption s'est faite finalement.

◆ **go through with** *vt insep*: **to go through with sthg** aller jusqu'au bout de qqch, exécuter qqch; **he'll never go through with it** il n'ira jamais jusqu'au bout; **they went through with their plan/threat** ils ont exécuté leur projet/leur menace.

◆ **go together** *vi insep* -**1.** [colours, flavours] aller bien ensemble; [characteristics, ideas] aller de pair; **the two things often go together** les deux choses vont souvent de pair. -**2.** *Am* [people] sortir ensemble.

◆ **go towards** *vt insep* -**1.** [move towards] aller vers. -**2.** [effort, money] être consacré à; **all her energy went towards fighting illiteracy** elle a dépensé toute son énergie à combattre l'analphabétisme.

◆ **go under** ◇ *vi insep* -**1.** [go down - ship] couler, sombrer; [- person] couler, disparaître (sous l'eau). -**2.** *fig* [fail - business] couler, faire faillite; [- project] couler, échouer; [- person] échouer, sombrer.

◇ *vt insep* passer par-dessous.

◆ **go up** ◇ *vi insep* -**1.** [ascend, climb - person] monter, aller en haut; [- lift] monter; **to go up to town** aller en ville; **I'm going up to bed** je monte me coucher; **have you ever gone up in an aeroplane?** êtes-vous déjà monté en avion?; **going up!** on monte! -**2.** [reach as far as] aller, s'étendre; **the road goes up to the house** la route mène OR va à la maison. -**3.** [increase - amount, numbers] augmenter, croître; [- price] monter, augmenter; [- temperature] monter, s'élever; **rents are going up** les loyers sont en hausse; **meat is going up (in price)** (le prix de) la viande augmente. -**4.** [sudden noise] s'élever; **a shout went up** un cri s'éleva. -**5.** [appear - notices, posters] apparaître; [be built] être construit; **new buildings are going up all over town** de nouveaux immeubles surgissent dans toute la ville. -**6.** [explode, be destroyed] sauter, exploser. -**7.** MUS [raise pitch] monter. -**8.** THEAT [curtain] se lever; **before the curtain goes up** avant le lever du rideau. -**9.** *Br* UNIV entrer à l'université; **she went up to Oxford in 1950** elle est entrée à Oxford en 1950. -**10.** ▽ *Am* [be sent to prison]: **he went up for murder** il a fait de la taule pour meurtre. -**11.** SPORT [be promoted]: **they look set to go up to the First Division** ils ont l'air prêts à entrer en première division.

◇ *vt insep* monter; **to go up a hill/ladder** monter une colline/sur une échelle; **the pianist went up an octave** MUS le pianiste a monté d'une octave; **to go up a class** *Br* SCH monter d'une classe.

◆ **go with** *vt insep* -**1.** [accompany, escort] accompagner, aller avec; *fig*: **to go with the crowd** suivre la foule OR le mouvement; **you have to go with the times** il faut vivre avec son temps. -**2.** [be compatible - colours, flavours] aller avec; **that hat doesn't go with your suit** ce chapeau ne va pas avec ton ensemble; **a white Burgundy goes well with snails** le bourgogne blanc se marie bien OR va bien avec les escargots. -**3.** [be part of] aller avec; **the flat goes with the job** l'appartement va avec le poste; **the sense of satisfaction that goes with having done a good job** le sentiment de satisfaction qu'apporte le travail bien fait. -**4.** *inf* [spend time with] sortir avec; *euph* [have sex with]: **he's been going with other women** il a été avec d'autres femmes.

◆ **go without** ◇ *vt insep* se passer de, se priver de; **he went without sleep OR without sleeping for two days** il n'a pas dormi pendant deux jours.

◇ *vi insep* s'en passer; **we'll just have to go without** il faudra s'en passer, c'est tout!

goad [gəʊd] ◇ *n* aiguillon *m*.

◇ *vt* -**1.** [cattle] aiguillonner, piquer. -**2.** [person] harceler, provoquer; **stop ~ing the poor child!** cesse de houspiller ce petit!; **to ~ sb into doing sthg** pousser qqn à faire qqch, harceler

qqn jusqu'à ce qu'il fasse qqch; he ~ed me into losing my temper il m'a harcelé jusqu'à ce que je me mette en colère; the threat of redundancy ~ed the men into action la peur d'un licenciement incita les hommes à l'action.
◆ **goad on** *vt sep* aiguillonner; she was ~ed on by the prospect of wealth and power elle était stimulée par la perspective des richesses et du pouvoir.

go-ahead ◇ *n* feu *m* vert; to give sb the ~ to do sthg donner le feu vert à qqn pour (faire) qqch.
◇ *adj* [dynamic - person] dynamique, entreprenant, qui va de l'avant; [- attitude, business] dynamique.

goal [gəʊl] ◇ *n* -**1.** [aim] but *m*, objectif *m*; what's your ~ in life? quel est ton but OR quelle est ton ambition dans la vie?; she had achieved OR attained her ~ of becoming Prime Minister elle avait atteint OR réalisé son but de devenir Premier ministre; commercial and financial ~s need to be clearly defined les objectifs commerciaux et financiers doivent être clairement définis. -**2.** SPORT but *m*; to score a ~ marquer un but; they won by five ~s to two ils ont gagné par cinq buts à deux; who plays in OR keeps ~ for Liverpool? qui est gardien de but dans l'équipe de Liverpool?; ~! but!
◇ *comp* de but.

goal area *n* (zone *f* des) six mètres *mpl*.

goal average *n* goal-average *m*.

goal difference *n* différence *f* de buts.

goalie *inf* ['gəʊlɪ] *n* SPORT goal *m*, gardien *m* (de but).

goalkeeper ['gəʊl,kiːpəʳ] *n* gardien *m* (de but), goal *m*.

goalkeeping ['gəʊl,kiːpɪŋ] *n* jeu *m* du gardien de but; we saw some great ~ on both sides les deux gardiens de but ont très bien joué.

goal kick *n* coup *m* de pied de but, dégagement *m* aux six mètres.

goalless ['gəʊllɪs] *adj*: a ~ draw un match sans but marqué OR zéro à zéro.

goal line *n* ligne *f* de but.

goalminder ['gəʊl,maɪndəʳ] *n* gardien *m* (de but).

goalmouth ['gəʊl,maʊθ, *pl* -,maʊðz] *n*: in the ~ directement devant le but; a ~ scuffle un cafouillage devant le but.

goalpost ['gəʊlpəʊst] *n* poteau *m* (de but); to move the ~s *fig* changer les règles du jeu.

goalscorer ['gəʊl,skɔːrəʳ] *n* buteur *m*.

go-around *n*: to give sb the ~ faire une réponse de Normand OR répondre en Normand à qqn.

goat [gəʊt] *n* -**1.** ZOOL chèvre *f*. -**2.** *inf* [lecher]: old ~ vieux satyre *m*. -**3.** *inf dated* [foolish person] andouille *f*; you silly ~! espèce d'andouille!; to act OR to play the (giddy) ~ faire l'andouille. -**4.** *phr*: to get sb's ~ *inf* taper sur les nerfs OR le système à qqn; it gets my ~ ça me tape sur les nerfs.

goatee [gəʊ'tiː] *n* barbiche *f*, bouc *m*.

goatherd ['gəʊthɜːd] *n* chevrier *m*, -ère *f*.

goatskin ['gəʊtskɪn] *n* -**1.** [hide] peau *f* de chèvre. -**2.** [container] outre *f* (en peau de chèvre).

goatsucker ['gəʊt,sʌkəʳ] *n* ORNITH engoulevent *m*, tète-chèvre *m*.

gob [gɒb] (*pt* & *pp* gobbed, *cont* gobbing)
◇ *n* -**1.** ▽ *Br* [mouth] gueule *f*; shut your ~! ferme-la! -**2.** *inf* [lump - of mud, clay] motte *f*; [- of spittle] crachat *m*, mollard *m*. -**3.** *inf* = **gobs**.
◇ *vi* ▽ [spit] mollarder.
◆ **gobs** *inf npl*: ~s of un tas de, des masses de.

gobbet *inf* ['gɒbɪt] *n* morceau *m*.

gobble ['gɒbl] ◇ *vi* [turkey] glouglouter.
◇ *vt inf* [eat greedily] enfourner, engloutir; he ~d (down OR up) his lunch il a englouti son déjeuner à toute vitesse; don't ~ your food! ne mange pas si vite!
◇ *n* glouglou *m*.

gobbledegook *inf*, **gobbledygook** *inf* ['gɒbldɪguːk] *n* charabia *m*.

gobbler *inf* ['gɒbləʳ] *n* [male turkey] dindon *m*.

go-between *n* intermédiaire *mf*.

gobful▽ ['gɒbfʊl] *n Br* [mouthful] bouchée *f* pleine.

Gobi ['gəʊbɪ] *pr n*: the ~ Desert le désert de Gobi.

goblet ['gɒblɪt] *n* coupe *f*, verre *m* à pied; HIST gobelet *m*.

goblin ['gɒblɪn] *n* esprit *m* maléfique, lutin *m*.

gobo ['gəʊbəʊ] *n* -**1.** [on camera lens, spotlight etc] volet *m* (coupe-flux), écran *m* (de protection). -**2.** [on microphone] bonnette *f* de micro.

gobsmacked *inf* ['gɒbsmækt] *adj*: I was ~ j'en suis resté baba.

gobstopper ['gɒb,stɒpəʳ] *n Br gros bonbon rond qui change de couleur à mesure qu'on le suce*.

goby ['gəʊbɪ] (*pl* gobies) *n* gobie *m*.

GOC (*abbr of* General Officer Commanding/ Commanding-in-Chief) *n général commandant en chef*.

go-cart *n* -**1.** = **go-kart**. -**2.** *Am* [toy wagon] chariot *m*. -**3.** *Am* [babywalker] trotteur *m*.

god [gɒd] *n* dieu *m*; the ~ of War le dieu de la Guerre; profit is their only ~ leur seul dieu, c'est le profit; ye ~s! *hum* grands dieux!
◆ **God** *n* -**1.** RELIG Dieu *m*; Almighty God Dieu Tout-Puissant; God the Father, the Son and the Holy Ghost Dieu le Père, le Fils, le Saint-Esprit ❑ God's acre *lit* cimetière *m*; God slot *inf expression humoristique désignant les émissions religieuses à la télévision*. -**2.** [in interjections and expressions]: God bless you! Dieu vous bénisse!; thank God! grâce à Dieu!, Dieu soit loué!; (my OR by) God! *inf* mon Dieu!; in the name of God! *inf* (nom de) Dieu!; for the love of God *inf* pour l'amour de Dieu; for God's sake, don't go! pour l'amour de Dieu, ne partez pas!; God knows why/how Dieu sait pourquoi/comment; God (only) knows Dieu seul le sait; God forbid! à Dieu ne plaise!; God forbid that it should rain tomorrow! plaise à Dieu qu'il ne pleuve pas demain!; God willing s'il plaît à Dieu.
◆ **gods** *npl Br* THEAT: the ~s *inf* le poulailler.

god-awful▽ *adj* atroce, affreux; what ~ weather! quel sale temps!

godchild ['gɒdtʃaɪld] (*pl* godchildren [-,tʃɪldrən]) *n* filleul *m*, -e *f*.

goddam(n)▽ ['gɒdæm] *Am* ◇ *interj*: ~! zut!
◇ *n*: he doesn't care OR give a ~ il s'en fout.
◇ *adj* sacré, fichu; that ~ dog! ce sacré chien!; you ~ fool! pauvre imbécile!
◇ *adv* vachement; it's ~ hot il fait vachement chaud.

goddamned▽ ['gɒdæmd] = **goddam(n)** *adj* & *adv*.

goddaughter ['gɒd,dɔːtəʳ] *n* filleule *f*.

goddess ['gɒdɪs] *n* déesse *f*.

godet ['gəʊdeɪ] *n* SEW godet *m*.

godetia [gə'diːʃə] *n* godetia *m*.

godfather ['gɒd,fɑːðəʳ] *n* parrain *m*; 'The Godfather' *Coppola* 'le Parrain'.

god-fearing *adj* croyant, pieux.

godforsaken *inf* ['gɒdfə,seɪkn] *adj* paumé.

godhead ['gɒdhed] *n* divinité *f*; the ~ Dieu.

godless ['gɒdlɪs] *adj* irréligieux, impie.

godlike ['gɒdlaɪk] *adj* divin, céleste.

godliness ['gɒdlɪnɪs] *n* sainteté *f* (de l'âme), dévotion *f*.

godly ['gɒdlɪ] *adj* -**1.** [pious] pieux. -**2.** [divine] divin.

godmother ['gɒd,mʌðəʳ] *n* marraine *f*.

godown ['gəʊdaʊn] *n* entrepôt *m (en Asie, surtout en Inde)*.

godparent ['gɒd,peərənt] *n* parrain *m*, marraine *f*.

godsend ['gɒdsend] *n* aubaine *f*, bénédiction *f*.

godson ['gɒdsʌn] *n* filleul *m*.

godspeed [,gɒd'spiːd] *interj arch*: ~! à-Dieu-vat!

godsquad *inf* ['gɒdskwɒd] *n pej*: the ~ les soldats de Dieu.

goer ['gəʊəʳ] *n Br* -**1.** *inf* [fast person, vehicle, animal] fonceur *m*, -euse *f*; this horse is a real ~ *inf* il file OR il fonce, ce cheval. -**2.** *inf* [sexually active person]: he's/she's a real ~ il/elle n'y va pas par quatre chemins *(pour séduire qqn)*.

gofer *inf* ['gəʊfəʳ] *n esp Am* [office employee] *personne qui fait les menues tâches dans un bureau*.

go-getter *inf* [-'getəʳ] *n* fonceur *m*, -euse *f*, battant *m*, -e *f*.

goggle ['gɒgl] ◇ *vi* ouvrir de grands yeux OR des yeux ronds; to ~ at sb/sthg regarder qqn/qqch avec des yeux ronds.
◇ *adj*: to have ~ eyes avoir les yeux saillants OR exorbités OR globuleux.
◆ **goggles** *npl* -**1.** [protective] lunettes *fpl* (de protection); [for motorcyclist] lunettes *fpl* (de motocycliste); [for diver] lunettes *fpl* de plongée; [for swimmer] lunettes *fpl*. -**2.** *inf* [glasses] bésicles *fpl*.

goggle box *inf n Br hum* télé *f*.

goggle-eyed *adj* les yeux saillants OR exorbités OR globuleux; to stare ~ regarder en écarquillant les yeux.

goggly ['gɒglɪ] = **goggle** *adj*.

go-go *adj* [music, dancing] go-go.

go-go dancer *n* danseur *m* de go-go.

Goidelic [gɔɪ'delɪk] ◇ *n* goïdélique *m*.
◇ *adj* relatif au goïdélique.

going ['gəʊɪŋ] ◇ *n* -**1.** [leaving] départ *m*. -**2.** [progress] progrès *m*; we made good ~ on the return journey on est allés vite pour le retour; that's pretty good ~! c'est plutôt rapide!; it was slow ~, but we got the work done il nous a fallu du temps, mais on a réussi à finir le travail. -**3.** [condition of ground] état *m* du terrain; the ~ was heavy at Ascot racecourse yesterday le terrain était lourd à l'hippodrome d'Ascot hier; it's rough OR heavy ~ on these mountain roads c'est dur de rouler sur ces routes de montagne; this novel is heavy ~ *fig* ce roman ne se lit pas facilement; he left while the ~ was good *fig* il est parti au bon moment.
◇ *adj* -**1.** [profitable]: her company is a ~ concern son entreprise est en pleine activité; 'for sale as a ~ concern' 'à vendre avec fonds'. -**2.** [current] actuel; the ~ price le prix actuel, le prix sur le marché; she's getting the ~ rate for the job elle touche le tarif en vigueur OR normal pour ce genre de travail; the best computer/novelist ~ le meilleur ordinateur/ romancier du moment.

going-over *inf* (*pl* goings-over) *n* -**1.** [checkup] révision *f*, vérification *f*; [cleanup] nettoyage *m*; the house needs a good ~ il faudrait nettoyer la maison à fond. -**2.** *fig*: to give sb a (good) ~ [scolding] passer un savon à qqn; [beating] passer qqn à tabac.

goings-on *inf npl* -**1.** *pej* [behaviour] conduite *f*, activités *fpl*; there are some funny ~ in that house il s'en passe de drôles dans cette maison; what ~! il s'en passe des choses! -**2.** [events] événements *mpl*.

goitre *Br*, **goiter** *Am* ['gɔɪtəʳ] *n* goitre *m*.

go-kart *n* kart *m*.

Golan Heights ['gəʊ,læn-] *pl pr n*: the ~ le plateau du Golan.

gold [gəʊld] ◇ *n* -**1.** [metal, colour] or *m*; 1,000 French francs in ~ 1 000 francs français en or ❑ to be as good as ~ être sage comme une image; he has a heart of ~ il a un cœur d'or; to be worth its weight in ~ valoir son pesant d'or. -**2.** [gold medal] médaille *f* d'or; we won two ~s and a silver nous avons remporté deux médailles d'or et une (médaille) d'argent; to go for ~ viser la médaille d'or.
◇ *adj* -**1.** [made of gold - coin, ingot, medal] d'or; [- tooth, watch] en or; ~ lettering lettres *fpl* d'or. -**2.** [gold-coloured] or *(inv)*, doré.

goldbeater ['gəʊld,biːtəʳ] *n* batteur *m* d'or.

gold braid *n* galon *m* d'or.

goldbrick *inf* ['gəʊldbrɪk] *n Am*: to sell sb a ~ rouler qqn.

gold bullion *n* or *m* en barre OR en lingots; ~ standard étalon-or-lingot *m*.
gold card *n* carte *f* de crédit illimité.
gold-coloured *adj* or *(inv)*, doré.
gold-digger *n* chercheur *m* d'or; *fig* & *pej* aventurier *m*, -ère *f*.
gold disc *n* disque *m* d'or.
gold dust *n* poudre *f* d'or; **jobs are like ~ around here** *fig* le travail est rare OR ne court pas les rues par ici.
golden ['gəʊldən] *adj* **-1.** *literal* & *fig* [made of gold] en or, d'or; **a ~ opportunity** une occasion en or; **~ hours** des heures précieuses OR merveilleuses ❑ 'The Golden Bowl' *James* 'la Coupe d'or'. **-2.** [colour] doré, (couleur) d'or; **she has long ~ hair** elle a de longs cheveux dorés; **~ yellow** jaune *m* d'or. **-3.** *inf* [very successful]: **~ boy** OR **girl** enfant *mf* prodige.
Golden Age *n*: **the ~** l'âge *m* d'or.
golden calf *n* veau *m* d'or.
Golden Delicious *(pl inv) n* golden *f*.
golden eagle *n* aigle *m* royal.
Golden Fleece *n*: **the ~** la Toison d'or.
golden handcuffs *inf npl* primes *fpl (versées à un cadre à intervalles réguliers pour le dissuader de partir)*.
golden handshake *inf n* gratification *f* de fin de service.
golden hello *inf n* gratification *f* de début de service.
golden jubilee *n* (fête *f* du) cinquantième anniversaire *m*.
golden mean *n*: **the ~** le juste milieu.
golden number *n* nombre *m* d'or.
golden oldie *inf n* vieux tube *m*.
golden oriole *n* loriot *m* (jaune).
golden parachute *inf n* COMM prime *f* de licenciement *(versé à certains cadres supérieurs en cas de rachat de l'entreprise)*.
golden pheasant *n* faisan *m* doré.
golden retriever *n* golden retriever *m*.
goldenrod ['gəʊldənrɒd] *n* verge *f* d'or, solidago *m*.
golden rule *n* règle *f* d'or.
golden section *n* section *f* d'or OR dorée.
golden share *n* participation *f* majoritaire *(souvent détenue par le gouvernement britannique dans les entreprises privatisées)*.
golden syrup *n Br* mélasse *f* raffinée.
golden triangle *n* triangle *m* d'or.
golden wedding *n* noces *fpl* d'or.
gold fever *n* fièvre *f* de l'or.
goldfield ['gəʊldfiːld] *n* terrain *m* aurifère.
gold filling *n* obturation *f* OR incrustation *f* en or.
goldfinch ['gəʊldfɪntʃ] *n* chardonneret *m*.
goldfish ['gəʊldfɪʃ] *n* **-1.** [as pet] poisson *m* rouge. **-2.** ZOOL cyprin *m* doré.
goldfish bowl *n* bocal *m* (à poissons rouges); **it's like living in a ~** *fig* on ne se sent OR on n'est plus chez soi.
Goldilocks ['gəʊldɪlɒks] *pr n* Boucles d'or.
gold leaf *n* or *m* en feuille.
gold lettering *n (U)* lettres *fpl* d'or.
gold medal *n* médaille *f* d'or.
goldmine ['gəʊldmaɪn] *n literal* & *fig* mine *f* d'or.
gold plate *n* **-1.** [utensils] orfèvrerie *f*, vaisselle *f* d'or. **-2.** [plating] plaque *f* d'or.
gold-plated *adj* plaqué or.
gold reserves *npl* réserves *fpl* d'or.
gold-rimmed *adj*: **~ spectacles** lunettes *fpl* à montures en or.
gold rush *n* ruée *f* vers l'or; **the Gold Rush** *Am* HIST la ruée vers l'or; 'The Gold Rush' *Chaplin* 'la Ruée vers l'or'.

THE GOLD RUSH:
Des milliers de personnes partirent pour la Californie, à la suite de la découverte de gisements d'or, en 1848. En un an, près de 80 000 pionniers atteignirent la côte ouest par terre ou par mer, échappant à la maladie et aux dangers du voyage.

---

goldsmith ['gəʊldsmɪθ] *n* orfèvre *m*.
gold standard *n* étalon-or *m*.
golf [gɒlf] ◇ *n* golf *m*.
◇ *vi* jouer au golf.
◇ *comp*: **~ bag** sac *m* de golf; **~ cart** caddie *m* (de golf).
golf ball *n* **-1.** SPORT balle *f* de golf. **-2.** [for typewriter] boule *f*; **~ typewriter** machine *f* à écrire à boule.
golf club *n* **-1.** [stick] club *m* OR crosse *f* OR canne *f* de golf. **-2.** [building, association] club *m* de golf.
golf course *n* (terrain *m* de) golf *m*.
golfer ['gɒlfə^r] *n* joueur *m*, -euse *f* de golf, golfeur *m*, -euse *f*.
golfing ['gɒlfɪŋ] *n* golf *m (activité)*.
golf links *npl* links *mpl*.
golf widow *inf n femme délaissée par un mari qui est toujours au golf*.
Golgotha ['gɒlgəθə] *pr n* Golgotha *m*.
Goliath [gə'laɪəθ] *pr n* Goliath.
golliwog ['gɒlɪwɒg] *n poupée de chiffon, au visage noir et aux cheveux hérissés*.
golly *inf* ['gɒlɪ] *(pl* **gollies)** ◇ *n Br* = **golliwog**.
◇ *interj dated*: (good) **~!** ciel!, mince (alors)!, flûte!
gollywog ['gɒlɪwɒg] = **golliwog**.
goloshes [gə'lɒʃɪz] = **galoshes**.
GOM *pr n abbr of* Grand Old Man.
gonad ['gəʊnæd] *n* gonade *f*.
gondola ['gɒndələ] *n* **-1.** [boat] gondole *f*. **-2.** [on airship or balloon, for window cleaner] nacelle *f*. **-3.** [in supermarket] gondole *f*. **-4.** [ski lift] cabine *f* (de téléphérique).
gondolier [,gɒndə'lɪə^r] *n* gondolier *m*.
Gondwanaland [gɒnd'wɑːnəlænd] *pr n* continent *m* du Gondwana.
gone [gɒn] ◇ *pp* → **go**.
◇ *adj* **-1.** [past] passé, révolu; **those days are ~ now** c'est bien fini tout ça; **~ is the time when...** le temps n'est plus où... **-2.** [away]: **be ~ with you!** disparaissez de ma vue! ❑ 'Gone with the Wind' *Mitchell* 'Autant en emporte le vent'. **-3.** *inf* [high] parti; **to be really ~** être parti, planer. **-4.** *inf* [pregnant]: **she is 4 months ~** elle est enceinte de 4 mois. **-5.** *inf* [infatuated]: **to be ~ on sb/sthg** être (complètement) toqué de qqn/qqch. **-6.** *euph* [dead] mort. **-7.** *phr*: **to be far ~** *inf* [weak] il est bien faible; [drunk] il est bien parti.
◇ *prep Br*: **it's ~ 11** il est 11 h passées OR plus de 11 h.
goner *inf* ['gɒnə^r] *n*: **to be a ~** être fichu OR cuit.
gong [gɒŋ] *n* **-1.** [instrument] gong *m*. **-2.** *inf Br hum* & MIL médaille *f*.
goniometer [,gəʊnɪ'ɒmɪtə^r] *n* goniomètre *m*.
gonna *inf* ['gɒnə] *esp Am* = **going to**.
gonorrh(o)ea [gɒnə'rɪə] *n* blennorragie *f*.
gonzo *inf* ['gɒnzəʊ] *adj Am* subjectif, partial.
goo *inf* [guː] *n* **-1.** [sticky stuff] matière *f* poisseuse. **-2.** *fig* & *pej* sentimentalisme *m*.
good [gʊd] *(compar* **better** ['betə^r], *superl* **best** [best]) ◇ *adj* **A. -1.** [enjoyable, pleasant - book, feeling, holiday] bon, agréable; [- weather] beau; **we had ~ weather during the holidays** il faisait beau pendant nos vacances; **we're ~ friends** nous sommes très amis; **we're just ~ friends** on est des amis, c'est tout; **she has a ~ relationship with her staff** elle a un bon contact avec ses employés; **they have a ~ sex life** sexuellement, tout va bien entre eux; **they had a ~ time** ils se sont bien amusés; **~ to eat/to hear** bon à manger/à entendre; **it's ~ to be home** ça fait du bien OR ça fait plaisir de rentrer chez soi; **it's ~ to be alive** il fait bon vivre ‖ [agreeable] bon; **wait until he's in a ~ mood** attendez qu'il soit de bonne humeur; **they took advantage of his ~ nature** ils ont profité de son bon naturel OR caractère; **to feel ~** être en forme; **he doesn't feel ~ about leaving her alone** [worried] ça le gêne de la laisser seule; [ashamed] il a honte de la laisser seule ❑ **it's too ~ to be true** c'est trop beau pour être vrai OR pour y croire; **the ~ life** la belle vie; **she's never had it so ~!** elle n'a jamais eu la vie si belle!; **have a ~ day!** bonne journée!; **you can have too much of a ~ thing** on se lasse de tout, même du meilleur. **-2.** [high quality - clothing, dishes] bon, de bonne qualité; [- painting, film] bon; [- food] bon; **it's a ~ school** c'est une bonne école; **he speaks ~ English** il parle bien anglais; **she put her ~ shoes on** elle a mis ses belles chaussures; **I need a ~ suit** j'ai besoin d'un bon costume; **this house is ~ enough for me** cette maison me suffit; **this isn't ~ enough** ça ne va pas; **this work isn't ~ enough** ce travail laisse beaucoup à désirer; **nothing is too ~ for her family** rien n'est trop beau pour sa famille; **it makes ~ television** c'est télévisuel. **-3.** [competent, skilful] bon, compétent; **do you know a ~ lawyer?** connaissez-vous un bon avocat?; **she's a very ~ doctor** c'est un excellent médecin; **he's a ~ swimmer** c'est un bon nageur; **she's a ~ listener** c'est quelqu'un qui sait écouter; **to be ~ at sthg** être doué pour OR bon en qqch; **they're ~ at everything** ils sont bons en tout; **he's ~ with children** il sait s'y prendre avec les enfants; **to be ~ with one's hands** être habile OR adroit de ses mains; **they're not ~ enough to direct the others** ils ne sont pas à la hauteur pour diriger les autres; **you're as ~ as he is** tu le vaux bien, tu vaux autant que lui; **she's as ~ an artist as you are** elle vous vaut en tant qu'artiste; **the ~ gardening guide** le guide du bon jardinier. **-4.** [useful] bon; **to be ~ for nothing** être bon à rien; **this product is also ~ for cleaning windows** ce produit est bien aussi pour nettoyer les vitres.
B. -1. [kind] bon, gentil; [loyal, true] bon, véritable; [moral, virtuous] bon; **~ behaviour** OR **conduct** bonne conduite *f*; **she's a ~ person** c'est quelqu'un de bien; **he's a ~ sort** c'est un brave type; **she proved to be a ~ friend** elle a prouvé qu'elle était une véritable amie; **he's been a ~ husband to her** il a été pour elle un bon mari; **you're too ~ for him** tu mérites mieux que lui; **he's a ~ Christian/communist** c'est un bon chrétien/communiste; **to lead a ~ life** [comfortable] avoir une belle vie; [moral] mener une vie vertueuse OR exemplaire; **they've always been ~ to me** ils ont toujours été gentils avec moi; **that's very ~ of you** c'est très aimable de votre part; **it's ~ of you to come** c'est aimable OR gentil à vous d'être venu; **would you be ~ enough to ask him?** auriez-vous la bonté de lui demander?, seriez-vous assez aimable pour lui demander?; **would you be ~ enough to reply by return of post?** voudriez-vous avoir l'obligeance de répondre par retour du courrier?; **and how's your ~ lady?** *dated* OR *hum* et comment va madame?; **~ men and true** *lit* des hommes vaillants. **-2.** [well-behaved] sage; **be ~!** sois sage!; **be a ~ boy and fetch Mummy's bag** sois mignon, va chercher le sac de maman; **~ dog!** t'es un gentil chien, toi!
C. -1. [desirable, positive] bon, souhaitable; [cause] bon; **it's a ~ thing she's prepared to talk about it** c'est une bonne chose qu'elle soit prête à en parler; **she had the ~ fortune to arrive just then** elle a eu la chance d'arriver juste à ce moment-là; **it's a ~ job** OR **~ thing he decided not to go** c'est une chance qu'il ait décidé de OR heureusement qu'il a décidé de ne pas y aller; **all ~ wishes for the New Year** tous nos meilleurs vœux pour le nouvel an. **-2.** [favourable - contract, deal] avantageux, favorable; [- opportunity, sign] bon, favorable; **to buy sthg at a ~ price** acheter qqch bon marché OR à un prix avantageux; **she's in a ~ position to help**

us elle est bien placée pour nous aider; **there are ~ times ahead** l'avenir est prometteur; **he put in a ~ word for me with the boss** il a glissé un mot en ma faveur au patron. -**3.** [convenient, suitable - place, time] bon, propice; [- choice] bon, convenable; **it's a ~ holiday spot for people with children** c'est un lieu de vacances idéal pour ceux qui ont des enfants; **is this a ~ moment to ask him?** est-ce un bon moment pour lui demander?; **this is as ~ a time as any** autant le faire maintenant; **it's as ~ a way as any to do it** c'est une façon comme une autre de le faire. -**4.** [beneficial] bon, bienfaisant; **protein-rich diets are ~ for pregnant women** les régimes riches en protéines sont bons pour les femmes enceintes; **eat your spinach, it's ~ for you** mange tes épinards, c'est bon pour toi; **hard work is ~ for the soul!** le travail forme le caractère!; **whisky is ~ for a cold** le whisky est bon pour les rhumes; **this cold weather isn't ~ for your health** ce froid n'est pas bon pour ta santé OR est mauvais pour toi; **it's ~ for him to spend time outdoors** ça lui fait du bien OR c'est bon pour lui de passer du temps dehors; **he works more than is ~ for him** il travaille plus qu'il ne faudrait OR devrait; **he doesn't know what's ~ for him** *fig* il ne sait pas ce qui est bon pour lui; **if you know what's ~ for you, you'll listen** *fig* si tu as le moindre bon sens, tu m'écouteras.

D. -**1.** [sound, strong] bon, valide; **I can do a lot with my ~ arm** je peux faire beaucoup de choses avec mon bras valide; **my eyesight/hearing is ~** j'ai une bonne vue/l'ouïe fine. -**2.** [attractive - appearance] bon, beau; [- features, legs] beau, joli; **you're looking ~!** [healthy] tu as bonne mine!; [well-dressed] tu es très bien!; **that colour looks ~ on him** cette couleur lui va bien; **he has a ~ figure** il est bien fait. -**3.** [valid, well-founded] bon, valable; **she had a ~ excuse/reason for not going** elle avait une bonne excuse pour/une bonne raison de ne pas y aller; **I wouldn't have come without ~ reason** je ne serais pas venu sans avoir une bonne raison; **they made out a ~ case against drinking tap water** ils ont bien expliqué pourquoi il ne fallait pas boire l'eau du robinet. -**4.** [reliable, trustworthy - brand, car] bon, sûr; COMM & FIN [- cheque] bon; [- investment, securities] sûr; [- debt] bon, certain; **my passport is ~ for 5 years** mon passeport est bon OR valable pour 5 ans; **this coat is ~ for another year** ce manteau fera encore un an; **she's ~ for another ten years** *inf* elle en a bien encore pour dix ans; **he's always ~ for a laugh** *inf* il sait toujours faire rire; **how much money are you ~ for?** [do you have] de combien d'argent disposez-vous?; **they are OR their credit is ~ for £500** on peut leur faire crédit jusqu'à 500 livres. -**5.** [honourable, reputable] bon, estimé; **they live at a ~ address** ils habitent un quartier chic; **to protect their ~ name** pour défendre leur réputation; **the firm has a ~ name** la société a (une) bonne réputation; **she's from a ~ family** elle est de bonne famille; **a family of ~ standing** une famille bien.

E. -**1.** [ample, considerable] bon, considérable; **a ~ amount OR deal of money** beaucoup d'argent; **a ~-sized room** une assez grande pièce; **a ~ (round) sum** une somme rondelette; **take ~ care of your mother** prends bien soin de ta mère; **to make ~ money** bien gagner sa vie; **I make ~ money** je gagne bien ma vie; **we still have a ~ way to go** nous avons encore un bon bout de chemin à faire; **a ~ thirty years ago** il y a bien trente ans; **the trip will take you a ~ two hours** il vous faudra deux bonnes heures pour faire le voyage; **she's been gone a ~ while** ça fait un bon moment qu'elle est partie; **they came in a ~ second** ils ont obtenu une bonne deuxième place; **there's a ~ risk of it happening** il y a de grands risques que ça arrive. -**2.** [proper, thorough] bon, grand; **I gave the house a ~ cleaning** j'ai fait le ménage à fond; **have a ~ cry** pleure un bon coup; **we had a ~ laugh** on a bien ri; **I managed to get a ~ look at his face** j'ai pu bien regarder son visage; **take a ~ look at her** regardez-la bien; **he got a ~ spanking** il a reçu une bonne fessée ❑ **~ and: we were ~ and mad** *inf* on était carrément furax; **she'll call when she's ~ and ready** *inf* elle appellera quand elle le voudra bien; **I was ~ and sorry to have invited her** j'ai bien regretté de l'avoir invitée. -**3.** [acceptable] bon, convenable; **we made the trip in ~ time** le voyage n'a pas été trop long; **that's all very ~** OR **all well and ~ but...** c'est bien joli OR bien beau tout ça mais... -**4.** [indicating approval] bon, très bien; **I'd like a new suit – very ~, sir!** j'ai besoin d'un nouveau costume – (très) bien, monsieur!; **she left him – ~!** elle l'a quitté – tant mieux!; **he's feeling better – ~, let him go** il va mieux – très bien, laissez-le partir; **~, that's settled** bon OR bien, voilà une affaire réglée; **that's a ~ question** c'est une bonne question ❑ **that's a ~ one!** *inf* [joke] elle est (bien) bonne, celle-là!; *iron* [far-fetched story] à d'autres!; **~ for you** OR **on you!** *inf* bravo!, très bien!

◇ *adv* -**1.** [as intensifier] bien, bon; **a ~ hard bed** un lit bien dur; **I'd like a ~ hot bath** j'ai envie de prendre un bon bain chaud; **he needs a ~ sound spanking** il a besoin d'une bonne fessée; **the two friends had a ~ long chat** les deux amis ont longuement bavardé; **we took a ~ long walk** nous avons fait une bonne OR une grande promenade. -**2.** *inf (not standard)* [well] bien; **she writes ~** elle écrit bien; **the boss gave it to them ~ and proper** *inf* le patron leur a passé un de ces savons; **their team beat us ~ and proper** *inf* leur équipe nous a battus à plate couture OR à plates coutures. -**3.** *phr*: **to make ~** [succeed] réussir; [reform] changer de conduite, se refaire une vie; **a local boy made ~** un garçon du pays OR du coin qui a fait son chemin; **the prisoner made ~ his escape** le prisonnier est parvenu à s'échapper OR a réussi son évasion; **they made ~ their promise** ils ont tenu parole OR ont respecté leur promesse; **he made ~ his position as leader** il a assuré sa position de leader; **to make sthg ~** [mistake] remédier à qqch; [damages, injustice] réparer qqch; [losses] compenser qqch; [deficit] combler qqch; [wall, surface] apporter des finitions à qqch; **we'll make ~ any expenses you incur** nous vous rembourserons toute dépense; **to make ~ on sthg** *Am* honorer qqch.

◇ *n* -**1.** [morality, virtue] bien *m*; **they do ~** ils font le bien; **that will do more harm than ~** ça fera plus de mal que de bien; **to return ~ for evil** rendre le bien pour le mal; **that organization is a power for ~** cet organisme exerce une influence salutaire; **she recognized the ~ in him** elle a vu ce qu'il y avait de bon en lui; **to be up to no ~** préparer un mauvais coup; **their daughter came to no ~** leur fille a mal tourné; **for ~ or evil, for ~ or ill** pour le bien et pour le mal. -**2.** [use] : **this book isn't much ~ to me** ce livre ne me sert pas à grand-chose; **if it's any ~ to him** si ça peut lui être utile OR lui rendre service; **I was never any ~ at mathematics** je n'ai jamais été doué pour les maths, je n'ai jamais été bon OR fort en maths; **he'd be no ~ as a teacher** il ne ferait pas un bon professeur; **what's the ~?** à quoi bon?; **what ~ would it do to leave now?** à quoi bon partir maintenant?; **what ~ will it do you to see her?** ça te servira à quoi OR t'avancera à quoi de la voir?; **a fat lot of ~ that did you!** *inf* te voilà bien avancé maintenant!; **that will do you a lot of ~!** *iron* tu seras bien avancé!, ça te fera une belle jambe!; **it's no ~, I give up** ça ne sert à rien, j'abandonne; **it's no ~ worrying about it** ça ne sert à rien de OR ce n'est pas la peine de OR inutile de vous inquiéter; **I might as well talk to the wall for all the ~ it does** je ferais aussi bien de parler au mur, pour tout l'effet que ça fait. -**3.** [benefit, welfare] bien *m*; **I did it for your own ~** je l'ai fait pour ton (propre) bien; **a holiday will do her ~** des vacances lui feront du bien; **she resigned for the ~ of her health** elle a démissionné pour des raisons de santé; **it does my heart ~ to see you so happy** ça me réchauffe le cœur de vous voir si heureux; **much ~ may it do you!** grand bien vous fasse!; **the common ~** l'intérêt *m* commun.

◇ *npl* [people]: **the ~** les bons *mpl*, les gens *mpl* de bien; **the ~ and the bad** les bons et les méchants; **only the ~ die young** ce sont toujours les meilleurs qui partent les premiers ❑ **'the Good, the Bad and the Ugly'** *Leone* 'le Bon, la bête et le truand'.

◆ **as good as** *adv phr* pour ainsi dire, à peu de choses près; **I'm as ~ as blind without my glasses** sans lunettes je suis pour ainsi dire aveugle; **he's as ~ as dead** c'est comme s'il était mort; **the job is as ~ as finished** la tâche est pour ainsi dire OR est pratiquement finie; **it's as ~ as new** c'est comme neuf; **he as ~ as admitted he was wrong** il a pour ainsi dire reconnu qu'il avait tort; **they as ~ as called us cowards** ils n'ont pas dit qu'on était des lâches mais c'était tout comme.

◆ **for good** *adv phr* pour de bon; **she left for ~** elle est partie pour de bon; **they finally settled down for ~** ils se sont enfin fixés définitivement; **for ~ and all** une (bonne) fois pour toutes, pour de bon; **I'm warning you for ~ and all!** c'est la dernière fois que je te le dis!

◆ **to the good** *adv phr*: **that's all to the ~** tant mieux; **he finished up the card game £15 to the ~** il a fait 15 livres de bénéfice OR il a gagné 15 livres aux cartes.

Good Book *n*: **the ~** la Bible.

goodbye [gʊd'baɪ] ◇ *interj*: **~!** au revoir!; **~ for now** à bientôt, à la prochaine.

◇ *n* adieu *m*, au revoir *m*; **I hate ~s** j'ai horreur des adieux; **we said our ~s and left** on a fait nos adieux et on est partis; **to say ~ to sb** dire au revoir OR faire ses adieux à qqn, prendre congé de qqn; **if you fail these exams, you can say ~ to a career as a doctor** *fig* si tu rates ces examens, tu peux dire adieu à ta carrière de médecin ❑ **'Goodbye To All That'** *Graves* 'Adieu à tout cela'; **'Goodbye to Berlin'** *Isherwood* 'Adieux à Berlin'.

good day *interj* -**1.** *Br dated* OR *Am* [greeting] bonjour. -**2.** *Br dated* [goodbye] adieu.

good evening *interj*: **~!** [greeting or saying goodbye] bonsoir!

good-for-nothing ◇ *adj* bon OR propre à rien; **he's a ~ layabout!** c'est un bon à rien et un fainéant!; **that ~ husband of hers** son vaurien de mari.

◇ *n* vaurien *m*, -enne *f*, propre-à-rien *mf*.

Good Friday *n* le Vendredi saint.

GOOD FRIDAY:
En Grande-Bretagne, il est traditionnel, le jour du Vendredi saint, de manger des «hot cross buns» (petits pains ronds aux fruits secs, marqués d'une croix).

good-hearted *adj* [person] bon, généreux; [action] fait avec les meilleures intentions.

good-humoured *adj* [person] qui a bon caractère; [discussion] amical; [joke, remark] sans malice.

good-humouredly *adv* avec bonne humeur.

goodie *inf* ['gʊdɪ] = **goody**.

good looker *inf n* [man] bel homme *m*; [younger] beau garçon *m*; [woman] belle femme *f*; [younger] belle fille *f*.

good-looking *adj* [person] beau; **a ~ woman** une belle OR jolie femme.

good looks *npl* [attractive appearance] beauté *f*.

goodly ['gʊdlɪ] *adj* -**1.** *dated* [amount, size] considérable, important; **a ~ sum of money** une belle somme d'argent. -**2.** *arch* [attractive] charmant, gracieux.

good morning *interj*: **~!** [greeting] bonjour!; [goodbye] au revoir!, bonne journée!

good-natured *adj* [person] facile à vivre, qui a un bon naturel; [face, smile] bon enfant *(inv)*; [remark] sans malice.

good-naturedly *adv* avec bonne humeur, avec bonhomie.

goodness [ˈgʊdnɪs] *n* -**1.** [of person] bonté *f*, bienveillance *f*, bienfaisance *f*; [of thing] (bonne) qualité *f*, excellence *f*, perfection *f*; **he believes in people's essential ~** il croit en la bonté naturelle des gens; **she didn't even have the ~ to say thank you!** elle n'a même pas eu la bonté de dire merci! -**2.** [nourishment] valeur *f* nutritive; **there's a lot of ~ in fresh vegetables** les légumes frais sont pleins de bonnes choses. -**3.** *inf* [in interjections]: **(my) ~!** mon Dieu!; **~ gracious (me)!** Seigneur!, mon Dieu!; **for ~' sake** pour l'amour de Dieu, par pitié; **~ knows!** Dieu seul le sait!; **~ knows why** Dieu sait pourquoi; **I wish to ~ he would shut up!** si seulement il pouvait se taire!

good night ◇ *interj*: **~!** [when leaving] bonsoir!; [when going to bed] bonne nuit!
◇ *n*: **they said ~ and left** ils ont dit bonsoir et sont partis; **she kissed her mother ~ and went to bed** elle a dit bonsoir à sa mère et est allée se coucher.
◇ *comp*: **give your mother a ~ kiss** embrasse ta mère *(pour lui dire bonsoir)*.

goods [gʊdz] *npl* -**1.** [possessions] biens *mpl*; **he gave up all his worldly ~** il a renoncé à tous ses biens matériels ❑ **~ and chattels** biens et effets *mpl*. -**2.** COMM marchandises *fpl*, articles *mpl*; **send us the ~ by rail** envoyez-nous la marchandise par chemin de fer; **these ~ are not for sale** ces articles ne sont pas à vendre; **leather ~** articles de cuir, maroquinerie *f* ❑ **to deliver the ~** *inf* tenir parole; **have you got the ~?** vous avez ce qu'il faut?; **he thinks she's the ~** *inf* il pense qu'elle est géniale. -**3.** *inf Am* [information] renseignements *mpl*; **can you give me the ~ on him?** pouvez-vous me rencarder sur lui?

good Samaritan *n* bon Samaritain *m*, bonne Samaritaine *f*; **she's a real ~** elle a tout du bon Samaritain; **the ~ laws** *Am* JUR *lois qui protègent un sauveteur de toutes poursuites éventuelles engagées par le blessé*.
◆ **Good Samaritan** *n* BIBLE: **the Good Samaritan** le bon Samaritain.

Good Shepherd *n*: **the ~** le bon Pasteur.

goods train *n* train *m* de marchandises.

goods wagon *n* wagon *m* de marchandises.

goods yard *n* dépôt *m* de marchandises.

good-tempered *adj* [person] qui a bon caractère, d'humeur égale.

good-time girl *inf n pej* fille *f* qui ne pense qu'à se donner du bon temps, noceuse *f*.

goodwill [ˌgʊdˈwɪl] ◇ *n* -**1.** [benevolence] bienveillance *f*; **to show ~ towards sb** faire preuve de bienveillance à l'égard de qqn. -**2.** [willingness] bonne volonté *f*; **there needs to be ~ on both sides** il faut que chacun fasse preuve de bonne volonté OR y mette du sien. -**3.** COMM clientèle *f*, (biens *mpl*) incorporels *mpl*.
◇ *comp* d'amitié, de bienveillance; **a ~ gesture** un geste OR témoignage d'amitié; **a ~ mission** OR **visit** une visite d'amitié.

Goodwood [ˈgʊdwʊd] *pr n champ de courses en Angleterre*.

goody *inf* [ˈgʊdɪ] (*pl* **goodies**) ◇ *interj*: **~!** génial!, chouette!, chic!
◇ *n (usu pl)* -**1.** [good thing] bonne chose *f*; [sweet] bonbon *m*, friandise *f*; **her latest film's a ~** son dernier film est un régal. -**2.** [good person] bon *m*; **the goodies and the baddies** les bons et les méchants.

goody-goody *inf* (*pl* **goody-goodies**) *pej*
◇ *adj*: **he's too ~** il est trop parfait.
◇ *n* âme *f* charitable *hum*, modèle *m* de vertu *hum*.

gooey *inf* [ˈguːɪ] *adj* -**1.** [substance] gluant, visqueux, poisseux; [sweets] qui colle aux dents. -**2.** [sentimental] sentimental; **she goes all ~ over babies** elle devient gâteuse quand elle voit un bébé.

goof *inf* [guːf] ◇ *n* -**1.** [fool] imbécile *mf*, andouille *f*. -**2.** [blunder] gaffe *f*.
◇ *vi* [blunder] faire une gaffe.
◆ **goof off** *inf vi insep Am* [waste time] flemmarder; [malinger] tirer au flanc.
◆ **goof on** *inf vt insep Am* se moquer de.
◆ **goof up** *inf vt sep* bousiller, saloper; **he ~ed the job up** il a salopé le travail.

goofball▽ [ˈguːfbɔːl] *Am* ◇ *n* -**1.** [drug] barbiturique *m*. -**2.** [fool] crétin *m*, -e *f*, andouille *f*.
◇ *vi* gaffer, mettre les pieds dans le plat.

goof-off *n Am* tire-au-flanc *m inv*.

goofy *inf* [ˈguːfɪ] (*compar* **goofier**, *superl* **goofiest**) *adj* -**1.** [stupid] dingo. -**2.** *Br* [teeth] en avant.

googly [ˈguːglɪ] *n* [in cricket] balle *f* déviée; **to bowl a ~** *literal* faire dévier une balle; **the boss bowled us a ~** *fig* le patron nous a joué un sale tour.

googol [ˈguːgɒl] *n* dix *m* puissance cent.

goo-goo *inf adj*: **to make ~ eyes at sb** faire des yeux de velours OR les yeux doux à qqn.

gook▼ [guːk] *n Am terme raciste désignant un Asiatique*.

goolies▽ [ˈguːlɪ] *npl* roupettes *fpl*.

goon *inf* [guːn] *n* -**1.** [fool] abruti *m*, -e *f*; **the Goons** *groupe de comédiens loufoques très populaires dans les années 50 en Grande-Bretagne*. -**2.** *Am* [hired thug] casseur *m (au service de quelqu'un)*; **~ squad** [strike-breakers] milice *f* patronale.

Goonhilly [ˌguːnˈhɪlɪ] *pr n station de communications par satellite en Angleterre*.

goosander [guːˈsændəʳ] *n* harle *m*.

goose [guːs] (*pl* **geese** [giːs]) ◇ *n* -**1.** [bird] oie *f*; **~ egg** *inf Am* zéro *m*; **to kill the ~ that lays the golden egg** tuer la poule aux œufs d'or. -**2.** *inf* [fool]: **don't be such a ~!** ne sois pas si bête!; **what a little ~ she is!** quelle petite dinde!
◇ *vt inf Am* [prod]: **to ~ sb** *donner un petit coup sur les fesses de quelqu'un pour le faire sursauter*.

gooseberry [ˈgʊzbərɪ] *n* -**1.** BOT groseille *f* à maquereau. -**2.** [unwanted person]: **to be** OR **to play ~** tenir la chandelle.

gooseberry bush *n* groseillier *m*; **we found you under a ~** *hum* on t'a trouvé dans un chou.

goose bumps *inf esp Am* = **goose pimples**.

goose fat *n* graisse *f* d'oie.

gooseflesh [ˈguːsfleʃ] *n (U)* = **goose pimples**.

goosegog *inf* [ˈguːzgɒg] *n Br* groseille *f* à maquereau.

goose grass *n* grateron *m*, potentille *f*, ansérine *f*.

gooseneck [ˈguːsnek] *n* -**1.** [shape] col *m* de cygne. -**2.** NAUT [joint] vit-de-mulet *m*.

goose pimples *npl Br* la chair de poule; **to get** OR **to come out in ~** avoir la chair de poule; **horror films give me ~** les films d'horreur me donnent la chair de poule.

goosestep [ˈguːsˌstep] (*pt* & *pp* **goosestepped**, *cont* **goosestepping**) ◇ *n* pas *m* de l'oie.
◇ *vi* faire le pas de l'oie; **they goosestepped across the parade ground** ils ont traversé le terrain de manœuvres au pas de l'oie.

GOP (*abbr of* Grand Old Party) *pr n le parti républicain aux États-Unis*.

gopher [ˈgəʊfəʳ] *n* -**1.** [pocket gopher] gaufre *m*, gauphre *m*. -**2.** [ground squirrel] spermophile *m*. -**3.** [tortoise] *espèce de tortues qui s'enfouissent dans le sol*. -**4.** *inf* = **gofer**.

Gorbachov [ˈgɔːbətʃɒf] *pr n*: **Mikhail ~** Mikhaïl Gorbatchev.

Gorbals [ˈgɔːblz] *pl pr n*: **the ~** *quartier du sud de Glasgow autrefois connu pour ses taudis*.

gorblimey *inf* [gɔːˈblaɪmɪ] *Br* ◇ *interj*: **~!** mon Dieu!, mince!
◇ *n*: **he's got a real ~ accent** il a un bon accent cockney.

Gordian knot [ˈgɔːdjən-] *n* nœud *m* gordien; **to cut the ~** couper OR trancher le nœud gordien.

Gordonstoun [ˈgɔːdnstən] *pr n*: **~ (School)** *école privée en Écosse, fréquentée notamment par la famille royale*.

gore [gɔːʳ] ◇ *n* -**1.** [blood] sang *m* (coagulé); **his films are always full of blood and ~** il y a beaucoup de sang dans ses films. -**2.** SEW godet *m*; NAUT pointe *f* (de voile); [land] langue *f* de terre.
◇ *vt* -**1.** [wound] blesser à coups de cornes, encorner; **the matador was ~d by the bull** le matador a été encorné par le taureau; **he was ~d to death** il a été tué d'un coup de corne. -**2.** NAUT [sail] mettre une pointe à.

gored [gɔːd] *adj* [skirt] à godets.

gorge [gɔːdʒ] ◇ *n* -**1.** GEOG défilé *m*, gorge *f*. -**2.** *arch* [throat] gorge *f*, gosier *m*; **it made my ~ rise** *fig* cela m'a rendu malade OR m'a soulevé le cœur.
◇ *vt*: **to ~ o.s.** se gaver, se gorger, se bourrer; **don't ~ yourself with** OR **on sweets** ne vous bourrez OR gavez pas de bonbons.

gorgeous [ˈgɔːdʒəs] *adj* -**1.** *inf* [wonderful - person, weather] magnifique, splendide, superbe; [- flat, clothing] magnifique, très beau; [- food, meal] délicieux. -**2.** [magnificent - fabric, clothing] somptueux.

Gorgon [ˈgɔːgən] *pr n* MYTH: **the ~s** les Gorgones *fpl*.
◆ **gorgon** *n* [fierce woman] harpie *f*, dragon *m*.

gorilla [gəˈrɪlə] *n* -**1.** ZOOL gorille *m*. -**2.** *inf* [thug] voyou *m*; [bodyguard] gorille *m*.

Gorki, Gorky [ˈgɔːkɪ] *pr n* Gorki.

Gorky [ˈgɔːkɪ] *pr n*: **Maxim ~** Maxime Gorki.

gormandize, -ise [ˈgɔːməndaɪz] *vi fml* engloutir, dévorer.

gormless *inf* [ˈgɔːmlɪs] *adj Br* [person, expression] stupide, abruti; **don't look so ~!** ne prends pas cet air d'abruti!

gorse [gɔːs] *n (U)* ajoncs *mpl*; **a ~ bush** un ajonc.

gory [ˈgɔːrɪ] (*compar* **gorier**, *superl* **goriest**) *adj* [battle, scene, sight, death] sanglant; **a ~ film** un film sanglant OR très violent; **give me all the ~ details** *hum* vas-y, raconte-moi tout; **spare me all the ~ details** *hum* épargne-moi les détails.

gosh *inf* [gɒʃ] *interj*: **~!** oh dis donc!, ça alors!, hé ben!

goshawk [ˈgɒshɔːk] *n* autour *m*.

gosling [ˈgɒzlɪŋ] *n* oison *m*.

go-slow *n Br* grève *f* du zèle, grève *f* perlée.

gospel [ˈgɒspl] ◇ *n* -**1.** *fig*: **to take sthg as ~** prendre qqch pour parole d'évangile. -**2.** MUS gospel *m*.
◇ *comp* -**1.** *fig*: **the ~ truth** la vérité vraie. -**2.** MUS: **~ music** gospel *m*; **~ song** negro spiritual *m*.
◆ **Gospel** ◇ *n* BIBLE: **the Gospel** l'Évangile *m*; **the Gospel according to St Mark** l'Évangile selon saint Marc.
◇ *comp*: **Gospel book** évangéliaire *m*.

gospel(l)er [ˈgɒspələʳ] *n* évangéliste *m*.

gospel oath *n* serment *m* prêté sur l'Évangile.

gossamer [ˈgɒsəməʳ] ◇ *n (U)* [cobweb] fils *mpl* de la vierge, filandres *fpl*; [gauze] gaze *f*; [light cloth] étoffe *f* transparente.
◇ *comp* arachnéen, très léger, très fin.

gossip [ˈgɒsɪp] ◇ *n* -**1.** *(U)* [casual chat] bavardage *m*, papotage *m*; *pej* [rumour] commérage *m*, ragots *mpl*, racontars *mpl*; [in newspaper] potins *mpl*; **to have a good ~** bien papoter; **have you heard the latest (bit of) ~?** vous connaissez la dernière (nouvelle)?; **that's just (idle) ~** ce ne sont que des bavardages (futiles); **don't listen to ~** n'écoutez pas les racontars; **the paper gives all the local ~** il y a tous les petits potins du coin dans le journal. -**2.** *pej* [person] bavard *m*, -e *f*, pie *f*, commère *f*; **he's such a ~!** quelle commère!
◇ *vi* bavarder, papoter; [maliciously] faire des commérages, dire du mal des gens; **people are always ~ing about their neighbours** les gens ont toujours des ragots à raconter sur leurs voisins.

gossip column *n* échos *mpl*; **in the ~s** dans les échos.

gossip columnist *n* échotier *m*, -ère *f*.

gossiping [ˈgɒsɪpɪŋ] ◇ *adj* bavard; *pej* cancanier.
◇ *n (U)* bavardage *m*, papotage *m*; *pej* commérage *m*.

gossip writer = **gossip columnist**.

gossipy *inf* ['gɒsɪpɪ] *adj* [person] bavard; *pej* cancanier; [style] anecdotique; a ~ letter une lettre pleine de bavardages.

got [gɒt] *pt* & *pp* → **get**.

gotcha *inf* ['gɒtʃə] *interj* -**1.** [I understand]: ~! pigé! -**2.** [cry of success]: ~! ça y est (je l'ai)!; [cry when catching sb] je te tiens!

Goth [gɒθ] *n*: the ~s les Goths *mpl*.

Gothenburg ['gɒθən,bɜːg] *pr n* Göteborg.

Gothic ['gɒθɪk] ◇ *adj* [ARCHIT & gen] gothique; ~ type PRINT caractère *m* gothique; ~ novel roman *m* gothique.
◇ *n* [ARCHIT & gen] gothique *m*; LING gotique *m*, gothique *m*.

GOTHIC NOVEL:
Le roman gothique est une histoire d'horreur pseudoromantique ayant généralement pour cadre un château gothique; le genre fut popularisé au XVIIIe siècle par Walpole.

gotta *inf* ['gɒtə] *Am* -**1.** [have got a]: I ~ dog j'ai un chien. -**2.** [have got to]: I ~ work Saturday je dois bosser samedi.

gotten ['gɒtn] *Am* & *Scot pp* → **get**.

gouache [gʊ'ɑːʃ] *n* gouache *f*.

gouge [gaʊdʒ] ◇ *n* gouge *f*.
◇ *vt* [with gouge] gouger; to ~ a hole [intentionally] creuser un trou; [accidentally] faire un trou; you've ~d a great hole in the top of the table! vous avez fait un gros trou sur le dessus de la table!
◆ **gouge out** *vt sep* [with gouge] gouger, creuser (à la gouge); [with thumb] évider, creuser; to ~ sb's eyes out crever les yeux à qqn.

goulash ['guːlæʃ] *n* goulache *m*, goulasch *m*.

gourd [gʊəd] *n* [plant] gourde *f*, cucurbitacée *f*; [fruit] gourde *f*, calebasse *f*; [container] gourde *f*, calebasse *f*.

gourmand ['gʊəmənd] *n* [glutton] gourmand *m*, -e *f*; [gourmet] gourmet *m*.

gourmet ['gʊəmeɪ] ◇ *n* gourmet *m*, gastronome *mf*.
◇ *comp* gastronomique; ~ food cuisine *f* gastronomique; a ~ restaurant un restaurant gastronomique.

gout [gaʊt] *n* -**1.** *(U)* MED goutte *f*. -**2.** *fml* OR *lit* [blob] goutte *f*.

gouty ['gaʊtɪ] *adj* [leg, person] goutteux.

gov *inf* [gʌv] *abbr of* governor **2**.

govern ['gʌvən] ◇ *vt* -**1.** [country] gouverner, régner sur; [city, region, bank etc] gouverner; [affairs] administrer, gérer; [company, organization] diriger, gérer; the politicians who ~ Britain les politiciens qui gouvernent la Grande-Bretagne; when Louis XIV ~ed France quand Louis XIV gouvernait la France OR régnait sur la France. -**2.** [determine - behaviour, choice, events, speed] déterminer. -**3.** [restrain - passions] maîtriser, dominer. -**4.** GRAMM [case, mood] gouverner, régir. -**5.** TECH régler.
◇ *vi* COMM & POL gouverner, commander, diriger.

governable ['gʌvnəbl] *adj* gouvernable.

governance ['gʌvnəns] *n* gouvernement *m*, régime *m*.

governess ['gʌvənɪs] *n* gouvernante *f*.

governing ['gʌvənɪŋ] *adj* -**1.** COMM & POL gouvernant, dirigeant; the ~ party le parti au pouvoir; ~ body conseil *m* d'administration. -**2.** [factor] dominant; the ~ principle le principe directeur.

government ['gʌvnmənt] ◇ *n* -**1.** [process of governing - country] gouvernement *m*, direction *f*; [- company] administration *f*, gestion *f*; [- affairs] conduite *f*. -**2.** POL [governing authority] gouvernement *m*; [type of authority] gouvernement *m*, régime *m*; [the State] gouvernement *m*, État *m*; the Conservative ~ le gouvernement conservateur; to form a ~ constituer OR former un gouvernement; the ~ has fallen le gouvernement est tombé; the socialists have joined the coalition ~ les socialistes sont entrés dans le gouvernement de coalition; democratic ~ la démocratie; a stable ~ un gouvernement stable; the project is financed by the ~ le projet est financé par l'État OR le gouvernement.
◇ *comp* [measure, policy] gouvernemental, du gouvernement; [borrowing, expenditure] de l'État, public; [minister, department] du gouvernement; a ~-funded project un projet subventionné par l'État ❑ ~ bonds obligations *fpl* d'État, bons *mpl* du Trésor; ~ health warning *avertissement officiel contre les dangers du tabac figurant sur les paquets de cigarettes et dans les publicités pour le tabac*; 'The Government Inspector' *Gogol* 'le Revizor'.

governmental [,gʌvn'mentl] *adj* gouvernemental, du gouvernement; ~ responsibilities des responsabilités gouvernementales; a ~ organization une organisation gouvernementale.

Government House *n Br* palais *m* du gouverneur.

government issue *n* émission *f* d'État OR par le gouvernement; ~ uniform uniforme *m* fourni par l'État.

governor ['gʌvənə^r] *n* -**1.** [of bank, country] gouverneur *m*; *Br* [of prison] directeur *m*, -trice *f*; *Br* [of school] membre *m* du conseil d'établissement; State ~ *Am* gouverneur *m* d'État. -**2.** *inf Br* [employer] patron *m*, boss *m*. -**3.** TECH régulateur *m*.

governor-general, Governor-General (*pl* governor-generals) *n* gouverneur *m* général.

governor-generalship *n* poste *m* de gouverneur général.

governorship ['gʌvənəʃɪp] *n* fonctions *fpl* de gouverneur.

govt (*written abbr of* government) gvt.

gown [gaʊn] *n* -**1.** [gen] robe *f*. -**2.** SCH & UNIV toge *f*.

goy [gɔɪ] (*pl* goys OR goyim ['gɔɪɪm]) *n* goy *mf*, goï *mf*.

GP (*abbr of* general practitioner) *n* (médecin *m*) généraliste *m*.

GPMU (*abbr of* Graphical, Paper and Media Union) *pr n syndicat britannique des ouvriers du livre*.

GPO (*abbr of* General Post Office) *pr n* -**1.** [in Britain]: the ~ *titre officiel de la Poste britannique avant 1969*. -**2.** [in US]: the ~ *les services postaux américains*.

gr. *written abbr of* gross.

grab [græb] (*pt* & *pp* grabbed, *cont* grabbing) ◇ *vt* -**1.** [with hands] saisir; he grabbed the book out of my hand il m'a arraché le livre des mains; he grabbed my purse and ran il s'est emparé de mon porte-monnaie et est parti en courant. -**2.** *fig* [opportunity] saisir; [power] prendre; [land] s'emparer de; [quick meal] avaler, prendre (en vitesse); I'll ~ a sandwich and work through the lunch hour je vais me prendre un sandwich en vitesse et je travaillerai pendant l'heure du déjeuner ❑ how does that ~ you? *inf* qu'est-ce que tu en dis?; the film didn't really ~ me le film ne m'a pas vraiment emballé.
◇ *vi*: to ~ at sb/sthg essayer d'agripper qqn/qqch; don't ~! pas touche!; I grabbed at the chance *fig* j'ai sauté sur l'occasion.
◇ *n* -**1.** [movement] mouvement *m* vif; [sudden theft] vol *m* (à l'arraché); to make a ~ at OR for sthg essayer de saisir OR faire un mouvement vif pour saisir qqch ❑ to be up for ~s *inf* être disponible. -**2.** *Br* TECH benne *f* preneuse.

grab bag *n Am* -**1.** = **lucky dip**. -**2.** [assortment] fourre-tout *m inv*.

grabber ['græbə^r] *n* -**1.** [greedy person] personne *f* qui se précipite sur tout. -**2.** [attention-seeker] personne *f* qui cherche à attirer l'attention.

grabby *inf* ['græbɪ] *adj pej* radin, pingre; don't be so ~ ne sois pas aussi pingre.

grace [greɪs] ◇ *n* -**1.** [physical] grâce *f*; [decency, politeness, tact] tact *m*; social ~s bonnes manières *fpl*; to do sthg with good/bad ~ faire qqch de bonne/mauvaise grâce; at least he had the (good) ~ to apologize il a au moins eu la décence de s'excuser. -**2.** RELIG grâce *f*; by the ~ of God par la grâce de Dieu; in a state of ~ en état de grâce ❑ to fall from ~ RELIG perdre la grâce; *fig* tomber en disgrâce; to be in sb's good/bad ~s être bien/mal vu par qqn; there but for the ~ of God (go I) ça aurait très bien pu m'arriver aussi. -**3.** [amnesty] grâce *f*; [respite] grâce *f*, répit *m*; as an act of ~, the King... JUR en exerçant son droit de grâce, le Roi...; we have two days' ~ nous disposons de deux jours de répit; days of ~ COMM jours *mpl* de grâce. -**4.** [prayer]: to say ~ [before meals] dire le bénédicité; [after meals] dire les grâces.
◇ *vt* -**1.** [honour] honorer; she ~d us with her presence *hum* elle nous a honorés de sa présence. -**2.** [adorn] orner, embellir; some exquisite watercolours ~d the walls les murs étaient ornés de très jolies aquarelles.
◆ **Grace** *n* [term of address]: Your Grace [to Archbishop] Monseigneur OR (Votre) Excellence (l'Archevêque); [to Duke] Monsieur le duc; [to Duchess] Madame la duchesse; His Grace the Duke Monsieur le duc; Her Grace the Duchess Madame la duchesse; His Grace the Archbishop Monseigneur OR Son Excellence l'Archevêque.
◆ **Graces** *npl* MYTH: the three Graces les trois Grâces *fpl*.

grace-and-favour *adj Br*: ~ residence *logement appartenant à la Couronne et prêté à une personne que le souverain souhaite honorer*.

graceful ['greɪsfʊl] *adj* [person, movement] gracieux; [language, style] élégant.

gracefully ['greɪsfʊlɪ] *adv* [dance, move] avec grâce, gracieusement.

gracefulness ['greɪsfʊlnɪs] *n* grâce *f*, élégance *f*.

graceless ['greɪslɪs] *adj* [behaviour, person, movement] gauche.

gracelessly ['greɪslɪslɪ] *adv* avec maladresse, de façon peu élégante.

grace note *n* note *f* d'agrément, ornement *m*.

gracious ['greɪʃəs] ◇ *adj* -**1.** [generous, kind - gesture, smile] gracieux, bienveillant; [- action] généreux; to be ~ to OR towards sb faire preuve de bienveillance envers qqn; Your Gracious Majesty Votre gracieuse Majesté; by the ~ consent of... par la grâce de...; God has been ~ to us Dieu s'est montré miséricordieux OR bienveillant envers nous. -**2.** [luxurious]: ~ living vie *f* facile.
◇ *interj*: (good) ~ (me)! mon Dieu!, bonté divine!; goodness ~! Seigneur Dieu!, bonté divine!

graciously ['greɪʃəslɪ] *adv* [smile] gracieusement; [accept, agree, allow] avec bonne grâce; *fml* gracieusement; RELIG miséricordieusement.

graciousness ['greɪʃəsnɪs] *n* [of person] bienveillance *f*, générosité *f*, gentillesse *f*; [of action] grâce *f*, élégance *f*; [of lifestyle, surroundings] élégance *f*, raffinement *m*; RELIG miséricorde *f*, clémence *f*.

grackle [grækl] *n* -**1.** [American songbird] quiscale *m*. -**2.** [starling] mainate *m*.

grad *inf* [græd] *n abbr of* graduate.

gradable ['greɪdəbl] *adj* -**1.** [capable of being graded] qui peut être classé. -**2.** LING comparatif.

gradate [grə'deɪt] ◇ *vt* graduer.
◇ *vi* être gradué.

gradation [grə'deɪʃn] *n* gradation *f*, progression *f*, échelonnement *m*; [stage] gradation *f*, degré *m*, palier *m*; LING alternance *f* (vocalique), apophonie *f*.

gradational [grə'deɪʃənl] *adj* -**1.** [gen] graduel, progressif, échelonné. -**2.** LING comparatif.

grade [greɪd] ◇ *n* -**1.** [level] degré *m*, niveau *m*; [on scale] échelon *m*, grade *m*; [on salary scale] indice *m*; the top ~s of the civil service les échelons supérieurs OR les plus élevés de la fonction publique. -**2.** MIL grade *m*, rang *m*, échelon *m*; [in hierarchy] échelon *m*, catégorie *f*. -**3.** [quality - of product] qualité *f*, catégorie *f*; [- of petrol] grade *m*; [size of products] calibre *m*; a high ~ of coal un charbon de haute qualité; there are two ~s of eggs il y a des œufs de deux calibres; **grade A potatoes** pommes de terre de qualité A. -**4.** *Am* SCH [mark] note *f*; [year] année *f*, classe *f*; **she gets good ~s at school** elle a de bonnes notes à l'école; **a ~ A student** un excellent élève; **he's in fifth ~** ≃ il est en CM2. -**5.** *Am* = **grade school**. -**6.** MATH grade *m*. -**7.** *Am* [gradient] déclivité *f*, pente *f*; RAIL rampe *f*. -**8.** *phr*: **to make the ~** être à la hauteur; **do you think she'll make the ~?** vous pensez qu'elle est OR sera à la hauteur?

◇ *vt* -**1.** [classify - by quality] classer; [- by size] calibrer; [arrange in order] classer; **to ~ food/questions** classer de la nourriture/des questions. -**2.** SCH [mark] noter. -**3.** [cross - livestock] améliorer par sélection. -**4.** [level] niveler; **to ~ the ground** niveler le terrain.

◆ **grade down** *vt sep* mettre dans une catégorie inférieure.

◆ **grade up** *vt sep* -**1.** mettre dans une catégorie supérieure. -**2.** [level] = **grade** *vt* **4.**

grade crossing *n Am* RAIL passage *m* à niveau.

grader ['greɪdəʳ] *n* -**1.** *Am* SCH [marker of exams] correcteur *m*, -trice *f*; [member of a grade]: **fourth ~** élève *mf* de 4ᵉ année *(CM1)*. -**2.** TECH grader *m*, niveleuse *f*.

grade school *n Am* école *f* primaire.

grade separation *n Am* AUT séparation *f* des niveaux de circulation.

grade teacher *n Am* instituteur *m*, -trice *f*.

gradient ['greɪdjənt] *n* -**1.** *Br* [road] déclivité *f*, pente *f*, inclinaison *f*; RAIL rampe *f*, pente *f*, inclinaison *f*; **a steep ~** une ligne à forte pente; **a ~ of three in ten** OR **30%** une pente de 30%. -**2.** METEOR & PHYS gradient *m*; **pressure ~** gradient de pression.

gradient post *n* RAIL indicateur *m* de pente.

grading ['greɪdɪŋ] *n* [classification] classification *f*; [by size] calibration *f*; SCH notation *f*.

gradiometer [ˌgreɪdɪ'ɒmɪtəʳ] *n* clinomètre *m*.

gradual ['grædʒʊəl] ◇ *adj* [change, improvement, movement] graduel, progressif; [slope] doux.

◇ *n* RELIG graduel *m*.

gradualism ['grædʒʊəlɪzm] *n* gradualisme *m*; POL réformisme *m*.

gradually ['grædʒʊəlɪ] *adv* progressivement, petit à petit, peu à peu.

gradualness ['grædʒʊəlnɪs] *n* progressivité *f*.

graduand ['grædʒʊənd] *n Br* UNIV candidat *m*, -e *f*, postulant *m*, -e *f*, prétendant *m*, -e *f*.

graduate [*n* 'grædʒʊət, *vb* 'grædjʊeɪt] ◇ *n* -**1.** UNIV licencié *m*, -e *f*, diplômé *m*, -e *f*; *Am* SCH bachelier *m*, -ère *f*; **she's an Oxford ~** OR **a ~ of Oxford** elle a fait ses études à Oxford ❑ 'The Graduate' *Nichols* 'le Lauréat'. -**2.** *Am* [container] récipient *m* gradué.

◇ *adj* UNIV diplômé, licencié; **~ school** *Am école où l'on poursuit ses études après la licence*; **~ student** étudiant de deuxième/troisième cycle.

◇ *vi* -**1.** UNIV ≃ obtenir son diplôme/sa licence; *Am* SCH ≃ obtenir le OR être reçu au baccalauréat; **she ~d from the Sorbonne** elle a un diplôme de la Sorbonne; **he ~d in linguistics** il a une licence de linguistique. -**2.** [gain promotion] être promu, passer; **he ~d from the post of foreman to that of manager** il est passé du poste de contremaître à celui de directeur; **I've ~d from cheap plonk to good wines** *inf* je suis passé du gros rouge aux bons vins.

◇ *vt* -**1.** [calibrate] graduer; **the ruler is ~d in millimetres** la règle est graduée en millimètres. -**2.** [change, improvement, movement] graduer; **the teacher ~d the exercises** le professeur a gradué les exercices. -**3.** *Am* SCH & UNIV conférer OR accorder un diplôme à.

graduated ['grædjʊeɪtɪd] *adj* [tax] progressif; [measuring container, exercise, thermometer] gradué; [colours] dégradé.

graduation [ˌgrædʒʊ'eɪʃn] ◇ *n* -**1.** [gen] graduation *f*. -**2.** UNIV & *Am* SCH [ceremony] (cérémonie *f* de) remise *f* des diplômes.

◇ *comp*: **~ day** jour *m* de la remise des diplômes.

Graeco-, **Greco-** [ˌgriːkəʊ] *in cpds* gréco-; **~ Latin** gréco-latin; **~Roman** gréco-romain; **~Roman wrestling** SPORT lutte *f* gréco-romaine.

graffiti [grə'fiːtɪ] *n* OU *npl* graffiti *mpl*.

graft [grɑːft] ◇ *n* -**1.** HORT greffe *f*, greffon *m*; MED greffe *f*; **they performed a cornea ~** ils ont effectué une greffe de la cornée; **skin ~** greffe de la peau. -**2.** *inf (U)* [corruption] magouilles *fpl*. -**3.** *inf (U) Br* [hard work] travail *m* pénible.

◇ *vt* -**1.** HORT & MED greffer; **they ~ed a piece of skin onto his face** ils lui ont greffé un bout de peau sur le visage. -**2.** [obtain by corruption] obtenir par la corruption.

◇ *vi* -**1.** [be involved in bribery] donner OR recevoir des pots-de-vin. -**2.** HORT & MED: **pears ~ fairly easily** les poires se greffent assez facilement. -**3.** *inf Br* [work hard] bosser dur.

grafter ['grɑːftəʳ] *n* -**1.** BOT [instrument] greffoir *m*. -**2.** *inf* [hard worker] bourreau *m* de travail. -**3.** *inf* [corrupt person] corrupteur *m*, escroc *m*; [corrupt official] fonctionnaire *m* corrompu, concussionnaire *m*.

graham flour ['greɪəm-] *n Am* farine *f* brute.

grail [greɪl] *n*: **the Holy Grail** le Saint-Graal.

grain [greɪn] ◇ *n* -**1.** *(U)* [seeds of rice, wheat] grain *m*; [cereal] céréales *fpl*; *Am* blé *m*; **a cargo of ~** une cargaison de céréales. -**2.** [single] grain *m*; **~s of rice/wheat** grains *mpl* de riz/de blé ‖ [particle] grain *m*; **a ~ of salt/sand** un grain de sel/de sable. -**3.** *fig* [of madness, sense, truth etc] grain *m*, brin *m*; **a few ~s of comfort** une petite consolation. -**4.** [in leather, stone, wood etc] grain *m*; PHOT grain *m*; **I'll help you, but it goes against the ~** je vous aiderai, mais ce n'est pas de bon cœur; **it goes against the ~ for him to accept that they are right** ce n'est pas dans sa nature d'admettre qu'ils aient raison. -**5.** *Br* [weight] ≃ grain *m (poids)*.

◇ *vt* -**1.** [salt] cristalliser. -**2.** [leather, paper] greneler; [to paint to imitate wood] veiner.

◇ *vi* se cristalliser.

grain alcohol *n* alcool *m* de grains.

grained [greɪnd] *adj* -**1.** [salt] cristallisé. -**2.** [leather, paper] grenu, grené; [painted imitation of wood] veiné.

grain elevator *n* silo *m* à céréales.

grainy ['greɪnɪ] (*compar* **grainier**, *superl* **grainiest**) *adj* [surface, texture - of wood] veineux; [- of stone] grenu, granuleux; [- of leather, paper] grenu, grené; PHOT qui a du grain.

gram [græm] *n* -**1.** [metric unit] gramme *m*. -**2.** BOT [plant] pois *m*; [seed] pois *m*, graine *f* de pois; **~ flour** farine *f* de pois chiches.

gram atom *n* atome-gramme *m*.

gramineous [grə'mɪnɪəs] *adj* BOT graminée.

grammar ['græməʳ] *n* -**1.** LING grammaire *f*; **that's not very good ~** ce n'est pas très correct du point de vue grammatical. -**2.** [book] grammaire *f*; **a German ~** une grammaire OR un livre de grammaire allemande.

grammarian [grə'meərɪən] *n* grammairien *m*, -enne *f*.

grammar school *n* [in UK] *type d'école secondaire*; [in US] *école primaire*.

GRAMMAR SCHOOL:
En Grande-Bretagne, ce terme désigne une école secondaire recevant une aide de l'État mais pouvant être privée, réputée dispenser un enseignement de qualité de type traditionnel et préparant aux études supérieures. L'admission se fait sur concours («eleven-plus») ou sur dossier. Moins de cinq pour cent des élèves du pays fréquentent ce type d'école.

grammatical [grə'mætɪkl] *adj* grammatical.

grammaticality [grəˌmætɪ'kælətɪ] *n* grammaticalité *f*.

grammatically [grə'mætɪklɪ] *adv* grammaticalement, du point de vue grammatical.

grammaticalness [grə'mætɪkəlnɪs] = **grammaticality**.

gramme [græm] = **gram 1**.

gram molecule *n* molécule-gramme *f*.

Grammy ['græmɪ] *n*: **~ (award)** *distinction récompensant les meilleures œuvres musicales américaines de l'année (classique exclu)*.

gramophone ['græməfəʊn] *Br dated* ◇ *n* gramophone *m*, phonographe *m*.

◇ *comp*: **~ needle** aiguille *f* de phonographe OR de gramophone; **~ record** disque *m*.

gramps *inf* [græmps] *n* grand-père *m*, papy *m*, pépé *m*.

grampus ['græmpəs] *n* épaulard *m*, orque *f*.

gran *inf* [græn] *n esp Br* grand-mère *f*, mamie *f*, mémé *f*.

Granada [grə'nɑːdə] *pr n* Grenade.

granary ['grænərɪ] ◇ *n* grenier *m* à blé, silo *m* (à céréales).

◇ *comp*: **~ bread**, **~ loaf** pain *m* aux céréales.

grand [grænd] ◇ *adj* -**1.** [impressive - house] magnifique; [- style] grand, noble; [- music, occasion] grand; [pretentious, self-important] suffisant, prétentieux; [dignified, majestic] majestueux, digne; **to do sthg in ~ style** faire qqch en grande pompe; **to live in ~ style** mener la grande vie; **she likes to do things on a ~ scale** elle aime faire les choses en grand; **that dress is a bit too ~ for me** cette robe est un peu trop chic pour moi ❑ **the Grand Old Man** *surnom de William Gladstone*. -**2.** *inf Br dated* OR *dial* [wonderful] super; **I had a ~ time last night** je me suis super bien amusé hier soir. -**3.** *phr*: **that comes to a ~ total of £536** ça fait en tout 536 livres.

◇ *n* *inf Br* mille livres *fpl*; *Am* mille dollars *mpl*.

grandad *inf* ['grændæd] *n* grand-père *m*, pépé *m*, papy *m*.

grandaddy *inf* [ˌgræn'dædɪ] *n* -**1.** = **grandad**. -**2.** [most ancient] ancêtre *m*; **it's the ~ of them all** c'est leur ancêtre à tous.

Grand Canary *pr n* Grande Canarie *f*; **in ~** à la Grande Canarie.

Grand Canyon *pr n*: **the ~** le Grand Canyon.

grandchild ['grændtʃaɪld] (*pl* **grandchildren** [-ˌtʃɪldrən]) *n* petit-fils *m*, petite-fille *f*; **is it your first ~?** vous étiez déjà grand-père/grand-mère?; **she has six grandchildren** elle a six petits-enfants.

granddad *inf* ['grændæd] = **grandad**.

granddaddy *inf* [ˌgræn'dædɪ] = **grandaddy**.

granddaughter ['grænˌdɔːtəʳ] *n* petite-fille *f*.

grand duchess *n* grande-duchesse *f*.

grand duchy *n* grand-duché *m*.

grand duke *n* grand-duc *m*.

grandee [græn'diː] *n* grand *m* d'Espagne.

grandeur ['grændʒəʳ] *n* [of person] grandeur *f*, noblesse *f*; [of building, scenery] splendeur *f*, magnificence *f*; **an air of ~** un air de grandeur.

grandfather ['grændˌfɑːðəʳ] *n* grand-père *m*.

grandfather clause *n aux États-Unis, clause de la constitution de plusieurs États du sud qui, jusqu'en 1915, n'accordait le droit de vote qu'à ceux dont un parent votait avant le 1er janvier 1861, excluant ainsi les Noirs puisqu'ils n'étaient pas encore affranchis à cette date*.

grandfather clock *n* horloge *f* (de parquet).

grandfatherly ['grændˌfɑːðəlɪ] *adj* de grand-père.

grandiloquence [græn'dɪləkwəns] *n fml* grandiloquence *f*.

grandiloquent [græn'dɪləkwənt] *adj fml* grandiloquent.

grandiose ['grændɪəʊz] *adj pej* [building, style, plan] grandiose.

grand jury *n* [in US] jury *m* d'accusation.

grand larceny *n Am* vol *m* qualifié.

grandly ['grændlɪ] *adv* [behave, say] avec grandeur; [live] avec faste; [dress] avec panache.

grandma *inf* ['grænmɑː], **grandmama** *inf* ['grænməˌmɑː] *n* grand-mère *f*, mémé *f*, mamie *f*.

grandmaster ['grændˌmɑːstəʳ] *n* [of chess] grand maître *m*.

Grand Master *n* [of masonic lodge] Grand Maître *m*.

grandmother ['grænˌmʌðəʳ] *n* grand-mère *f*.

grandmother clock *n* petite horloge *f*.
grandmotherly ['græn,mʌðəlɪ] *adj* de grand-mère.
Grand National *pr n*: the ~ *la plus importante course d'obstacles de Grande-Bretagne, qui se déroule à Aintree, dans la banlieue de Liverpool*.
grandnephew ['græn,nefju:] *n* petit-neveu *m*.
grandness ['grændnɪs] *n* [of behaviour] grandeur *f*, noblesse *f*; [of lifestyle] faste *m*; [of appearance] panache *m*.
grandniece ['grænni:s] *n* petite-nièce *f*.
grand opera *n* grand opéra *m*.
grandpa *inf* ['grænpɑ:], **grandpapa** *inf* ['grænpə,pɑ:] = **grandad**.
grandparent ['græn,peərənt] *n*: my ~s mes grands-parents *mpl*.
grand piano *n* piano *m* à queue.
grand prix *n* grand prix *m*; ~ racing course *f* de grand prix; last year's ~ winner le vainqueur du dernier grand prix.
grandsire ['græn,saɪə^r] *n arch* OR *lit* [grandfather] grand-père *m*, aïeul *m*; [forefather] aïeul *m*.
grand slam *n* grand chelem *m*.
grandson ['grænsʌn] *n* petit-fils *m*.
grandstand ['grændstænd] ◇ *n* tribune *f*.
◇ *vi Am* faire l'intéressant.
grandstand view *n*: to have a ~ (of sthg) être aux premières loges (pour voir qqch).
grand tour *n*: she did OR went on a ~ of Italy *inf* elle a fait OR visité toute l'Italie ❑ the Grand Tour le tour d'Europe.
grand vizier *n* HIST Grand Vizir *m*.
grange [greɪndʒ] *n* -**1.** *Br* [country house] manoir *m*; [farmhouse] ferme *f*. -**2.** *Am* [farm] ferme *f*. -**3.** *arch* [granary] grenier *m* à blé, grange *f*.
granger ['greɪndʒə^r] *n Am* fermier *m*.
granite ['grænɪt] ◇ *n* granit *m*, granite *m*.
◇ *comp* de granit OR granite.
granitic [græ'nɪtɪk] *adj* granitique, graniteux.
granny *inf*, **grannie** *inf* ['grænɪ] *n* grand-mère *f*, mamie *f*, mémé *f*.
granny bond *inf n Br type d'obligation visant le marché des retraités*.
granny dumping *n abandon d'une personne âgée qu'on a à charge*.
granny flat *n Br* appartement *m* indépendant *(dans une maison)*.
granny knot *n* nœud *m* de vache.
Granny Smith *n* granny-smith *f inv*.
granola [grə'nəʊlə] *n Am* muesli *m*.
grant [grɑ:nt] ◇ *vt* -**1.** [permission, wish] accorder; [request] accorder, accéder à; [goal, point] SPORT accorder; [credit, loan, pension] accorder; [charter, favour, privilege, right] accorder, octroyer, concéder; [property] céder; to ~ sb permission to do sthg accorder à qqn l'autorisation de faire qqch; to ~ sb their request accéder à la requête de qqn; God ~ you good fortune *lit* que Dieu vous protège. -**2.** [accept as true] accorder, admettre, concéder; ~ed, he's not very intelligent, but... d'accord, il n'est pas très intelligent, mais...; will you at least ~ that he is honest? admettrez-vous au moins qu'il est honnête?; I ~ you I made an error of judgement je vous accorde que j'ai fait une erreur de jugement; I'll ~ you that point je vous concède ce point; ~ed! d'accord!, soit! -**3.** *phr*: to take sthg for ~ed considérer que qqch va de soi, tenir qqch pour certain OR établi; you seem to take it for ~ed he'll agree/help you vous semblez convaincu qu'il sera d'accord/vous aidera; to take sb for ~ed ne plus faire cas de qqn; he takes her for ~ed il la traite comme si elle n'existait pas; you take me too much for ~ed vous ne vous rendez pas compte de tout ce que je fais pour vous.
◇ *n* -**1.** [money given] subvention *f*, allocation *f*; [to student] bourse *f*. -**2.** [transfer - of property] cession *f*; [- of land] concession *f*; [permission] octroi *m*; ~ of probate validation *f* OR homologation *f* d'un testament.
grant-aided *adj* = **grant-maintained**.
grant-in-aid *n* subvention *f (de l'État)*.
grant-maintained *adj* subventionné *(par l'État)*; ~ school école privée *f* subventionnée *(acceptant en échange un droit de regard de l'État sur la gestion de ses affaires)*.
grantor [grɑ:n'tɔ:^r] *n* cessionnaire *mf*.
granular ['grænjʊlə^r] *adj* [surface] granuleux, granulaire; [structure] grenu.
granulate ['grænjʊleɪt] *vt* [lead, powder, tin] granuler; [salt, sugar] grener, grainer; [surface] grener, greneler, rendre grenu.
granulated sugar ['grænjʊleɪtɪd] *n* sucre *m* semoule.
granulation [,grænjʊ'leɪʃn] *n* [texture] granulation *f*; [action] granulation *f*, grenage *m*.
granule ['grænju:l] *n* granule *m*.
grape [greɪp] *n* -**1.** [fruit] grain *m* de raisin; black/white ~s du raisin noir/blanc ❑ 'The Grapes of Wrath' *Steinbeck* 'les Raisins de la colère'. -**2.** *(U)* = **grapeshot**.
grapefruit ['greɪpfru:t] *n* pamplemousse *m or f*.
grape harvest *n* vendanges *fpl*.
grape hyacinth *n* muscari *m*.
grape juice *n* jus *m* de raisin.
grapeshot ['greɪpʃɒt] *n* mitraille *f*.
grapevine ['greɪpvaɪn] *n* vigne *f*; to hear sthg through OR on the ~ entendre dire qqch.
grapey ['greɪpɪ] = **grapy**.
graph [grɑ:f] ◇ *n* -**1.** [diagram] graphique *m*, courbe *f*. -**2.** LING graphie *f*.
◇ *vt* mettre en graphique, tracer.
grapheme ['græfi:m] *n* LING graphème *m*.
graphic ['græfɪk] *adj* -**1.** MATH graphique. -**2.** [vivid] imagé.
◆ **graphics** ◇ *n (U)* [drawing] art *m* graphique.
◇ *npl* MATH (utilisation *f* des) graphiques *mpl*; [drawings] représentations *fpl* graphiques; COMPUT infographie *f*.
graphical ['græfɪkl] = **graphic**.
graphically ['græfɪklɪ] *adv* -**1.** MATH graphiquement. -**2.** [vividly] de façon très imagée.
graphic arts *npl* arts *mpl* graphiques.
graphic design *n* conception *f* graphique.
graphic designer *n* graphiste *mf*, maquettiste *mf*.
graphic display *n* graphisme *m*.
graphic equalizer *n* égaliseur *m* graphique.
graphics card ['græfɪks-] *n* COMPUT carte *f* graphique.
graphic solution *n* analyse *f* OR évaluation *f* graphique.
graphite ['græfaɪt] *n* graphite *m*, plombagine *f*, mine *f* de plomb.
graphologist [græ'fɒlədʒɪst] *n* graphologue *mf*.
graphology [græ'fɒlədʒɪ] *n* graphologie *f*.
graph paper *n* papier *m* quadrillé; [in millimetres] papier *m* millimétré.
grapnel ['græpnl] *n* grappin *m*.
grapple ['græpl] ◇ *n* TECH grappin *m*.
◇ *vt* -**1.** TECH saisir avec un grappin. -**2.** *Am* [person]: to ~ sb saisir qqn contre soi.
◇ *vi* -**1.** [physically]: to ~ with sb en venir aux mains avec qqn. -**2.** *fig*: to ~ with a problem être aux prises avec un problème.
grappling iron ['græplɪŋ-] = **grapnel**.
grapy ['greɪpɪ] *adj* [wine] fruité.
grasp [grɑ:sp] ◇ *vt* -**1.** [physically] saisir; to ~ (hold of) sthg saisir qqch; to ~ (hold of) sb's hand saisir la main de qqn ‖ [opportunity] saisir; [power] se saisir de, s'emparer de; to ~ the nettle prendre le taureau par les cornes. -**2.** [understand] saisir, comprendre; I didn't quite ~ what she meant je n'ai pas bien compris OR saisi ce qu'elle a voulu dire.
◇ *n* -**1.** [grip] (forte) poigne *f*; [action of holding] prise *f*, étreinte *f*; to have sb in one's ~ *fig* avoir OR tenir qqn en son pouvoir; to have sthg in one's ~ avoir prise sur qqch. -**2.** *fig* [reach] portée *f*; within sb's ~ à la portée de qqn; beyond sb's ~ hors de (la) portée de qqn; success is now within her ~ le succès est désormais à sa portée. -**3.** [understanding] compréhension *f*; she has a thorough ~ of the subject elle a une connaissance approfondie de la question. -**4.** [handle] poignée *f*.
◆ **grasp at** *vt insep* [attempt to seize] chercher à saisir, essayer de saisir; [accept eagerly] saisir; to ~ at an opportunity sauter sur OR saisir l'occasion ❑ to ~ at straws se raccrocher à n'importe quoi.
grasping ['grɑ:spɪŋ] *adj* avare, avide.
grass [grɑ:s] ◇ *n* -**1.** [gen] herbe *f*; a blade of ~ un brin d'herbe ‖ [lawn] pelouse *f*, gazon *m*; 'keep off the ~' 'défense de marcher sur la pelouse', 'pelouse interdite'; to cut OR to mow the ~ tondre la pelouse; to put a field down to OR under ~ mettre en pré OR enherber un champ ❑ to put out to ~: to put cattle/sheep out to ~ mettre le bétail/les moutons au pré; to put sb out to ~ mettre qqn au repos; he doesn't let the ~ grow under his feet il ne perd pas de temps; the ~ is always greener (on the other side of the fence) *prov* on n'est jamais content de son sort, on jalouse toujours le sort du voisin. -**2.** BOT: ~es graminées *fpl*. -**3.** ▽ [marijuana] herbe *f*. -**4.** ▽ *Br* [informer] mouchard *m*, indic *m*.
◇ *vt* -**1.** to ~ (over) [field] enherber, mettre en pré; [garden] gazonner, engazonner. -**2.** *Am* [animals] mettre au vert. -**3.** TEX herber, blanchir au pré.
◇ *vi* ▽ *Br* cafarder; to ~ on sb donner OR vendre qqn.
grass court *n* court *m* (en gazon).
grasshopper ['grɑ:s,hɒpə^r] *n* sauterelle *f*, grillon *m*.
grassland ['grɑ:slænd] *n* prairie *f*, pré *m*.
grassless ['grɑ:slɪs] *adj* sans herbe.
grass roots POL ◇ *npl*: the ~ la base.
◇ *comp*: at (the) ~ level au niveau de la base; ~ opposition/support résistance *f*/soutien *m* de la base.
grass skirt *n* pagne *m (de feuilles)*.
grass snake *n* couleuvre *f*.
grass widow *n femme séparée de son mari*.
grass widower *n homme séparé de sa femme*.
grassy ['grɑ:sɪ] *adj* herbu, herbeux.
grate [greɪt] ◇ *n* [fireplace] foyer *m*, âtre *m*; [for holding coal] grille *f* de foyer.
◇ *vt* -**1.** CULIN râper. -**2.** [chalk, metal] faire grincer.
◇ *vi* -**1.** [machine, metal] grincer; to ~ on the ears écorcher les oreilles. -**2.** *fig*: the baby's crying began to ~ les pleurs du bébé ont commencé à l'agacer; his behaviour ~s after a while son comportement est agaçant au bout d'un moment.
grateful ['greɪtfʊl] *adj* reconnaissant; to be ~ towards OR to sb for sthg être reconnaissant envers qqn de qqch; I am extremely ~ to you je vous suis extrêmement reconnaissant; I am ~ for your help je vous suis reconnaissant de votre aide; I would be most OR very ~ if you would help me je vous serais très reconnaissant de m'aider; a ~ letter une lettre de remerciements; with ~ thanks avec toute ma reconnaissance, avec mes sincères remerciements; be ~ for what you've got estime-toi heureux avec ce que tu as.
gratefully ['greɪtfʊlɪ] *adv* avec reconnaissance OR gratitude.
gratefulness ['greɪtfʊlnɪs] *n* reconnaissance *f*, gratitude *f*.
grater ['greɪtə^r] *n* râpe *f*; cheese ~ râpe *f* à fromage.
graticule ['grætɪkju:l] *n* [on map] quadrillage *m* cartographique; [in microscope, telescope] croisée *f* de fils.
gratification [,grætɪfɪ'keɪʃn] *n* [state or action] satisfaction *f*, plaisir *m*; PSYCH gratification *f*; he has the ~ of knowing that... il a la satisfaction OR le plaisir de savoir que...; I noticed to my ~ that... à ma grande satisfaction, j'ai remarqué que...; sexual ~ plaisir *m* sexuel, satisfaction *f* sexuelle.

gratify ['grætɪfaɪ] *vt* -**1.** [person] faire plaisir à, être agréable à; it gratified him OR he was gratified to learn that... ça lui a fait plaisir OR lui a été agréable d'apprendre que...; I was gratified with OR at the result j'ai été très content OR satisfait du résultat. -**2.** [whim, wish] satisfaire.

gratifying ['grætɪfaɪɪŋ] *adj* agréable, plaisant; PSYCH gratifiant; it's ~ to know that... c'est agréable OR ça fait plaisir de savoir que...

gratifyingly ['grætɪfaɪɪŋlɪ] *adv* [with pleasure] agréablement; [with attention] de manière flatteuse.

grating ['greɪtɪŋ] ◇ *n* grille *f*, grillage *m*.
◇ *adj* [irritating] agaçant, irritant, énervant; [sound] grinçant, discordant; [voice] discordant.

gratis ['grætɪs] ◇ *adj* gratuit.
◇ *adv* gratuitement.

gratitude ['grætɪtju:d] *n* gratitude *f*, reconnaissance *f*; to show/to express one's ~ towards sb for sthg témoigner/exprimer sa gratitude envers qqn pour qqch.

gratuitous [grə'tju:ɪtəs] *adj* -**1.** [unjustified] gratuit, sans motif, injustifié; ~ violence violence *f* gratuite. -**2.** *arch* [costing nothing] gratuit.

gratuitously [grə'tju:ɪtəslɪ] *adv* -**1.** [without good reason] gratuitement, sans motif. -**2.** *arch* [at no charge] gracieusement, gratuitement.

gratuity [grə'tju:ətɪ] *n* -**1.** *fml* [tip] gratification *f*, pourboire *m*. -**2.** *Br* [payment to employee] prime *f*; MIL peine *f* de démobilisation.

grave[1] [greɪv] ◇ *n* [hole] fosse *f*; [burial place] tombe *f*; when I'm in my ~ quand je serai mort et enterré; a mass ~ une fosse commune; from beyond the ~ d'outre-tombe ❑ to turn in one's ~ se retourner dans sa tombe; somebody has just walked over my ~ j'ai le frisson.
◇ *adj* grave, sérieux.

grave[2] [grɑ:v] LING ◇ *n* accent *m* grave.
◇ *adj* grave.

gravedigger ['greɪv,dɪgəʳ] *n* fossoyeur *m*.

gravel ['grævl] (*Br pt* & *pp* gravelled, *cont* gravelling, *Am pt* & *pp* graveled, *cont* graveling)
◇ *n* gravier *m*; [finer] gravillon *m*; MED gravelle *f*.
◇ *vt* gravillonner, répandre du gravier sur.
◇ *comp*: ~ path chemin *m* de gravier; ~ pit gravière *f*, carrière *f* de gravier.

gravelled *Br*, **graveled** *Am* ['grævld] *adj* couvert de gravier.

gravelly ['grævəlɪ] *adj* -**1.** [like or containing gravel] graveleux; [road] de gravier; [riverbed] caillouteux. -**2.** [voice] rauque, râpeux.

gravely ['greɪvlɪ] *adv* -**1.** [speak] gravement, sérieusement. -**2.** [as intensifier]: she is ~ ill/wounded elle est gravement malade/grièvement blessée.

graven ['greɪvn] *adj arch* OR *lit*: ~ on my memory gravé dans ma mémoire.

graveness ['greɪvnɪs] *n* gravité *f*.

graven image *n* RELIG idole *f*, image *f*.

grave robber [greɪv-] *n* voleur *m* de cadavres *(qui les déterre et les vend pour dissection)*.

graveside ['greɪvsaɪd] *n*: at sb's ~ sur la tombe de qqn.

gravestone ['greɪvstəʊn] *n* pierre *f* tombale.

graveyard ['greɪvjɑ:d] *n literal* & *fig* cimetière *m*.

gravid ['grævɪd] *adj* gravide.

gravimetric(al) [,grævɪ'metrɪk(l)] *adj* gravimétrique.

graving dock ['greɪvɪŋ-] *n* NAUT bassin *m* de radoub.

gravitate ['grævɪteɪt] *vi* graviter; to ~ towards sthg/sb graviter vers qqch/qqn; many young people ~ to the big cities beaucoup de jeunes sont attirés par les grandes villes.

gravitation [,grævɪ'teɪʃn] *n* gravitation *f*.

gravitational [,grævɪ'teɪʃənl] *adj* gravitationnel, de gravitation.

gravitational field *n* champ *m* de gravitation.

gravitational force *n* force *f* de gravitation OR gravitationnelle.

gravity ['grævətɪ] *n* -**1.** [seriousness] gravité *f*; I don't think you appreciate the ~ of the situation je n'ai pas l'impression que tu te rendes compte de OR que tu réalises la gravité de la situation. -**2.** PHYS [force] pesanteur *f*; [phenomenon] gravitation *f*; the law of ~ la loi de la pesanteur.

gravity feed *n* alimentation *f* par gravité.

gravy ['greɪvɪ] *n* -**1.** CULIN sauce *f* *(au jus de viande)*. -**2.** ▽ *Am* [easy money] bénef *m*; it's ~ [easy] c'est du gâteau.

gravy boat *n* saucière *f*.

gravy train *inf n* assiette *f* au beurre; to get on the ~ être à la recherche d'un bon filon.

gray *etc Am* = **grey**.

grayling ['greɪlɪŋ] *n* [fish] ombre *m*.

graze [greɪz] ◇ *vi* [animals] brouter, paître, pâturer.
◇ *vt* -**1.** [touch lightly] frôler, effleurer, raser; the boat just ~d the bottom le bateau a effleuré le fond. -**2.** [skin] érafler, écorcher; the bullet ~d his cheek la balle lui a éraflé la joue; she ~d her elbow on the wall elle s'est écorché le coude sur le mur. -**3.** [animals] faire paître; [grass] brouter, paître; [field] pâturer.
◇ *n* écorchure *f*, éraflure *f*; it's just a ~ c'est juste un peu écorché.

grazier ['greɪzjəʳ] *n* herbager *m*.

grazing ['greɪzɪŋ] *n* [grass for animals] pâturage *m*; [land] pâture *f*, pâturage *m*.

grease [gri:s] ◇ *n* [gen] graisse *f*; [lubricant] AUT graisse *f*, lubrifiant *m*; [used lubricant] cambouis *m*; [dirt] crasse *f*; to remove ~ from sthg dégraisser qqch; a collar covered in ~ un col couvert de crasse.
◇ *vt* [gen] graisser; AUT graisser, lubrifier; to ~ sb's palm *inf* graisser la patte à qqn; like ~d lightning en quatrième vitesse, à toute allure.

grease gun *n* (pistolet *m*) graisseur *m*, pompe *f* à graisse.

grease monkey *inf n* mécano *m*.

grease nipple *n* graisseur *m*.

greasepaint ['gri:speɪnt] *n* THEAT fard *m* (gras); a stick of ~ un crayon gras.

greaseproof ['gri:spru:f] *adj Br* imperméable à la graisse; ~ paper CULIN papier *m* sulfurisé.

greaser *inf* ['gri:səʳ] *n* -**1.** [mechanic] graisseur *m*, mécano *m*. -**2.** *Br* [rocker] rocker *m*. -**3.** ▼ *Am* *terme injurieux désignant une personne d'origine latino-américaine*.

grease-stained *adj* taché de graisse, graisseux.

greasiness ['gri:zɪnɪs] *n* -**1.** [gen] état *m* graisseux, nature *f* graisseuse; [of cosmetics] onctuosité *f*; [of hair, hands] nature *f* grasse. -**2.** [of road] surface *f* glissante.

greasy ['gri:zɪ] *adj* -**1.** [food, substance] graisseux, gras; [tools] graisseux; [cosmetics, hair, hands] gras; the ~ pole SPORT & *fig* le mât de cocagne. -**2.** [pavement, road] gras, glissant. -**3.** [clothes - dirty] crasseux, poisseux; [- covered in grease marks] taché de graisse, plein de graisse. -**4.** [obsequious] obséquieux; a ~ manner des manières obséquieuses; a ~ smile un sourire obséquieux.

greasy spoon *inf n* gargote *f*.

great [greɪt] (*compar* greater, *superl* greatest)
◇ *adj* -**1.** [in size, scale] grand; the ~ fire of London le grand incendie de Londres; he made a ~ effort to be nice il a fait un gros effort pour être agréable. -**2.** [in degree]: a ~ friend un grand ami; they're ~ friends ce sont de grands amis; ~ ignorance une grande ignorance, une ignorance complète; there's ~ ignorance about the problem les gens ne sont pas conscients du problème; ~ willpower une grande OR forte volonté; she's got ~ willpower elle est très volontaire; to my ~ satisfaction à ma grande satisfaction; a ~ surprise une grande surprise; with ~ care avec grand soin, avec beaucoup de soin; with ~ pleasure avec grand plaisir; to be in ~ pain souffrir (beaucoup); to have a ~ opinion of avoir une haute opinion de; I have a ~ liking for that country j'aime beaucoup ce pays. -**3.** [in quantity]: a ~ quantity of une grande quantité de; a ~ number of un grand nombre de; a ~ crowd une grande OR grosse foule, une foule nombreuse; to a ~ extent en grande partie; the ~ majority la grande majorité. -**4.** [important - person, event]: a ~ man un grand homme; Alfred the Great Alfred le Grand; the Great War la Grande Guerre; a ~ poet un grand poète; a ~ lady une grande dame; a ~ moment un grand moment; a ~ occasion une grande occasion. -**5.** [main]: the ~ hall la grande salle, la salle principale; France's ~est footballer le plus grand footballeur français. -**6.** [term of approval]: she has a ~ voice elle a une voix magnifique; he's a ~ guy *inf* c'est un type super OR génial; she's ~! [nice person] elle est super!, je l'adore!; we had a ~ holiday nous avons passé des vacances merveilleuses; what's that film like? — ~! *inf* comment est ce film? — génial!; it would be ~ to have lots of money ce serait super d'avoir beaucoup d'argent; you look ~ tonight! [appearance] tu es magnifique ce soir!; he's coming too — oh, ~ *iron* il vient aussi — oh, génial OR super! -**7.** [keen]: she's a ~ reader elle adore lire, elle lit beaucoup; she's a ~ one for television elle adore la télévision. -**8.** [good at or expert on]: he's ~ at languages il est très doué pour les langues; she's ~ on sculpture elle s'y connaît vraiment en sculpture. -**9.** [in exclamations]: Great Scott! grands dieux! -**10.** ZOOL: the ~ apes les grands singes.
◇ *n*: it's one of the all-time ~s c'est un des plus grands classiques; she's one of the all-time ~s c'est une des plus grandes stars.
◇ *adv* [as intensifier]: a ~ big fish un énorme poisson; an enormous ~ house une maison immense.

great auk *n* manchot *m* royal.

great-aunt *n* grand-tante *f*.

Great Australian Bight *pr n* Grande Baie *f* Australienne.

Great Barrier Reef *pr n*: the ~ la Grande Barrière.

Great Basin *pr n*: the ~ le Grand Bassin.

Great Bear *pr n*: the ~ la Grande Ourse.

Great Bear Lake *pr n* le grand lac de l'Ours.

Great Britain *pr n* Grande-Bretagne *f*; in ~ en Grande-Bretagne.

great circle *n* grand cercle *m*.

greatcoat ['greɪtkəʊt] *n* pardessus *m*, manteau *m*; MIL manteau *m*, capote *f*.

Great Dane *n* danois *m*.

great divide *n*: the ~ [significant point of division] la grande différence.
◆ **Great Divide** *pr n* GEOG: the Great Divide *ligne de partage des montagnes Rocheuses*.

greater ['greɪtəʳ] *compar* → **great**.

Greater Antilles *pl pr n*: the ~ les Grandes Antilles *fpl*.

Greater London *pr n* le Grand Londres.

greatest ['greɪtɪst] *superl* → **great**.

greatest common divisor *n* plus grand commun diviseur *m*.

great-grandchild *n* arrière-petit-fils *m*, arrière-petite-fille *f*; great-grandchildren arrière-petits-enfants *mpl*.

great-granddaughter *n* arrière-petite-fille *f*.

great-grandfather *n* arrière-grand-père *m*.

great-grandmother *n* arrière-grand-mère *f*.

great-grandparents *npl* arrière-grands-parents *mpl*.

great-grandson *n* arrière-petit-fils *m*.

great-great-granddaughter *n* arrière-arrière-petite-fille *f*.

great-great-grandfather *n* arrière-arrière-grand-père *m*.

great-great-grandmother *n* arrière-arrière-grand-mère *f*.

great-great-grandparents *npl* arrière-arrière-grands-parents *mpl*.

great-great-grandson *n* arrière-arrière-petit-fils *m*.

great-hearted *adj lit* au grand cœur, magnanime.

Great Lakes *pl pr n*: the ~ les Grands Lacs *mpl*.

greatly ['greɪtlɪ] *adv* très, beaucoup, fortement; I was ~ impressed by her work j'ai été très impressionné par son travail, son travail m'a beaucoup impressionné; ~ improved beaucoup amélioré; you'll be ~ missed vous nous manquerez beaucoup; ~ irritated très irrité; ~ surprised très OR énormément surpris.

great-nephew *n* petit-neveu *m*.

greatness ['greɪtnɪs] *n* -**1.** [size] grandeur *f*, énormité *f*, immensité *f*; [intensity] intensité *f*. -**2.** [eminence] grandeur *f*, importance *f*; he never achieved ~ as an artist il n'est jamais devenu un grand artiste.

great-niece *n* petite-nièce *f*.

great organ *n* grand orgue *m*; [in church] grandes orgues *fpl*.

Great Plains *pl pr n*: the ~ les Grandes Plaines *fpl*.

great power *n* grande puissance *f*; the Great Powers les grandes puissances.

Great Salt Lake *pr n*: the ~ le Grand Lac Salé.

great tit *n* mésange *f* charbonnière.

great-uncle *n* grand-oncle *m*.

Great Wall of China *pr n*: the ~ la Grande Muraille (de Chine).

Great War *n*: the ~ la Grande Guerre, la guerre de 14 OR de 14-18.

grebe [gri:b] *n* grèbe *m*.

Grecian ['gri:ʃn] ◇ *adj* grec; a ~ profile un profil grec.
◇ *n* Grec *m*, Grecque *f*.

Greco ['grekəʊ] *pr n*: El ~ le Greco; a painting by El ~ un tableau du Greco.

Greco- [ˌgri:kəʊ] = **Graeco-**.

Greece [gri:s] *pr n* Grèce *f*; in ~ en Grèce.

greed [gri:d] *n* [for fame, power, wealth] avidité *f*; [for food] gloutonnerie *f*.

greedily ['gri:dɪlɪ] *adv* [gen] avidement; [consume food] gloutonnement, voracement.

greediness ['gri:dɪnɪs] = **greed**.

greedy ['gri:dɪ] *adj* [for food] glouton, gourmand; [for fame, power, wealth] avide; ~ for money avide d'argent; ~ for power avide de pouvoir; don't be so ~! ne sois pas si gourmand!

greedy-guts *inf n* glouton *m*, -onne *f*, goinfre *mf*.

Greek [gri:k] ◇ *n* -**1.** [person] Grec *m*, Grecque *f*; 'Zorba the ~' *Kazantzakis* 'Alexis Zorba'. -**2.** LING grec *m*; ancient ~ grec ancien; modern ~ grec moderne; it's all ~ to me *inf* tout ça, c'est du chinois OR de l'hébreu pour moi.
◇ *adj* grec; the ~ Islands les îles *fpl* grecques.

Greek cross *n* croix *f* grecque.

Greek Orthodox ◇ *n* orthodoxe grec *m*, orthodoxe grecque *f*.
◇ *comp*: the ~ Church l'Église *f* orthodoxe grecque.

green [gri:n] ◇ *adj* -**1.** [colour] vert; [field, valley] vert, verdoyant; the wall was painted ~ le mur était peint en vert; to go OR to turn ~ [tree] devenir vert, verdir; [traffic light] passer au vert; [person] devenir blême, blêmir; to be OR to go ~ with envy être vert de jalousie ☐ as ~ as grass vert cru; Green Shield stamps *timbres donnant droit à des cadeaux, distribués par certains magasins en fonction du montant des achats*; ~ wellies *inf bottes de caoutchouc vertes (le terme évoque les classes bourgeoises ou aristocratiques habitant à la campagne)*. -**2.** [unripe fruit] vert, pas mûr; [undried timber] vert; [unsmoked bacon] frais, non fumé. -**3.** [naive] naïf; [inexperienced] inexpérimenté; I'm not as ~ as I might seem je ne suis pas aussi naïf que j'en ai l'air; a ~ young reporter un jeune reporter inexpérimenté. -**4.** [ecological] écologique, vert; to go ~ virer écolo. -**5.** *lit* [alive] vivant, vivace; to keep sb's memory ~ chérir la mémoire de qqn.
◇ *n* -**1.** [colour] vert *m*; ~ suits you le vert te va bien; the girl in ~ la fille en vert; dressed in ~ habillé de OR en vert. -**2.** [grassy patch] pelouse *f*, gazon *m*; village ~ ≃ place *f* du village, ≃ terrain *m* communal. -**3.** *Br*: (bowling) ~ ≃ terrain *m* de boules *(sur gazon)*. -**4.** GOLF green *m*; on the ~ sur le green.
◆ **Green** *adj Br* ECON & POL vert; the Green party le parti écologiste, les Verts *mpl*; Green politics la politique des Verts.
◆ **greens** *npl* -**1.** [vegetables] légumes *mpl* verts; you should eat more ~s tu devrais manger plus de légumes verts. -**2.** *Am* [foliage] feuillage *m (dans un bouquet)*.
◆ **Greens** *npl Br* POL: the Greens les Verts *mpl*, les écologistes *mpl*.

greenback *inf* ['gri:nbæk] *n Am* dollar *m*.

green bean *n* haricot *m* vert.

green belt *n* ceinture *f* verte.

Green Beret *n* marine *m*; the ~s les bérets *mpl* verts.

green card *n* -**1.** [insurance] carte *f* verte *(prouvant qu'un véhicule est assuré pour un voyage à l'étranger)*. -**2.** [work permit] carte *f* de séjour *(temporaire, aux États-Unis)*.

green cross code *n Br*: the ~ le code de sécurité routière *(pour apprendre aux piétons à traverser la route avec moins de risques d'accident)*.

greenery ['gri:nərɪ] *n* verdure *f*.

green-eyed *adj* aux yeux verts; [jealous] jaloux.

greenfield ['gri:nfi:ld] *comp*: ~ site *terrain jamais construit*.

greenfinch ['gri:nfɪntʃ] *n* verdier *m*.

green-fingered [-'fɪŋgəd] *adj Br* qui a la main verte.

green fingers *npl Br*: to have ~ avoir le pouce vert, avoir la main verte.

greenfly ['gri:nflaɪ] *n* puceron *m* (vert).

greengage ['gri:ngeɪdʒ] *n* reine-claude *f*.

greengrocer ['gri:nˌgrəʊsəʳ] *n Br* marchand *m* de fruits et légumes; to go to the ~'s aller chez le marchand de fruits et légumes.

Greenham Common ['gri:nəm-] *pr n village en Angleterre*.

GREENHAM COMMON:
La base aérienne qui se trouve près de ce village a été le siège de nombreuses manifestations (menées notamment par des groupes de femmes) hostiles aux armements nucléaires.

---

greenhorn *inf* ['gri:nhɔ:n] *n* blanc-bec *m*.

greenhouse ['gri:nhaʊs, *pl* -haʊzɪz] ◇ *n* serre *f*.
◇ *comp*: ~ plants plantes *fpl* de serre; ~ gases gaz *mpl* à effet de serre.

greenhouse effect *n*: the ~ l'effet *m* de serre.

greenish ['gri:nɪʃ] *adj* tirant sur le vert; *pej* verdâtre.

greenkeeper ['gri:nˌki:pəʳ] *n personne qui entretient les pelouses des terrains de sport*.

Greenland ['grinlənd] *pr n* Groenland *m*; in ~ au Groenland.

Greenlander ['gri:nləndəʳ] *n* Groenlandais *m*, -e *f*.

green light *n literal* & *fig* feu *m* vert; to give the ~ to sb/sthg donner le feu vert à qqn/pour qqch; to get the ~ from sb obtenir le feu vert de qqn.

greenmail ['gri:nmeɪl] *n Am* chantage *m* à coup de dollars.

greenness ['gri:nnɪs] *n* -**1.** [colour] couleur *f* verte, vert *m*; [of field, valley] verdure *f*; [of fruit] verdeur *f*. -**2.** [of person - inexperience] inexpérience *f*, manque *m* d'expérience; [- naivety] naïveté *f*. -**3.** ECON & POL côté *m* écologique.

green onion *n Am* ciboule *f*, cive *f*.

green paper *n* POL *document formulant des propositions destinées à orienter la politique gouvernementale*.

green peas *npl* petits pois *mpl*.

green pepper *n* poivron *m* vert.

green pound *n* ECON livre *f* verte.

greenroom ['gri:nrʊm] *n* THEAT foyer *m* des artistes.

green salad *n* salade *f* (verte).

greenshank ['gri:nʃæŋk] *n* chevalier *m*.

greenstick fracture *n* MED fracture *f* incomplète.

greenstuff ['gri:nstʌf] *n* -**1.** *(U)* [vegetables] légumes *mpl* verts. -**2.** *inf Am* [money] fric.

greensward ['gri:nswɔ:d] *n arch* OR *lit* pelouse *f*, gazon *m*, tapis *m* de verdure.

green tea *n* thé *m* vert.

green thumb *Am* = **green fingers**.

green-thumbed [-'θʌmd] *Am* = **green-fingered**.

green vegetables *npl* légumes *mpl* verts.

Greenwich Mean Time ['grenɪdʒ-] *n* heure *f* (du méridien) de Greenwich.

greenwood ['gri:nwʊd] *n arch* forêt *f* verdoyante.

green woodpecker *n* pivert *m*, pic-vert *m*.

greet [gri:t] ◇ *vt* [meet, welcome] saluer, accueillir; to ~ sb with a wave of the hand saluer qqn de la main; to ~ sb/sthg with open arms accueillir qqn/qqch les bras ouverts; the news was ~ed with a sigh of relief les nouvelles furent accueillies avec un soupir de soulagement; a strange sound ~ed our ears un son étrange est parvenu à nos oreilles; the sight that ~ed her (eyes) defied description la scène qui s'offrit à ses regards défiait toute description.
◇ *vi Scot* [weep] pleurer.
◇ *n Scot*: to have a ~ pleurer.

greeting ['gri:tɪŋ] *n* salut *m*, salutation *f*; [welcome] accueil *m*.
◆ **greetings** *npl* [good wishes] compliments *mpl*, salutations *fpl*; to send one's ~s to sb envoyer son bon souvenir OR le bonjour à qqn; birthday ~s vœux *mpl* d'anniversaire.

greetings card *Br*, **greeting card** *Am n* carte *f* de vœux.

gregarious [grɪ'geərɪəs] *adj* [animal, bird] grégaire; [person] sociable.

gregariousness [grɪ'geərɪəsnɪs] *n* [of animal, bird] grégarisme *m*; [of person] sociabilité *f*.

Gregorian [grɪ'gɔ:rɪən] *adj* grégorien.

Gregorian calendar *n*: the ~ le calendrier grégorien.

Gregorian chant *n* chant *m* grégorien.

Gregory ['gregərɪ] *pr n*: Saint ~ saint Grégoire; ~ the Great Grégoire le Grand.

gremlin *inf* ['gremlɪn] *n hum diablotin malfaisant que l'on dit responsable de défauts mécaniques ou d'erreurs typographiques*.

Grenada [grə'neɪdə] *pr n* Grenade *f*; in ~ à la Grenade.

grenade [grə'neɪd] *n* MIL grenade *f*.

Grenadian [grə'neɪdɪən] ◇ *n* Grenadin *m*, -e *f*.
◇ *adj* grenadin.

grenadier [ˌgrenə'dɪəʳ] *n* [soldier] grenadier *m*.

Grenadier Guards *pl pr n*: the ~ *régiment d'infanterie de la Garde Royale britannique*.

grenadine ['grenədi:n] *n* grenadine *f*.

Gretna Green ['gretnə-] *pr n village en Écosse*.

GRETNA GREEN:
Le forgeron de ce village écossais fut, jusqu'en 1940, habilité à célébrer les mariages sans formalités juridiques.

---

grew [gru:] *pt* → **grow**.

grey *Br*, **gray** *Am* [greɪ] ◇ *adj* -**1.** [colour, weather] gris; to paint sthg ~ peindre qqch en gris; ~ weather temps gris; ~ skies ciel gris OR couvert; a cold ~ day un jour de froid et de grisaille. -**2.** [hair] gris, grisonnant; to go ~ grisonner; it's enough to make your hair go OR turn ~ il y a de quoi se faire des cheveux blancs. -**3.** [complexion] gris, blême; she looked ~ and ill elle avait un teint gris de malade. -**4.** [life, situation] morne; John leads a very ~ existence John mène une vie très morne.
◇ *n* -**1.** [colour] gris *m*. -**2.** [horse] (cheval *m*) gris *m*.
◇ *vi* [hair] grisonner, devenir gris; Jacques is beginning to ~ at the temples Jacques commence à avoir les tempes grisonnantes.

grey area *n* zone *f* d'incertitude OR de flou; the ~ between right and wrong la frontière indistincte qui sépare le bien du mal.

greybeard *Br*, **graybeard** *Am* ['greɪ,bɪəd] *n lit* vieil homme *m*.

Grey Friar *n* franciscain *m*.

grey-haired *adj* aux cheveux gris, grisonnant.

greyhound ['greɪhaʊnd] *n* lévrier *m*, levrette *f*; ~ racing course *f* de lévriers; a ~ (racing) track un cynodrome.

Greyhound® *pr n*: ~ buses *réseau d'autocars couvrant tous les États-Unis*.

greying *Br*, **graying** *Am* ['greɪɪŋ] *adj* grisonnant.

greyish *Br*, **grayish** *Am* ['greɪɪʃ] *adj* tirant sur le gris; [beard] grisonnant; *pej* grisâtre.

greylag ['greɪlæg] *n*: ~ (goose) oie *f* cendrée.

grey matter *n* matière *f* grise.

grey mullet *n* muge *m*.

greyness *Br*, **grayness** *Am* ['greɪnɪs] *n* [of paint, skin] teinte *f* grise; [of sky, weather] grisaille *f*.

grey seal *n* phoque *m* gris.

grey squirrel *n* écureuil *m* gris, petit-gris *m*.

grey whale *n* baleine *f* grise.

grey wolf *n* loup *m* (gris).

grid [grɪd] ◇ *n* **-1.** [grating] grille *f*, grillage *m*. **-2.** [electrode] grille *f*; *Br* ELEC réseau *m*; the national ~ le réseau (électrique national). **-3.** [on chart, map] grille *f*; [lines on map] quadrillage *m*; the earth's ~ le quadrillage terrestre. **-4.** [in nuclear reactor] grille *f*. **-5.** THEAT gril *m*. **-6.** *Am* AUT zone quadrillée; 'do not enter ~ unless exit is clear' ne pas s'arrêter dans la zone quadrillée.
◇ *comp*: the city was built on a ~ pattern la ville était construite en quadrillé.

gridded ['grɪdɪd] *adj* **-1.** [grating] grillé, grillagé. **-2.** [chart, map] quadrillé.

griddle ['grɪdl] ◇ *n* [iron plate] plaque *f* en fonte; [on top of stove] plaque *f* chauffante.
◇ *vt* cuire sur une plaque *(à galette)*.

griddle cake *n sorte de galette épaisse*.

grid(iron) ['grɪd-] *n* **-1.** CULIN gril *m*. **-2.** THEAT gril *m*. **-3.** *Am* [game] football *m* américain; [football] terrain *m* de football.

gridlock ['grɪdlɒk] *n Am literal* embouteillage *m*; *fig* blocage *m*.

grid marking *n* [on charts, maps] repères *mpl* de quadrillage.

grid reference *n* coordonnées *fpl* de la grille.

grief [gri:f] *n* **-1.** [sorrow] chagrin *m*, peine *f*, (grande) tristesse *f*; he was driven almost mad with ~ son chagrin l'a presque rendu fou; to die of ~ mourir de chagrin. **-2.** *phr*: to come to ~ [person] avoir de graves ennuis; [project, venture] échouer, tomber à l'eau. **-3.** [as interjection]: good ~! mon Dieu!, ciel!

grief-stricken *adj* accablé de chagrin OR de douleur, affligé.

grievance ['gri:vns] *n* **-1.** [cause for complaint] grief *m*, sujet *m* de plainte; [complaint] réclamation *f*, revendication *f*; my only ~ (against him) is... le seul grief que j'ai (contre lui), c'est...; the workers put forward a list of ~s les travailleurs ont présenté un cahier de revendications ❑ ~ procedure *procédure permettant aux salariés de faire part de leurs revendications*. **-2.** [grudge]: to nurse a ~ entretenir OR nourrir une rancune OR un ressentiment. **-3.** [injustice] injustice *f*, tort *m*; to redress a ~ redresser un tort OR une injustice. **-4.** [discontent] mécontentement *m*; they voiced their ~s ils ont exprimé leur mécontentement.

grieve [gri:v] ◇ *vt* peiner, chagriner; it ~d me to see him so ill/unhappy ça m'a fait de la peine de le voir si malade/si malheureux; I was ~d to discover that... cela m'a fait beaucoup de peine d'apprendre que..
◇ *vi* [feel grief] avoir de la peine OR du chagrin, être peiné; to ~ at OR over OR about sthg avoir de la peine à cause de qqch || [express grief] pleurer; to ~ for the dead pleurer les morts; the grieving process le (processus de) deuil.

grievous ['gri:vəs] *adj* **-1.** *fml* [causing pain] affreux, cruel, atroce; a ~ loss une perte cruelle. **-2.** *lit* [grave, serious] grave, sérieux; ~ injury des blessures graves; he committed a ~ error il a commis une grave erreur. **-3.** JUR: ~ bodily harm coups *mpl* et blessures *fpl*.

grievously ['gri:vəslɪ] *adv fml* gravement, sérieusement; ~ mistaken tout à fait dans l'erreur; ~ wounded grièvement blessé.

griffin ['grɪfɪn] *n* MYTH griffon *m*.

griffon ['grɪfn] *n* MYTH & ZOOL griffon *m*.

grift▽ [grɪft] *Am* ◇ *n* [graft] corruption *f*; [cunning trickery] escroquerie *f*, filouterie *f*.
◇ *vi* filouter, vivre de l'arnaque.

grifter▽ ['grɪftəʳ] *n Am* arnaqueur *m*, -euse *f*, escroc *m*.

grill [grɪl] ◇ *vt* **-1.** CULIN (faire) griller. **-2.** *inf* [interrogate] cuisiner.
◇ *vi* CULIN griller.
◇ *n* CULIN [device] gril *m*; [dish] grillade *f*; to cook sthg under the ~ faire cuire qqch au gril.

grill(e) [grɪl] *n* **-1.** [grating] grille *f*, grillage *m*. **-2.** AUT: (radiator) ~ calandre *f*.

grillroom ['grɪlrʊm] *n* grill *m (restaurant)*.

grilse [grɪls] *n* grilse *m*.

grim [grɪm] *adj* **-1.** [hard, stern] sévère; a ~ look un regard sévère; to look ~ avoir l'air sévère; the ~ reality/necessity la dure réalité/nécessité; the ~ truth la dure vérité; with ~ determination avec une volonté inflexible. **-2.** [gloomy] sinistre, lugubre; ~ prospects de sombres perspectives; a ~ story une histoire sinistre OR macabre; it was a ~ reminder of his years in prison c'était un sinistre souvenir de ses années en prison; the economic situation is looking pretty ~ la situation économique n'est pas très encourageante ❑ to hold on to sthg like ~ death tenir à qqch de toutes ses forces. **-3.** [unpleasant]: his new film is pretty ~ son nouveau film n'est pas terrible || [unwell] patraque; [depressed] déprimé, abattu; I felt pretty ~ this morning [unwell] je ne me sentais pas bien du tout ce matin; [depressed] je n'avais vraiment pas le moral ce matin.

grimace [grɪ'meɪs] ◇ *n* grimace *f*; to make a ~ faire une grimace.
◇ *vi* [in disgust, pain] grimacer, faire la grimace; [to amuse] faire des grimaces.

grime [graɪm] *n (U)* crasse *f*, saleté *f*.

grimly ['grɪmlɪ] *adv* **-1.** [threateningly] d'un air menaçant; [unhappily] d'un air mécontent. **-2.** [defend, struggle] avec acharnement; [hold on] inflexiblement, fermement; [with determination] d'un air résolu, fermement.

grimness ['grɪmnɪs] *n* **-1.** [sternness] sévérité *f*, gravité *f*. **-2.** [of story] côté *m* sinistre OR macabre; [of prospects, situation] côté *m* difficile.

grimy ['graɪmɪ] *adj* sale, crasseux.

grin [grɪn] ◇ *n* grand sourire *m*; a broad ~ un large sourire.
◇ *vi* sourire; to ~ at sb faire OR adresser un grand sourire à qqn; what are you grinning at? qu'est-ce que tu as à sourire comme ça? ❑ we'll just have to ~ and bear it il faudra le prendre avec le sourire; to ~ like a Cheshire cat avoir un sourire jusqu'aux oreilles.

grind [graɪnd] (*pt* & *pp* ground [graʊnd])
◇ *n* **-1.** *inf* [monotonous work] corvée *f*; the daily ~ le train-train quotidien; what a ~! quelle corvée!, quelle barbe! **-2.** *inf Am* [hard worker] bûcheur *m*, -euse *f*, bosseur *m*, -euse *f*. **-3.** ▼ [copulation]: to have a good ~ bien baiser.
◇ *vt* **-1.** [coffee, corn, pepper] moudre; [stones] concasser; [meat] *Am* hacher; [into powder] pulvériser, réduire en poudre; [crush] broyer, écraser; he ground his feet into the sand il a enfoncé ses pieds dans le sable. **-2.** [rub together] écraser l'un contre l'autre; to ~ one's teeth grincer des dents; to ~ sthg between one's teeth broyer qqch entre ses dents; to ~ the gears AUT faire grincer les vitesses. **-3.** [polish - lenses] polir; [- stones] polir, égriser; [sharpen - knife] aiguiser OR affûter (à la meule). **-4.** [turn handle] tourner; to ~ a pepper mill tourner un moulin à poivre; to ~ a barrel-organ tourner la manivelle de OR jouer de l'orgue de Barbarie.
◇ *vi* **-1.** [crush]: this barley ~s well cet orge est facile à moudre; this pepper mill doesn't ~ very well ce moulin à poivre ne moud pas très bien. **-2.** [noisily] grincer; to ~ to a halt/to a standstill [machine, vehicle] s'arrêter/s'immobiliser en grinçant; [company, economy, production] s'immobiliser peu à peu, s'arrêter progressivement. **-3.** *inf Am* [work hard and long] bûcher OR bosser (dur). **-4.** ▼ [copulate] baiser.
◆ **grind away** *inf vi insep*: I've been ~ing away at this essay all weekend j'ai bûché sur cette dissertation tout le week-end.
◆ **grind down** *vt sep* **-1.** *literal* pulvériser, réduire en poudre; [lens] meuler. **-2.** *fig* [oppress] opprimer, écraser; don't let your job ~ you down ne te laisse pas abattre par ton boulot; the people were ground down by years of poverty la population était écrasée par des années de misère.
◆ **grind in** *vt sep*: to ~ in a valve roder une soupape.
◆ **grind on** *inf vi insep* [speaker] parler à n'en plus finir; [lecture, week] traîner en longueur.
◆ **grind out** *vt sep* **-1.** [extinguish by grinding]: she ground out her cigarette in the ashtray elle a écrasé sa cigarette dans le cendrier. **-2.** *fig* [produce slowly]: to ~ out a tune on the barrel-organ jouer un air sur l'orgue de Barbarie; she's just ground out another blockbuster elle vient de pondre un nouveau best-seller.
◆ **grind up** *vt sep* pulvériser; to ~ sthg up into powder réduire qqch en poudre.

grinder ['graɪndəʳ] *n* **-1.** [tooth] molaire *f*. **-2.** [person - of minerals] broyeur *m*, -euse *f*; [- of knives, blades etc] rémouleur *m*. **-3.** [machine - for crushing] moulin *m*, broyeur *m*; [- for sharpening] affûteuse *f*, machine *f* à aiguiser.

grinding ['graɪndɪŋ] ◇ *n* [sound] grincement *m*.
◇ *adj* **-1.** [sound]: a ~ noise un bruit grinçant. **-2.** [oppressive]: ~ poverty misère *f* écrasante.

grindstone ['graɪndstəʊn] *n* meule *f*; to keep one's nose to the ~ travailler sans relâche.

gringo▽ ['grɪŋgəʊ] (*pl* gringos) *n offensive* gringo *m*.

grip [grɪp] (*pt* & *pp* gripped, *cont* gripping)
◇ *n* **-1.** [strong hold] prise *f*, étreinte *f*; [on racket] tenue *f*; [of tyres on road] adhérence *f*; to lose one's ~ lâcher prise; he tightened his ~ on the rope il a serré la corde plus fort; to get a ~ of sthg/sb empoigner qqch/qqn. **-2.** [handclasp] poigne *f*; a strong ~ une forte poigne; she held his hand in a vice-like ~ elle lui serrait la main comme un étau OR tenait la main d'une poigne d'acier. **-3.** *inf* [self-control]: he's losing his ~ il perd les pédales; Grandad is starting to lose his ~ grand-père commence à baisser; get a ~ (of yourself)! secoue-toi un peu! **-4.** [understanding]: he has a good ~ of the subject il connaît OR domine bien son sujet. **-5.** [handle] poignée *f*. **-6.** CIN & THEAT machiniste *mf*. **-7.** *dated* [bag] sac *m* de voyage. **-8.** *phr*: to come OR to get to ~s with a problem s'attaquer à un problème; to come OR to get to ~s with the enemy être confronté à l'ennemi, être aux prises avec l'ennemi.
◇ *vt* **-1.** [grasp - rope, rail] empoigner, saisir; he gripped my arm il m'a saisi le bras. **-2.** [hold tightly] serrer, tenir serré; he gripped my hand il m'a serré la main très fort. **-3.** [subj: tyres] adhérer; to ~ the road [car] coller à la route. **-4.** [hold interest] passionner; the trial gripped the nation le procès a passionné OR captivé le pays.
◇ *vi* [tyres] adhérer.

gripe [graɪp] ◇ *n* **-1.** *inf* [complaint] ronchonnements *mpl*. **-2.** MED = **gripes**.
◇ *vi inf* [complain] ronchonner, rouspéter; he's been griping at me all day il a ronchonné contre moi toute la journée.
◆ **gripes** *npl* MED coliques *fpl*.

gripe water *n* calmant *m (pour coliques)*.

griping *inf* ['graɪpɪŋ] *n (U)* ronchonnements *mpl*, rouspétance *f*.

gripping ['grɪpɪŋ] *adj* [story, play] captivant, passionnant, palpitant.

grippingly ['grɪpɪŋlɪ] *adv* [written, told] de manière captivante OR passionnante.

grisly ['grɪzlɪ] *adj* épouvantable, macabre, sinistre.

grist [grɪst] *n* blé *m* (à moudre); it's all ~ to the mill c'est toujours ça de pris.

gristle ['grɪsl] *n (U)* [cartilage] cartilage *m*, tendons *mpl*; [in meat] nerfs *mpl*.

gristly ['grɪslɪ] *adj pej* nerveux, tendineux.

grit [grɪt] (*pt* & *pp* gritted, *cont* gritting) ◇ *n* -**1.** [gravel] gravillon *m*. -**2.** [sand] sable *m*. -**3.** [for fowl] gravier *m*. -**4.** = **gritstone**. -**5.** [dust] poussière *f*; I have a piece of ~ in my eye j'ai un grain de poussière dans l'œil. -**6.** *inf* [courage] cran *m*; she's got real ~ elle a vraiment du cran.
◇ *vt* -**1.** [road, steps] gravillonner, répandre du gravillon sur. -**2.** *phr*: to ~ one's teeth serrer les dents.
◆ **grits** *npl Am* gruau *m* de maïs.

gritstone ['grɪtstəʊn] *n* grès *m*.

gritting ['grɪtɪŋ] *n* [of roads] sablage *m*; ~ lorry camion *m* de sablage.

gritty ['grɪtɪ] (*compar* grittier, *superl* grittiest) *adj* -**1.** [road] couvert de gravier. -**2.** *inf* [person] qui a du cran. -**3.** [incisive - remark, comment] incisif, mordant. -**4.** [play, film] naturaliste.

grizzle *inf* ['grɪzl] *vi Br* -**1.** [cry fretfully] pleurnicher, geindre. -**2.** [complain] ronchonner.

grizzled ['grɪzld] *adj* [person, beard] grisonnant.

grizzly ['grɪzlɪ] (*compar* grizzlier, *superl* grizzliest) ◇ *adj* [greyish] grisâtre; [hair] grisonnant.
◇ *n* = **grizzly bear**.

grizzly bear *n* grizzli *m*, grizzly *m*, ours *m* brun *(des montagnes Rocheuses)*.

groan [grəʊn] ◇ *n* -**1.** [of pain] gémissement *m*, plainte *f*. -**2.** [of disapproval] grognement *m*; he gave a ~ of annoyance il a poussé un grognement d'exaspération. -**3.** [complaint] ronchonnement *m*.
◇ *vi* -**1.** [in pain] gémir. -**2.** [in disapproval] grogner; everybody ~ed at his corny jokes tout le monde levait les yeux au ciel quand il sortait ses plaisanteries éculées. -**3.** [be weighed down by] gémir; the table ~ed under the weight of the food la table ployait sous le poids de la nourriture. -**4.** [complain] ronchonner.

groat [grəʊt] *n ancienne pièce de monnaie britannique*.

groats [grəʊts] *npl* gruau *m* (d'avoine).

grocer ['grəʊsəʳ] *n* épicier *m*; at the ~'s (shop) à l'épicerie, chez l'épicier.

grocery ['grəʊsərɪ] (*pl* groceries) *n* [shop] épicerie *f*.
◆ **groceries** *npl* [provisions] épicerie *f (U)*, provisions *fpl*; what groceries do we need? qu'est-ce qu'il nous faut comme épicerie OR provisions?

grog [grɒg] *n* grog *m*.

groggily *inf* ['grɒgɪlɪ] *adv* -**1.** [weakly] faiblement. -**2.** [unsteadily - from exhaustion, from blows] de manière chancelante OR groggy.

groggy *inf* ['grɒgɪ] (*compar* groggier, *superl* groggiest) *adj* -**1.** [weak] faible, affaibli; ~ with flu affaibli par la grippe. -**2.** [unsteady - from exhaustion] groggy *(inv)*, vacillant, chancelant; [- from blows] groggy *(inv)*, sonné.

groin [grɔɪn] *n* -**1.** ANAT aine *f*. -**2.** *Br euph* [testicles] bourses *fpl*. -**3.** ARCHIT arête *f*. -**4.** *Am* = **groyne**.

groined vault [grɔɪnd-] *n* ARCHIT voûte *f* d'arête.

grommet ['grɒmɪt] *n* -**1.** [metal eyelet] œillet *m*. -**2.** MECH virole *f*, rondelle *f*. -**3.** NAUT erse *f*, estrope *f*, bague *f* en corde.

Groningen ['grəʊnɪŋən] *pr n* Groningue.

groom [gru:m] ◇ *n* -**1.** [for horses] palefrenier *m*, -ère *f*, valet *m* d'écurie. -**2.** = **bridegroom**.
◇ *vt* -**1.** [clean - horse] panser; [- dog] toiletter; [- subj: monkeys, cats]: cats ~ themselves les chats font leur toilette. -**2.** [prepare - candidate] préparer, former; Ray is being ~ed for an executive position on prépare OR forme Ray pour un poste de cadre; I'm ~ing him to take over from me c'est mon poulain.

groomed [gru:md] *adj* soigné; to be well-~ être soigné (de sa personne).

grooming ['gru:mɪŋ] *n* -**1.** [of person] toilette *f*; [neat appearance] présentation *f*. -**2.** [of horse] pansage *m*; [of dog] toilettage *m*.

groove [gru:v] ◇ *n* -**1.** [for pulley, in column] cannelure *f*, gorge *f*; [in folding knife] onglet *m*. -**2.** [in piston] gorge *f*. -**3.** [for sliding door] rainure *f*. -**4.** [on record] sillon *m*. -**5.** [notch] encoche *f*. -**6.** [of sword] gouttière *f*. -**7.** *inf* [rut]: to get into OR to be stuck in a ~ s'encroûter, être pris dans la routine.
◇ *vt* [make a groove] canneler, rainurer, rainer.
◇ *vi inf dated* [enjoy oneself] s'éclater.

groovy *inf* ['gru:vɪ] (*compar* groovier, *superl* grooviest) *dated* ◇ *adj* -**1.** [excellent] sensationnel, sensass, super. -**2.** [trendy] dans le vent.
◇ *interj*: ~! chouette!, génial!, super!

grope [grəʊp] ◇ *vi* [seek - by touch] tâtonner, aller à l'aveuglette; [- for answer] chercher; to ~ (about OR around) for sthg chercher qqch à tâtons OR à l'aveuglette; to ~ for words chercher ses mots.
◇ *vt* -**1.** to ~ one's way in the dark avancer à tâtons dans l'obscurité; to ~ one's way in/out entrer/sortir à tâtons. -**2.** *inf* [sexually] tripoter, peloter.

grosgrain ['grəʊgreɪn] *n* gros-grain *m*.

gross [grəʊs] (*pl sense 1* grosses, *pl sense 2 inv*) ◇ *adj* -**1.** [vulgar, loutish - person] grossier, fruste; [- joke] cru, grossier. -**2.** [flagrant - inefficiency, incompetence]: ~ injustice injustice *f* flagrante; ~ ignorance ignorance *f* crasse. -**3.** [fat] obèse, énorme. -**4.** [overall total] brut; ~ profits bénéfices *mpl* bruts; ~ wage salaire *m* brut. -**5.** *inf* [disgusting] dégueulasse.
◇ *n* -**1.** [whole amount]: the ~ le gros. -**2.** [twelve dozen] grosse *f*, douze douzaines *fpl*.
◇ *vt* COMM faire OR obtenir une recette brute de; our firm ~ed $800,000 last year notre société a fait OR obtenu une recette brute de 800 000 dollars l'année dernière.
◆ **gross out** *inf vt sep Am* dégoûter, débecter; it really ~ed me out ça m'a vraiment débecté.

gross domestic product *n* produit *m* intérieur brut.

grossly ['grəʊslɪ] *adv* -**1.** [coarsely] grossièrement. -**2.** [as intensifier] outre mesure, excessivement; ~ unfair extrêmement injuste.

gross national product *n* produit *m* national brut.

Grosvenor Square ['grəʊvnəʳ-] *pr n grande place à Londres où se trouve notamment l'ambassade des États-Unis*.

grot *inf* [grɒt] *n Br* crasse *f*, saleté *f*.

grotesque [grəʊ'tesk] ◇ *adj* grotesque.
◇ *n* grotesque *m*.

grotesquely [grəʊ'tesklɪ] *adv* grotesquement, absurdement.

grotto ['grɒtəʊ] (*pl* grottos OR grottoes) *n* grotte *f*.

grotty *inf* ['grɒtɪ] (*compar* grottier, *superl* grottiest) *adj Br* -**1.** [unattractive] moche; [unsatisfactory] nul. -**2.** [unwell]: to feel ~ ne pas se sentir bien, être mal fichu.

grouch *inf* [graʊtʃ] ◇ *vi* rouspéter, ronchonner, grogner; to ~ about sthg rouspéter OR ronchonner après qqch, grogner contre qqch.
◇ *n* rouspéteur *m*, -euse *f*.

grouchy *inf* ['graʊtʃɪ] (*compar* grouchier, *superl* grouchiest) *adj* grincheux, ronchon, grognon.

ground [graʊnd] ◇ *pt* & *pp* → **grind**.
◇ *n* -**1.** [earth] terre *f*; [surface] sol *m*; the ~ is often frozen in winter la terre est souvent gelée en hiver; at ~ level au niveau du sol; the children sat on the ~ les enfants se sont assis par terre; drive the stakes firmly into the ~ enfoncez solidement les pieux dans le sol; above ~ en surface; below ~ sous terre; to burn sthg to the ~ réduire qqch en cendres; to fall to the ~ tomber par OR à terre ❑ to go to ~ se terrer; to be on firm ~ être sûr de son fait; to get off the ~ *literal* [aeroplane] décoller; *fig* [project] démarrer; to have one's feet (firmly) on the ~ avoir (bien) les pieds sur terre; it suits him down to the ~ ça lui va à merveille, ça lui convient parfaitement; to run a car into the ~ utiliser une voiture jusqu'à ce qu'elle rende l'âme; to run a company into the ~ faire couler une entreprise. -**2.** *(U)* [land] terrain *m*; [region] région *f*, coin *m*; there's a lot of hilly ~ in Scotland il y a beaucoup de coins vallonnés en Écosse. -**3.** *Br* [piece of land] terrain *m*; [stadium] stade *m*; football/cricket ~ terrain de foot/cricket; the crowds are leaving the ~ la foule des spectateurs sort du stade. -**4.** [area used for specific purpose]: fishing ~s zones *fpl* réservées à la pêche; training ~ terrain *m* d'entraînement OR d'exercice. -**5.** MIL terrain *m*; to give/to lose ~ céder/perdre du terrain; to stand OR to hold one's ~ tenir bon; firm ~ terrain bien assis, terre ferme ❑ to gain ~ [in battle] gagner du terrain; [idea, concept] faire son chemin, progresser; [news] se répandre. -**6.** = **ground floor**. -**7.** *(U)* [area of reference] domaine *m*, champ *m*; his article covers a lot of ~ dans son article, il aborde beaucoup de domaines; this is new ~ for me pour moi, c'est un domaine nouveau; they were unable to find any common ~ [for discussion] ils n'ont pas pu trouver un terrain d'entente; [in interests] ils n'ont pas pu trouver un intérêt commun. -**8.** [subject] terrain *m*, sujet *m*; you're on dangerous ~ vous êtes sur un terrain glissant; for them, politics is forbidden ~ pour eux, la politique est un sujet tabou OR un domaine interdit. -**9.** [background] fond *m*; on a green ~ [of painting] sur fond vert; the middle ~ le second plan. -**10.** [of sea] fond *m*. -**11.** *Am* ELEC terre *f*, masse *f*; a ~ connection une prise de terre. -**12.** MUS: ~ (bass) basse *f* contrainte.
◇ *comp* au sol; ~ cover végétation *f* basse; ~ crew équipe *f* au sol; ~ fire *feu de forêt ne consumant que les broussailles*; ~ frost gelée blanche; ~ staff *personnel qui s'occupe de l'entretien d'un terrain de sport*.
◇ *vt* -**1.** [base] fonder, baser; my fears proved well ~ed mes craintes se sont révélées fondées, il s'est avéré que mes craintes étaient fondées. -**2.** [train] former; the students are well ~ed in computer sciences les étudiants ont une bonne formation OR de bonnes bases en informatique. -**3.** [plane, pilot]: to be ~ed être interdit de vol; the plane was ~ed for mechanical reasons l'avion a été interdit de vol à cause d'un incident mécanique. -**4.** [ship] échouer. -**5.** *Am* ELEC mettre à la terre OR à la masse. -**6.** *inf* [child] interdire de sortie.
◇ *vi* [ship] échouer; the submarine had ~ed on a sandbank le sous-marin s'était échoué OR avait échoué sur un banc de sable.
◇ *adj* [wheat, coffee] moulu; [pepper] concassé; [steel] meulé; [meat] haché.
◆ **grounds** *npl* -**1.** [around house] parc *m*, domaine *m*; [around block of flats, hospital] terrain *m*; [more extensive] parc *m*; the house has extensive ~s la maison est entourée d'un grand parc; the ~s are patrolled by dogs le terrain est gardé par des chiens. -**2.** [reason] motif *m*, raison *f*; [cause] cause *f*, raison *f*; [basis] base *f*, raison *f*; [pretext] raison *f*, prétexte *m*; you have no ~s for believing that he's lying vous n'avez aucune raison de croire qu'il ment; there are ~s for suspecting arson il y a lieu de penser qu'il s'agit d'un incendie criminel; he was excused on the ~s of poor health il a été exempté en raison de sa mauvaise santé; on medical/moral ~s pour (des) raisons médicales/morales || JUR: ~s for appeal voies *fpl* de recours; ~s for complaint grief *m*; ~s for divorce motifs *mpl* de divorce. -**3.** [of coffee] marc *m*.

groundcloth ['graʊndklɒθ] *Am* = **groundsheet**.

ground control *n* AERON contrôle *m* au sol.

ground floor *n* rez-de-chaussée *m*.

ground glass *n* -**1.** [glass] verre *m* dépoli. -**2.** [as abrasive] verre *m* pilé.

ground hog *n* marmotte *f* d'Amérique; Ground Hog Day *Am le 2 février, jour où les marmottes sont censées avoir fini leur hibernation.*

grounding ['graʊndɪŋ] *n* -**1.** [training] formation *f*; [knowledge] connaissances *fpl*, bases *fpl*. -**2.** [of argument] assise *f*. -**3.** *Am* ELEC mise *f* à la terre OR à la masse. -**4.** NAUT échouage *m*. -**5.** [of balloon] atterrissage *m*. -**6.** [of plane] interdiction *f* de vol.

groundless ['graʊndlɪs] *adj* sans fondement, sans motif; her fears proved ~ ses craintes s'avérèrent sans fondement.

groundlessly ['graʊndlɪslɪ] *adv* sans raison.

ground level *n* -**1.** [ground floor] rez-de-chaussée *m*. -**2.** [lowest level in organization] base *f*.

groundling ['graʊndlɪŋ] *n* -**1.** [fish] poisson *m* de fond. -**2.** [plant] plante *f* rampante. -**3.** THEAT ≃ spectateur *m*, -trice *f* du parterre; *fig* personne *f* sans culture, philistin *m*.

groundnut ['graʊndnʌt] = **peanut**.

ground plan *n* -**1.** [plan of ground floor] plan *m* au sol. -**2.** [plan of action] plan *m* d'action.

ground rent *n* redevance *f* foncière.

ground rice *n* farine *f* de riz.

ground rule *n* procédure *f*, règle *f*; to lay down the ~s établir les règles du jeu *fig*.

groundsel ['graʊnsl] *n* séneçon *m*.

groundsheet ['graʊndʃiːt] *n* tapis *m* de sol.

groundsman ['graʊndzmən] (*pl* groundsmen [-mən]) *n* gardien *m* de stade.

ground stroke *n* TENNIS: to hit a ~ frapper la balle au rebond.

groundswell ['graʊndswel] *n* lame *f* de fond; there was a ~ of public opinion in favour of the president *fig* l'opinion publique a basculé massivement en faveur du président.

groundwork ['graʊndwɜːk] *n* (*U*) travail *m* préparatoire, canevas *m*.

group [gruːp] ◇ *n* -**1.** [of people] groupe *m*; POL [party] groupement *m*; [literary] groupe *m*, cercle *m*. -**2.** [of objects] groupe *m*, ensemble *m*; [of mountains] massif *m*. -**3.** [in business] groupe *m*; they're in OR part of the Larousse ~ ils font partie du groupe Larousse. -**4.** [blood] groupe *m*; what (blood) ~ are you? – ~ AB quel est votre groupe sanguin? – le groupe AB. -**5.** MUS groupe *m*; a pop/rock ~ un groupe pop/rock. -**6.** LING groupe *m*, syntagme *m*. -**7.** MIL groupe *m*.
◇ *comp* [work] de groupe; ~ action/decision action/décision collective.
◇ *vt* -**1.** [bring together] grouper, réunir; [put in groups] disposer en groupes; the teacher ~ed all the eight-year-olds together l'institutrice a groupé OR regroupé tous les enfants de huit ans. -**2.** [combine] combiner.
◇ *vi* se grouper, se regrouper; they all ~ed round their leader ils se groupèrent tous autour de leur chef.

group captain *n* colonel *m* de l'armée de l'air; Group Captain Ross le colonel Ross.

groupie *inf* ['gruːpɪ] *n* groupie *f*.

grouping ['gruːpɪŋ] *n* groupement *m*.

group practice *n* MED cabinet *m* médical; to be in ~ faire partie d'un cabinet médical.

group therapy *n* thérapie *f* de groupe.

grouse [graʊs] ◇ *n* -**1.** [bird] grouse *f*, lagopède *m* d'Écosse. -**2.** *inf* [grumble] rouspétance *f*; [complaint] grief *m*; we were just having a ~ about work/the boss on était en train de rouspéter contre le travail/le patron.
◇ *vi inf* rouspéter, râler; what are you grousing about? pourquoi rouspètes-tu?
◇ *comp*: ~ beating rabattage *m*; ~ moor chasse *f* réservée (à la chasse à la grouse); ~ shooting chasse *f* à la grouse.

grouser *inf* ['graʊsəʳ] *n* [complainer] grognon *m*, rouspéteur *m*, -euse *f*.

grout [graʊt] ◇ *n* coulis *m* au ciment.
◇ *vt* jointoyer.

grouting ['graʊtɪŋ] *n* jointoiement *m*.

grove [grəʊv] *n* bosquet *m*; olive ~ oliveraie *f* ❑ the ~s of Academe le milieu *m* universitaire, l'Université *f*.

grovel ['grɒvl] (*Br pt* & *pp* grovelled, *cont* grovelling, *Am pt* & *pp* groveled, *cont* groveling) *vi* -**1.** [act humbly] ramper, s'aplatir; to ~ to sb (for sthg) s'aplatir devant qqn (pour obtenir qqch); to ~ before sb ramper devant qqn. -**2.** [crawl on floor] se vautrer OR se traîner par terre; stop grovelling around on the floor arrête de te traîner par terre.

groveller *Br*, **groveler** *Am* ['grɒvləʳ] *n* flagorneur *m*, -euse *f fml*, lèche-bottes *mf inv*.

grovelling *Br*, **groveling** *Am* ['grɒvlɪŋ] ◇ *adj* rampant, servile; a ~ letter une lettre obséquieuse; a ~ apology de viles excuses.
◇ *n* (*U*) flagornerie *f*.

grovellingly *Br*, **grovelingly** *Am* ['grɒvlɪŋlɪ] *adv* servilement, en rampant.

grow [grəʊ] (*pt* grew [gruː], *pp* grown [grəʊn]) ◇ *vi* -**1.** [plants] croître, pousser; [hair] pousser; [seeds] germer; orange trees ~ best in a warm climate les orangers poussent mieux en climat chaud; money doesn't ~ on trees l'argent ne pousse pas sur les arbres. -**2.** [person – in age, height] grandir; hasn't he grown! qu'est-ce qu'il a grandi! || [develop]: to ~ in wisdom/understanding devenir plus sage/compréhensif. -**3.** [originate]: this custom grew from OR out of a pagan ceremony cette coutume est née d'une OR a pour origine une cérémonie païenne. -**4.** [increase] s'accroître, augmenter; the crime rate in the big cities is ~ing le taux de criminalité augmente dans les grandes villes; our love/friendship grew over the years notre amour/amitié a grandi au fil des ans; he has grown in my esteem il a grandi OR est monté dans mon estime; the town grew in importance la ville a gagné en importance. -**5.** [become] devenir; to ~ angry se mettre en colère; to ~ bigger grandir, s'agrandir; it's beginning to ~ dark il commence à faire nuit; to ~ old devenir vieux, vieillir. -**6.** (*+ infin*) [come gradually]: I've grown to respect him j'ai appris à le respecter; to ~ to like/to dislike finir par aimer/détester.
◇ *vt* -**1.** [crops, plants] cultiver. -**2.** [beard, hair] laisser pousser; he's trying to ~ a beard il essaye de se laisser pousser la barbe; she's ~ing her hair (long) elle se laisse pousser les cheveux.
◆ **grow apart** *vi insep* [couple] s'éloigner l'un de l'autre.
◆ **grow away** *vi insep*: they began to ~ away from each other ils ont commencé à s'éloigner l'un de l'autre *fig*.
◆ **grow back** *vi insep* [hair, nail] repousser.
◆ **grow into** *vt insep* -**1.** [become] devenir (en grandissant); both her sons grew into fine-looking men ses deux fils sont devenus de beaux jeunes gens. -**2.** [clothes]: the pullover's too big for him, but he'll ~ into it le pull est trop grand pour lui, mais il pourra le mettre un jour; he'll soon ~ into those shoes il pourra bientôt mettre ces chaussures, bientôt ces chaussures lui iront. -**3.** [become used to]: to ~ into a job s'habituer à OR s'adapter à un travail.
◆ **grow on** *vt insep* plaire de plus en plus à; the song began to ~ on him after a while au bout d'un certain temps, la chanson commença à lui plaire de plus en plus; it ~s on you on s'y fait.
◆ **grow out of** *vt insep* -**1.** [clothes]: he's grown out of most of his clothes la plupart de ses vêtements ne lui vont plus, il ne rentre plus dans la plupart de ses vêtements. -**2.** [habit] perdre (avec le temps); he never grew out of (the habit of) biting his nails il n'a jamais perdu cette habitude de se ronger les ongles.
◆ **grow up** *vi insep* -**1.** [person] grandir, devenir adulte; what do you want to be when you ~ up? que veux-tu faire quand tu seras grand?; I hope he won't ~ up to be a liar/thief j'espère qu'il ne sera pas un menteur/voleur plus tard; ~ up! sois un peu adulte!; when are you going to ~ up? quand est-ce que tu seras un peu raisonnable? -**2.** [emotions, friendship] naître, se développer; a strong feeling of hatred grew up between them un puissant sentiment de haine est né entre eux.

grow bag *n sac plastique rempli d'engrais dans lequel on fait pousser une plante.*

grower ['grəʊəʳ] *n* -**1.** [producer] producteur *m*, -trice *f*; [professional] cultivateur *m*, -trice *f*; [amateur gardener] amateur *m* de jardinage; vegetable ~ maraîcher *m*, -ère *f*; rose ~ [professional] rosiériste *mf*; [amateur]: he's a keen rose ~ il se passionne pour la culture des roses. -**2.** [plant, tree]: a slow ~ une plante qui pousse lentement.

growing ['grəʊɪŋ] ◇ *adj* -**1.** [plant] croissant, qui pousse; [child] grandissant, en cours de croissance; a ~ child needs a well balanced diet un enfant en pleine croissance a besoin d'une alimentation bien équilibrée. -**2.** [increasing – debt] qui augmente; [– amount, number] grandissant, qui augmente; [– friendship, impatience] grandissant; ~ numbers of people are out of work de plus en plus de gens sont OR un nombre croissant de gens est au chômage; a ~ population une population qui s'accroît; there are ~ fears of a nuclear war on craint de plus en plus une guerre nucléaire.
◇ *comp*: wine ~ region région vinicole; wheat/potato ~ region région qui produit du blé/de la pomme de terre, région à blé/pommes de terre.
◇ *n* [of agricultural products] culture *f*.

growing pains *npl* -**1.** [of children] douleurs *fpl* de croissance. -**2.** [of business, project] difficultés *fpl* de croissance, problèmes *mpl* de départ.

growing season *n* saison *f* nouvelle.

growl [graʊl] ◇ *vi* [animal] grogner, gronder; [person] grogner, grommeler; [thunder] tonner, gronder; to ~ at sb grogner contre qqn.
◇ *vt* [answer, instructions] grommeler, grogner.
◇ *n* grognement *m*, grondement *m*.

grown [grəʊn] ◇ *pp* → **grow**.
◇ *adj* -**1.** [person] adulte; you don't expect ~ adults to behave so stupidly on ne s'attend pas à ce que des adultes se comportent de manière si stupide; he's a ~ man il est adulte; the children are fully ~ now les enfants sont grands maintenant. -**2.** [garden]: the garden is all ~ over le jardin est tout envahi par les mauvaises herbes.

-grown *in cpds* -**1.** [of size, development] grand, qui a fini sa croissance, qui est arrivé à maturité; half~ à mi-croissance. -**2.** [of plants] que l'on fait pousser, que l'on cultive; tub~ en bac.

grown-up ◇ *n* adulte *mf*, grande personne *f*.
◇ *adj* adulte; our children are ~ now nos enfants sont grands maintenant.

growth [grəʊθ] *n* -**1.** (*U*) [development – of child, plant] croissance *f*; [– of friendship] développement *m*, croissance *f*; [– of organization] développement *m*; lack of certain vitamins can hinder ~ la carence en certaines vitamines peut entraver la croissance; intellectual/spiritual ~ développement intellectuel/spirituel. -**2.** (*U*) [increase – in numbers, amount] augmentation *f*, croissance *f*; [– of market, industry] croissance *f*, expansion *f*; [– of influence, knowledge] développement *m*, croissance *f*; the experts predict a 2% ~ in tourism/imports les experts prédisent une croissance du tourisme/des importations de 2 % ❑ economic ~ développement OR croissance économique; population ~ croissance de la population. -**3.** [of beard, hair, weeds] pousse *f*; two days' ~ of beard une barbe de deux jours. -**4.** MED excroissance *f*, tumeur *f*, grosseur *f*.

growth factor *n* facteur *m* de croissance.

growth hormone *n* hormone *f* de croissance.

growth industry *n* industrie *f* en plein essor OR de pointe.

growth ring *n* anneau *m* de croissance.

growth shares *npl*, **growth stock** *n* ST. EX *actions susceptibles d'une hausse rapide.*

groyne *Br*, **groin** *Am* [grɔɪn] *n* brise-lames *m inv*.

grub [grʌb] ◇ *vi* -**1.** [animal] fouir. -**2.** [rummage] fouiller; they grubbed around for clues *fig* ils fouinaient à la recherche d'indices.
◇ *n* -**1.** [insect] asticot *m*. -**2.** *inf* [food] bouffe *f*; ~ OR ~'s **up**! à la soupe!
◆ **grub up** *vt sep* [bone] déterrer; [root] extirper; [plant] déraciner; [insects] déloger.
grubbiness *inf* ['grʌbɪnɪs] *n* (*U*) saleté *f*.
grubby ['grʌbɪ] *adj* sale, crasseux, malpropre.
grub-kick *n* [in rugby] coup *m* qui reste au sol.
grub screw *n* vis *f* noyée, vis *f* sans tête.
grubstake *inf* ['grʌbsteɪk] *n Am* investissement *m*.
grudge [grʌdʒ] ◇ *n* rancune *f*; to bear OR to hold a ~ against sb en vouloir à qqn, avoir de la rancune contre qqn; he still bears me a ~ il m'en veut toujours.
◇ *vt* = **begrudge**.
grudging ['grʌdʒɪŋ] *adj* [compliment, praise] fait OR donné à contrecœur; [agreement] réticent.
grudgingly ['grʌdʒɪŋlɪ] *adv* à contrecœur, avec réticence.
gruel [grʊəl] *n* bouillie *f* d'avoine.
gruelling *Br*, **grueling** *Am* ['grʊəlɪŋ] *adj* [race] éreintant, épuisant; [punishment] sévère; [experience] très difficile, très dur.
gruellingly *Br*, **gruelingly** *Am* ['grʊəlɪŋlɪ] *adv* de manière épuisante.
gruesome ['gru:səm] *adj* horrible, macabre; a ~ discovery une découverte macabre; a ~ sight un spectacle horrible.
gruff [grʌf] *adj* -**1.** [of manner] brusque. -**2.** [of speech, voice] bourru; a ~ voice une grosse voix.
gruffly ['grʌflɪ] *adv* -**1.** [of manner] avec brusquerie. -**2.** [of speech, voice] : to speak ~ parler d'un ton bourru.
gruffness ['grʌfnɪs] *n* -**1.** [of manner] brusquerie *f*. -**2.** [of speech, voice] ton *m* bourru.
grumble ['grʌmbl] ◇ *vi* -**1.** [complain] grogner, grommeler; he's always grumbling about something il rouspète constamment contre quelque chose; why are you grumbling at me? pourquoi rouspètes-tu contre moi?; stop grumbling! arrête de te plaindre!; how are you? — oh, mustn't ~! ça va? — on fait aller! -**2.** [thunder, artillery] gronder; my stomach kept grumbling loudly mon estomac n'arrêtait pas de gargouiller bruyamment.
◇ *n* -**1.** [complaint] ronchonnement *m*, sujet *m* de plainte; what's his latest ~? pourquoi se plaint-il cette fois? -**2.** [of thunder, artillery] grondement *m*; a distant ~ of thunder un lointain grondement de tonnerre.
grumbler ['grʌmbləʳ] *n* grincheux *m*, -euse *f*, mécontent *m*, -e *f*.
grumbling ['grʌmblɪŋ] ◇ *adj* grincheux, grognon; a ~ stomach un estomac qui gargouille; ~ appendix MED appendicite *f* chronique.
◇ *n* plaintes *fpl*, protestations *fpl*.
grummet ['grʌmɪt] = **grommet**.
grump *inf* [grʌmp] *n* bougon *m*, -onne *f*, ronchon *m*, -onne *f*; you are an old ~ this morning! t'es qu'un vieux ronchon, ce matin!; to have the ~s être de mauvais poil.
grumpily *inf* ['grʌmpɪlɪ] *adv* en ronchonnant, d'un ton OR air ronchon.
grumpiness *inf* ['grʌmpɪnɪs] *n* mauvaise humeur *f*, maussaderie *f*, caractère *m* désagréable.
grumpy *inf* ['grʌmpɪ] *adj* ronchon, bougon; a ~ old woman une vieille grincheuse; don't be so ~! ne sois pas si ronchon!
grunge *inf* [grʌndʒ] *n* -**1.** *Am* [dirt] crasse *f*. -**2.** [fashion] grunge *m*.
grungy *inf* ['grʌndʒɪ] *adj Am* crasseux.
grunt [grʌnt] ◇ *vi* grogner, pousser un grognement.
◇ *vt* [reply] grommeler, grogner; "what?", he ~ed «quoi?», grogna-t-il.
◇ *n* -**1.** [sound] grognement *m*; to give a ~ pousser un grognement; the pig gave a loud ~ le cochon grogna bruyamment. -**2.** *inf Am* [soldier] troufion *m*.

Gruyère ['gru:jeəʳ] *n* gruyère *m*.
gryphon ['grɪfn] *n* griffon *m*.
GS *n abbr of* General Staff.
G-string *n* -**1.** MUS (corde *f* de) sol *m*. -**2.** [item of clothing] cache-sexe *m*, string *m*.
GU *written abbr of* Guam.
guac(h)amole [ˌgwɑ:kə'məʊlɪ] *n* (*U*) guacamole *m*, purée *f* d'avocat.
Guadeloupe [ˌgwɑ:də'lu:p] *pr n* Guadeloupe *f*; in ~ à la OR en Guadeloupe.
guaiac ['gwaɪæk] *n* gaïac *m*.
guaiacum ['gwaɪəkəm] *n* bois *m* de gaïac.
Guam [gwɑ:m] *pr n* Guam; in ~ à Guam.
guano ['gwɑ:nəʊ] *n* guano *m*.
guarantee [ˌgærən'ti:] ◇ *n* -**1.** COMM garantie *f*; a ~ against defective workmanship une garantie contre les malfaçons; money-back ~ remboursement *m* garanti; to be under ~ être sous garantie; this washing machine has a five-year ~ cette machine à laver est garantie cinq ans. -**2.** JUR [pledge] caution *f*, garantie *f*, gage *m*; to give sthg as a ~ donner qqch en caution OR en gage. -**3.** [person] garant *m*, -e *f*; to act as ~ se porter garant. -**4.** [firm promise] garantie *f*; what ~ do I have that you'll bring it back? comment puis-je être sûr que vous le rapporterez?; there's no ~ it will arrive today il n'est pas garanti OR dit que ça arrivera aujourd'hui.
◇ *vt* -**1.** [goods] garantir; the watch is ~d waterproof la montre est garantie étanche; the car is ~d against rust for 10 years la voiture est garantie contre la rouille pendant 10 ans. -**2.** [loan, cheque] garantir, cautionner; to ~ sb against loss garantir des pertes de qqn. -**3.** [assure] certifier, assurer; I can't ~ that everything will go to plan je ne peux pas vous certifier OR garantir que tout se passera comme prévu; our success is ~d notre succès est garanti ❑ ~d seat *Am place assurée sur le vol suivant pour un passager en stand-by qui cède sa place à quelqu'un payant plein tarif mais n'ayant pas réservé*.
◇ *comp*: ~ agreement garantie *f*; ~ form formulaire *m* OR fiche *f* de garantie.
guarantor [ˌgærən'tɔ:ʳ] *n* garant *m*, -e *f*; to stand ~ for sb se porter garant pour qqn.
guaranty ['gærəntɪ] *n* -**1.** [security] caution *f*, garantie *f*. -**2.** [guarantor] garant *m*, -e *f*. -**3.** [written guarantee] garantie *f*.
guard [gɑ:d] ◇ *n* -**1.** [person] gardien *m*, garde *m*; [group] garde *f*; prison ~ gardien de prison; call out the ~! appelez la garde!; ~ of honour garde *f* d'honneur. -**2.** [watch] garde *f*; to be on ~ (duty) être de garde; to mount (a) ~ monter la garde; the military kept ~ over the town les militaires gardaient la ville; to stand ~ monter la garde; the changing of the ~ la relève de la garde; there was a heavy police ~ for the president's visit il y avait d'importantes forces de police pour la visite du président. -**3.** [supervision] garde *f*, surveillance *f*; to keep a prisoner under ~ garder un prisonnier sous surveillance; to put a ~ on sb/sthg faire surveiller qqn/qqch; the prisoners were taken under ~ to the courthouse les prisonniers furent emmenés sous escorte au palais de justice. -**4.** [attention] garde *f*; on ~! [in fencing] en garde!; to be on one's ~ être sur ses gardes; we must warn him to be on ~ against robbers nous devons lui dire de faire attention aux voleurs; how can you put him on (his) ~? comment le mettre en garde?; to catch sb off ~ prendre qqn au dépourvu; keep your ~ up! méfiez-vous!; to drop OR to lower one's ~ relâcher sa surveillance. -**5.** *Br* RAIL chef *m* de train. -**6.** [protective device - on machine] dispositif *m* de sûreté OR de protection; [- personal] protection *f*.
◇ *vt* -**1.** [watch over - prisoner] garder; ~ your tongue! surveille ta langue! -**2.** [defend - fort, town] garder, défendre; the house was heavily ~ed la maison était étroitement surveillée. -**3.** [protect - life, reputation] protéger; to ~ sb against danger protéger qqn d'un danger; ~ the letter with your life veille bien sur cette lettre. -**4.** GAMES garder.
◆ **Guards** *npl* MIL [regiment] garde *f* royale *(britannique)*; he's in the Guards il est dans les régiments de la Garde Royale.
◆ **guard against** *vt insep* se protéger contre OR de, se prémunir contre; to ~ against doing sthg se garder de faire qqch; plastic sheets help ~ against frost des housses en plastique aideront à protéger du gel; how can we ~ against such accidents (happening)? comment éviter OR empêcher (que) de tels accidents (arrivent)?
guard dog *n* chien *m* de garde.
guard duty *n*: to be on ~ être de garde OR de faction.
guarded ['gɑ:dɪd] *adj* prudent, circonspect, réservé; to give a ~ reply répondre avec réserve.
guardedly ['gɑ:dɪdlɪ] *adv* avec réserve OR circonspection, prudemment.
guardhouse ['gɑ:dhaʊs, *pl* -haʊzɪz] *n* MIL [for guards] corps *m* de garde; [for prisoners] salle *f* de garde.
guardian ['gɑ:djən] *n* -**1.** [gen] gardien *m*, -enne *f*; [of museum] conservateur *m*, -trice *f*; the Guardian PRESS *quotidien britannique de qualité, plutôt de gauche*; Guardian reader *lecteur du Guardian (représentatif de la gauche intellectuelle)*. -**2.** JUR [of minor] tuteur *m*, -trice *f*.
guardian angel *n* ange *m* gardien.
guardianship ['gɑ:djənʃɪp] *n* -**1.** [gen] garde *f*. -**2.** JUR tutelle *f*; the child was put under the ~ of his aunt l'enfant fut placé sous la tutelle de sa tante.
guardrail ['gɑ:dreɪl] *n* -**1.** [on ship] bastingage *m*, garde-corps *m inv*. -**2.** RAIL contre-rail *m*. -**3.** *Am* [on road] barrière *f* de sécurité.
guardroom ['gɑ:drʊm] *n* -**1.** MIL [for guards] corps *m* de garde. -**2.** [for prisoners] salle *f* de garde.
guardsman ['gɑ:dzmən, *pl* -mən] *n* MIL *Br* soldat *m* de la garde royale; *Am* soldat *m* de la garde nationale.
guard's van *n Br* fourgon *m* du chef de train.
Guatemala [ˌgwɑ:tə'mɑ:lə] *pr n* Guatemala *m*; in ~ au Guatemala.
Guatemalan [ˌgwɑ:tə'mɑ:lən] ◇ *n* Guatémaltèque *mf*.
◇ *adj* guatémaltèque.
guava ['gwɑ:və] *n* [tree] goyavier *m*; [fruit] goyave *f*.
gubbins *inf* ['gʌbɪnz] *n* -**1.** (*U*) [rubbish] déchets *mpl*, saletés *fpl*. -**2.** [thing] truc *m*, machin *m*.
gubernatorial [ˌgu:bənə'tɔ:rɪəl] *adj Am* de OR du gouverneur; ~ elections élections des gouverneurs.
gudgeon ['gʌdʒn] *n* -**1.** [socket] tourillon *m*. -**2.** [fish] goujon *m*.
gudgeon pin *n* axe *m* de piston.
guelder rose [ˌgeldəʳ-] *n* [shrub] boule-de-neige *f*, obier *m*.
guer(r)illa [gə'rɪlə] ◇ *n* guérillero *m*.
◇ *comp*: ~ band OR group guérilla *f*, groupe *m* de guérilleros; ~ strike grève *f* sauvage; ~ warfare guérilla *f (combat)*.
Guernsey ['gɜ:nzɪ] ◇ *pr n* [island] Guernesey; in ~ à Guernesey.
◇ *n* -**1.** [cow] vache *f* de Guernesey. -**2.** [sweater] jersey *m*, tricot *m*. -**3.** *inf Austr phr*: to get a ~ être sélectionné.
guess [ges] ◇ *n* -**1.** [at facts, figures] : to have *Br* OR to take *Am* a ~ at sthg (essayer de) deviner qqch; if you don't know, have a ~ si tu ne sais pas, essaie de deviner; at a (rough) ~, I'd say 200 à vue de nez, je dirais 200; he made a good/a wild ~ il a deviné juste/à tout hasard; I'll give you three ~es devine un peu. -**2.** [hypothesis] supposition *f*, conjecture *f*; it's anybody's ~ Dieu seul le sait, impossible de prévoir; my ~ is that he won't come à mon avis il ne viendra pas, je pense qu'il ne viendra pas; your ~ is as good as mine tu en sais autant que moi, je n'en sais pas plus que toi.

◇ *vt* -**1.** [attempt to answer] deviner; ~ **what!** devine un peu!; ~ **who!** devine qui c'est!; ~ **who I saw in town** devine (un peu) qui j'ai vu en ville; **I ~ed as much** je m'en doutais, c'est bien ce que je pensais ❑ **'Guess Who's Coming to Dinner?'** *Kramer* 'Devine qui vient dîner?'. -**2.** [imagine] croire, penser, supposer; **I ~ you're right** je suppose que vous avez raison; **I ~ he isn't coming** je suppose qu'il ne viendra pas; **I ~ so** je pense que oui; **I ~ not** je ne crois pas.
◇ *vi* deviner; **to ~ at sthg** deviner qqch; **how did you ~?** comment avez-vous deviné?; **try to ~!** devine un peu!; **you'll never ~** tu ne devineras jamais; **the police ~ed right** la police a deviné OR vu juste; **we ~ed wrong** nous nous sommes trompés; **to keep sb ~ing** laisser qqn dans le doute; **don't keep me ~ing!** ne me laissez pas dans le doute!

guesstimate *inf* ['gestɪmət] *n* calcul *m* au pifomètre.

guesswork ['geswɜːk] *n (U)* conjecture *f*, hypothèse *f*; **to do sthg by ~** faire qqch au hasard; **it's pure** OR **sheer ~** c'est une simple hypothèse OR supposition.

guest [gest] *n* -**1.** [visitor - at home] invité *m*, -e *f*, hôte *mf*; [at table] invité *m*, -e *f*, convive *mf*; **~ of honour** invité d'honneur, invitée d'honneur; **be my ~!** fais donc!, je t'en prie! -**2.** [in hotel] client *m*, -e *f*; [in boarding-house] pensionnaire *mf*.

guest artist *n* vedette *f* invitée.

guest book *n* livre *m* d'or.

guesthouse ['gesthaus, *pl* -hauzɪz] *n* pension *f* de famille.

guest list *n* liste *f* des invités.

guestroom ['gestrum] *n* chambre *f* d'amis.

guest speaker *n* conférencier *m*, -ère *f (invité à parler par une organisation, une association)*.

guest worker *n* travailleur immigré *m*, travailleuse immigrée *f*.

guff *inf* [gʌf] *n (U)* bêtises *fpl*, idioties *fpl*.

guffaw [gʌ'fɔː] ◇ *n* gros éclat *m* de rire.
◇ *vi* rire bruyamment, s'esclaffer.
◇ *vt*: **"of course!", he ~ed** «bien sûr!», s'esclaffa-t-il.

Guiana [gaɪ'ænə] *pr n* Guyane *f*; **the ~s** les Guyanes ; **in ~** en Guyane ❑ **French ~** Guyane française; **Dutch ~** Guyane hollandaise.

Guianan [gaɪ'ɑːnən], **Guianese** [gaɪə'niːz]
◇ *n* Guyanais *m*, -e *f*.
◇ *adj* guyanais.

guidance ['gaɪdəns] *n* -**1.** [advice] conseils *mpl*; **she needs ~ concerning her education** elle a besoin de conseils pour son éducation; **vocational ~** orientation *f* professionnelle. -**2.** [instruction] direction *f*, conduite *f*; [supervision] direction *f*, supervision *f*; **to do sthg under ~** faire qqch avec les conseils OR sous la direction de qqn; **he's writing the book under the ~ of his former professor** il écrit ce livre sous la direction de son ancien professeur. -**3.** [information] information *f*; **electrical diagrams are given for your ~** les schémas électriques sont donnés à titre d'information OR à titre indicatif. -**4.** AERON guidage *m*.

guide [gaɪd] ◇ *n* -**1.** [for tourists] guide *mf*; **Gino was our ~ during our tour of Rome** Gino nous servait de guide pendant notre visite de Rome. -**2.** [influence, direction] guide *m*, indication *f*; **let your conscience be your ~** laissez-vous guider par votre conscience; **to take sthg as a ~** prendre qqch comme règle de conduite. -**3.** [indication] indication *f*, idée *f*; **as a rough ~** en gros, approximativement; **are these tests a good ~ to intelligence?** ces tests fournissent-ils une bonne indication OR donnent-ils une bonne idée de l'intelligence?; **conversions are given as a ~** les conversions sont données à titre indicatif. -**4.** [manual] guide *m*, manuel *m* pratique; **a ~ to better French** un guide pour améliorer votre français; **a ~ to France** un guide de la France. -**5.** *Br* [girl scout]: **(Girl) Guide** éclaireuse *f*; **she's in the Guides** elle est éclaireuse. -**6.** [machine part] guide *m*.
◇ *vt* -**1.** [show the way] guider, conduire; **to ~ sb in/out** conduire qqn jusqu'à l'entrée/la sortie; **to ~ sb upstairs** conduire qqn en haut; **the children ~d us through the old city** les enfants nous ont guidés à travers la vieille ville. -**2.** [instruct] diriger, conduire. -**3.** [advise] conseiller, guider, orienter; **he ~d the country through some difficult times** il a su conduire le pays durant des périodes difficiles; **I'll be ~d by you** je me laisserai guider par vous. -**4.** AERON guider.

guidebook ['gaɪdbʊk] *n* guide *m* touristique *(manuel)*.

guided ['gaɪdɪd] *adj* guidé, sous la conduite d'un guide.

guided missile *n* missile *m* téléguidé.

guide dog *n* chien *m* d'aveugle.

guided tour *n* visite *f* guidée.

guideline ['gaɪdlaɪn] *n* -**1.** [for writing] ligne *f*. -**2.** [hint, principle] ligne *f* directrice, directives *fpl*.

guide movement *n mouvement féminin de scoutisme*.

guidepost ['gaɪdpəʊst] *n* poteau *m* indicateur.

guide rope *n* [for hoist] corde *f* de guidage; [for hot-air balloon] guiderope *m*.

guiding ['gaɪdɪŋ] ◇ *adj* [principle] directeur; **she gave me a ~ hand** *fig* elle m'a donné un coup de main; **he's been a ~ light in my career** il m'a toujours guidé dans ma carrière ❑ **~ star** guide *m*.
◇ *n* guidage *m*, conduite *f*.

guild [gɪld] *n* -**1.** [professional] guilde *f*, corporation *f*; **the ~ of goldsmiths** la guilde des orfèvres. -**2.** [association] confrérie *f*, association *f*, club *m*; **women's/church ~** cercle *m* féminin/paroissial.

guilder ['gɪldə^r] *n* florin *m* (hollandais).

guildhall ['gɪldhɔːl] *n* palais *m* des corporations; **The Guildhall** *l'hôtel de ville de la City de Londres, célèbre pour sa grande salle de réception*.

guile [gaɪl] *n (U) fml* [trickery] fourberie *f*, tromperie *f*; [cunning] ruse *f*, astuce *f*.

guileful ['gaɪlful] *adj fml* [deceitful] fourbe, trompeur; [cunning] rusé, astucieux.

guileless ['gaɪllɪs] *adj fml* [innocent, ingenuous] candide, ingénu.

guillemot ['gɪlɪmɒt] (*pl inv* OR **guillemots**) *n* guillemot *m*.

guillotine [gɪlə'tiːn] ◇ *n* -**1.** [for executions] guillotine *f*. -**2.** [for paper] massicot *m*. -**3.** POL *procédure parlementaire consistant à fixer des délais stricts pour l'examen de chaque partie d'un projet de loi*.
◇ *vt* -**1.** [person] guillotiner. -**2.** [paper] massicoter. -**3.** [discussion] clôturer.

guilt [gɪlt] *n* culpabilité *f*; **a sense of ~** un sentiment de culpabilité; **~ drove him to suicide** un sentiment de culpabilité l'a poussé au suicide.

guilt complex *n* complexe *m* de culpabilité.

guiltily ['gɪltɪlɪ] *adv* d'un air coupable.

guiltless ['gɪltlɪs] *adj* innocent.

guilty ['gɪltɪ] (*compar* **guiltier**, *superl* **guiltiest**) *adj* coupable; **~ of murder** coupable de meurtre; **to plead ~/not ~** plaider coupable/non coupable; **the judge found her ~** le juge l'a déclarée coupable; **a verdict of ~/not ~** un verdict de culpabilité/d'acquittement; **they're ~ of an appalling lack of sensitivity** ils font preuve d'un manque terrible de sensibilité; **to have a ~ conscience** avoir mauvaise conscience; **there's no need to feel ~** il n'y a pas de raison de culpabiliser; **she gave me a ~ look** elle me jeta un regard coupable; **I'm sure she has some ~ secret** je suis sûr qu'elle a un secret inavouable ❑ **the ~ party** le coupable, la coupable.

guinea ['gɪnɪ] *n* [money] guinée *f (ancienne monnaie britannique)*.

Guinea ['gɪnɪ] ◇ *pr n* Guinée *f*; **in ~** en Guinée ❑ **Equatorial ~** Guinée-Équatoriale *f*.
◇ *n* ▼ *Am terme injurieux désignant un Italien*, ≃ Rital *m*.

Guinea-Bissau [-bɪ'səʊ] *pr n* Guinée-Bissau *f*; **in ~** en Guinée-Bissau.

guinea fowl (*pl inv*) *n* pintade *f*.

guinea hen *n* pintade *f* (femelle).

Guinean ['gɪnɪən] ◇ *n* Guinéen *m*, -enne *f*.
◇ *adj* guinéen.

guinea pig *n* cochon *m* d'Inde, cobaye *m*; [used in experiments] cobaye *m*; **to use sb as a ~** se servir de qqn comme d'un cobaye, prendre qqn comme cobaye.

guise [gaɪz] *n* -**1.** [appearance] apparence *f*, aspect *m*; **the same old policies in a new ~** la même politique sous des dehors différents; **under** OR **in the ~ of** sous l'apparence de. -**2.** *arch* [costume] costume *m*.

guitar [gɪ'tɑː^r] *n* guitare *f*; **electric ~** guitare *f* électrique.

guitarist [gɪ'tɑːrɪst] *n* guitariste *mf*.

Gujarati [guːdʒə'rɑːtɪ] *n* gujarati *m*.

gulag ['guːlæg] *n* goulag *m*; **'The Gulag Archipelago'** *Solzhenitzyn* 'l'Archipel du goulag'.

gulch [gʌlʃ] *n Am* ravin *m*.

gulf [gʌlf] ◇ *n* -**1.** [bay] golfe *m*; **the Gulf of Aden** le golfe d'Aden; **the Gulf of Bothnia** le golfe de Botnie; **the Gulf of California** le golfe de Californie; **the Gulf of Mexico** le golfe du Mexique; **the Gulf of Siam** le golfe de Thaïlande. -**2.** [chasm] gouffre *m*, abîme *m*; **a huge ~ has opened up between the two parties** *fig* il y a désormais un énorme fossé entre les deux partis. -**3.** GEOG: **the Gulf** le golfe Persique.
◇ *comp* [country, oil] du Golfe; **the Gulf War** la guerre du Golfe.

Gulf States *pl pr n*: **the ~** [in US] les États du golfe du Mexique; [round Persian Gulf] les États du Golfe.

Gulf Stream *pr n*: **the ~** le Gulf Stream.

gulfweed ['gʌlfwiːd] *n* sargasse *f*.

gull [gʌl] ◇ *n* -**1.** [bird] mouette *f*, goéland *m*; **black headed ~** mouette rieuse; **herring ~** goéland argenté. -**2.** *arch* [dupe] dupe *f*.
◇ *vt arch* duper.

gullet ['gʌlɪt] *n* [œsophagus] œsophage *m*; [throat] gosier *m*.

gulley ['gʌlɪ] (*pl* **gulleys**) = **gully**.

gullibility [gʌlə'bɪlətɪ] *n* crédulité *f*, naïveté *f*.

gullible ['gʌləbl] *adj* crédule, naïf.

gull-wing *adj* AUT: **~ door** portière *f* en papillon.

gully ['gʌlɪ] (*pl* **gullies**) *n* -**1.** [valley] ravin *m*. -**2.** [drain] caniveau *m*, rigole *f*.

gulp [gʌlp] ◇ *vt*: **to ~ (down)** [food] engloutir; [drink] avaler à pleine gorge; [air] avaler.
◇ *vi* [with emotion] avoir un serrement de gorge; **he ~ed in surprise** la surprise lui a serré la gorge.
◇ *n* [act of gulping]: **she swallowed it in one ~** elle l'a avalé d'un seul coup ‖ [with emotion] serrement *m* de gorge; **"oh dear", he said with a ~** «mon Dieu», dit-il, la gorge serrée.
◆ **gulp back** *vt sep* avaler; **she ~ed back her tears** elle a ravalé OR refoulé ses larmes.

gum [gʌm] (*pt* & *pp* **gummed**, *cont* **gumming**)
◇ *n* -**1.** [chewing gum] chewing-gum *m*; **to chew ~** mâcher du chewing-gum. -**2.** [adhesive] gomme *f*, colle *f*. -**3.** BOT [substance] gomme *f*. -**4.** *Br* = **gumdrop**. -**5.** ANAT gencive *f*.
◇ *vt* -**1.** [cover with gum] gommer; **gummed paper** papier gommé. -**2.** [stick] coller; **~ down the flap** collez le rabat; **~ the two edges together** collez les deux bords ensemble.
◇ *vi* BOT exsuder de la gomme.
◇ *interj inf Br dated*: **by ~!** nom d'un chien!, mince alors!
◆ **gum up** *inf vt sep* [mechanism] bousiller; [plan] ficher en l'air; **that's gummed up the works!** ça a tout fichu en l'air!; **the kitten's eyes were all gummed up** les yeux du chaton étaient tout collés.

gum arabic *n* gomme *f* arabique.

gumbo [ˈgʌmbəʊ] (*pl* gumbos) *n* -**1.** [dish] *soupe épaisse aux fruits de mer.* -**2.** *Am* [okra] gombo *m*.

gumboil [ˈgʌmbɔɪl] *n* parulie *f*, abcès *m* gingival.

gumboot [ˈgʌmbuːt] *n Br* botte *f* de caoutchouc.

gumdrop [ˈgʌmdrɒp] *n* boule *f* de gomme.

gummy [ˈgʌmɪ] (*compar* gummier, *superl* gummiest) *adj* -**1.** [sticky] collant, gluant. -**2.** [gumlike] gommeux.

gumption *inf* [ˈgʌmpʃn] *n (U)* -**1.** *Br* [common sense] jugeote *f*; **he didn't even have the ~ to call the police** il n'a même pas eu la présence d'esprit d'appeler la police. -**2.** [initiative] initiative *f*; **at least he had the ~ to start up business on his own** au moins il a pris l'initiative de monter sa propre affaire.

gum resin *n* gomme-résine *f*.

gumshield [ˈgʌmʃiːld] *n* protège-dents *m inv*.

gumshoe▽ [ˈgʌmʃuː] *Am dated* ◇ *n* [detective] privé *m*.

◇ *vi* aller à pas feutrés.

◆ **gumshoes** *npl* [overshoes] caoutchoucs *mpl*.

gum tree *n* gommier *m*; **to be up a ~** *inf* être dans le pétrin.

gun [gʌn] (*pt* & *pp* gunned, *cont* gunning)

◇ *n* -**1.** arme *f* à feu; [pistol] pistolet *m*; [revolver] revolver *m*; [rifle] fusil *m*; [cannon] canon *m*; **the burglar had a ~** le cambrioleur était armé; **to draw a ~ on sb** braquer une arme sur qqn; **a 21-~ salute** une salve de 21 coups de canon; **the ~s** MIL l'artillerie *f* ❑ **machine ~** mitrailleuse *f*; **to be going great ~s** *inf* [enterprise] marcher à merveille; **she's going great ~s** ça boume pour elle; **the big ~s** *inf* les huiles *fpl*; **to bring out one's big ~s** *inf* mettre le paquet; **to jump the ~** brûler le feu; **to spike sb's ~s** mettre des bâtons dans les roues de qqn; **to stick to one's ~s** tenir bon. -**2.** [hunter] fusil *m*. -**3.** *inf* [gunman] gangster *m*; **hired ~** tueur *m* à gages. -**4.** [dispenser] pistolet *m*; **paint ~** pistolet *m* à peinture. -**5.** ELECTRON canon *m*.

◇ *vt* AUT: **to ~ the engine** accélérer.

◆ **gun down** *vt sep* abattre.

◆ **gun for** *vt insep* -**1.** [look for] chercher; **the boss is gunning for you** le patron te cherche OR est après toi. -**2.** [try hard for] faire des pieds et des mains pour obtenir.

gunboat [ˈgʌnbəʊt] *n* cannonière *f*.

gunboat diplomacy *n* diplomatie *f* imposée par la force, politique *f* de la cannonière.

gun carriage *n* affût *m* de canon.

gun cotton *n* fulmicoton *m*, coton-poudre *m*.

gun crew *n* servants *mpl* de pièce.

gundog [ˈgʌndɒg] *n* chien *m* de chasse.

gunfight [ˈgʌnfaɪt] *n* fusillade *f*.

gunfire [ˈgʌnfaɪəʳ] *n (U)* coups *mpl* de feu, fusillade *f*; [of cannon] tir *m* d'artillerie.

gunge *inf* [gʌndʒ] *n (U)* substance *f* collante, amas *m* visqueux.

gung-ho [ˌgʌŋˈhəʊ] *adj* tout feu tout flamme, enthousiaste.

gungy *inf* [ˈgʌndʒɪ] *adj* poisseux.

gunk *inf* [gʌnk] *n (U)* substance *f* visqueuse, amas *m* répugnant.

gun licence *n* permis *m* de port d'armes.

gunman [ˈgʌnmən] (*pl* gunmen [-mən]) *n* gangster *m* (armé); [terrorist] terroriste *m* (armé).

gunmetal [ˈgʌnˌmetl] *n* -**1.** [metal] bronze *m* à canon. -**2.** [colour] vert-de-gris *m inv*.

gun-metal grey ◇ *adj* vert-de-gris *(inv)*.

◇ *n* vert-de-gris *m inv*.

gunnel [ˈgʌnl] = **gunwale**.

gunner [ˈgʌnəʳ] *n* artilleur *m*, canonnier *m*.

gunnery [ˈgʌnərɪ] *n (U)* artillerie *f*.

gunnery officer *n* officier *m* d'artillerie.

gunnery sergeant *n* sergent *m* d'artillerie.

gunny [ˈgʌnɪ] *n* toile *f* de jute (grossière).

gunnysack [ˈgʌnɪsæk] *n* sac *m* de jute.

gunplay [ˈgʌnpleɪ] *n Am* échange *m* de coups de feu.

gunpoint [ˈgʌnpɔɪnt] *n*: **to have** OR **to hold sb at ~** menacer qqn d'un pistolet OR d'un revolver OR d'un fusil; **a confession obtained at ~** une confession obtenue sous la menace d'un revolver.

gunpowder [ˈgʌnˌpaʊdəʳ] *n* poudre *f* à canon.

Gunpowder Plot *n*: **the~** *Br* HIST la conspiration des poudres.

THE GUNPOWDER PLOT:

Complot organisé par des catholiques, menés par Guy Fawkes, pour faire sauter le Parlement britannique et tuer le roi Jacques Ier et sa famille, le 5 novembre 1605, en réaction au refus royal d'instaurer la liberté de culte. Le complot fut déjoué. On commémore cette journée, appelée «Guy Fawkes' Day», par des feux d'artifice et des feux de joie.

---

gun room *n* [in house] armurerie *f*; [on warship] poste *m* des aspirants.

gunrunner [ˈgʌnˌrʌnəʳ] *n* trafiquant *m*, -e *f* d'armes.

gunrunning [ˈgʌnˌrʌnɪŋ] *n (U)* trafic *m* d'armes.

gunsel *inf* [ˈgʌnsəl] *n Am* -**1.** [criminal] criminel *m* armé. -**2.** [boy] *jeune homme qui a des rapports sexuels avec un homme plus âgé.*

gunship [ˈgʌnʃɪp] *n* [helicopter] hélicoptère *m* armé.

gunshot [ˈgʌnʃɒt] *n* -**1.** [shot] coup *m* de feu; **a ~ wound** une blessure de OR par balle. -**2.** [range]: **to be out of/within ~** être hors de portée de/à portée de fusil.

gunshy [ˈgʌnʃaɪ] *adj*: **to be ~** avoir peur des coups de feu.

gunslinger *inf* [ˈgʌnˌslɪŋəʳ] *n* bandit *m* armé.

gunsmith [ˈgʌnsmɪθ] *n* armurier *m*.

gun turret *n* tourelle *f*.

gunwale [ˈgʌnl] *n* NAUT plat-bord *m*.

guppy [ˈgʌpɪ] (*pl* guppies) *n* guppy *m*.

gurgle [ˈgɜːgl] ◇ *vi* [liquid] glouglouter, gargouiller; [stream] murmurer; [person - with delight] glousser, roucouler; [baby] gazouiller.

◇ *n* [of liquid] glouglou *m*, gargouillis *m*; [of stream] murmure *m*, gazouillement *m*; [of laughter] gloussement *m*, roucoulement *m*; [of baby] gazouillis.

Gurkha [ˈgɜːkə] *n* Gurkha *m*.

gurnard [ˈgɜːnəd] *n* grondin *m*.

guru [ˈgʊruː] *n* gourou *m*.

gush [gʌʃ] ◇ *vi* -**1.** [flow] jaillir; **blood was ~ing from his arm** le sang jaillissait de son bras; **water ~ed forth** OR **out** l'eau jaillissait. -**2.** [talk effusively] parler avec animation; **everyone was ~ing over the baby** tout le monde se répandait en compliments sur le bébé; **"darling, you were wonderful", he ~ed** «chérie, tu as été formidable», lança-t-il avec exubérance.

◇ *n* -**1.** [of liquid, gas] jet *m*, flot *m*; **a ~ of words** *fig* un flot de paroles. -**2.** [of emotion] vague *f*, effusion *f*; **a sudden ~ of enthusiasm** une soudaine vague d'enthousiasme.

gusher [ˈgʌʃəʳ] *n* [oil well] puits *m* jaillissant OR éruptif.

gushing [ˈgʌʃɪŋ] *adj* -**1.** [liquid] jaillissant, bouillonnant. -**2.** [person] trop exubérant; **~ compliments/praise** compliments/éloges sans fin.

gushy *inf* [ˈgʌʃɪ] (*compar* gushier, *superl* gushiest) *adj pej* [person] exubérant.

gusset [ˈgʌsɪt] *n* -**1.** SEW soufflet *m*. -**2.** CONSTR gousset *m*.

gust [gʌst] ◇ *n*: **a ~ (of wind)** un coup de vent, une rafale; **a ~ of anger** *fig* un accès de colère.

◇ *vi* [wind] souffler en bourrasques; [rain] faire des bourrasques; **winds ~ing up to 50 mph were recorded** on a enregistré des pointes de vent à 80 km/h.

gustatory [ˈgʌstətrɪ] *adj* gustatif.

Gustav [ˈgʊstɑːv] *pr n* Gustave.

Gustavus Adolphus [gʊsˈtɑːvəsəˈdɒlfəs] *pr n* Gustave Adolphe.

gusto [ˈgʌstəʊ] *n* délectation *f*, enthousiame *m*; **to do sthg with ~** faire qqch avec enthousiasme.

gusty [ˈgʌstɪ] (*compar* gustier, *super* gustiest) *adj*: **it's a bit ~ out** il y a des rafales (de vent, OR des bourrasques dehors; **a ~ wind** un vent qui souffle en rafales, des rafales de vent; **a ~ day** un jour de grand vent.

gut [gʌt] ◇ *n* -**1.** *(usu pl)* ANAT boyau *m*, intestin *m*; **~s** instestins *mpl*, boyaux *mpl*, entrailles *fpl*; **I've got a pain in the ~** *inf* j'ai mal au bide ❑ **~ feeling** pressentiment *m*; **~ reaction** réaction *f* instinctive OR viscérale. -**2.** *inf (usu pl)* [of machine] intérieur *m*. -**3.** *(U)* [thread - for violins] corde *f* de boyau; [- for rackets] boyau *m*. -**4.** [in sea port] goulet *m*, passage *m* étroit.

◇ *vt* -**1.** [fish, poultry etc] étriper, vider. -**2.** [building] ne laisser que les quatre murs de. -**3.** [book] résumer, extraire l'essentiel de.

◆ **guts** *inf* ◇ *n* [glutton] morfal *m*, -e *f*; **don't be such a (greedy) ~s** ne sois pas si morfal

◇ *npl phr*: **to have ~s** avoir du cran OR du cœur au ventre; **he has no ~s** il n'a rien dans le ventre; **to work** OR **to sweat one's ~s out** se casser les reins, se tuer au travail; **to hate sb's ~s** ne pas pouvoir blairer qqn; **I'll have your ~s for garters** je vais faire de toi de la chair à pâté.

gutless *inf* [ˈgʌtlɪs] *adj* [cowardly] trouillard, dégonflé.

gutsy *inf* [ˈgʌtsɪ] (*compar* gutsier, *superl* gutsiest) *adj* -**1.** [courageous] qui a du cran; **she's one ~ woman** c'est vraiment une femme qui a du cran. -**2.** [powerful - film, language, novel] qui a du punch, musclé; **a ~ singer** un chanteur qui a des tripes.

gutta-percha [ˌgʌtəˈpɜːtʃə] *n* gutta-percha *f*.

gutted▽ [ˈgʌtɪd] *adj Br*: **to be** OR **to feel ~** en être malade.

gutter [ˈgʌtəʳ] ◇ *n* -**1.** [on roof] gouttière *f*; [in street] caniveau *m*, ruisseau *m*; *fig*: **to end up in the ~** tomber OR rouler dans le ruisseau; **to rescue sb from** OR **to drag sb out of the ~** tirer qqn du ruisseau; **to speak the language of the ~** parler le langage des rues. -**2.** [ditch] rigole *f*, sillon *m (creusé par la pluie)*; [in bookbinding] petits fonds *mpl*.

◇ *vi* [candle flame] vaciller, trembler.

guttering [ˈgʌtərɪŋ] *n (U)* [of roof] gouttières *fpl*

gutter press *n pej* presse *f* de bas étage, presse à scandale.

guttersnipe [ˈgʌtəsnaɪp] *n pej* gosse *mf* des rues.

guttural [ˈgʌtərəl] ◇ *adj* guttural.

◇ *n* LING gutturale *f*.

guv *inf* [gʌv], **guvnor** [ˈgʌvnəʳ] *n Br*: **the ~** [boss] le chef, le boss; *dated* [my father] le pater, le paternel; **got a fag, ~?** n'auriez pas un mégot, patron?

guy [gaɪ] *n* -**1.** *inf* [man] gars *m*, type *m*; **a good ~** un mec OR un type bien; **tough ~** dur *m*; **ok ~s, let's go** allez les gars, on y va; *Am* [to both men and women] allez les copains, on y va; **are you ~s ready?** vous êtes prêts, les gars?; *Am* [to both men and women] tout le monde est prêt? -**2.** *Br* [for bonfire] *effigie de Guy Fawkes.* -**3.** [for tent] corde *f* de tente.

Guyana [gaɪˈænə] *pr n* Guyana *m*; **in ~** au Guyana.

Guyanese [ˌgaɪəˈniːz] ◇ *adj* guyanais.

◇ *n* Guyanais *m*, -e *f*.

Guy Fawkes' Night [-ˈfɔːks-] *pr n fête célébrée le 5 novembre en commémoration de la conspiration des poudres.*

GUY FAWKES' NIGHT:

Cette fête se déroule en plein air autour d'un grand feu de joie sur lequel on est censé brûler une effigie («the Guy») de Guy Fawkes, l'instigateur de la conspiration des poudres. Des feux d'artifice sont également organisés.

---

guy rope = **guy 3**.

guzzle *inf* [ˈgʌzl] ◇ *vt* [food] bouffer, bâfrer, [drink] siffler; **he's ~d the whole lot!** [food] il a tout bouffé OR bâfré!; [drink] il a tout sifflé! **this car really ~s the gas** cette voiture bouffe vraiment beaucoup (d'essence).

◇ *vi* [eat] s'empiffrer, se goinfrer; [drink] boire trop vite.
◇ *n*: I had a good ~ je me suis bien empiffré.

guzzler *inf* ['gʌzləʳ] *n* [person] goinfre *mf*; [car] → **gas guzzler**.

gym [dʒɪm] *n* [hall, building] gymnase *m*; [activity] gymnastique *f*, gym *f*.

gymkhana [dʒɪm'kɑːnə] *n* gymkhana *m*.

gymnasium [dʒɪm'neɪzjəm] (*pl* gymnasiums OR gymnasia [-zɪə]) *n* gymnase *m*.

gymnast ['dʒɪmnæst] *n* gymnaste *mf*; I've never been much of a ~ je n'ai jamais été très fort en gymnastique.

gymnastic [dʒɪm'næstɪk] *adj* [exercises] de gymnastique; [ability] de gymnaste.

gymnastics [dʒɪm'næstɪks] *n (U)* gymnastique *f*; ~ display exhibition *f* de gymnastique; mental ~ gymnastique cérébrale.

gym shoe *n* chaussure *f* de gymnastique OR gym.

gymslip ['dʒɪm,slɪp], **gym tunic** *n* [part of uniform] blouse *f* d'écolière.

gynaecology *etc* [,gaɪnə'kɒlədʒɪ] *Br* = **gynecology**.

gynecological [,gaɪnəkə'lɒdʒɪkl] *adj* gynécologique.

gynecologist [,gaɪnə'kɒlədʒɪst] *n* gynécologue *mf*.

gynecology [,gaɪnə'kɒlədʒɪ] *n* gynécologie *f*.

gyp *inf* [dʒɪp] (*pt* & *pp* gypped, *cont* gypping)
◇ *n Br* - **1.** to give sb ~ [cause pain] dérouiller qqn. - **2.** UNIV [cleaning lady] femme *f* de ménage.
◇ *vt* [cheat] rouler; you've been gypped tu t'es fait rouler OR avoir.

gyppo▼ ['dʒɪpəʊ] (*pl* gyppos) = **gippo**.

gypsum ['dʒɪpsəm] *n* gypse *m*.

gypsy ['dʒɪpsɪ] (*pl* gypsies) = **gipsy**.

gyrate [dʒaɪ'reɪt] *vi* tournoyer.

gyration [dʒaɪ'reɪʃən] *n* giration *f*.

gyratory ['dʒaɪrətrɪ] *adj* giratoire.

gyro ['dʒaɪrəʊ] = **gyrocompass**, **gyroscope**.

gyrocompass ['dʒaɪrəʊ,kʌmpəs] *n* gyrocompas *m*.

gyromagnetic [,dʒaɪrəʊmæg'netɪk] *adj* gyromagnétique.

gyroscope ['dʒaɪrəskəʊp] *n* gyroscope *m*.

gyroscopic [,dʒaɪrəʊ'skɒpɪk] *adj* gyroscopique.

gyrostabilizer [,dʒaɪrəʊ'steɪbɪlaɪzəʳ] *n* stabilisateur *m* gyroscopique.

gyrostat ['dʒaɪrəʊstæt] *n* gyrostat *m*.

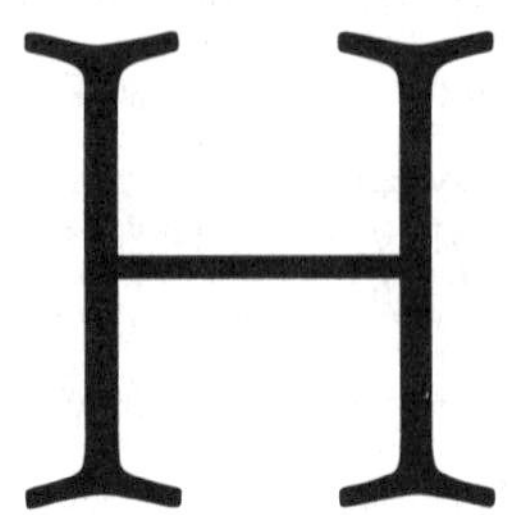

h (*pl* h's OR hs), **H** (*pl* H's OR Hs) [eɪtʃ] *n* [letter] h *m*, H *m*; to drop one's h's avaler ses h *(et révéler par là ses origines populaires)*.

ha [hɑː] *interj* [in triumph, sudden comprehension] ha!, ah!; [in contempt] peuh!; ~ ~, very funny! *iron* ha ha ha, très drôle!

habeas corpus [ˌheɪbjəs'kɔːpəs] *n* JUR habeas corpus *m*; to issue a writ of ~ délivrer un (acte d') habeas corpus.

THE HABEAS CORPUS ACT:
Loi votée en Angleterre en 1679 et selon laquelle toute personne arrêtée est en droit de faire examiner par un juge la légalité de son emprisonnement. Complétée par plusieurs lois postérieures (1816 et 1960), la procédure est encore applicable en Grande-Bretagne et dans tous les pays soumis à la «Common Law» (sauf l'Écosse). Elle fut également intégrée à la Constitution américaine.

---

haberdasher ['hæbədæʃəʳ] *n* -**1.** *Br* mercier *m*, -ère *f*. -**2.** *Am* chemisier *m*, -ère *f*.

haberdashery ['hæbədæʃərɪ] *n* -**1.** *Br* mercerie *f*. -**2.** *Am* marchand *m*, -e *f* de vêtements d'hommes *(en particulier de gants et de chapeaux)*.

habit ['hæbɪt] *n* -**1.** [custom] habitude *f*; to be in the ~ of doing sthg avoir l'habitude de faire qqch; to get into the ~ of doing sthg prendre l'habitude de faire qqch; you'd better get into the ~ of being more punctual il vaudrait mieux que tu prennes l'habitude d'être plus ponctuel; to get sb into the ~ of doing sthg faire prendre à qqn OR donner à qqn l'habitude de faire qqch, habituer qqn à faire qqch; to make a ~ of sthg/of doing sthg prendre l'habitude de qqch/de faire qqch; don't worry, I'm not going to make a ~ of it ne t'en fais pas, cela ne deviendra pas une habitude; just don't make a ~ of it! ne recommence pas!, que cela ne se reproduise pas!; to get out of a ~ perdre une habitude; to get sb out of the ~ of doing sthg faire perdre à qqn l'habitude de faire qqch; he has a very strange ~ of pulling his ear when he talks il a un tic très étrange consistant à se tirer l'oreille quand il parle; from force of ~ par habitude; it's just force of ~ c'est l'habitude; he's very much a creature of ~ il est esclave de ses habitudes. -**2.** *inf* [drug dependency] : to have a ~ être accro; to have a heroin ~ être accro à l'héroïne; he steals to pay for his ~ il vole pour payer sa drogue; to kick the ~ [drugs, tobacco] décrocher. -**3.** [dress - of monk, nun] habit *m*; [- for riding] tenue *f* de cheval.

habitable ['hæbɪtəbl] *adj* habitable.

habitat ['hæbɪtæt] *n* habitat *m*.

habitation [ˌhæbɪ'teɪʃn] *n* -**1.** [occupation] habitation *f*; there were signs of recent ~ l'endroit semblait avoir été habité dans un passé récent; fit for ~ habitable; unfit for ~ inhabitable; [from sanitary point of view] salubre/insalubre. -**2.** [place] habitation *f*, résidence *f*, demeure *f*.

habit-forming [-ˌfɔːmɪŋ] *adj* [drug] qui crée une accoutumance OR une dépendance; I'd better not have another, it could be ~ *hum* il vaut mieux que je n'en prenne pas d'autre, je risquerais de ne plus pouvoir m'en passer.

habitual [hə'bɪtʃʊəl] *adj* [customary - generosity, lateness, good humour] habituel, accoutumé; [- liar, drinker] invétéré; ~ offender JUR récidiviste *mf*.

habitually [hə'bɪtʃʊəlɪ] *adv* habituellement, ordinairement.

habituate [hə'bɪtʃʊeɪt] *vt fml*: to ~ o.s./sb to sthg s'habituer/habituer qqn à qqch; to become ~d to sthg s'habituer à qqch.

hack [hæk] ◇ *n* -**1.** [sharp blow] coup *m* violent; [kick] coup *m* de pied; to take a ~ at sb [kick] donner un coup de pied à qqn. -**2.** [cut] entaille *f*. -**3.** *pej* [writer] écrivaillon *m*; [politician] politicard *m*. -**4.** [horse for riding] cheval *m* de selle; [horse for hire] cheval *m* de louage; [old horse, nag] rosse *f*, carne *f*. -**5.** [ride] : to go for a ~ aller faire une promenade à cheval. -**6.** [cough] toux *f* sèche. -**7.** *inf Am* [car] tacot *m*.
◇ *comp*: ~ writer écrivaillon *m*, écrivain *m* médiocre; ~ writing travail *m* d'écrivaillon.
◇ *vt* -**1.** [cut] taillader, tailler; to ~ sb/sthg to pieces tailler qqn/qqch en pièces; *fig* [opponent, manuscript] mettre OR tailler qqn/qqch en pièces; to ~ sb to death tuer qqn à coups de couteau OR de hache; he ~ed his way through the jungle il s'est taillé un passage à travers la jungle à coups de machette. -**2.** [kick - ball] donner un coup de pied sec dans; to ~ sb on the shins donner un coup de pied dans les tibias à qqn. -**3.** COMPUT: to ~ one's way into a system entrer dans un système par effraction. -**4.** *inf phr*: I can't ~ it [can't cope] je n'en peux plus, je craque; the new guy can't ~ it le nouveau ne tient pas le choc.
◇ *vi* -**1.** [cut] donner des coups de couteau *(de hache etc)*; to ~ (away) at sthg taillader qqch. -**2.** [kick]: to ~ at the ball donner un coup de pied sec dans le ballon; to ~ at sb's shins donner des coups de pied dans les tibias à qqn. -**3.** COMPUT: to ~ into a system entrer dans un système par effraction. -**4.** [on horseback] aller à cheval; to go ~ing aller faire une promenade à cheval.

◆ **hack down** *vt sep* [tree] abattre à coups de hache; [person] massacrer à coups de couteau *(de hache etc)*.

◆ **hack into** *vt sep* [body, corpse] taillader; *fig* [text, article] massacrer.

◆ **hack off** *vt sep* [branch, sb's head] couper.

◆ **hack out** *vt sep* [centre of fruit, rotten parts] couper; [hole, clearing] tailler.

◆ **hack up** *vt sep* [meat, wood] tailler OR couper en menus morceaux; [body, victim] mettre en pièces, découper en morceaux.

hacker ['hækəʳ] *n* COMPUT pirate *m* informatique.

hacking ['hækɪŋ] ◇ *n* *(U)* -**1.** [in football, rugby etc] coups *mpl* de pied dans les tibias. -**2.** [coughing] toux *f* sèche. -**3.** COMPUT piratage *m* *(informatique)*.
◇ *adj*: ~ cough toux *f* sèche.

hacking jacket *n* veste *f* de cheval.

hackle ['hækl] *n* [of bird] plume *f* du cou.

hackles ['hæklz] *npl* [of dog] poils *mpl* du cou; when a dog has its ~ up quand un chien a le poil hérissé || *fig*: my ~ rose ça m'a hérissé le poil; it gets my ~ up, it makes my ~ rise ça me hérisse; don't go getting your ~ up ne t'énerve pas.

hackney ['hæknɪ] = **hackney carriage 1**.

hackney carriage *n* -**1.** [horse-drawn] fiacre *m*. -**2.** *fml* [taxi] *taxi officiellement agréé*.

hackneyed ['hæknɪd] *adj* [subject] réchauffé, rebattu; [turn of phrase] banal, commun; ~ expression cliché *m*, lieu *m* commun.

hacksaw ['hæksɔː] *n* scie *f* à métaux.

hackwork ['hækwɜːk] *n* écrivaillerie *f*.

had [*weak form* həd, *strong form* hæd] *pt* & *pp* → **have**.

haddock ['hædək] *n* aiglefin *m*, églefin *m*; [smoked] haddock *m*.

Hades ['heɪdiːz] *pr n* Hadès.

hadn't ['hædnt] = **had not**.

Hadrian ['heɪdrɪən] *pr n* Hadrien; ~'s Wall le Mur d'Hadrien.

haematological *Br*, **hematological** *Am* [ˌhiːmətə'lɒdʒɪkl] *adj* hématologique.

haematologist *Br*, **hematologist** *Am* [ˌhiːmə'tɒlədʒɪst] *n* hématologiste *mf*, hématologue *mf*.

haematology *Br*, **hematology** *Am* [ˌhiːmə'tɒlədʒɪ] *n* hématologie *f*.

haematoma *Br*, **hematoma** *Am* [ˌhiːmə'təʊmə] *n* hématome *m*.

haemoglobin *Br*, **hemoglobin** *Am* [ˌhiːmə'gləʊbɪn] *n* hémoglobine *f*.

haemophilia *Br*, **hemophilia** *Am* [ˌhiːmə'fɪlɪə] *n* hémophilie *f*.

haemophiliac *Br*, **hemophiliac** *Am* [ˌhiːmə'fɪlɪæk] *n* hémophile *mf*.

haemorrhage *Br*, **hemorrhage** *Am* ['hemərɪdʒ] ◇ *n* hémorragie *f*.
◇ *vi* faire une hémorragie; there's still some haemorrhaging l'hémorragie n'est pas encore arrêtée.

haemorrhoids *Br*, **hemorrhoids** *Am* ['hemərɔɪdz] *npl* hémorroïdes *fpl*.

hafnium ['hæfnɪəm] *n* CHEM hafnium *m*.

haft [hæft] *n* [of knife] manche *m*; [of sword] poignée *f*.

hag [hæg] *n* [witch] sorcière *f*; *pej* [old woman] vieille sorcière *f*, vieille chouette *f*; [unpleasant woman] harpie *f*; **she's a real old ~** ce n'est qu'une vieille chouette.

Hagar ['heɪgɑːʳ] *pr n* Agar.

Haggai ['hægaɪ] *pr n* Aggée.

haggard ['hægəd] *adj* [tired, worried] hâve.

haggis ['hægɪs] *n plat typique écossais fait d'une panse de brebis farcie, le plus souvent servie avec des navets et des pommes de terre.*

haggle ['hægl] ◇ *vi* -**1.** [bargain] marchander; **to ~ over the price** marchander sur le prix. -**2.** [argue over details] chicaner, chipoter; **to ~ over** OR **about sthg** chicaner OR chipoter sur qqch.
◇ *n*: **after a long ~ over the price** après un long marchandage sur le prix.

haggler ['hægləʳ] *n* -**1.** [over price] marchandeur *m*, -euse *f*. -**2.** [over details, wording] chicaneur *m*, -euse *f*, chipoteur *m*, -euse *f*.

haggling ['hæglɪŋ] *n* *(U)* -**1.** [over price] marchandage *m*. -**2.** [about details, wording etc] chicanerie *f*, chipotage *m*.

hagiographer [ˌhægɪ'ɒgrəfəʳ] *n* hagiographe *mf*.

hagiography [ˌhægɪ'ɒgrəfɪ] *n* hagiographie *f*.

hag-ridden *adj lit* [tormented] tourmenté, ravagé; *hum* [tormented by women] persécuté par les femmes.

Hague [heɪg] *pr n*: **The ~** La Haye.

hah [hɑː] = **ha**.

ha-ha ◇ *interj* [mock amusement] ha ha; [representing laughter: in comic, novel] ha ha ha, hi hi hi.
◇ *n* [wall, fence] *mur ou clôture installé dans un fossé.*

hahnium ['hɑːnɪəm] *n* CHEM hahnium *m*.

Haifa ['haɪfə] *pr n* Haïfa, Haiffa.

hail [heɪl] ◇ *n* -**1.** METEOR grêle *f*; *fig* [of stones] grêle *f*, pluie *f*; [of abuse] avalanche *f*, déluge *m*; **he went down under a ~ of blows** il est tombé sous une grêle de coups; **he died in a ~ of bullets** il est tombé sous une pluie de balles. -**2.** *lit* [call] appel *m*; **within ~** à portée de voix.
◇ *vi* METEOR grêler.
◇ *vt* -**1.** [call to – taxi, ship, person] héler; **within ~ing distance** à portée de voix. -**2.** [greet – person] acclamer, saluer. -**3.** [acclaim – person, new product, invention etc] acclamer, saluer; **her book has been ~ed as the most significant new novel this year** son livre a été acclamé comme le nouveau roman le plus marquant de cette année; **to ~ sb emperor** proclamer qqn empereur. -**4.** *phr*: **to ~ blows on sb** faire pleuvoir les coups sur qqn; **to ~ insults on sb** accabler qqn d'injures.
◇ *interj arch* salut à vous OR toi.
◆ **hail down** ◇ *vi insep* [blows, stones etc] pleuvoir; **blows/rocks were ~ing down on us** des coups/pierres nous pleuvaient dessus.
◇ *vt sep*: **to ~ down curses on sb** *lit* déverser un déluge de malédictions sur qqn.
◆ **hail from** *vt insep* [ship] être en provenance de; [person] venir de, être originaire de; **where does she ~ from?** [ship] quelle est sa provenance?

hail-fellow-well-met *adj dated & pej*: **he's always very ~** il fait toujours montre d'une familiarité joviale.

Hail Mary *n* RELIG [prayer] Je vous salue Marie *m inv*, Ave (Maria) *m inv*; **to say five ~s** dire cinq Je vous salue Marie, dire cinq Ave (Maria).

hailstone ['heɪlstəʊn] *n* grêlon *m*.

hailstorm ['heɪlstɔːm] *n* averse *f* de grêle.

hair [heəʳ] ◇ *n* -**1.** *(U)* [on person's head] cheveux *mpl*; **to have long/short ~** avoir les cheveux longs/courts; **she's got such beautiful ~** elle a vraiment de beaux cheveux; **to get one's ~ cut** se faire couper les cheveux; **to get one's ~ done** se faire coiffer; **who does your ~?** qui vous coiffe?; **I like the way you've done your ~** j'aime bien la façon dont tu t'es coiffé; **to wash one's ~** se laver les cheveux OR la tête; **to brush one's ~** se brosser (les cheveux); **to comb one's ~** se peigner (les cheveux); **she put her ~ up** elle a relevé ses cheveux; **she let her ~ down** elle a défait ses cheveux; **your ~ looks nice** tu es bien coiffée; **my ~'s a mess** je suis vraiment mal coiffé. -**2.** [single hair – on person's head] cheveu *m*; [– on person's or animal's face or body] poil *m*; **move it a ~ over to the right** *inf Am* déplace-le un chouia vers la droite. -**3.** *(U)* [on body, face] poils *mpl*; **to remove unwanted ~** épiler les poils superflus ‖ [on animal] poils *mpl*; **a dog with smooth ~** un chien au pelage lisse. -**4.** *phr*: **it makes your ~ stand on end** [is frightening] c'est à vous faire dresser les cheveux sur la tête; **it would make your ~ curl** *inf* [ride, journey] c'est à vous faire dresser les cheveux sur la tête; [prices, bad language] c'est à vous faire tomber à la renverse; [drink] ça arrache; **keep your ~ on!** *inf Br* ne t'excite pas!; **to let one's ~ down** se laisser aller, se défouler; **to get in sb's ~** *inf* taper sur les nerfs de qqn; **keep him out of my ~** *inf* fais en sorte que je ne l'aie pas dans les jambes; **I'll keep out of your ~** *inf* je ne vais pas t'embêter; **to have a ~ of the dog (that bit you)** reprendre un verre (pour faire passer sa gueule de bois); **here, a ~ of the dog is what you need** bois ça, il faut guérir le mal par le mal; **to split ~s** couper les cheveux en quatre, chercher la petite bête; **not one ~ of her head was harmed** elle s'en est sortie sans une égratignure; **if you harm one single ~ of his head** si tu touches à un seul de ses cheveux; **she never has a ~ out of place** [is immaculate] elle n'a jamais un cheveu de travers; **to win by a ~** gagner d'un cheveu OR d'un quart de poil; **to lose by a ~** perdre d'un cheveu OR à un quart de poil près; **she didn't turn a ~** elle n'a pas cillé; **this will put ~s on your chest** *inf hum* [strong drink, good steak etc] ça va te redonner du poil de la bête.
◇ *comp* -**1.** [cream, conditioner, lotion] capillaire, pour les cheveux; **~ appointment** rendez-vous *m* chez le coiffeur; **~ lacquer** laque *f* (pour les cheveux); **~ straightener** produit *m* défrisant. -**2.** [colour] de cheveux. -**3.** [mattress] de crin.

hairball ['heəbɔːl] *n* [of cat's fur] boule *f* de poils.

hairband ['heəbænd] *n* bandeau *m*.

hairbreadth ['heəbretθ] = **hair's breadth**.

hairbrush ['heəbrʌʃ] *n* brosse *f* à cheveux.

hairclip ['heəklɪp] *n* barrette *f*.

hair clippers *npl* tondeuse *f*; **a pair of ~** une tondeuse.

hair curlers *npl Br* bigoudis *mpl*.

haircut ['heəkʌt] *n* coupe *f* (de cheveux); **I like your ~** j'aime bien ta coupe (de cheveux); **I need a ~** j'ai besoin de me faire couper les cheveux; **to have a ~** se faire couper les cheveux; **to give sb a ~** couper les cheveux à qqn; **where did you get that ~!** où est-ce que tu t'es fait couper les cheveux!; **some ~!** quelle drôle de coupe!

hairdo *inf* ['heəduː] *n* coiffure *f*.

hairdresser ['heəˌdresəʳ] *n* [shop] salon *m* de coiffure; **to go to the ~'s** aller chez le coiffeur.

hairdressing ['heəˌdresɪŋ] *n* -**1.** [skill] coiffure *f*; **~ salon** salon *m* de coiffure. -**2.** [product for the hair] produit *m* capillaire.

hair drier, **hair dryer** *n* [hand-held] sèche-cheveux *m inv*, séchoir *m*; [over the head] casque *m*.

-haired [heəd] *in cpds*: **long/short~** [person] aux cheveux longs/courts; [animal] à poil(s) long(s)/court(s); **wire~** [dog] à poil(s) dur(s).

hair follicle *n* follicule *m* pileux.

hair gel *n* gel *m* pour les cheveux.

hairgrip ['heəgrɪp] *n Br* pince *f* à cheveux.

hairless ['heəlɪs] *adj* [head] chauve, sans cheveux; [face] glabre; [body] peu poilu; [animal] sans poils; [leaf] glabre.

hairline ['heəlaɪn] ◇ *n* -**1.** [of the hair] naissance *f* des cheveux; **to have a receding ~** [above forehead] avoir le front qui se dégarnit; [at temples] avoir les tempes qui se dégarnissent. -**2.** [in telescope, gun sight] fil *m*. -**3.** TYPO filet *m* ultra-fin; [in calligraphy] délié *m*.
◇ *comp*: **~ crack** fêlure *f*; **~ fracture** MED fêlure *f*.

hairnet ['heənet] *n* résille *f*, filet *m* à cheveux.

hair oil *n* huile *f* capillaire.

hairpiece ['heəpiːs] *n* [toupee] perruque *f (pour hommes)*; [extra hair] postiche *m*.

hairpin ['heəpɪn] *n* -**1.** [for hair] épingle *f* à cheveux. -**2.** **~ (bend)** virage *m* en épingle à cheveux.

hair-raising *inf* [-ˌreɪzɪŋ] *adj* [adventure, experience, story, account] à faire dresser les cheveux sur la tête, effrayant; [prices, expenses] affolant, exorbitant; **driving in London traffic can be a ~ experience** conduire à Londres peut être une expérience terrifiante; **it was pretty ~** c'était à vous faire dresser les cheveux sur la tête.

hair remover *n* crème *f* dépilatoire.

hair restorer *n* produit *m* pour la repousse des cheveux.

hair's breadth *n*: **the truck missed us by a ~** le camion nous a manqués d'un cheveu OR de justesse; **we came within a ~ of going bankrupt/of winning first prize** nous avons été à deux doigts de la faillite/de gagner le premier prix.

hair shirt *n* haire *f*, cilice *m*.

hair slide *n* barrette *f*.

hairsplitting ['heəˌsplɪtɪŋ] ◇ *adj*: **that's a ~ argument** OR **distinction** c'est de la chicanerie, c'est couper les cheveux en quatre.
◇ *n (U)* chicanerie *f*; **that's just ~** tu es vraiment en train de couper les cheveux en quatre.

hair spray *n* laque *f* OR spray *m* (pour les cheveux).

hairspring ['heəsprɪŋ] *n* [in clock] spiral *m (de montre)*.

hairstyle ['heəstaɪl] *n* coiffure *f*.

hairstyling salon ['heəˌstaɪlɪŋ-] *n* salon *m* de coiffure.

hairstylist ['heəˌstaɪlɪst] *n* styliste *mf* en coiffure.

hair transplant *n* implant *m* de cheveux.

hair trigger *n* [in firearm] détente *f* OR gâchette *f* sensible.
◆ **hair-trigger** *adj fig*: **to have a hair-trigger temper** [lose one's temper easily] s'emporter facilement.

hairy ['heərɪ] (*compar* hairier, *superl* hairiest) *adj* -**1.** [arms, chest] poilu, velu; [person, animal] poilu; [stalk of plant] velu. -**2.** *inf* [frightening] à faire dresser les cheveux sur la tête; [difficult, daunting] qui craint; **"that was a bit ~", he said** «j'ai eu un peu la frousse», dit-il; **there were a few ~ moments when the brakes seemed to be failing** il y a eu des moments craignos où les freins semblaient lâcher; **he gave a pretty ~ description of his two hours at the dentist** il a fait une description assez horrible OR atroce des deux heures qu'il a passées chez le dentiste; **he did some pretty ~ stunts** il a fait quelques cascades assez impressionnantes; **things are getting a bit ~ at the office** [because of workload] ça devient un peu la folie au bureau; [because of personal or financial tension] ça commence à craindre au bureau.

Haiti ['heɪtɪ] *pr n* Haïti; **in ~** à Haïti.

Haitian ['heɪʃn] ◇ *adj* haïtien.
◇ *n* Haïtien *m*, -enne *f*.

hake [heɪk] *n* merlu *m*, colin *m*.

halal [hə'lɑːl] ◇ *n* [meat] viande *f* halal.
◇ *adj* halal.

halberd ['hælbɜːd] *n* hallebarde *f*.

halcyon ['hælsɪən] *adj*: **in those ~ days** *lit* en ces temps heureux.

hale [heɪl] *adj*: **~ and hearty** en pleine santé.

half [*Br* hɑːf, *Am* hæf] (*pl* halves [*Br* hɑːvz, *Am* hævz]) ◇ *n* -**1.** moitié *f*; [of standard measured amount] demi *m*, -e *f*; [of ticket, coupon] souche *f*; **to cut/to break sthg in ~** couper/casser qqch en deux; what's ~ of 13.72? quelle est la moitié de 13,72?; two and two halves, please [on bus, train etc] deux billets tarif normal et deux billets demi-tarif, s'il vous plaît; you can have the smaller ~ la plus petite moitié est pour toi; it cuts the journey time in ~ cela diminue la durée du voyage de moitié; three and a ~ pieces trois morceaux et demi; three and a ~ years old trois ans et demi; bigger by ~ *Br* plus grand de moitié; two halves make a whole deux moitiés OR demis font un tout; to go halves with sb partager avec qqn; we'll go halves on partage; they don't do things by halves ils ne font pas les choses à moitié ❑ he always was too clever by ~ *Br* il a toujours été un peu trop malin; you're too cheeky by ~! *Br* tu es bien trop effronté OR culotté!; that was a walk and a ~! *inf* c'était une sacrée promenade!; I've got a headache and a ~ this morning! *inf* j'ai un sacré mal de tête ce matin!; and that's not the ~ of it et ce n'est que le début; it's sort of ~ and ~ c'est un peu de chaque; my better OR other ~ *hum* ma (chère) moitié; to see how the other ~ lives *hum* voir comment on vit de l'autre côté de la barrière, voir comment vivent les autres. -**2.** [period of sports match] mi-temps *f inv*; France was in the lead in the first ~ la France menait pendant la première mi-temps. -**3.** [area of football or rugby pitch] camp *m*. -**4.** [rugby or football player] demi *m*. -**5.** *Br* [half pint of beer] demi *m* (de bière).

◇ *pron*: leave ~ of it for me laisse-m'en la moitié; ~ of us were students la moitié d'entre nous étaient des étudiants.

◇ *adj*: a ~ chicken un demi-poulet; at ~ speed au ralenti; at ~ price à moitié prix; ~ fare demi-tarif *m*; to travel ~ fare voyager à demi-tarif.

◇ *predet*: ~ the time he seems to be asleep on a l'impression qu'il est endormi la moitié du temps; he's ~ a year older than me il a six mois de plus que moi; ~ a minute! *inf* une (petite) minute!; I'll be down in ~ a second *inf* je suis en bas dans une seconde; I'll be there in ~ an hour j'y serai dans une demi-heure; just ~ a cup for me juste une demi-tasse pour moi ❑ he's not ~ the man he used to be il n'est plus que l'ombre de lui-même; to have ~ a mind to do sthg *inf* avoir bien envie de faire qqch.

◇ *adv* -**1.** [finished, asleep, dressed] à moitié; [full, empty, blind] à moitié, à demi; to be ~ full of sthg être à moitié rempli de qqch; you're only ~ right tu n'as qu'à moitié raison; a strange colour, ~ green, ~ blue une couleur bizarre, entre le vert et le bleu; to be ~ English and ~ French être moitié anglais moitié français; I ~ think that... je suis tenté de penser que...; for a minute I ~ thought that... pendant une minute, j'ai presque pensé que...; I was ~ afraid you wouldn't understand j'avais un peu peur que vous ne compreniez pas; I was only ~ joking je ne plaisantais qu'à moitié. -**2.** *inf Br* [as intensifier]: they're not ~ fit ils sont en superforme; he's not ~ lazy il est drôlement OR rudement paresseux; it's not ~ cold today! il fait rudement OR sacrément froid aujourd'hui!; he didn't ~ yell il a hurlé comme un fou; she can't ~ run elle court comme un lièvre; you don't ~ put your foot in it sometimes! tu mets vraiment les pieds dans le plat parfois!; they didn't ~ complain ils se sont plaints, et pas qu'un peu; did you complain? – I didn't ~! OR not ~! est-ce que vous vous êtes plaint? – et comment! OR pas qu'un peu!; he's/it's not ~ bad il est/c'est vraiment bon. -**3.** [time]: it's ~ past two *Br*, it's ~ two *inf* il est deux heures et demie; ~ after six *Am* six heures et demie. -**4.** *phr*: to be ~ as big/fast as sb/sthg être moitié moins grand/rapide que qqn/qqch; the radio was only ~ as loud as before le son de la radio était moitié moins fort qu'avant; to earn ~ as much as sb gagner moitié moins que qqn; to be ~ as big again (as sb/sthg) être moitié plus grand (que qqn/qqch); he earns ~ as much again as you do il gagne moitié plus que toi.

half-a-crown *n Br* demi-couronne *f*.

half-and-half ◇ *n Br* [beer] *mélange de deux bières*; *Am* [for coffee] *mélange de crème et de lait*.
◇ *adv* moitié-moitié; it's ~ c'est moitié-moitié.

half-arsed▽ *Br* [-ˈɑːst], **half-assed**▽ *Am* [-ˈæst] *adj* [incompetent] nul à chier.

halfback [ˈhɑːfbæk] *n* [hockey, rugby, soccer player] demi *m*.

half-baked *inf* [-ˈbeɪkt] *adj fig* [scheme, proposal] qui ne tient pas debout; [person] niais.

half-binding *n* demi-reliure *f*.

half-blood *n* métis *m*, -isse *f*.

half-board *Br* ◇ *n* demi-pension *f*.
◇ *adv* en demi-pension.

half-breed ◇ *n* -**1.** [animal] hybride *m*; [horse] cheval *m* demi-sang. -**2.** *dated & offensive* [person] métis *m*, -isse *f*.
◇ *adj* -**1.** [animal] hybride; [horse] demi-sang. -**2.** *dated & offensive* [person] métis.

half-brother *n* demi-frère *m*.

half-caste *dated & offensive* ◇ *n* [person] métis *m*, -isse *f*.
◇ *adj* métis.

half-century *n* demi-siècle *m*.

half-circle *n* demi-cercle *m*.

half-cock *n*: to go off at ~ [plan, arrangements] avorter; we don't want to go off at ~ on this one il ne faut pas nous laisser prendre au dépourvu cette fois-ci.

half-cocked [-ˈkɒkt] *adj* [gun, pistol] à moitié armé.

half-crazy *adj* à moitié fou.

half-crown *n Br arch* demi-couronne *f*.

half-cup *adj*: ~ bra soutien-gorge *m* à balconnet.

half-day ◇ *n* [at school, work] demi-journée *f*; tomorrow is my ~ [work] demain c'est ma demi-journée de congé; to work ~s faire des demi-journées.
◇ *adj*: a ~ holiday une demi-journée de congé.

half-dead *inf adj Br* [very tired] complètement crevé.

half-deck *n* NAUT demi-pont *m*.

half-dollar *n* pièce *f* de 50 cents.

half-dozen *n* demi-douzaine *f*; a ~ eggs une demi-douzaine d'œufs.

half-drowned [-ˈdraʊnd] *adj* à moitié OR à demi noyé.

half-eaten *adj* à moitié mangé.

half-fill *vt* [glass] remplir à moitié OR à demi.

half-full *adj* à moitié OR à demi plein.

half-grown *adj* à mi-croissance.

half-hardy *adj* BOT semi-rustique.

half-hearted *adj* [attempt, attitude] qui manque d'enthousiasme OR de conviction, timide, hésitant; [acceptance] tiède, qui manque d'enthousiasme OR de conviction; he was very ~ about it il était vraiment peu enthousiaste à ce propos; they were very ~ about accepting ils ont accepté sans grand enthousiasme OR du bout des lèvres.

half-heartedly [-ˈhɑːtɪdlɪ] *adv* [accept, agree, say] sans enthousiasme OR conviction, du bout des lèvres.

half-hitch *n* demi-clef *f*.

half-holiday *n* demi-journée *f* de congé.

half-hour ◇ *n* [period] demi-heure *f*; I'll wait a ~ *Am* j'attendrai une demi-heure; on the ~ à la demie.
◇ *comp*: at ~ intervals toutes les demi-heures.

half-hourly *adj & adv* toutes les demi-heures.

half-joking *adj* mi-figue, mi-raisin.

half-jokingly *adv* d'un air mi-figue, mi-raisin.

half-landing *n* [on staircase] palier *m (entre deux étages)*.

half-length *adj* [portrait] en buste.

half-life *n* PHYS demi-vie *f*, période *f*.

half-light *n* demi-jour *m*.

half-marathon *n* semi-marathon *m*.

half-mast *n*: at ~ [flag] en berne; *hum* [trousers] arrivant à mi-mollet.

half measure *n* demi-mesure *f*.

half-miler *n* [runner] coureur *m*, -euse *f* de demi-mile.

half-moon *n* demi-lune *f*; [on fingernail] lunule *f*.

half-naked *adj* à moitié nu.

half-nelson *n* clef *f* de cou.

half-note *n Am* [minim] blanche *f*.

half-open ◇ *adj* [eyes, door, window] entrouvert.
◇ *vt* [eyes, door, window] entrouvrir.

half-pay *n* demi-salaire *m*; [in civil service] demi-traitement *m*; MIL demi-solde *f*; to be on ~ toucher un demi-salaire OR un demi-traitement; MIL toucher une demi-solde.

halfpenny [ˈheɪpnɪ] (*pl* **halfpennies**) *Br dated*
◇ *n* demi-penny *m*.
◇ *comp* d'un demi-penny.

halfpennyworth [ˈheɪpəθ] *n Br dated*: a ~ of ice cream ≃ de la glace pour un sou.

half-pint ◇ *n* -**1.** [measurement] ≃ quart *m* de litre; I'll just have a ~ [of beer] je prendrai juste un demi. -**2.** *inf* [small person] demi-portion *f*.
◇ *comp*: a ~ glass ≃ un verre de 25 cl.

half-price ◇ *n* demi-tarif *m*; reduced to ~ réduit de moitié; these goods are going at ~ ces produits sont vendus à moitié prix.
◇ *adj* [goods] à moitié prix; [ticket] (à) demi-tarif.
◇ *adv*: children get in ~ les enfants payent demi-tarif; I got it ~ [purchase] je l'ai eu à moitié prix.

half-rest *n Am* MUS demi-pause *f*.

half-seas over *inf adj dated* [drunk] pompette, rond.

half-shut *adj* [eyes, door, window] mi-clos, à moitié fermé.

half-sister *n* demi-sœur *f*.

half-size ◇ *adj* [model] réduit de moitié.
◇ *n* [in shoes] demi-pointure *f*; [in clothing] demi-taille *f*.

half-staff *Am* = **half-mast**.

half-starved *adj* à moitié mort de faim, affamé.

half step *n Am* MUS demi-ton *m*.

half term *n Br* SCH *congé scolaire en milieu de trimestre*.
◆ **half-term** *adj*: half-term holiday petites vacances *fpl*.

half-timbered [-ˈtɪmbəd] *adj* [house] à colombages, à pans de bois.

half-time ◇ *n* -**1.** SPORT mi-temps *f inv*; at ~ à la mi-temps; that's the whistle for ~ on siffle la mi-temps. -**2.** [in work] mi-temps *m*; to put sb on ~ mettre qqn à mi-temps; to be on ~ être OR travailler à mi-temps.
◇ *comp* SPORT [whistle] de la mi-temps; [score] à la mi-temps.

half-title *n* faux-titre *m*.

halftone [ˈhɑːftəʊn] *n* -**1.** ART & PHOT similigravure *f*. -**2.** *Am* MUS demi-ton *m*.

half-track *n* [vehicle] half-track *m*.

half-truth *n* demi-vérité *f*.

half-volley ◇ *n* [in tennis] demi-volée *f*.
◇ *vt* [in tennis]: he ~ed the ball to the baseline d'une demi-volée, il a envoyé la balle sur la ligne de fond.
◇ *vi* [in tennis] faire une demi-volée.

halfway [hɑːfweɪ] ◇ *adv* -**1.** [between two places] à mi-chemin; it's ~ between Rennes and Cherbourg c'est à mi-chemin entre Rennes et Cherbourg; we had got ~ to Manchester nous étions arrivés à mi-chemin de Manchester; they have now travelled ~ to the moon ils sont maintenant à mi-chemin de leur voyage vers la lune; we had climbed ~ up the mountain nous avions escaladé la moitié de la montagne; we had got ~ down the mountain nous avions descendu la moitié de la montagne; the path stops ~ up le chemin s'arrête à mi-côte; there's a blockage ~ up the pipe il y

a un bouchon à mi-hauteur du tuyau; **the ivy reaches ~ up the wall** le lierre monte jusqu'à la moitié du mur; **her hair hangs ~ down her back** ses cheveux lui arrivent jusqu'au milieu du dos; **he kicked the ball ~ into the French half** il a shooté dans le ballon et l'a envoyé à la moitié du camp français; **I've got ~ through chapter six** je suis arrivé à la moitié du chapitre six; **~ through the programme/film** à la moitié de l'émission/du film; **to meet sb ~** retrouver qqn à mi-chemin; *fig* couper la poire en deux, faire un compromis; **I'm willing to meet you ~** *fig* je veux bien couper la poire en deux, je suis prêt à t'accorder un compromis; **we're almost ~ there** [in travelling, walking etc] nous sommes presque à mi-chemin, nous avons fait presque la moitié du chemin; [in work, negotiations] nous sommes presque à mi-chemin; **this will go ~ towards covering the costs** cela couvrira la moitié des dépenses; **it's ~ between an alsatian and a collie** c'est (à mi-chemin) entre le berger allemand et le colley. **-2.** *inf* [more or less]: **a ~ decent salary** un salaire à peu près décent; **don't you have something ~ presentable to wear?** tu n'as rien d'à peu près présentable à porter?
◇ *comp*: **work has reached the ~ stage** le travail est à mi-chemin; **at the ~ point of his career** au milieu de sa carrière; **they're at the ~ mark** [in race] ils sont à mi-course; **~ line** SPORT ligne *f* médiane.

halfway house *n* **-1.** [on journey] (auberge *f*) relais *m*. **-2.** [for rehabilitation] centre *m* de réadaptation *(pour anciens détenus, malades mentaux, drogués etc)*. **-3.** *fig* [halfway stage] (stade *m* de) transition *f*; [compromise] compromis *m*.

half-wit *n* faible *m* OR simple *m* d'esprit; **some ~ has parked right in front of the gate** il y a un imbécile qui s'est garé juste devant la grille; **only a ~ would do something like that** il faut être débile pour faire un truc comme ça.

half-witted *adj* [person] faible OR simple d'esprit; [idea, suggestion, behaviour] idiot; **sometimes I think he's ~** parfois je le trouve débile.

half-yearly ◇ *adj* semestriel.
◇ *adv* tous les six mois.

halibut ['hælɪbət] *n* flétan *m*.

halitosis [,hælɪ'təʊsɪs] *n (U)* mauvaise haleine *f*; MED halitose *f*.

hall [hɔːl] *n* **-1.** [of house] entrée *f*, vestibule *m*; [of hotel, very large house] hall *m*; [corridor] couloir *m*. **-2.** [large room] salle *f*; **dining ~** SCH & UNIV réfectoire *m*; [of stately home] salle *f* à manger; **to eat in ~** *Br* UNIV *manger à la cantine ou au restaurant universitaire*; **(assembly) ~** SCH *grande salle où se rassemblent tous les élèves et les professeurs*; **prayers were held in ~ every morning** toute l'école se réunissait chaque matin dans la grande salle pour prier. **-3.** [building]: **town ~** mairie *f*, hôtel *m* de ville; **village ~** salle *f* des fêtes, salle *f* polyvalente; **~ of residence** *Br* UNIV résidence *f* universitaire; **I'm living in ~** *Br* UNIV je loge à l'université; **~ of fame** *fig* panthéon *m*; **baseball's ~ of fame** le panthéon de l'histoire du baseball; **his name will go down in the ~ of fame** son nom entrera au panthéon. **-4.** [mansion, large country house] château *m*, manoir *m*; **she works up at the ~** elle travaille au château OR au manoir; **Fotheringham Hall** le château OR le manoir de Fotheringham.

hallelujah [,hælɪ'luːjə] ◇ *interj* alléluia.
◇ *n* alléluia *m*; **the Hallelujah Chorus** MUS l'Alléluia.

hallmark ['hɔːlmɑːk] ◇ *n* **-1.** *literal* poinçon *m*. **-2.** *fig* marque *f*; **it carries his ~** cela porte sa marque; **the ~ of a creative mind** la marque OR le sceau d'un esprit créatif; **to have the ~ of genius** porter la marque OR le sceau OR l'empreinte *f* du génie; **the ~ of any good author** ce qui caractérise tout bon auteur.
◇ *vt* [precious metals] poinçonner.

hallo [hə'ləʊ] *interj* = **hello**.

halloo [hə'luː] (*pl* halloos, *pt* & *pp* hallooed, *cont* hallooing) HUNT ◇ *interj* taïaut, tayaut.
◇ *vi* crier taïaut OR tayaut.
◇ *n* taïaut *m*, tayaut *m*.

hallow ['hæləʊ] *vt fml* sanctifier, consacrer; **~ed be Thy name** que Ton nom soit sanctifié.

hallowed ['hæləʊd] *adj* saint, béni; **~ ground** RELIG terre *f* sainte OR bénie; *fig* lieu *m* de culte.

Hallowe'en [,hæləʊ'iːn] *pr n veille de la Toussaint, où les enfants se déguisent en fantômes et en sorcières.*

hall porter *n* [in hotel] portier *m*.

hallstand ['hɔːlstænd] *n* portemanteau *m*.

hall tree *Am* = **hallstand**.

hallucinate [hə'luːsɪneɪt] *vi* avoir des hallucinations; **it made her ~** cela lui a donné des hallucinations; **I must be hallucinating!** je dois avoir des hallucinations!

hallucination [hə,luːsɪ'neɪʃn] *n* hallucination *f*.

hallucinatory [hə'luːsɪnətrɪ] *adj* hallucinatoire.

hallucinogen [,hæluː'sɪnədʒən] *n* hallucinogène *m*.

hallucinogenic [hə,luːsɪnə'dʒenɪk] *adj* hallucinogène.

hallway ['hɔːlweɪ] *n* [of house] vestibule *m*, entrée *f*; [corridor] couloir *m*.

halo ['heɪləʊ] (*pl* halos OR haloes) *n* [of saint] auréole *f*, nimbe *m*; ASTRON halo *m*; *fig* auréole *f*; **her ~ never slips** *hum* c'est un modèle de vertu.

halogen ['hælədʒen] *n* CHEM halogène *m*; **~ headlights/lamps** phares *mpl*/lampes *fpl* à halogène.

halt [hɔːlt] ◇ *n* **-1.** [stop] halte *f*; **to bring to a ~** [vehicle] arrêter, immobiliser; [horse] arrêter; [production, project] interrompre; **the strike has brought production to a complete ~** la grève a complètement interrompu la production; **to call a ~ to sthg** mettre fin à qqch; **let's call a ~ for today** arrêtons-nous pour aujourd'hui; **to come to a ~** [vehicle, horse] s'arrêter, s'immobiliser; **the project has come to a ~** [temporarily] le projet s'est interrompu; [for good] le projet s'est définitivement arrêté; **until the aircraft comes to a complete ~** jusqu'à l'arrêt complet de l'appareil; **this decline in education standards must come to a ~** cette baisse des niveaux scolaires doit cesser. **-2.** *Br* [small railway station] halte *f*.
◇ *npl* BIBLE: **the ~ and the lame** les estropiés *mpl*.
◇ *vi* **-1.** [stop] s'arrêter; **~! (, who goes there?)** MIL halte! (, qui va là?). **-2.** *arch* [limp] boiter; *fig* [style, writing, verse] être boiteux.
◇ *vt* arrêter; [troops] faire faire halte à, stopper; [production - temporarily] interrompre, arrêter; [- for good] arrêter définitivement.

halter ['hɔːltəʳ] *n* **-1.** [for horse] licou *m*, collier *m*. **-2.** [on women's clothing] = **halter neck**. **-3.** *arch* [noose] corde *f* (de pendaison).

halter neck *n*: **a dress with a ~** une robe dos nu OR bain de soleil.
◆ **halter-neck** *comp* [dress] dos nu, bain de soleil.

halter top *n* bain *m* de soleil.

halting ['hɔːltɪŋ] *adj* [verse, style] boiteux, heurté; [voice, step, progress] hésitant; [growth] discontinu.

haltingly ['hɔːltɪŋlɪ] *adv* [say, speak] de façon hésitante.

halt sign *n* AUT stop *m*.

halve [*Br* hɑːv, *Am* hæv] *vt* **-1.** [separate in two - apple, cake etc] couper OR diviser OR partager en deux. **-2.** [reduce by half - workload, pay, journey time etc] réduire OR diminuer de moitié.

halves [*Br* hɑːvz, *Am* hævz] *pl* → **half**.

halyard ['hæljəd] *n* NAUT drisse *f*.

ham [hæm] (*pt* & *pp* hammed, *cont* hamming) ◇ *n* **-1.** [meat] jambon *m*; **a ~** un jambon; **~ and eggs** œufs *mpl* au jambon; **~ sandwich** sandwich *m* au jambon. **-2.** [radio operator] radioamateur *m*; **~ licence** permis *m* de radioamateur. **-3.** [actor] cabot *m*, cabotin *m*, -e *f*. **-4.** [of leg] cuisse *f*.
◇ *comp*: **~ acting** cabotinage *m*.
◇ *vi* = **ham up**.
◆ **ham up** *vt sep*: **to ~ it up** *inf* en faire trop.

Ham [hæm] *pr n* BIBLE Cham.

Hamburg ['hæmbɜːg] *pr n* Hambourg.

hamburger ['hæmbɜːgəʳ] *n* **-1.** [beefburger] hamburger *m*. **-2.** *Am* [minced beef] viande *f* hachée.

Hamburger University *pr n centre mondial de formation du personnel de la société MacDonald's, situé dans la banlieue de Chicago.*

ham-fisted [-'fɪstɪd], **ham-handed** [-'hændɪd] *adj* [person] empoté, maladroit; [behaviour] maladroit.

Hamitic [hæ'mɪtɪk] *adj* chamitique.

hamlet ['hæmlɪt] *n* [small village] hameau *m*; **'Hamlet'** *Shakespeare* 'Hamlet'.

hammer ['hæməʳ] ◇ *n* **-1.** [tool] marteau *m*; **(throwing the) ~** SPORT (lancer *m* du) marteau ❑ **the ~ and sickle** [flag] la faucille et le marteau; **to come** OR **to go under the ~** être vendu aux enchères; **to be** OR **to go at it ~ and tongs** [argue] se disputer comme des chiffonniers; [in work, match] y aller à fond OR de bon cœur, mettre le paquet. **-2.** [of piano] marteau *m*; [of firearm] chien *m*. **-3.** [in ear] marteau *m*.
◇ *vt* **-1.** [nail, spike etc] enfoncer au marteau; [metal] marteler; **to ~ a nail into sthg** enfoncer un clou dans qqch; **to ~ sthg flat/straight** aplatir/redresser qqch à coups de marteau; **to ~ home** [nail] enfoncer à fond au marteau; *fig* [point of view] insister lourdement sur; **she ~ed it home with the heel of her shoe** elle l'a enfoncé avec le talon de sa chaussure; **I had it ~ed into me that I mustn't do that type of thing** on m'a enfoncé dans la tête que je ne devais pas faire ce genre de choses; **they're always ~ing it into us that...** ils nous rabâchent sans arrêt que...; **to ~ an agreement into shape** réussir à mettre un accord au point. **-2.** *inf* [defeat] battre à plate couture; [criticize] descendre en flammes.
◇ *vi* **-1.** frapper OR taper au marteau; *fig* [heart] battre fort; **the rain ~ed at the window** la pluie tambourinait contre la fenêtre; **to ~ on the table** [with fist] taper du poing sur la table; **to ~ at the door** tambouriner à la porte. **-2.** *inf* [go fast, drive fast] foncer, aller à fond de train; **he came ~ing round the final bend** il a débouché à fond de train du dernier virage; **the French champion was really ~ing along the track when he tripped** le champion français était en pleine vitesse quand il a trébuché.
◆ **hammer away** *vi insep* [with hammer] donner des coups de marteau; **to ~ away at sthg** taper sur qqch avec un marteau, donner des coups de marteau sur qqch; *fig* [at agreement, contract] travailler avec acharnement à la mise au point de qqch; [problem] travailler avec acharnement à la solution de qqch; **he ~ed away at the door** [with fists] il a tambouriné à la porte; **to ~ away at the piano/on the typewriter** marteler le piano/la machine à écrire.
◆ **hammer down** *vt sep* [nail, spike] enfoncer (au marteau); [door] défoncer.
◆ **hammer in** *vt sep* [nail, spike] enfoncer (au marteau); **it's no good telling him just once, you'll have to ~ it in** *fig* le lui dire une bonne fois ne suffira pas, il faudra le lui répéter sans cesse.
◆ **hammer out** *vt sep* [dent] aplatir au marteau; *fig* [solution, agreement] mettre au point, élaborer; [tune, rhythm] marteler.

hammer drill *n* perceuse *f* à percussion.

hammerhead ['hæməhed] *n* [shark] requin-marteau *m*.

hammering ['hæmərɪŋ] *n* **-1.** [noise] martèlement *m*; *fig* [of heart] battement *m*; [of rain] tambourinement *m*. **-2.** *inf fig* [defeat] raclée *f*, pâtée *f*; **to give sb a ~** battre qqn à plate couture, mettre une raclée OR une pâtée à qqn;

to take a ~ se faire battre à plate couture, prendre une raclée OR pâtée.

hammerlock ['hæməlɒk] *n* [in wrestling] clé *f* de bras; to get sb in a ~ faire une clé de bras à qqn.

hammertoe ['hæmətəʊ] *n* orteil *m* en marteau.

hammock ['hæmək] *n* hamac *m*.

hammy *inf* ['hæmɪ] (*compar* hammier, *superl* hammiest) *adj* [acting] de cabot, exagéré.

hamper ['hæmpəʳ] ◇ *vt* [impede - work, movements, person] gêner; [- project] gêner la réalisation de, entraver.

◇ *n* [for picnic] panier *m*; [for laundry] panier *m* à linge sale; a Christmas ~ un panier de friandises de Noël.

hamster ['hæmstəʳ] *n* hamster *m*.

hamstring ['hæmstrɪŋ] (*pt* & *pp* hamstrung [-strʌŋ]) ◇ *n* tendon *m*; to pull a ~ se claquer un tendon.

◇ *vt* [cripple - animal, person] couper les tendons à; *fig* handicaper; the project is hamstrung le projet est bloqué; we are hamstrung nous sommes bloqués.

hand [hænd] ◇ *n* -**1.** [of person] main *f*; to hold sb's ~ tenir la main de qqn; I held her ~ je lui ai tenu la main; she's asked me to go along and hold her ~ *fig* elle m'a demandé de l'accompagner pour lui donner du courage; to hold ~s se tenir par la main; to take sb's ~, to take sb by the ~ prendre qqn par la main, prendre la main de qqn; to lead sb by the ~ conduire qqn par la main; to put one's ~s over one's eyes se couvrir les yeux de ses mains; to be on one's ~s and knees être à quatre pattes; to go down on one's ~s and knees *fig* se mettre à genoux OR à plat ventre; to put one's ~ in one's pocket *fig* mettre la main au portefeuille; to be good with one's ~s être adroit de ses mains; my ~s are full j'ai les mains occupées OR prises; to have one's ~s full *fig* avoir beaucoup à faire, avoir du pain sur la planche; to lay one's ~s on sthg [find] mettre la main sur qqch; to get OR to lay one's ~s on sthg [obtain] dénicher qqch; just wait till I get OR lay my ~s on her! *fig* attends un peu que je l'attrape!; to lift OR to raise a ~ to sb lever la main sur qqn; he never lifts a ~ to help il ne lève jamais le petit doigt pour aider; ~s off! bas les pattes!, pas touche!; ~s off the unions/education system! pas touche aux syndicats/au système éducatif!; he can't keep his ~s to himself il a la main baladeuse; take your ~s off me! ne me touche pas!; (put your) ~s up! les mains en l'air!, haut les mains!; ~s up anyone who knows the answer SCH que ceux qui connaissent la réponse lèvent le doigt OR la main; ~s up all those who agree que ceux qui sont d'accord lèvent la main; to tie sb's ~s attacher les mains de qqn; to sit on one's ~s [applaud half-heartedly] applaudir sans enthousiasme; [do nothing] ne rien faire; to ask for sb's ~ in marriage demander la main de qqn, demander qqn en mariage; at ~, near OR close at ~ [about to happen] proche; [nearby] à proximité; to suffer at the ~s of sb souffrir aux mains OR dans les mains de qqn; to pass sthg from ~ to ~ faire passer qqch de mains en mains; ~ in ~ la main dans la main; to go ~ in ~ (with sthg) *fig* aller de pair (avec qqch) ❑ the motion was adopted by a show of ~s la motion a été adoptée après un vote à main levée; to be ~ in glove with sb travailler en étroite collaboration avec qqn; to make money ~ over fist gagner de l'argent par millions; my ~s are tied j'ai les mains liées; she doesn't do a ~'s turn *inf Br* elle n'en fiche pas une; to live from ~ to mouth arriver tout juste à joindre les deux bouts; I could do it with one ~ tied behind my back je pourrais le faire sans aucun effort OR les doigts dans le nez; many ~s make light work *prov* à beaucoup d'ouvriers la tâche devient aisée; on the one ~... but on the other ~... [used in the same sentence] d'un côté... mais de l'autre...; on the other ~ [when beginning new sentence] d'un autre côté. -**2.** [assistance]: to give sb a ~ (with sthg) donner un coup de main à qqn; do you need a ~ (with that)? as-tu besoin d'un coup de main? -**3.** [control, management]: to need a firm ~ avoir besoin d'être sérieusement pris en main; to take sb/sthg in ~ prendre qqn/qqch en main; to be out of ~ [dog, child] ne rien écouter; to get out of ~ [dog, child] devenir indocile; [meeting, situation] échapper à tout contrôle; the garden is getting out of ~ le jardin à l'air d'une vraie jungle; to change ~s [company, restaurant etc] changer de propriétaire; it's out of my ~s cela ne m'appartient plus, ce n'est plus ma responsabilité OR de mon ressort; the matter is in the ~s of the headmaster la question relève maintenant OR est maintenant du ressort du principal; I have put the matter in the ~s of a lawyer j'ai mis l'affaire entre les mains d'un avocat; the answer lies in your own ~s la solution est entre tes mains; to have too much time on one's ~s avoir trop de temps à soi; to have sthg/sb on one's ~s avoir qqch/qqn sur les bras; now that that's off my ~s à présent que je suis débarrassé de cela; to fall into the ~s of the enemy tomber entre les mains de l'ennemi; to fall into the wrong ~s [information, secret, document etc] tomber en de mauvaises mains; in the right ~s en de bonnes mains; to be in good ~s être en de bonnes mains; they/it will be safe in my ~s avec moi, ils seront/ce sera en de bonnes mains; can I leave this in your ~s? puis-je te demander de t'en occuper?; it leaves too much power in the ~s of the police cela laisse trop de pouvoir à la police ❑ to give sb a free ~ donner carte blanche à qqn; to take the law into one's own ~s faire justice soi-même; to take matters into one's own ~s prendre les choses en main. -**4.** [applause]: to give sb a (big) ~ applaudir qqn (bien fort). -**5.** [influence, involvement]: to have a ~ in sthg avoir quelque chose à voir dans qqch; I had no ~ in it je n'avais rien à voir là-dedans, je n'y étais pour rien; I see OR detect your ~ in this j'y vois ta marque. -**6.** [skill, ability]: to have a light ~ with pastry réussir une pâte légère ❑ she can turn her ~ to anything elle peut tout faire; to keep one's ~ in garder la main; I was never much of a ~ at it je n'ai jamais été très doué pour cela; to try one's ~ at sthg s'essayer à qqch. -**7.** [in cards - cards held] main *f*, jeu *m*; [- round, game] partie *f*; to show OR to reveal one's ~ *fig* dévoiler son jeu; to throw in one's ~ *fig* jeter l'éponge. -**8.** [of clock] aiguille *f*. -**9.** [handwriting] écriture *f*; to have a good ~ avoir une belle écriture. -**10.** [measurement of horse] paume *f*. -**11.** [worker] ouvrier *m*, -ère *f*; [on ship] homme *m*, membre *m* de l'équipage; she was lost with all ~s [ship] il a coulé avec tous les hommes à bord OR tout l'équipage; old ~ expert *m*, vieux *m* de la vieille; to be an old ~ at sthg avoir une vaste expérience de qqch ❑ all ~s to the pump *literal* & *fig* tout le monde à la rescousse. -**12.** CULIN [of bananas] régime *m*; ~ of pork jambonneau *m*.

◇ *vt* passer, donner; to ~ sthg to sb passer OR donner qqch à qqn; you have to ~ it to her, she IS a good mother *fig* c'est une bonne mère, il faut lui accorder cela.

◆ **by hand** *adv phr* [written] à la main; [made, knitted, sewn] (à la) main; to wash sthg by ~ laver qqch à la main; to send sthg by ~ faire porter qqch; to rear an animal by ~ élever un animal au biberon.

◆ **in hand** *adv phr* -**1.** [available money] disponible; [- time] devant soi; do we have any time in ~? *Br* avons-nous du temps devant nous? -**2.** [being dealt with] en cours; the matter is in ~ on s'occupe de l'affaire; I have the situation well in ~ j'ai la situation bien en main; keep your mind on the job in ~ concentre-toi sur le travail en cours.

◆ **on hand** *adj phr* [person] disponible.

◆ **out of hand** *adv phr* [immediately] sur-le-champ.

◆ **to hand** *adv phr* [letter, information etc] sous la main; use what comes to ~ prends ce que tu as sous la main; he took the first one that came to ~ il a pris le premier qui lui est tombé sous la main.

◆ **hand around** = **hand round**.

◆ **hand back** *vt sep* [return] rapporter, rendre ❑ I now ~ you back to the studio/John Smith RAD & TV je rends maintenant l'antenne au studio/John Smith.

◆ **hand down** *vt sep* -**1.** [pass, give from high place] passer, donner; ~ me down the hammer passe-moi OR donne-moi le marteau (qui est là-haut). -**2.** [heirloom, story] transmettre; the necklace/property has been ~ed down from mother to daughter for six generations le collier est transmis/la propriété est transmise de mère en fille depuis six générations. -**3.** JUR [decision, sentence] annoncer; [judgment] rendre; to ~ down the budget *Am* annoncer le budget.

◆ **hand in** *vt sep* [return, surrender - book] rendre; [- ticket] remettre; [- exam paper] rendre, remettre; [something found - to authorities, police etc] déposer, remettre; to ~ in one's resignation remettre sa démission.

◆ **hand off** *vt sep* RUGBY raffûter.

◆ **hand on** *vt sep* -**1.** [give to someone else] passer; to ~ sthg on to sb passer qqch à qqn. -**2.** = **hand down 2**.

◆ **hand out** *vt sep* [distribute] distribuer; we ~ out 200 free meals a day nous servons 200 repas gratuits par jour; he's very good at ~ing out advice il est très fort pour ce qui est de distribuer des conseils; the French boxer ~ed out a lot of punishment le boxeur français a frappé à coups redoublés.

◆ **hand over** ◇ *vt sep* -**1.** [pass, give - object] passer, donner; we now ~ you over to the weather man/Bill Smith in Moscow RAD & TV nous passons maintenant l'antenne à notre météorologue/Bill Smith à Moscou; I'm ~ing him over now TELEC je te le passe tout de suite. -**2.** [surrender - weapons, hostage] remettre; [- criminal] livrer; [- power, authority] transmettre; he was ~ed over to the French police il a été livré à la OR aux mains de la police française; to ~ over the reins passer les rênes; ~ it over! donne!

◇ *vi insep*: to ~ over to [government minister, chairman etc] passer le pouvoir à; [in meeting] donner la parole à ‖ TELEC passer OR donner le combiné à.

◆ **hand round** *vt sep* [distribute] distribuer.

◆ **hand up** *vt sep* [pass, give from low place] passer, donner; ~ me up the hammer passe-moi OR donne-moi le marteau (qui est là en bas).

hand- *in cpds* (à la) main; ~stitched cousu main; ~knitted tricoté à la main.

handbag ['hændbæg] *n* sac à main.

hand-baggage = **hand-luggage**.

handball [*sense 1* 'hændbɔːl, *sense 2* hænd'bɔːl] *n* -**1.** [game] handball *m*. -**2.** FTBL main *f*.

handbasin ['hændbeɪsn] *n* lavabo *m*.

handbell ['hændbel] *n* clochette *f*.

handbill ['hændbɪl] *n Br* prospectus *m*.

handbook ['hændbʊk] *n* [for car, machine] guide *m*, manuel *m*; [for tourist's use] guide *m*.

handbrake ['hændbreɪk] *n Br* frein *m* à main.

handcart ['hændkɑːt] *n* charrette *f* à bras.

handclap ['hændklæp] *n*: to get the slow ~ *Br* [performer] se faire siffler; to give sb the slow ~ *Br* siffler qqn.

handclasp ['hændklɑːsp] *n Am* poignée *f* de main.

handcraft ['hændkrɑːft] *vt* fabriquer à la main.

hand cream *n* crème *f* pour les mains.

handcuff ['hændkʌf] *vt* passer les menottes à; to ~ sb to sthg attacher qqn à qqch avec des menottes; he was ~ed il avait les menottes aux poignets.

handcuffs ['hændkʌfs] *npl* menottes *fpl*; to be in ~ avoir les menottes (aux mains).

hand-drier *n* sèche-mains *m inv*.

hand-drill *n* perceuse *f* à main.

-handed ['hændɪd] *in cpds*: right~ droitier; single~ tout seul; empty~ les mains vides, bredouille; two~ sword épée *f* (que l'on tient) à deux mains; four~ game of cards jeu *m* de cartes pour quatre personnes; one~ catch interception *f* à une main.

Handel ['hændl] *pr n* Haendel.

-hander ['hændəʳ] *in cpds*: two-/three-~ [play] pièce *f* pour deux/trois personnes.

handfeed [hænd'fi:d] (*pt* & *pp* handfed [-'fed]) *vt* nourrir à la main.

handful ['hændfʊl] *n* -**1.** [amount] poignée *f*; a ~ of *fig* [a few] quelques; a ~ of people quelques personnes; how many people were there? – only a ~ combien de personnes y avait-il? – seulement quelques-unes ❑ 'A Handful of Dust' *Waugh* 'Une poignée de cendre'. -**2.** *inf* [uncontrollable person] : to be a ~ être difficile; he's proving to be a real ~ for the defence il donne du fil à retordre à la défense adverse.

hand grenade *n* grenade *f* à main.

handgrip ['hændgrɪp] *n* -**1.** [on racket] grip *m*; [on bicycle] poignée *f*. -**2.** [handshake] poignée *f* de main. -**3.** [holdall] fourre-tout *m inv*.

handgun ['hændgʌn] *n Am* revolver *m*, pistolet *m*.

hand-held *adj* [appliance] à main; [camera] portatif.

handhold ['hændhəʊld] *n* prise *f* (de main).

handicap ['hændɪkæp] (*pt* & *pp* handicapped) ◇ *n* -**1.** [physical, mental] handicap *m*; *fig* [disadvantage] handicap *m*, désavantage *m*; people with a (physical/mental) ~ les gens qui souffrent d'un handicap (physique/mental); do you find it a ~ being so small? trouvez-vous que c'est un handicap OR un désavantage d'être aussi petit? -**2.** SPORT handicap *m*.
◇ *vt* -**1.** *fig* handicaper, désavantager; they were always handicapped by a lack of money ils ont toujours été handicapés par le manque d'argent. -**2.** SPORT handicaper.

handicapped ['hændɪkæpt] ◇ *adj* handicapé; to be mentally/physically ~ être handicapé mental/physique; '~ parking' *Am* 'parking réservé aux handicapés'.
◇ *npl*: the ~ les handicapés *mpl*.

handicraft ['hændɪkrɑ:ft] *n* -**1.** [items] objets *mpl* artisanaux, artisanat *m*. -**2.** [skill] artisanat *m*.

handily ['hændɪlɪ] *adv* -**1.** [conveniently] de façon commode OR pratique; the shop is ~ situated only 100 metres from the house le magasin n'est qu'à 100 mètres de la maison, ce qui est pratique OR commode. -**2.** *Am* [easily] : to win ~ gagner haut la main.

handiwork ['hændɪwɜ:k] *n (U)* [work] travail *m* manuel; [result] œuvre *f*; the graffiti is the ~ of vandals les graffiti sont l'œuvre de vandales; this is YOUR ~, is it? c'est toi qui as fait ça?

handkerchief ['hæŋkətʃɪf] *n* mouchoir *m*.

hand-knitted *adj* tricoté main, tricoté à la main.

handle ['hændl] ◇ *n* -**1.** [of broom, knife, screwdriver] manche *m*; [of suitcase, box, drawer, door] poignée *f*; [of cup] anse *f*; [of saucepan] queue *f*; [of stretcher] bras *m*; starting ~ AUT manivelle *f*; to fly off the ~ (at sb) *inf Br* piquer une colère (contre qqn). -**2.** *inf* [name - of citizens band user] nom *m* de code; [- which sounds impressive] titre *m* de noblesse. -**3.** *inf phr*: to get a ~ on sthg piger qqch; I'll get back to you once I've got a ~ on the situation je vous recontacterai quand j'aurai la situation en main; the first thing to do is to get a ~ on the export market la première chose à faire est de nous familiariser avec le marché à l'exportation.
◇ *vt* -**1.** [touch] toucher à, manipuler; 'please do not ~ the goods' 'ne pas toucher'; '~ with care!' 'manipuler avec précaution'; pesticides should be ~d with caution les pesticides doivent être manipulés avec précaution; to ~ the ball [in football] faire une main. -**2.** [control, operate - ship] manœuvrer, gouverner; [- car] conduire; [- gun] se servir de, manier; [- words, numbers] manier; have you any experience of handling horses? savez-vous vous y prendre avec les chevaux? -**3.** [cope with - crisis, problem] traiter; [- situation] faire face à; [- crowd, traffic, death] supporter; you ~d that very well tu as réglé la chose comme un chef; I couldn't have ~d it better myself je n'aurais pas mieux fait; he's good at handling people il sait s'y prendre avec les gens; I don't know how to ~ her je ne sais pas comment la prendre; leave this to me, I'LL ~ him laisse-moi m'en occuper, je me charge de lui; four babies are a lot for one person to ~ quatre bébés, cela fait beaucoup pour une seule personne; do you think you can ~ the job? penses-tu être capable de faire le travail?; I couldn't ~ it if Dad died si papa mourait, je ne le supporterais pas; how is she handling it? comment s'en sort-elle?; he can't ~ his drink *inf* il ne tient pas l'alcool; it's nothing I can't ~ je me débrouille. -**4.** [manage, process] s'occuper de; [address - topic, subject] aborder, traiter; she ~s my tax for me elle s'occupe de mes impôts; we're too small to ~ an order of that size notre entreprise est trop petite pour traiter une commande de cette importance; could you ~ this task as well? pourriez-vous également vous charger de ce travail?; the airport ~s two hundred planes a day chaque jour deux cents avions passent par l'aéroport; to ~ stolen goods receler des objets volés.
◇ *vi* [car, ship] répondre; how does she ~? [car] est-ce qu'elle répond bien?

handlebar ['hændlbɑ:ʳ] *comp*: ~ moustache moustache *f* en guidon de vélo; ~ tape Guidoline® *f*.
◆ **handlebars** *npl* guidon *m*; she went right over the ~s elle est passée par-dessus le guidon.

-handled ['hændld] *in cpds* [broom, screwdriver, knife] à manche de; [suitcase, box, drawer, door] à poignée de; a short-~ screwdriver un tournevis à manche court; ivory-~ knives des couteaux à manche d'ivoire.

handler ['hændləʳ] *n* [of dogs] maître-chien *m*; [of baggage] bagagiste *m*.

handling ['hændlɪŋ] ◇ *n* -**1.** [of pesticides, chemicals] manipulation *f*; a penalty was awarded for ~ FTBL un penalty a été accordé pour main; ~ of stolen goods recel *m* d'objets volés. -**2.** [of tool, weapon] maniement *m*; the size of the car makes for easy ~ la taille de la voiture permet une grande maniabilité. -**3.** [of situation, operation] : my ~ of the problem la façon dont j'ai traité le problème; her ~ of the interview was very professional elle a conduit OR mené l'entretien en professionnelle. -**4.** [of order, contract] traitement *m*, exécution *f*; [of goods, baggage] manutention *f*.
◇ *comp*: ~ charges frais *mpl* de traitement; [for physically shifting goods] frais *mpl* de manutention.

handloom ['hændlu:m] *n* métier *m* à tisser.

hand lotion *n* lotion *f* pour les mains.

hand luggage *n (U)* bagages *mpl* à main.

handmade [,hænd'meɪd] *adj* fabriqué OR fait (à la) main.

handmaid(en) ['hændmeɪd(n)] *n arch* servante *f*, bonne *f*; *fig* bonne *f*.

hand-me-down *inf* ◇ *n* vêtement *m* de seconde main; this suit is a ~ from my father ce costume appartenait à mon père; why do I always have to wear his ~s? pourquoi dois-je toujours porter ses vieux vêtements?
◇ *adj* [clothes] de seconde main; *fig* [ideas] reçu.

hand-off *n* RUGBY raffut *m*.

handout ['hændaʊt] *n* -**1.** [donation] aide *f*, don *m*; to live off ~s vivre de dons; it's not a ~ ce n'est pas de la charité; government ~s subventions *fpl* gouvernementales. -**2.** [printed sheet or sheets] polycopié *m*; press ~ communiqué *m* pour la presse. -**3.** [leaflet] prospectus *m*.

handover ['hændəʊvəʳ] *n* [of power] passation *f*, transmission *f*, transfert *m*; [of territory] transfert *m*; [of hostage, prisoner] remise *f*; [of baton] transmission *f*, passage *m*.

handpick [hænd'pɪk] *vt* -**1.** [fruit, vegetables] cueillir à la main. -**2.** *fig* [people] sélectionner avec soin, trier sur le volet.

handpicked [,hænd'pɪkt] *adj* [people] trié sur le volet.

handrail ['hændreɪl] *n* [on bridge] rambarde *f*, garde-fou *m*; NAUT rambarde *f*; [of stairway - gen] rampe *f*; [- against wall] main *f* courante.

handsaw ['hændsɔ:] *n* scie *f* à main; [small] (scie *f*) égoïne *f*.

handset ['hændset] *n* TELEC combiné *m*.

handsewn [,hænd'səʊn] *adj* cousu main, cousu à la main.

handshake ['hændʃeɪk] *n* -**1.** poignée *f* de main. -**2.** COMPUT établissement *m* de liaison, poignée *f* de main.

handshaking ['hændʃeɪkɪŋ] = **handshake 2**.

hand signal *n* signal *m* de la main.

hands-off [hændz'ɒf] *adj* [policy] non interventionniste, de non-intervention; [manager] non interventionniste.

handsome ['hænsəm] *adj* -**1.** [good-looking - person, face, room] beau; [- building, furniture] élégant; a ~ man un bel homme; a ~ woman une belle femme. -**2.** [generous - reward, compliment] beau; [- conduct, treatment] généreux; [- apology] sincère; that's very ~ of you c'est très généreux de votre part, vous êtes bien bon. -**3.** [substantial - profit, price] bon; [- fortune] joli; a ~ amount une coquette OR jolie somme, une somme rondelette.

handsomely ['hænsəmlɪ] *adv* -**1.** [beautifully] avec élégance, élégamment. -**2.** [generously] généreusement, avec générosité; [sincerely] sincèrement. -**3.** [substantially] : to win ~ gagner haut la main.

hands-on [hændz'ɒn] *adj* [training, experience] pratique; [exhibition] *où le public peut toucher les objets exposés*; I go for a ~ style of management je suis le genre de patron à contribuer concrètement au fonctionnement de mon entreprise OR à mettre la main à la pâte.

handspring ['hændsprɪŋ] *n* saut *m* de mains.

handstand ['hændstænd] *n* appui *m* renversé, équilibre *m* sur les mains.

handstitched [hænd'stɪtʃt] *adj* cousu main.

hand-to-hand *adj* & *adv* au corps à corps.

hand-to-mouth ◇ *adj*: to lead OR to have a ~ existence tirer le diable par la queue.
◇ *adv*: to live ~ tirer le diable par la queue.

hand towel *n* serviette *f*, essuie-mains *m inv*.

handwash ['hændwɒʃ] ◇ *vt* laver à la main.
◇ *n*: to do a ~ faire une lessive à la main.

handwork ['hændwɜ:k] *n* travail *m* à la main.

handwoven [,hænd'wəʊvn] *adj* tissé main.

handwriting ['hænd,raɪtɪŋ] *n* écriture *f*; ~ expert graphologue *mf*.

handwritten ['hænd,rɪtn] *adj* manuscrit, écrit à la main.

handy *inf* ['hændɪ] (*compar* handier, *superl* handiest) *adj* -**1.** [near at hand] proche; I always keep my glasses ~ je range toujours mes lunettes à portée de main; have you got a pen and paper ~? as-tu un stylo et du papier sous la main? -**2.** [person - good with one's hands] adroit de ses mains; he's ~ about the house il est bricoleur; he's not the handiest man in the world ce n'est pas un très bon bricoleur; to be ~ at doing sthg être doué pour faire qqch, bien savoir faire qqch; she's ~ with a drill elle sait se servir d'une perceuse; he's a bit ~ with his fists il sait se servir de ses poings. -**3.** [convenient, useful] commode, pratique; living in the centre is ~ for work pour le travail c'est pratique d'habiter en ville; that's ~! c'est pratique OR commode!; he's a ~ guy to have around il peut rendre des tas de services; she's a ~ person to have around in a crisis c'est quelqu'un qu'il est bon d'avoir OR c'est quelqu'un d'utile en cas de crise; a ~ piece of advice un conseil utile; to come in ~ être utile; don't throw it away, it might come in ~ one day ne le jette pas, ça pourrait servir un jour.

handyman ['hændɪmæn] (*pl* handymen [-men]) *n* [employee] homme *m* à tout faire; [odd job expert] bricoleur *m*.

hang [hæŋ] (*pt* & *pp vt* & *vi senses 1* & *2* hung [hʌŋ], *pt* & *pp vt sense 3* hanged) ◇ *vt* -**1.** [suspend - curtains, coat, decoration, picture] accrocher, suspendre; [- door] fixer, monter; [- art exhibition] mettre en place; [- wallpaper] coller, poser; CULIN [- game, meat] faisander; to ~ sthg from OR on sthg accrocher qqch à qqch; to ~ one's head (in shame) baisser la tête (de honte) □ to ~ one on sb *inf Am* [punch] balancer un coup de poing à qqn; to ~ fire [project] être en suspens; [person] mettre les choses en suspens. -**2.** *(usu pass)* [adorn] décorer; a tree hung with lights un arbre décoré OR orné de lumières. -**3.** [criminal] pendre; to be ~ed for one's crime être pendu pour son crime; to ~ o.s. se pendre; ~ed OR hung, drawn and quartered pendu, éviscéré et écartelé □ ~ him! *inf* qu'il aille se faire voir!; I'll be ~ed if I know *inf Br* je veux bien être pendu si je le sais; I'll be ~ed if I'm going out in that weather *inf* il n'y a pas de danger que je sorte par ce temps; ~ it (all)! *inf Br* ras le bol!; (you) might as well be ~ed for a sheep as a lamb *Br* quitte à être puni, autant l'être pour quelque chose qui en vaille la peine. -**4.** *Am* [turn]: to ~ a left prendre à gauche.

◇ *vi* -**1.** [be suspended - rope, painting, light] être accroché, être suspendu; [- clothes on clothes line] être étendu, pendre; to ~ from sthg être accroché OR suspendu à qqch; to ~ on sb's arm être accroché au bras de qqn; her pictures are now ~ing in several art galleries ses tableaux sont maintenant exposés dans plusieurs galeries d'art; his suit ~s well son costume tombe bien; the way her hair ~s down her back la façon dont ses cheveux lui tombent le long du dos; time ~s heavy (on my/his hands) le temps me/lui semble long □ how's it ~ing? *inf Am* ça gaze? -**2.** [float - mist, smoke etc] flotter, être suspendu; the ball seemed to ~ in the air le ballon semblait suspendu en l'air. -**3.** [criminal] être pendu; you'll ~ for your crime vous serez pendu pour votre crime □ she can go ~ *inf Br* elle peut aller se faire voir.

◇ *n inf* -**1.** [knack, idea]: to get the ~ of doing sthg prendre le coup pour faire qqch; I never did get the ~ of skiing je n'ai jamais réussi à prendre le coup pour skier; to get the ~ of sthg [understand] piger qqch; I can't get the ~ of this computer je n'arrive pas à piger comment marche cet ordinateur; are you getting the ~ of your new job? est-ce que tu te fais à ton nouveau travail?; you'll soon get the ~ of it tu vas bientôt t'y faire. -**2.** *phr*: he doesn't give OR care a ~ *Br* [couldn't care less] il n'en a rien à taper OR à cirer.

◆ **hang about** *inf Br*, **hang around** *inf* ◇ *vi insep* -**1.** [wait] attendre; he kept me ~ing about OR around for half an hour il m'a fait poireauter pendant une demi-heure; I've been ~ing about OR around, waiting for her to come je tourne en rond à l'attendre; I hate all this ~ing about OR around je déteste toute cette attente, je déteste attendre comme ça; ~ about (a bit)! *Br* attends!; ~ about, that's not what I mean! attends OR doucement, ce n'est pas ce que je veux dire! -**2.** [be idle, waste time] traîner (à ne rien faire); to ~ about OR around on street corners traîner dans les rues; we can't afford to ~ about if we want that contract nous ne pouvons pas nous permettre de traîner si nous voulons obtenir ce contrat; she doesn't ~ about OR around [soon gets what she wants] elle ne perd pas de temps. -**3.** [be an unwanted presence]: Mum doesn't want me ~ing around when the guests arrive Maman ne veut pas que je sois là quand les invités arriveront; that kid's been ~ing around for the past hour ça fait une heure que ce gamin traîne dans les parages.

◇ *vt insep*: to ~ about OR around a place traîner dans un endroit.

◆ **hang about with** *inf vt insep Br* traîner avec; I don't like the boys she ~s about with je n'aime pas les garçons avec qui elle traîne.

◆ **hang back** *vi insep* [wait behind] rester un peu plus longtemps; [not go forward] se tenir OR rester en arrière; he hung back from saying what he really thought *Br fig* il s'est retenu de dire ce qu'il pensait vraiment.

◆ **hang down** *vi insep* [light] pendre; [hair] descendre, tomber.

◆ **hang in** *inf vi insep*: ~ in there! tiens bon!, accroche-toi!

◆ **hang on** ◇ *vi insep* -**1.** [hold tight] se tenir, s'accrocher; ~ on tight tiens-toi OR accroche-toi bien. -**2.** *inf* [wait] attendre; ~ on! [wait] attends!; [indicating astonishment, disagreement etc] une minute!; ~ on and I'll get him for you [on phone] ne quitte pas, je te le passe; do you mind ~ing on for a minute or two? ça ne te dérange pas de patienter quelques minutes?; I've been ~ing on for the past quarter of an hour! [on phone] ça fait un quart d'heure que j'attends! -**3.** [hold out, survive] résister, tenir (bon); ~ on in there! *inf* [don't give up] tiens bon!, tiens le coup!

◇ *vt insep* -**1.** [listen to]: she hung on his every word elle buvait ses paroles, elle était suspendue à ses lèvres. -**2.** [depend on] dépendre de; it all ~s on whether we get the loan pour nous, tout dépend de l'obtention ou non du prêt; this is what it all ~s on tout dépend de cela.

◆ **hang onto** *vt insep* -**1.** [cling to] s'accrocher à. -**2.** *inf* [keep] garder, conserver; I'd ~ onto that table if I were you à ta place, je garderais cette table.

◆ **hang out** ◇ *vi insep* -**1.** [protrude] pendre; his shirt tails were ~ing out sa chemise pendait; to ~ out of the window [flags] être déployé à la fenêtre; [person] se pencher par la fenêtre □ to let it all ~ out *inf* [person] se relâcher complètement, se laisser aller; [speak without restraint] se défouler. -**2.** *inf* [frequent] traîner; where does she ~ out? quels sont les endroits qu'elle fréquente? -**3.** [survive, not give in] résister, tenir bon; they won't be able to ~ out for more than another two days ils ne résisteront OR ne tiendront pas plus de deux jours; the strikers are ~ing out in their demands les grévistes tiennent bon dans leurs revendications; they're ~ing out for 10% ils insistent pour obtenir 10 %.

◇ *vt sep* [washing] étendre; [flags] déployer.

◆ **hang out with** *inf vt insep* fréquenter; she ~s out with a group of artists elle fréquente un groupe d'artistes.

◆ **hang over** *vt insep* être suspendu au-dessus de, planer sur; (a) thick fog hung over the town un brouillard épais flottait au-dessus de la ville; a question mark ~s over his future/the project un point d'interrogation plane sur son avenir/le projet; she has got the threat of redundancy ~ing over her head OR her une menace de licenciement plane sur elle; I can't go out with exams ~ing over me avec les examens qui approchent, je ne peux pas sortir.

◆ **hang together** *vi insep* -**1.** [be united - people] se serrer les coudes. -**2.** [be consistent - alibi, argument, plot etc] (se) tenir; [- different alibis, statements] concorder.

◆ **hang up** ◇ *vt sep* [coat, hat etc] accrocher; TELEC [receiver] raccrocher; to ~ up one's boots/skates/dancing shoes [retire] raccrocher ses chaussures de foot/patins/chaussons de danse.

◇ *vi insep* -**1.** TELEC raccrocher; to ~ up on sb raccrocher au nez de qqn. -**2.** COMPUT [cease functioning] s'arrêter.

◆ **hang with** *inf vt insep Am*: to ~ with sb traîner avec qqn.

hangar ['hæŋəʳ] *n* AERON hangar *m*.

hangdog ['hæŋdɒg] *adj*: to have a ~ look OR expression avoir un air penaud OR de chien battu.

hanger ['hæŋəʳ] *n* [hook] portemanteau *m*; [coat hanger] portemanteau *m*, cintre *m*; [loop on garment] cordon *m* OR ganse *f* d'accrochage *(à l'intérieur d'un vêtement)*.

hanger-on (*pl* hangers-on) *n pej* parasite *m*.

hang-glide *vi* faire du deltaplane; to ~ down Mont Blanc descendre le mont Blanc en deltaplane.

hang-glider *n* [aircraft] deltaplane *m*; [person] libériste *mf*, adepte *mf* du deltaplane.

hang-gliding *n* deltaplane *m*.

hanging ['hæŋɪŋ] ◇ *adj* -**1.** [suspended] suspendu; ~ wardrobe penderie *f*; the Hanging Gardens of Babylon les jardins suspendus de Babylone. -**2.** JUR: ~ judge juge *m* à la main lourde; ~ offence crime *m* passible de pendaison; it's not a ~ offence *fig* ce n'est pas une affaire d'État.

◇ *n* -**1.** [death penalty] pendaison *f*; ~'s too good for him la pendaison, c'est encore trop bon pour lui. -**2.** [of wallpaper] pose *f*; [of decorations, pictures] accrochage *m*, mise *f* en place. -**3.** [tapestry]: wall ~s tentures *fpl* (murales).

hangman ['hæŋmən] (*pl* hangmen [-mən]) *n* [executioner] bourreau *m*; to play ~ [word game] jouer au pendu.

hangnail ['hæŋneɪl] *n* envie *f (peau)*.

hang-out *inf n*: this is one of my favourite ~s j'adore traîner dans ce coin; this is one of his ~s c'est l'un des endroits où on le trouve le plus souvent.

hangover ['hæŋ,əʊvəʳ] *n* -**1.** [from alcohol] gueule *f* de bois; to have a ~ avoir la gueule de bois. -**2.** [relic] reste *m*, vestige *m*, survivance *f*.

hang-up *n* -**1.** *inf* [complex] complexe *m*, blocage *m*; she has a ~ about flying elle a peur de prendre l'avion. -**2.** COMPUT blocage *m*, interruption *f*; ~ loop boucle *f* sans fin.

hank [hæŋk] *n* pelote *f*.

hanker ['hæŋkəʳ] *vi*: to ~ after OR for sthg rêver de qqch, avoir énormément envie de qqch; to ~ after an easy life rêver d'une vie tranquille.

hankering ['hæŋkərɪŋ] *n* rêve *m*, envie *f*; to have a ~ after OR for sthg rêver de qqch, avoir énormément envie de qqch.

hankie *inf*, **hanky** *inf* ['hænkɪ] (*pl* hankies) *n abbr of* handkerchief.

hanky-panky *inf* [-'pæŋkɪ] *n (U)* -**1.** [sexual activity] galipettes *fpl*; to have a bit of OR a little ~ faire des galipettes. -**2.** [mischief] entourloupettes *fpl*, blagues *fpl*; to get up to (a bit of) ~ faire des entourloupettes OR des blagues.

Hannah ['hænə] *pr n* BIBLE Anne.

Hannibal ['hænɪbl] *pr n* Hannibal, Annibal.

Hanoi [hæ'nɔɪ] *pr n* Hanoi.

Hanover ['hænəvəʳ] *pr n* Hanovre.

Hanoverian [,hænə'vɪərɪən] ◇ *adj* hanovrien. ◇ *n* Hanovrien *m*, -enne *f*.

Hansard ['hænsɑːd] *pr n Br* POL *compte rendu quotidien des débats de la Chambre des communes*.

Hanseatic [,hænsɪ'ætɪk] *adj* HIST: the ~ League la ligue hanséatique.

hansom (cab) ['hænsəm-] *n* fiacre *m*.

Hants *written abbr of* Hampshire.

ha'penny *inf* ['heɪpnɪ] (*pl* ha'pence [-pəns]) *Br* = **halfpenny**.

haphazard [,hæp'hæzəd] *adj* mal organisé; it was done in a ~ fashion ça a été fait un peu n'importe comment; the whole thing was a bit ~ c'était un peu n'importe quoi; the city grew in a ~ fashion la ville s'est agrandie au gré des circonstances; to choose in a ~ fashion choisir au petit bonheur la chance, choisir au hasard.

haphazardly [,hæp'hæzədlɪ] *adv* sans organisation, n'importe comment; there were objects lying ~ on the table des choses traînaient sur la table; to choose ~ choisir au petit bonheur la chance, choisir au hasard.

hapless ['hæplɪs] *adj lit* malchanceux.

ha'p'orth ['heɪpəθ] *Br* = **halfpennyworth**.

happen ['hæpən] ◇ *vi* -**1.** [occur] arriver, se passer, se produire; what's ~ed? qu'est-il

arrivé?, que s'est-il passé?; **when did this ~?** quand cela s'est-il produit OR passé?, quand cela est-il arrivé?; **where did the accident ~?** où l'accident s'est-il produit OR est-il arrivé OR a-t-il eu lieu?; **don't let it ~ again** faites en sorte que cela ne se reproduise pas; **as if nothing had ~ed** comme si de rien n'était; **I pulled the lever, but nothing ~ed** j'ai tiré sur le manche, mais il ne s'est rien passé OR ça n'a rien fait; **whatever ~s** quoi qu'il arrive OR advienne; **as (so) often ~s** comme c'est bien souvent le cas; **it all ~ed so quickly** tout s'est passé si vite; **these things ~** ce sont des choses qui arrivent; **what ~ed next?** que s'est-il passé ensuite?; **to find out what ~s next...** RAD & TV pour connaître la suite...; **it's all been ~ing this morning** ça n'a pas arrêté ce matin; **it's all ~ing here** ça bouge ici; **I wonder what has ~ed to her** [what has befallen her] je me demande ce qui a bien pu lui arriver; [what she is doing now] je me demande ce qu'elle est devenue; **whatever ~ed to him?** qu'est-il devenu?; **if anything ~s** OR **should ~ to me** s'il m'arrivait quelque chose; **it couldn't ~ to a nicer person** elle le mérite bien; **a funny thing ~ed to me last night** il m'est arrivé une drôle d'aventure hier soir; **what's ~ed to my coat?** [cannot be found] où est passé mon manteau?; **what's ~ing to us?** qu'est-ce qui nous arrive? -**2.** [chance]: **do you ~ to have his address?** auriez-vous son adresse, par hasard?; **it just so ~s that I do** eh bien justement, oui; **you wouldn't ~ to know where I could find him, would you?** vous ne sauriez pas où je pourrais le trouver?; **as it ~s** justement; **I ~ to know her, it so ~s that I know her, I know her, as it ~s** il se trouve que je la connais; **the man you're talking about ~s to be my father** il se trouve que l'homme dont vous parlez est mon père; **if you ~ to see him** si jamais tu le vois.
◇ *adv inf Br dial* [maybe] peut-être.
◆ **happen along** *inf*, **happen by** *inf vi insep Am* passer par hasard.
◆ **happen on, happen upon** *vt insep*: **I ~ed on an old friend/a good pub** je suis tombé sur un vieil ami/un bon pub.

happening ['hæpənɪŋ] ◇ *n* [occurrence] événement *m*; THEAT happening *m*.
◇ *adj* ▽: **he's a ~ kind of guy** avec lui on ne s'ennuie pas une minute; **this is a ~ kind of place** il se passe toujours des tas de trucs ici.

happenstance ['hæpənstæns] *n Am* hasard *m*; **we met by ~** nous nous sommes rencontrés par hasard.

happily ['hæpɪlɪ] *adv* -**1.** [contentedly - say, smile] d'un air heureux; [- play, chat] tranquillement; **I could live here very ~** je serais très heureux ici; **they lived ~ ever after** ≃ ils vécurent heureux et eurent beaucoup d'enfants; **I thought that when you got married you lived ~ ever after** je croyais que quand on se mariait, on vivait heureux jusqu'à la fin de ses jours; **to be ~ married** [man] être un mari comblé; [woman] être une épouse comblée; **I always thought you two were ~ married** j'ai toujours pensé que vous étiez un couple heureux. -**2.** [gladly] volontiers; **she said she would ~ give her consent** elle a dit qu'elle donnerait volontiers son accord OR qu'elle serait heureuse de donner son accord; **I could quite ~ live here** je me verrais très bien vivre ici; **I could quite ~ strangle him** j'ai bien envie de l'étrangler. -**3.** [luckily] heureusement, par chance. -**4.** [appropriately] heureusement, avec bonheur; **a very ~ chosen turn of phrase** une tournure de phrase très heureuse.

happiness ['hæpɪnɪs] *n* bonheur *m*; **money can't buy you ~** l'argent ne fait pas le bonheur *prov*.

happy ['hæpɪ] (*compar* **happier**, *superl* **happiest**) *adj* -**1.** [content] heureux; **to make sb ~** rendre qqn heureux; **I want you to be ~** je veux que tu sois heureux, je veux ton bonheur; **I'm the happiest man in the world** je suis l'homme le plus heureux du monde; **I hope you'll both be very ~** je vous souhaite beaucoup de bonheur OR d'être très heureux; **I'm very ~ for you** je suis très heureux pour toi; **if you're ~, I'm ~** si tu es satisfait, moi aussi; **would you be ~ living here?** serais-tu heureux ici?; **in happier times** à une époque plus heureuse; **in happier circumstances** dans des circonstances plus heureuses; **those were ~ days** c'était le bon temps; **I'm not at all ~ about your decision** je ne suis pas du tout content de votre décision; **I'm still not ~ about it** je n'en suis toujours pas content; **that should keep the kids ~** cela devrait occuper les enfants; **their ~ smiling faces** leurs visages heureux et souriants; **it's a ~ office** il y a une bonne ambiance dans ce bureau; **~ ending** [in book, film] fin *f* heureuse, dénouement *m* heureux; **to have a ~ ending** [book, film] bien finir; **~ birthday** OR **anniversary!** joyeux anniversaire!; **Happy Christmas!** Joyeux Noël!; **Happy New Year!** Bonne Année! ❑ **~ families** [card game] jeu *m* des sept familles; **many ~ returns (of the day)!** joyeux anniversaire!; **to be as ~ as a lark** OR **a sandboy** *Br* être heureux comme tout. -**2.** [willing]: **I'm only too ~ to help** je suis ravi de rendre service; **I would be ~ to do it** je le ferais volontiers; **we'd be ~ to put you up** nous serions heureux de vous loger, nous vous logerions volontiers; **I'd be ~ to live here/move to Scotland** j'aimerais bien habiter ici/aller habiter en Écosse. -**3.** [lucky, fortunate - coincidence] heureux; **the ~ few** les privilégiés *mpl*. -**4.** [apt, appropriate - turn of phrase, choice of words] heureux. -**5.** *inf* [drunk] gris, pompette.

happy event *n* [birth] heureux événement *m*.

happy-go-lucky *adj* décontracté; *pej* insouciant.

happy hour *n* [in pub, bar] *heure, généralement en début de soirée, pendant laquelle les boissons sont moins chères.*

happy hunting ground *n* paradis *m* des Indiens; *fig* mine *f* d'or; **the market is a ~ for collectors** le marché est une vraie mine d'or pour les collectionneurs.

happy medium *n* équilibre *m*, juste milieu *m*; **to strike a ~** trouver un équilibre OR un juste milieu.

hara-kiri [,hærə'kiːrɪ] *n* hara-kiri *m*; **to commit ~** faire hara-kiri.

harangue [hə'ræŋ] ◇ *vt* [person, crowd etc] haranguer; **to ~ sb about sthg** haranguer qqn au sujet de qqch.
◇ *n* harangue *f*.

Harare [hə'rɑːrɪ] *pr n* Harare.

harass ['hærəs] *vt* [torment] tourmenter; [with questions, demands] harceler; MIL harceler; **he claimed that the police had ~ed him** il a déclaré que la police l'avait harcelé; **to sexually ~ an employee** harceler une employée sexuellement.

harassed ['hærəst] *adj* stressé; **to be sexually ~** être victime de harcèlement sexuel.

harassment ['hærəsmənt] *n* [tormenting] tracasserie *f*; [with questions, demands] harcèlement *m*; [stress] stress *m*; MIL harcèlement *m*; **police ~** harcèlement policier; **sexual ~** harcèlement sexuel.

harbinger ['hɑːbɪndʒə^r] *n lit* signe *m* avant-coureur; **swallows are a ~ of spring** les hirondelles annoncent le printemps; **a ~ of doom** [event, incident etc] un mauvais présage; [person] un oiseau de malheur.

harbour *Br*, **harbor** *Am* ['hɑːbə^r] ◇ *n* [for boats] port *m*; *fig* havre *m*.
◇ *comp*: **~ dues** droits *mpl* de port; **~ master** capitaine *m* de port.
◇ *vt* -**1.** [person] abriter, héberger; [criminal] donner asile à, receler. -**2.** [grudge, suspicion] nourrir, entretenir en soi; **to ~ a grudge against sb** garder rancune à qqn, nourrir de la rancune envers qqn. -**3.** [conceal - fleas, dirt, germs] renfermer, receler.

hard [hɑːd] ◇ *adj* -**1.** [not soft - substance, light, colour] dur; LING [consonant] dur; **to get** OR **to become ~** durcir ❑ **~ drug** drogue *f* dure; **~ water** eau *f* calcaire OR dure; **a ~ nut** *inf* OR **man** un dur; **he's a ~ nut to crack** [difficult to persuade] il n'est pas facile à convaincre; **it's a ~ nut to crack** [difficult to solve] c'est dur à résoudre; **a glass of wine, or would you prefer a drop of the ~ stuff?** un verre de vin, ou bien préféreriez-vous une goutte de quelque chose de plus fort?; **keep off the ~ stuff** évitez les boissons fortes; **she is (as) ~ as nails** [emotionally] elle est dure, elle n'a pas de cœur; [physically] c'est une dure à cuire; **rock ~, (as) ~ as rock** dur comme la pierre; **his muscles are rock ~** OR **(as) ~ as rock** ses muscles sont durs comme le fer, il a des muscles d'acier; **no ~ feelings?** sans rancune? -**2.** [concrete - facts] concret, tangible; [- evidence] tangible; **the ~ fact is that...** le fait est que...; **~ news** PRESS nouvelles *fpl* sûres OR vérifiées. -**3.** [difficult - question, problem etc] difficile, dur; **it's ~ to explain** c'est difficile OR dur à expliquer; **I find it ~ to understand/believe that...** je n'arrive pas à comprendre/croire que...; **it's ~ to say** c'est difficile à dire; **he's ~ to get on with** il n'est pas facile à vivre; **she is ~ to please** [never satisfied] elle est difficile; [difficult to buy gifts for etc] c'est difficile de lui faire plaisir; **it's ~ to beat** [value for money] pour le prix, c'est imbattable; **it's ~ to beat a good Bordeaux** il n'y a rien de meilleur qu'un bon bordeaux; **life is ~** c'est dur, la vie; **these are ~ times for all of us** c'est une période difficile pour tout le monde; **to fall on ~ times** [financially] connaître des temps difficiles OR une période de vaches maigres; [have difficult times] connaître des temps difficiles, en voir de dures ❑ **to give sb a ~ time** en faire voir de dures à qqn; **the boss has just been giving me a ~ time** le patron vient de me faire passer un mauvais quart d'heure; **come on, don't give me a ~ time!** allez, laisse-moi tranquille!; **you'll have a ~ time (of it) persuading him to do that** tu vas avoir du mal à le convaincre de faire cela; **she had a ~ time of it after her mother's death** elle a traversé une période difficile après la mort de sa mère; **she had a ~ time of it when she was a child** la vie n'était pas drôle pour elle quand elle était enfant; **she had a ~ time of it** [in childbirth, operation] elle a souffert; **to learn sthg the ~ way** [involving personal loss, suffering etc] apprendre qqch à ses dépens; [in a difficult way] faire le rude apprentissage de qqch; **I learnt the ~ way not to be underinsured** j'ai appris à mes dépens qu'il ne faut pas être sous-assuré; **I learnt skiing the ~ way** j'ai appris à skier à la dure; **I learnt my seamanship the ~ way** j'ai fait le rude apprentissage du métier de marin; **some people always have to do things the ~ way** il y a des gens qui choisissent toujours la difficulté; **to play ~ to get** [flirt] jouer les insaisissables; **their financial expert is playing ~ to get** *hum* leur expert financier semble jouer à cache-cache; **'Hard Times'** *Dickens* 'les Temps difficiles'. -**4.** [severe - voice, face, eyes] dur, froid; [- climate, winter] rigoureux, rude; [- frost] fort, rude; **to be ~ on sb** être dur avec qqn; **children are ~ on their shoes** les enfants font subir de mauvais traitements à leurs chaussures; **it's ~ on the nerves** c'est dur pour les nerfs; **it was ~ on the others** ça a été dur pour les autres; **it will be ~ luck if he doesn't get the job** ça ne sera pas de veine OR de bol s'il n'obtient pas le travail; **don't give me any of your ~ luck stories** ne me raconte pas tes malheurs; **he gave me some ~ luck story about having lost his investments** il a essayé de m'apitoyer en me racontant qu'il avait perdu l'argent qu'il avait investi; **to be a ~ taskmaster** être dur à la tâche; **to take a long ~ look at sthg** examiner qqch de près; **you should take a long ~ look at yourself** tu devrais bien te regarder; **the ~ left/right** POL l'extrême gauche/droite ❑ **he's taken a few ~ knocks** *literal* il a pris quelques mauvais coups; *fig* il en a vu de dures; **~ cheese!** *Br*, **~ lines!** *inf Br*, **~ luck!** pas de chance!, pas de veine!, pas de bol! -**5.** [strenuous]: **it's ~ work** c'est dur; **it's been a long ~**

day la journée a été longue; she's ~ work [difficult to get on with] elle n'est pas facile à vivre; [difficult to make conversation with] elle n'est pas causante; she's not afraid of ~ work le travail ne lui fait pas peur; she's a ~ worker c'est un bourreau de travail; he's a ~ drinker c'est un gros buveur, il boit beaucoup; he's a ~ charger c'est un fonceur; the climb was ~ going la montée était rude; it's ~ going making conversation with him c'est difficile de discuter avec lui; give it a good ~ shove pousse-le un bon coup, pousse-le fort. -**6.** TYPO [hyphen, return] imposé.

◇ *adv* -**1.** [strenuously - pull, push, hit, breathe] fort; [- work] dur; [- run] à toutes jambes; [- listen] attentivement; to work ~ at sthg beaucoup travailler qqch; to work ~ at improving one's service/French beaucoup travailler pour améliorer son service/français; to work sb ~ faire travailler qqn dur; work ~, play ~, that's what I say! beaucoup travailler pour beaucoup s'amuser, telle est ma devise!; you'll have to try ~er il faudra que tu fasses plus d'efforts; to try ~ to do sthg essayer de son mieux de faire qqch; try ~! fais de ton mieux!; to think ~ beaucoup réfléchir; think ~! réfléchis bien!; think ~er! réfléchis un peu plus!; to look ~ at sb regarder qqn bien en face; to look ~ at sthg examiner qqch; as ~ as possible, as ~ as one can [work, try] le plus qu'on peut; [push, hit, squeeze] de toutes ses forces; ~ astern! NAUT arrière, toute!; she hauled the wheel ~ over AUT elle a braqué à fond ❑ they're ~ at it *Br* [working] ils sont plongés dans leur travail; [engaged in sex] *inf* ils s'en donnent à cœur joie. -**2.** [with difficulty] difficilement; to be ~ put (to it) to do sthg avoir du mal à faire qqch; old habits die ~ les vieilles habitudes ont la vie dure. -**3.** [harshly, severely - treat sb] durement, sévèrement; he's feeling ~ done by il a l'impression d'avoir été injustement traité ‖ [heavily, strongly - rain] à verse; [- freeze, snow] fort; to be ~ hit by sthg être durement touché par qqch; she took the news/his death pretty ~ la nouvelle/sa mort l'a beaucoup éprouvée; it'll go ~ with him if he keeps telling lies ça va aller mal pour lui s'il continue à raconter des mensonges. -**4.** [solid]: the ground was frozen ~ le gel avait complètement durci la terre; to set ~ [concrete, mortar] prendre. -**5.** [close]: to follow ~ on the heels of sb être sur les talons de qqn; to follow OR to come ~ on the heels of sthg suivre qqch de très près.

◇ *n phr*: to try one's ~est faire de son mieux.

◆ **hard by** *prep phr* près de.

hard-and-fast *adj* [rule] strict, absolu; [information] correct, vrai; there's no ~ rule about it il n'existe pas de règle absolue là-dessus.

hardassed▽ ['hɑːdæst] *adj Am* vache.

hardback ['hɑːdbæk] ◇ *n* [book] livre *m* cartonné; available in ~ disponible en version cartonnée.

◇ *adj* cartonné.

hardball ['hɑːdbɔːl] *n Am* [game] baseball *m*; [ball] balle *f* de baseball; to play ~ *inf fig* employer les grands moyens.

hard-bitten [-'bɪtən] *adj* endurci.

hardboard ['hɑːdbɔːd] *n* panneau *m* de fibres; a sheet of ~ un panneau dur.

hard-boil *vt*: to ~ an egg faire un œuf dur.

hard-boiled [-'bɔɪld] *adj* -**1.** [egg] dur. -**2.** *inf* [person] dur.

hard case *inf n* dur *m* à cuire.

hard cash *n* (argent *m*) liquide *m*.

hard cider *n Am* cidre *m*.

hard coal *n* anthracite *m*.

hard copy *n* COMPUT copie *f* papier.

hardcore ['hɑːdkɔːʳ] *n* [for roads, buildings] blocaille *f*.

hard core *n* -**1.** [nucleus] noyau *m* dur. -**2.** MUS hard rock *m*, hard *m*. -**3.** [pornography] porno *m* hard.

◆ **hard-core** *adj* [belief in political system] dur; [believer] endurci; [support] ferme; [pornography, rock music] hard.

hard court *n Br* [for tennis] court *m* en ciment.

hardcover ['hɑːd,kʌvəʳ] = **hardback**.

hard currency *n* monnaie *f* OR devise *f* forte; a ~ shop un magasin où on paye en devises.

hard disk *n* COMPUT disque *m* dur.

hard-drinking *adj* qui boit beaucoup.

hard-earned [-'ɜːnt] *adj* [money] durement gagné; [victory] durement OR difficilement remporté; [reputation] durement acquis; [holiday, reward] bien mérité.

harden ['hɑːdn] ◇ *vt* [person - physically, emotionally] endurcir; [steel] tremper; LING [consonant] durcir; MED [arteries] durcir, scléroser; to ~ o.s. to sthg s'endurcir à qqch; to ~ one's heart endurcir son cœur; she ~ed her heart against him elle lui a fermé son cœur.

◇ *vi* -**1.** [snow, skin, steel] durcir; [concrete, mortar] prendre; MED [arteries] durcir, se scléroser; [person - emotionally] s'endurcir, se durcir; [- physically] s'endurcir; [attitude] se durcir. -**2.** FIN [prices, market] s'affermir.

◆ **harden off** ◇ *vt sep* [plant] mettre en jauge, habituer à des conditions plus dures.

◇ *vi insep* [plant] s'habituer à des conditions plus dures.

◆ **harden up** ◇ *vi insep* FIN [shares] se raffermir.

◇ *vt sep* [toughen - person] endurcir.

hardened ['hɑːdnd] *adj* [snow, skin] durci; [steel] trempé, durci; [arteries] sclérosé; a ~ criminal un criminel endurci OR invétéré; to become ~ to sthg se blinder contre qqch.

hardener ['hɑːdnəʳ] *n* [for glue, fingernails] durcisseur *m*.

hardening ['hɑːdnɪŋ] *n* [of snow, skin, attitudes] durcissement *m*; [of steel] trempe *f*; [of person - physical] endurcissement *m*; [- emotional] durcissement *m*; FIN [of prices] affermissement *m*; ~ of the arteries MED durcissement OR sclérose *f* des artères.

hard-faced [-'feɪst] *adj* au visage dur.

hard-fought [-'fɔːt] *adj* [game, competition, battle] rudement disputé.

hard hat ◇ *n* -**1.** [of construction worker] casque *m*. -**2.** *inf Am* [construction worker] ouvrier *m* du bâtiment.

◇ *comp*: ~ area *zone où le port du casque est obligatoire*; '~ area' 'port du casque obligatoire'.

◆ **hard-hat** *adj Am caractéristique des attitudes conservatrices des ouvriers du bâtiment.*

hard-headed [-'hedɪd] *adj* -**1.** [tough, shrewd - person] à la tête froide; [- realism] froid, brut; [- bargaining] dur; [- decision] froid. -**2.** *Am* [stubborn - person] qui a la tête dure; [- attitude] entêté.

hardhearted [,hɑːd'hɑːtɪd] *adj* [person] insensible, dur, au cœur de pierre; [attitude] dur; to be ~ towards sb être dur avec OR envers qqn.

hard-hitting [-'hɪtɪŋ] *adj* -**1.** [verbal attack] rude; [speech, report] implacable, sans indulgence. -**2.** [boxer] qui frappe dur.

hardiness ['hɑːdɪnɪs] *n* [of person] résistance *f*, robustesse *f*; [of plant, tree] résistance *f*.

hard labour *n (U)* travaux *mpl* forcés.

hardline ['hɑːdlaɪn] *n* ligne *f* de conduite dure; to take a ~ on sb/sthg adopter une ligne de conduite dure avec qqn/sur qqch.

◆ **hard-line** *adj* [policy, doctrine] dur; [politician] intransigeant, endurci, intraitable.

hardliner [,hɑːd'laɪnəʳ] *n* partisan *m*, -e *f* de la manière forte.

hardly ['hɑːdlɪ] *adv* -**1.** [barely] à peine, ne... guère; he can ~ read il sait à peine OR tout juste lire; you can ~ move in here for furniture c'est à peine si on peut bouger ici tellement il y a de meubles; I have ~ started je viens à peine OR tout juste de commencer; I ~ get a minute to myself these days c'est tout juste si j'ai une minute à moi ces jours-ci; I can ~ believe it j'ai du mal à le croire; ~ had I said these words when he arrived *lit* à peine eus-je *lit* OR avais-je prononcé ces mots qu'il arriva; ~ anyone presque personne; ~ anywhere presque nulle part; I ~ ever see you these days je ne te vois presque jamais ces temps-ci; there's ~ anything in the fridge il n'y a presque rien dans le frigo; I paid ~ anything for it ça m'a coûté trois fois rien; you've ~ touched your food tu n'as presque rien mangé; I can ~ wait to see her je suis très impatient de la voir; I can ~ wait! *iron* j'en frémis d'avance!; she ~ ever goes out elle ne sort presque jamais; ~ a week goes by without a telephone call from her il se passe rarement une semaine sans qu'elle téléphone; I need ~ say that... ai-je besoin de vous dire que... ?, je n'ai pas besoin de vous dire que... -**2.** [expressing negative opinion]: it's ~ MY fault! ce n'est quand même pas de ma faute!; it's ~ any of your business cela ne te regarde absolument pas; this is ~ the time to be selling your house ce n'est vraiment pas le moment de vendre votre maison; it's ~ surprising, is it? ça n'a rien de surprenant, ce n'est guère surprenant; it's ~ surprising that she left him ce n'est pas surprenant qu'elle l'ait quitté, il n'est guère surprenant qu'elle l'ait quitté; ~! [not in the slightest] bien au contraire!, loin de là!; she's ~ likely to agree elle ne risque pas d'accepter; he'd ~ have said that cela m'étonnerait qu'il ait dit cela.

hard-mouthed [-'maʊθd] *adj* -**1.** [horse] qui ne prend pas le mors OR la bride. -**2.** [person] têtu.

hardness ['hɑːdnɪs] *n* -**1.** [of snow, skin, water] dureté *f*; [of steel] trempe *f*, dureté *f*. -**2.** [difficulty] difficulté *f*; ~ of hearing MED surdité *f* partielle. -**3.** [severeness - of personality] dureté *f*; [- of heart] dureté *f*, froideur *f*. -**4.** [strenuousness] difficulté *f*. -**5.** FIN affermissement *m*.

hard-nosed *inf* [-'nəʊzd] = **hard-headed**.

hard of hearing ◇ *npl*: the ~ les malentendants *mpl*.

◇ *adj*: to be ~ être dur d'oreille.

hard-on▼ *n*: to have OR to get a ~ bander.

hard-packed [-'pækt] *adj* [snow, soil] tassé.

hard pad *n* VETER coussinet *m* dur.

hard palate *n* voûte *f* du palais, palais *m* dur.

hard-pressed [-'prest], **hard-pushed** [-'pʊʃt] *adj*: to be ~ for money/ideas/suggestions être à court d'argent/d'idées/de suggestions; to be ~ for time manquer de temps; to be ~ to do sthg avoir du mal à faire qqch.

hard rock *n* hard rock *m*, hard *m*.

hard sauce *n* CULIN sauce *f* au cognac.

hard sell ◇ *n* vente *f* agressive; the salesman gave us the ~ le vendeur a essayé de nous forcer la main.

◇ *comp*: ~ approach OR tactics méthode *f* de vente agressive.

hardship ['hɑːdʃɪp] ◇ *n* épreuves *fpl*; to go through a time of ~ traverser de terribles épreuves; to suffer great ~ OR ~s subir OR traverser de rudes épreuves; a life of ~ une vie pleine d'épreuves; further ~ is in store d'autres épreuves nous attendent.

◇ *comp*: ~ allowance [for student] *aide accordée à un étudiant en cas de graves problèmes financiers*.

hard shoulder *n* AUT bande *f* d'arrêt d'urgence.

hardtack ['hɑːdtæk] *n* NAUT biscuit *m* sans sel.

hardtop ['hɑːdtɒp] *n* AUT [of car] hard-top *m*; [car] voiture *f* à hard-top.

hard up *inf adj* [short of money] fauché, à sec; to be ~ for ideas manquer d'idées, être à court d'idées; to be ~ for volunteers manquer de volontaires; you must be ~ if you're going out with him! *fig* il faut vraiment que tu n'aies rien à te mettre sous la dent pour sortir avec lui!

hardware ['hɑːdweəʳ] ◇ *n (U)* -**1.** COMM quincaillerie *f*. -**2.** COMPUT matériel *m*, hardware *m*. -**3.** MIL matériel *m* de guerre, armement *m*. -**4.** *inf* [guns] armes *fpl*; he wasn't carrying any ~ il ne portait pas d'armes, il n'était pas armé.

◇ *comp* COMPUT [company, manufacturer] de matériel informatique; [problem] de matériel OR hardware.

hardware shop, hardware store *n* quincaillerie *f*.

hardwearing [ˌhɑːdˈweərɪŋ] *adj* robuste, résistant.

hard-wired [-ˈwaɪəd] *adj* COMPUT câblé.

hard-won [-ˈwʌn] *adj* [victory, trophy, independence] durement gagné; [reputation] durement acquis.

hardwood [ˈhɑːdwʊd] ◇ *n* [wood] bois *m* dur; [tree] arbre *m* à feuilles caduques.
◇ *comp* [floor] en bois dur.

hard-working *adj* travailleur; [engine, machine, printer] robuste.

hardy [ˈhɑːdɪ] (*comp* hardier, *superl* hardiest) *adj* -**1.** [strong - person, animal] robuste, résistant; [- plant] résistant; ~ **annual** BOT plante *f* annuelle; ~ **perennial** BOT plante vivace; *fig* serpent *m* de mer. -**2.** [intrepid - explorer, pioneer] intrépide, courageux.

hare [heəʳ] (*pl inv* OR hares) ◇ *n* -**1.** CULIN & ZOOL lièvre *m*; to raise OR to start a ~ *Br* mettre une question sur le tapis; 'The Hare and the Tortoise' *La Fontaine* 'le Lièvre et la tortue'. -**2.** SPORT [at dog race] lièvre *m*. -**3.** *Br* GAMES: ~ and hounds jeu *m* de piste.
◇ *vi inf*: to ~ across/down/out traverser/descendre/sortir à toutes jambes; she came haring down the stairs elle a dévalé les escaliers à fond de train.
◆ **hare off** *inf vi insep* prendre ses jambes à son cou, s'enfuir à toutes jambes.

harebell [ˈheəˌbel] *n* campanule *f*.

harebrained [ˈheəˌbreɪnd] *adj* [reckless, mad - person] écervelé; [- scheme] insensé, fou.

harelip [ˌheəˈlɪp] *n* bec-de-lièvre *m*.

harem [*Br* hɑːˈriːm, *Am* ˈhærəm] *n literal* & *fig* harem *m*.

haricot (bean) [ˈhærɪkəʊ-] *n* haricot *m* blanc.

hark [hɑːk] *vi lit* prêter l'oreille, ouïr; ~, I hear voices! écoutez OR chut, j'entends des voix!; just ~ at him! *inf Br* écoutez-le donc!
◆ **hark back to** *vt insep* [recall] revenir à; to ~ back to sthg revenir (tout le temps) à qqch; the style ~s back to the 1940s le style rappelle celui des années 40.

harken [ˈhɑːkn] *vi lit* prêter l'oreille.

Harlequin [ˈhɑːlɪkwɪn] *pr n* Arlequin.
◆ **harlequin** *adj* [costume] bigarré; [dog's coat] tacheté.

harlequinade [ˌhɑːlɪkwɪˈneɪd] *n* arlequinade *f*.

Harley Street [ˈhɑːlɪ-] *pr n rue du centre de Londres célèbre pour ses spécialistes en médecine*.

harlot [ˈhɑːlət] *n arch* prostituée *f*.

harm [hɑːm] ◇ *n (U)* [physical] mal *m*; [psychological] tort *m*, mal *m*; to do sb ~ faire du mal à qqn; I hope Ed won't come to (any) ~ j'espère qu'il n'arrivera rien à Ed; a bath wouldn't do him any ~ un bain ne lui ferait pas de mal; she has done you no ~ elle ne vous a fait aucun mal; they didn't mean any ~ ils ne voulaient pas (faire) de mal; Ted means no ~ Ted n'est pas méchant; I know you didn't mean any ~ when you said it je sais que tu ne l'as pas dit méchamment; the incident did a great deal of ~ to his reputation cet incident a beaucoup nui à sa réputation; no ~ done il n'y a pas de mal; there's no ~ in trying il n'y a pas de mal à essayer, on ne perd rien à essayer; I see no ~ in their going je ne vois pas d'inconvénient à ce qu'ils y aillent; what ~ is there in it? qu'est-ce qu'il y a de mal (à cela)?; no ~ will come of it ça n'est pas grave; too much adverse publicity will do their cause a great deal of ~ trop de mauvaise publicité nuira énormément à leur cause; to do more ~ than good faire plus de mal que de bien ❑ out of ~'s way [person] en sûreté, en lieu sûr; [things] en lieu sûr.
◇ *vt* -**1.** [person - physically] faire du mal à; [- psychologically] faire du tort à, nuire à; Clive wouldn't ~ a hair on her head Clive ne lui ferait aucun mal; he wasn't ~ed by the experience ça ne lui a pas fait de mal. -**2.** [surface] abîmer, endommager; [crops] endommager. -**3.** [cause, interests] causer du tort à, être préjudiciable à; [reputation] salir.

harmful [ˈhɑːmfʊl] *adj* -**1.** [person, influence] nuisible, malfaisant. -**2.** [chemicals] nocif; [effects] nuisible; ~ to plants nuisible pour les plantes.

harmless [ˈhɑːmlɪs] *adj* -**1.** [person] inoffensif, qui n'est pas méchant; [animal] inoffensif. -**2.** [joke] sans malice, anodin; [pastime] innocent.

harmlessly [ˈhɑːmlɪslɪ] *adv* sans faire de mal, sans dommage OR dommages.

harmonic [hɑːˈmɒnɪk] ◇ *n* MATH & MUS harmonique *m*.
◇ *adj* [gen, MATH & MUS] harmonique.

harmonica [hɑːˈmɒnɪkə] *n* harmonica *m*.

harmonic analysis *n* analyse *f* harmonique.

harmonic mean *n* moyenne *f* harmonique.

harmonic progression *n* progression *f* harmonique.

harmonics [hɑːˈmɒnɪks] *n (U)* harmoniques *mpl*.

harmonic series *n* série *f* harmonique.

harmonious [hɑːˈməʊnjəs] *adj* harmonieux.

harmoniously [hɑːˈməʊnjəslɪ] *adv* harmonieusement.

harmonist [ˈhɑːmənɪst] *n* harmoniste *mf*.

harmonium [hɑːˈməʊnjəm] *n* harmonium *m*.

harmonization [ˌhɑːmənaɪˈzeɪʃn] *n* harmonisation *f*.

harmonize, -ise [ˈhɑːmənaɪz] ◇ *vt* -**1.** MUS [instrument, melody] harmoniser. -**2.** [colours] harmoniser, assortir. -**3.** [views, statements] harmoniser, faire concorder; [people] concilier, amener à un accord.
◇ *vi* -**1.** MUS [sing in harmony] chanter en harmonie; [be harmonious] être harmonieux OR en harmonie; [write harmony] harmoniser, faire des harmonies. -**2.** [colours] aller (bien) ensemble, se marier (bien); choose colours that ~ with the background choisissez des couleurs qui soient assorties au décor.

harmony [ˈhɑːmənɪ] (*pl* harmonies) *n* -**1.** MUS harmonie *f*; to study ~ étudier l'harmonie; to sing in ~ chanter en harmonie; a three-part ~ une harmonie en trois parties; unusual harmonies des harmonies inhabituelles. -**2.** [agreement - of colours] harmonie *f*; [- of temperaments] harmonie *f*, accord *m*; to live in ~ with sb vivre en harmonie avec qqn; her choice is in perfect ~ with mine ses choix sont parfaitement en harmonie OR en accord avec les miens; the scene was one of perfect ~ une harmonie parfaite se dégageait de cette scène.

harness [ˈhɑːnɪs] ◇ *n* -**1.** [for horse, oxen] harnais *m*, harnachement *m*; [for parachute, car seat] harnais *m*; [for child] harnais *m*. -**2.** *phr*: to get OR to be back in ~ reprendre le collier.
◇ *vt* -**1.** [horse] harnacher, mettre le harnais à; [oxen, dogs] atteler; the pony was ~ed to the cart le poney était attelé à la charrette. -**2.** *fig* [resources] exploiter, maîtriser.

harness racing *n (U)* course *f* de trotteurs.

Harold [ˈhærəld] *pr n* Harold.

harp [hɑːp] MUS ◇ *n* harpe *f*.
◇ *vi* jouer de la harpe.
◆ **harp on** *inf* ◇ *vi insep* chanter (toujours) le même refrain OR la même rengaine; to ~ on about sthg rabâcher qqch, revenir sans cesse sur qqch; to ~ on at sb about sthg rebattre les oreilles à qqn au sujet de qqch; don't keep ~ing on! arrêtez de rabâcher!
◇ *vt insep*: to ~ on sthg revenir sans cesse sur qqch, rabâcher qqch.

harpist [ˈhɑːpɪst] *n* harpiste *mf*.

harpoon [hɑːˈpuːn] ◇ *n* harpon *m*.
◇ *vt* harponner.

harpsichord [ˈhɑːpsɪkɔːd] *n* clavecin *m*.

harpsichordist [ˈhɑːpsɪˌkɔːdɪst] *n* claveciniste *mf*.

harpy [ˈhɑːpɪ] (*pl* harpies) *n fig* harpie *f*, mégère *f*.
◆ **Harpy** *n* MYTH: the Harpies les Harpyes *fpl* OR Harpies *fpl*.

harpy eagle *n* harpie *f* ORNITH.

harridan [ˈhærɪdn] *n* harpie *f*, vieille sorcière *f*.

harried [ˈhærɪd] *adj* [person] tracassé, harcelé; a ~ husband un mari harcelé (par sa femme) ‖ [expression, look] tourmenté.

harrier [ˈhærɪəʳ] *n* -**1.** [dog] harrier *m*. -**2.** SPORT [runner] coureur *m* (de cross); Plymouth Harriers l'équipe d'athlétisme de Plymouth. -**3.** ORNITH busard *m*.

Harris tweed® [ˈhærɪs-] ◇ *n* tweed *m* (des Hébrides).
◇ *comp* [jacket] en tweed.

Harrovian [həˈrəʊvjən] *n Br* SCH [present] élève *m* de Harrow; [past] ancien élève *m* de Harrow.

harrow [ˈhærəʊ] ◇ *n* herse *f*.
◇ *vt* -**1.** AGR labourer à la herse. -**2.** *fig* torturer, déchirer le cœur à. -**3.** RELIG: Christ ~ing Hell la descente aux enfers du Christ.
◆ **Harrow** *pr n prestigieuse «public school» dans la banlieue de Londres*.

harrowing [ˈhærəʊɪŋ] ◇ *adj* [story] poignant, navrant, angoissant; [cry] déchirant; [experience] pénible, angoissant; the report makes ~ reading le rapport raconte des faits pénibles à lire.
◇ *n* hersage *m*; the ~ of Hell RELIG la descente aux enfers du Christ.

harrumph [həˈrʌmf] ◇ *n* & *onomat bruit que l'on fait en se raclant la gorge*.
◇ *vi* se racler la gorge.

harry [ˈhærɪ] (*pt* & *pp* harried) *vt* -**1.** [harass - person] harceler, tourmenter; he was harried by creditors il était harcelé par ses créanciers. -**2.** [pillage - village] dévaster, mettre à sac. -**3.** MIL [enemy, troops] harceler.

harsh [hɑːʃ] *adj* -**1.** [cruel, severe - person] dur, sévère, cruel; [- punishment, treatment] dur, sévère; [- fate] cruel; [- criticism, judgement, words] dur, sévère; to be ~ with sb être dur envers OR avec qqn. -**2.** [conditions, weather] rude, rigoureux. -**3.** [bitter - struggle] âpre, acharné. -**4.** [cry, voice] criard, strident; [tone] dur. -**5.** [colour, contrast] choquant; [light] cru. -**6.** [bleak - landscape, desert] dur, austère.

harshly [ˈhɑːʃlɪ] *adv* -**1.** [treat, punish] sévèrement, avec rigueur. -**2.** [answer, speak] avec rudesse OR dureté; [judge] sévèrement, durement; don't speak so ~ of him ne parlez pas de lui si durement. -**3.** [cry, shout] d'un ton strident.

harshness [ˈhɑːʃnɪs] *n* -**1.** [of person] dureté *f*, sévérité *f*; [of punishment, treatment] sévérité *f*; [of judgement] dureté *f*, sévérité *f*; [of statement, words, tone] dureté *f*. -**2.** [of climate] rigueur *f*, rudesse *f*. -**3.** [of cry, voice] discordance *f*. -**4.** [of light, contrast] dureté *f*.

hart [hɑːt] (*pl inv* OR harts) *n* cerf *m*.

harum-scarum *inf* [ˌheərəmˈskeərəm] *adj* [wild, reckless] casse-cou *(inv)*.

harvest [ˈhɑːvɪst] ◇ *n* -**1.** [gathering - of cereal, crops] moisson *f*; [- of fruit, mushrooms] récolte *f*, cueillette *f*; [- of grapes] vendange *f*, vendanges *fpl*. -**2.** [yield] récolte *f*. -**3.** *fig* [from experience, research] moisson *f*; a bitter ~ une moisson amère.
◇ *vt* -**1.** AGR [cereal, crops] moissonner; [fruit, mushrooms] cueillir, récolter; [grapes] vendanger. -**2.** *fig* [benefits] moissonner; [consequences] récolter.
◇ *vi* [for cereal, crops] moissonner, faire la moisson; [for fruit] faire les récoltes; [for grapes] vendanger.

harvester [ˈhɑːvɪstəʳ] *n* -**1.** [machine] moissonneuse *f*. -**2.** [person] moissonneur *m*, -euse *f*.

harvest festival *n* fête *f* des moissons.

HARVEST FESTIVAL:
A l'occasion de cette célébration de la moisson, les églises en Grande-Bretagne sont souvent décorées de fruits, de légumes etc.

---

harvest home *n* -**1.** *Br* [supper] fête *f* de la moisson. -**2.** [harvesting] moisson *f*.

harvesting ['hɑːvɪstɪŋ] ◇ *n (U)* moisson *f*, moissons *fpl*.
◇ *adj* [season] des moissons.

harvestman ['hɑːvɪstmæn] (*pl* harvestmen [-men]) *n* -**1.** AGR moissonneur *m*. -**2.** ENTOM faucheur *m*.

harvest mite *n* aoûtat *m*.

harvest moon *n* pleine lune *f* (de l'équinoxe d'automne).

harvest mouse *n* rat *m* des champs.

harvest supper *n* *en Grande-Bretagne, dîner réunissant une communauté villageoise à la fin de la moisson*.

Harvest Thanksgiving *n Am* fête *f* des moissons.

harvest time *n* période *f* de la moisson; at ~ à la moisson.

has [*weak form* həz, *strong form* hæz] → **have**.

has-been *inf* ['hæzbiːn] *n* has been *m inv*.

hash [hæʃ] ◇ *n* -**1.** *inf Br* [muddle, mix-up] pagaille *f*, embrouillamini *m*; [mess, botch] gâchis *m*; to make a ~ of sthg bousiller qqch, ficher qqch en l'air; **he certainly made a ~ of putting that shelf up!** il a certainement fait un beau gâchis en installant cette étagère!; **I made a real ~ of the interview** j'ai complètement merdé à l'entretien. -**2.** CULIN hachis *m*. -**3.** *inf* [marijuana] hasch *m*. -**4.** *inf phr*: **to fix** OR **to settle sb's ~** *Br* [in revenge, punishment] régler son compte à qqn; [reduce to silence] clouer le bec à qqn.
◇ *vt* CULIN hacher.
◆ **hash up** *vt sep* -**1.** *inf Br* [mess up] bâcler, bousiller; **I'm afraid I completely ~ed up the interview** j'ai bien peur d'avoir complètement merdé à l'entretien. -**2.** CULIN hacher.

hash browns *npl sorte de croquettes de pommes de terre*.

hash house *inf n Am* gargote *f*.

hashish ['hæʃiːʃ] *n* haschisch *m*.

hash mark *n symbole typographique ressemblant au dièse servant à indiquer un espace ou, aux États-Unis, un numéro*.

hash slinger *inf* [-ˌslɪŋəʳ] *n Am* serveur *m*, -euse *f* dans une gargote.

hash-up *inf n Br* [mess] gâchis *m*; to make a ~ of sthg bousiller OR gâcher qqch.

haslet ['hæzlɪt] *n (U)* abats *mpl (de porc)*, fressure *f*.

hasn't ['hæznt] = **has not**.

hasp [hɑːsp] ◇ *n* [for door] loquet *m*, loqueteau *m*, moraillon *m*; [for jewellery, lid, clothing] fermoir *m*.
◇ *vt* [door] fermer au loquet; [lid] fermer; [with padlock] cadenasser.

hassle *inf* ['hæsl] ◇ *n* -**1.** [difficulty, irritation] embêtement *m*, emmerdement *m*; **I don't want any ~** je ne veux pas d'embêtements; **it's too much ~** c'est trop compliqué; **it won't be any ~** ça ne posera pas de problèmes; **finding their house was quite a ~** trouver leur maison n'a pas été de la tarte, on a eu un mal fou à trouver leur maison. -**2.** [quarrel] dispute *f*, chamaillerie *f*; **there was a big ~ over who should drive** il y a eu une grosse dispute OR bagarre pour savoir qui allait conduire.
◇ *vt* [annoy, nag] embêter, harceler; **don't ~ me about it** ne m'embête pas avec ça; **Yvonne's always hassling him to stop smoking** Yvonne est toujours après lui pour qu'il arrête de fumer.
◇ *vi* [argue] se quereller, se chamailler.

hassock ['hæsək] *n* -**1.** RELIG coussin *m* d'agenouilloir. -**2.** [of grass] touffe *f* d'herbe. -**3.** *Am* [pouffe] pouf *m*.

hast [*weak form* həst, *strong form* hæst] *arch* OR BIBLE *2nd pers sing* → **have**.

haste [heɪst] *n* [speed] hâte *f*; [rush] précipitation *f*; **to do sthg in ~** faire qqch à la hâte, se dépêcher de faire qqch; **to act in ~** agir à la hâte OR précipitamment; **to make ~** se hâter, se dépêcher; **in my ~, I forgot my hat** dans ma hâte, j'ai oublié mon chapeau ❑ **more ~ less speed** *prov* hâtez-vous lentement.

hasten ['heɪsn] ◇ *vt* -**1.** [speed up - event, decline] précipiter, hâter; **the accident ~ed his death** l'accident précipita OR accéléra sa mort; **stress can ~ the ageing process** le stress peut accélérer le vieillissement. -**2.** [urge on - person] presser; **we were ~ed along a corridor** on nous a entraînés précipitamment dans un couloir. -**3.** [say quickly]: **she ~ed to assure us that all would be well** elle s'empressa de nous assurer que tout irait bien; **it wasn't me, I ~ed to add** ce n'était pas moi, m'empressai-je d'ajouter.
◇ *vi lit* [verb of movement]: **to ~ away** partir à la hâte, se hâter de partir; **to ~ back** revenir à la hâte, se dépêcher de revenir.

hastily ['heɪstɪlɪ] *adv* -**1.** [hurriedly] précipitamment, avec précipitation, à la hâte. -**2.** [impetuously, rashly] hâtivement, sans réfléchir.

Hastings ['heɪstɪŋz] *pr n* Hastings; **the Battle of ~** la bataille de Hastings.

hasty ['heɪstɪ] *adj* -**1.** [quick, hurried] précipité, à la hâte; **they made a ~ departure** ils sont partis à la hâte OR précipitamment; **she beat a ~ retreat** elle a rapidement battu en retraite. -**2.** [rash] irréfléchi, hâtif; **a ~ decision** une décision prise à la hâte OR à la légère; **let's not jump to any ~ conclusions** ne concluons pas à la légère OR hâtivement; **let's not be over-~** ne nous précipitons pas.

hasty pudding *n Br* semoule *f* au lait; *Am* bouillie *f* de maïs *(servie avec de la mélasse)*.

hat [hæt] *n* -**1.** chapeau *m*; **he always wears a ~** il porte toujours le OR un chapeau ❑ **keep your ~ on!** *inf* ne t'énerve pas!; **keep this under your ~** *inf* gardez ceci pour vous, n'en soufflez mot à personne; **to pass the ~ round** faire la quête; **to throw one's ~ into the ring** POL se mettre sur les rangs; **my ~!** *inf* mon œil!; **that's old ~** *inf* c'est dépassé; **I take my ~ off to him!** chapeau! -**2.** *fig* [role] rôle *m*, casquette *f*; **I'm wearing three different ~s at the moment** je porte trois casquettes différentes OR j'ai trois rôles différents en ce moment.

hatband ['hætbænd] *n* ruban *m* de chapeau.

hatbox ['hætbɒks] *n* boîte *f* à chapeau.

hatch [hætʃ] ◇ *vt* -**1.** ZOOL [eggs] faire éclore. -**2.** *fig* [plan, plot] tramer, manigancer. -**3.** ART hachurer.
◇ *vi* [eggs] éclore; [chicks] sortir de l'œuf.
◇ *n* -**1.** [hatching of egg] éclosion *f*. -**2.** [brood] couvée *f*. -**3.** NAUT écoutille *f*; **to batten down the ~es** *literal* fermer les descentes; *fig* se préparer *(pour affronter une crise)*; **down the ~!** *inf* à la vôtre! -**4.** [trapdoor] trappe *f*; [for inspection, access] trappe, panneau *m*; [in aircraft, spaceship] sas *m*; [in dam, dike] vanne *f (d'écluse)*. -**5.** [hatchway - for service] passe-plat *m*.
◆ **hatch up** *vt sep* [plot, scheme] tramer, manigancer.

hatchback ['hætʃbæk] *n* -**1.** [door] hayon *m*. -**2.** [model] voiture *f* à hayon, cinq portes *f*.

hatcheck girl ['hættʃek-] *n* fille *f* du vestiaire.

hatchery ['hætʃərɪ] (*pl* hatcheries) *n* -**1.** [for chickens, turkeys] couvoir *m*. -**2.** [for fish] station *f* d'alevinage.

hatchet ['hætʃɪt] *n* hachette *f*, hache *f* (à main).

hatchet-faced *adj* au visage en lame de couteau.

hatchet job *inf n*: **to do a ~ on sb/sthg** démolir qqn/qqch.

hatchet man *inf n* -**1.** [killer] tueur *m* à gages. -**2.** INDUST & POL homme *m* de main.

hatching ['hætʃɪŋ] *n* -**1.** [of eggs] éclosion *f*. -**2.** [brood] couvée *f*. -**3.** *(U)* ART hachures *fpl*.

hatchling ['hætʃlɪŋ] *n* [bird] oisillon *m*; [chick] poussin *m*; [duckling] caneton *m*.

hatchway ['hætʃweɪ] *n* NAUT écoutille *f*; [gen] trappe *f*.

hate [heɪt] ◇ *vt* (*no cont*) [gen] détester, avoir horreur de; [intensely] haïr, abhorrer; **I ~ Sundays** je déteste les dimanches; **I ~ getting up early** j'ai horreur de me lever tôt; **she ~s having to wear school uniform** elle a horreur d'avoir à porter un uniforme scolaire; **I ~ his guts** *inf* je ne peux pas le sentir; **I ~ her for what she has done** je lui en veux vraiment pour ce qu'elle a fait; **I ~ myself for letting them down** je m'en veux beaucoup de les avoir laissés tomber ‖ [polite use]: **I would ~ you to think I was avoiding you** je ne voudrais surtout pas vous donner l'impression que je cherchais à vous éviter; **I ~ to mention it, but you still owe me £5** je suis désolé d'avoir à vous le faire remarquer, mais vous me devez toujours 5 livres; **I ~ to bother you, but could I use your phone?** je ne voudrais surtout pas vous déranger, mais puis-je utiliser votre téléphone?
◇ *n* -**1.** [emotion] haine *f*; **I feel nothing but ~ for him** je ne ressens que de la haine pour lui. -**2.** [person hated] personne *f* que l'on déteste; [thing hated] chose *f* que l'on déteste; **it's one of my pet ~s** c'est une de mes bêtes noires.

hated ['heɪtɪd] *adj* détesté.

hateful ['heɪtful] *adj* odieux, détestable, abominable; **the very idea is ~ to him** l'idée même lui est insupportable.

hatesheet *inf* ['heɪtʃiːt] *n Am* PRESS torchon *m* qui incite à la haine.

Hatfields and McCoys ['hætfiːldz-] *pl pr n Am*: **the ~** *noms fictifs représentant des familles rivales*.

hath [hæθ] *arch* OR BIBLE = **has**.

hatless ['hætlɪs] *adj* tête nue, sans chapeau.

hatmaker ['hætˌmeɪkəʳ] *n* [for men] chapelier *m*, -ère *f*; [for women] modiste *mf*.

hatpin ['hætpɪn] *n* épingle *f* à chapeau.

hat rack *n* porte-chapeaux *m inv*.

hatred ['heɪtrɪd] *n* haine *f*; **to feel ~ for sb** avoir de la haine pour qqn, haïr qqn; **he had an intense ~ of the police** il avait une haine profonde de la police.

hat stand *n* portemanteau *m*.

hatter ['hætəʳ] *n* chapelier *m*, -ère *f*.

hat trick *n Br* [three goals] hat-trick *m*; [three wins] trois victoires *fpl* consécutives.

haughtily ['hɔːtɪlɪ] *adv* avec arrogance, de manière hautaine.

haughtiness ['hɔːtɪnɪs] *n* arrogance *f*, caractère *m* hautain.

haughty ['hɔːtɪ] (*compar* haughtier, *superl* haughtiest) *adj* hautain, arrogant.

haul [hɔːl] ◇ *vt* -**1.** [pull] tirer, traîner; [tow] tirer, remorquer; **they ~ed the boat out of the water** ils ont tiré le bateau hors de l'eau; **she has to ~ her little brother everywhere with her** *fig* elle doit traîner son petit frère partout avec elle; **they were ~ed in front of** OR **before a judge** on les traîna devant un tribunal ❑ **to ~ sb over the coals** passer un savon à qqn. -**2.** [transport] transporter; [by truck] camionner, transporter. -**3.** [move with effort] hisser; **he ~ed himself out of bed** il s'est péniblement sorti du lit; **he ~ed himself into a sitting position** il s'est hissé en position assise. -**4.** ▽ *Am phr*: **to ~ ass** se magner.
◇ *vi* -**1.** [pull] tirer; **they ~ed on the cable** ils ont tiré sur le câble. -**2.** NAUT [boat] lofer.
◇ *n* -**1.** [catch, takings - of fisherman, customs] prise *f*, coup *m* de filet; [- of robbers] butin *m*; **the thieves have made a good ~** les voleurs ont rapporté un beau butin. -**2.** [pull]: **to give a ~ on a rope/fishing net** tirer sur une corde/un filet de pêche. -**3.** [distance] parcours *m*, trajet *m*; **it was a long ~ from Madrid to Paris** la route fut longue de Madrid à Paris; **long-/short-~ flights** vols *mpl* long courrier/moyen courrier. -**4.** [in time]: **training to be a doctor is a long ~** les études de médecine sont très longues.
◆ **haul down** *vt sep* -**1.** [pull down] descendre, faire descendre; **his parents had to ~ him down from the tree** ses parents ont dû le faire descendre de l'arbre. -**2.** [lower - flag, sail] descendre, amener.

◆ **haul in** *vt sep* [catch, net, rope] tirer, amener; **the ship was ~ed in for repairs** le bateau a été mis en cale pour réparations; **Tom was ~ed in** *inf* **on a drink-driving charge** Tom a été épinglé pour conduite en état d'ivresse.

◆ **haul off** ◇ *vt sep* [take away] conduire, amener; **her mother ~ed her off to the dentist's** sa mère l'a traînée chez le dentiste; **he was ~ed off to prison** on l'a flanqué en prison. ◇ *vi insep inf Am* lever le bras OR le poing; **she ~ed off and slugged him** elle a levé le bras et lui a asséné un coup de poing.

◆ **haul up** *vt sep* [pull up] tirer, hisser; **the boat was ~ed up onto the beach** on a tiré le bateau sur le sable; **to ~ sb up before a judge** traîner qqn devant le tribunal OR le juge.

haulage ['hɔːlɪdʒ] ◇ *n (U)* -**1.** [as business] transports *mpl*, transport *m* (routier). -**2.** [act] transport *m*. -**3.** [cost] (frais *mpl* de) transport *m*. ◇ *comp* [company] de transport routier, de transports routiers; **she's in the ~ business** elle travaille dans le transport routier.

haulier ['hɔːljəʳ] *Br*, **hauler** ['hɔːləʳ] *Am n* -**1.** [business] entreprise *f* de transports routiers. -**2.** [owner] entrepreneur *m* de transports routiers. -**3.** [driver] routier *m*, camionneur *m*.

haunch [hɔːntʃ] *n* CULIN [of venison] cuissot *m*; [of beef] quartier *m*.

◆ **haunches** *npl* -**1.** [of human] hanche *f*; **to squat down on one's ~es** s'accroupir. -**2.** *(usu pl)* [of animal] arrière-train *m*, derrière *m*.

haunt [hɔːnt] ◇ *vt* -**1.** [subj: ghost, spirit] hanter. -**2.** [subj: problems] hanter, tourmenter; **the memory still ~s me** le souvenir me hante encore; **she is ~ed by her unhappy childhood** elle est hantée OR tourmentée par son enfance malheureuse; **his past continues to ~ him** son passé ne cesse de le poursuivre OR hanter. -**3.** *inf* [frequent - bar] hanter, fréquenter; [- streets] hanter, traîner dans.
◇ *n* -**1.** [place] lieu *m* que l'on fréquente beaucoup, lieu *m* de prédilection; **it's one of his favourite ~s** c'est un des endroits qu'il préfère; **we couldn't find her in any of her usual ~s** nous ne l'avons pas trouvée dans les endroits qu'elle fréquente d'habitude. -**2.** [refuge - for animals, criminals] repaire *m*.

haunted ['hɔːntɪd] *adj* -**1.** [house, castle] hanté. -**2.** [look] hagard, égaré.

haunting ['hɔːntɪŋ] *adj* [memory, sound] obsédant; [tune] qui vous trotte dans la tête; **she has a ~ beauty** elle est d'une beauté obsédante.

Hausa ['haʊsə] *(pl inv* OR **Hausas**) ◇ *n* -**1.** [person]: **the ~** les Haoussas *mpl*, les Hausas *mpl*. -**2.** LING haoussa *m*.
◇ *comp* des Haoussas.

Havana [hə'vænə] ◇ *pr n* [city] la Havane.
◇ *n* [cigar] havane *m*, cigare *m* de Havane; [tobacco] havane *m*.
◇ *comp* [tobacco, cigar] de Havane.

have [hæv] *(3rd pers sing pres* **has** [hæz], *pt & pp* **had** [hæd]) ◇ *aux vb* -**1.** [used to form perfect tenses] avoir, être; **to ~ finished** avoir fini; **to ~ left** être parti; **to ~ sat down** s'être assis; **to ~ been/had** avoir été/eu; **has she slept?** a-t-elle dormi?; **~ they arrived?** sont-ils arrivés?; **he has been ill** il a été malade; **when you've calmed down** quand vous vous serez calmé; **I will ~ forgotten by next week** j'aurai oublié d'ici la semaine prochaine; **the children will ~ gone to bed by the time we arrive** les enfants seront couchés quand nous arriverons; **you were silly not to ~ accepted** tu es bête de ne pas avoir accepté; **after** OR **when you ~ finished, you may leave** quand vous aurez fini, vous pourrez partir; **she was ashamed of having lied** elle avait honte d'avoir menti; **she felt she couldn't change her mind, having already agreed to go** elle sentait qu'elle ne pouvait pas changer d'avis, étant donné qu'elle avait dit être d'accord pour y aller; **I ~ been thinking** j'ai réfléchi; **he has been working here for two months** il travaille ici depuis deux mois, il y a deux mois qu'il travaille ici; **I ~ known her for three years/since childhood** je la connais depuis trois ans/depuis mon enfance; **I had known her for years** cela faisait des années que je la connaissais, je la connaissais depuis des années; **she claimed she hadn't heard the news** elle a prétendu ne pas avoir entendu la nouvelle; **I had already gone to bed when he arrived** j'étais déjà couché quand il est arrivé; **we had gone to bed early** nous nous étions couchés de bonne heure; **when he had given his speech, I left** une fois qu'il eut terminé son discours, je partis; **had I known I wouldn't ~ insisted** si j'avais su, je n'aurais pas insisté; **if I had known, I wouldn't ~ said anything** si j'avais su, je n'aurais rien dit; **they would ~ been happy if it hadn't been for the war** ils auraient vécu heureux si la guerre n'était pas survenue; **why don't you just leave him and ~ done with it?** pourquoi donc est-ce que vous ne le quittez pas, pour en finir? ❑ **I'd as soon not** j'aimerais mieux pas; **he'd rather** OR **sooner stay at home than go out dancing** il aimerait mieux rester OR il préférerait rester à la maison qu'aller danser; **he's had it** *inf* [is in trouble] il est fichu OR foutu; [is worn out] il est à bout; **I've had it with all your complaining!** *inf* j'en ai jusque-là de tes jérémiades!; **this plant has had it** *inf* cette plante est fichue. -**2.** [elliptical uses]: **~ you ever had the measles? – yes, I ~/no, I haven't** avez-vous eu la rougeole? – oui/non; **she hasn't finished – yes, she has!** elle n'a pas fini – (mais) si!; **you've forgotten his birthday – no, I haven't!** tu as oublié son anniversaire – mais non!; **~ you ever considered going into politics? if you ~.../if you haven't...** avez-vous déjà envisagé de rentrer dans la vie politique? si oui.../si non... -**3.** [in tag questions]: **you've read "Hamlet", haven't you?** vous avez lu «Hamlet», n'est-ce pas?; **he hasn't arrived, has he?** il n'est pas arrivé, si?; **so she's got a new job, has she?** elle a changé de travail alors?
◇ *vt* **A.** -**1.** [be in possession of, own] avoir, posséder; **do you ~** OR **~ you got a car?** avez-vous une voiture?; **they ~ (got) a lot of friends/money** ils ont beaucoup d'amis/d'argent; **they don't ~** OR **they haven't got any more** ils n'en ont plus; **she shares everything she has (got) with them** elle partage tout ce qu'elle a avec eux; **he has (got) £10 left** il lui reste 10 livres; **we ~ (got) six of them left** il nous en reste six; **do you ~ any children? if you ~...** avez-vous des enfants? si vous en avez OR si oui...; **they ~ a 50% interest in the business** ils ont OR détiennent 50 % des intérêts dans l'affaire; **do we ~ any milk in the house?** est-ce qu'on a du lait OR est-ce qu'il y a du lait à la maison?; **she has a baker's shop/bookshop** elle tient une boulangerie/librairie; **do you ~** OR **~ you got the time?** avez-vous l'heure?; **he has no job** il n'a pas de travail, il est sans travail ❑ **give it all you ~** OR **all you've got!** *inf* mets-y le paquet!; **I've got it!** ça y est, j'ai trouvé OR j'y suis!; **paper, envelopes and what ~ you** du papier, des enveloppes et je ne sais quoi encore; **you can't ~ your cake and eat it** on ne peut pas avoir le beurre et l'argent du beurre. -**2.** [enjoy the use of] avoir, disposer de; **we had a couple of hours to do our errands** nous disposions de OR nous avions quelques heures pour faire nos courses; **I don't ~ time** OR **I haven't got time to stop for lunch** je n'ai pas le temps de m'arrêter pour déjeuner; **he has (got) a month to finish** il a un mois pour finir; **he hasn't (got) long to live** il ne lui reste pas longtemps à vivre; **do you ~** OR **~ you (got) a minute (to spare)?** tu as une minute?; **she had the house to herself** elle avait la maison pour elle toute seule; **such questions ~ an important place in our lives** ce genre de questions occupe une place importante dans notre vie. -**3.** [possess as quality or attribute] avoir; **she has (got) red hair** elle a les cheveux roux, elle est rousse; **you ~ beautiful eyes** tu as de beaux yeux; **the ticket has a name on it** il y a un nom sur le billet; **to ~ good taste/a bad temper** avoir bon goût/mauvais caractère; **she has a reputation for being difficult** elle a la réputation d'être difficile; **the house has a beautiful view of the mountains** de la maison, on a une belle vue sur les montagnes; **she has what it takes** OR **she has it in her to succeed** elle a ce qu'il faut pour réussir; **you've never had it so good!** vous n'avez jamais eu la vie si belle! -**4.** [possess knowledge or understanding of]: **do you ~ any experience of teaching?** avez-vous déjà enseigné?; **she has a clear sense of what matters** elle sait très bien ce qui est important; **he has some Greek and Latin** il connaît un peu le grec et le latin; **I ~ a little Spanish** je parle un peu espagnol.
B. -**1.** [indicating experience of a specified situation]: **to ~ a dream/nightmare** faire un rêve/cauchemar; **I ~ no regrets** je n'ai aucun regret OR pas de regrets; **we ~ nothing** OR **we don't ~ anything against dogs** on n'a rien contre les chiens; **I've had my appendix taken out** je me suis fait opérer de l'appendicite; **he had all his money stolen** il s'est fait voler OR on lui a volé tout son argent; **I love having my back rubbed** j'adore qu'on me frotte le dos; **they had some strange things happen to them** il leur est arrivé de drôles de choses. -**2.** [be infected with, suffer from] avoir; **to ~ a cold** avoir un rhume, être enrhumé; **do you ~** OR **~ you got a headache?** avez-vous mal à la tête?; **he has (got) problems with his back** il a des problèmes de dos. -**3.** *(delexicalized use)* [perform, take part in - bath, lesson] prendre; [- meeting] avoir; **to ~ an effect on sthg** agir sur qqch; **we had our first argument last night** nous nous sommes disputés hier soir pour la première fois; **to ~ a stroll** se promener, faire un tour; **I want to ~ a think about it** je veux y réfléchir; **to ~ a party** [organize] organiser une fête; [celebrate] faire la fête; **I'll ~ no part in it** je refuse de m'en mêler. -**4.** [pass, spend] passer, avoir; **I had a horrible day at work** j'ai passé une journée atroce au travail; **~ a nice day!** bonne journée!; **to ~ a good time** s'amuser; **did you ~ a good time?** c'était bien?; **a good time was had by all** tout le monde s'est bien amusé; **she's had a hard time of it lately** elle vient de traverser une mauvaise passe. -**5.** [exhibit, show] avoir, montrer; **~ mercy on us!** ayez pitié de nous!; **he had the nerve to refuse** il a eu le culot de refuser; **he didn't even ~ the decency to apologize** il n'a même pas eu la décence de s'excuser. -**6.** [feel obligation or necessity in regard to]: **I ~ (got) a lot of work to finish** j'ai beaucoup de travail à finir; **he has (got) nothing to do/to read** il n'a rien à faire/à lire; **we ~ (got) a deadline to meet** nous avons un délai à respecter.
C. -**1.** [obtain, receive] avoir, recevoir; **I'd like him to ~ this picture** j'aimerais lui donner cette photo; **I'd like to ~ your advice on something** j'aimerais que vous me donniez un conseil à propos de quelque chose; **we had a phone call from the mayor** nous avons reçu OR eu un coup de fil du maire; **they've still had no news of the lost plane** ils n'ont toujours pas de nouvelles de l'avion (qui a) disparu; **I ~ it on good authority** je le tiens de bonne source; **I must ~ your answer by tomorrow** il me faut votre réponse pour demain; **let me ~ your answer by next week** donnez-moi votre réponse avant la semaine prochaine; **let me ~ the book back when you've finished** rends-moi le livre quand tu auras fini; **she let them ~ the wardrobe for £300** elle leur a laissé OR cédé l'armoire pour 300 livres; **there are plenty of nice flats to be had** il y a plein de jolis appartements; **stamps can be had at any newsagent's** on peut acheter des timbres chez le marchand de journaux ❑ **I let him ~ it** *inf* [attacked him] je lui ai réglé son compte; [told him off] je lui ai passé un savon; **you had it coming!** *inf* tu ne l'as pas volé! -**2.** [invite] recevoir, avoir; **she's having some people (over) for** OR **to dinner** elle reçoit OR elle a du monde à dîner; **let's ~ him round for a drink** et si on l'invitait à prendre un pot?; **did you ~**

any visitors? avez-vous eu de la visite?; we're having his family down for the weekend sa famille vient passer le week-end chez nous. -**3.** [accept, take] vouloir; he'd like to marry but nobody will ~ him! il aimerait se marier mais personne ne veut de lui!; do what you want, I'm having nothing more to do with your schemes fais ce que tu veux, je ne veux plus être mêlé à tes combines.

D. -**1.** [clutch] tenir; the teacher had (got) him by the arm/the ear le maître le tenait par le bras/l'oreille; he had (got) his assailant round the neck/by the throat il tenait son agresseur au cou/à la gorge. -**2.** *fig* [gain control or advantage of]: you ~ me there! là vous me tenez!; I ~ (got) you right where I want you now! je vous tiens! ❑ the Celtics ~ it! SPORT les Celtics ont gagné! -**3.** [bewilder, perplex]: who won? — you've got me there qui a gagné? — là, tu me poses une colle.

E. -**1.** [cause to be]: the news had me worried la nouvelle m'a inquiété; I'll ~ this light fixed in a minute j'en ai pour une minute à réparer cette lampe; we'll ~ everything ready tout sera prêt. -**2.** *(with past participle)* [cause to be done]: to ~ sthg done faire faire qqch; I had my hair cut je me suis fait couper les cheveux; we must ~ the curtains cleaned nous devons faire nettoyer les rideaux OR donner les rideaux à nettoyer; she had coffee brought up to the room elle a fait monter du café dans la chambre. -**3.** *(with infinitive)* [cause to do]: to ~ sb do sthg faire faire qqch à qqn; she had him invite all the neighbours round elle lui a fait inviter tous les voisins; ~ them come in faites-les entrer; the boss had him up to his office le patron l'a convoqué dans son bureau; he soon had them all laughing il eut tôt fait de les faire tous rire; I had the children go to bed early j'ai couché les enfants de bonne heure; as he would ~ us believe comme il voudrait nous le faire croire.

F. -**1.** [consume - food, meal] avoir, prendre; we were having lunch nous étions en train de déjeuner; we're having dinner out tonight nous sortons dîner ce soir; to ~ breakfast in bed prendre le petit déjeuner au lit; would you like to ~ coffee? voulez-vous (prendre) un café?; do you ~ coffee or tea in the morning? prenez-vous du café ou du thé le matin?; I had tea with her j'ai pris le thé avec elle; we stopped and had a drink nous nous sommes arrêtés pour boire quelque chose; what will you ~? — I'll ~ the lamb [in restaurant] qu'est-ce que vous prenez? — je vais prendre de l'agneau; we had fish for dinner nous avons mangé OR eu du poisson au dîner; he always has a cigarette after dinner il fume toujours une cigarette après le dîner; will you ~ a cigarette? voulez-vous une cigarette? -**2.** [indicating location, position] placer, mettre; we'll ~ the wardrobe here and the table in there nous mettrons l'armoire ici et la table par là; she had her arm around his shoulders elle avait mis le bras autour de ses épaules; I had my back to the window je tournais le dos à la fenêtre; he had his head down il avait la tête baissée. -**3.** [be accompanied by]: she had her mother with her sa mère était avec elle; I can't talk right now, I ~ someone with me je ne peux pas parler, je ne suis pas seul OR je suis avec quelqu'un. -**4.** [give birth to]: she's had a baby elle a eu un bébé; she had her baby last week elle a accouché la semaine dernière; she's going to ~ a baby elle attend OR elle va avoir un bébé; he's had three children by her il a eu trois enfants d'elle; our dog has just had puppies notre chien vient d'avoir des petits. -**5.** [assert, claim] soutenir, maintenir; rumour has it that they're married le bruit court qu'ils sont mariés; as the government would ~ it comme dirait le gouvernement. -**6.** *(with 'will' or 'would')* [wish for] vouloir; what would you ~ me do? que voudriez-vous que je fasse?; I'll ~ you know I ~ a degree in French je vous fais remarquer que j'ai une licence de français; as luck would ~ it her father was there la chance voulut que son père fût là. -**7.** *(in negative)* [allow, permit]: I will not ~ him in my house! il ne mettra pas les pieds chez moi!; I won't ~ it! ça ne va pas se passer comme ça!; we can't ~ you sleeping on the floor nous ne pouvons pas vous laisser dormir par terre. -**8.** *inf (in passive)* [cheat, outwit] avoir; you've been had! tu t'es fait avoir! -**9.** *inf* [sleep with] avoir.

G. WITH INFINITIVE -**1.** [indicating obligation]: to ~ (got) to do sthg devoir faire qqch, être obligé de faire qqch; do you ~ to OR ~ you got to leave so soon? êtes-vous obligé de partir OR faut-il que vous partiez si tôt?; I ~ (got) to go to the meeting il faut que j'aille OR je dois aller OR je suis obligé d'aller à la réunion; don't you ~ to OR haven't you got to phone the office? est-ce que tu ne dois pas appeler le bureau?; he'll do it if he's got to il le fera s'il est obligé de le faire; you don't ~ to OR you haven't got to go tu n'es pas obligé d'y aller; we had to take physics at school nous étions obligés de suivre des cours de physique à l'école; she had to take a blood test elle a été obligée de OR elle a dû faire un examen sanguin; I hate having to get up early j'ai horreur de devoir me lever tôt; I won't apologize — you ~ to je ne m'excuserai pas — il le faut || [expressing disbelief, dismay etc]: you've got to be joking! vous plaisantez!, c'est une plaisanterie!; you didn't ~ to tell your father what happened! tu n'avais pas besoin d'aller dire à ton père ce qui s'est passé!; the train would ~ to be late today of all days! il fallait que le train soit en retard aujourd'hui!; that has (got) to be the stupidest idea I've ever heard! *inf* ça doit être l'idée la plus idiote que j'aie jamais entendue! -**2.** [indicating necessity] devoir; you ~ (got) to get some rest il faut que vous vous reposiez, vous devez vous reposer; I'll ~ to think about it il va falloir que j'y réfléchisse; I ~ to know il faut que je le sache; we ~ to be careful about what we say on doit faire attention OR il faut qu'on fasse attention à ce qu'on dit; some problems still ~ to be worked out il reste encore des problèmes à résoudre; if you finish the report this evening you won't ~ to come in to work tomorrow si vous finissez le rapport ce soir, vous n'aurez pas besoin de venir travailler demain; the plumbing has to be redone la plomberie a besoin d'être refaite; you'd ~ to be deaf not to hear that noise il faudrait être sourd pour ne pas entendre ce bruit; do you ~ to turn the music up so loud? vous ne pourriez pas baisser un peu la musique? -**3.** *phr*: the book has to do with archaeology ce livre traite de l'archéologie; their argument had to do with money ils se disputaient à propos d'argent; this has nothing to do with you ça ne te concerne OR regarde pas; I'll ~ nothing more to do with her je ne veux plus avoir affaire à elle; they had nothing to do with her being fired ils n'avaient rien à voir avec son licenciement.

◆ **haves** *npl*: the ~s les riches *mpl*, les nantis *mpl*; the ~s and the ~-nots les riches et les pauvres, les nantis et les démunis.

◆ **have at** *vt insep Br* FENCING attaquer.

◆ **have away** *vt sep Br phr*: to ~ it away with sb ▽ coucher avec qqn.

◆ **have in** *vt sep* -**1.** [cause to enter] faire entrer; she had him in for a chat elle l'a fait entrer pour discuter. -**2.** [invite]: to ~ friends in for a drink inviter des amis à prendre un pot. -**3.** [doctor, plumber] faire venir; they've got workmen in at the moment ils ont des ouvriers en ce moment. -**4.** *phr*: to ~ it in for sb *inf* avoir une dent contre qqn.

◆ **have off** *vt sep Br phr*: to ~ it off with sb ▽ coucher avec qqn.

◆ **have on** *vt sep* -**1.** [wear] porter; what does she ~ on? qu'est-ce qu'elle porte?, comment est-elle habillée?; the child had nothing on l'enfant était tout nu. -**2.** [radio, television]: ~ you got the radio on? avez-vous allumé la radio?, est-ce que la radio est allumée?; he has the radio/television on all night sa radio/sa télévision est allumée toute la nuit. -**3.** [commitment, engagement]: we ~ a lot on today nous avons beaucoup à faire aujourd'hui; do you ~ anything on for tonight? avez-vous des projets pour OR êtes-vous pris ce soir?; I ~ nothing on for the weekend je n'ai rien de prévu ce week-end. -**4.** *inf Br* [tease, trick] faire marcher; you're having me on! tu me fais marcher! -**5.** *phr*: they ~ nothing on me ils n'ont aucune preuve contre moi; she must ~ something on the boss elle doit savoir quelque chose de compromettant sur le patron.

◆ **have out** *vt sep* -**1.** [tooth] se faire arracher. -**2.** [settle]: to ~ it out with sb s'expliquer avec qqn; she had it OR the matter OR the whole thing out with him elle a eu une longue explication avec lui.

◆ **have over** *vt sep* -**1.** [invite] inviter. -**2.** *phr*: to ~ one over on sb avoir le dessus sur qqn.

◆ **have up** *inf vt sep* [bring before the authorities]: I'll ~ you up for blackmail je vais vous poursuivre (en justice) pour chantage; they were had up by the police for vandalism ils ont été arrêtés pour vandalisme; he was had up (before the court) for breaking and entering il a comparu (devant le tribunal) pour effraction.

haven ['heɪvn] *n* -**1.** [refuge] abri *m*, refuge *m*; a safe ~ un abri sûr; the garden is a ~ of peace and tranquillity *lit* le jardin est un havre de paix et de tranquillité. -**2.** *arch* OR *lit* [harbour] havre *m*.

have-nots *npl*: the ~ les démunis *mpl*, les défavorisés *mpl*.

haven't ['hævnt] = **have not**.

haver ['heɪvəʳ] *vi Br* -**1.** [dither] tergiverser. -**2.** *dial* [talk nonsense] dire des sottises.

haversack ['hævəsæk] *n* havresac *m*.

havoc ['hævək] *n (U)* ravages *mpl*, chaos *m*; to wreak ~ on sthg ravager qqch; the strike played ~ with our plans la grève a mis nos projets par terre; a scene of ~ un vrai capharnaüm.

haw [hɔː] ◇ *n* BOT [berry] baie *f* d'aubépine, cenelle *f*; [shrub] aubépine *f*.
◇ *vi*: to hum and ~ tergiverser, tourner autour du pot.
◇ *interj*: ~! euh!

Hawaii [hə'waɪiː] *pr n* Hawaii; in ~ à Hawaii.

Hawaiian [hə'waɪən] ◇ *n* -**1.** [person] Hawaïen *m*, -enne *f*. -**2.** LING hawaïen *m*.
◇ *adj* hawaïen.

Hawaiian guitar *n* guitare *f* hawaïenne.

Hawaiian Standard Time *n* heure *f* de Hawaii.

haw-haw *interj*: ~! ha, ha!

hawk [hɔːk] ◇ *n* -**1.** [bird] faucon *m*; to watch sb/sthg like a ~ regarder qqn/qqch d'un œil perçant. -**2.** POL faucon *m*. -**3.** [cough] raclement *m* de gorge. -**4.** = **mortarboard 2**.
◇ *vi* -**1.** HUNT chasser au faucon. -**2.** [clear throat] se racler la gorge.
◇ *vt* -**1.** [sell - from door to door] colporter; [- in market, street] vendre à la criée. -**2.** *fig* [news, gossip] colporter. -**3.** [cough up] cracher.

hawker ['hɔːkəʳ] *n* [street vendor] marchand *m* ambulant; [door-to-door] démarcheur *m*, colporteur *m*; 'no ~s' 'démarchage interdit'.

hawk-eyed *adj* -**1.** [keen-sighted] au regard d'aigle. -**2.** *fig* [vigilant] qui a l'œil partout.

hawking ['hɔːkɪŋ] *n* HUNT chasse *f* au faucon.

hawkish ['hɔːkɪʃ] *adj* POL dur.

hawkmoth ['hɔːk,mɒθ] *n* sphinx *m* ENTOM.

hawksbill ['hɔːks,bɪl] *n* tortue *f* (à écailles).

hawse [hɔːz] *n* NAUT écubier *m*.

hawser ['hɔːzəʳ] *n* NAUT grelin *m*, aussière *f*.

hawthorn ['hɔːθɔːn] ◇ *n* aubépine *f*.
◇ *comp* [hedge, berry] d'aubépine.

hay [heɪ] *n* foin *m*; to make ~ AGR faire les foins ❑ to make ~ while the sun shines *prov* battre le fer pendant qu'il est chaud *prov*.

hay fever *n* rhume *m* des foins; to suffer from/to have ~ souffrir du/avoir le rhume des foins.

hayloft ['heɪlɒft] *n* grenier *m* à foin.

haymaker ['heɪ,meɪkəʳ] *n* -**1.** AGR [worker] faneur *m*, -euse *f*; [machine] faneuse *f*. -**2.** [punch] grand coup *m*.

haymaking ['heɪ,meɪkɪŋ] *n (U)* fenaison *f*, foins *mpl*.

hayrack ['heɪ,ræk] *n* [in barn] râtelier *m*; [on cart] ridelle *f*.

hayrick ['heɪ,rɪk] *n* meule *f* de foin.

hayseed ['heɪ,siːd] *n* -**1.** BOT graine *f* de foin. -**2.** *inf Am pej* [yokel] péquenaud *m*, -e *f*.

haystack ['heɪ,stæk] *n* meule *f* de foin.

haywain ['heɪ,weɪn] *n*: 'The Haywain' *Constable* 'la Charrette à foin'.

haywire *inf* ['heɪ,waɪəʳ] *adj* [system, person] détraqué; to go ~ [machine] débloquer, se détraquer; [plans] mal tourner.

hazard ['hæzəd] ◇ *n* -**1.** [danger, risk] risque *m*, danger *m*; the ~s of smoking les dangers du tabac; the ~s of life as a soldier les risques OR dangers de la vie de militaire; a health/fire ~ un risque pour la santé/d'incendie. -**2.** [in golf] obstacle *m*.
◇ *vt* -**1.** [risk - life] risquer, hasarder; [- reputation] risquer. -**2.** [venture - statement, advice, suggestion] hasarder, se risquer à faire; to ~ a guess: would you care to ~ a guess as to the weight? voulez-vous essayer de deviner combien ça pèse? -**3.** [stake, bet - fortune] risquer, miser.
◆ **hazards** *npl* AUT feux *mpl* de détresse.

hazardous ['hæzədəs] *adj* -**1.** [dangerous] dangereux, risqué; ~ waste déchets *mpl* dangereux; a ~ stretch of road une partie de la route qui est dangereuse. -**2.** [uncertain] hasardeux, incertain.

hazard warning AUT ◇ *n* signal *m* de danger.
◇ *comp*: ~ triangle triangle *m* de présignalisation; ~ lights feux *mpl* de détresse.

haze [heɪz] ◇ *n* -**1.** METEOR brume *f*; a heat ~ une brume de chaleur. -**2.** *(U)* [steam] vapeur *f*, vapeurs *fpl*; [smoke] nuage *m*. -**3.** [confusion] brouillard *m*; to be in a ~ être dans le brouillard.
◇ *vt Am* -**1.** [harass] harceler. -**2.** MIL faire subir des brimades à; SCH bizuter.
◆ **haze over** *vi insep* [sky] s'embrumer, devenir brumeux.

hazel ['heɪzl] ◇ *n* noisetier *m*.
◇ *adj* [colour] noisette *(inv)*; ~ eyes yeux *mpl* (couleur) noisette.

hazel grove *n* coudraie *f*.

hazelnut ['heɪzl,nʌt] ◇ *n* [nut] noisette *f*; [tree] noisetier *m*.
◇ *comp* [flavour] de noisette; [ice cream, yoghurt] à la noisette.

hazelwood ['heɪzl,wʊd] *n* (bois *m* de) noisetier *m*.

haziness ['heɪzɪnɪs] *n* -**1.** [of sky, weather] état *m* brumeux. -**2.** [of memory, thinking] flou *m*, imprécision *f*. -**3.** PHOT flou *m*.

hazing ['heɪzɪŋ] *n (U) Am* MIL brimades *fpl*; SCH bizutage *m*; ~ week (semaine *f* du) bizutage.

hazy ['heɪzɪ] (*compar* hazier, *superl* haziest) *adj* -**1.** [weather, sky] brumeux. -**2.** [memory] flou, vague; [thinking, ideas] flou, embrouillé; she's rather ~ about the details of what happened elle n'a qu'un vague souvenir de ce qui s'est passé. -**3.** PHOT flou. -**4.** [colour] pâle.

HB (*abbr of* hard-black) *n Br* [on pencils] HB.

H-block *n*: the ~s *les bâtiments construits en forme de H faisant partie de la prison de Maze, près de Belfast.*

H-bomb (*abbr of* hydrogen bomb) *n* bombe *f* H.

h & c *written abbr of* hot and cold (water).

HCF *abbr of* highest common factor.

he [hiː] ◇ *pron* il; he works in London il travaille à Londres; he and I lui et moi; there he is! le voilà!; she is older than he is *fml* elle est plus âgée que lui; every politician should do what he thinks best chaque homme politique devrait faire ce qu'il pense être le mieux; that's what HE thinks! c'est ce qu'il croit!
◇ *n* [animal] mâle *m*; [boy] garçon *m*.

HE -**1.** *written abbr of* high explosive. -**2.** (*written abbr of* His/Her Excellency) S Exc, SE.

head [hed] (*pl sense 12 inv, pl other senses* heads)
◇ *n* -**1.** [of human, animal] tête *f*; she has a lovely ~ of hair elle a de très beaux cheveux OR une très belle chevelure; he's already a ~ taller than his mother il dépasse déjà sa mère d'une tête; Sea Biscuit won by a ~ [in horseracing] Sea Biscuit a gagné d'une tête; from ~ to toe OR foot de la tête aux pieds; he was covered in mud from ~ to foot il était couvert de boue de la tête aux pieds; she was dressed in black from ~ to foot elle était tout en noir OR entièrement vêtue de noir; to fall ~ over heels tomber la tête la première; to fall ~ over heels in love with sb tomber éperdument amoureux de qqn; to have one's ~ in the clouds avoir la tête dans les nuages; he wanders around with his ~ in the clouds il est toujours dans les nuages; to give a horse its ~ lâcher la bride à un cheval; wine always goes to my ~ le vin me monte toujours à la tête; all this praise has gone to his ~ toutes ces louanges lui ont tourné la tête ❑ give him his ~ and put him in charge lâchez-lui la bride et laissez-le prendre des responsabilités; I could do it standing on my ~ c'est simple comme bonjour; she's got her ~ screwed on (the right way) elle a la tête sur les épaules; she's ~ and shoulders above the rest les autres ne lui arrivent pas à la cheville; to keep one's ~ above water s'en sortir; to laugh one's ~ off rire à gorge déployée; to shout OR to scream one's ~ off crier à tue-tête; ~s will roll des têtes tomberont. -**2.** [mind, thoughts] tête *f*; to take it into one's ~ to do sthg se mettre en tête de faire qqch; the idea never entered my ~ ça ne m'est jamais venu à l'esprit; don't put silly ideas into his ~ ne lui mettez pas des idées stupides en tête; I can't get these dates into my ~ je n'arrive pas à retenir ces dates; she got it into her ~ that she was being persecuted elle s'est mis en tête OR dans l'idée qu'on la persécutait; the answer has gone right out of my ~ j'ai complètement oublié la réponse; use your ~! fais travailler tes méninges! ❑ it's doing my ~ in! *inf* ça me tape sur le système!; I just can't get my ~ round the idea that she's gone *inf* je n'arrive vraiment pas à me faire à l'idée qu'elle est partie; to get one's ~ straight *inf* se ressaisir. -**3.** [aptitude]: in my job, you need a good ~ for figures pour faire mon métier, il faut savoir manier les chiffres; she has no ~ for business elle n'a pas le sens des affaires; to have a (good) ~ for heights ne pas avoir le vertige; I've no ~ for heights j'ai le vertige. -**4.** [clear thinking, common sense]: keep your ~! gardez votre calme!, ne perdez pas la tête!; to keep a cool ~ garder la tête froide; you'll need a clear ~ in the morning vous aurez besoin d'avoir l'esprit clair demain matin ❑ he's off his ~ *inf Br* il est malade, il est pas net. -**5.** [intelligence, ability] tête *f*; we'll have to put our ~s together and find a solution nous devrons nous y mettre ensemble pour trouver une solution ❑ off the top of my ~: off the top of my ~, I'd say it would cost about £1,500 à vue de nez, je dirais que ça coûte dans les 1 500 livres; I don't know off the top of my ~ je ne sais pas, il faudrait que je vérifie; her lecture was completely over my ~ sa conférence m'a complètement dépassé; to talk over sb's ~ s'exprimer de manière trop compliquée pour qqn; two ~s are better than one *prov* deux avis valent mieux qu'un. -**6.** *inf* [headache] mal *m* de tête; I've got a bit of a ~ this morning j'ai un peu mal à la tête ce matin. -**7.** [chief, boss - of police, government] chef *m*; [- of school, of company] directeur *m*, -trice *f*; the European ~s of government les chefs de gouvernement européens; the crowned ~s of Europe les têtes couronnées de l'Europe. -**8.** [authority, responsibility]: she went over my ~ to the president elle est allée voir le président sans me consulter; they were promoted over my ~ ils ont été promus avant moi ❑ on your (own) ~ be it! c'est toi qui en prends la responsabilité!, à tes risques et périls! -**9.** [top, upper end, extremity - of racquet, pin, hammer] tête *f*; [- of staircase] haut *m*, tête *f*; [- of bed] chevet *m*, tête *f*; [- of arrow] pointe *f*; [- of page] tête *f*; [- of letter] en-tête *m*; [- of cane] pommeau *m*; [- of valley] tête *f*; [- of river] source *f*; at the ~ of the procession/queue en tête de (la) procession/de (la) queue; sitting at the ~ of the table assis au bout de la OR en tête de table. -**10.** BOT & CULIN [of corn] épi *m*; [of garlic] tête *f*, gousse *f*; [of celery] pied *m*; [of asparagus] pointe *f*; a ~ of cauliflower un chou-fleur. -**11.** [of coin] côté *m* pile; ~s or tails? pile ou face? ❑ I can't make ~ nor tail of this pour moi ça n'a ni queue ni tête. -**12.** [of livestock] tête *f*; 50 ~ of cattle 50 têtes de bétail. -**13.** [in prices, donations]: tickets cost £50 a ~ les billets valent 50 livres par personne. -**14.** ELECTRON [of tape recorder, VCR] tête *f*. -**15.** [title - of chapter] tête *f*; under this ~ sous ce titre. -**16.** [on beer] mousse *f*. -**17.** [of pressure] pression *f*; to get up OR to work up a ~ of steam *fig* s'énerver. -**18.** [of drum] peau *f*. -**19.** [of ship] proue *f*. -**20.** GRAMM tête *f*. -**21.** MED [of abscess, spot] tête *f*; to come to a ~ [abscess, spot] mûrir; *fig* [problem] arriver au point critique; his resignation brought things to a ~ sa démission a précipité les choses. -**22.** ▼ [fellatio]: to give sb ~ tailler une pipe à qqn. -**23.** *inf Am* [toilet] toilettes *fpl*; I'm going to the ~ je vais pisser.
◇ *comp* chef; ~ porter chef-portier *m*.
◇ *vt* -**1.** [command - group, organization] être à la tête de; [- project, revolt] diriger, être à la tête de; [chair - discussion] mener; [- commission] présider. -**2.** [be first] être OR venir en tête de; Madrid ~s the list of Europe's most interesting cities Madrid vient OR s'inscrit en tête des villes les plus intéressantes d'Europe; she ~ed the pack from the start SPORT elle était en tête du peloton dès le départ. -**3.** [steer - vehicle] diriger; [- person] guider, diriger; we ~ed the sheep down the hill nous avons fait descendre les moutons de la colline; to ~ a ship westwards NAUT mettre le cap à l'ouest. -**4.** [provide title for] intituler; [be title of] être en tête de; the essay is ~ed "Democracy" l'essai s'intitule OR est intitulé «Démocratie». -**5.** FTBL: he ~ed the ball into the goal il a marqué de la tête. -**6.** [plant] écimer, étêter.
◇ *vi* [car, crowd, person] aller, se diriger; NAUT mettre le cap sur; where are you ~ed? où vas-tu?; we ~ed back to the office nous sommes retournés au bureau; I'm going to ~ home je vais rentrer; when are you ~ing back? quand comptez-vous rentrer?; the train ~ed into/out of a tunnel le train est entré dans un/sorti d'un tunnel.
◇ *adj* -**1.** [main - person] principal; [- office] central, principal; the ~ cook/gardener le cuisinier/jardinier en chef; send it to ~ office *Br* OR the ~ office *Am* envoyez-le au siège social OR au bureau central. -**2.** [first in series] premier.
◆ **head for** *vt insep* [car, person] se diriger vers; NAUT mettre le cap sur; she ~ed for home elle rentra (à la maison); he's ~ing for trouble il va (tout droit) à la catastrophe; to be ~ing for a fall *fig* courir à l'échec ❑ to ~ for the hills *inf* filer.
◆ **head off** ◇ *vt sep* -**1.** [divert - animal, vehicle, person] détourner de son chemin; [- enemy] forcer à reculer; she ~ed off all questions about her private life *fig* elle a éludé toute question sur sa vie privée. -**2.** [crisis, disaster] prévenir, éviter; [rebellion, revolt, unrest] éviter.
◇ *vi insep* partir; the children ~ed off to school les enfants sont partis pour OR à l'école.

headache ['hedeɪk] *n* -**1.** [pain] mal *m* de tête; [migraine] migraine *f*; to have a ~ [gen] avoir mal à la tête, avoir la migraine; white wine gives me a ~ le vin blanc me donne mal à la tête; he suffers a lot from ~s il a souvent des maux de tête OR mal à la tête. -**2.** *fig* [problem] problème *m*; the trip was one big ~ le voyage a été un casse-tête du début à la fin; convincing her is your ~ pour ce qui est de la convaincre, c'est ton problème.

headachy *inf* ['hedeɪkɪ] *adj*: I'm feeling a bit ~ j'ai un peu mal à la tête.

headband ['hedbænd] *n* bandeau *m*.

headboard ['hed,bɔːd] *n* tête *f* de lit.

head boy *n Br élève chargé d'un certain nombre de responsabilités et qui représente son école aux cérémonies publiques*.

headbutt ['hedbʌt] ◇ *n* coup *m* de tête, coup *m* de boule.
◇ *vt* donner un coup de tête OR de boule à.

head case *inf n* dingue *mf*.

headcheese ['hed,tʃiːz] *n Am* fromage *m* de tête.

head cold *n* rhume *m* de cerveau.

head count *n* vérification *f* du nombre de personnes présentes; the teacher did a ~ la maîtresse a compté les élèves.

headdress ['hed,dres] *n* [gen] coiffure *f*; [belonging to regional costume] coiffe *f*.

-headed ['hedɪd] *in cpds* à tête...; a silver~ cane une canne à pommeau d'argent; a three~ dragon un dragon à trois têtes.

headed notepaper ['hedɪd-] *n Br* papier *m* à en-tête.

header ['hedəʳ] *n* -**1.** [fall] chute *f* (la tête la première); [dive] plongeon *m* (la tête la première); he took a ~ into the ditch il est tombé la tête la première dans le fossé. -**2.** FTBL (coup *m* de) tête *f*; he scored with a ~ il a marqué de la tête. -**3.** COMPUT en-tête *m*; ~ block en-tête; ~ card carte *f* en-tête. -**4.** *Br* AUT: ~ (tank) collecteur *m* de tête. -**5.** CONSTR (pierre *f* en) boutisse *f*.

headfirst [,hed'fɜːst] *adv* -**1.** [dive, fall, jump] la tête la première; he dived ~ into the pool il a piqué une tête dans la piscine. -**2.** [rashly] sans réfléchir, imprudemment; to jump ~ into sthg se jeter tête baissée dans qqch.

headgear ['hed,gɪəʳ] *n* (*U*) coiffure *f*; they were wearing some very odd ~ *hum* ils avaient tous un drôle de chapeau.

head girl *n Br élève chargée d'un certain nombre de responsabilités et qui représente son école aux cérémonies publiques*.

headhunt ['hedhʌnt] ◇ *vi* recruter des cadres (pour une entreprise).
◇ *vt*: to be ~ed être recruté par un chasseur de têtes.

headhunter ['hed,hʌntəʳ] *n* ANTHR & *fig* chasseur *m* de têtes.

headhunting ['hed,hʌntɪŋ] *n* ANTHR & *fig* chasse *f* aux têtes; [recruiting] chasse *f* aux têtes, recrutement *m* de cadres.

headiness ['hedɪnɪs] *n* -**1.** [of wine] bouquet *m* capiteux; the ~ of her perfume son parfum capiteux; the ~ of sudden success la griserie OR l'ivresse qu'apporte un succès imprévu. -**2.** [excitement] exaltation *f*, excitation *f*; the ~ of the early sixties l'euphorie du début des années 60.

heading ['hedɪŋ] *n* -**1.** [title - of article, book] titre *m*; [- of chapter] titre *m*, intitulé *m*; page ~ tête *f* de page. -**2.** [subject] rubrique *f*; their latest record comes under the ~ of jazz leur dernier disque se trouve sous la rubrique jazz. -**3.** [letterhead] en-tête *m*. -**4.** AERON & NAUT [direction] cap *m*. -**5.** MIN [tunnel] galerie *f* d'avancement.

headlamp ['hedlæmp] *n* -**1.** *Br* = **headlight**. -**2.** MIN lampe-chapeau *f*.

headland ['hedlənd] *n* promontoire *m*, cap *m*.

headless ['hedlɪs] *adj* -**1.** [arrow, body, screw] sans tête; he was running around like a ~ chicken *hum* il courait dans tous les sens. -**2.** [company, commission] sans chef.

headlight ['hedlaɪt] *n* [on car] phare *m*; [on train] fanal *m*, feu *m* avant.

headline ['hedlaɪn] ◇ *n* -**1.** [in newspaper] (gros) titre *m*, manchette *f*; the hijacking made all the ~s le détournement a fait la une de tous les journaux; I just glanced at the ~s j'ai juste jeté un coup d'œil sur les gros titres; news of their marriage hit the ~s l'annonce de leur mariage a fait les gros titres OR a défrayé la chronique. -**2.** RADIO & TV [news summary] grand titre *m*; here are today's news ~s voici les principaux titres de l'actualité.
◇ *vt* -**1.** PRESS mettre en manchette. -**2.** [provide heading for] intituler; the article was ~d "The New Poor" l'article avait pour titre «Les Nouveaux Pauvres». -**3.** *Am* [have top billing in] avoir le rôle principal dans; headlining the show is Jane Brown Jane Brown est la vedette du spectacle.
◇ *vi Am* [have top billing] avoir le rôle principal.

headliner ['hedlaɪnəʳ] *n Am* vedette *f*.

headlock ['hedlɒk] *n* cravate *f*.

headlong ['hedlɒŋ] ◇ *adv* -**1.** [dive, fall] la tête la première; she dived ~ into the lake elle a piqué une tête dans le lac. -**2.** [rush - head down] tête baissée; [- at great speed] à toute allure OR vitesse; he threw himself ~ against the door il s'est littéralement jeté contre la porte. -**3.** [rashly] sans réfléchir, imprudemment; she rushed ~ to her downfall elle courait tout droit à sa perte; he plunged ~ into the story il s'est lancé dans l'histoire.
◇ *adj* -**1.** [dive, fall] la tête la première. -**2.** [impetuous - action] imprudent, impétueux; ~ flight sauve-qui-peut *m inv*, débandade *f*; the crowd made a ~ dash for the exit la foule s'est ruée vers la sortie.

headman ['hedmæn] (*pl* headmen [-men]) *n* chef *m*.

headmaster [,hed'mɑːstəʳ] *n* SCH proviseur *m*, directeur *m*, chef *m* d'établissement.

headmastership [,hed'mɑːstəʃɪp] *n* SCH poste *m* de proviseur OR de directeur.

headmistress [,hed'mɪstrɪs] *n* SCH directrice *f*, chef *m* d'établissement.

head office *n* siège *m* social, bureau *m* central.

head-on ◇ *adv* -**1.** [collide, hit] de front, de plein fouet; he ran ~ into the tree il a heurté l'arbre de plein fouet; the ship ran ~ into the wharf le navire a heurté le quai par l'avant. -**2.** [confront, meet] de front; to meet a problem ~ aborder un problème de front; management confronted the union ~ la direction a affronté le syndicat.
◇ *adj* -**1.** [collision - of car, plane] de front, de plein fouet; [- of ships] par l'avant. -**2.** [confrontation, disagreement] violent.

headphones ['hedfəʊnz] *npl* casque *m* (*à écouteurs*).

headpiece ['hedpiːs] *n* -**1.** [helmet] casque *m*. -**2.** TYPO vignette *f*, en-tête *m*.

headpin ['hedpɪn] *n* quille *f* de tête.

headquarters [,hed'kwɔːtəz] *npl* -**1.** [base - of bank, office] siège *m* social, bureau *m* central; [- of army, police] quartier *m* général; police ~ le quartier général de la police. -**2.** MIL [commanding officers] quartier *m* général; ~ staff état-major *m*.

headrest ['hedrest] *n* appuie-tête *m*, repose-tête *m*.

head restraint *n Br* appuie-tête *m*, repose-tête *m*.

headroom ['hedrʊm] *n* place *f*, hauteur *f*; there's not much ~ in the attic le plafond du grenier n'est pas très haut, le grenier n'est pas très haut de plafond; does the car have enough ~? est-ce qu'il y a assez de place dans la voiture pour ne pas se cogner la tête?; 'max ~ 10 metres' 'hauteur limite 10 mètres'.

headsail ['hedseɪl] *n* foc *m*.

headscarf ['hedskɑːf] (*pl* headscarves [-skɑːvz]) *n* foulard *m*.

headset ['hedset] *n* [with microphone] casque *m* (*à écouteurs et à micro*); *Am* [headphones] casque *m* (*à écouteurs*).

headship ['hedʃɪp] *n* -**1.** [leadership] direction *f*; under the ~ of sous la direction de. -**2.** SCH poste *m* de directeur OR de directrice.

headshrinker ['hed,ʃrɪŋkəʳ] *n* -**1.** ANTHR réducteur *m* de têtes. -**2.** *inf* [psychiatrist] psy *mf*.

headsquare ['hedskweəʳ] *n* foulard *m*, carré *m*.

headstand ['hedstænd] *n*: to do a ~ faire le poirier.

head start *n* -**1.** [lead] avance *f*; he had a ten-minute ~ over the others il a commencé dix minutes avant les autres; I got a ~ j'ai pris de l'avance sur les autres; go on, I'll give you a ~ allez, vas-y, je te donne un peu d'avance. -**2.** [advantage] avantage *m*; being bilingual gives her a ~ over the others étant bilingue, elle est avantagée par rapport aux autres.

headstone ['hedstəʊn] *n* -**1.** [of grave] pierre *f* tombale. -**2.** ARCHIT [keystone] clef *f* de voûte.

headstream ['hedstriːm] *n* source *f* (d'un fleuve).

headstrong ['hedstrɒŋ] *adj* -**1.** [wilful] têtu, entêté. -**2.** [rash] impétueux, imprudent.

head teacher *n* [man] proviseur *m*, directeur *m*, chef *m* d'établissement; [woman] directrice *f*, chef *m* d'établissement.

head-up *adj* [in aeroplane, car]: ~ display affichage *m* tête-haute.

head waiter *n* maître *m* d'hôtel.

headwaters ['hed,wɔːtəz] *npl* sources *fpl* (d'un fleuve).

headway ['hedweɪ] *n* -**1.** [progress]: to make ~ [gen] avancer, faire des progrès; NAUT faire route; they're making some/no ~ in their plans leurs projets avancent/n'avancent pas; I'm not making much ~ with this guest list je n'avance pas dans la préparation de cette liste d'invités, je n'ai toujours pas fini cette liste d'invités. -**2.** [headroom] place *f*, hauteur *f*. -**3.** [between buses, trains]: there is a ten-minute ~ between buses il y a dix minutes d'attente entre les bus.

headwind ['hedwɪnd] *n* [gen & AERON] vent *m* contraire; NAUT vent *m* debout.

headword ['hedwɜːd] *n* entrée *f*, adresse *f*.

heady ['hedɪ] (*compar* headier, *superl* headiest) *adj* -**1.** [intoxicating - wine] capiteux, qui monte à la tête; [- perfume] capiteux; the punch was a ~ blend of wines and spirits le punch était un mélange capiteux de vins et d'alcools; she breathed in a ~ draught of mountain air elle respira l'air grisant OR enivrant des montagnes. -**2.** [intoxicated] grisé, enivré; he felt quite ~ with success il se sentait complètement grisé par le succès. -**3.** [exciting - experience, time] excitant, passionnant; [- atmosphere] excitant, enivrant; she recalled her ~ days as a young reporter elle se rappelait l'époque excitante où elle était jeune reporter.

heal [hiːl] ◇ *vt* -**1.** [make healthy - person] guérir; [- wound] guérir, cicatriser; time ~s all wounds le temps guérit toutes les blessures. -**2.** [damage, division] remédier à, réparer; [disagreement] régler; I'd do anything to ~ the breach between them je ferais n'importe quoi pour les réconcilier OR pour les raccommoder.
◇ *vi* [person] guérir; [wound] se cicatriser, se refermer; [fracture] se consolider.
◆ **heal over** *vi insep* se cicatriser.
◆ **heal up** *vi insep* [wound] se cicatriser, guérir; [burn] guérir; [fracture] se consolider.

healer ['hiːləʳ] *n* guérisseur *m*, -euse *f*.

healing ['hiːlɪŋ] ◇ *n* [of person] guérison *f*; [of wound] cicatrisation *f*, guérison *f*; [of fracture] consolidation *f*.
◇ *adj* -**1.** [remedy, treatment] curatif; [ointment] cicatrisant; ~ hands mains *fpl* de guérisseur. -**2.** [wound] qui se cicatrise, qui guérit; [fracture] qui se consolide, qui guérit. -**3.** [soothing - influence] apaisant.

health [helθ] *n* -**1.** [general condition] santé *f*; to be in good/poor ~ être en bonne/mauvaise santé; his ~ has never been good il a toujours été fragile; smoking is bad for your ~ le tabac est mauvais pour OR nuisible à ta santé; the economic ~ of the nation *fig* la (bonne) santé économique de la nation ❑ mental ~ santé mentale; Health and Safety Executive ≃ inspection *f* du travail; Department of Health and Social Security *Br*, Department of Health and Human Services *Am* ≃ ministère de la Santé et des Affaires sociales. -**2.** [good condition] (bonne) santé *f*; **has he regained his ~?** s'est-il remis?, a-t-il recouvré la santé?, a-t-il guéri?; **she's the picture of ~** elle respire la santé; **I'm not doing this (just) for the good of my ~!** *hum* je ne fais pas ça pour le plaisir OR pour m'amuser! -**3.** [in toast]: **(to your) good ~!** à votre santé!; **we drank (to) the ~ of the bride and groom** nous avons porté un toast en l'honneur des mariés.

ealth centre *n* centre *m* médico-social.

ealth farm *n* centre *m* de remise en forme.

ealth food *n* aliments *mpl* diététiques OR biologiques.

ealthful ['helθfʊl] *dated* OR *lit* = **healthy 1, 4.**

ealth hazard *n* risque *m* pour la santé.

ealthily ['helθɪlɪ] *adv* [eat, live] sainement.

ealth insurance *n* assurance *f* maladie.

ealth risk *n* risque *m* pour la santé.

ealth service *n* -**1.** [of firm, school] infirmerie *f*. -**2.** = **national health service.**

ealthy ['helθɪ] (*compar* **healthier**, *superl* **healthiest**) *adj* -**1.** [in good health - person] sain, en bonne santé; [- animal, plant] en bonne santé; **he's very ~** il se porte très bien, il est bien portant. -**2.** [showing good health - colour, skin] sain; [appetite] robuste, bon. -**3.** [beneficial - air, climate] salubre; [- diet, food] sain; [- exercise] bon pour la santé, salutaire. -**4.** [thriving - economy] sain; [- business] prospère, bien assis; **the new measures are designed to make the economy healthier** les nouvelles lois sont destinées à assainir l'économie. -**5.** [substantial - profits] considérable; [- sum] considérable, important; [- difference] appréciable. -**6.** [sensible - attitude] sain; [- respect] salutaire; **he shows a ~ disrespect for opinion polls** il fait montre d'un dédain salutaire pour les sondages.

eap [hiːp] ◇ *n* -**1.** [pile] tas *m*, amas *m*; **her things were piled in a ~** ses affaires étaient (mises) en tas; **he collapsed in a ~ on the floor** il s'écroula OR tomba par terre comme une masse; **he started at the bottom of the ~ and worked his way up** il a commencé au bas de l'échelle et a peu à peu grimpé les échelons ❑ **to be struck** OR **knocked all of a ~** *inf Br dated* être soufflé, en rester comme deux ronds de flan. -**2.** *inf* [large quantity] tas *m*, masse *f*; **a ~** OR **~s of money** un paquet de fric; **I have a ~** OR **~s of work to do** j'ai un boulot monstre; **you've got ~s of time** tu as largement le temps OR tout ton temps; **he's helped us out ~s of times** il nous a rendu service mille fois OR des tas de fois; **they have ~s of room** ils ont de la place à ne plus savoir qu'en faire. -**3.** *inf* [old car] vieux clou *m*.

◇ *vt* -**1.** [collect into a pile] entasser, empiler; **she ~ed roast beef onto his plate** elle l'a généreusement servi en (tranches de) rosbif. -**2.** *fig* [lavish] couvrir de; **her fiancé ~ed flowers on her** son fiancé l'a couverte de fleurs; **to ~ praise on** OR **upon sb** couvrir OR combler qqn d'éloges OR de compliments; **the teacher ~ed homework on the students** le professeur a submergé ses élèves de devoirs.

◆ **heap up** *vt sep* [pile - books, furniture] entasser, empiler; [- money, riches] amasser; **she ~ed up our plates with food** elle a rempli nos assiettes.

eaped [hiːpt] *Br*, **heaping** ['hiːpɪŋ] *Am adj* gros; **a ~ teaspoonful** une cuiller à café bombée OR pleine.

eaps *inf* [hiːps] *adv* drôlement; **it's ~ faster to go by train** ça va drôlement plus vite en train; **I feel ~ better** je me sens drôlement OR rudement mieux.

ear [hɪəʳ] (*pt* & *pp* **heard** [hɜːd]) ◇ *vt* -**1.** [perceive with sense of hearing] entendre; **can you ~ me?** m'entendez-vous (bien)?; **we can't ~ you** nous ne vous entendons pas, nous n'entendons pas ce que vous dites; **he could ~ someone crying** il entendait (quelqu'un) pleurer; **I can ~ someone at the door** j'entends sonner à la porte; **a shout was heard** un cri se fit entendre; **he was heard to observe** OR **remark that he was against censorship** *fml* on l'a entendu dire qu'il était opposé à la censure; **I've heard it said that...** j'ai entendu dire que...; **I've heard tell that they're engaged** j'ai entendu dire qu'ils étaient fiancés; **I've heard tell of such things** j'ai entendu parler de choses de ce genre; **I couldn't make myself heard above the noise** je n'arrivais pas à me faire entendre dans le bruit; **to ~ my sister talk you'd think we were poor** à entendre ma sœur, vous pourriez croire que nous sommes pauvres; **he went on and on about it — I can just ~ him!** il n'a pas arrêté d'en parler — c'est comme si j'y étais OR pas la peine de me faire un dessin; **don't believe everything you ~** n'écoutez pas tous les bruits qui courent, ne croyez pas tout ce qu'on raconte; **you're ~ing things** tu t'imagines des choses; **I can hardly ~ myself think** je n'arrive pas à me concentrer (tant il y a de bruit) ❑ **you could have heard a pin drop** on aurait pu entendre une mouche voler; **let's ~ it for the Johnson sisters!** un grand bravo pour les sœurs Johnson!, et on applaudit bien fort les sœurs Johnson! -**2.** [listen to - music, person] écouter; [- concert, lecture, mass] assister à, écouter; **be quiet, d'you ~!** taisez-vous, vous entendez!; **let's ~ what you think** dites voir OR un peu ce que vous pensez; **so let's ~ it!** allez, dis ce que tu as à dire!; **I've never heard such nonsense!** qu'est-ce qu'il ne faut pas entendre!; **I heard her rehearse her lines** je l'ai fait répéter OR réciter son rôle; **the Lord heard our prayers** le Seigneur a écouté OR exaucé nos prières. -**3.** [subj: authority, official]: **the priest ~s confession on Saturdays** le prêtre confesse le samedi; **the court will ~ the first witness today** JUR la cour entendra le premier témoin aujourd'hui; **the case will be heard in March** l'affaire se plaidera au mois de mars. -**4.** [understand, be told] entendre, apprendre; **I ~ you're leaving** j'ai appris OR j'ai entendu (dire) que tu partais; **I ~ you've lived in Thailand** il paraît que tu as vécu en Thaïlande; **have you heard the latest?** connaissez-vous la dernière?; **have you heard anything more about the accident?** avez-vous eu d'autres nouvelles de l'accident? ❑ **have you heard the one about the Scotsman and the Irishman?** connaissez-vous l'histoire de l'Écossais et de l'Irlandais?; **I've heard that one before!** on ne me la fait plus!; **she's heard it all before** elle connaît la musique; **I've heard good things about that school** j'ai eu des échos favorables de cette école; **you haven't heard the last of this!** [gen] vous n'avez pas fini d'en entendre parler!; [threat] vous aurez de mes nouvelles!

◇ *vi* -**1.** [able to perceive sound] entendre; **she doesn't ~ very well** elle n'entend pas très bien, elle est un peu dure d'oreille. -**2.** [be aware of] être au courant; **haven't you heard? he's dead** vous n'êtes pas au courant? il est mort. -**3.** *phr*: **~, ~!** bravo!

◆ **hear about** *vt insep* -**1.** [learn] entendre; **have you heard about the accident?** êtes-vous au courant pour OR de l'accident?; **yes, I heard about that** oui, je suis au courant; **have you heard about the time she met Churchill?** connaissez-vous l'histoire de sa rencontre avec Churchill? -**2.** [have news of] avoir OR recevoir des nouvelles de; **I ~ about her through her sister** j'ai de ses nouvelles par sa sœur.

◆ **hear from** *vt insep* -**1.** [receive news of] avoir OR recevoir des nouvelles de; **they'd be delighted to ~ from you** ils seraient ravis d'avoir de tes nouvelles; **he never heard from her again** il n'a plus jamais eu de ses nouvelles; **you'll be ~ing from me** [gen] je vous donnerai de mes nouvelles; [threat] vous allez avoir de mes nouvelles, vous allez entendre parler de moi; **(I am) looking forward to ~ing from you** [in letters] dans l'attente de vous lire. -**2.** [listen to] écouter; **we ~ first from one of the survivors** nous allons d'abord écouter OR entendre l'un des survivants.

◆ **hear of** *vt insep* -**1.** [know of] entendre parler de, connaître; **I've never heard of her** je ne la connais pas. -**2.** [receive news of] entendre parler de; **the whole town had heard of his success** la ville entière était au courant de son succès OR sa réussite; **the director was never heard of again** on n'a plus jamais entendu parler du directeur; **the missing boy was never heard of again** on n'a jamais retrouvé la trace du garçon qui avait disparu; **have you ever heard of such a thing?** avez-vous déjà entendu parler d'une chose pareille?; **who ever heard of eating pizza for breakfast!** quelle (drôle d') idée de manger de la pizza au petit déjeuner!; **we ~ of nothing these days but rocketing interest rates!** ces temps-ci, on nous rebat les oreilles avec la montée en flèche OR la croissance folle des taux d'intérêt! -**3.** (*usu neg*) [accept, allow]: **her father won't ~ of it** son père ne veut pas en entendre parler OR ne veut rien savoir; **I won't ~ of you walking home** je ne veux absolument pas que tu rentres à pied; **may I pay for dinner? — I wouldn't ~ of it!** puis-je payer OR vous offrir le dîner? — (il n'en est) pas question!

◆ **hear out** *vt sep* écouter sans interruption; **at least ~ me out before you refuse my offer** au moins écoutez-moi jusqu'au bout avant de refuser ma proposition.

heard [hɜːd] *pt* & *pp* → **hear.**

hearer ['hɪərəʳ] *n* auditeur *m*, -trice *f*.

hearing ['hɪərɪŋ] *n* -**1.** [sense of] ouïe *f*; **to have good/bad ~** entendre bien/mal; **a keen sense of ~** l'oreille *f* OR l'ouïe fine; **his ~ gradually deteriorated** petit à petit il est devenu dur d'oreille; **cats have better ~ than humans** les chats entendent mieux OR ont l'ouïe plus fine que les humains. -**2.** [earshot]: **within ~** à portée de voix; **you shouldn't have said that in** OR **within ~ of his mother** tu n'aurais pas dû le dire devant OR en présence de sa mère. -**3.** [act of listening] audition *f*; **I didn't enjoy the symphony at (the) first ~** je n'ai pas aimé la symphonie à la première audition OR la première fois que je l'ai écoutée. -**4.** [chance to be heard] audition *f*; **they were the only ones to get a ~** ils furent les seuls à être entendus; **at least give me a ~** laissez-moi au moins parler; **they judged the architect without a ~** ils ont jugé l'architecte sans l'entendre OR sans entendre sa défense; **to give sb a fair ~** laisser parler qqn, écouter ce que qqn a à dire. -**5.** JUR audition *f*; **the ~ of witnesses** l'audition des témoins; **the ~ of a trial** l'audience *f*; **the case will come up for ~ in March** l'affaire sera entendue OR plaidée en mars. -**6.** [official meeting] séance *f*.

hearing aid *n* appareil *m* acoustique, audiophone *m*.

hearken ['hɑːkn] *vi dated* OR *lit*: **to ~ to sthg** écouter qqch.

hearsay ['hɪəseɪ] *n* ouï-dire *m inv*, rumeur *f*; **it's only ~** ce ne sont que des rumeurs; **I only know it by** OR **from ~** je ne le sais que par ouï-dire.

hearsay evidence *n* déposition *f* sur la foi d'un tiers OR d'autrui.

hearse [hɜːs] *n* corbillard *m*, fourgon *m* mortuaire.

heart [hɑːt] ◇ *n* -**1.** ANAT [organ] cœur *m*; **he has a weak ~** il est cardiaque, il a le cœur malade ‖ *fig*: **when she heard the news her ~ leapt** en apprenant la nouvelle, son cœur a bondi; **her ~ sank** elle eut un serrement de cœur; **my ~ sinks every time I think about leaving** j'ai un pincement au cœur OR un serrement de cœur chaque fois que je pense au départ; **two ~s that beat as one** *lit* deux cœurs qui battent à l'unisson ❑ **he sat there, his ~ in his boots** *Br* il était là, la mort dans l'âme; **she waited, her ~ in her mouth** elle attendait, son cœur battant la chamade OR rongée par l'angoisse. -**2.** [bosom] poitrine *f*; **she clutched him to her ~** elle l'a serré contre sa poitrine OR sur son cœur. -**3.** [seat of feelings, love] cœur *m*; **he has a ~ of gold/of stone** il a un cœur d'or/de pierre; **it does my ~ good to see them together** cela me réchauffe le cœur de les voir ensemble; to lose one's ~ to sb donner son cœur à qqn, tomber amoureux de qqn; her words went straight to his ~ ses paroles lui sont allées droit au cœur; the letter was written straight from the ~ la lettre était écrite du fond du cœur; to have one's ~ set on sthg s'être mis qqch dans la tête; he has his ~ set on winning il veut à tout prix gagner; they have their ~ set on that house ils ont jeté leur dévolu sur cette maison; they have your welfare at ~ ils ne pensent qu'à ton bien, c'est pour ton bien qu'ils font cela; they have everything their ~s could desire ils ont tout ce qu'ils peuvent désirer; my ~'s desire is to see Rome again *lit* mon plus cher désir est OR ce que je désire le plus au monde c'est de revoir Rome; she hardened OR steeled her ~ against him elle s'est endurcie contre lui; dear ~ *arch* OR *hum* mon cœur, mon chéri ❑ to wear one's ~ on one's sleeve montrer OR laisser paraître ses sentiments. -**4.** [innermost thoughts] fond *m*; in his ~ of ~s au fond de lui-même OR de son cœur, en son for intérieur; in my ~ I knew it was true au fond de moi-même je savais que c'était la vérité; there's a woman/a man after my own ~ voilà une femme/un homme selon mon cœur; I thank you from the bottom of my ~ OR with all my ~ je vous remercie du fond du cœur OR de tout mon cœur; do you love him? – with all my ~ vous l'aimez? – de tout mon cœur; to take sthg to ~ prendre qqch à cœur; she takes criticism too much to ~ elle prend les critiques trop à cœur; don't take it to ~ ne le prenez pas trop à cœur; she opened OR poured out her ~ to me elle m'a dévoilé son cœur. -**5.** [disposition, humour]: to have a change of ~ changer d'avis. -**6.** [interest, enthusiasm]: I worked hard but my ~ wasn't in it j'ai beaucoup travaillé mais je n'avais pas le cœur à l'ouvrage OR le cœur n'y était pas; I can tell that your ~ isn't in it je vois bien que tu n'y tiens pas tellement; she read to her ~'s content elle a lu tout son soûl; a subject close to one's ~ un sujet qui tient à cœur; she puts her ~ OR she throws herself ~ and soul into her work elle se donne à son travail corps et âme. -**7.** [courage]: to lose ~ perdre courage, se décourager; take ~! courage!; she took ~ from the fact that others shared her experience elle était encouragée par le fait que d'autres partageaient son expérience; the prospect of winning the prize put new ~ into them la perspective de gagner le prix leur a redonné du courage OR du cœur (au ventre); to be in good ~ [person] avoir bon moral; *Br* [land] être fécond OR productif. -**8.** [compassion] cœur *m*; he has no ~ il n'a pas de cœur, il manque de cœur; she didn't have the ~ to refuse, she couldn't find it in her ~ to refuse elle n'a pas eu le courage OR le cœur de refuser; can you find it in your ~ to forgive me? est-ce que vous pourrez jamais me pardonner? ❑ her ~'s in the right place elle a bon cœur; have a ~! pitié! -**9.** [core, vital part - of matter, topic] fond *m*, vif *m*; [- of city, place] centre *m*, cœur *m*; the ~ of the matter le fond du problème; the speaker went straight to the ~ of the matter le conférencier est allé droit au cœur du sujet OR du problème; the law strikes at the ~ of the democratic system la loi porte atteinte aux fondements du régime démocratique; in the ~ of the financial district au centre OR au cœur du quartier financier; in the ~ of winter en plein hiver, au cœur de l'hiver; in the ~ of the forest au cœur OR au beau milieu OR au fin fond de la forêt, en pleine forêt ❑ the Heart of Dixie *Am* l'Alabama *m*; 'Heart of Darkness' *Conrad* 'Au cœur des ténèbres'; 'The Heart of the Matter' *Greene* 'le Fond du problème'. -**10.** [of cabbage, celery, lettuce] cœur *m*; [of artichoke] cœur *m*, fond *m*. -**11.** CARDS cœur *m*; the king of ~s le roi de cœur; to play a ~ jouer un OR du cœur; ~s are trumps atout cœur; have you got any ~s? avez-vous du cœur?; game of ~s *jeu de cartes dont l'objet est de faire des plis ne comprenant ni des cœurs ni la dame de pique*. -**12.** [shape] cœur *m*; a pattern of little red ~s un motif de petits cœurs rouges; she had drawn ~s all over the letter elle avait dessiné des cœurs sur toute la lettre.

◇ *comp*: ~ disease maladie *f* de cœur, maladie *f* cardiaque; ~ is on the increase les maladies de cœur OR cardiaques sont en augmentation; smoking increases the incidence of ~ le tabagisme augmente le taux de maladies de cœur OR cardiaques; ~ patient cardiaque *mf*; ~ surgeon chirurgien *m* cardiologue; ~ surgery chirurgie *f* du cœur; ~ transplant greffe *f* du cœur; ~ trouble *(U)* maladie *f* du cœur, troubles *mpl* cardiaques; to have OR to suffer from ~ trouble souffrir du cœur, être cardiaque.

◆ **at heart** *adv phr* au fond; at ~ she was a good person elle avait un bon fond; my sister's a gypsy at ~ ma sœur est une bohémienne dans l'âme; to feel sad at ~ avoir le cœur triste; to be sick at ~ avoir la mort dans l'âme.

◆ **by heart** *adv phr* par cœur; to learn/to know sthg by ~ apprendre/savoir qqch par cœur.

heartache ['hɑːteɪk] *n* chagrin *m*, peine *f*; he caused her a lot of ~ il lui a causé beaucoup de chagrin.

heart attack *n* MED crise *f* cardiaque; to have a ~ avoir une crise cardiaque, faire un infarctus; she nearly had a ~ when she heard about it *fig* en apprenant la nouvelle, elle a failli avoir une attaque.

heartbeat ['hɑːtbiːt] *n* battement *m* de cœur, pulsation *f*; an irregular ~ un battement arythmique OR irrégulier; to be a ~ away from sthg être à deux doigts de qqch.

heartbreak ['hɑːtbreɪk] *n* [grief - gen] (immense) chagrin *m*, déchirement *m*; [- in love] chagrin *m* d'amour; 'Heartbreak House' *Shaw* 'la Maison des cœurs brisés'.

heartbreaker ['hɑːtˌbreɪkəʳ] *n* bourreau *m* des cœurs.

heartbreaking ['hɑːtˌbreɪkɪŋ] *adj* qui fend le cœur, déchirant, navrant; it was ~ to see children starving c'était à vous fendre le cœur de voir des enfants mourir de faim; ~ scenes des scènes déchirantes OR navrantes.

heartbroken ['hɑːtˌbrəʊkn] *adj* [person - gen] qui a un immense chagrin; [- stronger] qui a le cœur brisé; [sigh, sob] à fendre le cœur; she's ~ over losing the job elle n'arrive pas à se consoler OR à se remettre d'avoir perdu ce travail; the child was ~ l'enfant avait un gros chagrin.

heartburn ['hɑːtbɜːn] *n* *(U)* brûlures *fpl* d'estomac.

heart condition *n* maladie *f* de cœur; to have a ~ souffrir du cœur, être cardiaque.

-hearted [ˌhɑːtɪd] *in cpds* qui a le cœur...; cold~ impitoyable, sans pitié; kind~ bon, qui a bon cœur; faint~ pusillanime, timide.

hearten ['hɑːtn] *vt* encourager, donner du courage à; we were ~ed to learn of the drop in interest rates nous avons été contents d'apprendre que les taux d'intérêt avaient baissé.

heartening ['hɑːtnɪŋ] *adj* encourageant, réconfortant; I found the news ~ la nouvelle m'a donné du courage OR m'a encouragé.

heart failure *n* [condition] défaillance *f* cardiaque; [cessation of heartbeat] arrêt *m* du cœur; I nearly had ~ when they told me I'd got the job *fig* j'ai failli me trouver mal OR avoir une syncope quand ils m'ont dit que j'avais le poste.

heartfelt ['hɑːtfelt] *adj* [apology, thanks] sincère; a ~ wish un souhait qui vient (du fond) du cœur; she expressed a ~ wish to see her country again elle exprima le souhait sincère de revoir son pays; with our ~ wishes for a speedy recovery avec nos vœux sincères de prompt rétablissement.

hearth [hɑːθ] *n* -**1.** [of fireplace] foyer *m*, âtre *m*; a fire was burning in the ~ il y avait du feu dans la cheminée. -**2.** [home] foyer *m*; to leave ~ and home quitter le foyer.

hearthrug ['hɑːθrʌg] *n* devant *m* de foyer.

hearthstone ['hɑːθstəʊn] *n* foyer *m*, âtre *m*.

heartily ['hɑːtɪlɪ] *adv* -**1.** [enthusiastically - joke, laugh] de tout son cœur; [- say, thank, welcome] chaleureusement, de tout cœur; they ate ~ ils ont mangé de bon appétit OR avec appétit. -**2.** [thoroughly]: I ~ recommend it je vous le conseille vivement; she ~ dislikes him elle le déteste cordialement; to be ~ disgusted with sthg être on ne peut plus dégoûté de qqch; they were ~ sick of the work ils en avaient par-dessus la tête OR ils en avaient plus qu'assez du travail.

heartiness ['hɑːtɪnɪs] *n* -**1.** [of thanks, welcome] cordialité *f*, chaleur *f*; [of agreement] sincérité *f*; [of appetite] vigueur *f*; [of dislike] ardeur *f*. -**2.** [enthusiasm] zèle *m*, empressement *m*.

heartland ['hɑːtlænd] *n* cœur *m*, centre *m*; the ~ of France la France profonde; the industrial ~ of Europe le principal centre industriel de l'Europe; the Socialist ~ le fief des socialistes.

heartless ['hɑːtlɪs] *adj* [person] sans cœur, impitoyable; [laughter, treatment] cruel.

heartlessly ['hɑːtlɪslɪ] *adv* sans pitié.

heartlessness ['hɑːtlɪsnɪs] *n* [of person] manque *m* de cœur, caractère *m* impitoyable; [of laughter, treatment] cruauté *f*.

heart-lung machine *n* cœur-poumon *m* artificiel.

heart murmur *n* souffle *m* au cœur.

heartrending ['hɑːtˌrendɪŋ] *adj* déchirant, qui fend le cœur; ~ scenes of homeless refugees des images navrantes OR déchirantes de réfugiés sans abri.

heart-searching [-ˌsɜːtʃɪŋ] *n* examen *m* de conscience; you need to do some ~ before deciding tu ferais mieux de réfléchir avant de te décider; after much ~ she decided to leave après s'être longuement interrogée OR tâtée, elle décida de partir.

heart-shaped *adj* en forme de cœur.

heartsick ['hɑːtsɪk] *adj* découragé, démoralisé; a ~ lover un amoureux transi; to be ~ avoir la mort dans l'âme; ~ and disillusioned, he gave up his search démoralisé OR abattu et désenchanté, il abandonna ses recherches.

heartstrings ['hɑːtstrɪŋz] *npl*: to play on OR to pull on OR to tug at sb's ~ faire vibrer OR toucher la corde sensible de qqn; he certainly knows how to play on an audience's ~ il n'y a pas de doute, il sait faire vibrer la corde sensible d'un auditoire OR il sait toucher la sensibilité d'un auditoire; that song always tugs at my ~ cette chanson me serre toujours le cœur.

heartthrob ['hɑːtθrɒb] *n* coqueluche *f*, idole *f*; he's her ~ elle a le béguin pour lui; he's the office ~ il est la coqueluche des secrétaires.

heart-to-heart ◇ *adj* & *adv* à cœur ouvert *fig*. ◇ *n* conversation *f* intime OR à cœur ouvert; it's time we had a ~ il est temps qu'on se parle (à cœur ouvert).

heartwarming ['hɑːtˌwɔːmɪŋ] *adj* réconfortant, qui réchauffe le cœur.

heartwood ['hɑːtwʊd] *n* cœur *m* du bois, bois *m* de cœur, duramen *m spec*.

hearty ['hɑːtɪ] (*pl* hearties, *compar* heartier, *superl* heartiest) ◇ *adj* -**1.** [congratulations, welcome] cordial, chaleureux; [thanks] sincère; [approval, recommendation] sans réserves; [laugh] gros, franc; [knock, slap] vigoureux; they're ~ eaters ils ont un bon coup de fourchette, ce sont de gros mangeurs. -**2.** [person - robust] vigoureux, robuste, solide; [- cheerful] jovial; they're a bit too ~ for my liking ils sont un peu trop bruyants OR tapageurs à mon goût. -**3.** [meal] copieux, abondant. -**4.** [thorough] absolu; I have a ~ dislike of hypocrisy j'ai horreur de l'hypocrisie. ◇ *n* *inf* -**1.** *arch* & NAUT: my hearties! les gars! -**2.** [loud person] chahuteur *m*, -euse *f*.

heat [hiːt] ◇ *n* -**1.** [gen & PHYSIOL] chaleur *f*; [of fire, sun] ardeur *f*, chaleur *f*; you should avoid excessive ~ and cold il faudrait que vous évitiez les trop grosses chaleurs et les trop grands froids; the radiator gives off a lot of ~

le radiateur chauffe bien; **you shouldn't go out in this ~** tu ne devrais pas sortir par cette chaleur; **the ~ of summer** le plus fort de l'été; **in the ~ of the day** au (moment le) plus chaud de la journée; **the ~ of the day has passed** le plus chaud de la journée est passé; **I couldn't take the ~ of the tropics** je ne pourrais pas supporter la chaleur des tropiques ❑ **if you can't stand** OR **take the ~, get out of the kitchen** que ceux qui ne sont pas contents s'en aillent; **'In The Heat of the Night'** *Jewison* 'Dans la chaleur de la nuit'. -**2.** [temperature] température *f*, chaleur *f*; **body ~** chaleur animale || CULIN: **turn up the ~** mettre le feu plus fort; **reduce the ~** réduire le feu OR la chaleur; **cook at a high/low ~** faire cuire à feu vif/doux. -**3.** [heating] chauffage *m*; **to turn the ~ on** allumer OR mettre le chauffage; **to turn off the ~** éteindre OR arrêter le chauffage; **the building was without ~ all week** l'immeuble est resté toute la semaine sans chauffage OR n'a pas été chauffé de toute la semaine. -**4.** [intensity of feeling, fervour] feu *m*, passion *f*; **she replied with (some) ~** elle a répondu avec feu OR avec passion. -**5.** [high point of activity] fièvre *f*, feu *m*; **in the ~ of argument** dans le feu de la discussion; **in the ~ of the moment she forgot herself and kissed him** dans l'agitation OR l'excitation du moment, elle l'a spontanément embrassé; **in the ~ of battle** dans le feu du combat. -**6.** *inf* [coercion, pressure]: **the mafia turned the ~ on the mayor** la mafia a fait pression sur le maire; **I'm lying low until the ~ is off** je me tiens à carreau jusqu'à ce que les choses se calment; **the new deadline took the ~ off him** le nouveau délai lui a permis de souffler un peu. -**7.** SPORT [round of contest] manche *f*; [preliminary round] (épreuve *f*) éliminatoire *f*. -**8.** ZOOL chaleur *f*, rut *m*; **on ~** *Br*, **in ~** *Am* en chaleur, en rut. -**9.** ▽ *Am* [police]: **the ~** les flics *mpl*.
◇ *vi* [food, liquid] chauffer; [air, house, room] se réchauffer.
◇ *vt* -**1.** [gen & PHYSIOL] chauffer; [overheat] échauffer; **wine ~s the blood** le vin échauffe le sang. -**2.** *fig* [inflame] échauffer, enflammer.
◆ **heat up** ◇ *vt sep* réchauffer.
◇ *vi insep* [food, liquid] chauffer; [air, house, room] se réchauffer; *fig* [situation] se dégrader, s'aggraver.

heat capacity *n* capacité *f* calorifique.

heated ['hiːtɪd] *adj* -**1.** [room, swimming pool] chauffé. -**2.** [argument, discussion] passionné; [words] vif; [person] échauffé; **he became quite ~ about it** il s'est emporté OR échauffé à ce propos; **the discussion became ~** le ton de la conversation a monté; **she made a ~ reply** elle a répondu avec emportement; **there were a few ~ exchanges** ils échangèrent quelques propos vifs.

heatedly ['hiːtɪdlɪ] *adv* [debate, talk] avec passion; [argue, deny, refuse] avec passion OR emportement, farouchement.

heater ['hiːtə^r] *n* -**1.** [for room] appareil *m* de chauffage; [for water] chauffe-eau *m inv*; [for car] (appareil de) chauffage *m*; **I turned the ~ on this morning** j'ai mis le chauffage ce matin. -**2.** ▽ *Am* [gun] flingue *m*.

heat exhaustion *n* épuisement *m* dû à la chaleur.

heath [hiːθ] *n* -**1.** [moor] lande *f*. -**2.** [plant] bruyère *f*.

heat haze *n* brume *f* de chaleur.

heathen ['hiːðn] (*pl inv* OR **heathens**) ◇ *n* [pagan] païen *m*, -enne *f*; [barbaric person] barbare *mf*.
◇ *adj* [pagan] païen; [barbaric] barbare.

heathenish ['hiːðənɪʃ] *adj pej* -**1.** [pagan - beliefs, rites] païen, barbare, idolâtre. -**2.** [barbaric] barbare, grossier.

heathenism ['hiːðənɪzm] *n* paganisme *m*.

heather ['heðə^r] *n* bruyère *f*.

heathery ['heðərɪ] *adj* de bruyère.

heathland ['hiːθlænd] *n* lande *f*.

Heath Robinson [hiːθ'rɒbɪnsn] ◇ *pr n nom évoquant une machine d'une complexité absurde (d'après le nom d'un dessinateur qui imagina de nombreux dispositifs de ce genre)*.
◇ *adj* alambiqué.

heating ['hiːtɪŋ] ◇ *n* chauffage *m*.
◇ *comp* [apparatus, appliance, system] de chauffage.

heating element *n* [burner on stove] plaque *f* chauffante; [in dishwasher, kettle] élément *m* chauffant, résistance *f*.

heating engineer *n* chauffagiste *m*.

heat loss *n* perte *f* OR déperdition *f* de chaleur.

heatproof ['hiːtpruːf] *adj* [gen] résistant à la chaleur; [dish] qui va au four.

heat rash *n* irritation *f* OR inflammation *f* due à la chaleur.

heat-resistant *adj* [gen] résistant à la chaleur, thermorésistant *spec*; [dish] qui va au four.

heat-seeking [-ˌsiːkɪŋ] *adj* [missile] thermoguidé.

heat shield *n* AERON bouclier *m* thermique.

heatstroke ['hiːtstrəʊk] *n* (*U*) coup *m* de chaleur.

heat-treat *vt* traiter par la chaleur.

heat treatment *n* traitement *m* par la chaleur, thermothérapie *f spec*.

heat wave *n* vague *f* de chaleur, canicule *f*.

heave [hiːv] (*pt & pp vt all senses + vi senses 1-3* **heaved**, *pt & pp vi sense 4* **hove** [həʊv], *cont* **heaving**) ◇ *vt* -**1.** [lift] lever OR soulever avec effort; [pull] tirer fort; [drag] traîner avec effort; **I ~d myself out of the chair** je me suis arraché OR extirpé de ma chaise. -**2.** [throw] jeter, lancer; **he ~d a rock at the bear** il a lancé une pierre sur l'ours. -**3.** *fig*: **to ~ a sigh of relief** pousser un soupir de soulagement.
◇ *vi* -**1.** [rise and fall - sea, waves, chest] se soulever; [- ship] tanguer; **his shoulders ~d with suppressed laughter** il était secoué par un rire étouffé. -**2.** [lift] lever, soulever; [pull] tirer; **~! ho! hisse!** -**3.** [retch] avoir des haut-le-cœur; [vomit] vomir; **the sight made my stomach ~** le spectacle m'a soulevé le cœur OR m'a donné des nausées. -**4.** NAUT aller, se déplacer; **the ship hove alongside the quay** le navire a accosté le quai; **to ~ into sight** OR **into view** NAUT & *fig* paraître OR poindre *lit* à l'horizon.
◇ *n* -**1.** [attempt to move]: **one more ~ and we're there** encore un coup OR un petit effort et ça y est; **I gave the rope one more ~** j'ai tiré une fois de plus sur la corde; **with a ~ he dragged the table against the door** dans un effort il traîna la table jusqu'à la porte ❑ **to give sb the ~** OR **~-ho** *inf* [subj: employer] virer qqn; [boyfriend, girlfriend] plaquer qqn. -**2.** [retching] haut-le-cœur *m inv*, nausée *f*; [vomiting] vomissement *m*.
◆ **heaves** *npl* VETER pousse *f*; **this horse has the ~s** ce cheval a la pousse OR est poussif; **John had the ~s** *inf fig* John avait des haut-le-cœur.
◆ **heave down** ◇ *vt sep* mettre OR abattre en carène, caréner.
◇ *vi insep* caréner.
◆ **heave to** ◇ *vi insep* se mettre en panne.
◇ *vt sep* mettre en panne.

heaven ['hevn] *n* -**1.** RELIG ciel *m*, paradis *m*; **to go to ~** aller au ciel, aller au OR en paradis; **in ~** au ciel, au OR en paradis; **Our Father, who art in Heaven** notre Père qui es aux cieux. -**2.** *fig*: **the Caribbean was like ~ on earth** les Caraïbes étaient un véritable paradis sur terre; **this is sheer ~!** c'est divin OR merveilleux!, c'est le paradis!; **I wish to ~ I'd never said it** comme je regrette de l'avoir dit || [in interjections]: **~ forbid!** pourvu que non!, j'espère bien que non!; **~ forbid that I should see her** que Dieu me garde de la voir; **~ help us if they catch us** que le ciel nous vienne en aide s'ils nous attrapent; **~ knows I've tried!** Dieu sait si j'ai essayé!; **she bought books, magazines and ~ knows what (else)** elle a acheté des livres, des revues et je ne sais OR Dieu sait quoi encore; **what in ~'s name is that?** au nom du ciel, qu'est-ce que c'est que ça?; **who in ~'s name told you that?** qui diable vous a dit ça?, mais qui a donc pu vous dire cela?; **good ~s!** ciel!, mon dieu!; **(good) ~s, is that the time?** mon dieu OR juste ciel, il est si tard que ça?; **for ~'s sake!** [in annoyance] mince!; [in pleading] pour l'amour du ciel! ❑ **it smells** OR **stinks to high ~ in here!** qu'est-ce que ça peut puer ici!; **she's in ~** OR **in seventh ~ when she's with him** elle est au septième ciel OR aux anges quand elle est avec lui; **to move ~ and earth to do sthg** remuer ciel et terre pour faire qqch.
◆ **heavens** *npl* [sky]: **the ~s** *lit* le ciel, le firmament *lit*; **the ~s opened** il s'est mis à pleuvoir à torrents.

heavenly ['hevnlɪ] *adj* -**1.** [of space] céleste, du ciel; [holy] divin; **Heavenly Father** Père *m* céleste. -**2.** [wonderful] divin, merveilleux.

heavenly body *n* corps *m* céleste.

heaven-sent *adj* providentiel; **a ~ opportunity** une occasion providentielle OR qui tombe à pic.

heavenward ['hevnwəd] ◇ *adv* [ascend, point] vers le ciel; [glance] au ciel.
◇ *adj* vers le ciel; **with a ~ glance** en levant les yeux au ciel.

heavenwards ['hevnwədz] *Br* = **heavenward** *adv*.

heavily ['hevɪlɪ] *adv* -**1.** [fall, land] lourdement, pesamment; [walk] d'un pas lourd OR pesant, lourdement; **she leaned ~ on my arm** elle s'appuya de tout son poids sur mon bras || *fig*: **time hangs ~ on her** elle trouve le temps long, le temps lui pèse; **it weighed ~ on my conscience** cela me pesait sur la conscience. -**2.** [laboriously - move] avec difficulté, péniblement; [- breathe] péniblement, bruyamment. -**3.** [deeply - sleep] profondément; **she left the room, sighing ~** en poussant un énorme OR gros soupir, elle a quitté la pièce. -**4.** [as intensifier - bet, drink, smoke] beaucoup; [- fine, load, tax] lourdement; [- stress] fortement, lourdement; **it was raining ~** il pleuvait des cordes; **it was snowing ~** il neigeait très fort OR dru OR à gros flocons; **they lost ~** [team] ils se sont fait écraser; [gamblers] ils ont perdu gros; **they're ~ into yoga** *inf* ils donnent à fond dans le yoga; **they're ~ dependent on foreign trade** ils sont fortement tributaires du commerce extérieur; **~ populated** très peuplé, à forte densité de population; **~ wooded** très boisé.

heavily-built *adj* solidement bâti; **a ~ man** un homme costaud OR bien charpenté.

heavily-laden *adj* lourdement chargé; **~ with books** lourdement chargé de livres.

heaviness ['hevɪnɪs] *n* -**1.** [weight - of object, physique] lourdeur *f*, pesanteur *f*, poids *m*; [- of movement, step] lourdeur, pesanteur; **a feeling of ~** une lourdeur, des lourdeurs. -**2.** [depression] abattement *m*, découragement *m*; [sadness] tristesse *f*; **~ of heart** tristesse. -**3.** [of weather] lourdeur *f*. -**4.** [of humour] manque *m* de subtilité; [of style] lourdeur *f*. -**5.** [of food] caractère *m* indigeste; **what I don't like about their cooking is its ~** ce que je n'aime pas dans leur cuisine, c'est qu'elle est lourde.

heavy ['hevɪ] (*compar* **heavier**, *superl* **heaviest**, *pl* **heavies**) ◇ *adj* -**1.** [in weight] lourd; [box, parcel] lourd, pesant; **how ~ is he?** combien pèse-t-il?; **it's too ~ for me to lift** je ne peux pas le soulever, c'est OR ça pèse trop lourd; **~ luggage** gros bagages, bagages lourds; **~ machinery** matériel *m* lourd ❑ **~ (goods) vehicle** *Br* poids *m* lourd. -**2.** [burdened, laden] chargé, lourd; **the branches were ~ with fruit** les branches étaient chargées OR lourdes de fruits; **her eyes were ~ with sleep** elle avait les yeux lourds de sommeil; **she was ~ with child** *arch* OR *lit* elle était enceinte; **~ with young** ZOOL gravide, grosse. -**3.** [in quantity - expenses, payments] important, considérable; [- fine, losses] gros, lourd; [- taxes] lourd; [- casualties, damages] énorme, important; [- crop] abondant, gros; [- dew] abondant; **she has a ~ cold** elle a un gros rhume, elle est fortement enrhumée;

there's a ~ demand for teachers il y a une forte OR grosse demande d'enseignants; her students make ~ demands on her ses étudiants sont très exigeants avec elle OR exigent beaucoup d'elle; ~ rain forte pluie; ~ seas grosse mer; ~ showers grosses OR fortes averses; ~ sleep sommeil profond OR lourd; ~ snow neige abondante, fortes chutes de neige; to be a ~ sleeper avoir le sommeil profond OR lourd; they expect ~ trading on the Stock Exchange ils s'attendent à ce que le marché soit très actif; ~ traffic circulation dense, grosse circulation. -**4.** [using large quantities]: he's a ~ drinker/smoker il boit/fume beaucoup, c'est un grand buveur/fumeur; a ~ gambler un flambeur; the car's very ~ on petrol *inf Br* la voiture consomme énormément d'essence; you've been a bit ~ on the pepper *inf* tu as eu la main un peu lourde avec le poivre. -**5.** [ponderous - movement] lourd; [- step] pesant, lourd; [- sigh] gros, profond; [- thud] gros; he was dealt a ~ blow [hit] il a reçu un coup violent; [from fate] ça a été un rude coup OR un gros choc pour lui; ~ breathing [from effort, illness] respiration *f* pénible; [from excitement] respiration haletante; ~ fighting is reported in the Gulf on signale des combats acharnés dans le Golfe; we could hear his ~ tread on the stairs nous l'entendions monter l'escalier d'un pas lourd; a ~ landing un atterrissage brutal ❑ ~ breather *personne qui donne des coups de téléphone anonymes obscènes*. -**6.** [thick - coat, sweater] gros; [- soil] lourd, gras; ~ cream *Am* CULIN crème *f* fraîche épaisse. -**7.** [person - fat] gros, corpulent; [- solid] costaud, fortement charpenté; a man of ~ build un homme solidement bâti. -**8.** [coarse, solid - line, lips] gros, épais; [thick - beard] gros, fort; ~ features gros traits, traits épais OR lourds; ~ type TYPO caractères gras. -**9.** [grave, serious - news] grave; [- responsibility] lourd; [- defeat] lourd, grave; things got a bit ~ *inf* ça commençait à tourner mal. -**10.** [depressed - mood, spirits] abattu, déprimé; with a ~ heart, ~ at heart le cœur gros. -**11.** [tiring - task] lourd, pénible; [- work] pénible; [- day, schedule, week] chargé, difficile; I've got a ~ day ahead of me j'ai une journée chargée devant moi; ~ going [in horseracing] terrain lourd; *fig*: they found it ~ going ils ont trouvé cela pénible OR difficile; the rain made the trip ~ going la pluie a rendu le voyage pénible; it was ~ going getting them to agree j'ai eu du mal à le leur faire accepter; I found his last novel very ~ going j'ai trouvé son dernier roman très indigeste. -**12.** [difficult to understand - not superficial] profond, compliqué, sérieux; [- tedious] indigeste; the report makes for ~ reading le rapport n'est pas d'une lecture facile OR est ardu. -**13.** [clumsy - humour, irony] peu subtil, lourd; [- style] lourd. -**14.** [food, meal] lourd, indigeste; [wine] corsé, lourd; these scones are a bit on the ~ side ces scones sont un peu lourds OR indigestes. -**15.** [ominous, oppressive - air, cloud, weather] lourd; [- sky] couvert, chargé, lourd; [- silence] lourd, pesant, profond; [- smell, perfume] lourd, fort; to make ~ weather of sthg se compliquer l'existence; don't make such ~ weather of it! ne te complique pas tant l'existence! -**16.** [important] important; she was getting ready for a ~ date elle se préparait pour le rendez-vous de sa vie. -**17.** [stress] accentué; [rhythm] aux accents marqués. -**18.** MIL: ~ artillery artillerie *f* lourde OR de gros calibre. -**19.** ST. EX: the market is ~ le marché est lourd OR orienté vers la baisse. -**20.** THEAT [part - difficult] lourd, difficile; [- dramatic] tragique.

◇ *adv* -**1.** [lie, weigh] lourd, lourdement; the lie weighed ~ on her conscience le mensonge pesait lourd sur sa conscience; time hangs ~ on his hands il trouve le temps long. -**2.** [harshly]: to come on ~ with sb être dur avec qqn.

◇ *n* -**1.** THEAT [serious part] rôle *m* tragique; [part of villain] rôle du traître; he usually plays the ~ d'habitude il joue des rôles de traître. -**2.** *inf* [tough guy] dur *m*; he sent round the heavies il a envoyé les brutes OR les casseurs; don't come the ~ with me ne joue pas au dur avec moi. -**3.** *inf* [boxer, wrestler] (poids *m*) lourd *m*. -**4.** MIL gros calibre *m*. -**5.** *Scot* [beer] bière *f* très alcoolisée. -**6.** *inf Br* PRESS: the heavies *les quotidiens de qualité*.

heavy-duty *adj* -**1.** [clothing, furniture] résistant; [cleanser, equipment] à usage industriel. -**2.** *inf* [serious] sérieux; we've got to do some ~ socialising nous sommes obligés d'assister à de nombreuses réceptions.

heavy-footed *adj* qui marche lourdement, au pas lourd.

heavy-handed *adj* -**1.** [clumsy - person] maladroit; [- style, writing] lourd. -**2.** [tactless - remark] qui manque de tact; [- joke] lourd, qui manque de subtilité; [- compliment] lourd, (trop) appuyé. -**3.** [harsh - person] dur, sévère; [- action, policy] arbitraire.

heavy-handedness [-ˈhændɪdnɪs] *n* -**1.** [clumsiness - of person] maladresse *f*; [- of style, writing] lourdeur *f*. -**2.** [harshness - of person] caractère *m* dur OR sévère; [- of action, policy] caractère arbitraire. -**3.** [of remark] manque *m* de tact; [of joke] manque *m* de subtilité; [of compliment] lourdeur *f*, maladresse *f*.

heavyhearted [ˌhevɪˈhɑːtɪd] *adj* abattu, découragé; she felt sad and ~ elle se sentait triste et avait le cœur gros.

heavy hydrogen *n* hydrogène *m* lourd, deutérium *m*.

heavy industry *n* industrie *f* lourde.

heavy-laden *adj* [physically] très chargé; [emotionally] accablé; ~ with worries accablé de soucis; come unto me all those who are ~ BIBLE venez à moi vous qui souffrez.

heavy metal *n* -**1.** PHYS métal *m* lourd. -**2.** MUS heavy metal *m*.

heavy mob *inf n*: the ~ les casseurs *mpl*, les durs *mpl*.

heavy oil *n* huile *f* lourde.

heavy petting [-ˈpetɪŋ] *n* *(U)* caresses *fpl* très poussées.

heavy-set *adj* [solidly built - woman] fort; [- man] bien charpenté, costaud; [fat] gros, corpulent.

heavy water *n* eau *f* lourde.

heavyweight [ˈhevɪweɪt] ◇ *n* -**1.** [large person, thing] colosse *m*; *fig inf* [important person] personne *f* de poids OR d'envergure, ponte *m*; a literary ~ un écrivain profond OR sérieux, un grand écrivain. -**2.** SPORT poids *m* lourd.

◇ *adj* -**1.** [cloth, wool] lourd; [coat, sweater] gros. -**2.** *inf fig* [important] important; a ~ industrialist un grand OR gros industriel. -**3.** SPORT [championship, fight] poids lourd; the ~ title le titre (des) poids lourds; he's a ~ fighter c'est un poids lourd.

Hebraic [hiːˈbreɪɪk] *adj* hébraïque.

Hebrew [ˈhiːbruː] ◇ *n* -**1.** [person] Hébreu *m*, Israélite *mf*; the ~s les Hébreux *mpl*; the Epistle of Paul to the ~s l'Épître de saint Paul aux Hébreux. -**2.** LING Hébreu *m*.

◇ *adj* hébreu *m only*, hébraïque.

Hebrides [ˈhebrɪdiːz] *pl pr n*: the ~ les (îles *fpl*) Hébrides; in the ~ aux Hébrides.

Hebron [ˈhebrɒn] *pr n* Hébron.

hecatomb [ˈhekətuːm] *n* hécatombe *f*.

heck *inf* [hek] ◇ *n*: that's a ~ of a lot of money! c'est une sacrée somme d'argent!; what the ~ are you doing here? qu'est-ce que tu fous là?; where the ~ did he go? où diable est-il allé?; we saw a ~ of a good film on a vu un vachement bon film; I went just for the ~ of it j'y suis allé, histoire de rire OR de rigoler; oh, what the ~! et puis flûte!

◇ *interj* zut, flûte.

heckle [ˈhekl] ◇ *vt* [interrupt] interrompre bruyamment; [shout at] interpeller, harceler.

◇ *vi* crier *(pour gêner un orateur)*.

heckler [ˈheklər] *n* chahuteur *m*, -euse *f*.

heckling [ˈheklɪŋ] ◇ *n* *(U)* harcèlement *m*, interpellations *fpl*.

◇ *adj* qui fait du harcèlement, qui interpelle.

hectare [ˈhekteər] *n* hectare *m*.

hectic [ˈhektɪk] *adj* -**1.** [turbulent] agité, bousculé; [eventful] mouvementé; I've had a ~ day j'ai eu une journée mouvementée, j'ai été bousculé toute la journée; we spent three ~ weeks preparing the play ç'a été la course folle pendant les trois semaines où on préparait la pièce; they lead a ~ life [busy] ils mènent une vie trépidante; [eventful] ils mènent une vie très mouvementée. -**2.** [flushed] fiévreux; MED [fever, flush] hectique.

hectically [ˈhektɪklɪ] *adv* fiévreusement.

hectogram(me) [ˈhektəgræm] *n* hectogramme *m*.

hectolitre *Br*, **hectoliter** *Am* [ˈhektəˌliːtər] *n* hectolitre *m*.

hector [ˈhektər] ◇ *vt* harceler, tyranniser.

◇ *vi* être tyrannique, être une brute.

◇ *n* brute *f*, tyran *m*.

◆ **Hector** *pr n* Hector.

hectoring [ˈhektərɪŋ] ◇ *n* *(U)* harcèlement *m*, torture *f*.

◇ *adj* [behaviour] tyrannique; [tone, voice] impérieux, autoritaire.

he'd [hiːd] = **he had, he would**.

hedge [hedʒ] ◇ *n* -**1.** [shrubs] haie *f*; hawthorn ~ haie d'aubépine. -**2.** *fig* [protection] sauvegarde *f*; a ~ against inflation une sauvegarde OR une couverture contre l'inflation. -**3.** [statement] déclaration *f* évasive.

◇ *comp* [clippers, saw] à haie.

◇ *vt* -**1.** [enclose] entourer d'une haie, enclore; the field was ~d with beech le champ était entouré d'une haie de hêtres. -**2.** [guard against losing] couvrir; to ~ one's bets se couvrir.

◇ *vi* -**1.** [plant] planter une haie; [trim] tailler une haie. -**2.** [in action] essayer de gagner du temps, atermoyer; they are hedging slightly on the trade agreement ils essaient de gagner du temps avant de conclure l'accord commercial || [in answering] éviter de répondre, répondre à côté; [in explaining] expliquer avec des détours; stop hedging! dis-le franchement!, au fait! -**3.** [protect] se protéger; it's a way of hedging against inflation c'est un moyen de vous protéger OR vous couvrir contre l'inflation.

◆ **hedge about** *Br*, **hedge around** *vt sep* entourer; the offer was ~d about with conditions *fig* l'offre était assortie de conditions.

◆ **hedge in** *vt sep* entourer d'une haie, enclore; ~d in by restrictions *fig* assorti de restrictions; I'm feeling ~d in je ne me sens pas libre.

◆ **hedge off** *vt sep* [area] entourer d'une haie; [part of area] séparer par une haie.

hedgehog [ˈhedʒhɒg] *n* hérisson *m*.

hedgehop [ˈhedʒhɒp] (*pt* & *pp* **hedgehopped**, *cont* **hedgehopping**) *vi* voler en rase-mottes, faire du rase-mottes.

hedgehopper [ˈhedʒhɒpər] *n* [pilot] pilote *m* qui vole en rase-mottes; [aeroplane] avion *m* qui fait du rase-mottes.

hedgerow [ˈhedʒrəʊ] *n* haies *fpl*.

hedge sparrow *n* (accenteur *m*) mouchet *m*.

hedonism [ˈhiːdənɪzm] *n* hédonisme *m*.

hedonist [ˈhiːdənɪst] *n* hédoniste *mf*.

hedonistic [ˌhiːdəˈnɪstɪk] *adj* hédoniste.

heebie-jeebies *inf* [ˌhiːbɪˈdʒiːbɪz] *npl*: to have the ~ avoir la frousse OR les chocottes; the film gave me the ~ [revulsion] le film m'a donné la chair de poule; [fright] le film m'a donné la trouille OR la frousse; he gives me the ~ il me met mal à l'aise.

heed [hiːd] ◇ *n*: to take ~ of sthg, to pay OR to give ~ to sthg tenir bien compte de qqch; he pays little ~ to criticism il ne se soucie guère OR il ne fait pas grand cas des critiques; I took no ~ of her advice je n'ai pas écouté OR je n'ai tenu aucun compte de ses conseils; pay no ~ to him ne faites pas attention à lui; take ~! prenez garde!

◇ *vt* -**1.** [warning, words] faire bien attention à, tenir compte de, prendre garde à. -**2.** [person - listen to] bien écouter; [- obey] obéir à.

heedful [ˈhiːdfʊl] *adj* attentif; she's ~ of the importance of secrecy elle est consciente qu'il est important de garder le secret; they seemed ~ of what they were doing ils semblaient attentifs à ce qu'ils faisaient.

heedless ['hiːdlɪs] *adj*: ~ of: ~ of the danger sans se soucier du danger; ~ of my warning sans tenir compte de mon avertissement; she seemed ~ of what was going on around her elle ne semblait pas prêter attention à ce qui se passait autour d'elle.

heedlessly ['hiːdlɪslɪ] *adv* -**1.** [without thinking] sans faire attention, à la légère. -**2.** [inconsiderately] avec insouciance, négligemment.

hee-haw [ˌhiː'hɔː] ◇ *n* -**1.** [of donkey] hi-han *m*. -**2.** [guffaw] gros rire *m*.
◇ *vi* -**1.** [donkey] braire, faire hi-han. -**2.** [person] rire bruyamment.
◇ *interj* hi-han.

heel [hiːl] ◇ *n* -**1.** ANAT talon *m*; she spun OR turned on her ~ and walked away elle a tourné les talons; under the ~ of fascism *fig* sous le joug OR la botte du fascisme ❑ we followed hard on her ~s [walked] nous lui emboîtâmes le pas; [tracked] nous étions sur ses talons; famine followed hard on the ~s of drought la sécheresse fut suivie de près par la famine; he brought the dog to ~ il a fait venir le chien à ses pieds; to bring sb to ~ mettre qqn au pas; to take to one's ~s, to show a clean pair of ~s se sauver à toutes jambes, prendre ses jambes à son cou. -**2.** [of shoe] talon *m*. -**3.** [of glove, golf club, hand, knife, sock, tool] talon *m*. -**4.** [of bread] talon *m*, croûton *m*; [of cheese] talon *m*, croûte *f*. -**5.** ▽ *dated* [contemptible man] salaud *m*. -**6.** NAUT [of keel] talon *m*; [of mast] caisse *f*. -**7.** [incline - of ship] bande *f*; [- of vehicle, tower] inclinaison *f*.
◇ *vt* -**1.** [boot, shoe] refaire le talon de. -**2.** SPORT [ball] talonner.
◇ *vi* -**1.** [to dog]: ~! au pied! -**2.** [ship] gîter, donner de la bande; [vehicle, tower] s'incliner, se pencher.
◆ **heel over** *vi insep* [ship] gîter, donner de la bande; [vehicle, tower] s'incliner, se pencher; [cyclist] se pencher.

heel-and-toe ◇ *adj* -**1.** [walking]: ~ walking *façon de marcher où le talon d'un pied est posé avant que les doigts de l'autre pied quittent le sol*. -**2.** [driving]: ~ driving *façon de conduire utilisant le talon et les orteils du même pied pour actionner l'accélérateur et le frein*.
◇ *vi* AUT *conduire en se servant du talon et des orteils du même pied pour appuyer sur l'accélérateur et le frein*.

heel bar *n* talon-minute *m*, réparations-minute *fpl*.

heels [hiːlz] = **high heels**.

heft *inf* [heft] ◇ *n* -**1.** [weight] poids *m*. -**2.** *Am* [main part] gros *m*.
◇ *vt* -**1.** [lift] soulever; [hoist] hisser. -**2.** [test weight of] soupeser.

hefty *inf* ['heftɪ] (*compar* **heftier**, *superl* **heftiest**) *adj* -**1.** [package - heavy] lourd; [- bulky] encombrant, volumineux; [book] épais, gros; [person] costaud. -**2.** [part, profit] gros; a ~ sum une jolie somme; he paid a ~ price for them il les a payés drôlement cher; she earns a ~ salary elle se fait une bonne OR sacrée paie. -**3.** [blow, slap] puissant.

Hegelian [heɪ'giːljən] *adj* hégélien.

hegemony [hɪ'gemənɪ] *n* hégémonie *f*.

Hegira, Hejira ['hedʒɪrə] *n* hégire *f*.

heifer ['hefəʳ] *n* génisse *f*.

heigh-ho ['heɪ'həʊ] *interj* -**1.** [weariness] eh bien; [sadness] hélas. -**2.** *dated* & *lit* [of surprise] ça alors, ça par exemple; [of happiness] chouette alors.

height [haɪt] *n* -**1.** [tallness - of person] taille *f*, grandeur *f*; [- of building, tree] hauteur *f*; what ~ are you? combien mesurez-vous?; ~: 1 m 80 [on form] taille: 1 m 80; I'm of average ~ je suis de taille moyenne; redwoods grow to a ~ of 100 metres les séquoias peuvent atteindre 100 mètres (de haut). -**2.** [distance above ground - of mountain, plane] altitude *f*; [- of ceiling, river, stars] hauteur *f*; to be at a ~ of 3 metres above the ground être à 3 mètres au-dessus du sol ❑ ~ of land *Am* ligne *f* de partage des eaux. -**3.** [high position] hauteur *f*; to fall from a great ~ tomber de haut; the ~s GEOG les hauteurs; fear of ~s [gen] vertige *m*; MED acrophobie *f*; I'm afraid of ~s j'ai le vertige; to reach new ~s *fig* augmenter encore ❑ 'Wuthering Heights' *Emily Brontë* 'les Hauts de Hurlevent'. -**4.** *fig* [peak - of career, success] point *m* culminant; [- of fortune, fame] apogée *m*; [- of arrogance, stupidity] comble *m*; at the ~ of her powers en pleine possession de ses moyens; at its ~ the group had 300 members à son apogée, le groupe comprenait 300 membres; the tourist season is at its ~ la saison touristique bat son plein; at the ~ of summer en plein été, au plus chaud de l'été; at the ~ of the battle/storm au plus fort de la bataille/de l'orage; to dress in the ~ of fashion s'habiller à la dernière mode; it's the ~ of fashion c'est le dernier cri.

heighten ['haɪtn] ◇ *vt* -**1.** [make higher - building, ceiling, shelf] relever, rehausser. -**2.** [increase - effect, fear, pleasure] augmenter, intensifier; [- flavour] relever; MED [fever] faire monter, aggraver; the incident has ~ed public awareness of environmental problems l'incident a sensibilisé encore plus le public aux problèmes de l'environnement; the colour ~ed the deathly pallor of her skin cette couleur faisait ressortir OR accentuait sa pâleur cadavérique.
◇ *vi* [fear, pleasure] augmenter, monter.

heightened ['haɪtnd] *adj* -**1.** [building, ceiling, shelf] relevé, rehaussé. -**2.** [fear, pleasure] intensifié; [colour] plus vif.

heightening ['haɪtnɪŋ] *n* -**1.** [of building, ceiling] rehaussement *m*, surélévation *f*. -**2.** [of fear, pleasure] accroissement *m*, intensification *f*.

heinie▽ ['hiːnɪ] *n Am* fesses *fpl*.

heinous ['heɪnəs] *adj lit* OR *fml* odieux, atroce; a ~ crime un crime abominable OR odieux.

heir [eəʳ] *n* [gen] héritier *m*; JUR héritier *m*, légataire *mf*; he is ~ to a vast fortune il est l'héritier d'une immense fortune; the ~ to the throne l'héritier du trône OR de la couronne ❑ ~ apparent JUR héritier *m* présomptif; ~ at law, rightful ~ JUR héritier légitime OR naturel; ~ presumptive JUR héritier présomptif *(sauf naissance d'un héritier en ligne directe)*.

heiress ['eərɪs] *n* héritière *f*.

heirloom ['eəluːm] *n* -**1.** [family property] objet *m* de famille; a family ~ un objet de famille. -**2.** JUR [legacy] legs *m*.

heist *inf* [haɪst] *Am* ◇ *n* [robbery] vol *m*; [in bank] braquage *m*; [stolen objects] butin *m*.
◇ *vt* [steal] voler; [commit armed robbery] braquer.

held [held] *pt* & *pp* → **hold**.

Helen ['helɪn] *pr n* [of Troy] Hélène.

helical ['helɪkl] *adj* hélicoïdal.

helical gear *n* engrenage *m* hélicoïdal.

helicoid(al) ['helɪkɔɪd(l)] ◇ *adj* [gen] hélicoïdal; GEOM hélicoïde.
◇ *n* hélicoïde *m*.

helicopter ['helɪkɒptəʳ] ◇ *n* hélicoptère *m*; the wounded were transported by ~ les blessés on été héliportés.
◇ *vt* transporter en hélicoptère; they managed to ~ in provisions ils ont réussi à amener des provisions par hélicoptère.
◇ *vi* voyager en hélicoptère.
◇ *comp* [patrol, rescue] en hélicoptère; [pilot] d'hélicoptère; ~ transfer OR transport héliportage *m*.

helidrome ['helɪdrəʊm] *n* hélidrome *m*.

heliocentric [ˌhiːlɪəʊ'sentrɪk] *adj* héliocentrique.

heliograph ['hiːlɪəʊgrɑːf] ◇ *n* -**1.** [transmitter] héliographe *m*. -**2.** [camera] photohéliographe *m*.
◇ *vt* transmettre par héliographe.

heliometer [ˌhiːlɪ'ɒmɪtəʳ] *n* héliomètre *m*.

Helios ['hiːlɪɒs] *pr n* Hélios.

heliostat ['hiːlɪəʊstæt] *n* héliostat *m*.

heliotrope ['heljətrəʊp] ◇ *n* -**1.** BOT héliotrope *m*. -**2.** [colour] violet *m* clair.
◇ *adj* violet clair.

heliotropism [ˌhiːlɪəʊ'trəʊpɪzm] *n* héliotropisme *m*.

helipad ['helɪpæd] *n* héliport *m*.

heliport ['helɪpɔːt] *n* héliport *m*.

helistop ['helɪstɒp] *n* héliport *m*.

helium ['hiːlɪəm] *n* hélium *m*.

helix ['hiːlɪks] (*pl* **helices** ['helɪsiːz] OR **helixes**) *n* -**1.** ARCHIT & GEOM [spiral] hélice *f*. -**2.** ANAT & ZOOL hélix *m*.

hell [hel] *n* -**1.** RELIG enfer *m*; MYTH [underworld] les enfers; to go to ~ [Christianity] aller en enfer; MYTH descendre aux enfers ❑ it's (as) hot as ~ in there il fait une chaleur de tous les diables OR infernale là-dedans; go to ~! *inf* va te faire voir!; to ~ with society! *inf* au diable la société!; to ~ with what they think! *inf* leur avis, je m'assois dessus!; come ~ or high water *inf* contre vents et marées, envers et contre tout; when ~ freezes over à la saint-glinglin; it'll be a cold day in ~ before I apologize je m'excuserai quand les poules auront des dents; it was the journey from ~ *inf* ce voyage, c'était l'horreur; all ~ broke loose *inf* ça a bardé; to give sb ~ *inf* passer un savon OR faire sa fête à qqn; give them ~! *inf* rentre-leur dedans!, fais-leur en baver!; the damp weather plays ~ with my arthritis *inf* ce temps humide me fait rudement souffrir de mon arthrite!, par ces temps humides, qu'est-ce que je déguste avec mon arthrite!; there'll be ~ to pay when he finds out *inf* ça va barder OR chauffer quand il l'apprendra; they went into town to raise (a little) ~ *inf* ils sont allés faire la bringue en ville; the boss raised ~ when he saw the report *inf* le patron a fait une scène de tous les diables en voyant le rapport; I went along just for the ~ of it *inf* j'y suis allé histoire de rire OR de rigoler; he ran off ~ for leather *inf* il est parti ventre à terre; to ride ~ for leather aller au triple galop OR à bride abattue; ~'s bells!, ~'s teeth! *inf* mince alors! -**2.** [torture] enfer *m*; it's ~ in here c'est infernal ici; working there was ~ on earth c'était l'enfer de travailler là-bas; he made her life ~ il lui a fait mener une vie infernale. -**3.** *inf* [used as emphasis]: it's colder/hotter than ~ il fait vachement froid/chaud; he's as happy/tired as ~ il est vachement heureux/fatigué; the government is in a ~ of a mess le gouvernement est dans un sacré pétrin; a ~ of a wind un vent du diable OR de tous les diables; a ~ of a lot of books tout un tas OR un paquet de livres; we had a ~ of a good time nous nous sommes amusés comme des fous; they had a ~ of a time getting the car started ils en ont bavé pour faire démarrer la voiture; my arm started to hurt like ~ mon bras a commencé à me faire vachement mal; he worked like ~ il a travaillé comme une brute OR une bête; to run/to shout like ~ courir/crier comme un fou; will you lend me £50? – like ~ I will! peux-tu me prêter 50 livres? – tu peux toujours courir!; I'm leaving – like ~ you are! je pars – n'y compte pas!; I just hope to ~ he leaves j'espère de tout mon cœur qu'il partira; get the ~ out of here! fous OR fous-moi le camp!; what the ~ are you doing? qu'est-ce que tu fous?; why the ~ did you go? qu'est-ce qui t'a pris d'y aller?; how the ~ would I know? comment veux-tu que je le sache?; where the ~ are my keys? où diable sont mes clefs?; who the ~ do you think you are? mais tu te prends pour qui?; oh well, what the ~! oh qu'est-ce que ça peut bien faire?; did you agree? – ~, no! as-tu accepté? – tu plaisantes! -**4.** *inf Am* [high spirits]: there's ~ in that boy ce garçon respire la joie de vivre; full of ~ plein d'entrain OR de vivacité.
◆ **Hell** = **hell 1**.

he'll [hiːl] = **he will**.

hell-bent *inf adj* acharné; he's ~ on going il veut à tout prix y aller, il veut y aller coûte que coûte; society seems ~ on self-destruction la société semble décidée à aller tout droit à sa propre destruction.

hellcat ['helkæt] *n* harpie *f*, mégère *f*.

hellebore ['helɪbɔːʳ] *n* ellébore *m*.

Hellene ['heliːn] *n* Hellène *mf*.

Hellenic [he'liːnɪk] ◇ *adj* hellène, hellénique.
◇ *n* langue *f* hellénique.

hellfire ['helfaɪəʳ] ◇ *n literal* feu *m* de l'enfer; *fig* [punishment] châtiment *m* divin.
◇ *interj inf*: ~! bon sang!, sacré nom de Dieu!
◇ *comp*: ~ **preacher** prédicateur *m*.

hellhole *inf* ['helhəʊl] *n* bouge *m*.

hellhound ['helhaʊnd] *n literal* chien *m* des Enfers; *fig* [fiend] monstre *m*, démon *m*.

hellion *inf* ['heljən] *n Am* [child] galopin *m*, polisson *m*, -onne *f*; [adult] chahuteur *m*, trublion *m*.

hellish ['helɪʃ] ◇ *adj* -1. [cruel - action, person] diabolique. -2. *inf* [dreadful] infernal; **she's had a pretty ~ life** elle a eu une vie absolument infernale, sa vie a été un véritable enfer.
◇ *adv inf* = **hellishly**.

hellishly *inf* ['helɪʃlɪ] *adv Br* atrocement, épouvantablement.

hello [hə'ləʊ] (*pl* hellos) ◇ *interj* -1. [greeting] bonjour, salut; [in the evening] bonsoir; [on answering telephone] allô. -2. [to attract attention] hé, ohé. -3. [in surprise] tiens.
◇ *n* [greeting] bonjour *m*, salutation *f*; **he gave me a cheery ~** il m'a salué joyeusement OR avec entrain; **say ~ to the lady** dis bonjour à la dame; **he asked me to say ~ to you** il m'a demandé de vous donner le bonjour.

Hell's Angels *pl pr n nom d'un groupe de motards au comportement violent.*

helluva *inf* ['heləvə] *adj*: **a ~ noise** un sacré boucan; **a ~ wind** un de ces vents; **a ~ lot of money** un paquet de fric; **a ~ lot of kids** des tas d'enfants; **he's a ~ guy** c'est un type vachement bien; **I had a ~ time** [awful] je me suis emmerdé; [wonderful] je me suis vachement marré; **they had a ~ time convincing her** ils ont eu vachement de mal à la convaincre.

helm [helm] ◇ *n* -1. NAUT barre *f*, gouvernail *m*; **to be at the ~** *literal* tenir la barre OR le gouvernail; *fig* tenir la barre OR les rênes; **to take the ~** *literal & fig* prendre la barre, prendre la direction des opérations; **he's at the ~ of the company now** c'est lui qui dirige la société maintenant. -2. *arch* [helmet] casque *m*.
◇ *vt* -1. NAUT gouverner, barrer; *fig* diriger. -2. *arch* [supply with helmet] coiffer d'un casque.

helmet ['helmɪt] *n* [gen] casque *m*; [medieval] heaume *m*.

helmeted ['helmɪtɪd] *adj* casqué, portant un casque.

helmsman ['helmzmən] (*pl* helmsmen [-mən]) *n* timonier *m*, homme *m* de barre.

helot ['helət] *n* ilote *mf*.

help [help] ◇ *vt* -1. [assist, aid - gen] aider, venir en aide à; [- elderly, poor, wounded] secourir, venir en aide à; **come and ~ me** viens m'aider; **can I ~ you with the dishes?** puis-je t'aider à faire la vaisselle?; **they got their neighbours to ~ them move** ils se sont fait aider par leurs voisins pour le déménagement; **they ~ one another take care of the children** ils s'entraident pour s'occuper des enfants; **we want to ~ poorer countries to ~ themselves** nous voulons aider les pays sous-développés à devenir autonomes OR à se prendre en main; **he ~ed me on/off with my coat** il m'a aidé à mettre/enlever mon manteau; **she ~ed the old man to his feet/across the street** elle a aidé le vieux monsieur à se lever/à traverser la rue; **let me ~ you up/down** laissez-moi vous aider à monter/descendre; **it might ~ if you took more exercise** ça irait peut-être mieux si tu faisais un peu plus d'exercice ❑ **so ~ me God!** je le jure devant Dieu!; **I'll get you for this, so ~ me** *inf* j'aurai ta peau, je le jure!; **God ~s those who ~ themselves** *prov* aide-toi, le ciel t'aidera *prov*. -2. [contribute to] contribuer à; [encourage] encourager, favoriser; **the rain ~ed firefighters to bring the flames under control** la pluie a permis aux pompiers de maîtriser l'incendie. -3. [remedy - situation] améliorer; [- pain] soulager; **it ~ed to ease my headache** cela a soulagé mon mal de tête; **to ~ matters, it started to pour with rain** *iron* pour tout arranger, il s'est mis à pleuvoir des cordes; **crying won't ~ anyone** cela ne sert à rien OR n'arrange rien de pleurer. -4. [serve] servir; **she ~ed me to more rice** elle m'a servi du riz une deuxième fois; **I ~ed myself to the cheese** je me suis servi en fromage; **~ yourself!** servez-vous!; **they ~ed themselves to more meat** ils ont repris de la viande; **he ~ed himself to the petty cash** *euph* il a pioché OR il s'est servi dans la caisse. -5. (*with can, usu neg*) [avoid, refrain from]: **I can't ~ thinking that we could have done more** je ne peux pas m'empêcher de penser qu'on aurait pu faire plus; **we couldn't ~ laughing** OR **but laugh** nous ne pouvions pas nous empêcher de rire; **I tried not to laugh but I couldn't ~ myself** j'essayais de ne pas rire mais c'était plus fort que moi; **she never writes any more than she can ~** elle ne se foule pas pour écrire, elle écrit un minimum de lettres OR le moins possible. -6. (*with can, usu neg*) [control]: **he can't ~ it if she doesn't like it** il n'y est pour rien OR ce n'est pas de sa faute si cela ne lui plaît pas; **can he ~ it if the train is late?** est-ce que c'est de sa faute si le train est en retard?; **she can't ~ her temper** elle ne peut rien à ses colères; **I can't ~ it** je n'y peux rien, ce n'est pas de ma faute; **it can't be ~ed** tant pis! on n'y peut rien OR on ne peut pas faire autrement; **are they coming? — not if I can ~ it!** est-ce qu'ils viennent? — pas si j'ai mon mot à dire!
◇ *vi* être utile; **she ~s a lot around the house** elle se rend très utile à la maison, elle rend souvent service à la maison; **is there anything I can do to ~?** puis-je être utile?; **losing your temper isn't going to ~** ça ne sert à rien OR n'arrange rien de perdre ton calme; **every little bit ~s** les petits ruisseaux font les grandes rivières *prov*; **every penny ~s** il n'y a pas de petites économies.
◇ *n* -1. [gen] aide *f*, assistance *f*; [to drowning or wounded person] secours *m*, assistance *f*; **thank you for your ~** merci de votre aide; **can I be of any ~?** puis-je faire quelque chose pour vous?, puis-je vous rendre service?; **we're happy to have been of ~** nous sommes contents d'avoir pu rendre service; **he went to get ~** il est allé chercher du secours; **we yelled for ~** nous avons crié au secours; **we moved house with the ~ of a neighbour** nous avons déménagé avec l'aide d'un voisin; **he opened the window with the ~ of a crowbar** il a ouvert la fenêtre à l'aide d'un levier; **she did it without any ~** elle l'a fait toute seule; **I could never have done it without your ~** jamais je n'aurais pu le faire sans vous OR votre aide; **she needs ~ going upstairs** il faut qu'elle se fasse aider pour OR elle a besoin qu'on l'aide à monter l'escalier; **the situation is now beyond ~** la situation est désespérée OR irrémédiable maintenant; **there's no ~ for it** on n'y peut rien. -2. [something that assists] aide *f*, secours *m*; **you've been a great ~** vous m'avez été d'un grand secours, vous m'avez beaucoup aidé; **he's a great ~!** *iron* il est d'un précieux secours *iron*. -3. (*U*) *Am* [employees] personnel *m*, employés *mpl*; **it's hard to get good ~** il est difficile de trouver des employés sérieux; '**~ wanted**' 'cherchons employés'. -4. [domestic aid] femme *f* de ménage.
◇ *interj*: ~! [in distress] au secours!, à l'aide!; [in dismay] zut!, mince!

◆ **help along** *vt sep* [person] aider à marcher OR avancer; [plan, project] faire avancer.

◆ **help out** ◇ *vt sep* [gen] aider, venir en aide à; [with supplies, money] dépanner; **the scholarship really ~ed her out** la bourse lui a été d'un grand secours; **she ~s us out in the shop from time to time** elle vient nous donner un coup de main au magasin de temps en temps; **they ~ each other out** ils s'entraident; **she ~s him out with his homework** elle l'aide à faire ses devoirs.
◇ *vi insep* aider, donner un coup de main.

helper ['helpəʳ] *n* -1. [gen] aide *mf*, assistant *m*, -e *f*; [professional] auxiliaire *mf*. -2. *Am* [home help] femme *f* de ménage.

helpful ['helpfʊl] *adj* -1. [person] obligeant, serviable; **his secretary was very ~** sa secrétaire nous a été très utile OR nous a été d'un grand secours. -2. [advice, suggestion] utile; [gadget, information, map] utile; [medication] efficace, salutaire; **it's often ~ to talk to your doctor about it** il peut s'avérer utile d'en parler à votre médecin; **this book isn't very ~** ce livre ne sert pas à grand-chose; **~ hints** conseils utiles.

helpfully ['helpfʊlɪ] *adv* avec obligeance, obligeamment.

helpfulness ['helpfʊlnɪs] *n* -1. [of person] obligeance *f*, serviabilité *f*. -2. [of gadget, map etc] utilité *f*.

helping ['helpɪŋ] *n* portion *f*; **to ask for a second ~** demander à en reprendre; **who's for a second ~?** qui en reprend?; **he had four ~s** il en a repris trois fois.

helping hand *n* main *f* secourable; **to give** OR **lend (sb) a ~** donner un coup de main OR prêter main-forte (à qqn).

helpless ['helplɪs] *adj* -1. [vulnerable] désarmé, sans défense; **~ children** des enfants sans défense. -2. [physically] faible, impotent; [mentally] impuissant; **he lay ~ on the ground** il était allongé par terre sans pouvoir bouger. -3. [powerless - person] impuissant, sans ressource; [- anger, feeling] impuissant; [- situation] sans recours, désespéré; **he gave me a ~ look** il m'a jeté un regard désespéré; **he was ~ to stop her leaving** il était incapable de l'empêcher de partir; **I feel so ~** je ne sais vraiment pas quoi faire, je me sens vraiment désarmé; **I'm ~ in the matter** je n'y peux rien; **they were ~ with laughter** ils n'en pouvaient plus de rire, ils étaient morts de rire.

helplessly ['helplɪslɪ] *adv* -1. [without protection] sans défense, sans ressource. -2. [unable to react] sans pouvoir réagir; [argue, struggle, try] en vain; **he looked on ~** il a regardé sans pouvoir intervenir; **she was lying ~ on the floor** elle était allongée par terre sans pouvoir bouger; **she smiled ~** elle a eu un sourire où se lisait son impuissance; **"I don't know what to say" he said ~** «je ne sais pas quoi vous dire» dit-il d'un ton où se sentait OR qui trahissait son impuissance; **they giggled ~** ils n'ont pas pu s'empêcher de glousser.

helplessness ['helplɪsnɪs] *n* -1. [defencelessness] incapacité *f* de se défendre, vulnérabilité *f*. -2. [physical] incapacité *f*, impotence *f*; [mental] incapacité. -3. [powerlessness - of person] impuissance *f*, manque *m* de moyens; [- of anger, feeling] impuissance *f*; **a feeling of ~** un sentiment d'impuissance.

helpline ['helplaɪn] *n* service *m* d'assistance téléphonique; **AIDS ~** SOS SIDA.

helpmate ['helpmeɪt] *n* [companion] compagnon *m*, compagne *f*; [helper] aide *mf*, assistant *m*, -e *f*; [spouse] époux *m*, épouse *f*.

helpmeet ['helpmiːt] *arch* = **helpmate**.

Helsinki ['helsɪŋkɪ] *pr n* Helsinki.

helter-skelter [,heltə'skeltəʳ] ◇ *adv* [run, rush] en désordre, à la débandade; [organize, throw] pêle-mêle, en vrac.
◇ *adj* [rush] à la débandade; [account, story] désordonné.
◇ *n Br* [ride in fairground] toboggan *m*.

Helvetia [hel'viːʃjə] *pr n* Suisse *f*, Helvétie *f*.

Helvetian [hel'viːʃjən] ◇ *n* Suisse *m*, Suissesse *f*; **the ~s** les Suisses *mpl*, les Helvètes *mpl*.
◇ *adj* suisse, helvétique; HIST helvète.

hem [hem] (*pt & pp* **hemmed**, *cont* **hemming**) ◇ *n* -1. [of trousers, skirt] ourlet *m*; [of handkerchief, sheet] bord *m*, ourlet *m*; **she let the ~ down on her skirt** elle a défait l'ourlet pour rallonger OR elle a rallongé sa jupe; **your ~'s coming down** ton ourlet s'est défait OR dé

cousu. -**2.** [hemline] (bas *m* de l') ourlet *m*. -**3.** METALL ourlet *m*.
◇ *vt* ourler, faire l'ourlet de.
◇ *interj*: ~! [to call attention] hem!; [to indicate hesitation, pause] euh!
◇ *vi* faire hem; to ~ and haw bafouiller; he hemmed and hawed before getting to the point il a bafouillé OR hésité avant d'en venir au fait.
◆ **hem about** *vt sep* entourer, encercler; hemmed about by trees entouré d'arbres.
◆ **hem in** *vt sep* [house, people] entourer, encercler; [enemy] cerner; he felt hemmed in [in room] il faisait de la claustrophobie, il se sentait oppressé; [in relationship] il se sentait prisonnier OR pris au piège; hemmed in by rules *fig* entravé par des règles OR règlements.

he-man *inf* ['hi:mæn] *n* homme *m* viril; he thinks he's a real ~ il se croit viril.

hematological *Am* = **haematological**.

hematologist *Am* = **haematologist**.

hematology *Am* = **haematology**.

hemicycle ['hemɪˌsaɪkl] *n* hémicycle *m*.

hemidemisemiquaver ['hemɪˌdemɪ'semɪˌkweɪvəʳ] *n Br* quadruple croche *f*.

hemiplegia [ˌhemɪ'pli:dʒɪə] *n* hémiplégie *f*.

hemiplegic [ˌhemɪ'pli:dʒɪk] ◇ *adj* hémiplégique.
◇ *n* hémiplégique *mf*.

hemisphere ['hemɪˌsfɪəʳ] *n* hémisphère *m*.

hemispheric(al) [ˌhemɪ'sferɪk(l)] *adj* hémisphérique.

hemistich ['hemɪstɪk] *n* hémistiche *m*.

hemline ['hemlaɪn] *n* (bas *m* de l') ourlet *m*; ~s are going up les jupes vont raccourcir.

hemlock ['hemlɒk] *n* -**1.** [poison & BOT] ciguë *f*. -**2.** = **hemlock spruce**.

hemlock spruce *n* sapin *m* du Canada, sapin-ciguë *m*.

hemoglobin *Am* = **haemoglobin**.

hemophilia *Am* = **haemophilia**.

hemorrhage *Am* = **haemorrhage**.

hemorrhoids *Am* = **haemorrhoids**.

hemp [hemp] *n* -**1.** [fibre, plant] chanvre *m*. -**2.** [marijuana] marijuana *f*; [hash] haschisch *m*, hachisch *m*.

hemstitch ['hemstɪtʃ] ◇ *n* [stitch] jour *m*; a row of ~ un jour.
◇ *vt* ourler à jour.

hen [hen] *n* -**1.** [chicken] poule *f*. -**2.** [female] femelle *f*; ~ bird oiseau *m* femelle; ~ lobster homard *m* femelle; ~ pheasant poule *f* faisane. -**3.** *inf* [woman] mémère *f*. -**4.** *inf Scot dial* [term of address]: hello, ~ bonjour, ma poule OR cocotte.

henbane ['henbeɪn] *n* jusquiame *f* (noire), herbe *f* à poules.

hence [hens] *adv* -**1.** [therefore] donc, d'où; they are cheaper and ~ more popular ils sont moins chers et donc plus demandés; he was born on Christmas Day, ~ the name Noël il est né le jour de Noël, d'où son nom. -**2.** *fml* [from this time] d'ici; three days ~ dans OR d'ici trois jours. -**3.** *fml* [from here] d'ici; 5 kilometres ~ à 5 kilomètres d'ici; (get thee) ~! *arch* OR *hum* hors d'ici OR de ma vue!

henceforward [ˌhens'fɔ:wəd], **henceforth** [ˌhens'fɔ:θ] *adv* dorénavant, désormais.

henchman ['hentʃmən] (*pl* henchmen [-mən]) *n* -**1.** [follower] partisan *m*, adepte *m pej*; [right-hand man] homme *m* de main, suppôt *m pej*. -**2.** [squire, page] écuyer *m*.

hen coop *n* mue *f*, cage *f* à poules.

hen house *n* poulailler *m*.

Henley ['henlɪ] *pr n ville dans le Oxfordshire*; ~ Regatta *importante épreuve internationale d'aviron*.

HENLEY REGATTA:
Cette compétition, qui a lieu chaque année sur la Tamise à Henley, au mois de juin, est une manifestation autant mondaine que sportive.

---

henna ['henə] ◇ *n* henné *m*.
◇ *vt* teindre au henné.

hennaed ['henəd] *adj* teint au henné.

hen party, hen night *inf n* [gen] soirée *f* entre copines; [before wedding]: she's having a ~ elle enterre sa vie de célibataire.

henpecked ['henpekt] *adj* dominé; a ~ husband un mari dominé par sa femme; he's very ~ sa femme le mène par le bout du nez.

henry ['henrɪ] (*pl* henrys OR henries) *n* ELEC henry *m*.

Henry ['henrɪ] *pr n* Henri.

hep *inf* [hep] (*compar* hepper, *superl* heppest) *adj dated* dans le coup; he's ~ to your plan il est au courant de tes projets.

hepatic [hɪ'pætɪk] *adj* hépatique.

hepatitis [ˌhepə'taɪtɪs] *n* *(U)* hépatite *f*; infectious ~ hépatite A OR infectieuse; serum ~ hépatite B OR sérique.

hepcat *inf* ['hepkæt] *n dated* jeune homme *m* dans le vent, jeune femme *f* dans le vent.

heptagon ['heptəgən] *n* heptagone *m*.

heptagonal [hep'tægənl] *adj* heptagonal.

heptameter [hep'tæmɪtəʳ] *n* heptamètre *m*.

heptane ['hepteɪn] *n* heptane *m*.

heptathlon [hep'tæθlɒn] *n* heptathlon *m*.

her [hɜ:ʳ] ◇ *det* son *m*, sa *f*, ses *mfpl*; ~ book son livre; ~ secretary sa secrétaire; ~ glasses ses lunettes; ~ university son université; she has broken ~ arm/~ leg elle s'est cassé le bras/la jambe.
◇ *pron* -**1.** [direct object - unstressed] la, l' *(before vowel)*; [- stressed] elle; I recognize ~ je la reconnais; I heard ~ je l'ai entendue; why did you have to choose HER? pourquoi l'as-tu choisie elle? -**2.** [indirect object - unstressed] lui; [- stressed] à elle; give ~ the money donne-lui l'argent; he only told ~, no-one else il ne l'a dit qu'à elle, c'est tout; why do they always give HER the interesting jobs? pourquoi est-ce que c'est toujours à elle qu'on donne le travail intéressant? -**3.** [after preposition] elle; I was in front of ~ j'étais devant elle; as rich as/richer than ~ aussi riche/plus riche qu'elle; she closed the door behind ~ elle a fermé la porte derrière elle. -**4.** [with 'to be']: it's ~ c'est elle; if I were ~ si j'étais elle, si j'étais à sa place. -**5.** *fml* [with relative pronoun] celle; (to) ~ whom we adore (à) celle que nous adorons.

Hera ['hɪərə] *pr n* Héra.

Heracles ['herəkli:z] *pr n* Héraclès.

Heraclitus [ˌherə'klaɪtəs] *pr n* Héraclite.

Heraklion [hɪ'ræklɪən] *pr n* Héraklion.

herald ['herəld] ◇ *vt* -**1.** [announce] annoncer, proclamer; his rise to power ~ed a new era son ascension au pouvoir a annoncé une nouvelle ère. -**2.** [hail] acclamer.
◇ *n* -**1.** [medieval messenger] héraut *m*; the ~ of morn *lit* le messager de l'aube. -**2.** [forerunner] héraut *m*, avant-coureur *m*.

heraldic [he'rældɪk] *adj* héraldique.

heraldry ['herəldrɪ] *n* -**1.** [system, study] héraldique *f*. -**2.** [coat of arms] blason *m*. -**3.** [pageantry] faste *m*, pompe *f* (héraldique).

herb [hɜ:b, *Am* ɜ:rb] *n* -**1.** BOT & CULIN herbe *f*; ~s CULIN fines herbes, herbes aromatiques; medicinal ~s herbes médicinales OR officinales, simples *mpl*. -**2.** *inf* [marijuana] herbe *f*.

herbaceous [hɜ:'beɪʃəs, *Am* ɜ:r'beɪʃəs] *adj* [plant, stem] herbacé.

herbaceous border *n* bordure *f* de plantes herbacées.

herbage ['hɜ:bɪdʒ, *Am* 'ɜ:rbɪdʒ] *n (U)* [herbaceous plants] plantes *fpl* herbacées, herbages *mpl*; [vegetation] herbage *m*.

herbal ['hɜ:bl, *Am* 'ɜ:rbl] ◇ *adj* aux herbes; ~ tea tisane *f*; ~ medicine [practice] phytothérapie *f*; [medication] médicament *m* à base de plantes.
◇ *n* traité *m* sur les plantes, herbier *m arch*.

herbalist ['hɜ:bəlɪst, *Am* 'ɜ:rbəlɪst] *n* herboriste *mf*.

herbarium [hɜ:'beərɪəm, *Am* ɜ:r'beərɪəm] (*pl* herbaria [-rɪə]) *n* herbier *m (collection)*.

herb garden *n* jardin *m* d'herbes aromatiques.

herbicide ['hɜ:bɪsaɪd, *Am* 'ɜ:rbɪsaɪd] *n* herbicide *m*.

herbivore ['hɜ:bɪvɔ:ʳ, *Am* 'ɜ:rbɪvɔ:ʳ] *n* herbivore *m*.

herbivorous [hɜ:'bɪvərəs, *Am* ɜ:r'bɪvərəs] *adj* herbivore.

herculean, Herculean [ˌhɜ:kjʊ'li:ən] *adj* herculéen; a ~ task un travail de Titan OR herculéen.

Hercules ['hɜ:kjʊli:z] *pr n* Hercule; he's a veritable ~ *fig* c'est un vrai OR véritable hercule.

herd [hɜ:d] ◇ *n* -**1.** [of cattle, goats, sheep] troupeau *m*; [of wild animals] troupe *f*; [of horses] troupe *f*, bande *f*; [of deer] harde *f*. -**2.** *inf* [of people] troupeau *m pej*, foule *f*; the ~ *pej* le peuple, la populace. -**3.** *arch* OR *dial* [herdsman] gardien *m* de troupeau, pâtre *m lit*.
◇ *vt* -**1.** [bring together] rassembler (en troupeau); [look after] garder. -**2.** [drive] mener, conduire; he ~ed the students back into the classroom il a reconduit les élèves dans la salle de cours.
◇ *vi* s'assembler en troupeau, s'attrouper.
◆ **herd together** ◇ *vi insep* s'assembler en troupeau, s'attrouper.
◇ *vt sep* rassembler en troupeau.
◆ **herd up** *vt sep* rassembler en troupeau.

herd instinct *n* instinct *m* grégaire.

herdsman ['hɜ:dzmən] (*pl* herdsmen [-mən]) *n* [gen] gardien *m* de troupeau; [of cattle] vacher *m*, bouvier *m*; [of sheep] berger *m*.

here [hɪəʳ] ◇ *adv* -**1.** [at, in this place]: she left ~ yesterday elle est partie d'ici hier; I've lived ~ for two years ça fait deux ans que j'habite ici, j'habite ici depuis deux ans; is Susan ~? est-ce que Susan est là?; he won't be ~ next week il ne sera pas là la semaine prochaine; they're ~ [I've found them] ils sont ici; [they've arrived] ils sont arrivés; winter is ~ c'est l'hiver, l'hiver est arrivé; the miniskirt is ~ to stay la minijupe n'est pas près de disparaître; where do I switch on the light? — ~ où est l'interrupteur? — ici; sign ~ signez ici; it is a question ~ of finances il s'agit ici d'argent; '~ lies Tom Smith' 'ci-gît Tom Smith' ‖ *(after preposition)*: around ~ par ici; it's 2 km from ~ c'est à 2 km d'ici; from ~ to ~ d'ici jusqu'ici; bring them in ~ apportez-les (par) ici; I'm in ~ je suis là OR ici; they're over ~ ils sont ici; where are you? — over ~! où êtes-vous? — (par) ici!; the water came up to ~ l'eau est montée jusqu'ici ❑ I've had it up to ~ j'en ai jusque là; ~ today, gone tomorrow tout passe; any money he gets is ~ today and gone tomorrow tout l'argent qu'il gagne disparaît au fur et à mesure. -**2.** [drawing attention to sthg] voici; ~'s the key! voilà la clef!; ~ they come! les voilà!; ~'s a man who knows what he wants voilà un homme qui sait ce qu'il veut; ~ we are in San Francisco nous voici à San Francisco; have you got the paper? — ~ you are vous avez le journal? — le voilà ❑ ~ goes *inf*, ~ goes nothing *inf Am* allons-y!; ~ we go! [excitedly] c'est parti!; [wearily] et voilà, c'est reparti!; ~ we go again! ça y est, c'est reparti pour un tour! -**3.** [emphasizing specified object, person etc]: ask the lady ~ demandez à cette dame ici; it's this one ~ that I want c'est celui-ci que je veux; my friend ~ saw it mon ami (que voici) l'a vu; this ~ book *inf* [that I am pointing to] ce livre-ci; this ~ book you've all been talking about *inf* ce bouquin dont vous n'arrêtez pas de parler tous. -**4.** [at this point] maintenant; [at that point] alors, à ce moment-là; ~ I should like to remind you... maintenant je voudrais vous rappeler...; ~ she paused à ce moment-là, elle s'est arrêtée. -**5.** *phr*: ~'s to [in toasts] à; ~'s to the newlyweds! aux nouveaux mariés!; ~'s to your exams! à tes examens!; ~'s to us! à nous!, à nos amours!
◇ *interj* -**1.** [present]: Alex Perrin? — ~! Alex Perrin? — présent!; Emma Lindsay? ~! Emma Lindsay? — présente! -**2.** [giving, taking etc]: ~! tiens!, tenez!; ~, give me that! tiens, donne-moi ça! -**3.** [protesting]: ~! what do you think

you're doing? hé! qu'est-ce que tu fais?; ~, I never said that! mais dites donc, je n'ai jamais dit ça!

◆ **here and now** *adv phr* sur-le-champ; *(as noun)*: the ~ and now le présent.

◆ **here and there** *adv phr* ça et là; the paintwork needs retouching ~ and there la peinture a besoin d'être refaite par endroits.

◆ **here, there and everywhere** *adv phr hum* un peu partout; her things were scattered ~, there and everywhere ses affaires étaient éparpillées un peu partout.

hereabouts ['hɪərə,baʊts] *Br*, **hereabout** ['hɪərə,baʊt] *Am adv* par ici, près d'ici, dans les environs; it must be somewhere ~ ça doit être quelque part par ici.

hereafter [,hɪər'ɑːftəʳ] ◇ *n* -**1.** [life after death] au-delà *m inv*; in the ~ dans l'autre monde. -**2.** *lit* [future] avenir *m*, futur *m*.
◇ *adv* -**1.** *fml* & JUR [in document] ci-après. -**2.** *lit* [after death] dans l'au-delà. -**3.** *lit* [in the future] désormais, dorénavant.

hereby [,hɪə'baɪ] *adv fml* & JUR [in statement] par la présente (déclaration); [in document] par le présent (document); [in letter] par la présente; [in act] par le présent acte, par ce geste; [in will] par le présent testament; I ~ declare you man and wife en vertu des pouvoirs qui me sont conférés, je vous déclare mari et femme.

hereditament [,herɪ'dɪtəmənt] *n tout bien qui peut être transmis par héritage*.

hereditary [hɪ'redɪtrɪ] *adj* héréditaire.

heredity [hɪ'redətɪ] *n* hérédité *f*.

herein [,hɪər'ɪn] *adv fml* -**1.** [in this respect] en ceci, en cela. -**2.** JUR [in this document] ci-inclus.

hereinafter [,hɪərɪn'ɑːftəʳ] *adv fml* ci-après; JUR ci-après, dans la suite des présentes.

hereof [,hɪər'ɒv] *adv fml* de ceci, de cela; JUR des présentes.

hereon [,hɪər'ɒn] *adv fml* sur ce, là-dessus.

heresy ['herəsɪ] (*pl* heresies) *n* hérésie *f*; an act of ~ une hérésie.

heretic ['herətɪk] *n* hérétique *mf*.

heretical [hɪ'retɪkl] *adj* hérétique.

hereto [,hɪə'tuː] *adv fml* à ceci, à cela; JUR aux présentes.

heretofore [,hɪətʊ'fɔːʳ] *adv fml* jusqu'ici, auparavant; JUR ci-devant.

hereunder [,hɪər'ʌndəʳ] *adv fml* & JUR -**1.** [hereafter] ci-après. -**2.** [under the authority of this] selon les modalités de ceci OR des présentes.

hereupon [,hɪərə'pɒn] *adv fml* -**1.** [immediately following] sur ce, là-dessus. -**2.** [on this point] sur ce point, là-dessus.

herewith [,hɪə'wɪð] *adv fml* -**1.** [enclosed] ci-joint, ci-inclus; I enclose my curriculum vitae ~ veuillez trouver ci-joint mon curriculum vitae. -**2.** = **hereby**.

heritable ['herɪtəbl] *adj* JUR [property] dont on peut hériter; [person] qui peut hériter.

heritage ['herɪtɪdʒ] *n* héritage *m*, patrimoine *m*; the national ~ le patrimoine national.

hermaphrodite [hɜː'mæfrədaɪt] ◇ *adj* hermaphrodite.
◇ *n* hermaphrodite *m*.

hermaphroditism [hɜː'mæfrədaɪtɪzm] *n* hermaphrodisme *m*.

hermeneutic(al) [,hɜːmə'njuːtɪk(l)] *adj* herméneutique.

hermeneutics [,hɜːmə'njuːtɪks] *n (U)* herméneutique *f*.

Hermes ['hɜːmiːz] *pr n* Hermès.

hermetic [hɜː'metɪk] *adj* hermétique.

hermetically [hɜː'metɪkəlɪ] *adv* hermétiquement.

Hermione [hɜː'maɪənɪ] *pr n* Hermione.

hermit ['hɜːmɪt] *n* [gen] ermite *m*, solitaire *m*; RELIG ermite *m*.

hermitage ['hɜːmɪtɪdʒ] *n* ermitage *m*.

hermit crab *n* bernard-l'ermite *m inv*, pagure *m*.

hernia ['hɜːnɪə] (*pl* hernias OR herniae [-nɪiː]) *n* hernie *f*.

herniated ['hɜːnɪeɪtɪd] *adj* hernié.

hero ['hɪərəʊ] (*pl* heroes) *n* -**1.** [person] héros *m*. -**2.** *Am* [sandwich] *sorte de gros sandwich*.

◆ **Hero** *pr n* Héro.

Herod ['herəd] *pr n* Hérode.

Herodias [he'rəʊdɪæs] *pr n* Hérodiade.

Herodotus [hɪ'rɒdətəs] *pr n* Hérodote.

heroic(al) [hɪ'rəʊɪk(l)] *adj* -**1.** [act, behaviour, person] héroïque. -**2.** *lit* épique, héroïque.

heroically [hɪ'rəʊɪklɪ] *adv* héroïquement.

heroic couplet *n* distique *m* héroïque.

heroics [hɪ'rəʊɪks] *npl* -**1.** [language] emphase *f*, déclamation *f*; [behaviour] affectation *f*, emphase *f*; none of your ~ inutile de chercher à nous impressionner. -**2.** LITERAT [heroic verse] (vers *m*) héroïques *m*.

heroic stanza *n* quatrain *m* en vers croisés.

heroic verse *n (U)* vers *m* héroïque, (vers *m*) décasyllabe *m*.

heroin ['herəʊɪn] ◇ *n* héroïne *f*.
◇ *comp*: ~ addict OR user héroïnomane *mf*; ~ addiction héroïnomanie *f*.

heroine ['herəʊɪn] *n* héroïne *f (femme)*.

heroism ['herəʊɪzm] *n* héroïsme *m*.

heron ['herən] (*pl inv* OR herons) *n* héron *m*.

hero worship *n* [admiration] adulation *f*, culte *m* (du héros); ANTIQ culte *m* des héros.

◆ **hero-worship** *vt* aduler, idolâtrer.

hero-worshipper *n personne qui voue une admiration excessive aux idoles*.

herpes ['hɜːpiːz] *n (U)* herpès *m*; to have ~ avoir de l'herpès.

herpes simplex *n (U)* herpès *m*.

herring ['herɪŋ] (*pl inv* OR herrings) ◇ *n* hareng *m*; pickled ~ rollmops *m inv*.
◇ *comp*: ~ boat harenguier *m*.

herringbone ['herɪŋbəʊn] ◇ *n* -**1.** [bone] arête *f* de hareng. -**2.** TEX [pattern] (dessin *m* à) chevrons *mpl*; [fabric] tissu *m* à chevrons. -**3.** CONSTR appareil *m* en épi. -**4.** [in skiing] montée *f* en ciseaux OR en pas de canard.
◇ *comp*: ~ tweed tweed *m* à chevrons.
◇ *vt* -**1.** SEW & TEX faire au point d'épine (en chevron). -**2.** ARCHIT faire un appareil en épi.
◇ *vi* monter en ciseaux OR en pas de canard.

herringbone stitch *n* point *m* d'épine (en chevron).

herring gull *n* goéland *m* argenté.

hers [hɜːz] *pron* -**1.** [gen] le sien *m*, la sienne *f*, les siens *mpl*, les siennes *fpl*; this is my book, ~ is over there ça, c'est mon livre, le sien est là-bas; this car is ~ cette voiture lui appartient OR est à elle; ~ was the best photograph sa photographie était la meilleure; most speeches lasted 10 minutes, but ~ lasted half an hour la plupart des gens ont fait un discours de 10 minutes, mais le sien a duré une demi-heure; ~ is not an easy task elle n'a pas la tâche facile. -**2.** [after preposition]: she took his hand in ~ elle a pris sa main dans la sienne; he's an old friend of ~ c'est un vieil ami à elle, c'est un de ses vieux amis; no suggestion of ~ could possibly interest him aucune suggestion venant d'elle ne risquait de l'intéresser; when's that book of ~ coming out? quand est-ce qu'il sort, son livre?; I blame that husband of hers *pej* moi je dis que c'est de la faute de son sacré mari; I can't stand that boyfriend/dog of ~ je ne supporte pas son copain/chien; that (dreadful) voice of ~ sa voix (insupportable); that (dreadful) habit of ~ cette habitude (insupportable) qu'elle a. -**3.** [indicating authorship] d'elle; are these paintings ~? ces tableaux sont-ils d'elle?

herself [hɜː'self] *pron* -**1.** [reflexive form] se, s' *(before vowel)*; she introduced ~ elle s'est présentée; she bought ~ a car elle s'est acheté une voiture; she considers ~ lucky elle considère qu'elle a de la chance. -**2.** [emphatic form] elle-même; she built the shelves ~ elle a monté les étagères elle-même; I spoke with the teacher ~ j'ai parlé au professeur en personne. -**3.** [with preposition] elle; she took it upon ~ to tell us elle a pris sur elle de nous le dire; she has a room to ~ elle a sa propre chambre OR sa chambre à elle; the old woman was talking t[o] ~ la vieille femme parlait toute seule; "that's odd", she thought to ~ «c'est bizarre», s[e] dit-elle; she did it all by ~ elle l'a fait tout[e] seule. -**4.** [her usual self]: she isn't quite ~ ell[e] n'est pas dans son état habituel; she's feeling more ~ now elle va mieux maintenant.

Herts *written abbr of* Hertfordshire.

hertz [hɜːts] (*pl inv*) *n* hertz *m*.

hertzian, Hertzian ['hɜːtsɪən] *adj* hertzien.

hertzian wave, Hertzian wave *n* onde hertzienne.

he's [hiːz] = **he is, he has**.

hesitance ['hezɪtəns], **hesitancy** ['hezɪtənsɪ] *n* hésitation *f*, indécision *f*.

hesitant ['hezɪtənt] *adj* -**1.** [person - uncertain] hésitant, indécis; [- cautious] réticent; I'm ~ about sending her to a new school j'hésite à l'envoyer dans une nouvelle école. -**2.** [attempt, speech, voice] hésitant.

hesitantly ['hezɪtəntlɪ] *adv* [act, try] avec hésitation, timidement; [answer, speak] d'une voix hésitante.

hesitate ['hezɪteɪt] *vi* hésiter; don't ~ to call me n'hésitez pas à m'appeler; she wrote to them after hesitating for some time elle leur a écrit après avoir longuement hésité; he will ~ at nothing il ne recule devant rien, rien ne l'arrête ❑ he who ~s is lost *prov* un moment d'hésitation peut coûter cher.

hesitation [,hezɪ'teɪʃn] *n* hésitation *f*; after much ~ après bien des hésitations, après avoir longuement hésité; she answered with some ~ elle a répondu d'une voix hésitante; I would have no ~ in recommending him for promotion je n'hésiterais pas à le recommander pour de l'avancement; she accepted without a moment's ~ elle a accepté sans la moindre hésitation.

Hesperides [he'sperɪdiːz] *pl pr n*: the ~ les Hespérides.

Hesperus ['hespərəs] *pr n* [evening star] étoile *f* du berger; [Venus] Vénus.

Hesse [hes] *pr n* Hesse *f*.

hessian ['hesɪən] ◇ *n* (toile *f* de) jute *m*.
◇ *comp* [fabric, sack] de jute.

het[▽] [het] ◇ *adj* hétéro.
◇ *n* hétéro *mf*.

hetero *inf* ['hetərəʊ] (*pl* heteros) ◇ *adj* hétéro.
◇ *n* hétéro *mf*.

heteroclite ['hetərəklaɪt] ◇ *adj* hétéroclite.
◇ *n* mot *m* hétéroclite.

heterodox ['hetərədɒks] *adj* hétérodoxe.

heterodoxy ['hetərədɒksɪ] *n* hétérodoxie *f*.

heterodyne ['hetərədaɪn] ◇ *adj* hétérodyne.
◇ *n* hétérodyne *f*.

heterogeneous [,hetərə'dʒiːnjəs] *adj* hétérogène.

heteromorphic [,hetərə'mɔːfɪk], **heteromorphous** [,hetərə'mɔːfəs] *adj* hétéromorphe.

heteronym ['hetərənɪm] *n* homographe *m* à prononciation différente.

heterosexual [,hetərə'sekʃʊəl] ◇ *adj* hétérosexuel.
◇ *n* hétérosexuel *m*, -elle *f*.

heterosexuality ['hetərə,sekʃʊ'ælətɪ] *n* hétérosexualité *f*.

het up *inf adj* [angry] énervé; [excited] excité, agité; to get all ~ (about sthg) se mettre dans tous ses états OR s'énerver (pour qqch).

heuristic [hjʊə'rɪstɪk] *adj* heuristique.

heuristics [hjʊə'rɪstɪks] *n (U)* heuristique *f*.

hew [hjuː] (*pt* hewed, *pp* hewed OR hewn [hjuːn]) ◇ *vt* [wood] couper; [stone] tailler; [coal] abattre; to ~ away OR off a branch élaguer une branche; to ~ down a tree abattre un arbre; they ~ed a path through the undergrowth ils se sont taillé OR frayé un chemin à travers le sous-bois (à coups de hache); he ~ed a statue out of the marble il a taillé une statue dans le marbre.
◇ *vi* -**1.** [strike with blows] frapper (à coups de

hache). -**2.** *Am* [conform] se conformer; they ~ed to the company line ils se sont pliés à la politique de la société.

HEW (*abbr of* (Department of) Health, Education and Welfare) *pr n ancien ministère américain de l'Éducation et de la Santé publique*.

hewer ['hjuːəʳ] *n* [of tree] abatteur *m*; [of stone, wood] tailleur *m*; [of coal] haveur *m*.

hex [heks] *Am* ◇ *n* -**1.** [spell] sort *m*, sortilège *m*; to put a ~ on sb jeter un sort à qqn. -**2.** [witch] sorcière *f*.
◇ *vt* jeter un sort à.

hexachlorophene [,heksə'klɔːrəfiːn] *n* hexachlorophène *m*.

hexachord ['heksəkɔːd] *n* hexacorde *m*.

hexadecimal (notation) [,heksə'desɪml-] *n* COMPUT codes *mpl* hexadécimaux, notation *f* hexadécimale.

hexagon ['heksəgən] *n* hexagone *m*.

hexagonal [hek'sægənl] *adj* hexagonal.

hexahedron [,heksə'hedrən] (*pl* **hexahedrons** OR **hexahedra** [-drə]) *n* hexaèdre *m*.

hexameter [hek'sæmɪtəʳ] *n* hexamètre *m*.

hexapod ['heksəpɒd] *n* hexapode *m*.

hey [heɪ] *interj*: ~! [to draw attention] hé!, ohé!; [to show surprise] tiens!; ~ presto! [magician] passez muscade!, et hop!

heyday ['heɪdeɪ] *n* [of cinema, movement] âge *m* d'or, beaux jours *mpl*; [of nation, organization] zénith *m*, apogée *m*; in her ~ [youth] quand elle était dans la force de l'âge; [success] à l'apogée de sa gloire, au temps de sa splendeur; Hollywood in its ~ l'âge d'or d'Hollywood; the ~ of British theatre l'âge d'or du théâtre britannique.

Hezekiah [,hezɪ'kaɪə] *pr n* Ézéchias.

HF (*abbr of* high frequency) HF.

HGV (*abbr of* heavy goods vehicle) *n Br* PL *m*; an ~ licence un permis PL.

hi *inf* [haɪ] *interj* -**1.** [hello] salut. -**2.** [hey] hé, ohé.

HI *written abbr of* Hawaii.

hiatus [haɪ'eɪtəs] (*pl inv* OR **hiatuses**) *n* ANAT, LING & LITERAT hiatus *m*; [in manuscript] lacune *f*; [break, interruption] pause *f*, interruption *f*.

hiatus hernia *n* hernie *f* hiatale.

hibernal [haɪ'bɜːnl] *adj* hibernal.

hibernate ['haɪbəneɪt] *vi* hiberner.

hibernation [,haɪbə'neɪʃn] *n* hibernation *f*.

Hibernian [haɪ'bɜːnjən] ◇ *adj* irlandais.
◇ *n* Irlandais *m*, -e *f*.

hibiscus [hɪ'bɪskəs] *n* hibiscus *m*.

hiccough ['hɪkʌp], **hiccup** ['hɪkʌp] ◇ *n* -**1.** [sound] hoquet *m*; to have (the) ~s avoir le hoquet; it gave me the ~s cela m'a donné le hoquet. -**2.** [problem] contretemps *m*.
◇ *vi* hoqueter.

hick *inf* [hɪk] *Am* ◇ *n* péquenaud *m*, -e *f*, plouc *mf*.
◇ *adj* de péquenaud; ~ town bled *m pej*.

hickey *inf* ['hɪkɪ] *n Am* -**1.** [gadget] bidule *m*. -**2.** [lovebite] suçon *m*.

hickory ['hɪkərɪ] (*pl* **hickories**) ◇ *n* [tree] hickory *m*, noyer *m* blanc d'Amérique; [wood] (bois *m* de) hickory.
◇ *comp* en (bois de) hickory; a ~ table une table en hickory; ~ nut fruit *m* du hickory, noix *f* d'Amérique.

hid [hɪd] *pt* → **hide**.

hidden ['hɪdn] ◇ *pp* → **hide**.
◇ *adj* caché; ~ from sight à l'abri des regards indiscrets, caché; a village ~ away in the mountains un village caché OR niché dans les montagnes; a ~ meaning un sens caché; she has ~ talents elle a des talents cachés; a ~ agenda un plan secret ❑ ~ tax impôt *m* indirect OR déguisé.

hide [haɪd] (*pt* hid [hɪd], *pp* hidden ['hɪdn]) ◇ *vt* -**1.** [conceal - person, thing] cacher; [- disappointment, dismay, fright] dissimuler; to ~ sthg from sb [ball, letter] cacher qqch à qqn; [emotion] dissimuler qqch à qqn; we have nothing to ~ nous n'avons rien à cacher OR à dissimuler; the boy hid himself behind the door le garçon s'est caché derrière la porte; she hid her face elle s'est caché le visage; he hid it from sight il l'a dissimulé OR l'a dérobé aux regards ❑ to ~ one's light under a bushel cacher ses talents; she doesn't ~ her light under a bushel ce n'est pas la modestie qui l'étouffe. -**2.** [keep secret] taire, dissimuler; to ~ the truth (from sb) taire OR dissimuler la vérité (à qqn).
◇ *vi* se cacher; he's hiding from the police il se cache de la police; the ambassador hid behind his diplomatic immunity *fig* l'ambassadeur s'est réfugié derrière son immunité diplomatique.
◇ *n* -**1.** *Br* cachette *f*; [in hunting] affût *m*. -**2.** [animal skin - raw] peau *f*; [- tanned] cuir *m*. -**3.** *fig inf* [of person] peau *f*; I'll have your ~ for that tu vas me le payer cher ❑ I haven't seen ~ nor hair of them je n'ai eu aucune nouvelle d'eux.
◇ *adj* de OR en cuir.
◆ **hide away** ◇ *vi insep* se cacher; to ~ away (from sb/sthg) se cacher (de qqn/qqch).
◇ *vt sep* cacher.
◆ **hide out** *vi insep* se tenir caché; he's hiding out from the police il se cache de la police.

hide-and-seek *n* cache-cache *m*; to play (at) ~ jouer à cache-cache.

hideaway ['haɪdəweɪ] *n* cachette *f*.

hidebound ['haɪdbaʊnd] *adj* [person] obtus, borné; [attitude, view] borné, rigide.

hideous ['hɪdɪəs] *adj* -**1.** [physically ugly] hideux, affreux. -**2.** [ghastly - conditions, situation] atroce, abominable.

hideously ['hɪdɪəslɪ] *adv* -**1.** [deformed, wounded] hideusement, atrocement, affreusement. -**2.** *fig* [as intensifier] terriblement, horriblement; ~ expensive horriblement cher.

hideout ['haɪdaʊt] *n* cachette *f*.

hidey-hole *inf* ['haɪdɪhəʊl] *n* planque *f*.

hiding ['haɪdɪŋ] *n* -**1.** [concealment]: to be in ~ se tenir caché; to go into ~ [criminal] se cacher, se planquer; [spy, terrorist] entrer dans la clandestinité. -**2.** *inf* [thrashing] rossée *f*; to give sb a good ~ donner une bonne raclée à qqn. -**3.** [defeat] raclée *f*, dérouillée *f*; they got a good ~ in the election ils ont pris une raclée aux élections. -**4.** *Br phr*: to be on a ~ to nothing être voué à l'échec.

hiding place *n* cachette *f*.

hidy-hole *inf* ['haɪdɪhəʊl] = **hidey-hole**.

hie [haɪ] (*cont* **hieing** OR **hying**) *arch* OR *hum*
◇ *vi* se hâter, se presser.
◇ *vt* hâter, presser; ~ thee hence! hors d'ici!

hierarchic(al) [,haɪə'rɑːkɪk(l)] *adj* hiérarchique.

hierarchically [,haɪə'rɑːkɪklɪ] *adv* hiérarchiquement.

hierarchy ['haɪərɑːkɪ] (*pl* **hierarchies**) *n* -**1.** [organization into grades] hiérarchie *f*; [of animals, plants] classification *f*, classement *m*. -**2.** [upper levels of authority] dirigeants *mpl*, autorités *fpl*.

hieratic [,haɪə'rætɪk] *adj* hiératique.

hieroglyph ['haɪərəglɪf] *n* hiéroglyphe *m*.

hieroglyphic [,haɪərə'glɪfɪk] ◇ *adj* hiéroglyphique.
◇ *n* hiéroglyphe *m*.

hieroglyphics [,haɪərə'glɪfɪks] *npl* écriture *f* hiéroglyphique.

hi-fi *inf* ['haɪfaɪ] (*abbr of* high fidelity) ◇ *n* -**1.** *(U)* hi-fi *f inv*. -**2.** [stereo system] chaîne *f* (hi-fi); [radio] radio *f* (hi-fi).
◇ *comp* [equipment, recording, system] hi-fi *(inv)*; a ~ set OR system une chaîne (hi-fi).

higgledy-piggledy *inf* [,hɪgldɪ'pɪgldɪ] ◇ *adv* pêle-mêle, en désordre.
◇ *adj* en désordre, pêle-mêle.

high [haɪ] ◇ *adj* -**1.** [tall] haut; how ~ is that building? quelle est la hauteur de ce bâtiment?; the walls are three metres ~ les murs ont OR font trois mètres de haut, les murs sont hauts de trois mètres; the building is eight storeys ~ c'est un immeuble de OR à huit étages; when I was only so ~ quand je n'étais pas plus grand que ça. -**2.** [above ground level - river, tide] haut; [- altitude, shelf] haut, élevé; the sun was ~ in the sky le soleil était haut. -**3.** [greater than normal - number] grand, élevé; [- speed, value] grand; [- cost, price, rate] élevé; [- salary] élevé, gros; [- pressure] élevé, haut; [- polish] brillant; to the ~est degree au plus haut degré, à l'extrême; she suffers from ~ blood pressure elle a de la tension; the equipment is built to withstand ~ temperatures le matériel est conçu pour résister à des températures élevées; he has a ~ temperature il a beaucoup de température OR fièvre; he paid a ~ price for refusing *fig* il a payé cher le fait d'avoir refusé; areas of ~ unemployment des régions à fort taux de chômage; milk is ~ in calcium le lait contient beaucoup de calcium; ~ winds des vents violents, de grands vents; the ~est common factor MATH le plus grand facteur commun. -**4.** [good, better than average - quality] grand, haut; [- standard] haut, élevé; [- mark, score] élevé, bon; [- reputation] bon; ~-quality goods articles de qualité supérieure OR de première qualité; our chances of success remain ~ nos chances de succès restent très bonnes; to have a ~ opinion of sb avoir une bonne OR haute opinion de qqn; he has a ~ opinion of himself il a une haute idée de lui-même; she speaks of you in the ~est terms elle dit beaucoup de bien OR le plus grand bien de vous; one of the ~est honours in the arts l'un des plus grands honneurs dans le monde des arts. -**5.** [honourable - ideal, thought] noble, élevé; [- character] noble; a man of ~ principles un homme qui a des principes (élevés); he took a very ~ moral tone il prit un ton très moralisateur. -**6.** [of great importance or rank] haut, important; a ~ official un haut fonctionnaire; we have it on the ~est authority nous le tenons de la source la plus sûre; to have friends in ~ places avoir des relations haut placées, avoir le bras long; of ~ rank de haut rang. -**7.** [sound, voice] aigu; MUS [note] haut. -**8.** [at peak, zenith]: ~ summer plein été *m*; it was ~ summer c'était au cœur de l'été OR en plein été; it's ~ time we were leaving il est grand temps qu'on parte ❑ the High Middle Ages le Haut Moyen Âge. -**9.** [intensely emotional]: resentment was ~ il y avait énormément de ressentiment; moments of ~ drama des moments extrêmement dramatiques; ~ adventure grande aventure; ~ tragedy THEAT grande tragédie. -**10.** *Br* [complexion] rougeaud, rubicond; to have a ~ colour être haut en couleur. -**11.** [elaborate, formal - language, style] élevé, soutenu; ~ register language langage élevé OR soutenu. -**12.** [prominent - cheekbones] saillant. -**13.** CARDS haut; the ~est card la carte maîtresse. -**14.** *Br* [meat] avancé, faisandé; [butter, cheese] rance. -**15.** [remote] haut; High Antiquity Haute Antiquité. -**16.** GEOG [latitude] haut. -**17.** [conservative]: a ~ Tory un tory ultra-conservateur; a ~ Anglican un anglican de tendance conservatrice. -**18.** LING [vowel] fermé. -**19.** [excited] excité, énervé; [cheerful] plein d'entrain, enjoué; spirits are ~ amongst the staff la bonne humeur règne parmi le personnel; we had a ~ old time *dated* on s'est amusés comme des fous. -**20.** *inf* [drunk] parti, éméché; he gets ~ on sailing *fig* il prend son pied en faisant de la voile; they were feeling (as) ~ as kites [drunk] ils étaient bien partis; [drugged] ils planaient; [happy] ils avaient la pêche.
◇ *adv* -**1.** [at, to a height] haut, en haut; [at a great altitude] à haute altitude, à une altitude élevée; up ~ en haut; ~er up plus haut; ~er and ~er de plus en plus haut; he raised both hands ~ il a levé les deux mains en l'air; the kite flew ~ up in the sky le cerf-volant est monté très haut dans le ciel; she threw the ball ~ into the air elle a lancé le ballon très haut; the geese flew ~ over the fields les oies volaient très haut au-dessus des champs; the shelf was ~ above her head l'étagère était bien au-dessus de sa tête; he rose ~ in the company

il a accédé aux plus hauts échelons de la société || *fig*: **we looked ~ and low for him** nous l'avons cherché partout; **to set one's sights ~**, **to aim ~** viser haut; **they're flying ~** ils visent haut, ils voient grand ❑ **to hold one's head ~** *literal & fig* porter la tête haute; **to leave sb ~ and dry** laisser qqn en plan. -**2.** [at, to a greater degree than normal] haut; **they set the price/standards too ~** ils ont fixé un prix/niveau trop élevé; **I turned the heating up ~** j'ai mis le chauffage à fond; **he rose ~er in my esteem** il est monté encore plus dans mon estime; **salaries can go as ~ as £30,000** les salaires peuvent monter jusqu'à OR atteindre 30 000 livres; **I had to go as ~ as £50** il a fallu que j'aille OR que je monte jusqu'à 50 livres; **the card players played ~** les joueurs de cartes ont joué gros (jeu); **to run ~** [river] être en crue; [sea] être houleuse OR grosse; **feelings were running ~** les esprits se sont échauffés. -**3.** *inf Am phr*: **to live ~ off** OR **on the hog** vivre comme un roi OR nabab.

◇ *n* -**1.** [height] haut *m*; **on ~** [at a height] en haut; *fig* [in heaven] au ciel; **the decision came from on ~** *hum* la décision fut prononcée en haut lieu. -**2.** [great degree or level] haut *m*; **the stock market reached a new ~** la bourse a atteint un nouveau record OR maximum; **prices are at an all-time ~** les prix ont atteint leur maximum OR un record; **the ~s and lows** ST. EX les hausses et les baisses. -**3.** [setting - on iron, stove]: **I put the oven on ~** j'ai mis le four sur très chaud. -**4.** AUT [fourth gear] quatrième *f*; [fifth gear] cinquième *f*. -**5.** METEOR [anticyclone] anticyclone *m*. -**6.** *inf* [state of excitement]: **she's been on a permanent ~ since he came back** elle voit tout en rose depuis son retour; **to be on a ~** [drunk] être (complètement) parti; [on drugs] planer (complètement).

◆ **High** *n* RELIG: **the Most High** le Très-Haut.

-high *in cpds* à la hauteur de...; **shoulder~** à la hauteur de l'épaule; **waist~** à la hauteur de la taille.

high altar *n* maître-autel *m*.

high-and-mighty *adj* arrogant, impérieux; **to be ~** se donner de grands airs; **don't act so ~** descends de tes grands chevaux, ne prends pas tes airs de grand seigneur/grande dame.

highball ['haɪ,bɔːl] *Am* ◇ *n boisson à base d'alcool avec de l'eau et des glaçons.*

◇ *vi* aller grand train OR à toute vitesse, foncer.

◇ *vt* conduire à toute vitesse OR à toute allure.

high board *n* plongeoir *m* le plus haut.

highborn ['haɪbɔːn] *adj* bien né, de bonne OR haute naissance.

highboy ['haɪbɔɪ] *n Am* commode *f* (haute).

highbrow ['haɪbraʊ] ◇ *adj* [literature, film] pour intellectuels; [taste] intellectuel.

◇ *n* intellectuel *m*, -elle *f*, grosse tête *f*.

high camp *n* -**1.** [affectation] affectation *f*, cabotinage *m*. -**2.** [effeminate behaviour] manières *fpl* efféminées. -**3.** [style] kitsch *m*.

high chair *n* chaise *f* haute (pour enfants).

High Church ◇ *n fraction de l'Église d'Angleterre accordant une grande importance à l'autorité du prêtre, au rituel etc.*

◇ *adj de tendance conservatrice dans l'Église anglicane.*

High Churchman *n membre du mouvement conservateur à l'intérieur de l'Église anglicane.*

high-class *adj* [person] de la haute société, du grand monde; [flat, neighbourhood] de grand standing; [job, service] de premier ordre; [car, hotel, restaurant] de luxe; **a ~ prostitute** une prostituée de luxe.

high-coloured *adj* rougeaud, rubicond.

high comedy *n* THEAT comédie *f* au dialogue brillant; **the debate ended in scenes of ~** le débat se termina par des scènes du plus haut comique.

high command *n* haut commandement *m*.

high commissioner *n* [gen & ADMIN] haut commissaire *m*.

High Court ◇ *n*: **the ~ (of Justice)** ≃ le tribunal de grande instance *(principal tribunal civil en Angleterre et au pays de Galles).*

◇ *comp*: **~ judge** ≃ juge *m* du tribunal de grande instance.

high-density *adj* -**1.** [housing] à grande densité de population. -**2.** COMPUT haute densité.

high-energy *adj* à haut rendement énergétique; **a ~ diet** un régime hypercalorique OR riche en calories.

higher ['haɪəʳ] ◇ *adj* -**1.** [at greater height] plus haut. -**2.** [advanced] supérieur; **~ animals** animaux supérieurs; **any sum ~ than 50** toute somme supérieure à 50; **people in the ~ income brackets** les gens appartenant aux tranches de revenus supérieurs; **institute of ~ learning** institut *m* de hautes études; **the ~ forms** OR **classes** SCH les grandes classes, les classes supérieures.

◇ *adv* plus haut.

◇ *n Scot* = **Higher Grade**.

higher degree *n* diplôme *m* d'études supérieures.

higher education *n* enseignement *m* supérieur; **to go on to ~** faire des études supérieures.

Higher Grade *n Scot* diplôme *m* de fin d'études secondaires, ≃ baccalauréat *m*.

higher mathematics *n (U)* mathématiques *fpl* supérieures.

Higher National Certificate *n brevet de technicien en Grande-Bretagne*, ≃ BTS *m*.

Higher National Diploma *n brevet de technicien supérieur en Grande-Bretagne*, ≃ DUT *m*.

higher-up *inf n* supérieur *m*, -e *f*.

highest ['haɪɪst] *superl* → **high**.

high explosive *n* explosif *m* puissant.

highfalutin *inf* [,haɪfə'luːtɪn] *adj* affecté, prétentieux; **I'm tired of her ~ ways** j'en ai assez de ses airs de grande dame.

high fashion *n* haute couture *f*.

high fidelity *n* haute-fidélité *f*.

◆ **high-fidelity** *adj* haute-fidélité; **~ equipment** matériel *m* hi-fi.

high finance *n* haute finance *f*.

high-five *inf n geste que font deux personnes pour se féliciter ou se dire bonjour et qui consiste à se taper dans la main.*

high-flier *n* [ambitious person] ambitieux *m*, -euse *f*, jeune loup *m*; [talented person] cerveau *m*, grosse tête *f*, crack *m*.

high-flown *adj* -**1.** [ideas, plans] extravagant. -**2.** [language] ampoulé, boursouflé; [style] ampoulé.

high-flyer = **high-flier**.

high-flying *adj* -**1.** [aircraft] qui vole à haute altitude; [birds] qui vole haut. -**2.** [person] ambitieux; [behaviour, goal] extravagant.

high frequency *n* haute fréquence *f*.

◆ **high-frequency** *adj* à OR de haute fréquence.

high gear *n* AUT [fourth] quatrième *f* (vitesse *f*); [fifth] cinquième *f* (vitesse *f*); **they moved into ~** *fig* ils se sont dépêchés.

High German *n* haut allemand *m*.

high-grade *adj* de haute qualité, de premier ordre; **~ beef/fruit** bœuf/fruits de premier choix; **~ minerals** minéraux *mpl* à haute teneur; **a ~ idiot** *fig* un imbécile de premier ordre.

high-handed *adj* [overbearing] autoritaire, despotique; [inconsiderate] cavalier.

high-handedness [-'hændɪdnɪs] *n* [overbearing attitude - of person] caractère *m* autoritaire, despotisme *m*; [- of behaviour] caractère *m* arbitraire; [lack of consideration] caractère *m* cavalier.

high-hat *inf* ◇ *adj* snob, hautain.

◇ *vt Am* snober, traiter de haut.

◇ *n* snob *m*.

high-heeled [-'hiːld] *adj* à talons hauts, à hauts talons.

high heels *npl* hauts talons *mpl*.

highjack *etc* ['haɪdʒæk] = **hijack**.

high jinks *inf npl* chahut *m*; **they're up to their usual ~** ils font les imbéciles comme d'habitude; **there were some ~ at the party last night** on s'est amusés comme des fous à la soirée d'hier.

high jump *n* SPORT saut *m* en hauteur; **you're for the ~ when he finds out!** *inf Br fig* qu'est-ce que tu vas prendre quand il l'apprendra!

high jumper *n* sauteur *m (qui fait du saut en hauteur).*

high-key *adj* comprenant peu de contraste, high-key.

highland ['haɪlənd] ◇ *n* région *f* montagneuse.

◇ *adj* des montagnes.

◆ **Highland** *adj Br* [air, scenery] des Highlands; [holiday] dans les Highlands.

◆ **Highlands** *npl Scot* GEOG: **the Highlands** les Highlands *fpl*.

Highland cattle *npl* race *f* bovine des Highlands.

Highland Clearances *npl aux XVIII*[e] *et XIX*[e] *siècles, déplacement souvent forcé des populations d'une partie des Highlands d'Écosse dans le but d'affecter les terres à l'élevage de moutons.*

highlander ['haɪləndəʳ] *n* [mountain dweller] montagnard *m*, -e *f*.

◆ **Highlander** *n Scot* habitant *m*, -e *f* des Highlands, Highlander *m*.

Highland fling *n danse des Highlands traditionnellement exécutée en solo.*

Highland games *npl* jeux *mpl* écossais.

HIGHLAND GAMES:
En Écosse, sorte de kermesse locale en plein air où se déroulent simultanément toutes sortes de concours (danse, cornemuse) et d'épreuves sportives (courses, lancer du marteau, mais aussi «tossing the caber», «tug o' war» etc).

---

high-level *adj* -**1.** [discussion, meeting] à un haut niveau; [diplomat, official] de haut niveau, de rang élevé; **~ officers** [of company] cadres supérieurs; MIL officiers supérieurs. -**2.** COMPUT **~ language** langage *m* évolué OR de haut niveau.

high life *n*: **the ~** la grande vie; **she has a taste for the ~** elle a des goûts de luxe; **to lead** OR **to live the ~** mener la grande vie.

highlight ['haɪlaɪt] ◇ *vt* -**1.** [emphasize] souligner, mettre en relief; **the report ~s the desperate plight of the refugees** le rapport fait ressortir OR souligne la situation désespérée des réfugiés. -**2.** [with pen] surligner. -**3.** ART & PHOT rehausser. -**4.** [hair] faire des mèches dans.

◇ *n* -**1.** [major event - of news] événement *m* le plus marquant; [- of evening, holiday] point *m* culminant, grand moment *m*; **the news ~s** les grands titres *mpl* de l'actualité; **the ~ of the party** le clou de la soirée. -**2.** [in hair - natural] reflet *m*; [- bleached] mèche *f*; **she has had ~s (put in her hair)** elle s'est fait faire des mèches. -**3.** ART & PHOT rehaut *m*.

highlighter ['haɪlaɪtəʳ] *n* surligneur *m*.

highly ['haɪlɪ] *adv* -**1.** [very] très, extrêmement; **it's ~ improbable** c'est fort peu probable; **a ~ polished table** une table d'un beau poli; **the dish was ~ seasoned** le plat était fortement relevé OR épicé. -**2.** [very well] très bien; **his employees are very ~ paid** ses employés sont très bien payés OR touchent de gros salaires. -**3.** [favourably]: **to speak/think ~ of sb** dire, penser beaucoup de bien de qqn; **he praised her work ~** il a chanté (haut) les louanges de son travail; **I ~ recommend it** je vous le conseille vivement OR chaudement. -**4.** [at an important level] haut; **a ~ placed source** une source haut placée; **a ~ placed official** [gen] un officiel de haut rang; ADMIN un haut fonctionnaire.

highly-strung *adj* nerveux, tendu.

high mass, High Mass *n* grand-messe *f*.

high-minded *adj* de caractère noble, qui a des principes (élevés).

high-necked [-nekt] *adj* à col haut OR montant.

highness ['haɪnɪs] *n* [of building, wall] hauteur *f*.

◆ **Highness** *n* [title]: **His/Her Highness** son Altesse *f*.

high noon *n* plein midi *m*; at ~ à midi pile; 'High Noon' *Zinnemann* 'le Train sifflera trois fois'.

high-octane *adj* à haut degré d'octane; ~ petrol supercarburant *m*, super *m*.

high-performance *adj* performant.

high-pitched *adj* -**1.** [sound, voice] aigu; MUS [note] haut. -**2.** [argument, discussion] passionné; [style] ampoulé; [excitement] intense. -**3.** [roof] à forte pente.

high place *n* RELIG haut lieu *m*.

high point *n* [major event - of news] événement *m* le plus marquant; [- of evening, holiday] point *m* culminant, grand moment *m*; [- of film, novel] point *m* culminant; the ~ of the party le clou de la soirée.

high-powered [-'paʊəd] *adj* -**1.** [engine, rifle] puissant, de forte puissance; [microscope] à fort grossissement. -**2.** [dynamic - person] dynamique, entreprenant; [- advertising, course, method] dynamique. -**3.** [important] très important.

high-pressure ◇ *adj* -**1.** [cylinder, gas] à haute pression; ~ area METEOR anticyclone *m*, zone *f* de hautes pressions (atmosphériques). -**2.** *fig* [methods, selling] agressif; [job, profession] stressant; a ~ salesman un vendeur de choc.
◇ *vt inf Am* forcer la main à; she ~d me to do it OR into doing it elle m'a forcé la main pour que je le fasse.

high priest *n* grand prêtre *m*; the ~s of fashion *fig* les gourous de la mode.

high priestess *n* grande prêtresse *f*; the ~ of rock *fig* la grande prêtresse du rock.

high profile *n*: to have a ~ être très en vue.
◆ **high-profile** *adj* [job, position] qui est très en vue; [campaign] qui fait beaucoup de bruit.

high-ranking *adj* de haut rang, de rang élevé; a ~ official ADMIN un haut fonctionnaire.

high relief *n* haut-relief *m*.

high-resolution *adj* à haute résolution.

high-rise *adj* [flat] qui est dans une tour; [skyline] composé de tours.
◆ **high rise** *n* tour *f* *(immeuble)*.

high-risk *adj* à haut risque, à hauts risques.

high road *n* -**1.** [main road] route *f* principale, grand-route *f*. -**2.** *fig* [most direct route] bonne voie *f*; he's on the ~ to success il est en bonne voie de réussir; the ~ to fame la voie de la gloire.

high roller *inf n Am* [spendthrift] dépensier *m*, -ère *f*; [gambler] flambeur *m*.

high school ◇ *n* [in UK] lycée *m*; [in US] établissement *m* d'enseignement secondaire; she's still at ~ elle est toujours scolarisée OR va toujours au lycée.
◇ *comp* [diploma] de fin d'études secondaires.

high seas *npl* haute mer *f*; on the ~ en haute OR pleine mer.

high season *n* haute OR pleine saison *f*; during the ~ en haute OR pleine saison.
◆ **high-season** *comp* [prices] de haute saison.

high sign *n Am* signe *m*; to give sb the ~ faire signe à qqn.

high society *n* haute société *f*, grand monde *m*.

high-sounding *adj* [ideas] grandiloquent, extravagant; [language, title] grandiloquent, ronflant *pej*.

high-speed *adj* ultra-rapide; ~ train train *m* à grande vitesse, TGV *m*.

high-spirited *adj* -**1.** [person] plein d'entrain OR de vivacité; [activity, fun] plein d'entrain. -**2.** [horse] fougueux, nerveux.

high spirits *npl* pétulance *f*, vitalité *f*, entrain *m*; to be in ~ avoir de l'entrain, être plein d'entrain; to put sb in ~ mettre qqn de bonne humeur.

high spot *n* -**1.** = **high point**. -**2.** *Am* [place] endroit *m* intéressant; we hit all the ~s [tourists] nous avons vu toutes les attractions touristiques.

high-stepping *adj* -**1.** [horse] qui lève haut les pieds. -**2.** *fig* [person] qui aime se divertir; [town] qui offre beaucoup de divertissements.

high street *n Br*: the ~ la grand-rue, la rue principale; the ~ has been badly hit by the recession les commerçants ont été durement touchés par la récession.
◆ **high-street** *comp Br*: the high-street banks les grandes banques *(britanniques)*; high-street shops le petit commerce; high-street fashion prêt-à-porter *m*.

high-strung = **highly-strung**.

high table *n Br* [for guests of honour] table *f* d'honneur; SCH & UNIV table *f* des professeurs.

hightail *inf* ['haɪteɪl] *vt esp Am* filer; I ~ed it out of there j'ai foutu le camp; you'd better ~ it back home tu as intérêt à rentrer le plus vite possible.

high tea *n repas léger pris en début de soirée et accompagné de thé (surtout dans le nord de l'Angleterre et en Écosse)*.

high tech *n* -**1.** [technology] technologie *f* avancée OR de pointe. -**2.** [style] hi-tech *m*.
◆ **high-tech** *comp* -**1.** [industry, sector] de pointe; [equipment] de haute technicité. -**2.** [furniture, style] hi-tech *(inv)*.

high-tension *adj* à haute tension.

high tide *n* -**1.** [of ocean, sea] marée *f* haute; at ~ à marée haute. -**2.** *fig* [of success] point *m* culminant.

high-tops *npl chaussures de sport montantes*.

high treason *n* haute trahison *f*.

high-up *inf* ◇ *n* [important person] gros bonnet *m*, huile *f*; [hierarchical superior] supérieur *m*, -e *f*.
◇ *adj* haut placé.

high water *n* [of ocean, sea] marée *f* haute; [of river] crue *f*; the river is at ~ le fleuve est en crue.

high water mark *n* -**1.** [of ocean, river] niveau *m* des hautes eaux. -**2.** *fig* [of success] point *m* culminant.

highway ['haɪweɪ] *n* [road] route *f*; *Am* [main road] grande route, route nationale; [public road] voie *f* publique; [interstate] autoroute *f*; all the ~s and byways tous les chemins.

Highway Code *n Br*: the ~ le code de la route.

highwayman ['haɪweɪmən] (*pl* **highwaymen** [-mən]) *n* bandit *m* de grand chemin.

highway robbery *n* banditisme *m* de grand chemin; that's ~! *inf fig* c'est du vol!

high wire *n* corde *f* raide OR de funambule; to walk the ~ marcher sur la corde raide.

hijack ['haɪdʒæk] ◇ *vt* -**1.** [plane] détourner; [car, train] s'emparer de, détourner. -**2.** [rob] voler.
◇ *n* détournement *m*.

hijacker ['haɪdʒækəʳ] *n* -**1.** [of plane] pirate *m* (de l'air); [of car, train] gangster *m*. -**2.** [robber] voleur *m*.

hijacking ['haɪdʒækɪŋ] *n* -**1.** [of car, plane, train] détournement *m*. -**2.** [robbery] vol *m*.

hike [haɪk] ◇ *vi* faire de la marche à pied; we went hiking in the mountains nous avons fait des excursions OR des randonnées à pied dans les montagnes; he ~d through Spain il a parcouru l'Espagne à pied.
◇ *vt* -**1.** [walk] faire à pied, marcher; to ~ 5 kilometres faire 5 kilomètres à pied; we ~d all the way home on a dû faire tout le chemin du retour à pied. -**2.** [price] augmenter (brusquement).
◇ *n* -**1.** [gen & MIL] marche *f* à pied; [long walk] randonnée *f* à pied, marche *f* à pied; [short walk] promenade *f*; they went for a four-hour ~ ils ont fait une excursion OR une randonnée de quatre heures à pied; it's a bit of a ~ into town *inf* ça fait une petite trotte pour aller en ville. -**2.** [increase] hausse *f*, augmentation *f*; price ~ hausse des prix.
◆ **hike up** *vt sep* -**1.** [hitch up - skirt] relever; [- trousers] remonter; she ~d herself up over the wall elle s'est hissée au-dessus du mur. -**2.** [price, rent] augmenter (brusquement).

hiker ['haɪkəʳ] *n* [gen & MIL] marcheur *m*, -euse *f*; [in mountains, woods] randonneur *m*, -euse *f*, promeneur *m*, -euse *f*.

hiking ['haɪkɪŋ] *n (U)* [gen & MIL] marche *f* à pied; [in mountains, woods] randonnée *f*, trekking *m*.

hilarious [hɪ'leərɪəs] *adj* [funny - person, joke, story] hilarant; his stories are ~ ses histoires sont à se tordre de rire; we had a ~ time last night nous nous sommes amusés comme des fous hier soir.

hilariously [hɪ'leərɪəslɪ] *adv* joyeusement, gaiement; the film's ~ funny le film est à se tordre de rire OR désopilant.

hilarity [hɪ'lærətɪ] *n* hilarité *f*.

Hilary term ['hɪlərɪ-] *n Br* UNIV trimestre *m* de printemps *(à Oxford)*.

hill [hɪl] *n* -**1.** colline *f*, coteau *m*; we walked up the ~ nous avons gravi la colline ❑ up ~ and down dale, over ~ and dale par monts et par vaux; the soldiers fought up ~ and down dale les soldats ont mené le combat avec force et persévérance; as old as the ~s vieux comme le monde OR Mathusalem. -**2.** [slope] côte *f*, pente *f*; 'steep ~' [up] montée OR côte raide; [down] 'descente abrupte OR raide'. -**3.** [mound - of earth] levée *f* de terre, remblai *m*; [- of things] tas *m*, monceau *m*; that car isn't worth a ~ of beans *inf Am* cette voiture ne vaut rien OR ne vaut pas un clou; on the Hill *Am* au parlement *(par allusion à Capitol Hill, siège du Congrès)*.

hillbilly ['hɪl,bɪlɪ] (*pl* **hillbillies**) *Am* ◇ *n* montagnard *m*, -e *f* des Appalaches; *pej* péquenaud *m*, -e *f*, plouc *mf*.
◇ *adj* des Appalaches; ~ music folk *m* (des Appalaches).

hill climb *n* course *f* de côtes.

hill farmer *n* éleveur *m* de moutons dans les alpages.

hillfort ['hɪlfɔːt] *n endroit fortifié se trouvant au sommet d'une colline*.

hilliness ['hɪlɪnɪs] *n* vallonnement *m*, caractère *m* accidenté.

hillock ['hɪlək] *n* [small hill] mamelon *m*, butte *f*; [artificial hill] monticule *m*, amoncellement *m*.

hillside [,hɪl'saɪd] *n* (flanc *m* de) coteau *m*; vines grew on the ~ des vignes poussaient à flanc de coteau.

hilltop ['hɪl,tɒp] ◇ *n* sommet *m* de la colline; they built their house on the ~ ils ont construit leur maison au sommet OR en haut de la colline.
◇ *adj* [village] au sommet OR en haut de la colline; [view] d'en haut de la colline.

hilly ['hɪlɪ] (*compar* **hillier**, *superl* **hilliest**) *adj* [country, land] vallonné; [road] accidenté, à fortes côtes.

hilt [hɪlt] *n* [of dagger, knife] manche *m*; [of sword] poignée *f*, garde *f*; [of gun] crosse *f*; (up) to the ~ au maximum; to back sb up to the ~ soutenir qqn à fond; to be up to the ~ in debt être endetté jusqu'au cou.

him [hɪm] *pron* -**1.** [direct object - unstressed] le, l' *(before vowel)*; [- stressed] lui; I recognize ~ je le reconnais; I heard ~ je l'ai entendu; why did you have to choose HIM? pourquoi l'as-tu choisi lui? -**2.** [indirect object - unstressed] lui; [- stressed] à lui; give ~ the money donne-lui l'argent; she only told ~, no one else elle ne l'a dit qu'à lui, c'est tout; why do they always give HIM the interesting jobs? pourquoi est-ce toujours à lui qu'on donne le travail intéressant? -**3.** [after preposition] lui; I was in front of ~ j'étais devant lui; as rich as/richer than ~ aussi riche/plus riche que lui; he closed the door behind ~ il a fermé la porte derrière lui. -**4.** [with 'to be']: it's ~ c'est lui; if I were ~ si j'étais lui, si j'étais à sa place. -**5.** *fml* [with relative pronoun] celui; ~ who hesitates... celui qui hésite...

Himalayan [,hɪmə'leɪən] *adj* himalayen.

Himalayas [,hɪmə'leɪəz] *pl pr n*: the ~ l'Himalaya *m*; in the ~ dans l'Himalaya.

himself [hɪm'self] *pron* -**1.** [reflexive form] se, s' *(before vowel)*; he introduced ~ il s'est présenté; he bought ~ a car il s'est acheté une voiture; he considers ~ lucky il considère qu'il a de la chance. -**2.** [emphatic form] lui-même; **he built the shelves ~** il a monté les étagères lui-même; **I spoke with the teacher ~** j'ai parlé au professeur en personne. -**3.** [with preposition] lui; **he took it upon ~ to tell us** il a pris sur lui de nous le dire; **he has a room to ~** il a sa propre chambre OR sa chambre à lui; **the old man was talking to ~** le vieil homme parlait tout seul; **"that's odd", he thought to ~** «c'est bizarre», se dit-il; **he did it all by ~** il l'a fait tout seul. -**4.** [his usual self] : **he isn't quite ~** il n'est pas dans son état habituel; **he's feeling more ~ now** il va mieux maintenant.

hind [haɪnd] ◇ *n* [deer] biche *f*.
◇ *adj* de derrière; **~ leg** patte *f* de derrière; **he could talk the ~ legs off a donkey** *hum* il est bavard comme une pie; **to get up on one's ~ legs** prendre la parole.

Hindenburg [ˈhɪndən,bɜːg] *pr n*: **the ~** le Hindenburg.

THE HINDENBURG:
Dirigeable américain ayant inauguré, en 1936, la traversée transatlantique par les airs. Le 6 mai 1937, à son arrivée aux États-Unis, il prit feu et se désintégra en quelques secondes, tragédie qui mit définitivement fin à l'utilisation de ce moyen de transport.

---

hinder [ˈhɪndəʳ] *vt* [obstruct - person] gêner; [- progress] entraver, gêner; **to ~ sb in his/her work** gêner qqn dans son travail; **to ~ sb from doing sthg** empêcher qqn de faire qqch.

Hindi [ˈhɪndɪ] ◇ *n* LING hindi *m*.
◇ *adj* hindi.

hindmost [ˈhaɪndməʊst] *adj* dernier, du bout.

hindquarters [ˈhaɪndkwɔːtəz] *npl* arrière-train *m*.

hindrance [ˈhɪndrəns] *n* -**1.** [person, thing] obstacle *m*, entrave *f*; **you'll be more of a ~ than a help** tu vas gêner plus qu'autre chose. -**2.** *(U)* [action] : **without any ~ from the authorities** [referring to person] sans être gêné par les autorités; [referring to project] sans être entravé par les autorités; **without any ~ from the children/my husband** sans avoir les enfants/mon mari dans les jambes; **his illness has been something of a ~ to the project** sa maladie a quelque peu retardé le projet.

hindsight [ˈhaɪndsaɪt] *n* sagesse *f* acquise après coup; **with the benefit** OR **wisdom of ~** avec du recul, après coup.

Hindu [ˈhɪnduː] ◇ *n* Hindou *m*, -e *f*.
◇ *adj* hindou.

Hinduism [ˈhɪnduːɪzm] *n* hindouisme *m*.

Hindustan [,hɪndʊˈstɑːn] *pr n* Hindoustan *m*; **in ~** dans l'Hindoustan.

Hindustani [,hɪndʊˈstɑːnɪ] ◇ *n* LING hindoustani *m*.
◇ *adj* hindoustani.

hinge [hɪndʒ] ◇ *n* [of door] gond *m*, charnière *f*; [of box] charnière *f*; **the door has come off its ~s** la porte est sortie de ses gonds.
◇ *vt* [door] munir de gonds OR charnières; [box] munir de charnières; **the door can be ~d to open either left or right** la porte peut être montée de façon à s'ouvrir soit à gauche soit à droite.
◆ **hinge on, hinge upon** *vt insep* dépendre de; **the company's future ~s on whether we get the contract** l'avenir de l'entreprise dépend de OR tient à OR repose sur ce contrat.

hinged [hɪndʒd] *adj* à charnière OR charnières; **~ flap** [of counter] abattant *m*.

hint [hɪnt] ◇ *n* -**1.** [indirect suggestion] allusion *f*; [clue] indice *m*; **to drop a ~ (about sthg)** faire une allusion (à qqch); **you could try dropping a ~ that if his work doesn't improve...** tu pourrais essayer de lui faire comprendre que si son travail ne s'améliore pas...; **he can't take a ~** il ne comprend pas les allusions; **OK, I can take a ~** oh ça va, j'ai compris; **I took the ~** j'ai saisi ce qu'on essayait de me faire comprendre; **give me a ~** donne-moi un indice ❑ **I just love plain chocolate, ~, ~** j'adore le chocolat noir, si tu vois où je veux en venir. -**2.** [helpful suggestion, tip] conseil *m*, truc *m*. -**3.** [small amount, trace - of emotion] note *f*; [- of colour] touche *f*; [- of flavouring] soupçon *m*; **there's a ~ of spring/rain in the air** ça sent le printemps/la pluie, il y a du printemps/de la pluie dans l'air.
◇ *vt* insinuer; **that was what he ~ed** c'est ce qu'il a insinué OR laissé entendre.
◇ *vi*: **to ~ at sthg** faire allusion à qqch; **what are you ~ing at?** qu'est-ce que tu insinues?; [in neutral sense] à quoi fais-tu allusion?; **the speech seemed to ~ at the possibility of agreement being reached soon** le discours semblait laisser entendre qu'un accord pourrait être conclu prochainement; **remember, no ~ing in this game** souvenez-vous que vous n'avez droit à aucun indice dans ce jeu.

hinterland [ˈhɪntəlænd] *n* arrière-pays *m*.

hip [hɪp] ◇ *n* -**1.** [part of body] hanche *f*; **with one's hands on one's ~s** les mains sur les hanches; **to be big/small around the ~s** avoir les hanches larges/étroites; **to break one's ~** se casser le col du fémur. -**2.** [berry] fruit *m* de l'églantier/du rosier, cynorhodon *m*, gratte-cul *m*.
◇ *comp*: **~ measurement** OR **size** tour *m* de hanches.
◇ *interj*: **~ ~, hooray!** hip hip hip, hourra!
◇ *adj inf* [fashionable] branché; **to be ~ to sthg** être branché sur qqch.

hip bath *n* bain *m* de siège.

hipbone [ˈhɪpbəʊn] *n* os *m* iliaque.

hip flask *n* flasque *f*.

hiphuggers [ˈhɪp,hʌgəz] *npl Am* pantalon *m* à taille basse.

hip joint *n* articulation *f* de la hanche.

hippie [ˈhɪpɪ] ◇ *n* hippie *mf*, hippy *mf*.
◇ *adj* hippie, hippy.

hippo *inf* [ˈhɪpəʊ] *n* hippopotame *m*.

hip pocket *n* poche *f* revolver.

Hippocrates [hɪˈpɒkrətiːz] *pr n* Hippocrate.

Hippocratic [,hɪpəˈkrætɪk] *adj*: **the ~ oath** le serment d'Hippocrate.

Hippolyta [hɪˈpɒlɪtə] *pr n* Hippolyté.

Hippolytus [hɪˈpɒlɪtəs] *pr n* Hippolyte.

hippopotamus [,hɪpəˈpɒtəməs] (*pl* **hippopotamuses** OR **hippopotami** [-maɪ]) *n* hippopotame *m*.

hippy [ˈhɪpɪ] (*pl* **hippies**) = **hippie**.

hip replacement *n* [operation] remplacement *m* de la hanche par une prothèse; [prosthesis] prothèse *f* de la hanche.

hipsters [ˈhɪpstəz] *npl Br* pantalon *m* à taille basse.

hire [ˈhaɪəʳ] ◇ *n* -**1.** *Br* [of car, room, suit etc] location *f*; **'for ~'** 'à louer'; [taxi] 'libre'; **it's out on ~** il a été loué. -**2.** [cost - of car, boat etc] (prix *m* de) location *f*; [- of worker] paye *f*.
◇ *comp*: **~ charges** (frais *mpl* OR prix *m* de) location *f*.
◇ *vt* -**1.** *Br* [car, room, suit etc] louer; **to ~ sb's services** employer les services de qqn; **to ~ sthg from sb** louer qqch à qqn. -**2.** [staff] engager; [labourer] embaucher, engager; **~d hand** *Am* [on farm] ouvrier *m*, -ère *f* agricole; [employee] employé *m*, -e *f*; **~d killer** OR **assassin** tueur *m* à gages.
◇ *vi* engager du personnel, embaucher (des ouvriers); **with authority to ~ and fire** qui a pouvoir en matière d'embauche et de licenciement.
◆ **hire out** *vt sep Br* [car, room, suit etc] louer; **to ~ out one's services** offrir OR proposer ses services; **to ~ o.s. out** se faire engager; [labourer] se faire engager OR embaucher.

hire car *n Br* voiture *f* de location.

hireling [ˈhaɪəlɪŋ] *n pej* [menial] larbin *m*; [illegal or immoral] mercenaire *mf*.

hire purchase *n Br* location-vente *f*, vente *f* à tempérament; **to buy** OR **to get sthg on ~** acheter qqch en location-vente; **I don't own it, it's on ~** ce n'est pas encore à moi, je l'achète en location-vente; **~ agreement** contrat *m* de location; **~ goods** biens achetés en location vente OR à tempérament.

hiring [ˈhaɪərɪŋ] *n* -**1.** [of car] location *f*. -**2.** [o employee] embauche *f*.

Hiroshima [hɪˈrɒʃɪmə] *pr n* Hiroshima.

hirsute [ˈhɜːsjuːt] *adj fml* poilu, velu.

his [hɪz] ◇ *det* son *m*, sa *f*, ses *mfpl*; **~ table** s table; **~ glasses** ses lunettes; **~ university** so université; **it's HIS fault not mine** c'est de s faute à lui, pas de la mienne; **he has broken ~ arm/~ leg** il s'est cassé le bras/la jambe; **wit ~ hands in ~ pockets** les mains dans le poches; **everyone must do ~ best** *fml* chacu doit faire de son mieux; **one has ~ pride** *Am* on a sa fierté.
◇ *pron* -**1.** [gen] le sien *m*, la sienne *f*, le siens *mpl*, les siennes *fpl*; **it's ~** c'est à lui, c'es le sien; **the responsibility is ~** c'est lui qui es responsable, la responsabilité lui revient; **is thi coat ~?** ce manteau est-il à lui?, ce mantea est-il le sien?; **no, THIS one is ~** non, le sie c'est celui-ci; **whose fault is it? — ~!** qui est l responsable? — lui! -**2.** [after preposition]: **a friend of ~** un de ses amis; **that dog of ~ i a nuisance** son sacré chien est vraiment embê tant; **it's always been a fault of ~** ça a toujour été son défaut OR un de ses défauts; **everyon wants what is ~** *fml* chacun veut ce qui lu revient.

Hispanic [hɪˈspænɪk] ◇ *n* Hispano-Améri cain *m*, -e *f*.
◇ *adj* hispanique.

Hispaniola [,hɪspænɪˈəʊlə] *pr n* Hispaniola *f* **in ~** en Hispaniola.

Hispano-American [hɪˈspɑːnəʊ-] ◇ *n* Hispano-Américain *m*, -e *f*.
◇ *adj* hispano-américain.

hiss [hɪs] ◇ *n* [of gas, steam] sifflement *m*, chuin tement *m*; [of person, snake] sifflement *m*; [o cat] crachement *m*; **"be quiet", she said in a ~** «tais-toi!», dit-elle nerveusement; **there was a angry ~ from the bystanders** l'assistance émi un sifflement de colère; **he was greeted wit ~es** il est arrivé sous les sifflets (du public); **th cat backed away with a ~** le chat a reculé e crachant.
◇ *vt* [say quietly] souffler; [bad performer speaker etc] siffler; **the audience ~ed its dis approval** les spectateurs ont sifflé en signe d mécontentement; **the speaker was ~ed of the platform** l'orateur quitta la tribune sous le sifflets (du public).
◇ *vi* [gas, steam] siffler, chuinter; [snake] siffler [cat] cracher; [person - speak quietly] souffler [- in disapproval, anger] siffler; **there was a lou ~ing noise** il y a eu un bruit ressemblant à u fort sifflement; **why is the radiator making a these ~ing noises?** pourquoi est-ce que l radiateur siffle comme ça?

hist [hɪst] *interj dated* chut.

histamine [ˈhɪstəmiːn] *n* histamine *f*.

histogram [ˈhɪstəgræm] *n* histogramme *m*.

histologist [hɪsˈtɒlədʒɪst] *n* histologiste *mf*.

histology [hɪˈstɒlədʒɪ] *n* histologie *f*.

historian [hɪˈstɔːrɪən] *n* historien *m*, -enne *f*.

historic [hɪˈstɒrɪk] *adj* -**1.** [memorable - day, oc casion, meeting etc] historique. -**2.** [of time past révolu, passé; [fear] ancestral; **in ~ times** e des temps révolus; **~ building** monument historique.

historical [hɪˈstɒrɪkəl] *adj* historique; **it's a ~ fact** c'est un fait historique; **to be of ~ interes** présenter un intérêt historique ❑ **~ linguis tics** linguistique *f* diachronique; **~ presen** GRAMM présent *m* historique.

historically [hɪˈstɒrɪklɪ] *adv* historiquement [traditionally] traditionnellement.

historiographer [,hɪstɔːrɪˈɒgrəfəʳ] *n* historio graphe *mf*.

historiography [,hɪstɔːrɪˈɒgrəfɪ] *n* historic graphie *f*.

history [ˈhɪstərɪ] (*pl* **histories**) ◇ *n* -**1.** *(U)* [th past] histoire *f*; **ancient/modern ~** histoir ancienne/moderne; **the ~ of France, Frenc**

~ l'histoire de France; to study ~ étudier l'histoire; I find ~ fascinating l'histoire me fascine; a character in ~ un personnage historique OR de l'histoire; throughout ~ tout au long de l'histoire; the ~ plays of Shakespeare les pièces historiques de Shakespeare; tell me news, not ~! tu n'aurais pas de nouvelles un peu plus fraîches?; to make ~ entrer dans l'histoire; a day that has gone down in ~ une journée qui est entrée dans l'histoire ❑ that's ancient ~ [forgotten, in the past] c'est de l'histoire ancienne; [everyone knows that] c'est bien connu; the rest is ~ tout le monde connaît la suite. -**2.** *(U)* [development, lifespan] histoire *f*; the worst disaster in aviation ~ OR in the ~ of aviation le plus grand désastre de l'histoire de l'aviation. -**3.** [account] histoire *f*; Shakespeare's histories les pièces historiques de Shakespeare. -**4.** *(U)* [record]: employment ~ expérience *f* professionnelle; medical ~ antécédents *mpl* médicaux; there is a ~ of heart disease in my family il y a des antécédents de maladie cardiaque dans ma famille; the entire family has a ~ of political activity toute la famille a fait de la politique; he has a ~ of attempted rape il a plusieurs tentatives de viol à son actif.

◇ *comp* [book, teacher, lesson] d'histoire.

histrionic [ˌhɪstrɪ'ɒnɪk] *adj pej* [person, behaviour, gesture] théâtral.

histrionics [ˌhɪstrɪ'ɒnɪks] *npl pej* comédie *f*, simagrées *fpl*.

hit [hɪt] (*pt* & *pp* hit, *cont* hitting) ◇ *n* -**1.** [blow] coup *m*; we scored a direct ~ on the palace nous avons touché le palais en plein dans le mille; the tank won't withstand a direct ~ le char ne résistera pas à un coup direct OR s'il est touché de plein fouet; that was a ~ at me *fig* ça m'était destiné, c'est moi qui étais visé. -**2.** SPORT [in ball game] coup *m*; [in shooting] tir *m* réussi; [in fencing] touche *f*; to score a ~ [in shooting] faire mouche, toucher la cible; [in fencing] faire OR marquer une touche; he got three ~s and one miss il a réussi trois tirs et en a manqué un; it only counts as a ~ if the bullet goes inside the red line le tir ne compte que si la balle se trouve à l'intérieur de la ligne rouge; that was a ~ [in fencing] il y a eu touche; we sent the mailshot to fifty companies and got thirteen ~s *fig* nous avons contacté cinquante entreprises par publipostage et avons eu treize réponses favorables. -**3.** [success - record, play, book] succès *m*; [- song] succès *m*, hit *m*, tube *m*; to be a big ~ [book, record etc] faire OR être un grand succès; a ~ with the public/the critics un succès auprès du public/des critiques; to make a ~ with sb [person] conquérir qqn; she's a ~ with everyone elle a conquis tout le monde; I think you've made a ~ with him je crois que tu l'as conquis; [romantically] je crois que tu as fait une touche. -**4.** ▽ [murder] meurtre *m*, liquidation *f*; a ~ by the Mafia un meurtre perpétré par la Mafia. -**5.** *drugs sl* [injection of heroin] dose *f*, shoot *m*.

◇ *comp*: ~ record (disque *m* à) succès *m*; ~ single OR song succès, hit *m*, tube *m*; ~ tune air *m* à succès.

◇ *vt* -**1.** [strike with hand, fist, stick etc - person] frapper; [- ball] frapper OR taper dans; [- nail] taper sur; to ~ sb in the face/on the head frapper qqn au visage/sur la tête; they ~ him over the head with a baseball bat ils lui ont donné un coup de batte de baseball sur la tête; to ~ a ball over the net envoyer un ballon par-dessus le filet; to ~ sb where it hurts most *fig* toucher qqn là où ça fait mal ❑ to ~ a man when he's down *literal* & *fig* frapper un homme quand il est à terre; to ~ the nail on the head mettre le doigt dessus. -**2.** [come or bring forcefully into contact with - subj: ball, stone] heurter; [- subj: bullet, arrow] atteindre, toucher; the bottle ~ the wall and smashed la bouteille a heurté le mur et s'est cassée; the bullet ~ him in the shoulder la balle l'a atteint OR touché à l'épaule; I've been ~! j'ai été touché!; the boat was ~ by a missile le bateau a été touché par un missile; the windscreen was ~ by a stone une pierre a heurté le pare-brise; he was ~ by a stone il a reçu une pierre; the car ~ a tree la voiture a heurté OR est rentrée dans un arbre; the dog was ~ by a car le chien a été heurté par une voiture; to ~ one's head/knee (against sthg) se cogner la tête/le genou (contre qqch); to ~ sb's head against sthg frapper OR cogner la tête de qqn contre qqch; it suddenly ~ me that... *fig* il m'est soudain venu à l'esprit que... -**3.** [attack - enemy] attaquer. -**4.** [affect] toucher; the company has been ~ by the recession l'entreprise a été touchée par la récession; how badly did the postal strike ~ you? dans quelle mesure avez-vous été touchés par la grève des postes?; the region worst ~ by the earthquake la région la plus sévèrement touchée par le tremblement de terre; the child's death has ~ them all very hard la mort de l'enfant les a tous beaucoup éprouvés OR durement touchés OR frappés; it ~s everyone in the pocket *inf* tout le monde en subit financièrement les conséquences, tout le monde le sent passer. -**5.** *inf* [reach] arriver à; the new model can ~ 130 mph on the straight le nouveau modèle peut atteindre les 210 (km/h) OR faire des pointes à 210 (km/h) en ligne droite; to ~ a problem se heurter à un problème OR une difficulté; to ~ a note MUS [singer] chanter une note; [instrumentalist] jouer une note; he didn't quite ~ the note cleanly la note n'est pas sortie tout à fait nettement; we'll stop for dinner when we ~ town *Am* nous nous arrêterons pour dîner quand nous arriverons dans la ville; when it ~s the shops [product] quand il sera mis en vente; to ~ an all-time high/low [unemployment, morale etc] atteindre son plus haut/bas niveau; you'll ~ the rush hour traffic tu vas te retrouver en plein dans la circulation de l'heure de pointe. -**6.** SPORT [score - runs] marquer; [in fencing] toucher; to ~ three runs [cricket] marquer trois points; to ~ a home-run [baseball] faire un tour complet de circuit. -**7.** ▽ [kill] descendre, liquider. -**8.** *inf Am* [borrow money from] taper; to ~ sb for $10 taper qqn de 10 dollars; to ~ sb for a loan emprunter de l'argent à qqn. -**9.** *phr*: to ~ the books *inf Am* se mettre à étudier; to ~ the bottle *inf* [drink] picoler; [start to drink] se mettre à picoler; to ~ the ceiling *inf* OR roof *inf* sortir de ses gonds, piquer une colère folle; to ~ the deck *inf* [lie down] se mettre à terre; ~ the deck! tout le monde à terre!; [get out of bed] debout là-dedans!; to ~ the gas *inf Am* appuyer sur le champignon; to ~ the hay *inf* OR the sack *inf* aller se mettre au pieu, aller se pieuter; to ~ the headlines faire les gros titres; if ever this ~s the headlines we're in trouble si jamais cela paraît dans les journaux nous aurons des problèmes; to ~ home [remark, criticism] faire mouche; to ~ the jackpot gagner le gros lot; to ~ the road se mettre en route; ~ the road! [go away] fiche le camp!; that really ~s the spot [food, drink] c'est juste ce dont j'avais besoin.

◇ *vi* -**1.** frapper, taper; don't ~ so hard, we're only playing ne frappe OR tape pas si fort, ce n'est qu'un jeu; the door was hitting against the wall la porte cognait contre le mur; the two cars didn't actually ~ en fait les deux voitures ne se sont pas heurtées; the atoms ~ against each other les atomes se heurtent. -**2.** [inflation, recession etc] se faire sentir.

◆ **hit back** ◇ *vi insep* [reply forcefully, retaliate] riposter, rendre la pareille; he ~ back with accusations that they were giving bribes il a riposté en les accusant de verser des pots-de-vin; to ~ back at sb/sthg [in speech] répondre à qqn/qqch; to ~ back at the enemy riposter, répondre à l'ennemi; our army ~ back with a missile attack notre armée a riposté en envoyant des missiles.

◇ *vt sep*: to ~ the ball back renvoyer le ballon; he ~ me back il m'a rendu mon coup.

◆ **hit off** *vt sep* -**1.** [in words] décrire OR dépeindre à la perfection; [in paint] représenter de manière très ressemblante; [in mimicry] imiter à la perfection. -**2.** *phr*: to ~ it off [get on well] bien s'entendre; to ~ it off with sb bien s'entendre avec qqn; we ~ it off immediately le courant est tout de suite passé entre nous.

◆ **hit on** *vt insep* -**1.** [find - solution, plan etc] trouver. -**2.** *inf Am* [try to pick up] draguer.

◆ **hit out** *vi insep* -**1.** [physically - once] envoyer un coup; [- repeatedly] envoyer des coups; he started hitting out at me il s'est mis à envoyer des coups dans ma direction. -**2.** [in speech, writing]: to ~ out at OR against s'en prendre à, attaquer; he ~s out in his new book il lance l'offensive dans son nouveau livre.

◆ **hit upon** *vt insep* = **hit on 1**.

hit-and-miss = **hit-or-miss**.

hit-and-run *n* accident *m* avec délit de fuite; a child died in a ~ (accident) yesterday un enfant est mort hier dans un accident causé par un chauffard qui a pris la fuite; he's confessed to the ~ il s'est reconnu coupable du délit de fuite; ~ driver conducteur *m*, -trice *f* coupable de délit de fuite; ~ attack MIL attaque *f* éclair; ~ suit *Am* JUR poursuites *fpl* pour délit de fuite *(après avoir provoqué un accident de la route)*.

hitch [hɪtʃ] ◇ *vt* -**1.** *inf* to ~ a lift [gen] se faire emmener en voiture; [hitchhiker] se faire prendre en stop; can I ~ a lift, Dad? tu m'emmènes, papa?; I ~ed a lift from the woman next door je me suis fait emmener par la voisine; she has ~ed her way round Europe elle a fait toute l'Europe en stop OR auto-stop. -**2.** [railway carriage] attacher, atteler; [horse - to fence] attacher; [- to carriage] atteler; [rope] attacher, nouer. -**3.** *inf phr*: to get ~ed [one person] se caser; [couple] passer devant Monsieur le Maire.

◇ *vi* = **hitchhike**.

◇ *n* -**1.** [difficulty] problème *m*, anicroche *f*; there's been a ~ il y a eu un problème; a technical ~ un incident technique; it went off without a ~ OR any ~es tout s'est passé sans anicroche. -**2.** *inf Am* MIL: he's doing a five year ~ in the navy il s'est engagé pour cinq ans dans la marine. -**3.** [knot] nœud *m*. -**4.** [pull]: to give sthg a ~ (up) remonter OR retrousser qqch.

◆ **hitch up** *vt sep* -**1.** [trousers, skirt etc] remonter, retrousser. -**2.** [horse, oxen etc] atteler.

hitcher *inf* ['hɪtʃəʳ] = **hitchhiker**.

hitchhike ['hɪtʃhaɪk] ◇ *vi* faire du stop OR de l'auto-stop; to ~ to London aller à Londres en stop; I spent the summer hitchhiking in the South of France j'ai passé l'été à voyager dans le sud de la France en auto-stop.

◇ *vt*: to ~ one's way round Europe faire l'Europe en auto-stop.

hitchhiker ['hɪtʃhaɪkəʳ] *n* auto-stoppeur *m*, -euse *f*, stoppeur *m*, -euse *f*; I picked up a couple of ~s on the way j'ai pris quelques auto-stoppeurs OR stoppeurs en chemin.

hitchhiking ['hɪtʃhaɪkɪŋ] *n* auto-stop *m*, stop *m*.

hi-tech, **hitech** ['haɪˌtek] ◇ *n* -**1.** [in industry] technologie *f* de pointe. -**2.** [style of interior design] high-tech *m*.

◇ *adj* -**1.** [equipment, industry] de pointe. -**2.** [design, furniture] high-tech.

hither ['hɪðəʳ] *adv arch* ici; ~ and thither *lit* & *hum* çà et là, de ci de là.

hitherto [ˌhɪðə'tuː] *adv fml* jusqu'ici, jusqu'à présent; a ~ incurable disease une maladie jusqu'ici OR jusqu'à présent incurable; the man who had ~ been considered guilty l'homme qui avait jusqu'alors été tenu pour coupable.

hit list *inf n* liste *f* noire; to be on sb's ~ être sur la liste noire de qqn.

hitman *inf* ['hɪtmæn] (*pl* hitmen [-men]) *n* tueur *m* à gages.

hit-or-miss *inf adj* [method, approach] basé sur le hasard; [work] fait n'importe comment OR à la va comme je te pousse; the service here is a bit ~ le service ici est fait un peu n'importe comment.

hit parade *n dated* hit-parade *m*.

hit rate *n* MIL taux *m* de tirs réussis; *fig* taux *m* de réussite.

hit squad *inf n* commando *m* de tueurs.

Hittite ['hıtaıt] ◇ *n* -**1.** [person] Hittite *mf*. -**2.** LING hittite *m*.
◇ *adj* hittite.

HIV (*abbr of* human immunodeficiency virus) *n* VIH *m*, HIV *m*; to be ~ positive être séropositif.

hive [haıv] ◇ *n* [for bees] ruche *f*; [group of bees] essaim *m*; a ~ of industry OR activity *fig* une vraie OR véritable ruche.
◇ *vt* mettre en ruche.
◇ *vi* entrer dans une ruche.
◆ **hive off** ◇ *vt sep* transférer.
◇ *vi insep inf* [go away, slip off] se tirer, se casser.

hives [haıvz] *n* (U) MED urticaire *f*; to have ~ avoir de l'urticaire.

hiya *inf* ['haıjə] *interj* salut.

hl (*written abbr of* hectolitre) hl.

h'm [hm] *interj* hum, mmm.

HM (*abbr of* His/Her Majesty) SM.

HMG (*abbr of* His/Her Majesty's Government) *n expression utilisée sur des documents officiels en Grande-Bretagne*.

HMI (*abbr of* His/Her Majesty's Inspector) *n inspecteur de l'éducation nationale en Grande-Bretagne*.

HMO (*abbr of* Health Maintenance Organization) *n aux États-Unis, clinique de médecine préventive où l'on peut aller lorsqu'on a certains contrats d'assurance*.

HMS (*abbr of* His/Her Majesty's Ship) *n dénomination officielle précédant le nom de tous les bâtiments de guerre de la marine britannique*.

HMSO (*abbr of* His/Her Majesty's Stationery Office) *pr n maison d'édition publiant les ouvrages ou documents approuvés par le Parlement, les ministères et autres organismes officiels*, ≃ l'Imprimerie nationale.

HNC *n abbr of* Higher National Certificate.

HND *n abbr of* Higher National Diploma.

ho [həʊ] *interj* -**1.** [attracting attention] hé ho. -**2.** [imitating laughter]: ~ ~! ha ha ha!

hoagie ['həʊgı] *n Am sorte de gros sandwich*.

hoar [hɔːʳ] = **hoarfrost**.

hoard [hɔːd] ◇ *n* [of goods] réserve *f*, provisions *fpl*; [of money] trésor *m*, magot *m*.
◇ *vt* [goods] faire provision OR des réserves de, stocker; [money] accumuler, thésauriser.
◇ *vi* faire des réserves, stocker.

hoarder ['hɔːdə] *n* [gen] *personne ou animal qui fait des réserves*; [of money] thésauriseur *m*, -euse *f*; you're such a ~! quel conservateur tu fais!

hoarding ['hɔːdıŋ] *n* -**1.** *(U)* [of goods] mise *f* en réserve OR en stock; [of money] thésaurisation *f*, accumulation *f*; ~ is forbidden il est interdit de faire des réserves OR des stocks. -**2.** *Br* [fence] palissade *f*. -**3.** *Br* [billboard] panneau *m* publicitaire OR d'affichage.

hoarfrost ['hɔːfrɒst] *n* givre *m*.

hoarse [hɔːs] *adj* [person] enroué; [voice] rauque, enroué; to sound ~ être enroué, avoir la voix enrouée; to shout o.s. ~ s'enrouer à force de crier.

hoarsely ['hɔːslı] *adv* d'une voix rauque OR enrouée.

hoary ['hɔːrı] (*compar* hoarier, *superl* hoariest) *adj* -**1.** [greyish white - hair] blanc; [- person] aux cheveux blancs, chenu. -**2.** [old - problem, story] vieux; a ~ old joke une blague usée.

hoax [həʊks] ◇ *n* canular *m*; to play a ~ on sb jouer un tour à qqn, monter un canular à qqn; (bomb) ~ fausse alerte *f* à la bombe.
◇ *comp*: ~ (telephone) call canular *m* téléphonique.
◇ *vt* jouer un tour à, monter un canular à.

hoaxer ['həʊksəʳ] *n* mauvais plaisant *m*.

hob [hɒb] *n* [on stove top] plaque *f* (chauffante); [by open fire] plaque *f*.

hobble ['hɒbl] ◇ *vi* boitiller; she ~d across the street elle a traversé la rue en boitillant.
◇ *vt* [horse] entraver.
◇ *n* -**1.** [limp] boitillement *m*; to walk with a ~ marcher en boitillant. -**2.** [for horse] entrave *f*.
◇ *comp*: ~ skirt jupe *f* entravée.

hobbledehoy [ˌhɒbldı'hɔı] *n arch* dadais *m*, empoté *m*.

hobby ['hɒbı] (*pl* hobbies) *n* passe-temps *m*, hobby *m*.

hobbyhorse ['hɒbıhɔːs] *n* -**1.** [toy] cheval *m* de bois *(composé d'une tête sur un manche)*. -**2.** [favourite topic] sujet *m* favori, dada *m*; she's off on her ~ again la voilà repartie sur son sujet favori OR son dada; to get sb on his/her ~ brancher qqn sur son sujet favori OR dada.

hobgoblin [hɒb'gɒblın] *n* diablotin *m*.

hobnail ['hɒbneıl] *n* clou *m* à grosse tête, caboche *f*; ~ boots chaussures *fpl* ferrées.

hobnob ['hɒbnɒb] (*pt* & *pp* hobnobbed, *cont* hobnobbing) *vi*: to ~ with sb frayer avec qqn, fréquenter qqn.

hobo *inf* ['həʊbəʊ] (*pl* hobos OR hoboes) *n Am* -**1.** [tramp] clochard *m*, -e *f*, vagabond *m*, -e *f*. -**2.** [itinerant labourer] saisonnier *m*, -ère *f*.

Hobson's choice ['hɒbsnz-] *n*: it's (a case of) ~ il n'y a pas vraiment le choix.

Ho Chi Minh ['həʊˌtʃiː'mın] *pr n* Hô Chi Minh.

Ho Chi Minh City *pr n* Hô Chi Minh-Ville.

hock [hɒk] ◇ *n* -**1.** [joint] jarret *m*. -**2.** [wine] vin *m* du Rhin. -**3.** *inf phr*: in ~ [in pawn] au clou; [in debt] endetté; how much are you in ~ for? de combien es-tu endetté?; I'm in ~ for $500 j'ai 500 dollars de dettes; I'm in ~ to him for $500 je lui dois 500 dollars; to get sthg out of ~ retirer qqch du clou; he was finally out of ~ enfin il n'avait plus de dettes.
◇ *vt* [pawn] mettre au clou.

hockey ['hɒkı] ◇ *n* -**1.** *Br* hockey *m* sur gazon. -**2.** *Am* hockey *m* sur glace.
◇ *comp* [ball, match, pitch, team] *Br* de hockey; *Am* de hockey sur glace; ~ player *Br* joueur *m*, -euse *f* de hockey, hockeyeur *m*, -euse *f*; *Am* joueur *m*, -euse *f* de hockey sur glace; ~ stick *Br* crosse *f* de hockey; *Am* crosse de hockey sur glace.

hocus-pocus [ˌhəʊkəs'pəʊkəs] *n* -**1.** [of magician] tours *mpl* de passe-passe. -**2.** [trickery] tricherie *f*, supercherie *f*; [deceptive talk] paroles *fpl* trompeuses; [deceptive action] trucage *m*, supercherie *f*; it's just ~ ce n'est que de la supercherie.

hod [hɒd] ◇ *n* [for bricks] *ustensile utilisé par les maçons pour porter les briques*; [for mortar] auge *f*, oiseau *m*; [for coal] seau *m* à charbon.
◇ *comp*: ~ carrier apprenti *m* OR aide *m* maçon.

hodgepodge ['hɒdʒpɒdʒ] *Am* = **hotchpotch**.

hoe [həʊ] ◇ *n* houe *f*, binette *f*.
◇ *vt* biner, sarcler.

hoedown ['həʊdaʊn] *n Am* bal *m* populaire.

hog [hɒg] (*pt* & *pp* hogged, *cont* hogging) ◇ *n* [castrated pig] cochon *m* OR porc *m* châtré; *Am* [pig] cochon *m*, porc *m*; *fig* [greedy person] goinfre *mf*; [dirty person] porc *m*; to go the whole ~ *inf* ne pas faire les choses à moitié; why don't we go the whole ~ and order champagne? pourquoi ne pas faire les choses en grand et commander du champagne?; to live high on OR off the ~ *inf Am* mener la grande vie.
◇ *vt inf* monopoliser; to ~ the limelight accaparer OR monopoliser l'attention, se mettre en vedette; to ~ the middle of the road prendre toute la route; stop hogging all the wine for yourself ne garde pas tout le vin pour ta poire.

hoggish ['hɒgıʃ] *adj* [habits] de porc; [person - dirty] sale; [- greedy] goulu; he's very ~ c'est un vrai porc.

Hogmanay ['hɒgməneı] *n Scot les fêtes de la Saint-Sylvestre en Écosse*.

hogshead ['hɒgzhed] *n* tonneau *m*, barrique *f*.

hogtie ['hɒgtaı] *vt Am*: this has ~d us nous voici pieds et poings liés; to be ~d être pieds et poings liés.

hogwash ['hɒgwɒʃ] *n* *(U)* -**1.** *inf* [nonsense] bêtises *fpl*, imbécillités *fpl*; to talk ~ raconter des bêtises; ~! n'importe quoi! -**2.** [pigswill] eaux *fpl* grasses.

hogweed ['hɒgwiːd] *n* berce *f*.

hoick *inf* [hɔık] *vt* soulever; to ~ o.s. up onto a wall se hisser sur un mur; the helicopter ~ed him out of the sea l'hélicoptère l'a tiré de la mer avec une secousse.

hoi polloi [ˌhɔıpə'lɔı] *npl pej*: the ~ la populace.

hoist [hɔıst] ◇ *vt* [sails, flag] hisser; [load, person] lever, hisser; to be ~ with one's own petard être pris à son propre piège.
◇ *n* -**1.** [elevator] monte-charge *m*; [block and tackle] palan *m*. -**2.** [upward push, pull]: to give sb a ~ up [lift] soulever qqn; [pull] tirer qqn.

hoity-toity *inf* [ˌhɔıtı'tɔıtı] *adj pej* prétentieux, péteux; she's very ~ c'est une vraie bêcheuse; to go all ~ prendre ses grands airs.

hoke up [həʊk-] *vt sep Am* agrémenter.

hokey ['həʊkı] *adj Am* à l'eau de rose.

hokey cokey [-'kəʊkı] *n Br danse et chanson traditionnelles londoniennes*.

hokum *inf* ['həʊkəm] *n (U) Am* [nonsense] fadaises *fpl*, foutaises *fpl*; [sentimentality in play, film etc] niaiseries *fpl*, sentimentalisme *m*.

hold [həʊld] (*pt* & *pp* held [held]) ◇ *vt*
A. -**1.** [clasp, grasp] tenir; to ~ sthg in one's hand [book, clothing, guitar] avoir qqch à la main; [key, money] tenir qqch dans la main; to ~ sthg with both hands tenir qqch à deux mains; will you ~ my coat a second? peux-tu prendre OR tenir mon manteau un instant?; to ~ the door for sb tenir la porte à OR pour qqn; to ~ sb's hand *literal* & *fig* tenir la main à qqn; to ~ hands se donner la main, se tenir (par) la main; ~ my hand while we cross the street donne-moi la main pour traverser la rue; to ~ sb in one's arms tenir qqn dans ses bras; to ~ sb close OR tight serrer qqn contre soi; ~ it tight and don't let go tiens-le bien et ne le lâche pas; to ~ one's nose se boucher le nez. -**2.** [keep, sustain]: to ~ sb's attention retenir l'attention de qqn; to ~ an audience tenir un auditoire; to ~ one's serve [in tennis] défendre son service; to ~ a seat POL [to be an MP] occuper un siège de député; [to be re-elected] être réélu ❑ to ~ one's own tenir bon OR ferme; the Prime Minister held her own during the debate le Premier ministre a tenu bon OR ferme pendant le débat; she is well able to ~ her own elle sait se défendre; he can ~ his own in chess il se défend bien aux échecs; our products ~ their own against the competition nos produits se tiennent bien par rapport à la concurrence; to ~ the floor: the senator held the floor for an hour le sénateur a gardé la parole pendant une heure. -**3.** [have, possess - degree, permit, ticket] avoir, posséder; [- job, position] avoir, occuper; do you ~ a clean driving licence? avez-vous déjà été sanctionné pour des infractions au code de la route?; she ~s the post of treasurer elle occupe le poste de trésorière; to ~ office [chairperson, deputy] être en fonction, remplir sa fonction; [minister] détenir OR avoir un portefeuille; [political party, president] être au pouvoir OR au gouvernement; to ~ a living RELIG jouir d'un bénéfice; to ~ stock FIN détenir OR avoir des actions; to ~ a record *literal* & *fig* détenir un record; she ~s the world record for the javelin elle détient le record mondial du javelot. -**4.** [keep control of, authority over]: the guerrillas held the bridge for several hours MIL les guérilleros ont tenu le pont plusieurs heures durant ❑ to ~ centre stage *fig* & THEAT occuper le centre de la scène; ~ it!, ~ everything! [stop and wait] attendez!; [stay still] arrêtez!, ne bougez plus!; ~ your horses! *inf* pas si vite! -**5.** [reserve, set aside] retenir, réserver; we'll ~ the book for you until next week nous vous réserverons le livre OR nous vous mettrons le livre de côté jusqu'à la semaine prochaine; will the restaurant ~ the table for us? est-ce que le restaurant va nous garder la table? -**6.** [contain] contenir, tenir; this bottle ~s two litres cette bouteille contient deux litres; will this suitcase ~ all our clothes? est-ce que cette valise sera assez grande pour tous nos vêtements?; the car is to

small to ~ us all la voiture est trop petite pour qu'on y tienne tous; **the hall ~s a maximum of 250 people** la salle peut accueillir OR recevoir 250 personnes au maximum, il y a de la place pour 250 personnes au maximum dans cette salle; **to ~ one's drink** bien supporter l'alcool; **the letter ~s the key to the murder** la lettre contient la clé du meurtre. -**7.** [have, exercise] exercer; **the subject ~s a huge fascination for some people** le sujet exerce une énorme fascination sur certaines personnes. -**8.** [have in store] réserver; **who knows what the future may ~?** qui sait ce que nous réserve l'avenir? -**9.** [conserve, store] conserver, détenir; COMPUT stocker; **we can't ~ this data forever** nous ne pouvons pas conserver OR stocker ces données éternellement; **how much data will this disk ~?** quelle quantité de données cette disquette peut-elle stocker?; **the commands are held in the memory/in a temporary buffer** les instructions sont gardées en mémoire/sont enregistrées dans une mémoire intermédiaire; **my lawyer ~s a copy of my will** mon avocat détient OR conserve un exemplaire de mon testament; **this photo ~s fond memories for me** cette photo me rappelle de bons souvenirs. -**10.** AUT: **the new car ~s the road well** la nouvelle voiture tient bien la route.

B. -**1.** [maintain in position] tenir, maintenir; **she held her arms by her sides** elle avait les bras le long du corps; **her hair was held in place with hairpins** des épingles (à cheveux) retenaient OR maintenaient ses cheveux; **what's ~ing the picture in place?** qu'est-ce qui tient OR maintient le tableau en place?; **~ the picture a bit higher** tenez le tableau un peu plus haut. -**2.** [carry] tenir; **to ~ o.s. upright** OR **erect** se tenir droit.

C. -**1.** [confine, detain] détenir; **the police are ~ing him for questioning** la police l'a gardé à vue pour l'interroger; **they're ~ing him for murder** ils l'ont arrêté pour meurtre. -**2.** [keep back, retain] retenir; **to ~ sthg in trust for sb** tenir qqch par fidéicommis pour qqn; **the post office will ~ my mail for me while I'm away** la poste gardera mon courrier pendant mon absence; **once she starts talking politics there's no ~ing her!** *fig* dès qu'elle commence à parler politique, rien ne peut l'arrêter!; **one burger, ~ the mustard!** *Am* [in restaurant] un hamburger, sans moutarde! -**3.** [delay]: **don't ~ dinner for me** ne m'attendez pas pour dîner; **they held the plane another thirty minutes** ils ont retenu l'avion au sol pendant encore trente minutes; **~ all decisions on the project until I get back** attendez mon retour pour prendre des décisions concernant le projet; **~ the front page!** ne lancez pas la une tout de suite! -**4.** [keep in check]: **we have held costs to a minimum** nous avons limité nos frais au minimum; **inflation has been held at the same level for several months** le taux d'inflation est maintenu au même niveau depuis plusieurs mois; **they held their opponents to a goalless draw** ils ont réussi à imposer le match nul.

D. -**1.** [assert, claim] maintenir, soutenir; [believe] croire, considérer; **I ~ that teachers should be better paid** *fml* je considère OR j'estime que les enseignants devraient être mieux payés; **the Constitution ~s that all men are free** la Constitution stipule que tous les hommes sont libres; **to ~ a belief** croire; **she ~s strong views on the subject** elle a une opinion bien arrêtée sur le sujet; **her statement is held to be true** sa déclaration passe pour vraie. -**2.** [consider, regard] tenir, considérer; **to ~ sb responsible for sthg** tenir qqn pour responsable de qqch; **I'll ~ you responsible if anything goes wrong** je vous tiendrai pour responsable OR je vous considérerai responsable s'il y a le moindre incident; **the president is to be held accountable for his actions** le président doit répondre de ses actes; **to ~ sb in contempt** mépriser OR avoir du mépris pour qqn; **to ~ sb in high esteem** avoir beaucoup d'estime pour qqn, tenir qqn en haute estime. -**3.** JUR [judge] juger; **the appeal court held the evidence to be insufficient** la cour d'appel a considéré que les preuves étaient insuffisantes.

E. -**1.** [carry on, engage in - conversation, meeting] tenir; [- party] donner; [organize] organiser; **to ~ an election/elections** procéder à une élection/à des élections; **the book fair is held in Frankfurt** la foire du livre se tient OR a lieu à Francfort; **the classes are held in the evening** les cours ont lieu le soir; **interviews will be held in early May** les entretiens auront lieu au début du mois de mai OR début mai; **to ~ talks** être en pourparlers; **the city is ~ing a service for Armistice Day** la ville organise un office pour commémorer le 11 Novembre; **mass is held at 11 o'clock** la messe est célébrée à 11 h. -**2.** [continue without deviation] continuer; **we held our southerly course** nous avons maintenu le cap au sud, nous avons continué notre route vers le sud; **to ~ a note** MUS tenir une note. -**3.** TELEC: **will you ~ (the line)?** voulez-vous patienter?; **~ the line!** ne quittez pas!; **the line's busy just now — I'll ~** le poste est occupé pour le moment — je patiente OR je reste en ligne.

◇ *vi* -**1.** [cling - person] se tenir, s'accrocher; **she held tight to the railing** elle s'est cramponnée OR accrochée à la rampe; **~ fast!, ~ tight!** accrochez-vous bien!; **their resolve held fast** OR **firm in the face of fierce opposition** *fig* ils ont tenu bon face à une opposition acharnée || [remain in place - nail, fastening] tenir bon; **the rope won't ~ for long** la corde ne tiendra pas longtemps. -**2.** [last - luck] durer; [- weather] durer, se maintenir; **prices held at the same level as last year** les prix se sont maintenus au même niveau que l'année dernière; **the pound held firm against the dollar** la livre s'est maintenue par rapport au dollar; **we might buy him a guitar if his interest in music ~s** nous lui achèterons peut-être une guitare s'il continue à s'intéresser à la musique. -**3.** [remain valid - invitation, offer] tenir; [- argument, theory] valoir, être valable; **to ~ good** [invitation, offer] tenir; [promises] tenir, valoir; [argument, theory] rester valable; **the principle still ~s good** le principe tient OR vaut toujours; **that theory only ~s if you consider...** cette théorie n'est valable que si vous prenez en compte...; **the same ~s for Spain** il en est de même pour l'Espagne. -**4.** [stay, remain]: **~ still!** *inf* ne bougez pas!

◇ *n* -**1.** [grasp, grip] prise *f*; [in wrestling] prise *f*; **to catch** OR **to grab** OR **to seize** OR **to take ~ of sthg** se saisir de OR saisir qqch; **she caught ~ of the rope** elle a saisi la corde; **grab (a) ~ of that towel** tiens! prends cette serviette; **there was nothing for me to grab ~ of** il n'y avait rien à quoi m'accrocher OR me cramponner; **get a good** OR **take a firm ~ on** OR **of the railing** tenez-vous bien à la balustrade; **I still had ~ of his hand** je le tenais toujours par la main; **to get ~ of sthg** [find] se procurer qqch; **we got ~ of the book you wanted** nous avons trouvé le livre que tu voulais; **where did you get ~ of that idea?** où est-ce que tu es allé chercher cette idée?; **to get ~ of sb** trouver qqn; **I've been trying to get ~ of you all week!** je t'ai cherché toute la semaine!; **just wait till the newspapers get ~ of the story** attendez un peu que les journaux s'emparent de la nouvelle; **she kept ~ of the rope** elle n'a pas lâché la corde; **you'd better keep ~ of the tickets** tu ferais bien de garder les billets; **get a ~ on yourself** ressaisis-toi, ne te laisse pas aller; **to take ~** [fire] prendre; [idea] se répandre ❑ **no ~s barred** SPORT & *fig* tous les coups sont permis. -**2.** [controlling force or influence] prise *f*, influence *f*; **the church still exerts a strong ~ on the country** l'Église a toujours une forte mainmise sur le pays; **to have a ~ over sb** avoir de l'influence sur qqn; **I have no ~ over him** je n'ai aucune prise OR influence sur lui; **the mafia obviously has some kind of ~ over him** de toute évidence, la mafia le tient d'une manière ou d'une autre. -**3.** [in climbing] prise *f*. -**4.** [delay, pause] pause *f*, arrêt *m*; **the company has put a ~ on all new orders** l'entreprise a suspendu OR gelé toutes les nouvelles commandes. -**5.** *Am* [order to reserve] réservation *f*; **the association put a ~ on all the hotel rooms** l'association a réservé toutes les chambres de l'hôtel. -**6.** [prison] prison *f*; [cell] cellule *f*; [fortress] place *f* forte. -**7.** [store - in plane] soute *f*; [- in ship] cale *f*. -**8.** MUS point *m* d'orgue.

◆ **on hold** *adv phr* [gen & TELEC] en attente; **we've put the project on ~** nous avons mis le projet en attente; **the operator kept me on ~ for ten minutes** le standardiste m'a mis en attente pendant dix minutes.

◆ **hold against** *vt sep*: **to ~ sthg against sb** en vouloir à qqn de qqch; **his collaboration with the enemy will be held against him** sa collaboration avec l'ennemi lui sera préjudiciable; **he lied to her and she still ~s it against him** il lui a menti et elle lui en veut toujours; **I hope you won't ~ it against me if I decide not to accept** j'espère que tu ne m'en voudras pas si je décide de ne pas accepter.

◆ **hold back** ◇ *vt sep* -**1.** [control, restrain - animal, person] retenir, tenir; [- crowd, enemy forces] contenir; [- anger, laughter, tears] retenir, réprimer; **the government has succeeded in ~ing back inflation** le gouvernement a réussi à contenir l'inflation. -**2.** [keep - money, supplies] retenir; *fig* [- information, truth] cacher, taire; **she's ~ing something back from me** elle me cache quelque chose. -**3.** *Am* SCH: **they held her back a year** ils lui ont fait redoubler une classe, ils l'ont fait redoubler. -**4.** [prevent progress of] empêcher de progresser; **his difficulties with maths are ~ing him back** ses difficultés en maths l'empêchent de progresser.

◇ *vi insep literal* [stay back] rester en arrière; *fig* [refrain] se retenir; **he has held back from making a commitment** il s'est abstenu de s'engager; **the president held back before sending in the army** le président a hésité avant d'envoyer les troupes; **don't ~ back, tell me everything** vas-y, dis-moi tout.

◆ **hold down** *vt sep* -**1.** [keep in place - paper, carpet] maintenir en place; [- person] forcer à rester par terre, maintenir au sol; **it took four men to ~ him down** il a fallu quatre hommes pour le maîtriser OR pour le maintenir au sol. -**2.** [keep to limit] restreindre, limiter; **they're ~ing unemployment down to 4%** ils maintiennent le taux de chômage à 4 %; **to ~ prices down** empêcher les prix de monter, empêcher la montée des prix. -**3.** [employee]: **to ~ down a job** garder un emploi; **he's never managed to ~ down a job** il n'a jamais pu garder un emploi bien longtemps.

◆ **hold forth** *vi insep* pérorer, disserter; **he held forth on the evils of drink** il a fait un long discours sur les conséquences néfastes de l'alcool.

◆ **hold in** *vt sep* [emotion] retenir; **I don't know how I managed to ~ in my anger** je ne sais pas comment j'ai réussi à contenir ma colère; **~ your stomach in!** rentre ton ventre!

◆ **hold off** ◇ *vt sep* -**1.** [keep at distance] tenir à distance OR éloigné; **the troops held off the enemy** les troupes ont tenu l'ennemi à distance; **they managed to ~ off the attack** ils ont réussi à repousser l'attaque; **I can't ~ the reporters off any longer** je ne peux plus faire attendre OR patienter les journalistes. -**2.** [delay, put off] remettre à plus tard; **he held off going to see the doctor until May** il a attendu le mois de mai pour aller voir le médecin; **I held off making a decision** j'ai remis la décision à plus tard.

◇ *vi insep* -**1.** [rain]: **at least the rain held off** au moins il n'a pas plu. -**2.** [abstain] s'abstenir; **~ off from smoking for a few weeks** abstenez-vous de fumer OR ne fumez pas pendant quelques semaines.

◆ **hold on** ◇ *vi insep* -**1.** [grasp, grip] tenir bien, s'accrocher; **to ~ on to sthg** bien tenir qqch, s'accrocher à qqch, se cramponner à qqch; **~ on!** accrochez-vous!; **~ on to your hat!** tenez votre chapeau (sur la tête)! -**2.** [keep possession

of] garder; ~ on to this contract for me [keep it] garde-moi ce contrat; all politicians try to ~ on to power tous les hommes politiques essaient de rester au pouvoir; ~ on to your dreams/ideals accrochez-vous à vos rêves/ idéaux. -3. [continue, persevere] tenir, tenir le coup; how long can you ~ on? combien de temps pouvez-vous tenir (le coup)?; I can't ~ on much longer je ne peux pas tenir (le coup) beaucoup plus longtemps. -4. [wait] attendre; [stop] arrêter; ~ on just one minute! [stop] arrêtez!; [wait] attendez!, pas si vite!; ~ on, how do I know I can trust you? attends un peu! qu'est-ce qui me prouve que je peux te faire confiance? || TELEC: ~ on please! ne quittez pas!; I had to ~ on for several minutes before he answered j'ai dû patienter plusieurs minutes avant qu'il ne réponde.
◇ *vt sep* [maintain in place] tenir OR maintenir en place; her hat is held on with pins son chapeau est maintenu (en place) par des épingles.
◆ **hold out** ◇ *vi insep* -1. [last - supplies, stocks] durer; will the car ~ out till we get home? la voiture tiendra-t-elle (le coup) jusqu'à ce qu'on rentre? -2. [refuse to yield] tenir bon, tenir le coup; the garrison held out for weeks la garnison a tenu bon pendant des semaines; the management held out against any suggested changes la direction a refusé tous les changements proposés.
◇ *vt sep* [extend] tendre; she held out the book to him elle lui a tendu le livre; to ~ out one's hand to sb *literal & fig* tendre la main à qqn; I held out my hand j'ai tendu la main; his mother held her arms out to him sa mère lui a ouvert OR tendu les bras.
◇ *vt insep* [offer, present] offrir; I can't ~ out any promise of improvement je ne peux promettre aucune amélioration; the doctors ~ out little hope for him les médecins ont peu d'espoir pour lui; science ~s out some hope for cancer patients la science offre un espoir pour les malades du cancer.
◆ **hold out for** *vt insep* exiger; the workers held out for a shorter working week les ouvriers réclamaient une semaine de travail plus courte.
◆ **hold out on** *inf vt insep*: you're ~ing out on me! tu me caches quelque chose!
◆ **hold over** *vt sep* -1. [position] tenir sur; she held the glass over the sink elle tenait le verre au-dessus de l'évier; they ~ the threat of redundancy over their workers *fig* ils maintiennent la menace de licenciement sur leurs ouvriers. -2. [postpone] remettre, reporter; we'll ~ these items over until the next meeting on va remettre ces questions à la prochaine réunion. -3. [retain] retenir, garder; they're ~ing the show over for another month ils vont laisser le spectacle à l'affiche encore un mois. -4. MUS tenir.
◆ **hold to** ◇ *vt insep* [promise, tradition] s'en tenir à, rester fidèle à; [decision] maintenir, s'en tenir à; you must ~ to your principles vous devez rester fidèle à vos principes.
◇ *vt sep*: we held him to his promise nous lui avons fait tenir parole; if I win, I'll buy you lunch – I'll ~ you to that! si je gagne, je t'invite à déjeuner – je te prends au mot!
◆ **hold together** *vt sep* [book, car] maintenir; [community, family] maintenir l'union de; we need a leader who can ~ the workers together il nous faut un chef qui puisse rallier les ouvriers.
◆ **hold up** ◇ *vt sep* -1. [lift, raise] lever, élever; I held up my hand j'ai levé la main; ~ the picture up to the light tenez la photo à contre-jour; to ~ up one's head redresser la tête; she felt she would never be able to ~ her head up again *fig* elle pensait qu'elle ne pourrait plus jamais marcher la tête haute. -2. [support] soutenir; my trousers were held up with safety pins mon pantalon était maintenu par des épingles de sûreté. -3. [present as example]: they were held up as an example of efficient local government on les présentaient comme un exemple de gouvernement local compétent; to ~ sb up to ridicule tourner qqn en ridicule. -4. [delay] retarder; [stop] arrêter; the traffic held us up la circulation nous a mis en retard; the accident held up traffic for an hour l'accident a bloqué la circulation pendant une heure; I was held up j'ai été retenu; the project was held up for lack of funds [before it started] le projet a été mis en attente faute de financement; [after it started] le projet a été interrompu faute de financement. -5. [rob] faire une attaque à main armée; to ~ up a bank faire un hold-up dans une banque.
◇ *vi insep* [clothing, equipment] tenir; [supplies] tenir, durer; [weather] se maintenir; the car held up well during the trip la voiture a bien tenu le coup pendant le voyage.
◆ **hold with** *vt insep Br* [agree with] être d'accord avec; [approve of] approuver; I don't ~ with her ideas on socialism je ne suis pas d'accord avec OR je ne partage pas ses idées concernant le socialisme; his mother doesn't ~ with private schools sa mère est contre OR désapprouve les écoles privées.

holdall ['həʊldɔːl] *n Br* (sac *m*) fourre-tout *m inv*.

holder ['həʊldəʳ] *n* -1. [for lamp, plastic cup etc] support *m*; cigarette ~ fume-cigarette *m inv*; candle ~ bougeoir *m*. -2. [person - of ticket] détenteur *m*, -trice *f*; [- of passport, post, diploma] titulaire *mf*; [- of lease] locataire *mf*; SPORT [- of record, cup] détenteur *m*, -trice *f*; [- of title] détenteur *m*, -trice *f*, tenant *m*, -e *f*; FIN [- of stock] porteur *m*, -euse *f*, détenteur *m*, -trice *f*.

holding ['həʊldɪŋ] ◇ *n* -1. [of meeting] tenue *f*. -2. [in boxing]: ~ is against the rules il est contraire au règlement de tenir son adversaire. -3. [land] propriété *f*. -4. FIN participation *f*; ~s [lands] propriétés *fpl*, terres *fpl*; [stocks] participation *f*, portefeuille *m*.
◇ *comp*: ~ company FIN (société *f* en) holding *m*; ~ operation opération *f* de maintien; we were in a ~ pattern over Heathrow for two hours AERON nous avons eu une attente de deux heures au-dessus de Heathrow.

holdover ['həʊld,əʊvəʳ] *n Am* vestige *m*; CIN & THEAT *film ou pièce de théâtre qui reste à l'affiche plus longtemps que prévu*; a ~ from the war un vestige de la guerre.

hold-up *n* -1. [robbery] hold-up *m*, vol *m* à main armée. -2. [delay - on road, railway track etc] ralentissement *m*; [- in production, departure etc] retard *m*.

hole [həʊl] ◇ *n* -1. [in the ground] trou *m*; [in wall, roof etc] trou *m*; [in clouds] éclaircie *f*; to dig a ~ creuser un trou; his socks were full of OR in ~s ses chaussettes étaient pleines de trous; his sock's got a ~ in it il a un trou à sa chaussette; to wear a ~ in sthg faire un trou à qqch; to make a ~ in one's savings/a bottle of whisky *fig* bien entamer ses économies/une bouteille de whisky; money burns a ~ in my pocket l'argent me file entre les doigts; to pick ~s in an argument trouver des failles à une argumentation; to try to pick ~s in an argument chercher des failles à une argumentation; his argument's full of ~s son argumentation est pleine de défauts OR failles ❑ a ~ in the wall un café OR restaurant minuscule; [cash dispenser] un distributeur de billets; I need that like a ~ in the head *inf* c'est vraiment la dernière chose dont j'aie besoin; you're talking through a ~ in your head *inf* tu racontes n'importe quoi; that's filled a ~! *inf* ça m'a bien calé! -2. *inf pej* [boring place] trou *m*; what a ~! [town] quel trou!; this is an awful ~! [house, pub, disco] c'est mortel ici! -3. *inf* [tricky situation] pétrin *m*; to be in a ~ être dans le pétrin; to get sb out of a ~ sortir qqn du pétrin. -4. SPORT [in golf] trou *m*; to get a ~ in one faire un trou en un; an 18-~ (golf) course un parcours de 18 trous; we played a few ~s of golf together nous avons fait quelques trous ensemble au golf.
◇ *vt* -1. [make hole in] trouer. -2. [in golf]: to ~ the ball faire le trou; he ~d the fourteenth in four il a fait le quatorzième trou en quatr (coups).
◇ *vi* -1. [sock, stocking] se trouer. -2. [in golf] faire le trou; to ~ in four faire le trou en quatr (coups).
◆ **hole out** *vi insep* [in golf] finir le trou.
◆ **hole up** ◇ *vi insep* -1. [animal] se terrer -2. *inf* [hide] se planquer.
◇ *vt sep (usu pass)*: they're ~d up in a hote ils se planquent OR ils sont planqués dans u hôtel.

hole-and-corner *inf adj* [meeting, love affair etc] clandestin, secret.

hole in the heart *n* malformation *f* du cœur; to have a ~ avoir une malformation du cœur avoir la maladie bleue; a baby born with a ~ un enfant bleu.
◆ **hole-in-the-heart** *adj* [baby] bleu; a hole-in the-heart operation une opération d'une mal formation du cœur.

holey ['həʊlɪ] *adj* troué, plein de trous.

holiday ['hɒlɪdeɪ] ◇ *n* -1. *Br* [period withou work] vacances *fpl*; Christmas ~ vacances de Noël; summer ~ OR ~s vacances d'été; SC grandes vacances; on ~ en vacances; to go on ~ aller OR partir en vacances; to go on camping ~ aller passer ses vacances en cam ping; I'm going on ~ in a week je pars e vacances dans une semaine; we went to Greece for our ~s last year nous sommes allés passe nos vacances en Grèce l'année dernière; to take a ~/two months' ~ prendre des vacances, deux mois de vacances; how much OR how long a ~ do you get? combien de vacance as-tu?; ~ with pay, paid ~s congés *mpl* payés I need OR could do with a ~ j'ai besoin de vacances; take a ~ from the housework oublie un peu les travaux ménagers; I wish I could take a ~ from the children for a few days s seulement je pouvais passer quelques jours sans les enfants; it's no ~! ce n'est pas des vacan ces! -2. [day off] jour *m* de congé; tomorrow is a ~ demain c'est férié; public ~ jour *m* férié
◇ *comp* [mood, feeling, destination] de vacances [pay] versé pendant les vacances; the ~ traffic la circulation des départs en vacances; the ~ rush has started la folie OR cohue des départs en vacances a commencé.
◇ *vi Br* passer les vacances.

holiday camp *n Br centre de vacances familia (avec animations et activités diverses)*.

holiday home *n Br* maison *f* de vacances, résidence *f* secondaire.

holidaymaker ['hɒlɪdeɪ,meɪkəʳ] *n Br* vacancier *m*, -ère *f*.

holiday resort *n Br* lieu *m* de vacances OR de séjour.

holiday season *n Br* saison *f* des vacances.

holier-than-thou ['həʊlɪəðən'ðaʊ] *adj pej* [attitude, tone, person] moralisateur; to be ~ towards other people se comporter en pharisien avec les autres.

holiness ['həʊlɪnɪs] *n* sainteté *f*; His/Your Holiness Sa/Votre Sainteté.

holism ['həʊlɪzm] *n* MED & PHILOS holisme *m*

holistic [həʊ'lɪstɪk] *adj* MED & PHILOS holistique.

holland ['hɒlənd] *n* TEX hollande *f*.

Holland ['hɒlənd] *pr n* -1. [country] Hollande *f*, Pays-Bas *mpl*; in ~ en Hollande, aux Pays-Bas -2. *arch* [gin]: ~s genièvre *m* de Schiedam.

holler *inf* ['hɒləʳ] ◇ *vi* brailler, beugler.
◇ *vt* brailler.
◇ *n* braillement *m*; to give OR to let out a ~ brailler.
◆ **holler out** *inf vi insep & vt sep* = **holler**.

hollow ['hɒləʊ] ◇ *adj* -1. [not solid - tree, container] creux; to have a ~ feeling in one's stomach avoir une sensation de vide dans l'estomac ❑ to feel ~ [hungry] avoir le ventre OR l'estomac creux; you must have ~ legs! *inf* [able to eat a lot] tu dois avoir le ver solitaire!; [able to drink a lot] qu'est-ce que tu peux boire!, tu as une sacrée descente! -2. [sunken - eyes, cheeks] creux, cave. -3. [empty - sound] creux, caverneux; [- laugh, laughter] faux, forcé; in a ~

voice d'une voix éteinte; she gave a ~ laugh elle a ri d'un air un peu faux OR forcé, elle a ri jaune. -**4.** [worthless - promise, words] vain; it was a ~ victory for her cette victoire lui semblait dérisoire.
◇ *adv*: to sound ~ [tree, wall] sonner creux; [laughter, excuse, promise] sonner faux ❑ to beat sb ~ *inf Br* battre qqn à plate couture.
◇ *n* -**1.** [in tree] creux *m*, cavité *f*. -**2.** [in ground] enfoncement *m*, dénivellation *f*. -**3.** [in hand, back] creux *m*.
◇ *vt* creuser.
◆ **hollow out** *vt sep* creuser.

Holloway ['hɒləweɪ] *pr n*: ~ (Prison) *grande prison pour femmes dans le nord de Londres*.

hollow-cheeked *adj* aux joues creuses.

hollow-eyed *adj* aux yeux caves OR enfoncés.

hollowness ['hɒləʊnɪs] *n* -**1.** [of tree] creux *m*, cavité *f*. -**2.** [of features]: the ~ of his eyes ses yeux enfoncés; the ~ of his cheeks ses joues creuses. -**3.** [of sound] timbre *m* caverneux; [of laughter] fausseté *f*; the ~ of her voice sa voix éteinte. -**4.** [of promise, excuse] fausseté *f*, manque *m* de sincérité; the ~ of a victory une victoire qui ne veut rien dire.

holly ['hɒlɪ] ◇ *n* [tree, leaves] houx *m*.
◇ *comp*: ~ berry baie *f* de houx, cenelle *f*; ~ tree houx *m*.

hollyhock ['hɒlɪhɒk] *n* rose *f* trémière.

Hollywood ['hɒlɪwʊd] ◇ *pr n* Hollywood.
◇ *adj* hollywoodien.

holm [həʊm] = **holm oak**.

holmium ['hɒlmɪəm] *n* holmium *m*.

holm oak *n* chêne *m* vert, yeuse *f*.

holocaust ['hɒləkɔːst] *n* holocauste *m*; the Holocaust l'Holocauste.

hologram ['hɒləgræm] *n* hologramme *m*.

holograph ['hɒləgræf] ◇ *n* document *m* olographe OR holographe.
◇ *adj* olographe, holographe.

holography [hɒ'lɒgrəfɪ] *n* holographie *f*.

hols *inf* [hɒlz] *npl Br* SCH vacances *fpl*.

Holstein ['hɒlstaɪn] *n Am* [cow] frisonne *f*.

holster ['həʊlstəʳ] *n* [for gun - on waist, shoulder] étui *m* de revolver; [- on saddle] fonte *f*; [for piece of equipment] étui *m*.

holy ['həʊlɪ] (*compar* holier, *superl* holiest) ◇ *adj* -**1.** [sacred - bread, water] bénit; [- place, ground, day] saint; the Holy Bible la Sainte Bible; the Holy City [Jerusalem] la Ville sainte; to take Holy Communion communier, recevoir la Sainte Communion; the Holy Family la Sainte Famille; the Holy Father le saint-père; the Holy Ghost OR Spirit le Saint-Esprit, l'Esprit saint; the Holy Grail le Graal OR Saint-Graal; the quest for the Holy Grail la quête du Graal OR Saint-Graal; a quest for the Holy Grail *fig* une quête du Graal, une croisade; the Holy Land la Terre sainte; ~ orders ordres *mpl*; to take ~ orders entrer dans les ordres; the Holy Roman Empire le Saint-Empire romain; the Holy Rood la Sainte Croix; Holy Saturday Samedi *m* saint; Holy Scripture OR Writ Écriture *f* sainte, les Saintes Écritures; it's not ~ writ! *fig* ce n'est pas parole d'évangile!; the Holy See le Saint-Siège; the Holy Sepulchre le Saint-Sépulcre; the Holy Synod le saint-synode; the Holy Trinity la Sainte Trinité; ~ war guerre *f* sainte; Holy Week Semaine *f* sainte; to swear by all that is ~ jurer par tous les saints. -**2.** [devout] saint; Holy Joe *inf* bigot *m*. -**3.** *inf* [as intensifier]: that child is a ~ terror [mischievous] cet enfant est un vrai démon; the new headmaster is a ~ terror [intimidating] le nouveau principal est redoutable; to have a ~ fear of sthg avoir une sainte peur de qqch ❑ ~ smoke!, ~ mackerel!, ~ cow! mince alors!, ça alors!, Seigneur!
◇ *n*: the Holy of Holies RELIG le saint des saints; *hum* & *fig* [inner sanctum] sanctuaire *m*, antre *m* sacré; [special place] lieu *m* saint.

homage ['hɒmɪdʒ] *n* hommage *m*; to pay OR to do ~ to sb, to do sb ~ rendre hommage à qqn; in silent ~ en hommage silencieux.

homburg ['hɒmbɜːg] *n* chapeau *m* mou, feutre *m* souple.

home [həʊm] ◇ *n* -**1.** [one's house] maison *f*; [more subjectively] chez-soi *m inv*; a ~ from ~ un second chez-soi; I left ~ at 16 j'ai quitté la maison à 16 ans; her ~ is not far from mine sa maison n'est pas loin de chez moi; to have a ~ of one's own avoir un foyer OR un chez-soi; how long has he been missing from ~? depuis combien de temps a-t-il disparu de la maison?; he was found far away from ~ on l'a trouvé loin de chez lui; his ~ is in Nice il habite Nice; New York will always be ~ for me! c'est toujours à New York que je me sentirai chez moi!; when did she make her ~ in Hollywood? quand s'est-elle installée à Hollywood?; emigrants came to make their ~s in Canada des émigrés sont venus s'installer au Canada; to give sb a ~ recueillir qqn chez soi; they have a lovely ~! c'est très agréable chez eux! ❑ at ~ chez soi, à la maison; come and see me at ~ passez me voir à la maison; Mrs Carr is not at ~ on Mondays *fml* Mme Carr ne reçoit pas le lundi; make yourself at ~ faites comme chez vous; he made himself at ~ in the chair il s'est mis à l'aise dans le fauteuil; she feels at ~ everywhere! elle est à l'aise partout!; to be OR to feel at ~ with sb se sentir à l'aise avec qqn; he doesn't yet feel at ~ with the machine il n'est pas encore à l'aise avec la machine; I work out of OR at ~ je travaille à domicile OR chez moi; there's no place like ~ *prov* on n'est vraiment bien que chez soi; ~ is where the heart is *prov* où le cœur aime, là est le foyer. -**2.** [family unit] foyer *m*; ADMIN habitation *f*, logement *m*; the father left ~ le père a abandonné le foyer; to start OR to set up a ~ fonder un foyer; are you having problems at ~? est-ce que tu as des problèmes chez toi?; he comes from a good ~ il vient d'une famille comme il faut. -**3.** [native land] patrie *f*, pays *m* natal; it's the same at ~ c'est la même chose chez nous OR dans notre pays ‖ *fig*: this discussion is getting a bit close to ~! on aborde un sujet dangereux!; let's look at a situation closer to OR nearer ~ examinons une situation qui nous concerne plus directement; Kentucky, the ~ of bourbon Kentucky, le pays du bourbon; the ~ of jazz le berceau du jazz. -**4.** BOT & ZOOL habitat *m*. -**5.** [mental hospital] maison *f* de repos; [old people's home] maison *f* de retraite; [children's home] foyer *m* pour enfants. -**6.** GAMES & SPORT [finishing line] arrivée *f*; [on board game] case *f* départ; [goal] but *m*; they play better at ~ ils jouent mieux sur leur terrain; to be at ~ to recevoir; the Rams meet the Braves at ~ les Rams jouent à domicile contre les Braves.
◇ *adv* -**1.** [to or at one's house] chez soi, à la maison; to go OR to get ~ rentrer (chez soi OR à la maison); she'll be ~ tonight elle sera à la maison ce soir; to see sb ~ raccompagner qqn jusque chez lui/elle; to take sb ~ ramener qqn chez lui; Fido, ~! Fido, rentre OR à la maison! ❑ it's nothing to write ~ about *inf* il n'y a pas de quoi en faire un plat; ~ and dry *Br*, ~ free *inf Am* sauvé. -**2.** [from abroad] au pays natal, au pays; when did you get OR come ~? quand es-tu rentré?; to send sb ~ rapatrier qqn; the grandparents want to go OR to return ~ les grands-parents veulent rentrer dans leur pays. -**3.** [all the way] à fond; to drive a nail ~ enfoncer un clou jusqu'au bout; the remark really went ~ le commentaire a fait mouche; to bring sthg ~ to sb faire comprendre OR voir qqch à qqn.
◇ *adj* -**1.** [concerning family, household - life] de famille, familial; [- for family consumption] familial, à usage familial; ~ remedy remède *m* de bonne femme; ~ comforts confort *m* du foyer. -**2.** [to, for house] à OR pour la maison; ~ visit/delivery visite *f*/livraison *f* à domicile; ~ banking la banque à domicile; ~ decorating décoration *f* intérieure; ~ cleaning products produits *mpl* ménagers. -**3.** [national - gen] national, du pays; [- market, policy, sales] intérieur. -**4.** SPORT [team - national] national; [- local] local; the ~ team today is... l'équipe qui reçoit aujourd'hui est...; ~ game match *m* à domicile.
◇ *vi* [person, animal] revenir OR rentrer chez soi; [pigeon] revenir au colombier.
◆ **home in on** *vt insep* -**1.** [subj: missile] se diriger (automatiquement) sur OR vers; [proceed towards - goal] se diriger vers; *fig* mettre le cap sur. -**2.** [direct attention to - problem, solution] mettre l'accent sur; [- difficulty, question] viser, cerner.
◆ **home on to** = **home in on**.

home address *n* [on form] domicile *m* (permanent); [not business address] adresse *f* personnelle.

home automation *n* domotique *f*.

home-baked *adj* -**1.** [in home] maison *(inv)*, fait à la maison; ~ bread pain *m* fait à la maison. -**2.** [on premises] maison *(inv)*, fait maison.

homebody *inf* ['həʊm,bɒdɪ] (*pl* homebodies) *n* pantouflard *m*, -e *f*.

homebound ['həʊmbaʊnd] *adj* -**1.** [going home] sur le chemin du retour. -**2.** [confined to home] obligé de rester à la maison; [of sick people] qui garde la chambre.

homebred ['həʊmbred] *adj* -**1.** *literal* élevé à la maison; [homemade] fait à la maison. -**2.** [manner] naturel, rustique; [humour, language, tastes] peu raffiné, populaire. -**3.** [not foreign] du pays; he's a ~ version of Sinatra *inf* c'est notre Sinatra à nous.

home brew *n* [beer] bière *f* faite à la maison; [wine] vin *m* fait à la maison.

home brewing [-'bruːɪŋ] *n Am* [illegal distilling] *distillation clandestine d'alcool à domicile*.

homecoming ['həʊm,kʌmɪŋ] *n* [to family] retour *m* au foyer OR à la maison; [to country] retour *m* au pays; 'The Homecoming' *Pinter* 'le Retour'.
◆ **Homecoming** *Am* SCH & UNIV *fête donnée en l'honneur de l'équipe de football d'une université ou d'une école et à laquelle sont invités les anciens élèves*.

home computer *n* ordinateur *m* personnel, micro-ordinateur *m*.

home cooking *n* cuisine *f* familiale.

Home Counties *pl pr n*: the ~ *l'ensemble des comtés limitrophes de Londres*.

home country *n* pays *m* natal; the ~ le pays.

home economics *n (U)* économie *f* domestique.

home fries *npl Am* CULIN pommes de terre *fpl* sautées.

home front *n* -**1.** [during war] arrière *m*; on the ~ à l'arrière. -**2.** [in the home country]: what's the news on the ~? quelles sont les nouvelles du pays? -**3.** [at home]: how are things on the ~? comment ça va à la maison?

home ground *n* -**1.** to be on ~ [near home] être en pays de connaissance; *fig* [familiar subject] être sur son terrain. -**2.** SPORT: our ~ notre terrain; when they play at their ~ quand ils jouent sur leur terrain, quand ils reçoivent.

homegrown [,həʊm'grəʊn] *adj* [not foreign] du pays; [from own garden] du jardin.

Home Guard *n*: the ~ *les volontaires pour la défense du territoire en Grande-Bretagne en 1940-45, 1951-57*.

home help *n Br* aide *f* ménagère.

homeland ['həʊmlænd] *n* -**1.** [native country] patrie *f*. -**2.** [South African political territory] homeland *m*; the ~s policy la politique des homelands.

home leave *n Br* congé *m* au foyer.

homeless ['həʊmlɪs] ◇ *adj* sans foyer; [pet] abandonné, sans foyer.
◇ *npl*: the ~ les sans-abri *mpl*.

homelessness ['həʊmlɪsnəs] *n*: the problem of ~ le problème des sans-abri; ~ is an increasing problem les sans-abri représentent un problème de plus en plus grave.

home life *n* vie *f* de famille.

home loan *n* prêt *m* immobilier.

home-lover *n* casanier *m*, -ère *f*; [woman] femme *f* d'intérieur.

home-loving *adj* casanier.

homely ['həʊmlɪ] (*compar* homelier, *superl* homeliest) *adj* -**1.** [unpretentious] simple, modeste; they offer good but ~ fare on y mange bien mais sans façon; they're ~ folk ce sont des gens sans prétention. -**2.** [kind] aimable, plein de bonté; my aunt was a ~ old sort *inf* ma tante était une de ces bonnes vieilles dames. -**3.** *Am* [ugly - person]: what a ~ baby! il n'est vraiment pas beau ce bébé!

homemade [,həʊm'meɪd] *adj* -**1.** [made at home] fait à la maison *(inv)*; it's hard to believe your dress is ~ c'est difficile à croire que tu as fait ta robe toi-même; a ~ bomb une bombe de fabrication artisanale. -**2.** [made on premises] maison *(inv)*, fait maison; ~ apple pie [on menu] tarte *f* aux pommes (fait) maison.

homemaker ['həʊm,meɪkə] *n* femme *f* au foyer.

home movie *n* film *m* d'amateur.

Home Office *n*: the ~ *le ministère britannique de l'Intérieur*.

homeopath ['həʊmɪəʊpæθ] *n* homéopathe *mf*.

homeopathic [,həʊmɪəʊ'pæθɪk] *adj* homéopathique; a ~ doctor un (médecin) homéopathe; a ~ remedy un remède homéopathique.

homeopathy [,həʊmɪ'ɒpəθɪ] *n* homéopathie *f*.

homeostasis [,həʊmɪəʊ'steɪsɪs] *n* homéostasie *f*.

homeowner ['həʊm,əʊnəʳ] *n* propriétaire *mf*.

home plate *n* [in baseball] *plaque qui marque le début et la fin du parcours que doit effectuer le batteur pour marquer un point*.

home port *n* NAUT port *m* d'attache.

Homer ['həʊməʳ] *pr n* Homère.

Homeric [həʊ'merɪk] *adj* homérique.

homeroom ['həʊm,ruːm] *n Am* -**1.** [place] *salle où l'on fait l'appel*. -**2.** [group] *élèves rassemblés pour l'appel*.

Home Rule *pr n* [in Ireland] *gouvernement autonome de l'Irlande*.

HOME RULE:
Régime d'autonomie revendiqué par l'Irlande entre 1870 et 1914. Après plusieurs tentatives, une loi sur l'autonomie fut votée en 1914, établissant un Parlement composé de deux chambres chargées des affaires locales, mais cette mesure ne satisfaisait plus l'Irlande, qui réclamait l'indépendance.

---

home run *n* -**1.** [in baseball] *coup de batte qui permet au batteur de marquer un point en faisant un tour complet en une seule fois*. -**2.** [last leg of trip] dernière étape *f* du circuit; the ship/the delivery truck is on its ~ le navire/le camion rentre à son port d'attache/au dépôt.

Home Secretary *n* ministre *m* de l'Intérieur en Grande-Bretagne.

Home Show *n Am* ≃ salon *m* des arts ménagers et de la décoration.

homesick ['həʊmsɪk] *adj* nostalgique; to be ~ avoir le mal du pays; to be ~ for sb s'ennuyer de qqn; to be ~ for sthg avoir la nostalgie de qqch; he's ~ for his family sa famille lui manque.

homesickness ['həʊm,sɪknɪs] *n* mal *m* du pays.

homespun ['həʊmspʌn] ◇ *adj* -**1.** [wool] filé à la maison, de fabrication domestique; [cloth] de homespun. -**2.** [simple] simple, sans recherche. ◇ *n* homespun *m*.

homestead ['həʊmsted] ◇ *n* -**1.** *Am* HIST *terre dont la propriété est attribuée à un colon sous réserve qu'il y réside et l'exploite*; the Homestead Act *décret de 1862 par lequel le Congrès américain donnait 160 acres de terre à tout nouvel arrivant qui s'engageait à s'installer dans l'ouest*. -**2.** [buildings and land] propriété *f*; [farm] ferme *f*; *Austr* & *NZ* [house] maison *f (d'un ranch)*. -**3.** *Am* [birthplace]: he's returning to the ~ after a ten-year absence il rentre au pays après dix ans d'absence. ◇ *vt Am* [acquire] acquérir; [settle] s'installer à, coloniser. ◇ *vi Am s'installer sur une terre pour en devenir propriétaire*.

homesteader ['həʊmstedəʳ] *n* -**1.** *Am* HIST *personne qui acquiert une propriété en vertu du Homestead Act*. -**2.** [farm-owner] propriétaire *mf* d'une ferme; [ranch-owner] propriétaire *mf* d'un ranch.

home straight, home stretch *n* SPORT & *fig* dernière ligne *f* droite; they're on OR in the ~ ils sont dans la dernière ligne droite.

home time *n heure où l'on rentre à la maison*.

home town *n* -**1.** [of birth] ville *f* natale. -**2.** [of upbringing]: his ~ la ville où il a grandi.

home truth *n* vérité *f* désagréable; to tell sb a few ~s dire ses (quatre) vérités à qqn; I learnt some ~s about myself j'ai appris quelques vérités désagréables sur moi-même.

homeward ['həʊmwəd] ◇ *adj* du retour; on the ~ trip, he took the bus pour son (voyage de) retour, il a pris le bus. ◇ *adv* = **homewards**.

homeward-bound *adj* [commuters] qui rentre chez soi; [ship] sur le chemin du retour; to be homeward bound être sur le chemin du retour.

homewards ['həʊmwədz] *adv* -**1.** [to house] vers la maison; to head ~ se diriger vers la maison. -**2.** [to homeland] vers la patrie; to be ~ bound prendre le chemin du retour; the plane flew ~ l'avion faisait route vers sa base; the ship sailed ~ le navire faisait route vers son port d'attache.

home waters *npl* [territorial] eaux *fpl* territoriales; [near home port] eaux *fpl* voisines du port d'attache.

homework ['həʊmwɜːk] ◇ *n (U)* SCH devoirs *mpl* (à la maison); [research] travail *m* préparatoire; the minister hadn't done his ~ le ministre n'avait pas préparé son sujet. ◇ *comp*: a ~ exercise un devoir (à la maison).

homeworker ['həʊm,wɜːkəʳ] *n* travailleur *m*, -euse *f* à domicile.

homey *inf* ['həʊmɪ] (*pl* homies, *compar* homier, *superl* homiest) ◇ *n Am* -**1.** *Noir originaire du Sud récemment arrivé dans le Nord*. -**2.** [friend] pote *m*. ◇ *adj* = **homy**.

homicidal [,hɒmɪ'saɪdl] *adj* JUR homicide; a ~ maniac un maniaque à tendances homicides OR meurtrières.

homicide ['hɒmɪsaɪd] *n* JUR -**1.** [act] homicide *m*; accidental ~ homicide par imprudence; felonious/justifiable ~ homicide prémédité/par légitime défense. -**2.** [person] homicide *mf*.

homie *inf* ['həʊmɪ] = **homey** *n*.

homily ['hɒmɪlɪ] (*pl* homilies) *n* -**1.** RELIG homélie *f*. -**2.** *pej* [lecture] sermon *m*, homélie *f*; to read sb a ~ sermonner qqn.

homing ['həʊmɪŋ] *adj* [pre-programmed] autoguidé; [heat-seeking] à tête chercheuse; ~ device mécanisme *m* d'autoguidage; ~ guidance systems systèmes *mpl* d'autoguidage; ~ missile missile *m* à tête chercheuse.

homing pigeon *n* pigeon *m* voyageur.

hominid ['hɒmɪnɪd] ◇ *n* hominidé *m*. ◇ *adj* hominidien; the ~ family les hominidés.

hominoid ['hɒmɪnɔɪd] ◇ *n* humanoïde *m*. ◇ *adj* humanoïde.

hominy ['hɒmɪnɪ] *n Am* bouillie *f* de semoule de maïs.

homo▽ ['həʊməʊ] *pej* ◇ *n* pédé *m*, homo *mf*. ◇ *adj* pédé, homo.

homoeopath *etc* ['həʊmɪəʊpæθ] = **homeopath**.

homoeotasis [,həʊmɪəʊ'steɪsɪs] = **homeostasis**.

homogamy [hə'mɒgəmɪ] *n* homogamie *f*.

homogenate [həʊ'mɒdʒəneɪt] *n* résultat *m* de l'homogénéisation.

homogeneity [,hɒməʊdʒə'niːɪtɪ] *n* homogénéité *f*.

homogeneous [,hɒmə'dʒiːnjəs] *adj* homogène; a ~ population une population homogène.

homogenization [hə,mɒdʒənaɪ'zeɪʃən] *n* homogénéisation *f*.

homogenize, -ise [hə'mɒdʒənaɪz] *vt* homogénéiser, homogénéifier; ~d milk lait *m* homogénéisé.

homogenous [hə'mɒdʒənɪs] = **homogeneous**.

homogeny [hə'mɒdʒənɪ] *n ressemblance due à un ancêtre génétique commun*.

homograph ['hɒməgrɑːf] *n* LING homographe *m*.

homographic [hɒmə'græfɪk] *adj* LING homographe.

homologate [hɒ'mɒləgeɪt] *vt* homologuer.

homologous [hɒ'mɒləgəs] *adj* homologue.

homologue ['hɒməlɒg] *n* BIOL & CHEM homologue *m*.

homonym ['hɒmənɪm] *n* homonyme *m*; the words are ~s (of each other) ces mots sont homonymes (entre eux).

homonymous [hɒ'mɒnɪməs] *adj* homonyme.

homonymy [hɒ'mɒnɪmɪ] *n* homonymie *f*.

homophile ['hɒməfaɪl] *adj* homosexuel.

homophobe ['həʊməʊ,fəʊb] *n* homophobe *mf*.

homophobia [,həʊməʊ'fəʊbjə] *n intolérance vis-à-vis des homosexuels*.

homophobic [,həʊməʊ'fəʊbɪk] *adj intolérant vis-à-vis des homosexuels*.

homophone ['hɒməfəʊn] *n* LING homophone *m*.

homophonic [,hɒmə'fɒnɪk] *adj* MUS homophonique.

homophonous [hɒ'mɒfənəs] *adj* LING homophone.

homophony [hɒ'mɒfənɪ] (*pl* homophonies) *n* MUS homophonie *f*.

homosexual [,hɒmə'sekʃʊəl] ◇ *n* homosexuel *m*, -elle *f*. ◇ *adj* homosexuel.

homosexuality [,hɒmə,sekʃʊ'ælətɪ] *n* homosexualité *f*; male/female ~ homosexualité masculine/féminine.

homunculus [hɒ'mʌŋkjʊləs] (*pl* homunculi [-laɪ]) *n* -**1.** [small man] homuncule *m*, homoncule *m*. -**2.** [in alchemy] homuncule *m*, homunculus *m*.

homy *inf* ['həʊmɪ] (*compar* homier, *superl* homiest) *adj* -**1.** [comfortable] accueillant, confortable; you've made your place very ~ tu t'es fait un vrai chez-toi. -**2.** *Br* [home-loving] casanier; he's the ~ type c'est un pantouflard. -**3.** *Br* [private] intime; a ~ little chat une conversation intime.

hon *inf* [hʌn] *n Am* chéri *m*, -e *f*.

hon. *written abbr of* honorary.

Hon. *written abbr of* honourable.

Honduran [hɒn'djʊərən] ◇ *n* Hondurien *m*, -enne *f*. ◇ *adj* hondurien.

Honduras [hɒn'djʊərəs] *pr n* Honduras *m*; in ~ au Honduras.

hone [həʊn] ◇ *vt* -**1.** [sharpen] aiguiser, affûter, affiler; [re-sharpen] repasser; he ~d the knife to a razor sharp edge il a affûté le couteau pour qu'il coupe comme un rasoir. -**2.** [refine - analysis, thought] affiner; finely ~d arguments arguments *mpl* d'une grande finesse; practice will ~ your reflexes la pratique OR l'entraînement améliorera tes réflexes. ◇ *n* pierre *f* à aiguiser.
◆ **hone down** *vt sep* [reduce] tailler; [make slim] faire maigrir.

honest ['ɒnɪst] ◇ *adj* -**1.** [not deceitful] honnête, probe; [trustworthy] intègre; an ~ answer une réponse honnête; the ~ truth la pure vérité; it pays to be ~ ça paie d'être honnête; they are ~ workers ce sont des ouvriers consciencieux

❑ **he's (as) ~ as the day is long** il n'y a pas plus honnête que lui. -**2.** [decent, upright] droit; [virtuous] honnête; **he's an ~ bloke** *inf Br* c'est un brave type ❑ **he's decided to make an ~ woman of her** *hum* il a décidé de régulariser sa situation. -**3.** [not fraudulent] honnête; **he charges an ~ price** ses prix ne sont pas excessifs; **an ~ day's work** une bonne journée de travail; **they just want to make an ~ profit** ils ne veulent qu'un profit légitime; **to earn an ~ living** gagner honnêtement sa vie. -**4.** [frank - face] franc, sincère; **let's be ~ with each other** allons, soyons francs; **to be ~, I don't think it will work** à vrai dire, je ne crois pas que ça marchera; **give me your ~ opinion** dites-moi sincèrement ce que vous en pensez.
◇ *adv inf*: **I didn't mean it, ~!** je plaisantais, je te le jure!; **~ to goodness** OR **to God!** parole d'honneur!

honest broker *n Br* médiateur *m*, -trice *f* neutre.

honestly ['ɒnɪstlɪ] *adv* honnêtement; **quite ~, I don't see the problem** très franchement, je ne vois pas le problème; **it's not my fault, ~!** ce n'est pas ma faute, je te le jure!; **~?** c'est vrai?

honest-to-goodness *adj*: **a cup of ~ English tea** une tasse de bon thé anglais.

honesty ['ɒnɪstɪ] *n* -**1.** [truthfulness - of person] honnêteté *f*; [- of text, words] véracité *f*, exactitude *f*; **~ is the best policy** *prov* l'honnêteté paie toujours. -**2.** [incorruptibility] intégrité *f*; **we have never doubted his ~** nous n'avons jamais douté de son intégrité. -**3.** [upright conduct] droiture *f*; **a man of irreproachable ~** un homme d'une droiture irréprochable. -**4.** [sincerity] sincérité *f*, franchise *f*; **the ~ of his intentions is self-evident** la sincérité de ses intentions est évidente; **in all ~** en toute sincérité. -**5.** BOT monnaie-du-pape *f*.
◆ **in all honesty** *adv phr* en toute sincérité.

honey ['hʌnɪ] (*pl* honies) ◇ *n* -**1.** miel *m*; **clear/wildflower ~** miel liquide/de fleurs sauvages ‖ *fig* miel, douceur *f*. -**2.** *inf Am* [sweetheart] chou *m*; [addressing man] mon chéri; [addressing woman] ma chérie; **you're such a ~!** tu es un chou!; **OK, ~!** OK, chéri!; **a ~ of a dress** *inf* une super robe; **a ~ of a boat** un amour de bateau.
◇ *adj* miellé; **~-coloured** couleur de miel; **~ cake** gâteau *m* d'épices au miel.

honey bear *n* -**1.** [in Europe, Asia] ours *m* brun *(d'Europe et d'Asie)*. -**2.** [in South America] kinkajou *m*.

honeybee ['hʌnɪbiː] *n* abeille *f*.

honeybun(ch) ['hʌnɪbʌn(tʃ)] *n inf* [person] chou *m* (à la crème).

honeycomb ['hʌnɪkəʊm] ◇ *n* -**1.** [in wax] rayon *m* OR gâteau *m* de miel. -**2.** [material] structure *f* alvéolaire. -**3.** [pattern] nid *m* d'abeille; TEX nid *m* d'abeille. -**4.** METALL soufflure *f*.
◇ *vt* -**1.** [surface] cribler. -**2.** [interior] miner; **the hills are ~ed with secret tunnels** les collines sont truffées de passages secrets.

honeydew ['hʌnɪdjuː] *n* BOT [produced by insects] miellat *m*; [produced by plants] miellée *f*.

honeydew melon *n* melon *m* d'hiver OR d'Espagne.

honeyed ['hʌnɪd] *adj fig* mielleux; **he spoke in ~ tones** il parlait d'un ton mielleux.

honeymoon ['hʌnɪmuːn] ◇ *n* -**1.** [period] lune *f* de miel; [trip] voyage *m* de noces; **they're on ~** ils sont en voyage de noces. -**2.** *fig* état *m* de grâce; **the new Prime Minister's ~ is over** l'état de grâce du nouveau Premier ministre est terminé.
◇ *comp* [couple, suite] en voyage de noces; **a ~ period** *fig* une lune de miel, un état de grâce.
◇ *vi* passer sa lune de miel.

honeymooner ['hʌnɪmuːnəʳ] *n* nouveau OR jeune marié *m*, nouvelle OR jeune mariée *f*.

honeypot ['hʌnɪpɒt] *n* -**1.** [container] pot *m* à miel; **to have one's fingers in the ~** *inf* se sucrer. -**2.** ▼ *Am* [vagina] chatte *f*.

honeysuckle ['hʌnɪˌsʌkl] *n* chèvrefeuille *m*.

Hong Kong [ˌhɒŋ'kɒŋ] *pr n* Hong Kong, Hongkong; **in ~** à Hongkong.

honied ['hʌnɪd] = **honeyed**.

honk [hɒŋk] ◇ *vi* -**1.** [car] klaxonner. -**2.** [goose] cacarder.
◇ *vt*: **to ~ one's horn** donner un coup de Klaxon; **~ your horn at him!** klaxonne-le!
◇ *n* -**1.** [of car horn] coup *m* de Klaxon; **~, ~!** tut-tut! -**2.** [of geese] cri *m*; **~, ~!** couin-couin!

honkie▽, **honky**▽ ['hɒŋkɪ] (*pl* honkies) *n Am terme injurieux désignant un Blanc*.

honky-tonk ['hɒŋkɪˌtɒŋk] ◇ *n* -**1.** MUS musique *f* de bastringue. -**2.** *inf Am* [brothel] maison *f* close, clandé *m*; *dated* [nightclub] beuglant *m*; [bar] bouge *m*; [gambling den] tripot *m*.
◇ *adj* -**1.** MUS de bastringue. -**2.** *Am* [unsavoury] louche; **a ~ district** un quartier chaud; **a ~ woman** une putain; **a ~ bar/night club** un bar/une boîte de nuit louche.

Honolulu [ˌhɒnə'luːluː] *pr n* Honolulu.

honor *etc Am* = **honour**.

honorarium [ˌɒnə'reərɪəm] (*pl* honorariums OR honoraria [-rɪə]) *n* honoraires *mpl*.

honorary [*Br* 'ɒnərərɪ, *Am* ɒnə'reərɪ] *adj* [titular position] honoraire; [in name only] à titre honorifique, honoraire; [unpaid position] à titre gracieux; **~ member/professor** membre/professeur honoraire; **~ degree** grade honoris causa; **~ secretary** secrétaire honoraire.

honorary diploma *n* diplôme *m* honoris causa.

honorific [ˌɒnə'rɪfɪk] ◇ *adj* honorifique.
◇ *n* [general] témoignage *m* d'honneur; [title] titre *m* d'honneur.

honor roll *n Am* tableau *m* d'honneur.

honour *Br*, **honor** *Am* ['ɒnəʳ] ◇ *n* -**1.** [personal integrity] honneur *m*; **on my ~!** parole d'honneur!; **he's on his ~ to behave himself** il s'est engagé sur l'honneur OR sur son honneur à bien se tenir; **it's a point of ~ (with me) to pay my debts on time** je me fais un point d'honneur de OR je mets un OR mon point d'honneur à rembourser mes dettes; **the affair cost him his ~** l'affaire l'a déshonoré ❑ **(there is) ~ amongst thieves** *prov* les loups ne se mangent pas entre eux *prov*. -**2.** [public, social regard] honneur *m*; **they came to do her ~** ils sont venus pour lui faire OR rendre honneur; **peace with ~!** la paix sans le déshonneur! -**3.** *fml* [pleasure]: **it is a great ~ to introduce Mr Reed** c'est un grand honneur pour moi de vous présenter Monsieur Reed; **may I have the ~ of your company/the next dance?** pouvez-vous me faire l'honneur de votre compagnie/de la prochaine danse? ❑ **to do the ~s** [serve drinks, food] faire le service; [make introductions] faire les présentations (entre invités). -**4.** [credit] honneur *m*, crédit *m*; **she's an ~ to her profession** elle fait honneur à sa profession. -**5.** [mark of respect] honneur *m*; **military ~s** honneurs militaires; **to receive sb with full ~s** recevoir qqn avec tous les honneurs; **all ~ to him!** honneur à lui!; **Your Honour** Votre Honneur; JUR ≃ Monsieur le Juge, ≃ Monsieur le Président. -**6.** GAMES [face card] honneur *m*; **it's your ~** [starter's right] à vous l'honneur.
◇ *vt* -**1.** [person] honorer, faire honneur à; **she ~ed him with her friendship** elle l'a honoré de son amitié; **my ~ed colleague** mon cher collègue; **I'm most ~ed to be here tonight** *fml* je suis très honoré d'être parmi vous ce soir. -**2.** [fulfil the terms of] honorer; [observe - boycott, rule] respecter; **he always ~s his obligations** il honore toujours ses obligations. -**3.** [pay - debt] honorer. -**4.** [dance partner] saluer.
◆ **honours** *npl Br* UNIV [degree] ≃ licence *f*; **to take ~s in History** ≃ faire une licence d'histoire; **he was an ~s in university/in high school** *Am* ≃ il a toujours eu mention très bien/le tableau d'honneur; **she got first-/second-class ~s** elle a eu sa licence avec mention très bien/mention bien.
◆ **in honour of** *prep phr* en honneur de.

honourable *Br*, **honorable** *Am* ['ɒnrəbl] *adj* -**1.** honorable; **the profession is still an ~ one** la profession reste en honneur; **he got an ~ discharge** il a été rendu à la vie civile. -**2.** [title]: **the (Right) Honourable** le (très) honorable; **my ~ friend the member for Calderdale** mon collègue l'honorable député du Calderdale; **the ~ member will no doubt recall...** mon honorable collègue se rappellera sans doute...

HONOURABLE:

Cet appellatif s'utilise avant le nom de certains membres de l'aristocratie britannique: «the Honourable James Porter» ou «the Hon. James Porter». Il est également employé à la Chambre des communes lorsqu'un député parle d'un autre député: «the honourable member for Oxford». Lorsqu'un député désigne un collègue du même parti, il emploie l'expression «my honourable friend»; lorsque son interlocuteur appartient au parti opposé, le terme consacré est «the honourable gentleman ou lady».

---

honourable mention *n* mention *f (décernée par un jury à un bon projet qui ne gagne pas de prix)*.

honourably *Br*, **honorably** *Am* ['ɒnərəblɪ] *adv* honorablement.

honour-bound *adj*: **to be ~ (to)** être tenu par l'honneur (à).

honours degree *n diplôme universitaire obtenu avec mention*.

honours list *n Br liste de distinctions honorifiques conférées par le monarque deux fois par an*.

Hons. *written abbr of* **honours degree**.

Hon. Sec. *written abbr of* **honorary secretary**.

hooch▽ [huːtʃ] *n Am* -**1.** [drink] gnôle *f*. -**2.** [marijuana] herbe *f*.

hood [hʊd] ◇ *n* -**1.** [garment] capuchon *m*; [with collar] capuche *f*; [with eye-holes] cagoule *f*; UNIV épitoge *f*; **a rain ~** une capuche ❑ **Little Red Riding Hood** le Petit Chaperon rouge. -**2.** *Br* AUT [cover] capote *f*; *Am* AUT capot *m*; [of pram] capote *f*; [for fumes, smoke] hotte *f*; **lens ~** PHOT pare-soleil *m*. -**3.** [of animals, plants] capuchon *m*; [for falcons] chaperon *m*, capuchon *m*. -**4.** *Am crime sl* [gangster] gangster *m*, truand *m*. -**5.** *inf* = **hoodlum**.
◇ *vt* mettre le capuchon; [falcon] chaperonner, enchaperonner.

hooded ['hʊdɪd] *adj* [clothing] à capuchon; [person] encapuchonné; **~ eyes** *fig* yeux *mpl* tombants.

hooded crow *n* corneille *f* mantelée.

hoodlum *inf* ['huːdləm] *n* voyou *m*; **a young ~** un (petit) loubar OR loubard, un blouson noir.

hoodoo *inf* ['huːduː] ◇ *n Am* porte-malheur *mf inv*.
◇ *vt* porter la poisse OR la guigne à.

hoodwink ['hʊdwɪŋk] *vt* tromper, avoir; **he ~ed me into coming** par un tour de passe-passe il m'a fait venir.

hooey *inf* ['huːɪ] *n* foutaise *f*; **that's ~** c'est du bidon; **to talk a load of ~** raconter des bêtises.

hoof [huːf, hʊf] (*pl* hoofs OR hooves [huːvz])
◇ *n* sabot *m (d'animal)*; **on the ~** [alive] sur pied.
◇ *vt inf phr*: **to ~ it** [go on foot] aller à pinces; [flee] se cavaler; [dance] guincher.

hoofbeat ['hʊfbiːt] *n* bruit *m* de sabots *(d'animal)*; **the (horse's) ~s came closer** on entendait s'approcher des pas (de cheval).

hoofed [huːft] *adj* à sabots; ZOOL ongulé.

hoofer *inf* ['huːfəʳ] *n* danseur *m*, -euse *f (de music-hall)*.

hoofprint ['hʊfprɪnt] *n* empreinte *f* de sabot *(d'animal)*.

hoo-ha *inf* ['huːˌhɑː] *n* -**1.** [noise] boucan *m*, potin *m*; [chaos] pagaille *f*, tohu-bohu *m*; [fuss] bruit *m*, histoires *fpl*; **there was a lot of ~ about it** ça en a fait des histoires. -**2.** *Am* [party] fête *f* charivarique.

hook [hʊk] ◇ *n* -**1.** [gen] crochet *m*; [for coats] patère *f*; [on clothes] agrafe *f*; NAUT gaffe *f*; ~s and eyes agrafes (et œillets); the phone is off the ~ le téléphone est décroché ❑ by ~ or by crook coûte que coûte. -**2.** [fishing] hameçon *m*; he swallowed the story, ~, line and sinker *inf* il a gobé tout le paquet. -**3.** [in advertising] accroche *f*. -**4.** *inf phr*: to get sb off the ~ tirer qqn d'affaire; to let OR to get sb off the ~ [obligation] libérer qqn de sa responsabilité; I'll let you off the ~ this time je laisse passer cette fois-ci. -**5.** *inf Am* [dismissal]: to give sb the ~ flanquer qqn à la porte, vider qqn; he'll get the ~ one day il sera flanqué à la porte OR vidé un jour. -**6.** [in golf] hook *m*; [in cricket] coup *m* tourné; a right/left ~ [in boxing] un crochet (du) droit/gauche.
◇ *vt* -**1.** [snag] accrocher; [seize - person, prey] attraper; [- floating object] gaffer, crocher; he ~ed his arm through hers il lui a pris le bras. -**2.** [loop]: ~ the rope around the tree passez la corde autour de l'arbre; she ~ed one leg round the leg of the chair elle passa OR enroula une jambe autour du pied de la chaise. -**3.** FISHING [fish] prendre; TECH hameçonner. -**4.** [in golf] hooker; [in boxing] donner un crochet à; [in rugby] talonner *(le ballon)*; [in cricket] renvoyer *(la balle)* d'un coup tourné. -**5.** *inf* [steal] piquer. -**6.** *inf hum* [marry] passer la corde au cou à. -**7.** SEW [rug] fabriquer *(un tapis)* en nouant au crochet.
◇ *vi* -**1.** [fasten] s'agrafer. -**2.** GOLF hooker.
◆ **hook on** ◇ *vi insep* s'accrocher; this strap ~s on at the back cette bride s'accroche OR s'agrafe par derrière.
◇ *vt sep* accrocher.
◆ **hook up** ◇ *vt sep* -**1.** [trailer] accrocher; [dress] agrafer; [boat] amarrer; they ~ed up an extra coach to the train on a accroché un wagon supplémentaire au train. -**2.** *inf* [install] installer; [plug in] brancher. -**3.** RADIO & TV faire un duplex entre. -**4.** = **hitch up**.
◇ *vi insep* -**1.** [dress] s'agrafer. -**2.** *inf Am* [meet] se rencontrer, se donner rendez-vous; [work together] faire équipe. -**3.** *inf Am* [be in relationship]: to ~ up with sb sortir avec qqn. -**4.** RADIO & TV: to ~ up with faire une émission en duplex avec.

hookah ['hʊkə] *n* narguilé *m*, houka *m*.

hooked [hʊkt] *adj* -**1.** [hook-shaped] recourbé; a ~ nose un nez crochu. -**2.** [having hooks] muni de crochets; [fishing line] muni d'un hameçon. -**3.** *inf fig* [addicted]: he got ~ on hard drugs il est devenu accro aux drogues dures; she's really ~ on TV soaps c'est une mordue des feuilletons télévisés; to get ~ on chess/computers devenir fana d'échecs/d'informatique.

hooker ['hʊkə[r]] *n* -**1.** RUGBY talonneur *m*. -**2.** ▽ *Am* [prostitute] pute *f*.

hookey *inf*, **hooky** *inf* ['hʊkɪ] *n Am, Austr & NZ*: to play ~ sécher les cours, faire l'école buissonnière.

hook-nosed *adj* au nez recourbé OR crochu.

hook shot *n* [in basketball] bras roulé *m*; [in cricket] coup *m* tourné.

hookup *inf* ['hʊkʌp] *n* RADIO & TV relais *m* temporaire.

hookworm ['hʊkwɜːm] *n* anylostome *m*.

hooligan ['huːlɪgən] *n* hooligan *m*, vandale *m*.

hooliganism ['huːlɪgənɪzm] *n* vandalisme *m*.

hoop [huːp] ◇ *n* cerceau *m*; I had to jump through ~s to get the job j'ai dû faire des pieds et des mains pour obtenir ce travail; to put sb through the ~s *inf* [interrogate] mettre qqn sur la sellette; [test] mettre qqn à l'épreuve.
◇ *comp*: ~ earrings (anneaux *mpl*) créoles *fpl*.

hooped [huːpt] *adj* [barrel] cerclé; [skirt] à cerceaux; [earrings] en anneau.

hoopla ['huːplɑː] *n* -**1.** *Br* jeu *m* d'anneaux *(dans les foires)*. -**2.** *inf Am* = **hoo-ha 1**. -**3.** *inf Am* [advertising] publicité *f* tapageuse.

hoopoe ['huːpuː] *n* huppe *f*.

hooray [hʊ'reɪ] *interj* hourra, hurrah.

Hooray Henry *n Br BCBG bruyant et malappris*.

hoosegow▽ ['huːsgaʊ] *n Am* tôle *f*, bloc *m*.

hoot [huːt] ◇ *n* -**1.** [shout - of delight, pain] cri *m*; [jeer] huée *f*; ~s of laughter éclats *mpl* de rire. -**2.** [of owl] hululement *m*. -**3.** AUT coup *m* de klaxon; [of train] sifflement *m*; [of siren] mugissement *m*. -**4.** *inf* [least bit]: I don't give OR care a ~ OR two ~s je m'en fiche, mais alors complètement, je m'en contrefiche. -**5.** *inf* [amusing event] bonne partie *f* de rigolade; he's a real ~! *inf* c'est un sacré rigolo!, il est tordant!
◇ *vi* -**1.** *inf* [person]: to ~ with laughter s'esclaffer; to ~ with anger rugir de colère. -**2.** [owl] hululer. -**3.** AUT klaxonner; [train] siffler; [siren] mugir.
◆ **hoot down** *inf vt sep* [person, show] huer, conspuer; they ~ed him down ils l'ont fait taire par leurs huées.

hootch▽ [huːtʃ] = **hooch**.

hootenanny ['huːtnænɪ] (*pl* **hootenannies**) *n Am fête populaire animée par des chanteurs de chansons folkloriques*.

hooter ['huːtə[r]] *n esp Br* -**1.** [car horn] klaxon *m*; [in factory, ship] sirène *f*. -**2.** [party toy] mirliton *m*. -**3.** *inf* [nose] pif *m*.

Hoover® ['huːvə[r]] *n* aspirateur *m*.
◆ **hoover** *vt Br*: to ~ a carpet passer l'aspirateur sur un tapis; he ~ed the whole house il a passé l'aspirateur dans toute la maison.

hoovering ['huːvrɪŋ] *n Br*: to do the ~ passer l'aspirateur.

hooves [huːvz] *pl* → **hoof**.

hop [hɒp] (*pt* & *pp* **hopped**, *cont* **hopping**) ◇ *n* -**1.** [jump] saut *m*; [in rapid series] sautillement *m*; the ~, skip OR step and jump SPORT le triple saut; to catch sb on the ~ *Br* prendre qqn au dépourvu. -**2.** AERON étape *f*; it's just a short ~ from New York to Boston by plane Boston n'est qu'à quelques minutes d'avion de New York. -**3.** *inf dated* [dance] sauterie *f*; [for young people] boum *f*, surpatte *f vieilli*. -**4.** BOT houblon *m*; to pick ~s cueillir le houblon.
◇ *vt* -**1.** [jump] sauter; to ~ it *inf* décamper, décaniller; ~ it! *inf* allez, dégage! -**2.** *inf Am* [bus, subway etc - legally] sauter dans; [- illegally] prendre en resquillant.
◇ *vi* -**1.** [jump] sauter; [in rapid series] sautiller; to ~ on/off the bus *inf* sauter dans le/du bus; birds hopped about in the garden les oiseaux sautillaient dans le jardin. -**2.** [jump on one leg] sauter à cloche-pied; he hopped over to the door il est allé à cloche-pied jusqu'à la porte. -**3.** *inf* [travel by plane] aller en avion; we hopped across to Paris for the weekend nous sommes allés à Paris en avion pour le week-end.
◆ **hop off** *inf vi insep* [leave] décamper.
◆ **hop up** *vt sep Am* -**1.** [excite] exciter, stimuler; all that coffee hopped him up tout ce café l'a excité; the crowd is really hopped up le public est vraiment exubérant. -**2.** [make angry, nervy] énerver, exciter. -**3.** [drug user] défoncer; [athlete, racehorse] doper. -**4.** AUT = **hot up**.

hope [həʊp] ◇ *n* -**1.** [desire, expectation] espoir *m*; *fml* espérance *f*; his ~ is that... ce qu'il espère OR son espoir c'est que...; in the ~ of a reward/of leaving early dans l'espoir d'une récompense/de partir tôt; I have every ~ (that) he'll come j'ai bon espoir qu'il viendra; there's ~ for him yet il reste de l'espoir en ce qui le concerne; don't get your ~s up ne comptez pas là-dessus; to give up ~ (of) perdre l'espoir (de); the situation is past OR beyond ~ la situation est sans espoir; she is past OR beyond all ~ *euph* [of dying person] il n'y a plus aucun espoir; to raise sb's ~s [for first time] susciter OR faire naître l'espoir de qqn OR chez qqn; [anew] faire renaître l'espoir de qqn; [increase] renforcer l'espoir de qqn; don't raise his ~s too much ne lui donne pas trop d'espoir; with high ~s avec un grand espoir ❑ the Cape of Good Hope le cap de Bonne Espérance; some ~! *inf iron* tu parles! -**2.** [chance] espoir *m*, chance *f*; he's got little ~ of winning il a peu de chances OR d'espoir de gagner; one's last/only ~ le dernier/l'unique espoir de quelqu'un. -**3.** RELIG espérance *f*.
◇ *vi* espérer; to ~ for sthg espérer qqch; to ~ against ~ espérer contre toute attente; we just have to ~ for the best espérons que tout finira OR se passera bien; you shouldn't ~ for a high return vous ne devez pas vous attendre à un rendement élevé.
◇ *vt* espérer; he ~s OR is hoping to go il espère y aller; he's hoping (that) she'll be there il espère qu'elle sera là; hoping OR I ~ to hear from you soon j'espère avoir de tes nouvelles bientôt; I really ~ so! je l'espère bien!; I ~ not j'espère que non; I ~ you don't mind me calling j'espère que cela ne te dérange pas si je passe (te voir).

hope chest *n Am literal* coffre *m* à trousseau; *fig* trousseau *m*.

hopeful ['həʊpfʊl] ◇ *adj* -**1.** [full of hope] plein d'espoir; we're ~ that we'll reach an agreement nous avons bon espoir d'aboutir à un accord; he's still ~ that she'll come il garde bon espoir qu'elle viendra; he says he'll come, but I'm not that ~ il dit qu'il viendra mais je n'y compte pas trop; I am ~ about the outcome je suis optimiste quant au résultat. -**2.** [inspiring hope] encourageant, prometteur; the news is ~ les nouvelles sont encourageantes OR laissent de l'espoir; the situation/weather looks ~ la situation/le temps s'annonce meilleure/meilleur.
◇ *n* aspirant *m*, candidat *m*; a young ~ un jeune loup; Davis Cup ~s les prétendants à la coupe Davis.

hopefully ['həʊpfəlɪ] *adv* -**1.** [smile, speak, work] avec espoir, avec optimisme. -**2.** [with luck] on espère que...; ~, they'll leave tomorrow on espère qu'ils partiront demain; will you get it finished today? — ~! est-ce que tu l'auras terminé pour aujourd'hui? — je l'espère! OR oui, avec un peu de chance!

hopeless ['həʊplɪs] *adj* -**1.** [desperate - person] sans espoir, désespéré; [- situation] désespéré, irrémédiable, qui ne laisse aucun espoir; it's ~! c'est impossible OR désespérant! -**2.** [incurable - addiction, ill person] incurable; a ~ case un cas désespéré. -**3.** [inveterate - drunk, liar] invétéré, incorrigible. -**4.** *inf* [incompetent - person] nul; [- at job] incompétent; he's a ~ dancer il est nul comme danseur; she's ~! c'est un cas désespéré!; a ~ case un bon à rien, un fainéant; I'm ~ at this je n'y arriverai jamais; he's ~ at swimming il est nul en natation. -**5.** [pointless]: it's ~ trying to explain to him il est inutile d'essayer de lui expliquer.

hopelessly ['həʊplɪslɪ] *adv* -**1.** [speak] avec désespoir. -**2.** [irremediably]: they are ~ in debt/in love ils sont complètement endettés/éperdument amoureux; by this time we were ~ late/lost nous étions maintenant irrémédiablement en retard/complètement perdus.

hopelessness ['həʊplɪsnɪs] *n* -**1.** [despair] désespoir *m*. -**2.** [of position, situation] caractère *m* désespéré. -**3.** [pointlessness] inutilité *f*.

hopfield ['hɒpfiːld] *n* houblonnière *f*.

hophead▽ ['hɒphed] *n Am* défoncé *m*, -e *f*.

hopper ['hɒpə[r]] *n* -**1.** [jumper] sauteur *m*, -euse *f*; *Austr inf* kangourou *m*. -**2.** [feeder bin] trémie *f*; grain ~ trémie à blé; ~ car RAIL wagon-trémie *m*; ~ barge marie-salope *f*. -**3.** = **hop picker**.

hop picker *n* cueilleur *m*, -euse *f* de houblon.

hop picking *n* cueillette *f* du houblon.

hopping *inf* ['hɒpɪŋ] *adv* [as intensifier]: he was ~ mad il était fou furieux.

-hopping *in cpds*: to go bar~ aller de bar en bar, faire la tournée des bars; to go island~ aller d'île en île, faire le tour des îles.

hopscotch ['hɒpskɒtʃ] *n* marelle *f*.

Horace ['hɒrɪs] *pr n* Horace.

horde [hɔːd] *n* -**1.** [nomadic] horde *f*. -**2.** *fig* [crowd] essaim *m*; [of agitators] horde *f*; ~s of tourists des hordes de touristes; the ~ *pej* la horde, la foule.

horizon [hə'raɪzn] *n* horizon *m*; the sun was sinking below the ~ le soleil descendait au-dessous de l'horizon; we saw a boat on the ~

nous vîmes un bateau à l'horizon; a new star on the political ~ *fig* une nouvelle vedette à OR sur l'horizon politique.

◆ **horizons** *npl* [perspectives] horizons *mpl*; to broaden one's ~s élargir ses horizons; a man of limited ~s un homme aux vues étroites OR à l'esprit étroit; China presents new ~s for investment la Chine offre de nouveaux horizons pour les investisseurs.

horizontal [ˌhɒrɪ'zɒntl] ◇ *adj* -**1.** horizontal; turn the lever to the ~ position mettez le levier à l'horizontale. -**2.** ADMIN & COMM [communication, integration] horizontal; he asked for a ~ move il a demandé une mutation.
◇ *n* horizontale *f*.

horizontal bar *n* SPORT barre *f* fixe.

horizontally [ˌhɒrɪ'zɒntəlɪ] *adv* horizontalement; extend your arms ~ tendez vos bras à l'horizontale; to move sb ~ (to) ADMIN & COMM muter qqn (à).

hormonal [hɔː'məʊnl] *adj* hormonal.

hormone ['hɔːməʊn] *n* hormone *f*; ~ replacement therapy traitement *m* hormonal substitutif.

Hormuz [ˌhɔː'muːz] *pr n* Hormuz, Ormuz; the Strait of ~ le détroit d'Ormuz.

horn [hɔːn] ◇ *n* -**1.** [gen] corne *f*; [pommel] pommeau *m*; the ~ of plenty la corne d'abondance; the Horn of Africa la Corne de l'Afrique, la péninsule des Somalis; to draw OR to pull in one's ~s *Br* [back off] se calmer; [spend less] restreindre son train de vie; to be on the ~s of a dilemma *Br* être pris dans un dilemme. -**2.** MUS cor *m*; he blows a mean ~▽ [jazz trumpet] il touche à la trompette; [saxophone] il touche au saxo; ~ section les cors *mpl*. -**3.** AUT klaxon *m*; [manual] corne *f*; to sound OR to blow the ~ klaxonner, corner. -**4.** NAUT sirène *f*; to sound OR to blow the ~ donner un coup de sirène. -**5.** HUNT corne *f*, cor *m*, trompe *f*. -**6.** *Br* CULIN cornet *m*; a cream ~ *pâtisserie en forme de cornet remplie de crème*.
◇ *adj* [handle, bibelot] en corne.
◆ **horn in** *inf vi insep* [on conversation] mettre son grain de sel; [on a deal] s'immiscer.

hornbeam ['hɔːnbiːm] *n* charme *m*.

hornbill ['hɔːnbɪl] *n* calao *m*.

horned ['hɔːnd] *adj* cornu; a two-~ rhinoceros un rhinocéros (d'Afrique) à deux cornes.

horned owl *n* duc *m*.

horned toad *n* crapaud *m* cornu.

horned viper *n* vipère *f* cornue (d'Égypte).

hornet ['hɔːnɪt] *n* frelon *m*; to stir up a ~'s nest *fig* mettre le feu aux poudres.

hornless ['hɔːnlɪs] *adj* sans cornes.

hornpipe ['hɔːnpaɪp] *n* matelote *f (danse)*; to dance a ~ danser une matelote.

horn-rimmed *adj* à monture d'écaille.

hornswoggle▽ ['hɔːnˌswɒgl] *vt* blouser, embobiner.

horny ['hɔːnɪ] *adj* -**1.** [calloused - nail, skin] calleux; VETER encorné. -**2.** ▽ [randy] excité (sexuellement); he's ~ as a toad *Am* il est en rut. -**3.** ▽ [having sex appeal] sexy.

horology [hɔː'rɒlədʒɪ] *n* horlogerie *f*.

horoscope ['hɒrəskəʊp] *n* horoscope *m*.

horrendous [hɒ'rendəs] *adj* -**1.** *literal* terrible. -**2.** *fig* [very bad] affreux, horrible.

horrendously [hɒ'rendəslɪ] *adv* horriblement.

horrible ['hɒrəbl] *adj* -**1.** [horrific] horrible, affreux; [morally repulsive] abominable; a ~ tragedy/scream une tragédie/un cri horrible. -**2.** [dismaying] horrible, effroyable; in a ~ mess dans une effroyable OR horrible confusion; I've a ~ feeling that things are going to go wrong j'ai l'horrible pressentiment que les choses vont mal se passer. -**3.** [very unpleasant] horrible, atroce; [food] infect.

horribly ['hɒrəblɪ] *adv* -**1.** [nastily] horriblement, atrocement, affreusement; he treated her ~ il se conduisit d'une manière atroce OR atrocement mal envers elle; the story of a woman who was ~ murdered l'histoire d'une femme qui fut assassinée de manière atroce. -**2.** [as intensifier] affreusement; it's ~ extravagant but... c'est de la folie douce mais...; things went ~ wrong les choses ont affreusement mal tourné.

horrid ['hɒrɪd] *adj* -**1.** [unkind] méchant; [ugly] vilain; he was ~ to me il a été méchant avec moi. -**2.** = **horrible 3**.

horridly ['hɒrɪdlɪ] *adv* [as intensifier] atrocement, affreusement.

horrific [hɒ'rɪfɪk] *adj* -**1.** *literal* horrible, terrifiant; *lit* horrifique. -**2.** *fig* [very unpleasant] horrible.

horrifically [hɒ'rɪfɪklɪ] *adv* -**1.** [gruesomely] atrocement. -**2.** [as intensifier]: ~ expensive affreusement cher.

horrify ['hɒrɪfaɪ] (*pt* & *pp* horrified) *vt* -**1.** [terrify] horrifier. -**2.** [weaker use] horrifier, scandaliser.

horrifying ['hɒrɪfaɪɪŋ] *adj* -**1.** [terrifying] horrifiant, terrifiant. -**2.** [weaker use] scandaleux.

horror ['hɒrəʳ] *n* -**1.** [feeling] horreur *f*; he has a ~ of snakes il a horreur des serpents || [weaker use]: to my ~, I discovered... c'est avec horreur que j'ai découvert... ❑ he OR it gives me the ~s! *inf Br* il OR ça me donne le frisson!; ~ story *literal* histoire *f* d'horreur; they told some real ~ stories about their holiday *inf fig* ils ont raconté quelques histoires effrayantes sur leurs vacances; Chamber of Horrors Chambre *f* des horreurs. -**2.** [unpleasantness] horreur *f*; I began to see the ~ of it all j'ai commencé à en mesurer toute l'horreur. -**3.** *inf* [person, thing] horreur *f*; that child is a little ~ cet enfant est un petit monstre; ~ of ~s! l'horreur!; oh, ~s! *inf Br* quelle horreur!

horror film, **horror movie** *n* film *m* d'épouvante.

horror-stricken, **horror-struck** *adj* glacé OR frappé d'horreur.

hors d'œuvre [ɔː'dɜːvr] *n* hors-d'œuvre *m inv*; [cocktail snack] amuse-gueule *m*; for OR as an ~, a salad en hors-d'œuvre, une salade.

horse [hɔːs] ◇ *n* -**1.** [animal] cheval *m*; to ride a ~ monter à cheval; he fell off his ~ il a fait une chute de cheval; to play the ~s jouer aux courses ❑ to back the wrong ~ *fig* & *literal* miser sur le mauvais cheval; I could eat a ~! *inf* j'ai une faim de loup!; to eat like a ~ manger comme quatre; (straight) from the ~'s mouth de source sûre; that's a ~ of a different colour *Br* c'est une autre paire de manches; to get on one's high ~ monter sur ses grands chevaux; wild ~s couldn't drag it out of me je serai muet comme une tombe. -**2.** [trestle] tréteau *m*; GYMNASTICS cheval *m* d'arçons. -**3.** *drugs sl* [heroin] neige *f*, blanche *f*.
◇ *comp*: ~ breeder éleveur *m*, -euse *f* de chevaux; ~ butcher boucher *m* hippophagique; ~ manure crottin *m* de cheval; [as fertilizer] fumier *m* de cheval; ~ race course *f* de chevaux; ~ show OR trials concours *m* hippique.
◇ *npl* MIL cavalière *f*.
◆ **horse about** *inf Br*, **horse around** *inf vi insep* [noisily] chahuter.

horse-and-buggy *adj Am* qui date d'avant l'automobile; [old-fashioned] vieillot.

horseback ['hɔːsbæk] ◇ *n*: on ~ à cheval.
◇ *comp Am*: ~ riding équitation *f*; do you like ~ riding? tu aimes monter à cheval?

horsebox ['hɔːsbɒks] *n Br* [van] fourgon *m* à chevaux; [stall] box *m*.

horse brass *n* médaillon *m* de bronze *(fixé à une martingale)*.

horsebreaker ['hɔːsˌbreɪkəʳ] *n Br* dresseur *m*, -euse *f* de chevaux.

horsecar ['hɔːskɑːʳ] *n Am* fourgon *m* à chevaux.

horse chestnut *n* [tree] marronnier *m* (d'Inde); [nut] marron *m* (d'Inde).

horse doctor *inf n* vétérinaire *m*.

horse-drawn *adj* tiré par des chevaux, à chevaux.

horseflesh *inf* ['hɔːsfleʃ] *n (U)* -**1.** [horses] chevaux *mpl*; he's a good judge of ~ il s'y connaît bien en chevaux. -**2.** = **horsemeat**.

horsefly ['hɔːsflaɪ] (*pl* horseflies) *n* taon *m*.

Horse Guards *pl pr n*: the ~ [regiment] *régiment de cavalerie attaché à la reine et remplissant certaines fonctions officielles*; [building] *le bâtiment de Whitehall où se fait chaque jour la relève de la garde*.

horsehair ['hɔːsheəʳ] ◇ *n* crin *m* (de cheval).
◇ *adj* de crin (de cheval); a ~ sofa/mattress un canapé/un matelas de crin (de cheval).

horse latitudes *npl* NAUT pot *m* au noir.

horselaugh ['hɔːslɑːf] *n* gros rire *m*, rire *m* tonitruant.

horseman ['hɔːsmən] (*pl* horsemen [-mən]) *n* -**1.** [rider] cavalier *m*, écuyer *m*. -**2.** [breeder] éleveur *m* de chevaux.

horsemanship ['hɔːsmənʃɪp] *n* -**1.** [activity] équitation *f*. -**2.** [skill] talent *m* de cavalier.

horsemeat ['hɔːsmiːt] *n* viande *f* de cheval.

horse nuts *npl* avoine *f* enrichie *(pour l'alimentation des chevaux)*.

horse opera *inf n Am hum* western *m*.

horseplay ['hɔːspleɪ] *n (U)* chahut *m* brutal, jeux *mpl* tapageurs OR brutaux.

horsepower ['hɔːsˌpaʊəʳ] *n* [unit] cheval-vapeur *m*, cheval *m*; a 10-~ motor un moteur de 10 chevaux; it's a 4-~ car c'est une 4 chevaux.

horse racing *n (U)* courses *fpl* (de chevaux).

horseradish ['hɔːsˌrædɪʃ] ◇ *n* BOT raifort *m*, radis *m* noir.
◇ *comp*: ~ sauce sauce *f* au raifort.

horse riding *n* équitation *f*.

horse sense *inf n* (gros) bon sens *m*.

horseshit▼ ['hɔːsˌʃɪt] *n (U)* connerie *f*, conneries *fpl*; he's full of ~ il déconne complètement.

horseshoe ['hɔːsʃuː] *n* fer *m* à cheval.
◆ **horseshoes** *n* [game] jeu *m* de fer à cheval.

horse trader *n* -**1.** *literal* maquignon *m*. -**2.** *inf Br* [hard bargainer] négociateur *m*, -trice *f* redoutable.

horse trading *inf n Br* négociation *f* dure; *pej* maquignonnage *m*; after much ~ an agreement was reached un accord a été obtenu à l'arraché.

horsewhip ['hɔːswɪp] (*pt* & *pp* horsewhipped, *cont* horsewhipping) ◇ *n* cravache *f*.
◇ *vt* cravacher; I'll have him horsewhipped je le ferai fouetter.

horsewoman ['hɔːsˌwʊmən] (*pl* horsewomen [-ˌwɪmɪn]) *n* cavalière *f*, écuyère *f*; [sidesaddled] amazone *f*; she's a good ~ elle est bonne cavalière, elle monte bien.

horsey *inf*, **horsy** *inf* ['hɔːsɪ] *adj* -**1.** [horse-like] chevalin. -**2.** [fond of horses] féru de cheval; he mixes with a very ~ crowd il fréquente des (gens) passionnés de chevaux; the ~ set le monde OR le milieu du cheval.

horticultural [ˌhɔːtɪ'kʌltʃərəl] *adj* horticole; ~ show exposition *f* horticole OR d'horticulture.

horticulturalist [ˌhɔːtɪ'kʌltʃərəlɪst] = **horticulturist**.

horticulture ['hɔːtɪkʌltʃəʳ] *n* horticulture *f*.

horticulturist [ˌhɔːtɪ'kʌltʃərɪst] *n* horticulteur *m*, -trice *f*.

hosanna [həʊ'zænə] ◇ *n* hosanna *m*.
◇ *interj*: ~! hosanna!

hose [həʊz] ◇ *n* -**1.** [tube] tuyau *m*; AUT Durit® *f*; a length of rubber ~ un bout de tuyau en caoutchouc; turn off the ~ arrêtez le jet; fire ~ tuyau d'incendie; TECH manche *f* à incendie; garden ~ tuyau d'arrosage. -**2.** *(U)* [stockings] bas *mpl*; [tights] collant *m*, collants *mpl*; COMM articles *mpl* chaussants *(de bonneterie)*; HIST chausses *fpl*; [knee breeches] haut-de-chausse *m*, haut-de-chausses *m*, culotte *f* courte.
◇ *vt* [lawn] arroser au jet; [fire] arroser à la lance.
◆ **hose down** *vt sep* -**1.** [wash] laver au jet. -**2.** [with fire hose] arroser à la lance.
◆ **hose out** *vt sep* = **hose down 1**.

hosepipe ['həʊzpaɪp] ◇ *n* tuyau *m*.
◇ *comp*: a ~ ban une interdiction d'arroser.

hosier ['həʊzɪəʳ] *n* bonnetier *m*, -ère *f*.

hosiery ['həʊzɪərɪ] *n (U)* -**1.** [trade] bonneterie *f*. -**2.** [stockings] bas *mpl*; [socks] chaussettes *fpl*; COMM articles *mpl* chaussants *(de bonneterie)*; the (women's) ~ department le rayon des bas; the (men's) ~ department le rayon des chaussettes.

hospice ['hɒspɪs] *n* -**1.** [for travellers] hospice *m*. -**2.** [for the terminally ill] *hôpital pour grands malades en phase terminale*.

hospitable [hɒ'spɪtəbl] *adj* hospitalier; a ~ climate *fig* un climat hospitalier.

hospitably [hɒ'spɪtəblɪ] *adv* avec hospitalité.

hospital ['hɒspɪtl] ◇ *n* hôpital *m*; in ~ à l'hôpital; to ~ *Br*, to the ~ *Am* à l'hôpital; to go into ~ aller à l'hôpital; a children's ~ un hôpital pour enfants.
◇ *comp* [centre, service, staff, treatment] hospitalier; [bed, ward] d'hôpital; ~ care soins *mpl* hospitaliers; a ~ case un patient hospitalisé; ~ doctor médecin *m* hospitalier; ~ nurse infirmier *m*, -ère *f (d'hôpital)*; ~ train train *m* sanitaire.

hospitality [,hɒspɪ'tælətɪ] *n* -**1.** hospitalité *f*; thank you for your ~ merci pour votre hospitalité. -**2.** [room for guests] salon *m*.

hospitalization [,hɒspɪtəlaɪ'zeɪʃn] *n* hospitalisation *f*; does he have ~ insurance? *Am* a-t-il une assurance couvrant l'hospitalisation?

hospitalize, -ise ['hɒspɪtəlaɪz] *vt* hospitaliser.

hospital ship *n* navire-hôpital *m*.

host [həʊst] ◇ *n* -**1.** [person] hôte *m (qui reçoit)*; TV animateur *m*, -trice *f*; [innkeeper] aubergiste *mf*; he acted as our ~ for the evening il a été notre hôte pour la soirée; Japan will be the next ~ for the conference c'est le Japon qui accueillera la prochaine conférence. -**2.** BIOL & ZOOL hôte *m*. -**3.** [large number] foule *f*; a ~ of complaints toute une série de plaintes. -**4.** *lit* RELIG armée *f*; the Lord God of Hosts le Dieu des armées. -**5.** *lit* [denizen] hôte *m*.
◇ *adj* [cell, country] hôte; [team] qui reçoit; the ~ city for the Olympic Games la ville organisatrice des jeux Olympiques; ~ computer ordinateur *m* principal; [in network] serveur *m*.
◇ *vt* [TV show] animer; [event] organiser; she adores ~ing dinner parties elle adore recevoir à dîner.
◆ **Host** *n* RELIG: the Host l'hostie *f*.

hostage ['hɒstɪdʒ] *n* otage *m*; to take OR to hold sb ~ prendre qqn en otage; they released the parents but kept the child as (a) ~ ils ont libéré les parents et gardé l'enfant en otage ▫ a ~ to fortune le jouet du hasard.

hostel ['hɒstl] *n* -**1.** [residence] foyer *m*; (youth) ~ auberge *f* de jeunesse. -**2.** *arch* [inn] auberge *f*.

hosteller *Br*, **hosteler** *Am* ['hɒstələʳ] *n* -**1.** [youth] ≃ ajiste *mf*. -**2.** *arch* [innkeeper] aubergiste *mf*.

hostelling ['hɒstəlɪŋ] *n Br* mouvement *m* des auberges de jeunesse.

hostelry ['hɒstəlrɪ] *n* hôtellerie *f*; *arch* hostellerie *f*; the local ~ *inf hum* le bistrot du coin.

hostess ['həʊstes] *n* -**1.** [at home] hôtesse *f*; the ~ with the mostest *inf hum* la plus chouette des hôtesses. -**2.** [in nightclub] entraîneuse *f*; a ~ agency une agence d'hôtesses. -**3.** [inkeeper] hôtelière *f*, aubergiste *f*.

Hostess Trolley® *n table roulante avec chauffe-plats*.

hostile [*Br* 'hɒstaɪl, *Am* 'hɒstl] ◇ *adj* hostile; he's ~ to our plans il est hostile à nos projets; people who are ~ to change les gens qui n'aiment pas le changement.
◇ *n inf Am* ennemi *m*.

hostility [hɒs'tɪlətɪ] (*pl* hostilities) *n* hostilité *f*; to show ~ to OR towards sb manifester de l'hostilité OR faire preuve d'hostilité envers qqn; the outbreak/cessation of hostilities l'ouverture/la cessation des hostilités; we want to avoid further hostilities nous voulons éviter de nouvelles hostilités OR la poursuite des hostilités.

hostler ['ɒsləʳ] = **ostler**.

hot [hɒt] (*compar* hotter, *superl* hottest, *pt* & *pp* hotted, *cont* hotting) ◇ *adj* -**1.** [high in temperature] chaud; to be ~ avoir (très OR trop) chaud; a ~, stuffy room une pièce où il fait une chaleur étouffante OR où l'on étouffe; the engine/glass/oven is ~ le moteur/verre/four est chaud; I'm getting ~ je commence à avoir chaud; the water is getting ~ l'eau devient chaude; how ~ should the oven be? le four doit être à quelle température?; it was ~ work le travail donnait chaud; there's ~ and cold running water il y a l'eau courante chaude et froide; we sat in the ~ sun nous étions assis sous un soleil brûlant; I'd like a ~ bath j'aimerais prendre un bain bien chaud; the doctor said not to have any ~ drinks le médecin m'a conseillé de ne pas boire chaud OR m'a déconseillé les boissons chaudes; keep the meat ~ tenez la viande au chaud; serve the soup while it's ~ servez la soupe bien chaude; the bread was ~ from the oven le pain sortait tout chaud du four; '~ food always available' 'plats chauds à toute heure'; you're getting ~! *fig* [in guessing game] tu brûles! ▫ I've done this job more times than you've had ~ dinners! *inf Br* j'ai fait ce boulot plus souvent que tu ne changes de chemise!; to be OR to get (all) ~ and bothered about sthg *inf* être dans tous ses états OR se faire du mauvais sang au sujet de qqch; to be OR to get ~ under the collar (about sthg) *inf* être en colère OR en rogne au sujet de qqch; too ~ to handle *literal* trop chaud pour le prendre OR saisir avec les mains; *fig* brûlant; the books were selling like ~ cakes les livres se vendaient comme des petits pains. -**2.** METEOR: it's ~ il fait très chaud; it's really ~! il fait vraiment très chaud!; it's getting hotter il commence à faire très chaud; I can't sleep when it's so ~ je ne peux pas dormir par cette chaleur; it was very ~ that day il faisait très chaud ce jour-là, c'était un jour de grande OR forte chaleur; one ~ afternoon in August (par) une chaude après-midi d'août; in (the) ~ weather pendant les chaleurs; we had a ~ spell last week c'était la canicule la semaine dernière; the hottest day of the year la journée la plus chaude de l'année. -**3.** [clothing] qui tient chaud; this jacket's too ~ cette veste tient trop chaud. -**4.** [colour] chaud, vif. -**5.** [pungent, spicy - food] épicé, piquant, relevé; [- spice] fort; a ~ curry un curry relevé OR épicé. -**6.** [fresh, recent] tout frais; the news is ~ off the presses ce sont des informations de toute dernière minute; this book is ~ off the press ce livre vient juste de paraître. -**7.** [close, following closely]: to be ~ on the trail être sur la bonne piste; the police were ~ on their heels OR on their trail la police les talonnait OR était à leurs trousses; he fled with the police in ~ pursuit il s'est enfui avec la police à ses trousses. -**8.** [fiery, vehement] violent; she has a ~ temper elle s'emporte facilement, elle est très soupe au lait. -**9.** [intense - anger, shame] intense, profond. -**10.** [keen] enthousiaste, passionné; he's ~ on my sister *inf Am* il en pince pour ma sœur. -**11.** *inf* [exciting] chaud; the reporter was onto a ~ story le journaliste était sur un coup (fumant); this book is ~ stuff c'est un livre très audacieux. -**12.** *inf* [difficult, unpleasant] chaud, difficile; we could make it OR things very ~ for you if you don't cooperate nous pourrions vous mener la vie dure OR vous en faire voir de toutes les couleurs si vous ne vous montrez pas coopératif; the town had got too ~ for the drug dealers l'atmosphère de la ville était devenue irrespirable pour les trafiquants de drogue; this issue is ~ stuff, I wouldn't touch it c'est un sujet brûlant, je n'y toucherais pas. -**13.** *inf Br* [severe, stringent] sévère, dur; the police are really ~ on drunk driving la police ne badine vraiment pas avec la conduite en état d'ivresse. -**14.** *inf* [very good] génial, terrible; [skilful] fort, calé; how is he? — not so ~ [unwell] comment va-t-il? — pas trop bien; I don't feel so ~ je ne suis pas dans mon assiette; I'm not so ~ at maths je ne suis pas très calé en maths; she's ~ stuff at golf c'est un as OR un crack au golf; his latest book isn't so ~ son dernier livre n'est pas terrible OR fameux; a ~ tip un tuyau sûr OR increvable; a ~ favourite SPORT un grand favori. -**15.** *inf* [in demand, popular] très recherché; she's really ~ just now elle a vraiment beaucoup de succès en ce moment; windsurfing is ~ stuff in this area la planche à voile est très en vogue dans cette région. -**16.** *inf* MUS: ~ jazz (jazz *m*) hot *m*. -**17.** *inf* [sexually attractive]: to be ~ (stuff) être sexy *(inv)*; he's ~ [sexually aroused] il a le feu au derrière; to be ~ to trot *Am* avoir le feu aux fesses. -**18.** *inf* [stolen] volé. -**19.** *inf Br* [sought by police] recherché par la police. -**20.** ELEC [wire] sous tension. -**21.** METALL: ~ drawing/rolling tirage *m*/laminage *m* à chaud. -**22.** NUCL [atom] chaud; [radioactive] *inf* chaud, radioactif.
◇ *adv* chaudement; I went ~ and cold at the thought of what might have happened je me faisais un sang d'encre à l'idée de OR rien que de penser à ce qui aurait pu arriver.
◆ **hots** *inf npl*: to have the ~s for sb craquer pour qqn.
◆ **hot up** *inf Br* ◇ *vt sep* -**1.** [intensify - argument, contest] échauffer; [- bombing, fighting] intensifier; [- party] mettre de l'animation dans; [- music] faire balancer, faire chauffer; they hotted up the pace ils ont forcé l'allure. -**2.** AUT: to ~ up a car gonfler le moteur d'une voiture; a hotted-up car une voiture au moteur gonflé.
◇ *vi insep* [intensify - discussion] s'échauffer; [- fighting, situation] chauffer, s'intensifier; the price war has hotted up les prix sont montés en flèche.

hot air *inf n*: he's full of ~ c'est une grande gueule; all her promises are just a lot of ~ toutes ses promesses ne sont que des paroles en l'air; that's nothing but ~! tout ça n'est que du vent!

hot-air balloon *n* montgolfière *f*.

hotbed ['hɒtbed] *n* HORT couche *f* chaude, forcerie *f*; *fig* pépinière *f*, foyer *m*; a ~ of crime/intrigue un foyer de crime/d'intrigue.

hot-blooded *adj* -**1.** [person - excitable, passionate] fougueux, au sang chaud. -**2.** [horse - thoroughbred] de sang pur.

hotcake ['hɒtkeɪk] *n Am* crêpe *f*.

hotchpotch ['hɒtʃpɒtʃ] *n Br* -**1.** [jumble] fatras *m*, salmigondis *m*; a ~ of ideas un fatras d'idées. -**2.** CULIN ≃ hochepot *m*, ≃ salmigondis *m*.

hot cross bun *n petit pain brioché aux raisins secs et marqué d'une croix que l'on vend traditionnellement aux environs de Pâques*.

hot damn▽ *interj*: ~! *Am* [in excitement] bon sang!, nom d'un chien!; [in anger] merde!

hot dog ◇ *n* -**1.** [sausage] hot-dog *m*, frankfurter *m*. -**2.** [in skiing] ski *m* acrobatique; [in surfing] surf *m* acrobatique. -**3.** *inf Am* [show-off] m'as-tu-vu *mf inv*.
◇ *vi* -**1.** [in skiing] faire du ski acrobatique; [in surfing] faire du surf acrobatique. -**2.** *inf Am* [show off] crâner, poser (pour la galerie).
◇ *interj Am*: ~! génial!, super!

hotel [həʊ'tel] ◇ *n* hôtel *m*; a two-star ~ un hôtel deux étoiles; a luxury ~ un hôtel de luxe.
◇ *comp* [prices, reservation, room] d'hôtel; ~ accommodation hébergement *m* en hôtel; ~ accommodation not included frais d'hôtel non inclus; the town needs more ~ accommodation la ville a besoin d'augmenter sa capacité hôtelière OR de développer ses ressources hôtelières; the ~ business l'hôtellerie *f*; ~ chain chaîne *f* d'hôtels; ~ desk réception *f (d'un hôtel)*; leave a message at OR with the ~ desk laissez un message à la réception; the ~ industry OR trade l'industrie *f* hôtelière; ~ staff personnel *m* hôtelier OR de l'hôtel.

hotelier [həʊ'telɪeɪ] *n* hôtelier *m*, -ère *f*.

hotelkeeper [həʊ'tel,kiːpəʳ] *n* hôtelier *m*, -ère *f*.

hotel management *n* -**1.** [training] gestion *f* hôtelière. -**2.** [people] direction *f (de l'hôtel)*.

hotel manager *n* gérant *m*, -e *f* d'hôtel, directeur *m*, -trice *f* d'hôtel.

hot flush *Br*, **hot flash** *Am n* bouffée *f* de chaleur.

hotfoot ['hɒt,fʊt] ◇ *adv inf* à toute vitesse.
◇ *vt phr*: to ~ it galoper à toute vitesse.

hot gospeller *n prêcheur évangéliste qui harangue les foules*.

hothead ['hɒthed] *n* tête *f* brûlée, exalté *m*, -e *f*.

hotheaded [,hɒt'hedɪd] *adj* [person] impétueux, exalté; [attitude] impétueux; she's very ~ c'est une exaltée OR une tête brûlée.

hothouse ['hɒthaʊs, *pl* -haʊzɪz] ◇ *n* -**1.** HORT serre *f* (chaude). -**2.** *fig* [hotbed] foyer *m*; a ~ of creativity/of decadence un foyer de création/de décadence.
◇ *adj* de serre (chaude); ~ tomatoes tomates *fpl* de serre; a ~ plant *literal* & *fig* une plante de serre (chaude).

hot line *n* TELEC *ligne directe ouverte vingt-quatre heures sur vingt-quatre*; POL téléphone *m* rouge; he has a ~ to the president il a une ligne directe avec le président; she's on the ~ to the director elle téléphone au directeur; the ~ to the Kremlin la ligne rouge avec le Kremlin.

hotly ['hɒtlɪ] *adv* [dispute] vivement; [pursue] avec acharnement; [say] avec flamme; it was a ~ debated issue c'était une question très controversée.

hot money *inf n (U)* [stolen] argent *m* volé; FIN capitaux *mpl* flottants OR fébriles.

hot pants *npl* mini-short *m (très court et moulant)*.

hot pepper *n* piment *m*.

hotplate ['hɒtpleɪt] *n* [on stove] plaque *f* chauffante; [portable] chauffe-plats *m inv*.

hotpot ['hɒtpɒt] *n Br ragoût de viande et de pommes de terre*.

hot potato *n literal* pomme de terre *f* chaude; *fig inf* sujet *m* brûlant et délicat; a political ~ un sujet brûlant OR une question brûlante de politique.

hot rod *inf n* AUT voiture *f* gonflée.

hot seat *inf n* -**1.** [difficult situation]: to be in the ~ être sur la sellette. -**2.** *Am* [electric chair] chaise *f* électrique.

hot shoe *n* griffe *f* du flash, pied-sabot *m*.

hotshot *inf* ['hɒtʃɒt] ◇ *n* [expert] as *m*, crack *m*; [VIP] gros bonnet *m*.
◇ *adj* super; they've hired some ~ lawyer ils ont pris un as du barreau.

hot spot *n* -**1.** [dangerous area] point *m* chaud OR névralgique. -**2.** *inf* [night club] boîte *f* de nuit; let's hit the town's ~s si on faisait la tournée des boîtes? -**3.** TECH point *m* chaud.

hot spring *n* source *f* chaude.

hot-tempered *adj* colérique, emporté; he's very ~ il est très soupe au lait.

Hottentot ['hɒtntɒt] ◇ *n* -**1.** [person] Hottentot *m*, -e *f*. -**2.** LING hottentot *m*.
◇ *adj* hottentot.

hot tub *n sorte de Jacuzzi® qu'on installe dehors*.

hot war *n* guerre *f* chaude OR ouverte.

hot water *n literal* eau *f* chaude; *fig*: their latest prank got them into ~ OR landed them in ~ leur dernière farce leur a attiré des ennuis; you'll be in ~ when she finds out tu passeras un mauvais quart d'heure quand elle s'en apercevra.

hot-water bottle *n* bouillotte *f*.

hot wire *n* fil *m* sous tension.
◆ **hot-wire** *inf vt*: to hot-wire a car *faire démarrer une voiture en bricolant les fils de contact*.

houmous, houmus ['hʊməs] = **hummus**.

hound [haʊnd] ◇ *n* -**1.** [dog - gen] chien *m*; [- for hunting] chien *m* courant, chien *m* de meute; the ~s, a pack of ~s HUNT la meute; to ride to OR to follow the ~s HUNT chasser à courre ❑ 'The Hound of the Baskervilles' *Conan Doyle* 'le Chien des Baskerville'. -**2.** *pej* & *dated* [person] canaille *f*, crapule *f*.
◇ *vt* -**1.** [give chase] traquer, pourchasser. -**2.** [harass] s'acharner sur, harceler; she was ~ed by reporters elle était pourchassée OR harcelée par les journalistes.
◆ **hound down** *vt sep* prendre dans des rets, coincer; HUNT forcer.
◆ **hound out** *vt sep* chasser de; he was ~ed out of town il a été chassé de la ville.

houndstooth, hound's-tooth ['haʊndztu:θ] *n* TEX pied-de-poule *m*; a ~ (check) jacket une veste en pied-de-poule.

hour ['aʊəʳ] *n* -**1.** [unit of time] heure *f*; a quarter of an ~ un quart d'heure; half an ~, a half ~ une demi-heure; an ~ and three-quarters une heure trois quarts; at 60 km an OR per ~ à 60 km à l'heure; check it at least three times an ~ vérifie-le au moins trois fois par heure; it's a two-~ drive/walk from here c'est à deux heures de voiture/de marche d'ici; the play is an ~ long la pièce dure une heure, c'est une pièce d'une heure; he gets £10 an ~ il touche 10 livres (de) l'heure; are you paid by the ~? êtes-vous payé à l'heure?; a 35-~ week une semaine de 35 heures; the shop is open 24 ~s a day le magasin est ouvert 24 heures sur 24; he was an ~ late il était en retard d'une heure; we arrived with ~s to spare nous sommes arrivés avec plusieurs heures devant nous OR en avance de plusieurs heures; the situation is deteriorating by the ~ la situation s'aggrave d'heure en heure; it will save you ~s cela te fera gagner des heures; we waited for ~s and ~s on a attendu des heures; Miami is three ~s ahead of Fresno Miami a trois heures d'avance sur Fresno; output per ~ TECH puissance *f* horaire. -**2.** [time of day] heure *f*; it chimes on the ~ ça sonne à l'heure juste; every ~ on the ~ toutes les heures justes; in the early OR small ~s (of the morning) au petit matin, au petit jour; at this late ~ vu l'heure avancée. -**3.** *fig* [specific moment] heure *f*, moment *m*; the ~ has come l'heure est venue, c'est l'heure OR le moment; the man of the ~ l'homme de l'heure; in one's ~ of need quand on est dans le besoin; the burning questions of the ~ l'actualité brûlante.
◆ **hours** *npl* heures *fpl*; flexible working ~s INDUST des horaires mobiles OR souples; opening ~s heures d'ouverture; you'll have to make up the ~s next week il faudra que vous rattrapiez la semaine prochaine; do you work long ~s? as-tu de longues journées de travail?; he keeps late ~s c'est un couche-tard, il veille tard; to keep regular ~s avoir une vie réglée ❑ he was out until all ~s il est rentré à une heure indue; after ~s *Br* [in a pub, shops] après l'heure de fermeture; [offices] après les heures de bureau; they were convicted for after-~s drinking *Br* ils ont été condamnés pour avoir consommé de l'alcool dans un pub après l'heure légale de fermeture; an after-~s bar *Am* un bar de nuit.

hourglass ['aʊəglɑ:s] ◇ *n* sablier *m*.
◇ *adj* en forme d'amphore; an ~ figure une taille de guêpe.

hour hand *n* petite aiguille *f*.

hour-long *adj* d'une heure.

hourly ['aʊəlɪ] ◇ *adj* -**1.** [each hour - flights, trains]: ~ departures départs toutes les heures ‖ COMM & TECH horaire; the ~ wage has been increased le salaire horaire a été augmenté. -**2.** [continual - anticipation] constant, perpétuel.
◇ *adv* -**1.** [each hour] une fois par heure, chaque heure, toutes les heures; ~ paid workers ouvriers *mpl* payés à l'heure. -**2.** [continually] sans cesse; we expect them ~ on les attend d'une minute à l'autre OR à tout moment.

house [*n* haʊs, *vb* haʊz] (*pl* houses ['haʊzɪz]) ◇ *n* -**1.** maison *f*; at OR to his ~ chez lui; '~ for sale' 'propriété à vendre'; a ~ of cards un château de cartes; to clean the ~ faire le ménage; does he look after the ~ himself? est-ce que c'est lui qui s'occupe de son ménage?; to keep ~ (for sb) tenir la maison OR le ménage (de qqn); to move ~ *Br* déménager; to set up ~ monter son ménage, s'installer; they set up ~ together ils se sont mis en ménage; don't wake up the whole ~! ne réveille pas toute la maison! ❑ detached ~ pavillon *m*; semi-detached ~ maison *f* jumelée OR double; we got on OR along like a ~ on fire nous nous entendions à merveille OR comme larrons en foire; to set OR to put one's ~ in order mettre de l'ordre dans ses affaires. -**2.** COMM [establishment] maison *f (de commerce)*, compagnie *f*; RELIG maison *f* religieuse; *Br* SCH maison *f*; banking ~ établissement *m* bancaire; publishing ~ maison *f* d'édition; a bottle of ~ red (wine) une bouteille de (vin) rouge de la maison OR de l'établissement; drinks are on the ~! la tournée est aux frais de la maison! -**3.** [family line] maison *f*; the House of York la maison de York. -**4.** THEAT salle *f*, auditoire *m*; is there a good ~ tonight? est-ce que la salle est pleine ce soir?; a decent ~ une salle moyenne; they played to an empty ~ ils ont joué devant les banquettes (vides); there wasn't a soul in the ~ il n'y avait personne dans la salle; to have a full ~ jouer à guichets fermés OR à bureaux fermés; '~ full' 'complet'; the second ~ *Br* la deuxième séance ❑ to bring the ~ down faire crouler la salle sous les applaudissements; *fig* casser la baraque. -**5.** the House *Br* POL la Chambre; *Am* POL la Chambre des représentants; ST. EX la Bourse. -**6.** [in debate]: this ~ believes... la motion à débattre est la suivante...
◇ *vt* [accommodate - subj: organization, person] héberger, loger; [- subj: building] recevoir; we can ~ them temporarily in tents nous pouvons les loger provisoirement dans des tentes; many families are still badly ~d de nombreuses familles sont encore mal logées; this wing ~s a laboratory/five families cette aile abrite un laboratoire/cinq familles; the library cannot ~ any more books la bibliothèque ne peut pas abriter plus de livres; his boat is ~d in the garage during winter son bateau est (remisé) au garage pendant l'hiver; the archives are ~d in the basement on garde les archives dans les caves.
◇ *interj* [in bingo]: ~! ≃ carton!

HOUSE:
Dans certaines écoles en Grande-Bretagne (particulièrement dans les «grammar schools» et les «public schools»), les élèves sont répartis en plusieurs «houses», désignées chacune par un nom, entre lesquelles se développe un certain esprit de compétition.

---

house agent *n Br* agent *m* immobilier.

house arrest *n* assignation *f* à domicile OR à résidence; to put sb under ~ assigner qqn à domicile OR à résidence; he is under ~ il est assigné à domicile, il est en résidence surveillée.

houseboat ['haʊsbəʊt] *n* house-boat *m*, péniche *f* (aménagée).

housebound ['haʊsbaʊnd] *adj* qui ne peut quitter la maison.

houseboy ['haʊsbɔɪ] *n* domestique *m*, valet *m*; [colonial] boy *m*.

housebreaker ['haʊs,breɪkəʳ] *n* cambrioleur *m*, -euse *f*.

housebreaking ['haʊs,breɪkɪŋ] *n* cambriolage *m*.

housebroken ['haʊs,brəʊkn] *adj Am* [pet] propre.

housecoat ['haʊskəʊt] *n* robe *f* d'intérieur.

housecraft ['haʊskrɑ:ft] *n* économie *f* ménagère.

house detective *n* responsable *m* de la sécurité, détective *m* de l'hôtel.

housefather ['haʊs,fɑ:ðəʳ] *n* responsable *m* (de groupe) *(dans un foyer)*.

housefly ['haʊsflaɪ] (*pl* houseflies) *n* mouche *f* (commune OR domestique).

houseful ['haʊsfʊl] *n*: a ~ of guests une pleine maisonnée d'invités; we've got a real ~ this weekend la maison est vraiment pleine (de monde) ce week-end.

houseguest ['haʊsgest] *n* invité *m*, -e *f*.

household ['haʊshəʊld] ◇ *n* ménage *m*, (gens *mpl* de la) maison *f*, maisonnée *f*; ADMIN

& ECON ménage; **she grew up as part of a large ~** elle a grandi au sein d'une famille nombreuse; **the head of the ~** le chef de famille; **indicate your relationship to the other members of your ~** indiquez les liens de parenté existant entre vous et les autres personnes qui résident avec vous OR de votre foyer; **~s with more than two children** ménages OR familles de plus de deux enfants; **95 per cent of ~s have a television set** 95 pour cent des ménages possèdent un poste de télévision ❑ **the Royal Household** la maison royale.
◇ *adj* [products, expenses] de ménage; ADMIN & ECON des ménages; **'for ~ use only'** 'à usage domestique seulement'; **~ appliance** appareil *m* ménager; **~ chores** travaux *mpl* ménagers, tâches *fpl* ménagères; **label your boxes "~ goods"** accolez l'étiquette «objets personnels» sur vos cartons.

Household Cavalry *pr n* *division de cavalerie de la Garde Royale britannique*.

householder ['haʊs,həʊldəʳ] *n* [occupant] occupant *m*, -e *f*; [owner] propriétaire *mf*; [tenant] locataire *mf*.

household gods *npl* HIST dieux *mpl* du foyer.

household name *n* mot *m* que tout le monde connaît; **we want to make our brand a ~** nous voulons que notre marque soit connue de tous; **the TV series made her a ~** depuis cette série télévisée, tout le monde la connaît OR sait qui elle est.

household troops *npl* garde *f* personnelle; HIST garde *f* du palais; [in UK] Garde *f* Royale.

household word = **household name**.

house-hunt *vi* chercher un OR être à la recherche d'un logement; **I spent two months ~ing** j'ai passé deux mois à chercher une maison OR à la recherche d'une maison.

house husband *n* père *m* au foyer.

house journal *n* journal *m* interne, bulletin *m*.

housekeeper ['haʊs,kiːpəʳ] *n* [institutional] économe *f*, intendante *f*; [private] gouvernante *f*.

housekeeping ['haʊs,kiːpɪŋ] *n* *(U)* **-1.** [of household - skill] économie *f* domestique; [- work] ménage *m*; **~ (money)** argent *m* du ménage. **-2.** [of organization] services *mpl* généraux. **-3.** COMPUT opérations *fpl* de nettoyage et d'entretien.

house lights *npl* THEAT lumières *fpl* OR éclairage *m* de la salle.

house magazine = **house journal**.

housemaid ['haʊsmeɪd] *n* bonne *f*, femme *f* de chambre.

housemaid's knee *n* MED inflammation *f* du genou.

houseman ['haʊsmən] (*pl* **housemen** [-mən]) *n* **-1.** *Br* MED ≃ interne *m*. **-2.** = **houseboy**.

house manager *n* THEAT directeur *m*, -trice *f* de théâtre.

house martin *n* hirondelle *f* de fenêtre.

housemaster ['haʊs,mɑːstəʳ] *n* *Br* SCH *professeur responsable d'une «house»*.

housemen ['haʊsmən] *pl* → **houseman**.

housemistress ['haʊs,mɪstrɪs] *n* *Br* SCH *professeur responsable d'une «house»*.

housemother ['haʊs,mʌðəʳ] *n* responsable *f* (de groupe) *(dans un foyer)*.

house music *n* house *f* (music).

House of Commons *pr n*: **the ~** la Chambre des communes.

HOUSE OF COMMONS:
La Chambre des communes est composée de 650 députés («MPs») élus pour cinq ans et qui siègent environ 175 jours par an.

House of God *n* maison *f* de Dieu, église *f*, chapelle *f*.

House of Lords *pr n*: **the ~** la Chambre des lords.

HOUSE OF LORDS:
La Chambre des lords est composée de pairs et d'hommes d'Église. Il s'agit de la plus haute cour au Royaume-Uni (en excluant l'Écosse). Elle a le pouvoir d'amender certains projets de loi qui ont été votés par la Chambre des communes.

House of Representatives *pr n*: **the ~** la Chambre des représentants *(aux États-Unis)*.

HOUSE OF REPRESENTATIVES:
La Chambre des représentants constitue, avec le Sénat, l'organe législatif américain; ses membres sont élus par le peuple, en proportion de la population de chaque État.

---

house painter *n* peintre *m* en bâtiment.

houseparent ['haʊs,peərənt] *n* responsable *mf* (de groupe) *(dans un foyer)*.

house party *n* **-1.** [social occasion] fête *f* de plusieurs jours *(dans une maison de campagne)*. **-2.** [guests] invités *mpl*.

house physician *n* [in hospital] ≃ interne *m*; [in hotel] médecin *m* *(attaché à un hôtel)*.

houseplant ['haʊsplɑːnt] *n* plante *f* d'intérieur.

house-proud *adj*: **he's very ~** il attache beaucoup d'importance à l'aspect intérieur de sa maison, tout est toujours impeccable chez lui.

houseroom ['haʊsrʊm] *n* *Br* place *f* *(pour loger qqn ou qqch)*; **he has ~ for two** il a de la place pour deux; **I wouldn't give that table ~!** je ne voudrais pas de cette table chez moi!

house rule *n* règle *f* de la maison; GAMES règle du jeu particulière.

house-sit *vi*: **to ~ for sb** *s'occuper de la maison de qqn pendant son absence*.

Houses of Parliament *pl pr n*: **the ~** le Parlement *m* (britannique) *(où se réunissent la Chambre des communes et la Chambre des lords)*.

house sparrow *n* moineau *m* domestique.

house surgeon *n* chirurgien *m* de garde.

house-to-house *adj* [enquiry] de porte en porte; **to make a ~ search for sb/sthg** aller de porte en porte à la recherche de qqn/qqch, fouiller chaque maison à la recherche de qqn/qqch.

housetop ['haʊstɒp] *n* toit *m*; **to shout** OR **to proclaim sthg from the ~s** crier qqch sur les toits.

house trailer *n* *Am* caravane *f*.

house-train *vt* dresser à la propreté; **has the dog been ~ed?** est-ce que le chien est propre?; **he used to be really untidy, but she soon got him ~ed!** *inf hum* avant, il était très brouillon, mais elle a eu tôt fait de le dresser!

housewarming ['haʊs,wɔːmɪŋ] *n* pendaison *f* de crémaillère; **to give** OR **to have a ~ (party)** pendre la crémaillère.

housewife ['haʊswaɪf] (*pl* **housewives** [-waɪvz]) *n* ménagère *f*; [not career woman] femme *f* au foyer.

housewifely ['haʊs,waɪflɪ] *adj* de ménagère.

housewifery ['haʊswɪfərɪ] *n* économie *f* domestique.

house wine *n* vin *m* de la maison.

housewives ['haʊswaɪvz] *pl* → **housewife**.

housework ['haʊswɜːk] *n* (travaux *mpl* de) ménage *m*; **to do the ~** faire le ménage; **we share the ~** nous nous partageons le ménage, nous faisons le ménage à tour de rôle.

housey-housey [,haʊzɪ'haʊzɪ] *n* *Br* ≃ loto *m* *(joué pour de l'argent)*.

housing ['haʊzɪŋ] ◇ *n* **-1.** [accommodation] logement *m*; **the government has promised to provide more low-cost ~** le gouvernement a promis de fournir plus de logements à loyer modéré; **the budget allocation for ~ has been cut** la part du budget réservée au logement a été réduite; **two per cent still live in substandard ~** deux pour cent habitent encore des logements qui ne sont pas aux normes; **there's a lot of new ~ going up in the area** il y a beaucoup de logements nouveaux en construction dans le quartier; **four ~ units** quatre logements *mpl* OR habitations *fpl*. **-2.** TECH [of mechanism] carter *m*; PHOT boîtier *m*; **wheel ~** boîte *f* de roue; **watch ~** boîtier de montre. **-3.** CONSTR encastrement *m*.
◇ *comp*: **~ shortage** crise *f* du logement; **the local ~ department** ≃ l'antenne logement (de la commune); **the government has no long-term ~ strategy** le gouvernement n'a aucune stratégie à long terme en matière de logement.

housing association *n* *association britannique à but non lucratif qui construit ou rénove des logements pour les louer à ses membres*.

housing benefit *n* *Br* *allocation de logement versée par l'État aux familles justifiant de revenus faibles*.

housing development *n* **-1.** [estate] lotissement *m*. **-2.** [activity] construction *f* de logements.

housing estate *n* *Br* [of houses] lotissement *m*; [of flats] cité *f*.

housing list *n* *Br* *liste d'attente pour bénéficier d'un logement social*.

housing project *n* **-1.** *Am* = **housing estate**. **-2.** [plan] plan *m* d'aménagement immobilier.

housing scheme *n* **-1.** [plan] programme *m* municipal de logement. **-2.** [houses] = **housing estate**.

hove [həʊv] *pt & pp* → **heave**.

hovel ['hɒvl] *n* taudis *m*, masure *f*.

hover ['hɒvəʳ] *vi* **-1.** [in air - smoke] stagner; [- balloon, scent] flotter; [- insects] voltiger; [- helicopter, hummingbird] faire du surplace; **bees ~ed around the roses** des abeilles voltigeaient autour des roses. **-2.** [linger - person] rôder; [- smile] flotter; [- danger] planer; **the waitress ~ed over/round him** la serveuse rôdait/tournait autour de lui; **it's no use ~ing over the phone like that** ce n'est pas la peine de guetter la sonnerie du téléphone comme ça; **she was ~ing between life and death** elle restait suspendue entre la vie et la mort. **-3.** [hesitate] hésiter; **his finger ~ed over the button** son doigt hésita à appuyer sur le bouton; **I'm ~ing between the two possible options** j'hésite entre les deux options possibles.

hovercraft ['hɒvəkrɑːft] *n* aéroglisseur *m*.

hoverfly ['hɒvəflaɪ] (*pl* **hoverflies**) *n* syrphe *m*.

hoverport ['hɒvəpɔːt] *n* hoverport *m*.

hovertrain ['hɒvətreɪn] *n* train *m* à coussin d'air.

Hovis® ['həʊvɪs] *n* *marque de pain complet*.

how [haʊ] ◇ *adv* **-1.** [in what way] comment; **~ do you write it?** comment est-ce que ça s'écrit?; **~ shall we go about it?** comment faire?; **~ could you be so careless?** comment as-tu pu être aussi étourdi? ❑ **~ is it that...?** comment se fait-il que...?; **~ so?**, **~ can that be?** comment cela (se fait-il)?; **~'s that (again)?** comment?; **~'s that for results?** alors ces résultats, qu'est-ce que vous en pensez?; **~ the heck should I know?** *inf* mais enfin, comment veux-tu que je sache? **-2.** [in greetings, friendly enquiries etc] comment; **~ are you?** comment allez-vous?; **~ are you doing?** comment ça va?; **~ are things?** ça marche?; **~ did it go?** comment ça s'est passé?; **~'s the dollar (doing)?** comment va le dollar?; **~ did you like** OR **~ was the film?** comment as-tu trouvé le film?; **~ was your trip?** avez-vous fait bon voyage?; **~'s the water?** l'eau est bonne? ❑ **~ do you do?** bonjour!; **~'s tricks?** *inf* ça gaze? **-3.** [in exclamations] que, comme; **~ sad she is!** qu'elle est triste!, comme elle est triste!; **~ nice of you!** comme c'est aimable à vous!; **~ decadent!** quelle décadence!; **~ incredible!** c'est incroyable!; **~ easily they forget!** comme ils oublient facilement!; **~ I wish I could!** si seulement je pouvais! ❑ **~ stupid can you get!** *inf* est-il possible d'être bête à ce point-là! **-4.** *(with adj, adv)* [referring to measurement, rate, degree]: **~ wide is the room?** quelle est la largeur de la pièce?; **~ tall are you?** combien mesures-tu?; **~ old is she?** quel âge a-t-elle?; **~ well can you see it?** est-ce que tu le vois bien?; **~ angry**

is he? il est vraiment fâché?; ~ fast/slowly was he walking? à quelle vitesse marchait-il? || [referring to time, distance, quantity]: ~ far is it from here to the sea? combien y a-t-il d'ici à la mer?; ~ much does this bag cost? combien coûte ce sac?; ~ much is it/do I owe you? combien est-ce que ça coûte/vous dois-je?; ~ often did she come? – about three or four times combien de fois est-elle venue? – trois ou quatre fois; ~ often did he write? – every week est-ce qu'il écrivait souvent? – toutes les semaines; ~ long has he been here? depuis quand OR depuis combien de temps est-il ici?; ~ soon can you deliver it? à partir de quand pouvez-vous le livrer?; ~ late will you stay? jusqu'à quelle heure resteras-tu?
◇ *conj* -**1.** [in what way] comment; tell me ~ you do it dites-moi comment vous faites; he's learning ~ to read il apprend à lire; we know ~ to extract it nous savons comment l'extraire; I need more information on ~ the network functions j'ai besoin de plus de renseignements sur le fonctionnement du réseau. -**2.** [the fact that] que; he told us ~ he had seen his child born il nous a raconté qu'il avait vu naître son enfant; you know ~ he always gets his own way tu sais bien comment il est, il finit toujours par obtenir ce qu'il veut; we all know ~ smell can influence taste tout le monde sait que l'odorat peut avoir une influence sur le goût; I remember ~ he always used to turn up late je me souviens qu'il était toujours en retard. -**3.** *inf* [however] comme; arrange the furniture ~ you like installe les meubles comme tu veux ❑ did you like it? – and ~! ça t'a plu? – et comment!
◇ *n* comment *m inv*; the ~ and the why of it don't interest me le pourquoi et le comment ne m'intéressent pas.
◇ *interj hum* [greeting]: ~! salut!
◆ **how about** *inf adv phr*: ~ about a beer? et si on prenait une bière?; ~ about going out tonight? si on sortait ce soir?; ~ about you: what do you think? et toi, qu'est-ce que tu en penses?
◆ **how come** *inf adv phr*: ~ come? comment ça se fait?; ~ come you left? comment ça se fait que tu sois parti?

howbeit [ˌhaʊ'biːɪt] *arch conj* bien que.

howdy *inf* ['haʊdɪ] *interj Am*: ~! salut!

however [haʊ'evəʳ] ◇ *adv* -**1.** [indicating contrast or contradiction] cependant, pourtant, toutefois; I didn't see him, ~ cependant OR pourtant je ne l'ai pas vu; if, ~, you have a better suggestion... si toutefois vous avez une meilleure suggestion (à faire)... -**2.** *(with adj or adv)* [no matter how] si... que, quelque... que; ~ nice he tries to be... si gentil qu'il essaie d'être...; all contributions will be welcome, ~ small si petites soient-elles, toutes les contributions seront les bienvenues; he'll never do it, ~ much OR hard he tries quelque effort qu'il fasse, il n'y arrivera jamais; ~ cold/hot the weather même quand il fait très froid/chaud; ~ late/early you arrive, call me quelle que soit l'heure à laquelle tu arrives, appelle-moi; ~ long it takes (you) quel que soit le temps que cela (te) prend; ~ much he complains même s'il se plaint beaucoup. -**3.** *(in questions)* [emphatic use] comment; ~ did he find it? comment a-t-il bien pu le trouver?
◇ *conj* [in whatever way] de quelque manière que; it'll be fine, ~ you do it de quelque manière que vous le fassiez, ça ira; we can present it ~ you like OR want on peut le présenter comme vous voulez.

howitzer ['haʊɪtsəʳ] *n* obusier *m*.

howl [haʊl] ◇ *n* -**1.** [of person, animal] hurlement *m*; [of child] braillement *m*, hurlement *m*; [of wind] mugissement *m*; to let out a ~ of pain pousser un hurlement de douleur; the speech was greeted with ~s of derision le discours a été accueilli par des huées. -**2.** ELECTRON effet *m* Larsen.
◇ *vi* -**1.** [person, animal] hurler; [child] brailler; [wind] mugir; to ~ with laughter hurler de rire; to ~ in OR with rage hurler de rage. -**2.** *inf* [cry] chialer; [complain] gueuler.
◇ *vt* crier, hurler; they ~ed their defiance at the guards ils ont hurlé leur colère aux gardes.
◆ **howl down** *vt sep* [speaker]: they ~ed him down ils l'ont réduit au silence par leurs huées.
◆ **howl out** *vt sep* crier, hurler.

howler ['haʊləʳ] *n* -**1.** *inf* [blunder] gaffe *f*, bourde *f*. -**2.** [monkey] hurleur *m*, alouate *m*.

howling ['haʊlɪŋ] ◇ *n* [of person, animal] hurlement *m*, hurlements *mpl*; [of child] braillement *m*, braillements *mpl*; [of wind] mugissement *m*, mugissements *mpl*.
◇ *adj inf* [error] énorme; a ~ success un succès fou.

howsoever [ˌhaʊsəʊ'evəʳ] = **however** *adv*.

howzat *inf* [haʊ'zæt] *interj* [in cricket]: ~! sortez le batteur!

hoy [hɔɪ] *interj Br*: ~! [to people] ohé!, hep!; [to animals] hue!

hoyden ['hɔɪdn] *n* garçon *m* manqué.

hoydenish ['hɔɪdənɪʃ] *adj* garçonnier.

hp, HP ◇ *n* (*abbr of* hire purchase): to buy sthg on ~ acheter qqch à crédit.
◇ (*written abbr of* horsepower) CV.

HP Sauce® *n sauce épicée vendue en bouteille.*

HQ (*abbr of* headquarters) *n* QG *m*.

hr(s) (*written abbr of* hour(s)) h.

HRH (*written abbr of* His/Her Royal Highness) SAR.

HRT *n abbr of* hormone replacement therapy.

HS *Am written abbr of* high school.

HST *n* -**1.** (*abbr of* high speed train) ≃ TGV *m*. -**2.** *abbr of* Hawaiian Standard Time.

hub [hʌb] *n* [of wheel] moyeu *m*; *fig* centre *m*.

hub airport *n Am* aéroport important.

hubble-bubble ['hʌblˌbʌbl] *n Br* -**1.** = **hookah**. -**2.** = **hubbub**. -**3.** [bubbling sound] glouglou *m*.

hubbub ['hʌbʌb] *n* [of voices] brouhaha *m*; [uproar] vacarme *m*, tapage *m*.

hubby *inf* ['hʌbɪ] (*pl* **hubbies**) *n* bonhomme *m*, petit mari *m*.

hubcap ['hʌbkæp] *n* AUT enjoliveur *m* (de roue).

hubris ['hjuːbrɪs] *n* orgueil *m* (démesuré).

huckleberry ['hʌklbərɪ] (*pl* **huckleberries**) *n* airelle *f*, myrtille *f*; 'The Adventures of Huckleberry Finn' *Twain* 'les Aventures de Huckleberry Finn'.

huckster ['hʌkstəʳ] *n* -**1.** [pedlar] colporteur *m*, -euse *f*. -**2.** *Am pej* [in advertising] publicitaire *m* agressif; political ~ politicard *m*, -e *f*.

HUD (*abbr of* Department of Housing and Urban Development) *pr n ancien ministère américain de l'Urbanisme et du Logement.*

huddle ['hʌdl] ◇ *n* -**1.** [of people] petit groupe *m* (serré); [of objects] tas *m*, amas *m*; [of roofs] enchevêtrement *m*; to go into a ~ *inf* se réunir en petit comité. -**2.** *Am* SPORT concentration *f (d'une équipe)*.
◇ *vi* -**1.** [crowd together] se blottir; the sheep ~d under the trees les moutons se blottissaient les uns contre les autres sous les arbres; they ~d round the fire ils se sont blottis autour du feu. -**2.** [crouch] se recroqueviller, se blottir; he ~d in a corner of his cell il s'est recroquevillé dans un coin de sa cellule; she was huddling under a blanket elle était blottie sous une couverture.
◆ **huddle down** *vi insep* -**1.** [hunch] se recroqueviller; [out of the way] se faire tout petit. -**2.** [nestle] se blottir, se pelotonner.
◆ **huddle together** *vi insep* se serrer OR se blottir les uns contre les autres; [for talk] se mettre en petit groupe OR cercle serré; they ~d together for warmth ils se serraient OR se blottissaient les uns contre les autres pour se tenir chaud.

huddled ['hʌdld] *adj* -**1.** [for shelter] blotti; [curled up] pelotonné; I found him ~ in a ditch je l'ai trouvé blotti dans un fossé; they lay ~ under the blanket ils étaient blottis OR pelotonnés les uns contre les autres sous la couverture; the houses lay ~ in the valley les maisons étaient blotties dans la vallée. -**2.** [hunched] recroquevillé; he spends hours ~ over those maps il passe des heures penché sur ces cartes.

Hudson Bay ['hʌdsn-] *pr n* la baie d'Hudson.

Hudson River *pr n*: the ~ l'Hudson *m*.

hue [hjuː] *n* -**1.** [colour] teinte *f*, nuance *f*. -**2.** [aspect] nuance *f*; that puts a different ~ on the matter cela donne à l'affaire une autre coloration, cela fait voir l'affaire sous un autre jour. -**3.** *phr*: a ~ and cry *Br* une clameur (de haro); to raise a ~ and a cry against sb/sthg crier haro sur qqn/qqch.

-hued [hjuːd] *in cpds*: dark/light~ de couleur foncée/claire; many~ multicolore, bigarré.

huff [hʌf] ◇ *vi phr*: to ~ and puff [with exertion] haleter; [with annoyance] maugréer; they'll ~ and puff a bit but they won't stop us *Br fig* ils protesteront, mais ils nous laisseront faire.
◇ *vt* GAMES souffler (un pion).
◇ *n inf*: to be in a ~ être froissé OR fâché; to take the ~ *Br* prendre la mouche, s'offusquer; it's no use getting into a ~ about it ça ne vaut pas la peine de t'en offusquer; he went off in a ~ il est parti froissé OR fâché.

huffed *inf* [hʌft] *adj* froissé, fâché.

huffily ['hʌfɪlɪ] *adv* [reply] d'un ton vexé OR fâché; [behave] avec (mauvaise) humeur.

huffy ['hʌfɪ] *adj* [piqued] froissé, vexé; [touchy] susceptible.

hug [hʌg] (*pt & pp* hugged, *cont* hugging) ◇ *vt* -**1.** [in arms] serrer dans ses bras, étreindre; to ~ o.s. with delight (over OR about sthg) *fig* se réjouir vivement (de qqch), jubiler. -**2.** *fig* [idea] tenir à, chérir; she hugged the memory of that moment to herself elle chérissait le souvenir de cet instant. -**3.** [keep close to] serrer; to ~ the shore serrer la côte; don't ~ the kerb AUT ne serrez pas le trottoir; this car ~s the corners well cette voiture prend bien les virages; to ~ the ground AERON suivre le relief du terrain.
◇ *n* étreinte *f*; to give sb a ~ serrer qqn dans ses bras, étreindre qqn; they greeted each other with ~s and kisses ils se sont accueillis avec de grandes embrassades.

huge [hjuːdʒ] *adj* [in size, degree] énorme, immense; [in extent] vaste, immense; [in volume] énorme, gigantesque.

hugely ['hjuːdʒlɪ] *adv* [a lot] énormément; [as intensifier] énormément, extrêmement; the project has been ~ successful/expensive le projet a été un succès complet/a coûté extrêmement cher.

hugeness ['hjuːdʒnɪs] *n* immensité *f*; [of error, demands] énormité *f*.

hugger-mugger ['hʌgəˌmʌgəʳ] *arch* ◇ *n* -**1.** [disorder] fatras *m*, fouillis *m*, désordre *m*. -**2.** [secrecy] secret *m*.
◇ *adj* désordonné.
◇ *adv* en désordre.

Huguenot ['hjuːgənəʊ] ◇ *n* Huguenot *m*, -e *f*.
◇ *adj* huguenot.

huh [hʌ] *interj* [surprise]: ~? hein? || [scepticism]: ~! hum!

hula ['huːlə], **hula-hula** *n* danse *f* polynésienne; a ~ skirt une jupe en paille.

Hula-Hoop® *n* Hula-Hoop® *m*.

hulk [hʌlk] *n* -**1.** [ship] épave *f*; *pej* vieux rafiot *m*; [used as prison, storehouse] ponton *m*; to be sent to the ~s être envoyé au ponton. -**2.** [person, thing] mastodonte *m*; a great ~ of a man un malabar *m*.

hulking ['hʌlkɪŋ] *adj* [person] balourd, massif; [thing] gros, imposant; [as intensifier]: you ~ great oaf! espèce de malotru!

hull [hʌl] ◇ *n* -**1.** [of ship] coque *f*; MIL [of tank] caisse *f*. -**2.** [of peas, beans] cosse *f*, gousse *f*; [of nut] écale *f*; [of strawberry] pédoncule *m*.
◇ *vt* -**1.** [peas] écosser; [nuts] écaler, décortiquer; [grains] décortiquer; [strawberries] équeuter. -**2.** [ship] percer la coque de.

hullabaloo *inf* [ˌhʌləbə'luː] *n* raffut *m*, chambard *m*, barouf *m*; the press made a real ~ about it la presse en a fait tout un foin.

hullo [hə'ləʊ] *interj Br* **-1.** ~! [on meeting] salut!; [on phone] allô! **-2.** [for attention]: ~! ohé!, holà!; ~ **there!** holà, vous! **-3.** [in surprise]: ~! tiens!

hum [hʌm] (*pt* & *pp* **hummed**, *cont* **humming**) ◇ *vi* **-1.** [audience, bee, wires] bourdonner; [person] fredonner, chantonner; [top, fire] ronfler; ELECTRON ronfler; [air conditioner] ronronner; **the motors hummed into action** les moteurs se sont mis à ronfler OR vrombir; **everything was humming along nicely** *fig* tout marchait comme sur des roulettes. **-2.** [be lively] grouiller; **the airport/town was humming with activity** l'aéroport/la ville bourdonnait d'activité; **to make things ~** mener les choses rondement; **the party was just beginning to ~ when the police arrived** la fête commençait à s'animer quand la police est arrivée. **-3.** *inf Br* [stink] cocotter. **-4.** *phr*: **to ~ and haw** *literal* bafouiller; *fig* hésiter.
◇ *vt* [tune] fredonner, chantonner.
◇ *n* **-1.** [of bees, voices] bourdonnement *m*; [of vehicle] vrombissement *m*; [of fire, top] ronflement *m*; ELECTRON ronflement; [of machine] ronronnement *m*; **the distant ~ of traffic** le ronronnement lointain de la circulation. **-2.** *inf Br* [stench] puanteur *f*, mauvaise odeur *f*; **there's a bit of a ~ in here!** ça cocotte là-dedans!
◇ *interj*: ~! hem!, hum!

human ['hju:mən] ◇ *adj* humain; **the ~ race** le genre humain; **they were treated as less than ~** ils étaient traités comme des bêtes; **he's only ~** personne n'est parfait; **I can't do all that work alone, I'm only ~!** je ne peux pas faire tout ce travail tout seul, je ne suis pas une bête de somme!; **the crash was found to have been caused by ~ error** on a découvert que l'accident était dû à une erreur OR défaillance humaine; **it's those little ~ touches that make all the difference** ce sont les petites touches personnelles qui font toute la différence ❑ 'Of Human Bondage' *Maugham* 'Servitude humaine'.
◇ *n* (être *m*) humain *m*.

human being *n* être *m* humain.

humane [hju:'meɪn] *adj* **-1.** [compassionate - action, person] humain, plein d'humanité; [- treatment] humain; **a ~ method of killing animals** une façon humaine de tuer les animaux. **-2.** *fml* & *dated* [education] humaniste.

humanely [hju:'meɪnlɪ] *adv* humainement.

human engineering *n* INDUST gestion *f* des relations humaines; [ergonomics] ergonomie *f*.

humane society *n* [for animals] société *f* protectrice des animaux; [for good works] société *f* OR association *f* humanitaire.

human interest *n* PRESS dimension *f* humaine; **a ~ story** un reportage qui met l'accent sur OR privilégie la dimension humaine.

humanism ['hju:mənɪzm] *n* humanisme *m*.

humanist ['hju:mənɪst] ◇ *n* humaniste *m*.
◇ *adj* humaniste.

humanistic [,hju:mə'nɪstɪk] *adj* humaniste.

humanitarian [hju:,mænɪ'teərɪən] ◇ *n* humanitaire *mf*.
◇ *adj* humanitaire.

humanitarianism [hju:,mænɪ'teərɪənɪzm] *n* [philanthropy] humanitarisme *m*; [in theology] monophysisme *m*.

humanity [hju:'mænətɪ] *n* **-1.** [mankind] humanité *f*; **for the good of ~** pour le bien de l'humanité. **-2.** [compassion] humanité *f*; **to treat sb with ~** traiter qqn avec humanité; **the prison camps stripped the inmates of their ~** les détenus perdaient toute humanité dans les camps de prisonniers.
◆ **humanities** *npl* [arts] lettres *fpl*; [classical culture] lettres *fpl* classiques; **humanities students** étudiants en lettres OR humanités.

humanize, -ise ['hju:mənaɪz] *vt* humaniser.

humankind [,hju:mən'kaɪnd] *n* l'humanité *f*, le genre humain.

humanly ['hju:mənlɪ] *adv* humainement; **I'll do all that is ~ possible to help her** je ferai tout ce qui est humainement possible pour l'aider.

human nature *n* nature *f* humaine; **it's only ~ to be jealous** c'est normal OR humain d'être jaloux.

humanoid ['hju:mənɔɪd] ◇ *n* humanoïde *mf*.
◇ *adj* humanoïde.

human rights *npl* droits *mpl* de l'homme; **a ~ organization** une organisation pour les droits de l'homme.

humble ['hʌmbl] ◇ *adj* **-1.** [meek] humble; **in my ~ opinion** à mon humble avis; **please accept my ~ apologies** veuillez accepter mes humbles excuses; **your ~ servant** [in letters] veuillez agréer, Monsieur, l'assurance de mes sentiments les plus respectueux ❑ **to eat ~ pie** faire de plates excuses, faire amende honorable; **to force sb to eat ~ pie** forcer qqn à se rétracter. **-2.** [modest] modeste; **she came from ~ origins** elle a des origines modestes; **to come from a ~ background** venir d'un milieu modeste; **welcome to my ~ abode** *hum* bienvenue dans mon humble OR ma modeste demeure; **the ~ violet** *lit* l'humble violette.
◇ *vt* humilier, mortifier; **to ~ o.s. before sb** s'humilier devant qqn; **a severe defeat may ~ his pride** un échec sérieux servira peut-être à le rendre moins orgueilleux; **it was a humbling experience** c'était une expérience humiliante.

humbleness ['hʌmblnɪs] *n* humilité *f*.

humbly ['hʌmblɪ] *adv* **-1.** [speak, ask] humblement, avec humilité; **most ~** en toute humilité. **-2.** [live] modestement; **~ born** d'origine modeste OR humble.

humbug ['hʌmbʌg] (*pt* & *pp* **humbugged**, *cont* **humbugging**) ◇ *n* **-1.** [person] charlatan *m*, fumiste *mf*; *(U)* [deception] charlatanisme *m*. **-2.** *(U)* [nonsense] balivernes *fpl*. **-3.** *Br* [sweet] berlingot *m*.
◇ *vt* tromper.

humdinger *inf* [,hʌm'dɪŋəʳ] *n* **-1.** [person]: **she's a real ~!** elle est vraiment extra OR sensass OR terrible! **-2.** [thing]: **that was a ~ of a game!** quel match extraordinaire!; **they had a real ~ of a row!** ils se sont engueulés, quelque chose de bien!

humdrum ['hʌmdrʌm] ◇ *adj* [person, story] banal; [task, life] monotone, banal, routinier; **I'm sick of this ~ routine** j'en ai marre de ce traintrain.
◇ *n* monotonie *f*, banalité *f*.

humectant [hjʊ'mektənt] *n* hydratant *m*.

humeral ['hju:mərəl] *adj* huméral.

humerus ['hju:mərəs] (*pl* **humeri** [-raɪ]) *n* humérus *m*.

humid ['hju:mɪd] *adj* humide.

humidifier [hju:'mɪdɪfaɪəʳ] *n* humidificateur *m*.

humidify [hju:'mɪdɪfaɪ] (*pt* & *pp* **humidified**) *vt* humidifier.

humidity [hju:'mɪdətɪ] *n* humidité *f*.

humidor ['hju:mɪdɔ:ʳ] *n* humidificateur *m*.

humiliate [hju:'mɪlɪeɪt] *vt* humilier; **he refused to ~ himself by apologizing to them** il a refusé de s'humilier en leur présentant des excuses.

humiliating [hju:'mɪlɪeɪtɪŋ] *adj* humiliant.

humiliatingly [hju:'mɪlɪeɪtɪŋlɪ] *adv* d'une façon humiliante; **they were ~ close to failure** ils étaient au bord d'un échec humiliant.

humiliation [hju:,mɪlɪ'eɪʃn] *n* humiliation *f*.

humility [hju:'mɪlətɪ] *n* humilité *f*.

humming ['hʌmɪŋ] *n* [of bees, voices] bourdonnement *m*; [of air conditioner, traffic] ronronnement *m*; [of tune] fredonnement *m*.

hummingbird ['hʌmɪŋbɜ:d] *n* oiseau-mouche *m*, colibri *m*.

humming top *n* toupie *f* ronflante.

hummock ['hʌmək] *n* [knoll] monticule *m*, mamelon *m*, tertre *m*; [in ice field] hummock *m*.

hummus ['hʊmʊs] *n* houmous *m*.

humor *etc Am* = **humour**.

humorist ['hju:mərɪst] *n* humoriste *mf*.

humorous ['hju:mərəs] *adj* [witty - remark] plein d'humour, amusant; [- person] plein d'humour, drôle; **he replied in (a) ~ vein** il a répondu sur le mode humoristique.

humorously ['hju:mərəslɪ] *adv* avec humour.

humour *Br*, **humor** *Am* ['hju:məʳ] ◇ *n* **-1.** [wit, fun] humour *m*; **the play is devoid of ~** la pièce est dénuée OR dépourvue d'humour; **I like her sense of ~** j'aime son sens de l'humour; **he's got no sense of ~** il n'a aucun sens de l'humour; **he has a very dry sense of ~** il est très pince-sans-rire. **-2.** *fml* [mood] humeur *f*, disposition *f*; **in a good/bad ~** de bonne/mauvaise humeur; **he's in no ~ to talk to anybody** il n'est pas d'humeur à parler à qui que ce soit; **to be out of ~** *lit* être de mauvaise humeur. **-3.** *arch* & MED humeur *f*; **the four ~s** les quatre humeurs.
◇ *vt* [person - indulge, gratify] faire plaisir à; [- treat tactfully] ménager; [whim, fantasy] se prêter à; **don't try to ~ me** n'essaie pas de m'amadouer.

-humoured *Br*, **-humored** *Am* ['hju:məd] *in cpds*: **he's a pleasant good~ man** c'est un homme plaisant et d'humeur agréable; **he responded in a good~ enough way** il a répondu plutôt avec bonne humeur; **she seemed unpleasant and ill~** elle paraissait déplaisante et de mauvaise humeur.

humourless *Br*, **humorless** *Am* ['hju:məlɪs] *adj* [person] qui manque d'humour; [book, situation, speech] sans humour; **totally ~** totalement dépourvu d'humour; **a ~ smile** un sourire pincé.

hump [hʌmp] ◇ *n* **-1.** [on back of animal or person] bosse *f*; [hillock] bosse *f*, mamelon *m*; [bump] tas *m*; **we're over the ~ now** *inf* on a fait le plus dur OR gros maintenant. **-2.** *inf Br phr*: **to get the ~** avoir le cafard OR le bourdon; **he gives me the ~** il me donne le cafard OR le bourdon.
◇ *vt* **-1.** [back] arrondir, arquer. **-2.** *inf Br* [carry] trimbaler, trimballer. **-3.** ▽ [have sex with] baiser. **-4.** *inf phr*: **to ~ it** tenir le coup; **he hasn't the nerve to ~ it through to the end** il n'a pas le cran de tenir le coup jusqu'au bout.
◇ *vi* ▽[have sex] baiser.

humpback ['hʌmpbæk] *n* **-1.** = **hunchback**. **-2.** = **humpback whale**.

humpback(ed) bridge *n* pont *m* en dos d'âne.

humpbacked ['hʌmpbækt] = **hunchbacked**.

humpback whale *n* baleine *f* à bosse.

humph [mm, hʌmf] *interj*: ~! hum!

Humpty Dumpty [,hʌmptɪ'dʌmptɪ] *pr n* *personnage en forme d'oeuf figurant dans une comptine (désigne métaphoriquement une chose impossible à réparer)*.

humus ['hju:məs] *n* humus *m*.

Hun [hʌn] (*pl inv* OR **Huns**) *n* **-1.** ANTIQ Hun *m*. **-2.** ▽ *dated* & *offensive* Boche *m*.

hunch [hʌntʃ] ◇ *n* [inkling] pressentiment *m*, intuition *f*; **I have a ~ we'll meet again** j'ai comme un pressentiment que nous nous reverrons; **to play** OR **to follow one's ~** suivre son intuition; **to act on a ~** suivre son instinct; **my ~ paid off, he was there** mon intuition s'est vérifiée, il était là; **it's only a ~** c'est une idée que j'ai.
◇ *vt* [back] arrondir; [shoulders] voûter; **he was ~ed against the cold** il se recroquevillait sur lui-même pour se protéger du froid; **he sat ~ed in a corner** il était assis recroquevillé dans un coin; **don't ~ (up) your shoulders like that!** ne rentre pas la tête dans les épaules comme ça!; **she was sitting ~ed (up) over her papers** elle était assise penchée sur ses papiers.

hunchback ['hʌntʃbæk] *n* **-1.** [person] bossu *m*, -e *f*; 'The Hunchback of Notre Dame' *Hugo* 'Notre-Dame de Paris'. **-2.** ANAT bosse *f*.

hunchbacked ['hʌntʃbækt] *adj* bossu.

hundred ['hʌndrəd] ◇ *adj* cent; **a ~ guests** cent invités; **six ~ pages** six cents pages; **about a ~ metres** une centaine de mètres; **if I've told you once, I've told you a ~ times!** je te l'ai dit cent fois! ❑ 'One Hundred Years of Solitude' *Garciá Márquez* 'Cent ans de solitude'.

◇ *n* cent *m*; he has a ~ (of them) il en a cent; ~ and one cent un; two ~ deux cents; two ~ and one deux cent un; about a ~, a ~ odd une centaine; one OR a ~ per cent cent pour cent; in nineteen ~ en dix-neuf cents; in nineteen ~ and ten en dix-neuf cent dix; I'll never forget him (even) if I live to be a ~ même si je deviens centenaire, je ne l'oublierai jamais; the theatre seats five ~ la salle contient cinq cents places (assises); in the ~'s place MATH dans la colonne des centaines; give me $500 in ~s donnez-moi 500 dollars en billets de cent; the temperature is in the ~s today il fait plus de 30 aujourd'hui; in the seventeen ~s au dix-septième siècle; ~s of des centaines de; I've asked you ~s of times! je te l'ai demandé cent fois!; ~s and thousands of people des milliers de gens; they were dying in their ~s OR by the ~ ils mouraient par centaines; to be ~ per cent behind sb *fig* soutenir qqn à fond; to give a ~ per cent *fig* se donner à fond.

Hundred Days *npl*: the ~ les Cent Jours *mpl*.

hundredfold ['hʌndrədfəʊld] ◇ *adj* centuple.
◇ *adv* au centuple; he has increased his initial investment a ~ il a multiplié par cent son investissement initial.

hundred-percenter *inf* [-pə'sentəʳ] *n Am* nationaliste *mf* extrémiste.

hundreds and thousands *npl paillettes de sucre colorées servant à décorer les gâteaux*.

hundredth ['hʌndrədθ] ◇ *n* centième *mf*; [fraction] centième *m*.
◇ *adj* centième.

hundredweight ['hʌndrədweɪt] *n Br* (poids *m* de) cent douze livres *(50,8 kg)*; *Am* (poids *m* de) cent livres *(45,4 kg)*; a metric ~ un poids de 50 kg.

hundred-year-old *adj* centenaire.

Hundred Years' War *n*: the ~ la guerre de Cent Ans.

hung [hʌŋ] ◇ *pt* & *pp* → **hang**.
◇ *adj* [situation] bloqué; a ~ parliament/jury un parlement/un jury sans majorité.

Hungarian [hʌŋ'geərɪən] ◇ *n* -**1.** [person] Hongrois *m*, -e *f*. -**2.** LING hongrois *m*.
◇ *adj* hongrois; 'Hungarian Rhapsodies' *Liszt* 'Rhapsodies hongroises'.

Hungary ['hʌŋgərɪ] *pr n* Hongrie *f*; in ~ en Hongrie.

hunger ['hʌŋgəʳ] ◇ *n* faim *f*; a conference on world ~ une conférence sur la faim dans le monde; to satisfy one's ~ (for sthg) satisfaire sa faim (de qqch); he was driven by a ~ for truth/knowledge *fig* il était poussé par une soif de vérité/de savoir.
◇ *vi fig*: to ~ after OR for sthg avoir faim OR soif de qqch; he ~ed for revenge il avait faim OR soif de vengeance.

hunger march *n* marche *f* de la faim.

hunger strike *n* grève *f* de la faim; to go on (a) ~ faire la grève de la faim.

hunger striker *n* gréviste *mf* de la faim.

hung over *inf adj*: to be ~ avoir une OR la gueule de bois; he was too ~ to go to work il avait une telle gueule de bois qu'il ne pouvait pas aller au travail.

hungrily ['hʌŋgrəlɪ] *adv* [eat] voracement, avidement; *fig* [read, listen] avidement; she eyed his lunch ~ elle jeta un regard de convoitise sur son déjeuner.

hungry ['hʌŋgrɪ] (*compar* hungrier, *superl* hungriest) *adj* -**1.** [for food]: to be ~ avoir faim; we're very ~ nous avons très faim, nous sommes affamés; he still felt ~ il avait encore faim; she looked tired and ~ elle avait l'air fatiguée et affamée; are you getting ~? est-ce que tu commences à avoir faim?; to go ~ souffrir de la faim; he'd rather go ~ than cook for himself il se passerait de manger plutôt que de faire la cuisine; that night he went ~ cette nuit-là il est resté sur sa faim ❑ this is ~ work! ce travail donne faim! -**2.** *fig* [desirous] avide; a child ~ for affection un enfant avide d'affection; she was ~ for news of her family elle attendait avec impatience des nouvelles de sa famille; you have to be ~ to make it to the top *inf fig* ce sont les battants qui réussissent.

hung-up *adj* bourré de complexes.

hunk [hʌŋk] *n* -**1.** [piece] gros morceau *m*. -**2.** *inf* [man] beau mec *m* OR mâle *m*; he's a real ~ il est beau mec.

hunker ['hʌŋkəʳ] *vi*: to ~ (down) [crouch] s'accroupir; [squat] s'asseoir sur ses talons, s'accroupir; [animal] se tapir; I have to ~ down and work this term *fig* je dois donner un bon coup de collier ce trimestre.

hunkers *inf* ['hʌŋkəz] *npl* hanches *fpl*; sitting on his ~ assis sur ses talons.

hunky ['hʌŋkɪ] (*pl* hunkies) ◇ *n* ▼ *Am terme injurieux désignant un travailleur d'origine slave, balte ou hongroise*.
◇ *adj inf*: she likes ~ men elle aime les costauds.

hunky-dory *inf* [,hʌŋkɪ'dɔːrɪ] *adj*: to be ~ être au poil; everything is just ~! tout baigne (dans l'huile)!

hunt [hʌnt] ◇ *vt* -**1.** [for food, sport - subj: person] chasser, faire la chasse à; [- subj: animal] chasser; to ~ whales pêcher la baleine; they were ~ed to extinction ils ont été chassés jusqu'à extinction de l'espèce. -**2.** *Br* SPORT [area] chasser dans; to ~ the pack diriger la meute; he ~s his horse all winter il monte son cheval à la chasse tout l'hiver. -**3.** [pursue] pourchasser, poursuivre; he was being ~ed by the police il était pourchassé OR recherché par la police. -**4.** [search] fouiller; I've ~ed the whole office for it j'ai retourné tout le bureau pour le retrouver. -**5.** [drive out] chasser; people were ~ed from their homes des gens étaient chassés de leurs foyers. -**6.** *phr*: to play ~ the slipper OR thimble ≃ jouer à cache-tampon.
◇ *vi* -**1.** [for food, sport] chasser; they ~ by night/in packs ils chassent la nuit/en bande; to go ~ing aller à la chasse; do you ~? chassez-vous?; to ~ for sthg [person] chasser OR faire la chasse à qqch; [animal] chasser qqch. -**2.** [search] chercher (partout); she ~ed (around OR about) in her bag for her keys elle a fouillé dans son sac à la recherche de ses clefs; you'll just have to ~ until you find it vous n'aurez qu'à chercher jusqu'à ce que vous le trouviez; I've ~ed for it high and low j'ai remué ciel et terre pour le retrouver; I've ~ed all over town for a linen jacket j'ai parcouru OR fait toute la ville pour trouver une veste en lin. -**3.** TECH [gauge] osciller; [engine] pomper.
◇ *n* -**1.** SPORT [activity] chasse *f*; [hunters] chasse *f*, chasseurs *mpl*; [area] chasse *f*; [fox-hunt] chasse *f* au renard; a tiger/bear ~ une chasse au tigre/à l'ours; ~ ball *bal réunissant les notables locaux amateurs de chasse*. -**2.** [search] chasse *f*, recherche *f*; the ~ is on for the terrorists la chasse aux terroristes est en cours; the ~ for the assassin continues la chasse à l'assassin se poursuit; I've had a ~ for your scarf j'ai cherché ton écharpe partout, j'ai tout retourné pour trouver ton écharpe.
◆ **hunt down** *vt sep* [animal] forcer, traquer; [person] traquer; [thing, facts] dénicher; [abuses, errors] faire la chasse à; [truth] débusquer.
◆ **hunt out** *vt sep Br* dénicher, découvrir; I've ~ed out that book you wanted to borrow j'ai déniché le livre que vous vouliez emprunter.
◆ **hunt up** *vt sep Br* [look up] rechercher; I'm going to the library to ~ up that article she mentioned je vais à la bibliothèque rechercher cet article dont elle parlait.

hunted ['hʌntɪd] *adj* traqué; he has a ~ look about him il a un air persécuté OR traqué.

hunter ['hʌntəʳ] *n* -**1.** SPORT [person] chasseur *m*; [horse] cheval *m* de chasse, hunter *m*; [dog] chien *m* courant OR de chasse. -**2.** [gen] chasseur *m*; [pursuer] poursuivant *m*; an autograph ~ un chasseur d'autographes; bargain ~s des dénicheurs *mpl* de bonnes affaires. -**3.** [watch] (montre *f* à) savonnette *f*.

hunter-gatherer *n* chasseur-cueilleur *m*.

hunter-killer *adj* MIL d'attaque; a ~ submarine un sous-marin d'attaque.

hunter's moon *n pleine lune qui suit celle de l'équinoxe d'automne*.

hunting ['hʌntɪŋ] ◇ *n* -**1.** SPORT chasse *f*; *Br* [fox-hunting] chasse *f* au renard; HIST [mounted deer-hunt] chasse *f* à courre; HIST [as an art] vénerie *f* ❑ huntin' shootin' and fishin' *expression employée pour parodier l'aristocratie rurale, en insinuant que sa principale activité est la chasse et la pêche*. -**2.** [pursuit] chasse *f*, poursuite *f*; bargain ~ la chasse aux soldes; to be/to go job-~ être/aller à la recherche d'un emploi.
◇ *adj* [boots, gun, knife, licence] de chasse; he's a ~ man c'est un grand chasseur.

hunting ground *n* SPORT & *fig* terrain *m* de chasse.

hunting horn *n* cor *m* OR trompe *f* de chasse.

hunting lodge *n* pavillon *m* de chasse.

hunting pink ◇ *adj* rouge chasseur *inv*.
◇ *n* *(U) Br* habit *m* rouge de chasse à courre.

hunting season *n* saison *f* de la chasse.

Huntington's chorea ['hʌntɪŋtənz-] *n* chorée *f* de Huntington.

huntress ['hʌntrɪs] *n* chasseuse *f*; Diana the Huntress *lit* Diane chasseresse.

huntsman ['hʌntsmən] (*pl* huntsmen [-mən]) *n* -**1.** [hunter] chasseur *m*. -**2.** [master of hounds] veneur *m*.

hurdle ['hɜːdl] ◇ *n* -**1.** SPORT haie *f*; the 400 metre ~s le 400 mètres haies; to run a ~ OR ~s race faire OR courir une course de haies; she's the British ~s champion elle est la championne britannique de course de haies; to take OR to clear a ~ franchir une haie. -**2.** *fig* obstacle *m*; she took that ~ in her stride elle a franchi cet obstacle sans le moindre effort; the next ~ will be getting funding for the project la prochaine difficulté sera d'obtenir des fonds pour le projet. -**3.** [for fences] claie *f*.
◇ *vt* [jump] sauter, franchir; [overcome] franchir.
◇ *vi* SPORT faire de la course de haies.

hurdler ['hɜːdləʳ] *n* coureur *m*, -euse *f (qui fait des courses de haies)*.

hurdy-gurdy ['hɜːdɪ,gɜːdɪ] *n* -**1.** [barrel organ] orgue *m* de Barbarie; a ~ man un joueur d'orgue de Barbarie. -**2.** [medieval instrument] vielle *f*.

hurl [hɜːl] *vt* -**1.** [throw] lancer, jeter (avec violence); to ~ o.s. at sb/sthg se ruer sur qqn/qqch; he ~ed a vase at him il lui a lancé un vase à la figure; they were ~ed to the ground ils ont été précipités OR jetés à terre; she ~ed herself off the top of the tower elle s'est précipitée OR jetée (du haut) de la tour; he ~ed himself into the fight il s'est jeté dans la bagarre; the boat was ~ed onto the rocks le bateau a été projeté sur les rochers; they were ~ed into the crisis *fig* ils ont été précipités dans la crise. -**2.** [yell] lancer, jeter; to ~ abuse at sb lancer des injures à qqn, accabler qqn d'injures.

hurling ['hɜːlɪŋ] *n* SPORT *jeu irlandais voisin du hockey sur gazon*.

hurly-burly ['hɜːlɪ,bɜːlɪ] *Br* ◇ *n* tohu-bohu *m*; the ~ of city life le tourbillon de la vie urbaine.
◇ *adj* turbulent.

hurrah *Br* [hʊ'rɑː], **hurray** [hʊ'reɪ] ◇ *n* hourra *m*.
◇ *interj*: ~! hourra!; ~ for the cook! pour le chef, hip hip hip hourra!

hurricane ['hʌrɪkən] *n* ouragan *m*; [in Caribbean] hurricane *m*; Hurricane Mabel l'ouragan Mabel.

hurricane force *n* force *f* douze (sur l'échelle Beaufort).
◆ **hurricane-force** *comp*: hurricane-force winds TECH des vents de force douze.

hurricane lamp *n* lampe-tempête *f*.

hurried ['hʌrɪd] *adj* [meeting, reply, gesture, trip] rapide; [departure, steps] précipité; [judgment, decision] hâtif; [work] fait à la hâte; to have a ~ meal manger à la hâte; I wrote a ~ note to reassure her j'ai écrit un mot à la hâte OR un mot bref pour la rassurer; they only had time for a few ~ words ils ont juste eu le temps d'échanger quelques mots rapides.

hurriedly ['hʌrɪdlɪ] *adv* [examine] à la hâte; [leave] précipitamment; she passed ~ over the unpleasant details elle passa en vitesse sur les détails désagréables; he ~ excused himself il s'est empressé de s'excuser.

hurry ['hʌrɪ] (*pl* hurries, *pt* & *pp* hurried) ◇ *n* -1. [rush] hâte *f*, précipitation *f*; to be in a ~ to do sthg avoir hâte de faire qqch; not now, I'm in (too much of) a ~ pas maintenant, je suis (trop) pressé; he needs it in a ~ il en a besoin tout de suite; to be in a tearing OR an awful ~ être très pressé; in his OR the ~ to leave he forgot his umbrella dans sa hâte de partir il a oublié son parapluie; there's no big OR great ~ rien ne presse; there's no ~ for it cela ne presse pas; what's the OR your ~? qu'est-ce qui (vous) presse?; it was obviously written in a ~ de toute évidence, cela a été écrit à la hâte; he won't try that again in a ~! *inf Br* il ne ressaiera pas de sitôt!, il n'est pas près de ressayer! -2. [eagerness] empressement *m*; he's in no ~ to see her again il n'est pas pressé OR il n'a aucune hâte de la revoir; a young man in a ~ *Br* un jeune homme pressé de réussir OR ambitieux.
◇ *vi* se dépêcher, se presser, se hâter; he's ~ing to finish some work il se dépêche OR se presse OR se hâte de finir un travail; I must OR I'd better ~ il faut que je me dépêche; you don't have to ~ over that report vous pouvez prendre votre temps pour faire ce rapport; he hurried into/out of the room il est entré dans/sorti de la pièce en toute hâte OR précipitamment; he hurried down the stairs il a descendu l'escalier en toute hâte OR précipitamment; don't ~ back, I'll take care of everything ne te presse pas de revenir, je me chargerai de tout; he hurried (over) to the bank il s'est précipité à la banque, il s'est rendu à la banque en toute hâte; ~! it's already started dépêche-toi! c'est déjà commencé.
◇ *vt* -1. [chivvy along] faire se dépêcher, presser, bousculer; don't ~ him ne le bouscule pas; he was hurried into making a choice on l'a pressé de faire un choix; she won't be hurried, you can't ~ her vous ne la ferez pas se dépêcher; they hurried him through customs ils lui ont fait passer la douane à la hâte. -2. [preparations, work] activer, presser, hâter; this decision can't be hurried cette décision exige d'être prise sans hâte. -3. [transport hastily] emmener d'urgence; aid was hurried to the stricken town des secours ont été envoyés d'urgence à la ville sinistrée.
◆ **hurry along** ◇ *vi insep* marcher d'un pas pressé; ~ along now! pressons, pressons!; we'd better be ~ing along on ferait mieux de se presser.
◇ *vt sep* [person] faire presser le pas à, faire se dépêcher OR s'activer; [work] activer, accélérer; he wants the investigation hurried along il veut faire accélérer OR faire avancer plus rapidement l'enquête.
◆ **hurry on** *vi insep* se dépêcher, continuer à la hâte OR en hâte; he hurried on to the next shelter il s'est pressé de gagner l'abri suivant; can we ~ on to the next item on the agenda? peut-on vite passer OR passer sans tarder à la prochaine question inscrite à l'ordre du jour?
◆ **hurry up** ◇ *vi insep* se dépêcher, se presser; ~ up! dépêchez-vous!
◇ *vt sep* [person] faire se dépêcher; [production, work] activer, pousser.

hurt [hɜːt] (*pt* & *pp* hurt) ◇ *vt* -1. [cause physical pain to] faire mal à; to ~ o.s. se faire mal; mind you don't ~ yourself faites attention de ne pas vous faire mal OR vous blesser; I ~ my elbow on the door je me suis fait mal au coude contre la porte; is your back ~ing you today? est-ce que tu as mal au dos aujourd'hui?; where does it ~ you? où est-ce que vous avez mal?, où cela vous fait-il mal?; it hardly ~s (me) at all! ça ne me fait presque pas mal!; the fall didn't ~ him il ne s'est pas fait mal en tombant. -2. [injure] blesser; two people were ~ in the crash deux personnes ont été blessées dans la collision; no one was ~ in the accident personne n'a été blessé dans l'accident; do as I say and no one gets ~! *inf* faites ce que je dis et il n'y aura pas de casse! ☐ he wouldn't ~ a fly il ne ferait pas de mal à une mouche. -3. [upset] blesser, faire de la peine à; he was very ~ by your criticism il a été très blessé par vos critiques; it ~ her pride to have to ask him for money ça la blessait dans son amour-propre d'avoir à lui demander de l'argent; to ~ sb's feelings blesser OR froisser qqn; what ~ me most was his silence on the subject ce qui me faisait le plus mal c'était son silence à ce propos. -4. [disadvantage] nuire à; the new tax will ~ the middle classes most ce sont les classes moyennes qui seront les plus touchées par le nouvel impôt; it won't ~ you to miss the next meeting cela ne vous nuira pas de manquer la prochaine réunion; a bit of fresh air won't ~ him un peu d'air frais OR de grand air ne lui fera pas de mal. -5. [damage - crops, machine] abîmer, endommager; [- eyesight] abîmer.
◇ *vi* faire mal; my head ~s ma tête me fait mal; where does it ~? où est-ce que vous avez mal?; a holiday certainly wouldn't ~ ça ne ferait certainement pas de mal de prendre des vacances; he's ~ing *Am* il a mal; nothing ~s like the truth il n'y a que la vérité qui blesse.
◇ *n* -1. [physical pain] mal *m*; [wound] blessure *f*. -2. [mental pain] peine *f*; he wanted to make up for the ~ he had caused them il voulait réparer la peine qu'il leur avait faite. -3. [damage] tort *m*.
◇ *adj* -1. [physically] blessé; he's more frightened than ~ il a eu plus de peur que de mal; several people were seriously/slightly ~ plusieurs personnes ont été sérieusement/légèrement blessées. -2. [offended] froissé, blessé; I'm deeply ~ that you didn't tell me first que vous ne me l'ayez pas dit en premier m'a profondément blessé; a ~ expression un regard meurtri OR blessé; don't feel ~ ne le prends pas mal; he's feeling a bit ~ about it all il se sent quelque peu peiné par tout ça. -3. *Am* [damaged]: ~ books livres endommagés.

hurtful ['hɜːtfʊl] *adj* [event] préjudiciable, nuisible; [memory] pénible; [remark] blessant, offensant; they ended up saying ~ things to each other ils ont fini par se dire des méchancetés; what a ~ thing to say! comme c'est méchant OR cruel de dire cela!

hurtle ['hɜːtl] *vi*: to ~ along avancer à toute vitesse OR allure; the cars ~d round the track les voitures tournaient autour de la piste à toute allure; he went hurtling down the stairs il dévala les escaliers; the motorbike came hurtling towards him la moto fonça sur lui à toute vitesse; a rock ~d through the air une pierre a fendu l'air.

husband ['hʌzbənd] ◇ *n* mari *m*, époux *m*; are they ~ and wife? sont-ils mari et femme?; they lived (together) as ~ and wife ils vivaient maritalement OR comme mari et femme.
◇ *vt* [resources, strength] ménager, économiser.

husbandry ['hʌzbəndrɪ] *n* -1. AGR agriculture *f*; [as science] agronomie *f*; animal ~ élevage *m*. -2. *fml* [thrift] économie *f*; good ~ bonne gestion *f*.

hush [hʌʃ] ◇ *n* silence *m*, calme *m*; a ~ fell over the room un silence s'est installé OR s'est fait dans la salle; in the ~ of the early morning dans le silence du petit matin.
◇ *interj*: ~! [gen] silence!; [stop talking] chut!
◇ *vt* -1. [silence] faire taire; she ~ed the murmurs/the crowd with a gesture elle a fait taire les murmures/la foule d'un geste. -2. [appease] apaiser, calmer.
◇ *vi* se taire.
◆ **hush up** *vt sep* -1. [affair] étouffer; [witness] faire taire, empêcher de parler. -2. [noisy person] faire taire.

hushed [hʌʃt] *adj* [whisper, voice] étouffé; [silence] profond, grand; to speak in ~ tones parler à voix basse.

hush-hush *inf adj* secret, archi-secret; it's all very ~ tout cela c'est archi-secret OR top secret

hush money *inf n (U)* pot-de-vin *m (pour acheter le silence)*; to pay sb ~ acheter le silence de qqn

husk [hʌsk] ◇ *n* [of wheat, oats] balle *f*; [of corn, rice] enveloppe *f*; [of nut] écale *f*.
◇ *vt* [oats, barley] monder; [corn] éplucher; [rice] décortiquer; [wheat] vanner; [nuts] écaler.

huskily ['hʌskɪlɪ] *adv* [speak] d'une voix rauque; [sing] d'une voix voilée.

huskiness ['hʌskɪnɪs] *n* enrouement *m*.

husky ['hʌskɪ] (*compar* huskier, *superl* huskiest, *pl* huskies) ◇ *adj* -1. [of voice - hoarse] rauque, enroué; [- breathy] voilé; his voice was ~ with emotion il avait la voix voilée par l'émotion. -2. *inf* [burly] costaud.
◇ *n* [dog] chien *m* esquimau OR de traîneau

hussar [hʊ'zɑːʳ] *n* hussard *m*.

hussy ['hʌsɪ] (*pl* hussies) *n arch* OR *hum* [shameless woman] garce *f*, gourgandine *f dated*; you shameless OR brazen ~! espèce de garce!

hustings ['hʌstɪŋz] *npl Br* -1. [campaign] campagne *f* électorale; to go/to be out on the ~ partir/être en campagne électorale. -2. [occasion for speeches] ≃ débat *m* public *(pendant la campagne électorale)*; at the ~ au cours du débat public.

hustle ['hʌsl] ◇ *vt* -1. [cause to move - quickly] presser; [- roughly] bousculer, pousser; to ~ sb in/out faire entrer/sortir qqn énergiquement; they ~d him into an alley ils l'ont poussé dans une ruelle; he ~d us into the president's office il nous a pressés d'entrer chez le président; after that, I was ~d off to boarding school après cela, j'ai été expédié au pensionnat; the doctor was ~d through the crowd on a frayé un chemin au médecin dans la foule; he was ~d away OR off by two men il a été emmené de force par deux hommes. -2. *inf* [obtain - resourcefully] faire tout pour avoir; [- underhandedly] magouiller pour avoir; he's been hustling jobs since he was 16 il s'est décarcassé OR bagarré pour trouver des boulots depuis l'âge de 16 ans; they ~d that building permit ils ont magouillé pour obtenir ce permis de construire. -3. *inf Am* [swindle] rouler, arnaquer; he ~d me out of $100 il m'a roulé OR arnaqué de 100 dollars; he ~d the old lady for her savings il a arnaqué la vieille dame de ses économies ‖ [pressure]: to ~ sb into doing sthg forcer la main à qqn pour qu'il fasse qqch. -4. *inf Am* [steal] piquer. -5. ▽ *Am* [subj: prostitute] racoler; she ~s the bars elle racole dans les bars.
◇ *vi* -1. *Br* [shove] bousculer; don't ~ in the back! ne bousculez pas derrière! -2. = **hurry**. -3. *inf Am* [work hard] se bagarrer (pour réussir); they want that market and they're ready to ~ for it ils veulent ce marché et ils sont prêts à tout (faire) OR à se bagarrer pour l'avoir. -4. ▽ *Am* [engage in suspect activity] monter des coups, trafiquer; [politically] magouiller; so he's hustling in Washington now? alors il magouille à Washington maintenant? -5. ▽ *Am* [prostitute] faire le tapin, tapiner.
◇ *n* -1. [crush] bousculade *f*. -2. [bustle] grande activité *f*; the ~ and bustle of the big city le tourbillon d'activité des grandes villes. -3. ▽ *Am* [swindle] arnaque *f*.
◆ **hustle through** *inf vt sep* [deal rapidly with] expédier; they ~d the legislation through in a single day ils ont expédié le vote de la loi en une seule journée.
◆ **hustle up** *inf Am* ◇ *vt sep* [prepare quickly] préparer en cinq sec.
◇ *vi insep* & *vt sep* = **hurry up**.

hustler *inf* ['hʌsləʳ] *n* -1. [dynamic person] type *m* dynamique, débrouillard *m*, -e *f*, magouilleur *m*, -euse *f*. -2. [swindler] arnaqueur *m*, -euse *f*. -3. ▽ *Am* [prostitute] belle *f* de nuit OR de jour.

hut [hʌt] *n* [primitive dwelling] hutte *f*; [shed] cabane *f*, baraque *f*; [alpine] refuge *m*, chalet-refuge *m*; MIL baraquement *m*.

hutch [hʌtʃ] *n* **-1.** [cage] cage *f*; rabbit ~ *literal* & *fig* clapier *m*. **-2.** [chest] coffre *m*. **-3.** TECH [kneading trough] pétrin *m*, huche *f*. **-4.** MIN [wagon] wagonnet *m*, benne *f* (roulante).

hutment ['hʌtmənt] *n* MIL baraquements *mpl*.

hyacinth ['haɪəsɪnθ] *n* **-1.** BOT jacinthe *f*; wild ~ jacinthe sauvage OR des bois, endymion *m*. **-2.** [gem] hyacinthe *f*. **-3.** [colour] bleu jacinthe *inv*, bleu violet *inv*.

Hyades ['haɪədiːz] *pl pr n*: the ~ les Hyades.

hyaena [haɪ'iːnə] = **hyena**.

hybrid ['haɪbrɪd] ◇ *n* hybride *m*.
◇ *adj* hybride.

hybrid bill *n Br* POL *loi dont certaines dispositions sont d'application générale et d'autres d'application restreinte*.

hybridize, -ise ['haɪbrɪdaɪz] ◇ *vt* hybrider.
◇ *vi* s'hybrider.

hydra ['haɪdrə] (*pl* **hydras** OR **hydrae** [-driː]) *n fig* & ZOOL hydre *f*.
◆ **Hydra** *pr n* MYTH Hydre *f* (de Lerne).

hydra-headed *adj* à tête d'hydre.

hydrangea [haɪ'dreɪndʒə] *n* hortensia *m*.

hydrant ['haɪdrənt] *n* prise *f* d'eau; (fire) ~ bouche *f* d'incendie.

hydrate ['haɪdreɪt] ◇ *n* hydrate *m*.
◇ *vt* hydrater.
◇ *vi* s'hydrater.

hydration [haɪ'dreɪʃn] *n* hydratation *f*.

hydraulic [haɪ'drɔːlɪk] *adj* hydraulique; ~ engineer ingénieur *m* hydraulicien, hydraulicien *m*, -enne *f*.

hydraulic brake *n* frein *m* hydraulique.

hydraulic press *n* presse *f* hydraulique.

hydraulics [haɪ'drɔːlɪks] *n (U)* hydraulique *f*.

hydraulic suspension *n* suspension *f* hydraulique.

hydro ['haɪdrəʊ] ◇ *n* **-1.** *Br* [spa] établissement *m* thermal *(hôtel)*. **-2.** *Can* [power] énergie *f* hydro-électrique; [plant] centrale *f* hydro-électrique.
◇ *adj* hydro-électrique; my ~ bill has gone up *Can* ma facture d'électricité a augmenté.

hydrocarbon [ˌhaɪdrə'kɑːbən] *n* hydrocarbure *m*.

hydrocephalic [ˌhaɪdrəsɪ'fælɪk] *adj* hydrocéphale.

hydrochloric [ˌhaɪdrə'klɒrɪk] *adj* chlorhydrique.

hydrochloride [ˌhaɪdrə'klɔːraɪd] *n* chlorhydrate *m*.

hydrocortisone [ˌhaɪdrə'kɔːtɪzəʊn] *n* hydrocortisone *f*.

hydrodynamics [ˌhaɪdrədaɪ'næmɪks] *n (U)* hydrodynamique *f*.

hydroelectric [ˌhaɪdrəɪ'lektrɪk] *adj* hydroélectrique; ~ power énergie *f* hydro-électrique.

hydroelectricity [ˌhaɪdrəɪlek'trɪsətɪ] *n* hydroélectricité *f*.

hydrofoil ['haɪdrəfɔɪl] *n* hydrofoil *m*, hydroptère *m*.

hydrogen ['haɪdrədʒən] *n* hydrogène *m*.

hydrogenate [haɪ'drɒdʒɪneɪt], **hydrogenize, -ise** [haɪ'drɒdʒənaɪz] ◇ *vt* hydrogéner.
◇ *vi* s'hydrogéner.

hydrogen bomb *n* bombe *f* à hydrogène.

hydrogen bond *n* liaison *f* hydrogène.

hydrogen peroxide *n* eau *f* oxygénée.

hydrogen sulphide *n* acide *m* sulfhydrique, hydrogène *m* sulfuré.

hydrography [haɪ'drɒgrəfɪ] *n* hydrographie *f*.

hydrologist [haɪ'drɒlədʒɪst] *n* hydrologiste *mf*, hydrologue *mf*.

hydrology [haɪ'drɒlədʒɪ] *n* hydrologie *f*.

hydrolysis [haɪ'drɒlɪsɪs] *n* hydrolyse *f*.

hydrometer [haɪ'drɒmɪtəʳ] *n* hydromètre *m*.

hydrometry [haɪ'drɒmɪtrɪ] *n* hydrométrie *f*.

hydropathic [ˌhaɪdrə'pæθɪk] *adj* hydrothérapique.

hydropathy [haɪ'drɒpəθɪ] *n* hydropathie *f*.

hydrophobia [ˌhaɪdrə'fəʊbjə] *n* hydrophobie *f*.

hydroplane ['haɪdrəpleɪn] ◇ *n* **-1.** [boat] hydroglisseur *m*. **-2.** [seaplane] hydravion *m*. **-3.** [pontoon] flotteur *m (d'un hydravion)*. **-4.** [on submarine] stabilisateur *m* d'assiette *(d'un sous-marin)*.
◇ *vi* se dresser comme un hydroglisseur.

hydroponics [ˌhaɪdrə'pɒnɪks] *n (U)* culture *f* hydroponique.

hydrosphere ['haɪdrəˌsfɪəʳ] *n* hydrosphère *f*.

hydrostatics [ˌhaɪdrə'stætɪks] *n (U)* hydrostatique *f*.

hydrotherapy [ˌhaɪdrə'θerəpɪ] *n* hydrothérapie *f*.

hydrous ['haɪdrəs] *adj* CHEM hydraté; [gen - containing water] aqueux.

hydroxide [haɪ'drɒksaɪd] *n* hydroxyde *m*.

hyena [haɪ'iːnə] *n* hyène *f*.

hygiene ['haɪdʒiːn] *n* hygiène *f*; personal ~ hygiène personnelle OR corporelle.

hygienic [haɪ'dʒiːnɪk] *adj* hygiénique.

hygienically [haɪ'dʒiːnɪklɪ] *adv* de façon hygiénique.

hygienics [haɪ'dʒiːnɪks] *n (U)* hygiène *f*.

hygienist [haɪ'dʒiːnɪst] *n* hygiéniste *mf*; (dental) ~ ≃ assistant *m* OR assistante *f* dentaire *(qui s'occupe du détartrage etc)*.

hygrograph ['haɪgrəgrɑːf] *n* hygromètre *m* enregistreur.

hygrometer [haɪ'grɒmɪtəʳ] *n* hygromètre *m*.

hygrometry [haɪ'grɒmɪtrɪ] *n* hygrométrie *f*.

hymen ['haɪmen] *n* ANAT hymen *m*.
◆ **Hymen** *pr n* Hymen.

hymn [hɪm] ◇ *n* **-1.** RELIG hymne *f*, cantique *m*. **-2.** [gen - song of praise] hymne *m*; a ~ to nature un hymne à la nature.
◇ *vt lit* chanter un hymne à la gloire de.

hymnal ['hɪmnəl], **hymn book** *n* livre *m* de cantiques.

hype [haɪp] ◇ *n* **-1.** *inf (U)* [publicity] battage *m* publicitaire; the film got a lot of ~ il y a eu une publicité monstre autour de ce film; it's all ~ ce n'est que du bla-bla; I was put off by all the ~ toute cette pub me dégoûtait. **-2.** *inf Am* [put-on] baratin *m*; don't give me any ~ ne me baratine pas, ne me fais pas d'esbroufe. **-3.** ▽ *Am* [hypodermic] shooteuse *f*. **-4.** ▽ *Am* [addict] camé *m*, -e *f*.
◇ *vt inf* **-1.** [falsify] baratiner. **-2.** [publicize] monter un gros coup de pub autour de; her latest novel has been heavily ~d son dernier roman a été lancé à grand renfort de publicité.

hyped up *inf* [haɪpt-] *adj* speed *(inv)*, speedé.

hyper *inf* ['haɪpəʳ] *adj* **-1.** = **hyperactive**. **-2.** [angry] furax *(inv)*; he got OR went really ~ about it ça l'a mis dans une colère noire.

hyperacidity [ˌhaɪpərə'sɪdətɪ] *n* hyperacidité *f*.

hyperactive [ˌhaɪpər'æktɪv] *adj* hyperactif.

hyperactivity [ˌhaɪpəræk'tɪvətɪ] *n* hyperactivité *f*.

hyperaemia *Br*, **hyperemia** *Am* [ˌhaɪpər'iːmɪə] hyperémie *f*.

hyperbola [haɪ'pɜːbələ] *n* MATH hyperbole *f*.

hyperbole [haɪ'pɜːbəlɪ] *n* hyperbole *f*.

hyperbolic(al) [ˌhaɪpə'bɒlɪk(l)] *adj* hyperbolique.

hyperboloid [haɪ'pɜːbəlɔɪd] *n* hyperboloïde *m*.

hypercharge ['haɪpətʃɑːdʒ] *n* hypercharge *f*.

hyperconscious *inf* [ˌhaɪpə'kɒnʃəs] *adj Am* [aware] hyperconscient; [sensitive] hypersensible.

hypercritical [ˌhaɪpə'krɪtɪkl] *adj* hypercritique.

hyperglycaemia *Br*, **hyperglycemia** *Am* [ˌhaɪpəglaɪ'siːmɪə] *n* hyperglycémie *f*.

hypergolic [ˌhaɪpə'gɒlɪk] *adj* hypergolique.

hyperinflation [ˌhaɪpərɪn'fleɪʃn] *n* hyperinflation *f*.

Hyperion [haɪ'pɪərɪən] *pr n* Hypérion.

hypermarket [ˌhaɪpə'mɑːkɪt] *n Br* hypermarché *m*.

hypermetropia [ˌhaɪpəme'trəʊpɪə], **hypermetropy** [ˌhaɪpə'metrəpɪ] *n* hypermétropie *f*.

hyperon ['haɪpərɒn] *n* hypéron *m*.

hyperrealism [ˌhaɪpə'rɪəlɪzm] *n* hyperréalisme *m*.

hyperrealist [ˌhaɪpə'rɪəlɪst] ◇ *n* hyperréaliste *mf*.
◇ *adj* hyperréaliste.

hypersensitive [ˌhaɪpə'sensɪtɪv] *adj* hypersensible.

hypersensitivity ['haɪpəˌsensɪ'tɪvətɪ] *n* hypersensibilité *f*.

hypersonic [ˌhaɪpə'sɒnɪk] *adj* hypersonique.

hyperspace ['haɪpəspeɪs] *n* hyperespace *m*.

hypertension [ˌhaɪpə'tenʃn] *n* hypertension *f*.

hypertext ['haɪpətekst] *n* COMPUT hypertexte *m*.

hyperthyroid [ˌhaɪpə'θaɪrɔɪd] *adj* hyperthyroïdien.

hypertrophy [haɪ'pɜːtrəfɪ] (*pl* **hypertrophies**)
◇ *n* hypertrophie *f*.
◇ *vt* hypertrophier.
◇ *vi* s'hypertrophier.

hyperventilate [ˌhaɪpə'ventɪleɪt] *vi* faire de l'hyperventilation OR de l'hyperpnée.

hyperventilation ['haɪpəˌventɪ'leɪʃn] *n* hyperventilation *f*, hyperpnée *f*.

hyphen ['haɪfn] ◇ *n* trait *m* d'union.
◇ *vt* = **hyphenate**.

hyphenate ['haɪfəneɪt] *vt* mettre un trait d'union à; a ~ed word un mot à trait d'union.

hypnosis [hɪp'nəʊsɪs] *n* hypnose *f*; to be under ~ être en état hypnotique OR d'hypnose; to put sb under ~ mettre qqn sous hypnose.

hypnotherapy [ˌhɪpnəʊ'θerəpɪ] *n* hypnothérapie *f*.

hypnotic [hɪp'nɒtɪk] ◇ *adj* hypnotique.
◇ *n* [drug] hypnotique *m*; [person] hypnotique *mf*.

hypnotism ['hɪpnətɪzm] *n* hypnotisme *m*.

hypnotist ['hɪpnətɪst] *n* hypnotiseur *m*, -euse *f*.

hypnotize, -ise ['hɪpnətaɪz] *vt* hypnotiser.

hypoallergenic ['haɪpəˌælə'dʒenɪk] *adj* hypoallergique.

hypocentre *Br*, **hypocenter** *Am* ['haɪpəʊˌsentəʳ] *n* **-1.** [of earthquake] hypocentre *m*. **-2.** NUCL *point de la surface terrestre à la verticale d'une explosion atomique atmosphérique*.

hypochondria [ˌhaɪpə'kɒndrɪə] *n* hypocondrie *f*.

hypochondriac [ˌhaɪpə'kɒndrɪæk] ◇ *adj* hypocondriaque.
◇ *n* hypocondriaque *mf*, malade *mf* imaginaire; she's such a ~ c'est une véritable malade imaginaire.

hypocoristic [ˌhaɪpəkɔː'rɪstɪk] *adj* LING hypocoristique.

hypocrisy [hɪ'pɒkrəsɪ] (*pl* **hypocrisies**) *n* hypocrisie *f*.

hypocrite ['hɪpəkrɪt] *n* hypocrite *mf*.

hypocritical [ˌhɪpə'krɪtɪkl] *adj* hypocrite; a ~ remark une remarque hypocrite; it would be ~ of me to get married in church ce serait hypocrite de ma part de me marier à l'église.

hypocritically [ˌhɪpə'krɪtɪklɪ] *adv* hypocritement.

hypodermic [ˌhaɪpə'dɜːmɪk] ◇ *adj* hypodermique; ~ needle aiguille *f* hypodermique; ~ syringe seringue *f* hypodermique.
◇ *n* **-1.** [syringe] seringue *f* hypodermique. **-2.** [injection] injection *f* hypodermique.

hypoglycaemia *Br*, **hypoglycemia** *Am* [ˌhaɪpəʊglaɪ'siːmɪə] *n* hypoglycémie *f*.

hypoglycaemic *Br*, **hypoglycemic** *Am* [ˌhaɪpəʊglaɪ'siːmɪk] *adj* hypoglycémiant.

hypostasis [haɪ'pɒstəsɪs] (*pl* **hypostases** [-siːz]) *n* MED, PHILOS & RELIG hypostase *f*.

hypotension [ˌhaɪpəʊ'tenʃn] *n* hypotension *f*.

hypotenuse [haɪ'pɒtənjuːz] *n* hypoténuse *f*.

hypothalamus [ˌhaɪpəʊ'θæləməs] *n* hypothalamus *m*.

hypothermia [ˌhaɪpəʊ'θɜːmɪə] *n* hypothermie *f*.

hypothesis [haɪ'pɒθɪsɪs] (*pl* hypotheses [-siːz]) *n* hypothèse *f*; according to your ~ selon OR suivant votre hypothèse; to put forward OR to advance a ~ émettre OR énoncer une hypothèse; this confirms my ~ that... cela confirme mon hypothèse selon OR d'après laquelle...

hypothesize, **-ise** [haɪ'pɒθɪsaɪz] ◇ *vt* supposer; let's ~ the following faisons les hypothèses suivantes; he ~d that she was not in fact the killer il a formulé l'hypothèse selon laquelle ce ne serait pas elle l'assassin.
◇ *vi* faire des hypothèses OR des suppositions.

hypothetical [ˌhaɪpə'θetɪkl] *adj* hypothétique; it's purely ~ c'est purement hypothétique.

hypothetically [ˌhaɪpə'θetɪklɪ] *adv* hypothétiquement.

hypothyroid [ˌhaɪpəʊ'θaɪrɔɪd] *adj* hypothyroïdien.

hypsography [hɪp'sɒgrəfɪ] (*pl* hypsographies) *n* -**1.** [science of mapping] hypsométrie *f*, hypsographie *f*. -**2.** [relief - of a region] hypsométrie *f*. -**3.** [representation] carte *f* hypsographique.

hypsometer [hɪp'sɒmɪtə'] *n* GEOG hypsomètre *m*.

hypsometry [hɪp'sɒmɪtrɪ] *n* hypsométrie *f*.

hysterectomy [ˌhɪstə'rektəmɪ] (*pl* hysterectomies) *n* hystérectomie *f*.

hysteresis [ˌhɪstə'riːsɪs] *n* hystérésis *f*.

hysteria [hɪs'tɪərɪə] *n* -**1.** PSYCH hystérie *f*. -**2.** [hysterical behaviour] crise *f* de nerfs; his voice betrayed his mounting ~ sa voix trahissait la montée d'une crise de nerfs; an atmosphere of barely controlled ~ reigned in the office une atmosphère de folie à peine contenue régnait dans le bureau; the crowd was on the edge OR verge of ~ *fig* la foule était au bord de l'hystérie; a country in the grip of war ~ un pays en proie à une hystérie guerrière; mass ~ hystérie collective.

hysteric [hɪs'terɪk] *n* PSYCH hystérique *mf*.

hysterical [hɪs'terɪk(l)] *adj* -**1.** PSYCH hystérique. -**2.** [sobs, voice] hystérique; [laugh] hystérique, nerveux; ~ passengers fought to reach the emergency exits des passagers hystériques se battaient pour atteindre la sortie de secours; he's the ~ type c'est un grand nerveux; he was ~ with grief il était fou de chagrin. -**3.** [overexcited]: it's nothing to get ~ about! ce n'est pas la peine de faire une crise (de nerfs)! -**4.** *inf* [very funny] tordant, hilarant.

hysterically [hɪs'terɪklɪ] *adv* hystériquement; it was ~ funny! c'était super drôle!

hysterics [hɪs'terɪks] *npl* -**1.** = **hysteria 1.** -**2.** [fit] (violente) crise *f* de nerfs; to go into OR to have ~ avoir une (violente) crise de nerfs. -**3.** *inf* [laughter] crise *f* de rire; to go into OR to have ~ attraper un OR avoir le fou rire; we were in ~ about OR over it on était pliés en deux de rire; he had me in ~ il m'a fait mourir de rire.

Hz (*written abbr of* hertz) Hz.

I

i (*pl* i's OR is), **I** (*pl* I's OR Is) [aɪ] *n* [letter] i *m*, I *m*; I as in Ivor ≃ I comme Irma.

I [aɪ] *pron* [gen] je, j' (*before vowel or mute 'h'*); [emphatic] moi; I like skiing j'aime skier; Ann and I have known each other for years Ann et moi nous connaissons depuis des années; I found it, not you c'est moi qui l'ai trouvé, pas vous; it is I who should be apologizing *fml* c'est moi qui devrais m'excuser.

I. *written abbr of* island.

IA *written abbr of* Iowa.

IAEA (*abbr of* International Atomic Energy Agency) *pr n* AIEA *f*.

iambic [aɪ'æmbɪk] *adj* iambique; ~ pentameter pentamètre *m* iambique.

IATA [aɪ'ɑːtə] (*abbr of* International Air Transport Association) *pr n* IATA *f*.

iatrogenic [aɪˌætrəʊ'dʒenɪk] *adj* iatrogène, iatrogénique.

IBA (*abbr of* Independent Broadcasting Authority) *pr n organisme d'agrément et de coordination des stations de radio et chaînes de télévision du secteur privé en Grande-Bretagne*.

I beam *n* CONSTR fer *m* en I OR en double T.

Iberia [aɪ'bɪərɪə] *pr n* Ibérie *f*; in ~ en Ibérie.

Iberian [aɪ'bɪərɪən] ◇ *n* -**1.** [person] Ibère *mf*. -**2.** LING ibère *m*.
◇ *adj* ibérique.

Iberian Peninsula *pr n*: the ~ la péninsule Ibérique.

IBEW (*abbr of* International Brotherhood of Electrical Workers) *pr n syndicat international d'électriciens*.

ibex ['aɪbeks] (*pl inv* OR ibexes) *n* bouquetin *m*.

ibis ['aɪbɪs] (*pl* ibis OR ibises) *n* ibis *m*.

Ibiza [ɪ'biːθə] *pr n* Ibiza; in ~ à Ibiza.

i/c *written abbr of* in charge.

IC (*abbr of* integrated circuit) *n* CI *m*.

ICA (*abbr of* Institute of Contemporary Arts) *pr n centre d'art moderne à Londres*.

Icarus ['ɪkərəs] *pr n* Icare.

ICBM (*abbr of* intercontinental ballistic missile) *n* ICBM *m*.

ICC *pr n* -**1.** (*abbr of* International Chamber of Commerce) CCI *f*. -**2.** (*abbr of* Interstate Commerce Commission) *commission fédérale américaine réglementant le commerce entre les États*.

ice [aɪs] ◇ *n* -**1.** (*U*) [frozen water] glace *f*; [ice cube] glaçon *m*, glaçons *mpl*; her feet were like ~ elle avait les pieds gelés ❑ to put sthg on ~: the reforms have been put on ~ les réformes ont été gelées; to walk OR to be on thin ~ avancer en terrain miné. -**2.** [on road] verglas *m*. -**3.** [in ice rink] glace *f*; come out onto the ~ venez patiner OR sur la piste. -**4.** [ice-cream] glace *f*. -**5.** ▽ (*U*) *Am* [diamonds] diams *mpl*, cailloux *mpl*.
◇ *vt* -**1.** [chill - drink] rafraîchir; [- with ice cubes] mettre des glaçons dans. -**2.** [cake] glacer. -**3.** ▽ *Am* [kill] liquider.
◇ *vi* (se) givrer.
◆ **ice over** ◇ *vi insep* [lake, river etc] geler; [window, propellers] (se) givrer.
◇ *vt sep*: to be ~d over [lake, river etc] être gelé; [window, propellers] être givré.
◆ **ice up** ◇ *vi insep* -**1.** [lock, windscreen, propellers] (se) givrer, se couvrir de givre. -**2.** [road] se couvrir de verglas.
◇ *vt sep*: to be ~d up [lock, windscreen, propellers] être givré; [road] être verglacé.

ice age *n* période *f* glaciaire.
◆ **ice-age** *adj* (datant) de la période glaciaire.

ice axe *n* piolet *m*.

ice bag *n* sac *m* à glaçons.

iceberg ['aɪsbɜːg] *n* -**1.** iceberg *m*. -**2.** *inf* [cold person] glaçon *m*.

iceberg lettuce *n salade aux feuilles serrées et croquantes très répandue en Grande-Bretagne*.

ice blue ◇ *n* bleu métallique *m*.
◇ *adj* bleu métallique (*inv*).

iceboat ['aɪsbəʊt] *n* -**1.** [ice yacht] char *m* à voile (sur patins). -**2.** [icebreaker] brise-glace *m inv*.

icebound ['aɪsbaʊnd] *adj* bloqué par les glaces.

icebox ['aɪsbɒks] *n* -**1.** *Br* [freezer compartment] freezer *m*. -**2.** *Am dated* [refrigerator] réfrigérateur *m*, frigo *m*. -**3.** [coolbox] glacière *f*. -**4.** *fig* glacière *f*; their house is like an ~ c'est une vraie glacière OR on gèle chez eux.

icebreaker ['aɪsˌbreɪkəʳ] *n* -**1.** [vessel] brise-glace *m inv*. -**2.** [at party] façon *f* de briser la glace.

ice bucket *n* seau *m* à glace.

ice cap *n* calotte *f* glacière.

ice-cold *adj* [hands, drink] glacé; [house, manners] glacial.

ice cream *n* glace *f*; chocolate/strawberry ~ glace au chocolat/à la fraise.

ice-cream cone, ice-cream cornet *n* cornet *m* de glace.

ice-cream parlour *n* salon *m* de dégustation de glaces.

ice-cream soda *n* soda *m* avec de la glace.

ice-cream van *n* camionnette *f* de vendeur de glaces.

icecube ['aɪskjuːb] *n* glaçon *m*.

iced [aɪst] *adj* -**1.** [chilled - drink] glacé. -**2.** [decorated - cake, biscuit] glacé.

ice dancing *n* danse *f* sur glace.

icefield ['aɪsfiːld] *n* champ *m* de glace, icefield *m*.

ice floe *n* glace *f* flottante.

ice hockey *n* hockey *m* sur glace.

icehouse ['aɪshaʊs, *pl* -haʊzɪz] *n* glacière *f* (*local*).

Iceland ['aɪslənd] *pr n* Islande *f*; in ~ en Islande.

Icelander ['aɪsləndəʳ] *n* Islandais *m*, -e *f*.

Icelandic [aɪs'lændɪk] ◇ *n* islandais *m*.
◇ *adj* islandais.

ice lolly (*pl* ice lollies) *n Br* ≃ sucette *f* glacée.

ice machine *n* machine *f* à glace.

iceman ['aɪsmæn] (*pl* icemen [-men]) *n Am* livreur *m* de glace à domicile.

ice pack *n* -**1.** [pack ice] banquise *f*. -**2.** [ice bag] sac *m* à glaçons; MED poche *f* à glace.

ice pick *n* pic *m* à glace.

ice point *n* point *m* de congélation.

ice rink *n* patinoire *f*.

ice sheet *n* nappe *f* de glace.

ice show *n* spectacle *m* sur glace.

ice skate *n* patin *m* (à glace).
◆ **ice-skate** *vi* patiner; [professionally] faire du patinage (sur glace); [for pleasure] faire du patin (à glace).

ice-skater *n* patineur *m*, -euse *f*.

ice-skating *n* patinage *m* (sur glace); to go ~ faire du patin (à glace).

ice-tray *n* bac *m* à glace OR à glaçons.

ice water *n Am* eau *f* glacée.

ice yacht *n Br* char *m* à voile (sur patins).

I Ching [ˌiː'tʃɪŋ] *n* Yijing *m*, Yi-king *m*.

ichthyology [ˌɪkθɪ'ɒlədʒɪ] *n* ichtyologie *f*.

ichthyosaurus [ˌɪkθɪə'sɔːrəs] *n* (*pl inv* OR ichthyosauri [-raɪ]) ichtyosaure *m*.

icicle ['aɪsɪkl] *n* glaçon *m* (*qui pend d'une gouttière etc*).

icily ['aɪsɪlɪ] *adv* d'une manière glaciale; to answer ~ répondre d'un ton OR sur un ton glacial; he looked at her ~ il lui lança un regard glacial.

icing ['aɪsɪŋ] *n* -**1.** CULIN glace *f* (*de sucre*); it's the ~ on the cake c'est la cerise sur le gâteau. -**2.** [on aeroplane - process] givrage *m*; [- ice] givre *m*.

icing sugar *n Br* sucre *m* glace.

ICJ (*abbr of* International Court of Justice) *pr n* CIJ *f*.

ick *inf* [ɪk] *Am* ◇ *n* (*U*) cochonneries *fpl*.
◇ *interj* beurk.

icky *inf* ['ɪkɪ] (*compar* ickier, *superl* ickiest) *adj* [revolting] dégueulasse.

icon ['aɪkɒn] *n* icône *f*.

iconoclasm [aɪ'kɒnəklæzm] *n* iconoclasme *m*.

iconoclast [aɪ'kɒnəklæst] *n* iconoclaste *mf*.

iconoclastic [aɪˌkɒnə'klæstɪk] *adj* iconoclaste.

iconography [ˌaɪkɒ'nɒgrəfɪ] *n* iconographie *f*.

ICR (*abbr of* Institute for Cancer Research) *pr n institut américain de recherche sur le cancer*.

ICU *n abbr of* intensive care unit.

icy ['aɪsɪ] (*compar* icier, *superl* iciest) *adj* -**1.** [weather] glacial; [hands] glacé; [ground] gelé. -**2.** [covered in ice - road] verglacé; [- window, propeller] givré, couvert de givre; RAIL [points] gelé. -**3.** *fig* [reception, stare] glacial; his ~ manner sa froideur.

id [ɪd] *n* PSYCH ça *m*.

I'd [aɪd] = **I had, I would**.

ID ◇ *n* *(U)* *(abbr of* identification) papiers *mpl*; do you have any ~? vous avez une pièce d'identité?
◇ *vt*: to be OR to get ID'd subir un contrôle d'identité.
◇ *written abbr of* Idaho.

Idaho ['aɪdəhəʊ] *pr n* Idaho *m*; in ~ dans l'Idaho.

ID card *n* carte *f* d'identité.

IDD (*abbr of* international direct dialling) *n* indicatif *m* du pays.

idea [aɪ'dɪə] *n* -**1.** [plan, suggestion, inspiration] idée *f*; what a good ~! quelle bonne idée!; I've had an ~ j'ai une idée; it wasn't MY ~! l'idée n'était pas de moi!; the ~ of leaving you never entered my head l'idée de te quitter ne m'a jamais effleuré; where did you get the ~ for your book? d'où vous est venue l'idée de votre livre? ❑ that's an ~! ça, c'est une bonne idée!; that's the ~! c'est ça!; what's the ~? [showing disapproval] qu'est-ce que ça veut dire OR signifie?; the very ~! en voilà une idée! -**2.** [notion] idée *f*; our ~s about the universe notre conception de l'univers; he has some strange ~s il a de drôles d'idées; I have my own ~s on the subject j'ai mes idées personnelles sur la question; sorry, but this is not my ~ of fun désolé, mais je ne trouve pas ça drôle OR ça ne m'amuse pas; don't put ~s into his head ne va pas lui fourrer OR lui mettre des idées dans la tête; she hasn't an ~ in her head elle n'a pas un grain de jugeote; it was a nice ~ to phone c'est gentil d'avoir pensé à téléphoner; you've no ~ how difficult it was tu n'imagines pas à quel point c'était difficile; you've no ~ of the conditions in which they lived tu ne peux pas t'imaginer les conditions dans lesquelles ils vivaient; has anyone any ~ how the accident occurred? est-ce qu'on a une idée de la façon dont l'accident est arrivé?; I have a rough ~ of what happened je m'imagine assez bien ce qui est arrivé; she had no ~ what the time was elle n'avait aucune idée de l'heure; I haven't the slightest OR foggiest ~ je n'en ai pas la moindre idée; I've no ~ where it came from je ne sais vraiment pas d'où ça vient; what gave him the ~ that it would be easy? qu'est-ce qui lui a laissé croire que ce serait facile? -**3.** [estimate] indication *f*, idée *f*; can you give me an ~ of how much it will cost? est-ce que vous pouvez m'indiquer à peu près combien ça va coûter? -**4.** [suspicion] soupçon *m*, idée *f*; she had an ~ that something was going to happen elle se doutait que quelque chose allait arriver; I've an ~ that he'll succeed j'ai dans l'idée qu'il finira par réussir. -**5.** [objective, intention] but *m*; the ~ of the game le but du jeu; the ~ is to provide help for people in need il s'agit d'aider ceux qui sont dans le besoin.

ideal [aɪ'dɪəl] ◇ *adj* idéal; an ~ couple un couple idéal; that's ~! c'est parfait! ❑ the Ideal Home Exhibition ≃ le salon de l'habitat.
◇ *n* idéal *m*.

idealism [aɪ'dɪəlɪzm] *n* idéalisme *m*.

idealist [aɪ'dɪəlɪst] ◇ *n* idéaliste *mf*.
◇ *adj* idéaliste.

idealistic [aɪ,dɪə'lɪstɪk] *adj* idéaliste.

idealize, -ise [aɪ'dɪəlaɪz] *vt* idéaliser.

ideally [aɪ'dɪəlɪ] *adv* -**1.** [perfectly] parfaitement; they're ~ suited c'est un couple parfaitement assorti; the shop is ~ situated l'emplacement du magasin est idéal. -**2.** [in a perfect world] dans l'idéal; ~, this wine should be served at room temperature normalement, ce vin doit être servi chambré; ~, accidents like this wouldn't happen l'idéal serait que de tels accidents ne se produisent pas; ~, I would like to work in advertising mon rêve ce serait de travailler dans la publicité.

identical [aɪ'dentɪkl] *adj* identique; your hairstyle is ~ to OR with Jean's tu as exactement la même coiffure que Jean; they were wearing ~ dresses elles portaient la même robe.

identically [aɪ'dentɪklɪ] *adv* identiquement.

identical twins *npl* vrais jumeaux *mpl*, vraies jumelles *fpl*.

identifiable [aɪ'dentɪfaɪəbl] *adj* identifiable.

identification [aɪ,dentɪfɪ'keɪʃn] *n* -**1.** [gen] identification *f*. -**2.** *(U)* [identity papers] papiers *mpl*; the police asked me for ~ la police m'a demandé mes papiers OR une pièce d'identité.

identification card *n* carte *f* d'identité.

identification papers *npl* papiers *mpl* d'identité.

identification parade *n Br* séance *f* d'identification *(au cours de laquelle on demande à un témoin de reconnaître une personne)*.

identifier [aɪ'dentɪfaɪə^r] *n* COMPUT identificateur *m*, identifieur *m*.

identify [aɪ'dentɪfaɪ] (*pt* & *pp* identified) ◇ *vt* -**1.** [recognize, name] identifier; he was identified as one of the ringleaders il fut identifié comme étant l'un des meneurs; the winner has asked not to be identified le gagnant a tenu à garder l'anonymat. -**2.** [distinguish - subj: physical feature, badge etc]: she wore a red rose to ~ herself elle portait une rose rouge pour se faire reconnaître OR pour qu'on la reconnaisse; his accent immediately identified him to the others les autres l'ont immédiatement reconnu à son accent. -**3.** [acknowledge - difficulty, issue etc] relever; the report identifies two major problems le rapport met en lumière deux problèmes principaux. -**4.** [associate - people, ideas etc]: he has long been identified with right-wing groups il y a longtemps qu'il est assimilé OR identifié aux groupuscules de droite; she identifies herself with the activists elle s'identifie avec les militants.
◇ *vi*: to ~ with s'identifier à OR avec.

Identikit® [aɪ'dentɪkɪt] *n*: ~ (picture) portrait-robot *m*.

identity [aɪ'dentətɪ] (*pl* identities) ◇ *n* -**1.** [name, set of characteristics] identité *f*; only afterwards did they reveal his ~ ce n'est qu'après qu'ils ont révélé son identité; it was a case of mistaken ~ il y a eu erreur sur la personne. -**2.** [sense of belonging] identité *f*.
◇ *comp* [bracelet, papers] d'identité.

identity card *n* carte *f* d'identité.

identity crisis *n* crise *f* d'identité.

identity parade = **identification parade**.

ideogram ['ɪdɪəʊgræm], **ideograph** ['ɪdɪəʊgrɑːf] *n* idéogramme *m*.

ideographic [,ɪdɪəʊ'græfɪk] *adj* idéographique.

ideological [,aɪdɪə'lɒdʒɪkl] *adj* idéologique.

ideologically [,aɪdɪə'lɒdʒɪklɪ] *adv* du point de vue idéologique; ~ sound [idea] défendable sur le plan idéologique; [person] dont les idées sont défendables sur le plan idéologique.

ideologist [,aɪdɪ'ɒlədʒɪst] *n* idéologue *mf*.

ideologue ['aɪdɪəlɒg] *n* idéologue *mf*.

ideology [,aɪdɪ'ɒlədʒɪ] (*pl* ideologies) *n* idéologie *f*.

ides [aɪdz] *n* ides *fpl*.

idiocy ['ɪdɪəsɪ] *n* -**1.** [stupidity] stupidité *f*, idiotie *f*. -**2.** PSYCH & *arch* [mental retardation] idiotie *f*.

idiolect ['ɪdɪəlekt] *n* idiolecte *m*.

idiom ['ɪdɪəm] *n* -**1.** [expression] locution *f*, expression *f* idiomatique. -**2.** [language] idiome *m*. -**3.** [style - of music, writing etc] style *m*.

idiomatic [,ɪdɪə'mætɪk] *adj* idiomatique; ~ expression expression *f* idiomatique; his Italian is fluent and ~ il parle un italien tout à fait idiomatique.

idiomatically [,ɪdɪə'mætɪklɪ] *adv* de manière idiomatique.

idiosyncrasy [,ɪdɪə'sɪŋkrəsɪ] (*pl* idiosyncrasies) *n* [peculiarity] particularité *f*; [foible] manie *f*.

idiosyncratic [,ɪdɪəsɪŋ'krætɪk] *adj* [style, behaviour] caractéristique.

idiot ['ɪdɪət] *n* -**1.** [fool] idiot *m*, -e *f*, imbécile *mf*; (you) stupid ~! espèce d'idiot!; don't be an ~! ne sois pas idiot!; to behave like an ~ se comporter comme un imbécile OR un idiot; that ~ Harry cet imbécile de Harry ❑ 'The Idiot' *Dostoevsky* 'l'Idiot'. -**2.** PSYCH & *arch* idiot *m*, -e *f*.

idiot board *inf n* prompteur *m*, téléprompteur *m*, télésouffleur *m*.

idiot box *inf n pej* télé *f*.

idiotic [,ɪdɪ'ɒtɪk] *adj* idiot; he looks absolutely ~! il a l'air complètement idiot!

idiotically [,ɪdɪ'ɒtɪklɪ] *adv* stupidement, bêtement; he behaved ~ il s'est comporté comme un imbécile; he smiled ~ il a souri bêtement.

idiot-proof *inf* ◇ *adj* COMPUT à l'épreuve de toute fausse manœuvre.
◇ *vt* rendre infaillible.

idle ['aɪdl] ◇ *adj* -**1.** [person - inactive] inoccupé, désœuvré; [- lazy] oisif, paresseux; in her ~ moments à ses moments perdus; 1,500 men have been made ~ 1 500 hommes ont été mis au chômage; he's an ~ good-for-nothing c'est un fainéant et un bon à rien; the ~ rich les riches désœuvrés OR oisifs. -**2.** [not in use - factory, equipment] arrêté, à l'arrêt; to stand ~ [machine] être arrêté OR au repos; to lie ~ [factory] chômer; [money] dormir, être improductif. -**3.** [futile, pointless] inutile, vain; [empty - threat, promise etc] vain, en l'air; it would be ~ to speculate il ne servirait à rien de se livrer à de vaines conjectures ‖ [casual]: an ~ glance un regard distrait; ~ gossip ragots *mpl*; out of ~ curiosity par pure curiosité; ~ pleasure plaisir *m* futile; an ~ rumour une rumeur sans fondement.
◇ *vi* [engine] tourner au ralenti.
◇ *vt Am* [make unemployed - permanently] mettre au chômage; [- temporarily] mettre en chômage technique.
◆ **idle about, idle around** *vi insep Br* traîner.
◆ **idle away** *vt sep*: to ~ away one's time tuer le temps.

idleness ['aɪdlnɪs] *n* -**1.** [laziness] oisiveté *f*, paresse *f*; [inactivity] désœuvrement *m*; to live in ~ vivre dans l'oisiveté, mener une vie oisive. -**2.** [futility] futilité *f*.

idler ['aɪdlə^r] *n* -**1.** [lazy person] paresseux *m*, -euse *f*, fainéant *m*, -e *f*. -**2.** TECH [pulley] poulie *f* folle; [wheel] roue *f* folle.

idling speed ['aɪdlɪŋ-] *n* ralenti *m*.

idly ['aɪdlɪ] *adv* -**1.** [lazily] paresseusement. -**2.** [casually] négligemment; why not? she said ~ pourquoi pas? dit-elle négligemment. -**3.** [unresponsively] sans réagir; we will not stand ~ by nous n'allons pas rester sans réagir OR sans rien faire.

idol ['aɪdl] *n* idole *f*; a 1970s pop ~ une idole (pop) des années 1970.

idolater [aɪ'dɒlətə^r] *n* idolâtre *mf*.

idolatrous [aɪ'dɒlətrəs] *adj* idolâtre.

idolatry [aɪ'dɒlətrɪ] *n* idolâtrie *f*.

idolize, -ise ['aɪdəlaɪz] *vt* idolâtrer.

Idomeneus [aɪ'dɒmɪnjuːs] *pr n* Idoménée.

idyll ['ɪdɪl] *n* idylle *f*.

idyllic [ɪ'dɪlɪk] *adj* idyllique.

i.e. *adv* c'est-à-dire, à savoir.

if [ɪf] ◇ *conj* -**1.** [supposing that] si; if he comes, we'll ask him s'il vient, on lui demandera; if possible si (c'est) possible; have it done by Tuesday, if at all possible faites-le pour mardi si possible; if necessary si (c'est) nécessaire; if so si c'est le cas; if all goes well, we'll be there by midnight si tout va bien, nous y serons pour minuit; if anyone wants me, I'm OR I'll be in my office si quelqu'un veut me voir, je suis dans mon bureau; if she hadn't introduced herself, I would never have recognized her si elle ne s'était pas présentée, je ne l'aurais pas reconnue; if I'd known you were coming, I'd have baked a cake si j'avais su que tu venais, j'aurais fait un gâteau; if you'd told me the truth, this would never have happened si tu m'avais dit la vérité, ça ne serait jamais arrivé; if I was older, I'd leave home si j'étais plus âgé,

je quitterais la maison; if you could have anything you wanted, what would you ask for? si tu pouvais avoir tout ce que tu désires, qu'est-ce que tu demanderais?; if I were a millionaire, I'd buy a yacht si j'étais millionnaire, j'achèterais un yacht; would you mind if I invited Angie too? ça te dérangerait si j'invitais aussi Angie? -**2.** [whenever] si; if you mix blue and yellow you get green si on mélange du bleu et du jaune, on obtient du vert; if you ever come OR if ever you come to London, do visit us si jamais tu passes à Londres, viens nous voir; if you are gratified by something, you are pleased by it si (on dit que) quelque chose nous «satisfait», cela veut dire que ça nous fait plaisir; he gets angry if I so much as open my mouth si j'ai seulement le malheur d'ouvrir la bouche, il se fâche. -**3.** [given that] si; if Paul was the brains in the family, then Anne was the organizer si Paul était le cerveau de la famille, alors Anne en était l'esprit organisateur. -**4.** [whether]: to ask/to know/to wonder if demander/savoir/se demander si; it doesn't matter if he comes or not peu importe qu'il vienne ou (qu'il ne vienne) pas; I'll see if she's up yet je vais voir si elle est levée. -**5.** [with verbs or adjectives expressing emotion]: I'm sorry if I upset you je suis désolé si je t'ai fait de la peine; if I gave you that impression, I apologize je m'excuse si c'est l'impression que je vous ai donnée; we'd be so pleased if you could come ça nous ferait tellement plaisir si vous pouviez venir. -**6.** [used to qualify a statement]: few, if any, readers will have heard of him peu de lecteurs auront entendu parler de lui, ou même aucun; he was intelligent if a little arrogant il était intelligent, mais quelque peu arrogant. -**7.** [introducing comments or opinions]: if I could just come in here... si je puis me permettre d'intervenir...; it's rather good, if I say so myself c'est assez bon, sans fausse modestie; I'll leave it there, if I may, and go on to my next point j'en resterai là, si vous voulez bien et passerai au point suivant; I thought you were rather rude, if you don't mind my saying so je vous ai trouvé assez grossier, si je peux me permettre; well, if you want my opinion OR if you ask me, I thought it was dreadful eh bien, si vous voulez mon avis, c'était affreux; if you think about it, it is rather odd si vous y réfléchissez, c'est plutôt bizarre; if I remember rightly, she was married to a politician si j'ai bonne mémoire, elle était mariée à un homme politique. -**8.** [in polite requests] si; if you could just write your name here... si vous voulez bien inscrire votre nom ici...; if you could all just wait in the hall, I'll be back in a second si vous pouviez tous attendre dans l'entrée, je reviens tout de suite; would you like me to wrap it for you? — if you would, please vous voulez que je vous l'emballe? — oui, s'il vous plaît. -**9.** [expressing surprise, indignation] tiens, ça alors; well, if it isn't my old mate Jim! tiens OR ça alors, c'est ce vieux Jim!
◇ *n* si *m*; if you get the job - and it's a big if - you'll have to move to London si tu obtiens cet emploi, et rien n'est moins sûr, tu devras aller t'installer à Londres; no ifs and buts, we're going il n'y a pas de «mais» qui tienne OR pas de discussions, on y va.
◆ **if and when** *conj phr* au cas où; if and when he phones, I'll simply tell him to leave me alone au cas où il appellerait, je lui dirais tout simplement de me laisser tranquille.
◆ **if anything** *adv phr* plutôt; he doesn't look any slimmer, if anything, he's put on weight il n'a pas l'air plus mince, il a même plutôt grossi; I am, if anything, even keener to be involved j'ai peut-être encore plus envie d'y participer.
◆ **if ever** *conj phr*: there's a hopeless case if ever I saw one! voilà un cas désespéré s'il en est!; if ever I saw a man driven by ambition, it's him si quelqu'un est poussé par l'ambition, c'est bien lui.
◆ **if I were you** *adv phr* à ta place; if I were you I'd accept the offer si j'étais toi OR à ta place, j'accepterais la proposition.
◆ **if not** *conj phr* sinon; I'm happy to eat out if you want to, if not, I'll just rustle something up here on peut aller manger quelque part si tu veux, sinon je préparerai juste quelque chose ici; are you going to read this book? if not, I will tu vas lire ce livre? sinon, je vais le lire moi; did you finish on time? and if not, why not? avez-vous terminé à temps? sinon, pourquoi?
◆ **if only** *conj phr* -**1.** [providing a reason] au moins; I think I should come along too, if only to make sure you don't get into mischief je crois que je devrais venir aussi, au moins pour m'assurer que vous ne faites pas de bêtises; all right, I'll let you go to the party, if only to keep you quiet bon d'accord, tu peux aller à la fête, comme ça au moins, j'aurai la paix. -**2.** [expressing a wish] si seulement; if only I could drive si seulement je savais conduire; if only someone would tell us what has happened si seulement quelqu'un nous disait ce qui s'est passé; if only we'd known si seulement nous avions su.

iffy *inf* ['ɪfɪ] (*compar* iffier, *superl* iffiest) *adj* incertain, tangent.

if-then operation *n* COMPUT inclusion *f*.

igloo ['ɪgluː] *n* igloo *m*, iglou *m*.

igneous ['ɪgnɪəs] *adj* igné.

ignite [ɪg'naɪt] ◇ *vt* [set fire to] mettre le feu à, enflammer; [light] allumer.
◇ *vi* [catch fire] prendre feu, s'enflammer; [be lit] s'allumer.

ignition [ɪg'nɪʃn] *n* -**1.** AUT allumage *m*; to turn on/off the ~ mettre/couper le contact. -**2.** PHYS & CHEM ignition *f*.

ignition coil *n* bobine *f* d'allumage.

ignition key *n* clef *f* de contact.

ignition switch *n* contact *m*.

ignoble [ɪg'nəʊbl] *adj* infâme.

ignominious [,ɪgnə'mɪnɪəs] *adj* ignominieux.

ignominiously [,ɪgnə'mɪnɪəslɪ] *adv* ignominieusement.

ignominy ['ɪgnəmɪnɪ] *n* ignominie *f*.

ignoramus [,ɪgnə'reɪməs] (*pl* ignoramuses) *n* ignare *mf*.

ignorance ['ɪgnərəns] *n* -**1.** [lack of knowledge, awareness] ignorance *f*; out of OR through sheer ~ par pure ignorance; they kept him in ~ of his sister's existence ils lui ont caché l'existence de sa sœur; forgive my ~, but... excuse mon ignorance, mais...; ~ of the law is no excuse nul n'est censé ignorer la loi. -**2.** *pej* [bad manners] grossièreté *f*.

ignorant ['ɪgnərənt] *adj* -**1.** [uneducated] ignorant; I'm really ~ about classical music/politics je ne connais absolument rien à la musique classique/la politique. -**2.** [unaware] ignorant; I was ~ as to his whereabouts j'ignorais où il se trouvait; he was ~ of the facts il ignorait les faits. -**3.** *pej* [bad-mannered] mal élevé; don't be so ~, take your hat off! tiens-toi bien, enlève ton chapeau!

ignorantly ['ɪgnərəntlɪ] *adv* [behave] d'une manière grossière.

ignore [ɪg'nɔːʳ] *vt* -**1.** [pay no attention to - person, remark] ne pas prêter attention à, ignorer; she completely ~d me elle a fait semblant de ne pas me voir; ~ him and he'll go away fais comme s'il n'était pas là et il te laissera tranquille; we can't continue to ~ these objections on ne peut pas continuer à ne tenir aucun compte de ces objections. -**2.** [take no account of - warning, request etc] ne pas tenir compte de; he ~d the doctor's advice and continued smoking il n'a pas suivi les conseils de son médecin et a continué de fumer. -**3.** [overlook]: they can no longer ~ what is going on here il ne leur est plus possible d'ignorer OR de fermer les yeux sur ce qui se passe ici; the report ~s certain crucial facts le rapport passe sous silence des faits cruciaux; they seemed to ~ the fact that I was there ils semblaient ignorer ma présence.

ignore character *n* COMPUT caractère *m* d'effacement.

Iguaçu Falls [,iːgwə'suː-] *pl pr n*: the ~ les chutes *fpl* d'Iguaçu.

iguana [ɪ'gwɑːnə] *n* iguane *m*.

ikon ['aɪkɒn] = **icon**.

IL *written abbr of* Illinois.

ILA (*abbr of* International Longshoremen's Association) *pr n* *syndicat international de dockers*.

ILEA ['ɪlɪə] (*abbr of* Inner London Education Authority) *pr n*: (the) ~ *organisme qui, jusqu'en 1990, était chargé de gérer les services londoniens de l'enseignement*.

ileum ['ɪlɪəm] *n* iléon *m*.

ilex ['aɪleks] (*pl* ilexes) *n* yeuse *f*, chêne *m* vert.

ILGWU (*abbr of* International Ladies' Garment Workers Union) *pr n* *syndicat des employés de l'habillement féminin*.

Iliad ['ɪlɪəd] *pr n*: 'The ~' *Homer* 'l'Iliade'.

ilk [ɪlk] *n* [type]: people of that ~ ce genre de personnes; books of that ~ des livres de ce genre.

ill [ɪl] ◇ *adj* -**1.** [sick, unwell] malade; to fall OR to be taken ~ tomber malade; seriously ~ gravement malade; the smell makes me ~ l'odeur me rend malade; I feel ~ just thinking about it rien que d'y penser, j'en suis malade. -**2.** *Br* [injured]: he is critically ~ with stab wounds il est dans un état critique après avoir reçu de nombreux coups de couteau. -**3.** *lit* [bad] mauvais, néfaste; ~ fortune malheur *m*, malchance *f*; the ~ effects of alcohol les effets néfastes de l'alcool; ~ deeds méfaits *mpl*; a house of ~ repute une maison mal famée ❑ it's an ~ wind that blows nobody any good *prov* à quelque chose malheur est bon *prov*.
◇ *n* -**1.** *lit* [evil] mal *m*; to think/speak ~ of sb penser/dire du mal de qqn; for good or ~ [better or worse] pour le meilleur et pour le pire; [whatever happens] quoi qu'il arrive. -**2.** [difficulty, trouble] malheur *m*; the nation's ~s les malheurs du pays.
◇ *adv* -**1.** [hardly] à peine, difficilement; we can ~ afford these luxuries ce sont des luxes que nous pouvons difficilement nous permettre; we can ~ afford to wait nous ne pouvons vraiment pas nous permettre d'attendre. -**2.** *fml* [badly] mal; it ~ becomes OR befits you to criticize il vous sied mal de critiquer; to augur OR to bode ~ être de mauvais augure.

ill. (*written abbr of* illustration) ill.

I'll [aɪl] = **I shall, I will**.

ill-advised *adj* [remark, action] peu judicieux; he was ~ to go away il a eu tort de partir.

ill-assorted *adj* mal assorti.

ill-at-ease *adj* gêné, mal à l'aise.

illative [ɪ'leɪtɪv] ◇ *adj* illatif.
◇ *n* illatif *m*.

ill-bred *adj* mal élevé.

ill-breeding *n* manque *m* de savoir-vivre.

ill-concealed *adj* mal dissimulé.

ill-conceived [-kən'siːvd] *adj* mal pensé.

ill-considered *adj* [hasty] hâtif; [thoughtless] irréfléchi.

ill-defined [-dɪ'faɪnd] *adj* mal défini.

ill-disposed [-dɪs'pəʊzd] *adj* mal disposé; they are ~ towards young people ils ne portent pas les jeunes dans leur cœur.

illegal [ɪ'liːgl] *adj* -**1.** JUR illégal; ~ entry violation *f* de domicile; ~ immigrant immigré *m*, -e *f*, clandestin *m*, -e *f*; ~ substances stupéfiants *mpl*. -**2.** COMPUT interdit; ~ character caractère *m* interdit; ~ instruction instruction *f* erronée.

illegality [,ɪliː'gælətɪ] (*pl* illegalities) *n* illégalité *f*.

illegally [ɪ'liːgəlɪ] *adv* illégalement, d'une manière illégale; to be ~ parked être en stationnement interdit.

illegible [ɪ'ledʒəbl] *adj* illisible.

illegibly [ɪ'ledʒəblɪ] *adv* illisiblement.

illegitimacy [,ɪlɪ'dʒɪtɪməsɪ] *n* illégitimité *f*.

illegitimate [ˌɪlɪ'dʒɪtɪmət] ◇ *adj* -**1.** [child] naturel, illégitime JUR. -**2.** [activity] illégitime, interdit. -**3.** [argument] illogique.
◇ *n* enfant naturel *m*, enfant naturelle *f*.
illegitimately [ˌɪlɪ'dʒɪtɪmətlɪ] *adv* -**1.** [outside marriage] hors du mariage. -**2.** [illegally] illégitimement.
ill-equipped *adj* -**1.** [lacking equipment] mal équipé, mal préparé. -**2.** [lacking qualities - for job, situation]: to be ~ (for) ne pas être à la hauteur (de); he felt ~ to cope with the pressures of the job il ne se sentait pas capable d'affronter les problèmes posés par son travail.
ill-fated *adj* [action] malheureux, funeste; [person] qui joue de malheur, malheureux; [day] néfaste, de malchance; [journey] funeste, fatal.
ill-favoured *Br*, **ill-favored** *Am adj* -**1.** [ugly] laid. -**2.** [unpleasant] désagréable.
ill feeling *n* ressentiment *m*, animosité *f*.
ill-founded *adj* [hopes, confidence] mal fondé; [suspicions] sans fondement.
ill-gotten *adj*: ~ gains biens *mpl* mal acquis.
ill-health *n* mauvaise santé *f*; to suffer from ~ être en mauvaise santé; because of ~ pour des raisons de santé.
illiberal [ɪ'lɪbərəl] *adj* -**1.** [bigoted, intolerant] intolérant; POL [regime] arbitraire, oppressif; [legislation] restrictif. -**2.** [mean] avare.
illicit [ɪ'lɪsɪt] *adj* illicite.
illicitly [ɪ'lɪsɪtlɪ] *adv* illicitement.
illicitness [ɪ'lɪsɪtnɪs] *n* caractère *m* illicite.
illimitable [ɪ'lɪmɪtəbl] *adj* illimité, infini.
ill-informed *adj* [person] mal renseigné; [remark] inexact, faux.
Illinois [ˌɪlɪ'nɔɪ] *pr n* Illinois *m*; in ~ dans l'Illinois.
illiteracy [ɪ'lɪtərəsɪ] *n* illétrisme *m*, analphabétisme *m*.
illiterate [ɪ'lɪtərət] ◇ *adj* -**1.** [unable to read] analphabète, illettré. -**2.** [uneducated] ignorant, sans éducation; many young people are scientifically ~ de nombreux jeunes gens n'ont aucune formation OR connaissance scientifique.
◇ *n* analphabète *mf*.
ill-judged [-dʒʌdʒd] *adj* [remark, attempt] peu judicieux.
ill-mannered *adj* [person] mal élevé, impoli; [behaviour] grossier, impoli.
ill-natured [-neɪtʃəd] *adj* qui a mauvais caractère.
illness ['ɪlnɪs] *n* maladie *f*.
illocution [ˌɪlə'kjuːʃn] *n* illocution *f*, acte *m* illocutoire.
illocutionary [ˌɪlə'kjuːʃnrɪ] *adj* illocutoire, illocutionnaire.
illogical [ɪ'lɒdʒɪkl] *adj* illogique; that's ~ ce n'est pas logique; she knew it was ~, but she felt very bitter elle savait que c'était absurde, mais elle éprouvait une vive amertume.
illogicality [ˌɪlɒdʒɪ'kælətɪ] (*pl* illogicalities) *n* illogisme *m*.
illogically [ɪ'lɒdʒɪklɪ] *adv* d'une manière illogique; he assumed, ~, that he meant nothing to her il supposait, sans raison, qu'il n'était rien pour elle.
ill-prepared *adj* mal préparé.
ill-starred [-stɑːd] *adj lit* [person] né sous une mauvaise étoile; [day] néfaste, funeste.
ill-tempered *adj* [by nature] grincheux, qui a mauvais caractère; [temporarily] de mauvaise humeur; [remark, outburst etc] plein de mauvaise humeur.
ill-timed *adj* [arrival, visit] inopportun, intempestif, qui tombe mal; [remark, question] déplacé, mal à propos *(inv)*; the meeting was very ~ cette réunion ne pouvait plus mal tomber.
ill-treat *vt* maltraiter.
ill-treatment *n* mauvais traitement *m*.
illuminate [ɪ'luːmɪneɪt] ◇ *vt* -**1.** [light up] illuminer, éclairer. -**2.** [make clearer] éclairer; this book ~s many difficult problems ce livre éclaire de nombreux problèmes complexes. -**3.** [manuscript] enluminer.
◇ *vi* s'illuminer.
illuminated [ɪ'luːmɪneɪtɪd] *adj* -**1.** [lit up - sign, notice] lumineux. -**2.** [decorated - manuscript] enluminé.
illuminati [ɪˌluːmɪ'nɑːtiː] *npl* illuminés *mpl*.
illuminating [ɪ'luːmɪneɪtɪŋ] *adj* [book, speech] éclairant.
illumination [ɪˌluːmɪ'neɪʃn] *n* -**1.** [light] éclairage *m*; [of building] illumination *f*; a candle was the only means of ~ il n'y avait pour tout éclairage qu'une bougie. -**2.** [of manuscript] enluminure *f*.
◆ **illuminations** *npl* [coloured lights] illuminations *fpl*.
illuminator [ɪ'luːmɪneɪtə^r] *n* -**1.** ELEC source *f* lumineuse. -**2.** [artist] enlumineur *m*, -euse *f*.
illumine [ɪ'luːmɪn] *vt lit* illuminer.
ill-use [*vb* ˌɪl'juːz, *n* ˌɪl'juːs] *lit* ◇ *vt* [ill-treat] maltraiter.
◇ *n* [cruel treatment] mauvais traitement *m*.
illusion [ɪ'luːʒn] *n* -**1.** [false impression] illusion *f*; mirrors give an ~ of space les miroirs donnent une illusion d'espace ❑ optical ~ illusion d'optique. -**2.** [false belief] illusion *f*; we were living under an ~ nous étions victimes d'une illusion; she has no ~s about her chances of success elle ne se fait aucune illusion sur ses chances de succès OR de réussir. -**3.** [magic trick] illusion *f*.
illusionist [ɪ'luːʒənɪst] *n* [conjurer, magician] illusionniste *mf*.
illusory [ɪ'luːsərɪ] *adj* illusoire.
illustrate ['ɪləstreɪt] *vt* -**1.** [with pictures] illustrer; an ~d children's book un livre pour enfants illustré. -**2.** [show, demonstrate] illustrer; it clearly ~s the need for improvement cela montre bien que des améliorations sont nécessaires.
illustration [ˌɪlə'streɪʃn] *n* -**1.** [picture] illustration *f*. -**2.** [demonstration] illustration *f*; it's a clear ~ of a lack of government interest cela illustre bien un manque d'intérêt de la part du gouvernement; by way of ~ à titre d'exemple.
illustrative ['ɪləstrətɪv] *adj* [picture, diagram] qui illustre, explicatif; [action, event, fact] qui démontre, qui illustre; the demonstrations are ~ of the need for reform les manifestations montrent que des réformes sont nécessaires; ~ examples des exemples illustratifs.
illustrator ['ɪləstreɪtə^r] *n* illustrateur *m*, -trice *f*.
illustrious [ɪ'lʌstrɪəs] *adj* illustre.
ill will *n* malveillance *f*; I bear them no ~ je ne leur garde pas rancune, je ne leur en veux pas.
ILO (*abbr of* International Labour Organization) *pr n* OIT *f*.
ILWU (*abbr of* International Longshoremen's and Warehousemen's Union) *pr n syndicat international de dockers et de magasiniers*.
I'm [aɪm] = **I am**.
image ['ɪmɪdʒ] *n* -**1.** [mental picture] image *f*; I still have an ~ of her as a child je la vois encore comme une enfant; many people have the wrong ~ of her/of life in New York beaucoup de gens se font une fausse idée d'elle/de la vie à New York. -**2.** [public appearance]: (public) ~ image *f* de marque; the party tried to change its ~ le parti a essayé de changer son image de marque. -**3.** [likeness] image *f*; man was made in God's ~ l'homme a été créé à l'image de Dieu ❑ you are the (spitting *inf* OR very OR living) ~ of your mother tu es tout le portrait OR le portrait craché de ta mère. -**4.** [in literature, painting] image *f*; I tried to create an ~ of wartime Britain j'ai essayé de brosser un tableau de la vie en Grande-Bretagne pendant la guerre. -**5.** OPT & PHOT image *f*.
image file *n* COMPUT fichier *m* vidéo OR image.
image intensifier *n* intensificateur *m* d'image, amplificateur *m* de luminance.
image processing *n* COMPUT traitement *m* des images.
image processor *n* COMPUT unité *f* de traitement d'images.
imagery ['ɪmɪdʒrɪ] *n* *(U)* -**1.** [in literature] images *fpl*. -**2.** [visual images] imagerie *f*.
imaginable [ɪ'mædʒɪnəbl] *adj* imaginable; the worst thing ~ happened ce qu'on pouvait imaginer de pire est arrivé.
imaginary [ɪ'mædʒɪnrɪ] *adj* -**1.** [in one's imagination - sickness, danger] imaginaire. -**2.** [fictional - character, situation] fictif.
imagination [ɪˌmædʒɪ'neɪʃn] *n* [creativity] imagination *f*; [mind]: she tends to let her ~ run away with her elle a tendance à se laisser emporter par son imagination; it's all in her ~ elle se fait des idées; don't worry, it was only (my) ~ ne t'inquiète pas, c'est mon imagination qui me jouait des tours.
imaginative [ɪ'mædʒɪnətɪv] *adj* [person] imaginatif; [writing, idea, plan] original.
imaginatively [ɪ'mædʒɪnətɪvlɪ] *adv* avec imagination; an ~ illustrated book un livre illustré avec beaucoup d'imagination.
imaginativeness [ɪ'mædʒɪnətɪvnɪs] *n* imagination *f*.
imagine [ɪ'mædʒɪn] *vt* -**1.** [picture - scene, person] imaginer, s'imaginer, se représenter; I'd ~d him to be a much smaller man je l'imaginais plus petit; I can't ~ (myself) getting the job je n'arrive pas à imaginer que je puisse être embauché; ~ yourself in his situation imaginez-vous dans sa situation, mettez-vous à sa place; you can't ~ how awful it was vous ne pouvez pas (vous) imaginer OR vous figurer combien c'était horrible; just ~ my disgust imaginez combien j'étais dégoûté; (you can) ~ his delight! vous pensez s'il était ravi!; just ~! tu t'imagines!; you're imagining things tu te fais des idées. -**2.** [suppose, think] supposer, imaginer; I ~ you're tired je suppose OR j'imagine que vous êtes fatigué; an intelligent child, I'd ~ un enfant intelligent, j'imagine; ~ (that) you're on a beach imagine-toi sur une plage; ~ (that) you've won imagine que tu as gagné, suppose que tu aies gagné; don't ~ I'll help you again ne t'imagine pas que je t'aiderai encore.
imagines [ɪ'meɪdʒɪniːz] *pl* → **imago**.
imaginings [ɪ'mædʒɪnɪŋz] *npl* [fears, dreams]: never in my worst ~ did I think it would come to this je n'aurais jamais pensé que les choses en arriveraient là.
imagism ['ɪmədʒɪzm] *n* LITERAT imagisme *m*.
imago [ɪ'meɪgəʊ] (*pl* imagoes OR imagines [-dʒɪniːz]) *n* -**1.** ZOOL imago *m*. -**2.** PSYCH imago *f*.
imam [ɪ'mɑːm] *n* imam *m*.
imbalance [ˌɪm'bæləns] ◇ *n* déséquilibre *m*.
◇ *vt* déséquilibrer; ~d growth ECON croissance *f* déséquilibrée.
imbecile ['ɪmbɪsiːl] ◇ *n* -**1.** [idiot] imbécile *mf*, idiot *m*, -e *f*; to act the ~ faire l'imbécile; you ~! espèce d'imbécile OR d'idiot! -**2.** PSYCH imbécile *mf*.
◇ *adj* imbécile, idiot.
imbecility [ˌɪmbɪ'sɪlətɪ] (*pl* imbecilities) *n* -**1.** [stupidity] idiotie *f*, imbécillité *f*. -**2.** [stupid action] idiotie *f*, imbécillité *f*. -**3.** PSYCH imbécillité *f*.
imbed [ɪm'bed] = **embed**.
imbibe [ɪm'baɪb] ◇ *vt* -**1.** *fml* OR *hum* [drink] absorber. -**2.** *lit* [knowledge] assimiler. -**3.** PHYS absorber.
◇ *vi hum* boire.
imbroglio [ɪm'brəʊlɪəʊ] *n* imbroglio *m*.
imbue [ɪm'bjuː] *vt*: her parents had ~d her with high ideals ses parents lui avaient inculqué de nobles idéaux; his words were ~d with resentment ses paroles étaient pleines de ressentiment.
IMF (*abbr of* International Monetary Fund) *pr n* FMI *m*.
imitable ['ɪmɪtəbl] *adj* imitable.
imitate ['ɪmɪteɪt] *vt* imiter.

imitation [ˌɪmɪˈteɪʃn] ◇ *n* -**1.** [copy] imitation *f*; it's a cheap ~ c'est du toc; a poor ~ of the real thing une pâle imitation de l'original; 'beware of ~s' 'méfiez-vous des contrefaçons'. -**2.** [act of imitating] imitation *f*; to learn by ~ apprendre par mimétisme; he does everything in ~ of his brother il imite OR copie son frère en tout ❑ 'The Imitation of Christ' *Thomas à Kempis* 'l'Imitation de Jésus-Christ'.
◇ *comp* faux; an ~ diamond necklace un collier en faux diamants; ~ fur fourrure *f* synthétique; ~ jewellery bijoux *mpl* (de) fantaisie; ~ leather imitation *f* cuir, similicuir *m*.

imitative [ˈɪmɪtətɪv] *adj* [behaviour, sound] imitatif; [person, style] imitateur.

imitator [ˈɪmɪteɪtəʳ] *n* imitateur *m*, -trice *f*.

immaculate [ɪˈmækjʊlət] *adj* -**1.** [clean - house, clothes] impeccable, d'une propreté irréprochable; he's always ~ il est toujours impeccable OR tiré à quatre épingles. -**2.** [faultless - work, behaviour etc] parfait, impeccable. -**3.** [morally pure] irréprochable.

Immaculate Conception *n*: the ~ l'Immaculée Conception *f*.

immaculately [ɪˈmækjʊlətlɪ] *adv* -**1.** [spotlessly - clean, tidy] impeccablement; ~ dressed tiré à quatre épingles; ~ clean/white d'une propreté parfaite/blancheur éclatante. -**2.** [faultlessly - behave, perform etc] d'une manière irréprochable, impeccablement; she played ~ throughout the match elle a joué d'une manière remarquable pendant tout le match.

immanence [ˈɪmənəns] *n* immanence *f*.

immanent [ˈɪmənənt] *adj* immanent.

immaterial [ˌɪməˈtɪərɪəl] *adj* -**1.** [unimportant] sans importance; whether I was there or not is ~ que j'aie été présent ou non est sans importance; that point is ~ to what we are discussing cela n'a rien à voir avec ce dont nous sommes en train de parler; the truth is ~ to him la vérité est sans importance à ses yeux. -**2.** PHILOS immatériel.

immature [ˌɪməˈtjʊəʳ] *adj* -**1.** [childish] immature; she's very ~ elle manque vraiment de maturité. -**2.** BOT & ZOOL immature, jeune.

immaturity [ˌɪməˈtjʊərətɪ] *n* -**1.** [of person] manque *m* de maturité, immaturité *f*. -**2.** PSYCH, BOT & ZOOL immaturité *f*.

immeasurable [ɪˈmeʒrəbl] *adj* -**1.** *literal* incommensurable. -**2.** *fig* illimité, incommensurable.

immeasurably [ɪˈmeʒrəblɪ] *adv* -**1.** [long, high] incommensurablement. -**2.** [as intensifier] infiniment, extrêmement.

immediacy [ɪˈmiːdjəsɪ] *n* impact *m* immédiat; the ~ of the famine as seen on television l'impact immédiat des images de la famine montrées à la télévision; the ~ of the crisis les effets immédiats de la crise.

immediate [ɪˈmiːdjət] *adj* -**1.** [instant] immédiat, urgent; the problem needs ~ attention il est urgent de régler le problème; we need an ~ answer il nous faut une réponse immédiate; this pill gives ~ relief ce cachet soulage instantanément, l'effet de ce cachet est instantané ‖ [close in time] immédiat; in the ~ future dans les heures OR les jours qui viennent. -**2.** [nearest] immédiat, proche; my ~ relatives mes parents les plus proches; my ~ neighbours mes voisins immédiats ❑ ~ constituent LING constituant *m* immédiat. -**3.** [direct - cause, influence] immédiat, direct.

immediate access *n* COMPUT accès *m* direct.

immediately [ɪˈmiːdjətlɪ] ◇ *adv* -**1.** [at once] tout de suite, immédiatement; come ~ viens tout de suite; I left ~ after je suis parti tout de suite après. -**2.** [directly] directement. -**3.** [just] juste; ~ above the window juste au-dessus de la fenêtre.
◇ *conj Br* dès que; let me know ~ he arrives dès qu'il sera là, prévenez-moi.

immemorial [ˌɪmɪˈmɔːrɪəl] *adj* immémorial; from time ~ de temps immémorial.

immense [ɪˈmens] *adj* immense, considérable.

immensely [ɪˈmenslɪ] *adv* immensément, extrêmement; I'm ~ grateful to you je vous suis extrêmement reconnaissant.

immensity [ɪˈmensətɪ] *n* immensité *f*.

immerse [ɪˈmɜːs] *vt* -**1.** [plunge into liquid] immerger, plonger; I'm going to ~ myself in a hot bath je vais me plonger dans un bain chaud. -**2.** *fig*: I ~d myself in my work je me suis plongé dans mon travail; they were ~d in a game of chess ils étaient plongés dans une partie d'échecs; she went to London to ~ herself in the English language elle est allée à Londres en séjour linguistique. -**3.** RELIG baptiser par immersion.

immerser *inf* [ɪˈmɜːsəʳ] *Br* = **immersion heater**.

immersion [ɪˈmɜːʃn] *n* -**1.** [in liquid] immersion *f*. -**2.** *fig* [in reading, work] absorption *f*. -**3.** ASTRON & RELIG immersion *f*.

immersion heater *n* chauffe-eau *m inv* électrique.

immigrant [ˈɪmɪgrənt] ◇ *n* immigré *m*, -e *f*.
◇ *adj* immigré; ~ children enfants d'immigrés ❑ ~ worker travailleur *m* immigré.

immigrate [ˈɪmɪgreɪt] *vi* immigrer.

immigration [ˌɪmɪˈgreɪʃn] ◇ *n* -**1.** [act of immigrating] immigration *f*; the government wants to reduce ~ le gouvernement veut restreindre l'immigration ❑ the Immigration Control Act *loi de 1986 permettant aux immigrés illégaux résidant aux États-Unis depuis 1982 de recevoir un visa*. -**2.** [control section]: ~ (control) services *mpl* de l'immigration; to go through ~ (control) passer l'immigration.
◇ *comp* de l'immigration; ~ authorities services *mpl* de l'immigration; ~ regulations réglementation *f* relative à l'immigration.

imminence [ˈɪmɪnəns] *n* imminence *f*.

imminent [ˈɪmɪnənt] *adj* imminent.

immiscible [ɪˈmɪsəbl] *adj* non miscible.

immobile [ɪˈməʊbaɪl] *adj* immobile.

immobility [ˌɪməˈbɪlətɪ] *n* immobilité *f*.

immobilization [ɪˌməʊbɪlaɪˈzeɪʃn] *n* [gen & FIN] immobilisation *f*.

immobilize, -ise [ɪˈməʊbɪlaɪz] *vt* [gen & FIN] immobiliser.

immoderate [ɪˈmɒdərət] *adj* immodéré, excessif.

immoderately [ɪˈmɒdərətlɪ] *adv* immodérément.

immodest [ɪˈmɒdɪst] *adj* -**1.** [indecent] impudique. -**2.** [vain] prétentieux.

immodestly [ɪˈmɒdɪstlɪ] *adv* -**1.** [indecently] impudiquement, de façon indécente. -**2.** [vainly] sans modestie; he rather ~ claims to be the best il déclare non sans prétention qu'il est le meilleur.

immodesty [ɪˈmɒdɪstɪ] *n* -**1.** [indecency] indécence *f*, impudeur *f*. -**2.** [vanity] manque *m* de modestie, prétention *f*.

immolate [ˈɪməleɪt] *vt lit* immoler.

immoral [ɪˈmɒrəl] *adj* immoral.

immorality [ˌɪməˈrælətɪ] *n* immoralité *f*.

immorally [ɪˈmɒrəlɪ] *adv* immoralement.

immortal [ɪˈmɔːtl] ◇ *adj* immortel.
◇ *n* immortel *m*, -elle *f*.

immortality [ˌɪmɔːˈtælətɪ] *n* immortalité *f*.

immortalize, -ise [ɪˈmɔːtəlaɪz] *vt* immortaliser.

immov(e)able [ɪˈmuːvəbl] *adj* -**1.** [fixed] fixe; [impossible to move] impossible à déplacer. -**2.** [determined - person] inébranlable. -**3.** JUR: ~ property biens *mpl* immeubles OR immobiliers.
◆ **immovables** *npl* JUR biens *mpl* immobiliers.

immune [ɪˈmjuːn] *adj* -**1.** MED immunisé; ~ to measles immunisé contre la rougeole ❑ ~ serum immun-sérum *m*, antisérum *m*. -**2.** *fig*: ~ to [unaffected by] à l'abri de, immunisé contre; to be ~ to temptation/flattery être immunisé contre les tentations/la flatterie ‖ [exempt]: ~ from exempt de, exonéré de; ~ from taxation exonéré d'impôts; ~ from prosecution inviolable JUR.

immune response *n* réaction *f* immunitaire.

immune system *n* système *m* immunitaire.

immunity [ɪˈmjuːnətɪ] *n* -**1.** MED immunité *f*, résistance *f*; ~ to OR against measles immunité contre la rougeole. -**2.** [exemption]: ~ from exonération *f* de, exemption *f* de; ~ from taxation exonération d'impôts. -**3.** [diplomatic, parliamentary] immunité *f*; ~ from prosecution immunité, inviolabilité *f*.

immunization [ˌɪmjuːnaɪˈzeɪʃn] *n* immunisation *f*.

immunize, -ise [ˈɪmjuːnaɪz] *vt* immuniser, vacciner.

immunochemistry [ˌɪmjuːnəʊˈkemɪstrɪ] *n* immunochimie *f*.

immunodeficiency [ˌɪmjuːnəʊdɪˈfɪʃənsɪ] *n* immunodéficience *f*.

immunodeficient [ˌɪmjuːnəʊdɪˈfɪʃnt] *adj* immunodéficitaire.

immunodepressant [ˌɪmjuːnəʊdɪˈpresnt] *n* immunodépresseur *m*.

immunodepressive [ˌɪmjuːnəʊdɪˈpresɪv] *adj* immunodépressif.

immunogenic [ˌɪmjuːnəʊˈdʒenɪk] *adj* immunogène.

immunoglobulin [ˌɪmjuːnəʊˈglɒbjʊlɪn] *n* immunoglobuline *f*.

immunological [ˌɪmjuːnəʊˈlɒdʒɪkl] *adj* immunologique.

immunologist [ˌɪmjuːnˈɒlədʒɪst] *n* immunologiste *mf*.

immunology [ˌɪmjuːnˈɒlədʒɪ] *n* immunologie *f*.

immunopathology [ˌɪmjuːnəʊpəˈθɒlədʒɪ] *n* immunopathologie *f*.

immunoreaction [ˌɪmjuːnəʊrɪˈækʃn] *n* réaction *f* immunitaire, immunoréaction *f*.

immunosuppressant [ˌɪmjuːnəʊsəˈpresnt] ◇ *adj* immunosuppresseur.
◇ *n* immunosuppresseur *m*.

immunosuppressive [ˌɪmjuːnəʊsəˈpresɪv] *adj* immunosuppressif.

immunotherapy [ˌɪmjuːnəʊˈθerəpɪ] *n* immunothérapie *f*.

immure [ɪˈmjʊəʳ] *vt* emmurer; to ~ o.s. in silence *fig* se murer OR s'enfermer dans le silence.

immutability [ɪˌmjuːtəˈbɪlətɪ] *n* immuabilité *f*.

immutable [ɪˈmjuːtəbl] *adj* immuable.

immutably [ɪˈmjuːtəblɪ] *adv* immuablement.

imp [ɪmp] *n* [devil] lutin *m*; [child] coquin *m*, -e *f*; she's a little ~! c'est une petite coquine!, elle est très espiègle!

impact [*n* ˈɪmpækt, *vb* ɪmˈpækt] ◇ *n* -**1.** *literal* impact *m*; on ~ au moment de l'impact. -**2.** *fig* impact *m*, impression *f*; the scandal had little ~ on the election results le scandale n'a eu que peu d'impact sur les résultats de l'élection; you made OR had quite an ~ on him vous avez fait une forte impression sur lui; she made quite an ~ (at the meeting) son intervention (lors de la réunion) a été très remarquée.
◇ *vt* -**1.** [collide with] entrer en collision avec. -**2.** [influence] avoir un impact sur.
◇ *vi* -**1.** [affect]: to ~ on produire un effet sur. -**2.** COMPUT frapper.

impact adhesive *n Br* colle *f* instantanée.

impacted [ɪmˈpæktɪd] *adj* [tooth] inclus; [fracture] avec impaction.

impact printer *n* COMPUT imprimante *f* à impact.

impair [ɪmˈpeəʳ] *vt* -**1.** [weaken] diminuer, affaiblir. -**2.** [damage] détériorer, endommager.

impaired [ɪmˈpeəd] *adj* -**1.** [weakened] affaibli, diminué. -**2.** [damaged] détérioré, endommagé; ~ hearing/vision ouïe *f*/vue *f* affaiblie. -**3.** *Can*: ~ driving conduite *f* en état d'ivresse.

impairment [ɪmˈpeəmənt] *n* -**1.** [weakening] affaiblissement *m*, diminution *f*. -**2.** [damage] détérioration *f*.

impala [ɪmˈpɑːlə] *n* impala *m*.

impale [ɪmˈpeɪl] *vt* empaler; to ~ o.s. on sthg s'empaler sur qqch.

impalpable [ɪmˈpælpəbl] *adj* impalpable.

impanel [ɪm'pænl] *Am* = **empanel**.

impart [ɪm'pɑːt] *vt* -**1.** [communicate - news, truth] apprendre. -**2.** [transmit - knowledge, wisdom] transmettre. -**3.** [give - quality, flavour] donner.

impartial [ɪm'pɑːʃl] *adj* impartial.

impartiality [ɪm,pɑːʃɪ'ælətɪ] *n* impartialité *f*.

impartially [ɪm'pɑːʃəlɪ] *adv* impartialement.

impassable [ɪm'pɑːsəbl] *adj* [road] impraticable; [stream, frontier] infranchissable.

impasse [æm'pɑːs] *n* impasse *f*; **the talks have reached an ~** les pourparlers sont dans une impasse; **there's no way out of this ~** c'est une situation sans issue.

impassioned [ɪm'pæʃnd] *adj* passionné; [plea] fervent.

impassive [ɪm'pæsɪv] *adj* impassible.

impassively [ɪm'pæsɪvlɪ] *adv* impassiblement; **to look at sb/sthg ~** regarder qqn/qqch d'un air impassible.

impasto [ɪm'pæstəʊ] *n* ART empâtement *m*.

impatience [ɪm'peɪʃns] *n* -**1.** [lack of patience] impatience *f*; **with ~** avec impatience, impatiemment. -**2.** [irritation] irritation *f*; **I fully understand your ~ at the delay** je comprends parfaitement que ce retard vous irrite. -**3.** [intolerance] intolérance *f*.

impatient [ɪm'peɪʃnt] *adj* -**1.** [eager, anxious] impatient; **I'm ~ to see her again** je suis impatient de la revoir; **they were ~ for the results** ils attendaient les résultats avec impatience; **the people were ~ for reform** le peuple réclamait des réformes. -**2.** [easily irritated]: **she's ~ with her children** elle n'a aucune patience avec ses enfants; **I'm getting ~** je commence à m'impatienter OR à perdre patience. -**3.** [intolerant] intolérant; **he's ~ with people who always ask the same questions** il ne supporte pas les gens qui lui posent toujours les mêmes questions.

impatiently [ɪm'peɪʃntlɪ] *adv* impatiemment, avec impatience.

impeach [ɪm'piːtʃ] *vt* -**1.** [accuse] accuser, inculper. -**2.** ADMIN & POL [in US] entamer une procédure d'impeachment contre. -**3.** *Br fml* [doubt - motives, honesty] mettre en doute; [- character] attaquer. -**4.** JUR: **to ~ a witness** récuser un témoin.

impeachable [ɪm'piːtʃəbl] *adj* qui peut donner lieu à une procédure d'impeachment.

impeachment [ɪm'piːtʃmənt] *n* JUR [accusation] mise *f* en accusation; [in US] *mise en accusation d'un élu devant le Congrès.*

impeccable [ɪm'pekəbl] *adj* impeccable.

impeccably [ɪm'pekəblɪ] *adv* impeccablement; **~ dressed** tiré à quatre épingles.

impecunious [,ɪmpɪ'kjuːnjəs] *adj fml* nécessiteux.

impedance [ɪm'piːdəns] *n* impédance *f*.

impede [ɪm'piːd] *vt* -**1.** [obstruct - traffic, player] gêner. -**2.** [hinder - progress] ralentir; [- plan] faire obstacle à; [- person] gêner.

impediment [ɪm'pedɪmənt] *n* -**1.** [obstacle] obstacle *m*. -**2.** [handicap] défaut *m* (physique); **speech ~** défaut d'élocution. -**3.** JUR empêchement *m*.

impedimenta [ɪm,pedɪ'mentə] *npl fig* & MIL impedimenta *mpl*.

impel [ɪm'pel] (*pt* & *pp* **impelled**, *cont* **impelling**) *vt* -**1.** [urge, incite] inciter; [compel] obliger, contraindre; **I felt impelled to intervene** je me sentais obligé d'intervenir. -**2.** [propel] pousser.

impend [ɪm'pend] *vi* [be imminent] être imminent; [threaten - subj: danger] menacer.

impending [ɪm'pendɪŋ] *adj* (*before n*) imminent; **the ~ visit by the President** la visite imminente du Président; **the ~ arrival of all my relations** l'arrivée prochaine de ma famille au grand complet; **the ~ crisis** la crise imminente OR qui couve; **there was an atmosphere of ~ doom** il planait une atmosphère de désastre imminent.

impenetrable [ɪm'penɪtrəbl] *adj* -**1.** [wall, forest, fog] impénétrable; *fig* [mystery] insondable, impénétrable. -**2.** [incomprehensible - jargon, system etc] incompréhensible.

impenitence [ɪm'penɪtəns] *n* impénitence *f*.

impenitent [ɪm'penɪtənt] *adj* impénitent; **he is still utterly ~** il n'a toujours pas le moindre remords.

impenitently [ɪm'penɪtəntlɪ] *adv* avec impénitence.

imperative [ɪm'perətɪv] ◇ *adj* -**1.** [essential] (absolument) essentiel, impératif; **it's ~ that you reply immediately** il faut absolument que vous répondiez tout de suite; **it was ~ to finalize the deal** il fallait impérativement conclure l'affaire. -**2.** [categorical - orders, voice] impérieux, impératif. -**3.** GRAMM impératif.
◇ *n* impératif *m*; **in the ~** à l'impératif.

imperatively [ɪm'perətɪvlɪ] *adv* -**1.** [absolutely] impérativement. -**2.** [imperiously] impérieusement, impérativement.

imperceptible [,ɪmpə'septəbl] *adj* imperceptible; **~ to the human eye/ear** invisible/inaudible (pour l'homme).

imperceptibly [,ɪmpə'septəblɪ] *adv* imperceptiblement.

imperceptive [,ɪmpə'septɪv] *adj* peu perspicace.

imperfect [ɪm'pɜːfɪkt] ◇ *adj* -**1.** [flawed - work, argument] imparfait; [faulty - machine] défectueux; [- goods] de second choix. -**2.** [incomplete] incomplet, inachevé. -**3.** GRAMM imparfait. -**4.** JUR inapplicable (pour vice de forme).
◇ *n* GRAMM imparfait *m*; **in the ~** à l'imparfait.

imperfection [,ɪmpə'fekʃn] *n* [imperfect state] imperfection *f*; [fault] imperfection *f*, défaut *m*.

imperfective [,ɪmpə'fektɪv] ◇ *adj* imperfectif.
◇ *n* imperfectif *m*.

imperfectly [ɪm'pɜːfɪktlɪ] *adv* imparfaitement.

imperial [ɪm'pɪərɪəl] ◇ *adj* -**1.** [in titles] impérial; **His Imperial Majesty** Sa Majesté Impériale. -**2.** [majestic] majestueux, auguste. -**3.** [imperious] impérieux. -**4.** [size - of clothes] grande taille *(inv)*; [- of paper] grand format *(inv) (Br = 762 mm x 559 mm, Am = 787 mm x 584 mm)*. -**5.** *Br* [measure]: **~ pint** pinte *f* (britannique).
◇ *n* [beard] impériale *f*, barbe *f* à l'impériale.

imperial gallon *n Br* gallon *m* (britannique).

imperialism [ɪm'pɪərɪəlɪzm] *n* impérialisme *m*.

imperialist [ɪm'pɪərɪəlɪst] ◇ *adj* impérialiste.
◇ *n* impérialiste *mf*.

imperialistic [ɪm,pɪərɪəl'ɪstɪk] *adj* impérialiste.

imperially [ɪm'pɪərɪəlɪ] *adv* [majestically] majestueusement; [authoritatively] impérieusement.

imperil [ɪm'perəl] (*Br pt* & *pp* **imperilled**, *cont* **imperilling**, *Am pt* & *pp* **imperiled**, *cont* **imperiling**) *vt* mettre en péril.

imperious [ɪm'pɪərɪəs] *adj* [authoritative] impérieux, autoritaire.

imperiously [ɪm'pɪərɪəslɪ] *adv* [authoritatively] impérieusement, autoritairement.

imperishable [ɪm'perɪʃəbl] *adj* [quality, truth] impérissable; [goods] non perissable.

impermanence [ɪm'pɜːmənəns] *n* fugacité *f*.

impermanent [ɪm'pɜːmənənt] *adj* fugace.

impermeable [ɪm'pɜːmɪəbl] *adj* [soil, cell, wall] imperméable; [container] étanche.

impersonal [ɪm'pɜːsnl] *adj* -**1.** [objective] objectif. -**2.** [cold] froid, impersonnel. -**3.** GRAMM impersonnel.

impersonally [ɪm'pɜːsnəlɪ] *adv* de façon impersonnelle.

impersonate [ɪm'pɜːsəneɪt] *vt* -**1.** [imitate] imiter. -**2.** [pretend to be] se faire passer pour.

impersonation [ɪm,pɜːsə'neɪʃn] *n* -**1.** [imitation] imitation *f*. -**2.** [pretence of being] imposture *f*.

impersonator [ɪm'pɜːsəneɪtəʳ] *n* -**1.** [mimic] imitateur *m*, -trice *f*. -**2.** [impostor] imposteur *m*.

impertinence [ɪm'pɜːtɪnəns] *n* impertinence *f*.

impertinent [ɪm'pɜːtɪnənt] *adj* -**1.** [rude] impertinent, insolent; **to be ~ to sb** être impertinent envers qqn. -**2.** [irrelevant] hors de propos.

impertinently [ɪm'pɜːtɪnəntlɪ] *adv* avec impertinence.

imperturbable [,ɪmpə'tɜːbəbl] *adj* imperturbable.

imperturbably [,ɪmpə'tɜːbəblɪ] *adv* imperturbablement.

impervious [ɪm'pɜːvjəs] *adj* -**1.** [unreceptive, untouched - person] imperméable, fermé; **they are ~ to new ideas** ils sont imperméables OR inaccessibles aux idées nouvelles; **~ to criticism** imperméable à la critique; **he was ~ to her charm** il était insensible à son charme; **he remained ~ to our suggestions** il est resté sourd à nos propositions. -**2.** [resistant - material]: **~ to heat** résistant à la chaleur; **~ to water** imperméable.

impetigo [,ɪmpɪ'taɪgəʊ] *n* impétigo *m*.

impetuosity [ɪm,petjʊ'ɒsətɪ] *n* impétuosité *f*.

impetuous [ɪm'petʃʊəs] *adj* impétueux.

impetuously [ɪm'petʃʊəslɪ] *adv* avec impétuosité.

impetuousness [ɪm'petʃʊəsnɪs] = **impetuosity**.

impetus ['ɪmpɪtəs] *n* -**1.** [force] force *f* d'impulsion; [speed] élan *m*; [weight] poids *m*; **to be carried by** OR **under one's own ~** être entraîné par son propre élan OR par son propre poids. -**2.** *fig* [incentive, drive] impulsion *f*, élan *m*; **to give new ~ to sthg** donner un nouvel élan à qqch, relancer qqch.

impiety [ɪm'paɪətɪ] (*pl* **impieties**) *n* -**1.** RELIG impiété *f*. -**2.** [disrespect] irrévérence *f*.

impinge [ɪm'pɪndʒ] *vi* -**1.** [affect]: **to ~ on** OR **upon** affecter. -**2.** [encroach]: **to ~ on** OR **upon** empiéter sur; **to ~ on sb's rights/time** empiéter sur les droits/le temps de qqn.

impingement [ɪm'pɪndʒmənt] *n* empiètement *m*.

impious ['ɪmpɪəs] *adj lit* impie.

impish ['ɪmpɪʃ] *adj* espiègle, taquin, malicieux.

implacable [ɪm'plækəbl] *adj* implacable.

implacably [ɪm'plækəblɪ] *adv* implacablement.

implant [*vb* ɪm'plɑːnt, *n* 'ɪmplɑːnt] ◇ *vt* -**1.** [instil - idea, feeling] inculquer; **they tried to ~ their own beliefs in their children's minds** ils ont essayé d'inculquer leurs propres convictions à leurs enfants. -**2.** MED [graft] greffer; [place under skin] implanter.
◇ *n* [under skin] implant *m*; [graft] greffe *f*.

implausible [ɪm'plɔːzəbl] *adj* invraisemblable.

implement [*n* 'ɪmplɪmənt, *vb* 'ɪmplɪment] ◇ *n* -**1.** [tool] outil *m*; **agricultural ~s** matériel *m* agricole; **gardening ~s** outils de jardinage; **kitchen ~s** ustensiles *mpl* de cuisine. -**2.** *fig* [means] instrument *m*.
◇ *vt* [plan, orders] exécuter; [ideas, policies] appliquer, mettre en œuvre.

implementation [,ɪmplɪmen'teɪʃn] *n* [of ideas, policies] application *f*, mise *f* en œuvre; [of plan, orders] exécution *f*.

implicate ['ɪmplɪkeɪt] *vt* impliquer; **to be ~d in sthg** être impliqué dans qqch.

implication [,ɪmplɪ'keɪʃn] *n* -**1.** [possible repercussion] implication *f*; **what are the ~s of the survey?** quelles sont les implications de ce sondage?; **I don't think you understand the ~s of what you are saying** je ne suis pas sûr que vous mesuriez la portée de vos propos; **the full ~s of the report are not yet clear** il est encore trop tôt pour mesurer pleinement les implications de ce rapport. -**2.** [suggestion] suggestion *f*; [insinuation] insinuation *f*; [hidden meaning] sous-entendu *m*; **by ~** par voie de conséquence; **the ~ was that we would be punished** tout portait à croire que nous serions punis. -**3.** [involvement] implication *f*.

implicit [ɪm'plɪsɪt] *adj* -**1.** [implied] implicite; **his feelings were ~ in his words** ses paroles laissaient deviner ses sentiments. -**2.** [total - confidence, obedience] total, absolu.

implicitly [ɪm'plɪsɪtlɪ] *adv* -**1.** [by implication] implicitement. -**2.** [totally] absolument.

implied [ɪm'plaɪd] *adj* implicite, sous-entendu.

implode [ɪm'pləʊd] ◇ *vi* imploser.
◇ *vt* LING: ~d consonant consonne *f* implosive.

implore [ɪm'plɔːʳ] *vt* supplier; he ~d me to give him the money il m'a supplié de lui donner l'argent; I ~ you! je vous en supplie!

imploring [ɪm'plɔːrɪŋ] *adj* suppliant.

imploringly [ɪm'plɔːrɪŋlɪ] *adv*: he looked at me ~ il me suppliait du regard.

implosion [ɪm'pləʊʒn] *n* implosion *f.*

implosive [ɪm'pləʊsɪv] ◇ *adj* implosif.
◇ *n* implosive *f.*

imply [ɪm'plaɪ] (*pt* & *pp* implied) *vt* -**1.** [insinuate] insinuer; [give impression] laisser entendre OR supposer; are you ~ing that I'm mistaken? voulez-vous insinuer que je me trompe?; she implied that it wouldn't take long elle a laissé entendre que cela ne prendrait pas longtemps. -**2.** [presuppose] impliquer; [involve] comporter; it implies that one of them is lying cela implique OR veut dire que l'un d'eux ment; it implies a lot of hard work cela implique beaucoup de travail.

impolite [,ɪmpə'laɪt] *adj* impoli; to be ~ to sb être OR se montrer impoli envers qqn.

impolitely [,ɪmpə'laɪtlɪ] *adv* impoliment.

impoliteness [,ɪmpə'laɪtnɪs] *n* impolitesse *f.*

impolitic [ɪm'pɒlətɪk] *adj* peu OR mal avisé, maladroit.

imponderable [ɪm'pɒndrəbl] ◇ *adj* impondérable.
◇ *n* impondérable *m.*

import [*n* 'ɪmpɔːt, *vb* ɪm'pɔːt] ◇ *n* -**1.** COMM importation *f.* -**2.** [imported article] importation *f*, article *m* importé; the government has put a tax on ~s le gouvernement a instauré une taxe sur les produits d'importation OR les produits importés. -**3.** *fml* [meaning - of speech, action] signification *f*; [content] teneur *f.* -**4.** *fml* [importance] importance *f.*
◇ *vt* -**1.** COMM importer; lamb ~ed from New Zealand into Britain agneau de Nouvelle-Zélande importé en Grande-Bretagne. -**2.** [imply] signifier.
◇ *comp* [licence, surcharge] d'importation; [duty] de douane, sur les importations; [trade] des importations.

importance [ɪm'pɔːtns] *n* importance *f*; to be of ~ avoir de l'importance; it is of great ~ to act now il est très important d'agir maintenant; it's of no ~ whatsoever cela n'a aucune espèce d' importance; to give ~ to sthg attacher de l'importance à qqch; to be promoted to a position of ~ être promu à un poste important
❑ 'The Importance of Being Earnest' *Wilde* 'De l'importance d'être constant'.

important [ɪm'pɔːtnt] *adj* -**1.** [essential] important; it's not ~ ça n'a pas d'importance; it is ~ that you (should) get the job il est important que vous obteniez cet emploi OR ce boulot; it is ~ for her to know the truth il est important pour elle de connaître OR il est important qu'elle connaisse la vérité; my job is ~ to me mon travail compte beaucoup pour moi; to play an ~ part jouer un rôle important OR capital; stop trying to look ~ cesse de te donner des airs importants. -**2.** [influential]: an ~ book/writer un livre-/écrivain-clef.

importantly [ɪm'pɔːtntlɪ] *adv* d'un air important; and, more ~... et, ce qui est plus important...

importation [,ɪmpɔː'teɪʃn] *n* importation *f.*

importer [ɪm'pɔːtəʳ] *n* -**1.** [person] importateur *m*, -trice *f.* -**2.** [country] pays *m* importateur; an oil ~ un pays importateur de pétrole.

import-export *n* import-export *m*; an ~ company une société d'import-export.

importunate [ɪm'pɔːtjʊnət] *adj fml* [visitor, beggar] importun; [demands, questions] incessant.

importune [ɪm'pɔːtjuːn] *fml* ◇ *vt* -**1.** [gen] importuner, harceler; to ~ sb with questions harceler OR presser qqn de questions. -**2.** *Br* [subj: prostitute] racoler.
◇ *vi Br* [prostitute] racoler.

importunity [,ɪmpɔː'tjuːnətɪ] *n* [harassment] sollicitation *f.*

impose [ɪm'pəʊz] ◇ *vt* [price, tax, attitude, belief] imposer; [fine, penalty] infliger; to ~ a task on sb imposer une tâche à qqn; to ~ sanctions on sb infliger des sanctions à qqn; he tried to ~ his opinions on us il a essayé de nous imposer ses opinions; to ~ o.s. on sb imposer sa présence à qqn.
◇ *vi* s'imposer; I'm sorry to ~ je suis désolé de vous déranger; to ~ on sb abuser de la gentillesse de qqn; they ~ upon his hospitality ils abusent de son hospitalité.

imposing [ɪm'pəʊzɪŋ] *adj* [person, building] impressionnant; of ~ stature d'une taille imposante OR impressionnante.

imposingly [ɪm'pəʊzɪŋlɪ] *adv* d'une manière imposante.

imposition [,ɪmpə'zɪʃn] *n* -**1.** [of tax, sanction] imposition *f.* -**2.** [burden] charge *f*, fardeau *m*; I don't want to be an ~ (on you) je ne veux pas abuser de votre gentillesse OR de votre bonté. -**3.** TYPO imposition *f.* -**4.** *Br* SCH punition *f.*

impossibility [ɪm,pɒsə'bɪlətɪ] (*pl* impossibilities) *n* impossibilité *f*; it's a physical ~ for us to arrive on time nous sommes dans l'impossibilité matérielle d'arriver à l'heure; it's a total ~ c'est totalement impossible.

impossible [ɪm'pɒsəbl] ◇ *adj* -**1.** [not possible] impossible; it's ~ for me to leave work before 6 p.m. il m'est impossible de quitter mon travail avant 18 h; you make it ~ for me to be civil to you tu me mets dans l'impossibilité d'être poli envers toi; I'm afraid that's quite ~ je regrette, mais ça n'est vraiment pas possible. -**2.** [difficult to believe - story, adventure] impossible, invraisemblable; but that's ~! mais ce n'est pas possible!; it is ~ that he should be lying il est impossible qu'il mente. -**3.** [unbearable] impossible, insupportable; he's absolutely ~ il est vraiment impossible OR insupportable; he made their lives ~ il leur a rendu la vie insupportable OR impossible; you're putting me in an ~ situation vous me mettez dans une situation impossible.
◇ *n* impossible *m*; to attempt/to ask the ~ tenter/demander l'impossible.

impossibly [ɪm'pɒsəblɪ] *adv* -**1.** [extremely] extrêmement; ~ difficult extrêmement difficile; the film is ~ long le film n'en finit pas; the coach was travelling ~ slowly le car roulait incroyablement lentement. -**2.** [unbearably] insupportablement; they behave ~ ils sont totalement insupportables.

impost ['ɪmpəʊst] *n* -**1.** FIN impôt *m.* -**2.** ARCHIT imposte *f.*

impostor, imposter [ɪm'pɒstəʳ] *n* imposteur *m.*

imposture [ɪm'pɒstʃəʳ] *n fml* imposture *f.*

impotence ['ɪmpətəns] *n* [gen & MED] impuissance *f.*

impotent ['ɪmpətənt] *adj* -**1.** [powerless] faible. -**2.** [sexually] impuissant.

impound [ɪm'paʊnd] *vt* [gen] saisir; [car] mettre en fourrière.

impoverish [ɪm'pɒvərɪʃ] *vt* appauvrir.

impoverished [ɪm'pɒvərɪʃt] *adj* appauvri, très pauvre.

impoverishment [ɪm'pɒvərɪʃmənt] *n* appauvrissement *m.*

impracticable [ɪm'præktɪkəbl] *adj* [not feasible] irréalisable, impraticable.

impractical [ɪm'præktɪkl] *adj* [plan] irréaliste; [person] qui manque d'esprit pratique.

imprecation [,ɪmprɪ'keɪʃn] *n fml* imprécation *f.*

imprecise [,ɪmprɪ'saɪs] *adj* imprécis.

imprecision [,ɪmprɪ'sɪʒn] *n* imprécision *f.*

impregnable [ɪm'pregnəbl] *adj* -**1.** [fortress] imprenable. -**2.** *fig* [argument] irréfutable; his position is ~ sa position est inattaquable.

impregnate ['ɪmpregneɪt] *vt* -**1.** [fill] imprégner; ~d with water/smoke imprégné d'eau/de fumée. -**2.** *fml* [make pregnant] féconder.

impregnation [,ɪmpreg'neɪʃn] *n* -**1.** *fml* [fertilization] fécondation *f.* -**2.** [saturation] imprégnation *f.*

impresario [,ɪmprɪ'sɑːrɪəʊ] (*pl* impresarios) *n* impresario *m.*

imprescriptible [,ɪmprə'skrɪptəbl] *adj fml* imprescriptible.

impress [*vb* ɪm'pres, *n* 'ɪmpres] ◇ *vt* -**1.** [influence, affect - mind, person] faire impression sur, impressionner; I was favourably ~ed by her appearance son apparence m'a fait bonne impression; I'm not in the least ~ed ça ne m'impressionne pas du tout; he ~ed the jury il a fait une forte impression sur le jury; I wasn't ~ed by her friend son ami ne m'a pas fait grande impression. -**2.** to ~ sthg on sb [make understand] faire comprendre qqch à qqn. -**3.** [print] imprimer, marquer; the clay was ~ed with a design, a design was ~ed onto the clay un motif était imprimé dans l'argile; her words are ~ed on my memory *fig* ses paroles sont gravées dans ma mémoire.
◇ *n* empreinte *f.*

impression [ɪm'preʃn] *n* -**1.** [impact - on person, mind, feelings] impression *f*; he made a strong ~ on them il leur a fait une forte impression; he always tries to make an ~ il essaie toujours d'impressionner les gens; my words made no ~ on him whatsoever mes paroles n'ont eu absolument aucun effet sur lui; they got a good ~ of my brother mon frère leur a fait bonne impression. -**2.** [idea, thought] impression *f*; you should never trust first ~s il ne faut pas se fier aux premières impressions; it's my ~ OR I have the ~ that she's rather annoyed with us j'ai l'impression qu'elle est en colère contre nous; what were your ~s of Tokyo? quelles ont été vos impressions de Tokyo?; I was under the ~ that you were unable to come j'étais persuadé que vous ne pouviez pas venir. -**3.** [mark, imprint] marque *f*, empreinte *f.* -**4.** [printing] impression *f*; [edition] tirage *m.* -**5.** [impersonation] imitation *f*; to do ~s faire des imitations; she does a very good ~ of the Queen elle imite très bien la reine.

impressionable [ɪm'preʃnəbl] *adj* impressionnable; he is at a very ~ age il est à l'âge où on se laisse facilement impressionner; an ~ young man un jeune homme impressionnable.

Impressionism [ɪm'preʃənɪzm] *n* ART & LITERAT impressionnisme *m.*

impressionist [ɪm'preʃənɪst] *n* [entertainer] imitateur *m*, -trice *f*; ART & LITERAT impressionniste.
◆ **Impressionist** ◇ *n* impressionniste *mf.*
◇ *adj* impressionniste.

impressionistic [ɪm,preʃə'nɪstɪk] *adj* [vague] vague, imprécis.

impressive [ɪm'presɪv] *adj* impressionnant.

impressively [ɪm'presɪvlɪ] *adv* remarquablement.

imprimatur [,ɪmprɪ'meɪtəʳ] *n* imprimatur *m inv.*

imprint [*n* 'ɪmprɪnt, *vb* ɪm'prɪnt] ◇ *n* -**1.** [mark] empreinte *f*, marque *f*; the ~ of a hand l'empreinte d'une main; the ~ of suffering on her face les marques de la souffrance sur son visage; the war had left its ~ on all of us la guerre nous avait tous marqués. -**2.** TYPO [name]: published under the Larousse ~ édité chez Larousse. -**3.** [design] logo *m.*
◇ *vt* -**1.** [print] imprimer. -**2.** [in sand, clay, mud] imprimer; to be ~ed in être imprimé dans. -**3.** *fig* [fix] implanter, graver; her face was ~ed on my mind son visage est resté gravé dans mon esprit.

imprinting [ɪm'prɪntɪŋ] *n* ZOOL empreinte *f.*

imprison [ɪm'prɪzn] *vt* -**1.** [put in prison] mettre en prison, incarcérer; he has been ~ed several times il a fait plusieurs séjours en prison. -**2.** [sentence] condamner; she was ~ed for 15 years elle a été condamnée à 15 ans de prison OR de réclusion criminelle.

imprisonment [ɪm'prɪznmənt] *n* emprisonnement *m*; to be sentenced to six months'

~ être condamné à six mois de prison ❑ a sentence of life ~ une condamnation à perpétuité OR à vie.

improbability [ɪm,prɒbə'bɪlətɪ] (*pl* improbabilities) *n* -**1.** [of event] improbabilité *f*. -**2.** [of story] invraisemblance *f*.

improbable [ɪm'prɒbəbl] *adj* -**1.** [unlikely] improbable; **I think it highly ~ that he ever came here** il me paraît fort peu probable qu'il soit jamais venu ici. -**2.** [hard to believe] invraisemblable; **an ~ story** une histoire invraisemblable.

improbably [ɪm'prɒbəblɪ] *adv* invraisemblablement.

impromptu [ɪm'prɒmptjuː] ◇ *adj* impromptu; **an ~ speech** un discours improvisé. ◇ *adv* impromptu; **to speak ~** *Br* parler impromptu.
◇ *n* impromptu *m*.

improper [ɪm'prɒpəʳ] *adj* -**1.** [rude, shocking - words, action] déplacé; **his behaviour was most ~** il a eu un comportement tout à fait déplacé; **to make ~ suggestions (to sb)** faire des propositions malhonnêtes (à qqn). -**2.** [unsuitable] peu convenable. -**3.** [dishonest] malhonnête. -**4.** [incorrect - method, equipment] mauvais, inadéquat.

improperly [ɪm'prɒpəlɪ] *adv* -**1.** [indecently] de manière déplacée; **he behaved most ~** il s'est comporté d'une manière tout à fait déplacée. -**2.** [unsuitably]: **he was ~ dressed** il n'était pas habillé comme il faut. -**3.** [dishonestly] malhonnêtement. -**4.** [incorrectly] incorrectement, de manière incorrecte.

impropriety [ɪmprə'praɪətɪ] (*pl* improprieties) *n* -**1.** [of behaviour] inconvenance *f*; **to commit an ~** commettre une indélicatesse. -**2.** [of language] impropriété *f*.

improvable [ɪm'pruːvəbl] *adj* perfectible.

improve [ɪm'pruːv] ◇ *vt* -**1.** [make better - work, facilities, result] améliorer; **to ~ one's chances** augmenter ses chances; **if you cut your hair it would ~ your looks** tu serais mieux avec les cheveux plus courts; **a little basil will greatly ~ the flavour** ce sera nettement meilleur avec un peu de basilic; **she's gone to Madrid to ~ her Spanish** elle est allée à Madrid pour améliorer son espagnol. -**2.** [increase - knowledge, productivity] accroître, augmenter. -**3.** [cultivate]: **to ~ one's mind** se cultiver l'esprit; **reading ~s the mind** on se cultive en lisant.
◇ *vi* [get better] s'améliorer; [increase] augmenter; [make progress] s'améliorer, faire des progrès; **her health is improving** son état (de santé) s'améliore; **business is improving** les affaires reprennent; **your maths has ~d** vous avez fait des progrès en maths; **to ~ with age/use** s'améliorer en vieillissant/à l'usage; **he ~s on acquaintance** il gagne à être connu.
◆ **improve on, improve upon** *vt insep* -**1.** [result, work] améliorer; **it's difficult to see how the performance can be ~d on** il semble difficile d'améliorer cette performance. -**2.** [offer]: **to ~ on sb's offer** enchérir sur qqn.

improved [ɪm'pruːvd] *adj* [gen] amélioré; [services] amélioré, meilleur; [offer, performance] meilleur.

improvement [ɪm'pruːvmənt] *n* -**1.** amélioration *f*; [in person's work, performance] progrès *m*; **what an ~!** c'est nettement mieux!; **this is a great ~ on her previous work** c'est bien mieux que ce qu'elle faisait jusqu'à présent; **there has been some ~** il y a un léger mieux; **there has been a slight ~ in his work** son travail s'est légèrement amélioré; **there is no ~ in the weather** le temps ne s'est pas arrangé; **to show some ~** [in condition] aller un peu mieux; [in work] faire quelques progrès; **there's room for ~** on peut faire mieux. -**2.** [in building, road etc] rénovation *f*, aménagement *m*; (home) **~s** travaux *mpl* de rénovation; **to carry out ~s** effectuer des travaux de rénovation; **motorway ~s** travaux de réfection des autoroutes.

improvidence [ɪm'prɒvɪdəns] *n fml* imprévoyance *f*.

improvident [ɪm'prɒvɪdənt] *adj fml* [thriftless] dépensier; [heedless - person] imprévoyant; [- life] insouciant.

improvidently [ɪm'prɒvɪdəntlɪ] *adv fml* [thriftlessly] dispendieusement; [heedlessly] avec imprévoyance.

improvisation [,ɪmprəvaɪ'zeɪʃn] *n* improvisation *f*.

improvise ['ɪmprəvaɪz] *vt* & *vi* improviser.

imprudence [ɪm'pruːdəns] *n* imprudence *f*.

imprudent [ɪm'pruːdənt] *adj* imprudent.

imprudently [ɪm'pruːdəntlɪ] *adv* imprudemment.

impudence ['ɪmpjʊdəns] *n* effronterie *f*, impudence *f*.

impudent ['ɪmpjʊdənt] *adj* effronté, impudent; **he is ~ to his teachers** il est effronté avec ses professeurs.

impudently ['ɪmpjʊdəntlɪ] *adv* effrontément, impudemment.

impugn [ɪm'pjuːn] *vt fml* contester.

impulse ['ɪmpʌls] *n* -**1.** [desire, instinct] impulsion *f*, besoin *m*, envie *f*; **I felt an irresistible ~ to hit him** j'ai éprouvé une irrésistible envie de le frapper; **to act on ~** agir par impulsion; **I bought it on ~** je l'ai acheté sur un coup de tête; **I'm sorry, I did it on ~** je m'excuse, je l'ai fait sans réfléchir; **on a sudden ~, he kissed her** pris d'une envie irrésistible, il l'a embrassée. -**2.** *fml* [impetus] impulsion *f*, poussée *f*; **government grants have given an ~ to trade** les subventions gouvernementales ont relancé les affaires. -**3.** ELEC & PHYSIOL impulsion *f*.

impulse buy *n* achat *m* impulsif.

impulse buyer *n* acheteur *m* impulsif, acheteuse *f* impulsive.

impulse buying *n (U)* achats *mpl* impulsifs.

impulsion [ɪm'pʌlʃn] *n* impulsion *f*.

impulsive [ɪm'pʌlsɪv] *adj* -**1.** [instinctive, spontaneous] impulsif; [thoughtless] irréfléchi. -**2.** [force] impulsif.

impulsively [ɪm'pʌlsɪvlɪ] *adv* par OR sur impulsion, impulsivement; **he kissed her ~** pris d'une envie irrésistible, il l'embrassa; **I acted ~** j'ai agi par impulsion.

impulsiveness [ɪm'pʌlsɪvnɪs] *n* caractère *m* impulsif.

impunity [ɪm'pjuːnətɪ] *n fml* impunité *f*; **to act with ~** agir en toute impunité OR impunément.

impure [ɪm'pjʊəʳ] *adj* -**1.** [unclean - air, milk] impur. -**2.** *lit* [sinful - thought] impur, mauvais; [- motive] bas. -**3.** ARCHIT [style] bâtard.

impurity [ɪm'pjʊərətɪ] (*pl* impurities) *n* impureté *f*.

imputable [ɪm'pjuːtəbl] *adj* imputable.

imputation [,ɪmpjuː'teɪʃn] *n fml* -**1.** [attribution] attribution *f*. -**2.** [accusation] imputation *f*.

impute [ɪm'pjuːt] *vt fml* [attribute] imputer, attribuer; **the blame must be ~d to them** la responsabilité leur en revient.

in [ɪn] ◇ *prep* **A.** -**1.** [within a defined area or space] dans; **in a box** dans une boîte; **what have you got in your pockets?** qu'est-ce que tu as dans tes poches?; **she was sitting in an armchair** elle était assise dans un fauteuil; **in the house** dans la maison; **in Catherine's house** chez Catherine; **they're playing in the garden/living room/street** ils jouent dans le jardin/le salon/la rue; **we live in a village** nous habitons un village; **he's still in bed/in the bath** il est encore au lit/dans son bain; **she shut herself up in her bedroom** elle s'est enfermée dans sa chambre; **the light's gone in the fridge** la lumière du réfrigérateur ne marche plus. -**2.** [within an undefined area or space] dans; **she trailed her hand in the water** elle laissait traîner sa main dans l'eau; **there's a smell of spring in the air** ça sent le printemps; **we swam in the sea** nous nous sommes baignés dans la mer. -**3.** [indicating movement] dans; **put it in your pocket** mets-le dans ta poche; **throw the letter in the bin** jette la lettre à la poubelle; **we headed in the direction of the port** nous nous sommes dirigés vers le port. -**4.** [contained by a part of the body] dans; **he had a knife in his hand** il avait un couteau dans OR à la main; **she held her tight in her arms** elle la serrait dans ses bras; **with tears in his eyes** les larmes aux yeux. -**5.** [on or behind a surface] dans; **a hole in the wall** un trou dans le mur; **there were deep cuts in the surface** la surface était marquée de profondes entailles; **a reflection in the mirror** un reflet dans la glace; **how much is that pullover in the window?** combien coûte ce pull dans la vitrine?; **who's that man in the photo?** qui est cet homme sur la photo? -**6.** [in a specified institution]: **she's in hospital/in prison** elle est à l'hôpital/en prison; **he teaches in a language school** il enseigne dans une école de langues. -**7.** [with geographical names]: **in Paris** à Paris; **in France** en France; **in Afghanistan** en Afghanistan; **in the States** aux États-Unis; **in Portugal** au Portugal; **in the Pacific** dans l'océan Pacifique; **in the Third World** dans les pays du tiers-monde. -**8.** [wearing] en; **he was in a suit** il était en costume; **she was still in her dressing gown** elle était encore en robe de chambre; **he always dresses in green** il s'habille toujours en vert; **who's that woman in the hat?** qui est la femme avec le OR au chapeau?; **in uniform/mourning** en uniforme/deuil. -**9.** [covered by]: **sardines in tomato sauce** des sardines à la sauce tomate; **we were up to our waists in mud** nous étions dans la boue jusqu'à la taille.
B. -**1.** [during a specified period of time] en; **in 1992** en 1992; **in March** en mars, au mois de mars; **in (the) summer/autumn/winter** en été/automne/hiver; **in (the) spring** au printemps; **he doesn't work in the afternoon/morning** il ne travaille pas l'après-midi/le matin; **I'll come in the afternoon/morning** je viendrai l'après-midi/le matin; **at 5 o'clock in the afternoon/morning** à 5 h de l'après-midi/du matin; **in the future** un jour; **in the past** autrefois. -**2.** [within a specified period of time] en; **he cooked the meal in ten minutes** il prépara le repas en dix minutes. -**3.** [after a specified period of time] dans; **I'll be back in five minutes** je reviens dans cinq minutes, j'en ai pour cinq minutes. -**4.** [indicating a long period of time]: **we haven't had a proper talk in ages** nous n'avons pas eu de véritable conversation depuis très longtemps; **I hadn't seen her in years** ça faisait des années que je ne l'avais pas vue. -**5.** [during a specified temporary situation]: **in my absence** en OR pendant mon absence; **in the ensuing chaos** OR **confusion** dans la confusion qui s'ensuivit.
C. -**1.** [indicating arrangement, shape] en; **in five rows/parts** en cinq rangées/parties; **stand in a ring** mettez-vous en cercle; **cut the cake in three/in half** coupe le gâteau en trois/en deux; **she had her hair up in a ponytail** ses cheveux étaient relevés en queue de cheval. -**2.** [indicating form, method]: **in cash** en liquide; **in English/French/code** en anglais/français/code; **written in ink** écrit à l'encre. -**3.** [indicating state of mind]: **she's in a bit of a state** elle est dans tous ses états; **to be in love/in despair** être amoureux/désespéré; **don't keep us in suspense** ne nous tiens pas en haleine plus longtemps; **he watched in wonderment** il regardait avec émerveillement. -**4.** [indicating state, situation] dans, en; **in the present circumstances** dans les circonstances actuelles; **in the dark** dans l'obscurité; **in this weather** par OR avec ce temps; **in the sun** au soleil; **in the rain/snow** sous la pluie/neige; **in danger/silence** en danger/silence; **in my presence** en ma présence; **she's got her leg in plaster** elle a une jambe plâtrée OR dans le plâtre. -**5.** [referring to plants and animals]: **in blossom** en fleur OR fleurs; **in pup/calf/cub** plein; **in heat** *Am* en chaleur. -**6.** [among] chez; **a disease common in five-year-olds** une maladie très répandue chez les enfants de cinq ans; **the sense of smell is more developed in dogs** l'odorat est plus développé chez les chiens.
D. -**1.** [forming part of] dans; **in chapter six** dans le chapitre six; **we were standing in a queue**

nous faisions la queue; **she's appearing in his new play/film** elle joue dans sa nouvelle pièce/son nouveau film; **he has two Picassos in his collection** il a deux Picasso dans sa collection; **the best player in the team** le meilleur joueur de l'équipe; **how many feet are there in a metre?** combien de pieds y a-t-il dans un mètre?; **service is included in the charge** le service est inclus dans le prix. **-2.** [indicating a personality trait]: **she hasn't got it in her to be nasty** elle est bien incapable de méchanceté; **it's the Irish in me** c'est mon côté irlandais. **-3.** [indicating feelings about a person or thing]: **she has no confidence in him** elle n'a aucune confiance en lui; **they showed no interest in my work** mon travail n'a pas eu l'air de les intéresser le moins du monde. **-4.** [according to]: **in my opinion** OR **view** à mon avis.

E. -1. [indicating purpose, cause]: **he charged the door in an effort to get free** dans un effort pour se libérer, il donna un grand coup dans la porte; **in reply** OR **response to your letter...** en réponse à votre lettre...; **there's no point in complaining** il est inutile de OR ça ne sert à rien de se plaindre. **-2.** [as a result of] en; **in doing so, you only encourage him** en faisant cela, vous ne faites que l'encourager; **in attempting to save her son's life, she almost died** en essayant de sauver son fils, elle a failli mourir. **-3.** [as regards]: **it's five feet in length** ça fait cinq pieds de long; **the town has grown considerably in size** la ville s'est beaucoup agrandie; **a change in direction** un changement de direction; **he's behind in maths** il ne suit pas en maths; **spinach is rich in iron** les épinards sont riches en fer; **we've found the ideal candidate in Richard** nous avons trouvé en Richard le candidat idéal. **-4.** [indicating source of discomfort]: **I've got a pain in my arm** j'ai une douleur au OR dans le bras.

F. -1. [indicating specified field, sphere of activity] dans; **to be in the army/navy** être dans l'armée/la marine; **she's in advertising** elle est dans la publicité; **he's in business with his sister** il dirige une entreprise avec sa sœur; **there have been tremendous advances in the treatment of cancer** de grands progrès ont été faits dans le traitement du cancer; **a degree in Italian and French** un diplôme d'italien et de français. **-2.** [indicating activity engaged in]: **our days were spent in swimming and sailing** nous passions nos journées à nager et à faire de la voile; **they spent hours (engaged) in complex negotiations** ils ont passé des heures en négociations difficiles; **you took your time in getting here!** tu en as mis du temps à venir!

G. -1. [indicating approximate number, amount]: **people arrived in droves/in dribs and drabs** les gens sont arrivés en foule/par petits groupes; **they came in their thousands** ils sont venus par milliers; **he's in his forties** il a la quarantaine. **-2.** [in ratios] sur; **one child in three** un enfant sur trois; **a one-in-five hill** une pente de 20 %.

◇ *adv* **A. -1.** [into an enclosed space] à l'intérieur, dedans; **she opened the door and looked in** elle ouvrit la porte et regarda à l'intérieur; **he jumped in** il sauta dedans. **-2.** [indicating movement from outside to inside]: **breathe in then out** inspirez puis expirez; **we can't take in any more refugees** nous ne pouvons pas accueillir plus de réfugiés; **she's been in and out of mental hospitals all her life** elle a passé presque toute sa vie dans des hôpitaux psychiatriques. **-3.** [at home or place of work]: **is your wife/the boss in?** est-ce que votre femme/le patron est là?; **it's nice to spend an evening in** c'est agréable de passer une soirée chez soi; **to eat/to stay in** manger/rester à la maison; **he usually comes in about 10 o'clock** en général, il est là vers 10 h.

B. -1. [indicating entry]: **to go in** entrer; **come in!** entrez!; **to saunter/to run in** entrer d'un pas nonchalant/en courant; **in we go!** on y va! **-2.** [indicating arrival]: **the bus isn't in yet** le bus n'est pas encore arrivé; **what time does your train get in?** quand est-ce que votre train arrive? **-3.** [towards the centre]: **the walls fell in** les murs se sont écroulés; **the edges bend in** le bord est recourbé. **-4.** [towards the shore]: **the tide is in** la marée est haute.

C. -1. [indicating transmission]: **write in for further information** écrivez-nous pour plus de renseignements; **entries must be in by May 1st** les bulletins doivent nous parvenir avant le 1er mai; **offers of help poured in** les propositions d'aide sont arrivées en masse. **-2.** [indicating participation, addition]: **we asked if we could join in** nous avons demandé si nous pouvions participer; **stir in the chopped onions** ajouter les oignons en lamelles; **fill in the blanks** remplissez les espaces vides.

D. -1. SPORT [within area of court]: **the umpire said that the ball was in** l'arbitre a dit que la balle était bonne. **-2.** [in cricket] à l'attaque; **the other side went in first** c'est l'autre équipe qui était d'abord à l'attaque.

E. -1. POL [elected]: **he failed to get in at the last election** il n'a pas été élu aux dernières élections. **-2.** [in fashion] à la mode; **short skirts are coming back in** les jupes courtes reviennent à la mode.

F. *phr*: to be in for sthg: **you're in for a bit of a disappointment** tu vas être déçu; **he's in for a surprise/shock** il va avoir une surprise/un choc; **they don't know what they're in for** *inf* ils ne savent pas ce qui les attend; **now he's really in for it** *inf* cette fois-ci, il va y avoir droit; **to be in on sthg** *inf* [involved] être dans le coup; [informed] être au courant; **we were all in on the plot** on était tous au courant; **I wasn't in on that particular conversation** je n'étais pas là pendant cette conversation; **to be in with sb** *inf* être en bons termes avec qqn; **he's trying to get in with the boss** il essaie de se faire bien voir du patron.

◇ *adj* **-1.** [fashionable] à la mode, branché; **that nightclub is very in** cette boîte est très à la mode; **it's the in place to go** c'est l'endroit branché du moment; **to be the in thing** être à la mode. **-2.** [for a select few]: **it's an in joke** c'est une plaisanterie entre nous/elles *etc*.

◆ **ins** *npl*: **the ins and outs (of an affair/of a situation)** les tenants et les aboutissants (d'une affaire/d'une situation).

◆ **in all** *adv phr* en tout; **there are 30 in all** il y en a 30 en tout.

◆ **in between** ◇ *adv phr* **-1.** [in intermediate position]: **a row of bushes with little clumps of flowers in between** une rangée d'arbustes séparés par des petites touffes de fleurs; **he's neither right nor left but somewhere in between** il n'est ni de droite ni de gauche mais quelque part entre les deux; **she either plays very well or very badly, never in between** elle joue très bien ou très mal, jamais entre les deux. **-2.** [in time] entretemps, dans l'intervalle.
◇ *prep phr* entre.

◆ **in itself** *adv phr* en soi; **the town is not in itself beautiful but it has style** la ville n'est pas belle en soi mais elle a de l'allure; **this was in itself an achievement** c'était déjà un exploit en soi.

◆ **in that** *conj phr* puisque; **I'm not badly off in that I have a job and a flat but...** je ne peux pas me plaindre puisque j'ai un emploi et un appartement mais...; **we are lucky in that there are only a few of us** nous avons de la chance d'être si peu nombreux.

-in *in cpds exprime l'aspect collectif d'une activité*; **love-in** célébration *f* de l'amour en commun.

in- *in cpds*: **in-car** installé dans la voiture; **in-flight** pendant le vol; **in-house** interne.

in. *written abbr of* inch(es).

IN *written abbr of* Indiana.

inability [ˌɪnəˈbɪlətɪ] *n* incapacité *f*; **our ~ to help them** notre incapacité à les aider.

in absentia [ˌɪnæbˈsentɪə] *adv* in absentia; JUR par contumace.

inaccessibility [ˈɪnəkˌsesɪˈbɪlətɪ] *n* inaccessibilité *f*.

inaccessible [ˌɪnəkˈsesəbl] *adj* **-1.** [impossible to reach] inaccessible; **the ~ parts of Antarctica** les régions inaccessibles de l'Antarctique; **the village is ~ by car** le village n'est pas accessible en voiture. **-2.** [unavailable – person] inaccessible, inabordable; [– information] inaccessible. **-3.** [obscure – film, book, music] inaccessible, incompréhensible.

inaccuracy [ɪnˈækjʊrəsɪ] (*pl* **inaccuracies**) *n* [of translation, calculation, information] inexactitude *f*; [of word, expression] inexactitude *f*, impropriété *f*.

inaccurate [ɪnˈækjʊrət] *adj* [incorrect – figures] inexact; [– term] impropre; [– result] erroné; [– description] inexact.

inaccurately [ɪnˈækjʊrətlɪ] *adv* inexactement; **the events have been ~ reported** les événements ont été présentés de façon inexacte.

inaction [ɪnˈækʃn] *n* inaction *f*.

inactivate [ɪnˈæktɪveɪt] *vt* rendre inactif, désactiver.

inactive [ɪnˈæktɪv] *adj* **-1.** [person, animal – resting] inactif, peu actif; [– not working] inactif. **-2.** [lazy] paresseux, oisif. **-3.** [inoperative – machine] au repos, à l'arrêt. **-4.** [dormant – volcano] qui n'est pas en activité; [– disease, virus] inactif. **-5.** CHEM & PHYS inerte.

inactivity [ˌɪnækˈtɪvətɪ] *n* inactivité *f*, inaction *f*.

inadequacy [ɪnˈædɪkwəsɪ] (*pl* **inadequacies**) *n* **-1.** [of resources, facilities] insuffisance *f*. **-2.** [social] incapacité *f*, inadaptation *f*; [sexual] impuissance *f*, incapacité *f*; **feelings of ~** un sentiment d'impuissance. **-3.** [failing] défaut *m*, faiblesse *f*.

inadequate [ɪnˈædɪkwət] *adj* **-1.** [insufficient] insuffisant; **our resources are ~ to meet our needs** nos ressources ne correspondent pas à nos besoins. **-2.** [unsatisfactory] médiocre; **his performance in the test was ~** il n'a pas bien réussi son examen; **their response to the problem was ~** ils n'ont pas su trouver de réponse satisfaisante au problème. **-3.** [unsuitable – equipment] inadéquat; **our machinery is ~ for this type of work** notre outillage n'est pas adapté à ce genre de travail. **-4.** [incapable] incapable; [sexually] impuissant; **he's hopelessly ~ for the job** il n'est vraiment pas fait pour ce travail; **being unemployed often makes people feel ~** les gens au chômage se sentent souvent inutiles; **he's socially ~** c'est un inadapté.

inadequately [ɪnˈædɪkwətlɪ] *adv* de manière inadéquate; [fund, invest] insuffisamment.

inadmissible [ˌɪnədˈmɪsəbl] *adj* inacceptable; **~ evidence** JUR témoignage *m* irrecevable.

inadvertence [ˌɪnədˈvɜːtəns] *n* manque *m* d'attention, étourderie *f*, inadvertance *f*; **by ~** par mégarde OR inadvertance.

inadvertent [ˌɪnədˈvɜːtnt] *adj* **-1.** [not deliberate] accidentel, involontaire. **-2.** [careless]: **an ~ error** une erreur commise par inadvertance.

inadvertently [ˌɪnədˈvɜːtəntlɪ] *adv* par mégarde OR inadvertance.

inadvisability [ˈɪnədˌvaɪzəˈbɪlətɪ] *n* inopportunité *f*.

inadvisable [ˌɪnədˈvaɪzəbl] *adj* déconseillé; **this plan is ~** ce projet est à déconseiller; **it's ~ to invest all your money in one place** il est déconseillé d'investir tout son argent dans une seule entreprise.

inalienable [ɪnˈeɪljənəbl] *adj* inaliénable.

inamorata [ɪnˌæməˈrɑːtə] *n lit* OR *hum* amoureuse *f*.

inamorato [ɪnˌæməˈrɑːtəʊ] *n lit* OR *hum* amoureux *m*.

inane [ɪˈneɪn] *adj* [person] idiot, imbécile; [behaviour] stupide, inepte; [remark] idiot, stupide, inepte.

inanely [ɪˈneɪnlɪ] *adv* de façon idiote OR stupide OR inepte.

inanimate [ɪnˈænɪmət] *adj* inanimé.

inanition [ˌɪnəˈnɪʃn] *n* **-1.** [debility] inanition *f*. **-2.** [lethargy] léthargie *f*, torpeur *f*.

inanity [ɪˈnænətɪ] (*pl* **inanities**) *n* **-1.** [stupidity] stupidité *f*. **-2.** [stupid remark] ineptie *f*, bêtise *f*.

inapplicable [ˌɪnəˈplɪkəbl] *adj* inapplicable; **the rule is ~ to this case** dans ce cas, la règle ne s'applique pas.

inapposite [ɪnˈæpəzɪt] *adj* inopportun, inapproprié.

inappropriate [ˌɪnəˈprəʊprɪət] *adj* [unsuitable - action, remark] inopportun, mal à propos; [- time, moment] inopportun; [- clothing, equipment] peu approprié, inadéquat; [- name] mal choisi; **you've come at an ~ time** vous arrivez au mauvais moment, vous tombez mal; **principles which are ~ to modern life** des principes qui ne sont pas adaptés à la vie moderne.

inappropriately [ˌɪnəˈprəʊprɪətlɪ] *adv* de manière peu convenable OR appropriée; **she was ~ dressed** elle n'était pas vêtue pour la circonstance.

inapt [ɪnˈæpt] *adj* **-1.** [unsuitable - remark] mal choisi; [- behaviour] peu convenable. **-2.** [incapable] inapte, incapable.

inaptitude [ɪnˈæptɪtjuːd] *n* **-1.** [unsuitability - of remark] manque *m* d'à-propos; [- of dress, behaviour] inconvenance *f*. **-2.** [incapability] incapacité *f*, inaptitude *f*.

inarticulate [ˌɪnɑːˈtɪkjʊlət] *adj* **-1.** [person] qui bredouille; **an ~ old man** un vieil homme qui a du mal à s'exprimer; **to be ~ with fear/rage** bégayer de peur/de rage; **his ~ suffering** la souffrance qu'il ne pouvait exprimer. **-2.** [words, sounds] indistinct; **~ expressions of love** des mots d'amour bredouillés. **-3.** ANAT & BIOL inarticulé.

inarticulately [ˌɪnɑːˈtɪkjʊlətlɪ] *adv* [express o.s.] de manière confuse OR peu claire; [mumble] de façon indistincte, indistinctement.

inartistic [ˌɪnɑːˈtɪstɪk] *adj* **-1.** [painting, drawing etc] dénué de toute valeur artistique. **-2.** [person - lacking artistic taste] sans goût artistique; [- unskilled] sans talent.

inasmuch as [ˌɪnəzˈmʌtʃ-] *conj fml* [given that] étant donné que, vu que; [insofar as] dans la mesure où.

inattention [ˌɪnəˈtenʃn] *n* manque *m* d'attention, inattention *f*; **your essay shows ~ to detail** il y a beaucoup d'erreurs de détail dans votre travail.

inattentive [ˌɪnəˈtentɪv] *adj* **-1.** [paying no attention] inattentif. **-2.** [neglectful] peu attentionné, négligent; **to be ~ towards sb** être peu attentionné envers qqn, négliger qqn.

inattentively [ˌɪnəˈtentɪvlɪ] *adv* sans prêter OR faire attention.

inaudible [ɪˈnɔːdɪbl] *adj* inaudible; **she spoke in an almost ~ whisper** elle s'exprimait de façon presque inaudible.

inaudibly [ɪˈnɔːdɪblɪ] *adv* indistinctement; **"yes" she answered ~** «oui» répondit-elle d'une voix inaudible.

inaugural [ɪˈnɔːgjʊrəl] ◇ *adj* inaugural, d'inauguration.
◇ *n Am* discours *m* inaugural *(d'un président des États-Unis)*.

inaugurate [ɪˈnɔːgjʊreɪt] *vt* **-1.** [open ceremoniously] inaugurer. **-2.** [commence formally] inaugurer; **to ~ a new policy** instaurer OR inaugurer une nouvelle politique. **-3.** [herald - era] inaugurer. **-4.** [instate - official] installer (dans ses fonctions), investir; [- king, bishop] introniser.

inauguration [ɪˌnɔːgjʊˈreɪʃn] *n* **-1.** [of building] inauguration *f*, cérémonie *f* d'ouverture; [of policy, era etc] inauguration. **-2.** [of official] investiture *f*.

Inauguration Day *n jour de l'investiture du président des États-Unis (le 20 janvier)*.

inauspicious [ˌɪnɔːˈspɪʃəs] *adj* défavorable, peu propice; **things got off to an ~ start** les choses ont pris un mauvais départ; **an ~ event** un événement de mauvais augure OR de sinistre présage.

inauspiciously [ˌɪnɔːˈspɪʃəslɪ] *adv* défavorablement; **to start ~** prendre un mauvais départ.

in-between *adj* intermédiaire.

inboard [ˈɪnbɔːd] *adj* NAUT: **~ motor** en-bord *m inv*.

inborn [ˌɪnˈbɔːn] *adj* [characteristic, quality] inné; MED congénital, héréditaire.

inbred [ˌɪnˈbred] *adj* **-1.** [characteristic, quality] inné; **their hatred of violence is ~** leur horreur de la violence est innée. **-2.** BIOL [trait] acquis par sélection génétique; [strain] produit par le croisement d'individus consanguins; [person] de parents consanguins; [family, group] consanguin.

inbreeding [ˌɪnˈbriːdɪŋ] *n* croisement *m* d'individus ayant les mêmes caractères génétiques; **generations of ~** des générations d'alliances consanguines.

in-built *adj* **-1.** [device] incorporé, intégré. **-2.** [quality, defect] inhérent.

inc. (*written abbr of* **inclusive**): **12-15 April ~** du 12 au 15 avril inclus.

Inc. (*written abbr of* **incorporated**) *Am* ≃ SARL.

Inca [ˈɪŋkə] (*pl inv* OR **Incas**) *n* Inca *mf*.

incalculable [ɪnˈkælkjʊləbl] *adj* incalculable.

in camera [ˌɪnˈkæmərə] *adj* & *adv fml* à huis clos; **'In Camera'** *Sartre* 'Huis clos'.

incandescence [ˌɪnkænˈdesns] *n* incandescence *f*.

incandescent [ˌɪnkænˈdesnt] *adj* incandescent.

incandescent lamp *n* lampe *f* à incandescence.

incantation [ˌɪnkænˈteɪʃn] *n* incantation *f*.

incapability [ɪnˌkeɪpəˈbɪlətɪ] *n* incapacité *f*.

incapable [ɪnˈkeɪpəbl] *adj* **-1.** [unable] incapable; **he's ~ of showing emotion** il est incapable de montrer ce qu'il ressent; **she's ~ of such an act** elle est incapable de faire une chose pareille; **he's ~ of speech** il ne peut pas parler; **feelings ~ of expression** *lit* des sentiments impossibles à exprimer. **-2.** [incompetent] incapable; **to be declared ~** JUR être déclaré incapable, être frappé d'incapacité juridique.

incapacitant [ˌɪnkəˈpæsɪtənt] *n* incapacitant *m*.

incapacitate [ˌɪnkəˈpæsɪteɪt] *vt* **-1.** [cripple] rendre infirme OR invalide; **he was temporarily ~d by the accident** à la suite de l'accident, il a été temporairement immobilisé. **-2.** JUR frapper d'incapacité légale.

incapacity [ˌɪnkəˈpæsətɪ] (*pl* **incapacities**) *n* [gen & JUR] incapacité *f*; **his ~ for work** son incapacité à travailler; **her ~ to adapt** son incapacité à s'adapter.

in-car *adj* AUT: **~ stereo** autoradio *f* (à cassette).

incarcerate [ɪnˈkɑːsəreɪt] *vt* incarcérer.

incarceration [ɪnˌkɑːsəˈreɪʃn] *n* incarcération *f*.

incarnate [ɪnˈkɑːneɪt] *lit* ◇ *adj* **-1.** incarné; **he's stupidity ~** c'est la bêtise incarnée OR personnifiée. **-2.** [colour] incarnat.
◇ *vt* incarner.

incarnation [ˌɪnkɑːˈneɪʃn] *n* incarnation *f*; **he's the very ~ of humility** il est l'incarnation même de l'humilité, il est l'humilité incarnée; **I must have known her in a previous ~** *hum* j'ai dû la connaître dans une vie antérieure.
◆ **Incarnation** *n*: **the Incarnation** l'Incarnation *f*.

incautious [ɪnˈkɔːʃəs] *adj* imprudent.

incautiously [ɪnˈkɔːʃəslɪ] *adv* imprudemment.

incendiarism [ɪnˈsendjərɪzm] *n* **-1.** [arson] incendie *m* volontaire OR criminel. **-2.** POL sédition *f*.

incendiary [ɪnˈsendjərɪ] (*pl* **incendiaries**) ◇ *n* **-1.** [arsonist] incendiaire *mf*. **-2.** [bomb] bombe *f* incendiaire. **-3.** *fig* [agitator] fauteur *m* de troubles.
◇ *adj* **-1.** [causing fires] incendiaire; **~ bomb/device** bombe *f*/dispositif *m* incendiaire. **-2.** [combustible] inflammable. **-3.** *fig* [speech, statement] incendiaire, séditieux.

incense [ˈɪnsens] ◇ *n* encens *m*.
◇ *vt* **-1.** [anger] rendre furieux, excéder; **he was ~d by** OR **at her indifference** son indifférence l'a rendu furieux; **I was absolutely ~d** j'étais hors de moi. **-2.** [perfume] encenser.

incense bearer *n* thuriféraire *m*.

incense burner *n* encensoir *m*.

incense stick *n* bâtonnet *m* d'encens.

incentive [ɪnˈsentɪv] ◇ *n* **-1.** [motivation] motivation *f*; **they have lost their ~** ils ne sont plus très motivés; **he has no ~ to work harder** rien ne le motive à travailler plus dur; **to give sb the ~ to do sthg** motiver qqn à faire qqch. **-2.** FIN & INDUST incitation *f*, encouragement *m*; **the firm offers various ~s** la société offre diverses primes; **tax ~s** avantages *mpl* fiscaux.
◇ *comp* incitateur, incitatif; **~ bonus** *Br* prime *f* de rendement; **~ scheme** *Br* programme *m* d'encouragement.

inception [ɪnˈsepʃn] *n* création *f*.

inceptive [ɪnˈseptɪv] ◇ *adj* **-1.** [beginning] initial. **-2.** LING inchoatif.
◇ *n* LING inchoatif *m*.

incertitude [ɪnˈsɜːtɪtjuːd] *n* incertitude *f*.

incessant [ɪnˈsesnt] *adj* incessant.

incessantly [ɪnˈsesntlɪ] *adv* continuellement, sans cesse.

incest [ˈɪnsest] *n* inceste *m*.

incestuous [ɪnˈsestjʊəs] *adj* incestueux; **publishing is a very ~ business** *fig* le monde de l'édition est très fermé.

incestuously [ɪnˈsestjʊəslɪ] *adv* incestueusement.

inch [ɪntʃ] ◇ *n* pouce *m*; **it's about 6 ~es wide** cela fait à peu près 15 centimètres de large; **it's a few ~es shorter** c'est plus court de quelques centimètres; **the car missed me by ~es** la voiture m'a manqué de peu; **every ~ of the wall was covered with posters** il n'y avait pas un centimètre carré du mur qui ne fût couvert d'affiches, le mur était entièrement couvert d'affiches ❑ **give him an ~ and he'll take a yard** OR **a mile** on lui donne le doigt et il vous prend le bras; **~ by ~** petit à petit, peu à peu; **we'll have to fight every ~ of the way** MIL nous devrons nous battre pour chaque pouce de terrain; *fig* nous ne sommes pas au bout de nos peines; **he's every ~ a Frenchman** il est français jusqu'au bout des ongles; **the unions won't budge** OR **give an ~** les syndicats ne céderont pas d'un pouce; **to be within an ~ of doing sthg** être à deux doigts de faire qqch.
◇ *vt*: **to ~ one's way in/out/past** entrer/sortir/passer petit à petit; **he ~ed his way to the door** petit à petit, il s'approcha de la porte; **she ~ed the car forward slowly** elle fit avancer la voiture très lentement.
◇ *vi*: **to ~ in/out/past** entrer/sortir/passer petit à petit; **he ~ed along the ledge** il avançait petit à petit le long du rebord.

-inch *in cpds*: **a five~ floppy disk** une disquette cinq pouces.

inchoate [ɪnˈkəʊeɪt] *adj fml* [incipient] naissant; [unfinished] inachevé.

inchoative [ˈɪnkəʊeɪtɪv] *adj* **-1.** LING inchoatif. **-2.** *fml* [incipient] naissant.

inchtape [ˈɪntʃteɪp] *n Br* mètre *m* (de couturier), mètre-ruban *m*.

inchworm [ˈɪntʃwɜːm] *n* arpenteuse *f*.

incidence [ˈɪnsɪdəns] *n* **-1.** [rate] taux *m*; **there is a higher/lower ~ of crime** le taux de criminalité est plus élevé/plus faible; **the ~ of the disease in adults** la fréquence de la maladie chez les adultes. **-2.** GEOM & PHYS incidence *f*; **angle/point of ~** angle *m*/point *m* d'incidence.

incident [ˈɪnsɪdənt] ◇ *n* incident *m*; **the meeting went off without ~** la réunion s'est déroulée sans incident; **the match was full of ~** de nombreux incidents ont eu lieu pendant le match ❑ **border** OR **frontier ~** incident de frontière; **diplomatic ~** incident diplomatique.
◇ *adj* **-1.** *fml* lié, attaché; **~ to** lié à. **-2.** PHYS incident.

incidental [ˌɪnsɪˈdentl] ◇ *adj* **-1.** [minor] secondaire, accessoire; [additional] accessoire; **the project will have other ~ benefits** ce projet aura encore d'autres avantages; **~ expenses** faux frais *mpl*. **-2.** [related]: **~ to** en rapport avec, occasionné par; **the fatigue ~ to such**

work la fatigue occasionnée par un tel travail.
◇ *n* [chance happening] événement *m* fortuit; [minor detail] détail *m* secondaire.
◆ **incidentals** *npl* [expenses] faux frais *mpl*.

incidentally [ˌɪnsɪ'dentəlɪ] *adv* -**1.** [by chance] incidemment, accessoirement. -**2.** [by the way] à propos. -**3.** [additionally] accessoirement.

incidental music *n* musique *f* d'accompagnement.

incident room *n* *Br* [in police station] salle *f* des opérations.

incinerate [ɪn'sɪnəreɪt] *vt* incinérer.

incineration [ɪnˌsɪnə'reɪʃn] *n* incinération *f*.

incinerator [ɪn'sɪnəreɪtəʳ] *n* incinérateur *m*.

incipient [ɪn'sɪpɪənt] *adj* naissant.

incised [ɪn'saɪzd] *adj* -**1.** ART gravé. -**2.** MED incisé. -**3.** BOT découpé, incisé.

incision [ɪn'sɪʒn] *n* incision *f*.

incisive [ɪn'saɪsɪv] *adj* [mind] perspicace, pénétrant; [wit, remark] incisif.

incisively [ɪn'saɪsɪvlɪ] *adv* [think] de façon incisive; [ask, remark] de manière perspicace OR pénétrante.

incisiveness [ɪn'saɪsɪvnɪs] *n* [of thought] perspicacité *f*, acuité *f*; [of remark, wit] perspicacité *f*.

incisor [ɪn'saɪzəʳ] *n* incisive *f*.

incite [ɪn'saɪt] *vt*: to ~ sb to do sthg inciter qqn à faire qqch; to ~ sb to violence inciter qqn à la violence; **they were accused of inciting racial hatred** on les accusa d'incitation à la haine raciale.

incitement [ɪn'saɪtmənt] *n* incitation *f*; ~ **to riot/violence** incitation à la révolte/à la violence.

incivility [ˌɪnsɪ'vɪlətɪ] (*pl* **incivilities**) *n* *fml* -**1.** [rudeness] impolitesse *f*, manque *m* de savoir-vivre, incivilité *f* *lit*. -**2.** [act, remark] impolitesse *f*, indélicatesse *f*.

incl. (*written abbr of* **including**): ~ VAT TTC.

inclemency [ɪn'klemənsɪ] *n* *lit* rigueur *f*, inclémence *f* *lit*.

inclement [ɪn'klemənt] *adj* *lit* [weather] rigoureux, inclément *lit*.

inclination [ˌɪnklɪ'neɪʃn] *n* -**1.** [tendency] disposition *f*, prédisposition *f*, tendance *f*; **a decided ~ towards laziness** une nette prédisposition à la paresse. -**2.** [liking] penchant *m*, inclination *f*; **you should follow your own ~ in the matter** tu devrais suivre ta propre inclination; **I do it from necessity, not from ~** je le fais par nécessité, pas par inclination OR par goût. -**3.** [slant, lean] inclinaison *f*; [of body] inclination *f*; **a slight ~ of the head** une légère inclination de la tête. -**4.** [hill] pente *f*, inclinaison *f*. -**5.** ASTRON & MATH inclinaison *f*.

incline [*vb* ɪn'klaɪn, *n* 'ɪnklaɪn] ◇ *vt* -**1.** [dispose] disposer, pousser; **it's unlikely to ~ them to work harder** il est peu probable que cela les pousse OR incite à travailler davantage; **his unhappy childhood ~d him towards cynicism** OR **to be cynical** c'est à cause de son enfance malheureuse qu'il a tendance à être cynique. -**2.** [lean, bend] incliner; **to ~ one's head** incliner la tête.
◇ *vi* -**1.** [tend] tendre, avoir tendance; **he ~s towards exaggeration** il a tendance à exagérer, il exagère facilement. -**2.** [lean, bend] s'incliner.
◇ *n* inclinaison *f*; [slope] pente *f*, déclivité *f*; RAIL rampe *f*.

inclined [ɪn'klaɪnd] *adj* -**1.** [tending, disposed]: **I'm ~ to agree** j'aurais tendance à être d'accord; **he's ~ to exaggeration** il a tendance à exagérer, il exagère facilement; **the drawers are ~ to stick** les tiroirs ont tendance à se coincer; **to be well ~ towards sb** être bien disposé envers qqn; **if you are so ~** si ça vous dit, si le cœur vous en dit; **I'm not that way ~** je ne suis pas comme ça. -**2.** [slanting, leaning] incliné.

inclined plane *n* plan *m* incliné.

inclined railway *n* *Am* (chemin *m* de fer) funiculaire *m*.

inclose [ɪn'kləʊz] = **enclose**.

inclosure [ɪn'kləʊʒəʳ] = **enclosure**.

include [ɪn'kluːd] *vt* comprendre, inclure; **each team ~s eight forwards** chaque équipe comprend huit avants; **the price ~s VAT** la TVA est comprise (dans le prix); **everyone was in favour, myself ~d** tout le monde était pour, moi y compris; **don't forget to ~ the cheque** n'oubliez pas de joindre le chèque; **batteries not ~d** les piles ne sont pas fournies; **my duties ~ sorting the mail** trier le courrier entre dans mes attributions OR fait partie de mon travail; **the children refused to ~ him in their games** les enfants ont refusé de l'inclure dans leurs jeux.
◆ **include in** *insep vt sep* *Br*: ~ **me in!** comptez-moi aussi!
◆ **include out** *inf vt sep* *Br*: **you can ~ me out** ne comptez pas sur moi.

included [ɪn'kluːdɪd] *adj*: **myself ~** y compris moi; **'service not ~'** 'service non compris'; **service charge ~** service *m* compris.

including [ɪn'kluːdɪŋ] *prep* (y) compris; **14 guests ~ the children** 14 invités y compris les enfants; **14 guests not ~ the children** 14 invités sans compter les enfants; **up to and ~ page 40** jusqu'à la page 40 incluse; **five books, ~ one I hadn't read** cinq livres, dont un que je n'avais pas lu.

inclusion [ɪn'kluːʒn] *n* [gen, GEOL & MATH] inclusion *f*.

inclusive [ɪn'kluːsɪv] *adj* -**1.** inclus, compris; ~ **of service charge** service *m* compris; ~ **of tax** taxes *fpl* comprises; **from July to September ~** de juillet à septembre inclus; ~ **prices** prix *mpl* nets; **all-~ holidays** voyages *mpl* organisés *(où tout est compris)*. -**2.** [list] exhaustif; [survey] complet, poussé. -**3.** PHILOS inclusif; ~ **or** ou *m* inclusif.

inclusively [ɪn'kluːsɪvlɪ] *adv* inclusivement.

incognito [ˌɪnkɒg'niːtəʊ] (*pl* **incognitos**)
◇ *adv* incognito; **to remain ~** [witness] garder l'anonymat; [star, politician] garder l'incognito.
◇ *n* incognito *m*.

incognizant [ɪn'kɒgnɪzənt] *adj* *fml* ignorant, inconscient; ~ **of the danger** inconscient du danger.

incoherence [ˌɪnkəʊ'hɪərəns] *n* incohérence *f*.

incoherency [ˌɪnkəʊ'hɪərənsɪ] (*pl* **incoherencies**) *n* incohérence *f*.

incoherent [ˌɪnkəʊ'hɪərənt] *adj* [person, argument] incohérent; [thought] incohérent, décousu.

incoherently [ˌɪnkəʊ'hɪərəntlɪ] *adv* de manière incohérente; **he was muttering ~** il marmonnait des paroles incohérentes.

income ['ɪnkʌm] *n* revenu *m*; **a high/low ~** un revenu élevé/faible; **to declare one's ~** déclarer ses revenus; **the ~ from her shares** les revenus de ses actions; **unearned ~** rente *f*, rentes *fpl*.

income bracket = **income tax**.

income group *n* tranche *f* de revenus; **most people in this area belong to the lower/higher ~** la plupart des habitants de ce quartier sont des économiquement faibles/ont des revenus élevés.

incomer ['ɪnˌkʌməʳ] *n* nouveau venu *m*, nouvelle venue *f*.

incomes policy *n* *Br* politique *f* des revenus OR des salaires.

income support *n* *prestation complémentaire en faveur des personnes justifiant de faibles revenus*.

income tax *n* impôt *m* sur le revenu (des personnes physiques); ~ **is deducted at source** les impôts sont prélevés à la source; ~ **inspector** inspecteur *m* des contributions directes OR des impôts; ~ **return** déclaration *f* de revenus, feuille *f* d'impôts.

incoming ['ɪnˌkʌmɪŋ] *adj* -**1.** [in direction]: ~ **train/flight** train *m*/vol *m* à l'arrivée; ~ **passengers** passagers *mpl* à l'arrivée; ~ **mail** courrier *m* (du jour); ~ **calls** appels *mpl* téléphoniques (reçus); **please make a note of any ~ calls** veuillez noter tous les appels que vous recevez; **the ~ tide** la marée montante. -**2.** [cash, interest] qui rentre. -**3.** [official, administration, tenant] nouveau.
◆ **incomings** *npl* [revenue] rentrée *f*, rentrées *fpl*, recettes *fpl*.

incommensurable [ˌɪnkə'menʃərəbl] ◇ *adj* [gen & MATH] incommensurable.
◇ *n* MATH quantité *f* incommensurable.

incommensurate [ˌɪnkə'menʃərət] *adj* *fml* -**1.** [disproportionate] disproportionné, inadéquat; **it is ~ with our needs** cela ne correspond pas à nos besoins. -**2.** = **incommensurable**.

incommode [ˌɪnkə'məʊd] *vt* *fml* incommoder, indisposer.

incommodious [ˌɪnkə'məʊdjəs] *adj* *fml* -**1.** [cramped] exigu, étriqué. -**2.** [troublesome] ennuyeux, fâcheux.

incommunicable [ˌɪnkə'mjuːnɪkəbl] *adj* incommunicable, indicible.

incommunicado [ˌɪnkəmjuːnɪ'kɑːdəʊ] *adj* & *adv* sans communication avec le monde extérieur; **the prisoners are being kept** OR **held ~** les prisonniers sont (gardés) au secret.

incomparable [ɪn'kɒmpərəbl] *adj* incomparable.

incomparably [ɪn'kɒmpərəblɪ] *adv* incomparablement, infiniment.

incompatibility ['ɪnkəmˌpætə'bɪlətɪ] *n* incompatibilité *f*; [grounds for divorce] incompatibilité *f* d'humeur.

incompatible [ˌɪnkəm'pætɪbl] *adj* incompatible.

incompetence [ɪn'kɒmpɪtəns], **incompetency** [ɪn'kɒmpɪtənsɪ] *n* incompétence *f*.

incompetent [ɪn'kɒmpɪtənt] ◇ *adj* incompétent.
◇ *n* incompétent *m*, -e *f*, incapable *mf*.

incomplete [ˌɪnkəm'pliːt] *adj* -**1.** [unfinished] inachevé. -**2.** [lacking something] incomplet.

incompletely [ˌɪnkəm'pliːtlɪ] *adv* incomplètement; **her plan was ~ thought out** son projet était incomplètement préparé.

incompleteness [ˌɪnkəm'pliːtnɪs] *n* -**1.** caractère *m* incomplet; **there's a feeling of ~ about his paintings** ses tableaux donnent l'impression de ne pas être finis OR achevés. -**2.** LOGIC incomplétude *f*.

incomprehensible [ˌɪnkɒmprɪ'hensəbl] *adj* incompréhensible.

incomprehensibly [ˌɪnkɒmprɪ'hensəblɪ] *adv* incompréhensiblement, de manière incompréhensible; **they were ~ absent** chose incompréhensible, ils étaient absents.

incomprehension [ˌɪnkɒmprɪ'henʃn] *n* incompréhension *f*.

inconceivable [ˌɪnkən'siːvəbl] *adj* inconcevable, inimaginable.

inconceivably [ˌɪnkən'siːvəblɪ] *adv* incroyablement; ~ **rich** incroyablement riche.

inconclusive [ˌɪnkən'kluːsɪv] *adj* peu concluant; **the results are ~** les résultats sont peu concluants; ~ **data** données *fpl* peu probantes; **the talks have been ~** les pourparlers n'ont pas abouti.

inconclusively [ˌɪnkən'kluːsɪvlɪ] *adv* de manière peu concluante; **the meeting ended ~** la réunion n'a abouti à aucune conclusion.

incongruent [ɪn'kɒŋgrʊənt] *fml* = **incongruous**.

incongruity [ˌɪnkɒŋ'gruːətɪ] (*pl* **incongruities**) *n* -**1.** [strangeness, discordancy] incongruité *f*. -**2.** [disparity, discrepancy] disparité *f*; **their statements were full of incongruities** leurs témoignages contenaient un grand nombre d'incohérences.

incongruous [ɪn'kɒŋgrʊəs] *adj* [strange, discordant] incongru; [disparate] incohérent; **he was an ~ figure among the factory workers** on le remarquait tout de suite au milieu des ouvriers de l'usine.

inconsequent [ɪn'kɒnsɪkwənt], **inconsequential** [ˌɪnkɒnsɪ'kwenʃl] *adj* sans importance; **an ~ detail** un détail insignifiant; **an ~ little man** un bonhomme sans importance.

inconsiderable [ˌɪnkən'sɪdərəbl] *adj* insignifiant, négligeable; a not ~ amount of money une somme d'argent non négligeable.

inconsiderate [ˌɪnkən'sɪdərət] *adj* [person] qui manque de prévenance; [action, remark] irréfléchi; he's ~ of other people's feelings peu lui importe ce que pensent les autres; that was very ~ of you vous avez agi sans aucun égard pour les autres; to be ~ towards sb manquer d'égards envers qqn.

inconsiderately [ˌɪnkən'sɪdərətlɪ] *adv* sans aucune considération.

inconsistency [ˌɪnkən'sɪstənsɪ] (*pl* inconsistencies) *n* -**1.** [incoherence] manque *m* de cohérence, incohérence *f*. -**2.** [contradiction] contradiction *f*; there are several inconsistencies in your argument votre argumentation présente OR laisse apparaître plusieurs contradictions.

inconsistent [ˌɪnkən'sɪstənt] *adj* -**1.** [person] incohérent *(dans ses comportements)*. -**2.** [performance] inégal. -**3.** [reasoning] incohérent. -**4.** [incompatible] incompatible; ~ with incompatible avec.

inconsolable [ˌɪnkən'səʊləbl] *adj* inconsolable.

inconsolably [ˌɪnkən'səʊləblɪ] *adv* de façon inconsolable; he cried ~ il était inconsolable.

inconspicuous [ˌɪnkən'spɪkjʊəs] *adj* [difficult to see] à peine visible, qui passe inaperçu; [discreet] peu voyant, discret; she tried to make herself as ~ as possible elle fit tout son possible pour passer inaperçue.

inconspicuously [ˌɪnkən'spɪkjʊəslɪ] *adv* discrètement.

inconstancy [ɪn'kɒnstənsɪ] *n* -**1.** [of phenomenon] variabilité *f*, instabilité *f*. -**2.** [of person] versatilité *f*, inconstance *f*.

inconstant [ɪn'kɒnstənt] *adj* -**1.** [weather] variable. -**2.** [person] inconstant, volage.

incontestable [ˌɪnkən'testəbl] *adj* incontestable.

incontestably [ˌɪnkən'testəblɪ] *adv* incontestablement, sans conteste.

incontinence [ɪn'kɒntɪnəns] *n* incontinence *f*.

incontinent [ɪn'kɒntɪnənt] *adj* incontinent.

incontrovertible [ˌɪnkɒntrə'vɜːtəbl] *adj* indiscutable; ~ evidence une preuve irréfutable.

incontrovertibly [ˌɪnkɒntrə'vɜːtəblɪ] *adv* indiscutablement, indéniablement.

inconvenience [ˌɪnkən'viːnjəns] ◇ *n* -**1.** [disadvantage] inconvénient *m*; the language barrier was a major ~ to the participants la barrière de la langue a beaucoup gêné les participants. -**2.** [trouble]: to cause ~ déranger, gêner; I hope it's not putting you to too much ~ j'espère que cela ne vous dérange pas trop ‖ [disadvantages] incommodité *f*, inconvénients *mpl*; the ~ of a small flat les désagréments d'un petit appartement.
◇ *vt* déranger, incommoder.

inconvenient [ˌɪnkən'viːnjənt] *adj* -**1.** [inopportune, awkward] inopportun; at an ~ time au mauvais moment; if it's not ~ si cela ne vous dérange pas; he has chosen to ignore any ~ facts il a choisi d'ignorer tout ce qui pouvait poser problème. -**2.** [impractical - tool, kitchen] peu pratique.

inconveniently [ˌɪnkən'viːnjəntlɪ] *adv* -**1.** [happen, arrive] au mauvais moment, inopportunément. -**2.** [be situated] de façon malcommode, mal; the switch was ~ placed above the door l'interrupteur était placé à un endroit très peu pratique au-dessus de la porte.

inconvertible [ˌɪnkən'vɜːtəbl] *adj* inconvertible, non convertible.

incorporate [ɪn'kɔːpəreɪt] ◇ *vt* incorporer; she ~d many folk tunes into her performance son programme comprenait de nombreux airs folkloriques; the territory was ~d into Poland le territoire fut incorporé OR annexé à la Pologne; ~ the butter into the flour incorporez le beurre à la farine; to ~ amendments into a text apporter des modifications à un texte.
◇ *vi* COMM [form a corporation] se constituer en société commerciale; [merge] fusionner.

incorporated [ɪn'kɔːpəreɪtɪd] *adj* constitué en société commerciale; Bradley & Jones Incorporated ≃ Bradley & Jones SARL.

incorporation [ɪnˌkɔːpə'reɪʃn] *n* -**1.** incorporation *f*, intégration *f*. -**2.** COMM constitution *f* en société commerciale.

incorporeal [ˌɪnkɔː'pɔːrɪəl] *adj lit* incorporel.

incorrect [ˌɪnkə'rekt] *adj* -**1.** [wrong - answer, result] erroné, faux; [- sum, statement] incorrect, inexact; ~ use of a word usage *m* impropre d'un mot. -**2.** [improper] incorrect; ~ behaviour comportement *m* déplacé.

incorrectly [ˌɪnkə'rektlɪ] *adv* -**1.** [wrongly]: she answered ~ elle a mal répondu; I was ~ quoted j'ai été cité de façon incorrecte; the illness was ~ diagnosed il y a eu erreur de diagnostic; you're using that tool ~ vous utilisez mal cet outil. -**2.** [improperly] incorrectement; he behaved most ~ il s'est conduit de façon déplacée, sa conduite était tout à fait déplacée.

incorrigible [ɪn'kɒrɪdʒəbl] *adj* incorrigible.

incorruptible [ˌɪnkə'rʌptəbl] *adj* incorruptible.

increase [*vb* ɪn'kriːs, *n* 'ɪnkriːs] ◇ *vi* augmenter, croître; to ~ by 10 % augmenter de 10 %; production/demand/inflation has ~d la production/la demande/l'inflation a augmenté; the growth rate is likely to ~ le taux de croissance va probablement augmenter OR s'accélérer; the attacks have ~d in frequency la fréquence des attaques a augmenté; to ~ in size grandir; to ~ in intensity s'intensifier.
◇ *vt* augmenter; to ~ output to 500 units a week augmenter OR faire passer la production à 500 unités par semaine; recent events have ~d speculation des événements récents ont renforcé les rumeurs.
◇ *n* augmentation *f*; the ~ in productivity/in the cost of living l'augmentation de la productivité/du coût de la vie; a 10 % pay ~ une augmentation de salaire de 10 %; an ~ in population un accroissement de la population; an ~ in the number of patients une augmentation OR un accroissement du nombre des malades.
◆ **on the increase** *adj phr*: tourism/crime is on the ~ le tourisme/la criminalité est en hausse; shoplifting is on the ~ les vols à l'étalage sont de plus en plus nombreux.

increased [ɪn'kriːst] *adj* accru; ~ investment will lead to ~ productivity un accroissement des investissements entraînera un accroissement OR une augmentation de la productivité.

increasing [ɪn'kriːsɪŋ] *adj* croissant, grandissant; there have been an ~ number of complaints les réclamations sont de plus en plus nombreuses; they make ~ use of computer technology ils ont de plus en plus souvent recours à OR ils font de plus en plus souvent appel à l'informatique.

increasingly [ɪn'kriːsɪŋlɪ] *adv* de plus en plus.

incredible [ɪn'kredəbl] *adj* -**1.** [unbelievable] incroyable, invraisemblable. -**2.** *inf* [fantastic, amazing] fantastique, incroyable.

incredibly [ɪn'kredəblɪ] *adv* -**1.** [amazingly]: ~, we were on time aussi incroyable que cela puisse paraître, nous étions à l'heure. -**2.** [extremely] incroyablement; she was ~ beautiful elle était incroyablement belle.

incredulity [ˌɪnkrɪ'djuːlətɪ] *n* incrédulité *f*.

incredulous [ɪn'kredjʊləs] *adj* incrédule; an ~ look un regard incrédule.

incredulously [ɪn'kredjʊləslɪ] *adv* avec incrédulité.

incredulousness [ɪn'kredjʊləsnɪs] = **incredulity**.

increment ['ɪnkrɪmənt] ◇ *n* -**1.** [increase] augmentation *f*; a salary with yearly ~s of £500 un salaire assorti d'augmentations annuelles de 500 livres. -**2.** COMPUT incrément *m*. -**3.** MATH accroissement *m*.
◇ *vt* COMPUT incrémenter.

incremental [ˌɪnkrɪ'mentl] *adj* -**1.** [increasing] croissant; ~ increases augmentations *fpl* régulières. -**2.** COMPUT incrémentiel, incrémental.

incriminate [ɪn'krɪmɪneɪt] *vt* incriminer, mettre en cause; to ~ o.s. se compromettre; all the evidence seems to ~ the maid tous les indices semblent accuser la bonne.

incriminating [ɪn'krɪmɪneɪtɪŋ] *adj* accusateur, compromettant; ~ evidence pièce *f* OR pièces *fpl* à conviction.

incrimination [ɪnˌkrɪmɪ'neɪʃn] *n* mise *f* en cause, incrimination *f*.

incriminatory [ɪn'krɪmɪnətrɪ] = **incriminating**.

in-crowd *inf n* coterie *f*; to be in with the ~ être branché.

incrust [ɪn'krʌst] = **encrust**.

incubate ['ɪnkjʊbeɪt] ◇ *vt* -**1.** BIOL [eggs - subj: bird] couver; [- subj: fish] incuber; [- in incubator] incuber. -**2.** *fig* [plot, idea] couver.
◇ *vi* -**1.** BIOL [egg] être en incubation. -**2.** MED [virus] incuber; the disease ~s for several days la maladie a une période d'incubation de plusieurs jours. -**3.** *fig* [plan, idea] couver.

incubation [ˌɪnkjʊ'beɪʃn] *n* [of egg, virus, disease] incubation *f*; ~ period (période *f* d') incubation.

incubator ['ɪnkjʊbeɪtə'] *n* [for premature baby] couveuse *f*, incubateur *m*; [for eggs, bacteria] incubateur *m*.

incubus ['ɪnkjʊbəs] (*pl* incubuses OR incubi [-baɪ]) *n* -**1.** [demon] incube *m*. -**2.** *lit* [nightmare] cauchemar *m*.

inculcate ['ɪnkʌlkeɪt] *vt* inculquer; to ~ sb with an idea, to ~ an idea in sb inculquer une idée à qqn.

inculcation [ˌɪnkʌl'keɪʃn] *n* inculcation *f*.

incumbency [ɪn'kʌmbənsɪ] (*pl* incumbencies) *n* [office] office *m*, fonction *f*; during my predecessor's ~ pendant l'exercice de mon prédécesseur.

incumbent [ɪn'kʌmbənt] ◇ *adj fml* -**1.** [obligatory]: it is ~ on OR upon the manager to check the takings il incombe OR il appartient au directeur de vérifier la recette. -**2.** [in office] en fonction, en exercice; the ~ mayor [current] le maire en exercice; [during election campaign] le maire sortant.
◇ *n* [office holder] titulaire *mf*.

incunabula [ˌɪnkjuː'næbjʊlə] *npl* incunables *mpl*.

incur [ɪn'kɜː'] (*pt* & *pp* incurred, *cont* incurring) *vt* [blame, loss, penalty] s'exposer à, encourir [debt] contracter; [losses] subir; the expenses incurred les dépenses encourues; to ~ sb's wrath s'attirer les foudres de qqn.

incurable [ɪn'kjʊərəbl] ◇ *adj* [illness] incurable inguérissable; *fig* [optimist] inguérissable infatigable.
◇ *n* incurable *mf*.

incurably [ɪn'kjʊərəblɪ] *adv*: to be ~ ill avoir une maladie incurable; to be ~ lazy *fig* être irrémédiablement paresseux.

incurious [ɪn'kjʊərɪəs] *adj lit* incurieux *lit*, sans curiosité.

incursion [*Br* ɪn'kɜːʃn, *Am* ɪn'kɜːʒn] *n* incursion *f*; an ~ into enemy territory une incursion en territoire ennemi.

indebted [ɪn'detɪd] *adj* -**1.** [for help] redevable; to be ~ to sb for sthg: I am greatly ~ to you for doing me this favour je vous suis extrêmement reconnaissant de m'avoir rendu ce service; I am ~ to you for your loyal support je vous suis reconnaissant de votre soutien loyal. -**2.** [owing money] endetté; heavily ~ fortement endetté.

indebtedness [ɪn'detɪdnɪs] *n* -**1.** [for help] dette *f*, obligation *f*; my ~ to her ma dette envers elle. -**2.** [owing of money] endettement *m*. -**3.** [amount owed] dette *f*, dettes *fpl*.

indecency [ɪn'diːsnsɪ] (*pl* indecencies) *n* indécence *f*; an act of gross ~ JUR un grave outrage à la pudeur.

indecent [ɪn'diːsnt] *adj* -**1.** [obscene] indécent; an ~ proposition une proposition indécente. -**2.** [unseemly] indécent, inconvenant, déplacé; with ~ haste avec une précipitation déplacée; an ~ display of wealth un étalage indécent de richesse.

indecent assault *n* attentat *m* à la pudeur.

indecent exposure *n* outrage *m* public à la pudeur.

indecently [ɪn'diːsntlɪ] *adv* indécemment.

indecipherable [ˌɪndɪ'saɪfərəbl] *adj* indéchiffrable.

indecision [ˌɪndɪ'sɪʒn] *n* indécision *f*.

indecisive [ˌɪndɪ'saɪsɪv] *adj* -**1.** [hesitating - person] indécis, irrésolu. -**2.** [inconclusive] peu concluant.

indecisively [ˌɪndɪ'saɪsɪvlɪ] *adv* -**1.** [hesitatingly] de manière indécise, avec hésitation. -**2.** [inconclusively] de manière peu convaincante OR concluante; the argument ended ~ la discussion s'est terminée de façon peu concluante.

indecisiveness [ˌɪndɪ'saɪsɪvnɪs] = **indecision**.

indeclinable [ˌɪndɪ'klaɪnəbl] *adj* indéclinable.

indecorous [ɪn'dekərəs] *adj* inconvenant, malséant.

indecorously [ɪn'dekərəslɪ] *adv* de manière inconvenante.

indeed [ɪn'diːd] *adv* -**1.** [used to confirm] effectivement, en effet; there was ~ a problem il y avait effectivement OR bien un problème; we are aware of the problem; ~, we are already investigating it nous sommes conscients du problème; en fait, nous sommes déjà en train de l'étudier. -**2.** [used to qualify]: the problem, if ~ there is one, is theirs c'est leur problème, si problème il y a; it is difficult, ~ virtually impossible, to get in il est difficile, pour ne pas dire impossible OR voire impossible, d'entrer. -**3.** [used as intensifier] vraiment; I'm very tired ~ je suis vraiment très fatigué; thank you very much ~ merci beaucoup; that's praise ~! ça, c'est un compliment!, voilà ce qui s'appelle un compliment! || [in replies] en effet; I believe you support their policy — I do ~ je crois que vous soutenez leur politique — en effet. -**4.** [as surprised, ironic response]: he asked us for a pay rise — ~! il nous a demandé une augmentation — eh bien! OR vraiment?; I've bought a new car — have you ~! j'ai acheté une nouvelle voiture — vraiment?

indefatigable [ˌɪndɪ'fætɪgəbl] *adj* infatigable.

indefatigably [ˌɪndɪ'fætɪgəblɪ] *adv* infatigablement, sans se fatiguer, inlassablement.

indefensible [ˌɪndɪ'fensəbl] *adj* -**1.** [conduct] injustifiable, inexcusable; [argument] insoutenable, indéfendable. -**2.** MIL indéfendable.

indefensibly [ˌɪndɪ'fensəblɪ] *adv* de façon indéfendable.

indefinable [ˌɪndɪ'faɪnəbl] *adj* indéfinissable.

indefinably [ˌɪndɪ'faɪnəblɪ] *adv* indescriptiblement.

indefinite [ɪn'defɪnɪt] *adj* [indeterminate] indéterminé, illimité; for an ~ period pour une période indéterminée; an ~ strike une grève illimitée; of ~ origin d'origine incertaine || [vague, imprecise] flou, peu précis; an ~ answer une réponse floue OR vague.

indefinite article *n* article *m* indéfini.

indefinitely [ɪn'defɪnətlɪ] *adv* -**1.** [without limit] indéfiniment; we can't go on ~ on ne peut pas continuer indéfiniment; 'closed ~' 'fermé jusqu'à nouvel avis OR ordre'. -**2.** [imprecisely] vaguement.

indefinite pronoun *n* pronom *m* indéfini.

indelible [ɪn'deləbl] *adj* [ink, stain] indélébile; [memory] impérissable; ~ marker *Br* marqueur *m* indélébile.

indelibly [ɪn'deləblɪ] *adv* de manière indélébile; her face remained ~ fixed in his memory son visage resta à jamais gravé dans sa mémoire.

indelicacy [ɪn'delɪkəsɪ] (*pl* indelicacies) *n* -**1.** [of behaviour, remark] indélicatesse *f*. -**2.** [tactless remark, action] manque *m* de tact.

indelicate [ɪn'delɪkət] *adj* [action] déplacé, indélicat; [person, remark] indélicat, qui manque de tact.

indemnification [ɪnˌdemnɪfɪ'keɪʃn] *n* -**1.** [act of compensation] indemnisation *f*, dédommagement *m*. -**2.** [sum reimbursed] indemnité *f*.

indemnify [ɪn'demnɪfaɪ] (*pt* & *pp* **indemnified**) *vt* -**1.** [compensate] indemniser, dédommager; you will be indemnified for any losses incurred vous serez indemnisé OR dédommagé de toutes les pertes subies. -**2.** [insure] assurer, garantir; to be indemnified for OR against sthg être assuré contre qqch.

indemnity [ɪn'demnətɪ] (*pl* **indemnities**) *n* -**1.** [compensation] indemnité *f*, dédommagement *m*; war indemnities réparations *fpl* de guerre. -**2.** [insurance] assurance *f*. -**3.** [exemption - from prosecution, liability] immunité *f*.

indent [*vb* ɪn'dent, *n* 'ɪndent] ◇ *vt* -**1.** [line of text] mettre en retrait; ~ the first line commencez la première ligne en retrait OR avec un alinéa. -**2.** [edge] denteler, découper; [more deeply] échancrer. -**3.** [surface] marquer, faire une empreinte dans. -**4.** *Br* COMM [goods] commander. -**5.** = **indenture**.
◇ *vi* -**1.** [at start of paragraph] faire un alinéa. -**2.** *Br* COMM passer commande; to ~ on sb for sthg commander qqch à qqn.
◇ *n* -**1.** *Br* COMM [order] commande *f*; [order form] bordereau *m* de commande. -**2.** = **indentation 1**.

indentation [ˌɪnden'teɪʃn] *n* -**1.** [in line of text] renfoncement *m*. -**2.** [in edge] dentelure *f*; [deeper] échancrure *f*; [in coastline] découpure *f*. -**3.** [on surface] empreinte *f*. -**4.** = **indenture**.

indented [ɪn'dentɪd] *adj* [edge] découpé, dentelé; [coastline] découpé.

indenture [ɪn'dentʃəʳ] ◇ *n* (*often pl*) contrat *m*; [of apprentice] contrat *m* d'apprentissage.
◇ *vt* engager par contrat; [apprentice] mettre OR placer comme apprenti; he was ~d to a carpenter on le mit comme apprenti OR en apprentissage chez un menuisier; ~d labour/labourer *Br* main-d'œuvre *f*/travailleur *m* sous contrat.

independence [ˌɪndɪ'pendəns] *n* [gen & POL] indépendance *f*; the country has recently gained its ~ le pays vient d'accéder à l'indépendance; the (American) War of Independence la guerre d'Indépendance (américaine).

THE AMERICAN WAR OF INDEPENDENCE:
Guerre menée par les 13 colonies de la Nouvelle-Angleterre pour accéder à l'indépendance, en réaction à la dureté de l'administration britannique, qui leur imposait de lourdes taxes. Marqué par la Déclaration d'indépendance du 4 juillet 1776, le conflit dura 5 ans et le nouvel État fut reconnu en 1783.

Independence Day *n* fête *f* nationale de l'Indépendance *(aux États-Unis)*.

independency [ˌɪndɪ'pendənsɪ] (*pl* independencies) *n* -**1.** [country] État *m* indépendant. -**2.** = **independence**.

independent [ˌɪndɪ'pendənt] ◇ *adj* -**1.** indépendant; to become ~ [country] accéder à l'indépendance; she is ~ of her parents elle ne dépend pas OR plus de ses parents; two ~ studies have been made deux études indépendantes ont été menées; two ~ sources have confirmed the rumour deux sources indépendantes ont confirmé la rumeur; he is incapable of ~ thought il est incapable de penser par lui-même ❑ ~ income revenus *mpl* indépendants, rentes *fpl*; a man of ~ means un rentier; an ~ inquiry has been set up une enquête indépendante a été ouverte. -**2.** GRAMM, PHILOS & MATH indépendant.
◇ *n* -**1.** [gen] indépendant *m*, -e *f*; The Independent PRESS *quotidien britannique de qualité sans affiliation politique particulière*. -**2.** POL indépendant *m*, -e *f*, non-inscrit *m*, -e *f*.

independently [ˌɪndɪ'pendəntlɪ] *adv* de manière indépendante, de manière autonome; ~ of indépendamment de; to be ~ wealthy vivre de sa fortune personnelle.

independent school *n Br* école *f* privée.

in-depth *adj* en profondeur.

indescribable [ˌɪndɪ'skraɪbəbl] *adj* indescriptible.

indescribably [ˌɪndɪ'skraɪbəblɪ] *adv* incroyablement.

indestructible [ˌɪndɪ'strʌktəbl] *adj* indestructible.

indeterminable [ˌɪndɪ'tɜːmɪnəbl] *adj* -**1.** [fact, amount, distance] indéterminable. -**2.** [controversy, problem] insoluble.

indeterminacy [ˌɪndɪ'tɜːmɪnəsɪ] *n* indétermination *f*.

indeterminate [ˌɪndɪ'tɜːmɪnət] *adj* -**1.** [undetermined, indefinite] indéterminé; for an ~ period pour une période indéterminée; ~ sentence peine *f* (de prison) de durée indéterminée. -**2.** [vague, imprecise] flou, vague. -**3.** LING, MATH & PHILOS indéterminé.

indeterminately [ˌɪndɪ'tɜːmɪnətlɪ] *adv* -**1.** [indefinitely] de façon indéterminée. -**2.** [vaguely] de manière floue, imprécisément.

indeterminism [ˌɪndɪ'tɜːmɪnɪzm] *n* indéterminisme *m*.

index ['ɪndeks] (*pl senses 1-3 & 7* **indexes**, *pl senses 4-6* **indices** [-dɪsiːz]) ◇ *n* -**1.** [in book, database] index *m*; name/subject ~ index des noms propres/matières. -**2.** [in library] catalogue *m*, répertoire *m*; [on index cards] fichier *m*. -**3.** [finger] index *m*. -**4.** ECON & PHYS indice *m*; the Dow-Jones ~ l'indice Dow Jones; the cost of living ~ l'indice du coût de la vie. -**5.** [pointer on scale] aiguille *f*, indicateur *m*; *fig* [sign] indice *m*, indicateur *m*; it is a good ~ of the current political mood c'est un bon indicateur du climat politique actuel. -**6.** MATH [subscript] indice *m*; [superscript] exposant *m*. -**7.** TYPO [pointing fist] renvoi *m*. -**8.** RELIG: Index Index *m*.
◇ *vt* -**1.** [word, book, database] indexer; all geographical names are ~ed tous les noms géographiques sont indexés; you'll find it ~ed under "science" vous trouverez ça indexé à «science» OR dans l'index sous (l'entrée) «science». -**2.** ECON indexer; ~ed to indexé sur. -**3.** MECH indexer.

indexation [ˌɪndek'seɪʃn] *n* indexation *f*.

index card *n* fiche *f*.

index finger *n* index *m*.

index-linked *adj Br* indexé.

index-linking *n Br* indexation *f*.

index number *n* [in statistics] indice *m*.

index register *n* registre *m* d'index.

India ['ɪndjə] *pr n* Inde *f*; in ~ en Inde.

India ink *Am* = **Indian ink**.

Indiaman ['ɪndjəmən] (*pl* **Indiamen** [-mən]) *n Br grand voilier assurant le commerce avec les Indes*.

Indian ['ɪndjən] ◇ *n* -**1.** [person - in America, Asia] Indien *m*, -enne *f*. -**2.** LING [in America] langue *f* amérindienne.
◇ *adj* [American or Asian] indien.

Indiana [ˌɪndɪ'ænə] *pr n* Indiana *m*; in ~ dans l'Indiana.

Indian agent *n Am* & *Can* délégué *m*, -e *f* aux affaires indiennes.

Indianapolis [ˌɪndɪə'næpəlɪs] *pr n* Indianapolis.

Indian club *n* massue *f (pour la gymnastique)*.

Indian corn *n Am* maïs *m*.

Indian elephant *n* éléphant *m* d'Asie.

Indian file *n*: in ~ en file *f* indienne.

Indian hemp *n Br* chanvre *m* indien, cannabis *m*.

Indian ink *n Br* encre *f* de Chine.

Indian Mutiny *pr n*: the ~ *grande révolte indienne contre les Britanniques en 1857*.

THE INDIAN MUTINY:
Cette violente révolte de la population indienne contre l'Empire britannique et l'occidentalisation du pays éclata en 1857 dans une garnison et se propagea dans tout le pays. Elle dura deux ans et aboutit principalement à la fin de l'influence politique de l'East India Company.

Indian Ocean *pr n*: the ~ l'océan *m* Indien.
Indian red *n* colcotar *m*, rouge *m* de Prusse.
Indian sign *n Am* sort *m (jeté sur qqn)*.
Indian summer *n* été *m* de la Saint-Martin, été *m* indien; *fig* vieillesse *f* heureuse.
Indian wrestling *n* bras *m* de fer.
India paper *n* papier *m* bible.
India rubber *n Br* [substance] caoutchouc *m*; [eraser] gomme *f*.
indicate ['ɪndɪkeɪt] ◇ *vt* -**1.** [show, point to] indiquer; to ~ the way indiquer OR montrer le chemin; the footprints would seem to ~ that someone has been here les traces de pas semblent indiquer que quelqu'un est passé par ici; this dial ~s the temperature ce cadran indique la température; all the pointers ~ a rise in unemployment tous les indicateurs font état d'une montée du chômage. -**2.** [make clear, point out] signaler, indiquer; as I have already ~d comme je l'ai déjà signalé OR fait remarquer; he ~d his willingness to help il nous a fait savoir qu'il était prêt à nous aider; she ~d that the interview was over elle a fait comprendre que l'entretien était terminé. -**3.** *Br* AUT: to ~ (that one is turning) left/right mettre son clignotant à gauche/à droite (pour tourner). -**4.** [recommend, require] indiquer; surgery is ~d l'opération semble tout indiquée.
◇ *vi Br* AUT mettre son clignotant.
indication [ˌɪndɪ'keɪʃn] *n* -**1.** [sign] indication *f*; she gave no ~ that she had seen me rien ne pouvait laisser supposer qu'elle m'avait vu; he gave us a clear ~ of his intentions il nous a clairement fait comprendre OR clairement indiqué ses intentions; all the ~s are that..., there is every ~ that... tout porte à croire que... -**2.** [act of indicating] indication *f*.
indicative [ɪn'dɪkətɪv] ◇ *adj* -**1.** [symptomatic] indicatif; ~ of: his handwriting is ~ of his mental state son écriture est révélatrice de OR en dit long sur son état mental; it is ~ of a strong personality cela témoigne d'une forte personnalité. -**2.** GRAMM indicatif; the ~ mood le mode indicatif, l'indicatif *m*.
◇ *n* GRAMM indicatif *m*; in the ~ à l'indicatif.
indicator ['ɪndɪkeɪtəʳ] *n* -**1.** [instrument] indicateur *m*; [warning lamp] voyant *m*; temperature ~ indicateur *m* de température. -**2.** AUT clignotant *m*. -**3.** [at station, in airport]: arrivals/departures ~ panneau *m* des arrivées/des départs. -**4.** *fig* indicateur *m*; economic ~s indicateurs *mpl* économiques. -**5.** CHEM indicateur *m*. -**6.** LING indicateur *m*.
indices ['ɪndɪsiːz] *pl* → **index**.
indict [ɪn'daɪt] *vt* JUR inculper, mettre en examen *spec*.
indictable [ɪn'daɪtəbl] *adj* JUR -**1.** [person] passible de poursuites. -**2.** [crime] passible des tribunaux.
indictment [ɪn'daɪtmənt] *n* -**1.** JUR inculpation *f*, mise *f* en examen *spec*; ~ for fraud inculpation pour fraude. -**2.** *fig*: a damning ~ of government policy un témoignage accablant contre la politique gouvernementale.
indie *inf* ['ɪndɪ] *adj* [band, charts] indépendant *(dont les disques sont produits par des maisons indépendantes)*.
Indies ['ɪndɪz] *npl*: the ~ les Indes *fpl*; in the ~ aux Indes.
indifference [ɪn'dɪfrəns] *n* -**1.** [unconcern] indifférence *f*; with total ~ avec une indifférence totale; his ~ towards any suggestion son manque d'intérêt face à toutes les suggestions qui lui sont faites. -**2.** [mediocrity] médiocrité *f*. -**3.** [unimportance] insignifiance *f*; it is a matter of great ~ to me c'est une question qui me laisse totalement indifférent. -**4.** PHILOS indifférence *f*.
indifferent [ɪn'dɪfrənt] *adj* -**1.** [unconcerned, cold] indifférent; she was ~ to the beauty of the landscape elle était indifférente à la beauté du paysage; he was ~ to her pleas il est resté sourd à ses suppliques; ~ to the danger insouciant du danger. -**2.** [unimportant] indifférent; it's ~ to me whether they go or stay qu'ils partent ou qu'ils restent, cela m'est égal. -**3.** [mediocre] médiocre, quelconque; good, bad or ~ bon, mauvais ou ni l'un ni l'autre. -**4.** BIOL [cell, tissue] indifférencié.
indifferently [ɪn'dɪfrəntlɪ] *adv* -**1.** [coldly, unconcernedly] indifféremment, avec indifférence. -**2.** [not well] médiocrement.
indigence ['ɪndɪdʒəns] *n fml* indigence *f*.
indigenous [ɪn'dɪdʒɪnəs] *adj* -**1.** [animal, plant, custom] indigène; [population] autochtone; rabbits are not ~ to Australia à l'origine, il n'y avait pas de lapins en Australie. -**2.** [innate] inné, natif *lit*.
indigent ['ɪndɪdʒənt] *fml* ◇ *adj* indigent, nécessiteux.
◇ *n* indigent *m*, -e *f*.
indigestible [ˌɪndɪ'dʒestəbl] *adj* indigeste.
indigestion [ˌɪndɪ'dʒestʃn] *n* indigestion *f*; to have ~ avoir une indigestion.
indignant [ɪn'dɪgnənt] *adj* indigné, outré; he was ~ at her attitude il était indigné par son attitude; an ~ look un regard outré.
indignantly [ɪn'dɪgnəntlɪ] *adv* avec indignation.
indignation [ˌɪndɪg'neɪʃn] *n* indignation *f*; public ~ indignation générale; righteous ~ indignation justifiée.
indignity [ɪn'dɪgnətɪ] (*pl* **indignities**) *n* indignité *f*; he suffered the ~ of having to ask for a loan il a dû s'abaisser à solliciter un prêt.
indigo ['ɪndɪgəʊ] (*pl* **indigos** OR **indigoes**) ◇ *n* -**1.** [dye, colour] indigo *m*. -**2.** [plant] indigotier *m*.
◇ *adj* indigo *(inv)*.
indigo blue = **indigo 1**.
indirect [ˌɪndɪ'rekt] *adj* indirect; by an ~ route par un chemin indirect OR détourné; the ~ effects of radioactivity les effets indirects OR secondaires de la radioactivité; an ~ reference une allusion voilée; ~ free kick FTBL coup *m* franc indirect.
indirectly [ˌɪndɪ'rektlɪ] *adv* indirectement; I heard about it ~ je l'ai appris indirectement OR par personnes interposées OR par un tiers; she felt ~ responsible elle se sentait indirectement responsable.
indirectness [ˌɪndɪ'rektnɪs] *n* caractère *m* indirect.
indirect object *n* objet *m* indirect.
indirect question *n* question *f* indirecte.
indirect speech *n* discours *m* indirect.
indirect tax *n* impôts *mpl* indirects.
indirect taxation *n* fiscalité *f* indirecte.
indiscernible [ˌɪndɪ'sɜːnəbl] *adj* indiscernable, imperceptible.
indiscipline [ɪn'dɪsɪplɪn] *n* indiscipline *f*.
indiscreet [ˌɪndɪ'skriːt] *adj* indiscret.
indiscreetly [ˌɪndɪ'skriːtlɪ] *adv* indiscrètement.
indiscretion [ˌɪndɪ'skreʃn] *n* indiscrétion *f*.
indiscriminate [ˌɪndɪ'skrɪmɪnət] *adj*: it was ~ slaughter ce fut un massacre aveugle; to distribute ~ punishment/praise distribuer des punitions/des éloges à tort et à travers; children are ~ in their television viewing les enfants regardent la télévision sans discernement; her ~ admiration for everything American son admiration inconditionnelle pour tout ce qui est américain.
indiscriminately [ˌɪndɪ'skrɪmɪnətlɪ] *adv*: he reads ~ il lit tout ce qui lui tombe sous la main; the plague struck rich and poor ~ la peste a frappé indifféremment les riches et les pauvres; she admired everything ~ elle admirait tout sans discernement; I use the two terms ~ j'utilise indifféremment les deux termes.
indiscrimination ['ɪndɪsˌkrɪmɪ'neɪʃn] *n* manque *m* de discernement.
indispensable [ˌɪndɪ'spensəbl] *adj* indispensable; ~ to indispensable à OR pour; to make o.s. ~ to sb se rendre indispensable à qqn.
indisposed [ˌɪndɪ'spəʊzd] *adj fml* -**1.** *euph* [sick] indisposé, souffrant. -**2.** [unwilling] peu enclin, peu disposé; to be ~ to do sthg être peu enclin OR peu disposé à faire qqch.
indisposition [ˌɪndɪspə'zɪʃn] *n fml* -**1.** *euph* [illness] indisposition *f*. -**2.** [unwillingness] dispositions *fpl* peu favorables, manque *m* d'empressement.
indisputable [ˌɪndɪ'spjuːtəbl] *adj* incontestable, indiscutable.
indisputably [ˌɪndɪ'spjuːtəblɪ] *adv* incontestablement, indiscutablement.
indissoluble [ˌɪndɪ'sɒljʊbl] *adj* indissoluble.
indissolubly [ˌɪndɪ'sɒljʊblɪ] *adv* indissolublement.
indistinct [ˌɪndɪ'stɪŋkt] *adj* indistinct.
indistinctly [ˌɪndɪ'stɪŋktlɪ] *adv* indistinctement.
indistinguishable [ˌɪndɪ'stɪŋgwɪʃəbl] *adj* -**1.** [alike] impossible à distinguer; his handwriting is ~ from his brother's son écriture est impossible à distinguer de celle de son frère; the twins are ~ les jumeaux se ressemblent à s'y méprendre. -**2.** [imperceptible] imperceptible.
indistinguishably [ˌɪndɪ'stɪŋgwɪʃəblɪ] *adv* imperceptiblement.
indium ['ɪndɪəm] *n* indium *m*.
individual [ˌɪndɪ'vɪdʒʊəl] ◇ *adj* -**1.** [for one person] individuel; ~ portions portions *fpl* individuelles OR pour une personne; she has ~ tuition elle prend des cours particuliers; ~ rights droits *mpl* de l'individu OR de la personne. -**2.** [single, separate] particulier; we cannot consider each ~ case nous ne pouvons pas considérer tous les cas particuliers OR chaque cas en particulier; it's impossible to investigate each ~ complaint il est impossible d'étudier séparément chaque réclamation; each ~ case is different chaque cas est différent; everyone will have his ~ copy chacun aura son exemplaire personnel OR son propre exemplaire. -**3.** [distinctive] personnel, particulier; she has a very ~ way of working elle a une façon très particulière OR personnelle de travailler.
◇ *n* [gen, BIOL & LOGIC] individu *m*; who's that strange ~? qui est cet individu bizarre?
individualism [ˌɪndɪ'vɪdʒʊəlɪzm] *n* [gen, PHILOS & POL] individualisme *m*.
individualist [ˌɪndɪ'vɪdʒʊəlɪst] *n* individualiste *mf*.
individualistic ['ɪndɪˌvɪdʒʊə'lɪstɪk] *adj* individualiste.
individuality ['ɪndɪˌvɪdʒʊ'ælətɪ] (*pl* **individualities**) *n* individualité *f*.
individualize, -ise [ˌɪndɪ'vɪdʒʊəlaɪz] *vt* individualiser.
individually [ˌɪndɪ'vɪdʒʊəlɪ] *adv* -**1.** [separately] individuellement; ~ wrapped fruit fruits emballés individuellement OR séparément. -**2.** [distinctively] de façon distinctive; he dresses very ~ il s'habille de façon très originale, il a une façon très personnelle de s'habiller.
individuate [ˌɪndɪ'vɪdʒʊeɪt] *vt* différencier.
indivisible [ˌɪndɪ'vɪzəbl] *adj* indivisible; 17 is ~ by 3 17 n'est pas divisible par 3.
Indo- ['ɪndəʊ] *in cpds* indo-; an ~Pakistani agreement un accord indo-pakistanais.
Indochina [ˌɪndəʊ'tʃaɪnə] *pr n* Indochine *f*; in ~ en Indochine.
Indochinese [ˌɪndəʊtʃaɪ'niːz] ◇ *n* Indochinois *m*, -e *f*.
◇ *adj* indochinois.
indoctrinate [ɪn'dɒktrɪneɪt] *vt* endoctriner; they were ~d with revolutionary ideas on leur a inculqué des idées révolutionnaires.
indoctrination [ɪnˌdɒktrɪ'neɪʃn] *n* endoctrinement *m*.

Indo-European [ˈɪndəʊˌjʊərəˈpiːən] ◇ *n* indo-européen *m*.
◇ *adj* indo-européen.

indolence [ˈɪndələns] *n* -**1.** [laziness] paresse *f*, indolence *f*. -**2.** MED indolence *f*.

indolent [ˈɪndələnt] *adj* -**1.** [lazy] paresseux, indolent. -**2.** MED indolent.

indolently [ˈɪndələntlɪ] *adv* paresseusement, indolemment.

Indology [ɪnˈdɒlədʒɪ] *n* étude *f* de la civilisation indienne.

indomitable [ɪnˈdɒmɪtəbl] *adj* indomptable, irréductible.

indomitably [ɪnˈdɒmɪtəblɪ] *adv* de façon indomptable, irréductiblement.

Indonesia [ˌɪndəˈniːzjə] *pr n* Indonésie *f*; in ~ en Indonésie.

Indonesian [ˌɪndəˈniːzjən] ◇ *n* -**1.** [person] Indonésien *m*, -enne *f*. -**2.** LING indonésien *m*.
◇ *adj* indonésien.

indoor [ˈɪnˌdɔːʳ] *adj* [toilet] à l'intérieur; [clothing] d'intérieur; [swimming pool, tennis court] couvert; [sport] pratiqué en salle; ~ **athletics** athlétisme *m* en salle; ~ **games** [sports] jeux *mpl* pratiqués en salle; [board-games, charades etc] jeux *mpl* d'intérieur; ~ **plants** plantes *fpl* d'intérieur OR d'appartement; ~ **scene** CIN & TV scène *f* tournée en intérieur.

indoors [ˌɪnˈdɔːz] *adv* à l'intérieur; **let's go** ~ rentrons (à l'intérieur); **it's much cooler** ~ il fait beaucoup plus frais à l'intérieur; **I don't like being** ~ **all day** je n'aime pas rester enfermée toute la journée.

indorse [ɪnˈdɔːs] = **endorse**.

indraught *Br*, **indraft** *Am* [ˈɪndrɑːft] *n* [of liquid, air] afflux *m*.

indrawn [ˌɪnˈdrɔːn] *adj* -**1.** [air]: ~ **breath** aspiration *f*, inspiration *f*. -**2.** [person] replié sur soi-même, renfermé.

indubitable [ɪnˈdjuːbɪtəbl] *adj* indubitable.

indubitably [ɪnˈdjuːbɪtəblɪ] *adv* assurément, indubitablement.

induce [ɪnˈdjuːs] *vt* -**1.** [cause] entraîner, provoquer; **this drug sometimes** ~**s sleepiness** ce médicament peut provoquer la somnolence. -**2.** [persuade] persuader, décider; **nothing will** ~ **me to change my mind** rien ne me décidera à OR ne me fera changer d'avis. -**3.** MED [labour] déclencher (artificiellement). -**4.** PHILOS [infer] induire. -**5.** ELEC induire.

induced [ɪnˈdjuːst] *in cpds*: **work**~ **injury** accident *m* du travail; **drug**~ **sleep** sommeil *m* provoqué par des médicaments.

inducement [ɪnˈdjuːsmənt] *n* -**1.** [encouragement] persuasion *f*. -**2.** [reward] incitation *f*, récompense *f*; [bribe] pot-de-vin *m*; **he was offered considerable financial** ~**s to leave his company** on lui a offert des sommes considérables pour l'inciter à quitter son entreprise.

induct [ɪnˈdʌkt] *vt* -**1.** [into office, post] installer. -**2.** [into mystery, unknown field] initier. -**3.** *Am* MIL appeler (sous les drapeaux). -**4.** ELEC = **induce 5**.

inductance [ɪnˈdʌktəns] *n* ELEC -**1.** [property] inductance *f*. -**2.** [component] inducteur *m*.

inductee [ˌɪndʌkˈtiː] *n Am* MIL conscrit *m*, appelé *m*.

induction [ɪnˈdʌkʃn] *n* -**1.** [into office, post] installation *f*; [into mystery, new field] initiation *f*. -**2.** [causing] provocation *f*, déclenchement *m*; ~ **of sleep by drugs** sommeil *m* provoqué par des médicaments. -**3.** MED [of labour] déclenchement *m* (artificiel). -**4.** PHILOS induction *f*. -**5.** *Am* MIL conscription *f*, appel *m* sous les drapeaux. -**6.** BIOL, ELEC & TECH induction *f*.

induction coil *n* bobine *f* d'inductance.

induction course *n* stage *m* préparatoire OR de formation.

induction motor *n* moteur *m* à induction.

inductive [ɪnˈdʌktɪv] *adj* inductif.

inductor [ɪnˈdʌktəʳ] *n* inducteur *m*.

indulge [ɪnˈdʌldʒ] ◇ *vi*: to ~ in se livrer à; **let us** ~ **in a little speculation** livrons-nous à quelques suppositions; **I occasionally** ~ **in a cigar/drink** je me permets un cigare/verre de temps en temps; **no thank you, I don't** ~ [drink] non merci, je ne bois pas; [smoke] non merci, je ne fume pas.
◇ *vt* -**1.** [person] gâter; **she** ~**s her children** elle gâte ses enfants, elle passe tout à ses enfants; **to** ~ **o.s.** se faire plaisir; **we really** ~**d ourselves** on s'est vraiment fait plaisir. -**2.** [desire, vice] assouvir; **she** ~**d her passion for skiing** elle a satisfait sa passion pour le ski; **he** ~**s her every whim** il se prête à OR il lui passe tous ses caprices. -**3.** COMM [debtor] accorder un délai de paiement à.

indulgence [ɪnˈdʌldʒəns] *n* -**1.** [tolerance, kindness] indulgence *f*. -**2.** [gratification] assouvissement *m*; **the** ~ **of his every desire** l'assouvissement de tous ses désirs; ~ **in bad habits** fait *m* de se complaire dans de mauvaises habitudes. -**3.** [privilege] privilège *m*; [treat] gâterie *f*; **we allow ourselves a few small** ~**s from time to time** nous nous offrons quelques petites gâteries de temps en temps; **smoking is my only** ~ mon seul vice, c'est le tabac. -**4.** RELIG indulgence *f*.

indulgent [ɪnˈdʌldʒənt] *adj* [liberal, kind] indulgent, complaisant; **you shouldn't be so** ~ **with your children** vous ne devriez pas vous montrer aussi indulgent envers vos enfants.

indulgently [ɪnˈdʌldʒəntlɪ] *adv* avec indulgence.

indulin [ˈɪndjʊlɪn], **induline** [ˈɪndjʊlaɪn] *n* induline *f*.

Indus [ˈɪndəs] *pr n*: **the (River)** ~ l'Indus *m*.

industrial [ɪnˈdʌstrɪəl] *adj* [gen] industriel; [unrest] social; **an** ~ **city** une ville industrielle ☐ ~ **accident** accident *m* du travail; ~ **archaeology** archéologie *f* industrielle; ~ **diamond** diamant *m* industriel OR de nature; ~ **dispute** conflit *m* social; ~ **espionage** espionnage *m* industriel; **the Industrial Revolution** la révolution industrielle; ~ **school** *Am* école *f* technique; ~ **workers** travailleurs *mpl* de l'industrie.
◆ **industrials** *npl* ST. EX titres *mpl* industriels.

THE INDUSTRIAL REVOLUTION:
Processus d'industrialisation qui, au XVIIIe siècle, apporta de profonds changements dans la société britannique en bouleversant ses structures et son fonctionnement traditionnel. Si la richesse nationale augmenta rapidement, transformant la Grande-Bretagne en phare économique mondial, elle fut synonyme de misère pour la classe ouvrière jusqu'au XIXe siècle.

---

industrial action *n (U) Br* grève *f*, grèves *fpl*; **they threatened (to take)** ~ ils ont menacé de faire grève.

industrial design *n* dessin *m* industriel.

industrial estate *n Br* zone *f* industrielle.

industrialism [ɪnˈdʌstrɪəlɪzm] *n* industrialisme *m*.

industrialist [ɪnˈdʌstrɪəlɪst] *n* industriel *m*.

industrialization [ɪnˌdʌstrɪəlaɪˈzeɪʃn] *n* industrialisation *f*.

industrialize, -ise [ɪnˈdʌstrɪəlaɪz] ◇ *vt* industrialiser.
◇ *vi* s'industrialiser.

industrialized [ɪnˈdʌstrɪəlaɪzd] *adj* industrialisé; **the** ~ **countries** les pays *mpl* industrialisés.

industrial relations *npl* relations *fpl* entre le patronat et les travailleurs; ~ **have deteriorated** le climat social s'est dégradé.

industrial tribunal *n* ≃ conseil *m* de prud'hommes.

industrious [ɪnˈdʌstrɪəs] *adj* travailleur.

industriously [ɪnˈdʌstrɪəslɪ] *adv* avec application, industrieusement *lit*.

industriousness [ɪnˈdʌstrɪəsnɪs] *n* application *f*, diligence *f*.

industry [ˈɪndʌstrɪ] (*pl* **industries**) *n* -**1.** [business] industrie *f*; **both sides of** ~ syndicats *mpl* et patronat *m*, les partenaires *mpl* sociaux; **the oil/film** ~ l'industrie pétrolière/cinématographique. -**2.** = **industriousness**.

inebriate [*vb* ɪˈniːbrɪeɪt, *adj* & *n* ɪˈniːbrɪət] *fml*
◇ *vt* enivrer, griser.
◇ *adj* ivre.
◇ *n* ivrogne *mf*, alcoolique *mf*.

inebriated [ɪˈniːbrɪeɪtɪd] *adj fml* ivre; ~ **by his success** *fig* grisé par son succès.

inebriation [ɪˌniːbrɪˈeɪʃn], **inebriety** [ˌɪniːˈbraɪətɪ] *n fml* enivrement *m*; [habitual] ivrognerie *f*, alcoolisme *m*.

inedible [ɪnˈedɪbl] *adj* -**1.** [unsafe to eat] non comestible; ~ **mushrooms** des champignons non comestibles. -**2.** [unpleasant to eat] immangeable.

ineducable [ɪnˈedjʊkəbl] *adj* inéducable.

ineffable [ɪnˈefəbl] *adj lit* ineffable, indicible.

ineffably [ɪnˈefəblɪ] *adv lit* ineffablement, indiciblement.

ineffective [ˌɪnɪˈfektɪv] *adj* -**1.** [person] inefficace, incapable, incompétent; **an** ~ **leader** un dirigeant incompétent. -**2.** [action] inefficace, sans effet; **the drug is** ~ **against the new virus** le médicament est inefficace OR n'a aucun effet contre le nouveau virus.

ineffectively [ˌɪnɪˈfektɪvlɪ] *adv* sans résultat.

ineffectiveness [ˌɪnɪˈfektɪvnɪs] *n* inefficacité *f*.

ineffectual [ˌɪnɪˈfektʃʊəl] *adj* incompétent.

inefficacious [ˌɪnefɪˈkeɪʃəs] *adj* inefficace, sans effet.

inefficacity [ˌɪnefɪˈkæsətɪ], **inefficacy** [ɪnˈefɪkəsɪ] *n* inefficacité *f*.

inefficiency [ˌɪnɪˈfɪʃnsɪ] (*pl* **inefficiencies**) *n* inefficacité *f*, manque *m* d'efficacité; **the** ~ **of the old machines** le manque de rendement OR le faible rendement des anciennes machines.

inefficient [ˌɪnɪˈfɪʃnt] *adj* inefficace; **an** ~ **use of resources** une mauvaise utilisation des ressources; **these old machines are too** ~ le rendement de ces vieilles machines est vraiment insuffisant.

inefficiently [ˌɪnɪˈfɪʃntlɪ] *adv* inefficacement.

inelastic [ˌɪnɪˈlæstɪk] *adj* -**1.** [material] rigide, inélastique; [schedule] rigide, inflexible. -**2.** PHYS [collision] inélastique.

inelegant [ɪnˈelɪgənt] *adj* inélégant.

inelegantly [ɪnˈelɪgəntlɪ] *adv* de façon peu élégante.

ineligibility [ɪnˌelɪdʒəˈbɪlətɪ] *n* -**1.** [gen]: **his** ~ **for unemployment benefit** le fait qu'il n'ait pas droit aux allocations de chômage; **the** ~ **of most of the applications** l'irrecevabilité *f* de la plupart des demandes. -**2.** [for election] inéligibilité *f*.

ineligible [ɪnˈelɪdʒəbl] *adj* -**1.** [unqualified] non qualifié; **he is** ~ **for the post** il n'est pas qualifié pour le poste; **to be** ~ **for military service** être inapte au service militaire; **they are** ~ **for unemployment benefit** ils n'ont pas droit aux allocations de chômage; **they are** ~ **to vote** ils n'ont pas le droit de voter. -**2.** [for election] inéligible.

ineluctable [ˌɪnɪˈlʌktəbl] *adj fml* inéluctable.

inept [ɪˈnept] *adj* inepte.

ineptitude [ɪˈneptɪtjuːd] *n* ineptie *f*.

ineptly [ɪˈneptlɪ] *adv* absurdement, stupidement.

ineptness [ɪˈneptnɪs] = **ineptitude**.

inequality [ˌɪnɪˈkwɒlətɪ] (*pl* **inequalities**) *n* inégalité *f*.

inequitable [ɪnˈekwɪtəbl] *adj* inéquitable.

inequity [ɪnˈekwətɪ] (*pl* **inequities**) *n fml* injustice *f*, iniquité *f*.

ineradicable [ˌɪnɪˈrædɪkəbl] *adj* indéracinable.

inert [ɪˈnɜːt] *adj* inerte.

inert gas *n* gaz *m* inerte.

inertia [ɪˈnɜːʃə] *n* inertie *f*.

inertial [ɪˈnɜːʃəl] *adj* inertiel.

inertia-reel seat belt *n* ceinture *f* de sécurité à enrouleur.

inertia selling *n (U) Br* vente *f* forcée.

inescapable [ˌɪnɪˈskeɪpəbl] *adj* [outcome] inévitable, inéluctable; [fact] indéniable.

inescapably [ˌɪnɪ'skeɪpəblɪ] *adv* inévitablement, indéniablement.

inessential [ˌɪnɪ'senʃl] *adj* non essentiel.

◆ **inessentials** *npl* superflu *m*; to do without ~s se passer du superflu.

inestimable [ɪn'estɪməbl] *adj* inestimable, incalculable.

inestimably [ɪn'estɪməblɪ] *adv*: they're ~ rich ils ont une fortune incalculable; he's been ~ lucky il a eu une chance absolument incroyable.

inevitability [ɪnˌevɪtə'bɪlətɪ] *n* inévitabilité *f*.

inevitable [ɪn'evɪtəbl] ◇ *adj* [outcome, consequence] inévitable, inéluctable; [end] inévitable, fatal; war seems ~ la guerre semble inévitable; it's ~ that someone will feel left out il est inévitable OR on ne pourra empêcher que quelqu'un se sente exclu; the ~ cigarette in his mouth l'éternelle OR l'inévitable cigarette au coin des lèvres.

◇ *n* inévitable *m*; we had to resign ourselves to the ~ il fallut nous résoudre à accepter l'inévitable.

inevitably [ɪn'evɪtəblɪ] *adv* inévitablement, fatalement.

inexact [ˌɪnɪg'zækt] *adj* [imprecise] imprécis; [wrong] inexact, erroné; our figures are still ~ nos chiffres sont encore imprécis.

inexactitude [ˌɪnɪg'zæktɪtjuːd] *n* -**1.** [imprecision] imprécision *f*; [incorrectness] inexactitude *f*. -**2.** [mistake] inexactitude *f*.

inexactly [ˌɪnɪg'zæktlɪ] *adv* [imprecisely] de façon imprécise; [incorrectly] inexactement, incorrectement.

inexcusable [ˌɪnɪk'skjuːzəbl] *adj* inexcusable, impardonnable.

inexcusably [ˌɪnɪk'skjuːzəblɪ] *adv*: ~ rude d'une grossièreté impardonnable; he behaved quite ~ at the party la façon dont il s'est comporté à la soirée est inexcusable.

inexhaustible [ˌɪnɪg'zɔːstəbl] *adj* -**1.** [source, energy, patience] inépuisable, illimité. -**2.** [person] infatigable.

inexorable [ɪn'eksərəbl] *adj* inexorable.

inexorably [ɪn'eksərəblɪ] *adv* inexorablement.

inexpedient [ˌɪnɪk'spiːdjənt] *adj* peu judicieux, malavisé.

inexpensive [ˌɪnɪk'spensɪv] *adj* bon marché *(inv)*, peu cher.

inexpensively [ˌɪnɪk'spensɪvlɪ] *adv* [sell] (à) bon marché, à bas prix; [live] à peu de frais.

inexperience [ˌɪnɪk'spɪərɪəns] *n* inexpérience *f*, manque *m* d'expérience.

inexperienced [ˌɪnɪk'spɪərɪənst] *adj* inexpérimenté.

inexpert [ɪn'ekspɜːt] *adj* inexpérimenté, inexpert *lit*.

inexpertly [ɪn'ekspɜːtlɪ] *adv* maladroitement.

inexplicable [ˌɪnɪk'splɪkəbl] *adj* inexplicable.

inexplicably [ˌɪnɪk'splɪkəblɪ] *adv* inexplicablement.

inexpressible [ˌɪnɪk'spresəbl] *adj* inexprimable, indicible.

inexpressive [ˌɪnɪk'spresɪv] *adj* inexpressif.

inextinguishable [ˌɪnɪk'stɪŋgwɪʃəbl] *adj* [fire] impossible à éteindre, inextinguible *lit*; [need, desire] insatiable; [thirst] inextinguible; [passion] irrépressible, incontrôlable.

in extremis [ɪnɪk'striːmɪs] *adv* in extremis, de justesse.

inextricable [ˌɪnɪk'strɪkəbl] *adj* inextricable.

inextricably [ˌɪnɪk'strɪkəblɪ] *adv* inextricablement.

infallibility [ɪnˌfælə'bɪlətɪ] *n* infaillibilité *f*.

infallible [ɪn'fæləbl] *adj* infaillible.

infallibly [ɪn'fæləblɪ] *adv* infailliblement, immanquablement.

infamous ['ɪnfəməs] *adj* -**1.** [notorious] tristement célèbre, notoire. -**2.** [shocking – conduct] déshonorant, infamant.

infamy ['ɪnfəmɪ] (*pl* **infamies**) *n* -**1.** [notoriety] triste notoriété *f*. -**2.** [notorious act, event] infamie *f*.

infancy ['ɪnfənsɪ] (*pl* **infancies**) *n* -**1.** [early childhood] petite enfance *f*; a child in its ~ un enfant en bas âge. -**2.** *fig* débuts *mpl*, enfance *f*; when electronics was still in its ~ quand l'électronique n'en était qu'à ses balbutiements. -**3.** JUR minorité *f* (légale).

infant ['ɪnfənt] ◇ *n* -**1.** [young child] petit enfant *m*, petite enfant *f*, enfant *mf* en bas âge; [baby] bébé *m*; [new-born] nouveau-né *m*. -**2.** *Br* SCH *élève dans les premières années d'école primaire*. -**3.** JUR mineur *m*, -e *f*.

◇ *adj* [organization] naissant; the ~ Church l'Église des origines OR des premiers jours.

◇ *comp* -**1.** [food] pour bébés; [disease, mortality] infantile. -**2.** *Br* [teacher, teaching] des premières années d'école primaire.

infanticide [ɪn'fæntɪsaɪd] *n* -**1.** [act] infanticide *m*. -**2.** [person] infanticide *mf*.

infantile ['ɪnfəntaɪl] *adj* -**1.** *pej* [childish] infantile, puéril. -**2.** [of, for infants] infantile.

infantile paralysis *n (U) dated* paralysie *f* infantile.

infantilism [ɪn'fæntɪlɪzm] *n* infantilisme *m*.

infantry ['ɪnfəntrɪ] ◇ *n* infanterie *f*.

◇ *adj* de l'infanterie.

infantryman ['ɪnfəntrɪmən] (*pl* **infantrymen** [-mən]) *n* soldat *m* d'infanterie, fantassin *m*.

infant school *n Br* école *f* maternelle *(5-7 ans)*.

infarct [ɪn'fɑːkt], **infarction** [ɪn'fɑːkʃn] *n* infarctus *m (du myocarde)*.

infatuate [ɪn'fætjʊeɪt] *vt*: he was ~d with her il s'était entiché d'elle.

infatuation [ɪnˌfætjʊ'eɪʃn] *n* engouement *m*; his ~ for OR with her son engouement pour elle.

infect [ɪn'fekt] *vt* -**1.** MED [wound, organ, person, animal] infecter; is the liver ~ed? est-ce que le foie est infecté OR atteint?; I hope that cut won't get ~ed j'espère que cette coupure ne s'infectera pas; to ~ sb with sthg transmettre qqch à qqn; he ~ed all his friends with the flu il a transmis OR donné sa grippe à tous ses amis. -**2.** [food, water] contaminer. -**3.** *fig* [subj: vice] corrompre, contaminer; [subj: emotion] se communiquer à; they ~ed us with their enthusiasm ils nous ont communiqué leur enthousiasme.

infected [ɪn'fektɪd] *adj* [wound] infecté; [area] contaminé.

infection [ɪn'fekʃn] *n* -**1.** MED infection *f*; a throat ~ une infection de la gorge, une angine. -**2.** *fig* contagion *f*, contamination *f*.

infectious [ɪn'fekʃəs] *adj* -**1.** MED [disease] infectieux; [person] contagieux. -**2.** *fig* contagieux, communicatif.

infectious hepatitis *n (U)* hépatite *f* infectieuse, hépatite *f* virale A.

infectious mononucleosis *n (U)* MED mononucléose *f* infectieuse.

infectiousness [ɪn'fekʃəsnɪs] *n* -**1.** MED caractère *m* infectieux. -**2.** *fig* caractère *m* contagieux OR communicatif, contagiosité *f lit*.

infelicitous [ˌɪnfɪ'lɪsɪtəs] *adj lit* malheureux, malchanceux.

infelicity [ˌɪnfɪ'lɪsɪtɪ] (*pl* **infelicities**) *n lit* -**1.** [state of misfortune] malchance *f*, infortune *f lit*. -**2.** [piece of bad luck] malchance *f*. -**3.** [remark] parole *f* malheureuse, maladresse *f*.

infer [ɪn'fɜːʳ] (*pt* & *pp* **inferred**, *cont* **inferring**) *vt* -**1.** [deduce] conclure, inférer, déduire; what are we to ~ from their absence? que devons-nous conclure de leur absence?; I inferred from his look that I had done something wrong à son regard, j'ai compris que j'avais fait quelque chose de mal. -**2.** [imply] suggérer, laisser supposer; what are you inferring by that? qu'insinuez-vous par là?

inference ['ɪnfrəns] *n* déduction *f*; LOGIC inférence *f*; what ~s can we draw from it? quelles conclusions pouvons-nous en tirer?, que pouvons-nous en déduire?

inferential [ˌɪnfə'renʃl] *adj* [reasoning] par inférence; [proof] déduit par inférence; [belief] basé sur l'inférence.

inferior [ɪn'fɪərɪəʳ] ◇ *adj* -**1.** [quality, worth, soc status] inférieur; he always felt ~ to h brother il a toujours éprouvé un sentime d'infériorité par rapport à son frère; to make s feel ~ donner un sentiment d'infériorité à qq ~ imported goods marchandises *fpl* importé de qualité inférieure. -**2.** [in rank] subalterne; sh holds an ~ position in the company elle a u poste subalterne dans la société. -**3.** ANAT & S [in space, position] inférieur; the ~ maxillary mâchoire inférieure. -**4.** TYPO: ~ charact (caractère *m* en) indice *m*. -**5.** BOT: ~ ovai ovaire *m* infère OR adhérent.

◇ *n* [in social status] inférieur *m*, -e *f*; [in rar hierarchy] subalterne *mf*, subordonné *m*, -e *f*; h never speaks to his ~s il n'adresse jamais parole à ses subordonnés.

inferior court *n* cour *f* de juridiction inférieur

inferiority [ɪnˌfɪərɪ'ɒrətɪ] (*pl* **inferioritie** *n* infériorité *f*.

inferiority complex *n* complexe *m* d'infériorité.

inferior planet *n* planète *f* inférieure.

infernal [ɪn'fɜːnl] *adj* -**1.** *inf* [awful] infernal; sto that ~ racket OR din! arrêtez ce raffut c boucan infernal!; that ~ fuse has blow again! ce satané fusible a encore sauté! -**2.** [hell] infernal; [diabolical] infernal, diabolique

infernally *inf* [ɪn'fɜːnəlɪ] *adv* terriblemen épouvantablement; it's ~ hot il fait une ch leur d'enfer.

inferno [ɪn'fɜːnəʊ] (*pl* **infernos**) *n* -**1.** [fire] br sier *m*; the hotel was a blazing ~ l'hôtel n'éta qu'un gigantesque brasier. -**2.** [hell] enfer *m*.

infertile [ɪn'fɜːtaɪl] *adj* [person, animal] stéril [land, soil] stérile, infertile *lit*.

infertility [ˌɪnfə'tɪlətɪ] *n* stérilité *f*, infertilité *f l*

infest [ɪn'fest] *vt* infester; ~ed with rats vermin infesté de rats/vermine; shark-~e waters eaux infestées de requins.

infestation [ˌɪnfe'steɪʃn] *n* infestation *f*.

infibulation [ɪnˌfɪbjʊ'leɪʃn] *n* infibulation *f*.

infidel ['ɪnfɪdəl] ◇ *n* infidèle *mf*.

◇ *adj* infidèle, incroyant.

infidelity [ˌɪnfɪ'delətɪ] (*pl* **infidelities**) *n* -**1.** [be trayal] infidélité *f*. -**2.** [lack of faith] incroyance irréligion *f*.

infield ['ɪnfiːld] *n* SPORT [in cricket, baseba champ *m* intérieur.

infighting ['ɪnˌfaɪtɪŋ] *n (U)* -**1.** *Br* [within grou conflits *mpl* internes, luttes *fpl* intestines. -**2.** [boxing] corps à corps *m*.

infill ['ɪnfɪl] ◇ *vt* remplir, combler.

◇ *n* matériau *m* de remplissage.

infiltrate ['ɪnfɪltreɪt] ◇ *vt* -**1.** [organization] i filtrer, noyauter; the police had ~d the te rorist group la police avait infiltré OR noyau le groupe terroriste; they ~d spies into th organization ils ont envoyé des espions po infiltrer l'organisation. -**2.** [subj: liquid] s'infiltr dans.

◇ *vi* s'infiltrer.

infiltration [ˌɪnfɪl'treɪʃn] *n* -**1.** [of group] infiltr tion *f*, noyautage *m*. -**2.** [by liquid] infiltration

infiltrator ['ɪnfɪltreɪtəʳ] *n* agent *m* infiltré; the are ~s in the party le parti a été infiltré c noyauté.

infinite ['ɪnfɪnət] ◇ *adj* -**1.** infini; ~ set MAT ensemble *m* infini. -**2.** *fig* infini, incalculable; will do ~ harm to us all cela nous fera à tou un mal incalculable; the government, in its ~ wisdom, has decided to close the factory *irc* le gouvernement, dans son infinie sagesse, décidé de fermer l'usine.

◇ *n* infini *m*.

infinitely ['ɪnfɪnətlɪ] *adv* infiniment.

infinitesimal [ˌɪnfɪnɪ'tesɪml] *adj* -**1.** MATH inf nitésimal. -**2.** [tiny] infinitésimal, infime.

infinitesimally [ˌɪnfɪnɪ'tesɪməlɪ] *adv* infir ment.

infinitival [ɪnˌfɪnɪ'taɪvl] *adj* infinitif; ~ claus proposition *f* infinitive.

infinitive [ɪn'fɪnɪtɪv] ◇ *n* infinitif *m*.

◇ *adj* infinitif.

infinity [ɪn'fɪnətɪ] (*pl* infinities) *n* -**1.** infinité *f*, infini *m*; there is an ~ of names to choose from *fig* on peut choisir parmi une infinité de noms; it stretches to ~ cela s'étend jusqu'à l'infini. -**2.** MATH & PHOT infini *m*.

infirm [ɪn'fɜːm] ◇ *adj* -**1.** [in health, body] invalide, infirme. -**2.** *lit* [in moral resolution] indécis, irrésolu; to be ~ of purpose manquer de détermination. -**3.** JUR invalide.
◇ *npl*: the ~ les infirmes *mpl*.

infirmary [ɪn'fɜːmərɪ] (*pl* infirmaries) *n* [hospital] hôpital *m*, dispensaire *m*; [sickroom] infirmerie *f*.

infirmity [ɪn'fɜːmətɪ] (*pl* infirmities) *n* -**1.** [physical] infirmité *f*. -**2.** [moral] défaut *m*, faiblesse *f*.

infix [*vb* ɪn'fɪks, *n* 'ɪnfɪks] ◇ *vt* -**1.** [instil] instiller, implanter. -**2.** LING insérer (comme infixe).
◇ *n* LING infixe *m*.

inflame [ɪn'fleɪm] ◇ *vt* -**1.** [rouse - person, crowd] exciter, enflammer; [anger, hatred, passion] attiser, exacerber; the argument became ~d la discussion s'est enflammée; she was ~d with anger/passion elle brûlait de colère/de passion. -**2.** MED [wound, infection] enflammer; [organ, tissue] irriter, infecter. -**3.** [set fire to] enflammer, mettre le feu à. -**4.** *lit* [redden] enflammer.
◇ *vi* -**1.** [person, heart, passion] s'enflammer. -**2.** MED [wound, infection] s'enflammer; [organ, tissue] s'irriter, s'infecter. -**3.** [catch fire] s'enflammer, s'embraser.

inflamed [ɪn'fleɪmd] *adj* -**1.** MED [eyes, throat, tendon] enflammé, irrité. -**2.** *fig* [passions, hatred] enflammé, ardent.

inflammable [ɪn'flæməbl] ◇ *adj* inflammable; an ~ situation *fig* une situation explosive.
◇ *n* matière *f* inflammable.

inflammation [ˌɪnflə'meɪʃn] *n* inflammation *f*.

inflammatory [ɪn'flæmətrɪ] *adj* -**1.** [speech, propaganda] incendiaire. -**2.** MED inflammatoire.

inflatable [ɪn'fleɪtəbl] ◇ *adj* [toy] gonflable; [mattress, boat] pneumatique.
◇ *n* [boat] canot *m* pneumatique, bateau *m* gonflable.

inflate [ɪn'fleɪt] ◇ *vt* -**1.** [tyre, balloon, boat] gonfler; [lungs] emplir d'air; [chest] gonfler, bomber. -**2.** [opinion, importance] gonfler, exagérer; to ~ the importance of an event exagérer OR grossir l'importance d'un événement. -**3.** ECON [prices] faire monter, augmenter; [economy] provoquer l'inflation de; to ~ the currency provoquer une inflation monétaire.
◇ *vi* -**1.** [tyre] se gonfler; [lungs] s'emplir d'air; [chest] se gonfler, se bomber. -**2.** ECON [prices, money] subir une inflation; the government decided to ~ le gouvernement a décidé d'avoir recours à des mesures inflationnistes.

inflated [ɪn'fleɪtɪd] *adj* -**1.** [tyre] gonflé. -**2.** [opinion, importance] exagéré; [style] emphatique, pompier; he has an ~ sense of his own importance il se fait une idée exagérée de sa propre importance. -**3.** [price] exagéré.

inflation [ɪn'fleɪʃn] *n* -**1.** ECON inflation *f*. -**2.** [of tyre, balloon, boat] gonflement *m*; [of idea, importance] grossissement *m*, exagération *f*.

inflationary [ɪn'fleɪʃnrɪ] *adj* inflationniste; ~ spiral spirale *f* inflationniste OR de l'inflation.

inflationism [ɪn'fleɪʃənɪzm] *n* inflationnisme *m*.

inflationist [ɪn'fleɪʃənɪst] *adj* inflationniste.

inflation-proof *adj* protégé contre les effets de l'inflation.

inflect [ɪn'flekt] ◇ *vt* -**1.** LING [verb] conjuguer; [noun, pronoun, adjective] décliner; ~ed form forme *f* fléchie. -**2.** [tone, voice] moduler. -**3.** [curve] infléchir.
◇ *vi* LING: adjectives do not ~ in English les adjectifs ne prennent pas de désinence en anglais.

inflection [ɪn'flekʃn] *n* -**1.** [of tone, voice] inflexion *f*, modulation *f*. -**2.** LING désinence *f*, flexion *f*. -**3.** [curve] flexion *f*, inflexion *f*, courbure *f*. -**4.** MATH inflexion *f*; point of ~ point *m* d'inflexion.

inflectional [ɪn'flekʃənl] *adj* flexionnel.

inflexibility [ɪnˌfleksə'bɪlətɪ] *n* inflexibilité *f*, rigidité *f*.

inflexible [ɪn'fleksəbl] *adj* inflexible, rigide.

inflexion *etc* [ɪn'flekʃn] *Br* = **inflection**.

inflict [ɪn'flɪkt] *vt* infliger; to ~ pain/suffering on sb faire mal à/faire souffrir qqn; to ~ a punishment/defeat on sb infliger un châtiment/une défaite à qqn; I don't want to ~ myself OR my company on you je ne veux pas vous imposer OR infliger ma compagnie.

in-flight *adj* en vol; ~ meals repas *mpl* servis à bord; ~ video vidéo *f* projetée en vol; ~ refuelling ravitaillement *m* en vol.

inflorescence [ˌɪnflə'resəns] *n* BOT -**1.** inflorescence *f*. -**2.** [blossoming] floraison *f*.

inflow ['ɪnfləʊ] *n* [of water, gas] arrivée *f*, afflux *m*; the ~ of capital/of cheap imports l'afflux de capitaux/de produits importés de mauvaise qualité; cash ~ rentrées *fpl* d'argent.

influence ['ɪnflʊəns] ◇ *n* influence *f*; to have ~ avoir de l'influence; to bring one's ~ to bear on sthg exercer son influence sur qqch; he is a man of ~ c'est un homme influent; foreign ~ in Africa l'influence étrangère en Afrique; I have no ~ over them je n'ai aucune influence sur eux; he is a bad ~ on them il a une mauvaise influence sur eux; she is a disruptive ~ c'est un élément perturbateur; you can see the ~ of Bacon in his paintings on voit l'influence de Bacon dans ses tableaux; his music has a strong reggae ~ sa musique est fortement influencée par le reggae; they acted under his ~ ils ont agi sous son influence; she was under the ~ of drink/drugs elle était sous l'emprise de l'alcool/de la drogue; driving under the ~ of alcohol conduite en état d'ivresse; to be under the ~ *inf* [drunk] être soûl.
◇ *vt* influencer, influer sur; ~d by cubism influencé par le cubisme; don't let yourself be ~d by them ne te laisse pas influencer par eux; to ~ sb to the good exercer une bonne influence sur qqn; he is easily ~d il se laisse facilement influencer, il est très influençable; how can the stars ~ our lives? comment les étoiles peuvent-elles influer sur notre vie?

influential [ˌɪnflʊ'enʃl] *adj* influent, puissant; [newspaper, TV programme] influent, qui a de l'influence; she's an ~ woman c'est une femme qui a de l'influence.

influenza [ˌɪnflʊ'enzə] *n* (U) *fml* grippe *f*; to have ~ avoir la grippe.

influx ['ɪnflʌks] *n* -**1.** [inflow] afflux *m*; an ~ of capital un afflux de capitaux. -**2.** [of river] embouchure *f*.

info *inf* ['ɪnfəʊ] *n* (U) tuyaux *mpl*.

infomercial [ˌɪnfəʊ'mɜːʃl] *n* *Am publicité télévisée sous forme de débat sur l'annonceur et son produit.*

inform [ɪn'fɔːm] ◇ *vt* informer; will you ~ him of your decision? allez-vous l'informer de votre décision?; I have been ~ed that the funds have arrived on m'a informé que les fonds étaient arrivés; I'll keep you ~ed je vous tiendrai au courant.
◇ *vi*: to ~ on OR against sb dénoncer qqn.

informal [ɪn'fɔːml] *adj* -**1.** [gathering, discussion, meeting] informel; [dinner] décontracté. -**2.** [clothes]: his dress was ~ il était habillé simplement; ~ or evening dress? tenue de ville ou tenue de soirée? -**3.** [unofficial - arrangement, agreement] officieux; [- visit] non officiel; they had ~ talks with the Russians ils ont eu des entretiens non officiels avec les Russes. -**4.** [colloquial] familier.

informality [ˌɪnfɔː'mælətɪ] (*pl* informalities) *n* -**1.** [of gathering, meal] simplicité *f*; [of discussion, interview] absence *f* de formalité; [of manners] naturel *m*. -**2.** [of expression, language] familiarité *f*, liberté *f*.

informally [ɪn'fɔːməlɪ] *adv* -**1.** [casually - entertain, discuss] sans cérémonie; [- behave] simplement, avec naturel; [- dress] simplement. -**2.** [unofficially] officieusement. -**3.** [colloquially] familièrement, avec familiarité.

informant [ɪn'fɔːmənt] *n* [gen, SOCIOL & LING] informateur *m*, -trice *f*.

informatics [ˌɪnfə'mætɪks] *n* (U) sciences *fpl* de l'information.

information [ˌɪnfə'meɪʃn] *n* -**1.** (U) [facts] renseignements *mpl*, informations *fpl*; a piece OR bit of ~ un renseignement, une information; if my ~ is correct si mes informations sont exactes; do you have any ~ on OR about the new model? avez-vous des renseignements concernant OR sur le nouveau modèle?; I'd like some ~ about train times je voudrais des renseignements sur les horaires des trains; for more ~, call this number pour plus de renseignements OR de précisions, appelez ce numéro; the government is operating an ~ blackout le gouvernement fait de la rétention d'information. -**2.** [communication] information *f*; they discussed the importance of ~ in our time ils ont parlé de l'importance de l'information à notre époque. -**3.** (U) [knowledge] connaissances *fpl*; her ~ on the subject is unequalled elle connaît ce sujet mieux que personne; for your ~, please find enclosed... ADMIN à titre d'information, vous trouverez ci-joint...; for your ~, it happened in 1938 je vous signale que cela s'est passé en 1938. -**4.** COMPUT & SCI information *f*; the transmission of genetic ~ la transmission de l'information génétique. -**5.** (U) [service, department] (service *m* des) renseignements *mpl*; ask at the ~ desk adressez-vous aux renseignements; to call ~ *Am* appeler les renseignements. -**6.** *Br* JUR acte *m* d'accusation; to lay an ~ against sb porter une accusation contre qqn.

information bureau *Br*, **information office** *n* bureau *m* OR service *m* des renseignements.

information processing *n* -**1.** [action] traitement *m* de l'information. -**2.** [domain] informatique *f*; ~ error erreur *f* dans le traitement de l'information.

information retrieval *n* recherche *f* documentaire; COMPUT recherche *f* d'information.

information science *n* science *f* de l'information.

information technology *n* technologie *f* de l'information, informatique *f*.

information theory *n* théorie *f* de l'information.

informative [ɪn'fɔːmətɪv] *adj* [lecture, book, TV programme] instructif; [person]: he wasn't very ~ about his future plans il ne nous a pas dit grand-chose de ses projets.

informed [ɪn'fɔːmd] *adj* -**1.** [having information] informé, renseigné; according to ~ sources selon des sources bien informées; she's very well ~ elle est très bien informée OR renseignée. -**2.** [based on information]: an ~ choice un choix fait en toute connaissance de cause; it will allow us to make ~ decisions cela nous permettra de prendre des décisions en toute connaissance de cause; he made an ~ guess il a essayé de deviner en s'aidant de ce qu'il sait. -**3.** [learned, cultured] cultivé.

informer [ɪn'fɔːmə^r] *n* -**1.** [denouncer] informateur *m*; police ~ indicateur (de police). -**2.** [information source] informateur *m*, -trice *f*.

infraction [ɪn'frækʃn] *n* infraction *f*; ~ of the code/regulations infraction au code/règlement.

infra dig *inf* [ˌɪnfrə'dɪg] *adj Br* dégradant.

infrared [ˌɪnfrə'red] ◇ *adj* infrarouge; ~ photography photographie *f* (à l') infrarouge.
◇ *n* infrarouge *m*.

infrasonic [ˌɪnfrə'sɒnɪk] *adj* infrasonore.

infrasound ['ɪnfrəˌsaʊnd] *n* infrason *m*.

infrastructure ['ɪnfrəˌstrʌktʃə^r] *n* infrastructure *f*.

infrequency [ɪn'friːkwənsɪ] *n* rareté *f*.

infrequent [ɪn'friːkwənt] *adj* [event] peu fréquent, rare; [visitor] épisodique.

infrequently [ɪnˈfriːkwəntlɪ] *adv* rarement, peu souvent.

infringe [ɪnˈfrɪndʒ] ◇ *vt* [agreement, rights] violer, enfreindre; [law] enfreindre, contrevenir à; [patent] contrefaire; to ~ copyright enfreindre les lois de copyright.
◇ *vi*: to ~ on OR upon empiéter sur.

infringement [ɪnˈfrɪndʒmənt] *n* [violation] infraction *f*, atteinte *f*; [encroachment] empiètement *m*; an ~ of the treaty conditions une violation des termes du traité; an ~ on freedom of speech une atteinte à la liberté d'expression; that's an ~ of my rights c'est une atteinte à mes droits.

infuriate [ɪnˈfjʊərɪeɪt] *vt* [enrage] rendre furieux; [exasperate] exaspérer.

infuriated [ɪnˈfjʊərɪeɪtɪd] *adj* furieux.

infuriating [ɪnˈfjʊərɪeɪtɪŋ] *adj* agaçant, exaspérant; it's/he's ~! c'est/il est exaspérant!

infuriatingly [ɪnˈfjʊərɪeɪtɪŋlɪ] *adv*: ~ stubborn d'un entêtement exaspérant; she remained ~ polite elle restait d'une politesse exaspérante.

infuse [ɪnˈfjuːz] ◇ *vt* -**1.** [inspire, instill] inspirer, insuffler, infuser *lit*; to ~ sb with sthg, to ~ sthg into sb inspirer OR insuffler qqch à qqn; her speech ~d them with courage son discours leur a inspiré OR insufflé du courage. -**2.** CULIN (faire) infuser.
◇ *vi* CULIN infuser.

infuser [ɪnˈfjuːzəʳ] *n*: tea ~ boule *f* à thé.

infusion [ɪnˈfjuːʒn] *n* infusion *f*.

ingenious [ɪnˈdʒiːnjəs] *adj* [person, idea, device] ingénieux, astucieux.

ingeniously [ɪnˈdʒiːnjəslɪ] *adv* ingénieusement.

ingenuity [ˌɪndʒɪˈnjuːətɪ] (*pl* **ingenuities**) *n* ingéniosité *f*.

ingenuous [ɪnˈdʒenjʊəs] *adj* [naive] ingénu; [frank] candide.

ingenuously [ɪnˈdʒenjʊəslɪ] *adv* [naively] ingénument; [frankly] franchement.

ingenuousness [ɪnˈdʒenjʊəsnɪs] *n* [naivety] ingénuité *f*, naïveté *f*; [frankness] franchise *f*, candeur *f*.

ingest [ɪnˈdʒest] *vt* [food, liquid] ingérer.

ingestion [ɪnˈdʒestʃn] *n* ingestion *f*.

inglenook [ˈɪŋglnʊk] *n* coin *m* du feu; ~ fireplace vaste cheminée *f* à l'ancienne.

inglorious [ɪnˈglɔːrɪəs] *adj* [shameful] déshonorant; an ~ defeat une défaite déshonorante OR ignominieuse.

ingloriously [ɪnˈglɔːrɪəslɪ] *adv* sans gloire.

ingoing [ˈɪnˌgəʊɪŋ] *adj* [tenant, president] nouveau.

ingot [ˈɪŋgət] *n* lingot *m*; gold/cast-iron ~ lingot d'or/de fonte.

ingrained [ˌɪnˈgreɪnd] *adj* [attitude, fear, prejudice] enraciné, inébranlable; [habit] invétéré, tenace; [belief] inébranlable; ~ dirt crasse *f*.

ingratiate [ɪnˈgreɪʃɪeɪt] *vt*: to ~ o.s. (with sb) s'insinuer dans les bonnes grâces (de qqn).

ingratiating [ɪnˈgreɪʃɪeɪtɪŋ] *adj* [manners, person] insinuant; [smile] mielleux.

ingratitude [ɪnˈgrætɪtjuːd] *n* ingratitude *f*.

ingredient [ɪnˈgriːdjənt] *n* -**1.** CULIN ingrédient *m*; '~s: fruit juice, water' 'composition: jus de fruit, eau'. -**2.** [element] élément *m*, ingrédient *m lit*.

ingress [ˈɪngres] *n* -**1.** *fml* OR *lit* entrée *f*; to have free ~ avoir accès libre. -**2.** ASTRON immersion *f*.

ingressive [ɪnˈgresɪv] *adj* LING ingressif.

in-group *n* groupe *m* d'initiés.

ingrowing toenail [ˈɪnˌgrəʊɪŋ-] *n Br* ongle *m* incarné.

ingrown [ˈɪnˌgrəʊn] *adj* -**1.** [toenail] incarné. -**2.** [ingrained - habit] enraciné, tenace. -**3.** [introverted] renfermé, réservé.

inhabit [ɪnˈhæbɪt] *vt* habiter; the island is no longer ~ed l'île n'est plus habitée OR est maintenant inhabitée.

inhabitable [ɪnˈhæbɪtəbl] *adj* habitable.

inhabitant [ɪnˈhæbɪtənt] *n* habitant *m*, -e *f*.

inhalant [ɪnˈheɪlənt] *n* inhalation *f*.

inhalation [ˌɪnhəˈleɪʃn] *n* -**1.** [of air] inspiration *f*. -**2.** [of gas, glue] inhalation *f*.

inhalator [ˈɪnhəleɪtəʳ] *n* inhalateur *m*.

inhale [ɪnˈheɪl] ◇ *vt* [fumes, gas] inhaler; [fresh air, scent] respirer; [smoke] avaler.
◇ *vi* [smoker] avaler la fumée; [breathe in] aspirer.

inhaler [ɪnˈheɪləʳ] = **inhalator**.

inhere [ɪnˈhɪəʳ] *vi fml* être inhérent; the powers that ~ in the state les pouvoirs (qui sont) inhérents OR propres à l'État.

inherent [ɪnˈhɪərənt, ɪnˈherənt] *adj* inhérent; ~ in OR to inhérent à.

inherently [ɪnˈhɪərəntlɪ, ɪnˈherəntlɪ] *adv* intrinsèquement, par nature; the system is ~ inefficient le système est inefficace par nature.

inherit [ɪnˈherɪt] ◇ *vt* -**1.** [property, right] hériter (de); [title, peerage] accéder à; she ~ed a million dollars elle a hérité d'un million de dollars. -**2.** [situation, tradition, attitude] hériter; the problems ~ed from the previous government les problèmes hérités du gouvernement précédent ‖ [characteristic, feature] hériter (de); she ~ed her father's intelligence elle a hérité (de) l'intelligence de son père.
◇ *vi* hériter; she stands to ~ when her aunt dies elle doit hériter à la mort de sa tante.

inheritance [ɪnˈherɪtəns] *n* -**1.** [legacy] héritage *m*; to come into an ~ faire OR toucher un héritage. -**2.** [succession] succession *f*; to claim sthg by right of ~ revendiquer qqch en faisant valoir son droit à la succession. -**3.** SCI hérédité *f*; genetic ~ does not explain this phenomenon ce phénomène ne peut s'expliquer par l'héritage génétique. -**4.** [heritage] héritage *m*, patrimoine *m*; our cultural ~ notre héritage culturel.

inheritance tax *n* droits *mpl* de succession.

inheritor [ɪnˈherɪtəʳ] *n* héritier *m*, -ère *f*.

inhibit [ɪnˈhɪbɪt] *vt* -**1.** [hinder - person, freedom] gêner, entraver; were you ~ed by him being there? est-ce que sa présence vous a gêné?; a law which ~s free speech une loi qui constitue une entrave à la liberté d'expression. -**2.** [check - growth, development] freiner, entraver; to ~ progress entraver la marche du progrès. -**3.** [suppress - desires, emotions] inhiber, refouler; PSYCH inhiber. -**4.** [forbid] interdire. -**5.** CHEM inhiber.

inhibited [ɪnˈhɪbɪtɪd] *adj* inhibé.

inhibiting [ɪnˈhɪbɪtɪŋ] *adj* inhibant.

inhibition [ˌɪnhɪˈbɪʃn] *n* [gen] inhibition *f*.

inhibitor, inhibiter [ɪnˈhɪbɪtəʳ] *n* inhibiteur *m*.

inhibitory [ɪnˈhɪbɪtərɪ] *adj* -**1.** CHEM & PSYCH inhibiteur. -**2.** [prohibitory] prohibitif.

inhospitable [ˌɪnhɒˈspɪtəbl] *adj* -**1.** [person] peu accueillant; I don't wish to appear ~, but... je ne voudrais pas vous mettre à la porte, mais... -**2.** [weather] rude, rigoureux.

inhospitably [ˌɪnhɒˈspɪtəblɪ] *adv* d'une manière peu accueillante.

in-house ◇ *adj* interne *(à une entreprise)*; ~ journal journal *m* interne; a very small ~ staff un personnel permanent très peu nombreux; ~ training formation *f* interne.
◇ *adv* sur place.

inhuman [ɪnˈhjuːmən] *adj* [behaviour] inhumain, barbare; [person, place, process] inhumain.

inhumane [ˌɪnhjuːˈmeɪn] *adj* cruel.

inhumanity [ˌɪnhjuːˈmænətɪ] (*pl* **inhumanities**) *n* -**1.** [quality] inhumanité *f*, barbarie *f*, cruauté *f*; man's ~ to man la cruauté de l'homme pour l'homme. -**2.** [act] atrocité *f*, brutalité *f*.

inhumation [ˌɪnhjuːˈmeɪʃn] *n fml* inhumation *f*.

inhume [ɪnˈhjuːm] *vt fml* inhumer.

inimical [ɪˈnɪmɪkl] *adj* -**1.** [unfavourable]: ~ to peu favorable à. -**2.** [unfriendly] inamical.

inimitable [ɪˈnɪmɪtəbl] *adj* inimitable.

inimitably [ɪˈnɪmɪtəblɪ] *adv* d'une façon inimitable.

iniquitous [ɪˈnɪkwɪtəs] *adj* inique.

iniquity [ɪˈnɪkwətɪ] *n* iniquité *f*.

initial [ɪˈnɪʃl] (*Br pt* & *pp* initialled, *cont* initialling, *Am pt* & *pp* initialed, *cont* initialing) ◇ *adj* initial; my ~ reaction ma première réaction; we expect a few problems in the ~ stages dans un premier temps, nous nous attendons à quelques difficultés; the project is still in its ~ stages le projet en est encore à ses débuts ❑ ~ letter initiale *f*.
◇ *n* -**1.** [letter] initiale *f*; it's got his ~s on it il y a ses initiales dessus. -**2.** TYPO [of chapter] lettrine *f*.
◇ *vt* [memo, page] parapher, parafer, signer de ses initiales.

initialization [ɪˌnɪʃəlaɪˈzeɪʃn] *n* COMPUT initialisation *f*.

initialize, -ise [ɪˈnɪʃəlaɪz] *vt* COMPUT initialiser.

initially [ɪˈnɪʃəlɪ] *adv* initialement, à l'origine; the carpet was white ~ à l'origine, le tapis était blanc.

initiate [*vb* ɪˈnɪʃɪeɪt, *n* ɪˈnɪʃɪət] ◇ *vt* -**1.** [talks, debate] amorcer, engager; [policy] lancer; [quarrel, reaction] provoquer, déclencher; the pilot has ~d landing procedures le pilote a entamé OR amorcé les procédures d'atterrissage; I find it hard to ~ conversation with him je trouve difficile d'engager la conversation avec lui. -**2.** [person] initier; to ~ sb into sthg initier qqn à qqch.
◇ *n* initié *m*, -e *f*.

initiation [ɪˌnɪʃɪˈeɪʃn] ◇ *n* -**1.** [start] commencement *m*, début *m*; he fought for the ~ of new policies il s'est battu pour la mise en œuvre de politiques différentes. -**2.** [of person] initiation *f*; her ~ into politics son initiation à la politique; his ~ into the world of crime sa première expérience de la pègre.
◇ *comp*: ~ ceremony cérémonie *f* d'initiation.

initiative [ɪˈnɪʃətɪv] ◇ *n* -**1.** [drive] initiative *f*; she's certainly got ~ elle a de l'initiative, il n'y a pas de doute; to act on one's own ~ agir de sa propre initiative; you'll have to use your ~ vous devrez prendre des initiatives ❑ citizen's ~ *Am* POL initiative *f* populaire. -**2.** [first step] initiative *f*; to take the ~ prendre l'initiative; some new ~s have been suggested de nouvelles initiatives ont été proposées. -**3.** [lead] initiative *f*; to have the ~ avoir l'initiative; they lost the ~ to foreign competition ils ont été dépassés par la concurrence étrangère.
◇ *adj* -**1.** [preliminary] préliminaire. -**2.** [ritual] initiatique.

initiator [ɪˈnɪʃɪeɪtəʳ] *n* initiateur *m*, -trice *f*, instigateur *m*, -trice *f*.

inject [ɪnˈdʒekt] *vt* MED & *fig* injecter; to ~ sb with penicillin injecter de la pénicilline à qqn; have you been ~ed against tetanus? êtes-vous vacciné contre le tétanos?; he ~ed novocaine into my gum il m'a fait une injection OR une piqûre de novocaïne dans la gencive; the resin is ~ed into the mould la résine est injectée dans le moule; they've ~ed billions of dollars into the economy *fig* ils ont injecté des milliards de dollars dans l'économie; he tried to ~ some humour into the situation *fig* il a tenté d'introduire un peu d'humour dans la situation.

injectant [ɪnˈdʒektənt] *n* substance *f* injectée.

injection [ɪnˈdʒekʃn] *n* MED & *fig* injection *f*; to give sb an ~ MED faire une injection OR une piqûre à qqn; an ~ of capital une injection de capitaux ❑ ~ moulding moulage *m* par injection.

injector [ɪnˈdʒektəʳ] *n* injecteur *m*.

injudicious [ˌɪndʒuːˈdɪʃəs] *adj* peu judicieux, imprudent.

injudiciously [ˌɪndʒuːˈdɪʃəslɪ] *adv* peu judicieusement.

Injun *inf* [ˈɪndʒən] *n Am offensive* Peau-Rouge *mf*; honest ~! *dated* parole de scout!, juré craché!

injunction [ɪnˈdʒʌŋkʃn] *n* -**1.** JUR ordonnance *f*. -**2.** [warning] injonction *f*, recommandation *f* formelle; she smokes despite her father's ~s against it elle fume malgré les injonctions de son père OR bien que son père lui ait enjoint de ne pas le faire.

injure ['ɪndʒəʳ] *vt* -**1.** [physically] blesser; **he ~d his knee skiing** il s'est blessé au genou en faisant du ski; **ten people were ~d in the accident** l'accident a fait dix blessés; **you could ~ yourself lifting that box** vous pourriez vous faire mal en soulevant cette caisse. -**2.** [damage - relationship, interests] nuire à. -**3.** [offend] blesser, offenser; **only his pride was ~d** seul son amour-propre a été blessé; **try not to ~ her feelings** faites en sorte de ne pas l'offenser OR la blesser. -**4.** [wrong] faire du tort à.

injured ['ɪndʒəd] ◇ *adj* -**1.** [physically - person, limb] blessé; **his ~ left foot** son pied gauche blessé; **her head is badly ~** elle est grièvement blessée à la tête. -**2.** [offended - person] offensé; **to feel ~** être offensé; **it's just his ~ pride** il est blessé dans son amour-propre, c'est tout ❑ **the ~ party** JUR la partie lésée.
◇ *npl*: **the ~** les blessés *mpl*.

injurious [ɪn'dʒʊərɪəs] *adj fml* -**1.** [detrimental] nuisible, préjudiciable; **a campaign that would be highly ~ to the party's image** une campagne qui porterait un grand préjudice à l'image du parti. -**2.** [insulting] offensant, injurieux.

injury ['ɪndʒərɪ] (*pl* injuries) *n* -**1.** [physical] blessure *f*; **to sustain internal injuries** MED subir des lésions internes; **the explosion caused serious injuries** l'explosion a fait des blessés graves; **the team has had very few injuries this season** SPORT il n'y a eu que très peu de blessés dans l'équipe cette saison; **he escaped without ~** il s'en est sorti indemne; **be careful, you'll do yourself an ~!** *Br* fais attention, tu vas te blesser! -**2.** *fml* OR *lit* [wrong] tort *m*, préjudice *m*; **you do him ~** vous lui faites du tort. -**3.** [offence] offense *f*. -**4.** JUR préjudice *m*.

injury time *n* *(U)* SPORT arrêts *mpl* de jeu; **to play ~** jouer les arrêts de jeu; **they scored during ~** ils ont marqué un but pendant les arrêts de jeu.

injustice [ɪn'dʒʌstɪs] *n* injustice *f*; **to do sb an ~** être injuste envers qqn.

ink [ɪŋk] ◇ *n* -**1.** encre *f*; **in ~** à l'encre ❑ **~ drawing** dessin *m* à l'encre. -**2.** [of squid, octopus etc] encre *f*, noir *m*.
◇ *vt* encrer.
◆ **ink in** *vt sep* [drawing] repasser à l'encre; [lines] retracer à l'encre; [writing] réécrire à l'encre.
◆ **ink up** *vt sep* -**1.** *Am* [stain with ink] faire une tache d'encre à OR sur. -**2.** TYPO encrer.

inkblot ['ɪŋkblɒt] *n* tache *f* d'encre, pâté *m*; **~ test** test *m* de Rorschach OR des taches d'encre.

ink cap *n* BOT coprin *m*.

ink eraser *n* gomme *f* à encre.

inkjet printer ['ɪŋkdʒet-] *n* TECH imprimante *f* à jet d'encre.

inkling ['ɪŋklɪŋ] *n* vague OR petite idée *f*; **I had some ~ of the OR as to the real reason** j'avais bien une petite idée de la véritable raison; **you must have an ~** tu dois bien avoir une petite idée; **I had no ~** je ne m'en doutais pas du tout; **she didn't have the slightest ~ that her husband had been unfaithful** elle était à cent lieues de se douter que son mari l'avait trompée.

inkpad ['ɪŋkpæd] *n* tampon *m* (encreur).

ink pen *n* stylo *m* à encre.

inkpot ['ɪŋkpɒt] *n* encrier *m*.

ink rubber *Br* = **ink eraser**.

inkslinger ['ɪŋk,slɪŋəʳ] *n pej* écrivaillon *m*.

inkstain ['ɪŋksteɪn] *n* tache *f* d'encre.

inkstand ['ɪŋkstænd] *n* encrier *m*.

inkwell ['ɪŋkwel] *n* encrier *m* (encastré).

inky ['ɪŋkɪ] (*compar* inkier, *superl* inkiest) *adj* -**1.** [inkstained] taché d'encre. -**2.** [dark] noir comme l'encre.

inlaid [,ɪn'leɪd] ◇ *pt* & *pp* → **inlay**.
◇ *adj* incrusté; [wood] marqueté, incrusté; **an ~ table** une table en marqueterie.

inland [*adj* 'ɪnlənd, *adv* ɪn'lænd] ◇ *adj* -**1.** [not coastal - town, sea] intérieur; **~ waterways** voies *fpl* navigables; **~ navigation** navigation *f* fluviale. -**2.** *Br* [not foreign] intérieur; **~ trade/mail** commerce *m*/courrier *m* intérieur.
◇ *adv* [travelling] vers l'intérieur; [located] à l'intérieur.

Inland Revenue *n* *Br*: **the ~** ≃ le fisc.

Inland Sea *pr n*: **the ~** la mer Intérieure.

in-laws *inf npl* [gen] belle-famille *f*; [parents-in-law] beaux-parents *mpl*.

inlay [*vb* 'ɪnleɪ, *n* ,ɪn'leɪ] (*pt* & *pp* inlaid) ◇ *n* -**1.** [gen] incrustation *f*; [in woodwork] marqueterie *f*; [in metalwork] damasquinage *m*; **the brooch has very fine ~ work** la broche a de très belles incrustations; **with ivory ~** incrusté d'ivoire. -**2.** MED incrustation *f*.
◇ *vt* incruster; **gold inlaid with rubies** or incrusté de rubis; **the table was inlaid with ivory** la table avait des incrustations OR était incrustée d'ivoire.

inlet ['ɪnlet] ◇ *n* -**1.** [in coastline] anse *f*, crique *f*; [between offshore islands] bras *m* de mer. -**2.** TECH [intake] arrivée *f*, admission *f*; **to regulate the ~ of steam** régler l'admission de (la) vapeur ‖ [opening] (orifice *m* d') entrée *f*; [for air] prise *f* (d'air).
◇ *comp* d'arrivée; **~ pipe** tuyau *m* d'arrivée; **~ valve** soupape *f* d'admission.

in loco parentis [ɪn,ləʊkəʊpə'rentɪs] *adv*: **to act ~** agir en lieu et place des parents.

inmate ['ɪnmeɪt] *n* [of prison] détenu *m*, -e *f*; [of mental institution] interné *m*, -e *f*; [of hospital] malade *mf*; [of house] occupant *m*, -e *f*, résident *m*, -e *f*.

in memoriam [,ɪnmɪ'mɔːrɪəm] *prep* à la mémoire de; [on gravestone] in memoriam.

inmost ['ɪnməʊst] = **innermost**.

inn [ɪn] *n* -**1.** [pub, small hotel] auberge *f*. -**2.** *Br* JUR: **the Inns of Court** *associations auxquelles appartiennent les avocats et les juges et dont le siège se trouve dans le quartier historique du même nom à Londres*.

innards *inf* ['ɪnədz] *npl* entrailles *fpl*.

innate [ɪ'neɪt] *adj* [inborn] inné, naturel; **her ~ gift for music** son don inné pour la musique.

innately [ɪ'neɪtlɪ] *adv* naturellement; **nobody is ~ evil** aucun être n'est naturellement méchant.

inner ['ɪnəʳ] ◇ *adj* -**1.** [interior - courtyard, pocket, walls, lane] intérieur; [- structure, workings] interne; **the ~ wall of the stomach** la paroi interne de l'estomac; **Inner London** *partie centrale de l'agglomération londonienne*. -**2.** [inward - feeling, conviction] intime; [- life, voice, struggle, warmth] intérieur; **~ calm** paix intérieure; **the ~ meaning** le sens profond; **the ~ man** OR **woman** [spiritual self] l'être *m* intérieur; *hum* [stomach] l'estomac *m*. -**3.** [privileged]: **in the ~ circles of power** dans les milieux proches du pouvoir; **her ~ circle of advisers/friends** le cercle de ses conseillers/amis les plus proches.
◇ *n* [in archery, darts] *zone rouge entourant le centre de la cible*; **he got three ~s** il a mis trois fois dans le rouge.

inner city (*pl* inner cities) *n* *quartier défavorisé à l'intérieur d'une grande ville*.

inner ear *n* oreille *f* interne.

Inner Mongolia *pr n* Mongolie-Intérieure *f*; **in ~** en Mongolie-Intérieure.

innermost ['ɪnəməʊst] *adj* -**1.** [feeling, belief] intime; **my ~ thoughts** mes pensées les plus secrètes; **in her ~ being** au plus profond d'elle-même. -**2.** [central - place, room] le plus au centre; **in the ~ depths of the cave** au plus profond de la grotte.

innerspring mattress ['ɪnə,sprɪŋ-] *n* *Am* matelas *m* à ressorts.

Inner Temple *pr n*: **the ~** *la plus ancienne des «Inns of Court»*.

inner tube *n* [of tyre] chambre *f* à air.

inning ['ɪnɪŋ] *n* [in baseball] tour *m* de batte.

innings ['ɪnɪŋz] (*pl inv*) ◇ *n* [in cricket] tour *m* de batte; **he's had a good ~** *Br fig* il a bien profité de la vie.
◇ *npl* [reclaimed land] polders *mpl*.

innkeeper ['ɪn,kiːpəʳ] *n* aubergiste *mf*.

innocence ['ɪnəsəns] *n* innocence *f*.

innocent ['ɪnəsənt] ◇ *adj* -**1.** [not guilty] innocent; **to be ~ of a crime** être innocent d'un crime; **to be proven ~ of sthg** être reconnu innocent de qqch. -**2.** [naïve] innocent, naïf; **an ~ remark** une remarque innocente. -**3.** *fml* [devoid]: **~ of** dépourvu de, sans.
◇ *n* innocent *m*, -e *f*; **what an ~ you are!** quel innocent tu fais!; **don't play the ~!** ne fais pas l'innocent! ❑ **'The Innocents Abroad'** *Twain* 'le Voyage des innocents'.

innocently ['ɪnəsəntlɪ] *adv* innocemment.

innocuous [ɪ'nɒkjʊəs] *adj* inoffensif.

innovate ['ɪnəveɪt] *vi* & *vt* innover.

innovation [,ɪnə'veɪʃn] *n* innovation *f*; **~s in management techniques** des innovations en matière de gestion.

innovative ['ɪnəvətɪv] *adj* innovateur, novateur.

innovator ['ɪnəveɪtəʳ] *n* innovateur *m*, -trice *f*, novateur *m*, -trice *f*.

innovatory ['ɪnəvətərɪ] = **innovative**.

Innsbruck ['ɪnzbrʊk] *pr n* Innsbruck.

innuendo [,ɪnjuː'endəʊ] (*pl* innuendos OR innuendoes) *n* [insinuation] insinuation *f*, sous-entendu *m*; [remark, taunt] allusion *f*, sous-entendu *m*; **sexual ~es** insinuations d'ordre sexuel.

innumerable [ɪ'njuːmərəbl] *adj* innombrable; **~ times** un nombre incalculable de fois.

innumeracy [ɪ'njuːmərəsɪ] *n* incapacité *f* à compter.

innumerate [ɪ'njuːmərət] ◇ *adj* qui ne sait pas compter; **he's completely ~** il est incapable d'additionner deux et deux.
◇ *n* personne *f* qui ne sait pas compter.

inoculate [ɪ'nɒkjʊleɪt] *vt* MED [person, animal] vacciner; **to ~ sb against sthg** vacciner qqn contre qqch; **they ~d guinea pigs with the virus** ils ont inoculé le virus à des cobayes.

inoculation [ɪ,nɒkjʊ'leɪʃn] *n* inoculation *f*.

in-off *n* [in billiards] *boule qui entre dans un trou après en avoir touché une autre*.

inoffensive [,ɪnə'fensɪv] *adj* inoffensif.

inoperable [ɪn'ɒprəbl] *adj* -**1.** MED inopérable. -**2.** [unworkable] impraticable.

inoperative [ɪn'ɒprətɪv] *adj* inopérant.

inopportune [ɪn'ɒpətjuːn] *adj* [remark] déplacé, mal à propos; [time] mal choisi, inopportun; [behaviour] inconvenant, déplacé.

inopportunely [ɪn'ɒpətjuːnlɪ] *adv fml* inopportunément *lit*, mal à propos.

inordinate [ɪn'ɔːdɪnət] *adj* [immense - size] démesuré; [- pleasure, relief] incroyable; [- amount of money] exorbitant; **they spent an ~ amount of time on it** ils y ont consacré énormément de temps.

inordinately [ɪn'ɔːdɪnətlɪ] *adv* démesurément, excessivement.

inorganic [,ɪnɔː'gænɪk] *adj* inorganique.

inorganic chemistry *n* chimie *f* inorganique OR minérale.

in-patient *n* hospitalisé *m*, -e *f*, malade *mf*.

input ['ɪnpʊt] (*pt* & *pp* input, *cont* inputting) ◇ *n* *(U)* -**1.** [during meeting, discussion] contribution *f*; **we'd like some ~ from marketing before committing ourselves** nous aimerions consulter le service marketing avant de nous engager plus avant. -**2.** COMPUT [data] données *fpl* (en entrée); [entering] entrée *f* (de données); **the program requires ~ from the user** ce programme exige que l'utilisateur entre des données. -**3.** ELEC énergie *f*, puissance *f*; **to reduce the voltage ~ to a circuit** réduire la tension d'un circuit. -**4.** ECON input *m*, intrant *m*.
◇ *vt* [gen] (faire) entrer, introduire; COMPUT saisir.
◇ *comp* [device, file, program] d'entrée.

input/output *n* COMPUT entrée-sortie *f*; ~ device périphérique d'entrée-sortie.

inquest ['ɪnkwest] *n* JUR enquête *f*; [into death] *enquête menée pour établir les causes des morts violentes, non naturelles ou mystérieuses.*

inquire [ɪn'kwaɪəʳ] ◇ *vt* [ask] demander; to ~ sthg of sb s'enquérir de qqch auprès de qqn; she ~d how to get to the park elle a demandé qu'on lui indique le chemin du parc; may I ~ what brings you here? puis-je vous demander l'objet de votre visite?
◇ *vi* [seek information] se renseigner, demander; '~ within' se renseigner à l'intérieur; to ~ about sthg demander des renseignements OR se renseigner sur qqch.
◆ **inquire after** *vt insep Br* demander des nouvelles de; she ~d after you elle a demandé de vos nouvelles.
◆ **inquire into** *vt insep* se renseigner sur; [investigate] faire des recherches sur; ADMIN & JUR enquêter sur; they should ~ into how the money was spent ils devraient enquêter sur la façon dont l'argent a été dépensé.

inquirer [ɪn'kwaɪərəʳ] *n* investigateur *m*, -trice *f*.

inquiring [ɪn'kwaɪərɪŋ] *adj* [voice, look] interrogateur; [mind] curieux.

inquiringly [ɪn'kwaɪərɪŋlɪ] *adv* d'un air interrogateur; she looked at him ~ elle le regarda d'un air interrogateur, elle l'interrogea du regard.

inquiry [*Br* ɪn'kwaɪərɪ, *Am* 'ɪnkwərɪ] (*pl* inquiries) *n* -**1.** [request for information] demande *f* (de renseignements); we have received hundreds of inquiries nous avons reçu des centaines de demandes de renseignements; to make inquiries about sthg se renseigner sur qqch; could you make a few discreet inquiries? pourriez-vous vous renseigner discrètement? -**2.** [investigation] enquête *f*; the management is holding OR conducting an ~ into the affair la direction fait une enquête sur l'affaire; the police are making inquiries la police enquête, une enquête (policière) est en cours; he is helping police with their inquiries la police est en train de l'interroger; upon further ~ après vérification ❑ commission OR court of ~ commission *f* d'enquête; public ~ enquête *f* officielle. -**3.** [questioning]: a look/tone of ~ un regard/ton interrogateur.
◆ **inquiries** *npl* [information desk, department] renseignements *mpl*.

inquiry agent *n* détective *m* (privé).

inquiry desk, inquiry office *n* accueil *m*.

inquisition [,ɪnkwɪ'zɪʃn] *n* -**1.** [gen & *pej*] inquisition *f*. -**2.** HIST: the Inquisition l'Inquisition *f*. -**3.** JUR enquête *f*.

inquisitive [ɪn'kwɪzətɪv] *adj* [curious] curieux; *pej* [nosy] indiscret.

inquisitively [ɪn'kwɪzətɪvlɪ] *adv* [curiously] avec curiosité; *pej* [nosily] de manière indiscrète; he stared ~ into the room il jeta dans la pièce un regard inquisiteur.

inquisitiveness [ɪn'kwɪzətɪvnɪs] *n* [curiosity] curiosité *f*; *pej* [nosiness] indiscrétion *f*.

inquisitor [ɪn'kwɪzɪtəʳ] *n* -**1.** [investigator] enquêteur *m*, -euse *f*; [interrogator] interrogateur *m*, -trice *f*. -**2.** HIST inquisiteur *m*.

inquisitorial [ɪn,kwɪzɪ'tɔːrɪəl] *adj* inquisitorial.

inquorate [ɪn'kwɔːreɪt] *adj Br* sans quorum; the meeting is ~ la réunion n'a pas atteint le quorum.

inroad ['ɪnrəʊd] *n* [raid] incursion *f*; [advance] avance *f*.
◆ **inroads** *npl* -**1.** MIL: to make ~s into enemy territory avancer en territoire ennemi. -**2.** *fig*: to make ~s in OR into OR on [supplies, popularity, funds] entamer; [spare time, sb's rights] empiéter sur; they have made significant ~s into our market share ils ont considérablement mordu sur notre part du marché; they've made great ~s on the work ils ont bien avancé le travail.

inrush ['ɪnrʌʃ] *n* afflux *m*.

insalubrious [,ɪnsə'luːbrɪəs] *adj fml* [district, climate] insalubre, malsain.

insane [ɪn'seɪn] ◇ *adj* -**1.** [mentally disordered] fou; temporarily ~ en état de démence temporaire; to go ~ perdre la raison. -**2.** *fig* [person] fou; it's driving me ~! ça me rend fou! ‖ [scheme, price] démentiel.
◇ *npl*: the ~ les malades *mpl* mentaux.

insanely [ɪn'seɪnlɪ] *adv* -**1.** [crazily - laugh, behave, talk] comme un fou; they clapped ~ ils applaudissaient comme des fous. -**2.** [as intensifier - funny, rich] follement; he was ~ jealous il était fou de jalousie.

insanitary [ɪn'sænɪtrɪ] *adj* insalubre, malsain.

insanity [ɪn'sænətɪ] *n* folie *f*, démence *f*; temporary ~ démence temporaire.

insatiable [ɪn'seɪʃəbl] *adj* insatiable.

inscribe [ɪn'skraɪb] *vt* -**1.** [on list] inscrire; [on plaque, tomb etc] graver, inscrire; he had the ring ~d with her name OR her name ~d on the ring il a fait graver son nom sur la bague; his cigar case was ~d with his name son étui à cigares était gravé à son nom; it's ~d on my memory *fig* c'est inscrit OR gravé dans ma mémoire. -**2.** [dedicate] dédicacer; an ~d copy of the book un exemplaire dédicacé du livre. -**3.** GEOM inscrire. -**4.** FIN: ~d securities titres *mpl* nominatifs.

inscription [ɪn'skrɪpʃn] *n* [on plaque, tomb] inscription *f*; [in book] dédicace *f*.

inscrutability [ɪn,skruːtə'bɪlətɪ] *n* impénétrabilité *f*.

inscrutable [ɪn'skruːtəbl] *adj* [person] énigmatique, impénétrable; [remark] énigmatique.

insect ['ɪnsekt] *n* insecte *m*; ~ bite piqûre *f* d'insecte; ~ repellent produit *m* insectifuge.

insecticide [ɪn'sektɪsaɪd] *n* insecticide *m*.

insectivore [ɪn'sektɪvɔːʳ] *n* insectivore *m*.

insectivorous [,ɪnsek'tɪvərəs] *adj* insectivore.

insecure [,ɪnsɪ'kjʊəʳ] *adj* -**1.** [person - temporarily] inquiet; [- generally] pas sûr de soi, qui manque d'assurance; he's so ~ il est vraiment mal dans sa peau. -**2.** [chair, nail, scaffolding etc] peu solide. -**3.** [place] peu sûr. -**4.** [future, market] incertain; [peace, job, relationship] précaire; recent events have made her position/the regime ~ les récents événements ont rendu sa position/le régime plus précaire.

insecurely [,ɪnsɪ'kjʊəlɪ] *adv*: ~ balanced en équilibre instable; ~ closed/bolted/attached mal fermé/verrouillé/attaché.

insecurity [,ɪnsɪ'kjʊərətɪ] (*pl* insecurities) *n* -**1.** [lack of confidence] manque *m* d'assurance; [uncertainty] incertitude *f*; job ~ précarité *f* de l'emploi. -**2.** [lack of safety] insécurité *f*.

inseminate [ɪn'semɪneɪt] *vt* inséminer.

insemination [ɪn,semɪ'neɪʃn] *n* insémination *f*.

insensate [ɪn'senseɪt] *adj fml* -**1.** [unfeeling] insensible. -**2.** [foolish] insensé.

insensibility [ɪn,sensə'bɪlətɪ] (*pl* insensibilities) *n fml* -**1.** [unconsciousness] inconscience *f*. -**2.** [indifference] insensibilité *f*; his ~ to music son manque de sensibilité pour la musique.

insensible [ɪn'sensəbl] *adj fml* -**1.** [unconscious] inconscient, sans connaissance; she was knocked ~ by her fall sa chute lui a fait perdre connaissance ‖ [numb] insensible; her body was ~ to any pain son corps était insensible à toute douleur. -**2.** [cold, indifferent] insensible, indifférent; ~ to the suffering of others insensible OR indifférent à la souffrance d'autrui. -**3.** [unaware] inconscient *fig*; ~ of the risks inconscient des risques. -**4.** [imperceptible] insensible, imperceptible.

insensitive [ɪn'sensətɪv] *adj* -**1.** [cold-hearted] insensible, dur; they are ~ brutes ce sont des brutes épaisses; the government's reaction was highly ~ le gouvernement a fait preuve d'une indifférence extrême. -**2.** [unaware] insensible; to be ~ to sthg être insensible à qqch. -**3.** [physically] insensible; ~ to pain insensible à la douleur.

insensitively [ɪn'sensətɪvlɪ] *adj* avec un grand manque de tact.

insensitivity [ɪn,sensə'tɪvətɪ], **insensitiveness** [ɪn'sensətɪvnɪs] *n* insensibilité *f*.

inseparable [ɪn'seprəbl] *adj* inséparable.

inseparably [ɪn'seprəblɪ] *adv* inséparablement.

insert [*vb* ɪn'sɜːt, *n* 'ɪnsɜːt] ◇ *vt* introduire, insérer; ~ your coin/card into the machine introduisez votre pièce/carte dans la machine; she ~ed a small ad in the local paper elle a mis une petite annonce dans le journal local; before ~ing your contact lenses avant de mettre vos verres de contact; to ~ a name on a list ajouter un nom à une liste.
◇ *n* -**1.** [gen] insertion *f*; [extra text] encart *m*. -**2.** SEW pièce *f* rapportée; [decorative] incrustation *f*.

insertion [ɪn'sɜːʃn] *n* -**1.** [act] insertion *f*. -**2.** [thing inserted] = **insert**. -**3.** ANAT & BOT insertion *f*; point of ~ point *m* d'insertion.

in-service *adj*: ~ training formation *f* permanente OR continue.

inset ['ɪnset] (*pt* & *pp* inset, *cont* insetting) ◇ *vt* -**1.** [detail, map, diagram] insérer en encadré; town plans are ~ in the main map des plans de ville figurent en encadrés sur la carte principale. -**2.** SEW [extra material] rapporter; ~ pocket poche *f* couture. -**3.** TYPO rentrer. -**4.** [jewel] incruster; ~ with diamonds incrusté de diamants.
◇ *n* -**1.** [in map, text] encadré *m*; [on video, TV screen] incrustation *f*. -**2.** [in newspaper, magazine - extra pages] encart *m*. -**3.** SEW panneau *m* rapporté; lace ~ incrustation *f* de dentelle.

inshore [*adj* 'ɪnʃɔːʳ, *adv* ɪn'ʃɔːʳ] ◇ *adj* -**1.** [near shore] côtier; ~ fishing pêche *f* côtière. -**2.** [towards shore]: ~ wind vent *m* de mer; ~ current courant *m* qui porte vers la côte.
◇ *adv* [near shore] près de la côte; [towards shore] vers la côte; the boat was keeping close ~ le bateau longeait OR restait près de la côte.

inside [ɪn'saɪd] ◇ *adv* -**1.** [within enclosed space] dedans, à l'intérieur; it's hollow ~ c'est creux à l'intérieur, l'intérieur est creux. -**2.** [indoors] à l'intérieur; bring the chairs ~ rentre les chaises; she opened the door and went ~ elle ouvrit la porte et entra; go and play ~ va jouer à l'intérieur ‖ *Br* [in bus]: plenty of room ~! il y a plein de place à l'intérieur!; move along ~ there! avancez jusqu'au fond! -**3.** *inf* [in prison] en taule; he's been ~ il a fait de la taule. -**4.** [in one's heart] au fond (de soi-même); ~ I was furious au fond de moi-même, j'étais furieux.
◇ *prep* -**1.** [within] à l'intérieur de, dans; ~ the house à l'intérieur de la maison ‖ *fig*: what goes on ~ his head? qu'est-ce qui se passe dans sa tête?; I'll be all right once I've got a few drinks ~ me *inf* tout ira bien quand j'aurai descendu quelques verres; a little voice ~ me kept saying "no" une petite voix intérieure n'arrêtait pas de me dire «non»; it's just ~ the limit c'est juste (dans) la limite; the attack took place ~ Turkey itself l'assaut a eu lieu sur le territoire turc même; someone ~ the company must have told them quelqu'un de l'entreprise a dû le leur dire. -**2.** [in less than] en moins de; I'll have it finished ~ 6 days je l'aurai terminé en moins de 6 jours.
◇ *n* -**1.** [inner part] intérieur *m*; the ~ of the box l'intérieur de la boîte; the door doesn't open from the ~ la porte ne s'ouvre pas de l'intérieur; she has a scar on the ~ of her wrist elle a une cicatrice à l'intérieur du poignet. -**2.** [of pavement, road]: walk on the ~ marchez loin du bord; to overtake on the ~ AUT [driving on left] doubler à gauche; [driving on right] doubler à droite; coming up on the ~ is Bob Green/Golden Boy Bob Green/Golden Boy remonte à la corde. -**3.** *fig*: on the ~: only someone on the ~ would know that seul quelqu'un de la maison saurait ça.
◇ *adj* -**1.** [door, wall] intérieur; ~ toilet toilettes *fpl* à l'intérieur; ~ leg measurement hauteur *f* de l'entrejambe; the ~ pages [of newspaper] les pages intérieures; the ~ lane [in athletics] la corde; [driving on left] la voie de gauche; [driving on right] la voie de droite; to be on the ~ track [in horse-racing] tenir la corde;

fig être bien placé. -**2.** *fig*: he has ~ information il a quelqu'un dans la place; find out the ~ story essaie de découvrir les dessous de l'histoire; it looks like an ~ job on dirait que c'est quelqu'un de la maison qui a fait le coup. -**3.** FTBL: ~ forward inter *m*, intérieur *m*; ~ left/right inter *m* gauche/droit. -**4.** AUT: the ~ wheel/door la roue/portière côté trottoir.

◆ **insides** *inf npl* [stomach] estomac *m*; [intestines] intestins *mpl*, tripes *fpl*.

◆ **inside of** *inf prep phr* -**1.** [in less than] en moins de. -**2.** *Am* [within] à l'intérieur de, dans.

◆ **inside out** *adv phr* -**1.** [with inner part outwards]: your socks are on ~ out tu as mis tes chaussettes à l'envers; he turned his pockets ~ out il a retourné ses poches; they turned the room ~ out *fig* ils ont mis la pièce sens dessus dessous. -**2.** [thoroughly]: he knows this town ~ out il connaît cette ville comme sa poche; she knows her job ~ out elle connaît parfaitement son travail.

insider [,ɪn'saɪdəʳ] *n* initié *m*, -e *f*; according to an ~ selon une source bien informée; I got a hot tip from an ~ quelqu'un dans la place m'a donné un bon tuyau.

insider dealing, insider trading *n* ST. EX opérations *fpl* d'initiés; to be accused of ~ être accusé de délit d'initié.

insidious [ɪn'sɪdɪəs] *adj* insidieux.

insidiously [ɪn'sɪdɪəslɪ] *adv* insidieusement.

insight ['ɪnsaɪt] *n* -**1.** [perspicacity] perspicacité *f*; she has great ~ elle est très fine; his book shows remarkable ~ into the problem son livre témoigne d'une compréhension très fine du problème. -**2.** [idea, glimpse] aperçu *m*, idée *f*; I managed to get OR gain an ~ into her real character j'ai pu me faire une idée de sa véritable personnalité; his book offers us new ~s into human behaviour son livre nous propose un nouveau regard sur le comportement humain.

insightful ['ɪnsaɪtfʊl] *adj* pénétrant, perspicace.

insignia [ɪn'sɪgnɪə] (*pl inv* OR **insignias**) *n* insigne *m*, insignes *mpl*; he wore the ~ of his office il portait les insignes de sa fonction.

insignificance [,ɪnsɪg'nɪfɪkəns] *n* insignifiance *f*.

insignificant [,ɪnsɪg'nɪfɪkənt] *adj* -**1.** [unimportant] insignifiant, sans importance. -**2.** [negligible] insignifiant, négligeable.

insincere [,ɪnsɪn'sɪəʳ] *adj* peu sincère; his grief turned out to be ~ il s'avéra que son chagrin n'était que feint; did you think I was being ~? croyais-tu que je n'étais pas sincère?

insincerely [,ɪnsɪn'sɪəlɪ] *adv* sans sincérité, de manière hypocrite.

insincerity [,ɪnsɪn'serətɪ] *n* manque *m* de sincérité.

insinuate [ɪn'sɪnjʊeɪt] *vt* -**1.** [imply] insinuer, laisser entendre; he ~d that you were lying il a insinué que vous mentiez. -**2.** [introduce] insinuer; he ~d himself into their favour il s'est insinué dans leurs bonnes grâces.

insinuation [ɪn,sɪnjʊ'eɪʃn] *n* -**1.** [hint] insinuation *f*, allusion *f*. -**2.** [act, practice] insinuation *f*.

insipid [ɪn'sɪpɪd] *adj* insipide, fade.

insipidity [,ɪnsɪ'pɪdətɪ] *n* insipidité *f*, fadeur *f*, manque *m* de saveur.

insist [ɪn'sɪst] ◇ *vi* -**1.** [demand] insister; if you ~ si tu insistes; to ~ on sthg/doing sthg: he ~ed on a new contract il a exigé un nouveau contrat; I ~ on seeing the manager j'exige de voir le directeur; she ~s on doing it her way elle tient à le faire à sa façon; he ~ed on my taking the money il a insisté pour que je prenne l'argent. -**2.** [maintain]: to ~ on maintenir; she ~s on her innocence elle maintient qu'elle est innocente. -**3.** [stress]: to ~ on insister sur; I must ~ on this point je dois insister sur ce point.

◇ *vt* -**1.** [demand] insister; I ~ that you tell no-one j'insiste pour que vous ne le disiez à personne; you should ~ that you be paid vous devriez exiger qu'on vous paye. -**2.** [maintain] maintenir, soutenir; she ~s that she locked the door elle maintient qu'elle a fermé la porte à clef.

insistence [ɪn'sɪstəns] *n*: their ~ on secrecy has hindered negotiations en exigeant le secret, ils ont entravé les négociations; her ~ on her innocence ses protestations d'innocence; his ~ on his rights la revendication répétée de ses droits; at OR on my ~ sur mon insistance; I came here at her ~ je suis venu ici parce qu'elle a insisté.

insistent [ɪn'sɪstənt] *adj* [person] insistant; [demand] pressant; [denial, refusal] obstiné; she was most ~ elle a beaucoup insisté; the child's ~ cries les pleurs incessants de l'enfant.

insistently [ɪn'sɪstəntlɪ] *adv* [stare, knock] avec insistance; [ask, urge] avec insistance, instamment.

in situ [,ɪn'sɪtjuː] *adv phr* sur place, in situ MÉD & BOT.

insobriety [,ɪnsə'braɪətɪ] *n fml* [drunkenness] ébriété *f*; [intemperance] intempérance *f*.

insofar as [,ɪnsəʊ'fɑːʳ-] *conj* dans la mesure où; I'll help her ~ I can je l'aiderai dans la mesure de mes capacités; ~ it's possible dans la limite OR mesure du possible.

insolation [,ɪnsəʊ'leɪʃn] *n* insolation *f*.

insole ['ɪnsəʊl] *n* semelle *f* intérieure.

insolence ['ɪnsələns] *n* insolence *f*.

insolent ['ɪnsələnt] *adj* insolent; he's ~ to his teachers il est insolent OR il fait preuve d'insolence envers ses professeurs.

insolently ['ɪnsələntlɪ] *adv* insolemment, avec insolence.

insolubility [ɪn,sɒljʊ'bɪlətɪ] *n* insolubilité *f*.

insoluble [ɪn'sɒljʊbl] *adj* [problem, substance] insoluble.

insolvable [ɪn'sɒlvəbl] *adj* insoluble.

insolvency [ɪn'sɒlvənsɪ] *n* insolvabilité *f*; they're going to declare ~ ils vont se déclarer insolvables; [firm] ils vont déposer leur bilan.

insolvency provision *n* fonds *m* de garantie salariale.

insolvent [ɪn'sɒlvənt] ◇ *adj* insolvable; he was ~ by ten million dollars il laissait une dette de dix millions de dollars.

◇ *n* insolvable *mf*.

insomnia [ɪn'sɒmnɪə] *n* (*U*) insomnie *f*.

insomniac [ɪn'sɒmnɪæk] ◇ *adj* insomniaque.

◇ *n* insomniaque *mf*.

insomuch as [,ɪnsəʊ'mʌtʃ-] = **inasmuch as**.

insouciant [ɪn'suːsjənt] *adj lit* insoucieux.

inspect [ɪn'spekt] ◇ *vt* -**1.** [scrutinize] examiner, inspecter; she ~ed her body for bruises elle examina son corps à la recherche de bleus. -**2.** [check officially - school, product, prison] inspecter; [- ticket] contrôler; [- accounts] contrôler; the customs officer ~ed our luggage le douanier a inspecté nos bagages. -**3.** MIL [troops] passer en revue.

◇ *vi* faire une inspection.

inspection [ɪn'spekʃn] *n* -**1.** [of object] examen *m* (minutieux); [of place] inspection *f*; on closer ~ en regardant de plus près. -**2.** [official check] inspection *f*; [of ticket, passport] contrôle *m*; [of school, prison] (visite *f* d') inspection *f*; customs ~ contrôle douanier; ~ tour, tour of ~ tournée *f* d'inspection; product quality ~ contrôle de qualité des produits. -**3.** MIL [of troops] revue *f*, inspection *f*.

inspection chamber *n* bouche *f* d'égout.

inspection pit *n* AUT fosse *f* (de réparations).

inspector [ɪn'spektəʳ] *n* -**1.** [gen] inspecteur *m*, -trice *f*; [on public transport] contrôleur *m*, -euse *f*; factory ~ inspecteur *m*, -trice *f* du travail; public health ~ inspecteur *m*, -trice *f* sanitaire OR de l'hygiène; ~ of taxes *Br* ≃ inspecteur *m*, -trice *f* des impôts; tax ~ *Br* [sent to firms] polyvalent *m*. -**2.** *Br* SCH inspecteur *m*, -trice *f*. -**3.** [in police force]: (police) ~ ≃ inspecteur *m* (de police) ❑ 'An Inspector Calls' *Priestley* 'Un inspecteur vous demande'.

inspectorate [ɪn'spektərət] *n* [body of inspectors] inspection *f*; [duties, term of office] inspection *f*, inspectorat *m*.

inspector general (*pl* inspectors general) *n* -**1.** [gen] inspecteur *m* général. -**2.** MIL ≃ général *m* inspecteur.

inspiration [,ɪnspə'reɪʃn] *n* -**1.** [source of ideas] inspiration *f*; her art draws OR takes its ~ from desert landscapes son art s'inspire des paysages désertiques; to be an ~ to sb être une source d'inspiration pour qqn; your generosity has been an ~ for us all votre générosité nous a tous inspirés; the ~ for her screenplay l'idée de son scénario. -**2.** [bright idea] inspiration *f*; hey, I've had an ~! hé! j'ai une idée géniale!

inspirational [,ɪnspə'reɪʃənl] *adj* -**1.** [inspiring] inspirant. -**2.** [inspired] inspiré.

inspire [ɪn'spaɪəʳ] *vt* inspirer; Moore's sculptures ~d her early work les sculptures de Moore lui ont inspiré ses œuvres de jeunesse; to ~ sb to do sthg inciter OR pousser qqn à faire qqch; he ~d her to become a doctor il suscita en elle une vocation de médecin; whatever ~d you to do that? qu'est-ce qui a bien pu te donner l'idée de faire ça?; the decision was ~d by the urgent need for funds la décision a dû être prise pour répondre à un besoin urgent de fonds; to ~ confidence/respect inspirer (la) confiance/le respect; a man who once ~d fear un homme qui jadis inspirait la crainte; his success ~d me with confidence sa réussite m'a donné confiance en moi; to ~ courage/hope in sb insuffler du courage/donner de l'espoir à qqn.

inspired [ɪn'spaɪəd] *adj* [artist, poem] inspiré; [moment] d'inspiration; [performance] extraordinaire; [choice, decision] bien inspiré, heureux; an ~ idea une inspiration; to make an ~ guess deviner OR tomber juste.

inspiring [ɪn'spaɪərɪŋ] *adj* [speech, book] stimulant; [music] exaltant; it wasn't a very ~ debate ce débat n'avait rien de bien passionnant.

inst. (*written abbr of* instant) COMM courant; of the 9th ~ du 9 courant OR de ce mois.

instability [,ɪnstə'bɪlətɪ] (*pl* instabilities) *n* instabilité *f*.

instal *Am* = **install**.

install [ɪn'stɔːl] *vt* -**1.** [machinery, equipment] installer; we're having central heating ~ed nous faisons installer le chauffage central. -**2.** [settle - person] installer; she ~ed herself in an armchair elle s'installa dans un fauteuil. -**3.** [appoint - manager, president] nommer; the Tories were ~ed with a huge majority les conservateurs ont été élus avec une écrasante majorité.

installation [,ɪnstə'leɪʃn] *n* installation *f*.

installment plan *n Am système de paiement à tempérament*; to buy sthg on an ~ acheter qqch à crédit.

instalment *Br*, **installment** *Am* [ɪn'stɔːlmənt] *n* -**1.** [payment] acompte *m*, versement *m* partiel; monthly ~s mensualités *fpl*; to pay in OR by ~s payer par versements échelonnés; to pay off a loan in OR by ~s rembourser un prêt en plusieurs versements OR tranches. -**2.** [of serial, story] épisode *m*; [of book] fascicule *m*; the last ~ of our special report on Brazil [on TV] le dernier volet de notre reportage spécial sur le Brésil; published in ~s publié par fascicules. -**3.** = **installation**.

instance ['ɪnstəns] ◇ *n* -**1.** [example] exemple *m*; as an ~ of comme exemple de || [case] occasion *f*, circonstance *f*; he agrees with me in most ~s la plupart du temps OR dans la plupart des cas il est d'accord avec moi; our policy, in that ~, was to raise interest rates notre politique en la circonstance a consisté à augmenter les taux d'intérêt; what would you have decided in that ~? qu'auriez-vous décidé en pareil cas? -**2.** [stage]: in the first/second ~ en premier/second lieu ❑ court of first ~ JUR tribunal *m* de première instance. -**3.** *fml* [request] demande *f*, instances *fpl*; at the ~ of à la demande de.

◇ *vt* donner OR citer en exemple.

◆ **for instance** *adv phr* par exemple.

instant ['ɪnstənt] ◇ *adj* -**1.** [immediate] immédiat; this wound needs ~ attention cette blessure doit être soignée immédiatement; for ~ weight loss pour perdre du poids rapidement; give yourself an ~ new look changez de look en un clin d'œil ❑ ~ replay TV ralenti *m*. -**2.** CULIN [coffee] instantané, soluble; [soup, sauce] instantané, en sachet; [milk] en poudre; [mashed potato] en flocons; [dessert] à préparation rapide.

◇ *n* instant *m*, moment *m*; at that ~ à ce moment-là; the next ~ he'd disappeared l'instant d'après il avait disparu; do it this ~ fais-le tout de suite OR immédiatement OR à l'instant; she read it in an ~ elle l'a lu en un rien de temps; I'll be with you in an ~ je serai à vous dans un instant; call me the ~ you arrive appelle-moi dès que OR aussitôt que tu seras arrivé; I didn't believe it for one ~ je ne l'ai pas cru un seul instant; he left on the ~ il est parti immédiatement OR sur-le-champ.

instantaneous [ˌɪnstən'teɪnjəs] *adj* instantané.

instantaneously [ˌɪnstən'teɪnjəslɪ] *adv* instantanément.

instantly ['ɪnstəntlɪ] *adv* [immediately] immédiatement, instantanément; he was killed ~ il a été tué sur le coup; cleans and refreshes ~! nettoie et rafraîchit instantanément!

instead [ɪn'sted] *adv*: he didn't go to the office, he went home ~ au lieu d'aller au bureau, il est rentré chez lui; I don't like sweet things, I'll have cheese ~ je n'aime pas les sucreries, je prendrai plutôt du fromage; since I'll be away, why not send Mary ~? puisque je ne serai pas là, pourquoi ne pas envoyer Mary à ma place?

◆ **instead of** *prep phr* au lieu de, à la place de; ~ of reading a book au lieu de lire un livre; her son came ~ of her son fils est venu à sa place; I had an apple ~ of lunch j'ai pris une pomme en guise de déjeuner.

instep ['ɪnstep] *n* -**1.** ANAT cou-de-pied *m*; to have a high ~ avoir le pied très cambré. -**2.** [of shoe] cambrure *f*.

instigate ['ɪnstɪgeɪt] *vt* -**1.** [initiate - gen] être à l'origine de; [- project] promouvoir; [- strike] provoquer; [- revolt] provoquer, fomenter; [- plot] ourdir. -**2.** [urge] inciter, pousser; to ~ sb to do sthg pousser OR inciter qqn à faire qqch.

instigation [ˌɪnstɪ'geɪʃn] *n* [urging] instigation *f*, incitation *f*; at her ~ à son instigation.

instigator ['ɪnstɪgeɪtəʳ] *n* instigateur *m*, -trice *f*.

instil *Br*, **instill** *Am* [ɪn'stɪl] *vt* [principles, ideals] inculquer; [loyalty, courage, fear] insuffler; [idea] faire comprendre.

instinct ['ɪnstɪŋkt] *n* instinct *m*; by ~ d'instinct; she has an ~ for business/for gambling elle a le sens des affaires/l'instinct du jeu; he has an ~ for the right word il a le don pour trouver le mot juste; her first ~ was to run away sa première réaction a été de s'enfuir; to follow one's ~ suivre OR obéir à son instinct.

instinctive [ɪn'stɪŋktɪv] *adj* instinctif.

instinctively [ɪn'stɪŋktɪvlɪ] *adv* instinctivement; animals are ~ afraid of fire les animaux ont une peur instinctive du feu.

institute ['ɪnstɪtjuːt] ◇ *vt* -**1.** [establish - system, guidelines] instituer, établir; [- change] introduire, apporter; [- committee] créer, constituer; [- award, organization] fonder, créer. -**2.** [take up - proceedings] engager, entamer; [- inquiry] ouvrir; he threatened to ~ legal action against them il a menacé de leur intenter un procès. -**3.** [induct] installer; RELIG instituer.

◇ *n* institut *m*; research ~ institut de recherche.

institution [ˌɪnstɪ'tjuːʃn] *n* -**1.** [of rules] institution *f*, établissement *m*; [of committee] création *f*, constitution *f*; [of change] introduction *f*; JUR [of action] début *m*; [of official] installation *f*. -**2.** [organization] organisme *m*, établissement *m*; [governmental] institution *f*; [educational, penal, religious] établissement *m*; [private school] institution *f*; [hospital] hôpital *m*, établissement *m* hospitalier; *euph* [mental hospital] établissement *m* psychiatrique. -**3.** [custom, political or social structure] institution *f*; the ~ of marriage l'institution du mariage. -**4.** *hum* [person] institution *f*; she's a national ~ elle est devenue une véritable institution nationale.

institutional [ˌɪnstɪ'tjuːʃənl] *adj* -**1.** [hospital, prison, school etc] institutionnel; ~ care soins *mpl* hospitaliers; he'd be better off in ~ care il serait mieux dans un établissement OR centre spécialisé; after years of ~ life they can't look after themselves après des années d'internement, ils sont incapables de se prendre en charge. -**2.** [belief, values] séculaire. -**3.** COMM institutionnel; ~ investors investisseurs *mpl* institutionnels; ~ advertising publicité *f* institutionnelle.

institutionalism [ˌɪnstɪ'tjuːʃənlɪzm] *n* institutionnalisme *m*.

institutionalize, -ise [ˌɪnstɪ'tjuːʃənˌlaɪz] *vt* -**1.** [establish] institutionnaliser; to become ~d s'institutionnaliser. -**2.** [place in a hospital, home] placer dans un établissement *(médical ou médico-social)*; to be ~d être interné; he's been ~d all his life il a passé toute sa vie dans des établissements spécialisés; to become ~d ne plus être capable de se prendre en charge *(après des années passées dans des établissements spécialisés)*.

instruct [ɪn'strʌkt] *vt* -**1.** [command, direct] charger; we have been ~ed to accompany you nous sommes chargés de OR nous avons mission de vous accompagner. -**2.** [teach] former; to ~ sb in sthg enseigner OR apprendre qqch à qqn. -**3.** [inform] informer; I have been ~ed that the meeting has been cancelled on m'a informé OR avisé que la réunion a été annulée. -**4.** JUR [jury, solicitor] donner des instructions à.

instruction [ɪn'strʌkʃn] *n* -**1.** [order] instruction *f*; follow my ~s carefully suis bien mes instructions OR indications; she gave ~s for the papers to be destroyed elle a donné des instructions pour qu'on détruise les documents; they were given ~s not to let him out of their sight ils avaient reçu l'ordre de ne pas le perdre de vue ❑ ~s (for use) mode *m* d'emploi; operating ~s mode *m* d'emploi. -**2.** *(U)* [teaching] instruction *f*, leçons *fpl*; MIL instruction *f*.

instruction book, instruction manual *n* COMM & TECH manuel *m* (d'utilisation et d'entretien).

instructive [ɪn'strʌktɪv] *adj* instructif.

instructor [ɪn'strʌktəʳ] *n* -**1.** [gen] professeur *m*; MIL instructeur *m*; music ~ professeur de musique; sailing ~ moniteur *m*, -trice *f* de voile; swimming ~ maître-nageur *m*. -**2.** *Am* UNIV ≃ assistant *m*, -e *f*.

instrument ['ɪnstrʊmənt] ◇ *n* -**1.** MED, MUS & TECH instrument *m*; to fly by OR on ~s naviguer à l'aide d'instruments ❑ ~ error erreur due aux instruments; precision ~ instrument de précision. -**2.** *fig* [means] instrument *m*, outil *m*; ~ of propaganda outil de propagande. -**3.** FIN effet *m*, titre *m*; JUR instrument *m*, acte *m* juridique; an ~ of payment un moyen de paiement.

◇ *vt* -**1.** MUS orchestrer. -**2.** TECH munir OR équiper d'instruments.

◇ *comp* AERON [flying, landing] aux instruments (de bord).

instrumental [ˌɪnstrʊ'mentl] ◇ *adj* -**1.** [significant]: her work was ~ in bringing about the reforms elle a largement contribué à faire passer les réformes; an ~ role un rôle déterminant. -**2.** MUS instrumental. -**3.** TECH d'instruments; ~ check [of devices] vérification des instruments; [by devices] vérification par instruments. -**4.** LING: ~ phrase complément *m* d'instrument; ~ case (cas *m*) instrumental *m*.

◇ *n* -**1.** MUS morceau *m* instrumental; they played a few ~s ils ont joué quelques morceaux de musique instrumentale. -**2.** LING instrumental *m*.

instrumentalist [ˌɪnstrʊ'mentəlɪst] *n* MUS instrumentiste *mf*.

instrumentation [ˌɪnstrʊmen'teɪʃn] *n* -**1.** [musical arrangement] orchestration *f*, instrumentation *f*; [musical instruments] instruments *mpl*. -**2.** TECH instrumentation *f*.

instrument panel, instrument board *n* AERON & AUT tableau *m* de bord; TECH tableau *m* de contrôle.

insubordinate [ˌɪnsə'bɔːdɪnət] *adj* insubordonné; ~ behaviour conduite *f* insubordonnée OR rebelle.

insubordination ['ɪnsəˌbɔːdɪ'neɪʃn] *n* insubordination *f*.

insubstantial [ˌɪnsəb'stænʃl] *adj* -**1.** [structure] peu solide; [book] facile, peu substantiel; [garment, snack, mist] léger; [claim] sans fondement; [reasoning] faible, sans substance. -**2.** [imaginary] imaginaire, chimérique.

insufferable [ɪn'sʌfərəbl] *adj* insupportable, intolérable.

insufferably [ɪn'sʌfərəblɪ] *adv* insupportablement, intolérablement; he's ~ arrogant il est d'une arrogance insupportable.

insufficiency [ˌɪnsə'fɪʃnsɪ] (*pl* **insufficiencies**) *n* insuffisance *f*.

insufficient [ˌɪnsə'fɪʃnt] *adj* insuffisant; there is ~ evidence les preuves sont insuffisantes.

insufficiently [ˌɪnsə'fɪʃntlɪ] *adv* insuffisamment.

insular ['ɪnsjʊləʳ] *adj* -**1.** [island - tradition, authorities] insulaire; [isolated] isolé; he leads a very ~ existence il vit comme un ermite. -**2.** *fig* & *pej* [mentality] limité, borné; she's very ~ elle est très bornée OR a l'esprit très étroit.

insularity [ˌɪnsjʊ'lærətɪ] *n* insularité *f*; [isolation] isolement *m*.

insulate ['ɪnsjʊleɪt] *vt* -**1.** [against cold, heat, radiation] isoler; [hot water pipes, tank] calorifuger; [soundproof] insonoriser; ~d sleeping bag sac de couchage isolant. -**2.** ELEC isoler; ~d screwdriver tournevis isolant. -**3.** *fig* [protect] protéger; they are no longer ~d from the effects of inflation ils ne sont plus à l'abri des effets de l'inflation; his cynicism ~s him from any feelings of pity son cynisme le protège contre tout sentiment de pitié.

insulating tape ['ɪnsjʊleɪtɪŋ-] *n* chatterton *m*.

insulation [ˌɪnsjʊ'leɪʃn] *n* -**1.** [against cold] isolation *f* (calorifuge), calorifugeage *m*; [soundproofing] insonorisation *f*, isolation *f*; loft ~ isolation thermique du toit. -**2.** ELEC isolation *f*. -**3.** [feathers, foam etc] isolant *m*. -**4.** *fig* [protection] protection *f*.

insulator ['ɪnsjʊleɪtəʳ] *n* [material] isolant *m*; [device] isolateur *m*.

insulin ['ɪnsjʊlɪn] *n* insuline; ~ reaction OR shock choc *m* insulinique.

insult [*vb* ɪn'sʌlt, *n* 'ɪnsʌlt] ◇ *vt* [abuse] insulter, injurier; [offend] faire (un) affront à, offenser; don't be ~ed if I don't tell you everything ne le prends pas mal OR ne t'offense pas si je ne te dis pas tout.

◇ *n* insulte *f*, injure *f*, affront *m*; they were hurling ~s at each other ils se lançaient des insultes à la figure; his remarks were an ~ to my intelligence ses commentaires étaient une insulte à mon intelligence; their ads are an ~ to women leurs pubs sont insultantes OR une insulte pour les femmes.

insulting [ɪn'sʌltɪŋ] *adj* [language] insultant, injurieux; [attitude] insultant, offensant; [behaviour] grossier.

insultingly [ɪn'sʌltɪŋlɪ] *adv* [speak] d'un ton insultant OR injurieux; [act] d'une manière insultante; he behaved most ~ towards her son comportement a été très injurieux à son égard.

insuperable [ɪn'suːprəbl] *adj* insurmontable.

insuperably [ɪn'suːprəblɪ] *adv* de façon insurmontable; ~ **difficult** d'une difficulté insurmontable.

insupportable [ˌɪnsə'pɔːtəbl] *adj* -**1.** [unbearable] insupportable, intolérable. -**2.** [indefensible] insoutenable.

insurable [ɪn'ʃɔːrəbl] *adj* assurable.

insurance [ɪn'ʃɔːrəns] ◇ *n* -**1.** *(U)* [against fire, theft, accident] assurance *f*; [cover] garantie *f* (d'assurance), couverture *f*; [premium] prime *f* (d'assurance); **to take out ~ (against sthg)** prendre OR contracter une assurance, s'assurer (contre qqch); **to have ~ against sthg** être assuré pour OR contre qqch; **extend the ~ when you renew the policy** faites augmenter le montant de la garantie quand vous renouvelez le contrat d'assurance; **he bought himself a stereo out of the ~** il s'est acheté une chaîne stéréo avec (une partie de) l'argent de l'assurance; **she got £2,000 in ~** elle a reçu 2 000 livres de l'assurance; **how much do you pay in ~?** combien payez-vous (de prime) d'assurance? -**2.** *fig* [means of protection] garantie *f*, moyen *m* de protection; **take Sam with you, just as an ~** emmenez Sam avec vous, on ne sait jamais OR au cas où.
◇ *comp* [premium, scheme] d'assurance; [company] d'assurances.

insurance broker *n* courtier *m* d'assurance OR d'assurances.

insurance claim *n* demande *f* d'indemnité.

insurance policy *n* police *f* d'assurance, contrat *m* d'assurance.

insure [ɪn'ʃɔːʳ] *vt* -**1.** [car, building, person] assurer; **he ~d himself** OR **his life** il a pris OR contracté une assurance-vie; **we're ~d against flooding** nous sommes assurés contre les inondations. -**2.** *fig* [protect]: **what strategy can ~ (us) against failure?** quelle stratégie peut nous prévenir contre l'échec OR nous garantir que nous n'échouerons pas?; **to ~ one's future** assurer son avenir.

insured [ɪn'ʃɔːd] (*pl inv*) ◇ *adj* assuré; ~ **risk** risque *m* couvert.
◇ *n* assuré *m*, -e *f*.

insurer [ɪn'ʃɔːrəʳ] *n* assureur *m*.

insurgency [ɪn'sɜːdʒənsɪ], **insurgence** [ɪn'sɜːdʒəns] *n* insurrection *f*.

insurgent [ɪn'sɜːdʒənt] ◇ *n* insurgé *m*, -e *f*.
◇ *adj* insurgé.

insurmountable [ˌɪnsə'maʊntəbl] *adj* insurmontable.

insurrection [ˌɪnsə'rekʃn] *n* insurrection *f*; **armed ~** soulèvement *m* armé, insurrection armée.

insurrectionary [ˌɪnsə'rekʃnərɪ] (*pl* **insurrectionaries**) ◇ *adj* insurrectionnel.
◇ *n* insurgé *m*, -e *f*.

insurrectionist [ˌɪnsə'rekʃnɪst] = **insurrectionary**.

intact [ɪn'tækt] *adj* intact.

intaglio [ɪn'tɑːlɪəʊ] (*pl* **intaglios** OR **intagli** [-ljiː]) *n* [gem] intaille *f*; [design] dessin *m* en intaille.

intake ['ɪnteɪk] *n* -**1.** SCH & UNIV admission *f*, inscription *f*; MIL recrutement *m*; **the ~ of refugees** l'accueil des réfugiés; **they've increased their ~ of medical students** ils ont décidé d'admettre davantage d'étudiants en médecine; **this year's ~ of pupils is** OR **are of a higher standard than usual** cette année les nouveaux élèves sont d'un niveau plus élevé que d'habitude ❑ ~ **class** *Br* cours *m* préparatoire. -**2.** TECH [of water] prise *f*, arrivée *f*; [of gas, steam] admission *f*; **an ~ rate of 10 litres per second** un débit d'admission de 10 litres par seconde; **a high energy ~** une consommation importante d'énergie ❑ **air ~** admission d'air; ~ **valve** soupape *f* d'admission. -**3.** [of food] consommation *f*; **a daily ~ of 2,000 calories** une ration quotidienne de 2 000 calories; **there was a sharp ~ of breath** tout le monde retint son souffle ❑ **oxygen ~** absorption *f* d'oxygène.

intangible [ɪn'tændʒəbl] ◇ *adj* [quality, reality] intangible, impalpable; [idea, difficulty] indéfinissable, difficile à cerner; ~ **assets** COMM immobilisations *fpl* incorporelles; ~ **property** JUR biens *mpl* incorporels.
◇ *n* impondérable *m*.

integer ['ɪntɪdʒəʳ] *n* MATH (nombre *m*) entier *m*; [whole unit] entier.

integral ['ɪntɪgrəl] ◇ *adj* -**1.** [essential - part, element] intégrant, constitutif; **it's an ~ part of your job** cela fait partie intégrante de votre travail. -**2.** [entire] intégral, complet. -**3.** MATH intégral.
◇ *n* MATH intégrale *f*.

integral calculus *n* calcul *m* intégral.

integrand ['ɪntɪgrænd] *n* expression *f* à intégrer.

integrate ['ɪntɪgreɪt] ◇ *vt* -**1.** [combine]: **the two systems have been ~d** on a combiné les deux systèmes. -**2.** [include in a larger unit] intégrer; **to ~ sb in a group** intégrer qqn dans un groupe; **his brief was to ~ the new building into the historic old quarter** il avait pour mission de concevoir un bâtiment qui soit en harmonie avec la vieille ville. -**3.** [end segregation of]: **the law was intended to ~ racial minorities** cette loi visait à l'intégration des minorités raciales; **to ~ a school** mettre fin à la ségrégation raciale dans une école. -**4.** MATH intégrer.
◇ *vi* -**1.** [fit in] s'intégrer; **to ~ into** s'intégrer dans; **at first they found it hard to ~ with the local community** au début, ils ont eu du mal à s'intégrer dans la collectivité locale. -**2.** [desegregate] ne plus pratiquer la ségrégation raciale.

integrated ['ɪntɪgreɪtɪd] *adj* [gen] intégré; **vertically ~ company** société à intégration verticale; ~ **port facilities** complexe portuaire intégré ❑ ~ **studies** SCH études *fpl* interdisciplinaires; ~ **neighborhood** *Am* quartier *m* multiracial; ~ **school** *Am école où se pratique l'intégration (raciale)*.

integrated circuit *n* circuit *m* intégré.

integration [ˌɪntɪ'greɪʃn] *n* intégration *f*; **racial ~** déségrégation *f*; **school ~** *Am* déségrégation des établissements scolaires; **vertical/horizontal ~** ECON intégration verticale/horizontale.

integrator ['ɪntɪgreɪtəʳ] *n* [device] intégrateur *m*.

integrity [ɪn'tegrətɪ] *n* -**1.** [uprightness] intégrité *f*, probité *f*; **she's a woman of great ~** c'est une femme d'une grande intégrité. -**2.** [wholeness] totalité *f*; **cultural ~** identité *f* culturelle.

integument [ɪn'tegjʊmənt] *n* tégument *m*.

intellect ['ɪntəlekt] *n* -**1.** [intelligence] intelligence *f*. -**2.** [mind, person] esprit *m*.

intellectual [ˌɪntə'lektjʊəl] ◇ *adj* [mental] intellectuel; [attitude, image] d'intellectuel; **an ~ set** un petit groupe d'intellectuels.
◇ *n* intellectuel *m*, -elle *f*.

intellectualism [ˌɪntə'lektjʊəlɪzm] *n* intellectualisme *m*.

intellectualize, -ise [ˌɪntə'lektjʊəlaɪz] ◇ *vt* intellectualiser.
◇ *vi* tenir des discours intellectuels.

intellectually [ˌɪntə'lektjʊəlɪ] *adv* intellectuellement.

intelligence [ɪn'telɪdʒəns] *n* *(U)* -**1.** [mental ability] intelligence *f*; **to have the ~ to do sthg** avoir l'intelligence de faire qqch; **her decision shows ~** elle a fait preuve d'intelligence en prenant cette décision; **use your ~!** réfléchis un peu! -**2.** [information] renseignements *mpl*, information *f*, informations *fpl*; ~ **is** OR **are working on it** les services de renseignements y travaillent ❑ **army ~** service *m* de renseignements de l'armée. -**3.** [intelligent being] intelligence *f*.

intelligence officer *n* officier *m* de renseignements.

intelligence quotient *n* quotient *m* intellectuel.

intelligence service *n* POL service *m* de renseignements.

intelligence test *n* test *m* d'aptitude intellectuelle.

intelligent [ɪn'telɪdʒənt] *adj* intelligent.

intelligent card *n Br* carte *f* à mémoire OR à puce.

intelligently [ɪn'telɪdʒəntlɪ] *adv* intelligemment.

intelligentsia [ɪnˌtelɪ'dʒentsɪə] *n* intelligentsia *f*.

intelligibility [ɪnˌtelɪdʒə'bɪlətɪ] *n* intelligibilité *f*.

intelligible [ɪn'telɪdʒəbl] *adj* intelligible.

intelligibly [ɪn'telɪdʒəblɪ] *adj* intelligiblement.

intemperance [ɪn'tempərəns] *n fml* [overindulgence] intempérance *f*, manque *m* de modération.

intemperate [ɪn'tempərət] *adj fml* -**1.** [overindulgent] intempérant; ~ **drinking** consommation excessive d'alcool. -**2.** [uncontrolled - behaviour, remark] excessif, outrancier; **her ~ refusal** la violence de son refus. -**3.** [harsh - climate] rigoureux, rude.

intend [ɪn'tend] *vt* -**1.** [plan, have in mind]: **to ~ to do sthg, to ~ doing** OR **on doing** *Am* **sthg** avoir l'intention de OR projeter de faire qqch; **how do you ~ to do it?** comment avez-vous l'intention de vous y prendre?; **we arrived later than (we had) ~ed** nous sommes arrivés plus tard que prévu; **his statement was ~ed to mislead** la déclaration visait à induire en erreur; **I had ~ed staying** OR **to stay longer** j'avais l'intention OR prévu de rester plus longtemps; **he didn't ~ her to see the letter** il n'avait pas l'intention de lui laisser voir la lettre; **we ~ to increase our sales** nous entendons développer nos ventes; **the board ~s her to become managing director** le conseil d'administration souhaite qu'elle soit nommée P-DG; **to ~ marriage** *lit* avoir l'intention de se marier; **no harm was ~ed** c'était sans mauvaise intention; **I'm sorry, no criticism/insult was ~ed** je suis désolé, je ne voulais pas vous critiquer/offenser; **I ~ed it to be a joke!** je voulais plaisanter!; **no pun ~ed!** sans jeu de mots! -**2.** [destine] destiner; **a book ~ed for the general public** un livre destiné OR qui s'adresse au grand public; **the funds were ~ed for disabled children** les fonds étaient destinés à l'enfance handicapée; **the device is ~ed to reduce pollution** ce dispositif a été mis au point dans le but de réduire la pollution; **the reform is ~ed to limit the dumping of toxic waste** cette réforme vise à limiter le déversement de déchets toxiques.

intended [ɪn'tendɪd] ◇ *adj* -**1.** [planned - event, trip] prévu; [- result, reaction] voulu; [- market, public] visé. -**2.** [deliberate] intentionnel, délibéré.
◇ *n arch* OR *hum*: **his ~** sa future, sa promise *arch*; **her ~** son futur, son promis *arch*.

intense [ɪn'tens] *adj* -**1.** [gen] intense; [battle, debate] acharné; [hatred] violent, profond; [enthusiasm] vif; **a period of ~ activity** une période d'activité intense; **to my ~ satisfaction/dissatisfaction** à ma très grande satisfaction/mon grand déplaisir. -**2.** [person] extrême, passionné; **he's so ~** [serious] il prend tout très au sérieux; [emotional] il prend tout très à cœur.

intensely [ɪn'tenslɪ] *adv* -**1.** [with intensity - work, stare] intensément, avec intensité; [- love] profondément, passionnément. -**2.** [extremely - hot, painful, curious] extrêmement; [- moving, affected, bored] profondément.

intensification [ɪnˌtensɪfɪ'keɪʃn] *n* intensification *f*.

intensifier [ɪn'tensɪfaɪəʳ] *n* -**1.** LING intensif *m*. -**2.** PHOT renforçateur *m*.

intensify [ɪn'tensɪfaɪ] (*pt* & *pp* **intensified**) ◇ *vt* [feeling, impression, colour] renforcer; [sound] intensifier; **the police have intensified their search for the child** la police redouble d'efforts pour retrouver l'enfant.
◇ *vi* s'intensifier, devenir plus intense.

intensity [ɪn'tensətɪ] (*pl* **intensities**) *n* intensité *f*; **the emotional ~ of his paintings** la force des sentiments exprimés dans ses tableaux; **the ~ of the debate** la véhémence du débat.

intensive [ɪn'tensɪv] ◇ *adj* intensif; ~ **security measures** mesures de sécurité draconiennes ❑ ~ **farming** culture *f* intensive; ~ **security prison** *Am* prison *f* où la surveillance est renforcée.
◇ *n* LING intensif *m*.

-intensive *in cpds* qui utilise beaucoup de...; **labour~** qui nécessitent une main-d'œuvre importante; **capital~** qui mobilise beaucoup de capitaux; **energy~** qui consomme beaucoup d'énergie.

intensive care *n* *(U)* MED soins *mpl* intensifs; **in ~** en réanimation.

intensive care unit *n* unité *f* de soins intensifs.

intensively [ɪn'tensɪvlɪ] *adv* intensivement.

intent [ɪn'tent] ◇ *n* intention *f*, but *m*; **with good/evil ~** dans une bonne/mauvaise intention; **with criminal ~** JUR dans un but délictueux ❑ **declaration of ~** déclaration *f* d'intention.
◇ *adj* -**1.** [concentrated] attentif, absorbé; **with ~ application** avec une concentration extrême; **he was silent, ~ on the meal** il était silencieux, tout à son repas. -**2.** [determined] résolu, déterminé; **to be ~ on doing sthg** être déterminé OR résolu à faire qqch.
◆ **to all intents and purposes** *adv phr* en fait.

intention [ɪn'tenʃn] *n* intention *f*; **despite my ~ to say** OR **of saying nothing** malgré mon intention de ne rien dire; **I have absolutely no ~ of spending my life here** je n'ai aucune intention de passer ma vie ici; **he went to Australia with the ~ of making his fortune** il est parti en Australie dans l'intention de OR dans le but de faire fortune; **it was with this ~ that I wrote to him** c'est dans cette intention OR à cette fin que je lui ai écrit.

intentional [ɪn'tenʃənl] *adj* intentionnel, voulu.

intentionally [ɪn'tenʃənəlɪ] *adv* intentionnellement.

intently [ɪn'tentlɪ] *adv* [alertly - listen, watch] attentivement; [thoroughly - question, examine] minutieusement.

inter [ɪn'tɜːʳ] (*pt* & *pp* **interred**, *cont* **interring**) *vt fml* enterrer, inhumer.

interact [ˌɪntər'ækt] *vi* -**1.** [person]: **they ~ very well together** le courant passe bien (entre eux), ils s'entendent très bien. -**2.** [forces] interagir; [substances] avoir une action réciproque; **the cold air ~s with the warm** il se produit une réaction entre l'air chaud et l'air froid. -**3.** COMPUT dialoguer.

interaction [ˌɪntər'ækʃn] *n* interaction *f*.

interactive [ˌɪntər'æktɪv] *adj* interactif; ~ **mode** COMPUT mode conversationnel OR interactif.

inter alia [ˌɪntər'eɪlɪə] *adv phr fml* notamment.

interbreed [ˌɪntə'briːd] (*pt* & *pp* **interbred** [-bred]) ◇ *vt* [crossbreed - animals] croiser; [- races] métisser.
◇ *vi* -**1.** [crossbreed - animals] se croiser; [- races] se métisser. -**2.** [within family, community] contracter des mariages consanguins.

interbreeding [ˌɪntə'briːdɪŋ] *n* -**1.** [crossbreeding - of animals] croisement *m*; [- of races] métissage *m*. -**2.** [within breed] croisement *m* d'animaux de même souche; [within family, community] union *f* consanguine, unions *fpl* consanguines.

intercalate [ɪn'tɜːkəleɪt] *vt* intercaler.

intercalation [ɪnˌtɜːkə'leɪʃn] *n* intercalation *f*.

intercede [ˌɪntə'siːd] *vi* intercéder; **she ~d with the boss on my behalf** elle a intercédé en ma faveur auprès du patron.

intercellular [ˌɪntə'seljʊləʳ] *adj* intercellulaire.

intercept [*vb* ˌɪntə'sept, *n* 'ɪntəsept] ◇ *vt* intercepter; **to ~ a blow** parer un coup.
◇ *n* interception *f*.

intercepter [ˌɪntə'septəʳ] = **interceptor**.

interception [ˌɪntə'sepʃn] *n* interception *f*.

interceptor [ˌɪntə'septəʳ] *n* [plane] intercepteur *m*.

intercession [ˌɪntə'seʃn] *n* intercession *f*.

interchange [*vb* ˌɪntə'tʃeɪndʒ, *n* 'ɪntətʃeɪndʒ] ◇ *vt* -**1.** [exchange - opinions, information] échanger. -**2.** [switch round] intervertir, permuter; **these tyres can be ~d** ces pneus sont interchangeables.
◇ *n* -**1.** [exchange] échange *m*. -**2.** [road junction] échangeur *m*.

interchangeable [ˌɪntə'tʃeɪndʒəbl] *adj* interchangeable.

intercity [ˌɪntə'sɪtɪ] (*pl* **intercities**) *adj* [travel] d'une ville à l'autre, interurbain; ~ **train** *Br* (train *m*) rapide *m*.

intercollegiate [ˌɪntəkə'liːdʒɪət] *adj* entre collèges; *Am* [between universities] interuniversitaire.

intercom ['ɪntəkɒm] *n* Interphone® *m*; **to call sb on** OR **over the ~** appeler qqn à OR par l'Interphone.

intercommunicate [ˌɪntəkə'mjuːnɪkeɪt] *vi* communiquer.

intercommunication ['ɪntəkəˌmjuːnɪ'keɪʃn] *n* intercommunication *f*.

intercommunion [ˌɪntəkə'mjuːnjən] *n* RELIG intercommunion *f*.

interconnect [ˌɪntəkə'nekt] ◇ *vt* [gen] connecter; ~**ed corridors** couloirs *mpl* communicants; **the buildings are ~ed by underground walkways** les immeubles sont reliés par des passages souterrains; **the ~ing wall** le mur mitoyen; ~**ed ideas** *fig* idées étroitement reliées.
◇ *vi* [rooms, buildings] communiquer; [circuits] être connecté.

interconnection [ˌɪntəkə'nekʃn] *n* connection *f*, lien *m*; ELEC interconnexion *f*.

intercontinental ['ɪntəˌkɒntɪ'nentl] *adj* intercontinental.

intercontinental ballistic missile *n* missile *m* balistique intercontinental.

intercostal [ˌɪntə'kɒstl] *adj* intercostal; ~ **muscles** muscles *mpl* intercostaux.

intercourse ['ɪntəkɔːs] *n* -**1.** [sexual intercourse] rapports *mpl* (sexuels); **to have ~ (with sb)** avoir des rapports sexuels (avec qqn). -**2.** *fml* [communication] relations *fpl*, rapports *mpl*; **commercial ~** relations commerciales; **social ~** communication *f*.

interdenominational ['ɪntədɪˌnɒmɪ'neɪʃənl] *adj* interconfessionnel.

interdepartmental ['ɪntəˌdiːpɑːt'mentl] *adj* [in company, hospital] entre services; [in university, ministry] interdépartemental.

interdependence [ˌɪntədɪ'pendəns] *n* interdépendance *f*.

interdependent [ˌɪntədɪ'pendənt] *adj* interdépendant.

interdict [*n* 'ɪntədɪkt, *vb* ˌɪntə'dɪkt] ◇ *vt* -**1.** JUR interdire. -**2.** RELIG jeter l'interdit sur.
◇ *n* -**1.** JUR interdiction *f*. -**2.** RELIG interdit *m*.

interdiction [ˌɪntə'dɪkʃn] *n* JUR & RELIG interdiction *f*.

interdisciplinary [ˌɪntə'dɪsɪˌplɪnərɪ] *adj* interdisciplinaire.

interest ['ɪntrəst] ◇ *n* -**1.** [curiosity, attention] intérêt *m*; **centre of ~** centre *m* d'intérêt; **she takes a great/an active ~ in politics** elle s'intéresse beaucoup/activement à la politique; **he has** OR **takes no ~ whatsoever in music** il ne s'intéresse absolument pas à la musique; **to show (an) ~ in sthg** manifester de l'intérêt pour qqch; **he lost all ~ in his work** il a perdu tout intérêt pour son travail; **pupils can often lose ~** il arrive souvent que les élèves décrochent; **to hold sb's ~** retenir l'attention de qqn. -**2.** [appeal] intérêt *m*; **of no ~** sans intérêt; **politics has** OR **holds no ~ for me** la politique ne présente aucun intérêt pour moi; **to be of ~ to sb** intéresser qqn; **this information would be of great ~ to the police** cette information intéresserait sûrement la police. -**3.** [pursuit, hobby] centre d'intérêt *m*; **we share the same ~s** nous avons les mêmes centres d'intérêt; **his only ~s are television and comic books** la télévision et les bandes dessinées sont les seules choses qui l'intéressent. -**4.** [advantage, benefit] intérêt *m*; **it's in your own ~** OR **~s** c'est dans votre propre intérêt; **she helps us purely out of ~** elle ne nous aide que par intérêt; **to act against one's own ~s** agir à l'encontre de ses propres intérêts; **I have your ~s at heart** tes intérêts me tiennent à cœur; **a conflict of ~s** un conflit d'intérêts; **of public ~** d'intérêt public; **in the ~s of hygiene** par mesure d'hygiène; **in the ~s of accuracy** par souci d'exactitude. -**5.** [group with common aim] intérêt *m*; **big business ~s** de gros intérêts commerciaux; ~ **group** groupe *m* d'intérêt. -**6.** [share, stake] intérêts *mpl*; **he has an ~ in a sawmill** il a des intérêts dans une scierie; **our firm's ~s in Europe** les intérêts de notre société en Europe. -**7.** FIN intérêts *mpl*; **to pay ~ on a loan** payer des intérêts sur un prêt; **the investment will bear 6 % ~** le placement rapportera 6 %; **he'll get it back with ~!** *fig* il va le payer cher! ❑ **simple/compound ~** intérêts simples/composés.
◇ *vt* intéresser; **to be ~ed in sthg** s'intéresser à qqch; **she is ~ed in fashion** elle s'intéresse à la mode, la mode l'intéresse; **would you be ~ed in meeting him?** ça t'intéresserait de le rencontrer?; **can I ~ you in our new model?** puis-je attirer votre attention sur notre nouveau modèle?; **I'm ~ed to see how they do it** je suis curieux de voir comment ils le font.

interest-bearing *adj* productif d'intérêts.

interested ['ɪntrestɪd] *adj* -**1.** [showing interest] intéressé; **she seems ~ in the offer** elle semble intéressée par la proposition; **a group of ~ passers-by** un groupe de passants curieux. -**2.** [involved, concerned] intéressé; ~ **party** partie *f* intéressée.

interest-free *adj* FIN sans intérêt.

interesting ['ɪntrəstɪŋ] *adj* intéressant.

interestingly ['ɪntrəstɪŋlɪ] *adv* de façon intéressante; ~ **enough, they were out** chose intéressante, ils étaient sortis.

interest rate *n* taux *m* d'intérêt.

interface [*n* 'ɪntəfeɪs, *vb* ˌɪntə'feɪs] ◇ *n* [gen & COMPUT] interface *f*.
◇ *vt* -**1.** [connect] connecter. -**2.** SEW entoiler.

interfacing [ˌɪntə'feɪsɪŋ] *n* SEW entoilage *m*.

interfere [ˌɪntə'fɪəʳ] *vi* -**1.** [intrude] s'immiscer, s'ingérer; **to ~ in sb's life** s'immiscer OR s'ingérer dans la vie de qqn; **I warned him not to ~** je l'ai prévenu de ne pas s'en mêler OR de rester à l'écart; **I hate the way he always ~s** je déteste sa façon de se mêler de tout; **don't ~ between them** ne vous mêlez pas de leurs affaires. -**2.** [clash, conflict]: **to ~ with** entraver; **to ~ with the course of justice** entraver le cours de la justice; **it ~s with my work** cela me gêne dans mon travail; **he lets his pride ~ with his judgment** il laisse son orgueil troubler son jugement. -**3.** [meddle]: **to ~ with** toucher (à); **don't ~ with those wires!** laisse ces fils tranquilles!; **to ~ with a child** *euph* se livrer à des attouchements sur un enfant. -**4.** PHYS interférer. -**5.** LING interférence *f*; **local radio sometimes ~s with police transmissions** la radio locale brouille OR perturbe parfois les transmissions de la police.

interference [ˌɪntə'fɪərəns] *n* -**1.** [gen] ingérence *f*, intervention *f*; **she won't tolerate ~ in** OR **with her plans** elle ne supportera pas qu'on s'immisce dans ses projets. -**2.** PHYS interférence *f*. -**3.** *(U)* RADIO parasites *mpl*, interférence *f*. -**4.** LING interférence *f*.

interfering [ˌɪntə'fɪərɪŋ] *adj* [person] importun.

interferometer [ˌɪntəfə'rɒmɪtəʳ] *n* interféromètre *m*.

intergalactic [ˌɪntəgə'læktɪk] *adj* intergalactique.

intergovernmental ['ɪntəˌgʌvən'mentl] *adj* intergouvernemental.

interim ['ɪntərɪm] ◇ *n* intérim *m*.
◇ *adj* [government, measure, report] provisoire; [post, function] intérimaire; **the ~ minister** le ministre par intérim OR intérimaire; ~ **payment** versement *m* provisionnel.
◆ **in the interim** *adv phr* entretemps.

interior [ɪn'tɪərɪəʳ] ◇ *adj* intérieur; ~ **doors** portes *fpl* intérieures; ~ **monologue** monologue *m* intérieur; ~ **angle** MATH angle *m* interne; ~ **shot** CIN intérieur *m*, scène *f* d'intérieur.
◇ *n* -**1.** [gen] intérieur *m*; **the French Minister of the Interior** le ministre français de l'Intérieur; **Secretary/Department of the Interior** *ministre/ministère chargé de l'administration des domaines et des parcs nationaux aux États-Unis*. -**2.** ART (tableau *m* d') intérieur *m*.

interior decoration *n* décoration *f* (d'intérieurs).

interior decorator *n* décorateur *m*, -trice *f* (d'intérieurs).

interior design *n* architecture *f* d'intérieurs.

interior designer *n* architecte *mf* d'intérieurs.

interiorize, -ise [ɪn'tɪərɪəraɪz] *vt* intérioriser.

interior-sprung mattress *n Br* matelas *m* à ressorts.

interject [,ɪntə'dʒekt] *vt* [question, comment] placer; **"not like that", he ~ed** «pas comme ça», coupa-t-il.

interjection [,ɪntə'dʒekʃn] *n* -**1.** LING interjection *f*. -**2.** [interruption] interruption *f*.

interlace [,ɪntə'leɪs] ◇ *vt* -**1.** [entwine] entrelacer. -**2.** [intersperse] entremêler.
◇ *vi* s'entrelacer, s'entrecroiser.

interlanguage ['ɪntə,læŋgwɪdʒ] *n* LING interlangue *f*.

interlard [,ɪntə'lɑːd] *vt* entrelarder.

interleaf ['ɪntəliːf] (*pl* **interleaves** [-liːvz]) *n* feuillet *m* intercalé.

interleave [,ɪntə'liːv] *vt* [book] interfolier; [sheet] intercaler.

interline [,ɪntə'laɪn] *vt* -**1.** [text] interligner. -**2.** SEW poser une doublure intermédiaire à.

interlining [,ɪntə'laɪnɪŋ] *n* SEW doublure *f* intermédiaire.

interlinked [,ɪntə'lɪŋkt] *adj*: **the problems are ~** les problèmes sont liés.

interlock [*vb* ,ɪntə'lɒk, *n* 'ɪntəlɒk] ◇ *vt* -**1.** TECH enclencher. -**2.** [entwine] entrelacer.
◇ *vi* -**1.** TECH [mechanism] s'enclencher; [cogwheels] s'engrener; **~ing chairs** *chaises qui s'accrochent les unes aux autres*. -**2.** [groups, issues] s'imbriquer.
◇ *n* -**1.** TECH enclenchement *m*. -**2.** TEX interlock *m*.

interlocutor [,ɪntə'lɒkjʊtəʳ] *n* interlocuteur *m*, -trice *f*.

interloper ['ɪntələʊpəʳ] *n* intrus *m*, -e *f*.

interlude ['ɪntəluːd] *n* -**1.** [period of time] intervalle *m*; **a brief ~** un bref intervalle; **a pleasant ~ in her troubled life** un moment de répit dans sa vie mouvementée. -**2.** THEAT intermède *m*; MUS & TV interlude *m*.

intermarriage [,ɪntə'mærɪdʒ] *n* -**1.** [within family, clan] endogamie *f*. -**2.** [between different groups] mariage *m* mixte; **~ between Jews and Christians** mariage mixte entre juifs et chrétiens.

intermarry [,ɪntə'mærɪ] (*pt* & *pp* **intermarried**) *vi* -**1.** [within family, clan] pratiquer l'endogamie; **the tribe no longer intermarries** la tribu ne pratique plus l'endogamie. -**2.** [between different groups]: **members of different religions intermarried freely** les mariages mixtes se pratiquaient librement.

intermediary [,ɪntə'miːdjərɪ] (*pl* **intermediaries**) ◇ *adj* intermédiaire.
◇ *n* intermédiaire *mf*.

intermediate [,ɪntə'miːdjət] ◇ *adj* -**1.** [gen] intermédiaire; **~ range missile** missile *m* de moyenne portée OR de portée intermédiaire. -**2.** SCH [class] moyen; **~ students** étudiants *mpl* de niveau moyen OR intermédiaire; **an ~ English course** un cours d'anglais de niveau moyen OR intermédiaire; **~ school** *NZ école qui ne comprend que les classes de sixième et de cinquième*.
◇ *n* -**1.** *Am* [car] voiture *f* de taille moyenne. -**2.** CHEM produit *m* intermédiaire.

interment [ɪn'tɜːmənt] *n* enterrement *m*, inhumation *f*.

intermezzo [,ɪntə'metsəʊ] (*pl* **intermezzos** OR **intermezzi** [-'metsiː]) *n* THEAT intermède *m*; MUS intermezzo *m*.

interminable [ɪn'tɜːmɪnəbl] *adj* interminable.

interminably [ɪn'tɜːmɪnəblɪ] *adv* interminablement; **the play seemed ~ long** la pièce semblait interminable; **the discussions dragged on ~** les discussions s'éternisaient.

intermingle [,ɪntə'mɪŋgl] *vi* se mêler; **the different groups ~d freely** les différents groupes se mêlaient librement.

intermission [,ɪntə'mɪʃn] *n* -**1.** [break] pause *f*, trêve *f*; [in illness, fever] intermission *f*; **without ~** sans relâche. -**2.** CIN & THEAT entracte *m*.

intermittent [,ɪntə'mɪtənt] *adj* intermittent; **~ rain** pluies *fpl* intermittentes, averses *fpl*.

intermittently [,ɪntə'mɪtəntlɪ] *adv* par intervalles, par intermittence; **the journal has been published only ~** la revue n'a connu qu'une parution irrégulière.

intermodal [,ɪntə'məʊdl] *adj* [container] intermodal; **~ transport system** réseau *m* de transport intermodal; **~ points** points *mpl* de rupture de charge.

intermolecular [,ɪntəmə'lekjʊləʳ] *adj* intermoléculaire.

intern [*vb* ɪn'tɜːn, *n* 'ɪntɜːn] ◇ *vt* POL interner.
◇ *vi Am* MED faire son internat; SCH faire son stage pédagogique; [with firm] faire un stage en entreprise.
◇ *n* -**1.** MED interne *mf*; *Am* SCH (professeur *m*) stagiaire *mf*; *Am* [in firm] stagiaire *mf*. -**2.** [internee] interné *m*, -e *f* (politique).

internal [ɪn'tɜːnl] ◇ *adj* -**1.** [gen] interne, intérieur; **~ bleeding** hémorragie *f* interne; **~ examination** MED examen *m* interne; **~ injuries** lésions *fpl* internes; **~ rhyme** rime *f* intérieure. -**2.** [inside country] intérieur; **~ affairs** affaires *fpl* intérieures. -**3.** [inside organization, institution] interne; **~ memo** note *f* à circulation interne; **~ disputes are crippling the party** des luttes intestines paralysent le parti; **~ examiner** SCH examinateur *m*, -trice *f* d'un établissement scolaire.
◇ *n* MED examen *m* gynécologique.

internal-combustion engine *n* moteur *m* à explosion OR à combustion interne.

internalization [ɪn,tɜːnəlaɪ'zeɪʃn] *n* [of values, behaviour] intériorisation *f*.

internalize, -ise [ɪn'tɜːnəlaɪz] *vt* -**1.** [values, behaviour] intérioriser. -**2.** INDUST & FIN internaliser.

internally [ɪn'tɜːnəlɪ] *adv* intérieurement; **'not to be taken ~'** PHARM 'à usage externe', 'ne pas avaler'.

Internal Revenue Service *pr n Am* fisc *m*.

international [,ɪntə'næʃənl] ◇ *adj* international; **an ~ singing star** une vedette internationale de la chanson ❑ **~ law** droit *m* international; **~ relations** relations *fpl* internationales; **~ waters** eaux *fpl* internationales.
◇ *n* -**1.** SPORT [match] match *m* international; [player] international *m*, -e *f*. -**2.** POL: **the International** l'Internationale *f*; **the First International** la Première Internationale.

International Court of Justice *pr n* Cour *f* internationale de justice.

International Date Line *pr n* ligne *f* de changement de date.

Internationale [,ɪntənæʃə'nɑːl] *n*: **the ~** l'Internationale *f*.

internationalism [,ɪntə'næʃnəlɪzm] *n* internationalisme *m*.

internationalist [,ɪntə'næʃnəlɪst] ◇ *adj* internationaliste.
◇ *n* internationaliste *mf*.

internationalization ['ɪntə,næʃnəlaɪ'zeɪʃn] *n* internationalisation *f*.

internationalize, -ise [,ɪntə'næʃnəlaɪz] *vt* internationaliser.

International Labour Organization *pr n* Bureau *m* international du travail.

internationally [,ɪntə'næʃnəlɪ] *adv* internationalement; **~ famous** de renommée internationale; **~ (speaking), the situation is improving** sur le OR au plan international, la situation s'améliore.

International Monetary Fund *pr n* Fonds *m* monétaire international.

internecine [*Br* ,ɪntə'niːsaɪn, *Am* ,ɪntər'niːsn] *adj fml* [within a group] intestin; **~ struggles** luttes *fpl* intestines; **~ warfare** guerre *f* qui ravage les deux camps.

internee [,ɪntɜː'niː] *n* interné *m*, -e *f* (politique).

internist [ɪn'tɜːnɪst] *n Am* MED interniste *mf*, spécialiste *mf* de médecine interne.

internment [ɪn'tɜːnmənt] *n* -**1.** [gen] internement *m* (politique); **~ without trial** internement sans jugement; **~ camp** camp *m* d'internement. -**2.** [in Ireland] *système de détention des personnes suspectées de terrorisme en Irlande du Nord*.

INTERNMENT:
En Irlande du Nord, ce terme désigne l'emprisonnement forcé de terroristes présumés, méthode employée par les autorités britanniques pour tenter de contrôler les activités de l'IRA (Irish Republican Army), au début des années 70; cette mesure fut abandonnée en 1975.

---

internship ['ɪntɜːnʃɪp] *n Am* MED internat *m*; [with firm] stage *m* en entreprise.

interpellate [ɪn'tɜːpeleɪt] *vt* POL interpeller.

interpenetrate [,ɪntə'penɪtreɪt] *vt* [permeate] imprégner, pénétrer.

interpenetration ['ɪntə,penɪ'treɪʃn] *n* [permeation] imprégnation *f*, pénétration *f*.

interpersonal [,ɪntə'pɜːsənl] *adj* interpersonnel; **~ relationships** relations *fpl* interpersonnelles; **~ skills** qualités *fpl* relationnelles.

interplanetary [,ɪntə'plænɪtrɪ] *adj* interplanétaire.

interplay ['ɪntəpleɪ] *n* [between forces, events, people] interaction *f*; **the ~ of colours** le jeu des couleurs.

Interpol ['ɪntəpɒl] *pr n* Interpol.

interpolate [ɪn'tɜːpəleɪt] *vt* -**1.** *fml* [passage of text] interpoler; **he ~d several revised passages into the new edition** dans la nouvelle édition, il a interpolé plusieurs passages révisés. -**2.** *fml* [interrupt] interrompre; **"that's utter nonsense" she ~d** «c'est complètement absurde» interrompit-elle. -**3.** MATH interpoler.

interpolation [ɪn,tɜːpə'leɪʃn] *n* -**1.** *fml* [gen] interpolation *f*. -**2.** MATH interpolation *f*.

interpose [,ɪntə'pəʊz] ◇ *vt* -**1.** [between objects] interposer, intercaler. -**2.** [interject] lancer; **he ~d a few apt comments** il lança OR plaça quelques remarques pertinentes.
◇ *vi* intervenir, s'interposer; **"that simply isn't true!" he ~d** «c'est tout simplement faux!» lança-t-il.

interpret [ɪn'tɜːprɪt] ◇ *vt* interpréter.
◇ *vi* servir d'interprète, interpréter.

interpretation [ɪn,tɜːprɪ'teɪʃn] *n* interprétation *f*; **she puts quite a different ~ on the facts** l'interprétation qu'elle donne des faits est assez différente; **his comments were very much open to ~** ses remarques donnaient vraiment lieu à interprétation.

interpretative [ɪn'tɜːprɪtətɪv] *adj* interprétatif.

interpreter [ɪn'tɜːprɪtəʳ] *n* -**1.** [person] interprète *mf*. -**2.** COMPUT interpréteur *m*.

interpretive [ɪn'tɜːprɪtɪv] = **interpretative**.

interracial [,ɪntə'reɪʃl] *adj* [relations] interracial; **~ harmony** harmonie interraciale.

interregnum [,ɪntə'regnəm] (*pl* **interregnums** OR **interregna** [-'regnə]) *n* interrègne *m*; **the Interregnum** *Br* HIST l'Interrègne *m* *(intervalle (1649-1660) pendant lequel l'Angleterre, sous l'autorité de Cromwell, fut une république)*.

interrelate [,ɪntərɪ'leɪt] ◇ *vt* mettre en corrélation; **~d questions** questions interdépendantes OR intimement liées.
◇ *vi* être interdépendant, interagir.

interrelation [ˌɪntərɪ'leɪʃn], **interrelationship** [ˌɪntərɪ'leɪʃnʃɪp] *n* corrélation *f*; there's an ~ between poverty levels and inflation il y a une corrélation entre les niveaux de pauvreté et l'inflation.

interrogate [ɪn'terəgeɪt] *vt* [gen & COMPUT] interroger.

interrogation [ɪnˌterə'geɪʃn] *n* [gen, LING & COMPUT] interrogation *f*; [by police] interrogatoire *m*; to undergo (an) ~ subir un interrogatoire; she's been under ~ elle a subi un interrogatoire.

interrogation mark *n* point *m* d'interrogation.

interrogative [ˌɪntə'rɒgətɪv] ◇ *adj* -**1.** [inquiring] interrogateur. -**2.** LING interrogatif.
◇ *n* [word] interrogatif *m*; [grammatical form] interrogative *f*; in the ~ à la forme interrogative.

interrogatively [ˌɪntə'rɒgətɪvlɪ] *adv* -**1.** [look] interrogativement, d'un air interrogateur; [remark] d'un OR sur un ton interrogateur. -**2.** LING interrogativement.

interrogator [ɪn'terəgeɪtə'] *n* -**1.** [person] interrogateur *m*, -trice *f*. -**2.** *dated* & RADIO intervieweur *m*, journaliste *mf*.

interrogatory [ˌɪntə'rɒgətrɪ] *adj* interrogateur.

interrupt [ˌɪntə'rʌpt] ◇ *vt* -**1.** [person, lecture, conversation] interrompre; don't ~ me when I'm speaking to you! ne m'interromps pas lorsque je te parle! -**2.** [process, activity] interrompre; work on the project has been ~ed les travaux sur le projet ont été interrompus; we ~ this programme for a news flash nous interrompons notre émission pour un flash d'information. -**3.** [uniformity] rompre; only an occasional tree ~ed the monotony of the landscape seul un arbre ici et là venait rompre la monotonie du paysage.
◇ *vi* interrompre; he tried to explain but you kept ~ing il a essayé de s'expliquer mais vous n'avez cessé de l'interrompre OR de lui couper la parole; sorry to ~ but... désolé de vous interrompre mais...
◇ *n* COMPUT interruption *f*.

interrupter [ˌɪntəˌrʌptə'] = **interruptor**.

interruption [ˌɪntə'rʌpʃn] *n* interruption *f*; without ~ sans interruption, sans arrêt; he hates ~s il a horreur d'être interrompu.

interruptor [ˌɪntə'rʌptə'] *n* ELECTRON interrupteur *m*.

intersect [ˌɪntə'sekt] ◇ *vi* se couper, se croiser; ~ing lines MATH lignes intersectées.
◇ *vt* couper, croiser; the valley is ~ed by a network of small roads la vallée est quadrillée d'innombrables petites routes.

intersection [ˌɪntə'sekʃn] *n* -**1.** [road junction] carrefour *m*, croisement *m*. -**2.** MATH intersection *f*; point of ~ point *m* d'intersection.

interspace [ˌɪntə'speɪs] *vt* TYPO espacer.

intersperse [ˌɪntə'spɜːs] *vt* parsemer, semer; our conversation was ~d with long silences notre conversation était ponctuée de longs silences; there were small blue flowers ~d amongst the daisies les marguerites étaient parsemées de petites fleurs bleues; sunny weather ~d with the odd shower temps ensoleillé entrecoupé de quelques averses.

interstate ['ɪntəsteɪt] ◇ *adj* [commerce, railway] entre États.
◇ *n Am* autoroute *f*.

interstellar [ˌɪntə'stelə'] *adj* interstellaire; ~ space espace *m* interstellaire.

interstice [ɪn'tɜːstɪs] *n* interstice *m*.

interstitial [ˌɪntə'stɪʃl] *adj* interstitiel.

intertwine [ˌɪntə'twaɪn] ◇ *vt* entrelacer; their lives are inextricably ~d leurs vies sont inextricablement liées.
◇ *vi* s'entrelacer; intertwining branches branches entrelacées.

interurban [ˌɪntə'ɜːbn] *adj* interurbain.

interval ['ɪntəvl] *n* -**1.** [period of time] intervalle *m*; there was an ~ of three months between applying for the job and being accepted trois mois se sont écoulés entre la candidature et l'embauche; I saw him again after an ~ of six months je l'ai revu après un intervalle de six mois; at ~s par intervalles, de temps en temps; at regular ~s à intervalles réguliers; at short ~s à intervalles rapprochés; at weekly ~s toutes les semaines, chaque semaine. -**2.** [interlude] pause *f*; *Br* THEAT entracte *m*; SPORT mi-temps *f*. -**3.** [distance] intervalle *m*, distance *f*; trees planted at regular ~s des arbres plantés à intervalles réguliers. -**4.** METEOR: sunny ~s éclaircies *fpl*. -**5.** MATH & MUS intervalle *m*.

interval ownership *n Am* multipropriété *f*.

intervene [ˌɪntə'viːn] *vi* -**1.** [person, government] intervenir; they were unwilling to ~ in the conflict ils ne souhaitaient pas intervenir dans le conflit; I warned him not to ~ [in fight] je lui avais bien dit de ne pas intervenir OR s'interposer; [in argument] je lui avais bien dit de ne pas s'en mêler; the government ~d to save the dollar from falling le gouvernement est intervenu pour arrêter la chute du dollar. -**2.** [event] survenir; he was about to go to college when war ~d il allait entrer à l'université lorsque la guerre a éclaté. -**3.** [time] s'écouler; three months ~d between the agreement and actually signing the contract trois mois se sont écoulés entre l'accord et la signature du contrat. -**4.** [interrupt] intervenir; if I might just ~ here... si je peux me permettre d'intervenir sur ce point...

intervening [ˌɪntə'viːnɪŋ] *adj* [period of time] intermédiaire; during the ~ period dans l'intervalle, entre-temps.

intervention [ˌɪntə'venʃn] *n* intervention *f*; armed ~ intervention armée; ~ price ECON prix *m* d'intervention.

interventionism [ˌɪntə'venʃənɪzm] *n* interventionnisme *m*.

interventionist [ˌɪntə'venʃənɪst] ◇ *adj* interventionniste.
◇ *n* interventionniste *mf*.

intervertebral [ˌɪntə'vɜːtəbrəl] *adj* intervertébral.

interview ['ɪntəvjuː] ◇ *n* -**1.** [for job, university place etc] entrevue *f*, entretien *m*; ~s will be held at our London offices les entretiens se dérouleront dans nos bureaux de Londres; he's already had several ~s il a déjà eu plusieurs entretiens; to invite OR to call sb for ~ convoquer qqn pour une entrevue. -**2.** PRESS, RADIO & TV interview *f*; she gave him an exclusive ~ elle lui a accordé une interview en exclusivité.
◇ *vt* -**1.** [for university place, job etc] avoir une entrevue OR un entretien avec; shortlisted applicants will be ~ed in March les candidats sélectionnés seront convoqués pour un entretien en mars; we have ~ed ten people for the post nous avons déjà vu dix personnes pour ce poste || [for opinion poll] interroger, sonder; 900 voters were ~ed 900 électeurs ont été interrogés, l'enquête a été effectuée auprès de 900 électeurs. -**2.** PRESS, RADIO & TV interviewer; she's being ~ed by their top reporter leur meilleur journaliste l'interviewe OR l'interroge en ce moment. -**3.** [subj: police] interroger, questionner; he is being ~ed in connection with a series of thefts on l'interroge pour une série de vols.
◇ *vi* faire passer un entretien; I'm ~ing all day je fais passer des entretiens toute la journée.

interviewee [ˌɪntəvjuː'iː] *n* interviewé *m*, -e *f*.

interviewer ['ɪntəvjuːə'] *n* -**1.** [for media] intervieweur *m*, intervieweur *m*, -euse *f*; [for opinion poll] enquêteur *m*, -euse OR -trice *f*. -**2.** [for job]: the ~ asked me what my present salary was la personne qui m'a fait passer l'entretien OR l'entrevue m'a demandé quel était mon salaire actuel.

intervocalic [ˌɪntəvə'kælɪk] *adj* intervocalique.

interwar [ˌɪntə'wɔː'] *adj*: the ~ period OR years l'entre-deux-guerres *m*.

interweave [ˌɪntə'wiːv] (*pt* interwove [-'wəʊv] OR interweaved, *pp* interwoven [-'wəʊvn] OR interwove OR interweaved) ◇ *vt* entrelacer; the red and gold threads were interwoven with silver les fils rouge et or étaient entrelacés de fil d'argent; our lives have become closely interwoven *fig* nos deux vies sont devenues intimement liées.
◇ *vi* s'entrelacer, s'entremêler.

intestate [ɪn'testeɪt] ◇ *adj* intestat *(inv)*; to die ~ décéder intestat.
◇ *n* intestat *mf*.

intestinal [ɪn'testɪnl] *adj* intestinal.

intestine [ɪn'testɪn] *n (usu pl)* intestin *m*; an infection of the ~ OR ~s une infection intestinale ❑ large ~ gros intestin; small ~ intestin grêle.

intimacy ['ɪntɪməsɪ] (*pl* **intimacies**) *n* -**1.** [closeness, warmth] intimité *f*. -**2.** [privacy] intimité *f*; in the ~ of one's own home dans l'intimité du foyer. -**3.** *(U) euph* & *fml* [sexual relations] relations *fpl* sexuelles, rapports *mpl*; ~ took place on more than one occasion ils ont eu des rapports à plusieurs reprises.
◆ **intimacies** *npl* [familiarities] familiarités *fpl*; they never really exchanged intimacies ils ont toujours gardé une certaine réserve l'un envers l'autre.

intimate[1] ['ɪntɪmət] ◇ *adj* -**1.** [friend, relationship] intime; we were never very ~ nous n'avons jamais été (des amis) intimes; we're on ~ terms with them nous sommes très amis, ils font partie de nos amis intimes. -**2.** [small and cosy] intime; an ~ little bar un petit bar intime; an ~ dinner for two [lovers] un dîner en amoureux; an ~ (little) dinner party un dîner en tête-à-tête, un petit dîner à deux. -**3.** *euph* & *fml* [sexually]: they were ~ on more than one occasion ils ont eu des rapports (intimes) à plusieurs reprises; he admitted to having had ~ relations with her il a reconnu avoir eu des rapports avec elle. -**4.** [personal, private] intime; spare me the ~ details! *hum* fais-moi grâce de tous ces détails! -**5.** [thorough] profond, approfondi; she has an ~ knowledge of the field elle connaît le sujet à fond. -**6.** [close, direct] étroit; an ~ link un lien étroit.
◇ *n* intime *mf*.

intimate[2] ['ɪntɪmeɪt] *vt* [hint, imply] laisser entendre, insinuer; he ~d that he had had an affair with her il a laissé entendre qu'il avait eu une liaison avec elle; her speech ~d strong disapproval son discours laissait paraître son profond désaccord.

intimately ['ɪntɪmətlɪ] *adv* -**1.** [talk, behave - in a friendly way] intimement; to know sb ~ connaître qqn intimement. -**2.** [know - thoroughly] à fond; [- closely, directly] étroitement; the two questions are ~ related les deux questions sont intimement liées; I am ~ acquainted with the details of the matter je connais l'affaire dans ses moindres détails.

intimation [ˌɪntɪ'meɪʃn] *n fml* [suggestion] suggestion *f*; [sign] indice *m*, indication *f*; [premonition] pressentiment *m*; we had no ~ that disaster was imminent rien ne laissait pressentir l'imminence d'une catastrophe; her letter was the first ~ we had that she was in any danger sa lettre a été pour nous le premier indice du danger qu'elle courait.

intimidate [ɪn'tɪmɪdeɪt] *vt* intimider; don't let him ~ you ne le laisse pas t'intimider, ne te laisse pas intimider par lui.

intimidating [ɪn'tɪmɪdeɪtɪŋ] *adj* intimidant.

intimidation [ɪnˌtɪmɪ'deɪʃn] *n (U)* intimidation *f*, menaces *fpl*.

into ['ɪntʊ] *prep* -**1.** [indicating direction, movement etc] dans; come ~ my office venez dans mon bureau; to run/stroll ~ a room entrer dans une pièce en courant/d'un pas nonchalant; they sank deeper ~ debt ils se sont endettés de plus en plus; Britain's entry ~ the Common Market l'entrée de la Grande-Bretagne dans le Marché commun; to feed data ~ a computer entrer des données dans un ordinateur; planes take off ~ the wind les avions décollent face au vent. -**2.** [indicating collision] dans; the truck ran OR **crashed ~ the wall** le camion est rentré dans OR s'est écrasé contre le mur. **-3.** [indicating transformation] en; **the frog changed ~ a prince** la grenouille s'est transformée en prince; **he's grown ~ a man** c'est un homme maintenant; **mix the ingredients ~ a paste** mélangez les ingrédients jusqu'à ce qu'ils forment une pâte. **-4.** [indicating result]: **to frighten sb ~ confessing** faire avouer qqn en lui faisant peur; **they were shocked ~ silence** le choc leur a fait perdre la parole. **-5.** [indicating division] en; **cut it ~ three** coupe-le en trois; **7 ~ 63 goes 9** 63 divisé par 7 donne 9; **6 ~ 10 won't go** on ne peut pas diviser 10 par 6. **-6.** [indicating elapsed time]: **we worked well ~ the night** nous avons travaillé (jusque) tard dans la nuit; **he must be well ~ his forties** il doit avoir la quarantaine bien passée OR sonnée; **a week ~ her holiday and she's bored already** il y a à peine une semaine qu'elle est en vacances et elle s'ennuie déjà. **-7.** *inf* [fond of]: **to be ~ sthg** être passionné par qqch; **I was never really ~ pop music** je n'ai jamais été un fana de musique pop; **is he ~ drugs?** est-ce qu'il se drogue? **-8.** [curious about]: **the baby's ~ everything** le bébé est curieux de tout.

intolerable [ɪn'tɒlrəbl] *adj* intolérable, insupportable; **I find it ~ that...** je trouve intolérable que...

intolerably [ɪn'tɒlrəblɪ] *adv* intolérablement, insupportablement; **he had been ~ rude** il avait été d'une grossièreté intolérable.

intolerance [ɪn'tɒlərəns] *n* [gen & MED] intolérance *f*.

intolerant [ɪn'tɒlərənt] *adj* intolérant; **she is very ~ of fools** elle ne supporte absolument pas les imbéciles.

intolerantly [ɪn'tɒlərəntlɪ] *adv* avec intolérance.

intonation [ˌɪntə'neɪʃn] *n* intonation *f*; **~ pattern** LING intonation.

intone [ɪn'təʊn] *vt* entonner; **the priest ~d a hymn** le prêtre entonna un cantique.

intoxicant [ɪn'tɒksɪkənt] ◇ *n fml* [alcohol] alcool *m*, boisson *f* alcoolisée; [drug] stupéfiant *m*.
◇ *adj* enivrant, grisant.

intoxicate [ɪn'tɒksɪkeɪt] *vt* **-1.** *literal & fig* enivrer, griser. **-2.** MED [poison] intoxiquer.

intoxicated [ɪn'tɒksɪkeɪtɪd] *adj* **-1.** [drunk] ivre, en état d'ébriété *fml*. **-2.** *fig* ivre; **he was ~ with joy** il était ivre de joie; **she was ~ by success** son succès l'avait grisée OR lui avait fait tourner la tête.

intoxicating [ɪn'tɒksɪkeɪtɪŋ] *adj literal* enivrant; *fig* grisant, enivrant, excitant; **~ liquor** boisson *f* alcoolisée; **an ~ perfume** un parfum enivrant OR capiteux.

intoxication [ɪnˌtɒksɪ'keɪʃn] *n* **-1.** *literal & fig* ivresse *f*. **-2.** MED [poisoning] intoxication *f*.

intractability [ɪnˌtræktə'bɪlətɪ] *n* **-1.** [of person] intransigeance *f*, fermeté *f*, opiniâtreté *f*. **-2.** [of problem] insolubilité *f*.

intractable [ɪn'træktəbl] *adj* **-1.** [person] intraitable, intransigeant. **-2.** [problem] insoluble; [situation] inextricable, sans issue.

intramural [ˌɪntrə'mjʊərəl] *adj* SCH & UNIV [courses, sports] interne (à l'établissement); **~ teams** *équipes sportives d'un même établissement jouant les unes contre les autres.*

intramuscular [ˌɪntrə'mʌskjʊlə^r] *adj* intramusculaire.

intransigence [ɪn'trænzɪdʒəns] *n* intransigeance *f*.

intransigent [ɪn'trænzɪdʒənt] ◇ *adj* intransigeant.
◇ *n* intransigeant *m*, -e *f*.

intransitive [ɪn'trænzətɪv] ◇ *adj* intransitif.
◇ *n* intransitif *m*.

intransitively [ɪn'trænzətɪvlɪ] *adv* intransitivement.

intrastate [ˌɪntrə'steɪt] *adj* à l'intérieur d'un même État.

intrauterine [ˌɪntrə'juːtəraɪn] *adj* intra-utérin.

intrauterine device *n* stérilet *m*.

intravenous [ˌɪntrə'viːnəs] *adj* intraveineux; **~ drugs user** toxicomane *mf* qui s'injecte sa drogue; **~ injection** (injection *f*) intraveineuse *f*.

intravenously [ˌɪntrə'viːnəslɪ] *adv* par voie intraveineuse; **he's being fed ~** on l'alimente par perfusion; **to take drugs ~** s'injecter de la drogue.

in-tray *n* corbeille *f* de courrier à traiter OR «arrivée»; **put it in my ~** posez-ça sur le courrier à traiter.

intrepid [ɪn'trepɪd] *adj* intrépide.

intrepidly [ɪn'trepɪdlɪ] *adv* intrépidement.

intricacy ['ɪntrɪkəsɪ] (*pl* **intricacies**) *n* **-1.** [complicated detail] complexité *f*; **he knows all the legal intricacies** il connaît toutes les subtilités du droit; **I couldn't follow all the intricacies of her argument** je n'ai pas suivi toutes les subtilités de son raisonnement. **-2.** [complexity] complexité *f*; **I admire the ~ of her drawings** je suis en admiration devant la complexité de ses dessins.

intricate ['ɪntrɪkət] *adj* complexe, compliqué; **~ patterns** des motifs complexes OR très élaborés; **an ~ argument** un raisonnement complexe.

intricately ['ɪntrɪkətlɪ] *adv* de façon complexe OR compliquée; **an ~ carved chair** une chaise aux sculptures complexes OR très travaillées.

intrigue [ɪn'triːg] ◇ *n* **-1.** [plotting] intrigue *f*; **the boardroom was rife with ~** la salle du conseil d'administration sentait l'intrigue. **-2.** [plot, treason] complot *m*; **he was involved in various ~s against the state** il a participé à plusieurs complots contre l'État.
◇ *vt* intriguer; **her silence ~s me** son silence m'intrigue; **I'd be ~d to know where they met** je serais curieux de savoir où ils se sont rencontrés.
◇ *vi* intriguer, comploter; **they ~d with republicans against the throne** ils ont comploté avec des Républicains contre le roi.

intriguing [ɪn'triːgɪŋ] *adj* bizarre, curieux; **I find the whole thing most ~** tout cela me paraît très bizarre; **it's an ~ idea!** c'est une idée bizarre!

intriguingly [ɪn'triːgɪŋlɪ] *adv* bizarrement, curieusement; **did he turn up on time? — ~ enough, he did** est-il arrivé à l'heure? — curieusement, oui.

intrinsic [ɪn'trɪnsɪk] *adj* intrinsèque; **the picture has little ~ value** ce tableau a peu de valeur en soi; **such ideas are ~ to my argument** de telles idées sont essentielles OR inhérentes à mon raisonnement.

intrinsically [ɪn'trɪnsɪklɪ] *adv* intrinsèquement.

intro *inf* ['ɪntrəʊ] (*pl* **intros**) *n* introduction *f*, intro *f*.

introduce [ˌɪntrə'djuːs] *vt* **-1.** [present - one person to another] présenter; **she ~d me to her sister** elle m'a présenté à sa sœur; **may I ~ you?** permettez-moi de OR laissez-moi vous présenter; **let me ~ myself, I'm John** je me présente, John; **has everyone been ~d?** les présentations ont été faites?; **I don't think we've been ~d, have we?** nous n'avons pas été présentés, je crois?; **to ~ a speaker** présenter un conférencier. **-2.** [radio or TV programme] présenter. **-3.** [bring in] introduire; **when were rabbits ~d into Australia?** quand a-t-on introduit les lapins en Australie?; **I'd like to ~ a new topic into the debate, if I may** si vous le permettez, j'aimerais introduire dans le débat un nouveau sujet; **her arrival ~d a note of sadness into the festivities** son entrée mit une note de tristesse dans la fête. **-4.** [laws, legislation] déposer, présenter; **the government hopes to ~ the new bill next week** le gouvernement espère déposer son nouveau projet de loi la semaine prochaine; **to ~ a reform** introduire une réforme. **-5.** [initiate] initier; **she ~d me to the pleasures of French cooking** elle m'a initié aux OR révélé les délices de la cuisine française; **it was my sister who ~d me to yoga** c'est ma sœur qui m'a initiée au yoga OR fait découvrir le yoga. **-6.** [start] ouvrir, donner le départ; **a fanfare ~d the start of the ceremony** une fanfare a ouvert la cérémonie. **-7.** *fml* [insert, put in] introduire; **~ the wire carefully into the cavity** introduisez doucement le fil dans le trou.

introduction [ˌɪntrə'dʌkʃn] *n* **-1.** [of one person to another] présentation *f*; **would you make** OR **do** *inf* **the ~s?** peux-tu faire les présentations?; **our next guest needs no ~** inutile de vous présenter l'invité suivant. **-2.** [first part - of book, speech, piece of music] introduction *f*. **-3.** [basic textbook, course] introduction *f*, initiation *f*; **an ~ to linguistics** une introduction à la linguistique; **the short stories provide an easy ~ to his more difficult work** les nouvelles constituent une introduction facile aux parties difficiles de son œuvre. **-4.** [bringing in] introduction *f*; **the ~ of computer technology into schools** l'introduction de l'informatique à l'école. **-5.** [of bill, law] introduction *f*, présentation *f*. **-6.** [insertion] introduction *f*.

introductory [ˌɪntrə'dʌktrɪ] *adj* [remarks] préliminaire; [chapter, course] d'introduction; **~ offer** COMM offre *f* de lancement.

introit ['ɪntrɔɪt] *n* MUS & RELIG introït *m*.

intron ['ɪntrɒn] *n* intron *m*.

introspection [ˌɪntrə'spekʃn] *n* introspection *f*.

introspective [ˌɪntrə'spektɪv] *adj* introspectif.

introversion [ˌɪntrə'vɜːʃn] *n* introversion *f*.

introvert ['ɪntrəvɜːt] ◇ *n* PSYCH introverti *m*, -e *f*.
◇ *vt* introvertir.

introverted ['ɪntrəvɜːtɪd] *adj* PSYCH introverti.

intrude [ɪn'truːd] ◇ *vi* **-1.** [disturb] déranger, s'imposer; **I hope I'm not intruding** j'espère que je ne vous dérange pas. **-2.** [interfere with]: **I don't let my work ~ on my private life** je ne laisse pas mon travail empiéter sur ma vie privée; **they're intruding on our private lives** ils se mêlent de OR ils s'immiscent dans notre vie privée; **she didn't let the news ~ on her good mood** elle ne laissa pas cette nouvelle gâcher sa bonne humeur; **I felt I was intruding on their grief** j'ai eu l'impression de les déranger dans leur chagrin.
◇ *vt fml* [gen] imposer; **a doubt ~d itself into my mind** un doute m'est venu à l'esprit.

intruder [ɪn'truːdə^r] *n* [criminal] cambrioleur *m*; [outsider] intrus *m*, -e *f*, importun *m*, -e *f*; **they made us feel like ~s** nous avons eu l'impression de déranger OR d'être de trop.

intrusion [ɪn'truːʒn] *n* **-1.** [gen] intrusion *f*, ingérence *f*; **it's an ~ into our privacy** c'est une intrusion dans notre vie privée. **-2.** GEOL intrusion *f*.

intrusive [ɪn'truːsɪv] *adj* **-1.** [person] importun; **he was an ~ presence in the house** sa présence dans la maison était importune; **far away from the ~ sounds of the city** loin de la rumeur importune de la ville. **-2.** GEOL intrusif. **-3.** LING: **~ consonant** consonne *f* d'appui.

INTUC ['ɪntʌk] (*abbr of* **Indian National Trade Union Congress**) *pr n confédération de syndicats indiens.*

intuit [ɪn'tjuːɪt] *vt fml* savoir OR connaître intuitivement; **I could only ~ what had happened between them** je n'ai pu que deviner ce qui s'était passé entre eux.

intuition [ˌɪntjuː'ɪʃn] *n* intuition *f*; **(my) ~ tells me he won't be coming** mon intuition me dit qu'il ne viendra pas; **I had an ~ something was wrong** j'avais le sentiment que quelque chose n'allait pas.

intuitive [ɪn'tjuːɪtɪv] *adj* intuitif; **an ~ understanding** une connaissance intuitive; **he's very ~** c'est un intuitif.

intuitively [ɪn'tjuːɪtɪvlɪ] *adv* intuitivement; **I knew ~ that she was lying** je savais intuitivement qu'elle mentait, je sentais bien qu'elle ne disait pas la vérité.

intumescence [ˌɪntjuː'mesns] *n* intumescence *f*.

Inuit ['ɪnʊɪt] (*pl inv* OR **Inuits**) ◇ *n* Inuit *mf*.
◇ *adj* inuit.

inundate [ˈɪnʌndeɪt] *vt literal* & *fig* inonder; the whole area was ~d toute la région a été inondée; we've been ~d with phone calls/letters nous avons été submergés de coups de fil/courrier; I'm ~d with work just now pour l'instant je suis débordé (de travail) OR je croule sous le travail.

inundation [ˌɪnʌnˈdeɪʃn] *n* inondation *f*.

inure [ɪˈnjʊəʳ] ◇ *vt* aguerrir; he became ~d to the pain il s'est habitué OR fait à la douleur.
◇ *vi* [law] entrer en vigueur.

invade [ɪnˈveɪd] *vt* -**1.** MIL envahir. -**2.** *fig* envahir; the village was ~d by reporters les journalistes ont envahi le village; her mind was ~d by sudden doubts le doute s'empara soudain de son esprit; to ~ sb's privacy s'immiscer dans la vie privée de qqn.

invader [ɪnˈveɪdəʳ] *n* envahisseur *m*, -euse *f*; to repel ~s repousser l'envahisseur.

invading [ɪnˈveɪdɪŋ] *adj* -**1.** [army] d'invasion; the ~ barbarians l'envahisseur barbare. -**2.** [plants, insects] envahissant.

invalid¹ [*n* & *adj* ˈɪnvəlɪd, *vb* ˈɪnvəliːd]
◇ *n* [disabled person] infirme *mf*, invalide *mf*; [ill person] malade *mf*.
◇ *adj* [disabled] infirme, invalide; [ill] malade; he has to look after his ~ mother il doit s'occuper de sa mère infirme; ~ chair fauteuil *m* roulant.
◇ *vt* -**1.** [disable] rendre infirme. -**2.** *Br* MIL: he was ~ed home il a été rapatrié pour raisons médicales.
◆ **invalid out** *vt sep* MIL: to ~ sb out of the army réformer qqn pour raisons médicales.

invalid² [ɪnˈvælɪd] *adj* -**1.** [passport, ticket] non valide, non valable; your passport will soon be ~ votre passeport sera bientôt périmé. -**2.** [law, marriage, election] nul. -**3.** [argument] non valable; your reasoning is ~ votre raisonnement n'est pas valable OR ne tient pas.

invalidate [ɪnˈvælɪdeɪt] *vt* -**1.** [contract, agreement etc] invalider, annuler. -**2.** [argument] infirmer.

invalid car, **invalid carriage** *n Br* voiture *f* d'infirme.

invalidity [ˌɪnvəˈlɪdətɪ] *n* -**1.** MED invalidité *f*. -**2.** [of contract, agreement etc] manque *m* de validité, nullité *f*. -**3.** [of argument] manque *m* de fondement; to demonstrate the ~ of an argument prouver qu'un argument n'est pas valable.

invalidity benefit *n Br* prestation *f* d'invalidité.

invaluable [ɪnˈvæljʊəbl] *adj* inestimable, très précieux; your help has been ~ (to me) votre aide m'a été très précieuse; she's an ~ asset (to the company) elle représente un atout inestimable (pour l'entreprise).

invariable [ɪnˈveərɪəbl] ◇ *adj* invariable.
◇ *n* MATH constante *f*.

invariably [ɪnˈveərɪəblɪ] *adv* invariablement; she was almost ~ dressed in black elle était presque toujours habillée en noir.

invariant [ɪnˈveərɪənt] ◇ *adj* invariant.
◇ *n* invariant *m*.

invasion [ɪnˈveɪʒn] *n* -**1.** MIL invasion *f*, envahissement *m*; the Roman ~ of England l'invasion de l'Angleterre par les Romains. -**2.** *fig* invasion *f*, intrusion *f*; we expect the usual ~ of tourists this summer nous nous attendons à l'habituelle invasion de touristes cet été; he considered it an ~ of privacy il l'a ressenti comme une intrusion dans sa vie privée.

invasive [ɪnˈveɪsɪv] *adj* MIL [armies] d'invasion; *fig* envahissant.

invective [ɪnˈvektɪv] *n (U)* invective *f*, invectives *fpl*; he let out a stream of ~ il a lâché un torrent d'invectives.

inveigh [ɪnˈveɪ] *vi fml*: to ~ against sb/sthg invectiver qqn/qqch, pester contre qqn/qqch.

inveigle [ɪnˈveɪgl] *vt* manipuler; he had been ~d into letting them in on l'avait adroitement manipulé pour qu'il les laisse entrer; she ~d him into giving her a lift elle l'a habilement persuadé de la conduire en voiture.

invent [ɪnˈvent] *vt* -**1.** [new machine, process] inventer. -**2.** [lie, excuse] inventer.

invention [ɪnˈvenʃn] *n* -**1.** [discovery, creation] invention *f*; television is a wonderful ~ la télévision est une invention merveilleuse; she has great powers of ~ elle a de grandes facultés d'invention. -**2.** [untruth] invention *f*, fabrication *f*; the whole thing was an ~ of the press la presse a inventé OR monté cette histoire de bout en bout; it was pure ~ ce n'était que pure invention, c'était complètement faux.

inventive [ɪnˈventɪv] *adj* [person, mind] inventif; [plan, solution] ingénieux.

inventiveness [ɪnˈventɪvnɪs] *n* esprit *m* d'invention, inventivité *f*.

inventor [ɪnˈventəʳ] *n* inventeur *m*, -trice *f*.

inventory [ˈɪnvəntrɪ] (*pl* inventories, *pt* & *pp* inventoried) ◇ *n* -**1.** [list] inventaire *m*; to draw up OR to make an ~ dresser un inventaire; to take the ~ faire l'inventaire. -**2.** *(U) Am* [stock] stock *m*, stocks *mpl*; our ~ is low nos stocks sont bas; ~ control OR management gestion *f* des stocks.
◇ *vt* inventorier.

inverse [ɪnˈvɜːs] ◇ *adj* inverse; to be in ~ proportion to être inversement proportionnel à; in ~ video COMPUT en vidéo inverse.
◇ *n* inverse *m*, contraire *m*; MATH inverse *m*.

inversely [ɪnˈvɜːslɪ] *adv* inversement.

inversion [ɪnˈvɜːʃn] *n* -**1.** [gen] inversion *f*; [of roles, relations] renversement *m*. -**2.** MUS [of chord] renversement *m*; [in counterpoint] inversion *f*. -**3.** ANAT, ELEC & MATH inversion *f*.

invert [*vb* ɪnˈvɜːt, *n* ˈɪnvɜːt] ◇ *vt* -**1.** [turn upside down or inside out] inverser, retourner; [switch around] intervertir; [roles] intervertir, renverser; the two letters have been ~ed les deux lettres ont été interverties. -**2.** MUS [chord] renverser; [interval] inverser. -**3.** CHEM [sugar] invertir.
◇ *n* PSYCH inverti *m*, -e *f*.

invertebrate [ɪnˈvɜːtɪbreɪt] ◇ *adj* invertébré.
◇ *n* invertébré *m*.

inverted commas [ɪnˈvɜːtɪd-] *npl Br* guillemets *mpl*; in ~ entre guillemets; her "best friend", in ~, ran off with her husband sa «meilleure amie», entre guillemets, est partie avec son mari.

inverted snob *n Br personne d'origine modeste qui affiche du mépris pour les valeurs bourgeoises*.

inverter, **invertor** [ɪnˈvɜːtəʳ] *n* -**1.** ELEC onduleur *m* (de courant). -**2.** COMPUT inverseur *m*.

invert sugar *n* sucre *m* inverti.

invest [ɪnˈvest] ◇ *vi* investir; to ~ in shares/in the oil industry investir en actions/dans l'industrie pétrolière; she's been ~ing on the stock market elle a investi en Bourse; they decided to ~ in an automated system ils ont décidé d'investir dans un système automatisé; you ought to ~ in a new coat *inf* tu devrais t'offrir OR te payer un nouveau manteau.
◇ *vt* -**1.** [money] investir, placer; they ~ed five million dollars in new machinery ils ont investi cinq millions de dollars dans de nouveaux équipements. -**2.** [time, effort] investir; we've ~ed a lot of time and energy in this project nous avons investi beaucoup de temps et d'énergie dans ce projet. -**3.** *fml* [confer on] investir; ~ed with the highest authority investi de la plus haute autorité. -**4.** MIL [besiege, surround] investir. -**5.** *arch* OR *lit* [clothe, cover] revêtir.

investigate [ɪnˈvestɪgeɪt] ◇ *vt* [allegation, crime, accident] enquêter sur; [problem, situation] examiner, étudier.
◇ *vi* enquêter, mener une enquête.

investigation [ɪnˌvestɪˈgeɪʃn] *n* [into crime, accident] enquête *f*; [of problem, situation] examen *m*, étude *f*; months of ~ turned up no clues après des mois d'enquête, aucun indice n'a été découvert; his activities are under ~ une enquête a été ouverte sur ses activités; your case is currently under ~ nous étudions actuellement votre cas.

investigative [ɪnˈvestɪgətɪv] *adj* PRESS, RADIO & TV d'investigation; ~ journalism journalisme *m* d'investigation OR d'enquête; ~ reporter journaliste *mf* OR reporter *m* d'investigation.

investigator [ɪnˈvestɪgeɪtəʳ] *n* enquêteur *m*, -euse OR -trice *f*.

investigatory [ɪnˈvestɪgeɪtərɪ] *adj* d'investigation.

investiture [ɪnˈvestɪtʃəʳ] *n* investiture *f*.

investment [ɪnˈvestmənt] *n* -**1.** [of money, capital] investissement *m*, placement *m*; are these shares a good ~? ces actions sont-elles un bon placement?; property is no longer such a safe ~ l'immobilier n'est plus un placement aussi sûr; I'd prefer a better return on ~ je préférerais un investissement plus rentable; the company has ~s all over the world la société a des capitaux investis dans le monde entier. -**2.** [of time, effort] investissement *m*. -**3.** = **investiture**. -**4.** MIL [of fortress] investissement *m*.

investment account *n* compte *m* d'investissement.

investment analyst *n* analyste *mf* en placements.

investment bank *n* ≃ banque *f* d'affaires.

investment trust *n* société *f* de placement.

investor [ɪnˈvestəʳ] *n* investisseur *m*; [shareholder] actionnaire *mf*.

inveterate [ɪnˈvetərət] *adj* -**1.** [habit, dislike] invétéré; [hatred] tenace. -**2.** [drinker, gambler] invétéré; [bachelor, liar, smoker] impénitent.

invidious [ɪnˈvɪdɪəs] *adj* [unfair] injuste; ~ comparisons des comparaisons injustes || [unpleasant] ingrat, pénible; an ~ task une tâche pénible.

invigilate [ɪnˈvɪdʒɪleɪt] *vi* & *vt* *Br* SCH & UNIV surveiller *(pendant un examen)*.

invigilator [ɪnˈvɪdʒɪleɪtəʳ] *n Br* SCH & UNIV surveillant *m*, -e *f (d'un examen)*.

invigorate [ɪnˈvɪgəreɪt] *vt* revigorer, vivifier; she felt ~d by the cold wind le vent frais la revigorait.

invigorating [ɪnˈvɪgəreɪtɪŋ] *adj* revigorant, vivifiant, tonifiant; an ~ climate un climat vivifiant; it's ~ just talking to her il suffit de lui parler pour se sentir revigoré; an ~ walk une promenade revigorante.

invincibility [ɪnˌvɪnsɪˈbɪlətɪ] *n* invincibilité *f*.

invincible [ɪnˈvɪnsɪbl] *adj* [army, troops] invincible; [belief] inébranlable.

inviolability [ɪnˌvaɪələˈbɪlətɪ] *n* inviolabilité *f*.

inviolable [ɪnˈvaɪələbl] *adj* inviolable.

inviolate [ɪnˈvaɪələt] *adj lit* inviolé.

invisibility [ɪnˌvɪzɪˈbɪlətɪ] *n* invisibilité *f*.

invisible [ɪnˈvɪzɪbl] *adj* -**1.** invisible; ~ to the naked eye invisible à l'œil nu ❑ ~ mending stoppage *m*; 'The Invisible Man' *Wells* 'l'Homme invisible'. -**2.** COMM [unrecorded]: ~ imports importations *fpl* invisibles; ~ earnings revenus *mpl* occultes.

invisible ink *n* encre *f* invisible OR sympathique.

invisibly [ɪnˈvɪzɪblɪ] *adv* invisiblement.

invitation [ˌɪnvɪˈteɪʃn] *n* invitation *f*; have you sent out the wedding ~s? as-tu envoyé les invitations au mariage?; she's here at my ~ c'est moi qui l'ai invitée; we went to the congress at the ~ of the President himself nous sommes allés au congrès à l'invitation du président en personne; by ~ only sur invitation seulement; your son is included in the ~ votre fils est invité lui aussi; a standing ~ une invitation permanente; prison conditions are an (open) ~ to violence *fig* les conditions de détention sont une véritable incitation à la violence.

invite [*vb* ɪnˈvaɪt, *n* ˈɪnvaɪt] ◇ *vt* -**1.** [ask to come] inviter; to ~ sb for lunch inviter qqn à déjeuner; the Thomsons have ~d us over les Thomson nous ont invités chez eux; I ~d him up for a coffee je l'ai invité à monter prendre un café; the discussion took place in front of a specially ~d audience la discussion s'est déroulée devant un public spécialement invité OR invité pour l'occasion. -2. [ask to do sthg] demander, solliciter; they ~d her to become president ils lui ont demandé de devenir présidente; I've been ~d for interview j'ai été convoqué à un entretien. -3. [solicit]: he ~d comment on his book il a demandé aux gens leur avis sur son livre; we ~ applications from all qualified candidates nous invitons tous les candidats ayant le profil requis à postuler; we ~ suggestions from readers toute suggestion de la part de nos lecteurs est la bienvenue. -4. [trouble, defeat, disaster] aller au devant de; you're just inviting failure tu vas au devant de l'échec || [doubt, sympathy] appeler, attirer; his garbled answers simply ~d disbelief ses réponses embrouillées ne faisaient que susciter la méfiance.

◇ *n* *inf* invitation *f*.

◆ **invite out** *vt sep* inviter (à sortir); she's ~d me out tonight elle m'a invité à sortir (avec elle) ce soir; he's always getting ~d out il est toujours invité quelque part.

inviting [ɪnˈvaɪtɪŋ] *adj* [gesture] d'invitation; [eyes, smile] engageant; [display] attirant, attrayant; [idea] tentant, séduisant; [place, fire] accueillant.

invitingly [ɪnˈvaɪtɪŋlɪ] *adv* d'une manière attrayante; the page was ~ blank la blancheur de la page OR la page blanche était une invitation; he gestured ~ il eut un geste d'invitation; she spoke ~ of blue seas and white sand elle parlait de mer bleue et de sable blanc, c'était plutôt tentant.

in vitro [ɪnˈviːtrəʊ] ◇ *adj* in vitro; ~ fertilization fécondation *f* in vitro.
◇ *adv* in vitro.

invocation [ˌɪnvəˈkeɪʃn] *n* -1. JUR & POL invocation *f*. -2. RELIG invocation *f*; ~s to the gods l'invocation des dieux.

invoice [ˈɪnvɔɪs] ◇ *n* COMM facture *f*; to make out an ~ établir une facture; ~s should be settled within 30 days les factures doivent être réglées sous 30 jours.
◇ *vt* [goods] facturer; to ~ sb for sthg facturer qqch à qqn.

invoice clerk *n* facturier *m*, -ère *f*.

invoke [ɪnˈvəʊk] *vt* -1. [cite] invoquer; they ~d the non-intervention treaty ils ont invoqué le traité de non-intervention; she ~d the principle of free speech elle a invoqué le principe de la liberté d'expression. -2. [call upon] en appeler à, faire appel à; to ~ sb's help requérir l'aide de qqn; they ~d the might of the gods ils invoquèrent la puissance des dieux. -3. [conjure up] invoquer; to ~ evil spirits invoquer les mauvais esprits.

involuntarily [ɪnˈvɒləntrəlɪ] *adv* involontairement; she smiled ~ elle ne put réprimer un sourire OR s'empêcher de sourire.

involuntary [ɪnˈvɒləntrɪ] *adj* involontaire.

involute(d) [ˈɪnvəluːt(ɪd)] *adj* -1. [intricate] compliqué. -2. BOT involuté.

involution [ˌɪnvəˈluːʃn] *n* -1. [intricacy] complexité *f*. -2. BOT, MATH, MED & ZOOL involution *f*.

involve [ɪnˈvɒlv] *vt* -1. [entail] impliquer, comporter; it ~s a lot of work cela implique OR nécessite OR veut dire beaucoup de travail; what does the job ~? en quoi consiste le travail?; a job which ~s meeting people un travail où l'on est amené à rencontrer beaucoup de gens; it won't ~ you in much expense cela ne t'entraînera pas dans de grosses dépenses; there's a lot of work ~d in launching a new product le lancement d'un nouveau produit implique beaucoup de travail. -2. [concern, affect] concerner, toucher; there are too many accidents involving children il y a trop d'accidents dont les enfants sont les victimes. -3. [bring in, implicate] impliquer; it was a huge operation involving thousands of helpers c'était une opération gigantesque qui a nécessité l'aide de milliers de gens; several vehicles were ~d in the accident plusieurs véhicules étaient impliqués dans cet accident; it's not necessary to ~ anyone else in this matter il n'est pas nécessaire d'impliquer quelqu'un d'autre dans OR d'associer quelqu'un d'autre à cette affaire; we try to ~ the parents in the running of the school nous essayons de faire participer les parents à la vie de l'école; I'm not going to ~ myself in their private affairs je ne vais pas me mêler de leur vie privée OR de leurs affaires. -4. [absorb, engage] absorber; a book which really ~s the reader un livre dont le lecteur n'arrive pas à se détacher OR qui passionne le lecteur.

involved [ɪnˈvɒlvd] *adj* -1. [complicated] compliqué, complexe; I can't explain, it's all terribly ~ je ne peux pas expliquer, c'est terriblement compliqué. -2. [implicated] impliqué; were the CIA ~? est-ce que la CIA était impliquée?; I don't want to get ~ je ne veux pas être impliqué, je ne veux rien avoir à faire avec cela; they became ~ in a long war ils se sont trouvés entraînés dans une longue guerre; the amount of work ~ is enormous la quantité de travail à fournir est énorme; there are important principles ~ les principes en cause OR en jeu sont importants; he had no idea of the problems ~ il n'avait aucune idée des problèmes en jeu OR en cause; over 100 companies are ~ in the scheme plus de 100 sociétés sont associées à OR parties prenantes dans ce projet; I think he's ~ in advertising je crois qu'il est dans la publicité; to be ~ in politics prendre part à la vie politique. -3. [absorbed] absorbé; she's always too deeply ~ in her work to notice elle est bien trop absorbée par son travail pour remarquer quoi que ce soit. -4. [emotionally]: to be ~ with sb avoir une liaison avec qqn; she's heavily ~ with him elle est très éprise de lui, elle est très accrochée; he doesn't want to get ~ il ne veut pas s'engager.

involvement [ɪnˈvɒlvmənt] *n* -1. [participation] participation *f*; my ~ in the project is strictly limited ma participation au projet est strictement limitée; they were against American ~ in the war ils étaient opposés à toute participation américaine au conflit. -2. [commitment] investissement *m*, engagement *m*; she's looking for work that requires total ~ elle cherche un emploi qui demanderait un investissement total. -3. [relationship] liaison *f*; their ~ was short-lived leur liaison fut de courte durée; he's frightened of emotional ~ il a peur de s'engager sentimentalement, il redoute tout engagement affectif. -4. [complexity] complexité *f*, complication *f*.

invulnerability [ɪnˌvʌlnərəˈbɪlətɪ] *n* invulnérabilité *f*.

invulnerable [ɪnˈvʌlnərəbl] *adj* invulnérable; she seems ~ to attack elle semble invulnérable à toute attaque OR inattaquable.

inward [ˈɪnwəd] ◇ *adj* -1. [thoughts, satisfaction] intime, secret. -2. [movement] vers l'intérieur.
◇ *adv Am* = **inwards**.

inward-bound *adj* [flight] à l'arrivée; [traffic] en direction de la ville.

inward-looking *adj* [introspective] introverti, refermé sur soi; he's become very ~ lately il s'est beaucoup refermé OR replié sur lui-même ces derniers temps; it tends to be an ~ philosophy c'est une philosophie plutôt introspective.

inwardly [ˈɪnwədlɪ] *adv* [pleased, disgusted] secrètement; she said nothing but was ~ rejoicing elle n'a rien dit mais elle se réjouissait secrètement; he smiled ~ il sourit intérieurement; ~ I was still convinced that I was right en mon for intérieur, j'étais toujours convaincu d'avoir raison; we all groaned ~ at the thought à cette idée nous avons tous réprimé un mouvement d'humeur.

inwards [ˈɪnwədz] *adv* -1. [turn, face] vers l'intérieur; the doors open ~ les portes s'ouvrent vers l'intérieur. -2. [into one's own heart, soul etc]: my thoughts turned ~ je me suis replié sur moi-même; he said we should look ~ to find our true selves il a dit que c'est en nous-mêmes qu'il fallait chercher notre véritable identité.

Io [ˈaɪəʊ] *pr n* Io.

I/O (*written abbr of* input/output) E/S.

IOC (*abbr of* International Olympic Committee) *pr n* CIO *m*.

iodine [*Br* ˈaɪədiːn, *Am* ˈaɪədaɪn] *n* iode *m*; PHARM teinture *f* d'iode.

iodize, -ise [ˈaɪədaɪz] *vt* ioder.

iodoform [aɪˈɒdəfɔːm] *n* iodoforme *m*.

IOM *written abbr of* Isle of Man.

ion [ˈaɪən] *n* ion *m*.

ion accelerator *n* accélérateur *m* d'ions.

ion engine *n* moteur *m* ionique.

Ionian [aɪˈəʊnjən] ◇ *n* -1. [person] Ionien *m*, -enne *f*. -2. LING ionien *m*.
◇ *adj* ionien; ~ mode MUS mode *m* ionien.

Ionian Islands *pl pr n*: the ~ les îles *fpl* Ioniennes; in the ~ aux îles Ioniennes.

Ionian Sea *pr n*: the ~ la mer Ionienne.

ionic [aɪˈɒnɪk] *adj* CHEM & PHYS ionique.

Ionic [aɪˈɒnɪk] *adj* ARCHIT ionique.

ion implantation *n* implantation *f* d'ions.

ionize, -ise [ˈaɪənaɪz] *vt* ioniser.

ionizer [ˈaɪənaɪzəʳ] *n* ioniseur *m*.

ionosphere [aɪˈɒnəˌsfɪəʳ] *n* ionosphère *f*.

iota [aɪˈəʊtə] *n* -1. [Greek letter] iota *m*. -2. [tiny bit] brin *m*, grain *m*, iota *m*; she doesn't have an ~ of sense elle n'a pas un sou OR une once de jugeotte; there's not one ~ of truth in the letter il n'y a pas un mot de vrai dans cette lettre; I don't care one ~ cela m'est complètement égal, je m'en fiche complètement; they haven't changed one ~ ils n'ont absolument pas changé.

IOU (*abbr of* I owe you) *n reconnaissance de dette*.

IOW *written abbr of* Isle of Wight.

Iowa [ˈaɪəʊə] *pr n* Iowa *m*; in ~ dans l'Iowa.

IPA (*abbr of* International Phonetic Alphabet) *n* API *m*.

Iphigenia [ɪˌfɪdʒɪˈnaɪə] *pr n* Iphigénie; '~ in Tauris' *Euripides* 'Iphigénie en Tauride'.

IQ (*abbr of* intelligence quotient) *n* QI *m*.

IRA ◇ *pr n* (*abbr of* Irish Republican Army) IRA *f*.
◇ *n Am* (*abbr of* individual retirement account) *compte d'épargne retraite (à avantages fiscaux)*.

IRA:
L'IRA est une organisation qui lutte pour la réunification de l'Irlande. En 1969, elle s'est scindée en deux factions: la «Provisional IRA», qui a recours à la violence, et la «Official IRA», qui utilise des moyens politiques.

Iran [ɪˈrɑːn] *pr n* Iran *m*; in ~ en Iran.

Irangate [ɪˈrɑːngeɪt] *pr n*: the ~ scandal *scandale politique sous le mandat Reagan: le Président aurait autorisé la vente d'armes à l'Iran contre la mise en liberté d'otages américains, et versé une partie des revenus de ces opérations aux contras du Nicaragua*.

Iranian [ɪˈreɪnjən] ◇ *n* -1. [person] Iranien *m*, -enne *f*. -2. LING iranien *m*.
◇ *adj* iranien.

Iraq [ɪˈrɑːk] *pr n* Iraq *m*, Irak *m*; in ~ en Iraq.

Iraqi [ɪˈrɑːkɪ] ◇ *n* Irakien *m*, -enne *f*, Iraquien *m*, -enne *f*.
◇ *adj* irakien.

irascibility [ɪˌræsəˈbɪlətɪ] *n* irascibilité *f*.

irascible [ɪˈræsəbl] *adj* irascible, coléreux.

irate [aɪˈreɪt] *adj* furieux; she got most ~ about it cela l'a rendue furieuse; an ~ letter une lettre courroucée.

IRBM (*abbr of* intermediate range ballistic missile) *n* IRBM *m*.

ire [ˈaɪəʳ] *n lit* colère *f*, courroux *m lit*.

Ireland [ˈaɪələnd] *pr n* Irlande *f*; in ~ en Irlande; the Republic of ~ la République d'Irlande.

iridescence [ˌɪrɪˈdesəns] *n* irisation *f*.

iridescent [ˌɪrɪˈdesənt] *adj* irisé, iridescent *lit.*
iridium [ɪˈrɪdɪəm] *n* iridium *m.*
iridology [ˌɪrɪˈdɒlədʒɪ] *n* iridologie *f*, iridodiagnostic *m.*
iris [ˈaɪərɪs] (*pl sense 1* irises OR irides [-rɪdiːz], *pl sense 2* irises) *n* -**1.** ANAT iris *m.* -**2.** BOT iris *m.*
Iris [ˈaɪərɪs] *pr n* MYTH Iris.
Irish [ˈaɪrɪʃ] ◇ *npl*: the ~ les Irlandais.
◇ *n* LING irlandais *m.*
◇ *adj* irlandais; the ~ Free State l'État *m* libre d'Irlande.

THE IRISH FREE STATE:
En 1922, la division administrative de l'Irlande donna naissance, en même temps qu'à l'Irlande du Nord, à cet État autonome mais néanmoins membre du Commonwealth qui devint la République d'Irlande en 1949.

Irish coffee *n* irish-coffee *m.*
Irishism [ˈaɪrɪʃɪzm] *n* [idiom] locution *f* irlandaise; [custom] coutume *f* irlandaise.
Irishman [ˈaɪrɪʃmən] (*pl* Irishmen [-mən]) *n* Irlandais *m.*
Irish Sea *pr n*: the ~ la mer d'Irlande.
Irish setter *n* setter *m* irlandais.
Irish stew *n* ≃ ragoût *m* de mouton.
Irish wolfhound *n* lévrier *m* irlandais.
Irishwoman [ˈaɪrɪʃˌwʊmən] (*pl* Irishwomen [-ˌwɪmɪn]) *n* Irlandaise *f.*
irk [ɜːk] *vt* irriter, agacer; it really ~s me that he won't do the washing up cela m'agace vraiment qu'il ne fasse jamais la vaisselle.
irksome [ˈɜːksəm] *adj* irritant, agaçant.
IRN (*abbr of* Independent Radio News) *pr n agence de presse radiophonique.*
IRO (*abbr of* International Refugee Organization) *pr n organisation humanitaire pour les réfugiés.*
iron [ˈaɪən] ◇ *adj* -**1.** [made of, containing iron] de fer, en fer; an ~ grating une grille en fer; spinach has a high ~ content les épinards contiennent beaucoup de fer; ~ deficiency MED carence *f* en fer. -**2.** *fig* [strong] de fer, d'acier; an ~ will une volonté de fer; ~ discipline une discipline de fer ☐ the Iron Lady *Br* POL la Dame de Fer; the ~ hand OR fist in a velvet glove une main de fer dans un gant de velours.
◇ *vt* [laundry] repasser.
◇ *vi* [laundry] se repasser.
◇ *n* -**1.** [mineral] fer *m*; made of ~ de OR en fer; she has a will of ~ elle a une volonté de fer ☐ the ~ and steel industry la sidérurgie; (as) hard as ~ dur comme OR aussi dur que le fer. -**2.** [for laundry] fer *m* (à repasser); steam ~ fer à vapeur ‖ [action]: your shirt needs an ~ ta chemise a besoin d'un coup de fer OR d'être repassée. -**3.** [tool, appliance] fer *m*; branding ~ fer à marquer; to have many ~s in the fire avoir plusieurs fers au feu, jouer sur plusieurs tableaux. -**4.** [golf club] fer *m*; try a (number) five ~ essayez un (fer) cinq.
◆ **irons** *npl* [chains] fers *mpl*; clap them in ~s! mettez-les aux fers!
◆ **iron out** *vt sep* -**1.** [crease] repasser. -**2.** *fig* [problem, difficulty] aplanir; they've ~ed out their differences ils ont fait disparaître les différences qui existaient entre eux.
Iron Age *n*: the ~ l'âge *m* du fer; an ~ tool un outil de l'âge du fer.
ironbound [ˈaɪənbaʊnd] *adj* -**1.** [cask] cerclé de fer. -**2.** [rule, tradition] sévère, inflexible.
ironclad [ˈaɪənklæd] ◇ *adj* -**1.** [ship] cuirassé. -**2.** [argument] inattaquable. -**3.** [rule] inflexible.
◇ *n* cuirassé *m.*
Iron Curtain ◇ *n*: the ~ le rideau *m* de fer.
◇ *adj*: the ~ countries les pays *mpl* de l'Est.
iron foundry *n* fonderie *f (de fonte).*
iron-grey *adj* gris acier.
ironic(al) [aɪˈrɒnɪk(l)] *adj* ironique.
ironically [aɪˈrɒnɪklɪ] *adv* -**1.** [smile, laugh] ironiquement. -**2.** [paradoxically]: ~ enough, he was the only one to remember paradoxalement, il était le seul à s'en souvenir.
ironing [ˈaɪənɪŋ] *n* repassage *m*; she does the ~ on Sundays elle fait son repassage OR elle repasse le dimanche.
ironing board *n* planche *f* OR table *f* à repasser.
ironize, -ise [ˈaɪrənaɪz] *vi* ironiser.
iron lung *n* MED poumon *m* d'acier.
ironmonger [ˈaɪənˌmʌŋgəʳ] *n Br* quincailler *m*; available at the ~'s disponible en quincaillerie.
ironmongery [ˈaɪənˌmʌŋgərɪ] *n Br* quincaillerie *f.*
iron ore *n* minerai *m* de fer.
iron oxide *n* oxyde *m* de fer.
iron pyrites *n (U)* pyrite *f* (de fer).
ironstone [ˈaɪənstəʊn] *n* minerai *m* de fer.
iron tablet *n* MED comprimé *m* de fer.
ironwork [ˈaɪənwɜːk] *n* ferronnerie *f.*
ironworker [ˈaɪənwɜːkəʳ] *n* [in plant] (ouvrier *m*, -ère *f*) métallurgiste *mf*; [in wrought iron] ferronnier *m*, -ère *f.*
ironworks [ˈaɪənwɜːks] *n* usine *f* sidérurgique.
irony [ˈaɪrənɪ] (*pl* ironies) *n* [gen & LITERAT] ironie *f*; the ~ is that it might be true ce qui est ironique OR ce qu'il y a d'ironique, c'est que cela pourrait être vrai.
Iroquois [ˈɪrəkwɔɪ] ◇ *n* -**1.** [person] Iroquois *m*, -e *f*; the ~ les Iroquois. -**2.** LING iroquois *m.*
◇ *adj* iroquois.
irradiate [ɪˈreɪdɪeɪt] *vt* -**1.** MED & PHYS [expose to radiation] irradier; [food] irradier. -**2.** [light up] illuminer, éclairer.
irradiation [ɪˌreɪdɪˈeɪʃn] *n* -**1.** MED & PHYS [exposure to radiation] irradiation *f*; [X-ray therapy] radiothérapie *f*; [of food] irradiation *f*. -**2.** OPTICS irradiation *f.*
irrational [ɪˈræʃənl] *adj* -**1.** [person, behaviour, feeling] irrationnel; [fear] irraisonné; [creature, being] incapable de raisonner; don't be so ~! sois raisonnable! -**2.** MATH irrationnel.
irrationality [ɪˌræʃəˈnælətɪ] *n* irrationalité *f.*
irrationally [ɪˈræʃnəlɪ] *adv* irrationnellement.
irrational number *n* nombre *m* irrationnel.
irreconcilable [ɪˈrekənsaɪləbl] *adj* -**1.** [aims, views, beliefs] inconciliable, incompatible; his beliefs are ~ with his work ses convictions sont incompatibles avec son travail. -**2.** [conflict, disagreement] insoluble; to be ~ enemies être ennemis jurés.
irrecoverable [ˌɪrɪˈkʌvərəbl] *adj* -**1.** [thing lost] irrécupérable; [debt] irrécouvrable. -**2.** [loss, damage, wrong] irréparable.
irredeemable [ˌɪrɪˈdiːməbl] *adj* -**1.** [share, bond] non remboursable; [paper money] non convertible. -**2.** [person] incorrigible, impénitent. -**3.** [loss, damage, wrong] irréparable.
irredeemably [ˌɪrɪˈdiːməblɪ] *adv* irrémédiablement; to be ~ wicked être foncièrement méchant.
irreducible [ˌɪrɪˈdjuːsəbl] *adj* irréductible.
irrefutable [ˌɪrɪˈfjuːtəbl] *adj* [argument, proof] irréfutable; an ~ fact un fait certain OR indéniable.
irregular [ɪˈregjʊləʳ] ◇ *adj* -**1.** [object, shape etc] irrégulier; [surface] inégal; an ~ polygon un polygone irrégulier. -**2.** [intermittent, spasmodic] irrégulier; her visits became increasingly ~ ses visites se firent de plus en plus irrégulières; she works ~ hours elle a des horaires de travail irréguliers; ~ breathing respiration irrégulière OR saccadée. -**3.** *fml* [unorthodox] irrégulier; ~ conduct conduite irrégulière; your request is highly ~ votre demande n'est absolument pas régulière. -**4.** LING irrégulier.
◇ *n* -**1.** MIL irrégulier *m*. -**2.** *Am* COMM article *m* de second choix.
irregularity [ɪˌregjʊˈlærətɪ] (*pl* irregularities) *n* [of surface, work, breathing] irrégularité *f.*
◆ **irregularities** *npl* JUR irrégularités *fpl*; there were some irregularities in the paperwork il y avait quelques irrégularités dans les écritures.
irregularly [ɪˈregjʊləlɪ] *adv* -**1.** [spasmodically] irrégulièrement. -**2.** [unevenly] inégalement; ~ shaped triangles des triangles aux formes irrégulières.
irrelevance [ɪˈreləvəns] *n* -**1.** [of fact, comment] manque *m* de rapport, non-pertinence *f*; the ~ of your remarks on the subject is all too obvious il est évident que vos remarques n'ont pas de rapport avec le sujet. -**2.** [pointless fact or matter] inutilité *f*; don't waste your time on ~s ne perdez pas votre temps avec des choses sans importance; the committee has become an ~ le comité n'a plus de raison d'être.
irrelevancy [ɪˈreləvənsɪ] (*pl* irrelevancies) = **irrelevance.**
irrelevant [ɪˈreləvənt] *adj* sans rapport, hors de propos; your question is totally ~ to the subject in hand votre question n'a aucun rapport OR n'a rien à voir avec le sujet qui nous intéresse; ~ information information non pertinente; our personal feelings on the matter are ~ nos sentiments personnels n'ont rien à voir ici; age is ~ l'âge est sans importance OR n'est pas un critère.
irreligious [ˌɪrɪˈlɪdʒəs] *adj* irréligieux.
irremediable [ˌɪrɪˈmiːdjəbl] *adj* irrémédiable; ~ damage dégâts *mpl* irrémédiables.
irremediably [ˌɪrɪˈmiːdjəblɪ] *adv* irrémédiablement.
irreparable [ɪˈrepərəbl] *adj* irréparable; he's done ~ harm to his career il a compromis sa carrière de façon irréparable.
irreparably [ɪˈrepərəblɪ] *adv* irréparablement.
irreplaceable [ˌɪrɪˈpleɪsəbl] *adj* irremplaçable.
irrepressible [ˌɪrɪˈpresəbl] *adj* -**1.** [need, desire] irrépressible; [good humour] à toute épreuve. -**2.** [person] jovial, plein d'entrain.
irreproachable [ˌɪrɪˈprəʊtʃəbl] *adj* irréprochable; his behaviour has always been ~ sa conduite a toujours été irréprochable.
irresistible [ˌɪrɪˈzɪstəbl] *adj* irrésistible; she's got an ~ smile elle a un sourire irrésistible; the ~ force of their argument la force irrésistible de leur argument.
irresistibly [ˌɪrɪˈzɪstəblɪ] *adv* irrésistiblement.
irresolute [ɪˈrezəluːt] *adj* irrésolu, indécis.
irrespective [ˌɪrɪˈspektɪv]
◆ **irrespective of** *prep phr* sans tenir compte de; ~ of race or religion sans discrimination de race ou de religion; ~ of what has been said before indépendamment de ce qui a été dit auparavant.
irresponsibility [ˈɪrɪˌspɒnsəˈbɪlətɪ] *n* irresponsabilité *f.*
irresponsible [ˌɪrɪˈspɒnsəbl] *adj* [person] irresponsable; [act] irréfléchi; you're so ~! tu n'as aucun sens des responsabilités!
irresponsibly [ˌɪrɪˈspɒnsəblɪ] *adv* -**1.** [act, behave] de manière irresponsable. -**2.** JUR irresponsablement.
irretrievable [ˌɪrɪˈtriːvəbl] *adj* [object] introuvable; [loss, harm] irréparable; the damage is ~ les dégâts sont irréparables.
irretrievably [ˌɪrɪˈtriːvəblɪ] *adv* irréparablement, irrémédiablement; ~ lost perdu pour toujours OR à tout jamais.
irreverence [ɪˈrevərəns] *n* irrévérence *f.*
irreverent [ɪˈrevərənt] *adj* irrévérencieux; ~ remarks remarques irrévérencieuses OR insolentes; an ~ sense of humour un sens de l'humour insolent OR impertinent.
irreverently [ɪˈrevərəntlɪ] *adv* irrévérencieusement.
irreversible [ˌɪrɪˈvɜːsəbl] *adj* irréversible.
irreversibly [ˌɪrɪˈvɜːsəblɪ] *adv* irréversiblement.
irrevocable [ɪˈrevəkəbl] *adj* irrévocable.
irrevocably [ɪˈrevəkəblɪ] *adv* irrévocablement.
irrigable [ˈɪrɪgəbl] *adj* irrigable.
irrigate [ˈɪrɪgeɪt] *vt* [gen & MED] irriguer.
irrigation [ˌɪrɪˈgeɪʃn] *n* [gen & MED] irrigation *f*; ~ canal canal *m* d'irrigation.
irritability [ˌɪrɪtəˈbɪlətɪ] *n* irritabilité *f.*
irritable [ˈɪrɪtəbl] *adj* [gen & MED] irritable.
irritably [ˈɪrɪtəblɪ] *adv* avec irritation.
irritant [ˈɪrɪtənt] ◇ *adj* irritant.
◇ *n* irritant *m.*

irritate [ˈɪrɪteɪt] *vt* **-1.** [annoy] irriter, contrarier, énerver. **-2.** MED irriter.

irritated [ˈɪrɪteɪtɪd] *adj* **-1.** [annoyed] irrité, agacé; don't get ~! ne t'énerve pas! **-2.** MED [eyes, skin] irrité.

irritating [ˈɪrɪteɪtɪŋ] *adj* **-1.** [annoying] irritant, contrariant, énervant. **-2.** MED irritant, irritatif.

irritatingly [ˈɪrɪteɪtɪŋlɪ] *adv* de façon agaçante OR irritante; he's ~ slow il est d'une lenteur irritante.

irritation [ɪrɪˈteɪʃn] *n* **-1.** [annoyance] irritation *f*, agacement *m*; she tried to hide her ~ elle tenta de cacher son agacement; it's just one of life's little ~s ce n'est qu'une de ces petites choses énervantes de la vie. **-2.** MED irritation *f*.

irruption [ɪˈrʌpʃn] *n* irruption *f*.

IRS (*abbr of* Internal Revenue Service) *pr n*: the ~ *le fisc américain*.

is [ɪz] → **be**.

Isaac [ˈaɪzək] *pr n* Isaac.

Isaiah [aɪˈzaɪə] *pr n* Isaïe.

isallobar [aɪˈsæləbɑːʳ] *n* isallobare *f*.

ISBN (*abbr of* International Standard Book Number) *n* ISBN *m*.

ISDN (*abbr of* integrated services data network) *n* RNIS *m*.

Isfahan [ˌɪsfəˈhɑːn] *pr n* Ispahan.

isinglass [ˈaɪzɪŋglɑːs] *n* **-1.** [glue] ichtyocolle *f*. **-2.** [mica] mica *m*.

Isis [ˈaɪsɪs] *pr n* Isis.

Islam [ˈɪzlɑːm] *n* Islam *m*.

Islamabad [ɪzˈlɑːməbæd] *pr n* Islamabad.

Islamic [ɪzˈlæmɪk] *adj* islamique.

Islamize, -ise [ˈɪzləmaɪz] *vt* islamiser.

island [ˈaɪlənd] ◇ *n* **-1.** GEOG île *f*; the Channel Islands les îles Anglo-Normandes; they are an ~ race c'est une race insulaire; an ~ of peace *fig* une oasis de tranquillité. **-2.** TRANSP: (traffic) ~ [for pedestrians] refuge *m*; [roundabout] rond-point *m*; [centre of roundabout] terre-plein *m* central.
◇ *vt* [isolate] isoler.

islander [ˈaɪləndəʳ] *n* insulaire *mf*; the Channel Islanders les habitants *mpl* des îles Anglo-Normandes.
◆ **Islander** *n NZ* habitant *m*, -e *f* des îles du Pacifique.

isle [aɪl] *n* île *f*; the British Isles les îles Britanniques.

Isle of Man *pr n*: the ~ l'île *f* de Man; in the ~, on the ~ à l'île de Man.

Isle of Wight [-waɪt] *pr n*: the ~ l'île *f* de Wight; in OR on the ~ à l'île de Wight.

islet [ˈaɪlɪt] *n* îlot *m*.

ism *inf* [ˈɪzm] *n pej* doctrine *f*, idéologie *f*.

isn't [ˈɪznt] = **is not**.

isobar [ˈaɪsəbɑːʳ] *n* isobare *f*.

isochronal [aɪˈsɒkrənl], **isochronous** [aɪˈsɒkrənəs] *adj* isochrone, isochronique.

isogloss [ˈaɪsəʊglɒs] *n* isoglosse *f*.

isolate [ˈaɪsəleɪt] *vt* [gen & MED] isoler.

isolated [ˈaɪsəleɪtɪd] *adj* **-1.** [alone, remote] isolé. **-2.** [single] unique, isolé; an ~ incident un incident isolé.

isolation [aɪsəˈleɪʃn] *n* isolement *m*; a sense of complete ~ un sentiment d'isolement total; in ~ en soi, isolément; you cannot consider the problem in ~ on ne peut pas considérer le problème isolément.

isolation hospital *n* hôpital *m* d'isolement.

isolationism [ˌaɪsəˈleɪʃənɪzm] *n* isolationnisme *m*.

isolationist [ˌaɪsəˈleɪʃənɪst] *adj* isolationniste.

isolation ward *n* service *m* des contagieux.

isomer [ˈaɪsəməʳ] *n* isomère *m*.

isomerism [aɪˈsɒmərɪzm] *n* isomérie *f*.

isometric [ˌaɪsəʊˈmetrɪk] *adj* isométrique; ~ exercises exercices *mpl* isométriques.

isometrics [ˌaɪsəʊˈmetrɪks] *n* (*U*) exercices *mpl* isométriques.

isomorph [ˈaɪsəmɔːf] *n* isomorphe *m*.

isomorphism [ˌaɪsəˈmɔːfɪzm] *n* isomorphisme *m*.

isosceles [aɪˈsɒsɪliːz] *adj* isocèle; an ~ triangle un triangle isocèle.

isotherm [ˈaɪsəθɜːm] *n* isotherme *f*.

isotope [ˈaɪsətəʊp] *n* isotope *m*.

I-spy *n jeu d'enfant où l'un des joueurs donne la première lettre d'un objet qu'il voit et les autres doivent deviner de quoi il s'agit*.

Israel [ˈɪzreɪəl] *pr n* Israël; in ~ en Israël.

Israeli [ɪzˈreɪlɪ] (*pl inv* OR **Israelis**) ◇ *n* Israélien *m*, -enne *f*.
◇ *adj* israélien.

Israelite [ˈɪzrəlaɪt] *n* Israélite *mf*.

issue [ˈɪʃuː] ◇ *n* **-1.** [matter, topic] question *f*, problème *m*; where do you stand on the abortion ~? quel est votre point de vue sur (la question de) l'avortement?; the ~ was raised at the meeting le problème a été soulevé à la réunion; your personal feelings are not the ~ vos sentiments personnels n'ont rien à voir là-dedans; that's not the ~ il ne s'agit pas de ça; it's become an international ~ le problème a pris une dimension internationale; the important ~s of the day les grands problèmes du moment; at ~ en question; the point at ~ is not the coming election le problème n'est pas l'élection à venir; her competence is not at ~ sa compétence n'est pas en cause; to cloud OR confuse the ~ brouiller les cartes; to avoid OR duck OR evade the ~ esquiver la question; to force the ~ forcer la décision. **-2.** [cause of disagreement] différend *m*; the subject has now become a real ~ between us ce sujet est maintenant source de désaccord entre nous; they are at ~ with the Japanese over import quotas ils sont en désaccord avec les Japonais au sujet des quotas d'importations; to make an ~ of sthg monter qqch en épingle; don't make such an ~ of it! inutile d'en faire toute une histoire!; to take ~ with sb/sthg s'inscrire en faux contre qqn/qqch; I take ~ with him on only one point je suis en désaccord avec lui sur un point seulement. **-3.** [edition - of newspaper, magazine etc] numéro *m*; the latest ~ of the magazine le dernier numéro du magazine; back ~ vieux OR ancien numéro. **-4.** [distribution - of supplies] distribution *f*; [- of tickets, official document] délivrance *f*; [- of shares, money, stamps] émission *f*; write your passport number and date of ~ écrivez le numéro et la date de délivrance de votre passeport ❑ standard ~ modèle *m* standard; army ~ modèle *m* de l'armée. **-5.** *fml* [result, outcome] issue *f*, résultat *m*; I hope your request has a favourable ~ j'espère que votre demande connaîtra une issue OR recevra une réponse favorable. **-6.** *arch* OR JUR [progeny] descendance *f*, progéniture *f lit*; he died without ~ il est mort sans héritiers.
◇ *vt* **-1.** [book, newspaper] publier, sortir; [record] sortir; the magazine is ~d on Wednesdays le magazine sort OR paraît le mercredi || [official document] délivrer; JUR [warrant, writ] lancer; where was the passport ~d? où le passeport a-t-il été délivré? || [statement, proclamation] publier; the government has ~d a denial le gouvernement a publié un démenti || [shares, money, stamps] émettre; the Bank of Scotland ~s its own notes la Bank of Scotland émet ses propres billets. **-2.** [distribute - supplies, tickets etc] distribuer; the magazine is ~d free to every household le magazine est distribué gratuitement à OR dans tous les foyers; we were all ~d with rations on nous a distribué à tous des rations.
◇ *vi fml* **-1.** [come or go out] sortir; delicious smells ~d from the kitchen des odeurs délicieuses provenaient de la cuisine. **-2.** [result, originate]: to ~ from provenir de; all our difficulties ~ from that first mistake c'est de cette première erreur que proviennent tous nos ennuis.
◆ **issue forth** *vi insep lit* jaillir.

issuing [ˈɪʃuɪŋ] *adj* FIN [company] émetteur; ~ bank *Br* banque *f* d'émission OR émettrice.

Istanbul [ˌɪstænˈbʊl] *pr n* Istanbul.

isthmus [ˈɪsməs] (*pl* isthmuses OR isthmi [-maɪ]) *n* isthme *m*.

it [ɪt] ◇ *pron* **-1.** [referring to specific thing, animal etc - as subject] il, elle; [- as direct object] le, la, l' (*before vowel* OR *mute 'h'*); [- as indirect object] lui; is it a boy or a girl? c'est un garçon ou une fille?; the building's dangerous, it should be pulled down le bâtiment est dangereux, il devrait être démoli; I'd lend you my typewriter but it's broken je te prêterais bien ma machine à écrire mais elle est cassée; I took my hat off and now I can't find it j'ai enlevé mon chapeau et je ne le trouve plus; take this plate and put it on the table prends cette assiette et mets-la sur la table; give it a tap with a hammer donnez un coup de marteau dessus. **-2.** [after preposition]: he told me all about it il m'a tout raconté; there was nothing inside it il n'y avait rien dedans OR à l'intérieur; he walked on it il a marché dessus; I went over to it je m'en suis approché; I left the bag under it j'ai laissé le sac dessous. **-3.** [impersonal uses]: it's me! c'est moi!; it's raining/snowing il pleut/neige; it's cold/dark today il fait froid/sombre aujourd'hui; it's Friday today nous sommes OR c'est vendredi aujourd'hui; it seemed like a good idea cela OR ça semblait être une bonne idée; it's 500 miles from here to Vancouver Vancouver est à 800 kilomètres d'ici; I like it here je me plais beaucoup ici; I love it when we go on a picnic j'adore quand on va pique-niquer; I couldn't bear it if she left je ne supporterais pas qu'elle parte; she found it easy to make new friends ça lui a été facile de se faire de nouveaux amis; it's not easy for me to say this, but... je n'aime pas dire ce genre de chose, mais...; it'll take us hours to get there on va mettre des heures pour y arriver; it'll cost (us) a fortune to have it repaired ça va (nous) coûter une fortune pour le faire réparer; it was agreed that we should move out il a été convenu que nous déménagerions; it's vital to plan ahead il est indispensable de prévoir les choses à l'avance; it might look rude if I don't go si je n'y vais pas cela pourrait être considéré comme une impolitesse; it seems OR appears OR would appear that there's been some trouble il semble qu'il y ait eu des problèmes; it's the Johnny Carson Show! voici le Johnny Carson Show!; it's a goal! but!; it was tipping it down *inf* il pleuvait des cordes; it's his constant complaining I can't stand ce que je ne supporte pas c'est sa façon de se plaindre constamment.
◇ *n inf* **-1.** [in games]: you're it! c'est toi le chat!, c'est toi qui y es! **-2.** [most important person]: he thinks he's it il s'y croit. **-3.** [with drinks]: gin and it martini-gin *m*.

IT *n abbr of* information technology.

ITA (*abbr of* Initial Teaching Alphabet) *n*: the ~ *alphabet en partie phonétique parfois utilisé pour l'enseignement de la lecture*.

Italian [ɪˈtæljən] ◇ *n* **-1.** [person] Italien *m*, -enne *f*. **-2.** LING italien *m*.
◇ *adj* italien; the ~ embassy l'ambassade *f* d'Italie.

Italianate [ɪˈtæljəneɪt] *adj* italianisant.

Italianize, -ise [ɪˈtæljənaɪz] *vt* italianiser.

italic [ɪˈtælɪk] ◇ *adj* italique; in ~ script en italique.
◇ *n* italique *m*; in ~s en italique.
◆ **Italic** ◇ *adj* [of ancient Italy] italique.
◇ *n* LING italique *m*.

italicize, -ise [ɪˈtælɪsaɪz] *vt* mettre en italique; the ~d words les mots en italique.

Italo- [ɪˈtæləʊ] *in cpds* italo-; ~American italo-américain.

Italy [ˈɪtəlɪ] *pr n* Italie *f*; in ~ en Italie.

itch [ɪtʃ] ◇ *n* **-1.** *literal* démangeaison *f*; I've got an ~ between my shoulder blades ça me démange OR me gratte entre les omoplates. **-2.** *inf fig* [desire] envie *f*; to have the ~ to do sthg brûler OR mourir d'envie de faire qqch.
◇ *vi* **-1.** [physically] avoir des démangeaisons; I'm ~ing all over j'ai des démangeaisons

partout, je suis couvert de démangeaisons || [insect bite, part of body] : does it ~ ? est-ce que cela te démange ?; my back ~es mon dos me démange OR me gratte; that sweater ~es ce pull me gratte. -2. *inf fig* [desire] : to ~ to do sthg: I was ~ing to tell her ça me démangeait de lui dire; we're ~ing to go nous ne tenons plus en place.

itching ['ɪtʃɪŋ] *n* démangeaison *f*.

itching powder *n* poil *m* à gratter.

itchy ['ɪtʃɪ] (*compar* itchier, *superl* itchiest) *adj* qui gratte, qui démange; an ~ pullover un pull qui gratte; I've got an ~ leg ma jambe me démange ❑ to have ~ feet *inf* avoir la bougeotte.

it'd ['ɪtəd] -1. = **it would**. -2. = **it had**.

item ['aɪtəm] *n* -1. [object] article *m*; the ~s in the shop window les articles en vitrine; the only ~ he bought was a lighter la seule chose qu'il ait achetée, c'est un briquet; an ~ of clothing un vêtement. -2. [point, issue] point *m*, question *f*; there are two important ~s on the agenda il y a deux points importants à l'ordre du jour; I've several ~s of business to attend to j'ai plusieurs affaires à régler. -3. [in newspaper] article *m*; an ~ in the Times un article dans le «Times» || [on T.V. or radio] point *m* OR sujet *m* d'actualité; and here are today's main news ~s et voici les principaux points de l'actualité. -4. COMPUT article *m*. -5. LING item *m*; lexical ~ item lexical. -6. [in book-keeping] écriture *f*.

itemize, -ise ['aɪtəmaɪz] *vt* détailler; an ~d list une liste détaillée.

iterative ['ɪtərətɪv] *adj* [gen, LING & MATH] itératif.

Ithaca ['ɪθəkə] *pr n* Ithaque.

itinerant [ɪ'tɪnərənt] ◇ *adj* itinérant; [actors] ambulant, itinérant; ~ preacher prédicateur *m* itinérant; ~ teacher *Am* professeur *m* remplaçant.
◇ *n* nomade *mf*.

itinerary [aɪ'tɪnərərɪ] (*pl* itineraries) *n* itinéraire *m*.

it'll [ɪtl] = **it will**.

ITN (*abbr of* Independent Television News) *pr n service d'actualités télévisées pour les chaînes relevant de l'IBA*.

its [ɪts] *det* son *m*, sa *f*, ses *mfpl*; the committee has ~ first meeting on Friday le comité se réunit pour la première fois vendredi; the dog wagged ~ tail le chien a remué la queue; the jug's lost ~ handle le pichet n'a plus de poignée.

it's [ɪts] -1. = **it is**. -2. = **it has**.

itself [ɪt'self] *pron* -1. [reflexive use] se; the cat was licking ~ clean le chat faisait sa toilette. -2. [emphatic use] lui-même *m*, elle-même *f*; the town ~ is quite small la ville elle-même est assez petite; she's kindness ~ c'est la gentillesse même. -3. [after preposition] : it switches off by ~ ça s'éteint tout seul; it's not dangerous in ~ ce n'est pas dangereux en soi; working with her was in ~ fascinating le seul fait de travailler avec elle était fascinant.

itsy-bitsy *inf* [,ɪtsɪ'bɪtsɪ], **itty-bitty** *inf* [,ɪtɪ'bɪtɪ] *adj* tout petit, minuscule.

ITV (*abbr of* Independent Television) *pr n sigle désignant les programmes diffusés par les chaînes relevant de l'IBA*.

IUCD (*abbr of* intrauterine contraceptive device) *n* stérilet *m*.

IUD (*abbr of* intrauterine device) *n* stérilet *m*.

Ivan ['aɪvn] *pr n*: ~ the Great Ivan le Grand; ~ the Terrible Ivan le Terrible.

Ivanhoe ['aɪvnhəʊ] *pr n* Ivanhoé.

I've [aɪv] = **I have**.

IVF (*abbr of* in vitro fertilization) *n* FIV *f*.

ivied ['aɪvɪd] *adj* couvert de lierre.

Ivorian [aɪ'vɔːrɪən] ◇ *n* Ivoirien *m*, -enne *f*.
◇ *adj* ivoirien.

ivory ['aɪvərɪ] (*pl* ivories) ◇ *adj* -1. [made of ivory] d'ivoire, en ivoire; an ~ carving une sculpture d'ivoire. -2. [ivory-coloured] (couleur) ivoire *(inv)*.
◇ *n* -1. [substance] ivoire *m*. -2. [object] ivoire *m*.
◆ **ivories** *inf npl* [piano keys] touches *fpl*; to tickle the ivories *hum* toucher du piano.

Ivory Coast *pr n*: the ~ la Côte-d'Ivoire; in the ~ en Côte-d'Ivoire.

ivory tower *n* tour *f* d'ivoire.

ivy ['aɪvɪ] (*pl* ivies) *n* lierre *m*.

Ivy League *n groupe des huit universités les plus prestigieuses du nord-est des États-Unis*.
◆ **Ivy-League** *adj*: he had an Ivy-League education il a fait ses études dans une grande université; her boyfriend's very Ivy-League *inf* son petit ami est très BCBG.

IWW (*abbr of* Industrial Workers of the World) *pr n ancien syndicat luttant contre le capitalisme*.

Izmir ['ɪzmɪəʳ] *pr n* Izmir.

J

j (*pl* j's OR js), **J** (*pl* J's OR Js) [dʒeɪ] *n* j *m*, J *m*.

JA *n* (*abbr of* judge advocate).

J/A *written abbr of* joint account.

jab [dʒæb] (*pt* & *pp* jabbed, *cont* jabbing) ◇ *vt* [pierce] piquer; **he jabbed my arm with a needle, he jabbed a needle into my arm** il m'a piqué le bras avec une aiguille, il m'a enfoncé une aiguille dans le bras ‖ [poke] pousser; **you almost jabbed me in the eye with that knife!** tu as failli m'éborgner avec ce couteau! ‖ [brandish] pointer, brandir *(d'une façon menaçante)*; **she kept jabbing her finger at the defendant** elle ne cessait de pointer le doigt vers l'accusé OR de désigner l'accusé du doigt.
◇ *vi* -**1.** [stick] s'enfoncer; **something jabbed into my ribs** j'ai reçu un coup sec dans les côtes. -**2.** [gesture]: **he jabbed at me with his umbrella** il essaya de me donner un coup de parapluie; **she jabbed wildly at the buttons** elle appuyait frénétiquement sur les boutons. -**3.** [in boxing]: **he's jabbing with (his) right and left** il lui envoie un direct du droit et du gauche.
◇ *n* -**1.** [poke] coup *m (donné avec un objet pointu)*; [in boxing] (coup *m*) droit *m* OR direct *m*. -**2.** *inf* MED piqûre *f*; **I've got to get a tetanus ~** je dois me faire vacciner contre le tétanos.

jabber *inf* [ˈdʒæbəʳ] ◇ *vi* [idly] jacasser, caqueter *pej*; [inarticulately] bredouiller, bafouiller; **they ~ (away) for hours on the phone** ils passent des heures à jacasser au téléphone; **they were all ~ing away in different languages** chacun baragouinait dans sa langue.
◇ *vt*: **to ~ (out)** bredouiller, bafouiller; **I managed to ~ a few words of thanks** j'ai réussi à bredouiller OR bafouiller quelques mots de remerciements.
◇ *n* (*U*) brouhaha *m*.

jabbering *inf* [ˈdʒæbərɪŋ] *n* [idle chatter] bavardage *m*, papotage *m*; [in foreign tongue] baragouin *m*.

jacaranda [ˌdʒækəˈrændə] *n* jacaranda *m*.

jack [dʒæk] ◇ *vt* MECH soulever avec un vérin; AUT mettre sur cric.
◇ *n* -**1.** [tool] MECH & MIN vérin *m*; AUT cric *m*. -**2.** [playing card] valet *m*. -**3.** [in bowls] cochonnet *m*. -**4.** ELEC [male] = **jack plug**; [female] = **jack socket**. -**5.** *phr*: **every man ~ (of them)** *inf Br* tous autant qu'ils sont; **I didn't understand ~ shit**▽ *Am* j'ai pigé que dalle.
◆ **Jack** *pr n*: **Jack the Ripper** Jack l'Éventreur; **I'm all right Jack** *inf Br* moi ça va; **hey, Jack!** *Am* [to call stranger] hé, vous là-bas!
◆ **jacks** *n* (*U*) [game] osselets *mpl*.
◆ **jack in** *inf vt sep Br* plaquer; **I've ~ed my job in** j'ai plaqué mon boulot; **oh, ~ it in, will you!** oh, ferme-la, tu veux!
◆ **jack up** *vt sep* -**1.** [car] lever avec un cric. -**2.** *inf* [price, wage] augmenter, monter.

jackal [ˈdʒækəl] *n literal* & *fig* chacal *m*.

jackanapes [ˈdʒækəneɪps] *n arch* OR *lit* [arrogant person] fat *m*, arrogant *m*, -e *f*, faquin *m lit*; [mischievous child] polisson *m*, -onne *f*, galopin *m*.

jackass [ˈdʒækæs] *n* -**1.** [donkey] âne *m*, baudet *m*. -**2.** *inf* [imbecile] imbécile *mf*.

jackboot [ˈdʒækbuːt] *n* botte *f* (de militaire); **life under the ~** *fig* la vie sous la botte de l'ennemi; **~ tactics** des tactiques dictatoriales.

jackbooted [ˈdʒækbuːtɪd] *adj* botté.

jackdaw [ˈdʒækdɔː] *n* choucas *m*.

jacket [ˈdʒækɪt] *n* -**1.** [for men] veste *f*; [for women] veste *f*, jaquette *f*; **leather ~** blouson *m* de cuir. -**2.** [of book] jaquette *f*; *Am* [of record] pochette *f*. -**3.** CULIN: **~ potato, potato (cooked) in its ~** pomme de terre *f* en robe des champs OR en robe de chambre. -**4.** TECH [of boiler] chemise *f*.

Jack Frost *n personnage imaginaire symbolisant l'hiver*.

jackfruit [ˈdʒækfruːt] *n* jaque *m*.

jackhammer [ˈdʒækˌhæməʳ] *n* marteau-piqueur *m*.

jack-in-office *n Br pej* petit chef *m*.

jack-in-the-box *n* diable *m* (à ressort).

jackknife [ˈdʒæknaɪf] (*pl* jackknives [-naɪvz]) ◇ *n* couteau *m* de poche.
◇ *vi*: **the truck ~d** le camion s'est mis en travers de la route.

jack-of-all-trades *n pej* homme *m* à tout faire; **~ and master of none** *prov* propre à tout et bon à rien.

jack-o'-lantern *n* feu follet *m*.

jack plug *n* jack *m* (mâle), fiche *f* jack.

jackpot [ˈdʒækpɒt] *n* gros lot *m*; [in cards] pot *m*; **you hit the ~!** tu as décroché le gros lot!

jack rabbit *n gros lièvre d'Amérique*.

Jack Robinson *inf n Br*: **before you could say ~** avant d'avoir pu dire «ouf».

Jack Russell [-ˈrʌsl] *n* Jack Russell (terrier) *m*.

jack socket *n* jack *m* (femelle), prise *f* jack.

jackstraws [ˈdʒækstrɔːz] *n* jonchets *mpl*.

jack tar *inf n dated* marin *m*, matelot *m*.

Jack-the-Lad *inf n* jeune frimeur *m*.

Jacob [ˈdʒeɪkəb] *pr n* Jacob.

Jacobean [ˌdʒækəˈbɪən] *adj* jacobéen *m*, -enne *f*, de l'époque de Jacques Iᵉʳ (d'Angleterre).

Jacobin [ˈdʒækəbɪn] ◇ *n* Jacobin *m*, -e *f*.
◇ *adj* jacobin.

Jacobite [ˈdʒækəbaɪt] ◇ *adj* jacobite.
◇ *n* Jacobite *mf*.

THE JACOBITES:
Membres du parti légitimiste anglais qui soutint, après la révolution de 1688, d'abord la cause de Jacques II contre Guillaume d'Orange, puis celle des derniers Stuarts contre la maison des Hanovre.

Jacuzzi® [dʒəˈkuːzɪ] (*pl* Jacuzzis) *n* Jacuzzi® *m*, bain *m* à remous.

jade [dʒeɪd] ◇ *n* -**1.** [stone] jade *m*. -**2.** [colour] vert jade *m inv*. -**3.** *arch* [horse] rosse *f*, haridelle *f*. -**4.** *arch* [woman - shrewish] mégère *f*; [- disreputable] friponne *f*.
◇ *adj* -**1.** [made of jade] de OR en jade. -**2.** [colour] vert jade *(inv)*.

jaded [ˈdʒeɪdɪd] *adj* [person] désabusé, blasé, éreinté; [appetite] écœuré, saturé; **I'm feeling a bit ~ today** je ne suis pas très en forme aujourd'hui.

jadeite [ˈdʒeɪdaɪt] *n* jadéite *f*.

jag [dʒæg] (*pt* & *pp* jagged, *cont* jagging) ◇ *vt* déchiqueter; [fabric] taillader.
◇ *n* -**1.** pointe *f*, aspérité *f*; [of saw] dent *f*. -**2.** *Am inf* [party] orgie *f*; **to go on a drinking ~** faire les bars.

JAG *n abbr of* judge advocate general.

jagged [ˈdʒægɪd] *adj* [edge, coastline] déchiqueté; [tear] irrégulier; [rock] râpeux, rugueux; **pieces of ~ metal** des bouts de métal déchiqueté.

jaguar [ˈdʒægjʊəʳ] *n* jaguar *m*.

jai alai [ˌhaɪəˈlaɪ] *n jeu qui ressemble à la pelote basque, pratiqué surtout en Floride*.

jail [dʒeɪl] ◇ *n* prison *f*; **to be in ~** être en prison; **the burglar was sent to ~** le cambrioleur a été incarcéré OR emprisonné; **sentenced to 15 years in ~** condamné à 15 ans de prison.
◇ *vt* emprisonner, mettre en prison, incarcérer; **to be ~ed for life** être condamné à perpétuité OR à vie.

jailbait *inf* [ˈdʒeɪlbeɪt] *n* (*U*) *Am* mineur *m*, -e *f*; **she's ~** c'est un coup à se retrouver en taule *(pour détournement de mineur)*.

jailbird *inf* [ˈdʒeɪlbɜːd] *n* récidiviste *mf*.

jailbreak [ˈdʒeɪlbreɪk] *n* évasion *f*.

jailbreaker [ˈdʒeɪlˌbreɪkəʳ] *n* évadé *m*, -e *f*.

jailer [ˈdʒeɪləʳ] *n* geôlier *m*, -ère *f*.

jailhouse [ˈdʒeɪlhaʊs, *pl* -haʊzɪz] *n Am* prison *f*.

Jain [dʒaɪn] ◇ *n* jaïn *m*, -e *f*.
◇ *adj* jaïn.

Jaipur [ˌdʒaɪˈpʊəʳ] *pr n* Jaipur.

Jakarta [dʒəˈkɑːtə] *pr n* Djakarta, Jakarta.

jakes▽ [dʒeɪks] *npl Br arch* [toilet]: **the ~** les cabinets *mpl*.

jalopy *inf* [dʒəˈlɒpɪ] (*pl* jalopies) *n* tacot *m*, guimbarde *f*.

jam [dʒæm] (*pt* & *pp* jammed, *cont* jamming) ◇ *n* -**1.** [preserve] confiture *f*; **strawberry ~**

confiture de fraises; **he wants ~ on it** *inf Br* et avec ça, on est difficile!; **it's a case of ~ tomorrow** *inf Br* ce sont des promesses en l'air. **-2.** [congestion] encombrement *m*; **there was a ~ of people at the exit** ça se bousculait à la sortie; **traffic ~** embouteillage *m*. **-3.** *inf* [predicament] pétrin *m*; **I'm in a bit of a ~** je suis plutôt dans le pétrin. **-4.** *inf* = **jam session**.
◇ *comp* [tart, pudding, sandwich] à la confiture.
◇ *vt* **-1.** [crowd, cram] entasser, tasser; **we were jammed in like sardines** on était entassés OR serrés comme des sardines; **all my clothes are jammed into one drawer** tous mes vêtements sont entassés dans un seul tiroir; **I was jammed (up) against the wall** j'étais coincé contre le mur|| [push roughly, ram] fourrer; **he jammed the gun into his pocket** il fourra le pistolet dans sa poche; **she jammed her hat on** elle enfonça OR vissa son chapeau sur sa tête. **-2.** [make stick] coincer, bloquer; **she jammed the window shut with a wedge** elle coinça OR bloqua la fenêtre avec une cale. **-3.** [congest] encombrer, bloquer, boucher; **a crowd of late arrivals jammed the entrance** une foule de retardataires bloquait l'entrée; **the streets were jammed with cars** les rues étaient embouteillées. **-4.** RADIO brouiller.
◇ *vi* **-1.** [crowd] se tasser, s'entasser; **thousands of people jammed in for the concert** des milliers de personnes se sont entassées pour assister au concert. **-2.** [become stuck - gen] se coincer, se bloquer; [- gun] s'enrayer; [- brakes] se bloquer. **-3.** *inf* [play in a jam session] faire un bœuf.
◆ **jam on** *inf vt sep*: **to ~ on the brakes** piler.

Jamaica [dʒəˈmeɪkə] *pr n* Jamaïque *f*; **in ~** à la Jamaïque; **~ rum** rhum *m* jamaïquain OR jamaïcain OR de la Jamaïque.

Jamaican [dʒəˈmeɪkn] ◇ *n* Jamaïcain *m*, -e *f*, Jamaïquain *m*, -e *f*.
◇ *adj* jamaïcain, jamaïquain.

jamb(e) [dʒæm] *n* montant *m*.

jambalaya [ˌdʒæmbəˈlaɪə] *n plat cajun à base de fruits de mer et de poulet*.

jamboree [ˌdʒæmbəˈriː] *n* **-1.** [gathering] grande fête *f*. **-2.** [scout rally] jamboree *m*.

James [dʒeɪmz] *pr n* Jacques; **Saint ~** saint Jacques.

jam-full *inf adj* bourré, archiplein.

jamjar [ˈdʒæmdʒɑːʳ] *n* pot *m* à confiture.

jamming [ˈdʒæmɪŋ] *n* **-1.** coincement *m*; [of brakes] blocage *m*. **-2.** RADIO brouillage *m*.

jammy *inf* [ˈdʒæmɪ] (*compar* **jammier**, *superl* **jammiest**) *adj Br* **-1.** [sticky with jam] poisseux; **~ fingers** des doigts poisseux de confiture. **-2.** [lucky] chanceux; **you ~ beggar!** espèce de veinard!

jam-packed = **jam-full**.

jampot [ˈdʒæmpɒt] = **jamjar**.

jam session *inf n* bœuf *m*, jam-session *f*.

Jan. (*written abbr of* **January**) janv.

jangle [ˈdʒæŋgl] ◇ *vi* retentir (avec un bruit métallique OR avec fracas); [more quietly] cliqueter; **his keys ~d in his pocket** ses clés cliquetaient dans sa poche.
◇ *vt* faire retentir; [more quietly] faire cliqueter; **my nerves are all ~d** *fig* j'ai les nerfs en boule OR en pelote.
◇ *n*: **the ~ of bells** le tintamarre des cloches; **the ~ of keys** le cliquetis des clés; **the ~ of loose change** le bruit OR cliquetis des pièces de monnaie.

jangling [ˈdʒæŋglɪŋ] ◇ *adj* [bells] retentissant; [keys] qui tintent; **a ~ noise** un bruit métallique.
◇ *n* vacarme *m*, tintamarre *m*; [quieter] bruit *m*; **a ~ of keys** un bruit de clés.

janitor [ˈdʒænɪtəʳ] *n* [caretaker] *Am* & *Scot* gardien *m*, concierge *m*; [doorkeeper] *dated* portier *m*.

janitress [ˈdʒænɪtrɪs] *n* [caretaker] *Am* & *Scot* concierge *f*, gardienne *f*; [doorkeeper] *dated* portière *f*.

Jansenism [ˈdʒænsənɪzm] *n* jansénisme *m*.

Jansenist [ˈdʒænsənɪst] ◇ *adj* janséniste.
◇ *n* janséniste *mf*.

January [ˈdʒænjʊərɪ] *n* janvier *m*.

Janus [ˈdʒeɪnəs] *pr n* Janus.

Janus-faced *adj* à deux visages, hypocrite.

Jap *inf* [dʒæp] *n offensive* Jap *n*.

JAP *inf* (*abbr of* **Jewish American princess**) *n Am pej riche Juive américaine*.

japan [dʒəˈpæn] ◇ *n* ART laque *f*.
◇ *vt* laquer.

Japan [dʒəˈpæn] *pr n* Japon *m*; **in ~** au Japon.

Japanese [ˌdʒæpəˈniːz] (*pl inv*) ◇ *n* **-1.** [person] Japonais *m*, -e *f*. **-2.** LING japonais *m*.
◇ *adj* japonais; **the ~ embassy** l'ambassade *f* du Japon.

jape *inf* [dʒeɪp] *n dated* farce *f*, blague *f*.

japonica [dʒəˈpɒnɪkə] *n* cognassier *m* du Japon.

jar [dʒɑːʳ] (*pt* & *pp* **jarred**, *cont* **jarring**)
◇ *n* **-1.** [container - glass] bocal *m*; [- for jam] pot *m*; [- earthenware] pot *m*, jarre *f*. **-2.** *inf Br* [drink] pot *m*; **to have a few ~s with the lads** aller prendre un pot OR un verre avec les copains. **-3.** [jolt] secousse *f*, choc *m*.
◇ *vi* **-1.** [make harsh noise] grincer, crisser; **there's something about her voice which really ~s** sa voix a quelque chose qui vous écorche les oreilles. **-2.** [not be in harmony - note] détonner; [- colour] jurer; **it ~s with your red dress** cela jure avec ta robe rouge; **his constant complaining ~s on my nerves** ses lamentations continuelles me hérissent.
◇ *vt* [shake - structure] secouer, ébranler; **the fall jarred my bones** cette chute m'a secoué.
◆ **on the jar** *adj phr* [door] entrouvert.

jargon [ˈdʒɑːgən] *n* jargon *m*.

jarring [ˈdʒɑːrɪŋ] *adj* [sound] discordant; [colour] criard; **a loud ~ noise** un bruit discordant.

Jarrow Marches [ˈdʒærəʊˈmɑːtʃɪz] *pl pr n*: **the ~** *«marches de la faim», du nord-est de l'Angleterre à Londres, organisées par les chômeurs pour protester contre leur condition, au milieu des années trente*.

Jas. *written abbr of* **James**.

jasmine [ˈdʒæzmɪn] *n* jasmin *m*.

Jason [ˈdʒeɪsn] *pr n* Jason.

jasper [ˈdʒæspəʳ] *n* jaspe *m*.

jaundice [ˈdʒɔːndɪs] *n* **-1.** (*U*) MED jaunisse *f*. **-2.** *fig* [bitterness] amertume *f*.

jaundiced [ˈdʒɔːndɪst] *adj* [bitter] aigri, cynique; [disapproving] désapprobateur; **she has a very ~ view of English society** elle a une vision très négative de la société anglaise.

jaunt [dʒɔːnt] ◇ *n* balade *f*.
◇ *vi* se balader; **she's always ~ing off to Paris** elle est toujours en balade entre ici et Paris.

jauntily [ˈdʒɔːntɪlɪ] *adv* [cheerfully] joyeusement, jovialement; [in a sprightly way] lestement; **he was walking ~ down the street** il descendait la rue d'un pas leste OR allègre.

jauntiness [ˈdʒɔːntɪnɪs] *n* [cheerfulness] joie *f*, jovialité *f*; [sprightliness] légèreté *f*.

jaunty [ˈdʒɔːntɪ] (*compar* **jauntier**, *superl* **jauntiest**) *adj* [cheerful] joyeux, enjoué, jovial; [sprightly] leste, allègre.

Java [ˈdʒɑːvə] *pr n* Java; **in ~** à Java.

Javanese [ˌdʒɑːvəˈniːz] (*pl inv*) ◇ *n* **-1.** [person] Javanais *m*, -e *f*. **-2.** LING javanais *m*.
◇ *adj* javanais.

javelin [ˈdʒævlɪn] *n* [weapon] javelot *m*, javeline *f*; SPORT javelot *m*; **~ thrower** lanceur *m*, -euse *f* de javelot.

jaw [dʒɔː] ◇ *n* **-1.** ANAT mâchoire *f*; **she has a very square ~** elle a une mâchoire très carrée; **his ~ dropped in astonishment** il en est resté bouche bée; **snatched from the ~s of death** *fig* arraché aux griffes de la mort; **the ~s of hell** *fig* les portes *fpl* de l'enfer; **upper/lower ~** mâchoire supérieure/inférieure ❑ **'Jaws'** *Spielberg* 'les Dents de la mer'. **-2.** [of tool] mâchoire *f*. **-3.** *inf* [chat]: **to have a good old ~** tailler une petite bavette, papoter. **-4.** *inf* [moralizing speech] sermon *m*.
◇ *vi* *inf* [chat] papoter, tailler une bavette.
◇ *vt* *inf* [remonstrate with] sermonner.

jawbone [ˈdʒɔːbəʊn] ◇ *n* maxillaire *m*.
◇ *vt* *inf Am* POL exercer des pressions sur.

jawbreaker *inf* [ˈdʒɔːˌbreɪkəʳ] *n* **-1.** [word] mot *m* difficile à prononcer; [name] nom *m* à coucher dehors. **-2.** *Am* [sweet] *sorte de bonbon dur*.

jawline [ˈdʒɔːlaɪn] *n* menton *m*; **a strong ~** un menton saillant.

jay [dʒeɪ] *n* ORNITH geai *m*.

jaywalk [ˈdʒeɪwɔːk] *vi Am marcher en dehors des passages pour piétons*.

jaywalker [ˈdʒeɪwɔːkəʳ] *n Am piéton qui traverse en dehors des passages pour piétons*.

jaywalking [ˈdʒeɪwɔːkɪŋ] *n Am délit mineur qui consiste à traverser une rue en dehors des clous ou au feu vert*.

jazz [dʒæz] ◇ *n* **-1.** MUS jazz *m*; **the Jazz Age** *l'âge d'or du jazz américain*; **'The Jazz Singer'** *Crosland* 'le Chanteur de jazz'. **-2.** *inf* [rigmarole] baratin *m*, blabla *m*; **don't give me that ~!** ne me raconte pas de salades! ❑ **and all that ~** et tout le bataclan.
◇ *comp* [club, record, singer] de jazz; **~ band** jazz-band *m*; **they've done a ~ version of her song** ils ont fait une version jazz de sa chanson.
◇ *vt* ▽ *Am* [have sex with] baiser avec.
◆ **jazz up** *vt sep* **-1.** MUS: **to ~ up a song** mettre une chanson sur un rythme (de) jazz; **it's ~ed up Beethoven** c'est du Beethoven sur un rythme de jazz. **-2.** *inf* [enliven] égayer; **they've ~ed the hotel up** ils ont refait la déco de l'hôtel.

jazzman [ˈdʒæzmæn] (*pl* **jazzmen** [-men]) *n* musicien *m* de jazz.

jazz rock *n* jazz-rock *m*.

jazzy [ˈdʒæzɪ] (*compar* **jazzier**, *superl* **jazziest**) *adj* **-1.** [music] (de) jazz *(inv)*, sur un rythme de jazz; **a ~ version of "Carmen"** une version jazz de «Carmen». **-2.** *inf* [gaudy] tapageur, voyant; [smart, snazzy] chic *(inv)*.

JCB® *n* tractopelle *f*.

JCR (*abbr of* **junior common room**) *n Br* UNIV ≃ foyer *m* des étudiants.

JCS *pl pr n abbr of* **Joint Chiefs of Staff**.

JD *pr n abbr of* **Justice Department**.

jealous [ˈdʒeləs] *adj* **-1.** [envious] jaloux; **he gets terribly ~** il a des crises de jalousie terribles; **she's ~ of her sister** elle est jalouse de sa sœur; **he became very ~ of her sudden success** sa réussite soudaine l'a rendu très jaloux. **-2.** [possessive] jaloux, possessif; **to be ~ of one's reputation** être jaloux de OR veiller à sa réputation.

jealously [ˈdʒeləslɪ] *adv* jalousement.

jealousy [ˈdʒeləsɪ] (*pl* **jealousies**) jalousie *f*.

jeans [dʒiːnz] *npl* jean *m*, blue-jean *m*; **a pair of ~** un jean.

Jedda [ˈdʒedə] *pr n* Djedda.

Jeep® [dʒiːp] *n* Jeep® *f*.

jeepers *inf* [ˈdʒiːpəz] *interj Am*: **~ (creepers)!** oh la la!

jeer [dʒɪəʳ] ◇ *vi* [scoff] railler, se moquer; [boo, hiss] pousser des cris hostiles OR de dérision; **everybody ~ed at me** ils se sont tous moqués de moi.
◇ *vt* huer, conspuer.
◇ *n* [scoffing] raillerie *f*; [boo, hiss] huée *f*.

jeering [ˈdʒɪərɪŋ] ◇ *adj* railleur, moqueur.
◇ *n (U)* [scoffing] railleries *fpl*; [boos, hisses] huées *fpl*.

Jehovah [dʒɪˈhəʊvə] *pr n* Jéhovah; **~'s Witness** témoin de Jéhovah.

jejune [dʒɪˈdʒuːn] *adj lit* **-1.** [puerile] naïf, puéril. **-2.** [dull] ennuyeux, morne; [unrewarding] ingrat.

Jekyll and Hyde [ˌdʒekɪləndˈhaɪd] *n*: **he's a real ~** c'est un véritable docteur Jekyll.

jell [dʒel] ◇ *vi* = **gel**.
◇ *n* *inf Am* = **jelly**.

jellied [ˈdʒelɪd] *adj* CULIN en gelée; **~ eels** anguilles *fpl* en gelée.

Jell-o® ['dʒeləʊ] *n Am* = **jelly 2**.

jelly ['dʒelɪ] (*pl* jellies) ◇ *n* -**1.** [gen] gelée *f*; royal ~ gelée royale; my legs feel like ~ j'ai les jambes en coton OR comme du coton; my legs just turned to ~ j'en ai eu les jambes coupées, je n'avais plus de jambes. -**2.** *Br* CULIN [dessert] ≃ gelée *f*. -**3.** *Am* CULIN [jam] confiture *f*. -**4.** *mil sl* [gelignite] gélignite *f*.
◇ *vt* gélifier.

jelly baby (*pl* jelly babies) *n Br* bonbon *m (en forme de bébé)*.

jelly bean *n* dragée *f* à la gelée de sucre.

jellyfish ['dʒelɪfɪʃ] (*pl inv* OR jellyfishes) *n* méduse *f*.

jelly roll *n Am* (gâteau *m*) roulé *m*.

jemmy *inf* ['dʒemɪ] (*pl* jemmies, *pt* & *pp* jemmied) *Br* ◇ *n* pince-monseigneur *f*.
◇ *vt*: to ~ a door (open) ouvrir une porte avec une pince-monseigneur.

jenny ['dʒenɪ] (*pl* jennies) *n* -**1.** [female of bird or animal]: ~ wren roitelet *m* femelle; ~ (ass) ânesse *f*. -**2.** [machine] = **spinning jenny**.

jeopardize, -ise ['dʒepədaɪz] *vt* compromettre, mettre en péril.

jeopardy ['dʒepədɪ] *n* danger *m*, péril *m*; our future is in ~ notre avenir est en péril OR menacé OR compromis.

Jerba ['dʒɜːbə] = **Djerba**.

jerbil ['dʒɜːbɪl] = **gerbil**.

jerboa [dʒɜː'bəʊə] *n* gerboise *f*.

jeremiad [,dʒerɪ'maɪəd] *n lit* jérémiade *f*, lamentation *f*.

Jeremiah [,dʒerɪ'maɪə] ◇ *pr n* BIBLE Jérémie.
◇ *n fig* prophète *m* de malheur.

Jericho ['dʒerɪkəʊ] *pr n* Jéricho.

jerk [dʒɜːk] ◇ *vt* -**1.** [pull] tirer d'un coup sec, tirer brusquement; the door was ~ed open la porte s'ouvrit brusquement OR d'un coup sec. -**2.** [shake] secouer.
◇ *vi* -**1.** [jolt] cahoter, tressauter; the train began to ~ violently le train se mit à cahoter OR bringuebaler dans tous les sens; to ~ to a halt s'arrêter en cahotant. -**2.** [person - jump] sursauter; to ~ awake se réveiller en sursaut ‖ [person, muscle - twitch] se contracter; her hand ~ed up instinctively instinctivement, elle leva la main.
◇ *n* -**1.** [bump] secousse *f*, saccade *f*; the train came to a halt with a ~ le train s'arrêta brutalement. -**2.** [wrench] coup *m* sec; she gave the handle a ~ elle a tiré d'un coup sec sur la poignée. -**3.** [brusque movement] mouvement *m* brusque; with a ~ of his head he indicated that I should leave d'un brusque signe de la tête, il me fit comprendre qu'il me fallait partir; to wake up with a ~ se réveiller en sursaut. -**4.** ▽ [person] con *m*. -**5.** = **jerky** *n*.
◆ **jerk off**▼ *vi insep* se branler.

jerkily ['dʒɜːkɪlɪ] *adv* par à-coups.

jerkin ['dʒɜːkɪn] *n* blouson *m*; HIST pourpoint *m*.

jerkoff▼ ['dʒɜːkɒf] *n* branleur *m*.

jerky ['dʒɜːkɪ] (*compar* jerkier, *superl* jerkiest) ◇ *n* viande *f* séchée; beef ~ bœuf *m* séché.
◇ *adj* -**1.** [bumpy] saccadé; a ~ ride un trajet cahotant; we got off to a ~ start *fig* nos débuts ont été houleux. -**2.** ▽ *Am* [stupid] imbécile, con.

jeroboam [,dʒerə'bəʊəm] *n* jéroboam *m*.

Jeroboam [,dʒerə'bəʊəm] *pr n* Jéroboam.

Jerome [dʒə'rəʊm] *pr n*: Saint ~ saint Jérôme.

jerry *inf* ['dʒerɪ] (*pl* jerries) *n Br* pot *m* de chambre.

Jerry▽ ['dʒerɪ] (*pl* Jerries) *n dated* & *offensive* [German] Fritz *m*, Boche *m*.

jerry-builder *n pej marchand de biens peu scrupuleux qui fait construire des maisons de mauvaise qualité*.

jerry-built *adj pej* [house, building] construit en carton-pâte, peu solide.

jerry can *n* jerrican *m*.

jersey ['dʒɜːzɪ] *n* -**1.** [pullover] pull-over *m*, tricot *m*; SPORT maillot *m*. -**2.** [fabric] jersey *m*.

Jersey ['dʒɜːzɪ] ◇ *pr n* Jersey; in ~ à Jersey.
◇ *n* = **Jersey cow**.

Jersey cow *n* vache *f* jersiaise.

Jerusalem [dʒə'ruːsələm] *pr n* Jérusalem.

Jerusalem artichoke *n* topinambour *m*.

jest [dʒest] ◇ *n* plaisanterie *f*; to say sthg in ~ dire qqch pour rire OR pour plaisanter ❑ there's many a true word spoken in ~ *prov* il n'y a pas de meilleures vérités que celles dites en riant.
◇ *vi* plaisanter.

jester ['dʒestəʳ] *n* bouffon *m*, fou *m* (du roi); court ~ bouffon de cour.

jesting ['dʒestɪŋ] *n (U)* plaisanterie *f*, plaisanteries *fpl*.

Jesuit ['dʒezjʊɪt] ◇ *n* jésuite *m*.
◇ *adj* jésuite; ~ priest prêtre *m* jésuite.

jesuitic(al) [,dʒezjʊ'ɪtɪk(l)] *adj* jésuitique.

jesuitism ['dʒezjʊɪtɪzm] *n* jésuitisme *m*.

jesuitry ['dʒezjʊɪtrɪ] *n pej* jésuitisme *m*.

Jesus ['dʒiːzəs] ◇ *pr n* Jésus; ~ Christ Jésus-Christ.
◇ *interj*: ~ (Christ)!, ~ wept!▽ nom de Dieu!

Jesus creepers▽ *npl Br* sandales *fpl*.

jet [dʒet] (*pt* & *pp* jetted, *cont* jetting)
◇ *n* -**1.** [aircraft] avion *m* à réaction, jet *m*. -**2.** [stream - of liquid] jet *m*, giclée *f*; [- of gas, steam] jet *m*. -**3.** [nozzle, outlet] gicleur *m*; [on gas cooker] brûleur *m*. -**4.** [gem] jais *m*.
◇ *vi* -**1.** *inf* [travel by jet] voyager en avion (à réaction); they jetted (over) to Paris for the weekend ils ont pris l'avion pour passer le week-end à Paris. -**2.** [issue forth - liquid] gicler, jaillir.
◇ *vt* -**1.** [transport by jet] transporter par avion (à réaction); supplies are being jetted into OR to the disaster area des avions apportent des vivres à la zone sinistrée. -**2.** [direct - liquid] faire gicler.
◇ *comp* -**1.** [fighter, bomber] à réaction; [transport, travel] en avion (à réaction); ~ fuel kérosène *m*. -**2.** [made of jet - earrings, necklace] en jais.

jet black *adj* jais *(inv)*, noir de jais.

jet engine *n* moteur *m* à réaction.

jetfoil ['dʒetfɔɪl] *n* hydroglisseur *m*.

jetlag ['dʒetlæg] *n* fatigue *f* due au décalage horaire; I'm still suffering from ~ je suis encore sous le coup du décalage horaire.

jet-lagged [-lægd] *adj* fatigué par le décalage horaire; I'm still a bit ~ je ne suis pas complètement remis du décalage horaire.

jetliner ['dʒetlaɪnəʳ] *n* avion *m* de ligne.

jet plane *n* avion *m* à réaction.

jet-powered, jet-propelled *adj* à réaction.

jetsam ['dʒetsəm] *n (U)* jet *m* à la mer.

jet set *inf n* jet-set *m*.

jet-setter *inf n* membre *m* du jet-set.

jet stream *n* jet-stream *m*, courant-jet *m*.

jettison ['dʒetɪsən] *vt* -**1.** NAUT jeter à la mer, jeter par-dessus bord; AERON [bombs, cargo] larguer. -**2.** *fig* [unwanted possession] se débarrasser de; [theory, hope] abandonner.

jetty ['dʒetɪ] (*pl* jetties) *n* [landing stage] embarcadère *m*, débarcadère *m*; [breakwater] jetée *f*, môle *m*.

Jew [dʒuː] *n* Juif *m*, -ive *f*; the Wandering ~ le Juif errant.

jewel ['dʒuːəl] *n* -**1.** [precious stone] bijou *m*, joyau *m*, pierre *f* précieuse; ~ box coffret *m* à bijoux ‖ [in clockmaking] rubis *m*; a three-~ wristwatch une montre trois rubis. -**2.** *fig* [person, thing] bijou *m*, perle *f*; the new receptionist is an absolute ~ la nouvelle réceptionniste est une vraie perle.

jeweled *Am* = **jewelled**.

jeweler *Am* = **jeweller**.

jewelled *Br*, **jeweled** *Am* ['dʒuːəld] *adj* orné de bijoux; [watch] à rubis.

jeweller *Br*, **jeweler** *Am* ['dʒuːələʳ] *n* bijoutier *m*, -ère *f*, joaillier *m*, -ère *f*; ~'s (shop) bijouterie *f*.

jewellery *Br*, **jewelry** *Am* ['dʒuːəlrɪ] *n (U)* bijoux *mpl*; a piece of ~ un bijou.

Jewess ['dʒuːɪs] *n* Juive *f*.

Jewish ['dʒuːɪʃ] *adj* juif.

Jewry ['dʒʊərɪ] *n* [Jews collectively] la communauté juive.

jew's-harp *n* guimbarde *f*.

Jezebel ['dʒezə,bl] ◇ *pr n* BIBLE Jézabel.
◇ *n lit* OR *hum* dévergondée *f*.

JFK (*abbr of* John Fitzgerald Kennedy International Airport) *pr n aéroport de New York*.

jib [dʒɪb] (*pt* & *pp* jibbed, *cont* jibbing) ◇ *n* -**1.** NAUT foc *m*; I don't like the cut of his ~ [look] je n'aime pas son allure; [manner, behaviour] je n'aime pas ses façons de faire. -**2.** [of crane] flèche *f*, bras *m*.
◇ *vi Br* [horse] regimber; [person]: to ~ (at sthg) regimber OR rechigner (à qqch); to ~ at doing sthg rechigner à faire qqch.

jib boom *n* bâton *m* de foc.

jibe [dʒaɪb] ◇ *vi* -**1.** *inf Am* [agree] s'accorder, coller. -**2.** = **gibe**.
◇ *n* = **gibe**.

Jibouti [dʒɪ'buːtɪ] = **Djibouti**.

Jidda ['dʒɪdə] = **Jedda**.

jiffy *inf* ['dʒɪfɪ] (*pl* jiffies), **jiff** *inf* [dʒɪf] *n*: to do sthg in a ~ faire qqch en un rien de temps OR en moins de deux; I'll be back in a ~ je serai de retour dans une minute; half a ~ une petite minute.

Jiffy bag® *n* enveloppe *f* matelassée.

jig [dʒɪg] (*pt* & *pp* jigged, *cont* jigging)
◇ *n* -**1.** [dance] gigue *f*. -**2.** TECH gabarit *m*. -**3.** FISHING leurre *m*.
◇ *vi* -**1.** [dance] danser allègrement. -**2.** *Br*: to ~ (around OR about) sautiller, se trémousser.
◇ *vt* [shake] secouer (légèrement).

jigger ['dʒɪgəʳ] *n* -**1.** [spirits measure] mesure *f (42 ml)*; a ~ of gin/whisky un petit verre de gin/whisky. -**2.** [golf club] fer *m* quatre. -**3.** [in billiards] chevalet *m*, appui-queue *m inv*. -**4.** NAUT tapecul *m*. -**5.** *inf Am* [thing] machin *m*, truc *m*. -**6.** *Br* [flea] chique *f*, puce-chique *f*.

jiggered *inf* ['dʒɪgəd] *adj* -**1.** [exhausted] crevé, vidé. -**2.** *Br* [as expletive]: well, I'll be ~! mince alors!; I'm ~ if I'll do it! pas question que je le fasse!

jiggery-pokery *inf* [,dʒɪgərɪ'pəʊkərɪ] *n (U) Br* micmacs *mpl*; there's some ~ going on il se passe des choses pas très catholiques.

jiggle ['dʒɪgl] ◇ *vt* secouer (légèrement); you have to ~ the key a bit to get it in il faut tourner et retourner un peu la clef pour la faire entrer dans la serrure.
◇ *vi*: to ~ (about OR around) se trémousser.
◇ *n* secousse *f*; give it a ~ secoue-le un peu.

jigsaw ['dʒɪgsɔː] *n* -**1.** [game]: the pieces of the ~ were beginning to fall into place *fig* peu à peu tout devenait clair ❑ ~ (puzzle) puzzle *m*. -**2.** [tool] scie *f* sauteuse.

jihad [dʒɪ'hɑːd] *n* djihad *m*.

jilt [dʒɪlt] *vt* quitter; he ~ed her for someone else il l'a plaquée pour une autre.

Jim Crow *n Am* -**1.** ▼ [person] *terme raciste et vieilli désignant un Noir*, ≃ nègre *m*. -**2.** [policy] politique *f* raciste; ~ laws lois *fpl* ségrégationnistes.

jim-dandy *inf adj Am dial* chouette.

jimjams ['dʒɪmdʒæmz] *npl Br* -**1.** ▽ [excitement] agitation *f*; [nervousness] frousse *f*; to have the ~ [excited] être excité comme une puce; [nervous] avoir la frousse OR les foies. -**2.** *inf* [pyjamas] *baby talk* pyjama *m*.

jimmy *inf* ['dʒɪmɪ] (*pl* jimmies, *pt* & *pp* jimmied) *Am* = **jemmy**.

jimson weed ['dʒɪmsn-] *n Am* stramoine *f*.

jingle ['dʒɪŋgl] ◇ *n* -**1.** [sound] tintement *m*. -**2.** RADIO & TV jingle *m*.
◇ *vi* tinter.
◇ *vt* faire tinter.

jingo *inf* ['dʒɪŋgəʊ] *n dated*: by ~! crénom de nom!

jingoism ['dʒɪŋgəʊɪzm] *n pej* chauvinisme *m*.

jingoist [ˈdʒɪŋgəʊɪst] *pej* ◇ *n* chauvin *m*, -e *f*, cocardier *m*, -ère *f*.
◇ *adj* = **jingoistic**.

jingoistic [ˌdʒɪŋgəʊˈɪstɪk] *adj pej* chauvin, cocardier.

jink [dʒɪŋk] ◇ *n* [movement] esquive *f*.
◇ *vi* zigzaguer, se faufiler; **he ~ed through the defence** SPORT il s'est faufilé à travers la défense adverse.

jinni [ˈdʒɪnɪ] (*pl* jinn [dʒɪn]) *n* djinn *m*.

jinx *inf* [dʒɪŋks] ◇ *n* malchance *f*, sort *m*; **there's a ~ on this car** cette voiture porte malheur OR la guigne; **to put a ~ on sb** jeter un sort à qqn.
◇ *vt* porter malheur à, jeter un sort à; **to be ~ed** être frappé par le sort OR poursuivi par le mauvais sort.

jitterbug [ˈdʒɪtəbʌg] ◇ *n* -**1.** [dance] jitterbug *m*. -**2.** *inf* [nervous person] nerveux *m*, -euse *f*.
◇ *vi* [dance] danser le jitterbug.

jitters *inf* [ˈdʒɪtəz] *npl* frousse *f*; **to have the ~** avoir la frousse OR le trac; **to give sb the ~** flanquer la frousse à qqn.

jittery *inf* [ˈdʒɪtərɪ] *adj* [person] nerveux; [situation] tendu, délicat; **he's always ~ before exams** il a toujours le trac avant un examen.

jiu-jitsu [dʒuːˈdʒɪtsuː] = **ju-jitsu**.

Jivaro [ˈhiːvərəʊ] (*pl inv*) *n* Jivaro *mf*.

jive [dʒaɪv] ◇ *n* -**1.** [dance] swing *m*. -**2.** [slang]: **~ (talk)** argot *m (employé par les Noirs américains, surtout les musiciens de jazz)*. -**3.** ▽ *Am* [lies, nonsense] baratin *m*, blabla *m*; **don't give me all that ~** arrête ton char.
◇ *vt* ▽ *Am* [deceive, mislead] baratiner, charrier; **stop jiving him** arrête de le charrier.
◇ *vi* -**1.** [dance] danser le swing. -**2.** ▽ *Am* [fool around] déconner; **stop jiving and get to work!** assez déconné, au boulot!
◇ *adj* ▽ *Am* [phoney, insincere] bidon *(inv)*.

Jnr (*written abbr of* Junior): **Michael Roberts ~** Michael Roberts fils.

Joan of Arc [ˌdʒəʊnəvˈɑːk] *pr n* Jeanne d'Arc.

job [dʒɒb] (*pt & pp* jobbed, *cont* jobbing)
◇ *n* -**1.** [occupation, employment] emploi *m*, travail *m*; **to find a ~** trouver du travail OR un emploi; **to look for a ~** chercher un emploi OR du travail; **to be out of a ~** être sans emploi OR au chômage; **a Saturday/summer ~** un boulot OR un job pour le samedi/l'été; **what's your ~?** quelle est votre profession?, que faites-vous (dans la vie)?; **what kind of ~ does she do?** qu'est-ce qu'elle fait comme travail?; **she's got a very good ~** elle a une très bonne situation OR place; **he took a ~ as a rep** il a pris un emploi de représentant; **hundreds of ~s have been lost** des centaines d'emplois ont été supprimés, des centaines de personnes ont été licenciées; **he really knows his ~** il connaît bien son métier OR son boulot; **he was sleeping on the ~** il dormait pendant le travail OR à son poste; **it's more than my ~'s worth** je risquerais ma place (si je faisais ça) ❑ **~s for the boys** *Br* copinage *m*. -**2.** [piece of work, task] travail *m*, tâche *f*; **the ~ took longer than expected** le travail a pris plus longtemps qu'on ne pensait; **to do a good ~** faire du bon travail OR du bon boulot; **try to do a better ~ next time** essayez de faire mieux la prochaine fois; **she made a good ~ of fixing the car** elle s'en est bien sortie pour réparer la voiture; **we need to concentrate on the ~ in hand** il faut se concentrer sur ce que nous sommes en train de faire; **the car needs a paint ~** *inf* la voiture aurait besoin d'un (bon) coup de peinture; **it's not perfect but it does the ~** *fig* ce n'est pas parfait mais ça fera l'affaire ❑ **to be on the ~** [working] être en train (de travailler); ▽ *Br* [having sex] être en train de faire l'amour. -**3.** [role, responsibility] travail *m*; **he was only doing his ~** il ne faisait que son travail; **it's not my ~** ce n'est pas mon travail; **it's not my ~ to answer questions** je ne suis pas là pour répondre à des questions; **she had the ~ of breaking the bad news** c'est elle qui était chargée d'annoncer les mauvaises nouvelles; **it's the children's ~ to do the dishes** c'est aux enfants de faire la vaisselle. -**4.** [difficult time]: **to have a ~ doing sthg** avoir du mal à faire qqch; **you've got quite a ~ ahead of you** tu as du travail en perspective OR de quoi faire. -**5.** [state of affairs]: **he's left the company, and a good ~ too!** il a quitté la société et personne ne s'en plaindra!; **it's a good ~ they were home** heureusement qu'ils étaient à la maison; **thanks for the map, it's just the ~** merci pour la carte, c'est exactement ce qu'il me fallait; **to give sb/sthg up as a bad ~** laisser tomber qqn/qqch qui n'en vaut pas la peine; **we decided to make the best of a bad ~** nous avons décidé de faire avec ce que nous avions. -**6.** *inf* [crime] coup *m*; **to pull a ~** faire un casse; **to do a ~ on sb** passer qqn à tabac; **the police think he was in on the ~** la police croit qu'il était dans le coup. -**7.** *inf* [item, specimen]: **he drives a flashy Italian ~** il conduit un petit bolide italien. -**8.** COMPUT tâche *f*.
◇ *vi* -**1.** [do piecework] travailler à la pièce; [work irregularly] faire des petits travaux OR boulots. -**2.** *Br* COMM: **he ~s in used cars** il revend des voitures d'occasion.
◇ *vt* -**1.** *Br* ST. EX négocier; **she ~s government securities** elle négocie des fonds d'État. -**2.** ▽ *Am* [swindle] arnaquer, truander; [betray] vendre.
◆ **job out** *vt sep* sous-traiter; **they jobbed out the work to three different firms** ils ont confié le travail à trois sous-traitants.

Job [dʒəʊb] *pr n* BIBLE Job; **she has the patience of ~** elle a une patience à toute épreuve ❑ **he's a real ~'s comforter** pour remonter le moral, tu peux lui faire confiance *iron*; **as poor as ~** pauvre comme Job.

job analysis *n* analyse *f* des tâches OR du travail.

jobber [ˈdʒɒbəʳ] *n Br* -**1.** ST.EX courtier *m*, -ère *f* (en Bourse). -**2.** [pieceworker] ouvrier *m*, -ère *f* à la pièce; [casual worker] journalier *m*, -ère *f*. -**3.** COMM [wholesaler] grossiste *mf*.

jobbery [ˈdʒɒbərɪ] *n Br* concussion *f*.

jobbing [ˈdʒɒbɪŋ] *adj Br*: **~ gardener** jardinier *m* à la journée; **~ tailor** tailleur *m* à façon; **~ workman** ouvrier *m* à la tâche.

Jobcentre [ˈdʒɒbˌsentəʳ] *n Br agence locale pour l'emploi*, ≃ ANPE *f*.

job creation *n* création *f* d'emplois; **~ scheme** programme *m* de création d'emplois.

job description *n* description *f* de poste.

job evaluation *n* ADMIN analyse *f* des postes.

jobholder [ˈdʒɒbˌhəʊldəʳ] *n* salarié *m*, -e *f*.

job hunting *n* recherche *f* d'un emploi.

jobless [ˈdʒɒblɪs] ◇ *adj* au chômage, sans emploi.
◇ *npl*: **the ~** les chômeurs *mpl*, les demandeurs *mpl* d'emploi.

joblessness [ˈdʒɒblɪsnɪs] *n* chômage *m*.

job lot *n Br* COMM lot *m*; **they sold off the surplus as a ~** ils ont vendu tout l'excédent en un seul lot.

job queue *n Br* COMPUT file *f* d'attente des tâches.

job satisfaction *n* satisfaction *f* professionnelle.

job security *n* sécurité *f* de l'emploi.

job sharing *n* partage *m* du travail.

job spec *inf n* description *f* d'emploi.

jobsworth *inf* [ˈdʒɒbzwəθ] *n Br* petit chef *m (qui invoque le règlement pour éviter toute initiative)*.

job title *n* titre *m* (de fonction).

Joburg, Jo'burg [ˈdʒəʊbɜːg] *abbr of* Johannesburg.

Jocasta [dʒəˈkæstə] *pr n* Jocaste.

jock *inf* [dʒɒk] *n* -**1.** *Am* sportif *m*. -**2.** [jockey] jockey *m*. -**3.** [disc jockey] disc-jockey *m*, animateur *m*, -trice *f*.

Jock *inf* [dʒɒk] *n* -**1.** *Scot* [term of address]: **hello, ~!** salut, vieux! -**2.** [Scottish soldier] soldat *m* écossais.

jockey [ˈdʒɒkɪ] ◇ *n* -**1.** SPORT jockey *m*. -**2.** *inf Am* [driver] conducteur *m*, -trice *f*; [operator] opérateur *m*, -trice *f*; **desk ~** *hum* rond-de-cuir *m*; **elevator ~** liftier *m*; **truck ~** routier *m*.
◇ *vt* -**1.** [horse] monter. -**2.** [trick] manipuler, manœuvrer; **they ~ed him into lending them money** ils l'ont adroitement OR habilement amené à leur prêter de l'argent.
◇ *vi*: **to ~ for position** [in race] essayer de se placer avantageusement; **the companies were all ~ing for position** *fig* toutes les entreprises essayaient de se placer.

jockey cap *n* casquette *f* de jockey.

Jockey shorts® *npl* caleçon *m*.

jockstrap [ˈdʒɒkstræp] *n* suspensoir *m*.

jocose [dʒəˈkəʊs] *lit* = **jocular 1**.

jocular [ˈdʒɒkjʊləʳ] *adj* -**1.** [jovial] gai, jovial, enjoué. -**2.** [facetious] facétieux, badin; **a ~ remark** une remarque facétieuse.

jocularity [ˌdʒɒkjʊˈlærətɪ] *n* jovialité *f*.

jocularly [ˈdʒɒkjʊləlɪ] *adv* jovialement.

jocund [ˈdʒɒkənd] *adj lit* gai, jovial.

Jodhpur [ˌdʒɒdˈpʊəʳ] *pr n* Jodhpur.

jodhpurs [ˈdʒɒdpəz] *npl* jodhpurs *mpl*.

Joe *inf* [dʒəʊ] *n Am* -**1.** [man] type *m*, gars *m*. -**2.** [GI] soldat *m*, GI *m*.

Joe Bloggs *inf* [-blɒgz] *Br*, **Joe Blow** *inf Am & Austr n* Monsieur Tout le Monde.

Joe College *inf n Am* UNIV l'étudiant *m* type.

Joe Public *inf n* Monsieur Tout le Monde.

Joe Six-pack *n* l'Américain *m* moyen.

Joe Soap *inf n Br* Monsieur Tout le Monde.

joey *inf* [ˈdʒəʊɪ] *n Austr* -**1.** [kangaroo] jeune kangourou *m*. -**2.** [child] môme *mf*, marmot *m*.

jog [dʒɒg] (*pt & pp* jogged, *cont* jogging) ◇ *n* -**1.** [slow run] jogging *m*; EQUIT petit trot *m*; **to go for a ~** aller faire un jogging. -**2.** [push] légère poussée *f*; [nudge] coup *m* de coude.
◇ *vi* -**1.** [run] courir à petites foulées; [for fitness] faire du jogging; **she ~s to work every morning** tous les matins, elle va travailler en joggant. -**2.** [bump] se balancer; **his rifle jogged against his back** son fusil se balançait dans son dos.
◇ *vt* [nudge] donner un léger coup à; **to ~ sb's memory** *fig* rafraîchir la mémoire de qqn.
◆ **jog along** *vi insep* -**1.** EQUIT trottiner, aller au petit trot. -**2.** *fig* suivre son cours; **my work is jogging along pretty steadily** mon travail avance assez bien.

jogger [ˈdʒɒgəʳ] *n* jogger *mf*, joggeur *m*, -euse *f*.

jogging [ˈdʒɒgɪŋ] *n* jogging *m*; **to go ~** faire du jogging ❑ **~ suit** jogging *m*.

joggle [ˈdʒɒgl] ◇ *vt* -**1.** [shake] secouer (légèrement). -**2.** CONSTR fixer, assembler *(au moyen d'une cheville ou d'un goujon)*.
◇ *vi* cahoter, ballotter; **the truck ~d along the track** le camion cahotait sur la piste.
◇ *n* -**1.** [shake, jolt] secousse *f*. -**2.** CONSTR cheville *f*, goujon *m*.

jog trot *n* petit trot *m*.
◆ **jog-trot** *vi* trottiner, aller au petit trot.

Johannesburg [dʒəˈhænɪsbɜːg] *pr n* Johannesburg.

john [dʒɒn] *n Am* -**1.** *inf* [lavatory] waters *mpl*, W-C *mpl*. -**2.** ▽ [prostitute's client] micheton *m*.

John [dʒɒn] *pr n*: **Saint ~** saint Jean; **the Gospel According to (Saint) ~** l'Évangile selon saint Jean; **(Saint) ~ the Baptist** (saint) Jean-Baptiste; **~ Lackland** Jean sans Terre.

John Birch Society [-bɜːtʃ-] *pr n organisation conservatrice américaine, particulièrement hostile au communisme, influente dans les années 50-60*.

John Bull *pr n* John Bull *(personnification de la nation anglaise, du peuple anglais)*.

John Doe [-dəʊ] *pr n Am* l'Américain *m* moyen.

John Dory [-ˈdɔːrɪ] *n* saint-pierre *m inv*.

John Hancock *inf* [-ˈhænkɒk] *n Am* signature *f*; **to lay one's ~** *apposer sa signature au bas d'un document*.

johnny [ˈdʒɒnɪ] (*pl* johnnies) *n Br* -**1.** *inf dated* [man] type *m*, gars *m*. -**2.** ▽ *Br* [condom]: **(rubber) ~** capote *f* anglaise.

Johnny-come-lately *inf n* [newcomer] nouveau venu *m*; *pej* [upstart] parvenu *m*.

John o'Groats [-ə'grəʊts] *pr n village d'Écosse qui marque le point le plus septentrional de la Grande-Bretagne continentale*.

join [dʒɔɪn] ◇ *vt* -**1.** [political party, club etc] adhérer à; so you've been burgled too? ~ **the club!** alors, toi aussi tu as été cambriolé? tu n'es pas le seul! || [armed forces] s'engager dans; ~ **the army!** engagez-vous! -**2.** [join company with, meet] rejoindre; **I'll ~ you later** je vous rejoindrai OR retrouverai plus tard; **she ~ed the procession** elle se joignit au cortège; **I ~ed the queue at the ticket office** j'ai fait la queue au guichet; **to ~ one's ship** rallier son navire; **to ~ one's regiment** rejoindre son régiment; **they ~ed us for lunch** ils nous ont retrouvés pour déjeuner; **will you ~ me for** OR **in a drink?** vous prendrez bien un verre avec moi? || [in activity or common purpose] se joindre à; **he didn't want to ~ the dancing** il n'a pas voulu se joindre OR se mêler aux danseurs; **my wife ~s me in offering our sincere condolences** ma femme se joint à moi pour vous adresser nos sincères condoléances. -**3.** [attach, fasten] joindre, raccorder; **to ~ (up) the two ends of a rope** nouer les deux bouts d'une corde; **you have to ~ these two electric wires** il faut raccorder ces deux fils électriques; **the workmen ~ed the pipes (together)** les ouvriers ont raccordé les tuyaux. -**4.** [unite] relier, unir; **to be ~ed in marriage** OR **matrimony** être uni par les liens du mariage; **to ~ hands** [in prayer] joindre les mains; [link hands] se donner la main; **we must ~ forces (against the enemy)** nous devons unir nos forces (contre l'ennemi); **she ~ed forces with her brother** elle s'est alliée à son frère; **to ~ battle (with)** entrer en lutte (avec), engager le combat (avec). -**5.** [intersect with] rejoindre; **does this path ~ the main road?** est-ce que ce chemin rejoint la grand-route?; **we camped where the stream ~s the river** nous avons campé là où le ruisseau rejoint la rivière.
◇ *vi* -**1.** [become a member] devenir membre. -**2.** [meet, come together] se rejoindre. -**3.** [form an alliance] s'unir, se joindre; **they ~ed together to fight drug trafficking** ils se sont unis pour lutter contre le trafic de drogue; **we all ~ with you in your sorrow** [sympathize] nous nous associons tous à votre douleur.
◇ *n* [in broken china, wallpaper] (ligne *f* de) raccord *m*; SEW couture *f*.
◆ **join in** ◇ *vi insep*: **she started singing and the others ~ed in** elle a commencé à chanter et les autres se sont mis à chanter avec elle.
◇ *vt insep* participer à; **she never ~s in the conversation** elle ne participe jamais à la conversation; **he ~ed in the protest** il s'associa aux protestations; **all ~ in the chorus!** reprenez tous le refrain en chœur!
◆ **join on** ◇ *vi insep* s'attacher; **where does this part ~ on?** où cette pièce vient-elle se rattacher?
◇ *vt sep* attacher, ajouter; **we got off the train while they were ~ing on more coaches** nous sommes descendus du train pendant que l'on accrochait de nouveaux wagons.
◆ **join up** ◇ *vi insep* MIL s'engager.
◇ *vt sep* = **join** *vt* **3**.

joiner ['dʒɔɪnəʳ] *n* -**1.** [carpenter] menuisier *m*. -**2.** *inf* [member of many clubs]: **he's a real ~** il est de toutes les bonnes causes; **he's not really a ~** il n'est pas très sociable.

joinery ['dʒɔɪnərɪ] *n* menuiserie *f*.

joint [dʒɔɪnt] ◇ *n* -**1.** [gen & CONSTR] assemblage *m*; MECH joint *m*. -**2.** ANAT articulation *f*, jointure *f*; **to put one's shoulder out of ~** se démettre OR se déboîter l'épaule; **the change in schedule has put everything out of ~** *fig* le changement de programme a tout chamboulé. -**3.** *Br* CULIN rôti *m*. -**4.** *inf* [night club] boîte *f*; [bar] troquet *m*, boui-boui *m*; [gambling house] tripot *m pej*. -**5.** *inf Am* [house] baraque *f*; **nice ~ you have here!** c'est pas mal chez toi! -**6.** *drugs sl* joint *m*.
◇ *adj* -**1.** [united, combined] conjugué, commun; **to take ~ action** mener une action commune; **thanks to their ~ efforts...** grâce à leurs efforts conjugués... -**2.** [shared, collective] joint, commun; ~ **account** BANK compte *m* joint; ~ **agreement** [gen] accord *m* commun; INDUST convention *f* collective; ~ **committee** [gen] commission *f* mixte; INDUST comité *m* paritaire; ~ **custody** JUR garde *f* conjointe; ~ **ownership** copropriété *f*; ~ **property** biens *mpl* communs; ~ **resolution** *Am* POL ≃ projet *m* de loi; ~ **responsibility** OR **liability** responsabilité *f* conjointe; ~ **tenancy** location *f* commune; ~ **venture** entreprise *f* commune, joint-venture *m*. -**3.** [associate]: ~ **author** coauteur *m*; ~ **heir** cohéritier *m*; ~ **owner** copropriétaire *mf*.
◇ *vt* -**1.** MECH assembler, emboîter. -**2.** *Br* CULIN découper.

Joint Chiefs of Staff *pl pr n*: **the ~** *organe consultatif du ministère américain de la Défense, composé des chefs d'état-major des trois armes*.

jointed ['dʒɔɪntɪd] *adj* articulé.

join-the-dots *n (U) Br jeu qui consiste à relier des points numérotés pour découvrir un dessin*.

jointly ['dʒɔɪntlɪ] *adv* conjointement; **the house is ~ owned** la maison est en copropriété; ~ **liable** JUR coresponsable, conjointement responsable.

joint-stock company *n Br* société *f* par actions.

jointure ['dʒɔɪntʃəʳ] *n* JUR douaire *m*.

joist [dʒɔɪst] *n* solive *f*.

jojoba [həʊ'həʊbə] *n* jojoba *m*.

joke [dʒəʊk] ◇ *n* -**1.** [verbal] plaisanterie *f*; **to tell a ~** raconter une plaisanterie; **to make a ~ of** OR **about sthg** plaisanter sur OR à propos de qqch; **we did it for a ~** nous l'avons fait pour rire OR pour rigoler; **I don't get** OR **see the ~** je ne comprends pas l'astuce; **he can't take a ~** il ne comprend pas la plaisanterie; **it's gone beyond a ~** la plaisanterie a assez duré; **it's a private ~** c'est une plaisanterie entre nous/eux; **the test was a ~!** [easy] ce test, c'était de la rigolade!; **it was no ~ climbing that cliff!** escalader cette falaise, ce n'était pas de la tarte OR de la rigolade!; **the new legislation is just a ~** la nouvelle législation est une plaisanterie. -**2.** [prank] plaisanterie *f*, farce *f*; **to play a ~ on sb** jouer un tour à qqn, faire une farce à qqn; **the ~ is on you** la plaisanterie s'est retournée contre toi. -**3.** [laughing stock] risée *f*; **his staff just regard him as a ~** il est la risée de tous ses employés.
◇ *vi* plaisanter; **I was only joking** je ne faisais que plaisanter; **you must be joking, you have (got) to be joking!** vous plaisantez!, vous n'êtes pas sérieux!; **Tom's passed his driving test – you're joking!** Tom a eu son permis de conduire – sans blague! OR tu veux rire?; **they often ~ about his accent** ils se moquent souvent de son accent.

joker ['dʒəʊkəʳ] *n* -**1.** [funny person] farceur *m*, -euse *f*; *pej* [frivolous person] plaisantin *m*. -**2.** [in cards] joker *m*. -**3.** ▽ [man] type *m*, mec *m*. -**4.** [clause] clause *f* contradictoire; **the contract contained a ~** le contrat contenait une clause piège.

jokey *inf* ['dʒəʊkɪ] (*compar* jokier, *superl* jokiest) *adj* comique.

joking ['dʒəʊkɪŋ] ◇ *adj* badin.
◇ *n (U)* plaisanterie *f*, plaisanteries *fpl*; ~ **apart** OR **aside** plaisanterie mise à part, blague à part.

jokingly ['dʒəʊkɪŋlɪ] *adv* en plaisantant, pour plaisanter.

joky *inf* ['dʒəʊkɪ] = **jokey**.

jollifications [dʒɒlɪfɪ'keɪʃnz] *npl hum* réjouissances *fpl*.

jollify ['dʒɒlɪfaɪ] (*pt & pp* jollified) *vt* égayer.

jollity ['dʒɒlətɪ] (*pl* jollities) *n* entrain *m*, gaieté *f*.

jolly ['dʒɒlɪ] (*compar* jollier, *superl* jolliest, *pt & pp* jollied) ◇ *adj* -**1.** [person] gai, joyeux, jovial; **what are you so ~ about?** qu'est-ce qui te met de si bonne humeur? -**2.** *Br* [enjoyable] agréable, plaisant; **we had a very ~ time** nous nous sommes bien amusés ❑ ~ **hockey sticks** *expression parodique utilisée en parlant d'une femme bourgeoise, éduquée dans une public school, caractérisée par un enthousiasme débordant et une certaine naïveté*.
◇ *adv Br* rudement, drôlement; **it's a ~ good thing he came** c'est rudement bien qu'il soit venu; **a ~ good fellow** un chic type; **you'll ~ well do what you're told!** tu feras ce qu'on te dit de faire, un point c'est tout!; **it ~ well serves them right!** c'est vraiment bien fait pour eux!
◇ *vt Br* [coax] enjôler, entortiller; **she jollied me into going** avec ses paroles enjôleuses, elle a fini par me convaincre d'y aller; **he'll come if you ~ him along a bit** il viendra si tu le pousses un peu.
◆ **jolly up** *vt sep Br* égayer; **we jollied up the room with some posters** nous avons égayé la pièce avec des affiches.

jolly boat ['dʒɒlɪ-] *n* chaloupe *f*, canot *m*.

Jolly Roger [-'rɒdʒəʳ] *n* pavillon *m* noir, drapeau *m* de pirate.

jolt [dʒəʊlt] ◇ *vt* -**1.** [physically] secouer; **the passengers were ~ed about in the bus** les passagers étaient secoués dans le bus. -**2.** [mentally] secouer, choquer; **to ~ sb into action** pousser qqn à agir.
◇ *vi* cahoter; **the jeep ~ed along the track** la jeep avançait en cahotant sur la piste.
◇ *n* -**1.** [jar] secousse *f*, coup *m*; **the fall gave his spine a ~** dans sa chute, il a reçu un choc à la colonne vertébrale. -**2.** [start] sursaut *m*, choc *m*; **to wake up with a ~** se réveiller en sursaut.

Jonah ['dʒəʊnə] *pr n* Jonas.

Jonathan ['dʒɒnəθən] *pr n* Jonathan.

Joneses ['dʒəʊnzɪz] *npl*: **to keep up with the ~** *inf* vouloir faire aussi bien que le voisin, ne pas vouloir être en reste.

jonquil ['dʒɒŋkwɪl] *n* (petite) jonquille *f*.

Jordan ['dʒɔːdn] *pr n* Jordanie *f*; **in ~** en Jordanie; **the (River) ~** le Jourdain.

Jordanian [dʒɔː'deɪnjən] ◇ *n* Jordanien *m*, -enne *f*.
◇ *adj* jordanien.

Joseph ['dʒəʊzɪf] *pr n* Joseph; ~ **of Aramathea** Joseph d'Arimathie.

Josephine ['dʒəʊzəfiːn] *pr n*: **the Empress ~** l'impératrice *f* Joséphine.

josh *inf* [dʒɒʃ] ◇ *vi* blaguer; **I'm only ~ing** je plaisante.
◇ *vt* charrier.
◇ *n* quolibet *m*, moquerie *f*.

Joshua ['dʒɒʃʊə] *pr n* Josué.

Josiah [dʒəʊ'saɪə] *pr n* Josias.

joss stick [dʒɒs-] *n* bâtonnet *m* d'encens.

jostle ['dʒɒsl] ◇ *vi* se bousculer; **they were jostling for seats** ils se bousculaient pour avoir des places.
◇ *vt* bousculer, heurter; **she was ~d by the demonstrators** elle a été bousculée par les manifestants.
◇ *n* bousculade *f*.

jot [dʒɒt] (*pt & pp* jotted, *cont* jotting) *n*: **it won't change his mind one ~** ça ne le fera absolument pas changer d'avis; **there isn't a ~ of truth in what he says** il n'y a pas un brin de vérité dans ce qu'il raconte; **it doesn't matter a ~** cela n'a pas la moindre importance; **not one ~ or tittle** pas un iota.
◆ **jot down** *vt sep* noter, prendre note de; **she jotted a few ideas down before the meeting** elle a rapidement noté quelques idées avant la réunion.

jotter ['dʒɒtəʳ] *n Br* [exercise book] cahier *m*, carnet *m*; [pad] bloc-notes *m*.

jotting ['dʒɒtɪŋ] *n* note *f*; **her private ~s** ses notes personnelles.

joual [ʒwɑːl] *n* joual *m*.

joule [dʒuːl] *n* joule *m*.

journal ['dʒɜːnl] *n* -**1.** [publication] revue *f.* -**2.** [diary] journal *m* intime. -**3.** NAUT [logbook] journal *m* de bord. -**4.** JUR procès-verbal *m.* -**5.** MECH tourillon *m;* ~ **bearing** palier *m* (de tourillon).

journalese [,dʒɜːnə'liːz] *n pej* jargon *m* journalistique.

journalism ['dʒɜːnəlɪzm] *n* journalisme *m.*

journalist ['dʒɜːnəlɪst] *n* journaliste *mf.*

journalistic [dʒɜːnə'lɪstɪc] *adj* journalistique.

journey ['dʒɜːnɪ] ◇ *n* -**1.** [gen] voyage *m;* **to set out on a ~** partir en voyage; **she went on a ~ to Europe** elle a fait un voyage en Europe; **the ~ back** OR **home** le (voyage du) retour; **to break one's ~** [in plane, bus] faire escale; [in car] faire une halte, s'arrêter; **to reach (one's) ~'s end** [arrive] arriver à destination; [die] arriver au bout du voyage; **the ~ into adulthood** *fig* le passage à l'âge adulte. -**2.** [shorter distance] trajet *m;* **a short tube ~** un court trajet en métro; **the ~ to work takes me ten minutes** je mets dix minutes pour aller à mon travail.
◇ *vi fml* voyager.

journeyman ['dʒɜːnɪmən] (*pl* **journeymen** [-mən]) *n* -**1.** [qualified apprentice] compagnon *m.* -**2.** *arch* [day-worker] journalier *m.*

journo *inf* ['dʒɜːnəʊ] *n abbr of* **journalist.**

joust [dʒaʊst] ◇ *n* joute *f.*
◇ *vi* jouter.

Jove [dʒəʊv] *pr n* Jupiter; **by ~!** *inf Br dated* par Jupiter!

jovial ['dʒəʊvjəl] *adj* jovial, enjoué.

joviality [,dʒəʊvɪ'ælətɪ] *n* jovialité *f,* entrain *m.*

jovially ['dʒəʊvjəlɪ] *adv* jovialement.

jowl [dʒaʊl] *n* -**1.** [jaw] mâchoire *f.* -**2.** [cheek] joue *f;* **he has heavy ~s** il a les joues flasques.

-jowled [dʒaʊld] *in cpds:* **a heavy~ man** un homme aux joues flasques.

joy [dʒɔɪ] *n* -**1.** [pleasure] joie *f;* **to shout with** OR **for ~** crier de joie; **she moved out, to the great ~ of her neighbours** elle a déménagé, à la grande joie de ses voisins; **her grandchildren are a great ~ to her** ses petits-enfants sont la joie de sa vie; **it was a ~ to see him laughing again** c'était un plaisir de le voir rire à nouveau; **the ~s of gardening** les plaisirs OR les charmes du jardinage. -**2.** *inf* [luck, satisfaction]: **they had no ~ at the casino** ils n'ont pas eu de chance au casino; **any ~ at the job centre?** tu as trouvé quelque chose à l'agence pour l'emploi?; **you'll get no ~ out of her** tu n'as pas grand-chose à attendre d'elle.

Joycean ['dʒɔɪsɪən] *adj* de (James) Joyce.

joyful ['dʒɔɪfʊl] *adj* joyeux, enjoué.

joyfully ['dʒɔɪfʊlɪ] *adv* joyeusement.

joyfulness ['dʒɔɪfʊlnɪs] *n* joie *f,* allégresse *f.*

joyless ['dʒɔɪlɪs] *adj* [unhappy] triste, sans joie; [dull] morne, maussade.

joyous ['dʒɔɪəs] *adj lit* joyeux.

joyously ['dʒɔɪəslɪ] *adv* joyeusement.

joyride ['dʒɔɪraɪd] ◇ *n*: **they went for a ~** ils ont volé une voiture pour aller faire un tour.
◇ *vi*: **to go joyriding** faire une virée dans une voiture volée; **they were had up for joyriding** ils ont été convoqués devant les tribunaux pour vol de voiture.

joyrider ['dʒɔɪraɪdəʳ] *n personne qui vole une voiture pour faire un tour.*

joystick ['dʒɔɪstɪk] *n* -**1.** AERON manche *m* à balai. -**2.** COMPUT manette *f* (de jeux).

JP (*abbr of* Justice of the Peace) *n Br* ≃ juge d'instance.

JUSTICE OF THE PEACE:
Les «JPs» sont nommés par le Lord Chancellor. Ce sont en général des notables locaux (médecins, propriétaires terriens) jouissant d'une bonne réputation.

Jr. (*written abbr of* Junior) junior, fils.

jubilant ['dʒuːbɪlənt] *adj* débordant de joie, radieux; **the Prime Minister was ~ at the election results** le Premier ministre fut transporté de joie à la vue des résultats du scrutin; **the ~ champion** le champion radieux; **he gave a ~ shout** il poussa un cri de joie.

jubilation [,dʒuːbɪ'leɪʃn] *n (U)* [rejoicing] joie *f,* jubilation *f;* [celebration] réjouissances *fpl.*

jubilee ['dʒuːbɪliː] *n* jubilé *m;* **the Queen's silver ~** les 25 ans de règne de la Reine.

Judaea [dʒuː'dɪə] *pr n* Judée *f;* **in ~** en Judée.

Judaeo-Christian [dʒuː'diːəʊ-] *adj* judéo-chrétien.

Judah ['dʒuːdə] *pr n* Juda.

Judaic [dʒuː'deɪɪk] *adj* judaïque.

Judaica [dʒuː'deɪɪkə] *npl* [literature] littérature *f* judaïque; [objects] objets *mpl* ayant trait à la culture judaïque.

Judaism ['dʒuːdeɪɪzm] *n* judaïsme *m.*

judas ['dʒuːdəs] *n* [peephole] judas.

Judas ['dʒuːdəs] ◇ *pr n* BIBLE Judas; ~ **Iscariot** Judas Iscariote.
◇ *n* [traitor] judas *m.*

Judas tree *n* arbre *m* de Judée, gainier *m.*

judder ['dʒʌdəʳ] ◇ *vi Br* [gen] vibrer; [brakes, clutch] brouter; **the bus ~ed to a halt** le bus s'est arrêté en cahotant.
◇ *n* trépidation *f;* [of vehicle, machine] broutement *m.*

Jude [dʒuːd] *pr n* Jude; '~ **the Obscure**' *Hardy* 'Jude l'obscur'.

Judea [dʒuː'dɪə] = **Judaea.**

Judeo-Christian [dʒuː'diːəʊ-] = **Judaeo-Christian.**

judge [dʒʌdʒ] ◇ *n* -**1.** JUR juge *m;* **presiding ~** président *m* du tribunal. -**2.** [in a competition] membre *m* du jury; SPORT juge *m;* **the ~s were divided** le jury était partagé. -**3.** *fig* juge *m;* **I'll let you be the ~ of that** je vous laisse juge; **he's a bad ~ of character** il manque de psychologie; **Bob is an excellent ~ of** OR **in such matters** Bob est un excellent juge en la matière.
◇ *vt* -**1.** [pass judgment on, adjudicate] juger; **the case will be ~d tomorrow** l'affaire sera jugée demain; **a panel of critics ~d the competition** le concours a été jugé par un panel de critiques; **don't ~ him too harshly** ne le juge pas trop sévèrement. -**2.** [consider] juger, considérer; **she ~d it her duty to protest** elle a considéré qu'il était de son devoir de protester‖ [estimate] juger de, estimer; **can you ~ the distance?** peux-tu estimer OR évaluer la distance?; **I'd ~ him to be about thirty** je lui donnerais la trentaine.
◇ *vi* juger; **if you don't believe me, ~ for yourself** si vous ne me croyez pas, jugez-en par vous-même; **it isn't for me to ~** ce n'est pas à moi d'en juger; **you're in no position to ~** vous n'êtes pas en mesure d'en juger; **as far as I can ~** pour autant que je puisse en juger; **judging from** OR **by what he said** si j'en juge par ce qu'il a dit; **to ~ from** OR **by her accent** à en juger par son accent, d'après son accent.
◆ **Judges** *n*: (the book of) Judges BIBLE (le livre des) Juges.

judge advocate (*pl* **judge advocates**) *n* MIL assesseur *m (d'un tribunal militaire)*; ~ **general** assesseur *m* général.

judgement *etc* ['dʒʌdʒmənt] = **judgment.**

judgment ['dʒʌdʒmənt] *n* -**1.** JUR & RELIG jugement *m;* **to pass ~ on sb/sthg** porter un jugement sur qqn/qqch; **to pass ~ on a prisoner** juger un prisonnier; **to sit in ~ on a case** juger une affaire; **they have no right to sit in ~ over us!** ils n'ont pas le droit de nous juger! ❑ '**The Judgment**' *Kafka* 'le Verdict'. -**2.** [opinion] jugement *m,* opinion *f,* avis *m;* **we will have to reserve ~ on the new arrangements** *fig* nous devrons attendre avant de nous prononcer sur les nouvelles dispositions; **against my better ~ we decided to go** malgré mon avis, nous avons décidé d'y aller. -**3.** [discernment] jugement *m,* discernement *m;* **he is a man of ~** c'est un homme perspicace.

judgmental [dʒʌdʒ'mentl] *adj* [person - by nature] enclin à juger OR à critiquer; **I'm not being ~** ce n'est pas une critique que je vous fais.

Judgment Day *n* (jour *m* du) Jugement *m* dernier.

judicature ['dʒuːdɪkətʃəʳ] *n* JUR -**1.** [judge's authority] justice *f.* -**2.** [court's jurisdiction] juridiction *f;* **court of ~** cour *f* de justice. -**3.** [judges collectively] magistrature *f.*

judicial [dʒuː'dɪʃl] *adj* -**1.** JUR judiciaire; **to take** OR **to bring ~ proceedings against sb** attaquer qqn en justice ❑ ~ **inquiry** enquête *f* judiciaire; ~ **review** *Am* [of ruling] examen *m* d'une décision de justice *(par une juridiction supérieure)*; [of law] examen de la constitutionnalité d'une loi; ~ **separation** séparation *f* de corps. -**2.** [impartial] impartial, critique; **a ~ mind** un esprit critique.

judicially [dʒuː'dɪʃəlɪ] *adv* judiciairement.

judiciary [dʒuː'dɪʃərɪ] ◇ *adj* judiciaire.
◇ *n* -**1.** [judicial authority] pouvoir *m* judiciaire. -**2.** [judges collectively] magistrature *f.*

judicious [dʒuː'dɪʃəs] *adj* judicieux.

judiciously [dʒuː'dɪʃəslɪ] *adv* judicieusement.

Judith ['dʒuːdɪθ] *pr n* Judith.

judo ['dʒuːdəʊ] *n* judo *m.*

judoka ['dʒuːdəʊkə] *n* judoka *mf.*

Judy▽ ['dʒuːdɪ] (*pl* **Judies**) *n Br dated* nana *f,* gonzesse *f.*

jug [dʒʌg] (*pt* & *pp* **jugged,** *cont* **jugging**)
◇ *n* -**1.** *Br* [small - for milk] pot *m;* [- for water] carafe *f;* [- for wine] pichet *m,* carafe *f;* [large - earthenware] cruche *f;* [- metal, plastic] broc *m;* **a ~ of wine** une carafe de vin ❑ **wine ~** carafe *f* à vin. -**2.** ▽ *Br* [jail] tôle *f,* taule *f,* cabane *f;* **five years in ~** cinq ans en tôle. -**3.** *Am* [narrow-necked] bonbonne *f.*
◇ *vt* -**1.** CULIN cuire à l'étouffée OR à l'étuvée. -**2.** ▽[imprison] mettre en taule OR en cabane, coffrer.

jug band *n Am* orchestre *m* de folk ou de jazz *(jouant avec des instruments de fortune)*.

jugful ['dʒʌgfʊl] *n* (contenu *m* d'un) pot *m,* (contenu *m* d'une) carafe *f;* **he drank a whole ~ of water** il a bu toute une carafe d'eau.

jugged hare [dʒʌgd-] *n* lièvre *m* à l'étouffée.

juggernaut ['dʒʌgənɔːt] *n* -**1.** *Br* [large lorry] gros poids lourd *m.* -**2.** [force] force *f* fatale; **the ~ of history** la force aveugle de l'histoire; **the ~ of war** le pouvoir destructeur de la guerre.

juggle ['dʒʌgl] ◇ *vi* [as entertainment] jongler; **to ~ with** [figures, dates] jongler avec.
◇ *vt literal* & *fig* jongler avec; **he ~d all the different possibilities** *fig* il envisagea toutes les possibilités.
◇ *n* jonglerie *f.*

juggler ['dʒʌgləʳ] *n* -**1.** [entertainer] jongleur *m,* -euse *f.* -**2.** [deceitful person] tricheur *m,* -euse *f.*

juggling ['dʒʌglɪŋ], **jugglery** ['dʒʌglərɪ] *n literal* & *fig* jonglerie *f.*

Jugoslavia *etc* [,juːgəʊ'slaːvjə] = **Yugoslavia.**

jugular ['dʒʌgjʊləʳ] ◇ *adj* jugulaire; ~ **vein** jugulaire *f.*
◇ *n* jugulaire *f;* **to go for the ~** *inf* attaquer qqn sur ses points faibles.

juice [dʒuːs] ◇ *n* -**1.** CULIN jus *m;* **apple ~** jus de pomme; **meat ~** jus de viande. -**2.** BIOL suc *m;* **gastric ~** suc gastrique. -**3.** *inf* [electricity] jus *m;* [petrol] essence *f.* -**4.** *inf Am* [spirits] tord-boyaux *m;* [wine] pinard *m.*
◇ *vt* [fruit] presser.
◆ **juice up** *vt sep Am* -**1.** *inf* [battery] recharger. -**2.** *inf* [enliven] égayer, animer. -**3.** ▽ [intoxicate] soûler; **he got ~d up on whisky** il s'est soûlé au whisky.

juice extractor *n* presse-fruits *m inv.*

juicer ['dʒuːsəʳ] *n* presse-fruits *m inv.*

juiciness ['dʒuːsɪnɪs] *n* -**1.** [of fruit]: **I chose these oranges for their ~** j'ai choisi ces oranges parce qu'elles sont juteuses. -**2.** *inf* [of story] piquant *m.*

juicy ['dʒuːsɪ] (*compar* **juicier,** *superl* **juiciest**) *adj* -**1.** [fruit] juteux. -**2.** *inf* [profitable] juteux; **a ~ deal** une affaire juteuse. -**3.** *inf* [racy] savoureux; **a ~ story** une histoire osée OR piquante; **let's hear all the ~ details** raconte-nous les détails croustillants.

ju-jitsu [dʒuː'dʒɪtsuː] *n* jiu-jitsu *m inv.*

juju ['dʒuːdʒuː] *n* [charm] amulette *f.*

jujube ['dʒuːdʒuːb] *n* jujube *m*.
jukebox ['dʒuːkbɒks] *n* juke-box *m*.
Jul. (*written abbr of* July) juill.
julep ['dʒuːlɪp] *n* -**1.** [soft drink] boisson *f* sucrée. -**2.** [alcoholic drink]: (mint) ~ cocktail *m* à la menthe. -**3.** PHARM julep *m*.
Julian ['dʒuːljən] *pr n*: ~ the Apostate Julien l'Apostat.
Julian calendar *n* calendrier *m* julien.
Julius Caesar [,dʒuːljəs'siːzəʳ] *pr n* Jules César.
July [dʒuː'laɪ] *n* juillet *m*.
jumble ['dʒʌmbl] ◇ *n* -**1.** [confusion, disorder] fouillis *m*, désordre *m*; my things are all in a ~ mes affaires sont tout en désordre; a ~ of colours un kaléidoscope de couleurs. -**2.** *Br* [articles for jumble sale] bric-à-brac *m*.
◇ *vt* -**1.** [objects, belongings] mélanger; her clothes were all ~d (up OR together) in a suitcase ses vêtements étaient fourrés pêle-mêle dans une valise. -**2.** [thoughts, ideas] embrouiller; his essay was just a collection of ~d ideas sa dissertation n'était qu'un fourre-tout d'idées confuses.
jumble sale *n Br vente de charité où sont vendus des articles d'occasion et des produits faits maison.*
jumbo *inf* ['dʒʌmbəʊ] (*pl* jumbos) ◇ *n* -**1.** [elephant] éléphant *m*, pachyderme *m*. -**2.** = **jumbo jet**.
◇ *adj* énorme, géant; a ~(-sized) packet of washing powder un paquet de lessive familial.
jumbo jet *n* (avion *m*) gros-porteur *m*, jumbo *m*, jumbo-jet *m*.
jump [dʒʌmp] ◇ *vi* -**1.** [leap] sauter, bondir; they ~ed across the crevasse ils ont traversé la crevasse d'un bond; to ~ back faire un bond en arrière; can you ~ over the hedge? peux-tu sauter par-dessus la haie?; she ~ed into/out of her car elle a sauté dans/hors de sa voiture; he ~ed (down) off the train il a sauté du train; she ~ed off [from wall, bicycle] elle a sauté; he ~ed off the bridge il s'est jeté du haut du pont; he ~ed up, he ~ed to his feet il se leva d'un bond; the frog ~ed from stone to stone la grenouille bondissait de pierre en pierre; why did he ~ out of the window? pourquoi a-t-il sauté par la fenêtre? || *fig*: the answer suddenly ~ed out at me la réponse m'a subitement sauté aux yeux; this record ~s ce disque saute; the lecturer ~ed from one topic to another le conférencier passait rapidement d'un sujet à un autre; to ~ for joy sauter de joie; she was ~ing up and down with rage elle trépignait de rage; to ~ to conclusions tirer des conclusions hâtives ❑ ~ to it! *inf* grouille!; to ~ down sb's throat *inf* houspiller OR enguirlander qqn; when she saw me she nearly ~ed out of her skin quand elle m'a vu elle a failli sauter au plafond. -**2.** [start] sursauter, tressauter; the noise made her ~ le bruit l'a fait sursauter; when the phone rang his heart ~ed il tressaillit en entendant la sonnerie du téléphone. -**3.** [rise abruptly] grimper OR monter en flèche; prices ~ed dramatically in 1974 les prix ont grimpé de façon spectaculaire en 1974. -**4.** *inf Am* [be lively] être très animé; by nightfall the joint was ~ing à la tombée de la nuit, ça chauffait dans la boîte.
◇ *vt* -**1.** [leap over] sauter; to ~ a fence sauter OR franchir un obstacle; to ~ rope *Am* sauter à la corde; to ~ a piece [in draughts] prendre un pion. -**2.** [horse] faire sauter; she ~ed her horse over the stream elle a fait sauter OR franchir le ruisseau à son cheval. -**3.** [omit, skip] sauter; to ~ a line sauter une ligne. -**4.** *inf* [attack] sauter sur, agresser; two men ~ed him in the park deux hommes lui ont sauté dessus dans le parc. -**5.** *inf* [leave, abscond from]: to ~ ship abandonner son navire; to ~ bail ne pas comparaître au tribunal *(après avoir été libéré sous caution)*; the fugitive ~ed town *Am* le fugitif a réussi à quitter la ville. -**6.** [not wait one's turn at]: to ~ the queue ne pas attendre son tour, resquiller; she ~ed the lights elle a grillé OR brûlé le feu (rouge). -**7.** *inf* [not pay for, take illegally]: to ~ a train *esp Am* voyager sans billet; he ~ed a (mining) claim *Am* il s'est approprié une concession (minière).
◇ *n* -**1.** [leap, bound] saut *m*, bond *m*; she got up with a ~ elle se leva d'un bond; we need to keep one ~ ahead of the competition *fig* nous devons garder une longueur d'avance sur nos concurrents ❑ to get the ~ on sb *inf* devancer qqn; to be on the ~ *inf Am* être pressé OR débordé. -**2.** [sharp rise] bond *m*, hausse *f*; there has been a sudden ~ in house prices il y a eu une flambée des prix de l'immobilier. -**3.** EQUIT [fence, obstacle] obstacle *m*. -**4.** COMPUT saut *m*. -**5.** GAMES prise *f* (de pion).
◆ **jump about** *Br*, **jump around** *vi insep* sautiller.
◆ **jump at** *vt insep* sauter sur, saisir; he ~ed at the chance to go abroad il sauta sur l'occasion de partir à l'étranger.
◆ **jump in** *vi insep* -**1.** *literal* [into vehicle] monter; go on, ~ in! vas-y, monte!; if you want a lift, ~ in! si tu veux que je te dépose, monte! || [into water, hole] sauter. -**2.** *inf fig* [intervene] intervenir; he ~ed in to defend her il est intervenu pour la défendre, il est venu à sa rescousse.
◆ **jump on** *inf vt insep literal & fig* sauter sur; the boss ~s on every little mistake aucune faute n'échappe au patron.
jump ball *n* [in basketball] entre-deux *m inv*.
jumped-up *inf adj Br* parvenu; she's just a ~ shop assistant ce n'est qu'une petite vendeuse qui se donne de grands airs OR qui se prend au sérieux.
jumper ['dʒʌmpəʳ] *n* -**1.** *Br* [sweater] pullover *m*. -**2.** *Am* [dress] robe-chasuble *f*. -**3.** [person] sauteur *m*, -euse *f*.
jumper cables *Am* = **jump leads**.
jumping ['dʒʌmpɪŋ] *n* EQUIT jumping *m*.
jumping bean *n* pois *m* sauteur.
jumping jack *n* -**1.** [firework] pétard *m* mitraillette. -**2.** [puppet] pantin *m*.
jumping-off point, jumping-off place *n* point *m* de départ, tremplin *m*; his success could be a ~ for a new career *fig* sa réussite pourrait être le point de départ d'une nouvelle carrière.
jumping rope *n Am* corde *f* à sauter.
jump-jet *n Br* avion *m* à décollage vertical.
jump leads *npl Br* câbles *mpl* de démarrage.
jump-off *n* EQUIT dernière épreuve *f (d'un concours hippique)*.
jump rope *n Am* corde *f* à sauter.
jump seat *n Br* strapontin *m*.
jump-start *vt*: to ~ a car [by pushing or rolling] faire démarrer une voiture en la poussant OR en la mettant dans une pente; [with jump leads] faire démarrer une voiture avec des câbles *(branchés sur la batterie d'une autre voiture)*.
jump suit *n* combinaison-pantalon *f*.
jumpy ['dʒʌmpɪ] (*compar* jumpier, *superl* jumpiest) *adj* -**1.** *inf* [edgy] nerveux. -**2.** ST.EX instable, fluctuant.
Jun. -**1.** *written abbr of* June. -**2.** (*written abbr of* Junior) junior, fils.
junction ['dʒʌŋkʃn] *n* -**1.** [of roads] carrefour *m*, croisement *m*; [of railway lines, traffic lanes] embranchement *m*; [of rivers, canals] confluent *m*. -**2.** ELEC [of wires] jonction *f*, raccordement *m*.
junction box *n Br* boîte *f* de dérivation.
juncture ['dʒʌŋktʃəʳ] *n* -**1.** *fml* [moment] conjoncture *f*; at this ~ dans la conjoncture actuelle, dans les circonstances actuelles; at a crucial ~ à un moment critique. -**2.** LING joncture *f*, jointure *f*, frontière *f*. -**3.** TECH jointure *f*.
June [dʒuːn] *n* juin *m*.
June beetle, June bug *n* hanneton *m*.
Jungian ['jʊŋɪən] ◇ *adj* jungien.
◇ *n* jungien *m*, -enne *f*.
jungle ['dʒʌŋgl] ◇ *n* -**1.** [tropical forest] jungle *f*; 'The Jungle Book' *Kipling* 'le Livre de la jungle'. -**2.** *fig*: the world of business is a real ~ le monde des affaires est une véritable jungle; it's a ~ out there c'est la jungle là-bas; the ~ of tax laws le labyrinthe du droit fiscal.
◇ *comp* [animal] de la jungle.
jungle fever *n (U)* paludisme *m*.
jungle gym *n Am* cage *f* d'écureuil.
jungle juice *inf n* gnôle *f*.
junior ['dʒuːnjəʳ] ◇ *n* -**1.** [younger person] cadet *m*, -ette *f*; he is five years her ~ il est de cinq ans son cadet, il a cinq ans de moins qu'elle. -**2.** [subordinate] subordonné *m*, -e *f*, subalterne *mf*. -**3.** *Br* [pupil] écolier *m*, -ère *f (entre 7 et 11 ans)*; she teaches ~s elle est institutrice. -**4.** *Am* SCH élève *mf* de troisième année; *Am* UNIV étudiant *m*, -e *f* de troisième année. -**5.** *inf Am* [term of address] fiston *m*.
◇ *adj* -**1.** [younger] cadet, plus jeune. -**2.** [lower in rank] subordonné, subalterne; a ~ member of staff un employé subalterne; he's ~ to her in the department il est son subalterne dans le service ❑ ~ executive cadre *m* débutant, jeune cadre; the ~ faculty *Am* UNIV les enseignants non titulaires; ~ minister sous-secrétaire *m* d'État; ~ partner associé *m* adjoint. -**3.** [juvenile] jeune.
◇ *comp Br* [teaching, teacher] dans le primaire.
◆ **Junior** = **Jnr**.
Junior College *n* [in US] *établissement d'enseignement supérieur où l'on obtient un diplôme en deux ans.*
junior common room *n Br* UNIV salle *f* des étudiants.
Junior League *pr n association américaine de jeunes femmes de droite.*
junior school *n Br* école *f* élémentaire *(pour les enfants de 7 à 11 ans)*.
juniper ['dʒuːnɪpəʳ] *n* genévrier *m*; ~ berry baie *f* de genièvre.
junk [dʒʌŋk] ◇ *n* -**1.** *inf (U)* [anything poor-quality or worthless] pacotille *f*, camelote *f*; this watch is a real piece of ~ cette montre, c'est vraiment de la camelote OR c'est de la vraie camelote; all his so-called antiques were just a pile of ~ ses prétendues antiquités n'étaient en fait qu'un ramassis de vieilleries; his latest film is utter ~ *fig* son dernier film est absolument nul OR un vrai navet. -**2.** *(U)* [second-hand, inexpensive goods] bric-à-brac *m*. -**3.** *inf (U)* [stuff] trucs *mpl*, machins *mpl*; can you get your ~ off the table? tu peux enlever tes trucs OR ton bazar de la table?; what's all that ~ in the hall? qu'est-ce que c'est que ce bric-à-brac OR ce bazar dans l'entrée? -**4.** [boat] jonque *f*. -**5.** *(U) drugs sl* came *f*.
◇ *vt inf* jeter (à la poubelle), balancer.
junk bond *n* junk bond *m*.
junket ['dʒʌŋkɪt] ◇ *n* -**1.** *inf pej* [official journey] voyage *m* aux frais de la princesse. -**2.** *inf* [festive occasion] banquet *m*, festin *m*. -**3.** CULIN ≃ fromage *m* frais (sucré et parfumé).
◇ *vi inf* voyager aux frais de la princesse.
junketing *inf* ['dʒʌŋkɪtɪŋ] *n (U) pej* voyages *mpl* OR réceptions *fpl* aux frais de la princesse.
junk food *inf n* nourriture *f* de mauvaise qualité; their kids eat nothing but ~ leurs gosses ne mangent que des cochonneries.
junk heap *n* dépotoir *m*.
junkie *inf* ['dʒʌŋkɪ] *n* -**1.** [drug addict] drogué *m*, -e *f*, junkie *mf*. -**2.** *fig* dingue *mf*, accro *mf*; a television/football ~ un dingue de la télé/du football.
junk jewellery *n (U)* bijoux *mpl* fantaisie.
junk mail *n* publicité *f* (reçue par courrier).
junkman ['dʒʌŋkmæn] (*pl* junkmen [-men]) *n Am* [dealer in old furniture] brocanteur *m*; [ragman] chiffonnier *m*; [scrap metal dealer] ferrailleur *m*, marchand *m* de ferraille.
junk shop *n* magasin *m* de brocante; at the ~ chez le brocanteur.
junky ['dʒʌŋkɪ] = **junkie**.
junkyard ['dʒʌŋkjɑːd] *n* -**1.** [for scrap metal] entrepôt *m* de ferraille; at the ~ chez le ferrailleur. -**2.** [for discarded objects] dépotoir *m*.
Juno ['dʒuːnəʊ] *pr n* Junon.

junoesque [ˌdʒuːnəʊ'esk] *adj* [woman] imposant.

junta [*Br* 'dʒʌntə, *Am* 'hʊntə] *n* junte *f*.

Jupiter ['dʒuːpɪtəʳ] *pr n* -**1.** ASTRON Jupiter *f*. -**2.** MYTH Jupiter.

Jurassic [dʒʊ'ræsɪk] ◇ *adj* jurassique.
◇ *n* jurassique *m*.

juridical [dʒʊə'rɪdɪkl] *adj* juridique.

jurisdiction [ˌdʒʊərɪs'dɪkʃn] *n* JUR & ADMIN juridiction *f*; **the federal government has no ~ over such cases** de tels cas ne relèvent pas de la compétence OR des attributions du gouvernement fédéral; **to come** OR **to fall within the ~ of** relever de la juridiction de; **it comes within our ~** *fig* cela relève de nos compétences, c'est de notre ressort; **this territory is within the ~ of the United States** ce territoire est soumis à l'autorité judiciaire des États-Unis.

jurisdictional [ˌdʒʊərɪs'dɪkʃənl] *adj* juridictionnel; **~ dispute** *Am* querelle *f* d'attributions.

jurisprudence [ˌdʒʊərɪs'pruːdəns] *n* jurisprudence *f*.

jurist ['dʒʊərɪst] *n* juriste *mf*.

juror ['dʒʊərəʳ] *n* juré *m*.

jury ['dʒʊərɪ] (*pl* **juries**) ◇ *n* -**1.** JUR jury *m*; **to serve on a ~** faire partie d'un jury; **Ladies and Gentlemen of the ~** Mesdames et Messieurs les jurés ❑ **the ~ is still out on that one** ça reste à voir. -**2.** [in contest] jury *m*.
◇ *adj* NAUT de fortune, improvisé.

jury box *n* sièges *mpl* des jurés; **she was in the ~** elle faisait partie des jurés.

juryman ['dʒʊərɪmən] (*pl* **jurymen** [-mən]) *n* juré *m*.

jury-rigged *adj* NAUT avec un gréement de fortune.

jury-rigging *n* JUR truquage *m* d'un jury.

jury shopping *n Am* choix *m* vétilleux des jurés (par les avocats de la défense).

jurywoman ['dʒʊərɪˌwʊmən] (*pl* **jurywomen** [-ˌwɪmɪn]) *n* jurée *f*.

just[1] [dʒʌst] *adv* -**1.** [indicating immediate past] juste; **~ the other day** pas plus tard que l'autre jour; **~ last week** pas plus tard que la semaine dernière; **she has ~ gone out** elle vient juste de sortir; **they had (only) ~ arrived** ils venaient (tout) juste d'arriver; **I've ~ been speaking to him on the phone** je viens juste de lui parler au téléphone, je lui parlais au téléphone à l'instant; **she's ~ this moment** OR **minute left the office** elle vient de sortir du bureau à l'instant; **he's ~ been to Mexico** il revient OR rentre du Mexique. -**2.** [indicating present or immediate future] juste; **I was ~ going to phone you** j'allais juste OR justement te téléphoner, j'étais sur le point de te téléphoner; **I'm ~ off** *inf* je m'en vais; **~ coming!** *inf* j'arrive tout de suite!; **I was ~ about to tell you** j'allais justement te le dire; **I'm ~ making tea, do you want some?** je suis en train de faire du thé, tu en veux? -**3.** [only, merely] juste, seulement; **~ a few** quelques-uns/quelques-unes seulement; **~ a little** juste un peu; **~ a minute** OR **a moment** OR **a second, please** une (petite) minute OR un (petit) instant, s'il vous plaît; **do you want some whisky? — ~ a drop** est-ce que tu veux du whisky? — juste une goutte; **it was ~ a dream** ce n'était qu'un rêve; **he's ~ a clerk** ce n'est qu'un simple employé; **we're ~ friends** nous sommes amis, c'est tout; **he was ~ trying to help** il voulait juste OR simplement rendre service; **if he could ~ work a little harder!** si seulement il pouvait travailler un peu plus!; **if the job is so unpleasant you should ~ leave** si le travail est désagréable à ce point, tu n'as qu'à démissionner; **don't argue, ~ do it!** ne discute pas, fais-le, c'est tout!; **~ because I'm your friend, it doesn't mean I have to agree with you** ce n'est pas parce que je suis ton ami que je dois être d'accord avec toi; **if you can ~ sign here please** juste une petite signature ici, s'il vous plaît; **you can't ask ~ anybody to present the prizes** tu ne peux pas demander au premier venu de présenter les prix; **this is not ~ any horse race, this is the Derby!** ça n'est pas n'importe quelle course de chevaux, c'est le Derby! -**4.** [exactly, precisely] exactement, juste; **~ here/there** juste ici/là; **~ at that moment** juste à ce moment-là; **that's ~ what I needed** c'est exactement OR juste ce qu'il me fallait; *iron* il ne me manquait plus que ça; **~ what are you getting at?** où veux-tu en venir exactement?; **he's ~ like his father** c'est son père tout craché; **she's ~ the person for the job** elle a exactement le profil requis pour ce poste; **that dress is ~ the same as yours** cette robe est exactement la même que la tienne; **oh, I can ~ picture it!** oh, je vois tout à fait!; **that hat is ~ you** ce chapeau te va à merveille; **you speak French ~ as well as I do** ton français est tout aussi bon que le mien; **I'd ~ as soon go tomorrow** j'aimerais autant y aller demain; **(it's) ~ my luck!** *iron* c'est bien ma chance!; **don't come in ~ yet** n'entre pas tout de suite. -**5.** [barely] (tout) juste, à peine; **I could ~ make out what they were saying** je parvenais tout juste à entendre ce qu'ils disaient; **you came ~ in time!** tu es arrivé juste à temps!; **I ~ missed a lorry** j'ai failli heurter un camion; **the trousers ~ fit me** je rentre tout juste dans le pantalon ‖ [a little]: **it costs ~ over £50** ça coûte un tout petit peu plus de 50 livres; **it's ~ after/before two o'clock** il est un peu plus/moins de deux heures; **~ afterwards** juste après; **it's ~ to the right of the painting** c'est juste à droite du tableau. -**6.** [possibly]: **I may** OR **might ~ be able to do it** il n'est pas impossible que je puisse le faire; **his story might** OR **could ~ be true** son histoire pourrait être vraie, il est possible que son histoire soit vraie. -**7.** [emphatic use]: **~ think what might have happened!** imagine un peu ce qui aurait pu arriver!; **~ wait till I find the culprit!** attends un peu que je trouve le coupable!; **now ~ you wait a minute, John!** hé, une petite minute, John!; **I ~ won't do it** il n'est pas question que je le fasse; **it ~ isn't good enough** c'est loin d'être satisfaisant, c'est tout; **he looks terrible in that suit — doesn't he ~!** ce costume ne lui va pas du tout — je ne te le fais pas dire!; **don't you ~ love that hat?** adorable, ce chapeau, non? ‖ [with adjective]: **the meal was ~ delicious** le repas était tout simplement OR vraiment délicieux; **everything is ~ fine** tout est parfait; **this is ~ ridiculous** c'est vraiment ridicule.

◆ **just about** *adv phr* -**1.** [very nearly] presque, quasiment; **dinner is ~ about ready** le dîner est presque prêt; **she's ~ about as tall as you** elle est presque aussi grande que toi; **I've ~ about had enough of your sarcasm!** j'en ai franchement assez de tes sarcasmes! -**2.** [barely] (tout) juste; **can you reach the shelf? — ~ about!** est-ce que tu peux atteindre l'étagère? — (tout) juste!; **his handwriting is ~ about legible** son écriture est tout juste OR à peine lisible. -**3.** [approximately]: **their plane should be taking off ~ about now** leur avion devrait être sur le point de décoller.

◆ **just as** *conj phr* -**1.** [at the same time as] juste au moment où; **they arrived ~ as we were leaving** ils sont arrivés juste au moment où nous partions. -**2.** [exactly as]: **he did steal the money, ~ as I thought** il a bien volé l'argent comme je le pensais; **~ as you like** OR **wish** comme vous voulez OR voudrez; **why not come ~ as you are?** pourquoi ne viens-tu pas comme tu es?

◆ **just in case** ◇ *conj phr* juste au cas où; **~ in case we don't see each other** juste au cas où nous ne nous verrions pas.
◇ *adv phr* au cas où; **take a sandwich, ~ in case** apporte un sandwich, on ne sait jamais OR au cas où.

◆ **just like that** *inf adv phr* comme ça; **he told me to clear off, ~ like that!** il m'a dit de me tirer, carrément!

◆ **just now** *adv phr* -**1.** [at this moment]: **I'm busy ~ now** je suis occupé pour le moment; **not ~ now** pas en ce moment. -**2.** [a short time ago]: **I heard a noise ~ now** je viens juste d'entendre un bruit; **I've ~ now come from there** j'en viens à l'instant; **when did this happen? — ~ now** quand cela s'est-il passé? — à l'instant.

◆ **just on** *adv phr Br* exactement; **they've been married ~ on thirty years** ça fait exactement trente ans qu'ils sont mariés; **the fish weighed ~ on three kilos** le poisson pesait exactement trois kilos.

◆ **just so** ◇ *adv phr fml* [expressing agreement]: **are you a magistrate? — ~ so** vous êtes magistrat? — c'est exact.
◇ *adj phr Br* [properly arranged] parfait; **she likes everything (to be) ~ so** elle aime que tout soit parfait.

◆ **just then** *adv phr* à ce moment-là; **I was ~ then getting ready to go out** je me préparais justement à sortir; **~ then a strange figure appeared** à ce moment-là une silhouette étrange apparut.

◆ **just the same** *adv phr* [nonetheless] quand même; **~ the same, it's as well to check** il vaut quand même mieux vérifier.

just[2] [dʒʌst] ◇ *adj* -**1.** [fair, impartial] juste, équitable; **a ~ law** une loi juste OR équitable; **a ruler who was ~ to** OR **towards all men** un souverain qui a su faire preuve d'équité (envers tous) ‖ [reasonable, moral] juste, légitime; **a ~ cause** une juste cause; **he has ~ cause for complaint** il a de bonnes raisons pour se plaindre. -**2.** [deserved] juste, mérité; **a ~ reward** une juste récompense, une récompense bien méritée ❑ **he got his ~ deserts** il n'a eu que ce qu'il méritait, ce n'est que justice. -**3.** [accurate] juste, exact; **a ~ account of the facts** un compte-rendu exact des faits. -**4.** RELIG [righteous] juste.
◇ *npl*: **the ~** les justes *mpl*; **to sleep the sleep of the ~** dormir du sommeil du juste.

justice ['dʒʌstɪs] *n* -**1.** JUR justice *f*; **a court of ~** une cour de justice; **to dispense ~** rendre la justice; **to bring sb to ~** traduire qqn en justice ❑ **the Justice Department, the Department of Justice** *Am* ≃ le ministère de la Justice. -**2.** [fairness] justice *f*, équité *f*; **where's your sense of ~?** qu'est-il advenu de ton sens de la justice?; **they believe in the ~ of their cause** ils croient à la justesse de leur cause; **there's no ~ in their claim** leur demande est dénuée de fondement; **to do sb/sthg ~** [represent fairly] rendre justice à qqn/qqch; **the portrait didn't do her ~** son portrait ne lui rendait pas justice; **to do him ~, he wasn't informed of the decision** il faut lui rendre cette justice que OR il faut reconnaître que l'on ne l'avait pas mis au courant de la décision; **to do ~ to a meal** faire honneur à un repas. -**3.** [punishment, vengeance] justice *f*; **the whole town called for ~** la ville entière réclamait vengeance. -**4.** [judge] juge *m*; **Justice of the Peace** → **JP**.

justifiable ['dʒʌstɪˌfaɪəbl] *adj* justifiable; JUR légitime.

justifiable homicide *n* -**1.** [killing in self-defence] légitime défense *f*. -**2.** [state execution] application *f* de la peine de mort.

justifiably ['dʒʌstɪˌfaɪəblɪ] *adv* légitimement, à juste titre; **she was ~ angry** elle était fâchée, et à juste titre.

justification [ˌdʒʌstɪfɪ'keɪʃn] *n* -**1.** [gen] justification *f*; **what ~ do you have for such a statement?** comment justifiez-vous une telle affirmation?; **poverty is no ~ for theft** la pauvreté ne saurait justifier le vol; **he was accused of cheating, with some ~** il fut accusé d'avoir triché, non sans raison; **he spoke out in ~ of his actions** il a parlé pour justifier ses actes. -**2.** COMPUT & TYPO justification *f*; **left/right ~** justification à gauche/à droite.

justified ['dʒʌstɪfaɪd] *adj* -**1.** [right, fair - action] justifié, légitime; [- person]: **to be ~ in doing sthg** avoir raison de faire qqch. -**2.** COMPUT & TYPO [aligned] justifié.

justify ['dʒʌstɪfaɪ] (*pt* & *pp* **justified**) *vt* -**1.** [gen] justifier; **nothing can ~ such cruelty** rien ne saurait excuser OR justifier une telle cruauté; **she**

tried to ~ her behaviour to her parents elle a essayé de justifier son comportement aux yeux de ses parents. -**2.** COMPUT & TYPO justifier. -**3.** JUR: to ~ a lawsuit justifier une action en justice.

justly ['dʒʌstlɪ] *adv* -**1.** [fairly] justement, avec justice. -**2.** [accurately, deservedly] à juste titre; a ~ **unpopular decision** une décision impopulaire à juste titre.

jut [dʒʌt] (*pt* & *pp* **jutted**, *cont* **jutting**) *vi*: to ~ out dépasser, faire saillie; a **rocky peninsula** ~s **(out) into the sea** une péninsule rocheuse avance dans la mer; a **large rock jutted out over the path** un gros rocher surplombait le sentier.

jute [dʒuːt] *n* [textile] jute *m*.

Jute [dʒuːt] *n* Jute *mf*.

Jutland ['dʒʌtlənd] *pr n* Jütland *m*, Jylland *m*; **in** ~ dans le Jütland.

juvenile ['dʒuːvənaɪl] ◇ *adj* -**1.** [young, for young people] jeune, juvénile *fml*; ~ **literature** livres *mpl* pour enfants OR pour la jeunesse. -**2.** [immature] puéril, enfantin; **don't be so** ~! ne sois pas si puéril!
◇ *n* -**1.** *fml* mineur *m*, -e *f*. -**2.** THEAT jeune acteur *m*, -trice *f*.

juvenile court *n* tribunal *m* pour enfants *(10-16 ans)*.

juvenile delinquency *n* délinquance *f* juvénile.

juvenile delinquent *n* jeune délinquant *m*, -e *f*, mineur *m* délinquant, mineure *f* délinquante.

juvenilia [ˌdʒuːvə'nɪlɪə] *npl* œuvres *fpl* de jeunesse.

juxtapose [ˌdʒʌkstə'pəʊz] *vt* juxtaposer.

juxtaposition [ˌdʒʌkstəpə'zɪʃn] *n* juxtaposition *f*.

K

k (*pl* k's OR **ks**), **K** (*pl* K's OR Ks) [keɪ] *n* [letter] k *m*, K *m*.

K ◇ -**1.** (*written abbr of* kilobyte) K, Ko. -**2.** *written abbr of* Knight.
◇ *n* (*abbr of* thousand) K.

K2 [ˌkeɪ'tuː] *pr n* K2 *m*; they climbed ~ ils ont escaladé le (pic) K2.

kabob [kə'bɒb] = **kebab**.

Kabul ['kɑːbl] *pr n* Kaboul, Kabul.

Kabyle [kə'baɪl] (*pl inv* OR Kabyles) *n* -**1.** [person] Kabyle *mf*. -**2.** LING kabyle *m*.

Kabylia [kə'bɪlɪə] *pr n* Kabylie *f*.

Kabylian [kə'bɪlɪən] *adj* kabyle.

Kaf(f)ir ['kæfə^r] *n* -**1.** ▼ *SAfr terme raciste désignant un Noir*, ≃ nègre *m*, négresse *f*. -**2.** ETHN Cafre *mf*.

Kafkaesque [ˌkæfkə'esk] *adj* kafkaïen.

kaftan ['kæftæn] *n* caftan *m*, cafetan *m*.

kail [keɪl] = **kale**.

kainite ['kaɪnaɪt] *n* kaïnite *f*.

Kaiser ['kaɪzə^r] *n* Kaiser *m*.

Kalahari Desert [ˌkælə'hɑːrɪ-] *pr n*: the ~ le (désert du) Kalahari.

kale [keɪl] *n* chou *m* frisé.

kaleidoscope [kə'laɪdəskəʊp] *n literal & fig* kaléidoscope *m*.

kaleidoscopic [kəˌlaɪdə'skɒpɪk] *adj* kaléidoscopique.

Kalinin [kə'lɪnɪn] *pr n* Kalinine.

kamikaze [ˌkæmɪ'kɑːzɪ] ◇ *n* kamikaze *m*.
◇ *adj* -**1.** *literal*: ~ **pilot** kamikaze *m*; ~ **plane** kamikaze *m*, avion-suicide *m*. -**2.** *fig* suicidaire.

Kampala [kæm'pɑːlə] *pr n* Kampala.

Kampuchea [ˌkæmpuː'tʃɪə] *pr n* Kampuchéa *m*; in ~ au Kampuchéa.

Kampuchean [ˌkæmpuː'tʃɪən] ◇ *n* Cambodgien *m*, -enne *f*.
◇ *adj* cambodgien.

Kandinsky [kæn'dɪnskɪ] *pr n* Kandinsky.

kangaroo [ˌkæŋgə'ruː] *n* kangourou *m*.

kangaroo court *n* tribunal *m* illégal; [held by strikers, prisoners etc] ≃ tribunal *m* populaire.

kangaroo rat *n* rat-kangourou *m*.

Kansas ['kænzəs] *pr n* Kansas *m*; in ~ dans le Kansas.

Kantian ['kæntɪən] *adj* kantien.

kaolin ['keɪəlɪn] *n* kaolin *m*.

kaon ['keɪɒn] *n* kaon *m*.

kapok ['keɪpɒk] ◇ *n* kapok *m*.
◇ *comp* de kapok.

kaput *inf* [kə'pʊt] *adj* fichu, foutu.

Karachi [kə'rɑːtʃɪ] *pr n* Karachi.

karat *Am* = **carat**.

karate [kə'rɑːtɪ] *n* karaté *m*; ~ **chop** coup *m* de karaté *(donné avec le tranchant de la main)*.

Karelia [kə'riːlɪə] *pr n* Carélie *f*.

karma ['kɑːmə] *n* karma *m*, karman *m*.

Karnak ['kɑːnæk] *pr n* Carnac, Karnac.

kart [kɑːt] ◇ *n* kart *m*.
◇ *vi*: to go ~**ing** faire du karting.

karyotype ['kærɪətaɪp] *n* caryotype *m*.

Kashmir [ˌkæʃ'mɪə^r] *n* GEOG Cachemire *m*, Kashmir *m*.

Kashmiri [kæʃ'mɪərɪ] ◇ *n* -**1.** [person] Cachemirien *m*, -enne *f*. -**2.** LING kashmiri *m*.
◇ *adj* cachemirien.

Katar ['kætɑː^r] *pr n* Katar *m*, Qatar *m*; in ~ au Qatar.

Katmandu [ˌkætmæn'duː] *pr n* Katmandou, Katmandu.

katydid ['keɪtɪdɪd] *n* sauterelle *f* (d'Amérique du Nord).

kauri ['kaʊrɪ] *n* kauri *m*, kaori *m*.

kayak ['kaɪæk] *n* kayak *m*.

kayo *inf* [keɪ'əʊ] (*pl* kayos, *pt & pp* kayoed)
◇ *n* SPORT K-O *m*.
◇ *vt* mettre K-O.

Kazakh [kæ'zæk] ◇ *n* Kasakh *m*, -e *f*.
◇ *adj* kasakh.

Kazakhstan [ˌkæzæk'stɑːn] *pr n* Kazakhstan *m*; in ~ au Kazakhstan.

kazoo [kə'zuː] *n* mirliton *m*.

KC (*abbr of* King's Counsel) *n Br avocat de la Couronne*.

kcal (*written abbr of* kilocalorie) Kcal.

kd (*abbr of* knocked down) *adj livré en kit, à monter soi-même*.

kebab [kɪ'bæb] *n* chiche-kebab *m*; ~ **house** *restaurant grec ou turc*.

keck *inf* [kek] *vi Am* avoir des haut-le-cœur, avoir mal au cœur.

kedge [kedʒ] ◇ *n* ancre *f* à jet.
◇ *vt* haler, touer.
◇ *vi* se haler, se touer.

kedgeree ['kedʒəriː] *n Br plat à base de riz, de poisson et d'œufs*.

keel [kiːl] ◇ *n* -**1.** NAUT quille *f*; on an even ~ *literal* à tirant d'eau égal; *fig* en équilibre. -**2.** *lit* [ship] navire *m*.
◇ *vi* chavirer.
◇ *vt* faire chavirer, cabaner.
◆ **keel over** ◇ *vi insep* -**1.** NAUT chavirer. -**2.** [fall] s'effondrer; [faint] s'évanouir.
◇ *vt sep* NAUT faire chavirer, cabaner.

keelhaul ['kiːlhɔːl] *vt* -**1.** NAUT faire passer sous la quille. -**2.** *inf fig* [rebuke] houspiller, enguirlander.

keen [kiːn] ◇ *adj* -**1.** *Br* [eager, enthusiastic] passionné, enthousiaste; **she's a ~ gardener** c'est une passionnée de jardinage; **he was ~ to talk to her** il tenait à OR voulait absolument lui parler; **I'm ~ that they should get a second chance** je tiens à ce qu'ils aient une deuxième chance; **I'm not so ~ on the idea** l'idée ne m'enchante OR ne m'emballe pas vraiment; **they aren't so ~ on going out tonight** ils n'ont pas (très) envie OR ça ne leur dit pas grand-chose de sortir ce soir; **Susan is really ~ on Tom** Susan a vraiment le béguin pour Tom ❑ **to be as ~ as mustard** *inf* [enthusiastic] être très enthousiaste; [clever] avoir l'esprit vif. -**2.** [senses, mind, wit] fin, vif; **to have a ~ sense of smell** avoir un odorat subtil; **to have a ~ eye** avoir le coup d'œil. -**3.** [fierce - competition, rivalry] acharné. -**4.** *Br* [cold - wind] glacial. -**5.** *Br* [sharp - blade, knife] affilé. -**6.** [intense] intense, profond; **she felt a ~ desire to break free** elle ressentit une profonde envie de partir. -**7.** *Br* [very competitive]: ~ **prices** des prix *mpl* imbattables.
◇ *vi & vt dial* [mourn] pleurer.
◇ *n dial* [dirge] mélopée *f* funèbre.

keenly ['kiːnlɪ] *adv Br*. -**1.** [deeply, intensely] vivement, profondément; **she's ~ interested in the project** elle s'intéresse vivement OR elle porte un vif intérêt au projet; **he felt her death ~** sa mort l'a profondément affecté || [fiercely] âprement; **a ~ contested game** un match âprement disputé. -**2.** [eagerly] ardemment, avec enthousiasme; [attentively] attentivement.

keenness ['kiːnnɪs] *n* -**1.** *Br* [enthusiasm] enthousiasme *m*, empressement *m*, ardeur *f*; **there's no doubting her ~ to help** son empressement à rendre service ne fait aucun doute. -**2.** [sharpness - of blade, senses] acuité *f*, finesse *f*; ~ **of eye** acuité *f* visuelle; ~ **of mind** perspicacité *f*, finesse *f*. -**3.** [intensity, fierceness] intensité *f*, âpreté *f*.

keep [kiːp] (*pt & pp* kept [kept]) ◇ *vt* **A.** -**1.** [retain - receipt, change] garder; **she's kept her English accent** elle a gardé son accent anglais; **please ~ your seats** veuillez rester assis; **he's never kept a job for more than a year** il n'a jamais gardé OR conservé le même emploi plus d'un an; **to ~ a secret** garder un secret; **to ~ one's temper** garder son calme; **to ~ sthg to o.s.** garder qqch pour soi; **they kept the discovery to themselves** ils ont gardé la découverte pour eux; **~ it to yourself!** garde-ça pour toi!; **you can ~ your snide remarks to yourself!** tu peux garder tes remarques déplaisantes pour toi! ❑ **to ~ o.s. to o.s.** rester dans son coin; **they ~ themselves very much to themselves** ce sont des gens plutôt discrets; **if that's your idea of a holiday, you can ~ it!** *inf* si c'est ça ton idée des vacances, tu peux te la garder!; **tell him he can ~ his rotten job!** *inf* dis-lui qu'il peut se le garder, son sale boulot! -**2.** [save] garder; **we've kept some cake for you** on t'a gardé du gâteau; **can you ~ my seat?** pouvez-vous (me) garder ma place?; **we'll ~ the tickets for you until Wednesday** nous vous garderons les tickets jusqu'à mercredi; **I'm ~ing this cigar for later** je garde ce cigare pour plus tard. -**3.** [store, put] mettre, garder; **she ~s**

her money in the bank elle met son argent à la banque; I ~ my comb in my pocket je mets toujours mon peigne dans ma poche; how long can you ~ fish in the freezer? combien de temps peut-on garder OR conserver du poisson au congélateur?; where do you ~ the playing cards? où est-ce que vous rangez les cartes à jouer?; I've got nowhere to ~ my books je n'ai nulle part où mettre mes livres.
B. -**1.** *(with adj complement)* [maintain in the specified state or place]: to ~ sb quiet faire tenir qqn tranquille; to ~ sthg warm garder qqch au chaud; the noise kept me awake le bruit m'a empêché de dormir, le bruit m'a tenu éveillé; the doors are kept locked les portes sont toujours fermées à clef; to ~ sthg up to date tenir qqch à jour || *(with adv complement)*: a well-/badly-kept office un bureau bien/mal tenu; the weather kept us indoors le temps nous a empêchés de sortir; he kept his hands in his pockets il a gardé les mains dans les poches; ~ your eyes on the red dot ne quittez pas le point rouge des yeux; ~ the noise to a minimum essayez de ne pas faire trop de bruit || *(with present participle)*: to ~ sb waiting faire attendre qqn; ~ the engine running n'arrêtez pas le moteur; we kept the fire burning all night nous avons laissé le feu allumé toute la nuit; to ~ sthg going [organization, business] faire marcher qqch; [music, conversation] ne pas laisser qqch s'arrêter; alcohol is the only thing that ~s me going l'alcool est la seule chose qui me permette de tenir. -**2.** [delay] retenir; I hope I've not kept you j'espère que je ne vous ai pas retenu; what kept you? qu'est-ce qui t'a retenu? || [distract]: I don't want to ~ you from your work je ne veux pas vous empêcher de travailler. -**3.** [not allow to leave] garder; to ~ sb in hospital/prison garder qqn à l'hôpital/en prison.
C. -**1.** [support]: he hardly earns enough to ~ himself il gagne à peine de quoi vivre; she has a husband and six children to ~ elle a un mari et six enfants à nourrir; it ~s me in cigarette money ça paie mes cigarettes. -**2.** [have as dependant or employee] avoir; he ~s a mistress il a une maîtresse; they ~ a maid and a gardener ils ont une bonne et un jardinier. -**3.** [run - shop, business] tenir; to ~ house for sb tenir la maison de qqn. -**4.** COMM [have in stock] vendre; I'm afraid we don't ~ that article je regrette, nous ne vendons pas OR nous ne faisons pas cet article. -**5.** [farm animals] élever; they ~ pigs/bees ils élèvent des porcs/des abeilles. -**6.** [diary, list etc] tenir; my secretary ~s my accounts ma secrétaire tient OR s'occupe de ma comptabilité.
D. -**1.** [fulfil - a promise, one's word] tenir. -**2.** [observe - silence] observer; [- the Sabbath] respecter; [- law] respecter, observer. -**3.** [uphold, maintain] maintenir; to ~ order/the peace maintenir l'ordre/la paix; to ~ a lookout faire le guet. -**4.** [guard] garder; to ~ goal être gardien de but; God ~ you! *arch* Dieu vous garde!
E. -**1.** [prevent]: to ~ sb from doing sthg empêcher qqn de faire qqch; nothing will ~ me from going rien ne m'empêchera d'y aller. -**2.** [withhold]: to ~ sthg from sb cacher qqch à qqn; to ~ information from sb dissimuler des informations à qqn; I can't ~ anything from her je ne peux rien lui cacher; they deliberately kept the news from his family ils ont fait exprès de cacher les nouvelles à sa famille.
◇ *vi* -**1.** *(with present participle)* [continue] continuer; letters ~ pouring in les lettres continuent d'affluer; don't ~ apologizing arrête de t'excuser; they ~ teasing him ils n'arrêtent pas de le taquiner; she had several failures but kept trying elle a essuyé plusieurs échecs mais elle a persévéré; to ~ going: ~ going till you get to the crossroads allez jusqu'au croisement; she kept going when everyone else had given up elle a continué alors que tous les autres avaient abandonné; with so few customers, it's a wonder the shop ~s going avec si peu de clients, c'est un miracle que le magasin ne ferme pas. -**2.** [stay, remain] rester, se tenir; ~ calm! restez calmes!, du calme!; she kept warm by jumping up and down elle se tenait chaud en sautillant sur place; ~ to the path ne vous écartez pas du chemin; to ~ in touch with sb rester en contact avec qqn; to ~ to o.s. se tenir à l'écart. -**3.** [last, stay fresh] se conserver, se garder; it will ~ for a week in the refrigerator vous pouvez le garder OR conserver au réfrigérateur pendant une semaine; the news will ~ (until tomorrow) *fig* la nouvelle peut attendre (jusqu'à demain). -**4.** [in health] aller; how are you ~ing? comment allez-vous?, comment ça va?; I'm ~ing well je vais bien, ça va (bien).
◇ *n* -**1.** [board and lodging]: the grant is supposed to be enough to pay your ~ la bourse est censée vous permettre de vous nourrir et de vous loger; he gives his mother £50 a week for his ~ il donne 50 livres par semaine à sa mère pour sa pension; to earn one's ~ *payer ou travailler pour être nourri et logé*; our cat certainly earns his ~ notre chat vaut bien ce qu'il nous coûte. -**2.** [in castle] donjon *m*. -**3.** *phr*: for ~s *inf* pour de bon.
◆ **keep at** ◇ *vt insep* -**1.** [pester] harceler; she kept at him until he agreed elle l'a harcelé jusqu'à ce qu'il accepte. -**2.** *phr*: to ~ at it persévérer; he kept at it until he found a solution il a persévéré jusqu'à trouver une solution.
◇ *vt sep*: to ~ sb at it: the sergeant kept us hard at it all morning le sergent nous a fait travailler toute la matinée.
◆ **keep away** ◇ *vt sep* tenir éloigné, empêcher d'approcher; ~ the baby away (from the fire) empêche le bébé d'approcher (du feu); spectators were kept away by the fear of violence la peur de la violence tenait les spectateurs à distance.
◇ *vi insep* ne pas s'approcher; ~ away from the cooker ne t'approche pas de la cuisinière; I'd ~ away from those people if I were you j'éviterais ces gens-là si j'étais vous; I felt my visits were unwelcome and so I kept away je n'avais pas l'impression que mes visites étaient bienvenues, alors je n'y suis plus allé.
◆ **keep back** ◇ *vt sep* -**1.** [keep at a distance - crowd, spectators] tenir éloigné, empêcher de s'approcher. -**2.** [not reveal - names, facts] cacher; I'm sure he's ~ing something back (from us) je suis sûr qu'il (nous) cache quelque chose. -**3.** [retain] retenir; part of our salary is kept back every month une partie de notre salaire est retenue tous les mois. -**4.** [detain] retenir; to be kept back after school être en retenue. -**5.** [restrain] retenir; he struggled to ~ back the tears il s'est efforcé de retenir ses larmes.
◇ *vi insep* rester en arrière, ne pas s'approcher; ~ back! restez où vous êtes!, n'approchez pas!
◆ **keep behind** *vt sep* [after meeting, class] retenir.
◆ **keep down** ◇ *vt sep* -**1.** [not raise] ne pas lever; ~ your head down! ne lève pas la tête!, garde la tête baissée!; ~ your voices down! parlez doucement! -**2.** [prevent from increasing] limiter; we must ~ our expenses down il faut que nous limitions nos dépenses; our aim is to ~ prices down notre but est d'empêcher les prix d'augmenter; to ~ one's weight down garder la ligne. -**3.** [repress] réprimer; the army kept the population/the revolt down l'armée a tenu la population en respect/a maté la révolte || [control - vermin, weeds] empêcher de proliférer; you can't ~ a good man down rien n'arrêtera un homme de mérite. -**4.** [food] garder; she can't ~ solid foods down son estomac ne garde aucun aliment solide. -**5.** SCH faire redoubler; to be kept down a year redoubler une année.
◇ *vi insep* ne pas se lever; ~ down! ne vous relevez pas!
◆ **keep from** *vt insep* s'empêcher de, se retenir de; I couldn't ~ from laughing je n'ai pas pu m'empêcher de rire.
◆ **keep in** ◇ *vt sep* -**1.** [not allow out] empêcher de sortir; SCH donner une consigne à, garder en retenue; the bad weather kept us in le mauvais temps nous a empêchés de sortir. -**2.** [fire] entretenir. -**3.** [stomach] rentrer.
◇ *vi insep* [not go out] ne pas sortir, rester chez soi.
◆ **keep in with** *vt insep*: to ~ in with sb rester en bons termes avec qqn.
◆ **keep off** ◇ *vt sep* -**1.** [dogs, birds, trespassers] éloigner; [rain, sun]: this cream will ~ the mosquitoes off cette crème vous/le/te *etc* protégera contre les moustiques; ~ your hands off! pas touche!, bas les pattes! -**2.** [coat, hat] ne pas remettre.
◇ *vt insep* -**1.** [avoid] éviter; ~ off drink and tobacco évitez l'alcool et le tabac; we tried to ~ off the topic on a essayé d'éviter le sujet. -**2.** [keep at a distance from] ne pas s'approcher de; '~ off the grass' 'pelouse interdite'.
◇ *vi insep* -**1.** [keep at a distance] ne pas s'approcher; that's mine, ~ off! c'est à moi, n'y touchez pas! -**2.** [weather]: the rain/snow kept off il n'a pas plu/neigé; if the storm ~s off si l'orage n'éclate pas.
◆ **keep on** ◇ *vt sep* -**1.** [coat, hat] garder. -**2.** [employee] garder.
◇ *vi insep* -**1.** [continue] continuer; ~ on until you come to a crossroads continuez jusqu'à ce que vous arriviez à un carrefour; they kept on talking ils ont continué à parler; I ~ on making the same mistakes je fais toujours les mêmes erreurs. -**2.** *inf* [talk continually] parler sans cesse; he ~s on about his wife and kids il n'arrête pas de parler de sa femme et de ses gosses; don't ~ on about it! ça suffit, j'ai compris!
◆ **keep on at** *vt insep* [pester] harceler.
◆ **keep out** ◇ *vt sep* empêcher d'entrer; a guard dog to ~ intruders out un chien de garde pour décourager les intrus; a scarf to ~ the cold out une écharpe pour vous protéger du froid.
◇ *vi insep* ne pas entrer; '~ out' 'défense d'entrer', 'entrée interdite'; to ~ out of an argument ne pas intervenir dans une discussion.
◆ **keep to** *vt insep* -**1.** [observe, respect] respecter; you must ~ to the deadlines vous devez respecter les délais. -**2.** [not deviate from] ne pas s'écarter de; ~ to the point OR the subject! ne vous écartez pas du sujet! -**3.** [stay in] garder; to ~ to one's room/bed garder la chambre/le lit.
◆ **keep together** ◇ *vt sep* ne pas séparer; I'd like them to be kept together j'aimerais qu'ils ne soient pas séparés.
◇ *vi insep* rester ensemble.
◆ **keep under** *vt sep* -**1.** [repress] réprimer. -**2.** [with drug]: he's being kept under with Penthotal® on le garde sous Penthotal®.
◆ **keep up** ◇ *vt sep* -**1.** [prevent from falling - shelf, roof] maintenir; I need a belt to ~ my trousers up j'ai besoin d'une ceinture pour empêcher mon pantalon de tomber || *fig*: it will ~ prices up ça empêchera les prix de baisser; it's to ~ the troops' morale up c'est pour maintenir le moral des troupes; ~ your spirits up! ne te laisse pas abattre! -**2.** [maintain - attack, bombardment] poursuivre; [- correspondence, contacts, conversation] entretenir; you have to ~ up the payments on ne peut pas interrompre les versements; she kept up a constant flow of questions elle ne cessait de poser des questions; it's a tradition which hasn't been kept up c'est une tradition qui s'est perdue ❑ ~ up the good work! c'est du bon travail, continuez!; you're doing well, ~ it up! c'est bien, continuez!; once they start talking politics, they can ~ it up all night une fois lancés sur la politique, ils sont capables d'y passer la nuit. -**3.** [prevent from going to bed] empêcher de dormir; the baby kept us up all night nous n'avons pas pu fermer l'œil de la nuit à cause du bébé. -**4.** [not allow to deteriorate - house,

garden] entretenir; the lawns haven't been kept up les pelouses n'ont pas été entretenues; she goes to evening classes to ~ up her French elle suit des cours du soir pour entretenir son français.

◇ *vi insep* -**1.** [continue] continuer; if this noise ~s up much longer, I'll scream si ce bruit continue, je crois que je vais hurler. -**2.** [not fall] se maintenir; if prices ~ up si les prix se maintiennent; how are their spirits ~ing up? est-ce qu'ils gardent le moral? -**3.** [not fall behind] suivre; he's finding it hard to ~ up in his new class il a du mal à suivre dans sa nouvelle classe; things change so quickly I can't ~ up les choses bougent si vite que j'ai du mal à suivre.

◆ **keep up with** *vt insep* -**1.** [stay abreast of]: to ~ up with the news se tenir au courant de OR suivre l'actualité. -**2.** [keep in touch with] rester en contact avec; have you kept up with your cousin in Australia? est-ce que tu es resté en contact avec ton cousin d'Australie?

keeper ['kiːpəʳ] *n* -**1.** [gen] gardien *m*, -enne *f*; [in museum] conservateur *m*, -trice *f*; am I my brother's ~? BIBLE suis-je le gardien de mon frère? -**2.** [goal keeper] goal *m*, gardien *m* de but. -**3.** TECH [safety catch] cran *m* de sûreté.

-keeper *in cpds*: shop~ commerçant *m*, -e *f*; bee~ apiculteur *m*, -trice *f*.

keep-fit *n* culture *f* physique, gymnastique *f* (d'entretien); she goes to ~ (classes) every week toutes les semaines elle va à son cours de gymnastique.

keeping ['kiːpɪŋ] *n* -**1.** [care, charge] garde *f*; he left the manuscript in his wife's ~ il a confié le manuscrit à son épouse; in safe ~ en sécurité, sous bonne garde. -**2.** [observing - of rule, custom etc] observation *f*, observance *f*.

◆ **in keeping** *adj phr* conforme à; their dress was not at all in ~ with the seriousness of the occasion leur tenue ne convenait pas du tout à la gravité de la circonstance.

◆ **in keeping with** *prep phr* conformément à; in ~ with government policy conformément à la politique du gouvernement.

◆ **out of keeping** *adj phr*: to be out of ~ with être en désaccord avec.

keepsake ['kiːpseɪk] *n* souvenir *m*.

kef [kef] = **kif**.

keg [keg] *n* -**1.** [barrel] tonnelet *m*, baril *m*; [of fish] baril; [of beer] tonnelet; [of herring] caque *f*. -**2.** [beer] bière *f* (à la) pression.

kelly-green ['kelɪ-] *adj Am* vert-pomme.

kelp [kelp] *n* varech *m*.

kelvin ['kelvɪn] *n* kelvin *m*.

Kempton Park ['kemptən-] *pr n* *champ de courses dans le Surrey*.

ken [ken] (*pt* & *pp* kenned, *cont* kenning) ◇ *n dated* OR *hum*: it is beyond my ~ cela dépasse mon entendement.

◇ *vi* & *vt Scot* connaître, savoir.

Kennedy ['kenɪdɪ] *pr n* Kennedy; the ~ assassination l'assassinat *m* de Kennedy.

THE KENNEDY ASSASSINATION:

Assassinat, le 22 novembre 1963, du jeune président américain J.F. Kennedy, à Dallas, dans le Texas. Le meurtrier présumé, Lee Harvey Oswald, fut arrêté mais assassiné à son tour deux jours plus tard. Bien qu'officiellement close, cette affaire suscite encore aujourd'hui une controverse, en particulier de la part de ceux qui y voient un complot mettant en cause la CIA.

---

kennel ['kenl] (*Br pt* & *pp* kennelled, *Am pt* & *pp* kenneled) ◇ *n* -**1.** *Br* [doghouse] niche *f*. -**2.** *Am* [for boarding or breeding] chenil *m*.

◇ *vt* mettre dans un chenil.

◆ **kennels** *n Br* [for boarding or breeding] chenil *m*.

Kentish ['kentɪʃ] *adj* du Kent.

Kent State ['kent,steɪt] *pr n* Kent State.

THE KENT STATE INCIDENT:

Incident qui eut lieu le 4 mai 1970 sur le campus de Kent State University (dans l'Ohio) entre des étudiants manifestant contre la guerre du Viêt-nam et la Garde nationale américaine. Celle-ci riposta par balles aux jets de pierres, tuant quatre personnes et en blessant une dizaine.

Kentucky [ken'tʌkɪ] *pr n* Kentucky *m*; in ~ dans le Kentucky.

Kenya ['kenjə] *pr n* Kenya *m*; in ~ au Kenya.

Kenyan ['kenjən] ◇ *n* Kenyan *m*, -e *f*.

◇ *adj* kenyan.

kepi ['keɪpɪ] *n* képi *m*.

kept [kept] ◇ *pt* & *pp* → **keep**.

◇ *adj hum* OR *pej*: a ~ man un homme entretenu; a ~ woman une femme entretenue.

keratin ['kerətɪn] *n* kératine *f*.

kerb [kɜːb] *n* bord *m* du trottoir; he stepped off the ~ il est descendu du trottoir; the bus pulled into the ~ l'autobus s'est arrêté le long du trottoir.

kerb crawler *n personne qui longe le trottoir en voiture à la recherche d'une prostituée*.

kerb crawling *n recherche d'une prostituée en voiture*.

kerb market *n* ST. EX marché *m* officieux *(où les valeurs sont échangées en dehors des heures d'ouverture de la Bourse)*.

kerbstone ['kɜːbstəʊn] *n* bordure *f* de trottoir.

kerb weight *n* poids *m* à vide.

kerchief ['kɜːtʃɪf] *n dated* foulard *m*, fichu *m*.

kerfuffle *inf* [kə'fʌfl] *n Br* [disorder] désordre *m*, chahut *m*; [fight] bagarre *f*; there was a ~ at the exit il y a eu des remous à la sortie.

kernel ['kɜːnl] *n* -**1.** [of nut, fruit stone] amande *f*; [of cereal] graine *f*. -**2.** *fig* [heart, core] cœur *m*, noyau *m*.

kerosene, kerosine ['kerəsiːn] ◇ *n Am* [for aircraft] kérosène *m*; [for lamps, stoves] pétrole *m*.

◇ *comp* [lamp, stove] à pétrole.

kestrel ['kestrəl] *n* crécerelle *f*.

ketch [ketʃ] *n* ketch *m*.

ketchup ['ketʃəp] *n* ketchup *m*.

ketone ['kiːtəʊn] *n* cétone *f*.

kettle ['ketl] *n* -**1.** [for water] bouilloire *f*; to put the ~ on mettre de l'eau à chauffer; the ~'s boiling l'eau bout. -**2.** [for fish] poissonnière *f*; that's another OR a different ~ of fish *inf* c'est une autre paire de manches; this is a fine OR pretty ~ of fish! *inf Br* quelle salade!, quel sac de nœuds!

kettledrum ['ketldrʌm] *n* timbale *f*.

key [kiː] ◇ *n* -**1.** [for lock] clé *f*, clef *f*; [for clock, mechanism etc] clé *f*, remontoir *m*; the ~ to the drawer la clé du tiroir; where are the car ~s? où sont les clés de la voiture?; he was given the ~s to the city on lui a remis les clés de la ville ❑ to have the ~ of the door atteindre sa majorité; the (House of) Keys *une des deux chambres du parlement de l'île de Man*. -**2.** *fig* [means] clé *f*, clef *f*; the ~ to happiness la clé du bonheur; communication is the ~ to a good partnership la communication est la clef d'une bonne association. -**3.** [on typewriter, computer, piano, organ] touche *f*; [on wind instrument] clé *f*, clef *f*. -**4.** MUS ton *m*; in the ~ of B minor en si mineur; to play in/off ~ jouer dans le ton/dans le mauvais ton; to sing in/off ~ chanter juste/faux. -**5.** [on map, diagram] légende *f*. -**6.** [answers] corrigé *m*, réponses *fpl*; the ~ to the exercises is on page 155 le corrigé des exercices se trouve page 155. -**7.** TECH clé *f* OR clef *f* (de serrage). -**8.** [island] îlot *m*; [reef] (petit) récif *m (au large de la Floride)*. -**9.** *drugs sl* kilo *m (de marijuana)*.

◇ *adj* clé, clef; ~ industries industries clés, industries-clés; she was appointed to a ~ post elle a été nommée à un poste clé; a ~ factor un élément décisif; the ~ conspirator la cheville ouvrière du complot; one of the ~ issues in the election un des enjeux fondamentaux de ces élections.

◇ *vt* -**1.** [data, text] saisir, entrer. -**2.** [adjust, adapt] adapter; his remarks were ~ed to the occasion ses commentaires étaient adaptés aux circonstances.

◆ **key in** *vt sep* COMPUT [word, number] entrer; [data, text] saisir.

key bar *n* [in shop] stand *m* de clef-minute.

keyboard ['kiːbɔːd] ◇ *n* [of instrument, typewriter, computer] clavier *m*; who's on ~s? qui est aux claviers? ❑ ~ instrument instrument *m* à clavier; ~ operator claviste *mf*.

◇ *vt* saisir.

keyboarder ['kiːbɔːdəʳ] *n* TYPO claviste *mf*.

keyboardist ['kiːbɔːdɪst] *n* [pianist] pianiste *mf*; [on synthesizer] joueur *m*, -euse *f* de synthétiseur.

keyed up [kiːd-] *adj* surexcité; the fans were all ~ for the match les supporters attendaient le match dans un état de surexcitation.

key grip *n* CIN technicien *m*, -enne *f* en chef *(chargé(e) de l'installation des décors et des rails de caméra au cinéma)*.

keyhole ['kiːhəʊl] *n* trou *m* de serrure; he looked through the ~ il regarda par le trou de la serrure.

keying ['kiːɪŋ] *n* saisie *f*.

key money *n* pas *m* de porte.

Keynesian ['keɪnzɪən] *adj* keynésien.

keynote ['kiːnəʊt] ◇ *n* -**1.** [main point] point *m* capital; industrial recovery is the ~ of government policy le redressement industriel constitue l'axe central de la politique gouvernementale. -**2.** MUS tonique *f*.

◇ *adj* [address] introductif; [speaker] principal; ~ speech discours *m* introductif OR liminaire.

◇ *vt* insister sur, mettre en relief; she ~d the need for party unity elle a insisté sur la nécessité de cohésion au sein du parti.

keypad ['kiːpæd] *n* pavé *m* numérique.

keyphone ['kiːfəʊn] *n* téléphone *m* à touches.

keypunch ['kiːpʌntʃ] *n* perforatrice *f* à clavier.

key ring *n* porte-clés *m inv*.

key signature *n* MUS armature *f*, armure *f*.

keystone ['kiːstəʊn] *n* CONSTR & *fig* clé *f* OR clef *f* de voûte.

keystroke ['kiːstrəʊk] *n* touche *f*; codes are entered with a single ~ une seule touche suffit pour entrer les codes.

key word *n* mot-clef *m*.

kg (*written abbr of* kilogram) kg.

KGB *pr n* KGB *m*.

khaki ['kɑːkɪ] ◇ *adj* kaki *(inv)*.

◇ *n* [colour] kaki *m*; [material] treillis *m*.

khaki election *n Br élection dont la date est fixée dans la foulée d'une victoire militaire, assurant le succès du gouvernement au pouvoir*.

khan [kɑːn] *n* khan *m*.

Khania [xɑː'njə] *pr n* Khania, La Canée.

Khartoum [kɑː'tuːm] *pr n* Khartoum.

Khmer [kmeəʳ] ◇ *n* -**1.** [person] Khmer *m* -ère *f*; ~ Rouge Khmer rouge. -**2.** LING khmer *m*.

◇ *adj* khmer.

kibbutz [kɪ'bʊts] (*pl* kibbutzes OR kibbutzim [kɪbʊt'sɪm]) *n* kibboutz *m*.

kibitz *inf* ['kɪbɪts] *vi Am* [gen] mettre son grain de sel; [during card game] *commenter une partie sans y avoir été invité*.

kibitzer *inf* ['kɪbɪtsəʳ] *n Am* [gen] mouche *f* du coche; he's a real ~ il fourre son nez partout ‖ [at card game] donneur *m*, -euse *f* de conseils.

kibosh *inf* ['kaɪbɒʃ] *n*: to put the ~ on sthg ficher qqch en l'air.

kick [kɪk] ◇ *vt* -**1.** donner un coup de pied à OR dans; she ~ed the ball over the wall elle a envoyé la balle par-dessus le mur (d'un coup de pied); I ~ed the door open j'ai ouvert la porte d'un coup de pied; he had been ~ed to death il avait été tué à coups de pieds; the dancers ~ed their legs in the air les danseurs lançaient les jambes en l'air; to ~ a penalty [in rugby] marquer OR réussir une pénalité; to ~ a ba into touch mettre la balle en touche, botter (la balle) en touche ❑ to ~ the bucket *inf* passer l'arme à gauche, casser sa pipe; to ~ sb into touch *inf Br* mettre qqn sur la touche; you shouldn't ~ a man when he's down il ne faut pas s'attaquer à quelqu'un sans défense; I could have ~ed myself! je me serais donné des gifles!; they must be ~ing themselves ils doivent s'en mordre les doigts; he was ~ed upstairs *inf Br* [promoted] on l'a promu pour se débarrasser de lui; *Br* POL on s'est débarrassé de lui en l'envoyant siéger à la chambre des Lords; to ~ one's heels *inf* faire le pied de grue, poireauter. -**2.** *phr*: to ~ the habit *inf*: I used to smoke but I've managed to ~ the habit je fumais, mais j'ai réussi à m'arrêter.

◇ *vi* -**1.** donner OR lancer un coup de pied; I told you not to ~! je t'ai dit de ne pas donner de coups de pied!; they dragged him away ~ing and screaming il se débattait comme un beau diable quand ils l'ont emmené; the baby lay on its back ~ing le bébé gigotait, allongé sur le dos || [in rugby]: to ~ for touch chercher une touche ❑ to ~ over the traces *Br* ruer dans les brancards. -**2.** [in dance] lancer les jambes en l'air. -**3.** [gun] reculer.

◇ *n* -**1.** coup *m* de pied; a long ~ upfield un long coup de pied en avant; to aim a ~ at sb/sthg lancer OR donner un coup de pied en direction de qqn/qqch ❑ it was a real ~ in the teeth for him *inf* ça lui a fait un sacré coup; she needs a ~ up the backside *inf* OR in the pants *inf* elle a besoin d'un coup de pied aux fesses. -**2.** *inf* [thrill] plaisir *m*; to get a ~ from OR out of doing sthg prendre son pied à faire qqch; to do sthg for ~s faire qqch pour rigoler OR pour s'amuser. -**3.** *inf* [strength - of drink]: his cocktail had quite a ~ son cocktail était costaud; this beer's got no ~ in it cette bière est un peu plate OR manque de vigueur. -**4.** *inf* [vitality, force] entrain *m*, allant *m*; she's still got plenty of ~ in her elle a encore du ressort. -**5.** *inf* [fad] engouement *m*; she's on a yoga ~ at the moment elle est emballée OR elle ne jure que par le yoga en ce moment. -**6.** [recoil - of gun] recul *m*.

◆ **kick about** ◇ *vi insep inf Br* traîner; don't just leave your clothes ~ing about anywhere ne laisse donc pas traîner tes vêtements n'importe où.

◇ *vt sep* = **kick around**.

◆ **kick against** *inf vt insep* regimber contre; he was always trying to ~ against the system il n'arrêtait pas de regimber contre le système ❑ to ~ against the pricks se rebeller en pure perte.

◆ **kick around** ◇ *vt sep* -**1.** *literal*: to ~ a ball around jouer au ballon; they were ~ing a tin can around ils jouaient au foot avec une boîte de conserves. -**2.** *inf fig* [idea] débattre; we ~ed a few ideas around on a discuté à bâtons rompus. -**3.** *inf fig* [mistreat] malmener, maltraiter; I'm not going to let her ~ me around any more je ne vais plus me laisser faire par elle.

◇ *vi insep inf* traîner; who are you ~ing around with these days? avec qui tu traînes en ce moment?; I know my old overalls are ~ing around here somewhere je suis sûr que mon vieux bleu de travail traîne quelque part par là.

◆ **kick at** = **kick against**.

◆ **kick back** *vt sep* -**1.** [ball] renvoyer du pied. -**2.** *inf Am* [money] verser; he got 10 % ~ed back on the contract il a touché 10 % du contrat en dessous-de-table.

◆ **kick down** *vt sep* [person] abattre OR faire tomber à coups de pied; [door] défoncer à coups de pied.

◆ **kick in** ◇ *vt sep* défoncer à coups de pied; I'll ~ his teeth in! *inf* je vais lui casser la figure!

◇ *vi insep inf* entrer en action.

◆ **kick off** ◇ *vt sep* -**1.** [shoes] enlever d'un coup de pied. -**2.** *inf fig* [start] démarrer. -**3.** SPORT donner le coup d'envoi à.

◇ *vi insep* -**1.** SPORT donner le coup d'envoi; they ~ed off an hour late le match a commencé avec une heure de retard. -**2.** *inf fig* [start] démarrer, commencer.

◆ **kick out** ◇ *vt sep inf* [person] *literal* chasser à coups de pied; *fig* foutre dehors.

◇ *vi insep* -**1.** [person] lancer des coups de pieds; [horse, donkey] ruer. -**2.** *inf* [complain] râler, rouspéter; [revolt] se révolter.

◆ **kick over** *vt sep* renverser du pied OR d'un coup de pied.

◆ **kick up** *vt sep* -**1.** [dust, sand] faire voler (du pied). -**2.** *inf fig*: to ~ up a fuss OR a row (about sthg) faire toute une histoire OR tout un plat (au sujet de qqch); to ~ up a din OR a racket faire un boucan d'enfer.

kickback ['kɪkbæk] *n* -**1.** *inf* [bribe] dessous-de-table *m inv*, pot-de-vin *m*. -**2.** TECH recul *m*. -**3.** [backlash] contrecoup *m*.

kickoff ['kɪkɒf] *n* -**1.** SPORT coup *m* d'envoi; the ~ is at 3pm le coup d'envoi sera donné à 15h. -**2.** *inf Br fig*: for a ~ pour commencer.

kickpleat ['kɪkpliːt] *n* [in skirt] pli *m* d'aisance.

kickstand ['kɪkstænd] *n* béquille *f* (de moto).

kick-start ◇ *n* = **kick-starter**.

◇ *vt* démarrer (au kick); measures to ~ the economy *fig* des mesures pour faire repartir l'économie.

kick-starter *n* kick *m*, kick-starter *m*.

kick turn *n* [in skiing] conversion *f*.

kid [kɪd] (*pt* & *pp* **kidded**, *cont* **kidding**) ◇ *n* -**1.** *inf* [child, young person] gosse *mf*, môme *mf*, gamin *m*, -e *f*; she's just a ~ ce n'est qu'une gamine OR enfant; listen to me, ~! écoute-moi bien, petit!; that's ~s' stuff c'est pour les bébés; college ~s *Am* étudiants *mpl* ❑ 'The Kid' *Chaplin* 'le Gosse'; 'Butch Cassidy and the Sundance Kid' *Hill* 'Butch Cassidy et le kid'. -**2.** [young goat] chevreau *m*, chevrette *f*. -**3.** [hide] chevreau *m*.

◇ *adj* -**1.** *inf* [young]: ~ brother petit frère *m*, frérot *m*; ~ sister petite sœur *f*, sœurette *f*. -**2.** [coat, jacket] en chevreau.

◇ *vi inf* [joke] blaguer; I won it in a raffle — no kidding! OR you're kidding! je l'ai gagné dans une tombola — sans blague! OR tu rigoles!; don't get upset, I was just kidding ne te fâche pas, je plaisantais OR c'était une blague.

◇ *vt inf* -**1.** [tease] taquiner, se moquer de; they kidded him about his accent ils se moquaient de lui à cause de son accent. -**2.** [deceive, mislead] charrier, faire marcher; don't ~ yourself! il ne faut pas te leurrer OR te faire d'illusions!; who do you think you're kidding? tu te fous de moi?; you're not kidding! je ne te le fais pas dire!; I ~ you not *inf* sans blague, sans rigoler.

◆ **kid around** *inf vi insep* raconter des blagues, rigoler.

◆ **kid on** *inf Br* ◇ *vi insep* faire semblant; they were kidding on that I'd won ils voulaient me faire croire que j'avais gagné.

◇ *vt sep* charrier, faire marcher.

kiddie *inf* ['kɪdɪ] = **kiddy**.

kidding *inf* ['kɪdɪŋ] *n (U)* plaisanterie *f*, plaisanteries *fpl*, blague *f*, blagues *fpl*; ~ aside blague à part, sans rigoler.

kiddy *inf* ['kɪdɪ] (*pl* **kiddies**) *n* gosse *mf*, gamin *m*, -e *f*.

kid gloves *npl* gants *mpl* de chevreau; to handle OR to treat sb with ~ prendre des gants avec qqn.

kidnap ['kɪdnæp] (*Br pt* & *pp* **kidnapped**, *cont* **kidnapping**, *Am pt* & *pp* **kidnaped**, *cont* **kidnaping**) ◇ *vt* enlever, kidnapper; 'Kidnapped' *Stevenson* 'Enlevé'.

◇ *n* enlèvement *m*, rapt *m*, kidnapping *m*.

kidnaping ['kɪdnæpɪŋ] *Am* = **kidnapping**.

kidnapper ['kɪdnæpəʳ] *n* ravisseur *m*, -euse *f*, kidnappeur *m*, -euse *f*.

kidnapping ['kɪdnæpɪŋ] *n* enlèvement *m*, rapt *m*, kidnapping *m*.

kidney ['kɪdnɪ] ◇ *n* -**1.** ANAT rein *m*. -**2.** CULIN rognon *m*; pork ~s rognons de porc. -**3.** *Br lit* [temperament] nature *f*, caractère *f*; a man of (quite) a different ~ un homme d'un (tout) autre caractère.

◇ *comp* ANAT [ailment, trouble] des reins, rénal; ~ specialist néphrologue *mf*; ~ transplant greffe *f* du rein.

kidney bean *n* haricot *m* rouge OR de Soissons.

kidney machine *n* rein *m* artificiel; he's on a ~ il est sous rein artificiel OR en dialyse OR en hémodialyse.

kidology *inf* [kɪ'dɒlədʒɪ] *n Br* esbroufe *f*, bluff *m*.

kidskin ['kɪdskɪn] *n* (peau *f* de) chevreau *m*.

Kiev ['kiːev] *pr n* Kiev.

kif *inf* [kɪf, kiːf] *n* kif *m*.

kike▼ [kaɪk] *n Am terme antisémite désignant un juif*, ≃ youpin *m*, -e *f*.

Kilimanjaro [ˌkɪlɪmən'dʒɑːrəʊ] *pr n* Kilimandjaro *m*.

kill [kɪl] ◇ *vt* -**1.** [person, animal] tuer; to ~ o.s. se tuer, se donner la mort *fml*; they ~ed him in cold blood ils l'ont tué OR abattu de sang-froid; the frost ~ed the flowers le gel a tué les fleurs || *fig* tuer; I'll finish it even if it ~s me j'en viendrai à bout même si je dois me tuer à la tâche; don't ~ yourself working ne te tue pas au travail; he didn't exactly ~ himself to find a job *hum* il ne s'est pas trop fatigué pour trouver du travail; don't ~ yourself! *hum* ne te fatigue pas trop!, ne te tue pas à la tâche!; if you tell them, I'll ~ you! si tu leur dis, je te tue!; this joke will ~ you cette plaisanterie va te faire mourir de rire; they were ~ing themselves laughing OR with laughter ils étaient morts de rire ❑ to ~ two birds with one stone *prov* faire d'une pierre deux coups; to ~ time tuer le temps. -**2.** *inf fig* [cause pain to] faire très mal à; these shoes are ~ing me ces chaussures me font souffrir le martyre; my back's ~ing me j'ai très OR horriblement mal au dos; the heat will ~ you tu vas crever de chaleur. -**3.** [put an end to] tuer, mettre fin à; the accident ~ed all his hopes of becoming a dancer avec son accident ses espoirs de devenir danseur se sont évanouis OR envolés. -**4.** [alleviate, deaden] atténuer, soulager; this injection should ~ the pain cette piqûre devrait atténuer la douleur; to ~ the sound étouffer OR amortir le son. -**5.** *inf* POL [defeat] rejeter, faire échouer; the Senate ~ed the appropriations bill le Sénat a fait échouer le projet de loi de finances. -**6.** *inf* [cancel, remove] supprimer, enlever; [computer file] effacer; the editor had to ~ the story PRESS le rédacteur en chef a dû supprimer l'article. -**7.** *inf* [switch off] arrêter, couper; to ~ the engine arrêter le moteur; to ~ the lights éteindre les lumières.

◇ *vi* tuer; to shoot to ~ tirer dans l'intention de tuer; thou shalt not ~ BIBLE tu ne tueras point ❑ she was dressed to ~ *inf* elle était sur son trente et un; it's a case of ~ or cure c'est un remède de cheval.

◇ *n* -**1.** mise *f* à mort; the tiger had made three ~s that week le tigre avait tué à trois reprises OR avait fait trois victimes cette semaine-là ❑ to be in at the ~ assister au coup de grâce; to move in for the ~ donner OR porter le coup de grâce. -**2.** [prey - killed by animal] proie *f*; [- killed by hunter] chasse *f*; the ~ was plentiful la chasse a été bonne.

◆ **kill off** *vt sep* tuer, exterminer; high prices could ~ off the tourist trade *fig* des prix élevés pourraient porter un coup fatal au tourisme.

killer ['kɪləʳ] ◇ *n* -**1.** *literal* tueur *m*, -euse *f*; a convicted ~ une personne reconnue coupable d'homicide; tuberculosis was once a major ~ jadis, la tuberculose faisait de nombreuses victimes OR des ravages. -**2.** *phr*: a real ~ *inf*: the exam was a real ~ l'examen était d'une difficulté incroyable; that walk was a real ~ cette promenade était vraiment crevante; this joke is a real ~ cette histoire est à mourir de rire.

◇ *comp* [disease] meurtrier; a ~ shark un requin tueur.

killer instinct *n fig*: he's got the ~ c'est un battant; he lacks the ~ il manque d'agressivité OR de combativité, il a trop de scrupules.

killer whale *n* épaulard *m*, orque *m*.

killing ['kɪlɪŋ] ◇ *n* -**1.** assassinat *m*, meurtre *m*; **a wave of ~s** une vague d'assassinats; **the ~ of endangered species is forbidden** il est interdit de tuer un animal appartenant à une espèce en voie de disparition. -**2.** *inf* [profit] : **to make a ~** se remplir les poches, s'en mettre plein les poches.
◇ *adj inf Br* -**1.** [tiring] crevant, tuant. -**2.** *dated* [hilarious] tordant, bidonnant; **it was absolutely ~** c'était à se tordre OR à mourir de rire.

killingly *inf* ['kɪlɪŋlɪ] *adv Br*: **it was ~ funny** c'était à se tordre OR à mourir de rire.

killjoy ['kɪldʒɔɪ] *n* trouble-fête *mf inv*; **don't be such a ~!** ne sois pas rabat-joie!

kiln [kɪln] *n* four *m (à céramique, à briques etc)*.

Kilner jar® ['kɪlnəʳ-] *n Br* bocal *m* (à conserves).

kilo ['kiːləʊ] (*pl* **kilos**) (*abbr of* **kilogram**) *n* kilo *m*.

kilobyte ['kɪləbaɪt] *n* kilobyte *m*, kilo-octet *m*.

kilocalorie ['kɪləˌkælərɪ] *n* kilocalorie *f*, grande calorie *f*.

kilocycle ['kɪləˌsaɪkəl] *n* kilocycle *m*, kilohertz *m*.

kilogram(me) *Br*, **kilogram** *Am* ['kɪləgræm] *n* kilogramme *m*.

kilohertz ['kɪləˌhɜːts] *n* kilohertz *m*.

kilolitre *Br*, **kiloliter** *Am* ['kɪləˌliːtəʳ] *n* kilolitre *m*.

kilometre *Br*, **kilometer** *Am* ['kɪləˌmiːtəʳ, kɪ'lɒmɪtəʳ] *n* kilomètre *m*.

kiloton ['kɪləˌtʌn] *n* kilotonne *f*.

kilovolt ['kɪləˌvəʊlt] *n* kilovolt *m*.

kilowatt ['kɪləˌwɒt] *n* kilowatt *m*.

kilowatt-hour *n* kilowatt-heure *m*.

kilt [kɪlt] *n* kilt *m*.

kilted ['kɪltɪd] *adj* -**1.** [person] en kilt. -**2.** [pleated] : **~ skirt** kilt *m*.

kilter ['kɪltəʳ]
◆ **out of kilter** *adj phr* en dérangement, en panne.

kimono [kɪ'məʊnəʊ] (*pl* **kimonos**) *n* kimono *m*.

kin [kɪn] *npl* parents *mpl*, famille *f*.

kind[1] [kaɪnd] *n* -**1.** [sort, type] sorte *f*, type *m*, genre *m*; **hundreds of different ~s of books** des centaines de livres de toutes sortes; **they have every ~ of bird imaginable** ils ont tous les oiseaux possibles et imaginables; **have you got any other ~?** en avez-vous d'autres?; **all ~s of people** toutes sortes de gens; **what ~ of people go there? – oh, all ~s** quel type de gens y va? – oh, des gens très différents; **the place was packed with paintings of all ~s** il y avait là toutes sortes de tableaux; **it's a different ~ of problem** c'est un tout autre problème, c'est un problème d'un autre ordre; **I think he's some ~ of specialist** OR **a specialist of some ~** je crois que c'est un genre de spécialiste; **are you some ~ of nut?** *inf* tu es malade ou quoi?; **what ~ of fish is this?** quel type OR quelle sorte de poisson est-ce?; **what ~ of computer have you got?** qu'est-ce que vous avez comme (marque d') ordinateur?; **what ~ of person do you think I am?** pour qui me prenez-vous?; **it's all right, if you like that ~ of thing** c'est bien si vous aimez ce genre de choses; **his books are not the ~ to become best-sellers** ses livres ne sont pas du genre à devenir des best-sellers; **he's not the ~ that would betray his friends** il n'est pas du genre à trahir ses amis; **they're not our ~ of people** [not the sort we mix with] nous ne sommes pas du même monde; **Las Vegas is my ~ of town** Las Vegas est le genre de ville que j'aime; **she's not the marrying ~** elle n'est pas du genre à se marier ❑ **I said nothing of the ~!** je n'ai rien dit de pareil OR de tel!; **you were drunk last night – I was nothing of the ~!** tu étais ivre hier soir – absolument pas OR mais pas du tout!; **'A Kind of Loving'** *Barstow, Schlesinger* 'Un amour pas comme les autres'. -**2.** [class of person, thing] : **he's a traitor to his ~** il a trahi les siens; **it's one of the finest of its ~** [animal] c'est l'un des plus beaux spécimens de son espèce; [object] c'est l'un des plus beaux dans son genre. -**3.** *phr*: **a ~ of** une sorte de, une espèce de; **a hat with a ~ of (a) veil** un chapeau avec une espèce de voilette; **she had a ~ of fit** elle a eu une sorte d'attaque; **I had a ~ of (a) feeling you'd come** j'avais comme l'impression que tu viendrais; **~ of** plutôt; **it's ~ of big and round** c'est plutôt OR dans le genre grand et rond; **I'm ~ of sad about it** ça me rend un peu triste; **did you hit him? – well, ~ of** tu l'as frappé? – oui, si on veut; **we just ~ of wandered about** on s'est un peu baladés; **of a ~**: **they're two of a ~** ils sont de la même espèce; **one of a ~** unique (en son genre); **did he give you any tips? – of a ~** vous a-t-il donné des conseils? – si on peut appeler ça des conseils; **it's work of a ~, but only as a stopgap** c'est un emploi, d'accord, mais pas pour très longtemps.
◆ **in kind** *adv phr* -**1.** [with goods, services] en nature; **to pay sb in ~** payer qqn en nature. -**2.** [in similar fashion] de même; **he insulted me, and I replied in ~** il m'a insulté, et je lui ai rendu la monnaie de sa pièce.

kind[2] [kaɪnd] *adj* -**1.** [good-natured, considerate] gentil, aimable; **she's a very ~ woman** c'est une femme très gentille OR une femme d'une grande bonté; **to be ~ to sb** être gentil avec qqn; **it's very ~ of you to take an interest** c'est très gentil à vous de vous y intéresser; **how ~!** comme c'est gentil!; **she was ~ enough to say nothing** elle a eu la gentillesse de ne rien dire; **would you be so ~ as to post this for me?** auriez-vous l'amabilité de mettre ceci à la poste pour moi?; **most of the reviews were ~ to the actors** la plupart des critiques étaient favorables aux acteurs ❑ **'Kind Hearts and Coronets'** *Hamer* 'Noblesse oblige'. -**2.** [delicate, not harmful] doux; **a detergent that is ~ to your hands** une lessive qui n'abîme pas les mains.

kinda▽ ['kaɪndə] *Am* = **kind of**.

kindergarten ['kɪndəˌgɑːtn] *n* jardin *m* d'enfants, (école *f*) maternelle *f*.

kind-hearted *adj* bon, généreux; **she's very ~** elle a bon cœur, elle est d'une grande générosité.

kind-heartedly [-'hɑːtɪdlɪ] *adv* avec bonté, généreusement.

kind-heartedness [-'hɑːtɪdnɪs] *n* bonté *f*, générosité *f*.

kindle ['kɪndl] ◇ *vt* -**1.** [wood] allumer, faire brûler. -**2.** *fig* [interest] susciter; [passion] embraser, enflammer; [hatred, jealousy] attiser, susciter.
◇ *vi* -**1.** [wood] s'enflammer, brûler. -**2.** *fig* [passion, desire] s'embraser, s'enflammer; [interest] s'éveiller.

kindliness ['kaɪndlɪnɪs] *n* gentillesse *f*, amabilité *f*, bonté *f*.

kindling ['kɪndlɪŋ] *n* petit bois *m*, bois *m* d'allumage.

kindly ['kaɪndlɪ] (*compar* **kindlier**, *superl* **kindliest**) ◇ *adv* -**1.** [affably, warmly] chaleureusement, affablement; **he has always treated me ~** il a toujours été gentil avec moi. -**2.** [obligingly] gentiment, obligeamment; **she ~ offered to help us** elle a gentiment offert de nous aider. -**3.** [favourably] : **to look ~ on sthg** voir qqch d'un bon œil; **they don't take ~ to people arriving late** ils n'apprécient pas beaucoup OR tellement qu'on arrive en retard; **I have always thought ~ of him** j'ai toujours eu une bonne opinion de lui. -**4.** [in polite requests] : **would** OR **will you ~ pass the salt?** auriez-vous la gentillesse OR l'amabilité de me passer le sel?; **~ reply by return of post** prière de répondre par retour du courrier; **~ refrain from smoking** prière de ne pas fumer ‖ [in anger or annoyance] : **will you ~ sit down!** asseyez-vous, je vous prie!
◇ *adj* [person, attitude] gentil; [smile] bienveillant.

kindness ['kaɪndnɪs] *n* -**1.** [thoughtfulness] bonté *f*, gentillesse *f*; **an act of ~** un acte de bonté; **she did it out of the ~ of her heart** elle l'a fait par bonté d'âme. -**2.** *Br* [considerate act] service *m*; **to do sb a ~** rendre service à qqn; **please do me the ~ of replying** *fml* pourriez-vous être assez gentil pour OR pourriez-vous avoir l'amabilité de me donner une réponse?

kindred ['kɪndrɪd] ◇ *n arch* OR *lit* [relationship] parenté *f*; [family] famille *f*, parents *mpl*.
◇ *adj* [related] apparenté; [similar] similaire analogue; **~ spirits** âmes *fpl* sœurs.

kinematics [ˌkɪnɪ'mætɪks] *n (U)* cinématique *f*.

kinesics [kɪ'niːzɪks] *n (U)* kinésique *f*.

kinetic [kɪ'netɪk] *adj* cinétique.

kinetic art *n* art *m* cinétique.

kinetic energy *n* énergie *f* cinétique.

kinetics [kɪ'netɪks] *n (U)* cinétique *f*.

kinfolk ['kɪnfəʊk] *Am* = **kinsfolk**.

king [kɪŋ] *n* -**1.** roi *m*; **King Henry the Eighth** le roi Henri VIII; **the King of Spain/Belgium** le roi d'Espagne/des Belges; **the Three Kings** les trois Mages, les Rois mages; **the ~ of (the) beasts** *fig* le roi des animaux; **the fast-food ~** *fig* le roi OR magnat de la restauration rapide ❑ **to live like a ~** vivre en grand seigneur; **to pay a ~'s ransom (for sthg)** payer une fortune OR un prix fou (pour qqch); **I'm the ~ of the castle!** *inf* [in children's games] c'est moi le plus fort!; **'King John'** *Shakespeare* 'le Roi Jean'; **'King Lear'** *Shakespeare* 'le Roi Lear'; **'King Solomon's Mines'** *Haggard* 'les Mines du roi Salomon'. -**2.** [in cards & chess] roi *m*; [in draughts] dame *f*; **the ~ of hearts** le roi de cœur.
◆ **Kings** *n*: **(the book of) Kings** BIBLE (le livre des) Rois.

kingbolt ['kɪŋbəʊlt] *n* MECH pivot *m*.

King Charles spaniel *n* king-charles *m (inv)*.

king cobra *n* cobra *m* royal, hamadryade *f*.

kingcup ['kɪŋkʌp] *n Br* populage *m*, souci *m* d'eau.

kingdom ['kɪŋdəm] *n* -**1.** [realm] royaume *m*; **the ~ of God/Heaven** BIBLE le royaume de Dieu/des cieux ❑ **till ~ come** jusqu'à la fin des temps; **they were blown to ~ come** ils ont été expédiés dans l'autre monde OR dans l'au-delà. -**2.** [division] règne *m*; **the animal/vegetable/mineral ~** le règne animal/végétal/minéral.

kingfisher ['kɪŋˌfɪʃəʳ] *n* martin-pêcheur *m*.

kingly ['kɪŋlɪ] (*compar* **kinglier**, *superl* **kingliest**) *adj* royal, majestueux; **to behave in a ~ manner** [be like a king] se conduire en roi; [be generous] se conduire comme un prince.

kingmaker ['kɪŋˌmeɪkəʳ] *n* HIST faiseur *m* de rois; *fig* & POL *personne qui fait ou défait les candidats politiques*.

king penguin *n* manchot *m* royal.

kingpin ['kɪŋpɪn] *n* -**1.** TECH pivot *m*. -**2.** *fig* pivot *m*, cheville *f* ouvrière.

king prawn *n* (grosse) crevette *f*.

King's Bench (Division) *n* ≃ cour *f* d'assises *(en Grande-Bretagne et au Canada)*.

King's Counsel *n* avocat *m* de la couronne *(en Grande-Bretagne)*.

King's English *n Br*: **the ~** le bon anglais.

King's evidence *n Br*: **to turn ~** témoigner contre ses complices.

King's highway *n Br*: **the ~** la voie publique.

kingship ['kɪŋʃɪp] *n* royauté *f*.

king-size(d) *adj* [bed, mattress] (très) grand; [cigarette] long; [packet, container] géant; **I've got a ~ hangover** *inf fig* j'ai une gueule de bois carabinée.

kink [kɪŋk] ◇ *n* -**1.** [in rope, wire] nœud *m*; [in hair] boucle *f*, frisette *f*. -**2.** *inf fig* [sexual deviation] perversion *f*, aberration *f*; [quirk] bizarrerie *f*, excentricité *f*. -**3.** *inf Am* [flaw] problème *m*.
◇ *vt* [rope, cable] entortiller, emmêler.
◇ *vi* [rope, cable] s'entortiller, s'emmêler.

kinky ['kɪŋkɪ] (*compar* **kinkier**, *superl* **kinkiest**) *adj* -**1.** *inf* [behaviour] farfelu; [sexually] vicieux, pervers; **he likes ~ sex** il a des goûts sexuels un peu spéciaux; **she wears ~ clothes** elle a une façon très spéciale de s'habiller. -**2.** [rope, cable] entortillé, emmêlé; [hair] crépu, frisé.

kinsfolk ['kɪnzfəʊk] *npl* parents *mpl*, famille *f*.
Kinshasa [kɪn'ʃæsə] *pr n* Kinshasa.
kinship ['kɪnʃɪp] *n* [relationship] parenté *f*; *fig* [closeness] intimité *f*; I feel no real ~ with my colleagues je ne me sens pas du tout proche de mes collègues.
kinsman ['kɪnzmən] (*pl* kinsmen [-mən]) *n* parent *m*.
kinswoman ['kɪnz,wʊmən] (*pl* kinswomen [-,wɪmɪn]) *n* parente *f*.
kiosk ['ki:ɒsk] *n* [for newspapers, magazines] kiosque *m*; *Am* [for advertisements] ≃ colonne *f* Morris; telephone ~ *Br* cabine *f* téléphonique.
kip *inf* [kɪp] (*pt* & *pp* kipped, *cont* kipping) ◇ *n Br* [sleep] roupillon *m*; to have a OR to get some ~ faire OR piquer un roupillon; I got no ~ last night je n'ai pas fermé l'œil de la nuit.
◇ *vi* roupiller.
◆ **kip down** *inf vi insep Br* se pieuter.
kipper ['kɪpəʳ] ◇ *n* hareng *m* fumé, kipper *m*.
◇ *vt* [fish] fumer; ~ed herring hareng *m* fumé, kipper *m*.
kipper tie *n* large cravate *f*.
KIPS [kɪps] (*abbr of* kilo instructions per second) *n* COMPUT *millier d'instructions par seconde*.
Kirgizia [kɜ:'gɪzɪə] *pr n* Kirghizie *f*; in ~ en Khirgizie.
kirk [kɜ:k] *n Scot* église *f*.
kirsch [kɪəʃ] *n* Kirsch *m*.
kiss [kɪs] ◇ *n* -**1.** baiser *m*; they gave her a ~ ils l'ont embrassée; give us a ~! *inf* fais-moi un (gros) bisou!; she gave him a goodnight ~ elle lui a souhaité une bonne nuit en l'embrassant, elle l'a embrassé pour lui souhaiter (une) bonne nuit ❑ to give sb the ~ of life faire du bouche-à-bouche à qqn; it could be the ~ of life for the building trade cela pourrait permettre à l'industrie du bâtiment de retrouver un OR son second souffle; ~ of death coup fatal; the new supermarket was the ~ of death for local shopkeepers l'ouverture du supermarché a entraîné la ruine des petits commerçants; 'The Kiss' *Rodin* 'le Baiser'. -**2.** [sweet]: chocolate ~ (petit) bonbon *m* au chocolat. -**3.** [in snooker] touche *f*, contre *m*.
◇ *vt* -**1.** embrasser; he ~ed her on the lips/forehead il l'embrassa sur la bouche/sur le front; he ~ed her hand il lui a baisé la main, il lui a fait le baise-main *lit*; to ~ sb goodnight: I ~ed her goodnight je l'ai embrassée OR je lui ai fait une bise pour lui souhaiter (une) bonne nuit; ~ your dad goodnight! embrasse ton père OR fais une bise à ton père avant d'aller te coucher! ❑ you can ~ your money goodbye! *inf* tu peux faire ton deuil de OR tu peux faire une croix sur ton fric!; 'Kiss me, Kate!' *Porter* 'Embrasse-moi, Kate!'. -**2.** *lit* [touch lightly] caresser; the sunlight ~ed her hair le soleil lui caressait les cheveux. -**3.** [in snooker] toucher.
◇ *vi* -**1.** s'embrasser; they ~ed goodbye ils se sont dit au revoir en s'embrassant; to ~ and make up s'embrasser et faire la paix. -**2.** [in snooker] se toucher.
◆ **kiss away** *vt sep*: she ~ed away my tears ses baisers ont séché mes larmes.
◆ **kiss off**▽ *Am* ◇ *vt sep* -**1.** [dismiss] envoyer promener. -**2.** [kill] descendre, buter.
◇ *vi insep*: ~ off! va te faire voir!
kissagram ['kɪsəgræm] *n* baiser *m* par porteur spécial *(service utilisé à l'occasion d'un anniversaire etc)*.
kiss-and-tell *adj* PRESS: another ~ story by an ex-girlfriend encore des révélations intimes faites OR des secrets d'alcôve dévoilés par une ancienne petite amie.
kiss curl *n Br* accroche-cœur *m*.
kisser ['kɪsəʳ] *n* -**1.** [person]: is he a good ~? est-ce qu'il embrasse bien? -**2.** *inf* [face, mouth] tronche *f*.
kiss-off▽ *n Am*: to give sb the ~ envoyer promener qqn.
kit [kɪt] (*pt* & *pp* kitted, *cont* kitting) *n* -**1.** [set] trousse *f*; tool/sewing ~ trousse à outils/à couture. -**2.** [equipment] affaires *fpl*, matériel *m*; have you got your squash ~? as-tu tes affaires de squash?; get your ~ off!▽ *hum* à poil! ❑ the whole ~ and caboodle *inf* tout le bazar OR bataclan. -**3.** [soldier's gear] fourniment *m*; in full battle ~ en tenue de combat; ~ inspection revue *f* de détail. -**4.** [parts to be assembled] kit *m*; it's sold in ~ form c'est vendu en kit; model aircraft ~ maquette *f* d'avion.
◆ **kit out** *inf*, **kit up** *inf vt sep Br* équiper; we kitted ourselves out for a long trip nous nous sommes équipés pour un long voyage; he was kitted out for golf il était en tenue de golf.
kit bag *n Br* musette *f*, sac *m* de toile.
kitchen ['kɪtʃɪn] ◇ *n* cuisine *f*.
◇ *comp* [salt, scissors, table] de cuisine.
kitchen cabinet *n* -**1.** [furniture] buffet *m* (de cuisine). -**2.** *Br* POL cabinet *m* restreint *(conseillers proches du chef du gouvernement)*.
kitchenette [,kɪtʃɪ'net] *n* kitchenette *f*, cuisinette *f offic*.
kitchen foil *n* aluminium *m* ménager, papier *m* d'aluminium OR d'alu.
kitchen garden *n Br* (jardin *m*) potager *m*.
kitchen paper *n Br* essuie-tout *m*, Sopalin® *m*.
kitchen sink *n* évier *m*; everything but the ~ *fig* & *hum* tout sauf les murs; ~ drama *théâtre et cinéma réalistes des années 50-60 ayant pour thème l'ennui et la misère des gens ordinaires*.
kitchen unit *n* élément *m* (de cuisine).
kitchenware ['kɪtʃɪnweəʳ] *n* vaisselle *f* et ustensiles *mpl* de cuisine.
kite [kaɪt] ◇ *n* -**1.** [toy] cerf-volant *m*; to fly a ~ *literal* faire voler un cerf-volant; *fig* lancer un ballon d'essai. -**2.** ORNITH milan *m*. -**3.** *inf Br dated* [aeroplane] zinc *m*.
◇ *vi* s'envoler.
Kite mark *n label représentant un petit cerf-volant apposé sur les produits conformes aux normes officielles britanniques*.
kith [kɪθ] *npl*: ~ and kin amis *mpl* et parents *mpl*; he's one of our own ~ and kin il est l'un des nôtres.
kitsch [kɪtʃ] ◇ *adj* kitsch.
◇ *n* kitsch *m*.
kitschy ['kɪtʃɪ] (*compar* kitschier, *superl* kitschiest) = **kitsch** *adj*.
kitten ['kɪtn] *n* chaton *m*; our cat has had ~s notre chatte a eu des petits ❑ he was having ~s *inf Br* il était dans tous ses états OR aux cent coups.
kittenish ['kɪtənɪʃ] *adj* [playful] joueur, espiègle; [flirtatious] coquet.
kittiwake ['kɪtɪweɪk] *n* mouette *f* tridactyle.
kitty ['kɪtɪ] (*pl* kitties) *n* -**1.** *inf* [kitten] chaton *m*; here, ~ ~ viens, mon minou OR minet. -**2.** [funds held in common] cagnotte *f*, caisse *f* (commune); [in gambling] cagnotte *f*.
kiwi ['ki:wi:] *n* -**1.** ORNITH kiwi *m*, aptéryx *m*. -**2.** [fruit] kiwi *m*.
◆ **Kiwi** *inf* [New Zealander] Néo-Zélandais *m*, -e *f*; the Kiwis [rugby team] les Kiwis.
kiwi fruit *n* kiwi *m*.
KKK *pr n abbr of* Ku Klux Klan.
Klan [klæn] = **Ku Klux Klan**.
Klansman ['klænzmən] (*pl* Klansmen [-mən]) *n* membre *m* du Ku Klux Klan.
Klaxon® ['klæksn] *n Br* AUT Klaxon® *m*.
Kleenex® ['kli:neks] *n* Kleenex® *m inv*, mouchoir *m* en papier.
kleptomania [,kleptə'meɪnɪə] *n* kleptomanie *f*, cleptomanie *f*.
kleptomaniac [,kleptə'meɪnɪæk] ◇ *adj* kleptomane, cleptomane.
◇ *n* kleptomane *mf*, cleptomane *mf*.
klieg light [kli:g-] *n Am* lampe *f* à arc.
Klondike ['klɒndaɪk] *pr n*: the ~ (River) le Klondike; the ~ gold rush *la ruée vers l'or, aux États-Unis*.
klutz *inf* [klʌts] *n Am* balourd *m*, -e *f*, godiche *f*.
klystron ['klaɪstrɒn] *n* klystron *m*.
km (*written abbr of* kilometre) km.
km/h (*written abbr of* kilometres per hour) km/h.
knack [næk] *n* tour *m* de main, truc *m*; it's easy, once you get the ~ (of it) c'est facile, une fois qu'on a compris le truc; she's got a ~ of finding the right word elle sait toujours trouver le mot juste; he's got a ~ of turning up at meal-times *hum* il a le chic pour arriver aux heures des repas.
knacker ['nækəʳ] *Br* ◇ *vt* ▽ crever; that run completely ~ed me cette course m'a mis sur les genoux.
◇ *n* -**1.** [slaughterer] équarrisseur *m*; ~'s yard équarrissoir *m*, abattoir *m*. -**2.** [in real estate] démolisseur *m*.
◆ **knackers**▼ *npl Br* [testicles] couilles *fpl*.
knackered▽ ['nækəd] *adj* [tired] crevé; [engine] mort.
knapsack ['næpsæk] *n* havresac *m*, sac *m* à dos.
knave [neɪv] *n* -**1.** *arch* [rogue] fripon *m lit*, canaille *f*. -**2.** CARDS valet *m*.
knavery ['neɪvərɪ] (*pl* knaveries) *n arch* friponnerie *f*, canaillerie *f*, malhonnêteté *f*.
knavish ['neɪvɪʃ] *adj arch* [person] fripon; [trick, deed] de fripon, de canaille.
knead [ni:d] *vt* [dough, clay] pétrir, malaxer; [massage - body] pétrir, malaxer.
knee [ni:] ◇ *n* -**1.** ANAT genou *m*; the snow was up to our ~s, we were up to our ~s in snow on avait de la neige jusqu'aux genoux; to go down on one's ~s, to fall to one's ~s se mettre à genoux ❑ to be on one's ~s *literal* & *fig* être à genoux; to bring sb to his/her ~s faire capituler qqn; the war nearly brought the country to its ~s la guerre a failli entraîner la ruine du pays. -**2.** [of trousers] genou *m*; worn at the ~s usé aux genoux. -**3.** [lap] genoux *mpl*; come and sit on my ~ viens t'asseoir sur mes genoux; to put sb over one's ~ donner la fessée à OR corriger qqn ❑ I learnt it at my mother's ~ c'est ma mère qui me l'a appris lorsque je n'étais qu'un enfant; on bended ~ à genoux; to go down on bended ~ se mettre à genoux. -**4.** TECH [in a pipe] genou *m*, coude *m*; [device] rotule *f*.
◇ *vt* donner un coup de genou à; he ~d me in the groin il m'a donné un coup de genou dans l'aine.
knee breeches *npl Br* knickers *mpl*.
kneecap ['ni:kæp] (*pt* & *pp* kneecapped, *cont* kneecapping) ◇ *n* ANAT rotule *f*.
◇ *vt*: he was kneecapped on lui a brisé les rotules.
kneecapping ['ni:kæpɪŋ] *n* mutilation *f* des rotules.
knee-deep *adj*: the snow was ~ on avait de la neige jusqu'aux genoux; the water was only ~ l'eau ne nous arrivait qu'aux genoux; we were ~ in water l'eau nous arrivait OR nous étions dans l'eau jusqu'aux genoux; he was ~ in trouble *fig* il était dans les ennuis jusqu'au cou.
knee drop *n* [in wrestling] projection *f* sur le genou.
knee-high *adj* [grass] à hauteur de genou; ~ socks chaussettes *fpl* montantes; the grass was ~ l'herbe nous arrivait (jusqu') aux genoux ❑ ~ to a grasshopper *inf hum* haut comme trois pommes.
knee jerk *n* réflexe *m* rotulien.
◆ **knee-jerk** *adj* automatique; ~ reaction *fig* & *pej* réflexe *m*, automatisme *m*; ~ support POL soutien *m* systématique OR inconditionnel.
knee joint *n* articulation *f* du genou.
kneel [ni:l] (*pt* & *pp* knelt [nelt] OR kneeled) *vi* s'agenouiller, se mettre à genoux; she was ~ing on the floor elle était agenouillée OR à genoux par terre; to ~ in prayer s'agenouiller pour prier; to ~ before sb se mettre à genoux devant qqn.
◆ **kneel down** *vi insep* se mettre à genoux, s'agenouiller.
knee-length *adj*: a ~ skirt une jupe qui descend jusqu'au genou.
knee level *n*: at ~ à hauteur du genou.
kneeling ['ni:lɪŋ] *adj* agenouillé, à genoux; in a ~ position à genoux.

knee pad *n* genouillère *f.*
kneepan ['niːpæn] *n* ANAT patelle *f,* rotule *f.*
knee reflex *n* réflexe *m* rotulien.
kneeroom ['niːrʊm] *n*: have you got enough ~? avez-vous assez de place pour vos genoux OR vos jambes?
knees-up *inf n Br* [dance] danse *f* (agitée); [party] fête *f.*
knell [nel] *n lit* glas *m*; to toll the ~ sonner le glas.
knelt [nelt] *pt* & *pp* → **kneel**.
knew [njuː] *pt* → **know**.
knickerbocker glory ['nɪkəbɒkər-] *n coupe de glace avec fruits et crème Chantilly.*
knickerbockers ['nɪkəbɒkəz] *npl* knickers *mpl*; [for golf] culotte *f* de golf.
knickers ['nɪkəz] ◇ *npl* -**1.** *Br* [underwear] culotte *f,* slip *m (de femme)*; don't get your ~ in a twist! *inf* [don't panic] ne t'affole pas!; [don't get angry] du calme!, calme-toi! -**2.** *Am* = **knickerbockers**.
◇ *interj inf Br dated*: ~! mon œil!
knick-knack ['nɪknæk] *n* [trinket] bibelot *m*; [brooch] colifichet *m.*
knife [naɪf] (*pl* knives [naɪvz]) ◇ *n* -**1.** [for eating] couteau *m*; a ~ and fork une fourchette et un couteau; her words cut me like a ~ ses paroles m'ont piqué au vif OR profondément blessé ❑ fish ~ couteau *m* à poisson; like a ~ through butter comme dans du beurre; to be OR to go under the ~ *inf* passer sur le billard. -**2.** [as a weapon] couteau *m*; to carry a ~ porter un couteau sur soi ❑ she really got her ~ into them elle en avait drôlement après eux, elle leur en voulait drôlement; the knives are out ils sont à couteaux tirés OR en guerre ouverte; you really stuck the ~ in! *inf* tu ne l'as pas loupé!; to turn OR to twist the ~ (in the wound) retourner le couteau dans la plaie.
◇ *comp*: a ~ wound/attack une blessure/une attaque à coups de couteau.
◇ *vt* donner un coup de couteau à; to ~ sb to death tuer qqn à coups de couteau; he was ~d il a reçu un coup de couteau; he was ~d in the back *literal* il a reçu un coup de couteau OR on lui a planté un couteau dans le dos; *fig* on lui a tiré dans le dos OR dans les pattes.
knife-edge *n* -**1.** [blade] fil *m* d'un couteau; we were on a ~ *fig* on était sur des charbons ardents; his decision was (balanced) on a ~ sa décision ne tenait qu'à un fil. -**2.** [of scales] couteau *m.*
knife-grinder *n* rémouleur *m.*
knife pleat *n* pli *m* plat.
knife-point *n*: at ~ sous la menace du couteau.
knife-rest *n* porte-couteau *m.*
knife-sharpener *n* [automatic] aiguisoir *m*; [manual] fusil *m* (à aiguiser).
knifing ['naɪfɪŋ] *n* agression *f* à coups de couteau.
knight [naɪt] ◇ *n* -**1.** HIST chevalier *m*; the Knights of the Round Table les Chevaliers de la Table ronde; a ~ in shining armour [romantic hero] un prince charmant; [saviour] un sauveur, un redresseur de torts. -**2.** *Br* [honorary title] chevalier *m*; Laurence Olivier was made a ~ Laurence Olivier a été anobli OR fait chevalier. -**3.** [chess piece] cavalier *m.*
◇ *vt* faire chevalier.
knight-errant (*pl* knights-errant) *n* HIST & *lit* chevalier *m* errant.
knighthood ['naɪthʊd] *n* -**1.** *Br* [title] titre *m* de chevalier; to receive a ~ être fait chevalier, être anobli. -**2.** HIST chevalerie *f.*
knightly ['naɪtlɪ] *adj* chevaleresque.
Knightsbridge ['naɪtsbrɪdʒ] *pr n quartier chic de Londres connu pour ses magasins de luxe.*
Knight Templar (*pl* Knights Templar) *n* Templier *m.*
knit [nɪt] (*pt* & *pp* knit OR knitted, *cont* knitting) ◇ *vt* -**1.** tricoter; he knitted himself a scarf il s'est tricoté une écharpe. -**2.** [in instructions]: ~ 2 purl 2 (tricoter) 2 mailles à l'endroit, 2 mailles à l'envers; ~ 2 together tricoter 2 mailles ensemble. -**3.** [unite] unir. -**4.** *phr*: to ~ one's brows froncer les sourcils.
◇ *vi* tricoter; I like to ~ in the evenings j'aime bien tricoter OR faire du tricot le soir.
◆ **knit together** ◇ *vi insep* [heal - bones] se souder.
◇ *vt sep* [unite] unir; MED [bones] souder.
◆ **knit up** ◇ *vi insep* [yarn]: this wool ~s up easily cette laine se tricote facilement.
◇ *vt sep* [garment] tricoter; she knitted up a scarf from the spare wool elle a fait une écharpe avec la laine qui restait.
-knit *in cpds* -**1.** [of woollen garment]: a chunky~ sweater un gros pull, un pull en grosse laine. -**2.** [united]: a close~ family une famille très unie.
knitted ['nɪtɪd] *adj* tricoté, en tricot.
knitter ['nɪtər] *n* tricoteur *m,* -euse *f*; she's a good/a quick ~ elle tricote bien/vite.
knitting ['nɪtɪŋ] ◇ *n* -**1.** [garment] tricot *m*; have you seen my ~? avez-vous vu mon tricot? -**2.** [activity] tricot *m*; [on industrial scale] tricotage *m*; to do some ~ faire du tricot; ~ helps me relax le tricot m'aide à me détendre ❑ machine ~ tricots faits à la machine.
◇ *comp* [wool] à tricoter; [pattern] de tricot; [factory] de tricotage.
knitting machine *n* machine *f* à tricoter.
knitting needle, **knitting pin** *n* aiguille *f* à tricoter.
knitwear ['nɪtweər] *n* [garments] tricots *mpl,* pulls *mpl*; [in department store] rayon *m* pulls.
knives [naɪvz] *pl* → **knife**.
knob [nɒb] *n* -**1.** [handle - of door, drawer] poignée *f,* bouton *m*; the same to you with ~s on! *inf Br* toi-même! -**2.** [control - on appliance] bouton *m.* -**3.** [ball-shaped end - of walking stick] pommeau *m*; [- on furniture] bouton *m.* -**4.** [of butter] noix *f.* -**5.** [hillock] monticule *m.* -**6.** ▼ *Br* [penis] queue *f,* bite *f.*
knobbly *Br* ['nɒblɪ], **knobby** *Am* ['nɒbɪ] (*Br compar* knobblier, *superl* knobbliest, *Am compar* knobbier, *superl* knobbiest) *adj* noueux; ~ knees genoux couverts de bosses.
knock [nɒk] ◇ *vt* -**1.** [hit]: to ~ a nail in enfoncer un clou; she ~ed a nail into/she ~ed a hole in the wall elle a planté un clou/elle a fait un trou dans le mur; I ~ed the vase off the shelf j'ai fait tomber le vase de l'étagère; he was ~ed off his bicycle le choc l'a fait tomber de sa bicyclette; he was ~ed into the ditch il a été projeté dans le fossé; the boy was ~ing the ball against the wall le garçon lançait OR envoyait la balle contre le mur; the force of the explosion ~ed us to the floor la force de l'explosion nous a projetés à terre; to ~ sb unconscious OR cold *inf* assommer qqn; the boom ~ed him off balance la bôme, en le heurtant, l'a déséquilibré OR lui a fait perdre l'équilibre; the news ~ed me off balance *fig* la nouvelle m'a sidéré OR coupé le souffle ‖ [bump] heurter, cogner; I ~ed my head on OR against the low ceiling je me suis cogné la tête contre le OR au plafond. -**2.** *fig*: to ~ holes in a plan/an argument démolir un projet/un argument; maybe it will ~ some sense into him cela lui mettra peut-être du plomb dans la cervelle, cela le ramènera peut-être à la raison; the crisis has ~ed the bottom out of the market COMM la crise a entraîné l'effondrement du marché; he ~ed all our hopes on the head *Br* il a réduit nos espoirs à néant; it really ~ed me sideways *inf* OR for six *inf* cela m'a scié OR soufflé; he can ~ spots off me at chess/tennis *Br* il me bat à plate couture aux échecs/au tennis. -**3.** *inf* [criticize - author, film] éreinter; [- driving, cooking] critiquer; ~ing your colleagues isn't going to help ce n'est pas en débinant vos collègues OR en cassant du sucre sur le dos de vos collègues que vous changerez quoi que ce soit; they're always ~ing the trade unions ils n'arrêtent pas de taper sur les syndicats. -**4.** ▽ *Br* [have sex with] se faire, se taper.
◇ *vi* -**1.** [hit] frapper; to ~ on OR at the door frapper (à la porte); she came in without ~in[g] elle est entrée sans frapper; they ~ on the wa[ll] when we're too noisy ils tapent OR cognen[t] contre le mur quand on fait trop de bruit; it wa[s] a branch ~ing against the window c'était un[e] branche qui cognait contre la fenêtre. -**2.** [bump]: to ~ against OR into heurter, cogner; she ~ed into the desk elle s'est heurté[e] OR cognée contre le bureau; my elbow ~e[d] against the door frame je me suis cogné O[R] heurté le coude contre le chambranle de l[a] porte. -**3.** [make symptomatic sound] cogner; m[y] heart was ~ing je sentais mon cœur cogne[r] dans ma poitrine, j'avais le cœur qui cognait; the car engine is ~ing le moteur cogne; th[e] pipes ~ when you run the taps les tuyau[x] cognent quand on ouvre les robinets.
◇ *n* -**1.** [blow] coup *m*; give it a ~ with [a] hammer donne un coup de marteau dessus; there was a ~ at the door/window on [a] frappé à la porte/fenêtre; she gave three ~s o[n] the door elle a frappé trois fois OR coups à l[a] porte; no one answered my ~ personne n'[a] répondu quand j'ai frappé; ~! ~! toc! toc! can you give me a ~ tomorrow morning est-ce que vous pouvez (venir) frapper à m[a] porte demain matin? ‖ [bump] coup *m*; I got [a] nasty ~ on the elbow [in fight, accident] j'ai reç[u] un sacré coup au coude; [by one's own clumsiness] je me suis bien cogné le coude; the car's had [a] few ~s, but nothing serious la voiture est u[n] peu cabossée mais rien de grave. -**2.** [setback] coup *m*; his reputation has taken a hard ~ s[a] réputation en a pris un sérieux coup; I've take[n] a few ~s in my time *inf* j'ai encaissé des coup[s] moi aussi. -**3.** *inf* [criticism] critique *f*; she'[s] taken a few ~s from the press la presse n'a pa[s] toujours été très tendre avec elle. -**4.** AUT [i[n] engine] cognement *m.*
◆ **knock about** *Br*, **knock around** ◇ *vi insep inf* -**1.** [associate]: to ~ about with sb fréquente[r] qqn. -**2.** [loiter] traîner; Ray must be ~in[g] about here somewhere Ray doit traîner que[l]que part dans le coin; I ~ed about in Australi[a] for a while j'ai bourlingué OR roulé ma bosse e[n] Australie pendant quelque temps.
◇ *vt insep inf* traîner dans; I ~ed about tow[n] all day j'ai traîné en ville toute la journée; sh[e] spent a year ~ing about Europe elle a pass[é] une année à se balader en Europe; these clothe[s] are OK for ~ing about the house in ce[s] vêtements, ça va pour traîner à la maison.
◇ *vt sep* -**1.** [beat] battre; [ill-treat] malmener; he used to ~ his wife about a lot il tapait su[r] sa femme; the old car's been ~ed about a bi[t] la vieille voiture a pris quelques coups ici et là. -**2.** [jolt, shake] balloter; we were really ~e[d] about in the back of the truck nous étion[s] ballotés à l'arrière du camion. -**3.** *inf* [discuss] débattre; we ~ed the idea about for a whil[e] nous en avons vaguement discuté pendant u[n] certain temps.
◆ **knock back** *inf vt sep* -**1.** [drink] descendre; she could ~ back five cognacs in an hour ell[e] pouvait s'envoyer cinq cognacs en une heure; he certainly ~s it back! qu'est-ce qu'il des[cend]! -**2.** [cost] coûter; that car must have ~e[d] him back a few thousand pounds cette voitur[e] a bien dû lui coûter quelques milliers de livres. -**3.** [surprise, shock] secouer, bouleverser; th[e] news really ~ed me back la nouvelle m'[a] vraiment abasourdi OR m'a laissé pantois.
◆ **knock down** *vt sep* -**1.** [person] renverser; [in fight] envoyer par terre, étendre; she wa[s] ~ed down by a bus elle a été renversée par u[n] bus; he ~ed the champion down in the firs[t] round il a envoyé le champion au tapis OR il [a] mis le champion knock-down dans la premièr[e] reprise ❑ you could have ~ed me dow[n] with a feather! *inf* j'en suis resté assis OR comm[e] deux ronds de flan! -**2.** [hurdle, vase, pile of books] faire tomber, renverser. -**3.** [demolish - building] démolir; [- wall] démolir, abattre; to ~ dow[n] sb's argument démolir l'argument de qq[n]. -**4.** [price] baisser; [salesman] faire baisser; [I] managed to ~ him down to $500 j'ai réussi

le faire baisser jusqu'à 500 dollars. -**5.** *Br* [at auction] adjuger; it was ~ed down to her for £300 on le lui a adjugé pour 300 livres.

◆ **knock off** ◇ *vt sep* -**1.** [from shelf, wall etc] faire tomber; **the statue's arm had been ~ed off** la statue avait perdu un bras; **he ~ed the earth off the spade** il fit tomber la terre qui était restée collée à la bêche ❑ **to ~ sb's block off** *inf* casser la figure à qqn. -**2.** [reduce by] faire une réduction de; **the salesman ~ed 10 % off (for us)** le vendeur nous a fait un rabais OR une remise de 10 %. -**3.** *inf* [write rapidly] torcher; **she can ~ off an article in half an hour** elle peut pondre un article en une demi-heure. -**4.** ▽ [kill] descendre, buter. -**5.** ▽ *Br* [steal] piquer, faucher; [rob] braquer; **they ~ed off a bank** ils ont braqué une banque. -**6.** *inf phr*: **~ it off!** [stop] arrête tes conneries OR ton char! -**7.** ▼ *Br* [have sex with] baiser.

◇ *vi insep inf* [stop work] cesser le travail; **we ~ off at 5** on finit à 17 h.

◆ **knock on** ◇ *vi insep* -**1.** RUGBY faire un en-avant. -**2.** ▽ *Br* [age]: **my dad's ~ing on a bit now** mon père commence à prendre de la bouteille.

◇ *vt sep* RUGBY: **to ~ the ball on** faire un en-avant.

◇ *vt insep inf Br*: **he's ~ing on 60** il va sur la soixantaine; **there were ~ing on 50 people in the hall** il n'y avait pas loin de 50 personnes dans la salle.

◆ **knock out** *vt sep* -**1.** [nail] faire sortir; [wall] abattre; **one of his teeth was ~ed out** il a perdu une dent. -**2.** [make unconscious] assommer; [in boxing] mettre K-O; **the sleeping pill ~ed her out for ten hours** *inf* le somnifère l'a assommée OR mise K-O pendant dix heures. -**3.** *inf* [astound] épater; **her performance really ~ed me out!** *inf* son interprétation m'a vraiment épaté! -**4.** [eliminate] éliminer; **our team was ~ed out in the first round** notre équipe a été éliminée au premier tour. -**5.** [put out of action] mettre hors service; **it can ~ out a tank at 2,000 metres** cela peut mettre un tank hors de combat à 2 000 mètres. -**6.** *inf* [exhaust] crever; **I'm not going to ~ myself out working for him** je ne vais pas m'esquinter à travailler pour lui. -**7.** [pipe]: **he ~ed out his pipe** il a débourré sa pipe.

◆ **knock over** *vt sep* renverser, faire tomber; **I ~ed a pile of plates over** j'ai renversé OR fait tomber une pile d'assiettes; **she was ~ed over by a bus** elle a été renversée par un bus.

◆ **knock together** ◇ *vt sep* [hit together] cogner l'un contre l'autre; **they make music by ~ing bamboo sticks together** ils font de la musique en frappant des bambous l'un contre l'autre; **they need their heads ~ing together, those two** *inf* ces deux-là auraient bien besoin qu'on leur secoue les puces.

◇ *vi insep* s'entrechoquer.

◆ **knock up** ◇ *vt sep* -**1.** *inf* [make hurriedly] faire à la hâte; **these buildings were ~ed up after the war** ces bâtiments ont été construits à la hâte après la guerre; **he ~ed up a delicious meal in no time** en un rien de temps, il a réussi à nous préparer quelque chose de délicieux. -**2.** *Br* [waken] réveiller (en frappant à la porte). -**3.** *inf Br* [exhaust] crever; **that walk yesterday really ~ed me up** la promenade d'hier m'a complètement crevé ‖ [make ill] rendre malade; **he's ~ed up with the flu** il a chopé la grippe. -**4.** *inf Am* [damage] esquinter; **the furniture is pretty ~ed up** les meubles sont plutôt esquintés OR amochés. -**5.** ▽ [make pregnant] mettre en cloque; **she got ~ed up** elle s'est fait mettre en cloque. -**6.** [in cricket] marquer; **he ~ed up 50 runs before tea** il a marqué 50 points avant le thé.

◇ *vi insep Br* [in ball games] faire des balles.

knockabout ['nɒkəbaʊt] ◇ *adj* turbulent, violent; **a ~ comedy** OR **farce** une grosse farce; **a ~ comedian** un clown.

◇ *n* NAUT dériveur *m*.

knockdown ['nɒk,daʊn] ◇ *adj* -**1.** [forceful]: **a ~ blow** un coup à assommer un bœuf; **a ~ argument** un argument massue. -**2.** *Br* [reduced]: **for sale at ~ prices** en vente à des prix imbattables OR défiant toute concurrence; **I got it for a ~ price** je l'ai eu pour trois fois rien. -**3.** [which can be dismantled] démontable; **sold in ~ form** vendu en kit.

◇ *n* -**1.** [in boxing] knock-down *m*. -**2.** *inf Am dated* [introduction] présentation *f*; **I'll give you a ~ to him** je te le présenterai.

knocker ['nɒkəʳ] *n* -**1.** [on door] heurtoir *m*, marteau *m* (de porte). -**2.** *inf* [critic] débineur *m*, -euse *f*.

◆ **knockers**▽ *npl* [breasts] nichons *mpl*.

knocker-up (*pl* **knockers-up**) *n Br autrefois, personne qui réveillait les gens en frappant à leur porte.*

knock-for-knock *adj* [in insurance]: **~ agreement** *accord à l'amiable selon lequel, lors d'un accident, chaque compagnie d'assurance paie les dégâts de son propre assuré.*

knocking ['nɒkɪŋ] *n* -**1.** [noise] bruit *m* de coups, cognement *m*; AUT cognement *m*, cliquetis *m*. -**2.** *inf Br* [injury, defeat]: **to take a ~** [in fight] se faire rouer de coups; [in match] se faire battre à plate couture OR plates coutures; **their prestige took a ~** leur prestige en a pris un coup.

knocking copy *n (U)* contre-publicité *f*.

knocking-off time *inf n Br*: **it's ~** c'est l'heure de se tirer.

knocking shop▽ *n Br* bordel *m*.

knock-kneed [-'niːd] *adj* cagneux.

knock-knees *npl*: **to have ~** avoir les genoux cagneux.

knock-on ◇ *n* RUGBY en-avant *m inv*.

◇ *adj*: **~ effect** répercussion *f*; **to have a ~ effect** déclencher une réaction en chaîne.

knockout ['nɒkaʊt] ◇ *n* -**1.** [in boxing] knock-out *m*, K-O *m*; **to win by a ~** gagner par K-O; **technical ~** knock-out technique. -**2.** *inf* [sensation]: **to be a ~** être sensationnel OR génial. -**3.** SPORT tournoi *m* (par élimination directe).

◇ *adj* -**1.** **~ blow** coup *m* qui met K-O; **~ drops** *inf* soporifique *m*, somnifère *m*. -**2.** SPORT: **~ competition** tournoi *m* par élimination.

knock-up *n Br* SPORT [in ball games] échauffement *m*; **to have a ~** faire des balles.

knoll [nəʊl] *n* monticule *m*, tertre *m*.

Knossos ['knɒsəs] *pr n* Cnossos, Knossos.

knot [nɒt] (*pt & pp* **knotted**, *cont* **knotting**) ◇ *n* -**1.** [fastening] nœud *m*; *fig* [bond] lien *m*; **to tie sthg in a ~** nouer qqch; **to tie/to untie a ~** faire/défaire un nœud ❑ **to tie the (marriage) ~** se marier. -**2.** [tangle] nœud *m*; **the wool is full of ~s** la laine est toute emmêlée; **my stomach was in ~s** *fig* j'avais l'estomac noué. -**3.** [in wood] nœud *m*. -**4.** ANAT & MED nœud *m*, nodule *m*. -**5.** [cluster of people] petit groupe *m*. -**6.** NAUT nœud *m*; **we are doing 15 ~s** nous filons 15 nœuds ❑ **at a rate of ~s** à toute allure, à un train d'enfer.

◇ *vt* [string] nouer, faire un nœud dans; [tie] nouer; **he knotted the rope around his waist** il s'est attaché OR noué la corde autour de la taille.

◇ *vi* [stomach] se nouer; [muscles] se contracter, se raidir; **my stomach knotted up with fear** j'avais l'estomac noué par la peur.

knothole ['nɒthəʊl] *n* trou *m (laissé par un nœud dans du bois)*.

knotted ['nɒtɪd] *adj* noué; **get ~!**▽ va te faire voir!

knotty ['nɒtɪ] (*compar* **knottier**, *superl* **knottiest**) *adj* [wood, hands] noueux; [wool, hair] plein de nœuds; [problem] épineux.

knout [naʊt] *n* knout *m*.

know [nəʊ] (*pt* **knew** [njuː], *pp* **known** [nəʊn]) ◇ *vt* -**1.** [person] connaître; **to ~ sb by sight/by reputation** connaître qqn de vue/de réputation; **we've known each other for years** ça fait des années que nous nous connaissons; **I don't ~ him to speak to** je ne le connais pas assez pour lui parler; **~ing him, he'll still be in bed** tel que je le connais, il sera encore au lit; **to get to ~ sb**: **you'll like her once you get to ~ her better** elle vous plaira une fois que vous la connaîtrez mieux. -**2.** [place] connaître; **I ~ Budapest well** je connais bien Budapest. -**3.** [fact, information]: **do you ~ her phone number?** vous connaissez son numéro de téléphone?; **civilization as we ~ it** la civilisation telle que nous la connaissons; **how was I to ~ she wouldn't come?** comment aurais-je pu savoir OR deviner qu'elle ne viendrait pas?; **I ~ for a fact that he's lying** je sais pertinemment qu'il ment; **I don't ~ that it's the best solution** je ne suis pas certain OR sûr que ce soit la meilleure solution; **you don't ~** OR **you'll never ~ how glad I am that it's over** tu ne peux pas savoir combien OR à quel point je suis content que ce soit terminé; **I ~ what I'm talking about** je sais de quoi je parle; **I'll let you ~ how it turns out** je te dirai comment ça s'est passé; **any problems, let me ~** au moindre problème, n'hésitez pas; **do you ~ anything about him that could help us?** est-ce que vous savez quelque chose à son sujet qui pourrait nous aider?; **she ~s a lot about politics** elle s'y connaît en politique; **she ~s a thing or two about business** *inf* elle s'y connaît en affaires; **she ~s her own mind** elle sait ce qu'elle veut ❑ **it's not an easy job — don't I ~ it!** *inf* ce n'est pas un travail facile — à qui le dis-tu!; **you ~ what I mean** tu vois ce que je veux dire; **he was just sort of lying there, ~ what I mean?** *inf* il était allongé là, tu vois; **well, what do you ~!** *inf* ça alors!, ça par exemple!; **you ~ what you can do with it!**▽ tu sais où tu peux te le mettre!; **there's no ~ing how he'll react** on ne peut pas savoir comment il réagira; **God** OR **Heaven ~s why!** *inf* Dieu sait pourquoi! -**4.** [language, skill]: **he ~s French** il comprend le français; **I ~ a few words of Welsh** je connais quelques mots de gallois; **she really ~s her job/subject** elle connaît son boulot/sujet; **to ~ how to do sthg** savoir faire qqch; **does he ~ how to cook?** sait-il cuisiner?; **they knew how to make cars in those days!** en ce temps-là, les voitures, c'était du solide! -**5.** [recognize] reconnaître; **I knew her the moment I saw her** je l'ai reconnue dès que je l'ai vue; **the town centre has changed so much you wouldn't ~ it** le centre ville a tellement changé que vous auriez du mal à le reconnaître; **she ~s a bargain when she sees one** elle sait reconnaître une bonne affaire; **he wouldn't ~ a good novel if it hit him** il est tout à fait incapable de reconnaître un bon roman. -**6.** [distinguish] distinguer, discerner; **she doesn't ~ right from wrong** elle ne sait pas discerner le bien du mal OR faire la différence entre le bien et le mal. -**7.** [experience] connaître; **I've known poverty/failure** j'ai connu la pauvreté/l'échec; **I've never known him to be wrong** je ne l'ai jamais vu se tromper; **such coincidences have been known** de telles coïncidences se sont déjà vues. -**8.** [nickname, call]: **Ian White, known as "Chalky"** Ian White, connu sous le nom de «Chalky»; **they're known as June bugs in America** on les appelle des «June bugs» en Amérique. -**9.** [regard] considérer; **she's known as one of our finest singers** elle est considérée comme l'une de nos meilleures chanteuses. -**10.** *arch* OR BIBLE [have sex with] connaître.

◇ *vi* savoir; **who ~s?** qui sait?; **not that I ~** pas que je sache; **you never ~** on ne sait jamais; **he might** OR **should have known better** ce n'était pas très sage de sa part; **he always thinks he ~s best** il croit toujours avoir raison; **Mother ~s best** maman sait de quoi elle parle; **to ~ about sthg** être au courant de qqch; **I've known about it for a week** je le sais OR je suis au courant depuis une semaine; **do you ~ about the new arrangements?** est-ce que vous êtes au courant OR avez-vous entendu parler des nouvelles dispositions?; **he ~s about cars** il s'y connaît en voitures; **I don't ~ about you, but I'm exhausted** toi, je ne sais pas, mais moi, je suis épuisé; **to ~ of sb/sthg** avoir entendu parler de qqn/qqch; **do you ~ her? — well, I**

~ of her est-ce que tu la connais? – non, mais j'ai entendu parler d'elle; do you ~ of a good bookshop? vous connaissez une bonne librairie?; have they got much money? – not that I ~ of ont-ils beaucoup d'argent? – pas que je sache; it's just so difficult – oh, I ~ c'est tellement difficile – oh, je sais; it's difficult, I ~, but not impossible c'est difficile, je sais, mais pas impossible; what's his name? – I don't ~ comment s'appelle-t-il? – je ne sais pas; are you going to accept? – I don't ~ tu vas accepter? – je ne sais pas.
◇ *n phr*: to be in the ~ *inf* être au courant.
◆ **as far as I know** *adv phr* (pour) autant que je sache; not as far as I ~ pas que je sache; as far as I ~, he lives in London autant que je sache, il vit à Londres.
◆ **you know** *adv phr* -**1.** [for emphasis]: I was right, you ~ j'avais raison, tu sais. -**2.** [indicating hesitancy]: he was just, you ~, a bit boring il était juste un peu ennuyeux, si tu vois ce que je veux dire. -**3.** [to add information]: it was that blonde woman, you ~, the one with the dog c'était la femme blonde, tu sais, celle qui avait un chien. -**4.** [to introduce a statement]: you ~, sometimes I wonder why I do this tu sais, parfois je me demande pourquoi je fais ça.

knowable ['nəʊəbl] *adj* connaissable.

know-all *inf Br*, **know-it-all** *inf Am n pej* je-sais-tout *mf*, monsieur *m* OR madame *f* OR mademoiselle *f* je-sais-tout; she's a real ~ c'est une vraie (madame) je-sais-tout.

know-how *n* savoir-faire *m*, know-how *m*.

knowing ['nəʊɪŋ] *adj* [look, laugh] entendu, complice; she gave him a ~ look elle l'a regardé d'un air entendu.

knowingly ['nəʊɪŋlɪ] *adv* -**1.** [act] sciemment, consciemment. -**2.** [smile, laugh] d'un air entendu.

know-it-all *inf Am* = **know-all**.

knowledgable ['nɒlɪdʒəbl] = **knowledgeable**.

knowledge ['nɒlɪdʒ] *n* -**1.** [learning] connaissance *f*, savoir *m*; [total learning] connaissances *fpl*; she has a good ~ of English elle a une bonne connaissance de l'anglais; he has a basic ~ of computing il a un minimum de connaissances en informatique; to have a thorough ~ of sthg connaître qqch à fond. -**2.** [awareness] connaissance *f*; I have no ~ of what happened je ne sais absolument rien de OR j'ignore totalement ce qui s'est passé; it has come to my ~ that... j'ai appris que...; he brought the theft to my ~ il a porté le vol à ma connaissance, il m'a fait part du vol; to (the best of) my ~ (pour) autant que je sache, à ma connaissance; not to my ~ pas que je sache; without my ~ à mon insu, sans que je le sache; it's (a matter of) common ~ c'est de notoriété publique, personne ne l'ignore.

knowledgeable ['nɒlɪdʒəbl] *adj* -**1.** [well researched] bien documenté. -**2.** [expert] bien informé; he's very ~ about computing il connaît bien l'informatique, il s'y connaît en informatique.

knowledgeably ['nɒlɪdʒəblɪ] *adv* en connaisseur; he speaks very ~ about art il parle d'art en connaisseur.

knowledge engineer *n* COMPUT cogniticien *m*, -ienne *f*.

known [nəʊn] ◇ *pp* → **know**.
◇ *adj* [notorious] connu, notoire; he's a ~ drugs dealer c'est un revendeur de drogue notoire ‖ [recognized] reconnu; she's a ~ expert in the field c'est un expert reconnu OR qui fait autorité dans ce domaine; it's a ~ fact c'est un fait établi; to make o.s. ~ se faire connaître; to let it be ~ faire savoir.

knuckle ['nʌkl] *n* -**1.** [of human] articulation *f* OR jointure *f* (du doigt); [of animal] première phalange *f*; I grazed my ~s on the wall je me suis écorché les doigts contre le mur ❑ near the ~ [joke, remark] osé. -**2.** [joint of meat] jarret *m*.
◆ **knuckles** *npl Am* = **knuckle-duster**.
◆ **knuckle down** *vi insep Br* s'y mettre; we'd better ~ down to some work il vaudrait mieux se mettre OR s'atteler au travail.
◆ **knuckle under** *vi insep* céder, se soumettre; don't ~ under to the pressure/management ne cédez pas à la pression/la direction.

knucklebone ['nʌklbəʊn] *n* articulation *f* du doigt.

knuckle-duster *n* coup-de-poing *m* américain.

knucklehead *inf* ['nʌklhed] *n* andouille *f*.

knuckle sandwich▽ *n* coup *m* de poing; I gave him a ~ je lui ai mis mon poing sur la gueule.

knurl [nɜːl] ◇ *n* -**1.** [in wood] nœud *m*. -**2.** [on screw] moletage *m*.
◇ *vt* TECH moleter; ~ed ring bague *f* moletée.

KO (*pl* KO's, *pt* & *pp* KO'd, *cont* KO'ing) (*abbr of* knockout) ◇ *vt* mettre K-O; [in boxing] battre par K-O.
◇ *n* K-O *m*.

koala [kəʊ'ɑːlə] *n*: ~ (bear) koala *m*.

kohl [kəʊl] *n* kohol *m*, khôl *m*.

kohlrabi [kəʊl'rɑːbɪ] *n* chou-rave *m*.

koine ['kɔɪneɪ] *n* koinè *f*.

kola ['kəʊlə] = **cola**.

kook *inf* [kuːk] *n Am* dingo *m*, cinglé *m*, -e *f*.

kookaburra ['kʊkəbʌrə] *n* martin-chasseur *m* (australien), kookaburra *m*.

kookie *inf*, **kooky** *inf* ['kuːkɪ] (*compar* kookier, *superl* kookiest) *adj Am* fêlé, malade.

kopeck, **kopek** ['kəʊpek] *n* kopeck *m*.

Koran [kɒ'rɑːn] *n*: the ~ le Coran.

Koranic [kɒ'rænɪk] *adj* coranique.

Korea [kə'rɪə] *pr n* Corée *f*; in ~ en Corée; the Democratic People's Republic of ~ la République démocratique populaire de Corée.

Korean [kə'rɪən] ◇ *n* -**1.** [person] Coréen *m*, -enne *f*. -**2.** LING coréen *m*.
◇ *adj* coréen; the ~ War la guerre de Corée.

THE KOREAN WAR:
Conflit qui opposa, de 1950 à 1953, la Corée du Nord (régime communiste) aux forces des Nations unies (soutenant la Corée du Sud) qui, dirigées par le général MacArthur, étaient largement composées d'Américains. Un traité mit fin à cette guerre en établissant la frontière entre les deux pays sur la ligne de front.

kosher ['kəʊʃəʳ] ◇ *adj* -**1.** RELIG kasher, cacher (*inv*). -**2.** *inf* [honest] honnête, régulier; it's not ~ c'est louche, c'est pas catholique.
◇ *n* nourriture *f* kasher.

Kowait [kə'weɪt] = **Kuwait**.

kowtow [,kaʊ'taʊ] *vi*: to ~ to sb faire des courbettes à qqn.

kph (*written abbr of* kilometres per hour) km/h

kraal [krɑːl] *n* kraal *m*.

Krakow ['krækɒv] = **Cracow**.

K ration *n Am* MIL ration *f* (alimentaire).

Kraut▽ [kraʊt] *offensive* ◇ *n* Boche *mf*.
◇ *adj* boche.

Kremlin ['kremlɪn] *pr n* Kremlin *m*.

krill [krɪl] *n* krill *m*.

kris(s) [krɪs] *n* kriss *m*, criss *m*.

krona ['krəʊnə] *n* couronne *f* suédoise.

krone ['krəʊnə] *n* [in Norway] couronne *f* norvégienne; [in Denmark] couronne *f* danoise.

Krugerrand ['kruːgərænd] *n* Krugerrand *m*.

Krushchev ['krʊstʃɒf] *pr n*: Nikita ~ Nikita Khrouchtchev.

krypton ['krɪptɒn] *n* krypton *m*.

KS *written abbr of* Kansas.

KT *written abbr of* Knight.

Kuala Lumpur [,kwɑːlə'lʊm,pʊəʳ] *pr n* Kuala Lumpur.

kudos ['kjuːdɒs] *n* gloire *f*, prestige *m*.

kudzu vine ['kʊdzuː-] *n plante fourragère très envahissante qui pousse dans le sud des États-Unis*

Ku Klux Klan [,kuːklʌks'klæn] *pr n* Ku Klux Klan *m*.

kumquat ['kʌmkwɒt] *n* kumquat *m*.

kung fu [,kʌŋ'fuː] *n* kung-fu *m*.

Kurd [kɜːd] *n* Kurde *mf*.

Kurdish ['kɜːdɪʃ] ◇ *n* LING kurde *m*.
◇ *adj* kurde.

Kurdistan [,kɜːdɪ'stɑːn] *pr n* Kurdistan *m*; in ~ au Kurdistan.

Kuril Islands, **Kurile Islands** [kʊ'riːl-] *pl pr n*: the ~ les îles *f* Kouriles; in the ~ aux îles Kouriles.

Kuwait [kʊ'weɪt] *pr n* -**1.** [country] Koweït *m*; in ~ au Koweït. -**2.** [town] Koweït City.

Kuwaiti [kʊ'weɪtɪ] ◇ *n* Koweïtien *m*, -enne *f*.
◇ *adj* koweïtien.

kvetch *inf* [kvetʃ] *vi* rouspéter.

kW (*written abbr of* kilowatt) kW.

kwashiorkor [,kwɒʃɪ'ɔːkɔːʳ] *n* kwashiorkor *m*.

KY *written abbr of* Kentucky.

kymograph ['kaɪməgrɑːf] *n* LING & MED kymographe *m*; AERON indicateur *m* de virage.

Kyoto ['kjəʊtəʊ] *pr n* Kyoto.

Kyrgyzstan [,kɜːgɪ'stɑːn] *pr n*: the Republic of ~ la république du Kyrghyzstan.

l (*pl* l's OR ls), **L** (*pl* L's OR Ls) [el] *n* [letter] l *m*, L *m*.

l (*written abbr of* litre) l.

L -**1.** *written abbr of* lake. -**2.** *written abbr of* large. -**3.** (*written abbr of* left) g. -**4.** (*written abbr of* learner) *lettre apposée sur une voiture et signalant un apprenti conducteur (en Grande-Bretagne)*.

la [lɑː] *n* MUS la *m*.

LA ◇ *pr n abbr of* Los Angeles.
◇ *written abbr of* Louisiana.

laager [ˈlɑːgəʳ] *n* MIL camp *m*.

lab *inf* [læb] ◇ *n* (*abbr of* laboratory) labo *m*.
◇ *comp* [book, coat] de laboratoire; a ~ assistant un laborantin, une laborantine, un assistant de laboratoire, une assistante de laboratoire.

Lab [læb] *written abbr of* Labour/Labour Party.

label [ˈleɪbl] (*Br pt* & *pp* labelled, *cont* labelling, *Am pt* & *pp* labeled, *cont* labeling) ◇ *n literal* & *fig* étiquette *f*; they brought out the record on the Mega ~ ils ont sorti le disque chez Mega; it's a good ~ c'est une bonne marque ❑ designer ~ marque *f*, griffe *f*.
◇ *vt* -**1.** [suitcase, jar] étiqueter; you must ~ your clothes clearly tous vos vêtements doivent être clairement marqués à votre nom; the bottle was labelled "shake before use" la bouteille portait l'étiquette «agiter avant de s'en servir OR avant l'emploi». -**2.** *fig* [person] étiqueter, cataloguer; he's been labelled (as) a troublemaker on l'a étiqueté OR catalogué comme fauteur de troubles.

labelling *Br*, **labeling** *Am* [ˈleɪblɪŋ] *n* étiquetage *m*.

labia [ˈleɪbɪə] *npl* ANAT lèvres *fpl*; ~ minora/majora petites/grandes lèvres.

labial [ˈleɪbjəl] LING ◇ *adj* labial.
◇ *n* labiale *f*.

labile [ˈleɪbaɪl] *adj* labile.

labiodental [ˌleɪbɪəʊˈdentl] LING ◇ *adj* labiodental.
◇ *n* labiodentale *f*.

labionasal [ˌleɪbɪəʊˈneɪzl] LING ◇ *adj* labionasal.
◇ *n* labionasale *f*.

labiovelar [ˌleɪbɪəʊˈviːləʳ] LING ◇ *adj* labiovélaire.
◇ *n* labiovélaire *f*.

labor *etc Am* = **labour**.

laboratory [*Br* ləˈbɒrətrɪ, *Am* ˈlæbrəˌtɔːrɪ] (*pl* laboratories) ◇ *n* laboratoire *m*.
◇ *comp* [assistant, equipment] de laboratoire.

Labor Code *n* code *m* du travail *(aux États-Unis)*.

Labor Day *n* fête *f* du travail *(aux États-Unis, célébrée le premier lundi de Septembre)*.

laborious [ləˈbɔːrɪəs] *adj* laborieux.

laboriously [ləˈbɔːrɪəslɪ] *adv* laborieusement.

labor union *n Am* syndicat *m*.

labour *Br*, **labor** *Am* [ˈleɪbəʳ] ◇ *n* -**1.** [work] travail *m*; [hard effort] labeur *m*; a ~ of love un travail fait pour le plaisir; her book was the result of five years' hard ~ son livre était le fruit de cinq ans de dur labeur OR de travail acharné. -**2.** INDUST [manpower] main-d'œuvre *f*; [workers] ouvriers *mpl*, travailleurs *mpl*. -**3.** POL: Labour le parti travailliste britannique; to vote Labour voter travailliste. -**4.** MED travail *m*; to be in ~ être en travail; to go into ~ commencer le travail ❑ ~ pains douleurs *fpl* de l'accouchement; ~ ward salle *f* d'accouchement.
◇ *vi* -**1.** [work] travailler dur. -**2.** [struggle - person]: he ~ed up the stairs il monta péniblement l'escalier; to ~ under a misapprehension OR a delusion *fig* se méprendre, être dans l'erreur ‖ [move with difficulty - vehicle] peiner; the car ~ed up the slope la voiture peinait dans la montée; the ship was ~ing through heavy seas le bateau avançait péniblement dans la mer démontée.
◇ *vt* [stress] insister sur; to ~ a point insister OR s'étendre sur un point.
◇ *comp* -**1.** [dispute, movement] social; [market] du travail; [shortage] de main-d'œuvre. -**2.** POL [government, victory] travailliste.

labour camp *n* camp *m* de travail.

laboured *Br*, **labored** *Am* [ˈleɪbəd] *adj* -**1.** [breathing] pénible, difficile. -**2.** [clumsy] lourd, laborieux.

labourer *Br*, **laborer** *Am* [ˈleɪbərəʳ] *n* [gen] ouvrier *m*, -ère *f*; [on building site] manœuvre *m*.

labour exchange *n Br dated* agence *f* pour l'emploi.

labour force *n* [in country] population *f* active; [in firm] main-d'œuvre *f*.

labour-intensive *adj*: a ~ industry une industrie à forte main-d'œuvre; craftwork is very ~ le travail artisanal nécessite une main-d'œuvre considérable.

Labourite [ˈleɪbəraɪt] ◇ *adj* POL travailliste.
◇ *n* travailliste *mf*.

Labour Party *n* parti *m* travailliste.

labour relations *npl* relations *fpl* sociales.

laboursaving *Br*, **laborsaving** *Am* [ˈleɪbəˌseɪvɪŋ] *adj*: ~ device [in home] appareil *m* ménager; [at work] appareil permettant un gain de temps.

Labrador [ˈlæbrədɔːʳ] *pr n* GEOG Labrador *m*; in ~ au Labrador.
◆ **labrador** *n* [dog] labrador *m*.

laburnum [ləˈbɜːnəm] *n*: ~ (tree) cytise *m*, faux ébénier *m*.

labyrinth [ˈlæbərɪnθ] *n* labyrinthe *m*, dédale *m*.

labyrinthine [ˌlæbəˈrɪnθaɪn] *adj* labyrinthique.

lace [leɪs] ◇ *n* -**1.** TEX dentelle *f*. -**2.** [in shoe, corset] lacet *m*.
◇ *vt* -**1.** [tie] lacer; [put laces in] mettre des lacets à; he's already learned to ~ his own shoes il a déjà appris à lacer ses souliers. -**2.** [add alcohol to]: he ~d my orange juice with gin il a mis du gin dans mon jus d'orange.
◇ *comp* [handkerchief, tablecloth etc] en dentelle.
◆ **lace into** *inf vt insep Br* [physically] rosser; [in criticism] attaquer violemment.
◆ **lace up** *vt sep Br* [shoes] lacer.

lacemaker [ˈleɪsˌmeɪkəʳ] *n* dentellier *m*, -ère *f*.

lacemaking [ˈleɪsˌmeɪkɪŋ] *n* industrie *f* dentellière.

lacerate [ˈlæsəreɪt] ◇ *vt* lacérer; his hands were ~d by the broken glass il avait les mains lacérées par le verre brisé; the encounter left her emotions ~d *fig* la rencontre lui avait déchiré le cœur OR l'avait meurtrie.
◇ *adj* BOT: ~ leaves feuilles *fpl* dentées OR dentelées.

laceration [ˌlæsəˈreɪʃn] *n* -**1.** [action] lacération *f*. -**2.** MED [gash]: he had deep ~s on his back il avait le dos profondément lacéré OR entaillé.

lace-up *adj* [shoe, boot] à lacets.
◆ **lace-ups** *npl Br* chaussures *fpl* à lacets.

lachrymal [ˈlækrɪml] *adj* lacrymal.

lachrymose [ˈlækrɪməʊs] *adj lit* larmoyant.

lacing [ˈleɪsɪŋ] *n* -**1.** [on shoe, garment] laçage *m*. -**2.** *inf Br* [beating] raclée *f*; he took a real ~ il a pris une bonne raclée.

lack [læk] ◇ *n* manque *m*; through OR for ~ of par manque de, faute de; there's no ~ of volunteers ce ne sont pas les volontaires qui manquent.
◇ *vt* manquer de; they certainly don't ~ confidence ils ne manquent certes pas de confiance en eux; we ~ the necessary resources nous n'avons pas les ressources nécessaires.
◆ **lack for** *vt insep* manquer de; he ~s for nothing il ne manque de rien, il a tout ce qu'il lui faut.

lackadaisical [ˌlækəˈdeɪzɪkl] *adj* [person - apathetic] apathique; [- lazy] indolent; [work] tranquille.

lackaday [ˈlækədeɪ] *interj arch* hélas!

lackey [ˈlækɪ] ◇ *n* laquais *m*; *pej* larbin *m*.
◇ *vi*: I refuse to ~ for him je refuse d'être son larbin.

lacking [ˈlækɪŋ] *adj* -**1.** [wanting] qui manque de; ~ in confidence qui manque de confiance en soi; originality is sadly ~ in his new novel son nouveau roman manque malheureusement d'originalité. -**2.** *inf euph* [stupid] demeuré, simple d'esprit.

lacklustre *Br*, **lackluster** *Am* [ˈlækˌlʌstəʳ] *adj* terne.

laconic [ləˈkɒnɪk] *adj* laconique.

laconically [ləˈkɒnɪklɪ] *adv* laconiquement.

lacquer ['lækəʳ] ◇ *n* **-1.** [varnish, hairspray] laque *f*. **-2.** [varnished object] laque *m*.
◇ *vt* [wood] laquer; [hair] mettre de la laque sur; she ~s her hair elle se met de la laque (sur les cheveux).

lacquered ['lækəd] *adj* laqué; a ~ box une boîte laquée.

lacquerware ['lækəweəʳ] *n (U)* laques *mpl*.

lacrimal ['lækrɪml] = **lachrymal**.

lacrosse [lə'krɒs] ◇ *n* lacrosse *f*, crosse *f*; ~ stick crosse.
◇ *comp* [player] de crosse.

lactase ['lækteɪz] *n* lactase *f*.

lactate [*n* 'lækteɪt, *vb* læk'teɪt] ◇ *n* CHEM lactate *m*.
◇ *vi* sécréter du lait.

lactation [,læk'teɪʃn] *n* lactation *f*.

lacteal ['læktɪəl] ◇ *adj* lacté.
◇ *n* ANAT & MED veine *f* lactée.

lactic acid ['læktɪk-] *n* CHEM acide *m* lactique.

lactobacillus [,læktəʊbə'sɪləs] (*pl* **lactobacilli** [-laɪ]) *n* lactobacille *m*, lactobacillus *m*.

lactogenic [,læktə'dʒenɪk] *adj* lactogène.

lactose ['læktəʊs] *n* lactose *m*.

lacuna [lə'kju:nə] (*pl* **lacunas** OR **lacunae** [-ni:]) *n* lacune *f*.

lacustrine [lə'kʌstraɪn] *adj* lacustre.

lacy ['leɪsɪ] (*compar* lacier, *superl* laciest) *adj* [lace-like] semblable à de la dentelle; [made of lace] en dentelle.

lad [læd] *n* **-1.** [young boy] garçon *m*; [son] fils *m*; he's only a ~ c'est seulement un gamin; when I was a ~ quand j'étais jeune; come here, ~ viens ici, mon gars OR mon garçon. **-2.** *inf Br* [friend] copain *m*; he went out for a drink with the ~s il est allé boire un coup avec des copains ‖ [colleague] collègue *m*, gars *m*; the ~s from work les copains de travail; morning ~s! salut les gars! **-3.** *inf Br* [rake] noceur *m*; he was a bit of a ~ when he was young il a eu une jeunesse assez tumultueuse.

ladder ['lædəʳ] ◇ *n* **-1.** *literal & fig* échelle *f*; to be at the top of the ~ *literal & fig* être arrivé au sommet OR en haut de l'échelle. **-2.** *Br* [in stocking] maille *f* filée; you've got a ~ in your stocking ton bas a filé, tu as filé ton bas.
◇ *vi & vt Br* filer.

ladder back *n* chaise *f* à barrettes.

ladderproof ['lædəpru:f] *adj Br* indémaillable.

laddie *inf* ['lædɪ] *n Scot* gars *m*; come here, ~ viens là, mon petit gars.

lade [leɪd] (*pt* laded, *pp* laden ['leɪdn] OR laded) *vt fml* [ship] charger.

laden ['leɪdn] ◇ *pp* → **lade**.
◇ *adj* chargé; ~ with chargé de; apple-~ trees arbres couverts de pommes; a heavily ~ ship un navire à forte charge.

la-di-da *inf* [,lɑ:dɪ'dɑ:] *adj pej* [manner] snob, prétentieux; [voice] maniéré; she speaks in a very ~ way elle est assez pimbêche.

ladies ['leɪdɪz] *n Br* toilettes *fpl* pour dames.

ladies fingers *n* okra *m*.

ladies' man *n* don Juan *m*, homme *m* à femmes.

ladies room *Am* = **ladies**.

lading ['leɪdɪŋ] *n* [cargo] cargaison *f*, chargement *m*.

ladle ['leɪdl] ◇ *n* louche *f*.
◇ *vt* servir (à la louche).
◆ **ladle out** *vt sep Br* **-1.** [soup] servir (à la louche). **-2.** *inf fig* [money] distribuer à gogo; he's always ladling out advice il n'arrête pas de distribuer des conseils à droite et à gauche.

lady ['leɪdɪ] (*pl* ladies) ◇ *n* **-1.** [woman] dame *f*; Ladies and Gentlemen Mesdames et Messieurs; the ~ of the house la maîtresse de maison; young ~ [girl] jeune fille; [young woman] jeune femme; ask the young ~ over there [in shop] demandez à la demoiselle que vous voyez là-bas; well, young ~, what have you got to say for yourself? eh bien, ma fille, qu'avez-vous à répondre?; his young ~ *dated* sa petite amie ‖ [by birth or upbringing] dame *f*; she's a real ~ c'est une vraie dame; she's no ~ elle n'a aucune classe ‖ [term of address]: my Lady Madame ‖ [as title]: Lady Patricia Lady Patricia ❑ the Lady of the Lake la Dame du lac; the Lady of the Lamp la Dame à la Lampe *(Florence Nightingale, célèbre infirmière anglaise)*; 'Lady and the Tramp' *Disney* 'la Belle et le clochard'; 'Lady Chatterley's Lover' *Lawrence* 'l'Amant de Lady Chatterley'; 'Lady Windermere's Fan' *Wilde* 'l'Éventail de Lady Windermere'; 'The Lady of the Camelias' *Dumas* 'la Dame aux camélias'; 'The Lady's Not for Burning' *Fry* 'la Dame ne brûlera pas'; 'The Lady Vanishes' *Hitchcock* 'Une femme disparaît'. **-2.** *inf Am* [term of address] madame *f*; hey ~! eh, ma petite dame! **-3.** RELIG: Our Lady Notre-Dame *f*.
◇ *comp* femme; a ~ doctor une femme médecin.

ladybird ['leɪdɪbɜ:d] *n Br* coccinelle *f*.

lady bountiful *n pej* OR *hum* généreuse bienfaitrice *f*.

ladybug ['leɪdɪbʌg] *n Am* coccinelle *f*.

Lady Chapel *n* chapelle *f* de la Sainte-Vierge.

Lady Day *n* (fête *f* de) l'Annonciation *f*.

ladyfriend ['leɪdɪfrend] *n dated* petite amie *f*.

lady-in-waiting *n* dame *f* d'honneur.

ladykiller *inf* ['leɪdɪ,kɪləʳ] *n* bourreau *m* des cœurs; 'The Ladykillers' *Mackendrick* 'Tueurs de dames'.

ladylike ['leɪdɪlaɪk] *adj* [person] distingué, bien élevé; [manners] raffiné, élégant; it's not very ~ to smoke in the street! une fille comme il faut ne fume pas dans la rue!

ladylove ['leɪdɪlʌv] *n lit*: his ~ sa bien-aimée.

Lady Mayoress *n Br* femme *f* du maire.

Lady Muck *n Br pej se dit d'une femme qui se prend pour une grande dame*.

ladyship ['leɪdɪʃɪp] *n*: Your OR Her Ladyship *literal* Madame (la baronne/la vicomtesse/la comtesse); *fig* OR *hum* la maîtresse de ces lieux.

lady's maid *n* femme *f* de chambre.

lag [læg] (*pt & pp* lagged, *cont* lagging) ◇ *n* **-1.** [gap] décalage *m*; there is a two-hour time-~ il y a un décalage horaire de deux heures; there was a ~ between completion and publication il y a eu un décalage entre l'achèvement de l'œuvre et sa publication. **-2.** ▽ *Br* [convict] taulard *m*, -e *f*; [habitual offender] récidiviste *mf*; an old ~ un cheval de retour.
◇ *vi* rester en arrière, traîner.
◇ *vt* [pipe] calorifuger.
◆ **lag behind** ◇ *vi insep* [dawdle] traîner, lambiner; [be at the back] rester derrière; the youngest children were lagging behind les enfants les plus jeunes restaient en arrière ‖ [be outdistanced] se laisser distancer; our country is lagging behind in medical research notre pays a du retard en matière de recherche médicale.
◇ *vt insep* [competitor] traîner derrière, avoir du retard sur.

lager ['lɑ:gəʳ] *n* **-1.** = **laager**. **-2.** *Br* bière *f* blonde; ~ lout *jeune qui, sous l'influence de l'alcool, cherche la bagarre ou commet des actes de vandalisme*.

laggard ['lægəd] *n* traînard *m*, -e *f*.

lagging ['lægɪŋ] *n* isolant *m*, calorifuge *m*.

lagniappe ['lænjæp] *n Am* COMM prime *f*.

lagoon [lə'gu:n] *n* [gen] lagune *f*; [in coral reef] lagon *m*.

Lagos ['leɪgɒs] *pr n* Lagos.

lah [lɑ:] = **la**.

lah-di-dah [,lɑ:dɪ'dɑ:] = **la-di-da**.

laic(al) ['leɪɪk(l)] *adj* laïque.

laicism ['leɪɪsɪzm] *n* laïcisme *m*.

laicize, -ise ['leɪɪsaɪz] *vt* laïciser.

laid [leɪd] *pt & pp* → **lay**.

laid-back *inf adj* décontracté, cool.

lain [leɪn] *pp* → **lie**.

lair [leəʳ] *n* [for animals] tanière *f*; *fig* repaire *m*, tanière *f*.

laird [leəd] *n* laird *m*, propriétaire *m* foncier *(en Écosse)*.

laity ['leɪətɪ] *n (U)* **-1.** RELIG laïcs *mpl*. **-2.** [non-specialists] profanes *mpl*.

lake [leɪk] *n* **-1.** lac *m*; the Lakes *Br* = **Lake District**; a wine ~ *fig* des excédents *mpl* de vin ❑ go jump in a ~! *inf* va te faire cuire un œuf! **-2.** [pigment] laque *f*.

LAKES:
Lake Baikal le lac Baïkal;
Lake Balaton le lac Balaton;
Lake Constance le lac de Constance;
Lake Como le lac de Côme;
Lake Erie le lac Érié;
Lake Garda le lac de Garde;
Lake Geneva le lac Léman or de Genève;
Lake Huron le lac Huron;
Lake Ladoga le lac Ladoga;
Lake Maggiore le lac Majeur;
Lake Malawi le lac Malawi;
Lake Michigan le lac Michigan;
Lake Nasser le lac Nasser;
Lake Ontario le lac Ontario;
Lake Superior le lac Supérieur;
Lake Tanganyika le lac Tanganyika;
Lake Tiberias le lac de Tibériade;
Lake Titicaca le lac Titicaca;
Lake Victoria le lac Victoria;
Lake Winnipeg le lac Winnipeg.

Lake District *pr n* Lake District *m*, région *f* des lacs *(dans le nord-ouest de l'Angleterre)*.

lake dwelling *n* habitation *f* lacustre.

Lakeland ['leɪklənd] *adj* [of or in Lake District] de la région des lacs.

Lake Poets *npl* lakistes *mpl (poètes anglais du début du XIXe siècle, dont Wordsworth et Coleridge)*.

lakeside ['leɪksaɪd] ◇ *n* rive *f* OR bord *m* d'un lac.
◇ *comp* [hotel] (situé) au bord d'un lac.

la-la land *inf pr n Los Angeles*.

Lallans ['lælənz] *n* lallans *m (dialecte du sud de l'Écosse)*.

lallation [læ'leɪʃn] *n* LING lallation *f*, lambdacisme *m*.

lallygag *inf* ['lælɪgæg] (*pt & pp* lallygagged, *cont* lallygagging) *vi Am* traîner.

lam [læm] (*pt & pp* lammed, *cont* lamming) ◇ *vt inf* [beat] rosser.
◇ *n* ▽ *Am* [escape] cavale *f*; on the ~ en cavale; to take it on the ~ faire la belle.
◆ **lam into** *inf vt insep Br* **-1.** [physically] rentrer dans; he lammed into me il m'est rentré dedans. **-2.** [verbally] enguirlander, sonner les cloches à.

lama ['lɑ:mə] *n* RELIG lama *m*.

lamb [læm] ◇ *n* **-1.** ZOOL agneau *m*; like ~s to the slaughter comme des veaux à l'abattoir. **-2.** [meat] agneau *m*. **-3.** *fig* [innocent person] agneau *m*; [lovable person]: she's a ~ c'est un ange, elle est adorable; be a ~ and fetch my glasses sois un ange OR sois gentil, va me chercher mes lunettes; you poor little ~! mon pauvre chou! **-4.** RELIG: the Lamb of God l'Agneau de Dieu.
◇ *vi* agneler, mettre bas.
◇ *comp* [chop, cutlet] d'agneau.

lambast [læm'bæst], **lambaste** [læm'beɪst] *vt* [scold] réprimander; [thrash] battre, rosser.

lambda ['læmdə] *n* lambda *m*.

lambent ['læmbənt] *adj lit* [glowing] chatoyant, brillant; [sparkling] étincelant.

lambert ['læmbət] *n* PHYS lambert *m*.

Lambeth Palace ['læmbəθ-] *pr n résidence londonienne de l'archevêque de Cantorbéry*.

lambing ['læmɪŋ] *n* agnelage *m*; at ~ time au moment de l'agnelage.

lambkin ['læmkɪn] *n* agnelet *m*; [term of affection]: my little ~ mon petit chou.

lambskin ['læmskɪn] ◇ *n* (peau *f* d')agneau *m*.
◇ *comp* [coat, gloves] en agneau.

lambswool ['læmzwʊl] *comp* [scarf, sweater etc] en laine d'agneau, en lambswool.

lame [leɪm] ◇ *adj* -**1.** [person, horse] boiteux; to be ~ boiter; to go ~ se mettre à boiter; his left leg is ~, he's ~ in his left leg il boite de la jambe gauche. -**2.** [weak - excuse] piètre, bancal; [- argument, reasoning] boiteux; [- plot] boiteux, bancal; what a ~ joke! quelle blague idiote!, quelle astuce vaseuse! -**3.** *inf Am* [conventional] vieux jeu *(inv)*.
◇ *vt* estropier.
◇ *npl*: the ~ les boiteux *mpl*.

lamé ['lɑːmeɪ] *n* lamé *m*.

lamebrain *inf* ['leɪmbreɪn] *n* crétin *m*, -e *f*.

lame duck *n fig* -**1.** [gen & INDUST] canard *m* boiteux. -**2.** *Am* POL *candidat sortant non réélu qui attend l'arrivée de son successeur*.
◆ **lame-duck** *comp*: a lame-duck president *un président sortant non réélu*.

lamella [lə'melə] (*pl* lamellas OR lamellae [-liː]) *n* ANAT & BOT lame *f*.

lamely ['leɪmlɪ] *adv* de façon peu convaincante, maladroitement.

lameness ['leɪmnɪs] *n* -**1.** [limping] boiterie *f*, claudication *f spec*; his ~ is the result of a childhood accident il boite à la suite d'un accident qu'il a eu dans son enfance. -**2.** [weakness - of excuse, argument etc] faiblesse *f*.

lament [lə'ment] ◇ *vt* [feel sorrow for] regretter, pleurer; [complain about] se lamenter sur, se plaindre de; she ~ed the passing of her youth elle pleurait sa jeunesse perdue; "I'll never finish in time!", she ~ed «je n'aurai jamais fini à temps!», gémit-elle.
◇ *vi* se lamenter; she was ~ing loudly over the loss of her jewels elle se lamentait bruyamment OR à grands cris d'avoir perdu ses bijoux.
◇ *n* -**1.** [lamentation, complaint] lamentation *f*. -**2.** [poem] élégie *f*; [song] complainte *f*.

lamentable ['læməntəbl] *adj* [regrettable] regrettable; [poor] lamentable; the ~ state of the economy l'état lamentable OR déplorable de l'économie.

lamentably ['læməntəblɪ] *adv* lamentablement.

lamentation [,læmen'teɪʃn] *n* lamentation *f*; the Lamentations (of Jeremiah) les Lamentations (de Jérémie).

lamina ['læmɪnə] (*pl* laminas OR laminae [-niː]) *n* ANAT & BOT lame *f*.

laminal ['læmɪnl] *adj* LING laminal.

laminate ['læmɪneɪt] ◇ *vt* TECH [bond in layers] laminer; [veneer] plaquer.
◇ *n* stratifié *m*; a table covered in white ~ une table recouverte de stratifié blanc.

laminated ['læmɪneɪtɪd] *adj* [wood] stratifié; [glass] feuilleté; ~ windscreen pare-brise *m inv* (en verre) feuilleté.

lamp [læmp] *n* -**1.** [gen] lampe *f*; [street-lamp] réverbère *m*; [on car, train] lumière *f*, feu *m*. -**2.** MED lampe *f*; infrared ~ lampe à infrarouges.

lampblack ['læmpblæk] *n* noir *m* de carbone OR de fumée.

lamp bracket *n* applique *f*.

lamplight ['læmplaɪt] *n*: her hair shone in the ~ la lumière de la lampe faisait briller ses cheveux; to read by ~ lire à la lumière d'une OR de la lampe.

lamplighter ['læmplaɪtəʳ] *n* -**1.** [person] allumeur *m* de réverbères. -**2.** *Am* [device] programmeur *m* d'éclairage.

lamplit ['læmplɪt] *adj* éclairé par une lampe.

lampoon [læm'puːn] ◇ *n* [satire] satire *f*; [written] pamphlet *m*.
◇ *vt* ridiculiser, tourner en dérision.

lampoonist [læm'puːnɪst] *n* [satirist] satiriste *mf*; [in writings] pamphlétaire *mf*.

lamppost ['læmppəʊst] *n* réverbère *m*.

lamprey ['læmprɪ] *n* lamproie *f*.

lampshade ['læmpʃeɪd] *n* abat-jour *m inv*.

lampstand ['læmpstænd] *n* pied *m* de lampe.

lamp standard *n* lampadaire *m*.

Lancaster ['læŋkəstəʳ] *pr n* -**1.** GEOG Lancaster *m*. -**2.** HIST Lancastre *f*.

Lancastrian [læŋ'kæstrɪən] *n* -**1.** GEOG habitant *m*, -e *f* de Lancaster. -**2.** HIST lancastrien *m*, -enne *f*.

lance [lɑːns] ◇ *n* -**1.** [weapon] lance *f*; to break a ~ with sb *Br fig* se disputer avec qqn. -**2.** MED lancette *f*, bistouri *m*.
◇ *vt* MED percer, inciser.

lance corporal *n* caporal *m (dans l'armée britannique)*.

Lancelot ['lɑːnslɒt] *pr n* Lancelot.

lancer ['lɑːnsəʳ] *n* HIST & MIL lancier *m*.
◆ **lancers** *npl* [dance] (quadrille *m* des) lanciers *mpl*.

lancet ['lɑːnsɪt] *n* MED lancette *f*, bistouri *m*.

lancet arch *n* arc *m* lancéolé OR en lancette.

lancet window *n* fenêtre *f* en ogive.

Lancs *written abbr of* Lancashire.

land [lænd] ◇ *vi* -**1.** AERON & ASTRONAUT atterrir; they ~ at 7 pm ils atterrissent OR leur avion arrive à 19 h; to ~ on the moon atterrir sur la Lune, alunir; to ~ in the sea amerrir; to ~ on an aircraft carrier apponter (sur un porte-avions). -**2.** NAUT [boat] arriver à quai; [passengers] débarquer. -**3.** [ball, high jumper] tomber, retomber; [falling object, bomb, parachutist] tomber; [bird] se poser; an apple ~ed on her head elle a reçu une pomme sur la tête ❑ to ~ on one's feet *literal* & *fig* retomber sur ses pieds. -**4.** *inf* [finish up] finir, atterrir; I hope that problem doesn't ~ on my desk j'espère que ce problème ne va pas atterrir sur mon bureau; the car ~ed (up) in the ditch la voiture a terminé sa course dans le fossé; he ~ed in jail il s'est retrouvé en prison; you'll ~ up in jail! tu finiras en prison!; the letter ~ed up in Finland la lettre a atterri en Finlande; I ~ed up at a friend's house j'ai atterri OR échoué chez un ami.
◇ *vt* -**1.** [plane] poser; [cargo, passengers] débarquer; they have succeeded in ~ing men on the moon ils ont réussi à envoyer des hommes sur la lune. -**2.** [fish - onto bank] hisser sur la rive; [- onto boat] hisser dans le bateau. -**3.** *inf* [job, contract] décrocher. -**4.** *inf* [put, place] ficher; he caught me a blow that nearly ~ed me in the lake il m'a flanqué un tel coup que j'ai bien failli me retrouver dans le lac; this could ~ us in real trouble ça pourrait nous attirer de gros ennuis OR nous mettre dans le pétrin; it will ~ you in prison! tu finiras en prison! -**5.** [blow] flanquer; I ~ed him a blow OR ~ed him one on the nose je lui ai flanqué OR collé mon poing dans la figure. -**6.** *inf* [encumber]: to get ~ed with sthg: I got ~ed with the job of organizing the party c'est moi qui me suis retrouvé avec la fête à organiser, c'est moi qui me suis tapé l'organisation de la fête; we got ~ed with their children for the weekend ils nous ont refilé leurs gosses OR il a fallu se farcir leurs gosses tout le week-end; as usual, I got ~ed with all the work comme d'habitude, c'est moi qui me suis tapé tout le travail; they ~ed me with the bill c'est moi qui ai écopé de l'addition.
◇ *n* -**1.** [for farming, building etc] terre *f*; he works on the ~ il travaille la terre; this is good farming ~ c'est de la bonne terre; building ~ terrain constructible; '~ for sale' 'terrain à vendre'; a piece of ~ [for farming] un lopin de terre; [for building] un terrain (à bâtir); to live off the ~ vivre des ressources naturelles de la terre ❑ to see how the ~ lies, to find out the lie OR lay of the ~ tâter le terrain. -**2.** [property] terre *f*, terres *fpl*; their ~s were confiscated leurs terres ont été confisquées; get off my ~! sortez de mes terres! -**3.** [area, region] région *f*; the desert ~s of Northern Australia les régions désertiques du nord de l'Australie. -**4.** [not sea] terre *f*; they sighted ~ ils aperçurent la terre; we travelled by ~ to Cairo nous sommes allés au Caire par la route; over ~ and sea sur terre et sur mer. -**5.** [nation, country] pays *m*; to travel in distant ~s voyager dans des pays lointains; the victory was celebrated throughout the ~ le pays tout entier a fêté la victoire. -**6.** *fig* [realm] royaume *m*, pays *m*; he is no longer in the ~ of the living il n'est plus de ce monde; she lives in a ~ of make-believe elle vit dans un monde de chimères.
◇ *comp* [prices - in town] du terrain; [- in country] de la terre; [reform] agraire; [tax, ownership] foncier; *Br* HIST [army] de terre; [worker] agricole.
◆ **lands** *npl* = **land 2, 3**.
◆ **land up** *vi insep* = **land** *vi* **4**.

land agent *n* -**1.** [administrator] régisseur *m*, intendant *m*, -e *f*. -**2.** *Br* [estate agent] agent *m* immobilier.

landau ['lændɔː] *n* landau *m*.

land-based *adj* -**1.** ECON basé sur la propriété terrienne. -**2.** MIL: ~ forces forces *fpl* terrestres, armée *f* de terre.

land breeze *n* brise *f* de terre.

landed ['lændɪd] *adj Br* foncier; the ~ gentry la noblesse terrienne.

landfall ['lændfɔːl] *n* NAUT: to make ~ apercevoir la terre, arriver en vue d'une côte.

landfill ['lændfɪl] *n* ensevelissement *m* de déchets.

landholder ['lænd,həʊldəʳ] *n* propriétaire *m* terrien, propriétaire *f* terrienne.

landholding ['lænd,həʊldɪŋ] ◇ *adj* foncier.
◇ *n* propriété *f*.

landing ['lændɪŋ] *n* -**1.** [of plane, spacecraft] atterrissage *m*; [on moon] alunissage *m*; [of passengers, foods] débarquement *m*; the plane made a crash/emergency ~ l'avion s'est posé en catastrophe/a fait un atterrissage forcé ‖ SPORT [of skier, high jumper] réception *f*; he made a bad ~ il s'est mal reçu ❑ the Normandy ~s HIST le Débarquement (de Normandie). -**2.** [in staircase] palier *m*; [floor] étage *m*. -**3.** [jetty] débarcadère *m*, embarcadère *m*.

landing beacon *n* AERON balise *f* d'atterrissage.

landing card *n* carte *f* de débarquement.

landing craft *n* navire *m* de débarquement.

landing field = **landing strip**.

landing gear *n* AERON train *m* d'atterrissage.

landing lights *npl* [on plane] phares *mpl* d'atterrissage; [at airport] balises *fpl* (d'atterrissage).

landing net *n* épuisette *f*.

landing stage *n* débarcadère *m*.

landing strip *n* piste *f* d'atterrissage.

landlady ['lænd,leɪdɪ] (*pl* landladies) *n* [owner] propriétaire *f*; [in lodgings] logeuse *f*; [in pub, guesthouse] patronne *f*.

landless ['lændlɪs] *adj* sans terre.

land-line *n* TELEC ligne *f* terrestre.

landlocked ['lændlɒkt] *adj* [country] enclavé, sans accès à la mer; [sea] intérieur.

landlord ['lændlɔːd] *n* [owner] propriétaire *m*; [in lodgings] logeur *m*; [in pub, guesthouse] patron *m*.

landlubber *inf* ['lænd,lʌbəʳ] *n hum* & *pej* marin *m* d'eau douce.

landmark ['lændmɑːk] ◇ *n* -**1.** *literal* point *m* de repère; major Paris ~s les principaux monuments de Paris. -**2.** *fig* étape *f* décisive, jalon *m*; the trial was a ~ in legal history *fig* le procès a fait date dans les annales juridiques.
◇ *comp* [decision] qui fait date.

landmass ['lændmæs] *n* zone *f* terrestre; the American ~ le continent américain.

landmine ['lændmaɪn] *n* mine *f* (terrestre).

landowner ['lænd,əʊnəʳ] *n* propriétaire *m* foncier, propriétaire *f* foncière.

landowning ['lænd,əʊnɪŋ] *adj*: the ~ classes la classe des propriétaires fonciers.

land reform *n* réforme *f* agraire.

land registry *n* cadastre *m*.

Land Rover® *n* Land-Rover® *f*.

landscape ['lændskeɪp] ◇ *n* -**1.** [gen] paysage *m*; the political ~ *fig* le paysage politique. -**2.** PRINT: to print in ~ imprimer à l'italienne.
◇ *adj* PRINT à l'italienne.
◇ *vt* [garden] dessiner; [waste land] aménager; they had their garden ~d ils ont fait dessiner leur jardin par un paysagiste.

landscape architect *n* architecte *mf* paysagiste.
landscape gardener *n* jardinier *m* paysagiste, jardinière *f* paysagiste.
landscape gardening *n* paysagisme *m*.
landscape painter *n* (peintre *m*) paysagiste *mf*.
landscaping ['lænd,skeɪpɪŋ] *n* aménagement *m* paysager.
Land's End *pr n pointe en Cornouailles qui marque l'extrémité sud-ouest de la Grande-Bretagne.*
landslide ['lændslaɪd] ◇ *n* glissement *m* de terrain.
◇ *comp* [election victory] écrasant.
landslip ['lændslɪp] *n* éboulement *m*.
land tax *n* impôt *m* foncier.
landward ['lændwəd] ◇ *adj* du côté de la terre; on the ~ side du côté terre; ~ breeze vent *m* marin OR qui souffle de la mer.
◇ *adv* = **landwards**.
landwards ['lændwədz] *adv* NAUT en direction de la terre; [on land] vers l'intérieur (des terres).
lane [leɪn] *n* -**1.** [road - in country] chemin *m*; [- in street names] rue *f*, allée *f*. -**2.** [for traffic] voie *f*; [line of vehicles] file *f*; [for shipping, aircraft] couloir *m*; [in athletics, swimming] couloir *m*; get into the right-hand ~ mettez-vous dans la file OR sur la voie de droite; keep in ~ ne changez pas de file; a 4-~ road une route à 4 voies; to be in the wrong ~ être dans la mauvaise file.
lane closure *n* fermeture *f* de voies; the traffic was held up by ~s la circulation a été ralentie par des rétrécissements (dûs à des travaux).
lane markings *npl* -**1.** [on road] signalisation *f* au sol OR horizontale des voies. -**2.** SPORT [on track] lignes *fpl* de marquage des couloirs; [in swimming-pool] lignes *fpl* d'eau.
lang [læŋ] SCH & UNIV *written abbr of* language.
langlauf ['læŋlaʊf] *n* ski *m* de fond.
language ['læŋgwɪdʒ] ◇ *n* -**1.** langage *m*; I prefer ~ to literature je préfère l'étude des langues à celle de la littérature; the child's acquisition of ~ l'acquisition du langage par l'enfant; spoken/written ~ expression *f* parlée/écrite. -**2.** [specific tongue] langue *f*; SCH & UNIV [area of study] langue *f*; the French ~ la langue française; to study ~s faire des études de langue; she speaks three ~s fluently elle parle trois langues couramment ❑ modern ~s langues vivantes; to speak the same ~ parler le même langage; you speak my ~ nous parlons le même langage. -**3.** [code] langage *m*; a computer ~ un langage machine; the ~ of love/flowers le langage de l'amour/des fleurs. -**4.** [terminology] langue *f*, langage *m*; medical/legal ~ langage médical/juridique; the ~ of diplomacy [jargon] le langage diplomatique || [manner of expression] expression *f*, langue *f*; I find his ~ very pompous je trouve qu'il s'exprime avec emphase OR de façon très pompeuse || [rude words] gros mots *mpl*, grossièretés *fpl*; mind your ~! surveille ton langage!; to use bad OR strong ~ dire des gros mots OR des grossièretés.
◇ *comp* [acquisition] du langage; [course] de langues; [barrier] linguistique; [student] en langues.
language laboratory, **language lab** *n* laboratoire *m* de langues.
languid ['læŋgwɪd] *adj* langoureux, alangui.
languidly ['læŋgwɪdlɪ] *adv* langoureusement.
languish ['læŋgwɪʃ] *vi* -**1.** [suffer] languir; to ~ in prison croupir en prison. -**2.** [become weak] dépérir; to ~ in the heat [plant] dépérir à la chaleur; [person] souffrir de la chaleur; the project was ~ing for lack of funds le projet traînait, faute d'argent. -**3.** *lit* [pine] languir; he ~ed for love of his lady il languissait d'amour pour sa bien-aimée.
languishing ['læŋgwɪʃɪŋ] = **languid**.
languor ['læŋgəʳ] *n* langueur *f*.
languorous ['læŋgərəs] *adj* langoureux.
languorously ['læŋgərəslɪ] *adv* langoureusement.
laniard ['lænjəd] = **lanyard**.
lank [læŋk] *adj* [hair] terne, mou; [plant] étiolé, grêle.
lanky ['læŋkɪ] (*compar* lankier, *superl* lankiest) *adj* dégingandé.
lanolin(e) ['lænəlɪn] *n* lanoline *f*.
lantern ['læntən] *n* lanterne *f*.
lantern fish *n* poisson-lanterne *m*.
lantern-jawed [-dʒɔːd] *adj* aux joues creuses.
lanternslide ['læntənslaɪd] *n* plaque *f* de lanterne magique.
lanthanide series ['lænθənaɪd-] *n* lanthanides *mpl*.
lanthanum ['lænθənəm] *n* lanthane *m*.
lanyard ['lænjəd] *n* corde *f*, cordon *m*; NAUT ride *f*.
Lanzarote [,lænzə'rɒtɪ] *pr n* Lanzarote; in ~ à Lanzarote.
Lao [laʊ] = **Laotian**.
Laos ['lɑːɒs] *pr n* Laos *m*; in ~ au Laos.
Laotian ['lɑːɒʃn] ◇ *n* -**1.** [person] Laotien *m*, -enne *f*. -**2.** LING laotien *m*.
◇ *adj* laotien.
lap [læp] (*pt* & *pp* lapped, *cont* lapping) ◇ *n* -**1.** [knees] genoux *mpl*; come and sit on my ~ viens t'asseoir sur mes genoux ❑ don't think it's just going to fall into your ~! *inf* ne t'imagine pas que ça va te tomber tout cuit dans le bec!; it's in the ~ of the gods c'est entre les mains des dieux; the ~ of luxury le grand luxe; to live in the ~ of luxury vivre dans le plus grand luxe. -**2.** SPORT tour *m* de piste; we ran 2 ~s nous avons fait 2 tours de piste; a 30-~ race une course sur 30 tours. -**3.** [of journey] étape *f*; to be on the last ~: we're on the last ~ *literal* c'est le dernier tour; *fig* on arrive au bout de nos peines.
◇ *vt* -**1.** SPORT [competitor, car] dépasser, prendre un tour d'avance sur; the slower drivers were soon lapped by the leaders les pilotes les plus rapides n'ont pas tardé à prendre un tour d'avance sur les autres concurrents || [time] chronométrer; Kelly was lapped at over 200 mph Kelly a été chronométré sur un tour à plus de 300 km/h. -**2.** [wrap] enrouler, envelopper. -**3.** [milk] laper. -**4.** [subj: waves] clapoter contre; the waves lapped the hull les vagues clapotaient contre la coque.
◇ *vi* -**1.** SPORT tourner, faire un tour de circuit; Kelly was lapping at over 200 mph Kelly tournait à plus de 300 km/h de moyenne. -**2.** [waves] clapoter; the waves lapped against the boat les vagues clapotaient contre le bateau.
◆ **lap over** ◇ *vt insep* [tiles] chevaucher sur.
◇ *vi insep* se chevaucher.
◆ **lap up** *vt sep* -**1.** [milk] laper. -**2.** *inf fig* [praise] boire; [information] avaler, gober; he ~s up every word she says il gobe tout ce qu'elle dit; to ~ it up: he told a joke and the audience lapped it up il a raconté une blague et le public était suspendu à ses lèvres.
laparoscope ['læpərəskəʊp] *n* endoscope *m*.
laparoscopy [,læpə'rɒskəpɪ] *n* laparoscopie *f*, péritonéoscopie *f*.
La Paz [læ'pæz] *pr n* La Paz.
lapdog ['læpdɒg] *n* -**1.** *literal* petit chien *m* d'appartement. -**2.** *pej* toutou *m*, caniche *m*.
lapel [lə'pel] *n* revers *m*; he grabbed me by the ~s il m'a saisi par le revers de ma veste.
lap-held *adj* [typewriter, computer] portatif *(que l'on peut poser sur ses genoux)*.
lapidary ['læpɪdərɪ] (*pl* lapidaries) ◇ *adj* [cut in stone] lapidaire.
◇ *n* lapidaire *m*.
lapidate ['læpɪdeɪt] *vt lit* lapider.
lapis lazuli [,læpɪs'læzjʊlaɪ] *n* lapis *m*, lapis-lazuli *m inv*.
lap joint *n* enchevauchure *f*, assemblage *m* par recouvrement.
Lapland ['læplænd] *pr n* Laponie *f*; in ~ en Laponie.
Laplander ['læplændəʳ] *n* Lapon *m*, -one *f*.
lap of honour *n* SPORT tour *m* d'honneur.
Lapp [læp] ◇ *n* -**1.** [person] Lapon *m*, -one *f*. -**2.** LING lapon *m*.
◇ *adj* lapon *m*.
lapping ['læpɪŋ] *n* [of waves] clapotis *m*.
lapse [læps] ◇ *n* -**1.** [failure]: ~ of memory trou *m* de mémoire; ~ in concentration moment *m* d'inattention. -**2.** [in behaviour] écart *m* (de conduite); she has occasional ~s elle fait des bêtises de temps en temps; the slightest ~ was punished harshly la moindre faute était sévèrement punie; a ~ from virtue un manquement à la vertu. -**3.** [interval] laps *m* de temps, intervalle *m*; after a ~ of six months au bout de six mois. -**4.** [of contract] expiration *f*; [of custom] disparition *f*; [of legal right] déchéance *f*.
◇ *vi* -**1.** [decline] baisser, chuter; to ~ from grace RELIG pécher. -**2.** [drift] tomber; she ~d into a coma elle est tombée dans le coma; to ~ into bad habits prendre de mauvaises habitudes; to ~ into silence garder le silence, s'enfermer dans le silence; she kept lapsing into Russian elle se remettait sans cesse à parler russe. -**3.** [pass - time] passer; weeks ~d before I saw her again il se passa plusieurs semaines avant que je ne la revoie. -**4.** [law, custom] tomber en désuétude; [licence, passport] se périmer; [subscription] prendre fin, expirer; he let his insurance ~ il a laissé périmer son assurance. -**5.** RELIG [lose faith] abandonner OR perdre la foi.
lapsed [læpst] *adj* [law] caduc; [passport] périmé; a ~ Catholic un catholique qui ne pratique plus.
laptop ['læptɒp] *adj* [typewriter, computer] portable.
lapwing ['læpwɪŋ] *n* vanneau *m*.
larboard ['lɑːbəd] *n arch* bâbord *m*.
larceny ['lɑːsənɪ] (*pl* larcenies) *n* JUR vol *m* simple.
larch [lɑːtʃ] *n* mélèze *m*.
lard [lɑːd] ◇ *n* saindoux *m*.
◇ *vt* larder; an essay ~ed with quotations *fig* une rédaction truffée de citations.
larder ['lɑːdəʳ] *n* [room] cellier *m*; [cupboard] garde-manger *m inv*; to raid the ~ *inf* faire une razzia dans le garde-manger.
large [lɑːdʒ] ◇ *adj* -**1.** [in size] grand; [family] grand, nombreux; [person] gros, grand; [organization] gros, grand; [of clothes] la grande taille; [of product] le grand modèle; a ~ coat un grand manteau; on a ~ scale à grande échelle; to a ~ extent dans une large mesure; he lives in a ~ house il habite une grande maison; she's a ~ woman c'est une femme plutôt grosse OR forte || [in number, amount] grand, important; a ~ proportion une grande proportion, une part importante; she wrote him a ~ cheque elle lui a fait un chèque pour une somme importante OR une grosse somme; a ~ helping of potatoes/apple pie une grosse portion de pommes de terre/part de tarte aux pommes; there are a ~ number of entrants this year il y a beaucoup de participants OR candidats cette année, les participants OR candidats sont nombreux cette année; to get ~ grossir ❑ he was standing there as ~ as life il était là, en chair et en os; larger than life exagéré, outrancier. -**2.** [extensive - changes] considérable, important. -**3.** [liberal - views, ideas] libéral, large; [generous - heart] grand, généreux.
◇ *adv*: to loom ~ menacer, sembler imminent; to be writ ~ être évident.
◆ **at large** ◇ *adj phr* [at liberty] en liberté; [prisoner] en fuite; the rapist is at ~ somewhere in the city le violeur se promène en (toute) liberté quelque part dans cette ville.
◇ *adv phr* [as a whole] dans son ensemble; the country at ~ le pays dans son ensemble.
◆ **by and large** *adv phr* de manière générale, dans l'ensemble.
large-hearted *adj* au grand cœur.
large intestine *n* gros intestin *m*.
largely ['lɑːdʒlɪ] *adv* [mainly] en grande partie, pour la plupart; [in general] en général, en gros.

large-minded *adj* large d'esprit, ouvert.

largeness ['lɑːdʒnɪs] *n* [in size] grandeur *f*, (grande) taille *f*; [of sum] importance *f*; [of number] grandeur *f*, importance *f*.

large-scale *adj* à grande échelle.

large-size(d) *adj* [clothes] grande taille; [product] grand modèle; [envelope] grand format.

largesse [lɑː'dʒes] *n (U)* largesse *f*, largesses *fpl*.

large white *n* ENTOM piéride *f* (du chou).

largish ['lɑːdʒɪʃ] *adj* [in size] assez grand; [in amount] assez grand, assez gros; [in number] assez nombreux.

largo ['lɑːgəʊ] ◇ *n* largo *m*.
◇ *adj* & *adv* largo.

lariat ['lærɪət] *Am* ◇ *n* lasso *m*.
◇ *vt* prendre au lasso.

lark [lɑːk] *n* -**1.** ZOOL alouette *f*; to rise OR to be up with the ~ se lever avec les poules OR au chant du coq. -**2.** *inf* [joke] rigolade *f*; [prank] blague *f*, farce *f*; for a ~ pour blaguer, pour rigoler; what a ~! quelle rigolade!, quelle bonne blague! -**3.** *inf* [rigmarole, business] histoire *f*; I don't like the sound of this fancy dress ~ je n'aime pas beaucoup cette histoire de déguisement, cette idée de déguisement ne me dit rien qui vaille.
◆ **lark about** *inf*, **lark around** *inf vi insep Br* faire le fou; stop ~ing about! arrêtez de faire les fous OR les imbéciles!

larkspur ['lɑːkspɜːʳ] *n* pied-d'alouette *m*, delphinium *m*.

larva ['lɑːvə] (*pl* larvae [-viː]) *n* larve *f*.

larval ['lɑːvl] *adj* larvaire.

laryng(e)al [,lærɪn'dʒiːəl] *adj* MED laryngé, laryngien; LING laryngal, glottal.

laryngectomy [,lærɪn'dʒektəmɪ] (*pl* laryngectomies) *n* laryngectomie *f*.

laryngitis [,lærɪn'dʒaɪtɪs] *n (U)* laryngite *f*; to have ~ avoir une laryngite.

laryngoscope [lə'rɪŋgəskəʊp] *n* laryngoscope *m*.

larynx ['lærɪŋks] *n* larynx *m*.

lasagne [lə'zænjə] *n* lasagnes *fpl*.

lascar ['læskəʳ] *n* matelot *m* indien.

lascivious [lə'sɪvɪəs] *adj* lascif, lubrique.

lasciviously [lə'sɪvɪəslɪ] *adv* lascivement.

laser ['leɪzəʳ] *n* laser *m*; ~ surgery chirurgie *f* (au) laser.

laser beam *n* rayon *m* OR faisceau *m* laser.

laser card *n* carte *f* à puce.

laser printer *n* imprimante *f* (à) laser.

lash [læʃ] ◇ *n* -**1.** [whip] lanière *f*; [blow from whip] coup *m* de fouet; he was given 60 ~es on lui a donné OR il a reçu 60 coups de fouet. -**2.** *fig* [of scorn, criticism]: he'd often felt the ~ of her tongue il avait souvent été la cible de ses propos virulents. -**3.** [of rain, sea]: the ~ of the rain on the windows le bruit de la pluie qui fouette les vitres; the ~ of the waves against the shore le déferlement des vagues sur la grève. -**4.** [eyelash] cil *m*.
◇ *vt* -**1.** [with whip] fouetter. -**2.** [subj: rain, waves] battre, fouetter; the waves ~ed the shore les vagues venaient se fracasser sur la grève; the cold rain ~ed my face la pluie froide me cinglait OR me fouettait le visage; the hail ~ed the window la grêle s'abattait sur la vitre; he ~ed them with his tongue *fig* il leur adressa quelques remarques cinglantes. -**3.** [move]: the tiger ~ed its tail le tigre fouettait l'air de sa queue. -**4.** [tie] attacher; they ~ed him to the chair ils l'ont attaché solidement à la chaise; they ~ed the cargo to the deck ils arrimèrent la cargaison sur le pont.
◇ *vi*: its tail ~ed wildly il fouettait l'air furieusement de sa queue; the hail ~ed against the window la grêle cinglait la vitre.
◆ **lash down** ◇ *vt sep* [cargo] arrimer, fixer; the crates were ~ed down les caisses étaient solidement arrimées.
◇ *vi insep* [rain, hail] s'abattre, tomber avec violence.
◆ **lash into** *vt insep Br* [criticize] se déchaîner contre; she really ~ed into them elle était véritablement déchaînée contre eux.
◆ **lash out** *vi insep* -**1.** [struggle - with fists] donner des coups de poing; [- with feet] donner des coups de pied; she ~ed out in all directions elle se débattit de toutes ses forces. -**2.** *fig* [verbally]: he ~ed out at his critics il a fustigé ses détracteurs. -**3.** *inf Br* [spend]: to ~ out (on sthg) dépenser un fric monstre (pour qqch); he ~ed out and bought himself a new suit il a claqué son fric pour s'acheter un nouveau costume.

lashing ['læʃɪŋ] *n* -**1.** [with whip] flagellation *f*, fouet *m*; to give sb a ~ donner des coups de fouet à qqn. -**2.** *fig* [scolding] réprimandes *fpl*, correction *f*. -**3.** [rope] corde *f*; NAUT amarre *f*.
◆ **lashings** *npl Br* [in amount] des montagnes; with ~s of chocolate sauce couvert de sauce au chocolat.

Las Palmas [,læs'pælməs] *pr n* Las Palmas.

lass [læs] *n Scot* [girl] fille *f*.

Lassa ['læsə] = **Lhasa**.

Lassa fever *n* fièvre *f* de Lhassa.

lassie ['læsɪ] *n Scot* & *Ir* fillette *f*, gamine *f*.

lassitude ['læsɪtjuːd] *n* lassitude *f*.

lasso, lassoo [læ'suː] ◇ *n* lasso *m*.
◇ *vt* prendre au lasso.

last[1] [lɑːst] ◇ *adj* -**1.** [with dates, times of day] dernier; ~ Monday lundi dernier; ~ week/year la semaine/l'année dernière; ~ July en juillet dernier, l'année dernière au mois de juillet; ~ night [at night] cette nuit; [in the evening] hier soir. -**2.** [final] dernier; the ~ train le dernier train; that was the ~ time I saw him c'était la dernière fois que je le voyais; that's the ~ time I do him a favour c'est la dernière fois que je lui rends service; it's your ~ chance c'est votre dernière chance; at the ~ minute OR moment à la dernière minute; it's our ~ day here c'est notre dernière journée ici; I'm down to my ~ cigarette il ne me reste plus qu'une seule cigarette; they were down to their ~ few bullets il ne leur restait pratiquement plus de munitions; one of the ~ few survivors un des tout derniers survivants; the ~ two pages les deux dernières pages; I'll sack every ~ one of them! je vais les virer tous!; she used up every ~ ounce of energy elle a utilisé tout ce qui lui restait d'énergie; to the ~ detail dans les moindres détails; they were prepared to fight to the ~ man ils étaient prêts à se battre jusqu'au dernier ❑ she was on her ~ legs elle était au bout du rouleau; your car is on its ~ legs votre voiture ne va pas tarder à vous lâcher; the regime is on its ~ legs le régime vit ses derniers jours OR est au bord de l'effondrement; I'll get my money back if it's the ~ thing I do je récupérerai mon argent coûte que coûte; I always clean my teeth ~ thing at night je me brosse toujours les dents juste avant de me coucher; we finished the work ~ thing on Tuesday afternoon on a terminé le travail juste avant de partir mardi après-midi. -**3.** [most recent]: you said that ~ time c'est ce que tu as dis la dernière fois; I've been here for the ~ five years je suis ici depuis cinq ans, cela fait cinq ans que je suis ici; I didn't like her ~ film je n'ai pas aimé son dernier film. -**4.** [least likely]: he's the ~ person I expected to see c'est bien la dernière personne que je m'attendais à voir; that's the ~ place I'd have looked c'est bien le dernier endroit où j'aurais cherché; that's the ~ thing I wanted je n'avais vraiment pas besoin de ça.
◇ *adv* -**1.** [finally]: she arrived ~ elle est arrivée la dernière OR en dernier; ~ but not least enfin. -**2.** [most recently]: when did you ~ see him? quand l'avez-vous vu pour la dernière fois?; they ~ came to see us in 1989 leur dernière visite remonte à 1989; it's ~ in, first out dernier entré, premier sorti. -**3.** = **lastly**.◇ *n* & *pron* -**1.** [final one] dernier *m*, -ère *f*; the ~ in the class le dernier de la classe; she was the ~ to arrive elle est arrivée la dernière; the ~ of the Romanovs le dernier des Romanov; the next to ~, the ~ but one l'avant-dernier. -**2.** [previous one]: each more handsome than the ~ tous plus beaux les uns que les autres; the day before ~ avant-hier; the night before ~ [at night] la nuit d'avant-hier; [in the evening] avant-hier soir; the winter before ~ l'hiver d'il y a deux ans; the Prime Minister before ~ l'avant-dernier Premier ministre. -**3.** [end]: that was the ~ I saw of her c'était la dernière fois que je la voyais; I hope that's the ~ we see of them j'espère qu'on ne les reverra plus; I'll never see the ~ of this! je n'en verrai jamais la fin!, je n'en viendrai jamais à bout!; you haven't heard the ~ of this! vous aurez de mes nouvelles! ❑ till ~: leave the pans till ~ gardez les casseroles pour la fin, lavez les casseroles en dernier. -**4.** [remainder] reste *m*; we drank the ~ of the wine on a bu ce qui restait de vin.
◆ **at last** *adv phr* enfin; free at ~ enfin libre; at long ~ she's found a job she enjoys elle a enfin trouvé un emploi qui lui plaît; at ~! where on earth have you been? enfin! mais où étais-tu donc?; at ~ he said: "do you forgive me?" enfin il demanda: «tu me pardonnes?».
◆ **at the last** *adv phr fml* à la dernière minute; at the ~ the judges came out in her favour à la dernière minute, les juges ont décidé en sa faveur; she was there at the ~ elle est restée jusqu'au bout.
◆ **to the last** *adv phr* jusqu'au bout; she insisted to the ~ that she was not guilty elle a dit jusqu'au bout qu'elle n'était pas coupable.

last[2] [lɑːst] ◇ *vi* -**1.** [continue to exist or function] durer; it ~ed (for) ten days cela a duré dix jours; how long did the film ~? combien de temps le film a-t-il duré?, quelle était la durée du film?; how long can we ~ without water? combien de temps tiendrons-nous sans eau?; he didn't ~ more than a year as a singer il n'a pas tenu plus d'un an dans la chanson; their romance didn't ~ (for) long leur idylle n'a pas duré longtemps; he won't ~ long [in job] il ne tiendra pas longtemps; [will soon die] il n'en a plus pour longtemps; the batteries didn't ~ (for) long les piles n'ont pas duré longtemps; built/made to ~ construit/fait pour durer. -**2.** [be enough]: we've got enough food to ~ another week nous avons assez à manger pour une semaine encore. -**3.** [keep fresh - food] se conserver; these flowers don't ~ (long) ces fleurs ne tiennent OR ne durent pas (longtemps).
◇ *vt*: his money didn't ~ him to the end of the holiday il n'a pas eu assez d'argent pour tenir jusqu'à la fin des vacances; have we got enough to ~ us until tomorrow? en avons-nous assez pour tenir OR aller jusqu'à demain?; my camera's ~ed me ten years mon appareil photo a duré dix ans; that fountain pen will ~ you a lifetime vous pourrez garder ce stylo-plume toute votre vie.
◇ *n* [for shoes] forme *f*.
◆ **last out** ◇ *vi insep* -**1.** [survive] tenir; I'm not sure I'll ~ out at this job je ne sais pas si je pourrai faire ce travail longtemps; how long will he ~ out? combien de temps peut-il tenir? -**2.** [be enough] suffire; will our supplies ~ out till the end of the month? les provisions suffiront-elles jusqu'à la fin du mois?
◇ *vt sep*: he didn't ~ the night out il n'a pas passé la nuit, il est mort pendant la nuit; will the play ~ out the month? est-ce que la pièce tiendra le mois?

last-ditch *adj* [ultimate] ultime; [desperate] désespéré; a ~ attempt OR effort un ultime effort.

lasting ['lɑːstɪŋ] *adj* durable; to their ~ regret/shame à leur plus grand regret/plus grande honte.

Last Judgment *n*: the ~ le Jugement dernier.

lastly ['lɑːstlɪ] *adv* enfin, en dernier lieu.

last-minute *adj* de dernière minute.

last post *n Br* MIL [at night] extinction *f* des feux; [at funeral] sonnerie *f* aux morts.

last rites *npl* derniers sacrements *mpl*.

Last Supper *n*: the ~ la (sainte) Cène.

last word *n* -**1.** [final decision] dernier mot *m*; the Treasury has the ~ on defence spending le ministère des Finances a le dernier mot en matière de dépenses militaires. -**2.** [latest style] dernier cri *m*; she was wearing the very ~ in hats elle portait un chapeau du dernier cri.

Las Vegas [,læs'veɪgəs] *pr n* Las Vegas.

latch [lætʃ] ◇ *n* loquet *m*; leave the door on the ~ ne fermez pas la porte à clé; the door was on the ~ la porte n'était pas fermée à clé.
◇ *vt* fermer au loquet.
◇ *vi* se fermer.
◆ **latch on** *inf vi insep* piger.
◆ **latch onto** *inf vt insep* -**1.** [seize] s'accrocher à; to ~ onto an idea s'accrocher à une idée ‖ [attach o.s. to]: she always ~es onto older children elle s'accroche toujours à des enfants plus âgés. -**2.** *Br* [understand] piger; I suddenly ~ed onto the fact that they were following me d'un seul coup j'ai pigé qu'ils me suivaient. -**3.** *Am* [obtain] se procurer, obtenir.

latchkey ['lætʃki:] *n* clef *f* (de la porte d'entrée).

latchkey child *n enfant dont les parents travaillent et ne sont pas là quand il rentre de l'école.*

late [leɪt] ◇ *adj* -**1.** [behind schedule] en retard; to be ~ être en retard; to be 10 minutes ~ avoir 10 minutes de retard; she's often ~ elle est OR elle arrive souvent en retard; to make sb ~ retarder qqn, mettre qqn en retard; we apologize for the ~ arrival of flight 906 nous vous prions d'excuser le retard du vol 906. -**2.** [in time] tardif; at a ~ hour à une heure tardive; to keep ~ hours veiller, se coucher tard; in the ~ afternoon tard dans l'après-midi; she's in her ~ fifties elle approche la soixantaine; in the ~ seventies à la fin des années soixante-dix; in ~ 1970 fin 1970; at this ~ date à cette date avancée; at this ~ stage à ce stade avancé; to have a ~ lunch déjeuner tard; he was a ~ developer [physically] il a eu une croissance tardive; [intellectually] son développement intellectuel fut un peu tardif ‖ [news, edition] dernier; there have been some ~ developments in the talks il y a du nouveau dans les discussions. -**3.** [former] ancien, précédent; [deceased]: the ~ lamented president le regretté président; the ~ Mr Fox le défunt M. Fox, feu M. Fox *fml*; her ~ husband son défunt mari, feu son mari *fml*; his ~ wife feue sa femme *fml*. -**4.** [recent] récent, dernier.
◇ *adv* -**1.** [in time] tard; to arrive/to go to bed ~ arriver/se coucher tard; to arrive 10 minutes ~ arriver avec 10 minutes de retard; it's getting ~ il se fait tard; ~ in the afternoon tard dans l'après-midi; she came to poetry ~ in life elle est venue à la poésie sur le tard; they came too ~ ils sont arrivés trop tard ❑ ~ in the day *literal* vers la fin de la journée; it's rather ~ in the day to be thinking about that *fig* c'est un peu tard pour penser à ça. -**2.** [recently] récemment; even as ~ as last year he was still painting pas plus tard que l'année dernière, il peignait encore. -**3.** *fml* [formerly] autrefois, anciennement; Mr Fox, ~ of Delhi M. Fox, anciennement domicilié à Delhi.
◆ **of late** *adv phr* récemment; I haven't seen him of ~ je ne l'ai pas vu récemment OR ces derniers temps.

latecomer ['leɪt,kʌmə^r] *n* retardataire *mf*; ~s must wait in the foyer les retardataires doivent attendre dans le foyer; he was a ~ to football il est venu au football sur le tard.

lateen [lə'ti:n] *n*: ~ (sail) voile *f* latine.

lateen-rigged [-rɪgd] *adj* gréé avec une voile latine; ~ boat bâtiment *m* latin.

lately ['leɪtlɪ] *adv* récemment, ces derniers temps, dernièrement; until ~ jusqu'à ces derniers temps, jusqu'à récemment.

latency ['leɪtənsɪ] *n* latence *f*.

lateness ['leɪtnɪs] *n* -**1.** [of bus, train, person] retard *m*; I find persistent ~ infuriating les gens qui sont toujours en retard m'exaspèrent. -**2.** [late time] heure *f* tardive; given the ~ of the hour étant donné OR vu l'heure tardive.

late-night *adj* [play, show, film] ≃ de minuit; what's tonight's ~ movie? [on TV] qu'est-ce qu'il y a au ciné-club ce soir?; a ~ film [in cinema] une séance de minuit; a ~ bus service un bus de nuit; ~ opening COMM nocturne *f*; ~ shopping courses *fpl* en nocturne.

latent ['leɪtənt] *adj* latent.

latent heat *n* chaleur *f* latente.

latent image *n* image *f* latente.

latent period *n* -**1.** MED incubation *f*. -**2.** = **latent time**.

latent time *n* latence *f*, état *m* latent, temps *m* de latence.

later ['leɪtə^r] (*compar of* late) ◇ *adj* ultérieur; we can always catch a ~ train on peut toujours prendre un autre train, plus tard; a collection of her ~ poems un recueil de ses derniers poèmes; at a ~ date à une date ultérieure; at a ~ stage à un stade plus avancé; in ~ life plus tard dans la vie.
◇ *adv* plus tard; ~ that day plus tard dans la journée; ~ on plus tard; see you ~! à plus tard!; no ~ than tomorrow demain dernier délai, demain au plus tard.

lateral ['lætərəl] ◇ *adj* latéral.
◇ *n* LING (consonne *f*) latérale *f*.

laterally ['lætrəlɪ] *adv* latéralement.

lateral thinking *n* approche *f* originale; we need a bit of ~ on this problem il nous faut adopter une approche du problème plus originale.

laterite ['lætəraɪt] *n* latérite *f*.

latest ['leɪtɪst] ◇ *adj* (*superl of* late) dernier; the ~ date/time la date/l'heure limite; the ~ news les dernières nouvelles; the ~ model le dernier modèle; let's hope her ~ novel won't be her last espérons que le roman qu'elle vient de publier ne sera pas le dernier.
◇ *n* -**1.** [most recent - news]: have you heard the ~? vous connaissez la dernière?; what's the ~ on the trial? qu'y a-t-il de nouveau sur le procès?; tune in at 7 p.m. for the ~ on the elections soyez à l'écoute à 19 h pour les dernières informations sur les élections; have you met his/her ~? [boyfriend, girlfriend] avez-vous fait la connaissance de sa dernière conquête? -**2.** [in time]: at the ~ au plus tard; when is the ~ you can come? jusqu'à quelle heure pouvez-vous venir?

latex ['leɪteks] *n* latex *m*.

lath [lɑ:θ] *n* [wooden] latte *f*; [in venetian blind] lame *f*.

lathe [leɪð] ◇ *n* tour *m (à bois ou à métal)*; ~ operator tourneur *m*.
◇ *vt* tourner.

lather ['lɑ:ðə^r] ◇ *n* -**1.** [from soap] mousse *f*. -**2.** [foam - on horse, seawater] écume *f*; to get into a ~ about OR over sthg *Br* s'énerver OR se mettre dans tous ses états à propos de qqch; he got into a real ~ over the unpaid bills les factures impayées l'ont mis dans tous ses états.
◇ *vt* [clean] savonner.
◇ *vi* -**1.** [soap] mousser. -**2.** [horse] écumer.

Latin ['lætɪn] ◇ *n* -**1.** [person] Latin *m*, -e *f*; the ~s [in Europe] les Latins; [in US] les Latino-américains *mpl*. -**2.** LING latin *m*.
◇ *adj* latin; [alphabet] latin; the ~ Quarter le Quartier latin.

Latin America *pr n* Amérique *f* latine; in ~ en Amérique latine.

Latin American ◇ *n* Latino-américain *m*, -e *f*.
◇ *adj* latino-américain.

Latinate ['lætɪneɪt] *adj* [vocabulary] d'origine latine; [style] empreint de latinismes.

Latinist ['lætɪnɪst] *n* latiniste *mf*.

Latinize, -ise ['lætɪnaɪz] *vt* latiniser.

Latino [læ'ti:nəʊ] (*pl* Latinos) *n Am* Latino *mf*.

latish ['leɪtɪʃ] ◇ *adj*: at a ~ hour à une heure assez avancée OR tardive.
◇ *adv*: it was getting ~ il commençait à se faire tard.

latitude ['lætɪtju:d] *n* -**1.** ASTRON & GEOG latitude *f*; at a ~ of 50° south à 50° de latitude sud; few animals live in these ~s rares sont les animaux qui vivent sous ces latitudes. -**2.** [freedom] latitude *f*; they don't allow OR give the children much ~ for creativity ils n'encouragent pas les enfants à être créatifs.

latitudinal [,lætɪ'tju:dɪnl] *adj* latitudinal.

latitudinarian [,lætɪtju:dɪ'neərɪən] ◇ *adj* latitudinaire.
◇ *n* latitudinaire *mf*.

Latium ['leɪʃjəm] *pr n* Latium.

latrines [lə'tri:nz] *npl* latrines *fpl*.

latter ['lætə^r] ◇ *adj* -**1.** [in relation to former] dernier, second; the ~ proposal is unrealistic la seconde OR cette dernière proposition est irréaliste; the ~ half of the book was better la seconde moitié du livre était meilleure. -**2.** [later] dernier, second; in the ~ years of her life au cours des dernières années de sa vie; the ~ part of the holiday la seconde partie des vacances.
◇ *n*: the former... the ~ le premier... le second, celui-là... celui-ci; the ~ is definitely the better book le second livre est sans aucun doute le meilleur; of tigers and cheetahs, the ~ are by far the faster runners des tigres et des guépards, ces derniers sont de loin les plus rapides.

latter-day *adj* d'aujourd'hui; a ~ St Francis un saint François moderne; Church of the ~ Saints Église *f* de Jésus-Christ des saints des derniers jours.

latterly ['lætəlɪ] *adv* [recently] récemment, dernièrement; [towards the end] vers la fin.

lattice ['lætɪs] *n* [fence, frame] treillage *m*; [design] treillis *m*.

latticed ['lætɪst] *adj* [fence] à claire-voie; [ceramics] treillissé; [pastry] en croisillons; [dress] ajouré.

lattice window *n* fenêtre *f* à croisillons.

latticework ['lætɪswɜ:k] *n (U)* treillis *m*.

Latvia ['lætvɪə] *pr n* Lettonie *f*; in ~ en Lettonie.

Latvian ['lætvɪən] ◇ *n* -**1.** [person] Letton *m*, -onne *f*. -**2.** LING letton *m*.
◇ *adj* letton.

laud [lɔ:d] *vt fml* OR *lit* louer, chanter les louanges de, glorifier.

laudable ['lɔ:dəbl] *adj* louable, digne de louanges.

laudably ['lɔ:dəblɪ] *adv* de manière louable; you behaved ~ votre comportement a été admirable.

laudanum ['lɔ:dənəm] *n* laudanum *m*.

laudatory ['lɔ:dətrɪ] *adj fml* laudatif, élogieux.

laugh [lɑ:f] ◇ *vi* -**1.** [in amusement] rire; she was ~ing about his gaffe all day sa gaffe l'a fait rire toute la journée; you have to ~ mieux vaut en rire; to burst out ~ing éclater de rire; we ~ed until we cried on a ri aux larmes, on a pleuré de rire; we ~ed about it afterwards après coup, cela nous a fait bien rire, on en a ri après coup; it's easy for you to ~! vous pouvez rire!; to ~ aloud OR out loud rire aux éclats; he was ~ing to himself il riait dans sa barbe; they didn't know whether to ~ or cry ils ne savaient pas s'ils devaient en rire ou en pleurer ❑ to ~ one's head off rire comme un fou; to ~ up one's sleeve *Br* rire sous cape; I'll make him ~ on the other side of his face *Br* je lui ferai passer l'envie de rire, moi; he who ~s last ~s longest *Br* OR best *Am prov* rira bien qui rira le dernier *prov*; 'The Laughing Cavalier' *Hals* 'le Chevalier souriant'. -**2.** [in contempt, ridicule] rire; they ~ed in my face ils m'ont ri au nez; he ~ed about his mistakes il a ri de ses erreurs. -**3.** *fig* [be confident]: once we get the contract, we're ~ing une fois qu'on aura empoché le contrat, on sera tranquilles; she's ~ing all the way to the bank elle s'en met plein les poches.
◇ *vt* -**1.** [in amusement]: to ~ o.s. silly se tordre de rire, être plié en deux de rire. -**2.** [in ridicule]: he was ~ed off the stage/out of the room il a quitté la scène/la pièce sous les rires mo-

queurs; they ~ed him to scorn ils se sont moqués de lui ❑ to ~ sthg out of court tourner qqch en dérision. -3. [express]: she ~ed her scorn elle eut un petit rire méprisant.

◇ *n* -1. [of amusement] rire *m*; [burst of laughter] éclat *m* de rire; to give a ~ rire; we had a good ~ about it ça nous a bien fait rire; she left the room with a ~ elle sortit en riant OR dans un éclat de rire ‖ [of contempt] rire *m*; we all had a good ~ at his expense nous nous sommes bien moqués de lui ❑ to have the last ~ avoir le dernier mot. -2. *inf Br* [fun] rigolade *f*; to have (a bit of) a ~ rigoler OR se marrer un peu; he's always good for a ~ avec lui, on se marre bien; he's a ~ a minute il est très marrant. -3. *inf* [joke]: we did it for a ~ OR just for ~s on l'a fait pour rigoler; what a ~! qu'est-ce qu'on s'est marré!; home-made cakes? – that's a ~! *iron* gâteaux faits maison? – c'est une blague OR ils plaisantent!

◆ **laugh at** *vt insep* -1. [in amusement] rire de; we all ~ed at the joke la blague nous a tous fait rire. -2. [mock] se moquer de, rire de; to ~ at someone else's misfortunes se moquer des malheurs des autres; to ~ at one's own mistakes rire de ses propres erreurs. -3. [disregard] rire de, rester indifférent à; they ~ed at the dangers ils (se) riaient des dangers.

◆ **laugh away** *vt sep*: she ~ed away her tears/cares ça l'a amusée et elle a séché ses larmes/oublié ses soucis.

◆ **laugh down** *vt sep* [objection] ridiculiser.

◆ **laugh off** *vt sep* [difficulty] rire de, se moquer de; I managed to ~ off an awkward situation j'ai réussi à éviter une situation fâcheuse en plaisantant; how can they just ~ it off like that? comment osent-ils prendre ça à la légère?; he tried to ~ off the defeat il s'efforça de ne pas prendre sa défaite trop au sérieux.

laughable ['lɑːfəbl] *adj* ridicule, dérisoire; the whole situation is just ~ tout ça est parfaitement ridicule; he made a ~ attempt at reconciliation il fit une tentative de réconciliation pitoyable.

laughing ['lɑːfɪŋ] *adj* [eyes] riant, rieur; this is no ~ matter il n'y a pas de quoi rire.

laughing gas *n* gaz *m* hilarant.

laughing hyena *n* hyène *f* tachetée.

laughing jackass *n* martin-chasseur *m (d'Australie)*, kookaburra *m*.

laughingly ['lɑːfɪŋlɪ] *adv* -1. [cheerfully] en riant. -2. [inappropriately]: this noise is ~ called folk music c'est ce bruit qu'on appelle le plus sérieusement du monde de la musique folk.

laughing stock *n*: they were the ~ of the whole neighbourhood ils étaient la risée de tout le quartier; they made ~s of themselves ils se sont couverts de ridicule.

laughter ['lɑːftəʳ] *n (U)* rire *m*, rires *mpl*; a burst of ~ un éclat de rire; to roar with ~ rire aux éclats; there was much ~ over the misunderstanding le malentendu provoqua des éclats de rire; she continued to speak amid loud ~ elle a continué à parler au milieu des éclats de rire.

launch [lɔːntʃ] ◇ *n* -1. [boat] vedette *f*; [long boat] chaloupe *f*; (pleasure) ~ bateau *m* de plaisance. -2. [of ship, spacecraft, new product] lancement *m*; a book ~ le lancement d'un livre; the ~ of a new job creation scheme le lancement d'un nouveau programme de création d'emplois.

◇ *vt* -1. [boat - from ship] mettre à la mer; [- from harbour] faire sortir; [- for first time] lancer. -2. COMM lancer; FIN [shares] émettre; our firm has ~ed a new perfume on OR onto the market notre société a lancé un nouveau parfum. -3. [start]: that was the audition that ~ed me on my career cette audition a donné le coup d'envoi de ma carrière; to ~ a military offensive déclencher OR lancer une attaque.

◆ **launch forth** *vi insep* -1. [set off]: to ~ forth on a new career se lancer dans une nouvelle carrière. -2. [start speaking]: he ~ed forth into a long explanation il s'est lancé dans une longue explication.

◆ **launch into** *vt insep* [start] se lancer dans; she ~ed into her work with vigour elle s'est lancée dans son travail avec énergie.

◆ **launch out** *vi insep* se lancer; Blakes have ~ed out into distilling Blakes s'est lancé dans la distillation; she's just ~ed out on her own elle vient de se mettre à son compte.

launch complex *n* ASTRONAUT base *f* OR station *f* de lancement.

launcher ['lɔːntʃəʳ] *n* ASTRONAUT & MIL lanceur *m*.

launching ['lɔːntʃɪŋ] *n* -1. [of ship, spacecraft] lancement *m*; [of lifeboat - from ship] mise *f* à la mer; [- from shore] sortie *f*. -2. [of new product] lancement *m*.

launching ceremony *n* cérémonie *f* de lancement.

launching pad = **launch pad**.

launching site *n* aire *f* de lancement.

launching vehicle = **launch vehicle**.

launch pad *n* rampe *f* de lancement.

launch vehicle *n* fusée *f* de lancement.

launder ['lɔːndəʳ] *vt* -1. [clothes] laver; [at laundry] blanchir; the sheets have been freshly ~ed [at home] les draps viennent d'être lavés; [at laundry] les draps reviennent de chez le blanchisseur OR le teinturier. -2. *fig* [money] blanchir.

Launderette® [,lɔːndə'ret] = **laundrette**.

laundering ['lɔːndrɪŋ] *n* -1. [of clothes] blanchissage *m*. -2. *fig* [of money] blanchiment *m*.

laundress ['lɔːndrɪs] *n* blanchisseuse *f*.

laundrette [lɔːn'dret] *n Br* laverie *f* automatique.

Laundromat® ['lɔːndrəmæt] *n Am* laverie *f* automatique.

laundry ['lɔːndrɪ] (*pl* laundries) *n* -1. [shop] blanchisserie *f*; [in house] buanderie *f*. -2. [washing] linge *m*; to do the ~ faire la lessive.

laundry basket *n* panier *m* à linge.

laundryman ['lɔːndrɪmən] (*pl* laundrymen [-mən]) *n* -1. [van-driver] livreur *m* de blanchisserie. -2. [worker in laundry] blanchisseur *m*.

laundry mark *n* étiquette *f* de la blanchisserie.

laundry van *n* camionnette *f* du blanchisseur.

laundrywoman ['lɔːndrɪ,wʊmən] (*pl* laundrywomen [-,wɪmɪn]) *n* blanchisseuse *f*.

laureate ['lɔːrɪət] *n* -1. [prize winner] lauréat *m*; a Nobel ~ un prix Nobel. -2. [poet] poète *m* lauréat.

laurel ['lɒrəl] ◇ *n* [tree] laurier *m*.

◇ *comp* [crown, wreath] de lauriers.

◆ **laurels** *npl* [honours] lauriers *mpl*; to look to one's ~s ne pas s'endormir sur ses lauriers; to rest on one's ~s se reposer sur ses lauriers.

lav *inf* [læv] *n Br* cabinets *mpl*, W-C *mpl*.

lava ['lɑːvə] *n* lave *f*; ~ bed champ *m* de lave.

lavage [læ'vɑːʒ] *n* MED lavement *m*.

lavalier(e) [læ,vælɪ'eəʳ] *n Am* pendentif *m*.

lavatorial [,lævə'tɔːrɪəl] *adj* [style, humour] scatologique.

lavatory ['lævətrɪ] (*pl* lavatories) ◇ *n Br* toilettes *fpl*, cabinets *mpl*; [bowl] cuvette *f*; to go to the ~ aller aux toilettes.

◇ *adj* des W-C; [humour] scatologique.

lavatory bowl, lavatory pan *n Br* cuvette *f* (de W-C).

lavatory paper *n Br* papier *m* hygiénique.

lavender ['lævəndəʳ] ◇ *n* lavande *f*.

◇ *adj* [colour] lavande.

lavender bag *n* sachet *m* de lavande.

lavender blue ◇ *n* bleu lavande *m inv*.

◇ *adj* bleu lavande *(inv)*.

lavender water *n* eau *f* de lavande.

laver ['leɪvəʳ] *n* porphyra *f*.

laver bread ['lɑːvəʳ-] *n* galette *f* d'algues.

lavish ['lævɪʃ] ◇ *adj* -1. [abundant] copieux, abondant; [luxurious] somptueux, luxueux. -2. [generous] généreux, magnanime; he can afford to be ~ il peut se permettre d'être généreux; he was ~ in his praise il ne tarissait pas d'éloges.

◇ *vt* prodiguer; they ~ all their attention on their son ils sont aux petits soins pour leur fils; he ~ed praise on the book il ne tarissait pas d'éloges sur le livre.

lavishly ['lævɪʃlɪ] *adv* -1. [generously, extravagantly] généreusement, sans compter; she spends ~ elle dépense sans compter, elle ne regarde pas à la dépense; he praised us ~ il n'a pas tari d'éloges à notre égard. -2. [luxuriously] luxueusement, avec luxe; ~ decorated/furnished somptueusement décoré/meublé.

lavishness ['lævɪʃnɪs] *n* -1. [generosity] générosité *f*; [extravagance] extravagance *f*. -2. [luxuriousness] luxe *m*, somptuosité *f*.

law [lɔː] ◇ *n* -1. [legal provision] loi *f*; a ~ against gambling une loi qui interdit les jeux d'argent; there's no ~ against it! il n'y a pas de mal à cela!; there ought to be a ~ against it *hum* ça devrait être interdit par la loi ❑ Law Lords *membres de la chambre des Lords siégeant en tant que cour d'appel de dernière instance*; the Law Society *conseil de l'ordre des avocats chargé de faire respecter la déontologie*; to be a ~ unto o.s. ne connaître ni foi ni loi. -2. [legislation] loi *f*; it's against the ~ to sell alcohol la vente d'alcool est illégale; by ~ selon la loi; in OR under British ~ selon la loi britannique; to break/to uphold the ~ enfreindre/respecter la loi; the bill became ~ le projet de loi a été voté OR adopté; the ~ of the land la loi, les lois; the ~ of the jungle la loi de la jungle; to lay down the ~ *fig* imposer sa loi, faire la loi; her word is ~ *fig* ses décisions sont sans appel. -3. [legal system] droit *m*; a student of ~ un étudiant en droit; constitutional/civil ~ le droit constitutionnel/civil. -4. [justice] justice *f*, système *m* juridique; to go to ~ *Br* aller en justice; to take a case to ~ *Br* porter une affaire en justice OR devant les tribunaux; to take the ~ into one's own hands (se) faire justice soi-même ‖ [police]: the ~ *inf* les flics *mpl*; the ~ soon arrived les flics n'ont pas tardé à rappliquer; I'll have the ~ on you! je vais appeler les flics! -5. [rule - of club, sport] règle *f*; the ~s of rugby les règles du rugby. -6. SCI [principle] loi *f*; the ~s of gravity les lois de la pesanteur; the ~ of supply and demand ECON la loi de l'offre et de la demande.

◇ *comp* [faculty, school] de droit; he's a ~ student il est étudiant en droit.

law-abiding *adj* respectueux de la loi; a ~ citizen un honnête citoyen.

law and order *n* l'ordre public *m*; law-and-order issues questions *fpl* d'ordre public; he presents himself as the law-and-order candidate il se présente comme le candidat de l'ordre (public).

law-breaker *n* personne *f* qui transgresse la loi.

law-breaking *n* infraction *f* à la loi.

law centre *n* bureau *m* d'aide judiciaire.

law court *n* tribunal *m*, cour *f* de justice.

law-enforcement *adj Am* chargé de faire respecter la loi; ~ officer *représentant d'un service chargé de faire respecter la loi*.

lawful ['lɔːfʊl] *adj* [legal] légal; [legitimate] légitime; [valid] valide; by all ~ means par tous les moyens légaux; my ~ wedded wife mon épouse légitime.

lawfully ['lɔːfʊlɪ] *adv* légalement, de manière légale; did you come by that money ~? est-ce que vous avez gagné cet argent par des moyens légaux?

lawgiver ['lɔː,gɪvəʳ] *n* législateur *m*, -trice *f*.

lawless ['lɔːlɪs] *adj* [person] sans foi ni loi; [activity] illégal; [country] livré à l'anarchie; a ~ frontier territory un territoire sauvage situé aux confins du monde civilisé.

lawlessness ['lɔːlɪsnɪs] *n* non-respect *m* de la loi; [anarchy] anarchie *f*; [illegality] illégalité *f*.

lawmaker ['lɔː,meɪkəʳ] *n* législateur *m*, -trice *f*.

lawman ['lɔːmæn] (*pl* lawmen [-men]) *n Am* [policeman] policier *m*; [sheriff] shérif *m*.

lawn [lɔːn] *n* -1. [grass] pelouse *f*, gazon *m*. -2. TEX linon *m*.

lawn chair *n Am* chaise *f* de jardin.

lawnmower ['lɔːn,maʊəʳ] *n* tondeuse *f* (à gazon).

lawn party *n Am* garden party *f*.

lawn tennis ◇ *n* tennis *m* sur gazon.
◇ *comp* [club] de tennis.

Lawrence ['lɒrəns] *pr n*: ~ of Arabia Lawrence d'Arabie.

lawrencium [lə'rensɪəm] *n* lawrencium *m*.

Lawrentian [lə'renʃɪən] *adj* lawrencien.

lawsuit ['lɔːsuːt] *n* action *f* en justice; to bring a ~ against sb intenter une action (en justice) contre qqn.

lawyer ['lɔːjəʳ] *n* -**1.** [barrister] avocat *m*, homme *m* de loi. -**2.** [solicitor - for wills, conveyancing etc] notaire *m*. -**3.** [legal expert] juriste *mf*; [adviser] conseil *m* juridique.

lax [læks] *adj* -**1.** [person] négligent; [behaviour, discipline] relâché; [justice] laxiste; to be ~ about sthg négliger qqch. -**2.** [not tense - string] lâche, relâché; LING [phoneme] lâche, relâché; MED [bowels] relâché. -**3.** [imprecise - definition] imprécis, vague.

laxative ['læksətɪv] ◇ *adj* laxatif.
◇ *n* laxatif *m*.

laxity ['læksətɪ], **laxness** ['læksnɪs] *n* [slackness] relâchement *m*; [negligence] négligence *f*; moral ~ relâchement moral.

lay [leɪ] (*pt* & *pp* laid [leɪd]) ◇ *pt* → **lie**.
◇ *vt* -**1.** [in specified position] poser, mettre; ~ the cards face upwards posez les cartes face en l'air; ~ the photos on the shelf to dry mettez les photos à plat sur l'étagère pour qu'elles sèchent; he laid the baby on the bed il a couché l'enfant sur le lit; she laid her head on my shoulder elle a posé sa tête sur mon épaule; to ~ sb to rest *euph* enterrer qqn ‖ [spread out] étendre; she laid the blanket on the ground elle a étendu la couverture par terre ❑ to ~ it on the line *inf* ne pas y aller par quatre chemins. -**2.** [tiles, bricks, pipes, cable, carpet] poser; [foundations] poser; [wreath] déposer; [mine] poser, mouiller; to ~ lino on the floor, to ~ the floor with lino poser du linoléum; a roof laid with zinc un toit recouvert de zinc; the plan ~s the basis OR the foundation for economic development *fig* le projet jette les bases du développement économique. -**3.** [set - table] mettre; ~ the table for six mettez la table pour six (personnes), mettez six couverts; they hadn't laid enough places ils n'avaient pas mis assez de couverts, il manquait des couverts. -**4.** [prepare, arrange - fire] préparer; to ~ a trail tracer un chemin; they laid a trap for him ils lui ont tendu un piège. -**5.** [egg] pondre; 'new-laid eggs' 'œufs frais'. -**6.** [impose - burden, duty] imposer; to ~ emphasis OR stress on sthg mettre l'accent sur qqch. -**7.** JUR [lodge] porter; to ~ an accusation against sb porter une accusation contre qqn; charges have been laid against five men cinq hommes ont été inculpés. -**8.** [present, put forward]: she laid the scheme before him elle lui soumit le projet. -**9.** [allay - fears] dissiper; [exorcize - ghost] exorciser; [refute - rumour] démentir. -**10.** [bet] parier; I'll ~ you ten to one that she won't come je te parie à dix contre un qu'elle ne viendra pas. -**11.** ▼ [have sex with] baiser; to get laid baiser. -**12.** *lit* [strike]: to ~ a whip across sb's back fouetter qqn. -**13.** *lit* [cause to settle] faire retomber; the rain helped to ~ the dust la pluie a fait retomber la poussière. -**14.** [with adjective complements]: to ~ o.s. open to criticism s'exposer à la critique.
◇ *vi* -**1.** [bird, fish etc] pondre. -**2.** *inf* = **lie** *vi* **2**.
◇ *adj* -**1.** [non-clerical] laïque; in ~ dress en habit laïque. -**2.** [not professional] profane, non-spécialiste; ~ people les profanes *mpl*; the book is intended for a ~ audience le livre est destiné à un public de profanes.
◇ *n* -**1.** *phr*: the ~ of the land la configuration du terrain. -**2.** ▼ [person]: he's/she's a good ~ il/elle baise bien. -**3.** [poem, song] lai *m*.

◆ **lay about** *vt insep lit* attaquer, taper sur; she laid about him with her umbrella elle l'a attaqué à coups de parapluie, elle lui a tapé dessus avec son parapluie.

◆ **lay aside** *vt sep* -**1.** [put down] mettre de côté; she laid her knitting aside to watch the news elle posa son tricot pour regarder les informations; you should ~ aside any personal opinions you might have *fig* vous devez faire abstraction de toute opinion personnelle. -**2.** [save] mettre de côté; we have some money laid aside nous avons de l'argent de côté.

◆ **lay by** *vt sep Br* [provisions] mettre de côté.

◆ **lay down** *vt sep* -**1.** [put down] poser; she laid her knife and fork down elle posa son couvert; to ~ down one's arms déposer les armes. -**2.** [renounce, relinquish] renoncer à; to ~ down one's life se sacrifier. -**3.** [formulate, set out - plan, rule] formuler, établir; [- condition] imposer; as laid down in the contract, the buyer keeps exclusive rights il est stipulé OR il est bien précisé dans le contrat que l'acheteur garde l'exclusivité. -**4.** [store - wine] mettre en cave. -**5.** *inf* MUS [record - song, track] enregistrer. -**6.** AGR [field, land]: he has laid down five acres of barley il a semé deux hectares et demi d'orge.

◆ **lay in** *vt sep* [stores] faire provision de.

◆ **lay into** *inf vt insep* -**1.** [attack - physically] tomber (à bras raccourcis) sur; [- verbally] prendre à partie, passer un savon à; he really laid into his opponent il est tombé à bras raccourcis sur son adversaire; she laid into the government for their hard-line attitude elle a pris le gouvernement à partie pour son attitude intransigeante. -**2.** *inf* [eat greedily] se jeter sur.

◆ **lay off** ◇ *vt sep* -**1.** [employees] licencier. -**2.** [in gambling - bet] couvrir.
◇ *vt insep* laisser tomber; ~ off it, will you! laisse tomber, tu veux!; I told her to ~ off my husband je lui ai dit de laisser mon mari tranquille.
◇ *vi insep inf* laisser tomber.

◆ **lay on** *vt sep* -**1.** [provide] fournir; drinks will be laid on les boissons seront fournies; the meal was laid on by our hosts le repas nous fut offert par nos hôtes; they had transport laid on for us ils s'étaient occupés de nous procurer un moyen de transport. -**2.** *Br* [install] installer, mettre; the caravan has electricity laid on la caravane a l'électricité. -**3.** [spread - paint, plaster] étaler; to ~ it on thick *inf fig* en rajouter. -**4.** ▽ *Am*: to ~ sthg on sb [give] filer qqch à qqn; [tell] raconter qqch à qqn; let me ~ some advice on you je vais te filer un bon conseil; did she ~ a heavy one on me! elle n'a pas mâché ses mots! -**5.** *phr*: if you're not careful, I'll ~ one on you! ▽ [hit] fais gaffe ou je t'en mets une!

◆ **lay out** *vt sep* -**1.** [arrange, spread out] étaler; he laid his wares out on the ground il a étalé OR déballé sa marchandise sur le sol. -**2.** [present, put forward] exposer, présenter; her ideas are clearly laid out in her book ses idées sont clairement exposées dans son livre. -**3.** [design] concevoir; the house is badly laid out la maison est mal conçue. -**4.** [corpse] faire la toilette de. -**5.** *inf* [spend] mettre; we've already laid out a fortune on the project nous avons déjà mis une fortune dans ce projet. -**6.** *inf* [knock out] assommer, mettre K-O; he was laid out cold il a été mis K-O. -**7.** TYPO faire la maquette de, monter.

◆ **lay over** *vi insep Am* [stop off] faire une halte, faire escale.

◆ **lay to** NAUT ◇ *vi insep* se mettre en panne.
◇ *vt sep* mettre en panne.

◆ **lay up** *vt sep Br* -**1.** [store, save] mettre de côté; you're just ~ing up trouble for yourself *fig* tu te prépares des ennuis. -**2.** *inf* [confine to bed] aliter; she's laid up with mumps elle est au lit avec les oreillons. -**3.** [ship] désarmer; [car] mettre au garage; my car is laid up ma voiture est au garage.

layabout *inf* ['leɪəbaʊt] *n Br* paresseux *m*, -euse *f*, fainéant *m*, -e *f*.

lay analyst *n* psychanalyste *mf* sans diplôme de médecin.

lay brother *n* frère *m* lai.

lay-by (*pl* lay-bys) *n* -**1.** *Br* AUT aire *f* de stationnement. -**2.** RAIL voie *f* de garage. -**3.** *Austr, Can* & *NZ* [deposit] arrhes *fpl*; to buy sthg on ~ retenir qqch en versant des arrhes.

layer ['leɪəʳ] ◇ *n* -**1.** [of skin, paint, wood] couche *f*; [of fabric, clothes] épaisseur *f*; the poem has many ~s of meaning *fig* le poème peut être lu de différentes façons. -**2.** GEOL strate *f*, couche *f*. -**3.** HORT marcotte *f*. -**4.** [hen] pondeuse *f*.
◇ *vt* [hair] couper en dégradé; HORT marcotter.

layer cake *n* génoise *f*; chocolate ~ génoise au chocolat.

layered ['leɪəd] *adj* SEW: a ~ skirt une jupe à volants.

layette [leɪ'et] *n* layette *f*.

lay figure *n* ART mannequin *m*.

laying ['leɪɪŋ] ◇ *n* -**1.** [of egg] ponte *f*. -**2.** [of cables, carpets] pose *f*; [of mine] pose *f*, mouillage *m*; [of wreath] dépôt *m*; a wreath-~ ceremony un dépôt de gerbe ❑ ~ on of hands RELIG imposition *f* des mains.
◇ *adj*: ~ hen poule *f* pondeuse.

layman ['leɪmən] (*pl* laymen [-mən]) *n* -**1.** [non-specialist] profane *mf*, non-initié *m*, -e *f*; the book is incomprehensible to the ~ le livre est incompréhensible pour le profane; a ~'s guide to the stock market un manuel d'initiation au système boursier. -**2.** [non-clerical] laïc *m*, laïque *f*.

lay-off *n* -**1.** [sacking] licenciement *m*. -**2.** [inactivity] chômage *m* technique.

layout ['leɪaʊt] *n* -**1.** [gen] disposition *f*; [of building, park] disposition *f*, agencement *m*; [of essay] plan *m*; the ~ of the controls is very straightforward la disposition des commandes est très simple; you've got quite a ~ here! *inf* c'est pas mal chez vous! -**2.** TYPO maquette *f*; ~ artist maquettiste *mf*. -**3.** [diagram] schéma *m*.

layover ['leɪəʊvəʳ] *n Am* escale *f*, halte *f*; we had a 3-hour ~ in Miami nous avons eu OR fait une escale de 3 heures à Miami.

lay person *n* profane *mf*, non-initié *m*, -e *f*.

lay preacher *n* prédicateur *m* laïque.

lay reader *n* prédicateur *m* laïque.

lay sister *n* sœur *f* converse.

laywoman ['leɪ,wʊmən] (*pl* laywomen [-,wɪmɪn]) *n* [non-clerical clergywoman] laïque *f*.

Lazarus ['læzərəs] *pr n* Lazare.

laze [leɪz] ◇ *vi* [relax] se reposer; [idle] paresser; to ~ in bed traîner au lit; we spent the holidays lazing on the beach nous avons passé nos vacances à paresser sur la plage.
◇ *n* farniente *m*; to have a ~ in bed traîner au lit.

◆ **laze about** *Br*, **laze around** *vi insep* paresser, fainéanter; we just ~d about on n'a rien fait de spécial.

◆ **laze away** *vt sep*: to ~ one's time away passer son temps à ne rien faire.

lazily ['leɪzɪlɪ] *adv* paresseusement, avec paresse.

laziness ['leɪzɪnɪs] *n* paresse *f*, fainéantise *f*.

lazy ['leɪzɪ] (*compar* lazier, *superl* laziest) *adj* -**1.** [idle] paresseux, fainéant; [relaxed] indolent, nonchalant; he's always been ~ about getting up il a toujours eu du mal à se lever; we spent a ~ afternoon on the beach on a passé l'après-midi à paresser sur la plage. -**2.** [movement] paresseux, lent.

lazybones *inf* ['leɪzɪbəʊnz] *n* fainéant *m*, -e *f*; come on, ~! allez, secoue-toi OR remue-toi un peu!

lazy eye *n* amblyopie *f*; to have a ~ être amblyope.

lazy Susan *n* [on table] plateau *m* tournant.

lb (*written abbr of* pound): 3 ~ OR ~s 3 livres.

LB *written abbr of* Labrador.

lbw (*abbr of* leg before wicket) *n au cricket, faute d'un joueur qui met une jambe devant le guichet*.

lc (*written abbr of* lower case) bdc.
LC *pr n abbr of* Library of Congress.
L/C *written abbr of* letter of credit.
LCD (*abbr of* liquid crystal display) *n* LCD *m*.
LCM (*abbr of* lowest common multiple) *n* PPCM *m*.
Ld *written abbr of* lord.
L-dopa [ˌel'dəʊpə] *n* L-dopa *f*, lévo-dopa *f*.
L-driver (*abbr of* learner-driver) *n Br personne qui apprend à conduire.*

L-DRIVER:
En Grande-Bretagne, la lettre «L» apposée sur l'arrière d'un véhicule indique que le conducteur n'a pas encore son permis mais qu'il est en conduite accompagnée.

LDS (*abbr of* Licentiate in Dental Surgery) *n (titulaire d'un) diplôme en chirurgie dentaire.*
lea [liː] *n lit* pré *m*.
LEA *n abbr of* local education authority.
leach [liːtʃ] *vt* -**1.** TECH lessiver, extraire par lessivage. -**2.** CHEM & PHARM lixivier.
leaching ['liːtʃɪŋ] *n* -**1.** TECH lessivage *m*. -**2.** CHEM & PHARM lixiviation *f*.
lead[1] [liːd] (*pt & pp* led [led]) ◇ *vt* -**1.** [take, guide] mener, emmener, conduire; to ~ sb somewhere mener OR conduire qqn quelque part; I was led into the garden on m'a emmené OR conduit dans le jardin; he led them across the lawn il leur fit traverser la pelouse; she led him down the stairs elle lui fit descendre l'escalier; to ~ an army into battle mener une armée au combat; the captain led the team onto the field le capitaine a conduit son équipe sur le terrain; she led them through the garden [to get out] elle les fit passer par le jardin; [to visit] elle leur fit visiter le jardin; he led her to the altar *lit* il la prit pour épouse; to ~ the way montrer le chemin; police motorcyclists led the way des motards de la police ouvraient la route; to ~ sb astray [misinform] mettre OR diriger qqn sur une fausse piste; [morally] détourner qqn du droit chemin ❑ to ~ sb a merry dance *Br* mener la vie dure à qqn; to ~ sb by the nose mener qqn par le bout du nez; to ~ sb up the garden path mener qqn en bateau. -**2.** [be leader of] être à la tête de, diriger; SPORT [be in front of] mener; to ~ the prayers/singing diriger la prière/les chants; Stardust is ~ing Black Beauty by 10 lengths Stardust a pris 10 longueurs d'avance sur Black Beauty ❑ to ~ the field *literal* [in race] être en tête; *fig* [in research, development etc] être à l'avant-garde. -**3.** [induce] amener; to ~ sb to do sthg amener qqn à faire qqch; despair led him to commit suicide le désespoir l'a poussé au suicide; he led me to believe (that) he was innocent il m'a amené à croire qu'il était innocent; everything ~s us to believe (that) she is still alive tout porte à croire OR nous avons toutes les raisons de croire qu'elle est encore en vie; he is easily led il se laisse facilement influencer ‖ *fig*: subsequent events led the country into war des événements ultérieurs ont entraîné le pays dans la guerre; this ~s me to my second point ceci m'amène à mon second point; he led the conversation round to money again il a ramené la conversation sur la question de l'argent. -**4.** [life] mener. -**5.** [in cards] demander, jouer; to ~ trumps demander OR jouer atout; what was led? qu'est-ce qui a été demandé? -**6.** JUR [witness] influencer.
◇ *vi* -**1.** [go] mener; this path ~s to the village ce chemin mène au village; where does this door ~ to? sur quoi ouvre cette porte?; the stairs lead to the cellar l'escalier mène OR conduit à la cave; take the street that ~s away from the station prenez la rue qui part de la gare; that road ~s nowhere cette route ne mène nulle part; this is ~ing nowhere! *fig* cela ne rime à rien! -**2.** SPORT mener, être en tête; to ~ by 2 metres avoir 2 mètres d'avance; to ~ by 3 points to 1 mener par 3 points à 1; Black Beauty is ~ing Black Beauty est en tête ‖ [in cards]: hearts led cœur (a été) demandé; Peter to ~ c'est à Peter de jouer. -**3.** [go in front] aller devant; if you ~, I'll follow allez-y, je vous suis. -**4.** *Br* PRESS: to ~ with sthg mettre qqch à la une; the "Times" led with news of the plane hijack le détournement d'avion faisait la une OR était en première page du «Times». -**5.** [in boxing]: he ~s with his right il attaque toujours du droit OR de la droite. -**6.** [in dancing] conduire.
◇ *n* -**1.** SPORT tête *f*; to be in the ~ être en tête, mener; to go into OR to take the ~ [in race] prendre la tête; [in match] mener; to have a 10-point/10-length ~ avoir 10 points/10 longueurs d'avance; to have a good ~ over the rest of the field avoir une bonne avance sur les autres concurrents. -**2.** [initiative] initiative *f*; he took the ~ in asking questions il fut le premier à poser des questions; take your ~ from me prenez exemple sur moi; to follow sb's ~ suivre l'exemple de qqn; it's up to the government to give a ~ on housing policy c'est au gouvernement (qu'il revient) de donner l'exemple en matière de politique du logement. -**3.** [indication, clue] indice *m*, piste *f*; the police have several ~s la police tient plusieurs pistes. -**4.** *Br* PRESS gros titre *m*; the news made the ~ in all the papers la nouvelle était à la une de tous les journaux; the "Telegraph" opens with a ~ on the Middle East crisis le «Telegraph» consacre sa une à la crise au Proche-Orient. -**5.** CIN & THEAT [role] rôle *m* principal; [actor] premier rôle *m* masculin; [actress] premier rôle *m* féminin. -**6.** [in cards] première carte *f* demandée; whose ~ is it? c'est à qui de jouer?; you must follow the ~ il faut fournir à la couleur demandée; a heart ~ une ouverture à cœur. -**7.** [for dog] laisse *f*; 'dogs must be kept on a ~' 'les chiens doivent être tenus en laisse'. -**8.** ELEC fil *m*; extension ~ *Br* rallonge *f*.
◇ *adj* [actor, singer] principal, premier; PRESS [article] de tête.
◆ **lead away** *vt sep* emmener; the guards led him away les gardes l'ont emmené; he led her away from the scene of the accident il l'éloigna du lieu de l'accident.
◆ **lead back** ◇ *vt sep* ramener, reconduire; they led him back to his room ils l'ont ramené OR reconduit à sa chambre; she led the conversation back to the question of money elle a ramené la conversation sur la question de l'argent.
◇ *vi insep*: this path ~s back to the beach ce chemin ramène à la plage.
◆ **lead off** ◇ *vi insep* [in conversation] commencer, débuter; [at dance] ouvrir le bal.
◇ *vt insep* -**1.** [begin] commencer, entamer. -**2.** [go from] partir de; several avenues ~ off the square plusieurs avenues partent de la place.
◇ *vt sep* conduire; they were led off to jail ils ont été conduits OR emmenés en prison.
◆ **lead on** ◇ *vi insep* aller OR marcher devant; ~ on! allez-y!
◇ *vt sep* -**1.** [trick]: to ~ sb on faire marcher qqn; you shouldn't ~ him on like that vous ne devriez pas le faire marcher comme ça. -**2.** [bring on] faire entrer; ~ on the horses! faites entrer les chevaux! -**3.** [in progression] amener; this ~s me on to my second point ceci m'amène à mon deuxième point.
◆ **lead to** *vt insep* [result in, have as consequence] mener OR aboutir à; what's all this ~ing to? sur quoi tout ceci va-t-il déboucher?; the decision led to panic on Wall Street la décision a semé la panique à Wall Street; one thing led to another une chose en amenait une autre; a course ~ing to a degree un cursus qui débouche sur un diplôme; several factors led to his decision to leave plusieurs facteurs le poussèrent OR l'amenèrent à décider de partir; this could ~ to some confusion ça pourrait provoquer une certaine confusion; her research led to nothing ses recherches n'ont abouti à rien OR n'ont rien donné.
◆ **lead up to** *vt insep* -**1.** [path, road] conduire à, mener à; a narrow path led up to the house un étroit sentier menait jusqu'à la maison; those stairs ~ up to the attic cet escalier mène au grenier. -**2.** [in reasoning]: she's ~ing up to something je me demande où elle veut en venir; what are you ~ing up to? où voulez-vous en venir? -**3.** [precede, cause]: the events ~ing up to the war les événements qui devaient déclencher la guerre; in the months ~ing up to her death pendant les mois qui précédèrent sa mort.
lead[2] [led] ◇ *n* -**1.** [metal] plomb *m*; it's made of ~ c'est en plomb; ~ oxide oxyde *m* de plomb. -**2.** *inf* [bullets] plomb *m*; they pumped him full of ~ ils l'ont flingué. -**3.** [in pencil] mine *f*; black ~ mine de plomb. -**4.** [piece of lead - for sounding] plomb *m* (de sonde); [- on car wheel, fishing line] plomb *m*; TYPO interligne *m*.
◇ *vt* -**1.** [seal] plomber. -**2.** TYPO interligner.
◇ *adj* [made of lead] de OR en plomb; [containing lead] plombifère; ~ pipe/shot tuyau *m*/grenaille *f* de plomb; red ~ paint minium *m*.
◆ **leads** *npl* [on roof] plombs *mpl* (de couverture); [on window] plombures *fpl*, plombs *mpl*.
leaded ['ledɪd] *adj* -**1.** [door, box, billiard cue] plombé; ~ window fenêtre *f* avec verre cathédrale. -**2.** [petrol] au plomb. -**3.** TYPO interligné.
leaden ['ledn] *adj* -**1.** [made of lead] de OR en plomb. -**2.** [dull - sky] de plomb, plombé; [heavy - sleep] de plomb; [- heart] lourd; he walked with ~ steps il marchait d'un pas lourd ‖ [oppressive - atmosphere] lourd, pesant; there was a ~ silence il régnait un silence de mort.
leaden-eyed *adj* aux yeux ternes OR morts.
leader ['liːdəʳ] *n* -**1.** [head] chef *m*; POL chef *m*, leader *m*, dirigeant *m*, -e *f*; [of association] dirigeant *m*, -e *f*; [of strike, protest] meneur *m*, -euse *f*; the ~s of the march were arrested les organisateurs de la manifestation ont été arrêtés ❑ the Leader of the House [in the Commons] *parlementaire de la majorité chargé de certaines fonctions dans la mise en place du programme gouvernemental*; [in the Lords] *porte-parole du gouvernement*; the Leader of the Opposition *chef du principal parti d'opposition à la Chambre des communes*. -**2.** SPORT [horse] cheval *m* de tête; [athlete] coureur *m* de tête; [in championship] leader *m*; she was up with the ~s elle était parmi les premiers OR dans le peloton de tête ‖ [main body or driving force]: the institute is a world ~ in cancer research l'institut occupe une des premières places mondiales en matière de recherche contre le cancer; the ~s of fashion ceux qui font la mode. -**3.** MUS: ~ of the orchestra *Br* premier violon *m*; *Am* chef *m* d'orchestre. -**4.** [in newspapers - editorial] éditorial *m*. -**5.** COMM produit *m* d'appel. -**6.** [for film, tape] amorce *f*. -**7.** [in climbing] premier *m* de cordée.
leaderless ['liːdəlɪs] *adj* sans chef, dépourvu de chef.
leadership ['liːdəʃɪp] *n* -**1.** [direction] direction *f*; during OR under her ~ sous sa direction; he was offered the party ~ on lui a offert la direction du parti; she is clearly cut out for ~ elle est manifestement née pour diriger; he has great ~ qualities c'est un excellent meneur d'hommes; they looked to us for ~ ils comptaient sur nous pour leur montrer le chemin. -**2.** [leaders] direction *f*, dirigeants *mpl*; the ~ of the movement is divided on this issue les chefs OR les dirigeants du mouvement sont divisés sur cette question.
leader writer *n Br* éditorialiste *mf*.
lead-free [led-] *adj* [paint, petrol] sans plomb; [toy] (garanti) sans plomb.
lead glass [led-] *n* verre *m* de OR au plomb.
lead-in [liːd-] *n Br* -**1.** [introductory remarks] introduction *f*, remarques *fpl* préliminaires. -**2.** [wire] descente *f* d'antenne.
leading[1] ['liːdɪŋ] *adj* -**1.** [prominent] premier, de premier plan; [major] majeur, principal; he was a ~ figure in the resistance movement c'était un des principaux OR grands chefs de la résistance; they played a ~ part in the discussions ils ont joué un rôle prépondérant dans le débat;

he is the ~ actor in the company c'est le meilleur acteur de la troupe; to play the ~ role in a film être la vedette d'un film; ~ technology technologie *f* de pointe. -**2.** SPORT [in race] de tête; [in championship] premier; to be in the ~ position être en tête; the ~ runners/riders les coureurs/cavaliers de tête; the ~ cyclists, the ~ motorcyclists le peloton de tête. -**3.** MATH [coefficient] premier.

leading[2] ['ledɪŋ] *n* TYPO [process] interlignage *m*; [space] interligne *m*.

leading article ['li:dɪŋ-] *n Br* éditorial *m*; *Am* article *m* leader OR de tête.

leading edge ['li:dɪŋ-] *n* -**1.** AERON bord *m* d'attaque. -**2.** *fig*: they are on OR at the ~ of technology ils sont à la pointe de la technologie.

◆ **leading-edge** *comp* de pointe.

leading lady ['li:dɪŋ-] *n* CIN & THEAT premier rôle *m* (féminin); Vivian Leigh was the ~ Vivian Leigh tenait le premier rôle féminin.

leading light ['li:dɪŋ-] *n* personnage *m* (de marque).

leading man ['li:dɪŋ-] *n* CIN & THEAT premier rôle *m* (masculin); he was the ~ il tenait le premier rôle masculin.

leading note ['li:dɪŋ-] *n* MUS sensible *f*.

leading question ['li:dɪŋ-] *n* question *f* orientée.

leading reins ['li:dɪŋ-] *npl Br* harnais *m (pour enfant)*.

lead pencil [led-] *n* crayon *m* noir OR à papier OR à mine de plomb.

lead poisoning [led-] *n* -**1.** MED intoxication *f* par le plomb, saturnisme *m*. -**2.** ▽ *Am* [death] mort *f* par balles; [injury] blessure *f* par balles.

lead time [li:d-] *n* INDUST délai *m* de préparation; COMM délai *m* de livraison.

leaf [li:f] (*pl* leaves [li:vz]) ◇ *n* -**1.** [on plant, tree] feuille *f*; to come into ~ se couvrir de feuilles; the tree has lost its leaves l'arbre a perdu son feuillage OR ses feuilles; the trees are in ~ les arbres sont en feuilles. -**2.** [page] feuillet *m*, page *f*; to take a ~ out of sb's book prendre exemple OR modèle sur qqn. -**3.** [on table - dropleaf] abattant *m*; [- inserted board] allonge *f*, rallonge *f*. -**4.** [of metal] feuille *f*.

◇ *vi* [tree] se feuiller.

◆ **leaf through** *vt insep* [book, magazine] feuilleter, parcourir.

leaf beet *n* bette *f*.

leafless ['li:flɪs] *adj* sans feuilles; the ~ trees les arbres dénudés.

leaflet ['li:flɪt] ◇ *n* -**1.** [brochure] prospectus *m*, dépliant *m*; [political] tract *m*; ~ drop largage *m* de prospectus OR de tracts *(par avion)*. -**2.** [instruction sheet] notice *f* (explicative), mode *m* d'emploi. -**3.** BOT foliole *f*.

◇ *vt* distribuer des prospectus OR des tracts à; has the area been ~ed? est-ce qu'on a distribué des tracts dans le quartier?

leaf mould *n* terreau *m* de feuilles.

leaf spot *n (U)* (maladie *f* des) taches *fpl* noires.

leaf spring *n* ressort *m* à lames; ~ suspension suspension *f* à lames.

leafy ['li:fɪ] (*compar* leafier, *superl* leafiest) *adj* [tree] feuillu; [woodland] boisé, vert; a ~ avenue une avenue bordée d'arbres.

league [li:g] ◇ *n* -**1.** [alliance] ligue *f*; to be in ~ (with sb) être de mèche (avec qqn); they are in ~ together ils sont complices OR de mèche; they're all in ~ against me ils se sont tous ligués contre moi ❑ the League of Nations HIST la Société des Nations. -**2.** SPORT [competition] championnat *m*; United are ~ leaders at the moment United est en tête du championnat en ce moment || [division] division *f*. -**3.** *fig* [class] classe *f*; he's not in the same ~ as his father il n'a pas la classe de son père; to be in the top ~ être parmi les meilleurs. -**4.** *arch* [distance] lieue *f*.

◇ *vi* se liguer.

◇ *vt*: to be ~d with sb être allié à OR avec qqn.

league champion *n* champion *m*; to become ~s remporter le championnat.

league championship *n* championnat *m*; ~ match match *m* de championnat OR comptant pour le championnat.

league table *n* (classement *m* du) championnat *m*.

Leah ['lɪə] *pr n* Lia.

leak [li:k] ◇ *n* -**1.** [in pipe, tank, roof] fuite *f*; [in boat] voie *f* d'eau. -**2.** [disclosure - of information, secret] fuite *f*. -**3.** *phr*: to go for OR to take a ~ ▽ [urinate] pisser un coup.

◇ *vi* [pen, pipe, roof] fuir; [boat, shoe] prendre l'eau; the roof ~s il y a une fuite dans le toit; his pen ~ed in his pocket son stylo a fui OR coulé dans sa poche || [gas, liquid] fuir, s'échapper; the rain ~s through the ceiling la pluie s'infiltre par le plafond.

◇ *vt* -**1.** [liquid] répandre, faire couler; the can ~ed oil onto my trousers de l'huile du bidon s'est répandue sur mon pantalon. -**2.** [information] divulguer; to ~ news to the press divulguer des informations à la presse; the budget details were ~ed il y a eu des fuites sur le budget; the documents had been ~ed to a local councillor quelqu'un avait communiqué OR avait fait parvenir les documents à un conseiller municipal.

◆ **leak in** *vi insep* s'infiltrer; the rain had ~ed in through a crack in the wall la pluie s'était infiltrée par une lézarde dans le mur.

◆ **leak out** *vi insep* -**1.** [liquid, gas] fuir, s'échapper. -**2.** [news, secret] filtrer, transpirer; the truth finally ~ed out la vérité a fini par se savoir.

leakage ['li:kɪdʒ] *n (U)* fuite *f*; damage caused by ~ des dégâts dus à des fuites.

leakproof ['li:kpru:f] *adj* étanche.

leaky ['li:kɪ] (*compar* leakier, *superl* leakiest) *adj* [boat, shoes] qui prend l'eau; [pen, roof, bucket] qui fuit.

lean [li:n] (*Br pt* & *pp* leaned OR leant [lent], *Am pt* & *pp* leaned) ◇ *vi* [be on incline] pencher, s'incliner; she/a ladder was ~ing (up) against the wall elle/une échelle était appuyée contre le mur; he was ~ing with his back to OR against the wall il était adossé au mur; she leant down to speak to me elle s'est penchée pour me parler; to ~ in through the window pencher la tête par la fenêtre; ~ on my arm appuyez-vous OR prenez appui sur mon bras; she was ~ing with her elbows on the window sill elle était accoudée à la fenêtre.

◇ *vt* -**1.** [prop - ladder, bicycle] appuyer; he leant the ladder/bike (up) against the tree il appuya l'échelle/le vélo contre un arbre. -**2.** [rest - head, elbows] appuyer; to ~ one's elbows on sthg s'accouder à qqch; she leant her head on his shoulder elle posa sa tête sur son épaule. -**3.** [incline] pencher; to ~ one's head to one side pencher OR incliner la tête.

◇ *adj* -**1.** [animal, meat] maigre; [person - thin] maigre; [- slim] mince. -**2.** [poor - harvest] maigre, pauvre; [- period of time] difficile. -**3.** [deficient - ore, mixture] pauvre.

◇ *n* -**1.** [slope] inclinaison *f*. -**2.** [meat] maigre *m*.

◆ **lean back** ◇ *vi insep* -**1.** [person] se pencher en arrière; he ~ed back against the wall il s'est adossé au mur; don't ~ back on your chair! ne te balance pas sur ta chaise!; he ~t back in his armchair il s'est renversé dans son fauteuil. -**2.** [chair] basculer; this chair ~s back if you pull that lever on peut incliner OR faire basculer le siège en poussant ce levier.

◇ *vt sep* pencher en arrière; to ~ one's head back pencher OR renverser la tête en arrière; to ~ one's chair back pencher sa chaise en arrière.

◆ **lean forward** ◇ *vi insep* se pencher en avant.

◇ *vt sep* pencher en avant.

◆ **lean on, lean upon** *vt insep* -**1.** [depend] s'appuyer sur; to ~ on sb's advice/friendship compter sur les conseils/l'amitié de qqn; she ~s heavily on her family for elle dépend beaucoup de sa famille. -**2.** *inf Br* [pressurize] faire pression sur; they ~ed on him for more information ils ont fait pression sur lui pour qu'il parle; they kept ~ing on him until they got him to agree ils ne l'ont pas lâché avant qu'il ait dit oui.

◆ **lean out** ◇ *vi insep* se pencher au dehors; don't ~ out of the window! ne te penche pas par la fenêtre!; 'do not ~ out of the window' 'interdiction de se pencher au dehors'.

◇ *vt sep* pencher au dehors; he ~ed his head out of the window il a passé la tête par la fenêtre.

◆ **lean over** *vi insep* [person] se pencher en avant; [tree, wall] pencher, être penché; he ~ed over to speak to me il s'est penché vers moi pour me parler ❑ to ~ over backwards *literal* se pencher en arrière; *fig* remuer ciel et terre, se mettre en quatre.

◆ **lean towards** *vt insep* [tend] pencher pour; I rather ~ towards the view that we should sell je pencherais plutôt pour la vente, j'ai tendance à penser que nous devrions vendre; politically she ~s towards the right politiquement, elle se situe plutôt à droite.

lean-burn *adj* [engine] fonctionnant avec un mélange pauvre.

leaning ['li:nɪŋ] ◇ *n (usu pl)* tendance *f*, penchant *m*; she has communist/literary ~s elle a des penchants communistes/aimerait être écrivain.

◇ *adj* [tree, wall] penché; the Leaning Tower of Pisa la tour de Pise.

leanness ['li:nnɪs] *n* maigreur *f*.

leant [lent] *Br pt* & *pp* → **lean**.

lean-to *n Br*: a ~ (shed) un appentis.

leap [li:p] (*Br pt* & *pp* leaped OR leapt [lept], *Am pt* & *pp* leaped) ◇ *vi* -**1.** [person, animal] bondir, sauter; [flame] jaillir; she leapt a good four feet elle a sauté un bon mètre vingt; to ~ to one's feet se lever d'un bond; to ~ for joy [person] sauter de joie; [heart] faire un bond; we leapt back in fright de frayeur, nous fîmes un bond en arrière; to ~ into the air sauter en l'air; the cat leapt off the chair onto the table le chat sauta de la chaise sur la table; we had to ~ over the stream nous avons dû sauter par-dessus le ruisseau ❑ look before you ~ il faut réfléchir à deux fois avant d'agir. -**2.** *fig* faire un bond; the price of petrol leapt by 10% le prix du pétrole a fait un bond de 10 %; the answer almost leapt off the page at me la réponse m'a pour ainsi dire sauté aux yeux; the idea suddenly leapt into my mind l'idée m'est soudain venue à l'esprit; she leapt to the wrong conclusion elle a conclu trop hâtivement.

◇ *vt* -**1.** [fence, stream] sauter (par-dessus), franchir d'un bond. -**2.** [horse] faire sauter.

◇ *n* -**1.** [jump] saut *m*, bond *m*; to take a ~ forward *literal* & *fig* faire un bond en avant, sauter en avant; it's a great ~ forward in medical research c'est un grand bond en avant pour la recherche médicale ❑ by ~s and bounds à pas de géant; a ~ in the dark un saut dans l'inconnu. -**2.** [in prices] bond *m*.

◆ **leap about** *Br*, **leap around** ◇ *vt insep* gambader dans; he kept ~ing about the room il n'a cessé de gambader dans la pièce.

◇ *vi insep* gambader.

◆ **leap at** *vt insep* -**1.** [in attack] sauter sur; the dog leapt at me le chien m'a sauté dessus. -**2.** *fig*: to ~ at an opportunity sauter sur l'occasion; she leapt at the chance elle a sauté sur l'occasion.

◆ **leap out** *vi insep* bondir; to ~ out at sb bondir sur qqn; they leapt out from behind the bushes ils ont surgi de derrière les buissons || *fig*: a familiar face leapt out at me from the newspaper soudain, je remarquai dans le journal un visage que je connaissais; he almost leapt out of his skin il a failli tomber à la renverse.

◆ **leap up** *vi insep* [into the air] sauter (en l'air); [to one's feet] se lever d'un bond; to ~ up in surprise sauter au plafond, sursauter; to ~ up in indignation bondir d'indignation; the dog leapt up at him le chien lui a sauté dessus.

leapfrog ['li:pfrɒg] (*pt* & *pp* leapfrogged, *cont* leapfrogging) ◇ *n* saute-mouton *m*; to play ~ jouer à saute-mouton.

◇ *vi Br*: to ~ over sb sauter par-dessus qqn; to ~ into the computer age *fig* se trouver propulsé à l'ère de l'informatique.

◇ *vt Br fig* dépasser.

leapt [lept] *Br pt* & *pp* → **leap**.

leap year *n* année *f* bissextile.

learn [lɜ:n] (*Br pt* & *pp* learned OR learnt [lɜ:nt], *Am pt* & *pp* learned) ◇ *vt* -**1.** [by instruction] apprendre; to ~ (how) to do sthg apprendre à faire qqch; to ~ sthg by heart apprendre qqch par cœur; he's learnt his lesson now *fig* cela lui a servi de leçon. -**2.** [discover, hear] apprendre; I subsequently learnt that he wouldn't be coming j'ai appris par la suite qu'il ne viendrait pas. -**3.** *hum* [teach] apprendre; that'll ~ you! ça t'apprendra!

◇ *vi* -**1.** [by instruction, experience] apprendre; to ~ about sthg apprendre qqch; to ~ by OR from one's mistakes tirer la leçon de ses erreurs; they learnt the hard way ils ont été à dure école; it's never too late to ~ il n'est jamais trop tard pour apprendre. -**2.** [be informed]: to ~ of sthg apprendre qqch; we only learnt of her death today ce n'est qu'aujourd'hui que nous avons appris sa mort.

◆ **learn off** *vt sep Br* apprendre par cœur.

◆ **learn up** *inf vt sep Br* bûcher, potasser; I've been ~ing up all about the town's history j'ai potassé tout ce qui a trait à l'histoire de la ville.

learned [*senses 1 and 2* 'lɜ:nɪd, *sense 3* lɜ:nd] *adj* -**1.** [erudite - person] savant, érudit; [- subject, book, society] savant. -**2.** JUR [lawyer]: my ~ friend mon éminent confrère. -**3.** PSYCH [behaviour] acquis.

learnedly ['lɜ:nɪdlɪ] *adv* savamment, avec érudition.

learner ['lɜ:nəʳ] *n* apprenti *m*, -e *f*, débutant *m*, -e *f*; to be a quick ~ apprendre vite ❑ ~ (driver) *Br* conducteur *m* débutant, conductrice *f* débutante.

learning ['lɜ:nɪŋ] *n* -**1.** [erudition] érudition *f*, savoir *m*; a man of great ~ [in sciences] un grand savant; [in arts] un homme d'une grande érudition OR culture. -**2.** [acquisition of knowledge] étude *f*; language ~ l'étude OR l'apprentissage *m* des langues ❑ adults/children with ~ difficulties adultes *mpl*/enfants *mpl* inadaptés (à la vie en société).

learning curve *n* courbe *f* d'assimilation.

learnt [lɜ:nt] *Br* ◇ *pt* & *pp* → **learn**.

◇ *adj* PSYCH acquis.

lease [li:s] ◇ *n* -**1.** JUR bail *m*; a 99-year ~ un bail de 99 ans; to take (out) a ~ on a house, to take a house on ~ prendre une maison à bail; to sign a ~ signer un bail. -**2.** *phr*: the trip has given her a new ~ of *Br* OR on *Am* life le voyage l'a remise en forme OR lui a redonné du tonus; to take on a new ~ of life retrouver une nouvelle jeunesse.

◇ *vt* [house] louer à bail; [car, sailboard] louer.

◆ **lease out** *vt sep* = **lease** *vt*.

leaseback ['li:sbæk] *n* cession-bail *f*.

leasehold ['li:shəʊld] ◇ *n* [lease] bail *m*; [property] location *f* à bail.

◇ *adj* loué à bail.

leaseholder ['li:s,həʊldəʳ] *n* [tenant] locataire *mf*.

leash [li:ʃ] *n* [for dog] laisse *f*; 'dogs must be kept on a ~' 'les chiens doivent être tenus en laisse'.

leasing ['li:sɪŋ] *n* crédit-bail *m*, leasing *m*.

least [li:st] ◇ *det* & *pron* (*superl of* little) -**1.** [in quantity, size]: he's the one who drank the ~ (wine) c'est lui qui a bu le moins (de vin); he's got the ~ c'est lui qui en a le moins. -**2.** [slightest]: I haven't the ~ idea je n'en ai pas la moindre idée; the ~ thing upsets her un rien la contrarie; I'm not the ~ bit interested cela ne m'intéresse pas le moins du monde; it was the ~ we could do c'était la moindre des choses ❑ that's the ~ of our worries c'est le moindre OR c'est le cadet de nos soucis; ~ said, soonest mended *prov* moins on en parle, mieux on se porte.

◇ *adv* (le) moins; which do you find (the) ~ useful? à votre avis, lequel est le moins utile?; it's just about the ~ interesting film I've ever seen je crois que c'est le film le moins intéressant que j'aie jamais vu; it's what we ~ expected c'est ce à quoi nous nous attendions le moins.

◆ **at least** *adv phr* -**1.** [not less than] au moins; at ~ $500 au moins 500 dollars; he smokes at ~ forty cigarettes a day il fume au moins quarante cigarettes par jour; she's at ~ as tall as you elle est au moins aussi grande que toi. -**2.** [as a minimum] au moins; you could at ~ have phoned vous auriez pu au moins téléphoner; at the very ~ he might have phoned us la moindre des choses aurait été de nous téléphoner. -**3.** [indicating an advantage] au moins, du moins; at ~ we've got an umbrella au moins OR du moins on a un parapluie. -**4.** [used to qualify] du moins; I didn't like him, at ~ not at first il ne m'a pas plu, en tout cas OR du moins pas au début; I understand now, at ~ I think I do ça y est, je comprends, du moins je crois.

◆ **in the least** *adv phr (with negative)*: not in the ~ pas du tout, pas le moins du monde; am I boring you? — not in the ~ je t'ennuie? — pas du tout; she's not in the ~ angry elle n'est pas du tout fâchée; she didn't seem to mind in the ~ ça ne semblait pas la déranger le moins du monde.

◆ **least of all** *adv phr* surtout pas; nobody could understand it, Jim ~ of all OR ~ of all Jim personne ne comprenait, surtout pas Jim OR Jim encore moins que les autres.

◆ **not least** *adv phr*: many politicians, not ~ the Foreign Secretary, are in favour of nombreux hommes politiques, le ministre des Affaires étrangères le premier, y sont favorables.

least common denominator *n Br*: the ~ le plus petit dénominateur commun.

leastways *inf* ['li:stweɪz] *adv* du moins.

leastwise *inf* ['li:stwaɪz] *Am* = **leastways**.

leather ['leðəʳ] ◇ *n* -**1.** [material] cuir *m*; real ~ cuir véritable; made of ~ de OR en cuir. -**2.** [for polishing]: (wash OR window) ~ peau *f* de chamois. -**3.** *inf* [sexual fetish]: he's into ~ c'est un fétichiste du cuir.

◇ *comp* -**1.** [jacket, shoes, sofa, bag] de OR en cuir; ~ goods [ordinary] articles *mpl* en cuir; [finer] maroquinerie *f*. -**2.** [bar, club] cuir *(inv)*.

◇ *vt inf* [punish] tanner le cuir à.

leatherback ['leðəbæk] *n* tortue *f* luth, fausse tortue *f*.

leatherbound ['leðəbaʊnd] *adj* relié (en) cuir.

leatherette [,leðə'ret] ◇ *n* similicuir *m*.

◇ *adj* en similicuir.

leathering *inf* ['leðərɪŋ] *n Br* raclée *f*; to give sb a ~ tanner le cuir à qqn.

leatherjacket ['leðə,dʒækɪt] *n* ZOOL larve *f* de la tipule.

leatherneck *inf* ['leðənek] *n Am* marine *m (américain)*.

leathery ['leðərɪ] *adj* [meat] coriace; [skin] parcheminé, tanné.

leave[1] [li:v] (*pt* & *pp* left [left]) ◇ *vi* -**1.** [depart] partir; my flight ~s at ten mon avion part à dix heures; when did you ~? quand est-ce que vous êtes partis?; we're leaving for Mexico tomorrow nous partons pour le Mexique demain; which station do you ~ from? vous partez de quelle gare?; he's just left for lunch il vient de partir déjeuner; if you'd rather I left... si vous voulez que je vous laisse... -**2.** [quit] partir; half of the staff have left la moitié du personnel est partie; fewer schoolchildren are now leaving at 16 les élèves sont aujourd'hui moins nombreux à quitter l'école à 16 ans. -**3.** [end relationship]: Charles, I'm leaving! Charles, je te quitte!

◇ *vt* -**1.** [depart from - place] quitter; she left London yesterday elle est partie de OR elle a quitté Londres hier; he left the room il est sorti de OR il a quitté la pièce; I ~ home at 8 every morning je pars OR je sors de chez moi tous les matins à 8 h; to ~ the table se lever de table; the boat finally left port at 6 le bateau quitta finalement le port à 6 h; his brakes failed and the car left the road ses freins ont lâché et la voiture a quitté la route. -**2.** [quit - job, institution] quitter; she left the firm last year elle a quitté l'entreprise l'année dernière; I left home at 18 je suis parti de chez moi OR de chez mes parents à 18 ans; to ~ school quitter l'école. -**3.** [in specified place or state] laisser; you can't ~ them alone for a minute on ne peut pas les laisser seuls une minute; he left her asleep on the sofa elle était endormie sur le canapé lorsqu'il la quitta; I left him to his reading je l'ai laissé à sa lecture; I left him to himself je l'ai laissé seul; just ~ me alone! laissez-moi tranquille! -**4.** [abandon - person] quitter; she left him (for another man) after 15 years of marriage elle l'a quitté (pour un autre) après 15 ans de mariage; the prisoners were left to die les prisonniers furent abandonnés à la mort ‖ *fml* [take leave of - person] quitter; it's getting late, I must ~ you now il se fait tard, je dois vous laisser; you may ~ us now vous pouvez disposer maintenant. -**5.** [deposit, set down] laisser; it's no trouble to ~ you at the station ça ne me dérange pas de vous laisser OR déposer à la gare. -**6.** [for sb's use, information etc] laisser; I've left your dinner in the oven for you je t'ai laissé de quoi dîner dans le four; ~ your name with the receptionist laissez votre nom à la réception; he's out, do you want to ~ a message? il n'est pas là, voulez-vous laisser un message?; she left word for you to call her back elle a demandé que vous la rappeliez. -**7.** [forget] laisser, oublier; I must have left my gloves at the café j'ai dû oublier mes gants au café. -**8.** [allow or cause to remain] laisser; ~ some cake for your brother laisse du gâteau pour ton frère; if you don't like your dinner, then ~ it si tu n'aimes pas ton dîner, laisse-le; ~ enough space for the address laissez assez de place pour l'adresse; ~ the stew to cook for two hours laissez mijoter le ragoût pendant deux heures; ~ yourself an hour to get to the airport prévoyez une heure pour aller à l'aéroport; I only left myself £20 a week to live on je n'avais plus que 20 livres par semaine pour me nourrir; don't ~ things to the last minute n'attendez pas la dernière minute (pour faire ce que vous avez à faire); he left his work unfinished il n'a pas terminé son travail; please ~ the windows closed veuillez laisser les fenêtres fermées; to ~ sthg unsaid passer qqch sous silence; their behaviour ~s a lot to be desired leur conduite laisse beaucoup à désirer; her words left me curious to know more le peu qu'elle a dit m'a donné l'envie d'en savoir plus; the decision ~s me in a bit of a quandary cette décision me place devant un dilemme; I want to be left on/off the list je veux que mon nom reste/je ne veux pas que mon nom figure sur la liste; I was left with the bill c'est moi qui ai dû payer l'addition ‖ *(passive use)*: to be left rester; we finished what was left of the cake on a fini ce qui restait du gâteau; there's nothing left il ne reste (plus) rien; there wasn't enough left to go round il n'en restait pas assez pour tout le monde; I've got £10/10 minutes left il me reste 10 livres/10 minutes; there's no doubt left in my mind il n'y a plus le moindre doute dans mon esprit; he had nothing left to do but lock up the house il ne lui restait (plus) qu'à fermer la maison ‖ [mark, trace] laisser; the wine left a stain le vin a fait une tache. -**9.** [allow]: can I ~ you to deal with it, then? vous vous en chargez, alors?; she ~s me to get on with things elle me laisse faire; right then, I'll ~ you to it bon, eh bien, je te laisse. -**10.** [entrust] laisser; can I ~ my suitcase with you for a few minutes? puis-je vous confier ma valise quelques instants?; she left the detailed arrangements to her secretary elle a laissé à sa secrétaire le soin de régler les détails; you should ~ such tasks to a specialist vous devriez laisser OR confier ce genre de travail à un spécialiste; I'll ~ it to you to finish it off je vous laisse (le soin de) finir; ~ it to me! je m'en occupe!, je m'en charge!; ~ it with me laissez-moi faire, je m'en charge. -**11.** *Br* MATH: 9 from 16 ~s 7 16 moins 9 égale 7; what does 29 from 88 ~? 29 ôté de 88 égale combien? -**12.** [bequeath] léguer; she left all her money to charity elle légua toute sa fortune à des œuvres de charité. -**13.** [be survived by]: he ~s a wife and two children il laisse une femme et deux enfants.

◇ *n* -**1.** [from work] congé *m*; MIL permission *f*; to be/to go on ~ [gen] être/partir en congé; MIL être/partir en permission ❑ sick ~ congé (de) maladie; ~ of absence congé (exceptionnel); [without pay] congé sans solde. -**2.** [permission] permission *f*, autorisation *f*; he asked ~ to address the meeting il a demandé la permission de prendre la parole devant l'assemblée; by OR with your ~ avec votre permission. -**3.** [farewell] congé *m*; to take one's ~ (of sb) prendre congé (de qqn); to take ~ of sb prendre congé de qqn; to take ~ of one's senses *fig* perdre la tête OR la raison.

◆ **leave about** *Br*, **leave around** *vt sep* laisser traîner.

◆ **leave aside** *vt sep* laisser de côté; leaving aside the question of cost for the moment si on laisse de côté pour le moment la question du coût.

◆ **leave behind** *vt sep* -**1.** [not take] laisser; it's hard to ~ all your friends and relations behind c'est dur de laisser tous ses amis et sa famille derrière soi || [forget] laisser, oublier; somebody left their watch behind quelqu'un a laissé OR oublié sa montre. -**2.** [leave as trace] laisser; the cyclone left behind a trail of destruction le cyclone a tout détruit sur son passage. -**3.** [outstrip] distancer, devancer; she soon left the other runners behind elle a vite distancé tous les autres coureurs; if you don't work harder you'll soon get left behind si tu ne travailles pas plus, tu vas vite te retrouver loin derrière les autres.

◆ **leave in** *vt sep* [word, paragraph] garder, laisser.

◆ **leave off** ◇ *vi insep* [stop] s'arrêter; we'll carry on from where we left off nous allons reprendre là où nous nous étions arrêtés; ~ off, will you! *inf Br* arrête, tu veux!

◇ *vt insep inf Br* [stop]: to ~ off doing sthg s'arrêter de faire qqch; if it ~s off raining, we'll go for a walk s'il s'arrête de pleuvoir OR si la pluie cesse, nous irons nous promener.

◇ *vt sep* -**1.** [not put on] ne pas remettre; who left the top of the toothpaste off? qui a laissé le tube de dentifrice débouché?; you can ~ your jacket off ce n'est pas la peine de remettre ta veste. -**2.** [not switch or turn on - tap, gas] laisser fermé; [- light] laisser éteint; [not plug in - iron] laisser débranché; we left the heating off while we were away nous avons arrêté OR coupé le chauffage pendant notre absence.

◆ **leave on** *vt sep* -**1.** [not take off - garment] garder; [- top, cover] laisser; don't ~ the price tag on enlève l'étiquette. -**2.** [not switch or turn off - tap, gas] laisser ouvert; [- light] laisser allumé; [not unplug - iron] laisser branché; I hope I didn't ~ the gas on j'espère que j'ai éteint le gaz.

◆ **leave out** *vt sep* -**1.** [omit] omettre; several names have been left out plusieurs noms ont été omis; ~ out any reference to her husband in your article dans votre article, évitez toute allusion à son mari. -**2.** [exclude] exclure; I felt completely left out at the party j'ai eu le sentiment d'être totalement tenu à l'écart OR exclu de leur petite fête. -**3.** [not put away - by accident] ne pas ranger; [- on purpose] laisser sorti, ne pas ranger; he left a meal out for the children il a laissé un repas tout prêt pour les enfants || [leave outdoors] laisser dehors; to ~ the washing out to dry mettre le linge à sécher (dehors). -**4.** *phr*: ~ it out!▽ *Br* lâche-moi!

◆ **leave over** *vt sep* [allow or cause to remain] laisser; to be left over rester; there are still one or two left over il en reste encore un ou deux.

leave[2] [liːv] (*pt* & *pp* leaved, *cont* leaving) *vi* BOT [produce leaves] feuiller.

leaven ['levn] ◇ *n* [yeast] levain *m*; he brought a ~ of humour to the dullest occasion *fig* il apportait une touche OR pointe d'humour dans les occasions les plus sinistres.

◇ *vt* -**1.** CULIN faire lever. -**2.** *fig* [occasion] égayer.

leavened bread ['levnd-] *n* pain *m* au levain.

leavening ['levnɪŋ] *n literal* & *fig* levain *m*.

leaves [liːvz] *pl* → **leaf**.

leave-taking *n (U)* adieux *mpl*.

leaving ['liːvɪŋ] *n* départ *m*.

leavings ['liːvɪŋz] *npl* restes *mpl*.

Lebanese [,lebə'niːz] (*pl inv*) ◇ *n* Libanais *m*, -e *f*.

◇ *adj* libanais.

Lebanon ['lebənən] *pr n* Liban *m*; in (the) ~ au Liban.

lech *inf* [letʃ] *vi*: stop ~ing! ne prends pas ce regard lubrique!; he's always ~ing after my secretary il n'arrête pas de reluquer ma secrétaire.

lecher ['letʃəʳ] *n* débauché *m*, obsédé *m* (sexuel).

lecherous ['letʃərəs] *adj* lubrique.

lecherously ['letʃərəslɪ] *adv* lubriquement, avec lubricité; to look at sb ~ regarder qqn d'un œil lubrique.

lechery ['letʃərɪ] *n* lubricité *f*.

lectern ['lektən] *n* lutrin *m*.

lector ['lektəʳ] *n* RELIG & UNIV lecteur *m*, -trice *f*.

lecture ['lektʃəʳ] ◇ *n* -**1.** [talk] conférence *f*, exposé *m*; UNIV [as part of course] cours *m* (magistral); she gave a very good ~ on Yeats elle a fait un très bon cours sur Yeats; have you been to his linguistics ~s? avez-vous suivi ses cours de linguistique? -**2.** *fig* [sermon] sermon *m*, discours *m*; I'm tired of his ~s about the virtues of healthy living j'en ai assez de ses discours OR de ses sermons sur les vertus d'une vie saine; to give sb a ~ sermonner qqn, faire des remontrances à qqn; she gave the children a ~ on how to behave elle a donné aux enfants une leçon de bonne conduite.

◇ *vi* [talk] faire OR donner une conférence; [teach] faire (un) cours; he ~s twice a week il fait cours deux fois par semaine; she ~s in linguistics elle enseigne la OR donne des cours de linguistique; she ~s on Dante elle donne des cours sur Dante.

◇ *vt* [reprimand] réprimander, sermonner; he's always lecturing his children about their manners il est toujours à sermonner OR réprimander ses enfants sur leurs manières.

◇ *comp* [notes] de cours.

lecture hall *n* salle *f* de cours, amphithéâtre *m*.

lecturer ['lektʃərəʳ] *n* [speaker] conférencier *m*, -ère *f*; UNIV [teacher] assistant *m*, -e *f*; she's a ~ in English at the University of Dublin elle est professeur d'anglais à l'université de Dublin ❑ assistant ~ ≃ maître-assistant *m*; senior ~ ≃ maître *m* de conférences.

lecture room *n* salle *f* de cours OR de conférences.

lectureship ['lektʃəʃɪp] *n* UNIV poste *m* d'assistant; he got a ~ at the University of Oxford il a été nommé assistant à l'université d'Oxford ❑ senior ~ ≃ poste de maître de conférences.

led [led] *pt* & *pp* → **lead** *(guide)*.

LED (*abbr of* light-emitting diode) *n* LED *f*; ~ display affichage *m* (par) LED.

ledge [ledʒ] *n* -**1.** [shelf] rebord *m*; (window) ~ rebord de fenêtre. -**2.** GEOG [on mountain] saillie *f*; [on rock or cliff face] corniche *f*; [on seabed] haut-fond *m*. -**3.** GEOL [vein] filon *m*.

ledger ['ledʒəʳ] *n* -**1.** COMM & FIN grand livre *m*. -**2.** TECH longrine *f*.

ledger line *n* MUS ligne *f* supplémentaire.

lee [liː] ◇ *n* -**1.** NAUT bord *m* sous le vent. -**2.** [shelter] abri *m*; in the ~ of a rock à l'abri d'un rocher.

◇ *adj* sous le vent.

leech [liːtʃ] ◇ *n literal* & *fig* sangsue *f*; to cling to sb like a ~ s'accrocher OR coller à qqn comme une sangsue.

◇ *vt* MED saigner (avec des sangsues).

leek [liːk] *n* poireau *m*.

leer [lɪəʳ] ◇ *n* [malevolent] regard *m* méchant; [lecherous] regard *m* concupiscent OR lubrique.

◇ *vi*: to ~ at sb lorgner qqn.

leery *inf* ['lɪərɪ] (*compar* leerier, *superl* leeriest) *adj* méfiant; to be ~ of sthg se méfier de qqch.

lees [liːz] *npl* [sediment] lie *f*; to drink OR to drain sthg to the ~ *fig* boire qqch jusqu'à la lie.

leeward ['liːwəd] ◇ *adj* sous le vent.

◇ *n* bord *m* sous le vent; to ~ NAUT sous le vent.

Leeward Islands *pl pr n*: the ~ les îles *fpl* Sous-le-Vent; in the ~ aux îles Sous-le-Vent.

leeway ['liːweɪ] *n (U)* -**1.** [margin] marge *f* (de manœuvre); it doesn't give us much ~ cela ne nous laisse pas une grande marge de manœuvre; a quarter of an hour should be enough ~ une marge de sécurité d'un quart d'heure devrait suffire. -**2.** [lost time] retard *m*. -**3.** AERON & NAUT [drift] dérive *f*.

left[1] [left] *pt* & *pp* → **leave**.

left[2] [left] ◇ *adj* [foot, eye] gauche; on the ~ side sur la gauche, du côté gauche; I always sleep on my ~ side je dors toujours sur le côté gauche; with her ~ hand de la main gauche; ~ hand down a bit! AUT braquez un peu à gauche!; to make a ~ turn tourner à gauche; take the ~ fork prenez à gauche à l'embranchement ❑ ~ back/half SPORT arrière *m*/demi *m* gauche; ~ hook crochet *m* du gauche.

◇ *adv* -**1.** [gen] à gauche; turn ~ at the junction tournez OR prenez à gauche au croisement; eyes ~! MIL tête à gauche!; ~ turn! MIL à gauche! gauche! -**2.** POL à gauche; to vote ~ voter à gauche.

◇ *n* -**1.** [gen] gauche *f*; on the ~ sur la gauche, à gauche; to drive on the ~ rouler à gauche; the building on the ~ le bâtiment de gauche; on your ~ à OR sur votre gauche; it's to the ~ of the fireplace c'est à gauche de la cheminée; it's to OR on the ~ of the picture [in the picture] c'est sur la gauche du tableau; [next to the picture] c'est à gauche du tableau; move a bit to the ~ déplacez-vous un peu vers la gauche; to keep to the ~ tenir sa gauche; the second figure from the ~ le deuxième chiffre en partant de la gauche; he doesn't know his ~ from his right il ne reconnaît pas sa droite de sa gauche. -**2.** POL gauche *f*; the far OR extreme ~ l'extrême gauche; the parties of the ~ les partis de (la) gauche; she is further to the ~ than her husband elle est (politiquement) plus à gauche que son mari. -**3.** [in boxing] gauche *m*; he knocked him out with a ~ to the chin il l'a étendu d'un gauche au menton.

left-footed [-'fʊtɪd] *adj* gaucher (du pied).

left-hand *adj* gauche; on the ~ side à gauche, sur la gauche; on my ~ side, the Grand Palace à OR sur ma gauche, le Grand Palais; a ~ bend un virage à gauche; ~ drive conduite *f* à gauche; my car is ~ drive ma voiture a le volant à gauche.

left-handed [-'hændɪd] ◇ *adj* -**1.** [person] gaucher; she's ~ elle est gauchère. -**2.** [scissors, instrument, golf club] pour gauchers. -**3.** *Am*: a ~ compliment un faux compliment.

◇ *adv* de la main gauche.

left-handedness [-'hændɪdnɪs] *n* gaucherie *f*, latéralité *f* de gauche; do you find ~ a problem? est-ce qu'être gaucher vous pose des problèmes?

left-hander [-'hændəʳ] *n* [person] gaucher *m*, -ère *f*; [blow] coup *m* (donné de la main gauche).

leftie *inf* ['leftɪ] = **lefty**.

leftism ['leftɪzm] *n* [gen] idées *fpl* de gauche; [extreme left] gauchisme *m*.

leftist ['leftɪst] ◇ *n* [gen] homme *m* de gauche, femme *f* de gauche; [extreme left-winger] gauchiste *mf*.
◇ *adj* [gen] de gauche; [extremely left-wing] gauchiste.
left luggage *n (U) Br* [cases] bagages *mpl* en consigne; [office] consigne *f*.
left-luggage office *n* consigne *f*.
left-of-centre *adj* POL de centre-gauche; his views are slightly ~ ses opinions sont plutôt de centre-gauche.
leftover ['leftəʊvəʳ] ◇ *adj* [food, material] qui reste; [stock] en surplus; she used the ~ wool to knit a scarf elle a tricoté une écharpe avec la laine qui restait.
◇ *n* [throwback, vestige] vestige *m*; the gun is a ~ from the war le fusil est un souvenir de la guerre.
leftovers ['leftəʊvəz] *npl* [food] restes *mpl*.
leftward ['leftwəd] ◇ *adj* de gauche.
◇ *adv Am* = **leftwards**.
leftwards ['leftwədz] *adv* à gauche.
left wing *n* -1. POL gauche *f*; the ~ of the party l'aile *f* gauche du parti. -2. SPORT [position] aile *f* gauche; [player] ailier *m* gauche.
◆ **left-wing** *adj* POL de gauche; a left-wing publication une publication de gauche; she's very left-wing elle est très à gauche.
left-winger *n* -1. POL homme *m* de gauche, femme *f* de gauche. -2. SPORT ailier *m* gauche.
lefty *inf* ['leftɪ] (*pl* lefties) *n* -1. *pej* homme *m* de gauche, femme *f* de gauche. -2. *Am* [left-handed person] gaucher *m*, -ère *f*.
leg [leg] (*pt* & *pp* legged, *cont* legging) ◇ *n* -1. ANAT [of human, horse] jambe *f*; [of smaller animals and birds] patte *f*; his ~s went from under him ses jambes se sont dérobées sous lui ❑ he hasn't got a ~ to stand on sa position est indéfendable; to get one's ~ over▽ se faire quelqu'un; to pull sb's ~ faire marcher qqn. -2. CULIN [of lamb] gigot *m*; [of pork, beef] rôti *m*; [of chicken] cuisse *f*; frog's ~s cuisses de grenouille. -3. [of chair, table] pied *m*; [of compasses] branche *f*. -4. [of trousers, pyjamas] jambe *f*. -5. [stage - of journey] étape *f*; [- of competition] manche *f*; they won the first/second ~ SPORT ils ont gagné le match aller/retour.
◇ *vt*: to ~ it *inf* [run] courir; [walk] aller à pied; [flee] se sauver, se tirer.
legacy ['legəsɪ] (*pl* legacies) *n* -1. JUR legs *m*; to leave sb a ~ faire un legs OR laisser un héritage à qqn; the money is a ~ from my aunt j'ai hérité cet argent de ma tante, ma tante m'a légué cet argent. -2. *fig* héritage *m*.
legal ['li:gl] *adj* -1. [lawful] légal; [legitimate] légal, légitime; they're below the ~ age ils n'ont pas atteint l'âge légal; to be above the ~ limit [for drinking] dépasser le taux légal (d'alcoolémie); to make sthg ~ légaliser qqch ❑ '~, decent, honest, truthful' *devise de la Advertising Standards Authority*. -2. [judicial - mind, matter, question] juridique; [- power, investigation, error] judiciaire; to take ~ action engager des poursuites judiciaires, intenter un procès; to take ~ advice consulter un juriste OR un avocat; he's a member of the ~ profession c'est un homme de loi; this is the ~ procedure c'est la procédure à suivre; ~ system système *m* juridique.
legal adviser *n* conseil *m* juridique.
legal aid *n* assistance *f* judiciaire.
legal department *n* [in bank, company] (service *m* du) contentieux *m*.
legal eagle *inf n hum* avocat *m*, -e *f*.
legalese [,li:gə'li:z] *n pej* jargon *m* juridique.
legal holiday *n Am* jour *m* férié, fête *f* légale.
legalism ['li:gəlɪzm] *n* -1. [strict respect of law] légalisme *m*. -2. [technicality] argutie *f* juridique.
legalistic [,li:gə'lɪstɪk] *adj* légaliste, formaliste.
legalistically [,li:gə'lɪstɪklɪ] *adv* avec légalisme, de façon légaliste.
legality [li:'gælətɪ] *n* légalité *f*.
legalization [,li:gəlaɪ'zeɪʃn] *n* légalisation *f*.
legalize, -ise ['li:gəlaɪz] *vt* légaliser, rendre légal.
legally ['li:gəlɪ] *adv* légalement; to act ~ agir légalement OR dans la légalité; to be ~ binding avoir force de loi, être juridiquement contraignant; to be held ~ responsible for sthg être tenu légalement OR juridiquement responsable de qqch; ~ you're not responsable légalement OR du point de vue légal, vous n'êtes pas responsable; they were not ~ married ils vivaient maritalement.
legal medicine *n* médecine *f* légale.
legal tender *n* monnaie *f* légale; these coins are no longer ~ ces pièces n'ont plus cours OR ont été démonétisées.
legate ['legɪt] *n* RELIG légat *m*; [gen] messager *m*, -ère *f*.
legatee [,legə'ti:] *n* légataire *mf*.
legation [lɪ'geɪʃn] *n* légation *f*.
legend ['ledʒənd] *n* -1. [myth] légende *f*; she became a ~ in her own lifetime elle est entrée dans la légende de son vivant. -2. [inscription] légende *f*.
legendary ['ledʒəndrɪ] *adj* légendaire.
legerdemain [,ledʒədə'meɪn] *n (U)* [conjuring] (tours *mpl* de) prestidigitation *f*; [cunning] tours *mpl* de passe-passe.
-legged ['legɪd] *in cpds* aux jambes...; bare~ aux jambes nues; to sit cross~ s'asseoir en tailleur; two~ bipède.
leggings ['legɪŋz] *npl* caleçon *m (porté comme pantalon)*.
leggo▽ [le'gəʊ] *interj* = **let go**.
leggy ['legɪ] (*compar* leggier, *superl* leggiest) *adj* [person] tout en jambes; [colt, young animal] haut sur pattes.
Leghorn [,leg'hɔ:n] *pr n* Livourne.
legibility [,ledʒɪ'bɪlətɪ] *n* lisibilité *f*.
legible ['ledʒəbl] *adj* lisible.
legibly ['ledʒəblɪ] *adv* lisiblement.
legion ['li:dʒən] ◇ *n* MIL & *fig* légion *f*.
◇ *adj fml* légion *(inv)*.
legionary ['li:dʒənərɪ] (*pl* legionaries) ◇ *n* légionnaire *m*.
◇ *adj* de la légion.
legionnaire [,li:dʒə'neəʳ] *n* légionnaire *m*.
legionnaire's disease *n* maladie *f* du légionnaire.
leg iron *n* MED appareil *m* orthopédique.
legislate ['ledʒɪsleɪt] *vi* légiférer; to ~ in favour of/against sthg légiférer en faveur de/contre qqch; you can't ~ for everything *fig* on ne peut pas tout prévoir.
legislation [,ledʒɪs'leɪʃn] *n* législation *f*; the ~ on immigration la législation sur l'immigration; a piece of ~ une loi; to bring in ~ in favour of/against sthg légiférer en faveur de/contre qqch.
legislative ['ledʒɪslətɪv] *adj* législatif; ~ assembly assemblée *f* législative.
legislator ['ledʒɪsleɪtəʳ] *n* législateur *m*, -trice *f*.
legislature ['ledʒɪsleɪtʃəʳ] *n* (corps *m*) législatif *m*.
legit *inf* [lə'dʒɪt] *adj* réglo.
legitimacy [lɪ'dʒɪtɪməsɪ] *n* légitimité *f*.
legitimate [*adj* lɪ'dʒɪtɪmət, *vb* lɪ'dʒɪtɪmeɪt] ◇ *adj* -1. [legal, lawful] légitime; ~ child enfant *mf* légitime. -2. [valid] légitime, valable; his criticisms are perfectly ~ ses critiques sont parfaitement légitimes OR fondées; it would be perfectly ~ to ask them to pay on serait tout à fait en droit d'exiger qu'ils paient. -3. [theatre] sérieux.
◇ *vt* légitimer.
legitimately [lɪ'dʒɪtɪmətlɪ] *adv* -1. [legally, lawfully] légitimement; both ~ and effectively de droit comme de fait. -2. [justifiably] légitimement, avec raison; it could ~ be argued that... on peut soutenir, non sans raison, que...
legitimize, -ise [lɪ'dʒɪtəmaɪz] *vt* légitimer.
legless ['leglɪs] *adj* -1. [without legs] cul-de-jatte. -2. *inf Br* [drunk] bourré, soûl.
leg-pull *inf n* canular *m*, farce *f*; it was only a ~! on te faisait marcher!
leg-pulling *inf n (U)* blagues *fpl*, mise *f* en boîte; he got a lot of ~ about his marriage on l'a beaucoup charrié sur son mariage.
legroom ['legrʊm] *n* place *f* pour les jambes.
leg show *inf n* revue *f* légère.
legume [le'gju:m] *n* légumineuse *f*.
leguminous [le'gju:mɪnəs] *adj* légumineux.
leg-up *n*: to give sb a ~ *literal* faire la courte échelle à qqn; *fig* donner un coup de main OR de pouce à qqn.
legwarmer ['leg,wɔ:məʳ] *n* jambière *f*.
legwork *inf* ['legwɜ:k] *n*: who's going to do the ~? qui va se taper la marche?
Leicester Square ['lestəʳ-] *pr n place populaire de Londres connue pour ses grands cinémas*.
Leics *written abbr of* Leicestershire.
Leipzig ['laɪpzɪg] *pr n* Leipzig.
leisure [*Br* 'leʒəʳ, *Am* 'li:ʒər] ◇ *n (U)* -1. [spare time] loisir *m*, loisirs *mpl*, temps *m* libre; during my ~ (time) pendant mes loisirs, à mes heures perdues; to be at ~ to do sthg avoir (tout) le loisir de faire qqch; I'll read it at (my) ~ je le lirai à tête reposée. -2. [relaxation] loisir *m*; to lead a life of ~ mener une vie oisive; he's a man of ~ il mène une vie de rentier.
◇ *comp* [activity, clothes] de loisir OR loisirs; ~ industry industrie *f* des loisirs.
leisure centre *n* centre *m* de loisirs.
leisured [*Br* 'leʒəd, *Am* 'li:ʒərd] *adj* oisif, qui mène une vie oisive.
leisurely [*Br* 'leʒəlɪ, *Am* 'li:ʒərlɪ] ◇ *adj* [gesture] mesuré, nonchalant; [lifestyle] paisible, indolent; we went for a ~ stroll through the park nous sommes allés faire une petite balade dans le parc; at a ~ pace sans se presser; he spoke in a ~ way il parlait en prenant son temps.
◇ *adv* [calmly] paisiblement, tranquillement; [unhurriedly] sans se presser.
leitmotiv, leitmotif ['laɪtməʊ,ti:f] *n* [gen & MUS] leitmotiv *m*.
LEM [lem] (*abbr of* lunar excursion module) *n* module *m* lunaire.
lemma ['lemə] (*pl* lemmas OR lemmata [-mətə]) *n* lemme *m*.
lemmatize, -ise ['lemətaɪz] *vt* lemmatiser.
lemme▽ ['lemɪ] *interj* = **let me**.
lemming ['lemɪŋ] *n* lemming *m*.
lemon ['lemən] ◇ *n* -1. [fruit] citron *m*; [tree] citronnier *m*; ~ juice jus *m* de citron; [lemon squash] citronnade *f*; [freshly squeezed] citron pressé; ~ squash citronnade *f*, sirop *m* de citron; ~ tea thé *m* au citron. -2. [colour] jaune citron *m inv*. -3. *inf Br* [awkward person] idiot *m*, -e *f*; I'm going to look a right ~ je vais avoir l'air plutôt débile. -4. *inf* [useless object]: she got sold a ~ elle s'est fait rouler.
◇ *adj* [colour] (jaune) citron *(inv)*; [flavour] citron *(inv)*; ~ ice cream glace *f* au citron.
lemonade [,lemə'neɪd] *n Br* limonade *f*; *Am* citron *m* pressé.
lemon balm *n* BOT mélisse *f*, citronnelle *f*.
lemon cheese, lemon curd *n* lemon curd *m*, crème *f* au citron.
lemon drop *n* bonbon *m* au citron.
lemongrass ['lemənɡrɑ:s] *n* lemon-grass *m*.
lemon sole *n* limande-sole *f*.
lemon squeezer *n* presse-citron *m*.
lemon thyme *n* thym *m* citronné.
lemon verbena *n* verveine *f* citronnelle.
lemur ['li:məʳ] *n* lémur *m*, maki *m*.
lend [lend] (*pt* & *pp* lent [lent]) ◇ *vt* -1. [money, book] prêter; to ~ sthg to sb, to ~ sb sthg prêter qqch à qqn. -2. [contribute] apporter, conférer; her presence lent glamour to the occasion sa présence a conféré un certain éclat à l'événement; the bright uniforms lent colour to the ceremony les uniformes éclatants apportaient une touche de couleur à la cérémonie. -3. [give - support] apporter; [- name] prêter; to ~ sb a hand donner un coup de main à qqn; you can't expect me to ~ my name to such an

enterprise ne comptez pas sur moi pour prêter mon nom à OR cautionner cette affaire; to ~ an ear *fig* prêter l'oreille. -**4.** [adapt - to circumstances, interpretation]: the novel doesn't ~ itself to being filmed le roman ne se prête pas à une adaptation cinématographique.
◇ *n inf Br*: can I have a ~ of your book? tu peux me prêter ton livre?

lender ['lendəʳ] *n* prêteur *m*, -euse *f*.

lending ['lendɪŋ] *n* prêt *m*.

lending library *n* bibliothèque *f* de prêt.

lending rate *n* taux *m (d'un prêt)*.

length [leŋθ] *n* -**1.** [measurement, distance] longueur *f*; what ~ is the room? quelle est la longueur de la pièce?; the room is 20 metres in ~ la pièce fait 20 mètres de long OR de longueur; a river 200 kilometres in ~ un fleuve long de 200 kilomètres; we walked the ~ of the garden nous sommes allés jusqu'au bout du jardin; flower beds ran the ~ of the boulevard il y avait des massifs de fleurs tout le long du boulevard; the ship can turn in its own ~ *Br* le navire peut virer sur place; throughout the ~ and breadth of the continent partout sur le continent; what ~ skirts are in this year? [in fashion] quelle est la longueur des jupes cette année? -**2.** [effort]: to go to considerable OR great ~s to do sthg se donner beaucoup de mal pour faire qqch; he would go to any ~s to meet her il ferait n'importe quoi pour la rencontrer. -**3.** [duration] durée *f*, longueur *f*; the ~ of time required to do sthg le temps qu'il faut pour faire qqch; the wine is kept in casks for a great ~ of time le vin séjourne très longtemps dans des fûts; bonuses are given for ~ of service les primes sont accordées selon l'ancienneté. -**4.** [of written material] longueur *f*; articles must be less than 5,000 words in ~ les articles doivent faire moins de 5 000 mots. -**5.** SPORT [in racing, rowing] longueur *f*; to win by a ~ gagner d'une longueur; to have a three-~ lead avoir trois longueurs d'avance || [in swimming] longueur *f* (de bassin); I swam ten ~s j'ai fait dix longueurs. -**6.** [piece - of string, tubing] morceau *m*, bout *m*; [- of wallpaper] lé *m*; [- of fabric] pièce *f*; a ~ of curtain material une pièce de tissu pour faire des rideaux. -**7.** LING [of syllable, vowel] longueur *f*.
◆ **at length** *adv phr* [finally] finalement, enfin; [in detail, for a long time] longuement; she went on OR spoke at some ~ about her experience elle a parlé assez longuement de son expérience.

-length *in cpds* à hauteur de; knee~ socks chaussettes *fpl* (montantes), mi-bas *mpl*.

lengthen ['leŋθən] ◇ *vi* [shadow] s'allonger; [day] rallonger; [holiday, visit] se prolonger.
◇ *vt* [garment] allonger, rallonger; [holiday, visit] prolonger; LING [vowel] allonger.

lengthily ['leŋθɪlɪ] *adv* longuement.

lengthways ['leŋθweɪz], **lengthwise** ['leŋθwaɪz] ◇ *adv* dans le sens de la longueur, longitudinalement.
◇ *adj* en longueur, longitudinal.

lengthy ['leŋθɪ] (*compar* lengthier, *superl* lengthiest) *adj* (très) long; after a ~ wait après avoir attendu très longtemps, après une attente interminable; his speech was a bit ~ son discours n'en finissait plus.

lenience ['liːnjəns], **leniency** ['liːnjənsɪ] *n* clémence *f*, indulgence *f*.

lenient ['liːnjənt] *adj* [jury, sentence] clément; [attitude, parent] indulgent; his parents are too ~ with him ses parents sont trop indulgents avec lui; you shouldn't be so ~ with them vous devriez être plus strict avec eux.

leniently ['liːnjəntlɪ] *adv* avec clémence OR indulgence; the magistrate had treated him ~ le magistrat s'était montré indulgent OR avait fait preuve d'indulgence à son égard.

Lenin ['lenɪn] *pr n* Lénine.

Leningrad ['lenɪngræd] *pr n* Leningrad.

Leninism ['lenɪnɪzm] *n* léninisme *m*.

Leninist ['lenɪnɪst] ◇ *adj* léniniste.
◇ *n* léniniste *mf*.

lenitive ['lenɪtɪv] ◇ *adj* lénitif.
◇ *n* lénitif *m*.

lenity ['lenətɪ] (*pl* **lenities**) *n lit* clémence *f*.

lens [lenz] *n* -**1.** OPT [in microscope, telescope] lentille *f*; [in spectacles] verre *m*; [in camera] objectif *m*; [contact lens] lentille *f* OR verre *m* (de contact). -**2.** ANAT [in eye] cristallin *m*.

lens cap *n* bouchon *m* d'objectif.

lens hood *n* pare-soleil *m inv*.

lens paper *n* papier *m* pour surfaces optiques.

lent [lent] *pt* & *pp* → **lend**.

Lent [lent] *n* RELIG le carême; to keep ~ faire carême, observer le carême; I've given up sugar for ~ j'ai renoncé au sucre pour le carême.

Lenten ['lentən] *adj* de carême.

lentil ['lentɪl] *n* BOT & CULIN lentille *f*; ~ soup soupe *f* aux lentilles.

Lent term *n Br* UNIV deuxième trimestre *m (de janvier à Pâques)*.

Leo ['liːəʊ] ◇ *pr n* ASTROL & ASTRON Lion *m*.
◇ *n*: he's a ~ il est (du signe du) Lion.

Leonardo da Vinci [ˌliːəˈnɑːdəʊdəˈvɪntʃɪ] *pr n* Léonard de Vinci.

leonine ['liːənaɪn] *adj lit* léonin *lit*, de lion.

leopard ['lepəd] *n* léopard *m*; a ~ cannot change its spots *prov* chassez le naturel, il revient au galop *prov*.

leopardess ['lepədɪs] *n* léopard *m* femelle.

leopard moth *n* zeuzère *f*.

leopard skin ◇ *n* peau *f* de léopard.
◇ *adj* [coat, rug] en (peau de) léopard.

Leopold ['lɪəpəʊld] *pr n* [emperor] Léopold.

leotard ['liːətɑːd] *n* body *m (pour le sport)*.

leper ['lepəʳ] *n* lépreux *m*, -euse *f*; *fig* pestiféré *m*, -e *f*; ~ colony léproserie *f*.

lepidopteran [ˌlepɪ'dɒptərən] (*pl* **lepidopterans** OR **lepidoptera** [-rə]) ◇ *adj* lépidoptère.
◇ *n* lépidoptère *m*.

lepidopterist [ˌlepɪ'dɒptərɪst] *n* lépidoptériste *mf*.

leprechaun ['leprəkɔːn] *n* lutin *m*.

leprosarium [ˌleprə'seərɪəm] (*pl* **leprosaria** [-rɪə]) *n* léproserie *f*.

leprosy ['leprəsɪ] *n* lèpre *f*.

leprous ['leprəs] *adj* lépreux.

lepton ['leptɒn] *n* PHYS lepton *m*.

Lermontov ['leəmɒntɒf] *pr n* Lermontov.

lesbian ['lezbɪən] ◇ *adj* lesbien.
◇ *n* lesbienne *f*.

lesbianism ['lezbɪənɪzm] *n* lesbianisme *m*.

lese majesty [ˌliːz'mædʒɪstɪ] *n* (crime *m* de) lèse-majesté *f inv*.

lesion ['liːʒn] *n* lésion *f*.

Lesotho [lə'suːtuː] *pr n* Lesotho *m*; in ~ au Lesotho.

less [les] ◇ *det* moins de; ~ money/time/bread moins d'argent/de temps/de pain; of ~ importance/value de moindre importance/valeur; that's one ~ cup to wash up! voilà une tasse de moins à laver!; I seem to have ~ and ~ energy on dirait que j'ai de moins en moins d'énergie.
◇ *pron* moins; there was ~ than I expected il y en avait moins que je m'y attendais; he eats ~ than he used to il mange moins qu'avant; a bit ~ un peu moins; we found we had ~ and ~ to say to each other nous nous sommes rendu compte que nous avions de moins en moins de choses à nous dire ❑ ~ of: the evening was ~ of a success than she had hoped la soirée était moins réussie qu'elle ne l'avait espéré; let's hope we see ~ of them in future espérons que nous les verrons moins souvent à l'avenir; ~ of your noise! faites moins de bruit!; ~ of that!, ~ of it! *inf* ça suffit!; ~ than: it took me ~ than five minutes ça m'a pris moins de cinq minutes; you won't get another one like it for ~ than $1,000 vous n'en retrouverez pas un comme ça à moins de 1 000 dollars; nothing ~ than a four-star hotel is good enough for them il leur faut au moins un quatre étoiles; in ~ than no time en un rien de temps, en moins de deux; the weather was rather ~ than ideal le temps était vraiment loin d'être idéal; it would have been ~ than fair to have kept it from her ça aurait été vraiment injuste de le lui cacher.
◇ *adv* moins; they couldn't be ~ friendly if they tried il leur serait difficile d'être plus désagréables; the blue dress costs ~ la robe bleue coûte moins cher; he was ~ amusing than I remembered il était moins drôle que dans mes souvenirs; we saw his books ~ as literature than as propaganda nous considérions ses livres moins comme de la littérature que comme de la propagande; ~ and ~ interesting de moins en moins intéressant ❑ I don't think any (the) ~ of her OR I think no ~ of her because of what happened ce qui s'est passé ne l'a pas fait baisser dans mon estime; we don't like her any the ~ for all her faults nous ne l'aimons pas moins à cause de ses défauts; the more I see of her the ~ I like her plus je la vois moins elle me plaît.
◇ *prep*: that's £300 ~ tax ça fait 300 livres moins les impôts; 8 ~ 3 is 5 8 moins 3 OR 3 ôté de 8 égale 5.
◆ **much less** *conj phr* encore moins; he wouldn't even phone her, much ~ visit her il ne voulait même pas l'appeler, encore moins aller la voir; I hadn't really thought about it, much ~ talked to anyone else je n'y avais pas vraiment réfléchi, et j'en avais encore moins parlé à qui que ce soit.
◆ **no less** *adv phr* rien de moins; he won the Booker prize, no ~! il a obtenu le Booker prize, rien de moins que ça!; she married a duke, no ~! elle a épousé un duc, ni plus ni moins!; she had invited no ~ a person than the President himself elle avait invité rien moins que le président lui-même.
◆ **no less than** *adv phr* pas moins de; taxes rose by no ~ than 15% les impôts ont augmenté de 15 %, ni plus ni moins; no ~ than 5,000 people wrote in pas moins de 5 000 personnes ont écrit.
◆ **still less** = **much less**.

lessee [le'siː] *n* preneur *m*, -euse *f* (à bail).

lessen ['lesn] ◇ *vt* [cost, importance] diminuer, réduire; [impact, effect] atténuer, amoindrir; [shock] amortir.
◇ *vi* s'atténuer, s'amoindrir.

lessening ['lesənɪŋ] *n (U)* [of cost, importance] diminution *f*; [of value, rate] réduction *f*, diminution *f*, baisse *f*; [of powers] réduction *f*, baisse *f*; [of impact, effect] amoindrissement *m*; [of shock] amortissement *m*.

lesser ['lesəʳ] *adj* -**1.** [gen] moindre; to be of ~ intelligence être moins intelligent; Wordsworth, Coleridge and their ~ contemporaries Wordsworth, Coleridge et leurs contemporains de moindre envergure; to a ~ extent dans une moindre mesure; she treats them as though they were ~ mortals elle les traite de haut; ~ mortals like me *hum* les simples mortels comme moi. -**2.** BOT, GEOG & ZOOL petit; the ~ panda le petit panda.

lesser-known *adj* moins connu.

lesson ['lesn] *n* -**1.** [gen] leçon *f*; SCH leçon *f*, cours *m*; an English ~ une leçon OR un cours d'anglais; a dancing/driving ~ une leçon de danse/de conduite; to give a ~ donner un cours OR une leçon; ~s start at half past eight les cours commencent à huit heures et demie; private ~s cours *mpl* particuliers. -**2.** [example] leçon *f*; her downfall was a ~ to us all sa chute nous a servi de leçon à tous; to teach sb a ~ donner une (bonne) leçon à qqn; that'll teach him a ~! cela lui servira de leçon!; the experience has taught me a ~ I won't forget! cette expérience m'a servi de leçon, croyez-moi! -**3.** RELIG leçon *f*, lecture *f*.

lessor [le'sɔːʳ] *n* bailleur *m*, -eresse *f*.

lest [lest] *conj lit* de peur que, de crainte que; they whispered ~ the children should hear ils parlèrent à voix basse de peur OR de crainte que les enfants ne les entendent; she wrote it down, ~ she forget OR ~ she might forget elle l'a noté, de peur d'oublier.

let[1] [let] (*pt* & *pp* **let**, *cont* **letting**) ◇ *vt* -**1.** [rent] louer; 'to ~' 'à louer'. -**2.** *arch* OR *lit* MED: **to ~ (sb's) blood** faire une saignée (à qqn).
◇ *n* -**1.** [rental] location *f*; **she took a six-month ~ on a house** elle a loué une maison pour six mois. -**2.** SPORT [in tennis, squash]: ~ **(ball)** let *m*; **the ball was a ~** la balle était let; **to play a ~** jouer un let. -**3.** *fml* [hindrance] empêchement *m*; **without ~ or hindrance** librement, sans entrave.

let[2] [let] (*pt* & *pp* **let**, *cont* **letting**) *vt* -**1.** [permit] laisser, permettre; **she ~ them watch the programme** elle les a laissés regarder l'émission; **I couldn't come because my parents wouldn't ~ me** je ne suis pas venu parce que mes parents ne me l'ont pas permis ‖ [allow] laisser; **I ~ the cakes burn** j'ai laissé brûler les gâteaux; ~ **me buy you all a drink** laissez-moi vous offrir un verre; **don't ~ me stop you going** je ne veux pas t'empêcher d'y aller; ~ **me see the newspaper** fais-moi voir le journal; **to ~ sb past** laisser passer qqn; **they don't ~ anyone near the reactor** ils ne laissent personne approcher du réacteur; **don't ~ it get you down!** *inf* ne te laisse pas abattre pour ça!; **don't ~ him get to you** ne te soucie pas de lui; **to ~ sb have sthg** donner qqch à qqn; **don't be selfish, ~ him have a cake!** ne sois pas égoïste, donne-lui un gâteau!; **I'll ~ you have a copy of the report** je vous ferai parvenir une copie du rapport; **she ~ him know what she thought of him** elle lui a fait savoir ce qu'elle pensait de lui; **please ~ me know if there's any change** veuillez me prévenir s'il y a du changement; **please God don't ~ anything happen to her!** faites qu'il ne lui arrive rien!; **to ~ sthg pass** laisser passer qqch ❑ **to ~ sb have it** *inf* [physically] casser la figure à qqn; [verbally] dire ses quatre vérités à qqn. -**2.** [followed by 'go']: **to ~ sb go** [allow to leave] laisser partir qqn; [release] relâcher qqn; [dismiss, fire] *euph* licencier qqn; **they ~ the hostages go** ils ont relâché les otages; **she ~ her assistant go** elle a licencié son assistant; **to ~ sb/sthg go** [allow to escape] laisser échapper qqn/qqch; **to ~ sb/sthg go, to ~ go of sb/sthg** [stop holding] lâcher qqn/qqch; **hold the rope and don't ~ go (of it)!** tiens la corde et ne la lâche pas!; ~ **me go!**, ~ **go of me!** lâchez-moi!; **to ~ o.s. go** [neglect o.s., relax] se laisser aller; **he's really ~ the garden go** il a vraiment négligé le jardin; **that remark was uncalled-for but ~ it go** cette réflexion était déplacée mais restons-en là; **give me £5 and we'll ~ it go at that** donne-moi 5 livres et on n'en parle plus. -**3.** [in making suggestions]: ~**'s go to bed** allons nous coucher; ~**'s go!** allons-y!; **don't ~'s go out** OR ~**'s not go out tonight** ne sortons pas ce soir; **shall we have a picnic? — yes, ~'s!** si on faisait un pique-nique? — d'accord!; ~ **us pray** *fml* prions ensemble. -**4.** [to focus attention]: ~ **me start by saying** OR ~ **me just say how pleased I am to be here** laissez-moi d'abord vous dire combien je suis ravi d'être ici; ~ **me put it another way** attends, je vais être plus clair; ~ **me try and explain** attendez que je vous explique. -**5.** [in hesitation]: ~ **me think** attends, voyons voir; ~ **me see**, ~**'s see** voyons. -**6.** [to express criticism or defiance]: **if she doesn't want my help, ~ her do it herself!** si elle ne veut pas de mon aide, qu'elle le fasse toute seule!; ~ **them talk!** laisse-les dire! -**7.** [in threats]: **don't ~ me catch you at it again!** que je ne t'y reprenne plus!; ~ **me catch you doing that again and you're for it!** *inf* si je te reprends à faire ça, ça va être ta fête! -**8.** [in commands]: ~ **there be light** BIBLE que la lumière soit; ~ **the festivities begin!** que la fête commence!; ~ **them be!** laisse-les tranquilles!, fiche-leur la paix! -**9.** [in making assumptions]: ~ **us suppose that...** supposons que...; ~ **x equal 17** MATH soit x égal à 17; ~ **ABC be a right-angled triangle** MATH soit un triangle rectangle ABC.

◆ **let alone** *conj phr*: **I wouldn't go out with him, ~ alone marry him** je ne sortirais même pas avec lui, alors pour ce qui est de l'épouser...

◆ **let down** *vt sep* -**1.** [disappoint] décevoir; **I felt really ~ down** j'étais vraiment déçu; **our old car has never ~ us down** notre vieille voiture ne nous a jamais laissés tomber; **she ~ us down badly** elle nous a proprement laissés tomber. -**2.** [lower, let fall - object] baisser, (faire) descendre; [- hair] dénouer; **to ~ sb down gently** *fig* traiter qqn avec ménagement. -**3.** SEW rallonger; **to ~ (the hem of) a dress down** rallonger une robe. -**4.** [deflate] dégonfler.

◆ **let in** *vt sep* -**1.** [person, animal] laisser entrer; **to ~ sb in** ouvrir (la porte) à qqn, faire entrer qqn; **his mother ~ me in** sa mère m'a fait entrer OR m'a ouvert (la porte); **here's the key to ~ yourself in** voici la clé pour entrer; **she ~ herself in with a pass key** elle est entrée avec un passe. -**2.** [air, water] laisser passer; **the roof ~s the rain in** le toit laisse entrer OR passer la pluie; **my shoes ~ in water** mes chaussures prennent l'eau. -**3.** AUT: **to ~ in the clutch** embrayer.

◆ **let in for** *vt sep*: **he didn't realize what he was letting himself in for** il ne savait pas à quoi il s'engageait.

◆ **let in on** *vt sep*: **to ~ sb in on sthg** mettre qqn au courant de qqch; **have you ~ him in on the secret?** lui avez-vous confié le secret?

◆ **let into** *vt sep* -**1.** [allow to enter] laisser entrer; **my mother ~ her into the flat** ma mère l'a laissée entrer dans l'appartement. -**2.** [allow to know]: **I'll ~ you into a secret** je vais te confier un secret. -**3.** [insert] encastrer; **the pipes are ~ into the wall** les tuyaux sont encastrés dans le mur; **to ~ a door/window into a wall** percer une porte/fenêtre dans un mur.

◆ **let off** ◇ *vt sep* -**1.** [excuse] dispenser; **to ~ sb off doing sthg** dispenser qqn de faire qqch; **I've been ~ off work** je suis dispensé de travailler. -**2.** [allow to leave] laisser partir; [allow to disembark] laisser descendre; **we were ~ off an hour early** on nous a laissés partir une heure plus tôt; **they ~ us off the bus** on nous a laissés descendre du bus. -**3.** [criminal, pupil, child] ne pas punir; **the judge ~ him off lightly** le juge a fait preuve d'indulgence à son égard; **she was ~ off with a reprimand/a fine** elle s'en est tirée avec une réprimande/une amende; **I'll ~ you off this once** pour cette fois, je passe. -**4.** [bomb, explosive] faire exploser; [firework] faire partir; [gun] laisser partir. -**5.** [release - steam, liquid] laisser échapper. -**6.** [rent] louer; **the whole building is ~ off as offices** tout l'immeuble est loué en bureaux.
◇ *vi insep inf* [break wind] péter.

◆ **let on** *inf* ◇ *vi insep*: **she never ~ on** elle ne l'a jamais dit; **somebody ~ on about the wedding to the press** quelqu'un a parlé du mariage à OR a révélé le mariage à la presse.
◇ *vt sep* [allow to embark] laisser monter; **they ~ us on the train** on nous a laissés monter dans le train.

◆ **let out** *vt sep* -**1.** [allow to leave] laisser sortir; **the teacher ~ us out early** le professeur nous a laissés sortir plus tôt; **my secretary will ~ you out** ma secrétaire va vous reconduire; **don't get up, I'll ~ myself out** ne vous levez pas, je connais le chemin. -**2.** [water, air] laisser échapper; **someone's ~ the air out of the tyres** quelqu'un a dégonflé les pneus. -**3.** [shout, oath, whistle] laisser échapper. -**4.** [secret] révéler; **who ~ it out that they're getting married?** qui est allé raconter qu'ils allaient se marier? -**5.** SEW [dress, trousers] élargir. -**6.** AUT: **to ~ out the clutch** débrayer. -**7.** [rent] louer; **they ~ out boats by the hour** ils louent des bateaux à l'heure.

◆ **let up** *vi insep* -**1.** [stop] arrêter; [diminish] diminuer; **the rain didn't ~ up all day** il n'a pas cessé OR arrêté de pleuvoir de toute la journée. -**2.** [relax]: **he never ~s up** il ne s'accorde aucun répit; **don't ~ up now, you're in the lead** ce n'est pas le moment de faiblir, tu es en tête.

◆ **let up on** *inf vt insep*: **to ~ up on sb** lâcher la bride à qqn.

letch *inf* [letʃ] = **lech**.

letdown *inf* ['letdaʊn] *n* déception *f*; **the party was a bit of a ~** la fête a été plutôt décevante.

lethal ['li:θl] *adj* fatal, mortel; MED létal; **a ~ weapon** une arme meurtrière; **in the hands of a child, a plastic bag can be ~** dans les mains d'un enfant, un sac en plastique peut être dangereux; **this substance is ~ to rats** c'est une substance mortelle pour les rats; **this vodka's ~** *inf fig* cette vodka est redoutable ❑ ~ **dose** dose *f* mortelle OR létale; ~ **gene** gène *m* létal.

lethally ['li:θəlɪ] *adv* mortellement.

lethargic [lə'θɑ:dʒɪk] *adj* [person, sleep] léthargique; [atmosphere] soporifique; **I feel really ~ today** je me sens complètement à plat aujourd'hui.

lethargy ['leθədʒɪ] *n* léthargie *f*; **to fall into a state of ~** tomber en léthargie.

let-out *n Br* [excuse] prétexte *m*; [way out] échappatoire *f*; **I've been invited but I'm looking for a ~** j'ai été invité, mais je cherche un prétexte pour ne pas y aller.

let's [lets] = **let us**.

Lett [let] *n* Letton *m*, -on(n)e *f*.

letter ['letəʳ] ◇ *n* -**1.** [of alphabet] lettre *f*; **in capital ~s** en (lettres) majuscules; **the ~ B** la lettre B; **a six-~ word** un mot de six lettres; **he's got a lot of ~s after his name** il est bardé de diplômes. -**2.** *fig* [exact meaning] lettre *f*; **the ~ of the law** la lettre de la loi; **to keep** OR **to stick to the ~ of the law** respecter la loi au pied de la lettre OR à la lettre; **she obeyed the instructions to the ~** elle a suivi les instructions à la lettre OR au pied de la lettre. -**3.** [communication] lettre *f*; [mail] courrier *m*; **by ~** par lettre OR courrier; **he's a good ~ writer** il écrit régulièrement; **I'm a bad ~ writer** je n'écris pas souvent; **to post ~s** *Br* poster des lettres OR du courrier; **a ~ of introduction** une lettre de recommandation; ~**s to the editor** [in newspapers, magazines] courrier des lecteurs; **the ~s of D. H. Lawrence** la correspondance de D. H. Lawrence ❑ ~ **of credit** COMM lettre de crédit; ~**s of credence** ADMIN lettres de créance.
◇ *vt* [write] inscrire des lettres sur; [engrave] graver (des lettres sur); [manuscript] enluminer; **the title was ~ed in gilt** le titre était inscrit en lettres dorées; **the rooms are ~ed from A to K** les salles portent des lettres de A à K.

◆ **letters** *npl fml* [learning] belles-lettres *fpl*; **a man of ~s** [scholar] un lettré; [writer] un homme de lettres; **English ~s** *Br* littérature *f* anglaise.

letter bomb *n* lettre *f* piégée.

letter box *n Br* boîte *f* à OR aux lettres.

letter card *n* carte-lettre *f*.

lettered ['letəd] *adj* -**1.** *fml* [person] lettré. -**2.** [inscribed]: ~ **in gold** inscrit en lettres d'or.

letterhead ['letəhed] *n* en-tête *m inv (de lettre)*.

lettering ['letərɪŋ] *n (U)* [inscription] inscription *f*; [characters] caractères *mpl*; **written in gold ~** écrit en lettres d'or.

letter-opener *n* coupe-papier *m inv*.

letter-perfect *adj Am* [person] qui connait son texte parfaitement; [text] parfait.

letterpress ['letəpres] *n* [technique] typographie *f*; [text] texte *m* (imprimé).

letter quality *n* COMPUT qualité *f* courrier; **near ~** qualité quasi-courrier *(pour une imprimante)*.

◆ **letter-quality** *adj* qualité courrier *(inv)*.

letter rack *n* porte-lettres *m inv*.

letterset ['letəset] *n* offset *m* sec.

letters patent *npl* patente *f*.

letting ['letɪŋ] *n* [of house, property] location *f*.

lettuce ['letɪs] *n* [gen & CULIN] salade *f*; BOT laitue *f*; ~ **leaf** feuille *f* de salade OR de laitue.

let-up *n* [stop] arrêt *m*, pause *f*; [abatement] répit *m*; **it's been raining for days without a ~** ça fait des jours qu'il n'arrête pas de pleuvoir OR qu'il pleut sans arrêt.

leucin ['lu:sɪn], **leucine** ['lu:si:n] *n* leucine *f*.

leucocyte ['luːkəsaɪt] *n* leucocyte *m.*

leucoma ['luːkəʊmə] *n* leucome *m.*

leucotomy [luː'kɒtəmɪ] (*pl* leucotomies) *n* leucotomie *f.*

leukaemia *Br*, **leukemia** *Am* [luː'kiːmɪə] *n (U)* leucémie *f*; **he has ~** il a une leucémie, il est atteint de leucémie.

leukocyte ['luːkəsaɪt] = **leucocyte**.

Levant [lɪ'vænt] *n*: **the ~** le Levant.

Levantine ['levəntaɪn] ◇ *n* Levantin *m*, -e *f.* ◇ *adj* levantin.

levee ['levɪ] *n* -**1.** *Am* [embankment] levée *f*; [surrounding field] digue *f.* -**2.** *Am* [landing place] quai *m.* -**3.** HIST [in royal chamber] lever *m* (du roi); *Br* [at court] réception *f* à la cour.

level ['levl] (*Br pt & pp* levelled, *cont* levelling, *Am pt & pp* leveled, *cont* leveling) ◇ *n* -**1.** [height - in a horizontal plane] niveau *m*; [- in a vertical plane] hauteur *f*; **at ground ~** au niveau du sol; **water seeks its own ~** c'est le principe des vases communicants; **the ~ of the river has risen overnight** le niveau de la rivière a monté pendant la nuit; **the flood waters have reached the ~ of the bridge** la crue a atteint le niveau du pont; **the sink is on a ~ with the work surface** l'évier est au niveau du OR de niveau avec le plan de travail; **the house and garden are on the same ~** la maison et le jardin sont au même niveau. -**2.** [amount] niveau *m*; [percentage] taux *m*; **noise ~s are far too high** le niveau sonore est bien trop élevé; **a low ~ of sugar in the bloodstream** un faible taux de sucre dans le sang; **inflation has reached new ~s** l'inflation a atteint de nouveaux sommets; **check the oil ~** [in car] vérifiez le niveau d'huile. -**3.** [rank] niveau *m*, échelon *m*; **at cabinet/national ~** à l'échelon ministériel/national; **at a regional ~** au niveau régional; **talks are being held at the highest ~** on négocie au plus haut niveau. -**4.** [standard] niveau *m*; **her ~ of English is poor** elle n'a pas un très bon niveau en anglais; **students at beginners' ~** étudiants *mpl* au niveau débutant; **a high ~ of competence/intelligence** un haut niveau de compétence/d'intelligence; **they're not on the same ~ at all** ils ne sont pas du tout du même niveau, ils n'ont absolument pas le même niveau; **she's on a different ~ from the others** elle n'est pas au même niveau que les autres; **to come down to sb's ~** se mettre au niveau de qqn; **don't descend** OR **sink to their ~** ne t'abaisse pas à leur niveau. -**5.** [point of view]: **on a personal ~, I really like him** sur le plan personnel, je l'aime beaucoup; **on a practical ~** du point de vue pratique. -**6.** [storey] niveau *m*, étage *m*; **the library is on ~ three** la bibliothèque est au niveau trois OR au troisième étage. -**7.** [flat land] plat *m*; **100 km/h on the ~** 100 km/h sur le plat. -**8.** [for woodwork, building etc]: **(spirit) ~** niveau *m* (à bulle). -**9.** *inf phr*: **on the ~** [honest] honnête, réglo; **do you think he's on the ~?** tu crois qu'il est réglo OR que c'est un type réglo?; **I'm giving it to you on the ~** je te dis ça franchement OR sans détours; **this deal is definitely on the ~** cette affaire est tout ce qu'il y a de plus réglo.

◇ *adj* -**1.** [flat] plat; **a ~ spoonful** une cuillerée rase; **to make sthg ~** aplanir qqch. -**2.** [at the same height] au même niveau, à la même hauteur; [at the same standard] au même niveau; **the terrace is ~ with the pool** la terrasse est au même niveau que OR de plain-pied avec la piscine; **his head is just ~ with my shoulder** sa tête m'arrive exactement à l'épaule. -**3.** [in horizontal position]: **hold the tray ~** tenez le plateau à l'horizontale OR bien à plat; **to fly ~** AERON voler en palier. -**4.** [equal] à égalité; **the leading cars are almost ~** les voitures de tête sont presque à la même hauteur; **to draw ~** se trouver à égalité; **the other runners drew ~ with me** les autres coureurs m'ont rattrapé. -**5.** [calm, steady] calme, mesuré; **to speak in a ~ voice** parler d'une voix calme OR posée; **she gave me a ~ look** elle me regarda posément; **to keep a ~ head** garder la tête froide. -**6.** *inf* [honest] honnête, réglo; **you're not being ~ with me** tu ne joues pas franc jeu avec moi. -**7.** *inf phr*: **to do one's ~ best** faire de son mieux; **she did her ~ best to irritate me** elle a tout fait pour me mettre en colère; **~ pegging** *inf Br* à égalité.

◇ *vt* -**1.** [flatten] aplanir, niveler. -**2.** [aim]: **to ~ a gun at sb** braquer une arme sur qqn; **a lot of criticism has been levelled at me** on m'a beaucoup critiqué.

◇ *vi inf*: **to ~ with sb** être franc avec qqn, jouer franc jeu avec qqn.

◆ **level down** *vt sep* [surface] aplanir, niveler; [standard] niveler par le bas.

◆ **level off** ◇ *vi insep* -**1.** [production, rise, development] s'équilibrer, se stabiliser; **the curve on the graph ~s off at this point** la courbe du graphique se stabilise à partir d'ici; **the team's performance has levelled off this season** les résultats de l'équipe se sont stabilisés cette saison. -**2.** AERON amorcer un palier. ◇ *vt sep* [flatten] aplatir, niveler.

◆ **level out** ◇ *vi insep* -**1.** [road, surface] s'aplanir. -**2.** [stabilize] se stabiliser. ◇ *vt sep* niveler.

◆ **level up** *vt sep* niveler (par le haut).

level crossing *n Br* passage *m* à niveau.

leveler *Am* = **leveller**.

level-headed *adj* équilibré, pondéré, réfléchi; **he's a ~ boy** c'est un garçon qui a la tête sur les épaules.

leveling *Am* = **levelling**.

leveller *Br*, **leveler** *Am* ['levələʳ] *n* POL égalitariste *mf*, niveleur *m*, -euse *f*; **death is a great ~** nous sommes tous égaux devant la mort.

◆ **the Levellers** *npl* HIST les niveleurs *mpl.*

THE LEVELLERS:

Mouvement de républicains acharnés apparu en 1647 pendant la guerre civile en Angleterre. Les «niveleurs» réclamaient un renforcement des pouvoirs du Parlement ainsi qu'une plus large représentation populaire, mais furent durement réprimés par Cromwell.

---

levelling *Br*, **leveling** *Am* ['levəlɪŋ] ◇ *n* nivellement *m*, aplanissement *m*; **earth ~** nivellement du terrain; **a ~ up/down of salaries is desirable** un nivellement des salaires par le haut/par le bas est souhaitable; **a ~ off of prices** une stabilisation des prix. ◇ *adj* de nivellement; **~ screw** vis *f* d'ajustement (de niveau); **~ staff** mire *f* (parlante).

lever [*Br* 'liːvəʳ, *Am* 'levər] ◇ *n literal & fig* levier *m*; [smaller] manette *f.* ◇ *vt* manœuvrer à l'aide d'un levier; **they ~ed the engine into position** ils installèrent le moteur à l'aide d'un levier.

◆ **lever out** *vt sep* extraire OR extirper (à l'aide d'un levier); *fig*: **he ~ed himself out of bed** il s'extirpa du lit; **they ~ed the president out of office** ils ont délogé le président de son poste.

◆ **lever up** *vt sep* soulever (au moyen d'un levier); **she ~ed herself up onto the rock** *fig* elle se hissa sur le rocher.

leverage [*Br* 'liːvərɪdʒ, *Am* 'levərɪdʒ] *n* -**1.** MECH force *f* (de levier); **I can't get enough ~** je n'ai pas assez de prise. -**2.** [influence]: **he has no ~ with the management** il n'a aucun moyen de pression sur la direction; **the committee's findings give us considerable (political) ~** les conclusions de la commission constituent pour nous des moyens de pression considérables (sur le plan politique). -**3.** *Am* ECON effet *m* de levier.

leveret ['levərɪt] *n* levraut *m.*

Levi ['liːvaɪ] *pr n* Lévi.

leviathan [lɪ'vaɪəθn] *n* [ship] navire *m* géant; [institution, organization] institution *f* OR organisation *f* géante.

◆ **Leviathan** *pr n* Léviathan.

Levi's® ['liːvaɪz] *npl* jean *m* OR jeans *mpl* (Levi's)®.

levitate ['levɪteɪt] ◇ *vi* léviter. ◇ *vt* faire léviter, soulever par lévitation.

levitation [,levɪ'teɪʃn] *n* lévitation *f.*

Levite ['liːvaɪt] *n* lévite *m.*

Leviticus [lɪ'vɪtɪkəs] *pr n* le Lévitique.

levity ['levətɪ] (*pl* levities) *n* légèreté *f*, manque *m* de sérieux.

levy ['levɪ] (*pl* levies, *pt & pp* levied) ◇ *n* -**1.** [levying] prélèvement *m*; **tax ~** prélèvement *m* fiscal; **a capital ~ of 10%** un prélèvement de 10 % sur le capital. -**2.** [tax, duty] impôt *m*, taxe *f*; **to impose a ~ on sugar imports** taxer les importations de sucre. -**3.** MIL levée *f.*

◇ *vt* -**1.** [impose - tax] prélever; [- fine] imposer, infliger; **to ~ a duty on imports** prélever une taxe sur les importations. -**2.** [collect - taxes, fine] lever, percevoir. -**3.** MIL [troops] lever. -**4.** [wage]: **to ~ war on small states** faire la guerre à de petits États.

◆ **levy on** *vt insep fml* OR JUR: **to ~ on sb's property** saisir les biens de qqn.

lewd [ljuːd] *adj* [behaviour] lubrique; [speech] obscène.

lewdness ['ljuːdnɪs] *n* [of behaviour] lubricité *f*; [of speech] obscénité *f.*

Lewis gun ['luːɪs-] *n* mitrailleuse *f (utilisée pendant la Première Guerre mondiale).*

lexeme ['leksiːm] *n* lexème *m.*

lexical ['leksɪkl] *adj* lexical.

lexicalize, -ise ['leksɪkəlaɪz] *vt* lexicaliser.

lexicographer [,leksɪ'kɒgrəfəʳ] *n* lexicographe *mf.*

lexicographical [,leksɪkə'græfɪkl] *adj* lexicographique.

lexicography [,leksɪ'kɒgrəfɪ] *n* lexicographie *f.*

lexicologist [,leksɪ'kɒlədʒɪst] *n* lexicologue *mf.*

lexicology [,leksɪ'kɒlədʒɪ] *n* lexicologie *f.*

lexicon ['leksɪkən] *n* lexique *m.*

lexis ['leksɪs] *n* lexique *m.*

ley [leɪ] *n* pâturage *m.*

ley line *n ensemble de repères indiquant le tracé probable d'un chemin préhistorique.*

Lhasa ['lɑːsə] *pr n* Lhassa.

LI *written abbr of* Long Island.

liability [,laɪə'bɪlətɪ] (*pl* liabilities) *n* -**1.** *(U)* JUR [responsibility] responsabilité *f* (légale); **he refused to admit ~ for the damage** il refusa d'endosser la responsabilité des dégâts. -**2.** *(U)* [eligibility] assujettissement *m*; **~ for tax** assujettissement à l'impôt; **~ for military service** obligations *fpl* militaires. -**3.** [hindrance] gêne *f*, handicap *m*; **some qualifications are more of a ~ than an asset** certains diplômes sont un handicap plus qu'un atout; **the house he had inherited was a real ~** la maison dont il avait hérité lui coûtait une petite fortune OR lui revenait cher; **that man is a (total) ~** ce type est un vrai poids mort OR un véritable boulet.

◆ **liabilities** *npl* FIN [debts] passif *m*, engagements *mpl* financiers; **to meet one's liabilities** faire face à ses engagements; **liabilities on an estate** passif d'une succession.

liability suit *n Am* JUR procès *m* en responsabilité civile.

liable ['laɪəbl] *adj* -**1.** JUR [responsible] responsable; **to be held ~ for sthg** être tenu (pour) responsable de qqch; **employers are ~ for their staff's mistakes** les employeurs sont (civilement) responsables des erreurs de leur personnel; **to be ~ for sb's debts** répondre des dettes de qqn; **you'll be ~ for damages** on sera en droit de vous demander OR réclamer des dommages et intérêts. -**2.** [likely]: **~ to: the programme is ~ to change** le programme est susceptible d'être modifié, il se peut que le programme subisse des modifications; **he's ~ to arrive at any moment** il peut arriver d'une minute à l'autre; **the bomb is ~ to explode at any moment** la bombe risque d'exploser à tout instant; **we are all ~ to make mistakes** tout le monde peut se tromper; **if you don't remind him, he's ~ to forget** si on ne lui rappelle pas, il risque d'oublier; **~ to headaches** sujet aux maux de tête. -**3.** ADMIN: **to be ~ for tax** [person] être assujetti à OR redevable de l'impôt; [goods] être assujetti à une taxe; **offenders are**

~ to a fine les contrevenants sont passibles d'une amende; **he is ~ to be prosecuted** il s'expose à des poursuites judiciaires || MIL: **to be ~ for military service** être astreint au service militaire.

liaise [lɪ'eɪz] *vi*: **to ~ with sb** assurer la liaison avec qqn.

liaison [lɪ'eɪzɒn] *n* liaison *f*.

liaison officer *n* [between services, companies] agent *m* de liaison; MIL officier *m* de liaison.

liana [lɪ'ɑːnə] *n* liane *f*.

liar ['laɪəʳ] *n* menteur *m*, -euse *f*.

lib *inf* [lɪb] (*abbr of* **liberation**) *n*: **women's ~** le mouvement de libération des femmes, ≃ le MLF; **gay ~** le mouvement de libération gay OR des homosexuels.

Lib [lɪb] *abbr of* **Liberal**.

libation [laɪ'beɪʃn] *n lit* [offering] libation *f*; *hum* [drink] libations *fpl*.

libber *inf* ['lɪbəʳ] *n*: **women's ~** féministe *f*, ≃ adhérente *f* du MLF.

libel ['laɪbl] (*Br pt* & *pp* **libelled**, *cont* **libelling**, *Am pt* & *pp* **libeled**, *cont* **libeling**) ◇ *n* JUR [act of publishing] diffamation *f*; [publication] écrit *m* diffamatoire; *fig* [calumny] calomnie *f*, mensonge *m*; **the ~ laws** la législation en matière de diffamation; **~ suit** procès *m* en diffamation.
◇ *vt* JUR diffamer; *fig* calomnier.

libellee *Br*, **libelee** *Am* [ˌlaɪbə'liː] *n* personne *f* poursuivie pour diffamation.

libellous *Br*, **libelous** *Am* ['laɪbələs] *adj* diffamatoire.

liberal ['lɪbərəl] ◇ *adj* -**1.** [tolerant - person] libéral, large d'esprit; [- ideas, mind] libéral, large; **a ~ education** une éducation libérale ❑ **~ studies** ≃ programme *m* de culture générale. -**2.** [generous] libéral, généreux; [copious - helping, portion] abondant, copieux; **the cook was a bit too ~ with the salt** le cuisinier a eu la main un peu lourde avec le sel; **he was always very ~ with his praise** il n'était jamais avare de compliments.
◇ *n* [moderate]: **she's a ~** elle est de centre-gauche.
◆ **Liberal** ◇ *adj* POL [in 19th century] libéral; [nowadays] de centre-gauche; **the Liberal Party** le parti Libéral; **the Liberal Democrats** *parti centriste britannique*; **the Liberal-SDP Alliance** *alliance entre le parti Libéral et le SDP (en 1987) qui a donné lieu à la création du SLD*.
◇ *n* [party member] libéral *m*, -e *f*.

liberal arts *npl*: **the ~** les sciences humaines.

liberalism ['lɪbərəlɪzm] *n* libéralisme *m*.

liberality [ˌlɪbə'rælətɪ] (*pl* **liberalities**) *n* -**1.** [tolerance] libéralisme *m*. -**2.** [generosity] libéralité *f*, largesse *f*.

liberalize, -ise ['lɪbərəlaɪz] *vt* libéraliser.

liberally ['lɪbərəlɪ] *adv* libéralement; **a ~ spiced dish** un plat généreusement épicé.

liberate ['lɪbəreɪt] *vt* -**1.** [gen] libérer; CHEM libérer, dégager. -**2.** *hum* [steal] piquer.

liberated ['lɪbəreɪtɪd] *adj* libéré.

liberation [ˌlɪbə'reɪʃn] *n* libération *f*.

liberationist [ˌlɪbə'reɪʃənɪst] *n* [feminist] féministe *m* militant, féministe *f* militante.

liberation movement *n* mouvement *m* de libération.

liberation theology *n* théologie *f* de la libération.

liberator ['lɪbəreɪtəʳ] *n* libérateur *m*, -trice *f*.

Liberia [laɪ'bɪərɪə] *pr n* Liberia *m*; **in ~** au Liberia.

Liberian [laɪ'bɪərɪən] ◇ *n* Libérien *m*, -enne *f*.
◇ *adj* libérien.

libertarian [ˌlɪbə'teərɪən] ◇ *adj* libertaire.
◇ *n* libertaire *mf*.

libertarianism [ˌlɪbə'teərɪənɪzm] *n* [doctrine] doctrine *f* libertaire; [political ideas] convictions *fpl* libertaires.

libertine ['lɪbətiːn] ◇ *adj* libertin.
◇ *n* libertin *m*, -e *f*.

liberty ['lɪbətɪ] (*pl* **liberties**) *n* [in behaviour] liberté *f*; **to take liberties with sb** prendre OR se permettre des libertés avec qqn; **to take liberties with the truth/a text** prendre des libertés avec la vérité/un texte; **I took the ~ of inviting them** j'ai pris la liberté OR je me suis permis de les inviter || [cheek]: **what a ~!** quel toupet!
◆ **at liberty** *adj phr*: **the criminals are still at ~** les criminels sont toujours en liberté OR courent toujours; **you are at ~ to leave** vous êtes libre de partir; **I'm not at ~ to disclose my sources** il ne m'est pas possible OR permis de dévoiler mes sources; **I'm not at ~ to comment** je n'ai pas le droit de OR il ne m'est pas permis de faire de commentaires.

liberty cap *n* bonnet *m* phrygien OR d'affranchi.

liberty hall *inf n pej*: **it's ~ in this house** chacun fait ce qui lui plaît OR c'est la pétaudière dans cette maison.

libidinal [lɪ'bɪdɪnəl] *adj* libidinal.

libidinous [lɪ'bɪdɪnəs] *adj* libidineux.

libido [lɪ'biːdəʊ] (*pl* **libidos**) *n* libido *f*.

Lib-Lab *inf* ['lɪblæb] (*abbr of* **Liberal-Labour**) *adj Br* POL [agreement, talks] entre libéraux et travaillistes; **a ~ pact** un accord entre libéraux et travaillistes.

Libra ['liːbrə] ◇ *pr n* ASTROL & ASTRON Balance *f*.
◇ *n*: **he's a ~** il est (du signe de la) Balance.

Libran ['liːbrən] *n* (natif *m*, -ive *f* de la) Balance *f*.

librarian [laɪ'breərɪən] *n* bibliothécaire *mf*.

librarianship [laɪ'breərɪənʃɪp] *n* [science] bibliothéconomie *f*; **to study ~** faire des études de bibliothécaire OR de bibliothéconomie.

library ['laɪbrərɪ] (*pl* **libraries**) ◇ *n* -**1.** [gen] bibliothèque *f*; **the Library of Congress** la bibliothèque du Congrès *(équivalent américain de la Bibliothèque Nationale)*. -**2.** [published series] bibliothèque *f*, collection *f*. -**3.** COMPUT bibliothèque *f*.
◇ *comp* [book, card] de bibliothèque.

library edition *n* édition *f* de luxe.

library science *n* bibliothéconomie *f*; **she's studying ~** elle fait des études de bibliothécaire.

librettist [lɪ'bretɪst] *n* librettiste *mf*.

libretto [lɪ'bretəʊ] (*pl* **librettos** OR **libretti** [-tɪ]) *n* MUS livret *m*, libretto *m*.

Libreville ['liːbrəvɪl] *pr n* Libreville.

Librium® ['lɪbrɪəm] *n* Librium® *m*.

Libya ['lɪbɪə] *pr n* Libye *f*; **in ~** en Libye.

Libyan ['lɪbɪən] ◇ *n* Libyen *m*, -enne *f*.
◇ *adj* libyen; **the ~ Desert** le désert de Libye.

lice [laɪs] *pl* → **louse**.

licence *Br*, **license** *Am* ['laɪsəns] *n* -**1.** [permit] permis *m*; [for marriage] certificat *m* de publication des bans; [for trade, bar] licence *f*; [for TV, radio] redevance *f*; [for pilot] brevet *m*; [for driver] permis *m* (de conduire); **do you have a TV ~?** avez-vous payé la redevance (télé)?; **a ~ to sell alcoholic drinks** une licence de débit de boissons. -**2.** ADMIN & COMM [permission] licence *f*, autorisation *f*; **to manufacture sthg under ~** fabriquer qqch sous licence; **to marry by special ~** ≃ se marier sans publication de bans; **a ~ to print money** *fig*: **that job's a ~ to print money!** ce travail est une sinécure! -**3.** [liberty] licence *f*, liberté *f*; **the biographer has allowed himself a certain ~ in his interpretation** le biographe s'est permis certaines libertés d'interprétation; **artistic ~** licence artistique. -**4.** [immoral behaviour] licence *f*, débordements *mpl*; **sexual ~** débordements sexuels.

licence number *n* [on vehicle] numéro *m* d'immatriculation; [on driving licence] numéro *m* de permis de conduire.

license ['laɪsəns] ◇ *n Am* = **licence**.
◇ *vt* -**1.** ADMIN & COMM [premises, trader] accorder une licence OR une autorisation à; **~d to practise medicine** habilité à exercer la médecine; **to ~ a car** immatriculer une voiture; **is this vehicle ~d?** *Br* ce véhicule est-il immatriculé? -**2.** [allow]: **to ~ sb to do sthg** autoriser qqn à faire qqch, permettre à qqn de faire qqch.

licensed ['laɪsənst] *adj* -**1.** COMM fabriqué sous licence; [for alcohol]: **these premises are ~ to sell alcoholic drinks** cet établissement est autorisé à vendre des boissons alcoolisées ❑ **~ victualler** *fml* débitant *m* de boissons; **~ premises** [bar, pub] débit *m* de boissons; [restaurant, cafeteria] établissement *m* autorisé à vendre des boissons alcoolisées; **~ product** produit *m* sous licence. -**2.** [pilot] breveté; [driver] qui a son permis (de conduire).

licensed practical nurse *n Am* infirmier *m*, -ère *f*.

licensee [ˌlaɪsən'siː] *n* [gen] titulaire *mf* d'une licence OR d'un permis; [pub-owner, landlord] débitant *m*, -e *f* (de boissons).

license plate *n Am* plaque *f* minéralogique OR d'immatriculation.

licensing ['laɪsənsɪŋ] *n* [of car] immatriculation *f*; [of activity] autorisation *f*; **~ authority** *organisme chargé de la délivrance des licences*.

licensing hours *npl* [in UK] *heures d'ouverture des pubs*.

LICENSING HOURS:
Traditionnellement, les heures d'ouverture des pubs répondent à une réglementation très stricte (liée à la législation sur la vente des boissons alcoolisées), mais celle-ci a été assouplie en 1988. Au lieu d'ouvrir uniquement de 11 h 30 à 14 h 30 et de 18 h à 22 h 30, les pubs peuvent désormais rester ouverts de 11 h à 23 h.

---

licensing laws *npl* [in UK] *lois réglementant la vente d'alcools*.

licentiate [laɪ'senʃɪət] *n* diplômé *m*, -e *f*.

licentious [laɪ'senʃəs] *adj* licencieux.

lichee [ˌlaɪ'tʃiː] *n* litchi *m*, lychee *m*.

lichen ['laɪkən] *n* lichen *m*.

lich-gate ['lɪtʃ-] = **lych-gate**.

licit ['lɪsɪt] *adj* licite.

lick [lɪk] ◇ *vt* -**1.** [ice-cream] lécher; [stamp] humecter; **the dog ~ed its bowl clean** le chien a nettoyé sa gamelle à coups de langue; **the dog ~ed her hand** le chien lui a léché la main; **the cat ~ed (up) the milk from the plate** le chat a lapé le lait qui était dans l'assiette; **he ~ed the jam off the bread** il lécha la confiture de la tartine; **the dog ~ed the crumbs off the floor** le chien léchait les miettes par terre; **to ~ one's chops** *inf* se lécher les babines; **the flames ~ed the walls of the house** *fig* les flammes léchaient les murs de la maison ❑ **to ~ sb's boots** lécher les bottes à qqn; **to ~ one's lips** *literal* se lécher les lèvres; *fig* [with satisfaction, lust] se frotter les mains; [with eager anticipation] se lécher les babines; **to ~ one's wounds** panser ses blessures; **to ~ sb into shape** former OR entraîner qqn; **to ~ sthg into shape** arranger qqch, mettre au point qqch; **how long did it take to ~ the garden into shape?** combien de temps vous a-t-il fallu pour que le jardin prenne forme?; **a spell in the army will soon ~ him into shape** un séjour à l'armée lui fera le plus grand bien. -**2.** *inf* [defeat] battre à plate couture; [in fight] donner une raclée à; **this crossword has got me ~ed** ces mots croisés sont trop forts pour moi; **we've finally got the problem ~ed** nous sommes enfin venus à bout du problème.
◇ *n* -**1.** [with tongue] coup *m* de langue; **to give sthg a ~** lécher qqch; **can I have a ~ of your ice-cream?** je peux goûter ta glace?; **a ~ of paint** un (petit) coup de peinture ❑ **to give o.s. a ~ and a promise** faire un brin de toilette. -**2.** *inf Br* [speed]: **at a tremendous ~** à fond la caisse OR de train. -**3.** AGR pierre *f* à lécher.

lickety-split *inf* [ˌlɪkətɪ'splɪt] *adv Am* à toute pompe, à toutes pompes, à fond la caisse.

licking *inf* ['lɪkɪŋ] *n* [thrashing] raclée *f*, dégelée *f*; [defeat] déculottée *f*; **to get a good ~** prendre une raclée.

lickspittle *inf* ['lɪkˌspɪtl] *n* lèche-bottes *mf inv*.

licorice *Am* = **liquorice**.

lid [lɪd] *n* -**1.** [gen] couvercle *m*. -**2.** *inf phr*: **the scandal put the ~ on the Chicago operation**

le scandale mit fin à l'opération de Chicago; that puts the (tin) ~ on it! *Br* ça, c'est le bouquet!; to take OR to lift the ~ off sthg percer OR mettre qqch à jour. -**3.** ANAT [eyelid] paupière *f*. -**4.** *inf* [hat] galure *m*, galurin *m*; [helmet] casque *m*.

lidded [ˈlɪdɪd] *adj*: heavy ~ eyes des yeux aux paupières lourdes.

lidless [ˈlɪdlɪs] *adj* [container] sans couvercle; [eyes] sans paupières.

lido [ˈliːdəʊ] (*pl* lidos) *n* [pool] piscine *f* découverte; [resort] station *f* balnéaire.

lie [laɪ] (*cont* lying, *pt* & *pp sense 1* lied, *pt senses 2-10* lay [leɪ], *pp senses 2-10* lain [leɪn]) ◇ *vi* -**1.** [tell untruth] mentir; he ~d about his age il a menti sur son âge; "it wasn't me", she ~d «ce n'était pas moi», mentit-elle; the camera never ~s *fig* une photo ne ment pas. -**2.** [person, animal - recline] se coucher, s'allonger, s'étendre; she lay on the beach all day elle est restée allongée sur la plage toute la journée; she was lying on the couch elle était couchée OR allongée sur le divan; he lay helpless on the floor il gisait là sans pouvoir bouger; ~ on your back couchez-vous sur le dos; ~ still! ne bouge pas!; I like lying in bed on Sunday mornings j'aime rester au lit OR faire la grasse matinée le dimanche matin; they lay sound asleep ils dormaient profondément, ils étaient profondément endormis; she lay awake for hours elle resta plusieurs heures sans pouvoir s'endormir ❑ 'As I Lay Dying' *Faulkner* 'Tandis que j'agonise'. -**3.** [corpse] reposer; he OR his body ~s in the village graveyard il OR son corps repose au cimetière du village; he will ~ in state at Westminster Abbey son corps sera exposé solennellement à l'abbaye de Westminster; 'here ~s John Smith' 'ci-gît John Smith'. -**4.** [team, competitor - rank] être classé, se classer; France ~s second, after Italy la France est classée deuxième, après l'Italie; she was lying fourth [in race] elle était en quatrième position. -**5.** [thing - be, be placed]: a folder lay open on the desk before her un dossier était ouvert devant elle sur le bureau; a pile of ammunition lay ready des munitions étaient là, prêtes à servir; I found your watch lying on the floor j'ai trouvé ta montre qui traînait par terre; several boats lay in the harbour plusieurs bateaux étaient mouillés dans le port; thick fog lay over the plain un brouillard épais recouvrait la plaine; snow lay (thick) on the ground il y avait une (épaisse) couche de neige; the castle now ~s in ruins le château est aujourd'hui en ruines; all her hopes and dreams lay in ruins *fig* tous ses espoirs et ses rêves étaient anéantis OR réduits à néant. -**6.** [thing - remain, stay] rester; the jewel lay hidden for many years le bijou est resté caché pendant de nombreuses années; our machines are lying idle nos machines sont arrêtées OR ne tournent pas. -**7.** [place - be situated] se trouver, être; Texas ~s to the south of Oklahoma le Texas se trouve OR s'étend au sud de l'Oklahoma || [land - stretch, extend] s'étendre; the valley lay at our feet la vallée s'étendait à nos pieds; a vast desert lay before us un immense désert s'étendait devant nous. -**8.** [future event]: they didn't know what lay ahead of them ils ne savaient pas ce qui les attendait; who knows what may ~ in store for us qui sait ce qui nous attend OR ce que l'avenir nous réserve. -**9.** [answer, explanation, duty etc]: the problem ~s in getting them motivated le problème, c'est de réussir à les motiver; where do our real interests ~? qu'est-ce qui compte vraiment pour nous?; responsibility for the strike ~s with the management la responsabilité de la grève incombe à la direction; the onus of proof ~s with them c'est à eux qu'il incombe de fournir la preuve. -**10.** JUR [appeal, claim] être recevable.
◇ *n* -**1.** [untruth] mensonge *m*; to tell ~s dire des mensonges, mentir; a pack of ~s un tissu de mensonges; to give the ~ to sthg *lit* démentir qqch; it was in June, no, I tell a ~, in July c'était en juin, non, c'est faux, en juillet. -**2.** [of land] configuration *f*, disposition *f*. -**3.** SPORT [of golf ball] position *f*; he's got a bad ~ c'est une balle difficile.

◆ **lie about** *Br*, **lie around** *vi insep* -**1.** [person] traîner; I lay about all weekend doing nothing j'ai traîné tout le week-end à ne rien faire. -**2.** [thing] traîner; don't leave your things lying about ne laisse pas traîner tes affaires.

◆ **lie back** *vi insep*: he lay back in his armchair il s'est renversé dans son fauteuil; just ~ back and take it easy! *fig* repose-toi un peu!

◆ **lie behind** *vt insep* se cacher derrière; what can ~ behind this unexpected decision? qu'est-ce qui peut bien se cacher derrière cette décision soudaine?; deep insecurity lay behind his apparently successful life sa vie, en apparence réussie, cachait une profonde insécurité.

◆ **lie down** *vi insep* se coucher, s'allonger, s'étendre; go and ~ down for an hour va t'allonger une heure ❑ to take sthg lying down accepter qqch sans réagir OR sans broncher; I won't take this lying down! je ne vais pas me laisser faire comme ça!

◆ **lie in** *vi insep* -**1.** [sleep in] faire la grasse matinée. -**2.** *arch* & MED être en couches.

◆ **lie off** *vi insep* NAUT rester au large.

◆ **lie to** *vi insep* NAUT se tenir OR (se) mettre à la cape.

◆ **lie up** *vi insep* [person] rester au lit, garder le lit; [machine] ne pas tourner, être arrêté; [car] rester au garage.

lie-abed *n arch* paresseux *m*, -euse *f*.

Liechtenstein [ˈlɪktənstaɪn] *pr n* Liechtenstein *m*; in ~ au Liechtenstein.

lied [liːd] (*pl* lieder [ˈliːdəʳ]) *n* MUS lied *m*.

lie detector *n* détecteur *m* de mensonges.

lie-down *inf n Br*: to have a ~ se coucher, s'allonger; I think I'll go for a little ~ je crois que je vais aller m'allonger un peu; that ~ has done me good ça m'a fait du bien de m'allonger un peu.

lief [liːf] *adv arch* OR *lit*: I'd as ~ die as marry him plutôt mourir que de l'épouser.

liege [liːdʒ] *arch* ◇ *adj* -**1.** ~ lord seigneur *m*, suzerain *m*. -**2.** [vassal, homage] lige; ~ man homme *m* lige.
◇ *n* seigneur *m*, suzerain *m*.

lie-in *inf n Br* grasse matinée *f*; to have a ~ faire la grasse matinée.

lien [ˈlɪən] *n* JUR privilège *m*.

lieu [ljuː, luː]

◆ **in lieu** *adv phr*: take Monday off in ~ prends ton lundi pour compenser.

◆ **in lieu of** *prep phr* au lieu de, à la place de.

Lieut. (*written abbr of* lieutenant) lieut.

lieutenant [*Br* lefˈtenənt, *Am* luːˈtenənt] *n* -**1.** MIL [in army] lieutenant *m*; [in navy] lieutenant *m* de vaisseau. -**2.** [in US police] inspecteur *m* (de police). -**3.** *fig* lieutenant *m*, second *m*; the marketing director and his ~s le directeur du marketing et ses lieutenants. -**4.** *Br* HIST lieutenant *m*.

lieutenant colonel *n* lieutenant-colonel *m*.

lieutenant commander *n* capitaine *m* de corvette.

lieutenant general *n* [in army] général *m* de corps d'armée; [in US airforce] général *m* de corps aérien.

lieutenant governor *n* -**1.** [in Canada] lieutenant *m* gouverneur. -**2.** [in US] gouverneur *m* adjoint.

life [laɪf] (*pl* lives [laɪvz]) ◇ *n* -**1.** [existence] vie *f*; they believe in ~ after death ils croient à la vie après la mort; it's a matter of ~ and death c'est une question de vie ou de mort; I've worked hard all my ~ j'ai travaillé dur toute ma vie; ~ is hard la vie est dure; ~ has been good to us la vie nous a gâtés; he hasn't seen much of ~ il ne connaît pas grand-chose de la vie; there have been several attempts on her ~ elle a été victime de plusieurs attentats; he's in hospital fighting for his ~ il lutte contre la mort à l'hôpital; how's ~? *inf* comment ça va?; what a ~! quelle vie!; I began ~ as a labourer j'ai débuté dans la vie comme ouvrier; it began ~ as a car chassis à l'origine c'était un châssis de voiture; just relax and enjoy ~! profite donc un peu de la vie!; I want to live my own ~ je veux vivre ma vie; is ~ worth living? la vie vaut-elle la peine d'être vécue?; meeting him has made my ~ worth living le rencontrer OR notre rencontre a donné un sens à ma vie; to live ~ to the full *Br* OR fullest *Am* croquer la vie à belles dents; hundreds lost their lives des centaines de personnes ont trouvé la mort; he emigrated in order to make a new ~ for himself il a émigré pour commencer une nouvelle vie OR pour repartir à zéro; we don't want to spend the rest of our lives here on ne veut pas finir nos jours ici; to save sb's ~ sauver la vie à qqn; to risk one's ~ (to do sthg) risquer sa vie (à faire qqch); to take sb's ~ tuer qqn; she took her own ~ elle s'est donné la mort; I've never eaten snails in my ~ je n'ai jamais mangé d'escargots de ma vie; she's the only woman in his ~ c'est la seule femme dans sa vie; I ran the race of my ~! j'ai fait la course de ma vie!; it gave me the fright of my ~ je n'ai jamais eu aussi peur de ma vie ❑ my/her *etc* ~'s work l'œuvre *f* de toute ma/sa *etc* vie; the fire destroyed her ~'s work l'incendie a détruit l'œuvre de toute sa vie; to run for one's ~ OR for dear ~ s'enfuir à toutes jambes; run for your lives! sauve qui peut!; she was hanging on for dear ~ elle s'accrochait de toutes ses forces; for the ~ of me I can't remember where we met rien à faire, je n'arrive pas à me rappeler où nous nous sommes rencontrés; not on your ~! jamais de la vie!; to risk ~ and limb risquer sa peau; to have nine lives avoir l'âme chevillée au corps; I can't sing to save my ~ *inf* je suis absolument incapable de chanter; you take your ~ in your hands when cycling in London on risque sa vie quand on fait du vélo à Londres; that's ~! c'est la vie!; this is the ~! (ça, c'est) la belle vie!; I had the time of my ~ je ne me suis jamais autant amusé; upon my ~ *arch* seigneur!, mon Dieu! -**2.** [mode of existence] vie *f*; they lead a strange ~ ils mènent une drôle de vie; school ~ la vie scolaire; she's not used to city ~ elle n'a pas l'habitude de vivre en ville; married ~ la vie conjugale ❑ to live the ~ of Riley *inf* mener une vie de pacha; 'Life at the Top' *Braine* 'la Vie au sommet'. -**3.** [living things collectively] vie *f*; is there ~ on Mars? y a-t-il de la vie sur Mars? ❑ animal ~ faune *f*; plant ~ flore *f*. -**4.** (U) [physical feeling] sensation *f*; ~ began to return to her frozen fingers le sang se remit peu à peu à circuler dans ses doigts gelés. -**5.** [liveliness] vie *f*; she's still young and full of ~ elle est encore jeune et pleine de vie; there's a lot more ~ in Sydney than in Wellington Sydney est nettement plus animé que Wellington; to come to ~ s'animer; his arrival put new ~ into the firm son arrivée a donné un coup de fouet à l'entreprise; there's ~ in the old boy yet! il est encore vert, le bonhomme! ❑ she was the ~ and soul of the party c'est elle qui a mis de l'ambiance dans la soirée. -**6.** [living person] vie *f*; a phone call can save a ~ un coup de fil peut sauver une vie; 200 lives were lost in the disaster 200 personnes ont perdu la vie dans la catastrophe, la catastrophe a fait 200 morts. -**7.** [durability] (durée de) vie *f*; double the ~ of your batteries multipliez par deux la durée de vos piles; the average ~ of an isotope la durée de vie moyenne d'un isotope; during the ~ of the previous government sous le gouvernement précédent. -**8.** [biography] vie *f*; she's writing a ~ of James Joyce elle écrit une biographie de James Joyce. -**9.** ART nature *f*; to draw from ~ dessiner d'après nature || LITERAT réalité *f*; his novels are very true to ~ ses romans sont très réalistes ❑ that's her to the ~ c'est elle tout craché. -**10.** GAMES vie *f*; when you lose three lives you're out quand on perd trois vies, on est éliminé. -**11.** *inf* [imprisonment] prison *f* à vie; the kidnappers got ~ les ravisseurs ont été

condamnés à perpétuité OR à la prison à vie; he's doing ~ il purge une peine à perpétuité.
◇ *comp* [post, member, president] à vie.
◆ **for life** *adv phr*: he was crippled for ~ il a été estropié à vie; sent to prison for ~ condamné à perpétuité; if you help me, I'll be your friend for ~ si tu m'aides, je serai ton ami pour la vie; a job for ~ un emploi à vie.

life-and-death *adj*: a ~ matter une question de vie ou de mort; this is a ~ decision c'est une décision vitale; a ~ struggle un combat à mort, une lutte désespérée.

life assurance *Br* = **life insurance**.

life belt *n* bouée *f* de sauvetage.

lifeblood ['laɪfblʌd] *n* élément *m* vital.

lifeboat ['laɪfbəʊt] *n* [shore-based] canot *m* de sauvetage; [on ship] chaloupe *f* de sauvetage.

lifeboatman ['laɪfbəʊtmən] (*pl* **lifeboatmen** [-mən]) *n* sauveteur *m* (en mer).

life buoy *n* bouée *f* de sauvetage.

life class *n* cours *m* de dessin d'après nature.

life cycle *n* cycle *m* de vie.

life drawing *n* dessin *m* d'après nature.

life expectancy *n* [of human, animal] espérance *f* de vie; [of machine] durée *f* de vie probable.

life-force *n* force *f* vitale.

life-form *n* forme *f* de vie.

life-giving *adj* qui insuffle la vie, vivifiant.

lifeguard ['laɪfgɑːd] *n* maître *m* nageur.

Life Guard *pr n*: the ~s *régiment de cavalerie de la Garde Royale britannique*.

life history *n* vie *f*; the organism takes on many different forms during its ~ l'organisme prend de nombreuses formes au cours de sa vie OR de son existence; she told me her whole ~ elle m'a raconté l'histoire de sa vie.

life imprisonment *n* prison *f* à vie.

life insurance *n* assurance-vie *f*; to take out ~ contracter une assurance-vie.

life jacket *n* gilet *m* de sauvetage.

lifeless ['laɪflɪs] *adj* -**1.** [dead body] sans vie; his ~ form son corps sans vie. -**2.** [where no life exists] sans vie; a ~ desert un désert sans vie. -**3.** [dull - eyes] éteint; [- hair] terne; [- town] mort; [- style] sans énergie.

lifelessness ['laɪflɪsnɪs] *n* [of body] absence *f* de vie; [lack of vivacity] manque *m* de vigueur, mollesse *f*.

lifelike ['laɪflaɪk] *adj* -**1.** [portrait] ressemblant. -**2.** [seeming alive]: the new robots are extremely ~ ces nouveaux robots ont l'air OR paraissent vraiment vivants.

lifeline ['laɪflaɪn] *n* -**1.** NAUT [thrown to boat] remorque *f*; [stretched across deck] sauvegarde *f*, filière *f* de mauvais temps OR de sécurité; they threw the drowning man a ~ ils ont lancé un filin à l'homme qui se noyait. -**2.** [for diver] corde *f* de sécurité. -**3.** *fig* lien *m* vital; it's his ~ to the outside world c'est son lien avec le monde extérieur; to cut off sb's ~ couper les vivres à qqn.

lifelong ['laɪflɒŋ] *adj* de toute une vie; it's been my ~ ambition to meet her toute ma vie, j'ai espéré la rencontrer.

life-or-death = **life-and-death**.

life peer *n membre de la Chambre des lords dont le titre n'est pas héréditaire*.

life peerage *n* [in UK] pairie *f* personnelle.

life preserver *n Am* [life belt] bouée *f* de sauvetage; [life jacket] gilet *m* de sauvetage.

lifer *inf* ['laɪfəʳ] *n* condamné *m*, -e *f* à perpète.

life raft *n* radeau *m* de sauvetage.

lifesaver ['laɪf,seɪvəʳ] *n* -**1.** [lifeguard] maître nageur *m*. -**2.** *inf fig*: thank you, you're a ~! merci, tu m'as sauvé la vie!; that money was a ~ cet argent m'a sauvé la vie.

life science *n*: the ~s les sciences de la vie; anthropology is a ~ l'anthropologie fait partie des sciences de la vie.

life sentence *n* condamnation *f* à vie OR à perpétuité.

life-size(d) *adj* grandeur nature *(inv)*.

life span *n* durée *f* de vie.

life story *n* biographie *f*.

life-style *n* style *m* OR mode *m* de vie.

life-support system *n* MED respirateur *m* artificiel; AERON & ASTRON équipement *m* de vie.

life-threatening *adj* [illness] qui peut être mortel.

lifetime ['laɪftaɪm] *n* vie *f*; it won't happen during our ~ nous ne serons pas là pour voir ça; win the holiday of a ~! gagnez les vacances de votre vie!; a once-in-a-~ experience une expérience unique OR qui ne se renouvellera pas; it seems a ~ since we last met ça fait une éternité qu'on ne s'est pas vu.

life vest = **life jacket**.

lift [lɪft] ◇ *vt* -**1.** [object] soulever, lever; help me ~ the wardrobe aide-moi à soulever l'armoire; she ~ed the washing basket off OR from the table elle a soulevé le panier à linge de la table; I ~ed the books out of the crate j'ai sorti les livres de la caisse; she ~ed the suitcase down from the top of the wardrobe elle a descendu la valise de dessus l'armoire; I feel as if a burden has been ~ed from my shoulders j'ai l'impression qu'on m'a enlevé un poids des épaules ‖ [part of body] lever; she ~ed her eyes from her magazine elle leva les yeux de sa revue ‖ *fml* [voice] élever. -**2.** [spirits, heart] remonter; his music never fails to ~ my spirits sa musique me remonte toujours le moral. -**3.** [end - blockade, embargo etc] lever; [- control, restriction] supprimer. -**4.** *inf* [steal] piquer, faucher; [plagiarize] plagier, piquer. -**5.** AGR [bulbs, potatoes, turnips] arracher. -**6.** *Am* [debt] rembourser. -**7.** [face]: she's had her face ~ed elle s'est fait faire un lifting.
◇ *vi* -**1.** [rise] se lever, se soulever; our spirits ~ed at the news la nouvelle nous a remonté le moral. -**2.** [fog, mist] se lever, se dissiper; his bad mood didn't ~ all day sa mauvaise humeur ne s'est pas dissipée de la journée.
◇ *n* -**1.** [act of lifting]: to give sthg a ~ soulever qqch. -**2.** [in morale, energy]: to give sb a ~ remonter le moral à qqn; glucose tablets are good if you need a quick ~ les comprimés de glucose sont bons si vous avez besoin d'un coup de fouet. -**3.** *Br* [elevator] ascenseur *m*; goods ~ monte-charge *m inv*. -**4.** [free ride]: can I give you a ~ home? est-ce que je peux te raccompagner chez toi (en voiture)?; I got a ~ in a lorry j'ai été pris (en auto-stop) par un camion; the roundabout's the best place to get a ~ le meilleur endroit pour faire du stop, c'est le rond-point.
◆ **lift off** ◇ *vi insep* [plane, rocket] décoller.
◇ *vt sep* [hat, lid] enlever, ôter.
◆ **lift up** *vt sep* soulever, lever; ~ me up so I can see the parade soulève-moi pour que je puisse voir le défilé; she ~ed up the mat and found a key elle souleva le paillasson et trouva une clé ‖ [part of body] lever; to ~ up one's head lever la tête; *fml* [voice] élever; the choir ~ed up their voices in song le chœur s'est mis à chanter; *fml* [heart] élever; ~ up your hearts in prayer élevez vos âmes OR cœurs dans la prière.

lift attendant *n Br* liftier *m*, -ère *f*.

liftboy ['lɪftbɔɪ] *Br* = **liftman**.

liftgate ['lɪftgeɪt] *n Am* AUT hayon *m*.

lifting ['lɪftɪŋ] *n* -**1.** [of weight] levage *m*; ~ gear appareil *m* de levage; ~ jack cric *m* (de levage). -**2.** [of blockade, embargo etc] levée *f*; [of control, restriction] suppression *f*. -**3.** AGR arrachage *m*, récolte *f*.

liftman ['lɪftmæn] (*pl* **liftmen** [-men]) *n Br* liftier *m*.

lift-off *n* décollage *m*; we have ~! décollage!

lift shaft *n Br* cage *f* d'ascenseur.

ligament ['lɪgəmənt] *n* ligament *m*.

ligature ['lɪgətʃəʳ] ◇ *n* -**1.** [gen, MED & TYPO] ligature *f*. -**2.** MUS liaison *f*.
◇ *vt* ligaturer.

light [laɪt] (*pt* & *pp* **lit** [lɪt] OR *lit* **lighted**) ◇ *n* -**1.** [luminosity, brightness] lumière *f*; there's not enough ~ to read by il n'y a pas assez de lumière pour lire; it looks brown in this ~ on dirait que c'est marron avec cette lumière; by the ~ of our flashlamps à la lumière de nos lampes de poche; the ~ was beginning to fail le jour commençait à baisser; she took the picture against the ~ elle a pris la photo à contre-jour; at first ~ *lit* au point OR au lever du jour; you're (standing) in my ~ tu me fais de l'ombre; in the cold ~ of the morning dans la lueur pâle du matin ‖ *fig*: to bring to ~ mettre en lumière; to be brought OR to come to ~ être découvert OR révélé; to throw OR to cast ~ on sthg: the trial will throw OR cast ~ on their real motives le procès permettra d'en savoir plus sur OR de percer à jour leurs véritables mobiles; can you throw any ~ on this problem? peux-tu apporter tes lumières sur ce problème?, peux-tu éclaircir cette question? ❑ artificial ~ lumière artificielle, éclairage *m* artificiel; ~ wave onde *f* lumineuse; the ~ at the end of the tunnel le bout du tunnel; to see the ~ [understand] comprendre; [be converted] trouver le chemin de la vérité; [be born] venir au monde; to see the ~ of day voir le jour. -**2.** [light source] lumière *f*; [lamp] lampe *f*; the ~s of the city les lumières de la ville; a ~ went on in the window une lumière s'est allumée à la fenêtre; turn the ~ on/off allume/éteins (la lumière); put the ~s out before you go to bed éteins les lumières avant de te coucher; during the storm the ~s went out il y a eu une panne d'électricité OR de lumière pendant l'orage ❑ to go out like a ~ [fall asleep] s'endormir tout de suite; [faint] tomber dans les pommes. -**3.** *fig* [in sb's eyes] lueur *f*. -**4.** AUT [gen] feu *m*; [headlamp] phare *m*; we were dazzled by the ~s of the oncoming cars les phares des véhicules qui venaient en face nous éblouissaient ❑ parking/reversing ~s feux de stationnement/de recul. -**5.** [traffic light] feu *m* (rouge); turn left at the ~s tournez à gauche au feu rouge; she jumped the ~s elle a brûlé le feu rouge; the ~s were (on) amber le feu était à l'orange. -**6.** [aspect, viewpoint] jour *m*; I see the problem in a different ~ je vois le problème sous un autre jour; in a good/bad/new ~ sous un jour favorable/défavorable/nouveau ❑ to act according to one's ~s *fml* agir selon ses principes. -**7.** [flame] feu *m*; could you give me a ~? pouvez-vous me donner du feu?; to set ~ to sthg mettre le feu à qqch. -**8.** [window] fenêtre *f*, jour *m*.
◇ *adj* -**1.** [bright, well-lit] clair; a large, ~ room une grande pièce claire; it isn't ~ enough to read il n'y a pas assez de lumière pour lire; it's getting ~ already il commence déjà à faire jour; it stays ~ until 10 il fait jour jusqu'à 10 h du soir. -**2.** [pale] clair; she has ~ hair elle a des cheveux clairs; ~ yellow/brown jaune/marron clair *(inv)*. -**3.** LING [in phonetics] atone. -**4.** [in weight] léger; ~ clothes vêtements *mpl* légers ❑ a ~ aircraft un avion de tourisme; ~ soil terre *f* légère; ~ vehicle véhicule *m* léger; ~ weapons armes *fpl* légères; it's (as) ~ as a feather c'est léger comme une plume; to be ~ on one's feet être leste. -**5.** [comedy, music etc] léger, facile; take some ~ reading prends quelque chose de facile à lire; to trip the ~ fantastic *arch* OR *hum* danser. -**6.** [comedy, music] léger; take some ~ reading prends quelque chose de facile à lire; ~ conversation conversation peu sérieuse, propos anodins. -**7.** [not intense, strong etc] léger; there was a ~ tap at the door on frappa tout doucement à la porte; the traffic was ~ la circulation était fluide; I had a ~ lunch j'ai mangé légèrement à midi, j'ai déjeuné léger; a ~ rain was falling il tombait une pluie fine; I'm a ~ sleeper j'ai le sommeil léger; a ~ wine un vin léger; he can only do ~ work il ne peut faire que des travaux peu fatigants ❑ ~ industry industrie *f* légère; to make ~ of sthg prendre qqch à la légère.
◇ *adv*: to travel ~ voyager avec peu de bagages.
◇ *vt* -**1.** [illuminate] éclairer; the room was lit by a single bare bulb la pièce n'était éclairée que par une ampoule nue; I'll ~ the way for

you je vais t'éclairer le chemin. -**2.** [lamp, candle, cigarette] allumer; [match] craquer; to ~ a fire allumer un feu, faire du feu.
◇ *vi* -**1.** [lamp] s'allumer; [match] s'enflammer; [fire, coal] prendre. -**2.** *lit* [alight] se poser.
◆ **lights** *npl* [lungs] mou *m*.
◆ **in (the) light of** *prep phr*: in the ~ of these new facts à la lumière de ces faits nouveaux.
◆ **light on, light upon** *vt insep* tomber (par hasard) sur, trouver par hasard.
◆ **light out** *inf vi insep Am* se tirer.
◆ **light up** ◇ *vt sep* éclairer; the house was all lit up la maison était tout OR toute éclairée; joy lit up her face son visage rayonnait de bonheur.
◇ *vi insep* -**1.** [lamp] s'allumer. -**2.** [face, eyes] s'éclairer, s'illuminer. -**3.** *inf* [have a cigarette] allumer une cigarette.

light air *n* [on Beaufort scale] très légère brise *f*.

light ale *n Br bière brune légère*.

light breeze *n* [gen] petite brise *f*, brise *f* légère; [on Beaufort scale] légère brise *f*.

light bulb *n* ampoule *f* (électrique).

light-coloured *adj* clair, de couleur claire.

light-emitting diode [-ɪ'mɪtɪŋ-] *n* diode *f* électroluminescente.

lighten ['laɪtn] ◇ *vt* -**1.** [make brighter] éclairer, illuminer; a single candle ~ed the darkness seule une bougie trouait l'obscurité. -**2.** [make paler] éclaircir; ~ the blue with a little white éclaircissez le bleu avec un peu de blanc; to have one's hair ~ed se faire éclaircir les cheveux. -**3.** [make less heavy] alléger; having an assistant will ~ my workload avec un assistant ma charge de travail sera moins lourde.
◇ *vi* -**1.** [become light] s'éclairer, s'éclaircir; the sky has ~ed a little le ciel s'est légèrement éclairci; her mood ~ed sa mauvaise humeur se dissipa. -**2.** [load, burden] s'alléger.
◆ **lighten up** *inf vi insep* se remettre; oh come on, ~ up, it's not the end of the world! allez, remets-toi OR ne fais pas cette tête, ce n'est pas la fin du monde!

lighter ['laɪtəʳ] ◇ *n* -**1.** [for cigarettes] briquet *m*; [for gas] allume-gaz *m inv*. -**2.** [barge] allège *f*, chaland *m*. -**3.** → **firelighter**.
◇ *comp* [flint, fuel] à briquet.

lighterage ['laɪtərɪdʒ] *n* aconage *m*, acconage *m*.

lighter-than-air *adj* plus léger que l'air.

lightface ['laɪtfeɪs] *n* TYPO (caractère *m*) maigre *m*.

light-fingered [-'fɪŋgəd] *adj* chapardeur.

light fitting *n* applique *f* (électrique).

light-footed [-'fʊtɪd] *adj* au pied léger, à la démarche légère.

light-haired [-'heəd] *adj* aux cheveux clairs, blond.

light-headed [-'hedɪd] *adj* [dizzy] étourdi; [tipsy] ivre, énivré; to feel ~ avoir des vertiges OR la tête qui tourne; the wine had made me ~ le vin m'était monté à la tête OR m'avait tourné la tête.

light-headedness [-'hedɪdnɪs] *n* [dizziness] vertige *m*; [tipsiness] ivresse *f*.

light-hearted *adj* [person, atmosphere] enjoué, gai; [poem, irony] léger; a ~ remark une remarque bon enfant; this programme takes a ~ look at politics cette émission pose un regard amusé sur la politique.

light-heartedly [-'hɑːtɪdlɪ] *adv* joyeusement, gaiement.

light heavyweight ◇ *n* (poids *m*) mi-lourd *m*.
◇ *adj* mi-lourd.

lighthouse ['laɪthaʊs, *pl* -haʊzɪz] *n* phare *m*; ~ keeper gardien *m* de phare; 'To the Lighthouse' *Woolf* 'la Promenade au phare'.

lighting ['laɪtɪŋ] *n* -**1.** [gen] éclairage *m*; artificial/neon ~ éclairage *m* artificiel/au néon. -**2.** *(U)* THEAT éclairages *mpl*; ~ effects effets *mpl* d'éclairage OR de lumière; ~ engineer éclairagiste *mf*.

lighting-up time *n Br heure où les automobilistes doivent obligatoirement allumer leurs phares*.

lightly ['laɪtlɪ] *adv* -**1.** [not heavily] légèrement; ~ dressed légèrement vêtu; it was raining ~ il tombait une pluie fine; she stepped ~ onto the dance floor elle entra sur la piste de danse d'un pas léger. -**2.** [casually] légèrement, à la légère; to take sthg ~ prendre qqch à la légère; "I'm getting married tomorrow", he said ~ «je me marie demain», annonça-t-il d'un air détaché. -**3.** *phr*: to get off ~ s'en tirer à bon compte.

light meter *n* posemètre *m*.

light-middleweight ◇ *n* (poids *m*) mi-moyen *m*.
◇ *adj* mi-moyen.

lightness ['laɪtnɪs] *n* -**1.** [brightness, light] clarté *f*. -**2.** [of object, tone, step etc] légèreté *f*.

lightning ['laɪtnɪŋ] ◇ *n (U)* éclairs *mpl*, foudre *f*; ~ frightens me les éclairs me font peur; a flash of ~ un éclair; to be struck by ~ être frappé par la foudre OR foudroyé ❑ to go like (greased) ~ partir sur les chapeaux de roue.
◇ *adj* [raid, visit] éclair *(inv)*; with OR at ~ speed à la vitesse de l'éclair, en un éclair.

lightning arrester *n* parafoudre *m* (de surtension).

lightning bug *n Am* luciole *f*, ver *m* luisant.

lightning conductor, lightning rod *n* paratonnerre *m*.

lightning strike *n* grève *f* surprise *(inv)*.

light opera *n* opéra *m* comique, opérette *f*.

light pen *n* crayon *m* optique.

lightship ['laɪtʃɪp] *n* bateau-feu *m*, bateau-phare *m*.

light show *n* spectacle *m* de lumière; a laser ~ un spectacle laser.

lights-out *n* extinction *f* des feux.

lightweight ['laɪtweɪt] ◇ *n* -**1.** [in boxing] poids *m* léger; the world ~ championship le championnat du monde des poids légers. -**2.** [insignificant person] personne *f* sans envergure; he's a literary ~ c'est un écrivain sans envergure.
◇ *adj* -**1.** [clothes, equipment] léger. -**2.** [in boxing] poids léger *(inv)*.

light-year *n* année-lumière *f*; it seems ~s away ça paraît si loin.

ligneous ['lɪgnɪəs] *adj* ligneux.

lignify ['lɪgnɪfaɪ] *(pt & pp* **lignified**) *vi* se lignifier.

lignin ['lɪgnɪn] *n* lignine *f*.

lignite ['lɪgnaɪt] *n* lignite *m*.

likable ['laɪkəbl] = **likeable**.

like[1] [laɪk] *vt* -**1.** [find pleasant] aimer (bien); I ~ her, but I don't love her je l'aime bien, mais je ne suis pas amoureux d'elle; I don't ~ him je ne l'aime pas beaucoup, il ne me plaît pas; I ~ Anne better than Simon j'aime mieux Anne que Simon; I ~ Sally best c'est Sally que je préfère; what do you ~ about him? qu'est-ce qui te plaît chez lui?; do you ~ coffee? est-ce que tu aimes le café?; I ~ curry but it doesn't ~ me! *hum* j'aime le curry mais ça ne me réussit pas tellement! -**2.** [enjoy - activity]: to ~ doing OR to do sthg aimer faire qqch; I ~ dancing OR to dance j'aime danser; I ~ to spend my weekends at home j'aime passer mes week-ends à la maison; I don't ~ being talked at je n'aime pas qu'on me fasse des discours; how would HE ~ being kept waiting in the rain? ça lui plairait, à lui, qu'on le fasse attendre sous la pluie? -**3.** [approve of] aimer; I ~ people to be frank with me j'aime qu'on soit franc avec moi; I don't ~ you swearing, I don't ~ it when you swear je n'aime pas que tu dises des gros mots; they're not going to ~ it! ça ne va pas leur plaire!; whether you ~ it or not! que ça te plaise ou non!; well, I ~ that! *iron* ça, c'est le bouquet!; I ~ the way you say "don't worry" *hum* «ne t'inquiète pas», c'est facile à dire. -**4.** [want, wish] aimer, vouloir; take any dress you ~ prends la robe que tu veux OR qui te plaît; do what you ~ fais ce que tu veux OR ce qui te plaît; what I'd ~ to know is where he got the money from ce que je voudrais savoir, c'est où il a obtenu cet argent; I didn't ~ to say anything, but... je ne voulais rien dire mais...; I'd ~ your opinion on this wine j'aimerais savoir ce que tu penses de ce vin; I would OR I'd ~ to go out tonight j'aimerais (bien) sortir ce soir ‖ [in polite offers, requests]: would you ~ to go out tonight? ça te dirait de OR tu as envie de sortir ce soir?; would you ~ tea or coffee? voulez-vous du thé ou du café?; would you ~ to leave a message? voulez-vous laisser un message?; would you ~ me to do it for you? veux-tu que je le fasse à ta place?; I'd ~ to speak to Mr Smith, please je voudrais parler à M. Smith, s'il vous plaît; I'd ~ the soup followed by a salad je voudrais de la soupe puis une salade; I'd ~ my steak rare, please je voudrais mon steak saignant, s'il vous plaît. -**5.** [asking opinion]: how do you ~ my jacket? comment trouves-tu ma veste?; how would you ~ a trip to Paris? ça te dirait d'aller à Paris? -**6.** [asking preference]: how do you ~ your coffee, black or white? vous prenez votre café noir ou avec du lait? -**7.** [in generalizations]: I ~ to be in bed by 10 p.m. j'aime être couché pour 10 h; one doesn't ~ to interrupt c'est toujours délicat d'interrompre quelqu'un.

like[2] [laɪk] ◇ *prep* -**1.** [similar to] comme; there's a car ~ ours voilà une voiture comme la nôtre; their house is a bit ~ ours leur maison est un peu comme la nôtre; there's no place ~ home rien ne vaut son chez-soi; she's nothing ~ her sister elle ne ressemble pas du tout à sa sœur; he talks ~ his father il parle comme son père; it's shaped ~ an egg ça a la forme d'un œuf; do you have any more ~ this? en avez-vous d'autres?; it seemed ~ hours c'était comme si des heures entières s'étaient écoulées; it looks ~ rain on dirait qu'il va pleuvoir. -**2.** [asking for opinion or description]: what's your new boss ~? comment est ton nouveau patron?; what's the weather ~? quel temps fait-il?; what does it taste ~? quel goût ça a?; what was it ~? c'était comment? -**3.** [such as] comme; in a family ~ ours dans une famille comme la nôtre; I've had enough of people ~ him! j'en ai assez des gens comme lui!; cities ~ Toronto and Ottawa des villes comme Toronto et Ottawa; I'm useless at things ~ sewing je ne suis bon à rien quand il s'agit de couture et de choses comme ça. -**4.** [indicating typical behaviour]: kids are ~ that, what do you expect? les gosses sont comme ça, qu'est-ce que tu veux!; it's not ~ him to be rude ça ne lui ressemble pas OR ce n'est pas son genre d'être impoli; it's just ~ him not to show up! c'est bien son style OR c'est bien de lui de ne pas venir! ❑ ~ father ~ son tel père tel fils. -**5.** [in the same manner as] comme; you're acting ~ a fool tu te comportes comme un imbécile; they chattered ~ monkeys ils ont bavardé comme de vraies pipelettes; we, ~ everyone else, were forced to queue all night nous avons dû faire la queue toute la nuit, comme tout le monde; do it ~ this/that voici/voilà comment il faut faire; ~ so comme ça; sorry to interrupt you ~ this, but... désolé de vous interrompre ainsi, mais...; don't talk to me ~ that! ne me parle pas sur ce ton! -**6.** [in approximations]: it cost something ~ £200 ça a coûté dans les 200 livres; it was more ~ midnight when we got home il était plus près de minuit quand nous sommes arrivés à la maison ❑ that's more ~ it! voilà qui est mieux!; he ran ~ anything *inf* OR ~ hell *inf* OR ~ blazes *inf* il a couru comme un dératé OR comme s'il avait le feu aux fesses.
◇ *adj*: we were treated in ~ manner on nous a traités de la même façon.
◇ *conj inf* -**1.** [as] comme; ~ I was saying comme je disais; they don't make them ~ they used to! ils/elles ne sont plus ce qu'ils/elles étaient!; I wish I could dance ~ you! j'aimerais bien pouvoir danser comme toi!; it was just ~ in the films c'était exactement comme au cinéma; tell it ~ it is dis les choses comme elles sont. -**2.** [as if] comme si; he acted ~ he was in charge il se comportait comme si c'était lui le chef; she felt ~ she wanted to cry elle avait l'impression qu'elle allait pleurer.

◇ *adv* ▽ *Br*: I was hungry, ~, so I went into this café j'avais faim, tu vois, alors je suis entré dans un café.

◇ *n*: ~ attracts ~ qui se ressemble s'assemble; you can only compare ~ with ~ on ne peut comparer que ce qui est comparable; to give OR to return ~ for ~ rendre la pareille; she goes in for macramé, yoga and the ~ elle fait du macramé, du yoga et d'autres choses comme ça; I've never seen the ~ of it! je n'ai jamais rien vu de pareil!; he was a president the ~ OR ~s of which we will probably never see again *lit* c'était un président comme on n'en verra probablement plus jamais.

◆ **likes** *npl* -**1.** [preferences] goûts *mpl*; try to discover their ~s and dislikes esssayez de découvrir ce qu'ils aiment et ce qu'ils n'aiment pas. -**2.** *phr*: the ~s of us/them *etc inf* les gens comme nous/eux *etc*; it's not for the ~s of us ça n'est pas pour les gens comme nous.

◆ **(as) like as not** = **like enough**.

◆ **if you like** *adv phr* -**1.** [expressing willingness] si tu veux; I can do it, if you ~ je peux le faire, si tu veux; I'll get lunch, shall I? – if you ~ je vais chercher de quoi manger, d'accord? – si tu veux. -**2.** [as it were] si tu veux; it was a surprise, a shock, if you ~ ça m'a surpris, choqué si tu veux.

◆ **like enough** *inf adv phr* probablement; he's still at the office, ~ enough il y a des chances qu'il soit encore au bureau; (as) ~ as not, she hasn't even read it yet elle ne l'a probablement même pas encore lu.

◆ **like it or not** *adv phr*: ~ it or not, we're heading for a confrontation qu'on le veuille ou non, nous ne pouvons éviter une confrontation.

-like *in cpds*: dream~ onirique, de rêve; ghost~ fantomatique.

likeable ['laɪkəbl] *adj* sympathique, agréable; he's a ~ person c'est un type sympathique.

likelihood ['laɪklɪhʊd] *n* probabilité *f*; there's not much ~ of us moving il est peu probable que nous déménagions; there is little ~ of us still being here OR that we'll still be here in August il y a peu de chances (pour) que nous soyons encore là en août; there is every ~ of an agreement tout porte à croire qu'un accord sera conclu.

◆ **in all likelihood** *adv phr* vraisemblablement, selon toute vraisemblance.

likely ['laɪklɪ] (*compar* likelier, *superl* likeliest) ◇ *adj* -**1.** [probable] probable; what are the ~ consequences of this action? quelles sont les conséquences probables de cette mesure?; such an occurrence does not seem ~ il est peu probable que cela se produise; they're the likeliest candidates for the sack *inf* ce sont eux qui ont le plus de chances de faire partie de la prochaine charrette; it's more than ~ that it will snow il y a de grandes chances pour qu'il neige; it's not OR hardly ~ to happen il est peu probable OR il y a peu de chances que cela se produise; rain is ~ in the east il risque de pleuvoir dans l'est; they're not ~ to drop the case il est peu probable qu'ils abandonnent les poursuites; a ~ story! *iron* mon œil!, elle est bien bonne! -**2.** [promising] prometteur; we found a ~ OR ~-looking spot for a picnic on a trouvé un endroit qui a l'air idéal pour pique-niquer.

◇ *adv* probablement, sans doute; they'll very ~ OR most ~ forget ils vont très probablement oublier; as ~ as not she's already home elle est sûrement déjà rentrée ❑ would you do it again? – not ~! *inf* tu recommencerais? – ça risque pas OR y a pas de risque!

like-minded *adj*: ~ people des gens ayant la même vision des choses.

liken ['laɪkn] *vt* comparer; his style has been ~ed to that of Peter Wolfe on a comparé son style à celui de Peter Wolfe.

likeness ['laɪknɪs] *n* -**1.** [resemblance] ressemblance *f*; a family ~ un air de famille; she bears a strong ~ to her mother elle ressemble beaucoup à sa mère. -**2.** [portrait] portrait *m*; to paint sb's ~ faire le portrait de qqn; it's a very good ~ of him c'est tout à fait lui; it isn't a very good ~ of him ça ne lui ressemble pas beaucoup.

likewise ['laɪkwaɪz] *adv* -**1.** [similarly] de même; ~ in Israel, talks are in progress en Israël aussi, des pourparlers ont été entamés; he worked hard and expected his daughters to do ~ il travaillait beaucoup et attendait de ses filles qu'elles fassent de même;...and I suggest you do ~ ...et je suggère que tu en fasses autant; pleased to meet you – ~ ravi de vous rencontrer – moi de même. -**2.** [by the same token] de même.

liking ['laɪkɪŋ] *n* -**1.** [affection] sympathie *f*, affection *f*; I have a great ~ for Alan j'ai beaucoup de sympathie pour Alan; to take a ~ to sb se prendre d'amitié pour qqn; I took an instant ~ to Rome j'ai tout de suite aimé Rome. -**2.** [taste] goût *m*, penchant *m*; she has a ~ for expensive jewellery elle a un faible pour les bijoux de prix; is everything to your ~? est-ce que tout est à votre convenance?; it's too small for my ~ c'est trop petit à mon goût.

lilac ['laɪlək] ◇ *n* [colour, flower] lilas *m*.

◇ *adj* [colour] lilas *(inv)*.

Lilliputian [,lɪlɪ'pju:ʃn] ◇ *n* lilliputien *m*, -enne *f*.

◇ *adj* lilliputien.

Lilo® ['laɪləʊ] (*pl* Lilos) *n* matelas *m* pneumatique.

Lilongwe [lɪ'lɒŋweɪ] *pr n* Lilongwe.

lilt [lɪlt] *n* -**1.** [in voice] modulation *f*; her voice has a ~ to it sa voix a des inflexions mélodieuses. -**2.** [in music] rythme *m*, cadence *f*. -**3.** [in movement] balancement *m* harmonieux.

lilting ['lɪltɪŋ] *adj* -**1.** [voice, accent] mélodieux. -**2.** [music, tune] chantant, mélodieux. -**3.** [movement] souple, harmonieux.

lily ['lɪlɪ] (*pl* lilies) *n* lis *m*, lys *m*; ~ of the valley muguet *m*.

lily-livered *inf* [-'lɪvəd] *adj* froussard.

lily pad *n* feuille *f* de nénuphar.

lily-white *adj* d'une blancheur de lis, d'un blanc immaculé.

Lima ['li:mə] *pr n* Lima.

lima bean ['laɪmə-] *n* haricot *m* de Lima OR du Cap, pois *m* de sept ans.

limb [lɪm] *n* -**1.** ANAT membre *m*; let's rest our weary ~s! *hum* si on soufflait un peu!; I'll tear him ~ from ~! je le taillerai en pièces! -**2.** [of tree] (grosse) branche *f*; to be out on a ~ *inf* [alone] se trouver tout seul; [without support] être très exposé.

-limbed [lɪmd] *in cpds*: to be long~ avoir les membres longs, être élancé; to be loose~ être délié OR souple.

limber ['lɪmbə'] ◇ *adj* souple, agile.

◇ *n* [of gun carriage] avant-train *m*.

◆ **limber up** *vi insep* SPORT s'échauffer, faire des assouplissements; do some ~ing-up exercises first commencez par des exercices d'assouplissement; they're ~ing up for a fight with the unions *fig* ils se préparent à une bataille OR ils fourbissent leurs armes en vue d'une bataille avec les syndicats.

limbo ['lɪmbəʊ] (*pl sense 3* limbos) *n* -**1.** *(U)* RELIG limbes *mpl*. -**2.** COMPUT: ~ file fichier *m* temporaire. -**3.** DANCE limbo *m*. -**4.** *fig*: to be in (a state of) ~ être dans l'incertitude; they kept us in ~ for weeks ils nous ont laissés dans l'incertitude pendant des semaines.

lime [laɪm] ◇ *n* -**1.** AGR & CHEM chaux *f*; caustic/slaked ~ chaux vive/éteinte; burnt ~ chaux vive. -**2.** [fruit] citron *m* vert, lime *f*, limette *f*; lager and ~ bière *f* blonde au sirop de citron vert. -**3.** [citrus tree] limettier *m*. -**4.** [linden]: ~ (tree) tilleul *m*.

◇ *vt* -**1.** AGR [soil] chauler. -**2.** [with birdlime - branch, bird] engluer.

limeade [laɪ'meɪd] *n* boisson *f* au citron vert.

lime green *n* vert *m* citron.

◆ **lime-green** *adj* vert citron *(inv)*.

lime juice *n* jus *m* de citron vert.

lime kiln *n* four *m* à chaux.

limelight ['laɪmlaɪt] *n (U)* THEAT feux *mpl* de la rampe; to be in the ~ être sous les feux de la rampe, occuper le devant de la scène; '**Limelight**' *Chaplin* 'les Feux de la rampe'.

lime pit *n* [quarry] fosse *f* à chaux; [in tanning] pelain *m*.

limerick ['lɪmərɪk] *n* limerick *m (poème absurde ou indécent en cinq vers, dont les rimes doivent suivre un ordre précis)*.

limestone ['laɪmstəʊn] *n* calcaire *m*, roche *f* calcaire.

limewater ['laɪm,wɔ:tə'] *n* eau *f* de chaux.

limey *inf* ['laɪmɪ] *Am hum* OR *pej* ◇ *n* -**1.** [English person] ≃ Angliche *mf*. -**2.** [English sailor] matelot *m* anglais.

◇ *adj* ≃ angliche.

liminal ['lɪmɪnl] *adj* liminal.

limit ['lɪmɪt] ◇ *n* -**1.** [boundary, greatest extent, maximum] limite *f*; the eastern ~s of the empire les limites orientales de l'empire; I know my ~s je connais mes limites, je sais ce dont je suis capable; there is no ~ to his powers ses pouvoirs sont illimités; our resources are stretched to the ~ nous sommes au bout de nos ressources; within the ~s of the present regulations dans le cadre délimité par le présent règlement; I'd like to help but there are ~s je veux bien aider mais il y a des limites; I agree with you, within ~s je suis d'accord avec toi, jusqu'à un certain point ❑ off ~s interdit d'accès; the bar's off ~s to servicemen le bar est interdit aux militaires; that's the (absolute) ~! c'est le comble!; she really is the ~! elle dépasse vraiment les bornes! -**2.** [restriction] limitation *f*; the ~ on Japanese imports la limitation des importations japonaises; to put OR to set a ~ on sthg limiter qqch ❑ time ~ [duration] temps *m* maximum, durée *f* maximale; [deadline] délai *m*; weight ~ limitation de poids; to be over the ~ *Br* [driver] dépasser le taux d'alcoolémie autorisé.

◇ *vt* limiter; we're trying to ~ costs nous essayons de limiter les coûts; they are ~ing their research to one kind of virus ils limitent leurs recherches à un seul type de virus; she ~s herself to one visit a week elle se contente d'une visite par semaine.

limitation [,lɪmɪ'teɪʃn] *n* -**1.** [restriction, control] limitation *f*, restriction *f*; we will accept no ~ on our freedom nous n'accepterons aucune entrave à notre liberté ❑ arms ~ talks négociations *fpl* sur la limitation des armements. -**2.** [shortcoming] limite *f*; we all have our ~s nous avons tous nos limites; to know one's ~s connaître ses limites. -**3.** JUR prescription *f*.

limited ['lɪmɪtɪd] *adj* -**1.** [restricted] limité, restreint; the choice was rather ~ le choix était plutôt limité; only a ~ number of players will be successful seul un nombre limité OR un petit nombre de participants gagneront; the play met with only ~ success la pièce n'a connu qu'un succès relatif; to a ~ extent jusqu'à un certain point; they are of ~ intelligence ils ont une intelligence limitée. -**2.** *Am* [train, bus] semi-direct.

limited company *n* société *f* à responsabilité limitée, SARL *f*.

limited edition *n* édition *f* à tirage limité.

limited liability *n* responsabilité *f* limitée.

limiter ['lɪmɪtə'] *n* ELECTRON limiteur *m*.

limiting ['lɪmɪtɪŋ] *adj* contraignant.

limitless ['lɪmɪtlɪs] *adj* illimité; ~ resources des ressources illimitées OR inépuisables; the ~ sea *lit* la mer infinie.

limnology [lɪm'nɒlədʒɪ] *n* limnologie *f*.

limo *inf* ['lɪməʊ] (*pl* limos) = **limousine**.

limousine ['lɪməzi:n] *n* limousine *f*.

limp [lɪmp] ◇ *vi* boiter; [slightly] clopiner; he ~ed into the room il entra dans la pièce en boitant; she was ~ing badly elle boitait beaucoup; the convoy ~ed into harbour *fig* le convoi gagna le port tant bien que mal.

◇ *n*: to walk with a ~ boiter; the accident left him with a ~ depuis son accident il boite; a man with a ~ un boiteux.
◇ *adj* -**1.** [cloth, lettuce] mou; [skin] flasque; a ~ handshake une poignée de main molle; the plants had gone ~ through lack of water les plantes s'étaient étiolées faute d'être arrosées; his body went completely ~ il s'affaissa. -**2.** [book - cover, binding] souple.

limpet ['lɪmpɪt] *n* ZOOL patelle *f*, bernique *f*, chapeau *m* chinois; to hold on to sthg OR to cling to sthg like a ~ se cramponner à qqch de toutes ses forces.

limpet mine *n* mine-ventouse *f*.

limpid ['lɪmpɪd] *adj* limpide.

limply ['lɪmplɪ] *adv* mollement.

limpness ['lɪmpnɪs] *n* [of handshake, bearing] mollesse *f*; [of temperament] manque *m* de vigueur; [of attitude] manque *m* de fermeté.

limp-wristed [-'rɪstɪd] *adj pej* efféminé.

limy ['laɪmɪ] (*compar* limier, *superl* limiest) *adj* -**1.** [containing lime] calcaire. -**2.** [smeared with lime] englué, gluant.

linchpin ['lɪntʃpɪn] *n* -**1.** TECH esse *f* (d'essieu). -**2.** *fig* [person] pivot *m*; it's the ~ of government policy c'est l'axe central de la politique du gouvernement.

Lincoln's Inn ['lɪŋkənz-] *pr n une des quatre «Inns of Court»*.

Lincs. *written abbr of* Lincolnshire.

linctus ['lɪŋktəs] *n* sirop *m* (pour la toux).

Lindbergh ['lɪndbɜːg] *pr n* Lindbergh; the ~ kidnapping le kidnapping Lindbergh.

THE LINDBERGH KIDNAPPING:
Enlèvement et meurtre, en 1932, du fils, âgé de deux ans, de l'aviateur américain Charles Lindbergh. À la suite de cette affaire, qui fut largement exploitée par la presse de l'époque, le kidnapping devint un crime fédéral puni de mort aux États-Unis.

---

linden ['lɪndən] *n*: ~ (tree) tilleul *m*.

line [laɪn] ◇ *n* -**1.** [mark, stroke] ligne *f*, trait *m*; [wrinkle] ride *f*; MATH, SPORT & TV ligne; to draw a ~ tracer OR tirer une ligne; below the ~ ACCTS hors bilan; to score 50 points above/below the ~ [in bridge] marquer 50 points d'honneur/de marche; straight ~ MATH droite *f*; [gen] ligne *f* droite; the first to cross the (finishing) ~ le premier à franchir la ligne d'arrivée; there are five ~s to a stave une portée est constituée de cinq lignes ❑ he parked on a double yellow ~ ≃ il s'est garé en stationnement interdit. -**2.** [path] ligne *f*; light travels in a straight ~ la lumière se propage en ligne droite; it's on a ~ between Houston and Dallas c'est sur la ligne qui va de Houston à Dallas; the two grooves must be exactly in ~ les deux rainures doivent être parfaitement alignées ❑ I don't follow your ~ of thinking je ne suis pas ton raisonnement; ~ of fire ligne de tir; ~ of sight OR of vision ligne de visée; let's try a different ~ of attack essayons une approche différente; it's all in the ~ of duty cela fait partie de mes fonctions; the problems I meet in the ~ of duty les problèmes auxquels je suis confronté dans l'exercice de mes fonctions; to take the ~ of least resistance *Br* choisir la solution de facilité; there's been a terrible mistake somewhere along the ~ il s'est produit une erreur grave quelque part; I'll support them all along OR right down the ~ je les soutiendrai jusqu'au bout OR sur toute la ligne; the population is split along religious ~s la population est divisée selon des critères religieux; he reorganized the company along more rational ~s il a réorganisé l'entreprise sur une base plus rationnelle; we shall take action along the ~s suggested nous agirons dans le sens de ce qui a été proposé; another idea along the same ~s une autre idée dans le même genre; to be on the right ~s être sur la bonne voie. -**3.** [row - side by side] ligne *f*, rang *m*, rangée *f*; [- one behind another] rang *m*, file *f*; stand in ~, children mettez-vous en rang, les enfants; to step into ~ se mettre en rang; a ~ of trees une rangée d'arbres ‖ *Am* [queue] file *f* (d'attente), queue *f*; we joined the ~ at the bus stop nous avons fait la queue à l'arrêt de bus; they wanted to be first in ~ ils voulaient être les premiers dans la file d'attente ‖ *fig*: he's in ~ for promotion il est sur les rangs pour une promotion; he's next in ~ for promotion la prochaine promotion sera pour lui; he's first in ~ for the throne c'est l'héritier du trône. -**4.** *fig* [conformity]: it's in/out of ~ with company policy c'est conforme/ce n'est pas conforme à la politique de la société; it's more or less in ~ with what we'd expected cela correspond plus ou moins à nos prévisions; to bring wages into ~ with inflation actualiser les salaires en fonction de l'inflation; the dissidents have been brought into ~ les dissidents ont été mis au pas; to fall into ~ with government policy accepter la politique gouvernementale; to step out of ~ s'écarter du droit chemin. -**5.** [of writing, text] ligne *f*; a 20-~ program COMPUT un programme de 20 lignes; she gave me 100 ~s SCH elle m'a donné 100 lignes (à faire) ‖ [of poem, song] vers *m*; she quoted a ~ from Wordsworth elle a cité un vers de Wordsworth ‖ THEAT réplique *f*; I only have two ~s in the whole play! je n'ai que deux répliques dans toute la pièce!; he forgot his ~s il a oublié son texte; he gave me the usual ~ about his wife not understanding him il m'a fait son numéro habituel comme quoi sa femme ne le comprend pas; to shoot a ~ *inf* [boast] frimer; [smooth talk] baratiner. -**6.** *inf* [letter] mot *m*; to drop sb a ~ envoyer un mot à qqn. -**7.** [rope] corde *f*; NAUT bout *m*; FISHING ligne *f*; to hang the washing on the ~ mettre le linge à sécher, étendre le linge; clothes OR washing ~ corde à linge. -**8.** [pipe] tuyau *m*; [pipeline] pipeline *m*. -**9.** *Br* RAIL [track] voie *f*; [single rail] rail *m*; the train left the ~ le train a déraillé. -**10.** [travel route] ligne *f*; underground ~ ligne de métro; there's a new coach ~ to London il y a un nouveau service d'autocars pour Londres; to keep the ~s of communication open maintenir ouvertes les lignes de communication ‖ [transport company] compagnie *f*; shipping ~ compagnie de navigation. -**11.** ELEC ligne *f*; the power ~s have been cut les lignes électriques ont été coupées; the ~s are still down after the gale les lignes n'ont pas été rétablies depuis la tempête; the power station comes on ~ in June la centrale entre en service en juin. -**12.** TELEC ligne *f*; the ~ went dead la communication a été coupée; I was on the ~ to Paris je téléphonais à Paris; then a voice came on the other end of the ~ alors une voix a répondu à l'autre bout du fil ❑ a direct ~ to Washington une ligne directe avec Washington; hold the ~ ne quittez pas; on ~ COMPUT en ligne. -**13.** [outline] ligne *f*; the graceful ~ OR ~s of the new model la ligne harmonieuse du nouveau modèle; can you explain the main OR broad ~s of the project to me? pouvez-vous m'expliquer les grandes lignes du projet? -**14.** [policy] ligne *f*; they took a hard OR tough ~ on terrorism ils ont adopté une politique de fermeté envers le terrorisme; the opposition takes a harder ~ on this issue l'opposition a une politique plus dure sur cette question ❑ to follow OR to toe the party ~ suivre la ligne du parti. -**15.** MIL ligne *f*; they struggled vainly to hold the ~ ils ont vainement tenté de maintenir leur position ❑ battle ~s lignes de bataille; to infiltrate enemy ~s infiltrer les lignes ennemies; regiment/ship of the ~ régiment *m*/navire *m* de ligne. -**16.** [boundary] frontière *f*, limite *f*; the distant ~ of the horizon la ligne lointaine de l'horizon ❑ the (dividing) ~ between frankness and rudeness la limite entre la franchise et l'impolitesse; the poverty ~ le seuil de pauvreté; they crossed the state ~ into Nevada ils ont franchi la frontière du Nevada; to cross the Line [equator] traverser l'équateur. -**17.** [field of activity] branche *f*; [job] métier *m*; she's in the same ~ (of work) as you elle travaille dans la même branche que toi; what ~ (of business) are you in?, what's your ~ (of business)? qu'est-ce que vous faites dans la vie?; if you need anything doing in the plumbing ~ si vous avez besoin de faire faire des travaux de plomberie ‖ [field of interest] domaine *m*; that's more in Katy's ~ c'est plus du domaine de Katy; opera isn't really my ~ l'opéra n'est pas vraiment mon genre. -**18.** [range - of products] ligne *f*; a new ~ of office furniture une nouvelle ligne de meubles de bureau; they produce OR do an interesting ~ in chairs ils produisent une gamme intéressante de chaises ❑ product ~ gamme *f* OR ligne de produits. -**19.** [production line] chaîne *f*; the new model will be coming off the ~ in May le nouveau modèle sortira de l'usine en mai. -**20.** [lineage, ancestry] lignée *f*; the Windsor ~ la lignée des Windsor; the title is transmitted by the male ~ le titre se transmet par les hommes; he comes from a long ~ of doctors il est issu d'une longue lignée de médecins. -**21.** *inf* [information]: I'll try and get a ~ on what actually happened j'essaierai d'avoir des tuyaux sur ce qui s'est réellement passé; the police have got a ~ on him la police sait des trucs sur lui.
◇ *vt* -**1.** [road, river] border; the avenue is ~d with trees l'avenue est bordée d'arbres; crowds ~d the streets la foule était OR s'était massée sur les trottoirs. -**2.** [paper] régler, ligner. -**3.** [clothes, curtains] doubler; [container, drawer, cupboard] tapisser, garnir; [brakes] garnir; ~d with silk doublé de soie; the tissue that ~s the digestive tract la paroi interne de l'appareil digestif; the tubes are ~d with plastic l'intérieur des tubes est revêtu d'une couche de plastique; walls ~d with books des murs tapissés de livres ❑ to ~ one's pockets *inf* s'en mettre plein les poches.
◆ **line up** ◇ *vt sep* -**1.** [put in line] aligner, mettre en ligne; he ~d up the troops for inspection il fit aligner les hommes pour passer l'inspection. -**2.** [bring into alignment] aligner; the two grooves must be exactly ~d up les deux rainures doivent être parfaitement alignées; he had the pheasant ~d up in his sights il avait le faisan dans sa ligne de mire. -**3.** *inf* [prepare, arrange] préparer, prévoir; I've got a treat ~d up for the kids j'ai préparé une surprise pour les gosses; he's ~d up an all-star cast for his new film la distribution de son nouveau film ne comprend que des stars.
◇ *vi insep* [stand in line] s'aligner, se mettre en ligne; *Am* [queue up] faire la queue; the Liberals ~d up behind the government *fig* les Libéraux ont apporté leur soutien au gouvernement.

lineage ['lɪnɪɪdʒ] *n* [ancestry] ascendance *f*, famille *f*; [descendants] lignée *f*, descendance *f*; of noble ~ de famille OR d'ascendance noble.

lineal ['lɪnɪəl] *adj* en ligne directe.

lineament ['lɪnɪəmənt] *n lit* trait *m*, linéament *m lit*.

linear ['lɪnɪəʳ] *adj* linéaire.

linear equation *n* équation *f* linéaire.

linear measure *n* mesure *f* linéaire, mesure *f* de longueur.

linear perspective *n* perspective *f* linéaire.

line block *n* TYPO cliché *m* au trait.

line call *n* SPORT décision *f* du juge de ligne.

lined [laɪnd] *adj* -**1.** [paper] réglé. -**2.** [face, skin] ridé. -**3.** [jacket] doublé; [box] tapissé.

line drawing *n* dessin *m* au trait.

line fence *n Am* clôture *f*.

line gauge *n* TYPO typomètre *m*.

line judge *n* SPORT juge *m* de ligne.

lineman ['laɪnmən] (*pl* linemen [-mən]) *n Am* ELEC & TELEC monteur *m* OR ouvrier *m* de ligne.

linen ['lɪnɪn] ◇ *n* -**1.** [fabric] (toile *f* de) lin *m*. -**2.** [sheets, tablecloths, towels etc] linge *m* (de maison); [underclothes] linge *m* (de corps); dirty ~ linge sale; table ~ linge de table.
◇ *comp* de fil, de lin; ~ sheets draps *mpl* de fil; ~ thread fil *m* de lin.

linen basket *n* corbeille *f* à linge.

linen cupboard *n* armoire *f* OR placard *m* à linge.

line-out *n* SPORT touche *f*.

line printer *n* imprimante *f* ligne à ligne.

liner ['laɪnəʳ] *n* -**1.** [ship] paquebot *m* (de grande ligne). -**2.** [eyeliner] eye-liner *m*. -**3.** [for clothing] doublure *f*. -**4.** [plastic bag]: bin OR dustbin ~ sac *m* poubelle. -**5.** TECH chemise *f*.

linesman ['laɪnzmən] (*pl* **linesmen** [-mən]) *n* -**1.** SPORT [in rubgy, football] juge *m* OR arbitre *m* de touche; [in tennis] juge *m* de ligne. -**2.** *Br* ELEC & TELEC monteur *m* OR ouvrier *m* de ligne.

line-up *n* -**1.** [identity parade] séance *f* d'identification; [line of suspects] rangée *f* de suspects. -**2.** [composition]: **a jazz band with a traditional ~** une formation de jazz traditionnelle; **the England ~ for tonight's match** la composition de l'équipe anglaise pour le match de ce soir; **we have an all-star ~ for tonight's programme** nous avons un plateau de vedettes pour l'émission de ce soir.

ling [lɪŋ] *n* -**1.** [sea fish] lingue *f*, julienne *f*; [freshwater fish] lotte *f*. -**2.** [heather] bruyère *f*.

linger ['lɪŋgəʳ] *vi* -**1.** [persist] persister, subsister; **a doubt ~ed (on) in my mind** il subsistait un doute dans mon esprit. -**2.** [tarry] s'attarder, traîner; **we ~ed over lunch** nous nous sommes attardés à table; **a few students ~ed outside the classroom** quelques étudiants s'attardaient devant la salle de cours. -**3.** [stay alive]: **she might ~ on for years yet** il se pourrait qu'elle tienne encore des années.

lingerie ['lænʒərɪ] *n* lingerie *f*.

lingering ['lɪŋgrɪŋ] *adj* [long] long; **he gave her a long ~ look** il lui lança un long regard langoureux; **they had no time for ~ goodbyes** ils n'avaient pas le temps d'échanger des adieux prolongés ‖ [persistent] persistant; **a ~ feeling of dissatisfaction** un irréductible sentiment d'insatisfaction; **a ~ doubt** un doute persistant ‖ [slow] lent; **a ~ death** une mort lente.

lingo *inf* ['lɪŋgəʊ] (*pl* **lingoes**) *n*: **I don't speak the ~** je ne parle pas la langue du pays.

lingua franca [,lɪŋgwə'fræŋkə] (*pl* **lingua francas** OR **linguae francae** [,lɪŋgwiː'fræŋkiː]) *n* lingua franca *f*, langue *f* véhiculaire.

linguist ['lɪŋgwɪst] *n* -**1.** [in foreign languages - student] étudiant *m*, -e *f* en langues étrangères; [- specialist] spécialiste *mf* en langues étrangères; **to be a good ~** être doué pour les langues. -**2.** [in linguistics] linguiste *mf*.

linguistic [lɪŋ'gwɪstɪk] *adj* linguistique.

linguistically [lɪŋ'gwɪstɪklɪ] *adv* linguistiquement.

linguistics [lɪŋ'gwɪstɪks] *n (U)* linguistique *f*.

liniment ['lɪnɪmənt] *n* pommade *f*.

lining ['laɪnɪŋ] *n* -**1.** [of clothes, curtains] doublure *f*. -**2.** [of container, bearing] revêtement *m*; [of brake, clutch] garniture *f*. -**3.** ANAT paroi *f* interne; **the stomach ~** la paroi de l'estomac.

link [lɪŋk] ◇ *n* -**1.** [of chain] chaînon *m*, maillon *m*. -**2.** [bond, relationship] lien *m*; **she's severed all ~s with her family** elle a coupé les ponts avec sa famille; **Britain's trade ~s with Spain** les relations commerciales entre la Grande-Bretagne et l'Espagne; **the ~ between inflation and unemployment** le lien OR rapport entre l'inflation et le chômage. -**3.** [physical connection] liaison *f*; **a road/rail/radio ~** une liaison routière/ferroviaire/radio.
◇ *vt* -**1.** [relate] lier; **the two crimes are ~ed** les deux crimes sont liés; **how would you ~ these two theories?** quel rapport voyez-vous entre ces deux théories? -**2.** [connect physically] relier; **it can be ~ed (up) to a computer** on peut le relier OR connecter à un ordinateur; **they ~ed arms** ils se prirent le bras.
◆ **link up** ◇ *vi insep* -**1.** [meet - persons] se rejoindre; [- troops] effectuer une jonction; [- spacecraft] s'arrimer. -**2.** [form a partnership] s'associer. -**3.** [be connected] se relier; **it can ~ up to a computer** on peut le relier OR connecter à un ordinateur.
◇ *vt sep* relier.

linkage ['lɪŋkɪdʒ] *n* lien *m*, rapport *m*.

linkman ['lɪŋkmən] (*pl* **linkmen** [-mən]) *n* RADIO & TV journaliste *m (qui annonce les reportages des envoyés spéciaux)*.

link road *n* route *f* de jonction.

links [lɪŋks] *npl* (terrain *m* OR parcours *m* de) golf *m*, links *mpl*.

linkup ['lɪŋkʌp] *n* -**1.** [physical connection] liaison *f*; **a telephone/satellite ~** une liaison téléphonique/par satellite. -**2.** [of spacecraft, troops] jonction *f*.

linkwoman ['lɪŋk,wʊmən] (*pl* **linkwomen** [-,wɪmɪn]) *n* journaliste *f (qui annonce les reportages des envoyés spéciaux)*.

linnet ['lɪnɪt] *n* linotte *f*.

lino ['laɪnəʊ] *n Br* lino *m*.

linocut ['laɪnəʊkʌt] *n* linogravure *f*, gravure *f* sur linoléum.

linoleum [lɪ'nəʊljəm] *n* linoléum *m*.

lino tile *n Br* dalle *f* de linoléum.

Linotype ®['laɪnəʊtaɪp] *n* Linotype® *f*.

linseed ['lɪnsiːd] *n* graine *f* de lin.

linseed oil *n* huile *f* de lin.

lint [lɪnt] *n (U)* -**1.** [fabric] tissu *m* gratté; **~ bandage** charpie *f*. -**2.** [fluff] peluches *fpl*.

lintel ['lɪntl] *n* linteau *m*.

lion ['laɪən] *n* -**1.** ZOOL lion *m*; **~ hunter** chasseur *m* de lions ❑ **the ~'s den** l'antre *m* du lion; **to fight like a ~** se battre comme un lion; **to put one's head in the ~'s mouth** se jeter dans la gueule du loup; **the ~'s share** la part du lion. -**2.** *fig* [courageous person] lion *m*, lionne *f*; [celebrity] célébrité *f*; **a literary ~** un grand nom de la littérature.

lion cub *n* lionceau *m*.

lioness ['laɪənes] *n* lionne *f*.

lionhearted ['laɪən,hɑːtɪd] *adj* courageux comme un lion.

lionize, -ise ['laɪənaɪz] *vt* [make a celebrity] célébrer; [treat like a celebrity] porter aux nues.

lion-tamer *n* dompteur *m*, -euse *f* (de lions).

lip [lɪp] *n* -**1.** [human] lèvre *f*; [animal] lèvre *f*, babine *f*; **my ~s are sealed** je ne dirai rien; **her name is on everyone's ~s** son nom est sur toutes les lèvres; **they only pay ~ service to the ideal of solidarity** ils ne souscrivent qu'en paroles à l'idéal de solidarité. -**2.** [of jug] bec *m*; [of cup, bowl] rebord *m*; [of wound] lèvre *f*, bord *m*; [of crater] bord *m*. -**3.** *inf* [impertinence] culot *m*; **enough of your ~!** ne sois pas insolent!

lip gloss *n* brillant *m* à lèvres.

lipid(e) ['lɪpɪd] *n* lipide *m*.

lipoid ['lɪpɔɪd] *adj* lipoïde, lipoïdique.

liposome ['lɪpəsəʊm] *n* liposome *m*.

liposuction ['lɪpəʊ,sʌkʃn] *n* liposuccion *f*.

-lipped [lɪpt] *in cpds*: **thin~** aux lèvres minces.

lip pencil *n* crayon *m* à lèvres.

lippy *inf* ['lɪpɪ] (*compar* **lippier**, *superl* **lippiest**) *adj* insolent, culotté.

lip-read ['lɪpriːd] (*pt* & *pp* **lip-read** [-red]) ◇ *vi* lire sur les lèvres.
◇ *vt* lire sur les lèvres de.

lip-reading *n* lecture *f* sur les lèvres.

lip salve *n* pommade *f* OR baume *m* pour les lèvres.

lip-smacking *inf adj* appétissant, qui met l'eau à la bouche.

lipstick ['lɪpstɪk] *n* -**1.** [substance] rouge *m* à lèvres. -**2.** [stick] (tube *m* de) rouge *m* à lèvres.

liquefaction [,lɪkwɪ'fækʃn] *n* liquéfaction *f*.

liquefy ['lɪkwɪfaɪ] (*pt* & *pp* **liquefied**) ◇ *vt* liquéfier.
◇ *vi* se liquéfier.

liqueur [lɪ'kjʊəʳ] *n* liqueur *f*; **cherry ~** liqueur aux cerises.

liqueur chocolate *n* chocolat *m* à la liqueur.

liqueur glass *n* verre *m* à liqueur.

liquid ['lɪkwɪd] ◇ *adj* -**1.** [fluid] liquide; **~ air/nitrogen/fuel/oxygen** air *m*/azote *m*/combustible *m*/oxygène *m* liquide; **to have a ~ lunch** *hum* boire de l'alcool en guise de déjeuner. -**2.** FIN liquide; **~ assets** liquidités *fpl*. -**3.** [clear - eyes, sound] limpide. -**4.** LING [consonant] liquide.
◇ *n* -**1.** [fluid] liquide *m*. -**2.** LING [consonant] liquide *f*.

liquidate ['lɪkwɪdeɪt] ◇ *vt* -**1.** *euph* [kill, eliminate] liquider, éliminer. -**2.** FIN & JUR [debt, company, estate] liquider; [capital] mobiliser.
◇ *vi* FIN & JUR entrer en liquidation, déposer son bilan.

liquidation [,lɪkwɪ'deɪʃn] *n* -**1.** *euph* [killing, elimination] liquidation *f*. -**2.** FIN & JUR [of debt, company, estate] liquidation *f*; [of capital] mobilisation *f*; **to go into ~** entrer en liquidation, déposer son bilan.

liquidator ['lɪkwɪdeɪtəʳ] *n* liquidateur *m*, -trice *f*.

liquid crystal *n* cristal *m* liquide.

liquid crystal display *n* affichage *m* à cristaux liquides.

liquidity [lɪ'kwɪdətɪ] *n* liquidité *f*.

liquidize, -ise ['lɪkwɪdaɪz] *vt* -**1.** CULIN passer au mixeur. -**2.** PHYS liquéfier.

liquidizer ['lɪkwɪdaɪzəʳ] *n Br* mixer *m*, mixeur *m*.

liquid paraffin *n* huile *f* de paraffine.

liquor ['lɪkəʳ] *n* -**1.** *Am* [alcohol] alcool *m*, boissons *fpl* alcoolisées; **he never touches ~** il ne touche jamais à l'alcool; **to be the worse for ~** être ivre. -**2.** CULIN jus *m*, bouillon *m*. -**3.** PHARM solution *f* aqueuse.
◆ **liquor up** ▽ *Am* ◇ *vt sep* saouler; **to get ~ed up** se pinter OR se beurrer (la gueule).
◇ *vi insep* se biturer.

liquorice *Br*, **licorice** *Am* ['lɪkərɪs] *n* [plant, root] réglisse *f*; [sweet] réglisse *f*; **~ allsorts** *bonbons au réglisse de différentes couleurs*.

liquor store *n Am* magasin *m* de vins et spiritueux; **state ~** *magasin de vins et spiritueux agréé par l'État*.

lira ['lɪərə] (*pl* **lire** [-rɪ] OR **liras**) *n* lire *f*.

Lisbon ['lɪzbən] *pr n* Lisbonne.

lisle [laɪl] *n*: **~ (thread)** fil *m* d'Écosse.

lisp [lɪsp] ◇ *vi* parler avec un cheveu sur la langue, zézayer.
◇ *vt* dire en zézayant.
◇ *n*: **to speak with** OR **to have a ~** avoir un cheveu sur la langue, zézayer.

lissom(e) ['lɪsəm] *adj lit* souple, agile.

list [lɪst] ◇ *n* -**1.** [record] liste *f*; **to make** OR **write a ~** faire OR dresser une liste; **address ~** liste d'adresses; **are you on our mailing ~?** est-ce que vous figurez sur notre fichier? -**2.** [lean] inclinaison *f*; NAUT gîte *f*, bande *f*.
◇ *vt* -**1.** [make list of] dresser la liste de; [enumerate] énumérer; [enter in a list] inscrire (sur une liste); **I've ~ed the things to be done** j'ai dressé une liste de choses à faire; **she ~ed the reasons for her decision** elle a énuméré les raisons pour lesquelles elle avait pris cette décision; **my name isn't ~ed** mon nom ne figure pas sur la liste. -**2.** [classify] classer; **they are ~ed by family name** ils sont classés par nom de famille; **it was officially ~ed as suicide** ce fut officiellement classé comme un suicide. -**3.** COMPUT lister. -**4.** ST. EX [shares] coter.
◇ *vi* [lean] pencher, être incliné; NAUT [ship] gîter, donner de la bande.

listed building ['lɪstɪd-] *n Br* monument *m* classé.

listed securities *npl* valeurs *fpl* cotées en bourse.

listen ['lɪsn] ◇ *vi* -**1.** [to sound] écouter; **~ carefully** écoutez bien; **to ~ to sb/sthg** écouter qqn/qqch; **did you ~ to the news?** as-tu écouté les informations? -**2.** [take notice - of advice] écouter; **if only I'd ~ed to my mother!** si seulement j'avais écouté ma mère OR suivi les conseils de ma mère!; **I told him but he wouldn't ~** je le lui ai dit, mais il ne voulait rien entendre.
◇ *n inf*: **have a ~ to their latest record** écoute un peu leur dernier disque.

◆ **listen (out) for** *vt insep* guetter; she ~s (out) for his steps on the stairs every evening elle guette le bruit de ses pas dans l'escalier tous les soirs; he was ~ing (out) for mistakes il était à l'affût des fautes.

◆ **listen in** *vi insep* -**1.** [to radio] écouter, être à l'écoute; ~ in tomorrow at the same time soyez à l'écoute demain à la même heure. -**2.** [eavesdrop] écouter; it's rude to ~ in on other people's conversations c'est impoli d'écouter les conversations.

◆ **listen up** *inf vi insep Am*: hey you guys, ~ up! hé, écoutez un peu!

listener ['lɪsnəʳ] *n* -**1.** personne *f* qui écoute; he's a good/bad ~ il sait/il ne sait pas écouter (les autres). -**2.** RADIO auditeur *m*, -trice *f*.

listening post ['lɪsnɪŋ-] *n* poste *m* d'écoute.

listing ['lɪstɪŋ] *n* -**1.** [gen - list] liste *f*; [- entry] entrée *f*; I found no ~ for the company in the directory je n'ai pas trouvé la société dans l'annuaire. -**2.** COMPUT listing *m*, listage *m*.

◆ **listings** *npl*: cinéma/TV ~s programme *m* des films/émissions de la semaine.

listless ['lɪstlɪs] *adj* [torpid, unenergetic] apathique, endormi, avachi; [weak] mou, inerte; [bored] indolent, alangui; [indifferent] indifférent, insensible.

listlessly ['lɪstlɪslɪ] *adv* [without energy] sans énergie OR vigueur, avec apathie; [weakly] mollement; [without interest] d'un air absent.

listlessness ['lɪstlɪsnɪs] *n* [lack of energy] manque *m* d'énergie OR de vigueur, apathie *f*; [weakness] mollesse *f*; [boredom] langueur *f*, indolence *f*; [indifference] indifférence *f*.

list price *n* prix *m* du catalogue; I can get 20% off (the) ~ je peux avoir un rabais de 20 % sur le prix de vente.

lists [lɪsts] *npl* lice *f*; to enter the ~ *literal* & *fig* entrer en lice.

lit [lɪt] ◇ *pt* & *pp* → **light**.

◇ *adj* éclairé; the room is well/badly ~ la pièce est bien/mal éclairée.

◇ *n inf* (*abbr of* literature): she teaches English ~ elle enseigne la littérature anglaise.

litany ['lɪtənɪ] (*pl* litanies) *n literal* & *fig* litanie *f*.

liter *Am* = **litre**.

literacy ['lɪtərəsɪ] *n* [of individual] capacité *f* de lire et d'écrire; [of population] alphabétisation *f*; a ~ campaign une campagne d'alphabétisation OR contre l'illettrisme; the work requires a high degree of ~ le poste exige une solide culture générale ❑ adult ~ l'alphabétisation des adultes; computer ~ connaissances *fpl* en informatique.

literal ['lɪtərəl] *adj* [meaning] propre, littéral; [translation] littéral; there was a ~ invasion of tourists il y a eu une véritable invasion de touristes.

literally ['lɪtərəlɪ] *adv* -**1.** [not figuratively] littéralement, au sens propre; [word for word] littéralement; to take sthg ~ prendre qqch au pied de la lettre OR à la lettre; to translate ~ faire une traduction littérale; he was ~ bleeding to death il se vidait de son sang. -**2.** [in exaggeration] littéralement; we've had ~ hundreds of letters nous avons reçu littéralement des centaines de lettres.

literal-minded *adj* sans imagination, terre à terre.

literary ['lɪtərərɪ] *adj* -**1.** [style, work etc] littéraire; a ~ man un homme de lettres; ~ criticism critique *f* littéraire. -**2.** [formal, written - language] littéraire.

literary agent *n* agent *m* littéraire.

literate ['lɪtərət] *adj* -**1.** [able to read and write] capable de lire et d'écrire; only 20% of the population is ~ seuls 20 % de la population savent lire et écrire; to be computer-~ avoir des connaissances en informatique. -**2.** [educated] instruit, cultivé.

-literate *in cpds*: to be computer~ s'y connaître en informatique.

literati [,lɪtə'rɑːtɪ] *npl fml* gens *mpl* de lettres, lettrés *mpl*.

literature ['lɪtrətʃəʳ] *n* (*U*) -**1.** [creative writing] littérature *f*. -**2.** [printed material] documentation *f*; scientific/medical ~ la documentation scientifique/médicale; can you give me some ~? pouvez-vous me donner de la documentation?; sales ~ documentation *f*, brochures *fpl* de vente.

lithe [laɪð] *adj* [movement, person] agile; [body] souple.

lithium ['lɪθɪəm] *n* lithium *m*.

lithograph ['lɪθəgrɑːf] ◇ *n* lithographie *f* (*estampe*).

◇ *vt* lithographier.

lithographic [,lɪθə'græfɪk] *adj* lithographique.

lithography [lɪ'θɒgrəfɪ] *n* lithographie *f* (*procédé*).

Lithuania [,lɪθjʊ'eɪnjə] *pr n* Lituanie *f*; in ~ en Lituanie.

Lithuanian [,lɪθjʊ'eɪnjən] ◇ *n* -**1.** [person] Lituanien *m*, -enne *f*. -**2.** LING lituanien *m*.

◇ *adj* lituanien.

litigant ['lɪtɪgənt] JUR ◇ *n* plaideur *m*, -euse *f*, partie *f*.

◇ *adj* en litige; the ~ parties les parties plaidantes OR en litige.

litigate ['lɪtɪgeɪt] JUR ◇ *vt* contester (en justice).

◇ *vi* plaider, intenter une action en justice.

litigation [,lɪtɪ'geɪʃn] *n* JUR litige *m*; the case went to ~ le cas est passé en justice; they are in ~ ils sont en procès; the issue is still in ~ l'affaire est toujours devant OR entre les mains de la justice.

litigious [lɪ'tɪdʒəs] *adj* -**1.** *fml* & *pej* [fond of lawsuits] procédurier. -**2.** *fml* & *pej* [given to arguing] chicaneur, chicanier. -**3.** JUR litigieux, contentieux.

litmus ['lɪtməs] *n* tournesol *m*.

litmus paper *n* papier *m* de tournesol.

litmus test *n* CHEM réaction *f* au tournesol; *fig* épreuve *f* de vérité.

litotes ['laɪtəʊtiːz] (*pl inv*) *n* litote *f*.

litre *Br*, **liter** *Am* ['liːtəʳ] *n* litre *m*.

litter ['lɪtəʳ] ◇ *n* -**1.** (*U*) [rubbish] détritus *mpl*, ordures *fpl*; [dropped in street] papiers *mpl* (gras); 'no ~' respectez la propreté des lieux. -**2.** [clutter] fouillis *m*; his desk was covered in a ~ of papers son bureau était envahi par les papiers. -**3.** ZOOL portée *f*. -**4.** [material - to bed animals] litière *f*; [- to protect plants] paille *f*, paillis *m*; cat ~ litière pour chats. -**5.** [sedan chair] litière *f*, palanquin *m*.

◇ *vt* -**1.** [make untidy - public place] laisser des détritus dans; [- house, room] mettre du désordre dans; don't ~ the table (up) with your tools n'encombre pas la table avec tes outils. -**2.** (*usu pass*) [cover, strew] joncher, couvrir; *fig* parsemer; beer cans ~ed the dance floor la piste de danse était jonchée de cannettes de bière; his life is ~ed with failed love affairs sa vie est jalonnée d'échecs amoureux.

◇ *vi* ZOOL mettre bas.

litter bin *n Br* poubelle *f*.

litterbug ['lɪtəbʌg] *Am*, **litter lout** *inf Br* *n personne qui jette des papiers ou des détritus par terre*.

little[1] ['lɪtl] *adj* -**1.** [in size, quantity] petit; a ~ group of children un petit groupe d'enfants; would you like a ~ drop of gin? tu veux un peu de gin?; he has a ~ antiques shop il a une petite boutique d'antiquités; a ~ smile/sob/cry un petit sourire/sanglot/cri; would you like a ~ something to eat? voudriez-vous manger un petit quelque chose? ❑ the ~ hand [of clock] la petite aiguille. -**2.** [young - child, animal] petit; a ~ boy un petit garçon; a ~ girl une petite fille; when I was ~ quand j'étais petit ‖ [younger] petit; my ~ sister ma petite sœur. -**3.** [short - time, distance]: we spent a ~ time in France nous avons passé quelque temps en France; a ~ while ago [moments ago] il y a quelques instants; [days, months ago] il y a quelque temps; she only stayed (for) a ~ while elle n'est pas restée très longtemps; the shop is a ~ way along the street le magasin se trouve un peu plus loin dans la rue. -**4.** [unimportant] petit; we had a ~ difference of opinion nous avons eu un petit différend; they had a ~ argument ils se sont un peu disputés. -**5.** [expressing affection, pleasure, irritation] petit; what a nice ~ garden! quel joli petit jardin!; I've got my own ~ house in Oxford now j'ai ma petite maison à moi à Oxford maintenant; a ~ old lady une petite vieille; poor ~ thing! pauvre petit!; she's a ~ horror! c'est une petite peste!; you're a filthy ~ pig! *inf* espèce de petit cochon!; I'm used to his ~ ways je connais ses petites habitudes; I've sussed his ~ game! *inf* j'ai compris son petit jeu!

little[2] ['lɪtl] (*compar* less [les], *superl* least [liːst])

◇ *det* [opposite of 'much'] peu de; very ~ time/money/water très peu de temps/d'argent/d'eau; I had ~ time to relax je n'ai guère eu le temps de me détendre; I watch very ~ television je regarde très peu la télévision; I'm afraid there's ~ hope left je crains qu'il n'y ait plus beaucoup d'espoir; to have ~ chance of doing sthg avoir peu de chances de faire qqch; they have so ~ freedom ils ont si peu de liberté; there was too ~ money il y avait trop peu d'argent; with no ~ difficulty *fml* non sans peine.

◇ *pron* -**1.** [small amount] pas grand-chose; there's ~ one can say il n'y a pas grand-chose à dire; I see very ~ of him now je ne le vois plus que très rarement; very ~ is known about his childhood on ne sait pas grand-chose OR on ne sait que très peu de choses sur son enfance; I gave her as ~ as possible je lui ai donné le minimum; you may be paid as ~ as £3 an hour tu ne seras peut-être payé que 3 livres de l'heure; so ~ si peu; you know so ~ about me tu ne sais presque rien de moi; too ~ trop peu; to make ~ of [fail to understand] ne pas comprendre grand-chose à; [not emphasize] minimiser; [scorn] faire peu de cas de. -**2.** [certain amount]: a ~ of everything un peu de tout; the ~ I saw looked excellent le peu que j'en ai vu paraissait excellent.

◇ *adv* -**1.** [to a limited extent]: it's ~ short of madness ça frise la folie; he's ~ more than a waiter il n'est rien de plus qu'un simple serveur. -**2.** [rarely] peu; we go there as ~ as possible nous y allons le moins possible; we talk very ~ now nous ne nous parlons presque plus. -**3.** [never] *fml*: I ~ thought OR ~ did I think we would be friends one day jamais je n'aurais cru que nous serions amis un jour.

◆ **a little** ◇ *det phr* un peu de; there's still a ~ time/bread left il reste encore un peu de temps/pain; I speak a ~ French je parle quelques mots de français ❑ a ~ learning is a dangerous thing *prov* il est moins dangereux de ne rien savoir que d'en savoir trop peu.

◇ *pron phr* un peu.

◇ *adv phr* -**1.** [slightly] un peu; he laughed a ~ il a ri un peu; I'm a ~ tired je suis un peu fatigué; a ~ too late un peu trop tard; a ~ less/more sugar un (petit) peu moins/plus de sucre; not even a ~ interested pas le moins du monde intéressé. -**2.** [for a short time or distance] un peu; I walked on a ~ j'ai marché encore un peu; I paused there (for) a ~ and then said... j'ai marqué un petit temps d'arrêt, puis j'ai dit...

◆ **a little bit** *inf adv phr* = **a little**.

◆ **little by little** *adv phr* peu à peu, petit à petit; he pieced the story together ~ by ~ il reconstitua l'histoire peu à peu.

little- *in cpds*: a ~understood phenomenon un phénomène (encore) mal compris; a ~explored area une zone presque inexplorée OR (encore) peu explorée.

Little Bear *pr n Br* ASTRON: the ~ la Petite Ourse.

Little Bighorn ['lɪtl'bɪg,hɔːn] *pr n*: the battle of the ~ la bataille de Little Bighorn.

THE BATTLE OF THE LITTLE BIGHORN: Ultime bataille du général américain Custer, qui lança sa cavalerie aux trousses des Indiens Sioux de Sitting Bull et Crazy Horse dans l'État du Montana, en 1876. Custer ayant sous-estimé les forces indiennes, celles-ci firent face et massacrèrent la troupe entière. Cet épisode est également connu sous le nom de «Custer's last stand».

little-boy *adj* de petit garçon, de garçonnet; [haircut] à la garçonne.

Little Dipper *Am* ASTRON = **Little Bear**.

little end *n Br* AUT pied *m* de bielle.

little Englander *n Anglais borné*.

little finger *n* auriculaire *m*, petit doigt *m*.

little-girl *adj* de petite fille, de fillette.

little-known *adj* peu connu.

Little League *pr n Am* SPORT *championnat de baseball pour les jeunes de 8 à 12 ans*.

little owl *n* chevêche *f*.

little people *npl Ir*: the ~ les lutins *mpl*.

little toe *n* petit orteil *m*.

little woman *n* -**1.** *dated* [wife]: the ~ ma/ta/sa tendre moitié *f*. -**2.** *pej* [helpless woman]: she plays the ~ elle joue les faibles femmes.

littoral ['lɪtərəl] ◇ *adj* littoral.
◇ *n* littoral *m*.

liturgic(al) [lɪ'tɜːdʒɪk(l)] *adj* liturgique.

liturgy ['lɪtədʒɪ] (*pl* **liturgies**) *n* liturgie *f*.

livable ['lɪvəbl] *adj* -**1.** [inhabitable] habitable; **we're trying to make the house ~ (in)** nous essayons de rendre la maison habitable. -**2.** [bearable] supportable; **his visits made her life ~** ses visites lui ont rendu la vie supportable; **she's not ~ with** *inf* elle est invivable.

live¹ [lɪv] ◇ *vi* -**1.** [be or stay alive] vivre; **plants need oxygen to ~** les plantes ont besoin d'oxygène pour vivre; **as long as I ~** tant que je vivrai, de mon vivant; **was she still living when her grandson was born?** est-ce qu'elle était encore en vie quand son petit-fils est né?; **he hasn't long to ~** il ne lui reste pas beaucoup de temps à vivre; **she didn't ~ long after her son died** elle n'a pas survécu longtemps à son fils; **the doctors think she'll ~** les médecins pensent qu'elle vivra; **you'll ~!** *iron* tu n'en mourras pas!; **I won't ~ to see them grow up** je ne vivrai pas assez vieux pour les voir grandir; **to ~ on borrowed time** être en sursis *fig*; **to ~ to a ripe old age** vivre vieux OR jusqu'à un âge avancé || *fig*: **the dialogue is what makes the characters ~** ce sont les dialogues qui donnent de la vie aux personnages; **your words will ~ in our hearts/memories** vos paroles resteront à jamais dans nos cœurs/notre mémoire. -**2.** [have a specified way of life] vivre; **to ~ dangerously** vivre dangereusement; **they ~d happily ever after** ils vécurent heureux jusqu'à la fin de leurs jours; **he ~s by the rules** il mène une vie bien rangée; **the rules we all ~ by** les règles auxquelles nous nous plions tous; **she ~d by her wits** elle vivait d'expédients; **she ~s for her children/for skiing** elle ne vit que pour ses enfants/que pour le ski; **he ~d for music** il ne vivait que pour la musique; **to ~ in poverty/luxury** vivre dans la pauvreté/le luxe; **to ~ in fear** vivre dans la peur; **he ~s in the past** il vit dans le passé; **we ~ in uncertain times** nous vivons une époque incertaine; **he ~s in that shirt!** *hum* il a cette chemise sur le dos en permanence! ❑ **~ and let ~!** *prov* laisse faire!; **well, you ~ and learn!** on en apprend tous les jours! -**3.** [reside] habiter; **where does she ~?** où habite-t-elle?; **they have nowhere to ~** ils sont à la rue; **the giant tortoise ~s mainly in the Galapagos** la tortue géante vit surtout aux Galapagos; **they ~ in Rome** ils habitent (à) Rome, ils vivent à Rome; **to ~ in a flat/a castle** habiter (dans) un appartement/un château; **I ~ in OR on Bank Street** j'habite Bank Street; **they ~ in OR on my street** ils habitent (dans) ma rue; **she ~s on the ground floor** elle habite au rez-de-chaussée; **he practically ~s in OR at the library** il passe sa vie à la bibliothèque; **do you ~ with your parents?** habitez-vous chez vos parents?; **to ~ in sin with sb** *dated* OR *hum* vivre dans le péché avec qqn. -**4.** [support o.s.] vivre; **they don't earn enough to ~** ils ne gagnent pas de quoi vivre; **he ~s by teaching** il gagne sa vie en enseignant; **the tribe ~s by hunting** la tribu vit de la chasse; **how does she ~ on that salary?** comment s'en sort-elle avec ce salaire? -**5.** [obtain food] se nourrir; **we've been living out of cans OR tins lately** on se nourrit de conserves depuis quelque temps; **he was reduced to living out of rubbish bins** il en était réduit à fouiller les poubelles pour se nourrir. -**6.** [exist fully, intensely] vivre; **she really knows how to ~** elle sait vraiment profiter de la vie; **let's ~ for the moment OR for today!** vivons l'instant présent!; **if you haven't been to New York, you haven't ~d!** si tu n'es jamais allé à New York tu n'as rien vu!
◇ *vt* vivre; **to ~ a life of poverty** vivre dans la pauvreté; **to ~ a solitary life** mener une vie solitaire; **to ~ a lie** être dans une situation fausse; **she ~d the life of a film star for six years** elle a vécu comme une star de cinéma pendant six ans ❑ **to ~ it up** *inf* faire la fête; **my father ~s and breathes golf** mon père ne vit que pour le golf.
◆ **live down** *vt sep* [recover from - error, disgrace]: **they'll never let him ~ that down** ils ne lui passeront OR pardonneront jamais cela; **if I forget her birthday, I'll never ~ it down!** si j'oublie son anniversaire, elle ne me le pardonnera jamais!; **you'll never ~ this down!** [ridicule] tu n'as pas fini d'en entendre parler!
◆ **live in** *vi insep* -**1.** [domestic] être logé et nourri; [worker, nurse] être logé OR habiter sur place; **all their farm hands ~ in** tous leurs ouvriers agricoles sont logés sur place. -**2.** [pupil] être interne.
◆ **live off** *vt insep* -**1.** [sponge off] vivre aux crochets de; **he ~s off his parents** il vit aux crochets de ses parents. -**2.** [savings] vivre de; [nuts, berries] se nourrir de; **they ~ off the fruit of other people's labours** ils vivent du produit du travail d'autrui; **to ~ off the land** vivre de la terre.
◆ **live on** ◇ *vi insep* [person] continuer à vivre; [custom, ideal] persister; **she ~d on to the end in the same house** elle a vécu dans la même maison jusqu'à sa mort; **his memory ~s on** son souvenir est encore vivant.
◇ *vt insep* -**1.** [food] vivre de, se nourrir de; **to ~ on fruit and vegetables** vivre de fruits et de légumes. -**2.** [salary] vivre de; **his pension is all they have to ~ on** ils n'ont que sa retraite pour vivre; **to ~ on $800 a month** vivre avec 800 dollars par mois. -**3.** *fig*: **to ~ on one's wits** vivre d'expédients; **to ~ on one's name** vivre sur sa réputation.
◆ **live out** ◇ *vt sep* -**1.** [survive]: **will we ~ out the century?** verrons-nous la fin de ce siècle? -**2.** [spend] passer; **she ~d out the rest of her life in Spain** elle a passé le reste de sa vie en Espagne. -**3.** [fulfil] vivre; **he ~d out his destiny** sa destinée s'est accomplie, il a suivi son destin; **to ~ out one's fantasies** réaliser ses rêves.
◇ *vi insep*: **the maid ~s out** la bonne ne loge pas sur place; **he studies here but ~s out** il est étudiant ici mais il n'habite pas sur le campus.
◆ **live through** *vt insep* connaître; **they've ~d through war and famine** ils ont connu la guerre et la famine.
◆ **live together** *vi insep* [as a couple] vivre ensemble, cohabiter.
◆ **live up to** *vt insep* [name, reputation] se montrer à la hauteur de, mériter; [expectation] répondre à; **we have a reputation to ~ up to!** nous avons une réputation à défendre!; **the holiday didn't ~ up to our expectations** les vacances n'étaient pas à la hauteur de nos espérances.
◆ **live with** *vt insep* -**1.** [cohabit with] vivre avec; **she ~d with him for a couple of years before they got married** elle a vécu avec lui pendant quelques années avant qu'ils se marient. -**2.** [put up with]: **she's not easy to ~ with** elle n'est pas facile à vivre; **I don't like the situation, but I have to ~ with it** cette situation ne me plaît pas, mais je n'ai pas le choix; **I couldn't ~ with myself if I didn't tell him the truth** je ne supporterais pas de ne pas lui dire la vérité.

live² [laɪv] ◇ *adj* -**1.** [alive - animal, person] vivant; **the ~ weight of the animal** le poids de l'animal sur pied; **a real ~ cowboy** *inf* un cowboy, un vrai de vrai ❑ **~ births** naissances *fpl* viables; **~ yoghurt** yaourt *m* actif. -**2.** MUS, RADIO & TV [programme, interview, concert] en direct; **~ pictures from Mars** des images en direct de Mars; **Sinatra ~ at the Palladium** Sinatra en concert au Palladium; **recorded before a ~ audience** enregistré en public ❑ **~ music** musique *f* live; **~ recording** enregistrement *m* live OR public. -**3.** ELEC [connected] sous tension; **~ circuit** circuit *m* alimenté OR sous tension. -**4.** [unexploded] non explosé; **~ ammunition** balles *fpl* réelles. -**5.** [still burning - coals, embers] ardent. -**6.** [not extinct - volcano] actif. -**7.** [controversial] controversé; **a ~ issue** un sujet controversé.
◇ *adv* en direct; **to perform ~** [singer, group] chanter en direct; **the match can be seen/is going out ~ at 3.30 p.m.** on peut suivre le match/le match est diffusé en direct à 15 h 30.

liveable ['lɪvəbl] = **livable**.

livebait ['laɪvbeɪt] *n* [in fishing] vif *m*, appât *m* vivant.

lived-in ['lɪvdɪn] *adj* [comfortable] confortable; [occupied] habité; **the room had a nice ~ feel** on sentait que la pièce était habitée.

live-in ['lɪvɪn] *adj* [maid] logé et nourri; [nurse, governess] à demeure; **his ~ girlfriend** sa compagne, la femme avec qui il vit; **she has a ~ lover** son ami habite chez elle.

livelihood ['laɪvlɪhʊd] *n (U)* moyens *mpl* d'existence, gagne-pain *m inv*; **to lose one's ~** perdre son gagne-pain; **writing isn't a hobby, it's my ~** écrire n'est pas un passe-temps, c'est mon gagne-pain OR mon métier.

liveliness ['laɪvlɪnɪs] *n* [of person] vivacité *f*; [of conversation, party] animation *f*; [of debate, style] vigueur *f*; [of music, dance] gaieté *f*, allégresse *f*; [of colours] éclat *m*, gaieté *f*.

livelong ['lɪvlɒŋ] *adj lit*: **all the ~ day** toute la journée, tout au long du jour.

lively ['laɪvlɪ] (*compar* **livelier**, *superl* **liveliest**) *adj* -**1.** [full of life - person] vif, plein d'entrain; [- kitten, puppy] plein de vie, espiègle; [- horse] fringant; [- music] gai, entraînant; **she's ~ company** on ne s'ennuie pas avec elle. -**2.** [keen - mind, curiosity, imagination] vif; **to take a ~ interest in sthg** s'intéresser vivement à qqch. -**3.** [exciting - place, event, discussion] animé; **a very ~ debate** un débat très animé; **the town gets a bit livelier in summer** la ville s'anime un peu en été; **a ~ performance** une interprétation très enlevée. -**4.** [eventful - day, time] mouvementé, agité; **things got ~ when the police arrived** il y a eu de l'animation quand la police est arrivée; **look ~!** *inf Br* grouille-toi! -**5.** [brisk - pace] vif. -**6.** [vivid - colour] vif, éclatant.

liven ['laɪvn] *vi Am* [respond]: **I didn't ~ to his plan** son projet n'a pas éveillé mon intérêt.
◆ **liven up** ◇ *vt sep* -**1.** [make cheerful - person, room] égayer. -**2.** [stimulate, make interesting] animer; **her arrival ~ed the party up** son arrivée a mis un peu d'animation dans la soirée; **they need to ~ up their image** ils auraient besoin de rafraîchir leur image de marque.
◇ *vi insep* s'animer.

live oak *n* chêne *m* vert.

liver ['lɪvəʳ] *n* -**1.** ANAT foie *m*; **~ complaint** maladie *f* du foie. -**2.** CULIN foie *m*; **~ pâté** pâté *m* de foie. -**3.** [colour] rouge brun *m inv*, brun roux *m inv*. -**4.** [person]: **fast OR high ~** fêtard *m*, -e *f*, noceur *m*, -euse *f*.

liver fluke *n* VETER grande douve *f*.

liveried ['lɪvərɪd] *adj* en livrée.

liverish ['lɪvərɪʃ] *adj* -**1.** *inf* [ill]: to be OR to feel ~ avoir mal au foie. -**2.** [peevish] irritable, bilieux.

Liverpool ['lɪvəpu:l] *pr n* Liverpool.

Liverpudlian [,lɪvə'pʌdlɪən] ◇ *n habitant de Liverpool.*
◇ *adj* de Liverpool.

liver salts *npl* lithiné *m.*

liver sausage *n* pâté *m* de foie.

liver spot *n* tache *f* de vieillesse.

liverwort ['lɪvəwɜ:t] *n* BOT hépatique *f.*

liverwurst ['lɪvəwɜ:st] *Am* = **liver sausage**.

livery ['lɪvərɪ] (*pl* **liveries**) *n* -**1.** [uniform] livrée *f.* -**2.** [of company] couleurs *fpl*; the cars have been painted in the new company ~ les voitures ont été peintes aux nouvelles couleurs de la maison.

livery company *n Br* confrérie *f (de la cité de Londres).*

liveryman ['lɪvərɪmən] (*pl* **liverymen** [-mən]) *n Br* [member of livery company] membre *m* d'une confrérie londonienne.

livery stable *n* [for boarding] écurie *f* prenant des chevaux en pension; [for hiring] écurie *f* de chevaux de louage.

lives [laɪvs] *pl* → **life**.

livestock ['laɪvstɒk] *n* bétail *m*, cheptel *m.*

live wire *n* -**1.** ELEC fil *m* sous tension. -**2.** *inf fig*: she's a real ~ elle déborde d'énergie.

livid ['lɪvɪd] *adj* -**1.** [blue-grey] livide; he went ~ with rage il a blêmi de rage; a ~ sky un ciel de plomb. -**2.** *inf* [angry] furax.

living ['lɪvɪŋ] ◇ *n* -**1.** [livelihood] vie *f*; I have to work for a ~ je suis obligé de travailler pour vivre; what do you do for a ~? qu'est-ce que vous faites dans la vie?; she made a (good) ~ as a pianist elle gagnait (bien) sa vie comme pianiste; you can't make a decent ~ in this business on gagne mal sa vie OR on a du mal à gagner sa vie dans ce métier. -**2.** [life, lifestyle] vie *f*; come to California where the ~ is easy venez en Californie, la vie y est facile; plain ~ la vie simple. -**3.** *Br* RELIG bénéfice *m.*
◇ *adj* -**1.** [alive] vivant; the study of ~ organisms l'étude des organismes vivants; he has no ~ relatives il n'a plus de famille; who's the greatest ~ boxer? quel est le plus grand boxeur vivant? ❑ it was the worst storm in ~ memory de mémoire d'homme on n'avait jamais vu une tempête aussi violente; I didn't see a ~ soul je n'ai pas vu âme qui vive; she's ~ proof that the treatment works elle est la preuve vivante que le traitement est efficace; they made her life a ~ hell ils lui ont rendu la vie infernale; the ~ dead les morts vivants *mpl*; ~ death vie *f* de souffrances; his life became a ~ death sa vie ne fut plus qu'une longue souffrance; to be the ~ image of sb être le portrait vivant de qqn. -**2.** GEOL: the ~ rock la roche non exploitée; sculpted from the ~ rock taillé à même le roc.
◇ *npl*: the ~ les vivants *mpl.*
◇ *comp* -**1.** [conditions] de vie; ~ standards niveau *m* de vie. -**2.** [place]: the ~ area is separated from the bedrooms la partie séjour est séparée des chambres; ~ quarters partie *f* habitée; these are the crew's ~ quarters ce sont les quartiers de l'équipage.

living-in *adj Br* [maid, cook] logé sur place.

living room *n* (salle *f* de) séjour *m.*

living space *n* espace *m* vital.

living wage *n*: a ~ le minimum vital; £400 a month isn't a ~ on ne peut pas vivre avec 400 livres par mois.

Livy ['lɪvɪ] *pr n* Tite-Live.

lizard ['lɪzəd] ◇ *n* lézard *m.*
◇ *comp* [belt, shoes] en lézard.

llama ['lɑ:mə] *n* ZOOL lama *m.*

LLB (*abbr of* Bachelor of Laws) *n (titulaire d'une) licence de droit.*

LLD (*abbr of* Doctor of Laws) *n docteur en droit.*

LMT (*abbr of* Local Mean Time) *n heure locale.*

lo [ləʊ] *interj* -**1.** *arch* OR *lit* regardez!, voyez! -**2.** *phr*: and ~ and behold there he was! et voilà, il était là!

loach [ləʊtʃ] *n* loche *f.*

load [ləʊd] ◇ *vt* -**1.** [person, animal, vehicle] charger; to ~ sthg with sthg charger qqch sur qqch; ~ the bags into the car chargez OR mettez les sacs dans la voiture; the ship is ~ing grain on est en train de charger le navire de céréales; she left ~ed with presents elle est repartie les bras chargés de cadeaux; he's trying to ~ the work (off) onto me il essaie de se décharger de son travail sur moi. -**2.** [camera, gun, machine] charger; ~! take aim! fire! chargez! en joue! feu!; to ~ a film/tape mettre une pellicule/une cassette; ~ the cassette into the recorder introduisez la cassette dans le magnétophone; to ~ a program (into memory) COMPUT charger un programme (en mémoire). -**3.** [insurance premium] majorer, augmenter. -**4.** *phr*: to ~ the dice piper les dés; to ~ the dice against sb *fig* défavoriser qqn; the dice are ~ed against us nous n'aurons pas la partie facile.
◇ *vi* -**1.** [receive freight] charger; the ship is ~ing le navire est en cours de chargement; the tankers ~ off shore les pétroliers font le chargement en mer. -**2.** [camera, gun] se recharger; [computer program] se charger.
◇ *n* -**1.** [cargo] charge *f*, chargement *m*; [carrying capacity] charge *f*; 'maximum ~ 5 tonnes' 'charge maximum 5 tonnes'; a ~ of gravel un chargement de gravier; one horse can't pull such a heavy ~ un seul cheval ne peut pas tirer une charge aussi lourde; a lorry-~ of supplies un (plein) camion d'approvisionnements; we moved all the stuff in ten ~s nous avons tout transporté en dix voyages. -**2.** *fig* [burden] fardeau *m*, charge *f*; the reforms should lighten the ~ of classroom teachers les réformes devraient faciliter la tâche des enseignants; hire somebody to share the ~ embauchez quelqu'un pour vous faciliter la tâche ❑ that's a ~ off my mind! me voilà soulagé d'un poids! -**3.** [batch of laundry] machine *f*; I've two more ~s to do j'ai encore deux machines à faire. -**4.** ELEC, CONSTR & TECH charge *f*. -**5.** *phr*: get a ~ of this *inf* [look] vise un peu ça; [listen] écoute-moi ça; he has a ~ on, he's carrying a ~ ▽ *Am* il est complètement bourré; to shoot one's ~ ▼ [ejaculate] décharger.
◇ *comp* COMPUT [program] de chargement; [module] chargeable; ~ mode mode *m* chargement.

◆ **a load of** *inf det phr*: what a ~ of rubbish! *inf Br* c'est vraiment n'importe quoi!

◆ **loads** *inf adv* beaucoup.

◆ **loads of** *inf det phr* des tas OR des masses de; it'll be ~s of fun ça va être super marrant; it'll be ~s of work on va bosser comme des malades; she's got ~s of money elle est bourrée de fric, elle a un fric monstre.

◆ **load down** *vt sep* charger (lourdement); he was ~ed down with packages il avait des paquets plein les bras; I'm ~ed down with work je suis surchargé de travail.

◆ **load up** ◇ *vt sep* charger; ~ the wheelbarrow up with bricks remplissez la brouette de briques.
◇ *vi insep* charger.

load-bearing *adj* [wall] porteur.

loaded ['ləʊdɪd] *adj* -**1.** [laden] chargé; is the lorry fully ~? le camion est-il vraiment plein? -**2.** *fig*: to be ~ with être chargé de OR plein de; his writing is ~ with metaphors ses textes sont pleins de métaphores; she's ~ with talent elle est bourrée de talent. -**3.** [gun, camera] chargé. -**4.** [dice] pipé. -**5.** [statement, comment] insidieux; ~ question question *f* piège. -**6.** *inf* [rich] plein aux as. -**7.** ▽ [drunk] plein, bourré; [high on drugs] défoncé, cassé.

loader ['ləʊdə^r] *n* -**1.** [person] chargeur *m*, -euse *f*. -**2.** ELEC, MIL & PHOT [device] chargeur *m*. -**3.** CONSTR [machine] chargeuse *f*, loader *m*. -**4.** COMPUT (programme *m*) chargeur *m*.

loading ['ləʊdɪŋ] *n* [of vehicle, machine, gun, computer program] chargement *m*.

loading bay *n* aire *f* de chargement.

load line *n* NAUT ligne *f* de charge.

loads *inf* [ləʊdz] *adv* vachement; it's ~ easier than I thought c'est vachement plus facile qu[e] je croyais; it'll cost ~ ça va coûter un max o[u] vachement cher.

loadstar ['ləʊdstɑ:^r] = **lodestar**.

loadstone ['ləʊdstəʊn] = **lodestone**.

loaf [ləʊf] (*pl* **loaves** [ləʊvz]) ◇ *n* -**1.** [of bread] pain *m*; [large round loaf] miche *f*; two loaves (o[f] bread) please deux pains, s'il vous plaît. -**2.** *ph[r]*: use your ~! *inf Br* fais travailler tes méninges.
◇ *vi inf* fainéanter, traîner; I spent the da[y] ~ing about OR around the house j'ai passé l[a] journée à traîner chez moi.

loafer ['ləʊfə^r] *n* -**1.** *inf* [person] fainéant *m*, -e -**2.** [shoe] mocassin *m*.

loam [ləʊm] *n* -**1.** AGR & HORT terreau *m* -**2.** CONSTR pisé *m*.

loamy ['ləʊmɪ] (*compar* **loamier**, *superl* **loamiest**) *adj* [soil] riche en terreau.

loan [ləʊn] ◇ *n* -**1.** [money lent] prêt *m*; [money borrowed] emprunt *m*; a £500 ~ un prêt d[e] 500 livres; he asked me for a ~ il m'a demand[é] de lui prêter de l'argent; student ~s des prêt[s] aux étudiants. -**2.** [act of lending]: may I have th[e] ~ of your typewriter? *Br* peux-tu me prêter t[a] machine à écrire?; give me a ~ of your scissor[s] *inf Br* prête-moi tes ciseaux; I have three book[s] on ~ from the library j'ai emprunté trois livre[s] à la bibliothèque; the book you want is out o[n] ~ le livre que vous voulez est sorti; the pictur[e] is on ~ to an American museum le tableau [a] été prêté à un musée américain; she's on ~ from head office le siège l'a envoyée chez nou[s] pour un temps. -**3.** = **loanword**.
◇ *vt* prêter; he asked me to ~ him £20/m[y] car il m'a demandé de lui prêter 20 livres/m[a] voiture.

loan collection *n* collection *f* en prêt.

loan shark *n pej* usurier *m*, -ère *f*.

loan translation *n* LING calque *m*.

loanword ['ləʊnwɜ:d] *n* LING (mot *m* d') em[-]prunt *m*.

loath [ləʊθ] *adj*: to be ~ to do sthg ne pas êtr[e] disposé à faire qqch; I'm very ~ to admit it j'[a] beaucoup de mal à l'admettre; they were ~ t[o] leave ils étaient peu disposés à partir; I am somewhat ~ to contradict you, but... [j]e n'aime pas vous contredire, mais...; nothing ~ avec plaisir, très volontiers.

loathe [ləʊð] *vt* détester; I ~ having to get u[p] in the mornings j'ai horreur d'être obligé de m[e] lever le matin; I ~ being mistaken for a touris[t] je déteste OR j'ai horreur qu'on me prenne pou[r] un touriste; you know how much I ~ him t[u] sais à quel point je le déteste.

loathing ['ləʊðɪŋ] *n* aversion *f*, répugnance *f*; have an absolute ~ for people like them j'[a]i horreur des gens comme eux; it fills me with ~ ça me révolte.

loathsome ['ləʊðsəm] *adj* [behaviour] abomina[-]ble; [person] détestable.

loaves [ləʊvz] *pl* → **loaf**.

lob [lɒb] (*pt* & *pp* **lobbed**, *cont* **lobbing**)
◇ *n* SPORT lob *m*.
◇ *vt* -**1.** [throw] lancer; he lobbed the ston[e] into the air il envoya la pierre en l'air; ~ m[e] those cigarettes *inf* balance-moi ces cigarettes -**2.** SPORT [ball] envoyer haut; [opponent] lober she lobbed the ball over my head elle m'a lobé to ~ a goalkeeper lober un gardien de but.
◇ *vi* SPORT [player] faire un lob.

lobby ['lɒbɪ] (*pl* **lobbies**, *pt* & *pp* **lobbied**
◇ *n* -**1.** [in hotel] hall *m*; THEAT foyer *m*; [in larg[e] house, apartment block] entrée *f*. -**2.** POL [pressur[e] group] groupe *m* de pression, lobby *m*; the eco[l]ogy ~ le lobby écologiste || [action] pression [f] yesterday's ~ of parliament la pression exe[r]cée hier sur le parlement; the nurses' ~ fo[r] increased pay la pression exercée par les infi[r]mières pour obtenir une augmentation de sa[-]laire. -**3.** *Br* POL [hall] salle *f* des pas perdus.

◇ *vi*: ecologists are ~ing for the closure of the plant les écologistes font pression pour obtenir la fermeture de la centrale; he's being paid to ~ on behalf of the dairy farmers il est payé par les producteurs laitiers pour faire pression en leur faveur.
◇ *vt* [person, parliament] exercer une pression sur; a group of teachers came to ~ the minister un groupe d'enseignants est venu faire pression sur le ministre.

lobby correspondent *n Br* POL journaliste *mf* parlementaire.

lobbying ['lɒbɪɪŋ] *n (U)* POL pressions *fpl*; there has been intense ~ against the bill il y a eu de fortes pressions pour que le projet de loi soit retiré.

lobbyist ['lɒbɪɪst] *n* lobbyiste *mf*, membre *m* d'un groupe de pression.

lobe [ləʊb] *n* ANAT, BOT & RADIO lobe *m*.

lobectomy [ləʊ'bektəmɪ] (*pl* lobectomies) *n* lobectomie *f*.

lobelia [lə'biːljə] *n* BOT lobélie *f*.

lobotomize, -ise [lə'bɒtəmaɪz] *vt* pratiquer une lobotomie sur.

lobotomized *inf* [lə'bɒtəmaɪzd] *adj Am* apathique, éteint; he acts like he's ~ on dirait qu'il est tombé sur la tête.

lobotomy [lə'bɒtəmɪ] (*pl* lobotomies) *n* lobotomie *f*, leucotomie *f*.

lobster ['lɒbstəʳ] (*pl inv* OR lobsters) *n* homard *m*; (spiny) ~ langouste *f*.

lobsterpot ['lɒbstəpɒt] *n* casier *m* à homards OR à langoustes.

lobster thermidor [-'θɜːmɪdɔːʳ] *n* homard *m* OR langouste *f* thermidor.

lobule ['lɒbjuːl] *n* lobule *m*.

local ['ləʊkl] ◇ *adj* -**1.** [of the immediate area - tradition, phone call] local; [- hospital, shop] de quartier; [- inhabitants] du quartier, du coin; a ~ woman une femme du quartier OR du coin; ~ traders les commerces *mpl* de proximité. -**2.** ADMIN & POL [services, council] local, communal, municipal; ~ authority administration *f* locale; [in town] municipalité *f*. -**3.** MED [infection, pain] localisé.
◇ *n* -**1.** [person] habitant *m*, -e *f* (du lieu); the ~s les gens *m* du pays OR du coin; ask one of the ~s demande à quelqu'un du coin. -**2.** *inf Br* [pub] troquet *m* du coin; it used to be our ~ c'est là qu'on allait boire un pot. -**3.** *Am* [train] omnibus *m*; [bus] bus *m* local. -**4.** *Am* [union branch] section *f* syndicale. -**5.** *inf* MED anesthésie *f* locale. -**6.** *Can* TELEC poste *m*; ~ 476 please le poste 476, s'il vous plaît. -**7.** *Am* PRESS [item] nouvelle *f* locale.

local anaesthetic *n* anesthésie *f* locale.

local area network *n* COMPUT réseau *m* local.

local colour *n* couleur *f* locale.

locale [ləʊ'kɑːl] *n* [place] endroit *m*, lieu *m*; [scene, setting] cadre *m*; a rural ~ un cadre champêtre.

local education authority *n* direction *f* régionale de l'enseignement *(en Angleterre et au pays de Galles)*.

local government *n* administration *f* municipale; ~ elections élections *fpl* municipales; ~ official fonctionnaire *mf* de l'administration municipale.

locality [lə'kælətɪ] (*pl* localities) *n* -**1.** [neighbourhood] voisinage *m*, environs *mpl*; [general area] région *f*; he was seen in the (general) ~ of the station on l'a vu dans le quartier de la gare. -**2.** [location - of building, place] lieu *m*, site *m*; [- of species] localité *f*.

localize, -ise ['ləʊkəlaɪz] *vt* -**1.** [pinpoint, locate] localiser, situer; the source of the problem has been ~d on a réussi à localiser l'origine du problème. -**2.** [confine] localiser, limiter; they have tried to ~ the effect of the strike ils ont essayé de limiter l'effet de la grève. -**3.** [concentrate - power, money] concentrer. -**4.** [acclimatize - species, plant] acclimater.

localized ['ləʊkəlaɪzd] *adj* localisé.

locally ['ləʊkəlɪ] *adv* localement; she is well known ~ [in region] elle est très connue dans la région; [in neighbourhood] elle est très connue dans le quartier; there have been no disturbances ~ [in region] il n'y a pas eu de troubles dans la région; [in neighbourhood] il n'y a pas eu de troubles dans le quartier; he lives ~ il vit par ici; we shop ~ nous faisons nos courses dans le quartier; many issues have to be decided ~, not nationally de nombreux problèmes doivent être résolus au niveau local, et non au niveau national; '~ grown potatoes/carrots' 'pommes de terre/carottes du pays'; ~ manufactured goods articles *mpl* de fabrication locale.

local time *n* heure *f* locale.

locate [*Br* lə'keɪt, *Am* 'ləʊkeɪt] ◇ *vt* -**1.** [find] repérer, trouver, localiser; they have ~d the cause of the trouble ils ont localisé la cause du problème; the police are trying to ~ possible witnesses la police recherche des témoins éventuels; we are trying to ~ his sister nous essayons de savoir où se trouve sa sœur; he had hoped to ~ precisely the site of Troy il avait espéré repérer l'emplacement exact de Troie. -**2.** *(usu pass)* [situate] situer; the house is conveniently ~d for shops and public transport la maison est située à proximité des magasins et des transports en commun.
◇ *vi* -**1.** COMM [company, factory] s'établir, s'implanter. -**2.** *Am* [settle] s'installer, s'établir.

location [ləʊ'keɪʃn] *n* -**1.** [place, site] emplacement *m*, site *m*; what a beautiful ~ for a campus! quel site magnifique pour un campus universitaire!; the firm has moved to a new ~ la société a déménagé || [whereabouts]: what is your present ~? où te trouves-tu en ce moment?; show me the exact ~ of the tower montrez-moi l'emplacement exact de la tour. -**2.** CIN extérieurs *mpl*; shot on ~ tourné en extérieur. -**3.** [finding, discovery] repérage *m*, localisation *f*; ~ of the wreckage is proving difficult l'endroit exact du naufrage s'avère difficile à localiser. -**4.** COMPUT position *f*; memory ~ position (en) mémoire. -**5.** *SAfr* [township] township *m*; [reservation] réserve *f* (noire).

locative ['lɒkətɪv] LING ◇ *adj* locatif.
◇ *n* locatif *m*.

loc. cit. (*written abbr of* loco citato) loc. cit.

loch [lɒk, lɒx] *n Scot* loch *m*, lac *m*.

lochia ['lɒkɪə] *n (U)* lochies *fpl*.

loci ['ləʊsaɪ, 'ləʊkaɪ] *pl* → **locus**.

lock [lɒk] ◇ *vt* -**1.** [door, drawer, car etc] fermer à clef; check that all the doors and windows are ~ed vérifiez que toutes les portes et les fenêtres sont bien fermées. -**2.** [valuables, person] enfermer; ~ all these papers in the safe enfermez tous ces papiers dans le coffre-fort || *fig*: they were ~ed into the agreement ils étaient tenus par l'accord. -**3.** [hold tightly] serrer; they were ~ed in a passionate embrace ils étaient unis OR enlacés dans une étreinte passionnée; to ~ arms [police cordon] former un barrage; the armies were ~ed in battle les armées étaient engagées à fond dans la bataille; the unions were ~ed in a dispute with the management les syndicats étaient aux prises avec la direction; to be ~ed in combat être engagé dans un combat; *fig* être aux prises ❑ to ~ horns [stags] s'entremêler les bois; *fig* être aux prises. -**4.** [device, wheels, brakes] bloquer. -**5.** COMPUT [file] verrouiller.
◇ *vi* -**1.** [door, drawer, car etc] (se) fermer à clef. -**2.** [engage] se joindre; push the lever back until it ~s into place pousse le levier jusqu'à ce qu'il s'enclenche. -**3.** [wheels, brakes, nut] se bloquer.
◇ *n* -**1.** [on door, drawer etc] serrure *f*; steering ~ antivol *m*; under ~ and key [object] sous clef; the whole gang is now safely under ~ and key toute la bande est désormais sous les verrous. -**2.** [on canal] écluse *f*. -**3.** [grip - gen] prise *f*; [in wrestling] clef *f*, prise *f*. -**4.** *Br* AUT (rayon *m* de) braquage *m*; on full ~ braqué à fond; the car has a good/poor ~ la voiture a un bon/médiocre rayon de braquage. -**5.** TECH [device - gen] verrou *m*; [- on gun] percuteur *m*; [- on keyboard]: shift OR caps ~ touche *f* de verrouillage majuscule. -**6.** COMPUT verrouillage *m*. -**7.** RUGBY: ~ (forward) deuxième ligne *m*. -**8.** [curl] boucle *f*; [stray strand] mèche *f*. -**9.** *phr*: ~, stock and barrel en entier; she bought the company ~, stock and barrel elle a acheté la société en bloc; his essay was lifted, ~, stock and barrel from a textbook il a copié sa rédaction telle quelle OR mot pour mot dans un manuel scolaire; the family has moved ~, stock and barrel to Canada la famille est partie avec armes et bagages s'installer au Canada.

◆ **locks** *npl lit* chevelure *f*.

◆ **lock away** *vt sep* [valuables] mettre sous clef; [criminal] incarcérer, mettre sous les verrous; we keep the alcohol ~ed away nous gardons l'alcool sous clef.

◆ **lock in** *vt sep* enfermer; he ~ed himself in il s'est enfermé (à l'intérieur).

◆ **lock onto** *vt insep* [subj: radar] capter; [subj: homing device] se caler sur; to ~ onto a signal capter un signal; the missile ~ed onto its target le missile s'est fixé OR verrouillé sur sa cible.

◆ **lock out** *vt sep* -**1.** [accidentally] enfermer dehors; [deliberately] laisser dehors; her father threatened to ~ her out if she was late home son père a menacé de la laisser à la porte OR dehors si elle rentrait en retard; I've ~ed myself out j'ai fermé la porte en laissant les clés à l'intérieur, je me suis enfermé dehors. -**2.** INDUST [workers] lock-outer.

◆ **lock up** ◇ *vt sep* -**1.** [house, shop] fermer à clef. -**2.** [valuables, criminal] = **lock away**. -**3.** [capital] immobiliser. -**4.** TYPO [type] caler; [forme] serrer.
◇ *vi insep* fermer à clef; the last to leave ~s up le dernier à partir ferme la porte à clef.

locker ['lɒkəʳ] *n* -**1.** [for clothes, valuables etc] casier *m*, petit placard *m*; where are the left-luggage ~s? où se trouve la consigne automatique? -**2.** *Am* [freezer] congélateur *m*.

locker room *n Am* vestiaire *m (avec casiers)*.

◆ **locker-room** *adj* [humour, joke] corsé, salé.

locket ['lɒkɪt] *n* pendentif *m*.

lock gate *n* porte *f* d'écluse.

locking ['lɒkɪŋ] *adj* [door, briefcase] à serrure, qui ferme à clef; there was a fault in the ~ mechanism il y avait un défaut dans le mécanisme de verrouillage.

lockjaw ['lɒkdʒɔː] *n* tétanos *m*.

lock keeper *n* éclusier *m*, -ère *f*.

locknut ['lɒknʌt] *n* [supplementary nut] contre-écrou *m*; [self-locking] écrou *m* autobloquant.

lockout ['lɒkaʊt] *n* [of workers] lock-out *m inv*.

locksmith ['lɒksmɪθ] *n* serrurier *m*.

lockstitch ['lɒkstɪtʃ] *n* SEW point *m* de piqûre.

lockup ['lɒkʌp] *n* -**1.** *Am* [jail] prison *f*; [cell] cellule *f*. -**2.** *Br* [garage] garage *m*. -**3.** [act of locking up] fermeture *f*.

lock-up garage *n Br* garage *m*.

lock-up shop *n Br* & *NZ* (petite) boutique *f (sans logement attenant)*.

loco ['ləʊkəʊ] (*pl* locos) ◇ *adj* ▽ *Am* dingue, cinglé.
◇ *n inf* RAIL loco *f*.

locomotion [,ləʊkə'məʊʃn] *n* locomotion *f*.

locomotive [,ləʊkə'məʊtɪv] ◇ *n* locomotive *f*.
◇ *comp*: ~ roundhouse rotonde *f* RAIL; ~ works usine *f* de construction de machines.
◇ *adj* automobile; ANAT locomoteur.

locomotor [,ləʊkə'məʊtəʳ] *adj* locomoteur.

locomotor ataxia *n* MED ataxie *f* locomotrice.

locoweed ['ləʊkəʊwiːd] *n* astragale *m* toxique.

locum ['ləʊkəm] *n Br* remplaçant *m*, -e *f (de prêtre ou de médecin)*.

locum tenens [,ləʊkəm'tiːnenz] (*pl* locum tenentes [-tɪ'nentiːz]) *Br fml* = **locum**.

locus ['ləʊkəs] (*pl* loci [-saɪ, -kaɪ]) *n* -**1.** *fml* [place] lieu *m*; JUR lieux *mpl*. -**2.** MATH lieu *m* (géométrique). -**3.** BIOL [of gene] locus *m*.

locust ['ləʊkəst] ◇ *n* -**1.** [insect] locuste *f*, criquet *m* migrateur. -**2.** = **locust tree**.
◇ *comp*: ~ bean caroube *f*.
locust tree *n* -**1.** [false acacia] robinier *m* (faux acacia). -**2.** [carob tree] caroubier *m*.
locution [lə'kjuːʃn] *n fml* -**1.** [phrase] locution *f*. -**2.** [style] style *m*, phraséologie *f*; [manner of speech] élocution *f*.
locutionary act [ləʊ'kjuːʃənrɪ-] *n* acte *m* de parole.
lode [ləʊd] *n* [vein - of metallic ore] veine *f*; [- of gold, copper, silver] filon *m*.
lodestar ['ləʊdstɑːʳ] *n* (étoile *f*) Polaire *f*; *fig* guide *m*, point *m* de repère.
lodestone ['ləʊdstəʊn] *n* MINER pierre *f* à aimant, magnétite *f*; *fig* aimant *m*.
lodge [lɒdʒ] ◇ *vt* -**1.** [house] héberger, loger; **the rescued passengers were ~d overnight in schools** les rescapés ont été hébergés pour la nuit dans des écoles; **the hotel can ~ 65 people** l'hôtel peut accueillir 65 personnes. -**2.** [stick, embed] loger; **a fish bone had ~d itself in his throat** une arête s'était logée dans sa gorge; **his words were ~d in my memory** ses paroles étaient gravées dans ma mémoire. -**3.** [make, file - claim] déposer; **to ~ a complaint** porter plainte; **she ~d a formal complaint with the authorities** elle a déposé une plainte officielle auprès de l'administration; **to ~ an accusation against sb** JUR porter plainte contre qqn. -**4.** [deposit for safekeeping] déposer, mettre en sûreté. -**5.** [invest - power, authority etc] investir.
◇ *vi* -**1.** [stay] loger, être logé; **he is lodging at Mrs Smith's** OR **with Mrs Smith** il loge chez Mme Smith; [with board] il est en pension chez Mme Smith. -**2.** [stick, become embedded] se loger.
◇ *n* -**1.** [cabin - for hunters] pavillon *m*; [- for skiers] chalet *m*. -**2.** *Br* [on country estate] maison *f* du gardien; [of porter] loge *f*. -**3.** *Am* [in park, resort] bâtiment *m* central. -**4.** [Masonic] loge *f*. -**5.** [hotel] hôtel *m*, relais *m*. -**6.** [beavers'] hutte *f*.
lodgement ['lɒdʒmənt] = **lodgment**.
lodger ['lɒdʒəʳ] *n* locataire *mf*; [with board] pensionnaire *mf*.
lodging ['lɒdʒɪŋ] *n* hébergement *m*; **they offered the family free ~** ils ont offert d'héberger gratuitement la famille.
◆ **lodgings** *npl Br* chambre *f* meublée OR chambres *fpl* meublées *(chez un particulier)*; **most of the students live in ~s** la plupart des étudiants habitent dans des chambres meublées.
lodging house *n* meublé *m*.
lodgment ['lɒdʒmənt] *n fml* -**1.** [placing] emplacement *m*. -**2.** [accumulation] accumulation *f*; [obstruction] bouchon *m*.
loess ['ləʊɪs] *n* lœss *m*.
loft [lɒft] ◇ *n* -**1.** [attic] grenier *m*; **~ conversion** combles *mpl* aménagés; **they spent a lot of money on the ~ conversion** ils ont dépensé beaucoup d'argent pour aménager les combles. -**2.** [elevated space - in church] tribune *f*, galerie *f*; **organ ~** tribune d'orgue. -**3.** *Am* [warehouse space] loft *m*.
◇ *vt* SPORT [hit] lancer très haut; **he ~ed the ball clear of the bushes** il a envoyé la balle loin au-dessus des buissons.
loftily ['lɒftɪlɪ] *adv* avec mépris, dédaigneusement.
lofty ['lɒftɪ] (*compar* loftier, *superl* loftiest) *adj* -**1.** [high - summit, building etc] haut, élevé; **the ~ peaks of the Alps** les hauts sommets des Alpes; **a ~ interior** des pièces hautes (de plafond). -**2.** [supercilious - manner] hautain, dédaigneux, méprisant. -**3.** [exalted - in spirit] noble, élevé; [- in rank, position] éminent. -**4.** [elevated - style, prose] élevé, noble.
log [lɒg] (*pt* & *pp* logged, *cont* logging) ◇ *n* -**1.** [of wood] rondin *m*; [for firewood] bûche *f*; **a ~ fire** un feu de bois. -**2.** [record] journal *m*, registre *m*; NAUT journal *m* OR livre *m* de bord; AERON carnet *m* de vol; [lorry driver's] carnet *m* de route; **keep a ~ of all the phone calls** notez tous les appels téléphoniques. -**3.** NAUT [apparatus] loch *m*. -**4.** (*abbr of* logarithm) log *m*; **~ tables** MATH tables *fpl* de logarithmes. -**5.** [cake]: **Yuletide** OR **Christmas ~** bûche *f* de Noël.
◇ *comp*: **~ cabin** cabane *f* en rondins.
◇ *vt* -**1.** [information - on paper] consigner, inscrire; [- in computer memory] entrer. -**2.** [speed, distance, time]: **he has logged 2,000 hours flying time** il a 2 000 heures de vol à son actif, il totalise 2 000 heures de vol. -**3.** [tree] tronçonner; [forest] mettre en coupe.
◇ *vi Am* [company] exploiter une forêt; [person] travailler comme bûcheron.
◆ **log in** ◇ *vi insep* COMPUT entrer dans le système, ouvrir une session.
◇ *vt sep* [user name, password] entrer, introduire.
◆ **log off** = **log out**.
◆ **log on** = **log in**.
◆ **log out** *vi insep* COMPUT sortir du système, fermer une session.
◆ **log up** *vt sep Br* -**1.** [do, achieve] avoir à son actif; **I've logged up three extra days' work** j'ai fait trois journées de travail supplémentaires; **they managed to ~ up 80 miles a day** ils ont réussi à faire 130 km par jour; **he has logged up yet another victory** il a remporté une nouvelle victoire. -**2.** [write up] consigner, inscrire.
loganberry ['ləʊgənbərɪ] (*pl* **loganberries**) *n* [plant] framboisier *m* (hybride); [fruit] mûre-framboise *f*.
logarithm ['lɒgərɪðm] *n* logarithme *m*.
logarithmic [,lɒgə'rɪðmɪk] *adj* logarithmique; **~ function** fonction *f* logarithme.
logbook ['lɒgbʊk] *n* -**1.** [record] journal *m*; NAUT journal *m* OR livre *m* de bord; AERON carnet *m* de vol. -**2.** *Br* AUT ≃ carte *f* grise.
loge [ləʊʒ] *n* THEAT [box] loge *f*; [gallery] galerie *f*, balcon *m*.
logger ['lɒgəʳ] *n* -**1.** *Am* [lumberjack] bûcheron *m*. -**2.** *Br* [tractor] tracteur *m* forestier.
loggerhead ['lɒgəhed] *n*: **~ (turtle)** ZOOL caouanne *f*.
loggerheads ['lɒgəhedz] *npl*: **to be at ~ (with sb)**: **he's at ~ with the management over the issue** il est en complet désaccord avec la direction sur cette question.
loggerhead shrike *n* pie-grièche *f*.
loggia ['ləʊdʒə] (*pl* loggias OR loggie [-dʒe]) *n* loggia *f*; THEAT galerie *f*.
logging ['lɒgɪŋ] *n* exploitation *f* forestière.
logic ['lɒdʒɪk] *n* [gen & COMPUT] logique *f*; **if you follow my ~** si tu suis mon raisonnement; **that's typical male ~!** c'est un raisonnement typiquement masculin!
logical ['lɒdʒɪkl] *adj* logique; **it's a ~ impossibility** c'est logiquement impossible; **he is incapable of ~ argument** il est incapable d'avoir un raisonnement logique; **a ~ conclusion** une conclusion logique.
logical form *n* LING forme *f* logique.
logically ['lɒdʒɪklɪ] *adv* logiquement; **if you think about it ~** si on y réfléchit bien; **~, he should win** logiquement OR normalement, il devrait gagner.
logical positivism *n* PHILOS positivisme *m* logique, néopositivisme *m*.
logical positivist *n* logicopositiviste *mf*.
logic circuit *n* COMPUT circuit *m* logique.
logician [lə'dʒɪʃn] *n* logicien *m*, -enne *f*.
logistic(al) [lə'dʒɪstɪk(l)] *adj* logistique.
logistically [lə'dʒɪstɪklɪ] *adv* sur le plan logistique.
logistics [lə'dʒɪstɪks] *npl* logistique *f*.
logjam ['lɒgdʒæm] *n* -**1.** [in river] bouchon *m* de bois flottés. -**2.** *fig* [deadlock] impasse *f*.
logo ['ləʊgəʊ] (*pl* logos) *n* logo *m*.
logogram ['lɒgəgræm], **logograph** ['lɒgəgrɑːf] *n* logogramme *m*.
logorrhoea *Br*, **logorrhea** *Am* [,lɒgə'rɪə] *n* logorrhée *f*.
logos ['lɒgɒs] *n* PHILOS logos *m*.
◆ **Logos** *n* RELIG Logos *m*.
logotype ['lɒgətaɪp] *n* TYPO logotype *m*.
logrolling ['lɒgrəʊlɪŋ] *n Am pej* échange *m* de faveurs *(accord entre hommes politiques selon lequel on se rend mutuellement des services)*.
log tables *npl* tables *fpl* de logarithmes.
logy *inf* ['ləʊgɪ] (*compar* logier, *superl* logiest) *adj Am* patraque; **you look a bit ~** tu n'as pas l'air en forme.
loin [lɔɪn] *n* CULIN [of pork] longe *f*, échine *f*, filet *m*; [of beef] aloyau *m*; [of veal] longe *f*; [of lamb] carré *m*.
◆ **loins** *npl* ANAT reins *mpl*; *euph* [genitals] parties *fpl*.
loincloth ['lɔɪnklɒθ] *n* pagne *m*.
loiter ['lɔɪtəʳ] *vi* -**1.** [hang about] traîner; [lurk] rôder; **there was someone ~ing in the carpark** il y avait quelqu'un qui rôdait dans le parking; **'no ~ing'** zone sous surveillance *(où il est interdit de s'attarder)*; **~ing with intent** JUR délit *m* d'intention. -**2.** [dawdle] traîner; [lag behind] traîner (en route).
loll [lɒl] *vi* -**1.** [lounge] se prélasser; **he was ~ing against the wall** il était nonchalamment appuyé contre le mur. -**2.** [dangle] dodeliner; [hang heavily] pendre.
◆ **loll about** *Br*, **loll around** *vi insep* [in grass, armchair etc] se prélasser; **I just ~ed about** OR **around all day** j'ai paressé toute la journée.
◆ **loll out** *vi insep* [tongue] pendre (mollement).
lollapalooza▽ [,lɒləpə'luːzə] *n Am* merveille *f*, phénomène *m*; **her last film's a ~** son dernier film est vraiment prodigieux.
lollipop ['lɒlɪpɒp] *n* -**1.** [sweet] sucette *f*. -**2.** *Br* [ice lolly] esquimau *m*, sucette *f* glacée.
lollipop lady *inf*, **lollipop man** *inf n en Grande-Bretagne, personne chargée d'aider les enfants à traverser une rue en arrêtant la circulation à l'aide d'un panneau en forme de sucette*.
lollop ['lɒləp] *vi* [person] marcher lourdement; [animal] galoper.
lolly ['lɒlɪ] (*pl* lollies) *n* -**1.** *inf Br* = **lollipop**. -**2.** ▽ *Br* [money] fric *m*, pognon *m*. -**3.** *inf Austr* & *NZ* [sweet] bonbon *m*.
lollypop ['lɒlɪpɒp] = **lollipop**.
Lombard ['lɒmbəd] ◇ *n* Lombard *m*, -e *f*.
◇ *adj* Lombard.
Lombardy ['lɒmbədɪ] *pr n* Lombardie *f*; **in ~** en Lombardie.
Lombardy poplar *n* peuplier *m* d'Italie.
Lomé ['ləʊmeɪ] *pr n* Lomé.
Lomond ['ləʊmənd] *pr n*: **Loch ~** le loch Lomond.
London ['lʌndən] ◇ *pr n* Londres.
◇ *comp* [museums, shops, traffic] londonien; [life] à Londres; **~ (Regional) Transport** *régie des transports publics londoniens*.
Londonderry [,lʌndən'derɪ] *pr n* Londonderry.
Londoner ['lʌndənəʳ] *n* Londonien *m*, -enne *f*, habitant *m*, -e *f* de Londres.
London pride *n* BOT saxifrage *f* à feuilles en coin, désespoir-des-peintres *m*.
lone [ləʊn] *adj* [unaccompanied - rider, stag] solitaire; [isolated - house] isolé; [single, unique] unique, seul; **a ~ fishing boat on the horizon** un seul bateau de pêche à l'horizon ❑ **~ parent** parent *m* unique.
loneliness ['ləʊnlɪnɪs] *n* [of person] solitude *f*, isolement *m*; [of place] isolement *m*; **'The Loneliness of the Long Distance Runner'** *Sillitoe* 'la Solitude du coureur de fond'.
lonely ['ləʊnlɪ] (*compar* lonelier, *superl* loneliest) *adj* -**1.** [sad - person] seul; [- life] solitaire; **to be** OR **to feel ~** se sentir seul; **the house seems ~ without you** la maison paraît vide sans toi; **he went home to his ~ room** il regagna la solitude de sa chambre; **the loneliest hour of the day** l'heure de la journée où l'on se sent le plus seul. -**2.** [unfrequented - spot] isolé; [- street] peu fréquenté, vide; **I find the village too ~** je trouve le village trop isolé.

lonely hearts *adj*: ~ club club *m* de rencontres; ~ column rubrique *f* rencontres *(des petites annonces)*.

loner *inf* ['ləʊnəʳ] *n* [person] solitaire *mf*; he's a bit of a ~ il est un peu sauvage OR farouche.

lonesome ['ləʊnsəm] ◇ *adj Am* = **lonely**.
◇ *n inf*: on one's ~ tout seul.

lone wolf = **loner**.

long [lɒŋ] (*compar* longer ['lɒŋgəʳ], *superl* longest ['lɒŋgɪst]) ◇ *adj* -**1.** [in space - road, garment, letter] long; how ~ is the pool? quelle est la longueur de la piscine?, la piscine fait combien de long?; the pool's 33 metres ~ la piscine fait 33 mètres de long; the article is 80 pages ~ l'article fait 80 pages; is it a ~ way (away)? est-ce loin (d'ici)?; it's a ~ way to the beach la plage est loin; she can throw a ~ way elle lance loin; to take the ~ way round prendre le chemin le plus long; to get OR grow ~er [shadows] s'allonger; [hair, beard] pousser ❑ the Long March HIST la Longue Marche; ~ trousers OR *Am* pants pantalon *m* long; ~ dress [for evening wear] robe *f* longue; why the ~ face? pourquoi est-ce que tu fais cette tête de six pieds de long? -**2.** [in time - pause, speech, separation] long; how ~ will the flight be/was the meeting? combien de temps durera le vol/a duré la réunion?; the film is three hours ~ le film dure trois heures; her five-year-~ battle with the authorities sa lutte de cinq années contre les autorités; to have a ~ memory avoir une bonne mémoire OR une mémoire d'éléphant; to get ~er [days, intervals] devenir plus long; they want ~er holidays ils veulent des vacances plus longues; she took a ~ swig of beer elle a bu une grande gorgée de bière; they took a ~ look at the view ils restèrent longtemps à regarder la vue qui s'offrait à eux; it was a ~ two months ces deux mois ont été longs; I've had a ~ day j'ai eu une journée bien remplie; I've known her (for) a ~ time OR while je la connais depuis longtemps, cela fait longtemps que je la connais ❑ at ~ last! enfin! -**3.** GRAMM [vowel, syllable] long. -**4.** ST. EX: they are ~ on copper, they have taken a ~ position on copper ils ont investi dans le cuivre. -**5.** *inf* SPORT [in tennis]: that serve was ~ ce service était trop long. -**6.** *phr*: she's ~ on good ideas elle n'est pas à court de bonnes idées, ce ne sont pas les bonnes idées qui lui manquent; his speeches are ~ on rhetoric but short on substance ce n'est pas la rhétorique qui manque dans ses discours, c'est la substance.
◇ *n* -**1.** *phr*: the ~ and the short of it is that I got fired *inf* enfin bref, j'ai été viré. -**2.** GRAMM [vowel, syllable] longue *f*.
◇ *adv* -**1.** [a long time] longtemps; they live ~er than humans ils vivent plus longtemps que les êtres humains; he won't keep you ~/much ~er il ne vous gardera pas longtemps/beaucoup plus longtemps; I haven't been here ~ je viens d'arriver, j'arrive juste; they haven't been married ~ ça ne fait pas longtemps qu'ils sont mariés, ils ne sont pas mariés depuis longtemps; how ~ will he be/was he in jail? (pendant) combien de temps restera-t-il/est-il resté en prison?; how ~ has he been in jail? ça fait combien de temps qu'il est en prison?, depuis combien de temps est-il en prison?; how ~ is it since we last visited them? quand sommes-nous allés les voir pour la dernière fois?; it happened ~ ago/not ~ ago cela s'est passé il y a longtemps/il n'y a pas longtemps; as ~ ago as 1937 déjà en 1937; ~ before you were born bien avant que tu sois né; not ~ before/after their divorce peu avant/après leur divorce; the decision had been taken ~ before la décision avait été prise depuis longtemps; ~ after OR afterwards, when these events were mostly forgotten... bien après, alors que ces évènements étaient presque complètement oubliés...; colleagues ~ since promoted des collègues promus depuis longtemps; a law which had come into force not ~ since une loi qui était entrée en vigueur depuis peu; we talked ~ into the night nous avons parlé jusque tard dans la nuit || [with 'be', 'take']: will you be ~? tu en as pour longtemps?; I won't be ~ je n'en ai pas pour longtemps; please wait, she won't be ~ attendez, s'il vous plaît, elle ne va pas tarder; don't be OR take too ~ fais vite; it wasn't ~ before he realized, it didn't take ~ for him to realize il n'a pas mis longtemps à s'en rendre compte, il s'en est vite rendu compte; he took OR it took him so ~ to make up his mind... il a mis si longtemps à se décider..., il lui a fallu tellement de temps pour se décider...; how ~ does it take to get there? combien de temps faut-il pour y aller?; this won't take ~ ça va être vite fait; this won't take ~er than five minutes ça sera fait en moins de cinq minutes || [in wishes, toasts etc]: ~ may our partnership continue! à notre collaboration!; ~ live the Queen! vive la reine! -**2.** [for a long time] depuis longtemps; it has ~ been known that... on sait depuis longtemps que...; I have ~ suspected that he was involved in it cela fait longtemps que je le soupçonne OR je le soupçonne depuis longtemps d'être impliqué là-dedans; the ~est-running TV series le plus long feuilleton télévisé. -**3.** [throughout]: all day/week ~ toute la journée/la semaine; all my life ~ toute ma vie. -**4.** *phr*: so ~! *inf* salut!, à bientôt!
◇ *vi*: to ~ for sb/sthg: I ~ for him il me manque énormément; she was ~ing for a letter from you elle attendait impatiemment que vous lui écriviez; we were ~ing for a cup of tea nous avions très envie d'une tasse de thé; to ~ OR to be ~ing to do sthg être impatient OR avoir hâte de faire qqch; he's ~ing to go back to Italy il meurt d'envie de retourner en Italie; I was ~ing to tell her the truth je mourais d'envie de lui dire la vérité; I've been ~ing to meet you for years cela fait des années que je souhaite faire votre connaissance.
◆ **as long as** *conj phr* -**1.** [during the time that] aussi longtemps que, tant que; as ~ as he's in power, there will be no hope tant qu'il sera au pouvoir, il n'y aura aucun espoir. -**2.** [providing] à condition que, pourvu que; you can have it as ~ as you give me it back vous pouvez le prendre à condition que OR pourvu que vous me le rendiez; I'll do it as ~ as I get paid for it je le ferai à condition d'être payé; you can go out as ~ as you're back before midnight tu peux sortir à condition de rentrer avant minuit. -**3.** *inf Am* [seeing that] puisque; as ~ as you're going to the post office get me some stamps puisque tu vas à la poste, achète-moi des timbres.
◆ **before long** *adv phr* [soon] dans peu de temps, sous peu; [soon afterwards] peu (de temps) après; she'll be back before ~ elle sera de retour dans peu de temps OR sous peu; before ~, everything had returned to normal tout était rapidement rentré dans l'ordre.
◆ **for long** *adv phr* longtemps; he's still in charge here, but not for ~ c'est encore lui qui s'en occupe, mais plus pour longtemps.
◆ **no longer** *adv phr* ne... plus; not any ~er plus maintenant; she no ~er loves him elle ne l'aime plus; I can't wait any ~er je ne peux pas attendre plus longtemps, je ne peux plus attendre; they used to live there, but not any ~er ils habitaient là autrefois, mais plus maintenant.
◆ **so long as** = **as long as**.

long. (*written abbr of* longitude) long.

long-awaited [-ə'weɪtɪd] *adj* très attendu.

longboat ['lɒŋbəʊt] *n* chaloupe *f*.

longbow ['lɒŋbəʊ] *n* arc *m*.

long-chain *adj* CHEM [molecule] à longue chaîne.

long-dated *adj* ST. EX à long terme.

long-distance ◇ *adj* -**1.** [phone call] interurbain. -**2.** [runner, race] de fond; [pilot, lorry driver] au long cours; [journey] vers un pays lointain. -**3.** [device] (à) longue portée; [aircraft] long-courrier.
◇ *adv*: to call OR phone ~ appeler OR téléphoner par l'interurbain; I'm phoning ~ from Aberdeen c'est un appel interurbain, j'appelle d'Aberdeen.

long division *n* MATH division *f* posée; to do ~/a ~ faire des divisions/une division *(sans calculatrice)*.

long-drawn-out *adj* très long, interminable, qui n'en finit pas.

long drink *n* long drink *m*; [non-alcoholic] *grand verre de jus de fruit, de limonade etc*.

long-eared *adj* aux grandes oreilles.

longed-for ['lɒŋd-] *adj* très attendu.

longeron ['lɒndʒərən] *n* AERON longeron *m*.

long-established *adj* [tradition] qui existe depuis longtemps.

longevity [lɒn'dʒevətɪ] *n* longévité *f*.

long-forgotten *adj* oublié depuis longtemps; a ~ tradition une tradition tombée en désuétude.

long hair *inf n Am pej* hippie *mf*, baba (cool) *mf*.

long-haired *adj* [person] aux cheveux longs; [animal] à poil long.

longhand ['lɒŋhænd] *n* écriture *f* courante; he writes everything out in ~ [not on a typewriter] il écrit tout à la main; [not in shorthand] il écrit tout en entier, il ne prend jamais de notes en sténo.

long-haul *adj* [aircraft] long-courrier.

longheaded [,lɒŋ'hedɪd] *adj* [shrewd] astucieux, malin.

longhorn ['lɒŋhɔːn] *n* AGR longhorn *m*.

longhouse ['lɒŋhaʊs, *pl* -haʊzɪz] *n* long house *f*.

longing ['lɒŋɪŋ] ◇ *n* envie *f*, désir *m*; I had a ~ to see the sea j'avais très envie de voir la mer; the sight of her filled him with ~ en la voyant le désir s'empara de lui.
◇ *adj* d'envie, de désir; a ~ look un regard plein d'envie.

longingly ['lɒŋɪŋlɪ] *adv* [with desire] avec désir OR envie; [with regret] avec regret; to think ~ of the past penser au passé avec nostalgie.

longish ['lɒŋɪʃ] *adj* assez long.

Long Island *pr n* Long Island; in ~ à Long Island.

longitude ['lɒndʒɪtjuːd] *n* longitude *f*; at a ~ of 60° east par 60° de longitude est.

longitudinal [,lɒndʒɪ'tjuːdɪnl] *adj* longitudinal; ~ section coupe *f* longitudinale.

longitudinally [,lɒndʒɪ'tjuːdɪnəlɪ] *adv* longitudinalement.

long johns *inf npl* caleçon *m* long, caleçons *mpl* longs.

long jump *n Br* SPORT saut *m* en longueur.

long jumper *n Br* sauteur *m (qui fait du saut en longueur)*.

long-lasting *adj* durable, qui dure longtemps.

long-legged *adj* [person] aux jambes longues; [animal] aux pattes longues.

long-life *adj* [milk] longue conservation *(inv)*; [lightbulb, battery] longue durée *(inv)*.

long-limbed *adj* aux longs membres.

long-lived [-lɪvd] *adj* [family, species] d'une grande longévité; [friendship, idea] durable; [prejudice] tenace, qui a la vie dure.

long-lost *adj* [friend, cousin] perdu de vue depuis longtemps; [object] perdu depuis longtemps.

long-nosed *adj* au nez long.

Long Parliament *pr n*: the ~ *Parlement convoqué par Charles Ier en 1640, renvoyé par Cromwell en 1653 et dissous en 1660*.

long pig *n* chair *f* humaine.

long player, long-playing record *n* 33 tours *m inv*, microsillon *m*.

long-range *adj* -**1.** [weapon] à longue portée; [vehicle, aircraft] à long rayon d'action. -**2.** [forecast, plan] à long terme.

long-running *adj* qui tient l'affiche.

longship ['lɒŋʃɪp] *n* drakkar *m*.

longshoreman ['lɒŋʃɔːmən] (*pl* longshoremen [-mən]) *n Am* docker *m*.

long shot *n* -**1.** [in race - runner, horse] *concurrent qui ne figure pas parmi les favoris*. -**2.** [bet] pari *m* risqué. -**3.** CIN plan *m* éloigné. -**4.** *fig* entreprise *f* hasardeuse; **it's a bit of a ~, but we may be successful** c'est une entreprise hasardeuse mais nous réussirons peut-être; **I haven't finished by a ~** je n'ai pas fini, loin de là.

longsighted [ˌlɒŋˈsaɪtɪd] *adj* -**1.** MED hypermétrope, presbyte. -**2.** *fig* [well-judged] prévoyant.

longsightedness [ˌlɒŋˈsaɪtɪdnɪs] *n* -**1.** MED hypermétropie *f*, presbytie *f*. -**2.** *fig* [good judgement] prévoyance *f*, discernement *m*.

long-sleeved *adj* à manches longues.

long-standing *adj* de longue date.

long-suffering *adj* (extrêmement) patient, d'une patience à toute épreuve; [resigned] résigné; **she gave a ~ sigh** elle poussa un soupir résigné OR de résignation.

long-tailed [-teɪld] *adj* à longue queue.

long term

◆ **long-term** *adj* à long terme; [situation] prolongé; [unemployment] longue durée; **long-term car park** *Br* parking *m* longue durée; **long-term memory** mémoire *f* à long terme.

◆ **in the long term** *adv phr* à long terme.

long-time *adj* [friend, acquaintance] de longue date; [interest, affiliation] ancien, qui dure depuis longtemps.

long ton *n* TECH tonne *f* (anglaise), long ton *f*.

long vacation *n* UNIV grandes vacances *fpl*, vacances *fpl* d'été.

long view *n* prévisions *fpl* à long terme.

long-waisted [-ˈweɪstɪd] *adj* [garment] à taille basse; [person] au buste long.

long wave *n* RADIO grandes ondes *fpl*; **on (the) ~** sur les grandes ondes.

◆ **long-wave** *adj*: **long-wave broadcasts** émissions *fpl* sur grandes ondes.

longways [ˈlɒŋweɪz] *adv* longitudinalement, dans le sens de la longueur.

longwearing [ˌlɒŋˈweərɪŋ] *adj Am* solide, résistant.

long weekend *n* week-end *m* prolongé; **to take a ~** prendre un week-end prolongé.

long-winded *adj* [person] prolixe, bavard; [article, essay, lecture] interminable; [style] verbeux, diffus.

longwise [ˈlɒŋwaɪz] = **longways**.

long-woolled [-wʊld] *adj* [sheep] à grosse laine.

Lonsdale Belt [ˈlɒnzdeɪl-] *n la plus haute distinction pour les boxeurs professionnels en Grande-Bretagne*.

loo [luː] *n* -**1.** *inf Br* cabinets *mpl*, petit coin *m*. -**2.** [card game] *jeu de cartes*.

loofa(h) [ˈluːfə] *n* luffa *m*, loofa *m*.

look [lʊk] ◇ *vi* -**1.** [gen] regarder; **~, there's Brian!** regarde, voilà Brian!; **what's happening outside? let me ~** qu'est-ce qui se passe dehors? laissez-moi voir; **have you cut yourself? let me ~** tu t'es coupé? montre-moi OR laisse-moi voir; **go on, nobody's ~ing** vas-y, personne ne regarde; **they crept up on me while I wasn't ~ing** ils se sont approchés de moi pendant que j'avais le dos tourné; **I'm just ~ing** [in shop] je jette un coup d'œil; **~ and see if there's anyone there** regarde voir s'il y a quelqu'un; **if you ~ very carefully you can see a tiny crack in it** si tu regardes bien, tu verras une toute petite fissure; **~ this way** regardez par ici; **she ~ed along the row/down the list** elle a parcouru la rangée/la liste du regard; **he was ~ing out of the window/over the wall/up the chimney** il regardait par la fenêtre/par-dessus le mur/dans la cheminée ❑ **to ~ over sb's shoulder** *literal* regarder par-dessus l'épaule de qqn; *fig* surveiller ce que fait qqn; **~ before you leap** *prov* n'agis pas sans réfléchir. -**2.** [search] chercher; **you can't have ~ed hard enough** tu n'as pas dû beaucoup chercher. -**3.** [in imperative - listen, pay attention] écouter; **~, I can't pay you back just yet** écoute, je ne peux pas te rembourser tout de suite; **now ~, Paul, I've had enough of this!** bon écoute, Paul, ça suffit maintenant!; **~ here!** dites donc! -**4.** [seem, appear] avoir l'air; **that ~s delicious!** ça a l'air délicieux!; **you ~ OR are ~ing better today** tu as l'air (d'aller) mieux aujourd'hui; **how do I ~?** comment tu me trouves?; **you ~ absolutely stunning in that dress** tu es vraiment ravissante dans cette robe; **it makes him ~ ten years older/younger** ça le vieillit/rajeunit de dix ans; **he's 70, but he doesn't ~ it** il a 70 ans mais il n'en a pas l'air OR mais il ne les fait pas; **I can't hang the picture there, it just doesn't ~ right** je ne peux pas mettre le tableau là, ça ne va pas; **it ~s all right to me** moi, je trouve ça bien; **how does the situation ~ to you?** que pensez-vous de la situation?; **that's not how it ~s to the man in the street** ce n'est pas comme ça que l'homme de la rue voit les choses; **things will ~ very different when you leave school** les choses te sembleront très différentes quand tu quitteras l'école; **it'll ~ bad if I don't contribute** ça fera mauvaise impression si je ne contribue pas; **things are ~ing black for the economy** les perspectives économiques sont assez sombres; **I must have ~ed a fool** j'ai dû passer pour un imbécile; **to make sb ~ a fool OR an idiot** tourner qqn en ridicule; **he makes the rest of the cast ~ very ordinary** à côté de lui, les autres acteurs ont l'air vraiment quelconques; **to ~ like sb/sthg** [resemble] ressembler à qqn/qqch; **she ~s like her mother** elle ressemble à sa mère; **what does she ~ like?** [describe her] comment est-elle?; [she looks a mess] non mais, à quoi elle ressemble!; **it ~s like an oil refinery** ça ressemble à une raffinerie de pétrole, on dirait une raffinerie de pétrole; **I don't know what it is, but it ~s like blood** je ne sais pas ce que c'est, mais on dirait OR ça ressemble à du sang ❑ **it ~s like rain** on dirait qu'il va pleuvoir; **it ~s (to me) like he was lying** j'ai l'impression qu'il mentait; **is this our room? – it ~s like it** c'est notre chambre? – ça m'en a tout l'air; **the meeting ~ed like going on all day** la réunion avait l'air d'être partie pour durer toute la journée; **you ~ as if you've seen a ghost** on dirait que tu as vu un revenant; **it ~s as if Wayne's going to resign** Wayne a l'air de vouloir démissionner; **it doesn't ~ as if they're coming** on dirait qu'ils ne vont pas venir; **to ~ good: you're ~ing good** tu as l'air en forme; **he ~s good in jeans** les jeans lui vont bien; **that hat ~s very good on you** ce chapeau te va très bien; **it'll ~ good on your CV** ça fera bien sur ton curriculum; **things are ~ing pretty good here** les choses ont l'air de se présenter plutôt bien ici. -**5.** [face - house, window]: **to ~ (out) onto a park** donner sur un parc; **to ~ north/west** être exposé au nord/à l'ouest. -**6.** [intend]: **to be ~ing to do sthg** chercher à faire qqch; **she'll be ~ing to improve on her previous best time** elle cherchera à améliorer son meilleur temps; **we're ~ing to expand our export business** nous cherchons à développer nos exportations.

◇ *vt* -**1.** *phr*: **to ~ one's last on sthg** jeter un dernier regard à qqch; **to ~ sb up and down** regarder qqn de haut en bas, toiser qqn du regard. -**2.** [in imperative]: **~ who's coming!** regarde qui arrive!; **~ who's talking!** tu peux parler, toi!; **~ what you're doing/where you're going!** regarde un peu ce que tu fais/où tu vas!

◇ *n* -**1.** [gen] coup *m* d'œil; **to have OR to take a ~ (at sthg)** jeter un coup d'œil (sur OR à qqch), regarder (qqch); **would you like a ~ through my binoculars?** voulez-vous regarder avec mes jumelles?; **one ~ at him is enough to know he's a crook** on voit au premier coup d'œil que c'est un escroc; **it's worth a quick ~** ça vaut le coup d'œil; **we need to take a long hard ~ at our image abroad** il est temps que nous examinions de près notre image de marque à l'étranger; **did the mechanic have a proper ~ at the car?** est-ce que le mécanicien a bien regardé la voiture?; **and now a ~ ahead to next week's programmes** et maintenant, un aperçu des programmes de la semaine pr[ochaine]; **do you mind if I take a ~ around?** ç[a] vous gêne si je jette un coup d'œil?; **we'll jus[t] have a quick ~ round the garden** nous allon[s] jeter un coup d'œil dans le jardin; **I took a quic[k] ~ through the drawers** j'ai jeté un rapide cou[p] d'œil dans les tiroirs. -**2.** [search]: **to have a ~ for sthg** chercher qqch; **have another ~** che[r]che encore. -**3.** [glance] regard *m*; **she gave me [a] dirty ~** elle m'a jeté un regard mauvais; **you should have seen the ~s we got fro[m] passers-by!** si tu avais vu la façon dont le[s] passants nous regardaient! ❑ **he didn't sa[y] anything, but if ~s could kill!** il n'a pas dit u[n] mot, mais il y a des regards qui tuent. -**4.** [appearance, air] air *m*; [expression]: **he had [a] strange ~ in his eyes** il avait un drôle d[e] regard; **the old house has a neglected ~** l[a] vieille maison a l'air négligé; **she has the ~ o[f] someone who's going places** elle a l'air d[e] quelqu'un qui réussira dans la vie; **by the ~ o[f it] OR ~s of her, I'd say she failed the exam** à la voi[r] OR rien qu'en la voyant, je dirais qu'elle a ra[té] son examen; **there's trouble brewing by the ~ of it** OR **things** on dirait que quelque chose s[e] trame; **I quite like the ~ of the next candidat[e]** j'aime assez le profil du prochain candidat; **[I] don't like the ~ of it** ça ne me dit rien de bo[n] OR rien qui vaille; **I didn't like the ~ of her a[t] all** son allure ne m'a pas du tout plu. -**5.** [fashion] mode *f*, look *m*; **the hippie ~** le look hippie.

◆ **looks** *npl* [beauty]: **she's got everything[:] ~s, intelligence, youth...** elle a tout pour elle[:] elle est belle, intelligente, jeune...; **he's kept hi[s] ~s** il est resté beau; **he's lost his ~s** il n'es[t] plus aussi beau qu'avant.

◆ **look after** *vt insep* -**1.** [take care of] s'occupe[r] de; **my mother's ~ing after the kids/cat thi[s] week-end** ma mère va s'occuper des en[fants]/du chat ce week-end; **she has a sic[k] mother to ~ after** elle a une mère malade [à] charge; **you should ~ after your clothes mor[e] carefully** tu devrais prendre plus grand soin d[e] tes vêtements; **he helps me to ~ after th[e] garden** il m'aide à m'occuper du jardin ‖ *fig*: **~ after yourself!** fais bien attention à toi!; **don['t] worry, he can ~ after himself** ne t'inquièt[e] pas, il est capable de se débrouiller tout seul. -**2.** [be responsible for] s'occuper de; **they ~ after our interests in Europe** ils s'occupent d[e] nos affaires en Europe. -**3.** [take charge of] garder, surveiller; **Grandma can ~ after th[e] children while we're away** grand-mère peu[t] garder les enfants pendant notre absence; **ca[n] you ~ after my luggage for a few minutes** pouvez-vous surveiller mes bagages quelque[s] instants?

◆ **look ahead** *vi insep* regarder vers l'aveni[r]; **~ing ahead three or four years** dans trois o[u] quatre ans; **let's ~ ahead to the next cen[tury]/to next month's meeting** pensons a[u] siècle prochain/à la réunion du mois prochain.

◆ **look around** = **look round**.

◆ **look at** *vt insep* -**1.** *literal* regarder; **she ~e[d] at herself in the mirror** elle se regarda dans l[a] glace; **they ~ed at each other** ils ont échang[é] un regard; **oh dear, ~ at the time!** oh la la[,] regardez l'heure!; **it's not much to ~ at** c[e] n'est pas beau à regarder; **you wouldn't think to ~ at him, that he's a multi-millionaire** à l[e] voir on ne croirait pas avoir affaire à u[n] multi-millionnaire. -**2.** [consider] considérer; **~ at the problem from my point of view** consi[dé]rez le problème de mon point de vue; **that['s] not the way I ~ at it** ce n'est pas comme ça qu[e] je vois les choses; **they won't even ~ at th[e] idea** ils refusent même de prendre cette idée e[n] considération; **if you don't have money, h[e] won't even ~ at you** si vous n'avez pa[s d']l'argent, il ne vous regardera même pas; **m[y] brother can't ~ at an egg** *inf* mon frère n[e] supporte pas OR déteste les œufs. -**3.** [check] vérifier, regarder; **could you ~ at the tyres** pouvez-vous regarder les pneus?; **to have one['s] teeth ~ed at** se faire examiner les dents.

◆ **look away** *vi insep* détourner les yeux.

◆ **look back** *vi insep* -**1.** [in space] regarder derrière soi; **she walked away without ~ing back** elle est partie sans se retourner. -**2.** [in time] regarder en arrière; **there's no point in ~ing back** ça ne sert à rien de regarder en arrière; **the author ~s back on the war years** l'auteur revient sur les années de guerre; **it seems funny now we ~ back on it** ça semble drôle quand on y pense aujourd'hui; **we can ~ back on some happy times** nous avons connu de bons moments; **after she got her first job she never ~ed back** *fig* à partir du moment où elle a trouvé son premier emploi, tout lui a réussi.

◆ **look down** *vi insep* regarder en bas; [in embarrassment] baisser les yeux; **we ~ed down on** OR **at the valley** nous regardions la vallée en-dessous.

◆ **look down on** *vt insep* [despise] mépriser.

◆ **look for** *vt insep* -**1.** [seek] chercher; **she's still ~ing for a job** elle est toujours à la recherche d'un emploi; **are you ~ing for a fight?** tu cherches la bagarre? -**2.** [expect] attendre; **it's not the result we were ~ing for** ce n'est pas le résultat que nous attendions.

◆ **look forward to** *vt insep* attendre avec impatience; **we're ~ing forward to the end of term** nous attendons la fin du trimestre avec impatience; **to ~ forward to doing sthg** être impatient de faire qqch; **they had been ~ing forward to this moment for months** cela faisait des mois qu'ils attendaient cet instant; **I ~ forward to hearing from you soon** [in letter] dans l'attente de votre réponse.

◆ **look in** *vi insep* -**1.** [inside] regarder à l'intérieur. -**2.** [pay a visit] passer; **to ~ in on sb** rendre visite à OR passer voir qqn; **he ~ed in at the pub on the way home** il s'est arrêté au pub en rentrant chez lui. -**3.** [watch TV] regarder la télévision.

◆ **look into** *vt insep* examiner, étudier; **it's a problem that needs ~ing into** c'est un problème qu'il faut examiner OR sur lequel il faut se pencher.

◆ **look on** ◇ *vi insep* regarder; **the passers-by just ~ed on** les passants se sont contentés de regarder.
◇ *vt insep* considérer; **I ~ on him as my brother** je le considère comme mon frère; **to ~ on sb/sthg with favour/disfavour** voir qqn/qqch d'un œil favorable/défavorable.

◆ **look out** ◇ *vi insep* -**1.** [person] regarder dehors. -**2.** [room, window]: **the bedroom ~s out on** OR **over the garden** la chambre donne sur le jardin. -**3.** [be careful] faire attention; **~ out, it's hot!** attention, c'est chaud!; **you'll be in trouble if you don't ~ out** tu vas t'attirer des ennuis si tu ne fais pas attention.
◇ *vt sep Br*: **I'll ~/I've ~ed that book out for you** je te chercherai/je t'ai trouvé ce livre.

◆ **look out for** *vt insep* -**1.** [be on watch for] guetter; **I'll ~ out for you at the station** je te guetterai à la gare; **~ out for the sign to Dover** guettez le panneau pour Douvres; **she's always ~ing out for bargains** elle est toujours à la recherche OR à l'affût d'une bonne affaire; **you have to ~ out for snakes** il faut faire attention OR se méfier, il y a des serpents. -**2.** *inf phr*: **to ~ out for o.s.** OR **for number one** ne penser qu'à soi; **you've got to ~ out for number one!** chacun pour soi!

◆ **look over** *vt insep* [glance over] jeter un coup d'œil sur; [examine] examiner, étudier.

◆ **look round** ◇ *vi insep* -**1.** [look at surroundings] regarder (autour de soi); **I'm just ~ing round** je ne fais que jeter un coup d'œil, je jette simplement un coup d'œil; **I'd rather ~ round on my own than take the guided tour** je préférerais faire le tour moi-même plutôt que de suivre la visite guidée; **I ~ed round for an exit** j'ai cherché une sortie. -**2.** [look back] regarder derrière soi, se retourner.
◇ *vt insep* [museum, cathedral, factory] visiter; [shop, room] jeter un coup d'œil dans.

◆ **look through** *vt insep* -**1.** [window, screen] regarder à travers. -**2.** [book, report] jeter un coup d'œil sur OR à, regarder. -**3.** *fig* [person]: **he ~ed straight through me** il m'a regardé comme si je n'étais pas là.

◆ **look to** *vt insep* -**1.** [turn to] se tourner vers; **it's best to ~ to an expert** il est préférable de consulter un expert OR de demander l'avis d'un expert; **don't ~ to her for help** ne compte pas sur elle pour t'aider; **they are ~ing to us to find a solution to this problem** ils comptent sur nous pour trouver une solution à ce problème. -**2.** *fml* [attend to] veiller à; **he should ~ to his reputation** il devrait veiller à sa réputation; **~ to it that discipline is properly maintained** veillez à ce que la discipline soit bien maintenue.

◆ **look up** ◇ *vi insep* -**1.** [raise one's eyes] lever les yeux. -**2.** [improve] s'améliorer; **things are ~ing up for the economy** les perspectives économiques semblent meilleures.
◇ *vt sep* -**1.** [in reference work, directory etc] chercher; **~ the word up in the dictionary** cherche le mot dans le dictionnaire. -**2.** [visit] passer voir, rendre visite à; **~ us up when you're in New York** passe nous voir quand tu seras à New York.

◆ **look upon** = **look on** *vt insep*.

◆ **look up to** *vt insep* respecter, avoir du respect pour.

look-ahead *adj Am* tourné vers l'avenir.

lookalike ['lʊkəˌlaɪk] *n* [double] sosie *m*; **a John Major ~** un sosie de John Major.

looked-for ['lʊkd-] *adj* recherché, attendu.

looker *inf* ['lʊkəʳ] *n* canon *m*; **she's/he's quite a ~** elle/il n'est pas mal (du tout).

looker-on (*pl* **lookers-on**) *n* [spectator] spectateur *m*, -trice *f*.

look-in *inf n Br* -**1.** [chance]: **she talked so much that I didn't get a ~** elle ne m'a pas laissé le temps de placer un mot OR d'en placer une; **the other people applying for the job don't have a ~** les autres candidats n'ont aucune chance. -**2.** [visit]: **to give sb a ~** passer voir qqn, faire un saut chez qqn.

-looking ['lʊkɪŋ] *in cpds*: **a kind~ nurse** une infirmière qui a l'air gentille; **filthy~** (d'aspect) très sale OR répugnant.

looking glass *n dated* miroir *m*, glace *f*; **a looking-glass world** *fig* un monde à l'envers.

lookout ['lʊkaʊt] *n* -**1.** [watcher - gen] guetteur *m*; MIL guetteur *m*, sentinelle *f*; NAUT vigie *f*. -**2.** [watch] guet *m*; **they left a man outside the bank to keep (a) ~** ils ont laissé un homme devant la banque pour faire le guet; **to keep a ~** OR **to be on the ~ for sthg** guetter qqch, être à l'affût de qqch; **keep a good ~ for them** guette-les bien; **I'm on the ~ for a better job** je suis à la recherche d'un meilleur emploi; **~ post/tower** poste *m*/tour *f* de guet. -**3.** [observation post] MIL poste *m* de guet; NAUT poste *m* de vigie. -**4.** *inf Br* [prospect]: **it's a poor ~ when even doctors are on the dole** il y a de quoi s'inquiéter quand même les médecins sont au chômage ❑ **that's your/his ~!** c'est ton/son problème!

look-over *inf n* coup *m* d'œil; **I've given the report a ~** j'ai jeté un coup d'œil sur le rapport.

look-see *inf n*: **to have** OR **to take a ~** jeter un petit coup d'œil.

look-up *n* COMPUT recherche *f*, consultation *f*.

loom [luːm] ◇ *vi* -**1.** [appear] surgir; **an iceberg ~ed out of** OR **through the fog** un iceberg a soudain surgi du brouillard; **a figure ~ed in the doorway** une silhouette est apparue dans l'encadrement de la porte; **above us ~ed a high cliff** une falaise se dressait au-dessus de nos têtes. -**2.** [approach] être imminent; **a sinister-looking character was ~ing up towards them** un personnage à l'air sinistre s'avançait vers eux de façon menaçante; **the deadline was ~ing nearer and nearer** la date fatidique approchait; **he's getting worried with the elections ~ing ahead** l'approche des élections l'inquiète. -**3.** **to ~ large** [threaten] menacer; **the idea of eviction ~ed large in their minds** l'idée d'être expulsés ne les quittait pas.
◇ *n* TEX métier *m* à tisser; **hand/power ~** métier manuel/mécanique.

◆ **loom up** *vi insep* apparaître indistinctement, surgir.

LOOM [luːm] (*abbr of* Loyal Order of the Moose) *pr n association caritative américaine*.

loon [luːn] ◇ *n* -**1.** *inf* [lunatic] dingue *mf*; [simpleton] idiot *m*, -e *f*. -**2.** *arch* [commoner] roturier *m*, -ère *f*; **lord and ~** seigneur et vilain. -**3.** *Am* ORNITH plongeon *m*.
◇ *vi inf Br*: **to ~ (about)** faire le fou OR l'imbécile.

looney *inf* ['luːnɪ] = **loony**.

loon pants = **loons**.

loons [luːnz] *npl pantalon taille basse à pattes d'éléphant*.

loony *inf* ['luːnɪ] (*compar* **loonier**, *superl* **looniest**, *pl* **loonies**) ◇ *adj* dingue, loufoque; **the ~ left** *pej l'aile gauche extrémiste du parti travailliste*.
◇ *n* dingue *mf*, malade *mf*.

loony bin *inf n hum* asile *m*; **he's ready for the ~** il est bon pour l'asile.

loop [luːp] ◇ *n* -**1.** [in string, rope] boucle *f*; [in river] méandre *m*; [in drainpipe] siphon *m*; **a ~ of string served as a handle** une ficelle servait de poignée; **the film/the tape runs in a ~** le film/la bande défile en continu; **the Loop** *quartier des affaires de Chicago (délimité par une ligne de métro faisant une boucle)*. -**2.** COMPUT boucle *f*. -**3.** ELEC [closed circuit] circuit *m* fermé. -**4.** [contraceptive device] stérilet *m*.
◇ *vt* -**1.** [in string, rope etc] faire une boucle à; **~ the rope around your waist/through the ring** passez la corde autour de votre taille/dans l'anneau; **streamers were ~ed across the room** la pièce était tendue de guirlandes. -**2.** AERON: **to ~ the ~** faire un looping.
◇ *vi* [road] zigzaguer; [river] faire des méandres OR des boucles; **the path ~ed round the side of the mountain** le sentier montait en lacet à flanc de montagne.

loop aerial *n* RADIO cadre *m*.

looper ['luːpəʳ] *n* ENTOM chenille *f* arpenteuse.

loopey ['luːpɪ] = **loopy**.

loophole ['luːphəʊl] *n* -**1.** [gap, defect] lacune *f*, faille *f*; **a ~ in the law** un vide législatif. -**2.** ARCHIT meurtrière *f*.

loop stitch *n* point *m* de chaînette.

loopy ['luːpɪ] (*compar* **loopier**, *superl* **loopiest**) *adj* -**1.** [curly] bouclé; [knotted] plein de nœuds. -**2.** *inf* [crazy] dingue, cinglé.

loose [luːs] ◇ *adj* -**1.** [not tightly fixed - nail] mal enfoncé; [- screw, bolt] desserré; [- button] qui pend, mal cousu; [- knot] qui se défait; [- floor tile] décollé; [- shelf] mal fixé; [- handle, brick] branlant; **your button's ~** ton bouton est décousu; **I've got a ~ tooth** j'ai une dent qui bouge; **he prised a brick ~** il a réussi à faire bouger une brique; **a ~ slate fell off the roof** une ardoise mal fixée est tombée du toit; **remove all the ~ plaster** enlève tout le plâtre qui se détache; **the steering seems ~** il y a du jeu dans la direction; **a ~ board creaked** une planche disjointe a craqué; **to work ~** [nail] sortir; [screw, bolt] se desserrer; [knot] se défaire; **the wind blew some slates ~** le vent a déplacé quelques ardoises; **to have a ~ cough** *Br* avoir une toux grasse; **~ connection** ELEC mauvais contact *m*. -**2.** [free, unattached] libre; **tie the ~ end of the rope to the post** attache le bout libre de la corde au poteau; **she picked up all the ~ newspapers** elle a ramassé tous les journaux qui traînaient; **a ~ sheet of paper** une feuille volante; **the cutlery was ~ in the drawer** les couverts étaient en vrac dans le tiroir; **her hair hung ~ about her shoulders** ses cheveux flottaient librement sur ses épaules; **several pages have come ~** plusieurs pages se sont détachées; **I got one hand ~** j'ai réussi à dégager une de mes mains; **if I manage to tear myself ~** si je réussis à me libérer OR à me dégager; **he decided to cut ~ from his family and friends** il a décidé de couper les ponts avec sa famille et ses amis; **all the cows were ~ in**

the village toutes les vaches se promenaient OR étaient en liberté dans les rues du village; **a lion got ~ from the zoo** un lion s'est échappé du zoo; **he set** OR **let** OR **turned a mouse ~ in the kitchen** il a lâché une souris dans la cuisine; **he let ~ a torrent of abuse** *fig* il a lâché un torrent d'injures || COMM [not packaged] en vrac; **~ coal** charbon *m* en vrac; **~ cheese** fromage *m* à la coupe; **I always buy vegetables ~** je n'achète jamais de légumes préemballés. -**3.** [slack - grip, hold] mou; [- skin, flesh] flasque; [- bowstring, rope] lâche; **she tied the ribbon in a ~ bow** elle noua le ruban sans le serrer; **his arms hung ~ at his sides** il avait les bras ballants || *fig* [discipline] relâché; **to have a ~ tongue** ne pas savoir tenir sa langue; **~ talk** des propos lestes. -**4.** [not tight-fitting - dress, jacket] ample, flottant. -**5.** [weak - connection, link] vague; **they have ~ ties with other political groups** ils sont vaguement liés à d'autres groupes politiques || [informal - organization] peu structuré; **a ~ political grouping** un regroupement politique peu organisé; **we have a ~ arrangement** nous avons passé un accord officieux. -**6.** [imprecise, broad - thinking, application] peu rigoureux; [- translation, terminology] approximatif; **we can make a ~ distinction between the two phenomena** nous pouvons faire une vague distinction entre les deux phénomènes. -**7.** *pej* [woman] facile; [morals] léger; **~ living** débauche *f*, vie *f* dissolue. -**8.** [not dense or compact - earth] meuble; [- knit, weave] lâche. -**9.** [relaxed - muscles] détendu, relâché, au repos; **to have ~ bowels** avoir la diarrhée. -**10.** FIN disponible; **~ money** argent *m* disponible, liquidités *fpl*. -**11.** *Am phr*: **to keep** OR **to stay ~**▽ rester cool; **hang** OR **stay ~!**▽ relax!, du calme!

◇ *n* [in rugby]: **in the ~** dans la mêlée ouverte.

◇ *vt lit* -**1.** [unleash - dogs] lâcher; [- panic, chaos] semer; **she ~d her tongue** OR **fury upon me** elle s'est déchaînée contre moi || [let fly - bullet] tirer; [- arrow] décocher; **he ~d a volley of threats/abuse at her** *fig* il s'est répandu en menaces/invectives contre elle. -**2.** [undo - knot] défaire; [- hair] détacher; [unfasten - boat, raft] démarrer, détacher.

◆ **on the loose** *adj phr*: **to be on the ~** [gen] être en liberté; [on the run] être en fuite; **a gang of hooligans on the ~** une bande de jeunes voyous qui rôdent; **there was a gunman on the ~ in the neighbourhood** il y avait un homme armé qui rôdait dans le quartier.

◆ **loose off** ◇ *vt sep* [bullet] tirer; [arrow] décocher; [gun] décharger; [curses] lâcher.

◇ *vi insep* [with gun] tirer; **he ~d off into the crowd** il tira au hasard dans la foule || *Am fig* [with insults, criticism etc]: **to ~ off at sb** se déchaîner contre qqn, s'en prendre violemment à qqn.

loosebox ['lu:sbɒks] *n Br* EQUIT box *m*.

loose change *n* petite monnaie *f*.

loose cover *n Br* [for armchair, sofa] housse *f*.

loose end *n*: **I have a few ~s to tie up** j'ai encore quelques petits détails à régler ❑ **to be at a ~** *Br* OR **at ~s** *Am* être dans un moment creux.

loose-fitting *adj* [garment] ample, large, flottant.

loose-jointed *adj* [supple] souple; [gangling] dégingandé.

loose-leaf(ed) *adj* à feuilles mobiles OR volantes; **~ binder** classeur *m* (à feuilles mobiles); **~ paper** feuillets *mpl* mobiles.

loose-limbed *adj* souple, agile.

loosely ['lu:slɪ] *adv* -**1.** [not firmly - pack, fit, hold, wrap] sans serrer; [not closely - knit, weave] lâchement; **the dress was ~ gathered at the waist** la robe était vaguement froncée à la taille; **the rope hung ~** [unattached] la corde pendait; [slackly] la corde était lâche. -**2.** [apply, interpret] mollement; **~ translated** [freely] traduit librement; [inaccurately] mal traduit; **~ speaking, I'd say...** en gros, je dirais... -**3.** [vaguely - connect, relate] vaguement; **the book is only ~ based on my research** le livre n'a qu'un rapport lointain avec mes recherches; **the exhibition is ~ organized around four themes** l'exposition tourne autour de quatre grands thèmes.

loosen ['lu:sn] ◇ *vt* -**1.** [make less tight - knot, screw, lid] desserrer; [- rope, cable] détendre; [- grip, reins] relâcher; **he ~ed his grip** il relâcha OR desserra son étreinte; **I ~ed my belt a notch** j'ai desserré ma ceinture d'un cran; **the accident ~ed the front wheels** depuis l'accident, il y a du jeu dans le train avant; **the punch had ~ed several of his teeth** le coup lui a déchaussé plusieurs dents; **~ the cake from the sides of the tin** détachez le gâteau des bords du moule; **it ~s the bowels** c'est un laxatif; **~ the soil with a hoe** ameublissez le sol avec une binette; **the wine soon ~ed his tongue** le vin eut vite fait de lui délier la langue || [weaken] affaiblir; **they have ~ed their ties with Moscow** leurs liens avec Moscou se sont relâchés. -**2.** [liberalize - rules, restrictions] assouplir.

◇ *vi* [become less tight - knot, screw] se desserrer; [- grip] se relâcher, se desserrer; **one of the bolts had ~ed during the flight** un des boulons s'était desserré pendant le vol.

◆ **loosen up** ◇ *vi insep* -**1.** [get less severe] se montrer moins sévère; **to ~ up on discipline** relâcher la discipline; **will they ~ up on immigration?** vont-ils adopter une position plus souple vis-à-vis de l'immigration? -**2.** [relax socially] se détendre; **~ up a bit!** détends-toi un peu!; **he began to ~ up once the meal was served** il commença à se détendre quand le repas fut servi. -**3.** [limber up - athlete, musician] s'échauffer.

◇ *vt sep* [muscles] échauffer.

looseness ['lu:snɪs] *n* -**1.** [of screw, nail, lever] jeu *m*; [of rope] relâchement *m*, mou *m*. -**2.** [of clothing] ampleur *f*. -**3.** [of thinking, interpretation] manque *m* de rigueur; [of translation, terminology] manque *m* de précision; **he shows a certain ~ in his interpretation of the rules** il interprète le règlement de façon assez fantaisiste. -**4.** *pej* [of way of life] débauche *f*, licence *f*; **a growing ~ of morals** un relâchement croissant des mœurs.

loose scrum *n* RUGBY mêlée *f* ouverte.

loose strife *n* lysimaque *f* commune, souci *m* d'eau.

loose-tongued *adj* bavard.

loose-weave *adj* [fabric] lâche, à mailles lâches.

loot [lu:t] ◇ *vt* [town, goods, tomb] piller; **state coffers were ~ed to finance the war** *fig* les coffres de l'État ont été pillés pour financer la guerre.

◇ *vi* piller, se livrer au pillage.

◇ *n* -**1.** [stolen goods] butin *m*. -**2.** ▽ [money] pognon *m*, fric *m*; **where's the ~ stashed?** où est planqué le fric?; **he's got plenty of ~** il est plein aux as.

looter ['lu:təʳ] *n* [in war, riot] pillard *m*, -e *f*; [of tombs, churches] pilleur *m*, -euse *f*.

looting ['lu:tɪŋ] *n* pillage *m*.

lop [lɒp] (*pt* & *pp* lopped, *cont* lopping) *vt* -**1.** [tree] élaguer, tailler; [branch] couper; **farmers have to ~ and top all trees and hedges** les agriculteurs doivent tailler tous les arbres et toutes les haies. -**2.** *fig* [budget] élaguer, faire des coupes sombres dans; [sum of money, item of expenditure] retrancher, supprimer.

◆ **lop off** *vt sep* -**1.** [branch] couper, tailler. -**2.** *fig* [price, time] réduire; **they could easily ~ another ten per cent off fares** ils pourraient facilement baisser le prix des billets de dix pour cent; **the new motorway will ~ 30 minutes off travelling time** la nouvelle autoroute va raccourcir le trajet de 30 minutes.

lope [ləʊp] ◇ *vi* [runner] courir à grandes foulées; [animal] courir en bondissant.

◇ *n* [of runner] pas *m* de course *(rapide et souple)*; [of animal] course *f (avec des bonds)*.

lop-eared *adj Br* aux oreilles tombantes.

lop-sided *adj* -**1.** [crooked - nose, grin] de travers; [out of line - wall, roof, building] de travers; [asymmetric] asymétrique; [of uneven proportions] disproportionné; **her handwriting is all ~** son écriture part dans tous les sens. -**2.** [unevenly weighted] mal équilibré; [unequal - debate, contest] inégal, déséquilibré; **the article presents a rather ~ picture of events** l'article présente les événements de façon plutôt partiale.

loquacious [lə'kweɪʃəs] *adj fml* loquace, volubile.

loquacity [lə'kwæsətɪ] *n fml* volubilité *f*, loquacité *f*.

lor▽ [lɔ:ʳ] *interj Br dated* crénom!, nom d'une pipe!

loran ['lɔ:rən] *n* loran *m*.

lord [lɔ:d] *n* -**1.** [master] seigneur *m*; [nobleman] noble *m*; **the ~s of industry** les barons de l'industrie; **to live like a ~** mener grand train, vivre en grand seigneur; **she mixes with ~s and ladies** elle fréquente la haute société; **~ of the manor** châtelain *m*, maître *m* de céans; **her ~ and master** *hum* son seigneur et maître. -**2.** ASTROL maître *m*.

◆ **Lord** ◇ *n Br* [title] lord *m*; **Lord (Peter) Snow** lord (Peter) Snow || [term of address]: **my Lord** [to noble] Monsieur le Marquis, Monsieur le Baron; [to judge] Monsieur le juge; [to bishop] Monseigneur, Excellence ❑ **'Lord Jim'** *Conrad* 'Lord Jim'; **'The Lord of the Flies'** *Golding* 'Sa Majesté des Mouches'; **'The Lord of the Rings'** *Tolkien* 'le Seigneur des anneaux'.

◇ *pr n* RELIG: **the Lord** le Seigneur; **Our Lord Jesus Christ** Notre Seigneur Jésus-Christ; **in the year of our Lord 1897** en l'an de grâce 1897; **the Lord's Supper** l'eucharistie *f* || [in interjections and expressions]: **Good Lord!** *inf* Seigneur!; **oh Lord!** *inf* mon Dieu!; **Lord (only) knows!** Dieu seul le sait!; **Lord love a duck!** *inf Br* crénom de nom!

◇ *vt*: **to ~ it over sb** *Br* prendre des airs supérieurs avec qqn.

◆ **Lords** *pl pr n*: **the (House of) Lords** la Chambre des lords.

Lord Advocate *n* ≃ procureur *m* de la République, ≃ procureur *m* général *(en Écosse)*.

Lord Chamberlain *n* grand chambellan *m (en Grande-Bretagne)*.

Lord Chancellor *n* lord *m* chancelier, ≃ ministre *m* de la Justice *(en Grande-Bretagne)*.

Lord Chief Justice (*pl* Lords Chief Justice) *n* ≃ président *m* de la Haute Cour *(en Grande-Bretagne)*.

Lord High Chancellor = **Lord Chancellor**.

Lord Justice of Appeal (*pl* Lords Justices of Appeal) *n* ≃ président *m* de la cour d'appel.

Lord Lieutenant (*pl* Lords Lieutenant OR Lord Lieutenants) *n* lord-lieutenant *m (en Grande-Bretagne)*.

lordly ['lɔ:dlɪ] *adj* -**1.** [arrogant] arrogant, hautain; **with ~ indifference** avec une indifférence souveraine. -**2.** [noble - gesture] noble, auguste; [splendid - feast, occasion, life style] somptueux; **he lives in a ~ mansion** il vit dans une maison princière.

Lord Mayor *n* lord-maire *m*, maire *m*.

Lord Privy Seal (*pl* Lords Privy Seal) *n*: **the ~** *titre du doyen du gouvernement britannique*.

Lord Provost *n*: **the ~** le maire *(dans les villes d'Aberdeen, Dundee, Edimbourg et Glasgow)*.

Lord's [lɔ:dz] *pr n célèbre terrain de cricket dans le nord de Londres*.

lordship ['lɔ:dʃɪp] *n* -**1.** [form of address]: **Your/His Lordship** [to noble] Monsieur le Marquis, Monsieur le Baron; [to judge] Monsieur le juge; [to bishop] Excellence, Son Excellence; **if His Lordship would care to sit down** *hum* si votre Altesse daigne s'asseoir. -**2.** [lands, rights] seigneurie *f*; [power] autorité *f*.

Lord's Prayer *n*: **the ~** le Notre Père.

Lords Spiritual *pl pr n membres ecclésiastiques de la Chambre des lords*.

Lords Temporal *pl pr n membres laïques de la Chambre des lords*.

lore [lɔ:ʳ] *n* -**1.** [folk legend] tradition *f*, traditions *fpl*, coutume *f*, coutumes *fpl*; **according to Celtic ~, it was built by fairies** la tradition celtique veut qu'il ait été construit par des fées. -**2.** [traditional knowledge] science *f*, savoir *m*; she **knows all the countryside ~** elle connaît tous les us et coutumes du pays.

lorgnette [lɔːˈnjet] *n* -**1.** [spectacles] lorgnon *m*, face-à-main *m*. -**2.** [opera glasses] jumelles *fpl* de théâtre, lorgnette *f*.

Lorraine [lɒˈreɪn] *pr n* Lorraine *f*; in **~** en Lorraine.

lorry [ˈlɒrɪ] (*pl* lorries) *n Br* camion *m*, poids lourd *m*; **~ park** aire *f* de stationnement pour poids lourds; **it fell off the back of a ~** *inf* c'est de la marchandise volée.

lorry driver *n Br* chauffeur *m* de camion, routier *m*.

lorry-load *n Br* chargement *m*; **he had a ~ of bricks to deliver** il avait un chargement de briques à livrer.

Los Angeles [lɒsˈændʒɪliːz] *pr n* Los Angeles.

lose [luːz] (*pt* & *pp* lost [lɒst]) ◇ *vt* -**1.** [gen - limb, job, money, patience etc] perdre; **I've lost my umbrella again** j'ai encore perdu mon parapluie; **to ~ one's way** se perdre, s'égarer; **what have you got to ~?** qu'est-ce que tu as à perdre?; **you've got nothing to ~** tu n'as rien à perdre; **we haven't got a moment to ~** il n'y a pas une seconde à perdre; **his shop is losing money** son magasin perd de l'argent; **they are losing their markets to the Koreans** ils sont en train de perdre leurs marchés au profit des Coréens; **he lost no time in telling her she was wrong** il ne s'est pas gêné pour lui dire qu'elle avait tort; **we lost 80 days in strikes last year** l'année dernière, nous avons perdu 80 journées de travail à cause des grèves; **don't talk so fast, you've lost me** ne parle pas si vite, je n'arrive pas à te suivre; **the hint/the suggestion was not lost on him** l'allusion/la suggestion ne lui a pas échappé; **your compliment was lost on her** elle ne s'est pas rendu compte que tu lui faisais un compliment; **at what age did he ~ his mother?** à quel âge a-t-il perdu sa mère?; **they lost their homes in the flood** ils ont perdu leur maison dans l'inondation; **30 lives were lost in the fire** 30 personnes ont péri dans l'incendie, l'incendie a fait 30 morts; **she lost a leg/her eyesight in an accident** elle a perdu une jambe/la vue dans un accident; **to ~ one's voice** avoir une extinction de voix; **to ~ one's appetite** perdre l'appétit; **it made me ~ my appetite** ça m'a coupé l'appétit; **the plane is losing altitude** OR **height** l'avion perd de l'altitude; **to ~ one's balance** perdre l'équilibre; **to ~ consciousness** perdre connaissance; **to ~ face** perdre la face; **to ~ ground** perdre du terrain; **to ~ one's head** perdre la tête; **I've lost interest in it** ça ne m'intéresse plus; **he lost his nerve at the last minute** le courage lui a manqué au dernier moment. -**2.** [not win] perdre; **he lost four games to Karpov** il a perdu quatre parties contre Karpov. -**3.** [shed, get rid of] perdre; **to ~ weight** perdre du poids; **I've lost several pounds** j'ai perdu plusieurs kilos; **the trees ~ their leaves in winter** les arbres perdent leurs feuilles en hiver || [elude, shake off] semer; **she managed to ~ the detective** elle a réussi à semer le détective. -**4.** [cause to lose] coûter, faire perdre; **it lost him his job** ça lui a fait perdre son emploi; **it lost us the contract** cela nous a fait perdre le contrat; **his attitude lost him our respect** à cause de son attitude, il a perdu notre estime. -**5.** [subj: clock, watch]: **my watch ~s five minutes a day** ma montre prend cinq minutes de retard par jour.
◇ *vi* -**1.** perdre; **they lost by one goal** ils ont perdu d'un but; **either way, I can't ~** je suis gagnant à tous les coups; **the dollar is losing in value (against the deutschmark)** le dollar baisse (par rapport au Deutsche Mark); **his work ~s a lot in translation** son œuvre se prête très mal à la traduction; **the play didn't ~ much in the television version** la pièce n'a pas perdu beaucoup en étant adaptée pour la télévision; **if you sell the house now you'll ~ on it** si tu vends la maison maintenant tu vas perdre de l'argent; **I lost on the deal** j'ai été perdant dans l'affaire. -**2.** [clock, watch] retarder.
◆ **lose out** *vi insep* perdre, être perdant; **to ~ out on a deal** être perdant dans une affaire; **will the Americans ~ out to the Japanese in computers?** les Américains vont-ils perdre le marché de l'informatique au profit des Japonais?

loser [ˈluːzəʳ] *n* -**1.** [gen & SPORT] perdant *m*, -e *f*; **he's not a very good ~** il est mauvais perdant OR joueur; **they're the ~s by it** *Br fig* ce sont eux les perdants dans cette affaire. -**2.** *inf* [failure - person] raté *m*, -e *f*; **he's a born ~** c'est un vrai raté, il échoue dans tout ce qu'il entreprend.

losing [ˈluːzɪŋ] *adj* -**1.** [gen & SPORT] perdant; **to fight a ~ battle** engager une bataille perdue d'avance. -**2.** [unprofitable]: **the business was a ~ concern** cette entreprise n'était pas viable; **it's a ~ proposition** ce n'est pas rentable.
◆ **losings** *npl* [losses] pertes *fpl*.

loss [lɒs] *n* -**1.** [gen] perte *f*; **have you reported the ~ to the police?** avez-vous signalé cette perte à la police?; **it's your gain and their ~** c'est vous qui y gagnez et eux qui y perdent; **it's your ~!** tant pis pour vous!; **her retirement will be a great ~ to us all** son départ à la retraite sera une grande perte pour nous tous; **it's no great ~ to me** ce n'est pas une grosse perte pour moi; **he would be no great ~ to the firm** ce ne serait pas une grande perte pour l'entreprise; **it can cause temporary ~ of vision** cela peut provoquer OR entraîner une perte momentanée de la vue; **the ~ of a close relative** la perte OR la mort d'un parent proche; **the party suffered heavy ~es in the last elections** le parti a subi de lourdes pertes OR a perdu de nombreux sièges lors des dernières élections; **the company announced ~es of** OR **a ~ of a million pounds** la société a annoncé un déficit d'un million de livres; **we made a ~ of 10% on the deal** nous avons perdu 10 % dans l'affaire; **to sell at a ~** vendre à perte; **the closure will cause the ~ of hundreds of jobs** la fermeture provoquera la disparition de centaines d'emplois; **fortunately there was little ~ of life** heureusement, il n'y eut que peu de victimes; **there was terrible ~ of life in the last war** la dernière guerre a coûté beaucoup de vies humaines; **they inflicted heavy ~es on the enemy** ils infligèrent de lourdes pertes à l'ennemi; **heat ~** perte OR déperdition *f* de chaleur. -**2.** [feeling of pain, unhappiness] malheur *m*, chagrin *m*; **his family rallied round him in his ~** sa famille l'a beaucoup entouré dans son chagrin; **she tried to hide her sense of ~ from her friends** elle essayait de cacher son chagrin à ses amis; **a tremendous feeling of ~ overcame him** il réalisa avec angoisse ce qu'il avait perdu. -**3.** [in insurance] sinistre *m*; **the following ~es are not covered by the policy** les sinistres suivants ne sont pas couverts par cette police. -**4.** *phr*: **to be at a ~** ne pas savoir quoi faire, être déconcerté OR dérouté; **he's never at a ~** il ne se laisse jamais déconcerter; **I was at a ~ for words** je ne savais pas quoi dire, les mots me manquaient; **I'm at a ~ as to how to tell him the truth** je ne sais pas comment m'y prendre pour lui dire la vérité; **she was at a ~ to explain why she'd done it** elle était dans l'incapacité d'expliquer son comportement.

loss adjuster *n* [for insurance] expert *m*; NAUT dispatcheur *m*.

loss leader *n* COMM *article vendu à perte dans le but d'attirer la clientèle*.

lossmaker [ˈlɒsmeɪkəʳ] *n* gouffre *m* financier.

lost [lɒst] ◇ *pt* & *pp* → **lose**.
◇ *adj* -**1.** [keys, money etc] perdu; **all is not yet ~** tout n'est pas perdu; **they have discovered a ~ masterpiece** ils ont découvert un chef-d'œuvre disparu; **the ~ city of Atlantis** Atlantide, la ville engloutie; **the ~ and found department** le bureau des objets trouvés; **I put an advert in the ~ and found column** j'ai mis une annonce dans la rubrique des objets trouvés. -**2.** [person - in direction] perdu, égaré; **can you help me, I'm ~** pouvez-vous m'aider, je me suis perdu OR égaré; **to get ~** se perdre; **they got ~ on the way back** ils se sont perdus sur le chemin du retour; **~ in action** MIL mort au combat; **a ~ sheep** *literal* & *fig* une brebis égarée; **a ~ soul** une âme en peine; **a ~ woman** *dated* une femme perdue *(moralement)* ❑ **get ~!** *inf* va te faire voir! -**3.** *fig* [engrossed] perdu, plongé, absorbé; **she was ~ in her book** elle était plongée dans son livre; **~ in thought/in a daydream** perdu dans ses pensées/dans une rêverie. -**4.** [wasted - time] perdu; [- opportunity] perdu, manqué; [- youth] gâché; **the allusion was ~ on me** je n'ai pas compris OR saisi l'allusion; **your advice would be ~ on them** leur donner un conseil serait peine perdue. -**5.** [confused, bewildered] perdu; **I'm ~, start again!** je suis perdu OR je ne vous suis plus, recommencez! || [disconcerted] désorienté; **I felt quite ~ in the new job** je me sentais complètement perdu dans mon nouveau travail; **I'm ~ for words** je ne sais pas quoi dire. -**6.** [oblivious] insensible; **he was ~ to the world** il avait l'esprit ailleurs.

lost cause *n* cause *f* perdue.

lost generation *n* génération *f* perdue.

lost property *n* objets *mpl* trouvés.

lost property office *n Br* bureau *m* des objets trouvés.

lot [lɒt] *n* -**1.** *inf* [group of people]: **this ~ are leaving today and another ~ are arriving tomorrow** ce groupe part aujourd'hui et un autre (groupe) arrive demain; **the new recruits are quite an interesting ~** les nouveaux sont tous assez intéressants; **I don't want you getting mixed up with that ~** je ne veux pas que tu traînes avec cette bande; **I'm taking my ~ to the cinema** j'emmène les miens au cinéma; **come here, you ~!** venez ici, vous autres! ❑ **he's a bad ~** c'est un sale type. -**2.** [group of things]: **most of the last ~ of fans we had in were defective** presque tous les ventilateurs du dernier lot étaient défectueux; **take all this ~ and dump it in my office** prends tout ça et mets-le dans mon bureau; **I've just been given another ~ of letters to sign** on vient de me donner un autre paquet de lettres à signer. -**3.** [item in auction, in lottery] lot *m*; **~ 49 is a set of five paintings** le lot 49 est un ensemble de cinq tableaux; **the winner of ~ 20** le gagnant du lot 20. -**4.** [destiny, fortune] sort *m*, destin *m*; **to be content with one's ~** être content de son sort; **it was his ~ in life to be the underdog** il était destiné à rester un sous-fifre ❑ **it fell to my ~ to be the first to try** le sort a voulu que je sois le premier à essayer; **to throw in one's ~ with sb** se mettre du côté de qqn. -**5.** [random choice]: **the winners are chosen by ~** les gagnants sont choisis par tirage au sort; **to draw** OR **cast ~s** tirer au sort. -**6.** *Am* [plot of land] terrain *m*; **a vacant ~** un terrain vague; **a used car ~** un parking de voitures d'occasion. -**7.** *Am* CIN studio *m* (de cinéma).
◆ **lots** *inf* ◇ *pron* beaucoup; **do you need any paper/envelopes? I've got ~s** est-ce que tu as besoin de papier/d'enveloppes? j'en ai plein; **there are ~s to choose from** il y a du choix.
◇ *adv* beaucoup; **are you feeling better now? – oh, ~s, thank you** vous vous sentez mieux maintenant? – oh, beaucoup mieux, merci; **this is ~s easier than the last exam** c'est vachement plus facile que le dernier exam.
◆ **lots of** *det phr* beaucoup de; **we had ~s of fun** on s'est bien marrés; **I've been there ~s of times** j'y suis allé plein de fois; **~s and ~s of lovely money** tout plein de sous; **~s of love** [at end of letter] ≃ je t'embrasse, grosses bises; **they've got money, and ~s of it!** ils ont de l'argent, et pas qu'un peu!
◆ **a lot** ◇ *pron phr* beaucoup; **there's a ~ still to be done** il y a encore beaucoup à faire; **there's an awful ~ wrong with the plan** il y a beaucoup de choses qui ne vont pas dans ce projet; **there's not a ~ you can do about it** tu n'y peux pas grand-chose; **I'd give a ~ to know** je donnerais beaucoup OR cher pour savoir; **it did me a ~ of good** ça m'a fait beaucoup de

bien; a ~ of people think it's true beaucoup de gens pensent que c'est vrai; what a ~ of people! quelle foule!, que de monde!; there's an awful ~ of work still to be done il reste encore beaucoup de travail à faire; I've had such a ~ of cards from well-wishers j'ai vraiment reçu beaucoup de cartes de sympathie; she takes a ~ of care over her appearance elle fait très attention à son apparence; we see a ~ of them nous les voyons beaucoup OR souvent; a (fat) ~ of help you were! *iron*, you were a (fat) ~ of help! *iron* ça, pour être utile, tu as été utile! *iron*.

◇ *adv phr* beaucoup; a ~ better/more beaucoup mieux/plus; their house is a ~ bigger leur maison est beaucoup plus grande; he's changed a ~ since I last saw him il a beaucoup changé depuis la dernière fois que je l'ai vu; she travels a ~ on business elle voyage beaucoup pour ses affaires; thanks a ~! merci beaucoup!; a (fat) ~ she cares! *iron* elle s'en fiche pas mal!

◆ **the lot** *pron phr* le tout; there isn't much, take the ~ il n'y en a pas beaucoup, prenez tout; there aren't many, take the ~ il n'y en a pas beaucoup, prenez-les tous; she ate the (whole) ~ elle a tout mangé; the (whole) ~ of them came ils sont tous venus; clear off, the ~ of you débarrassez-moi tous le plancher; it only cost me a pound for the ~ le tout ne m'a coûté qu'une livre; that's the ~ tout est là; that's the OR your ~ for tonight *inf* c'est tout pour ce soir.

Lot [lɒt] *pr n* BIBLE Lot, Loth.

loth [ləʊθ] = **loath**.

Lothario [lə'θɑːrɪəʊ] (*pl* Lotharios) *n* don Juan *m*, libertin *m*.

Lothian Region ['ləʊðjən-] *pr n* la région du Lothian *(Écosse)*.

lotion ['ləʊʃn] *n* lotion *f*; aftershave ~ lotion après-rasage; hand/suntan ~ crème pour les mains/bronzante.

lottery ['lɒtərɪ] *n* -**1.** loterie *f*; ~ ticket billet *m* de loterie. -**2.** *fig* [matter of luck] loterie *f*.

lotto ['lɒtəʊ] *n* loto *m (jeu de société)*.

lotus ['ləʊtəs] *n* lotus *m*.

lotus-eater *n* MYTH lotophage *m*; *fig* doux rêveur *m*.

lotus position *n* position *f* du lotus.

loud [laʊd] ◇ *adj* -**1.** [noise, shout] grand, puissant; [voice, music] fort; [explosion] fort, violent; the television is too ~ la télévision est trop forte, le son de la télévision est trop fort; the door slammed with a ~ bang la porte a claqué très fort; a ~ argument was going on in the next room on se disputait bruyamment dans la pièce voisine; "come tomorrow", he said in a ~ whisper «venez demain», chuchota-t-il, assez fort pour qu'on l'entende || [vigorous - protest, applause] vif; there were ~ protests among politicians de vives protestations se sont élevées dans la classe politique, la classe politique a vivement protesté; they were ~ in their support/condemnation of the project ils ont vigoureusement soutenu/condamné le projet || *pej* [loudmouthed, brash] bruyant, tapageur; he's a bit ~, isn't he? ce n'est pas le genre discret! -**2.** [garish - colour] criard, voyant; [- pattern] voyant; he wore a suit with a ~ check il portait un costume à carreaux très voyant.

◇ *adv* fort; can you speak a little ~er? pouvez-vous parler un peu plus fort?; the music was turned up ~ on avait mis la musique à fond; to read out ~ lire à haute voix; I was thinking out ~ je pensais tout haut; receiving you ~ and clear je vous reçois cinq sur cinq.

loudhailer [,laʊd'heɪlə^r] *n Br* porte-voix *m inv*, mégaphone *m*; they spoke to him by ~ ils lui ont parlé à l'aide d'un porte-voix.

loudly ['laʊdlɪ] *adv* -**1.** [noisily - speak] d'une voix forte; [- laugh] bruyamment; our neighbour banged ~ on the wall notre voisin a donné de grands coups contre le mur; the supporters cheered ~ les supporters ont applaudi bruyamment || [vigorously] avec force OR vigueur; we protested ~ nous avons protesté vigoureusement. -**2.** [garishly] de façon tapageuse OR voyante.

loudmouth *inf* ['laʊdmaʊθ, *pl* -maʊðz] *n* -**1.** [noisy person] braillard *m*, -e *f*, gueulard *m*, -e *f*. -**2.** [boaster] crâneur *m*, -euse *f*, frimeur *m*, -euse *f*. -**3.** [gossip] commère *f*.

loudmouthed *inf* ['laʊdmaʊðd] *adj* -**1.** [noisy] fort en gueule. -**2.** [boastful] crâneur; [gossipy] bavard, frimeur.

loudness ['laʊdnɪs] *n* -**1.** [of sound] intensité *f*, force *f*; [of voice] intensité *f*; [of cheers] vigueur *f*; the ~ of the music makes conversation impossible la musique est tellement forte qu'on ne s'entend pas. -**2.** [on hi-fi system]: ~ control bouton *m* de compensation physiologique. -**3.** [of colours, dress] violence *f*, éclat *m*.

loud pedal *n* MUS pédale *f* forte.

loudspeaker [,laʊd'spiːkə^r] *n* haut-parleur *m*; [on stereo] enceinte *f*, baffle *m*.

lough [lɒk] *n Ir* [lake] lac *m*; [inlet] lagune *f*.

louis ['luːɪ] (*pl inv* [-iːz]) *n* [coin] louis *m* (d'or).

Louis ['luːɪ] *pr n* Louis; Saint ~ saint Louis.

Louisiana [luː,iːzɪ'ænə] *pr n* Louisiane *f*; in ~ en Louisiane.

Louisiana Purchase *pr n*: the ~ l'achat *m* de la Louisiane.

THE LOUISIANA PURCHASE:
Cession par la France aux États-Unis du territoire de la Louisiane, en 1803. Craignant l'expansion de l'empire napoléonien, Thomas Jefferson négocia avec la France, qui céda facilement l'immense territoire contre de l'argent liquide. La surface du pays s'en trouva doublée.

lounge [laʊndʒ] ◇ *n* -**1.** [room - in private house, on ship, in hotel] salon *m*; [- at airport] salle *f* d'attente; [bar] (salle *f* de) bar *m*; *Br* [- in pub] = **lounge bar**. -**2.** [rest]: to have a ~ in the sun paresser OR se prélasser au soleil. -**3.** [seat] méridienne *f*.

◇ *vi* -**1.** [recline] s'allonger, se prélasser; [sprawl] être allongé; he spent the afternoon lounging on the sofa reading il a passé l'après-midi à lire allongé sur le canapé; he ~d against the counter il était appuyé nonchalamment contre le comptoir. -**2.** [laze] paresser; [hang about] traîner; gangs of kids were lounging on street corners des bandes de gosses traînaient au coin des rues || [stroll] flâner; I spent the afternoon lounging round the shops j'ai passé l'après-midi à flâner dans les magasins.

◆ **lounge about** *Br*, **lounge around** = **lounge** *vi* **2**.

lounge bar *n Br salon dans un pub (plus confortable et plus cher que le «public bar»)*.

lounge lizard *inf n dated* salonnard *m*, -e *f*.

lounger ['laʊndʒə^r] *n* -**1.** [sunbed] lit *m* de plage. -**2.** [person] paresseux *m*, -euse *f*.

lounge suit *n Br* costume *m* de ville; [on invitation] tenue *f* de ville.

lour ['laʊə^r] = **lower** *(sky, weather)*.

louse [laʊs] (*pl sense 1* lice [laɪs], *pl sense 2* louses)
◇ *n* -**1.** [insect] pou *m*. -**2.** ▽ [person] salaud *m*, chienne *f*.

◇ *vt* [remove lice from] épouiller.

◆ **louse up**▽ *vt sep* [spoil] foutre en l'air.

lousy ['laʊzɪ] (*compar* lousier, *superl* lousiest) *adj* -**1.** *inf* [appalling - film, singer] nul; [- weather] pourri; we had a ~ holiday! bonjour les vacances!; I've got a ~ hangover! j'ai une de ces gueules de bois!; I feel ~ this morning je suis mal fichu ce matin; I'm ~ at tennis, I'm a ~ tennis player je suis nul au tennis, je joue au tennis comme un pied; it's in ~ condition il est en très mauvais état; you're a ~ liar [lie badly] tu ne sais pas mentir; [as intensifier] tu n'es qu'un sale menteur || [annoying] fichu, sacré; I've got these ~ letters to write! j'ai ces fichues lettres à écrire! -**2.** *inf* [mean] vache; that was a ~ trick! tu parles d'une vacherie!; I feel ~ about what happened ça m'embête, ce qui est arrivé. -**3.** *inf* [full]: the town was ~ with police la ville grouillait de flics; they're ~ with money ils sont bourrés de fric OR pleins aux as. -**4.** [lice-infested] pouilleux.

lout [laʊt] *n* [bumpkin] rustre *m*; [hooligan] voyou *m*; you ignorant ~! espèce de brute épaisse!

loutish ['laʊtɪʃ] *adj* [behaviour] grossier; [manners] de rustre, mal dégrossi.

louvre *Br*, **louver** *Am* ['luːvə^r] *n* [slat] lamelle *f*; [window] jalousie *f*, volet *m* à claire-voie, persienne *f*.

louvred *Br*, **louvered** *Am* ['luːvəd] *adj* à claire-voie.

lovable ['lʌvəbl] *adj* charmant, sympathique, attachant.

lovage ['lʌvɪdʒ] *n* BOT livèche *f*, levisticum *m*.

lovat ['lʌvət] *n couleur bleu-vert ou jaune-vert qu'on trouve en particulier dans les lainages et dans les tweeds*.

love [lʌv] ◇ *vt* -**1.** [sweetheart] aimer; [friends, relatives] aimer beaucoup OR bien; I like you but I don't ~ you je t'aime bien mais je ne suis pas amoureux de toi; I ~ my brother but... j'aime beaucoup mon frère, mais... ❑ I'll have to ~ you and leave you *inf* ce n'est pas tout mais il faut que j'y aille. -**2.** [enjoy] aimer, adorer; don't you just ~ that little dress? cette petite robe est vraiment adorable, tu ne trouves pas?; I love lying OR to lie in bed on Sunday mornings j'adore faire la grasse matinée le dimanche; she ~s to hear you sing elle adore vous entendre chanter; I'd ~ to come j'aimerais beaucoup venir; I'd ~ you to come j'aimerais beaucoup que OR cela me ferait très plaisir que tu viennes; would you like to come too? – I'd ~ to voudriez-vous venir aussi? – avec grand plaisir. -**3.** [prize - one's country, freedom etc] aimer.

◇ *n* -**1.** [for person] amour *m*; motherly ~ amour maternel; we didn't marry for ~ nous n'avons pas fait un mariage d'amour; he did it out of ~ for her il l'a fait par amour pour elle; it was ~ at first sight ce fut le coup de foudre; to be in ~ être amoureux; he's in ~ with Patricia il est amoureux de Patricia; they were deeply in ~ ils s'aimaient profondément; to fall in ~ (with sb) tomber amoureux (de qqn); to make ~ faire l'amour; to make ~ to sb [have sex with] faire l'amour à qqn; *arch* [court] faire la cour à qqn; make ~ not war! faites l'amour, pas la guerre!; for the ~ of God OR *Br* Mike *inf*! pour l'amour du ciel!; Harry sends OR gives you his ~ Harry t'embrasse; give my ~ to Harry embrasse Harry de ma part OR pour moi; (lots of) ~ from Jane, all my ~, Jane [in letter] affectueusement, Jane ❑ I wouldn't do it for ~ nor money *inf* je ne le ferais pas pour tout l'or du monde, je ne le ferais pour rien au monde; you can't get a taxi for ~ nor money round here *inf* pas moyen de trouver un taxi par ici; there's no ~ lost between them ils se détestent cordialement; 'All For Love' *Dryden* 'Tout pour l'amour'; 'Love's Labours Lost' *Shakespeare* 'Peines d'amour perdues'. -**2.** [for jazz, one's country etc] amour *m*; his ~ of good food sa passion pour la bonne chère; she fell in ~ with the house immediately elle a eu le coup de foudre pour la maison; I don't do this job for the ~ of it je ne fais pas ce travail pour le OR par plaisir. -**3.** [beloved person] amour *m*; he's one of her many ~s c'est un des nombreux hommes qu'elle a aimés; she's the ~ of his life c'est la femme de sa vie; isn't he a ~! *inf Br* ce qu'il est mignon OR chou! || [favourite activity] passion *f*; music is his great ~ la musique est sa grande passion. -**4.** [term of address]: thank you, (my) ~ *inf* merci, mon chou ‖ [to stranger]: wait a minute, ~! *inf Br* [woman to child] attends une minute, mon petit!; [woman to man] attendez une minute, Monsieur!; [to woman] attendez une minute, Madame! -**5.** SPORT zéro *m*; 40 ~ 40 zéro.

loveable [ˈlʌvəbl] = **lovable**.

love affair *n* liaison *f* (amoureuse); *fig* passion *f*; his ~ with Paris sa passion pour Paris.

lovebird [ˈlʌvbɜːd] *n* -**1.** ORNITH perruche *f*; ~s inséparables *mpl*. -**2.** *hum* [lover] amoureux *m*, -euse *f*; the ~s are in the other room les amoureux OR les tourtereaux sont dans l'autre pièce.

lovebite [ˈlʌvbaɪt] *n Br* suçon *m*.

love child *n* enfant *mf* de l'amour.

love-in-a-mist *n* BOT *(U)* cheveux *mpl* de Vénus, nigelle *f* de Damas.

love knot *n* lacs *m* d'amour.

loveless [ˈlʌvlɪs] *adj* [marriage] sans amour; [person - unloved] mal aimé; [- unloving] sans cœur, incapable d'aimer.

love letter *n* lettre *f* d'amour, billet *m* doux.

love life *n* vie *f* sentimentale; how's your ~? *inf* comment vont tes amours?

loveliness [ˈlʌvlɪnɪs] *n* charme *m*, beauté *f*.

lovelorn [ˈlʌvlɔːn] *adj* malheureux en amour; to be ~ avoir le mal d'amour.

lovely [ˈlʌvlɪ] (*compar* lovelier, *superl* loveliest)
◇ *adj* -**1.** [beautiful] beau, très joli; [- child] joli, mignon; [home, scenery] joli. -**2.** [view, evening, weather] beau; [holiday] (très) agréable; [dress] joli; what a ~ day! quelle belle journée!; that was a ~ meal nous avons fait un excellent repas; we had a ~ day at the beach nous avons passé une très agréable journée à la plage; it's a ~ idea c'est une très bonne idée; it's ~ to see you je suis enchanté OR ravi de vous voir; this wool is ~ and soft *Br* cette laine est très douce au toucher; it's ~ and warm by the fire *Br* il fait bon près de la cheminée; it sounds ~ cela a l'air très bien ❑ 'Oh! What a Lovely War' *Attenborough* 'Ah! Dieu que la guerre est jolie'. -**3.** [in character] charmant, très aimable; her parents are ~ people ses parents sont des gens charmants.
◇ *n inf* mignonne *f*.

lovemaking [ˈlʌvˌmeɪkɪŋ] *n* -**1.** [sexual intercourse] ébats *mpl* (amoureux); during their ~ pendant qu'ils faisaient l'amour. -**2.** *arch* [courtship] cour *f*.

love match *n* mariage *m* d'amour.

love nest *n* nid *m* d'amour.

love potion *n* philtre *m*.

lover [ˈlʌvəʳ] *n* -**1.** [sexual partner] amant *m*, -e *f*; he fancies himself as a great ~ il se considère comme un merveilleux amant ❑ 'The Lover' *Pinter* 'l'Amant'. -**2.** *dated* [suitor] amoureux *m*, soupirant *m*; the young ~s les jeunes amoureux *mpl*. -**3.** [enthusiast] amateur *m*, -trice *f*; he's a real music ~ c'est un mélomane; I'm not a dog ~ myself moi-même je n'aime pas beaucoup les chiens; for all ~s of good food pour tous les amateurs de bonne cuisine; she's a great ~ of the cinema elle adore le cinéma, c'est une grande cinéphile.

lover-boy *inf n hum* OR *pej* [womanizer] don Juan *m*, tombeur *m*, séducteur *m*.

love scene *n* scène *f* d'amour.

lovesick [ˈlʌvsɪk] *adj*: to be ~ se languir d'amour.

love song *n* chanson *f* d'amour.

love story *n* histoire *f* d'amour.

love token *n* gage *m* d'amour.

lovey-dovey *inf* [ˈlʌvɪdʌvɪ] *adj hum & pej* doucereux.

loving [ˈlʌvɪŋ] *adj* [affectionate] affectueux; [tender] tendre; ~ kindness bonté *f*.

-loving *in cpds*: wine~ qui aime le vin, amateur de vin; music~ amateur de musique, mélomane; money~ qui aime l'argent, cupide.

loving cup *n* coupe *f* de l'amitié.

lovingly [ˈlʌvɪŋlɪ] *adv* [affectionately] affectueusement; [tenderly] tendrement; [passionately] avec amour, amoureusement; [with great care] soigneusement, avec soin.

low [ləʊ] ◇ *adj* -**1.** [in height] bas; this room has a ~ ceiling cette pièce est basse de plafond; ~ hills collines peu élevées; a ~ neckline un décolleté; the sun was already ~ in the sky le soleil était déjà bas dans le ciel; the houses are built on ~ ground les maisons sont bâties dans une cuvette; the river is ~ today la rivière est basse aujourd'hui; '~ bridge' AUT 'hauteur limitée'. -**2.** [in scale - temperature] bas; [- level] faible; the temperature is in the ~ twenties il fait un peu plus de vingt degrés; old people are given very ~ priority les personnes âgées ne sont absolument pas considérées comme prioritaires; I've reached a ~ point in my career j'ai atteint un creux dans ma carrière; their relationship is at a ~ ebb leurs relations sont au plus bas; a ~ blood count une numération globulaire basse; ~ gear *Am* première (vitesse) *f*; 'engage ~ gear' AUT 'utilisez le frein moteur' ‖ [in degree, intensity - probability, visibility] faible; [- fire] bas; [- lighting] faible, tamisé; cook on a ~ heat faire cuire à feu doux; a ~ pressure area METEOR une zone de basse pression ‖ [in value, amount - figure, price] bas, faible; [- profit] faible, maigre; ~ economic growth faible croissance économique; attendance was ~ il y avait peu de monde; we're only playing for ~ stakes nous ne jouons que de petites mises, nous ne jouons pas de grosses sommes; we're rather ~ on whisky on n'a plus beaucoup de whisky; we're getting ~ on kerosene nous allons bientôt être à court de kérosène; the ammunition is getting ~ nous aurons bientôt épuisé les munitions; ~ in calories pauvre en calories; the soil is very ~ in nitrogen la terre est très pauvre en azote; to play a ~ trump CARDS jouer un petit atout ❑ ~ tar cigarettes cigarettes *fpl* à faible teneur en goudron. -**3.** [poor - intelligence] faible; [- opinion] faible, piètre; [- in health] mauvais, médiocre; he's very ~ at the moment il est bien bas OR bien affaibli en ce moment; I'm in rather ~ spirits, I feel rather ~ je n'ai pas le moral, je suis assez déprimé; [- in quality] mauvais; the pupils in this school have a ~ standard of reading les élèves de cette école ont un niveau faible en lecture; a ~ quality carpet une moquette de mauvaise qualité. -**4.** [in rank] bas, inférieur; to be of ~ birth être de basse extraction OR d'origine modeste; ~ ranking officials petits fonctionnaires *mpl*, fonctionnaires *mpl* subalternes. -**5.** [vulgar - behaviour] grossier; [- tastes] vulgaire; to keep ~ company fréquenter des gens peu recommandables; that was a ~ trick c'était un sale tour; a man of ~ cunning un homme d'une ruse ignoble ❑ ~ comedy farce *f* THÉÂT. -**6.** [primitive]: ~ forms of life des formes de vie inférieures OR peu évoluées. -**7.** [soft - voice, music] bas, faible; [- light] faible; keep your voice ~ ne parlez pas trop fort; turn the radio down ~ mettez la radio moins fort; turn the lights down ~ baissez les lumières; she gave a ~ groan elle poussa un faible gémissement; we heard a ~ moan nous avons entendu une plainte étouffée. -**8.** [deep - note, voice] bas.
◇ *adv* -**1.** [in height] bas; ~er down plus bas; aim ~ visez bas; I can't bend down that ~ je ne peux pas me pencher si bas; a helicopter flew ~ over the town un hélicoptère a survolé la ville à basse altitude; the sun sank ~ on the horizon le soleil est descendu très bas sur l'horizon; she was sitting very ~ in her chair elle était avachie sur sa chaise; he bowed ~ il s'inclina profondément; to lie ~ [hide] se cacher; [keep low profile] adopter un profil bas; to be laid ~ [ill] être immobilisé. -**2.** [in intensity] bas; the fire had burnt ~ le feu avait baissé; stocks are running ~ les réserves baissent; the batteries are running ~ les piles sont usées. -**3.** [in price]: to buy ~ acheter à bas prix; ST. EX acheter quand les cours sont bas. -**4.** [morally]: I wouldn't stoop OR sink so ~ as to tell lies je ne m'abaisserais pas à mentir.
◇ *n* -**1.** [in height] bas *m*; [in intensity] minimum *m*; the heating is on ~ le chauffage est au minimum. -**2.** [low point] niveau *m* bas, point *m* bas; the dollar has reached a record ~ le dollar a atteint son niveau le plus bas; relations between them are at an all-time ~ leurs relations n'ont jamais été si mauvaises. -**3.** METEOR dépression *f*. -**4.** *Am* AUT: in ~ en première OR seconde. -**5.** *lit* [of cattle] meuglement *m*, beuglement *m*.
◇ *vi* meugler, beugler.

low-born *adj* d'origine modeste, de basse extraction.

lowboy [ˈləʊbɔɪ] *n* commode *f* (basse).

lowbrow [ˈləʊbraʊ] ◇ *n pej* personne *f* sans prétentions intellectuelles OR terre à terre.
◇ *adj* [person] peu intellectuel, terre à terre; [book, film] sans prétentions intellectuelles; ~ literature littérature *f* de hall de gare.

low-budget *adj* économique.

low-calorie *adj* (à) basses calories.

Low Church *adj* à tendance évangélique *(dans l'Église anglicane)*.

low-cost *adj* (à) bon marché.

Low Countries *pl pr n*: the ~ les Pays-Bas *mpl*; in the ~ aux Pays-Bas.

low-cut *adj* décolleté.

lowdown *inf* [ˈləʊdaʊn] *n (U)* renseignements *mpl*; can you give me the ~ on what happened? tu peux me mettre au courant de ce qui s'est passé?
◆ **low-down** *adj* -**1.** [shameful] honteux, bas; [mean] mesquin; that was a dirty low-down trick c'était un sale tour. -**2.** *Am* [depressed] cafardeux; I'm feeling low-down j'ai le cafard.

lower[1] [ˈləʊəʳ] ◇ *adj (compar of* low*)* inférieur, plus bas; the ~ deck [of ship] le pont inférieur; the ~ House OR Chamber *Br* POL la Chambre basse OR des communes; the ~ classes les classes inférieures; the ~ middle class la petite bourgeoisie; ~ vertebrates vertébrés inférieurs; 'The Lower Depths' *Gorky, Renoir* 'les Bas-Fonds'.
◇ *adv (compar of* low*)*: the ~ paid la tranche inférieure du salariat.
◇ *vt* -**1.** [blind] baisser; [eyes] baisser; [sails] abaisser, amener; ~ your aim a bit visez un peu plus bas; the lifeboats were ~ed into the sea les canots de sauvetage ont été mis à la mer; supplies were ~ed down to us on a rope on nous a descendu des provisions au bout d'une corde; she ~ed herself into the water elle se laissa glisser dans l'eau ❑ ~ed control button *Am dans un ascenseur, bouton accessible aux personnes en fauteuil roulant*; to ~ one's guard [in boxing] baisser sa garde; *fig* prêter le flanc; to ~ one's sights: he's ~ed his sights since then il est un peu moins ambitieux depuis. -**2.** [reduce - price, pressure, standard] baisser, diminuer; ~ your voice parlez moins fort, baissez la voix. -**3.** [morally]: she wouldn't ~ herself to talk to them elle ne s'abaisserait pas au point de leur adresser la parole.
◇ *vi* [diminish - pressure] diminuer; [- price] baisser.
◆ **lower away** *vi insep*: ~ away! laissez descendre!

lower[2] [ˈlaʊəʳ] *vi* -**1.** [sky, weather] se couvrir; a ~ing sky un ciel menaçant OR couvert. -**2.** [person] regarder d'un air menaçant; he sat in the corner and ~ed at me il s'assit dans un coin et il me regarda d'un œil OR d'un air menaçant.

lower-case [ˈləʊəʳ-] ◇ *adj* TYPO en bas de casse.
◇ *n* bas *m* de casse.

lower-class [ˈləʊəʳ-] *adj* populaire.

lowering[1] [ˈləʊərɪŋ] ◇ *n* -**1.** [of flag] abaissement *m*; [of boat] mise *f* à la mer; the ~ of the coffin into the grave la descente du cercueil dans la tombe. -**2.** [reduction - of temperature, standards, prices] baisse *f*.
◇ *adj* humiliant.

lowering[2] [ˈlaʊərɪŋ] *adj* [sky] sombre, couvert; [clouds] menaçant.

lowermost ['ləʊəməʊst] *adj fml* le plus bas.

lowest ['ləʊɪst] *adj* (*superl of* low) le plus bas; **the sun was at its ~** le soleil était très bas sur l'horizon; **the ~ of the low** le dernier des derniers; **the newspaper panders to the views of the ~ in society** *fig* ce journal flatte les instincts les plus bas de la société ❑ **the ~ common multiple** le plus petit commun multiple; **the ~ common denominator** le plus petit dénominateur commun.

low-flying *adj* volant à basse altitude.

low-frequency *adj* (à) basse fréquence.

Low German *n* bas allemand *m*.

low-grade *adj* [in quality] de qualité inférieure; [in rank] (de rang) inférieur, subalterne.

low-heeled *adj* à talons plats.

lowing ['ləʊɪŋ] *n* (*U*) *lit* meuglement *m*, beuglement *m*, mugissement *m*.

low-key *adj* [style] discret; [person] réservé; **the meeting was a very ~ affair** la réunion s'est tenue dans la plus grande discrétion; **a ~ approach** une approche discrète.

lowland ['ləʊlənd] *n* plaine *f*, basse terre *f*; **the Lowlands** les Basses Terres.

Low Latin *n* bas latin *m*.

low-level *adj* [talks] à bas niveau; [operation] de faible envergure; **~ flying** AERON vol *m* à basse altitude; **~ language** COMPUT langage *m* non évolué OR de bas niveau; **~ radiation** NUCL irradiation *f* de faible intensité.

low life *n*: **scenes from London ~** des scènes de la vie des bas-fonds londoniens.

lowliness ['ləʊlɪnɪs] *n* humilité *f*.

low-loader *n* RAIL wagon *m* à plate-forme surbaissée; AUT camion *m* à plate-forme surbaissée.

lowly ['ləʊlɪ] (*compar* lowlier, *superl* lowliest) *adj* [modest] modeste; [meek] humble; [simple] sans prétention OR prétentions; **of ~ birth** issu d'un milieu humble.

low-lying *adj* [land - gen] bas; [- below sea level] au-dessous du niveau de la mer; [cloud] bas.

Low Mass *n* RELIG messe *f* basse.

low-minded *adj* vulgaire, grossier.

low-necked *adj* décolleté.

lowness ['ləʊnɪs] *n* **-1.** [of wall, building] faible hauteur *f*; [of land] faible élévation *f*. **-2.** [of wages, prices] modicité *f*. **-3.** [of temperature] faible élévation *f*. **-4.** [of voice - softness] douceur *f*; [- in pitch] profondeur *f*.

low-paid ◇ *adj* mal payé.
◇ *npl*: **the ~** les petits salaires *mpl*.

low-pitched *adj* **-1.** [voice, note] bas, grave. **-2.** [roof] à faible pente.

low-pressure *adj* **-1.** [gas] sous faible pression, de basse pression; [tyre] à basse pression. **-2.** [job] peu stressant.

low-price(d) *adj* bon marché, peu cher.

low profile *n*: **to keep a ~** garder un profil bas.
◆ **low-profile** *adj* **-1.** = **low-key**. **-2.** AUT: **low-profile tyre** pneu *m* à profil bas.

low-rise *adj* [buildings] de faible hauteur, bas.

low season *n*: **the ~** la basse saison; **~ holidays** vacances *fpl* hors saison.

low-spirited *adj* déprimé, démoralisé.

low-tech *adj* rudimentaire.

low-tension *adj* ELEC (de) basse tension.

low tide *n* marée *f* basse; **at ~** à marée basse.

low water *n* (*U*) basses eaux *fpl*.

lox [lɒks] *n* **-1.** *abbr of* **liquid oxygen**. **-2.** CULIN saumon *m* fumé.

loyal ['lɔɪəl] *adj* loyal, fidèle; **to be ~ to sb** être loyal envers qqn, faire preuve de loyauté envers qqn; **a ~ friend** un ami fidèle; **~ supporters** partisans fidèles ❑ **the ~ toast** *toast porté à la reine d'Angleterre à la fin d'un dîner*.

loyalism ['lɔɪəlɪzm] *n* loyalisme *m*.

loyalist ['lɔɪəlɪst] ◇ *n* loyaliste *mf*.
◇ *adj* loyaliste.

◆ **Loyalist** *n* loyaliste *mf*.

LOYALIST:
Dans le contexte britannique, le mot «Loyalist» désigne un protestant d'Irlande du Nord souhaitant rester au sein du Royaume-Uni.

---

loyally ['lɔɪəlɪ] *adv* loyalement, fidèlement.

loyalty ['lɔɪəltɪ] (*pl* loyalties) *n* **-1.** [faithfulness] loyauté *f*, fidélité *f*; **she's always shown great ~** elle a toujours fait preuve d'une grande loyauté; **the party demands ~ to the principles of democracy** le parti exige le respect des principes de la démocratie; **her ~ to the cause is not in doubt** son dévouement à la cause n'est pas mis en doute. **-2.** [tie]: **tribal loyalties** liens *mpl* tribaux; **my loyalties are divided** je suis déchiré (entre les deux), entre les deux mon cœur balance *hum*.

Loyola [lɔɪ'əʊlə] *pr n*: **Saint Ignatius ~** saint Ignace de Loyola.

lozenge ['lɒzɪndʒ] *n* **-1.** [sweet] pastille *f*; **throat ~** pastille pour la gorge. **-2.** [rhombus] losange *m*.

LP (*abbr of* **long-player**) *n*: **an ~** un 33 tours.

L-plate *n Br plaque apposée sur la voiture d'un conducteur qui n'a pas encore son permis (L signifie «learner», apprenti)*.

LPN (*abbr of* **licensed practical nurse**) *n aide infirmière diplômée*.

LRAM (*abbr of* **Licentiate of the Royal Academy of Music**) *n membre de la Royal Academy of Music*.

LSAT (*abbr of* **Law School Admissions Test**) *n test d'admission aux études de droit*.

LSD¹ (*abbr of* **lysergic acid diethylamide**) *n* LSD *m*.

LSD², **£.s.d.**, **lsd** *written abbr symboles représentant les pounds, les shillings et les pence de l'ancienne monnaie britannique avant l'adoption du système décimal en 1971*.

LSE (*abbr of* **London School of Economics**) *pr n grande école de sciences économiques et politiques à Londres*.

L-shaped *adj* en (forme de) L.

LSI (*abbr of* **large scale integration**) *n* intégration *f* à grande échelle.

LSO (*abbr of* **London Symphony Orchestra**) *pr n orchestre symphonique de Londres*.

Lt. (*written abbr of* **lieutenant**) Lieut.

LT (*written abbr of* **low tension**) BT.

Ltd, **ltd** (*written abbr of* **limited**) ≃ SARL; **Smith and Sons, ~** ≃ Smith & Fils, SARL.

Luanda [luː'ændə] *pr n* Luanda.

lubricant ['luːbrɪkənt] ◇ *adj* lubrifiant.
◇ *n* lubrifiant *m*.

lubricate ['luːbrɪkeɪt] *vt* [gen] lubrifier; [mechanism] lubrifier, graisser, huiler.

lubricated *inf* ['luːbrɪkeɪtɪd] *adj fig* & *hum* [drunk] beurré.

lubrication [ˌluːbrɪ'keɪʃn] *n* [gen] lubrification *f*; [of mechanism] lubrification *f*, graissage *m*, huilage *m*.

lubricator ['luːbrɪkeɪtəʳ] *n* graisseur *m*.

lubricious [luː'brɪʃəs] *adj lit* lubrique.

lubricity [luː'brɪsətɪ] *n* **-1.** *lit* [lewdness] lubricité *f*. **-2.** TECH onctuosité *f*.

lucerne [luː'sɜːn] *n Br* AGR luzerne *f (cultivée)*.

Lucerne [luː'sɜːn] *pr n* Lucerne.

lucid ['luːsɪd] *adj* **-1.** [clear-headed] lucide; **he has his ~ moments** il a des moments de lucidité. **-2.** [clear] clair, limpide; **a ~ narrative style** un style d'une grande clarté; **she gave a ~ account of events** elle donna un compte rendu net et précis des événements.

lucidity [luː'sɪdətɪ] *n* **-1.** [of mind] lucidité *f*. **-2.** [of style, account] clarté *f*, limpidité *f*.

lucidly ['luːsɪdlɪ] *adv* lucidement, avec lucidité.

Lucifer ['luːsɪfəʳ] *pr n* Lucifer.

Lucius ['luːsjəs] *pr n* Lucius.

luck [lʌk] *n* **-1.** [fortune] chance *f*; **to have good ~** avoir de la chance; **good ~!** bonne chance!; **good ~ to you!** *iron* je vous souhaite bien du plaisir!; **good ~ in your new job!** bonne chance pour ton nouveau travail! ‖ [good fortune]: **that's a bit of ~!** c'est de la chance!; **~ was with us** OR **on our side** la chance était avec nous; **you're in ~, your ~'s in** vous avez de la chance; **we're out of ~** on n'a pas de chance; **one more for ~** et un pour le pot; **better ~ next time** vous aurez plus de chance la prochaine fois; **any ~?** alors, ça a marché?; **some people have all the ~!** il y en a qui ont vraiment de la chance!; **it would be just my ~ to bump into my boss** *iron* ce serait bien ma veine de tomber sur mon patron ‖ [bad fortune]: **we had a bit of bad ~ with the car** on a eu un pépin avec la voiture; **you've brought me nothing but bad ~** tu ne m'as causé que des malheurs; **it's bad ~ to spill salt** renverser du sel porte malheur; **bad** OR **hard** OR **tough ~!** pas de chance!; **we thought the exam was cancelled – no such ~** nous croyions que l'examen était annulé – ç'aurait été trop beau; **to be down on one's ~** avoir la poisse OR la guigne; **to push one's ~** jouer avec le feu; **with (any) ~** avec un peu de chance; **worse ~** tant pis; **no, he hasn't asked me out, worse ~!** non, il ne m'a pas invitée à sortir, tant pis! **-2.** [chance, opportunity] hasard *m*; **it's the ~ of the draw** c'est une question de chance; **to try one's ~** tenter sa chance; **as ~ would have it** [by chance] par hasard; [by good luck] par bonheur; [by bad luck] par malheur; **as ~ would have it I'd forgotten my keys** et comme par hasard, j'avais oublié mes clés.
◆ **luck out** *inf vi insep Am* **-1.** [succeed] avoir de la veine. **-2.** [fail] avoir la poisse.

luckily ['lʌkɪlɪ] *adv* heureusement, par chance; **~ for him, he escaped** heureusement pour lui, il s'échappé.

luckless ['lʌklɪs] *adj* [person] malchanceux; [escapade, attempt] malheureux.

lucky ['lʌkɪ] (*compar* luckier, *superl* luckiest) *adj* **-1.** [fortunate - person] chanceux; [- encounter, winner] heureux; **to be ~** avoir de la chance; **to get ~** *inf* avoir un coup de bol; **you're ~ to have escaped with your life** vous avez eu de la chance de vous en tirer vivant; **what a ~ escape!** on l'a échappé belle!; **it was ~ for them that we were there** heureusement pour eux que nous étions là ❑ **a ~ break** *inf* un coup de pot OR de bol; **it's my ~ day** c'est mon jour de chance; **you ~ devil** OR **thing!** *inf* sacré veinard!; **I'd like a pay rise – you'll be ~** OR **you should be so ~!** j'aimerais une augmentation – tu peux toujours courir!; **~ you!** vous en avez de la chance!; **'Lucky Jim'** *Amis* 'Jim-la-Chance'. **-2.** [token, number] porte-bonheur (*inv*). **-3.** [guess] heureux.

lucky dip *n Br jeu d'enfant consistant à chercher des cadeaux enfouis dans une caisse remplie de sciure*; **the job-market is a real ~ at the moment** *fig* de nos jours, trouver un emploi, c'est vraiment une question de chance.

lucrative ['luːkrətɪv] *adj* [job] bien rémunéré, lucratif; [activity, deal] lucratif, rentable.

lucre ['luːkəʳ] *n hum* & *pej*: **(filthy) ~** lucre *m*.

Lucretia Borgia [luː'kriːʃə'bɔːdʒə] *pr n* Lucrèce Borgia.

Lucretius [luː'kriːʃəs] *pr n* Lucrèce.

lucubration [ˌluːkjuː'breɪʃn] *n fml* [studying] travail *m* laborieux, élucubration *f*; *lit* [literary work] élucubration *f*.

Luddite ['lʌdaɪt] ◇ *n* luddite *m*.
◇ *adj* luddite; **the ~ Riots** les émeutes *fpl* luddites.

THE LUDDITE RIOTS:
Émeutes ouvrières en Grande-Bretagne pendant la dépression de 1811-1813, au cours desquelles des chômeurs parcoururent le nord du pays en détruisant les nouvelles machines textiles, jugées responsables de leur sort. Ces émeutes furent durement réprimées par le gouvernement.

---

ludicrous ['luːdɪkrəs] *adj* ridicule, absurde.

ludicrously ['luːdɪkrəslɪ] *adv* ridiculement.

ludo ['luːdəʊ] *n* ≃ (jeu *m* des) petits chevaux *mpl*.
Ludwig ['lʊdvɪg] *pr n*: ~ of Bavaria Louis de Bavière.
luff [lʌf] NAUT ◇ *n* bord *m* d'une voile aurique.
◇ *vi* lofer, venir au lof.
luffa ['lʌfə] = **loofa(h)**.
lug [lʌg] (*pt* & *pp* **lugged**, *cont* **lugging**) ◇ *vt inf* [carry, pull] trimbaler; I had to ~ my bags all the way from the station j'ai dû trimbaler mes bagages de la gare jusqu'ici; he lugged his bicycle up the stairs il s'est trimbalé sa bicyclette jusqu'en haut des escaliers.
◇ *n* -**1.** [for fixing] ergot *m*, (petite) patte *f*; [handle] anse *f*, poignée *f*. -**2.** ▽ *Br* = **lughole**.
◆ **lug about, lug around** *inf vt sep* trimbaler; he always has to ~ his little sister about with him il doit toujours trimbaler OR traîner sa petite sœur à droite et à gauche.
luggage ['lʌgɪdʒ] *n* (*U*) bagages *mpl*; ~ trolley chariot *m* à bagages.
luggage handler *n* bagagiste *mf*.
luggage rack *n* RAIL [shelf] porte-bagages *m inv*; [net] filet *m* (à bagages); AUT galerie *f* (de toit).
luggage van *n* RAIL fourgon *m* (à bagages).
lugger ['lʌgəʳ] *n* lougre *m*.
lughole ▽ ['lʌghəʊl] *n Br* [ear] esgourde *f*.
lug screw *n* vis *f* sans tête.
lugubrious [luː'guːbrɪəs] *adj* lugubre.
lugubriously [luː'guːbrɪəslɪ] *adv* lugubrement, de façon lugubre.
lugworm ['lʌgwɜːm] *n* arénicole *f*.
Luke [luːk] *pr n* Luc; Saint ~ saint Luc; the Gospel According to (Saint) ~ l'Évangile selon saint Luc.
lukewarm ['luːkwɔːm] *adj* [water, soup] tiède; a ~ reception *fig* [of person] un accueil peu chaleureux; [of book, film] un accueil mitigé.
lull [lʌl] ◇ *n* [in weather] accalmie *f*; [in fighting] accalmie *f*, pause *f*; [in conversation] pause *f*; the ~ before the storm le calme avant la tempête.
◇ *vt* [calm - anxiety, person] calmer, apaiser; she ~ed the child to sleep elle berça l'enfant jusqu'à ce qu'il s'endorme; the sound of the engine ~ed me to sleep le ronronnement du moteur m'a endormi; they were ~ed into a false sense of security ils ont fait l'erreur de se laisser rassurer par des propos lénifiants.
lullaby ['lʌləbaɪ] (*pl* **lullabies**) *n* berceuse *f*.
lulu ▽ ['luːluː] *n Am*: it's a ~! c'est du tonnerre!; her latest film's a real ~ son dernier film est champion.
lumbago [lʌm'beɪgəʊ] *n* (*U*) lumbago *m*, lombalgie *f*.
lumbar ['lʌmbəʳ] *adj* lombaire.
lumbar puncture *n* ponction *f* lombaire, rachicentèse *f*.
lumber ['lʌmbəʳ] ◇ *n* -**1.** *Am* [cut wood] bois *m* (d'œuvre); [ready for use] bois *m* de construction OR de charpente. -**2.** *Br* [junk] bric-à-brac *m inv*.
◇ *vt Am* [logs] débiter; [tree] abattre, couper.
◇ *vi* -**1.** [large person, animal] marcher pesamment; I could hear him ~ing down the stairs je l'entendais descendre l'escalier d'un pas pesant; she ~ed into the room elle entra dans la pièce d'un pas lourd || [heavy vehicle]: the tanks ~ed into the centre of the town la lourde colonne de chars avançait vers le centre de la ville. -**2.** *Am* [fell trees] abattre des arbres (*pour le bois*).
◆ **lumber with** *inf vt sep* (*usu pass*) [encumber]: to ~ sb with sthg refiler qqch à qqn; I'll get ~ed with it ça va me retomber dessus.
lumbering ['lʌmbərɪŋ] ◇ *n Am* exploitation *f* forestière.
◇ *adj* [heavy - step] pesant, lourd; [- person] lourd, maladroit.
lumberjack ['lʌmbədʒæk] *n* bûcheron *m*, -onne *f*.
lumber-jacket *n* grosse veste *f* de bûcheron.
lumberman ['lʌmbəmən] (*pl* **lumbermen** [-mən]) *Am* = **lumberjack**.
lumber room *n Br* débarras *m*.
lumberyard ['lʌmbəjɑːd] *n Am* dépôt *m* de bois.
lumen ['luːmɪn] *n* PHYS lumen *m*; ANAT lumière *f*.
luminance ['luːmɪnəns] *n* luminance *f*.
luminary ['luːmɪnərɪ] (*pl* **luminaries**) *n* -**1.** [celebrity] lumière *f*, sommité *f*. -**2.** *lit* [heavenly body] astre *m*.
luminescence [,luːmɪ'nesəns] *n* luminescence *f*.
luminescent [,luːmɪ'nesənt] *adj* luminescent.
luminosity [,luːmɪ'nɒsətɪ] *n* luminosité *f*.
luminous ['luːmɪnəs] *adj* [paint, colour, sky] lumineux; *fig* [explanation, argument] lumineux, limpide.
lumme *inf* ['lʌmɪ] *interj Br dated* ben mon vieux.
lummox *inf* ['lʌməks] *n* empoté *m*, -e *f*.
lummy ['lʌmɪ] = **lumme**.
lump [lʌmp] ◇ *n* -**1.** [of sugar] morceau *m*; one ~ or two? un ou deux sucres? -**2.** [of solid matter - small] morceau *m*; [- large] masse *f*; [in food] grumeau *m*; a huge ~ of marble un énorme bloc de marbre; a shapeless ~ of melted plastic une masse informe de plastique fondu ☐ to have a ~ in one's throat avoir une boule dans la gorge, avoir la gorge serrée; you've got to take your ~s *inf Am* tout n'est pas toujours rose. -**3.** [bump] bosse *f*; I've got a ~ on my forehead j'ai une bosse au front; there are lots of ~s in this mattress ce matelas est plein de bosses. -**4.** MED [swelling] grosseur *f*, protubérance *f*; she has a ~ in her breast elle a une grosseur au sein. -**5.** [of money]: you don't have to pay it all in one ~ vous n'êtes pas obligé de tout payer en une seule fois. -**6.** *inf pej* [clumsy person] empoté *m*, -e *f*. -**7.** *Br* CONSTR: to work on the ~ *inf* travailler au noir; ~ labour main-d'œuvre *f* non déclarée.
◇ *vt inf* [put up with]: if that's her final decision, we'll just have to ~ it! puisque c'est sa décision définitive, on n'a plus qu'à s'écraser!; if you don't like it you can ~ it! si ça ne te plaît pas, tant pis pour toi!
◆ **lump together** *vt sep* -**1.** [gather together] réunir, rassembler; couldn't you ~ all these paragraphs together under one heading? ne pourrais-tu pas réunir OR regrouper tous ces paragraphes sous un même titre? -**2.** [consider the same] mettre dans la même catégorie.
lumpectomy [,lʌmp'ektəmɪ] *n* ablation *f* d'une tumeur au sein.
lumpenproletariat ['lʌmpən,prəʊlɪ'teərɪət] *n* lumpenprolétariat *m*.
lumpfish ['lʌmpfɪʃ] (*pl inv* OR **lumpfishes**) *n* lump *m*, lompe *m*.
lumpish ['lʌmpɪʃ] *adj* [clumsy] maladroit; [dull-witted] idiot, abruti.
lump-sucker = **lumpfish**.
lump sugar *n* sucre *m* en morceaux.
lump sum *n* somme *f* forfaitaire; they pay me a ~ je touche une somme forfaitaire; to work for a ~ travailler à forfait; to be paid in a ~ être payé en une seule fois.
lumpy ['lʌmpɪ] (*compar* **lumpier**, *superl* **lumpiest**) *adj* [sauce] plein de grumeaux; [mattress] plein de bosses, défoncé.
lunacy ['luːnəsɪ] (*pl* **lunacies**) *n* -**1.** [madness] démence *f*, folie *f*. -**2.** [folly] folie *f*; it would be ~ to accept such a proposal ce serait de la folie d'accepter pareille proposition; it's sheer ~! c'est de la folie pure et simple!
lunar ['luːnəʳ] *adj* [rock, month, cycle] lunaire; [eclipse] de la Lune; ~ landing alunissage *m*; ~ module module *m* lunaire.
lunatic ['luːnətɪk] ◇ *n* -**1.** [madman] aliéné *m*, -e *f*, dément *m*, -e *f*. -**2.** *inf* [fool] cinglé *m*, -e *f*; he's a complete ~! il est fou à lier!, il est complètement cinglé!
◇ *adj* -**1.** [insane] fou, dément. -**2.** *inf* [crazy - person] cinglé, dingue; [- idea] dément, démentiel.
lunatic asylum *n* asile *m* d'aliénés.
lunatic fringe *n pej* extrémistes *mpl* fanatiques.
lunch [lʌntʃ] ◇ *n* déjeuner *m*; to have ~ déjeuner; after ~ après le déjeuner; she's gone out for ~ elle est partie déjeuner; I've invited him for ~ on Tuesday je l'ai invité à déjeuner mardi prochain; I have a ~ date je déjeune avec quelqu'un, je suis pris pour le déjeuner; [for business] j'ai un déjeuner d'affaires; what did you have for ~? qu'est-ce que tu as mangé à midi?; they're giving a ~ at the Savoy ils donnent un déjeuner au Savoy ☐ he's out to ~ ▽ il débloque.
◇ *vi* déjeuner.
lunchbox ['lʌntʃbɒks] *n boîte dans laquelle on transporte son déjeuner*.
luncheon ['lʌntʃən] *n fml* déjeuner *m*; a literary ~ un déjeuner littéraire.
luncheonette [,lʌntʃə'net] *n Am* snack *m*, snack-bar *m*.
luncheon meat *n bloc de viande de porc en conserve*.
luncheon voucher *n Br* Ticket-Restaurant® *m*.
lunch hour *n* heure *f* du déjeuner; she's not here, it's her ~ elle n'est pas là, c'est l'heure à laquelle elle déjeune.
lunchpail ['lʌntʃpeɪl] *Am* = **lunchbox**.
lunchtime ['lʌntʃtaɪm] *n* heure *f* du déjeuner; I saw him at ~ je l'ai vu à midi OR à l'heure du déjeuner; it's ~ c'est l'heure de déjeuner.
lung [lʌŋ] ◇ *n* poumon *m*; he filled his ~s with air il inspira profondément.
◇ *comp* [artery, congestion, disease] pulmonaire; [transplant] du poumon; ~ cancer cancer *m* du poumon; ~ specialist pneumologue *mf*.
lunge [lʌndʒ] ◇ *n* -**1.** [sudden movement]: to make a ~ for sthg se précipiter vers qqch. -**2.** FENCING fente *f* (avant). -**3.** EQUIT longe *f*.
◇ *vi* [move suddenly] faire un mouvement brusque en avant; she ~d at him with a knife elle se précipita sur lui avec un couteau; he ~d at his opponent FENCING il allongea une botte à son adversaire.
◇ *vt* [horse] mener à la longe.
◆ **lunge forward** *vi insep* se jeter en avant; FENCING se fendre.
lungfish ['lʌŋfɪʃ] (*pl inv* OR **lungfishes**) *n* dipneuste *m*.
lungful ['lʌŋfʊl] *n*: she breathed in a ~ of cold air elle aspira l'air froid à pleins poumons, elle aspira une grande bouffée d'air froid; take a ~ of air inspirez à fond.
lunisolar [,luːnɪ'səʊləʳ] *adj* luni-solaire.
lunula ['luːnjʊlə], **lunule** ['luːnjuːl] *n* lunule *f*.
lupin ['luːpɪn] *n* lupin *m*.
lupine ['luːpaɪn] ◇ *n Am* = **lupin**.
◇ *adj* de loup.
lurch [lɜːtʃ] ◇ *vi* [person] tituber, chanceler; he ~ed into the room il entra dans la pièce en titubant || [car - swerve] faire une embardée; [- jerk forwards] avancer par à-coups; [ship] tanguer; the car ~ed out of control la voiture livrée à elle-même fit une embardée; his opinions ~ from one extreme to another *fig* dans ses opinions, il passe d'un extrême à l'autre.
◇ *n*: the car gave a sudden ~ and left the road la voiture fit une embardée et quitta la route ☐ to leave sb in the ~ laisser qqn en plan.
lurcher ['lɜːtʃəʳ] *n chien bâtard, croisement de lévrier et de colley*.
lure [ljʊəʳ] ◇ *n* -**1.** [attraction] attrait *m*; [charm] charme *m*; [temptation] tentation *f*. -**2.** FISHING & HUNT leurre *m*.
◇ *vt* [person] attirer (sous un faux prétexte); he ~d them into a trap il les a attirés dans un piège.
◆ **lure away** *vt sep*: he ~d me away from my friends il a fait en sorte que je ne voie plus mes amis, il m'a éloigné de mes amis; she invited me over in order to ~ me away from the office elle m'a invité pour m'éloigner du bureau.
Lurex® ['lʊəreks] *n* [thread] Lurex® *m*; [cloth] tissu *m* en Lurex®.

lurgy *inf* ['lɜːgɪ] *n Br hum*: I've got the dreaded ~ j'ai attrapé quelque chose.

lurid ['ljʊərɪd] *adj* -**1.** [sensational - account, story] macabre, atroce, horrible; [salacious] salace, malsain; many newspapers go in for ~ sensationalism de nombreux journaux exploitent le goût du public pour le sensationnel; he gave me a ~ account of the plane crash il m'a décrit l'accident d'avion sans m'épargner le moindre détail; the book gives a ~ description of life at the castle le livre donne une description haute en couleur de la vie au château. -**2.** [glaring - sky, sunset] sanglant, rougeoyant; [- wallpaper, shirt] criard, voyant; a ~ green dress une robe d'un vert criard.

luridly ['ljʊərɪdlɪ] *adv* [garishly] violemment, tapageusement.

lurk [lɜːk] *vi* [person, animal] se tapir; [danger] se cacher, menacer; [doubt, worry] persister; the burglar was ~ing behind the trees le cambrioleur était tapi derrière les arbres.

lurking ['lɜːkɪŋ] *adj* [suspicion, fear] vague; [danger] menaçant.

Lusaka [luː'sɑːkə] *pr n* Lusaka.

luscious ['lʌʃəs] *adj* -**1.** [fruit] succulent; [colour] riche. -**2.** [woman] séduisant; ~ lips lèvres pulpeuses OR appétissantes.

lush [lʌʃ] ◇ *adj* -**1.** [vegetation] riche, luxuriant; [fruit] succulent; *fig* [description] riche. -**2.** [luxurious] luxueux.
◇ *n* ▽ poivrot *m*, -e *f*.

Lusitania [,luːsɪ'teɪnjə] *pr n* Lusitanie *f*; in ~ en Lusitanie.

Lusitanian [,luːsɪ'teɪnjən] ◇ *n* Lusitanien *m*, -enne *f*.
◇ *adj* lusitanien.

lust [lʌst] *n* -**1.** [sexual desire] désir *m* sexuel, concupiscence *f*; [as sin] luxure *f*. -**2.** [greed] soif *f*, convoitise *f*; ~ for power soif de pouvoir.
◆ **lust after** *vt insep* [person] désirer, avoir envie de, convoiter; [money, property] convoiter.
◆ **lust for** *vt insep* [money] convoiter; [revenge, power] avoir soif de.

luster *Am* = **lustre**.

lustful ['lʌstfʊl] *adj* -**1.** [lecherous] concupiscent, lascif. -**2.** [greedy] avide.

lustfully ['lʌstfʊlɪ] *adv* -**1.** [lecherously] lascivement. -**2.** [greedily] avidement.

lustily ['lʌstɪlɪ] *adv* [sing, shout] à pleine gorge, à pleins poumons.

lustre *Br*, **luster** *Am* ['lʌstəʳ] *n* -**1.** [sheen] lustre *m*, brillant *m*. -**2.** *fig* [glory] éclat *m*.

lustreless ['lʌstəlɪs] *adj* terne, sans éclat.

lustrous ['lʌstrəs] *adj* -**1.** [shiny - pearls, stones] lustré, chatoyant; [eyes] brillant; [cloth] lustré; ~ black hair cheveux d'un noir de jais. -**2.** *lit* [illustrious - career] illustre; [name] glorieux.

lusty ['lʌstɪ] (*compar* **lustier**, *superl* **lustiest**) *adj* [strong - person, baby] vigoureux, robuste; [- voice, manner] vigoureux.

lute [luːt] *n* MUS luth *m*.

lutecium [luː'tiːʃəm] = **lutetium**.

luteinizing hormone ['luːtɪɪnaɪzɪŋ-] *n* hormone *f* lutéinisante.

Lutetia [luː'tiːʃə] *pr n* Lutèce.

lutetium [luː'tiːʃəm] *n* lutécium *m*.

Lutheran ['luːθərən] ◇ *n* Luthérien *m*, -enne *f*.
◇ *adj* luthérien.

Lutheranism ['luːθərənɪzm] *n* luthéranisme *m*.

luv *inf* [lʌv] *n* & *vt Br* = **love**.

luvvie *inf* ['lʌvɪ] *n hum* acteur *m* prétentieux, actrice *f* prétentieuse.

lux [lʌks] *n* PHYS lux *m*.

luxate [lʌk'seɪt] *vt* luxer.

Luxembourg ['lʌksəmbɜːg] *pr n* -**1.** [country] Luxembourg *m*; in ~ au Luxembourg. -**2.** [town] Luxembourg.

Luxemburger ['lʌksəmbɜːgəʳ] *n* Luxembourgeois *m*, -e *f*.

Luxor ['lʌksɔːʳ] *pr n* Louqsor, Louxor.

luxuriance [lʌg'ʒʊərɪəns] *n* -**1.** [luxury] luxe *m*, somptuosité *f*. -**2.** [of vegetation] luxuriance *f*, richesse *f*; [of plants] exubérance *f*, abondance *f*; [of hair] abondance *f*.

luxuriant [lʌg'ʒʊərɪənt] *adj* -**1.** [luxurious - surroundings] luxueux, somptueux. -**2.** [vegetation] luxuriant; [crops, undergrowth] abondant, riche; [countryside] couvert de végétation, luxuriant; *fig* [style] luxuriant, riche. -**3.** [flowing - hair, beard] abondant.

luxuriate [lʌg'ʒʊərɪeɪt] *vi* -**1.** [take pleasure]: to ~ in sthg se délecter de qqch; to ~ in the sun/in a hot bath se prélasser au soleil/dans un bain chaud. -**2.** *lit* [proliferate, flourish] proliférer.

luxurious [lʌg'ʒʊərɪəs] *adj* -**1.** [opulent - house, clothes] luxueux, somptueux; [- car] luxueux; to have ~ tastes avoir des goûts de luxe. -**2.** [voluptuous] voluptueux.

luxuriously [lʌg'ʒʊərɪəslɪ] *adv* -**1.** [with, in luxury] luxueusement; ~ furnished luxueusement OR richement meublé; to live ~ vivre dans le luxe OR dans l'opulence. -**2.** [voluptuously] voluptueusement; she stretched out ~ on the grass elle s'allongea voluptueusement sur l'herbe.

luxuriousness [lʌg'ʒʊərɪəsnɪs] *n* luxe *m*.

luxury ['lʌkʃərɪ] (*pl* **luxuries**) ◇ *n* -**1.** [comfort] luxe *m*; to live in ~, to lead a life of ~ vivre dans le luxe. -**2.** [treat] luxe *m*; whisky is the one ~ I still allow myself le whisky est le seul luxe que je me permette encore; one of life's little luxuries un des petits plaisirs de la vie; it's a ~ for them to eat meat manger de la viande est, pour eux, un luxe.
◇ *comp* [car, restaurant, kitchen] de luxe; [apartment] de luxe, de standing.

luxury goods *npl* articles *mpl* de luxe.

LV *written abbr of* luncheon voucher.

LW (*written abbr of* long wave) GO.

LWT (*abbr of* London Weekend Television) *pr n chaîne de télévision relevant de l'IBA*.

lycanthropy [laɪ'kænθrəpɪ] *n* lycanthropie *f*.

lyceum [laɪ'sɪəm] *n* -**1.** [in names of public buildings] théâtre *m*. -**2.** *Am* [hall] salle *f* publique; [organization] association *f* culturelle.

lychee [,laɪ'tʃiː] *n* litchi *m*.

lych-gate ['lɪtʃ-] *n* porche *m* de cimetière.

Lycra® ['laɪkrə] *n* Lycra® *m*.

lye [laɪ] *n* CHEM lessive *f*.

lying ['laɪɪŋ] ◇ *cont* → **lie**.
◇ *adj* -**1.** [reclining] couché, étendu, allongé. -**2.** [dishonest - person] menteur; [- story] mensonger, faux; you ~ bastard!▽ sale menteur!
◇ *n* -**1.** [corpse]: ~ in state exposition *f* du corps. -**2.** *(U)* [dishonesty] mensonges *mpl*.

lying-in *n* MED couches *fpl*.

lyme grass [laɪm-] *n* elymus *m*.

lymph [lɪmf] *n* lymphe *f*.

lymphatic [lɪm'fætɪk] *adj* lymphatique; ~ system système *m* lymphatique.

lymph gland, lymph node *n* ganglion *m* lymphatique.

lymphocyte ['lɪmfəsaɪt] *n* lymphocyte *m*.

lynch [lɪntʃ] *vt* lyncher.

lynching ['lɪntʃɪŋ] *n* lynchage *m*.

lynch law *n* loi *f* de Lynch.

lynchpin ['lɪntʃpɪn] = **linchpin**.

lynx [lɪŋks] (*pl inv* OR **lynxes**) *n* lynx *m inv*.

lynx-eyed *adj* aux yeux de lynx.

Lyon [liːɔ̃], **Lyons** ['laɪənz] *pr n* Lyon.

lyophilize, -ise [laɪ'ɒfɪlaɪz] *vt* lyophiliser.

lyre ['laɪəʳ] *n* lyre *f*.

lyrebird ['laɪəbɜːd] *n* oiseau-lyre *m*.

lyric ['lɪrɪk] ◇ *adj* lyrique.
◇ *n* [poem] poème *m* lyrique; ~s writer parolier *m*, -ère *f*.
◆ **lyrics** *npl* [of song] paroles *fpl*.

lyrical ['lɪrɪkl] *adj* -**1.** *literal* lyrique. -**2.** *fig* passionné; he was positively ~ about his visit to China son séjour en Chine l'a véritablement enthousiasmé.

lyrically ['lɪrɪklɪ] *adv* [poetically] avec lyrisme; [enthusiastically] avec enthousiasme; she spoke/wrote ~ of her voyage to Africa elle a évoqué son voyage en Afrique avec beaucoup d'enthousiasme.

lyricism ['lɪrɪsɪzm] *n* lyrisme *m*.

lyricist ['lɪrɪsɪst] *n* [of poems] poète *m* lyrique; [of song, opera] parolier *m*, -ère *f*.

Lysander [laɪ'sændəʳ] *pr n* Lysandre.

lysergic [laɪ'sɜːdʒɪk] *adj* lysergique; ~ acid acide *m* lysergique.

lysine ['laɪsiːn] *n* lysine *f*.

lysozyme ['laɪsəzaɪm] *n* lysozyme *m*, muramidase *f*.

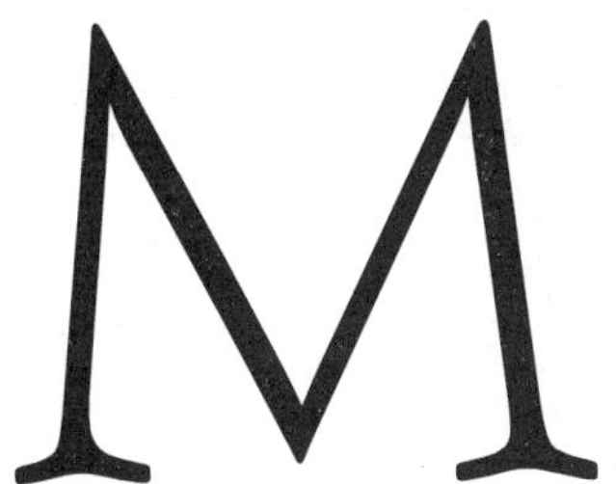

m (*pl* m's OR ms), **M** (*pl* M's OR Ms) [em] *n* [letter] m *m*, M *m*.

m -**1.** (*written abbr of* metre) m. -**2.** (*written abbr of* million) M. -**3.** *written abbr of* mile.

M ◇ *Br* (*abbr of* motorway): the M5 l'autoroute M5.
◇ (*written abbr of* medium) M.

ma *inf* [mɑː] *n* maman *f*; Ma Baker *hum* la mère Baker.

MA ◇ *n* -**1.** (*abbr of* Master of Arts) [in England, Wales and US] *(titulaire d'une) maîtrise de lettres*; [in Scotland] *premier examen universitaire, équivalent de la licence*. -**2.** *abbr of* military academy.
◇ *written abbr of* Massachusetts.

ma'am [mæm] *n* madame *f*.

Maastricht ['mɑːstrɪkt] *pr n* Maastricht.

mac *inf* [mæk] -**1.** *Br* (*abbr of* macintosh) imper *m*. -**2.** *Am* & *Scot*: come here ~! amène-toi, mec!

macabre [mə'kɑːbrə] *adj* macabre.

macadam [mə'kædəm] ◇ *n* macadam *m*.
◇ *comp* [road] macadamisé, en macadam.

macadamize, -ise [mə'kædəmaɪz] *vt* macadamiser.

Macao [mə'kaʊ] *pr n* Macao; in ~ à Macao.

macaroni [,mækə'rəʊnɪ] *n (U)* macaronis *mpl*; ~ cheese gratin *m* de macaronis.

macaronic [,mækə'rɒnɪk] ◇ *n* vers *m* macaronique, poésie *f* macaronique.
◇ *adj* macaronique.

macaroon [,mækə'ruːn] *n* CULIN macaron *m*.

macassar [mə'kæsəʳ] *n* macassar *m*; ~ oil huile *f* de macassar.

macaw [mə'kɔː] *n* ara *m*.

mace [meɪs] *n* -**1.** [spice] macis *m*. -**2.** [club] massue *f*, masse *f* d'armes; [ceremonial] masse *f*; ~ bearer massier *m*.

Mace® [meɪs] ◇ *n* [spray] gaz *m* lacrymogène.
◇ *vt* *inf Am* bombarder au gaz lacrymogène.

Macedonia [,mæsɪ'dəʊnjə] *pr n* Macédoine *f*; in ~ en Macédoine.

Macedonian [,mæsɪ'dəʊnjən] ◇ *n* -**1.** [person] Macédonien *m*, -enne *f*. -**2.** LING macédonien *m*.
◇ *adj* macédonien.

macerate ['mæsəreɪt] *vi* & *vt* macérer.

maceration [,mæsə'reɪʃn] *n* macération *f*.

Mach [mæk] *n* Mach; to fly at ~ 3 voler à Mach 3.

machete [mə'ʃetɪ] *n* machette *f*.

Machiavelli [,mækɪə'velɪ] *pr n* Machiavel.

Machiavellian [,mækɪə'velɪən] *adj* machiavélique.

Machiavellianism [,mækɪə'velɪənɪzm] *n* machiavélisme *m*.

machinable [mə'ʃiːnəbl] *adj* usinable.

machinate ['mækɪneɪt] *vt* machiner.

machination [,mækɪ'neɪʃn] *n* machination *f*.

machine [mə'ʃiːn] ◇ *n* -**1.** [mechanical device] machine *f*; to do sthg by ~ OR on a ~ faire qqch à la machine || *fig* & *pej* [person] machine *f*, automate *m*; he thinks she's just a ~ for doing housework il la considère comme une machine à faire le ménage; a thinking ~ une machine à penser. -**2.** [organization] machine *f*, appareil *m*; the party ~ l'appareil du parti. -**3.** [car, motorbike] machine *f*; [plane] appareil *m*.
◇ *vt* SEW coudre à la machine; INDUST [manufacture] fabriquer à la machine; [work on machine] usiner.
◇ *comp*: the ~ age l'ère *f* de la machine.

machine code *n* code *m* machine.

machine-finished *adj* [paper] apprêté, calandré.

machine gun *n* mitrailleuse *f*.
◆ **machine-gun** *vt* mitrailler.

machine-gunner *n* mitrailleur *m*.

machine-gunning [-'gʌnɪŋ] *n* mitraillage *m*.

machine intelligence *n* intelligence *f* artificielle.

machine language *n* langage *m* machine.

machine-made *adj* fait OR fabriqué à la machine.

machine operator *n* opérateur *m*, -trice *f* (sur machine).

machine pistol *n* mitraillette *f*, pistolet *m* mitrailleur.

machine-readable *adj* COMPUT exploitable par machine.

machinery [mə'ʃiːnərɪ] (*pl* machineries) *n* -**1.** *(U)* [machines] machines *fpl*, machinerie *f*; [mechanism] mécanisme *m*. -**2.** *fig* rouages *mpl*; the ~ of state/of government les rouages de l'État/du gouvernement.

machine shop *n* atelier *m* d'usinage.

machine-stitch ◇ *n* point *m* (de piqûre) à la machine.
◇ *vt* piquer (à la machine).

machine tool *n* machine-outil *f*.

machine translation *n* traduction *f* automatique.

machine washable *adj* lavable à la OR en machine.

machinist [mə'ʃiːnɪst] *n* INDUST opérateur *m*, -trice *f* (sur machine); SEW mécanicien *m*, -enne *f*.

machismo [mə'tʃɪzməʊ, mə'kɪzməʊ] *n* machisme *m*.

machmeter ['mæk,miːtəʳ] *n* machmètre *m*.

Mach number *n* nombre *m* de Mach.

macho *inf* ['mætʃəʊ] ◇ *adj* macho.
◇ *n* macho *m*.

mack [mæk] = **mac 1**.

mackerel ['mækrəl] (*pl inv*) *n* maquereau *m*.

mackerel sky *n* ciel *m* pommelé.

mackintosh ['mækɪntɒʃ] *n* *Br* imperméable *m*.

macramé [mə'krɑːmɪ] *n* macramé *m*.

macro ['mækrəʊ] (*pl* macros) *n* macro-instruction *f*.

macrobiotic [,mækrəʊbaɪ'ɒtɪk] *adj* macrobiotique.
◆ **macrobiotics** *n (U)* macrobiotique *f*.

macroclimate ['mækrəʊ,klaɪmət] *n* macroclimat *m*.

macrocosm ['mækrəʊkɒzm] *n* macrocosme *m*.

macrocosmic [,mækrəʊ'kɒzmɪk] *adj* macrocosmique.

macroeconomics ['mækrəʊ,iːkə'nɒmɪks] *n (U)* macroéconomie *f*.

macroglobulin [,mækrəʊ'glɒbjʊlɪn] *n* macroglobuline *f*.

macroinstruction [,mækrəʊɪn'strʌkʃn] = **macro**.

macromolecule [,mækrəʊ'mɒlɪkjuːl] *n* macromolécule *f*.

macron ['mækrɒn] *n* TYPO macron *m*.

macroscopic [,mækrəʊ'skɒpɪk] *adj* macroscopique.

macrostructure ['mækrəʊ,strʌktʃəʳ] *n* macrostructure *f*.

maculation [,mækjʊ'leɪʃn] *n* maculation *f*, maculage *m*.

mad [mæd] ◇ *adj* -**1.** *esp Br* [crazy] fou; to go ~ devenir fou; you must have been ~ to do it il fallait être fou pour faire ça; that's a ~ idea c'est une idée folle OR insensée; to be ~ with joy/grief être fou de joie/douleur; it's a case of patriotism gone ~ c'est du patriotisme poussé à l'extrême OR qui frise la folie; to drive sb ~ rendre qqn fou; it's enough to drive you ~ il y a de quoi devenir fou, c'est à vous rendre fou; you're driving me ~ with all your questions tu me rends fou avec toutes tes questions ❑ to be as ~ as a hatter OR a March hare être fou à lier; MAD (magazine) PRESS *magazine satirique américain très populaire*. -**2.** [absurd - ambition, plan] fou, insensé; he's always full of ~ schemes for making money il a toujours des plans insensés pour se faire de l'argent. -**3.** [angry] en colère, furieux; he went ~ when he saw them il s'est mis dans une colère noire en les voyant; to be ~ at OR with sb être en colère OR fâché contre qqn; she makes me ~ elle m'énerve; don't get ~ ne vous fâchez pas. -**4.** [frantic]: there was a ~ rush for the door tous les gens se sont rués vers la porte comme des fous; I'm in a ~ rush *inf* je suis très pressé, je suis à la bourre; there was a ~ panic to sell les gens n'avaient plus qu'une idée en tête, vendre; don't go ~ and try to do it all yourself

fig tu ne vas pas te tuer à essayer de tout faire toi-même? ❑ like ~ *inf*: to run like ~ courir comme un fou OR un dératé; they were arguing like ~ ils discutaient comme des perdus; the kettle was boiling away like ~ la bouilloire s'emballait. -**5.** *inf esp Br* [enthusiastic, keen] fou; to be ~ about OR on sthg être fou de qqch; she's ~ about cats elle adore les chats; he's ~ about her il est fou d'elle; I can't say I'm ~ about going je ne peux pas dire que ça m'emballe OR que je meure d'envie d'y aller. -**6.** [dog] enragé; [bull] furieux.
◇ *n Am* accès *m* de colère.
◇ *adv Br*: to be ~ keen on OR about sthg *inf* être dingue OR être un mordu de qqch.

MAD [mæd] (*abbr of* mutual assured destruction) *n équilibre de la terreur*.

Madagascan [ˌmædəˈgæskn] ◇ *n* Malgache *mf*.
◇ *adj* malgache.

Madagascar [ˌmædəˈgæskəʳ] *pr n* Madagascar; in ~ à Madagascar.

madam [ˈmædəm] *n* -**1.** *fml* madame *f*; Dear Madam (Chère) Madame; ~ Chairman Madame la Présidente. -**2.** *pej*: she's a little ~ c'est une petite effrontée. -**3.** [in brothel] tenancière *f*.

madcap [ˈmædkæp] ◇ *adj* fou, insensé; a ~ scheme un projet insensé.
◇ *n* fou *m*, folle *f*, hurluberlu *m*, -e *f*.

madden [ˈmædn] *vt* [drive insane] rendre fou; [exasperate] exaspérer, rendre fou; her silence ~ed him son silence l'exaspérait.

maddening [ˈmædnɪŋ] *adj* exaspérant; a ~ noise un bruit à vous rendre fou.

maddeningly [ˈmædnɪŋlɪ] *adv* de façon exaspérante; ~ slow d'une lenteur exaspérante.

madder [ˈmædəʳ] *n* BOT & TEX garance *f*.

madding [ˈmædɪŋ] *adj lit & arch* effréné, frénétique.

made [meɪd] *pt & pp* → **make**.

-made *in cpds*: factory~ industriel; British~ fabriqué au Royaume-Uni; man~ [gen] artificiel; [fabric, fibre] synthétique.

Madeira [məˈdɪərə] ◇ *pr n* [island] Madère; in ~ à Madère.
◇ *n* [wine] madère *m*.

Madeira cake *n* ≃ quatre-quarts *m inv*.

made-to-measure *adj* (fait) sur mesure.

made-to-order *adj* (fait) sur commande.

made-up *adj* -**1.** [wearing make-up] maquillé; a heavily ~ face un visage très maquillé. -**2.** [invented - story] fabriqué; [- evidence] faux.

madhouse *inf* [ˈmædhaʊs, *pl* -haʊzɪz] *n* asile *m* d'aliénés, maison *f* de fous; *fig* maison de fous; the place was a complete ~ when we arrived lorsque nous sommes arrivés, on se serait crus dans une maison de fous.

Madison Avenue [ˈmædɪsn-] *pr n rue de New York dont le nom évoque le milieu de la publicité*.

madly [ˈmædlɪ] *adv* -**1.** [passionately] follement; ~ excited surexcité; ~ in love éperdument OR follement amoureux; ~ jealous fou de jalousie. -**2.** [frantically] comme un fou, frénétiquement; [wildly] comme un fou, follement; to run/to shout ~ courir/crier comme un fou; the dog was barking ~ le chien aboyait frénétiquement ‖ [desperately] désespérément; she was ~ trying to contact her parents elle essayait désespérément de contacter ses parents.

madman [ˈmædmən] (*pl* madmen [-mən]) *n* fou *m*, aliéné *m*.

madness [ˈmædnɪs] *n* -**1.** [insanity] folie *f*, démence *f*. -**2.** [folly] folie *f*; it's ~ even to think of going away now il faut être fou pour songer à partir maintenant.

Madonna [məˈdɒnə] *pr n* RELIG Madone *f*; [image] madone *f*; '~ and Child' 'Vierge à l'enfant'.

madras [məˈdrɑːs] *n* madras *m*.

Madras [məˈdrɑːs] *pr n* Madras.

Madrid [məˈdrɪd] *pr n* Madrid.

madrigal [ˈmædrɪgl] *n* MUS madrigal *m*.

madwoman [ˈmædˌwʊmən] (*pl* madwomen [-ˌwɪmɪn]) *n* folle *f*, aliénée *f*.

Maecenas [miːˈsiːnæs] *pr n* Mécène.

maelstrom [ˈmeɪlstrɒm] *n* maelström *m*; a ~ of violence *fig* un ouragan de violence.

Maenad [ˈmiːnæd] *n* ménade *f*; the ~s les ménades.

maestro [ˈmaɪstrəʊ] (*pl* maestros) *n* maestro *m*; he's a real ~ on the violin c'est un vrai virtuose du violon.

Mae West *inf* [ˌmeɪˈwest] *n Am* gilet *m* de sauvetage (gonflable).

maf(f)ia [ˈmæfɪə] *n literal & fig* mafia *f*, maffia *f*.

mafioso [ˌmæfɪˈəʊsəʊ] (*pl* **mafiosi** [-siː]) *n* mafioso *m*, maffioso *m*.

mag *inf* [mæg] *n abbr of* magazine.

magazine [ˌmægəˈziːn] *n* -**1.** [publication] magazine *m*, revue *f*; TV magazine *m*. -**2.** [in gun] magasin *m*; [cartridges] chargeur *m*. -**3.** MIL [store] magasin *m*; [for weapons] dépôt *m* d'armes; [munitions] munitions *fpl*. -**4.** PHOT magasin *m*; [for slides] panier *m*, magasin *m*.

Magellan [məˈgelən] *pr n* Magellan.

Magellan Strait *pr n*: the ~ le détroit de Magellan.

magenta [məˈdʒentə] ◇ *n* magenta *m*.
◇ *adj* magenta *(inv)*.

maggot [ˈmægət] *n* asticot *m*.

maggoty [ˈmægətɪ] *adj* [food] véreux.

Maghreb [ˈmɑːgrəb] *pr n*: the ~ le Maghreb; in the ~ au Maghreb.

Magi [ˈmeɪdʒaɪ] *pl pr n*: the ~ les Rois *mpl* mages.

magic [ˈmædʒɪk] ◇ *n* -**1.** [enchantment] magie *f*; like OR as if by ~ *fig* comme par enchantement OR magie; the medicine worked like ~ le remède a fait merveille ‖ [conjuring] magie *f*, prestidigitation *f*. -**2.** [special quality] magie *f*; the ~ of Greta Garbo la magie OR le charisme de Greta Garbo; discover the ~ of Greece découvrez les merveilles de la Grèce.
◇ *adj* -**1.** [supernatural] magique; a ~ spell un sortilège; just say the ~ words il suffit de dire la formule magique ❑ ~ number/square nombre *m*/carré *m* magique; 'The Magic Flute' *Mozart* 'la Flûte enchantée'; 'The Magic Mountain' *Mann* 'la Montagne magique'. -**2.** [special - formula, moment] magique. -**3.** *inf* [marvellous] génial.
◆ **magic away** *vt sep* faire disparaître comme par enchantement.

magical [ˈmædʒɪkl] *adj* magique; her songs had a ~ quality ses chansons avaient quelque chose de magique.

magically [ˈmædʒɪklɪ] *adv* magiquement; don't think it will just happen ~ ne t'imagine pas que cela va se produire comme par enchantement.

magic carpet *n* tapis *m* volant.

magic eye *n* cellule *f* photoélectrique.

magician [məˈdʒɪʃn] *n* magicien *m*, -enne *f*.

magic lantern *n* lanterne *f* magique.

magic mushroom *n drugs sl* champignon *m* hallucinogène.

magic wand *n* baguette *f* magique.

magisterial [ˌmædʒɪˈstɪərɪəl] *adj* JUR de magistrat; *fig* magistral.

magisterially [ˌmædʒɪˈstɪərɪəlɪ] *adv* magistralement.

magistracy [ˈmædʒɪstrəsɪ] (*pl* magistracies) *n* magistrature *f*.

magistral [məˈdʒɪstrəl] *adj* magistral.

magistrate [ˈmædʒɪstreɪt] *n* magistrat *m*.

magistrates' court *n* tribunal *m* de première instance.

magma [ˈmægmə] *n* magma *m*.

Magna Carta, Magna Charta [ˌmægnəˈkɑːtə] *pr n Br* HIST la Grande Charte.

MAGNA CARTA:
Souvent prise pour le symbole de la lutte contre l'oppression, cette charte, imposée en 1215 au roi Jean sans Terre par les barons anglais, énonce les droits et privilèges des nobles, de l'Église et des «hommes libres» («freemen») face à l'arbitraire royal.

---

magna cum laude [ˌmægnəkʊmˈlaʊdeɪ] *adv* UNIV avec mention très bien.

magnanimity [ˌmægnəˈnɪmətɪ] *n* magnanimité *f*.

magnanimous [mægˈnænɪməs] *adj* magnanime.

magnanimously [mægˈnænɪməslɪ] *adv* avec magnanimité, magnanimement.

magnate [ˈmægneɪt] *n* magnat *m*; a press ~ un magnat de la presse.

magnesia [mægˈniːʃə] *n* magnésie *f*.

magnesium [mægˈniːzɪəm] *n* magnésium *m*; ~ oxide magnésie *f*, oxyde *m* de magnésium.

magnet [ˈmægnɪt] *n* aimant *m*.

magnetic [mægˈnetɪk] *adj* magnétique; a ~ personality *fig* une personnalité fascinante OR charismatique.

magnetically [mægˈnetɪklɪ] *adv* magnétiquement.

magnetic field *n* champ *m* magnétique.

magnetic needle *n* aiguille *f* aimantée.

magnetic north *n* nord *m* magnétique.

magnetic storm *n* orage *m* magnétique.

magnetic tape *n* bande *f* magnétique.

magnetism [ˈmægnɪtɪzm] *n* magnétisme *m*.

magnetize, -ise [ˈmægnɪtaɪz] *vt* aimanter, magnétiser; *fig* [charm] magnétiser.

magneton [ˈmægnɪtɒn] *n* magnéton *m*.

magnificat [mægˈnɪfɪkæt] *n* magnificat *m inv*; the Magnificat le Magnificat.

magnification [ˌmægnɪfɪˈkeɪʃn] *n* -**1.** OPT grossissement *m*; ACOUST amplification *f*. -**2.** RELIG glorification *f*.

magnificence [mægˈnɪfɪsəns] *n* magnificence *f*, splendeur *f*.

magnificent [mægˈnɪfɪsənt] *adj* magnifique, splendide; Lorenzo the Magnificent Laurent le Magnifique ❑ 'The Magnificent Ambersons' *Welles* 'la Splendeur des Amberson'; 'The Magnificent Seven' *Sturges* 'les Sept Mercenaires'.

magnificently [mægˈnɪfɪsəntlɪ] *adv* magnifiquement.

magnifico [mægˈnɪfɪkəʊ] (*pl* **magnificos** OR magnificoes) *n* grand seigneur *m*.

magnify [ˈmægnɪfaɪ] (*pt & pp* **magnified**) *vt* -**1.** OPT grossir; ACOUST amplifier. -**2.** [exaggerate] exagérer, grossir; the incident was magnified out of all proportion on a terriblement exagéré l'importance de cet incident. -**3.** *lit* [exalt] exalter, magnifier; RELIG glorifier.

magnifying glass [ˈmægnɪfaɪɪŋ-] *n* loupe *f*.

magniloquence [mægˈnɪləkwəns] *n fml* grandiloquence *f*, emphase *f*, pompe *f*.

magniloquent [mægˈnɪləkwənt] *adj fml* grandiloquent, emphatique, pompeux.

magnitude [ˈmægnɪtjuːd] *n* [scale] ampleur *f*, étendue *f*, ASTRON & GEOL magnitude *f*; ~ 7 on the Richter scale magnitude 7 sur l'échelle (de) Richter; the ~ of the problem [importance] l'importance du problème; [size] l'ampleur du problème.

magnolia [mægˈnəʊljə] ◇ *n* magnolia *m*.
◇ *adj* couleur magnolia *(inv)*, blanc rosé *(inv)*.

magnum [ˈmægnəm] *n* [wine bottle, gun] magnum *m*.

magnum opus *n* œuvre *f* maîtresse, chef-d'œuvre *m*.

magpie [ˈmægpaɪ] *n* -**1.** ORNITH pie *f*. -**2.** *inf fig* [chatterbox] pie *f*, moulin *m* à paroles; *Br* [hoarder] chiffonnier *m*, -ère *f fig*.

magus [ˈmeɪgəs] (*pl* magi [-dʒaɪ]) *n* mage *m*.

Magyar [ˈmægjɑː] ◇ *n* -**1.** [person] Magyar *m*, -e *f*. -**2.** LING magyar *m*.
◇ *adj* magyar.

maharaja(h) [ˌmɑːhəˈrɑːdʒə] *n* maharaja *m*, maharadjah *m*.

maharani [ˌmɑːhəˈrɑːniː] *n* maharani *f*.

maharishi [ˌmɑːhəˈriːʃi] *n* maharishi *m*.

mahatma [məˈhɑːtmə] *n* mahatma *m*.

mah-jong(g) [mɑːˈdʒɒŋ] *n* mah-jong *m*.

mahogany [məˈhɒgənɪ] (*pl* **mahoganies**) ◇ *n* acajou *m*; ~ tree acajou *m*.
◇ *adj* -**1.** ~ (coloured) acajou *(inv)*; ~ brown brun acajou *(inv)*. -**2.** [furniture] en acajou.

Mahomet [məˈhɒmɪt] = **Mohammed**.

Mahometan [məˈhɒmɪtn] *dated* ◇ *adj* mahométan.
◇ *n* Mahométan *m*, -e *f*.

maid [meɪd] *n* -**1.** [servant] bonne *f*, domestique *f*; [in hotel] femme *f* de chambre; ~ of all work bonne à tout faire; ~ of honour demoiselle *f* d'honneur. -**2.** *lit* jeune fille *f*, demoiselle *f*; the Maid of Orleans la pucelle d'Orléans. -**3.** *pej*: old ~ vieille fille *f*.

maiden [ˈmeɪdn] *n* [young girl] jeune fille *f*; [virgin] vierge *f*.

maiden aunt *n* tante *f* célibataire.

maidenhair [ˈmeɪdnheəʳ] *n*: ~ (fern) capillaire *m*, cheveu-de-Vénus *m*.

maidenhead [ˈmeɪdnhed] *n lit* [hymen] hymen *m*; [virginity] virginité *f*.

maidenhood [ˈmeɪdnhʊd] *n* virginité *f*.

maiden name *n* nom *m* de jeune fille.

maiden over *n au cricket, série de balles où aucun point n'a été marqué*.

maiden speech *n Br premier discours prononcé par un parlementaire nouvellement élu*.

maiden voyage *n* voyage *m* inaugural.

maid-in-waiting (*pl* **maids-in-waiting**) *n* dame *f* d'honneur.

maidservant [ˈmeɪdˌsɜːvənt] *n* servante *f*.

mail [meɪl] ◇ *n* -**1.** [postal service] poste *f*; to send a letter by ~ envoyer une lettre par la poste; the parcel got lost in the ~ le colis a été égaré par la poste; your cheque is in the ~ votre chèque a été posté. -**2.** [letters] courrier *m*; has the ~ arrived? est-ce que le courrier est arrivé?; the ~ is only collected twice a week il n'y a que deux levées par semaine. -**3.** *(U)* [armour] mailles *fpl*; coat of ~ cotte *f* de mailles.
◇ *vt Am* [parcel, goods, cheque] envoyer OR expédier par la poste; [letter] poster; I've just ~ed some money home je viens d'expédier OR d'envoyer de l'argent à ma famille.
◆ **Mail** *pr n*: the Mail PRESS *nom abrégé du Daily Mail*.

mailable [ˈmeɪləbl] *adj Am* conforme aux règlements postaux.

mailbag [ˈmeɪlbæg] *n* sac *m* postal.

mailboat [ˈmeɪlbəʊt] *n* navire *m* postal.

mail bomb *n Am* [letter] lettre *f* piégée; [parcel] colis *m* piégé.

mailbox [ˈmeɪlbɒks] *n* -**1.** *esp Am* [postbox] boîte *f* à lettres. -**2.** *Am* [letterbox] boîte *f* aux lettres.

mail clerk *n Am* employé *m*, -e *f* responsable du courrier.

mailcoach [ˈmeɪlkəʊtʃ] *n* RAIL voiture-poste *f*; [horse-drawn] malle-poste *f*.

mail drop *n* boîte *f* à OR aux lettres.

mailed [meɪld] *adj* [armour] maillé.

mailing [ˈmeɪlɪŋ] *n* -**1.** [posting] expédition *f*, envoi *m* par la poste; our prices are correct up to the time of ~ nos prix sont valables au moment où nous vous les adressons. -**2.** COMM & COMPUT mailing *m*, publipostage *m*.

mailing list *n* fichier *m* d'adresses.

mailing shot = **mailshot**.

mailman [ˈmeɪlmən] (*pl* **mailmen** [-mən]) *n Am* facteur *m*.

mail order *n* vente *f* par correspondance; to buy sthg by ~ acheter qqch par correspondance OR sur catalogue.
◆ **mail-order** *adj*: mail-order catalogue catalogue *m* de vente par correspondance; mail-order firm maison *f* de vente par correspondance; mail-order goods marchandises *fpl* vendues OR achetées par correspondance.

mailshot [ˈmeɪlʃɒt] *n* mailing *m*, publipostage *m*.

mail train *n* train *m* postal.

mail van *n Br* AUT camionnette *f* OR fourgon *m* des postes; RAIL voiture-poste *f*.

maim [meɪm] *vt* [disable] mutiler, estropier; [injure] blesser; people were badly ~ed in the attack des gens ont été grièvement blessés au cours de l'attaque ‖ [psychologically] marquer, perturber; the experience ~ed her for life l'expérience l'a marquée pour la vie.

main [meɪn] ◇ *adj* -**1.** [principal] principal; [largest] principal, plus important; [essential - idea, theme, reason] principal, essentiel; the ~ body of public opinion le gros de l'opinion publique; the ~ points les points principaux; the ~ thing we have to consider is his age la première chose à prendre en compte, c'est son âge; you're safe, that's the ~ thing tu es sain et sauf, c'est le principal; that's the ~ thing to remember c'est ce dont il faut se souvenir avant tout ❑ he always has an eye to the ~ chance *inf* il ne perd jamais de vue ses propres intérêts; ~ course plat *m* de résistance; ~ office [gen] bureau *m* principal; [headquarters] siège *m*. -**2.** *lit* [sheer]: to do sthg by ~ force employer la force pour faire qqch.
◇ *n* -**1.** [for gas, water - public] canalisation *f* principale; [- domestic]: gas ~ conduite *f* de gaz; water ~ conduite *f* d'eau ‖ [for electricity] conducteur *m* principal. -**2.** *arch*: the (Spanish) Main [sea] la mer des Antilles. -**3.** NAUT grand mât *m*.
◆ **in the main** *adv phr* en gros, dans l'ensemble.

main beam *n* -**1.** AUT feux *mpl* de route; to be on ~ rouler pleins phares. -**2.** CONSTR poutre *f* maîtresse.

main bearing *n* palier *m (dans un moteur)*.

mainbrace [ˈmeɪnbreɪs] *n* grand bras *m*.

main clause *n* GRAMM proposition *f* principale.

main deck *n* NAUT pont *m* principal.

main drag▽ *Am* = **main street**.

Maine [meɪn] *pr n* le Maine; in ~ dans le Maine.

mainframe [ˈmeɪnfreɪm] *n*: ~ (computer) gros ordinateur *m*.

mainland [ˈmeɪnlənd] ◇ *n* continent *m*; she sailed back to the ~ elle regagna le continent en bateau; the Danish ~ le Danemark continental; the British ~ la Grande-Bretagne *(le Royaume-Uni sans l'Irlande du Nord)*.
◇ *adj* continental; in ~ Europe en Europe continentale; in ~ Britain en Grande-Bretagne proprement dite *(par opposition aux îles qui l'entourent)*.

mainlander [ˈmeɪnləndəʳ] *n* habitant *m*, -e *f* du continent, continental *m*, -e *f*.

mainline [ˈmeɪnlaɪn] *drugs sl* ◇ *vi* se piquer, se shooter.
◇ *vt*: to ~ heroin se shooter à l'héroïne.

main line *n* RAIL grande ligne *f*; *Am* [road] grande route *f*.
◆ **main-line** *adj* [train, station] de grande ligne.

mainliner [ˈmeɪnlaɪnəʳ] *n drugs sl* drogué *m*, -e *f (qui se pique)*.

mainly [ˈmeɪnlɪ] *adv* [chiefly] principalement, surtout; [in the majority] pour la plupart, dans l'ensemble.

main mast *n* grand mât *m*.

main road *n* grande route *f*, route à grande circulation, ≃ nationale *f*.

mains [meɪnz] ◇ *n (with sg or pl verb)* -**1.** [main supply] réseau *m*; where's the ~? où est la conduite principale?; did you turn the electricity/gas off at the ~? as-tu fermé l'arrivée de gaz/d'électricité? -**2.** ELEC secteur *m*; my shaver works on battery or ~ mon rasoir marche sur piles ou sur (le) secteur.
◇ *comp*: the village doesn't have ~ electricity le village n'est pas raccordé au réseau électrique; ~ gas gaz *m* de ville; ~ razor rasoir *m* fonctionnant sur secteur; ~ set poste *m* secteur; ~ supply réseau *m* de distribution de gaz OR d'eau OR d'électricité; ~ water eau *f* courante.

mainsail [ˈmeɪnseɪl, ˈmeɪnsəl] *n* NAUT grand-voile *f*.

main sewer *n* égout *m* collecteur.

mainsheet [ˈmeɪnshiːt] *n* écoute *f* de (la) grand-voile.

mains-operated *adj* fonctionnant sur secteur.

mainspring [ˈmeɪnsprɪŋ] *n* -**1.** TECH ressort *m* principal. -**2.** *fig* moteur *m*; his courage was the ~ of his success son courage était la raison profonde de son succès.

main squeeze▽ *n Am* [girlfriend] petite copine *f*; [boyfriend] petit copain *m*.

mainstay [ˈmeɪnsteɪ] *n* -**1.** NAUT étai *m* (de grand mât). -**2.** *fig* soutien *m*, point *m* d'appui; maize is the ~ of their diet le maïs constitue la base de leur alimentation.

mainstream [ˈmeɪnstriːm] ◇ *adj*: ~ French politics le courant dominant de la politique française; ~ America la majorité des américains; their music is hardly what you'd call ~! leur musique se démarque de ce qu'on entend habituellement!
◇ *n* courant *m*; the ~ of modern European literature la tendance qui prédomine dans la littérature européenne moderne; he is in the ~ of politics en politique, il suit la plus forte pente OR la tendance générale; to live outside the ~ of society vivre en marge de la société.

main street *n* -**1.** *literal* rue *f* principale. -**2.** *Am fig*: Main Street *les petits commerçants*.

mainstreeting [ˈmeɪnstriːtɪŋ] *n (U) Can* POL bains *mpl* de foule; to go ~ prendre un bain de foule.

maintain [meɪnˈteɪn] ◇ *vt* -**1.** [retain - institution, tradition] conserver, préserver; the old rules have been ~ed les anciennes règles ont été conservées ‖ [preserve - peace, standard] maintenir; to ~ law and order maintenir l'ordre; we must ~ our output nous devons maintenir notre niveau de production; to ~ a position MIL & *fig* tenir une position ‖ [look after - roads, machinery] entretenir; the grounds are well ~ed les jardins sont bien entretenus OR tenus. -**2.** [uphold, keep - correspondence, friendship] entretenir; [- silence, advantage] garder; he had difficulty ~ing his composure il avait du mal à garder son sang-froid; I have my reputation to ~ j'ai une réputation à défendre. -**3.** [financially - dependents] entretenir; they have two children at university to ~ ils ont deux enfants à charge à l'université; he has a wife and 7 children to ~ il a une femme et 7 enfants à nourrir. -**4.** [assert - opinion] soutenir, défendre; [- innocence] affirmer; I still ~ she's innocent je soutiens OR je maintiens toujours qu'elle est innocente.
◇ *vi Am*: I'm ~ing! [I'm fine] ça va!

maintainable [meɪnˈteɪnəbl] *adj* [attitude, opinion, position] soutenable, défendable.

maintained [meɪnˈteɪnd] *adj Br*: ~ school ≃ école *f* publique.

maintainer [meɪnˈteɪnəʳ] *n* [of opinion, cause] défenseur *m*.

maintenance [ˈmeɪntənəns] ◇ *n* -**1.** [of roads, building] entretien *m*; [of machinery, computer] maintenance *f*. -**2.** [financial support] entretien *m*; he has very little money left for his own ~ il lui reste très peu d'argent pour vivre. -**3.** JUR [alimony] pension *f* alimentaire. -**4.** [of order] maintien *m*; [of regulations] application *f*; [of situation] maintien *m*; ~ of a reasonable standard of living le maintien d'un niveau de vie correct.
◇ *comp* [costs, crew] d'entretien; ~ contract contract *m* de maintenance OR d'entretien; ~ man ouvrier *m* chargé de l'entretien OR de la maintenance.

maintenance allowance *n* [to student] bourse *f* d'études; [to businessman] indemnité *f* pour frais de déplacement.

maintenance-free *adj* sans entretien, sans maintenance.

maintenance grant = **maintenance allowance**.

maintenance order *n* obligation *f* alimentaire; **she got a ~ against him** elle a obtenu du tribunal qu'il lui verse une pension alimentaire.

maintop ['meɪntɒp] *n* grande hune *f*.

Mainz [maɪnts] *pr n* Mayence.

maisonette [,meɪzə'net] *n Br* [small house] maisonnette *f*; [flat] duplex *m*.

maître d' [,metrə'diː] *n* maître *m* d'hôtel.

maître d'hôtel [,metrədəʊ'tel] *n* maître *m* d'hôtel.

maize [meɪz] *n* maïs *m*.

Maj. (*written abbr of* Major) ≃ Cdt.

majestic [mə'dʒestɪk] *adj* majestueux.

majestically [mə'dʒestɪklɪ] *adv* majestueusement.

majesty ['mædʒəstɪ] (*pl* **majesties**) *n* majesté *f*; **His Majesty the King** Sa Majesté le Roi; **Her Majesty the Queen** Sa Majesté la Reine.

majolica [mə'jɒlɪkə] *n* majolique *f*.

major ['meɪdʒə^r] ◇ *adj* -**1.** [main] : **the ~ part of our research** l'essentiel de nos recherches; **the ~ portion of my time is devoted to politics** la majeure partie OR la plus grande partie de mon temps est consacrée à la politique ❑ **~ premise** PHILOS majeure *f*; **~ road** route *f* principale OR à grande circulation, ≃ nationale *f*; **~ subject** UNIV matière *f* principale. -**2.** [significant - decision, change, factor, event] majeur; **we shouldn't have any ~ problems** nous ne devrions pas rencontrer de problèmes majeurs; **don't worry, it's not a ~ problem** ne t'inquiète pas, ce n'est pas très grave; **of ~ importance** d'une grande importance, d'une importance capitale; **a ~ role** [in play, film] un grand rôle; [in negotiations, reform] un rôle capital OR essentiel; **to launch a ~ offensive** lancer une vaste offensive. -**3.** [serious - obstacle, difficulty] majeur; **the roof is in need of ~ repair work** la toiture a grand besoin d'être remise en état; **she underwent ~ surgery** elle a subi une grosse opération. -**4.** MUS majeur; **a sonata in E ~** une sonate en mi majeur ❑ **in a ~ key** en (mode) majeur; **a ~ third** une tierce majeure. -**5.** *Br* SCH [elder] : **Smith ~** Smith aîné. -**6.** CARDS majeur; **~ suit** majeure *f*.
◇ *n* -**1.** MIL [in air force] commandant *m*; [in infantry] chef *m* de bataillon; [in cavalry] chef *m* d'escadron. -**2.** *fml* [person over 18] personne *f* majeure. -**3.** *Am* UNIV [subject] matière *f* principale; **Tina is a physics ~** Tina fait des études de physique. -**4.** MUS (mode *m*) majeur *m*. -**5.** *Am* [big company] : **the oil ~s** les grandes compagnies pétrolières; **the Majors** [film companies] *les cinq compagnies de production les plus importantes à Hollywood*.
◇ *vi Am* UNIV [specialize] se spécialiser; **Fred ~s in chemistry** Fred se spécialise en chimie ‖ [be a student] : **she ~ed in sociology** elle a fait des études de sociologie.

Majorca [mə'dʒɔːkə, mə'jɔːkə] *pr n* Majorque; **in ~** à Majorque.

Majorcan [mə'dʒɔːkn, mə'jɔːkn] ◇ *n* Majorquin *m*, -e *f*.
◇ *adj* majorquin.

majordomo [,meɪdʒə'dəʊməʊ] (*pl* **majordomos**) *n* majordome *m*.

majorette [,meɪdʒə'ret] *n* majorette *f*.

major general *n* général *m* de division.

majority [mə'dʒɒrətɪ] (*pl* **majorities**) ◇ *n* -**1.** [of a group] majorité *f*, plupart *f*; **the ~ of people** la plupart des gens; **in the ~ of cases** dans la plupart des cas; **the ~ was** OR **were in favour** la majorité OR la plupart d'entre eux était pour; **the vast ~ of the tourists were Japanese** les touristes, dans leur très grande majorité, étaient des Japonais ‖ [in voting, opinions] majorité *f*; **to be in a ~** être majoritaire; **the proposition had an overwhelming ~** la proposition a recueilli une écrasante majorité; **she was elected by a ~ of 6** elle a été élue avec une majorité de 6 voix OR par 6 voix de majorité. -**2.** JUR [voting age] majorité *f*.
◇ *comp* majoritaire; **a ~ government/verdict** un gouvernement/verdict majoritaire.

major league *n Am* -**1.** [in baseball] *une des deux principales divisions de baseball professionnel aux États-Unis*. -**2.** [gen] première division *f*; **~ team** grande équipe *(sportive)*.

make [meɪk] (*pt* & *pp* **made** [meɪd]) ◇ *vt*
A. -**1.** [construct, create, manufacture] faire, fabriquer; **to ~ one's own clothes** faire ses vêtements soi-même; **to ~ a meal** préparer un repas; **I'll ~ some tea** je vais préparer du thé; **they ~ computers** ils fabriquent des ordinateurs; **'made in Japan'** 'fabriqué au Japon'; **a vase made of** OR **from clay** un vase en OR de terre cuite; **what's it made of?** en quoi est-ce que c'est fait?; **what do you ~ aluminium from?** à partir de quoi est-ce qu'on fabrique l'aluminium?; **he ~s models out of matchsticks** il fait des maquettes avec des allumettes ❑ **they're made for each other** ils sont faits l'un pour l'autre; **we're not made of money!** on n'a pas d'argent à jeter par les fenêtres!; **I'll show them what I'm made of!** je leur montrerai de quel bois je me chauffe OR qui je suis! -**2.** [cause to appear or happen - hole, tear, mess, mistake, noise] faire; **it made a dent in the bumper** ça a cabossé le pare-chocs; **he's always making trouble** il faut toujours qu'il fasse des histoires. -**3.** [establish - law, rule] établir, faire; **I don't ~ the rules** ce n'est pas moi qui fais les règlements. -**4.** [form - circle, line] former. -**5.** CIN & TV [direct] faire; [act in] faire; **she's making a documentary** elle fait un documentaire; **he's made several films with Scott** il a fait plusieurs films avec Scott. -**6.** *(delexical use)* [indicating action performed] : **to ~ a decision** prendre une décision; **to ~ an offer** faire une offre; **to ~ a request** faire une demande; **to ~ a note of sthg** prendre note de qqch; **to ~ a speech** faire un discours; **to ~ a phone call** passer un coup de fil; **the Queen will ~ an official visit to Japan** la reine va se rendre en visite officielle au Japon; **we've made a few changes** nous avons fait OR apporté quelques modifications; **the police are making inquiries** la police procède à une enquête; **I have no further comments to ~** je n'ai rien à ajouter. -**7.** [tidy] : **to ~ one's bed** faire son lit.
B. -**1.** *(with adj or pp complement)* [cause to be] rendre; **to ~ sb happy/mad** rendre qqn heureux/fou; **this will ~ things easier** cela facilitera les choses; **it ~s her tired** ça la fatigue; **what ~s the sky blue?** qu'est-ce qui fait que le ciel est bleu?; **I'd like to ~ it clear that it wasn't my fault** je voudrais qu'on comprenne bien que je n'y suis pour rien; **~ yourselves comfortable** mettez-vous à l'aise; **it was hard to ~ myself heard/understood** j'ai eu du mal à me faire entendre/comprendre; **a child would ~ our happiness complete** il ne nous manque qu'un enfant pour que notre bonheur soit parfait. -**2.** *(with noun complement or with 'into')* [change into] faire; **the film made her (into) a star** le film a fait d'elle une vedette; **to ~ a success of sthg** réussir qqch; **he was made president for life** il a été nommé président à vie; **they made Bonn the capital** ils ont choisi Bonn pour capitale; **they made Strasbourg the capital of Europe** ils ont fait de Strasbourg la capitale de l'Europe; **he ~s a joke of everything** il tourne tout en plaisanterie; **the building has been made into offices** l'immeuble a été réaménagé OR converti en bureaux; **I'll ~ you a present of it** je t'en ferai cadeau; **the latest cheque ~s the total £10,000** le dernier chèque porte la somme totale à 10 000 livres; **I can't come in the morning, shall we ~ it 2 p.m.?** je ne peux pas venir le matin, est-ce que 14 h vous conviendrait? -**3.** *(with verb complement)* [cause] faire; **what ~s you think they're wrong?** qu'est-ce qui te fait penser qu'ils ont tort?; **peeling onions ~s my eyes water** les oignons me font pleurer; **I can't ~ the coffee machine work** je n'arrive pas à faire marcher la machine à café; **you ~ it look easy** à vous voir, on croirait que c'est facile; **the hat/photo ~s you look ridiculous** tu as l'air ridicule avec ce chapeau/sur cette photo; **don't ~ me laugh!** ne me fais pas rire! -**4.** [force, oblige] : **to ~ sb do sthg** faire faire qqch à qqn; [stronger] forcer OR obliger OR contraindre qqn à faire qqch; **they made me wait** ils m'ont fait attendre; **if he doesn't want to do it you can't ~ him** s'il ne veut pas le faire, tu ne peux pas l'y obliger OR forcer; **she made herself keep running** elle s'est forcée à continuer à courir.
C. -**1.** [attain, achieve - goal] atteindre; **we made all our production targets** nous avons atteint tous nos objectifs de production; **their first record made the top ten** leur premier disque est rentré au top ten; **you won't ~ the team if you don't train** tu n'entreras jamais dans l'équipe si tu ne t'entraînes pas; **the story made the front page** l'histoire a fait la une des journaux. -**2.** [arrive at, get to - place] atteindre; **we should ~ Houston/port by evening** nous devrions arriver à Houston/atteindre le port d'ici ce soir; **did you ~ your train?** as-tu réussi à avoir ton train? -**3.** [be available for] : **I won't be able to ~ lunch** je ne pourrai pas déjeuner avec toi/elle/vous *etc*; **can you ~ Friday afternoon?** vendredi après-midi, ça vous convient? -**4.** [earn, win] faire, gagner; **to ~ a profit** faire un profit; **how much do you ~ a month?** combien gagnes-tu par mois?; **she made her first million selling beauty products** elle a gagné son premier million en vendant des produits de beauté; **what do they ~ out of the deal?** qu'est-ce qu'ils gagnent dans l'affaire?, qu'est-ce que l'affaire leur rapporte?
D. -**1.** [amount to, add up to] faire; **17 and 19 ~** OR **~s 36** 17 plus 19 font OR égalent 36; **if Kay comes, that will ~ eight** si Kay vient, ça fera huit; **that ~s £4, Madam** ça fait OR fera 4 livres, Madame; **that ~s the third time you've been late this week** c'est la troisième fois que vous êtes en retard cette semaine; **how old does that ~ him?** quel âge ça lui fait? -**2.** [reckon to be] : **I ~ the answer 257** d'après moi, ça fait 257; **I ~ it $14 each** si je compte bien, ça fait 14 dollars par personne; **what time do you ~ it?** quelle heure as-tu? -**3.** *(with noun complement)* [fulfil specified role, function etc] faire; **these shoes will ~ an excellent Christmas present** ces chaussures feront un très beau cadeau de Noël; **he'll ~ somebody a good husband** ce sera un excellent mari; **he'd ~ a good teacher** il ferait un bon enseignant; **they ~ a handsome couple** ils forment un beau couple; **her reminiscences ~ interesting reading** ses souvenirs sont intéressants à lire. -**4.** [score] marquer; **Smith made his second century** Smith a marqué deux cents points.
E. -**1.** [make successful] faire le succès de; **it's her performance that ~s the film** tout le film repose sur son interprétation; **if this deal comes off we're made!** si ça marche, on touche le gros lot! ❑ **you've got it made!** tu n'as plus de souci à te faire!; **what happens today will ~ or break us** notre avenir dépend entièrement de ce qui va se passer aujourd'hui. -**2.** *inf* [seduce] draguer; [have sex with] se faire. -**3.** *Am* [in directions] : **~ a right/left** tournez à droite/à gauche. -**4.** *phr*: **to ~ it** [arrive] arriver; [be successful] réussir; [be able to attend] être là; **I'll never ~ it for 10 o'clock** je ne pourrai jamais y être pour 10 h; **we made it to the airport with an hour to spare** nous sommes arrivés à l'aéroport avec une heure d'avance; **if he doesn't ~ it back in 10 minutes, start without him** s'il n'est pas revenu dans 10 minutes, commencez sans lui; **I hope she ~s it through the winter** j'espère qu'elle passera l'hiver; **he'll never ~ it as a businessman** il ne réussira jamais dans les affaires; **I can't ~ it for supper tomorrow** je ne peux pas dîner avec eux/toi *etc* demain ❑ **to ~ it with sb** *inf* se faire qqn.
◇ *vi* [act] : **to ~ (as if) to** faire mine de; **she made (as if) to stand up** elle fit mine de se lever; **I walked in trying to ~ like a businessman** *inf*

je suis entré en essayant d'avoir l'air d'un homme d'affaires; ~ like you're asleep! *inf* fais semblant de dormir!; I didn't know what it was all about but I made like I did *inf* je ne savais pas de quoi il était question, mais j'ai fait comme si ❑ to ~ believe imaginer; ~ believe you're a bird imagine que tu es un oiseau; to ~ do (with) [manage] se débrouiller (avec); [be satisfied] se contenter (de); it's broken but we'll just have to ~ do c'est cassé mais il faudra faire avec OR nous débrouiller avec.

◇ *n* -**1.** [brand] marque *f*; what ~ of washing machine have you got? quelle est la marque de votre machine à laver?, qu'est-ce que vous avez comme machine à laver? -**2.** *phr*: to be on the ~ *inf* [financially] chercher à se faire du fric. -**3.** [in bridge] contrat *m*.

◆ **make away with** = **make off with**.

◆ **make for** *vt insep* -**1.** [head towards] se diriger vers; [hastily] se précipiter vers; the plane is making for Berlin l'avion se dirige sur Berlin; he made straight for the fridge il se dirigea tout droit vers le frigo; when it started to rain everyone made for the trees quand il s'est mis à pleuvoir, tout le monde s'est précipité vers les arbres; the truck was making right for him le camion fonçait droit sur lui; he made for his gun il fit un geste pour saisir son pistolet. -**2.** [contribute to] mener à; the treaty should ~ for a more lasting peace le traité devrait mener OR aboutir à une paix plus durable; this layout ~s for easier reading cette mise en page permet une lecture plus facile; a good diet ~s for healthier babies un bon régime alimentaire donne des bébés en meilleure santé.

◆ **make of** ◇ *vt sep* -**1.** [understand] comprendre à; can you ~ anything of these instructions? est-ce que tu comprends quelque chose à ce mode d'emploi? -**2.** [give importance to]: I think you're making too much of a very minor problem je pense que tu exagères l'importance de ce petit problème; do you want to ~ something of it, then? *inf* [threat] tu cherches des histoires ou quoi?

◇ *vt insep* [think of] penser de; what do you ~ of the Smiths? qu'est-ce que tu penses des Smith?

◆ **make off** *vi insep* partir.

◆ **make off with** *vt insep* partir avec; he made off with the cash il est parti avec l'argent.

◆ **make out** ◇ *vt sep* -**1.** [see] distinguer; [hear] comprendre; I could just ~ out the outline of the castle je distinguais juste la silhouette du château; I couldn't ~ out what he said je ne comprenais pas ce qu'il disait; I can't ~ out the address je n'arrive pas à déchiffrer l'adresse. -**2.** [understand] comprendre; I couldn't ~ out how to fit it together je ne comprenais pas comment l'assembler; I can't ~ her out at all je ne la comprends pas du tout. -**3.** [claim] prétendre; she made out that she was busy elle a fait semblant d'être occupée; don't ~ yourself out to be something you're not ne prétends pas être ce que tu n'es pas; it's not as bad as everyone ~s out ce n'est pas aussi mauvais qu'on le prétend. -**4.** [fill out - form, cheque] remplir; who shall I ~ the cheque out to? je fais le chèque à quel ordre? -**5.** [draw up - list] dresser, faire; [- will, contract] faire, rédiger, établir; could you ~ me out a receipt? pourriez-vous me faire un reçu?

◇ *vi insep* -**1.** *inf* [manage, get along] se débrouiller; I'm sure she'll ~ out whatever happens je suis sûr qu'elle se débrouillera quoi qu'il arrive; how did you ~ out at work today? comment ça s'est passé au boulot aujourd'hui? -**2.** ▽ [neck, pet] se peloter; to ~ out with sb [have sex] s'envoyer qqn.

◆ **make over** *vt sep* -**1.** [transfer] transférer, céder. -**2.** *Am* [convert - room, house] réaménager; the garage had been made over into a workshop le garage a été transformé en atelier.

◆ **make up** ◇ *vi insep* -**1.** [put on make-up] se maquiller. -**2.** [become reconciled] se réconcilier.

◇ *vt sep* -**1.** [put make-up on] maquiller; to ~ o.s. up se maquiller; he was heavily made up il était très maquillé OR fardé. -**2.** [prepare] faire, préparer; we can ~ up a bed for you in the living room nous pouvons vous faire un lit dans le salon; the chemist made up the prescription le pharmacien a préparé l'ordonnance; the fire needs making up il faut remettre du charbon/du bois sur le feu. -**3.** [invent] inventer; I'm sure he made the story up je suis sûr qu'il a inventé cette histoire (de toutes pièces). -**4.** TYPO mettre en pages. -**5.** *phr*: to ~ it up with sb se réconcilier avec qqn; have you made it up with him? est-ce que vous vous êtes réconciliés?

◇ *vt insep* -**1.** [constitute] composer, constituer; the different ethnic groups that ~ up our organization les différents groupes ethniques qui constituent notre organisation; the cabinet is made up of 11 ministers le cabinet est composé de 11 ministres; it is made up of a mixture of different types of tobacco c'est un mélange de plusieurs tabacs différents. -**2.** [compensate for - losses] compenser; to ~ up lost ground regagner le terrain perdu; he's making up time il rattrape son retard. -**3.** [complete]: this cheque will help you ~ up the required sum ce chèque vous aidera à atteindre le montant requis; we need two more players to ~ up the team nous avons besoin de deux joueurs de plus pour que l'équipe soit au complet; I'll ~ up the difference je mettrai la différence.

◆ **make up for** *vt insep* compenser; the pay doesn't ~ up for the poor conditions le salaire ne compense pas les piètres conditions de travail; how can I ~ up for all the trouble I've caused you? que puis-je faire pour me faire pardonner tous les ennuis que je vous ai causés?; she's making up for lost time now! *literal & fig* elle est en train de rattraper le temps perdu!

◆ **make up to** ◇ *vt insep*: to ~ up to sb [try to win favour] essayer de se faire bien voir par qqn; [make advances] faire du plat à qqn.

◇ *vt sep phr*: to ~ it up to sb (for sthg): I promise I'll ~ it up to you someday tu peux être sûr que je te revaudrai ça (un jour).

◆ **make with** *inf vt insep Am*: ~ with the drinks! à boire!; ~ with the music! musique!

make-believe ◇ *n*: it's only ~ ce n'est qu'illusion; a world of ~ un monde d'illusions; to play at ~ jouer à faire semblant.

◇ *adj* imaginaire; a ~ friend un ami imaginaire; they turned the bed into a ~ raft ils imaginèrent que le lit était un radeau.

maker ['meɪkə^r] *n* -**1.** [craftsman] fabricant *m*, -e *f*. -**2.** RELIG: Maker Créateur *m*; to go to meet one's Maker *euph* OR *hum* passer de vie à trépas.

-maker *in cpds* -**1.** [manufacturer] fabricant *m*; dress~ couturière *f*; shoe~ [manufacturer] fabricant *m*, -e *f* de chaussures; [craftsman] bottier *m*. -**2.** [machine]: electric coffee~ cafetière *f* électrique; ice cream~ sorbetière *f*.

makeshift ['meɪkʃɪft] ◇ *adj* de fortune; a ~ shelter un abri de fortune; the accommodation was very ~ le logement était plutôt improvisé.

◇ *n* expédient *m*.

make-up *n* -**1.** [cosmetics] maquillage *m*, fard *m*; she had a lot of ~ on elle était très maquillée; eye ~ fard pour les yeux ❑ ~ artist maquilleur *m*, -euse *f*; ~ bag trousse *f* de maquillage; ~ remover démaquillant *m*. -**2.** [constitution] constitution *f*; she changed the ~ of the cabinet elle a procédé à un remaniement ministériel. -**3.** [nature, character] nature *f*, caractère *m*; spontaneous generosity is not really in her ~ elle n'est pas généreuse de nature. -**4.** TYPO mise *f* en pages. -**5.** *Am* [test, exam]: ~ (test) examen *m* de rattrapage.

makeweight ['meɪkweɪt] *n* [on scales] complément *m* de poids; I'm only here as a ~ *fig* je ne suis là que pour faire nombre.

making ['meɪkɪŋ] *n* -**1.** [manufacture, creation] fabrication *f*; the situation is entirely of his own ~ il est entièrement responsable de la situation dans laquelle il se trouve; the incident was to be the ~ of his career as a politician l'incident devait être à l'origine de sa carrière d'homme politique; the two years she spent abroad were the ~ of her success les deux années qu'elle a passées à l'étranger ont été la clé de sa réussite. -**2.** [preparation - of cake] confection *f*, préparation *f*; [- of film] tournage *m*.

◆ **in the making** *adj phr* [idea] en gestation; [plan] à l'étude; [building] en construction; it's history in the ~ c'est une page d'histoire qui s'écrit sous nos yeux.

◆ **makings** *npl* [essential elements] ingrédients *mpl*; his war stories have the ~s of a good film il y a de quoi faire un bon film avec ses récits de guerre; the affair has all the ~s of a national scandal il y a dans cette affaire largement de quoi déclencher un scandale national ‖ [potential]: that child has the ~s of a genius cet enfant présente toutes les caractéristiques du génie.

-making *in cpds*: cake~ fabrication *f* de gâteaux; decision~ prise *f* de décisions; film~ tournage *m* d'un film; it's absolutely sick~ *inf Br* c'est à vous donner la nausée.

Malabar Coast ['mæləbɑː-] *pr n*: the ~ la côte de Malabar.

malabsorption [,mæləb'sɔːpʃn] *n* malabsorption *f*.

Malachi ['mæləkaɪ] *pr n* Malachie.

malachite ['mæləkaɪt] *n* malachite *f*.

maladapted [,mælə'dæptɪd] *adj* inadapté.

maladjusted [,mælə'dʒʌstɪd] *adj* -**1.** PSYCH [child] inadapté; ~ children l'enfance *f* inadaptée; to be socially ~ être socialement inadapté. -**2.** [engine, TV picture] mal réglé; [mechanism] mal ajusté.

maladjustment [,mælə'dʒʌstmənt] *n* -**1.** [psychological or social] inadaptation *f*; [emotional] déséquilibre *m*. -**2.** [of engine, TV] mauvais réglage *m*; [of mechanism] mauvais réglage *m*, mauvais ajustement *m*.

maladminister [,mæləd'mɪnɪstə^r] *vt* mal administrer, mal gérer.

maladministration ['mæləd,mɪnɪs'treɪʃn] *n* [of country, economy] mauvaise administration *f*; [of business] mauvaise gestion *f*.

maladroit [,mælə'drɔɪt] *adj* maladroit, gauche, malhabile.

maladroitly [,mælə'drɔɪtlɪ] *adv* maladroitement, gauchement.

maladroitness [,mælə'drɔɪtnɪs] *n* maladresse *f*.

malady ['mælədɪ] (*pl* **maladies**) *n lit* maladie *f*, affection *f*, mal *m*.

Malaga ['mæləgə] *pr n* Malaga.

Malagasy [,mælə'gæsɪ] ◇ *n* -**1.** [person] Malgache *mf*. -**2.** LING malgache *m*.

◇ *adj* malgache.

malaise [mæ'leɪz] *n* malaise *m*.

malapropism ['mæləprɒpɪzm] *n* lapsus *m*.

malaria [mə'leərɪə] *n* malaria *f*, paludisme *m*.

malarial [mə'leərɪəl] *adj* [disease, fever] paludéen.

malarkey *inf* [mə'lɑːkɪ] *n (U)* bêtises *fpl*, sottises *fpl*.

Malawi [mə'lɑːwɪ] *pr n* Malawi *m*; in ~ au Malawi.

Malawian [mə'lɑːwɪən] ◇ *n* Malawite *mf*.

◇ *adj* malawite.

Malay [mə'leɪ] ◇ *n* -**1.** [person] Malais *m*, -e *f*. -**2.** LING malais *m*.

◇ *adj* malais.

Malaya [mə'leɪə] *pr n* Malaisie *f*, Malaysia *f* Occidentale; in ~ en Malaisie.

Malayan [mə'leɪən] ◇ *n* Malais *m*, -e *f*.

◇ *adj* malais.

Malay Peninsula *pr n*: the ~ (la presqu'île de) Malacca, la presqu'île Malaise.

Malaysia [mə'leɪzɪə] *pr n* Malaysia *f*; in ~ en Malaysia.

Malaysian [mə'leɪzɪən] ◇ *n* Malais *m*, -e *f*.

◇ *adj* malais.

malcontent ['mælkən,tent] *n fml* mécontent *m*, -e *f*.

Maldives ['mɔːldaɪvz] *pl pr n*: the ~ les (îles *fpl*) Maldives *fpl*; in the ~ aux Maldives.

Maldivian [mɔːl'dɪvɪən] ◇ *n habitant ou natif des Maldives*.
◇ *adj* des Maldives.

male [meɪl] ◇ *adj* -**1.** ZOOL & BOT mâle; ~ attitudes l'attitude des hommes; ~ child enfant mâle; when I phoned her, a ~ voice answered quand je l'ai appelée, c'est une voix d'homme qui a répondu; the ~ sex le sexe masculin ❑ ~ voice choir chœur *m* d'hommes. -**2.** [virile] mâle, viril. -**3.** TECH [plug] mâle.
◇ *n* ZOOL & BOT mâle *m*; [gen - man] homme *m*.

Malé ['mɑːleɪ] *pr n* Malé.

male chauvinism *n* phallocratie *f*.

male chauvinist *n* phallocrate *m*; ~ pig! sale phallocrate!

malediction [,mælɪ'dɪkʃn] *n lit* malédiction *f*.

malefactor ['mælɪfæktəʳ] *n fml* malfaiteur *m*.

maleficent [mə'lefɪsnt] *adj lit* maléfique.

maleic [mə'leɪɪk] *adj* maléique; ~ acid acide *m* maléique.

maleness ['meɪlnɪs] *n* masculinité *f*.

malevolence [mə'levələns] *n* malveillance *f*.

malevolent [mə'levələnt] *adj* malveillant.

malevolently [mə'levələntlɪ] *adv* avec malveillance.

malfeasance [mæl'fiːzns] *n* JUR méfait *m*, malversation *f*.

malformation [,mælfɔː'meɪʃn] *n* malformation *f*.

malformed [mæl'fɔːmd] *adj* difforme.

malfunction [mæl'fʌŋkʃn] ◇ *n* [fault] fonctionnement *m* défectueux; [breakdown] panne *f*, défaillance *f*.
◇ *vi* [go wrong] mal fonctionner; [break down] tomber en panne.

malfunction routine *n* COMPUT programme *m* de diagnostic.

Mali ['mɑːlɪ] *pr n* Mali *m*; in ~ au Mali.

Malian ['mɑːlɪən] ◇ *n* Malien *m*, -enne *f*.
◇ *adj* malien.

malic ['mælɪk] *adj* malique; ~ acid acide *m* malique.

malice ['mælɪs] *n* méchanceté *f*, malveillance *f*; to bear ~: I don't bear any ~ towards them, I don't bear them any ~ je ne leur en veux pas, je ne leur veux aucun mal; out of OR through ~ par méchanceté, par malveillance ❑ with ~ aforethought JUR avec préméditation.

malicious [mə'lɪʃəs] *adj* -**1.** [gen] méchant, malveillant; ~ gossip médisances *fpl*. -**2.** JUR criminel; ~ damage *Br*, ~ mischief *Am* ≃ dommage *m* causé avec intention de nuire.

maliciously [mə'lɪʃəslɪ] *adv* -**1.** [gen] méchamment, avec malveillance. -**2.** JUR avec préméditation, avec intention de nuire.

malign [mə'laɪn] ◇ *vt* [slander] calomnier; [criticize] critiquer, dire du mal de; the much-~ed government le gouvernement, dont on dit beaucoup de mal OR que l'on a souvent critiqué.
◇ *adj* -**1.** [evil] pernicieux, nocif. -**2.** MED malin.

malignancy [mə'lɪgnənsɪ] (*pl* **malignancies**) *n* -**1.** [ill will] malignité *f*, malveillance *f*, méchanceté *f*. -**2.** MED malignité *f*.

malignant [mə'lɪgnənt] *adj* -**1.** [person, behaviour, intentions] malveillant, malfaisant, méchant. -**2.** MED malin; ~ tumour tumeur *f* maligne.

malignity [mə'lɪgnətɪ] = **malignancy**.

malinger [mə'lɪŋgəʳ] *vi* simuler la maladie, faire semblant d'être malade.

malingerer [mə'lɪŋgərəʳ] *n* faux malade *m*, personne *f* qui fait semblant d'être malade.

mall [mɔːl] *n* -**1.** [avenue] mail *m*, avenue *f*. -**2.** *esp Am* [shopping precinct]: (shopping) ~ centre *m* commercial.

mallard ['mælɑːd] *n*: ~ (duck) colvert *m*.

malleability [,mælɪə'bɪlətɪ] *n* malléabilité *f*.

malleable ['mælɪəbl] *adj* [substance] malléable; [person] influençable, malléable.

mallet ['mælɪt] *n* maillet *m*.

mallow ['mæləʊ] *n* BOT mauve *f*.

malnourished [,mæl'nʌrɪʃt] *adj* sous-alimenté.

malnutrition [,mælnjuː'trɪʃn] *n* malnutrition *f*.

malodorous [mæl'əʊdərəs] *adj* malodorant, nauséabond.

malpractice [,mæl'præktɪs] *n (U)* [professional] faute *f* professionnelle; [financial] malversation *f*, malversations *fpl*; [political] fraude *f*.

malpractice suit *n Am* JUR *procès pour faute ou négligence professionnelle*.

malt [mɔːlt] ◇ *n* -**1.** [substance] malt *m*. -**2.** = **malt whisky**. -**3.** *Am* [milk shake] milk-shake *m* au malt.
◇ *comp* [extract, sugar, vinegar] de malt.
◇ *vt* malter.

Malta ['mɔːltə] *pr n* Malte; in ~ à Malte.

malted ['mɔːltɪd] *n*: ~ (milk) lait *m* malté.

Maltese [,mɔːl'tiːz] ◇ *n* -**1.** [person] Maltais *m*, -e *f*. -**2.** LING maltais *m*.
◇ *adj* maltais; ~ cat chat *m* maltais; the ~ Cross la croix de Malte ❑ 'The ~ Falcon' *Hammett, Huston* 'le Faucon maltais'.

Malthusian [mæl'θjuːzjən] *adj* malthusien.

Malthusianism [mæl'θjuːzjənɪzm] *n* malthusianisme *m*.

maltings ['mɔːltɪŋs] (*pl inv*) *n* malterie *f*.

malt liquor *n Am boisson alcoolisée tirée du malt*.

maltreat [,mæl'triːt] *vt* maltraiter.

maltreatment [,mæl'triːtmənt] *n (U)* mauvais traitement *m* OR traitements *mpl*, sévices *mpl*.

malt whisky *n* whisky *m* au malt.

malty ['mɔːltɪ] (*compar* **maltier**, *superl* **maltiest**) *adj* [in smell] qui sent le malt; [in taste] qui a un goût de malt; a ~ taste un goût de malt.

mam *inf* [mæm] *n* maman *f*.

mama[1] [mə'mɑː] *n Br dated* maman *f*.

mama[2] ['mɒmə] *n Am* maman *f*.

mama's boy *n inf Am* fils *m* à sa maman.

mamba ['mæmbə] *n* mamba *m*.

mambo ['mæmbəʊ] (*pl* **mambos**) *n* mambo *m*.

mamelon ['mæmələn] *n* mamelon *m*, butte *f*.

mamma ['mæmə] *n esp Am* -**1.** *inf* [mother] maman *f*. -**2.** ▽ [woman] môme *f*, nana *f*.

mammal ['mæml] *n* mammifère *m*.

mammalian [mə'meɪljən] *adj* mammalien.

mammary ['mæmərɪ] *adj* mammaire; ~ gland glande *f* mammaire.

mammography [mæ'mɒgrəfɪ] *n* mammographie *f*.

Mammon ['mæmən] *pr n* Mammon *m*.

mammoth ['mæməθ] ◇ *n* mammouth *m*.
◇ *adj* immense, colossal, gigantesque; a ~ task un travail de Titan.

mammy *inf* ['mæmɪ] (*pl* **mammies**) *n* -**1.** [mother] maman. -**2.** *pej* & *dated* [black nanny] *bonne d'enfants noire*.

man [mæn] (*pl* men [men], *pt* & *pp* manned, *cont* manning) ◇ *n* -**1.** [adult male] homme *m*; a young ~ un jeune homme; an old ~ un vieillard; he seems a nice ~ il a l'air gentil; a blind ~ un aveugle; he's lived here, ~ and boy, for forty years c'est ici qu'il a grandi et vécu pendant quarante ans; I'm just a ~ je ne suis qu'un homme comme les autres; one move and you're a dead ~! un (seul) geste et tu es un homme mort! ❑ he's a ~'s ~ il aime bien être avec ses copains; he's a ~ of the world c'est un homme d'expérience; the ~ in the moon le visage de la lune. -**2.** [type] homme *m*; he's not a betting/drinking ~ ce n'est pas un homme qui parie/boit; he was never a ~ for taking risks il n'a jamais été homme à OR ce n'est pas le genre d'homme à prendre des risques; he's not a ~ to make a mistake il n'est pas homme à se tromper. -**3.** [appropriate person] homme *m*; he's the ~ for the job c'est l'homme qu'il faut pour faire ce travail; I'm your ~ je suis votre homme; he's not the ~ for that kind of work il n'est pas fait pour ce genre de travail. -**4.** [professional]: a medical ~ un médecin; a ~ of learning un savant; a ~ of letters un homme de lettres. -**5.** [with manly qualities] homme *m*; to act like a ~ se comporter en homme; he took the news like a ~ il a pris la nouvelle avec courage; he's not ~ enough to own up il n'aura pas le courage d'avouer; the army will make him a ~! l'armée en fera un homme!; a holiday will make a new ~ of me des vacances me feront le plus grand bien; this will separate OR sort the men from the boys c'est là qu'on verra les vrais hommes. -**6.** [person, individual] homme *m*, individu *m*; what more can a ~ do? qu'est-ce qu'on peut faire de plus?; any ~ would have reacted in the same way n'importe qui aurait réagi de la même façon; all men are born equal tous les hommes naissent égaux; the ~ must be mad! il doit être fou!; I've never met the ~ je n'ai jamais rencontré l'individu en question ❑ to be one's own ~ être indépendant OR son propre maître; to the last ~ [without exception] sans exception; [until defeat] jusqu'au dernier; it's every ~ for himself c'est chacun pour soi; the ~ in the street l'homme de la rue; one ~'s meat is another ~'s poison *prov* le malheur des uns fait le bonheur des autres *prov*. -**7.** [as husband, father] homme *m*; ~ and wife mari et femme; to live as ~ and wife vivre maritalement OR en concubinage; he's a real family ~ c'est un vrai père de famille; the ~ of the house l'homme de la maison; *hum* le pater familias; my old ~ *inf* [husband] mon homme; [father] mon vieux. -**8.** [boyfriend, lover] homme *m*; there's a new ~ in her life il y a un nouvel homme dans sa vie; have you met her young ~? [boyfriend] avez-vous rencontré son petit ami?; [fiancé] avez-vous rencontré son fiancé? -**9.** [inhabitant, native]: I'm a Dublin ~ je suis de Dublin; he's a local ~ c'est un homme du pays. -**10.** [student]: he's a Harvard ~ [at present] il fait ses études à Harvard; [in the past] il a fait ses études à Harvard. -**11.** [servant] valet *m*, domestique *m*. -**12.** [employee - in industry, on farm] ouvrier *m*; [- in business, shop] employé *m*; the men have gone on strike les hommes se sont mis en grève; a TV repair ~ un réparateur télé; we'll send a ~ round to look at it nous vous envoyons quelqu'un pour voir; our ~ in Paris [representative] notre représentant à Paris; [journalist] notre correspondant à Paris; [diplomat] notre envoyé diplomatique à Paris. -**13.** [in armed forces - soldier] soldat *m*, homme *m* (de troupe); [- sailor] matelot *m*, homme *m* (d'équipage); officers and men [in army] officiers et hommes de troupe; [in navy] officiers et matelots. -**14.** [player] joueur *m*, équipier *m*; a 3-~ team une équipe de 3 joueurs; twelfth ~ [in cricket] remplaçant *m*. -**15.** [mankind] homme *m*; primitive/modern ~ l'homme primitif/moderne; one of the most deadly poisons known to ~ un des plus dangereux poisons connus de l'homme ❑ ~ proposes, God disposes *prov* l'homme propose, Dieu dispose *prov*; ~ cannot live by bread alone *prov* l'homme ne vit pas que de pain. -**16.** [as term of address]: come on, ~! allez, viens!; hey, ~, how are you doing?▽ salut, mon vieux, comment tu vas?; what can I do for you, young ~? que puis-je faire pour vous, jeune homme?; my good ~ *dated* mon cher monsieur; good ~! c'est bien!; how are you, old ~? *dated* comment tu vas, mon vieux? -**17.** [in chess] pièce *f*; [in draughts] pion *m*.
◇ *vt* -**1.** MIL [ship] armer, équiper; [pumps] armer; [cannon] servir; the tanker was manned by Greek seamen le pétrolier avait un équipage grec; ~ the lifeboats! mettez les canots à la mer!; manned space-flight vol *m* spatial habité; the sentries manned the battlements il y avait des sentinelles sur les remparts; the fort was manned by 20 soldiers le fort était tenu par une garnison de 20 soldats; can you ~ the fort while I'm at lunch? *hum* pouvez-vous prendre la relève OR me remplacer pendant que je vais déjeuner? -**2.** [staff - machine] faire tourner, s'occuper de; [- switchboard] assurer le service OR la permanence de; who's manning the

telephone? qui assure la permanence téléphonique?; the office is manned by a skeleton staff le bureau tourne à effectif réduit.
◇ *interj inf Am*: ~, was it big! bon sang, qu'est-ce que c'était grand!
◆ **as one man** *adv phr* comme un seul homme.
◆ **to a man** *adv phr* sans exception; they agreed to a ~ ils ont accepté à l'unanimité.

man-about-town (*pl* men-about-town) *n Br* homme *m* du monde, mondain *m*.

manacle ['mænəkl] *vt* [shackle] enchaîner; [handcuff] mettre OR passer les menottes à; his wrists were ~d il portait des menottes.
◆ **manacles** *npl* [shackles] fers *mpl*, chaînes *fpl*; [handcuffs] menottes *fpl*.

manage ['mænɪdʒ] ◇ *vt* -**1.** [business, hotel, shop] gérer, diriger; [property, estate] gérer; she ~s a shoe shop elle est gérante d'une boutique de chaussures; he ~s his father's company il dirige la société de son père || [team] être le manager de, diriger; he ~s Melchester United c'est le manager de OR il manage Melchester United || [finances, resources] s'occuper de; he needs somebody to ~ his affairs il a besoin de quelqu'un pour s'occuper de ses affaires; I'm very bad at managing money je suis incapable de gérer un budget || [crisis, illness] gérer. -**2.** [accomplish] réussir; you'll ~ it ça ira; she ~d a smile elle trouva la force de sourire; to ~ to do sthg réussir OR parvenir OR arriver à faire qqch; he ~d to keep a straight face il est parvenu à garder son sérieux; did you ~ to get anything to eat? as-tu finalement trouvé quelque chose à manger?; he always ~s to arrive at meal times il se débrouille toujours pour arriver OR il trouve toujours le moyen d'arriver à l'heure des repas. -**3.** [handle - person, animal] savoir s'y prendre avec; she's a difficult child to ~ c'est une enfant difficile, c'est une enfant dont on ne fait pas ce qu'on veut; he doesn't know how to ~ people il ne sait pas s'y prendre avec les gens || [manipulate - machine, tool] manier; I can't ~ these new typewriters je ne sais pas bien me servir de ces nouvelles machines à écrire. -**4.** [be available for]: can you ~ 9 o'clock/next Saturday? pouvez-vous venir à 9 h/samedi prochain?; can you ~ lunch tomorrow? pouvez-vous déjeuner avec moi demain? -**5.** [cope with]: I can't ~ all this extra work je ne peux pas faire face à ce surcroît de travail; can you ~ that rucksack? pouvez-vous porter ce sac à dos?; he can't ~ the stairs any more il n'arrive plus à monter l'escalier; we can't ~ any more guests nous ne pouvons pas accueillir plus de gens || [eat or drink]: I think I could ~ another slice j'en reprendrais volontiers une tranche; I couldn't ~ another thing je ne peux plus rien avaler || [financially]: can you ~ £10? pouvez-vous aller jusqu'à 10 livres?
◇ *vi* [cope] se débrouiller, y arriver; we'll have to ~ on our own nous devrons nous débrouiller tout seuls; can you ~? ça ira?; give me a fork, I can't ~ with chopsticks donne-moi une fourchette, je ne m'en sors pas avec des baguettes; we had to ~ without heating nous avons dû nous passer de chauffage || [financially] se débrouiller, s'en sortir; they just about ~ on the dole ils arrivent tout juste à s'en sortir avec les allocations de chômage; how am I going to ~ without a job? comment vais-je faire OR m'en sortir sans travail?

manageable ['mænɪdʒəbl] *adj* [size, amount] raisonnable; [tool, car, boat] maniable; [hair] facile à coiffer; this new shampoo leaves your hair shiny and ~ ce nouveau shampooing rendra vos cheveux brillants et faciles à coiffer; cut the wood into ~ pieces coupez le bois en morceaux faciles à manipuler.

management ['mænɪdʒmənt] *n* -**1.** [control - of firm, finances, property] gestion *f*, direction *f*; the ~ of the country's economy la gestion de l'économie du pays; all their problems are due to bad ~ tous leurs problèmes sont dus à une mauvaise gestion; under Gordon's ~ sales have increased significantly depuis que c'est Gordon qui s'en occupe, les ventes ont considérablement augmenté; who looks after the ~ of the farm? qui s'occupe de l'exploitation de la ferme? || [handling]: she was praised for her ~ of the situation on a applaudi la façon dont elle s'est comportée dans cette situation || [of crisis, illness etc] gestion *f*; man ~ *Br* gestion des ressources humaines. -**2.** [of shop, hotel etc] direction *f*; 'the ~ cannot accept responsibility for any loss or damage' 'la direction décline toute responsabilité en cas de perte ou de dommage'; 'under new ~' 'changement de direction OR de propriétaire'; they're on the ~ ils font partie de la direction || INDUST patronat *m*; negotiations between ~ and unions have broken down les négociations entre le patronat et les syndicats ont échoué.

management buyout *n Br* rachat *m* d'une entreprise par les salariés.

management committee *n* comité *m* de direction.

management consultancy *n* [activity] conseil *m* en gestion (d'entreprise); [firm] cabinet *m* (de) conseil.

management consultant *n* conseiller *m*, -ère *f* en OR de gestion (d'entreprise).

management studies *n (U)* études *fpl* de gestion.

manager ['mænɪdʒəʳ] *n* -**1.** [of firm, bank] directeur *m*, -trice *f*; [of shop] directeur *m*, -trice *f*, gérant *m*; [of restaurant] gérant *m*, -e *f*; [of pop star, football team] manager *m*; FIN directeur *m*, -trice *f*; fund ~ directeur financier; he's been made ~ il est passé cadre. -**2.** [organizer]: she's a good home ~ elle sait tenir une maison.

manageress [,mænɪdʒə'res] *n* [of shop] directrice *f*, gérante *f*; [of restaurant] gérante *f*; [of bank] directrice *f*.

managerial [,mænɪ'dʒɪərɪəl] *adj* gestionnaire; ~ staff cadres *mpl*, encadrement *m*; ~ skills qualités *fpl* de gestionnaire.

managing director ['mænɪdʒɪŋ-] *n* directeur *m* général, directrice *f* générale, P-DG *m*.

managing editor *n* rédacteur *m*, -trice *f* en chef.

Managua [mə'nægwə] *pr n* Managua.

man-at-arms (*pl* men-at-arms) *n* HIST homme *m* d'armes.

manatee [,mænə'tiː] *n* lamantin *m*.

man-child (*pl* man-children) *n lit* enfant *m* mâle.

Manchu [mæn'tʃuː] ◇ *n* Mandchou *m*, -e *f*.
◇ *adj* mandchou.

Manchuria [mæn'tʃʊərɪə] *pr n* Mandchourie *f*; in ~ en Mandchourie.

Manchurian [mæn'tʃʊərɪən] ◇ *n* -**1.** [person] Mandchou *m*, -e *f*. -**2.** LING mandchou *m*.
◇ *adj* mandchou.

manciple ['mænsɪpl] *n* intendant *m*.

Mancunian [mæŋ'kjuːnjən] ◇ *n* [inhabitant] habitant *m*, -e *f* de Manchester; [native] natif *m*, -ive *f* de Manchester.
◇ *adj* de Manchester.

Mandalay [,mændə'leɪ] *pr n* Mandalay.

mandarin ['mændərɪn] *n* -**1.** HIST & *fig* mandarin *m*. -**2.** BOT [tree] mandarinier *m*. -**3.** [fruit]: ~ (orange) mandarine *f*.
◆ **Mandarin** *n* LING: Mandarin (Chinese) mandarin *m*.

mandarin collar *n* col *m* Mao.

mandarin duck *n* (canard *m*) mandarin *m*.

mandate [*n* 'mændeɪt, *vt* ,mæn'deɪt] ◇ *n* -**1.** POL mandat *m*; the government receives its ~ from the electorate c'est l'électorat qui mandate les membres du gouvernement; the government has no ~ to introduce the new tax le gouvernement n'a pas été mandaté pour mettre en place ce nouvel impôt. -**2.** [country] (territoire *m* sous) mandat *m*; under British ~ sous mandat britannique. -**3.** [task] tâche *f*, mission *f*.
◇ *vt* -**1.** [give authority] mandater; to ~ sb to do sthg donner mandat à qqn de faire qqch. -**2.** [country] mettre sous mandat, administrer par mandat.

mandatory ['mændətrɪ] (*pl* mandatories) ◇ *adj* -**1.** [obligatory] obligatoire; participation is ~ la participation est obligatoire. -**2.** [of a mandate] découlant d'un mandat; ~ powers pouvoirs *mpl* donnés par mandat.
◇ *n* mandataire *mf*.

man-day *n Br* jour-homme *m*; 30 ~s 30 journées *fpl* de travail.

mandible ['mændɪbl] *n* mandibule *f*.

mandolin(e) ['mændəlɪn] *n* mandoline *f*.

mandrake ['mændreɪk] *n* mandragore *f*.

mandrel ['mændrəl] *n* TECH mandrin *m*.

mandrill ['mændrɪl] *n*: ~ (ape) mandrill *m*.

mane [meɪn] *n* [of horse, lion] crinière *f*; a ~ of golden hair une crinière blonde.

man-eater *n* [animal] anthropophage *m*; [cannibal] cannibale *m*, anthropophage *m*; *hum* [woman] dévoreuse *f* d'hommes, mante *f* religieuse.

man-eating *adj* [animal] mangeur d'hommes, anthropophage; [people] cannibale, anthropophage; *fig* [woman] mangeuse d'hommes.

manege, **manège** [mæ'neɪʒ] *n* [training] manège *m*; [school] école *f* d'équitation, centre *m* hippique.

maneuver *etc Am* = **manoeuvre**.

man-for-man *adj Br* SPORT: ~ marking marquage *m* individuel.

man Friday *n* [servant] fidèle serviteur *m*.
◆ **Man Friday** *pr n* Vendredi.

manful ['mænfʊl] *adj* [courageous] vaillant, ardent.

manfully ['mænfʊlɪ] *adv* [courageously] vaillamment, courageusement.

manganese ['mæŋgəniːz] *n* manganèse *m*.

manganese steel *n* acier *m* au manganèse.

mange [meɪndʒ] *n* gale *f*.

mangel-wurzel ['mæŋgl,wɜːzl] *n* betterave *f* fourragère.

manger ['meɪndʒəʳ] *n* [trough] mangeoire *f*; RELIG crèche *f*.

mangetout [,mɑ̃ʒ'tuː] *n* mange-tout *m*.

mangey ['meɪndʒɪ] = **mangy**.

mangle ['mæŋgl] ◇ *vt* -**1.** [body] mutiler, déchiqueter; [vehicle] rendre méconnaissable; [quotation, text] estropier, mutiler; the ~d wreckage of the two cars les carcasses déchiquetées des deux voitures. -**2.** [laundry, linen] essorer.
◇ *n* essoreuse *f* (à rouleaux).

mango ['mæŋgəʊ] (*pl* mangos OR mangoes) *n* -**1.** [fruit] mangue *f*. -**2.** [tree] manguier *m*.

mangold(-wurzel) ['mæŋgəld(,wɜːzl)] = **mangel-wurzel**.

mangrove ['mæŋgrəʊv] *n* manglier *m*, palétuvier *m*; ~ swamp mangrove *f*.

mangy ['meɪndʒɪ] (*compar* mangier, *superl* mangiest) *adj* -**1.** [having mange - animal] galeux. -**2.** [shabby - coat, carpet] miteux, pelé.

manhandle ['mæn,hændl] *vt* -**1.** [treat roughly] maltraiter, malmener. -**2.** [move] porter OR transporter (à bras d'homme).

Manhattan [mæn'hætn] ◇ *pr n* GEOG Manhattan.
◇ *n* [cocktail] manhattan *m*.

manhole ['mænhəʊl] *n* regard *m*; [into sewer] bouche *f* d'égout; ~ cover plaque *f* d'égout.

manhood ['mænhʊd] *n* -**1.** [age] âge *m* d'homme; he has reached ~ c'est un homme maintenant. -**2.** [virility] virilité *f*. -**3.** [men collectively] hommes *mpl*, population *f* masculine.

man-hour *n Br* heure-homme *f*; 300 ~s 300 heures *fpl* de travail.

manhunt ['mænhʌnt] *n* chasse *f* à l'homme.

mania ['meɪnjə] *n* -**1.** PSYCH manie *f*; [obsession] obsession *f*. -**2.** [zeal] manie *f pej*, passion *f*; he has a ~ for collecting old photographs il a la manie de collectionner les vieilles photos; he's got football ~ c'est un passionné de football.

maniac ['meɪnɪæk] ◇ *n* -**1.** [dangerous person] fou *m*, folle *f*; [sexual] obsédé *m*, -e *f*; I've been working like a ~ for the past two months ça fait deux mois que je travaille comme un fou; to drive like a ~ conduire comme un fou. -**2.** [fan] fou *m*, folle *f*; he's a football ~ c'est un fan OR un mordu de football. -**3.** PSYCH maniaque *mf*.
◇ *adj* -**1.** [gen] fou. -**2.** PSYCH maniaque.

maniacal [mə'naɪəkl] *adj* -**1.** [crazy] fou; ~ laughter rire *m* hystérique. -**2.** PSYCH maniaque.

maniacally [mə'naɪəklɪ] *adv* de manière hystérique.

manic ['mænɪk] ◇ *adj* -**1.** [crazy] fou. -**2.** PSYCH maniaque.
◇ *n* maniaque *mf*.

manic depression *n* psychose *f* maniacodépressive.

manic-depressive ◇ *adj* maniaco-dépressif.
◇ *n* maniaco-dépressif *m*, -ive *f*.

Manichean [,mænɪ'kiːən] ◇ *adj* manichéen.
◇ *n* manichéen *m*, -enne *f*.

manicure ['mænɪ,kjʊəʳ] ◇ *n* soins *mpl* des mains; to give sb a ~ faire les mains de qqn, manucurer qqn.
◇ *vt* faire les mains à, manucurer; she was manicuring her nails elle était en train de se faire les ongles; a ~d lawn *fig* une pelouse impeccable.
◇ *comp* [case, scissors] de manucure, à ongles.

manicurist ['mænɪ,kjʊərɪst] *n* manucure *mf*.

manifest ['mænɪfest] ◇ *adj fml* manifeste, évident.
◇ *vt* manifester; to ~ open hostility manifester une franche hostilité; how did this mania ~ itself? comment cette obsession s'est-elle manifestée?
◇ *vi* [ghost, spirit] se manifester.
◇ *n* [of ship, plane] manifeste *m*.

manifestation [,mænɪfes'teɪʃn] *n* manifestation *f*.

manifestly ['mænɪfestlɪ] *adv* manifestement, à l'évidence.

manifesto [,mænɪ'festəʊ] (*pl* manifestos OR manifestoes) *n* manifeste *m*.

manifold ['mænɪfəʊld] ◇ *adj fml* [numerous] multiple, nombreux; [varied] varié, divers.
◇ *n* AUT: inlet ~ tubulure *f* d'admission; exhaust ~ collecteur *m* d'échappement.

manikin ['mænɪkɪn] = **mannikin**.

Manila [mə'nɪlə] *pr n* Manille.

manil(l)a [mə'nɪlə] *adj* en chanvre de Manille.

manil(l)a hemp *n* chanvre *m* de Manille.

manil(l)a paper *n* papier *m* kraft.

manioc ['mænɪɒk] *n* manioc *m*.

manipulate [mə'nɪpjʊleɪt] *vt* -**1.** [equipment] manœuvrer, manipuler; [tool] manier; [vehicle] manœuvrer. -**2.** *pej* [person] manipuler, manœuvrer; [facts, figures] manipuler; he skilfully ~d situations (to his own end) il avait l'art de tirer profit de toutes les situations. -**3.** MED: to ~ bones pratiquer des manipulations.

manipulation [mə,nɪpjʊ'leɪʃn] *n* [of equipment] manœuvre *f*, manipulation *f*; *pej* [of people, facts, situation] manipulation *f*; MED manipulation *f*.

manipulative [mə'nɪpjʊlətɪv] *adj pej*: he can be very ~ il n'hésite pas à manipuler les gens; that's so ~ [remark, action] c'est de la manipulation.

manipulator [mə'nɪpjʊleɪtəʳ] *n* manipulateur *m*, -trice *f*.

Manitoba [,mænɪ'təʊbə] *pr n* Manitoba *m*; in ~ dans le Manitoba.

man jack *inf n Br*: every ~ of them chacun d'eux sans exception.

mankind [mæn'kaɪnd] *n* -**1.** [species] humanité *f*, espèce *f* humaine; for the good of ~ pour le bien de l'humanité. -**2.** [men in general] hommes *mpl*.

manky▽ ['mæŋkɪ] (*compar* mankier, *superl* mankiest) *adj Br* [worthless] nul; [dirty] miteux, pourri.

manlike ['mænlaɪk] *adj* -**1.** [virile] viril, masculin. -**2.** [woman] masculin.

manliness ['mænlɪnɪs] *n* virilité *f*.

manly ['mænlɪ] (*compar* manlier, *superl* manliest) *adj* viril, mâle.

man-mad *adj* obsédé par les hommes, nymphomane.

man-made *adj* [fibre] synthétique; [construction, lake] artificiel; the landscape is entirely ~ le paysage a été entièrement modelé OR façonné par l'homme.

manna ['mænə] *n* manne *f*; ~ from heaven *fig* manne céleste.

manned [mænd] *adj* [ship, machine] ayant un équipage; ~ spacecraft vaisseau *m* spatial habité.

mannequin ['mænɪkɪn] *n* mannequin *m*.

manner ['mænəʳ] *n* -**1.** [way] manière *f*, façon *f*; in the same ~ de la même manière OR façon; it's just a ~ of speaking c'est juste une façon de parler; it was the ~ in which he did it that upset me c'est la manière OR la façon dont il s'y est pris qui m'a blessé; she dealt with them in a very gentle ~ elle a été d'une grande douceur avec eux. -**2.** [attitude] attitude *f*, manière *f*; [behaviour] comportement *m*, manière *f* de se conduire; to have a pleasant ~ avoir des manières agréables; I don't like his ~ je n'aime pas ses façons; he has a good telephone ~ il fait bonne impression au téléphone; there was something in his ~ that made me suspicious quelque chose dans son comportement a éveillé mes soupçons ❑ in a ~ of speaking pour ainsi dire, dans un certain sens; by all ~ of means [of course] bien entendu; not by any ~ of means en aucune manière, aucunement; to the ~ born vraiment fait pour ça. -**3.** [style] manière *f*; in the ~ of Rembrandt dans le style OR à la manière de Rembrandt; painted in the Italian ~ peint à la manière italienne. -**4.** [kind] sorte *f*, genre *m*; all ~ of rare books toutes sortes de livres rares; what ~ of man is he? *arch* quel genre d'homme est-ce?
◆ **manners** *npl* -**1.** [social etiquette] manières *fpl*; good/bad ~s bonnes/mauvaises manières; to have good table ~s savoir se tenir à table; it's bad ~s to talk with your mouth full c'est mal élevé OR ce n'est pas poli de parler la bouche pleine; she has no ~s elle n'a aucune éducation, elle est mal élevée; where are your ~s? [say thank you] qu'est-ce qu'on dit quand on est bien élevé?; [behave properly] est-ce que c'est une façon de se tenir? -**2.** *lit* [social customs] mœurs *fpl*, usages *mpl*.

mannered ['mænəd] *adj* maniéré, affecté, précieux.

-mannered *in cpds*: mild~ aux manières douces; well/bad~ bien/mal élevé.

mannerism ['mænərɪzm] *n* tic *m*, manie *f*.
◆ **Mannerism** *n* ART maniérisme *m*.

Mannerist ['mænərɪst] ART ◇ *adj* maniériste.
◇ *n* maniériste *mf*.

mannerly ['mænəlɪ] *adj* bien élevé, courtois, poli.

mannikin ['mænɪkɪn] *n* -**1.** [dwarf] nain *m*. -**2.** = **mannequin**.

mannish ['mænɪʃ] *adj* [woman] masculin.

mannishly ['mænɪʃlɪ] *adv* comme un homme.

manoeuvrability *Br*, **maneuverability** *Am* [mə,nuːvrə'bɪlətɪ] manœuvrabilité *f*, maniabilité *f*.

manoeuvrable *Br*, **maneuvrable** *Am* [mə'nuːvrəbl] *adj* manœuvrable, maniable.

manoeuvre *Br*, **maneuver** *Am* [mə'nuːvəʳ]
◇ *n* manœuvre *f*; to be on ~s MIL être en manœuvres; it was only a ~ to get him to resign ce n'était qu'une manœuvre pour l'amener à démissionner; room for ~ marge *f* de manœuvre.
◇ *vt* -**1.** [physically] manœuvrer; he ~d the ladder through the window il a manœuvré pour faire passer l'échelle par la fenêtre; they ~d the animal into the pen ils ont fait entrer l'animal dans l'enclos. -**2.** [by influence, strategy] manœuvrer; she ~d her way to the top elle a réussi à se hisser jusqu'au sommet; they ~d him into resigning ils l'ont poussé à démissionner.
◇ *vi* manœuvrer; to ~ for position manœuvrer pour se placer avantageusement.

man-of-war [,mænə'wɔːʳ] (*pl* men-of-war [,men-]) *n* bâtiment *f* de guerre.

manometer [mə'nɒmɪtəʳ] *n* manomètre *m*.

manor ['mænəʳ] *n* -**1.** [house]: ~ (house) manoir *m*, château *m*. -**2.** HIST seigneurie *f*, domaine *m* seigneurial; lord of the ~ châtelain *m*, lady of the ~ châtelaine *f*. -**3.** ▽ *Br* [of police local] secteur *m*.

manorial [mə'nɔːrɪəl] *adj* seigneurial.

man-o'-war [,mænə'wɔːʳ] = **man-of-war**.

manpower ['mæn,paʊəʳ] *n* (*U*) [personnel] main-d'œuvre *f*; MIL effectifs *mpl*; we don't have the necessary ~ nous ne disposons pas des effectifs nécessaires.

Manpower Services Commission *n agence britannique pour l'emploi, aujourd'hui remplacée par la Training Agency*, ≃ ANPE *f*.

mansard ['mænsɑːd] *n* [roof] toit *m* mansardé; [attic] mansarde *f*.

manse [mæns] *n* presbytère *m*.

manservant ['mænsɜːvənt] *n* [gen] domestique *m*; [valet] valet *m* (de chambre).

mansion ['mænʃn] *n* [in town] hôtel *m* particulier; [in country] château *m*, manoir *m*; their house is more like a ~ leur maison est un vrai château; ~ block résidence *f*.

Mansion House *pr n*: the ~ *la résidence officielle du maire de Londres*.

man-size(d) *adj* [job, task] ardu, difficile; [meal] copieux; ~ tissues grands mouchoirs *mpl* (en papier).

manslaughter ['mæn,slɔːtəʳ] *n* homicide *m* involontaire.

mantel ['mæntl] *n* [shelf] (tablette *f* de) cheminée *f*; [frame] manteau *m*.

mantelpiece ['mæntlpiːs] *n* -**1.** [surround] (manteau *m* de) cheminée *f*. -**2.** [shelf] (tablette *f* de) cheminée *f*.

mantelshelf ['mæntlʃelf] (*pl* mantelshelves [-ʃelvz]) = **mantelpiece 2**.

mantic ['mæntɪk] *adj* divinatoire, prophétique.

mantilla [mæn'tɪlə] *n* mantille *f*.

mantis ['mæntɪs] *n* mante *f*.

mantissa [mæn'tɪsə] *n* mantisse *f*.

mantle ['mæntl] *n* -**1.** [cloak] cape *f*; *fig* manteau *m*; a ~ of fog un manteau de brume; to take on OR to assume the ~ of *fig* assumer le rôle de. -**2.** ZOOL & GEOL manteau *m*. -**3.** [of gas-lamp] manchon *m*; turn up the ~ *Br* montez le gaz. -**4.** = **mantel**.

man-to-man ◇ *adj* -**1.** [discussion] entre hommes, d'homme à homme. -**2.** SPORT = **man-for-man**.
◇ *adv* entre hommes, d'homme à homme.

mantra ['mæntrə] *n* mantra *m inv*.

mantrap ['mæntræp] *n* piège *m* à hommes.

Mantua ['mæntʊə] *pr n* Mantoue.

manual ['mænjʊəl] ◇ *adj* manuel; ~ worker travailleur *m* manuel; ~ labour travail *m* manuel; ~ dexterity dextérité *f*, habileté *f* manuelle.
◇ *n* -**1.** [handbook] manuel *m*. -**2.** [of organ] clavier *m*.

manually ['mænjʊəlɪ] *adv* manuellement, à la main.

manufacture [,mænjʊ'fæktʃəʳ] ◇ *n* -**1.** [making] fabrication *f*; [of clothes] confection *f*. -**2.** TECH [product] produit *m* manufacturé.
◇ *vt* -**1.** [produce] fabriquer, produire; [clothes] confectionner; ~d goods produits *mpl* manufacturés. -**2.** [invent - news, story] inventer; [- evidence] fabriquer.

manufacturer [,mænjʊ'fæktʃərəʳ] *n* fabricant *m*, -e *f*.

manufacturing [ˌmænjʊˈfæktʃərɪŋ] ◇ *adj* [city, area] industriel; ~ industry les industries *fpl* de transformation.
◇ *n* fabrication *f*.

manumission [ˌmænjʊˈmɪʃn] *n* manumission *f*.

manumit [ˌmænjʊˈmɪt] (*pt* & *pp* manumitted, *cont* manumitting) *vt* affranchir, émanciper.

manure [məˈnjʊəʳ] ◇ *n* [farmyard] fumier *m*; [fertilizer] engrais *m*; liquid ~ purin *m*, lisier *m*; ~ heap tas *m* de fumier.
◇ *vt* [with dung] fumer; [with fertilizer] répandre de l'engrais sur.

manuscript [ˈmænjʊskrɪpt] ◇ *n* manuscrit *m*; I read the book in ~ j'ai lu le manuscrit du livre || [for music]: ~ (paper) papier *m* à musique.
◇ *adj* manuscrit, (écrit) à la main.

Manx [mæŋks] ◇ *npl*: the ~ les Manxois *mpl*.
◇ *n* LING manx *m*.
◇ *adj* manxois.

Manx cat *n* chat *m* (sans queue) de l'île de Man.

Manxman [ˈmæŋksmən] (*pl* Manxmen [-mən]) *n* Manxois *m*.

Manxwoman [ˈmæŋksˌwʊmən] (*pl* Manxwomen [-ˌwɪmɪn]) *n* Manxoise *f*.

many [ˈmenɪ] (*compar* more [mɔːʳ], *superl* most [məʊst]) ◇ *det* & *pron* beaucoup de, de nombreux; ~ people beaucoup de OR bien des gens; ~ years bien des années, de nombreuses années; ~ times souvent, bien des fois; she had cards from all her ~ admirers elle a reçu des cartes de ses nombreux admirateurs; ~ of the audience were children il y avait de nombreux enfants OR beaucoup d'enfants dans l'assistance; ~ of them beaucoup d'entre eux; ~ a time, ~'s the time bien des fois; ~ a child would be glad of it bien des enfants s'en contenteraient; ~'s the holiday I spent there j'y ai passé bien des vacances; take as ~ books as you like prenez autant de livres OR tous les livres que vous voudrez; they admitted as ~ (people) as they could ils ont laissé entrer autant de gens que possible; as ~ again encore autant; twice/three times as ~ deux/trois fois plus; we visited six cities in as ~ days nous avons visité six villes en autant de jours; as ~ as 8,000 students enrolled jusqu'à OR près de 8 000 étudiants se sont inscrits; how ~? combien?; how ~ students came? combien d'étudiants sont venus?; how ~ were there? combien étaient-ils?; so ~ people tant de gens; we can only fit in so ~ nous n'avons de place que pour un certain nombre de personnes; too ~ people trop de gens; don't give me too ~ ne m'en donne pas trop; a good ~ un bon nombre; we met a good ~ times on s'est vus bien des fois; a great ~ un grand nombre; I've received a great ~ applications j'ai reçu de très nombreuses OR un grand nombre de candidatures.
◇ *npl* [masses]: the ~ la majorité; the ~ who loved her tous ceux qui l'aimaient.

many-coloured *adj Br* multicolore.

many-sided *adj* -**1.** [figure, shape] qui a de nombreux côtés. -**2.** [problem] aux aspects multiples, multiforme. -**3.** [personality] qui a de nombreuses facettes; [individual] aux talents multiples.

Maoism [ˈmaʊɪzm] *n* maoïsme *m*.

Maoist [ˈmaʊɪst] ◇ *adj* maoïste.
◇ *n* maoïste *mf*.

Maori [ˈmaʊrɪ] (*pl inv* OR Maoris) ◇ *n* -**1.** [person] Maori *m*, -e *f*. -**2.** LING maori *m*.
◇ *adj* maori.

Mao Tse-Tung, Mao Zedong [ˈmaʊtseˈtʊŋ] *pr n* Mao Tsé-toung, Mao Zedong.

map [mæp] (*pt* & *pp* mapped, *cont* mapping) ◇ *n* -**1.** [of country] carte *f*; [of town, network] plan *m*; to read a ~ lire une carte; a ~ of India une carte de l'Inde; it doesn't look far on the ~ ça n'a pas l'air loin sur la carte; the city was wiped off the ~ *fig* la ville a été rayée de la carte ❑ to put sthg on the ~ faire connaître qqch; the election results put them firmly on the political ~ le résultat des élections leur assure une place sur l'échiquier politique; the legend of the monster put Loch Ness on the ~ la légende du monstre a rendu le loch Ness célèbre. -**2.** MATH fonction *f*, application *f*.
◇ *vt* -**1.** [country, region] faire OR dresser la carte de; [town] faire OR dresser le plan de. -**2.** MATH: to ~ sthg onto sthg else représenter qqch sur qqch.
◆ **map out** *vt sep* [itinerary] tracer; [essay] faire le plan de; [plan] établir les grandes lignes de; [career, future] organiser, prévoir; they have Laura's future all mapped out for her ils ont déjà planifié l'avenir de Laura; to ~ out one's time organiser son emploi du temps.

MAP (*abbr of* Modified American Plan) *n dans un hôtel américain, séjour en demi-pension*.

maple [ˈmeɪpl] *n* érable *m*.

maple leaf *n* feuille *f* d'érable.

maple sugar *n* sucre *m* d'érable.

maple syrup *n* sirop *m* d'érable.

mapmaker [ˈmæpˌmeɪkəʳ] *n* cartographe *mf*.

mapmaking [ˈmæpˌmeɪkɪŋ] *n* cartographie *f*.

mapping [ˈmæpɪŋ] *n* MATH application *f*, fonction *f*.

mapping pen *n* plume *f* à dessin.

map reading *n* lecture *f* de carte.

Maputo [məˈpuːtəʊ] *pr n* Maputo.

mar [mɑːʳ] (*pt* & *pp* marred, *cont* marring) *vt* gâter, gâcher; today will make or ~ their future c'est aujourd'hui que se décide OR se joue leur avenir.

Mar. *written abbr of* March.

maraca [məˈrækə] *n* maraca *f*.

maraschino [ˌmærəˈskiːnəʊ] (*pl* maraschinos) *n* marasquin *m*; ~ cherry cerise *f* au marasquin.

marathon [ˈmærəθn] ◇ *n* SPORT marathon *m*; dance ~ *fig* marathon de danse.
◇ *comp*: ~ race marathon *m*; ~ runner coureur *m*, -euse *f* de marathon, marathonien *m*, -enne *f*.
◇ *adj* marathon *(inv)*; a ~ exam un examen-marathon.

marauder [məˈrɔːdəʳ] *n* [person] maraudeur *m*, -euse *f*; [animal, bird] maraudeur *m*, prédateur *m*.

marauding [məˈrɔːdɪŋ] *adj* maraudeur, en maraude; ~ soldiers des soldats en maraude.

marble [ˈmɑːbl] ◇ *n* -**1.** [stone, sculpture] marbre *m*. -**2.** [for game] bille *f*; to play ~s jouer aux billes ❑ to lose one's ~s *inf* perdre la boule.
◇ *comp* [fireplace, staircase, statue] de OR en marbre; [industry] marbrier; ~ quarry marbrière *f*, carrière *f* de marbre.
◇ *vt* marbrer.

marble cake *n* gâteau *m* marbré.

marbled [ˈmɑːbld] *adj* marbré.

marbling [ˈmɑːblɪŋ] *n* [gen] marbrure *f*; [in meat] marbré *m*.

marcasite [ˈmɑːkəˌsaɪt] *n* marcassite *f*.

march [mɑːtʃ] ◇ *n* -**1.** MIL marche *f*; troops on the ~ des troupes en marche; the ~ on Versailles la marche sur Versailles; a ~ of 20 km une marche de 20 km; their camp was a day's ~ away leur camp était à une journée de marche; the ~ of time/events *fig* la marche du temps/des événements ❑ Sherman's ~ to the sea *Am* HIST la marche vers l'océan du général Sherman. -**2.** [demonstration] manifestation *f*, marche *f*; to go on a ~ manifester, descendre dans la rue; peace ~ marche pour la paix. -**3.** [music] marche *f*; slow/quick ~ marche lente/rapide. -**4.** *(usu pl)* [frontier] frontière *f*; the Welsh Marches les marches *fpl* galloises.
◇ *vi* -**1.** MIL marcher (au pas); the soldiers ~ed for three days and nights les soldats ont marché pendant trois jours et trois nuits; to ~ against the enemy marcher contre l'ennemi; to ~ off to war/into battle partir à la guerre/au combat; to ~ on a city marcher sur une ville || [at a ceremony, on parade] défiler; the regiment ~ed past the President le régiment défila devant le Président || *fig* [time, seasons] avancer, s'écouler; time ~es on le temps s'écoule inexorablement. -**2.** [walk briskly] avancer d'un pas ferme OR résolu; to ~ down the street/into a room descendre la rue/entrer dans une pièce d'un pas résolu; they ~ed off in a huff ils partirent furieux; she ~ed up to him and slapped him across the face elle se dirigea droit sur lui et le gifla; he ~ed impatiently up and down the station platform il arpentait le quai impatiemment; he ~ed upstairs il monta l'escalier d'un air décidé. -**3.** [in demonstration] manifester; the students ~ed alongside the workers les étudiants manifestèrent aux côtés des ouvriers.
◇ *vt* -**1.** MIL faire marcher au pas; the troops were ~ed out of the citadel on fit sortir les troupes de la citadelle. -**2.** [lead forcibly]: the prisoner was ~ed away/back to his cell on conduisit/ramena le prisonnier dans sa cellule; the shoplifter was ~ed into the manager's office on conduisit le voleur dans le bureau du directeur; the children were ~ed off to bed les enfants ont été expédiés au lit (au pas de gymnastique).

SHERMAN'S MARCH TO THE SEA:
Opération menée en 1864 par le général nordiste Sherman en Géorgie pendant la guerre de Sécession. A la tête de 60 000 hommes et après avoir incendié la ville d'Atlanta, Sherman rejoignit la côte en détruisant sur son passage toute l'infrastructure sudiste: voies de chemin de fer, cultures, bétail, bâtiments etc.

March [mɑːtʃ] *n* (mois *m* de) mars *m*; ~ hare lièvre *m* en rut.

marcher [ˈmɑːtʃəʳ] *n* [in demonstration] manifestant *m*, -e *f*.

marching [ˈmɑːtʃɪŋ] ◇ *n* [gen & MIL] marche *f*.
◇ *adj* cadencé; the sound of ~ feet le bruit de pas cadencés.

marching orders *npl* -**1.** MIL ordre *m* de route. -**2.** *inf Br fig*: to give sb his/her ~ flanquer qqn à la porte; she got her ~ elle a été virée.

marchioness [ˈmɑːʃənes] *n* [aristocrat] marquise *f*.

march-past *n* défilé *m* (militaire).

Marcus Aurelius [ˈmɑːkəsɔːˈriːljəs] *pr n* Marc Aurèle.

mare [meəʳ] *n* jument *f*.

mare's nest *n* [illusion] illusion *f*; [disappointment] déception *f*.

margarine [ˌmɑːdʒəˈriːn, ˌmɑːgəˈriːn] *n* margarine *f*.

margarita [ˌmɑːgəˈriːtə] *n* margarita *f*.

marge *inf* [mɑːdʒ] *Br* = **margarine**.

margin [ˈmɑːdʒɪn] *n* -**1.** [on page] marge *f*; written in the ~ écrit dans la OR en marge. -**2.** [leeway] marge *f*; a ~ of error/of safety une marge d'erreur/de sécurité; the ~ of error is negligible la marge d'erreur est négligeable || [distance, gap] marge *f*; the opposition candidate won by a 10% ~ le candidat de l'opposition a gagné avec une marge de 10 %; they won by a narrow/wide ~ ils ont gagné de justesse/avec une marge confortable. -**3.** COMM: profit ~ marge *f* (bénéficiaire). -**4.** [periphery - of field, lake] bord *m*; [- of wood] lisière *f*, orée *f*; on the ~ OR ~s of society en marge de la société.

marginal [ˈmɑːdʒɪnl] ◇ *adj* -**1.** [slight - improvement] léger; [- effect] minime, insignifiant; [- importance] mineur, secondaire; a ~ case un cas limite; a ~ problem un problème d'ordre secondaire ❑ ~ land AGR terre *f* de faible rendement. -**2.** COMM [business, profit] marginal. -**3.** [in margin - notes] marginal, en marge.
◇ *n* POL = **marginal seat**.

marginalia [ˌmɑːdʒɪˈneɪljə] *npl* annotations *fpl* OR notes *fpl* en marge.

marginalize, -ise [ˈmɑːdʒɪnəlaɪz] *vt* marginaliser.

marginally [ˈmɑːdʒɪnəlɪ] *adv* à peine, légèrement; his health has improved only ~ son état ne s'est guère amélioré.

marginal seat *n* POL *en Grande-Bretagne, circonscription dont le député ne dispose que d'une majorité très faible*.
margin release *n* déclenche-marge *m inv*.
marguerite [,mɑːgəˈriːt] *n* marguerite *f* BOT.
Maria [məˈraɪə] → **Black Maria**.
Maria de Medici [məˈrɪədeˈmedɪtʃiː] *pr n* Marie de Médicis.
Mariana Islands [,mærɪˈɑːnə-] *pl pr n*: the ~ les îles *fpl* Mariannes; in the ~ aux îles Mariannes.
Marie-Antoinette [ˈmærɪ,æntwəˈnet] *pr n* Marie-Antoinette.
marigold [ˈmærɪgəʊld] *n*: African ~ rose *f* d'Inde; (French) ~ œillet *m* d'Inde; (pot) ~ souci *m* (des jardins).
marihuana, marijuana [,mærɪˈwɑːnə] *n* marihuana *f*, marijuana *f*.
marina [məˈriːnə] *n* marina *f*.
marinade [,mærɪˈneɪd] ◇ *n* CULIN marinade *f*.
◇ *vt* mariner.
marinate [ˈmærɪneɪt] *vt & vi* CULIN mariner.
marine [məˈriːn] ◇ *adj* -**1.** [underwater] marin; ~ **biology** biologie *f* marine; ~ **life** vie *f* marine. -**2.** [naval] maritime; ~ **engineering** mécanique *f* navale; ~ **insurance** assurance *f* maritime.
◇ *n* -**1.** [ships collectively] marine *f*. -**2.** [soldier] fusilier *m* marin; [British or American] marine *m*; go tell it to the ~s! *inf* mon œil!, à d'autres!
Marine Corps *pr n Am* MIL Marines *mpl*.
mariner [ˈmærɪnəʳ] *n fml* OR *lit* marin *m*.
Mariolatry [,meərɪˈɒlətrɪ] *n* culte *m* excessif de la Vierge.
Mariology [,meərɪˈɒlədʒɪ] *n* mariologie *f*.
marionette [,mærɪəˈnet] *n* marionnette *f*.
marital [ˈmærɪtl] *adj* [vows, relations, duty] conjugal; [problem] conjugal, matrimonial; ~ **rights** droits *mpl* conjugaux; ~ **status** situation *f* de famille.
maritime [ˈmærɪtaɪm] *adj* maritime; ~ **climate/law** climat *m*/droit *m* maritime.
Maritime Provinces, Maritimes *pl pr n*: the ~ les Provinces *fpl* Maritimes.
marjoram [ˈmɑːdʒərəm] *n* marjolaine *f*, origan *m*.
mark [mɑːk] ◇ *n* -**1.** [symbol, sign] marque *f*, signe *m*; **to make a ~ on sthg** faire une marque sur qqch, marquer qqch; **punctuation** ~ signe *m* de ponctuation ‖ [on scale, in number, level] marque *f*, niveau *m*; **sales topped the 5 million** ~ les ventes ont dépassé la barre des 5 millions; **to reach the half-way** ~ arriver à mi-course; **don't go beyond the 50-metre** ~ ne dépassez pas les 50 mètres; **gas ~ 6** *Br* CULIN thermostat 6 ‖ [model]: ~ **3** COMM modèle *m* OR série *f* 3 ‖ [feature] marque *f*; **the town bears the ~ of Greek classicism** la ville porte la marque du classicisme grec ‖ [token] marque *f*, signe *m*; **a ~ of affection** une marque d'affection; **as a ~ of my esteem/friendship** en témoignage de mon estime/de mon amitié; **as a ~ of respect** en signe de respect. -**2.** [trace] trace *f*, marque *f*; **to leave ~s in the snow** [car] laisser des traces dans la neige; **there are finger ~s on the mirror** il y a des traces OR des marques de doigts sur la glace; **there are muddy ~s on the carpet** il y a des traces de boue sur la moquette; **the years she spent in prison have left their ~** ses années en prison l'ont marquée ‖ [stain, blemish] tache *f*, marque *f*; **the cup has left a ~ on the table** la tasse a laissé une marque sur la table ‖ [wound] trace *f* de coups; **there wasn't a ~ on the body** le corps ne portait aucune trace de coups. -**3.** SCH [grade] note *f*; **the ~ is out of 100** la note est sur 100; **to get full ~s** obtenir la meilleure note (possible) ‖ [point] point *m*; **you need ten more ~s** il vous faut encore dix points ‖ *fig*: **it will be a black ~ against his name** ça va jouer contre lui, ça ne va pas jouer en sa faveur; **she deserves full ~s for imagination** il faut saluer son imagination; **no ~s for guessing the answer!** il ne faut pas être sorcier pour deviner la réponse! -**4.** [impact] empreinte *f*, impression *f*; **to make one's ~** s'imposer, se faire un nom; **she made her ~ as a singer** elle s'est imposée OR elle s'est fait un nom dans la chanson; **they left their ~ on 20th-century history** ils ont profondément marqué l'histoire du XXᵉ siècle ‖ [distinction] marque *f*; **to be of little ~** *Br* avoir peu d'importance. -**5.** *Br* [standard]: **to be up to the ~** [be capable] être à la hauteur; [meet expectations] être satisfaisant; **I'm afraid the work just isn't up to the ~** malheureusement le travail laisse à désirer ‖ [in health]: **I still don't feel quite up to the ~** je ne suis pas encore en pleine forme. -**6.** *Br* [target] but *m*, cible *f*; **to hit/to miss the ~** atteindre/manquer la cible. -**7.** SPORT: **on your ~s, (get) set, go!** à vos marques, prêts, partez! ‖ *Br fig*: **she is quick/slow off the ~** [clever] elle est/n'est pas très maligne, elle a/n'a pas l'esprit très vif; [in reactions] elle est/n'est pas très rapide; **you have to be quick off the ~** il faut réagir tout de suite OR immédiatement; **he's sometimes a bit too quick off the ~ in his criticism** il lui arrive d'avoir la critique un peu trop facile. -**8.** RUGBY arrêt *m* de volée; **to call for a ~** crier «marque» (en faisant un arrêt de volée). -**9.** [currency] mark *m*.
◇ *vt* -**1.** [label] marquer; **the towels were ~ed with his name** les serviettes étaient à son nom, son nom était marqué sur les serviettes; ~ **the text with your initials** inscrivez vos initiales sur ce texte; **shall I ~ her absent?** est-ce que je la marque absente?; **the table was ~ed "sold"** la table portait l'étiquette «vendue». -**2.** [stain] tacher, marquer; **the red wine ~ed the carpet** le vin rouge a taché la moquette ‖ [face, hands] marquer; **his face was ~ed by suffering** son visage était marqué par la souffrance; **the scandal ~ed him for life** [mentally] le scandale l'a marqué pour la vie ‖ ZOOL tacheter; **brown wings ~ed with blue** des ailes brunes tachetées de bleu. -**3.** [indicate] indiquer, marquer; **X ~s the spot** l'endroit est marqué d'un X; **today ~s a turning point in our lives** aujourd'hui marque un tournant dans notre vie. -**4.** [celebrate - anniversary, event] célébrer, marquer; **let's have some champagne to ~ the occasion** ouvrons une bouteille de champagne pour fêter l'événement. -**5.** [distinguish] marquer; **he has all the qualities that ~ a good golfer** il possède toutes les qualités d'un bon golfeur; **the period was ~ed by religious persecution** cette époque fut marquée par des persécutions religieuses. -**6.** SCH [essay, homework] corriger; [student] noter; **the exam was ~ed out of 100** l'examen a été noté sur 100; **to ~ sthg wrong/right** marquer qqch comme étant faux/juste. -**7.** [pay attention to]: **(you) ~ my words!** souvenez-vous de ce que je vous dis!; ~ **how he does it** *Br* observez bien la façon dont il s'y prend; ~ **you, I didn't believe him** *Br* remarquez, je ne l'ai pas cru. -**8.** SPORT [opponent] marquer. -**9.** *phr*: **to ~ time** MIL marquer le pas; *fig* attendre son heure OR le moment propice; **the government are just ~ing time until the elections** le gouvernement fait traîner les choses en attendant les élections.
◇ *vi* [garment] être salissant, se tacher facilement; **this material ~s easily** ce tissu est salissant.
◆ **mark down** *vt sep* -**1.** [write] noter, prendre note de, inscrire; ~ **the address down in your diary** notez l'adresse dans votre agenda. -**2.** [reduce - price] baisser; [- article] baisser le prix de; ~**ed down shirts** chemises démarquées OR soldées; **prices were ~ed down in early trading** ST. EX les valeurs étaient en baisse OR ont reculé en début de séance ‖ SCH [essay, student] baisser la note de; **he was ~ed down for bad grammar** il a perdu des points à cause de la grammaire. -**3.** [single out] désigner; **my brother was ~ed down for the managership** mon frère a été désigné pour le poste de directeur; **I ~ed him down as a troublemaker** j'avais remarqué qu'il n'était bon qu'à créer des ennuis.
◆ **mark off** *vt sep* -**1.** [divide, isolate - area, period of time] délimiter; **one corner of the field had been ~ed off by a fence** un coin du champ avait été isolé par une barrière. -**2.** [measure - distance] mesurer. -**3.** *Br* [distinguish] distinguer; **his intelligence ~ed him off from his school friends** il se distinguait de ses camarades d'école par son intelligence. -**4.** [on list] cocher.
◆ **mark out** *vt sep* -**1.** [with chalk, paint - court, pitch] tracer les lignes de; [with stakes] jalonner; [with lights, flags] baliser; **his path in life is clearly ~ed out** *fig* son avenir est tout tracé. -**2.** [designate] désigner; **Brian was ~ed out for promotion** Brian était désigné pour obtenir une promotion; **they were ~ed out for special treatment** ils ont bénéficié d'un régime particulier. -**3.** *Br* [distinguish] distinguer; **her ambition ~s her out from her colleagues** son ambition la distingue de ses collègues.
◆ **mark up** *vt sep* -**1.** [on notice] marquer; **the menu is ~ed up on the blackboard** le menu est sur le tableau. -**2.** [increase - price] augmenter, majorer; [- goods] augmenter le prix de, majorer; **prices at last began to be ~ed up** ST. EX les cours sont enfin à la hausse. -**3.** [annotate] annoter; **I've ~ed the manuscript up** j'ai annoté le manuscrit.
Mark [mɑːk] *pr n* Marc; ~ **Antony** Marc Antoine; **Saint** ~ saint Marc; **the Gospel According to (Saint)** ~ l'Évangile selon saint Marc.
markdown [ˈmɑːkdaʊn] *n* démarque *f*.
marked [mɑːkt] *adj* -**1.** [noticeable] accentué, marqué, sensible; **he has a very ~ German accent** il a un accent allemand très prononcé; **in ~ contrast** en contraste total. -**2.** [bearing a mark] marqué; **he's a ~ man** c'est l'homme à abattre. -**3.** LING marqué.
markedly [ˈmɑːkɪdlɪ] *adv* d'une façon marquée, sensiblement, ostensiblement.
marker [ˈmɑːkəʳ] ◇ *n* -**1.** [pen] feutre *m*, marqueur *m*. -**2.** [indicator, landmark] jalon *m*, balise *f*. -**3.** [scorekeeper] marqueur *m*, -euse *f*. -**4.** SCH correcteur *m*, -trice *f*; **to be a hard ~** noter sévèrement. -**5.** [page marker] marque-page *m*, signet *m*. -**6.** SPORT marqueur *m*; **to lose one's ~** se démarquer (d'un adversaire). -**7.** LING marque *f*.
◇ *comp* [pen, buoy]: ~ **pen** marqueur *m*; ~ **buoy** bouée *f* de balisage.
market [ˈmɑːkɪt] ◇ *n* -**1.** [gen] marché *m*; **to go to (the) ~** aller au marché, aller faire son marché; ~ **square** place *f* du marché. -**2.** ECON marché *m*; **home and foreign ~** marché intérieur et extérieur; **the job ~** le marché de l'emploi; **the property ~** le marché immobilier; **a buyer's/seller's ~** un marché acheteur/vendeur; **to put sthg on the ~** mettre qqch en vente OR sur le marché; **they've just put their house on the ~** ils viennent de mettre leur maison en vente; **new products are always coming onto the ~** de nouveaux produits apparaissent constamment sur le marché; **a new electric car has been brought onto the ~** une nouvelle voiture électrique a été mise sur le marché; **to be on the open ~** être sur le marché libre; **she's in the ~ for Persian rugs** elle cherche à acheter des tapis persans, elle est acheteuse de tapis persans ‖ [demand] demande *f*, marché *m*; **there's always a (ready) ~ for computer software** il y a toujours une forte demande pour les logiciels ‖ [outlet] débouché *m*, marché *m*; **he's unable to find a ~ for his products** il ne trouve pas de débouchés pour ses produits ‖ [clientele] marché *m*, clientèle *f*; **we hope to conquer the Australian ~** nous espérons conquérir le marché australien; **this ad should appeal to the teenage ~** cette pub devrait séduire les jeunes. -**3.** ST. EX marché *m*; [index] indice *m*; [prices] cours *mpl*; **the ~ has risen 10 points** l'indice est en hausse de 10 points; **to play the ~** jouer en bourse, spéculer.
◇ *vt* [sell] vendre, commercialiser; [launch] lancer OR mettre sur le marché.
◇ *vi Am* [go shopping] faire le marché; **to go ~ing** aller faire ses courses.

marketability [ˌmɑːkɪtəˈbɪlətɪ] *n* possibilité *f* de commercialisation.

marketable [ˈmɑːkɪtəbl] *adj* vendable, commercialisable; ST. EX négociable.

market economy *n* économie *f* de marché OR libérale.

marketeer [ˌmɑːkəˈtɪəʳ] *n* -**1.** black ~ trafiquant *m*, -e *f* (au marché noir). -**2.** *Br* POL: pro-~ partisan *m*, -e *f* du Marché commun; anti-~ adversaire *mf* du Marché commun.

market forces *npl* les forces *fpl* du marché.

market garden *n Br* jardin *m* maraîcher.

market gardener *n Br* maraîcher *m*, -ère *f*.

market gardening *n Br* culture *f* maraîchère.

marketing [ˈmɑːkɪtɪŋ] *n* [selling] commercialisation *f*, distribution *f*; [promotion, research] marketing *m*; ~ **strategy** stratégie *f* de commercialisation.

marketing consultant *n* conseil *m* en marketing.

market leader *n* [product] premier produit *m* sur le marché; [firm] leader *m* du marché.

market maker *n* FIN teneur *m* de marché.

marketplace [ˈmɑːkɪtpleɪs] *n* -**1.** [in town] place *f* du marché. -**2.** COMM marché *m*; the ethics of the ~ l'éthique *f* du marché; the international/European ~ le marché international/européen.

market price *n* COMM prix *m* marchand; ST. EX cours *m* du marché.

market research *n* étude *f* OR études *fpl* de marché; ~ has shown that the idea is viable des études de marché ont montré que l'idée a des chances de réussir; he works in ~ il travaille dans le marketing.

market researcher *n personne qui fait des études de marché*.

market share *n* part *f* de marché.

market town *n* bourg *m*.

market value *n* COMM valeur *f* marchande; ST. EX valeur *f* boursière OR en bourse.

marking [ˈmɑːkɪŋ] *n* -**1.** ZOOL tache *f*, marque *f*. -**2.** SCH correction *f*. -**3.** SPORT marquage *m*.

marking ink *n* encre *f* indélébile.

marksman [ˈmɑːksmən] (*pl* **marksmen** [-mən]) *n* tireur *m* d'élite; police marksmen des tireurs d'élite de la police.

marksmanship [ˈmɑːksmənʃɪp] *n* habileté *f* au tir.

markswoman [ˈmɑːksˌwʊmən] (*pl* **markswomen** [-ˌwɪmɪn]) *n* tireuse *f* d'élite.

mark-up *n* majoration *f*, augmentation *f* (de prix).

marl [mɑːl] ◇ *n* marne *f*.
◇ *vt* marner AGR.

marlin [ˈmɑːlɪn] *n* -**1.** [fish] makaire *m*. -**2.** = **marline**.

marline [ˈmɑːlɪn] *n* NAUT merlin *m*.

marlinspike [ˈmɑːlɪnspaɪk] *n* épissoir *m*.

marly [ˈmɑːlɪ] *adj* marneux.

marmalade [ˈmɑːməleɪd] ◇ *n* confiture *f* d'agrumes; (orange) ~ marmelade *f* d'orange; ~ orange orange *f* amère, bigarade *f*.
◇ *adj* [cat] roux.

Marmite® [ˈmɑːmaɪt] *n pâte à tartiner végétale à base d'extrait de levure*.

marmoreal [mɑːˈmɔːrɪəl] *adj lit* marmoréen.

marmoset [ˈmɑːməzet] *n* ouistiti *m*.

marmot [ˈmɑːmət] *n* marmotte *f*.

Maronite [ˈmærənaɪt] ◇ *adj* maronite.
◇ *n* Maronite *mf*.

maroon [məˈruːn] ◇ *vt* [abandon] abandonner *(sur une île ou une côte déserte)*; to be ~ed [shipwrecked] faire naufrage; he felt ~ed in his suburban flat *fig* il se sentait abandonné dans son appartement de banlieue.
◇ *adj* [colour] bordeaux *(inv)*.
◇ *n* -**1.** [colour] bordeaux *m*. -**2.** [rocket] fusée *f* de détresse.

Marplan [ˈmɑːplæn] *pr n nom d'un institut de sondage*.

marque [mɑːk] *n* [brand] marque *f*.

marquee [mɑːˈkiː] *n* -**1.** *Br* [tent] grande tente *f*; [for circus] chapiteau *m*. -**2.** *Am* [canopy at hotel, theatre] marquise *f*.

Marquesas Islands [mɑːˈkeɪsæs-] *pl pr n*: the ~ les îles *fpl* Marquises; in the ~ aux îles Marquises.

marquess [ˈmɑːkwɪs] *n* marquis *m*.

marquetry [ˈmɑːkɪtrɪ] ◇ *n* marqueterie *f*.
◇ *adj* [table] en marqueterie.

marquis [ˈmɑːkwɪs] = **marquess**.

Marrakech, Marrakesh [ˌmærəˈkeʃ] *pr n* Marrakech.

marriage [ˈmærɪdʒ] ◇ *n* -**1.** mariage *m*; [ceremony] mariage *m*, noces *fpl*; to ask for sb's hand in ~ *fml* demander la main de qqn, demander qqn en mariage; to make an offer of ~ faire une proposition de mariage; to give sb in ~ donner qqn en mariage; to take sb in ~ prendre qqn pour époux/épouse, épouser qqn; he's my uncle by ~ c'est mon oncle par alliance ❑ 'The Marriage at Cana' *Veronese* 'les Noces de Cana'; 'The Marriage of Figaro' *Beaumarchais* 'le Mariage de Figaro'; *Mozart* 'les Noces de Figaro'. -**2.** *fig* [union] mariage *m*, alliance *f*.
◇ *comp* conjugal, matrimonial; ~ **bed** lit *m* conjugal; ~ **ceremony** cérémonie *f* de mariage; ~ **vows** vœux *mpl* de mariage.

marriageable [ˈmærɪdʒəbl] *adj* mariable; to be of ~ age être en âge de se marier.

marriage broker *n* agent *m* matrimonial.

marriage bureau *n* agence *f* matrimoniale.

marriage certificate *n* extrait *m* d'acte de mariage.

marriage guidance *n* conseil *m* conjugal; ~ counsellor conseiller *m* conjugal, conseillère *f* conjugale.

marriage licence *n* ≃ certificat *m* de non-opposition au mariage.

marriage lines *inf npl Br dated* = **marriage certificate**.

marriage of convenience *n* mariage *m* de raison.

marriage settlement *n* [dowry] dot *f*; [between couple] ≃ contrat *m* de mariage, ≃ régime *m* matrimonial.

married [ˈmærɪd] *adj* [man, woman] marié, mariée; [life] conjugal; 'just ~' 'jeunes mariés'; he's ~ to his work *fig* il passe son temps à travailler ❑ ~ **couple** couple *m* marié; ~ **name** nom *m* d'épouse.

marrow [ˈmærəʊ] *n* -**1.** BIOL & *fig* moelle *f*; frozen OR chilled to the ~ gelé jusqu'à la moelle des os. -**2.** [vegetable] courge *f*.

marrowbone [ˈmærəʊbəʊn] *n* os *f* à moelle.

marrowfat pea [ˈmærəʊfæt] *n* pois *m* carré.

marry [ˈmærɪ] (*pt* & *pp* **married**) ◇ *vt* -**1.** [subj: fiancé] épouser, se marier avec; to get married se marier; to be married (to sb) être marié (avec qqn); will you ~ me? veux-tu m'épouser?; to ~ money faire un mariage d'argent. -**2.** [subj: priest] marier; they were married by the archbishop ils ont été mariés par l'archevêque. -**3.** *fig* [styles] marier, allier.
◇ *vi* se marier; he's not the ~ing type ce n'est pas le genre à se marier; she married beneath herself/above herself elle s'est mésalliée/a fait un beau mariage; to ~ for money faire un mariage d'argent; she married into a farming family elle a épousé un agriculteur.
◆ **marry off** *vt sep* marier; she married off her daughter to an aristocrat elle a marié sa fille à un aristocrate.
◆ **marry up** ◇ *vt sep* [join together] marier.
◇ *vi insep* s'associer.

Mars [mɑːz] *pr n* ASTRON & MYTH Mars.

Marseille, Marseilles [mɑːˈseɪ] *pr n* Marseille.

marsh [mɑːʃ] *n* marais *m*, marécage *m*.

marshal [ˈmɑːʃl] (*Br pt* & *pp* **marshalled**, *cont* **marshalling**, *Am pt* & *pp* **marshaled**, *cont* **marshaling**) ◇ *n* -**1.** MIL maréchal *m*. -**2.** [at public event] membre *m* du service d'ordre; [in law court] huissier *m*; [at race-track] commissaire *m*. -**3.** *Am* [police chief] commissaire *m* de police; [fire chief] capitaine *m* des pompiers; [district police officer] commissaire *m*.
◇ *vt* -**1.** MIL [troops] masser, rassembler; the troops were marshalled into the square on rassembla les troupes sur la place || [people, group] canaliser, diriger; she marshalled the children out of the room elle dirigea les enfants vers la porte. -**2.** [organize - arguments, thoughts] rassembler; he's trying to ~ support for his project il essaie d'obtenir du soutien pour son projet.

marshalling yard [ˈmɑːʃəlɪŋ-] *n Br* centre *m* OR gare *f* de triage.

Marshall Islands [ˈmɑːʃl-] *pl pr n*: the ~ les îles *fpl* Marshall; in the ~ aux îles Marshall.

Marshall Plan [ˈmɑːʃl-] *pr n*: the ~ le Plan Marshall.

MARSHALL PLAN:
Le Plan Marshall, du nom du général et secrétaire d'État américain l'ayant élaboré, est le programme américain d'aide à la reconstruction économique de l'Europe d'après-guerre.

---

marsh fever *n* fièvre *f* des marais, paludisme *m*.

marsh gas *n* gaz *m* des marais, méthane *m*.

marsh hen *n* poule *f* d'eau, râle *m* d'eau.

marshland [ˈmɑːʃlænd] *n* marais *m*, terrain *m* marécageux.

marshmallow [*Br* mɑːʃˈmæləʊ, *Am* ˈmarʃˌmeləʊ] *n* BOT guimauve *f*; CULIN [sweet] guimauve *f*.

marsh marigold *n* souci *m* d'eau, populage *m*.

marshy [ˈmɑːʃɪ] (*compar* marshier, *superl* marshiest) *adj* marécageux.

Marston Moor [ˈmɑːstənˈmɔːr] *pr n première grande victoire, en 1644, des armées alliées du Parlement anglais et de l'Écosse contre les royalistes, pendant la guerre civile en Angleterre*.

marsupial [mɑːˈsuːpjəl] ◇ *adj* marsupial.
◇ *n* marsupial *m*.

mart [mɑːt] *n* -**1.** [market] marché *m*; second-hand car ~ magasin *m* de voitures d'occasion. -**2.** [auction room] salle *f* des ventes.

marten [ˈmɑːtɪn] *n* marte *f*, martre *f*.

Martha [ˈmɑːθə] *pr n* Marthe.

martial [ˈmɑːʃl] *adj* [military] martial; [warlike] martial, guerrier; ~ **music** musique *f* militaire.

martial art *n* art *m* martial.

martial law *n* loi *f* martiale.

Martian [ˈmɑːʃn] ◇ *n* Martien *m*, -enne *f*.
◇ *adj* martien.

martin [ˈmɑːtɪn] *n* martinet *m*; house ~ hirondelle *f* de fenêtre.

martinet [ˌmɑːtɪˈnet] *n* tyran *m*.

martingale [ˈmɑːtɪŋgeɪl] *n* [of horse] martingale *f*.

martini ® [mɑːˈtiːnɪ] *n* martini *m*.

Martinique [ˌmɑːtɪˈniːk] *pr n* Martinique *f*; in ~ à la OR en Martinique.

Martinmas [ˈmɑːtɪnməs] *n* Saint-Martin *f*; at ~ à la Saint-Martin.

martyr [ˈmɑːtəʳ] ◇ *n* martyr *m*, -e *f*; to die a ~ mourir en martyr || *fig*: she's always making a ~ of herself elle joue toujours les martyres; he's a ~ to rheumatism ses rhumatismes lui font souffrir le martyre.
◇ *vt* martyriser; to put on a ~ed look *fig* prendre des airs de martyr.

martyrdom [ˈmɑːtədəm] *n* RELIG martyre *m*; *fig* martyre *m*, calvaire *m*.

martyrize, -ise [ˈmɑːtəraɪz] *vt* martyriser.

MARV [mɑːv] (*abbr of* manoeuvrable re-entry vehicle) *n* MARV *m*.

marvel [ˈmɑːvl] (*Br pt* & *pp* **marvelled**, *cont* **marvelling**, *Am pt* & *pp* **marveled**, *cont* **marveling**) ◇ *n* -**1.** [miracle] merveille *f*, miracle *m*, prodige *m*; to do OR to work ~s faire des merveilles; it's a ~ to me that she managed to survive pour moi, c'est un miracle qu'elle ait survécu. -**2.** [marvellous person]: you're a ~! tu es une vraie petite merveille!
◇ *vi*: to ~ at sthg s'émerveiller de qqch; I ~

at the speed they get things done je suis émerveillé par la vitesse à laquelle ils font les choses.
◇ *vt*: he marvelled that she had kept so calm il n'en revenait pas qu'elle ait pu rester si calme.
marvellous *Br*, **marvelous** *Am* ['mɑːvələs] *adj* [amazing] merveilleux, extraordinaire; [miraculous] miraculeux.
marvellously *Br*, **marvelously** *Am* ['mɑːvələslɪ] *adv* merveilleusement, à merveille.
Marxism ['mɑːksɪzm] *n* marxisme *m*.
Marxism-Leninism *n* marxisme-léninisme *m*.
Marxist ['mɑːksɪst] ◇ *adj* marxiste.
◇ *n* marxiste *mf*.
Marxist-Leninist ◇ *adj* marxiste-léniniste.
◇ *n* marxiste-léniniste *mf*.
Mary ['meərɪ] *pr n* Marie; ~ **Magdalene** Marie Madeleine; **the Virgin** ~ la Vierge Marie.
Maryland ['meərɪlənd] *pr n* Maryland *m*; in ~ dans le Maryland.
marzipan ['mɑːzɪpæn] ◇ *n* pâte *f* d'amandes.
◇ *comp* [cake, sweet etc] à la pâte d'amandes.
mascara [mæs'kɑːrə] *n* mascara *m*.
mascaraed [mæs'kɑːrəd] *adj*: **she had heavily ~ eyelashes** elle portait beaucoup de mascara.
mascon ['mæskɒn] *n* mascon *m*, réplétion *f*.
mascot ['mæskət] *n* mascotte *f*.
masculine ['mæskjʊlɪn] ◇ *adj* masculin.
◇ *n* GRAMM masculin *m*.
masculinity [,mæskjʊ'lɪnətɪ] *n* masculinité *f*.
maser ['meɪzə^r] *n* maser *m*.
mash [mæʃ] ◇ *n* -**1**. *inf Br* CULIN purée *f* (de pommes de terre); **bangers and ~** saucisses-purée *fpl*. -**2**. [for horses] mash *m*. -**3**. [in brewing] moût *m*. -**4**. *inf* [pulp] pulpe *f*, bouillie *f*.
◇ *vt* -**1**. [crush] écraser, broyer; ~ **it all together** écraser le tout; ~ **it (up) well** bien écraser. -**2**. CULIN faire une purée de; **~ed potato** OR **potatoes** purée *f* (de pommes de terre). -**3**. [in brewing] brasser.
MASH [mæʃ] (*abbr of* **mobile army surgical hospital**) *n hôpital militaire de campagne*.
masher ['mæʃə^r] *n* broyeur *m*; [for potatoes] presse-purée *m inv*.
mask [mɑːsk] ◇ *n* -**1**. *literal* & *fig* masque *m*; PHOT cache *m*. -**2**. COMPUT masque *m*.
◇ *vt* -**1**. [face] masquer. -**2**. [truth, feelings] masquer, cacher, dissimuler. -**3**. [house] masquer, cacher; [view] boucher, masquer; [flavour, smell] masquer, recouvrir. -**4**. [in painting, photography] masquer, cacher.
◆ **mask out** *vt sep* PHOT masquer, cacher.
◆ **mask up** *vi insep* [surgeon] se masquer, se mettre un masque.
masked [mɑːskt] *adj* [face, man] masqué.
masked ball *n* bal *m* masqué.
masking ['mɑːskɪŋ] *n* masquage *m*.
masking tape *n* papier *m* à maroufler.
masochism ['mæsəkɪzm] *n* masochisme *m*.
masochist ['mæsəkɪst] ◇ *adj* masochiste.
◇ *n* masochiste *mf*.
masochistic [,mæsə'kɪstɪk] *adj* masochiste.
mason ['meɪsn] *n* [stoneworker] maçon *m*.
◆ **Mason** *n* [Freemason] Maçon *m*, franc-maçon *m*.
Mason-Dixon Line [,meɪsn'dɪksn-] *pr n frontière sud de la Pennsylvanie qui marquait aussi la limite entre les États esclavagistes et les États anti-esclavagistes*.
Masonic [mə'sɒnɪk] *adj* maçonnique, franc-maçonnique; ~ **lodge** loge *f* maçonnique.
masonry ['meɪsnrɪ] ◇ *n* [stonework, skill] maçonnerie *f*; **a large piece of ~** un gros bloc de pierre.
◇ *comp*: ~ **drill** perçeuse *f*.
◆ **Masonry** *n* [Freemasonry] Maçonnerie *f*, franc-maçonnerie *f*.
masque [mɑːsk] *n* THEAT masque *m*.
masquerade [,mæskə'reɪd] ◇ *n literal* & *fig* mascarade *f*.
◇ *vi*: to ~ as [pretend to be] se faire passer pour; [disguise o.s. as] se déguiser en.
mass [mæs] ◇ *n* -**1**. PHYS masse *f*; **dyed in the ~** TEX teinté dans la masse. -**2**. [large quantity or amount] masse *f*, quantité *f*; **a ~ of documents** une masse de documents; **a ~ of work** une quantité de travail; **the streets were a solid ~ of people/traffic** les rues regorgeaient de monde/de voitures || [bulk] masse *f*; **the dark ~ of the mountains** la masse sombre des montagnes. -**3**. [majority] majorité *f*, plupart *f*; **the ~ of the people are in favour of this policy** la majorité des gens est favorable à cette politique; **in the ~** dans l'ensemble. -**4**. GEOG: **land ~** masse *f* continentale.
◇ *adj* [for all - communication, education] de masse; [large-scale - starvation, unemployment] à OR sur une grande échelle; [involving many - resignation] massif, en masse; [collective - funeral] collectif; **this product will appeal to a ~ audience** ce produit plaira à un large public; ~ **consumption/culture** consommation *f*/culture *f* de masse; ~ **demonstration** grande manifestation *f*; ~ **execution** exécution *f* en masse; ~ **grave** charnier *m*; ~ **meeting** grand rassemblement *m*; ~ **hypnosis/hysteria** hypnose *f*/hystérie *f* collective; ~ **suicide** suicide *m* collectif; ~ **murder** tuerie *f*; ~ **murderer** tueur *m* fou.
◇ *vi* [people] se masser; [clouds] s'amonceler; **the crowds were ~ing in the square** des milliers de personnes se massaient sur la place.
◇ *vt* [troops] masser.
Mass [mæs] *n* RELIG -**1**. [music] messe *f*; ~ **in B Minor** messe en si mineur. -**2**. [ceremony] messe *f*; **to go to ~** aller à la messe; **to say ~** dire la messe.
Mass. *written abbr of* Massachusetts.
Massachusetts [,mæsə'tʃuːsɪts] *pr n* Massachusetts *m*; in ~ dans le Massachusetts.
massacre ['mæsəkə^r] ◇ *vt* -**1**. [kill] massacrer. -**2**. *inf* SPORT écraser.
◇ *n* massacre *m*; **the Massacre of the Innocents** le Massacre des Innocents.
massage [*Br* 'mæsɑːʒ, *Am* mə'sɑːʒ] ◇ *n* massage *m*.
◇ *vt literal* masser; *fig* [statistics, facts] manipuler.
massage parlour *n* salon *m* de massage.
masse [mæs] *n* → **en masse**.
massed [mæst] *adj* -**1**. [crowds, soldiers] massé, regroupé; ~ **bands** *Br* ensemble *m* de fanfares. -**2**. [collective] de masse; **the ~ weight of public opinion** le poids de l'opinion publique.
mass-energy *comp*: ~ **equation** OR **relation** relation *f* masse-énergie.
masses ['mæsɪz] *npl* -**1**. **the ~** les masses *fpl*; **culture for the ~** la culture à la portée de tous OR à la portée du plus grand nombre. -**2**. *inf* [large amount]: **we've got ~** on en a plein; ~ **of** des masses de, plein de; **we ate ~ of sweets** on a mangé plein de bonbons.
masseur [*Br* mæ'sɜː^r, *Am* mæ'sʊər] *n* masseur *m*.
masseuse [*Br* mæ'sɜːz, *Am* mæ'suːz] *n* masseuse *f*.
massif ['mæsiːf] *n* massif *m* (montagneux).
massive ['mæsɪv] *adj* [in size] massif, énorme; [dose, increase] massif; [majority] écrasant; [change, explosion] énorme; [sound] retentissant; **the general was a ~ man** le général était un homme massif.
massively ['mæsɪvlɪ] *adv* massivement; **he's ~ built** il est solidement bâti.
mass-market *adj* grand public *inv*.
mass media *n* OU *npl* mass media *mpl*.
mass noun *n* nom *m* non comptable.
mass number *n* nombre *m* de masse.
mass-produce *vt* fabriquer en série.
mass production *n* fabrication *f* OR production *f* en série.
mast [mɑːst] *n* -**1**. [on ship, for flag] mât *m*; [for radio or TV aerial] pylône *m*. -**2**. [animal food] faine *f (destinée à l'alimentation animale)*.
mastectomy [mæs'tektəmɪ] (*pl* mastectomies) *n* mastectomie *f*, mammectomie *f*.
master ['mɑːstə^r] ◇ *n* -**1**. [of household, dog, servant, situation] maître *m*; **the ~ of the house** le maître de maison; **to be ~ in one's own house** être maître chez soi; **to be one's own ~** être son propre maître; **to be (the) ~ of one's fate** être maître de son destin; **he's ~ of the situation** il est maître de la situation ❑ ~ **of ceremonies** [at reception] maître des cérémonies; [on TV show] présentateur *m*; ~ **of hounds** OR **foxhounds** maître d'équipage; **Master of the Rolls** ≃ président *m* de la cour d'appel *(en Grande-Bretagne)*. -**2**. [expert] maître *m*; **chess ~** maître; **he's a ~ at the art of ducking questions** il est maître dans l'art d'éluder les questions. -**3**. SCH [in primary school] instituteur *m*, maître *m* d'école; [in secondary school] professeur *m*; [private tutor] maître *m*; **history ~** professeur d'histoire. -**4**. UNIV: **Master of Arts/Science** [diploma] ≃ maîtrise *f* ès lettres/ès sciences; [person] ≃ titulaire *mf* d'une maîtrise de lettres/de sciences; **she's doing a ~'s (degree) in philosophy** elle prépare une maîtrise de philosophie. -**5**. *dated* & *fml* [boy's title] monsieur *m*. -**6**. ART maître *m*. -**7**. NAUT [of ship] capitaine *m*; [of fishing boat] patron *m*. -**8**. UNIV [head of college] principal *m*. -**9**. [original copy] original *m*; [standard] étalon *m*.
◇ *vt* -**1**. [person, animal] maîtriser, dompter; [problem, difficulty] surmonter, venir à bout de; [emotions] maîtriser, surmonter; [situation] maîtriser, se rendre maître de; **to ~ o.s.** se maîtriser, se dominer. -**2**. [subject, technique] maîtriser; **she ~ed Portuguese in only 6 months** 6 mois lui ont suffi pour maîtriser le portugais.
◇ *adj* -**1**. [overall] directeur, maître; ~ **plan** stratégie *f* globale. -**2**. [in trade] maître; ~ **baker/chef/craftsman** maître boulanger *m*/chef *m*/artisan *m*; **a ~ thief/spy** un voleur/un espion de génie. -**3**. [controlling] principal; ~ **switch** interrupteur *m* général. -**4**. [original] original; ~ **tape** bande *f* originale; ~ **copy** original *m*.
master-at-arms (*pl* masters-at-arms) *n* capitaine *m* d'armes.
master beam *n* poutre *f* maîtresse.
master bedroom *n* chambre *f* principale.
master builder *n* maître *m* bâtisseur.
master card *n* carte *f* maîtresse.
master class *n* cours *m* de maître; MUS master class *m*.
master cylinder *n* maître-cylindre *m*.
master file *n* COMPUT fichier *m* principal OR maître.
masterful ['mɑːstəfʊl] *adj* -**1**. [dominating] autoritaire. -**2**. = **masterly**.
masterfully ['mɑːstəfʊlɪ] *adv* -**1**. [dominatingly] fermement, autoritairement; **to speak ~** parler sur un ton autoritaire. -**2**. [skilfully] magistralement.
master key *n* passe-partout *m inv*.
masterly ['mɑːstəlɪ] *adj* magistral; **a ~ performance** une performance magistrale; **in a ~ fashion** magistralement, avec maestria.
master mariner *n* capitaine *m*.
mastermind ['mɑːstəmaɪnd] ◇ *n* [genius] cerveau *m*, génie *m*; [of crime, operation] cerveau *m*.
◇ *vt* diriger, organiser; **she ~ed the whole operation** c'est elle qui a dirigé toute l'opération, c'est elle le cerveau de toute l'opération.
◆ **Mastermind** *pr n jeu télévisé britannique portant sur des questions de culture générale*.
masterpiece ['mɑːstəpiːs] *n literal* & *fig* chef d'œuvre *m*.
master race *n* race *f* supérieure.
masterstroke ['mɑːstəstrəʊk] *n* coup *m* de maître.
mastery ['mɑːstərɪ] (*pl* masteries) *n* -**1**. [domination, control] maîtrise *f*, domination *f*; ~ **of** OR **over a situation** maîtrise d'une situation; ~ **of an opponent** supériorité *f* sur un adversaire. -**2**. [of art, subject, language] maîtrise *f*, connaissance *f*. -**3**. [masterly skill] maestria *f*, brio *m*.
masthead ['mɑːsthed] *n* -**1**. NAUT tête *f* de mât. -**2**. PRESS titre *m*.

mastic ['mæstɪk] *n* [resin] mastic *m* de Chio; [filler, seal] mastic *m*; ~ tree lentisque *m*, arbre *m* à mastic.

masticate ['mæstɪkeɪt] *vi* & *vt* mastiquer, mâcher.

mastication [,mæstɪ'keɪʃn] *n* mastication *f*.

masticatory ['mæstɪkətrɪ] ◇ *n* MED masticatoire *m*.
◇ *adj* [muscle] masticateur; [function] masticatoire.

mastiff ['mæstɪf] *n* mastiff *m*.

mastodon ['mæstədɒn] *n* mastodonte *m*.

mastoid ['mæstɔɪd] ◇ *adj* ANAT mastoïdien.
◇ *n* -**1.** [bone] mastoïde *f*. -**2.** *inf* = **mastoiditis**.

mastoiditis [,mæstɔɪ'daɪtɪs] *n (U)* mastoïdite *f*.

masturbate ['mæstəbeɪt] ◇ *vi* se masturber.
◇ *vt* masturber.

masturbation [,mæstə'beɪʃn] *n* masturbation *f*.

masturbatory [,mæstə'beɪtərɪ] *adj* masturbatoire.

mat [mæt] (*pt* & *pp* matted, *cont* matting) ◇ *adj* = **matt**.
◇ *n* -**1.** [floor covering] (petit) tapis *m*, carpette *f*; [doormat] paillasson *m*; [in gym] tapis *m*; to be on the ~ *inf* être sur la sellette; to have sb on the ~ *inf* faire passer un mauvais quart d'heure à qqn. -**2.** [for sleeping on] natte *f*. -**3.** [on table] set *m* de table; [for hot dishes] dessous-de-plat *m inv*.
◇ *vi* -**1.** [hair] s'emmêler. -**2.** [material] (se) feutrer.

matador ['mætədɔːʳ] *n* matador *m*.

match [mætʃ] ◇ *n* -**1.** SPORT match *m*, rencontre *f*; a rugby/boxing ~ un match de rugby/de boxe; game, set and ~ TENNIS jeu, set et match; to play a ~ jouer un match. -**2.** [equal] égal *m*, -e *f*; he's found OR met his ~ (in Pauline) il a trouvé à qui parler (avec Pauline); he's a ~ for her any day il est de taille à lui faire face; Dave is no ~ for Rob Dave ne fait pas le poids contre Rob; they were more than a ~ for us nous ne faisions pas le poids contre eux. -**3.** [couple] couple *m*; [marriage] mariage *m*; they are a good ~ ils vont bien ensemble; to make a ~ arranger un mariage; to find a (good) ~ for sb trouver un (beau) parti à qqn. -**4.** [combination]: these colours are a good ~ ces couleurs se marient bien OR vont bien ensemble; the new paint's not quite a perfect ~ la nouvelle peinture n'est pas exactement de la même couleur que la précédente. -**5.** [for lighting] allumette *f*; to light OR to strike a ~ frotter OR craquer une allumette; to put OR to set a ~ to sthg mettre le feu à qqch; a box/book of ~es une boîte/une pochette d'allumettes. -**6.** [fuse] mèche *f*.
◇ *vt* -**1.** [be equal to] être l'égal de, égaler; his arrogance is ~ed only by that of his father son arrogance n'a d'égale que celle de son père. -**2.** [go with - subj: clothes, colour] s'assortir à, aller (bien) avec, se marier (harmonieusement) avec; the gloves ~ the scarf les gants sont assortis à l'écharpe. -**3.** [coordinate]: I'm trying to ~ this paint je cherche une peinture identique à celle-ci; can you ~ the names with the photographs? pouvez-vous attribuer à chaque photo le nom qui lui correspond?; I tried to ~ my gestures to theirs j'ai essayé d'imiter leurs gestes; he and his wife are well ~ed lui et sa femme vont bien ensemble. -**4.** [oppose]: to ~ sb against sb opposer qqn à qqn; he ~ed his skill against the champion's il mesura son habileté à celle du champion; the two teams are well ~ed les deux équipes sont de force égale. -**5.** [find equal to] égaler; to ~ an offer égaler une offre; this restaurant can't be ~ed for quality ce restaurant n'a pas son pareil pour ce qui est de la qualité.
◇ *vi* aller (bien) ensemble, être bien assorti; these colours don't ~ ces couleurs ne vont pas très bien ensemble; a red scarf with a bonnet to ~ un foulard rouge avec un bonnet assorti; I can't find two socks that ~ je ne parviens pas à trouver deux chaussettes identiques; none of the glasses ~ed les verres étaient tous dépareillés.
◆ **match up** ◇ *vt sep* = **match** *vt* **3**.
◇ *vi insep* [dates, figures] correspondre; [clothes, colours] aller (bien) ensemble, être bien assorti.
◆ **match up to** *vt insep* valoir; his jokes don't ~ (up to) Mark's ses plaisanteries ne valent pas celles de Mark; the hotel didn't ~ (up to) our expectations l'hôtel nous a déçus OR ne répondait pas à notre attente.

matchboard ['mætʃbɔːd] *n (U)* [for floor] lames *fpl* de parquet; [for walls, ceiling] lambris *mpl*.

matchbook ['mætʃbʊk] *n* pochette *f* d'allumettes.

matchbox ['mætʃbɒks] *n* boîte *f* d'allumettes.

match-fit *adj Br*: they only have ten ~ players ils n'ont que dix joueurs en état de jouer.

match fitness *n Br*: I haven't reached full ~ yet je n'ai pas encore retrouvé ma forme (pour jouer).

matching ['mætʃɪŋ] *adj* assorti; a blue suit with a ~ tie un costume bleu avec une cravate assortie.

matchless ['mætʃlɪs] *adj lit* sans égal, sans pareil.

matchlock ['mætʃlɒk] *n* fusil *m* à mèche.

matchmaker ['mætʃ,meɪkəʳ] *n* -**1.** [gen] entremetteur *m*, -euse *f*; [for marriage] marieur *m*, -euse *f*. -**2.** [manufacturer] fabricant *m* d'allumettes.

matchmaking ['mætʃ,meɪkɪŋ] *n*: he loves ~ [gen] il adore jouer les entremetteurs; [for marriage] il adore jouer les marieurs.

match-play *adj* GOLF: ~ tournament match-play *m*.

match point *n* TENNIS balle *f* de match.

matchstick ['mætʃstɪk] *n Br* allumette *f*; ~ men personnages *mpl* stylisés *(dessinés de simples traits)*.

match-winner *n* atout *m* pour gagner, joker *m*; he is the possible ~ in the team il est sans doute le meilleur atout de l'équipe (pour gagner).

matchwood ['mætʃwʊd] *n* bois *m* d'allumettes; smashed OR reduced to ~ *Br* réduit en miettes.

mate[1] [meɪt] ◇ *n* -**1.** *inf Br* & *Austr* [friend] pote *m*, copain *m*; [term of address]: listen, ~! *inf* écoute, mon vieux! -**2.** [colleague] camarade *mf* (de travail). -**3.** [workman's helper] aide *mf*; plumber's ~ aide-plombier *m*. -**4.** NAUT [in navy] second maître *m*; [on merchant vessel]: (first) ~ second *m*; second ~ lieutenant *m*. -**5.** ZOOL mâle *m*, femelle *f*; *hum* [husband] époux *m*; [wife] épouse *f*; [lover] partenaire *mf*; some animals pine when separated from their ~ certains animaux dépérissent quand on les sépare de leur compagnon. -**6.** [in chess] mat *m*.
◇ *vt* -**1.** ZOOL accoupler; to ~ a cow with a bull accoupler une vache à un taureau. -**2.** [in chess] mettre échec et mat, mater.
◇ *vi* s'accoupler.

mate[2], **maté** ['mæteɪ] *n* -**1.** [tree] (variété *f* de) houx *m*. -**2.** [drink] maté *m*.

mater ['meɪtəʳ] *n Br dated* & *hum* mère *f*, maman *f*.

material [mə'tɪərɪəl] ◇ *n* -**1.** [wood, plastic, stone etc] matière *f*, substance *f*; [as constituent] matériau *m*; building ~s matériaux de construction; raw ~s matières *fpl* premières. -**2.** [cloth] tissu *m*, étoffe *f*; curtain ~ tissu pour faire des rideaux. -**3.** *(U)* [ideas, data] matériaux *mpl*, documentation *f*; I'm collecting ~ for a novel je rassemble des matériaux pour un roman; background ~ documentation de base. -**4.** [finished work]: written ~ des textes *mpl*; published ~ des publications *fpl*; a comic who writes his own ~ un comique qui écrit ses propres textes OR sketches; a singer who writes his own ~ un auteur-compositeur; publicity ~ publicité *f*; reading ~ lecture *f*. -**5.** [necessary equipment] matériel *m*; writing ~ matériel pour écrire; teaching ~s SCH supports *mpl* pédagogiques; reference ~s documents *mpl* de référence. -**6.** [suitable person or persons]: is he officer/university ~? a-t-il l'étoffe d'un officier/universitaire?; they're not first division ~ ils ne sont pas de taille à jouer en première division.
◇ *adj* -**1.** [concrete] matériel; the ~ world le monde matériel; ~ comforts confort *m* matériel; ~ possessions biens *mpl* matériels; of ~ benefit d'un apport capital. -**2.** *fml* [relevant] pertinent; that is not ~ to the present discussion cela n'a aucun rapport OR n'a rien à voir avec ce dont nous discutons; the facts ~ to the investigation les faits qui présentent un intérêt pour l'enquête ❑ ~ evidence JUR preuve *f* matérielle OR tangible.

materialism [mə'tɪərɪəlɪzm] *n* matérialisme *m*.

materialist [mə'tɪərɪəlɪst] ◇ *adj* matérialiste.
◇ *n* matérialiste *mf*.

materialistic [mə,tɪərɪə'lɪstɪk] *adj* matérialiste.

materialization [mə,tɪərɪəlaɪ'zeɪʃn] *n* matérialisation *f*.

materialize, -ise [mə'tɪərɪəlaɪz] ◇ *vi* -**1.** [become fact] se matérialiser, se réaliser; [take shape] prendre forme; the promised pay rise never ~d l'augmentation promise ne s'est jamais concrétisée. -**2.** *inf* [arrive]: he eventually ~d around ten il a fini par se pointer vers dix heures. -**3.** [ghost, apparition] se matérialiser.
◇ *vt* matérialiser.

materially [mə'tɪərɪəlɪ] *adv* matériellement.

maternal [mə'tɜːnl] *adj* [motherly] maternel; ~ grandfather grand-père *m* maternel.

maternity [mə'tɜːnətɪ] ◇ *n* maternité *f*.
◇ *comp* [dress] de grossesse; [ward] de maternité; ~ home OR hospital maternité *f*.

maternity allowance *n allocation de maternité versée par l'État à une femme n'ayant pas droit à la «maternity pay»*.

maternity benefit *n* ≃ allocations *fpl* de maternité.

maternity leave *n* congé *m* (de) maternité.

maternity pay *n allocation de maternité versée par l'employeur*.

matey *inf* ['meɪtɪ] ◇ *n Br* pote *m*; [term of address]: all right, ~? ça va, mon vieux?
◇ *adj* [pally] copain; he's very ~ with me il est très copain avec moi.

mateyness ['meɪtɪnɪs] = **matiness**.

math [mæθ] *Am* = **maths**.

mathematical [,mæθə'mætɪkl] *adj* mathématique; a ~ genius un génie en mathématiques; I haven't got a ~ mind je n'ai pas l'esprit mathématique ❑ ~ linguistics/logic linguistique *f*/logique *f* mathématique.

mathematically [,mæθə'mætɪklɪ] *adv* mathématiquement.

mathematician [,mæθəmə'tɪʃn] *n* mathématicien *m*, -enne *f*.

mathematics [,mæθə'mætɪks] ◇ *n (U)* [science, subject] mathématiques *fpl*.
◇ *npl* [calculations involved]: can you explain the ~ of it to me? pouvez-vous m'expliquer comment on parvient à ce résultat?

maths [mæθs] (*abbr of* mathematics) *n (U) Br* maths *fpl*.

matinee, matinée ['mætɪneɪ] *n* CIN & THEAT matinée *f*.

matinee coat *n Br* veste *f* de bébé.

matinee idol *n dated* OR *hum* idole *f* (romantique).

matinee jacket *Br* = **matinee coat**.

matiness *inf* ['meɪtɪnɪs] *n Br* camaraderie *f*.

mating ['meɪtɪŋ] ◇ *n* accouplement *m*.
◇ *comp*: ~ call appel *m* du mâle OR de la femelle; ~ instinct instinct *m* sexuel; ~ season saison *f* des amours.

matins ['mætɪnz] = **mattins**.

matriarch ['meɪtrɪɑːk] *n* [ruler, head of family] chef *m* de famille *(dans un système matriarcal)*; [old woman] matrone *f*.

matriarchal [,meɪtrɪ'ɑːkl] *adj* matriarcal.

matriarchy ['meɪtrɪɑːkɪ] (*pl* matriarchies) *n* matriarcat *m*.

matric *inf* [mə'trɪk] *n Br abbr of* matriculation.

matrices ['meɪtrɪsiːz] *pl* → **matrix**.

matricide ['mætrɪsaɪd] *n* -**1.** [act] matricide *m*. -**2.** [person] matricide *mf*.

matriculate [mə'trɪkjʊleɪt] *vi* -**1.** [register] s'inscrire, se faire immatriculer; [at university] s'inscrire. -**2.** *Br* SCH ≃ obtenir son baccalauréat.

matriculation [mə,trɪkjʊ'leɪʃn] *n* -**1.** [registration] inscription *f*, immatriculation *f*; [at university] inscription *f*; ~ fees droits *mpl* d'inscription. -**2.** *Br* SCH *ancien examen équivalent au baccalauréat*.

matrilineal [,mætrɪ'lɪnɪəl] *adj* matrilinéaire.

matrimonial [,mætrɪ'məʊnjəl] *adj* matrimonial, conjugal.

matrimony ['mætrɪmənɪ, *Am* 'mætrɪməʊnɪ] (*pl* matrimonies) *n fml* mariage *m*.

matrix ['meɪtrɪks] (*pl* matrixes OR matrices [-trɪsiːz]) *n* matrice *f*.

matron ['meɪtrən] *n* -**1.** *Br* [in hospital] infirmière *f* en chef; [in school] infirmière *f*. -**2.** *lit* [married woman] matrone *f*, mère *f* de famille. -**3.** [in retirement home] surveillante *f*. -**4.** *Am* [in prison] gardienne *f*, surveillante *f*.

matronly ['meɪtrənlɪ] *adj*: she looks very ~ elle a tout de la matrone.

matron of honour (*pl* matrons of honour) *n* dame *f* d'honneur.

matt [mæt] *adj* mat; ~ **paint** peinture *f* mate.

matte [mæt] ◇ *adj* = **matt**.
◇ *n* METALL matte *f*, maton *m*.

matted ['mætɪd] *adj* [material] feutré; [hair] emmêlé; [vegetation, roots] enchevêtré.

matter ['mætə^r] ◇ *n* -**1.** [affair] affaire *f*; [subject] sujet *m*; **I reported the** ~ **to the police** j'ai rapporté les faits à la police; **business** ~**s** affaires *fpl*; **money** ~**s** questions *fpl* d'argent; **the** ~ **in hand** les faits qui nous préoccupent; **I consider the** ~ **closed** pour moi, c'est une affaire classée; **this is no laughing** ~ il n'y a pas de quoi rire; **it is no easy** ~ c'est une question difficile OR un sujet délicat; **I think we should let the** ~ **drop** je pense que nous devrions laisser tomber le sujet; **you're not going out, and that's the end of** OR **there's an end to the** ~! tu ne sortiras pas, un point c'est tout! -**2.** [question] question *f*; **there's the small** ~ **of the £100 you owe me** il y a ce petit problème des 100 livres que tu me dois; **a** ~ **of life and death** une question de vie ou de mort; **that's quite another** ~, **that's a different** ~ **altogether** ça c'est une (tout) autre affaire; **a** ~ **of taste** une question de goût; **that's a** ~ **of opinion** ça c'est une question d'opinion; **as a** ~ **of course** tout naturellement; **as a** ~ **of principle** par principe; **as a** ~ **of urgency** d'urgence; **she'll do it in a** ~ **of minutes** cela ne lui prendra que quelques minutes; **it'll be a** ~ **of days rather than weeks before we get a result** obtenir le résultat sera une question de jours plutôt que de semaines; **it's only** OR **just a** ~ **of time** ce n'est qu'une question de temps; **it's only** OR **just a** ~ **of filling in a few forms** il ne s'agit que de remplir quelques formulaires. -**3.** [physical substance] matière *f*; **organic/inorganic** ~ matière organique/inorganique. -**4.** [written material]: **advertising** ~ matériel *m* publicitaire; **printed** ~ texte *m* imprimé; [sent by post] imprimés *mpl*; **reading** ~ de la lecture, quelque chose à lire. -**5.** MED [pus] pus *m*. -**6.** *phr*: **what's the** ~? qu'est-ce qu'il y a?, qu'est-ce qui ne va pas?; **what's the** ~ **with you?** qu'est-ce que tu as?, qu'est-ce qui ne va pas?; **what's the** ~ **with Jim?** qu'est-ce qu'il a, Jim?; **what's the** ~ **with your eyes?** qu'est-ce que vous avez aux yeux?; **what's the** ~ **with the television?** qu'est-ce qu'elle a, la télévision?; **what's the** ~ **with the way I dress?** qu'est-ce que vous reprochez à ma façon de m'habiller?; **what's the** ~ **with telling him the truth?** quel mal y a-t-il à lui dire la vérité?; **there's something the** ~ **with my leg** j'ai quelque chose à la jambe; **there's something the** ~ **with the aerial** il y a un problème avec l'antenne; **is there something** OR **is anything the** ~? il y a quelque chose qui ne va pas?, il y a un problème?; **something must be the** ~ il doit y avoir quelque chose; **nothing's the** OR **there's nothing the** ~ il n'y a rien, tout va bien; **nothing's the** ~ **with me** je vais parfaitement bien; **there's nothing the** ~ **with the engine** le moteur est en parfait état de marche; **no** ~! peu importe!; **no** ~ **what I do** quoi que je fasse; **no** ~ **what the boss thinks** peu importe ce qu'en pense le patron; **don't go back, no** ~ **how much he begs you** même s'il te le demande à genoux, n'y retourne pas; **no** ~ **what** quoi qu'il arrive; **I'll be there tomorrow no** ~ **what** j'y serai demain quoi qu'il arrive; **we've got to win, no** ~ **what** il faut que nous gagnions à tout prix; **no** ~ **how hard I try** quels que soient les efforts que je fais; **I must speak to her, no** ~ **how ill she is** je dois lui parler, quel que soit son état de santé; **no** ~ **when it happens** peu importe quand ça arrivera; **no** ~ **where I am** où que je sois.
◇ *vi* importer, avoir de l'importance; **what does it** ~? quelle importance est-ce que ça a?, qu'importe?; **it** ~**s a lot** cela a beaucoup d'importance, c'est très important; **it doesn't** ~ cela n'a pas d'importance, ça ne fait rien; **it doesn't** ~ **to me what you do with your money** ce que tu fais de ton argent m'est égal; **money is all that** ~**s to him** il n'y a que l'argent qui l'intéresse; **I forgot to tell him, not that it** ~**s, he'll find out soon enough** j'ai oublié de le lui dire mais c'est sans importance, il s'en rendra vite compte; **she** ~**s a lot to him** il tient beaucoup à elle, elle compte beaucoup pour lui; **she knows all the people who** ~ elle connaît tous les gens qui comptent.
◆ **matters** *npl*: **as** ~**s stand** les choses étant ce qu'elles sont; **getting angry won't help** ~**s at all** se mettre en colère n'arrangera pas les choses; ~**s have taken a turn for the worse** les choses ont pris un tour plus alarmant.
◆ **as a matter of fact** *adv phr* en fait, à vrai dire, en réalité.
◆ **for that matter** *adv phr* d'ailleurs.

Matterhorn ['mætəhɔːn] *pr n*: **the** ~ le mont Cervin.

matter-of-fact *adj* [down-to-earth] terre-à-terre (*inv*); [prosaic] prosaïque; [unemotional] neutre; **Frank has a very** ~ **approach** Frank a une vision très pratique des choses; **he has a very** ~ **way of speaking** il dit les choses comme elles sont; **in a** ~ **voice** d'une voix neutre; **she took the news in a very** ~ **way** elle a pris les nouvelles avec beaucoup de sang-froid.

Matthew ['mæθjuː] *pr n* Matthieu; **the Gospel According to (Saint)** ~ l'Évangile selon saint Matthieu.

Matthias [mə'θaɪəs] *pr n* Matthias, Mathias.

matting ['mætɪŋ] *n* (*U*) [used as mat] natte *f*, tapis *m*; **there was rush** ~ **on the floor** le sol était couvert d'un tapis tressé.

mattins ['mætɪnz] *n* (*U*) RELIG matines *fpl*.

mattock ['mætək] *n* pioche *f*.

mattress ['mætrɪs] *n* matelas *m*.

maturation [,mætjʊ'reɪʃn] *n* BOT & BIOL maturation *f*; *fig* mûrissement *m*.

mature [mə'tjʊə^r] ◇ *adj* -**1.** [person - physically] mûr; [- mentally] mûr, mature; **a man of** ~ **years** un homme d'âge mûr; **her style is not yet** ~ son style n'est pas encore arrivé à maturité. -**2.** [cheese] fait; [wine, spirits] arrivé à maturité. -**3.** FIN échu.
◇ *vi* -**1.** [person, attitude] mûrir; **he has** ~**d into a very sensible young man** c'est maintenant un jeune homme plein de bon sens. -**2.** [wine] arriver à maturité; [cheese] se faire. -**3.** FIN arriver à échéance, échoir.
◇ *vt* [cheese] faire mûrir, affiner; [wine, spirits] faire vieillir.

mature student *n* UNIV *adulte qui fait des études*.

maturity [mə'tjʊərətɪ] *n* -**1.** [gen] maturité *f*; **to reach** ~ [person] devenir majeur. -**2.** FIN: ~ (date) échéance *f*.

matzo [mætsəʊ] (*pl* matzos) *n* pain *m* azym

maudlin ['mɔːdlɪn] *adj* larmoyant, sen timental.

maul [mɔːl] ◇ *vt* -**1.** [attack - subj: anima mutiler; [- subj: person, crowd] malmener; h **was** ~**ed to death by a lion** il a été mis e pièces par un lion. -**2.** *inf* [handle clumsily] trip ter. -**3.** [criticize] démolir, mettre en pièces.
◇ *vi* RUGBY faire un maul.
◇ *n* RUGBY maul *m*.

maulers^▽ ['mɔːləz] *npl Br* [hands] pattes *fpl*.

maunder ['mɔːndə^r] *vi Br* -**1.** [talk] divague parler à tort et à travers; **what's he** ~**ing** o **about?** qu'est-ce qu'il raconte? -**2.** [walk] erre

Maundy money ['mɔːndɪ-] *n* (*U*) *pièces d monnaie spéciales offertes par le souverain britann que à certaines personnes âgées le jour du jeudi sain*

Maundy Thursday ['mɔːndɪ-] *n* RELIG jeudi saint.

Mauritania [,mɒrɪ'teɪnjə] *pr n* Mauritanie *f*; **i** ~ en Mauritanie.

Mauritanian [,mɒrɪ'teɪnjən] ◇ *n* Maur tanien *m*, -enne *f*.
◇ *adj* mauritanien.

Mauritian [mə'rɪʃn] ◇ *n* Mauricien *m*, -enne
◇ *adj* mauricien.

Mauritius [mə'rɪʃəs] *pr n* l'île *f* Maurice; **in** ~ à l'île Maurice.

mausoleum [,mɔːsə'lɪəm] *n* mausolée *m*.

mauve [məʊv] ◇ *adj* mauve.
◇ *n* mauve *m*.

maven *inf* ['meɪvn] *n Am* expert *m*.

maverick ['mævərɪk] ◇ *n* -**1.** [person] fran tireur *m*, indépendant *m*, -e *f*. -**2.** [calf] veau non marqué.
◇ *adj* non-conformiste, indépendant; **a** ~ **Marxist** un franc-tireur du marxisme.

maw [mɔː] *n* ZOOL [of cow] caillette *f*; [of bir jabot *m*; *fig* gouffre *m*.

mawkish ['mɔːkɪʃ] *adj* [sentimental] mièvr [nauseating] écœurant; **a** ~ **smile** un souri niais.

mawkishness ['mɔːkɪʃnɪs] *n* mièvrerie *f*, nia serie *f*.

max. (*written abbr of* **maximum**) max.

maxi ['mæksɪ] ◇ *adj* [skirt, dress etc] maxi.
◇ *n* maxi *m*.

maxilla [mæk'sɪlə] (*pl* maxillae [-liː]) *n* ANA maxillaire *m*.

maxim ['mæksɪm] *n* maxime *f*.

maxima ['mæksɪmə] *pl* → **maximum**.

maximal ['mæksɪml] *adj* maximal.

maximalist ['mæksɪməlɪst] ◇ *adj* max maliste.
◇ *n* maximaliste *mf*.

maximize, -ise ['mæksɪmaɪz] *vt* maximise maximaliser.

maximum ['mæksɪməm] (*pl* **maximums** c maxima [-mə]) ◇ *n* maximum *m*; **a** ~ **of 4 people** un maximum de 40 personnes, 4 personnes au maximum; **the space has bee used to the** ~ l'espace a été utilisé a maximum.
◇ *adj* maximum, maximal; **what is the** ~ **speed?** quelle est la vitesse maximum?; ~ **loa** charge *f* maximale OR limite ❑ ~ **securit prison** prison *f* de haute sécurité.
◇ *adv* au maximum; **it happens twice a yea** ~ ça se produit deux fois par an au maximun **you can stay for two hours** ~ vous ne pouve pas rester plus de deux heures.

maxwell ['mækswel] *n* PHYS maxwell *m*.

may[1] [meɪ] *modal vb* -**1.** [expressing possibility **this** ~ **take some time** ça prendra peut-être c il se peut que ça prenne du temps; **sympton** ~ **disappear after a few days** les symptôme peuvent disparaître après quelques jours; **yo** ~ **be right** vous avez peut-être raison, il se pe que vous ayez raison; **you** ~ **well be right** il e fort possible OR il se peut bien que vous aye raison; **what he says** ~ **be true** ce qu'il dit e peut-être vrai; **it** ~ **well be that he misunde stood** il est fort possible OR il se peut bien qu' ait mal compris; I ~ live to regret this! il se peut que je le regrette un jour!; she ~ have missed the plane elle a peut-être manqué l'avion, il se peut qu'elle ait manqué l'avion; she ~ not have arrived yet il se peut OR il se pourrait qu'elle ne soit pas encore arrivée; he ~ have been right il avait peut-être raison. -2. [expressing permission]: you ~ sit down vous pouvez vous asseoir; only close relatives ~ attend seuls les parents proches sont invités à assister à la cérémonie; I will go home now, if I ~ je vais rentrer chez moi, si vous me le permettez; if I ~ say so si je peux OR puis me permettre cette remarque; you ~ well ask! bonne question! -3. [in polite questions, suggestions]: ~ I interrupt? puis-je vous interrompre?, vous permettez que je vous interrompe?; ~ I? vous permettez?; ~ I make a suggestion? puis-je me permettre de faire une suggestion?; ~ I help you? puis-je vous aider?; ~ I buy you ladies a drink? puis-je vous offir un verre, mesdames?; ~ I come too? – yes, you ~ puis-je venir aussi? – oui; and how, ~ I ask, did you find out? et comment vous en êtes-vous rendu compte, s'il vous plaît?; ~ I say how pleased we are that you could come permettez-moi de vous dire à quel point nous sommes ravis que vous ayez pu venir. -4. [contradicting a point of view]: you ~ think I'm imagining things, but I think I'm being followed tu vas croire que je divague mais je crois que je suis suivi; such facts ~ seem insignificant, but they could prove vital de telles choses peuvent paraître insignifiantes mais elles pourraient se révéler vitales; he ~ not be very bright, but he's got a heart of gold il n'est peut-être pas très brillant mais il a un cœur d'or; brilliant she ~ be, but is she reliable? elle est peut-être brillante, mais peut-on lui faire confiance? ❑ that's as ~ be c'est possible; that's as ~ be, but I still don't think you're right c'est possible mais je ne suis toujours pas convaincu que tu aies raison. -5. [giving additional information]: this, it ~ be said, is yet another example of government interference c'est là, on peut le dire, un autre exemple de l'interventionnisme de l'État. -6. *fml* [expressing purpose]: they work hard so that their children ~ have a better life ils travaillent dur pour que leurs enfants aient une vie meilleure. -7. [expressing wishes, hopes]: long ~ he reign vive le roi; ~ she rest in peace qu'elle repose en paix; ~ he rot in hell! qu'il aille au diable!; ~ the best man win! que le meilleur gagne! -8. *phr*: ~ as well: can I go home now? – you ~ as well est-ce que je peux rentrer chez moi maintenant? – tu ferais aussi bien; we ~ as well have another drink tant qu'à faire, autant prendre un autre verre.

may[2] [meɪ] *n* [hawthorn] aubépine *f*, épine *f* de mai.

May [meɪ] *n* mai *m*.

Maya(n) ['maɪə(n)] ◇ *n* -1. [person] Indien *m*, -enne *f* maya; the ~s les Mayas *mpl*. -2. LING maya *m*.
◇ *adj* maya.

May ball *n bal qui se tient au mois de juin à l'université de Cambridge*.

maybe ['meɪbiː] *adv* peut-être; ~ she'll come tomorrow elle viendra peut-être demain; ~ so peut-être bien que oui; ~ not peut-être bien que non; ~ so, but... peut-être bien, mais...

may blossom *n (U)* fleurs *fpl* d'aubépine.

May bug *n* hanneton *m*.

Mayday ['meɪdeɪ] *n* [SOS] SOS *m*; to send out a ~ signal envoyer un signal de détresse OR un SOS.

May Day *n* le Premier Mai.

Mayfair ['meɪfeəʳ] *pr n quartier chic de Londres*.

mayflower ['meɪflaʊəʳ] *n* [gen] fleur *f* printanière; *Br* [marsh marigold] souci *m* d'eau; *Br* [hawthorn] aubépine *f*.
◆ **Mayflower** *pr n*: the Mayflower *Am* HIST le Mayflower; the Mayflower Compact le covenant du Mayflower.

THE MAYFLOWER COMPACT:
Pacte conclu par les puritains pèlerins à bord du «Mayflower» en novembre 1620, avant de débarquer sur le site de Plymouth, par lequel ils s'engageaient à fonder une société civile régie par leurs propres lois. Cette convention est considérée comme la première Constitution de l'Amérique du Nord.

---

mayfly ['meɪflaɪ] (*pl* mayflies) *n* éphémère *m*.

mayhem ['meɪhem] *n* -1. [disorder] désordre *m*; it was absolute ~ in that office c'était le désordre le plus complet dans ce bureau; to create OR to cause ~ semer la panique. -2. JUR mutilation *f* du corps humain.

mayn't [meɪnt] *Br* = **may not**.

mayo *inf* ['meɪəʊ] *n Am* mayonnaise *f*.

mayonnaise [ˌmeɪə'neɪz] *n* mayonnaise *f*.

mayor [meəʳ] *n* maire *m*, mairesse *f*.

mayoralty ['meərəltɪ] (*pl* mayoralties) *n* mandat *m* de maire.

mayoress ['meərɪs] *n* femme *f* du maire.

maypole ['meɪpəʊl] *n* ≃ arbre *m* de mai *(mât autour duquel on danse le Premier mai)*.

May queen *n* reine *f* du Premier mai.

may've *inf* ['meɪəv] = **may have**.

May week *n semaine du mois de juin pendant laquelle se tiennent les «May balls»*.

maze [meɪz] *n literal* & *fig* labyrinthe *m*, dédale *m*; the hospital is a ~ of corridors cet hôpital est un vrai labyrinthe.
◆ **Maze** *pr n*: the ~ (Prison) *prison d'Irlande du Nord*.

mazuma▽ [mə'zuːmə] *n Am* fric *m*, oseille *f*.

mazurka [mə'zɜːkə] *n* mazurka *f*.

MB -1. (*written abbr of* megabyte) Mo. -2. *written abbr of* Manitoba.

MBA (*abbr of* Master of Business Administration) *n (titulaire d'une) maîtrise de gestion*.

MBBS (*abbr of* Bachelor of Medicine and Surgery) *n (titulaire d'une) licence de médecine et de chirurgie*.

MBE (*abbr of* Member of the Order of the British Empire) *n (membre de) l'ordre de l'Empire britannique (titre honorifique)*.

MBO (*abbr of* management buyout) *n Br* RES *m*.

MC *n* -1. *abbr of* master of ceremonies. -2. *Br abbr of* Military Cross. -3. *Am abbr of* Member of Congress. -4. *Am abbr of* Marine Corps.

MCAT (*abbr of* Medical College Admissions Test) *n test d'admission aux études de médecine*.

MCC (*abbr of* Marylebone Cricket Club) *pr n célèbre club de cricket de Londres*.

McCarthyism [mə'kɑːθɪɪzm] *n* POL maccartisme *m*, maccarthysme *m*.

McCARTHYISM:
Mouvement anti-communiste américain né dans les années 40-50, donnant lieu à une chasse aux sorcières dans les milieux artistique, professionnel et politique de l'époque.

McCarthyist [mə'kɑːθɪɪst], **McCarthyite** [mə'kɑːθɪaɪt] ◇ *n* partisan *m*, -e *f* du maccartisme.
◇ *adj* maccartiste.

McCoy *inf* [mə'kɔɪ] *n phr*: it's the real ~ c'est du vrai de vrai, c'est de l'authentique.

MCP *inf* (*abbr of* male chauvinist pig) *n* phallo *m*.

MD ◇ *n* -1. *abbr of* Doctor of Medicine. -2. *abbr of* managing director.
◇ *written abbr of* Maryland.

MDT *n abbr of* Mountain Daylight Time.

me[1] [miː] ◇ *pron* -1. [direct or indirect object – unstressed] me, m' (*before vowel*); [– stressed] moi; do you love me? tu m'aimes?; give me a light donne-moi du feu; what, me, tell a lie? moi, mentir? -2. [after preposition] moi; they're talking about me ils parlent de moi; come with me viens avec moi. -3. [used instead of 'I'] moi; it's me c'est moi; it's always me who pays c'est toujours moi qui paie; is it just me or is it cold in here? c'est moi, ou bien il fait froid ici?; she's bigger than me elle est plus grande que moi; this hairstyle isn't really me *fig* cette coiffure, ce n'est pas vraiment mon style. -4. [in interjections]: dear me! mon Dieu!; poor me! pauvre de moi!; silly me! que je suis bête!
◇ *n* moi *m*; now I'm going to show you the real me maintenant je vais te montrer qui je suis.
◇ *det inf* = **my**.

me[2] [miː] MUS = **mi**.

ME ◇ *n (U)* (*abbr of* myalgic encephalomyelitis) myélo-encéphalite *f*.
◇ *written abbr of* Maine.

mead [miːd] *n* -1. *lit* = **meadow**. -2. [drink] hydromel *m*.

meadow ['medəʊ] *n* pré *m*, prairie *f*.

meadow grass *n* pâturin *m*.

meadowland ['medəʊlænd] *n* prairie *f*, pâturages *mpl*.

meadow pipit *n* pipit *m* des prés, farlouse *f*.

meadow saffron *n* safran *m* des prés, colchique *m*.

meadowsweet ['medəʊswiːt] *n* reine-des-prés *f*.

meagre *Br*, **meager** *Am* ['miːgəʳ] *adj* maigre; I can't live on such a ~ salary je ne peux pas vivre avec un salaire aussi maigre.

meagrely *Br*, **meagerly** *Am* ['miːgəlɪ] *adv* maigrement.

meagreness *Br*, **meagerness** *Am* ['miːgənɪs] *n* maigreur *f*.

meal [miːl] *n* -1. repas *m*; he had an enormous ~ il a mangé comme un ogre; go to bed as soon as you've finished your ~ va te coucher dès que tu as fini de manger; children need three ~s a day les enfants ont besoin de trois repas par jour; have a nice ~!, enjoy your ~! bon appétit!; they've invited us round for a ~ ils nous ont invités à manger ❑ evening ~ dîner *m*; we have our evening ~ early nous dînons tôt; to make a ~ of sthg *inf* faire tout un plat de qqch. -2. [flour] farine *f*. -3. *(U) Scot* [oatmeal] flocons *mpl* d'avoine.

meals on wheels *n service de repas à domicile à l'intention des invalides et des personnes âgées*.

meal ticket *n* -1. *Am* ticket *m* restaurant. -2. *inf* [source of income] gagne-pain *m inv*; I can't leave Harry, he's my ~ je ne peux pas quitter Harry, c'est lui qui fait bouillir la marmite.

mealtime ['miːltaɪm] *n* [lunch] heure *f* du déjeuner; [dinner] heure *f* du dîner; at ~s aux heures des repas.

mealy ['miːlɪ] (*compar* mealier, *superl* mealiest) *adj* -1. [floury] farineux; ~ potatoes des pommes de terre farineuses. -2. [pale] pâle.

mealy bug *n* cochenille *f* farineuse.

mealy-mouthed *adj* doucereux, patelin.

mean [miːn] (*pt* & *pp* meant [ment]) ◇ *adj* -1. [miserly] avare, radin, pingre; he's ~ with his money il est près de ses sous; they're very ~ about pay rises ils accordent les augmentations de salaire au compte-gouttes. -2. [nasty, unkind] méchant, vache; don't be ~ to your sister! ne sois pas méchant avec ta sœur!; go on, don't be ~! allez, ne sois pas vache!; to play a ~ trick on sb jouer un sale tour à qqn; I feel ~ about not inviting her j'ai un peu honte de ne pas l'avoir invitée; he gets ~ after a few drinks *inf Am* il devient mauvais OR méchant après quelques verres; ~ weather *inf Am* sale temps; the sky was a ~ shade of gray *Am* le ciel était d'une méchante couleur grise. -3. [inferior]: it should be obvious even to the meanest intelligence cela devrait être évident même pour l'esprit le plus borné; he's no ~ architect/guitarist c'est un architecte/guitariste de talent; it was no ~ feat ce n'était pas un mince exploit. -4. [average] moyen; ~ deviation écart *m* moyen; ~ distance/duration distance *f*/durée *f* moyenne. -5. ▽ [excellent] terrible, super; she plays a ~ guitar comme guitariste, elle est super; he makes a ~ chocolate cake pas mal, son gâteau au chocolat. -6. [shabby] miteux, misérable; ~ slums taudis misérables. -**7.** *lit* [of lower rank or class] : of ~ birth de basse extraction.

◇ *n* -**1.** [middle point] milieu *m*, moyen terme *m*; the golden OR happy ~ le juste milieu. -**2.** MATH moyenne *f*.

◇ *vt* -**1.** [signify – subj : word, gesture] vouloir dire, signifier; [– subj : person] vouloir dire; what does this term ~? que signifie OR que veut dire ce terme?; what do you ~? qu'est-ce que tu veux dire?; what do you ~ by "superior"? qu'entendez-vous par «supérieur»?; what do you ~ you don't like the cinema? comment ça, vous n'aimez pas le cinéma?; do you ~ OR you ~ it's over already? tu veux dire que c'est déjà fini?; what, take them to court, you ~? tu veux dire les traîner en justice?; that film didn't ~ anything to me je n'ai rien compris à ce film; does the name Heathcliff ~ anything to you? est-ce que le nom de Heathcliff vous dit quelque chose?; that was when the word "friendship" still meant something c'était à l'époque où le mot «amitié» avait encore un sens; that doesn't ~ a thing! ça ne veut (strictement) rien dire! || [requesting or giving clarification] : when he says early afternoon he really ~s around four quand il dit en début d'après-midi, il veut dire vers quatre heures; do you ~ it? tu es sérieux?; she always says what she ~s elle dit toujours ce qu'elle pense; I'll never speak to you again, I ~ it OR I ~ what I say je ne t'adresserai plus jamais la parole, je suis sérieux ❑ I ~ [that's to say] je veux dire; I was with Barry, I ~ Harry j'étais avec Barry, je veux dire Harry; why diet? I ~, you're not exactly fat pourquoi te mettre au régime? on ne peut pas dire que tu sois grosse; I ~ to say ce que je veux dire c'est... -**2.** [imply, entail – subj : event, change] signifier; this will ~ more unemployment ça veut dire OR signifie qu'il y aura une augmentation du chômage; going to see a film ~s driving into town pour voir un film, nous sommes obligés de prendre la voiture et d'aller en ville; does that ~ we shouldn't wait for him? est-ce que cela veut dire OR signifie que nous ne devrions pas l'attendre?; she's never known what it ~s to be loved elle n'a jamais su ce que c'est que d'être aimée. -**3.** [matter, be of value] compter; this watch ~s a lot to me je suis très attaché à cette montre; your friendship ~s a lot to her votre amitié compte beaucoup pour elle; you ~ everything to me tu es tout pour moi; he ~s nothing to me il n'est rien pour moi; I can't tell you what this ~s to me je ne peux pas te dire ce que ça représente pour moi; $20 ~s a lot to me 20 dollars, c'est une grosse somme OR c'est beaucoup d'argent pour moi. -**4.** [refer to] : do you ~ us? tu veux dire nous?; it was you she meant when she said that c'était à vous qu'elle pensait OR qu'elle faisait allusion quand elle a dit ça. -**5.** [intend] avoir l'intention de, vouloir, compter; we ~ to win nous avons (bien) l'intention de gagner, nous comptons (bien) gagner; I meant to tell you about it j'avais l'intention de t'en parler; I meant to phone you last night je voulais OR j'avais l'intention de vous téléphoner hier soir; I didn't ~ to hurt you je ne voulais pas te faire de mal; I only meant to help je voulais seulement me rendre utile; I didn't ~ it! [action] je ne l'ai pas fait exprès!; [words] je n'étais pas sérieux!; I meant it as a joke c'était une plaisanterie; that remark was meant for you cette remarque s'adressait à vous; the present was meant for your brother le cadeau était destiné à ton frère; they're meant for each other ils sont faits l'un pour l'autre; what's this switch meant to be for? à quoi est censé servir cet interrupteur?; it's meant to be a horse c'est censé représenter un cheval; perhaps I was meant to be a doctor peut-être que j'étais fait pour être médecin; it was meant to be c'était écrit; he ~s well il a de bonnes intentions; he meant well il croyait bien faire. -**6.** [consider, believe] : it's meant to be good for arthritis il paraît que c'est bon pour l'arthrite; this painting is meant to be by Rembrandt ce tableau est censé être un Rembrandt. -**7.** [suppose] : that box isn't meant to be in here cette boîte n'est pas censée être ici; you're meant to bow when she comes in tu dois faire la révérence quand elle entre.

meander [mɪ'ændəʳ] ◇ *vi* -**1.** [river] serpenter, faire des méandres. -**2.** [person] errer (sans but), se promener au hasard; we ~ed off into the night nous sommes partis sans but dans la nuit.
◇ *n* méandre *m*.

meanie *inf* ['mi:nɪ] *n* radin *m*, -e *f*, pingre *mf*; you old ~! *inf* vieux radin!

meaning ['mi:nɪŋ] ◇ *n* sens *m*, signification *f*; double ~ double sens; hidden ~ sens caché; I don't know the ~ of this word je ne connais pas le sens de ce mot, je ne sais pas ce que veut dire ce mot; love? you don't know the ~ of the word! aimer? mais tu ne sais pas ce que ça veut dire!; he doesn't know the ~ of hard work il ne sait pas ce que c'est que de travailler dur; they're just good friends, if you get my ~ ils sont seulement bons amis, si vous voyez ce que je veux dire; what's the ~ of this? [in anger] qu'est-ce que ça veut dire?; the ~ of life le sens de la vie; our success gives ~ to what we're doing notre réussite donne un sens à ce que nous faisons.
◇ *adj* [look, smile] significatif, éloquent.

meaningful ['mi:nɪŋfʊl] *adj* -**1.** [expressive – gesture] significatif, éloquent; she gave him a ~ look elle lui adressa un regard qui en disait long. -**2.** [comprehensible – explanation] compréhensible; nobody had ever explained it to me in such a ~ way personne ne me l'avait jamais expliqué de façon aussi claire OR compréhensible || [significant] significatif; the experiment produced no ~ results l'expérience n'a donné aucun résultat significatif. -**3.** [profound – experience, relationship] profond; I wouldn't say we had a very ~ relationship je ne qualifierais pas notre relation de profonde.

meaningfully ['mi:nɪŋfʊlɪ] *adv* de façon significative.

meaningless ['mi:nɪŋlɪs] *adj* -**1.** [devoid of sense] dénué de sens, sans signification; the lyrics of this song are completely ~ les paroles de cette chanson n'ont absolument aucun sens; ~ poems des poèmes dénués de sens OR qui ne veulent rien dire. -**2.** [futile] futile, vain; they lead very ~ lives ils mènent une vie très futile; a ~ task une tâche inutile; ~ violence de la violence gratuite.

meanness ['mi:nnɪs] *n* -**1.** [stinginess] avarice *f*. -**2.** *Am* [nastiness, spitefulness] méchanceté *f*, mesquinerie *f*. -**3.** *lit* [poverty] pauvreté *f*.

means [mi:nz] (*pl inv*) ◇ *n* -**1.** [way, method] moyen *m*; a ~ of doing sthg un moyen de faire qqch; is there no ~ of doing it any faster? n'y a-t-il pas moyen de le faire plus vite?; he has no ~ of support il est sans ressources; it's just a ~ to an end ce n'est qu'un moyen d'arriver au but; the end justifies the ~ *prov* la fin justifie les moyens; by ~ of a screwdriver à l'aide d'un tournevis; they communicate by ~ of signs ils communiquent par signes; by what ~ may I send it to him? par quel moyen OR quels moyens puis-je le lui faire parvenir?; by some ~ or other OR another d'une façon ou d'une autre ❑ ~ of transport moyen de transport; ~ of production moyens de production. -**2.** *phr*: may I leave? – by all ~! puis-je partir? – je vous en prie OR mais bien sûr!; by no (manner of) ~ pas du tout; it's by no ~ easy c'est loin d'être facile; she's not his friend by any (manner of) ~ elle est loin d'être son amie.
◇ *npl* [money, resources] moyens *mpl*, ressources *fpl*; to have the ~ to do sthg avoir les moyens de faire qqch; to live within one's ~ vivre selon ses moyens; to live beyond one's ~ vivre au-dessus de ses moyens; the ~ at our disposal les moyens dont nous disposons; her family obviously has ~ il est évident qu'elle vient d'une famille aisée.

means test *n* enquête *f* sur les revenus *(d'une personne désirant bénéficier d'une allocation d'État)*; to undergo a ~ faire l'objet d'une enquête sur les revenus; the grant is subject to a ~ cette allocation est assujettie à des conditions de ressources.
◆ **means-test** *vt*: is unemployment benefit means-tested? les allocations de chômage sont-elles attribuées en fonction des ressources OR des revenus du bénéficiaire?; all applicants are means-tested tous les candidats font l'objet d'une enquête sur leurs revenus.

meant [ment] *pt* & *pp* → **mean**.

meantime ['mi:n,taɪm] *adv* pendant ce temps; ~ things were changing pendant ce temps, les choses étaient en train de changer.
◆ **in the meantime** *adv phr* entre-temps; in the ~ I had got married entre-temps, je m'étais marié.
◆ **for the meantime** *adv phr* pour l'instant; for the ~, at least, the situation is resolved le problème est résolu, au moins pour l'instant.

meanwhile ['mi:n,waɪl] *adv* entre-temps, pendant ce temps; I, ~, was stuck in the lift pendant ce temps, moi, j'étais coincé dans l'ascenseur; ~, another 2,000 people have lost their jobs entre-temps OR en attendant, 2 000 personnes de plus ont perdu leur emploi.

meany ['mi:nɪ] (*pl* meanies) = **meanie**.

measles ['mi:zlz] *n* rougeole *f*; to have (the) ~ avoir la rougeole.

measly *inf* ['mi:zlɪ] (*compar* measlier, *superl* measliest) *adj* minable, misérable; all I got was one ~ bar of chocolate! je n'ai eu qu'une misérable tablette de chocolat!; all that for a ~ £5! tout ça pour cinq malheureuses livres!

measurable ['meʒərəbl] *adj* -**1.** [rate, change, amount] mesurable. -**2.** [noticeable, significant] sensible, perceptible; we've made ~ progress nous avons sensiblement progressé.

measurably ['meʒərəblɪ] *adv* [noticeably, significantly] sensiblement, notablement.

measure ['meʒəʳ] ◇ *n* -**1.** [measurement] mesure *f*; the metre is a ~ of length le mètre est une mesure de longueur; weights and ~s les poids *mpl* et mesures; linear/square/cubic ~ mesure de longueur/de superficie/de volume; to give good OR full ~ [in length, quantity] faire bonne mesure; [in weight] faire bon poids; to give short ~ [in quantity] tricher sur la quantité; [in weight] tricher sur le poids; for good ~ *fig* pendant qu'il/elle y est; then he painted the door, just for good ~ et puis, pendant qu'il y était, il a peint la porte; to take OR to get the ~ of sb *fig* jauger qqn, se faire une opinion de qqn; this award is a ~ of their success ce prix ne fait que refléter leur succès; her joy was beyond ~ sa joie était incommensurable ❑ 'Measure for Measure' *Shakespeare* 'Mesure pour mesure'. -**2.** [degree] mesure *f*; in some ~ dans une certaine mesure, jusqu'à un certain point; in large ~ dans une large mesure, en grande partie. -**3.** [device – ruler] mètre *m*, règle *f*; [– container] mesure *f*; a pint ~ une mesure d'une pinte. -**4.** [portion] portion *f*, dose *f*; she poured me a generous ~ of gin elle m'a servi une bonne dose de gin. -**5.** [step, legislation] mesure *f*; as a precautionary ~ par mesure de précaution; parliament must draft ~s to halt this trade le parlement doit élaborer des mesures pour mettre fin à ce trafic; we have taken ~s to correct the fault nous avons pris des mesures pour rectifier l'erreur. -**6.** MUS & LITERAT mesure *f*.
◇ *vt* -**1.** [take measurement of] mesurer; he ~d me for a suit il a pris mes mesures pour me faire un costume; a thermometer ~s temperature un thermomètre sert à mesurer la température ❑ to ~ one's length s'étaler de tout son long. -**2.** [judge] jauger, mesurer, évaluer; to ~ oneself OR one's strength against sb se mesurer à qqn.
◇ *vi* mesurer; the room ~s 18 feet by 12 la pièce mesure 18 pieds sur 12.
◆ **measure off** *vt sep* mesurer; he ~d off a metre of ribbon il mesura un mètre de ruban.
◆ **measure out** *vt sep* mesurer; ~ out a pound of flour mesurez une livre de farine; he ~d out a double gin il versa un double gin.

◆ **measure up** ◇ *vt sep* mesurer; to ~ sb up *fig* jauger qqn, prendre la mesure de qqn.
◇ *vi insep* être à la hauteur; to ~ up to sb's expectations répondre aux espérances de qqn; the hotel didn't ~ up (to our expectations) l'hôtel nous a déçus.

measured ['meʒəd] *adj* -**1.** [distance, length etc] mesuré; the record over a ~ mile le record officiel sur un mile. -**2.** [careful, deliberate] mesuré; a ~ speech un discours mesuré OR modéré; with ~ steps à pas mesurés.

measureless ['meʒəlɪs] *adj* infini, incommensurable.

measurement ['meʒəmənt] *n* -**1.** [dimension] mesure *f*; to take (down) the ~s of a piece of furniture prendre les dimensions d'un meuble; he took my ~s il a pris mes mesures; waist/hip ~ tour *m* de taille/de hanches. -**2.** [act] mesurage *m*.

measurement ton *n* tonne *f* d'encombrement.

measuring ['meʒərɪŋ] *n* mesurage *m*.

measuring jug *n* verre *m* gradué, doseur *m*.

measuring tape *n* mètre *m* à ruban.

measuring worm *n* (chenille *f*) arpenteuse *f*.

meat [miːt] *n* -**1.** viande *f*; red/white ~ viande rouge/blanche; cooked OR cold ~s viande froide. -**2.** *lit* [food] nourriture *f*. -**3.** [substance, core] substance *f*; there's not much ~ in his report il n'y a pas grand-chose dans son rapport.

meatball ['miːtbɔːl] *n* -**1.** CULIN boulette *f* (de viande). -**2.** ▽ *Am* [idiot] imbécile *mf*, andouille *f*.

meat-eater *n* carnivore *mf*; we aren't big ~s nous ne mangeons pas beaucoup de viande, nous ne sommes pas de gros mangeurs de viande.

meat-eating *adj* carnivore.

meathead▽ ['miːthed] *n Am* imbécile *mf*.

meat hook *n* crochet *m* de boucherie.

meat loaf (*pl* meat loaves) *n* pain *m* de viande.

meat pie *n* pâté *m* de viande en croûte.

meat safe *n* garde-manger *m inv*.

meatus [mɪ'eɪtəs] *n* ANAT conduit *m*, méat *m*.

meaty ['miːtɪ] (*compar* meatier, *superl* meatiest) *adj* -**1.** [taste] de viande; a good, ~ meal [full of meat] un bon repas riche en viande. -**2.** [rich in ideas] substantiel, étoffé; a ~ novel un roman substantiel.

mebbe▽, **mebby**▽ ['mebɪ] = **maybe**.

Mecca ['mekə] *pr n* la Mecque.
◆ **mecca** *n fig*: it's a ~ for book lovers c'est la Mecque des bibliophiles; the ~ of country music le haut lieu de la country.

mechanic [mɪ'kænɪk] *n* mécanicien *m*.

mechanical [mɪ'kænɪkl] *adj* -**1.** [device, process] mécanique; ~ shovel pelle *f* mécanique, pelleteuse *f*. -**2.** [machine-like] machinal, mécanique; a ~ gesture un geste machinal.

mechanical drawing *n* dessin *m* aux instruments.

mechanical engineer *n* ingénieur *m* mécanicien.

mechanical engineering *n* [study] mécanique *f*; [industry] construction *f* mécanique; the ~ industries les industries *fpl* mécaniques.

mechanically [mɪ'kænɪklɪ] *adv* mécaniquement; *fig* machinalement, mécaniquement; he answered ~ il a répondu machinalement.

mechanics [mɪ'kænɪks] ◇ *n (U)* [study] mécanique *f*.
◇ *npl* [functioning] mécanisme *m*; the ~ of government les mécanismes gouvernementaux, les rouages du gouvernement; I haven't got to grips yet with the ~ of the system je n'ai pas encore compris comment fonctionne le système.

mechanism ['mekənɪzm] *n* mécanisme *m*.

mechanistic [,mekə'nɪstɪk] *adj* mécaniste.

mechanization [,mekənaɪ'zeɪʃn] *n* mécanisation *f*.

mechanize, -ise ['mekənaɪz] *vt* -**1.** [equip with machinery] mécaniser; a highly ~d industry une industrie fortement mécanisée. -**2.** MIL [motorize] motoriser.

mechanotherapy [,mekənəʊ'θerəpɪ] *n* mécanothérapie *f*.

meconium [mɪ'kəʊnɪəm] *n* méconium *m*.

Med *inf* [med] *pr n Br*: the ~ la Méditerranée.

MEd [,em'ed] (*abbr of* Master of Education) *n (titulaire d'une) maîtrise en sciences de l'éducation*.

medal ['medl] *n* médaille *f*; gold ~ médaille d'or.

medalist *Am* = **medallist**.

medallion [mɪ'dæljən] *n* médaillon *m*.

medallist *Br*, **medalist** *Am* ['medəlɪst] *n* [winner of medal] médaillé *m*, -e *f*; the bronze ~ le détenteur de la médaille de bronze.

meddle ['medl] *vi* -**1.** [interfere]: to ~ in sthg se mêler de qqch; stop meddling in my affairs! cessez de vous mêler de mes affaires!; he can't resist the temptation to ~ il ne peut pas s'empêcher de se mêler de tout OR de ce qui ne le regarde pas; I do try not to ~ j'essaie vraiment de ne pas m'occuper des affaires des autres. -**2.** [tamper]: to ~ with sthg toucher à qqch, tripoter qqch; someone's been meddling with the carburettor quelqu'un a touché au carburateur.

meddler ['medlə^r] *n* -**1.** [busybody]: she's such a ~ il faut toujours qu'elle fourre son nez partout. -**2.** [tamperer] touche-à-tout *mf inv*.

meddlesome ['medlsəm] *adj* indiscret, qui se mêle de tout.

Medea [mɪ'dɪə] *pr n* Médée.

medevac ['medɪvæk] *n* MIL hélicoptère *m* sanitaire *(qui évacue les blessés)*.

media ['miːdjə] ◇ *npl* -**1.** *(often sg)*: the ~ les médias *mpl*; he works in the ~ il travaille dans les médias; the power of the ~ la puissance des médias; the news ~ la presse; he knows how to handle the ~ il sait s'y prendre avec les journalistes; the ~ follow OR follows her everywhere les journalistes la suivent partout. -**2.** → **medium**.
◇ *comp* des médias; ~ person homme *m* de communication, femme *f* de communication; it aroused a lot of ~ interest cela a suscité un grand intérêt médiatique; ~ coverage couverture *f* médiatique; it got little ~ coverage les médias en ont très peu parlé.

mediaeval *etc* [,medɪ'iːvl] = **medieval**.

media event *n* événement *m* médiatique.

medial ['miːdjəl] ◇ *adj* -**1.** [average] moyen. -**2.** [middle] médian. -**3.** LING médial, médian.
◇ *n* LING médiale *f*.

median ['miːdjən] ◇ *adj* médian; ~ line ligne *f* médiane.
◇ *n* -**1.** MATH médiane *f*. -**2.** *Am* AUT = **median strip**.

median strip *n Am* bande *f* médiane *(qui sépare les deux côtés d'une grande route)*.

mediant ['miːdɪənt] *n* médiante *f*.

mediate ['miːdɪeɪt] ◇ *vi* [act as a peacemaker] servir de médiateur; to ~ in a dispute servir de médiateur dans un conflit; to ~ between servir d'intermédiaire entre.
◇ *vt* -**1.** [agreement, peace] obtenir par médiation; [dispute] servir de médiateur dans, se faire le médiateur de; the United States ~d an agreement between the two countries les États-Unis ont servi de médiateur pour qu'un accord soit conclu entre les deux pays; to ~ an industrial dispute servir de médiateur dans un conflit social. -**2.** [moderate] modérer.

mediating ['miːdɪeɪtɪŋ] *adj* médiateur.

mediation [,miːdɪ'eɪʃn] *n* médiation *f*.

mediator ['miːdɪeɪtə^r] *n* médiateur *m*, -trice *f*.

medic *inf* ['medɪk] *n* -**1.** [doctor] toubib *m*. -**2.** *Br* [medical student] étudiant *m* en médecine.

medicable ['medɪkəbl] *adj* guérissable, curable.

Medicaid ['medɪkeɪd] *pr n Am* assistance *f* médicale.

medical ['medɪkl] ◇ *adj* médical; the ~ profession le corps médical; ~ board commission *f* médicale; MIL conseil *m* de révision; ~ student étudiant *m*, -e *f* en médecine ❑ ~ officer INDUST médecin *m* du travail; MIL médecin *m* militaire; Medical Officer of Health directeur *m*, -trice *f* de la santé publique; ~ practitioner (médecin *m*) généraliste *mf*; ~ school faculté *f* de médecine.
◇ *n* visite *f* médicale; to have a ~ passer une visite médicale; to pass/fail a ~ être déclaré apte/inapte à un travail après un bilan de santé.

medical certificate *n* certificat *m* médical.

medical examination *n* visite *f* médicale.

medically ['medɪklɪ] *adv* médicalement; ~ speaking d'un point de vue médical; ~ approved approuvé par les autorités médicales; to be ~ examined passer une visite médicale.

medicament [mɪ'dɪkəment] *n* médicament *m*.

Medicare ['medɪkeə^r] *pr n aux États-Unis, programme fédéral d'assistance médicale pour personnes âgées qui a largement contribué à réhabiliter socialement le 3ème âge*.

medicated ['medɪkeɪtɪd] *adj* traitant; ~ soap/shampoo savon *m*/shampooing *m* traitant.

medication [,medɪ'keɪʃn] *n* médication *f*; to be on ~ être sous médicaments.

medicinal [me'dɪsɪnl] *adj* médicinal.

medicine ['medsɪn] *n* -**1.** [art] médecine *f*; preventive ~ médecine préventive; to practise ~ exercer la médecine; he studies ~ il est étudiant en médecine; she studied ~ elle a fait des études de médecine. -**2.** [substance] médicament *m*, remède *m*; don't forget to take your ~ n'oublie pas de prendre tes médicaments ❑ to take one's ~ *Br* avaler la pilule; to give sb a dose OR taste of his/her own ~ rendre à qqn la monnaie de sa pièce.

medicine ball *n* medicine-ball *m*, médecine-ball *m*.

medicine cabinet, **medicine chest** *n* (armoire *f* à) pharmacie *f*.

medicine man *n* sorcier *m*, medicine-man *m*.

medico *inf* ['medɪkəʊ] (*pl* medicos) *Br* = **medic**.

medieval [,medɪ'iːvl] *adj* médiéval.

medievalism [,medɪ'iːvəlɪzm] *n* médiévisme *m*.

medievalist [,medɪ'iːvəlɪst] *n* médiéviste *mf*.

Medieval Latin *n* latin *m* médiéval.

medina [me'diːnə] *n* médina *f*.

mediocre [,miːdɪ'əʊkə^r] *adj* médiocre.

mediocrity [,miːdɪ'ɒkrətɪ] (*pl* mediocrities) *n* -**1.** [gen] médiocrité *f*. -**2.** [mediocre person] médiocre *mf*, incapable *mf*.

meditate ['medɪteɪt] *vi* -**1.** [practise meditation] méditer. -**2.** [reflect, ponder] réfléchir, songer; to ~ on OR upon sthg réfléchir OR songer à qqch.

meditation [,medɪ'teɪʃn] *n* méditation *f*, réflexion *f*; to spend one's days in prayer and ~ passer ses journées en prière et en méditation.

meditative ['medɪtətɪv] *adj* méditatif.

meditatively ['medɪtətɪvlɪ] *adv* d'un air méditatif OR songeur.

Mediterranean [,medɪtə'reɪnjən] ◇ *pr n*: the ~ (Sea) la (mer) Méditerranée.
◇ *n* Méditerranéen *m*, -enne *f*.
◇ *adj* méditerranéen.

medium ['miːdjəm] (*pl sense 1* media [-djə], *pl senses 2 and 3* media [-djə] OR mediums, *pl senses 4 and 5* mediums) ◇ *n* -**1.** [means of communication] moyen *m* (de communication); the decision was made public through the ~ of the press la décision fut rendue publique par voie de presse OR par l'intermédiaire des journaux; television is a powerful ~ in education la télévision est un très bon instrument éducatif; his favourite ~ is watercolour son moyen d'expression favori est l'aquarelle. -**2.** PHYS [means of transmission] véhicule *m*, milieu *m*; sound travels through the ~ of air les sons sont propagés OR véhiculés par l'air; a refractive ~ un milieu réfringent. -**3.** BIOL [environment] milieu *m*; in its natural ~ dans son milieu naturel. -**4.** [spiritualist] médium *m*. -**5.** [middle course] milieu *m*; the happy ~ le juste milieu.

◇ *adj* -**1.** [gen] moyen; in the ~ term à moyen terme; she's of ~ height elle est de taille moyenne; ~ brown châtain. -**2.** CULIN [meat] à point.

medium-dry *adj* [wine] demi-sec.

medium-range *adj*: ~ missile missile *m* à moyenne portée.

medium-rare *adj* CULIN [meat] entre saignant et à point.

medium-sized *adj* moyen, de taille moyenne.

medium-term *adj* à moyen terme.

medium wave *n (U)* RADIO ondes *fpl* moyennes; on ~ sur (les) ondes moyennes.

◆ **medium-wave** *adj* [broadcast] sur ondes moyennes; [station, transmitter] émettant sur ondes moyennes.

medlar ['medlə^r] *n* [fruit] nèfle *f*; [tree] néflier *m*.

medley ['medlɪ] *n* -**1.** [mixture] mélange *m*. -**2.** MUS pot-pourri *m*. -**3.** [in swimming] quatre nages *m inv*.

medulla [mɪ'dʌlə] *n* -**1.** ANAT [part of organ, structure] moelle *f*; [part of brain] bulbe *m* rachidien. -**2.** BOT moelle *f*.

Medusa [mɪ'dju:zə] *pr n* Méduse.

meek [mi:k] *adj* doux, docile; ~ and mild doux comme un agneau.

meekly ['mi:klɪ] *adv* doucement, docilement.

meekness ['mi:knɪs] *n* douceur *f*, docilité *f*.

meerschaum ['mɪəʃəm] *n* -**1.** [pipe] pipe *f* en écume. -**2.** [mineral] écume *f* de mer, magnésite *f*.

meet [mi:t] (*pt* & *pp* met [met]) ◇ *vt* -**1.** [by chance] rencontrer; guess who I met this morning devine qui j'ai rencontré ce matin; to ~ sb on the stairs croiser qqn dans l'escalier; fancy ~ing you here! je ne m'attendais pas à vous trouver ici! || [by arrangement] rejoindre, retrouver; I'll ~ you on the platform in 20 minutes je te retrouve sur le quai dans 20 minutes; I'll ~ you after work je te retrouverai après le travail; I'm ~ing Gregory this afternoon j'ai rendez-vous avec Gregory cet après-midi; the train ~s the ferry at Dover le train assure la correspondance avec le ferry à Douvres. -**2.** [wait for, collect] attendre, aller OR venir chercher; nobody was at the station to ~ me personne ne m'attendait à la gare; I'll be there to ~ the bus je serai là à l'arrivée du car; he'll ~ us at the station il viendra nous chercher à la gare; I'll send a car to ~ you j'enverrai une voiture vous chercher OR vous prendre. -**3.** [greet]: she came to ~ us elle est venue à notre rencontre. -**4.** [make acquaintance of] rencontrer, faire la connaissance de; I met him last year je l'ai rencontré OR j'ai fait sa connaissance l'année dernière; I'd like you to ~ Mr Jones j'aimerais vous présenter M. Jones; ~ Mrs Dickens je vous présente Mme Dickens; (I'm very) glad OR pleased to ~ you enchanté (de faire votre connaissance); nice to have met you enchanté d'avoir fait votre connaissance. -**5.** [satisfy] satisfaire, répondre à; we couldn't ~ their needs nous n'avons pu répondre à leurs besoins; supply isn't ~ing demand l'offre est inférieure à la demande; to ~ sb halfway *fig* trouver un compromis avec qqn; they decided to ~ each other halfway ils décidèrent de couper la poire en deux || [settle] régler; I couldn't ~ the payments je n'ai pas pu régler OR payer les échéances. -**6.** [face] rencontrer, affronter; he ~s the champion on Saturday il rencontre le champion samedi; to ~ an obstacle se heurter à OR rencontrer un obstacle; to ~ the enemy affronter l'ennemi; how are we going to ~ the challenge? comment allons-nous relever le défi?; to ~ one's death trouver la mort. -**7.** [come in contact with] rencontrer; it's the first case of this sort I've met c'est la première fois que je vois un cas semblable; his hand met hers leurs mains se rencontrèrent; my eyes met his nos regards se croisèrent OR se rencontrèrent; he couldn't ~ her eye il ne pouvait pas la regarder dans les yeux ❑ there's more to OR in this than ~s the eye cette affaire nous réserve encore bien des surprises; there's more to her than ~s the eye elle gagne à être connue. -**8.** [treat] accueillir; his suggestion was met with howls of laughter sa proposition a été accueillie par des éclats de rire; we shall ~ violence with violence à la violence, nous répondrons par la violence.

◇ *vi* -**1.** [by chance] se rencontrer; we met on the stairs nous nous sommes croisés dans l'escalier || [by arrangement] se retrouver, se rejoindre, se donner rendez-vous; shall we ~ at the station? on se donne rendez-vous OR on se retrouve à la gare?; we arranged to ~ at the station nous nous sommes donné rendez-vous à la gare; they weren't to ~ again for a long time ils ne devaient pas se revoir avant longtemps; until we ~ again! à la prochaine!; I think they ~ every day je crois qu'ils se voient tous les jours. -**2.** [become acquainted] se rencontrer, faire connaissance; we first met in 1989 nous nous sommes rencontrés pour la première fois en 1989; have you two met? est-ce que vous vous connaissez déjà?, vous vous êtes déjà rencontrés? -**3.** [assemble] se réunir; the delegates will ~ in the conference room les délégués se réuniront dans la salle de conférence; the committee ~s once a month le comité se réunit une fois par mois. -**4.** [join - lines, wires] se rencontrer, se joindre; the cross stands where four roads ~ la croix se trouve à la jonction de quatre routes; their eyes met leurs regards se rencontrèrent OR se croisèrent. -**5.** [teams, opponents] se rencontrer, s'affronter; [armies] s'affronter, se heurter.

◇ *n* -**1.** *Br* [in hunting] rendez-vous *m* (de chasse). -**2.** *Am* SPORT rencontre *f*; athletics ~ rencontre *f* OR meeting *m* d'athlétisme.

◇ *adj arch* OR *fml* [suitable] séant, convenable; [right] juste; it is only ~ that they should be the ones to leave ce n'est que justice que ce soient eux qui partent.

◆ **meet up** *vi insep* [by chance] se rencontrer; [by arrangement] se retrouver, se donner rendez-vous; we met up with them in Paris nous les avons retrouvés à Paris.

◆ **meet with** *vt insep* -**1.** [encounter] rencontrer; they met with considerable difficulties ils ont rencontré d'énormes difficultés; the agreement met with general approval l'accord a reçu l'approbation générale; to ~ with a refusal se heurter à OR essuyer un refus; the play met with great success on Broadway la pièce a eu beaucoup de succès à Broadway; I'm afraid your dog has met with an accident j'ai bien peur que votre chien n'ait eu un (petit) accident. -**2.** *Am* = **meet** *vt* **1, 2**.

meeting ['mi:tɪŋ] *n* -**1.** [assembly] réunion *f*; POL assemblée *f*, meeting *m*; *Br* SPORT rencontre *f*, meeting *m*; to hold a ~ tenir une réunion; to call a ~ of the committee/the workforce convoquer les membres du comité/le personnel; the ~ voted in favour of the measure l'assemblée a voté la proposition; the (general) ~ of shareholders l'assemblée (générale) des actionnaires ❑ athletics ~ rencontre *f* OR meeting *m* d'athlétisme; committee ~ réunion du comité. -**2.** [encounter] rencontre *f*; a chance ~ in the street une rencontre fortuite dans la rue. -**3.** [arranged] rendez-vous *m*; I have a ~ with the boss this morning j'ai rendez-vous avec le patron ce matin; the Governor had a ~ with Church dignitaries le Gouverneur s'est entretenu avec OR a rencontré les dignitaires de l'Église. -**4.** [junction - of roads] jonction *f*, rencontre *f*; [- of rivers] confluent *m*. -**5.** RELIG [Quakers'] culte *m*; to go to ~ aller au culte.

meetinghouse ['mi:tɪŋhaʊs, *pl* -haʊzɪz] *n* RELIG temple *m*.

meeting place *n* [for gatherings] lieu *m* de réunion; [for rendez-vous] (lieu *m* de) rendez-vous *m*.

megabuck *inf* ['megəbʌk] *n Am* million *m* de dollars; we're talking ~s c'est de millions de dollars qu'il s'agit là, ce sont des millions de dollars qui sont en jeu.

megabyte ['megəbaɪt] *n* mégaoctet *m*.

megacycle ['megə,saɪkl] *n* mégacycle *m*.

megadeath ['megədeθ] *n* million *m* de morts; weapons capable of causing 100 ~s des armes capables de faire des centaines de millions de morts.

megadose *inf* ['megədəʊs] *n* superdose *f*.

megahertz ['megəhɜ:ts] (*pl inv*) *n* mégahertz *m*.

megalith ['megəlɪθ] *n* mégalithe *m*.

megalithic [,megə'lɪθɪk] *adj* mégalithique.

megalomania [,megələ'meɪnjə] *n* mégalomanie *f*.

megalomaniac [,megələ'meɪnɪæk] ◇ *adj* mégalomane.

◇ *n* mégalomane *mf*.

megalopolis [,megə'lɒpəlɪs] *n* mégapole *f*, mégalopole *f*.

megaphone ['megəfəʊn] *n* porte-voix *m inv*, mégaphone *m*.

megascopic [,megə'skɒpɪk] *adj* macroscopique.

megastar *inf* ['megəstɑ:^{r}] *n* superstar *f*.

megaton ['megətʌn] *n* mégatonne *f*; a 5 ~ bomb une bombe de 5 mégatonnes.

megawatt ['megəwɒt] *n* mégawatt *m*.

meiosis [maɪ'əʊsɪs] (*pl* **meioses** [-si:z] *n* -**1.** BIOL méiose *f*. -**2.** [in rhetoric] litote *f*.

meiotic [maɪ'ɒtɪk] *adj* BIOL méiotique.

Mekong [,mi:'kɒŋ] *pr n*: the ~ le Mékong.

melamine ['meləmi:n] *n* mélamine *f*.

melancholia [,melən'kəʊljə] *n* mélancolie PSYCH.

melancholic [,melən'kɒlɪk] ◇ *adj* mélancolique.

◇ *n* mélancolique *mf*.

melancholy ['melənkəlɪ] ◇ *n lit* mélancolie *f*.

◇ *adj* [person, mood] mélancolique; [news, sight, thought] sombre, triste.

Melanesia [,melə'ni:zjə] *pr n* Mélanésie *f*; in ~ en Mélanésie.

Melanesian [,melə'ni:zjən] ◇ *n* -**1.** [person] Mélanésien *m*, -enne *f*. -**2.** LING mélanésien *m*.

◇ *adj* mélanésien.

melanin ['melənɪn] *n* mélanine *f*.

melanism ['melənɪzm] *n* mélanisme *m*.

melanocyte ['melənəʊsaɪt] *n* mélanocyte *m*.

melanoma [,melə'nəʊmə] *n* mélanome *m*.

Melba ['melbə] *adj* CULIN Melba *(inv)*.

Melba toast *n tartine de pain grillé très fine*.

Melbourne ['melbən] *pr n* Melbourne.

Melchior ['melkɪ,ɔ:^{r}] *pr n* Melchior.

meld [meld] ◇ *n* CARDS pose *f*.

◇ *vi* poser ses cartes.

◇ *vt Am* [merge] fusionner, amalgamer.

melee, mêlée ['meleɪ] *n* mêlée *f*.

mellifluous [me'lɪfluəs], **mellifluent** [me'lɪfluənt] *adj lit* mélodieux, doux.

mellophone ['meləʊfəʊn] *n* cor *m* d'harmonie.

mellow ['meləʊ] ◇ *adj* -**1.** [fruit] mûr; [wine] velouté. -**2.** [bricks] patiné; [light] doux, tamisé; [colour] doux; [voice, music] doux, mélodieux. -**3.** [person, mood] serein, tranquille; to become OR to grow ~ s'adoucir; [with age] mûrir; ~ thoughts des pensées langoureuses. -**4.** *inf Am* [relaxed] cool, relax, relaxe. -**5.** *inf* [tipsy] éméché, gai.

◇ *vt* [subj: age, experience] adoucir, faire mûrir [subj: food, alcohol] détendre, décontracter.

◇ *vi* -**1.** [fruit] mûrir; [wine] devenir moelleux, se velouter. -**2.** [light, colour] s'adoucir; [stone, brick, building] se patiner; [sound, music] s'adoucir, devenir plus mélodieux; her voice has ~ed sa voix s'est adoucie. -**3.** [person - with age] mûrir, s'adoucir; I've ~ed a lot since those days j'ai mûri depuis cette époque || [with food, alcohol] se décontracter; after the second whisky he began to ~ après le deuxième whisky, il a commencé à se décontracter.

mellowing ['meləʊɪŋ] ◇ *n* -**1.** [of fruit, wine] maturation *f*. -**2.** [of person, mood, light] adoucissement *m*; [of stone] patine *f*.

◇ *adj* adoucissant; the alcohol had a ~ effect on them l'alcool les a détendus.

mellowness ['meləʊnɪs] *n* -**1.** [of fruit] douceur *f*; [of wine] moelleux *m*, velouté *m*. -**2.** [of light, colour] douceur *f*; [of voice, music] douceur *f*, mélodie *f*. -**3.** [of person, mood] douceur *f*, sérénité *f*.

melodic [mɪ'lɒdɪk] *adj* mélodique.

melodically [mɪ'lɒdɪklɪ] *adv* mélodiquement.

melodious [mɪ'ləʊdjəs] *adj* mélodieux.

melodiously [mɪ'ləʊdjəslɪ] *adv* mélodieusement.

melodrama ['melədrɑːmə] *n* mélodrame *m*.

melodramatic [,melədrə'mætɪk] *adj* mélodramatique.

melodramatically [,melədrə'mætɪklɪ] *adv* de façon mélodramatique; he spoke ~ of leaving her d'un air mélodramatique, il parla de la quitter.

melody ['melədɪ] (*pl* melodies) *n* mélodie *f*.

Melody Maker *pr n hebdomadaire britannique consacré à la musique pop*.

melon ['melən] *n* melon *m*.

melt [melt] ◇ *vi* -**1.** [become liquid] fondre; that chocolate ~s in your mouth ce chocolat fond dans la bouche; his heart ~ed ça l'a attendri. -**2.** [disappear]: to ~ (away) disparaître, s'évaporer; her anger ~ed away sa colère s'est évanouie; the crowd ~ed (away) la foule s'est dispersée; all my problems seemed to ~ away tous mes problèmes semblaient s'évanouir. -**3.** [blend] se fondre; he tried to ~ into the crowd il a essayé de se fondre OR de disparaître dans la foule; the green ~s into the blue le vert se fond dans le bleu OR se confond avec le bleu; the images ~ ed into one another les images se fondaient les unes dans les autres.

◇ *vt* [gen] (faire) fondre; [metal] fondre; the sun will ~ the ice le soleil fera fondre la glace; ~ the butter in a pan faire fondre le beurre dans une poêle; to ~ sb's heart attendrir (le cœur de) qqn.

◆ **melt down** *vt sep* & *vi insep* fondre.

meltdown ['meltdaʊn] *n* NUCL fusion *f* (du cœur).

melting ['meltɪŋ] ◇ *adj* -**1.** *literal* fondant; ~ ice/snow de la glace/neige qui fond. -**2.** *fig* attendrissant; she gave him a ~ look elle lui a lancé un regard attendrissant.

◇ *n* [of ice, snow] fonte *f*; [of metal] fusion *f*, fonte *f*.

melting point *n* point *m* de fusion.

melting pot *n* creuset *m*; a ~ of several cultures *fig* un mélange de plusieurs cultures; the American ~ *fig* le melting-pot américain.

member ['membəʳ] ◇ *n* -**1.** [of club, union, political party etc] membre *m*, adhérent *m*, -e *f*; to become a ~ of a club/society devenir membre d'un club/d'une association; he became a ~ of the party in 1985 il a adhéré au parti en 1985. -**2.** [of group, family, class] membre *m*; you're practically a ~ of the family now tu fais presque partie de la famille maintenant; it's a ~ of the cat family il fait partie de OR il appartient à la famille des félins; a ~ of the opposite sex un représentant du sexe opposé; he invited a ~ of the audience up on stage il a fait venir un spectateur sur scène; a ~ of the public un membre du public. -**3.** ANAT, ARCHIT & MATH membre *m*; (male) ~ ANAT membre (viril).

◇ *comp*: ~ country/state pays *m*/État *m* membre.

◆ **Member** *n* [of legislative body]: Member of Parliament membre *m* de la Chambre des communes, ≃ député *m*; the Member (of Parliament) for Leicester le député de Leicester; Member of Congress membre *m* du Congrès.

membership ['membəʃɪp] *n* -**1.** [condition] adhésion *f*; ~ of the union will entitle you to vote in meetings l'adhésion au syndicat vous donne le droit de voter lors des réunions; his country's ~ of UNESCO is in question l'adhésion de son pays à l'UNESCO est remise en question; to apply for ~ faire une demande d'adhésion; they have applied for ~ to the EC ils ont demandé à entrer dans OR à faire partie de la CEE; to take up party ~ prendre sa carte du OR adhérer au parti; it's hard to get ~ of the golf club il est difficile de devenir membre du club de golf ❑ ~ card carte *f* d'adhérent OR de membre; ~ fee cotisation *f*. -**2.** [body of members]: our club has a large ~ notre club compte de nombreux adhérents OR membres; ~ increased last year le nombre d'adhérents a augmenté l'année dernière; the rank and file ~ of the party la base militante du parti; we have a ~ of under 20 nous avons moins de 20 adhérents.

membrane ['membreɪn] *n* membrane *f*.

membranous ['membrənəs] *adj* membraneux.

memento [mɪ'mentəʊ] (*pl* mementos OR mementoes) *n* souvenir *m*; a ~ of our visit un souvenir de notre visite.

memo ['meməʊ] (*pl* memos) *n* note *f*.

memoir ['memwɑːʳ] *n* -**1.** [biography] biographie *f*. -**2.** [essay, monograph] mémoire *m*.

◆ **memoirs** *npl* [autobiography] mémoires *mpl*.

memoirist ['memwɑːrɪst] *n* mémorialiste *mf*.

memo pad *n* bloc-notes *m*.

memorabilia [,memərə'bɪlɪə] *npl* souvenirs *mpl*.

memorable ['memərəbl] *adj* mémorable, inoubliable.

memorably ['memərəblɪ] *adv*: a ~ hot summer un été torride dont on se souvient encore.

memorandum [,memə'rændəm] (*pl* memoranda [-də]) *n* -**1.** COMM note *f*; I've received a ~ from head office j'ai reçu une note (de service) du siège. -**2.** JUR sommaire *m*. -**3.** [diplomatic communication] mémorandum *m*.

memorial [mɪ'mɔːrɪəl] ◇ *n* -**1.** [monument] monument *m* (commémoratif), mémorial *m*; war ~ monument aux morts. -**2.** [diplomatic memorandum] mémorandum *m*; [petition] pétition *f*; [official request] requête *f*, mémoire *m*.

◇ *adj* -**1.** [commemorative] commémoratif; the Marcel Proust ~ prize le prix Marcel Proust; ~ service commémoration *f*. -**2.** [of memory] mémoriel.

Memorial Day *n Am dernier lundi du mois de mai (férié aux États-Unis en l'honneur des soldats américains morts pour la patrie)*.

memorize, -ise ['meməraɪz] *vt* mémoriser.

memory ['memərɪ] (*pl* memories) *n* -**1.** [capacity to remember] mémoire *f*; to have a good/bad ~ avoir (une) bonne/mauvaise mémoire; to have a short ~ avoir la mémoire courte; I've got a very good/bad ~ for names j'ai/je n'ai pas une très bonne mémoire des noms; to quote a figure from ~ citer un chiffre de mémoire OR de tête; to lose one's ~ perdre la mémoire; it will long remain in our memories nous nous en souviendrons longtemps; if (my) ~ serves me well OR right, to the best of my ~ si j'ai bonne mémoire, autant que je m'en souvienne; I've a ~ like a sieve je n'ai aucune mémoire; within living ~ de mémoire d'homme. -**2.** [recollection] souvenir *m*; childhood memories des souvenirs d'enfance; to have good/bad memories of sthg garder un bon/mauvais souvenir de qqch; I have very bad memories of that evening j'ai de très mauvais souvenirs OR j'ai (gardé) un très mauvais souvenir de cette soirée; to have no ~ of sthg/sb n'avoir aucun souvenir de qqch/qqn; to the ~ of à la mémoire de; to keep the ~ alive OR green garder vivant OR entretenir le souvenir (de); I cherish his ~ je chéris sa mémoire OR son souvenir ❑ to take a trip down ~ lane se rappeler, se souvenir. -**3.** COMPUT mémoire *f*; how much ~ does this computer have? cet ordinateur a combien de mémoire?; data is stored in the ~ les données sont (entrées) en mémoire.

◆ **in memory of** *prep phr* en souvenir de.

memory bank *n* bloc *m* de mémoire.

memory card *n* COMPUT carte *f* d'extension mémoire.

memory span *n* empan *m* mnémonique.

memory trace *n* trace *f* mnésique.

Memphis ['memfɪs] *pr n* Memphis.

memsahib ['mem,sɑːhɪb] *n dated* [in colonial India] Européenne *f*; [form of address] Madame *f*.

men [men] *pl* → **man**.

menace ['menəs] ◇ *n* -**1.** [source of danger] danger *m*; these steps are a real ~ at night ces escaliers sont vraiment dangereux la nuit; some drivers are a public ~ certains conducteurs constituent un véritable danger public OR sont de véritables dangers publics. -**2.** [threat] menace *f*; the new weapon is a ~ to world peace cette nouvelle arme constitue une menace pour la paix mondiale. -**3.** *inf* [annoying person or thing] plaie *f*.

◇ *vt* menacer.

menacing ['menəsɪŋ] *adj* menaçant.

menacingly ['menəsɪŋlɪ] *adv* [speak, act] de manière menaçante; [look] d'un air menaçant.

menagerie [mɪ'nædʒərɪ] *n* ménagerie *f*.

Mencap ['menkæp] *pr n association britannique pour les enfants et les adultes handicapés mentaux*.

mend [mend] ◇ *vt* -**1.** [repair - machine, television, broken vase] réparer; [- clothes] raccommoder; [- hem] recoudre; [darn - socks] repriser, ravauder; to get sthg ~ed faire réparer qqch. -**2.** [rectify] rectifier, réparer; to ~ matters arranger les choses; to ~ one's ways s'amender.

◇ *vi* [improve - patient] se remettre, être en voie de guérison; [- weather] s'améliorer.

◇ *n* -**1.** [darn] reprise *f*; [patch] pièce *f*. -**2.** *phr*: to be on the ~ *inf* s'améliorer; [patient] se remettre, être en voie de guérison.

mendacious [men'deɪʃəs] *adj fml* [statement, remark] mensonger, fallacieux; [person] menteur.

mendacity [men'dæsətɪ] (*pl* mendacities) *n fml (U)* mensonge *m*, mensonges *mpl*.

mendelevium [,mendɪ'liːvɪəm] *n* mendélévium *m*.

Mendelian [men'diːljən] *adj* mendélien.

Mendelianism [men'diːljənɪzm], **Mendelism** ['mendəlɪzm] *n* mendélisme *m*.

mendicant ['mendɪkənt] ◇ *n* mendiant *m*, -e *f*.

◇ *adj* mendiant; ~ order RELIG ordre *m* mendiant.

mendicity [men'dɪsətɪ] *n* mendicité *f*.

mending ['mendɪŋ] *n* raccommodage *m*; I've got a whole pile of ~ to do j'ai toute une pile de raccommodage (à faire).

Menelaus [,menɪ'leɪəs] *pr n* Ménélas.

menfolk ['menfəʊk] *npl* hommes *mpl*; all the ~ of the village tous les hommes du village.

menhir ['men,hɪəʳ] *n* menhir *m*.

menial ['miːnjəl] ◇ *adj*: ~ tasks tâches *fpl* ingrates OR sans intérêt; I find the work a bit ~ je trouve le travail un peu ingrat.

◇ *n* [subordinate] subalterne *mf*; [servant] domestique *mf*, laquais *m pej*.

meningitis [,menɪn'dʒaɪtɪs] *n* méningite *f*.

meniscus [mə'nɪskəs] (*pl* meniscuses OR menisci [-'nɪsaɪ]) *n* ménisque *m*.

menology [mɪ'nɒlədʒɪ] (*pl* menologies) *n* ménologe *m*.

menopausal [,menə'pɔːzl] *adj* ménopausique.

menopause ['menəpɔːz] *n* ménopause *f*; the male ~ l'andropause *f*.

Mensa ['mensə] *pr n association de personnes ayant un QI particulièrement élevé*.

mensch▽ [menʃ] *n Am* chic type *m*.

menses ['mensiːz] *npl* menstrues *fpl*, règles *fpl*.

Menshevik ['menʃəvɪk] ◇ *adj* menchévik.

◇ *n* menchévik *mf*.

Menshevism ['menʃəvɪzm] *n* menchévisme *m*.

Menshevist ['menʃəvɪst] ◇ *adj* menchéviste.

◇ *n* menchéviste *mf*.

men's room *n Am* toilettes *fpl (pour hommes)*.
menstrual ['menstrʊəl] *adj* menstruel; ~ cycle cycle *m* menstruel.
menstruate ['menstrʊeɪt] *vi* avoir ses règles.
menstruation [ˌmenstrʊ'eɪʃn] *n* menstruation *f*, règles *fpl*.
mensurable ['menʃərəbl] *adj* mesurable.
mensuration [ˌmenʃə'reɪʃn] *n* mesurage *m*, mensuration *f*.
menswear ['menzweəʳ] *n (U)* vêtements *mpl* pour hommes.
mental ['mentl] *adj* -**1.** [intellectual] mental; ~ **faculties** facultés *fpl* mentales OR intellectuelles; **he has a ~ age of seven** il a un âge mental de sept ans. -**2.** [in the mind] mental; **to make a ~ note of sthg** prendre note de qqch; **she made a ~ note to speak to him about the matter** elle se promit de lui en parler ❑ ~ **arithmetic** calcul *m* mental. -**3.** [psychiatric] mental; **it can cause great ~ strain** cela peut provoquer une grande tension nerveuse; **he had a ~ breakdown** il a fait une dépression nerveuse ❑ **to suffer from ~ handicap** être handicapé mental; ~ **health** santé *f* mentale; ~ **illness** maladie *f* mentale; ~ **nurse** infirmier *m*, -ère *f* psychiatrique; ~ **patient** malade *m* mental, malade *f* mentale; ~ **ward** service *m* psychiatrique. -**4.** ▽ [crazy] malade, timbré.
mental cruelty *n* cruauté *f* mentale.
mental home, **mental hospital** *n* hôpital *m* psychiatrique.
mentalism ['mentəlɪzm] *n* mentalisme *m* PHILOS.
mentality [men'tæləti] (*pl* **mentalities**) *n* mentalité *f*; **a civil servant ~** une mentalité de fonctionnaire.
mentally ['mentəlɪ] *adv* mentalement; **she's ~ and physically exhausted** elle est épuisée mentalement et physiquement; **the ~ disabled** OR **handicapped** les handicapés mentaux; ~ **ill** malade *(mentalement)*; ~ **defective** (mentalement) déficient; ~ **disturbed** déséquilibré (mental); ~ **retarded** (mentalement) arriéré.
menthol ['menθɒl] *n* menthol *m*; ~ **cigarette** cigarette *f* au menthol OR mentholée.
mentholated ['menθəleɪtɪd] *adj* au menthol, mentholé.
mention ['menʃn] ◇ *vt* [talk about] mentionner, faire mention de, parler de; **he didn't ~ his divorce** il n'a pas parlé de son divorce; **the newspapers didn't ~ it** les journaux n'en ont pas fait mention OR n'en ont pas parlé; **she never ~s her past** elle ne parle jamais de son passé; **how dare you ~ such a thing!** comment osez-vous parler d'une chose pareille!; **I shall never ~ it again** je n'en parlerai jamais plus; **I'll ~ it to him sometime** je lui en toucherai un mot à l'occasion; **thank you very much – don't ~ it!** merci beaucoup – il n'y a pas de quoi! OR je vous en prie!; **it's not worth ~ing** ça ne vaut pas la peine d'en parler ‖ [remark, point out] signaler; **I should ~ that it was dark at the time** il faut signaler OR je tiens à faire remarquer qu'il faisait nuit; **she did ~ a couple of good restaurants to me** elle m'a bien donné l'adresse de OR elle m'a bien signalé quelques bons restaurants ‖ [name, cite] mentionner, citer, nommer; **don't ~ any names** ne citez aucun nom; **someone, without ~ing any names, has broken my hairdryer** je ne citerai personne, mais quelqu'un a cassé mon séchoir à cheveux; **just ~ my name to her** dites-lui que c'est de ma part; **to ~ sb in one's will** coucher qqn sur son testament; **to be ~ed in dispatches** MIL être cité à l'ordre du jour.
◇ *n* mention *f*; **there's no ~ of it in the papers** les journaux n'en parlent pas; **it got a ~ in the local paper** le journal local en a parlé OR y a fait allusion; **special ~ should be made of all the people behind the scenes** n'oublions pas tous ceux qui ont travaillé dans l'ombre OR en coulisse ❑ **honourable ~** mention.
◆ **not to mention** *prep phr* sans parler de; **not to ~ the children** sans parler des enfants.
mentor ['mentɔːʳ] *n* mentor *m*.
◆ **Mentor** *pr n* Mentor.
menu ['menjuː] *n* -**1.** [in restaurant] menu *m*, carte *f*; **what's on the ~ tonight?** qu'est-ce qu'il y a au menu ce soir?; **they have a very varied ~** ils ont une carte très variée. -**2.** COMPUT menu *m*.
menu-driven *adj* COMPUT piloté par menus.
meow [miː'aʊ] = **miaow**.
MEP (*abbr of* Member of the European Parliament) *n* député *m* à l'Assemblée européenne, membre *m* du Parlement européen.
mephistophelean, **mephistophelian** [ˌmefɪstə'fiːljən] *adj* méphistophélique.
Mephistopheles [ˌmefɪ'stɒfɪliːz] *pr n* Méphistophélès.
meprobamate [mə'prəʊbəmeɪt] *n* méprobamate *m*.
mercantile ['mɜːkəntaɪl] *adj* -**1.** COMM: ~ **agreement** accord *m* commercial; ~ **company** société *f* commerciale; ~ **law** droit *m* commercial; ~ **nation** nation *f* commerçante; **the ~ system** le système marchand. -**2.** ECON [concerning mercantilism] mercantiliste.
mercantilism ['mɜːkəntɪlɪzm] *n* mercantilisme *m*.
mercantilist ['mɜːkəntɪlɪst] ◇ *adj* mercantiliste.
◇ *n* mercantiliste *mf*.
Mercator's projection [mɜː'keɪtɔːz-] *n* projection *f* de Mercator.
mercenarily ['mɜːsɪnərɪlɪ] *adv* de manière intéressée.
mercenary ['mɜːsɪnrɪ] (*pl* **mercenaries**) ◇ *n* mercenaire *m*.
◇ *adj* -**1.** *pej* intéressé. -**2.** MIL mercenaire.
mercer ['mɜːsəʳ] *n Br dated* négociant *m*, -e *f* en tissus.
mercerize, **-ise** ['mɜːsəraɪz] *vt* merceriser.
merchandise ['mɜːtʃəndaɪz] ◇ *n (U)* marchandises *fpl*.
◇ *vt* commercialiser.
merchandising ['mɜːtʃəndaɪzɪŋ] *n* merchandising *m*, marchandisage *m*.
merchant ['mɜːtʃənt] ◇ *n* -**1.** [trader] négociant *m*, -e *f*; [shopkeeper] marchand *m*, -e *f*; **wool ~** lainier *m*, négociant en laines; **wine ~** marchand de vin; **'The Merchant of Venice'** *Shakespeare* 'le Marchand de Venise'. -**2.** *fig*: ~ **of death** marchand de mort; **a doom ~** un prophète de malheur.
◇ *adj* marchand.
merchant bank *n* banque *f* d'affaires.
merchant banker *n* banquier *m* d'affaires.
merchantman ['mɜːtʃəntmən] (*pl* **merchantmen** [-mən]) = **merchant ship**.
merchant marine *n Am* marine *f* marchande.
merchant navy *n Br* marine *f* marchande.
merchant seaman *n* marin *m* de la marine marchande.
merchant ship *n* navire *m* de commerce.
merciful ['mɜːsɪfʊl] *adj* clément, miséricordieux; **to be ~ to** OR **towards sb** faire preuve de clémence OR de miséricorde envers qqn; **a ~ act** un geste charitable; **her death was a ~ release** sa mort a été une délivrance.
mercifully ['mɜːsɪfʊlɪ] *adv* -**1.** [luckily] heureusement, par bonheur; ~, **nobody was hurt** par bonheur il n'y a pas eu de blessés. -**2.** [with clemency] avec clémence; **he acted ~** il a fait preuve de clémence OR de miséricorde.
merciless ['mɜːsɪlɪs] *adj* impitoyable, implacable.
mercilessly ['mɜːsɪlɪslɪ] *adv* sans merci, impitoyablement, implacablement.
mercurial [mɜː'kjʊərɪəl] *adj* -**1.** [changeable] versatile, d'humeur inégale, changeant. -**2.** [lively] vif, plein de vie, gai. -**3.** CHEM mercuriel.
mercury ['mɜːkjʊrɪ] *n* -**1.** CHEM mercure *m*. -**2.** BOT mercuriale *f*.
◆ **Mercury** *pr n* ASTRON & MYTH Mercure.
Mercury program *n*: **the ~** *le programme spatial américain Mercury (1961-1963)*.
mercy ['mɜːsɪ] (*pl* **mercies**) ◇ *n* -**1.** [clemency] clémence *f*, pitié *f*, indulgence *f*; **without ~** sans pitié, sans merci; **she had** OR **showed no ~** elle n'a eu aucune pitié, elle a été sans pitié; **to have ~ on sb** avoir pitié de qqn; **(have) ~!** (ayez) pitié!; **I'll have him begging** OR **crying for ~!** il va le regretter! ‖ RELIG miséricorde *f*; **may God in his ~ forgive you** que Dieu vous pardonne en sa miséricorde. -**2.** [blessing] chance *f*, bonheur *m*; **it's a ~ that he doesn't know** heureusement qu'il ne sait pas, c'est une chance qu'il ne sache pas; **we must be thankful for small mercies** il faut savoir apprécier les moindres bienfaits; **it was really a ~ that she left** son départ fut un véritable soulagement ou une véritable délivrance. -**3.** [power] merci *f*; **to be at sb's/sthg's ~** être à la merci de qqn/qqch; **the ship was at the ~ of the storm** le navire était à la merci de la tempête; **I throw myself on your ~** *fml* je mets mon sort entre vos mains; **to leave sb to the tender mercies of sb** *iron* abandonner qqn aux bons soins de qqn.
◇ *comp* humanitaire, de secours; **on a ~ mission** en mission humanitaire; ~ **dash** course *f* contre la mort.
mercy killing *n* euthanasie *f*.
mere [mɪəʳ] ◇ *adj* seul, simple, pur; **I'm a ~ beginner** je ne suis qu'un débutant; **it's a ~ formality** ce n'est qu'une simple formalité; **the ~ thought of it disgusts her** rien que d'y penser ça lui répugne; **the ~ sight of fish makes me queasy** la seule vue du poisson me donne la nausée; **a ~ five per cent of the population** cinq pour cent seulement de la population; **his eyes light up at the merest mention of money** son regard s'allume dès qu'on commence à parler d'argent.
◇ *n* (petit) lac *m*, étang *m*.
merely ['mɪəlɪ] *adv* seulement, (tout) simplement; **I'm ~ a beginner** je ne suis qu'un débutant; **I was ~ wondering if this is the best solution** je me demandais seulement OR simplement si c'était la meilleure solution; **she ~ glanced at it** elle n'a fait qu'y jeter OR elle s'est contentée d'y jeter un coup d'œil.
meretricious [ˌmerɪ'trɪʃəs] *adj fml* [glamour, excitement] factice; [impression] faux; [ornamentation, design] clinquant, tape-à-l'œil; [style] ampoulé, pompier.
merganser [mɜː'gænsəʳ] *n* harle *m*.
merge [mɜːdʒ] ◇ *vi* -**1.** [join – rivers] se rejoindre, confluer; [– roads] se rejoindre; [– colours, voices] se confondre; [– cultures] se mélanger POL s'unir. -**2.** [vanish] se perdre; **the thief ~d into the crowd** le voleur s'est fondu dans la foule. -**3.** COMM fusionner; **they have ~d with their former competitor** ils ont fusionné avec leur ancien concurrent.
◇ *vt* joindre, fusionner; COMM & COMPUT fusionner; POL unifier.
merger ['mɜːdʒəʳ] *n* COMM fusion *f*.
meridian [mə'rɪdɪən] ◇ *n* -**1.** ASTRON, GEOG & MED méridien *m*; **the Greenwich ~** le méridien de Greenwich. -**2.** MATH méridienne *f*. -**3.** *fig* [zenith] zénith *m*, sommet *m*, apogée *m*.
◇ *adj* méridien.
meridional [mə'rɪdɪənl] ◇ *adj* -**1.** = **meridian**. -**2.** [southern] méridional.
◇ *n* méridional *m*, -e *f*.
meringue [mə'ræŋ] *n* meringue *f*.
merino [mə'riːnəʊ] (*pl* **merinos**) ◇ *n* [sheep, wool] mérinos *m*.
◇ *adj* en mérinos.
merit ['merɪt] ◇ *n* mérite *m*; **its great ~ is its simplicity** ça a le grand mérite d'être simple; **promotion is on ~ alone** l'avancement se fait uniquement au mérite; **I don't see much ~ in the idea** cette idée ne me paraît pas particulièrement intéressante; **a work of great ~** une œuvre remarquable; **the relative ~s of theatre and cinema** les avantages respectifs du théâtre et du cinéma; **the project has the further ~ of being cheap** le projet a de plus l'avantage d'être bon marché.

◇ *vt* mériter; the case ~s closer examination le cas mérite d'être examiné de plus près.

merit increase *n* augmentation *f* au mérite.

meritocracy [ˌmerɪ'tɒkrəsɪ] (*pl* meritocracies) *n* méritocratie *f*.

meritorious [ˌmerɪ'tɔːrɪəs] *adj* [person] méritant; [act] méritoire, louable.

merit system *n Am* ADMIN système *m* d'avancement fondé sur le mérite.

merlin ['mɜːlɪn] *n* émerillon *m*.

Merlin ['mɜːlɪn] *pr n* Merlin; ~ the Wizard Merlin l'Enchanteur.

mermaid ['mɜːmeɪd] *n* sirène *f* MYTH.

merman ['mɜːmæn] (*pl* mermen [-men]) *n* triton *m* MYTH.

Merovingian [ˌmerə'vɪndʒɪən] ◇ *n* Mérovingien *m*, -enne *f*.
◇ *adj* mérovingien.

merrily ['merɪlɪ] *adv* joyeusement, gaiement.

merriment ['merɪmənt] *n* [joy] joie *f*, gaieté *f*; [laughter] rire *m*, rires *mpl*, hilarité *f*; sounds of ~ came from the garden on entendait des éclats de rire venant du jardin.

merry ['merɪ] (*compar* merrier, *superl* merriest) *adj* -**1.** [happy] joyeux, gai; Merry Christmas! Joyeux Noël!; the more the merrier *prov* plus on est de fous, plus on rit *prov*. -**2.** *inf* [tipsy] éméché, pompette. -**3.** [good]: the ~ month of May le joli mois de mai; the Minister and his ~ men *hum* le ministre et son état-major ❑ Merry England la bonne vieille Angleterre; 'The Merry Widow' *Lehar* 'la Veuve joyeuse'; 'The Merry Wives of Windsor' *Shakespeare* 'les Joyeuses Commères de Windsor'.

merry-go-round *n* manège *m*; *fig* [whirl] tourbillon *m*.

merrymaker ['merɪˌmeɪkəʳ] *n* fêtard *m*, -e *f*.

merrymaking ['merɪˌmeɪkɪŋ] *n* (*U*) réjouissances *fpl*, festivités *fpl*.

mesa ['meɪsə] *n* mesa *f*.

mescal ['meskæl] *n* -**1.** BOT peyotl *m*. -**2.** [alcohol] mescal *m*, mezcal *m*.

mescaline ['meskəliːn], **mescalin** ['meskəlɪn] *n* mescaline *f*.

mesh [meʃ] ◇ *n* -**1.** [of net] mailles *fpl*; [of sieve] grille *f*; the ~ is too fine les mailles sont trop serrées; fine-~ stockings des bas à mailles fines; 3 cm ~ netting du filet à mailles de 3 cm; a ~ shopping bag un filet à provisions. -**2.** [fabric] tissu *m* à mailles; nylon ~ tulle *m* de nylon. -**3.** *fig* [trap] rets *mpl*, piège *m*; caught in a ~ of lies enfermé dans OR prisonnier de ses propres mensonges ‖ [network] réseau *m*; a ~ of intrigue un réseau d'intrigues. -**4.** MECH [of gears] engrenage *m*; in ~ en prise.
◇ *vi* -**1.** [be in harmony] s'harmoniser, s'accorder; our temperaments just don't ~ nos caractères ne s'accordent pas. -**2.** [tally, coincide] cadrer, concorder; this doesn't ~ with the information we have already ceci ne cadre OR concorde pas avec les informations dont nous disposons. -**3.** MECH [gears] s'engrener.

meshing ['meʃɪŋ] *n* (*U*) rets *mpl*, mailles *fpl*.

meshuga *inf* [mə'ʃʊgə] *adj* dingue.

mesmerism ['mezmərɪzm] *n* -**1.** [hypnotism] hypnotisme *m*. -**2.** [Mesmer's doctrine] mesmérisme *m*.

mesmerist ['mezmərɪst] *n* hypnotiseur *m*, -euse *f*.

mesmerize, -ise ['mezməraɪz] *vt* -**1.** [hypnotise] hypnotiser. -**2.** [entrance] ensorceler, envoûter.

mesoblast ['mesəʊblæst] *n* mésoblaste *m*.

mesoderm ['mesəʊdɜːm] *n* mésoderme *m*.

Mesolithic [ˌmesə'lɪθɪk] ◇ *adj* mésolithique.
◇ *n* mésolithique *m*.

mesomorph ['mesəʊmɔːf] *n* mésomorphe *m*.

meson ['miːzɒn] *n* méson *m*.

Mesopotamia [ˌmesəpə'teɪmjə] *pr n* Mésopotamie *f*; in ~ en Mésopotamie.

Mesopotamian [ˌmesəpə'teɪmjən] ◇ *n* Mésopotamien *m*, -enne *f*.
◇ *adj* mésopotamien.

Mesozoic [ˌmesə'zəʊɪk] *adj* mésozoïque.

mess [mes] ◇ *n* -**1.** [untidiness] désordre *m*, fouillis *m*; what a ~! quel désordre!, quelle pagaille!; Tom's room is (in) a real ~! il y a une de ces pagailles OR un de ces fouillis dans la chambre de Tom!; my papers are in a ~ mes papiers sont en désordre; clear up this ~! mets un peu d'ordre là-dedans!, range un peu tout ce fouillis!; your essay is a real ~! *inf* ta rédaction est un vrai torchon!; my hair's a ~! je suis coiffé comme l'as de pique!; I feel a ~ je suis dans un état lamentable; you're a ~, go and clean up tu n'es pas présentable, va t'arranger ‖ [dirtiness] saleté *f*, saletés *fpl*; clean up that ~! nettoie un peu ces saletés OR cette crasse!; the cooker is (in) a horrible ~ la cuisinière est vraiment sale OR dégoûtante; the dog has made a ~ on the carpet le chien a fait des saletés sur le tapis. -**2.** [muddle] gâchis *m*; to make a ~ of a job gâcher un travail; to make a ~ of one's life gâcher sa vie; I'm afraid I've made a ~ of the travel arrangements je suis désolé, je me suis trompé dans les préparatifs de voyage; this country is in a ~! la situation dans ce pays n'est pas vraiment réjouissante! -**3.** *inf* [predicament] pétrin *m*; he's got himself into a bit of a ~ il s'est fourré dans de beaux draps OR dans le pétrin; thanks for getting me out of that ~ merci de m'avoir sorti de ce mauvais pas OR tiré de ce pétrin. -**4.** MIL [canteen] mess *m*; the whole ~ got food poisoning tous ceux qui ont pris leur repas au mess ont été victimes d'une intoxication alimentaire. -**5.** MIL [food] ordinaire *m*, gamelle *f*. -**6.** *arch* [dish] plat *m*; a ~ of pottage BIBLE un plat de lentilles.
◇ *vt* [dirty] salir, souiller.
◇ *vi* -**1.** *inf* [meddle]: to ~ with sb embêter qqn; don't ~ with me! ne me cherche pas!; it's true, no ~ing! c'est vrai, je ne blague pas! -**2.** MIL manger OR prendre ses repas au mess; they don't ~ with the other officers ils ne mangent pas avec les autres officiers.
◆ **mess about** *inf*, **mess around** *inf* ◇ *vi insep Br* -**1.** [waste time] perdre son temps; [dawdle, hang around] traîner; get on with the job and stop ~ing about! mettez-vous au travail et que ça saute! ‖ [potter] bricoler; I spent the weekend ~ing about (in) the house j'ai passé le week-end à faire des bricoles dans la maison; he likes ~ing about in the garden il aime s'occuper dans le jardin ‖ [play the fool] faire l'imbécile; stop ~ing about and listen to me! arrête de faire l'imbécile et écoute-moi! -**2.** [meddle, fiddle] tripoter, tripatouiller; don't ~ about with my computer ne tripote pas mon ordinateur; to ~ about with sb *fig* embêter qqn; if I catch her ~ing about with my husband I'll kill her! si je l'attrape à faire du gringue à mon mari, je la tue!
◇ *vt sep inf* [person] embêter; I'm fed up with being ~ed about by men j'en ai marre des hommes qui se moquent de moi.
◆ **mess up** *vt sep* -**1.** [make disorderly - room, papers] mettre en désordre; stop it, you'll ~ my hair up! arrête, tu vas me décoiffer! -**2.** *inf* [spoil] ficher en l'air; that's really ~ed our plans up! ça a vraiment fichu nos projets en l'air! -**3.** [dirty] salir, souiller.

message ['mesɪdʒ] *n* -**1.** [communication] message *m*, commission *f*; [written] message *m*, mot *m*; to take/to leave a ~ prendre/laisser un message; can you give her a ~? pouvez-vous lui transmettre un message?; would you like to leave a ~ for him? voulez-vous (lui) laisser un message? -**2.** [theme - of book, advert] message *m*; [teaching - of prophet] message *m*, enseignement *m*; to get one's ~ across se faire comprendre; (do you) get the ~? *inf* tu piges? -**3.** *Scot* commission *f*, course *f*; to do a ~ for sb faire une commission pour qqn. -**4.** LING message *m*.
◆ **messages** *npl Ir & Scot* [shopping] courses *fpl*; he's out doing the ~s il est sorti faire les courses.

message switching [-'swɪtʃɪŋ] *n* COMPUT commutation *f* de messages.

messenger ['mesɪndʒəʳ] *n* [gen] messager *m*, -ère *f*; [errand boy - in office] coursier *m*; [in hotel] chasseur *m*, coursier *m*; [in post office] télégraphiste *mf*; by special ~ par porteur spécial ❑ ~ boy coursier *m*, garçon *m* de courses; ~ service messagerie *f*.

messenger RNA *n* ARN messager *m*.

messiah [mɪ'saɪə] *n* messie *m*.
◆ **Messiah** *n* Messie *m*.

messianic [ˌmesɪ'ænɪk] *adj* messianique.

messianism [me'saɪənɪzm] *n* messianisme *m*.

messily ['mesɪlɪ] *adv* -**1.** [untidily] mal, de façon peu soignée; [in a disorganized way] n'importe comment; she did it really ~ elle l'a vraiment fait n'importe comment; the affair ended ~ *fig* l'affaire s'est mal terminée. -**2.** [dirtily] comme un cochon.

Messina [me'siːnə] *pr n* Messine.

messiness ['mesɪnɪs] *n* -**1.** [disorder] désordre *m*, pagaille *f*. -**2.** [dirt] saleté *f*. -**3.** [unpleasant situation] difficultés *fpl*, confusion *f*.

mess jacket *n* MIL veston *m* de tenue de soirée; [civilian] veste *f* courte.

mess kit *n* -**1.** *inf Br* MIL [clothes] tenue *f* de soirée. -**2.** MIL [eating equipment] gamelle *f*.

messmate ['mesmeɪt] *n* commensal *m*, -e *f*.

mess-room *n* NAUT carré *m*.

Messrs, Messrs. ['mesəz] *abbr* MM, Messieurs.

mess tin *n* gamelle *f*.

messuage ['meswɪdʒ] *n* JUR propriété *f*, maison *f* avec ses dépendances.

mess-up *inf n* confusion *f*; there was a ~ over the dates on s'est embrouillé dans les dates.

messy ['mesɪ] (*compar* messier, *superl* messiest) *adj* -**1.** [dirty - hands, clothes] sale, malpropre; [- job] salissant; don't get all ~ ne te salis pas; he did some painting and got all ~ il a fait de la peinture et il s'en est mis partout. -**2.** [untidy - place] en désordre, désordonné, mal tenu; [- person] peu soigné, négligé, débraillé; [- hair] ébouriffé, en désordre, en bataille. -**3.** [badly done] bâclé; a ~ piece of homework un devoir bâclé. -**4.** *fig* [awkward, unpleasant] compliqué, embrouillé, délicat; a ~ situation une situation délicate OR difficile; a very ~ business une affaire très embrouillée; a ~ divorce un divorce difficile OR compliqué.

met [met] *pt & pp* → **meet**.

Met *inf* [met] *pr n* -**1.** *Am abbr of* Metropolitan Opera. -**2.** *Am abbr of* Metropolitan Museum. -**3.** *Br abbr of* Metropolitan Police.

metabolic [ˌmetə'bɒlɪk] *adj* métabolique.

metabolism [mɪ'tæbəlɪzm] *n* métabolisme *m*.

metabolize, -ise [mɪ'tæbəlaɪz] *vt* métaboliser.

metacarpal [ˌmetə'kɑːpl] ◇ *adj* métacarpien.
◇ *n* métacarpien *m*.

metacarpus [ˌmetə'kɑːpəs] (*pl* metacarpi [-paɪ]) *n* métacarpe *m*.

metal ['metl] (*Br pt & pp* metalled, *cont* metalling, *Am pt & pp* metaled, *cont* metaling) ◇ *n* -**1.** [gen & CHEM] métal *m*; the framework is made of ~ la structure est en métal. -**2.** TYPO plomb *m*. -**3.** [for road - building] cailloutis *m*, empierrement *m*. -**4.** [glass] pâte *f* de verre.
◇ *adj* en métal, métallique; a ~ box une boîte en métal.
◇ *vt* -**1.** [cover with metal] couvrir de métal. -**2.** [road] empierrer.
◆ **metals** *npl Br* RAIL voie *f* ferrée, rails *mpl*.

metalanguage ['metəˌlæŋgwɪdʒ] *n* métalangue *f*, métalangage *m*.

metal detector *n* détecteur *m* de métaux.

metaled *Am* = **metalled**.

metalinguistic [ˌmetəlɪŋ'gwɪstɪk] *adj* métalinguistique.

metalinguistics [ˌmetəlɪŋ'gwɪstɪks] *n* (*U*) métalinguistique *f*.

metalled *Br*, **metaled** *Am* ['metld] *adj* [road] revêtu (*de macadam, de pierres etc*).

metallic [mɪ'tælɪk] *adj* -**1.** CHEM métallique. -**2.** [colour]: ~ blue/grey bleu/gris métallisé;

~ paint peinture *f* métallisée. -**3.** [voice] métallique; [sound] métallique, grinçant.
metalling *Br*, **metaling** *Am* ['metəlɪŋ] *n* [of road] revêtement *m (en macadam, en pierre etc)*.
metallize, -ise ['metəlaɪz] *vt* métalliser.
metallurgist [me'tæləd͡ʒɪst] *n* métallurgiste *m*, ingénieur *m* en métallurgie.
metallurgy [me'tæləd͡ʒɪ] *n* métallurgie *f*.
metalware ['metəlweəʳ] *n* ustensiles *mpl* (domestiques) en métal.
metalwork ['metəlwɜːk] *n* -**1.** [objects] ferronnerie *f*. -**2.** [activity] travail *m* des métaux. -**3.** [metal framework] tôle *f*, métal *m*; [of crashed car, plane] carcasse *f*.
metalworker ['metəl,wɜːkəʳ] *n* -**1.** [in factory] métallurgiste *m*, métallo *m*. -**2.** [craftsman] ferronnier *m*.
metalworking ['metəl,wɜːkɪŋ] *n* travail *m* des métaux.
metamathematics [,metəmæθə'mætɪks] *n (U)* métamathématique *f*.
metamorphic [,metə'mɔːfɪk] *adj* métamorphique.
metamorphism [,metə'mɔːfɪzm] *n* métamorphisme *m*.
metamorphose [,metə'mɔːfəʊz] ◇ *vi* se métamorphoser; to ~ into sthg se métamorphoser en qqch.
◇ *vt* métamorphoser.
metamorphosis [,metə'mɔːfəsɪs, ,metəmɔː'fəʊsɪs] (*pl* metamorphoses [-siːz]) *n* métamorphose *f*.
metamorphous [,metə'mɔːfəs] = **metamorphic**.
metaphor ['metəfəʳ] *n* métaphore *f*; it's a ~ for loneliness c'est une métaphore de la solitude.
metaphoric(al) [,metə'fɒrɪk(l)] *adj* métaphorique.
metaphrase ['metəfreɪz] ◇ *vt* traduire littéralement OR mot à mot.
◇ *n* traduction *f* littérale OR mot à mot.
metaphysic [,metə'fɪzɪk] *n* métaphysique *f*.
metaphysical [,metə'fɪzɪkl] *adj* LITERAT OR PHILOS métaphysique; *fig* [abstract] métaphysique, abstrait.
metaphysically [,metə'fɪzɪklɪ] *adv* métaphysiquement.
metaphysician [,metəfɪ'zɪʃn] *n* métaphysicien *m*, -enne *f*.
metaphysics [,metə'fɪzɪks] *n (U)* métaphysique *f*.
metaplasm ['metəplæzm] *n* LING métaplasme *m*.
metapsychology [,metəsaɪ'kɒləd͡ʒɪ] *n* métapsychologie *f*.
metastable ['metəsteɪbl] *adj* métastable.
metastasis [me'tæstəsɪs] (*pl* metastases [-siːz]) *n* métastase *f*.
metatarsal [,metə'tɑːsl] ◇ *adj* métatarsien.
◇ *n* métatarsien *m*.
metatarsus [,metə'tɑːsəs] (*pl* metatarsi [-saɪ]) *n* métatarse *m*.
metatheory [,metə'θɪərɪ] (*pl* metatheories) *n* métathéorie *f*.
metathesis [mɪ'tæθəsɪs] (*pl* metatheses [-siːz]) *n* métathèse *f*.
metazoan [metə'zəʊən] *n* métazoaire *m*.
mete [miːt]
◆ **mete out** *vt sep* [punishment] infliger; [judgment, justice] rendre.
meteor ['miːtɪəʳ] *n* météore *m*; ~ shower pluie *f* de météores.
meteoric [miːtɪ'ɒrɪk] *adj* -**1.** ASTRON météorique. -**2.** *fig* fulgurant, très rapide; Hitler's ~ rise to power l'ascension fulgurante d'Hitler au pouvoir.
meteorite ['miːtjəraɪt] *n* météorite *f*.
meteorograph ['miːtjərəgrɑːf] *n* météorographe *m*.
meteoroid ['miːtjərɔɪd] *n* météoroïde *m*.
meteorological [,miːtjərə'lɒd͡ʒɪkl] *adj* météorologique; ~ office office *m* météorologique.
meteorologist [,miːtjə'rɒləd͡ʒɪst] *n* météorologue *mf*, météorologiste *mf*.
meteorology [,miːtjə'rɒləd͡ʒɪ] *n* météorologie *f*.
meter ['miːtəʳ] ◇ *n* -**1.** [for water, gas, electricity] compteur *m*; to read the ~ relever le compteur; to feed the ~ mettre des pièces dans le compteur ❑ (parking) ~ parcmètre *m*, parcomètre *m*; (taxi) ~ taximètre *m*, compteur *m*. -**2.** *Am* = **metre**.
◇ *vt* -**1.** [electricity, water, gas] mesurer à l'aide d'un compteur. -**2.** [mail] affranchir *(avec une machine)*.
meter maid *inf n* contractuelle *f*, pervenche *f*.
methadon ['meθədɒn], **methadone** ['meθədəʊn] *n* méthadone *f*.
methane ['miːθeɪn] *n* méthane *m*.
methane series *n* alcanes *mpl*.
methanol ['meθənɒl] *n* méthanol *m*.
methinks [mɪ'θɪŋks] (*pt* methought [-'θɔːt]) *vb arch* OR *hum* ce me semble.
method ['meθəd] *n* -**1.** [means] méthode *f*, moyen *m*; [manner] manière *f*; [instruction] méthode *f*, mode *m* d'emploi; ~ of doing sthg manière de faire qqch, méthode (employée) pour faire qqch. -**2.** [procedure] méthode *f*, procédé *m*; experimental ~s des méthodes expérimentales; their ~s of investigation have come under fire la façon dont ils mènent leurs enquêtes a été critiquée, on a critiqué leur façon d'enquêter ‖ [theory] théorie *f*, méthode *f*; the Montessori ~ la méthode Montessori. -**3.** [organization] organisation *f*, méthode *f*; his work lacks ~ son travail manque de méthode; there's ~ in her madness elle n'est pas aussi folle qu'elle en a l'air.
◆ **Method** *n*: Method acting la méthode Stanislavski.
methodic(al) [mɪ'θɒdɪk(l)] *adj* méthodique.
methodically [mɪ'θɒdɪklɪ] *adv* méthodiquement, de façon méthodique, avec méthode.
Methodism ['meθədɪzm] *n* méthodisme *m*.
Methodist ['meθədɪst] ◇ *adj* méthodiste.
◇ *n* méthodiste *mf*.
methodize, -ise ['meθədaɪz] *vt* systématiser.
methodological [,meθədə'lɒd͡ʒɪkl] *adj* méthodologique.
methodologically [,meθədə'lɒd͡ʒɪklɪ] *adv* méthodologiquement.
methodology [,meθə'dɒləd͡ʒɪ] (*pl* methodologies) *n* méthodologie *f*.
meths *inf* [meθs] (*abbr of* methylated spirits) *n Br* alcool *m* à brûler; ~ drinker *alcoolique qui boit de l'alcool à brûler*.
Methuselah [mɪ'θjuːzələ] ◇ *pr n* BIBLE Mathusalem; as old as ~ vieux comme Mathusalem.
◇ *n* [bottle] mathusalem *m*.
methyl ['meθɪl] *n* méthyle *m*.
methyl acetate *n* acétate *m* de méthyle.
methylal ['meθəlæl] *n* méthylal *m*.
methyl alcohol *n* méthanol *m*, alcool *m* méthylique.
methylate ['meθɪleɪt] *vt* méthyler.
methylated spirits ['meθɪleɪtɪd] *n* alcool *m* à brûler.
methylene ['meθəliːn] *n* méthylène *m*.
metic ['metɪk] *n* métèque *m* ANTIQ.
meticulous [mɪ'tɪkjʊləs] *adj* méticuleux.
meticulously [mɪ'tɪkjʊləslɪ] *adv* méticuleusement; ~ honest d'une honnêteté scrupuleuse.
meticulousness [mɪ'tɪkjʊləsnɪs] *n* minutie *f*, méticulosité *f lit*; with great ~ avec un soin tout particulier.
Met Office [met-] (*abbr of* Meteorological Office) *pr n les services météorologiques britanniques*.
metol ['miːtɒl] *n* métol *m*.
metonym ['metənɪm] *n* métonymie *f*.
metonymy [mɪ'tɒnɪmɪ] *n* métonymie *f*.
metre *Br*, **meter** *Am* ['miːtəʳ] *n* -**1.** [measurement] mètre *m*. -**2.** LITERAT mètre *m*; in iambic ~ en vers *mpl* iambiques. -**3.** MUS mesure *f*.
metric ['metrɪk] *adj* MATH métrique; to go ~ adopter le système métrique; ~ hundredweight 50 kilogrammes *mpl*; ~ ton tonne *f* the ~ system le système métrique.
metrical ['metrɪkl] *adj* métrique LITERAT.
metrically ['metrɪklɪ] *adv* -**1.** LITERAT en vers -**2.** MATH selon le système métrique.
metricate ['metrɪkeɪt] *vt* convertir au système métrique.
metrication [,metrɪ'keɪʃn] *n* conversion *f* au système métrique, métrisation *f*.
metrify ['metrɪfaɪ] (*pt* & *pp* **metrified**) *vt* LITERAT versifier.
metro ['metrəʊ] (*pl* metros) *n* métro *m*.
Metroliner® ['metrəʊ,laɪnəʳ] *pr n ligne de chemin de fer entre Boston et New York*.
metrology [me'trɒləd͡ʒɪ] *n* métrologie *f*.
metronome ['metrənəʊm] *n* métronome *m*.
metronymic [,metrə'nɪmɪk] ◇ *adj* matronymique.
◇ *n* matronyme *m*.
metropolis [mɪ'trɒpəlɪs] *n* métropole *f*, grande ville *f*, grand centre *m* urbain.
metropolitan [,metrə'pɒlɪtn] ◇ *adj* -**1.** GEOG métropolitain. -**2.** RELIG métropolitain; ~ bishop métropolitain *m*.
◇ *n* RELIG métropolitain *m*; [in orthodox church] métropolite *m*.
Metropolitan Police *n* -**1.** *Br* police *f* londonienne. -**2.** *Am* police *f* urbaine.
Mets [mets] *pl pr n*: the (New York) ~ *l'une des équipes de base-ball de New York*.
mettle ['metl] *n* courage *m*; to show OR to prove one's ~ montrer ce dont on est capable; this new challenge has really put him on his ~ ce nouveau défi l'a vraiment forcé à donner le meilleur de lui-même.
mettlesome ['metəlsəm] *adj lit* courageux.
mew [mjuː] ◇ *vi* [cat] miauler; [gull] crier.
◇ *n* -**1.** [of cat] miaulement *m*; [of gull] cri *m*. -**2.** [gull] mouette *f*.
mewl [mjuːl] *vi* vagir, geindre.
mews [mjuːz] ◇ *n Br* -**1.** [flat] *appartement chic aménagé dans une écurie rénovée*; she lives in a converted ~ (flat) elle habite un appartement aménagé dans une ancienne écurie. -**2.** [street] ruelle *f*.
◇ *npl arch* écurie *f*, écuries *fpl*.
mews flat = **mews** *n* **1**.
Mexican ['meksɪkn] ◇ *n* Mexicain *m*, -aine *f*.
◇ *adj* mexicain; the ~ War la guerre du Mexique.

THE MEXICAN WAR:
Conflit qui opposa, de 1846 à 1848, les États-Unis au Mexique. Vaincu, celui-ci renonça à ses prétentions sur le Texas et céda un vaste territoire comprenant plusieurs États américains actuels (y compris le Nouveau Mexique et la Californie).

Mexico ['meksɪkəʊ] *pr n* Mexique *m*; in ~ au Mexique.
Mexico City *pr n* Mexico.
mezzanine ['metsəniːn] *n* -**1.** mezzanine *f*. -**2.** *Am* [in theatre] corbeille *f*.
mezzo *inf* ['metsəʊ] (*pl* mezzos) = **mezzo-soprano**.
mezzo-soprano (*pl* mezzo-sopranos) *n* -**1.** [singer] mezzo-soprano *f*. -**2.** [voice] mezzo-soprano *m*.
mezzotint ['medzəʊtɪnt] *n* mezzotinto *m inv*.
MFA (*abbr of* Master of Fine Arts) *n (titulaire d'une) maîtrise en beaux-arts*.
mfr *written abbr of* manufacturer.
mg (*written abbr of* milligram) mg.
Mgr -**1.** (*written abbr of* Monseigneur, Monsignor) Mgr. -**2.** *written abbr of* manager.
mho [məʊ] (*pl* mhos) *n dated* MHO *m dated*, siemens *m*.
MHz (*written abbr of* megahertz) MHz.
mi [miː] *n* MUS mi *m inv*.
MI *written abbr of* Michigan.

MI5 (*abbr of* Military Intelligence 5) *pr n service de contre-espionnage britannique*.
MI6 (*abbr of* Military Intelligence 6) *pr n service de renseignements britannique*.
MIA (*abbr of* missing in action) *adj expression indiquant qu'une personne a disparu lors d'un combat*.
miaow [miːˈaʊ] *Br* ◇ *vi* miauler.
◇ *n* miaulement *m*.
◇ *interj* miaou.
miasma [mɪˈæzmə] *n lit* -**1.** [vapour] miasme *m*; [of smoke] bouffée *f*. -**2.** [evil influence] emprise *f*, empire *m*; the ~ of despair/of poverty l'emprise du désespoir/de la misère.
mica [ˈmaɪkə] *n* mica *m*.
Micah [ˈmaɪkə] *pr n* Michée.
mice [maɪs] *pl* → **mouse**.
Mich. *written abbr of* Michigan.
Michael [ˈmaɪkl] *pr n*: Saint ~ saint Michel; to take the ~ *inf Br hum*: are you taking the ~? tu me fais marcher ou quoi?
Michaelmas [ˈmɪkəlməs] *n* -**1.** RELIG Saint-Michel *f*; at ~ à la Saint-Michel. -**2.** *Br* UNIV: ~ (term) premier trimestre *m*.
Michaelmas daisy *n* aster *m* (d'automne).
Michelangelo [ˌmaɪkəlˈændʒɪləʊ] *pr n* Michel-Ange.
Michigan [ˈmɪʃɪgən] *pr n* Michigan *m*; in ~ dans le Michigan.
Mick▽ [mɪk] *n terme injurieux désignant un Irlandais*.
mickey [ˈmɪkɪ] *n Br*: to take the ~ out of sb *inf* se payer la tête de qqn; are you taking the ~? *inf* tu me fais marcher ou quoi?
Mickey Finn *n* boisson *f* droguée.
Mickey Mouse ◇ *pr n* Mickey.
◇ *adj inf* [trivial] de pacotille; a ~ job un boulot à la manque OR à la noix.
mickle [ˈmɪkl] *n Scot* & *N Eng*: many a ~ makes a muckle *prov* les petits ruisseaux font les grandes rivières *prov*.
MICR (*abbr of* magnetic ink character recognition) *n reconnaissance magnétique de caractères*.
micro [ˈmaɪkrəʊ] (*pl* micros) ◇ *adj* très petit, microscopique.
◇ *n* [microcomputer] micro-ordinateur *m*, micro *m*.
microanalysis [ˌmaɪkrəʊəˈnæləsɪs] (*pl* microanalyses [-siːz]) *n* micro-analyse *f*.
microbe [ˈmaɪkrəʊb] *n* microbe *m*.
microbial [maɪˈkrəʊbɪəl], **microbic** [maɪˈkrəʊbɪk] *adj* microbien.
microbiological [ˈmaɪkrəʊˌbaɪəˈlɒdʒɪkl] *adj* microbiologique.
microbiologist [ˌmaɪkrəʊbaɪˈɒlədʒɪst] *n* microbiologiste *mf*.
microbiology [ˌmaɪkrəʊbaɪˈɒlədʒɪ] *n* microbiologie *f*.
microchemistry [ˌmaɪkrəʊˈkemɪstrɪ] *n* microchimie *f*.
microchip [ˈmaɪkrəʊtʃɪp] *n* microprocesseur *m*.
microcircuit [ˈmaɪkrəʊˌsɜːkɪt] *n* microcircuit *m*.
microcircuitry [ˌmaɪkrəʊˈsɜːkɪtrɪ] *n (U)* microcircuits *mpl*.
microclimate [ˈmaɪkrəʊˌklaɪmət] *n* microclimat *m*.
micrococcus [ˌmaɪkrəʊˈkɒkəs] (*pl* micrococci [-kaɪ]) *n* microcoque *m*, micrococcus *m*.
microcode [ˈmaɪkrəʊkəʊd] *n* micro-code *m*.
microcoding [ˈmaɪkrəʊkəʊdɪŋ] *n* microprogrammation *f*.
microcomputer [ˌmaɪkrəʊkəmˈpjuːtəʳ] *n* micro-ordinateur *m*.
microcomputing [ˌmaɪkrəʊkəmˈpjuːtɪŋ] *n* micro-informatique *f*.
microcopy [ˈmaɪkrəʊˌkɒpɪ] (*pl* microcopies) *n* microcopie *f*.
microcosm [ˈmaɪkrəʊˌkɒzm] *n* microcosme *m*.
microcosmic [ˌmaɪkrəʊˈkɒzmɪk] *adj* microcosmique.
microdot [ˈmaɪkrəʊdɒt] *n* micropoint *m*, micro-image *f*.
microeconomic [ˈmaɪkrəʊˌiːkəˈnɒmɪk] *adj* microéconomique.
microeconomics [ˈmaɪkrəʊˌiːkəˈnɒmɪks] *n (U)* micro-économie *f*.
microelectronic [ˈmaɪkrəʊɪˌlekˈtrɒnɪk] *adj* microélectronique.
microelectronics [ˈmaɪkrəʊɪˌlekˈtrɒnɪks] *n* microélectronique *f*.
microfiche [ˈmaɪkrəʊfiːʃ] *n* microfiche *f*.
microfilm [ˈmaɪkrəʊfɪlm] ◇ *n* microfilm *m*.
◇ *vt* microfilmer, mettre sur microfilm.
micrograph [ˈmaɪkrəgrɑːf] ◇ *n* micrographie *f*.
◇ *vt* micrographier.
micrographic [ˌmaɪkrəˈgræfɪk] *adj* micrographique.
micrography [maɪˈkrɒgrəfɪ] *n* micrographie *f*.
microgroove [ˈmaɪkrəgruːv] *n* microsillon *m*.
microhabitat [ˌmaɪkrəʊˈhæbɪtæt] *n* microhabitat *m*.
microinstruction [ˌmaɪkrəʊɪnˈstrʌkʃn] *n* micro-instruction *f*.
microlight [ˈmaɪkrəlaɪt] *n* AERON ultra-léger motorisé *m*, ULM *m*.
microlinguistics [ˌmaɪkrəʊlɪŋˈgwɪstɪks] *n (U)* microlinguistique *f*.
microlith [ˈmaɪkrəʊlɪθ] *n* microlithe *m*.
micromesh [ˈmaɪkrəʊmeʃ] *adj* [tights] surfin.
micrometer [maɪˈkrɒmiːtəʳ] *n* [device] micromètre *m (appareil)*; ~ screw vis *f* micrométrique; ~ screw gauge palmer *m*.
micrometre *Br*, **micrometer** *Am* [ˈmaɪkrəʊˌmiːtəʳ] *n* micromètre *m (mesure)*.
micrometry [maɪˈkrɒmətrɪ] *n* micrométrie *f*.
microminiaturization [ˈmaɪkrəʊˌmɪnətʃəraɪˈzeɪʃn] *n* microminiaturisation *f*.
microminiaturize, -ise [ˌmaɪkrəʊˈmɪnətʃəraɪz] *vt* microminiaturiser.
micron [ˈmaɪkrɒn] (*pl* microns OR micra [-krə]) *n* micron *m*.
Micronesia [ˌmaɪkrəˈniːzjə] *pr n* Micronésie *f*; in ~ en Micronésie.
Micronesian [ˌmaɪkrəˈniːzjən] ◇ *n* -**1.** [person] Micronésien *m*, -enne *f*. -**2.** LING micronésien.
◇ *adj* micronésien.
microorganism [ˌmaɪkrəʊˈɔːgənɪzm] *n* micro-organisme *m*.
microphone [ˈmɪkrəfəʊn] *n* microphone *m*; to talk into a ~ parler dans un micro.
microphotograph [ˌmaɪkrəʊˈfəʊtəgrɑːf] *n* microphotographie *f*.
microphotography [ˌmaɪkrəʊfəˈtɒgrəfɪ] *n* microphotographie *f*.
microphysics [ˌmaɪkrəʊˈfɪzɪks] *n (U)* microphysique *f*.
microprobe [ˈmaɪkrəʊprəʊb] *n* microsonde *f*.
microprocessor [ˈmaɪkrəʊˌprəʊsesəʳ] *n* microprocesseur *m*.
microprogram [ˈmaɪkrəʊˌprəʊgræm] *n* microprogramme *m*.
microprogramming [ˌmaɪkrəʊˈprəʊgræmɪŋ] *n* microprogrammation *f*.
microreader [ˈmaɪkrəʊˌriːdəʳ] *n* microlecteur *m*, lecteur *m* de microformes.
microscope [ˈmaɪkrəskəʊp] *n* microscope *m*; to look at sthg under the ~ *literal* observer OR examiner qqch au microscope; *fig* examiner qqch de très près.
microscopic [ˌmaɪkrəˈskɒpɪk] *adj* -**1.** [tiny] microscopique. -**2.** [using a microscope] au microscope, microscopique.
microscopically [ˌmaɪkrəˈskɒpɪklɪ] *adv* [examine] au microscope; ~ small invisible à l'œil nu.
microscopy [maɪˈkrɒskəpɪ] *n* microscopie *f*.
microsecond [ˈmaɪkrəʊˌsekənd] *n* microseconde *f*.
microstructure [ˈmaɪkrəʊˌstrʌktʃəʳ] *n* microstructure *f*.
microsurgery [ˌmaɪkrəʊˈsɜːdʒərɪ] *n* microchirurgie *f*.
microsurgical [ˌmaɪkrəʊˈsɜːdʒɪkl] *adj* microchirurgical.
microwave [ˈmaɪkrəweɪv] ◇ *n* -**1.** PHYS micro-onde *f*. -**2.** = **microwave oven**.
◇ *vt* faire cuire au micro-ondes.
microwave oven *n* four *m* à micro-ondes.
microwriter [ˈmaɪkrəʊˌraɪtəʳ] *n* COMPUT micro-ordinateur *m* de traitement de texte.
micturate [ˈmɪktjʊəreɪt] *vi fml* uriner.
mid [mɪd] ◇ *adj* -**1.** [middle]: in ~ October à la mi-octobre, au milieu du mois d'octobre; he's in his ~ fifties il a environ 55 ans; she stopped in ~ sentence elle s'est arrêtée au milieu de sa phrase, sa phrase est restée en suspens. -**2.** [half]: ~ brown/green brun/vert ni clair ni foncé. -**3.** [central] central, du milieu; ~ Wales le centre OR la région centrale du pays de Galles; ~ vowels voyelles *fpl* centrales.
◇ *prep* = **amid**.
mid' [mɪd] = **amid**.
midair [mɪdˈeəʳ] ◇ *adj* en plein ciel.
◇ *n*: in ~ en plein ciel.
Midas [ˈmaɪdəs] *pr n* Midas; to have the ~ touch avoir le sens des affaires.
mid-Atlantic ◇ *adj* [accent] américanisé.
◇ *n*: in (the) ~ au milieu de l'Atlantique.
midbrain [ˈmɪdbreɪn] *n* ANAT mésencéphale *m*.
midcourse [ˈmɪdkɔːs] ◇ *n*: in ~ à mi-course.
◇ *adj* ASTRON: ~ corrections corrections *fpl* de trajectoire.
midday [ˈmɪddeɪ] *n* midi *m*; at ~ à midi; the ~ heat la chaleur de midi; ~ meal repas *m* de midi.
midden [ˈmɪdn] *n* -**1.** *dial* [dung heap] (tas *m* de) fumier *m*. -**2.** ARCHEOL ordures *fpl* ménagères, rejets *mpl* domestiques.
middle [ˈmɪdl] ◇ *n* -**1.** [in space] milieu *m*, centre *m*; in the ~ (of) au milieu (de), au centre (de); a square with a dot in the ~ un carré avec un point au milieu; two seats in the ~ of the row deux places en milieu de rangée; in the ~ of the crowd au milieu de la foule; in the ~ of London en plein Londres; right in the ~ of the target au beau milieu OR en plein centre de la cible; in the ~ of the road au milieu de la route; in the ~ of the Atlantic au milieu de l'Atlantique, en plein Atlantique ☐ they live in the ~ of nowhere ils habitent dans un trou perdu; we broke down in the ~ of nowhere on est tombés en panne dans un endroit perdu. -**2.** [in time] milieu *m*; in the ~ of the week/month au milieu de la semaine/du mois; in the ~ of October à la mi-octobre, au milieu (du mois) d'octobre; in the ~ of the night en pleine nuit, en plein milieu de la nuit; in the ~ of winter en plein hiver ‖ [in activity]: to be in the ~ of (doing) sthg être en train de faire qqch. -**3.** [stomach] ventre *m*; [waist] taille *f*; he's got rather fat around the ~ il a pris du ventre.
◇ *adj* -**1.** [in the centre] du milieu; the ~ book/shelf le livre/l'étagère du milieu; to take the ~ course OR way *fig* trouver le juste milieu; the ~ path *literal* le chemin du milieu; *fig* la voie de la modération; ~ C do *m* du milieu du clavier. -**2.** [average] moyen; of ~ height *Br* de taille moyenne ‖ [intermediate] moyen, intermédiaire; this car is in the ~ price range cette voiture se situe dans un ordre de prix moyen.
◇ *vt* -**1.** NAUT [sail] plier en deux. -**2.** FTBL centrer.
◆ **Middle** *adj* LING: Middle Irish/French moyen gaélique/français.
middle age *n* la cinquantaine; a man in ~ un homme d'un certain âge; to reach ~ avoir un certain âge; she's well into ~ elle a plus de 50 ans.
◆ **middle-age** *comp*: he's got middle-age spread il prend de l'embonpoint.
middle-aged *adj* d'une cinquantaine d'années; a ~ businessman un homme d'affaires d'un certain âge.

Middle Ages *npl* Moyen Âge *m*; in the ~ au Moyen Âge.

Middle America *pr n* -**1.** GEOG Amérique *f* centrale. -**2.** SOCIOL l'Amérique *f* moyenne; *pej* l'Amérique *f* bien pensante.

Middle American ◇ *n* -**1.** GÉOG Américain *m*, -e *f* du Middle-West. -**2.** *fig* Américain *m* moyen, Américaine *f* moyenne.
◇ *adj* -**1.** GÉOG du Middle-West. -**2.** *fig* de l'américain moyen.

middlebrow ['mɪdlbraʊ] ◇ *n pej* [reader] lecteur *m* moyen, lectrice *f* moyenne; [audience] spectateur *m* moyen, spectatrice *f* moyenne.
◇ *adj* [reader, audience] moyen; their music's very ~ leur musique s'adresse à un public moyen; ~ books livres sans prétentions; ~ programmes programmes s'adressant à un public moyen.

middle class *n*: the ~, the ~es les classes *fpl* moyennes; *pej* la bourgeoisie *f*.
◆ **middle-class** *adj* des classes moyennes; *pej* bourgeois.

middle distance *n*: in the ~ à mi-distance || [in picture] au second plan.
◆ **middle-distance** *adj* SPORT: middle-distance runner/race coureur *m*, -euse *f* / course *f* de demi-fond.

middle ear *n* ANAT oreille *f* moyenne.

Middle East *pr n*: the ~ le Moyen-Orient; in the ~ au Moyen-Orient.

Middle Eastern *adj* moyen-oriental.

Middle English *n* LING moyen anglais *m*.

middle finger *n* majeur *m*.

middle game *n* [in chess] milieu *m* de partie.

middle ground *n* -**1.** [in picture] second plan *m*. -**2.** *fig* terrain *m* neutre; to occupy the ~ adopter une position de compromis.

Middle High German *n le haut allemand de 1200 à 1500*.

middleman ['mɪdlmæn] (*pl* **middlemen** [-men]) *n* intermédiaire *mf*.

middle management *n (U)* cadres *mpl* moyens.

middlemost ['mɪdlməʊst] *adj* le plus proche du centre.

middle name *n* deuxième prénom *m*; *fig* trait *m* de caractère principal; honesty is her ~ c'est l'honnêteté même.

middle-of-the-road *adj* [opinions, policies] modéré; *pej* timide, circonspect; ~ music variétés *fpl* OR musique *f* passe-partout *pej*.

middle school *n Br école pour enfants de 8 à 13 ans; Am école pour enfants de 10 à 13 ans*, ≃ collège.

middle-sized *adj* de taille moyenne.

middle term *n* PHILOS moyen terme *m (d'un syllogisme)*.

middleweight ['mɪdlweɪt] ◇ *n* poids *m* moyen.
◇ *adj* [championship] de poids moyen; he's the world ~ champion c'est le champion du monde des poids moyens.

Middle West = **Midwest**.

middling *inf* ['mɪdlɪŋ] *adj* [average] moyen; [mediocre] médiocre; [in health]: he's only ~ ça va sans plus; how are you? – fair to ~ ça va? – on fait aller.

Middx *written abbr of* Middlesex.

Mideast [,mɪd'iːst] *Am* = **Middle East**.

midfield [,mɪd'fiːld] *n* SPORT milieu *m* du terrain; in ~ au milieu du terrain; ~ player (joueur *m* du) milieu *m* de terrain.

midge [mɪdʒ] *n* moucheron *m*.

midget ['mɪdʒɪt] ◇ *n* [dwarf] nain *m*, naine *f*.
◇ *adj* nain, minuscule.

midi ['mɪdɪ] *n* [coat] manteau *m* à mi-mollet; [skirt] jupe *f* à mi-mollet.

midiron ['mɪdaɪən] *n* [in golf] fer *m* moyen.

midi system *n* mini-chaîne *f*.

midland ['mɪdlənd] *adj* au centre du pays.

Midlands ['mɪdləndz] *pl pr n*: the ~ les Midlands *(comtés du centre de l'Angleterre)*.

midlife ['mɪdlaɪf] *n* la cinquantaine; in ~, it's hard to find a new job la cinquantaine passée, il est difficile de retrouver un emploi.

midlife crisis *n*: he's having OR going through a ~ il a du mal à passer le cap de la cinquantaine.

midmorning [,mɪd'mɔːnɪŋ] *n* milieu *m* de la matinée; we had a ~ snack nous avons mangé quelque chose vers 11 h.

midmost ['mɪdməʊst] *adj* le plus proche du centre.

midnight ['mɪdnaɪt] ◇ *n* minuit *m*; at ~ à minuit ❑ 'Midnight's Children' *Rushdie* 'les Enfants de minuit'.
◇ *adj* [mass, swim] de minuit; we had a ~ feast on a mangé quelque chose au milieu de la nuit; to burn the ~ oil travailler tard dans la nuit; the land of the ~ sun les pays du soleil de minuit *(au nord du cercle polaire arctique)*; 'Midnight Cowboy' *Schlesinger* 'Macadam cowboy'; the ~ ride *Am* HIST *épisode héroïque de la guerre d'Indépendance américaine*.

THE MIDNIGHT RIDE:
Nom donné à l'acte héroïque de Paul Revere, qui, en 1775, pendant la guerre d'Indépendance, parcourut au galop la distance de Boston à Lexington et Concord et parvint à alerter les patriotes américains du débarquement des troupes anglaises.

---

midnight blue *adj* bleu nuit *(inv)*.

mid-off *n au cricket, position du joueur le plus proche du lanceur, à gauche de celui-ci s'il est gaucher, à sa droite s'il est droitier*.

mid-on *n au cricket, position du joueur le plus proche du lanceur, à sa gauche de celui-ci s'il est droitier, à sa droite s'il est gaucher*.

midpoint ['mɪdpɔɪnt] *n* [in space, time] milieu *m*.

midrib ['mɪdrɪb] *n* nervure *f* centrale.

midriff ['mɪdrɪf] *n* -**1.** [stomach] ventre *m*; he's developed a bit of a ~ bulge il a pris du ventre. -**2.** ANAT diaphragme *m*.

midrise ['mɪdraɪz] *adj Am*: ~ apartment block immeuble *m* de hauteur moyenne *(10 étages au maximum)*.

midshipman ['mɪdʃɪpmən] (*pl* **midshipmen** [-mən]) *n* NAUT aspirant *m*, enseigne *m* de vaisseau (deuxième classe).

midst [mɪdst] *n* -**1.** [in space] milieu *m*, cœur *m*; in the ~ of au milieu OR au cœur de; there's a spy in our ~ il y a un espion parmi nous. -**2.** [in time]: in the ~ of the crisis en pleine crise.

midstream [mɪd'striːm] *n*: in ~ *literal* au milieu du courant; he stopped talking in ~ *fig* il s'arrêta au beau milieu d'une phrase.

midsummer ['mɪd,sʌmə'] *n*: in ~ au milieu de l'été, en été; a ~ night une nuit d'été ❑ ~ madness folie *f* estivale; 'A Midsummer Night's Dream' *Shakespeare* 'le Songe d'une nuit d'été'.

Midsummer Day, Midsummer's Day *n* le solstice d'été.

midterm [mɪd'tɜːm] *n* -**1.** SCH & UNIV milieu *m* du trimestre; at OR in ~ au milieu du trimestre; ~ exams examens *mpl* du milieu du trimestre. -**2.** MED [of pregnancy] milieu *m*. -**3.** POL: ~ elections *aux États-Unis, élections législatives qui ont lieu au milieu du mandat présidentiel*.

midtown ['mɪdtaʊn] *n Am partie d'une ville située à mi-chemin entre le centre et les quartiers périphériques*; a ~ apartment un appartement pas très loin du centre.

midway [*adv* ,mɪd'weɪ, *adj* 'mɪdweɪ] ◇ *adv* à mi-chemin; we broke our journey ~ nous avons interrompu notre voyage à mi-chemin; she was ~ through writing the first chapter elle avait déjà écrit la moitié du premier chapitre; ~ between à mi-chemin entre.
◇ *adj*: ~ point [in time, space] milieu *m*; we've now reached a ~ point in the negotiations nous avons maintenant parcouru la moitié du chemin dans les négociations.
◇ *n Am* [in fairground] allée *f* centrale.

midweek [*adv* mɪd'wiːk, *adj* 'mɪd'wiːk]
◇ *adv* [travel, arrive, meet] au milieu de la semaine; RAIL ≃ en période bleue.
◇ *adj* [travel, prices, performance] au milieu de la semaine; RAIL ≃ (en) période bleue.

Midwest [,mɪd'west] *pr n*: the ~ le Midwest; in the ~ dans le Midwest.

Midwestern [,mɪd'westən] *adj* du Midwest.

midwife ['mɪdwaɪf] (*pl* **midwives** [-waɪvz]) *n* sage-femme *f*.

midwifery ['mɪd,wɪfərɪ] *n* obstétrique *f*.

midwife toad *n* crapaud *m* accoucheur, alyte *m*.

midwinter [,mɪd'wɪntə'] *n* [solstice] solstice *m* d'hiver; in ~ au milieu de l'hiver; a ~ OR ~'s day un jour d'hiver.

midyear [,mɪd'jɪə'] ◇ *n* milieu *m* de l'année.
◇ *adj* du milieu de l'année.
◆ **midyears** *npl Am* UNIV ≃ partiels *mpl* du deuxième trimestre.

miffed *inf* [mɪft] *adj* [person] piqué, fâché; [expression] froissé, fâché.

miffy *inf* ['mɪfɪ] (*compar* **miffier**, *superl* **miffiest**) *adj* en rogne.

might[1] [maɪt] *modal vb* -**1.** [expressing possibility] you ~ well be right il se pourrait bien que vous ayez raison; I ~ be home late tonight je rentrerai peut-être tard ce soir; why not come with us? – I ~ pourquoi ne viens-tu pas avec nous? – peut-être; don't eat it, it ~ be poisonous n'en mange pas, tu pourrais t'empoisonner; hundreds of lives ~ have been lost unnecessarily des centaines de gens sont peut-être morts inutilement; she ~ well have decided to turn back il se pourrait OR il se peut bien qu'elle ait décidé de rentrer; they ~ have reached the summit by now ils ont peut-être déjà atteint le sommet; she ~ have decided not to go il se peut qu'elle ait décidé de ne pas y aller. -**2.** [past form of 'may']: I never considered that she ~ want to come je n'avais jamais pensé qu'elle pouvait avoir envie de venir; we feared you ~ be dead nous avons eu peur que vous ne soyez mort. -**3.** [in polite questions or suggestions]: ~ I interrupt? puis-je me permettre de vous interrompre?; and what, ~ I ask, was the reason? et puis-je savoir quelle en était la raison?; ~ I make a suggestion? puis-je me permettre de suggérer quelque chose?; you ~ try using a different approach altogether vous pourriez adopter une approche entièrement différente; I thought we ~ have tea together somewhere je m'étais dit que nous pourrions aller prendre un thé ensemble quelque part. -**4.** [commenting on a statement made]: that, I ~ add, was not my idea cela n'était pas mon idée, soit dit en passant; this, as one ~ expect, did not go down well with the government le gouvernement, est-il nécessaire de le préciser, n'a guère apprécié. -**5.** [ought to]: you ~ at least tidy up your room! tu pourrais au moins ranger ta chambre!; I ~ have known he'd be the last (to arrive) j'aurais dû savoir qu'il serait le dernier (à arriver); you ~ have warned me! tu aurais pu me prévenir! -**6.** [used to contradict or challenge]: they ~ say they support women, but they do nothing practical to help them ils disent peut-être qu'ils soutiennent les femmes mais ils ne font rien pour les aider sur le plan concret. -**7.** *fml* OR *hum* [in questions]: and who ~ you be? et qui êtes-vous donc?; and what ~ you be up to? et que faites-vous donc? -**8.** *phr*: we ~ as well go home (as stay here) nous ferions aussi bien de rentrer chez nous (plutôt que de rester ici); I ~ as well have stayed in bed j'aurais aussi bien fait de rester au lit; he's regretting it now, as well he ~! il le regrette maintenant, et pour cause!

might[2] [maɪt] *n* -**1.** [power - of nation] pouvoir *m*, puissance *f*; [- of army] puissance *f*. -**2.** [physical strength] force *f*; with all one's ~ de toutes ses forces; he started yelling with all his ~ il se mit à crier à tue-tête ❑ with ~ and main de toutes ses forces; ~ is right *prov* force fait loi *prov*.

might-have-been *n* **-1.** [opportunity] occasion *f* manquée; [hope] espoir *m* déçu. **-2.** *inf* [person] raté *m*, -e *f*.
mightily ['maɪtɪlɪ] *adv* **-1.** [with vigour] avec vigueur, vigoureusement. **-2.** [extremely] extrêmement.
mightn't ['maɪtənt] = **might not**.
might've ['maɪtəv] = **might have**.
mighty ['maɪtɪ] (*compar* **mightier**, *superl* **mightiest**) ◇ *adj* **-1.** [powerful] puissant. **-2.** [impressive] imposant; [enormous] énorme.
◇ *adv* *inf Am* rudement; that's ~ kind of you c'est rudement gentil de votre part.
mignonette [,mɪnjə'net] *n* mignonnette *f*, réséda *m*.
migraine ['mi:greɪn, 'maɪgreɪn] *n* migraine *f*; to suffer from ~ avoir des migraines; I've got a ~ j'ai la migraine.
migrant ['maɪgrənt] ◇ *n* **-1.** [bird, animal] migrateur *m*. **-2.** [worker - in agriculture] (travailleur *m*) saisonnier *m*; [- foreign] travailleur *m* immigré. **-3.** *Austr* immigré *m*, -e *f*.
◇ *adj* **-1.** [bird, animal] migrateur. **-2.** [person]: ~ worker [seasonal] (travailleur *m*) saisonnier *m*; [foreign] travailleur *m* immigré. **-3.** *Austr* [immigrant] immigrant; ~ accommodation logement *m* pour les immigrés.
migrate [*Br* maɪ'greɪt, *Am* 'maɪgreɪt] *vi* **-1.** [bird, animal] migrer. **-2.** [person, family] migrer, se déplacer, émigrer; the people ~d to the cities les gens ont migré vers les villes.
migration [maɪ'greɪʃn] *n* migration *f*.
migratory ['maɪgrətrɪ] *adj* **-1.** [bird, fish] migrateur. **-2.** [habit, movement] migratoire.
mikado [mɪ'kɑ:dəʊ] (*pl* **mikados**) *n* mikado *m* *(empereur)*.
mike *inf* [maɪk] (*abbr of* **microphone**) *n* micro *m*.
mil [mɪl] *n* **-1.** [unit of length] millième *m* de pouce. **-2.** [thousand] mille *m inv*.
milady [mɪ'leɪdɪ] (*pl* **miladies**) *n arch* madame *f*.
Milan [mɪ'læn] *pr n* Milan.
Milanese [,mɪlə'ni:z] ◇ *n* Milanais *m*, -e *f*.
◇ *adj* milanais.
milch cow ['mɪltʃ-] *n* vache *f* laitière; *fig* vache *f* à lait.
mild [maɪld] ◇ *adj* **-1.** [person, manner, voice] doux. **-2.** [in taste - cheese] doux; [- curry] pas très fort OR épicé; [soap, shampoo] doux; [in strength - sedative, cigarette] léger. **-3.** [clement - winter] doux; the weather's ~ for the time of year il fait (un temps) doux pour la saison. **-4.** [indulgent - punishment] léger; [- criticism] clément.
◇ *n Br bière moins riche en houblon et plus foncée que la «bitter»*.
mildew ['mɪldju:] ◇ *n* **-1.** [on cereals, flowers] rouille *f*; [on vines, potatoes, tomatoes] mildiou *m*. **-2.** [on paper, leather, food] moisissure *f*.
◇ *vi* **-1.** [cereals, flowers] se rouiller; [vines, potatoes, tomatoes] être atteint par le mildiou. **-2.** [paper, leather, food] moisir.
mildewed ['mɪldju:d] *adj* [cereals, flowers] rouillé; [vines] mildiousé; [paper, leather, food] moisi.
mildly ['maɪldlɪ] *adv* **-1.** [in manner, voice] doucement, avec douceur. **-2.** [slightly] modérément, légèrement; that's putting it ~! c'est le moins qu'on puisse dire!; it was rather silly, to put it ~ c'était plutôt idiot, c'est le moins qu'on puisse dire.
mild-mannered *adj* doux.
mildness ['maɪldnɪs] *n* **-1.** [of manner] douceur *f*. **-2.** [in taste]: she appreciated the ~ of the curry elle apprécia le fait que le curry n'était pas trop épicé. **-3.** [of weather] douceur *f*. **-4.** [of rebuke] indulgence *f*, clémence *f*.
mild steel *n* acier *m* doux.
mile [maɪl] *n* **-1.** [measurement] mille *m (1 609,33 m)*; [in athletics] mile *m*; it's 10 ~s away c'est à une quinzaine de kilomètres d'ici; she lives 30 ~s from Birmingham elle habite à une cinquantaine de kilomètres de Birmingham; the two towns are 50 ~s apart les deux villes sont (situées) à 80 kilomètres l'une de l'autre; it's 10 ~s back c'est à une quinzaine de kilomètres derrière nous; we passed a restaurant a few ~s back nous sommes passés devant un restaurant quelques kilomètres plus haut; a 100-~ journey un voyage de 160 kilomètres; a 10-~ tailback (of traffic) un bouchon d'une quinzaine de kilomètres. **-2.** [long distance]: you can see it a ~ off ça se voit de loin; they live ~s apart ils habitent à des kilomètres l'un de l'autre; the best doctor for ~s around le meilleur médecin à des kilomètres à la ronde; we're ~s from the nearest town on est à des kilomètres de la ville la plus proche; it's ~s from anywhere c'est un endroit complètement isolé; you can see for ~s and ~s on voit à des kilomètres à la ronde; we walked (for) ~s and ~s on a fait des kilomètres (à pied); I've had to use ~s of string il m'a fallu des kilomètres de ficelle. **-3.** *fig*: they're ~s ahead of their competitors ils ont une avance considérable sur leurs concurrents; the two judges are ~s apart on capital punishment les deux juges ont des points de vue OR des avis radicalement opposés sur la peine de mort ❑ he was ~s away il était dans la lune; you could see what was going to happen a ~ off on voyait d'ici ce qui allait arriver; your calculations are ~s out vous vous êtes complètement trompé dans vos calculs; not a million ~s from here tout près d'ici, parmi nous; it's not a million ~s from what we tried to do cela ressemble assez à ce que nous avons essayé de faire. **-4.** *inf (adverbial use)* [much]: she's ~s better than me at languages elle est bien plus forte que moi en langues; I'm feeling ~s better already je me sens déjà cent fois mieux.
mileage ['maɪlɪdʒ] *n* **-1.** AUT [distance] ≃ kilométrage *m*; the car's got a very high ~ la voiture a beaucoup roulé OR a un kilométrage élevé; the papers got tremendous ~ out of the scandal *fig* les journaux ont exploité le scandale au maximum. **-2.** [consumption] consommation *f* (d'essence); you get better ~ with a small car on consomme moins avec une petite voiture.
mileage allowance *n* indemnité *f* kilométrique.
Mile-High City *pr n* *surnom de la ville de Denver*.
mileometer [maɪ'lɒmɪtəʳ] *n* compteur *m* (kilométrique).
milepost ['maɪlpəʊst] *n* ≃ borne *f* (kilométrique).
miler ['maɪləʳ] *n* coureur *m*, -euse *f* du mile.
milestone ['maɪlstəʊn] *n* **-1.** *literal* ≃ borne *f* (kilométrique). **-2.** *fig* [important event] jalon *m*, étape *f* importante; a ~ in the history of aviation une étape importante dans l'histoire de l'aviation.
milieu [*Br* 'mi:ljɜ:, *Am* mi:l'ju:] *n* environnement *m* (social).
militancy ['mɪlɪtənsɪ] *n* militantisme *m*.
militant ['mɪlɪtənt] ◇ *adj* militant; she's a ~ feminist c'est une féministe militante.
◇ *n* **-1.** [gen] militant *m*, -e *f*. **-2.** *Br* = **Militant (Tendency)**.
◆ **Militant (Tendency)** *pr n* POL *tendance d'extrême gauche à l'intérieur du parti travailliste britannique*.
militarily [*Br* 'mɪlɪtərɪlɪ, *Am* ,mɪlə'terəlɪ] *adv* militairement.
militarism ['mɪlɪtərɪzm] *n* militarisme *m*.
militarist ['mɪlɪtərɪst] *n* militariste *mf*.
militaristic [,mɪlɪtə'rɪstɪk] *adj* militariste.
militarization [,mɪlɪtəraɪ'zeɪʃn] *n* militarisation *f*.
militarize, -ise ['mɪlɪtəraɪz] *vt* militariser.
military ['mɪlɪtrɪ] ◇ *adj* militaire; he's a ~ man c'est un militaire (de carrière) ❑ ~ academy école *f* militaire; ~ band fanfare *f* militaire; ~ service service *m* militaire.
◇ *n*: the ~ l'armée *f*.
military police *n* police *f* militaire.
military policeman *n membre de la police militaire*.
militate ['mɪlɪteɪt]
◆ **militate against** *vt insep* [facts, actions] militer contre; her temperament ~s against her son tempérament joue contre elle.
militia [mɪ'lɪʃə] *n* **-1.** [body of citizens] milice *f*. **-2.** *Am* [reserve army] réserve *f*.
militiaman [mɪ'lɪʃəmən] (*pl* **militiamen** [-mən]) *n* milicien *m*.
milk [mɪlk] ◇ *n* lait *m*; mother's ~ lait maternel; cow's ~ lait de vache; goat's ~ lait de chèvre; Milk of Magnesia® lait de magnésie; a land flowing with ~ and honey un pays de cocagne; the ~ of human kindness *fig* le lait de la tendresse humaine.
◇ *comp* [bottle, churn, jug etc - empty] à lait; [- full] de lait; ~ can *Am* bidon *m* de lait.
◇ *vt* **-1.** [cow, goat] traire. **-2.** [snake] extraire le venin de. **-3.** *fig*: to ~ a country of its resources dépouiller un pays de ses ressources; he really ~s his clients il plume ses clients; she ~ed the subject dry elle a épuisé le sujet.
◇ *vi*: the cow ~s well la vache donne beaucoup de lait.
milk bar *n* milk-bar *m*.
milk chocolate *n* chocolat *m* au lait.
milk duct *n* canal *m* galactophore.
milker ['mɪlkəʳ] *n* **-1.** [cow]: a good ~ une bonne laitière. **-2.** [dairy hand] trayeur *m*, -euse *f*. **-3.** [machine] trayeuse *f*.
milk fever *n* fièvre *f* lactée.
milk float *n Br* camionnette *f* du laitier.
milk gland *n* glande *f* lactéale OR mammaire OR galactophore.
milking ['mɪlkɪŋ] *n* traite *f*; to do the ~ traire les vaches; ~ time l'heure *f* de la traite.
milking machine *n* machine *f* à traire, trayeuse *f*.
milking parlour *n* salle *f* de traite.
milking stool *n* tabouret *m* à traire.
milk loaf *n* pain *m* brioché.
milkmaid ['mɪlkmeɪd] *n* vachère *f*, trayeuse *f*.
milkman ['mɪlkmən] (*pl* **milkmen** [-mən]) *n* [who delivers milk] laitier *m*; *Br* [who milks] vacher *m*, trayeur *m*.
milk powder *n* lait *m* en poudre.
milk pudding *n Br* entremets *m* au lait.
milk round *n Br* **-1.** [for milk delivery] tournée *f* du laitier. **-2.** UNIV *tournée des universités par les employeurs pour recruter des étudiants en fin d'études*.
milk run *n* **-1.** AERON vol *m* sans histoire, partie *f* de rigolade. **-2.** [regular journey] trajet *m* habituel, tournée *f* habituelle.
milk shake *n* milk-shake *m*.
milksop ['mɪlksɒp] *n* chiffe *f* molle; he's such a ~! c'est une vraie chiffe molle!
milk stout *n Br* bière *f* brune.
milk tooth *n* dent *f* de lait.
milk train *n* premier train *m*.
milkweed ['mɪlkwi:d] *n* asclépias *f*.
milk-white *adj* d'un blanc laiteux.
milky ['mɪlkɪ] (*compar* **milkier**, *superl* **milkiest**) *adj* **-1.** [taste] laiteux, de lait; [dessert] lacté, à base de lait; [tea, coffee] avec du lait; do you have your tea ~? est-ce que vous prenez beaucoup de lait dans votre thé? **-2.** [colour] laiteux; [skin] d'un blanc laiteux. **-3.** [cloudy - liquid] laiteux, lactescent.
Milky Way *pr n*: the ~ la Voie lactée.
mill [mɪl] ◇ *n* **-1.** [for flour] moulin *m*; [on industrial scale] meunerie *f*, minoterie *f*; she's been through the ~ elle a souffert; she put him through the ~ elle lui en a fait voir; 'The Mill on the Floss' *Eliot* 'le Moulin sur la Floss'. **-2.** [factory] usine *f*; steel ~ aciérie *f*; cotton ~ filature *f*. **-3.** [domestic - for coffee, pepper] moulin *m*. **-4.** TECH [for coins] machine *f* à créneler; [for metal] fraiseuse *f*.
◇ *vt* **-1.** [grain] moudre; [ore] broyer. **-2.** [mark - coin] créneler; [- screw] moleter; [- surface] strier, rainer; a coin with a ~ed edge une pièce crénelée.
◆ **mill about** *Br*, **mill around** *vi insep* [crowd, people] grouiller.

millboard ['mɪlbɔːd] *n* carton *m* gris.

millenarian [ˌmɪlɪ'neərɪən] ◇ *adj* millénariste.
◇ *n* millénariste *mf*.

millenarianism [ˌmɪlɪ'neərɪənɪzm] *n* millénarisme *m*, chiliasme *m*.

millenary [mɪ'lenərɪ] (*pl* **millenaries**) ◇ *adj* millénaire.
◇ *n* millénaire *m*.

millennial [mɪ'lenɪəl] *adj* du millenium.

millennium [mɪ'lenɪəm] (*pl* **millenniums** OR **millennia** [-nɪə]) *n* **-1.** [thousand years] millénaire *m*. **-2.** RELIG *fig*: the ~ le millénium.

millepede ['mɪlɪpiːd] = **millipede**.

miller ['mɪlə^r] *n* meunier *m*, -ère *f*.

millet ['mɪlɪt] *n* millet *m*.

mill hand *n dated* ouvrier *m*, -ère *f*.

milliard ['mɪljɑːd] *n Br* milliard *m*.

millibar ['mɪlɪbɑː^r] *n* millibar *m*.

milligram(me) ['mɪlɪgræm] *n* milligramme *m*.

millilitre *Br*, **milliliter** *Am* ['mɪlɪˌliːtə^r] *n* millilitre *m*.

millimetre *Br*, **millimeter** *Am* ['mɪlɪˌmiːtə^r] *n* millimètre *m*.

milliner ['mɪlɪnə^r] *n* modiste *mf*.

millinery ['mɪlɪnrɪ] *n* [manufacture] fabrication *f* de chapeaux de femmes; [sale] vente *f* de chapeaux de femmes.

milling ['mɪlɪŋ] *n* crénelage *m*.

milling machine *n* fraiseuse *f*.

million ['mɪljən] *n* **-1.** *literal* million *m*; two ~ dollars deux millions de dollars; ~s of pounds des millions de livres; the population of Scotland is five ~ l'Écosse a cinq millions d'habitants; the chance of that happening is one in a ~ il y a une chance sur un million que ça arrive; his secretary is one in a ~ sa secrétaire est une perle rare; that man is worth several ~ cet homme est plusieurs fois milliardaire ❑ I feel like a ~ dollars! je suis en pleine forme!; she looked (like) a ~ dollars elle était éblouissante. **-2.** [enormous number]: there were simply ~s of people at the concert! il y avait un monde fou au concert!; I've told you a ~ times not to do that je t'ai dit cent fois de ne pas faire ça; there are a ~ and one ways of cooking vegetables il y a mille et une façons de préparer les légumes.
◆ **millions** *npl* [masses] masses *fpl*; the nameless ~s who will come after us les millions d'inconnus qui nous succéderont.

millionaire [ˌmɪljə'neə^r] *n* ≃ milliardaire *mf*; he's a dollar ~ il possède des millions de dollars.

millionairess [ˌmɪljə'neərɪs] *n* millionnaire *f*.

millionth ['mɪljənθ] ◇ *adj* millionième.
◇ *n* **-1.** [ordinal] millionième *mf*. **-2.** [fraction] millionième *m*.

millipede ['mɪlɪpiːd] *n* mille-pattes *m inv*.

millisecond ['mɪlɪˌsekənd] *n* milliseconde *f*, millième *m* de seconde.

millpond ['mɪlpɒnd] *n* retenue *f* de moulin; the sea was like a ~ *fig* la mer était d'huile.

millrace ['mɪlreɪs] *n* bief *m*.

Mills and Boon® ['mɪlzn̩buːn] *pr n maison d'édition publiant des romans sentimentaux.*

millstone ['mɪlstəʊn] *n* **-1.** *literal* meule *f*. **-2.** *fig* fardeau *m*; another ~ round the taxpayer's neck une charge supplémentaire pour le contribuable.

millstream ['mɪlstriːm] *n* courant *m* du bief.

millwheel ['mɪlwiːl] *n* roue *f* (d'un moulin).

millwright ['mɪlraɪt] *n* constructeur *m* de moulins.

milometer [maɪ'lɒmɪtə^r] = **mileometer**.

milord [mɪ'lɔːd] *n arch* milord *m*.

milt [mɪlt] *n* [of fish - fluid] laitance *f*; [- organ] testicule *m*.

mim *inf* [mɪm] *adj Br dial* bégueule.

mime [maɪm] ◇ *n* [actor, play] mime *m*; to explain something in ~ expliquer quelque chose par gestes; to study ~ étudier l'art du mime.
◇ *vi* **-1.** THEAT faire du mime. **-2.** [pop singer] chanter en playback.
◇ *vt* mimer; [derisively] singer.

Mimeograph® ['mɪmɪəgrɑːf] ◇ *n* **-1.** [machine] Ronéo® *f*, duplicateur *m* (à stencil). **-2.** [text] polycopié *m*, texte *m* ronéotypé.
◇ *vt* ronéotyper, ronéoter.

mimesis [mɪ'miːsɪs] *n* BIOL mimétisme *m*.

mimetic [mɪ'metɪk] *adj* mimétique.

mimic ['mɪmɪk] (*pt* & *pp* **mimicked**, *cont* **mimicking**) ◇ *vt* **-1.** [gestures] mimer; [satirically] parodier, singer. **-2.** BIOL imiter (par mimétisme).
◇ *n* imitateur *m*, -trice *f*; she's an excellent ~ c'est une excellente imitatrice.
◇ *adj* **-1.** [mock - battle, warfare] simulé; ~ colouring mimétisme *m* des couleurs. **-2.** THEAT mimique.

mimicry ['mɪmɪkrɪ] *n* **-1.** [imitation] imitation *f*. **-2.** BIOL mimétisme *m*.

mimosa [mɪ'məʊzə] *n* mimosa *m*.

min. **-1.** (*written abbr of* **minute**) mn, min. **-2.** (*written abbr of* **minimum**) min.

Min. *written abbr of* **ministry**.

minaret [mɪnə'ret] *n* minaret *m*.

minatory ['mɪnətrɪ] *adj fml* comminatoire.

mince [mɪns] ◇ *vt* **-1.** CULIN hacher. **-2.** *phr*: he doesn't ~ his words il ne mâche pas ses mots.
◇ *vi* **-1.** [speak] parler avec affectation. **-2.** [move] marcher en se trémoussant; he ~d into the room il est entré dans la salle en se trémoussant.
◇ *n* viande *f* hachée, haché *m*.

mincemeat ['mɪnsmiːt] *n* **-1.** [meat] viande *f* hachée. **-2.** [sweet filling] *mélange de fruits secs et d'épices qui sert de garniture à des tartelettes.* **-3.** *phr*: to make ~ of sb *inf* réduire qqn en bouillie OR en chair à pâté.

mince pie *n tartelette fourrée avec un mélange de fruits secs et d'épices que l'on sert à Noël en Grande-Bretagne.*

mincer ['mɪnsə^r] *n* hachoir *m*, hache-viande *m inv*.

mincing ['mɪnsɪŋ] *adj* affecté, maniéré; he came in with ~ steps il est entré en se trémoussant.

mincingly ['mɪnsɪŋlɪ] *adv* en minaudant.

mincing machine = **mincer**.

mind [maɪnd] ◇ *n* **-1.** [reason] esprit *m*; the power of ~ over matter le pouvoir de l'esprit sur la matière; to be strong in ~ and body être physiquement et mentalement solide; to be of sound ~ être sain d'esprit; his ~ became unhinged il a perdu la raison, il est devenu fou; what state of ~ was he in? dans quel état d'esprit était-il? ❑ to be/to go out of one's ~ être/devenir fou; he was out of his ~ with worry il était fou d'inquiétude; he isn't in his right ~ il n'a pas tous ses esprits; no-one in their right ~ would do such a thing aucune personne sensée n'agirait ainsi. **-2.** [thoughts]: there's something on her ~ il y a quelque chose qui la tracasse; I have a lot on my ~ j'ai beaucoup de soucis; what's going on in her ~? qu'est-ce qui se passe dans son esprit OR sa tête?; at the back of my ~ was the fear that we would arrive too late au fond de moi-même, je craignais que nous n'arrivions trop tard; to put sthg to the back of one's ~ chasser qqch de son esprit; I just can't get him out of my ~ je n'arrive absolument pas à l'oublier; to have sb/sthg in ~ penser à qqn/qqch de précis; who do you have in ~ for the role? à qui songez-vous pour le rôle?, qui avez-vous en vue pour le rôle?; what kind of holiday did you have in ~? qu'est-ce que tu voulais OR voudrais faire pour les vacances?; you must put the idea out of your ~ tu dois te sortir cette idée de la tête; to set one's mind on doing sthg se mettre en tête de faire qqch; to have one's ~ set on sthg vouloir qqch à tout prix; a drink will take your ~ off the accident bois un verre, ça te fera oublier l'accident ❑ to see things in one's ~'s eye bien se représenter qqch. **-3.** [attention]: I can't seem to apply my ~ to the problem je n'arrive pas à me concentrer sur le problème; keep your ~ on the job ne vous laissez pas distraire; she does crosswords to keep her ~ occupied elle fait des mots croisés pour s'occuper l'esprit. **-4.** [memory]: my ~ has gone blank j'ai un trou de mémoire; it brings to ~ the time we were in Spain cela me rappelle l'époque où nous étions en Espagne; Churchill's words come to ~ on pense aux paroles de Churchill; it went clean OR right out of my ~ cela m'est complètement sorti de l'esprit OR de la tête; it puts me in ~ of Japan cela me fait penser au Japon, cela me rappelle le Japon; it must have slipped my ~ j'ai dû oublier ❑ time out of ~ I've warned him not to go there *Br* cela fait une éternité que je lui dis de ne pas y aller. **-5.** [intellect] esprit *m*; she has an outstanding ~ elle est d'une très grande intelligence; he has the ~ of a child il a l'esprit d'un enfant || [intelligent person, thinker] esprit *m*; the great ~s of our century les grands esprits OR cerveaux de notre siècle. **-6.** [way of thinking]: the Western ~ les modes de pensée occidentaux; he has a suspicious ~ il est soupçonneux de nature. **-7.** [opinion]: to be of the same OR of like ~ être du même avis; they're all of one ~ ils sont tous d'accord OR du même avis ❑ to be in two ~s about sthg: I'm in two ~s about where to go for my holidays je ne sais pas très bien où aller passer mes vacances; to make up one's ~ se décider, prendre une décision; my ~ is made up ma décision est prise; to make up one's ~ about sthg décider qqch; to make up one's ~ to do sthg se décider à faire qqch; she's made up her ~ to move house elle s'est résolue à déménager. **-8.** [desire]: I've half a ~ to give up j'ai à moitié envie de renoncer; I've a good ~ to tell him what I think j'ai bien envie de lui dire ce que je pense || [intention]: nothing was further from my ~ je n'en avais nullement l'intention; I've had it in ~ for some time now j'y songe depuis un moment.
◇ *vt* **-1.** [look after - children] garder; [- bags, possessions] garder, surveiller; [- shop, business] garder, tenir; [- plants, garden] s'occuper de, prendre soin de; can you ~ the house for us while we're away? [watch] pouvez-vous surveiller la maison pendant notre absence?; [look after] pouvez-vous vous occuper de la maison pendant notre absence? **-2.** [pay attention to] faire attention à; don't ~ the dog ne faites pas attention au chien; he didn't ~ my advice il n'a pas fait attention à OR n'a pas écouté mes conseils; ~ your own business! occupe-toi de ce qui te regarde!, mêle-toi de tes oignons!; ~ your language! surveille ton langage!; to ~ one's manners se surveiller; '~ the step' 'attention à la marche'; ~ the cat! attention au chat! ❑ never you ~! ce n'est pas votre affaire!; ~ your step *Br literal* & *fig* faites attention où vous mettez les pieds. **-3.** (+ *verb phrase*) [be sure of] faire attention à; ~ (that) you don't forget n'oubliez surtout pas; ~ you don't break it fais bien attention de ne pas le casser; ~ what you say [pay attention] réfléchissez à OR faites attention à ce que vous dites, [don't be rude] mesurez vos paroles; ~ what you're doing! regarde ce que tu fais! || [remember]: ~ you post my letter n'oubliez surtout pas de poster ma lettre. **-4.** [bother about] faire attention à, s'inquiéter de OR pour; don't ~ me, I'll just sit here quietly ne vous inquiétez pas de moi, je vais m'asseoir ici et je ne dérangerai personne; I really don't ~ what he says/thinks je me fiche de ce qu'il peut dire/penser. **-5.** [object to]: I don't ~ him il ne me dérange pas; you don't ~ me using the car, do you? — I ~ very much cela ne te dérange pas que je prenne la voiture? — cela me dérange beaucoup; do you ~ going out when the weather's cold? est-ce que cela vous ennuie de sortir quand il fait froid?; do you ~ me smoking? cela ne vous ennuie OR dérange pas que je fume?; did you ~ me inviting her? tu aurais peut-être préféré que je ne l'invite pas? ça t'ennuie que je l'aie invitée?; would you ~

turning out the light, please? [politely] pourriez-vous éteindre la lumière, s'il vous plaît?; [aggressively] est-ce que cela vous dérangerait beaucoup d'éteindre la lumière?; I wouldn't ~ a cup of tea je prendrais bien OR volontiers une tasse de thé. -**6.** *Scot & Ir* [remember] se rappeler, se souvenir de. -**7.** *phr*: ~ (you), I'm not surprised remarque OR tu sais, cela ne m'étonne pas; ~ you, he's a bit young ceci dit, il est un peu jeune; never ~ that now [leave it] ne vous occupez pas de cela tout de suite; [forget it] ce n'est plus la peine de s'en occuper; never ~ the consequences ne vous préoccupez pas des conséquences, peu importent les conséquences; never ~ what people say/think peu importe ce que disent/pensent les gens; never ~ his feelings, I've got a business to run! je n'ai que faire de ses états d'âme, j'ai une affaire à diriger!; never ~ him, just run for it! ne t'occupe pas de lui, fonce!

◇ *vi* -**1.** [object - esp in requests]: do you ~ if I open the window? cela vous dérange si j'ouvre la fenêtre?; would you ~ if I opened the window? est-ce que cela vous ennuierait si j'ouvrais la fenêtre?; do you ~ if I smoke? est-ce que cela vous gêne OR dérange que je fume?; I don't ~ in the least cela ne me dérange pas le moins du monde; if you don't ~ si vous voulez bien, si vous n'y voyez pas d'inconvénient; I can't say I really ~ je ne peux pas dire que cela m'ennuie OR me dérange vraiment; do you ~ if I take the car? – of course I don't (~) est-ce que cela vous ennuie que je prenne la voiture? – bien sûr que non; I don't ~ if I do [in reply to offer] volontiers, je ne dis pas non, ce n'est pas de refus. -**2.** [care, worry]: I don't ~ if people laugh at me – but you should ~! je ne me soucie guère que les gens se moquent de moi – mais vous devriez!; if you don't ~, I haven't finished si cela ne vous fait rien, je n'ai pas terminé; do you ~! *iron* [politely] vous permettez?; [indignantly] non mais!; never ~ [it doesn't matter] cela ne fait rien, tant pis; [don't worry] ne vous en faites pas; never ~ about the money now ne t'en fais pas pour l'argent, on verra plus tard. -**3.** *Br* [be careful] faire attention; ~ when you cross the road fais attention en traversant la route; ~! attention!

◆ **mind out** *vi insep Br* faire attention; ~ out! attention!; ~ out for (the) rocks! attention aux rochers!

MIND [maɪnd] *pr n organisme d'aide aux handicapés mentaux.*

mind-bending *inf adj* -**1.** [complicated] compliqué. -**2.** [drugs] hallucinogène, psychédélique.

mind-blowing *inf adj* [amazing] époustouflant.

mind-boggling *adj* extraordinaire, stupéfiant.

minded ['maɪndɪd] *adj fml* disposé; she could easily lend us the money, if she were ~ to do so elle pourrait facilement nous prêter l'argent, si elle y était disposée OR le voulait.

-minded *in cpds* -**1.** *(with adj)*: simple~ simple d'esprit; they're so narrow~ ils sont tellement étroits d'esprit. -**2.** *(with adv)*: to be politically~ s'intéresser beaucoup à la politique; many young people are scientifically~ beaucoup de jeunes ont l'esprit scientifique. -**3.** *(with n)*: my parents are very money~ mes parents ont un faible pour l'argent OR sont très portés sur l'argent; he's very sports~ c'est un passionné de sports.

minder ['maɪndəʳ] *n* -**1.** *inf Br* [bodyguard] gorille *m*. -**2.** [gen] gardien *m*, -enne *f*, surveillant *m*, -e *f*.

mind-expanding *adj* [drugs] hallucinogène, psychédélique.

mindful ['maɪndfʊl] *adj fml*: ~ of her feelings on the subject, he fell silent attentif à ce qu'elle ressentait à ce sujet, il se tut; he was always ~ of his children's future il a toujours été soucieux OR il s'est toujours préoccupé de l'avenir de ses enfants.

mindless ['maɪndlɪs] *adj* -**1.** [stupid - film, book] idiot, stupide; [senseless - cruelty, violence] insensé, sans nom. -**2.** [boring] bête, ennuyeux; a ~ job un travail ingrat OR stupide. -**3.** [heedless]: ~ of the danger, he dived into the river insouciant du danger, il plongea dans la rivière.

mind reader *n*: he must be a ~ il lit dans les pensées comme dans un livre; I'm not a ~ je ne suis pas devin.

mindset ['maɪndset] *n* façon *f* de voir les choses.

mine[1] [maɪn] ◇ *pron* le mien *m*, la mienne *f*, les miens *mpl*, les miennes *fpl*; is this pen ~? – no, it's ~! il est à moi ce stylo? – non, c'est le mien!; this bag is ~ ce sac m'appartient OR est à moi; the furniture is his but the house is ~ les meubles lui appartiennent mais la maison est à moi; he's an old friend of ~ c'est un vieil ami à moi; where did that brother of ~ get to? mais où est-ce que mon frère est encore passé?; I took her hands in ~ j'ai pris ses mains dans les miennes; ~ is an exceptional situation je me trouve dans une situation exceptionnelle; what's ~ is yours ce qui est à moi est à toi.

◇ *det arch* mon *m*, ma *f*, mes *pl*; ~ only hope mon seul espoir.

mine[2] [maɪn] ◇ *n* -**1.** [for coal, gold, salt etc] mine *f*; he went down the ~ OR mines at 16 il est descendu à la mine à 16 ans. -**2.** *fig* [valuable source] mine *f*; she's a ~ of information c'est une véritable mine de renseignements. -**3.** [explosive] mine *f*; to clear a road of ~s déminer une route.

◇ *vt* -**1.** GEOL [coal, gold etc] extraire; they ~ coal in the area il y a des mines de charbon dans la région. -**2.** MIL [road, sea] miner; the path was ~d le chemin était miné ‖ [destroy]: their jeep was ~d leur jeep a sauté sur une mine. -**3.** [undermine - fortification] saper.

◇ *vi* exploiter une mine; to ~ for uranium [prospect] chercher de l'uranium, prospecter pour trouver de l'uranium; [extract] exploiter une mine d'uranium.

mine detector *n* détecteur *m* de mines.

minefield ['maɪnfiːld] *n* -**1.** *literal* champ *m* de mines. -**2.** *fig*: the ~ of high-level diplomacy les chausse-trappes de la haute diplomatie; a medical/legal/political ~ une situation épineuse du point de vue médical/juridique/politique.

minehunter ['maɪn,hʌntəʳ] *n* NAUT chasseur *m* de mines.

minelayer ['maɪn,leɪəʳ] *n* mouilleur *m* de mines.

miner ['maɪnəʳ] *n* mineur *m* MIN.

mineral ['mɪnərəl] ◇ *n* -**1.** GEOL minéral *m*. -**2.** *Br* [soft drink] boisson *f* gazeuse (non alcoolique), soda *m*.

◇ *adj* minéral.

mineral jelly *n Br* vaseline *f*.

mineral kingdom *n*: the ~ le règne minéral.

mineralogical [,mɪnərə'lɒdʒɪkl] *adj* minéralogique.

mineralogist [,mɪnə'rælədʒɪst] *n* minéralogiste *mf*.

mineralogy [,mɪnə'rælədʒɪ] *n* minéralogie *f*.

mineral oil *n Br* huile *f* minérale; *Am* huile *f* de paraffine.

mineral ore *n* minerai *m*.

mineral water *n* eau *f* minérale.

Minerva [mɪ'nɜːvə] *pr n* Minerve.

mineshaft ['maɪnʃɑːft] *n* puits *m* de mine.

minestrone (soup) [,mɪnɪ'strəʊnɪ-] *n* minestrone *m*.

minesweeper ['maɪn,swiːpəʳ] *n* dragueur *m* de mines.

mineworker ['maɪn,wɜːkəʳ] *n* ouvrier *m*, -ère *f* de la mine, mineur *m*.

mingle ['mɪŋgl] ◇ *vt* mélanger, mêler; he ~d truth with lies il mélangeait le vrai et le faux; she read the letter with ~d sadness and relief elle lut la lettre avec un mélange de tristesse et de soulagement.

◇ *vi* se mêler (aux autres); people from all walks of life ~d together des gens de toutes conditions sociales se mêlaient les uns aux autres ‖ [at party]: excuse me, I must ~ excusez-moi, il faut que je salue d'autres invités.

mingy *inf* ['mɪndʒɪ] (*compar* **mingier**, *superl* **mingiest**) *adj Br* [mean - person] radin, pingre; [- portion, quantity] chiche, misérable, maigre.

mini ['mɪnɪ] ◇ *n* -**1.** *inf* [skirt] minijupe *f*. -**2.** *inf* COMPUT mini-ordinateur *m*, mini *m*.

◇ *adj* mini *(inv)*.

Mini® *n* [car] mini *f* (Austin®).

miniature ['mɪnətʃəʳ] ◇ *adj* [in miniature] en miniature; [model] miniature; [tiny] minuscule; a ~ Eiffel Tower une tour Eiffel miniature; ~ golf golf *m* miniature; ~ poodle caniche *m* nain; ~ railway chemin *m* de fer miniature.

◇ *n* [gen & ART] miniature *f*; in ~ en miniature.

miniaturist ['mɪnətʃərɪst] *n* miniaturiste *mf*.

miniaturization [,mɪnətʃəraɪ'zeɪʃn] *n* miniaturisation *f*.

miniaturize, -ise ['mɪnətʃəraɪz] *vt* miniaturiser.

miniaturized ['mɪnətʃəraɪzd] *adj* miniaturisé.

minibudget ['mɪnɪ,bʌdʒɪt] *n Br* POL *annexe à la loi de finances*.

minibus ['mɪnɪbʌs] (*pl* **minibuses**) *n* minibus *m*.

minicab ['mɪnɪkæb] *n Br voiture de série convertie en taxi*.

minicomputer [,mɪnɪkəm'pjuːtəʳ] *n* mini-ordinateur *m*.

minicourse ['mɪnɪkɔːs] *n Am* SCH stage *m* (intensif).

minidress ['mɪnɪdres] *n* mini-robe *f*.

minim ['mɪnɪm] *n* -**1.** *Br* MUS blanche *f*. -**2.** [measure] ≃ goutte *f (0,5 ml)*.

minima ['mɪnɪmə] *pl* → **minimum**.

minimal ['mɪnɪml] *adj* minimal; there has been only a ~ improvement il n'y a eu qu'une infime amélioration ❑ ~ art art *m* minimal; ~ pair LING paire *f* minimale.

minimalism ['mɪnɪməlɪzm] *n* minimalisme *m*.

minimalist ['mɪnɪməlɪst] *n* minimaliste *mf*.

minimalize, -ise ['mɪnɪməlaɪz] *vt* minimaliser.

minimally ['mɪnɪməlɪ] *adv* à peine; the new system is only ~ more efficient le nouveau système n'est guère plus efficace.

minimarket ['mɪnɪ,mɑːkɪt], **minimart** ['mɪnɪmɑːt] *n* supérette *f*, petit supermarché *m*.

minimax ['mɪnɪmæks] *n* MATH minimax *m*.

minimize, -ise ['mɪnɪ,maɪz] *vt* -**1.** [reduce - size, amount] réduire au minimum, diminuer le plus possible; they are trying to ~ the levels of CO_2 in the atmosphere on essaie de réduire les niveaux de CO_2 dans l'atmosphère. -**2.** [diminish - importance, achievement] minimiser; he tried to ~ her success as a novelist il essayait de minimiser son succès en tant que romancière.

minim rest *n Br* MUS demi-pause *f*.

minimum ['mɪnɪməm] (*pl* **minimums** OR **minima** [-mə]) ◇ *n* minimum *m*; costs were reduced to the OR a ~ les coûts furent réduits au minimum; there was only the ~ of damage il n'y a eu que des dégâts minimes; reduced to the very ~ réduit au strict minimum; keep expenses to a ~ limitez au minimum les dépenses, dépensez le moins possible; at the (very) ~ it will cost £2,000 (en mettant les choses) au mieux, cela coûtera 2 000 livres; we will need £50 each ~ OR a ~ of £50 each il nous faudra 50 livres chacun (au) minimum.

◇ *adj* minimum, minimal.

minimum lending rate *n Br* taux *m* d'escompte OR de base.

minimum safeguard price *n Br* prix *m* minimum de sauvegarde *(du pétrole)*.

minimum wage *n* salaire *m* minimum *(légal)*, ≃ SMIC *m*.

mining ['maɪnɪŋ] ◇ *n* -**1.** MIN exploitation *f* minière, extraction *f*. -**2.** MIL [on land] pose *f* de mines; [at sea] mouillage *m* de mines.

◇ *adj* [town, company, area] minier; [family] de mineurs.

mining engineer *n* ingénieur *m* des mines.

mining engineering *n* ingénierie *f* des mines.

minion ['mɪnjən] *n pej* laquais *m*.

minipill ['mɪnɪpɪl] *n* minipilule *f*.

miniscule ['mɪnɪskju:l] *adj* minuscule.

mini-series *n* TV mini-feuilleton *m*.

miniskirt ['mɪnɪskɜ:t] *n* minijupe *f*.

minister ['mɪnɪstəʳ] ◇ *n* -**1.** POL ministre *m*; **the Minister of Education/Defence** le ministre de l'Éducation/de la Défense; **junior ~** sous-secrétaire *m* d'État. -**2.** [diplomat] ministre *m*. -**3.** RELIG pasteur *m*, ministre *m*; **~ of God** ministre du culte.

◇ *vi* -**1.** [provide care]: **to ~ to sb** secourir qqn, donner des soins à qqn; **to ~ to sb's needs** pourvoir aux besoins de qqn; **he ~ed to the sick** il secourait les malades. -**2.** RELIG: **he ~ed to St. Luke's for 20 years** il a été le pasteur de l'église St-Luc pendant 20 ans.

ministerial [,mɪnɪ'stɪərɪəl] *adj* -**1.** POL [project, crisis] ministériel; [post] de ministre; **~ benches** banc *m* des ministres; **he held ~ office for six months** il fut ministre pendant six mois. -**2.** RELIG pastoral, sacerdotal.

ministering angel ['mɪnɪstrɪŋ-] *n fig* ange *m* de bonté.

ministration [,mɪnɪ'streɪʃn] *n* RELIG ministère *m*.

◆ **ministrations** *npl fml* soins *mpl*; **despite her ~s the animal died** malgré les soins qu'elle lui a prodigués, l'animal est mort.

ministry ['mɪnɪstrɪ] (*pl* **ministries**) *n* -**1.** POL [department] ministère *m*; [government] gouvernement *m*; **the Ministry of Defence** le ministère de la Défense. -**2.** RELIG [collective body] sacerdoce *m*, saint ministère *m*; **to join the ~** [Roman Catholic] se faire ordonner prêtre; [Protestant] devenir pasteur || [period of office] ministère *m*; **at the end of his ~ in London he moved away** il quitta Londres au terme de son ministère dans cette ville.

minium ['mɪnɪəm] *n* minium *m*.

mink [mɪŋk] ◇ *n* [animal, fur] vison *m*.

◇ *comp* [coat, stole] de OR en vison.

Minnesota [,mɪnɪ'səʊtə] *pr n* Minnesota *m*; **in ~** dans le Minnesota.

minnow ['mɪnəʊ] (*pl inv* OR **minnows**) *n* -**1.** [specific fish] vairon *m*; [any small fish] fretin *m* (*U*). -**2.** *Br fig* [insignificant person] (menu) fretin *m*.

Minoan [mɪ'nəʊən] ◇ *n* minoen *m*.

◇ *adj* minoen.

minor ['maɪnəʳ] ◇ *adj* -**1.** [secondary - road, role, position] secondaire; [- writer] mineur; [- importance, interest] secondaire, mineur; [- share] petit, mineur; **~ orders** ordres *mpl* mineurs; **~ planet** astéroïde *m*; **~ premise** LOGIC (proposition *f*) mineure *f*; **~ suit** CARDS couleur *f* mineure. -**2.** [unimportant - problem, worry] mineur, peu important. -**3.** [small - alteration, disagreement] mineur, petit; [- detail, expense] mineur, petit, menu. -**4.** [not serious - accident] mineur, petit; [- illness, injury] bénin; **~ offence** JUR délit *m* mineur; **to have a ~ operation** MED subir une petite intervention chirurgicale OR une intervention chirurgicale bénigne. -**5.** MUS mineur; **in A ~** en la mineur ❑ **in a ~ key** en mode mineur; **~ third** tierce *f* mineure. -**6.** *Br* SCH: **Jones ~** Jones junior. -**7.** *Am* UNIV [subject] facultatif.

◇ *n* -**1.** [in age] mineur *m*, -e *f*. -**2.** *Am* UNIV matière *f* secondaire. -**3.** *Am*: **the Minors** [film companies] *les trois compagnies de production secondaires (par rapport aux «Majors») à Hollywood: Universal, United Artists, Columbia*.

◇ *vi Am* UNIV: **she ~ed in economics** elle a pris les sciences économiques comme matière secondaire.

Minorca [mɪ'nɔ:kə] *pr n* Minorque; **in ~** à Minorque.

Minorcan [mɪ'nɔ:kn] ◇ *n* Minorquin *m*, -e *f*.

◇ *adj* minorquin.

minority [maɪ'nɒrətɪ] (*pl* **minorities**) ◇ *n* -**1.** [small group] minorité *f*; **to be in a** OR **the ~** être dans la minorité; **only a ~ (of people) watch late-night TV** seule une minorité (de gens) regarde la télé tard le soir; **I'm afraid you're in a ~ of one** *hum* j'ai bien peur que vous ne soyez le seul de cet avis; **the vocal ~** la minorité qui se fait entendre. -**2.** JUR [age] minorité *f*.

◇ *comp* [government, movement, tastes] minoritaire; **~ group** minorité *f*; **~ report** contre-rapport *m* *(soumis par une minorité)*; **a ~ TV programme** *une émission de télévision destinée à un public restreint*; **~ verdict** JUR verdict *m* de la minorité.

minor league ◇ *n Am* SPORT ≃ division *f* d'honneur.

◇ *adj fig* secondaire, de peu d'importance; **they're ~ compared with some American corporations** ils sont loin d'avoir l'envergure de certaines grandes sociétés américaines.

Minos ['maɪnɒs] *pr n* Minos.

Minotaur ['maɪnətɔ:ʳ] *n*: **the ~** le Minotaure.

Minsk [mɪnsk] *pr n* Minsk.

minster ['mɪnstəʳ] *n* [abbey church] (église *f*) abbatiale *f*; [cathedral] cathédrale *f*.

minstrel ['mɪnstrəl] *n* ménestrel *m*, troubadour *m*.

minstrel gallery *n* tribune *f* des musiciens.

minstrel show *n Br* spectacle *m* de variétés *(donné par des chanteurs déguisés en Noirs)*.

mint [mɪnt] ◇ *n* -**1.** BOT menthe *f*. -**2.** [sweet] bonbon *m* à la menthe. -**3.** [for coins]: **the Mint** l'Hôtel *m* de la Monnaie, la Monnaie. -**4.** *inf* [fortune] fortune *f*; **to make a ~** faire fortune; **it's worth a ~** cela vaut une fortune.

◇ *comp* [chocolate, sauce, tea] à la menthe.

◇ *adj* [stamps, coins] (tout) neuf; **in ~ condition** *fig* en parfait état, à l'état neuf.

◇ *vt* -**1.** [coins] fabriquer, frapper, battre. -**2.** [invent - word] inventer, créer; [- expression] forger.

mintage ['mɪntɪdʒ] *n* [process of minting] monnayage *m*, frappe *f* (de monnaie).

minuend ['mɪnjʊend] *n* MATH nombre *m* à diminuer.

minuet [,mɪnjʊ'et] *n* menuet *m*.

minus ['maɪnəs] (*pl* **minuses** OR **minusses**) ◇ *prep* -**1.** MATH moins; **seven ~ two leaves** OR **equals five** sept moins deux font cinq; **~ 12** moins 12. -**2.** [in temperature]: **it's ~ 5° outside** il fait moins 5° dehors. -**3.** *inf* [without]: **he came home ~ his shopping** il est rentré sans ses achats; **that chair is ~ a leg** cette chaise a un pied en moins.

◇ *n* -**1.** [sign] moins *m*; **put a ~ (sign) in front of the 12** mettez un moins devant le 12. -**2.** [drawback] inconvénient *m*; **one of the ~es is that we risk losing money** un des inconvénients est que nous risquons de perdre de l'argent.

◇ *adj* -**1.** [number] moins; **~ sign** signe *m* moins. -**2.** *fig* négatif; **the one ~ factor in the job is the low salary** le seul aspect négatif de ce poste est le salaire, qui est bas.

minuscule ['mɪnəskju:l] ◇ *adj* -**1.** [tiny] minuscule. -**2.** [lower-case] en (lettres) minuscules.

◇ *n* minuscule *f*.

minute¹ ['mɪnɪt] ◇ *n* -**1.** [period of 60 seconds] minute *f*; **for ten ~s** pendant dix minutes; **I'll be ready in ten ~s** je serai prêt dans dix minutes; **it's only a few ~s' walk (from here)** c'est seulement à quelques minutes (d'ici) à pied; **he got there with only a ~ to spare** il y est arrivé avec une seule minute d'avance || [in telling the time]: **two ~s past/to ten** dix heures deux/moins deux. -**2.** [moment] instant *m*, minute *f*; **I'll be back in a ~** je reviens dans une minute OR dans un instant OR tout de suite; **it only took him a ~** il en a eu pour une minute; **wait a ~, please** attendez un instant, s'il vous plaît; **just a ~!** un instant!; [aggressively] une minute!; **come here this ~!** viens ici tout de suite!; **I think of you every ~ of the day** je pense à vous à chaque instant de la journée; **I'll talk to him the ~ he arrives** je lui parlerai dès qu'il arrivera; **the weather here changes from one ~ to the next** ici, le temps change d'une minute à l'autre; **any ~ now** d'un instant à l'autre; **right up till the last ~** jusqu'à la toute dernière minute; **she left the house within ~s of his arrival** elle a quitté la maison dans les minutes qui ont suivi son arrivée; **the flight took two hours to the ~** le vol a duré deux heures à la minute près OR exactement; **she arrived at six o'clock to the ~** *Br* elle est arrivée à six heures précises OR à six heures pile. -**3.** GEOM [of degree] minute *f*.

◇ *vt* -**1.** [take down - fact, remark] inscrire au procès-verbal. -**2.** [time] minuter, chronométrer.

◆ **minutes** *npl* -**1.** [of meeting] procès-verbal *m*, compte rendu *m*. -**2.** [report] note *f*.

minute² [maɪ'nju:t] *adj* -**1.** [tiny] minuscule, infime; [very slight - difference, improvement] infime, minime. -**2.** [precise] minutieux, détaillé; **with ~ care** avec un soin minutieux; **in ~ detail** par le menu; **she described the accident in the minutest detail** elle a décrit l'accident dans les moindres détails.

minute book ['mɪnɪt-] *n* registre *m* des délibérations OR des procès-verbaux.

minute gun ['mɪnɪt-] *n canon dont les coups sont tirés à intervalles d'une minute, pour des funérailles par exemple*.

minute hand ['mɪnɪt-] *n* grande aiguille *f*, aiguille *f* des minutes.

minutely [maɪ'nju:tlɪ] *adv* -**1.** [carefully] minutieusement, avec un soin minutieux; [in detail] en détail, par le menu. -**2.** [fold] tout petit; [move] imperceptiblement, très légèrement.

Minuteman ['mɪnɪtmæn] (*pl* **Minutemen** [-men]) *n* -**1.** [soldier] homme-minute *m* *(soldat volontaire de la guerre d'indépendance américaine)*. -**2.** [missile] Minuteman *m* *(missile balistique)*.

MINUTEMEN:

Les «hommes-minute» doivent leur nom au fait qu'ils étaient prêts à rejoindre les troupes à tout moment pour se battre. Pendant la guerre froide, le nom de «Minuteman» fut donné à un type de missile américain.

minute steak ['mɪnɪt-] *n* entrecôte *f* minute.

minutiae [maɪ'nju:ʃɪaɪ] *npl* menus détails *mpl*, petits détails *mpl*; *pej* [trivialities] vétilles *fpl*, riens *mpl*.

minx [mɪŋks] *n dated & hum* coquine *f*, friponne *f*.

Miocene ['maɪəsi:n] ◇ *adj* miocène.

◇ *n* miocène *m*.

MIPS [mɪps] (*abbr of* **million instructions per second**) *npl* COMPUT MIPS.

miracle ['mɪrəkl] ◇ *n* -**1.** RELIG & *fig* miracle *m*; **to work ~s** faire OR accomplir des miracles; **she's worked ~s with those kids** elle a fait des miracles avec ces enfants; **by a ~ disaster was averted** la catastrophe a été évitée par miracle; **it was a ~ (that) she survived** c'est un miracle qu'elle ait survécu || [achievement]: **economic ~** miracle *m* économique; **a ~ of modern science** un prodige OR miracle de la science moderne. -**2.** = **miracle play**.

◇ *comp* [drug] miracle; [cure] miraculeux; **~ worker** faiseur *m*, -euse *f* de miracles.

miracle play *n* miracle *m* *(drame)*.

miraculous [mɪ'rækjʊləs] *adj* miraculeux; **they had a ~ escape** c'est un miracle qu'ils s'en soient tirés (vivants); **a ~ beauty** une beauté extraordinaire.

miraculously [mɪ'rækjʊləslɪ] *adv* -**1.** [by a miracle] miraculeusement, par miracle. -**2.** [extremely] merveilleusement, prodigieusement.

mirage [mɪ'rɑ:ʒ] *n* mirage *m*.

MIRAS ['maɪ,ræs] (*abbr of* **mortgage interest relief at source**) *n Br* *système d'exonération fiscale sur les intérêts des emprunts immobiliers*.

mire [maɪəʳ] *lit* ◇ *n* boue *f*; [deep] bourbier *m*; to drag sb's name through the ~ traîner le nom de qqn dans la boue.
◇ *vt (usu pass)* -**1.** *lit* [in debt, difficulty] empêtrer. -**2.** [in mud] embourber.

mirror [ˈmɪrəʳ] ◇ *n* -**1.** [looking glass] miroir *m*, glace *f*; AUT rétroviseur *m*; to hold up a ~ to sthg *fig* refléter qqch; the tabloid press is not necessarily a ~ of national opinion la presse à sensation ne reflète pas nécessairement l'opinion du pays. -**2.** PRESS: the Mirror *nom abrégé du Daily Mirror*.
◇ *vt* -**1.** [reflect] réfléchir, refléter; the water ~ed her face l'eau réfléchissait son visage; the stars were ~ed in the smooth surface of the lake les étoiles se réfléchissaient OR se reflétaient sur la surface lisse du lac. -**2.** [imitate] imiter; her career exactly ~ed her brother's sa carrière fut calquée exactement sur celle de son frère.

mirror image *n* image *f* en miroir, image *f* spéculaire; *fig* copie *f* conforme.

mirrorlike [ˈmɪrəlaɪk] *adj* [sea, lake] lisse comme un miroir.

mirror writing *n* écriture *f* spéculaire OR en miroir.

mirth [mɜːθ] *n (U)* rires *mpl*, hilarité *f*.

mirthful [ˈmɜːθfʊl] *adj lit* rieur, joyeux.

mirthless [ˈmɜːθlɪs] *adj lit* triste, sombre, morne; [laugh] faux, forcé.

mirthlessly [ˈmɜːθlɪslɪ] *adv lit* sans joie; she laughed ~ elle eut un rire forcé.

MIRV [mɜːv] (*abbr of* multiple independently targeted re-entry vehicle) *n* MIL MIRV *m*.

miry [ˈmaɪərɪ] (*compar* mirier, *superl* miriest) *adj* boueux, fangeux.

misadventure [ˌmɪsədˈventʃəʳ] *n* [accident] mésaventure *f*; [misfortune] malheur *m*.

misaligned [ˌmɪsəˈlaɪnd] *adj* mal aligné.

misalliance [ˌmɪsəˈlaɪəns] *n* mésalliance *f*.

misanthrope [ˈmɪsənθrəʊp] *n* misanthrope *mf*.

misanthropic [ˌmɪsənˈθrɒpɪk] *adj* [person] misanthrope; [thoughts] misanthropique.

misanthropist [mɪˈsænθrəpɪst] *n* misanthrope *mf*.

misanthropy [mɪˈsænθrəpɪ] *n* misanthropie *f*.

misapplication [ˈmɪsˌæplɪˈkeɪʃn] *n* mauvaise utilisation *f*, mauvaise application *f*; [of law] mauvaise application *f*; [of money] détournement *m*.

misapply [ˌmɪsəˈplaɪ] (*pt* & *pp* misapplied) *vt* [learning] mal utiliser, mal exploiter; [law] mal appliquer, appliquer à tort; [money] détourner.

misapprehend [ˈmɪsˌæprɪˈhend] *vt fml* se méprendre sur.

misapprehension [ˈmɪsˌæprɪˈhenʃn] *n fml* malentendu *m*; I'm afraid you are under a OR some ~ je crains que vous ne vous mépreniez.

misappropriate [ˌmɪsəˈprəʊprɪeɪt] *vt fml* [money, funds] détourner; [property] voler.

misappropriation [ˈmɪsəˌprəʊprɪˈeɪʃn] *n fml* détournement *m*.

misbegotten [ˌmɪsbɪˈgɒtn] *adj fml* -**1.** [plan] mal conçu, bâtard; [child] bâtard, illégitime. -**2.** [illegally obtained] d'origine douteuse.

misbehave [ˌmɪsbɪˈheɪv] *vi*: to ~ (o.s.) se conduire mal; stop misbehaving! sois sage!; he's misbehaving again! il fait encore des siennes!

misbehaviour *Br*, **misbehavior** *Am* [ˌmɪsbɪˈheɪvjəʳ] *n* mauvaise conduite *f*.

misc *written abbr of* miscellaneous.

miscalculate [ˌmɪsˈkælkjʊleɪt] ◇ *vt* [amount, distance] mal calculer; *fig* mal évaluer.
◇ *vi* MATH se tromper dans ses calculs; *fig* [judge wrongly] se tromper.

miscalculation [ˌmɪskælkjʊˈleɪʃn] *n* MATH erreur *f* de calcul; *fig* mauvais calcul *m*.

miscall [ˌmɪsˈkɔːl] *vt fml* appeler à tort.

miscarriage [ˌmɪsˈkærɪdʒ] *n* -**1.** MED fausse couche *f*; to have a ~ faire une fausse couche. -**2.** [failure] échec *m*; ~ of justice erreur *f* judiciaire. -**3.** *Br* [loss - of mail, cargo] perte *f*.

miscarry [ˌmɪsˈkærɪ] (*pt* & *pp* miscarried) *vi* -**1.** MED faire une fausse couche. -**2.** [fail - plan, hopes] échouer, avorter, mal tourner. -**3.** *Br* [mail, cargo] s'égarer, se perdre.

miscast [ˌmɪsˈkɑːst] (*pt* & *pp* miscast) *vt* CIN & THEAT [play] se tromper dans la distribution de; [actor] mal choisir le rôle de; Jim was hopelessly ~ as Romeo Jim n'était vraiment pas fait pour jouer le rôle de Roméo.

miscegenation [ˌmɪsɪdʒɪˈneɪʃn] *n fml* métissage *m (de races humaines)*.

miscellanea [ˌmɪsəˈleɪnɪə] *npl* miscellanées *fpl*.

miscellaneous [ˌmɪsəˈleɪnɪəs] *adj* [assorted] divers, varié; [jumbled] hétérogène, hétéroclite, disparate; ~ expenses frais *mpl* divers.

miscellany [*Br* mɪˈselənɪ, *Am* ˈmɪsəleɪnɪ] (*pl* miscellanies) *n* -**1.** [mixture, assortment] amalgame *m*, mélange *m*. -**2.** [anthology] recueil *m*, anthologie *f*.

mischance [ˌmɪsˈtʃɑːns] *n fml* malheur *m*, malchance *f*; by pure ~ par pure malchance; [stronger] par malheur.

mischief [ˈmɪstʃɪf] *n* -**1.** *(U)* [naughtiness] espièglerie *f*, malice *f*; to get up to ~ faire des bêtises OR sottises; to keep sb out of ~ occuper qqn; to do sthg out of sheer ~ faire qqch par pure espièglerie OR par pure malice; they're always up to (some) ~ ils trouvent toujours des bêtises à faire; a smile full of ~ un sourire espiègle; she looked at me with ~ in her eyes elle me regardait d'un air taquin OR malicieux. -**2.** *(U)* [trouble]: to make ~ semer la zizanie. -**3.** *(U) fml* [damage] dommages *mpl*, dégâts *mpl*. -**4.** *Br* [injury]: to do o.s. a ~ *inf* se blesser, se faire mal; he did himself a ~ carrying the suitcases il s'est fait mal en portant les valises. -**5.** *inf hum* [child] polisson *m*, -onne *f*, (petite) canaille *f*; come here, ~! viens ici, polisson!

mischief-maker *n* faiseur *m* d'histoires OR d'embarras; she's a terrible ~ [naughtiness] elle est toujours prête à jouer des tours; [nastiness] avec elle, on est sûr d'avoir des histoires.

mischievous [ˈmɪstʃɪvəs] *adj* -**1.** [child, trick] espiègle, malicieux; [look] taquin, narquois; [thought] malicieux. -**2.** [harmful] méchant, malveillant; ~ gossip médisances *fpl*.

mischievously [ˈmɪstʃɪvəslɪ] *adv* [naughtily, teasingly] malicieusement; [nastily] méchamment, avec malveillance.

mischievousness [ˈmɪstʃɪvəsnɪs] *n* [naughtiness] espièglerie *f*, malice *f*; [nastiness] malveillance *f*, méchanceté *f*.

misconceive [ˌmɪskənˈsiːv] *vt* [misunderstand] mal comprendre, mal interpréter; [have wrong idea of] se faire une idée fausse de.

misconceived [ˌmɪskənˈsiːvd] *adj* [plan] mal conçu; [idea] faux, erroné.

misconception [ˌmɪskənˈsepʃn] *n* [poor understanding] mauvaise compréhension *f*; [complete misunderstanding] idée fausse *f*, méprise *f*; the whole scheme is based on a basic ~ tout le projet repose sur une idée fausse; a popular ~ une fausse idée couramment répandue.

misconduct [*n* ˌmɪsˈkɒndʌkt, *vb* ˌmɪskənˈdʌkt] ◇ *n* -**1.** [bad behaviour] mauvaise conduite *f*; [immoral behaviour] inconduite *f*; [adultery] adultère *m*; (professional) ~ faute *f* professionnelle. -**2.** [bad management] mauvaise gestion *f*; they accused her of ~ of the company's affairs ils l'ont accusée d'avoir mal géré la société.
◇ *vt* [mismanage - business] mal gérer; [- affair] mal conduire.

misconstruction [ˌmɪskənˈstrʌkʃn] *n* -**1.** fausse interprétation *f*; the law is open to ~ la loi peut prêter à des interprétations erronées. -**2.** GRAMM mauvaise construction *f*.

misconstrue [ˌmɪskənˈstruː] *vt* mal interpréter.

miscount [*vb* ˌmɪsˈkaʊnt, *n* ˈmɪskaʊnt] ◇ *vt* mal compter, faire une erreur en comptant.
◇ *vi* se tromper dans le compte.
◇ *n* mécompte *m*; there was a ~ POL une erreur s'est produite dans le décompte des voix.

miscreant [ˈmɪskrɪənt] *n* -**1.** *lit* [villain] scélérat *m*, -e *f*, vaurien *m*, -enne *f*. -**2.** *arch* [unbeliever] mécréant *m*, -e *f*.

misdate [ˌmɪsˈdeɪt] *vt* mal dater; the letter was ~d la lettre ne portait pas la bonne date.

misdeal [ˌmɪsˈdiːl] (*pt* & *pp* misdealt [-ˈdelt])
◇ *vt*: to ~ the cards faire (une) maldonne.
◇ *vi* faire (une) maldonne.
◇ *n* maldonne *f*.

misdeed [ˌmɪsˈdiːd] *n fml* méfait *m*; JUR délit *m*.

misdemeanour *Br*, **misdemeanor** *Am* [ˌmɪsdɪˈmiːnəʳ] *n* méfait *m*; JUR délit *m*, infraction *f*.

misdiagnose [ˌmɪsˈdaɪəgnəʊz] *vt* MED & *fig* se tromper dans le diagnostic de.

misdiagnosis [ˌmɪsdaɪəgˈnəʊsɪs] (*pl* misdiagnoses [-siːz]) *n* MED & *fig* erreur *f* de diagnostic, mauvais diagnostic *m*.

misdirect [ˌmɪsdɪˈrekt] *vt* -**1.** [to destination - traveller] mal orienter, mal renseigner; [- letter] mal adresser. -**2.** [misuse - efforts, talents] mal employer, mal orienter. -**3.** JUR [jury] mal renseigner.

misdirection [ˌmɪsdɪˈrekʃn] *n* -**1.** [of traveller] mauvaise orientation *f*. -**2.** [of efforts, talents] mauvais emploi *m*, mauvais usage *m*.

misdoing [ˌmɪsˈduːɪŋ] *n* méfait *m*.

miser [ˈmaɪzəʳ] *n* -**1.** [person] avare *mf*; he's a real ~ c'est un vrai grippe-sou ❑ 'The Miser' *Molière* 'l'Avare'. -**2.** [tool] tarière *f* à gravier.

miserable [ˈmɪzrəbl] *adj* -**1.** [unhappy] malheureux, triste; to look ~ avoir l'air déprimé OR malheureux; I feel really ~ today je n'ai vraiment pas le moral aujourd'hui; to make sb ~ rendre qqn malheureux, faire de la peine à qqn; don't be so ~! allez! ne fais pas cette tête; they make her life ~ ils lui rendent OR mènent la vie dure. -**2.** [unpleasant - evening, sight] pénible; [- weather, summer] épouvantable, pourri; [- conditions, holiday] déplorable, lamentable; I've got a ~ cold j'ai un sale rhume; he had a ~ time of it at the dentist's il a passé un sale quart d'heure chez le dentiste; to have a ~ time passer un mauvais moment; we had a ~ time on holiday nous avons passé des vacances atroces OR détestables. -**3.** [poor - hotel] miteux; [- tenement] misérable; [- meal] maigre; all their efforts were a ~ failure tous leurs efforts ont échoué lamentablement. -**4.** [mean - reward] minable, misérable; [- salary] de misère; [- donation, amount] dérisoire; he was paid a ~ salary il avait un salaire de misère; they only gave us five ~ dollars ils ne nous ont donné que cinq malheureux OR misérables dollars. -**5.** *pej* méchant; you ~ brat! sale gosse! -**6.** *Scot* & *Austr* [stingy] pingre.

miserably [ˈmɪzrəblɪ] *adv* -**1.** [extremely - unhappy, cold] extrêmement; [very badly - play] de façon lamentable OR déplorable; [- fail] lamentablement; [- pay] très mal. -**2.** [unhappily] malheureusement, d'un air malheureux; she sat ~ at the back of the class elle était assise, l'air malheureux OR pitoyable, au fond de la classe. -**3.** [in poverty] misérablement, dans la misère; he died ~ in a garret il est mort pauvre dans une mansarde.

misère [mɪˈzeəʳ] *n* [in cards] misère *f*.

miserly [ˈmaɪzəlɪ] *adj* avare.

misery [ˈmɪzərɪ] (*pl* miseries) *n* -**1.** [unhappiness] malheur *m*, tristesse *f*; to make sb's life a ~ rendre la vie insupportable à qqn. -**2.** [suffering]: she begged to be put out of her ~ elle suppliait qu'on mît fin à ses souffrances; go on, put me out of my ~ and tell me the worst continue, mets fin à mon supplice, dis-moi tout; to put a sick animal out of its ~ *euph* achever un animal malade. -**3.** [misfortune] malheur *m*, misère *f*. -**4.** [poverty] misère *f*. -**5.** *inf Br* [gloomy person] rabat-joie *m inv*, grincheux *m*, -euse *f*; don't be such an old ~! cesse de jouer les rabat-joie!

misfile [*vb* ˌmɪsˈfaɪl, *n* ˈmɪsfaɪl] ◇ *vt* [papers, information] mal classer.
◇ *n* COMPUT erreur *f* de classement.

misfire [*vb* ˌmɪsˈfaɪəʳ, *n* ˈmɪsfaɪəʳ] ◇ *vi* -**1.** [gun] faire long feu; *fig* [plan, joke] rater, échouer.

-**2.** [engine] avoir des problèmes d'allumage OR des ratés.
◇ *n* MIL & AUT raté *m*.

misfit ['mɪsfɪt] *n* inadapté *m*, -e *f*, marginal *m*, -e *f*; **she was always a ~ at school** à l'école, elle n'a jamais été acceptée par les autres; **a social ~** un inadapté social.

misfortune [mɪs'fɔːtʃuːn] *n* -**1.** [bad luck] malchance *f*, infortune *f*; **allies** OR **companions in ~** compagnons *mpl* d'infortune; **I had the ~ to meet him in Paris** j'ai eu la malchance de le rencontrer à Paris. -**2.** [unfortunate event] malheur *m*; **to be plagued by ~s** jouer de malchance.

misgiving [mɪs'gɪvɪŋ] *n* doute *m*, appréhension *f*; **to have ~s about** avoir des doutes quant à, douter de; **the whole idea fills me with ~** l'idée même me remplit d'appréhension.

misgovern [,mɪs'gʌvən] *vi* & *vt* mal gouverner.

misgovernment [,mɪs'gʌvənmənt] *n* [of country] mauvais gouvernement *m*; [of affairs] mauvaise gestion *f*.

misguidance [,mɪs'gaɪdəns] *n* mauvaise influence *f*.

misguided [,mɪs'gaɪdɪd] *adj* [attempt] malencontreux; [decision] peu judicieux; **~ nationalism** nationalisme dévoyé; **they're just ~ idealists** ce sont des idéalistes égarés; **a ~ genius** un génie dévoyé; **a ~ attack on the government** une attaque malavisée OR maladroite contre le gouvernement; **it was very ~ of him to try to intervene** il a commis une grosse bévue en essayant d'intervenir.

misguidedly [,mɪs'gaɪdɪdlɪ] *adv* malencontreusement.

mishandle [,mɪs'hændl] *vt* -**1.** [equipment] mal utiliser, mal se servir de; [resources, information] mal exploiter; [affair] mal gérer; **the case was ~d from the outset** l'affaire a été mal menée depuis le début. -**2.** [treat insensitively - customer] malmener, traiter avec rudesse.

mishap ['mɪshæp] *n* [misadventure] mésaventure *f*, accident *m*; **he arrived without ~** il est arrivé sans encombre; **she had a slight ~ on the way here** il lui est arrivé une petite mésaventure en venant ici.

mishear [,mɪs'hɪəʳ] (*pt* & *pp* **misheard** [-'hɜːd]) *vt* mal entendre, mal comprendre.

mishit [*vb* ,mɪs'hɪt, *n* 'mɪshɪt] (*pt* & *pp* **mishit**)
◇ *vt* SPORT [ball] mal frapper.
◇ *vi* mal frapper la balle.
◇ *n* mauvais coup *m*, coup *m* manqué.

mishmash *inf* ['mɪʃmæʃ] *n* méli-mélo *m*, micmac *m*.

misinform [,mɪsɪn'fɔːm] *vt* [unintentionally] mal renseigner; [intentionally] donner de faux renseignements à, tromper.

misinformation [,mɪsɪnfə'meɪʃn] *n* *(U)* fausse information *f*.

misinterpret [,mɪsɪn'tɜːprɪt] *vt* mal comprendre, mal interpréter; **now don't ~ what I'm saying** surtout, ne vous méprenez pas sur le sens de mes propos; **she ~ed his silence as contempt** elle a pris à tort son silence pour du mépris.

misinterpretation ['mɪsɪn,tɜːprɪ'teɪʃn] *n* erreur *f* d'interprétation; **the rules are open to ~** l'interprétation du règlement prête à confusion.

misjudge [,mɪs'dʒʌdʒ] *vt* [distance, reaction] mal juger, mal évaluer; [person] mal juger; **I have ~d her** je me suis trompé sur son compte, je l'ai mal jugée.

misjudg(e)ment [,mɪs'dʒʌdʒmənt] *n* erreur *f* de jugement.

miskick [*vb* ,mɪs'kɪk, *n* 'mɪskɪk] ◇ *vt* SPORT: **he ~ed the ball** il a raté son coup de pied.
◇ *vi* rater le ballon.
◇ *n* coup *m* de pied raté.

mislay [,mɪs'leɪ] (*pt* & *pp* **mislaid** [-'leɪd]) *vt* égarer.

mislead [,mɪs'liːd] (*pt* & *pp* **misled** [-'led]) *vt* tromper, induire en erreur; **we were misled into believing he was dead** on nous a fait croire qu'il était mort.

misleading [,mɪs'liːdɪŋ] *adj* [false] trompeur, fallacieux; [confusing] équivoque; **~ advertising** publicité *f* mensongère; **the map is very ~** cette carte n'est pas claire du tout.

misleadingly [,mɪs'liːdɪŋlɪ] *adj* [falsely] trompeusement.

mismanage [,mɪs'mænɪdʒ] *vt* mal gérer.

mismanagement [,mɪs'mænɪdʒmənt] *n* mauvaise gestion *f*.

mismatch [*vb* ,mɪs'mætʃ, *n* 'mɪsmætʃ] ◇ *vt* -**1.** [colours, clothes] mal assortir. -**2.** [in marriage]: **they were totally ~ed** [socially] ils étaient vraiment mal assortis; [by temperament] ils n'étaient absolument pas faits pour s'entendre.
◇ *n* -**1.** [clash]: **the colours are a ~** ces couleurs ne vont vraiment pas ensemble OR sont vraiment mal assorties. -**2.** [in marriage] mésalliance *f*. -**3.** SPORT match *m* inégal. -**4.** COMPUT incohérence *f*.

misname [,mɪs'neɪm] *vt* mal nommer.

misnomer [,mɪs'nəʊməʳ] *n* nom *m* inapproprié; **to call it a democratic country is a complete ~** ce pays ne mérite vraiment pas le nom de démocratie.

miso ['miːsəʊ] *n* miso *m*.

misogamy [mɪ'sɒgəmɪ] *n* misogamie *f*.

misogynist [mɪ'sɒdʒɪnɪst] *n* misogyne *mf*.

misogyny [mɪ'sɒdʒɪnɪ] *n* misogynie *f*.

misoneism [,mɪsəʊ'niːɪzm] *n* misonéisme *m*.

misplace [,mɪs'pleɪs] *vt* -**1.** [put in wrong place] mal placer; **she's utterly ~d in social work** elle n'est vraiment pas à sa place dans le secteur social. -**2.** [mislay] égarer. -**3.** [trust, confidence] mal placer.

misplaced [,mɪs'pleɪst] *adj* [trust, confidence] mal placé.

misprint [*n* 'mɪsprɪnt, *vb* ,mɪs'prɪnt] ◇ *n* faute *f* d'impression, coquille *f*.
◇ *vt*: **my name was ~ed in the newspaper** il y a eu une coquille dans mon nom sur le journal.

mispronounce [,mɪsprə'naʊns] *vt* [word] mal prononcer, prononcer incorrectement; [name] estropier, écorcher.

mispronunciation ['mɪsprə,nʌnsɪ'eɪʃn] *n* faute *f* de prononciation.

misquotation [,mɪskwəʊ'teɪʃn] *n* citation *f* inexacte.

misquote [*vb* ,mɪs'kwəʊt, *n* 'mɪskwəʊt]
◇ *vt* [author, text] citer inexactement; [speaker] déformer les propos de; **on your programme you ~d me as saying...** dans votre émission vous m'avez incorrectement fait dire que ...
◇ *n* *inf* = **misquotation**.

misread [*vb* ,mɪs'riːd, *n* 'mɪsriːd] (*pt* & *pp* **misread** [-'red]) ◇ *vt* [word, text] mal lire; *fig* [actions, motives] mal interpréter, mal comprendre.
◇ *n* COMPUT erreur *f* de lecture.

misrepresent ['mɪs,reprɪ'zent] *vt* [facts, events] déformer; [person] donner une image fausse de; **I have been grossly ~ed by my opponents** mes adversaires donnent de moi une image entièrement fausse.

misrepresentation ['mɪs,reprɪzen'teɪʃn] *n* [of truth] déformation *f*; **what they say is a complete ~ of the facts** ils déforment complètement la réalité.

misrule [,mɪs'ruːl] ◇ *vt* mal gouverner.
◇ *n* -**1.** [misgovernment] mauvais gouvernement *m*. -**2.** [anarchy] désordre *m*, anarchie *f*.

miss [mɪs] ◇ *vt* -**1.** [bus, film, target] manquer, rater; [opportunity, turn] manquer, laisser passer; **we ~ed the train by five minutes** on a manqué le train de cinq minutes; **he ~ed breakfast** [too late] il a manqué le petit déjeuner; [didn't go] il a sauté le petit déjeuner; **this film is not to be ~ed** c'est un film à ne pas manquer OR à ne manquer sous aucun prétexte; **at that price, it's a bargain not to be ~ed** à ce prix, c'est une affaire à ne pas manquer; **you didn't ~ much** vous n'avez pas manqué grand-chose; **it's too good an opportunity to ~** c'est une occasion trop belle pour qu'on la manque ❑ **to ~ the boat** rater une occasion, manquer le coche; **you're going to ~ the boat if you delay your application** vous allez manquer le coche si vous tardez à poser votre candidature; **to ~ one's cue** THEAT manquer sa réplique; *fig* rater l'occasion. -**2.** [fail to do, find, see etc] manquer; **to ~ school** manquer l'école; **it's at the end of the street, you can't ~ it** c'est au bout de la rue, vous ne pouvez pas le manquer; **to ~ a turning** rater un tournant; **I'm sorry, I ~ed you in the crowd** désolé, je ne vous ai pas vu OR remarqué OR aperçu dans la foule; **I ~ed seeing them in Australia** [for lack of time] je n'ai pas eu le temps de les voir en Australie; [for lack of opportunity] je n'ai pas eu l'occasion OR la possibilité de les voir en Australie; **I ~ed the beginning of your question** je n'ai pas entendu le début de votre question; **they've ~ed my name off the list** ils ont oublié mon nom sur la liste; **you've ~ed** OR **you're ~ing the point!** vous n'avez rien compris!; **he ~ed the point of the exercise** il n'a pas compris OR saisi le but de l'exercice; **she ~ed her footing** OR **step** *Br* elle a glissé OR trébuché ❑ **they never** OR **don't ~ a trick** *Br* rien ne leur échappe. -**3.** [escape, manage to avoid]: **I narrowly** OR **just ~ed being killed** j'ai bien failli me faire tuer. -**4.** [regret the absence of]: **I ~ her** elle me manque; **you'll be ~ed when you retire** on vous regrettera OR vous nous manquerez quand vous serez à la retraite; **I ~ the warm weather/the sea** la chaleur/la mer me manque. -**5.** [be short of, lack] manquer de; **I'm ~ing two books from my collection** il me manque deux livres dans ma collection, deux livres de ma collection ont disparu. -**6.** [notice disappearance of]: **when did you first ~ your passport?** quand est-ce que vous vous êtes aperçu pour la première fois de la perte de OR que vous aviez perdu votre passeport?; **he disappeared for a week and no-one ever ~ed him** il a disparu pendant une semaine et personne ne s'en est aperçu; **he's got so many records he won't ~ one** il a tellement de disques qu'il ne s'apercevra pas qu'il lui en manque un.
◇ *vi* -**1.** [fail to hit target] manquer OR rater son coup; **~ed!** raté! -**2.** [engine] avoir des ratés. -**3.** *phr*: **to be ~ing** manquer; **there's a piece ~ing** il manque une pièce; **there's one ~ing, one is ~ing** il en manque un; **two of the children are still ~ing** il manque encore deux enfants, deux enfants manquent encore.
◇ *n* -**1.** [gen & SPORT] coup *m* raté OR manqué; AERON quasi-collision *f*; **it was a near ~** FTBL il s'en est fallu de peu qu'on marque OR on a failli marquer un but; [answer] la réponse était presque la bonne; [accident] on a frôlé l'accident; **the two cars had a near ~** les deux voitures ont bien failli se rentrer dedans; **that was a near ~!** [escape] on l'a échappé belle!; **a ~ is as good as a mile** *Br prov* rater de peu ou de beaucoup, c'est toujours rater. -**2.** *inf* [girl] jeune fille *f*; **everything for the modern ~** tout ce qu'il faut pour la jeune fille moderne; **impudent little ~!** petite effrontée! -**3.** TEX [size] junior. -**4.** *phr*: **to give sthg a ~** *Br* [do without] se passer de qqch; [avoid] éviter qqch; **I gave work a ~ yesterday** je ne suis pas allé travailler hier; **I'd like to give lessons a ~ this week** j'aimerais ne pas assister aux cours cette semaine; **why don't you give the TV a ~ tonight?** pourquoi ne pas te passer de (la) télé ce soir?

◆ **Miss** *n* [term of address] mademoiselle *f*; **Dear Miss Brett** Chère Mademoiselle Brett, Chère Mlle Brett; **the Misses Brett** *fml* Mesdemoiselles Brett; **the Miss Bretts** les demoiselles Brett; **Miss West Indies** Miss Antilles; **please Miss!** *Br* SCH Madame!

◆ **miss out** ◇ *vt sep* [omit] omettre, sauter; [forget] oublier; [in distribution] oublier, sauter; **they ~ed my first name out** on a oublié mon prénom; **you've ~ed out one important fact** vous avez omis OR oublié un fait important.
◇ *vi insep*: **he ~ed out because he couldn't**

afford to go to college il a été désavantagé parce qu'il n'avait pas les moyens de poursuivre ses études.

◆ **miss out on** *vt insep* [advantage, opportunity] manquer, rater; **you're ~ing out on all the fun** tu rates une occasion de bien t'amuser; **he ~ed out on a proper education** il n'a pas eu la possibilité de faire de vraies études; **we ~ed out on the deal** l'affaire nous est passée sous le nez OR nous a échappé.

missal ['mɪsl] *n* missel *m*.

misshapen [,mɪs'ʃeɪpn] *adj* difforme, tordu, déformé.

missile [*Br* 'mɪsaɪl, *Am* 'mɪsəl] *n* **-1.** MIL missile *m*; **~ base** base *f* de missiles. **-2.** [object thrown] projectile *m*.

missile carrier *n* porte-missiles *m inv*.

missile launcher *n* lance-missiles *m inv*.

missil(e)ry ['mɪsəlrɪ] *n* **-1.** [stocks] (ensemble *m* des) missiles *mpl*. **-2.** [science] étude *f* des missiles.

missing ['mɪsɪŋ] *adj* **-1.** [lacking] manquant; **the table had one leg ~** il manquait un pied à la table; **fill in the ~ words** complétez avec les mots manquants. **-2.** [lost - person] disparu; [- object] manquant, égaré, perdu; **to go ~** disparaître; [in war] être porté disparu; **the ~ diamonds were found in her suitcase** les diamants qui avaient disparu ont été retrouvés dans sa valise; **the ~ climbers are safe** les alpinistes dont on était sans nouvelles sont sains et saufs; **the expedition was reported ~** l'expédition a été portée disparue ❑ **~ person** personne *f* disparue; MIL & POL disparu *m*.

missing link *n* chaînon *m* manquant.

mission ['mɪʃn] *n* **-1.** [delegation] mission *f*; **~ of inquiry** mission d'enquête; **he was sent on a rescue ~** il fut envoyé en mission de sauvetage; **a Chinese trade ~** une mission commerciale chinoise. **-2.** [job, vocation] mission *f*; **she saw it as her ~ in life to provide for the homeless** elle s'est donné pour mission d'aider les sans-abris. **-3.** [organization, charity] mission *f*; **Mission to Seamen** Mission aux Marins. **-4.** RELIG [campaign, building] mission *f*; **~ station** mission. **-5.** MIL & ASTRONAUT mission *f*; **he had flown 20 ~s** il avait effectué 20 missions; **~ accomplished** mission accomplie.

missionary ['mɪʃənrɪ] (*pl* **missionaries**)

◇ *n* missionnaire *mf*.

◇ *adj* [work] missionnaire; [zeal] de missionnaire; **~ society** société *f* de missionnaires.

missionary position *n* position *f* du missionnaire.

mission control *n* centre *m* de contrôle.

mission controller *n* chef *m* du centre de contrôle.

missis ['mɪsɪz] = **missus**.

Mississippi [,mɪsɪ'sɪpɪ] *pr n* **-1.** [river]: **the ~ (River)** le Mississippi. **-2.** [state] Mississippi *m*; **in ~** dans le Mississippi.

missive ['mɪsɪv] *n fml* missive *f*.

Missouri [mɪ'zʊərɪ] *pr n* **-1.** [river]: **the ~ (river)** le Missouri. **-2.** [state] Missouri *m*; **in ~** dans le Missouri; **the ~ Compromise** le compromis du Missouri.

THE MISSOURI COMPROMISE:

Admission simultanée dans l'Union (des États américains), en 1820, de l'État libre du Maine et de l'État du Missouri. Ce dernier, bien qu'esclavagiste, se trouvait au nord de la ligne de séparation entre les États esclavagistes et les États non esclavagistes. Cette admission fit basculer l'équilibre numérique entre le Nord et le Sud au Congrès et souleva une violente opposition malgré le réajustement de la ligne de démarcation.

---

misspell [,mɪs'spel] (*pt & pp* **misspelt** [-'spelt] OR **misspelled**) *vt* [in writing] mal écrire, mal orthographier; [in speaking] mal épeler.

misspelling [,mɪs'spelɪŋ] *n* faute *f* d'orthographe.

misspend [,mɪs'spend] (*pt & pp* **misspent** [-'spent]) *vt* [money, talents] gaspiller, gâcher; **my misspent youth** mes folles années de jeunesse.

misstate [,mɪs'steɪt] *vt* [case, argument] rapporter OR exposer incorrectement; [truth] déformer.

misstatement [,mɪs'steɪtmənt] *n* [report] rapport *m* inexact; [mistake] inexactitude *f*.

missus *inf* ['mɪsɪz] *n Br* **-1.** [wife] bourgeoise *f*; **I'll have to ask the ~** je dois demander à la patronne. **-2.** [woman]: **eh, ~!** dites, m'dame OR ma p'tite dame!

missy *inf* ['mɪsɪ] (*pl* **missies**) *n dated* jeune fille *f*.

mist [mɪst] ◇ *n* **-1.** [fog] brume *f*; **the morning ~ will clear by noon** les brumes matinales se dissiperont avant midi; **the ~s of time** *fig* la nuit des temps. **-2.** [vapour - on window, glasses] buée *f*; [- from spray] brouillard *m*, nuage *m*.

◇ *vt*: **to ~ (over** OR **up)** embuer; **tears ~ed his eyes** ses yeux étaient brouillés par les larmes.

◇ *vi*: **to ~ (over** OR **up)** [window, glasses, eyes] s'embuer.

mistake [mɪ'steɪk] (*pt* **mistook** [-'stʊk], *pp* **mistaken** [-'steɪkn]) ◇ *n* **-1.** [error] erreur *f*; [in grammar, spelling] faute *f*; **to make a ~** faire une erreur OR une faute; **I made the ~ of losing my temper** j'ai commis l'erreur de OR j'ai eu le tort de me fâcher; **anybody can make a ~** tout le monde peut se tromper; **you're making a big ~** vous faites une grave erreur; **make no ~ (about it)** ne vous y trompez pas; **there must be some ~** il doit y avoir erreur OR un malentendu; **she knew it was a ~ ever to have married him** elle savait bien qu'elle n'aurait pas dû commettre l'erreur de l'épouser; **sorry, my ~** [my fault] excusez-moi, c'est (de) ma faute; [I got it wrong] excusez-moi, c'est moi qui me trompe. **-2.** [inadvertence]: **by** OR **in** *Br* **~** par mégarde OR erreur; **I took her scarf in ~ for mine** en croyant prendre mon écharpe, j'ai pris la sienne; **I went into the wrong room by ~** je suis entré par erreur dans la mauvaise pièce. **-3.** *phr*: **he's a big man and no ~!** *Br* pour être costaud, il est costaud!

◇ *vt* **-1.** [misunderstand - meaning, intention] mal comprendre, se tromper sur; **there's no mistaking what she said** on ne peut pas se méprendre sur le sens de ses propos. **-2.** [fail to distinguish] se tromper sur; **you can't ~ our house, it has green shutters** vous ne pouvez pas vous tromper OR il n'y a pas de confusion possible, notre maison a des volets verts; **there's no mistaking the influence of Brahms on his music** l'influence de Brahms sur sa musique est indéniable. **-3.** [date, route] se tromper de; [person]: **I'm often mistaken for my sister** on me prend souvent pour ma sœur; **I mistook his shyness for arrogance** j'ai pris sa timidité pour de l'arrogance.

mistaken [mɪ'steɪkn] ◇ *pp* → **mistake**.

◇ *adj* [wrong - idea, conclusion] erroné, faux; **to be ~** se tromper, être dans l'erreur; **I was ~ about the date** je faisais erreur en ce qui concerne la date; **if I'm not ~** si je ne me trompe, si je ne m'abuse; **it was a case of ~ identity** il y avait erreur sur la personne; **unless I'm very much ~, that's Nick's daughter** si je ne m'abuse, c'est la fille de Nick; **he proposed to her in the ~ belief that she loved him** il la demanda en mariage, croyant à tort qu'elle l'aimait.

mistakenly [mɪ'steɪknlɪ] *adv* [in error] par erreur; [wrongly] à tort; **they quite ~ believed that it would be easy** ils croyaient, tout à fait à tort, que ce serait facile.

mister *inf* ['mɪstəʳ] *n* monsieur *m*; **hey ~!** dites, m'sieur!; **~ knowall** *Br*, **~ know-it-all** *Am* monsieur je-sais-tout.

mistime [,mɪs'taɪm] *vt* mal calculer (le moment de); **the producer had ~d the release of the film** le producteur n'avait pas choisi le bon moment OR la bonne date pour sortir le film; **she ~d her volley** elle a mal calculé sa volée, le timing de sa volée était mauvais.

mistiness ['mɪstɪnɪs] *n* **-1.** [mist] brume *f*; [drizzle] bruine *f*; **there may be some ~ early on** on peut s'attendre à des brumes matinales. **-2.** [condensation] condensation *f*, buée *f*.

mistle thrush ['mɪsl-] *n* draine *f*.

mistletoe ['mɪsltəʊ] *n* gui *m*.

mistook [mɪ'stʊk] *pt* → **mistake**.

Mistra ['mɪstrə] *pr n* Mistra.

mistranslate [,mɪstræns'leɪt] ◇ *vt* mal traduire.

◇ *vi* faire des contresens.

mistranslation [,mɪstræns'leɪʃn] *n* **-1.** [mistake] contresens *m*, faute *f* OR erreur *f* de traduction. **-2.** [faulty text] traduction *f* inexacte, mauvaise traduction *f*.

mistreat [,mɪs'triːt] *vt* maltraiter.

mistreatment [,mɪs'triːtmənt] *n* mauvais traitement *m*.

mistress ['mɪstrɪs] *n* **-1.** maîtresse *f*; **she's her own ~** elle est sa propre maîtresse; **she was ~ of the situation** elle était maîtresse de la situation, elle maîtrisait la situation; **the ~ of the house** la maîtresse de maison. **-2.** [lover] maîtresse *f*; **he kept a ~ for years** il a eu une maîtresse pendant des années. **-3.** *Br* SCH [in primary school] maîtresse *f*; [in secondary school] professeur *m* *(femme)*; **the PE ~** le professeur de gymnastique. **-4.** *Br* [of servants] maîtresse *f*; **the ~ wouldn't like it** cela déplairait à Madame. **-5.** *arch*: **Mistress Bacon** Madame OR Mme Bacon. **-6.** [owner of pet] maîtresse *f*.

mistrial ['mɪstraɪəl] *n* erreur *f* judiciaire; *Am* [with hung jury] *procès annulé par manque d'unanimité parmi les jurés*.

mistrust [,mɪs'trʌst] ◇ *n* méfiance *f*, défiance *f*; **she has a natural ~ of doctors** elle éprouve une méfiance naturelle à l'égard des médecins.

◇ *vt* [be suspicious, wary of] se méfier de; [doubt] douter de, ne pas avoir confiance en; **he ~s his own abilities** il doute de ses propres capacités.

mistrustful [,mɪs'trʌstfʊl] *adj* méfiant; **to be ~ of sb** se méfier de qqn.

misty ['mɪstɪ] (*compar* **mistier**, *superl* **mistiest**) *adj* **-1.** [weather, morning] brumeux; **it was still ~** le temps était encore brumeux, la brume ne s'était toujours pas levée. **-2.** [window, eyes] embué; [horizon, mountain] embrumé; **her eyes were ~ with tears** ses yeux étaient embués OR voilés de larmes. **-3.** [vague - idea, memory] flou, nébuleux. **-4.** [like mist] vaporeux; **a ~ veil of cloud** un léger voile de nuages; **~ blue** bleu pâle.

mistype [,mɪs'taɪp] ◇ *vt* faire une faute de frappe dans; **the address has been ~d** il y a une faute de frappe dans l'adresse.

◇ *n* faute *f* de frappe.

misunderstand [,mɪsʌndə'stænd] (*pt & pp* **misunderstood** [-'stʊd]) *vt* **-1.** [misinterpret] mal comprendre, comprendre de travers; **I misunderstood the message** j'ai mal compris le message; **don't ~ me** comprenez-moi bien; **your irony could be misunderstood** votre ironie pourrait être mal interprétée. **-2.** *(usu passive)* [misjudge, underrate] méconnaître; **a misunderstood artist** un artiste méconnu; **he feels misunderstood** il se sent incompris.

misunderstanding [,mɪsʌndə'stændɪŋ] *n* **-1.** [misapprehension] méprise *f*, quiproquo *m*, malentendu *m*; **there seems to have been some ~** il semble qu'il y ait eu méprise OR une erreur; **his statement is open to ~** sa déclaration prête à confusion; **the whole dispute hinges on a ~** cette discussion repose toute entière sur un malentendu; **to clear up a ~** dissiper un malentendu; **through a ~** à cause d'un malentendu. **-2.** *euph* [quarrel] mésentente *f*, brouille *f*; **we've had a ~ with the neighbours** nous nous sommes brouillés avec les voisins.

misunderstood [,mɪsʌndə'stʊd] *pt & pp* → **misunderstand**.

misusage [,mɪs'juːsɪdʒ] = **misuse** *n*.

misuse [*vb* ,mɪs'juːz, *n* ,mɪs'juːs] ◇ *vt* **-1.** [privilege, position etc] abuser de; [word, phrase] employer abusivement; [equipment, gun] mal

employer, mal utiliser; [money, time] mal employer; **the government is misusing our natural resources** le gouvernement fait un mauvais usage de nos ressources naturelles. -**2.** [funds] détourner. -**3.** [ill-treat] maltraiter, malmener.
◇ *n* -**1.** [of privilege, one's position] abus *m*; [of word, phrase] emploi *m* abusif; [of equipment, gun] mauvais usage *m*, mauvaise utilisation *f*; [of money, time] mauvais emploi *m*. -**2.** [of funds] détournement *m*.

MIT (*abbr of* Massachusetts Institute of Technology) *pr n l'Institut de Technologie du Massachusetts.*

mite [maɪt] *n* -**1.** [insect] mite *f*. -**2.** *inf* [little bit] grain *m*, brin *m*, tantinet *m*; **I am a ~ tired after my journey** je me sens un tantinet fatigué après mon voyage. -**3.** *inf* [child] mioche *mf*; **poor little ~!** pauvre petit! -**4.** [coin] denier *m*; [donation] obole *f*.

miter *Am* = **mitre**.

mitigate [ˈmɪtɪgeɪt] *vt* [anger, grief, pain] adoucir, apaiser, alléger; [conditions, consequences, harm] atténuer, mitiger *dated*.

mitigating [ˈmɪtɪgeɪtɪŋ] *adj*: **~ circumstances** JUR circonstances *fpl* atténuantes.

mitigation [ˌmɪtɪˈgeɪʃn] *n fml* [of anger, grief, pain] adoucissement *m*, allègement *m*; [of conditions, consequences, harm] atténuation *f*, mitigation *f*; **in ~, it is obvious that she was provoked** il est évident qu'elle a été provoquée, ce qui constitue une circonstance atténuante.

mitosis [maɪˈtəʊsɪs] (*pl* mitoses [-siːz]) *n* mitose *f*.

mitre *Br*, **miter** *Am* [ˈmaɪtəʳ] ◇ *n* -**1.** RELIG mitre *f*; **bishop's ~** mitre d'évêque. -**2.** [in carpentry] onglet *m*.
◇ *vt* [in carpentry - cut] tailler en onglet; [join] assembler en onglet.

mitre block, mitre box *n* boîte *f* à onglet.

mitre joint *n* (assemblage *m* à OR en) onglet *m*.

mitre square *n* équerre *f* d'onglets.

mitt [mɪt] *n* -**1.** = **mitten**. -**2.** [glove] gant *m*; [boxing glove] gant *m* (de boxe); **oven/baseball ~** gant isolant/de baseball. -**3.** *inf* [hand] paluche *f*; **keep your ~s off my lunch!** touche pas à mon déjeuner!

mitten [ˈmɪtn] *n* [with fingers joined] moufle *f*; [with cut-off fingers] mitaine *f*; [boxing glove] gant *m* (de boxe), mitaine *f*.

mix [mɪks] ◇ *vt* -**1.** [combine, blend] mélanger; **~ the sugar and** OR **with the flour** mélangez le sucre et OR avec la farine; **~ the sugar into the batter** incorporez le sucre à la pâte; **the screws and nails were all ~ed together** les vis et les clous étaient tous mélangés; **I never ~ business and pleasure** je ne mélange jamais les affaires et le plaisir; **never ~ your drinks** ne faites jamais de mélanges de boissons; **to ~ metaphors** faire des amalgames de métaphores ❑ **to ~ it** *inf Br* [fight] chercher la bagarre, être bagarreur. -**2.** [prepare - cocktail, medicine] préparer; [- cement, plaster] malaxer; **sit down and I'll ~ you a drink** asseyez-toi, je vais te préparer un cocktail. -**3.** [stir - salad] tourner. -**4.** CIN, ELECTRON & MUS mixer.
◇ *vi* -**1.** [combine, blend] se mélanger; **oil and water don't ~** l'huile et l'eau ne se mélangent pas; **the fuel ~es with air in the carburettor** le mélange air carburant s'effectue dans le carburateur. -**2.** [go together] aller ensemble, faire bon ménage; **drinking and driving don't ~** l'alcool et le volant ne font pas bon ménage. -**3.** [socialize]: **she ~es well** elle est très sociable; **he ~es with a strange crowd** il fréquente de drôles de gens; **my friends and his just don't ~** mes amis et les siens ne sympathisent pas.
◇ *n* -**1.** [combination, blend] mélange *m*; **it's a ~ of gothic and baroque** c'est un mélange de gothique et de baroque; **a fascinating ~ of cultures** un mélange de cultures fascinant; **there's not enough cement in the ~** le mélange ne contient pas assez de ciment; **he's put together the right ~ of talent for the show** il est parvenu à réunir pour ce spectacle un superbe choix de talents. -**2.** *Br* [act of mixing]: **give the paint a (good) ~** mélangez (bien) la peinture. -**3.** CULIN [in package] préparation *f*; [batter] pâte *f*; **cake ~** préparation pour gâteau; **a packet of soup ~** un sachet de soupe instantanée. -**4.** CIN, ELECTRON & MUS mixage *m*.
◆ **mix in** ◇ *vt sep* mélanger; **add the sugar and ~ it in well** ajoutez le sucre et mélangez bien (la préparation).
◇ *vi insep*: **she makes no effort to ~ in** elle ne fait aucun effort pour se montrer sociable.
◆ **mix up** *vt sep* -**1.** [mistake] confondre; **I always ~ her up with her sister** je la confonds toujours avec sa sœur ‖ [baffle, confuse] embrouiller; **I'm ~ed up about how I feel about him** mes sentiments pour lui sont très confus ‖ [scramble]: **you've got the story completely ~ed up** tu t'es complètement embrouillé dans cette histoire. -**2.** (*usu pass*) [involve] impliquer; **he was ~ed up in a burglary** il a été impliqué OR mêlé à une affaire de cambriolage; **she got ~ed up with some awful people** elle s'est mise à fréquenter des gens épouvantables; **I got ~ed up in their quarrel** je me suis trouvé mêlé à leur querelle. -**3.** [disorder] mélanger; **you've ~ed all my papers up** tu as mélangé tous mes papiers. -**4.** [combine, blend] mélanger; **~ up all the ingredients** mélangez tous les ingrédients.

mixed [mɪkst] *adj* -**1.** [assorted] mélangé; **there was a very ~ crowd at the party** il y avait toutes sortes de gens à la fête; **a bag of ~ sweets** un sachet de bonbons assortis; **we had rather ~ weather** nous avons eu un temps assez variable ❑ **~ border** HORT *plate-bande composée de fleurs de variétés différentes*; **~ economy** économie *f* mixte; **~ fabric** tissu *m* mélangé; **~ farming** polyculture *f*; **~ grill** assortiment *m* de grillades, mixed grill *m*; **~ metaphor** mélange *m* de métaphores; **~ vegetables** jardinière *f* de légumes. -**2.** [not wholly positive] mitigé; **to meet with a ~ reception** recevoir un accueil mitigé; **I have ~ feelings about it** je ne sais pas très bien ce que j'en pense, je suis partagé à ce sujet ❑ **it's a bit of a ~ bag** *inf* il y a un peu de tout; **it's a ~ blessing** il y a du pour et du contre. -**3.** [sexually, racially] mixte; **it's not a proper topic for ~ company** ce n'est pas un sujet à aborder devant les dames; **man of ~ race** métis *m*; **woman of ~ race** métisse *f* ❑ **~ school/doubles** école *f*/double *m* mixte; **~ marriage** mariage *m* mixte. -**4.** MATH: **~ number** nombre *m* mixte (fractionnaire).

mixed-ability *adj* [class, teaching] sans niveaux.

mixed-media *adj* multimédia.

mixed-up *adj* [confused] désorienté, déboussolé; **she's a crazy ~ kid** *inf* elle est un peu paumée, cette gamine.

mixer [ˈmɪksəʳ] *n* -**1.** [device - gen] mélangeur *m*; CULIN [mechanical] batteur *m*; [electric] mixeur *m*, mixer *m*; CIN, ELECTRON & MUS mixeur *m*, mélangeur *m* de signaux; **cement** OR **concrete ~** bétonnière *f*. -**2.** [sociable person]: **to be a good/poor ~** être sociable/peu sociable. -**3.** *inf* [troublemaker] provocateur *m*, -trice *f*. -**4.** [soft drink] boisson *f* gazeuse *(servant à la préparation des cocktails)*.

mixer tap *n* (robinet *m*) mélangeur *m*.

mixing [ˈmɪksɪŋ] *n* -**1.** [gen] mélange *m*. -**2.** CIN, ELECTRON & MUS mixage *m*; **the ~ room** TV la régie; **~ desk** table *f* de mixage.

mixing bowl *n* [big] saladier *m*; [smaller] bol *m*.

mixture [ˈmɪkstʃəʳ] *n* -**1.** [gen] mélange *m*; **they speak a ~ of French and English** ils parlent un mélange de français et d'anglais. -**2.** MED mixture *f*.

mix-up *n* confusion *f*; **there was a ~ over the bookings** il y a eu confusion dans les réservations.

mizen, mizzen [ˈmɪzn] *n* artimon *m*.

mizzenmast [ˈmɪznmɑːst] *n* mât *m* d'artimon.

mk, MK *written abbr of* mark.

mkt *written abbr of* market.

ml (*written abbr of* millilitre) ml.

MLitt [emˈlɪt] (*abbr of* Master of Literature, Master of Letters) *n (titulaire d'une) maîtrise de lettres.*

MLR *n abbr of* minimum lending rate.

M'lud [mˈlʌd] *n manière conventionnelle de représenter la prononciation de «My Lord», terme utilisé lorsqu'on s'adresse à un juge.*

mm (*written abbr of* millimetre) mm.

MN ◇ *n abbr of* Merchant Navy.
◇ *written abbr of* Minnesota.

mnemonic [nɪˈmɒnɪk] ◇ *adj* -**1.** [aiding memory] mnémonique, mnémotechnique; **~ code** code *m* mnémotechnique. -**2.** [relating to memory] mnémonique.
◇ *n* formule *f* mnémotechnique, aide *f* à la mémoire; COMPUT mnémonique *m*.

mnemonics [nɪˈmɒnɪks] *n (U)* mnémotechnique *f*.

mo *inf*, **mo'** *inf* [məʊ] *n* moment *m*, instant *m*; **half a ~** un petit instant, une (petite) minute; **(I) won't be a ~** j'en ai pour une minute.

MO ◇ *n* -**1.** *abbr of* medical officer. -**2.** *abbr of* modus operandi.
◇ *written abbr of* Missouri.

m.o. *written abbr of* money order.

moan [məʊn] ◇ *vi* -**1.** [in pain, sadness] gémir; **he lay ~ing in the gutter** il était étendu dans le caniveau et gémissait; **the wind ~ed in the trees** le vent gémissait dans les arbres. -**2.** [grumble] ronchonner, grogner; **stop ~ing!** arrête de maugréer OR ronchonner!; **what are you ~ing about now?** de quoi te plains-tu encore?
◇ *vt* maugréer; **"I'm so bored!", she ~ed** «qu'est-ce que je m'ennuie!», maugréa-t-elle.
◇ *n* [of pain, sadness] gémissement *m*; [of complaint] plainte *f*; **she gave a ~** elle poussa un gémissement.

moaner *inf* [ˈməʊnəʳ] *n* grognon *m*, -onne *f*, râleur *m*, -euse *f*.

moaning [ˈməʊnɪŋ] ◇ *n (U)* -**1.** [in pain, sadness] gémissement *m*, gémissements *mpl*. -**2.** [complaining] plaintes *fpl*, jérémiades *fpl*; **stop your ~!** arrête de ronchonner!
◇ *adj* -**1.** [groaning] gémissant; **a ~ sound** un gémissement. -**2.** [complaining] grognon, râleur; **she's a real ~ Minnie** *inf Br* quelle râleuse, celle-là!

moat [məʊt] *n* douves *fpl*, fossé *m*, fossés *mpl*.

mob [mɒb] (*pt & pp* mobbed) ◇ *n* -**1.** [crowd] foule *f*, cohue *f*; **we were surrounded by an angry ~** nous étions cernés par une foule en colère; **~ hysteria** hystérie *f* collective; **~ rule** loi *f* de la rue. -**2.** *pej* [common people]: **the ~** la populace. -**3.** [of criminals] gang *m*; **the Mob** la Mafia. -**4.** *inf* [bunch, clique] bande *f*, clique *f pej*; **he was surrounded by the usual ~ of hangers-on** il était entouré par sa bande habituelle de parasites.
◇ *vt* [person] attaquer, agresser; [place] assiéger.

mob cap *n* charlotte *f (bonnet)*.

mobile [ˈməʊbaɪl] ◇ *adj* -**1.** mobile; **~ troops** troupes mobiles; **she's no longer ~** elle ne peut plus se déplacer seule ❑ **~ library** bibliobus *m*. -**2.** [features, face] mobile, expressif. -**3.** [socially]: **the middle classes tend to be particularly ~** les classes moyennes se déplacent plus facilement que les autres. -**4.** *inf* [having transport]: **are you ~?** tu es motorisé?
◇ *n* ART mobile *m*.

mobile home *n* caravane *f*.

mobile phone *n* téléphone *m* portable.

mobility [məˈbɪlətɪ] *n* mobilité *f*; **~ allowance** indemnité *f* de déplacement *(versée aux personnes handicapées)*.

mobilization [ˌməʊbɪlaɪˈzeɪʃn] *n* mobilisation *f*.

mobilize, -ise [ˈməʊbɪlaɪz] *vi & vt* mobiliser.

mobocracy [mɒbˈɒkrəsɪ] (*pl* mobocracies) *n Br* voyoucratie *f*.

mob rule *n* loi *f* de la rue.

mobster *inf* [ˈmɒbstəʳ] *n* gangster *m*.

moccasin [ˈmɒkəsɪn] *n* mocassin *m*.

mocha [ˈmɒkə] *n* moka *m*.

mock [mɒk] ◇ *vt* -**1.** [deride] se moquer de, tourner en dérision; **don't ~ the afflicted!** ne te moque pas des malheureux! -**2.** [imitate] singer, parodier. -**3.** *lit* [thwart] déjouer.
◇ *vi* se moquer; **you shouldn't ~** tu ne devrais pas te moquer.
◇ *adj* -**1.** [imitation] faux, factice; **~ turtle soup** consommé *m* à la tête de veau. -**2.** [feigned] feint; **~ horror/surprise** horreur/surprise feinte. -**3.** [as practice]: **~ battle** exercice *m* de combat; **~ examination** examen *m* blanc.
◇ *n* -**1.** *phr*: **to make a ~ of sb/sthg** *lit* tourner qqn/qqch en dérision. -**2.** *inf Br* [examination] examen *m* blanc.
◆ **mock up** *vt sep Br* faire une maquette de.
mock-epic = **mock-heroic**.
mocker ['mɒkəʳ] *n* moqueur *m*, -euse *f*.
mockers *inf* ['mɒkəz] *npl Br*: **to put the ~ on sthg** ficher qqch en l'air, bousiller qqch.
mockery ['mɒkərɪ] (*pl* **mockeries**) *n* -**1.** [derision] moquerie *f*, raillerie *f*; **to hold sthg up to ~** tourner qqch en ridicule OR en dérision; **he soldiered on despite the ~ of his colleagues** il persévéra en dépit des railleries de ses collègues. -**2.** [travesty] parodie *f*; **a ~ of justice** une parodie de justice; **the interview was a ~** l'entretien était une véritable caricature; **to make a ~ of sthg** rendre qqch ridicule, enlever toute crédibilité à qqch.
mock-heroic *adj* burlesque.
mocking ['mɒkɪŋ] ◇ *n* moquerie *f*, raillerie *f*.
◇ *adj* moqueur, railleur.
mockingbird ['mɒkɪŋbɜːd] *n* moqueur *m* ORNITH.
mockingly ['mɒkɪŋlɪ] *adv* de façon moqueuse.
mock orange *n* seringa *m*.
mock turtleneck *n Am* pull *m* à col cheminée.
mock-up *n* maquette *f*.
mod [mɒd] ◇ *adj inf dated* [fashionable] à la mode.
◇ *n* -**1.** *en Angleterre, membre d'un groupe de jeunes des années 60 qui s'opposaient aux rockers. Ils circulaient souvent en scooter, s'habillaient à la dernière mode et écoutaient de la musique noire américaine*. -**2.** [festival] *festival de littérature et de musique gaélique en Écosse*.
MoD, MOD *pr n Br abbr of* Ministry of Defence.
modal ['məʊdl] *adj* GRAMM, PHILOS & MATH modal; **~ auxiliary** OR **verb** auxiliaire *m* modal.
modality [mə'dælətɪ] (*pl* **modalities**) *n* modalité *f*.
modally ['məʊdəlɪ] *adv* de manière modale.
mod cons [-kɒnz] (*abbr of* **modern conveniences**) *npl inf*: **all ~** tout confort, tt. conf.
mode [məʊd] *n* -**1.** [manner] mode *m*, manière *f*; **~ of life** mode de vie; **~s of transport** moyens de transport. -**2.** GRAMM, PHILOS & MATH mode *m*. -**3.** COMPUT mode *m*; **access/control ~** mode d'accès/de contrôle. -**4.** [prevailing fashion] mode *f*; **the current ~ is for sixties fashion** le dernier cri, c'est la mode des années soixante.
model ['mɒdl] (*Br pt* & *pp* **modelled**, *cont* **modelling**, *Am pt* & *pp* **modeled**, *cont* **modeling**) ◇ *n* -**1.** [copy, representation] modèle *m*, maquette *f*; [theoretical pattern] modèle *m*; **a computer ~ of the US economy** un modèle informatique de l'économie américaine ❑ **scale ~** modèle réduit. -**2.** [perfect example] modèle *m*; **your essay is a ~ of concision** votre rédaction est un modèle de concision; **they always hold my brother up as a ~ of intelligence** ils citent toujours mon frère comme un modèle d'intelligence. -**3.** ART & PHOT [sitter] modèle *m*. -**4.** [in fashion show] mannequin *m*; **male ~** mannequin (homme). -**5.** COMM modèle *m*; **it's the latest ~** c'est le dernier modèle; **demonstration ~** modèle de démonstration. -**6.** *Am* [showhouse] résidence *f* témoin.
◇ *vt* -**1.** [shape] modeler; **to ~ clay** modeler l'argile; **to ~ figures out of clay** modeler des figures en argile; **to ~ o.s. on sb** prendre modèle sur qqn. -**2.** [in fashion show]: **she ~s clothes** elle est mannequin; **she ~s hats** elle présente des chapeaux dans des défilés de mode.
◇ *vi* [for artist, photographer] poser; [in fashion show] être mannequin; **she has modelled for Dior** elle a été mannequin chez Dior.
◇ *adj* -**1.** [miniature] (en) miniature; **~ aeroplane** maquette *f* d'avion; **~ car** [toy] petite voiture *f*; [for collectors] modèle *m* réduit. -**2.** [exemplary] modèle; **~ factory** usine modèle *f*, usine-pilote *f*; **he's a ~ pupil/husband** c'est un élève/mari modèle.
modelling *Br*, **modeling** *Am* ['mɒdəlɪŋ] *n* -**1.** [building models] modelage *m*; [as a hobby] construction *f* de maquettes. -**2.** [in fashion shows]: **~ is extremely well-paid** le travail de mannequin est très bien payé, les mannequins sont très bien payés; **to make a career in ~** faire une carrière de mannequin. -**3.** MATH modélisation *f*.
modem ['məʊdem] *n* modem *m*.
Modena ['mɒdɪnə] *pr n* Modène.
moderate [*adj* & *n* 'mɒdərət, *vb* 'mɒdəreɪt] ◇ *adj* -**1.** [restrained, modest] modéré; **a ~ wage increase** une augmentation raisonnable des salaires; **the candidate holds ~ views** le candidat défend des idées modérées; **he's a ~ drinker** il boit avec modération; **~ language** langage mesuré. -**2.** [average] moyen; **pupils of ~ ability** élèves moyens; **a ~ performance** une prestation moyenne. -**3.** METEOR tempéré.
◇ *n* POL modéré *m*, -e *f*.
◇ *vt* -**1.** [make less extreme] modérer; **they have since ~d their demands** depuis, ils ont modéré leurs exigences. -**2.** [preside over - meeting, group, debate] présider. -**3.** NUCL [slow down - neutrons] modérer, ralentir.
◇ *vi* -**1.** [lessen] se modérer. -**2.** [preside] présider, être président.
moderate breeze *n* [on Beaufort scale] jolie brise *f*.
moderate gale *n* [on Beaufort scale] grand frais *m*.
moderately ['mɒdərətlɪ] *adv* [with moderation] modérément, avec modération; **~ priced** d'un prix raisonnable ‖ [slightly] moyennement; **she was only ~ pleased with her new job** elle n'était que moyennement satisfaite de son nouvel emploi.
moderation [,mɒdə'reɪʃn] *n* modération *f*; **a slight ~ of temperature** un léger changement de température; **to drink in** OR **with ~** boire avec modération; **smoking is dangerous even in ~** il est dangereux de fumer même avec modération.
moderator ['mɒdəreɪtəʳ] *n* -**1.** [president] président *m*, -e *f*; [mediator] médiateur *m*, -trice *f*; RELIG modérateur *m*. -**2.** NUCL modérateur *m*, ralentisseur *m*.
modern ['mɒdən] ◇ *adj* moderne; **~ English/French/Greek** anglais *m*/français *m*/grec *m* moderne; **~ face** TYPO didot *m*; **~ jazz** jazz *m* moderne; **~ languages** langues *fpl* vivantes; **~ maths** mathématiques *fpl* modernes.
◇ *n* -**1.** [person] moderne *mf*. -**2.** TYPO didot *m*.
modern-day *adj* d'aujourd'hui; **a ~ Joan of Arc** la Jeanne d'Arc des temps modernes.
modernism ['mɒdənɪzm] *n* -**1.** modernisme *m*. -**2.** [expression, word] néologisme *m*.
modernist ['mɒdənɪst] ◇ *adj* moderniste.
◇ *n* moderniste *mf*.
modernistic [,mɒdə'nɪstɪk] *adj* moderniste.
modernity [mɒ'dɜːnətɪ] *n* modernité *f*.
modernization [,mɒdənaɪ'zeɪʃn] *n* modernisation *f*.
modernize, -ise ['mɒdənaɪz] ◇ *vt* moderniser.
◇ *vi* se moderniser.
modest ['mɒdɪst] *adj* -**1.** [unassuming] modeste; **she's very ~ about her success** son succès ne lui est pas monté à la tête. -**2.** [small, moderate, simple] modeste; [meagre] modique; **a ~ salary** un salaire modique; **we are very ~ in our needs** nous avons besoin de très peu. -**3.** [decorous] pudique.
modestly ['mɒdɪstlɪ] *adv* -**1.** [unassumingly] modestement, avec modestie. -**2.** [simply] modestement, simplement; **they live very ~** ils vivent très simplement, ils mènent une vie très simple. -**3.** [with decorum] avec pudeur, pudiquement; **to dress ~** s'habiller avec pudeur.
modesty ['mɒdɪstɪ] *n* -**1.** [lack of conceit] modestie *f*; **in all ~** en toute modestie; **false ~** fausse modestie. -**2.** [moderation] modestie *f*; [meagreness] modicité *f*. -**3.** [decorum] pudeur *f*; **she lowered her gaze out of ~** la pudeur lui a fait baisser les yeux.
modicum ['mɒdɪkəm] *n* minimum *m*; **she showed a ~ of common sense** elle a fait preuve d'un minimum de bon sens.
modifiable ['mɒdɪfaɪəbl] *adj* modifiable.
modification [,mɒdɪfɪ'keɪʃn] *n* modification *f*; **he made several ~s in** OR **to the text** il apporta plusieurs modifications au texte; **the rules need some ~** il faut modifier les règles.
modifier ['mɒdɪfaɪəʳ] *n* GRAMM modificateur *m*.
modify ['mɒdɪfaɪ] (*pt* & *pp* **modified**) *vt* -**1.** [alter] modifier; **once they had modified the engine it worked perfectly** après quelques modifications, le moteur était en parfait état de marche. -**2.** [moderate] modérer. -**3.** GRAMM modifier.
modish ['məʊdɪʃ] *adj* à la mode.
modishly ['məʊdɪʃlɪ] *adv* selon la mode.
Mods [mɒdz] (*abbr of* (Honour) Moderations) *npl premier examen universitaire à Oxford*.
modular ['mɒdjʊləʳ] *adj* modulaire; **~ degree** ≃ licence *f* à UV; **~ furniture** mobilier *m* modulaire OR à éléments; **~ programming** programmation *f* modulaire.
modularity [,mɒdjʊ'lærətɪ] *n* modularité *f*.
modulate ['mɒdjʊleɪt] *vt* -**1.** ELECTRON & MUS moduler; [voice] moduler. -**2.** [moderate, tone down] adapter, ajuster; **they ~ their prices to the US market** ils adaptent leurs prix au marché américain.
modulation [,mɒdjʊ'leɪʃn] *n* modulation *f*; **amplitude/frequency ~** modulation d'amplitude/de fréquence.
modulator ['mɒdjʊleɪtəʳ] *n* ELECTRON modulateur *m*.
module ['mɒdjuːl] *n* -**1.** [gen] module *m*; **lunar ~** module lunaire. -**2.** UNIV ≃ unité *f* de valeur, ≃ UV *f*.
modus operandi ['məʊdəs,ɒpə'rændiː] *n fml* OR *lit* méthode *f* (de travail), procédé *m*.
modus vivendi ['məʊdəsvɪ'vendiː] *n fml* OR *lit* modus vivendi *m*.
mog *inf* [mɒg] = **moggie**.
Mogadiscio, Mogadishu [,mɒgə'dɪʃuː] *pr n* Mogadiscio.
moggie, moggy *inf* ['mɒgɪ] (*pl* **moggies**) *n Br* minou *m*.
mogul ['məʊgl] *n* -**1.** [magnate] magnat *m*. -**2.** [on ski slope] bosse *f*.
◆ **Mogul** ◇ *n* Moghol *m*.
◇ *adj* moghol.
MOH (*abbr of* Medical Officer of Health) *n Br* directeur *m*, -trice *f* de la santé publique.
mohair ['məʊheəʳ] ◇ *n* mohair *m*.
◇ *adj* en OR de mohair.
Mohammed [mə'hæmɪd] *pr n* Mahommed.
Mohammedan [mə'hæmɪdn] ◇ *n* musulman *m*, -e *f*.
◇ *adj* musulman.
Mohawk ['məʊhɔːk] (*pl inv* OR **Mohawks**) *n* Mohawk *m*.
◆ **mohawk** *n* [in ice-skating] mohawk *m*.
Mohican [məʊ'hiːkən, 'məʊɪkən] (*pl inv* OR **Mohicans**) ◇ *n* -**1.** [person] Mohican *m*, -e *f*. -**2.** LING mohican *m*.
◇ *adj* mohican.
◆ **mohican** *n* [hairstyle] coupe *f* à l'iroquoise.
moiré ['mwɑːreɪ] ◇ *adj* moiré; **~ silk** moire *f* de soie.
◇ *n* moiré *m*.
moist [mɔɪst] *adj* [skin, air, heat] moite; [climate, soil, surface] humide; [cake] moelleux.

moisten ['mɔɪsn] ◇ *vt* humecter, mouiller; she ~ed her lips elle s'humecta les lèvres.
◇ *vi* [eyes] se mouiller; [palms] devenir moite.

moistness ['mɔɪstnɪs] *n* moiteur *f*, humidité *f*.

moisture ['mɔɪstʃəʳ] *n* humidité *f*; [on mirror, window etc] buée *f*; **he wiped the ~ from the window** il essuya la buée de la fenêtre; ~ **content** teneur *f* en humidité OR en eau.

moistureproof ['mɔɪstʃəpruːf] *adj* [clothing, shoes] imperméable; [watch, container] étanche; [finish, sealant] hydrofuge.

moisturize, -ise ['mɔɪstʃəraɪz] *vt* [skin] hydrater; [air] humidifier.

moisturizer ['mɔɪstʃəraɪzəʳ] *n* crème *f* hydratante.

moke *inf* [məʊk] *n Br* [donkey] bourricot *m*; *Austr* [horse] canasson *m*.

molar ['məʊləʳ] ◇ *adj* [quantity, solution] molaire.
◇ *n* [tooth] molaire *f*.

molasses [mə'læsɪz] *n (U)* mélasse *f*.

mold *etc Am* = **mould**.

Moldavia [mɒl'deɪvjə] *pr n* Moldavie *f*; in ~ en Moldavie.

Moldavian [mɒl'deɪvjən] ◇ *n* Moldave *mf*.
◇ *adj* moldave.

Moldova [ˌmɒl'dəʊvə] *pr n*: the Republic of ~ la république de Moldova.

mole [məʊl] *n* -**1.** [on skin] grain *m* de beauté. -**2.** ZOOL taupe *f*. -**3.** *fig* [spy] taupe *f*. -**4.** [breakwater] môle *m*, digue *f*. -**5.** [unit of substance] mole *f*.

molecular [mə'lekjʊləʳ] *adj* moléculaire; ~ **formula/weight** formule *f*/poids *m* moléculaire.

molecule ['mɒlɪkjuːl] *n* molécule *f*.

molehill ['məʊlhɪl] *n* taupinière *f*.

moleskin ['məʊlskɪn] *n* -**1.** [fur] (peau *f* de) taupe *f*. -**2.** [cotton] coton *m* sergé; ~ **trousers** pantalon en coton sergé.

molest [mə'lest] *vt* [bother] importuner, tracasser; [more violently] molester, malmener; [sexually] agresser (sexuellement).

molestation [ˌməʊle'steɪʃn] *n (U)* brutalité *f*, violences *fpl*; [sexual] attentat *m* à la pudeur.

molester [mə'lestəʳ] *n* agresseur *m*; **child ~** pédophile *mf*.

moll▽ [mɒl] *n* poule *f*, nana *f*.

mollification [ˌmɒlɪfɪ'keɪʃn] *n* apaisement *m*.

mollify ['mɒlɪfaɪ] (*pt & pp* **mollified**) *vt* apaiser, amadouer.

mollusc *Br*, **mollusk** *Am* ['mɒləsk] *n* mollusque *m*.

mollycoddle *inf* ['mɒlɪˌkɒdl] *vt Br pej* dorloter, materner.

Molotov cocktail ['mɒlətɒf-] *n* cocktail *m* Molotov.

molt *Am* = **moult**.

molten ['məʊltn] *adj* [metal, lava] en fusion.

Molucca [məʊ'lʌkə] *pl pr n*: the ~ **Islands**, the ~s les îles *fpl* Moluques.

molybdenite [mə'lɪbdənaɪt] *n* molybdénite *f*.

molybdenum [mə'lɪbdənəm] *n* molybdène *m*.

mom *inf* [mɒm] *n Am* maman *f*; ~ **and pop store** *petit magasin familial*.

moment ['məʊmənt] *n* -**1.** [period of time] moment *m*, instant *m*; **at the ~** en ce moment; **at that ~** à ce moment-là; **at this (very) ~** en ce moment même; **at this ~ in time** à l'heure qu'il est; **she's the idol of the ~** c'est elle l'idole du moment; **for the ~** pour le moment; **let me think (for) a ~** laissez-moi réfléchir un moment OR une seconde; **for a long ~ he remained silent** pendant un long moment il est resté sans parler; **I'll do it in a ~** je le ferai dans un instant; **I didn't believe them for a** OR **one ~** je ne les ai pas crus un seul instant; **one ~, please** un instant, s'il vous plaît; [on telephone] ne quittez pas; **just a ~, you haven't paid yet** un instant, vous n'avez pas encore payé; **she's just this ~ gone out** elle vient de sortir; **don't wait until the last ~** n'attendez pas la dernière minute; **the next ~ the phone rang** l'instant d'après le téléphone a sonné; **without a ~'s hesitation** sans la moindre hésitation; **he fell in love with her the ~ he saw her** il est tombé amoureux d'elle à l'instant même où il l'a vue; **it was her darkest ~** ce fut l'époque la plus sombre de sa vie; **the ~ of truth** l'heure de vérité; **in the heat of the ~** dans le feu de l'action; **the film has its ~s** le film est parfois intéressant OR a de bons passages. -**2.** *fml* [import, consequence] importance *f*, signification *f*; **an event of great historical ~** un événement d'une très grande portée historique. -**3.** PHYS moment *m*; **magnetic ~** moment magnétique.

momentarily [*Br* 'məʊməntərɪlɪ, *Am* ˌməʊmen'terɪlɪ] *adv* -**1.** [briefly, temporarily] momentanément. -**2.** *Am* [immediately] immédiatement, tout de suite; **I'll be with you ~** je suis à vous dans une seconde.

momentary ['məʊməntrɪ] *adj* -**1.** [brief, temporary] momentané; **there will be a ~ delay** il y aura un retard de quelques minutes. -**2.** *lit* [continual] constant, continuel.

momentous [mə'mentəs] *adj* capital, d'une importance capitale; **on this ~ occasion** en cette occasion mémorable; **a ~ decision** une décision d'une importance capitale.

momentousness [mə'mentəsnɪs] *n* importance *f* capitale.

momentum [mə'mentəm] *n* -**1.** [impetus] vitesse *f*, élan *m*; **the campaign soon gained ~** la campagne a rapidement atteint sa vitesse de croisière; **to lose ~** [vehicle] perdre de la vitesse; [campaign] s'essouffler. -**2.** MECH & PHYS moment *m*.

momma *inf* ['mɒmə] *n Am* maman *f*; **he's a ~'s boy** il est toujours fourré dans les jupons de sa mère.

mommy *inf* ['mɒmɪ] *Am* = **mummy 2**.

Mon. (*written abbr of* Monday) lun.

Monacan ['mɒnəkən] = **Monegasque**.

Monaco ['mɒnəkəʊ] *pr n* Monaco.

monad ['məʊnæd] (*pl* **monads** OR **monades** [-diːz]) *n* PHILOS monade *f*.

Mona Lisa ['məʊnə'liːzə] *pr n*: 'The ~' *Leonardo da Vinci* 'la Joconde'.

monarch ['mɒnək] *n* [gen & ENTOM] monarque *m*.

monarchic(al) [mə'nɑːkɪk(l)] *adj* monarchique.

monarchism ['mɒnəkɪzm] *n* monarchisme *m*.

monarchist ['mɒnəkɪst] ◇ *adj* monarchiste.
◇ *n* monarchiste *mf*.

monarchy ['mɒnəkɪ] (*pl* **monarchies**) *n* monarchie *f*.

monastery ['mɒnəstrɪ] (*pl* **monasteries**) *n* monastère *m*.

monastic [mə'næstɪk] *adj* monastique.

monasticism [mə'næstɪsɪzm] *n* monachisme *m*.

monatomic [ˌmɒnə'tɒmɪk] *adj* monoatomique.

monaural [mɒ'nɔːrəl] *adj* monaural.

Monday ['mʌndɪ] *n* lundi *m*; **I've got that ~ morning feeling** je me sens comme on peut se sentir un lundi matin.

Monegasque [ˌmɒnɪ'gæsk] ◇ *n* Monégasque *mf*.
◇ *adj* monégasque.

monetarism ['mʌnɪtərɪzm] *n* monétarisme *m*.

monetarist ['mʌnɪtərɪst] ◇ *adj* monétariste.
◇ *n* monétariste *mf*.

monetary ['mʌnɪtrɪ] *adj* monétaire; **a tight ~ policy** une politique monétaire stricte; ~ **unit** unité *f* monétaire.

money ['mʌnɪ] (*pl* **moneys** OR **monies**) ◇ *n* -**1.** [gen] argent *m*; **have you got any ~ on you?** est-ce que tu as de l'argent OR du liquide sur toi?; **they don't accept foreign ~** ils n'acceptent pas l'argent étranger OR les devises étrangères; **your ~ or your life!** la bourse ou la vie!; **to get one's ~'s worth** en avoir pour son argent; **they're unwilling to put any ~ into the project** ils ne veulent pas investir dans le projet; **it's ~ well spent** c'est une bonne affaire; **the best dictionary that ~ can buy** le meilleur dictionnaire qui existe OR qui soit; **the shop isn't making any ~** la boutique ne rapporte pas; **how did she make her ~?** comment a-t-elle gagné son argent?; ~ **is no object** peu importe le prix, l'argent n'entre pas en ligne de compte; **I'm no good with ~** je n'ai pas la notion de l'argent; **there's no ~ in translating** la traduction ne rapporte pas OR ne paie pas; **toys cost ~, you know** les jouets, ce n'est pas gratuit, tu sais; **we paid good ~ for it** cela nous a coûté cher; **you can earn big ~ selling carpets** on peut gagner beaucoup d'argent en vendant des tapis; **I'm not made of ~, you know** tu as l'air de croire que je roule sur l'or; **to put ~ on a horse** miser sur un cheval ❑ **to be in the ~** *inf* être plein aux as; **put your ~ where your mouth is** il est temps de joindre le geste à la parole; **to have ~ to burn** avoir de l'argent à jeter par les fenêtres; **it's ~ for old rope** *inf Br* c'est de l'argent vite gagné OR du fric vite fait; **for my ~, he's the best candidate** à mon avis, c'est le meilleur candidat; ~ **is the root of all evil** *prov* l'argent est la source de tous les maux. -**2.** FIN [currency] monnaie *f*; **to coin** OR **to mint ~** battre OR frapper de la monnaie; **counterfeit ~** fausse monnaie; **paper ~** papier-monnaie *m*.
◇ *comp* [problems, matters] d'argent, financier.
◆ **moneys, monies** *npl* JUR [sums] sommes *fpl* (d'argent); **public ~** deniers *mpl* publics.

moneybags *inf* ['mʌnɪbægz] (*pl inv*) *n* richard *m*, -e *f*, rupin *m*, -e *f*.

money belt *n* ceinture *f* portefeuille.

money box *n* tirelire *f*.

money changer *n* -**1.** [person] cambiste *mf*. -**2.** *Am* [machine] changeur *m* de monnaie.

moneyed ['mʌnɪd] *adj* riche, nanti.

money-grubber *inf* [-'grʌbəʳ] *n* radin *m*, -e *f*, pingre *mf*.

money-grubbing *inf* [-'grʌbɪŋ] ◇ *n* radinerie *f*.
◇ *adj* radin.

moneylender ['mʌnɪˌlendəʳ] *n* FIN prêteur *m*, -euse *f*; [usurer] usurier *m*, -ère *f*; [pawnbroker] prêteur *m*, -euse *f* sur gages.

money-maker *n* affaire *f* qui rapporte, mine *f* d'or *fig*.

money-making *adj* lucratif; **it's another of her ~ schemes** c'est encore une de ses idées pour faire fortune.

money market *n* marché *m* monétaire.

money order *n* mandat *m*.

money spider *n* araignée *f* porte-bonheur.

money-spinner *inf Br* = **money-maker**.

money-spinning *inf Br* = **money-making**.

money supply *n* masse *f* monétaire.

mongol ['mɒŋgəl] *dated & offensive* ◇ *n* mongolien *m*, -enne *f*.
◇ *adj* mongolien.

Mongol ['mɒŋgəl] ◇ *n* -**1.** [person] Mongol *m*, -e *f*. -**2.** LING mongol *m*.
◇ *adj* mongol.

Mongolia [mɒŋ'gəʊlɪə] *pr n* Mongolie *f*; in ~ en Mongolie; **Inner/Outer ~** Mongolie-Intérieure/Extérieure.

Mongolian [mɒŋ'gəʊlɪən] = **Mongol**.

Mongolic [mɒŋ'gɒlɪk] *adj* -**1.** LING mongol. -**2.** [people, customs etc] mongoloïde.

mongolism ['mɒŋgəlɪzm] *n dated & offensive* mongolisme *m*, trisomie *f*.

mongoloid ['mɒŋgəlɔɪd] *dated & offensive*
◇ *adj* mongoloïde.
◇ *n* mongoloïde *mf*.

Mongoloid ['mɒŋgəlɔɪd] ◇ *adj* mongol, mongolique.
◇ *n* mongol *m*, -e *f*, mongolique *mf*.

mongoose ['mɒŋguːs] *n* mangouste *f*.

mongrel ['mʌŋgrəl] ◇ *adj* [dog] bâtard; [other animal] hybride.
◇ *n* [dog] bâtard *m*; [other animal] hybride *m*.

mongst, 'mongst [mʌŋst] *poet* = **among(st)**.

monicker▽ ['mɒnɪkəʳ] = **moniker**.
monied ['mʌnɪd] = **moneyed**.
moniker▽ ['mɒnɪkəʳ] *n* [name] nom *m*; [nickname] surnom *m*.
monism ['mɒnɪzm] *n* monisme *m*.
monitor ['mɒnɪtəʳ] ◇ *n* -**1.** MED & TECH [checking device] moniteur *m*. -**2.** COMPUT & TV [screen] moniteur *m*. -**3.** SCH ≃ chef *m* de classe; **dinner ~** *élève chargé de veiller au bon déroulement des repas à la cantine*. -**4.** RADIO employé *m*, -e *f* d'un service d'écoute.
◇ *vt* -**1.** [check] suivre, surveiller; **their progress is carefully ~ed** leurs progrès sont suivis de près; **the FBI is ~ing his movements** le FBI surveille ses déplacements; **this instrument ~s the pulse rate** cet instrument surveille le pouls du patient. -**2.** [listen in to - broadcasts] écouter; **~ing station** station *f* d'écoute.
monitory ['mɒnɪtərɪ] *adj fml* [warning] d'avertissement; [reproving] d'admonition.
monk [mʌŋk] *n* moine *m*, religieux *m*.
monkey ['mʌŋkɪ] *n* -**1.** [animal] singe *m*; **female ~** guenon *f* ❑ **to make a ~ out of sb** *inf* se payer la tête de qqn; **to have a ~ on one's back** *inf Am* être accro. -**2.** *inf* [scamp] polisson *m*, -onne *f*, galopin *m*. -**3.** ▽ *Br* [£500] *cinq cents livres*.
◆ **monkey about** *inf Br*, **monkey around** *inf vi insep* -**1.** [play the fool] faire l'imbécile. -**2.** [tamper]: **to ~ about** OR **around with sthg** tripoter qqch; **don't ~ about with my tools** ne t'amuse pas avec mes outils.
monkey business *inf n (U)* [suspect activity] combines *fpl*; [mischief] bêtises *fpl*; **they're up to some ~** ils sont en train de préparer un sale tour.
monkey jacket *n* veste *f* courte.
monkey nut *n Br* cacahouète *f*, cacahuète *f*.
monkey-puzzle *n*: **~ (tree)** araucaria *m*, désespoir *m* des singes.
monkey suit *inf n* tenue *f* de soirée, habit *m*.
monkey wrench *n* clef *f* anglaise OR à molette.
monkfish ['mʌŋkfɪʃ] (*pl inv* OR **monkfishes**) *n* [angler fish] baudroie *f*, lotte *f*; [angel shark] ange *m* de mer.
monkhood ['mʌŋkhʊd] *n* -**1.** [institution] monachisme *m*; [life] vie *f* monastique; **to enter the ~** entrer dans les ordres (monastiques). -**2.** [monks collectively]: **the ~** les moines *mpl*.
monkish ['mʌŋkɪʃ] *adj* monacal, de moine.
monkshood ['mʌŋkshʊd] *n* aconit *m (normal)*.
mono ['mɒnəʊ] (*pl* **monos**) ◇ *adj* (*abbr of* **monophonic**) mono *(inv)*, monophonique; **~ record player** électrophone *m* mono.
◇ *n* -**1.** AUDIO monophonie *f*; **in ~** en monophonie. -**2.** *inf Am* MED mononucléose *f* (infectieuse).
monoacid [,mɒnəʊ'æsɪd] *n* monoacide *m*.
monobasic [,mɒnəʊ'beɪsɪk] *adj* monobasique.
monochromatic [,mɒnəkrə'mætɪk] *adj* monochromatique.
monochrome ['mɒnəkrəʊm] ◇ *adj* [photograph] en noir et blanc; [television set] en noir et blanc *(inv)*; [computer screen] monochrome; [painting] en camaïeu; **he leads a very ~ existence** *fig* il mène une existence très terne.
◇ *n* -**1.** [technique] monochromie *f*; PHOT & TV noir et blanc *m*; ART camaïeu *m*. -**2.** [photograph] photographie *f* en noir et blanc; [painting] camaïeu *m*; [in modern art] monochrome *m*.
monocle ['mɒnəkl] *n* monocle *m*.
monocled ['mɒnəkld] *adj* qui porte un monocle.
monocline ['mɒnəklaɪn] *n* monoclinal *m*.
monoclonal antibody [,mɒnə'kləʊnl-] *n* anticorps *m* monoclonal.
monocoque ['mɒnəkɒk] *n* AERON construction *f* monocoque; AUT monocoque *f*.
monocracy [mɒ'nɒkrəsɪ] (*pl* **monocracies**) *n* monocratie *f*.
monocratic [,mɒnəʊ'krætɪk] *adj* monocratique.
monocular [mɒ'nɒkjʊləʳ] *adj* monoculaire.
monoculture ['mɒnə,kʌltʃəʳ] *n* monoculture *f*.
monocyte ['mɒnəsaɪt] *n* monocyte *m*.
monody ['mɒnədɪ] (*pl* **monodies**) *n* monodie *f*.
monogamist [mɒ'nɒgəmɪst] *n* monogame *mf*.
monogamous [mɒ'nɒgəməs] *adj* monogame.
monogamy [mɒ'nɒgəmɪ] *n* monogamie *f*.
monogenesis [,mɒnəʊ'dʒenəsɪs] *n* -**1.** [of human race] monogénisme *m*. -**2.** BIOL [asexual reproduction] multiplication *f* asexuée.
monogram ['mɒnəgræm] (*pt & pp* **monogrammed**, *cont* **monogramming**) ◇ *n* monogramme *m*.
◇ *vt* marquer d'un monogramme; **monogrammed handkerchiefs** mouchoirs avec un monogramme brodé.
monogrammed *Br*, **monogramed** *Am* ['mɒnəgræmd] *adj* qui porte un monogramme.
monograph ['mɒnəgrɑːf] *n* monographie *f*.
monohull ['mɒnə,hʌl] *n* NAUT monocoque *m*.
monolingual [,mɒnə'lɪŋgwəl] *adj* monolingue.
monolith ['mɒnəlɪθ] *n* monolithe *m*.
monolithic [,mɒnə'lɪθɪk] *adj* monolithique.
monologue *Br*, **monolog** *Am* ['mɒnəlɒg]
◇ *n* monologue *m*.
◇ *vi* monologuer.
monomania [,mɒnə'meɪnjə] *n* monomanie *f*.
monomaniac [,mɒnə'meɪnɪæk] ◇ *adj* monomaniaque, monomane.
◇ *n* monomaniaque *mf*, monomane *mf*.
monomer ['mɒnəməʳ] *n* monomère *m*.
monomial [mɒ'nəʊmɪəl] ◇ *n* monôme *m* MATH.
◇ *adj* de OR en monôme; **~ function** fonction monôme.
monomorphic [,mɒnəʊ'mɔːfɪk] *adj* monomorphe.
monomorphism [,mɒnəʊ'mɔːfɪzm] *n* monomorphisme *m*.
mononuclear [,mɒnəʊ'njuːklɪəʳ] *adj* mononucléaire.
mononucleosis ['mɒnəʊ,njuːklɪ'əʊsɪs] *n* mononucléose *f*.
monophonic [,mɒnə'fɒnɪk] *adj* monophonique, monaural.
monophthong ['mɒnəfθɒŋ] *n* monophtongue *f*.
monoplane ['mɒnəpleɪn] *n* monoplan *m*.
monopolist [mə'nɒpəlɪst] *n* monopoliste *mf*, monopoleur *m*, -euse *f*.
monopolistic [mə,nɒpə'lɪstɪk] *adj* monopoliste, monopolistique.
monopolization [mə,nɒpəlaɪ'zeɪʃn] *n* monopolisation *f*.
monopolize, -ise [mə'nɒpəlaɪz] *vt* monopoliser.
monopoly [mə'nɒpəlɪ] (*pl* **monopolies**) *n* monopole *m*; **to have a ~ of** OR **in** OR **on sthg** avoir le monopole de qqch ❑ **state ~** monopole d'État; **the Monopolies and Mergers Commission** *commission veillant au respect de la législation antitrust en Grande-Bretagne*.
◆ **Monopoly**® *n* [game] Monopoly® *m*; **~ money** *fig* billets *mpl* de Monopoly.
monopsony [mə'nɒpsənɪ] (*pl* **monopsonies**) *n* monopsone *m*.
monorail ['mɒnəreɪl] *n* monorail *m*.
monosemic [,mɒnəʊ'siːmɪk] *adj* monosémique.
monosemy ['mɒnəʊ,siːmɪ] *n* monosémie *f*.
monosodium glutamate [,mɒnə'səʊdjəm'gluːtəmeɪt] *n* CULIN glutamate *m* (de sodium).
monostable ['mɒnəʊsteɪbl] *adj* monostable.
monosyllabic [,mɒnəsɪ'læbɪk] *adj* -**1.** LING monosyllabe, monosyllabique. -**2.** [person] qui s'exprime par monosyllabes; **he's very ~** il ne parle que par monosyllabes.
monosyllable ['mɒnə,sɪləbl] *n* monosyllabe *m*; **to speak in ~s** parler par monosyllabes.
monotheism ['mɒnəθiː,ɪzm] *n* monothéisme *m*.
monotheist ['mɒnəθiː,ɪst] ◇ *adj* monothéiste.
◇ *n* monothéiste *mf*.
monotheistic [,mɒnəθiː'ɪstɪk] *adj* monothéiste.
monotone ['mɒnətəʊn] ◇ *n* ton *m* monocorde; **to speak in a ~** parler d'un ton monocorde.
◇ *adj* monocorde.
monotonous [mə'nɒtənəs] *adj* monotone.
monotonously [mə'nɒtənəslɪ] *adv* de façon monotone; **he droned ~ on** il ânonnait d'un ton monotone.
monotony [mə'nɒtənɪ] (*pl* **monotonies**) *n* monotonie *f*; **her visits broke the ~ of his life** les visites qu'elle lui rendait rompaient la monotonie de son existence; **the ~ of the landscape** l'uniformité OR la monotonie du paysage.
monotype ['mɒnətaɪp] *n* ART & BIOL monotype *m*.
◆ **Monotype**® *n* TYPO [machine] Monotype® *f*.
monovalent [,mɒnəʊ'veɪlənt] *adj* monovalent, univalent.
monoxide [mɒ'nɒksaɪd] *n* monoxyde *m*; **carbon ~** monoxyde *m* de carbone; **nitrogen ~** protoxyde *m* d'azote.
Monroe Doctrine [mən'rəʊ-] *n*: **the ~** la doctrine Monroe.

MONROE DOCTRINE:
La doctrine Monroe, énoncée en 1823, inaugura une période isolationniste aux États-Unis, en interdisant le continent américain à l'Europe colonialiste, et en se détournant délibérément des affaires européennes.

Monrovia [mən'rəʊvɪə] *pr n* Monrovia.
monsignor [,mɒnsiː'njəʳ] (*pl* **monsignors** OR **monsignori** [-siː'njɔːrɪ]) *n* monseigneur *m*.
monsoon [mɒn'suːn] *n* mousson *f*; **the ~ season** la mousson.
monster ['mɒnstəʳ] ◇ *n* monstre *m*; **she's becoming a ~** elle devient un monstre; **it's a ~ of a machine** c'est un vrai monstre, cette machine.
◇ *adj* colossal, monstre.
monstrance ['mɒnstrəns] *n* ostensoir *m*.
monstrosity [mɒn'strɒsətɪ] (*pl* **monstrosities**) *n* -**1.** [monstrous nature] monstruosité *f*. -**2.** [ugly person, thing] horreur *f*; **the town hall is a huge Victorian ~** la mairie est une horreur de l'époque victorienne.
monstrous ['mɒnstrəs] *adj* -**1.** [appalling] monstrueux, atroce. -**2.** [enormous] colossal, énorme. -**3.** [abnormal] monstrueux.
monstrously ['mɒnstrəslɪ] *adv* affreusement.
montage ['mɒntɑːʒ] *n* ART, CIN & PHOT montage *m*.
Montana [mɒn'tænə] *pr n* Montana *m*; **in ~** dans le Montana.
Mont Blanc [,mɒm'blɒŋ] *pr n* mont Blanc *m*.
Monte Carlo [,mɒntɪ'kɑːləʊ] *pr n* Monte-Carlo.
Montenegro [,mɒntɪ'niːgrəʊ] *pr n* Monténégro *m*.
Montevideo [,mɒntɪvɪ'deɪəʊ] *pr n* Montevideo.
Montezuma [,mɒntɪ'zuːmə] *n*: **~'s revenge** *inf hum* la tourista.
month [mʌnθ] *n* mois *m*; **how much does she earn a ~?** combien gagne-t-elle par mois?; **he's six ~s old** il a six mois; **he got six ~s** *inf* il a été condamné à six mois de prison; **every ~** tous les mois; **in a ~'s time** dans un mois; **by the ~** au mois; **two ~s' holiday** OR **vacation** deux mois de vacances; **I can't keep it up ~ after ~** je ne pourrai pas tenir ce rythme éternellement; **~ by ~ you can see an improvement** on constate une amélioration de mois en mois ❑ **she hasn't heard from him in a ~ of Sundays** *inf* ça fait des siècles OR un bail

qu'elle n'a pas de nouvelles de lui; **never in a ~ of Sundays** à la saint-glinglin.

monthly ['mʌnθlɪ] (*pl* monthlies) ◇ *adj* mensuel; **~ instalment** OR **payment** mensualité *f*; **~ period** MED règles *fpl*.
◇ *n* [periodical] mensuel *m*.
◇ *adv* [meet, occur] tous les mois; [pay] mensuellement.
◆ **monthlies** *inf npl* [menstrual period] règles *fpl*.

Montreal [ˌmɒntrɪ'ɔːl] *pr n* Montréal.

monument ['mɒnjʊmənt] *n* -**1.** [memorial] monument *m*; **a ~ to the war dead** un monument aux morts; **it is a ~ to man's stupidity** c'est un monument à la bêtise humaine. -**2.** [historic building] monument *m* historique; **a national ~** un monument national.

monumental [ˌmɒnjʊ'mentl] *adj* monumental; **the film is a ~ failure** le film est un échec monumental OR complet; **he's a ~ bore** il est prodigieusement ennuyeux.

monumentally [ˌmɒnjʊ'mentəlɪ] *adv* -**1.** [build] de façon monumentale. -**2.** [extremely] extrêmement; **it was ~ boring** c'était extrêmement ennuyeux.

moo [muː] ◇ *n* -**1.** [sound] meuglement *m*, beuglement *m*, mugissement *m*. -**2.** *inf Br* [stupid woman] bécasse *f*; **silly ~!** bécasse!, vieille bique!
◇ *vi* meugler, beugler, mugir.
◇ *onomat* meuh.

mooch *inf* [muːtʃ] ◇ *vi* -**1.** *Br* [wander aimlessly] traîner; **he ~ed down the street** il descendit la rue en flânant. -**2.** *Am* [cadge]: **he's always ~ing off** OR **on people** il passe son temps à quémander, il est toujours en train de taper quelqu'un.
◇ *vt Am* -**1.** [cadge] taper; **to ~ $10 off** OR **from sb** taper qqn de 10 dollars; **can I ~ a cigarette off you?** est-ce que je peux te piquer une cigarette? -**2.** [steal] chiper, piquer.
◆ **mooch about** *inf*, **mooch around** *inf vi insep Br* [loaf] traîner; **I was just ~ing about at home** je traînais OR flemmardais à la maison.

mood [muːd] *n* -**1.** [humour] humeur *f*, disposition *f*; **to be in a good/bad ~** être de bonne/mauvaise humeur; **he's in a foul ~** il est d'une humeur exécrable; **it's hard to predict the ~ of the electorate** il est difficile de prédire l'état d'esprit OR l'humeur des électeurs; **she can be quite funny when the ~ takes her** elle peut être plutôt drôle quand l'envie lui en prend; **are you in the ~ for a hamburger?** un hamburger, ça te dit?; **I'm not in the ~** OR **I'm in no ~ to hear his life story** je ne suis pas d'humeur à l'écouter raconter (l'histoire de) sa vie. -**2.** [bad temper, sulk] mauvaise humeur *f*, bouderie *f*; **to be in a ~** être de mauvaise humeur; **she's in one of her ~s** elle est de mauvaise humeur, elle fait la tête. -**3.** [atmosphere] ambiance *f*, atmosphère *f*; **the ~ is one of cautious optimism** l'ambiance est à l'optimisme prudent. -**4.** GRAMM mode *m*; **imperative ~** impératif *m*; **subjunctive ~** subjonctif *m*.

moodily ['muːdɪlɪ] *adv* [behave] maussadement, d'un air morose; [talk, reply] d'un ton maussade; **"oh, do what you like" he said** «oh! faites ce que vous voulez» dit-il d'un ton maussade OR boudeur.

moodiness ['muːdɪnɪs] *n* -**1.** [sullenness] humeur *f* maussade, maussaderie *f*. -**2.** [volatility] humeur *f* changeante; **it's his ~ I can't stand** ce sont ses sautes d'humeur que je ne supporte pas.

moody ['muːdɪ] (*compar* moodier, *superl* moodiest) *adj* -**1.** [sullen] de mauvaise humeur, maussade, grincheux. -**2.** [temperamental] versatile, d'humeur changeante; **he's very ~** il est d'humeur très changeante, il est très lunatique.

moolah *inf* ['muːlə] *n Am* fric *m*.

moon [muːn] ◇ *n* -**1.** lune *f*; **Saturn has several ~s** Saturne a plusieurs lunes; **there's a ~ tonight** on voit la lune ce soir; **by the light of the ~** au clair de (la) lune ❑ **crescent ~** croissant *m* de lune; **full/new ~** pleine/nouvelle lune; **to cry for the ~** demander la lune; **many ~s ago** il y a bien des lunes; **to be over the ~** *inf* être aux anges; **he promised her the ~ (and the stars)** il lui promit la lune; **once in a blue ~** tous les trente-six du mois; '**The Moon and Sixpence**' *Maugham* 'l'Envoûté'. -**2.** *inf Am* [bare backside] lune *f*.
◇ *comp* [base, flight, rocket] lunaire.
◇ *vi inf* [show one's buttocks] montrer son derrière OR ses fesses.
◆ **moon about** *inf Br*, **moon around** *inf vi insep* [idly] paresser, traîner, flemmarder; [dreamily] rêvasser; [gloomily] se morfondre.
◆ **moon over** *inf vt insep* soupirer après; **she's still ~ing over her old boyfriend** elle soupire toujours après son ancien petit ami.

moonbeam ['muːnbiːm] *n* rayon *m* de lune.

moonboots ['muːnbuːts] *npl* après-skis *mpl*.

moon buggy (*pl* moon buggies) *n* Jeep® *f* lunaire.

moon-faced *adj* joufflu, aux joues rebondies.

Moonie *inf* ['muːnɪ] *n* adepte *m* de la secte Moon, mooniste *mf*.

moon landing *n* atterrissage *m* sur la lune, alunissage *m*.

moonless ['muːnlɪs] *adj* sans lune.

moonlight ['muːnlaɪt] ◇ *n* clair *m* de lune; **they took a walk by ~** ils se sont promenés au clair de (la) lune ❑ '**The Moonlight Sonata**' *Beethoven* 'la Sonate au clair de lune'.
◇ *adj* [walk] au clair de (la) lune.
◇ *vi inf* [have second job] avoir un deuxième emploi; [illegally] travailler au noir.

moonlighter ['muːnlaɪtə^r] *n* travailleur *m* non déclaré, travailleuse *f* non déclarée.

moonlight flit *inf n Br*: **to do a ~** déménager à la cloche de bois.

moonlighting ['muːnlaɪtɪŋ] *n* [illegal work] travail *m* au noir.

moonlit ['muːnlɪt] *adj* éclairé par la lune; **a ~ night** une nuit de lune; **a bright ~ night** une nuit très claire; **we walked through the ~ fields** nous avons marché à travers champs, au clair de lune.

moonrise ['muːnraɪz] *n* lever *m* de la lune.

moonscape ['muːnskeɪp] *n* paysage *m* lunaire.

moonshine ['muːnʃaɪn] *n* (*U*) -**1.** = **moonlight** *n*. -**2.** *inf* [foolishness] sornettes *fpl*, sottises *fpl*, bêtises *fpl*. -**3.** *Am* [illegally made spirits] alcool *m* de contrebande.

moonshining ['muːnʃaɪnɪŋ] *n Am fabrication clandestine d'alcool en milieu rural*.

moon shot *n* lancement *m* d'un vaisseau lunaire.

moonstone ['muːnstəʊn] *n* pierre *f* de lune, adulaire *f*; '**The Moonstone**' *Collins* 'la Pierre de lune'.

moonstruck ['muːnstrʌk] *adj* [dreamy] dans la lune; [mad] fou, détraqué.

moon walk *n* marche *f* sur la lune.

moony *inf* ['muːnɪ] (*compar* moonier, *superl* mooniest) *adj* -**1.** [dreamy] rêveur, dans la lune. -**2.** *Br* [crazy] dingue, timbré.

moor [mɔː^r] ◇ *vt* [boat] amarrer; [buoy] mouiller.
◇ *vi* mouiller.
◇ *n* lande *f*.

Moor [mɔː^r] *n* Maure *m*, Mauresque *f*.

moorhen ['mɔːhen] *n* -**1.** [waterfowl] poule *f* d'eau. -**2.** [female grouse] grouse *f* d'Écosse.

mooring ['mɔːrɪŋ] *n* -**1.** [act] amarrage *m*, mouillage *m*. -**2.** [place] mouillage *m*.
◆ **moorings** *npl* [cables, ropes etc] amarres *fpl*; **the boat was (riding) at her ~s** le bateau tirait sur ses amarres; **he's lost his ~s** *fig* il est à la dérive.

Moorish ['mɔːrɪʃ] *adj* maure.

moorland ['mɔːlənd] *n* lande *f*.

moose [muːs] (*pl inv*) *n* orignal *m*.

moot [muːt] ◇ *vt* [question, topic] soulever; **a change in the rules has been ~ed** il a été question de modifier le règlement.
◇ *n* -**1.** HIST assemblée *f*. -**2.** UNIV [in law faculties] tribunal *m* fictif.

moot point *n*: **will the legislation have any real effect? — well, that's a ~** really la législation sera-t-elle réellement efficace? — c'est discutable OR ce n'est pas sûr.

mop [mɒp] (*pt* & *pp* mopped, *cont* mopping) ◇ *n* -**1.** [for floor - string, cloth] lave-pont *m*, balai *m* (à franges); [- sponge] balai-éponge *m*; NAUT vadrouille *f*; [for dishes] lavette *f* (à vaisselle). -**2.** [of hair] tignasse *f*; **a ~ of blond hair** une tignasse blonde.
◇ *vt* [floor] laver; [table, face, spilt liquid] essuyer, éponger; **he mopped the sweat from his brow** il s'épongea le front.
◆ **mop up** *vt sep* -**1.** [floor, table, spilt liquid] essuyer, éponger; **have some bread to ~ up the sauce** prenez un morceau de pain pour saucer votre assiette. -**2.** *inf* [win, make off with] rafler; **they mopped up all the gold medals** ils ont raflé toutes les médailles d'or. -**3.** MIL [resistance] liquider.

mope [məʊp] *vi* broyer du noir; **he's been moping around** OR **about all week** il a passé la semaine à broyer du noir; **there's no use moping about** OR **over it** ça ne sert à rien de passer ton temps à ressasser ce qui s'est passé.

moped ['məʊped] *n Br* Mobylette® *f*, cyclomoteur *m*, vélomoteur *m*.

moppet *inf* ['mɒpɪt] *n* chou *m*.

mopping-up operation ['mɒpɪŋ-] *n* opération *f* de nettoyage.

moquette [mɒ'ket] *n* moquette *f (étoffe)*.

moraine [mɒ'reɪn] *n* moraine *f*.

moral ['mɒrəl] ◇ *adj* moral; **it's a very ~ story** c'est une histoire très morale; **he complains about the decline in ~ standards** il se plaint du déclin des valeurs morales OR du relâchement des mœurs; **we have a ~ duty to help them** nous sommes moralement obligés de les aider; **to give sb ~ support** soutenir qqn moralement ❑ **~ philosophy** morale *f*, éthique *f*; **~ victory** victoire *f* morale.
◇ *n* [lesson] morale *f*; **what's the ~ of the story?** quelle est la morale de l'histoire?
◆ **morals** *npl* [standards] sens *m* moral, moralité *f*; **he has no ~s** il n'a aucun sens moral.

morale [mə'rɑːl] *n* moral *m*; **~ is high/low among the troops** les troupes ont bon/mauvais moral, les troupes ont/n'ont pas le moral; **she tried to raise their ~** elle a essayé de leur remonter le moral OR de leur redonner (du) courage; **news of the defeat sapped the troops' ~** la nouvelle de la défaite a sapé le moral des troupes.

moralist ['mɒrəlɪst] *n* moraliste *mf*.

moralistic [ˌmɒrə'lɪstɪk] *adj* moraliste.

morality [mə'rælətɪ] (*pl* moralities) *n* -**1.** moralité *f*. -**2.** **~ (play)** THEAT moralité *f*.

moralize, -ise ['mɒrəlaɪz] ◇ *vi* moraliser; **to ~ about sthg** moraliser sur qqch; **he's forever moralizing about things** il passe son temps à faire la morale.
◇ *vt* moraliser.

moralizing ['mɒrəlaɪzɪŋ] ◇ *adj* moralisateur, moralisant.
◇ *n (U)* leçons *fpl* de morale, prêches *mpl péj*.

morally ['mɒrəlɪ] *adv* moralement; **the parents are ~ responsible** les parents sont moralement responsables; **~ wrong** contraire à la morale.

moral majority *n*: **the ~** les néo-conservateurs *mpl (surtout aux États-Unis)*.

Moral Rearmament *pr n mouvement international pour un renouveau moral et spirituel fondé en 1938*.

morass [mə'ræs] *n* -**1.** [disordered situation] bourbier *m*; **a ~ of conflicting information** un fouillis OR fatras d'informations contradictoires; **bogged down in a ~ of rules and regulations** empêtré dans un fatras de règles et de règlements. -**2.** [marsh] marais *m*, bourbier *m*.

moratorium [ˌmɒrə'tɔːrɪəm] (*pl* moratoriums OR moratoria [-rɪə]) *n* -**1.** [suspension of activity] moratoire *m*; **they are calling for a ~ on arms sales** ils appellent à un moratoire sur les ventes d'armes. -**2.** ECON & JUR moratoire *m*; [of debt] moratoire, suspension *f*.

Moravia [məˈreɪvjə] *pr n* Moravie *f*; in ~ en Moravie.

Moravian [məˈreɪvjən] ◇ *n* Morave *mf*.
◇ *adj* morave.

moray [ˈmɒreɪ] *n*: ~ (eel) murène *f*.

morbid [ˈmɔːbɪd] *adj* -**1.** [gen] morbide; he has a ~ outlook on life il voit les choses en noir; ~ thoughts pensées morbides; don't be so ~! chasse ces idées noires! -**2.** MED [state, growth] morbide; ~ anatomy anatomie *f* pathologique.

morbidity [mɔːˈbɪdətɪ] *n* -**1.** [gen] morbidité *f*. -**2.** ~ (rate) MED morbidité *f* (relative).

morbidly [ˈmɔːbɪdlɪ] *adv* maladivement.

morbidness [ˈmɔːbɪdnɪs] *n* morbidité *f*.

mordant [ˈmɔːdənt] *adj* mordant, caustique.

more [mɔːʳ] ◇ *det* -**1.** (*compar of* many & much) [greater in number, amount] plus de, davantage de; there were ~ boys than girls il y avait plus de garçons que de filles; there's much OR a lot OR far ~ room in the other building il y a beaucoup plus de place dans l'autre bâtiment. -**2.** [further, additional]: you should eat ~ fish tu devrais manger davantage de OR plus de poisson; I need ~ time j'ai besoin de plus de temps; three ~ people arrived trois autres personnes sont arrivées; do you have any ~ questions? avez-vous d'autres questions?; do you have any ~ stamps? est-ce qu'il vous reste des timbres?; is there any ~ butter? reste-t-il du beurre?; just wait a few ~ minutes patiente encore quelques instants; a little ~ sugar? encore un peu de sucre?; there are no ~ OR there aren't any ~ green lampshades il n'y a plus d'abat-jour verts; no ~ talking maintenant, taisez-vous OR silence!; there'll be no ~ skiing this winter le ski est fini pour cet hiver; there have been several ~ incidents in the same area plusieurs autres incidents se sont produits dans le même quartier; bring me some ~ potatoes, please apporte-moi encore des pommes de terre, s'il te plaît; there's some ~ paper in that drawer il y a encore du papier dans ce tiroir; would you like some ~ soup? voulez-vous un peu plus de soupe?
◇ *pron* -**1.** (*compar of* many & much) [greater amount] plus, davantage; [greater number] plus; he earns ~ than I do OR than me il gagne plus que moi; I wish I could do ~ for her j'aimerais pouvoir l'aider plus OR davantage; it'll take a lot ~ than that to persuade them il en faudra bien plus (que ça) OR bien davantage pour les convaincre; some opted for A, but many ~ chose B certains ont choisi A, mais ceux qui ont choisi B étaient bien plus nombreux; there are ~ of them than there are of us ils sont plus nombreux que nous; ~ of: he's even ~ of a coward than I thought il est encore plus lâche que je ne pensais; it's ~ of a problem now than it used to be ça pose plus de problèmes maintenant qu'avant; she's ~ of a singer than a dancer c'est une chanteuse plus qu'une danseuse. -**2.** [additional amount] plus, encore; there's ~ if you want it il y en a encore si tu veux; he asked for ~ il en redemanda; I couldn't eat any ~, thanks je ne pourrais plus rien avaler, merci; she just can't take any ~ elle n'en peut vraiment plus; please can I have some ~? [food] puis-je en reprendre, s'il vous plaît?; there are some ~ here that you haven't washed il en reste ici que tu n'as pas lavés; I could say ~, but... je pouvais en dire plus mais...; something/nothing ~ quelque chose/rien de plus; I have something/nothing ~ to say j'ai encore quelque chose/je n'ai plus rien à dire; what ~ do you want? que voulez-vous de plus?; but ~ of that later... mais nous reparlerons de ça plus tard...; I want no ~ of this defeatist talk je ne veux plus de ces discours défaitistes ❑ ~ of the same la même chose; the government simply promises ~ of the same le gouvernement se contente de refaire les mêmes promesses; there's plenty ~ where that came from si vous en revoulez, il n'y a qu'à demander. -**3.** *hum* [additional people]: any ~ for the ferry? qui d'autre prend le ferry?
◇ *adv* -**1.** [forming comparatives] plus; ~ intelligent plus intelligent; ~ comfortably plus confortablement. -**2.** [to a greater extent, degree] plus, davantage; you should read ~ tu devrais lire plus OR davantage; it worries me ~ than it used to ça m'inquiète plus qu'avant; I like wine ~ than beer je préfère le vin à la bière, j'aime mieux le vin que la bière; he's intelligent but his sister is ~ so il est intelligent mais sa sœur l'est davantage ‖ [rather] plutôt; she was ~ disappointed than angry elle était plus déçue que fâchée; do it ~ like this fais-le plutôt comme ceci; it's ~ a question of who foots the bill il s'agit plutôt de savoir qui paiera la facture. -**3.** [again]: once/twice ~ encore une/deux fois.
◆ **more and more** ◇ *det phr* de plus en plus; ~ and ~ people are using it de plus en plus de gens l'utilisent.
◇ *adv phr* de plus en plus; I was growing ~ and ~ tired j'étais de plus en plus fatigué.
◆ **more or less** *adv phr* -**1.** [roughly] plus ou moins; that's ~ or less what I expected c'est plus ou moins ce à quoi je m'attendais; is that correct? — well, ~ or less est-ce que c'est vrai? — plus ou moins, oui. -**2.** [almost] presque; we've ~ or less finished nous avons presque terminé.
◆ **more than** ◇ *prep phr* [with numbers, measurements etc] plus de; ~ than 500 people plus de 500 personnes; it costs much OR a lot ~ than $50 ça coûte bien plus de 50 dollars; for little ~ than £500 pour à peine plus de 500 livres; I won't be ~ than two hours je n'en ai pas pour plus de deux heures, j'en ai pour deux heures au maximum.
◇ *adv phr* plus que; I'd be ~ than happy to do it je serais ravi de le faire; you've been ~ than generous vous avez été plus que généreux; this ~ than makes up for his previous mistakes voilà qui rachète largement ses anciennes erreurs.
◆ **more than a little** *adv phr* vraiment; we were ~ than a little shocked nous étions vraiment choqués.
◆ **no more** *adv phr* -**1.** [neither] non plus; he doesn't believe the rumours and no ~ do I il ne croit pas les rumeurs et moi non plus. -**2.** [as little] pas plus; she's no ~ a spy than I am! elle n'est pas plus espionne que moi!; it's no ~ dangerous than crossing the street ce n'est pas plus dangereux que de traverser la rue; they can no ~ act than fly in the air *inf* ils jouent comme des pieds. -**3.** *lit* [no longer]: no ~ will she grace our company plus jamais elle ne nous tiendra compagnie; the Empire is no ~ l'Empire n'est plus.
◆ **not... any more** *adv phr*: we don't go there any ~ nous n'y allons plus; he still works here, doesn't he? — not any ~ (he doesn't) il travaille encore ici, n'est-ce pas? — non, plus maintenant.
◆ **the more** *adv phr fml* d'autant plus; I was the ~ disappointed j'étais d'autant plus déçu; they went the ~ willingly on that account ils y sont allés d'autant plus volontiers; the ~ so because... d'autant plus que...
◆ **the more... the more** *conj phr* plus... plus; the ~ they have, the ~ they want plus ils en ont, plus ils en veulent; the ~ I see him, the ~ I like him plus je le vois, plus il me plaît.
◆ **what is more, what's more** *adv phr* qui plus est.

moreish *inf* [ˈmɔːrɪʃ] *adj Br* appétissant; these peanuts are very ~ on en mangerait de ces cacahuètes, ces cacahuètes ont un petit goût de revenez-y.

morello [məˈreləʊ] (*pl* morellos) *n*: ~ (cherry) griotte *f*.

moreover [mɔːˈrəʊvəʳ] *adv* de plus.

mores [ˈmɔːreɪz] *npl fml* mœurs *fpl*.

morganatic [ˌmɔːgəˈnætɪk] *adj* morganatique.

morgue [mɔːg] *n* -**1.** [mortuary] morgue *f*. -**2.** *inf* PRESS archives *fpl*.

MORI [ˈmɒrɪ] (*abbr of* Market & Opinion Research Institute) *pr n institut de sondage*.

moribund [ˈmɒrɪbʌnd] *adj* moribond.

morish *inf* [ˈmɔːrɪʃ] = **moreish**.

Mormon [ˈmɔːmən] ◇ *n* mormon *m*, -e *f*.
◇ *adj* mormon.

Mormonism [ˈmɔːmənɪzm] *n* mormonisme *m*.

morn [mɔːn] *n* -**1.** *lit* [morning] matin *m*. -**2.** *Scot*: the ~ [tomorrow] demain.

morning [ˈmɔːnɪŋ] ◇ *n* -**1.** matin *m*, matinée *f*; at three/ten o'clock in the ~ à trois/dix heures du matin; I worked all ~ j'ai travaillé toute la matinée; one summer ~ un matin d'été; when I awoke it was ~ quand je me suis réveillé il faisait jour; every Saturday/Sunday ~ tous les samedis/dimanches matin; from ~ till night du matin jusqu'au soir; there's a flight in the ~ [before noon] il y a un vol le matin; [sometime during] il y a un vol dans la matinée; [tomorrow] il y a un vol demain matin; he's leaving in the ~ il s'en va dans la matinée; it's open in the ~ OR ~s c'est ouvert le matin; see you in the ~! à demain matin!; in the early/late ~ en début/fin de matinée; I'll be back on Monday ~ je serai de retour lundi matin; the cleaning lady comes on Monday ~s la femme de ménage vient le lundi matin; on the ~ of the twelfth le matin du douze, le douze au matin; do you work ~s? est-ce que vous travaillez le matin?; I'm on ~s this week je travaille le matin cette semaine; could I have the ~ off? puis-je avoir la matinée de libre?; (good) ~! [hello] bonjour!; [goodbye] au revoir!; this ~ ce matin; that ~ ce matin-là; tomorrow/yesterday ~ demain/hier matin; the previous ~, the ~ before la veille au matin; the next ~, the ~ after le lendemain matin ❑ the ~ after the night before *inf* un lendemain de cuite. -**2.** *lit* [beginning] matin *m*, aube *f*; in the ~ of one's life à l'aube de sa vie.
◇ *comp* [dew, sun, bath] matinal, du matin; [newspaper, broadcast] du matin; the ~ rush hour les heures de pointe du matin; cancel the Monday ~ meeting annulez le rendez-vous de lundi matin; we have ~ coffee around 11 nous faisons une pause-café vers 11 h du matin.

morning-after pill *n* pilule *f* du lendemain.

morning coat *n* queue-de-pie *f*.

morning dress *n* (*U*) -**1.** *Br habit porté lors des occasions importantes et comportant queue-de-pie, pantalon gris et haut-de-forme gris*. -**2.** *Am* robe *f* d'intérieur.

morning glory *n* ipomée *f*, volubilis *m*.

Morning Prayer *n* office *m* du matin (*Église anglicane*).

morning room *n* petit salon *m*.

mornings [ˈmɔːnɪŋz] *adv esp Am* le matin.

morning sickness *n* nausées *fpl* matinales OR du matin.

morning star *n* étoile *f* du matin.
◆ **Morning Star** *pr n*: the ~ PRESS *quotidien britannique d'obédience communiste*.

Moroccan [məˈrɒkən] ◇ *n* Marocain *m*, -e *f*.
◇ *adj* marocain.

Morocco [məˈrɒkəʊ] *pr n* Maroc *m*; in ~ au Maroc.
◆ **morocco** *n*: morocco (leather) maroquin *m*.

moron [ˈmɔːrɒn] *n* -**1.** ▽ [stupid person] imbécile *mf*, crétin *m*, -e *f*; you ~! pauvre imbécile! -**2.** *dated* [mentally retarded person] débile *m* léger, débile *f* légère.

Moroni [məˈrəʊnɪ] *pr n* Moroni.

moronic [məˈrɒnɪk] *adj* imbécile, stupide.

moronically [məˈrɒnɪklɪ] *adv* comme un imbécile.

morose [məˈrəʊs] *adj* morose.

morosely [məˈrəʊslɪ] *adv* avec morosité.

morph [mɔːf] *n* LING morphe *f*.

morpheme [ˈmɔːfiːm] *n* morphème *m*.

morphemics [mɔːˈfiːmɪks] *n* (*U*) morphématique *f*.

Morpheus [ˈmɔːfjuːs] *pr n* Morphée; in the arms of ~ dans les bras de Morphée.

morphine ['mɔːfiːn], **morphia** ['mɔːfjə] *n* morphine *f*; ~ addict morphinomane *mf*.

morphological [,mɔːfə'lɒdʒɪkl] *adj* BIOL & LING morphologique.

morphology [,mɔː'fɒlədʒɪ] *n* BIOL & LING morphologie *f*.

morphophoneme [,mɔːfəʊ'fəʊniːm] *n* LING morphophonème *m*.

morphophonemics [,mɔːfəʊfə'niːmɪks] *n (U)* morphophonémique *f*.

morris ['mɒrɪs] *n*: ~ dance *danse folklorique anglaise, exécutée par des hommes en costume blanc portant des grelots et des mouchoirs*; ~ dancer, ~ man *danseur folklorique anglais*; ~ dancing *danses folkloriques anglaises*.

morrow ['mɒrəʊ] *n* -**1.** *lit* [next day] lendemain *m*; on the ~ le lendemain. -**2.** *arch* OR *lit* [morning] matin *m*.

Morse [mɔːs] *n*: ~ alphabet alphabet *m* morse; ~ (code) morse *m*; ~ signals signaux *mpl* en morse.

morsel ['mɔːsl] *n* [gen] morceau *m*; [mouthful] bouchée *f*; a choice ~ un morceau de choix.

Mortadella [,mɔːtə'delə] *n* mortadelle *f*.

mortal ['mɔːtl] ◇ *adj* -**1.** [not immortal] mortel; all men are ~ tous les hommes sont mortels ❑ ~ remains *euph* dépouille *f* mortelle. -**2.** [fatal - blow, disease, injury] mortel, fatal; [deadly - enemy, danger] mortel. -**3.** *inf dated* [blessed, damned] sacré, satané; I've tried every ~ thing! j'ai absolument tout essayé! -**4.** [very great]: he lived in ~ fear of being found out il vivait dans une peur mortelle d'être découvert.
◇ *n* mortel *m*, -elle *f*; a mere ~ un simple mortel.

mortality [mɔː'tælətɪ] (*pl* mortalities) *n* -**1.** [loss of life] mortalité *f*; no mortalities have been reported on ne fait état d'aucun mort, aucun décès n'a été enregistré ❑ infant ~ la mortalité infantile; the ~ rate le taux de mortalité; ~ tables tables *fpl* de mortalité OR de létalité. -**2.** [mortal] mortalité *f*.

mortally ['mɔːtəlɪ] *adv* mortellement; ~ offended mortellement offensé; ~ wounded blessé à mort; to be ~ afraid être mort de peur *fig*.

mortal sin *n* péché *m* mortel.

mortar ['mɔːtə^r] ◇ *n* CONSTR, MIL & PHARM mortier *m*.
◇ *vt* CONSTR cimenter.

mortarboard ['mɔːtəbɔːd] *n* -**1.** SCH & UNIV ≃ mortier *m (couvre-chef de professeur, d'universitaire)*. -**2.** CONSTR taloche *f*.

mortgage ['mɔːgɪdʒ] ◇ *n* -**1.** [to buy house] prêt *m* (immobilier); a 25-year ~ at 13% un emprunt sur 25 ans à 13 % ❑ we can't meet our ~ repayments nous ne pouvons pas payer les mensualités de notre emprunt; second ~ hypothèque *f*. -**2.** [surety] hypothèque *f*.
◇ *vt literal & fig* hypothéquer, prendre une hypothèque sur; to be ~d to the hilt [person] crouler sous les remboursements.

mortgagee [,mɔːgɪ'dʒiː] *n* créancier *m*, -ère *f* hypothécaire, prêteur *m*, -euse *f* (sur une hypothèque).

mortgage rate *n* taux *m* de crédit immobilier.

mortgagor [,mɔːgɪ'dʒɔː^r] *n* débiteur *m*, -trice *f* hypothécaire, emprunteur *m*, -euse *f (sur une hypothèque)*.

mortice ['mɔːtɪs] = **mortise**.

mortician [mɔː'tɪʃn] *n Am* entrepreneur *m* de pompes funèbres.

mortification [,mɔːtɪfɪ'keɪʃn] *n* [gen, MED & RELIG] mortification *f*; ~ of the flesh mortification de la chair.

mortify ['mɔːtɪfaɪ] (*pt & pp* mortified) ◇ *vt* mortifier; I was absolutely mortified j'ai été profondément vexé.
◇ *vi* MED [become gangrenous] se gangrener; [undergo tissue death] se nécroser, se mortifier.

mortise ['mɔːtɪs] ◇ *n* mortaise *f*.
◇ *vt* mortaiser.

mortise lock *n* serrure *f* encastrée.

mortuary ['mɔːtʃʊərɪ] (*pl* mortuaries) ◇ *n* morgue *f*.
◇ *adj* mortuaire.

MOS (*abbr of* metal oxide semiconductor) *n* MOS *m*.

mosaic [mə'zeɪɪk] ◇ *n* mosaïque *f*.
◇ *adj* en mosaïque; ~ floor carrelage *m* en mosaïque.

Mosaic [məʊ'zeɪɪk] *adj* BIBLE mosaïque, de Moïse.

Moscow ['mɒskəʊ] *pr n* Moscou.

Mosel(le) [məʊ'zel] *n* -**1.** [region] Moselle *f*; in ~ en Moselle. -**2.** [wine] (vin *m* de) Moselle *m*.

Moses ['məʊzɪz] *pr n* Moïse; Holy ~! *inf* Seigneur!

Moses basket *n* couffin *m*.

mosey *inf* ['məʊzɪ] *vi Am* [amble] marcher d'un pas tranquille; to ~ along aller OR se promener sans se presser; let's ~ over to the pond allons faire un petit tour jusqu'à l'étang.

Moslem ['mɒzləm] ◇ *n* musulman *m*, -e *f*.
◇ *adj* musulman.

mosque [mɒsk] *n* mosquée *f*.

mosquito [mə'skiːtəʊ] (*pl* mosquitos OR mosquitoes) *n* moustique *m*; ~ bite piqûre *f* de moustique.

mosquito net *n* moustiquaire *f*.

moss [mɒs] *n* mousse *f* BOT; a rolling stone gathers no ~ *prov* pierre qui roule n'amasse pas mousse *prov*.

mossback ['mɒsbæk] *n Am* POL ultraconservateur *m*, -trice *f*, réactionnaire *mf*.

Moss Bros® ['mɒsbrɒs] *pr n célèbre entreprise britannique de location de vêtements (notamment de soirée)*.

moss green *n* vert *m* mousse.
◆ **moss-green** *adj* vert mousse *(inv)*.

moss-grown *adj* couvert de mousse, moussu.

moss rose *n* rose *f* moussue OR mousseuse.

moss stitch *n* point *m* de riz; double ~ point *m* de blé.

mossy ['mɒsɪ] (*compar* mossier, *superl* mossiest) *adj* moussu, couvert de mousse.

most [məʊst] ◇ *det* (*superl of* many & much) -**1.** [greatest in number, degree etc]: (the) ~ le plus de; the candidate who gets (the) ~ votes le candidat qui obtient le plus de voix OR le plus grand nombre de voix; which of your inventions gave you ~ satisfaction? laquelle de vos inventions vous a procuré la plus grande satisfaction? -**2.** [the majority of] la plupart de, la majorité de; ~ Europeans la plupart OR la majorité des Européens; I like ~ kinds of fruit j'aime presque tous les fruits; I go out ~ evenings je sors presque tous les soirs; I don't like ~ modern art en général, je n'aime pas l'art moderne; ~ French wine is excellent presque tous les vins français sont excellents.
◇ *pron* (*superl of* many & much) -**1.** [the greatest amount]: (the) ~ le plus; we all earn a lot but Diana earns (the) ~ nous gagnons tous beaucoup d'argent mais c'est Diana qui en gagne le plus; which of the three applicants has (the) ~ to offer? lequel des trois candidats a le plus à offrir?; that is the ~ one can say in his defence c'est tout ce qu'on peut dire en sa faveur ❑ her latest album is the ~! *inf Am* son dernier album est vraiment génial!; to make the ~ of [advantage, chance, good weather] profiter de; [bad situation, ill-luck] tirer le meilleur parti de; [resources, skills] employer OR utiliser au mieux; let's try and make the ~ of our last day essayons de profiter au maximum de notre dernière journée; he knows how to make the ~ of himself il sait se mettre en valeur. -**2.** [the greater part] la plus grande OR la majeure partie; [the greater number] la plupart OR majorité; ~ of my salary la majeure partie de mon salaire; ~ of the snow has melted presque toute la neige a fondu; ~ of the time la plupart du temps; ~ of my friends are on holiday presque tous OR la plupart de mes amis sont en vacances; ~ of us/them la plupart d'entre nous/eux.
◇ *adv* -**1.** [forming superlatives]: the ~ populated region in the world la région la plus peuplée du monde; it's the ~ beautiful house I've ever seen c'est la plus belle maison que j'aie jamais vue; she was the one who explained things ~ clearly c'est elle qui expliquait les choses le plus clairement. -**2.** [to the greatest extent, degree]: (the) ~ le plus; the people who complain (the) ~ les gens qui se plaignent le plus; what worries you ~?, what ~ worries you? qu'est-ce qui vous inquiète le plus?; it's the one I like ~ of all de tous, c'est celui que je préfère. -**3.** [as intensifier] bien, fort; a ~ interesting theory une théorie fort intéressante; we had the ~ awful weather nous avons eu un temps détestable; it's ~ kind of you to say so c'est extrêmement OR bien gentil à vous de dire ça; she sang ~ delightfully elle a chanté de façon exquise; ~ certainly you may! mais bien entendu! -**4.** *inf Am* [almost] presque; ~ everybody had heard of it presque OR pratiquement tout le monde était au courant.
◆ **at (the) most** *adv phr* au plus, au maximum; there's at ~ a 30% chance of success les chances de succès sont de 30 % tout au plus; at the very ~ tout au plus, au grand maximum.

most-favoured nation *n* nation *f* la plus favorisée; this country has ~ status ce pays bénéficie de la clause de la nation la plus favorisée.

mostly ['məʊstlɪ] *adv* -**1.** [mainly] principalement, surtout; it's ~ sugar c'est surtout du sucre; the soldiers were ~ young men il s'agissait pour la plupart OR surtout OR principalement de jeunes soldats; I've travelled a lot, ~ in Europe j'ai beaucoup voyagé, en Europe surtout. -**2.** [usually] le plus souvent, la plupart du temps; ~ I get home quite early la plupart du temps, je rentre assez tôt.

MOT (*pt & pp* MOT'd [,eməʊ'tiːd], *cont* MOT'ing [,eməʊ'tiːɪŋ]) (*abbr of* Ministry of Transport) *Br* ◇ *n* -**1.** *dated* [ministry] ministère *m* des Transports. -**2.** AUT: ~ (certificate) *en Grande-Bretagne, contrôle technique annuel obligatoire pour les véhicules de plus de trois ans*; that old car of yours will never pass its ~ ta vieille voiture n'obtiendra jamais son certificat de contrôle technique.
◇ *vt*: to have one's car ~'d soumettre sa voiture au contrôle technique.

mote [məʊt] *n lit* atome *m*, grain *m*, particule *f*; the ~ in thy brother's eye BIBLE la paille dans l'œil de ton frère.

motel [məʊ'tel] *n* motel *m*.

motet [məʊ'tet] *n* motet *m*.

moth [mɒθ] *n* -**1.** ENTOM papillon *m* (nocturne). -**2.** [in clothes] mite *f*.

mothball ['mɒθbɔːl] ◇ *n* boule *f* de naphtaline; it smells of ~s in here ça sent la naphtaline ici ❑ to put sthg in ~s mettre qqch au placard OR en sommeil.
◇ *vt* [project] mettre en suspens.

moth-eaten *adj* -**1.** *literal* [clothing] mité. -**2.** *inf fig* [shabby] miteux.

mother ['mʌðə^r] ◇ *n* -**1.** [parent] mère *f*; she's a ~ of three elle est mère de trois enfants; ~, this is John maman, je te présente John ❑ Mother Earth la Terre; ~'s milk lait *m* maternel; unmarried ~ mère célibataire; shall I be ~? *Br* c'est moi qui fait le service?; every ~'s son tous sans exception; 'Mother Courage and Her Children' *Brecht* 'Mère Courage et ses enfants'; 'Mother Goose Tales' *Perrault* 'Contes de ma mère l'Oye'. -**2.** RELIG [woman in authority] mère *f*; mother superior Mère *f* supérieure ‖ [Virgin Mary]: Mother of God Mère *f* de Dieu. -**3.** [original cause, source] mère *f*; the Mother of parliaments le Parlement britannique *(qui a servi de modèle à d'autres parlements)*; necessity is the ~ of invention *prov* nécessité est mère d'industrie OR d'invention. -**4.** ▽ *Am* [character] type *m*; he was a big ~ c'était une véritable armoire à glace. -**5.** ▽ *Am* = **motherfucker**.
◇ *adj* -**1.** [motherly] maternel; ~ love amour *m* maternel. -**2.** [as parent]: the ~ bird feeds her

young l'oiseau (femelle) nourrit ses petits ❑ ~ hen mère *f* poule; ~ lode MIN veine *f* principale; ~ ship MIL ravitailleur *m*.
◇ *vt* -**1.** [give birth to] donner naissance à. -**2.** [take care of] servir de mère à; [coddle] dorloter, materner; she ~s him too much elle le dorlote trop.

motherboard ['mʌðəbɔːd] *n* COMPUT carte *f* mère.

mother country *n* (mère) patrie *f*.

mothercraft ['mʌðəkrɑːft] *n* puériculture *f*.

mother figure *n* image *f* de la mère; she's a ~ to them all pour eux tous elle représente l'image de la mère.

motherfucker▼ ['mʌðəˌfʌkəʳ] *n Am* [person] enculé *m*, -e *f*; [thing] saloperie *f*.

Mother Goose rhyme *n Am* comptine *f*.

motherhood ['mʌðəhʊd] *n* maternité *f*; it's ~ and apple pie *esp Am* c'est quelque chose qui va de soi.

Mothering Sunday ['mʌðərɪŋ-] *n Br* la fête des Mères.

mother-in-law (*pl* mothers-in-law) *n* belle-mère *f*.

motherland ['mʌðəlænd] *n* (mère) patrie *f*, pays *m* natal.

motherless ['mʌðəlɪs] *adj* sans mère.

motherly ['mʌðəlɪ] *adj* maternel.

Mother Nature *n* la Nature.

mother-of-pearl *n* nacre *f*; ~ buttons boutons *mpl* en OR de nacre.

mother's boy *Br*, **mamma's boy** *Am n* fils *m* à sa maman, poule *f* mouillée.

Mother's Day *n* la fête des Mères.

mother-to-be (*pl* mothers-to-be) *n* future mère *f*.

mother tongue *n* langue *f* maternelle.

mother wit *n* bon sens *m*.

mothproof ['mɒθpruːf] ◇ *adj* traité à l'antimite.
◇ *vt* traiter à l'antimite.

motif [məʊ'tiːf] *n* ART, LITERAT & MUS motif *m*.

motile [*Br* 'məʊtaɪl, *Am* 'məʊtl] *adj* mobile.

motility [məʊ'tɪlətɪ] *n* motilité *f*.

motion ['məʊʃn] ◇ *n* -**1.** [movement] mouvement *m*; the gentle ~ of the boat le mouvement léger du bateau. -**2.** [gesture] geste *m*, mouvement *m*; he made a ~ as if to step back il esquissa un geste de recul; with a swaying ~ of the hips en ondulant des hanches ❑ to go through the ~s faire qqch machinalement; they just went through the ~s of applauding ils ont applaudi machinalement. -**3.** [proposal] motion *f*, résolution *f*; to propose OR to bring a ~ présenter une motion, soumettre une proposition; to table a ~ of no confidence déposer une motion de censure. -**4.** JUR [application] requête *f*. -**5.** MED [faeces] selles *fpl*; to have OR to pass a ~ aller à la selle. -**6.** MUS mouvement *m*; contrary ~ mouvement contraire.
◇ *vi*: to ~ to sb (to do sthg) faire signe à qqn (de faire qqch).
◇ *vt*: to ~ sb in/away/out faire signe à qqn d'entrer/de s'éloigner/de sortir.
◆ **in motion** ◇ *adj* [moving] en mouvement; [working] en marche; do not alight while the train is in ~ il est interdit de descendre du train avant l'arrêt complet.
◇ *adv phr*: he set the machine in ~ il mit la machine en marche; we'll be setting the new system in ~ next year nous mettrons le nouveau système en place l'année prochaine; to set the wheels in ~ démarrer.

motionless ['məʊʃənlɪs] *adj* immobile.

motion picture *n Am* CIN film *m*.

motion sickness *n Am* mal *m* des transports.

motivate ['məʊtɪveɪt] *vt* motiver; how can I ~ my pupils? comment puis-je motiver mes élèves?; what ~d your choice? qu'est-ce qui a motivé votre choix?; what ~d you to change your mind? qu'est-ce qui vous a poussé à changer d'avis?

motivated ['məʊtɪveɪtɪd] *adj* motivé; a highly ~ young woman une jeune femme extrêmement motivée OR débordant d'ardeur.

motivation [ˌməʊtɪ'veɪʃn] *n* motivation *f*; the pupils lack ~ les élèves sont peu motivés.

motivational [ˌməʊtɪ'veɪʃənl] *adj* motivationnel; ~ research études *fpl* de motivation.

motive ['məʊtɪv] ◇ *n* -**1.** [reason] motif *m*, raison *f*; the ~s for her behaviour ce qui explique sa conduite, les raisons de sa conduite; my ~ for asking is simple la raison pour laquelle je pose cette question est simple ‖ JUR mobile *m*; what could have been his ~ for committing the crime? quelles sont les raisons qui ont pu le pousser à commettre ce crime? -**2.** = **motif**.
◇ *adj* moteur; ~ energy/power énergie/force motrice.

motiveless ['məʊtɪvlɪs] *adj* immotivé, injustifié; an apparently ~ murder un meurtre sans mobile apparent.

motley ['mɒtlɪ] ◇ *adj* -**1.** [diverse, assorted] hétéroclite, composite, disparate; a ~ crew une foule bigarrée. -**2.** [multicoloured] multicolore, bariolé.
◇ *n* -**1.** [mixture] mélange *m* hétéroclite. -**2.** *arch* [jester's dress] livrée *f* de bouffon.

motocross ['məʊtəkrɒs] *n* moto-cross *m*.

motor ['məʊtəʳ] ◇ *n* -**1.** [engine] moteur *m*; electric ~ moteur électrique. -**2.** *inf Br* [car] auto *f*, automobile *f*, voiture *f* (automobile).
◇ *adj* -**1.** [equipped with motor] à moteur; ~ coach autocar *m*; ~ launch vedette *f*; ~ mower tondeuse *f* à moteur; ~ vehicle véhicule *m* automobile; ~ mouth *inf fig* & *hum* moulin *m* à paroles. -**2.** *Br* [concerning cars] automobile; the ~ industry l'industrie *f* automobile; ~ insurance assurance *f* automobile; she had a ~ accident elle a eu un accident de voiture ❑ ~ racing courses *fpl* automobiles; the ~ show le salon de l'automobile. -**3.** ANAT [nerve, muscle] moteur; ~ response réponse *f* motrice.
◇ *vi Br dated* aller en voiture; we ~ed up to London/across Europe nous sommes allés à Londres/nous avons traversé l'Europe en voiture.

Motorail ['məʊtəreɪl] *n* train *m* autocouchette OR autos-couchettes.

motorbike ['məʊtəbaɪk] *n* moto *f*.

motorboat ['məʊtəbəʊt] *n* canot *m* automobile OR à moteur.

motorbus ['məʊtəbʌs] *n* autobus *m*.

motorcade ['məʊtəkeɪd] *n* cortège *m* (de voitures).

motor car *n fml* automobile *f*, voiture *f*.

motorcycle ['məʊtəˌsaɪkl] ◇ *n* motocyclette *f*, moto *f*; ~ racing motocyclisme *m*; ~ cop *inf Am* motard *m (de la police)*.
◇ *vi* aller en moto.

motorcyclist ['məʊtəˌsaɪklɪst] *n* motocycliste *mf*.

motor home *n Am* camping-car *m*.

motoring ['məʊtərɪŋ] *n* l'automobile *f (U)*; a ~ trip un voyage en voiture; school of ~ auto-école *f*.

motor inn *n Am* motel *m*.

motorist ['məʊtərɪst] *n* automobiliste *mf*.

motorize, -ise ['məʊtəraɪz] *vt* motoriser; ~d troops troupes motorisées; a ~d wheelchair un fauteuil roulant à moteur.

motor lodge *n Am* motel *m*.

motorman ['məʊtəmən] (*pl* motormen [-mən]) *n* mécanicien *m*, conducteur *m*.

motor neurone disease *n* affection *f* des motoneurones.

motor scooter *n* scooter *m*.

motorway ['məʊtəweɪ] *n Br* autoroute *f*; ~ café restauroute *m*; ~ madness la folie de l'autoroute.

mottle ['mɒtl] *vt* tacheter, moucheter.

mottled ['mɒtld] *adj* tacheté, moucheté; [skin] marbré.

motto ['mɒtəʊ] (*pl* mottos OR mottoes) *n* -**1.** [maxim] devise *f*; the college ~ la devise du collège. -**2.** [in Christmas cracker – joke] blague *f*; [– riddle] devinette *f*.

mould *Br*, **mold** *Am* [məʊld] ◇ *vt* -**1.** [fashion – statue, vase] façonner, modeler; to ~ sthg in OR from OR out of clay sculpter qqch dans de l'argile; the waves have ~ed the cliff les vagues ont modelé la falaise; to ~ sb's character *fig* façonner OR former le caractère de qqn; they're trying to ~ public opinion *fig* ils essaient de façonner l'opinion publique. -**2.** ART & METALL [make in a mould] mouler; ~ed plastic chairs chaises *fpl* en plastique moulé. -**3.** [cling to – body, figure] mouler.
◇ *vi* [become mouldy] moisir.
◇ *n* -**1.** ART & METALL [hollow form] moule *m*; [prototype] modèle *m*, gabarit *m*; cake ~ moule à gâteau ‖ [moulded article] pièce *f* moulée; rice ~ gâteau *m* de riz. -**2.** *fig* [pattern] moule *m*; they're all cast in the same ~ ils sortent tous du OR ils ont tous été coulés dans le même moule; to break the ~ sortir des sentiers battus; when they made him they broke the ~ il n'y en a pas deux comme lui. -**3.** [mildew] moisissure *f*. -**4.** [soil] humus *m*, terreau *m*.

moulder *Br*, **molder** *Am* ['məʊldəʳ] *vi* -**1.** [decay – corpse, compost] se décomposer; [– house, beams] se délabrer; [– bread] moisir. -**2.** [languish – person, article] moisir; [– economy, institution] dépérir; he's ~ing away in prison il moisit OR croupit en prison.

moulding *Br*, **molding** *Am* ['məʊldɪŋ] *n* -**1.** ARCHIT [decorative] moulure *f*; [at join of wall and floor] baguette *f*, plinthe *f*. -**2.** [moulded article] objet *m* moulé, pièce *f* moulée. -**3.** [act of shaping] moulage *m*.

mouldy *Br*, **moldy** *Am* ['məʊldɪ] (*Br compar* mouldier, *superl* mouldiest, *Am compar* moldier, *superl* moldiest) *adj* -**1.** moisi; it smells ~ ça sent le moisi. -**2.** *inf* [measly] minable; [nasty] vache, rosse.

Mouli® ['muːlɪ] *Br* ◇ *n* moulin *m* à légumes.
◇ *vt* passer à la Moulinette®.

moult *Br*, **molt** *Am* [məʊlt] ◇ *vi* ZOOL muer; [cat, dog] perdre ses poils.
◇ *vt* [hair, feathers] perdre.
◇ *n* mue *f*.

mound [maʊnd] *n* -**1.** [of earth, stones] butte *f*, monticule *m*, tertre *m*; burial ~ tertre funéraire, tumulus *m*. -**2.** [heap] tas *m*; a huge ~ of junk mail une gigantesque pile de prospectus; he ate ~s of rice *inf* il a mangé une montagne de riz.

mount [maʊnt] ◇ *vt* -**1.** [climb – slope, steps] monter; [climb onto – horse, bicycle] monter sur, enfourcher; [– stage, throne etc] monter sur; a truck ~ed the pavement un camion monta sur le trottoir. -**2.** [organize, put on – exhibition, campaign etc] monter, organiser; they ~ed an attack on the party leadership ils montèrent une attaque contre la direction du parti; to ~ guard on OR over veiller sur; to ~ guard MIL monter la garde. -**3.** [fix, support] monter; to ~ a gem monter une pierre; to ~ photographs/stamps coller des photos/timbres (dans un album); they ~ed machine guns on the roofs ils installèrent des mitrailleuses sur les toits; an old sword ~ed in a glass case une épée de collection exposée dans une vitrine. -**4.** [mate with] monter, saillir, couvrir.
◇ *vi* -**1.** [onto horse] monter (à cheval), se mettre en selle. -**2.** [rise, increase] monter, augmenter, croître; her anger ~ed sa colère grandit.
◇ *n* -**1.** [mountain] mont *m*, montagne *f*. -**2.** GEOG: the Mount of Olives le mont des Oliviers. -**3.** [horse] monture *f*. -**4.** [support – of photo] carton *m*, support *m*; [– of gem, lens, tool] monture *f*; [– of machine] support *m*; [– for stamp in collection] charnière *f*; [– for object under microscope] lame *f*.
◆ **mount up** *vi insep* -**1.** [increase] monter, augmenter, s'accroître. -**2.** [accumulate] s'accumuler, s'amonceler; you'll be amazed how quickly the money ~s up vous serez stupéfait de voir la somme qu'on peut atteindre en si peu de temps.

MOUNTAINS BEGINNING WITH 'MOUNT':
Mount Ararat le mont Ararat;
Mount Athos le mont Athos;
Mount Etna le mont Etna, l'Etna;
Mount Everest le mont Everest, l'Everest;
Mount Fuji le (mont) Fuji-Yama;
Mount Kilimanjaro le Kilimandjaro;
Mount Olympus le mont Olympe, l'Olympe;
Mount Parnassus le mont Parnasse;
Mount Rushmore le mont Rushmore (dans lequel sont sculptés les visages des Présidents Washington, Jefferson, Lincoln et Th. Roosevelt);
Mount Sinaï le (mont) Sinaï;
Mount Vesuvius le (mont) Vésuve;
Mount Whitney le mont Whitney.

mountain ['maʊntɪn] ◇ *n* -**1.** montagne *f*; we spent a week in the ~s on a passé une semaine à la montagne ❑ to make a ~ out of a molehill se faire une montagne d'un rien; to move ~s déplacer des montagnes; you can't expect him to move ~s just to please you! il ne peut pas faire l'impossible uniquement pour te faire plaisir! -**2.** [heap, accumulation] montagne *f*, tas *m*; a ~ of papers une énorme pile de papiers; he had bought ~s of rice il avait acheté des montagnes de riz; I've got ~s of work to get through j'ai un travail fou OR monstre à terminer ❑ the butter ~ ECON la montagne de beurre.
◇ *comp* [people] montagnard; [resort, stream, guide] de montagne; [air] de la montagne; [life] en montagne; [flora, fauna] de montagne, des montagnes; a ~ rescue team une équipe de secours en montagne.

mountain ash *n* -**1.** [rowan] sorbier *m*. -**2.** [eucalyptus] eucalyptus *m*.

mountain bike *n* vélo *m* tout terrain, vélo-cross *m*.

mountain cat *n* [lynx] lynx *m*; [puma] puma *m*, cougouar *m*.

Mountain Daylight Time *n* heure *f* d'été des montagnes Rocheuses.

mountain dew *n Br* whisky *m* (produit illégalement).

mountaineer [,maʊntɪ'nɪə^r] *n* alpiniste *mf*.

mountaineering [,maʊntɪ'nɪərɪŋ] *n* alpinisme *m*.

mountain goat *n* chamois *m*.

mountain lion *n* puma *m*, cougouar *m*.

mountainous ['maʊntɪnəs] *adj* -**1.** [region] montagneux. -**2.** *fig* [huge] énorme, colossal; ~ seas vagues *f* énormes.

mountain pass *n* col *m*, défilé *m*.

mountain range *n* chaîne *f* de montagnes.

mountain sheep (*pl inv*) *n* bighorn *m*.

mountain sickness *n* mal *m* des montagnes.

mountainside ['maʊntɪnsaɪd] *n* flanc *m* OR versant *m* d'une montagne; a village perched on the ~ un village juché à flanc de montagne.

Mountain (Standard) Time *n* heure *f* d'hiver des montagnes Rocheuses.

mountain top *n* sommet *m*, cime *f*.

mountainy ['maʊntɪnɪ] *adj* -**1.** *Am* [terrain] montagneux. -**2.** *Am* & *Ir* [people] montagnard.

mountebank ['maʊntɪbæŋk] *n* charlatan *m*.

mounted ['maʊntɪd] *adj* [troops] monté, à cheval; the ~ police la police montée; ~ policeman [gen] policier *m* à cheval.

Mountie *inf*, **Mounty** *inf* ['maʊntɪ] (*pl* Mounties) *n* membre *m* de la police montée *(au Canada)*; the ~s la police montée *(au Canada)*.

mounting ['maʊntɪŋ] ◇ *n* = **mount 3**.
◇ *adj* [pressure, anxiety] croissant.

mourn [mɔːn] ◇ *vi* [feel, express grief] pleurer; [be in mourning] être en deuil, porter le deuil; to ~ over the loss of sb pleurer qqn, être en deuil de qqn; we ~ with you nous partageons votre douleur; he ~s for OR over his lost youth il se lamente sur OR il pleure sa jeunesse perdue.
◇ *vt* [person] pleurer, porter le deuil de; [death, loss] pleurer; the whole town ~s the tragedy cette tragédie a plongé la ville entière dans le malheur.

mourner ['mɔːnə^r] *n* [friend, relative] proche *mf* du défunt; the ~s followed the hearse le cortège funèbre suivait le corbillard; the streets were lined with ~s la foule en deuil s'était massée sur les trottoirs.

mournful ['mɔːnfʊl] *adj* [person, eyes, mood] triste, mélancolique; [tone, voice] lugubre; [place] lugubre, sinistre; a ~ occasion tristes OR douloureuses circonstances.

mournfully ['mɔːnfʊlɪ] *adv* mélancoliquement, tristement.

mournfulness ['mɔːnfʊlnɪs] *n* tristesse *f*, mélancolie *f*.

mourning ['mɔːnɪŋ] ◇ *n (U)* -**1.** [period] deuil *m*; [clothes] (vêtements *mpl* de) deuil *m*; to be in ~ être en deuil, porter le deuil; to be in ~ for sb porter le deuil de qqn; to go into/come out of ~ prendre/quitter le deuil; a day of ~ was declared une journée de deuil a été décrétée ❑ 'Mourning Becomes Electra' *O'Neill* 'le Deuil sied à Électre'. -**2.** [cries] lamentations *fpl*.
◇ *comp* [dress, suit] de deuil.

mouse [maʊs] (*pl* **mice** [maɪs]) ◇ *n* -**1.** souris *f*; 'Of Mice and Men' *Steinbeck* 'Des souris et des hommes'. -**2.** [shy person] timide *mf*, timoré *m*, -e *f*. -**3.** COMPUT souris *f*.
◇ *vi* [cat] chasser les souris.
◆ **mouse out** *inf vt sep Am* dénicher.

mousehole ['maʊshəʊl] *n* trou *m* de souris.

mouser ['maʊsə^r] *n* [cat] chasseur *m*, -euse *f* de souris.

mousetrap ['maʊstræp] *n* souricière *f*; ~ cheese *inf Br fromage de qualité inférieure* ❑ 'The Mousetrap' *Christie* 'la Souricière'.

mousey ['maʊsɪ] = **mousy**.

moussaka [muː'sɑːkə] *n* moussaka *f*.

mousse [muːs] *n* mousse *f*; chocolate ~ mousse au chocolat.

moustache [məs'tɑːʃ] *Br*, **mustache** ['mʌstæʃ] *Am n* moustache *f*, moustaches *fpl*; he's growing a ~ il se fait pousser la moustache.

mousy ['maʊsɪ] (*compar* mousier, *superl* mousiest) *adj* -**1.** *pej* [shy] timide, effacé. -**2.** *pej* [in colour - hair] châtain clair.

mouth [*n* maʊθ, *vb* maʊð] (*pl* mouths [maʊðz]) ◇ *n* -**1.** [of person] bouche *f*; [of animal] gueule *f*; don't talk with your ~ full! ne parle pas la bouche pleine!; breathe through your ~ respirez par la bouche; I have five ~s to feed j'ai cinq bouches à nourrir; the smell made her ~ water l'odeur lui fit venir l'eau à la bouche; 'to be taken by ~' PHARM 'à prendre par voie orale'; he didn't open his ~ once during the meeting il n'a pas ouvert la bouche OR il n'a pas dit un mot pendant toute la réunion; keep your ~ shut n'en parlez à personne, gardez-le pour vous; he's incapable of keeping his ~ shut il ne sait pas tenir sa langue ❑ he's all ~ *inf* c'est une grande gueule OR un fort en gueule; he's got a big ~ *inf* il ne peut pas s'empêcher de l'ouvrir; to be down in the ~ *inf* avoir le cafard; me and my big ~! j'ai encore perdu une occasion de me taire! -**2.** [of river] embouchure *f*, bouche *f*, bouches *fpl*. -**3.** [opening - gen] ouverture *f*, orifice *m*, bouche *f*; [- of bottle] goulot *m*; [- of cave] entrée *f*.
◇ *vt* -**1.** [silently - insults, obscenities] dire à voix basse, marmonner; don't talk/sing, just ~ the words ne parle/chante pas, fais seulement semblant. -**2.** [pompously] déclamer; [mechanically] débiter; [insincerely - excuses] dire qqch du bout des lèvres; [- regrets] formuler sans conviction; to ~ platitudes débiter des lieux communs.
◆ **mouth off** *inf vi insep* -**1.** [brag] la ramener. -**2.** [be insolent] se montrer insolent.

-mouthed [maʊðd] *in cpds*: open~ bouche bée; wide~ [bottle] à large goulot.

mouthful ['maʊθfʊl] *n* -**1.** [of food] bouchée *f*; [of liquid] gorgée *f*; I couldn't eat another ~! je ne pourrais rien avaler de plus! -**2.** *inf* [word] mot *m* difficile à prononcer; his name's a bit of a ~ il a un nom *m* à coucher dehors. -**3.** *Am* [important remark]: you said a ~! ça, tu peux le dire!, là tu as parlé d'or!

mouth organ *n* harmonica *m*.

mouthpiece ['maʊθpiːs] *n* -**1.** [of musical instrument] bec *m*, embouchure *f*; [of pipe] tuyau *m*; [of telephone] microphone *m*. -**2.** [spokesperson] porte-parole *m inv*; [newspaper, magazine] organe *m*, porte-parole *m inv*.

mouth-to-mouth *adj*: to give sb ~ resuscitation faire du bouche-à-bouche à qqn.

mouthwash ['maʊθwɒʃ] *n* [for cleansing] bain *m* de bouche; [for gargling] gargarisme *m*.

mouth-watering *adj* appétissant, alléchant; a ~ display of pastries un appétissant étalage de pâtisseries, un étalage de pâtisseries qui vous mettent l'eau à la bouche.

mouthy *inf* ['maʊðɪ] (*compar* mouthier, *superl* mouthiest) *adj* bavard, jaseur.

movable ['muːvəbl] ◇ *adj* mobile; ~ property JUR biens *mpl* meubles; ~ feast RELIG fête *f* mobile; 'A Movable Feast' *Hemingway* 'Paris est une fête'.
◇ *n*: ~s JUR effets *mpl* mobiliers, biens *mpl* meubles.

move [muːv] ◇ *vt* -**1.** [put elsewhere - object] déplacer; [- part of body] bouger, remuer; this key ~s the cursor towards the right cette touche déplace le curseur vers la droite; ~ the lever to the left poussez le levier vers la gauche; we ~d all the chairs indoors/outdoors nous avons rentré/sorti toutes les chaises; we've ~d the couch into the spare room nous avons mis le canapé dans la chambre d'amis; ~ all those papers off the table! enlève tous ces papiers de la table!, débarrasse la table de tous ces papiers!; don't ~ anything on my desk ne touche à rien sur mon bureau; I can't ~ my leg je n'arrive pas à bouger la jambe; he ~s his lips when he reads il remue les lèvres en lisant; ~ your head to the left inclinez la tête vers la gauche ‖ GAMES jouer; she ~d a pawn elle a joué un pion ❑ ~ it! *inf* grouille-toi! -**2.** [send elsewhere - prisoner, troops etc] transférer; ~ all these people out of the courtyard faites sortir tous ces gens de la cour; she's been ~d to the New York office/to accounts elle a été mutée au bureau de New York/affectée à la comptabilité; he asked to be ~d to a room with a sea-view il a demandé qu'on lui donne une chambre avec vue sur la mer; troops are being ~d into the area des troupes sont envoyées dans la région; he's decided to ~ his family to England [he is in England] il a décidé de faire venir sa famille en Angleterre; [he is elsewhere] il a décidé d'envoyer sa famille en Angleterre. -**3.** [change time or date of] déplacer; the meeting has been ~d to Friday [postponed] la réunion a été remise à vendredi; [brought forward] la réunion a été avancée à vendredi. -**4.** [to new premises, location]: the company that ~d us la firme qui s'est chargée de OR qui a effectué notre déménagement; to ~ house OR flat déménager. -**5.** [affect, touch] émouvoir; I was deeply ~d j'ai été profondément ému OR touché; he was ~d to tears il fut ému jusqu'aux larmes. -**6.** [motivate, prompt] pousser, inciter; to ~ sb to do sthg pousser OR inciter qqn à faire qqch; what ~d you to change your mind? qu'est-ce qui vous a fait changer d'avis? -**7.** *(usu passive & negative)* [cause to yield]: the Prime Minister will not be ~d le Premier ministre ne cédera pas d'un pouce; we shall not be ~d! nous ne céderons pas! -**8.** [propose] proposer; to ~ an amendment proposer un amendement; I ~ that we vote on it je propose que nous procédions au vote. -**9.** COMM [sell] écouler, vendre. -**10.** MED: to ~ one's bowels aller à la selle.
◇ *vi* -**1.** [shift, change position] bouger; I'm sure the curtains ~d je suis sûr d'avoir vu les rideaux bouger; I was so scared I couldn't ~ j'avais tellement peur que je n'osais pas faire un geste; the train was so crowded, I could barely ~ le train était tellement bondé que je pouvais à peine bouger OR faire un mouvement; you can't ~ for furniture in their flat il y a

tellement de meubles dans leur appartement qu'il n'y a pas la place de se retourner; **the handle won't ~** la poignée ne bouge pas; **she wouldn't ~ out of my way** elle ne voulait pas s'écarter de mon chemin || [be in motion - vehicle]: **the line of cars was moving slowly down the road** la file de voitures avançait lentement le long de la route; **I jumped off while the train was still moving** j'ai sauté avant l'arrêt du train; **the truck started moving backwards** le camion a commencé à reculer || [travel in specified direction]: **the guests ~d into/out of the dining room** les invités passèrent dans/sortirent de la salle à manger; **the depression is moving westwards** la dépression se déplace vers l'ouest; **the demonstrators were moving towards the embassy** les manifestants se dirigeaient vers l'ambassade; **the hands of the clock ~d inexorably towards midnight** les aiguilles de l'horloge s'approchaient inexorablement de minuit; **small clouds ~d across the sky** de petits nuages traversaient le ciel; **the earth ~s round the sun** la Terre tourne autour du Soleil; **public opinion is moving to the left/right** *fig* l'opinion publique évolue vers la gauche/droite ❑ **to ~ in high circles** fréquenter la haute société. -**2.** [leave] partir; **it's getting late, I ought to be** OR **get moving** il se fait tard, il faut que j'y aille OR que je parte. -**3.** GAMES [player] jouer; **you can't ~ until you've thrown a six** on ne peut pas jouer avant d'avoir fait sortir OR d'avoir amené un six; **white to ~ and mate in three** les blancs jouent et font mat en trois coups || [piece] se déplacer; **pawns can't ~ backwards** les pions ne peuvent pas reculer. -**4.** [to new premises, location] déménager; **when are you moving?** quand est-ce que vous déménagez?; **when are you moving to your new apartment?** quand est-ce que vous emménagez dans votre nouvel appartement?; **she's moving to San Francisco** elle va habiter (à) San Francisco; **the company has ~d to more modern premises** la société s'est installée dans des locaux plus modernes. -**5.** [change job, profession etc]: **he's ~d to a job in publishing** il travaille maintenant dans l'édition. -**6.** [develop, progress] avancer, progresser; **events have started moving now** les choses ont commencé à avancer; **the colonel knew how to get things moving** le colonel savait activer OR faire avancer les choses ❑ **to ~ with the times** évoluer OR vivre avec son temps. -**7.** *inf* [travel fast] filer, foncer; **that car can really ~!** cette voiture a quelque chose dans le ventre!; **she's really moving now** maintenant elle fonce vraiment. -**8.** [take action] agir; **if you want to succeed now is the time to ~** si vous voulez réussir, il vous faut agir maintenant OR dès à présent; **the town council ~d to have the school closed down** la municipalité a pris des mesures pour faire fermer l'école; **I'll get moving on it first thing tomorrow** je m'en occuperai demain à la première heure. -**9.** COMM [sell] se vendre, s'écouler. -**10.** MED: **have your bowels ~d today?** êtes-vous allé à la selle aujourd'hui?

◇ *n* -**1.** [movement] mouvement *m*; **with one ~ she was by his side** en un éclair, elle fut à ses côtés; **one ~ out of you and you're dead!** un seul geste et tu es mort!; **he made a ~ to take out his wallet** il s'apprêta à sortir son portefeuille; **she made a ~ to leave** elle se leva pour partir; **it's late, I ought to be making a ~** il se fait tard, il faut que j'y aille ❑ **get a ~ on!** *inf* grouille-toi!, active! -**2.** [change of home, premises] déménagement *m*; **how did the ~ go?** comment s'est passé le déménagement?; **we're considering a ~ to bigger premises** nous envisageons d'emménager dans des locaux plus spacieux. -**3.** [change of job] changement *m* d'emploi; **after ten years in the same firm she felt it was time for a ~** après dix ans dans la même société elle avait le sentiment qu'il était temps de changer d'air OR d'horizon. -**4.** [step, measure] pas *m*, démarche *f*; **she made the first ~** elle a fait le premier pas; **she wondered when he would make his ~** elle se demandait quand il allait se décider; **the new management's first ~ was to increase all salaries** la première mesure de la nouvelle direction a été de relever tous les salaires; **what do you think their next ~ will be?** selon vous, que vont-ils faire maintenant?; **they made an unsuccessful ~ to stop the war** ils firent une tentative infructueuse pour arrêter la guerre. -**5.** GAMES [turn to move] tour *m*; **it's my ~** c'est à moi (de jouer) || [act of moving] coup *m*; **white mates in two ~s** les blancs font mat en deux coups || [way piece moves] marche *f*; **in chess the first thing to learn is the ~s** la première chose à apprendre aux échecs, c'est la façon dont les pièces se déplacent sur l'échiquier OR le déplacement des pièces sur l'échiquier ❑ **to be on the ~** être en déplacement; **he's a travelling salesman, so he's always on the ~** c'est un représentant de commerce, voilà pourquoi il est toujours en déplacement OR il est toujours par monts et par vaux; **the enemy forces on the ~** les colonnes ennemies en marche OR en mouvement; **I've been on the ~ all day** je n'ai pas arrêté de la journée; **we're a firm on the ~** nous sommes une entreprise dynamique.

◆ **move about** *Br* ◇ *vi insep* se déplacer, bouger; **I can hear somebody moving about upstairs** j'entends des bruits de pas là-haut; **it's hard to ~ about on crutches** c'est dur de se déplacer avec des béquilles.
◇ *vt sep* déplacer.

◆ **move along** ◇ *vi insep* avancer; **the procession ~d along painfully slowly** le cortège avançait OR progressait terriblement lentement; **the policeman told them to ~ along** le policier leur ordonna de circuler; **~ along there, please!** circulez, s'il vous plaît!
◇ *vt sep* [bystanders, busker] faire circuler.

◆ **move around** = **move about**.

◆ **move away** ◇ *vi insep* -**1.** [go in opposite direction] s'éloigner, partir; **he held out his arms to her but she ~d away** il lui tendit les bras mais elle s'éloigna; **the train ~d slowly away** le train partit lentement. -**2.** [change address] déménager; **her best friend ~d away** sa meilleure amie a déménagé.
◇ *vt sep* éloigner.

◆ **move back** ◇ *vi insep* -**1.** [back away] reculer. -**2.** [return to original position] retourner; **they've ~d back to the States** ils sont retournés habiter OR ils sont rentrés aux États-Unis.
◇ *vt sep* -**1.** [push back - person, crowd] repousser; [- chair] reculer. -**2.** [return to original position] remettre; **you can change the furniture around as long as you ~ it back afterwards** vous pouvez déplacer les meubles à condition de les remettre ensuite à leur place OR là où ils étaient.

◆ **move down** ◇ *vi insep* -**1.** [from higher level, floor etc] descendre; **he ~d down a class** SCH on l'a fait descendre d'une classe. -**2.** [make room] se pousser; **~ down, there's plenty of room inside** poussez-vous, il y a de la place à l'intérieur.
◇ *vt insep*: **~ down the bus, please** avancez jusqu'au fond de l'autobus, s'il vous plaît.
◇ *vt sep* [from higher level, floor etc] descendre; **he was ~d down a class** SCH on l'a fait passer dans la classe inférieure.

◆ **move forward** ◇ *vi insep* avancer.
◇ *vt sep* avancer; **she ~d the clock forward one hour** elle a avancé l'horloge d'une heure.

◆ **move in** ◇ *vi insep* -**1.** [into new home, premises] emménager; **his mother-in-law has ~d in with them** sa belle-mère s'est installée OR est venue habiter chez eux. -**2.** [close in, approach] avancer, s'approcher; **the police began to ~ in on the demonstrators** la police a commencé à avancer OR à se diriger vers les manifestants; **the camera then ~s in on the bed** la caméra s'approche ensuite du lit. -**3.** [take control]: **another gang is trying to ~ in** un autre gang essaie de mettre la main sur l'affaire; **the unions ~d in and stopped the strike** les syndicats prirent les choses en main et mirent un terme à la grève.
◇ *vt sep*: **we've ~d most of the furniture in** nous avons déjà installé la plupart des meubles; **the landlord ~d another family in** le propriétaire a loué à une autre famille.

◆ **move off** *vi insep* s'éloigner, partir; **the train finally ~d off** le train partit OR s'ébranla enfin.

◆ **move on** ◇ *vi insep* -**1.** [proceed on one's way] poursuivre son chemin; **we spent a week in Athens, then we ~d on to Crete** on a passé une semaine à Athènes avant de partir pour la Crète; **a policeman told me to ~ on** un policier m'a dit de circuler. -**2.** [progress - to new job, new subject etc]: **she's ~d on to better things** elle a trouvé une meilleure situation; **after five years in the same job I feel like moving on** après avoir occupé le même emploi pendant cinq ans, j'ai envie de changer d'air; **can we ~ on to the second point?** pouvons-nous passer au deuxième point?
◇ *vt sep* [bystanders, busker] faire circuler.

◆ **move out** ◇ *vi insep* -**1.** [of home, premises] déménager; **when are you moving out of your room?** quand est-ce que tu déménages de OR tu quittes ta chambre?; **his girlfriend has ~d out** son amie l'a quitté. -**2.** MIL [troops] se retirer.
◇ *vt sep* MIL [troops] retirer.

◆ **move over** *vi insep* -**1.** [make room] se pousser; **~ over and let me sit down** pousse-toi pour que je puisse m'asseoir. -**2.** [stand down - politician] se désister; **it's time he ~d over to make way for a younger man** il serait temps qu'il laisse la place à un homme plus jeune. -**3.** [change over]: **we're moving over to mass production** nous passons à la fabrication en série.

◆ **move up** ◇ *vi insep* -**1.** [make room] se pousser; **~ up and let me sit down** pousse-toi pour que je puisse m'asseoir. -**2.** [in hierarchy] monter; [in company] avoir de l'avancement; **to ~ up a class** SCH passer dans la classe supérieure ❑ **you've ~d up in the world!** tu en as fait du chemin! -**3.** MIL [troops] avancer; **our battalion's moving up to the front** notre bataillon monte au front.
◇ *vt sep* -**1.** [in order to make room] pousser, écarter. -**2.** [in hierarchy] faire monter; **he's been ~d up a class** SCH on l'a fait passer dans la classe supérieure. -**3.** MIL [troops] faire avancer; **another division has been ~d up** une autre division a été envoyée sur place.

moveable ['muːvəbl] = **movable**.

movement ['muːvmənt] *n* -**1.** [change of position] mouvement *m*; **population/troop ~s** mouvements de populations/de troupes; **the ~ of goods** le transport des marchandises; **there was a general ~ towards the bar** tout le monde se dirigea vers le bar; **she heard ~ in the next room** elle a entendu des bruits dans la pièce voisine; **his ~s are being watched** ses déplacements sont surveillés; **I'm not sure what my ~s are going to be over the next few weeks** je ne sais pas exactement ce que je vais faire OR quel sera mon emploi du temps dans les quelques semaines à venir; **freedom of ~** la liberté de circulation || [gesture] mouvement *m*, geste *m*; **all her ~s were rapid and precise** tous ses gestes étaient rapides et précis. -**2.** [change, tendency] mouvement *m*, tendance *f*; **there's a growing ~ towards privatization** la tendance à la privatisation s'accentue; **his speeches over the last year show a ~ towards the right** les discours qu'il a prononcés depuis un an font apparaître un glissement vers la droite; **the upward/downward ~ of interest rates** la hausse/baisse des taux d'intérêts. -**3.** [group] mouvement *m*; **liberation ~** mouvement de libération. -**4.** TECHN [mechanism - of clock etc] mouvement *m*. -**5.** MUS [of symphony, sonata etc] mouvement *m*. -**6.** MED [faeces] selles *fpl*; **to have a (bowel) ~** aller à la selle.

mover ['muːvəʳ] *n* -**1.** [physical]: **sloths are extraordinarily slow ~s** les paresseux sont des animaux à mouvements extrêmement lents;

she's a lovely ~ *inf* elle bouge bien ❑ he's a fast ~ *inf* c'est un tombeur. -**2.** [of a proposal, motion] motionnaire *mf*; who was the ~ of this amendment? qui a proposé cet amendement?

movie ['muːvɪ] *esp Am* ◇ *n* film *m*.
◇ *comp* [actor, star] de cinéma; the ~ industry l'industrie *f* cinématographique OR du cinéma; ~ reviewer critique *mf* de cinéma.
◆ **movies** *npl esp Am*: to go to the ~s aller au cinéma; she's in the ~s elle travaille dans le cinéma.

movie camera *n Am* caméra *f*.

moviegoer ['muːvɪ,gəʊə^r] *n Am* cinéphile *mf*.

movie house, movie theatre *n Am* (salle *f* de) cinéma *m*.

moving ['muːvɪŋ] *adj* -**1.** [in motion] en mouvement; [vehicle] en marche; [target] mouvant; slow-/fast-~ qui se déplace lentement/rapidement. -**2.** [not fixed] mobile; ~ parts pièces *fpl* mobiles. -**3.** [touching] émouvant, touchant. -**4.** [motivating]: she's the ~ force OR spirit behind the project c'est elle l'instigatrice OR le moteur du projet. -**5.** [for moving house] de déménagement; on ~ day le jour du déménagement; ~ van *Am* camion *m* de déménageurs.

movingly ['muːvɪŋlɪ] *adv* de façon émouvante OR touchante.

moving pavement *n Br* trottoir *m* roulant.

moving picture *n Am dated* film *m*.

moving staircase *n* escalier *m* roulant, escalator *m*.

mow [məʊ] (*pt* mowed, *pp* mowed OR mown [məʊn]) *vt* [lawn] tondre; [hay] faucher.
◆ **mow down** *vt sep* faucher, abattre.

mower ['məʊə^r] *n* [person] faucheur *m*, -euse *f*; [machine - for lawn] tondeuse *f*; [- for hay] faucheuse *f*.

mowing ['məʊɪŋ] *n* AGR fauchage *m*; ~ machine faucheuse *f*.

mown [məʊn] *pp* → **mow**.

Mozambican [,məʊzæm'biːkn] ◇ *n* Mozambicain *m*, -e *f*.
◇ *adj* mozambicain.

Mozambique [,məʊzæm'biːk] *pr n* Mozambique *m*; in ~ au Mozambique.

Mozambique Channel *pr n*: the ~ le canal de Mozambique.

mozzarella [,mɒtsə'relə] *n* mozzarelle *f*.

MP *n* -**1.** (*abbr of* Military Police) PM *f*. -**2.** *Br & Can* (*abbr of* Member of Parliament) ≃ député; the ~ for Finchley le député de Finchley. -**3.** *Can abbr of* Mounted Police.

mpg (*abbr of* miles per gallon) *n* consommation *f* d'essence; my old car did 20 ~ mon ancienne voiture faisait OR consommait 3,5 litres au cent.

mph (*abbr of* miles per hour) *n* miles *mpl* à l'heure; 100 ~ 160 km/h.

MPhil [,em'fɪl] (*abbr of* Master of Philosophy) *n (titulaire d'une) maîtrise de lettres*.

MPS *n abbr of* Member of the Pharmaceutical Society.

Mr ['mɪstə^r] *abbr* M., Monsieur; ~ Brown M. Brown; ~ President Monsieur le Président ❑ 'Mr Deeds Goes To Town' *Capra* 'l'Extravagant M. Deeds'.

Mr Big *inf n* le chef, le patron.

MRC *pr n* (*abbr of* Medical Research Council) *institut de recherche médicale situé à Londres*.

MRCP *n abbr of* Member of the Royal College of Physicians.

MRCS *n abbr of* Member of the Royal College of Surgeons.

MRCVS *n abbr of* Member of the Royal College of Veterinary Surgeons.

MRP *n abbr of* manufacturer's recommended price.

Mr Right *inf n* l'homme idéal, le prince charmant; she's waiting for ~ elle attend le prince charmant OR l'homme de ses rêves.

Mrs ['mɪsɪz] *abbr* Mme, Madame; ~ Brown Mme Brown.

Mrs Mop *inf n Br* [cleaner] femme *f* de ménage; I'm not your ~, you know! hé, je ne suis pas ta bonne!

ms. (*pl* mss.) (*written abbr of* manuscript) ms.

Ms [məz] *abbr titre que les femmes peuvent utiliser au lieu de madame ou mademoiselle pour éviter la distinction entre les femmes mariées et les célibataires*.

MS ◇ *n* -**1.** (*abbr of* multiple sclerosis) SEP *f*. -**2.** *Am* (*abbr of* Master of Science) *(titulaire d'une) maîtrise de sciences*.
◇ -**1.** *written abbr of* Mississippi. -**2.** (*written abbr of* manuscript) ms.

MSA (*abbr of* Master of Science in Agriculture) *n (titulaire d'une) maîtrise en sciences agricoles*.

MSB (*abbr of* most significant bit/byte) *n bit de poids fort*.

MSc (*abbr of* Master of Science) *n (titulaire d'une) maîtrise de sciences*.

MSC *pr n abbr of* Manpower Services Commission.

MSF (*abbr of* Manufacturing, Science, Finance) *pr n confédération syndicale britannique*.

MSG *n abbr of* monosodium glutamate.

Msgr (*written abbr of* Monsignor) Mgr.

Mss *written abbr of* manuscripts.

MSS *pl* → **MS, ms.**

MST *n abbr of* Mountain Standard Time.

MSW (*abbr of* Master of Social Work) *n (titulaire d'une) maîtrise en travail social*.

Mt (*written abbr of* mount) Mt.

MT ◇ *n* (*abbr of* machine translation) TA *f*.
◇ *written abbr of* Montana.

much [mʌtʃ] ◇ *det* beaucoup de; we don't have ~ time on n'a pas beaucoup de temps; there isn't ~ cake/money left il ne reste pas beaucoup de gâteau/d'argent; the tablets didn't do ~ good les comprimés n'ont pas servi à grand-chose OR n'ont pas fait beaucoup d'effet; ~ good may it do you! *iron* grand bien vous fasse!
◇ *pron* beaucoup; is there ~ left? est-ce qu'il en reste beaucoup?; is there any left? – not ~ est-ce qu'il en reste? – pas beaucoup; there's still ~ to be decided il reste encore beaucoup de choses à décider; he hadn't ~ to say on the subject il n'avait pas grand-chose à dire à ce sujet; there's not ~ anyone can do about it personne n'y peut grand-chose; we have ~ to be thankful for nous avons beaucoup de raisons d'être reconnaissants; ~ of the time [long period] la majeure partie du temps; [very often] la plupart du temps; ~ of the coffee had to be thrown away on a dû jeter une grande partie du café; I agreed with ~ of what she said j'étais d'accord avec presque tout ce qu'elle a dit || [used to intensify]: I'm not ~ of a hiker je ne suis pas un très bon marcheur; it hasn't been ~ of a holiday ce n'était pas vraiment des vacances ❑ what he said didn't amount to ~ il n'avait pas grand-chose d'important à dire; his plans didn't come to ~ ses projets n'ont pas abouti à grand-chose; to make ~ of sb/sthg: the defence made ~ of the witness's criminal record la défense a beaucoup insisté sur le casier judiciaire du témoin; I couldn't make ~ of the figures je n'ai pas compris grand-chose aux chiffres; I don't think ~ of him/of his technique je n'ai pas une très haute opinion de lui/de sa technique; there's ~ to be said for the old-fashioned method la vieille méthode a beaucoup d'avantages; there's ~ to be said for his suggestions il y a des choses fort intéressantes dans ce qu'il propose; there's not ~ to choose between them ils se valent; there's not ~ in it il n'y a pas une grande différence; he doesn't want OR ask OR expect ~, does he? *inf iron* il n'est pas difficile, lui, au moins! *iron*.
◇ *adv* beaucoup; I don't drink ~ je ne bois pas beaucoup; ~ admired/appreciated très admiré/apprécié; ~ happier/more slowly beaucoup plus heureux/plus lentement; I feel very ~ better je me sens beaucoup mieux; it is ~ to be regretted that... *fml* il est fort regrettable que...; ~ to my surprise à mon grand étonnement; I'm not ~ good at making speeches je ne suis pas très doué pour faire des discours; thank you very ~ OR so ~ merci beaucoup; it's ~ the best/the fastest way to travel c'est de beaucoup le meilleur moyen/le moyen le plus rapide de voyager; it's ~ the best/the fastest c'est le meilleur/le plus rapide de beaucoup ❑ ~ the same presque pareil; she's still ~ the same as yesterday son état n'a pas changé depuis hier.
◆ **as much** ◇ *pron phr* [that, the same]: I thought/suspected as ~ c'est bien ce que je pensais/soupçonnais; I said as ~ to him yesterday c'est ce que je lui ai dit hier; would you do as ~ for me? en ferais-tu autant pour moi?
◇ *adv phr* [with multiples, fractions]: twice/three times as ~ deux/trois fois plus; half as ~ la moitié (de ça); a quarter as ~ un quart (de ça)
◆ **as much... as** ◇ *det phr* [the same amount as]: as ~... as autant de... que; I've got as ~ money as you j'ai autant d'argent que vous; take as ~ sugar as you like prenez autant de OR tout le sucre que vous voulez.
◇ *conj phr* autant que; he's as ~ to blame as her elle n'est pas plus responsable que lui, il est responsable autant qu'elle.
◆ **as much as** ◇ *pron phr* -**1.** [the same as]: it costs as ~ as the Japanese model ça coûte le même prix que le modèle japonais; that's as ~ as to say that I'm a liar ça revient à me traiter de menteur. -**2.** [all]: it was as ~ as I could do to keep a straight face j'ai failli éclater de rire.
◇ *conj phr* autant que; I hate it as ~ as you do ça me déplaît autant qu'à vous; as ~ as ever toujours autant; as ~ as before autant qu'avant; I don't dislike them as ~ as all that ils ne me déplaisent pas autant que ça.
◆ **however much** ◇ *det phr*: however ~ money you give him, it won't be enough vous pouvez lui donner autant d'argent que vous voulez, ça ne suffira pas.
◇ *pron phr*: however ~ they offer, take it quelle que soit la somme qu'ils proposent, acceptez-la.
◇ *adv phr*: however ~ you dislike the idea... quelle que soit votre aversion pour cette idée...; however ~ I try, it doesn't work j'ai beau essayer, ça ne marche pas.
◆ **how much** ◇ *det phr* combien de; how ~ flour have we got left? combien de farine nous reste-t-il?
◇ *pron phr* combien; how ~ do you want? [gen] combien en voulez-vous?; [money] combien voulez-vous?; how ~ is the record OR does the record cost? combien coûte ce disque?
◆ **much as** *conj phr*: ~ as I admire him, I have to admit that... malgré toute mon admiration pour lui, je dois admettre que...; ~ as I would like to, I can't come à mon grand regret, il m'est véritablement impossible de venir.
◆ **so much** ◇ *det phr* tant de, tellement de; it takes up so ~ time ça prend tellement de temps; it's just so ~ nonsense c'est tellement bête.
◇ *pron phr* -**1.** [such a lot] tant; I've learnt so ~ on this course j'ai vraiment appris beaucoup (de choses) en suivant ces cours; there's still so ~ to do il y a encore tant à faire. -**2.** [this amount]: there's only so ~ one can do il y a une limite à ce qu'on peut faire; how ~ water will I put in? – about so ~ combien d'eau est-ce que je dois mettre? – à peu près ça.
◇ *adv phr* tellement; I miss you so ~ tu me manques tellement; I wouldn't mind so ~, only he promised to do it ça ne me gêne pas tellement, mais il avait promis de le faire; it's not so ~ his unpunctuality, it's his rudeness I can't stand ce n'est pas tellement ses retards, c'est sa grossièreté que je ne supporte pas; thank you ever so ~ merci infiniment OR mille fois.
◆ **so much as** *adv phr* même; if you so ~ as breathe a word of this... si seulement tu répètes

un mot de tout ça...; without so ~ as asking permission sans même demander la permission.

◆ **so much for** *prep phr*: so ~ for the agenda; now let us consider... voilà pour ce qui est de l'ordre du jour; maintenant, je voudrais que nous nous penchions sur la question de...; so ~ for that idea! on peut oublier cette idée!

◆ **that much** ◇ *det phr*: there was that ~ food, we thought we'd never finish it il y avait tellement à manger qu'on pensait ne jamais arriver à finir.

◇ *pron phr*: was there ~ damage? – not that ~ y a-t-il eu beaucoup de dégâts? – pas tant que ça; did it cost that ~? ça a coûté autant que ça?; how ~ do you want? – about that ~ combien en veux-tu? – à peu près ça.

◇ *adv phr (with compar)* -**1.** [a lot] beaucoup plus; it'll be that ~ easier to organize ce sera d'autant plus facile à organiser; not that ~ better pas beaucoup mieux. -**2.** [this amount]: she's that ~ taller than me elle est plus grande que moi de ça.

◆ **this much** ◇ *det phr*: there was this ~ coffee left il restait ça de café.

◇ *pron phr* -**1.** [this amount]: I had to cut this ~ off the hem of my skirt j'ai dû raccourcir ma jupe de ça. -**2.** [one thing] une chose; this ~ is true... une chose au moins est vraie...; I'll say this ~ for her, she's got guts il faut reconnaître une chose, c'est qu'elle a du cran.

◆ **too much** ◇ *det phr* trop de.

◇ *pron phr* trop; there's too ~ to do il y a trop à faire; don't expect too ~ [be too demanding] ne soyez pas trop exigeant, n'en demandez pas trop; [be too hopeful] ne vous faites pas trop d'illusions; that's too ~! *inf* ça, c'est trop!

◇ *adv phr* [work, speak] trop.

muchness *inf* ['mʌtʃnɪs] *n Br phr*: I can't decide which curtains to get, they're all pretty much of a ~ je ne sais pas quels rideaux acheter, c'est vraiment du pareil au même; the candidates were all (pretty) much of a ~ tous les candidats se valaient.

mucilage ['mju:sɪlɪdʒ] *n* BOT mucilage *m*.

muck *inf* [mʌk] *(U)* ◇ *n* -**1.** [mud] boue *f*, gadoue *f*; [dirt] saletés *fpl*; [manure] fumier *m*; [dung - of horse] crottin *m*; [- of dog] crotte *f*; they think they're Lord and Lady Muck *Br hum* ils ne se prennent pas pour n'importe qui, ils se croient sortis de la cuisse de Jupiter; where there's ~, there's brass *Br prov* c'est peut-être sale, mais ça rapporte! *(fait référence aux travaux salissants mais rentables)*. -**2.** *fig* [inferior literature, films etc] saletés *fpl*; [bad food] cochonneries *fpl*. -**3.** *phr*: to make a ~ of sthg *Br* [bungle] foutre qqch par terre, bousiller qqch.

◇ *vt* AGR fumer.

◆ **muck about** *inf*, **muck around** *inf Br* ◇ *vi insep* -**1.** [waste time] traîner, perdre son temps. -**2.** [be stupid] faire l'imbécile; stop ~ing about! arrête de faire l'imbécile! -**3.** [interfere]: to ~ about with sthg [equipment] toucher à qqch, tripoter qqch; [belongings] déranger qqch, mettre la pagaille dans qqch.

◇ *vt sep* [person - waste time of] faire perdre son temps à; [- be inconsiderate to] malmener; [belongings, papers] déranger, toucher à.

◆ **muck in** *inf vi insep Br* [share task] mettre la main à la pâte, donner un coup de main; [share costs] participer aux frais.

◆ **muck out** *vt sep Br* [horse, stable] nettoyer, curer.

◆ **muck up** *inf vt sep* -**1.** [dirty] cochonner. -**2.** [ruin] bousiller, foutre en l'air.

mucker▽ ['mʌkəʳ] *n Br* [pal] copain *m*, copine *f*, pote *m*.

muckheap *inf* ['mʌkhi:p] *n Br* tas *m* de fumier.

muckraker ['mʌkreɪkəʳ] *n pej* fouineur *m*, -euse *f*.

muckraking ['mʌkreɪkɪŋ] *n pej*: it's the kind of paper that specializes in ~ c'est le type de journal spécialisé dans les scandales.

muckspreader ['mʌkspredəʳ] *n* AGR épandeur *m* (d'engrais).

muck-up *inf n Br* pagaille *f*, bordel *m*; to make a ~ of sthg foutre qqch en l'air, bousiller qqch.

mucky *inf* ['mʌkɪ] (*compar* muckier, *superl* muckiest) *adj* -**1.** [dirty, muddy - hands] sale, crasseux; [- shoes] sale, crotté; [- water, road] sale, boueux; the weather was ~ *Br* il faisait un sale temps. -**2.** [obscene - book, film] obscène.

mucous ['mju:kəs] *adj* muqueux; ~ membrane muqueuse *f*.

mucus ['mju:kəs] *n* mucus *m*, mucosité *f*; [from nose] morve *f*.

mud [mʌd] (*pt* & *pp* mudded, *cont* mudding) ◇ *n* [gen] boue *f*; [in river, lake] vase *f*; my car got stuck in the ~ ma voiture s'est embourbée ❑ here's ~ in your eye! *Am* à la tienne!; to drag sb OR sb's name through the ~ traîner qqn dans la boue; my name is ~ in certain circles *inf* je suis en disgrâce OR persona non grata dans certains milieux; to throw OR to sling ~ at sb couvrir qqn de boue.

◇ *vt* couvrir de boue, crotter.

mudbank ['mʌdbæŋk] *n* banc *m* de vase.

mudbath ['mʌdbɑ:θ] *n* bain *m* de boue.

muddle ['mʌdl] ◇ *n* [confusion] confusion *f*; [mess] désordre *m*, fouillis *m*; all her belongings were in a ~ toutes ses affaires étaient en désordre OR sens dessus dessous; my finances are in an awful ~ ma situation financière n'est pas claire du tout OR est complètement embrouillée; Peter was in a real ~ over the holiday plans Peter ne savait plus où il en était dans ses projets de vacances; let's try to sort out this ~ essayons de démêler cet écheveau *fig*; there must have been a ~ over the train times quelqu'un a dû se tromper dans les horaires de train.

◇ *vt* -**1.** [mix up - dates] confondre, mélanger; [- facts] embrouiller, mélanger; the dates got ~d il y a eu une confusion dans les dates. -**2.** [confuse - person] embrouiller (l'esprit OR les idées de); now you've got me ~d maintenant, je ne sais plus où j'en suis; she'll get ~d if you all talk at once vous allez lui embrouiller l'esprit si vous parlez tous à la fois.

◆ **muddle along** *vi insep* se débrouiller.

◆ **muddle through** *vi insep* se tirer d'affaire.

◆ **muddle up** *vt sep* = **muddle** *vt*.

muddleheaded [,mʌdl'hedɪd] *adj* [person] désordonné, brouillon, écervelé; [idea, speech, essay] confus.

muddler ['mʌdləʳ] *n* personne *f* désordonnée; he's such a ~! il est tellement brouillon!

muddle-up *n* -**1.** [misunderstanding] quiproquo *m*, malentendu *m*; there was a ~ over the dates il y a eu une confusion dans les dates. -**2.** [situation] embrouillement *m*, imbroglio *m*.

muddy ['mʌdɪ] (*compar* muddier, *superl* muddiest) ◇ *adj* -**1.** [hand, car] plein OR couvert de boue; [shoes] plein de boue, crotté; [road, stream] boueux. -**2.** *fig* [complexion] terreux; [colour] terne, sale; [flavour, drink] boueux; [liquid] boueux, trouble. -**3.** [indistinct - thinking, ideas] confus, embrouillé, peu clair; [out of focus - image] brouillé, trouble, flou.

◇ *vt* -**1.** [hands, shoes] salir, couvrir de boue; [road, stream] rendre boueux. -**2.** [situation] compliquer, embrouiller.

mudflap ['mʌdflæp] *n* [on car] bavette *f*; [on truck] pare-boue *m inv*.

mudflat ['mʌdflæt] *n* laisse *f* OR banc *m* de boue.

mudguard ['mʌdgɑ:d] *n* garde-boue *m inv*.

mud hut *n* case *f* en pisé OR en terre.

mudlark ['mʌdlɑ:k] *n lit* gamin *m*, -e *f* des rues, gavroche *mf*.

mudpack ['mʌdpæk] *n* masque *m* à l'argile.

mud pie *n* pâté *m* (de sable).

mudslinger ['mʌd,slɪŋəʳ] *n* fauteur *m*, -trice *f* de scandales; the ~s will be disappointed les amateurs de scandales en seront pour leurs frais.

mudslinging ['mʌd,slɪŋɪŋ] *n* calomnie *f*; a lot of ~ went on during the elections ils ont passé leur temps à se traîner les uns les autres dans la boue pendant les élections.

muesli ['mju:zlɪ] *n* muesli *m*; the ~ belt *Br pej quartiers où vit une certaine bourgeoisie de gauche, soucieuse de diététique etc*.

muezzin [mu:'ezɪn] *n* muezzin *m*.

muff [mʌf] ◇ *n* -**1.** [for hands] manchon *m*; [for ears] oreillette *f*. -**2.** ORNITH aigrette *f*. -**3.** [bungled attempt] coup *m* manqué.

◇ *vt* [bungle] rater, manquer; to ~ a catch rater une prise.

muffin ['mʌfɪn] *n* muffin *m*.

muffle ['mʌfl] *vt* -**1.** [quieten - sound] étouffer, assourdir; [- engine] étouffer le bruit de; the silencer ~s engine noise le silencieux étouffe le bruit du moteur; we could hear ~d cries coming from the next room on entendait des cris étouffés OR sourds qui venaient de la pièce voisine. -**2.** [repress - laughter] retenir, étouffer; there was a lot of ~d laughter on entendait de nombreux rires étouffés.

◆ **muffle up** ◇ *vt sep* (bien) emmitoufler.

◇ *vi insep* s'emmitoufler.

muffled ['mʌfld] *adj* [sound, voice] sourd, étouffé; [oars] assourdi; [drums] voilé.

muffler ['mʌfləʳ] *n* -**1.** *dated* [scarf] écharpe *f* de laine, cache-nez *m inv*. -**2.** *Am* AUT silencieux *m*.

mufti ['mʌftɪ] *n dated* tenue *f* civile; wearing ~, in ~ en civil.

mug [mʌg] (*pt* & *pp* mugged, *cont* mugging) ◇ *n* -**1.** [cup, beer glass] chope *f*. -**2.** ▽ [face] gueule *f*; shut your ugly ~! ferme ta sale gueule! -**3.** *inf Br* [dupe] poire *f*; [fool] nigaud *m*, -e *f*; it's a ~'s game [foolish] c'est de la connerie; [trap] c'est de l'arnaque. -**4.** *inf Am* [thug] gangster *m*, voyou *m*. -**5.** = **mug shot**.

◇ *vt* agresser.

◆ **mug up** *inf Br* ◇ *vi insep* bûcher, boulonner; he's mugging up for the test il bûche ferme en prévision de son examen; I'd better ~ up on my French je ferais mieux de potasser mon français.

◇ *vt sep* potasser, bosser.

mugful ['mʌgfʊl] *n* [of tea, coffee] tasse *f* (pleine); [of beer] chope *f* (pleine).

mugger ['mʌgəʳ] *n* agresseur *m*.

mugginess ['mʌgɪnɪs] *n* METEOR chaleur *f* lourde et humide.

mugging ['mʌgɪŋ] *n* agression *f*; he was the victim of a ~ il a été victime d'une agression; ~ is on the increase il y a une augmentation des agressions.

muggins *inf* ['mʌgɪnz] (*pl inv* OR **mugginses**) *n Br* idiot *m*, -e *f*, poire *f*; I suppose ~ will have to go je suppose que c'est bibi OR ma pomme qui devra y aller.

muggy ['mʌgɪ] (*compar* muggier, *superl* muggiest) *adj* METEOR lourd et humide.

mug shot *inf n* photo *f* d'identité judiciaire.

mugwort ['mʌgwɜ:t] *n* BOT armoise *f*.

mugwump ['mʌgwʌmp] *n Am* POL *péj* indépendant *m*, -e *f*.

Muhammedan, Muhammadan [mə'hæmɪdn] ◇ *n* Mahométan *m*, -e *f*.

◇ *adj* mahométan.

mujaheddin [,mu:dʒəhe'di:n] *n* moudjahid *m*.

mulatto [mju:'lætəʊ] (*pl* mulattos OR mulattoes) ◇ *adj* mulâtre.

◇ *n* mulâtre *m*, mûlatresse *f*.

mulberry ['mʌlbərɪ] ◇ *n* -**1.** [fruit] mûre *f*; [tree] mûrier *m*; white ~ mûrier blanc. -**2.** [colour] violet *m* foncé.

◇ *adj* violet foncé *(inv)*.

mulch [mʌltʃ] HORT ◇ *n* paillis *m*.

◇ *vt* pailler, couvrir de paillis.

mulct [mʌlkt] *fml* ◇ *n* amende *f*.

◇ *vt* -**1.** [fine] infliger une amende à. -**2.** [defraud] escroquer; [overcharge] escroquer.

mule [mju:l] *n* -**1.** [animal - male] mulet *m*; [- female] mule *f*; (as) stubborn as a ~ têtu comme un mulet OR une mule. -**2.** TECH mule-jenny *f*. -**3.** [slipper] mule *f*.

muleteer [,mju:lɪ'tɪəʳ] *n* muletier *m*, -ère *f*.

mulish ['mju:lɪʃ] *adj* têtu, entêté.
mulishness ['mju:lɪʃnɪs] *n* entêtement *m*, obstination *f*.
mull [mʌl] *vt* [wine, beer] chauffer et épicer; ~ed wine vin *m* chaud.
◆ **mull over** *vt sep* réfléchir (longuement) à.
mullah ['mʌlə] *n* mollah *m*.
mullet ['mʌlɪt] (*pl inv* OR **mullets**) *n* [grey] muge *m*, mulet *m* gris; [red] rouget *m*, mulet *m* rouge.
mulligan ['mʌlɪgən] *n Br*: ~ (stew) [of meat] ragoût *m*; [of fish] fricassée *f* de poisson.
mulligatawny [,mʌlɪgə'tɔ:nɪ] *n Br* mulligatawny *m*, soupe *f* au curry.
mullion ['mʌlɪən] *n* meneau *m*; ~ window fenêtre *f* à meneaux.
mullioned ['mʌlɪənd] *adj* [window] à meneaux.
multiaccess [,mʌltɪ'ækses] *adj* COMPUT multiaccès *(inv)*.
multicellular [,mʌltɪ'seljʊlə^r] *adj* multicellulaire.
multichannel [,mʌltɪ'tʃænl] *adj* multicanal.
multicoloured *Br*, **multicolored** *Am* ['mʌltɪ,kʌləd] *adj* multicolore.
multicultural [,mʌltɪ'kʌltʃərəl] *adj* multiculturel.
multiculturalism [,mʌltɪ'kʌltʃərəlɪzm] *n* multiculturalisme *m*.
multidirectional [,mʌltɪdɪ'rekʃənl] *adj* multidirectionnel.
multidisciplinary ['mʌltɪ,dɪsɪ'plɪnərɪ] *adj Br* pluridisciplinaire, multidisciplinaire.
multiethnic [,mʌltɪ'eθnɪk] *adj* pluriethnique.
multifaceted [,mʌltɪ'fæsɪtɪd] *adj* présentant de multiples facettes.
multifamily [,mʌltɪ'fæmɪlɪ] *adj Am* pour plusieurs familles.
multifarious [,mʌltɪ'feərɪəs] *adj* [varied] (très) divers OR varié; [numerous] (très) nombreux.
multifile ['mʌltɪfaɪl] *adj* à fichiers multiples.
multiform ['mʌltɪfɔ:m] *adj* multiforme.
multihull ['mʌltɪhʌl] ◇ *adj* multicoque.
◇ *n* multicoque *m*.
multilateral [,mʌltɪ'lætərəl] *adj* multilatéral.
multilaterally [,mʌltɪ'lætərəlɪ] *adv* de façon multilatérale.
multilingual [,mʌltɪ'lɪŋgwəl] *adj* multilingue.
multimedia [,mʌltɪ'mi:djə] *adj* multimédia.
multimeter ['mʌltɪ,mi:tə^r] *n* ELEC multimètre *m*.
multimillionaire ['mʌltɪ,mɪljə'neə^r] *n* multimillionnaire *mf*.
multinational [,mʌltɪ'næʃənl] ◇ *adj* multinational.
◇ *n* multinationale *f*.
multipartite [,mʌltɪ'pɑ:taɪt] *adj* -**1.** [talks] multipartite, multilatéral. -**2.** [in many parts] composé de plusieurs parties; [with many people] impliquant plusieurs personnes; [with many signatories] comportant de nombreux signataires.
multiparty ['mʌltɪ,pɑ:tɪ] *adj*: the ~ system le pluripartisme.
multiple ['mʌltɪpl] ◇ *n* -**1.** MATH multiple *m*; in ~s of 100 en OR par multiples de 100. -**2.** *Br* [store] chaîne *f* de magasins.
◇ *adj* -**1.** [gén] multiple; she suffered ~ injuries elle a été blessée en plusieurs endroits ‖ [ownership] collectif; ~ collision collision *f* multiple. -**2.** ELEC en parallèle.
multiple-access = **multiaccess**.
multiple-choice *adj* à choix multiples.
multiple sclerosis *n* sclérose *f* en plaques.
multiple shop, **multiple store** *n* grand magasin *m* à succursales, chaîne *f* de magasins.
multiplex ['mʌltɪpleks] TELEC ◇ *adj* multiplex.
◇ *n* multiplex *m*.
◇ *vt* multiplexer.
multiplexer, **multiplexor** ['mʌltɪ,pleksə^r] *n* TELEC multiplexeur *m*.
multiplicand [,mʌltɪplɪ'kænd] *n* multiplicande *m*.

multiplication [,mʌltɪplɪ'keɪʃn] *n* [gen & MATH] multiplication *f*.
multiplication sign *n* signe *m* de multiplication.
multiplication table *n* table *f* de multiplication.
multiplicity [,mʌltɪ'plɪsətɪ] *n* multiplicité *f*.
multiplier ['mʌltɪplaɪə^r] *n* -**1.** ECON, ELECTRON & MATH multiplicateur *m*. -**2.** COMPUT multiplieur *m*.
multiply ['mʌltɪplaɪ] (*pt & pp* **multiplied**) ◇ *vt* multiplier; it will ~ costs by eight ça va multiplier les coûts par huit.
◇ *vi* -**1.** MATH faire des multiplications. -**2.** [reproduce, increase] se multiplier.
multiprocessor [,mʌltɪ'prəʊsesə^r] *n* COMPUT multiprocesseur *m*.
multiprogramming [,mʌltɪ'prəʊgræmɪŋ] *n* COMPUT multiprogrammation *f*.
multipurpose [,mʌltɪ'pɜ:pəs] *adj* à usages multiples, polyvalent.
multiracial [,mʌltɪ'reɪʃl] *adj* multiracial.
multistage ['mʌltɪsteɪdʒ] *adj* -**1.** [procedure] à plusieurs étapes. -**2.** [rocket] à plusieurs étages.
multistorey [,mʌltɪ'stɔ:rɪ] *Br*, **multistoried** [,mʌltɪ'stɔ:rɪd] *Am adj*: ~ building grand immeuble *m*; ~ car park parking *m* à plusieurs niveaux.
multitasking [,mʌltɪ'tɑ:skɪŋ] ◇ *n* multitâche *f*.
◇ *comp* multitâche.
multitrack [,mʌltɪ'træk] *adj* multipiste.
multitude ['mʌltɪtju:d] *n* -**1.** [large number - of people, animals] multitude *f*; [- of details, reasons] multitude *f*, foule *f*; it covers a ~ of sins cela peut être interprété de diverses façons. -**2.** [ordinary people]: the ~ la multitude, la foule.
multitudinous [,mʌltɪ'tju:dɪnəs] *adj* [countless] innombrable.
multiuser [,mʌltɪ'ju:zə^r] *adj* multiutilisateurs *(inv)*.
multiwindow [,mʌltɪ'wɪndəʊ] *adj* COMPUT multifenêtre.
mum [mʌm] ◇ *adj*: to keep ~ garder le silence ❑ ~'s the word! *inf* motus et bouche cousue!
◇ *n inf Br* [mother] maman *f*.
mumble ['mʌmbl] ◇ *vi* marmonner; what are you mumbling about? qu'est-ce que tu as à marmonner comme ça?; to ~ to o.s. marmonner tout seul; he ~d on for half an hour il a radoté pendant une demi-heure.
◇ *vt* marmonner; to make a ~d apology, to ~ an apology marmonner des excuses.
◇ *n* paroles *fpl* indistinctes, marmonnement *m*, marmonnements *mpl*; he replied in a ~ il marmonna une réponse.
mumbo jumbo [,mʌmbəʊ'dʒʌmbəʊ] *n pej* langage *m* incompréhensible, charabia *m*; it's just a load of ~ tout ça, c'est du charabia; as far as I'm concerned astrology is just a load of ~ pour moi, l'astrologie n'est que de la superstition ridicule.
mummer ['mʌmə^r] *n* danseur *m*, -euse *f* folklorique.
mummery ['mʌmərɪ] (*pl* **mummeries**) *n* -**1.** *pej* [ceremony] cérémonie *f* pompeuse. -**2.** [dancing] spectacle *m* de danses folkloriques.
mummification [,mʌmɪfɪ'keɪʃn] *n* momification *f*.
mummify ['mʌmɪfaɪ] (*pt & pp* **mummified**) ◇ *vt* momifier.
◇ *vi* se momifier.
mummy ['mʌmɪ] (*pl* **mummies**) *n* -**1.** [body] momie *f*. -**2.** *inf Br* [mother] maman *f*.
mumps [mʌmps] *n (U)* oreillons *mpl*.
munch [mʌntʃ] ◇ *vt* [crunchy food] croquer; [food in general] mâcher.
◇ *vi*: to ~ on an apple croquer une pomme; she was ~ing away at some toast elle mâchonnait un toast; he sat there ~ing away il restait là à mâchonner.
munchies *inf* ['mʌntʃɪz] *npl*: to have the ~ avoir un petit creux; I've got a bad case of the ~ j'ai la dalle.

mundane [mʌn'deɪn] *adj* banal, ordinaire.
mung bean [mʌŋ-] *n* mungo *m*, ambérique
Munich ['mju:nɪk] *pr n* Munich.
municipal [mju:'nɪsɪpl] *adj* municipal, de ville.
municipality [mju:,nɪsɪ'pælətɪ] (*pl* **municipal**ties) *n* municipalité *f*.
munificence [mju:'nɪfɪsəns] *n* munificence
munificent [mju:'nɪfɪsənt] *adj* munificent.
munitions [mju:'nɪʃnz] *npl* munitions *fpl*; ~ dump dépôt *m* de munitions; ~ factory fabr que *f* de munitions; she was a ~ worker ell travaillait dans une fabrique de munitions.
muon ['mju:ɒn] *n* muon *m*.
mural ['mju:ərəl] ◇ *n* [painting] mural *m*, peinture *f* murale.
◇ *adj* mural.
Murcia ['mɜ:sɪə] *pr n* Murcie.
murder ['mɜ:də^r] ◇ *n* -**1.** *literal* meurtre *m*, assassinat *m*; he's up on a ~ charge il est accus de meurtre; ~ trial procès *m* pour meurtre; th ~ weapon l'arme *f* du crime ❑ to get awa with ~ faire n'importe quoi impunément they know their mother will let them ge away with ~ ils savent qu'avec leur mère i peuvent faire ce qu'ils veulent; 'Murder in th Cathedral' *Eliot* 'Meurtre dans la cathédrale' 'Murder on the Orient Express' *Christie, Lum* 'le Crime de l'Orient-Express'; 'The Murders i the Rue Morgue' *Poe* 'Double assassinat dans rue Morgue'. -**2.** *inf fig* calvaire *m*, enfer *m*; th traffic is ~ on Fridays il y a une circulatio épouvantable le vendredi; it's ~ trying to ge her to agree ce n'est pas une mince affaire qu d'obtenir son consentement.
◇ *vt* -**1.** [kill] tuer, assassiner; [slaughter] tue massacrer; I could ~ a beer! je me taperais bie une bière! -**2.** *fig* [language, play] massacrer.
◇ *interj*: ~! à l'assassin!
murderer ['mɜ:dərə^r] *n* meurtrier *m*, -ère *f*, assassin *m*.
murderess ['mɜ:dərɪs] *n* meurtrière *f*.
murderous ['mɜ:dərəs] *adj* -**1.** [deadly - regim attack, intention] meurtrier. -**2.** [hateful - loo expression] meurtrier, assassin, de haine -**3.** [dangerous - road, bend] meurtrier, redoutable. -**4.** *inf* [hellish] infernal, épouvantable.
murex ['mjʊəreks] (*pl* **murexes** OR **murice** [-rɪsi:z]) *n* murex *m*.
murk [mɜ:k] *n (U)* obscurité *f*, ténèbres *fpl*.
murkiness ['mɜ:kɪnɪs] *n* obscurité *f*.
murky ['mɜ:kɪ] (*compar* **murkier**, *superl* **murk**iest) *adj* -**1.** [dark - sky, night] noir, sombre [muddy - water] boueux, trouble; [dirty windows, weather] sale. -**2.** *fig* [shameful]: a ~ episode une histoire sombre OR trouble; he someone from my ~ past c'est quelqu'un qu appartient à mon passé trouble.
Murmansk [mɜ:'mænsk] *pr n* Mourmansk.
murmur ['mɜ:mə^r] ◇ *vi* murmurer; to ~ at o against sthg murmurer contre qqch.
◇ *vt* murmurer; to ~ excuses murmurer de excuses.
◇ *n* -**1.** [sound] murmure *m*; [of conversatior bruit *m*, bourdonnement *m*; there wasn't a ~ on aurait pu entendre une mouche vole without a ~ sans broncher. -**2.** MED [of hear souffle *m*.
murphy *inf* ['mɜ:fɪ] (*pl* **murphies**) *n Br* pomm de terre *f*, patate *f*.
Murphy bed ['mɜ:fɪ-] *n Am* lit *m* escamotabl
Murphy's law ['mɜ:fɪz-] *n* loi *f* de l'emmerdement maximum; that's ~! c'est la poisse!
Mururoa Atoll ['mʊrʊ,rəʊə'ætɒl] *pr* Mururoa; on ~ à Mururoa.
MusB ['mʌzbi:], **MusBac** ['mʌzbæk] (*abbr* Bachelor of Music) *n* (titulaire d'une) licenc de musique.
Muscat ['mʌskət] *pr n* Mascate; ~ and Oma Mascate et Oman.
muscatel [,mʌskə'tel] *n* muscat *m*.
muscle ['mʌsl] ◇ *n* -**1.** ANAT & ZOOL muscle *n* [strength] muscle *m*, force *f*; ~ power force

physique OR musculaire ☐ she didn't move a ~ elle est restée parfaitement immobile. -**2.** [influence, power] puissance *f*, poids *m*; the drink-driving laws have no ~ les lois contre l'alcoolisme au volant n'ont aucun poids OR impact.
◇ *vt* muscler; **well-~d arms** bras bien musclés.
◆ **muscle in** *inf vi insep* intervenir; to ~ in on sthg intervenir autoritairement dans qqch; to ~ one's way in entrer par la force.
muscle-bound *adj* -**1.** [muscular] extrêmement musclé. -**2.** [rigid] inflexible, rigide.
muscleman ['mʌslmæn] (*pl* **musclemen** [-men]) *n* [strongman] hercule *m*; [bodyguard] garde *m* du corps, homme *m* de main.
muscly ['mʌslɪ] *adj* musclé, plein de muscles.
Muscovite ['mʌskəvaɪt] ◇ *n* Moscovite *mf*.
◇ *adj* moscovite.
muscular ['mʌskjʊlə^r] *adj* -**1.** [body] musclé. -**2.** [pain, tissue] musculaire.
muscular dystrophy *n* (*U*) myopathie *f*.
musculature ['mʌskjʊlətʃə^r] *n* musculature *f*.
MusD ['mʌzdiː], **MusDoc** ['mʌzdɒk] (*abbr of* Doctor of Music) *n* (titulaire d'un) doctorat en musique.
muse [mjuːz] ◇ *n* muse *f*; the Muses les Muses.
◇ *vi* rêvasser, songer; to ~ on OR upon OR over sthg songer à qqch.
◇ *vt*: "I wonder what happened to him", she ~d «je me demande bien ce qu'il est devenu», dit-elle d'un air songeur.
museum [mjuː'ziːəm] *n* musée *m*.
museum piece *n literal* & *fig* pièce *f* de musée.
mush[1] [mʌʃ] *n* -**1.** [food] bouillie *f*; *Am* [porridge] bouillie *f* de maïs. -**2.** *inf fig* [sentimentality] mièvrerie *f*.
mush[2▽] [mʊʃ] *n Br* -**1.** [face] poire *f*, trombine *f*. -**2.** [term of address]: oi, ~![▽] eh, machin!
mushroom ['mʌʃrʊm] ◇ *n* BOT & NUCL champignon *m*.
◇ *vi* -**1.** [gather mushrooms]: to go ~ing aller aux champignons. -**2.** [spring up] pousser comme un champignon OR des champignons; video shops ~ed in almost every town les magasins de vidéo se sont multipliés dans presque toutes les villes. -**3.** [grow quickly] s'étendre, prendre de l'ampleur; the conflict ~ed into full-scale war le conflit a vite dégénéré en véritable guerre; a ~ing estate un lotissement qui s'étend rapidement.
◇ *comp* -**1.** [soup, omelette] aux champignons. -**2.** [in colour] beige. -**3.** *fig*: ~ growth poussée *f* OR croissance *f* rapide; ~ town ville *f* champignon.
mushroom cloud *n* champignon *m* atomique.
mushrooming ['mʌʃruːmɪŋ] *n* -**1.** [mushroom picking] cueillette *f* des champignons. -**2.** [sudden growth] croissance *f* exponentielle.
mushy ['mʌʃɪ] (*compar* **mushier**, *superl* **mushiest**) *adj* -**1.** [vegetables] ramolli; [fruit] trop mûr, blet; [ground] détrempé; ~ peas purée *f* de petits pois. -**2.** *inf fig* [sentimental] à l'eau de rose, mièvre.
music ['mjuːzɪk] ◇ *n* musique *f*; to set to ~ mettre en musique ‖ [score] partition *f*, musique *f*; to read ~ lire une partition ☐ the news was ~ to my ears la nouvelle m'a fait très plaisir OR m'a ravi.
◇ *comp* [teacher, lesson, festival] de musique.
musical ['mjuːzɪkl] ◇ *adj* -**1.** [evening, taste, exercise, composition] musical; [instrument] de musique. -**2.** [person] mélomane; they are a ~ people [liking music] c'est un peuple mélomane; [including musicians] c'est un peuple de musiciens; I'm not very ~ je n'ai pas tellement l'oreille musicale. -**3.** [pleasant - voice, chimes] musical.
◇ *n* = **musical comedy**.
musical box *Br* = **music box**.
musical chairs *n* -**1.** [game] jeu *m* des chaises musicales. -**2.** *fig* va-et-vient *m inv*, remue-ménage *m inv*; POL remaniements *mpl*.
musical comedy *n* comédie *f* musicale, musical *m*.
musical instrument *n* instrument *m* de musique.
musically ['mjuːzɪklɪ] *adv* [in a musical way] musicalement; [from a musical viewpoint] musicalement, d'un point de vue musical.
music box *n* boîte *f* à musique.
music case *n* porte-musique *m inv*.
music centre *n* chaîne *f* (midi).
music hall ◇ *n* -**1.** [theatre] théâtre *m* de variétés. -**2.** [entertainment] music-hall *m*.
◇ *comp* [song, artist] de music-hall.
musician [mjuː'zɪʃn] *n* musicien *m*, -enne *f*.
musicianship [mjuː'zɪʃnʃɪp] *n* sens *m* musical.
music-lover *n* mélomane *mf*.
musicologist [ˌmjuːzɪ'kɒlədʒɪst] *n* musicologue *mf*.
musicology [ˌmjuːzɪ'kɒlədʒɪ] *n* musicologie *f*.
music paper *n* papier *m* à musique.
music stand *n* pupitre *m* (à musique).
musing ['mjuːzɪŋ] ◇ *n* (*U*) songes *mpl*, rêverie *f*.
◇ *adj* songeur, rêveur.
musingly ['mjuːzɪŋlɪ] *adv* pensivement; "I don't know", she answered ~ «je ne sais pas», répondit-elle songeuse OR d'un air songeur.
musk [mʌsk] *n* musc *m*.
musk deer *n* porte-musc *m*.
musket ['mʌskɪt] *n* mousquet *m*.
musketeer [ˌmʌskɪ'tɪə^r] *n* mousquetaire *m*.
musketry ['mʌskɪtrɪ] *n* (*U*) -**1.** [muskets] mousquets *mpl*. -**2.** [musketeers] mousquetaires *mpl*.
muskmelon ['mʌskˌmelən] *n* melon *m*.
musk ox *n* bœuf *m* musqué, ovibus *m*.
muskrat ['mʌskræt] (*pl inv* OR **muskrats**) *n* -**1.** ZOOL rat *m* musqué, ondatra *m*. -**2.** [fur] rat *m* d'Amérique, loutre *f* d'Hudson.
musk rose *n* rosier *m* musqué.
musky ['mʌskɪ] (*compar* **muskier**, *superl* **muskiest**) *adj* musqué.
Muslim ['mʊzlɪm] ◇ *adj* musulman.
◇ *n* musulman *m*, -e *f*.
muslin ['mʌzlɪn] ◇ *n* mousseline *f* TEXT.
◇ *comp* de OR en mousseline.
musquash ['mʌskwɒʃ] = **muskrat**.
muss *inf* [mʌs] *vt* [rumple] friper, froisser; [dirty] salir; don't ~ my hair ne me décoiffe pas.
◆ **muss up** *inf vt sep Am* -**1.** = **muss**. -**2.** [upset - plans] ficher par terre.
mussel ['mʌsl] ◇ *n* moule *f*.
◇ *comp*: ~ farm moulière *f*; ~ bed parc *m* à moules.
Mussorgsky [mʊ'sɔːgskɪ] *pr n* Moussorgski.
must[1] [*weak form* məs, məst, *strong form* mʌst] ◇ *modal vb* -**1.** [expressing necessity, obligation] devoir; you ~ lock the door vous devez fermer OR il faut que vous fermiez la porte à clé; I ~ go now il faut que je parte (maintenant); the system ~ change il faut que le système change; I ~ admit the idea intrigues me je dois avouer que l'idée m'intrigue; if I/you *etc* ~ s'il le faut; I can't! – you ~! je ne peux pas! – mais il le faut!; if you ~ know, he's asked me out to dinner si tu veux tout savoir, il m'a invitée à dîner; this I ~ see! il faut que je voie ça!; you really ~ see his latest film il faut vraiment que tu voies son dernier film; ~ you be so rude? es-tu obligé d'être aussi grossier?; they told us we ~ leave ils nous ont dit qu'il fallait que nous partions, ils nous ont dit que nous devions partir; you mustn't smoke il est interdit de fumer; I mustn't say any more je n'ai pas le droit d'en dire plus; they told us we mustn't come before 10 o'clock ils nous ont dit de ne pas arriver avant 10 h; you mustn't forget to press this button n'oubliez (surtout) pas d'appuyer sur ce bouton. -**2.** [suggesting, inviting]: you ~ meet my wife il faut que vous rencontriez OR fassiez la connaissance de ma femme; you ~ come and see us il faut (absolument) que vous veniez nous voir. -**3.** [expressing likelihood] devoir; you ~ be Alison vous devez être Alison; you ~ be famished vous devez être morts de faim; it ~ be very hard for you ça doit être très dur pour toi; there ~ be thousands of them! il doit y en avoir des milliers!; you ~ be joking! tu plaisantes! -**4.** (*with 'have' + past participle*) [making assumptions]: she ~ have forgotten elle a dû oublier, elle a sans doute oublié; has she forgotten? – she ~ have elle a oublié? – sans doute OR certainement; you ~ have known! vous le saviez sûrement!; there ~ have been at least a thousand people il devait y avoir au moins un millier de personnes ‖ [stating requirements]: before applying candidates ~ have successfully completed all their exams les candidats doivent avoir obtenu tous leurs examens avant de se présenter.
◇ *n inf*: sunglasses are a ~ les lunettes de soleil sont absolument indispensables; this film/his new album is a ~ il faut absolument avoir vu ce film/acheter son dernier album; leggings are a ~ this year les caleçons sont un must cette année.
must[2] [mʌst] *n* -**1.** [mould] moisissure *f*. -**2.** [for wine] moût *m*.
mustache *Am* ['mʌstæʃ] = **moustache**.
mustachio [mə'stɑːʃɪəʊ] (*pl* **mustachios**) *n* (longue) moustache *f*.
mustachioed [mə'stɑːʃɪəʊd] *adj* moustachu.
mustang ['mʌstæŋ] *n* mustang *m*.
mustard ['mʌstəd] ◇ *n* moutarde *f*; ~ seed graine *f* de moutarde; ~ and cress *mélange de cresson alénois et de pousses de moutarde blanche utilisé en salade*; French ~ ≃ moutarde *f* de Dijon; ~ pot moutardier *m*, pot *m* à moutarde.
◇ *adj* [colour] moutarde (*inv*).
mustard gas *n* gaz *m* moutarde, ypérite *f*.
mustard plaster *n* sinapisme *m*.
muster ['mʌstə^r] ◇ *vt* -**1.** [gather - troops] rassembler, réunir; [- courage, energy] rassembler; [- finance, cash] réunir; they were unable to ~ enough support ils n'ont pas pu trouver suffisamment de gens pour soutenir leur initiative; to ~ one's courage to do sthg prendre son courage à deux mains pour faire qqch. -**2.** [take roll-call] faire l'appel de.
◇ *vi* se rassembler.
◇ *n* -**1.** MIL revue *f*, inspection *f*; to pass ~ *Br fig* [in dress, appearance] être présentable; [in content] être acceptable; I don't know whether your account of the facts will pass ~ je ne sais pas si votre version des faits sera acceptée OR si on acceptera votre version des faits. -**2.** [assembly] rassemblement *m*.
◆ **muster in** *vt sep Am* MIL incorporer, engager.
◆ **muster out** *vt sep Am* MIL libérer (des obligations militaires).
◆ **muster up** *vt insep* [courage] rassembler; to ~ up support chercher à obtenir un soutien OR un appui.
mustiness ['mʌstɪnɪs] *n* [of smell] odeur *f* de moisi; [of room] odeur *f* de renfermé.
musty ['mʌstɪ] (*compar* **mustier**, *superl* **mustiest**) *adj* -**1.** [smell] de moisi; [room] qui sent le renfermé. -**2.** *fig* [old-fashioned] suranné, vieux jeu (*inv*); ~ ideas idées *fpl* dépassées.
mutability [ˌmjuːtə'bɪlətɪ] *n* mutabilité *f*.
mutable ['mjuːtəbl] *adj* [gen] mutable; ASTROL mutable, commun.
mutagen ['mjuːtədʒən] *adj* mutagène.
mutant ['mjuːtənt] ◇ *adj* mutant.
◇ *n* mutant *m*, -e *f*.
mutate [mjuː'teɪt] *vi* & *vt* muter.
mutation [mjuː'teɪʃn] *n* mutation *f*.
mute [mjuːt] ◇ *adj* -**1.** MED muet. -**2.** LING [vowel, letter] muet. -**3.** [silent - person] muet, silencieux; to stand ~ rester muet OR silencieux ‖ [unspoken - admiration, protest] muet.
◇ *vt* [sound] amortir, atténuer; [feelings, colour] atténuer.
◇ *n* -**1.** MED muet *m*, -ette *f*. -**2.** MUS sourdine *f*.
muted ['mjuːtɪd] *adj* -**1.** [sound] assourdi, amorti, atténué; [voice] feutré, sourd; [colour] doux, pâle; [criticism, protest] voilé; [applause] faible. -**2.** MUS en sourdine.

mute swan *n* cygne *m* muet OR tuberculé OR domestique.

mutilate ['mju:tɪleɪt] *vt* -**1.** [maim - body] mutiler; [- face] défigurer. -**2.** [damage - property, thing] mutiler, dégrader, détériorer. -**3.** [adulterate - text] mutiler, estropier, altérer.

mutilation [,mju:tɪ'leɪʃn] *n* -**1.** [of body] mutilation *f*. -**2.** [of property] détérioration *f*, dégradation *f*. -**3.** [of text] mutilation *f*, altération *f*.

mutineer [,mju:tɪ'nɪəʳ] *n* mutin *m*, mutiné *m*, -e *f*.

mutinous ['mju:tɪnəs] *adj* -**1.** [rebellious - crew, soldiers] mutiné, rebelle; **the inmates of the prison were ~** les détenus étaient au bord de la rébellion. -**2.** [unruly - child] indiscipliné, rebelle.

mutiny ['mju:tɪnɪ] (*pl* mutinies) ◇ *n* [on ship] mutinerie *f*; [in prison, barracks] rébellion *f*, mutinerie *f*; [in city] soulèvement *m*, révolte *f*; '**Mutiny on the Bounty**' *Nordhoff, Hall* 'les Révoltés du Bounty'; '**The Caine Mutiny**' *Dmytryk* 'Ouragan sur le Caine'.
◇ *vi* se mutiner, se rebeller.

mutism ['mju:tɪzm] *n* [gen & PSYCH] mutisme *m*; MED mutité *f*.

mutt *inf* [mʌt] *n* -**1.** [dog] clébard *m*. -**2.** [fool] crétin *m*, -e *f*.

mutter ['mʌtəʳ] ◇ *vt* [mumble] marmonner, grommeler; **he ~ed a threat** il grommela OR marmonna une menace; **he ~ed something and left** il marmonna quelque chose et sortit.
◇ *vi* -**1.** [mumble] marmonner, parler dans sa barbe OR entre ses dents; **what are you ~ing about?** qu'est-ce que tu as à marmonner?; **to ~ to o.s.** marmonner tout seul. -**2.** [grumble] grommeler, grogner.
◇ *n* murmure *m*, murmures *mpl*, marmonnement *m*; **this provoked ~s of discontent** cela a provoqué un murmure de mécontentement; **to speak in a ~** marmonner dans sa barbe.

muttering ['mʌtərɪŋ] *n* marmottement *m*.

mutton ['mʌtn] ◇ *n* CULIN mouton *m*; **she's ~ dressed as lamb** elle joue les jeunesses.
◇ *comp* [chop, stew] de mouton.

muttonchops [,mʌtən'tʃɒps], **muttonchop whiskers** *npl* favoris *mpl (bien fournis)*.

muttonhead▽ ['mʌtənhed] *n* crétin *m*, -e *f*.

mutual ['mju:tʃʊəl] *adj* [reciprocal - admiration, help] mutuel, réciproque; [shared - friend, interest] commun; **by ~ consent** à l'amiable, par consentement mutuel; **the feeling is ~** c'est réciproque ❑ '**Our Mutual Friend**' *Dickens* 'Notre ami commun'.

mutual fund *n Am* [unit trust] fonds *m* commun de placement.

mutual insurance *n* (assurance *f*) mutuelle *f*.

mutuality [,mju:tjʊ'ælətɪ] *n* réciprocité *f*.

mutually ['mju:tʃʊəlɪ] *adv* mutuellement, réciproquement; **~ exclusive** OR **contradictory** qui s'excluent l'un l'autre, contradictoires.

Muzak ®['mju:zæk] *n* musique *f* de fond, fond *m* sonore.

muzziness ['mʌzɪnɪs] *n Br* -**1.** [of mind, ideas] confusion *f*, flou *m*. -**2.** [of picture, outline] flou *m*, manque *m* de netteté.

muzzle ['mʌzl] ◇ *n* -**1.** [for dog, horse] muselière *f*. -**2.** *fig* [censorship] bâillon *m*, censure *f*. -**3.** [of gun] canon *m*. -**4.** [mouth of animal] gueule *f*.
◇ *vt* -**1.** [dog, horse] museler, mettre une muselière à. -**2.** *fig* [speaker] museler, empêcher de s'exprimer librement; [press] bâillonner, museler.

muzzle-loader *n arme à feu dont le chargement s'opère par la bouche*.

muzzle velocity *n* vitesse *f* initiale.

muzzy ['mʌzɪ] (*compar* muzzier, *superl* muzziest) *adj Br* -**1.** [person] aux idées embrouillées; [mind, head] confus; [ideas] embrouillé, flou. -**2.** [picture] flou, indistinct.

MVP (*abbr of* **most valuable player**) *n Am titre décerné au meilleur joueur d'une équipe*.

MW (*written abbr of* **medium wave**) PO.

MX (*abbr of* **missile-experimental**) *n missile américain MX*.

my [maɪ] ◇ *det* -**1.** [belonging to me] mon *m*, ma *f*, mes *pl*; **my dog/car/ear** mon chien/ma voiture/mon oreille; **my dogs/cars/ears** mes chiens/voitures/oreilles; **I never use my own car** je n'utilise jamais ma voiture (personnelle); **I have a car of my own** j'ai une voiture (à moi); **this is MY chair** cette chaise est à moi; **I've broken my glasses** j'ai cassé mes lunettes; **I've broken my arm** je me suis cassé le bras; **she looked into my eyes** elle m'a regardé dans les yeux. -**2.** [in terms of affection]: **my dear** OR **darling** [to man] mon chéri; [to woman] ma chérie. -**3.** [in titles]: **my Lord** [to judge] Monsieur le juge; [to nobleman] Monsieur le Comte/le Duc; [to bishop] Monseigneur. -**4.** [in exclamations]: **oh, my God!** oh! mon Dieu!
◇ *interj* eh bien; **my, but you've grown!** eh bien dis donc, tu as poussé!

Myanmar [,maɪæn'mɑ:ʳ] *pr n* Myanmar *m*; **in ~** au Myanmar.

Mycenae [maɪ'si:ni:] *pr n* Mycènes.

Mycenaean [,maɪsɪ'ni:ən] ◇ *n* Mycénien *m*, -enne *f*.
◇ *adj* mycénien.

mycology [maɪ'kɒlədʒɪ] *n* mycologie *f*.

myelitis [,maɪə'laɪtɪs] *n* myélite *f*.

myeloma [,maɪə'ləʊmə] *n* myélome *m*.

myocardial [,maɪəʊ'kɑ:dɪəl] *adj*: **~ infarction** infarctus *m* du myocarde.

myopia [maɪ'əʊpjə] *n* myopie *f*.

myopic [maɪ'ɒpɪk] *adj* myope; **they have a ~ view of things** *fig* ils ne voient pas plus loin que le bout de leur nez.

myotonia [,maɪə'təʊnɪə] *n* myotonie *f*.

myriad ['mɪrɪəd] ◇ *adj lit* innombrable.
◇ *n* myriade *f*.

Myrmidon ['mɜ:mɪdən] *n* -**1.** MYTH Myrmidon *m*. -**2.** *fig* [follower] acolyte *m*.

myrrh [mɜ:ʳ] *n* myrrhe *f*.

myrtle ['mɜ:tl] *n* myrte *m*.

myself [maɪ'self] *pron* -**1.** [reflexive use]: **may I help ~?** puis-je me servir?; **I knitted ~ a cardigan** je me suis tricoté un gilet; **it tastes not bad, though I say it ~** *hum* sans fausse modestie, ça n'est pas mauvais; **I can see ~ reflected in the water** je vois mon reflet dans l'eau; **I can't see ~ going on holiday this year** je ne crois pas que je pourrai partir en vacances cette année; **I took it upon ~ to answer** j'ai pris sur moi de répondre. -**2.** [replacing 'me']: **the group included ~ and Jim** Jim et moi faisions partie du groupe; **it is meant for people like ~** c'est fait pour les gens comme moi ❑ **I'm not (feeling) ~ today** je ne me sens pas très bien OR je ne suis pas dans mon assiette aujourd'hui. -**3.** [emphatic use]: **I'm not a great fan of opera ~** personnellement, je ne suis pas un passionné d'opéra; **I'm a stranger here ~** je ne suis pas d'ici non plus; **I ~ saw him leave** je l'ai vu partir de mes propres yeux; **I ~** OR **~, I don't believe him** pour ma part, je ne le crois pas; **I was left all by ~** on m'a laissé tout seul. -**4.** [unaided, alone] moi-même; **I can do it ~** je peux le faire moi-même OR tout seul; **I made the pattern ~** j'ai fait le patron moi-même.

mysterious [mɪ'stɪərɪəs] *adj* mystérieux.

mysteriously [mɪ'stɪərɪəslɪ] *adv* mystérieusement.

mystery ['mɪstərɪ] (*pl* mysteries) ◇ *n* -**1.** [strange or unexplained event] mystère *m*; **it's a ~ to me why she came** la raison de sa venue est un mystère pour moi, je n'ai aucune idée de la raison pour laquelle elle est venue; **his past is a ~** son passé est bien mystérieux; **there's no ~ about that** ça n'a rien de mystérieux, cela n'est un mystère pour personne. -**2.** [strangeness] mystère *m*; **she has a certain ~ about her** il se dégage de sa personne une impression de mystère. -**3.** [story] = **mystery story**. -**4.** THEAT & RELIG mystère *m*.
◇ *comp* [man, voice] mystérieux.

mystery play *n* mystère *m* THEAT.

mystery story *n* mystère *m*, histoire *f* à suspense, intrigue *f* policière.

mystery tour *n excursion dont la destination est inconnue des participants*.

mystic ['mɪstɪk] ◇ *adj* mystique.
◇ *n* mystique *mf*.

mystical ['mɪstɪkl] *adj* -**1.** PHILOS & RELIG mystique. -**2.** [occult] occulte.

mysticism ['mɪstɪsɪzm] *n* mysticisme *m*.

mystification [,mɪstɪfɪ'keɪʃn] *n* mystification *f*.

mystified ['mɪstɪfaɪd] *adj* perplexe.

mystify ['mɪstɪfaɪ] (*pt* & *pp* mystified) *vt* [puzzle] déconcerter, laisser OR rendre perplexe; [deceive] mystifier.

mystique [mɪ'sti:k] *n* mystique *f*, côté *m* mystique.

myth [mɪθ] *n* mythe *m*.

mythic(al) ['mɪθɪk(l)] *adj* mythique.

mythmaker ['mɪθ,meɪkəʳ] *n* créateur *m*, -trice *f* de mythes.

mythological [,mɪθə'lɒdʒɪkl] *adj* mythologique.

mythology [mɪ'θɒlədʒɪ] (*pl* mythologies) *n* mythologie *f*.

mythomania [,mɪθə'meɪnjə] *n* mythomanie *f*.

mythomaniac [,mɪθə'meɪnɪæk] ◇ *adj* mythomane.
◇ *n* mythomane *mf*.

myxomatosis [,mɪksəmə'təʊsɪs] *n* myxomatose *f*.

n (*pl* **n's** OR **ns**), **N**(*pl* **N's** OR **Ns**) [en] *n* [letter] n *m*, N *m*.

n *n* MATH n *m*; **x to the power of ~** x puissance n; **there are ~ possible solutions** *inf* il y a 36 solutions possibles.

'n', 'n *inf* [(ə)n] (*abbr of* **and**) *conj* et; **fish ~ chips** poisson-frites *m*.

N (*written abbr of* **North**) N.

n/a, N/A (*written abbr of* **not applicable**) s.o.

NA (*abbr of* **Narcotics Anonymous**) *pr n* *association américaine d'aide aux toxicomanes*.

NAACP (*abbr of* **National Association for the Advancement of Colored People**) *pr n* *ligue américaine pour la défense des droits de la population noire*.

Naafi *n* ['næfɪ] (*abbr of* **Navy, Army, and Air Force Institutes**) ◇ *pr n* *organisme approvisionnant les forces armées britanniques en biens de consommation*.
◇ *n* [canteen] cantine *f* militaire; [shop] magasin *m* réservé aux militaires.

nab *inf* [næb] (*pt* & *pp* **nabbed**, *cont* **nabbing**) *vt* **-1.** [catch in wrongdoing] pincer, choper; **to be nabbed** se faire pincer. **-2.** [catch - to speak to] coincer, agrafer. **-3.** [steal, take] chiper, faucher; [occupy - seat] prendre, accaparer; [- parking place] piquer.

nabob ['neɪbɒb] *n* nabab *m*.

nacelle [næ'sel] *n* nacelle *f* AÉRON.

nachos ['nɑːtʃəʊz] *npl* *chips de maïs servis avec du fromage fondu*.

nacre ['neɪkəʳ] *n* nacre *f*.

nacreous ['neɪkrɪəs] *adj* nacré.

NACU (*abbr of* **National Association of Colleges and Universities**) *pr n* *association des établissements d'enseignement supérieur américains*.

nadir ['neɪˌdɪəʳ] *n* **-1.** ASTRON nadir *m*. **-2.** *fig* [lowest point] point *m* le plus bas OR profond; **to reach a ~** être au plus bas, toucher le fond, atteindre le niveau le plus bas.

naff *inf* [næf] *adj Br* nul, bidon.
◆ **naff off** *inf vi insep Br*: ~ **off!** [go away] tire-toi!; [as refusal] arrête ton char!

naffing▽ ['næfɪŋ] *Br* ◇ *adj* foutu; ~ **hell!** merde!
◇ *adv* sacrément; ~ **marvellous!** super!, génial!

nag [næg] (*pt* & *pp* **nagged**, *cont* **nagging**) ◇ *vt* **-1.** [pester] houspiller, harceler; **she's always nagging him** elle est toujours après lui; **he nagged me into buying him a hi-fi** il m'a harcelé jusqu'à ce que je lui achète une chaîne stéréo. **-2.** [subj: pain, sorrow] ronger, travailler; [subj: doubt] tourmenter, ronger; **his conscience nagged him perpetually** sa conscience ne cessait de le tourmenter OR ne lui accordait pas de répit.
◇ *vi* trouver à redire, maugréer; **his children nagged at him to buy a video** ses enfants lui ont cassé les pieds pour qu'il achète un magnétoscope.
◇ *n* **-1.** *inf* [person] rouspéteur *m*, -euse *f*, râleur *m*, -euse *f*; **he's an awful ~** [pesterer] il se pose là comme enquiquineur; [complainer] il est toujours en train de rouspéter, c'est un affreux râleur; **his wife's a real ~** sa femme est toujours sur son dos OR ne lui laisse pas une seconde de répit. **-2.** [horse] rosse *f*.

Nagasaki [ˌnægə'sɑːkɪ] *pr n* Nagasaki.

nagging ['nægɪŋ] ◇ *adj* **-1.** [wife, husband] grincheux, acariâtre. **-2.** [doubt, feeling] tenace, harcelant; [pain] tenace; **I have a ~ suspicion he won't come** je reste persuadé qu'il ne viendra pas.
◇ *n (U)* plaintes *fpl* continuelles.

naiad ['naɪæd] *n* naïade *f*.

nail [neɪl] ◇ *n* **-1.** [pin] clou *m*; **it's another ~ in his coffin** [ruin] pour lui, c'est un pas de plus vers la ruine; [death] pour lui, c'est un pas de plus vers la tombe. **-2.** ANAT ongle *m*; **to do one's ~s** se faire les ongles.
◇ *vt* **-1.** [attach] clouer; **~ the planks together** clouez les planches l'une à l'autre; **there was a notice ~ed to the door** il y avait un écriteau cloué sur la porte; **the windows are ~ed shut** les fenêtres ont été clouées OR sont condamnées; **he stood ~ed to the spot** *fig* il est resté cloué sur place ❑ **to ~ one's colours to the mast** exprimer clairement son opinion. **-2.** *inf* [catch, trap - person] pincer, coincer. **-3.** *inf* [expose - rumour] démentir; [- lie] dénoncer, révéler. **-4.** *inf* [shoot] descendre. **-5.** *inf* [stare at] fixer (des yeux).
◆ **nail down** *vt sep* **-1.** [fasten] clouer, fixer avec des clous. **-2.** [make definite - details, date] fixer (définitivement); [- agreement] parvenir à, arriver à; [- person] amener à se décider; **try to ~ her down to a definite date** essayez de faire en sorte qu'elle vous fixe une date précise; **he's difficult to ~ down** il est difficile d'obtenir son acceptation.
◆ **nail up** *vt sep* **-1.** [shut - door, window] condamner *(en fixant avec des clous)*; [- box] clouer; [- items in box]: **the pictures were ~ed up in a crate** les tableaux étaient placés dans une caisse fermée par des clous. **-2.** [fix to wall, door - picture, photo etc] fixer (avec un clou); [- notice] clouer, afficher.

nail-biting ◇ *n* [habit] manie *f* de se ronger les ongles; *fig* nervosité *f*, inquiétude *f*.
◇ *adj* [situation] angoissant, stressant; [finish] haletant.

nail bomb *n* bombe *f* à fragmentation *(bourrée de clous)*.

nailbrush ['neɪlbrʌʃ] *n* brosse *f* à ongles.

nail clippers *npl* coupe-ongles *m inv*, pince *f* à ongles.

nail file *n* lime *f* à ongles.

nail polish *n* vernis *m* à ongles.

nail scissors *npl* ciseaux *mpl* à ongles.

nail varnish *n Br* vernis *m* à ongles; **~ remover** dissolvant *m* (pour vernis à ongles).

Nairobi [naɪ'rəʊbɪ] *pr n* Nairobi.

naive, naïve [naɪ'iːv] *adj* naïf.

naively, naïvely [naɪ'iːvlɪ] *adv* naïvement, avec naïveté.

naivety [naɪ'iːvtɪ] *n* naïveté *f*.

naked ['neɪkɪd] *adj* **-1.** [unclothed - body, leg] nu; **the ~ ape** *fig* l'homme *m*, l'espèce *f* humaine ‖ [bare - tree] nu, dénudé, sans feuilles; [- landscape] nu, dénudé; [- wall, room] nu; [unprotected - flame, light, sword] nu; [- wire] nu, dénudé; **a ~ lightbulb lit the room** une simple ampoule électrique éclairait la pièce ❑ **'The Naked and the Dead'** *Mailer* 'les Nus et les morts'. **-2.** [undisguised - reality, truth] tout nu, tout cru; [- facts] brut; [- fear] pur et simple; [- aggression] délibéré; **an expression of ~ terror** une expression de pure terreur. **-3.** [eye] nu; **visible with** OR **to the ~ eye** visible à l'œil nu. **-4.** BOT & ZOOL nu.

nakedness ['neɪkɪdnɪs] *n* nudité *f*.

NALGO ['nælgəʊ] (*abbr of* **National and Local Government Officers' Association**) *pr n* *ancien syndicat de la fonction publique en Grande-Bretagne*.

Nam *inf* [nɑːm] *pr n Am* Vietnam *m*.

NAM (*abbr of* **National Association of Manufacturers**) *pr n* *organisation patronale américaine*.

namby-pamby *inf* [ˌnæmbɪ'pæmbɪ] ◇ *adj* [person] gnangnan *(inv)*, cucul *(inv)*; [style] à l'eau de rose, fadasse.
◇ *n* lavette *f*, gnangnan *mf*.

name [neɪm] ◇ *n* **-1.** nom *m*; **what's your ~?** quel est votre nom?, comment vous appelez-vous?; **my ~'s Richard** je m'appelle Richard; **the house is in his wife's ~** la maison est au nom de sa femme; **I know her only by ~** je ne la connais que de nom; **she knows all the children by ~** elle connaît le nom de tous les enfants; **he is known** OR **he goes by the ~ of Penn** il est connu sous le nom de Penn, il se fait appeler Penn; **someone by** OR **of the ~ of Penn** quelqu'un du nom de OR qui s'appelle Penn; **a guy ~ of Jones** *inf Am* un type du nom de Jones; **I know it by** OR **under a different ~** je le connais sous un autre nom; **he writes novels under the ~ of A. Penman** il écrit des romans sous le pseudonyme de A. Penman; **our dog answers to the ~ of Rip** notre chien répond au nom de Rip; **have you put your ~ down for evening classes/a council house?** est-ce que vous vous êtes inscrit aux cours du soir/sur la liste d'attente pour un logement dans une HLM?; **she was his wife in all but ~** ils n'étaient pas mariés, mais c'était tout comme; **he had his ~ taken** FTBL il a eu un carton jaune; **he is president in ~ only** il n'a de président que le nom, c'est un président sans pouvoir; **what's in a ~?** on n'a pas toujours le nom que l'on mérite ❑ **to call sb ~s** injurier OR insulter qqn; **money is the ~ of the game** c'est une affaire OR une question d'argent; **ah well, that's the ~ of the game** c'est comme ça!, c'est la vie!; **my ~ is mud since I broke the window** je suis en disgrâce OR je suis persona non grata depuis que j'ai cassé la fenêtre; **'The Name of the Rose'** *Eco* 'le Nom de la rose'. -**2.** [sake] nom *m*; **in the ~ of freedom/religion** au nom de la liberté/la religion; **in God's ~!, in the ~ of God!** pour l'amour de Dieu! ‖ [authority] nom; **in the ~ of the mayor/the law** au nom du maire/de la loi; **halt in the ~ of the King!** halte-là, au nom du Roi! -**3.** [reputation - professional or business] nom *m*, réputation *f*; **to make** OR **to win a ~ for o.s.** se faire un nom OR une réputation; **we have the company's (good) ~ to think of** il faut penser au renom de la société; **they have a ~ for efficiency** ils ont la réputation d'être efficaces; **to have a bad ~** avoir (une) mauvaise réputation. -**4.** [famous person] nom *m*, personnage *m*; **he's a big ~ in the art world** c'est une figure de proue du monde des arts; **all the great political ~s were there** tous les ténors de la scène politique étaient présents.

◇ *vt* -**1.** [give name to - person, animal] nommer, appeler, donner un nom à; [- ship, discovery] baptiser; **they ~d the baby Felix** ils ont appelé OR prénommé le bébé Felix; **she wanted to ~ her son after the President** elle voulait donner à son fils le prénom du Président, elle voulait que son fils porte le prénom du Président; **the building is ~d for Abraham Lincoln** *Am* on a donné au bâtiment le nom d'Abraham Lincoln; **the fellow ~d Chip** le dénommé Chip. -**2.** [give name of] désigner, nommer; **the journalist refused to ~ his source** le journaliste a refusé de révéler OR de donner le nom de son informateur; **whatever you need, just ~ it** vos moindres désirs seront exaucés; **you ~ it, we've got it** demandez-nous n'importe quoi, nous l'avons!; **~ the books of the Old Testament** citez les livres de l'Ancien Testament; **to ~ names** donner des noms; **let us ~ no names** ne nommons personne ‖ [cite] citer, mentionner; **he is ~d as one of the consultants** son nom est cité OR mentionné en tant que consultant. -**3.** [appoint] nommer, désigner; **she has been ~d as president** elle a été nommée présidente; **June 22nd has been ~d as the date for the elections** la date du 22 juin a été retenue OR choisie pour les élections; **~ your price** votre prix sera le mien, dites votre prix ❑ **they've finally ~d the day** ils ont enfin fixé la date de leur mariage. -**4.** *Br* POL: **to ~ an MP** ≃ suspendre un député.

◇ *comp* COMM [product] de marque.

name-calling *n (U)* insultes *fpl*, injures *fpl*.

-named [neɪmd] *in cpds* nommé; **first~** premier nommé.

name day *n* fête *f*; **today is his ~** c'est aujourd'hui sa fête.

name-dropper *n*: **she's an awful ~** à la croire, elle connaît tout le monde.

name-dropping *n allusion fréquente à des personnes connues dans le but d'impressionner.*

nameless ['neɪmlɪs] *adj* -**1.** [anonymous, unmentioned] sans nom, anonyme; [unknown - grave, writer] anonyme, inconnu; **a person who shall be ~** une personne que je ne nommerai pas; **to remain ~** garder l'anonymat. -**2.** [indefinable - fear, regret] indéfinissable, indicible. -**3.** [atrocious, extreme - crime] innommable, sans nom, inouï.

namely ['neɪmlɪ] *adv* c'est-à-dire, à savoir.

nameplate ['neɪmpleɪt] *n* plaque *f*; **manufacturer's ~** plaque du fabricant OR du constructeur.

namesake ['neɪmseɪk] *n* homonyme *m*; **she's my ~** nous portons toutes les deux le même nom.

nametape ['neɪmteɪp] *n* marque *f (sur des vêtements)*, griffe *f*.

Namib Desert [nə'mɪb-] *pr n*: **the ~** le désert du Namib.

Namibia [nə'mɪbɪə] *pr n* Namibie *f*; **in ~** en Namibie.

Namibian [nə'mɪbɪən] ◇ *n* Namibien *m*, -enne *f*.

◇ *adj* namibien.

naming ['neɪmɪŋ] *n* -**1.** [gen] attribution *f* d'un nom; [of ship] baptême *m*. -**2.** [citing] mention *f*, citation *f*. -**3.** [appointment] nomination *f*.

nan *inf* [næn] *n Br* [grandmother] mémé *f*.

nana¹ ['nænə] = **nan**.

nana² ['nɑːnə] *n inf* [banana] banane *f*.

nan bread [nɑːn-] *n pain plat indien*.

nancy▽ ['nænsɪ] ◇ *n*: **~ (boy)** pédale *f*, tapette *f*.

◇ *adj* efféminé.

Nanjing [ˌnæn'dʒɪŋ] *pr n* Nanjing, Nankin.

nankeen [næŋ'kiːn] *n* -**1.** [cloth] nankin *m*. -**2.** [colour] nankin *m*, jaune *m* clair.

Nanking [ˌnæn'kɪŋ] = **Nanjing**.

nanna ['nænə] *Br* = **nan**.

nannoplankton ['nænəʊˌplæŋktən] = **nanoplankton**.

nanny ['nænɪ] (*pl* **nannies**) *n* -**1.** [nurse] nurse *f*, bonne *f* d'enfants. -**2.** *inf Br* [grandma] grand-mère *f*, mémé *f*, mamie *f*.

nanny goat *n* chèvre *f*.

nanometre ['nænəʊˌmiːtəʳ] *n* nanomètre *m*.

nanoplankton ['nænəʊˌplæŋktən] *n (U) organismes microscopiques du plancton*.

nanosecond ['nænəʊˌsekənd] *n* nanoseconde *f*.

nap [næp] (*pt & pp* **napped**, *cont* **napping**)

◇ *n* -**1.** [sleep] somme *m*; **to take** OR **to have a ~** faire un (petit) somme; **to take an afternoon ~** faire la sieste. -**2.** TEX poil *m*. -**3.** [card game] *jeu de cartes ressemblant au whist*. -**4.** [in horse-racing] préféré *m*.

◇ *vi* [sleep - gen] faire un (petit) somme; [- in afternoon] faire la sieste.

◇ *vt* -**1.** TEX [cloth] lainer, gratter; [velvet] brosser. -**2.** [in horse-racing] désigner comme favori, donner gagnant.

NAPA (*abbr of* National Association of Performing Artists) *pr n syndicat américain des gens du spectacle*.

napalm ['neɪpɑːm] ◇ *n* napalm *m*; **~ bomb** bombe *f* au napalm.

◇ *vt* bombarder au napalm.

nape [neɪp] *n*: **the ~ of the neck** la nuque.

nap hand *n Br*: **to have** OR **to hold a ~** avoir tous les atouts en main.

naphtha ['næfθə] *n* naphta *m*.

naphthalene, naphthaline ['næfθəliːn] *n* CHEM naphtalène *m*; [for mothballs] naphtaline *f*.

napkin ['næpkɪn] *n* -**1.** [on table] serviette *f* (de table). -**2.** *Br* [for baby] couche *f*.

napkin ring *n* rond *m* de serviette.

Naples ['neɪplz] *pr n* Naples.

napoleon [nə'pəʊljən] *n* -**1.** [coin] napoléon *m*. -**2.** *Am* CULIN mille-feuille *m*.

Napoleon [nə'pəʊljən] *pr n* Napoléon; **~ Bonaparte** Napoléon Bonaparte.

Napoleonic [nəˌpəʊlɪ'ɒnɪk] *adj* napoléonien.

Napoleonic Code *n*: **the ~** le Code Napoléon.

Napoleonic Wars *npl*: **the ~** les guerres napoléoniennes.

napper ['næpəʳ] *n* -**1.** TEX laineur *m*, -euse *f*. -**2.** ▽ *Br* [head] caboche *f*.

nappy ['næpɪ] (*pl* **nappies**) *n Br* couche *f* (pour bébé).

nappy rash *n* érythème *m* fessier; **babies often get ~** les bébés ont souvent les fesses rouges et irritées.

narc▽ [nɑːk] *n Am* agent *m* de la brigade des stupéfiants OR des stups.

narcissi [nɑː'sɪsaɪ] *pl* → **narcissus**.

narcissism ['nɑːsɪsɪzm] *n* narcissisme *m*.

narcissist ['nɑːsɪsɪst] *n* narcissique *mf*.

narcissistic [ˌnɑːsɪ'sɪstɪk] *adj* narcissique.

narcissus [nɑː'sɪsəs] (*pl inv* OR **narcissuses** OR **narcissi** [-'sɪsaɪ]) *n* narcisse *m*.

Narcissus [nɑː'sɪsəs] *pr n* Narcisse.

narcosis [nɑː'kəʊsɪs] *n* narcose *f*.

narcotic [nɑː'kɒtɪk] ◇ *adj* narcotique.

◇ *n* -**1.** PHARM narcotique *m*. -**2.** *Am* [illegal drug] stupéfiant *m*.

narcotize, -ise ['nɑːkətaɪz] *vt* soumettre à un traitement aux narcotiques.

nark [nɑːk] ◇ *n* -**1.** *crime sl* [informer] indic *m*. -**2.** *inf Br* [gripe] râleur *m*, -euse *f*. -**3.** ▽ *Am* = **narc**.

◇ *vt inf* [annoy] mettre en boule OR en rogne.

◇ *vi* -**1.** *crime sl* [inform] moucharder. -**2.** *inf Br* [gripe] rouspéter, grogner.

narked *inf* [nɑːkt] *adj Br* furibard, furax; **don't get ~** ne te fous pas en boule OR en rogne.

narky *inf* ['nɑːkɪ] (*compar* **narkier**, *superl* **narkiest**) *adj Br* rouspéteur, grognon.

narrate [*Br* nə'reɪt, *Am* 'næreɪt] *vt* -**1.** [relate - story] raconter, narrer *lit*; [- event] faire le récit de, relater. -**2.** [read commentary for]: **the film was ~d by an American actor** le commentaire du film a été dit OR lu par un acteur américain.

narration [*Br* nə'reɪʃn, *Am* næ'reɪʃn] *n* -**1.** [narrative] narration *f*. -**2.** [commentary] commentaire *m*.

narrative ['nærətɪv] ◇ *adj* narratif.

◇ *n* -**1.** LITERAT narration *f*. -**2.** [story] histoire *f*, récit *m*.

narrator [*Br* nə'reɪtəʳ, *Am* 'næreɪtəʳ] *n* narrateur *m*, -trice *f*.

narrow ['nærəʊ] ◇ *adj* -**1.** [not wide - street, passage, valley] étroit; [tight - skirt, shoe] étroit, serré; [long - nose] mince; [- face] allongé; **to grow** OR **to become ~** se rétrécir; **to have ~ shoulders** être petit de carrure, ne pas être large d'épaules. -**2.** [scant, small - advantage, budget, majority] petit, faible; [close - result] serré; **it was another ~ victory/defeat for the French side** l'équipe française l'a encore emporté de justesse/a encore perdu de peu; **we had a ~ escape** on l'a échappé belle. -**3.** [restricted - scope, field, research] restreint, limité; [strict - sense, interpretation] restreint, strict; **in the ~est sense of the word** au sens strict du mot. -**4.** [bigoted, illiberal -mind, attitude] borné, étroit; [- person] borné. -**5.** *fml* [detailed - search] minutieux, détaillé; **we were subjected to ~ scrutiny** nous avons été soumis à un examen minutieux. -**6.** LING [vowel] tendu; [in phonetics]: **~ transcription** transcription *f* étroite.

◇ *vt* -**1.** [make narrow - road] rétrécir; **to ~ one's eyes** plisser les yeux. -**2.** [reduce - difference, gap] réduire, restreindre; [limit - search] limiter, restreindre; **the police have ~ed their search to a few streets in central Glasgow** la police concentre ses recherches sur quelques rues du centre de Glasgow.

◇ *vi* -**1.** [become narrow - road, space] se rétrécir, se resserrer; **the old man's eyes ~ed** le vieil homme plissa les yeux. -**2.** [be reduced - difference, choice] se réduire, se limiter; [number, majority] s'amenuiser, se réduire.

◇ *n (usu pl)* [gen] passage *m* étroit; [pass] col *m*; [strait] détroit *m*.

◆ **narrow down** ◇ *vt sep* [limit - choice, search] limiter, restreindre; [reduce - majority, difference] réduire.

◇ *vi insep* [search] se limiter, se restreindre; **the choice ~ed down to just two people** il ne restait que deux personnes en lice.

narrow-band *adj* à bande étroite.

narrow boat *n* péniche *f* (étroite).

narrow gauge *n* voie *f* étroite.

◆ **narrow-gauge** *adj* [track, line] à voie étroite.

narrowly ['nærəʊlɪ] *adv* -**1.** [barely] de justesse, de peu; **he ~ avoided capture** il s'en est fallu de peu qu'il (ne) soit capturé; **she ~ escaped with her life** elle a échappé à la mort de justesse. -**2.** [closely] de près, étroitement; **he watched**

her ~ il la surveillait de près. -**3.** *fml* [strictly] de manière stricte, rigoureusement.

narrow-minded *adj* [person] étroit d'esprit, borné; [attitude, opinions] borné.

narrow-mindedness [-'maɪndɪdnɪs] *n* étroitesse *f* d'esprit.

narrowness ['nærəʊnɪs] *n* étroitesse *f*.

narrow-shouldered [-'ʃəʊldəd] *adj* petit de carrure; he's rather ~ il n'est pas très large d'épaules.

narwal, narwhal ['nɑːwəl] *n* narval *m*.

nary ['neərɪ] *adj dial* pas un seul, aucun.

NAS (*abbr of* National Academy of Sciences) *pr n académie américaine des sciences*.

NASA (*abbr of* National Aeronautics and Space Administration) ['næsə] *pr n* NASA *f*.

nasal ['neɪzl] ◇ *adj* -**1.** ANAT & LING nasal. -**2.** [voice, sound] nasillard.
◇ *n* LING nasale *f*.

nasalization [,neɪzəlaɪ'zeɪʃn] *n* nasalisation *f*.

nasalize, -ise ['neɪzəlaɪz] *vt* nasaliser.

nasally ['neɪzəlɪ] *adv* LING de manière nasale; [speak] d'une voix nasillarde.

nascent ['neɪsənt] *adj* -**1.** [in early stages] naissant; a ~ **rebellion** un début de rébellion. -**2.** CHEM naissant.

nastily ['nɑːstɪlɪ] *adv* -**1.** [unpleasantly - answer, remark] méchamment, avec méchanceté. -**2.** [seriously - burnt, bitten] gravement; **she cut herself ~ on the knife** elle s'est fait une vilaine blessure avec le couteau.

nastiness ['nɑːstɪnɪs] *n* -**1.** [of character] méchanceté *f*. -**2.** [of injury] gravité *f*. -**3.** [obscenity] obscénité *f*, indécence *f*. -**4.** [unpleasantness - of smell, taste] caractère *m* très désagréable.

nasturtium [nəs'tɜːʃəm] *n* capucine *f*.

nasty ['nɑːstɪ] (*compar* **nastier**, *superl* **nastiest**, *pl* **nasties**) ◇ *adj* -**1.** [mean, spiteful - person] mauvais, méchant; [- remark, rumour] désagréable, désobligeant; **don't be ~ to your little brother!** ne sois pas méchant avec ton petit frère!; **that was a ~ thing to do** c'était vraiment méchant de faire ça; **he's got a ~ temper** il a un sale caractère; **what a ~ man!** quel homme désagréable OR déplaisant! ❑ **that woman is a ~ piece of work!** *Br* cette femme est une vraie vipère OR peste! -**2.** [unpleasant - smell, taste] mauvais, désagréable; [- impression, surprise] désagréable, déplaisant; [- weather, job] sale; **it was a very ~ moment!** on a passé un mauvais moment!; **things started to turn ~** la situation a pris une vilaine tournure ‖ [in child language - dragon, giant, wolf] vilain, méchant. -**3.** [ugly, in bad taste] vilain, laid; ~ **plastic flowers** d'horribles fleurs artificielles ❑ **everything they sell is cheap and ~** ils ne vendent que de la pacotille. -**4.** [serious - sprain, burn, disease] grave; **she had a ~ accident** elle a eu un grave accident. -**5.** [dangerous - bend, junction] dangereux. -**6.** [difficult - problem, question] difficile, épineux. -**7.** [book, film, scene - violent] violent, dur; [- obscene] obscène, indécent.
◇ *n* -**1.** [person] méchant *m*, -e *f*. -**2.** *inf* [obscene film] film *m* pornographique; [violent film] film *m* violent.

NAS/UWT (*abbr of* National Association of Schoolmasters/Union of Women Teachers) *pr n syndicat d'enseignants et de chefs d'établissement en Grande-Bretagne*.

natal ['neɪtl] *adj* natal.

Natal [nə'tæl] *pr n* Natal *m*; in ~ au Natal.

natality [neɪ'tælətɪ] (*pl* **natalities**) *n* (taux *m* de) natalité *f*.

natch *inf* [nætʃ] *adv* bien sûr, bien entendu.

Nathan ['neɪθən] *pr n* Nathan.

nation ['neɪʃn] *n* -**1.** [country] pays *m*, nation *f*; **the British ~** la nation britannique; **a ~ of shopkeepers** un pays de petits commerçants. -**2.** [people] nation *f*; **to go to the ~** *Br* POL s'en remettre à l'électorat *m*.

national ['næʃənl] ◇ *adj* national; **the ~ newspapers** la presse nationale; **he became a ~ hero** il est devenu un héros national; **the killings caused a ~ outcry** les assassinats ont scandalisé le pays; **on a ~ scale** à l'échelon national; **it's not in the ~ interest** ce n'est pas dans l'intérêt du pays ❑ **the National Council for Civil Liberties** *en Grande-Bretagne, ligue de défense des droits du citoyen luttant contre toute forme de discrimination*; **National Heritage Minister** ≃ ministre *m* de la Culture.
◇ *n* -**1.** [person] ressortissant *m*, -e *f*; **all EC ~s** tous les ressortissants des pays de la CEE. -**2.** [newspaper] journal *m* national.

national anthem *n* hymne *m* national.

national assistance *n Br dated* assistance *f* publique *dated*, ≃ allocations *fpl* de garantie de ressources.

national code *n Austr* football *m* australien.

National Convention *n Am* POL *grande réunion du parti démocrate ou républicain pour choisir le «ticket» (candidats à la présidence et à la vice-présidence)*.

national debt *n*: **the ~** la dette publique.

National Enterprise Board *pr n Br* ≃ Agence *f* nationale pour le développement industriel.

National Front *pr n* Front *m* national.

national government *n* gouvernement *m* de coalition.

national grid *n* -**1.** *Br* ELEC réseau *m* national d'électricité. -**2.** GEOG réseau *m*.

National Guard *pr n* [in the US] Garde *f* nationale *(armée nationale américaine composée de volontaires)*.

National Guardsman *n* membre *m* de la Garde nationale.

National Health Service, National Health *inf pr n système créé en 1946 en Grande-Bretagne et financé par l'État, assurant la gratuité des soins et des services médicaux*, ≃ Sécurité *f* sociale; ~ **glasses** *Br modèle de lunettes remboursé par la Sécurité sociale*.

national hunt *n*: ~ **(racing)** courses *fpl* d'obstacles.

national income *n* revenu *m* national.

national insurance *n Br système britannique de sécurité sociale (maladie, retraite) et d'assurance chômage*; ~ **contributions** cotisations *fpl* à la Sécurité sociale.

nationalism ['næʃnəlɪzm] *n* nationalisme *m*.

nationalist ['næʃnəlɪst] ◇ *adj* nationaliste.
◇ *n* nationaliste *mf*.

nationalistic [,næʃnə'lɪstɪk] *adj* nationaliste.

nationality [,næʃə'nælətɪ] (*pl* **nationalities**) *n* nationalité *f*.

nationalization [,næʃnəlaɪ'zeɪʃn] *n* nationalisation *f*.

nationalize, -ise ['næʃnəlaɪz] *vt* nationaliser.

National League *pr n l'une des deux ligues professionnelles de base-ball aux États-Unis*.

nationally ['næʃnəlɪ] *adv* nationalement; ~ **famous** connu dans OR à travers tout le pays.

national park *n* parc *m* national.

National Savings Bank *pr n* ≃ Caisse *f* nationale d'épargne.

national service *n Br* service *m* militaire.

national serviceman *n Br* appelé *m*, militaire *m* du contingent.

national socialism *n* national-socialisme *m*.

national socialist ◇ *adj* national-socialiste.
◇ *n* national-socialiste *mf*.

National Trust *pr n*: **the ~** *organisme non gouvernemental britannique assurant la conservation de certains paysages et monuments historiques*; ~ **property** ≃ site *m* protégé.

nationhood ['neɪʃənhʊd] *n* statut *m* de nation; **to attain ~** être reconnu en tant que nation.

nation-state *n* État-nation *m*.

nationwide ['neɪʃənwaɪd] ◇ *adj* national, à travers tout le pays; **a ~ strike** une grève nationale.
◇ *adv* à l'échelle nationale, dans tout le pays; **the speech was broadcast ~** le discours a été diffusé dans tout le pays.

native ['neɪtɪv] ◇ *n* -**1.** [of country] natif *m*, -ive *f*, autochtone *mf*; [of town] natif *m*, -ive *f*; **I'm a ~ of Portland** je suis originaire de Portland, je suis né à Portland; **she's a ~ of Belgium** elle est belge de naissance, elle est née en Belgique; **she speaks English like a ~** elle parle anglais comme si c'était sa langue maternelle OR comme les Anglais. -**2.** *pej* [primitive] indigène *m*. -**3.** BOT [plant] plante *f* indigène; ZOOL [animal] animal *m* indigène; [species] espèce *f* indigène.
◇ *adj* -**1.** [by birth] natif; ~ **Indians** Indiens *mpl* de naissance OR de souche; **Portland honours its ~ sons** Portland rend hommage à ses enfants ‖ [of birth - country] natal; [- language] maternel; ~ **land** pays *m* natal; **our ~ soil** OR **clay** notre sol *m* natif; **he always writes in his ~ Russian** il écrit toujours en russe, sa langue maternelle. -**2.** [indigenous - resources] du pays; [- tribe, customs] indigène; [- costume] du pays, national; **to go ~** adopter les us et coutumes locaux. -**3.** [innate - ability, attraction] inné, naturel. -**4.** BOT & ZOOL indigène, originaire; ~ **to India** originaire de l'Inde. -**5.** MINER [ore, silver] natif.

Native American *n* Indien *m*, -enne *f* d'Amérique, Amérindien *m*, -enne *f*.

native speaker *n* LING locuteur *m* natif, locutrice *f* native; **a ~ of Polish, a Polish ~** une personne de langue maternelle polonaise; **a ~ of French/German, a French/German ~** un francophone/germanophone, une personne de langue maternelle française/allemande.

nativity [nə'tɪvətɪ] (*pl* **nativities**) *n* -**1.** RELIG: **the Nativity** la Nativité. -**2.** [birth] horoscope *m*.

Nativity play *n pièce jouée par des enfants et représentant l'histoire de la Nativité*.

NATO ['neɪtəʊ] (*abbr of* North Atlantic Treaty Organization) *pr n* l'OTAN *f*.

natron ['neɪtrən] *n* natron *m*.

natter *inf* ['nætəʳ] ◇ *vi Br* papoter.
◇ *n* papotage *m*; **to have a ~** tailler une bavette, faire la causette OR un brin de causette.

natterer *inf* ['nætərəʳ] *n Br* bavard *m*, -e *f*; **what a ~!** quel moulin à paroles!

natterjack ['nætədʒæk] *n*: ~ **(toad)** crapaud *m* des roseaux, calamite *m*.

nattily ['nætɪlɪ] *adv*: ~ **dressed** sur son trente-et-un.

natty *inf* ['nætɪ] (*compar* **nattier**, *superl* **nattiest**) *adj* -**1.** [smart - person] bien sapé; [- dress] chic, qui a de l'allure; **he's a ~ dresser** il est toujours très bien sapé. -**2.** [clever - device] astucieux.

natural ['nætʃrəl] ◇ *adj* -**1.** [created by nature - scenery, resources] naturel; [wild - prairie, woodland] à l'état naturel, sauvage; **a ~ harbour** un port naturel; **in a ~ state** nature, à l'état naturel. -**2.** [not artificial - wood, finish] naturel; **she's a ~ redhead** ses cheveux sont naturellement roux. -**3.** [normal - explanation, reaction, wish] naturel, normal; **it's only ~ for her to be worried** OR **that she should be worried** il est tout à fait normal OR il est tout naturel qu'elle se fasse du souci; **death from ~ causes** mort *f* naturelle; **in the ~ course of events** dans le cours normal des choses. -**4.** [unaffected - person, manner] naturel, simple. -**5.** [innate - talent] inné, naturel; **she's a ~ organizer** c'est une organisatrice née, elle a un sens inné de l'organisation. -**6.** [free of additives] naturel; ~ **yoghurt** yaourt *m* nature. -**7.** [child] naturel. -**8.** [real - parents] naturel. -**9.** MUS naturel; [after accidental] bécarre *(inv)*; **G ~** sol bécarre. -**10.** MATH naturel. -**11.** ~ **wastage** *diminution du nombre d'employés qui consiste à ne pas remplacer ceux qui s'en vont*; ~ **person** JUR personne *f* physique OR naturelle.
◇ *adv inf*: **try to act ~!** soyez naturel!
◇ *n* -**1.** *inf* [gifted person]: **she's a ~** elle a ça dans le sang; **he's a ~ for the job** il est tout indiqué pour (faire) ce boulot; **he's a ~ for the part of Banquo** le rôle de Banquo lui irait comme un gant. -**2.** MUS bécarre *m*.

natural childbirth *n* accouchement *m* naturel.

natural gas *n* gaz *m* naturel.

natural history *n* histoire *f* naturelle.

naturalism ['nætʃrəlɪzm] *n* naturalisme *m*.

naturalist ['nætʃrəlɪst] *n* naturaliste *mf*.

naturalistic [ˌnætʃrə'lɪstɪk] *adj* naturaliste.

naturalization [ˌnætʃərəlaɪ'zeɪʃn] *n* naturalisation *f*.

naturalize, -ise ['nætʃrəlaɪz] ◇ *vt* [person, expression, custom] naturaliser; [plant, animal] acclimater.
◇ *vi* BIOL s'acclimater.

natural justice *n* droits *mpl* naturels.

natural language *n* langage *m* naturel, langue *f* naturelle.

natural law *n* loi *f* naturelle.

natural logarithm *n* logarithme *m* naturel OR népérien.

naturally ['nætʃrəlɪ] *adv* -**1.** [of course] naturellement, bien sûr, bien entendu; you have got the money? – ~! tu as l'argent? – cela va de soi!; I was ~ surprised évidemment, cela m'a surpris. -**2.** [by nature - lazy] de nature, par tempérament; [- difficult] naturellement, par sa nature; skiing comes ~ to her on dirait qu'elle a fait du ski toute sa vie. -**3.** [unaffectedly] naturellement, de manière naturelle; you answered very ~ vous avez répondu très naturellement OR de manière très naturelle. -**4.** [in natural state - occur] naturellement, à l'état naturel.

naturalness ['nætʃrəlnɪs] *n* -**1.** [unaffectedness] naturel *m*, simplicité *f*; he behaved with great ~ il s'est comporté avec beaucoup de naturel; his acting was impressive for its ~ le naturel de cet acteur était remarquable. -**2.** [natural appearance] naturel *m*.

natural number *n* nombre *m* naturel.

natural science *n* -**1.** *(U)* sciences *fpl* naturelles. -**2.** *(C)* botany is a ~ la botanique fait partie des sciences naturelles.

natural selection *n* sélection *f* naturelle.

nature ['neɪtʃə^r] *n* -**1.** nature *f*; Nature can be cruel la nature peut être cruelle; the wildest landscapes in ~ les paysages les plus sauvages que la nature puisse offrir; to go back OR to return to ~ retourner à la nature; the ~-nurture debate le débat sur l'inné et l'acquis; to let ~ take its course laisser faire la nature. -**2.** [character] nature *f*, caractère *m*; he has such a kind ~ il a une si bonne nature OR un si bon caractère; it's not in her ~ to struggle ce n'est pas dans sa nature de lutter; lazy by ~ paresseux de nature; to appeal to sb's better ~ faire appel aux bons sentiments de qqn; it's in the ~ of volcanoes to erupt il est dans la nature des volcans d'entrer en éruption; human beings are by ~ gregarious l'homme est, par nature, un être grégaire; war is by its very ~ destructive la guerre est destructrice par nature; in the ~ of things dans la nature des choses. -**3.** [type] nature *f*, type *m*, genre *m*; questions of a troublesome ~ des questions difficiles à résoudre; do you sell chocolates or anything of that ~? est-ce que vous vendez des chocolats ou ce genre de choses?
◆ **in the nature of** *prep phr* en guise de, à titre de.

nature cure *n* naturopathie *f*, naturothérapie *f*; to go on a ~ suivre une naturothérapie.

-natured ['neɪtʃəd] *in cpds* d'une nature..., d'un caractère...; she's good/ill~ elle a bon/mauvais caractère; gentle~ d'une nature douce.

nature lover *n* amoureux *m*, -euse *f* de la nature.

nature-loving *adj* qui adore la nature.

nature reserve *n* réserve *f* naturelle.

nature study *n* SCH sciences *fpl* naturelles, histoire *f* naturelle.

nature trail *n* sentier *m* (de découverte de la) nature.

naturism ['neɪtʃərɪzm] *n* naturisme *m*.

naturist ['neɪtʃərɪst] ◇ *adj* naturiste.
◇ *n* naturiste *mf*.

naturopathy [ˌneɪtʃə'rɒpəθɪ] *n* naturothérapie *f*, naturopathie *f*.

naught [nɔːt] ◇ *n* -**1.** = **nought 1.** -**2.** *arch* OR *lit* [nothing]: their plans came to ~ leurs projets ont échoué OR n'ont pas abouti; they set my ideas at ~ ils ne font aucun cas OR ils ne tiennent aucun compte de mes idées.
◇ *adv arch* OR *lit* nullement; it matters ~ cela n'a aucune importance; it serves you ~ cela ne vous sert nullement.

naughtily ['nɔːtɪlɪ] *adv* -**1.** [mischievously] avec malice, malicieusement; you have behaved very ~ tu as été très vilain. -**2.** [suggestively] avec grivoiserie.

naughtiness ['nɔːtɪnɪs] *n* -**1.** [disobedience] désobéissance *f*; [mischievousness] malice *f*; she will be punished for her ~ elle sera punie pour avoir désobéi. -**2.** [indecency] grivoiserie *f*, gaillardise *f*.

naughty ['nɔːtɪ] (*compar* naughtier, *superl* naughtiest) *adj* -**1.** [badly behaved - child] méchant, désobéissant, vilain; that was very ~ of you ce que tu as fait était très vilain; you ~ boy! petit vilain! || [mischievous] coquin, malicieux. -**2.** [indecent - postcard] grivois, paillard, osé; [- joke, story] osé, paillard, polisson; [- word] vilain, gros. -**3.** [sexy] sexy *(inv)*; ~ underwear dessous *mpl* sexy.

nausea ['nɔːsjə] *n* nausée *f*.

nauseate ['nɔːsɪeɪt] *vt literal* & *fig* donner la nausée à, écœurer; the sight of blood ~d him en voyant le sang, il eut un haut-le-cœur.

nauseating ['nɔːsɪeɪtɪŋ] *adj* [food, sight, idea] écœurant, qui donne la nausée; [smell] écœurant, nauséabond; [person, behaviour] écœurant, dégoûtant, répugnant; the stench was ~ la puanteur vous levait OR soulevait le cœur.

nauseatingly ['nɔːsɪeɪtɪŋlɪ] *adv* à vous donner la nausée, à vous écœurer; she was ~ smug elle prenait des airs écœurants de supériorité, elle était d'une supériorité écœurante.

nauseous [*Br* 'nɔːsjəs, *Am* 'nɔːʃəs] *adj* -**1.** [revolting - smell] nauséabond, qui donne la nausée, écœurant. -**2.** [unwell - person] écœuré; it made me feel ~ cela m'a levé OR soulevé le cœur. -**3.** *inf Am* [disgusting] dégueulasse.

Nausicaa [nɔː'sɪkɪə] *pr n* Nausicaa.

nautical ['nɔːtɪkl] *adj* nautique.

nautical mile *n* mille *m* marin.

nautilus ['nɔːtɪləs] *n* ZOOL nautile *m*.

navaid ['næveɪd] *n* radioguidage *m*, aide *f* à la navigation.

Navajo ['nævəhəʊ] (*pl inv* OR Navajos OR Navajoes) ◇ *n* -**1.** [person] Navajo *mf*; the ~ les Navajos. -**2.** LING navajo *m*.
◇ *adj* navajo.

naval ['neɪvl] *adj* [gen] naval; [power] maritime; ~ base base *f* navale; ~ forces forces *fpl* navales; ~ officer officier *m* de marine.

naval architect *n* architecte *m* naval, architecte *f* navale; [for warships] ingénieur *m* du génie maritime OR en construction navale.

naval architecture *n* construction *f* navale.

Navarre [nə'vɑː^r] *pr n* Navarre *f*.

nave [neɪv] *n* -**1.** [of church] nef *f*. -**2.** [hub] moyeu *m*.

navel ['neɪvl] *n* nombril *m*.

navel orange *n* navel *f*.

navigable ['nævɪgəbl] *adj* [water] navigable; [craft] dirigeable.

navigate ['nævɪgeɪt] ◇ *vt* -**1.** [chart course of - ship] calculer le parcours de; [- car, aircraft] être le navigateur de; she ~d us successfully through Bombay elle nous a fait traverser Bombay sans problèmes; he ~d the plane to the nearest airport il dirigea l'avion sur l'aéroport le plus proche. -**2.** [sail]: to ~ the Atlantic traverser l'Atlantique (en bateau); they ~d the seven seas ils naviguaient sur OR parcouraient toutes les mers du globe. -**3.** *fig*: the stairs are difficult to ~ in the dark cet escalier est difficile à monter/descendre dans l'obscurité; she ~d her way across the crowded room elle se fraya un chemin à travers la salle bondée.
◇ *vi* naviguer; to ~ by the stars naviguer aux étoiles || [in car]: can you ~ for me? peux-tu m'indiquer la route OR me piloter?

navigation [ˌnævɪ'geɪʃn] *n* -**1.** [act, skill of navigating] navigation *f*. -**2.** *Am* [shipping] navigation *f*, trafic *m* (maritime).

navigational [ˌnævɪ'geɪʃnl] *adj* de (la) navigation.

navigation lights *npl* AERON feux *mpl* de position; NAUT fanaux *mpl*, feux *mpl* de bord OR de route.

navigator ['nævɪgeɪtə^r] *n* navigateur *m*, -trice *f*.

navvy *inf* ['nævɪ] (*pl* navvies) *n Br* terrassier *m*.

navy ['neɪvɪ] (*pl* navies) ◇ *n* -**1.** [service] marine *f* (nationale); to be OR to serve in the ~ être dans la marine. -**2.** [warships collectively] marine *f* de guerre; [fleet] flotte *f*. -**3.** = **navy blue**.
◇ *adj* -**1.** de la marine. -**2.** = **navy-blue**.

navy blue *n* bleu *m* marine.
◆ **navy-blue** *adj* bleu marine *(inv)*.

Navy Cut® *n Br* tabac *m* haché fin.

Navy List *Br*, **Navy Register** *Am n* ≃ liste navale.

navy yard *n* arsenal *m* maritime.

nawab [nə'wɑːb] *n* nabab *m*.

nay [neɪ] ◇ *adv arch* OR *hum* voire, que dis-je; I was asked, ~ ordered to come on m'a demandé, ou plutôt donné l'ordre, de venir; for a few dollars, ~ a few cents pour quelques dollars, voire quelques cents.
◇ *n* vote *m* négatif; the ~s have it les non l'emportent.
◇ *interj* [in oral vote] non.

Nazarene [ˌnæzə'riːn] ◇ *n* Nazaréen *m*, -enne *f*.
◇ *adj* nazaréen.

Nazareth ['næzərəθ] *pr n* Nazareth.

Nazi ['nɑːtsɪ] ◇ *adj* nazi.
◇ *n* nazi *m*, -e *f*.

Nazism ['nɑːtsɪzm], **Naziism** ['nɑːtsɪˌɪzm] *n* nazisme *m*.

NB -**1.** (*written abbr of* nota bene) NB. -**2.** *written abbr of* New Brunswick.

NBA *pr n* -**1.** (*abbr of* National Basketball Association) *fédération américaine de basket-ball*. -**2.** (*abbr of* National Boxing Association) *fédération américaine de boxe*.

NBC ◇ *pr n* (*abbr of* National Broadcasting Company) *chaîne de télévision américaine*.
◇ *adj* (*abbr of* nuclear, biological and chemical) NBC.

nbg *inf* (*abbr of* no bloody good) *adj Br* nul.

NBS (*abbr of* National Bureau of Standards) *pr n service américain des poids et mesures*.

NC -**1.** *written abbr of* no charge. -**2.** *written abbr of* North Carolina.

NCB (*abbr of* National Coal Board) *pr n ancien nom des charbonnages britanniques*.

NCC (*abbr of* Nature Conservancy Council) *pr n organisme britannique de protection de la nature*.

NCCL *pr n abbr of* National Council for Civil Liberties.

NCO (*abbr of* non-commissioned officer) *n* sous-officier *m*.

NCU (*abbr of* National Communication Union) *pr n syndicat des salariés qui travaillent dans les télécommunications*.

ND *written abbr of* North Dakota.

N'Djamena [əndʒɑː'meɪnə] *pr n* N'Djamena.

NE -**1.** *written abbr of* Nebraska. -**2.** *written abbr of* New England. -**3.** (*written abbr of* north-east) N-E.

Neanderthal, neanderthal [nɪ'ændətɑːl] ◇ *adj* -**1.** ANTHR néandertalien, de Neandertal. -**2.** [uncivilized] fruste, inculte, primitif. -**3.** *inf* POL réac.
◇ *n* néandertalien *m*.

Neanderthal man *n* l'homme *m* de Neandertal.

neap [niːp] ◇ *adj* faible.
◇ *n* = **neap tide**.

Neapolitan [ˌnɪəˈpɒlɪtn] ◇ *n* Napolitain *m*, -e *f*.
◇ *adj* napolitain; ~ ice cream tranche *f* napolitaine.

neap tide *n* (marée *f* de) morte-eau *f*.

near [nɪəʳ] (*compar* nearer, *superl* nearest) ◇ *prep* -**1.** [in space] près de; ~ Paris près de Paris; don't go ~ the fire ne t'approche pas du feu; is there a chemist's ~ here? est-ce qu'il y a un pharmacien près d'ici OR dans le coin?; she likes to have her family ~ her elle aime avoir sa famille près d'elle OR auprès d'elle; ~ the end of the book vers la fin du livre; I haven't been ~ a horse since the accident je n'ai pas approché un cheval depuis l'accident; you can't trust him ~ a gun il est dangereux avec une arme à feu; she wouldn't let anyone ~ her [physically] elle ne voulait pas qu'on l'approche; [emotionally] elle ne voulait être proche de personne. -**2.** [in time] près de, proche de; it's getting ~ Christmas c'est bientôt Noël; ask me ~er the time repose-moi la question quand l'heure viendra; ~ the end of the film vers la fin du film. -**3.** [similar to] près de; that would be ~er the truth ce serait plus près de la vérité; your answer was ~est the mark c'est vous qui avez donné la meilleure réponse. -**4.** [in amount or number]: profits were ~ the 30% mark les bénéfices approchaient la barre des 30 %; it took us ~er three hours to finish en fait, nous avons mis presque trois heures à finir; it will cost ~er £5,000 ça coûtera plutôt dans les 5 000 livres. -**5.** [on the point of] près de, au bord de; the country's economy is ~ ruin le pays est au bord de la faillite; to be ~ tears être au bord des larmes; it's ~ freezing il ne fait pas loin de zéro, la température avoisine zéro degré.
◇ *adv* -**1.** [in space] près, à côté, à proximité; to draw ~ s'approcher; the heat was too great for us to get ~ la chaleur était trop intense pour que l'on puisse s'approcher ❑ so ~ and yet so far! c'est dommage, si près du but! -**2.** [in time] proche, près; as the time grew OR drew ~ à mesure que le moment approchait; midnight drew ~ minuit approchait, on approchait de minuit. -**3.** [with adjective] quasi; a ~ impossible task une tâche quasi OR quasiment OR pratiquement impossible; the show went ahead with ~ tragic consequences le spectacle a continué avec des conséquences quasi tragiques. -**4.** *phr*: as ~ as makes no difference à peu de chose près, à quelque chose près; £50 or as ~ as dammit *inf* 50 livres à peu de chose près; it's ~ enough ça va comme ça; it's ~ enough 50 lbs ça pèse dans les 50 livres; it's nowhere ~ good enough c'est loin d'être suffisant; there weren't anywhere ~ enough people il y avait bien trop peu de gens.
◇ *adj* -**1.** [in space] proche; the ~ edge le bord le plus proche; our ~ neighbours nos proches voisins; I knew you were ~ je savais que vous étiez dans les environs OR parages; the ~est post office le bureau de poste le plus proche; the ~ front wheel [driving on left] la roue avant gauche; [driving on right] la roue avant droite. -**2.** [in time] proche; when the time is ~ quand le moment approchera; in the ~ future dans un proche avenir. -**3.** [virtual]: it was a ~ disaster on a frôlé la catastrophe; he found himself in ~ darkness il s'est retrouvé dans une obscurité quasi totale ❑ it was a ~ thing on l'a échappé belle, il était moins une; I caught the train, but it was a ~ thing j'ai eu mon train de justesse; I missed the train, but it was a ~ thing j'ai manqué mon train de peu; he's the ~est thing we have to a national hero il est ce que nous avons de mieux en matière de héros national. -**4.** [in amount, number]: to the ~est £10 à 10 livres près; round it up/down to the ~est 10 francs arrondissez aux 10 francs supérieurs/inférieurs. -**5.** [closely related] proche; her ~est relatives ses parents les plus proches; your ~est and dearest *hum* vos proches.
◇ *vt* [approach - place, date, event] approcher de; [- state] être au bord de; the train was ~ing the station le train approchait de la gare; he was ~ing 70 when he got married il allait sur ses 70 ans quand il s'est marié; the book is ~ing completion le livre est sur le point d'être terminé; we're ~ing the point of no return il sera bientôt trop tard pour faire marche arrière, on atteindra bientôt le point de non-retour.
◇ *vi* [subj: date, place] approcher.
◆ **near to** *prep phr* -**1.** [in space] près de; they live ~ to us ils habitent près de OR à côté de chez nous || [emotionally] proche de. -**2.** [in time] près de, proche de; it's getting ~ to Christmas Noël approche. -**3.** [in similarity] près de. -**4.** [on the point of] près de, au bord de; to be ~ to death être sur le point de mourir; to be ~ to tears être au bord des larmes; I came ~ to leaving several times j'ai failli partir plusieurs fois.

near- *in cpds*: ~perfect pratiquement OR quasi parfait; ~complete pratiquement OR quasi complet.

near beer *n* bière *f* sans alcool.

nearby [*adv* ˌnɪəˈbaɪ, *adj* ˈnɪəbaɪ] ◇ *adv* [near here] près d'ici; [near there] près de là; I live just ~ j'habite tout près d'ici; is there a station ~? est-ce qu'il y a une gare près d'ici OR à proximité?
◇ *adj*: we stopped at a ~ post office nous nous sommes arrêtés dans un bureau de poste situé non loin de là; he threw it into a ~ dustbin il l'a jeté dans une poubelle non loin de là.

Near East *pr n*: the ~ le Proche-Orient; in the ~ au Proche-Orient.

near gale *n* [on Beaufort scale] grand frais *m*.

nearly [ˈnɪəlɪ] *adv* -**1.** [almost] presque, à peu près; I'm ~ ready je suis presque prêt; we're ~ there on y est presque; he's ~ 80 il a presque 80 ans; it's ~ 8 o'clock il est presque 8 h; I ~ fell j'ai failli tomber; I very ~ didn't come j'ai bien failli ne pas venir; I can ~ reach the shelf j'arrive presque à atteindre l'étagère; she ~ went bankrupt elle a failli faire faillite; he was ~ crying OR in tears il était au bord des larmes; I'm ~ as tall as my brother je suis presque aussi grand que mon frère. -**2.** [with negative]: I didn't buy ~ enough food for everyone je suis loin d'avoir acheté assez de provisions pour tout le monde; he's not ~ as important as he likes to think il est loin d'être aussi important qu'il le croit; it's not ~ as difficult as I thought c'est bien moins difficile que je ne l'imaginais.

nearness [ˈnɪənɪs] *n* proximité *f*.

nearside [ˈnɪəsaɪd] *Br* ◇ *adj* AUT [when driving on right] (du côté) droit, du côté trottoir; [when driving on left] (du côté) gauche, du côté trottoir.
◇ *n* [when driving on right] côté *m* droit; [when driving on left] côté *m* gauche; get out on the ~ descendez côté trottoir.

nearsighted [ˌnɪəˈsaɪtɪd] *adj Am* myope.

nearsightedness [ˌnɪəˈsaɪtɪdnɪs] *n Am* myopie *f*.

neat [niːt] *adj* -**1.** [tidy - in dress] net, soigné; [- desk, room] net, bien rangé; [- garden] bien tenu OR entretenu, soigné; her clothes are always ~ ses vêtements sont toujours impeccables || [careful - work, handwriting] soigné; to do a ~ job faire un travail soigné, soigner son travail ❑ as ~ as a new pin tiré à quatre épingles. -**2.** [smart, pretty] joli; a ~ little house une gentille petite maison. -**3.** [effective - organization] net, efficace; [- system, plan] bien conçu; [- solution] élégant. -**4.** *inf Am* [great] chouette; what a ~ outfit! chouettes fringues!; that's really ~ c'est vraiment chouette, c'est super. -**5.** [undiluted - spirits] sec, sans eau. -**6.** [tax-free]: we made a ~ £100 on a fait 100 livres net.

neaten [ˈniːtn] *vt* [room, house] remettre en ordre, ranger; [garden] ranger; [clothing] arranger, ajuster; [hair] arranger, mettre en ordre; you ought to ~ (up) the place before they arrive tu devrais mettre un peu d'ordre dans la maison avant qu'ils arrivent; go and ~ your hair va te recoiffer.

'neath, neath [niːθ] *lit* = **beneath**.

neatly [ˈniːtlɪ] *adv* -**1.** [tidily] avec soin OR ordre; [carefully - write, work] avec soin, soigneusement; put the papers ~ on the desk posez les papiers soigneusement sur le bureau; to dress ~ s'habiller avec soin. -**2.** [skilfully] habilement, adroitement; to solve a problem ~ résoudre un problème avec élégance; you put that very ~ vous l'avez très bien dit OR exprimé; he ~ avoided the issue il a habilement évité le sujet; you got out of the situation very ~ vous vous en êtes magnifiquement tiré.

neatness [ˈniːtnɪs] *n* -**1.** [tidiness - of dress] soin *m*, netteté *f*; [- of room] ordre *m*; a passion for ~ la passion de l'ordre || [carefulness - of work] soin *m*; the ~ of her writing l'élégance *f* de son écriture. -**2.** [skilfulness - of phrase, solution] élégance *f*; [- of scheme] habileté *f*. -**3.** [prettiness - of figure, legs] finesse *f*.

Nebraska [nɪˈbræskə] *pr n* Nebraska *m*; in ~ dans le Nebraska.

Nebuchadnezar [ˌnebjʊkədˈnezəʳ] ◇ *n* [bottle] nabuchodonosor *m*.
◇ *pr n* Nabuchodonosor.

nebula [ˈnebjʊlə] (*pl* nebulas OR nebulae [-liː]) *n* -**1.** ASTRON nébuleuse *f*. -**2.** MED [of cornea] nébulosité *f*; [of urine] aspect *m* trouble.

nebular [ˈnebjʊləʳ] *adj* -**1.** ASTRON nébulaire. -**2.** MED [cornea] nébuleux; [urine] trouble.

nebulize, -ise [ˈnebjʊlaɪz] *vt* nébuliser.

nebulosity [ˌnebjʊˈlɒsətɪ] (*pl* nebulosities) *n* nébulosité *f*.

nebulous [ˈnebjʊləs] *adj* -**1.** [vague] vague, flou, nébuleux. -**2.** ASTRON nébulaire. -**3.** MED [of cornea] nébuleux. -**4.** *lit* [misty] brumeux.

nebulousness [ˈnebjʊləsnɪs] = **nebulosity**.

NEC (*abbr of* National Exhibition Centre) *pr n parc d'expositions près de Birmingham en Angleterre*.

necessarily [*Br* ˈnesəsrəlɪ, *esp Am* ˌnesəˈserɪlɪ] *adv* nécessairement, forcément; we don't ~ have to go rien ne nous oblige à partir, nous ne sommes pas forcés de partir; it's not ~ so pas forcément, ce n'est pas obligé.

necessary [ˈnesəsrɪ] (*pl* necessaries) ◇ *adj* -**1.** [essential] nécessaire, essentiel; [indispensable] indispensable; [compulsory] obligatoire; water is ~ to OR for life l'eau est indispensable à la vie; is this visit really ~? est-ce que cette visite est vraiment indispensable?; it is ~ for him to come il est nécessaire qu'il vienne, il faut qu'il vienne; circumstances made it ~ to delay our departure les circonstances nous ont obligés à retarder notre départ; I'll do everything ~ to make her agree je ferai tout pour qu'elle accepte; he did no more than was ~ il n'a fait que le strict nécessaire; if ~ [if forced] s'il le faut; [if need arises] le cas échéant, si besoin est; a ~ condition [gen] une condition nécessaire OR sine qua non; PHILOS une condition nécessaire; will you make the ~ arrangements? pouvez-vous prendre les dispositions nécessaires?; he took the ~ measures il a pris les mesures nécessaires OR qui s'imposaient. -**2.** [inevitable] nécessaire, inéluctable; a ~ evil un mal nécessaire; you can draw the ~ conclusion yourself vous pouvez vous-même tirer les conclusions qui s'imposent.
◇ *n* -**1.** *inf Br*: to do the ~ faire le nécessaire. -**2.** *inf Br* [cash]: have you got the ~? tu as de quoi payer?

necessitate [nɪˈsesɪteɪt] *vt* nécessiter, rendre nécessaire; family problems have ~d his resignation des problèmes familiaux l'ont obligé OR contraint à démissionner.

necessitous [nɪˈsesɪtəs] *adj fml* nécessiteux, démuni, pauvre.

necessity [nɪˈsesətɪ] (*pl* necessities) *n* -**1.** [need] nécessité *f*, besoin *m*; there is no ~ for drastic measures il n'y a pas lieu de prendre des mesures draconiennes; there's no real ~ for us to go nous n'avons pas vraiment besoin d'y aller, il n'est pas indispensable que nous y allions; the ~ for OR of keeping careful records la nécessité de prendre des notes détaillées; if the ~ should arise si le besoin se faisait sentir; in case of absolute ~ en cas de force majeure; out of OR by OR through ~ par nécessité, par la force des choses ❑ ~ has no law *prov* nécessité fait loi *prov*; ~ is the mother of invention *prov* l'invention naît de la nécessité. -**2.** *fml* [poverty] besoin *m*, nécessité *f*. -**3.** [essential] chose *f* nécessaire OR essentielle; the basic OR bare necessities of life les choses qui sont absolument essentielles OR indispensables à la vie; it's one of life's necessities c'est un élément vital. -**4.** PHILOS nécessité *f*.

◆ **of necessity** *adv phr* nécessairement.

neck [nek] ◇ *n* -**1.** ANAT cou *m*; he threw his arms round her ~ il s'est jeté à son OR il lui a sauté au cou; the cat had a collar round its ~ le chat avait un collier au cou; water was dripping down my ~ l'eau me coulait dans le cou; to get a stiff ~ attraper le torticolis ‖ *fig*: he's always breathing down my ~ il est tout le temps sur mon dos; they were up to their ~s in debt ils étaient endettés jusqu'au cou; I'm up to my ~ in trouble j'ai des ennuis par-dessus la tête; the problem is still hanging round my ~ je n'ai toujours pas résolu ce problème; to risk one's ~ risquer sa peau; I could wring her ~! *inf* je lui tordrais le cou! ❑ she'll get it in the ~ *inf Br* ça va chauffer pour son matricule; he was thrown out ~ and crop OR on his ~ *Br* il a été mis à la porte avec pertes et fracas; it's ~ or nothing *inf Br* ça passe ou ça casse; to stick one's ~ out prendre des risques. -**2.** CULIN [of lamb] collet *m*; [of beef] collier *m*. -**3.** SPORT: to win by a ~ gagner d'une encolure ❑ to be ~ and ~ être à égalité; the two candidates are ~ and ~ les deux candidats sont au coude à coude. -**4.** [narrow part or extremity - of bottle, flask] goulot *m*, col *m*; [- of pipe] tuyau *m*; [- of womb, femur] col *m*; [- of violin] manche *m*; [- of bolt, tooth] collet *m*. -**5.** GEOG [peninsula] péninsule *f*, presqu'île *f*; [strait] détroit *m*; a ~ of land une langue de terre ❑ in our ~ of the woods par chez nous. -**6.** [of dress, pullover] col *m*, encolure *f*; a low ~ un décolleté; a dress with a low ~ une robe décolletée; what ~ size OR what size ~ do you take? combien faites-vous de tour de cou? -**7.** *inf Br* [cheek] toupet *m*, culot *m*; you've got a ~! tu ne manques pas de culot!

◇ *vi inf* se bécoter, se peloter.

neckband ['nekbænd] *n* bande *f* d'encolure; a lace ~ un col en dentelle.

-necked [nekt] *in cpds* à col...; swan~ en col de cygne; a V/round~ pullover un pull en V/ras du cou; stiff~ qui a le torticolis.

neckerchief ['nekətʃɪf] *n* foulard *m*.

necking *inf* ['nekɪŋ] *n* pelotage *m*.

necklace ['neklɪs] *n* collier *m*.

neckline ['neklaɪn] *n* col *m*, encolure *f*; her dress had a low/plunging ~ elle avait une robe décolletée/très décolletée.

necktie ['nektaɪ] *n Am* cravate *f*; ~ party *inf* lynchage *m*.

necrology [ne'krɒlədʒɪ] *n* nécrologie *f*.

necromancer ['nekrəmænsəʳ] *n* nécromancien *m*, -enne *f*.

necromancy ['nekrəmænsɪ] *n* nécromancie *f*.

necrophilia [,nekrə'fɪlɪə] *n* nécrophilie *f*.

necrophiliac [,nekrə'fɪlɪæk] *n* nécrophile *mf*.

necropolis [ne'krɒpəlɪs] *n* nécropole *f*.

necrosis [ne'krəʊsɪs] (*pl* necroses [-si:z]) *n* nécrose *f*.

nectar ['nektəʳ] *n* BOT & *fig* nectar *m*.

nectarine ['nektərɪn] *n* nectarine *f*.

NEDC (*abbr of* National Economic Development Council) *pr n agence nationale britannique de développement économique supprimée en 1992*.

neddy *inf* ['nedɪ] (*pl* neddies) *n* -**1.** *Br* [donkey] baudet *m*. -**2.** *Austr* [horse] canasson *m*.

◆ **Neddy** *inf pr n surnom de la NEDC*.

née, nee [neɪ] *adj fml*: Sarah James, ~ White Sarah James née White.

need [ni:d] ◇ *vt* -**1.** [as basic requirement] avoir besoin de; have you got everything you ~? est-ce que tu as tout ce qu'il te faut?; she ~s rest elle a besoin de repos OR de se reposer; I ~ more money/time j'ai besoin de plus d'argent/de temps; you take the car, I won't be ~ing it this evening prends la voiture, je n'en aurai pas besoin ce soir; he likes to feel ~ed il aime se sentir indispensable; a lot of money is ~ed if we are to save the company il va falloir beaucoup d'argent pour empêcher l'entreprise de couler; you only ~ to ask vous n'avez qu'à demander; you don't ~ me to tell you that vous devez le savoir mieux que moi; the carpet ~s cleaning la moquette a besoin d'être nettoyée. -**2.** [would benefit from]: I ~ a drink/a shower j'ai besoin de boire quelque chose/de prendre une douche; what he ~s is a good hiding ce qu'il lui faut, c'est une bonne correction; it's just what I ~ c'est exactement ce qu'il me faut; that's all we ~! *iron* il ne nous manquait plus que ça!; who ~s money anyway? de toute façon, l'argent n'a aucune importance; your hair ~s combing vos cheveux ont besoin d'un coup de peigne; I gave the car a much-~ed wash j'ai lavé la voiture, elle en avait bien besoin; liquid nitrogen ~s careful handling OR to be handled with care l'azote liquide demande à être manié avec précaution; there are still a few points that ~ to be made il reste encore quelques questions à soulever. -**3.** [expressing obligation]: to ~ to do sthg avoir besoin de OR être obligé de faire qqch; I ~ to be home by ten il faut que je sois rentré OR je dois être rentré pour 10 h; you ~ to try harder tu vas devoir faire OR il va falloir que tu fasses un effort supplémentaire; I'll help you – you don't ~ to je vais t'aider – tu n'es pas obligé.

◇ *modal vb*: you needn't come if you don't want to vous n'avez pas besoin de OR vous n'êtes pas obligé de venir si vous n'en avez pas envie; I needn't tell you how important it is je n'ai pas besoin de vous dire OR vous savez à quel point c'est important; I needn't have bothered je me suis donné bien du mal pour rien, ce n'était pas la peine que je me donne autant de mal; the accident ~ never have happened cet accident aurait pu être évité; no-one else ~ ever know ça reste entre nous; ~ I say more? ai-je besoin d'en dire davantage OR plus?; ~ that be the case? est-ce nécessairement OR forcément le cas?

◇ *n* -**1.** [necessity] besoin *m*; I have no ~ of your sympathy je n'ai que faire de votre sympathie; I feel the ~ of some fresh air OR to get some fresh air j'ai besoin d'air; phone me if you feel the ~ for a chat appelle-moi si tu as besoin de parler; there's no ~ to adopt that tone inutile d'employer ce ton; there's no ~ to hurry rien ne presse, inutile de se presser; there's no ~ to panic OR for any panic inutile de paniquer; I'll help with the dishes – no ~, I've done them already je vais vous aider à faire la vaisselle – inutile, c'est terminé; to be in ~ of sthg avoir besoin de qqch; I'm in ~ of help j'ai besoin d'aide OR qu'on m'aide; Fred is in urgent ~ of cash Fred a un besoin urgent d'argent; the ceiling is in ~ of repair le plafond a besoin d'être réparé; should the ~ arise si cela s'avérait nécessaire, si le besoin s'en faisait sentir; your ~ is greater than mine *hum* vous en avez plus besoin que moi. -**2.** [requirement] besoin *m*; their ~s can be easily satisfied leurs besoins sont faciles à satisfaire; he saw to her every ~ il subvenait à ses moindres besoins; £1,000 should be enough for our immediate ~s 1 000 livres devraient suffire pour répondre à nos besoins immédiats; the grant is ~s-based le montant de la bourse est établi selon les besoins du demandeur. -**3.** [poverty] besoin *m*, nécessité *f*; [adversity] adversité *f*, besoin *m*; to be in ~ être dans le besoin.

◆ **if need(s) be** *adv phr* si besoin est, le cas échéant.

needful ['ni:dfʊl] ◇ *adj fml* nécessaire, requi
◇ *n inf Br* -**1.** *phr*: to do the ~ faire
nécessaire. -**2.** [money]: to find the ~ trouver
fric.

needle ['ni:dl] ◇ *n* -**1.** MED & SEW aiguille *f*; [f
record player] pointe *f* de lecture, saphir *m*; [
pine-tree] aiguille *f*; [spine - of hedgehog] p
quant *m*; it's like looking for a ~ in a haystac
c'est comme si l'on cherchait une aiguille dar
une botte de foin. -**2.** [as indicator - in compass, c
dial] aiguille *f*. -**3.** GEOL [rocky outcrop] aiguille
pic *m*. -**4.** [monument] aiguille *f*, flèche *f*. -**5.** *inf*
[aggressiveness] agressivité *f*; a bit of ~ has cre
into the match les joueurs commencent
s'énerver OR disputent le match avec plu
d'âpreté ❑ to get the ~ prendre la mouch
to give sb the ~ [tease] chambrer qqn; [anno
taper sur les nerfs de qqn.

◇ *vt* -**1.** *inf* [annoy] asticoter; [tease] chambre
he's always needling her about her weight
passe son temps à la charrier à propos de sc
poids; they ~d him into retaliating à forc
d'être asticoté, il a fini par riposter. -**2.** *A*
[drink] corser. -**3.** SEW coudre.

needlecord ['ni:dlkɔ:d] *n* velours *m* côtelé;
trousers pantalon *m* en velours côtelé.

needlecraft ['ni:dlkrɑ:ft] *n* travaux *mpl* d'a
guille.

needle match *inf n Br* match *m* âprement di
puté.

needlepoint ['ni:dlpɔɪnt] ◇ *n* [embroider
broderie *f*, tapisserie *f*; [lace] dentelle *f*
l'aiguille.

◇ *comp*: ~ lace dentelle *f* brodée.

needle-sharp *adj* [point] acéré; [eyes] de lyn
[mind] fin, perspicace.

needless ['ni:dlɪs] *adj* [unnecessary - expens
effort, fuss] superflu, inutile; [- remark] inoppo
tun, déplacé; ~ to say I won't go il va sans di
que je n'irai pas; the war was a ~ waste
lives la guerre a provoqué beaucoup de mor
inutiles.

needlessly ['ni:dlɪslɪ] *adv* inutilement.

needle-threader *n* enfile-aiguilles *m inv*.

needle valve *n* soupape *f* à pointeau.

needlewoman ['ni:dl,wʊmən] (*pl* needl
women [-,wɪmɪn]) *n* couturière *f*; she's a goo
~ elle sait manier l'aiguille, c'est une bon
couturière.

needlework ['ni:dlwɜ:k] *n (U)* travaux *m*
d'aiguille, couture *f*.

needling ['ni:dlɪŋ] *n (U)* taquineries *fpl*.

needs [ni:dz] *adv arch* OR *hum*: ~ must il le fau
c'est indispensable; if ~ must, I shall go s'il
faut absolument OR si c'est indispensable, j'ir
❑ ~ must when the devil drives *prov* nécessi
fait loi *prov*.

needs test *n Br* examen *m* des conditions de v
(pour bénéficier d'une aide de l'État).

needy ['ni:dɪ] (*compar* needier, *superl* needies
◇ *adj* [financially] nécessiteux, dans le besoi
[emotionally] en manque d'affection.

◇ *npl*: the ~ les nécessiteux *mpl*.

ne'er [neəʳ] *lit* = **never** *adv*.

ne'er-do-well *n* bon *m* à rien, bonne *f* à rie
my ~ cousins mes vauriens *mpl* de cousins.

nefarious [nɪ'feərɪəs] *adj* infâme, vil.

Nefertiti [,nefə'ti:tɪ] *pr n* Néfertiti.

negate [nɪ'geɪt] *vt* -**1.** [nullify - law] abroge
[- order] annuler; [- efforts] réduire à néan
[- argument, theory] invalider, rendre invalid
-**2.** [deny] réfuter, nier.

negation [nɪ'geɪʃn] *n* négation *f*.

negative ['negətɪv] ◇ *adj* négatif; a ~ answ
une réponse négative; she's always so ~ abo
my plans elle trouve toujours quelque chose
redire à mes projets; the result of the test w
~ le résultat de l'examen était négatif ❑
earth ELEC négatif *m*, terre *f* reliée au moins.

◇ *n* -**1.** GRAMM négation *f*; in the ~ à la form
négative. -**2.** [answer] réponse *f* négative, non
to reply in the ~ répondre négativement
par la négative. -**3.** PHOT négatif *m*. -**4.** ELEC
PHYS (pôle *m*) négatif *m*.

◇ *vt* -**1.** [cancel - instruction] annuler; [nullify - effect] neutraliser, réduire à néant. -**2.** [reject - proposition, evidence] rejeter, repousser. -**3.** [deny] nier, réfuter.

negative feedback *n* -**1.** [in electronic circuit] contre-réaction *f*, réaction *f* négative; [in mechanical or cybernetic system] feedback *m* négatif, rétroaction *f* négative. -**2.** *fig*: **we got a lot of ~ from the questionnaire** ce questionnaire a révélé de nombreuses réactions négatives.

negatively ['negətɪvlɪ] *adv* négativement; **she replied ~** sa réponse a été négative.

negative reinforcement *n* renforcement *m* négatif.

negative sign *n* signe *m* moins OR négatif.

negativism ['negətɪvɪzm] *n* négativisme *m*.

negator [nɪ'geɪtəʳ] *n* -**1.** [gen] négateur *m*, -trice *f*. -**2.** ELECTRON inverseur *m*.

neglect [nɪ'glekt] ◇ *n* -**1.** [lack of attention, care - of building, garden] abandon *m*, manque *m* de soins OR d'entretien; [- of child, invalid] manque *m* de soins OR d'attention; [- of people's demands, needs] manque *m* d'égards; **through ~** par négligence *f*; **many people fall ill through ~** bien des gens tombent malades par négligence OR par manque de précautions; **the roof fell in through ~** le toit s'est effondré faute d'entretien; **to suffer from ~** [person] souffrir d'un manque de soins; [building, garden] être laissé à l'abandon; **his ~ of his appearance** le peu d'intérêt qu'il accorde à son apparence || [bad condition - of building, garden] délabrement *m*; **to be in a state of ~** être à l'abandon; **the buildings fell into ~** les bâtiments sont tombés en ruine; **the apparatus fell into ~** on cessa d'entretenir les appareils. -**2.** [disregard - of duty, promise, rules] manquement *m*; **he was reprimanded for ~ of duty/elementary safety rules** il a été réprimandé pour avoir manqué à ses devoirs/pour ne pas avoir respecté les règles élémentaires de sécurité.

◇ *vt* -**1.** [fail to attend to, to care for - building, garden] négliger, laisser à l'abandon; [- work] négliger; [- child, invalid, friend] délaisser, négliger; **he ~s himself** OR **his appearance** il se néglige OR se laisse aller; **you shouldn't ~ your health** vous devriez vous soucier un peu plus de votre santé; **the house has been ~ed for years** la maison est à l'abandon depuis des années; **he ~ed his wife all evening** il n'a pas prêté la moindre attention à sa femme de toute la soirée; **governments have ~ed the needs of the disabled for long enough** il est temps que les gouvernements cessent d'ignorer les besoins des invalides. -**2.** [disregard - duty, promise] manquer à; **don't ~ his advice** vous auriez tout intérêt à écouter ses conseils; **they ~ elementary rules** ils ne respectent pas les règles élémentaires || [omit, overlook] omettre, oublier; **don't ~ to feed the animals** n'oubliez pas de donner à manger aux animaux; **they ~ed to lock the door when they went out** ils ont oublié de fermer la porte à clé en sortant.

neglected [nɪ'glektɪd] *adj* -**1.** [uncared for - garden] (laissé) à l'abandon, mal entretenu; [- building] (laissé) à l'abandon, délabré; [- appearance] négligé, peu soigné. -**2.** [emotionally - child, wife] délaissé, abandonné; **to feel ~** se sentir abandonné, avoir l'impression d'être délaissé.

neglectful [nɪ'glektfʊl] *adj* [person, attitude] négligent; **it's very ~ of me** c'est très négligent de ma part; **to be ~ of one's duty** négliger ses devoirs; **he's very ~ of his appearance** il ne prend aucun soin de sa tenue.

neglectfully [nɪ'glektfʊlɪ] *adv* négligemment, avec négligence.

negligee, negligée, negligé ['neglɪʒeɪ] *n* négligé *m*, déshabillé *m*.

negligence ['neglɪdʒəns] *n* -**1.** [inattention] négligence *f*; **due to** OR **through ~** par négligence || [of duties, rules] négligence *f*, manquement *m*; **~ of basic precautions can be fatal** le non-respect des précautions élémentaires peut se révéler fatal. -**2.** *Br* [nonchalance] nonchalance *f*.

negligent ['neglɪdʒənt] *adj* -**1.** [neglectful] négligent; **to be ~ of one's duties** manquer à OR négliger ses devoirs; **teenagers are often ~ of their appearance** les adolescents négligent souvent leur mise. -**2.** [nonchalant - attitude, manner] nonchalant, négligent.

negligently ['neglɪdʒəntlɪ] *adv* -**1.** [carelessly] négligemment; **he acted ~** il a fait preuve de légèreté; **they behaved ~ towards their children** ils ont négligé leurs enfants. -**2.** [nonchalantly] négligemment, nonchalamment; **she leaned ~ against the car** elle s'appuya avec nonchalance contre la voiture.

negligible ['neglɪdʒəbl] *adj* négligeable, insignifiant.

negotiable [nɪ'gəʊʃjəbl] *adj* -**1.** FIN [bonds] négociable; [price, salary] négociable, à débattre. -**2.** [road] praticable; [river - navigable] navigable; [- crossable] franchissable.

negotiate [nɪ'gəʊʃɪeɪt] ◇ *vt* -**1.** [gen & FIN] négocier. -**2.** [manoeuvre round - bend] négocier; [- rapids, obstacle] franchir; *fig* [- difficulty] franchir, surmonter.

◇ *vi* négocier; **the unions will have to ~ with the management for higher pay** il faudra que les syndicats négocient une augmentation de salaire auprès de la direction; **we should ~ instead of preparing for war** nous ferions mieux de négocier au lieu de nous préparer à la guerre.

negotiating table [nɪ'gəʊʃɪeɪtɪŋ-] *n* table *f* des négociations.

negotiation [nɪ,gəʊʃɪ'eɪʃn] *n* -**1.** [discussion] négociation *f*, pourparlers *mpl*; **to enter into ~** OR **~s with sb** entamer des négociations avec qqn; **the project is under ~** le projet est en négociation; **the pay deal is subject to ~** l'accord salarial est sujet à négociation; **your salary is a matter of ~** nous devons débattre du montant de votre salaire. -**2.** [of bend, obstacle] franchissement *m*.

negotiator [nɪ'gəʊʃɪeɪtəʳ] *n* négociateur *m*, -trice *f*.

Negress ['niːgrɪs] *n* négresse *f* *(attention: le terme «Negress», comme son équivalent français, est considéré comme raciste)*.

negritude ['negrɪtjuːd] *n* négritude *f*.

Negro ['niːgrəʊ] (*pl* Negroes) ◇ *n* nègre *m* *(attention: le terme «Negro» est considéré comme raciste, sauf dans le domaine de l'anthropologie)*.

◇ *adj* nègre.

negroid ['niːgrɔɪd] ◇ *adj* négroïde.

◇ *n* négroïde *mf*.

Negro spiritual *n* négro-spiritual *m*, spiritual *m*.

Nehemiah [,niːɪ'maɪə] *pr n* Néhémie.

neigh [neɪ] ◇ *vi* hennir.

◇ *n* hennissement *m*.

neighbor *etc Am* = **neighbour**.

neighbour *Br*, **neighbor** *Am* ['neɪbəʳ]

◇ *n* -**1.** voisin *m*, -e *f*; **what will the ~s say?** que vont dire les voisins?; **Britain's nearest ~ is France** la France est le plus proche voisin de la Grande-Bretagne. -**2.** RELIG [fellow man] prochain *m*, -e *f*.

◇ *comp*: **~ states** pays *mpl* voisins.

◇ *vt Am* avoisiner; **their farm ~s mine** nos fermes sont voisines.

◆ **neighbour on** *vt insep* [adjoin] avoisiner, être contigu à.

◆ **neighbor with** *vt insep Am* vivre en bon voisinage avec, entretenir des relations de bon voisinage avec.

neighbourhood *Br*, **neighborhood** *Am* ['neɪbəhʊd] ◇ *n* -**1.** [district] voisinage *m*, quartier *m*; **you can get mugged in this ~** ce quartier n'est pas très sûr; **the whole ~'s talking about it** tout le quartier en parle; **they live in the ~ of the station** ils habitent tout près de la gare; **there's some nice scenery in the ~** il y a de jolis paysages dans les environs. -**2.** *fig*: **it'll cost you in the ~ of $1,000** cela vous coûtera dans les OR environ 1 000 dollars.

◇ *comp* [police, shop, school] du quartier.

Neighbourhood Watch *n système par lequel les habitants d'un quartier s'entraident pour en assurer la surveillance et la sécurité*.

neighbouring *Br*, **neighboring** *Am* ['neɪbərɪŋ] *adj* avoisinant, voisin.

neighbourliness *Br*, **neighborliness** *Am* ['neɪbəlɪnɪs] *n* (bons) rapports *mpl* de voisinage, sociabilité *f*, amabilité *f*.

neighbourly *Br*, **neighborly** *Am* ['neɪbəlɪ] *adj* amical, de bon voisin; **to pay someone a ~ visit** rendre une visite de bon voisinage à qqn; **to be ~** être bon voisin, entretenir de bonnes relations avec ses voisins.

neither [*Br* 'naɪðəʳ, *esp Am* 'niːðəʳ] ◇ *pron*: **~ of us** aucun de nous (deux); **~ (of them) eats fish** aucun des deux OR ni l'un ni l'autre ne mange de poisson; **which do you prefer? — ~!** lequel des deux préfères-tu? — ni l'un ni l'autre!

◇ *conj*: **~... nor...** ni... ni...; **it's ~ good nor bad** ce n'est ni bon ni mauvais; **I like ~ tea nor coffee** je n'aime ni le thé ni le café ❑ **that's ~ here nor there** [unimportant] c'est sans importance; [irrelevant] là n'est pas la question; **I ~ know nor care** c'est vraiment le cadet de mes soucis.

◇ *adv* non plus; **I don't like coffee, and ~ does my wife** je n'aime pas le café, (et) ma femme non plus; **Peter can't swim and ~ can I** Peter ne sait pas nager, (et) moi non plus; **~ did/do/were we** (et) nous non plus; **me ~!** *inf* moi non plus!

◇ *det* aucun (des deux), ni l'un ni l'autre; **~ bottle is big enough** aucune des deux bouteilles n'est assez grande; **~ one of them has accepted** ni l'un ni l'autre n'a accepté.

nekton ['nektɒn] *n* necton *m*.

nelly ['nelɪ] *n Br phr*: **not on your ~!** *inf* tu peux courir!

nelson ['nelsn] *n* [in wrestling] double clé *f*; **full ~** nelson *m*; **half ~** clé *f*.

nematode ['nemətəʊd] *n* nématode *m*.

nem con [,nem'kɒn] *adv* unanimement, à l'unanimité.

nemesia [nɪ'miːʒə] *n* némésia *m*.

nemesis ['neməsɪs] *n lit* -**1.** [retribution]: **it's ~** c'est un juste retour des choses. -**2.** [agency of retribution]: **she saw the British press as her ~** elle vit dans la presse britannique l'instrument de sa vengeance.

◆ **Nemesis** *pr n* MYTH Némésis.

neoclassical [,niːəʊ'klæsɪkl] *adj* néoclassique.

neoclassicism [,niːəʊ'klæsɪsɪzm] *n* néoclassicisme *m*.

neocolonial [,niːəʊkə'ləʊnɪəl] *adj* néocolonial.

neocolonialism [,niːəʊkə'ləʊnɪəlɪzm] *n* néocolonialisme *m*.

neocolonialist [,niːəʊkə'ləʊnɪəlɪst] ◇ *adj* néocolonialiste.

◇ *n* néocolonialiste *mf*.

neo-Darwinism [,niːəʊ'dɑːwɪnɪzm] *n* néodarwinisme *m*.

neodymium [,niːəʊ'dɪmɪəm] *n* néodyme *m*.

neofascism [,niːəʊ'fæʃɪzm] *n* néofascisme *m*.

neofascist [,niːəʊ'fæʃɪst] ◇ *adj* néofasciste.

◇ *n* néofasciste *mf*.

Neogene ['niːəʊdʒiːn] ◇ *adj* néogène.

◇ *n* néogène *m*.

Neo-Latin [,niːəʊ'lætɪn] ◇ *n* latin *m* scientifique.

◇ *adj* -**1.** [New Latin] du latin scientifique. -**2.** [Romance] néo-latin.

neolith ['niːəlɪθ] *n* (objet *m* de) pierre *f* polie.

neolithic, Neolithic [,niːə'lɪθɪk] ◇ *adj* néolithique.

◇ *n* néolithique *m*.

neologism [niː'ɒlədʒɪzm] *n* néologisme *m*.

neologistic [niː,ɒlə'dʒɪstɪk] *adj* néologique.

neology [niː'ɒlədʒɪ] (*pl* neologies) = **neologism**.

neomycin [,niːəʊ'maɪsɪn] *n* néomycine *f*.

neon ['niːɒn] ◇ *n* néon *m*.

◇ *comp* [lamp, lighting] au néon; **~ sign** enseigne *f* lumineuse (au néon).

neonatal [ˌniːəʊ'neɪtl] *adj* néonatal.
neonate ['niːəʊneɪt] *n* nouveau-né *m*.
neo-Nazi [ˌniːəʊ'nɑːtsɪ] ◇ *n* néonazi *m*, -e *f*.
◇ *adj* néonazi.
neophyte ['niːəfaɪt] *n* néophyte *mf*.
neoplasm ['niːəʊˌplæzm] *n* néoplasme *m*.
Neoplatonic [ˌniːəʊplə'tɒnɪk] *adj* néoplatonicien.
Neoplatonism [ˌniːəʊ'pleɪtənɪzm] *n* néoplatonisme *m*.
neorealism [ˌniːəʊ'riːəlɪzm] *n* CIN néoréalisme *m*.
Neozoic [ˌniːəʊ'zəʊɪk] ◇ *adj* néozoïque.
◇ *n* néozoïque *m*.
Nepal [nɪ'pɔːl] *pr n* Népal *m*; in ~ au Népal.
Nepalese [ˌnepə'liːz] (*pl inv*) ◇ *n* Népalais *m*, -e *f*.
◇ *adj* népalais.
Nepali [nɪ'pɔːlɪ] (*pl inv* OR **Nepalis**) ◇ *n* -**1.** [person] Népalais *m*, -e *f*. -**2.** HIST népalais *m*.
◇ *adj* népalais.
neper ['niːpəʳ] *n* néper *m*.
nephew ['nefjuː] *n* neveu *m*.
nephralgia [nɪ'frældʒə] *n* (*U*) néphralgie *f*.
nephrectomy [nɪ'frektəmɪ] (*pl* **nephrectomies**) *n* néphrectomie *f*.
nephritic [nɪ'frɪtɪk] *adj* néphrétique.
nephritis [nɪ'fraɪtɪs] *n* (*U*) néphrite *f*.
nepotism ['nepətɪzm] *n* népotisme *m*.
Neptune ['neptjuːn] *pr n* ASTRON & MYTH Neptune.
neptunium [nep'tjuːnɪəm] *n* neptunium *m*.
nerd *inf* [nɜːd] *n* crétin *m*.
Nereid ['nɪərɪɪd] (*pl* **Nereides** [nə'riːədiːz])
◇ *pr n* ASTRON Néréide.
◇ *n* MYTH Néréide *f*.
Nero ['nɪərəʊ] *pr n* Néron.
nerve [nɜːv] ◇ *n* -**1.** ANAT nerf *m*; **to touch a raw** ~ *fig* toucher une corde sensible. -**2.** [courage] courage *m*; [boldness] audace *f*; [self-control] assurance *f*, sang-froid *m*; **it takes** ~ **to say no to him** il faut du courage OR il faut avoir les nerfs solides pour lui dire non; **he didn't have the** ~ **to say no** il n'a pas osé dire non, il n'a pas eu le courage de dire non; **to get up enough** ~ **to jump** trouver le courage de sauter; **his** ~ **failed him, he lost his** ~ [backed down] le courage lui a manqué; [panicked] il a perdu son sang-froid. -**3.** [cheek, audacity] culot *m*; **he had the** ~ **to refuse** il a eu le culot de refuser; **you've got a** ~ **coming here!** *inf* tu es gonflé de venir ici!; **what a** ~! *inf* quel culot OR toupet! -**4.** [vein - in leaf, marble] veine *f*, nervure *f*.
◇ *vt fml*: **to** ~ **sb to do sthg** encourager OR inciter qqn à faire qqch; **he has to** ~ **himself to jump** il faut qu'il s'arme de courage pour sauter.
◆ **nerves** *npl* -**1.** [agitated state] nerfs *mpl*; [anxiety] nervosité *f*; [before concert, exam, interview] trac *m*; **to have a fit of** ~**s** avoir le trac; **to be in a state of** ~**s** être sur les nerfs; **I'm a bundle of** ~**s** je suis un paquet de nerfs; **I need a drink to steady my** ~**s** il faut que je boive un verre pour me calmer. -**2.** [self-control] nerfs *mpl*; **to have strong** ~**s/**~**s of steel** avoir les nerfs solides/des nerfs d'acier ❑ **he gets on my** ~**s** *inf* il me tape sur les nerfs OR sur le système.
nerve cell *n* cellule *f* nerveuse.
nerve centre *n* -**1.** ANAT centre *m* nerveux. -**2.** *fig* [headquarters] quartier *m* général, poste *m* de commandement.
nerve ending *n* terminaison *f* nerveuse.
nerve fibre *n* fibre *f* nerveuse.
nerve gas *n* gaz *m* neurotoxique.
nerve impulse *n* influx *m* nerveux.
nerveless ['nɜːvlɪs] *adj* -**1.** [numb] engourdi, inerte; **the revolver fell from his** ~ **fingers** le revolver tomba de ses doigts inertes. -**2.** [weak] sans force, mou. -**3.** [calm] impassible, imperturbable; [fearless] intrépide.
nerve-racking *inf*, **nerve-wracking** *inf* [-ˌrækɪŋ] *adj* angoissant, stressant; **after a** ~ **wait he was shown in** après une attente qui mit ses nerfs à rude épreuve, on le fit entrer.
nervous ['nɜːvəs] *adj* -**1.** [anxious, worried] anxieux, appréhensif; [shy] timide, intimidé; [uneasy] mal à l'aise; [agitated] agité, tendu; [tense] tendu; **I'm always** ~ OR **I always feel** ~ **when he's around** je suis toujours tendu lorsqu'il est dans les parages; **don't be** ~ détendez-vous, n'ayez pas peur; **you're making me** ~ vous m'intimidez, vous me faites perdre mes moyens; **you don't need to be** ~ **on my account** vous n'avez pas besoin de vous inquiéter pour moi; **he is** ~ **of Alsatians** les bergers allemands lui font peur; **he is** ~ **of failure** il a peur de l'échec; **I'm** ~ **about speaking in public** j'ai peur OR j'appréhende de parler en public; **I'm always** ~ **before exams** j'ai toujours le trac avant un examen; **he's a** ~ **wreck** *inf* il est à bout de nerfs, il est à cran. -**2.** ANAT [strain, illness] nerveux; **the** ~ **system** le système nerveux; ~ **tension** tension *f* nerveuse.
nervous breakdown *n* dépression *f* nerveuse; **to have a** ~ avoir OR faire une dépression nerveuse.
nervously ['nɜːvəslɪ] *adv* [anxiously] anxieusement, avec inquiétude; [tensely] nerveusement.
nervousness ['nɜːvəsnɪs] *n* -**1.** [worry] anxiété *f*, inquiétude *f*; [before exam] trac *m*. -**2.** [agitation] nervosité *f*, agitation *f* (nerveuse), fébrilité *f*. -**3.** [of writing, speech] nervosité *f*.
nervy *inf* ['nɜːvɪ] (*compar* **nervier**, *superl* **nerviest**) *adj* -**1.** *Br* [tense] énervé, excité. -**2.** *Am* [cheeky] culotté.
Ness [nes] *pr n*: **loch** ~ le Loch Ness; **the loch** ~ **monster** le monstre du Loch Ness.
Nessie *inf* ['nesɪ] *pr n surnom du monstre du loch Ness.*
nest [nest] ◇ *n* -**1.** [for birds, wasps, snakes etc] nid *m*; [occupants - esp birds] nichée *f*; *fig* [den - of brigands] nid *m*, repaire *m*; [for machine guns] nid *m*; **love** ~ nid d'amour. -**2.** [set]: ~ **of tables/boxes** (série *f* OR ensemble *m* de) tables *fpl*/boîtes *fpl* gigognes.
◇ *vi* -**1.** [bird] (se) nicher, faire son nid. -**2.** [person]: **to go** ~**ing** [find nests] aller chercher des nids; [steal young] aller dénicher des oisillons; [steal eggs] aller dénicher des œufs. -**3.** [fit together] s'emboîter; **the boxes** ~ **together neatly** les cartons s'emboîtent bien (les uns dans les autres).
◇ *vt* -**1.** [animal, bird] servir de nid à. -**2.** [tables, boxes] emboîter.
nest box *n* [in henhouse] pondoir *m*; [in birdhouse] nichoir *m*.
nest egg *n* économies *fpl*, bas *m* de laine, pécule *m*; **I've got a nice little** ~ **put by for when I retire** j'ai mis de côté un bon petit pécule en prévision de ma retraite.
nesting ['nestɪŋ] ◇ *n* nidification *f*.
◇ *comp* [bird] nicheur; [time, instinct] de (la) nidification.
nesting box = **nest box**.
nestle ['nesl] ◇ *vi* -**1.** [against person] se blottir; **she** ~**d (up) against me** elle s'est blottie contre moi ‖ [in comfortable place] se pelotonner; **to** ~ **down in bed/on the sofa** se pelotonner dans son lit/sur le canapé. -**2.** [land, house] être niché OR blotti; **their house** ~**s among the pines** leur maison est tapie OR blottie au milieu des sapins.
◇ *vt* blottir.
nestling ['neslɪŋ] *n* oisillon *m*.
Nestor ['nestɔːʳ] *pr n* Nestor.
net [net] (*pt* & *pp* **netted**, *cont* **netting**)
◇ *n* -**1.** [gen, for fishing, butterflies etc] filet *m*; *fig* [trap] filet *m*, piège *m*; **to fall into the** ~ tomber dans le piège; **to slip through the** ~ glisser OR passer à travers les mailles du filet. -**2.** SPORT filet *m*; **to put the ball in the (back of the)** ~ FTBL marquer un but, envoyer la balle au fond des filets. -**3.** [for hair] filet *m* à cheveux, résille *f*. -**4.** TEX tulle *m*, filet *m*. -**5.** [network] réseau *m*; **radio** ~ ensemble *m* du réseau radiophonique. -**6.** [income, profit, weight] net *m*.
◇ *vt* -**1.** [catch - fish, butterfly] prendre OR attraper (au filet); [- terrorist, criminal] arrêter; **the police have netted the gang leaders** la police a mis la main sur les chefs de la bande -**2.** [acquire - prize] ramasser, gagner; [- fortune] amasser. -**3.** SPORT: **to** ~ **the ball** [in tennis] envoyer la balle dans le filet; **he netted his service** [in tennis] son service échoua dans le filet; **to** ~ **a goal** FTBL marquer un but. -**4.** [fruit tree] recouvrir de filets OR d'un filet. -**5.** [income, salary] toucher OR gagner net; [profit] rapporter net; **we netted over $10,000** nous avons réalisé un bénéfice net de plus de 10 000 dollars.
◇ *vi* FTBL: **Barnes netted from 5 yards out** Barnes a marqué un but (depuis la ligne) de 6 mètres.
◇ *adj* -**1.** [income, price, weight] net; **we made a** ~ **loss/profit of £500** nous avons enregistré une perte sèche/réalisé un bénéfice net de 500 livres; **to earn £500** ~ gagner 500 livres net. -**2.** [result] final.
netball ['netbɔːl] *n* net-ball *m (sport féminin proche du basket-ball)*.
net curtain *n* rideau *m* (de tulle OR en filet), voilage *m*.
net domestic product *n* produit *m* intérieur net.
nether ['neðəʳ] *adj arch* OR *lit* bas, inférieur; [lip] inférieur; **the** ~ **regions** OR **world** *fig* l'enfer *m*; **the ball hit him in the** ~ **regions** *hum* le ballon l'a atteint dans les parties basses.
Netherlander ['neðəlændəʳ] *n* Néerlandais *m*, -e *f*.
Netherlands ['neðələndz] *pl pr n*: **the** ~ les Pays-Bas *mpl*; **in the** ~ aux Pays-Bas.
nethermost ['neðəməʊst] *adj lit* le plus bas OR profond.
nett [net] = **net** *n* **6**, *vt* **5**, *adj* **1**.
netting ['netɪŋ] *n* (*U*) -**1.** [for strawberries, trees] filet *m*, filets *mpl*; [fencing] treillis *m* (métallique), grillage *m*. -**2.** TEX [for curtains] tulle *m*, filet *m*. -**3.** [of fish, butterfly] prise *f* au filet.
nettle ['netl] ◇ *n* ortie *f*; **to grasp the** ~ *Br* prendre le taureau par les cornes.
◇ *vt Br* agacer, énerver.
nettled ['netld] *adj* agacé; **don't get** ~ ne t'énerve pas.
nettle rash *n* urticaire *f*.
network ['netwɜːk] ◇ *n* -**1.** [gen, ELEC & RAIL] réseau *m*; [of shops, hotels] réseau *m*, chaîne *f*; [of streets] lacis *m*; **road** ~ réseau routier. -**2.** TV [national] réseau *m*; [channel] chaîne *f*. -**3.** COMPUT réseau *m*.
◇ *vt* TV diffuser sur l'ensemble du réseau OR sur tout le territoire.
◇ *vi* -**1.** COMPUT faire partie du OR d'un réseau, être raccordé au OR à un réseau. -**2.** [make contacts] tenter d'établir un réseau de contacts professionnels.
networking ['netwɜːkɪŋ] *n* -**1.** COMPUT interconnexion *f* de réseaux. -**2.** [gen & COMM] établissement *m* d'un réseau de liens OR de contacts.
network TV *n* réseau *m* (de télévision) national.
neural ['njʊərəl] *adj* neural.
neuralgia [njʊə'rældʒə] *n* (*U*) névralgie *f*.
neurasthenia [ˌnjʊərəs'θiːnjə] *n* (*U*) neurasthénie *f*.
neurasthenic [ˌnjʊərəs'θenɪk] *adj* neurasthénique.
neuritis [njʊə'raɪtɪs] *n* (*U*) névrite *f*.
neurogenic [ˌnjʊərəʊ'dʒenɪk] *adj* neurogénique.
neuroleptic [ˌnjʊərəʊ'leptɪk] ◇ *adj* neuroleptique.
◇ *n* neuroleptique *m*.
neurolinguistic [ˌnjʊərəʊlɪŋ'gwɪstɪk] *adj* neurolinguistique.
neurolinguistics [ˌnjʊərəʊlɪŋ'gwɪstɪks] *n* (*U*) neurolinguistique *f*.
neurological [ˌnjʊərə'lɒdʒɪkl] *adj* neurologique.
neurologist [ˌnjʊə'rɒlədʒɪst] *n* neurologue *mf*.
neurology [ˌnjʊə'rɒlədʒɪ] *n* neurologie *f*.

neuroma [ˌnjʊəˈrəʊmə] (*pl* neuromas OR neuromata [-mətə]) *n* névrome *m*.

neuromuscular [ˌnjʊərəʊˈmʌskjʊləʳ] *adj* neuromusculaire.

neuron [ˈnjʊərɒn], **neurone** [ˈnjʊərəʊn] *n* neurone *m*.

neuropath [ˈnjʊərəˌpæθ] *n* névropathe *mf*.

neuropathic [ˌnjʊərəˈpæθɪk] *adj* neuropathique.

neuropathology [ˌnjʊərəʊpəˈθɒlədʒɪ] *n* neuropathologie *f*.

neuropathy [ˌnjʊəˈrɒpəθɪ] *n* neuropathie *f*.

neurophysiology [ˈnjʊərəʊˌfɪzɪˈɒlədʒɪ] *n* neurophysiologie *f*.

neuropsychiatric [ˈnjʊərəʊˌsaɪkɪˈætrɪk] *adj* neuropsychiatrique.

neuropsychiatry [ˌnjʊərəʊsaɪˈkaɪətrɪ] *n* neuropsychiatrie *f*.

neurosis [ˌnjʊəˈrəʊsɪs] (*pl* neuroses [-siːz]) *n* névrose *f*.

neurosurgeon [ˈnjʊərəʊˌsɜːdʒən] *n* neurochirurgien *m*, -enne *f*.

neurosurgery [ˌnjʊərəʊˈsɜːdʒərɪ] *n* neurochirurgie *f*.

neurosurgical [ˌnjʊərəʊˈsɜːdʒɪkl] *adj* neurochirurgical.

neurotic [ˌnjʊəˈrɒtɪk] ◇ *n* névrosé *m*, -e *f*.
◇ *adj* [person] névrosé; [disease] névrotique; **he's really ~ about his weight** *fig* il est littéralement obsédé par son poids; **don't be so ~ about it** *inf fig* tu ne vas pas en faire tout un plat OR une maladie.

neuroticism [ˌnjʊəˈrɒtɪsɪzm] *n* neurasthénie *f fig*.

neurotransmitter [ˌnjʊərəʊtrænzˈmɪtəʳ] *n* neurotransmetteur *m*.

neurovascular [ˌnjʊərəʊˈvæskjʊləʳ] *adj* neurovasculaire.

neuston [ˈnjuːstən] *n* neuston *m*.

neuter [ˈnjuːtəʳ] ◇ *adj* neutre.
◇ *n* -**1.** GRAMM neutre *m*. -**2.** [animal - asexual] animal *m* asexué; [- castrated] animal *m* châtré; [insect, plant] neutre *m*.
◇ *vt* châtrer.

neutral [ˈnjuːtrəl] ◇ *adj* neutre; [policy] de neutralité; **to remain ~** garder la neutralité, rester neutre.
◇ *n* -**1.** AUT point *m* mort; **in ~** au point mort. -**2.** POL [person] habitant *m*, -e *f* d'un pays neutre; [state] pays *m* neutre.

neutralism [ˈnjuːtrəlɪzm] *n* neutralisme *m*.

neutralist [ˈnjuːtrəlɪst] ◇ *adj* neutraliste.
◇ *n* neutraliste *mf*.

neutrality [njuːˈtrælətɪ] *n* neutralité *f*.

neutralization [ˌnjuːtrəlaɪˈzeɪʃn] *n* neutralisation *f*.

neutralize, -ise [ˈnjuːtrəlaɪz] *vt* neutraliser.

neutrino [njuːˈtriːnəʊ] (*pl* **neutrinos**) *n* neutrino *m*.

neutron [ˈnjuːtrɒn] *n* neutron *m*.

neutron bomb *n* bombe *f* à neutrons.

neutron star *n* étoile *f* à neutrons.

Nevada [nɪˈvɑːdə] *pr n* Nevada *m*; **in ~** dans le Nevada.

never [ˈnevəʳ] ◇ *adv* -**1.** [not ever] jamais; **I've ~ been there** je n'y suis jamais allé; **I ~ saw her again** je ne l'ai plus jamais OR jamais plus revue; **you ~ know** on ne sait jamais; **~ before** [until that moment] jamais auparavant OR avant OR jusque-là; [until now] jamais jusqu'ici OR jusqu'à présent; **I'll ~ ever speak to him again** plus jamais de ma vie je ne lui adresserai la parole; **~ again** jamais plus, plus jamais; **~ again!** plus jamais ça! -**2.** [used instead of 'did not']: **she ~ turned up** elle n'est pas venue; **they ~ said a word about it** ils n'en ont jamais dit mot; **I ~ knew you cared** je ne savais pas que tu m'aimais ‖ [as intensifier]: **~ a one** pas même un seul; **I ~ even asked if you wanted something to drink** je ne vous ai même pas offert (quelque chose) à boire; **he ~ so much as blinked** il n'a même pas cillé; **~ fear** ne craignez rien, n'ayez crainte ❑ **that will ~ do!** [it is unacceptable] c'est inadmissible!; [it is insufficient] ça ne va pas! -**3.** [in surprise, disbelief]: **you ~ did!** vous n'avez pas fait ça!; **you ~ asked him to dinner!** vous ne l'avez quand même pas OR tout de même pas invité à dîner!; **you've ~ lost your purse again!** ne me dis pas que tu as encore perdu ton porte-monnaie! ❑ **well I ~ (did)!** ça alors!, par exemple!; **well I ~, look who's coming!** ça alors OR par exemple, regarde qui arrive!
◇ *interj*: **~!** (ce n'est) pas possible!

never-ending *adj* interminable, qui n'en finit pas.

never-failing *adj* -**1.** [infallible] infaillible. -**2.** [enduring] inépuisable, intarissable.

nevermore [ˌnevəˈmɔːʳ] *adv lit* jamais plus, plus jamais.

never-never *inf* ◇ *n Br*: **to buy sthg on the ~** acheter qqch à crédit OR à tempérament.
◇ *adj* imaginaire, chimérique; **~ land** pays *m* de cocagne.

nevertheless [ˌnevəðəˈles] *adv* néanmoins; **a small, but ~ significant increase** une augmentation faible mais néanmoins significative; **we shall press on ~ and hope things get better** nous poursuivrons néanmoins nos efforts en espérant que les choses s'amélioreront; **she'd not skied before but she insisted on coming with us ~** elle n'avait jamais fait de ski mais elle a quand même tenu à nous accompagner ‖ [at start of clause or sentence] cependant; **he says he never wants to see her again, ~, I think he still loves her** il dit qu'il ne veut plus jamais la revoir, cependant je crois qu'il l'aime encore.

never-to-be-forgotten *adj* inoubliable.

new [njuː] (*compar* newer, *superl* newest) ◇ *adj* -**1.** [gen] nouveau; [different] nouveau, autre; [unused] neuf, nouveau; **a ~ tablecloth** [brand new] une nouvelle nappe, une nappe neuve; [fresh] une nouvelle nappe, une nappe propre; **~ evidence** de nouvelles preuves; **he's wearing his ~ suit for the first time** il porte son nouveau costume OR son costume neuf pour la première fois; **I don't want to get my ~ gloves dirty** je ne veux pas salir mes nouveaux gants OR gants neufs; **this dress isn't ~** ce n'est pas une robe neuve OR une nouvelle robe, cette robe n'est pas neuve; **have you seen their ~ house yet?** est-ce que tu as vu leur nouvelle maison?; **she needs a ~ sheet of paper** il lui faut une autre feuille de papier; **we need some ~ ideas** il nous faut de nouvelles idées OR des idées neuves; **a ~ application of an old theory** une nouvelle application d'une vieille théorie; **there are ~ people in the flat next door** il y a de nouveaux occupants dans l'appartement d'à côté; **she likes her ~ boss** elle aime bien son nouveau patron; **~ members are always welcome** nous sommes toujours ravis d'accueillir de nouveaux adhérents; **'under ~ management'** 'changement de propriétaire' ❑ **as** OR **like ~** comme neuf; [in advert] 'état neuf'; **as good as ~ (again)** [clothing, carpet] (à nouveau) comme neuf; [watch, electrical appliance] (à nouveau) en parfait état de marche; **to feel like a ~ woman/man** se sentir revivre; **to make a ~ woman/man of sb** transformer qqn complètement; **there's nothing ~ under the sun** *prov* (il n'y a) rien de nouveau sous le soleil. -**2.** [latest, recent - issue, recording, baby] nouveau; **the ~est fashions** la dernière mode; **is there anything ~ on the catastrophe?** est-ce qu'il y a du nouveau sur la catastrophe? ‖ [modern] nouveau, moderne; **~ maths** les maths modernes; **~ grammar** la nouvelle grammaire; **the New Right** POL la nouvelle droite; **her husband is a New Man** son mari est le type même de l'homme moderne ❑ **what's ~?** quoi de neuf?; (so) **what's ~!, what else is ~!** [dismissive] quelle surprise! -**3.** [unfamiliar - experience, environment] nouveau; **to be ~ to sb**: **everything's still very ~ to me here** tout est encore tout nouveau pour moi ici ❑ **that's a ~ one on me!** *inf* [joke] celle-là, on ne me l'avait jamais faite!; [news] première nouvelle!; [experience] on en apprend tous les jours! -**4.** [recently arrived] nouveau; [novice] novice; **you're ~ here, aren't you?** vous êtes nouveau ici, n'est-ce pas?; **those curtains are ~ in this room** ces rideaux n'étaient pas dans cette pièce; **she's ~ to the job** elle débute dans le métier; **we're ~ to this area** nous venons d'arriver dans la région. -**5.** CULIN [wine] nouveau; [potatoes, carrots] nouveau.
◇ *n* nouveau *m*; **the cult of the ~** le culte du nouveau.

new- *in cpds*: **~won freedom** une liberté toute neuve; **~mown** fraîchement coupé; **~built** nouvellement construit.

New Age *adj* New Age.

newborn [ˈnjuːbɔːn] ◇ *adj* nouveau-né; **a ~ baby girl** une (petite fille) nouveau-née.
◇ *npl*: **the ~** les nouveaux-nés *mpl*.

new boy *n* SCH nouveau *m*, nouvel élève *m*; [in office, team etc] nouveau *m*.

New Britain *pr n* Nouvelle-Bretagne *f*.

new broom *n* réformateur *m*, -trice *f*; **this company needs a manager who will be a ~** cette société a besoin d'un directeur qui soit un réformateur OR qui procède à d'importantes réformes.

New Brunswick *pr n* Nouveau-Brunswick *m*; **in ~** dans le Nouveau-Brunswick.

New Caledonia *pr n* Nouvelle-Calédonie *f*; **in ~** en Nouvelle-Calédonie.

New Caledonian ◇ *n* Néo-Calédonien *m*, -enne *f*.
◇ *adj* néo-calédonien.

newcomer [ˈnjuːˌkʌməʳ] *n* -**1.** [new arrival] nouveau venu *m*, nouvelle venue *f*; **she's a ~ to the town** elle vient d'arriver dans la ville. -**2.** [beginner] novice *mf*; **a good book for ~s to computing** un bon livre pour les débutants en informatique; **I'm a ~ to all this** tout cela est nouveau pour moi.

New Deal *pr n*: **the ~** le New Deal *(programme de réformes sociales mises en place aux États-Unis par le président Roosevelt au lendemain de la grande dépression des années 30)*.

New Delhi *pr n* New Delhi.

newel [ˈnjuːəl] *n* -**1.** [on ordinary staircase]: **~ (post)** pilastre *m*. -**2.** [in spiral staircase] noyau *m* (d'escalier).

New England *pr n* Nouvelle-Angleterre *f*; **in ~** en Nouvelle-Angleterre.

New Englander *n* habitant *m*, -e *f* de la Nouvelle-Angleterre.

New English Bible *n*: **the ~** *texte de la Bible révisé dans les années 60*.

newfangled [ˈnjuːˌfæŋgld] *adj pej* [idea, device] nouveau, dernier cri *(inv)*.

new-found *adj* nouveau, récent; **her ~ friends** ses amis de fraîche date.

Newfoundland [ˈnjuːfəndlənd] *pr n* -**1.** GEOG Terre-Neuve; **in ~** à Terre-Neuve. -**2.** [dog] terre-neuve *m inv*.

Newfoundlander [ˈnjuːfəndləndəʳ] *pr n* Terre-Neuvien *m*, -enne *f*.

new girl *n* SCH nouvelle (élève) *f*; [in office, team etc] nouvelle *f*.

New Guinea *pr n* Nouvelle-Guinée *f*; **in ~** en Nouvelle-Guinée.

New Hampshire [-ˈhæmpʃəʳ] *pr n* New Hampshire *m*; **in ~** dans le New Hampshire.

New Hebridean [-ˌhebrɪˈdiːən] ◇ *n* Néo-Hébridais *m*, -e *f*.
◇ *adj* néo-hébridais.

New Hebrides *pl pr n* Nouvelles-Hébrides *fpl*; **in the ~** aux Nouvelles-Hébrides.

New Ireland *pr n* Nouvelle-Irlande *f*; **in ~** en Nouvelle-Irlande.

newish [ˈnjuːɪʃ] *adj* assez neuf OR nouveau.

New Jersey *pr n* le New Jersey; **in ~** dans le New Jersey.

new-laid *adj Br*: **a ~ egg** un œuf extra-frais.

New Latin *n* latin *m* scientifique.

New Left *n* nouvelle gauche *f*.

newly ['nju:lɪ] *adv* nouvellement, récemment; ~ arrived récemment arrivé, arrivé de fraîche date; the gate has been ~ painted la barrière vient d'être peinte; the ~ elected mayor le nouveau maire, le maire nouvellement élu; a ~ discovered galaxy une galaxie qu'on vient de découvrir OR récemment découverte; their ~ won independence leur indépendance récemment conquise.

newlyweds ['nju:lɪwedz] *npl* jeunes mariés *mpl.*

newmarket ['nju:,mɑ:kɪt] *n Br jeu de cartes.*
◆ **Newmarket** *pr n ville du Suffolk célèbre pour ses courses de chevaux.*

New Mexico *pr n* Nouveau-Mexique *m*; in ~ au Nouveau-Mexique.

new-mown *adj Br* [grass] fraîchement coupé; [lawn] fraîchement tondu; [hay] fraîchement fauché.

newness ['nju:nɪs] *n* -**1.** [of building] nouveauté *f*; [of shoes, carpet] état *m* neuf. -**2.** [of ideas, experience, fashion] nouveauté *f*, originalité *f*.

New Orleans [-'ɔ:lɪənz] *pr n* La Nouvelle-Orléans.

New Quebec *pr n* Nouveau-Québec *m*; in ~ au Nouveau-Québec.

new rich *npl* nouveaux riches *mpl.*

news [nju:z] ◇ *n (U)* -**1.** [information] nouvelles *fpl*, informations *fpl*; a piece of ~ une nouvelle, une information; an interesting piece of ~ une nouvelle intéressante; is there any more ~ about OR on the explosion? est-ce qu'on en sait un peu plus OR est-ce qu'on a plus d'informations sur l'explosion?; that's good/bad ~ c'est une bonne/mauvaise nouvelle; to have ~ of sb avoir des nouvelles de qqn; have you had any ~ of her? avez-vous eu de ses nouvelles?; what's your ~? quoi de neuf (chez vous)? ❑ have I got ~ for you! j'ai du nouveau (à vous annoncer)!; it's ~ to me! première nouvelle!, je l'ignorais!; famine isn't ~ any more la famine ne fait plus la une (des journaux); to be in the ~, to make ~ défrayer la chronique, faire parler de soi; to break the ~ (of sthg) to sb annoncer la nouvelle (de qqch) à qqn; bad ~ travels fast les mauvaises nouvelles vont vite; he's bad ~ *inf* on a toujours des ennuis avec lui; no ~ is good ~ *prov* pas de nouvelles, bonnes nouvelles *prov*. -**2.** RADIO & TV actualités *fpl*, informations *fpl*; [bulletin] chronique *f*, journal *m*, page *f*; the 9 o'clock ~ TV le journal (télévisé) OR les informations de 21 h; RADIO le journal (parlé) OR les informations de 21 h; I heard it on the ~ je l'ai entendu aux informations; the sports/financial ~ la page sportive/financière.
◇ *comp*: ~ desk (salle *f*) de rédaction *f*; ~ editor rédacteur *m*, -trice *f*; ~ film film *m* d'actualités; ~ item information *f*; ~ value intérêt *m* médiatique.

news agency *n* agence *f* de presse.

newsagent *Br* ['nju:z,eɪdʒənt], **news dealer** *Am n* marchand *m*, -e *f* de journaux.

news analyst *n Am* RADIO & TV commentateur *m*.

newsboy ['nju:zbɔɪ] *n* [in street] crieur *m* de journaux; [delivery boy] livreur *m* de journaux.

news bulletin *n* bulletin *m* d'informations.

newscast ['nju:zkɑ:st] *n* bulletin *m* d'informations; TV journal *m* télévisé, informations *fpl*.

newscaster ['nju:zkɑ:stəʳ] *n* présentateur *m*, -trice *f* du journal.

news conference *n* conférence *f* de presse.

news dealer *Am* = **newsagent**.

newsflash ['nju:zflæʃ] *n* flash *m* d'informations.

newshawk *inf* ['nju:zhɔ:k] = **newshound**.

news headlines *npl* titres *mpl* de l'actualité.

newshound *inf* ['nju:zhaʊnd] *n* reporter *m*, journaliste *mf*.

newsletter ['nju:z,letəʳ] *n* lettre *f*, bulletin *m*; monthly ~ bulletin mensuel.

newsman ['nju:zmən] (*pl* newsmen [-mən]) *n* journaliste *m*.

newsmonger ['nju:z,mʌŋgəʳ] *n pej* pipelet *m*, -ette *f*.

newsocracy [,nju:z'ɒkrəsɪ] *n aux États-Unis, ensemble de la presse et du réseau télévisé à audience nationale.*

New South Wales *pr n* Nouvelle-Galles du Sud *f*; in ~ en Nouvelle-Galles du Sud.

newspaper ['nju:z,peɪpəʳ] ◇ *n* -**1.** [publication] journal *m*; I read it in the ~ je l'ai lu dans le journal; an evening ~ un journal du soir; a daily ~ un quotidien. -**2.** [paper]: wrapped in ~ enveloppé dans du papier journal.
◇ *comp* [article, report] de journal; ~ reporter reporter *m* (de la presse écrite).

newspaper clipping, newspaper cutting *n* coupure *f* de presse.

newspaperman ['nju:z,peɪpəmæn] (*pl* newspapermen [-men]) *n* journaliste *m* (de la presse écrite).

newspaper rack *n* porte-journaux *m*.

newspaperwoman ['nju:zpeɪpə,wʊmən] (*pl* newspaperwomen [-,wɪmɪn]) *n* journaliste *f* (de la presse écrite).

newspeak ['nju:spi:k] *n* jargon *m* bureaucratique, ≃ langue *f* de bois.

newsprint ['nju:zprɪnt] *n* papier *m* journal.

newsreader ['nju:z,ri:dəʳ] = **newscaster**.

newsreel ['nju:zri:l] *n* film *m* d'actualités.

news sheet = **newsletter**.

newsstand ['nju:zstænd] *n* kiosque *m* (à journaux).

newsvendor ['nju:z,vendəʳ] *n* [gen] marchand *m*, -e *f* de journaux; [in street] crieur *m*, -euse *f* de journaux.

newswoman ['nju:z,wʊmən] (*pl* newswomen [-,wɪmɪn]) *n* journaliste *f*.

newsworthiness ['nju:z,wɜ:ðɪnɪs] *n* intérêt *m* médiatique.

newsworthy ['nju:z,wɜ:ðɪ] *adj*: it's not ~ cela n'a aucun intérêt médiatique; political scandal is always ~ les médias sont toujours friands OR la presse est toujours friande de scandales politiques.

newsy *inf* ['nju:zɪ] (*compar* newsier, *superl* newsiest) *adj* [letter] plein de nouvelles.

newt [nju:t] *n* triton *m* ZOOL.

New Testament *pr n* Nouveau Testament *m*.

newton ['nju:tn] *n* newton *m*.

Newtonian [nju:'təʊnjən] *adj* newtonien.

new town *n Br* ville *f* nouvelle.

new wave *n* [in cinema] nouvelle vague *f*; [in pop music] new wave *f*.
◆ **new-wave** *adj* [cinema] nouvelle vague *(inv)*; [pop music] new-wave *(inv)*.

New World *pr n*: the ~ le Nouveau Monde ❑ 'The New World Symphony' *Dvorák* 'Symphonie du nouveau monde'.

New Year *n* Nouvel An *m*; happy ~! bonne année!; to see the ~ in réveillonner (le 31 décembre); ~'s resolutions résolutions *fpl* du nouvel an; the ~'s Honours List *titres et distinctions honorifiques décernés par la Reine à l'occasion de la nouvelle année et dont la liste est établie officieusement par le Premier ministre.*

New Year's *n Am* -**1.** [day] le premier de l'an. -**2.** [eve] le soir du réveillon OR du 31 décembre.

New Year's Day *n* jour *m* de l'an.

New Year's Eve *n* Saint-Sylvestre *f*.

New York *pr n* -**1.** [city]: ~ (City) New York; the ~ subway le métro new-yorkais. -**2.** [state]: ~ (State) l'État *m* de New York; in (the State of) ~, in ~ (State) dans l'État de New York.

New Yorker [-'jɔ:kəʳ] *n* New-Yorkais *m*, -e *f*.

New Zealand [-'zi:lənd] *pr n* Nouvelle-Zélande *f*; in ~ en Nouvelle-Zélande; ~ butter beurre néo-zélandais.

New Zealander [-'zi:ləndəʳ] *n* Néo-Zélandais *m*, -e *f*.

next [nekst] ◇ *adj* -**1.** [in time - coming] prochain; [- already past] suivant; keep quiet about it for the ~ few days n'en parlez pas pendant les quelques jours qui viennent; I had to stay i[n] bed for the ~ ten days j'ai dû garder le l[it] pendant les dix jours qui ont suivi; (the) ~ da[y] le lendemain; (the) ~ morning/evening [le] lendemain matin/soir; ~ Sunday, Sunday ~ dimanche prochain; the ~ Sunday le dima[n]che suivant; ~ year l'année prochaine; the ~ year l'année suivante; (the) ~ minute moment: ~ minute she was dashing off o[u] again *inf* une minute après, elle repartait; th[e] situation's changing from one moment to th[e] ~ la situation change sans arrêt; ~ time: (th[e]) ~ time I see him la prochaine fois que je le vo[is] OR verrai; (the) ~ time I saw him quand je l'[ai] revu; you may not be so lucky ~ time t[u] pourrais avoir moins de chance la OR u[ne] prochaine fois; there isn't going to be a ~ tim[e] il n'y aura pas de prochaine fois. -**2.** [in series - future] prochain; [- in past] suivant; the ~ episode [in future] le prochain épisode; [in past] l'épisode suivant; translate the ~ sentenc[e] traduisez la phrase suivante; their ~ child wa[s] a girl ensuite, ils eurent une fille; they wa[nt] their ~ child to be a girl ils veulent que le[ur] prochain enfant soit une fille, la prochaine fo[is] ils veulent une fille; the ~ 10 pages les 10 page[s] suivantes; the ~ before last l'avant-dernie[r]; ask the ~ person you meet demandez à [la] première personne que vous rencontrez; the ~ world l'au-delà *m*; this life and the ~ c[e] monde et l'autre ‖ [in space - house, stree[t]] prochain, suivant; take the ~ street on the le[ft] prenez la prochaine à gauche; after the kitche[n] it's the ~ room on your right après la cuisin[e] c'est la première pièce à votre droite ‖ [in queu[e], line]: I'm ~ c'est (à) mon tour, c'est à mo[i]; who's ~? à qui le tour?; I'm ~ after you j[e] suis (juste) après vous; Helen is ~ in line fo[r] promotion Helen est la suivante sur la liste d[e] promotions ❑ I can take a joke as well as th[e] ~ person, but... j'aime plaisanter comme to[ut] le monde, mais...; (the) ~ thing ensuite; I wa[s] walking down the stairs, and (the) ~ thing [I] knew, I woke up in hospital je descenda[is] l'escalier, et l'instant d'après je me suis réveil[lé] à l'hôpital; ~ thing, they'll be melting th[e] polar ice! un de ces quatre (matins), ils vont s[e] mettre à faire fondre les glaces du pôle!
◇ *adv* -**1.** [afterwards] ensuite, après; what di[d] you do with it ~? et ensuite, qu'en avez-vo[us] fait?; ~ on the agenda is the question o[f] finance la question suivante à l'ordre du jo[ur] est celle des finances; ~ came Henry VII pu[is] vint OR il y eut Henri VII; what will they thin[k] of ~? *hum* qu'est-ce qu'ils vont bien pouvo[ir] inventer maintenant?; what OR whatever ~ [indignantly or in mock indignation] et puis qu[oi] encore? -**2.** [next time - in future] la prochai[ne] fois; [- in past] la fois suivante OR d'après; whe[n] we ~ meet, when ~ we meet la prochai[ne] fois que nous nous verrons, lors de not[re] prochaine rencontre; when we ~ met quan[d] nous nous sommes revus. -**3.** [with superlati[ve] adj]: the ~ youngest/oldest child l'enfant [le] plus jeune/le plus âgé ensuite; the ~ large[st] size la taille juste au-dessus; you'll have t[o] make do with the ~ best il faudra vo[us] contenter de la qualité en-dessous; watchin[g] the match on TV was the ~ best thing [to] actually being there l'idéal aurait été de po[u]voir assister au match, mais ce n'était déjà pa[s] mal de le voir à la télé.
◇ *n* [next train, person, child] prochain *m*, -e [*f*]; ~ please! au suivant, s'il vous plaît!; ~ of ki[n] plus proche parent *m*; the ~ of kin have bee[n] informed la famille a été prévenue.
◇ *prep Am* = **next to**.
◆ **next to** *prep* -**1.** [near] à côté de; they live ~ to a hospital ils habitent à côté d'un hôpita[l]; come and sit ~ to me venez vous asseoir à cô[té] de OR près de moi; I love the feel of silk ~ t[o] my skin j'adore le contact de la soie sur m[a] peau; ~ to him, everybody looks tiny à cô[té] de lui, tout le monde a l'air minuscule ‖ [in series]: ~ to last avant-dernier; the ~ t[o] bottom shelf la deuxième étagère en partant d[u]

pas. -**2.** [in comparisons] après; ~ to red, Ted prefers white après le rouge, Ted préfère le blanc; ~ to you, he was the smartest après vous, c'était lui le plus élégant. -**3.** [almost] presque; ~ to impossible presque OR quasiment impossible; I bought it for ~ to nothing je l'ai acheté pour trois fois rien OR presque rien; they have ~ to no proof ils n'ont pratiquement aucune preuve.

next door ◇ *adv*: they live ~ to us ils habitent à côté de chez nous, ce sont nos voisins; I'm just going ~ je vais juste chez les voisins; the house ~ la maison d'à côté OR des voisins; the girl/boy ~ la fille/le garçon d'à côté; that's ~ to madness/absurdity *fig* ça frise la folie/l'absurde.
◇ *n* la maison d'à côté; ~'s children les enfants qui habitent à côté OR des voisins; it's the man from ~ c'est le voisin.
◆ **next-door** *adj*: next-door neighbour [in private house] voisin *m*, -e *f* (de la maison d'à côté); [in apartment building] voisin *m*, -e *f* de palier; the next-door garden le jardin des voisins.

nexus ['neksəs] (*pl inv* OR nexuses) *n* lien *m*, liaison *f*.

NF ◇ *pr n abbr of* National Front.
◇ *written abbr of* Newfoundland.

NFL (*abbr of* National Football League) *pr n fédération nationale de football américain*.

NFU (*abbr of* National Farmers' Union) *pr n syndicat britannique d'exploitants agricoles*.

NG *pr n Am abbr of* National Guard.

NGO (*abbr of* non-governmental organization) *n* ONG *f*.

NH *written abbr of* New Hampshire.

NHL (*abbr of* National Hockey League) *pr n fédération nationale américaine de hockey sur glace*.

NHS *pr n Br abbr of* National Health Service.

NI ◇ *n Br abbr of* national insurance.
◇ *written abbr of* Northern Ireland.

Niagara [naɪ'ægərə] *pr n*: ~ Falls les chutes *fpl* du Niagara.

nib [nɪb] *n* [of fountain pen] plume *f*; [of ballpoint, tool] pointe *f*.

nibbed [nɪbd] *in cpds*: gold~ avec une plume en or; fine~ [fountain pen] à plume fine; [ballpoint] à pointe fine.

nibble ['nɪbl] ◇ *vt* -**1.** [subj: person, caterpillar] grignoter; [subj: rodent] grignoter, ronger; [subj: goat, sheep] brouter; I'm not hungry, I'll just ~ a piece of bread je n'ai pas faim, je vais juste grignoter un morceau de pain; the mice have ~d the telephone wire les souris ont rongé OR grignoté le fil du téléphone; the fish ~d the bait le poisson a mordu à l'hameçon. -**2.** [playfully - ear] mordiller.
◇ *vi* -**1.** [eat]: to ~ at OR on sthg grignoter qqch; she ~d nervously at her food elle mangeait nerveusement du bout des dents; the mice have ~d through the wire les souris ont entièrement rongé le fil. -**2.** [bite]: to ~ at sthg mordiller qqch; the cat likes to ~ at my toes le chat aime bien me mordiller les orteils ❑ to ~ at the bait *literal* & *fig* mordre à l'hameçon. -**3.** *fig* [show interest]: to ~ at a suggestion/an offer être tenté par une proposition/une offre.
◇ *n* -**1.** FISHING touche *f*. -**2.** [snack]: to have a ~ grignoter quelque chose.

nibbler ['nɪbləʳ] *n* [person] grignoteur *m*, -euse *f*.

nibbling ['nɪblɪŋ] *n* grignotage *m*.

niblick ['nɪblɪk] *n* niblick *m*.

nibs *inf* [nɪbz] *n Br hum*: his ~ sa Majesté, son Altesse *hum*.

Nicaragua [,nɪkə'rægjʊə] *pr n* Nicaragua *m*; in ~ au Nicaragua.

Nicaraguan [,nɪkə'rægjʊən] ◇ *n* Nicaraguayen *m*, -enne *f*.
◇ *adj* nicaraguayen.

nice [naɪs] ◇ *adj* -**1.** [expressing approval - good] bien, chouette; [- attractive] beau; [- pretty] joli; [- car, picture] beau; [- food] bon; [- idea] bon; [- weather] beau; they have a ~ house ils ont une belle maison; very ~ [visually] très joli; [food] très bon; to taste ~ avoir bon goût; to smell ~ sentir bon; she was wearing a very ~ hat elle portait un très joli chapeau; she always looks ~ elle est toujours bien habillée OR mise; we had a ~ meal on a bien mangé; ~ work! beau travail!; ~ work if you can get it *hum* c'est un travail agréable, encore faut-il le décrocher ‖ [pleasant - gen] agréable, bien; [- person] bien, sympathique; she's very ~ elle est très sympa; have a ~ time amusez-vous bien; it's ~ to be back again cela fait plaisir d'être de retour; (it was) ~ meeting you (j'ai été) ravi de faire votre connaissance ❑ ~ one! bravo!, chapeau! -**2.** [kind] gentil, aimable; to be ~ to sb être gentil avec qqn; that's ~ of her c'est gentil OR aimable de sa part; she said some ~ things elle a dit des choses gentilles OR aimables; it's ~ of you to say so vous êtes bien aimable de le dire; he was ~ enough to carry my case il a eu la gentillesse OR l'obligeance de porter ma valise. -**3.** [respectable] bien (élevé), convenable; ~ people don't blow their noses at table les gens bien élevés ne se mouchent pas OR cela ne se fait pas de se moucher à table. -**4.** [ironic use]: he made a ~ mess of the job il a fait un travail de cochon; you're a ~ one to talk! toi, tu peux parler!; we're in a ~ mess nous sommes dans de beaux draps OR un beau pétrin; that's a ~ way to talk! en voilà une façon de parler! ❑ ~ one! *Br* bravo! -**5.** [subtle - distinction, point] subtil, délicat.
◇ *adv* [as intensifier]: ~ long holidays des vacances longues et agréables; a ~ cold drink une boisson bien fraîche; to have a ~ long nap faire une bonne sieste ‖ [with 'and']: take it ~ and easy allez-y doucement; ~ and warm bien chaud; it's ~ and warm in here il fait bon ici.

nice-looking *adj* joli, beau.

nicely ['naɪslɪ] *adv* -**1.** [well] bien; it's coming along ~ ça progresse bien; it fits her ~ cela lui va bien; ~ dressed bien habillé; ~ done! bien joué!, beau travail!; ~ put! bien dit!; this bag will do ~ ce sac fera très bien l'affaire; he's doing ~ [at school] il travaille bien; [after illness] il se remet bien; [financially] il s'en sort bien, il n'est pas à plaindre ‖ [pleasantly] gentiment, agréablement; she smiled at me ~ elle me sourit gentiment. -**2.** [politely - behave, eat] bien, comme il faut; ask ~ demandez gentiment. -**3.** [exactly] exactement, avec précision; [subtly] avec précision; they judged it ~ ils ne se sont pas trompés dans leur appréciation.

Nicene [naɪ'siːn] *adj*: the ~ Creed le symbole de Nicée.

nicety ['naɪsətɪ] (*pl* niceties) *n* -**1.** [precision] justesse *f*, précision *f*; to a ~ exactement, à la perfection. -**2.** [subtlety] subtilité *f*, finesse *f*; a distinction of some ~ une distinction assez subtile OR fine; the niceties of chess les subtilités des échecs; we haven't time for all these social niceties nous n'avons guère le temps de nous livrer à ces mondanités. -**3.** [refinement] raffinement *m*, agrément *m*; the niceties of a life of leisure les agréments d'une vie de loisirs.

niche [niːʃ] *n* -**1.** [recess - in church, cliff] niche *f*; to find one's ~ *fig* trouver sa voie. -**2.** COMM créneau *m*.

Nicholas ['nɪkələs] *pr n*: Saint ~ saint Nicolas; Saint ~' Day la Saint-Nicolas.

nick [nɪk] ◇ *n* -**1.** [notch] encoche *f*; [chip - in crockery] ébréchure *f*; [cut - on skin] (petite) coupure *f*. -**2.** ▽ *Br* [police station] poste *m* (de police); [prison] taule *f*; in the ~ en taule, au bloc; down the ~ au poste. -**3.** *inf Br* [condition] état *m*; in good/bad ~ en bon/mauvais état. -**4.** *phr*: in the ~ of time à point nommé.
◇ *vt* -**1.** [cut - deliberately] faire une entaille OR une encoche sur; [accidentally - crockery] ébrécher; [- metal, paint] faire des entailles dans; [- skin, face] entailler, couper (légèrement); he ~ed his chin shaving il s'est légèrement coupé le menton OR il s'est fait une légère coupure au menton en se rasant. -**2.** ▽ *Br* [arrest] épingler; he got ~ed outside the bank il s'est fait épingler OR pincer devant la banque. -**3.** *inf Br* [steal] faucher, chiper. -**4.** *inf Am* [cheat] arnaquer; they ~ed him for $1,000 il s'est fait arnaquer de 1 000 dollars.

Nick [nɪk] *pr n*: Old ~ le diable.

nickel ['nɪkl] (*Br pt* & *pp* nickelled, *cont* nickelling, *Am pt* & *pp* nickeled, *cont* nickeling) ◇ *n* -**1.** [metal] nickel *m*. -**2.** *Am* [coin] pièce *f* de 5 cents; it only costs a ~ ça ne coûte que 5 cents.
◇ *vt* nickeler.

nickel-and-dime store *n Am magasin à prix unique*.

nickel bag *n Am drugs sl sachet de drogue*.

nickelodeon [,nɪkl'əʊdɪən] *n Am dated* -**1.** [jukebox] juke-box *m*. -**2.** [cinema] cinéma *m* bon marché.

nickel-plated *adj* nickelé.

nickel-plating *n* nickelage *m*.

nickel silver *n* argentan *m*, maillechort *m*.

nicker ['nɪkəʳ] (*pl inv*) ◇ *vi Br* -**1.** [neigh] hennir doucement. -**2.** [snigger] ricaner.
◇ *n inf Br* livre *f* (sterling); five ~ cinq livres.

nick-nack ['nɪknæk] = **knick-knack**.

nickname ['nɪkneɪm] ◇ *n* [gen] surnom *m*, sobriquet *m*; [short form] diminutif *m*.
◇ *vt* surnommer.

Nicodemus [,nɪkə'diːməs] *pr n* Nicodème.

Nicosia [,nɪkə'siːə] *pr n* Nicosie.

nicotine ['nɪkətiːn] *n* nicotine *f*; ~ addiction tabagisme *m*; ~ poisoning tabagisme *m*, intoxication *f* nicotinique.

nicotine-stained *adj* jauni par la nicotine.

nicotinic acid [nɪkə'tɪnɪk] *n* acide *m* nicotinique.

niece [niːs] *n* nièce *f*.

Nietzschean ['niːtʃɪən] ◇ *n* nietzschéen *m*, -enne *f*.
◇ *adj* nietzschéen.

niff▽ [nɪf] ◇ *n Br* mauvaise odeur *f*, puanteur *f*; what a ~! ça schlingue!
◇ *vi* schlinguer.

niffy▽ ['nɪfɪ] (*compar* niffier, *superl* niffiest) *adj Br* puant.

nifty *inf* ['nɪftɪ] (*compar* niftier, *superl* niftiest) *adj* -**1.** [stylish] chouette, classe (*inv*); they've got a ~ house ils ont une chouette baraque; that's a ~ sweater il est chouette, ce pull. -**2.** [clever - solution] génial; a ~ piece of work du bon travail. -**3.** [quick] rapide; [agile] agile.

Niger [*sense 1* niː'ʒeəʳ, *sense 2* 'naɪdʒəʳ] *pr n* -**1.** [country] Niger *m*; in ~ au Niger. -**2.** [river]: the (River) ~ le Niger.

Nigeria [naɪ'dʒɪərɪə] *pr n* Nigeria *m*; in ~ au Nigeria.

Nigerian [naɪ'dʒɪərɪən] ◇ *n* Nigérian *m*, -e *f*.
◇ *adj* nigérian.

Nigerien [niː'ʒeərɪən] ◇ *n* Nigérien *m*, -enne *f*.
◇ *adj* nigérien.

niggard ['nɪgəd] *n* avare *m*.

niggardliness ['nɪgədlɪnɪs] *n* pingrerie *f*, avarice *f*.

niggardly ['nɪgədlɪ] ◇ *adj* [person] avare, pingre, ladre; [quantity] parcimonieux, chiche.
◇ *adv* chichement, parcimonieusement, avec parcimonie.

nigger▼ ['nɪgəʳ] *n terme raciste désignant un Noir*, ≃ nègre *m*, négresse *f*; there's a ~ in the woodpile *Br* [problem] il y a un hic; [person] il y a un empêcheur de tourner en rond; [secret] il y a anguille sous roche.

niggle ['nɪgl] ◇ *vi* -**1.** [fuss over details] ergoter; to ~ over OR about sthg ergoter sur qqch. -**2.** [nag] trouver à redire.
◇ *vt* -**1.** [worry - subj: conscience] harceler, travailler. -**2.** [nag] harceler.
◇ *n* -**1.** [small criticism] objection *f* mineure; I've got one slight ~ il y a un point de détail sur lequel je ne suis pas d'accord. -**2.** [small worry, doubt] léger doute *m*.

niggling [ˈnɪglɪŋ] ◇ *adj* -**1.** [petty - person] tatillon; [- details] insignifiant. -**2.** [fastidious - job] fastidieux. -**3.** [nagging - pain, doubt] tenace.
◇ *n* chicanerie *f*, pinaillerie *f*.

niggly *inf* [ˈnɪglɪ] (*compar* nigglier, *superl* niggliest) *adj* pinailleur.

nigh [naɪ] *lit* ◇ *adv*: well ~ 80 years près de 80 ans; well ~ impossible presque impossible.
◇ *adj* proche; the hour is ~ c'est bientôt OR presque l'heure; to be ~ unto death *arch* être à l'article de la mort.
◇ *prep* près de, proche de.
◆ **nigh on** *adv phr* presque; ~ on 6 o'clock presque 6 heures; it's ~ on sundown le soleil se couchera d'ici peu.

night [naɪt] ◇ *n* -**1.** [late] nuit *f*; [evening] soir *m*, soirée *f*; at ~ [evening] le soir; [late] la nuit; ten o'clock at ~ dix heures du soir; all ~ (long) toute la nuit; by ~ de nuit; during OR in the ~ pendant la nuit; (on) Tuesday ~ [evening] mardi soir; [during night] dans la nuit de mardi à mercredi; last ~ [evening] hier soir; [during night] cette nuit; the ~ before [evening] la veille au soir; [late] la nuit précédente; far OR late into the ~ jusqu'à une heure avancée de la nuit; it's weeks since we had a ~ out ça fait des semaines que nous ne sommes pas sortis le soir; it's the au pair's ~ off c'est le soir de sortie de la jeune fille au pair; Tuesday's our poker ~ le mardi, c'est notre soirée poker, le mardi soir-nous faisons un poker; to have a late ~ se coucher tard; we worked on the project day and ~ on a travaillé sur le projet jour et nuit; this has been going on ~ after ~ cela s'est prolongé des nuits durant; what you need is a good ~'s sleep ce qu'il vous faut, c'est une bonne nuit de sommeil OR de repos; I had a bad ~ j'ai passé une mauvaise nuit, j'ai mal dormi; let's make a ~ of it! [have fun] faisons la fête toute la nuit! □ the ~ of the long knives la nuit des longs couteaux; the ~ is young *literal* la nuit n'est pas très avancée; *hum* on a toute la nuit devant nous; 'It Happened One Night' *Capra* 'New York-Miami'; 'The Night of the Iguana' *Williams, Huston* 'la Nuit de l'iguane'; 'The Night Watch' *Rembrandt* 'la Ronde de nuit'. -**2.** [darkness] obscurité *f*; *fig* ténèbres *fpl*; ~ falls early il fait nuit tôt, la nuit tombe tôt. -**3.** THEAT soirée *f*; gala ~ soirée de gala; poetry ~ soirée poésie.
◇ *comp* [duty, flight, sky] de nuit.
◆ **nights** *adv* de nuit; to work ~s travailler de nuit; I'm on ~s next week je suis de nuit la semaine prochaine; to lie awake ~s *Am* ne pas dormir la nuit.

night bird *n* ORNITH oiseau *m* nocturne OR de nuit; *fig* noctambule *mf*, oiseau *m* de nuit.

night blindness *n* (*U*) héméralopie *f*.

nightcap [ˈnaɪtkæp] *n* -**1.** [drink - gen] boisson *f* *(que l'on prend avant d'aller se coucher)*; [- alcoholic] dernier verre *m (avant d'aller se coucher)*; I always have a ~ je bois toujours un petit quelque chose avant d'aller me coucher. -**2.** [headgear] bonnet *m* de nuit.

nightclothes [ˈnaɪtkləʊðz] *npl* [pyjamas] pyjama *m*; [nightdress] chemise *f* de nuit; the children were in their ~ les enfants étaient en pyjama.

nightclub [ˈnaɪtklʌb] *n* night-club *m*, boîte *f* de nuit.

nightclubber [ˈnaɪtklʌbəʳ] *n*: he's a bit of a ~ c'est un vrai pilier de boîtes de nuit.

nightclubbing [ˈnaɪtklʌbɪŋ] *n*: to go ~ sortir en boîte.

nightdress [ˈnaɪtdres] *n* chemise *f* de nuit.

night editor *n* rédacteur *m*, -trice *f* de nuit *(dans un journal)*.

nightfall [ˈnaɪtfɔːl] *n* tombée *f* de la nuit OR du jour; at ~ à la tombée de la nuit OR du jour; we must get there by ~ il faut que nous y arrivions avant la tombée de la nuit OR du jour.

night fighter *n* chasseur *m* de nuit.

nightgown [ˈnaɪtgaʊn] = **nightdress**.

nighthawk [ˈnaɪthɔːk] *n* ORNITH engoulevent *m* (d'Amérique); *fig* couche-tard *mf inv*, oiseau *m* de nuit.

nightie *inf* [ˈnaɪtɪ] *n* chemise *f* de nuit.

nightingale [ˈnaɪtɪŋgeɪl] *n* rossignol *m*.

nightjar [ˈnaɪtdʒɑːʳ] *n* engoulevent *m* (d'Europe).

night letter *n* *Am* télégramme *m (à tarif réduit, livré le lendemain matin)*.

nightlife [ˈnaɪtlaɪf] *n* vie *f* nocturne; what's the ~ like round here? qu'est-ce qu'on peut faire le soir, ici?

nightlight [ˈnaɪtlaɪt] *n* veilleuse *f*.

nightlong [ˈnaɪtlɒŋ] ◇ *adj* qui dure toute la nuit; a ~ vigil une nuit de veille.
◇ *adv* pendant toute la nuit, la nuit durant.

nightly [ˈnaɪtlɪ] ◇ *adj* [happening every night] de tous les soirs, de chaque nuit; he made his ~ call home comme chaque soir OR nuit, il téléphona chez lui; to make a ~ TV appearance passer tous les soirs à la télévision.
◇ *adv* tous les soirs, chaque soir; appearing ~ at the Odeon THEAT tous les soirs sur la scène de l'Odéon.

nightmare [ˈnaɪtmeəʳ] ◇ *n* *literal* & *fig* cauchemar *m*; I had a ~ j'ai fait un cauchemar; the first day of the sales was a ~ la première journée de soldes fut un cauchemar.
◇ *comp* [vision, experience] cauchemardesque, de cauchemar.

nightmarish [ˈnaɪtmeərɪʃ] *adj* cauchemardesque, de cauchemar.

night-night *inf interj*: ~! bonne nuit!

night nurse *n* infirmier *m*, -ère *f* de nuit.

night owl *inf n* couche-tard *mf inv*.

night porter *n* portier *m* de nuit.

night safe *n* coffre *m* de nuit.

night school *n* cours *mpl* du soir; to go to ~ suivre des cours du soir; in *Am* OR at *Br* ~ aux cours du soir.

nightshade [ˈnaɪtʃeɪd] *n* morelle *f*.

night shift *n* [work force] équipe *f* de nuit; [period of duty] poste *m* de nuit; to be on the ~ être de nuit.

nightshirt [ˈnaɪtʃɜːt] *n* chemise *f* de nuit.

night soil *n* fumier *m (d'excréments humains)*.

nightspot *inf* [ˈnaɪtspɒt] *n* boîte *f* (de nuit).

nightstick [ˈnaɪtstɪk] *n* *Am* matraque *f* (de policier).

night storage heater *n* radiateur *m* à accumulation (de chaleur).

night-time *n* nuit *f*; at ~ la nuit.

night vision *n* vision *f* nocturne; to have good/bad ~ avoir une bonne/mauvaise vision nocturne.

night watchman *n* veilleur *m* de nuit.

nightwear [ˈnaɪtweəʳ] *n* (*U*) = **nightclothes**.

nighty *inf* [ˈnaɪtɪ] (*pl* nighties) = **nightie**.

nighty-night *inf* = **night-night**.

nihilism [ˈnaɪɪlɪzm] *n* nihilisme *m*.

nihilist [ˈnaɪɪlɪst] ◇ *adj* nihiliste.
◇ *n* nihiliste *mf*.

nihilistic [ˌnaɪɪˈlɪstɪk] *adj* nihiliste.

Nijinsky [nɪˈdʒɪnskɪ] *pr n* Nijinski.

Nike [ˈnaɪkiː] *pr n* MYTH Nikê.

nil [nɪl] ◇ *n* [gen & SPORT] zéro *m*; [on written form] néant *m*.
◇ *adj* nul, zéro *(inv)*.

Nile [naɪl] *pr n*: the (River) ~ *Br*, the ~ River *Am* le Nil; the Blue ~ le Nil Bleu; the White ~ le Nil Blanc.

nimbi [ˈnɪmbaɪ] *pl* → **nimbus**.

nimble [ˈnɪmbl] *adj* -**1.** [agile - body, movements] agile; [- fingers] adroit, habile; she's very ~ for (someone of) her age elle est très alerte pour (quelqu'un de) son âge; a ~ climber/dancer un grimpeur/un danseur agile; he soon got to be ~ on his crutches il eut tôt fait d'apprendre à se déplacer avec ses béquilles || [skilful] habile; a ~ seamstress une habile couturière. -**2.** [quick - thought, mind] vif, prompt.

nimble-fingered *adj* aux doigts agiles, habile de ses doigts.

nimble-witted *adj* vif (d'esprit), à l'esprit vif rapide.

nimbly [ˈnɪmblɪ] *adv* agilement, lesteme prestement; he leapt ~ over the wall il sau lestement par-dessus le mur.

nimbostratus [ˌnɪmbəʊˈstreɪtəs] (*pl* nimb trati [-taɪ]) *n* nimbo-stratus *m*.

nimbus [ˈnɪmbəs] (*pl* nimbi [-baɪ] OR nimbus *n* -**1.** METEOR nimbus *m*. -**2.** [halo] nimbe auréole *f*.

nimby *inf* [ˈnɪmbɪ] (*abbr of* not in my backyar *n personne qui est d'accord pour quelque chose (exemple, projet de construction) mais pas à pro mité de chez elle*.

niminy-piminy *inf* [ˌnɪmɪnɪˈpɪmɪnɪ] *adj* cucul.

nincompoop *inf* [ˈnɪŋkəmpuːp] *n* cruche don't be such a ~ ne sois pas si bête.

nine [naɪn] ◇ *adj* neuf *(inv)*; a ~-hole g course un (parcours de) neuf trous; ~ tim out of ten neuf fois sur dix □ a ~ day wonder *Br* un feu de paille.
◇ *n* -**1.** neuf *m inv*; he was dressed up to t ~s il s'était mis sur son trente et un. -**2.** SPORT équipe *f* (de base-ball).

ninefold [ˈnaɪnfəʊld] ◇ *adj* neuf fois su rieur; there was a ~ increase in casualties nombre de victimes fut multiplié par neuf.
◇ *adv* neuf fois; to increase ~ (se) multipl par neuf.

ninepin [ˈnaɪnpɪn] *n* [skittle] quille *f*; to down like ~s *Br* tomber comme des mouch
◆ **ninepins** *n* [game] quilles *fpl*.

nineteen [ˌnaɪnˈtiːn] ◇ *adj* dix-neuf.
◇ *n* dix-neuf *m*; they were talking ~ to t dozen *Br* ils étaient intarissables, il n'y avait p moyen de les faire taire.

nineteenth [ˌnaɪnˈtiːnθ] ◇ *adj* dix-neuvièm the ~ hole *hum* [in golf] le bar (du club).
◇ *n* -**1.** [ordinal] dix-neuvième *mf*. -**2.** [fractic dix-neuvième *m*.

ninetieth [ˈnaɪntɪəθ] ◇ *adj* quatre-vin dixième.
◇ *n* -**1.** [ordinal] quatre-vingt-dixième *r* -**2.** [fraction] quatre-vingt-dixième *m*.

nine-to-five ◇ *adv* de neuf heures du matin cinq heures du soir; to work ~ avoir d horaires de bureau.
◇ *adj* -**1.** [job] routinier. -**2.** [mentality, attituc de gratte-papier.

ninety [ˈnaɪntɪ] (*pl* nineties) ◇ *adj* quat vingt-dix.
◇ *n* quatre-vingt-dix *m*; ~-one quatre-vin onze; ~-two quatre-vingt-douze; ~-ni quatre-vingt-dix-neuf; he's in his nineties il nonagénaire, il a quatre-vingt-dix ans passés; the nineties dans les années quatre-vingt-d

Nineveh [ˈnɪnɪvə] *pr n* Ninive.

ninny *inf* [ˈnɪnɪ] (*pl* ninnies) *n* empoté *m*, -e nigaud *m*, -e *f*, bêta *m*, -asse *f*.

ninth [naɪnθ] ◇ *adj* neuvième.
◇ *n* -**1.** [ordinal] neuvième *mf*. -**2.** [fractio neuvième *m*.

niobium [naɪˈəʊbɪəm] *n* niobium *m*.

nip [nɪp] (*pt* & *pp* nipped, *cont* nippin ◇ *n* -**1.** [pinch] pincement *m*; [bite] morsure that dog gave me a ~ on the leg ce chien m mordillé la jambe. -**2.** [cold] froid *m* piquar there's a ~ in the air ça pince. -**3.** [in tas goût *m* piquant; I like cheese with a ~ to j'aime le fromage un peu relevé OR fort. -**4.** alcohol] goutte *f*. -**5.** *phr*: to be ~ and tuck ê au coude à coude.
◇ *vt* -**1.** [pinch] pincer; [bite] mordre (légè ment), mordiller; she nipped her finger in t door elle s'est pincé le doigt dans la porte; t puppy nipped my leg le chiot m'a mordillé jambe. -**2.** HORT [plant, shoot] pincer; to ~ st in the bud *fig* tuer OR écraser OR étouffer qq dans l'œuf. -**3.** [numb, freeze] geler, piquer; t cold nipped our ears le froid nous piquait oreilles; the vines were nipped by the frost l vignes ont été grillées par le gel. -**4.** *inf Am* [ste piquer, faucher.

◇ *vi* -**1.** [try to bite]: the dog nipped at my ankles le chien m'a mordillé les chevilles. -**2.** *inf Br* [go] faire un saut; to ~ (across OR along OR over) to the butcher's faire un saut chez le boucher; she nipped in to say hello elle est passée en vitesse dire bonjour; to ~ in and out of the traffic se faufiler entre les voitures; we just nipped out for a drink on est sorti prendre un pot en vitesse.

◆ **nip off** ◇ *vt sep* [cut off] couper; HORT pincer.

◇ *vi insep inf Br* filer; she nipped off home elle a filé chez elle.

Jip▼ [nɪp] *n terme injurieux désignant un Japonais,* ≃ Jap *mf.*

ipper ['nɪpəʳ] *n* -**1.** [of crab, lobster] pince *f.* -**2.** *inf Br* [child] gosse *mf,* môme *mf.*

◆ **nippers** *npl* [tool] pince *f;* a pair of ~s une pince.

ipple ['nɪpl] *n* -**1.** [on breast] mamelon *m;* [on animal] tétine *f,* mamelle *f.* -**2.** [teat - on feeding bottle] tétine *f.* -**3.** *Am* [baby's dummy] tétine *f.* -**4.** TECH [of pump] embout *m;* [for greasing] graisseur *m;* [connector] raccord *m.*

ippy ['nɪpɪ] (*compar* nippier, *superl* nippiest) *adj* -**1.** *inf* [weather] frisquet; [cold] piquant; it's ~ (out) this morning ça pince ce matin. -**2.** *inf Br* [quick] vif, rapide; a ~ little car une petite voiture rapide. -**3.** *Br* [odour, flavour] piquant, âpre.

irvana [ˌnɪə'vɑːnə] *n* nirvana *m.*

Nisei [nɪ'seɪ] *n Am* Japonais *m,* -e *f* de la deuxième génération.

isi ['naɪsaɪ] → **decree nisi**.

Nissen hut ['nɪsn-] *n Br* MIL abri *m* (en tôle ondulée).

it [nɪt] *n* -**1.** ENTOM lente *f;* [in hair] pou *m.* -**2.** *inf Br* [idiot] andouille *f.*

iter *Am* = **nitre**.

itpick *inf* ['nɪtpɪk] *vi* couper les cheveux en quatre, chercher la petite bête, pinailler.

itpicking *inf* ['nɪtpɪkɪŋ] ◇ *n* chicanerie *f,* pinaillage *m.*

◇ *adj* chicanier.

itrate ['naɪtreɪt] *n* nitrate *m,* azotate *m.*

itration [naɪ'treɪʃn] *n* nitration *f.*

itre *Br,* **niter** *Am* ['naɪtəʳ] *n* nitre *m dated,* nitrate *m* de potassium.

itric acid ['naɪtrɪk-] *n* acide *m* nitrique.

itric oxide *n* oxyde *m* nitrique.

itrify ['naɪtrɪfaɪ] (*pt* & *pp* **nitrified**) *vt* -**1.** CHEM nitrifier. -**2.** AGR fertiliser avec des nitrates.

itrogen ['naɪtrədʒən] *n* azote *m.*

itrogen cycle *n* cycle *m* de l'azote.

itrogen fixation *n* fixation *f* de l'azote.

itrogenous [naɪ'trɒdʒɪnəs] *adj* azoté.

itrogen peroxide *n* protoxyde *m* d'azote.

itroglycerin(e) [ˌnaɪtrəʊ'glɪsəriːn] *n* nitroglycérine *f.*

itrous ['naɪtrəs] *adj* nitreux, azoteux.

itrous acid *n* acide *m* nitreux.

itty-gritty *inf* [ˌnɪtɪ'grɪtɪ] *n* essentiel *m;* let's get down to the ~ venons-en au cœur du problème.

itwit *inf* ['nɪtwɪt] *n* andouille *f.*

ix *inf* [nɪks] *Am* ◇ *interj* -**1.** [no] non; to say ~ to OR on sthg dire non à qqch. -**2.** [watch out] attention.

◇ *n* rien *m;* we got ~ out of the deal l'affaire ne nous a pas rapporté un radis.

◇ *vt* [refuse] rejeter, refuser; [veto] opposer un veto à.

NJ *written abbr of* New Jersey.

NLF (*abbr of* National Liberation Front) *pr n* FLN *m.*

NLQ (*abbr of* near letter quality) *n qualité quasi-courrier.*

NLRB (*abbr of* National Labor Relations Board) *pr n commission américaine d'arbitrage en matière d'emploi.*

NM *written abbr of* New Mexico.

NME (*abbr of* New Musical Express) *pr n hebdomadaire anglais de musique rock.*

no [nəʊ] (*pl* noes OR nos) ◇ *adv* -**1.** [expressing refusal, disagreement] non; do you like spinach? — no, I don't aimez-vous les épinards? — non; oh no you don't! [stopping, forbidding] oh que non!; to say no dire non; the answer's no la réponse est non ❑ they won't take no for an answer ils n'accepteront aucun refus. -**2.** [with comparative adj or adv]: I can go no further je ne peux pas aller plus loin; we'll go no further than three million on n'ira pas au-delà de OR nous ne dépasserons pas les trois millions; you're no better than he is vous ne valez pas mieux que lui; call me, if you're (feeling) no better in the morning appelez-moi si vous ne vous sentez pas mieux demain matin; this car is no more expensive than the other one cette voiture ne coûte pas plus cher que l'autre. -**3.** *lit* [not]: whether you wish it or no que vous le vouliez ou non.

◇ *det* -**1.** [not any, not one]: I have no family je n'ai pas de famille; she has no intention of leaving elle n'a aucune intention de partir; there are no letters for you today il n'y a pas de courrier OR aucune lettre pour toi aujourd'hui; no sensible person would dispute this quelqu'un de raisonnable ne discuterait pas; no other washing powder gets clothes so clean aucune autre lessive ne laisse votre linge aussi propre; it's of no importance/interest ça n'a aucune importance/aucun intérêt; no one company can handle all the orders une seule entreprise ne pourra jamais s'occuper de toutes les commandes; no two experts ever come up with the same answer il n'y a pas deux experts qui soient d'accord; there's no telling nul ne peut le dire; there's no denying it c'est indéniable. -**2.** [not a]: I'm no expert, I'm afraid malheureusement, je ne suis pas un expert; she's no friend of mine ce n'est pas une amie à moi; this is no time for arguments ce n'est pas le moment de se disputer; it will be no easy task persuading them ce ne sera pas une tâche facile que de les persuader; that's no bad thing ce n'est pas une mauvaise chose. -**3.** [introducing a prohibition]: 'no left turn' 'interdiction de tourner à gauche'; 'no smoking' 'défense de fumer'; 'no swimming' 'baignade interdite'.

◇ *n* non *m inv;* the noes have it les non l'emportent.

◇ *interj* non; I'm getting married — no! [surprise, dismay] je me marie — non!

No., no. (*written abbr of* number) No, no.

no-account *inf Am* ◇ *n* bon *m* à rien, bonne *f* à rien.

◇ *adj* bon à rien; her ~ husband son bon à rien de mari.

Noah ['nəʊə] *pr n* Noé; ~'s Ark l'arche de Noé.

nob *inf* [nɒb] *n* -**1.** *Br* [wealthy person] richard *m,* -e *f.* -**2.** [head] caboche *f.*

no-ball *n* SPORT balle *f* nulle.

nobble *inf* ['nɒbl] *vt Br* -**1.** [jury, witness - bribe] graisser la patte à; [- threaten] manipuler (avec des menaces). -**2.** [racehorse] mettre hors d'état de courir; [with drugs] droguer. -**3.** [grab, catch - person] accrocher (au passage), agrafer; he ~d me as I arrived il m'a accroché au moment où je suis arrivé. -**4.** [steal] faucher, barboter, chiper. -**5.** [kidnap] kidnapper, enlever.

Nobel [nəʊ'bel] *comp:* ~ prize prix *m* Nobel; ~ prizewinner lauréat *m,* -e *f* du prix Nobel.

nobelium [nəʊ'biːlɪəm] *n* nobélium *m.*

nobility [nə'bɪlətɪ] (*pl* **nobilities**) *n* -**1.** [aristocracy] noblesse *f,* aristocratie *f.* -**2.** [loftiness] noblesse *f,* majesté *f,* grandeur *f.*

noble ['nəʊbl] ◇ *adj* -**1.** [aristocratic] noble; of ~ birth de haute naissance, de naissance noble. -**2.** [fine, distinguished - aspiration, purpose] noble, élevé; [- bearing, manner] noble, gracieux, majestueux; [- person] noble, supérieur; [- animal] noble; [- wine] grand. -**3.** [generous - gesture] généreux, magnanime; that's very ~ of you *hum* c'est très généreux de votre part. -**4.** [brave - deed, feat] noble, héroïque; the ~ art OR science la boxe. -**5.** [impressive - monument] noble, majestueux. -**6.** CHEM [gas, metal] noble.

◇ *n* noble *mf,* aristocrate *mf.*

nobleman ['nəʊblmən] (*pl* noblemen [-mən]) *n* noble *m,* aristocrate *m.*

noble-minded *adj* magnanime, généreux.

noblewoman ['nəʊblˌwʊmən] (*pl* noblewomen [-ˌwɪmɪn]) *n* noble *f,* aristocrate *f.*

nobly ['nəʊblɪ] *adv* -**1.** [by birth] noblement; ~ born de haute naissance. -**2.** [majestically, superbly] majestueusement, superbement. -**3.** [generously] généreusement, magnanimement. -**4.** [bravely] noblement, courageusement.

nobody ['nəʊbədɪ] (*pl* **nobodies**) ◇ *pron* personne; ~ came personne n'est venu; ~ knows better than I do personne ne sait mieux que moi; ~ else knows personne d'autre ne sait; there's ~ here il n'y a personne ici; they found ~ ils n'ont trouvé personne; who was at the party? — ~ you know qui était à la fête? — personne que tu connais; ~ famous/important personne de célèbre/d'important ❑ she's ~'s fool elle n'est pas née d'hier OR tombée de la dernière pluie.

◇ *n* [insignificant person] moins que rien *mf.*

no-claim(s) bonus *n Br* [in insurance] bonus *m.*

nocturnal [nɒk'tɜːnl] *adj* nocturne.

nocturne ['nɒktɜːn] *n* nocturne *m.*

nod [nɒd] (*pt* & *pp* **nodded**, *cont* **nodding**)

◇ *vt:* to ~ one's head [as signal] faire un signe de (la) tête; [in assent] faire oui de la tête, faire un signe de tête affirmatif; [in greeting] saluer d'un signe tête; [with fatigue] dodeliner de la tête; she nodded her head in approval OR nodded her approval elle manifesta son approbation d'un signe de tête; the boss nodded him into the office le chef lui fit signe (de la tête) d'entrer dans le bureau.

◇ *vi* -**1.** [as signal] faire un signe de (la) tête; [in assent, approval] faire un signe de tête affirmatif, faire oui de la tête; [in greeting] saluer d'un signe de tête; she nodded at OR to him through the window elle lui fit un signe de tête de derrière la fenêtre. -**2.** [doze] somnoler; he was nodding in his chair il somnolait dans son fauteuil. -**3.** *fig* [flowers] danser, se balancer; [crops, trees] se balancer, onduler.

◇ *n* -**1.** [sign] signe *m* de (la) tête; to give sb a ~ [as signal] faire un signe de tête à qqn; [in assent] faire un signe de tête affirmatif à qqn; [in greeting] saluer qqn d'un signe de tête ❑ a ~ is as good as a wink (to a blind man) inutile d'en dire plus; to get the ~ *Br* OR a ~ *Am* [gen] obtenir le feu vert; [in boxing] gagner aux points; to give sb the ~ *Br* OR a ~ *Am* donner le feu vert à qqn; on the ~ *Br* [without formality]: to approve sthg on the ~ approuver qqch d'un commun accord. -**2.** [nap] somme *m;* [sleep] sommeil *m;* the land of Nod le pays des rêves.

◆ **nod off** *inf vi insep* s'endormir, s'assoupir.

◆ **nod out**▽ *vi insep* tomber dans les vapes.

nodal ['nəʊdl] *adj* nodal.

nodding ['nɒdɪŋ] *adj Br:* to have a ~ acquaintance with sb connaître qqn de vue OR vaguement; we're on ~ terms on se connaît de vue; a ~ acquaintance with marketing techniques *fig* quelques notions des techniques de marketing.

noddle *inf* ['nɒdl] *n* caboche *f;* use your ~! fais travailler tes méninges OR ta matière grise!

noddy *inf* ['nɒdɪ] (*pl* **noddies**) *Br* ◇ *n* bêta *m,* -asse *f.*

◇ *adj:* he's got a ~ job il fait un boulot peinard.

node [nəʊd] *n* ASTRON, BOT, LING & MATH nœud *m;* ANAT nodosité *f,* nodule *m.*

nodular ['nɒdjʊləʳ] *adj* nodulaire.

nodule ['nɒdjuːl] *n* nodule *m.*

Noel, Noël [nəʊ'el] *n lit* [Christmas] Noël *m.*

no-frills *adj* sans fioritures, (tout) simple, sommaire; a ~ hotel un hôtel sans confort superflu.

noggin ['nɒgɪn] *n* -**1.** [measure] quart *m* de pinte. -**2.** *inf* [drink] pot *m.* -**3.** *inf* [head]: use your ~!

fais marcher tes méninges!, sers-toi de ta cervelle!

no-go area *n* zone *f* interdite.

no-good *inf* ◇ *adj* propre à rien.
◇ *n* bon *m* à rien, bonne *f* à rien.

no-hoper *inf* [-'həʊpəʳ] *n* raté *m*, -e *f*, minable *mf*.

nohow *inf* ['nəʊhaʊ] *adv* aucunement, en aucune façon.

noise [nɔɪz] ◇ *n* -**1.** [sound] bruit *m*, son *m*; the clock is making a funny ~ la pendule fait un drôle de bruit; I thought I heard a ~ downstairs j'ai cru entendre du bruit en bas; the humming ~ of the engine le ronronnement du moteur ❑ ~s off THEAT instruments *mpl* OR dispositif *m* de bruitage. -**2.** [din] bruit *m*, tapage *m*, tintamarre *m*; [very loud] vacarme *m*; to make a ~ faire du bruit; do you call that ~ music? pour vous, ce vacarme c'est de la musique?; shut your ~! *inf Br* ferme-la! ❑ ~ abatement lutte *f* contre le bruit; ~ pollution nuisances *fpl* sonores, pollution *f* sonore. -**3.** ELEC & TELEC parasites *mpl*; [on line] friture *f*, sifflement *m*. -**4.** *inf phr*: to make a ~ about sthg faire du tapage OR beaucoup de bruit autour de qqch; the critics made a lot of ~ about the film les critiques ont fait beaucoup de bruit autour de ce film; they made a lot of ~ about banning the march ils ont remué ciel et terre pour faire interdire la manifestation.
◇ *vt*: to ~ sthg about OR abroad ébruiter qqch.
◆ **noises** *inf npl* [indications of intentions]: she made vague ~s about emigrating elle a vaguement parlé d'émigrer; he started making placatory ~s il se mit à marmonner quelques paroles d'apaisement; they made all the right ~s, but... ils ont fait semblant de marcher à fond OR d'être tout à fait d'accord, mais...

noiseless ['nɔɪzlɪs] *adj* silencieux.

noiselessly ['nɔɪzlɪslɪ] *adv* silencieusement, sans faire de bruit.

noisemaker ['nɔɪzmeɪkəʳ] *n Am* [rattle] crécelle *f*; [trumpet] trompe *f*.

noisily ['nɔɪzɪlɪ] *adv* bruyamment.

noisome ['nɔɪsəm] *adj lit* [repellent] répugnant, repoussant; [smelly] puant, méphitique *lit*; [noxious] nocif, nuisible; a ~ smell une odeur infecte OR pestilentielle.

noisy ['nɔɪzɪ] (*compar* noisier, *superl* noisiest) *adj* -**1.** [machine, engine, person] bruyant; my typewriter is very ~ ma machine à écrire est très bruyante OR fait beaucoup de bruit; London was too ~ for him Londres était trop bruyant à son goût. -**2.** [colour] criard.

nomad ['nəʊmæd] *n* nomade *mf*.

nomadic [nəʊ'mædɪk] *adj* nomade.

nomadism ['nəʊmædɪzm] *n* nomadisme *m*.

nomadize, -ise ['nəʊmædaɪz] ◇ *vi* nomadiser.
◇ *vt*: the desert has ~d them le désert les a contraints à se nomadiser OR à la nomadisation.

no-man's-land *n literal* & *fig* no man's land *m inv*.

nom de plume [,nɒmdə'pluːm] *n* pseudonyme *m*, nom *m* de plume.

nomenclature [*Br* nəʊ'menklətʃəʳ, *Am* 'nəʊmənkleɪtʃər] *n* nomenclature *f*.

nominal ['nɒmɪnl] ◇ *adj* -**1.** [in name only - owner, leader] de nom (seulement), nominal; [- ownership, leadership] nominal; he was the ~ president of the company il n'était le président de la société que de nom. -**2.** [negligible] insignifiant; a ~ amount une somme insignifiante ‖ [token] symbolique; a ~ contribution of one pound a year une contribution symbolique d'une livre par an. -**3.** GRAMM nominal.
◇ *n* GRAMM élément *m* nominal; [noun phrase] groupe *m* nominal; [pronoun] nominal *m*.

nominalism ['nɒmɪnəlɪzm] *n* nominalisme *m*.

nominalization [,nɒmɪnəlaɪ'zeɪʃn] *n* nominalisation *f*.

nominalize, -ise ['nɒmɪnəlaɪz] *vt* nominaliser.

nominally ['nɒmɪnəlɪ] *adv* -**1.** [in name only] nominalement. -**2.** [as token] pour la forme. -**3.** [theoretically] théoriquement.

nominal value *n* valeur *f* nominale.

nominate ['nɒmɪneɪt] ◇ *vt* -**1.** [propose] proposer (la candidature de); to ~ sb for a post proposer la candidature de qqn à un poste ‖ [for award] sélectionner, nominer; the film was ~d for an Oscar le film a été sélectionné OR nominé pour un Oscar. -**2.** [appoint] nommer, désigner; she was ~d to replace Mr Neill as minister elle a été nommée ministre en remplacement de M. Neill; he was ~d chairman OR to the chairmanship il fut nommé président.
◇ *vi Austr* se présenter (comme candidat).

nomination [,nɒmɪ'neɪʃn] *n* -**1.** [proposal] proposition *f*; who will get the Democratic ~ (for president)? qui obtiendra l'investiture démocrate (à l'élection présidentielle)? ‖ [for award] nomination *f*; the film got three Oscar ~s le film a obtenu trois nominations aux Oscars. -**2.** [appointment] nomination *f*.

nominative ['nɒmɪnətɪv] ◇ *n* GRAMM nominatif *m*; in the ~ au nominatif.
◇ *adj* -**1.** GRAMM nominatif; the ~ case le nominatif. -**2.** [appointed] désigné. -**3.** [name-bearing] nominatif.

nominator ['nɒmɪneɪtəʳ] *n* présentateur *m*, -trice *f* (*d'un candidat*).

nominee [,nɒmɪ'niː] *n* -**1.** [proposed] candidat *m*, -e *f*. -**2.** [appointed] personne *f* désignée OR nommée; the government ~s on the commission les membres de la commission nommés par le gouvernement.

nomogram ['nɒməgræm], **nomograph** ['nɒməgrɑːf] *n* nomogramme *m*.

non- [nɒn] *in cpds* -**1.** [not] non-; the ~application of this rule la non-application de cette règle; all ~French nationals tous les ressortissants de nationalité autre que française; his answers were ~answers ses réponses n'en étaient pas. -**2.** [against] anti-; ~rust antirouille (*inv*).

nonabsorbent [,nɒnəb'sɔːbənt] *adj* non absorbant.

nonacademic [,nɒnækə'demɪk] *adj* -**1.** [activity] SCH extrascolaire; UNIV extra-universitaire. -**2.** SCH & UNIV [staff] non enseignant. -**3.** [course] pratique, technique.

nonacceptance [,nɒnək'septəns] *n* nonacceptation *f*.

nonachiever [,nɒnə'tʃiːvəʳ] *n* élève *mf* qui ne réussit pas.

nonaddictive [,nɒnə'dɪktɪv] *adj* qui ne crée pas de phénomène d'accoutumance.

nonadmission [,nɒnəd'mɪʃn] *n* nonadmission *f*.

nonaffiliated [,nɒnə'fɪlɪeɪtɪd] *adj* non affilié, indépendant.

nonage ['nəʊnɪdʒ] *n* minorité *f*.

nonagenarian [,nəʊnədʒɪ'neərɪən] ◇ *adj* nonagénaire.
◇ *n* nonagénaire *mf*.

nonaggression [,nɒnə'greʃn] *n* nonagression *f*; ~ pact pacte *m* de non-agression.

nonalcoholic [,nɒnælkə'hɒlɪk] *adj* non alcoolisé, sans alcool; ~ beverages boissons *fpl* non alcoolisées.

nonaligned [,nɒnə'laɪnd] *adj* non-aligné; ~ countries pays *mpl* non-alignés.

nonalignment [,nɒnə'laɪnmənt] *n* nonalignement *m*.

nonappearance [,nɒnə'pɪərəns] *n* JUR noncomparution *f*; [gen]: how do you account for her ~? comment expliquez-vous le fait qu'elle ne soit pas venue?

nonarrival [,nɒnə'raɪvl] *n* non-arrivée *f*.

nonattendance [,nɒnə'tendəns] *n* absence *f*; ~ of lectures absence aux cours.

nonavailability ['nɒnə,veɪlə'bɪlətɪ] *n* nondisponibilité *f*.

nonbeliever [,nɒnbɪ'liːvəʳ] *n* non-croyant *m*, -e *f*, incroyant *m*, -e *f*.

nonbelligerent [,nɒnbɪ'lɪdʒərənt] *adj* non belligérant.

nonbinding [,nɒn'baɪndɪŋ] *adj* sans obligation non contraignant.

nonbiodegradable ['nɒn,baɪəʊdɪ'greɪdəb *adj* non biodégradable.

nonce [nɒns] *n lit* OR *hum*: for the ~ pou l'instant.

nonce word *n* mot *m* créé pour l'occasion.

nonchalance [*Br* 'nɒnʃələns, *Am* ,nɒnʃə'lɑːn *n* nonchalance *f*.

nonchalant [*Br* 'nɒnʃələnt, *Am* ,nɒnʃə'lɑːn *adj* nonchalant.

nonchalantly [*Br* 'nɒnʃələntlɪ, *A* ,nɒnʃə'lɑːntlɪ] *adv* nonchalamment, avec no chalance.

noncom *inf* ['nɒnkɒm] *n* sous-off *m*.

noncombatant [*Br* ,nɒn'kɒmbətənt, *A* ,nɒnkəm'bætənt] ◇ *n* non-combattant *m*, -e
◇ *adj* non-combattant.

noncombustible [,nɒnkəm'bʌstəbl] *a* incombustible.

noncommissioned officer [,nɒnkə'mɪʃnd *n* sous-officier *m*.

noncommittal [,nɒnkə'mɪtl] *adj* [statemen évasif, qui n'engage à rien; [attitude, person réservé; [gesture] peu révélateur; a ~ reply ur réponse évasive; she gave a ~ grunt elle ém un petit grognement qui ne l'engageait ni dar un sens, ni dans l'autre; he was very ~ abo his plans il s'est montré très réservé OR il a fa preuve d'une grande réserve quant à ses projet

noncompliance [,nɒnkəm'plaɪəns] non-respect *m*, non-observation *f*; ~ with th treaty le non-respect du traité; ~ with th orders of a superior refus d'obéir aux ordre d'un supérieur.

non compos mentis ['nɒn,kɒmpɒs'mentɪ *adj* fou, dément, irresponsable.

nonconductor [,nɒnkən'dʌktəʳ] *n* no conducteur *m*.

nonconformism [,nɒnkən'fɔːmɪzm] *n* [ge non-conformisme *m*.
◆ **Nonconformism** *n* RELIG non-confo misme *m*.

nonconformist [,nɒnkən'fɔːmɪst] ◇ *n* [ge non-conformiste *mf*.
◇ *adj* [gen] non-conformiste.
◆ **Nonconformist** RELIG ◇ *n* non-confo miste *mf*.
◇ *adj* non-conformiste.

nonconformity [,nɒnkən'fɔːmətɪ] *n* [ger non-conformité *f*.
◆ **Nonconformity** RELIG = **Nonconformism**

noncontributory [,nɒnkən'trɪbjʊtərɪ] *adj Br*: ~ pension scheme un régime de retraite sar retenues OR cotisations.

noncooperation ['nɒnkəʊ,ɒpə'reɪʃn] *n* refus de coopérer.

non-dairy *adj* qui ne contient aucun produ laitier; ~ cream *Am crème liquide d'origir végétale*.

non-dazzle *adj* anti-éblouissement (*inv*).

nondeductible [,nɒndɪ'dʌktəbl] *adj* non d ductible.

nondelivery [,nɒndɪ'lɪvərɪ] *n*: in the event c ~ dans l'éventualité où les marchandises n seraient pas livrées.

nondescript [*Br* 'nɒndɪskrɪpt, *A* ,nɒndɪ'skrɪpt] *adj* quelconque; a ~ little ma un petit homme que rien ne distingue de autres OR tout à fait anodin; the street was line with ~ buildings la rue était bordée de bât ments quelconques OR dépourvus de caractère

nondrinker [,nɒn'drɪŋkəʳ] *n* abstinent *m*, -e she's a ~ elle ne boit pas (d'alcool).

nondrip [,nɒn'drɪp] *adj* anti-goutte (*inv*).

nondriver [,nɒn'draɪvəʳ] *n* personne *f* qui n conduit pas; I'm a ~ [never learnt] je n'ai pa mon permis; [out of choice] je ne conduis pa

none [nʌn] *pron* -**1.** [with countable nouns] a cun *m*, -e *f*; ~ of the photos is OR are for sa aucune des photos n'est à vendre; he looke for clues but found ~ il chercha des indice mais n'en trouva aucun; there are ~ left il n'en reste plus; how many cigarettes have you got? – ~ at all combien de cigarettes as-tu? – aucune OR pas une seule ‖ [with uncountable nouns]: ~ of her early work has been published aucun de ses premiers textes n'a été publié; ~ of the mail is for you il n'y a rien pour vous au courrier; I've done a lot of work but you've done ~ j'ai beaucoup travaillé, mais toi tu n'as rien fait; she displayed ~ of her usual good humour elle était loin d'afficher sa bonne humeur habituelle; they'll get ~ of my money! ils n'auront pas un centime de moi!; more soup anyone? – ~ for me, thanks encore un peu de soupe? – pas pour moi, merci ❑ (I'll have) ~ of your cheek! je ne tolérerai pas vos insolences!; ~ of that! [stop it] pas de ça!; she would have ~ of it elle ne voulait rien savoir. -**2.** [not one person] aucun *m*, -e *f*; ~ of them works OR work hard enough aucun d'eux ne travaille suffisamment; ~ of us understood his explanation aucun de nous n'a compris son explication; ~ can tell what the future holds *lit* nul ne sait ce que l'avenir nous réserve; there was ~ braver than her *lit* nul n'était plus courageux qu'elle.

◆ **none but** *adv phr fml* OR *lit*: we use ~ but the finest ingredients nous n'utilisons que les meilleurs ingrédients; ~ but an expert would know the difference seul un expert serait à même de faire la différence; I love ~ but her je n'aime qu'elle.

◆ **none other than** *prep phr* personne d'autre que; he received a letter from ~ other than the Prime Minister himself il reçut une lettre dont l'auteur n'était autre que le Premier ministre en personne.

◆ **none the** *adv phr (with comparative adj)*: I feel ~ the better/worse for it je ne me sens pas mieux/plus mal pour autant; I like them ~ the better/worse for it je ne les en aime pas plus/moins; she's ~ the worse for her adventure son aventure ne lui a pas fait de mal; we're still ~ the wiser! nous ne sommes pas plus avancés pour autant!

◆ **none too** *adv phr*: he's ~ too bright il est loin d'être brillant OR d'être d'une intelligence exceptionnelle; I was ~ too pleased with them j'étais loin d'être content d'eux; he replied ~ too politely sa réponse ne fut pas particulièrement polie; and ~ too soon! ce n'est pas trop tôt!

nonentity [nɒn'entətɪ] (*pl* **nonentities**) *n* -**1.** [insignificant person] personne *f* insignifiante, nullité *f*. -**2.** [insignificance] inexistence *f*.

nonessential [ˌnɒnɪ'senʃl] ◇ *adj* accessoire, non essentiel; ~ details des détails superflus.
◇ *n*: the ~s l'accessoire *m*, le superflu; leave behind all ~s n'emportez que l'essentiel.

nonesuch ['nʌnsʌtʃ] *n* -**1.** *lit* OR *arch* personne *f* OR chose *f* incomparable. -**2.** BOT lupuline *f*, minette *f*.

nonetheless [ˌnʌnðə'les] = **nevertheless**.

non-event *n* non-événement *m*.

non-executive *adj* [director] externe.

nonexistent [ˌnɒnɪg'zɪstənt] *adj* non-existant, inexistant; his help has been almost ~ *inf* il ne s'est pas beaucoup foulé pour nous aider.

nonfat ['nɒnfæt] *adj* sans matière grasse OR matières grasses; ~ diet régime *m* sans matière grasse OR matières grasses.

nonfattening [ˌnɒn'fætnɪŋ] *adj* qui ne fait pas grossir.

nonfiction [ˌnɒn'fɪkʃn] ◇ *n (U)* ouvrages *mpl* non romanesques.
◇ *comp*: ~ section [of bookshop] rayon *m* des ouvrages généraux.

nonfigurative [ˌnɒn'fɪgjʊrətɪv] *adj* non-figuratif.

nonflammable [ˌnɒn'flæməbl] *adj* ininflammable.

non-habit-forming [-ˌfɔːmɪŋ] *adj* qui ne crée pas de phénomène d'accoutumance.

nonhuman [ˌnɒn'hjuːmən] *adj* non humain.

nonintervention [ˌnɒnɪntə'venʃn] *n* non-intervention *f*, non-ingérence *f*.

noninterventionist [ˌnɒnɪntə'venʃənɪst] *adj* [policy] non interventionniste, de non-intervention.

non-iron *adj* qui ne nécessite aucun repassage.

nonjudg(e)mental [ˌnɒndʒʌdʒ'mentl] *adj* neutre, impartial.

nonmember ['nɒnˌmembəʳ] *n* non-membre *m*; [of a club] personne *f* étrangère (au club); open to ~s ouvert au public.

nonmetal [ˌnɒn'metl] *n* non-métal *m*.

nonmetallic [ˌnɒnmɪ'tælɪk] *adj* non-métallique.

non-native *adj* non-indigène.

non-negotiable *adj* non négociable.

no-no *inf n* interdit *m*; that subject is a ~ ce sujet est tabou.

nonobservance [ˌnɒnəb'zɜːvəns] *n* [of rules] non observation *f*; [of treaty] non-respect *m*; RELIG inobservance *f*.

non obst. *written abbr of* non obstante.

no-nonsense *adj* [efficient] pratique; she's got a very ~ approach elle va droit au but.

nonpareil ['nɒnpərəl] *n lit* personne *f*/chose *f* incomparable OR unique.

nonparticipant [ˌnɒnpɑː'tɪsɪpənt] *n* non participant *m*, -e *f*.

nonpartisan ['nɒnˌpɑːtɪ'zæn] *adj* impartial, sans parti pris.

nonparty [ˌnɒn'pɑːtɪ] *adj* indépendant.

nonpayment [ˌnɒn'peɪmənt] *n* non-paiement *m*, défaut *m* de paiement.

nonperson [ˌnɒn'pɜːsən] *n* -**1.** [stateless person] *personne mise au ban de la société*. -**2.** [insignificant person] personne *f* insignifiante, nullité *f*; he treats his secretary like a ~ il se conduit envers sa secrétaire comme si elle n'existait pas.

nonplus [ˌnɒn'plʌs] (*Br pt & pp* **nonplussed**, *cont* **nonplussing**, *Am pt & pp* **nonplused**, *cont* **nonplusing**) *vt* déconcerter, dérouter.

nonplussed [ˌnɒn'plʌst] *adj* dérouté, perplexe.

nonpractising [ˌnɒn'præktɪsɪŋ] *adj* non pratiquant.

nonproductive [ˌnɒnprə'dʌktɪv] *adj* ECON [labour] improductif.

nonprofit [ˌnɒn'prɒfɪt] *Am* = **non-profit-making**.

non-profitmaking *adj Br* à but non lucratif.

nonproliferation ['nɒnprəˌlɪfə'reɪʃn] *n* non-prolifération *f*.

nonreader [ˌnɒn'riːdəʳ] *n* [who cannot read] personne *f* qui ne sait pas lire, illettré *m*, -e *f*; [who doesn't read] personne *f* qui ne lit pas; half the children are ~s la moitié des enfants ne savent pas lire.

nonresident [ˌnɒn'rezɪdənt] ◇ *n* -**1.** [of country] non-résident *m*, -e *f*. -**2.** [of hotel]: the dining room is open/closed to ~s le restaurant est ouvert au public/réservé aux clients.
◇ *adj* non résidant.

nonresistance [ˌnɒnrɪ'zɪstəns] *n* [nonviolence] non-violence *f*.

nonresistant [ˌnɒnrɪ'zɪstənt] *adj* non résistant.

nonreturnable [ˌnɒnrɪ'tɜːnəbl] *adj* [bottle, container] non consigné; sales goods are ~ les articles en solde ne sont pas repris.

nonrun [ˌnɒn'rʌn] *adj* indémaillable.

nonsectarian [ˌnɒnsek'teərɪən] *adj* tolérant, ouvert.

nonsense ['nɒnsəns] ◇ *n (U)* -**1.** [rubbish, absurdity] absurdités *fpl*, non-sens *m inv*, sottises *fpl*; the computer is outputting ~ l'ordinateur sort des âneries; you're talking ~! tu dis des bêtises!, tu racontes n'importe quoi!; his accusations are utter ~ ses accusations n'ont aucun sens; it's ~ to say that things will never improve il est absurde de dire que les choses n'iront jamais mieux; I've had enough of his ~ j'en ai assez de l'entendre raconter n'importe quoi; to make a ~ of sthg saboter qqch. -**2.** [foolishness] sottises *fpl*, bêtises *fpl*, enfantillages *mpl*; stop this OR no more of this ~! arrêtez de vous conduire comme des imbéciles!; she took no ~ from her subordinates elle ne tolérait pas le moindre OR elle ne tolérait aucun manquement de la part de ses subordonnés, elle menait ses subordonnés à la baguette; the maths teacher doesn't stand for any ~ le prof de maths ne se laisse pas marcher sur les pieds; there's no ~ about him c'est un homme très carré.
◇ *interj* taratata.
◇ *adj* dénué de sens; a ~ word un mot qui ne veut rien dire, un non-sens.

nonsense verse *n* vers *mpl* amphigouriques.

nonsensical [nɒn'sensɪkl] *adj* [talk, idea, action] absurde, qui n'a pas de sens, inepte; a ~ explanation une explication incohérente OR incompréhensible.

nonsensically [nɒn'sensɪklɪ] *adv* absurdement.

non sequitur [ˌnɒn'sekwɪtəʳ] *n* illogisme *m*; his argument was full of ~s son raisonnement était incohérent.

nonsexist [ˌnɒn'seksɪst] ◇ *adj* non-sexiste.
◇ *n* non-sexiste *mf*.

nonshrink [ˌnɒn'ʃrɪŋk] *adj* irrétrécissable.

nonskid [ˌnɒn'skɪd] *adj* antidérapant.

nonslip [ˌnɒn'slɪp] *adj* antidérapant.

nonsmoker [ˌnɒn'sməʊkəʳ] *n* -**1.** [person] non-fumeur *m*, -euse *f*. -**2.** RAIL compartiment *m* non-fumeurs.

nonsmoking [ˌnɒn'sməʊkɪŋ] *adj* [area] (pour les) non-fumeurs; we have a ~ office il est interdit de fumer dans notre bureau.

nonspecific urethritis [ˌnɒnspɪˌsɪfɪk-] *n (U)* urétrite *f* non spécifique OR non gonococcique.

nonstandard [ˌnɒn'stændəd] *adj* -**1.** LING [use of word] critiqué; in ~ English [colloquial] en anglais familier OR populaire; [dialectal] en anglais dialectal. -**2.** [product, size, shape etc] non-standard.

nonstarter [ˌnɒn'stɑːtəʳ] *n* -**1.** [horse] non-partant *m*. -**2.** *inf fig*: this project is a ~ ce projet n'est pas viable OR est voué à l'échec OR est condamné d'avance.

nonstick [ˌnɒn'stɪk] *adj* [coating] anti-adhérent, anti-adhésif; [pan] qui n'attache pas.

nonstop [ˌnɒn'stɒp] ◇ *adj* [journey] sans arrêt; [flight] direct, sans escale, non-stop; [train] direct; [radio programme] non-stop, sans interruption; they kept up a ~ conversation leur conversation se poursuivit sans interruption.
◇ *adv* sans arrêt; to fly ~ from Rome to Montreal faire Rome-Montréal sans escale.

nonsuch ['nʌnsʌtʃ] = **nonesuch**.

nontoxic [ˌnɒn'tɒksɪk] *adj* non-toxique.

nontransferable [ˌnɒntræns'fɜːrəbl] *adj* nominatif.

non-U *adj Br dated façon de désigner «ce qui ne se fait pas» selon le code des bonnes manières*.

nonunion [ˌnɒn'juːnjən] *adj* [worker, labour] non syndiqué; [firm] qui n'emploie pas de personnel syndiqué.

nonviolence [ˌnɒn'vaɪələns] *n* non-violence *f*.

nonviolent [ˌnɒn'vaɪələnt] *adj* non-violent.

nonwhite [ˌnɒn'waɪt] ◇ *n* personne *f* de couleur.
◇ *adj* de couleur; a ~ neighbourhood un quartier où vivent des gens de couleur (et très peu de blancs).

noodle ['nuːdl] *n* -**1.** CULIN nouille *f*; chicken ~ soup soupe *f* de poulet aux vermicelles. -**2.** *inf* [fool] andouille *f*, nouille *f*. -**3.** *inf Am* [head] tronche *f*.

nook [nʊk] *n* -**1.** [corner] coin *m*, recoin *m*; in every ~ and cranny dans le moindre recoin. -**2.** *lit* [secluded spot] retraite *f*; a shady ~ une retraite ombragée, un coin ombragé.

nookie *inf*, **nooky** *inf* ['nʊkɪ] *n hum*: a bit of ~ une partie de jambes en l'air.

noon [nu:n] ◇ *n* -**1.** [midday] midi *m*; come at ~ venez à midi. -**2.** *lit* [peak] zénith *m*.
◇ *comp* [break, heat, sun] de midi; ~ hour *Am* heure *f* du déjeuner.

noonday ['nu:ndeɪ] ◇ *n* midi *m*.
◇ *comp* [heat, sun] de midi.

no one, no-one = **nobody**.

noontide ['nu:ntaɪd] *lit* = **noontime**.

noontime ['nu:ntaɪm] *n* midi *m*; the ~ traffic la circulation à l'heure du déjeuner.

noose [nu:s] ◇ *n* [gen] nœud *m* coulant; [snare] collet *m*; [lasso] lasso *m*; to get the ~ être condamné à la potence; to put one's head in the ~, to put a ~ around one's neck creuser sa (propre) tombe.
◇ *vt* -**1.** [rope] faire un nœud coulant à. -**2.** [snare] prendre au collet; [lasso] attraper OR prendre au lasso.

no-par *adj Br* sans valeur nominale.

nope *inf* [nəʊp] *adv* non.

no-place *Am* = **nowhere**.

nor [nɔ:ʳ] ◇ *conj* [following 'neither', 'not'] ni; neither he ~ his wife has ever spoken to me ni lui ni sa femme ne m'ont jamais adressé la parole; I have neither the time ~ the inclination to do it je n'ai ni le temps ni l'envie de le faire; she neither drinks ~ smokes elle ne boit ni ne fume; not a wave, ~ even a ripple, disturbed the surface *lit* pas une vague ni même une ride ne troublait la surface.
◇ *adv*: I don't believe him, ~ do I trust him je ne le crois pas, et je n'ai pas confiance en lui non plus; it's not the first time, ~ will it be the last ce n'est ni la première ni la dernière fois; she couldn't see them, ~ (could) they (see) her elle ne les voyait pas, et eux non plus; I don't like fish – ~ do I je n'aime pas le poisson – moi non plus; she won't do it and ~ will he elle ne le fera pas et lui non plus.

Nordic ['nɔ:dɪk] ◇ *n* Nordique *mf*.
◇ *adj* nordique; ~ skiing ski *m* nordique.

nor'easter [,nɔ:r'i:stəʳ] NAUT = **northeaster**.

Norf *written abbr of* Norfolk.

norm [nɔ:m] *n* norme *f*; to deviate from the ~ s'écarter de la norme; unemployment has become the ~ in certain areas dans certaines régions, le chômage est devenu la règle.

normal ['nɔ:ml] ◇ *adj* -**1.** [common, typical, standard] normal; a perfectly ~ baby un bébé parfaitement normal; under ~ conditions of use dans des conditions normales d'utilisation; he's just a ~ kind of bloke *inf* c'est un type tout ce qu'il y a de (plus) banal; it's ~ for it to rain in April il est normal OR naturel qu'il pleuve en avril ‖ [habitual] habituel, normal; at the ~ time à l'heure habituelle. -**2.** MATH [in statistics, geometry] normal. -**3.** CHEM normal.
◇ *n* -**1.** [gen] normale *f*, état *m* normal; temperatures above ~ des températures au-dessus de la normale; the situation has returned to ~ la situation est redevenue normale. -**2.** GEOM normale *f*.

normality [nɔ:'mælətɪ] *Br*, **normalcy** ['nɔ:mәlsɪ] *Am n* normalité *f*; everything returned to ~ tout est revenu à la normale.

normalization [,nɔ:məlaɪ'zeɪʃn] *n* normalisation *f*.

normalize, -ise ['nɔ:məlaɪz] *vt* normaliser.

normally ['nɔ:məlɪ] *adv* -**1.** [in a normal manner] normalement; he's behaving ~ il se comporte normalement. -**2.** [ordinarily] en temps normal, d'ordinaire; I ~ get up at 7:30 d'ordinaire je me lève à 7 h 30.

Norman ['nɔ:mən] ◇ *n* -**1.** [person] Normand *m*, -e *f*. -**2.** LING normand *m*.
◇ *adj* GEOG & HIST normand; the ~ Conquest la conquête normande *(de l'Angleterre)* ‖ ARCHIT roman, anglo-normand.

THE NORMAN CONQUEST:
Conquête militaire de l'Angleterre par Guillaume le Conquérant, inaugurée par sa victoire sur le roi Harold à la bataille de Hastings, en 1066. Désormais gouverné et régi par des Normands, le pays subit de grands changements dans les domaines politique et social, se voyant notamment imposer le français comme langue officielle.

Normandy ['nɔ:məndɪ] *pr n* Normandie *f*; in ~ en Normandie.

normative ['nɔ:mətɪv] *adj* normatif.

Norse [nɔ:s] ◇ *npl* HIST: the ~ [Scandinavians] les Scandinaves *mpl*, les Nordiques *mpl*; [Norwegians] les Norvégiens *mpl*; [Vikings] les Vikings *mpl*.
◇ *n* LING norrois *m*, nordique *m*; Old ~ vieux norrois.
◇ *adj* [Scandinavian] scandinave, nordique; [Norwegian] norvégien; ~ legends légendes *fpl* scandinaves.

Norseman ['nɔ:smən] (*pl* Norsemen [-mən]) *n* Viking *m*.

north [nɔ:θ] ◇ *n* -**1.** GEOG nord *m*; the region to the ~ of Sydney la région au nord de Sydney; I was born in the North je suis né dans le Nord; in the ~ of India dans le nord de l'Inde; the wind is in the ~ le vent est au nord ❑ the ~-south divide *en Angleterre, ligne fictive de démarcation entre le nord frappé par le chômage et la délinquance, et le sud plus prospère*; the far ~ le Grand Nord; 'North by Northwest' *Hitchcock* 'la Mort aux trousses'. -**2.** CARDS nord *m*.
◇ *adj* -**1.** GEOG nord *(inv)*, du nord; the ~ coast la côte nord; in North London dans le nord de Londres; in North India dans le nord de l'Inde, en Inde du Nord; the North Atlantic/Pacific l'Atlantique/le Pacifique Nord. -**2.** [wind] du nord.
◇ *adv* au nord, vers le nord; the ranch lies ~ of the town le ranch est situé au nord de la ville; the trail headed ~ le chemin piquait vers le nord; this room faces ~ cette pièce est exposée au nord; go ~ until you come to a village allez vers le nord jusqu'à ce que vous arriviez à un village; I drove ~ for two hours j'ai roulé pendant deux heures en direction du nord; they live up ~ ils habitent dans le nord ❑ ~ of Watford *façon humoristique de désigner l'Angleterre provinciale, par opposition à Londres*.

North Africa *pr n* Afrique *f* du Nord; in ~ en Afrique du Nord.

North African ◇ *n* Nord-Africain *m*, -e *f*.
◇ *adj* nord-africain, d'Afrique du Nord.

North America *pr n* Amérique *f* du Nord.

North American ◇ *n* Nord-Américain *m*, -e *f*.
◇ *adj* nord-américain, d'Amérique du Nord; the ~ Indians les Indiens *mpl* d'Amérique du Nord.

Northants *written abbr of* Northamptonshire.

northbound ['nɔ:θbaʊnd] *adj* en direction du nord; there are roadworks on the ~ carriageway of the motorway *Br* il y a des travaux sur l'autoroute en direction du nord.

North Cape *pr n* le cap Nord.

North Carolina *pr n* Caroline *f* du Nord; in ~ en Caroline du Nord.

North Country *pr n* -**1.** [in England] Angleterre *f* du Nord; he's got a ~ accent il a un accent du nord. -**2.** [in America] *l'Alaska, le Yukon et les Territoires du Nord-Ouest*.

north-countryman (*pl* north-countrymen) *n* Anglais *m* du nord.

Northd *written abbr of* Northumberland.

North Dakota *pr n* Dakota *m* du Nord; in ~ dans le Dakota du Nord.

northeast [,nɔ:θ'i:st] ◇ *n* GEOG nord-est *m*; in the ~ of Scotland dans le nord-est de l'Écosse.
◇ *adj* -**1.** GEOL nord-est *(inv)*, du nord-est; in ~ Scotland dans le nord-est de l'Écosse. -**2.** [wind] de nord-est.
◇ *adv* au nord-est, vers le nord-est; it's 20 miles ~ of Birmingham c'est à 32 kilomètres au nord-est de Birmingham.

northeaster [,nɔ:θ'i:stəʳ] *n* vent *m* de nord-es[t] nordé *m*, nordet *m*.

northeasterly [,nɔ:θ'i:stəlɪ] (*pl* northeaste[rlies]) ◇ *adj* -**1.** GEOG nord-est *(inv)*, du nord-es[t]; go in a ~ direction allez vers le nord-est OR e[n] direction du nord-est. -**2.** [wind] de nord-est.
◇ *adv* au nord-est, vers le nord-est.
◇ *n* = **northeaster**.

northeastern [,nɔ:θ'i:stən] *adj* nord-est *(inv)*, du nord-est; the ~ suburbs la banlieue nor[d]-est.

northeastwards [,nɔ:θ'i:stwədz] *adv* vers [le] nord-est, en direction du nord-est.

northerly ['nɔ:ðəlɪ] (*pl* northerlies) ◇ *a[dj]* -**1.** GEOG nord *(inv)*, du nord; in these ~ latitudes sous ces latitudes boréales; in a ~ direction vers le nord; a room with a ~ aspec[t] une pièce exposée au nord. -**2.** [wind] du nor[d].
◇ *adv* vers le nord.
◇ *n* vent *m* du nord.

northern ['nɔ:ðən] *adj* -**1.** GEOG nord *(inv)*, d[u] nord; the ~ wing of the castle l'aile nord d[u] château; ~ tribes tribus du nord; she has a ~ accent elle a un accent du nord; in ~ Mexic[o] dans le nord du Mexique; the ~ migration o[f] swallows in spring la migration printanière de[s] hirondelles vers le nord. -**2.** [wind] du nord.

Northerner ['nɔ:ðənəʳ] *n* -**1.** [gen] homme *m*, femme *f* du nord; she is a ~ elle vient du nord; I find that ~s are more friendly je trouve qu[e] les gens du Nord sont plus accueillants. -**2.** *A[m]* HIST nordiste *mf*.

northern hemisphere *n* hémisphère *m* nor[d] OR boréal.

Northern Ireland *pr n* Irlande *f* du Nord; i[n] ~ en Irlande du Nord.

NORTHERN IRELAND:
Partie de l'Irlande à majorité protestante resté[e] rattachée à la Grande-Bretagne lors de la par[tition] du pays, en 1949. Depuis les émeute[s] sanglantes de Belfast et de Londonderry e[n] 1969, les affrontements entre nationalistes d[e] l'IRA, extrémistes protestants et représentant[s] de l'autorité britannique n'ont pas cessé, san[s] qu'une solution soit en vue, malgré l'accor[d] anglo-irlandais sur la gestion des affaires d[e] l'Ulster en 1985.

Northernism ['nɔ:ðənɪzm] *n Br* particularité linguistique (de l'anglais) du Nord.

northern lights *npl* aurore *f* boréale.

northernmost ['nɔ:ðənməʊst] *adj* le plus a[u] nord; the ~ island of Japan l'île du Japon la plu[s] au nord; the ~ limits of the Roman Empire le[s] limites septentrionales de l'Empire romain.

Northern Territory *pr n* Territoire *m* d[u] Nord; in ~ dans le Territoire du Nord.

north-facing *adj* [wall, building] (exposé) a[u] nord.

North Island *pr n* l'île *f* du Nord; in the ~ [à] l'île du Nord.

North Korea *pr n* Corée *f* du Nord.

North Korean ◇ *n* Nord-Coréen *m*, -enne *f*.
◇ *adj* nord-coréen.

Northman ['nɔ:θmən] (*pl* Northmen [-mən]) *n Br* Viking *m*.

north-northeast ◇ *n* nord-nord-est *m*.
◇ *adj* nord-nord-est *(inv)*, du nord-nord-est.
◇ *adv* au nord-nord-est, vers le nord-nord-est.

north-northwest ◇ *n* nord-nord-ouest *m*.
◇ *adj* nord-nord-ouest *(inv)*, du nord-nord-ouest.
◇ *adv* au nord-nord-ouest, vers le nord-nord-ouest.

North Pole *pr n*: the ~ le pôle Nord.

North Rhine-Westphalia *pr n* Rhénanie-du-Nord-Westphalie *f*; in ~ en Rhénanie-du-Nord-Westphalie.

North Sea ◇ *pr n*: the ~ la mer du Nord.
◇ *comp* [oil, gas] de la mer du Nord.

North Star *pr n*: the ~ l'étoile *f* Polaire.

Northumbrian [nɔ:'θʌmbrɪən] ◇ *adj* GEO[G] du Northumberland; HIST northumbrien, de l[a] Northumbrie.

◇ *n* GEOG habitant *m*, -e *f* du Northumberland; HIST habitant *m*, -e *f* de la Northumbrie.

North Vietnam *pr n* Nord Viêt-nam *m*; in ~ au Nord Viêt-nam.

North Vietnamese ◇ *n* Nord-Vietnamien *m*, -enne *f*.
◇ *adj* nord-vietnamien.

northward ['nɔːθwəd] ◇ *adj* au nord.
◇ *adv* = **northwards**.

northwards ['nɔːθwədz] *adv* vers le nord, en direction du nord.

northwest [,nɔːθ'west] ◇ *n* nord-ouest *m*; in the ~ of Canada dans le nord-ouest du Canada.
◇ *adj* -**1.** GEOG nord-ouest *(inv)*, du nord-ouest; in ~ Canada dans le nord-ouest du Canada. -**2.** [wind] de nord-ouest.
◇ *adv* au nord-ouest, vers le nord-ouest; it's ~ of London c'est au nord-ouest de Londres.

northwester [,nɔːθ'westəʳ] *n* vent *m* de nord-ouest, noroît *m*.

northwesterly [,nɔːθ'westəlɪ] (*pl* **northwesterlies**) ◇ *adj* -**1.** GEOG nord-ouest *(inv)*, du nord-ouest; in a ~ direction vers le nord-ouest. -**2.** [wind] du nord-ouest.
◇ *adv* au nord-ouest, vers le nord-ouest.
◇ *n* = **northwester**.

northwestern [,nɔːθ'westən] *adj* nord-ouest *(inv)*, du nord-ouest; the ~ frontier la frontière nord-ouest.

Northwest Passage *pr n* passage *m* du Nord-Ouest.

Northwest Territories *pl pr n* Territoires *mpl* du Nord-Ouest.

northwestwards [,nɔːθ'westwədz] *adv* vers le nord-ouest, en direction du nord-ouest.

North Yemen *pr n* Yemen *m* du Nord; in ~ au Yemen du Nord.

Norway ['nɔːweɪ] *pr n* Norvège *f*; in ~ en Norvège.

Norway lobster *n* langoustine *f*.

Norwegian [nɔː'wiːdʒən] ◇ *n* -**1.** [person] Norvégien *m*, -enne *f*. -**2.** LING norvégien *m*.
◇ *adj* norvégien.

nor'wester [,nɔː'westəʳ] NAUT = **northwester**.

Nos., nos. (*written abbr of* **numbers**) no.

nose [nəʊz] ◇ *n* -**1.** ANAT nez *m*; to hold one's ~ se pincer le nez; the dog has a wet ~ le chien a le nez OR la truffe humide; your ~ is bleeding tu saignes du nez; your ~ is running tu as le nez qui coule; to speak through one's ~ parler du nez; I punched him on OR in the ~ je lui ai donné un coup de poing en pleine figure; she's always got her ~ in a book elle a toujours le nez dans un livre; the favourite won by a ~ [in horseracing] le favori a gagné d'une demi-tête; I'll have £10 on the ~ je parie 10 livres qu'il va gagner; look, it's right under your ~! regarde, il est juste sous ton nez OR tu as le nez dessus!; it was (right) under my ~ all the time c'était en plein sous mon nez; they stole it from under the ~ of the police *fig* ils l'ont volé au nez et à la barbe de la police ❑ he can see no further than (the end of) his ~ il ne voit pas plus loin que le bout de son nez; he really gets OR he gets right up my ~! *inf* il me pompe l'air!; you've got OR hit it right on the ~ tu as mis en plein dans le mille; to keep one's ~ clean se tenir à carreau; try and keep your ~ clean tu ferais bien de te tenir peinard; keep your (big) ~ out of my business! *inf* mêle-toi de ce qui te regarde!; to keep OR to have one's ~ to the grindstone bosser (dur); to keep sb's ~ to the grindstone faire bosser OR trimer qqn; to lead sb by the ~ mener qqn par le bout du nez; to look down one's ~ at sb/sthg traiter qqn/qqch avec condescendance; to pay through the ~ (for sthg) payer (qqch) la peau des fesses; to put sb's ~ out of joint *inf Br* contrarier OR dépiter qqn; he's always sticking OR poking his ~ in *inf* il faut qu'il fourre son nez partout; she's always sticking OR poking her ~ into our affairs *inf* elle est toujours en train de fourrer son nez dans nos affaires; to turn up one's ~ at sthg faire la fine bouche devant qqch; he's always walking around with his ~ in the air il prend toujours un air hautain OR méprisant. -**2.** [sense of smell] odorat *m*, nez *m*; these dogs have an excellent ~ ces chiens ont un excellent flair OR le nez fin *spec*; she's got a (good) ~ for a bargain *fig* elle a le nez creux OR du nez pour dénicher les bonnes affaires. -**3.** [aroma - of wine] arôme *m*, bouquet *m*, nez *m*. -**4.** [forward part - of aircraft, ship] nez *m*; [- of car] avant *m*; [- of bullet, missile, tool] pointe *f*; [- of gun] canon *m*; the traffic was ~ to tail all the way to London *Br* les voitures étaient pare-chocs contre pare-chocs jusqu'à Londres.
◇ *vt* -**1.** [smell] flairer, renifler. -**2.** [push with nose] pousser du nez; the dog ~d the door open le chien a ouvert la porte en la poussant du nez.
◇ *vi* -**1.** [advance with care] avancer précautionneusement; the car ~d out into the traffic la voiture se frayait un chemin au milieu des embouteillages. -**2.** *inf* [snoop] fouiner.
◆ **nose about** *inf Br*, **nose around** *inf vi insep* [snoop] fureter, fouiner; two men came nosing about for information deux hommes sont venus fouiner pour avoir des renseignements; I don't want them nosing about in here! je ne veux pas qu'ils viennent fourrer leur nez ici!
◆ **nose out** *vt sep* -**1.** [discover - by smell] flairer; [- by cunning, intuition] dénicher, débusquer. -**2.** *inf* [beat narrowly] battre d'une courte tête; he was ~d out of first place by an outsider un outsider lui a soufflé la première place d'une courte tête.

nosebag ['nəʊzbæg] *n Br* musette *f*, mangeoire *f* portative.

noseband ['nəʊzbænd] *n* muserolle *f*.

nosebleed ['nəʊzbliːd] *n* saignement *m* de nez, épistaxis *f spec*; I've got a ~ je saigne du nez; do you often get ~s? est-ce que vous saignez souvent du nez?

nose cone *n* [of missile] ogive *f*; [of aircraft] nez *m*.

-nosed [nəʊzd] *in cpds* au nez...; snub~ au nez retroussé; red~ au nez rouge.

nose dive *n* -**1.** [of plane, bird] piqué *m*; I did a ~ onto the concrete *inf* je suis tombé la tête la première sur le béton. -**2.** *inf fig* [sharp drop] chute *f*, dégringolade *f*; prices took a ~ les prix ont considérablement chuté; his popularity has taken a ~ sa cote de popularité s'est littéralement effondrée.
◆ **nose-dive** *vi* -**1.** [plane] piquer, descendre en piqué. -**2.** *fig* [popularity, prices] être en chute libre, chuter.

nose drops *npl* gouttes *fpl* nasales OR pour le nez.

nosegay ['nəʊzgeɪ] *n lit* (petit) bouquet *m*.

nose job *inf n* intervention *f* de chirurgie esthétique sur le nez; she's had a ~ elle s'est fait refaire le nez.

nose ring *n* anneau *m* de nez.

nose wheel *n* roue *f* avant.

nosey *inf* ['nəʊzɪ] = **nosy**.

nosh *inf* [nɒʃ] *dated* ◇ *n* bouffe *f*.
◇ *vi* bouffer.

no-show *n* [for flight, voyage] *passager qui ne se présente pas à l'embarquement*; [for show] *spectateur qui a réservé sa place et qui n'assiste pas au spectacle*; there were so many ~s that they cancelled the flight il y a eu tellement de défections que le vol a été annulé.

nosh-up *inf n Br* gueuleton *m*.

no-side *n* [in rugby] fin *f* du match.

nosiness *inf* ['nəʊzɪnɪs] *n* curiosité *f*; his ~ really annoys me il m'agace sérieusement à fourrer son nez partout.

nosography [nɒ'sɒgrəfɪ] (*pl* **nosographies**) *n* nosographie *f*.

nosological [,nɒsə'lɒdʒɪkl] *adj* nosologique.

nosology [nɒ'sɒlədʒɪ] *n* nosologie *f*.

nostalgia [nɒ'stældʒə] *n* nostalgie *f*.

nostalgic [nɒ'stældʒɪk] *adj* nostalgique.

nostril ['nɒstrɪl] *n* [gen] narine *f*; [of horse, cow etc] naseau *m*.

nostrum ['nɒstrəm] *n literal & fig* panacée *f*.

nosy *inf* ['nəʊzɪ] (*compar* **nosier**, *superl* **nosiest**) *adj* curieux; don't be so ~! occupe-toi donc de tes affaires OR de tes oignons!; he's very ~ il fourre son nez partout; I didn't mean to be ~ je ne voulais pas être indiscret.

nosy parker *inf n Br pej* curieux *m*, -euse *f*.

not [nɒt] *adv* -**1.** [after verb or auxiliary] ne... pas; we are ~ OR aren't sure nous ne sommes pas sûrs; do ~ OR don't believe her ne la croyez pas; didn't he OR did he ~ hear you? ne vous a-t-il pas entendu?; you've been there already, haven't you OR *fml* have you ~? vous y êtes déjà allé, non OR n'est-ce pas? ‖ [with infinitive] ne pas; I'll try ~ to cry j'essaierai de ne pas pleurer; I asked them ~ to do it je leur ai demandé de ne pas le faire. -**2.** [as phrase or clause substitute] non, pas; we hope ~ nous espérons que non; are there any left? — I'm afraid ~ est-ce qu'il en reste? — j'ai bien peur que non; will it rain? — I think ~ *fml* est-ce qu'il va pleuvoir? — je crois que non OR je ne crois pas; whether they like it or ~ que ça leur plaise ou non OR ou pas. -**3.** [with adj, adv, noun etc] pas; it's Thomas, ~ Jake c'est Thomas, pas Jake; the water is green, ~ blue l'eau est verte, pas bleue; ~ a leaf stirred pas une feuille ne bougeait; ~ all her books are good ses livres ne sont pas tous bons, tous ses livres ne sont pas bons; ~ everyone would agree with you tout le monde ne serait pas d'accord avec toi; who wants some more? — ~ I *fml* qui en veut encore? — pas moi; ~ I *fml* pas moi. -**4.** [in double negatives]: ~ without some difficulty non sans quelque difficulté; a ~ insignificant amount of money une somme non négligeable; it's ~ unusual for him to be late il n'est pas rare qu'il soit en retard; the two events are ~ unconnected les deux événements ne sont pas tout à fait indépendants l'un de l'autre. -**5.** [less than] moins de; ~ five minutes later the phone rang moins de cinq minutes plus tard, le téléphone a sonné; ~ ten metres away à moins de dix mètres.

notability [,nəʊtə'bɪlətɪ] (*pl* **notabilities**) *n* -**1.** [importance] importance *f*. -**2.** [important person] notabilité *f*, notable *m*.

notable ['nəʊtəbl] ◇ *adj* [thing] notable, remarquable; [person] notable, éminent; ~ progress has been made des progrès notables ont été accomplis; the film was ~ for its lack of violence le film se distinguait par l'absence de scènes de violence.
◇ *n* notable *m*.

notably ['nəʊtəblɪ] *adv* -**1.** [particularly] notamment, en particulier; several officials were absent, ~ the mayor il manquait plusieurs personnalités, notamment le maire. -**2.** [markedly] manifestement, de toute évidence.

notarial [nəʊ'teərɪəl] *adj* [procedure, stamp] notarial; [deed] notarié.

notarize, -ise ['nəʊtəraɪz] *vt* certifier, officialiser; ~d deed acte *m* notarié; a ~d copy ≃ une copie certifiée conforme *(par un notaire)*.

notary ['nəʊtərɪ] (*pl* **notaries**) *n*: ~ (public) notaire *m*; signed in the presence of a ~ signé par-devant notaire.

notation [nəʊ'teɪʃn] *n* -**1.** [sign system] notation *f*; musical ~ notation musicale; mathematical ~ symboles *mpl* mathématiques; in binary ~ en numération binaire, en base 2. -**2.** *Am* [jotting] notation *f*, note *f*.

notch [nɒtʃ] ◇ *n* -**1.** [cut - in stick] entaille *f*, encoche *f*; [hole - in belt] cran *m*; he let out his belt a ~ il a desserré sa ceinture d'un cran. -**2.** [degree] cran *m*; he's gone up a ~ in my estimation il est monté d'un cran dans mon estime; turn the heating up a ~ monte un peu le chauffage; her novel is a ~ above the rest son roman est un peu meilleur que les autres. -**3.** *Am* [gorge] défilé *m*.

◇ *vt* -**1.** [make cut in - stick] entailler, encocher; [- gear wheel] cranter, denteler; [damage - blade] ébrécher. -**2.** *fig* = **notch up**.

◆ **notch up** *vt sep* [achieve] accomplir; they've ~ed up six wins in a row ils ont six victoires consécutives à leur palmarès.

note [nəʊt] ◇ *n* -**1.** [record, reminder] note *f*; to take OR to make ~s prendre des notes; she spoke from/without ~s elle a parlé en s'aidant/sans s'aider de notes; make a ~ of everything you spend notez toutes vos dépenses; I must make a ~ to myself to ask her about it *fig* il faut que je pense à le lui demander; he made a mental ~ to look for it later il se promit de le chercher plus tard; to compare ~s *fig* échanger ses impressions. -**2.** [short letter] mot *m*; she left a ~ to say she'd call back later elle a laissé un mot pour dire qu'elle repasserait plus tard. -**3.** [formal communication] note *f*; diplomatic ~ note diplomatique; a doctor's OR sick ~ un certificat OR une attestation du médecin (traitant); SCH un certificat (médical). -**4.** [annotation, commentary] note *f*, annotation *f*; ~s in the margin notes dans la OR en marge; editor's ~ note de la rédaction; see ~ 6 voir note 6 ❑ programme ~s notes sur le programme. -**5.** *Br* [banknote] billet *m* (de banque); ten-pound ~ billet de dix livres. -**6.** [sound, tone] ton *m*, note *f*; the piercing ~ of the siren le son strident de la sirène; there was a ~ of contempt in her voice il y avait du mépris dans sa voix ‖ *fig* [feeling, quality] note *f*; the meeting began on a promising ~ la réunion débuta sur une note optimiste; on a more serious/a happier ~ pour parler de choses plus sérieuses/plus gaies; the flowers add a ~ of colour les fleurs apportent une touche de couleur; her speech struck a warning ~ son discours était un signal d'alarme ❑ to strike the right/a false ~ [speech] sonner juste/faux; [behaviour] être/ne pas être dans le ton. -**7.** MUS note *f*; to hit a high ~ sortir un aigu ‖ *Br* [piano key] touche *f*; the black ~s les touches noires. -**8.** [notice, attention]: to take ~ of sthg prendre (bonne) note de qqch. -**9.** COMM: (promissory) ~, ~ of hand billet *m* à ordre.

◇ *vt* -**1.** [observe, notice] remarquer, noter; he ~d that the window was open il remarqua que la fenêtre était ouverte; we have ~d several omissions nous avons relevé plusieurs oublis; ~ that she didn't actually refuse notez (bien) qu'elle n'a pas vraiment refusé; please ~ that payment is now due veuillez effectuer le règlement dans les plus brefs délais. -**2.** [write down] noter, écrire; I ~d (down) her address j'ai noté son adresse; all sales are ~d in this book toutes les ventes sont enregistrées OR consignées dans ce carnet. -**3.** [mention] (faire) remarquer OR observer; as I ~d earlier comme je l'ai fait remarquer précédemment.

◆ **of note** *adj phr*: a musician of ~ un musicien éminent OR renommé; a musician of some ~ un musicien d'une certaine renommée; everyone of ~ was there tous les gens importants OR qui comptent étaient là; nothing of ~ has happened il ne s'est rien passé d'important, aucun événement majeur ne s'est produit; we have achieved little of ~ nous n'avons pas fait grand-chose d'important.

◆ **note down** *vt sep* = **note** *vt* **2**.

notebook ['nəʊtbʊk] *n* carnet *m*, calepin *m*; SCH cahier *m*, carnet *m*; ~ computer (petit) ordinateur *m* portable, notebook *m*.

notecase ['nəʊtkeɪs] *n Br dated* portefeuille *m*.

noted ['nəʊtɪd] *adj* [person] éminent, célèbre; [place, object] réputé, célèbre; [fact, idea] reconnu; to be ~ for one's integrity être connu pour son intégrité; he's not ~ for his flexibility il ne passe pas pour quelqu'un de particulièrement accommodant; a city ~ as a centre of culture une ville réputée pour sa vie culturelle; a region ~ for its parks une région réputée OR connue pour ses parcs.

notelet ['nəʊtlɪt] *n Br* carte-lettre *f*.

notepad ['nəʊtpæd] *n* [for notes] bloc-notes *m*; [for letters] bloc *m* de papier à lettres.

notepaper ['nəʊtpeɪpəʳ] *n* papier *m* à lettres.

noteworthiness ['nəʊt,wɜːðɪnɪs] *n* importance *f*.

noteworthy ['nəʊt,wɜːðɪ] *adj* notable, remarquable.

nothing ['nʌθɪŋ] ◇ *pron* ne... rien; she forgets ~ elle n'oublie rien; ~ has been decided rien n'a été décidé; I have ~ to drink je n'ai rien à boire; it's got ~ to do with you ça ne te concerne absolument pas; I told them ~ at all je ne leur ai rien dit du tout; I have ~ else to say je n'ai rien d'autre à dire; ~ serious rien de grave; there's ~ exceptional about him arriving late il n'y a rien d'exceptionnel à ce qu'il arrive en retard; there's ~ wrong with your car ta voiture est en parfait état de marche; I see ~ wrong with borrowing money je ne vois aucun mal à emprunter de l'argent; there's ~ the matter OR ~'s the matter with me je n'ai rien, je vais parfaitement bien; they're always fighting over ~ ils passent leur temps à se disputer pour des broutilles OR des riens; reduced to ~ réduit à néant; there's ~ for it but to start again il n'y a plus qu'à recommencer; there's ~ in OR to these rumours ces rumeurs sont dénuées de tout fondement; there's ~ to it! [it's easy] c'est simple (comme bonjour)!; she says he's ~ OR he means ~ to her elle dit qu'il n'est rien pour elle; the name means ~ to me le nom ne me dit rien; a thousand pounds is ~ to her mille livres, ce n'est rien pour elle; I'll take what's due to me, ~ more, ~ less je prendrai mon dû, ni plus ni moins ❑ what a physique! Charles Atlas has got ~ on you! *inf* quel physique! tu n'as rien à envier à Charles Atlas OR Charles Atlas peut aller se rhabiller!; our sacrifices were as ~ compared to his *lit* nos sacrifices ne furent rien auprès des siens.

◇ *n* -**1.** [trifle] rien *m*, vétille *f*; $500 may be a mere ~ to you 500 dollars ne représentent peut-être pas grand-chose pour vous. -**2.** *inf* [person] nullité *f*, zéro *m*. -**3.** MATH zéro *m*.

◇ *adj inf* [worthless] nul; it's a ~ play! c'est une pièce nulle!

◇ *adv lit* [in no way]: ~ daunted, he... pas le moindrement découragé, il...

◆ **for nothing** *adv phr* -**1.** [gratis] pour rien; I got it for ~ at the flea market je l'ai eu pour (trois fois) rien aux puces. -**2.** [for no purpose] pour rien; all that work for ~! tout ce travail pour rien OR en pure perte!; are you telling me I gave up my day off for ~? est-ce que tu veux dire que j'ai sacrifié ma journée de vacances pour rien? -**3.** [for no good reason] pour rien; the police say they don't arrest people for ~ la police dit qu'elle n'arrête personne sans raison; it's not for ~ that... ce n'est pas pour rien que...; they don't call him Einstein for ~ ce n'est pas pour rien qu'on le surnomme Einstein.

◆ **nothing but** *adv phr*: that car's been ~ but trouble cette voiture ne m'a attiré que des ennuis; ~ but a miracle can save us seul un miracle pourrait nous sauver; she wants ~ but the best elle ne veut que ce qu'il y a de meilleur; they do ~ but sleep ils ne font que dormir.

◆ **nothing if not** *adv phr* rien de moins que; she's ~ if not honest elle n'est rien de moins qu'honnête.

◆ **nothing less than** *adv phr* -**1.** [undoubtedly] rien de moins que, tout bonnement; it was ~ less than miraculous/a miracle c'était tout simplement miraculeux/un miracle. -**2.** [only] seul; ~ less than outright victory would satisfy him seule une victoire écrasante le satisferait.

◆ **nothing like** ◇ *prep phr* -**1.** [completely unlike]: she's ~ like her mother elle ne ressemble en rien à sa mère. -**2.** [nothing as good as]: there's ~ like a nice cup of tea! rien de tel qu'une bonne tasse de thé!; there's ~ like a cold shower for freshening OR to freshen you up rien de tel qu'une douche froide pour se rafraîchir.

◇ *adv phr inf* [nowhere near]: this box is ~ like big enough cette boîte est beaucoup trop OR bien trop petite.

◆ **nothing more than** *adv phr*: I want ~ more than a word of thanks from time to time tout ce que je demande, c'est un petit mot de remerciement de temps à autre; he's ~ more than a petty crook il n'est rien d'autre qu'un vulgaire escroc.

nothingness ['nʌθɪŋnɪs] *n* néant *m*; he stared out into the ~ il avait le regard perdu dans le vide.

notice ['nəʊtɪs] ◇ *n* -**1.** [written announcement] annonce *f*; [sign] écriteau *m*, pancarte *f*; [poster] affiche *f*; [in newspaper - article] entrefilet *m*; [- advertisement] annonce *f*; a ~ was pinned to the door il y avait une notice sur la porte; ~s went up telling people to stay indoors on placarda des affiches pour demander aux gens de rester chez eux. -**2.** [attention] attention *f*; to take ~ of faire OR prêter attention à; take no ~ (of him)! ne faites pas attention (à lui)!; you never take any ~ of what I say! tu ne fais jamais attention à ce que je dis!; she considers it beneath her ~ *fml* elle considère que ça ne vaut pas la peine qu'elle s'y arrête; to bring sthg to sb's ~ faire remarquer qqch à qqn, attirer l'attention de qqn sur qqch; certain facts have come to OR been brought to our ~ on a attiré notre attention sur certains faits; her book attracted a great deal of/little ~ son livre a suscité beaucoup/peu d'intérêt; to escape OR to avoid ~ passer inaperçu; my mistake did not escape his ~ mon erreur ne lui a pas échappé; has it escaped their ~ that something is seriously wrong? ne se sont-ils pas aperçu qu'il y a quelque chose qui ne va pas du tout? -**3.** [notification, warning] avis *m*, notification *f*; [advance notification] préavis *m*; please give us ~ of your intentions veuillez nous faire part préalablement de vos intentions; he was given ~ OR ~ was served on him *fml* to quit on lui a fait savoir qu'il devait partir; give me more ~ next time you come up préviens-moi plus tôt la prochaine fois que tu viens; legally, they must give you a month's ~ d'après la loi, ils doivent vous donner un mois de préavis; we require five days' ~ nous demandons un préavis de cinq jours; give me a few days' ~ prévenez-moi quelques jours à l'avance; without previous OR prior ~ sans préavis; he turned up without any ~ il est arrivé à l'improviste; at a moment's ~ sur-le-champ immédiatement; at short ~ très rapidement; it's impossible to do the work at such short ~ c'est un travail impossible à faire dans un déla[i] aussi court; until further ~ jusqu'à nouve[l] ordre OR avis. -**4.** [notifying document] avis *m*, notification *f*; [warning document] avertissement *m*; they sent three ~s before cutting of[f] the water ils ont envoyé trois avertissement[s] avant de couper l'eau ❑ ~ of receipt COMM accusé *m* de réception. -**5.** [intent to terminat[e] contract - by employer, landlord, tenant] congé *m*; [- by employee] démission *f*; fifty people have been given their ~ cinquante personnes on[t] été licenciées; to give in OR to hand in one's ~ remettre sa démission; has the landlord give[n] you ~? le propriétaire vous a-t-il donn[é] congé?; we are under ~ to quit nous avon[s] reçu notre congé. -**6.** [review] critique *f*; the film got excellent ~s le film a eu d'excellente[s] critiques.

◇ *vt* -**1.** [spot, observe] remarquer, s'apercevoi[r] de; he ~d a scratch on the table il remarqu[a] que la table était rayée; surely you ~d her? n[e] me dis pas que tu ne l'as pas vue!; hello, Sam, I didn't ~ you in the corner bonjour, Sam, j[e] ne t'avais pas vu dans le coin; so I've ~d! c'es[t] ce que j'ai remarqué!; he ~d that his watch was gone il s'est aperçu que sa montre avai[t] disparu; try and slip in without her noticin[g] essayez d'entrer sans qu'elle s'en aperçoive; I ~d her smiling j'ai remarqué qu'elle souriait. -2. [take notice of] faire attention à; he never ~s what I wear! il ne fait jamais attention à ce que je porte!

noticeable ['nəʊtɪsəbl] *adj* [mark, defect] visible; [affect, change] sensible; there has been a ~ improvement il y a eu une amélioration sensible; the stain is barely ~ la tache est à peine visible OR se voit à peine.

noticeably ['nəʊtɪsəblɪ] *adv* sensiblement.

noticeboard ['nəʊtɪsbɔːd] *n* panneau *m* d'affichage.

notifiable ['nəʊtɪfaɪəbl] *adj* [disease] à déclaration obligatoire.

notification [ˌnəʊtɪfɪ'keɪʃn] *n* notification *f*, avis *m*; you will receive ~ by mail vous serez averti par courrier.

notify ['nəʊtɪfaɪ] (*pt* & *pp* notified) *vt* notifier, avertir; to ~ sb of sthg avertir qqn de qqch, notifier qqch à qqn; have you notified the authorities? avez-vous averti OR prévenu les autorités?; winners will be notified within ten days les gagnants seront avisés dans les dix jours.

notion ['nəʊʃn] *n* -1. [concept] notion *f*, concept *m*; the ~ of evil la notion du mal; I lost all ~ of time j'ai perdu la notion du temps. -2. [opinion] idée *f*, opinion *f*; where did she get the ~ OR whatever gave her the ~ that we don't like her? où est-elle allée chercher que nous ne l'aimions pas? -3. [vague idea] notion *f*, idée *f*; have you any ~ of what it will cost? avez-vous une idée de ce que cela va coûter? -4. [thought, whim] idée *f*; he hit upon the ~ of buying a houseboat il eut soudain l'idée d'acheter une péniche aménagée || [urge] envie *f*, désir *m*; I've got a ~ to paint it red j'ai envie de le peindre en rouge.

◆ **notions** *npl Am* [haberdashery] mercerie *f*.

notional ['nəʊʃənl] *adj* -1. *Br* [hypothetical] théorique, notionnel; let's put a ~ price of $2 a kilo on it pour avoir un ordre d'idées, fixons-en le prix à 2 dollars le kilo. -2. [imaginary] imaginaire. -3. *Am* [fanciful] capricieux. -4. LING [word] sémantique, plein; ~ grammar grammaire *f* notionnelle.

notoriety [ˌnəʊtə'raɪətɪ] (*pl* notorieties) *n* [ill fame] triste notoriété *f*; [fame] notoriété *f*; these measures brought him ~ ces mesures l'ont rendu tristement célèbre.

notorious [nəʊ'tɔːrɪəs] *adj pej* [ill-famed - person] tristement célèbre; [- crime] célèbre; [- place] mal famé; a ~ miser/spy un avare/espion notoire; she's ~ for being late elle est connue pour ne jamais être à l'heure; his ~ past son passé chargé; the junction is a ~ accident spot ce croisement est réputé pour être très dangereux; the area is ~ for muggings il est bien connu que c'est un quartier où il y a beaucoup d'agressions.

notoriously [nəʊ'tɔːrɪəslɪ] *adv* notoirement; the trains here are ~ unreliable tout le monde sait qu'on ne peut pas se fier aux horaires des trains ici.

no-trump(s) *n* sans-atout *m inv*.

Notts *written abbr of* Nottinghamshire.

notwithstanding [ˌnɒtwɪθ'stændɪŋ] *fml*

◇ *prep* en dépit de; ~ the agreement, the agreement ~ en dépit de l'accord.

◇ *adv* malgré tout, néanmoins.

nougat ['nuːgɑː] *n* nougat *m*.

nought [nɔːt] *n* -1. *Br* [zero] zéro *m*; ~ point five zéro virgule cinq. -2. *arch* = **naught 2**.

noughts and crosses *n Br (U)* ≃ morpion *m (jeu)*.

noumenon ['nuːmənən] (*pl* noumena [-nə]) *n* noumène *m*.

noun [naʊn] *n* nom *m*, substantif *m*; common/proper ~ nom commun/propre; ~ phrase groupe *m* OR syntagme *m* nominal; ~ clause proposition *f*.

nourish ['nʌrɪʃ] *vt* -1. [feed] nourrir; ~ed on grain nourri au grain. -2. [entertain, foster] nourrir, entretenir.

nourishing ['nʌrɪʃɪŋ] *adj* nourrissant, nutritif.

nourishment ['nʌrɪʃmənt] *n (U)* -1. [food] nourriture *f*, aliments *mpl*; the patient has taken no ~ le malade ne s'est pas alimenté; brown rice is full of ~ le riz complet est très nourrissant. -2. [act of nourishing] alimentation *f*.

nous [naʊs] *n* -1. *inf Br* bon sens *m*, jugeote *f*. -2. PHILOS esprit *m*, intellect *m*.

Nov. (*written abbr of* November) nov.

nova ['nəʊvə] (*pl* novas OR novae [-viː]) *n* nova *f*.

Nova Scotia [ˌnəʊvə'skəʊʃə] *pr n* Nouvelle-Écosse *f*; in ~ en Nouvelle-Écosse.

Nova Scotian [ˌnəʊvə'skəʊʃn] ◇ *n* Néo-Écossais *m*, -e *f*.

◇ *adj* néo-écossais.

Novaya Zemlya [ˌnɒvəjəzem'ljɑː] *pr n* Nouvelle-Zemble *f*; in ~ en Nouvelle-Zemble.

novel ['nɒvl] ◇ *n* roman *m*; detective/spy ~ roman policier/d'espionnage.

◇ *adj* nouveau, original; what a ~ idea! quelle idée originale!; it was a ~ experience for me ce fut une expérience nouvelle pour moi.

novelette [ˌnɒvə'let] *n* -1. [short novel] nouvelle *f*. -2. *pej* [easy reading] roman *m* de hall de gare; [love story] roman *m* à l'eau de rose.

novelettish [ˌnɒvə'letɪʃ] *adj pej* [sentimental] à l'eau de rose.

novelist ['nɒvəlɪst] *n* romancier *m*, -ère *f*.

novella [nə'velə] (*pl* novellas OR novelle [-leɪ]) *n* ≃ nouvelle *f (texte plus court qu'un roman et plus long qu'une nouvelle)*.

novelty ['nɒvltɪ] (*pl* novelties) *n* -1. [newness] nouveauté *f*, originalité *f*; the ~ soon wore off l'attrait de la nouveauté n'a pas duré ❑ ~ value attrait *m* de la nouveauté. -2. [thing, idea] innovation *f*, nouveauté *f*; it was a real ~ c'était une nouveauté, c'était tout nouveau. -3. [trinket] nouveauté *f*, article *m* fantaisie; [gadget] gadget *m*; ~ jewellery bijoux *mpl* fantaisie.

November [nə'vembəʳ] *n* novembre *m*.

novena [nəʊ'viːnə] (*pl* novenae [-niː]) *n* neuvaine *f*.

novice ['nɒvɪs] *n* -1. [beginner] débutant *m*, -e *f*, novice *mf*; I'm still a ~ at golf en matière de golf, je ne suis encore qu'un novice; a ~ at skiing, a ~ skier un skieur débutant. -2. RELIG novice *mf*.

novitiate, noviciate [nə'vɪʃɪət] *n* RELIG -1. [period] noviciat *m*; *fig* noviciat *m*, apprentissage *m*. -2. [place] noviciat *m*.

Novocaine® ['nəʊvəkeɪn] *n* Novocaïne® *f*, procaïne *f*.

now [naʊ] ◇ *adv* -1. [at this time] maintenant; what shall we do ~? qu'est-ce qu'on fait maintenant?; he hasn't seen her for a week ~ ça fait maintenant une semaine qu'il ne l'a pas vue; she'll be here any moment OR any time ~ elle va arriver d'un moment OR instant à l'autre; don't stop ~! n'arrête pas maintenant!; we are ~ entering enemy territory nous sommes désormais en territoire ennemi; it's ~ or never c'est le moment ou jamais; ~ is the time to invest, the time to invest is ~ c'est maintenant le moment d'investir; ~ she tells me! *hum* c'est maintenant qu'elle me le dit!; (and) ~ for something completely different (et) voici à présent quelque chose de tout à fait différent; as of ~ I'm in charge désormais, c'est moi le responsable; I'd never met them before ~ je ne les avais jamais rencontrés auparavant; between ~ and next August/next year d'ici le mois d'août prochain/l'année prochaine; they must have got the letter by ~ ils ont dû recevoir la lettre à l'heure qu'il est; that's all for ~ c'est tout pour le moment; from ~ until Monday/next year d'ici (à) lundi prochain/l'année prochaine; in a few years from ~ d'ici quelques années; from ~ on désormais, dorénavant, à partir de maintenant; from ~ on you do as you're told! à partir de maintenant, tu vas obéir!; we've had no problems till ~ OR until ~ OR up to ~ nous n'avons eu aucun problème jusqu'ici. -2. [nowadays] maintenant, aujourd'hui, actuellement; he lives in London ~ il habite (à) Londres maintenant; her ~ famous first novel son premier roman, aujourd'hui célèbre. -3. [marking a specific point in the past] maintenant, alors, à ce moment-là; they were singing ~ ils chantaient maintenant; by ~ we were all exhausted nous étions alors tous épuisés; up to ~ I'd never agreed with him jusque-là OR jusqu'alors, je n'avais jamais été d'accord avec lui. -4. [introducing information] or; ~ a Jaguar is a very fast car or, la Jaguar est une voiture très rapide. -5. [to show enthusiasm]: ~ that's what I call a car! voilà ce que j'appelle une voiture! || [to show surprise]: well ~! ça alors! || [to mark a pause]: ~, what was I saying? voyons, où en étais-je?; ~ let me see voyons voir || [to comfort]: there ~ OR ~, ~, you mustn't cry allons, allons, il ne faut pas pleurer || [to cajole, warn]: ~ then, it's time to get up! allons, il est l'heure de se lever!; you be careful ~! fais bien attention, hein! || [to scold]: ~ that's just silly! arrête tes bêtises!

◇ *conj* maintenant que, à présent que; she's happier ~ (that) she's got a job elle est plus heureuse depuis qu'elle travaille; ~ you come to mention it maintenant que tu le dis.

◇ *adj inf* -1. [current] actuel; the ~ president le président actuel. -2. [fashionable]: a ~ style un style branché; she's a ~ person c'est une branchée; golf is the ~ thing to do pour être branché, il faut se mettre au golf.

◆ **now and again, now and then** *adv phr* de temps en temps, de temps à autre; we still see them ~ and again nous les voyons encore de temps en temps OR de temps à autre.

◆ **now... now** *conj phr* tantôt... tantôt; ~ happy, ~ sad tantôt gai, tantôt triste.

NOW [naʊ] (*abbr of* National Organization for Women) *pr n organisation féministe américaine*.

nowadays ['naʊədeɪz] *adv* aujourd'hui, de nos jours.

noway *inf* ['nəʊweɪ], **noways** *inf* ['nəʊweɪz] *adv Am* pas du tout.

nowhere ['nəʊweəʳ] *adv* -1. [no place] nulle part; he goes ~ without her il ne va nulle part sans elle; I've got ~ to go je n'ai nulle part où aller; there's ~ to hide il n'y a pas d'endroit où se cacher; ~ else nulle part ailleurs; where are you going? — ~ in particular où vas-tu? — je ne sais pas exactement; it's ~ on the map cela ne figure pas sur la carte; she's ~ in the building elle n'est pas dans l'immeuble; my watch is ~ to be found impossible de retrouver ma montre; she/the book was ~ to be seen elle/le livre avait disparu || *fig*: he appeared from ~ OR out of ~ il est apparu comme par enchantement; she rose to fame from ~ elle est devenue célèbre du jour au lendemain; without your help we would be ~ sans votre aide nous serions perdus; the horse I backed came ~ le cheval sur lequel j'ai parié est arrivé bon dernier OR loin derrière; lying will get you ~ mentir ne vous servira à OR ne mènera à rien; I got ~ trying to convince him mes tentatives pour le convaincre sont restées vaines OR se sont soldées par un échec; we're getting ~ fast *inf* on pédale dans la choucroute OR la semoule; he's going ~ fast il n'ira pas loin. -2. *phr*: ~ near: the hotel was ~ near the beach l'hôtel était bien loin de la plage; dinner is ~ near ready le dîner est loin d'être prêt; I've ~ near enough time je suis loin d'avoir assez de temps.

nowise *inf* ['nəʊwaɪz] *Am* = **noway**.

nowt *inf* [naʊt] *Br dial* = **nothing** *pron*.

noxious ['nɒkʃəs] *adj* [gas, substance] nocif; [influence] néfaste.

nozzle ['nɒzl] *n* [gen] bec *m*, embout *m*; [for hose, paint gun] jet *m*, buse *f*; [in carburettor] gicleur *m*; [in turbine] tuyère *f*.

NP *written abbr of* notary public.

nr *written abbr of* near.

NS *written abbr of* Nova Scotia.

NSC (*abbr of* National Security Council) *pr n organisme chargé de superviser la politique militaire de défense du gouvernement des États-Unis*.

NSF ◇ *pr n abbr of* National Science Foundation.
◇ *written abbr of* not sufficient funds.

NSPCC (*abbr of* National Society for the Prevention of Cruelty to Children) *pr n association britannique de protection de l'enfance*.

NSU *n abbr of* nonspecific urethritis.

NSW *written abbr of* New South Wales.

NT ◇ *n* (*abbr of* New Testament) NT.
◇ *pr n* -**1.** *abbr of* National Trust. -**2.** (*abbr of* (Royal) National Theatre) *grand théâtre londonien subventionné par l'État*.

nth [enθ] *adj* -**1.** MATH: to the ~ power à la puissance n. -**2.** *inf* [umpteenth] énième; for the ~ time pour la énième fois; to the ~ degree au énième degré.

NUAAW (*abbr of* National Union of Agricultural and Allied Workers) *pr n syndicat britannique des employés du secteur agricole*.

nuance [nju:'ɑ:ns] *n* nuance *f*.

nub [nʌb] *n* -**1.** [crux] essentiel *m*, cœur *m*; the ~ of the problem le cœur OR le nœud du problème; the ~ of the matter le vif du sujet. -**2.** [small piece] petit morceau *m*, (petit) bout *m*; coal ~s noisettes *fpl* de charbon ‖ [small bump] petite bosse *f*.

nubbin ['nʌbɪn] *n Am* [gen] (petit) bout *m*; [of corn] épi *m* (de maïs) rachitique.

nubby ['nʌbɪ] *adj Am* couvert de peluches.

Nubia ['nju:bjə] *pr n* Nubie *f*.

Nubian ['nju:bjən] ◇ *n* Nubien *m*, -enne *f*.
◇ *adj* nubien; the ~ Desert le désert de Nubie.

nubile [*Br* 'njubaɪl, *Am* 'nu:bəl] *adj* nubile.

nubility ['nju:bɪlətɪ] *n* nubilité *f*.

nuclear ['nju:klɪə'] *adj* -**1.** PHYS nucléaire; ~ power station centrale *f* nucléaire OR atomique. -**2.** MIL nucléaire; ~ war guerre *f* atomique; France's ~ deterrent la force de dissuasion nucléaire française; ~ testing essais *mpl* nucléaires; ~ disarmament désarmement *m* nucléaire; ~ weapons armes *fpl* nucléaires. -**3.** BIOL nucléaire.

nuclear energy *n* énergie *f* nucléaire.

nuclear family *n* SOCIOL famille *f* nucléaire.

nuclear fission *n* fission *f* nucléaire.

nuclear-free zone *n périmètre dans lequel une collectivité locale interdit l'utilisation, le stockage ou le transport des matières radioactives*.

nuclear fusion *n* fusion *f* nucléaire.

nuclear physics *n* (*U*) physique *f* nucléaire.

nuclear power *n* nucléaire *m*, énergie *f* nucléaire.

nuclear-powered *adj* à propulsion nucléaire; ~ submarine sous-marin *m* nucléaire.

nuclear reactor *n* réacteur *m* nucléaire.

nuclear winter *n* hiver *m* nucléaire.

nuclei ['nju:klɪaɪ] *pl* → **nucleus**.

nucleic acid [nju:'klɪɪk-] *n* acide *m* nucléique.

nucleon ['nju:klɪɒn] *n* nucléon *m*.

nucleus ['nju:klɪəs] (*pl* **nucleuses** OR **nuclei** [-klɪaɪ]) *n* -**1.** BIOL & PHYS noyau *m*. -**2.** *fig* [kernel] noyau *m*, cœur *m*; they form the ~ of the team ils forment le noyau de l'équipe; we have the ~ of an idea nous avons un début d'idée; a ~ for regional development un centre de développement régional.

nuclide ['nju:klaɪd] *n* nuclide *m*, nucléide *m*.

nude [nju:d] ◇ *adj* [naked] nu; ~ photos nus *mpl*; [soft pornography] photos *fpl* érotiques; is ~ sunbathing common here? est-ce qu'il y a beaucoup de nudistes par ici?
◇ *n* -**1.** ART nu *m*; a Matisse ~ un nu de Matisse. -**2.** [being nude]: I was in the ~ j'étais (tout) nu; to pose in the ~ poser nu.

nudge [nʌdʒ] ◇ *vt* -**1.** [with elbow] pousser du coude; she ~d her friend to wake her up elle donna un petit coup de coude à son amie pour la réveiller ❑ he didn't come home last night, ~ ~, wink wink *hum Br* il n'est pas rentré hier soir, si tu vois ce que je veux dire. -**2.** [push] pousser; he cautiously ~d the door open il poussa tout doucement la porte (pour l'ouvrir); the truck ~d its way through the crowd le camion se fraya un passage à travers la foule. -**3.** [encourage] encourager, pousser; to ~ sb into doing sthg encourager OR pousser qqn à faire qqch; to ~ sb's memory *Br* rafraîchir la mémoire de qqn. -**4.** [approach] approcher (de); he must be nudging fifty il doit approcher la cinquantaine; temperatures nudging 40° C des températures proches de 40° C.
◇ *n* -**1.** [with elbow] coup *m* de coude; [with foot, stick etc] petit coup *m* (de pied, de bâton etc); to give sb a ~ pousser qqn du coude. -**2.** [encouragement]: she agreed with a ~ from her friends ses amis l'ont encouragée à dire oui; he needs a ~ in the right direction il a besoin qu'on le pousse dans la bonne direction.

nudism ['nju:dɪzm] *n* nudisme *m*, naturisme *m*.

nudist ['nju:dɪst] ◇ *adj* nudiste, naturiste; ~ colony/beach camp *m*/plage *f* de nudistes.
◇ *n* nudiste *mf*, naturiste *mf*.

nudity ['nju:dətɪ] *n* nudité *f*.

nugatory ['nju:gətrɪ] *adj fml* -**1.** [trifling] insignifiant, sans valeur. -**2.** [not valid] non valable; [ineffective] inopérant, inefficace.

nugget ['nʌgɪt] *n* -**1.** [piece] pépite *f*; gold ~ pépite d'or. -**2.** *fig*: ~s of wisdom des trésors de sagesse; an interesting ~ of information un (petit) renseignement intéressant.

nuisance ['nju:sns] *n* -**1.** [annoying thing, situation]: that noise is a ~ ce bruit est énervant; it's (such) a ~ having to attend all these meetings c'est (vraiment) pénible de devoir assister à toutes ces réunions; what a ~! c'est énervant!; it's a ~ having to commute every day ce n'est pas drôle de devoir faire le trajet tous les jours ❑ to be of ~ value *Br* empoisonner le monde. -**2.** [annoying person] empoisonneur *m*, -euse *f f*; he's nothing but a ~ c'est un véritable empoisonneur; to make a ~ of o.s. embêter OR empoisonner le monde; stop being a ~ arrête de nous embêter. -**3.** [hazard] nuisance *f*; that rubbish dump is a public ~ cette décharge est une calamité.

NUJ (*abbr of* National Union of Journalists) *pr n syndicat britannique des journalistes*.

nuke *inf* [nju:k] ◇ *vt* lâcher une bombe atomique sur.
◇ *n* -**1.** [weapon] arme *f* nucléaire. -**2.** *Am* [power plant] centrale *f* nucléaire.

null [nʌl] *adj* -**1.** JUR [invalid] nul; [lapsed] caduc; ~ and void nul et non avenu; the contract was rendered ~ (and void) le contrat a été annulé OR invalidé. -**2.** [insignificant] insignifiant, sans valeur; [amounting to nothing] nul; the effect of the embargo was ~ l'embargo n'eut aucun effet. -**3.** MATH nul; ~ set ensemble *m* vide; ~ string COMPUT chaîne *f* vide.

nullification [,nʌlɪfɪ'keɪʃn] *n* annulation *f*, invalidation *f*.

nullify ['nʌlɪfaɪ] (*pt* & *pp* **nullified**) *vt* -**1.** JUR [claim, contract, election] annuler, invalider. -**2.** [advantage] neutraliser.

nullity ['nʌlətɪ] (*pl* **nullities**) *n* -**1.** [worthlessness] nullité *f*. -**2.** JUR nullité *f*; ~ suit demande *f* en nullité de mariage. -**3.** [person] nullité *f*.

NUM (*abbr of* National Union of Mineworkers) *pr n syndicat britannique des mineurs*.

numb [nʌm] ◇ *adj* engourdi; we were ~ with cold nous étions transis de froid; my arm has gone ~ mon bras est engourdi; is your jaw still ~? [anaesthetized] ta mâchoire est-elle encore anesthésiée?; ~ with terror *fig* paralysé par la peur; he was ~ with shock *fig* il était sous le choc.
◇ *vt* [person, limbs, senses] engourdir; [pain] atténuer, apaiser; opium ~s the senses l'opium engourdit les sens; the cold ~ed my ears il faisait tellement froid que je ne sentais plus mes oreilles; ~ed by grief *fig* prostré de douleur.

number ['nʌmbə'] ◇ *n* -**1.** [gen & MATH] nombre *m*; [figure, numeral] chiffre *m*; a six-figure ~ un nombre de six chiffres; the ~s on the keyboard les chiffres sur le clavier; in round ~s en chiffres ronds; to do sthg by ~s faire qqch en suivant des instructions précises; she taught him his ~s elle lui a appris à compter ❑ even/odd/prime/rational/whole ~ nombre pair/impair/premier/rationnel/entier. -**2.** [as identifier] numéro *m*; have you got my work ~? avez-vous mon numéro (de téléphone) au travail?; you're ~ six vous êtes (le) numéro six; the winning ~ le numéro gagnant; we live at ~ 80 nous habitons au (numéro) 80; he's the President's ~ two il est le bras droit du président; name, rank and ~! MIL nom, grade et matricule! ❑ did you get the car's (registration) ~? tu as relevé le numéro d'immatriculation de la voiture?; telephone ~ numéro *m* de téléphone; I've got your ~! *inf* toi, je te vois venir!; his ~'s up *inf* son compte est bon. -**3.** [quantity] nombre *m*; the ~ of tourists is growing le nombre de touristes va en augmentant; any ~ can participate le nombre de participants est illimité; they were eight in ~ ils étaient (au nombre de) huit; in equal ~s en nombre égal; to be equal in ~ être à nombre égal; we were many/few in ~ nous étions nombreux/en petit nombre; a ~ of people un certain nombre de gens; a (certain) ~ of you un certain nombre d'entre vous; a large ~ of people un grand nombre de gens, de nombreuses personnes; a small ~ of people un petit nombre de gens, peu de gens; in a good OR fair ~ of cases dans bon nombre de cas; times without ~ à maintes (et maintes) reprises; they defeated us by force of OR by sheer weight of ~s ils l'ont emporté sur nous parce qu'ils étaient plus nombreux. -**4.** [group]: one of their/our ~ un des leurs/des nôtres; she was not of our ~ elle n'était pas des nôtres OR avec nous. -**5.** [issue - of magazine, paper] numéro *m*; did you read last week's ~? avez-vous lu le numéro de la semaine dernière? -**6.** *inf* [job] boulot *m*; a cushy ~ une planque. -**7.** [song, dance, act] numéro *m*; a dance ~ un numéro de danse; they played some new ~s ils ont joué de nouveaux morceaux; they sang some new ~s ils ont chanté de nouvelles chansons; they only danced to the slow ~s ils n'ont dansé que les slows. -**8.** *inf* [thing, person]: this ~ is a hot seller ce modèle se vend comme des petits pains; she was wearing a little black ~ elle portait une petite robe noire; he was driving a little Italian ~ il était au volant d'un de ces petits bolides italiens; who's that blonde ~? qui est cette belle blonde? ❑ to do OR to pull a ~ on sb rouler qqn. -**9.** GRAMM nombre *m*.
◇ *vt* -**1.** [assign number to] numéroter; don't forget to ~ the pages n'oubliez pas de numéroter les pages. -**2.** [include] compter; I ~ him among the best jazz musicians je le compte parmi les meilleurs musiciens de jazz; I'm glad to ~ her among my closest friends je suis heureux de la compter parmi mes meilleurs amis. -**3.** [total] compter; each team ~s six players chaque équipe est composée de OR compte six joueurs; the crowd ~ed 5,000 il y avait une foule de 5 000 personnes. -**4.** [count] compter; who can ~ the stars? *lit* qui peut dire combien il y a d'étoiles?; now their options are ~ed désormais, leur choix est assez restreint ❑ his days are ~ed ses jours sont comptés.
◇ *vi*: she ~s among the great writers of the century elle compte parmi les grands écrivains de ce siècle; did he ~ among the ringleaders?

faisait-il partie des meneurs ?; the crowd ~ed in thousands il y avait des milliers de gens.

◆ **any number of** *adj phr*: there were any ~ of different dishes to choose from un très grand nombre de plats différents nous furent présentés.

◆ **numbers** *n Am* = **numbers game**.

◆ **number off** *vi insep* se numéroter.

number cruncher *inf n* COMPUT ordinateur *m* puissant *(pour le traitement de données numériques)*.

number crunching *inf n* COMPUT traitement *m* en masse des chiffres.

numbering ['nʌmbərɪŋ] *n* numérotation *f*, numérotage *m*.

numberless ['nʌmbəlɪs] *adj* -**1.** *fml* [countless] innombrable, sans nombre. -**2.** [without a number] sans numéro, qui ne porte pas de numéro, non numéroté.

number one ◇ *adj* premier; it's our ~ priority c'est la première de nos priorités; the ~ oil exporter le premier exportateur de pétrole; my ~ choice mon tout premier choix; the ~ hit in the charts le numéro un au hit-parade.

◇ *n* -**1.** *inf* [boss] boss *m*, patron *m*, -onne *f*. -**2.** *inf* [oneself]: to look out for ~, to take care of ~ ne se préoccuper que de soi-même. -**3.** [in hit parade]: her record got to ~ son disque a été classé numéro un au hit-parade. -**4.** *inf baby talk*: to do ~ faire pipi.

numberplate ['nʌmbəpleɪt] *n Br* AUT plaque *f* minéralogique OR d'immatriculation; the lorry had a foreign ~ le camion était immatriculé à l'étranger.

Numbers ['nʌmbəz] *n* BIBLE Nombres *mpl*; the book of ~ le livre des Nombres.

numbers game *n Am* loterie *f* clandestine.

Number Ten *pr n*: ~ (Downing Street) *résidence officielle du Premier ministre britannique*.

numbhead *inf* ['nʌmhed] *Am* = **numskull**.

numbness ['nʌmnɪs] *n* [physical] engourdissement *m*; [mental] torpeur *f*, engourdissement *m*.

numbskull ['nʌmskʌl] = **numskull**.

numeracy ['nju:mərəsɪ] *n (U) Br* notions *fpl* d'arithmétique; a high level of ~ de solides notions d'arithmétique.

numeral ['nju:mərəl] *n* chiffre *m*, nombre *m*; in Roman ~s en chiffres romains.

numerate ['nju:mərət] *adj Br* [skilled] bon en mathématiques; [having basics] sachant compter.

numerator ['nju:məreɪtə^r] *n* MATH numérateur *m*.

numeric(al) [nju:'merɪk(l)] *adj* numérique; ~ data données *fpl* numériques; in ~ order par ordre numérique.

numerical analysis *n* analyse *f* numérique.

numerical control *n* contrôle *m* numérique.

numerically [nju:'merɪklɪ] *adv* numériquement.

numeric keypad *n* COMPUT pavé *m* numérique.

numerology [,nju:mə'rɒlədʒɪ] *n* numérologie *f*, arithmosophie *f*.

numerous ['nju:mərəs] *adj* nombreux; for ~ reasons pour de nombreuses raisons; a ~ group un groupe important.

numinous ['nju:mɪnəs] *adj* [awe-inspiring] terrifiant.

numismatic [,nju:mɪz'mætɪk] *adj* numismatique.

numismatics [,nju:mɪz'mætɪks] *n (U)* numismatique *f*.

numismatist [nju:'mɪzmətɪst] *n* numismate *mf*.

numismatology [,nju:mɪzmə'tɒlədʒɪ] = **numismatics**.

numskull *inf* ['nʌmskʌl] *n* andouille *f*.

nun [nʌn] *n* religieuse *f*; to become a ~ prendre le voile.

nunciature ['nʌnsɪətʃə^r] *n* nonciature *f*.

nuncio ['nʌnsɪəʊ] (*pl* **nuncios**) *n* nonce *m*.

nunnery ['nʌnərɪ] (*pl* **nunneries**) *n* couvent *m* OR monastère *m* (de femmes).

NUPE ['nju:pɪ] (*abbr of* National Union of Public Employees) *pr n ancien syndicat britannique des employés de la fonction publique*.

nuptial ['nʌpʃl] *adj* nuptial; ~ blessing bénédiction *f* nuptiale; ~ vows vœux *mpl* du mariage.

◆ **nuptials** *npl lit* noce *f*, noces *fpl*.

nurd *inf* [nɜ:d] = **nerd**.

Nuremberg ['njʊərəmbɜ:g] *pr n* Nuremberg.

Nureyev ['njʊərɪef] *pr n*: Rudolph ~ Rudolph Noureïev.

nurse [nɜ:s] ◇ *n* -**1.** MED [in hospital] infirmier *m*, -ère *f*; [at home] infirmier *m*, -ère *f*, garde-malade *mf*; male ~ infirmier *m*; student ~ élève *m* infirmier, élève *f* infirmière. -**2.** *Br* [nanny] gouvernante *f*, nurse *f*. -**3.** [wet nurse] nourrice *f*.

◇ *vt* -**1.** MED soigner; he ~d her through the worst of it il l'a soignée pendant qu'elle était au plus mal; she ~d me back to health elle m'a guérie || *fig*: he was nursing a bad hangover il essayait de faire passer sa gueule de bois; to ~ one's pride panser ses blessures (d'amour-propre); she ~d the boat back into harbour elle ramena le bateau au port sans encombre; he ~d the company through the crisis il a permis à l'entreprise de traverser la crise. -**2.** [harbour, foster - grudge, hope, desire] entretenir; [- scheme] mijoter, couver. -**3.** [breast-feed] allaiter. -**4.** [hold] bercer (dans ses bras); he sat nursing his fourth whisky il sirotait son quatrième whisky.

◇ *vi* -**1.** MED être infirmier/infirmière; she spent a few years nursing elle a travaillé pendant quelques années comme infirmière. -**2.** [infant] téter.

nurseling ['nɜ:slɪŋ] = **nursling**.

nursemaid ['nɜ:smeɪd] *n* gouvernante *f*, nurse *f*; to play ~ to sb *fig* tenir qqn par la main.

nursery ['nɜ:sərɪ] (*pl* **nurseries**) *n* -**1.** [room] nursery *f*, chambre *f* d'enfants. -**2.** [day-care centre] crèche *f*, garderie *f*. -**3.** [school] école *f* maternelle; they go to the local ~ ils vont à l'école maternelle du quartier ❑ ~ education enseignement *m* de l'école maternelle; ~ teacher instituteur *m*, -trice *f* de maternelle. -**4.** [for plants, trees] pépinière *f*.

nurserymaid ['nɜ:srɪmeɪd] = **nursemaid**.

nurseryman ['nɜ:srɪmən] (*pl* **nurserymen** [-mən]) *n* pépiniériste *m*.

nursery nurse *n* puéricultrice *f*.

nursery rhyme *n* comptine *f*.

nursery school *n* école *f* maternelle; ~ teacher instituteur *m*, -trice *f* de maternelle.

nursery slopes *npl Br* pistes *fpl* pour débutants.

nursing ['nɜ:sɪŋ] ◇ *n* -**1.** [profession] profession *f* d'infirmier; when did she take up ~? quand a-t-elle commencé ses études d'infirmière ? -**2.** [care] soins *mpl*; he needs proper ~ il a besoin de soins professionnels. -**3.** [breast-feeding] allaitement *m*.

◇ *adj* -**1.** MED d'infirmier; the ~ staff le personnel soignant. -**2.** [suckling] allaitant.

nursing bottle *n Am* biberon *m*.

nursing bra *n* soutien-gorge *m* d'allaitement.

nursing home *n* -**1.** [for aged] maison *f* de retraite; [for convalescents] maison *f* de repos; [for mentally ill] maison *f* de santé. -**2.** *Br* [private clinic] hôpital *m* privé, clinique *f* privée.

nursing mother *n* mère *f* qui allaite.

nursing officer *n Br* infirmier *m*, -ère *f* en chef.

nursing order *n* ordre *m* de sœurs infirmières.

nursling ['nɜ:slɪŋ] *n* nourrisson *m*.

nurture ['nɜ:tʃə^r] ◇ *vt* -**1.** [bring up] élever, éduquer; [nourish] nourrir; a philosophy ~d on revolutionary principles une philosophie nourrie de principes révolutionnaires. -**2.** [foster - hope, desire] entretenir; [- plan, scheme] mijoter, couver.

◇ *n* -**1.** [upbringing] éducation *f*. -**2.** [food] nourriture *f*.

nut [nʌt] (*pt* & *pp* **nutted**, *cont* **nutting**) ◇ *n* -**1.** BOT & CULIN *terme générique pour les amandes, noisettes, noix etc*; ~s and raisins mélange *m* de noisettes et de raisins secs ❑ cashew ~ (noix *f* de) cajou *m*; she's a tough ~ to crack *inf* on n'en fait pas ce qu'on veut; the American market will be a hard ~ to crack *inf* ça ne sera pas facile de pénétrer le marché américain. -**2.** TECH écrou *m*; ~s and bolts des écrous et des boulons ❑ to learn the ~s and bolts of a department/business apprendre à connaître le fonctionnement d'un service/d'une entreprise. -**3.** *inf* [crazy person] dingue *mf*, timbré *m*, -e *f*, taré *m*, -e *f*; what a ~! il est complètement dingue! || [enthusiast] fana ;she's a golf ~ c'est une fana de golf. -**4.** *inf* [head] caboche *f*; it hit him right on the ~ il l'a reçu en pleine caboche ❑ you must be off your ~! tu es complètement cinglé !; to do OR to go off one's ~ piquer sa crise; she really did her OR went off her ~ elle a piqué une de ces crises. -**5.** [small lump of coal] noix *f*, tête-de-moineau *f*.

◇ *vt inf* donner un coup de boule à.

NUT (*abbr of* National Union of Teachers) *pr n syndicat britannique d'enseignants*.

nutation [nju:'teɪʃn] *n* ASTRON, BOT & MED nutation *f*.

nut-brown *adj* brun.

nutcase *inf* ['nʌtkeɪs] *n* dingue *mf*, timbré *m*, -e *f*, taré *m*, -e *f*.

nutcracker ['nʌt,krækə^r] *n*, **nutcrackers** ['nʌt,krækəz] *npl* casse-noix *m inv*, casse-noisettes *m inv*; '(The) Nutcracker (Suite)' *Tchaikovsky* 'Casse-Noisette'.

nuthatch ['nʌthætʃ] *n* grimpereau *m*.

nuthouse *inf* ['nʌthaʊs, *pl* -haʊzɪz] *n* maison *f* de fous; in the ~ chez les fous.

nutmeg ['nʌtmeg] *n* [nut] (noix *f* de) muscade *f*; [tree] muscadier *m*.

nut oil *n* [from walnuts] huile *f* de noix; [from hazelnuts] huile *f* de noisettes.

nutrient ['nju:trɪənt] ◇ *n* substance *f* nutritive.

◇ *adj* nutritif.

nutriment ['nju:trɪmənt] *n* [food] nourriture *f*.

nutrition [nju:'trɪʃn] *n* nutrition *f*; cereals have a high ~ content les céréales sont très nourrissantes OR nutritives.

nutritional [nju:'trɪʃənl] *adj* [disorder, process, value] nutritif; [science, research] nutritionnel.

nutritionist [nju:'trɪʃənɪst] *n* nutritionniste *mf*.

nutritious [nju:'trɪʃəs] *adj* nutritif, nourrissant.

nutritive ['nju:trətɪv] *adj* nutritif.

nuts [nʌts] ◇ *adj inf* dingue, timbré, fêlé; that noise is driving me ~ ce bruit me rend dingue; to go ~ [crazy, angry] piquer une crise; to be ~ about OR on être fou OR dingue de.

◇ *npl* ▽ [testicles] couilles *fpl*, roupettes *fpl*.

◇ *interj* ▽: ~! des clous !; ~ to them! *Am* oh! et puis zut!

nutshell ['nʌtʃel] *n* coquille *f* de noix *(de noisette etc)*; in a ~ en un mot; to put it in a ~ pour résumer l'histoire (en un mot).

nutter *inf* ['nʌtə^r] *n Br* malade *mf*, timbré *m*, -e *f*, taré *m*, -e *f*.

nutty ['nʌtɪ] (*compar* **nuttier**, *superl* **nuttiest**) *adj* -**1.** [tasting of or containing nuts] aux noix *(aux amandes, aux noisettes etc)*; a ~ flavour un goût de noix *(de noisette etc)*. -**2.** *inf* [crazy] dingue, timbré; what a ~ idea! c'est complètement débile comme idée! ❑ he's as ~ as a fruitcake il est complètement dingue.

nuzzle ['nʌzl] ◇ *vt* [push with nose] pousser du nez; [sniff at] renifler; the horse ~d my shoulder le cheval m'a poussé l'épaule du museau.

◇ *vi* -**1.** to ~ up against, to ~ at = **nuzzle** *vt*. -**2.** [nestle] se blottir; they ~d (up) against their mother ils se blottirent contre leur mère.

NV *written abbr of* Nevada.

NW (*written abbr of* north-west) N-O.

NWT *written abbr of* Northwest Territories.

NY *written abbr of* New York.

Nyasaland [naɪ'æsəlænd] *pr n* Nyassaland *m*.

NYC *written abbr of* New York City.

nyctalopia [ˌnɪktə'ləʊpɪə] *n* héméralopie *f*.

nylon ['naɪlɒn] ◇ *n* nylon *m*.

◇ *comp* [thread, shirt, stockings] de OR en nylon.

◆ **nylons** *npl* [stockings] bas *mpl* (de) nylon.

nymph [nɪmf] *n* MYTH & ZOOL nymphe *f*; sea ~ néréide *f*.

nymphet ['nɪmfət] *n* nymphette *f*.

nympho *inf* ['nɪmfəʊ] (*pl* nymphos) *n* nympho *f*.

nymphomania [ˌnɪmfə'meɪnɪə] *n* nymphomanie *f*.

nymphomaniac [ˌnɪmfə'meɪnɪæk] ◇ *adj* nymphomane.

◇ *n* nymphomane *f*.

NYSE *pr n abbr of* New York Stock Exchange.

NZ *written abbr of* New Zealand.

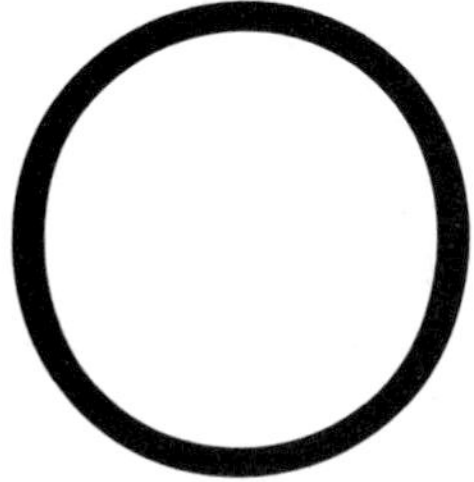

o (*pl* o's OR os), **O** (*pl* O's OR Os) [əʊ] *n* [letter] o *m*, O *m*; **O positive/negative** MED O positif/négatif.

o *interj* -**1.** *lit* [as vocative] ô; **o God!** ô mon Dieu! -**2.** [as exclamation] = **oh**.

o' [ə] *prep* [of] de; **(the) top ~ the morning to you!** *Ir* bien le bonjour!

O *n* [zero] zéro *m*; **agent double O seven** agent 007.

oaf [əʊf] *n* [dull, clumsy man] lourdaud *m*; [uncouth man] rustre *m*, goujat *m*; **get out of the way, you great ~!** pousse-toi, gros lourdaud!

oafish ['əʊfɪʃ] *adj* [dull, clumsy] lourdaud, balourd; [uncouth] rustre.

oak [əʊk] ◇ *n* chêne *m*.
◇ *comp* [furniture, door, panelling] de OR en chêne; **~ forest** forêt *f* de chênes; **~ tree** chêne *m*.

oak apple *n* noix *f* de galle.

oaken ['əʊkn] *adj lit* de OR en chêne.

oak-leaf cluster *n Am* MIL *barrette portée sur une première décoration en témoignage de mérite renouvelé*.

oakum ['əʊkəm] *n* étoupe *f*, filasse *f*.

OAP (*abbr of* **old age pensioner**) *n Br* retraité *m*, -e *f*; **'students and ~s half price'** ≃ 'étudiants et carte vermeille demi-tarif'.

oar [ɔːʳ] ◇ *n* -**1.** [instrument] rame *f*, aviron *m*; **to stick** OR **to put one's ~ in** *inf Br* mettre son grain de sel; **to rest on one's ~s** *literal* lever les rames; *fig* se reposer sur ses lauriers. -**2.** [person] rameur *m*, -euse *f*.
◇ *vi* & *vt lit* ramer.

oarlock ['ɔːlɒk] *n Am* [concave] dame *f* (de nage); [pin] tolet *m*.

oarsman ['ɔːzmən] (*pl* **oarsmen** [-mən]) *n* rameur *m*.

oarsmanship ['ɔːzmənʃɪp] *n (U)* compétences *fpl* de rameur.

oarswoman ['ɔːz,wʊmən] (*pl* **oarswomen** [-,wɪmɪn]) *n* rameuse *f*.

OAS *pr n* -**1.** (*abbr of* **Organization of American States**) OÉA *f*. -**2.** (*abbr of* **Organisation armée secrète**) OAS *f*.

oasis [əʊ'eɪsɪs] (*pl* **oases** [-siːz]) *n literal* & *fig* oasis *f*; **an ~ of calm** une oasis OR un havre de paix.

oast [əʊst], **oast house** *n Br* séchoir *m* à houblon.

oat [əʊt] *n* [plant] avoine *f*.
◆ **oats** *npl* avoine *f*; **a field of ~s** un champ d'avoine ❑ **he's feeling his ~s** *inf Am* il est gonflé à bloc; **to be off one's ~s** *inf Br* se sentir patraque, ne pas être dans son assiette; **is he getting his ~s?** *inf* est-ce que sa femme le satisfait?

oatcake ['əʊtkeɪk] *n* gâteau *m* sec (d'avoine).

oaten ['əʊtn] *adj* d'avoine.

oatflakes ['əʊtfleɪks] *npl* flocons *mpl* d'avoine.

oath [əʊθ, *pl* əʊðz] *n* -**1.** [vow] serment *m*; **he took** OR **swore an ~ never to return** il fit le serment OR il jura de ne jamais revenir; **to take the ~ of allegiance** faire (le) serment d'allégeance; **to swear on ~** jurer (sous serment); **it's true, on my ~!** c'est vrai, je vous le jure!; **to be on** OR **under ~** JUR être sous serment, être assermenté; **to put sb on** OR **under ~** JUR faire prêter serment à qqn. -**2.** [swearword] juron *m*; **he let out a string of ~s** il a laissé échapper un torrent d'injures.

oatmeal ['əʊtmiːl] ◇ *n (U)* [flakes] flocons *mpl* d'avoine; [flour] farine *f* d'avoine; **~ porridge** bouillie *f* d'avoine, porridge *m*.
◇ *adj* [colour] grège.

OAU (*abbr of* **Organization of African Unity**) *pr n* OUA *f*.

OB *n abbr of* **outside broadcast**.

Obadiah [,əʊbə'daɪə] *pr n* Abdias.

obbligato [,ɒblɪ'gɑːtəʊ] *adj* obligé.

obduracy ['ɒbdjʊrəsɪ] *n fml* -**1.** [hardheartedness] dureté *f* (de cœur), insensibilité *f*. -**2.** [obstinacy] obstination *f*, entêtement *m*; [inflexibility] inflexibilité *f*, intransigeance *f*.

obdurate ['ɒbdjʊrət] *adj fml* -**1.** [hardhearted] insensible, dur. -**2.** [obstinate] obstiné, entêté; [unyielding] inflexible; **we met with an ~ refusal** on nous opposa un refus catégorique.

OBE (*abbr of* **Officer of the Order of the British Empire**) *n distinction honorifique britannique*.

obedience [ə'biːdjəns] *n* -**1.** obéissance *f*; **to show ~ to sb** obéir à qqn; **to owe ~ to sb** *lit* devoir obédience à qqn; **in ~ to her wishes** conformément à ses vœux; **in ~ to his conscience** obéissant à sa conscience; **to command ~** savoir se faire obéir. -**2.** RELIG obédience *f*.

obedient [ə'biːdjənt] *adj* obéissant, docile; **to be ~ to sb** obéir à qqn; **your ~ servant** *fml* & *dated* [in letters] votre humble serviteur.

obediently [ə'biːdjəntlɪ] *adv* docilement; **they followed him ~** ils le suivirent sans discuter.

obeisance [əʊ'beɪsns] *n lit* -**1.** [homage] hommage *m*; **to make** OR **to pay ~ to sb** rendre hommage à qqn. -**2.** [bow] révérence *f*; [sign] geste *m* de respect.

obelisk ['ɒbəlɪsk] *n* -**1.** [column] obélisque *m*. -**2.** TYPO croix *f* (d'évêque), obel *m*.

Oberon ['əʊbərɒn] *pr n* Oberon.

obese [əʊ'biːs] *adj* obèse.

obesity [əʊ'biːsətɪ], **obeseness** [əʊ'biːsnɪs] *n* obésité *f*.

obey [ə'beɪ] ◇ *vt* obéir à; **he always ~ed his mother/his intuition/the law** il a toujours obéi à sa mère/à son intuition/aux lois; **an order which he refused to ~** un ordre auquel il refusa d'obéir; **the plane is no longer ~ing the controls** l'avion ne répond plus; **I want these instructions ~ed to the letter** je veux que ces instructions soient suivies à la lettre.
◇ *vi* obéir, obtempérer.

obfuscate ['ɒbfʌskeɪt] *vt fml* [obscure - issue] obscurcir, embrouiller; [- mind] embrouiller; [perplex - person] embrouiller, dérouter.

obfuscation [,ɒbfʌs'keɪʃn] *n fml* [of issue] obscurcissement *m*, embrouillement *m*; [of mind] embrouillement *m*; [of person] confusion *f*, embrouillement *m*.

obituarist [ə'bɪtʃʊərɪst] *n* nécrologue *mf*.

obituary [ə'bɪtʃʊərɪ] (*pl* **obituaries**) ◇ *n* nécrologie *f*, notice *f* nécrologique; **the ~ column, the obituaries** la rubrique nécrologique.
◇ *adj* nécrologique.

object¹ ['ɒbdʒɪkt] *n* -**1.** [thing] objet *m*, chose *f*; **an unidentified ~** un objet non identifié. -**2.** [aim] objet *m*, but *m*, fin *f*; **the real ~ of his visit** le véritable objet de sa visite; **with the sole ~ of pleasing you** dans le seul but de OR à seule fin de vous plaire; **with this ~ in mind** dans ce but, à cette fin; **that's the (whole) ~ of the exercise** c'est (justement là) le but de l'opération ❑ **money is no ~** peu importe le prix, le prix est sans importance; **money is no ~ to them** ils n'ont pas de problèmes d'argent; **time is no ~** peu importe le temps que cela prendra. -**3.** [focus] objet *m*; **an ~ of ridicule/interest** un objet de ridicule/d'intérêt; **the ~ of his love** l'objet de son amour; **~ of study** objet OR sujet *m* d'étude ❑ **sex ~** objet sexuel. -**4.** GRAMM [of verb] complément *m* d'objet; [of preposition] objet *m*; **direct/indirect ~** complément d'objet direct/indirect.

object² [əb'dʒekt] ◇ *vi* élever une objection; [stronger] protester; **to ~ to sthg** protester contre qqch; **many groups ~ed to the new law** de nombreux groupes ont protesté contre OR se sont opposés à la nouvelle loi; **they ~ to working overtime** ils ne sont pas d'accord pour faire des heures supplémentaires; **if you don't ~** si vous n'y voyez pas d'inconvénient; **you know how your father ~s to it!** tu sais combien ton père y est opposé!; **I ~!** je proteste!; **I ~ strongly to that remark!** je proteste vigoureusement contre cette remarque!; **I ~ strongly to your attitude** je trouve votre attitude proprement inadmissible; **I wouldn't ~ to a cup of tea** je ne dirais pas non à OR je prendrais volontiers une tasse de thé; **he ~s to her smoking** il désapprouve qu'elle fume; **she ~s to his coming** elle n'est pas d'accord pour qu'il vienne; **why do you ~ to all my friends?** pourquoi cette hostilité à l'égard de tous mes amis?; **it's not her I ~ to but her husband** ce n'est pas elle qui me déplaît, c'est son mari; **to ~ to a witness** JUR récuser un témoin.
◇ *vt* objecter; **I ~ed that it was too late** j'ai objecté qu'il était trop tard.

objection [əbˈdʒekʃn] *n* -**1.** [argument against] objection *f*; are there any ~s? y a-t-il des objections?; to make OR to raise an ~ faire OR soulever une objection; I have no ~ to his coming je ne vois pas d'objection à ce qu'il vienne; I have no ~ to his friends je n'ai rien contre ses amis; if you have no ~ si vous n'y voyez pas d'inconvénient; ~! JUR objection!; ~ overruled! JUR objection rejetée! -**2.** [opposition] opposition *f*; there was no ~ nous n'avons rencontré aucune opposition.

objectionable [əbˈdʒekʃnəbl] *adj* [unpleasant] désagréable; [blameworthy] répréhensible; a highly ~ smell/man une odeur/un homme insupportable; to use ~ language parler vulgairement; I find his views ~ je n'aime pas sa façon de penser; what is so ~ about her behaviour? qu'est-ce qu'on peut lui reprocher?

objective [əbˈdʒektɪv] ◇ *adj* -**1.** [unbiased] objectif, impartial; an ~ observer un observateur impartial. -**2.** [real, observable] objectif; ~ reality la réalité objective ❑ ~ symptoms MED signes *mpl*. -**3.** GRAMM objectif; the ~ case le cas objectif; ~ genitive génitif *m* objectif.
◇ *n* -**1.** [aim] objectif *m*, but *m*; to achieve OR to reach one's ~ atteindre son but. -**2.** GRAMM accusatif *m*, cas *m* objectif. -**3.** PHOT objectif *m*.

objectively [əbˈdʒektɪvlɪ] *adv* -**1.** [unbiasedly] objectivement, impartialement. -**2.** [really, externally] objectivement.

objectivism [əbˈdʒektɪvɪzm] *n* objectivisme *m*.

objectivist [əbˈdʒektɪvɪst] ◇ *adj* objectiviste.
◇ *n* objectiviste *mf*.

objectivity [ˌɒbdʒekˈtɪvətɪ] *n* objectivité *f*.

object lesson *n* -**1.** [example] demonstration *f*, illustration *f (d'un principe)*; it was an ~ in how to lose votes ce fut une illustration (parfaite) de la façon dont il faut s'y prendre pour perdre des voix; it was an ~ in persistence ce fut un parfait exemple de persévérance. -**2.** SCH leçon *f* de choses.

objector [əbˈdʒektəʳ] *n* opposant *m*, -e *f*; are there many ~s to the proposal? y a-t-il beaucoup de gens contre la proposition?

object program *n* COMPUT programme *m* objet.

oblate [ˈɒbleɪt] ◇ *adj* GEOM aplati (aux pôles).
◇ *n* RELIG oblat *m*, -e *f*.

oblation [əˈbleɪʃn] *n* RELIG [ceremony] oblation *f*; [thing offered] oblation *f*, oblats *mpl*.

obligate [ˈɒblɪgeɪt] *vt* -**1.** *Am* OR *fml* [compel] obliger, contraindre; to be/to feel ~d to do sthg être/se sentir obligé de faire qqch. -**2.** *Am* FIN [funds, credits] affecter.

obligation [ˌɒblɪˈgeɪʃn] *n* obligation *f*; to be under an ~ to do sthg être dans l'obligation de faire qqch; you are under no ~ to reply vous n'êtes pas tenu de répondre; I am under an ~ to her j'ai une dette envers elle; to put OR to place sb under an ~ to do sthg mettre qqn dans l'obligation de faire qqch; it is my ~ to inform you that... il est de mon devoir de OR je suis tenu de vous informer que...; family ~s obligations familiales; moral ~s compel me to refuse je suis moralement obligé de refuser; to meet one's ~s satisfaire à ses obligations, assumer ses engagements.

obligatory [əˈblɪgətrɪ] *adj* obligatoire; attendance is ~ la présence est obligatoire.

oblige [əˈblaɪdʒ] ◇ *vt* -**1.** [constrain] obliger; to ~ sb to do sthg obliger qqn à faire qqch; you're not ~d to come tu n'es pas obligé de venir. -**2.** [do a favour to] rendre service à, obliger; I would be ~d if you would refrain from smoking *fml* vous m'obligeriez beaucoup en ne fumant pas; could you ~ me with a match? *fml* auriez-vous l'amabilité OR l'obligeance de me donner une allumette?; much ~d! merci beaucoup!; to be ~d to sb for sthg savoir gré à qqn de qqch; she ~d the guests with a song elle a consenti à chanter pour les invités.
◇ *vi*: always ready to ~! toujours prêt à rendre service!; I would be only too glad to ~ je serais ravi de vous rendre service.

obligee [ˌɒblɪˈdʒiː] *n* COMM -**1.** [creditor] créancier *m*, -ère *f*. -**2.** [bondholder] obligataire *mf*.

obliging [əˈblaɪdʒɪŋ] *adj* serviable, obligeant; our neighbours are very ~ nos voisins sont très serviables; it was very ~ of him c'était très aimable à lui OR de sa part.

obligingly [əˈblaɪdʒɪŋlɪ] *adv* aimablement, obligeamment; the letter you ~ sent me la lettre que vous avez eu l'obligeance de m'envoyer; "any time", he said ~ «je vous en prie», dit-il aimablement.

oblique [əˈbliːk] ◇ *adj* -**1.** GEOM [slanted] oblique. -**2.** [indirect] indirect; an ~ reference une référence indirecte. -**3.** BOT oblique. -**4.** GRAMM oblique.
◇ *n* -**1.** GEOM oblique *f*; ANAT oblique *m*. -**2.** TYPO barre *f* oblique.

obliquely [əˈbliːklɪ] *adv* -**1.** obliquement, en biais. -**2.** [indirectly] indirectement.

obliqueness [əˈbliːknɪs], **obliquity** [əˈblɪkwətɪ] (*pl* **obliquities**) *n* -**1.** ASTRON & GEOM obliquité *f*. -**2.** [perversity] perversité *f*; [obscurity] obscurité *f*, manque *m* de clarté.

obliterate [əˈblɪtəreɪt] *vt* [destroy, erase] effacer; [cancel - stamp] oblitérer; the town was ~d la ville a été effacée de la carte; to ~ the past faire table rase du passé.

obliteration [əˌblɪtəˈreɪʃn] *n* [destruction, erasure] effacement *m*; [of stamp] oblitération *f*.

oblivion [əˈblɪvɪən] *n* -**1.** [being forgotten] oubli *m*; to fall OR to sink into ~ tomber dans l'oubli; to save sb/sthg from ~ tirer qqn/qqch de l'oubli, sauver qqn/qqch de l'oubli. -**2.** [unconsciousness] inconscience *f*, oubli *m*; he had drunk himself into ~ il était abruti par l'alcool.

oblivious [əˈblɪvɪəs] *adj* inconscient; she was ~ of OR to what was happening elle n'avait pas conscience de OR n'était pas consciente de ce qui se passait; he remained ~ to our comments il est resté sourd à nos remarques; he is ~ to the fact that millions of people are starving il n'est pas conscient du fait que des millions de gens meurent de faim.

oblong [ˈɒblɒŋ] ◇ *adj* [rectangular] rectangulaire; [elongated] allongé, oblong.
◇ *n* [rectangle] rectangle *m*.

obloquy [ˈɒbləkwɪ] (*pl* obloquies) *n* *(U) fml* -**1.** [abuse] insultes *fpl*, injures *fpl*; [defamation] diffamation *f*. -**2.** [disgrace] opprobre *m*.

obnoxious [əbˈnɒkʃəs] *adj* [person] odieux, ignoble; [behaviour] odieux; [smell] ignoble, infect.

o.b.o. (*written abbr of* or best offer) à déb.

oboe [ˈəʊbəʊ] *n* hautbois *m*.

oboist [ˈəʊbəʊɪst] *n* hautbois *m (musicien)*, hautboïste *mf*.

obscene [əbˈsiːn] *adj* obscène; an ~ gesture un geste obscène; an ~ publication une publication obscène; it's ~ to earn so much money *fig* c'est indécent de gagner autant d'argent.

obscenely [əbˈsiːnlɪ] *adv* d'une manière obscène; she gestured ~ elle fit un geste obscène; he's ~ rich *fig* il est tellement riche que ç'en est dégoûtant.

obscenity [əbˈsenətɪ] (*pl* obscenities) *n* -**1.** *(U)* [obscene language] obscénité *f*, obscénités *fpl*. -**2.** [obscene word] obscénité *f*, grossièreté *f*; to shout obscenities crier des obscénités. -**3.** *fig*: war is an ~ la guerre est une chose obscène.

obscurantism [ˌɒbskjʊəˈræntɪzm] *n fml* obscurantisme *m*.

obscurantist [ˌɒbskjʊəˈræntɪst] *fml* ◇ *adj* obscurantiste.
◇ *n* obscurantiste *mf*.

obscure [əbˈskjʊəʳ] ◇ *adj* -**1.** obscur; the meaning is rather ~ le sens n'est pas très clair; an ~ writer un écrivain obscur; an ~ feeling of unease un obscur OR vague sentiment de malaise; she comes from an ~ little village elle vient d'un petit village perdu; of ~ birth de naissance obscure. -**2.** [dark] obscur, sombre.
◇ *vt* -**1.** [hide] cacher; that building ~s the view ce bâtiment cache la vue; to ~ the truth cacher OR dissimuler la vérité || [confuse] obscurcir, embrouiller; to ~ the facts/the issue embrouiller les faits/la question. -**2.** [darken] obscurcir, assombrir.

obscurely [əbˈskjʊəlɪ] *adv* obscurément.

obscurity [əbˈskjʊərətɪ] (*pl* **obscurities**) *n* -**1.** [insignificance] obscurité *f*; to rise from ~ to fame passer de l'anonymat à la célébrité; to fall into ~ sombrer dans l'oubli. -**2.** [difficulty] obscurité *f*. -**3.** [darkness] obscurité *f*, ténèbres *fpl*.

obsequies [ˈɒbsɪkwɪz] *npl fml* obsèques *fpl*.

obsequious [əbˈsiːkwɪəs] *adj fml* obséquieux.

obsequiously [əbˈsiːkwɪəslɪ] *adv fml* obséquieusement.

obsequiousness [əbˈsiːkwɪəsnɪs] *n fml* obséquiosité *f*.

observable [əbˈzɜːvəbl] *adj* [visible] observable, visible; [discernible] perceptible, appréciable; behaviour ~ in humans un comportement observable OR que l'on peut observer chez les humains.

observably [əbˈzɜːvəblɪ] *adv* perceptiblement, visiblement.

observance [əbˈzɜːvəns] *n* -**1.** [recognition - of custom, law etc] observation *f*, observance *f*; [- of anniversary] célébration *f*. -**2.** RELIG [rite, ceremony] observance *f*.

observant [əbˈzɜːvnt] *adj* [alert] observateur; how ~ of him! comme il est observateur!, rien ne lui échappe!

observantly [əbˈzɜːvəntlɪ] *adv* perspicacement.

observation [ˌɒbzəˈveɪʃn] *n* -**1.** [study] observation *f*, surveillance *f*; the ~ of nature l'observation de la nature; to be under ~ [patient] être en observation; [by police] être surveillé par la police OR sous surveillance policière; they are keeping the house under ~ ils ont placé la maison sous surveillance. -**2.** [comment] observation *f*, remarque *f*; I have a few ~s to make j'ai quelques remarques à faire. -**3.** [perception] observation *f*; to have great powers of ~ avoir de grandes facultés d'observation. -**4.** NAUT relèvement *m*.

observational [ˌɒbzəˈveɪʃənl] *adj* [faculties, powers] d'observation; [technique, research] observationnel.

observation car *n* RAIL voiture *f* panoramique.

observation post *n* MIL poste *m* d'observation.

observation satellite *n* satellite *m* d'observation.

observation tower *n* tour *f* de guet, mirador *m*.

observatory [əbˈzɜːvətrɪ] (*pl* observatories) *n* observatoire *m*.

observe [əbˈzɜːv] *vt* -**1.** [see, notice] observer, remarquer; did you ~ anything strange? tu as remarqué quelque chose d'anormal? -**2.** [study, pay attention to] observer; he likes observing human behaviour il aime observer OR étudier le comportement humain; the police are observing his movements la police surveille ses allées et venues. -**3.** [comment, remark] (faire) remarquer, (faire) observer; "she seems worried" he ~d «elle a l'air inquiet» fit-il remarquer. -**4.** [abide by, keep] observer, respecter; to fail to ~ the law ne pas observer la loi; to ~ a minute's silence observer une minute de silence.

observer [əbˈzɜːvəʳ] *n* -**1.** [watcher] observateur *m*, -trice *f*; to the casual ~ pour un non-initié. -**2.** [at official ceremony, election] observateur *m*, -trice *f*; he attended as an ~ il était présent en tant qu'observateur. -**3.** [commentator] spécialiste *mf*, expert *m*; The Observer PRESS *journal de qualité politiquement indépendant, paraissant le dimanche et comprenant un supplément magazine*.

obsess [əbˈses] *vt* obséder; he's ~ed with punctuality c'est un maniaque de la ponctualité; she's ~ed with the idea of becoming an actress elle n'a qu'une idée, devenir actrice; he became ~ed by the horrific image cette vision d'horreur se mit à le hanter.

obsession [əb'seʃn] *n* [fixed idea] obsession *f*, idée *f* fixe; it's becoming an ~ with him ça devient une idée fixe OR une obsession chez lui; she has an ~ about punctuality c'est une maniaque de la ponctualité || [obsessive fear] hantise *f*; his ~ with death sa hantise de la mort.

obsessional [əb'seʃənl] *adj* obsessionnel.

obsessive [əb'sesɪv] ◇ *adj* -**1.** [person] obsédé, obsessionnel MED & PSYCH; [behaviour] obsessionnel. -**2.** [thought, image] obsédant.
◇ *n* obsessionnel *m*, -elle *f*.

obsessively [əb'sesɪvlɪ] *adv* d'une manière obsessionnelle; he's ~ cautious il est d'une prudence obsessionnelle; he is ~ attached to the toy il a un attachement maladif pour ce jouet; she is ~ attached to her mother elle est trop attachée à sa mère.

obsidian [ɒb'sɪdɪən] *n* obsidienne *f*.

obsolescence [,ɒbsə'lesns] *n* [of equipment, consumer goods] obsolescence *f*; planned OR built-in ~ COMM obsolescence planifiée, désuétude *f* calculée.

obsolescent [,ɒbsə'lesnt] *adj* qui tombe en désuétude; [equipment, consumer goods] obsolescent.

obsolete ['ɒbsəli:t] *adj* -**1.** [outmoded] démodé, désuet; [antiquated] archaïque; those machines have been ~ for years ces machines sont dépassées depuis des années. -**2.** LING obsolète. -**3.** BIOL atrophié.

obstacle ['ɒbstəkl] *n* obstacle *m*; what are the ~s to free trade? qu'est-ce qui fait obstacle au libre-échange?; to put ~s in sb's way mettre des bâtons dans les roues à qqn.

obstacle course, obstacle race *n* course *f* d'obstacles.

obstetric(al) [ɒb'stetrɪk(l)] *adj* obstétrical; [nurses] en obstétrique.

obstetrician [,ɒbstə'trɪʃn] *n* obstétricien *m*, -enne *f*.

obstetrics [ɒb'stetrɪks] *n (U)* obstétrique *f*.

obstinacy ['ɒbstɪnəsɪ] *n* -**1.** [stubbornness] obstination *f*, entêtement *m*; [tenacity] opiniâtreté *f*, ténacité *f*. -**2.** [persistence] persistance *f*; the ~ of an infection le caractère persistant d'une infection.

obstinate ['ɒbstənət] *adj* -**1.** [stubborn] obstiné, entêté, têtu; [tenacious] obstiné, tenace, acharné; an ~ refusal un refus obstiné; to meet with ~ resistance se heurter à une résistance obstinée OR acharnée. -**2.** [persistent] persistant, tenace; an ~ fever une fièvre persistante.

obstinately ['ɒbstənətlɪ] *adv* [stubbornly] obstinément, avec acharnement.

obstreperous [əb'strepərəs] *adj fml* OR *hum* [noisy] bruyant; [disorderly] turbulent; [recalcitrant] récalcitrant; don't (you) get ~ with me! tu ne vas pas me faire la vie!; a class of ~ children une classe d'enfants indisciplinés OR turbulents.

obstreperously [əb'strepərəslɪ] *adv fml* OR *hum* [noisily] bruyamment; [in a disorderly manner] avec turbulence; [recalcitrantly] à contre-cœur.

obstruct [əb'strʌkt] *vt* -**1.** [block - passage, road, traffic] bloquer, obstruer; [- pipe] boucher; [- vein, artery] obstruer, boucher; don't ~ the exits ne bloquez pas les sorties; the lane was ~ed by OR with fallen trees le chemin était bloqué par des arbres déracinés; her hat ~ed my view son chapeau m'empêchait de voir. -**2.** [impede - progress, measures] faire obstruction OR obstacle à, entraver; to ~ progress/justice entraver la marche du progrès/le cours de la justice; he was arrested for ~ing a policeman in the course of his duty on l'a arrêté pour avoir entravé un agent dans l'exercice de ses fonctions. -**3.** SPORT [opponent] faire obstruction à.

obstruction [əb'strʌkʃn] *n* -**1.** [impeding - of progress, measures] obstruction *f*; a policy of ~ une politique d'obstruction. -**2.** [blockage, obstacle] obstacle *m*; [- in vein, artery] obstruction *f*; [- in pipe] bouchon *m*; the accident caused an ~ in the road l'accident a bloqué la route. -**3.** SPORT obstruction *f*. -**4.** JUR obstruction *f* de la voie publique.

obstructionism [əb'strʌkʃənɪzm] *n* obstructionnisme *m*.

obstructionist [əb'strʌkʃənɪst] ◇ *adj* obstructionniste.
◇ *n* obstructionniste *mf*.

obstructive [əb'strʌktɪv] *adj*: they are being very ~ ils nous mettent constamment des bâtons dans les roues; to use ~ tactics POL user de tactiques obstructionnistes.

obtain [əb'teɪn] ◇ *vt* obtenir; [for oneself] se procurer; to ~ sthg for sb obtenir qqch pour qqn, procurer qqch à qqn; to ~ sthg from sb obtenir qqch de qqn; the book may be ~ed from the publisher on peut se procurer le livre chez l'éditeur; the party which ~s an absolute majority wins le parti qui obtient la majorité absolue l'emporte.
◇ *vi fml* [prevail] avoir cours, être en vigueur; this custom still ~s in Europe cette coutume est encore en vigueur en Europe; the situation ~ing in South Africa la situation en Afrique du Sud; practices ~ing in British banking des pratiques courantes dans le système bancaire britannique; this new system will ~ as from next week ce nouveau système entrera en vigueur dès la semaine prochaine.

obtainable [əb'teɪnəbl] *adj*: where is this drug ~? où peut-on se procurer ce médicament?; the catalogue is ~ in our branches le catalogue est disponible dans nos agences; ~ from your local supermarket en vente dans votre supermarché; this result is easily ~ ce résultat est facile à obtenir.

obtrude [əb'tru:d] *fml* ◇ *vt* -**1.** [impose] imposer. -**2.** [stick out] sortir.
◇ *vi* -**1.** [impose oneself] s'imposer. -**2.** [stick out] dépasser.

obtrusion [əb'tru:ʒn] *n fml* intrusion *f*.

obtrusive [əb'tru:sɪv] *adj* [intrusive - decor, advertising, hoarding, architecture] trop voyant; [- smell] tenace, envahissant, pénétrant; [- person, behaviour] envahissant, importun, indiscret.

obtrusively [əb'tru:sɪvlɪ] *adv* importunément.

obtuse [əb'tju:s] *adj* -**1.** *fml* [slow-witted] obtus; stop being so ~! ne sois pas si borné! -**2.** GEOM [angle] obtus; [triangle] obtusangle. -**3.** [indistinct] vague, sourd; an ~ pain une douleur sourde.

obtuseness [əb'tju:snɪs] *n fml* [slow-wittedness] lenteur *f* d'esprit; [stupidity] stupidité *f*.

obverse ['ɒbvɜ:s] ◇ *n* -**1.** [of coin] avers *m*, face *f*. -**2.** [of opinion, argument etc] contraire *m*, opposé *m*.
◇ *adj* the ~ side [of coin] le côté face OR l'avers d'une pièce; *fig* [of opinion, argument etc] le contraire.

obviate ['ɒbvɪeɪt] *vt fml* [difficulty, need] obvier à; this ~s the need for further action cela rend toute autre démarche inutile.

obvious ['ɒbvɪəs] ◇ *adj* -**1.** [evident] évident; it's ~ that he's wrong il est évident qu'il a tort; don't always go for the ~ solution n'opte pas toujours pour la solution qui semble la plus évidente; the ~ choice le choix évident OR qui s'impose; her ~ innocence son innocence manifeste; for ~ reasons pour des raisons évidentes; the ~ thing to do is to leave la seule chose à faire, c'est de partir; it was ~ that he was going to resign il était clair qu'il allait démissionner. -**2.** *pej* [predictable] prévisible; his symbolism is too ~ son symbolisme manque de subtilité; the ending was a bit ~ la fin était prévisible.
◇ *n*: to state the ~ enfoncer une porte ouverte; it would be stating the ~ to say that cela va sans dire.

obviously ['ɒbvɪəslɪ] *adv* -**1.** [of course] évidemment, de toute évidence; she's ~ not lying il est clair OR évident qu'elle ne ment pas; ~ not! il semble que non!; he ~ got the wrong number de toute évidence, il s'est trompé de numéro; they were ~ ill ils étaient manifestement malades. -**2.** [plainly, visibly] manifestement; she's not ~ lying il n'est pas sûr qu'elle mente.

ocarina [,ɒkə'ri:nə] *n* ocarina *m*.

OCAS (*abbr of* Organization of Central American States) *pr n* ODEAC *f*.

Occam's razor ['ɒkəmz-] *n* le rasoir d'Occam OR d'Ockham, le principe de parcimonie.

occasion [ə'keɪʒn] ◇ *n* -**1.** [circumstance, time] occasion *f*; he was perfectly charming on that ~ cette fois-là, il fut tout à fait charmant; on the ~ of her wedding à l'occasion de son mariage; I have been there on quite a few ~s j'y suis allé à plusieurs occasions OR à plusieurs reprises; if the ~ arises, should the ~ arise si l'occasion se présente, le cas échéant; it wasn't a suitable ~ les circonstances n'étaient pas favorables; this is no ~ for an argument ce n'est pas le moment de se disputer ❑ to rise to the ~ se montrer à la hauteur (de la situation). -**2.** [special event] événement *m*; his birthday is always a big ~ son anniversaire est toujours un événement important; to have a sense of ~ savoir marquer le coup. -**3.** [reason, cause] motif *m*, raison *f*, occasion *f*; I had no ~ to suspect her je n'avais aucune raison de la soupçonner; there is no ~ for worry il n'y a pas lieu de s'inquiéter; her return was the ~ for great rejoicing son retour donna lieu à de grandes réjouissances.
◇ *vt* occasionner, provoquer.
◆ **on occasion(s)** *adv phr* de temps en temps, de temps à autre.

occasional [ə'keɪʒənl] *adj* -**1.** occasionnel, épisodique; he's an ~ visitor/golfer il vient/joue au golf de temps en temps; during his ~ visits to her lorsqu'il allait la voir OR lui rendait visite; I like an OR the ~ cigar j'aime (fumer) un cigare à l'occasion OR de temps en temps; she writes me the ~ postcard elle m'envoie une carte postale de temps à autre; there will be ~ showers il y aura quelques averses OR pluies intermittentes. -**2.** [music, play etc] de circonstance.

occasionally [ə'keɪʒnəlɪ] *adv* de temps en temps, quelquefois, occasionnellement; I smoke only very ~ je ne fume que très rarement.

occasional table *n Br* table *f* volante.

occident ['ɒksɪdənt] *n lit* occident *m*, couchant *m*.
◆ **Occident** *n*: the Occident l'Occident *m*.

occidental [,ɒksɪ'dentl] *adj lit* occidental.
◆ **Occidental** ◇ *adj* occidental.
◇ *n* Occidental *m*, -e *f*.

occidentalize, -ise [,ɒksɪ'dentəlaɪz] *vt* occidentaliser.

occipital [ɒk'sɪpɪtl] ◇ *adj* occipital.
◇ *n* = **occipital bone**.

occipital bone *n* os *m* occipital.

occipital lobe *n* lobe *m* occipital.

occiput ['ɒksɪpʌt] (*pl* occiputs OR occipita [ɒk'sɪpɪtə]) *n* occiput *m*.

occlude [ɒ'klu:d] *vt* occlure.

occluded front [ɒ'klu:dɪd-] *n* METEOR front *m* occlus.

occlusion [ɒ'klu:ʒn] *n* occlusion *f*.

occlusive [ɒ'klu:sɪv] ◇ *adj* occlusif.
◇ *n* LING (consonne *f*) occlusive *f*.

occult [ɒ'kʌlt] ◇ *adj* occulte.
◇ *n*: the ~ [supernatural] le surnaturel; [mystical skills] les sciences *fpl* occultes.

occultism ['ɒkʌltɪzm] *n* occultisme *m*.

occupancy ['ɒkjʊpənsɪ] (*pl* occupancies) *n* occupation *f (d'un appartement etc)*.

occupant ['ɒkjʊpənt] *n* [gen] occupant *m*, -e *f*; [tenant] locataire *mf*; [of vehicle] passager *m*, -ère *f*; [of job] titulaire *mf*.

occupation [,ɒkjʊ'peɪʃn] *n* -**1.** [employment] emploi *m*, travail *m*; what's his ~? qu'est-ce qu'il fait comme travail OR dans la vie?; please state your name and ~ veuillez indiquer votre nom et votre profession; I'm not an actor by ~ je ne suis pas acteur de métier; **raising a family is a full-time ~** élever des enfants, c'est un travail à plein temps. -**2.** [activity, hobby] occupation *f*; **his favourite ~ is listening to music** ce qu'il aime faire par-dessus tout, c'est écouter de la musique; **the TV provides some ~ for the children** la télévision est un moyen d'occuper les enfants. -**3.** [of building, offices etc] occupation *f*; **during Mr Gray's ~ of the premises** lorsque M. Gray occupait les locaux; **the offices are ready for ~** les bureaux sont prêts à être occupés. -**4.** MIL & POL occupation *f*; **army of ~** armée *f* d'occupation; **the students have voted to continue their ~** les étudiants ont voté la poursuite de l'occupation des locaux; **under French ~** sous occupation française; **the Occupation** HIST l'Occupation.

occupational [ˌɒkjuːˈpeɪʃənl] *adj* professionnel; **~ disease** maladie *f* professionnelle; **~ hazard** risque *m* professionnel OR du métier.

occupational pension *n Br* retraite *f* complémentaire; **~ scheme** caisse *f* de retraite complémentaire.

occupational psychology *n* psychologie *f* du travail.

occupational therapist *n* ergothérapeute *mf*.

occupational therapy *n* ergothérapie *f*.

occupied [ˈɒkjʊpaɪd] *adj* [country, town] occupé; **in ~ France** dans la France occupée.

occupier [ˈɒkjʊpaɪəʳ] *n* [gen] occupant *m*, -e *f*; [tenant] locataire *mf*.

occupy [ˈɒkjʊpaɪ] (*pt* & *pp* **occupied**) *vt* -**1.** [house, room etc] occuper; **is this seat occupied?** est-ce que cette place est prise? -**2.** [keep busy - person, mind] occuper; **she occupies herself by doing crosswords** elle s'occupe en faisant des mots croisés; **to be occupied in** OR **with (doing) sthg** être occupé à (faire) qqch; **try to keep them occupied for a few minutes** essaie de les occuper quelques minutes; **find something to ~ your mind** trouvez quelque chose qui vous occupe l'esprit; **reading keeps him occupied** ça l'occupe de lire; **I like to keep my mind occupied** j'aime bien m'occuper l'esprit. -**3.** [fill, take up - time, space] occuper; **the sofa occupies half the room** le canapé occupe OR prend la moitié de la pièce; **how do you ~ your evenings?** comment OR à quoi occupez-vous vos soirées? -**4.** MIL & POL occuper; **~ing army** armée *f* d'occupation. -**5.** [hold - office, role, rank] occuper.

occur [əˈkɜːʳ] (*pt* & *pp* **occurred**, *cont* **occurring**) *vi* -**1.** [happen] arriver, avoir lieu, se produire; **misunderstandings often ~ over the phone** il y a souvent des malentendus au téléphone; **many changes have occurred since then** beaucoup de choses ont changé depuis ce temps-là; **if a difficulty/the opportunity ~s** si une difficulté/l'occasion se présente; **I promise it won't ~ again** je promets que ça ne se reproduira pas; **whatever ~s** quoi qu'il arrive. -**2.** [exist, be found] se trouver, se rencontrer; **the mistake ~s at the end** l'erreur se trouve à la fin; **such phenomena often ~ in nature** on rencontre souvent de tels phénomènes dans la nature. -**3.** [come to mind]: **to ~ to sb** venir à l'esprit de qqn; **another thought occurred to me** autre chose m'est venu à l'esprit; **it occurred to me later that he was lying** j'ai réalisé plus tard qu'il mentait; **it ~s to me now that something wasn't quite right** je réalise seulement maintenant que quelque chose n'allait pas; **didn't it ~ to you to call me?** ça ne t'est pas venu à l'idée de m'appeler?; **it would never ~ to me to use violence** il ne me viendrait jamais à l'idée d'avoir recours à la violence.

occurrence [əˈkʌrəns] *n* -**1.** [incident] événement *m*; **it's an everyday ~** ça arrive OR ça se produit tous les jours. -**2.** [fact or instance of occurring]: **the increasing ~ of racial attacks** le nombre croissant d'agressions racistes; **the ~ of the disease in adults is more serious** lorsqu'elle se déclare chez l'adulte, la maladie est plus grave; **of rare ~** qui arrive OR se produit rarement. -**3.** LING occurrence *f*.

ocean [ˈəʊʃn] *n* -**1.** GEOG océan *m*; **the ~** *Am* la mer ❑ **the Indian Ocean** l'océan Indien. -**2.** *fig*: **~s of** beaucoup de; **there's always ~s of drink at his parties** il y a toujours beaucoup d'alcool à ses soirées.

ocean bed, **ocean floor** *n* fond *m* océanique.

oceanfront [ˈəʊʃnfrʌnt] *n Am* bord *m* de mer.

ocean-going *adj* de haute mer.

Oceania [ˌəʊʃɪˈɑːnɪə] *pr n* Océanie *f*; **in ~** en Océanie.

Oceanian [ˌəʊʃɪˈɑːnɪən] ◇ *n* Océanien *m*, -enne *f*.
◇ *adj* océanien.

oceanic [ˌəʊʃɪˈænɪk] *adj* -**1.** [marine] océanique. -**2.** *fig* [huge] immense.

oceanographer [ˌəʊʃəˈnɒgrəfəʳ] *n* océanographe *mf*.

oceanography [ˌəʊʃəˈnɒgrəfɪ] *n* océanographie *f*.

ocelot [ˈəʊsɪlɒt] *n* ocelot *m*.

och [ɒx] *interj Scot* & *Ir* oh; **~ aye!** eh oui! *(parfois employé pour parodier les Écossais)*.

oche [ˈɒkɪ] *n ligne derrière laquelle le joueur de fléchettes doit se placer*.

ochre, **ocher** *Am* [ˈəʊkəʳ] ◇ *n* [ore] ocre *f*; [colour] ocre *m*.
◇ *adj* ocre *(inv)*.
◇ *vt* ocrer.

ochreous [ˈəʊkrɪəs] *adj* ocreux.

o'clock [əˈklɒk] *adv* -**1.** [time]: **it's one/two ~** il est une heure/deux heures; **at precisely 9 ~** à 9 h précises; **a flight at 4 ~ in the afternoon** un vol à 16 h; **the 8 ~ bus** le bus de 8 h; **at 12 ~** [midday] à midi; [midnight] à minuit. -**2.** [position]: **enemy fighter at 7 ~** chasseur ennemi à 7 h.

OCR *n* -**1.** *abbr of* **optical character reader**. -**2.** (*abbr of* **optical character recognition**) ROC.

Oct. (*written abbr of* **October**) oct.

octagon [ˈɒktəgən] *n* octogone *m*.

octagonal [ɒkˈtægənl] *adj* octogonal.

octahedron [ˌɒktəˈhiːdrən] *n* octaèdre *m*.

octal [ˈɒktl] ◇ *adj* octal.
◇ *n* octal *m*.

octameter [ɒkˈtæmɪtəʳ] *n* LITERAT vers *m* de huit pieds, octosyllabe *m*.

octane [ˈɒkteɪn] *n* octane *m*; **high-~ petrol** *Br* OR **gas** *Am* super *m*, supercarburant *m*; **low-~ petrol** *Br* OR **gas** *Am* ordinaire *m*, essence *f* ordinaire.

octane number, **octane rating** *n* indice *m* d'octane.

octave [ˈɒktɪv] *n* FENCING, MUS & RELIG octave *f*; LITERAT huitain *m*.

Octavian [ɒkˈteɪvjən] *pr n* Octave.

octavo [ɒkˈteɪvəʊ] (*pl* **octavos**) *n* in-octavo *m inv*.

octet [ɒkˈtet] *n* -**1.** [group] octuor *m*. -**2.** MUS octuor *m*. -**3.** LITERAT huitain *m*. -**4.** CHEM octet *m*.

October [ɒkˈtəʊbəʳ] *n* octobre *m*.

October Revolution *n*: **the ~** la révolution d'octobre.

octogenarian [ˌɒktəʊdʒɪˈneərɪən] ◇ *adj* octogénaire.
◇ *n* octogénaire *mf*.

octopus [ˈɒktəpəs] (*pl* **octopuses** OR **octopi** [-paɪ]) *n* -**1.** ZOOL pieuvre *f*, poulpe *m*; CULIN poulpe *m*. -**2.** *fig* pieuvre *f*.

octosyllabic [ˌɒktəʊsɪˈlæbɪk] *adj* octosyllabique, octosyllabe; **in ~ verse** en octosyllabes, en vers octosyllabiques.

octosyllable [ˈɒktəʊˌsɪləbl] *n* -**1.** [in poetry - line] octosyllabe *m*, vers *m* octosyllabique. -**2.** [word] mot *m* octosyllabique OR octosyllabe.

octuple [ˈɒktjuːpl] ◇ *adj* octuple.
◇ *n* octuple *m*.
◇ *vt* octupler.

ocular [ˈɒkjʊləʳ] ◇ *adj* oculaire.
◇ *n* oculaire *m*.

oculist [ˈɒkjʊlɪst] *n* oculiste *mf*.

OD *inf* (*pt* & *pp* **OD'd**) ◇ *n* (*abbr of* **overdose**) overdose *f*.
◇ *vi* être victime d'une overdose; **we rather ~'d on TV last night** *hum* on a un peu forcé sur la télé hier soir.
◇ *written abbr of* **overdrawn**.

odalisk, **odalisque** [ˈəʊdəlɪsk] *n* odalisque *f*.

odd [ɒd] *adj* -**1.** [weird] bizarre, étrange; **he's an ~ character** c'est un drôle d'individu; **the ~ thing is that the room was empty** ce qui est bizarre, c'est que la pièce était vide; **it felt ~ seeing her again** ça m'a fait (tout) drôle de la revoir; **he's a bit ~ in the head** *inf* il lui manque une case. -**2.** [occasional, incidental]: **at ~ moments** de temps en temps; **he has his ~ moments of depression** il lui arrive d'avoir ses moments de déprime; **I smoke the ~ cigarette** il m'arrive de fumer une cigarette de temps en temps; **we took the ~ photo** nous avons pris deux ou trois photos; **we did get the ~ enquiry** on a bien eu une ou deux demandes de renseignements; **just add any ~ carrots** ajoute simplement quelques carottes ❑ **~ jobs** petits boulots *mpl*; **she gives him a few ~ jobs from time to time** de temps en temps, elle lui donne une ou deux choses à faire. -**3.** [not matching] dépareillé; **he was wearing ~ socks** ses chaussettes étaient dépareillées, il portait des chaussettes dépareillées. -**4.** [not divisible by two] impair; **the ~ pages of a book** les pages impaires d'un livre ❑ **~ function** MATH fonction *f* impaire; **~ number** nombre *m* impair. -**5.** *inf (in combinations)* [or so]: **twenty ~** vingt et quelques; **thirty-~ pounds** trente livres et quelques, trente et quelques livres; **he must be forty-~** il doit avoir la quarantaine OR dans les quarante ans. -**6.** *phr*: **the ~ one** OR **man** OR **woman out** l'exception *f*; **everyone else was in evening dress, I was the ~ one out** ils étaient tous en tenue de soirée sauf moi; **which of these drawings is the ~ one out?** parmi ces dessins, lequel est l'intrus?; **when they chose the two teams, Jill was the ~ one out** lorsqu'ils ont formé les deux équipes, Jill s'est retrouvée toute seule; **they all knew each other so well that I felt the ~ one out** ils se connaissaient tous si bien que j'avais l'impression d'être la cinquième roue du carrosse OR de la charrette.

oddball *inf* [ˈɒdbɔːl] ◇ *n* excentrique *mf*, original *m*, -e *f*; **he's a real ~** c'est un drôle de numéro.
◇ *adj* excentrique, original.

odd bod *inf Br* = **oddball** *n*.

odd-even *adj* COMPUT: **~ check** contrôle *m* de parité.

oddity [ˈɒdɪtɪ] (*pl* **oddities**) *n* -**1.** [strange person] excentrique *mf*, original *m*, -e *f*; [strange thing] curiosité *f*; **she's a bit of an ~** elle est un peu bizarre; **being the only woman there makes her something of an ~** on la remarque du simple fait qu'elle est la seule femme. -**2.** [strangeness] étrangeté *f*, bizarrerie *f*.

odd-job man *n* homme *m* à tout faire, factotum *m*.

odd-looking *adj* à l'air bizarre.

odd lot *n* COMM lot *m* dépareillé; ST. EX lot *m* fractionné.

odd-lotter [-ˈlɒtəʳ] *n Am* ST. EX petit actionnaire *m*.

oddly [ˈɒdlɪ] *adv* bizarrement, curieusement; **~ shaped** d'une forme bizarre; **~ enough, he didn't recognize me** chose curieuse, il ne m'a pas reconnu.

oddment [ˈɒdmənt] *n* COMM [of matched set] article *m* dépareillé; [of lot, line] fin *f* de série; [of fabric] coupon *m*.

odds [ɒdz] *npl* -**1.** [in betting] cote *f*; **the ~ are ten to one against** la cote est de dix contre un; **the ~ are ten to one on** la cote est de un contre dix; **they're offering long/short ~ against Jackson** Jackson a une bonne/faible cote; **I'll lay** OR **give you ~ of twenty to one that she'll leave him** je te parie à vingt contre un qu'elle le quittera ❑ **I ended up paying over the ~** *Br* en fin de compte, je l'ai payé plus cher qu'il ne valait OR que sa valeur. -**2.** [chances] chances *fpl*;

the ~ are she's been lying to us all along il y a de fortes chances qu'elle nous ait menti depuis le début; the ~ are on/against her accepting il y a de fortes chances/il y a peu de chances (pour) qu'elle accepte; the ~ are in favour of the Tories winning il y a de fortes chances pour que les conservateurs l'emportent. -3. [great difficulties]: against all the ~ contre toute attente; they won against overwhelming ~ ils ont gagné alors que tout était contre eux. -4. *inf Br* [difference]: it makes no ~ ça ne change rien; it makes no ~ to me ça m'est égal. -5. *phr*: ~ and ends, ~ and sods *inf Br* [miscellaneous objects] objets *mpl* divers; [leftovers] restes *mpl*; her desk is always covered with ~ and ends son bureau est toujours encombré de tout un bric-à-brac.

◆ **at odds** *adj phr* en conflit; they're always at ~ with the neighbours ils sont constamment en conflit avec leurs voisins; the way she was dressed was completely at ~ with her personality ce qu'elle portait ne correspondait pas du tout à sa personnalité.

odds-on *adj Br*: it's ~ that he'll win il y a tout à parier qu'il gagnera ❑ ~ favourite grand favori *m*.

ode [əʊd] *n* ode *f*; 'Ode On a Grecian Urn' *Keats* 'Ode sur une urne grecque'; 'Ode To a Nightingale' *Keats* 'Ode à un rossignol'; 'Ode to Joy' *Beethoven* 'Hymne à la joie'.

Odessa [əʊ'desə] *pr n* Odessa.

odious ['əʊdjəs] *adj fml* odieux.

odium ['əʊdjəm] *n fml* [condemnation] réprobation *f*; [hatred] haine *f*.

odometer [əʊ'dɒmɪtə^r] *n Am* AUT compteur *m* kilométrique.

odontologist [ˌɒdɒn'tɒlədʒɪst] *n* odontologiste *mf*.

odontology [ˌɒdɒn'tɒlədʒɪ] *n* odontologie *f*.

odor *etc Am* = **odour**.

odoriferous [ˌəʊdə'rɪfərəs] *adj* odoriférant.

odorous ['əʊdərəs] *adj* [fragrant] odorant; [malodorous] malodorant.

odour *Br*, **odor** *Am* ['əʊdə^r] *n* -1. [smell] odeur *f*; guaranteed to get rid of unpleasant ~s! fini les mauvaises odeurs! -2. [pervasive quality] odeur *f*, parfum *m*, arôme *m*; ~ of sanctity RELIG odeur de sainteté. -3. *Br phr*: to be in good/bad ~ with sb *fml* être bien/mal vu de qqn.

odourless *Br*, **odorless** *Am* ['əʊdəlɪs] *adj* inodore.

Odysseus [ə'diːsɪəs] *pr n* Ulysse.

odyssey ['ɒdɪsɪ] *n* odyssée *f*; 'The Odyssey' *Homer* 'l'Odyssée'; '2001: A Space Odyssey' *Kubrick* '2001: l'odyssée de l'espace'.

OECD (*abbr of* Organization for Economic Cooperation and Development) *pr n* OCDE *f*.

oecumenical *etc* [ˌiːkjuː'menɪkl] = **ecumenical**.

oedema *Br*, **edema** *Am* [iː'diːmə] (*Br pl* oedemata [-mətə], *Am pl* edemata [-mətə]) *n* œdème *m*.

Oedipal ['iːdɪpl] *adj* œdipien.

Oedipus ['iːdɪpəs] *pr n* Œdipe; 'Oedipus at Colonus' *Sophocles* 'Œdipe à Colone'; 'Oedipus Rex' *Sophocles* 'Œdipe roi'.

Oedipus complex *n* complexe *m* d'Œdipe.

oenologist [iː'nɒlədʒɪst] *n* œnologue *mf*.

oenology [iː'nɒlədʒɪ] *n* œnologie *f*.

o'er ['əʊə^r] *lit* = **over** *adv* & *prep*.

oesophagus *Br*, **esophagus** *Am* [ɪ'sɒfəgəs] (*Br pl* oesophaguses OR oesophagi [-gaɪ], *Am pl* esophaguses OR esophagi [-gaɪ]) *n* œsophage *m*.

oestrogen *Br*, **estrogen** *Am* ['iːstrədʒən] *n* œstrogène *m*.

oestrous *Br*, **estrus** *Am* ['iːstrəs] *adj* œstral; ~ cycle cycle *m* œstral.

oestrus *Br*, **estrus** *Am* ['iːstrəs] *n* œstrus *m*.

of [*weak form* əv, *strong form* ɒv] *prep* -1. [after nouns expressing quantity, number, amount] de; a pound of onions une livre d'oignons; a loaf of bread un pain; a piece of cake un morceau de gâteau; a bottle of wine une bouteille de vin; a pair of trousers un pantalon; there are six of us nous sommes six; thousands of mosquitos des milliers de moustiques; some/many/few of us were present quelques-uns/beaucoup/peu d'entre nous étaient présents; half of them failed la moitié d'entre eux ont échoué. -2. [indicating age] de; a boy/a girl of three un garçon/une fille de trois ans; at the age of nineteen à dix-neuf ans, à l'âge de dix-neuf ans. -3. [indicating composition, content] de; a photo of Lily une photo de Lily; a map of Spain une carte d'Espagne; a report of events in Parliament un compte rendu de ce qui se passe au Parlement; a rise of 25% une augmentation de 25 %; a team of cricketers une équipe de cricket; a city of 120,000 une ville de 120 000 habitants; a series of programmes on Italy une série d'émissions sur l'Italie. -4. [created by] de; the poems of Byron les poèmes de Byron. -5. [with words expressing attitude or emotion] de; I'm ashamed of it j'en ai honte; I'm proud of it j'en suis fier; I'm afraid of the dark j'ai peur du noir; she dreamt of one day becoming Prime Minister elle rêvait de devenir Premier ministre un jour; I have no intention of leaving je n'ai aucune intention de partir. -6. [indicating possession, relationship] de; he's a friend of mine c'est un ami à moi; a friend of mine told me un de mes amis me l'a dit; I'd like a home of my own j'aimerais avoir mon chez-moi; the corner of the street le coin de la rue; the subject of the lecture le sujet du cours; cancer of the bowel cancer des intestins; the rights of man les droits de l'homme; she's head of department elle est chef de service. -7. [indicating subject of action]: it was kind/mean of him c'était gentil/méchant de sa part. -8. [with names of places] de; the city of New York la ville de New York; the people of Chile le peuple OR les habitants du Chili; the University of Cambridge l'université de Cambridge; the village of Carlton le village de Carlton. -9. [after nouns derived from verbs] de; the arrival/departure of Flight 556 l'arrivée/le départ du vol 556; we need the approval of the committee nous devons obtenir l'autorisation du comité; a lover of fine wine un amateur de bons vins; the success of the meeting le succès de la réunion; an outbreak of cholera une épidémie de choléra. -10. [describing a particular feeling or quality] de; a feeling of relief un sentiment de soulagement; she has the gift of mimicry elle a un talent d'imitatrice; a man of courage un homme de courage; a coat of many colours un manteau multicolore; a sort OR kind OR type of tree un type d'arbre ‖ *fml*: to be of sound mind être sain d'esprit; to be of a nervous disposition avoir une prédisposition à la nervosité. -11. [made from]: a ring of solid gold une bague en or massif; a heart of stone un cœur de pierre. -12. [after nouns of size, measurement etc] de; a width/length of sixty feet une largeur/longueur de soixante pieds; they reach a height of ten feet ils atteignent une hauteur de dix pieds. -13. [indicating cause, origin, source] de; the consequence/the effects of the explosion la conséquence/les effets de l'explosion; to die of cancer mourir du OR d'un cancer; of royal descent de lignée royale; of which/whom dont. -14. [indicating likeness, similarity] de; the colour of blood/of grass la couleur du sang/de l'herbe; the size of a tennis ball de la taille d'une balle de tennis; he reminds me of John Wayne il me rappelle John Wayne; it smells of coffee ça sent le café; a giant of a man un homme très grand; a huge barn of a house une énorme bâtisse. -15. [indicating specific point in time or space] de; the 3rd of May le 3 mai; in the middle of August à la mi-août; the crash of 1929 le krach de 1929; the day of our wedding le jour de notre mariage; it was the high point of the week ça a été le point culminant de la semaine; a quarter of nine *Am* neuf heures moins le quart; in the middle of the road au milieu de la chaussée; at the far end of the room à l'autre bout de la pièce. -16. [indicating deprivation or absence]: a lack of food un manque de nourriture; to get rid of sthg se débarrasser de qqch; to be cured of sthg être guéri de qqch; to rob sb of sthg voler qqch à qqn. -17. [indicating information received or passed on]: I've never heard of him je n'ai jamais entendu parler de lui; to learn of sthg apprendre qqch; her knowledge of French sa connaissance du français. -18. [as intensifier]: the best/the worst of all le meilleur/le pire de tout; today of all days! il fallait que ça arrive aujourd'hui! -19. *dated* OR *dial*: I like to listen to the radio of a morning/an evening j'aime écouter la radio le matin/le soir.

off [ɒf] ◇ *adv* -1. [indicating removal]: to take sthg ~ enlever OR ôter qqch; to come ~ [sticker, handle] se détacher; [lipstick, paint] partir; you can leave your jacket ~ ce n'est pas la peine de remettre votre veste; she kicked ~ her shoes elle ôta ses chaussures d'un coup de pied; the knob had broken ~ la poignée était cassée; peel ~ the wallpaper décollez le papier peint; she cut ~ her hair elle s'est coupé les cheveux; ~ with his head! coupez-lui la tête! -2. [indicating departure]: the truck drove ~ le camion démarra; to run ~ partir en courant; when are you ~ to Dublin? quand partez-vous pour Dublin?; we'd better be ~ on doit partir; they're ~! SPORT ils sont partis!; I'm ~! *inf* j'y vais!; ~ we go! c'est parti!; ~ to bed with you! au lit!; be ~ with you! va-t-en!; oh no, he's ~ again! *hum* ça y est, ça le reprend! -3. [indicating movement away from a surface]: the ball hit the wall and bounced ~ la balle a heurté le mur et a rebondi; I knocked the glass ~ with my elbow j'ai fait tomber le verre d'un coup de coude. -4. [indicating location]: it's ~ to the right c'est sur la droite; she's ~ playing tennis elle est partie jouer au tennis. -5. [indicating disembarkment, dismounting etc]: to get ~ descendre; to jump ~ sauter. -6. [indicating absence, inactivity]: to take a week ~ prendre une semaine de congé; Monday's my day ~ le lundi est mon jour de congé. -7. [indicating distance in time or space]: Paris/Christmas is still a long way ~ Paris/Noël est encore loin; it's a few miles ~ c'est à quelques kilomètres d'ici. -8. THEAT off; voice ~ voix *f* off; noises/voices ~ bruits *mpl*/voix *fpl* en coulisses. -9. [indicating disconnection]: to put OR switch OR turn the light ~ éteindre la lumière; to turn the tap ~ fermer le robinet; leave the lights ~ n'allume pas. -10. [indicating separation, partition]: the playing area is divided ~ by a low wall l'aire de jeu est délimitée par un petit mur; to fence ~ land clôturer un terrain; the police have cordoned ~ the area la police a bouclé le quartier. -11. [indicating price reduction]: 'special offer: £5 ~' 'offre spéciale: 5 livres de réduction'; the salesman gave me $20/20% ~ le vendeur m'a fait une remise de 20 dollars/ 20 %. -12. [indicating relief from discomfort]: to sleep/to walk sthg ~ faire passer qqch en dormant/marchant.

◇ *prep* -1. [indicating movement away from] de; he fell ~ his chair il est tombé de sa chaise; she knocked the vase ~ the table elle a fait tomber le vase de la table; take your elbows ~ the table enlève tes coudes de la table; couples started drifting ~ the dance floor les couples commencèrent à quitter la piste de danse; 'drinks must not be taken ~ the premises' 'les boissons doivent être consommées sur place'; it'll take your mind ~ it *fig* ça te changera les idées. -2. [indicating removal] de; take the top ~ the bottle enlève le bouchon de la bouteille; I've stripped the wallpaper ~ the walls j'ai décollé le papier peint des murs. -3. [from]: to buy sthg ~ sb acheter qqch à qqn; I bought it ~ a stall je l'ai acheté sur le marché; can I borrow £5 ~ you? je peux t'emprunter 5 livres? -4. [from the direction of] de; a cool breeze ~ the sea une brise fraîche venant du large. -5. [indicating location]: a few miles ~ the coast à quelques kilomètres de la côte; most students live ~ campus la plupart des étudiants vivent à l'extérieur du campus; we ate in a small restaurant ~ the main road nous avons mangé dans un petit restaurant à l'écart de la grand-route; the bathroom's ~ the bedroom la salle de bains donne dans la chambre; an alley ~ Oxford Street une ruelle qui donne sur Oxford Street; just ~ Oxford Street there's a pretty little square à deux pas d'Oxford Street il y a une petite place ravissante. -**6.** [absent from]: Mr Dale is ~ work today M. Dale est absent aujourd'hui; you need a few days ~ work vous avez besoin de quelques jours de congé; Wayne's ~ school with the flu Wayne est à la maison avec la grippe; I've been ~ work for over a year now voilà un an que je ne travaille plus. -**7.** [by means of]: it runs ~ gas/electricity/solar power ça marche au gaz/à l'électricité/à l'énergie solaire; the radio works ~ the mains la radio fonctionne sur secteur. -**8.** [indicating source of nourishment] de; to live ~ vegetables vivre de légumes; to live ~ the land vivre (des produits) de la terre. -**9.** [reduced from]: I can get $20/ 20% ~ the list price je peux avoir une remise de 20 dollars/20 % sur le prix de vente; they'll take OR knock *inf* something ~ it if you pay cash ils vous feront une remise si vous payez en liquide. -**10.** *inf* [no longer wanting or needing]: to be ~ one's food ne pas avoir faim; I'm ~ whisky je n'aime plus le whisky; I'm ~ him at the moment j'en ai marre de lui en ce moment; she's ~ antibiotics now elle ne prend plus d'antibiotiques maintenant; he's ~ heroin now il ne touche plus à l'héroïne maintenant.

◇ *adj* -**1.** [not working - electricity, light, radio, TV] éteint; [- tap] fermé; [- engine, machine] arrêté, à l'arrêt; [- handbrake] desserré; the gas is ~ [at mains] le gaz est fermé; [under saucepan] le gaz est éteint; [for safety reasons] le gaz est coupé; 'off' 'arrêt'; make sure the switches are in the ~ position vérifiez que les interrupteurs sont sur (la position) arrêt; the ~ button le bouton d'arrêt. -**2.** [bad, tainted] mauvais, avarié; the milk is ~ le lait a tourné; it smells/tastes ~ on dirait que ce n'est plus bon. -**3.** [cancelled] annulé; tonight's match is ~ le match de ce soir est annulé; if that's your attitude, the deal's ~! si c'est comme ça que vous le prenez, ma proposition ne tient plus! -**4.** *Br* [not available]: I'm afraid salmon's ~ je regrette, mais il n'y a plus de saumon. -**5.** [unwell]: I felt decidedly ~ the next morning le lendemain matin, je ne me sentais vraiment pas bien; everyone has their ~ days on a tous nos mauvais jours. -**6.** *inf* [unacceptable]: I say, that's a bit ~! dites donc, vous y allez un peu fort!; I thought it was a bit ~ the way she just ignored me je n'ai pas apprécié qu'elle m'ignore comme ça. -**7.** *Br* AUT [when driving on right] (du côté) gauche; [when driving on left] (du côté) droit. -**8.** [having a certain amount of]: how are we ~ for milk? combien de lait nous reste-t-il?

◇ *n inf* [start] départ *m*; they're ready for the ~ ils sont prêts à partir; right from the ~ dès le départ.

◇ *vt* ▽ [kill] *Am* buter.

◆ **off and on** *adv phr* par intervalles; we lived together ~ and on for three years on a plus ou moins vécu ensemble pendant trois ans.

offal ['ɒfl] *n (U)* -**1.** *Br* CULIN abats *mpl*. -**2.** [refuse] ordures *fpl*, déchets *mpl*. -**3.** [carrion] charogne *f*.

off-balance ◇ *adj* déséquilibré.
◇ *adv*: to throw OR to knock sb ~ *literal* faire perdre l'équilibre à qqn; *fig* couper le souffle à OR désarçonner qqn; her question caught me ~ sa question m'a pris au dépourvu.

offbeat ['ɒfbi:t] ◇ *adj* [unconventional] original, excentrique.
◇ *n* MUS temps *m* faible.

off-Broadway *adj Am*: an ~ show *spectacle new-yorkais non conventionnel qui se démarque du style de ceux de Broadway, et qui n'est pas présenté dans un 'Broadway Theatre'*; an ~ director un metteur en scène de pièces d'avant-garde.

off camera *adj* & *adv* CIN & TV hors champ, off.

off-campus *adv* UNIV à l'extérieur du campus; I prefer to live ~ je préfère habiter à l'extérieur du campus.

off-centre *Br*, **off-center** *Am* ◇ *adj* -**1.** [painting on wall] décentré; [rotation] désaxé; [gun sights] désaligné; the title is ~ le titre n'est pas centré. -**2.** *fig* [unconventional] original.
◇ *adv* de côté; aim slightly ~ visez légèrement de côté.

off chance *n*
◆ **on the off chance** *adv phr* au cas où; I phoned on the ~ of catching him at home j'ai appelé en espérant qu'il serait chez lui; she kept it on the ~ (that) it might prove useful elle l'a gardé pour le cas où cela pourrait servir.

off-colour *adj* -**1.** *Br* [ill] souffrant; she's looking a little ~ elle est un peu pâlotte. -**2.** [indelicate - film, story] de mauvais goût, d'un goût douteux.

offcut ['ɒfkʌt] *n* [of cloth, wood, paper] chute *f*; [of meat] reste *m*.

off-day *n*: he was having an ~ il n'était pas en forme; everyone has their ~s on a tous nos mauvais jours.

off-duty *adj* [policeman, soldier, nurse] qui n'est pas de service; I'm off duty at 6 je finis mon service à 6 h.

offence *Br*, **offense** *Am* [ə'fens] *n* -**1.** JUR délit *m*; it's his first ~ c'est la première fois qu'il commet un délit; second OR subsequent ~ récidive *f*; to commit a second OR subsequent ~ récidiver; arrested for drug ~s [dealing] arrêté pour trafic de drogue; [use] arrêté pour consommation de drogue ❑ capital ~ crime *m* capital; indictable/nonindictable ~ infraction *f* majeure/mineure; motoring OR driving ~ infraction *f* au Code de la route; parking ~ contravention *f* au stationnement; sex ~ ≃ attentat *m* à la pudeur. -**2.** [displeasure, hurt]: to give OR to cause ~ to sb blesser OR offenser qqn; to take ~ at sthg s'offenser OR s'offusquer de qqch; he's very quick to take ~ il se vexe pour un rien; I meant no ~ je ne voulais pas vous blesser; no ~ meant — none taken! je n'avais pas l'intention de te vexer — il n'y a pas de mal!; the factory is an ~ to the eye l'usine est une insulte au regard; it's an ~ against good taste c'est un outrage au bon goût. -**3.** MIL [attack] attaque *f*, offensive *f*. -**4.** SPORT [attackers] attaque *f*.

offend [ə'fend] ◇ *vt* [person] offenser, blesser; she's easily ~ed elle est susceptible, elle se vexe pour un rien; don't be ~ed if I leave early ne le prends pas mal si je pars de bonne heure; she was very ~ed when he didn't come to her party elle a été extrêmement vexée qu'il ne vienne pas à sa soirée; the film contains scenes which could ~ some viewers le film contient des scènes pouvant choquer certains spectateurs ‖ [eyes, senses, reason] choquer; his behaviour ~s my sense of fair play son comportement choque mon sens du fair-play.
◇ *vi* JUR violer la loi, commettre un délit; he is liable to ~ again il risque de récidiver.
◆ **offend against** *vt insep* [law, regulation] enfreindre, violer; [custom] aller à l'encontre de; [good manners, good taste] être un outrage à.

offender [ə'fendəʳ] *n* -**1.** JUR délinquant *m*, -e *f*; 13% of convicted ~s return to crime 13 % des condamnés récidivent ❑ drug ~ [dealer] trafiquant *m*, -e *f* de drogue; [user] toxicomane *mf*; sex ~ auteur *m* d'un délit sexuel; traffic ~s contrevenants *mpl* au Code de la route. -**2.** [gen - culprit] coupable *mf*; the chemical industry is the worst ~ l'industrie chimique est la première responsable.

offending [ə'fendɪŋ] *adj* blessant; the ~ word was omitted le mot choquant a été enlevé; the ~ object/article l'objet/l'article incriminé.

offense *Am* = **offence**.

offensive [ə'fensɪv] ◇ *adj* -**1.** [causing indignation, anger] offensant, choquant; to find sthg ~ être choqué par qqch; to be ~ to sb [person] injurier OR insulter qqn; this advertisement is ~ to Muslims/women cette publicité porte atteinte à la religion musulmane/à la dignité de la femme; ~ language propos *mpl* choquants. -**2.** [disgusting - smell] repoussant. -**3.** [aggressive] offensif; they took immediate ~ action ils sont immédiatement passés à l'offensive ❑ ~ weapon arme *f* offensive.
◇ *n* offensive *f*; to go over to OR to go on OR to take the ~ passer à OR prendre l'offensive; a military ~ une offensive militaire; a diplomatic/peace ~ une offensive diplomatique/de paix.

offensively [ə'fensɪvlɪ] *adv* -**1.** [behave, speak] d'une manière offensante OR blessante. -**2.** MIL & SPORT offensivement; ~, theirs is the stronger team en attaque, c'est leur équipe qui est la plus forte.

offer ['ɒfəʳ] ◇ *vt* -**1.** [present] offrir; to ~ sthg to sb, to ~ sb sthg offrir qqch à qqn; she ~ed me £800 for my car elle m'a proposé 800 livres pour ma voiture; he ~ed her a chair/his arm il lui offrit une chaise/son bras; can I ~ you a drink? puis-je vous offrir un verre?; to ~ sb one's sympathy présenter ses condoléances à qqn; to have a lot to ~ [town, person] avoir beaucoup à offrir; candidates may ~ one of the following foreign languages les candidats peuvent présenter une des langues étrangères suivantes. -**2.** [propose] proposer; to ~ to do sthg s'offrir pour faire qqch, proposer de faire qqch; I ~ed to help them je leur ai proposé mon aide; to ~ sb advice donner des conseils à qqn; may I ~ a little advice? puis-je vous donner un petit conseil?; nobody bothered to ~ any explanation personne ne s'est soucié de fournir une explication.
◇ *n* offre *f*; ~s of help are pouring in les offres d'aide affluent; I'll make you a final ~ je vous ferai une dernière offre; £500 or near OR nearest ~ 500 livres, à débattre; she wants £500, but she's open to ~s elle veut 500 livres, mais elle est prête à négocier; make me an ~! faites-moi une offre!; I made him an ~ he couldn't refuse je lui ai fait une offre qu'il ne pouvait pas refuser; take advantage of our latest special ~s profitez de nos dernières offres spéciales.
◆ **on offer** *adv phr*: these goods are on ~ this week ces articles sont en promotion cette semaine; there aren't many jobs on ~ les offres d'emploi sont peu nombreuses.
◆ **offer up** *vt sep* [hymn, sacrifice] offrir.

offering ['ɒfərɪŋ] *n* -**1.** [action] offre *f*. -**2.** [thing offered] offre *f*, don *m*; his latest ~ is a novel set in Ireland *fig* le dernier roman qu'il nous propose se déroule en Irlande. -**3.** RELIG offrande *f*.

offer price *n* ST. EX prix *m* demandé.

offertory ['ɒfətrɪ] (*pl* offertories) *n* -**1.** [prayers, ritual] offertoire *m*. -**2.** [collection] quête *f*.

off-guard *adj* [moment]: in an ~ moment dans un moment d'inattention.
◆ **off guard** *adv phr*: to catch OR to take sb off guard prendre qqn au dépourvu; his offer of help caught her off guard elle ne s'attendait pas à ce qu'il lui propose son aide.

offhand [,ɒf'hænd] ◇ *adj* -**1.** [nonchalant] désinvolte, cavalier. -**2.** [abrupt] brusque.
◇ *adv* spontanément, au pied levé; ~ I'd say it'll take a week à première vue, je dirais que cela prendra une semaine; I can't give you the figures ~ je ne peux pas vous citer les chiffres de mémoire OR de tête.

offhanded [,ɒf'hændɪd] *adj* = **offhand** *adj*.

offhandedly [,ɒf'hændɪdlɪ] *adv* [nonchalantly] de façon désinvolte OR cavalière, avec désinvolture; [with abruptness] brusquement, sans ménagement.

office ['ɒfɪs] ◇ *n* -**1.** [of firm] bureau *m*; people who work in ~s les gens qui travaillent dans les bureaux; the whole ~ knows tout le bureau est au courant; she's been transferred to the Paris ~ elle a été mutée au bureau de Paris; ~ space is cheaper in the suburbs les bureaux sont moins chers en banlieue ❑ doctor's ~ *Am* cabinet *m* médical; lawyer's ~

cabinet *m* d'avocat; ~ party *réception organisée dans un bureau à l'occasion des fêtes de fin d'année*. -**2.** [government department] bureau *m*, département *m*; I have to send this to the tax ~ je dois envoyer ça au centre des impôts ❑ the Office of Fair Trading *service britannique de la concurrence et des prix*. -**3.** [distribution point] bureau *m*, guichet *m*; ticket ~ guichet *m (de vente des billets)*. -**4.** [position, power] fonction *f*; a woman in high ~ une femme haut placée; he's one of the candidates seeking ~ c'est l'un des candidats qui se présentent aux élections; to be in OR to hold ~ [political party] être au pouvoir; [mayor, minister, official] être en fonctions; to be out of ~ avoir quitté ses fonctions; to take ~ [political party] arriver au pouvoir; [mayor, minister, official] entrer en fonctions; to resign/to leave ~ se démettre de/quitter ses fonctions; to run for OR to seek ~ se présenter aux élections; elected to the ~ of president élu à la présidence. -**5.** RELIG office *m*.

◇ *comp* [furniture, hours, job, staff] de bureau.

◆ **offices** *npl* -**1.** [help, actions]: I got the job through the (good) ~s of Mrs Katz j'ai obtenu ce travail grâce aux bons offices de Mme Katz. -**2.** *Br* [of large house, estate] office *m*.

office bearer *n Br* [in club, association] membre *m* du bureau.

office block *n Br* immeuble *m* de bureaux.

office boy *n dated* garçon *m* de bureau.

office building = **office block**.

officeholder ['ɒfɪs,həʊldəʳ] *n* -**1.** POL titulaire *mf* d'une fonction. -**2.** *Am* = **office bearer**.

office junior *n* stagiaire *mf (en secrétariat)*.

officer ['ɒfɪsəʳ] ◇ *n* -**1.** MIL officier *m*; naval ~ officier de marine. -**2.** [policeman] agent *m* de police; [as form of address - to policeman] Monsieur l'agent; [- to policewoman] Madame l'agent. -**3.** [official - in local government] fonctionnaire *mf*; [- of trade union] représentant *m* permanent; [- of company] membre *m* de la direction; [- of association, institution] membre *m* du bureau; the ~s of the association meet every month le bureau de l'association se réunit tous les mois ❑ careers ~ *Br* conseiller *m*, -ère *f* d'orientation; prison ~ gardien *m*, -enne *f* de prison.

◇ *vt* MIL encadrer; they were ~ed by young recruits ils étaient encadrés par de jeunes recrues.

official [ə'fɪʃl] ◇ *adj* -**1.** [formal] officiel; she's here on ~ business elle est ici en visite officielle; I can't understand this ~ language je ne comprends rien à ce jargon administratif; it's ~, they're getting a divorce c'est officiel, ils divorcent; his appointment will be made ~ tomorrow sa nomination sera (rendue) officielle demain; we decided to make it ~ (and get married) nous avons décidé de rendre notre liaison officielle (en nous mariant); to go through the ~ channels suivre la filière (habituelle); Spanish is the ~ language of Mexico l'espagnol est la langue officielle du Mexique ❑ ~ strike *grève soutenue par la direction du syndicat*; the Official Secrets Act *loi britannique sur le secret Défense*. -**2.** [alleged] officiel; the ~ reason for his visit is to discuss trade officiellement, il est là pour des discussions ayant trait au commerce.

◇ *n* [representative] officiel *m*; [civil servant] fonctionnaire *mf*; [subordinate employee] employé *m*, -e *f*; SPORT [referee] arbitre *m*; a bank/club/union ~ un représentant de la banque/du club/du syndicat; a government ~ un haut fonctionnaire.

officialdom [ə'fɪʃəldəm] *n pej* bureaucratie *f*.

officialese [ə,fɪʃə'li:z] *n pej* jargon *m* administratif.

officially [ə'fɪʃəlɪ] *adv* -**1.** [formally] officiellement; he's now been ~ appointed sa nomination est désormais officielle; we now have it ~ la nouvelle est maintenant officielle. -**2.** [allegedly] théoriquement, en principe; ~, he's at the dentist's en principe, il est chez le dentiste.

Official Receiver *n Br* ADMIN administrateur *m*, -trice *f* judiciaire; the ~ has been called in on a fait appel à l'administration judiciaire.

officiant [ə'fɪʃɪənt] *n* RELIG officiant *m*, célébrant *m*.

officiate [ə'fɪʃɪeɪt] *vi* -**1.** [gen]: to ~ as remplir les fonctions de; she ~d at the ceremony elle a présidé la cérémonie; the mayor will ~ at the opening of the stadium le maire inaugurera le stade. -**2.** RELIG officier.

officious [ə'fɪʃəs] *adj* -**1.** [overbearing] impérieux, autoritaire; [interfering] importun; [zealous] zélé, empressé. -**2.** [in diplomacy - unofficial] officieux; ~ talks pourparlers *mpl* officieux.

officiously [ə'fɪʃəslɪ] *adv* [overbearingly] impérieusement, de manière autoritaire; [interferingly] d'une manière importune; [zealously] avec zèle, avec empressement.

offing ['ɒfɪŋ] *n* -**1.** NAUT large *m*. -**2.** *phr*: to be in the ~ être imminent; a confrontation had long been in the ~ une confrontation couvait depuis longtemps.

offish *inf* ['ɒfɪʃ] *adj Br* [aloof] plutôt distant OR froid.

off-key ◇ *adj* -**1.** MUS faux. -**2.** *fig* [remark] hors de propos, sans rapport.

◇ *adv* faux; to play/to sing ~ jouer/chanter faux.

off-licence *n Br* -**1.** [shop] *magasin autorisé à vendre des boissons alcoolisées à emporter*; at the ~ chez le marchand de vins. -**2.** [licence] licence *f (autorisant la vente de boissons alcoolisées à emporter)*.

off-limits ◇ *adj* interdit; the bar is ~ to non-coms *inf* MIL le bar est interdit aux sous-offs.

◇ *adv* en dehors des limites autorisées; to go ~ sortir des limites autorisées.

off-line *adj* -**1.** COMPUT [storage, mode] autonome; [equipment] hors-circuit; ~ processing traitement *m* autonome. -**2.** INDUST [production] hors ligne.

off-load *vt* -**1.** [unload - passengers] débarquer; [- cargo] décharger. -**2.** [dump - work, blame]: she tends to ~ responsibility onto other people elle a tendance à se décharger de ses responsabilités sur les autres.

off-off-Broadway *adj Am* à l'avant-garde de l'avant-garde; ~ show spectacle *m* d'avant-garde.

off-peak *adj* [consumption, rate, train] aux heures creuses, en dehors des périodes d'affluence OR de pointe; ~ hours OR times heures *fpl* creuses.

off-piste *adj* & *adv* SPORT hors-piste.

offprint ['ɒfprɪnt] ◇ *n* tiré *m* à part.

◇ *vt*: to ~ an article faire un tiré à part.

off-putting *adj Br* [smell] repoussant; [manner] rébarbatif; [person, description] peu engageant; the idea of a five-hour stopover is very ~ l'idée d'une escale de cinq heures n'a rien d'enthousiasmant OR de réjouissant.

off sales *npl Br vente à emporter de boissons alcoolisées*.

offscourings ['ɒf,skaʊərɪŋz] *npl* [dregs] lie *f*; [scum] écume *f*.

offscreen [*adj* 'ɒfskri:n, *adv* ɒf'skri:n] CIN & TV

◇ *adj* [out of sight] hors champ, off; ~ narration commentaire *m* en voix off.

◇ *adv* -**1.** CIN & TV hors champ, off. -**2.** [in private life] dans le privé; he's less handsome ~ il est moins séduisant dans la réalité.

off-season ◇ *n* morte-saison *f*.

◇ *adj* hors saison *(inv)*.

offset ['ɒfset] (*pt* & *pp* offset, *cont* offsetting)

◇ *vt* -**1.** [make up for] contrebalancer, compenser; the advantages tend to ~ the difficulties les avantages compensent presque les inconvénients; any wage increase will be ~ by inflation avec l'inflation, les augmentations de salaire n'en seront plus vraiment; we'll have to ~ our research investment against long-term returns nous devons amortir notre investissement dans la recherche en faisant des bénéfices à long terme; his faults are ~ by his enthusiasm son enthousiasme fait oublier ses défauts. -**2.** PRINT imprimer en offset.

◇ *n* -**1.** [counterbalance] contrepoids *m*; [compensation] compensation *f*. -**2.** PRINT offset *m*. -**3.** BOT [shoot] rejeton *m*. -**4.** CONSTR ressaut *m*.

offshoot ['ɒfʃu:t] *n* -**1.** [spin-off] application *f* secondaire; it's an ~ of space technology c'est une application secondaire de la technologie spatiale ‖ [descendant]: French and Spanish are ~s of Latin le français et l'espagnol sont issus du latin ‖ [subsidiary]: the company has ~s in Asia la société a des succursales en Asie. -**2.** BOT rejeton *m*.

offshore ['ɒfʃɔ:ʳ] *adj* -**1.** [in or on sea] marin; [near shore - shipping, fishing, waters] côtier; [- island] près de la côte; PETR offshore *(inv)*, marin; ~ rig plate-forme *f* offshore. -**2.** [towards open sea - current, direction] vers le large; [- wind] de terre. -**3.** FIN: ~ fund placement *m* dans un paradis fiscal.

offside [*adj* & *adv* ,ɒf'saɪd, *n* 'ɒfsaɪd] ◇ *adj* & *adv* SPORT hors jeu *(inv)*; to play the ~ trap jouer le hors-jeu.

◇ *n Br* AUT [when driving on right] côté *m* gauche, côté *m* rue; [when driving on left] côté *m* droit, côté *m* rue.

offspring ['ɒfsprɪŋ] (*pl inv*) ◇ *n* -**1.** *arch* OR *hum* [son or daughter] rejeton *m*. -**2.** *fig* retombée *f*, conséquence *f*.

◇ *npl* [descendants] progéniture *f*.

offstage [*adv* ,ɒf'steɪdʒ, *adj* 'ɒf,steɪdʒ] ◇ *adv* -**1.** THEAT dans les coulisses; she ran ~ elle quitta la scène en courant. -**2.** [in private life] en privé; ~, she was surprisingly reserved en privé, elle était étonnamment réservée.

◇ *adj* dans les coulisses; an ~ row une querelle de coulisses.

off-street *adj*: ~ parking place *f* de parking *(située ailleurs que dans la rue)*.

off-the-cuff ◇ *adj* impromptu, improvisé.

◇ *adv* au pied levé, à l'improviste.

off-the-peg *adj* prêt à porter; ~ clothes prêt-à-porter *m*.

◆ **off the peg** *adv* en confection, en prêt-à-porter.

off-the-record *adj* [not to be made public] confidentiel; [not to be put in minutes] à ne pas faire figurer dans le compte-rendu.

off-the-wall *inf adj* [crazy] loufoque, dingue; [unexpected] original, excentrique.

off-white ◇ *adj* blanc cassé *(inv)*.

◇ *n* blanc *m* cassé.

off-year *n* POL *année présidentielle sans élection aux États-Unis*.

Ofgas ['ɒfgæs] (*abbr of* Office of Gas Supply) *pr n organisme britannique chargé de contrôler les activités des compagnies régionales de distribution du gaz*.

oft [ɒft] *adv lit* maintes fois, souvent.

oft- *in cpds*: ~repeated [warning] réitéré; [argument] ressassé; ~quoted souvent cité.

OFT *abbr of* Office of Fair Trading.

Oftel ['ɒftel] (*abbr of* Office of Telecommunications) *pr n agence gouvernementale britannique chargée de contrôler les activités des sociétés de télécommunications*.

often ['ɒfn, 'ɒftn] *adv* souvent; I've ~ thought of leaving j'ai souvent pensé à partir; I don't see her very ~ je ne la vois pas très souvent; it's not ~ you get an offer like that ce n'est pas souvent qu'on vous fait une offre pareille; do you come here ~? vous venez ici souvent?; how ~ do I have to tell you? combien de fois faudra-t-il que je te le répète?; how ~ does he write to you? est-ce qu'il t'écrit souvent?; she's said that once too ~ elle l'a dit une fois de trop.

◆ **as often as not** *adv phr* la plupart du temps.

◆ **every so often** *adv phr* de temps en temps, de temps à autre.

◆ **more often than not** *adv phr* la plupart du temps.

oftentimes ['ɒfəntaɪmz], **ofttimes** ['ɒftaɪmz] *adv arch* souventes fois.

Ofwat ['ɒfwɒt] (*abbr of* Office of Water Supply) *pr n organisme britannique chargé de contrôler les activités des compagnies régionales de distribution des eaux*.

ogival [əʊ'dʒaɪvəl] *adj* ogival, en ogive.

ogive ['əʊdʒaɪv] *n* ARCHIT & MATH ogive *f*.

ogle ['əʊgl] *vt* lorgner.

ogre ['əʊgəʳ] *n* ogre *m*.

ogress ['əʊgrɪs] *n* ogresse *f*.

oh [əʊ] *interj* oh, ah; ~, what a surprise! oh, quelle surprise!; ~ really? vraiment?, ah bon?

OH *written abbr of* Ohio.

oh arr [-ɑːʳ] *interj expression humoristique dénotant un parler paysan*.

Ohio [əʊ'haɪəʊ] *pr n* Ohio *m*; in ~ dans l'Ohio.

ohm [əʊm] *n* ohm *m*.

ohmmeter ['əʊm,miːtəʳ] *n* ohmmètre *m*.

OHMS (*written abbr of* On His/Her Majesty's Service) *tampon apposé sur le courrier administratif britannique*.

oho [ə'həʊ] *interj* oh, ah.

oidium [əʊ'ɪdɪəm] *n* [fungus, disease] oïdium *m*; [spore] oïdie *f*.

oik *inf* [ɔɪk] *n Br pej* pignouf *m*.

oil [ɔɪl] ◇ *n* -**1.** [petroleum] pétrole *m*; to drill for ~ effectuer des forages pour trouver du pétrole. -**2.** [in food, as lubricant] huile *f*; [as fuel] mazout *m*; sardines in ~ sardines *fpl* à l'huile; to change the ~ AUT faire la vidange ❑ lubricating ~ huile lubrifiante; ~ of lavender/turpentine essence *f* de lavande/de térébenthine; olive/cod-liver ~ huile d'olive/de foie de morue; to pour ~ on troubled waters ramener le calme; suntan ~ huile solaire. -**3.** ART [paint] (peinture *f* à l') huile *f*; [picture] huile *f*; a portrait in ~s un portrait (peint) à l'huile; she works in ~s elle travaille avec de la peinture à l'huile.
◇ *comp* -**1.** [industry, production, corporation] pétrolier; [drum, deposit, reserves] de pétrole; [magnate, sheikh] du pétrole. -**2.** [level, pressure] d'huile; [filter] à huile; [heating, burner] à mazout.
◇ *vt* [machine, engine] lubrifier, graisser; [hinge, wood] huiler; [skin] graisser, huiler; it will help to ~ the wheels *fig* cela facilitera les choses.
◆ **oils** *npl* ST. EX (valeurs *fpl*) pétrolières *fpl*.

oil-bearing *adj* pétrolifère.

oil-burning *adj* à mazout.

oil cake *n* tourteau *m* (pour bétail).

oilcan ['ɔɪlkæn] *n* [drum] bidon *m* d'huile; [oiler] burette *f* (à huile).

oilcloth ['ɔɪlklɒθ] *n* toile *f* cirée.

oiled [ɔɪld] *adj* -**1.** [machine] lubrifié, graissé; [hinge, silk] huilé. -**2.** *inf* [drunk]: to be well ~ être complètement bourré.

oiler ['ɔɪləʳ] *n* -**1.** [person] graisseur *m*, -euse *f*. -**2.** [tanker] pétrolier *m*. -**3.** [can] burette *f* (à huile). -**4.** [well] puits *m* de pétrole.

oilfield ['ɔɪlfiːld] *n* gisement *m* de pétrole OR pétrolier.

oil-fired [-,faɪəd] *adj* à mazout.

oil gauge *n* [for measuring level] jauge *f* OR indicateur *m* de niveau d'huile; [for measuring pressure] indicateur *m* de pression d'huile.

oiliness ['ɔɪlɪnɪs] *n* -**1.** [greasiness] nature *f* huileuse; the ~ of the dish makes it rather indigestible ce plat contient tellement d'huile qu'il en devient indigeste. -**2.** *fig* [obsequiousness] obséquiosité *f*, patelinerie *f*.

oil lamp *n* [burning oil] lampe *f* à huile; [burning paraffin] lampe *f* à pétrole.

oilman ['ɔɪlmən] (*pl* oilmen [-mən]) *n* pétrolier *m (personne)*.

oil paint *n* peinture *f* à l'huile *(substance)*.

oil painting *n* peinture *f* à l'huile; he's no ~ *inf Br* ce n'est pas une beauté rare.

oil-producing *adj* producteur de pétrole; the ~ countries les pays producteurs de pétrole.

oil refinery *n* raffinerie *f* de pétrole.

oil rig *n* [onshore] derrick *m*; [offshore] plate-forme *f* pétrolière.

oilskin ['ɔɪlskɪn] ◇ *n* -**1.** [cloth] toile *f* cirée. -**2.** [garment] ciré *m*.
◇ *comp* en toile cirée.

oil slick *n* nappe *f* de pétrole.

oil spill *n* -**1.** [event] marée *f* noire. -**2.** = **oil slick**.

oil stove *n Br* [using fuel oil] poêle *m* à mazout; [using paraffin, kerosene] réchaud *m* à pétrole.

oil tanker *n* [ship] pétrolier *m*, tanker *m*; [lorry] camion-citerne *m (pour le pétrole)*.

oil terminal *n* terminal *m* (pétrolier).

oil well *n* puits *m* de pétrole.

oily ['ɔɪlɪ] (*compar* oilier, *superl* oiliest) *adj* -**1.** [substance] huileux; [rag, fingers] graisseux; [cooking, hair, skin] gras; an ~ stain une tache de graisse. -**2.** *pej* [smile, person] mielleux, doucereux.

oink [ɔɪŋk] ◇ *n* grognement *m*, grommellement *m*.
◇ *onomat* krouik-krouik.

ointment ['ɔɪntmənt] *n* pommade *f*, onguent *m*.

oiro (*written abbr of* offers in the region of): ~ £100 100 livres à débattre.

OK (*pt & pp* OKed, *cont* OKing) ◇ *interj inf* OK, d'accord, d'ac; well ~, I'm not a specialist, but... bon, d'accord, je ne suis pas spécialiste, mais...; in five minutes, ~? dans cinq minutes, ça va? ❑ ~ yah *expression humoristique dénotant les milieux BCBG*.
◇ *adj inf*: you look very pale, are you ~? tu es très pâle, tu te sens bien?; don't worry about me, I'm ~ ne t'inquiète pas pour moi, je vais bien; that idea sounds ~ to me ça me semble être une bonne idée; is it a good film? — it's ~ est-ce un bon film? — pas mal; it's ~ but it could be better ce n'est pas mal, mais ça pourrait être mieux; I'll bring my husband if that's ~ with OR by you je viendrai avec mon mari, si ça ne vous gêne pas; thanks for your help — that's ~! merci de votre aide — de rien! OR il n'y a pas de quoi!; he's ~, he's an ~ guy *Am* c'est un type sympa.
◇ *adv inf* bien; is the engine working ~? le moteur, ça va?; everything is going ~ tout va bien OR marche bien; you're doing ~! tu t'en tires bien!
◇ *vt inf* [approve] approuver; [initial] parafer, parapher; his plan has been ~ed son projet a reçu le feu vert.
◇ *n inf* [agreement] accord *m*; [approval] approbation *f*; I gave him the ~ je lui ai donné le feu vert; did you get her ~ on the new plan? elle est d'accord pour le nouveau projet?
◇ *written abbr of* Oklahoma.

okapi [əʊ'kɑːpɪ] (*pl inv* OR okapis) *n* okapi *m*.

okay [,əʊ'keɪ] = **OK**.

okeydoke(y) *inf* [,əʊkɪ'dəʊk(ɪ)] *interj* d'ac, OK.

Okie▽ ['əʊkɪ] *n Am offensive* -**1.** [inhabitant] habitant *m*, -e *f* de l'Oklahoma. -**2.** HIST: the ~s *habitants de l'Oklahoma qui se sont déplacés vers la Californie dans les années 30 pour échapper à la pauvreté du «Dust Bowl»*.

Oklahoma [,əʊklə'həʊmə] *pr n* Oklahoma *m*; in ~ dans l'Oklahoma.

okra ['əʊkrə] *n* gombo *m*.

ol' *inf* [əʊl] = **old** *adj*.

old [əʊld] (*compar* older, *superl* oldest)
◇ *adj* -**1.** [not new or recent] vieux; the ~ traditions of the countryside les vieilles traditions campagnardes; there's an ~ saying that... il y a un vieux dicton qui dit que...; it's hard to shake off ~ habits on ne se débarrasse pas facilement de ses vieilles habitudes; not that ~ excuse again! tu ne vas pas/il ne va pas *etc* ressortir encore une fois la même excuse!; they're ~ friends ce sont de vieux amis OR des amis de longue date; the ~ country la mère patrie. -**2.** [not young] vieux; an ~ man un vieil homme; an ~ woman une vieille femme; I don't like that ~ man/woman je n'aime pas ce vieux/cette vieille; ~ people personnes *fpl* âgées; the ~ folks les vieux *mpl*; to get OR grow ~ vieillir; who will look after me in my ~ age? qui s'occupera de moi quand je serai vieux?; I've got a little money put aside for my ~ age j'ai quelques économies de côté pour mes vieux jours ❑ ~ people's home maison *f* de retraite. -**3.** [referring to a particular age]: how ~ is she? quel âge a-t-elle?; to be ~ enough to do sthg être en âge de faire qqch; she's ~ enough to know better elle ne devrait plus faire ce genre de chose à son âge; he's ~ enough to look after himself il est (bien) assez grand pour se débrouiller tout seul; he's ~ enough to be my father! il pourrait être mon père!; she's two years ~er than him elle a deux ans de plus que lui; my boy wants to be a soldier when he's ~er mon fils veut être soldat quand il sera grand; the ~er generation la vieille génération; my ~er sister ma sœur aînée; she's 6 months/25 years ~ elle a 6 mois/25 ans, elle est âgée de 6 mois/25 ans; they have a 14-year-~ boy ils ont un garçon de 14 ans; a 3-day-~ baby un bébé de 3 jours. -**4.** [former] ancien; that's my ~ address c'est mon ancienne adresse; an ~ admirer of hers un de ses anciens admirateurs ❑ in the ~ days autrefois, jadis; the good ~ days le bon vieux temps. -**5.** *inf* [expressing familiarity or affection] vieux, brave; ~ Jim wants to speak to you le vieux Jim veut te parler; good ~ Jack! ce (bon) vieux Jack!; hello, ~ thing OR chap! *dated* salut, mon vieux OR vieille branche! -**6.** *inf* [as intensifier]: it's a funny ~ life! la vie est drôle, quand même!; you ~ bastard!▽ espèce de salaud!; silly ~ bat *inf* espèce de vieille folle!; any ~ bit of wood will do n'importe quel vieux bout de bois fera l'affaire; any ~ how n'importe comment; I just wear any ~ thing to do the gardening je porte n'importe quel vieux truc pour jardiner; he's not just any ~ scientist, he's a Nobel prizewinner ce n'est pas n'importe quel scientifique, c'est un prix Nobel.
◇ *npl*: the ~ les vieux *mpl*; a game for ~ and young alike un jeu pour tous les âges.
◆ **of old** *adv phr* -**1.** *lit* [of former times]: in days of ~ autrefois, jadis; the knights of ~ les chevaliers du temps jadis OR de jadis. -**2.** [for a long time]: I know them of ~ je les connais depuis longtemps.

old age pension *n Br* (pension *f* de) retraite *f*.

old age pensioner *n Br* retraité *m*, -e *f*.

Old Bailey *pr n*: the ~ *la Cour d'assises de Londres*.

Old Bill▽ *npl Br*: the ~ les flics *mpl*.

old boy *n Br* -**1.** [ex-pupil of school] ancien élève *m*. -**2.** *inf* [old man] vieux *m*; he's a nice ~ c'est un vieux monsieur charmant. -**3.** *inf dated* [form of address] mon vieux.

old boy network *inf n Br contacts privilégiés entre anciens élèves d'un même établissement privé*; he got the job through the ~ il a obtenu ce poste en faisant jouer ses relations.

olde [əʊld, 'əʊldɪ] *adj* [in name of inn, shop] d'antan, d'autrefois; 'Ye Olde Sweet Shoppe' 'Aux Douceurs d'Autrefois'.

olden ['əʊldn] *adj arch* OR *lit* d'autrefois, d'antan; in ~ times OR days autrefois, jadis.

Old English *n* vieil anglais *m*.

Old English sheepdog *n* bobtail *m*.

olde-worlde [,əʊldɪ'wɜːldɪ] *Br* = **old-world 1**.

old-fashioned [-'fæʃnd] ◇ *adj* -**1.** [out-of-date] suranné, désuet, démodé; [idea] périmé, démodé; he's a bit ~ il est un peu vieux jeu. -**2.** [of the past] d'autrefois, ancien; he needs a good ~ kick in the pants *inf hum* ce qu'il lui faudrait, c'est un bon coup de pied aux fesses. -**3.** [quizzical]: to give sb an ~ look jeter un regard dubitatif à qqn.
◇ *n Am* old-fashioned *m (cocktail au whisky)*.

old flame *n* ancien béguin *m*.

Old French *n* ancien français *m*.

old girl *n Br* -**1.** [ex-pupil] ancienne élève *f*. -**2.** *inf* [old woman] vieille *f*; she's a nice ~ c'est une vieille dame charmante. -**3.** *inf dated* [form of address] ma chère, chère amie.

Old Glory *pr n Am surnom du drapeau américain*.

old guard *n* vieille garde *f*.

old hand *n* vieux routier *m*, vétéran *m*; he's an ~ at flying these planes cela fait des années qu'il pilote ces avions.
old hat *inf adj* dépassé, vieux.
oldie *inf* ['əʊldɪ] *n* -**1.** [show, song] vieux succès *m*; [pop song] vieux tube *m*; golden ~ *hum* vieux tube. -**2.** [old person] (petit) vieux *m*, (petite) vieille *f*.
oldish ['əʊldɪʃ] *adj* vieillot.
old lady *inf* = **old woman 1, 2**.
old maid *n* vieille fille *f*.
old-maidish [-'meɪdɪʃ] *adj* [habits] de vieille fille; to become ~ [man] prendre des habitudes de vieux garçon.
old man *inf n* -**1.** [husband] homme *m*. -**2.** [father] vieux *m*. -**3.** *Br dated* [form of address] mon cher, cher ami.
old master *n* [painter] grand maître *m* (de la peinture); [painting] tableau *m* de maître.
Old Nick *pr n* Satan *m*, Lucifer *m*.
old school *n*: of the ~ de la vieille école; a writer of the ~ un écrivain de la vieille école.
old school tie *n Br* -**1.** *literal* cravate *f* aux couleurs de son ancienne école. -**2.** *fig* & *pej* *attitudes et système de valeurs typiques des anciens élèves des écoles privées britanniques*.
old stager *n* vieux routier *m*, vétéran *m*.
oldster *inf* ['əʊldstəʳ] *n Am* ancien *m*, vieillard *m*.
Old Testament *n* Ancien Testament *m*.
old-time *adj* d'autrefois, ancien; ~ dancing danses anciennes.
old-timer *inf n Am* [old person] vieillard *m*, ancien *m*, -enne *f*; [veteran] vétéran *m*, vieux *m* de la vieille.
old wives' tale *n* conte *m* de bonne femme.
old woman *inf n* -**1.** [wife] patronne *f*, bourgeoise *f*. -**2.** [mother] vieille *f*. -**3.** *fig* & *pej*: he's such an ~ il est comme une petite vieille.
old-womanish *adj Br* [habits] de vieille femme; he's rather ~ il a des manies de petite vieille.
old-world *adj* -**1.** [of the past] d'antan, d'autrefois; [quaint] pittoresque; a village full of ~ charm un village au charme suranné. -**2.** [of the Old World] de l'Ancien Monde OR Continent.
Old World *pr n*: the ~ l'Ancien Monde.
ole *inf* [əʊl] = **old** *adj*.
oleaginous [,əʊlɪ'ædʒɪnəs] *adj* oléagineux.
oleander [,əʊlɪ'ændəʳ] *n* laurier-rose *m*.
oleic acid [əʊ'liːɪk-] *n* acide *m* oléique.
oleomargarine [,ɒlɪəʊ'mɑːdʒəriːn] *n Am* margarine *f*.
O level *n Br* SCH *examen qui sanctionnait autrefois la fin des études au niveau de la seconde*, ≃ BEPC *m*.
olfaction [ɒl'fækʃn] *n* olfaction *f*.
olfactory [ɒl'fæktərɪ] *adj* olfactif; ~ nerve nerf *m* olfactif.
oligarchic(al) [,ɒlɪ'gɑːkɪk(l)] *adj* oligarchique.
oligarchy ['ɒlɪgɑːkɪ] (*pl* **oligarchies**) *n* oligarchie *f*.
Oligocene [ɒ'lɪgəsiːn] ◇ *adj* oligocène.
◇ *n* oligocène *m*.
oligopoly [,ɒlɪ'gɒpəlɪ] *n* oligopole *m*.
oligopsony [,ɒlɪ'gɒpsənɪ] *n* oligopsone *m*.
olive ['ɒlɪv] ◇ *n* [fruit] olive *f*; [tree] olivier *m*; ~ (wood) bois *m* d'olivier; ~ grove olivaie *f*, oliveraie *f*.
◇ *adj* [colour] (vert) olive *(inv)*; he has an ~ complexion il a le teint olive.
olive branch *n* rameau *m* d'olivier; to hold out an ~ to sb proposer à qqn de faire la paix.
olive drab *Am* ◇ *adj* gris-vert (olive) *(inv)*.
◇ *n* [colour] gris-vert *m* (olive); [cloth] toile *f* gris-vert (olive); [uniform] uniforme *m* gris-vert *(surtout celui de l'Armée des États-Unis)*.
olive green *n* vert *m* olive.
◆ **olive-green** *adj* vert olive *(inv)*.
olive oil *n* huile *f* d'olive.
Olympia [ə'lɪmpɪə] *pr n* Olympie.
Olympiad [ə'lɪmpɪæd] *n* olympiade *f*.
Olympian [ə'lɪmpɪən] ◇ *n* -**1.** MYTH Olympien *m*, -enne *f*. -**2.** *Am* SPORT athlète *mf* olympique.
◇ *adj* olympien; it was an ~ task *fig* cela représentait un travail phénoménal.
Olympic [ə'lɪmpɪk] *adj* olympique; an ~ champion un champion olympique ❑ the ~ Games les jeux Olympiques.
◆ **Olympics** *npl*: the ~s les jeux Olympiques.
Olympus [əʊ'lɪmpəs] *pr n*: (Mount) ~ l'Olympe *m*.
OM *abbr of* Order of Merit.
O & M (*abbr of* organization and method) *n* O et M *f*.
Oman [əʊ'mɑːn] *pr n* Oman; in ~ à Oman.
Omani [əʊ'mɑːnɪ] ◇ *n* Omanais *m*, -e *f*.
◇ *adj* omanais.
OMB (*abbr of* Office of Management and Budget) *pr n organisme fédéral américain chargé de préparer le budget*.
ombudsman ['ɒmbʊdzmən] (*pl* **ombudsmen** [-mən]) *n* ombudsman *m*, médiateur *m*; [in Quebec] protecteur *m* du citoyen.
ombudswoman ['ɒmbʊdz,wʊmən] (*pl* **ombudswomen** [-,wɪmɪn]) *n* médiatrice *f*; [in Quebec] protectrice *f* du citoyen.
omega ['əʊmɪgə] *n* oméga *m*.
omelette *Br*, **omelet** *Am* ['ɒmlɪt] *n* omelette *f*; plain/mushroom ~ omelette nature/aux champignons ❑ you can't make an ~ without breaking eggs *prov* on ne fait pas d'omelette sans casser d'œufs *prov*.
omen ['əʊmen] *n* augure *m*, présage *m*; a good/bad ~ un bon/mauvais présage; the ~s aren't good cela ne laisse rien présager de bon; a bird of ill ~ un oiseau de mauvaise augure.
ominous ['ɒmɪnəs] *adj* [threatening] menaçant, inquiétant; [boding ill] de mauvais augure, de sinistre présage; an ~ silence un silence lourd de menaces; an ~ sign un signe inquiétant OR alarmant; ~ black clouds des nuages menaçants.
ominously ['ɒmɪnəslɪ] *adv* de façon inquiétante OR menaçante; the sea was ~ calm la mer était étrangement calme; he looked at her ~ il lui jeta un regard inquiétant.
omission [ə'mɪʃn] *n* -**1.** [exclusion - accidental] omission *f*, oubli *m*; [- deliberate] exclusion *f*; their mistakes were sins of ~ ils ont péché par omission; there are several major ~s in his report il y a plusieurs oublis importants dans son rapport. -**2.** TYPO [text omitted] bourdon *m*.
omit [ə'mɪt] (*pt* & *pp* **omitted**, *cont* **omitting**) *vt* omettre; a name was omitted from the list un nom a été omis sur la liste; to ~ to do sthg omettre de faire qqch; she omitted to say where she had been elle a omis de dire où elle était allée.
omnibus ['ɒmnɪbəs] ◇ *n* -**1.** *dated* [bus] omnibus *m*. -**2.** RADIO & TV *rediffusion des épisodes d'un feuilleton en continu*.
◇ *adj Br* [edition] complet; ~ volume anthologie *f*.
omnibus bill *n Am projet de loi englobant des mesures diverses*.
omnidirectional [,ɒmnɪdɪ'rekʃənl] *adj* omnidirectionnel.
omnifarious [,ɒmnɪ'feərɪəs] *adj* de toutes sortes, très varié.
omnipotence [ɒm'nɪpətəns] *n* omnipotence *f*.
omnipotent [ɒm'nɪpətənt] ◇ *adj* omnipotent, tout-puissant.
◇ *n*: the Omnipotent le Tout-Puissant.
omnipresence [,ɒmnɪ'prezəns] *n* omniprésence *f*.
omnipresent [,ɒmnɪ'prezənt] *adj* omniprésent.
omnirange ['ɒmnɪ,reɪndʒ] *n* radiophare *m* omnidirectionnel.
omniscience [ɒm'nɪsɪəns] *n* omniscience *f*.
omniscient [ɒm'nɪsɪənt] *adj* omniscient.
omnivore ['ɒmnɪvɔːʳ] *n* omnivore *m*.
omnivorous [ɒm'nɪvərəs] *adj* ZOOL omnivore; *fig* insatiable, avide.
on [ɒn] ◇ *prep* **A.** -**1.** [specifying position] sur; the vase is on the shelf le vase est sur l'étagère; put it on the shelf mets-le sur l'étagère; on the floor par terre; on the ceiling au plafond; there are posters on the walls il y a des affiches aux OR sur les murs; there was blood on the walls il y avait du sang sur les murs; a coat was hanging on the hook un manteau était accroché à la patère; to lie on one's back/side être allongé sur le dos/côté; on the left/right à gauche/droite. -**2.** [indicating writing or painting surface] sur; I had nothing to write on je n'avais rien sur quoi écrire; red on a green background rouge sur un fond vert. -**3.** [indicating general location, area]: he works on a building site il travaille sur un chantier; they live on a farm ils habitent une ferme; there's been an accident on the M1 il y a eu un accident sur la M1; we met on the way there on s'est rencontrés en chemin. -**4.** [indicating part of body touched] sur; I kissed him on the cheek je l'ai embrassé sur la joue; someone tapped me on the shoulder quelqu'un m'a tapé sur l'épaule. -**5.** [close to]: the village is right on the lake/sea le village est juste au bord du lac/de la mer. -**6.** [indicating movement, direction]: the mirror fell on the floor la glace est tombée par terre; they marched on the capital ils marchèrent sur la capitale.
B. -**1.** [indicating thing carried] sur; I only had £10 on me je n'avais que 10 livres sur moi; she's got a gun on her elle est armée. -**2.** [indicating facial expression]: he had a scornful smile on his face il affichait un sourire plein de mépris.
C. -**1.** [indicating purpose of money, time, effort spent] sur; I spent hours on that essay j'ai passé des heures sur cette dissertation; she spent £1,000 on her new stereo elle a dépensé 1 000 livres pour acheter sa nouvelle chaîne hi-fi; what are you working on at the moment? sur quoi travaillez-vous en ce moment? -**2.** [indicating activity undertaken]: to be on strike être en grève; he's off on a trip to Brazil il part pour un voyage au Brésil; to go on safari faire un safari; she was sent on a course on l'a envoyée suivre des cours; I'm on nights next week je suis de nuit la semaine prochaine; he's on lunch *Am* /a break *Am* il est en train de déjeuner/faire la pause; she's been on the committee for years ça fait des années qu'elle siège au comité. -**3.** [indicating special interest, pursuit]: she's keen on music elle a la passion de la musique; he's good on modern history il excelle en histoire moderne; she's very big on equal opportunities l'égalité des chances, c'est son cheval de bataille. -**4.** [indicating scale of activity]: on a large/small scale sur une grande/petite échelle. -**5.** [compared with] par rapport à; imports are up/down on last year les importations sont en hausse/en baisse par rapport à l'année dernière; it's an improvement on the old system c'est une amélioration par rapport à l'ancien système.
D. -**1.** [about, on the subject of] sur; a book/film on the French Revolution un livre/film sur la Révolution française; we all agree on that point nous sommes tous d'accord sur ce point; I need some advice on a legal matter j'ai besoin de conseils sur un point légal. -**2.** [indicating person, thing affected] sur; it has no effect on them cela n'a aucun effet sur eux; a tax on alcohol une taxe sur les boissons alcoolisées; try it on your parents essaie-le sur tes parents; the government must act on inflation le gouvernement doit prendre des mesures contre l'inflation; he has survived two attempts on his life il a échappé à deux tentatives d'assassinat; it's unfair on women c'est injuste envers les femmes; the joke's on you! c'est toi qui as l'air ridicule! -**3.** [indicating cause of injury]: I cut my finger on a piece of glass je me suis coupé le doigt sur un morceau de verre. -**4.** [according to] selon; everyone will be judged on their merits chacun sera jugé selon ses mérites; candidates are selected on their examination results les candidats sont choisis en fonction des résultats qu'ils ont obtenus à l'examen.

-**5.** [indicating reason, motive for action]: on **impulse** sur un coup de tête; **the police acted on information from abroad** la police est intervenue après avoir reçu des renseignements de l'étranger; **I shall refuse on principle** je refuserai par principe. -**6.** [included in, forming part of]: **your name isn't on the list** votre nom n'est pas sur la liste; **the books on the syllabus** les livres au programme; **on the agenda** à l'ordre du jour. -**7.** [indicating method, system]: **they work on a rota system** ils travaillent par roulement; **reorganized on a more rational basis** réorganisé sur une base plus rationnelle. -**8.** [indicating means of transport]: **on foot/horseback** à pied/cheval; **on the bus/train** dans le bus/train; **she arrived on the midday bus/train** elle est arrivée par le bus/train de midi. -**9.** [indicating instrument played]: **to play a tune on the flute** jouer un air à la flûte; **who's on guitar/on drums?** qui est à la guitare/à la batterie? -**10.** RAD, TV & THEAT: **I heard it on the radio/on television** je l'ai entendu à la radio/à la télévision; **it's the first time she's been on television** c'est la première fois qu'elle passe à la télévision; **what's on the other channel** OR **side?** qu'est-ce qu'il y a sur l'autre chaîne?; **on stage** sur scène. -**11.** [indicating where information is stored]: **it's all on computer** tout est sur ordinateur; **on file** sur fichier.

E. [indicating date, time etc]: **on the 6th of July** le 6 juillet; **on Christmas Day** le jour de Noël; **I'll see her on Monday** je la vois lundi; **on Monday morning** lundi matin; **I don't work on Mondays** je ne travaille pas le lundi; **on a Monday morning in February** un lundi matin (du mois) de février; **the train arrived on time** le train est arrivé à l'heure; **every hour on the hour** à chaque heure; **it's just on five o'clock** il est cinq heures pile.

F. -**1.** [indicating source of payment]: **have a drink on me** prenez un verre, c'est moi qui offre; **the drinks are on me/the house!** c'est ma tournée/la tournée du patron!; **you can get it on the National Health** ≃ c'est remboursé par la Sécurité sociale. -**2.** [indicating source or amount of income]: **you can't live on such a low wage** on ne peut pas vivre avec des revenus aussi modestes; **they're on the dole** *inf* OR **on unemployment benefit** ils vivent du chômage OR des allocations de chômage. -**3.** [indicating source of power] à; **it works on solar energy/on electricity** ça marche à l'énergie solaire/à l'électricité. -**4.** [indicating source of nourishment] de; **they live on cereals** ils se nourrissent de céréales; **we dined on oysters and champagne** nous avons dîné d'huîtres et de champagne. -**5.** [indicating drugs, medicine prescribed]: **is she on the pill?** est-ce qu'elle prend la pilule?; **I'm still on antibiotics** je suis toujours sous antibiotiques; **the doctor put her on tranquillizers** le médecin lui a prescrit des tranquillisants; **he's on drugs** il se drogue. -**6.** [at the same time as] à; **he'll deal with it on his return** il s'en occupera à son retour; **cash on delivery** paiement à la livraison; **looters will be shot on sight** les pillards seront abattus sans sommation || [with present participle] en; **on hearing the news** en apprenant la nouvelle.

◇ *adv* -**1.** [in place]: **the lid wasn't on** le couvercle n'était pas mis; **put the top back on afterwards** remets le capuchon ensuite. -**2.** [referring to clothes]: **why have you got your gloves on?** pourquoi as-tu mis tes gants?; **the woman with the blue dress on** la femme en robe bleue; **he's got nothing on** il est nu. -**3.** [indicating continued action]: **to read on** continuer à lire; **the car drove on** la voiture ne s'est pas arrêtée; **they walked on** ils poursuivirent leur chemin; **from now** OR **this moment** OR **this time on** désormais; **earlier/later/further on** plus tôt/tard/loin. -**4.** [indicating activity]: **I've got a lot on this week** je suis très occupé cette semaine; **have you got anything on tonight?** tu fais quelque chose ce soir?; **what's on at the cinema?** qu'est-ce qui passe au cinéma? -**5.** [functioning, running]: **put** OR **turn** OR **switch the television on** allume la télévision; **turn the tap on** ouvre le robinet; **the lights had been left on** les lumières étaient restées allumées; **the tap had been left on** le robinet était resté ouvert; **the car had its headlights on** les phares de la voiture étaient allumés. -**6.** *inf phr*: **to be** OR **go on about sthg** parler de qqch sans arrêt; **he's on about his new car again** le voilà reparti sur sa nouvelle voiture; **what's she on about?** qu'est-ce qu'elle raconte?; **to be** OR **go on at sb (about sthg)**: **my parents are always on at me about my hair** mes parents n'arrêtent pas de m'embêter avec mes cheveux.

◇ *adj* -**1.** [working - electricity, light, radio, TV] allumé; [- gas, tap] ouvert; [- engine, machine] en marche; [- handbrake] serré; **the radio was on very loud** la radio hurlait; **make sure the switches are in the on position** vérifiez que les interrupteurs sont sur (la position) «marche»; **the on button** le bouton de mise en marche. -**2.** [happening, under way]: **there's a conference on next week** il y a une conférence la semaine prochaine; **the match is still on** [on TV] le match n'est pas terminé; [going ahead] le match n'a pas été annulé; **it's on at the local cinema** ça passe au cinéma du quartier; **your favourite TV programme is on tonight** il y a ton émission préférée à la télé ce soir; **is our deal still on?** est-ce que notre affaire tient toujours?; **the kettle's on for tea** j'ai mis de l'eau à chauffer pour le thé; **hurry up, your dinner's on** dépêche-toi, ton dîner va être prêt. -**3.** [in betting]: **the odds are twenty to one on** la cote est de vingt contre un. -**4.** *inf* [acceptable]: **such behaviour just isn't on!** une telle conduite est tout à fait inadmissible! -**5.** *inf* [feasible, possible]: **we'll never be ready by tomorrow, it just isn't on** nous ne serons jamais prêts pour demain, c'est tout bonnement impossible. -**6.** *inf* [in agreement]: **are you still on for dinner tonight?** ça marche toujours pour le dîner de ce soir?; **shall we say £10? – you're on!** disons 10 livres? – d'accord OR tope là!

◆ **on and on** *adv phr* sans arrêt; **he goes on and on about his minor ailments** il nous rebat les oreilles avec ses petits problèmes de santé; **the play dragged on and on** la pièce n'en finissait plus.

◆ **on and off** *adv phr*: **we went out together on and off for three years** on a eu une relation irrégulière pendant trois ans.

ON *written abbr of* Ontario.

onanism ['əʊnənɪzm] *n* onanisme *m.*

onanist ['əʊnənɪst] ◇ *adj* onaniste.
◇ *n* onaniste *mf.*

once [wʌns] ◇ *adv* -**1.** [on a single occasion] une fois; **I've been there ~ before** j'y suis déjà allé une fois; **more than ~** plus d'une fois; **~ or twice** une ou deux fois; **~ a month/year** une fois par mois/an; **I see her ~ every three months** je la vois tous les trois mois ❑ **~ in a while** occasionnellement, une fois de temps en temps; **~ more** OR **again** encore une fois; **for ~ he isn't late** pour une fois, il n'est pas en retard; **~ a liar always a liar** qui a menti mentira; **I'll try anything ~** il faut bien tout essayer; **~ bitten twice shy** *prov* chat échaudé craint l'eau froide *prov.* -**2.** [formerly] jadis, autrefois, une fois; **people ~ believed that the world was flat** autrefois, on croyait que la terre était plate; **a ~ famous poet** un poète autrefois célèbre; **~ there was a little girl called Goldilocks** il était une fois une petite fille nommée Boucle d'or ❑ **~ upon a time there was...** il était une fois...

◇ *conj* une fois que, dès que; **it'll be easy ~ we've started** une fois qu'on aura commencé, ce sera facile; **give me a call ~ you get there** passe-moi un coup de fil quand tu arrives; **~ you've told her the truth there'll be no turning back** une fois que tu lui auras dit la vérité, il ne te sera plus possible de faire marche arrière.

◇ *n*: **(just) this ~** (juste) pour cette fois-ci, (juste) pour une fois; **she did it just the ~** elle ne l'a fait qu'une seule fois.

◆ **at once** *adv phr* -**1.** [at the same time] à la fois, en même temps; **it was at ~ fascinating and terrifying** c'était à la fois fascinant et terrifiant. -**2.** [immediately] tout de suite; **come here at ~!** viens ici tout de suite OR immédiatement!

◆ **once and for all** *adv phr* une fois pour toutes; **let's settle this matter ~ and for all!** réglons cette affaire une (bonne) fois pour toutes!

once-over *inf n* -**1.** [glance] coup *m* d'œil; **I gave the morning paper the ~** j'ai jeté un coup d'œil sur le journal du matin; **I could see her giving me the ~** je la voyais qui me regardait des pieds à la tête. -**2.** [clean]: **give the stairs/the bookcase a quick ~** passe un coup dans l'escalier/sur la bibliothèque. -**3.** [beating] raclée *f*; **to give sb the** OR **a ~** donner une bonne raclée à qqn.

oncogenesis [ˌɒŋkəʊ'dʒenɪsɪs] *n* oncogenèse *f.*

oncogenic [ˌɒŋkəʊ'dʒenɪk] *adj* oncogène.

oncologist [ɒŋ'kɒlədʒɪst] *n* oncologue *mf*, oncologiste *mf.*

oncology [ɒŋ'kɒlədʒɪ] *n* oncologie *f.*

oncoming ['ɒnˌkʌmɪŋ] ◇ *adj* -**1.** [traffic, vehicle] venant en sens inverse. -**2.** [year, season] qui arrive, qui approche; **the ~ generation of school-leavers** les jeunes qui vont quitter l'école à la fin de cette année scolaire.
◇ *n* approche *f.*

OND (*abbr of* Ordinary National Diploma) *n brevet de technicien supérieur en Grande-Bretagne.*

one [wʌn] ◇ *det* -**1.** *(as numeral)* [in expressions of age, date, measurement etc] un *m*, une *f*; **~ dollar** un dollar; **~ pound** une livre; **~ and a half kilos** un kilo et demi; **~ million** un million; **~ thousand** mille; **at ~ o'clock** à une heure; **he'll be ~ (year old) in June** il aura un an en juin; **on page ~** [of book] (à la) page un; [of newspaper] à la une ❑ **~ or two** [a few] un/une ou deux; **a million** OR **a thousand and ~** [a lot] un millier de. -**2.** [referring to a single object or person] un *m*, une *f*; **~ American in two** un Américain sur deux; **only ~ answer is correct** il n'y a qu'une seule bonne réponse; **at any ~ time** au même moment; **~ car looks much like another to me** pour moi, toutes les voitures se ressemblent; **take ~ half and give him the other** prends-en une moitié et donne-lui l'autre. -**3.** [only, single] seul, unique; **my ~ mistake** ma seule erreur; **the ~ woman who knows** la seule femme qui soit au courant; **no ~ man should have that responsibility** c'est trop de responsabilité pour un seul homme; **not ~ family was spared** pas une (seule) famille ne fut épargnée. -**4.** [same] même; **they all arrived on the ~ day** ils sont tous arrivés le même jour; **the two wanted men are in fact ~ and the same person** les deux hommes recherchés sont en fait une seule et même personne; **to be of ~ mind (with sb on sthg)** être du même avis (que qqn sur qqch). -**5.** [instead of 'a']: **if there's ~ thing I hate it's rudeness** s'il y a une chose que je n'aime pas, c'est bien la grossièreté; **for ~ thing it's too late** d'abord, c'est trop tard; **we had ~ customer once who wouldn't leave** une fois on a eu un client qui ne voulait pas partir. -**6.** [a certain]: **I was introduced to ~ Arthur Crown** on m'a présenté un certain Arthur Crown. -**7.** [indicating indefinite time]: **~ day you'll understand** un jour, tu comprendras; **~ evening in July** un soir de juillet; **early ~ morning** un matin de bonne heure. -**8.** *inf* [as intensifier]: **that's ~ fine car!** c'est une sacrée bagnole!; **the room was ~ big mess** il y avait une de ces pagailles dans la pièce!; **it's been ~ hell of a day!** quelle journée!

◇ *pron* **A.** -**1.** [person, thing]: **which ~** lequel *m*, laquelle *f*; **this ~** celui-ci *m*, celle-ci *f*; **the other ~** l'autre; **the right ~** le bon; **the wrong ~** le mauvais; **which ~s?** lesquels? *mpl*, lesquelles? *fpl*; **these ~s** ceux-ci *mpl*, celles-ci *fpl*; **which dog? – the ~ that's barking** quel chien? – celui qui aboie; **which cars? – the ~s you like** quelles voitures? – celles que tu aimes;

he's the ~ who did it c'est lui qui l'a fait; ~ of my colleagues is sick (l') un/(l') une de mes collègues est malade; ~ of the bulbs has fused (l') une des ampoules a grillé; she's ~ of us elle est des nôtres; that's ~ of my favourite restaurants c'est (l') un de mes restaurants préférés; he's ~ of my many admirers c'est un de mes nombreux admirateurs; I've only got ~ je n'en ai qu'un; have you seen ~? en avez-vous vu un/une?; ~ or other l'un d'eux, l'une d'elles; ~ after the other l'un/l'une après l'autre; take the new ~ prends le nouveau/la nouvelle; she's eaten all the ripe ~s elle a mangé tous ceux qui étaient mûrs; the mother and her little ~s la mère et ses petits; she's my littlest ~ c'est ma plus jeune OR ma petite dernière ❑ ooh, you are a ~! *inf* toi, alors!; he's a right ~ he is! *inf* lui alors!; I'm not much of a ~ OR I'm not a great ~ for cheese *inf* je ne cours pas après le fromage; she's a great ~ for computers c'est une mordue d'informatique; she's ~ in a million OR thousand c'est une perle rare; I'm not ~ to gossip but... je ne suis pas du genre commère mais...; ~ and all tous (sans exception); to get ~ over on sb *inf* avoir l'avantage sur qqn. **-2.** [joke, story, question etc]: have you heard the ~ about the two postmen? tu connais celle des deux facteurs?; that's a good ~! elle est bien bonne celle-là!; that's an easy ~ c'est facile; the question is ~ of great importance cette question est d'une grande importance; you'll have to solve this ~ yourself il faudra que tu règles ça tout seul. **-3.** *inf* [drink]: do you fancy a quick ~? on prend un verre en vitesse? ❑ to have ~ too many boire un verre de trop. **-4.** *inf* [blow]: to hit OR thump OR belt sb ~ en mettre une à qqn.

B. -1. *fml* [as subject] on; [as object or after preposition] vous; ~ can only do ~'s OR *Am* his best on fait ce qu'on peut; it certainly makes ~ think ça fait réfléchir, c'est sûr. **-2.** [with infinitive forms]: to wash ~'s hands se laver les mains; to put ~'s hands in ~'s pockets mettre ses OR les mains dans les poches.

◆ **at one** *adv phr fml*: to be at ~ with sb/sthg être en harmonie avec qqn/qqch; she felt at ~ with the world elle se sentait en harmonie avec le monde.

◆ **for one** *adv phr*: I for ~ am disappointed pour ma part, je suis déçu; I know that Eric for ~ is against it je sais qu'Éric est contre en tout cas.

◆ **in one** *adv phr* **-1.** [combined]: all in ~ à la fois; she's a writer, actress and director (all) in ~ elle est à la fois scénariste, actrice et metteur en scène; a useful three-in-~ kitchen knife un couteau de cuisine très utile avec ses trois fonctions. **-2.** [at one attempt] du premier coup; he did it in ~ il l'a fait en un seul coup; got it in ~! *inf* du premier coup!

◆ **in ones and twos** *adv phr*: they arrived in ~s and twos ils arrivèrent les uns après les autres; people stood around in ~s and twos les gens se tenaient là par petits groupes.

◆ **one another** *pron phr* l'un l'autre *m*, l'une l'autre *f*, les uns les autres *mpl*, les unes les autres *fpl*; they didn't dare talk to ~ another ils n'ont pas osé se parler; we love ~ another nous nous aimons; the group meet in ~ another's homes le groupe se réunit chez l'un ou chez l'autre; they respect ~ another [two people] ils ont du respect l'un pour l'autre; [more than two people] ils se respectent les uns les autres; you can copy ~ another's notes [two people] vous pouvez copier vos notes l'un sur l'autre; [more than two people] vous pouvez copier vos notes les uns sur les autres.

◆ **one by one** *adv phr* un par un, une par une.

one-act *adj*: ~ play pièce *f* en un (seul) acte.

one-armed *adj* manchot (d'un bras); a ~ man un manchot.

one-armed bandit *n* machine *f* à sous.

one-dimensional *adj* unidimensionnel.

one-eyed *adj* borgne.

one-handed ◇ *adj* **-1.** [person]: he's ~ il lui manque une main. **-2.** [shot, stroke, catch] fait d'une (seule) main; [tool] utilisable d'une seule main.
◇ *adv* d'une (seule) main.

one-horse *adj* **-1.** [carriage] à un cheval. **-2.** *phr*: a ~ town *inf* un (vrai) trou, un bled paumé.

oneiric [əʊˈnaɪərɪk] *adj* onirique.

one-legged *adj* unijambiste; a ~ man un unijambiste.

one-liner *n* [quip] bon mot *m*; she has some very good ~s ses boutades sont très drôles; there are some great ~s in the film il y a de très bonnes répliques dans ce film.

one-man *adj* [vehicle, canoe] monoplace; [task] pour un seul homme; [expedition] en solitaire; I'm a ~ woman je suis la femme d'un seul homme ❑ ~ show [by artist] exposition *f* individuelle; [by performer] spectacle *m* solo, one-man-show *m inv*.

one-man band *n* homme-orchestre *m*; the company is very much a ~ *fig* c'est une seule personne qui fait marcher cette entreprise.

oneness [ˈwʌnnɪs] *n* **-1.** [singleness] unité *f*; [uniqueness] unicité *f*. **-2.** [agreement] accord *m*. **-3.** [wholeness] intégrité *f*. **-4.** [sameness] identité *f*.

one-night stand *n* **-1.** MUS & THEAT représentation *f* unique. **-2.** *inf* [brief affair] aventure *f* (sans lendemain).

one-off ◇ *adj* unique; she wants a ~ payment elle veut être payée en une seule fois; I'll do it if it's a ~ job je veux bien le faire mais seulement à titre exceptionnel; this trip is definitely a ~ deal *Am* c'est la première et dernière fois que je fais ce voyage; ~ order COMM commande *f* ponctuelle.
◇ *n* [original]: he's a complete ~ il n'y en a pas deux comme lui.

one-on-one *Am* = **one-to-one**.

one-parent *adj*: ~ family famille *f* monoparentale.

one-party *adj* POL à parti unique.

one-piece ◇ *adj* une pièce *(inv)*; ~ swimsuit maillot *m* une pièce.
◇ *n* vêtement *m* une pièce.

one-room *adj* à une (seule) pièce; a ~ flat OR apartment un studio.

onerous [ˈəʊnərəs] *adj fml* lourd, pénible.

oneself [wʌnˈself] *pron* **-1.** [reflexive] se; [after preposition] soi, soi-même; [emphatic] soi-même; to wash ~ se laver; to enjoy ~ s'amuser; to live for ~ vivre pour soi; to be pleased with ~ être content de soi OR soi-même. **-2.** [one's normal self] soi-même; it's enough to be ~ il suffit d'être soi-même. **-3.** *phr*: to be (all) by ~ être tout seul.

one-shot *inf Am* = **one-off** *adj*.

one-sided *adj* **-1.** [unequal] inégal; a ~ match SPORT un match inégal; conversations with him tend to be pretty ~ avec lui, ce n'est pas une conversation: il n'y a que lui qui parle. **-2.** [biased] partial. **-3.** [unilateral] unilatéral.

one-stop *adj* [shop, service] *où l'on trouve tout ce dont on a besoin*.

one-time *adj* ancien; a ~ actor turned director un ancien acteur devenu metteur en scène.

one-to-one *adj* **-1.** [discussion, meeting] seul à seul, en tête-à-tête; I'd prefer to talk to you on a ~ basis je préférerais vous parler seul à seul; students receive ~ instruction le professeur travaille individuellement avec chaque étudiant. **-2.** [comparison, relationship] terme à terme, biunivoque MATH.

one-track *adj* **-1.** RAIL à voie unique. **-2.** *fig*: he's got a ~ mind *inf* [thinks only of one thing] il n'a qu'une idée en tête; [thinks only of sex] il ne pense qu'à ça.

one-two *n* **-1.** [in boxing] *direct suivi d'un crochet de l'autre main*. **-2.** FTBL une-deux *m inv*.

one-up (*pt* & *pp* one-upped, *cont* one-upping)
◇ *adj*: we're ~ on our competitors nous avons pris l'avantage sur nos concurrents.
◇ *vt inf Am* marquer un point sur.

one-upmanship [-ˈʌpmənʃɪp] *n comportement d'une personne qui ne supporte pas de voir d'autres faire mieux qu'elle*; it's pure ~ on her part elle veut uniquement prouver qu'elle est la meilleure.

one-way *adj* **-1.** [street] à sens unique; [traffic] en sens unique; ~ street (rue *f* à) sens *m* unique; he went the wrong way up a ~ street il a pris un sens interdit. **-2.** [ticket] simple; a ~ ticket to Rome un aller simple pour Rome. **-3.** [mirror] sans tain. **-4.** [reaction, current] irréversible; [decision] unilatéral. **-5.** [relationship, feeling] à sens unique.

one-woman *adj*: I'm a ~ man je suis l'homme d'une seule femme ❑ ~ show [by artist] exposition *f* individuelle; [by performer] spectacle *m* solo, one-woman-show *m inv*.

ongoing [ˈɒn,gəʊɪŋ] *adj* [continuing] continu; [current, in progress] en cours; the ~ debate between supporters and adversaries of the system le débat en cours entre partisans et adversaires du système.

onion [ˈʌnjən] *n* oignon *m*; ~ soup soupe *f* à l'oignon ❑ he knows his ~s *inf Br* il connaît son affaire.

onion dome *n* ARCHIT bulbe *m* (byzantin).

onionskin [ˈʌnjənskɪn] *n*: ~ (paper) pelure *f* d'oignon.

on-line *adj* & *adv* COMPUT en ligne.

onlooker [ˈɒn,lʊkəʳ] *n* [during event] spectateur *m*, -trice *f*; [after accident] badaud *m*, -e *f*, curieux *m*, -euse *f*.

onlooking [ˈɒn,lʊkɪŋ] *adj*: the ~ crowd [at state occasion, sporting event etc] la foule des spectateurs; [after accident] les badauds, la foule des badauds.

only [ˈəʊnlɪ] ◇ *adj* seul, unique; he's/she's an ~ child il est fils/elle est fille unique; she was the ~ woman there c'était la seule femme; the ~ coat I possess le seul manteau que je possède; he's the ~ one who believes me il est le seul à me croire; I'm fed up! – you're not the ~ one! j'en ai assez! – tu n'es pas le seul!; her ~ answer was to shrug her shoulders pour toute réponse, elle a haussé les épaules; it's our ~ chance c'est notre seule chance; the ~ thing is, I won't be there le seul problème, c'est que je ne serai pas là; her one and ~ friend son seul et unique ami; Ladies and Gentlemen, the one and ~ Billy Shears! Mesdames, Mesdemoiselles, Messieurs, le seul, l'unique Billy Shears!
◇ *adv* **-1.** [exclusively] seulement; there are ~ two people I trust il n'y a que deux personnes en qui j'aie confiance; 'for external use ~' 'usage externe'; 'staff ~' 'réservé au personnel'. **-2.** [just, merely]: he's ~ a child! *inf* ce n'est qu'un enfant!; after all, it's ~ money après tout, ce n'est que de l'argent; it's ~ me! c'est moi!; you've ~ ruined my best silk shirt (, that's all)! tu n'as fait qu'abîmer ma plus belle chemise en soie (, c'est tout)!; go on, ask him, he can ~ say no vas-y, demande-lui, ce qui peut t'arriver de pire c'est qu'il refuse; I was ~ trying to help je ne cherchais qu'à me rendre utile; it will ~ make him sad ça ne fera que l'attrister; it's ~ natural she should want to see him c'est tout naturel qu'elle veuille le voir; I ~ hope we're not too late j'espère seulement que nous n'arrivons pas trop tard; you ~ have to look at him to see he's guilty il suffit de le regarder pour voir qu'il est coupable; be quiet, you stupid dog, it's ~ the postman! tais-toi donc, le chien, ce n'est que le facteur! ❑ you're ~ young once il faut profiter de sa jeunesse. **-3.** [to emphasize smallness of amount, number etc] ne... que; it ~ cost me £5 ça ne m'a coûté que 5 livres; it ~ took me half an hour je n'ai mis qu'une demi-heure. **-4.** [to emphasize recentness of event]: it seems like ~ yesterday c'est comme si c'était hier; I ~ found out this morning je n'ai appris ça que ce matin. **-5.** [with infinitive]: I awoke ~ to find he was gone à mon réveil, il était parti.
◇ *conj inf* **-1.** [but, except] mais; it's like Spain, ~ cheaper c'est comme l'Espagne, mais en

moins cher; go on then, ~ hurry! vas-y alors, mais dépêche-toi! -**2.** [were it not for the fact that] mais, seulement; **I'd do it, ~ I don't have the time** je le ferais bien, seulement je n'ai pas le temps.

◆ **not only** *conj phr*: **she's not ~ bright, she's funny too** elle est non seulement intelligente, mais en plus elle est drôle; **not ~... but also** non seulement... mais aussi.

◆ **only if, only... if** *conj phr* seulement si; **I'll do it, but ~ if you say sorry first** je le ferai, mais seulement si vous vous excusez d'abord; **he'll ~ agree if the money's good enough** il n'acceptera que si on lui propose assez d'argent.

◆ **only just** *adv phr* -**1.** [not long before]: **I've ~ just woken up** je viens (tout) juste de me réveiller. -**2.** [barely] tout juste; **I ~ just finished in time** je n'ai fini qu'au dernier moment; **did she win? – yes, but ~ just** a-t-elle gagné? – oui, mais de justesse; **I've ~ just got enough** j'en ai tout juste assez.

◆ **only too** *adv phr*: **I was ~ too aware of my own shortcomings** je n'étais que trop conscient de mes propres imperfections; **I'd be ~ too delighted to come** je ne serai que trop heureux de venir; **I remember her ~ too well** je ne risque pas de l'oublier.

o.n.o. (*abbr of* or near/nearest offer) *adv Br*: **£100 ~** 100 livres à débattre.

on-off *adj* -**1.** ELEC: **~ button** bouton *m* de marche-arrêt. -**2.** [intermittent]: **they have a very ~ relationship** ils ont une relation très peu suivie.

onomastic [ˌɒnəˈmæstɪk] *adj* onomastique.

onomastics [ˌɒnəˈmæstɪks] *n (U)* onomastique *f*.

onomatopoeia [ˈɒnəˌmætəˈpiːə] *n* onomatopée *f*.

onomatopoeic [ˈɒnəˌmætəˈpiːɪk], **onomatopoetic** [ˈɒnəˌmætəpəʊˈetɪk] *adj* onomatopéique.

onrush [ˈɒnˌrʌʃ] *n* [of attackers, army] attaque *f*, assaut *m*; [of emotion, tears] crise *f*; **in a sudden ~ of anger** dans un accès subit de colère.

onset [ˈɒnˌset] *n* -**1.** [assault] attaque *f*, assaut *m*. -**2.** [beginning] début *m*, commencement *m*; **the ~ of winter** le début de l'hiver.

onshore [ˈɒnˈʃɔːʳ] *adj* -**1.** [on land] sur terre, terrestre; **~ oil production** production *f* pétrolière à terre. -**2.** [moving towards land]: **~ wind** vent *m* de mer.

onside [ˌɒnˈsaɪd] *adj* & *adv* SPORT qui n'est pas hors jeu OR en position de hors-jeu.

on-site *adj* sur place.

onslaught [ˈɒnˌslɔːt] *n* attaque *f*, assaut *m*; **the opposition's ~ on government policy** l'attaque violente de l'opposition contre la politique du gouvernement.

onstage [ˈɒnsteɪdʒ] *adj* & *adv* sur scène.

Ont. *written abbr of* Ontario.

Ontario [ɒnˈteərɪəʊ] *pr n* Ontario *m*; **in ~** dans l'Ontario.

on-the-job *adj* [training] en entreprise; [experience] sur le tas.

onto [ˈɒntuː] *prep* -**1.** [gen] sur; **the bedroom looks out ~ a garden** la chambre donne sur un jardin; **let's move ~ the next point** passons au point suivant; **get ~ the bus** montez dans le bus. -**2.** [indicating discovery]: **let's just hope the authorities don't get ~ us** espérons qu'on ne sera pas découverts par les autorités; **we're ~ something big** nous sommes sur le point de faire une importante découverte; **is he ~ the fact that they're having an affair?** est-il au courant de leur liaison?; **he'd better watch out, I'm ~ him!** qu'il fasse attention, je l'ai dans mon OR le collimateur! -**3.** [in contact with]: **you should get ~ head office** *Br* OR **the head office** *Am* **about this** vous devriez contacter le siège à ce sujet; **she's been ~ me about my poor marks** elle m'a enguirlandé à cause de mes mauvaises notes.

ontogeny [ɒnˈtɒdʒənɪ], **ontogenesis** [ˌɒntəˈdʒenəsɪs] *n* ontogénie *f*, ontogenèse *f*.

ontological [ˌɒntəˈlɒdʒɪkl] *adj* ontologique.

ontology [ɒnˈtɒlədʒɪ] *n* ontologie *f*.

onus [ˈəʊnəs] *n* [responsibility] responsabilité *f*; [burden] charge *f*; **the ~ is on you to make good the damage** c'est à vous qu'il incombe de réparer les dégâts.

onward [ˈɒnwəd] ◇ *adj*: **the ~ journey** la suite du voyage; **there is an ~ flight to Chicago** il y a une correspondance pour Chicago; **the ~ march of time** la fuite du temps.
◇ *adv Am* = **onwards**.
◇ *interj* en avant.

onwards [ˈɒnwədz] *adv* [forwards] en avant; [further on] plus loin; **to go ~** avancer; **a trip to Europe, and ~ into Asia** un voyage en Europe, qui se poursuit en Asie; **~ and upwards!** en avant!

◆ **from... onwards** *adv phr* à partir de; **from next July ~** à partir de juillet prochain; **from her childhood ~** dès OR depuis son enfance; **from now ~** désormais, dorénavant, à partir de maintenant; **from then ~** à partir de ce moment-là.

onyx [ˈɒnɪks] ◇ *n* onyx *m*.
◇ *comp* en onyx, d'onyx.

oo [uː] = **ooh**.

oocyte [ˈəʊəsaɪt] *n* ovocyte *m*.

oodles *inf* [ˈuːdlz] *npl* des masses *fpl*, des tas *mpl*; **there's ~ of food left** il reste un tas de bouffe.

oogonium [ˌəʊəˈgəʊnɪəm] (*pl* **oogoniums** OR **oogonia** [-nɪə]) *n* -**1.** BOT oogone *f*. -**2.** ANAT ovogonie *f*.

ooh [uː] ◇ *interj* oh!
◇ *vi*: **they were all ~ing and aahing over her baby** ils poussaient tous des cris d'admiration devant son bébé.

oolite [ˈəʊəlaɪt] *n* oolite *m*, oolithe *m*.

oolitic [ˌəʊəˈlɪtɪk] *adj* oolithique.

oompah [ˈuːmpɑː] *n* flonflon *m*.

oomph *inf* [ʊmf] *n* -**1.** [energy] punch; **he's certainly got plenty of ~!** en tout cas, il a un sacré punch! -**2.** [sex appeal] sex-appeal *m*.

oops *inf* [ʊps, uːps], **oops-a-daisy** *inf* [ˌʊpsəˈdeɪzɪ] *interj* oh la la!

oosphere [ˈəʊəsfɪəʳ] *n* oosphère *f*.

oospore [ˈəʊəspɔːʳ] *n* oospore *f*.

ooze [uːz] ◇ *vi* suinter; **blood ~d from the wound** du sang coulait de la blessure; **the new father fairly ~d with pride** *fig* le nouveau père débordait de fierté; **her courage was oozing slowly away** *fig* son courage l'abandonnait peu à peu.
◇ *vt*: **the walls ~ moisture** l'humidité suinte des murs; **she ~s good health** *fig* elle respire la bonne santé.
◇ *n* boue *f*, vase *f*.

op *inf* [ɒp] (*abbr of* **operation**) *n* MED & MIL opération *f*.

op. (*written abbr of* **opus**) op.

opacity [əˈpæsətɪ] *n* -**1.** *literal* opacité *f*. -**2.** *fig* [of text] inintelligibilité *f*, obscurité *f*; [of person] stupidité *f*.

opal [ˈəʊpl] ◇ *n* opale *f*.
◇ *comp* [brooch, ring] en opale.

opalescence [ˌəʊpəˈlesns] *n* opalescence *f*.

opalescent [ˌəʊpəˈlesnt] *adj* opalescent *lit*, opalin.

opaque [əʊˈpeɪk] *adj* -**1.** *literal* opaque. -**2.** *fig* [text] inintelligible, obscur; [person] stupide.

opaque projector *n Am* épiscope *m*, épidiascope *m*.

op art *n* op art *m*.

OPEC [ˈəʊpek] (*abbr of* **Organization of Petroleum Exporting Countries**) *pr n* OPEP *f*; **the ~ countries** les pays membres de l'OPEP.

open [ˈəʊpn] ◇ *adj* -**1.** [not shut – window, cupboard, suitcase, jar, box, sore, valve] ouvert; **her eyes were slightly ~/wide ~** ses yeux étaient entrouverts/grands ouverts; **he kicked the door ~** il a ouvert la porte d'un coup de pied; **the panels slide ~** les panneaux s'ouvrent en coulissant; **I can't get the bottle ~** je n'arrive pas à ouvrir la bouteille; **there's a bottle already ~ in the fridge** il y a une bouteille entamée dans le frigo; **you won't need the key, the door's ~** tu n'auras pas besoin de la clef, la porte est ouverte. -**2.** [not fastened – coat, fly, packet] ouvert; **his shirt was ~ to the waist** sa chemise était ouverte OR déboutonnée jusqu'à la ceinture; **her blouse hung ~** son chemisier était déboutonné; **the wrapping had been torn ~** l'emballage avait été arraché OR déchiré. -**3.** [spread apart, unfolded – arms, book, magazine, umbrella] ouvert; [– newspaper] ouvert, déplié; [– legs, knees] écarté; **the book lay ~ at page four** le livre était ouvert à la page quatre; **I dropped the coin into his ~ hand** OR **palm** j'ai laissé tomber la pièce de monnaie dans le creux de sa main; **the seams had split ~** les coutures avaient craqué; **he ran into my ~ arms** il s'est précipité dans mes bras; **to welcome sb/sthg with ~ arms** *fig* accueillir qqn/qqch à bras ouverts; **she** OR **her mind is an ~ book** *fig* on peut lire en elle comme dans un livre. -**4.** [for business] ouvert; **I couldn't find a bank ~** je n'ai pas pu trouver une banque qui soit ouverte; **are you ~ on Saturdays?** ouvrez-vous le samedi?; **we're ~ for business as usual** nous sommes ouverts comme à l'habitude. -**5.** [not covered – carriage, wagon, bus] découvert; [– car] décapoté; [– grave] ouvert; [– boat] ouvert, non ponté; [– courtyard, sewer] à ciel ouvert; **the passengers sat on the ~ deck** les passagers étaient assis sur le pont; **the wine should be left ~ to breathe** il faut laisser la bouteille ouverte pour que le vin puisse respirer. -**6.** [not enclosed – hillside, plain]: **the shelter was ~ on three sides** l'abri était ouvert sur trois côtés; **the hill was ~ to the elements** la colline était exposée à tous les éléments; **our neighbourhood lacks ~ space** notre quartier manque d'espaces verts; **the wide ~ spaces of Texas** les grands espaces du Texas; **shanty towns sprang up on every scrap of ~ ground** des bidonvilles ont surgi sur la moindre parcelle de terrain vague; **they were attacked in ~ country** ils ont été attaqués en rase campagne; **~ countryside stretched away to the horizon** la campagne s'étendait à perte de vue; **~ grazing land** pâturages non clôturés; **ahead lay a vast stretch of ~ water** au loin s'étendait une vaste étendue d'eau; **in the ~ air** en plein air; **nothing beats life in the ~ air** il n'y a rien de mieux que la vie au grand air; **he took to the ~ road** il a pris la route; **it'll do 150 on the ~ road** elle monte à 150 sur l'autoroute; **the ~ sea** la haute mer, le large. -**7.** [unobstructed – road, passage] dégagé; [– mountain pass] ouvert, praticable; [– waterway] ouvert à la navigation; [– view] dégagé; **only one lane on the bridge is ~** il n'y a qu'une voie ouverte à la circulation sur le pont. -**8.** [unoccupied, available – job] vacant; [– period of time] libre; **we have two positions ~** nous avons deux postes à pourvoir; **I'll keep this Friday ~ for you** je vous réserverai ce vendredi; **she likes to keep her weekends ~** elle préfère ne pas faire de projets pour le week-end; **it's the only course of action ~ to us** c'est la seule chose que nous puissions faire; **she used every opportunity ~ to her** elle a profité de toutes les occasions qui se présentaient à elle; **he wants to keep his options ~** il ne veut pas s'engager. -**9.** [unrestricted – competition] ouvert (à tous); [– meeting, trial] public; [– society] ouvert, démocratique; **the contest is not ~ to company employees** le concours n'est pas ouvert au personnel de la société; **club membership is ~ to anyone** aucune condition particulière n'est requise pour devenir membre du club; **there are few positions of responsibility ~ to immigrants** les immigrés ont rarement accès aux postes de responsabilité; **the field is wide ~ for someone with your talents** pour quelqu'un d'aussi doué que vous, ce domaine offre des possibilités quasi illimitées; **to extend an ~ invitation to sb** inviter qqn à venir chez soi quand il le souhaite; **Reno was a pretty ~ town in those days** *inf Am* à cette époque, Reno était aux mains des hors-la-loi ❑ ~ classroom SCOL classe *f* primaire à activités libres; **they have an ~ marriage** ils forment un couple très libre; **~ primary** POL *(élection) primaire américaine ouverte aux non-inscrits d'un parti*; **~ seating** AERON & THEAT places *fpl* non réservées; **~ ticket** billet *m* open; **~ tournament** SPORT (tournoi *m*) open *m*. **-10.** [unprotected, unguarded - flank, fire] ouvert; [- wiring] non protégé; **~ city** MIL & POL ville *f* ouverte; **the two countries share miles of ~ border** les deux pays sont séparés par des kilomètres de frontière non matérialisée; **he missed an ~ goal** SPORT il n'y avait pas de défenseurs, et il a raté le but; **to lay o.s. ~ to criticism** prêter le flanc à la critique. **-11.** [undecided - question] non résolu, non tranché; **the election is still wide ~** l'élection n'est pas encore jouée; **it's still an ~ question whether he'll resign or not** on ne sait toujours pas s'il va démissionner; **I prefer to leave the matter ~** je préfère laisser cette question en suspens; **he wanted to leave the date ~** il n'a pas voulu fixer de date. **-12.** [liable]: **his speech is ~ to misunderstanding** son discours peut prêter à confusion; **the prices are not ~ to negotiation** les prix ne sont pas négociables; **the plan is ~ to modification** le projet n'a pas encore été finalisé; **it's ~ to debate whether she knew about it or not** on peut se demander si elle était au courant. **-13.** [receptive]: **to be ~ to suggestions** être ouvert aux suggestions; **I don't want to go but I'm ~ to persuasion** je ne veux pas y aller mais je pourrais me laisser persuader; **I try to keep an ~ mind about such things** j'essaie de ne pas avoir de préjugés sur ces questions. **-14.** [candid - person, smile, countenance] ouvert, franc; [- discussion] franc; **let's be ~ with each other** soyons francs l'un avec l'autre; **they weren't very ~ about their intentions** ils se sont montrés assez discrets en ce qui concerne leurs intentions. **-15.** [blatant - contempt, criticism] ouvert; [- attempt] non dissimulé; [- scandal] public; [- rivalry] déclaré; **the country is in a state of ~ civil war** le pays est en état de véritable guerre civile; **they acted in ~ violation of the treaty** ce qu'ils ont fait constitue une violation flagrante du traité; **they showed an ~ disregard for the law** ils ont fait preuve d'un manque de respect flagrant face à la loi; **it's an ~ admission of guilt** cela équivaut à un aveu. **-16.** [loose - weave] lâche; **~ mesh** mailles *fpl* lâches; **~ pattern** motif *m* aéré. **-17.** LING [vowel, syllable] ouvert. **-18.** ELEC [circuit] ouvert. **-19.** *Br* FIN [cheque] non barré. **-20.** MUS [string] à vide.

◇ *vt* **-1.** [window, lock, shop, eyes, border] ouvrir; [wound] rouvrir; [bottle, can] ouvrir, déboucher; [wine] déboucher; **~ quotations** OR **inverted commas** ouvrez les guillemets; **she ~ed her eyes very wide** elle ouvrit grand les yeux, elle écarquilla les yeux; **they plan to ~ the border to refugees** ils projettent d'ouvrir la frontière aux réfugiés; **~ the aperture one more stop** PHOT ouvrez d'un diaphragme de plus; **to ~ the throttle** [car] accélérer; [plane] mettre les gaz ‖ *fig*: **to ~ one's heart to sb** se confier à qqn; **we must ~ our minds to new ideas** nous devons être ouverts aux idées nouvelles. **-2.** [unfasten - coat, envelope, gift, collar] ouvrir. **-3.** [unfold, spread apart - book, umbrella, penknife, arms, hand] ouvrir; [- newspaper] ouvrir, déplier; [- legs, knees] écarter. **-4.** [pierce - hole] percer; [- breach] ouvrir; [- way, passage] ouvrir, frayer; **to ~ a road through the jungle** ouvrir une route à travers la jungle; **the agreement ~s the way for peace** l'accord va mener à la paix. **-5.** [start - campaign, discussion, account, trial] ouvrir, commencer; [- negotiations] ouvrir, engager; [- conversation] engager, entamer; **her new film ~ed the festival** son dernier film a ouvert le festival; **to ~ a file on sb** ouvrir un dossier sur qqn; **to ~ fire (on** OR **at sb)** ouvrir le feu (sur qqn); **to ~ the bidding** [in bridge] ouvrir (les enchères); **to ~ the betting** [in poker] lancer les enchères. **-6.** [set up - shop, business] ouvrir; [inaugurate - hospital, airport, library] ouvrir, inaugurer. **-7.** [clear, unblock - road, lane, passage] dégager; [- mountain pass] ouvrir.

◇ *vi* **-1.** [door, window] (s') ouvrir; [suitcase, valve, padlock, eyes] s'ouvrir; **the window ~s outwards** la fenêtre (s') ouvre vers l'extérieur; **~ wide!** ouvrez grand!; **to ~, press down and twist** pour ouvrir, appuyez et tournez; **both rooms ~ onto the corridor** les deux chambres donnent OR ouvrent sur le couloir; **the heavens ~ed and we got drenched** *fig* il s'est mis à tomber des trombes d'eau et on s'est fait tremper. **-2.** [unfold, spread apart - book, umbrella, parachute] s'ouvrir; [- bud, leaf] s'ouvrir, s'épanouir; **a new life ~ed before her** une nouvelle vie s'ouvrait devant elle. **-3.** [gape - chasm] s'ouvrir. **-4.** [for business] ouvrir; **what time do you ~ on Sundays?** à quelle heure ouvrez-vous le dimanche?; **the doors ~ at 8 p.m.** les portes ouvrent à 20 h. **-5.** [start - campaign, meeting, discussion, concert, play, story] commencer; **the book ~s with a murder** le livre commence par un meurtre; **the hunting season ~s in September** la chasse ouvre en septembre; **she ~ed with a statement of the association's goals** elle commença par une présentation des buts de l'association; **the film ~s next week** le film sort la semaine prochaine; **when are you ~ing?** THEAT quand aura lieu la première?; **when it ~ed on Broadway, the play flopped** lorsqu'elle est sortie à Broadway, la pièce a fait un four; **the Dow Jones ~ed at 2461** le Dow Jones a ouvert à 2461; **to ~ with two clubs** [in bridge] ouvrir de deux trèfles.

◇ *n* **-1.** [outdoors, open air]: **(out) in the ~** [gen] en plein air, dehors; [in countryside] au grand air; **eating (out) in the ~ gives me an appetite** manger au grand air me donne de l'appétit; **to sleep in the ~** dormir à la belle étoile. **-2.** [public eye]: **to bring sthg (out) into the ~** parler ouvertement OR franchement de qqch; **the riot brought the instability of the regime out into the ~** l'émeute a révélé l'instabilité du régime; **the conflict between them finally came out into the ~** le conflit qui les opposait a finalement éclaté au grand jour. **-3.** SPORT: **the British Open** l'open *m* OR le tournoi open de Grande-Bretagne.

◆ **open out** ◇ *vi insep* **-1.** [unfold - bud, petals] s'ouvrir, s'épanouir; [- parachute] s'ouvrir; [- sail] se gonfler; **the sofa ~s out into a bed** le canapé est convertible en lit; **the doors ~ out onto a terrace** les portes donnent OR s'ouvrent sur une terrasse. **-2.** [lie - vista, valley] s'étendre, s'ouvrir; **miles of wheatfields ~ed out before us** des champs de blé s'étendaient devant nous à perte de vue. **-3.** [broaden, widen - path, stream] s'élargir; **the river ~s out into a lake** la rivière se jette dans un lac; **the trail finally ~s out onto a plateau** la piste débouche sur un plateau. **-4.** *Br fig* [become less reserved] s'ouvrir; **he ~ed out after a few drinks** quelques verres ont suffi à le faire sortir de sa réserve.

◇ *vt sep* [unfold - newspaper, deck chair, fan] ouvrir; **the peacock ~ed out its tail** le paon a fait la roue.

◆ **open up** ◇ *vi insep* **-1.** [unlock the door] ouvrir; **~ up or I'll call the police!** ouvrez, sinon j'appelle la police!; **~ up in there!** ouvrez, là-dedans! **-2.** [become available - possibility] s'ouvrir; **we may have a position ~ing up in May** il se peut que nous ayons un poste disponible en mai. **-3.** [for business - shop, branch etc] (s') ouvrir; **a new hotel ~s up every week** un nouvel hôtel ouvre ses portes chaque semaine. **-4.** [start firing - guns] faire feu, tirer; [- troops, person] ouvrir le feu, se mettre à tirer. **-5.** [become less reserved - person] s'ouvrir; [- discussion] s'animer; **he won't ~ up even to me** il ne s'ouvre pas, même à moi; **he needs to ~ up about his feelings** il a besoin de dire ce qu'il a sur le cœur OR de s'épancher; **I got her to ~ up about her doubts** j'ai réussi à la convaincre de me faire part de ses doutes. **-6.** [become interesting] devenir intéressant; **things are beginning to ~ up in my field of research** ça commence à bouger dans mon domaine de recherche; **the game ~ed up in the last half** le match est devenu plus ouvert après la mi-temps.

◇ *vt sep* **-1.** [crate, gift, bag, tomb] ouvrir; **we're ~ing up the summer cottage this weekend** nous ouvrons la maison de campagne ce week-end; **the sleeping bag will dry faster if you ~ it up** le sac de couchage séchera plus vite si tu l'ouvres. **-2.** [for business] ouvrir; **each morning Lucy ~ed up the shop** chaque matin, Lucy ouvrait la boutique; **he wants to ~ up a travel agency** il veut ouvrir une agence de voyages. **-3.** [for development - isolated region] désenclaver; [- quarry, oilfield] ouvrir, commencer l'exploitation de; [- new markets] ouvrir; **irrigation will ~ up new land for agriculture** l'irrigation permettra la mise en culture de nouvelles terres; **the airport ~ed up the island for tourism** l'aéroport a ouvert l'île au tourisme; **a discovery which ~s up new fields of research** une découverte qui crée de nouveaux domaines de recherche; **the policy ~ed up possibilities for closer cooperation** la politique a créé les conditions d'une coopération plus étroite. **-4.** *inf* [accelerate]: **he ~ed it** OR **her up in the straight** il a accéléré à fond dans la ligne droite.

open-air *adj* [market, concert] en plein air; [sports] de plein air; **~ swimming pool** piscine *f* découverte; **~ restaurant** restaurant *m* en terrasse; **~ museum** écomusée *m*.

open-and-shut *adj* [choice] simple, évident; **it's an ~ case** la solution est évidente OR ne fait pas l'ombre d'un doute.

opencast ['əʊpnkɑːst] *adj Br* MIN à ciel ouvert; **~ mining** extraction *f* à ciel ouvert.

open day *n Br* journée *f* portes ouvertes.

open-door *adj* [policy] de la porte ouverte.

open-ended *adj* [flexible - offer] flexible; [- plan] modifiable; [- question] ouvert; **an ~ discussion** une discussion libre; **~ contract** contrat *m* à durée indéterminée.

opener ['əʊpnəʳ] *n* **-1.** [tool] outil *m* OR dispositif *m* servant à ouvrir; [for cans] ouvre-boîtes *m inv*; **you need a special ~ for these tins** il faut un ouvre-boîtes spécial pour ces boîtes. **-2.** [person - in cards, games] ouvreur *m*, -euse *f*. **-3.** [first song, act etc] lever *m* de rideau; **she chose her latest hit single as an ~ for the show** elle a choisi son dernier tube pour ouvrir le spectacle. **-4.** *phr*: **for ~s** *inf Br* pour commencer; **I'm sacking the whole staff, and that's just for ~s** je licencie toute l'équipe et ce n'est qu'un début; **well, let's offer £100 for ~s** eh bien, proposons 100 livres pour commencer.

open-eyed ◇ *adj* (qui a) les yeux ouverts; **they watched in ~ amazement** ils ouvraient de grands yeux.

◇ *adv*: **to stare ~** regarder les yeux écarquillés.

open-faced *adj Am*: **~ sandwich** [gen] tartine *f*; [cocktail food] canapé *m*.

open-field *adj* HIST: **the ~ system** l'open-field *m*.

open-handed *adj* généreux.

open-hearted [-'hɑːtɪd] *adj* **-1.** [candid] franc, sincère. **-2.** [kind] bon, qui a bon cœur.

open-hearth *adj* METALL: **~ furnace** four *m* Martin; **~ process** procédé *m* Martin.

open-heart surgery *n* chirurgie *f* à cœur ouvert.

open house *n* **-1.** *Am* = **open day**. **-2.** *Am* [party] grande fête *f*. **-3.** *phr*: **to keep ~** *Br* tenir table ouverte.

opening ['əʊpnɪŋ] ◇ *adj* [part, chapter] premier; [day, hours] d'ouverture; [ceremony] d'ouverture, d'inauguration; [remark] préliminaire, préalable; **the play's ~ scene** le début de la pièce; **~ prices** ST. EX prix *mpl* à l'ouverture ❑ **~ gambit** CHESS gambit *m*; *fig* premier pas *m*.

◇ *n* **-1.** [act of opening] ouverture *f*; **the ~ of a new supermarket** l'ouverture d'un nouveau supermarché; **at the play's New York ~** lors de la première de la pièce à New York; **the ~ of negotiations has been postponed** l'ouverture des négociations a été ajournée. **-2.** [gap, hole, entrance] ouverture *f*; **we came to an ~ in the fence** nous avons trouvé un passage OR une ouverture dans la clôture; **an ~ in the clouds** une trouée OR une percée dans les nuages; **the ~ to the mine** l'entrée de la mine. **-3.** *Am* = **clearing 1.** **-4.** [start, first part] ouverture *f*, début *m*; **the ~ of the film is in black and white** le début du film est en OR les premières scènes du film sont en noir et blanc. **-5.** [opportunity - gen] occasion *f*; [- for employment] débouché *m*; **her remarks about the company gave me the ~ I needed** ses observations au sujet de l'entreprise m'ont fourni le prétexte dont j'avais besoin; **there are lots of good ~s in industry** l'industrie offre de nombreux débouchés intéressants; **there's an ~ with Smith & Co** il y a un poste vacant chez Smith & Co.

opening night *n* THEAT première *f*.

opening time *n* COMM heure *f* d'ouverture.

open letter *n* lettre *f* ouverte; **an ~ to the President** une lettre ouverte au Président.

openly ['əʊpənlɪ] *adv* visiblement; **drugs are on sale ~** la drogue est en vente libre; **she was ~ distressed about it** ça l'avait visiblement bouleversée; **he wept ~** il pleurait sans retenue.

open market *n* marché *m* libre; **to buy sthg on the ~** acheter qqch sur le marché libre.

open-minded *adj* [receptive] ouvert (d'esprit); [unprejudiced] sans préjugés; **my parents are pretty ~ about mixed marriages** mes parents n'ont aucun a priori contre les mariages mixtes.

open-mindedness [-'maɪndɪdnɪs] *n* ouverture *f* d'esprit.

open-mouthed ◇ *adj* [person] stupéfait, interdit; **he was sitting there in ~ astonishment** il était assis là, béat d'étonnement.
◇ *adv*: **to watch ~** regarder bouche bée.

open-neck(ed) *adj* à col ouvert.

openness ['əʊpənnɪs] *n* **-1.** [candidness] franchise *f*; **she spoke with refreshing ~ about her career** elle parlait de son métier avec une franchise qui faisait plaisir || [receptivity] ouverture *f*; **I admire her for her ~** ce que j'admire chez elle, c'est qu'elle est très ouverte. **-2.** [spaciousness] largeur *f*; **the picture window gives a feeling of ~ to the room** la baie vitrée agrandit la pièce.

open-plan *adj* ARCHIT [design, house] à plan ouvert, sans cloisons; **~ kitchen** cuisine *f* américaine; **~ office** bureau *m* paysager.

open prison *n* prison *f* ouverte.

open sandwich *n* [gen] tartine *f*; [cocktail food] canapé *m*.

open season *n* saison *f*; **the ~ for hunting** la saison de la chasse; **the tabloid papers have declared ~ on the private lives of rock stars** *fig* les journaux à scandale se sont mis à traquer les stars du rock dans leur vie privée.

open secret *n Br* secret *m* de Polichinelle; **it's an ~ that Smith will get the job** c'est Smith qui aura le poste, ce n'est un secret pour personne.

open sesame ◇ *interj*: **~!** sésame, ouvre-toi!
◇ *n Br* [means to success] sésame *m*; **good A level results aren't necessarily an ~ to university** de bons résultats aux A levels n'ouvrent pas forcément la porte de l'université.

open shop *n* INDUST **-1.** *Br* [open to non-union members] *entreprise ne pratiquant pas le monopole d'embauche*. **-2.** *Am* [with no union] établissement *m* sans syndicat.

Open University *n Br* ≃ Université *f* ouverte à tous (pratiquant le télé-enseignement).

open verdict *n* JUR verdict *m* de décès sans cause déterminée.

openwork ['əʊpənwɜːk] *n (U)* **-1.** SEW jours *mpl*, ajours *mpl*. **-2.** ARCHIT claire-voie *f*, ajours *mpl*.

opera ['ɒpərə] ◇ *fml pl* → **opus**.
◇ *n* **-1.** [musical play] opéra *m*. **-2.** [art of opera] opéra *m*; **she adores (the) ~** elle adore l'opéra ❑ **~ singer** chanteur *m*, -euse *f* d'opéra. **-3.** [opera house] opéra *m*.

operable ['ɒprəbl] *adj* MED opérable.

opera cloak *n* (grande) cape *f*.

opera glasses *npl* jumelles *fpl* de théâtre.

operagoer ['ɒprəˌgəʊəʳ] *n* amateur *m* d'opéra.

opera hat *n Br* gibus *m*, (chapeau *m*) claque *m*.

opera house *n* (théâtre *m* de l') opéra *m*; **the Sydney Opera House** l'Opéra de Sydney.

operand ['ɒpərænd] *n* opérande *m*.

operate ['ɒpəreɪt] ◇ *vt* **-1.** [machine, device etc] faire fonctionner, faire marcher; **my husband doesn't even know how to ~ the toaster!** mon mari ne sait même pas se servir du grille-pain!; **is it possible to ~ the radio off the mains?** peut-on brancher cette radio sur le secteur?; **this clock is battery-~d** cette horloge fonctionne avec des piles; **a circuit-breaker ~s the safety mechanism** un disjoncteur actionne OR déclenche le système de sécurité. **-2.** [business] gérer, diriger; [mine] exploiter; [drug ring] contrôler; **they ~ several casinos** ils tiennent plusieurs casinos; **she ~s her business from her home** elle fait marcher son affaire depuis son domicile; **they ~ a protection racket in the neighbourhood** ils rackettent les gens du quartier; **they ~ a system of rent rebates for poorer families** ils ont un système de loyers modérés pour les familles les plus démunies.
◇ *vi* **-1.** [machine, device] marcher, fonctionner; [system, process, network] fonctionner; **it ~s by itself** ça fonctionne tout seul; **this is how colonialism ~s** voici comment fonctionne le colonialisme; **the factory is operating at full capacity** l'usine tourne à plein rendement. **-2.** MED opérer; **to ~ on sb (for sthg)** opérer qqn (de qqch); **he was ~d on for cancer** on l'a opéré OR il a été opéré d'un cancer. **-3.** [be active] opérer; **military patrols ~ along the border** des patrouilles militaires opèrent le long de la frontière; **many crooks ~ in this part of town** de nombreux malfaiteurs sévissent dans ce quartier; **the company ~s out of Chicago** le siège de la société est à Chicago. **-4.** [produce an effect] opérer, agir; **the drug ~s on the nervous system** le médicament agit sur le système nerveux; **the decision has ~d against us** la décision a joué contre nous; **two elements ~ in our favour** deux éléments jouent en notre faveur || [be operative] s'appliquer; **the rule doesn't ~ in such cases** la règle ne s'applique pas à de tels cas.

operatic [ˌɒpə'rætɪk] *adj* d'opéra; **~ repertoire/role** répertoire/rôle lyrique.

operating ['ɒpəreɪtɪŋ] *adj* [costs, methods etc] d'exploitation; **the factory has reached full ~ capacity** l'usine a atteint sa pleine capacité de production ❑ **~ instructions** mode *m* d'emploi; **~ profit** bénéfice *m* d'exploitation; **~ system** COMPUT système *m* d'exploitation.

operating room *n Am* salle *f* d'opération.

operating table *n* table *f* d'opération.

operating theatre *n Br* salle *f* d'opération.

operation [ˌɒpə'reɪʃn] *n* **-1.** [functioning - of machine, device] fonctionnement *m*, marche *f*; [- of process, system] fonctionnement *m*; [- of drug, market force] action *f*; **to be in ~** [machine, train service] être en service; [firm, group, criminal] être en activité; [law] être en vigueur; **bus services are in ~ until midnight** les lignes de bus sont en service jusqu'à minuit; **the pit has been in ~ for two years** le puits est exploité depuis deux ans; **the plant is in ~ round the clock** l'usine fonctionne 24 heures sur 24; **to put into ~** [machine, train service] mettre en service; [plan] mettre en application OR en œuvre; [law] faire entrer en vigueur; **to come into ~** [machine, train service] entrer en service; [law] entrer en vigueur; **the old machines have been taken out of ~** les vieilles machines ont été retirées du service. **-2.** [running, management - of firm] gestion *f*; [- of mine] exploitation *f*; [- of process, system] application *f*; **~ of the new machines is simplicity itself** le fonctionnement de ces nouvelles machines est très simple. **-3.** [act activity, deal etc] opération *f*; **a police/rescue ~** une opération de police/de sauvetage; **they are to close down their ~s in Mexico** ils vont mettre un terme à leurs opérations OR activités au Mexique || MIL opération *f*; **peace-keeping ~s** opérations de pacification; **Operation Omega** Opération Oméga. **-4.** [company] entreprise *f*, société *f*; **she works for a mining ~** elle travaille pour une exploitation minière. **-5.** MED opération *f*, intervention *f*; **she had an ~ for cancer** elle s'est fait opérer d'un cancer; **he had a heart ~** il a subi une opération OR il a été opéré du cœur; **to perform an ~** réaliser une intervention. **-6.** COMPUT & MATH opération *f*.

operational [ˌɒpə'reɪʃənl] *adj* **-1.** [MIL & gen] opérationnel; **the design team was ~ within six months** en l'espace de six mois, l'équipe de dessinateurs fut opérationnelle ❑ **~ costs** frais *mpl* opérationnels; COMM frais *mpl* d'exploitation. **-2.** [equipment, engine, system] opérationnel; **the new missiles are not yet ~** les nouveaux missiles ne sont pas encore opérationnels; **as soon as the engine is ~** dès que le moteur sera en état de marche; **~ difficulties** difficultés d'ordre pratique; **we have an ~ malfunction** nous avons un problème de fonctionnement.

operations research *n* COMPUT recherche *f* opérationnelle.

operations room *n* base *f* d'opérations.

operative ['ɒprətɪv] ◇ *adj* **-1.** [law] en vigueur; **to become ~** entrer en vigueur, prendre effet; **parking restrictions became ~ last year** les limitations de stationnement ont pris effet l'an dernier. **-2.** [operational - system, scheme, skill] opérationnel; **the system will soon be ~** le système sera bientôt opérationnel. **-3.** MED opératoire. **-4.** *phr*: **the ~ word** le mot qui convient.
◇ *n* **-1.** opérateur *m*, -trice *f*; **machine ~** conducteur *m*, -trice *f* de machine; **textile ~** ouvrier *m*, -ère *f* du textile. **-2.** *Am* [secret agent] agent *m* secret; [detective] (détective *m*) privé *m*.

operator ['ɒpəreɪtəʳ] *n* **-1.** [technician] opérateur *m*, -trice *f*; **radio ~** radio *mf*. **-2.** TELEC opérateur *m*, -trice *f*; **(switchboard) ~** standardiste *mf*. **-3.** COMM OR *pej* [director] directeur *m*, -trice *f*, dirigeant *m*, -e *f*; [organizer] organisateur *m*, -trice *f*; **there are too many small ~s in real estate** l'immobilier compte trop de petites entreprises; **he's a big drug ~** c'est un grand caïd de la drogue ❑ **tour ~** tour-opérateur *m*, voyagiste *mf*; **he's a smooth ~** *inf fig* il sait s'y prendre OR se débrouiller, c'est un petit malin. **-4.** MATH opérateur *m*. **-5.** *Am* [in bus] machiniste *mf*.

operetta [ˌɒpə'retə] *n* opérette *f*.

ophthalmia [ɒf'θælmɪə] *n* ophtalmie *f*.

ophthalmic [ɒf'θælmɪk] *adj* ANAT [nerve] ophtalmique; MED [surgery] ophtalmologique.

ophthalmic optician *n* opticien *m*, -enne *f* (optométriste).

ophthalmologist [ˌɒfθæl'mɒlədʒɪst] *n* oculiste *mf*, ophtalmologiste *mf*, ophtalmologue *mf*.

ophthalmology [ˌɒfθæl'mɒlədʒɪ] *n* ophtalmologie *f*.

ophthalmoscope [ɒf'θælməskəʊp] *n* ophtalmoscope *m*.

ophthalmoscopy [ˌɒfθæl'mɒskəpɪ] *n* ophtalmoscopie *f*.

opiate ['əʊpɪət] ◇ *adj* opiacé.
◇ *n* opiacé *m*.

opine [əʊ'paɪn] *vt fml* OR *lit* (faire) remarquer.

opinion [ə'pɪnjən] *n* **-1.** [estimation] opinion *f*, avis *m*; [viewpoint] point *m* de vue; **in my ~** à mon avis; **in the ~ of her teachers** de l'avis de ses professeurs, selon ses professeurs; **I am of the ~ that we should wait** je suis d'avis que l'on attende; **what is your ~ on** OR **about the elections?** que pensez-vous des élections?; **everyone should be free to express an ~** chacun devrait être libre d'exprimer son opinion; **my personal ~ is that...** je suis d'avis que..., pour ma part, je pense que...; **well, if you want my honest ~, I'll tell you** puisque tu veux savoir le fond de ma pensée, je vais te le dire; **can you give us your ~ on the festival?** pouvez-vous nous dire ce que vous pensez du festival?; **to have a good/bad ~ of sthg** avoir une bonne/mauvaise opinion de qqch; **I have a rather low ~ of him** je n'ai pas beaucoup d'estime pour lui; **he has too high an ~ of himself** il a une trop haute opinion de lui-même. -**2.** [conviction, belief] opinion *f*; **to have strong ~s** avoir des opinions bien arrêtées OR tranchées; **world/international ~** l'opinion mondiale/internationale; **a matter of ~** une affaire d'opinion ‖ JUR avis *m*; **it is the ~ of the court that...** la cour est d'avis que... ❑ **public ~ is against them** ils ont l'opinion publique contre eux. -**3.** [advice] opinion *f*, avis *m*; **a medical/legal ~** un avis médical/juridique ❑ **to ask for a second ~** demander l'avis d'un tiers; [doctor] demander l'avis d'un autre médecin.

opinionated [əˈpɪnjəneɪtɪd] *adj pej* borné, têtu.

opinion poll *n* sondage *m* d'opinion.

opium [ˈəʊpjəm] *n* opium *m*; **~ addict** opiomane *mf*; **~ addiction** opiomanie *f*; **~ dream** rêve *m* d'opium.

opium den *n* fumerie *f* d'opium.

opium poppy *n* pavot *m* (somnifère).

Oporto [əˈpɔːtəʊ] *pr n* Porto.

opossum [əˈpɒsəm] (*pl inv* OR **opossums**) *n* opossum *m*.

opponent [əˈpəʊnənt] ◇ *n* -**1.** [gen, POL & SPORT] adversaire *mf*; [rival] rival *m*, -e *f*; [competitor] concurrent *m*, -e *f*; [in debate] adversaire *mf*; **political ~** [democratic] adversaire politique; [of regime] opposant *m*, -e *f* politique; **she has always been an ~ of blood sports** elle a toujours été contre les sports sanguinaires; **~s of the new marina held a rally** les opposants à la construction de la nouvelle marina ont organisé un meeting. -**2.** ANAT antagoniste *m*.
◇ *adj* ANAT [muscle] antagoniste.

opportune [ˈɒpətjuːn] *adj fml* -**1.** [coming at the right time] opportun; **a very ~ remark** une remarque tout à fait opportune. -**2.** [suitable for a particular purpose] propice; **the ~ moment** le moment opportun OR propice; **this seems an ~ moment to break for coffee** le moment semble propice pour faire une pause-café.

opportunely [ˈɒpətjuːnlɪ] *adv* opportunément, au moment opportun.

opportunism [ˌɒpəˈtjuːnɪzm] *n* opportunisme *m*.

opportunist [ˌɒpəˈtjuːnɪst] ◇ *adj* opportuniste.
◇ *n* opportuniste *mf*.

opportunistic [ˌɒpətjuːˈnɪstɪk] *adj* opportuniste.

opportunity [ˌɒpəˈtjuːnətɪ] (*pl* **opportunities**) *n* -**1.** [chance] occasion *f*; **to have an ~ to do** OR **of doing sthg** avoir l'occasion de faire qqch; **we don't have much ~ of practising hang-gliding** nous avons rarement l'occasion de faire du deltaplane; **if ever you get the ~** si jamais vous en avez l'occasion; **to give sb an ~ of doing sthg** OR **the ~ to do sthg** donner à qqn l'occasion de faire qqch; **I took every ~ of travelling** je n'ai manqué aucune occasion de OR j'ai saisi toutes les occasions de voyager; **you missed a golden ~** vous avez manqué OR laissé passer une occasion en or; **I'll leave at the first** OR **earliest ~** je partirai à la première occasion OR dès que l'occasion se présentera; **at every ~** à la moindre occasion. -**2.** [prospect] perspective *f*; **the opportunities for advancement are excellent** les perspectives d'avancement sont excellentes; **job opportunities** perspectives d'emploi.

opportunity cost *n* ECON coût *m* d'opportunité OR de renoncement.

opposable [əˈpəʊzəbl] *adj* opposable.

oppose [əˈpəʊz] *vt* -**1.** [decision, plan, bill etc] s'opposer à, être hostile à; [verbally] parler contre; **the family ~d their marriage** la famille s'opposa à leur mariage; **the construction of the power station was ~d by local people** la construction de la centrale s'est heurtée à l'hostilité de la population locale; **40% of voters are strongly ~d to the plan** 40 % des votants sont farouchement opposés au projet. -**2.** [in contest, fight] s'opposer à; [combat] combattre. -**3.** [contrast] opposer; **the social sciences are often ~d to pure science** on oppose souvent les sciences humaines aux sciences pures.

opposed [əˈpəʊzd] *adj* opposé, hostile; **to be ~ to sthg** être opposé OR hostile à qqch; **she is very much ~ to the idea** c'est une idée à laquelle elle est totalement opposée; **his views are diametrically ~ to mine** il a des idées radicalement opposées aux miennes.
◆ **as opposed to** *prep phr* par opposition à, plutôt que; **we will propose more science as ~ to arts courses** nous proposons de renforcer l'enseignement des sciences plutôt que celui des matières littéraires.

opposing [əˈpəʊzɪŋ] *adj* -**1.** [army] adverse; [factions] qui s'opposent; [party, minority] d'opposition; **the ~ team** l'équipe *f* adverse; **they're on ~ sides** ils sont adversaires, ils ne sont pas du même côté. -**2.** [contrasting - views] opposé, qui s'oppose.

opposite [ˈɒpəzɪt] ◇ *adj* -**1.** [facing] d'en face, opposé; **the ~ side of the road** l'autre côté de la rue; **'see illustration on ~ page'** 'voir illustration ci-contre'. -**2.** [opposing - direction, position] inverse, opposé; [rival - team] adverse; **the letter-box is at the ~ end of the street** la boîte à lettres se trouve à l'autre bout de la rue. -**3.** [conflicting - attitude, character, opinion] contraire, opposé; **I take the ~ view** je suis de l'avis contraire; **his words had just the ~ effect** ses paroles eurent exactement l'effet contraire. -**4.** BOT opposé. -**5.** MATH opposé.
◇ *adv* en face; **the houses ~** les maisons d'en face; **they live just ~** ils habitent juste en face; **the lady ~** la dame qui habite en face.
◇ *prep* -**1.** en face de; **he lives ~ us** il habite en face de chez nous; **our houses are ~ each other** nos maisons se font face OR sont en face l'une de l'autre; **they sat ~ each other** ils étaient assis l'un en face de l'autre; **we have a park ~ our house** nous avons un parc en face de chez nous; **the church is right ~ the school** l'église se trouve juste en face de l'école; **put a tick ~ the correct answer** mettre une croix en face de la bonne réponse, cocher la bonne réponse. -**2.** CIN & THEAT: **to play ~ sb** donner la réplique à qqn; **she played ~ Richard Burton in many films** elle fut la partenaire de Richard Burton dans de nombreux films. -**3.** NAUT en face de, à la hauteur de; **the ship was lying ~ Tobruk** le navire se trouvait à la hauteur de Tobrouk.
◇ *n* opposé *m*, contraire *m*; **I understood quite the ~** j'ai compris exactement le contraire; **she always does the ~ of what she's told** elle fait toujours le contraire de ce qu'on lui dit de faire; **Mary is the complete ~ of her sister** Mary est tout à fait l'opposé de sa sœur; **what's the ~ of "optimistic"?** quel est le contraire d'«optimiste»?

opposite number *n* homologue *mf*.

opposite sex *n* sexe *m* opposé; **a person** OR **member of the ~** une personne du sexe opposé.

opposition [ˌɒpəˈzɪʃn] ◇ *n* -**1.** [physical] opposition *f*, résistance *f*; **the army met with fierce ~** l'armée se heurta à une vive résistance; **the besieged city put up little ~** la ville assiégée n'opposa guère de résistance ‖ [moral] opposition *f*; **we found ourselves in ~ to everybody else** nous nous sommes retrouvés en opposition avec tout le monde; **the plans met with some ~** les projets suscitèrent une certaine opposition OR hostilité. -**2.** POL: **the ~** l'opposition *f*; **Labour spent the 1980s in ~** les travaillistes furent dans l'opposition pendant toutes les années 80; **the Opposition was** OR **were unable to decide** l'opposition fut incapable de prendre une décision ❑ **the leader of the Opposition** le chef de l'opposition; **the Opposition benches** les bancs *mpl* de l'opposition. -**3.** [rivals] adversaires *mpl*; SPORT adversaires *mpl*; COMM concurrents *mpl*, concurrence *f*; **don't underestimate the ~** SPORT ne sous-estimez pas vos adversaires; COMM ne sous-estimez pas vos concurrents OR la concurrence. -**4.** [contrast] (mise *f* en) opposition *f*.
◇ *comp* [committee, spokesperson etc] de l'opposition.

oppress [əˈpres] *vt* -**1.** [tyrannize] opprimer. -**2.** *lit* [torment - subj: anxiety, atmosphere] accabler, oppresser.

oppressed [əˈprest] *npl*: **the ~** les opprimés *mpl*.

oppression [əˈpreʃn] *n* -**1.** [persecution] oppression *f*; **the ~ of women** l'oppression des femmes. -**2.** [sadness] angoisse *f*, malaise *m*.

oppressive [əˈpresɪv] *adj* -**1.** POL [regime, government] oppressif, tyrannique; [law, tax] oppressif. -**2.** [hard to bear - debt, situation] accablant. -**3.** [weather] lourd, étouffant; **the heat was ~** il faisait une chaleur accablante.

oppressively [əˈpresɪvlɪ] *adv* d'une manière oppressante OR accablante; **it was ~ hot** il faisait une chaleur étouffante OR accablante.

oppressor [əˈpresəʳ] *n* oppresseur *m*.

opprobrious [əˈprəʊbrɪəs] *adj fml* -**1.** [scornful] méprisant. -**2.** [shameful] honteux, scandaleux.

opprobrium [əˈprəʊbrɪəm] *n fml* opprobre *m*.

opt [ɒpt] *vi*: **to ~ for sthg** opter pour qqch, choisir qqch; **she ~ed to study maths** elle a choisi d'étudier les maths.
◆ **opt out** *vi insep* -**1.** [gen] se désengager, retirer sa participation; **to ~ out of society** rejeter la société; **I'm ~ing out!** ne comptez plus sur moi!, je me retire de la partie!; **many ~ed out of joining the union** beaucoup ont choisi de ne pas adhérer au syndicat; **you can't just ~ out of paying bills** il faudra bien que vous payiez vos factures un jour ou l'autre. -**2.** POL [school, hospital] *choisir l'autonomie vis-à-vis des pouvoirs publics*.

optative [ˈɒptətɪv] ◇ *adj* optatif.
◇ *n* optatif *m*.

optic [ˈɒptɪk] *adj* optique; **~ nerve** nerf *m* optique.

optical [ˈɒptɪkl] *adj* [lens] optique; [instrument] optique; **~ art** art *m* optique; **~ glass** verre *m* optique.

optical character reader *n* lecteur *m* optique de caractères.

optical character recognition *n* reconnaissance *f* optique de caractères.

optical fibre *n* fibre *f* optique.

optical illusion *n* illusion *f* OR effet *m* d'optique.

optician [ɒpˈtɪʃn] *n* opticien *m*, -enne *f*; **at the ~'s** chez l'opticien.

optics [ˈɒptɪks] *n (U)* optique *f*.

optimal [ˈɒptɪml] *adj* optimal.

optimally [ˈɒptɪməlɪ] *adv* de façon optimale.

optimism [ˈɒptɪmɪzm] *n* optimisme *m*.

optimist [ˈɒptɪmɪst] *n* optimiste *mf*.

optimistic [ˌɒptɪˈmɪstɪk] *adj* [person, outlook] optimiste; [period] d'optimisme.

optimistically [ˌɒptɪˈmɪstɪklɪ] *adv* avec optimisme, d'une manière optimiste.

optimize, **-ise** [ˈɒptɪmaɪz] *vt* optimiser, optimaliser.

optimum [ˈɒptɪməm] (*pl* **optimums** OR *fml* **optima** [-mə]) ◇ *adj* optimum, optimal.
◇ *n* optimum *m*.

option [ˈɒpʃn] *n* -**1.** [alternative] choix *m*; **he has no ~** il n'a pas le choix; **I have no ~ but to refuse** je ne peux faire autrement que de refuser; **they were given the ~ of adopting a child** on leur a proposé d'adopter un enfant; **you leave me no ~** vous ne me laissez pas le choix; **she was given the ~ of bail** elle a pu être libérée sous caution ❑ **to take the soft ~**

choisir la solution de facilité. -**2.** [possible choice] option *f*, possibilité *f*; I prefer to keep OR leave my ~s open je préfère ne pas prendre de décision OR ne pas m'engager pour l'instant || SCH (matière *f* à) option *f*; she has to choose between three foreign language ~s elle doit choisir une option parmi trois langues étrangères; economics is an ~ in the third year en troisième année, l'économie politique est une option || [accessory] option *f*; power steering is an ~ la direction assistée est en option. -**3.** COMM & FIN option *f*; to take an ~ on sthg prendre une option sur qqch; the agency allowed her to take out an ~ on the house until Monday l'agence lui a laissé une option sur la maison jusqu'à lundi; to take up an ~ lever une option; Air France have an ~ to buy 15 planes Air France a une option d'achat sur 15 appareils.

optional ['ɒpʃənl] *adj* -**1.** facultatif; the tinted lenses are ~ les verres teintés sont en option ❑ ~ extra option *f*; the radio is an ~ extra la radio est en option OR en supplément. -**2.** SCH facultatif, optionnel; German is an ~ subject l'allemand est une matière optionnelle; linguistics is ~ la linguistique est facultative.

optionally ['ɒpʃənəlɪ] *adv* facultativement.

optoelectronics [,ɒptəʊɪlek'trɒnɪks] *n (U)* optoélectronique *f*.

optometrist [ɒp'tɒmətrɪst] *n* optométriste *mf*, réfractionniste *mf*.

optometry [ɒp'tɒmətrɪ] *n* optométrie *f*.

opulence ['ɒpjʊləns] *n* opulence *f*.

opulent ['ɒpjʊlənt] *adj* [lifestyle, figure] opulent; [abundant] abondant, luxuriant; [house, clothes] somptueux.

opus ['əʊpəs] (*pl* opuses OR *fml* opera ['ɒpərə]) *n* opus *m*.

or [ɔːʳ] *conj* -**1.** [in positive statements] ou; [in negative statements] ni; in New York or in London à New York ou à Londres; I can go today or tomorrow je peux y aller aujourd'hui ou demain; have you got any brothers or sisters? avez-vous des frères et sœurs?; he never laughs or smiles il ne rit ni ne sourit jamais; I go two or three times a week j'y vais deux ou trois fois par semaine; Norma Jean Baker, or Marilyn Monroe as she became known Norma Jean Baker ou Marilyn Monroe, puisque c'est le nom sous lequel elle est devenue célèbre; or so I thought du moins c'est ce que je pensais;...or not, as the case may be ...ou non, peut-être. -**2.** [otherwise - in negative statements] ou; [- in positive statements] sinon; don't hit it too hard or it'll break ne tape pas trop fort dessus ou ça va casser; she must have some talent or they wouldn't have chosen her elle doit avoir un certain talent sinon ils ne l'auraient pas choisie.

◆ **or else** ◇ *conj phr* -**1.** [otherwise] sinon; I'd better rush, or else I'll be late je ferais mieux de me dépêcher, sinon je serai en retard. -**2.** [offering an alternative] ou bien; Monday, or else Tuesday lundi, ou bien mardi.
◇ *adv phr inf*: give us the money, or else...! donne-nous l'argent, sinon...!

◆ **or no** *conj phr* ou pas; I'm taking a holiday, work or no work travail ou pas, je prends des vacances.

◆ **or other** *adv phr*: we stayed at San something or other on s'est arrêté à San quelque chose; somehow or other we made it home on a fini par réussir à rentrer, Dieu sait comment; somebody or other said that... quelqu'un, je ne sais plus qui, a dit que...; one or other of us will have to go il faudra bien que l'un de nous s'en aille; some actress or other une actrice (quelconque).

◆ **or so** *adv phr* environ; ten minutes or so environ dix minutes; fifty kilos or so cinquante kilos environ, dans les cinquante kilos; ten dollars or so dix dollars environ, à peu près dix dollars.

◆ **or something** *inf adv phr* ou quelque chose comme ça; she's a lawyer or something elle est avocate ou quelque chose comme ça; are you deaf or something? t'es sourd ou quoi?

◆ **or what** *inf adv phr* ou quoi; are you stupid or what? t'es bête ou quoi?

OR *written abbr of* Oregon.

oracle ['ɒrəkl] *n* oracle *m*.

◆ **Oracle®** *pr n système de télétexte en Grande-Bretagne*.

oracular [ɒ'rækjʊləʳ] *adj literal* prophétique; *fig* sibyllin.

oral ['ɔːrəl] ◇ *adj* -**1.** [spoken] oral; ~ exam (examen *m*) oral *m*; ~ literature/tradition littérature *f*/tradition *f* orale. -**2.** ANAT [of mouth] buccal, oral; ~ sex rapports *mpl* bucco-génitaux; the ~ stage PSYCH le stade oral || PHARM [medicine] à prendre par voie orale; ~ contraceptive contraceptif *m* oral. -**3.** LING [in phonetics] oral.
◇ *n* (examen *m*) oral *m*.

orally ['ɔːrəlɪ] *adj* -**1.** [verbally] oralement, verbalement, de vive voix. -**2.** SCH oralement; MED par voie orale; 'to be taken ~' à administrer par voie orale; 'not to be taken ~' 'ne pas avaler'.

Oran [ə'ræn] *pr n* Oran.

orange ['ɒrɪndʒ] ◇ *n* -**1.** [fruit] orange *f*. -**2.** [drink] boisson *f* à l'orange; vodka and ~ vodka-orange *f*. -**3.** [colour] orange *m*.
◇ *adj* -**1.** [colour] orange *(inv)*, orangé. -**2.** [taste] d'orange; [liqueur, sauce] à l'orange; ~ grove orangeraie *f*; ~ juice jus *m* d'orange; ~ marmalade marmelade *f* d'orange, confiture *f* d'orange OR d'oranges; ~ blossom fleur *f* OR fleurs *fpl* d'oranger; ~ peel écorce *f* OR peau *f* d'orange; *fig* [cellulite] peau *f* d'orange; ~ tree oranger *m*.

orangeade [,ɒrɪndʒ'eɪd] *n* [still] orangeade *f*; [fizzy] soda *m* à l'orange.

orange-flower water *n* eau *f* de fleur d'oranger.

Orange Free State *pr n* l'État *m* libre d'Orange; in ~ dans l'État libre d'Orange.

Orangeism ['ɒrɪndʒɪzm] *n* POL orangisme *m*.

Orange Lodge *n* association *f* d'orangistes.

Orangeman ['ɒrɪndʒmən] (*pl* Orangemen [-mən]) *n* -**1.** *Br* HIST Orangiste *m (partisan de la maison d'Orange)*. -**2.** [in Ireland] Orangiste *m (Protestant)*.

Orangeman's Day *n* fête annuelle des orangistes *(le 12 juillet)*.

orange pekoe *n* pekoe *m* orange.

orangery ['ɒrɪndʒərɪ] (*pl* orangeries) *n* orangerie *f*.

orange stick *n* bâtonnet *m* (de) manucure.

Orangewoman ['ɒrɪndʒwʊmən] (*pl* Orangewomen [-,wɪmɪn]) *n* orangiste *f*.

orangewood ['ɒrɪndʒwʊd] *n* (bois *m* d') oranger *m*.

orangey ['ɒrɪndʒɪ] *adj* -**1.** [taste] qui a un goût d'orange; [perfume] qui sent l'orange. -**2.** [colour] orangé.

orang(o)utan [ɔː,ræŋuː'tæn], **orang(o)utang** [ɔː,ræŋuː'tæŋ] *n* orang-outan *m*, orang-outang *m*.

orangy ['ɒrɪndʒɪ] = **orangey**.

orate [ɔː'reɪt] *vi fml* [make speech] prononcer un discours; [pompously] pérorer, discourir.

oration [ɔː'reɪʃn] *n* (long) discours *m*, allocution *f*; funeral ~ oraison *f* funèbre.

orator ['ɒrətəʳ] *n* orateur *m*, -trice *f*.

oratorical [,ɒrə'tɒrɪkl] *adj fml* oratoire.

oratorio [,ɒrə'tɔːrɪəʊ] (*pl* oratorios) *n* oratorio *m*.

oratory ['ɒrətrɪ] *n* -**1.** [eloquence] art *m* oratoire, éloquence *f*; a superb piece of ~ un superbe morceau de rhétorique. -**2.** RELIG oratoire *m*.

orb [ɔːb] *n* -**1.** [sphere] globe *m*. -**2.** ASTRON & *lit* orbe *m*.

orbit ['ɔːbɪt] ◇ *n* -**1.** ASTRON orbite *f*; to put a satellite into ~ mettre un satellite sur OR en orbite; in ~ en orbite. -**2.** [influence] orbite *f*; the countries within Washington's ~ les pays qui se situent dans la sphère d'influence de Washington. -**3.** ANAT & PHYS [of eye, electron] orbite *f*.
◇ *vt* [subj: planet, comet] graviter OR tourner autour de; [subj: astronaut]: the first man to ~ the Earth le premier homme à être placé OR mis en orbite autour de la Terre.
◇ *vi* décrire une orbite.

orbital ['ɔːbɪtl] *adj* orbital; ~ velocity vélocité orbitale; ~ motorway *Br* (autoroute *f*) périphérique *m*.

Orcadian [ɔː'keɪdjən] ◇ *adj* des Orcades.
◇ *n* habitant *m*, -e *f* des Orcades.

orchard ['ɔːtʃəd] *n* verger *m*.

orchestra ['ɔːkɪstrə] *n* -**1.** [band] orchestre *m*. -**2.** [in theatre, cinema] fauteuils *mpl* d'orchestre, parterre *m*.

orchestral [ɔː'kestrəl] *adj* d'orchestre, orchestral; ~ music musique *f* orchestrale.

orchestra pit *n* fosse *f* d'orchestre.

orchestra stalls *npl Am* = **orchestra 2**.

orchestrate ['ɔːkɪstreɪt] *vt* MUS & *fig* orchestrer; a superbly ~d advertising campaign une campagne publicitaire remarquablement orchestrée.

orchestration [,ɔːke'streɪʃn] *n* MUS & *fig* orchestration *f*.

orchid ['ɔːkɪd] *n* orchidée *f*.

orchis ['ɔːkɪs] *n* orchis *m*.

orchitis [ɔː'kaɪtɪs] *n* orchite *f*.

ordain [ɔː'deɪn] *vt* -**1.** RELIG ordonner; to be ~ed priest être ordonné prêtre. -**2.** [order] ordonner, décréter; the judge ~ed that the prisoner should be released le juge ordonna que le prisonnier soit relâché || [declare] décréter, déclarer; it is ~ed in the Bible c'est la Bible qui le dit || [decide] dicter, décider; fate ~ed that they should meet le destin a voulu qu'ils se rencontrent.

ordainment [ɔː'deɪnmənt] *n* ordination *f*.

ordeal [ɔː'diːl] *n* -**1.** épreuve *f*, calvaire *m*; to undergo an ~ subir une épreuve; she has been through some terrible ~s elle a traversé des moments très difficiles; it was quite an ~ for him ce fut une épreuve assez pénible pour lui; I always find family reunions an ~ j'ai toujours considéré les réunions de famille comme un (véritable) calvaire. -**2.** HIST ordalie *f*, épreuve *f* judiciaire; ~ by fire épreuve *f* du feu.

order ['ɔːdəʳ] ◇ *n* -**1.** [sequence, arrangement] ordre *m*; in alphabetical/chronological ~ par ordre alphabétique/chronologique; in ascending ~ of importance par ordre croissant d'importance; can you put the figures in the right ~? pouvez-vous classer les chiffres dans le bon ordre?; let's do things in ~ faisons les choses en ordre; what was the ~ of events? dans quel ordre les événements se sont-ils déroulés?; they have two boys and a girl, in that ~ ils ont deux garçons et une fille, dans cet ordre; in ~ of appearance THEAT par ordre d'entrée en scène CIN & TV par ordre d'apparition à l'écran; we were called to the platform, in ~ of precedence on était appelés à la tribune par ordre de préséance ❑ battle ~ ordre de bataille. -**2.** [organization, tidiness] ordre *m*; to put one's affairs/books in ~ mettre de l'ordre dans ses affaires/livres, ranger ses affaires/livres; the magazines are all out of ~ les magazines sont tous dérangés; to get one's ideas in ~ mettre de l'ordre dans ses idées; she needs to get some ~ into her life elle a besoin de mettre un peu d'ordre dans sa vie ❑ you should put your own house in ~ before criticizing other people il faut mettre de l'ordre dans ses propres affaires avant de critiquer les autres. -**3.** [command] ordre *m*; [instruction] instruction *f*; to give sb ~s to do sthg ordonner à qqn de faire qqch; the Queen gave the ~ for the prisoner to be executed la reine ordonna que le prisonnier soit exécuté; Harry loves giving ~s Harry adore donner des ordres; we have ~s to wait here on a reçu l'ordre d'attendre ici; I'm just following ~s je ne fais qu'exécuter les ordres; and that's an ~! et c'est un ordre!; I don't have

to take ~s from you je n'ai pas d'ordres à recevoir de vous; ~s are ~s les ordres sont les ordres; on my ~, line up in twos à mon commandement, mettez-vous en rangs par deux; on doctor's ~s sur ordre du médecin; to be under sb's ~s être sous les ordres de qqn; I am under ~s to say nothing j'ai reçu l'ordre de ne rien dire; until further ~s jusqu'à nouvel ordre ‖ MIL ordre *m*, consigne *f*; to give the ~ to open fire donner l'ordre d'ouvrir le feu. -**4.** COMM [request for goods] commande *f*; to place an ~ for sthg passer (une) commande de qqch; the books are on ~ les livres ont été commandés ‖ [goods ordered] marchandises *fpl* commandées; your ~ has now arrived votre commande est arrivée ‖ [in restaurant]: can I take your ~? avez-vous choisi? ‖ *Am* [portion] part *f*; an ~ of French fries une portion de frites. -**5.** FIN: (money) ~ mandat *m*; pay to the ~ of A. Jones payez à l'ordre de A. Jones; pay A. Jones or ~ payer à A. Jones ou à son ordre; cheque to ~ chèque *m* à ordre. -**6.** JUR ordonnance *f*, arrêté *m*; he was served with an ~ for the seizure of his property il a reçu une ordonnance pour la saisie de ses biens. -**7.** [discipline, rule] ordre *m*, discipline *f*; to keep ~ [police] maintenir l'ordre; SCH maintenir la discipline; children need to be kept in ~ les enfants ont besoin de discipline; to restore ~ rétablir l'ordre ‖ [in meeting, assembly] ordre *m*; to call sb to ~ rappeler qqn à l'ordre; to be ruled out of ~ être en infraction avec le règlement; he's out of ~ *fig* ce qu'il a dit était déplacé; ~! de l'ordre! -**8.** [system] ordre *m* établi; the old ~ l'ordre ancien; in the ~ of things dans l'ordre des choses ❑ to be the ~ of the day [common] être à l'ordre du jour; [fashionable] être au goût du jour. -**9.** [functioning state]: in working ~ en état de marche OR de fonctionnement; in good/perfect ~ en bon/parfait état. -**10.** [class] classe *f*, ordre *m*; the lower ~s les ordres inférieurs ‖ [rank] ordre *m*; research work of the highest ~ un travail de recherche de tout premier ordre; a crook of the first ~ *Br* un escroc de grande envergure ‖ [kind] espèce *f*, genre *m*; questions of a different ~ des questions d'un autre ordre. -**11.** [decoration] ordre *m*; the Order of the Garter/of Merit l'ordre de la Jarretière/du Mérite. -**12.** RELIG ordre *m*; to take (holy) ~s entrer dans les ordres; the Order of St Benedict l'ordre de saint Benoît. -**13.** ARCHIT, BOT & ZOOL ordre *m*.
◇ *vt* -**1.** [command] ordonner; to ~ sb to do sthg ordonner à qqn de faire qqch; the Queen ~ed that the prisoner (should) be executed la reine donna l'ordre d'exécuter le prisonnier; the doctor ~ed him to rest for three days le médecin lui a prescrit trois jours de repos; the government ~ed an inquiry into the disaster le gouvernement a ordonné l'ouverture d'une enquête sur la catastrophe; he was ~ed to pay costs JUR il a été condamné aux dépens; the minister ~ed the drug to be banned le ministre a ordonné de faire retirer le médicament de la vente; to ~ sb back/in/out donner à qqn l'ordre de reculer/d'entrer/de sortir; we were ~ed out of the room on nous a ordonné de quitter la pièce; she ~ed the children to bed elle a ordonné aux enfants d'aller se coucher ‖ MIL: to ~ sb to do sthg donner l'ordre à qqn de faire qqch; they were ~ed (to return) home on leur donna OR ils reçurent l'ordre de regagner leurs foyers; the troops were ~ed to the Mediterranean les troupes ont reçu l'ordre de gagner la Méditerranée ❑ it's just what the doctor ~ed! *hum* c'est exactement ce dont nous avions besoin! -**2.** COMM [meal, goods] commander; he ~ed himself a beer il a commandé une bière. -**3.** [organize - society] organiser; [- ideas, thoughts] mettre de l'ordre dans; [- affairs] régler, mettre en ordre; a peaceful, well-~ed existence une existence paisible et bien réglée. -**4.** BOT & ZOOL classer.
◇ *vi* commander, passer une commande; would you like to ~ now? [in restaurant] voulez-vous commander maintenant?

◆ **by order of** *prep phr* par ordre de; by ~ of the Court sur décision du tribunal.
◆ **in order** *adj phr* -**1.** [valid] en règle. -**2.** [acceptable] approprié, admissible; it is quite in ~ for you to leave rien ne s'oppose à ce que vous partiez; I think lunch is in ~ je pense qu'il est temps de faire une pause pour le déjeuner; an apology is in ~ des excuses s'imposent.
◆ **in order that** *conj phr* afin que; in ~ that no one goes home empty-handed afin que nul ne rentre chez soi les mains vides.
◆ **in order to** *conj phr* afin de; in ~ to simplify things afin de simplifier les choses; in ~ not to upset you pour éviter de vous faire de la peine.
◆ **in the order of** *Br*, **of the order of** *Br*, **on the order of** *Am prep phr* de l'ordre de; a sum in *Br* OR of *Br* OR on *Am* the ~ of £500 une somme de l'ordre de 500 livres.
◆ **out of order** *adj phr* [machine, TV] en panne; [phone] en dérangement; 'out of ~' 'hors service', 'en panne'.
◆ **to order** *adv phr* sur commande; she's one of these people who can cry to ~ *Br* elle fait partie de ces gens qui arrivent à pleurer sur commande; to be made to ~ *literal* & *fig* être fait sur commande; he had a suit made to ~ il s'est fait faire un costume sur mesures.
◆ **order about** *Br*, **order around** *vt sep* commander; he likes ~ing people about il adore régenter son monde; I refuse to be ~ed about! je n'ai pas d'ordres à recevoir!

order book *n* carnet *m* de commandes; our ~s are empty/full nos carnets de commandes sont vides/pleins.
order form *n* bon *m* de commande.
orderliness ['ɔːdəlɪnɪs] *n* -**1.** [of room, desk] (bon) ordre *m*. -**2.** [of person, lifestyle, behaviour] méticulosité *f*. -**3.** [of crowd] discipline *f*, bonne conduite *f*.
orderly ['ɔːdəlɪ] (*pl* orderlies) ◇ *adj* -**1.** [tidy - room] ordonné, rangé; a very ~ kitchen une cuisine très bien rangée. -**2.** [organized - person, mind, lifestyle] ordonné, méthodique; try to work in an ~ way essayez de travailler méthodiquement. -**3.** [well-behaved] ordonné, discipliné; an ~ crowd une foule disciplinée; in case of fire, leave the building in an ~ fashion en cas d'incendie, quitter les lieux sans précipitation.
◇ *n* -**1.** MIL officier *m* d'ordonnance. -**2.** MED aide-infirmier *m*.
orderly officer *n* officier *m* de jour.
order paper *n* POL (feuille *f* de l') ordre *m* du jour.
ordinal ['ɔːdɪnl] ◇ *adj* ordinal; ~ number nombre *m* ordinal.
◇ *n* ordinal *m*.
ordinance ['ɔːdɪnəns] *n* ordonnance *f*, décret *m*.
ordinand ['ɔːdɪnænd] *n* ordinand *m*.
ordinarily ['ɔːdənrəlɪ, *Am* ,ɔːrdn'erəlɪ] *adv* -**1.** [in an ordinary way] ordinairement, d'ordinaire; the questions were more than ~ difficult les questions étaient plus difficiles que d'ordinaire OR qu'à l'accoutumée. -**2.** [normally] normalement, en temps normal; isn't she due at 5 o'clock? — well, ~, she would be ne doit-elle pas être là OR arriver à 5 h? — oui, normalement.
ordinary ['ɔːdənrɪ] ◇ *adj* -**1.** [usual] ordinaire, habituel; [normal] normal; the ~ run of things le cours ordinaire OR normal des événements; she remembered it as just an ~ day elle s'en souvenait comme d'un jour ordinaire. -**2.** [average] ordinaire, moyen; Paul was just an ~ guy before he got involved in films *inf* Paul était un type comme les autres avant de faire du cinéma; Miss Brodie was no ~ teacher Miss Brodie était un professeur peu banal OR qui sortait de l'ordinaire. -**3.** [commonplace] ordinaire, quelconque *pej*; they're very ~ people ce sont des gens très ordinaires; it's a very ~-looking car c'est une voiture qui n'a rien de spécial; she's a very ~-looking girl c'est une fille quelconque.
◇ *n* -**1.** RELIG: the Ordinary of the mass l'ordinaire *m* de la messe. -**2.** ADMIN: physician in ~ to the king *Br* médecin *m* (attitré) du roi.
◆ **out of the ordinary** *adj phr*: as a pianist, she's really out of the ~ c'est vraiment une pianiste exceptionnelle OR hors du commun; nothing out of the ~ ever happens here il ne se passe jamais rien de bien extraordinaire ici.
ordinary degree *n Br* ≃ licence *f* sans mention OR avec la mention passable.
Ordinary level → **O level**.
ordinary seaman *n Br* matelot *m* breveté.
ordinary share *n* action *f* ordinaire.
ordinate ['ɔːdənət] *n* ordonnée *f*.
ordination [,ɔːdɪ'neɪʃn] *n* ordination *f*.
ordnance ['ɔːdnəns] *n* -**1.** [supplies] (service *m* de l') équipement *m* militaire. -**2.** [artillery] artillerie *f*.
ordnance corps *n* service *m* du matériel, ≃ train *m*.
ordnance factory *n* usine *f* d'artillerie.
Ordnance Survey *pr n Br* service *m* national de cartographie, ≃ IGN *m*; ~ map carte *f* d'état-major.
ordure ['ɔːdjʊəʳ] *n lit* excrément *m*.
ore [ɔːʳ] *n* minerai *m*; iron ~ minerai de fer.
oregano [,ɒrɪ'gɑːnəʊ] *n* BOT & CULIN origan *m*.
Oregon ['ɒrɪgən] *pr n* Oregon *m*; in ~ dans l'Oregon.
Oreo ['ɔːrɪəʊ] *n Am* -**1.** ~ (cookie)® *biscuit au chocolat fourré à la crème*. -**2.** ▼ *terme injurieux désignant un Noir qui fréquente les Blancs*.
Oresteia [,ɒre'staɪə] *pr n*: 'The ~' *Aeschylus* 'l'Orestie'.
Orestes [ɒ'restiːz] *pr n* Oreste.
orfe [ɔːf] (*pl inv*) *n* ide *m*, mélanote *m*; golden ~ ide rouge, orfe *m*.
organ ['ɔːgən] *n* -**1.** MUS orgue *m*; [large] (grandes) orgues *fpl*. -**2.** ANAT organe *m*; *euph* [penis] membre *m*; the ~s of speech les organes phonatoires OR de la parole. -**3.** *fig* [means] organe *m*, instrument *m*; the courts are the ~s of justice les tribunaux sont les organes OR les instruments de la justice ‖ [mouthpiece] organe *m*, porte-parole *m inv*; the official ~ of the Party le porte-parole officiel du Parti.
organdie *Br*, **organdy** *Am* ['ɔːgəndɪ] (*pl* organdies) ◇ *n* organdi *m*.
◇ *comp* d'organdi, en organdi.
organ grinder *n* joueur *m*, -euse *f* d'orgue de Barbarie.
organic [ɔː'gænɪk] *adj* -**1.** BIOL & CHEM organique; ~ life vie *f* organique; ~ disease maladie *f* organique. -**2.** [natural - produce] naturel, biologique. -**3.** [structural] organique; [fundamental] organique, fondamental; ~ change changement organique.
organically [ɔː'gænɪklɪ] *adv* -**1.** BIOL & CHEM organiquement; ~ grown cultivé sans engrais chimiques, biologique. -**2.** *fig* organiquement; the two ideas are ~ linked les deux idées sont organiquement liées.
organic chemistry *n* chimie *f* organique.
organic farming *n* culture *f* biologique.
organicism [ɔː'gænɪsɪzm] *n* organicisme *m*.
organism ['ɔːgənɪzm] *n* organisme *m* BIOL.
organist ['ɔːgənɪst] *n* organiste *mf*.
organization [,ɔːgənaɪ'zeɪʃn] *n* -**1.** [organizing] organisation *f*; to have a flair for ~ avoir le sens de l'organisation; we are unhappy with the ~ of the company l'organisation de la firme ne nous satisfait pas ❑ ~ and method INDUST organisation *f* scientifique du travail, OST *f*. -**2.** [association] organisation *f*, association *f*; a political ~ une organisation politique ‖ [official body] organisme *m*, organisation *f*; a charitable ~ une œuvre de bienfaisance. -**3.** ADMIN [personnel] cadres *mpl*.
organizational [,ɔːgənaɪ'zeɪʃnl] *adj* [skills, methods] organisationnel, d'organisation; [expenses] d'organisation; [change] dans l'organisation, structurel; the concert turned out to be

an ~ nightmare l'organisation du concert fut un véritable cauchemar.

organization chart *n* organigramme *m*.

organization man *n employé ou cadre qui se dévoue entièrement à la société pour laquelle il travaille*.

organize, -ise ['ɔːgənaɪz] ◇ *vt* -**1.** [sort out] organiser; to get ~d s'organiser; he doesn't know how to ~ himself il ne sait pas s'organiser; to ~ one's thoughts mettre de l'ordre dans ses idées; her colleagues ~d a farewell dinner for her ses collègues ont organisé un dîner d'adieu en son honneur; I've ~d a visit to a dairy for them j'ai organisé la visite d'une laiterie à leur intention; she's good at organizing people elle a le sens du commandement; who's organizing the drinks? qui est-ce qui s'occupe des boissons? -**2.** INDUST syndiquer.
◇ *vi* INDUST se syndiquer.

organized ['ɔːgənaɪzd] *adj* -**1.** organisé; we went on an ~ tour of Scottish castles nous avons visité les châteaux écossais en voyage organisé. -**2.** [unionized] syndiqué; ~ labour main-d'œuvre *f* syndiquée. -**3.** [orderly] organisé; [methodical] méthodique.

organized crime *n* le crime organisé, le grand banditisme.

organizer ['ɔːgənaɪzəʳ] *n* -**1.** [person] organisateur *m*, -trice *f*. -**2.** [diary] agenda *m*, Filofax® *m*. -**3.** BIOL organisateur *m*.

organ loft *n* tribune *f* d'orgue.

organogenesis [,ɔːgənəʊ'dʒenɪsɪs] *n* organogenèse *f*.

organoleptic [,ɔːgənəʊ'leptɪk] *adj* organoleptique.

organotherapy [,ɔːgənəʊ'θerəpɪ] *n* opothérapie *f*.

organ pipe *n* tuyau *m* d'orgue.

organ stop *n* jeu *m* d'orgue.

organza [ɔː'gænzə] *n* organza *m*.

orgasm ['ɔːgæzm] *n* orgasme *m*.

orgasmic [ɔː'gæzmɪk] *adj* orgasmique, orgastique.

orgiastic [,ɔːdʒɪ'æstɪk] *adj* orgiaque.

orgy ['ɔːdʒɪ] (*pl* **orgies**) *n* orgie *f*; a drunken ~ une beuverie; an ~ of killing *fig* une orgie de meurtres.

oriel ['ɔːrɪəl] *n* oriel *m*.

orient ['ɔːrɪənt] *vt* orienter; to ~ o.s. s'orienter; our firm is very much ~ed towards the American market notre société est très orientée vers le marché américain.

Orient ['ɔːrɪənt] *pr n*: the ~ l'Orient *m*.

oriental [,ɔːrɪ'entl] *adj* oriental; ~ rug tapis *m* d'Orient.
◆ **Oriental** *n* Asiatique *mf (attention: le substantif «Oriental» est considéré comme raciste)*.

orientalist [,ɔːrɪ'entəlɪst] *n* orientaliste *mf*.

orientate ['ɔːrɪenteɪt] *vt Br* orienter; to ~ o.s. s'orienter; the course is very much ~d towards the sciences le cours est très orienté vers OR axé sur les sciences.

-orientated ['ɔːrɪenteɪtɪd] *Br* = **-oriented**.

orientation [,ɔːrɪen'teɪʃn] *n* orientation *f*; James is in charge of student ~ James est responsable de l'orientation des étudiants; she's found a new ~ in life elle a trouvé une orientation nouvelle à sa vie.

oriented ['ɔːrɪentɪd] *adj* orienté.

-oriented *in cpds* orienté vers..., axé sur...; ours is a money~ society c'est l'argent qui mène notre société; she's very work~ elle est très axée sur son travail; pupil~ teaching enseignement adapté aux besoins des élèves.

orienteer [,ɔːrɪen'tɪəʳ] *n* orienteur *m*, -euse *f*.

orienteering [,ɔːrɪen'tɪərɪŋ] *n* exercice *m* d'orientation.

orifice ['ɒrɪfɪs] *n* orifice *m*.

origami [,ɒrɪ'gɑːmɪ] *n* origami *m*.

origin ['ɒrɪdʒɪn] *n* -**1.** [source] origine *f*; the ~ of the Nile la source du Nil; what's the ~ of that word? quelle est l'origine de ce mot?; country of ~ pays *m* d'origine; of unknown ~ d'origine inconnue; this wine is of Austrian ~ ce vin est d'origine autrichienne; the present troubles have their ~ in the proposed land reform le projet de réforme agraire est à l'origine des troubles actuels; the song is Celtic in ~ la chanson est d'origine celte ❑ 'The Origin of Species' *Darwin* 'De l'origine des espèces'. -**2.** [ancestry] origine *f*; he is of Canadian ~ il est d'origine canadienne; to be of humble ~s avoir des origines modestes; they can trace their ~s back to the time of the Norman conquest ils ont réussi à remonter dans leur arbre généalogique jusqu'à l'époque de la conquête normande.

original [ɒ'rɪdʒɪnl] ◇ *adj* -**1.** [initial] premier, d'origine, initial; the ~ inhabitants of the country les premiers habitants du pays; the ~ meaning of the word le sens originel du mot; my ~ intention was to drive there ma première intention OR mon intention initiale était d'y aller en voiture; the fabric has lost its ~ lustre l'étoffe a perdu son éclat d'origine; most of the ~ 600 copies have been destroyed la plupart des 600 exemplaires originaux ont été détruits; ~ edition édition originale; the ~ portrait by Rubens le portrait original peint par Rubens. -**2.** [unusual] original; based on an ~ idea by Sam Ford d'après une idée originale de Sam Ford || [strange] singulier; he has some ~ ideas il a des idées originales; she has an ~ approach to child-rearing sa conception de l'éducation est originale. -**3.** [new - play, writing] original, inédit.
◇ *n* -**1.** [painting, book] original *m*; the film was shown in the ~ le film a été projeté en version originale; I prefer to read Proust in the ~ je préfère lire Proust dans le texte. -**2.** [model - of hero, character]: Betty was the ~ of the novel's heroine Betty inspira le personnage de l'héroïne du roman. -**3.** [unusual person] original *m*, -e *f*, excentrique *mf*; she's a real ~ elle est vraiment spéciale OR originale.

originality [ə,rɪdʒə'nælətɪ] (*pl* **originalities**) *n* originalité *f*.

originally [ə'rɪdʒənəlɪ] *adv* -**1.** [initially] à l'origine, au début, initialement; this room was ~ the kitchen à l'origine, cette pièce servait de cuisine; ~, I had planned to go to Greece initialement OR au début, j'avais l'intention d'aller en Grèce. -**2.** [unusually, inventively] d'une façon OR d'une manière originale, originalement.

original sin *n* péché *m* originel.

originate [ə'rɪdʒəneɪt] ◇ *vi* [suggestion, rumour]: to ~ in avoir OR trouver son origine dans; to ~ from tirer son origine de; where did the rumour ~ from? qu'est-ce qui a donné naissance à cette rumeur?; this concept ~s from Freudian psychology ce concept est issu de la psychologie freudienne; the conflict ~d in the towns le conflit est né dans les villes; this information ~s from an official source le renseignement émane d'une source officielle; I wonder how that saying ~d je me demande d'où vient ce dicton || [goods] provenir; the cocaine ~s from South America la cocaïne provient d'Amérique du Sud || [person]: he ~s from Melbourne il est originaire de Melbourne.
◇ *vt* [give rise to] être à l'origine de, donner naissance à; [be author of] être l'auteur de; the experience ~d the story of the invisible man cette expérience donna naissance à l'histoire de l'homme invisible.

origination [ə,rɪdʒə'neɪʃn] *n* création *f*.

originator [ə'rɪdʒəneɪtəʳ] *n* [of crime] auteur *m*; [of idea] initiateur *m*, -trice *f*, auteur *m*.

Orinoco [,ɒrɪ'nəʊkəʊ] *pr n*: the (River) ~ l'Orénoque *m*.

oriole ['ɔːrɪəʊl] *n* loriot *m*.

Orion [ə'raɪən] *pr n* Orion.

orison ['ɒrɪzən] *n lit* oraison *f*.

Orkney Islands ['ɔːknɪ-], **Orkneys** ['ɔːknɪz] *pl pr n*: the ~ les Orcades *fpl*; in the ~ dans les Orcades.

Orlando [ɔː'lændəʊ] *pr n* Orlando.

Orlon® ['ɔːlɒn] ◇ *n* Orlon® *m*.
◇ *comp* en Orlon.

ormer ['ɔːməʳ] *n* ormeau *m* ZOOL.

ormolu ['ɔːməluː] ◇ *n* chrysocale *m*, bronze doré.
◇ *comp* [clock] en chrysocale, en bronze doré

Ormuz [ɔː'muːz] = **Hormuz**.

ornament [*n* 'ɔːnəmənt, *vb* 'ɔːnəment]
◇ *n* -**1.** [decorative object] objet *m* décorati[f] bibelot *m*; [jewellery] colifichet *m*. -**2.** [embellishment] ornement *m*; rich in ~ richement orn[é] -**3.** MUS ornement *m*.
◇ *vt* orner; the dress was ~ed with gol[d] braid la robe était ornée d'un liseré d'or; th[e] ceiling was ~ed with frescoes le plafond éta[it] orné de fresques; his style is highly ~ed il a u[n] style très fleuri.

ornamental [,ɔːnə'mentl] *adj* [decorative] orn[e]mental, décoratif; [plant] ornemental; [garden] d'agrément.

ornamentation [,ɔːnəmen'teɪʃn] *n* orneme[n]tation *f*.

ornate [ɔː'neɪt] *adj* [decoration] (très) orné [style] orné, fleuri; [lettering] orné.

ornately [ɔː'neɪtlɪ] *adv* d'une façon très orné[e] ~ decorated room pièce richement décorée ~ carved furniture meubles ornés OR rehau[s]sés de nombreuses sculptures.

ornery *inf* ['ɔːnərɪ] *adj Am* -**1.** [nasty] méchan[t] an ~ trick un sale tour. -**2.** [stubborn] obstin[é] entêté.

ornithologist [,ɔːnɪ'θɒlədʒɪst] *n* ornitho[logiste] logiste *mf*, ornithologue *mf*.

ornithology [,ɔːnɪ'θɒlədʒɪ] *n* ornithologie *f*.

orogenics [,ɒrə'dʒenɪks], **orogeny** [ɒ'rɒdʒən[ɪ]] *n (U)* orogénie *f*, orogenèse *f*.

orography [ɒ'rɒgrəfɪ] *n* orographie *f*.

orotund ['ɒrətʌnd] *adj fml* [voice] sonore; [style] ampoulé.

orphan ['ɔːfn] ◇ *n* orphelin *m*, -e *f*; to be le[ft] an ~ se retrouver OR devenir orphelin.
◇ *adj* orphelin.
◇ *vt*: to be ~ed se retrouver OR deven[ir] orphelin.

orphanage ['ɔːfənɪdʒ] *n* orphelinat *m*.

Orpheus ['ɔːfɪəs] *pr n* Orphée; '~ in the Un[d]erworld' *Offenbach* 'Orphée aux enfers'.

orphic ['ɔːfɪk] *adj* orphique.

Orphism ['ɔːfɪzm] *n* ART & HIST orphisme *m*.

orrery ['ɒrərɪ] (*pl* **orreries**) *n* planétaire *m*.

orthicon ['ɔːθɪkɒn] *n* orthicon *m*.

orthochromatic [,ɔːθəʊkrə'mætɪk] *a[dj]* orthochromatique.

orthodontic [,ɔːθə'dɒntɪk] *adj* orthodontique

orthodontics [,ɔːθə'dɒntɪks] *n (U)* orth[o]dontie *f*.

orthodontist [,ɔːθə'dɒntɪst] *n* ortho[dontiste] dontiste *mf*.

orthodox ['ɔːθədɒks] *adj* orthodoxe.

Orthodox Church *n*: the ~ l'Église *f* ortho[doxe] doxe.

orthodoxy ['ɔːθədɒksɪ] (*pl* **orthodoxies**) *n* orthodoxie *f*.

orthogenesis [,ɔːθə'dʒenɪsɪs] *n* orthogenèse

orthogenic [,ɔːθə'dʒenɪk] *adj* orthogénique.

orthogonal [ɔː'θɒgənl] *adj* orthogonal; ~ pro[jection] projection *f* orthogonale.

orthographic(al) [,ɔːθə'græfɪk(l)] *adj* ortho[graphique] graphique.

orthography [ɔː'θɒgrəfɪ] *n* orthographe *f*.

orthopaedic *etc* [,ɔːθə'piːdɪk] *Br* = **orthopedi[c]**

orthopedic [,ɔːθə'piːdɪk] *adj* orthopédique; ~ surgeon (chirurgien *m*, -enne *f*) orthop[é]diste *mf*; ~ surgery chirurgie *f* orthopédique

orthopedics [,ɔːθə'piːdɪks] *n (U)* orthopédie

orthopedist [,ɔːθə'piːdɪst] *n* orthopédiste *m*

orthoptics [ɔː'θɒptɪks] *n (U)* orthoptique *f*.

oryx ['ɒrɪks] (*pl inv* OR **oryxes**) *n* oryx *m*.

OS ◇ *n abbr of* ordinary seaman.
◇ *pr n* (*abbr of* Ordnance Survey) ≃ IGN *m*
◇ *written abbr of* outsize.

Osaka [əʊ'sɑːkə] *pr n* Osaka.

Oscar ['ɒskəʳ] *n* CIN Oscar *m*.
oscillate ['ɒsɪleɪt] ◇ *vi* -**1.** ELEC & PHYS osciller. -**2.** [person] osciller; his mood ~d between gloom and elation son humeur oscillait entre la mélancolie et l'exultation.
◇ *vt* faire osciller.
oscillation [,ɒsɪ'leɪʃn] *n* oscillation *f*.
oscillator ['ɒsɪleɪtəʳ] *n* oscillateur *m*.
oscillatory [ɒ'sɪlətrɪ] *adj* oscillatoire.
oscilloscope [ɒ'sɪləskəʊp] *n* oscilloscope *m*.
osculate ['ɒskjʊleɪt] *Br hum* ◇ *vt* donner un baiser à, embrasser.
◇ *vi* s'embrasser.
osculation [,ɒskjʊ'leɪʃn] *n Br hum* baiser *m*.
OSD (*abbr of* optical scanning device) *n* lecteur *m* optique.
OSHA (*abbr of* Occupational Safety and Health Administration) *pr n aux États-Unis, direction de la sécurité et de l'hygiène au travail*.
osier ['əʊzɪəʳ] *n* osier *m*.
Osiris [əʊ'saɪərɪs] *pr n* Osiris.
Oslo ['ɒzləʊ] *pr n* Oslo.
osmium ['ɒzmɪəm] *n* osmium *m*.
osmometer [ɒz'mɒmɪtəʳ] *n* osmomètre *m*.
osmose ['ɒzməʊs] *vi* subir une osmose.
osmosis [ɒz'məʊsɪs] *n* osmose *f*.
osmotic [ɒz'mɒtɪk] *adj* osmotique.
osprey ['ɒsprɪ] *n* [bird] balbuzard *m*; [feather] aigrette *f*.
osseous ['ɒsɪəs] *adj* osseux.
Ossianic [,ɒsɪ'ænɪk] *adj* ossianique, inspiré de la poésie d'Ossian.
ossicle ['ɒsɪkl] *n* osselet *m*.
ossiferous [ɒ'sɪfərəs] *adj* ossifère.
ossification [,ɒsɪfɪ'keɪʃn] *n* ossification *f*.
ossify ['ɒsɪfaɪ] (*pt* & *pp* **ossified**) ◇ *vt* ossifier.
◇ *vi* s'ossifier.
ossuary ['ɒsjʊərɪ] (*pl* **ossuaries**) *n* [vault] ossuaire *m*; [urn] urne *f* (funéraire).
Ostend [ɒs'tend] *pr n* Ostende.
ostensible [ɒ'stensəbl] *adj* [apparent] apparent; [pretended] prétendu; [so-called] soi-disant *(inv)*; her ~ reason for not coming was illness elle a prétendu être malade pour éviter de venir.
ostensibly [ɒ'stensəblɪ] *adv* [apparently] apparemment, prétendument, soi-disant; ~ they are diplomats ils se font passer pour des diplomates || [on the pretext]: he left early, ~ because he was sick il est parti tôt, prétextant une indisposition.
ostentation [,ɒstən'teɪʃn] *n* ostentation *f*.
ostentatious [,ɒstən'teɪʃəs] *adj* -**1.** [showy - display, appearance, decor] ostentatoire, plein d'ostentation; [manner, behaviour] prétentieux, ostentatoire. -**2.** [exaggerated] exagéré, surfait; with ~ dislike avec un mépris exagéré.
ostentatiously [,ɒstən'teɪʃəslɪ] *adv* avec ostentation.
osteoarthritis [,ɒstɪəʊɑː'θraɪtɪs] *n* ostéoarthrite *f*.
osteology [,ɒstɪ'ɒlədʒɪ] *n* ostéologie *f*.
osteopath ['ɒstɪəpæθ] *n* ostéopathe *mf*.
osteopathy [,ɒstɪ'ɒpəθɪ] *n* ostéopathie *f*.
osteoporosis [,ɒstɪəʊpɔː'rəʊsɪs] *n* ostéoporose *f*.
ostler ['ɒsləʳ] *n Br arch* valet *m* d'écurie.
ostracism ['ɒstrəsɪzm] *n* ostracisme *m*.
ostracize, -ise ['ɒstrəsaɪz] *vt* frapper d'ostracisme, ostraciser; he was ~d by his workmates ses collègues l'ont mis en quarantaine.
ostrich ['ɒstrɪtʃ] *n* autruche *f*.
Ostrogoth ['ɒstrəgɒθ] *n*: the ~s les Ostrogoths *mpl*.
OT *n* -**1.** (*abbr of* Old Testament) AT. -**2.** *abbr of* occupational therapy.
otalgia [əʊ'tældʒə] *n* otalgie *f*.
OTC ◇ *pr n* (*abbr of* Officer Training Corps) *section de formation des officiers en Grande-Bretagne*.
◇ *adj abbr of* over the counter.
Othello [ə'θeləʊ] *pr n* Othello.
other ['ʌðəʳ] ◇ *adj* -**1.** [different] autre, différent; it's the same in ~ countries c'est la même chose dans les autres pays; I had no ~ choice je n'avais pas le choix OR pas d'autre solution; by ~ means par d'autres moyens; he doesn't respect ~ people's property il ne respecte pas le bien d'autrui; it always happens to ~ people cela n'arrive qu'aux autres; can't we discuss it some ~ time? on ne peut pas en parler plus tard?; in ~ times autrefois, à une autre époque; the ~ world l'autre monde *m*, l'au-delà *m*. -**2.** [second of two] autre; give me the ~ one donnez-moi l'autre. -**3.** [additional] autre; can you get some ~ cups? pouvez-vous aller chercher d'autres tasses?; some ~ people came d'autres personnes sont arrivées; they have two ~ daughters ils ont deux autres filles. -**4.** [remaining] autre; the ~ three men les trois autres hommes. -**5.** [in expressions of time] autre; the ~ day/morning/month/week l'autre jour/matin/mois/semaine. -**6.** [opposite]: on the ~ side of the room/of the river de l'autre côté de la pièce/de la rivière; a voice at the ~ end (of the telephone) une voix à l'autre bout (du fil).
◇ *pron* -**1.** [additional person, thing] autre; he and two ~s got the sack lui et deux autres ont été renvoyés; some succeed, ~s fail certains réussissent, d'autres échouent. -**2.** [opposite, far end] autre; I stood at this end of the room and she stood at the ~ j'étais à ce bout-ci de la pièce et elle était à l'autre (bout). -**3.** [related person] autre; each thought the ~ the better writer chacun trouvait que l'autre était un meilleur écrivain.
◇ *n* [person, thing] autre *mf*; the ~ PHILOS l'autre; the three ~s les trois autres; wait for the ~s attendez les autres; politicians, industrialists and ~s les hommes politiques, les industriels et les autres; she cares nothing for ~s elle ne se soucie pas du tout des autres; can you show me some ~s? pouvez-vous m'en montrer d'autres?
◆ **other than** ◇ *conj phr* -**1.** [apart from, except] autrement que; she had never seen him ~ than on the screen elle ne l'avait jamais vu autrement qu'à l'écran; we had no alternative ~ than to accept their offer nous n'avions pas d'autre possibilité que celle d'accepter leur offre. -**2.** [differently from] différemment de; I think she should have behaved ~ than she did je pense qu'elle aurait dû se comporter différemment OR d'une autre façon; she can't be ~ than she is elle est comme ça, c'est tout.
◇ *prep phr* sauf, à part; ~ than that à part cela.
otherness ['ʌðənɪs] *n* [difference] altérité *f*, différence *f*; [strangeness] étrangeté *f*.
otherwise ['ʌðəwaɪz] ◇ *adv* -**1.** [differently] autrement; I think ~ [in a different way] je ne vois pas les choses de cette façon; [don't agree] je ne suis pas d'accord; she is ~ engaged elle a d'autres engagements; we'll have to invite everyone, we can hardly do ~ nous devrons inviter tout le monde, il nous serait difficile de faire autrement; except where ~ stated [on form] sauf indication contraire. -**2.** [in other respects] autrement, à part cela; [in other circumstances] sinon, autrement; an ~ excellent performance une interprétation par ailleurs excellente; it's a bit small, but ~ it's a very nice house c'est un peu petit, mais à part cela, c'est une maison très agréable; the weather was bad, ~ he might have stayed longer il faisait mauvais, sans cela OR sinon il aurait pu rester plus longtemps. -**3.** [in other words] autrement; Louis XIV, ~ known as the Sun King Louis XIV, surnommé le Roi-Soleil. -**4.** [in contrast, opposition]: through diplomatic channels or ~ par voie diplomatique ou autre.
◇ *conj* [or else] sinon, autrement; you'd better phone your father, ~ he'll worry tu devrais appeler ton père, sinon il va s'inquiéter.
◇ *adj* autre; the facts are ~ les faits sont autres.
◆ **or otherwise** *adv phr*: it is of no interest, financial or ~ ça ne présente aucun intérêt, que ce soit financier ou autre; she appeared to have no feelings about it, jealous or ~ elle ne semblait rien éprouver, que ce soit de la jalousie ou autre chose.
otherworldly [,ʌðə'wɜːldlɪ] *adj* -**1.** [unrealistic] peu réaliste. -**2.** [mystical] mystique. -**3.** [ethereal] éthéré.
otiose ['əʊtɪəʊs] *adj fml* oiseux, inutile.
otitis [əʊ'taɪtɪs] *n (U) fml* otite *f*.
otolaryngology ['əʊtəʊ,lærɪŋ'gɒlədʒɪ] *n* otorhino-laryngologie *f*.
OTT *inf* (*abbr of* over-the-top) *adj Br*: that's a bit ~! c'est pousser le bouchon un peu loin!, c'est un peu fort!
Ottawa ['ɒtəwə] *pr n* Ottawa.
otter ['ɒtəʳ] *n* loutre *f*.
ottoman ['ɒtəmən] *n* -**1.** [seat] ottomane *f*. -**2.** [fabric] ottoman *m*.
◆ **Ottoman** ◇ *n* Ottoman *m*, -e *f*.
◇ *adj* ottoman.
OU *pr n abbr of* Open University.
ouch [aʊtʃ] *interj*: ~! aïe!, ouille!, ouïe!
ought[1] [ɔːt] *modal vb* -**1.** [indicating morally right action]: you ~ to tell her vous devriez le lui dire; you ~ to talk to him tu devrais lui parler, il faudrait que tu lui parles; she thought she ~ to tell you elle a pensé qu'il valait mieux te le dire || [indicating sensible or advisable action]: perhaps we ~ to discuss this further peut-être devrions-nous en discuter plus longuement; I really ~ to be going il faut vraiment que je m'en aille; do you think I ~? *fml* pensez-vous que je doive le faire?; he ~ to know better il devrait être plus sensé; that's a nice car – it ~ to be, it cost me a fortune! c'est une belle voiture – j'espère bien, elle m'a coûté une fortune! -**2.** [expressing expectation, likelihood]: they ~ to be home now à l'heure qu'il est, ils devraient être rentrés; it ~ to be good ça devrait être bien; she ~ to beat him easily elle devrait le battre facilement OR sans difficulté; that oughtn't to be too difficult ça ne devrait pas être trop difficile. -**3.** [followed by 'to have']: you ~ to have told me! vous auriez dû me le dire!; you ~ to have seen her! si vous l'aviez vue!, il fallait la voir!; they ~ not to have been allowed in on n'aurait pas dû les laisser entrer.
ought[2] [ɔːt] = **aught**.
oughta *inf* ['ɔːtə] *Am* = **ought to**.
ouija ['wiːdʒə] *n*: ~ (board) oui-ja *m inv*.
ounce [aʊns] *n* -**1.** [weight] once *f*. -**2.** *fig*: there isn't an ~ of truth in what she says il n'y a pas une once de vérité dans ce qu'elle raconte; you haven't got an ~ of common sense tu n'as pas (pour) deux sous de bon sens; it took every ~ of strength she had cela lui a demandé toutes ses forces. -**3.** ZOOL once *f*.
OUP (*abbr of* Oxford University Press) *pr n maison d'édition de l'université d'Oxford*.
our ['aʊəʳ] *det* notre *(sg)*, nos *(pl)*; ~ house notre maison; this is OUR house cette maison est à nous; we have a car of ~ own nous avons une voiture à nous; how's ~ little boy, then? alors, comment va notre petit garçon?; ~ Agnes will be sixteen next week *inf* notre (petite) Agnès aura seize ans la semaine prochaine; have you seen ~ Peter? *inf* avez-vous vu Peter?; she's one of ~ finest poets c'est un de nos meilleurs poètes.
Our Father *n* [prayer] Notre Père *m*.
Our Lady *n* Notre-Dame *f*.
ours ['aʊəz] *pron* le nôtre *m*, la nôtre *f*, les nôtres *mfpl*; that house is ~ [we live there] cette maison est la nôtre; [we own it] cette maison est à nous OR nous appartient; those books are ~ ces livres sont à nous; it's ~ to spend as we like nous pouvons le dépenser comme nous voulons; it's all ~! tout cela nous appartient!; ~ was a curious relationship nous avions des rapports assez bizarres; ~ is a big family nous sommes une grande famille; it must be one of ~ ce doit être un des nôtres; she's a friend of ~ c'est une de nos amies; a friend of ~ told us c'est un ami à nous qui nous l'a dit; those

damned neighbours of ~ *inf* nos fichus voisins; that wretched dog of ~ notre saleté de chien.

ourself [aʊə'self] *pron fml* [regal or editorial plural] nous-même.

ourselves [aʊə'selvz] *pron* -**1.** [reflexive use] nous; we enjoyed ~ nous nous sommes bien amusés; we built ~ a log cabin nous avons construit une cabane en rondins; we said to ~, why not wait here? nous nous sommes dit OR on s'est dit: pourquoi ne pas attendre ici? -**2.** [emphatic use] nous-mêmes; we welcomed him ~ nous l'avons accueilli nous-mêmes; we'd love to help him, but we're not in very good health ~ nous aimerions beaucoup l'aider mais nous ne sommes pas en très bonne santé nous-mêmes OR non plus; we were able to visit the caves ~ nous avons eu la chance de pouvoir visiter les grottes; we ~ have much to learn nous-mêmes avons beaucoup à apprendre; we want to see for ~ nous avons envie de nous en rendre compte (par) nous-mêmes; (all) by ~ tout seuls; we had the flat to ~ nous avions l'appartement pour nous tout seuls. -**3.** [replacing 'us'] nous-mêmes; apart from our parents and ~, everyone was Russian en dehors de nos parents et de nous-mêmes, tout le monde était russe.

oust [aʊst] *vt* -**1.** [opponent, rival] évincer, chasser; the president was ~ed from power le président a été évincé du pouvoir; she has ~ed her sister in Arthur's affections elle a pris la place de OR a supplanté sa sœur dans le cœur d'Arthur. -**2.** [tenant, squatter] déloger, expulser; [landowner] déposséder.

ouster ['aʊstəʳ] *n* -**1.** JUR dépossession *f.* -**2.** *Am* [from country] expulsion *f*; [from office] renvoi *m.*

out [aʊt] ◇ *adv* **A.** -**1.** [indicating movement from inside to outside] dehors; to go ~ sortir; she ran/limped/strolled ~ elle est sortie en courant/en boîtant/sans se presser; the way ~ la sortie; I met her on my way ~ je l'ai rencontrée en sortant; the cork popped ~ le bouchon sauta; she took ~ a gun elle a sorti un révolver; I had my camera ~ ready j'avais sorti mon appareil; he drew ~ £50 [from bank] il a retiré 50 livres; [from pocket] il a sorti 50 livres. -**2.** [away from home, office etc] : Mr Powell's ~, do you want to leave a message? M. Powell est sorti, voulez-vous laisser un message?; a search party is ~ looking for them une équipe de secours est partie à leur recherche; to eat ~ aller au restaurant; it's a long time since we had an evening ~ ça fait longtemps que nous ne sommes pas sortis; he stayed ~ all night il n'est pas rentré de la nuit; the children are playing ~ in the street les enfants jouent dans la rue. -**3.** [no longer attending hospital, school etc] sorti; she's ~ of hospital now elle est sortie de l'hôpital maintenant; what time do you get ~ of school? à quelle heure sors-tu de l'école? -**4.** [indicating view from inside] : he was looking ~ at the people in the street il regardait les gens qui passaient dans la rue; I stared ~ of the window je regardais par la fenêtre; the bedroom looks ~ onto open fields la chambre donne sur les champs. -**5.** [in the open air] dehors; to sleep ~ dormir dehors; it's cold ~ il fait froid dehors. -**6.** [indicating distance from land, centre, town etc] : we were two days ~ from Portsmouth nous étions à deux jours de Portsmouth; on the trip ~ à l'aller; they live a long way ~ ils habitent loin du centre; she's ~ in Africa elle est en Afrique. -**7.** [indicating extended position] : she stuck her tongue ~ at me elle m'a tiré la langue; he lay stretched ~ on the bed il était allongé (de tout son long) sur le lit; hold your arms/your hand ~ tendez les bras/la main.

B. -**1.** [indicating distribution] : she handed ~ some photocopies elle a distribué des photocopies; the letter was sent ~ yesterday la lettre a été postée hier. -**2.** [indicating source of light, smell, sound etc] : it gives ~ a lot of heat ça dégage beaucoup de chaleur; music blared ~ from the radio la radio hurlait. -**3.** [loudly, audibly] : read ~ the first paragraph lisez le premier paragraphe à haute voix; I was thinking ~ loud je pensais tout haut.

C. -**1.** [indicating exclusion or rejection] : 'keep ~' 'défense d'entrer', 'entrée interdite'; traitors ~! les traîtres, dehors!; throw him ~! jetez-le dehors! -**2.** [indicating abandonment of activity] : get ~ before it's too late abandonne avant qu'il ne soit trop tard; you can count me ~ ne comptez plus sur moi; I want ~! *inf* je laisse tomber! -**3.** [extinguished] : put OR turn the lights ~ éteignez les lumières; to stub ~ a cigarette écraser une cigarette. -**4.** [unconscious] : to knock sb ~ assommer qqn, mettre qqn K-O; several people passed ~ plusieurs personnes se sont évanouies. -**5.** [indicating disappearance] : the stain will wash ~ la tache partira au lavage.

D. -**1.** [revealed, made public] : the secret is ~ le secret a été éventé; word is ~ that he's going to resign le bruit court qu'il va démissionner; we must stop the news getting ~ nous devons empêcher la nouvelle de s'ébruiter; ~ with it! *inf* alors, t'accouches? -**2.** [published, on sale] : is her new book/film/record ~? est-ce que son nouveau livre/film/disque est sorti?; the new model will be OR come ~ next month le nouveau modèle sort le mois prochain. -**3.** *inf (with superlative)* [in existence] : it's the best computer ~ c'est le meilleur ordinateur qui existe; she's the biggest liar ~ c'est la pire menteuse qui soit.

E. -**1.** SPORT : ~! TENNIS faute!, out! -**2.** [of tide] : the tide's on its way ~ la mer se retire, la marée descend.

◇ *adj* -**1.** [flowering] en fleurs; the daffodils/cherry trees are ~ les jonquilles/cerisiers sont en fleurs. -**2.** [shining] : the sun is ~ il y a du soleil; the moon is ~ la lune s'est levée; the stars are ~ on voit les étoiles. -**3.** [finished] : before the year is ~ avant la fin de l'année. -**4.** [on strike] en grève; the dockers have been ~ for a month les dockers sont en grève depuis un mois; everybody ~! tout le monde en grève! -**5.** GAMES & SPORT : if you score less than 3 points you're ~ si on marque moins de 3 points on est éliminé; the ball was ~ la balle était dehors OR sortie, la balle était faute; she went ~ in the first round elle a été éliminée au premier tour. -**6.** [tide] bas; the tide's ~ la marée est basse. -**7.** [wrong] : your calculations are (way) ~, you're (way) ~ in your calculations vous vous êtes (complètement) trompé dans vos calculs; I've checked the figures but I'm still £50 ~ j'ai vérifié les chiffres mais il manque toujours 50 livres; it's a few inches ~ [too long] c'est trop long de quelques centimètres; [too short] c'est trop court de quelques centimètres; it's only a few inches ~ c'est bon à quelques centimètres près. -**8.** *inf* [impossible] : that plan's ~ because of the weather ce projet est à l'eau à cause du temps. -**9.** *inf* [unfashionable] : long hair's (right) ~ les cheveux longs c'est (carrément) dépassé. -**10.** [indicating aim, intent] : to be ~ to do sthg avoir l'intention de faire qqch; we're ~ to win nous sommes partis pour gagner; to be ~ for sthg vouloir qqch; she's ~ for the presidency elle vise le poste de président; he's just ~ for himself il ne s'intéresse qu'à lui-même. -**11.** *inf* [unconscious] : to be ~ être K-O. -**12.** [extinguished] éteint; the fire was ~ le feu était éteint. -**13.** *inf* [openly gay] : to be ~ ne pas cacher son homosexualité.

◇ *n* -**1.** [way of escape] échappatoire *f.* -**2.** TYPO bourdon *m.* -**3.** → **in.**

◇ *interj* -**1.** [leave] : ~! dehors! -**2.** TELEC : (over and) ~! terminé!

◇ *prep inf* hors de; she went ~ that door elle est sortie par cette porte; look ~ the window regarde par la fenêtre.

◇ *vi lit* : the truth will ~ la vérité se saura.

◇ *vt* [expose] dénoncer.

◆ **out and about** *adv phr* : where have you been? – oh, ~ and about où étais-tu? – oh, je suis allé faire un tour; ~ and about in Amsterdam dans les rues d'Amsterdam.

◆ **out of** *prep phr* -**1.** [indicating movement fro inside to outside] hors de; she came ~ of th office elle est sortie du bureau; he ran/limped strolled ~ of the office il est sorti du bureau e courant/en boitant/sans se presser; to look/t fall ~ of a window regarder/tomber par un fenêtre; take your hands ~ of your pockets sors OR ôte tes mains de tes poches! -**2.** [ind cating location] : we drank ~ of china cups nou avons bu dans des tasses de porcelaine; sh works ~ of York elle opère à partir de York the company works ~ of Oxford l'entrepris est basée à Oxford; he's ~ of town il n'est pa en ville; it's a long way ~ of town c'est loi de la ville. -**3.** [indicating source - of feeling, profi money etc] : she did well ~ of the deal elle trouvé son compte dans l'affaire; what plea sure do they get ~ of it? quel plaisir e tirent-ils?; you won't get anything ~ of hir vous ne tirerez rien de lui; she paid for it ~ c company funds/~ of her own pocket elle l' payé avec l'argent de la société/payé de s poche. -**4.** [indicating raw material] : it's made ~ of mahogany c'est en acajou; plastic is mad ~ of petroleum on obtient le plastique à part du pétrole. -**5.** [indicating motive] par; he refuse ~ of sheer spite il a refusé par pur dépi -**6.** [indicating previous tendency, habit] : I've got ~ of the habit j'en ai perdu l'habitude; try an stay ~ of trouble essaie d'éviter les ennuis -**7.** [lacking] : I'm ~ of cigarettes je n'ai plus d cigarettes; ~ of work au chômage. -**8.** [i proportions, marks etc] sur; he got nine ~ of te in maths il a eu neuf sur dix en maths ninety-nine times ~ of a hundred quatre vingt-dix neuf fois sur cent; ~ of all the peopl there, only one spoke German parmi toutes le personnes présentes, une seule parlait all mand. -**9.** [indicating similarity to book, film etc] : was like something ~ of a Fellini film on s serait cru dans un film de Fellini. -**10.** [indicatir exclusion or rejection] : he's ~ of the race il n'es plus dans la course; you keep ~ of this mêlez-vous de ce qui vous regarde! -**11.** [ind cating avoidance] : come in ~ of the rain ne rest pas dehors sous la pluie; stay ~ of the sun n restez pas au soleil. -**12.** [indicating recently com pleted activity] : a young girl just ~ of universit une jeune fille tout juste sortie de l'université -**13.** *phr* : to be ~ of it *inf* [unaware of situation être à côté de la plaque; [drunk] être bourré; felt really ~ of it [excluded] je me sentai complètement exclu.

outa *inf* ['aʊtə] *Am* = **out of.**

outage ['aʊtɪdʒ] *n Am.* -**1.** [breakdown] panne ELEC coupure *f* OR panne *f* de courant. -**2.** [c service] interruption *f.* -**3.** COMM [missing goods marchandises *fpl* perdues *(pendant le stockage o le transport).*

out-and-out *adj* complet, total; it was an ~ disaster ce fut un désastre complet; that's ~ madness! c'est de la folie pure!; he's an ~ crook c'est un véritable escroc.

out-and-outer *inf n Am* jusqu'au-boutiste *mf.*

outasight *inf* ['aʊtəsaɪt] *adj Am dated* extra super, génial.

outback ['aʊtbæk] *n Austr* arrière-pays *m in* intérieur *m* du pays.

outbalance [,aʊt'bæləns] *vt literal* peser plu lourd que; *fig* dépasser.

outbid [aʊt'bɪd] (*pt* outbid, *pp* outbid OR ou bidden [-'bɪdn], *cont* outbidding) *vt* enchér sur; we were ~ for the Renoir quelqu'un surenchéri sur le Renoir et nous n'avons p l'acheter.

outboard ['aʊtbɔːd] ◇ *adj* [position, directior hors-bord; ~ motor moteur *m* hors-bord.
◇ *n* [motor, boat] hors-bord *m inv.*

outbound ['aʊtbaʊnd] *adj* qui quitte le centre ville.

outbreak ['aʊtbreɪk] *n* -**1.** [of fire, storm, wa début *m*; [of violence, disease, epidemic] éru tion *f*; there have been ~s of violenc throughout the country il y a eu des explosior de violence dans tout le pays; at the ~ of wa au début de la guerre, lorsque la guerre a éclaté; at the ~ of the strike dès le début de la grève; doctors fear an ~ of meningitis les médecins redoutent une épidémie de méningite; to have an ~ of spots avoir une éruption de boutons. -2. METEOR [sudden shower]: there will be ~s of rain/snow in many places il y aura des chutes de pluie/de neige un peu partout.

outbuilding ['aʊt,bɪldɪŋ] *n Br* (bâtiment *m*) annexe *f*; [shed] remise *f*; the ~s [on farm, estate] les dépendances *fpl*.

outburst ['aʊtbɜːst] *n* accès *m*, explosion *f*; a sudden ~ of violence [group] une soudaine explosion de violence; [individual] un accès de brutalité; a sudden ~ of temper un accès de mauvaise humeur; you must control these ~s il faut que vous appreniez à garder OR conserver votre sang-froid.

outcast ['aʊtkɑːst] ◇ *n* paria *m*.
◇ *adj* proscrit, banni.

outclass [,aʊt'klɑːs] *vt* surclasser, surpasser; she ~ed all of the other athletes elle a surclassé tous les autres athlètes.

outcome ['aʊtkʌm] *n* [of election, competition] résultat *m*; [of sequence of events] conséquence *f*; the ~ of it all was that they never visited us again résultat, ils ne sont jamais revenus chez nous.

outcrop [*n* 'aʊtkrɒp, *vb* ,aʊt'krɒp] (*pt* & *pp* outcropped, *cont* outcropping) ◇ *n* GEOL affleurement *m*.
◇ *vi* affleurer.

outcry ['aʊtkraɪ] (*pl* outcries) *n* tollé *m*; the government's decision was greeted by public ~ la décision du gouvernement fut accueillie par un tollé général.

outdated [,aʊt'deɪtɪd] *adj* [idea, attitude] démodé, dépassé; [clothes] démodé; [expression] désuet.

outdistance [,aʊt'dɪstəns] *vt* laisser derrière soi; she was easily ~d by the Nigerian elle fut facilement distancée par la Nigérienne.

outdo [,aʊt'duː] (*pt* outdid [-'dɪd], *pp* outdone [-'dʌn]) *vt* surpasser, faire mieux que, l'emporter sur; he's not easily outdone in an argument il n'est pas facile d'avoir le dernier mot quand on discute avec lui; Mark, not to be outdone, decided to be ill as well Mark, pour ne pas être en reste, décida d'être malade lui aussi; she wasn't to be outdone [in contest] elle refusait de s'avouer vaincue; she outdid all the other competitors elle l'a emporté sur tous les autres concurrents.

outdoor ['aʊtdɔːʳ] *adj* -1. [open-air - games, sports] de plein air; [- work] d'extérieur; [- swimming pool] en plein air, découvert. -2. [clothes] d'extérieur; ~ shoes [warm] grosses chaussures; [waterproof] chaussures imperméables; [for walking] chaussures de marche. -3. [person] qui aime le grand air; to lead an ~ life vivre au grand air; Kate is a real ~ type Kate aime la vie au grand air.

outdoors [aʊt'dɔːz] ◇ *n*: the great ~ les grands espaces naturels.
◇ *adv* dehors, au dehors; the scene takes place ~ la scène se déroule à l'extérieur; to sleep ~ coucher à la belle étoile; we were ~ for most of the holiday nous avons passé la plus grande partie de nos vacances au grand air.
◇ *adj* [activity] en OR de plein air.

outer ['aʊtəʳ] *adj* -1. [external] extérieur, externe; the ~ man l'homme dans son apparence extérieure; ~ garments vêtements *mpl* de dessus. -2. [peripheral] périphérique; the ~ suburbs la grande banlieue; ~ London la banlieue londonienne. -3. [furthest - limits] externe; [- planets] extérieur.

outer ear *n* oreille *f* externe.

Outer Mongolia *pr n* Mongolie-Extérieure *f*; in ~ en Mongolie-Extérieure.

outermost ['aʊtəməʊst] *adj* [most distant] le plus (à l') extérieur; [most isolated] le plus reculé OR isolé; the ~ limits of the galaxy les limites les plus reculées de la galaxie.

outer space *n* espace *m* intersidéral, cosmos *m*.

outface [,aʊt'feɪs] *vt* -1. [outstare] faire baisser les yeux à *(en dévisageant)*; *fig* décontenancer. -2. [defy] tenir tête à, défier.

outfield ['aʊtfiːld] *n* SPORT -1. [part of field] champ *m* OR terrain *m* extérieur. -2. [players] joueurs *mpl* de champ.

outfielder ['aʊtfiːldəʳ] *n Am* joueur *m* de champ *(au baseball)*.

outfit ['aʊtfɪt] (*pt* & *pp* outfitted, *cont* outfitting) ◇ *n* -1. [clothes] ensemble *m*, tenue *f*; Maggie appears in a new ~ every day Maggie porte une tenue différente chaque jour; riding/travelling ~ tenue d'équitation/de voyage; you should have seen the ~ he had on! tu aurais dû voir comment il était attifé OR fagoté! ‖ [child's disguise] panoplie *f*; cowboy's/nurse's ~ panoplie de cowboy/d'infirmière. -2. [equipment, kit - for camping, fishing] matériel *m*, équipement *m*; [tools] outils *mpl*, outillage *m*; [case] trousse *f*; repair ~ trousse de réparation; camera cleaning ~ nécessaire *m* de nettoyage pour appareil photo. -3. *inf* [group] équipe *f*, bande *f*; the whole ~ was there toute la bande OR l'équipe était là. -4. MIL équipe *f*.
◇ *vt* [with equipment] équiper.

outfitter ['aʊtfɪtəʳ] *n Br* [shop]: school ~ OR ~'s *magasin qui vend des uniformes et autres vêtements scolaires*; sports ~ OR ~'s magasin de vêtements de sport; (gentlemen's) ~ OR ~'s magasin de vêtements d'homme.

outflank [,aʊt'flæŋk] *vt* MIL déborder; *fig* [rival] déjouer les manœuvres de.

outflow ['aʊtfləʊ] *n* -1. [of fluid] écoulement *m*; [place of outflow] décharge *f*. -2. [of capital] sorties *fpl*, fuite *f*; [of population] exode *m*, sorties *fpl*, fuite *f*; the institute's aim is to ensure the continuous ~ of new ideas l'institut a pour but d'assurer un flux continu d'idées nouvelles.

outfox [,aʊt'fɒks] *vt* se montrer plus rusé que.

outgeneral [,aʊt'dʒenərəl] *vt* se montrer meilleur tacticien OR stratège que.

outgoing ['aʊt,gəʊɪŋ] *adj* -1. [departing - government, minister, tenant] sortant; [- following resignation] démissionnaire. -2. [train, ship] en partance; [letters] à expédier. -3. [tide] descendant. -4. [extrovert] extraverti, plein d'entrain; she's a very ~ person elle a une personnalité très ouverte.

outgoings ['aʊt,gəʊɪŋz] *npl* dépenses *fpl*, frais *mpl*.

outgrow [,aʊt'grəʊ] (*pt* outgrew [-'gruː], *pp* outgrown [-'grəʊn]) *vt* -1. [grow faster than] grandir plus (vite) que; that boy is ~ing his strength ce garçon a une croissance beaucoup trop rapide pour sa constitution; the world is ~ing its resources la population mondiale croît plus vite que les ressources dont elle dispose. -2. [clothes] devenir trop grand pour; she has outgrown three pairs of shoes this year elle a pris quatre pointures cette année. -3. [game, habit, hobby] ne plus s'intéresser à *(en grandissant)*; [attitude, behaviour, phase] abandonner (en grandissant OR en prenant de l'âge); Moira has outgrown dolls Moira est devenue trop grande pour s'intéresser aux poupées; they soon outgrew their first computer ils ont vite eu fait le tour (des possibilités) de leur premier ordinateur; he has outgrown his protest phase il a dépassé le stade de la contestation; I think I just outgrew our friendship je crois qu'avec l'âge, notre amitié a tout simplement perdu son intérêt pour moi; he has outgrown his reputation as a romantic il a fini par se défaire de sa réputation de romantique.

outgrowth ['aʊtgrəʊθ] *n literal* excroissance *f*; *fig* [consequence] conséquence *f*.

outgun [,aʊt'gʌn] (*pt* & *pp* outgunned, *cont* outgunning) *vt* MIL avoir une puissance de feu supérieure à; *fig* vaincre, l'emporter sur.

out-Herod *vt phr*: to ~ Herod en rajouter *(en cruauté, en violence etc)*.

outhouse ['aʊthaʊs, *pl* -haʊzɪz] *n* -1. *Br* [outbuilding] remise *f*. -2. *Am* [toilet] toilettes *fpl* extérieures.

outing ['aʊtɪŋ] *n* -1. [trip] sortie *f*; [organized] excursion *f*; to go on an ~ faire une excursion; to go for an ~ in the car partir faire une balade en voiture; it was an ~ for them cela leur a fait une sortie ❑ school ~ sortie scolaire. -2. [of homosexuals] *délation d'homosexuels dans le monde de la politique et du spectacle*.

outlandish [aʊt'lændɪʃ] *adj* [eccentric - appearance, behaviour, idea] bizarre, excentrique; *pej* [language, style] barbare.

outlast [,aʊt'lɑːst] *vt* [subj: person] survivre à; [subj: machine] durer plus longtemps que; the new exhaust will ~ the car le nouveau pot d'échappement durera plus longtemps que la voiture.

outlaw ['aʊtlɔː] ◇ *n* hors-la-loi *m inv*.
◇ *vt* [person] mettre hors la loi; [behaviour] proscrire, interdire; [organization] interdire.

outlay [*n* 'aʊtleɪ, *vb* aʊt'leɪ] (*pt* & *pp* outlaid [-'leɪd]) ◇ *n* [expense] dépense *f*; [investment] investissement *m*, mise *f* de fonds.
◇ *vt* [spend] dépenser; [invest] investir; to ~ $10,000 capital faire une mise de fonds de 10 000 dollars.

outlet ['aʊtlet] ◇ *n* -1. [for liquid, air, smoke] bouche *f*; [in reservoir, lock] déversoir *m*, dégorgeoir *m*; [tap] vanne *f* d'écoulement; air ~ bouche *f* d'aération; the pipe/channel provides an ~ for excess water le tuyau/le canal permet l'écoulement du trop-plein d'eau. -2. [mouth of river] embouchure *f*. -3. [for feelings, energy] exutoire *m*; children need an ~ for their energies les enfants ont besoin de se défouler; writing is an ~ for me l'écriture est pour moi un exutoire. -4. [for talent] débouché *m*; the programme provides an ~ for young talent l'émission permet à de jeunes talents de se faire connaître. -5. COMM [market] débouché *m*; there are not many sales ~s in Japan le Japon offre peu de débouchés commerciaux ‖ [sales point] point *m* de vente; our North American ~s notre réseau (de distribution) en Amérique du Nord. -6. *Am* ELEC prise *f* (de courant).
◇ *comp* [for liquid] d'écoulement; [for gas, smoke] d'échappement.

outline ['aʊtlaɪn] ◇ *n* -1. [contour, shape] silhouette *f*, contour *m*; [of building, of mountains] silhouette *f*; [of face, figure] profil *m*; ART [sketch] esquisse *f*, ébauche *f*; to draw sthg in ~ faire un croquis de qqch. -2. [plan - of project, essay] plan *m* d'ensemble, esquisse *f*; [- of book] canevas *m*; I've only written a rough ~ of the chapter je n'ai écrit que les grandes lignes du chapitre ‖ [general idea] idée *f* générale, grandes lignes *fpl*; [overall view] vue *f* d'ensemble; to give sb an ~ of sthg expliquer les grandes lignes de qqch à qqn; she gave us an ~ of OR she explained to us in ~ what she intended to do elle nous a expliqué dans les grandes lignes ce qu'elle avait l'intention de faire; An Outline of Modern History [as title] Éléments d'histoire moderne; an ~ history of Greece un précis d'histoire grecque.
◇ *vt* -1. [plan, theory] expliquer dans les grandes lignes; [facts] résumer, passer en revue; he ~d the situation briefly il dressa un bref bilan de la situation; could you ~ your basic reasons for leaving? pourriez-vous exposer brièvement les principales raisons de votre départ? -2. [person, building, mountain]: the trees were ~d against the blue sky les arbres se détachaient sur le fond bleu du ciel. -3. ART esquisser (les traits de), tracer; to ~ sthg in pencil faire le croquis de qqch; the figures are ~d in charcoal les personnages sont esquissés au fusain; to ~ one's eyes in black souligner le contour de ses yeux en noir.

outline drawing *n* dessin *m* au trait.

outlive [,aʊt'lɪv] *vt* survivre à; she ~d her husband by only six months elle n'a survécu à son mari que six mois; he'll ~ us all at this rate au train où il va, il nous enterrera tous; the measures have ~d their usefulness les mesures n'ont plus de raison d'être.

outlook ['aʊtlʊk] *n* **-1.** [prospect] perspective *f*; ECON & POL horizon *m*, perspectives *fpl* (d'avenir); the ~ for the New Year is promising cette nouvelle année s'annonce prometteuse; it's a bleak ~ for the unemployed pour les sans-emploi, les perspectives d'avenir ne sont guère réjouissantes; the ~ for the future is grim l'avenir est sombre ‖ METEOR prévision *f*, prévisions *fpl*; the ~ for March is cold and windy pour mars, on prévoit un temps froid avec beaucoup de vent. **-2.** [viewpoint] point de vue *m*, conception *f*; what's your ~ on life? quelle est votre conception de la vie?; she has rather a pessimistic ~ elle voit les choses plutôt en noir OR de manière pessimiste. **-3.** [view - from window] perspective *f*, vue *f*; we have a pleasant ~ onto a small park nous avons une vue agréable sur un petit parc.

outlying ['aʊt,laɪɪŋ] *adj* [remote - area, village] isolé, à l'écart; [far from centre - urban areas] périphérique; the ~ suburbs la grande banlieue.

outmanoeuvre *Br*, **outmaneuver** *Am* [,aʊtmə'nuːvəʳ] *vt* MIL se montrer meilleur tacticien que; *fig* déjouer les manœuvres de; we were ~d by the opposition l'opposition nous a pris de vitesse.

outmoded [,aʊt'məʊdəd] *adj* démodé, désuet.

outnumber [,aʊt'nʌmbəʳ] *vt* être plus nombreux que; they were ~ed by the enemy l'ennemi était supérieur en nombre; women ~ men by two to one il y a deux fois plus de femmes que d'hommes.

out-of-bounds *adj* **-1.** [barred] interdit; ~ to civilians interdit aux civils. **-2.** *Am* SPORT hors (du) terrain.

out-of-date *adj* **-1.** = **outdated**. **-2.** [expired] périmé; your passport is out of date votre passeport est périmé.

out-of-door *Br* = **outdoor**.

out-of-doors *Br* ◇ *adv* = **outdoors**.
◇ *adj* = **outdoor**.

out-of-pocket *adj*: I'm £5 out of pocket j'en suis pour 5 livres de ma poche ❑ ~ expenses frais *mpl*.

out-of-the-ordinary *adj* insolite.

out-of-the-way *adj* **-1.** [isolated] écarté, isolé; [unknown to most people] peu connu; [not popular] peu fréquenté. **-2.** [uncommon] insolite.

out-of-work *adj* au chômage.

outpace [,aʊt'peɪs] *vt* [run faster than] courir plus vite que; [overtake] dépasser, devancer.

outpatient ['aʊt,peɪʃnt] *n* malade *mf* en consultation externe; ~s' department service *m* des consultations externes.

outperform [,aʊtpə'fɔːm] *vt* avoir de meilleures performances que, être plus performant que.

outplacement ['aʊtpleɪsmənt] *n assistance offerte par certaines entreprises à leurs employés pour leur permettre de retrouver un emploi en cas de licenciement.*

outplay [,aʊt'pleɪ] *vt* jouer mieux que, dominer (au jeu).

outpost ['aʊtpəʊst] *n* avant-poste *m*; the last ~s of civilization les derniers bastions de la civilisation.

outpouring ['aʊt,pɔːrɪŋ] *n* épanchement *m*; ~s effusions *fpl*.

output ['aʊtpʊt] (*pt* & *pp* output, *cont* outputting) ◇ *n* **-1.** [production] production *f*; [productivity] rendement *m*; our ~ is not keeping pace with demand notre production est insuffisante pour répondre à la demande; his writing ~ is phenomenal c'est un auteur très prolifique ‖ [power - of machine] rendement *m*, débit *m*; this machine has an ~ of 6,000 items an hour cette machine débite 6 000 pièces à l'heure. **-2.** ELEC puissance *f*; [of amplifier] puissance *f* (de sortie); COMPUT [device] sortie *f*; [printout] sortie *f* papier, tirage *m*.
◇ *vt* COMPUT [data] sortir.
◇ *vi* COMPUT sortir des données.

output device *n* périphérique *m* de sortie.

output signal *n* signal *m* de sortie.

outrage ['aʊtreɪdʒ] ◇ *n* **-1.** [affront] outrage *m*, affront *m*; it's an ~ against public decency c'est un outrage aux bonnes mœurs; it's an ~ against humanity/society c'est un affront à l'humanité/la société ‖ [scandal] scandale *m*; it's an ~ that no-one came to their aid c'est un scandale OR il est scandaleux que personne ne soit venu à leur secours. **-2.** [indignation] indignation *f*. **-3.** [brutal act] atrocité *f*, acte *m* de brutalité OR de violence ❑ bomb ~ *Br* attentat *m* à la bombe.
◇ *vt* [person] outrager; [moral sensibility] outrager, faire outrage à; to be ~d at OR by sthg être outré OR scandalisé par qqch.

outrageous [aʊt'reɪdʒəs] *adj* **-1.** [scandalous - behaviour, manners] scandaleux; [atrocious - crime, attack etc] monstrueux, atroce; an ~ violation of human rights une violation scandaleuse des droits de l'homme; it's ~ that anyone should believe him guilty! il est scandaleux qu'on puisse le croire coupable! **-2.** [slightly offensive - humour, style] choquant; [- joke, remark] outrageant. **-3.** [extravagant - person, colour] extravagant; he wears the most ~ clothes il porte les vêtements les plus extravagants ‖ [price] exorbitant.

outrageously [aʊt'reɪdʒəslɪ] *adv* **-1.** [scandalously] de façon scandaleuse, scandaleusement; [atrociously] atrocement, monstrueusement; they behaved ~ ils se sont comportés de façon scandaleuse; we have been treated ~ on nous a traités d'une façon scandaleuse. **-2.** [extravagantly] de façon extravagante; she was ~ dressed elle était habillée de façon extravagante; the shop is ~ expensive les prix pratiqués dans ce magasin sont exorbitants.

outrageousness [aʊt'reɪdʒəsnɪs] *n* [of behaviour] caractère *m* scandaleux OR outrageant; [of crime, torture] atrocité *f*; [of dress] extravagance *f*; [of language] outrance *f*; [of prices] exagération *f*.

outrank [aʊt'ræŋk] *vt* avoir un rang plus élevé que; MIL avoir un grade supérieur à.

outré ['uːtreɪ] *adj Br fml* OR *hum* outrancier.

outreach [*vb* ,aʊt'riːtʃ, *n* 'aʊtriːtʃ] ◇ *vt* **-1.** [exceed] dépasser. **-2.** [in arm length] avoir le bras plus long que; [in boxing] avoir l'allonge supérieure à.
◇ *n* ADMIN *recherche des personnes qui ne demandent pas l'aide sociale dont elles pourraient bénéficier.*

outrider ['aʊt,raɪdəʳ] *n Br* [motorcyclist] motard *m* (d'escorte); [horseman] cavalier *m*.

outrigger ['aʊt,rɪgəʳ] *n* NAUT [gen] balancier *m*; [on racing boat] portant *m*, outrigger *m*.

outright [*adj* 'aʊtraɪt, *adv* aʊt'raɪt] ◇ *adj* **-1.** [absolute, utter - dishonesty, hypocrisy] pur (et simple), absolu; [- liar] fieffé; [- ownership] total, absolu; [frank - denial, refusal] net, catégorique; he's an ~ fascist! c'est un vrai fasciste!; she's an ~ opponent of capital punishment c'est une adversaire inconditionnelle de la peine de mort; it was ~ blackmail c'était purement et simplement du chantage OR du chantage, ni plus ni moins. **-2.** [clear - win, winner] incontesté; it's an ~ win for New Zealand la victoire revient incontestablement à la Nouvelle-Zélande. **-3.** COMM [sale - for cash] au comptant; [- total] en bloc.
◇ *adv* **-1.** [frankly - refuse] net, carrément; [- ask] carrément, franchement. **-2.** [totally - oppose] absolument; [- own] totalement. **-3.** [clearly - win] nettement, haut la main. **-4.** COMM [sell - for cash] au comptant; [- totally] en bloc. **-5.** [instantly]: they were killed ~ ils ont été tués sur le coup.

outrun [,aʊt'rʌn] (*pt* outran [-'ræn], *pp* outrun, *cont* outrunning) *vt* **-1.** [run faster than] courir plus vite que; [pursuer] distancer. **-2.** [ability, energy, resources] excéder, dépasser; our enthusiasm outran our financial resources notre enthousiasme dépassait nos ressources financières.

outsell [,aʊt'sel] (*pt* & *pp* outsold [-'səʊld]) *vt* [subj: article] se vendre mieux que; [subj: company] vendre davantage que; the brand of cigarettes that ~s all the others la marque de cigarettes la plus vendue; her book outsold all of this week's other publications son livre a été la meilleure vente de la semaine.

outset ['aʊtset] *n*: at the ~ au début, au départ; from the ~ dès le début, d'emblée.

outshine [,aʊt'ʃaɪn] (*pt* & *pp* outshone [-'ʃɒn]) *vt* [subj: star] briller plus que; *fig* [rival] éclipser, surpasser.

outside [*adv* & *prep* aʊt'saɪd, *adj* & *n* 'aʊtsaɪd] ◇ *adv* **-1.** [outdoors] dehors, à l'extérieur; it's cold ~ il fait froid dehors; put the box ~ mettez la boîte dehors; to go ~ sortir; seen from ~ vu de l'extérieur; the car is waiting ~ la voiture attend dehors; you'll have to park ~ il faudra vous garer dans la rue. **-2.** [on other side of door] dehors; can you wait ~? pouvez-vous attendre dehors?; there's a woman ~ in the hall il y a une femme dehors dans le vestibule. **-3.** [out of prison] dehors; after ten years, it's hard to imagine life ~ après dix ans, c'est dur d'imaginer la vie dehors.
◇ *prep* **-1.** [on or to the exterior] à l'extérieur de, hors de; nobody is allowed ~ the house personne n'a le droit de quitter la maison; your front foot must remain ~ the base line votre pied d'appel doit rester derrière la OR ne doit pas mordre sur la ligne; put the eggs ~ the window/door mettez les œufs sur le rebord de la fenêtre/devant la porte; she was wearing her shirt ~ her trousers elle portait sa chemise par-dessus son pantalon; nobody ~ the office must know personne ne doit être mis au courant en dehors du bureau; the troublemakers were people from ~ the group *fig* les fauteurs de troubles ne faisaient pas partie du groupe. **-2.** [away from]: we live some way ~ the town nous habitons assez loin de la ville; I don't think anybody ~ France has heard of him je ne pense pas qu'il soit connu ailleurs qu'en France. **-3.** [in front of] devant; they met ~ the cathedral [by chance] ils se sont rencontrés devant la cathédrale; [by arrangement] ils se sont retrouvés devant la cathédrale. **-4.** [beyond] en dehors de, au-delà de; it's ~ his field ce n'est pas son domaine; it's ~ my experience ça ne m'est jamais arrivé; the matter is ~ our responsibility la question ne relève pas de notre responsabilité; ~ office hours en dehors des heures de bureau.
◇ *adj* **-1.** [exterior] extérieur; the ~ world le monde extérieur; she has few ~ interests elle s'intéresse à peu de choses à part son travail; an ~ toilet des toilettes (situées) à l'extérieur; the ~ edge le bord extérieur; ~ lane [driving on left] file *f* OR voie *f* de droite; [driving on right] file *f* OR voie *f* de gauche; an ~ line [on telephone] une ligne extérieure. **-2.** [from elsewhere - help, influence] extérieur; to get an ~ opinion demander l'avis d'un tiers. **-3.** [poor - possibility] faible; she has only an ~ chance of winning elle n'a que très peu de chances de gagner. **-4.** [maximum - price] maximum; the ~ odds are 6 to 1 la cote maximum est de 6 contre 1. **-5.** [not belonging to a group] extérieur, indépendant; an ~ body un organisme indépendant.
◇ *n* **-1.** [exterior - of building, container] extérieur *m*, dehors *m*; the ~ of the house needs repainting l'extérieur de la maison a besoin d'être repeint; the door opens from (the) ~ la porte s'ouvre de l'extérieur OR du dehors; the arms were flown in from ~ les armes ont été introduites dans le pays par avion ‖ *fig*: looking at the problem from (the) ~ quand on considère le problème de l'extérieur. **-2.** [out of prison]: I've almost forgotten what life is like on the ~ j'ai presque oublié ce qu'est la vie dehors OR de l'autre côté des barreaux. **-3.** AUT: to overtake on the ~ [driving on left] doubler à droite; [driving on right] doubler à gauche. **-4.** [outer edge] extérieur *m*; begin at the ~ and work in commencez par les bords et allez vers l'intérieur.

◆ **at the outside** *adv phr* **-1.** [in number] tout au plus, au maximum; twenty people at the ~

vingt personnes tout au plus. -**2.** [in time] au plus tard; 6:30 at the ~ 6 h 30 au plus tard.
◆ **outside of** *esp Am* -**1.** = **outside** *prep.* -**2.** [except for] en dehors de; **nobody, ~ of a few close friends, was invited** personne, en dehors de OR à part quelques amis intimes, n'était invité. -**3.** [more than] au-delà de; **an offer ~ of 10 million** une offre de plus de OR supérieure à 10 millions.

outside broadcast *n* reportage *m.*

outside half *n* SPORT demi *m* d'ouverture.

outside left *n* SPORT ailier *m* gauche.

outsider [ˌaʊt'saɪdəʳ] *n* -**1.** [person] étranger *m*, -ère *f*; **he's always been a bit of an ~** il a toujours été plutôt marginal; **I'd be glad to have an ~'s viewpoint** je serais heureux d'avoir un point de vue extérieur. -**2.** SPORT outsider *m.*

outside right *n* SPORT ailier *m* droit.

outsize ['aʊtsaɪz] *Br* ◇ *n* [gen] grande taille *f*, grandes tailles *fpl*; [for men] très grand patron *m.*
◇ *adj* -**1.** [large] énorme, très grand. -**2.** [in clothes sizes] grande taille *(inv).*

outskirts ['aʊtskɜːts] *npl* [of town] banlieue *f*, périphérie *f*; [of forest] orée *f*, lisière *f*; **we live on the ~ of Copenhagen** nous habitons la banlieue de Copenhague.

outsmart [ˌaʊt'smɑːt] *vt* se montrer plus malin que.

outspend [ˌaʊt'spend] (*pt* & *pp* **outspent** [-'spent]) *vt* dépenser plus que.

outspoken [ˌaʊt'spəʊkn] *adj* franc; **to be ~** parler franchement, avoir son franc-parler; **she was ~ in her criticism of the project** elle a ouvertement critiqué le projet; **he has always been an ~ critic of the reforms** il a toujours ouvertement critiqué les réformes.

outspokenness [ˌaʊt'spəʊkənnɪs] *n* franc-parler *m.*

outspread [ˌaʊt'spred] *adj* étendu; **with ~ arms** les bras écartés; **with ~ wings** les ailes déployées; **with ~ fingers** les doigts écartés; **an ~ newspaper** un journal déplié.

outstanding [ˌaʊt'stændɪŋ] *adj* -**1.** [remarkable - ability, performance] exceptionnel, remarquable; [notable - event, feature] marquant, mémorable; **an ~ politician** un politicien hors pair OR exceptionnel. -**2.** [unresolved - problem] non résolu, en suspens; **there is still one ~ matter** il reste encore un problème à régler ‖ [unfinished - business, work] inachevé, en cours; ADMIN en souffrance, en attente; **there are about 20 pages ~** il reste environ 20 pages à faire ‖ [unpaid - bill] impayé; **~ payment** impayé *m*; **~ interest/rent** arriérés *mpl* d'intérêt/de loyer. -**3.** ST. EX émis.

outstandingly [ˌaʊt'stændɪŋlɪ] *adv* exceptionnellement, remarquablement.

outstare [ˌaʊt'steəʳ] *vt* faire baisser les yeux à *(en dévisageant).*

outstation ['aʊtsteɪʃn] *n* -**1.** [in colony, isolated region] avant-poste *m.* -**2.** RADIO station *f* extérieure OR satellite.

outstay [ˌaʊt'steɪ] *vt* -**1.** [subj: guests] rester plus longtemps que; **to ~ one's welcome** abuser de l'hospitalité de ses hôtes. -**2.** *Br* SPORT [competitor] tenir plus longtemps que.

outstretched [ˌaʊt'stretʃt] *adj* [limbs, body] étendu, allongé; [wings] déployé; **to lie ~** s'allonger; **with arms ~, with ~ arms** [gen] les bras écartés; [in welcome] à bras (grand) ouverts; **the beggar stood outside the church with ~ hands** le mendiant se tenait devant l'église, la main tendue.

outstrip [ˌaʊt'strɪp] (*pt* & *pp* **outstripped**, *cont* **outstripping**) *vt Br* dépasser, surpasser; **they outstripped all their rivals** ils l'ont emporté sur tous leurs concurrents.

outtake ['aʊtteɪk] *n* CIN & TV coupure *f.*

out tray *n* corbeille *f* sortie.

outvote [ˌaʊt'vəʊt] *vt* [bill, reform] rejeter (à la majorité des voix); **the bill was ~d** une majorité a voté contre le projet de loi ‖ [person] mettre en minorité; **I wanted to go to the cinema, but I was ~d** je voulais aller au cinéma, mais les autres ont voté contre.

outward ['aʊtwəd] ◇ *adj* -**1.** [external] extérieur, externe; [apparent] apparent; **to (all) ~ appearances, she's very successful** selon toute apparence, elle réussit très bien; **an ~ show of wealth** un étalage de richesses; **she showed no ~ signs of fear** elle ne montrait aucun signe de peur. -**2.** [in direction] vers l'extérieur; **the ~ journey** le voyage aller, l'aller *m.*
◇ *adv* vers l'extérieur; **~ bound** [ship, train] en partance.

outward bound course *n* école *f* d'aventure.

outwardly ['aʊtwədlɪ] *adv* en apparence; **she remained ~ calm** elle est restée calme en apparence; **~ they seem to get on** ils donnent l'impression de bien s'entendre.

outwards ['aʊtwədz] *adv* vers l'extérieur; **his feet turn ~** il marche les pieds en dehors; **the door opens ~** la porte s'ouvre vers l'extérieur.

outweigh [aʊt'weɪ] *vt* l'emporter sur; **the advantages easily ~ the disadvantages** les avantages l'emportent largement sur les inconvénients.

outwit [ˌaʊt'wɪt] (*pt* & *pp* **outwitted**, *cont* **outwitting**) *vt* se montrer plus malin que; **we've been outwitted** on nous a eus.

outwork ['aʊtwɜːk] *n Br* [work] travail *m* fait à l'extérieur.
◆ **outworks** *npl* MIL ouvrage *m* défensif avancé.

outworker ['aʊtˌwɜːkəʳ] *n Br* travailleur *m* à domicile.

outworn ['aʊtwɔːn] *adj* [clothes] usé; [custom, idea] dépassé, vieux-jeu.

ouzo ['uːzəʊ] *n* ouzo *m.*

ova ['əʊvə] *pl* → **ovum.**

oval ['əʊvl] ◇ *adj* (en) ovale.
◇ *n* ovale *m.*
◆ **Oval** *pr n*: **the Oval** *célèbre terrain de cricket dans le centre de Londres.*

Oval Office *pr n* [office] Bureau *m* ovale; [authority] présidence *f* des États-Unis.

ovarian [əʊ'veərɪən] *adj* ovarien.

ovariectomy [ˌəʊvərɪ'ektəmɪ] (*pl* **ovariectomies**) *n* ovariectomie *f.*

ovary ['əʊvərɪ] (*pl* **ovaries**) *n* ovaire *m.*

ovate ['əʊveɪt] *adj* oviforme.

ovation [əʊ'veɪʃn] *n* ovation *f*; **to give sb an ~** faire une ovation à qqn.

oven ['ʌvn] *n* four *m*; **to cook sthg in an ~** faire cuire qqch au four; **cook in a hot/medium ~** faire cuire à four chaud/à four moyen; **Athens is like an ~ in summer** *fig* Athènes est une vraie fournaise en été.

ovenable ['ʌvnəbl] *adj* allant au four.

oven glove *n* gant *m* isolant.

ovenproof ['ʌvnpruːf] *adj* allant OR qui va au four.

oven-ready *adj* prêt à cuire OR à mettre au four.

ovenware ['ʌvnweəʳ] *n* plats *mpl* allant au four.

over ['əʊvəʳ] ◇ *prep* **A.** -**1.** [above] au-dessus de; **a bullet whistled ~ my head** une balle siffla au-dessus de ma tête; **they live ~ the shop** ils habitent au-dessus du magasin; **the plane came down ~ France** l'avion s'est écrasé en France. -**2.** [on top of, covering] sur, par-dessus; **put a lace cloth ~ the table** mets une nappe en dentelle sur la table; **she wore a cardigan ~ her dress** elle portait un gilet par-dessus sa robe; **she wore a black dress with a red cardigan ~ it** elle avait une robe noire avec un gilet rouge par-dessus; **I put my hand ~ my mouth** j'ai mis ma main devant ma bouche; **he had his jacket ~ his arm** il avait sa veste sur le bras; **we painted ~ the wallpaper** nous avons peint par-dessus la tapisserie; **she was hunched ~ the wheel** elle était penchée sur la roue. -**3.** [across the top or edge of] par-dessus; **he was watching me ~ his newspaper** il m'observait par-dessus son journal; **I peered ~ the edge** j'ai jeté un coup d'œil par-dessus le rebord; **he fell/jumped ~ the cliff** il est tombé/a sauté du haut de la falaise. -**4.** [across the entire surface of]: **to cross ~ the road** traverser la rue; **they live ~ the road from me** ils habitent en face de chez moi; **there's a fine view ~ the valley** on a une belle vue sur la vallée; **he ran his eye ~ the article** il a parcouru l'article des yeux; **she ran her hand ~ the smooth marble** elle passa la main sur le marbre lisse; **we travelled for days ~ land and sea** nous avons voyagé pendant des jours par terre et par mer; **a strange look came ~ her face** son visage prit une expression étrange. -**5.** [on the far side of]: **the village ~ the hill** le village de l'autre côté de la colline; **they must be ~ the border by now** ils doivent avoir passé la frontière maintenant.
B. -**1.** [indicating position of control]: **to rule ~ a country** régner sur un pays; **I have no control/influence ~ them** je n'ai aucune autorité/influence sur eux; **she has some kind of hold ~ him** elle a une certaine emprise sur lui; **she watched ~ her children** elle surveillait ses enfants. -**2.** [indicating position of superiority, importance] sur; **a victory ~ the forces of reaction** une victoire sur les forces réactionnaires; **our project takes priority ~ the others** notre projet a priorité sur les autres.
C. -**1.** [with specific figure or amount - more than] plus de; **it took me well/just ~ an hour** j'ai mis bien plus/un peu plus d'une heure; **he must be ~ thirty** il doit avoir plus de trente ans; **children ~ (the age of) 7** les enfants (âgés) de plus de 7 ans; **think of a number ~ 100** pensez à un chiffre supérieur à 100. -**2.** [louder than]: **his voice rang out ~ the others** sa voix dominait toutes les autres; **I couldn't hear what she was saying ~ the music** la musique m'empêchait d'entendre ce qu'elle disait. -**3.** MATH [divided by]: **eight ~ two** huit divisé par deux. -**4.** [during]: **I've got a job ~ the long vacation** je vais travailler pendant les grandes vacances; **what are you doing ~ Easter?** qu'est-ce que tu fais pour Pâques?; **it's improved ~ the years** ça s'est amélioré au cours OR au fil des années; **~ the next few decades** au cours des prochaines décennies; **we discussed it ~ a drink/~ a game of golf** nous en avons discuté autour d'un verre/en faisant une partie de golf.
D. -**1.** [concerning] au sujet de; **a disagreement ~ working conditions** un conflit portant sur les conditions de travail; **they're always quarrelling ~ money** ils se disputent sans cesse pour des questions d'argent; **there's a big question mark ~ his future** nous n'avons aucune idée de ce qu'il va devenir. -**2.** [by means of, via]: **they were talking ~ the telephone** ils parlaient au téléphone; **I heard it ~ the radio** je l'ai entendu à la radio. -**3.** [recovered from]: **are you ~ your bout of flu?** est-ce que tu es guéri OR est-ce que tu t'es remis de ta grippe?; **he's ~ the shock now** il s'en est remis maintenant; **we'll soon be ~ the worst** le plus dur sera bientôt passé; **it took her a long time to get ~ his death** elle a mis longtemps à se remettre de sa mort.
◇ *adv* **A.** -**1.** [indicating movement or location, across distance or space]: **an eagle flew ~** un aigle passa au-dessus de nous; **she walked ~ to him and said hello** elle s'approcha de lui pour dire bonjour; **he must have seen us, he's coming ~** il a dû nous voir, il vient vers nous OR de notre côté; **pass my cup ~, will you** tu peux me passer ma tasse?; **she glanced ~ at me** elle jeta un coup d'œil dans ma direction; **she leaned ~ to whisper to him** elle se pencha pour lui chuchoter quelque chose à l'oreille; **~ in the States** aux États-Unis; **~ there** là-bas; **come ~ here!** viens (par) ici!; **has Bill been ~?** est-ce que Bill est passé?; **she drove ~ to meet us** elle est venue nous rejoindre en voiture; **let's have OR invite them ~ for dinner** si on les invitait à dîner?; **we have guests ~ from Morocco** nous avons des invités qui viennent du Maroc. -**2.** [everywhere]: **she's travelled the whole world ~** elle a voyagé dans le monde entier; **people the world ~ are watching the broad-**

cast live des téléspectateurs dans le monde entier assistent à cette retransmission en direct. -**3.** [indicating movement from a higher to a lower level]: I fell ~ je suis tombé (par terre); she knocked her glass ~ elle a renversé son verre; he flipped the pancake ~ il a retourné la crêpe; they rolled ~ and ~ in the grass ils se roulaient dans l'herbe. -**4.** [so as to cover]: we just whitewashed it ~ nous l'avons simplement passé à la chaux; the bodies were covered ~ with blankets les corps étaient recouverts avec des couvertures. -**5.** [into the hands of another person, group etc]: he's gone ~ to the other side/to the opposition il est passé de l'autre côté/dans l'opposition; they handed him ~ to the authorities ils l'ont remis aux autorités OR entre les mains des autorités || RADIO & TV: and now ~ to David Smith in Paris nous passons maintenant l'antenne à David Smith à Paris || TELEC: ~ (to you)! à vous!; ~ and out! terminé!

B. -**1.** [left, remaining]: there were/I had a few pounds (left) ~ il restait/il me restait quelques livres; seven into fifty-two makes seven with three ~ cinquante-deux divisé par sept égale sept, il reste trois. -**2.** [with specific figure or amount - more] plus; men of 30 and ~ les hommes âgés de 30 ans et plus; articles costing £100 or ~ les articles de 100 livres et plus. -**3.** [through]: read it ~ carefully lisez-le attentivement; do you want to talk the matter ~? voulez-vous en discuter? -**4.** [again, more than once] encore; I had to do the whole thing ~ *Am* j'ai dû tout refaire; she won the tournament five times ~ elle a gagné le tournoi à cinq reprises.

◇ *adj* fini; the party's ~ la fête est finie; I'm glad that's ~ (with)! je suis bien content que ça soit fini!

◆ **over and above** *prep phr* en plus de; ~ and above what we've already paid en plus de ce que nous avons déjà payé; and ~ and above that, he was banned from driving for life en plus, on lui a retiré son permis (de conduire) à vie.

◆ **over and over** *adv phr*: I've told you ~ and ~ (again) je te l'ai répété je ne sais combien de fois.

over- *in cpds* -**1.** [excessive]: ~activity suractivité *f*; ~cautious trop prudent, d'une prudence excessive. -**2.** [more than]: a club for the ~fifties un club pour les plus de cinquante ans.

overabundant [ˌəʊvərəˈbʌndənt] *adj* surabondant.

overachieve [ˌəʊvərəˈtʃiːv] *vi* réussir brillamment; children who ~ les enfants surdoués.

overachiever [ˌəʊvərəˈtʃiːvəʳ] *n* surdoué *m*, -e *f*.

overact [ˌəʊvərˈækt] *vi* forcer la note, avoir un jeu outré.

overage [ˈəʊvərɪdʒ] *n Am* [surplus] surplus *m*, excédent *m*.

over-age *adj* [too old] trop âgé.

overall [*adv* ˌəʊvərˈɔːl, *adj* & *n* ˈəʊvərɔːl]

◇ *adv* -**1.** [in general - consider, examine] en général, globalement. -**2.** [measure] de bout en bout, d'un bout à l'autre; [cost, amount] en tout. -**3.** [in competition, sport] au classement général; Britain finished third ~ la Grande-Bretagne a fini troisième au classement général.

◇ *adj* -**1.** [general] global, d'ensemble; my ~ impression mon impression d'ensemble. -**2.** [total - cost, amount] total; [- measurement] total, hors tout.

◇ *n* [protective coat] blouse *f*; *Am* [boiler suit] bleu *m* de travail.

◆ **overalls** *npl Br* [boiler suit] bleu *m* de travail; *Am* [dungarees] salopette *f*.

overambitious [ˌəʊvəræmˈbɪʃəs] *adj* trop ambitieux.

overanxious [ˌəʊvərˈæŋkʃəs] *adj* -**1.** [worried] trop inquiet; don't be ~ about the exam ne vous inquiétez pas trop au sujet de l'examen. -**2.** [keen] trop soucieux; he did not seem ~ to meet her il n'avait pas l'air tellement pressé de faire sa connaissance; she is ~ to please elle est trop désireuse OR soucieuse de plaire, elle en fait trop.

overarm [ˈəʊvərɑːm] ◇ *adv*: to throw a ball ~ lancer une balle par-dessus sa tête; to swim ~ nager à l'indienne.

◇ *adj*: ~ stroke brasse *f* indienne.

overate [ˌəʊvərˈet] *pt* → **overeat**.

overawe [ˌəʊvərˈɔː] *vt* intimider, impressionner; don't be ~d by what you are about to hear ne vous laissez pas impressionner par ce que vous allez entendre.

overbalance [ˌəʊvəˈbæləns] ◇ *vi* [person] perdre l'équilibre; [load, pile] basculer, se renverser; [car] capoter; [boat] chavirer.

◇ *vt* [person] faire perdre l'équilibre à; [pile, vehicle] renverser, faire basculer.

overbear [ˌəʊvəˈbeəʳ] (*pt* overbore [-ˈbɔːʳ], *pp* overborne [-ˈbɔːn]) *vt fml* [rival, victim] dominer, triompher de, vaincre; [objection, proposal] l'emporter sur, prévaloir contre.

overbearing [ˌəʊvəˈbeərɪŋ] *adj* autoritaire, impérieux.

overbid [*vb* ˌəʊvəˈbɪd, *n* ˈəʊvəbɪd] (*pt* & *pp* overbid, *cont* overbidding) ◇ *vt* enchérir sur.

◇ *vi* surenchérir.

◇ *n* surenchère *f*.

overblown [ˌəʊvəˈbləʊn] *adj* -**1.** [flower, beauty] qui commence à se faner. -**2.** *pej* [prose, style] boursouflé, ampoulé, pompier.

overboard [ˈəʊvəbɔːd] *adv* NAUT par-dessus bord; to fall ~ passer par-dessus bord; to jump ~ sauter à la mer; man ~! un homme à la mer! ❑ to throw sthg/sb ~ *literal* jeter qqch/qqn par-dessus bord; *fig* se débarrasser de qqch/qqn; to throw a project ~ abandonner un projet; to go ~ *inf* dépasser la mesure, exagérer; he has really gone ~ with his latest film il a vraiment dépassé les bornes avec son dernier film; he went ~ for a young waitress il est tombé amoureux fou d'une jeune serveuse; the critics went ~ about her first novel les critiques se sont enthousiasmés OR emballés pour son nouveau roman.

overbook [ˌəʊvəˈbʊk] ◇ *vt* [flight, hotel] surréserver.

◇ *vi* [airline, hotel] surréserver.

overbooking [ˌəʊvəˈbʊkɪŋ] *n* surréservation *f*, surbooking *m*.

overbore [ˌəʊvəˈbɔːʳ] *pt* → **overbear**.

overborne [ˌəʊvəˈbɔːn] *pp* → **overbear**.

overburden [ˌəʊvəˈbɜːdn] *vt* surcharger, accabler; ~ed with work submergé de travail; ~ed with debts criblé de dettes; ~ed with worries accablé de soucis.

overcall [*vb* ˌəʊvəˈkɔːl, *n* ˈəʊvəkɔːl] ◇ *vt* [in bridge] surenchérir sur.

◇ *n* [in bridge] surenchère *f*.

overcame [ˌəʊvəˈkeɪm] *pt* → **overcome**.

overcapitalize, **-ise** [ˌəʊvəˈkæpɪtəlaɪz] *vt* surcapitaliser.

overcast [*vb* ˌəʊvəˈkɑːst, *adj* & *n* ˈəʊvəkɑːst] (*pt* & *pp* overcast) ◇ *vt* SEW surfiler.

◇ *adj* [sky] sombre, couvert; [weather] couvert; it's getting ~ le temps se couvre; the sky became ~ le ciel s'assombrit.

◇ *n* nébulosité *f*.

overcautious [ˌəʊvəˈkɔːʃəs] *adj* trop prudent, prudent à l'excès.

overcharge [ˌəʊvəˈtʃɑːdʒ] ◇ *vt* -**1.** [customer] faire payer trop cher; I've been ~d! on m'a fait payer trop cher!, je me suis fait écorcher!; they ~d me for the coffee ils m'ont fait payer le café trop cher; they ~d me for the repair ils m'ont pris trop cher pour la réparation. -**2.** ELEC [circuit] surcharger. -**3.** *Br* [description, picture] surcharger; the painting was ~d with detail le tableau était surchargé de détails.

◇ *vi* faire payer trop cher; they ~d for the tomatoes ils ont fait payer les tomates trop cher.

overcloud [ˌəʊvəˈklaʊd] ◇ *vt*: the sky became ~ed le ciel se couvrit de nuages.

◇ *vi* se couvrir, devenir nuageux.

overcoat [ˈəʊvəkəʊt] *n* manteau *m*, pardessus *m*.

overcome [ˌəʊvəˈkʌm] (*pt* overcame [-ˈkeɪm], *pp* overcome) ◇ *vt* -**1.** [vanquish - enemy, opposition] vaincre, triompher de; [- difficulty, shyness] surmonter; [- fear, repulsion, prejudice] vaincre, surmonter, maîtriser; [master - nerves] maîtriser, contrôler. -**2.** [debilitate, weaken] accabler; the heat overcame me la chaleur finit par me terrasser; she was ~ by the fumes les émanations lui ont fait perdre connaissance; he felt sleep ~ him *lit* il sentait le sommeil le gagner. -**3.** *(usu pass)* [overwhelm]: to be ~ by the enemy succomber à l'ennemi; to be ~ by fear être paralysé par la peur; to be ~ with joy être comblé de joie; to be ~ with grief être accablé par la douleur; I was ~ by the news la nouvelle m'a bouleversé; in a voice ~ with emotion d'une voix tremblante d'émotion; how did he take the news? – he was quite ~ comment a-t-il pris la nouvelle? – il est resté muet.

◇ *vi* vaincre; 'We Shall Overcome' 'Nous triompherons' *(célèbre chanson du mouvement américain des droits civiques)*.

overcompensate [ˌəʊvəˈkɒmpənseɪt] *vt* surcompenser.

overcompensation [ˈəʊvəˌkɒmpənˈseɪʃn] *n* surcompensation *f*.

overcomplicated [ˌəʊvəˈkɒmplɪkeɪtɪd] *adj* trop OR excessivement compliqué.

overconfidence [ˌəʊvəˈkɒnfɪdəns] *n* -**1.** [arrogance] suffisance *f*, présomption *f*. -**2.** [trust] confiance *f* aveugle OR excessive.

overconfident [ˌəʊvəˈkɒnfɪdənt] *adj* -**1.** [arrogant] suffisant, présomptueux. -**2.** [trusting] trop confiant; I'm not ~ of his chances of recovery je ne crois pas trop en ses chances de guérison.

overcook [ˌəʊvəˈkʊk] ◇ *vt* faire trop cuire; the vegetables are ~ed les légumes sont trop cuits.

◇ *vi* trop cuire.

overcrowd [ˌəʊvəˈkraʊd] *vt* [bus, train, room] remplir au maximum, bourrer; [city, streets, prison] surpeupler; [class] surcharger.

overcrowded [ˌəʊvəˈkraʊdɪd] *adj* [bus, train, room] bondé, comble; [city, country, prison] surpeuplé; [streets] plein de monde; [class] surchargé; Paris is ~ with tourists in summer en été, Paris est envahi par les touristes; they live in very ~ conditions ils vivent très à l'étroit.

overcrowding [ˌəʊvəˈkraʊdɪŋ] *n* surpeuplement *m*, surpopulation *f*; [in housing] entassement *m*; [in bus, train etc] entassement *m* des voyageurs, affluence *f*; [in schools] effectifs *mpl* surchargés; [in prisons] surpeuplement *m*; ~ on trains means you sometimes have to stand les trains sont tellement bondés qu'on est parfois contraint de voyager debout; prison ~ is a growing problem le surpeuplement des prisons est un problème croissant.

overdevelop [ˌəʊvədɪˈveləp] *vt* [gen & PHOT] surdévelopper; parts of the coastline have been ~ed par endroits, le littoral est trop construit.

overdevelopment [ˌəʊvədɪˈveləpmənt] *n* surdéveloppement *m*.

overdo [ˌəʊvəˈduː] (*pt* overdid [-ˈdɪd], *pp* overdone [-ˈdʌn]) *vt* -**1.** [exaggerate] exagérer, pousser trop loin; he rather overdoes the penniless student (bit) il joue un peu trop l'étudiant pauvre; the battle scenes are a bit overdone les scènes de combat sont un peu exagérées; all that jewellery is really ~ing it! tous ces bijoux, c'est vraiment un peu trop!; Mabel rather overdoes the make-up Mabel se maquille un peu trop; you've overdone the curry powder tu as eu la main un peu lourde avec le curry. -**2.** [eat, drink too much of]: don't ~ the whisky n'abuse pas du whisky. -**3.** *phr*: to ~ it, to ~ things se surmener; I've been ~ing it again j'ai de nouveau un peu trop forcé. -**4.** CULIN trop cuire.

overdone [ˌəʊvəˈdʌn] ◇ *pp* → **overdo**.

◇ *adj* -**1.** [exaggerated] exagéré, excessif. -**2.** CULIN trop cuit.

overdose [*n* 'əʊvədəʊs, *vb* ˌəʊvə'dəʊs] ◇ *n literal* & *fig* overdose *f*, surdose *f*; an ~ of sleeping pills une dose massive de somnifères; she died from a drugs ~ elle est morte d'une overdose; I think I've had an ~ of culture today *hum* je crois que j'ai eu ma dose de culture pour aujourd'hui.
◇ *vi* prendre une overdose; he ~d on heroin/ LSD il a pris une overdose d'héroïne/de LSD; I've been overdosing on chocolate recently *hum* j'ai trop forcé sur le chocolat ces derniers temps.
◇ *vt* [patient] administrer une dose excessive à; [drug] prescrire une dose excessive de.

overdraft ['əʊvədrɑːft] *n* découvert *m* (bancaire); to have an ~ avoir un découvert; they live off an ~ ils sont en permanence à découvert; the bank gave me a £100 ~ la banque m'a accordé un découvert de 100 livres ❑ ~ facilities autorisation *f* de découvert.

overdramatic [ˌəʊvədrə'mætɪk] *adj* mélodramatique, exagéré.

overdraw [ˌəʊvə'drɔː] (*pt* overdrew [-'druː], *pp* overdrawn [-'drɔːn]) ◇ *vt* [account] mettre à découvert; to be OR to go overdrawn être OR se mettre à découvert; my account is overdrawn mon compte est à découvert; I'm overdrawn by £100 j'ai un découvert de 100 livres.
◇ *vi* mettre son compte à découvert.

overdress [*vb* ˌəʊvə'dres, *n* 'əʊvədres] ◇ *vi pej* s'habiller avec trop de recherche, porter des toilettes trop recherchées.
◇ *n* robe-chasuble *f*.

overdressed [ˌəʊvə'drest] *adj* habillé avec trop de recherche; to be ~ être trop bien habillé pour la circonstance; I felt ~ in my dinner suit j'avais la sensation d'être emprunté dans mon smoking.

overdrew [ˌəʊvə'druː] *pt* → **overdraw**.

overdrive ['əʊvədraɪv] *n* AUT (vitesse *f*) surmultipliée *f*, overdrive *m*; to go into ~ *fig* mettre les bouchées doubles.

overdub [*vb* ˌəʊvə'dʌb, *n* 'əʊvədʌb] (*pt* & *pp* overdubbed, *cont* overdubbing) ◇ *vt* [in recording] surimprimer.
◇ *n* surimpression *f*.

overdue [ˌəʊvə'djuː] *adj* -**1.** [bus, flight, person] en retard; she is long ~ elle devrait être là depuis longtemps; the flight from Panama is half an hour ~ le vol de Panama a une demi-heure de retard ‖ [payment, rent] en retard, impayé; [library book] non retourné; our repayments are two months ~ nous avons un retard de deux mois dans nos remboursements. -**2.** [apology] tardif; an explanation is ~ le moment semble venu de donner une explication, il est temps de donner une explication ‖ [change, reform] qui tarde, qui se fait attendre; this reform is long ~ cette réforme aurait dû être appliquée il y a longtemps; the car is ~ for a service la voiture a besoin d'être révisée. -**3.** [in pregnancy]: to be ~ être en retard.

overeager [ˌəʊvər'iːgə^r] *adj* trop empressé; he is ~ to please il est trop soucieux OR désireux de plaire; I can't say I'm ~ to go je ne peux pas dire que j'aie une envie folle d'y aller.

overeat [ˌəʊvər'iːt] (*pt* overate [-'et], *pp* overeaten [-'iːtn]) *vi* [once] trop manger, faire un repas trop copieux; [habitually] se suralimenter.

overeating [ˌəʊvər'iːtɪŋ] *n* [habitual] suralimentation *f*.

overelaborate [ˌəʊvərɪ'læbərɪt] *adj* [dress, style] trop recherché; [ornamentation] tarabiscoté; [explanation, excuse] tiré par les cheveux; [description] alambiqué, contourné.

overemotional [ˌəʊvərɪ'məʊʃənl] *adj* hyperémotif, trop émotif.

overemphasize, -ise [ˌəʊvər'emfəsaɪz] *vt* trop mettre l'accent sur, trop insister sur; I cannot ~ the need for discretion je n'insisterai jamais assez sur la nécessité de faire preuve de discrétion.

overemployment [ˌəʊvərɪm'plɔɪmənt] *n* suremploi *m*.

overenthusiastic ['əʊvərɪnˌθjuːzɪ'æstɪk] *adj* trop enthousiaste.

overestimate [ˌəʊvər'estɪmeɪt] *vt* surestimer.

overexaggerate [ˌəʊvərɪg'zædʒəreɪt] *vt* exagérer, attacher trop d'importance à.

overexcite [ˌəʊvərɪk'saɪt] *vt* surexciter; to become OR to get ~d (trop) s'énerver; don't get ~d, they haven't arrived yet ne vous excitez pas, ils ne sont pas encore arrivés; she got ~d and burst into tears elle s'est mise dans un état d'agitation extrême et a fondu en larmes.

overexcitement [ˌəʊvərɪk'saɪtmənt] *n* surexcitation *f*.

overexert [ˌəʊvərɪg'zɜːt] *vt* surmener; to ~ o.s. se surmener, s'éreinter.

overexertion [ˌəʊvərɪg'zɜːʃn] *n* surmenage *m*.

overexpose [ˌəʊvərɪk'spəʊz] *vt literal* & *fig* surexposer.

overexposure [ˌəʊvərɪk'spəʊʒə^r] *n literal* & *fig* surexposition *f*.

overfamiliar [ˌəʊvəfə'mɪljə^r] *adj* -**1.** [too intimate, disrespectful] trop familier. -**2.** [conversant]: I'm not ~ with the British electoral system je ne connais pas très bien le système électoral britannique.

overfamiliarity ['əʊvəfəˌmɪlɪ'ærətɪ] *n* familiarité *f* excessive.

overfeed [ˌəʊvə'fiːd] (*pt* & *pp* overfed [-'fed]) ◇ *vt* suralimenter.
◇ *vi* se suralimenter, trop manger.

overflew [ˌəʊvə'fluː] *pt* → **overfly**.

overflow [*vb* ˌəʊvə'fləʊ, *n* 'əʊvəfləʊ] ◇ *vi* -**1.** [with liquid - container, bath] déborder; [river] déborder, sortir de son lit; the glass is full to ~ing le verre est plein à ras bord; the river frequently ~s onto the surrounding plain la rivière inonde souvent la plaine environnante ‖ [with people - room, vehicle] déborder, être plein à craquer; the streets were ~ing with people les rues regorgeaient de monde; the demonstrators ~ed into the side streets les manifestants envahirent les rues adjacentes; the shop was full to ~ing le magasin était plein à craquer ‖ [with objects - box, wastebin] déborder; the contents of the bin ~ed onto the floor le contenu de la poubelle s'est répandu par terre; her desk was ~ing with papers son bureau disparaissait sous les papiers. -**2.** *fig* [with emotion] déborder; his heart was ~ing with joy son cœur débordait de joie.
◇ *vt* déborder de; the river ~ed its banks la rivière est sortie de son lit OR a débordé.
◇ *n* -**1.** [drain - from sink, cistern] trop-plein *m*; [- large-scale] déversoir *m*. -**2.** [excess - of population, production] excédent *m*, surplus *m*; [- of energy, emotion] trop-plein *m*, débordement *m*. -**3.** [flooding] inondation *f*; [excess] trop-plein *m*. -**4.** COMPUT dépassement *m* de capacité, débordement *m*.

overflown [ˌəʊvə'fləʊn] *pp* → **overfly**.

overflow pipe *n* trop-plein *m*, tuyau *m* d'écoulement.

overfly [ˌəʊvə'flaɪ] (*pt* overflew [-'fluː], *pp* overflown [-'fləʊn]) *vt* survoler.

overfond [ˌəʊvə'fɒnd] *adj*: she's not ~ of children on ne peut pas dire qu'elle ait une passion pour les enfants; he's not ~ of the cinema il n'est pas très porté sur le cinéma.

overfull [ˌəʊvə'fʊl] *adj* trop plein, qui déborde.

overgenerous [ˌəʊvə'dʒenərəs] *adj* [person, act] (trop) généreux, prodigue; [portion] trop copieux, excessif.

overground ['əʊvəgraʊnd] ◇ *adj* à la surface du sol, en surface; an ~ rail link une voie ferrée à l'air libre OR aérienne.
◇ *adv* à la surface du sol; the line goes ~ when it reaches the suburbs la ligne fait surface quand elle arrive en banlieue.

overgrown [ˌəʊvə'grəʊn] *adj* [garden, path etc]: the path was ~ with weeds/brambles le chemin était envahi par les mauvaises herbes/ronces; the garden has become very ~ le jardin est devenu une vraie jungle; a wall ~ with ivy un mur recouvert de lierre; he's just an ~ schoolboy *fig* c'est un grand enfant.

overhand ['əʊvəhænd] = **overarm**.

overhang [*vb* ˌəʊvə'hæŋ, *n* 'əʊvəhæŋ] (*pt* & *pp* overhung [-'hʌŋ]) ◇ *vt* -**1.** [subj: cliff, ledge, balcony] surplomber, faire saillie au-dessus de; [subj: cloud, mist, smoke] planer sur, flotter au-dessus de. -**2.** *fig* [subj: threat, danger] planer sur, menacer.
◇ *vi* être en surplomb, faire saillie.
◇ *n* surplomb *m*.

overhanging [ˌəʊvə'hæŋɪŋ] *adj* -**1.** [cliff, ledge, balcony] en surplomb, en saillie; we walked under the ~ branches nous marchions sous un dais OR une voûte de branches. -**2.** *fig* [threat] imminent.

overhaul [*n* 'əʊvəhɔːl, *vb* ˌəʊvə'hɔːl] ◇ *n* [of car, machine] révision *f*; [of institution, system] révision *f*, remaniement *m*; the education system needs a complete ~ le système scolaire a besoin d'être complètement remanié.
◇ *vt* -**1.** [car, machine] réviser; [system] revoir, remanier. -**2.** [catch up] rattraper; [overtake] dépasser; NAUT gagner.

overhead [*adv* ˌəʊvə'hed, *adj* & *n* 'əʊvəhed] ◇ *adv* au-dessus; we watched the hawk circling ~ nous regardions le faucon tournoyer dans le ciel OR au-dessus de nos têtes.
◇ *adj* -**1.** [cable, railway] aérien; [lighting] au plafond; SPORT [racket stroke] smashé; FTBL [kick] retourné. -**2.** COMM: ~ costs frais *mpl* généraux.
◇ *n Am* = **overheads**.
◆ **overheads** *npl Br* frais *mpl* généraux.

overhead camshaft *n* arbre *m* à cames en tête.

overhead door *n* porte *f* basculante.

overhead projector *n* rétroprojecteur *m*.

overhear [ˌəʊvə'hɪə^r] (*pt* & *pp* overheard [-'hɜːd]) *vt* [gen] entendre par hasard; [conversation] surprendre; I couldn't help ~ing what you were saying malgré moi, j'ai entendu votre conversation; she overheard them talking about her elle les a surpris à parler d'elle.

overheat [ˌəʊvə'hiːt] ◇ *vt* surchauffer.
◇ *vi* chauffer.

overheated [ˌəʊvə'hiːtɪd] *adj* -**1.** [too hot - room] surchauffé, trop chauffé; [- engine] qui chauffe. -**2.** *fig* [angry] passionné, violent, exalté; to become OR to get ~ [person] s'échauffer, s'énerver; [situation] devenir explosif; [discussion, conversation] s'animer.

overheating [ˌəʊvə'hiːtɪŋ] *n* échauffement *m* excessif.

overhung [ˌəʊvə'hʌŋ] *pt* & *pp* → **overhang**.

overimpress [ˌəʊvərɪm'pres] *vt*: she wasn't ~ed by the film le film ne l'a pas particulièrement impressionnée.

overindulge [ˌəʊvərɪn'dʌldʒ] ◇ *vt* -**1.** [appetite, desire] céder à, succomber à, se laisser aller à; she ~s her passion for chocolate elle cède OR succombe trop facilement à sa passion pour le chocolat. -**2.** [person] (trop) gâter; she ~s her children elle cède à tous les caprices de ses enfants; he has a tendency to ~ himself il a tendance à faire des excès OR à se laisser aller.
◇ *vi* [overeat] trop manger; [drink] trop boire; you mustn't ~ il ne faut pas abuser des bonnes choses.

overindulgence [ˌəʊvərɪn'dʌldʒəns] *n* -**1.** [in food and drink] excès *m*, abus *m*. -**2.** [towards person] indulgence *f* excessive, complaisance *f*.

overindulgent [ˌəʊvərɪn'dʌldʒənt] *adj* -**1.** [in food and drink]: he's ~ c'est un bon vivant; an ~ weekend un week-end de bombance. -**2.** [towards person] trop indulgent, complaisant.

overjoyed [ˌəʊvə'dʒɔɪd] *adj* comblé, transporté, ravi; she was ~ at being home again elle était ravie d'être rentrée; I was ~ at the news cette nouvelle m'a ravi OR transporté; I was ~ to see him after so long j'étais ravi de le voir après si longtemps.

overkill ['əʊvəkɪl] *n* -**1.** MIL surarmement *m*. -**2.** *fig* exagération *f*, excès *m*; media ~ médiatisation *f* excessive.

overladen [ˌəʊvəˈleɪdn] ◇ *pp* → **overload**.
◇ *adj* surchargé.

overlaid [ˌəʊvəˈleɪd] *pt* & *pp* → **overlay**.

overland [ˈəʊvəlænd] *adj* & *adv* par voie de terre; the ~ route to India le voyage en Inde par la route.

overlap [*vb* ˌəʊvəˈlæp, *n* ˈəʊvəlæp] (*pt* & *pp* overlapped, *cont* overlapping) ◇ *vi* [gen] (se) chevaucher, se recouvrir en partie; our visits overlapped nos visites ont plus ou moins coïncidé; my responsibilities ~ with hers mes responsabilités empiètent sur les siennes; the two systems ~ les deux systèmes font en partie double emploi.
◇ *vt* [in space] faire se chevaucher; [in time] empiéter sur; the edges/tiles ~ each other les bords/les tuiles se chevauchent.
◇ *n* -**1.** [gen] chevauchement *m*. -**2.** GEOL nappe *f* de charriage.

overlay [*vb* ˌəʊvəˈleɪ, *n* ˈəʊvəleɪ] (*pt* & *pp* overlaid [-ˈleɪd]) ◇ *vt* recouvrir; the shelf is overlaid with marble l'étagère est recouverte de marbre.
◇ *n* -**1.** [covering] revêtement *m*. -**2.** COMPUT recouvrement *m*; ~ segment segment *m* de recouvrement.

overleaf [ˌəʊvəˈliːf] *adv* au dos, au verso; 'see ~' 'voir au verso'; 'continued ~' [in book, magazine] 'suite page suivante'.

overload [*vb* ˌəʊvəˈləʊd, *n* ˈəʊvələʊd] (*pp sense 1* overloaded OR overladen [-ˈleɪdn], *pp sense 2* overloaded) ◇ *vt* -**1.** [animal, vehicle] surcharger. -**2.** [electric circuit] surcharger; [engine, machine] surmener; *fig* [with work] surcharger, écraser; she's ~ed with work elle est surchargée OR débordée de travail.
◇ *n* surcharge *f*.

overlong [ˌəʊvəˈlɒŋ] ◇ *adj* trop OR excessivement long.
◇ *adv* trop longtemps.

overlook [ˌəʊvəˈlʊk] *vt* -**1.** [have view of] avoir vue sur, donner sur; 'villa ~ing the sea' 'villa avec vue sur la mer'; the bedroom window ~s the garden la fenêtre de la chambre donne sur le jardin; our house is ~ed at the back il y a une maison qui a vue sur l'arrière de la nôtre. -**2.** [fail to notice - detail, small thing] laisser échapper, oublier; it's easy to ~ the small print on oublie souvent de lire ce qui est en petits caractères || [neglect]: they ~ed the language problem ils n'ont pas pris en compte le problème de la langue; he seems to have ~ed the fact that I might have difficulties l'idée que je puisse avoir des difficultés semble lui avoir échappé; his work has been ~ed for centuries cela fait des siècles que ses travaux sont ignorés || [ignore] laisser passer, passer sur; she decided to ~ the matter elle décida de fermer les yeux sur l'affaire; I'll ~ it this time je veux bien fermer les yeux cette fois-ci. -**3.** [supervise] surveiller.

overlord [ˈəʊvəlɔːd] *n* -**1.** HIST suzerain *m*. -**2.** *fig* grand patron *m*.

overly [ˈəʊvəlɪ] *adj* trop; she was not ~ friendly elle ne s'est pas montrée particulièrement aimable.

overmanned [ˌəʊvəˈmænd] *adj* [factory, production line] en sureffectif.

overmanning [ˌəʊvəˈmænɪŋ] *n (U)* sureffectifs *mpl*.

overmuch [ˌəʊvəˈmʌtʃ] *fml* ◇ *adj* trop de.
◇ *adv* outre mesure, trop.

overnice [ˌəʊvəˈnaɪs] *adj* [distinction] trop subtil; [person] trop méticuleux, pointilleux à l'excès.

overnight [*adv* ˌəʊvəˈnaɪt, *adj* & *vb* ˈəʊvənaɪt] ◇ *adv* -**1.** [during the night] pendant la nuit; to drive/to fly ~ rouler/voler de nuit || [until next day] jusqu'au lendemain; they stopped OR stayed ~ in Birmingham ils ont passé la nuit à Birmingham; the milk won't keep ~ le lait ne se conservera pas jusqu'à demain. -**2.** *fig* [suddenly] du jour au lendemain; her hair went grey ~ ses cheveux sont devenus gris du jour au lendemain; the situation grew worse ~ la situation a empiré du jour au lendemain OR a subitement empiré.
◇ *adj* -**1.** [stay, guest] d'une nuit; [clothes, journey] de nuit; an ~ stay une nuit; we had an ~ stay in Paris nous avons passé une nuit à Paris. -**2.** *fig* [sudden] soudain, subit; there has been an ~ improvement in the situation la situation s'est subitement améliorée.
◇ *vi* passer la OR une nuit.

overnight bag *n* sac *m* OR nécessaire *m* de voyage.

overpaid [ˌəʊvəˈpeɪd] *pt* & *pp* → **overpay**.

overpass [ˈəʊvəpɑːs] *n* AUT saut-de-mouton *m* *(route)*.

overpay [ˌəʊvəˈpeɪ] (*pt* & *pp* overpaid [-ˈpeɪd]) *vt* [bill, employee] surpayer, trop payer.

overpayment [ˌəʊvəˈpeɪmənt] *n* trop-perçu *m*.

overplay [ˌəʊvəˈpleɪ] ◇ *vt* [importance] exagérer; to ~ one's hand présumer de ses forces OR de ses capacités.
◇ *vi* exagérer son rôle.

overpopulated [ˌəʊvəˈpɒpjʊleɪtɪd] *adj* surpeuplé.

overpopulation [ˈəʊvəˌpɒpjʊˈleɪʃn] *n* surpeuplement *m*, surpopulation *f*.

overpower [ˌəʊvəˈpaʊəʳ] *vt* -**1.** [physically - enemy, opponent] maîtriser, vaincre. -**2.** [subj: smell] suffoquer; [subj: heat, emotion] accabler; they were ~ed by his charm ils furent ensorcelés OR subjugués par son charme.

overpowering [ˌəʊvəˈpaʊərɪŋ] *adj* -**1.** [heat, sensation] accablant, écrasant; [smell] suffocant; her perfume is ~ son parfum est envahissant. -**2.** [desire, passion] irrésistible; [grief] accablant; an ~ sense of guilt un sentiment irrépressible de culpabilité. -**3.** [force] irrésistible. -**4.** [personality, charisma] dominateur, irrésistible.

overprescribe [ˌəʊvəprɪˈskraɪb] ◇ *vi* MED prescrire trop de médicaments.
◇ *vt* [medicine, tablets] prescrire en trop fortes quantités.

overprice [ˌəʊvəˈpraɪs] *vt* vendre trop cher; those books are really ~d le prix de ces livres est vraiment excessif OR trop élevé.

overprint [*vb* ˌəʊvəˈprɪnt, *n* ˈəʊvəprɪnt] ◇ *vt* imprimer en surcharge; the old prices had been ~ed with new ones les nouveaux prix avaient été imprimés sur les anciens.
◇ *n* surcharge *f*.

overproduce [ˌəʊvəprəˈdjuːs] *vt* surproduire.

overproduction [ˌəʊvəprəˈdʌkʃn] *n* surproduction *f*.

overprotect [ˌəʊvəprəˈtekt] *vt* surprotéger, trop protéger; he was ~ed as a child il a été trop couvé lorsqu'il était enfant.

overprotective [ˌəʊvəprəˈtektɪv] *adj* trop protecteur, protecteur à l'excès; she is ~ of OR towards her son elle couve trop son fils.

overpublicize, -ise [ˌəʊvəˈpʌblɪsaɪz] *vt* faire trop de publicité pour, donner trop de publicité à.

overqualified [ˌəʊvəˈkwɒlɪfaɪd] *adj* surqualifié.

overran [ˌəʊvəˈræn] *pt* → **overrun**.

overrate [ˌəʊvəˈreɪt] *vt* [person] surestimer; he is rather ~d as a novelist sa réputation de romancier est assez surfaite || [book, film] surfaire; I think champagne is really ~d je pense que le champagne ne mérite pas sa réputation OR que la réputation du champagne est surfaite.

overreach [ˌəʊvəˈriːtʃ] *vt*: to ~ o.s. présumer de ses forces, viser trop haut.

overreact [ˌəʊvərɪˈækt] *vi* [gen] réagir de façon excessive, dramatiser; [panic] s'affoler; he has a tendency to ~ il a tendance à tout dramatiser; I thought she ~ed to the news d'après moi, la façon dont elle a réagi en apprenant la nouvelle avait quelque chose d'excessif OR de disproportionné.

overreaction [ˌəʊvərɪˈækʃn] *n* réaction *f* disproportionnée OR excessive; [panic] affolement *m*.

overridable [ˌəʊvəˈraɪdəbl] *adj* COMPUT annulable.

override [ˌəʊvəˈraɪd] (*pt* overrode [-ˈrəʊd], *pp* overridden [-ˈrɪdn]) *vt* -**1.** [instruction, desire, authority] passer outre à, outrepasser; [decision] annuler; [rights] fouler aux pieds, bafouer; my objection was overridden il n'a été tenu aucun compte de mon objection. -**2.** [fact, factor] l'emporter sur. -**3.** [controls, mechanism] annuler, neutraliser. -**4.** [horse] harasser.

overrider [ˈəʊvəˌraɪdəʳ] *n Br* AUT butoir *m* (de pare-chocs).

overriding [ˌəʊvəˈraɪdɪŋ] *adj* -**1.** [importance] primordial, capital; [belief, consideration, factor] prépondérant, premier, dominant; our ~ desire is to avoid conflict notre premier souci est d'éviter un conflit. -**2.** JUR [clause] dérogatoire.

overripe [ˌəʊvəˈraɪp] *adj* [fruit] trop mûr; [cheese] trop fait.

overrode [ˌəʊvəˈrəʊd] *pt* → **override**.

overrule [ˌəʊvəˈruːl] *vt* [decision] annuler; [claim, objection] rejeter; I was ~d mon avis a été rejeté.

overrun [*vb* ˌəʊvəˈrʌn, *n* ˈəʊvərʌn] (*pt* overran [-ˈræn], *pp* overrun, *cont* overrunning) ◇ *vt* -**1.** [invade] envahir; the enemy troops overran the country les troupes ennemies ont envahi le pays; the garden is ~ with weeds le jardin est envahi de mauvaises herbes; the building was ~ by rats l'immeuble était infesté de rats; the streets were ~ by holidaymakers les rues étaient envahies par les vacanciers. -**2.** [exceed - time limit] dépasser; the programme overran the allotted time by ten minutes l'émission a dépassé de dix minutes le temps qui lui était imparti || [overshoot] dépasser, aller au-delà de; the plane overran the runway l'avion a dépassé le bout de la piste d'atterrissage; to ~ a signal RAIL brûler un signal. -**3.** TYPO [word, sentence - over line] reporter à la ligne suivante; [- over page] reporter à la page suivante.
◇ *vi* [subj: - programme, speech] dépasser le temps alloué OR imparti; [- meeting] dépasser l'heure prévue; the speech overran by ten minutes le discours a duré dix minutes de plus que prévu.
◇ *n* [in time, space] dépassement *m*.

oversaw [ˌəʊvəˈsɔː] *pt* → **oversee**.

overscore [ˌəʊvəˈskɔːʳ] *vt* barrer, rayer.

overscrupulous [ˌəʊvəˈskruːpjʊləs] *adj* [morally] trop scrupuleux; [in detail] pointilleux.

overseas [*adv* ˌəʊvəˈsiːz, *adj* ˈəʊvəsiːz] ◇ *adv* à l'étranger; to go ~ partir à l'étranger; she prefers to live ~ elle préfère vivre à l'étranger; people who come back from ~ les gens qui reviennent de l'étranger.
◇ *adj* [student, tourist, market] étranger; [travel, posting] à l'étranger; [mail - from overseas] (en provenance) de l'étranger; [- to an overseas country] pour l'étranger; [trade] extérieur; [colony, possession] d'outre-mer; the Ministry of Overseas Development ≃ le ministère de la Coopération et du Développement; the French ~ territories les Territoires français d'outre-mer.

oversee [ˌəʊvəˈsiː] (*pt* oversaw [-ˈsɔː], *pp* overseen [-ˈsiːn]) *vt* [watch] surveiller, contrôler; [supervise] superviser.

overseer [ˈəʊvəˌsiːəʳ] *n* [foreman] contremaître *m*, chef *m* d'équipe; [in mine] porion *m*; [in printing works] prote *m*; HIST [of slaves] surveillant *m*, -e *f*.

oversell [*vb* ˌəʊvəˈsel, *n* ˈəʊvəsel] (*pt* & *pp* oversold [-ˈsəʊld]) ◇ *vt* -**1.** [exaggerate - person, quality] mettre trop en valeur, faire trop valoir; to ~ o.s. se mettre trop en avant; personally, I think the Costa Brava is oversold personnellement, je pense que la Costa Brava est surfaite. -**2.** COMM: the concert was oversold on a vendu plus de billets pour le concert qu'il n'y avait de places.
◇ *n* [exaggeration] éloge *m* excessif, panégyrique *m*.

oversensitive [ˌəʊvəˈsensɪtɪv] *adj* trop sensible OR susceptible, hypersensible.

oversew [ˈəʊvəsəʊ] (*pp* oversewn [-səʊn]) *vt* surjeter.

oversexed [ˌəʊvəˈsekst] *adj*: they're ~ ils ne pensent qu'au sexe.

vershadow [,əʊvə'ʃædəʊ] *vt* -**1.** [eclipse - person, event] éclipser; **the peace talks were ~ed by the presidential election** l'élection présidentielle a éclipsé les pourparlers de paix. -**2.** [darken] ombrager; **the house is ~ed by a huge flyover** la maison est assombrie par un immense autopont; **their lives had been ~ed by the death of their father** *fig* leur vie avait été endeuillée par la mort de leur père.

vershoe ['əʊvəʃuː] *n* galoche *f*; **rubber ~s** caoutchoucs *mpl*.

vershoot [*vb* ,əʊvə'ʃuːt, *n* 'əʊvəʃuːt] (*pt* & *pp* **overshot** [-'ʃɒt]) ◇ *vt* dépasser, aller au-delà de; **the plane overshot the runway** l'avion a dépassé la piste ☐ **to ~ the mark** aller trop loin.
◇ *vi* [aircraft] dépasser la piste.
◇ *n* dépassement *m*.

versight ['əʊvəsaɪt] *n* -**1.** [error] omission *f*, oubli *m*; **by** OR **through an ~** par mégarde, par négligence; **due to an ~ your tickets have been sent to your old address** vos billets ont été envoyés par erreur à votre ancienne adresse. -**2.** [supervision] surveillance *f*, supervision *f*.

versimplification ['əʊvə,sɪmplɪfɪ'keɪʃn] *n* simplification *f* excessive.

versimplify [,əʊvə'sɪmplɪfaɪ] (*pt* & *pp* **oversimplified**) *vt* simplifier à l'excès.

versize(d) [,əʊvə'saɪz(d)] *adj* -**1.** [very big] énorme, démesuré. -**2.** [too big] trop grand.

versleep [,əʊvə'sliːp] (*pt* & *pp* **overslept** [-'slept]) *vi* se réveiller en retard, ne pas se réveiller à temps.

versold [,əʊvə'səʊld] *pt* & *pp* → **oversell**.

verspend [,əʊvə'spend] (*pt* & *pp* **overspent** [-'spent]) ◇ *vi* trop dépenser; **I've been ~ing recently** j'ai trop dépensé OR j'ai dépensé trop d'argent récemment; **I've overspent by £5** j'ai dépensé 5 livres de trop.
◇ *vt* [allowance] dépasser.

verspill [*vb* ,əʊvə'spɪl, *n* 'əʊvəspɪl] ◇ *vi* déborder, se répandre.
◇ *n* excédent *m* de population (urbaine); **the London ~** l'excédent de la population londonienne.
◇ *comp*: **~ population** excédent *m* de population.

verstaffed [,əʊvə'stɑːft] *adj* en sureffectif; **the firm is ~** le personnel de la firme est trop nombreux, la firme connaît un problème de sureffectifs.

verstate [,əʊvə'steɪt] *vt* exagérer.

verstatement [,əʊvə'steɪtmənt] *n* exagération *f*; **to say that he's a singer would be an ~** il ne mérite pas vraiment le titre de chanteur.

verstay [,əʊvə'steɪ] *vt*: **to ~ one's welcome** abuser de l'hospitalité de ses hôtes; **to ~ one's leave** MIL dépasser la durée de sa permission.

versteer [*n* 'əʊvəstɪə^r, *vb* ,əʊvə'stɪə^r] ◇ *n* AUT survirage *m*.
◇ *vi* survirer.

verstep [,əʊvə'step] (*pt* & *pp* **overstepped**, *cont* **overstepping**) *vt* dépasser, outrepasser; **to ~ one's authority** outrepasser ses pouvoirs ☐ **to ~ the mark** OR **the limit** *fig* dépasser les bornes, aller trop loin.

verstocked [,əʊvə'stɒkt] *adj* -**1.** [warehouse] trop approvisionné; [market] encombré, surchargé; **the market is ~ with foreign goods** le marché regorge de marchandises étrangères. -**2.** [farm] qui a un excès de cheptel; [river] trop poissonneux.

verstrung [,əʊvə'strʌŋ] *adj* -**1.** [person] tendu, surexcité. -**2.** [piano] à cordes croisées.

verstuffed [,əʊvə'stʌft] *adj* rembourré.

versubscribe [,əʊvəsəb'skraɪb] *vt*: **to be ~d** [concert, play] être en surlocation; **the share issue was ~d** ST. EX la demande d'achats a dépassé le nombre de titres émis; **the school trip is ~d** il y a trop d'élèves inscrits à l'excursion organisée par l'école.

versubtle [,əʊvə'sʌtl] *adj* trop subtil.

vert ['əʊvɜːt] *adj* manifeste, évident.

vertake [,əʊvə'teɪk] (*pt* **overtook** [-'tʊk], *pp* **overtaken** [-'teɪkn]) *vt* -**1.** [pass beyond] dépasser, devancer; **he overtook all the other runners** il a dépassé tous les autres coureurs || *Br* AUT dépasser, doubler; **'no overtaking'** 'interdiction de dépasser'. -**2.** [surprise] surprendre; **overtaken by events** dépassé par les événements || [strike] frapper; **catastrophe overtook the community** la catastrophe a frappé OR s'est abattue sur la communauté; **~n by** OR **with panic** pris de panique. -**3.** *lit* [engulf - subj: emotion] s'emparer de.

overtaking lane [,əʊvə'teɪkɪŋ-] *n Br* AUT [when driving on right] voie *f* de gauche; [when driving on left] voie *f* de droite.

overtax [,əʊvə'tæks] *vt* -**1.** FIN [person] surimposer; [goods] surtaxer. -**2.** [strain - patience, hospitality] abuser de; [- person, heart] surmener; **don't ~ your strength** OR **yourself** ne te fatigue pas inutilement, ne te surmène pas; **don't ~ his brain!** ne lui usez pas la cervelle!

over-the-counter *adj* -**1.** [medicines] vendu sans ordonnance, en vente libre. -**2.** ST. EX: **~ market** marché *m* hors-cote.

overthrow [*vb* ,əʊvə'θrəʊ, *n* 'əʊvəθrəʊ] (*pt* **overthrew** [-'θruː], *pp* **overthrown** [-'θrəʊn])
◇ *vt* -**1.** [regime, government] renverser; [rival, enemy army] vaincre; [values, standards] bouleverser; [plans] réduire à néant. -**2.** [ball] envoyer trop loin.
◇ *n* -**1.** [of enemy] défaite *f*; [of regime, government] renversement *m*, chute *f*; [of values, standards] bouleversement *m*. -**2.** [in cricket - throw] *balle qui dépasse le guichet*; [- run] *point marqué par une balle hors jeu*.

overtime ['əʊvətaɪm] *n* (*U*) -**1.** [work] heures *fpl* supplémentaires; **to do** OR **to work ~** faire des heures supplémentaires; **he'll have to work ~ to get those two to agree!** *fig* s'il veut mettre ces deux-là d'accord, il a intérêt à se lever de bonne heure!; **your imagination seems to have been working ~** on dirait que tu as laissé ton imagination s'emballer. -**2.** [overtime pay] rémunération *f* des heures supplémentaires; **after 6pm we're on ~ (pay)** après 6 h, on nous paie en heures supplémentaires; **to be paid ~** être payé en heures supplémentaires. -**3.** *Am* SPORT prolongations *fpl*; **the match went into ~** ils ont joué les prolongations.

overtime pay = **overtime 2**.

overtired [,əʊvə'taɪəd] *adj* surmené.

overtly [əʊ'vɜːtlɪ] *adv* franchement, ouvertement.

overtone ['əʊvətəʊn] *n* -**1.** [nuance] nuance *f*, accent *m*; **there was an ~ of aggression in what she said** il y avait une pointe d'agressivité dans ses propos; **his speech was full of racist ~s** son discours était truffé de sous-entendus racistes. -**2.** MUS harmonique *m*.

overtook [,əʊvə'tʊk] *pt* → **overtake**.

overtrick ['əʊvətrɪk] *n* [in bridge] levée *f* de mieux.

overtrump [,əʊvə'trʌmp] *vt* surcouper.

overture ['əʊvə,tjʊə^r] *n* -**1.** MUS ouverture *f*. -**2.** *fig* [proposal] ouverture *f*, avance *f*; **to make ~s to sb** faire des avances à qqn; **romantic ~s** avances amoureuses. -**3.** *fig* [prelude] prélude *m*, début *m*.

overturn [,əʊvə'tɜːn] ◇ *vt* -**1.** [lamp, car, furniture] renverser; [ship] faire chavirer. -**2.** [overthrow - regime, government, plans] renverser; JUR [judgment, sentence] casser; **the bill was ~ed by the Senate** le projet de loi a été rejeté par le Sénat.
◇ *vi* [lamp, furniture] se renverser; [car] se retourner, capoter; [ship] chavirer.

overuse [*vb* ,əʊvə'juːz, *n* ,əʊvə'juːs] ◇ *vt* abuser de.
◇ *n* abus *m*, usage *m* excessif.

overvalue [,əʊvə'væljuː] *vt* -**1.** [currency] surévaluer; [house, painting] surestimer. -**2.** [overrate] surestimer, faire trop de cas de; **his influence has been ~d** son influence a été surestimée OR exagérée.

overview ['əʊvəvjuː] *n* vue *f* d'ensemble.

overweening [,əʊvə'wiːnɪŋ] *adj Br* -**1.** [pride, ambition etc] sans bornes, démesuré. -**2.** [person] outrecuidant, présomptueux.

overweight [*adj* & *vb* ,əʊvə'weɪt, *n* 'əʊvəweɪt]
◇ *adj* [person] (trop) gros; **~ people are more prone to heart disease** les personnes trop grosses OR fortes ont plus de risques d'avoir des maladies cardiaques; **I'm a few pounds ~** j'ai quelques kilos de trop || [luggage, parcel] trop lourd.
◇ *n* excès *m* de poids.
◇ *vt* -**1.** [overload] surcharger. -**2.** [overemphasize] accorder trop d'importance à, trop privilégier.

overwhelm [,əʊvə'welm] *vt* -**1.** [devastate] accabler, terrasser; [astound] bouleverser; **~ed with grief** accablé de chagrin; **grief ~ed us** le chagrin nous a terrassés; **your generosity ~s me** votre générosité me bouleverse OR me va droit au cœur. -**2.** *literal* & *fig* [submerge] submerger, engloutir; **our switchboard has been ~ed by the number of calls** notre standard a été submergé par les appels; **I'm completely ~ed with work** je suis débordé de travail. -**3.** [defeat] écraser; **the England team was finally ~ed** l'équipe d'Angleterre a finalement été écrasée; **we fought back but our attackers ~ed us** nous nous sommes débattus mais nos agresseurs ont eu le dessus.

overwhelming [,əʊvə'welmɪŋ] *adj* -**1.** [crushing - victory, defeat] écrasant; **to win by an ~ majority** gagner avec une majorité écrasante; **the ~ majority (of people) oppose these measures** la grande majorité des gens est opposée à ces mesures. -**2.** [extreme, overpowering - grief, heat] accablant; [- joy] extrême; [- love] passionnel; [- desire, urge, passion] irrésistible; **an ~ sense of frustration** un sentiment d'extrême frustration; **their friendliness is somewhat ~** leur amabilité a quelque chose d'excessif.

overwhelmingly [,əʊvə'welmɪŋlɪ] *adv* -**1.** [crushingly] de manière écrasante; **the House of Lords voted ~ against the bill** la Chambre des lords a voté contre le projet à une écrasante majorité. -**2.** [as intensifier] extrêmement; [predominantly] surtout.

overwind [,əʊvə'waɪnd] (*pt* & *pp* **overwound** [-'waʊnd]) *vt* [clock, watch] trop remonter.

overwork [*vb* ,əʊvə'wɜːk, *n* 'əʊvə,wɜːk]
◇ *vt* -**1.** [person] surmener; **he tends to ~ himself** il a tendance à se surmener; **don't ~ yourself** n'en fais pas trop; **to be ~ed and underpaid** être surchargé de travail et sous-payé. -**2.** [word] abuser de, utiliser trop souvent; **it's one of the most ~ed phrases in the English language** c'est une des expressions les plus utilisées de la langue anglaise.
◇ *vi* se surmener.
◇ *n* surmenage *m*.

overwound [,əʊvə'waʊnd] *pt* & *pp* → **overwind**.

overwrite [,əʊvə'raɪt] (*pt* **overwrote** [-'rəʊt], *pp* **overwritten** [-'rɪtn]) ◇ *vt* -**1.** [write on top of] écrire sur, repasser sur. -**2.** COMPUT [file] écraser.
◇ *vi* écrire dans un style ampoulé.

overwrought [,əʊvə'rɔːt] *adj* sur les nerfs, à bout.

overzealous [,əʊvə'zeləs] *adj* trop zélé.

Ovid ['ɒvɪd] *pr n* Ovide.

oviduct ['əʊvɪdʌkt] *n* oviducte *m*.

oviform ['əʊvɪfɔːm] *adj* oviforme.

ovine ['əʊvaɪn] *adj* ovin.

oviparous [əʊ'vɪpərəs] *adj* ovipare.

ovipositor [,əʊvɪ'pɒzɪtə^r] *n* ovipositeur *m*, tarière *f*.

ovoid ['əʊvɔɪd] ◇ *adj* ovoïde, ovoïdal.
◇ *n* figure *f* ovoïde.

ovulate ['ɒvjʊleɪt] *vi* ovuler.

ovulation [,ɒvjʊ'leɪʃn] *n* ovulation *f*.

ovule ['ɒvjuːl] *n* ovule *m*.

ovum ['əʊvəm] (*pl* **ova** [-və]) *n* BIOL ovule *m*.

ow [aʊ] *interj* aïe.

owe [əʊ] ◇ *vt* devoir; to ~ sthg to sb, to ~ sb sthg devoir qqch à qqn; you ~ me £10 tu me dois 10 livres; how much OR what do I ~ you? combien est-ce que OR qu'est-ce que je vous dois?; how much do we still ~ him for OR on the car? combien nous reste-t-il à lui payer pour la voiture?; I ~ you a beer je te dois une bière; he thinks society ~s him a living il s'imagine avoir le droit de vivre aux crochets de la société; I think you ~ him an explanation je pense qu'il a droit à une explication de ta part OR que tu lui dois une explication; we ~ them an apology nous leur devons des excuses; you ~ it to yourself to try again tu te dois d'essayer encore une fois; we ~ this discovery to a lucky accident nous devons cette découverte à un heureux hasard; to what do we ~ the honour of your visit? qu'est-ce qui nous vaut l'honneur de votre visite?; I ~ it all to my parents je suis redevable de tout cela à mes parents; he ~s his good looks to his mother il tient sa beauté de sa mère ❑ I ~ you one c'est OR à mon tour, je te dois bien cela.
◇ *vi* être endetté; he still ~s for OR on the house il n'a pas encore fini de payer la maison.

owing ['əʊɪŋ] *adj (after n)* dû; the sum ~ on the car la somme qui reste due sur le prix de la voiture; to have a lot of money ~ [to owe] devoir beaucoup d'argent; [to be owed] avoir beaucoup d'argent à récupérer.
◆ **owing to** *prep phr* à cause de, en raison de.

owl [aʊl] *n* hibou *m*, chouette *f*; he's a wise old ~ c'est la sagesse faite homme, c'est l'image même de la sagesse.

owlet ['aʊlɪt] *n* jeune hibou *m*, jeune chouette *f*.

owlish ['aʊlɪʃ] *adj*: those glasses give you an ~ look tu as l'air d'un hibou avec ces lunettes.

own [əʊn] ◇ *adj* propre; I have my ~ bedroom j'ai ma propre chambre; I have my very ~ bedroom j'ai une chambre pour moi tout seul; a flat with its ~ entrance un appartement avec une porte d'entrée indépendante; these are my ~ skis ces skis sont à moi OR m'appartiennent; I'll do it (in) my ~ way je le ferai à ma façon; it's all my ~ work c'est moi qui ai tout fait; she makes all her ~ clothes elle fait elle-même tous ses vêtements; 'how to build your ~ sauna' 'comment construire votre propre sauna'; it's your ~ fault! tu n'as à t'en prendre qu'à toi-même!; you'll have to make up your ~ mind c'est à toi et à toi seul de décider, personne ne pourra prendre cette décision à ta place; I saw it with my ~ eyes je l'ai vu de mes propres yeux; your ~ mother wouldn't recognize you! ta propre mère ne te reconnaîtrait pas!
◇ *pron*: is that car your ~? est-ce que cette voiture est à vous?; I don't need a pen, I've brought my ~ je n'ai pas besoin de stylo, j'ai apporté le mien; if you want a car, you'll have to buy your ~ si tu veux une voiture, tu n'as qu'à t'en acheter une; her opinions are identical to my ~ nous partageons exactement les mêmes opinions; a house/a room/a garden of one's (very) ~ une maison/une pièce/un jardin (bien) à soi; their son has a car of his ~ leur fils a sa propre voiture; I shan't be going for reasons of my ~ je n'irai pas pour des raisons personnelles; the town has a character of its ~ OR all (of) its ~ la ville possède un charme qui lui est propre OR un charme bien à elle; my time is not my ~ je ne suis pas maître de mon temps; I haven't a single thing I can call my ~ je n'ai rien à moi ❑ each to his ~ des goûts et des couleurs, on ne discute pas *prov*; to come into one's ~ [show one's capabilities] montrer de quoi on est capable; [inherit] toucher son héritage; on bad roads the four-wheel-drive model really comes into its ~ sur les mauvaises routes, le modèle à quatre roues motrices montre vraiment ses capacités; to get one's ~ back (on sb) se venger (de qqn); I'll get my ~ back on him for that je lui revaudrai ça; to look after one's ~ s'occuper des siens; to make sthg one's ~ s'approprier qqch; she has made the role her ~ elle en a fait son rôle.
◇ *vt* -**1.** [possess] posséder; I've lost everything I ~ j'ai perdu tout ce que je possède; they ~ 51% of the shares ils détiennent 51 % des actions; does she ~ the house? est-elle propriétaire de la maison?; who ~s this car? à qui appartient cette voiture?; the land ~ed by the Crown les terres qui appartiennent à la Couronne ❑ they walked in as if they ~ed the place *inf* ils sont entrés comme (s'ils étaient) chez eux. -**2.** *lit* [admit] admettre, reconnaître; she ~ed that I was right elle a reconnu que j'avais raison.
◆ **on one's own** *adj phr* (tout) seul; are you here on your ~? êtes-vous seul ici?; he left me on my ~ all evening il m'a laissé seul toute la soirée; I'm trying to get him on his ~ j'essaie de le voir seul à seul; I did it (all) on my ~ je l'ai fait tout seul; she's setting up in business on her ~ elle monte une affaire toute seule.
◆ **own to** *vt insep lit* avouer; she ~ed to a secret passion for Damian elle avoua une passion cachée pour Damian; nobody ~ed to having taken it personne n'a avoué l'avoir pris.
◆ **own up** *vi insep* avouer, faire des aveux; if the culprit doesn't ~ up... si le coupable n'avoue pas OR ne passe pas aux aveux...; to ~ up to sthg avouer qqch; he ~ed up to his mistake il a reconnu son erreur.

own-brand *adj*: ~ products *produits vendus sous la marque du distributeur*; the supermarket's ~ jam is cheaper la confiture que le supermarché vend sous sa propre marque coûte moins cher.

owner ['əʊnəʳ] *n* propriétaire *mf*; he is the rightful ~ c'est lui le propriétaire légitime; at the ~'s risk aux risques du propriétaire; who is the ~ of this jacket? à qui appartient cette veste?; they are all car ~s ils possèdent OR ils ont tous une voiture.

owner-driver *n* conducteur *m*, -trice *f* propriétaire du véhicule.

ownerless ['əʊnəlɪs] *adj* sans propriétaire.

owner-occupied *adj* occupé par son propriétaire.

owner-occupier *n* occupant *m*, -e *f* propriétaire.

ownership ['əʊnəʃɪp] *n* possession *f*; we require proof of ~ nous demandons un titre de propriété; the government encourages home ~ le gouvernement encourage l'accession à la propriété; change of ~ changement de propriétaire; 'under new ~' 'changement de propriétaire'.

own goal *n* FTBL but *m* marqué contre son camp; to score an ~ marquer contre son camp; the government scored another ~ *fig* le gouvernement a agi une nouvelle fois contre ses propres intérêts.

ownsome *inf* ['əʊnsəm], **owny-o** *inf* ['əʊnɪəʊ] *n Br*: (all) on one's ~ tout seul.

owt *inf* [aʊt] *pron Br dial* quelque chose.

ox [ɒks] (*pl* oxen ['ɒksn]) *n* bœuf *m*; (as) strong as an ~ fort comme un bœuf.

oxalic acid [ɒk'sælɪk-] *n* acide *m* oxalique.

oxblood ['ɒksblʌd] ◇ *n* [colour] rouge *m* sang.
◇ *adj* rouge sang *(inv)*.

oxbow (lake) ['ɒksbəʊ-] *n* bayou *m*.

Oxbridge ['ɒksbrɪdʒ] *pr n désignation collective des universités d'Oxford et de Cambridge*; ~ graduates diplômés des universités d'Oxford ou de Cambridge; the privileges of an ~ education les privilèges que confère un diplôme d'Oxford ou de Cambridge.

oxcart ['ɒkskɑːt] *n* char *m* à bœuf OR à bœufs.

oxen ['ɒksn] *pl* → **ox**.

oxeye daisy ['ɒksaɪ-] *n* marguerite *f* jaune OR des blés.

Oxfam ['ɒksfæm] (*abbr of* Oxford Committee for Famine Relief) *pr n association caritative britannique*.

Oxford ['ɒksfəd] *pr n* Oxford.

Oxford bags *npl* [trousers] pantalon *m* très large.

Oxford blue ◇ *n* -**1.** [colour] bleu *m* foncé. -**2.** [sportsperson] *sportif qui porte ou a porté les couleurs de l'université d'Oxford*.
◇ *adj* bleu foncé *(inv)*.

Oxford English *n* anglais *m* d'Oxford.

oxfords ['ɒksfədz] *npl* chaussures *fpl* à lacets.

Oxford Street *pr n une des grandes artères commerçantes de Londres*.

oxhide ['ɒkshaɪd] *n* cuir *m* de bœuf.

oxidant ['ɒksɪdənt] *n* oxydant *m*.

oxidation [,ɒksɪ'deɪʃn] *n* oxydation *f*.

oxide ['ɒksaɪd] *n* oxyde *m*.

oxidize, -ise ['ɒksɪdaɪz] ◇ *vt* oxyder.
◇ *vi* s'oxyder.

oxidizer ['ɒksɪdaɪzəʳ] *n* oxydant *m*.

oxidizing agent ['ɒksɪdaɪzɪŋ-] *n* oxydant *m*.

oxlip ['ɒkslɪp] *n sorte de primevère*.

Oxon *written abbr of* Oxfordshire.

Oxon. (*written abbr of* Oxoniensis) *de l'université d'Oxford*.

Oxonian [ɒk'səʊnjən] ◇ *n* [student] étudiant *m*, -e *f* de l'université d'Oxford; [townsperson] Oxfordien *m*, -enne *f*.
◇ *adj* oxfordien, d'Oxford.

oxtail ['ɒksteɪl] *n* queue *f* de bœuf; ~ soup soupe *f* de queue de bœuf.

oxyacetylene [,ɒksɪə'setɪliːn] *adj* oxyacétylénique; ~ burner OR lamp OR torch chalumeau *m* oxyacétylénique.

oxygen ['ɒksɪdʒən] *n* oxygène *m*.

oxygenate ['ɒksɪdʒəneɪt] *vt* oxygéner.

oxygenation [,ɒksɪdʒə'neɪʃn] *n* oxygénation *f*.

oxygen mask *n* masque *m* à oxygène.

oxygen tent *n* tente *f* à oxygène.

oxymoron [,ɒksɪ'mɔːrɒn] (*pl* oxymora [-rə]) *n* oxymoron *m*.

oyez [əʊ'jes] *interj arch* oyez.

oyster ['ɔɪstəʳ] *n* huître *f*; ~ basket bourriche *f*; ~ farming ostréiculture *f*; ~ knife couteau *m* à huîtres; the world is her ~ le monde lui appartient.

oyster bed *n* parc *m* à huîtres.

oystercatcher [,ɔɪstə'kætʃəʳ] *n* huîtrier-pie *m*.

oysterman ['ɔɪstəmən] (*pl* oystermen [-mən]) *n* -**1.** [cultivator] ostréiculteur *m*, -trice *f*; [seller] écailler *m*, -ère *f*. -**2.** [boat] bateau *m* huîtrier.

oyster pink *n* rose *m* nacré.
◆ **oyster-pink** *adj* rose nacré *(inv)*.

oyster white *n* blanc *m* nacré.
◆ **oyster-white** *adj* blanc nacré *(inv)*.

oz. *written abbr of* ounce.

Oz *inf* [ɒz] *pr n* Australie *f*.

Ozalid® ['ɒzəlɪd] *n* Ozalid® *m*.

ozone ['əʊzəʊn] *n* -**1.** [gas] ozone *m*; ~ depletion diminution *f* de l'ozone; ~ layer OR shield couche *f* d'ozone. -**2.** *inf* [sea air] bon air *m* marin.

ozone-friendly *adj* qui préserve la couche d'ozone.

p (*pl* p's OR ps), **P** (*pl* P's OR Ps) [piː] *n* [letter] p *m*, P *m*; **mind your p's and q's!** *inf Br* surveille ton langage!
p ◇ (*written abbr of* page) p.
◇ *n abbr of* penny, pence.
P -**1.** *written abbr of* president. -**2.** (*written abbr of* prince) Pce.
pa *inf* [pɑː] *n* papa *m*.
p.a. (*written abbr of* per annum) p.a.
PA ◇ *n* -**1.** *Br* (*abbr of* personal assistant) secrétaire *mf* de direction. -**2.** (*abbr of* public address system) système *m* de sonorisation, sono *f*; **departure times will be announced over the ~** les horaires de départ seront annoncés par haut-parleur.
◇ *pr n abbr of* Press Association.
◇ *written abbr of* Pennsylvania.
PABX (*abbr of* private automatic branch exchange) *n autocommutateur privé*.
PAC (*abbr of* political action committee) *pr n aux États-Unis, comité dont le rôle est de réunir des fonds pour soutenir une cause politique*.
pace¹ [peɪs] ◇ *n* -**1.** [speed] allure *f*, vitesse *f*, train *m*; **she quickened her ~** elle pressa le pas; **she slackened her ~** elle ralentit le pas; **we set off at a good** OR **brisk** OR **smart ~** nous sommes partis à vive allure; **the traffic slowed to (a) walking ~** on roulait au pas; **the slower ~ of country life** le rythme plus paisible de la vie à la campagne; **don't walk so fast, I can't keep ~ with you** ne marche pas si vite, je n'arrive pas à te suivre; **we try to keep ~ with new developments** nous essayons de nous tenir au courant des derniers développements; **output is keeping ~ with demand** la production se maintient au niveau de OR répond à la demande; **he couldn't stand** OR **take the ~** il n'arrivait pas à suivre le rythme; **do it at your own ~** faites-le à votre propre rythme; **to force the ~** forcer l'allure ❑ **to make** OR **to set the ~** SPORT donner l'allure, mener le train; *fig* donner le ton. -**2.** [step] pas *m*; **take two ~s to the left** faites deux pas à gauche; **he was a few ~s from me** il était à quelques pas de moi ❑ **to put sb through his/her ~s** *Br* mettre qqn à l'épreuve; **to go through** OR **to show one's ~s** montrer ce dont OR de quoi on est capable.
◇ *vi* marcher (à pas mesurés); **he ~d up and down the corridor** il arpentait le couloir.
◇ *vt* -**1.** [corridor, cage, room] arpenter. -**2.** [regulate] régler l'allure de; **she ~d the first two laps well** elle a trouvé le bon rythme pour les deux premiers tours de piste; **the action is well ~d** le suspense ne faiblit pas.
◆ **pace off, pace out** *vt sep* mesurer en pas; **she ~d out ten steps** elle compta dix pas.
pace² ['peɪsɪ] *prep fml* n'en déplaise à.
pacemaker ['peɪs,meɪkəʳ] *n* -**1.** SPORT meneur *m*, -euse *f* de train; *fig* [leader] leader *m*; **they've become the ~s in their field** ils sont devenus les leaders dans leur domaine. -**2.** MED pacemaker *m*, stimulateur *m* cardiaque.
pacer ['peɪsəʳ] *n* SPORT meneur *m*, -euse *f* de train.
pacesetter ['peɪs,setəʳ] = **pacemaker 1**.
pacey ['peɪsɪ] (*compar* pacier, *superl* paciest) *adj* [vehicle, runner, horse] rapide; [story, film] mouvementé, vivant.
pacha ['pæʃə] = **pasha**.
pachyderm ['pækɪdɜːm] *n* pachyderme *m*.
pacific [pə'sɪfɪk] *adj fml* pacifique.
Pacific [pə'sɪfɪk] ◇ *pr n*: **the ~ (Ocean)** le Pacifique, l'océan *m* Pacifique.
◇ *adj* du Pacifique.
pacifically [pə'sɪfɪklɪ] *adv fml* pacifiquement.
pacification [,pæsɪfɪ'keɪʃn] *n* -**1.** [of anger] apaisement *m*. -**2.** [of country, region] pacification *f*.
Pacific Daylight Time *n* heure *f* d'été du Pacifique.
Pacific Islands *pl pr n* îles *fpl* du Pacifique; **in the ~** dans les îles du Pacifique.
Pacific Rim *pr n*: **the ~** *groupe de pays situés au bord du Pacifique, particulièrement les pays industrialisés d'Asie*.
Pacific (Standard) Time *n* heure *f* d'hiver du Pacifique.
pacifier ['pæsɪfaɪəʳ] *n* -**1.** [person] pacificateur *m*, -trice *f*. -**2.** *Am* [for baby] tétine *f*, sucette *f*.
pacifism ['pæsɪfɪzm] *n* pacifisme *m*.
pacifist ['pæsɪfɪst] ◇ *adj* pacifiste.
◇ *n* pacifiste *mf*.
pacify ['pæsɪfaɪ] (*pt* & *pp* **pacified**) *vt* -**1.** [soothe] apaiser, calmer. -**2.** MIL [subdue] pacifier.
pack [pæk] ◇ *vt* -**1.** [bags] faire; **to ~ one's case** OR **suitcase** faire sa valise; **she ~ed her bags and left** elle a fait ses bagages et elle est partie, elle a plié bagage. -**2.** [container, crate] remplir. -**3.** [put in bags - clothes, belongings]: **I've already ~ed the towels** j'ai déjà mis les serviettes dans la valise; **shall I ~ the camera?** est-ce que j'emporte OR je prends l'appareil photo?; **I've ~ed a lunch for you** je t'ai préparé de quoi déjeuner. -**4.** [wrap up - goods for transport] emballer; **the equipment is ~ed in polystyrene** le matériel est emballé dans du polystyrène. -**5.** [cram tightly - cupboard, container] bourrer; [- belongings, people] entasser; **he ~ed his pockets with sweets, he ~ed sweets into his pockets** il a bourré ses poches de bonbons; **we managed to ~ a lot into a week's holiday** *fig* on a réussi à faire énormément de choses en une semaine de vacances; **she ~s the house every night** THEAT elle fait salle comble chaque soir. -**6.** [crowd into - subj: spectators, passengers] s'entasser dans; **commuters ~ the morning trains** les banlieusards s'entassent dans les trains du matin. -**7.** [compress - soil] tasser; **the wind had ~ed the snow against the wall** le vent avait tassé la neige contre le mur. -**8.** [fill with supporters]: **to ~ a jury** se composer un jury favorable. -**9.** *inf* [have, carry]: **he ~s a lot of influence in cabinet/ministerial circles** il a beaucoup d'influence au conseil des ministres/dans les milieux ministériels; **to ~ a gun** *Am* être armé. -**10.** [load - horse, donkey] charger.
◇ *vi* -**1.** [for journey] faire sa valise OR ses bagages; **have you finished ~ing?** as-tu fini tes bagages? -**2.** [fit - into container] rentrer; **the keyboard will ~ easily into a briefcase** on peut facilement faire tenir le clavier dans un attaché-case; **this dress ~s well** cette robe ne se froisse pas (même dans une valise). -**3.** [crowd together - spectators, passengers] s'entasser; **we all ~ed into her car** nous nous sommes tous entassés dans sa voiture.
◇ *n* -**1.** [for carrying - rucksack] sac *m* à dos; [- bundle] ballot *m*; [- bale] balle *f*; [- on animal] charge *f*; **parachute ~** sac *m* à parachute. -**2.** [packet] paquet *m*; **a ~ of washing powder** *Br* un paquet de lessive; **a ~ of cigarettes** *Am* un paquet de cigarettes. -**3.** *Br* [deck of cards] jeu *m*. -**4.** [group - of children, wolves] bande *f*; [- of cub scouts] meute *f*; [- of hunting hounds] meute *f*. -**5.** SPORT [in rugby] pack *m*, paquet *m* (d'avant). -**6.** MED compresse *f*. -**7.** *phr*: **that's a ~ of lies!** *Br* c'est un tissu de mensonges!
◆ **pack away** *vt sep* -**1.** [tidy up] ranger. -**2.** = **pack off**.
◆ **pack down** ◇ *vt sep* [soil] tasser.
◇ *vi insep* SPORT [in rugby] former une mêlée.
◆ **pack in** ◇ *vt sep Br* -**1.** [crowd in] entasser; **the play is ~ing them in** *inf* la pièce fait salle comble. -**2.** *inf* [task] arrêter; [job, boyfriend, girlfriend] plaquer; **you should ~ in smoking** tu devrais arrêter de fumer; **~ it in!** laisse tomber!, arrête!
◇ *vi insep* -**1.** [crowd in] s'entasser (à l'intérieur). -**2.** *inf Br* [break down - machine, engine] tomber en rade.
◆ **pack off** *inf vt sep* expédier; **I ~ed the kids off to bed/school** j'ai envoyé les gosses au lit/à l'école.
◆ **pack up** ◇ *vi insep* -**1.** [pack one's suitcase] faire sa valise OR ses bagages. -**2.** [tidy up] ranger. -**3.** *inf Br* [break down] tomber en rade. -**4.** *inf Br* [give up] laisser tomber; **I'm ~ing up for today** j'arrête pour aujourd'hui.
◇ *vt sep* -**1.** [suitcase, bags] faire. -**2.** [clothes, belongings, tools] ranger; **help me ~ up the tent** aide-moi à plier la tente.
package ['pækɪdʒ] ◇ *n* -**1.** [small parcel] paquet *m*, colis *m*; *Am* [packet] paquet *m*. -**2.** [set of proposals] ensemble *m*; **the offer is part of a larger ~** l'offre fait partie d'un ensemble plus important; **a new ~ of measures to halt inflation** un nouvel ensemble OR un nouveau train de mesures visant à stopper l'inflation; we

offered them a generous ~ worth over £100,000 nous leur avons proposé un contrat global très avantageux de plus de 100 000 livres. -**3.** = **package holiday**. -**4.** COMPUT: (software) ~ progiciel *m*.
◇ *vt* -**1.** [wrap] emballer, conditionner; **each item is individually ~d** chaque article est conditionné OR emballé séparément. -**2.** [in advertising - product, politician, pop star] fabriquer l'image (de marque) de.

package deal *n* transaction *f* globale, accord *m* global; **the ~ put forward by the management** l'ensemble des mesures proposées par la direction; **we bought up the lot in a ~** nous avons tout acheté en un seul lot.

package holiday *n* voyage *m* organisé OR à prix forfaitaire.

packager ['pækɪdʒəʳ] *n* [in advertising, publishing] packager *m*, packageur *m*.

package tour = **package holiday**.

packaging ['pækɪdʒɪŋ] *n* -**1.** [wrapping materials] emballage *m*, conditionnement *m*. -**2.** [in advertising, publishing] packaging *m*.

pack animal *n* bête *f* de somme.

pack drill *n* MIL exercice *m* avec paquetage.

packed [pækt] *adj* -**1.** [crowded - train, room] bondé; [- theatre] comble; **the cinema was ~ (out)** *Br* la salle était comble OR pleine à craquer; **the meeting was ~** la réunion a fait salle comble. -**2.** [packaged] emballé, conditionné. -**3.** [jury] favorable.

-packed *in cpds* [full of]: **a fun~ evening** une soirée pleine de divertissements; **an action~ first half** une première moitié pleine d'action.

packed lunch *n* panier-repas *m*, casse-croûte *m inv*.

packer ['pækəʳ] *n* [worker] emballeur *m*, -euse *f*, conditionneur *m*, -euse *f*; [machine] emballeuse *f*, conditionneuse *f*.

packet ['pækɪt] *n* -**1.** [box] paquet *m*; **a ~ of cigarettes** *Br* un paquet de cigarettes || [bag, envelope] sachet *m*; **a ~ of soup/seeds** un sachet de soupe/graines. -**2.** [parcel] paquet *m*, colis *m*. -**3.** *inf Br* [lot of money] paquet *m*; **to make a ~** gagner un fric fou OR monstre. -**4.** NAUT: ~ **(boat** OR **steamer)** paquebot *m*.

packet switching [-ˌswɪtʃɪŋ] *n* COMPUT commutation *f* par paquets.

packhorse ['pækhɔːs] *n* cheval *m* de bât.

pack ice *n* pack *m*, banquise *f*.

packing ['pækɪŋ] *n* *(U)* -**1.** [of personal belongings]: **have you done your ~?** as-tu fait tes bagages?; **the removal men will do the ~** les déménageurs se chargeront de l'emballage. -**2.** [of parcel] emballage *m*; [of commercial goods] emballage *m*, conditionnement *m*; **the fish/meat ~ industry** les conserveries de poisson/viande. -**3.** [wrapping material] emballage *m*. -**4.** TECH [of piston, joint] garniture *f*.

packing case *n* caisse *f* d'emballage.

pack rat *n Am* ZOOL rat *m* des bois, néotome *m*.

packsaddle ['pækˌsædl] *n* bât *m*.

pact [pækt] *n* pacte *m*; **we made a ~ to stop smoking** nous avons convenu de nous arrêter de fumer; **to make a ~ with the Devil** faire un pacte OR pactiser avec le Diable.

pacy ['peɪsɪ] = **pacey**.

pad [pæd] (*pt* & *pp* **padded**, *cont* **padding**) ◇ *n* -**1.** [to cushion shock] coussinet *m*; **the skaters wear ~s on their knees and elbows** les patineurs portent des genouillères et des protège-coudes; **shin-~** protège-tibia *m*. -**2.** [for garment]: **(shoulder)~** épaulette *f*. -**3.** [for absorbing liquid, polishing etc] tampon *m*; **a ~ of cotton wool** un tampon de coton hydrophile. -**4.** ZOOL [underside of foot] coussinet *m*. -**5.** [of paper] bloc *m*; **writing ~** bloc-notes *m*. -**6.** AERON & ASTRONAUT aire *f*; **helicopter ~** aire d'atterrissage pour hélicoptères. -**7.** *inf* [flat] appart *m*; [room] piaule *f*; **let's go to my ~** allons chez moi; **bachelor ~** garçonnière *f*. -**8.** BOT [leaf] feuille *f*; **(water) lily ~** feuille de nénuphar. -**9.** [noise]: **the ~ of footsteps behind me** des pas feutrés derrière moi; **the ~ of bare feet on marble** le bruit sourd de pieds nus sur le marbre. -**10.** *inf* [sanitary towel] serviette *f* hygiénique.
◇ *vt* -**1.** [clothing] matelasser; [shoulder] rembourrer; [door, wall] capitonner. -**2.** = **pad out 2**.
◇ *vi* [walk] avancer à pas feutrés; **he padded downstairs in his slippers** il descendit l'escalier en pantoufles; **the dog padded along beside the cyclist** le chien trottinait à côté du cycliste.
◆ **pad out** *vt sep* -**1.** = **pad** *vt* **1**. -**2.** *fig* [essay, article, speech] délayer; **he padded out the talk with anecdotes** il a allongé son discours en le truffant d'anecdotes.

padded ['pædɪd] *adj* -**1.** [door, bench, steering wheel] capitonné; [garment, envelope, oven glove] matelassé; [sofa] bien rembourré; **~ bra** soutien-gorge *m* à bonnets renforcés; **~ cell** cellule *f* capitonnée; **~ shoulders** épaules *fpl* rembourrées. -**2.** [fat]: **he's well ~** il est bien en chair.

padding ['pædɪŋ] *n* -**1.** [fabric] ouate *f*, ouatine *f*, garnissage *m*. -**2.** *fig* [in essay, speech] délayage *m*, remplissage *m*.

paddle ['pædl] ◇ *n* -**1.** [for boat, canoe] pagaie *f*. -**2.** [of waterwheel] palette *f*, aube *f*. -**3.** *Am* [table tennis bat] raquette *f* (de ping-pong). -**4.** [of turtle, seal] palette *f* natatoire. -**5.** [wade]: **to go for** OR **to have a ~** aller barboter.
◇ *vi* -**1.** [in canoe] pagayer; **he ~d across the lake** il a traversé le lac en pagayant. -**2.** [wade] barboter.
◇ *vt* -**1.** [boat]: **to ~ a canoe** pagayer; **to ~ one's own canoe** *fig* se débrouiller tout seul, mener sa barque. -**2.** *inf Am* [spank - child] donner une fessée à; **I'll ~ your ass!** tu vas prendre une fessée!

paddle boat *n* -**1.** = **paddle steamer**. -**2.** [pedalo] Pédalo® *m*.

paddle steamer *n* bateau *m* à roues.

paddle wheel *n* NAUT roue *f* à aubes.

paddling pool *n* pataugeoire *f*.

paddock ['pædək] *n* [gen] enclos *m*; [at racetrack] paddock *m*.

paddy ['pædɪ] (*pl* **paddies**) *n* -**1.** [field] rizière *f*. -**2.** [rice] paddy *m*, riz *m* non décortiqué. -**3.** *inf Br* [fit of temper] crise *f* de colère; **she was in a real ~** elle était furax.

Paddy *inf* ['pædɪ] (*pl* **Paddies**) *n offensive* Irlandais *m*.

paddy field *n* rizière *f*.

paddy wagon *inf n Am* panier *m* à salade.

padlock ['pædlɒk] ◇ *n* [for door, gate] cadenas *m*; [for bicycle] antivol *m*.
◇ *vt* [door, gate] cadenasser; [bicycle] mettre un antivol à; **she ~ed her bicycle to a lamppost** elle a attaché sa bicyclette à un réverbère avec son antivol.

padre ['pɑːdrɪ] *n* -**1.** MIL aumônier *m*. -**2.** [priest] prêtre *m*, curé *m*; [clergyman] pasteur *m*; [term of address] (mon) Père *m*.

Padua ['pædjʊə] *pr n* Padoue.

Paduan ['pædjʊən] ◇ *n* Padouan *m*, -e *f*.
◇ *adj* padouan.

paean ['piːən] *n* -**1.** HIST péan *m*. -**2.** *lit* [expressing praise] dithyrambe *m*.

paederast *etc* ['pedəræst] *Br* = **pederast**.

paediatric *etc* [ˌpiːdɪ'ætrɪk] *Br* = **pediatric**.

paedology [piː'dɒlədʒɪ] *Br* = **pedology**.

paedophile *etc* ['piːdəʊˌfaɪl] *Br* = **pedophile**.

paella [paɪ'elə] *n* paella *f*.

paeony ['pɪənɪ] *Br* = **peony**.

pagan ['peɪgən] ◇ *n* païen *m*, -enne *f*.
◇ *adj* païen.

paganism ['peɪgənɪzm] *n* paganisme *m*.

page [peɪdʒ] ◇ *n* -**1.** [of book, newspaper etc] page *f*; **on ~ two** [of book] (à la) page deux; [of newspaper] (en) page deux; **the sports ~** la page des sports, la page sportive; **a glorious ~ in our history** *lit* une page glorieuse de notre histoire ❑ **~ three** *la page 3 du «Sun», où figure chaque jour une pin-up*; **~ three girl** *nom que l'on donne aux jeunes femmes qui posent seins nus pour certains quotidiens populaires britanniques*. -**2.** [at court] page *m*; [in hotel] chasseur *m*, groom *m*; [at wedding] page *m*; [in legislative body] (jeune) huissier *m*.
◇ *vt* -**1.** [paginate] paginer. -**2.** [call] appeler (par haut-parleur); **paging Mrs Clark!** on demande Mme Clark!
◆ **page through** *vt insep* feuilleter.

pageant ['pædʒənt] *n* [historical parade, show] reconstitution *f* historique; [grand display] spectacle *m* fastueux.

pageantry ['pædʒəntrɪ] *n* apparat *m*, pompe *f*.

page boy *n* -**1.** [servant] page *m*; [in hotel] chasseur *m*, groom *m*; [at wedding] page *m*. -**2.** [hairstyle]: **~ (cut)** coupe *f* à la Jeanne d'Arc.

page proofs *npl* TYPO épreuves *fpl* en pages.

pager ['peɪdʒəʳ] *n* TELEC récepteur *m* d'appel OR de poche.

paginate ['pædʒɪneɪt] *vt* paginer.

pagination [ˌpædʒɪ'neɪʃn] *n* pagination *f*.

pagoda [pə'gəʊdə] *n* pagode *f*.

pah [pɑː] *interj*: **~!** pouah!

paid [peɪd] ◇ *pt* & *pp* → **pay**.
◇ *adj* -**1.** payé, rémunéré; **~ holidays** *Br* OR **vacation** *Am* congés *mpl* payés; **~ work** travail *m* rémunéré; **~ workers** travailleurs *mpl* salariés. -**2.** *phr*: **to put ~ to sthg** gâcher OR ruiner qqch.

paid-up *adj* -**1.** [member] à jour de ses cotisations; *fig* [committed]: **he's a (fully) ~ member of the Communist Party** il a sa carte au Parti Communiste. -**2.** FIN [capital] versé; [shares] libéré.

pail [peɪl] *n* -**1.** [bucket] seau *m*. -**2.** [bucketful] = **pailful**.

pailful ['peɪlfʊl] *n esp Am*: **a ~ of...** un plein seau de...

paillasse ['pælɪæs] = **palliasse**.

pain [peɪn] ◇ *vt* [cause distress to] peiner, faire de la peine à; [hurt] faire souffrir.
◇ *n* -**1.** [physical] douleur *f*; **he has a ~ in his ear** il a mal à l'oreille; **I have a ~ in my side** j'ai une douleur au côté; **are you in ~?** avez-vous mal?, est-ce que vous souffrez? -**2.** [emotional] peine *f*, douleur *f*, souffrance *f*; **the news will cause her great ~** cette nouvelle va lui faire de la peine; **he went through a lot of ~ when his son left home** il a eu beaucoup de peine quand son fils a quitté la maison. -**3.** *inf* [annoying person or thing]: **what a ~ he is!** qu'est-ce qu'il est enquiquinant!; **it's a (real)** OR **such a ~ trying to cross London during the rush hour** traverser Londres aux heures de pointe, c'est la galère ❑ **he's a ~ in the arse**▽ OR **backside** *inf Br* OR **ass**▽ *Am* il est chiant, c'est un emmerdeur; **she's a ~ in the neck** *inf* elle me casse les pieds. -**4.** JUR: **on ~ of death/banishment** sous peine de mort/de bannissement.
◆ **pains** *npl* [efforts] peine *f*, mal *m*; **he went to great ~s to help us** il s'est donné beaucoup de mal pour nous aider; **she took great ~s over her work/the dinner** elle s'est donné beaucoup de mal pour son travail/pour ce dîner; **is that all we get for our ~s?** c'est comme cela que nous sommes récompensés de nos efforts?; **he was at** OR **he took ~s to avoid her** il a tout fait pour l'éviter.

pained [peɪnd] *adj* peiné, affligé; **his face took on a ~ look** il a pris un air peiné.

painful ['peɪnfʊl] *adj* -**1.** [sore] douloureux; **my burns are still ~** mes brûlures me font toujours mal; **these shoes are really ~** ces chaussures me font vraiment mal; **is your back still ~?** avez-vous toujours mal au dos? -**2.** [upsetting] pénible; **it's ~ to have to admit it** c'est dur à admettre. -**3.** [laborious] pénible, difficile, laborieux. -**4.** *inf* [very bad] nul.

painfully ['peɪnfʊlɪ] *adv* -**1.** [hit, strike, rub] durement; [move, walk] péniblement. -**2.** [distressingly] douloureusement; [laboriously] laborieusement, avec difficulté. -**3.** [as intensifier] horriblement, affreusement; **a ~ boring speech** un discours mortellement ennuyeux; **it was ~ obvious that he didn't understand** il n'était que trop évident qu'il ne comprenait pas.

painkiller ['peɪn,kɪləʳ] *n* analgésique *m*, calmant *m*.

painkilling ['peɪn,kɪlɪŋ] *adj* analgésique, calmant; to give sb a ~ injection injecter un analgésique à qqn.

painless ['peɪnlɪs] *adj* -**1.** [injection, operation] sans douleur, indolore; [death] sans souffrance. -**2.** [unproblematic] facile; it was a ~ decision la décision n'a pas été dure à prendre; a ~ way to lose weight une manière facile de perdre du poids.

painlessly ['peɪnlɪslɪ] *adv* -**1.** [without hurting] sans douleur. -**2.** [unproblematically] sans peine, sans mal.

painstaking ['peɪnz,teɪkɪŋ] *adj* [research, care] rigoureux, méticuleux; [worker] assidu, soigneux.

painstakingly ['peɪnz,teɪkɪŋlɪ] *adv* soigneusement, méticuleusement.

paint [peɪnt] ◇ *n* -**1.** [for a room, furniture, picture] peinture *f*; a tin of ~ un pot de peinture; a set OR box of ~s une boîte de couleurs; the ~ was beginning to flake off la peinture commençait à s'écailler ☐ gloss/matt ~ peinture brillante/mate; oil/acrylic ~ peinture à l'huile/acrylique. -**2.** *pej* [make-up] peinture *f*, fard *m*.

◇ *vt* -**1.** [room, furniture, picture] peindre; the door was ~ed yellow la porte était peinte en jaune; to ~ one's nails se vernir les ongles; to ~ one's face se farder; *pej* [with make-up] se peinturlurer ☐ to ~ the town red *inf* faire la noce OR la foire. -**2.** [wound] badigeonner; [apply - varnish, layer] appliquer (au pinceau); [- antiseptic]: she ~ed iodine onto his elbow, she ~ed his elbow with iodine elle lui a mis de la teinture d'iode sur le coude. -**3.** *fig* [describe] dépeindre, décrire; the author ~s a bleak picture of suburban life l'auteur dresse un sombre portrait OR brosse un sombre tableau de la vie des banlieusards.

◇ *vi* peindre, faire de la peinture; to ~ in oils faire de la peinture à l'huile; to ~ in watercolours faire de l'aquarelle.

◆ **paint out, paint over** *vt sep* recouvrir (d'une couche) de peinture.

paintbox ['peɪntbɒks] *n* boîte *f* de couleurs.

paintbrush ['peɪntbrʌʃ] *n* pinceau *m*, brosse *f*.

painted ['peɪntɪd] *adj* -**1.** [with paint] peint; ~ blue peint en bleu. -**2.** *pej* [with make-up] maquillé, fardé.

painted lady *n* belle-dame *f*.

painter ['peɪntəʳ] *n* -**1.** [artist, decorator] peintre *m*; house ~ peintre en bâtiment; ~ and decorator peintre-décorateur; landscape ~ paysagiste *mf*; portrait ~ portraitiste *mf*. -**2.** NAUT amarre *f*.

painting ['peɪntɪŋ] *n* -**1.** [activity] peinture *f*. -**2.** [picture] peinture *f*, tableau *m*.

paint pot *n Br* pot *m* de peinture.

paint shop *n* INDUST atelier *m* de peinture.

paint stripper *n* décapant *m*.

paintwork ['peɪntwɜːk] *n (U)* peinture *f*; the house with the white ~ la maison avec les peintures blanches.

pair [peəʳ] ◇ *n* -**1.** [two related objects or people] paire *f*; a ~ of shoes/gloves une paire de chaussures/de gants; an odd-looking ~ un drôle de tandem; where's the ~ to this sock? où est la chaussette qui va avec celle-ci?; to work in ~s travailler par deux; line up in ~s! mettez-vous en rang (deux) par deux!; you're a ~ of idiots! vous faites une belle paire d'imbéciles!; I've only got one ~ of hands! je n'ai que deux mains! -**2.** [single object in two parts]: a ~ of trousers/shorts/tights un pantalon/short/collant; a ~ of pliers une pince; a ~ of scissors une paire de ciseaux. -**3.** [husband and wife] couple *m*. -**4.** [of birds, animals] paire *f*. -**5.** MATH paire *f*; ordered ~ paire ordonnée. -**6.** *Br* POL *deux membres de partis adverses qui se sont entendus pour ne pas participer à un vote ou pour s'abstenir de voter durant une période déterminée.* -**7.** [in cards, dice] paire *f*; a ~ of kings/sevens une paire de rois/de sept.

◇ *vt* [socks] assortir; [animal, birds] apparier, accoupler.

◇ *vi* [animals, birds] s'apparier, s'accoupler.

◆ **pair off** ◇ *vt sep* [arrange in couples - dancers] répartir en couples; [- team members, children in class] mettre deux par deux; I got ~ed off with Roger on m'a mis avec Roger; our parents are trying to ~ us off nos parents essaient de nous fiancer.

◇ *vi insep* [dancers] former des couples; [team members, children in class] se mettre deux par deux.

◆ **pair up** ◇ *vt sep* [socks] assortir.

◇ *vi insep* [people] se mettre par deux; he ~ed up with Bob for the car rally il a choisi Bob comme partenaire OR équipier pour le rallye.

pair royal *n* brelan *m*.

paisley ['peɪzlɪ] *n* [pattern] (impression *f*) cachemire *m*; [material] tissu *m* cachemire; a ~ tie une cravate impression cachemire.

pajama *Am* = **pyjama**.

Paki▼ ['pækɪ] *n Br terme raciste désignant un Pakistanais.*

Paki-bashing▼ [-,bæʃɪŋ] *n (U) Br terme raciste désignant des brutalités exercées contre les immigrés pakistanais,* ≃ ratonnades *fpl*.

Pakistan [*Br* ,pɑːkɪ'stɑːn, *Am* 'pækɪstæn] *pr n* Pakistan *m*; in ~ au Pakistan.

Pakistani [*Br* ,pɑːkɪ'stɑːnɪ, *Am* ,pækɪ'stænɪ] ◇ *n* Pakistanais *m*, -e *f*.

◇ *adj* pakistanais.

pal *inf* [pæl] (*pt* & *pp* palled, *cont* palling) *n* -**1.** [friend] copain *m*, copine *f*, pote *m*; we're great ~s nous sommes très copains; be a ~ and fetch my coat sois sympa, va me chercher mon manteau. -**2.** [term of address]: watch it, ~! fais gaffe, mec!; thanks, ~ merci mon pote.

◆ **pal about** *inf Br*, **pal around** *inf vi insep*: to ~ about with sb copiner avec qqn; they ~ about together ils sont toujours fourrés ensemble.

◆ **pal up** *inf vi insep Br*: they palled up [men] ils sont devenus copains; [women] elles sont devenues copines; he/she palled up with George il est devenu le copain/elle est devenue la copine de George.

PAL [pæl] (*abbr of* phase alternation line) *n* PAL *f*.

palace ['pælɪs] *n* palais *m*; royal/bishop's ~ palais royal/épiscopal; the Palace *Br* [Buckingham Palace] le palais de Buckingham *(et par extension ses habitants)* ☐ picture ~ *dated* cinéma *m*; the Palace of Westminster le palais de Westminster *(siège du Parlement britannique)*.

palace revolution *n* révolution *f* de palais.

paladin ['pælədɪn] *n* paladin *m*.

palaeo- *etc Br* = **paleo-**.

palatable ['pælətəbl] *adj* -**1.** [food, drink - tasty] savoureux; [- edible] mangeable. -**2.** *fig* [idea] acceptable.

palatal ['pælətl] ◇ *adj* -**1.** ANAT palatin. -**2.** LING palatal.

◇ *n* palatale *f*.

palatalize, -ise ['pælətəlaɪz] *vt* palataliser.

palate ['pælət] *n* -**1.** ANAT palais *m*. -**2.** [sense of taste] palais *m*; to have a delicate ~ avoir le palais fin.

palatial [pə'leɪʃl] *adj* grandiose, magnifique; she lives alone in a ~ house elle vit toute seule dans un véritable palais OR palace.

palatinate [pə'lætɪnət] *n* palatinat *m*.

◆ **Palatinate** *pr n*: the ~ le Palatinat.

palatine ['pælətaɪn] ◇ *adj* -**1.** HIST palatin; the Palatine (Hill) le mont Palatin. -**2.** ANAT palatin.

◇ *n* palatin *m*.

palatography [,pælə'tɒgrəfɪ] *n* palatographie *f*.

palaver *inf* [pə'lɑːvəʳ] *Br* ◇ *n (U)* -**1.** [rigmarole, fuss] chichis *mpl*, histoire *f*, histoires *fpl*; all the ~ of passports, customs and immigration toutes ces histoires de passeports, de formalités de douane et d'immigration; what a ~! quelle affaire!, que de chichis! -**2.** [discussion] palabre *m or f*; [tedious] palabres *mpl or fpl*.

◇ *vi* palabrer.

pale [peɪl] ◇ *adj* -**1.** [face, complexion] pâle; [from fright, shock, sickness] blême, blafard; he turned ~ il a pâli OR blêmi ☐ (as) ~ as death blanc comme un linge. -**2.** [colour] pâle, clair; [light] pâle, blafard; ~ pink ribbons des rubans rose pâle. -**3.** [feeble] pâle; it was a ~ imitation of the real thing c'était une pâle copie de l'original.

◇ *vi* [person, face] pâlir, blêmir; [sky, colour] pâlir; our problems ~ into insignificance beside hers nos problèmes sont insignifiants comparés aux siens OR à côté des siens.

◇ *n* -**1.** [post] pieu *m*. -**2.** [fence] palissade *f*; beyond the ~ *Br*: he's beyond the ~ il n'est pas fréquentable; I find such behaviour beyond the ~ je trouve un tel comportement inadmissible.

pale ale *n* pale-ale *f*, bière *f* blonde légère.

paleface ['peɪlfeɪs] *n pej* OR *hum* Visage *m* pâle.

palefaced ['peɪlfeɪst] *adj* (au teint) pâle.

paleness ['peɪlnɪs] *n* pâleur *f*.

Paleocene ['pælɪəʊsiːn] ◇ *adj* paléocène.

◇ *n* paléocène *m*.

paleographer [,pælɪ'ɒgrəfəʳ] *n* paléographe *m*.

paleography [,pælɪ'ɒgrəfɪ] *n* paléographie *f*.

paleolith ['pælɪəʊlɪθ] *n* outil *m* paléolithique.

Paleolithic [,pælɪəʊ'lɪθɪk] ◇ *adj* paléolithique.

◇ *n* paléolithique *m*.

paleontology [,pælɪɒn'tɒlədʒɪ] *n* paléontologie *f*.

Paleozoic [,pælɪəʊ'zəʊɪk] ◇ *adj* paléozoïque.

◇ *n* paléozoïque *m*.

Palermitan [pə'lɜːmɪtn] ◇ *n* Palermitain *m*, -e *f*.

◇ *adj* palermitain.

Palermo [pə'lɜːməʊ] *pr n* Palerme.

Palestine ['pælə,staɪn] *pr n* Palestine *f*; in ~ en Palestine.

Palestine Liberation Organization *pr n* Organisation *f* de libération de la Palestine.

Palestinian [,pælə'stɪnɪən] ◇ *n* Palestinien *m*, -enne *f*.

◇ *adj* palestinien.

palette ['pælət] *n* palette *f* BX-ARTS.

palette knife *n* ART couteau *m* (à palette); CULIN palette *f*.

palfrey ['pɔːlfrɪ] *n arch* palefroi *m*.

palimony ['pælɪmənɪ] *n* pension *f* alimentaire *(accordée à un ex-concubin ou une ex-concubine)*.

palimpsest ['pælɪmpsest] *n* palimpseste *m*.

palindrome ['pælɪndrəʊm] *n* palindrome *m*.

paling ['peɪlɪŋ] *n* [stake] pieu *m*; [fence] palissade *f*.

◆ **palings** *npl* [fence] palissade *f*.

palisade [,pælɪ'seɪd] *n* [fence] palissade *f*.

◆ **palisades** *npl Am* [cliffs] ligne *f* de falaises.

palish ['peɪlɪʃ] *adj* pâlot.

pall [pɔːl] ◇ *n* -**1.** [cloth] drap *m* mortuaire, poêle *m*. -**2.** [cloud - of smoke] voile *m*; *fig* voile *m*, manteau *m*; a ~ of silence hung over the room il régnait dans la pièce un silence profond. -**3.** *Am* [coffin] cercueil *m*.

◇ *vi Br* perdre son charme; it began to ~ on me after a few days après quelques jours, j'ai commencé à m'en lasser.

Palladian [pə'leɪdjən] *adj* palladien.

pallbearer ['pɔːl,beərəʳ] *n*: the ~s [carrying coffin] les porteurs *mpl* du cercueil; [accompanying coffin] le cortège funèbre.

pallet ['pælɪt] *n* -**1.** [bed] grabat *m*; [mattress] paillasse *f*. -**2.** [for loading, transportation] palette *f*. -**3.** [potter's instrument] palette *f*. -**4.** = **palette**.

pallet truck *n* chariot *m* élévateur, transpalette *m*.

palliasse ['pælɪæs] *n* paillasse *f*.

palliate ['pælɪeɪt] *vt* -**1.** MED pallier, lénifier. -**2.** *fml* [fault, offence] pallier, atténuer.

palliative ['pælɪətɪv] ◇ *adj* palliatif.
◇ *n* palliatif *m*.

pallid ['pælɪd] *adj* -**1.** [wan] pâle, blême, blafard; ~ light lumière blafarde. -**2.** [lacking vigour] insipide.

pallidness ['pælɪdnɪs] *n* pâleur *f*.

pallor ['pæləʳ] *n* pâleur *f*.

pally *inf* ['pælɪ] (*compar* pallier, *superl* palliest) *adj*: to be ~ with sb être copain/copine avec qqn; he's really ~ with all the shopkeepers il est à tu et à toi avec tous les commerçants.

palm [pɑːm] ◇ *n* -**1.** [of hand] paume *f*; to have sweaty ~s avoir les mains moites; to read sb's ~ lire les lignes de la main à qqn; he had them in the ~ of his hand il les tenait à sa merci OR sous sa coupe; to grease sb's ~ graisser la patte à qqn. -**2.** [tree] palmier *m*. -**3.** [branch] palme *f*; RELIG rameau *m*; the winner's ~ *Br fig* la palme du vainqueur; to carry off the ~ *Br* remporter la palme. -**4.** *arch* [measure] palme *m*.
◇ *vt* [coin] cacher dans le creux de la main.
◆ **palm off** *inf vt sep* [unwanted objects] refiler; [inferior goods] fourguer; to ~ sb off with sthg, to ~ sthg off on sb refiler qqch à qqn.

Palma (de Mallorca) [,pælmədəmə'jɔːkə] *pr n* Palma (de Majorque).

palmate ['pælmeɪt] *adj* BOT & ZOOL palmé.

palmist ['pɑːmɪst] *n* chiromancien *m*, -enne *f*.

palmistry ['pɑːmɪstrɪ] *n* chiromancie *f*.

palm oil *n* huile *f* de palme.

palm sugar *n* sucre *m* de palme.

Palm Sunday *n* (le dimanche des) Rameaux *mpl*.

palm tree *n* palmier *m*.

palm wine *n* vin *m* de palme.

palmy ['pɑːmɪ] (*compar* palmier, *superl* palmiest) *adj* -**1.** [pleasant] agréable, doux; in the ~ days of our youth aux jours heureux de notre jeunesse. -**2.** [beach, coast] bordé de palmiers.

Palmyra [pæl'maɪərə] *pr n* Palmyre.

palomino [,pælə'miːnəʊ] (*pl* palominos) *n* palomino *m*.

palooka *inf* [pə'luːkə] *n Am* balourd *m*, -e *f*.

palpable ['pælpəbl] *adj* -**1.** [tangible] palpable, tangible. -**2.** [obvious] évident, manifeste, flagrant; a ~ lie un mensonge grossier.

palpably ['pælpəblɪ] *adv* -**1.** [tangibly] tangiblement. -**2.** [obviously] manifestement.

palpate ['pælpeɪt] *vt* palper.

palpitate ['pælpɪteɪt] *vi* palpiter.

palpitating ['pælpɪteɪtɪŋ] *adj* MED palpitant.

palpitation [,pælpɪ'teɪʃn] *n* palpitation *f*; to have OR to get ~s MED avoir des palpitations; I get ~s whenever I see her *hum* mon cœur bat la chamade OR s'emballe chaque fois que je la vois.

palsied ['pɔːlzɪd] *adj* -**1.** [paralysed] paralysé. -**2.** [shaking, trembling] tremblant, tremblotant.

palsy ['pɔːlzɪ] *n* paralysie *f*; shaking ~ = **Parkinson's disease**.

paltry ['pɔːltrɪ] *adj* -**1.** [meagre - wage, sum] misérable, dérisoire; it'll cost you a ~ $100 ça vous coûtera cent malheureux dollars. -**2.** [worthless - person, attitude] insignifiant, minable; a ~ excuse une piètre excuse.

Pamirs [pə'mɪəz] *pl pr n*: the ~ le Pamir; in the ~ au Pamir.

pampas ['pæmpəz] *npl* pampa *f*.

pampas grass *n* herbe *f* de la pampa.

pamper ['pæmpəʳ] *vt* choyer, dorloter; to ~ o.s. se dorloter; ~ yourself with a bubble bath faites-vous plaisir, prenez un bain moussant.

pamphlet ['pæmflɪt] *n* [gen] brochure *f*; POL pamphlet *m*.

pamphleteer [,pæmflə'tɪəʳ] *n* [gen & POL] pamphlétaire *mf*.

Pamplona [pæm'pləʊnə] *pr n* Pampelune.

pan [pæn] (*pt* & *pp* panned, *cont* panning) ◇ *n* -**1.** CULIN casserole *f*; cake ~ *Am* moule *m* à gâteau. -**2.** MIN [for gold] batée *f*. -**3.** [on scales] plateau *m*. -**4.** *Br* [toilet bowl]: (lavatory) ~ cuvette *f* de W-C. -**5.** CIN & TV panoramique *m*. -**6.** *inf* [face] bouille *f*.
◇ *vi* -**1.** [miner]: to ~ for gold chercher de l'or. -**2.** [camera] faire un panoramique.
◇ *vt* -**1.** [camera]: to ~ the camera faire un panoramique, panoramiquer *spec*. -**2.** *inf* [criticize] descendre; the film was panned by the critics le film a été descendu par les critiques.
◆ **pan out** *inf vi insep Br* [work out] se dérouler, marcher; [succeed] réussir; if things ~ out as planned si tout marche comme prévu; our strategy is not panning out notre stratégie ne donne pas de résultats; things should start to ~ out around August les choses devraient commencer à s'arranger vers le mois d'août.

pan- *in cpds* pan-; Pan-Asian panasiatique.

Pan [pæn] *pr n* Pan.

panacea [,pænə'sɪə] *n* panacée *f*.

panache [pə'næʃ] *n* panache *m*.

Pan-African ◇ *adj* panafricain.
◇ *n* partisan *m*, -e *f* du panafricanisme.

Pan-Africanism *n* panafricanisme *m*.

Panama ['pænəmɑː] ◇ *pr n* Panama *m*; in ~ au Panama; the Isthmus of ~ l'isthme *m* de Panama.
◇ *n* = **Panama hat**.

Panama Canal *pr n*: the ~ le canal de Panama.

Panama City *pr n* Panama.

Panama hat *n* panama *m*.

Panamanian [,pænə'meɪnjən] ◇ *n* Panaméen *m*, -enne *f*.
◇ *adj* panaméen.

Pan-American *adj* panaméricain; the ~ Highway la route panaméricaine.

Pan-Americanism *n* panaméricanisme *m*.

Pan-Arab *adj* panarabe.

Pan-Arabism [-'ærəbɪzm] *n* panarabisme *m*.

Pan-Arabist *n* partisan *m*, -e *f* du panarabisme.

panatella [,pænə'telə] *n* panatela *m*, panatella *m*.

pancake ['pæŋkeɪk] ◇ *n* -**1.** CULIN [in UK] crêpe *f*; [in US] *sorte de petite galette épaisse servie au petit déjeuner*; ~ race *course traditionnelle du mardi gras britannique consistant à courir avec une poêle dans laquelle se trouve une crêpe qu'il faut retourner*; (as) flat as a ~ plat comme une galette. -**2.** *inf* [make-up] fond *m* de teint épais; ~ make-up tartine *f* de maquillage. -**3.** AERON = **pancake landing**.
◇ *vi* AERON atterrir sur le ventre.

Pancake Day *n Br* mardi gras *m*.

pancake landing *n* atterrissage *m* sur le ventre.

panchromatic [,pænkrəʊ'mætɪk] *adj* panchromatique.

pancreas ['pæŋkrɪəs] *n* pancréas *m*.

pancreatic [,pæŋkrɪ'ætɪk] *adj* pancréatique.

panda ['pændə] *n* panda *m*; ~ (car) *Br* voiture *f* de police.

pandemic [pæn'demɪk] ◇ *adj* -**1.** MED pandémique. -**2.** [universal] universel, général.
◇ *n* MED pandémie *f*.

pandemonium [,pændɪ'məʊnjəm] *n* *(U)* [chaos] chaos *m*; [uproar] tumulte *m*, tohu-bohu *m*; ~ broke out cela a déclenché un véritable tumulte; the whole office is in ~ le bureau est sens dessus dessous.

pander ['pændəʳ] ◇ *vi*: to ~ to [person, weaknesses] flatter (bassement).
◇ *n* [pimp] entremetteur *m*, -euse *f*, proxénète *mf*.

pandit ['pændɪt] *n* [wise man] sage *m*; [term of address] *titre donné à certains sages en Inde*.

Pandora [pæn'dɔːrə] *pr n* Pandore; ~'s box la boîte de Pandore.

pane [peɪn] *n* vitre *f*, carreau *m*; a ~ of glass un carreau; ~ glass window *Am* fenêtre *f* panoramique.

panegyric [,pænɪ'dʒɪrɪk] *n fml* panégyrique *m*; he launched into a ~ of OR about French cuisine il s'est lancé dans un éloge dithyrambique de la cuisine française.

panegyrize, -ise ['pænɪdʒɪraɪz] *vt fml* faire le panégyrique de.

panel ['pænl] (*Br pt* & *pp* panelled, *cont* panelling, *Am pt* & *pp* paneled, *cont* paneling) ◇ *n* -**1.** [flat section - of wood, glass etc] panneau *m*; sliding ~ panneau coulissant. -**2.** [group, committee - gen] comité *m*; [- to judge exam, contest] jury *m*; [- in radio or TV quiz] invités *mpl*; [- in public debate] panel *m*; [- in public inquiry] commission *f* (d'enquête); a ~ of experts un comité d'experts; our ~ for tonight's show nos invités à l'émission de ce soir; the ~ were unanimous in awarding her top marks le jury lui a accordé à l'unanimité la plus haute note. -**3.** [set of controls]: (control) ~ tableau *m* de bord; (instrument) ~ AERON & AUT tableau *m* de bord. -**4.** SEW panneau *m*, lé *m*. -**5.** JUR [selection list] liste *f* de jurés. -**6.** ART [backing] panneau *m*; [picture] (peinture *f* sur) panneau *m*.
◇ *vt* [wall, hall] lambrisser, revêtir de panneaux; a panelled door une porte à panneaux; the dining room is in panelled oak la salle à manger est lambrissée de chêne; one wall was panelled in pine un des murs était lambrissé de pin.

panel beater *n* carrossier *m*, tôlier *m* AUT.

panel discussion *n* débat *m*, tribune *f*.

panel doctor *n Br dated* ≃ médecin *m* conventionné.

panel game *n Br* RADIO jeu *m* radiophonique; TV jeu *m* télévisé.

panel heating *n* chauffage *m* à panneaux.

panelling *Br*, **paneling** *Am* ['pænəlɪŋ] *n (U)* panneaux *mpl*, lambris *m*.

panellist *Br*, **panelist** *Am* ['pænəlɪst] *n* [jury member] juré *m*; [in radio or TV quiz] invité *m*, -e *f*; [in public debate] panéliste *mf*.

panel pin *n* pointe *f* à tête d'homme, clou *m* à panneau.

panel truck *n Am* camionnette *f*.

Pan-European *adj* paneuropéen.

pan-fries *npl Am* pommes *fpl* (de terre) sautées.

pan-fry *vt Am* (faire) sauter; pan-fried eggs œufs sur le plat.

pang [pæŋ] *n* -**1.** [of emotion] coup *m* au cœur, pincement *m* de cœur; I felt a ~ of sadness j'ai eu un serrement de cœur; to feel ~s of conscience OR guilt éprouver des remords; he resigned without a ~ of regret il a démissionné sans l'ombre d'un remords OR regret. -**2.** [of pain] élancement *m*, douleur *f* lancinante; hunger ~s tiraillements *mpl* d'estomac.

Pan-Germanic *adj* pangermanique.

pangolin [pæŋ'gəʊlɪn] *n* pangolin *m*.

panhandle ['pæn,hændl] *Am* ◇ *n* GEOG *nom donné à la partie longue et étroite de certains États ou parcs américains*; the Alaska ~ la région sud de l'Alaska.
◇ *vi inf* faire la manche.
◇ *vt inf*: to ~ money from sb, to ~ sb taper qqn.

panhandler *inf* ['pæn,hændləʳ] *n Am* mendiant *m*, -e *f*.

panic ['pænɪk] (*pt* & *pp* panicked, *cont* panicking) ◇ *n* -**1.** [alarm, fear] panique *f*, affolement *m*; she was close to ~ elle était au bord de l'affolement; it started a ~ on the stock exchange cela a semé la panique à la Bourse; to throw sb into a ~ affoler qqn. -**2.** *inf* [rush] hâte *f*; I was in a mad ~ to get to the airport c'était la panique pour aller à l'aéroport; what's the ~? ne vous affolez pas!; there's no ~ il n'y a pas le feu. -**3.** *inf Am* [sthg funny]: it was a ~! c'était à hurler de rire!
◇ *vi* s'affoler; don't ~! ne vous affolez pas!; he's starting to ~ about the wedding il commence à s'affoler à la perspective de ce mariage.
◇ *vt* affoler.

panic bolt *n* barre *f* antipanique.

panic button *n* signal *m* d'alarme; to hit the ~ *inf* perdre les pédales.

panic buying *n* *(U)* achats *mpl* en catastrophe OR de dernière minute.

panicky *inf* ['pænɪkɪ] *adj* [person, crowd] paniqué; [voice, message] affolé; [feeling, reaction] de panique; [giggle] nerveux; I get ~ every time I have to speak to him je panique chaque fois que je dois lui parler.
panicmonger ['pænɪk,mʌŋgəʳ] *n* semeur *m*, -euse *f* de panique.
panic stations *inf npl*: it was ~! ça a été la panique générale!
panic-stricken *adj* affolé, pris de panique.
panjandrum *inf* [pæn'dʒændrəm] *n* grand manitou *m*, ponte *m*.
pannier ['pænɪəʳ] *n* -**1.** [bag - on bicycle, motorbike] sacoche *f*; [- on donkey] panier *m* de bât. -**2.** [basket] panier *m*, corbeille *f*.
panoply ['pænəplɪ] *n* panoplie *f*.
panorama [,pænə'rɑːmə] *n literal* & *fig* panorama *m*.
panoramic [,pænə'ræmɪk] *adj* panoramique; ~ screen CIN écran *m* panoramique; ~ view vue *f* panoramique.
panpipes ['pænpaɪps] *npl* flûte *f* de Pan.
pan scrubber *n* tampon *m* à récurer.
pansy ['pænzɪ] (*pl* **pansies**) *n* -**1.** BOT pensée *f*. -**2.** *inf Br pej* [sissy] poule *f* mouillée, femmelette *f*; [homosexual] tante *f*.
pant [pænt] ◇ *vi* [puff] haleter, souffler; he ~ed up the stairs il monta l'escalier en soufflant; to ~ for breath chercher son souffle.
◇ *vt* [say] dire en haletant OR d'une voix haletante.
◇ *n* [breath] halètement *m*.
◆ **pant for** *vt insep* mourir d'envie de.
Pantaloon [,pæntə'luːn] *pr n* THEAT Pantalon.
pantaloons [,pæntə'luːnz] *npl* pantalon *m* bouffant.
pantechnicon [pæn'teknɪkən] *n Br* -**1.** [van] camion *m* de déménagement. -**2.** [warehouse] garde-meubles *m*.
pantheism ['pænθiːɪzm] *n* panthéisme *m*.
pantheist ['pænθiːɪst] *n* panthéiste *mf*.
pantheistic [,pænθiː'ɪstɪk] *adj* panthéiste.
pantheon ['pænθɪən] *n* panthéon *m*.
panther ['pænθəʳ] (*pl inv* OR **panthers**) *n* -**1.** [leopard] panthère *f*. -**2.** *Am* [puma] puma *m*.
pantie girdle ['pæntɪ-] = **panty girdle**.
pantie hose = **panty hose**.
panties ['pæntɪz] *npl* (petite) culotte *f*; a pair of ~ un slip, une culotte.
pantihose *Am* = **panty hose**.
panting ['pæntɪŋ] *adj* [person, dog] haletant.
panto *inf* ['pæntəʊ] (*pl* **pantos**) *n Br* = **pantomime 1**.
pantograph ['pæntəgrɑːf] *n* pantographe *m*.
pantomime ['pæntəmaɪm] *n* -**1.** *Br* [Christmas show] *spectacle de Noël pour enfants*; ~ **dame** *rôle travesti outré et ridicule dans la «pantomime»*. -**2.** [mime] pantomime *f*. -**3.** *inf Br fig* comédie *f*, vaudeville *m*.

PANTOMIME:
Le genre typiquement britannique de la «pantomime» est très conventionnel; certains personnages-types («pantomime dame», «principal boy») et certaines rengaines («behind you!», «Oh yes he is! - Oh no he isn't!») apparaissent dans toutes les pièces. Ces pièces, qui se jouent au moment des fêtes de fin d'année, sont généralement inspirées d'un conte de fées.

---

pantry ['pæntrɪ] (*pl* **pantries**) *n* [cupboard] garde-manger *m inv*; [walk-in cupboard] cellier *m*, office *m*.
pants [pænts] *npl* -**1.** *Br* [underpants] slip *m*, culotte *f*. -**2.** *esp Am* [trousers] pantalon *m*; ~ leg jambe *f* de pantalon; a kick in the ~ un coup de pied aux fesses; he's still in short ~ il est encore à l'âge des culottes courtes ❑ to catch sb with his ~ down *inf* surprendre qqn dans une situation embarrassante; it's his wife who wears the ~ c'est sa femme qui porte la culotte; he bores the ~ off me *inf* il me rase; she scares the ~ off me *inf Br* elle me fiche la trouille.
pantsuit ['pæntsuːt] *n Am* tailleur-pantalon *m*.
panty ['pæntɪ] → **panties**.
panty girdle *n* gaine-culotte *f*.
panty hose *Br*, **pantihose** *Am* ['pæntɪ,həʊz] *npl* collant *m*, collants *mpl*.
pantywaist *inf* ['pæntɪweɪst] *n Am dated* poule *f* mouillée, femmelette *f*.
panzer ['pæn(t)zəʳ] *n* panzer *m*, blindé *m*.
pap [pæp] *n* -**1.** [mush] bouillie *f*. -**2.** *(U) fig* [drivel] bêtises *fpl*, imbécillités *fpl*; his films are ~ ses films sont stupides; what a load of ~! n'importe quoi! -**3.** *arch* OR *dial* [teat] mamelon *m*, téton *m*. -**4.** [hill] mamelon *m*, monticule *m*.
papa [pə'pɑː] *n* papa *m*.
papacy ['peɪpəsɪ] (*pl* **papacies**) *n* [system, institution] papauté *f*; [term of office] pontificat *m*.
papadum ['pɒpədəm] = **popadum**.
papal ['peɪpl] *adj* papal.
paparazzi [,pæpə'rætsɪ] *npl* paparazzi *mpl*.
papaw [pə'pɔː] *n* -**1.** = **papaya**. -**2.** [custard apple] anone *f*, pomme-cannelle *f*.
papaya [pə'paɪə] *n* -**1.** [fruit] papaye *f*. -**2.** [tree] papayer *m*.
paper ['peɪpəʳ] ◇ *n* -**1.** *(U)* [material] papier *m*; a piece/sheet of ~ un bout/une feuille de papier; he wants it on ~ il veut que ce soit écrit; don't put anything down on ~! ne mettez rien par écrit!; on ~, they're by far the better side sur le papier OR a priori, c'est de loin la meilleure équipe. -**2.** [newspaper] journal *m*; it's in all the morning ~s c'est dans tous les journaux du matin. -**3.** *(usu pl)* [document] papier *m*, document *m*; could you fill out this ~? pourriez-vous remplir ce formulaire?; once you've got the necessary ~s together une fois que vous aurez réuni les pièces nécessaires; Virginia Woolf's private ~s les écrits personnels de Virginia Woolf ❑ (identity) ~s papiers (d'identité); ship's ~s papiers de bord. -**4.** SCH & UNIV [exam paper] devoir *m*, épreuve *f*; you have an hour for each ~ vous avez une heure pour chaque épreuve ‖ [student's answers] copie *f*; hand in your ~s rendez vos copies. -**5.** [academic treatise - published] article *m*; [- oral] communication *f*; to write a ~ écrire un article; to give OR to read a ~ on sthg faire un exposé sur qqch. -**6.** [wallpaper] papier peint *m*. -**7.** POL → **green paper**, **white paper**.
◇ *adj* -**1.** [cup, napkin, towel] en OR de papier; ~ chains guirlandes *fpl* de papier; ~ currency billets *mpl* (de banque). -**2.** [theoretical] sur le papier, théorique; ~ profits profits *mpl* fictifs; ~ qualifications diplômes *mpl*. -**3.** *pej* [worthless] sans valeur; a ~ victory une victoire inutile.
◇ *vt* [room, walls] tapisser.
◆ **paper over** *vt sep* -**1.** *literal* recouvrir de papier peint. -**2.** *fig* [dispute, facts] dissimuler; they tried to ~ over the cracks ils ont essayé de masquer les désaccords.
paperback ['peɪpəbæk] ◇ *n* livre *m* de poche; it's coming out in ~ soon ça sort bientôt en (édition de) poche.
◇ *adj* [book, edition] de poche.
paperbacked ['peɪpəbækt] *adj* broché.
paper bag *n* sac *m* en papier.
paperboard ['peɪpəbɔːd] *n* carton *m*, carton-pâte *m*.
paperbound ['peɪpəbaʊnd] *adj* broché.
paperboy ['peɪpəbɔɪ] *n* [delivering papers] livreur *m* de journaux; [selling papers] vendeur *m* OR crieur *m* de journaux.
paper chase *n* rallye-papier *m*, ≃ jeu *m* de piste.
paper clip *n* trombone *m*.
◆ **paper-clip** *vt* attacher avec un trombone.
paper feed *n* COMPUT & TYPO alimentation *f* en papier.
papergirl ['peɪpəgɜːl] *n* [delivering papers] livreuse *f* de journaux; [selling papers] vendeuse *f* de journaux.
paperhanging ['peɪpə,hæŋɪŋ] *n* pose *f* de papiers peints.
paper knife *n* coupe-papier *m inv*.
paperless ['peɪpəlɪs] *adj* [electronic - communication, record-keeping] informatique; the ~ office le bureau entièrement informatisé.
papermill ['peɪpəmɪl] *n* papeterie *f*, usine *f* à papier.
paper money *n* papier-monnaie *m*.
paper round *n*: to do a ~ livrer les journaux à domicile.
paper shop *n* marchand *m* de journaux.
paper shredder *n* broyeur *m*.
paper tape *n* COMPUT bande *f* perforée.
paper-thin *adj* extrêmement mince OR fin.
paper tiger *n* tigre *m* de papier.
paperweight ['peɪpəweɪt] *n* presse-papiers *m inv*.
paperwork ['peɪpəwɜːk] *n* travail *m* de bureau; *pej* paperasserie *f*.
papery ['peɪpərɪ] *adj* [thin and dry - gen] comme du papier; [- skin] parcheminé.
papier-mâché [,pæpjeɪ'mæʃeɪ] *n* papier *m* mâché.
papilla [pə'pɪlə] (*pl* **papillae** [-liː]) *n* papille *f*.
papist ['peɪpɪst] ◇ *adj pej* papiste.
◇ *n pej* papiste *mf*.
papistry ['peɪpɪstrɪ] *n pej* papisme *m*.
papoose [pə'puːs] *n* papoose *m*.
pappy ['pæpɪ] (*pl* **pappies**, *compar* **pappier**, *superl* **pappiest**) ◇ *n inf Am dial* papa *m*.
◇ *adj* gluant.
paprika ['pæprɪkə] *n* paprika *m*.
Papua ['pæpjʊə] *pr n* Papouasie *f*; in ~ en Papouasie.
Papuan ['pæpjʊən] ◇ *n* -**1.** [person] Papou *m*, -e *f*. -**2.** LING langue *f* papoue.
◇ *adj* papou.
Papua New Guinea *pr n* Papouasie-Nouvelle-Guinée *f*; in ~ en Papouasie-Nouvelle-Guinée.
papyrus [pə'paɪərəs] (*pl* **papyruses** OR **papyri** [-raɪ]) *n* papyrus *m*.
par [pɑːʳ] (*pt* & *pp* **parred**, *cont* **parring**) ◇ *n* -**1.** [equality] égalité *f*; to be on a ~ (with sb/sthg) être au même niveau (que qqn/qqch); you can't put him on a ~ with Mozart! tu ne peux pas le comparer à Mozart! -**2.** [normal, average] normale *f*, moyenne *f*; I'm feeling a bit below OR under ~ these days je ne me sens pas en forme ces jours-ci; your work is below OR not up to ~ votre travail laisse à désirer ❑ that's about ~ for the course c'est normal OR dans les normes. -**3.** SPORT [in golf] par *m*; this hole is a ~ 5 ce trou est un par 5; she was two under/over ~ elle était à deux coups en-dessous/au-dessus du par.
◇ *vt* [in golf - hole] faire le par à.
para *inf* ['pærə] (*abbr of* **paratrooper**) *n Br* para *m*.
parable ['pærəbl] *n* parabole *f* RELIG.
parabola [pə'ræbələ] *n* parabole *f* MATH.
parabolic [,pærə'bɒlɪk] *adj* parabolique.
paraboloid [pə'ræbəlɔɪd] *n* paraboloïde *m*.
parabrake ['pærəbreɪk] *n* parachute *m* anti-vrille, parachute *m* de freinage.
paracetamol [,pærə'siːtəmɒl] *n* paracétamol *m*.
parachute ['pærəʃuːt] ◇ *n* parachute *m*; emergency ~ parachute de secours.
◇ *comp* [harness] de parachute; [troops, regiment] de parachutistes; ~ drop OR landing parachutage *m*; ~ jump saut *m* en parachute.
◇ *vt* parachuter; ~d candidate *Can* POL candidat *m* parachuté.
◇ *vi* sauter en parachute; they ~d into occupied France ils se sont fait parachuter en France occupée; to go parachuting SPORT faire du parachutisme.
parachutist ['pærəʃuːtɪst] *n* parachutiste *mf*.
Paraclete ['pærəkliːt] *n* Paraclet *m*.
paraclinical [,pærə'klɪnɪkl] *adj* paraclinique.
parade [pə'reɪd] ◇ *n* -**1.** [procession - gen] défilé *m*; MIL défilé *m*, parade *f*; fashion ~ défilé

de mode; to be on ~ MIL défiler. -**2.** [street - of shops] rangée *f* de magasins; [- public promenade] promenade *f*. -**3.** [show, ostentation] étalage *m*; to make a ~ of one's grief faire étalage de son chagrin; a ~ of force une démonstration de force. -**4.** FENCING parade *f*. -**5.** = **parade ground**.
◇ *vi* -**1.** [march - gen & MIL] défiler; supporters ~d through the streets les supporters défilaient dans les rues. -**2.** [strut] se pavaner, parader.
◇ *vt* -**1.** [troops, prisoners etc] faire défiler; the prisoners were ~d through the streets on fit défiler les prisonniers dans les rues. -**2.** [streets] défiler dans. -**3.** [show off] faire étalage de; he likes to ~ his knowledge il aime faire étalage de ses connaissances.

parade ground *n* terrain *m* de manœuvres.

paradigm ['pærədaɪm] *n* paradigme *m*.

paradigmatic [,pærədɪg'mætɪk] *adj* paradigmatique.

paradisaical [,pærədɪ'seɪɪkl(l)] = **paradisiac**.

paradise ['pærədaɪs] *n* -**1.** [heaven] paradis *m*; [Eden] le paradis terrestre; to go to Paradise aller OR monter au paradis ❑ 'Paradise Lost' *Milton* 'Paradis perdu'; 'Paradise Regained' *Milton* 'Paradis reconquis'. -**2.** *fig* paradis *m*; it's ~ (here) on earth c'est le paradis sur terre; a week away from the kids was ~! une semaine loin des enfants, quel paradis!; this river is a fisherman's ~ cette rivière est le paradis des pêcheurs.

paradisiac [,pærə'dɪsɪæk], **paradisiacal** [,pærədɪ'saɪəkl] *adj* paradisiaque, édénique *lit*.

paradox ['pærədɒks] *n* paradoxe *m*.

paradoxical [,pærə'dɒksɪkl] *adj* paradoxal.

paradoxically [,pærə'dɒksɪklɪ] *adv* paradoxalement.

paraffin ['pærəfɪn] ◇ *n* -**1.** *Br* [fuel - for lamp] pétrole *m*; [- for stove] mazout *m*; [- for aircraft] kérosène *m*. -**2.** CHEM [alkane] paraffine *f*, alcane *m*. -**3.** = **paraffin wax**.
◇ *comp* à pétrole, à mazout; ~ lamp lampe *f* à pétrole; ~ stove poêle *m* à mazout.

paraffin wax *n* paraffine *f*.

paragliding ['pærəglaɪdɪŋ] *n* parapente *m*; to go ~ faire du parapente.

paragon ['pærəgən] *n* modèle *m*; ~ of virtue modèle OR parangon *m lit* de vertu.

paragraph ['pærəgrɑːf] ◇ *n* -**1.** [in writing] paragraphe *m*, alinéa *m*; begin OR start a new ~ (allez) à la ligne; section A, ~ 3 (of the contract) article A, alinéa 3 (du contrat). -**2.** [short article] entrefilet *m*. -**3.** TYPO: ~ (mark) pied de mouche *m*, alinéa *m*.
◇ *vt* diviser en paragraphes OR en alinéas.

Paraguay ['pærəgwaɪ] *pr n* Paraguay *m*; in ~ au Paraguay.

Paraguayan [,pærə'gwaɪən] ◇ *n* Paraguayen *m*, -enne *f*.
◇ *adj* paraguayen.

parakeet ['pærəkiːt] *n* perruche *f*.

paralanguage ['pærə,læŋgwɪdʒ] *n* paralangage *m*.

paraldehyde [pə'rældɪhaɪd] *n* paraldéhyde *m*.

paralinguistic [,pærəlɪŋ'gwɪstɪk] *adj* paralinguistique.

paralinguistics [,pærəlɪŋ'gwɪstɪks] *n (U)* paralinguistique *f*.

paralipsis [,pærə'lɪpsɪs] (*pl* paralipses [-siːz]) *n* prétérition *f*.

parallax ['pærəlæks] *n* parallaxe *f*.

parallel ['pærəlel] ◇ *adj* -**1.** [gen & MATH] parallèle; ~ lines lignes *fpl* parallèles; there is a ditch ~ with OR to the fence il y a un fossé qui longe la clôture; to run ~ to sthg longer qqch. -**2.** [concomitant - change, event] parallèle; a ~ investigation was mounted in England and Scotland une enquête a été menée simultanément en Angleterre et en Écosse. -**3.** COMPUT [interface, operation] parallèle; ~ computer ordinateur *m* à traitement parallèle; ~ printer imprimante *f* en parallèle; ~ port port *m* parallèle. -**4.** ELEC: ~ circuit circuit *m* en parallèle.
◇ *n* -**1.** [equivalent] équivalent *m*; [similarity] ressemblance *f*, similitude *f*; there are obvious ~s between the two cases les deux cas présentent des similitudes frappantes; a tradition which has no ~ in our own culture une tradition qui n'a pas d'équivalent dans notre culture; the two industries have developed in ~ ces deux industries se sont développées en parallèle; the disaster is without ~ une telle catastrophe est sans précédent. -**2.** [comparison] parallèle *m*; to draw a ~ between faire OR établir un parallèle entre. -**3.** MATH (ligne *f*) parallèle *f*. -**4.** GEOG parallèle *m*; the 48th ~ le 48e parallèle. -**5.** ELEC parallèle *m*; in ~ en parallèle.
◇ *vt* -**1.** [run parallel to] être parallèle à, longer. -**2.** [match, equal] égaler; his career has ~ed his father's sa carrière a suivi une trajectoire semblable à celle de son père.
◇ *adv*: to ski ~, to ~ ski skier parallèle; to ~ park *Am* faire un créneau.

parallel bars *npl* barres *fpl* parallèles.

parallelism ['pærəlelɪzm] *n* parallélisme *m*.

parallelogram [,pærə'leləgræm] *n* parallélogramme *m*.

parallel turn *n* [in skiing] virage *m* parallèle.

paralysation *Br*, **paralyzation** *Am* [,pærəlaɪ'zeɪʃn] *n* [of traffic, industry etc] immobilisation *f*, paralysie *f*.

paralyse *Br*, **paralyze** *Am* ['pærəlaɪz] *vt* -**1.** MED paralyser; both his legs are ~d, he's ~d in both legs il est paralysé des deux jambes, il a les deux jambes paralysées. -**2.** *fig* [city, industry etc] paralyser, immobiliser; [person] paralyser, pétrifier; ~d with OR by shyness paralysé par la timidité.

paralysis [pə'rælɪsɪs] *n* -**1.** MED paralysie *f*. -**2.** *fig* [of industry, business, organization] immobilisation *f*; [of government] paralysie *f*.

paralytic [,pærə'lɪtɪk] ◇ *adj* -**1.** MED paralytique. -**2.** *inf Br* [drunk] ivre mort.
◇ *n* paralytique *mf*.

paralyze *etc Am* = **paralyse**.

paramedic [,pærə'medɪk] ◇ *n* aide-soignant *m*, -e *f membre du personnel paramédical*; 'paramedic' *Am* services *mpl* de secours, ≃ 'SAMU'.
◇ *adj* = **paramedical**.

paramedical [,pærə'medɪkl] *adj* paramédical.

parameter [pə'ræmɪtəʳ] *n* [gen, LING & MATH] paramètre *m*; we must take all the ~s into account il faut prendre en compte tous les paramètres; according to established ~s of evaluation selon les critères établis.

paramilitary [,pærə'mɪlɪtrɪ] (*pl* paramilitaries)
◇ *adj* paramilitaire.
◇ *n* [group] formation *f* paramilitaire; [person] membre *m* d'une formation paramilitaire.
◇ *npl*: the ~ la milice.

paramnesia [,pæræm'niːzjə] *n* paramnésie *f*.

paramount ['pærəmaʊnt] *adj* -**1.** [asset, concern] primordial; to be of ~ importance être de la plus haute importance; the children's interests are ~ l'intérêt des enfants passe avant tout. -**2.** [ruler] suprême.

paramour ['pærə,mʊəʳ] *n lit* OR *hum* amant *m*, maîtresse *f*.

paranoia [,pærə'nɔɪə] *n (U)* paranoïa *f*.

paranoiac [,pærə'nɔɪæk], **paranoic** [,pærə'nəʊɪk] ◇ *adj* paranoïaque.
◇ *n* paranoïaque *mf*.

paranoid ['pærənɔɪd] ◇ *adj* [disorders] paranoïde; [person] paranoïaque; you're getting ~! tu deviens paranoïaque!
◇ *n* paranoïaque *mf*.

paranormal [,pærə'nɔːml] ◇ *adj* paranormal.
◇ *n*: the ~ le paranormal.

parapet ['pærəpɪt] *n* ARCHIT parapet *m*, garde-fou *m*; MIL parapet *m*.

paraph ['pærəf] *n* paraphe *m (en fin de signature)*.

paraphernalia [,pærəfə'neɪljə] *n (U)* -**1.** [equipment] attirail *m*; [disordered belongings] fourbi *m*; his skis, poles and other ~ ses skis, ses bâtons et le reste de son attirail. -**2.** *inf* [trappings] tralala *m*; it was a society wedding with all the ~ ce fut un mariage mondain avec tout l[e] tralala. -**3.** *inf* [for drug taking] attirail *m (nécessaire à l'inhalation ou à l'injection de drogue)*. -**4.** JU[R] biens *mpl* paraphernaux.

paraphrase ['pærəfreɪz] ◇ *n* paraphrase *f*.
◇ *vt* paraphraser.

paraplegia [,pærə'pliːdʒə] *n* paraplégie *f*.

paraplegic [,pærə'pliːdʒɪk] ◇ *adj* paraplégique.
◇ *n* paraplégique *mf*.

parapraxis [,pærə'præksɪs] *n* PSYCH acte *m* manqué.

parapsychologist [,pærəsaɪ'kɒlədʒɪst] *n* parapsychologue *mf*.

parapsychology [,pærəsaɪ'kɒlədʒɪ] *n* parapsychologie *f*.

parasailing ['pærə,seɪlɪŋ] *n* parachute *m* ascensionnel.

parascending ['pærə,sendɪŋ] *n* parachute *m* tracté.

parascience ['pærə,saɪəns] *n (U)* études *fpl* parascientifiques.

parasite ['pærəsaɪt] *n* BOT & ZOOL parasite *m*; *fig* parasite *m*; he's such a ~! c'est un vrai parasite!

parasitic(al) [,pærə'sɪtɪk(l)] *adj* -**1.** [plant, animal] parasite; *fig* [person] parasite; [existence] de parasite. -**2.** [illness - caused by parasites] parasitaire; ~ disease maladie *f* parasitaire.

parasiticide [,pærə'sɪtɪsaɪd] *n* parasiticide *m*.

parasitism ['pærəsaɪ,tɪzm] *n* parasitisme *m*.

parasitize, -ise ['pærəsɪtaɪz] *vt* parasiter.

parasitologist [,pærəsaɪ'tɒlədʒɪst] *n* parasitologue *mf*.

parasitology [,pærəsaɪ'tɒlədʒɪ] *n* parasitologie *f*.

parasol ['pærəsɒl] *n* [for woman] ombrelle *f*; [for beach, table] parasol *m*.

parasol mushroom *n* coulemelle *f*.

parasympathetic ['pærə,sɪmpə'θetɪk] ◇ *adj* parasympathique; ~ nerve nerf *m* parasympathique.
◇ *n*: the ~ le parasympathique.

parasynthesis [,pærə'sɪnθəsɪs] *n* dérivation parasynthétique.

parataxis [,pærə'tæksɪs] *n* parataxe *f*, juxtaposition *f*.

parathyroid [,pærə'θaɪrɔɪd] ◇ *adj* parathyroïdien.
◇ *n* parathyroïde *f*.

paratroop ['pærətruːp] *comp* de parachutistes; [regiment] parachutiste, de parachutistes; [commander] parachutiste.
◆ **paratroops** *npl* MIL parachutistes *mpl*.

paratrooper ['pærətruːpəʳ] *n* MIL parachutiste *m*.

paratyphoid [,pærə'taɪfɔɪd] ◇ *n* paratyphoïde *f*.
◇ *adj* [bacillus] paratyphique; [fever] paratyphoïde.

parboil ['pɑːbɔɪl] *vt* CULIN blanchir.

parcel ['pɑːsl] (*Br pt* & *pp* parcelled, *cont* parcelling, *Am pt* & *pp* parceled, *cont* parceling)
◇ *n* -**1.** [package] colis *m*, paquet *m*; ~ delivery livraison *f* de colis à domicile. -**2.** [portion of land] parcelle *f*. -**3.** [group, quantity - gen] groupe *m*, lot *m*; [- of shares] paquet *m*; a ~ of rogues une bande de gredins. -**4.** [integral part] partie *f* (intégrante).
◇ *vt* -**1.** [wrap up] emballer, faire un colis de. -**2.** [divide up] diviser en parcelles.
◆ **parcel out** *vt sep* -**1.** [share out] distribuer, partager. -**2.** [divide up] diviser en parcelles, lotir.
◆ **parcel up** *vt sep* emballer, mettre en colis.

parcel bomb *n* colis *m* piégé.

parcel post *n*: to send sthg by ~ envoyer qqch par colis postal OR en paquet-poste.

parch [pɑːtʃ] *vt* -**1.** [scorch] dessécher, brûler; the sun had ~ed the hills le soleil avait brûlé les collines. -**2.** *(usu pass)* [make thirsty] assoiffer. -**3.** CULIN griller légèrement.

parched ['pɑːtʃt] *adj* -**1.** [very dry - grass, hills] desséché; [- throat, lips] sec. -**2.** *inf* [person]: I'm ~ je crève de soif.

parchment ['pɑːtʃmənt] *n* [material, document] parchemin *m*; skin like ~ peau parcheminée.

pard *inf* [pɑːd], **pardner** *inf* ['pɑːdnəʳ] *n Am* copain *m*, copine *f*, pote *m*.

pardon ['pɑːdn] ◇ *vt* -**1.** [forgive] pardonner; to ~ sb for sthg pardonner qqch à qqn; please ~ my rudeness veuillez excuser mon impolitesse; ~ me for asking, but... excusez-moi de vous poser cette question, mais...; ~ me for breathing! excuse-moi d'avoir osé ouvrir la bouche! ☐ he's a bastard, if you'll ~ the expression OR my French▽ c'est un salaud, si vous voulez bien me passer l'expression. -**2.** JUR gracier.
◇ *n* -**1.** [forgiveness] pardon *m*. -**2.** JUR grâce *f*; he was granted a (free) ~ il fut gracié. -**3.** RELIG indulgence *f*.
◇ *interj*: ~ (me)? [what?] pardon?, comment?; ~ (me)! [sorry] pardon!, excusez-moi!

pardonable ['pɑːdnəbl] *adj* pardonnable, excusable.

pardonably ['pɑːdnəblɪ] *adv* de façon bien pardonnable OR excusable.

pare [peəʳ] *vt* -**1.** [fruit, vegetable] peler, éplucher; [nails] ronger, couper; ~ the rind off the cheese enlever la croûte du fromage. -**2.** [reduce - budget] réduire; staff levels have already been ~d to the bone on a déjà réduit les effectifs au minimum.
◆ **pare down** *vt sep* [expenses, activity] réduire; [text, speech] raccourcir; we've got to ~ the report down to 50 pages il va falloir ramener le rapport à 50 pages.

parent ['peərənt] ◇ *n* -**1.** [mother] mère *f*; [father] père *m*; ~s parents *mpl*; Anne and Bob have become ~s Anne et Bob ont eu un enfant. -**2.** PHYS parent *m*.
◇ *comp* -**1.** [cooperation, participation] des parents, parental. -**2.** [organization] mère. -**3.** [plant] mère; cuttings from the ~ plant des boutures de la plante mère. -**4.** [animal] parent; one of the ~ birds/seals un des parents de l'oiseau/du phoque.

parentage ['peərəntɪdʒ] *n* origine *f*; a child of unknown ~ un enfant de père et mère inconnus; children of racially mixed ~ des enfants issus de mariages mixtes.

parental [pə'rentl] *adj* parental, des parents.

parent company *n* COMM société *f* OR maison *f* mère.

parenthesis [pə'renθɪsɪs] (*pl* **parentheses** [-siːz]) *n* parenthèse *f*; in ~ entre parenthèses.

parenthesize, -ise [pə'renθɪsaɪz] *vt* [word, explanation] mettre entre parenthèses.

parenthetic(al) [,pærən'θetɪk(l)] *adj* entre parenthèses.

parenthetically [,pærən'θetɪklɪ] *adv* entre parenthèses.

parenthood ['peərənthʊd] *n* [fatherhood] paternité *f*; [motherhood] maternité *f*; the responsibilities of ~ les responsabilités parentales.

parenting ['peərəntɪŋ] *n* fait *m* OR art *m* d'élever un enfant; the problems of ~ les problèmes qu'on a quand on est parent OR quand on a des enfants; I put it down to bad ~ d'après moi, c'est parce que les parents remplissent mal leur rôle.

parent-teacher association *n association regroupant les parents d'élèves et les enseignants.*

parer ['peərəʳ] *n* économe *m*.

parhelion [pɑː'hiːljən] (*pl* **parhelia** [-ljə]) *n* parélie *m*, parhélie *m*.

pariah [pə'raɪə] *n* paria *m*.

pariah dog *n* (chien *m*) paria *m*.

parietal [pə'raɪɪtl] ◇ *adj* ANAT & BOT pariétal.
◇ *n* ANAT pariétal *m*.

paring ['peərɪŋ] *n* [activity - of fruit, vegetables] épluchage *m*; [- of nails] fait *m* OR action *f* de ronger; ~ knife couteau *m* de cuisine.
◆ **parings** *npl* [of fruit, vegetables] épluchures *fpl*, pelures *fpl*; [of nails] rognures *fpl*.

Paris ['pærɪs] *pr n* -**1.** GEOG Paris *m*; the ~ Basin le Bassin parisien; the ~ Commune la Commune; 'An American in Paris' *Gershwin, Minnelli* 'Un Américain à Paris'. -**2.** MYTH Pâris.

parish ['pærɪʃ] ◇ *n* -**1.** RELIG paroisse *f*. -**2.** [local government area] ≃ commune *f (en Angleterre)*.
◇ *comp* [hall, funds] RELIG paroissial.

parish church *n* église *f* paroissiale.

parish clerk *n* bedeau *m*.

parish council *n* ≃ conseil *m* municipal *(d'une petite commune en Angleterre)*.

parishioner [pə'rɪʃənəʳ] *n* paroissien *m*, -enne *f*.

parish priest *n* [Catholic] curé *m*; [Protestant] pasteur *m*.

parish-pump *adj Br pej* [parochial - issue] d'intérêt purement local; [- outlook, mentality, quarrel] de clocher.

parish register *n* registre *m* paroissial.

parish school *n* école *f* communale.

Parisian [pə'rɪzjən] ◇ *n* Parisien *m*, -enne *f*.
◇ *adj* parisien.

parity ['pærətɪ] (*pl* **parities**) *n* -**1.** [equality] égalité *f*, parité *f*; women demanded wage ~ with men les femmes ont réclamé l'égalité de salaires avec les hommes. -**2.** ÉCON & FIN parité *f*; exchange parities parités de change; ~ value valeur *f* au pair. -**3.** COMPUT, MATH & PHYS parité *f*.

parity bit *n* COMPUT bit *m* de parité.

park [pɑːk] ◇ *n* -**1.** [public] parc *m*; [smaller] jardin *m* public; [private estate] parc *m*, domaine *m*. -**2.** AUT [on automatic gearbox] position *f* (de) stationnement. -**3.** *inf Br* FTBL: the ~ le terrain.
◇ *vt* -**1.** AUT garer; where can I ~ my car? où est-ce que je peux garer ma voiture OR me garer?; he was ~ed by a fire hydrant il s'était garé devant une bouche d'incendie; behind the ~ed coaches derrière les cars en stationnement. -**2.** *inf* [dump - person, box] laisser; she ~ed her bags in the entry elle a laissé ses sacs dans l'entrée; he ~ed himself on the sofa il s'installa sur le canapé.
◇ *vi* AUT se garer, stationner; I couldn't find anywhere to ~ je n'ai pas trouvé à me garer.

parka ['pɑːkə] *n* parka *m*.

park-and-ride *n système de contrôle de la circulation qui consiste à garer les voitures à l'extérieur des grandes villes, puis à utiliser les transports en commun.*

Parkhurst ['pɑːkhɜːst] *pr n*: ~ (Prison) *prison pour condamnés de longue durée située sur l'île de Wight.*

parkin ['pɑːkɪn] *n Br* ≃ pain *m* d'épice OR d'épices.

parking ['pɑːkɪŋ] ◇ *n* stationnement *m*; 'no ~' 'stationnement interdit', 'défense de stationner'; there's plenty of underground ~ il y a de nombreuses places dans les parkings souterrains; I'm not very good at ~ je ne suis pas très doué pour les créneaux.
◇ *comp* [area] de stationnement; to look for/to find a ~ place chercher/trouver à se garer.

parking attendant *n* [in car park] gardien *m*, -enne *f*; [at hotel] voiturier *m*.

parking brake *n Am* frein *m* à main.

parking garage *n Am* parking *m* couvert.

parking lights *npl* feux *mpl* de position.

parking lot *n Am* parking *m*, parc *m* de stationnement.

parking meter *n* parcmètre *m*, parcomètre *m*.

parking orbit *n* ASTRONAUT orbite *f* d'attente.

parking ticket *n* contravention *f* (pour stationnement irrégulier), P-V *m*.

Parkinson's disease ['pɑːkɪnsnz-] *n* maladie *f* de Parkinson.

Parkinson's law *n hum* principe *m* de Parkinson; it's a case of ~ plus on a de temps, plus on met de temps.

park keeper *n* gardien *m*, -enne *f* de jardin public.

parkland ['pɑːklænd] *n (U)* espace *m* vert, espaces *mpl* verts.

parkway ['pɑːkweɪ] *n Am* route *f* paysagère (à plusieurs voies).

parky *inf* ['pɑːkɪ] (*compar* **parkier**, *superl* **parkiest**) *adj Br* [cold] frisquet.

parlance ['pɑːləns] *n fml* langage *m*, parler *m*; in legal ~ en langage juridique.

parlay ['pɑːlɪ] *vt Am* -**1.** [winnings] remettre en jeu; he ~ed everything on the red il a tout misé sur le rouge. -**2.** *fig* [talent, project] mener à bien; [money] faire fructifier; she ~ed the local newspapers into a press empire elle a bâti un empire de presse à partir des journaux locaux.

parley ['pɑːlɪ] ◇ *vi* parlementer.
◇ *n* pourparlers *mpl*.

parleyvoo *inf* [,pɑːlɪ'vuː] *hum* ◇ *n* -**1.** [French language] français *m*. -**2.** [person] Français *m*, -e *f*.
◇ *vi*: I don't ~ je ne parle pas français.

parliament ['pɑːləmənt] *n* parlement *m*; she was elected to Parliament in 1988 elle a été élue député en 1988; the French Parliament l'Assemblée nationale (française).

parliamentarian [,pɑːləmen'teərɪən] ◇ *adj* parlementaire.
◇ *n* parlementaire *mf*.

parliamentarianism [,pɑːləmen'teərɪənɪzm] *n* parlementarisme *m*.

parliamentary [,pɑːlə'mentərɪ] *adj* [system, debate, democracy] parlementaire; ~ elections élections *fpl* législatives; ~ candidate candidat *m* aux (élections) législatives.

Parliamentary Commissioner (for Administration) *n Br* médiateur *m*, -trice *f*.

parliamentary private secretary *n en Grande-Bretagne, député qui assure la liaison entre un ministre et la Chambre des communes.*

parliamentary secretary *n Br* ≃ sous-secrétaire *m* d'État.

parlor *etc Am* = **parlour**.

parlor car *n Am* RAIL pullman *m (dans un train)*.

parlour *Br*, **parlor** *Am* ['pɑːləʳ] *n* -**1.** *dated* [in house] salon *m*. -**2.** *dated* [in hotel, club] salon *m*; [in pub] arrière-salle *f*. -**3.** [in convent] parloir *m*. -**4.** *Am* COMM: beauty ~ institut *m* de beauté; beer ~ bar *m*; billiard ~ salle *f* de billard.

parlour game *n Br* jeu *m* de société.

parlourmaid *Br*, **parlormaid** *Am* ['pɑːləmeɪd] *n* femme *f* de chambre.

parlous ['pɑːləs] *adj arch* OR *lit* [situation, state] précaire, instable.

Parma ['pɑːmə] *pr n* Parme; ~ ham jambon *m* de Parme.

Parmesan (cheese) [,pɑːmɪ'zæn-] *n* parmesan *m*.

Parnassian [pɑː'næsɪən] ◇ *adj* parnassien.
◇ *n* parnassien *m*, -enne *f*.

Parnassus [pɑː'næsəs] *pr n* Parnasse *m*; (Mount) ~ le (mont) Parnasse.

parochial [pə'rəʊkjəl] *adj* -**1.** RELIG paroissial. -**2.** *pej* borné; ~ attitudes attitudes de clocher OR bornées.

parochialism [pə'rəʊkjəlɪzm] *n pej* esprit *m* de clocher, étroitesse *f* d'esprit.

parodist ['pærədɪst] *n* parodiste *mf*.

parody ['pærədɪ] (*pl* **parodies**, *pt* & *pp* **parodied**)
◇ *n* parodie *f*.
◇ *vt* parodier.

parole [pə'rəʊl] ◇ *n* -**1.** JUR liberté *f* conditionnelle OR sur parole; she was released on ~ elle a été mise en liberté conditionnelle OR libérée sur parole; he's up for ~ next year il devrait être mis en liberté conditionnelle l'année prochaine. -**2.** *Am* MIL [password] mot *m* de passe. -**3.** LING parole *f*.
◇ *vt* mettre en liberté conditionnelle, libérer sur parole.

parole board *n* ≃ comité *m* de probation et d'assistance aux libérés.

paronym ['pærənɪm] *n* paronyme *m*.

parotid [pə'rɒtɪd] ◇ *adj* parotidien *m*.
◇ *n*: ~ (gland) (glande *f*) parotide *f*.

paroxysm ['pærəksɪzm] *n* -**1.** [outburst - of rage, despair] accès *m*; [- of tears] crise *f*; his answer sent them into ~s of laughter sa réponse provoqua l'hilarité générale OR déclencha un fou rire général. -**2.** MED paroxysme *m*.

parquet ['pɑːkeɪ] ◇ *n* -**1.** CONSTR: ~ (floor OR flooring) parquet *m*. -**2.** *Am* THEAT parterre *m*.
◇ *vt* parqueter.

parquetry ['pɑːkɪtrɪ] *n* parquetage *m*.

parr [pɑːʳ] (*pl inv* OR parrs) *n* saumoneau *m*, parr *m*.

parrakeet ['pærəkiːt] = **parakeet**.

parricide ['pærɪsaɪd] *n* -**1.** [act] parricide *m*. -**2.** [killer] parricide *mf*.

parrot ['pærət] ◇ *n* perroquet *m*.
◇ *vt* [words] répéter comme un perroquet; [person, actions] imiter.

parrot disease = **parrot fever**.

parrot fashion *adv* comme un perroquet.

parrot fever *n* psittacose *f*.

parrot fish *n* perroquet *m* de mer.

parry ['pærɪ] (*pt* & *pp* parried, *pl* parries)
◇ *vt* -**1.** [in boxing, fencing etc] parer; to ~ a blow parer un coup. -**2.** [problem] tourner, éviter; [question] éluder; [manœuvre] parer à, contrer.
◇ *vi* [in boxing, fencing] parer; he parried with his right il a paré l'attaque OR le coup d'une droite.
◇ *n* parade *f (en boxe, en escrime etc)*.

parse [pɑːz] *vt* faire l'analyse grammaticale de.

parsec ['pɑːsek] *n* parsec *m*.

Parsee, Parsi [,pɑː'siː] ◇ *n* Parsi *m*, -e *f*.
◇ *adj* parsi.

parser ['pɑːzəʳ] *n* COMPUT programme *m* d'analyse (grammaticale).

parsimonious [,pɑːsɪ'məʊnjəs] *adj fml* parcimonieux.

parsimoniously [,pɑːsɪ'məʊnjəslɪ] *adv fml* avec parcimonie, parcimonieusement.

parsimony ['pɑːsɪmənɪ] *n fml* parcimonie *f*.

parsing ['pɑːzɪŋ] *n* analyse *f* grammaticale.

parsley ['pɑːslɪ] *n* persil *m*; Chinese ~ coriandre *f*; ~ sauce sauce *f* au persil OR persillée.

parsnip ['pɑːsnɪp] *n* panais *m*.

parson ['pɑːsn] *n* [gen] ecclésiastique *m*; [Protestant] pasteur *m*.

parsonage ['pɑːsnɪdʒ] *n* presbytère *m*.

parson's nose *n* CULIN croupion *m*.

Parsons table ['pɑːsnz-] *n Am table carrée ou rectangulaire dont les pieds carrés semblent faire bloc avec le plateau*.

part [pɑːt] ◇ *n* -**1.** [gen - portion, subdivision] partie *f*; the exam is in two ~s l'examen est en deux parties; see ~ one, section two voir première partie, section deux; the different ~s of the body les différentes parties du corps; (a) ~ of the garden is flooded une partie du jardin est inondée; (a) ~ of me strongly agrees with them sur un certain plan, je suis tout à fait d'accord avec eux; that's only ~ of the problem ce n'est qu'un des aspects du problème; it's very much ~ of the game/of the process ça fait partie du jeu/du processus; it's very much ~ of the excitement c'est en partie pour ça que c'est amusant; we've finished the hardest ~ nous avons fait le plus dur; I haven't told you the best ~ yet je ne t'ai pas encore dit le plus beau OR la meilleure; to be (a) ~ of sthg [be involved with] faire partie de qqch; he desperately wants to be a ~ of her organization il veut à tout prix faire partie de son organisme; to form ~ of sthg faire partie de qqch ❑ to be ~ and parcel of sthg faire partie (intégrante) de qqch. -**2.** [role] rôle *m*; who played the ~ of Hamlet? qui a joué le rôle de Hamlet?; work plays a large ~ in our lives le travail joue un rôle important dans notre vie; to take ~ (in sthg) prendre part OR participer (à qqch); I had no ~ in that affair je n'ai joué aucun rôle dans cette affaire; he has no ~ in the running of the company il ne participe pas à OR il n'intervient pas dans la gestion de la société; Joe had no ~ in it Joe n'y était pour rien; I want no ~ in OR of their schemes je ne veux pas être mêlé à leurs projets; to do one's ~ y mettre du sien ❑ to dress the ~ se mettre en tenue de circonstance; to look the ~ avoir la tenue de circonstance; for my/his ~ pour ma/sa part. -**3.** [component - of machine] pièce *f*; oil the moving ~s lubrifiez les pièces mobiles. -**4.** [area - of country, town etc]: which ~ of England are you from? vous êtes d'où en Angleterre?, de quelle région de l'Angleterre venez-vous?; in some ~s of Sydney/Australia dans certains quartiers de Sydney/certaines régions de l'Australie; it's a dangerous ~ of town c'est un quartier dangereux; are you new to these ~s? vous êtes nouveau ici?; she's travelling in foreign ~s elle est en voyage à l'étranger. -**5.** [instalment - of encyclopedia] fascicule *m*; [- of serial] épisode *m*; don't miss ~ two! [of serial] ne manquez pas le deuxième épisode!; [of programme in two parts] ne manquez pas la deuxième partie! -**6.** [measure] mesure *f*; one ~ of pastis and four ~s of water une mesure de pastis et quatre mesures d'eau; a concentration of six ~s per million CHEM une concentration de six pour un million; the bottle was three ~s empty la bouteille était aux trois quarts vide. -**7.** [side] parti *m*, part *f*; he always takes his mother's ~ il prend toujours le parti de sa mère ❑ to take sthg in good ~ bien prendre qqch. -**8.** *Am* [in hair] raie *f*. -**9.** GRAMM partie *f*. -**10.** MUS partie *f*; the vocal/violin ~ la partie vocale/(pour) violon.
◇ *comp* [payment] partiel; ~ owner copropriétaire *mf*.
◇ *adv* en partie, partiellement; the jacket is ~ cotton, ~ polyester la veste est un mélange de coton et de polyester OR un mélange coton-polyester; he's ~ English, ~ Chinese il est moitié anglais, moitié chinois.
◇ *vi* -**1.** [move apart, open - lips, curtains] s'ouvrir; [- branches, legs, crowd] s'écarter; [disengage - fighters] se séparer; the clouds ~ed il y eut une éclaircie. -**2.** [leave one another] se quitter; they ~ed good friends ils se sont quittés bons amis. -**3.** [break - rope, strand] se casser; [tear - fabric] se déchirer.
◇ *vt* -**1.** [move apart, open - lips, curtains] ouvrir; [- branches, legs, crowd] écarter; her lips were slightly ~ed ses lèvres étaient entrouvertes. -**2.** [separate] séparer; the children were ~ed from their parents les enfants ont été séparés de leurs parents; he's not easily ~ed from his cash *hum* il ne se sépare pas facilement de son argent. -**3.** [hair] faire une raie à; her hair's ~ed in the middle elle a la raie au milieu.

◆ **parts** *npl* [talents] talents *mpl*; a man/woman of many ~s un homme/une femme de talent.

◆ **for the most part** *adv phr* dans l'ensemble; the day will be sunny for the most ~ la journée sera ensoleillée dans l'ensemble; for the most ~ we get along pretty well dans l'ensemble, nous nous entendons assez bien.

◆ **in part** *adv phr* en partie; it's true in ~ c'est en partie vrai; it's in large ~ true c'est en grande partie vrai; the problem stems in ~ from a misunderstanding le problème vient en partie d'un malentendu.

◆ **in parts** *adv phr* par endroits; the book is good in ~s le livre est bon par endroits, certains passages du livre sont bons; in ~s the text is almost illegible le texte est presque illisible par endroits.

◆ **on the part of** *prep phr* de la part de; it was negligence on the ~ of the landlord c'était une négligence de la part du propriétaire.

◆ **part with** *vt insep* se séparer de; we'll have to ~ with most of the furniture nous devrons nous séparer de presque tous les meubles; he hates ~ing with his money il a horreur de dépenser son argent.

partake [pɑː'teɪk] (*pt* partook [-'tʊk], *pp* partaken [-'teɪkn]) *vi arch* OR *fml* -**1.** [eat, drink]: to ~ of prendre; to ~ of a meal prendre un repas. -**2.** [participate]: to ~ in [event] participer à; [joy, grief] partager. -**3.** [share quality]: to ~ of relever de, tenir à.

part exchange *n* COMM reprise *f*; they'll take your old TV set in ~ ils vous font une reprise sur OR ils reprennent votre ancien téléviseur.

parthenogenesis [,pɑːθɪnəʊ'dʒenɪsɪs] *n* parthénogenèse *f*.

Parthenon ['pɑːθɪnən] *pr n*: the ~ le Parthénon.

Parthian ['pɑːθjən] *n* Parthe *mf*; ~ shot flèche *f* du Parthe.

partial ['pɑːʃl] *adj* -**1.** [incomplete] partiel; a ~ loss of hearing une perte partielle de l'ouïe; the exhibition was only a ~ success l'exposition n'a connu qu'un succès mitigé. -**2.** [biased] partial. -**3.** [fond]: to be ~ to sthg avoir un penchant OR un faible pour qqch.

partial eclipse *n* éclipse *f* partielle.

partial fraction *n* petite partie *f* d'une fraction.

partiality [,pɑːʃɪ'ælətɪ] (*pl* partialities) *n* -**1.** [bias] partialité *f*. -**2.** [fondness] faible *m*, penchant *m*.

partially ['pɑːʃəlɪ] *adv* -**1.** [partly] en partie, partiellement. -**2.** [in biased way] partialement, avec partialité.

partially sighted ◇ *adj* malvoyant.
◇ *npl*: the ~ les malvoyants *mpl*.

participant [pɑː'tɪsɪpənt] *n* participant *m*, -e *f*; the ~s in the debate les participants au débat.

participate [pɑː'tɪsɪpeɪt] *vi* participer, prendre part; to ~ in [race, discussion] prendre part à, participer à.

participation [pɑː,tɪsɪ'peɪʃn] *n* participation *f*; teachers should encourage greater student ~ les professeurs devraient encourager les étudiants à participer plus activement.

participatory [pɑː,tɪsɪ'peɪtərɪ] *adj* participatif.

participial [,pɑːtɪ'sɪpɪəl] *adj* participial.

participle ['pɑːtɪsɪpl] *n* participe *m*; present/past ~ participe présent/passé.

particle ['pɑːtɪkl] *n* -**1.** [tiny piece] particule *f*, parcelle *f*; [of dust] grain *m*; *fig* [jot] brin *m*, grain *m*; food ~s particules de nourriture. -**2.** LING particule *f*. -**3.** PHYS particule *f*. -**4.** RELIG hostie *f*.

particle accelerator *n* accélérateur *m* de particules.

particle beam *n* faisceau *m* de particules.

particle board *n* panneau *m* de particules.

particle physics *n (U)* physique *f* des particules.

parti-coloured ['pɑːtɪ-] *adj* bariolé, bigarré.

particular [pə'tɪkjʊləʳ] ◇ *adj* -**1.** [specific, distinct] particulier; for no ~ reason sans raison particulière; do you have a ~ day in mind? est-ce que vous avez un jour précis OR particulier en tête?; only that ~ colour will do il n'y a que cette couleur-là qui fasse l'affaire; I've got no ~ place to go je ne vais nulle part en particulier, je n'ai pas de destination précise; the problem is not ~ to this region le problème n'est pas particulier à OR spécifique à OR ne se limite pas à cette région. -**2.** [exceptional, special] particulier, spécial; it's an issue of ~ importance to us c'est une question qui revêt une importance toute particulière à nos yeux. -**3.** [fussy]: to be ~ about hygiene/manners attacher beaucoup d'importance à l'hygiène/aux bonnes manières; to be ~ about one's food être difficile pour la nourriture; he's very ~ about the way he dresses il attache beaucoup d'importance à sa tenue. -**4.** *fml* [detailed - description, account] détaillé.
◇ *n* -**1.** [specific]: from the general to the ~ du général au particulier. -**2.** [facts, details] détails *mpl*, points *mpl*; correct in all ~s correct en tout point; I won't go into the ~s je n'entrerai pas dans les détails; for further ~s phone this number pour de plus amples renseignements, appelez ce numéro.

◆ **in particular** *adv phr* en particulier; what are you thinking about? — nothing in ~ à quoi penses-tu? — à rien en particulier; what happened? — nothing in ~ que s'est-il passé? – rien de particulier OR rien de spécial; no one in ~ personne en particulier; where are you going? — nowhere in ~ où vas-tu? – je vais juste faire un tour.

particularity [pə,tɪkjʊ'lærətɪ] (*pl* particularities) *n* particularité *f.*

particularize, -ise [pə'tɪkjʊləraɪz] ◇ *vt* particulariser.
◇ *vi*: one can ~ from this general rule on peut particulariser cette règle générale.

particularly [pə'tɪkjʊləlɪ] *adv* particulièrement; I don't know him ~ well je ne le connais pas spécialement bien; it was a ~ vicious murder ce fut un meurtre extrêmement OR particulièrement sauvage.

parting ['pɑːtɪŋ] ◇ *n* -**1.** [leave-taking] séparation *f*; they had a tearful ~ at the station ils se quittèrent en larmes à la gare; ~ from his family was hard il a eu du mal à quitter sa famille ❑ we came to a ~ of the ways nous sommes arrivées à la croisée des chemins. -**2.** [opening - in clouds] trouée *f*; the ~ of the Red Sea le partage des eaux de la mer Rouge. -**3.** *Br* [in hair] raie *f.*
◇ *adj lit* [words, kiss] d'adieu; he gave me a ~ handshake il m'a serré la main en partant.

parting shot *n fig* flèche *f* du Parthe; that was his ~ et sur ces mots, il s'en alla.

partisan [,pɑːtɪ'zæn] ◇ *adj* partisan; ~ politics politique *f* partisane; a very ~ audience un auditoire très partisan.
◇ *n* partisan *m.*

partisanship [,pɑːtɪ'zænʃɪp] *n* partialité *f*, esprit *m* de parti.

partition [pɑː'tɪʃn] ◇ *n* -**1.** [wall] cloison *f*; [screen] paravent *m*; metal ~s cloisons *fpl* métalliques. -**2.** [of country] partition *f*; [of property] division *f*; [of power] répartition *f*, morcellement *m.*
◇ *vt* -**1.** [room] diviser, cloisonner. -**2.** [country] diviser, démembrer.
◆ **partition off** *vt sep* [part of room] cloisonner; a small office had been ~ed off on avait aménagé un petit bureau derrière une cloison.

partition wall *n* cloison *f.*

partitive ['pɑːtɪtɪv] ◇ *adj* partitif.
◇ *n* partitif *m.*

partly ['pɑːtlɪ] *adv* en partie, partiellement; it's ~ because of the view that I like this room so much c'est en partie à cause de la vue que j'aime tant cette pièce.

partner ['pɑːtnə'] ◇ *n* -**1.** [spouse] époux *m*, épouse *f*, conjoint *m*, -e *f*; [lover] ami *m*, -e *f*; sexual ~ partenaire *mf* (sexuel). -**2.** [in game, dance etc] partenaire *mf*; his ~ in the waltz sa partenaire OR sa cavalière pour la valse. -**3.** [in common undertaking] partenaire *mf*; [in firm, medical practice etc] associé *m*, -e *f*; our ~s in NATO nos partenaires de l'OTAN; to be ~s in crime être complices dans le crime.
◇ *vt* -**1.** [be the partner of] être partenaire de. -**2.** [dance with] danser avec; [play with] faire équipe avec, être le partenaire de.

partnership ['pɑːtnəʃɪp] *n* -**1.** [gen] association *f*; to work in ~ with sb/sthg travailler en association avec qqn/qqch; we work in ~ with relief organizations nous travaillons en association avec des organisations humanitaires; to go into ~ with sb s'associer avec qqn; they've gone into ~ together ils se sont associés; they offered him a ~ ils lui ont proposé de devenir leur associé. -**2.** [firm] ≃ société *f* en nom collectif.

part of speech *n* partie *f* du discours.

parton ['pɑːtn] *n* parton *m.*

partook [pɑː'tʊk] *pt* → **partake**.

part payment *n* acompte *m*; I received £500 in ~ for the car j'ai reçu un acompte de 500 livres pour la voiture.

partridge ['pɑːtrɪdʒ] (*pl inv* OR partridges) *n* perdrix *f*; [immature] perdreau *m.*

part-singing *n* chant *m* polyphonique OR à plusieurs voix.

part song *n* chant *m* polyphonique OR à plusieurs voix.

part-time *adj* & *adv* à temps partiel; she's got a ~ job elle travaille à temps partiel; a ~ teacher un professeur à temps partiel.

part-timer *n* travailleur *m*, -euse *f* à temps partiel.

parturition [,pɑːtjʊ'rɪʃn] *n fml* OR MED parturition *f.*

partway ['pɑːtweɪ] *adv* en partie, partiellement; ~ through the year, she resigned elle a démissionné en cours d'année; I'm only ~ through the book je n'ai pas fini le livre; I was ~ down the stairs when the phone rang j'étais dans l'escalier quand le téléphone a sonné.

part work *n Br série de périodiques destinés à être rassemblés en un seul ouvrage*; they published it as a ~ ils l'ont publié sous forme de fascicules.

party ['pɑːtɪ] (*pl* parties, *pt* & *pp* partied) ◇ *n* -**1.** [social event] fête *f*; [more formal] soirée *f*, réception *f*; to give a ~ [formal] donner une réception OR une soirée; [informal] faire une fête; to have OR to throw a ~ for sb organiser une fête en l'honneur de qqn; I'm having a little cocktail ~ on Friday je fais un petit cocktail vendredi; New Year's Eve ~ réveillon *m* de fin d'année. -**2.** POL parti *m*; the Conservative/Democratic Party le parti conservateur/démocrate; he joined the Socialist Party in 1936 il est entré au parti socialiste en 1936. -**3.** [group of people] groupe *m*; a tour ~ un groupe de touristes; the funeral ~ le cortège funèbre; the wedding ~ les invités *mpl (à un mariage)*; to make dinner reservations for a ~ of six réserver une table pour six personnes; working ~ équipe *f* de travail. -**4.** *fml* OR JUR [individual, participant] partie *f*; to be a ~ to [discussion] prendre part à; [crime] être complice de; [conspiracy, enterprise] être mêlé à, tremper dans; the guilty ~ le coupable; the injured ~ la partie lésée; (the) interested parties les intéressés *mpl.* -**5.** [person] individu *m.*
◇ *comp* -**1.** [atmosphere, clothes] de fête; ~ dress robe *f* habillée; ~ invitations invitations *fpl*; ~ snacks amuse-gueule *mpl.* -**2.** POL [leader, leadership, funds] du parti; [system] des partis.
◇ *vi* faire la fête; we partied all night nous avons fait la fête toute la nuit.

partying ['pɑːtɪɪŋ] *n*: she's a great one for ~ *inf* elle adore faire la fête.

party line *n* -**1.** POL ligne *f* du parti; to toe the ~ suivre la ligne du parti. -**2.** TELEC ligne *f* commune *(à plusieurs abonnés)*.

party piece *inf n* chanson *f* OR poème *m* de circonstance *(à l'occasion d'une fête)*.

party political *adj* [broadcast] réservé à un parti politique; [issue] de parti politique.

party politics *npl* politique *f* de parti; *pej* politique *f* politicienne.

party pooper *inf n* rabat-joie *m inv.*

party wall *n* mur *m* mitoyen.

par value *n* valeur *f* nominale.

parvenu ['pɑːvənjuː] ◇ *n* parvenu *m*, -e *f.*
◇ *adj* parvenu.

pascal ['pæskl] *n* pascal *m* PHYS.

PASCAL [pæ'skæl] *n* PASCAL *m.*

paschal, Paschal ['pæskl] *adj* pascal; ~ candle cierge *m* pascal.

Paschal Lamb *n* agneau *m* pascal.

pasha ['pæʃə] *n* pacha *m.*

pass [pɑːs] ◇ *vi* -**1.** [move in specified direction] passer; a cloud ~ed across the moon un nuage est passé devant la lune; the wires ~ under the floorboards les fils passent sous le plancher; alcohol ~es rapidly into the bloodstream l'alcool passe rapidement dans le sang; his life ~ed before his eyes il a vu sa vie défiler devant ses yeux. -**2.** [move past, go by] passer; let me ~ laissez-moi passer; the road was too narrow for two cars to ~ la route était trop étroite pour que deux voitures se croisent; I happened to be ~ing, so I thought I'd call in il s'est trouvé que je passais, alors j'ai eu l'idée de venir vous voir. -**3.** [overtake] dépasser, doubler. -**4.** [elapse - months, years] (se) passer, s'écouler; [- holiday] se passer; the weekend ~ed without surprises le week-end s'est passé sans surprises; time ~ed rapidly le temps a passé très rapidement. -**5.** [be transformed] passer, se transformer; it then ~es into a larval stage il se transforme par la suite en larve; the oxygen then ~es to a liquid state ensuite l'oxygène passe à l'état liquide; to ~ from joy to despair passer de la joie au désespoir. -**6.** [take place] se passer, avoir lieu; harsh words ~ed between them ils ont eu des mots; the party, if it ever comes to ~, should be quite something la fête, si elle a jamais lieu, sera vraiment un grand moment; and it came to ~ that... BIBLE et il advint que... -**7.** [end, disappear - pain, crisis, fever] passer; [- anger, desire] disparaître, tomber; [- dream, hope] disparaître; the moment of tension ~ed le moment de tension est passé. -**8.** [be transferred - power, responsibility] passer; [- inheritance] passer, être transmis; authority ~es to the Vice-President when the President is abroad c'est au vice-président que revient la charge du pouvoir lorsque le président se trouve à l'étranger; the turn ~es to the player on the left c'est ensuite au tour du joueur placé à gauche. -**9.** [get through, be approved - proposal] être approuvé; [- bill, law] être voté; [- motion] être adopté; SCH & UNIV [- student] être reçu OR admis. -**10.** [go unchallenged] passer; the insult ~ed unnoticed personne ne releva l'insulte; he let the remark/mistake ~ il a laissé passer la remarque/l'erreur sans la relever; I don't like it, but I'll let it ~ je n'aime pas ça, mais je préfère ne rien dire OR me taire. -**11.** [be adequate, acceptable - behaviour] convenir, être acceptable; [- repair job] passer; in a grey suit you might just ~ avec ton costume gris, ça peut aller. -**12.** [substitute]: don't try to ~ as an expert n'essaie pas de te faire passer pour un expert; you could easily ~ for your sister on pourrait très bien te prendre pour ta sœur; he could ~ for 35 on lui donnerait 35 ans; she could ~ for a Scandinavian on pourrait la prendre pour une Scandinave. -**13.** SPORT faire une passe. -**14.** GAMES passer; (I) ~! (je) passe!
◇ *vt* -**1.** [move past, go by - building] passer devant; [- person] croiser; if you ~ a chemist's, get some aspirin si tu passes devant une pharmacie, achète de l'aspirine; he ~ed my table without seeing me il est passé devant ma table sans me voir; I ~ed her on the stairs je l'ai croisée dans l'escalier; the ships ~ed each other in the fog les navires se sont croisés dans le brouillard. -**2.** [go beyond - finishing line, frontier] passer; [overtake] dépasser, doubler; we've ~ed the right exit nous avons dépassé la sortie que nous aurions dû prendre; contributions have ~ed the $100,000 mark les dons ont franchi la barre des 100 000 dollars; we've ~ed a major turning point nous avons franchi un cap important. -**3.** [move, run] passer; she ~ed her hand over her hair elle s'est passé la main dans les cheveux. -**4.** [hand] passer; ~ me the sugar, please passez-moi le sucre, s'il vous plaît ‖ [transmit - message] transmettre; ~ the list around the office faites passer OR circuler la liste dans le bureau; can you ~ her the message? pourriez-vous lui transmettre OR faire passer le message? -**5.** [spend - life, time, visit] passer; to ~ the time of day bavarder un peu. -**6.** [succeed in - exam, driving test] être reçu à, réussir; he didn't ~ his history exam il a échoué OR il a été recalé à son examen d'histoire. -**7.** [approve - bill, law] voter; [- motion, resolution] adopter; SCH & UNIV [- student] recevoir, admettre; the drug has not been ~ed by the Health Ministry le médicament n'a pas reçu l'autorisation de mise sur le marché du ministère de la Santé. -**8.** [pronounce - judgment, verdict, sentence] prononcer, rendre; [- remark, compliment] faire; to ~ judgment on sb/sthg *fig* porter un jugement sur qqn/qqch; he declined to ~ comment il s'est refusé à tout commentaire. -**9.** [counterfeit money, stolen

goods] écouler. -**10.** SPORT [ball, puck] passer. -**11.** GAMES: to ~ one's turn passer OR sauter son tour. -**12.** PHYSIOL: to ~ blood avoir du sang dans les urines; to ~ water uriner.

◇ *n* -**1.** [in mountains] col *m*, défilé *m*; the Brenner Pass le col du Brenner. -**2.** [authorization - for worker, visitor] laissez-passer *m inv*; THEAT invitation *f*, billet *m* de faveur; MIL [- for leave of absence] permission *f*; [- for safe conduct] sauf-conduit *m*; press ~ carte *f* de presse; rail/bus ~ carte *f* d'abonnement (de train/de bus). -**3.** SCH & UNIV [in exam] moyenne *f*, mention *f* passable; to get a ~ avoir la moyenne; I got three ~es j'ai été reçu dans trois matières. -**4.** [state of affairs] situation *f*; things have come to a pretty OR fine OR sorry ~ on est dans une bien mauvaise passe, la situation s'est bien dégradée. -**5.** SPORT [with ball, puck] passe *f*; [in fencing] botte *f*; [in bullfighting] passe *f*; to make a ~ at [in fencing] porter une botte à. -**6.** [by magician] passe *f*. -**7.** COMPUT passe *f*. -**8.** AERON [overflight] survol *m*; [attack] attaque *f*. -**9.** *inf phr*: to make a ~ at sb faire des avances à qqn.

◆ **pass around** *vt sep* [cake, cigarettes] (faire) passer; [petition] (faire) circuler; [supplies] distribuer; he ~ed around the tray of champagne il a fait passer le plateau avec les coupes de champagne.

◆ **pass away** ◇ *vi insep* -**1.** *euph* [die] s'éteindre *euph*, décéder. -**2.** [elapse - time] passer, s'écouler.

◇ *vt sep* [while away] passer; she ~ed away the morning painting elle a passé la matinée à peindre; we played cards to ~ the time away nous avons joué aux cartes pour tuer OR passer le temps.

◆ **pass back** *vt sep* -**1.** [give back] rendre; ~ the book back when you've finished rendez-moi le livre quand vous aurez fini. -**2.** RADIO & TV: I'll now ~ you back to the studio je vais rendre l'antenne au studio. -**3.** SPORT [to team mate] repasser; [backwards] passer en arrière.

◆ **pass by** ◇ *vi insep* -**1.** [move past, go by]: he ~ed by without a word! il est passé à côté de moi sans dire un mot! -**2.** [visit] passer; she ~ed by to say hello elle est passée dire bonjour.

◇ *vt sep* [disregard] ignorer, négliger; she felt life had ~ed her by elle avait le sentiment d'avoir raté sa vie.

◆ **pass down** *vt sep* -**1.** [reach down] descendre; he ~ed me down my suitcase il m'a tendu OR passé ma valise. -**2.** [transmit - inheritance, disease, tradition] transmettre, passer; the songs were ~ed down from generation to generation les chansons ont été transmises de génération en génération.

◆ **pass off** ◇ *vi insep* -**1.** [take place - conference, attack] se passer, se dérouler; the meeting ~ed off without incident la réunion s'est déroulée sans incident. -**2.** [end - fever, fit] passer; the effects of the drug had ~ed off les effets du médicament s'étaient dissipés.

◇ *vt sep* [represent falsely] faire passer; he ~es himself off as an actor il se fait passer pour un acteur.

◆ **pass on** ◇ *vi insep* -**1.** *euph* [die] trépasser, s'éteindre *euph*. -**2.** [proceed] passer; let's ~ on to the next question passons à la question suivante.

◇ *vt sep* -**1.** [hand on - box, letter] passer. -**2.** [transmit - disease, tradition] transmettre; they ~ the costs on to their customers ils répercutent les coûts sur leurs clients; we meet at 8, ~ it on nous avons rendez-vous à 8 h, dis-le aux autres OR fais passer (la consigne).

◆ **pass out** ◇ *vi insep* -**1.** [faint] s'évanouir, perdre connaissance; [from drunkenness] tomber ivre mort; [go to sleep] s'endormir. -**2.** MIL [cadet] ≃ finir ses classes.

◇ *vt sep* [hand out] distribuer.

◆ **pass over** ◇ *vt sep* [not take - opportunity] négliger, ignorer; [overlook - person]: he was ~ed over for promotion on ne lui a pas accordé la promotion qu'il attendait.

◇ *vt insep* -**1.** [overlook - fault, mistake] passer sur, ne pas relever. -**2.** [skip - paragraph] sauter; you can ~ over this section vous pouvez sauter ce passage.

◆ **pass round** = **pass around**.

◆ **pass through** ◇ *vi insep* passer; are you in Boston for some time or are you just ~ing through? êtes-vous à Boston pour quelque temps ou êtes-vous juste de passage?

◇ *vt insep* [difficult period] traverser; [barrier] franchir; the bullet ~ed through his shoulder la balle lui a traversé l'épaule; you ~ through a small village vous traversez un petit village; he ~ed through the checkpoint without any trouble il a passé le poste de contrôle sans encombre.

◆ **pass up** *vt sep* -**1.** [hand up] passer; ~ me up the light bulb passe-moi l'ampoule. -**2.** [forego - job, opportunity] manquer, laisser passer; I'll have to ~ up their invitation je vais devoir décliner leur invitation.

passable ['pɑːsəbl] *adj* -**1.** [acceptable] passable, acceptable; a very ~ little restaurant un petit restaurant très honnête OR correct. -**2.** [road] praticable; [river, canyon] franchissable. -**3.** [currency] ayant cours.

passably ['pɑːsəblɪ] *adv* passablement, pas trop mal.

passage ['pæsɪdʒ] *n* -**1.** [way through] passage *m*; the police cleared a ~ through the crowd les policiers ouvrirent un passage à travers la foule. -**2.** [corridor] passage *m*, couloir *m*; [alleyway] ruelle *f*; an underground ~ un passage souterrain. -**3.** [part of book, piece of music] passage *m*; selected ~s from Churchill's speeches morceaux choisis des discours de Churchill. -**4.** ANAT & TECH [duct] conduit *m*; nasal ~s conduits nasaux. -**5.** [passing - gen] passage *m*; [- of bill] adoption *f*; the trench did not block the ~ of the tanks la tranchée n'a pas empêché les chars de passer; their friendship has survived the ~ of time leur amitié a survécu au temps. -**6.** NAUT [voyage] voyage *m*; [crossing] traversée *f*; she worked her ~ to Rio elle a payé son voyage à Rio en travaillant à bord du navire ❑ 'A Passage to India' *Forster, Lean* 'la Route des Indes'. -**7.** *fml* [access] libre passage *m*; to grant sb safe ~ through a country accorder à qqn le libre passage à travers un pays. -**8.** *arch* OR *fig*: ~ of OR at arms passe *f* d'armes.

passageway ['pæsɪdʒweɪ] *n* [corridor] passage *m*, couloir *m*; [alleyway] ruelle *f*; don't block the ~! n'obstruez pas le passage!, laissez le passage libre!

passbook ['pɑːsbʊk] *n* -**1.** [bankbook] livret *m* (d'épargne). -**2.** *SAfr* laissez-passer *m inv*.

pass degree *n en Grande-Bretagne, licence obtenue avec mention passable (par opposition au «honours degree»).*

passé [*Br* 'pæseɪ, *Am* pæ'seɪ] *adj pej* dépassé, vieillot, désuet.

passenger ['pæsɪndʒəʳ] *n* -**1.** [in car, bus, aircraft, ship] passager *m*, -ère *f*; [in train] voyageur *m*, -euse *f*. -**2.** *Br pej* [worker, team member] poids *m* mort.

passenger coach *Br*, **passenger car** *Am n* RAIL wagon *m* OR voiture *f* de voyageurs.

passenger list *n* liste *f* des passagers.

passenger mile *n* AERON ≃ kilomètre-passager *m*; RAIL ≃ kilomètre-voyageur *m*.

passenger seat *n* AUT [in front] siège *m* du passager; [in back] siège *m* arrière.

passenger train *n* train *m* de voyageurs.

passe-partout [ˌpæspə'tuː] *n* -**1.** [mounting] passe-partout *m inv*. -**2.** = **passkey**.

passer-by [ˌpɑːsə'baɪ] (*pl* passers-by) *n* passant *m*, -e *f*.

passim ['pæsɪm] *adv* passim.

passing ['pɑːsɪŋ] ◇ *adj* -**1.** [going by] qui passe; she watched the ~ crowd elle regardait la foule qui passait; with each ~ day/second he grew more worried son inquiétude croissait de jour en jour/de seconde en seconde. -**2.** [fleeting] éphémère, passager; a ~ whim un caprice passager. -**3.** [cursory, casual] (fait) en passant; he didn't give her absence a ~ thought c'est tout juste s'il a remarqué son absence, il a à peine remarqué son absence; he made only a ~ reference to her absence il a fait mention de son absence en passant. -**4.** AUT: ~ lane voie *f* de dépassement.

◇ *n* -**1.** [of time] passage *m*, fuite *f*; [of youth, traditions, old ways] disparition *f*; she regretted the ~ of her beauty elle regrettait sa beauté envolée; with the ~ of time the pain will ease la douleur s'atténuera avec le temps. -**2.** [of train, crowd] passage *m*. -**3.** *euph* [death] trépas *m*, mort *f*.

◇ *adv arch* fort, extrêmement.

◆ **in passing** *adv phr* en passant.

passing bell *n* glas *m*.

passing-out parade *n* MIL défilé *m* de promotion.

passing place *n* voie *f* de dépassement, aire *f* de croisement.

passing shot *n* [in tennis] passing-shot *m*.

passion ['pæʃn] *n* -**1.** [love] passion *f*; to give in to one's ~ s'abandonner à sa passion; crime of ~ crime *m* passionnel; I have a ~ for Chinese food j'adore la cuisine chinoise; his latest ~ is Faulkner sa dernière passion, c'est Faulkner. -**2.** [emotion, feeling] passion *f*; she sings with great ~ elle chante avec beaucoup de passion; nationalist ~s passions nationalistes. -**3.** *lit* [fit of anger] (accès *m* de) colère *f*; he tore it up in a ~ il l'a déchiré dans un accès de colère.

◆ **Passion** *n* MUS & RELIG: the Passion la Passion; 'the St Matthew Passion' *Bach* 'la Passion selon saint Matthieu'.

passionate ['pæʃənət] *adj* passionné; to have a ~ interest in sthg s'intéresser passionnément à qqch; she's ~ about human rights elle est dévouée à la cause des droits de l'homme.

passionately ['pæʃənətlɪ] *adv* passionnément; he is ~ devoted to the cause il est dévoué à la cause corps et âme.

passionflower ['pæʃnˌflaʊəʳ] *n* passiflore *f*, fleur *f* de la Passion.

passion fruit *n* fruit *m* de la Passion.

passionless ['pæʃənlɪs] *adj* sans passion.

Passion play *n* mystère *m* de la Passion.

Passion Sunday *n* le dimanche de la Passion.

Passion Week *n* la semaine de la Passion.

passive ['pæsɪv] ◇ *adj* -**1.** [gen, CHEM & ELECTRON] passif. -**2.** GRAMM passif.

◇ *n* GRAMM passif *m*; in the ~ au passif.

passively ['pæsɪvlɪ] *adv* -**1.** [gen] passivement. -**2.** GRAMM au passif.

passiveness ['pæsɪvnɪs], **passivity** [pæ'sɪvətɪ] *n* passivité *f*.

passive resistance *n* résistance *f* passive.

passive smoker *n non-fumeur dans un environnement fumeur.*

passive smoking *n* tabagisme *m* passif.

passivization [ˌpæsɪvaɪ'zeɪʃn] *n* mise *f* au passif; the verb can undergo ~ on peut mettre le verbe au passif.

passivize, -ise ['pæsɪvaɪz] *vt* GRAMM passiver.

passkey ['pɑːskiː] *n* passe-partout *m inv*.

pass mark *n* SCH moyenne *f*.

Passover ['pɑːsˌəʊvəʳ] *n* Pâque *f* (juive), Pesah *m*.

passport ['pɑːspɔːt] *n* -**1.** passeport *m*; British ~ holders les détenteurs de passeports britanniques; ~ control contrôle *m* des passeports; ~ photo photo *f* d'identité. -**2.** *fig* clé *f*; the ~ to happiness la clé du bonheur.

pass-the-parcel *n Br jeu où l'on se passe un colis contenant soit un gage, soit un cadeau.*

password ['pɑːswɜːd] *n* mot *m* de passe.

past [pɑːst] ◇ *n* -**1.** [former time] passé *m*; to live in the ~ vivre dans le passé; the great empires of the ~ les grands empires de l'histoire; he's a man with a ~ il a un passé chargé ❑ politeness seems to have become a thing of the ~ la politesse semble être une chose démodée. -**2.** GRAMM passé *m*; in the ~ (tense) au passé.

◇ *adj* -**1.** [gone by - life] antérieur; [- quarrels, differences] vieux, d'autrefois; [- generation, cen-

turies, mistakes, event] passé; in ~ time OR times ~ autrefois, (au temps) jadis || [ended, over]: to be ~ être passé OR terminé; the crisis is now ~ la crise est maintenant passée. -2. [last] dernier; this ~ month has been very busy le mois qui vient de s'achever a été très chargé; I've not been feeling well for the ~ few days ça fait quelques jours que je ne me sens pas très bien; he has spent the ~ five years in China il a passé ces cinq dernières années en Chine. -3. [former] ancien; the ~ mayors of the town les anciens maires de la ville. -4. GRAMM passé.
◇ *prep* -1. [in time] après; it's ten/quarter/half ~ six il est six heures dix/et quart/et demie; it's quarter ~ the hour il est le OR et quart; it's already ~ midnight il est déjà plus de minuit OR minuit passé; it's long OR way ~ my bedtime je devrais être au lit depuis longtemps; he's ~ 50 il a plus de 50 ans, il a dépassé la cinquantaine; she's ~ the adolescent stage ce n'est plus une adolescente; these beans are ~ their best ces haricots ne sont plus très frais ☐ to be ~ it *inf* avoir passé l'âge. -2. [further than] plus loin que, au-delà de; it's a few miles ~ the lake c'est quelques kilomètres après le lac; turn right just ~ the school prenez à droite juste après l'école; he can't count ~ ten il ne sait compter que jusqu'à dix; I didn't manage to get ~ the first page je n'ai pas réussi à lire plus d'une page. -3. [by, in front of] devant; he walked right ~ my table il est passé juste devant ma table. -4. [beyond scope of] au-delà de; it's ~ all understanding ça dépasse l'entendement; their demands are ~ all reason leurs exigences sont totalement démesurées. -5. [no longer capable of]: I'm ~ caring ça ne me fait plus ni chaud ni froid ☐ I wouldn't put it ~ him il en est bien capable.
◇ *adv* -1. [by]: to go ~ passer; they ran ~ ils passèrent en courant; the years flew ~ les années passaient à une vitesse prodigieuse. -2. [ago]: one night about three years ~ une nuit il y a environ trois ans; it had long ~ struck midnight minuit avait sonné depuis longtemps.
◆ **in the past** *adv phr* autrefois, dans le temps.

pasta ['pæstə] *n (U)* pâtes *fpl* (alimentaires).

paste [peɪst] ◇ *n* -1. [substance - gen] pâte *f*; hard/soft ~ [in ceramics] pâte dure/tendre. -2. CULIN [dough] pâte *f*; [mashed meat, fish] pâté *m*; anchovy ~ beurre *m* d'anchois; tomato ~ concentré *m* de tomate. -3. [glue] colle *f*. -4. [for jewellery] strass *m*, stras *m*; ~ necklace/diamonds collier/diamants en stras OR strass.
◇ *vt* -1. [stick - stamp] coller; [spread glue on] encoller, enduire de colle; ~ the labels on the parcel collez les étiquettes sur le colis. -2. [cover - wall] recouvrir; the crate was ~d with stickers la caisse était couverte d'autocollants.
◆ **paste up** *vt sep* [poster] coller; [list] afficher; [wallpaper] poser.

pasteboard ['peɪstbɔːd] ◇ *n* -1. [cardboard] carton *m*. -2. *Am* [for pastry] planche *f* à pâtisserie.
◇ *adj* de OR en carton-pâte.

pastel ['pæstl] ◇ *n* pastel *m*; ~ (drawing) (dessin *m* au) pastel; a portrait in ~s un portrait au pastel; ~s suit her les couleurs OR teintes pastel lui vont bien.
◇ *adj* pastel *(inv)*; ~ pink skirts des jupes rose pastel; ~ shade ton *m* OR teinte *f* pastel.

pastern ['pæstɜːn] *n* paturon *m*.

paste-up *n* TYPO maquette *f*.

pasteurization [ˌpɑːstʃəraɪ'zeɪʃn] *n* pasteurisation *f*.

pasteurize, -ise ['pɑːstʃəraɪz] *vt* pasteuriser.

pasteurized ['pɑːstʃəraɪzd] *adj* -1. [milk, beer] pasteurisé. -2. *pej* [version, description] édulcoré, aseptisé.

pastiche [pæ'stiːʃ] *n* pastiche *m*.

pastille, pastil ['pæstɪl] *n* pastille *f*; cough ~s pastilles pour OR contre la toux.

pastime ['pɑːstaɪm] *n* passe-temps *m*.

pasting *inf* ['peɪstɪŋ] *n* [beating, defeat] raclée *f*; they got a ~ in the elections ils ont pris une raclée aux élections.

past master *n* expert *m*; he's a ~ at doing as little as possible *hum* il est passé maître dans l'art d'en faire le moins possible.

pastor ['pɑːstə^r] *n* pasteur *m* RELIG.

pastoral ['pɑːstərəl] *adj* -1. [gen, ART & LITERAT] pastoral; they are a ~ people c'est un peuple de bergers; a ~ idyll une idylle pastorale ☐ ~ land pâturages *mpl*; 'The Pastoral Symphony' *Beethoven* 'la Symphonie pastorale'. -2. RELIG pastoral; ~ visit visite *f* pastorale; ~ staff crosse *f* (d'évêque). -3. SCH: ~ care ≃ tutorat *m*; teachers also have a ~ role les enseignants ont également un rôle de conseillers.

past participle *n* participe *m* passé.

past perfect *n* plus-que-parfait *m*.

pastrami [pə'strɑːmɪ] *n* pastarmi *m*, pastermi *m*.

pastry ['peɪstrɪ] (*pl* pastries) *n* -1. [dough] pâte *f*. -2. [cake] pâtisserie *f*, gâteau *m*.

pastry board *n* planche *f* à pâtisserie.

pastry brush *n* pinceau *m* (à pâtisserie).

pastry case *n* croûte *f*.

pastry cook *n* pâtissier *m*, -ère *f*.

pastry cream, pastry custard *n* crème *f* pâtissière.

pastry shell *n* fond *m* de tarte.

past tense *n* passé *m*.

pasturage ['pɑːstjʊrɪdʒ] *n* pâturage *m*.

pasture ['pɑːstʃə^r] ◇ *n* pâture *f*, pré *m*, pâturage *m*; to put out to ~ [animal] mettre au pâturage; *hum* [person] mettre à la retraite; *hum* [car] mettre à la casse; he left for greener ~s il est parti vers des horizons plus favorables.
◇ *vt* [animal] faire paître.

pastureland ['pɑːstʃəlænd] *n* herbages *mpl*, pâturages *mpl*.

pasty¹ ['peɪstɪ] (*compar* pastier, *superl* pastiest) *adj* [texture] pâteux; [sallow] terreux; [whitish] blanchâtre.

pasty² ['pæstɪ] (*pl* pasties) *n Br* CULIN ≃ petit pâté *m*.

pasty-faced ['peɪstɪ-] *adj* au teint terreux.

pat [pæt] (*pt* & *pp* patted, *cont* patting) ◇ *vt* tapoter; "sit here", she said, patting the place beside her «assieds-toi ici», dit-elle, désignant la place à côté d'elle; ~ your face dry séchez-vous le visage en le tapotant; she patted her hair elle se tapota les cheveux; he patted the soil/sand down il a tassé la terre/le sable ☐ to ~ sb on the back *literal* tapoter qqn OR donner une petite tape à qqn dans le dos; *fig* féliciter OR complimenter qqn.
◇ *n* -1. [tap] (légère) tape *f*; he gave me a friendly ~ on the shoulder il m'a donné une tape amicale sur l'épaule; you deserve a ~ on the back *fig* tu mérites un coup de chapeau. -2. [lump]: a ~ of butter une noix de beurre.
◇ *adj* -1. [glib - remark] tout fait; [- answer] tout prêt; his story is a little too ~ son histoire colle un peu trop bien. -2. [in poker]: a ~ hand une main servie.
◇ *adv* -1. [exactly] parfaitement, avec facilité; to have sthg off ~ apprendre qqch à la perfection OR par cœur. -2. *Am* [unbending]: to stand ~ [on decision] rester intraitable; dealer stands ~ [in poker] pas de cartes pour le donneur, donneur servi.

Patagonia [ˌpætə'gəʊnjə] *pr n* Patagonie *f*; in ~ en Patagonie.

Patagonian [ˌpætə'gəʊnjən] ◇ *n* Patagon *m*, -onne *f*.
◇ *adj* patagon.

patch [pætʃ] ◇ *n* -1. [of fabric] pièce *f*; [on inner tube] Rustine® *f*; a jacket with suede ~es on the elbows une veste avec des pièces en daim aux coudes ☐ he's not a ~ on you il ne t'arrive pas à la cheville. -2. [over eye] bandeau *m*; he wore a black eye ~ il avait un bandeau noir sur l'œil. -3. [sticking plaster] pansement *m* (adhésif). -4. [beauty spot] mouche *f*. -5. MIL [on uniform] insigne *m*. -6. [plot of land] parcelle *f*, lopin *m*; cabbage/strawberry ~ carré *m* de choux/de fraises; cotton ~ champ *m* de coton; vegetable ~ potager *m*. -7. [small expanse - of light, colour] tache *f*; there were damp ~es on the ceiling il y avait des taches d'humidité au plafond; snow still lay in ~es on the slopes les pistes étaient encore enneigées par endroits; ~es of fog nappes OR poches de brouillard; we crossed a rough ~ of road nous sommes passés sur un tronçon de route défoncé; a bald ~ une (petite) tonsure. -8. *Br* [period] période *f*, moment *m*; to go through a bad OR sticky OR rough ~ traverser une période difficile OR une mauvaise passe; the company had a bad ~ in 1990 la firme a connu des moments difficiles en 1990. -9. *Br* [district, beat] secteur *m*. -10. COMPUT modification *f* (de programme).
◇ *vt* -1. [mend - clothes] rapiécer; [- tyre, canoe] réparer; his jeans were ~ed at the knees son jean avait des pièces OR était rapiécé aux genoux; they ~ed the hole in the roof ils ont colmaté OR bouché le trou dans la toiture. -2. COMPUT [program] modifier. -3. TELEC raccorder; I'll ~ you through je vous passe votre communication.
◆ **patch together** *vt sep*: they managed to ~ together a government/story ils sont parvenus à former un gouvernement de fortune/à construire une histoire de toutes pièces.
◆ **patch up** *vt sep* -1. [repair - clothes] rapiécer; [- car, boat] réparer; [- in makeshift way] rafistoler; they ~ed him up in hospital ils l'ont rafistolé à l'hôpital. -2. [relationship]: he's trying to ~ things up with his wife il essaie de se rabibocher avec sa femme; they've ~ed up their dispute ils se sont réconciliés.

patch board *n* tableau *m* de raccordement.

patchouli ['pætʃʊlɪ] *n* patchouli *m*; ~ oil patchouli.

patch pocket *n* poche *f* plaquée.

patch test *n* test *m* cutané.

patchwork ['pætʃwɜːk] *n* -1. SEW patchwork *m*; we flew over a ~ of fields *fig* nous avons survolé une mosaïque de champs. -2. [collection] collection *f*; the book is a ~ of previously published writings le livre rassemble des écrits déjà publiés.

patchy ['pætʃɪ] (*compar* patchier, *superl* patchiest) *adj* -1. [not uniform] inégal, irrégulier; ~ fog des nappes de brouillard. -2. [incomplete] incomplet; our knowledge of that period of history is very ~ nous n'avons qu'une connaissance imparfaite de cette période de l'histoire.

pate [peɪt] *n arch* OR *hum* tête *f*.

pâté ['pæteɪ] *n* pâté *m*.

patella [pə'telə] (*pl* patellas OR patellae [-liː]) *n* -1. ANAT rotule *f*. -2. ARCHEOL patelle *f*.

paten ['pætn] *n* patène *f*.

patent [*Br* 'peɪtənt, *Am* 'pætənt] ◇ *n* -1. [on invention] brevet *m*; to take out a ~ on sthg prendre un brevet sur qqch, faire breveter qqch; '~ pending' demande de brevet déposée. -2. = **patent leather**. -3. *Am* [on land] concession *f*.
◇ *adj* -1. [product, procedure] breveté. -2. [blatant] patent, manifeste.
◇ *vt* faire breveter.

patent agent *n* agent *m* en brevets.

patent application *n* demande *f* de brevet.

patentee [*Br* ˌpeɪtən'tiː, *Am* ˌpætən'tiː] *n* détenteur *m*, -trice *f* OR titulaire *mf* d'un brevet (d'invention).

patent leather *n* (cuir *m*) vernis *m*; ~ boots bottes *fpl* vernies OR en cuir verni.

patently [*Br* 'peɪtəntlɪ, *Am* 'pætəntlɪ] *adv* manifestement, de toute évidence.

patent medicine *n* médicament *m* vendu sans ordonnance; *pej* [cure-all] élixir *m* universel, remède *m* de charlatan *pej*.

Patent Office *n* ≃ Institut *m* national de la propriété industrielle.

pater *inf* ['peɪtə^r] *n Br dated* OR *hum* pater *m*, paternel *m*.

paterfamilias [ˌpeɪtəfə'mɪlɪæs] *n* paterfamilias *m*.
paternal [pə'tɜːnl] *adj* paternel.
paternalism [pə'tɜːnəlɪzm] *n* paternalisme *m*.
paternalistic [pəˌtɜːnə'lɪstɪk] *adj* paternaliste.
paternally [pə'tɜːnəlɪ] *adv* paternellement.
paternity [pə'tɜːnətɪ] *n* paternité *f*.
paternity leave *n* congé *m* de paternité.
paternity order *n* JUR (ordonnance *f* de) reconnaissance *f* de paternité.
paternity suit *n* action *f* en recherche de paternité.
paternity test *n* test *m* de recherche de paternité.
paternoster [ˌpætə'nɒstə^r] *n* **-1.** [rosary bead] pater *m*. **-2.** [fishing tackle, lift] pater-noster *m*.
◆ **Paternoster** *n* [prayer] Pater *m*.
path [pɑːθ] (*pl* paths [pɑːðz]) *n* **-1.** [in garden, park] allée *f*; [in country] chemin *m*, sentier *m*; [along road] trottoir *m*. **-2.** [way ahead or through] chemin *m*, passage *m*; to cut a ~ through sthg se tailler OR se frayer un chemin à travers qqch; the hurricane destroyed everything in its ~ l'ouragan a tout détruit sur son passage; the ~ to fame *fig* la route OR le chemin qui mène à la gloire. **-3.** [trajectory - of projectile, planet] trajectoire *f*; our ~s first crossed in 1965 nos chemins se sont croisés OR nous nous sommes rencontrés pour la première fois en 1965.
Pathan [pə'tɑːn] ◇ *n* Pathan *m*, -e *f*.
◇ *adj* pathan.
pathetic [pə'θetɪk] *adj* **-1.** [pitiable - lament, waif, smile, story] pitoyable; it was ~ to see how they lived cela serrait le cœur OR c'était un crève-cœur de voir dans quelles conditions ils vivaient; a ~ story une histoire pitoyable OR pathétique. **-2.** *pej* [worthless] minable, lamentable; you're a ~ lot! *inf* vous n'êtes que des minables!
pathetically [pə'θetɪklɪ] *adv* pitoyablement; she felt ~ lonely elle se sentait terriblement seule; he used to be ~ shy autrefois, il était d'une timidité qui faisait peine à voir.
pathetic fallacy *n* anthropomorphisme *m*.
pathfinder ['pɑːθˌfaɪndə^r] *n* **-1.** [scout] éclaireur *m*. **-2.** *fig* pionnier *m*. **-3.** AERON avion *m* éclaireur.
pathogenesis [ˌpæθə'dʒenɪsɪs] *n* pathogénie *f*.
pathogenic [ˌpæθə'dʒenɪk] *adj* pathogène.
pathogeny [pə'θɒdʒənɪ] = **pathogenesis**.
pathological [ˌpæθə'lɒdʒɪk(l)] *adj* pathologique; he's a ~ liar il ne peut pas s'empêcher de mentir.
pathologist [pə'θɒlədʒɪst] *n* pathologiste *mf*.
pathology [pə'θɒlədʒɪ] (*pl* **pathologies**) *n* pathologie *f*.
pathos ['peɪθɒs] *n* pathétique *m*.
pathway ['pɑːθweɪ] *n* [in garden] allée *f*; [in country] chemin *m*, sentier *m*; [beside road] trottoir *m*.
patience ['peɪʃns] *n* **-1.** patience *f*; to lose ~ (with sb) perdre patience (avec qqn); I haven't the ~ to redo it je n'ai pas la patience de le refaire; he has no ~ with children les enfants l'exaspèrent; don't try my ~ any further! ne mets pas davantage ma patience à l'épreuve!, n'abuse pas davantage de ma patience!; have a little ~! un peu de patience!; my ~ is wearing thin ma patience a des limites, je suis à bout de patience. **-2.** *Br* [card game] réussite *f*; she was playing ~ elle faisait des réussites.
patient ['peɪʃnt] ◇ *adj* patient; be ~! (un peu de) patience!, soyez patient!; if you'll be ~ a few moments longer veuillez patienter encore quelques instants; with a ~ smile avec un sourire empreint d'une grande patience.
◇ *n* MED malade *mf*, patient *m*, -e *f*.
patiently ['peɪʃntlɪ] *adv* patiemment.
patina ['pætɪnə] (*pl* patinas OR patinae [-niː]) *n* patine *f*.
patio ['pætɪəʊ] (*pl* patios) *n* patio *m*; ~ furniture meubles *mpl* de jardin.
patio doors *npl* portes *fpl* vitrées *(donnant sur un patio)*.
Patna rice ['pætnə-] *n variété de riz à grains longs*.
patois ['pætwɑː] (*pl inv* ['pætwɑːz]) *n* patois *m*.
patriarch ['peɪtrɪɑːk] *n* patriarche *m*.
patriarchal [ˌpeɪtrɪ'ɑːkl] *adj* patriarcal.
patriarchy ['peɪtrɪɑːkɪ] (*pl* **patriarchies**) *n* patriarcat *m*.
patrician [pə'trɪʃn] *n* patricien *m*, -enne *f*.
patricide ['pætrɪsaɪd] *n* **-1.** [killer] parricide *mf*. **-2.** [act] parricide *m*.
Patrick ['pætrɪk] *pr n*: Saint ~ saint Patrick; Saint ~'s Day la Saint-Patrick.
patrilineal [ˌpætrɪ'lɪnɪəl] *adj* patrilinéaire.
patrimony [*Br* 'pætrɪmənɪ, *Am* 'pætrɪməʊnɪ] (*pl* patrimonies) *n* patrimoine *m*.
patriot [*Br* 'pætrɪət, *Am* 'peɪtrɪət] *n* patriote *mf*.
patriotic [*Br* ˌpætrɪ'ɒtɪk, *Am* ˌpeɪtrɪ'ɒtɪk] *adj* [person] patriote; [song, action etc] patriotique.
patriotically [*Br* ˌpætrɪ'ɒtɪklɪ, *Am* ˌpeɪtrɪ'ɒtɪklɪ] *adv* patriotiquement, en patriote.
patriotism [*Br* 'pætrɪətɪzm, *Am* 'peɪtrɪətɪzm] *n* patriotisme *m*.
patrol [pə'trəʊl] (*pt* & *pp* **patrolled**, *cont* **patrolling**) ◇ *n* **-1.** [group] patrouille *f*; the ~ is OR are on the way la patrouille est en route; highway ~ *Am* police *f* des autoroutes. **-2.** [task] patrouille *f*; to be on ~ être de patrouille; they were sent out on ~ ils ont été envoyés en patrouille.
◇ *vi* patrouiller.
◇ *vt* [area, streets] patrouiller dans; the border is patrolled by armed guards des gardes armés patrouillent le long de la frontière.
patrol boat *n* NAUT patrouilleur *m*.
patrol car *n* voiture *f* de police.
patrol leader *n* chef *m* de patrouille.
patrolman [pə'trəʊlmən] (*pl* **patrolmen** [-mən]) *n* **-1.** *Am* agent *m* de police *(qui fait sa ronde)*. **-2.** *Br dépanneur employé par une association d'automobilistes*.
patrol wagon *n Am, Austr* & *NZ* voiture *f* OR fourgon *m* cellulaire.
patrolwoman [pə'trəʊlˌwʊmən] (*pl* **patrolwomen** [-ˌwɪmɪn]) *n Am* femme *f* agent de police *(qui fait sa ronde)*.
patron ['peɪtrən] *n* **-1.** [sponsor - of the arts] mécène *m*; [- of a festival] parrain *m*, sponsor *m*; many multinational companies are becoming ~s of the arts de nombreuses multinationales se lancent dans le mécénat; the mayor is one of the ~s of our association [supporter] le maire est une des personnes qui ont accordé leur patronage à notre association. **-2.** [customer - of restaurant, hotel, shop] client *m*, -e *f*; [- of library] usager *m*; [- of museum] visiteur *m*, -euse *f*; [- of theatre, cinema] spectateur *m*, -trice *f*; '~s only' 'réservé aux clients'. **-3.** [in ancient Rome] patron *m*.
patronage ['peɪtrənɪdʒ] *n* **-1.** [support, sponsorship] patronage *m*, parrainage *m*. **-2.** COMM clientèle *f*; I shall take my ~ elsewhere j'irai me fournir ailleurs. **-3.** POL pouvoir *m* de nomination; *pej* trafic *m* d'influence; he got the promotion through the Minister's ~ il a obtenu de l'avancement grâce à l'influence du ministre. **-4.** [condescension] condescendance *f*.
patronize, -ise ['pætrənaɪz] *vt* **-1.** [business] donner sa clientèle à; [cinema] fréquenter; we no longer ~ the local shops nous ne faisons plus nos courses dans le quartier. **-2.** [condescend to] traiter avec condescendance; don't ~ me! ne prenez pas ce ton condescendant avec moi! **-3.** [sponsor] patronner, parrainer.
patronizing ['pætrənaɪzɪŋ] *adj* condescendant.
patronizingly ['pætrənaɪzɪŋlɪ] *adv* [smile] avec condescendance; [say] d'un ton condescendant.
patron saint *n* (saint *m*) patron *m*, (sainte *f*) patronne *f*.
patronymic [ˌpætrə'nɪmɪk] ◇ *n* patronyme *m*.
◇ *adj* patronymique.
patsy^▽ ['pætsɪ] (*pl* patsies) *n Am* [gullible person] pigeon *m*, gogo *m*; [scapegoat] bouc *m* émissaire.
patten ['pætn] *n* socque *m (pour protéger les chaussures contre la boue)*.
patter ['pætə^r] ◇ *n* **-1.** [sound] crépitement *m*, (petit) bruit *m*; the ~ of rain on the windows le crépitement de la pluie sur les fenêtres ❑ the (pitter) ~ of tiny feet *hum* un heureux événement. **-2.** *inf* [of salesman] baratin *m*, boniment *m*; [of entertainer] bavardage *m*, baratin *m*. **-3.** *inf* [jargon] jargon *m*.
◇ *vi* **-1.** [raindrops] tambouriner. **-2.** [person, mouse] trottiner; she ~ed down the corridor in her slippers elle trottinait dans le couloir en pantoufles. **-3.** *inf* [talk] bavarder, baratiner.
pattern ['pætən] ◇ *n* **-1.** [design - decorative] motif *m*; [- natural] dessin *m*; [- on animal] marques *fpl*; a geometric/herringbone ~ un motif géométrique/à chevrons. **-2.** [physical arrangement] disposition *f*, configuration *f*; to form a ~ former un motif OR un dessin. **-3.** [abstract arrangement] système *m*, configuration *f*; sometimes there seems to be no ~ to our lives notre existence semble parfois être régie par le hasard; all the different elements fell into a ~ tous les éléments ont fini par s'emboîter les uns dans les autres OR s'articuler les uns aux autres; research has established that there is a ~ in OR to the data la recherche a établi que les données ne sont pas aléatoires; behaviour ~s in monkeys types de comportement chez les singes; there is a definite ~ to the burglaries on observe une constante bien précise dans les cambriolages; the ~ of TV viewing in the average household les habitudes du téléspectateur moyen; economic growth on the Japanese ~ croissance économique à la japonaise; voice ~ empreintes *fpl* vocales. **-4.** [diagram, shape which guides] TECH modèle *m*, gabarit *m*; SEW patron *m*; dress ~ patron de robe. **-5.** *fig* [model worth imitating, example] exemple *m*, modèle *m*; their methods set the ~ for other companies leurs méthodes ont servi de modèle à d'autres sociétés.
◇ *vt* **-1.** [mark - fabric] décorer d'un motif. **-2.** [copy] modeler; to ~ o.s. on OR after sb prendre modèle OR exemple sur qqn; their quality control is ~ed on Japanese methods leur contrôle de qualité est calqué sur les méthodes japonaises.
pattern designer *n* INDUST dessinateur *m*, -trice *f* de patrons.
patterned ['pætənd] *adj* à motifs; ~ wallpaper papier peint à motifs.
patterning ['pætənɪŋ] *n* **-1.** PSYCH & SOCIOL acquisition *f* des structures de pensée. **-2.** ZOOL [markings] marques *fpl*, taches *fpl*.
pattie, patty ['pætɪ] (*pl* patties) *n* **-1.** *Am*: (hamburger) ~ *portion de steak haché*. **-2.** [pasty] (petit) pâté *m*.
paucity ['pɔːsətɪ] *n fml* pénurie *f*.
Paul [pɔːl] *pr n*: Saint ~ saint Paul.
Pauline ['pɔːlaɪn] *adj* RELIG paulinien.
paunch [pɔːntʃ] *n* **-1.** *pej* OR *hum* [stomach] (gros) ventre *m*, bedaine *f*; he's getting a ~ il prend du ventre. **-2.** ZOOL panse *f*.
paunchy ['pɔːntʃɪ] (*compar* paunchier, *superl* paunchiest) *adj pej* OR *hum* ventru, pansu, bedonnant; he's getting ~ il prend du ventre.
pauper ['pɔːpə^r] *n* pauvre *mf*, pauvresse *f*, indigent *m*, -e *f*; to end up in a ~'s grave finir à la fosse commune.
pauperism ['pɔːpərɪzm] *n* indigence *f*, paupérisme *m*.
pauperize, -ise ['pɔːpəraɪz] *vt* paupériser.
pause [pɔːz] ◇ *n* **-1.** [break] pause *f*, temps *m* d'arrêt; 'pause' [on tape recorder, cassette player] 'pause'; there will be a ten minute ~ after the second lecture il y aura OR nous ferons une pause de dix minutes après le deuxième cours; without a ~ sans s'arrêter, sans interruption; there was a long ~ before she answered elle garda longtemps le silence avant de répondre; to give sb ~, to give ~ to sb *fml* donner

à réfléchir à qqn. -**2.** MUS point *m* d'orgue. -**3.** LITERAT césure *f*.
◇ *vi* faire OR marquer une pause; **the speaker ~d while the latecomer took his seat** le conférencier fit une pause pendant que le retardataire prenait place; **he ~d in the middle of his explanation** il s'arrêta OR s'interrompit au milieu de son explication; **I signed it without pausing to read the details** je l'ai signé sans prendre le temps d'en lire les détails; **without pausing for breath** sans même reprendre son souffle; **she ~d on the doorstep** elle hésita sur le pas de la porte.

pave [peɪv] *vt* [street, floor - with flagstones, tiles] paver; [- with concrete, asphalt] revêtir; **~d in** OR **with asphalt** revêtu d'asphalte; **the road isn't ~d yet** la route n'est pas encore goudronnée; **bricks ~d the courtyard** la cour était pavée de briques; **~d with gold** pavé d'or; **her career was ~d with success** *fig* sa carrière fut jalonnée de succès ❑ **to ~ the way for sthg** ouvrir la voie à OR préparer le terrain pour qqch.

pavement ['peɪvmənt] *n* -**1.** *Br* [footpath] trottoir *m*; **~ café** café *m*, terrasse *f* d'un café. -**2.** *Am* [roadway] chaussée *f*. -**3.** [surfaced area - of cobbles, stones] pavé *m*; [- of marble, granite] dallage *m*; [- of concrete] (dalle *f* de) béton *m*; [- of mosaic] pavement *m*.

pavement artist *n Br* artiste *mf* de trottoir.

pavilion [pə'vɪljən] *n* -**1.** [building] pavillon *m*; [at sports ground] vestiaires *mpl*; **the Japanese ~ at the exhibition** le pavillon du Japon à l'exposition ❑ **(cricket) ~** *bâtiment abritant les vestiaires et le bar sur un terrain de cricket*. -**2.** [tent] pavillon *m*, tente *f*.

paving ['peɪvɪŋ] ◇ *n* [cobbles, flagstones] pavé *m*; [tiles] carrelage *m*; [concrete] dallage *m*, béton *m*.
◇ *adj* [measure, legislation] préparatoire.

paving stone *n* pavé *m*.

pavlova [pæv'ləʊvə] *n* vacherin *m*.

Pavlovian [pæv'ləʊvɪən] *adj* pavlovien.

paw [pɔː] ◇ *n* -**1.** [of animal] patte *f*. -**2.** *inf* [hand] pince *f*, patte *f*.
◇ *vt* -**1.** [animal] donner un coup de patte à; **the horse ~ed the ground** le cheval piaffait. -**2.** *inf* [touch, maul] tripoter; [sexually] peloter.
◇ *vi*: **the dog ~ed at the door** le chien grattait à la porte.

pawky ['pɔːkɪ] *adj dial* pince-sans-rire *inv*.

pawl [pɔːl] *n* cliquet *m*.

pawn [pɔːn] ◇ *n* -**1.** [in chess] pion *m*; **they are mere ~s in the hands of the politicians** *fig* ils ne sont que des pions sur l'échiquier politique. -**2.** [at pawnbroker's]: **my watch is in ~** ma montre est en gage; **I got my watch out of ~** *Br* j'ai dégagé ma montre.
◇ *vt* mettre OR laisser en gage.

pawnbroker ['pɔːn,brəʊkə^r^] *n* prêteur *m* sur gages; **at the ~'s** au mont-de-piété.

pawnshop ['pɔːnʃɒp] *n* boutique *f* de prêteur sur gages, mont-de-piété *m*.

pawn ticket *n* reconnaissance *f* du mont-de-piété.

pawpaw ['pɔːpɔː] *n* papaye *f*.

pax [pæks] ◇ *n* RELIG [tablet] paix *f*; [kiss] baiser *m* de paix.
◇ *interj Br school sl*: **~!** pouce!

pay [peɪ] (*pt* & *pp* **paid** [peɪd]) ◇ *vt* -**1.** [person] payer; **she's paid £2,000 a month** elle est payée OR elle touche 2 000 livres par mois; **you should ~ someone to do it for you** vous devriez payer quelqu'un pour le faire à votre place. -**2.** [sum of money] payer; **you ~ £100 now, the rest later** vous payez 100 livres maintenant, le solde plus tard; **I paid her £20** je lui ai payé 20 livres; **he paid £20 for the watch** il a payé la montre 20 livres; **to ~ dividends** porter ses fruits, produire des dividendes; **shut up and ~ the man his money!** *inf* ferme-la et casque! -**3.** [bill, debt] payer, régler; [fine, taxes, fare] payer; **have you paid your union dues?** avez-vous payé vos cotisations syndicales?; **the rent is paid up until the end of May** le loyer est payé jusqu'à la fin mai; **they've paid their debt to society** ils ont payé leur dette envers la société ❑ **to ~ one's way** payer sa part; **is the business ~ing its way?** cette affaire est-elle rentable? -**4.** *fig* [benefit] rapporter à; **it ~s them to use immigrant labour** cela leur rapporte d'utiliser la main-d'œuvre immigrée; **it'll ~ you to start now** vous avez intérêt à commencer tout de suite; **it'll ~ you to keep quiet!** tu as intérêt à tenir ta langue! -**5.** [with various noun objects]: **~ attention!** faites attention!; **nobody ~s any attention to me** personne ne m'écoute; **to ~ a call on sb, to ~ sb a visit** rendre visite à qqn.
◇ *vi* payer; **to ~ by cheque** payer par chèque; **to ~ (by) cash** payer en espèces; **the job ~s very well** le travail est très bien payé; **after two years the business was beginning to ~** après deux ans, l'affaire était devenue rentable; **it ~s to be honest** ça rapporte d'être honnête; **crime doesn't ~** le crime ne paie pas ❑ **to ~ on the nail** payer rubis sur ongle.
◇ *n* paie *f*, paye *f*; **my first month's ~** ma première paie, mon premier salaire; **the ~ is good** c'est bien payé; **he's in the ~ of the enemy** il est à la solde de l'ennemi.
◇ *comp* -**1.** [demand, negotiations] salarial; [increase, cut] de salaire. -**2.** [not free] payant; **~ toilets** toilettes *fpl* payantes. -**3.** MIN [deposit] exploitable.

◆ **pay back** *vt sep* -**1.** [loan, lender] rembourser; **she paid her father back the sum she had borrowed** elle remboursa à son père la somme qu'elle avait empruntée. -**2.** [retaliate against] rendre la monnaie de sa pièce à; **I'll ~ you back for that!** tu me le paieras!

◆ **pay for** *vt insep* -**1.** [item, task] payer; **to ~ for sthg** payer qqch; **who paid for the drinks?** qui est-ce qui a payé les consommations?; **I paid good money for that!** ça m'a coûté cher!; **you get what you ~ for** la qualité est en rapport avec le prix (que vous payez); **double glazing ~s for itself after a few years** l'installation d'un double vitrage est amortie au bout de quelques années; **it seems a small price to ~ for peace of mind** c'est faire un bien petit sacrifice pour avoir sa tranquillité d'esprit ❑ **to ~ through the nose for sthg** payer qqch les yeux de la tête. -**2.** [crime, mistake] payer; **you'll ~ for this!** tu me le paieras!; **to ~ dearly for sthg** payer chèrement qqch; **he paid for his mistake with his life** il a payé son erreur de sa vie; **to make sb ~ for sthg** faire payer qqch à qqn.

◆ **pay in** *vt sep Br* [cheque] déposer sur un compte.

◆ **pay into** ◇ *vt sep* [money]: **I'd like to ~ this cheque into my account** j'aimerais déposer ce chèque sur mon compte.
◇ *vt insep*: **to ~ into a pension scheme** cotiser à un plan de retraite.

◆ **pay off** ◇ *vt sep* -**1.** [debt] payer, régler, s'acquitter de; [loan] rembourser; **it takes years to ~ off a mortgage** il faut des années pour rembourser un emprunt-logement. -**2.** [dismiss, lay off] licencier, congédier; **he threatened to ~ us all off** il a menacé de nous mettre tous à la porte. -**3.** *inf* [bribe] acheter; **they paid off the police chief** ils ont acheté le chef de la police.
◇ *vi insep* payer, rapporter; **moving the company out of London really paid off** le transfert de la société hors de Londres a été une affaire rentable.

◆ **pay out** *vt sep* -**1.** [money] payer, débourser. -**2.** [rope] laisser filer.

◆ **pay up** *vi insep* payer; **~ up or else!** payez, sinon...!

payable ['peɪəbl] *adj* payable; **~ in 24 monthly instalments/in advance** payable en 24 mensualités/d'avance; **refunds are ~ in certain cases** vous pouvez être remboursé sous certaines conditions; **cheques should be made ~ to Mr Brown** les chèques devraient être libellés OR établis à l'ordre de M. Brown.

pay-as-you-earn → **PAYE**.

pay bed *n Br* lit *m* (d'hôpital) privé.

pay check *Am* = **pay packet**.

payday ['peɪdeɪ] *n* jour *m* de paie; **tomorrow is ~** nous sommes payés demain.

pay dirt *inf n Am* -**1.** [earth] gisement *m*. -**2.** [discovery] trouvaille *f*; **to hit ~** trouver un bon filon.

PAYE (*abbr of* **pay-as-you-earn**) *n* prélèvement *m* à la source *(des impôts)*.

payee [peɪ'iː] *n* bénéficiaire *mf*.

pay envelope *Am* = **pay packet**.

payer ['peɪə^r^] *n* -**1.** [gen] payeur *m*, -euse *f*; **a good/bad ~** un bon/mauvais payeur. -**2.** [of cheque] tireur *m*, -euse *f*.

paying ['peɪɪŋ] ◇ *n* paiement *m*.
◇ *adj* -**1.** [who pays] payant. -**2.** [profitable] payant, rentable.

paying guest *n* hôte *m* payant.

paying-in book *n* carnet *m* de versement.

paying-in slip *n Br* bordereau *m* de versement.

payload ['peɪləʊd] *n* -**1.** [gen] chargement *m*; **he was transporting a ~ of cement** il transportait un chargement de ciment. -**2.** TECH [of vehicle, aircraft, rocket] charge *f* payante; [of missile, warhead] puissance *f*.

paymaster ['peɪ,mɑːstə^r^] *n* [gen] payeur *m*, -euse *f*, intendant *m*, -e *f*; [in school, institution] économe *mf*; [in army] payeur *m*; [in administration] trésorier-payeur *m*; **the World Bank acts as ~ of the project** la Banque mondiale fait office de bailleur de fonds pour ce projet.

Paymaster General *pr n*: **the ~** le Trésorier-payeur-général britannique.

payment ['peɪmənt] *n* -**1.** [sum paid, act of paying] paiement *m*, versement *m*; **48 monthly ~s** 48 versements mensuels, 48 mensualités; **on ~ of a deposit** moyennant des arrhes; **in ~ of your invoice** en règlement de votre facture; **they offered their services without ~** ils ont offert leurs services à titre gracieux. -**2.** [reward, compensation] récompense *f*.

payoff ['peɪɒf] *n* -**1.** [act of paying off] paiement *m*; **the ~ is set for tomorrow night** [gen] le paiement sera effectué demain soir; [ransom] la remise de la rançon est fixée à demain soir. -**2.** [profit] bénéfice *m*, profit *m*. -**3.** [consequence] conséquence *f*, résultat *m*; [reward] récompense *f*; **it's an unexpected but welcome ~ of this policy** ceci est une conséquence inattendue mais heureuse de cette politique. -**4.** *inf* [climax] dénouement *m*. -**5.** *inf* [bribe] pot-de-vin *m*.

payola *inf* [peɪ'əʊlə] *n (U)* pots-de-vin *mpl*, dessous-de-table *mpl*.

pay packet *n Br* [envelope] enveloppe *f* contenant le salaire; [money] paie *f*, salaire *m*.

payphone ['peɪfəʊn] *n* téléphone *m* à pièces.

pay rise *n* augmentation *f* de salaire.

payroll ['peɪrəʊl] *n* -**1.** [personnel] personnel *m*; **he's been on our ~ for years** il fait partie du personnel depuis des années; **they've added 500 workers to their ~** ils ont embauché 500 travailleurs supplémentaires. -**2.** [list] registre *m* du personnel; **to do the ~** faire la paie, établir les bulletins de paie.

payslip ['peɪslɪp] *n* fiche *f* OR feuille *f* OR bulletin *m* de paie.

pay television *n* chaîne *f* à péage.

PBS (*abbr of* **Public Broadcasting Service**) *pr n société américaine de production télévisuelle*.

PBX (*abbr of* **private branch exchange**) *n Br autocommutateur privé*.

pc -**1.** *written abbr of* **postcard**. -**2.** (*written abbr of* **per cent**) p. cent.

pc, PC (*abbr of* **personal computer**) *n* PC *m*, micro *m*.

p/c *written abbr of* **petty cash**.

PC ◇ *n* -**1.** *abbr of* **police constable**. -**2.** *abbr of* **privy councillor**.
◇ *adj abbr of* **politically correct**.

PCB *n abbr of* **printed circuit board**.

pcm (*written abbr of* **per calendar month**) par mois.

PCV (*abbr of* **passenger carrying vehicle**) *n Br* véhicule *m* de transport en commun.

pd *written abbr of* paid.

PD *Am abbr of* police department.

pdq *inf* (*abbr of* pretty damn quick) *adv* illico presto.

PDSA (*abbr of* People's Dispensary for Sick Animals) *pr n association de soins aux animaux malades.*

PDT *n abbr of* Pacific Daylight Time.

PE (*abbr of* physical education) *n* EPS *f*.

pea [piː] *n* BOT pois *m*; CULIN (petit) pois *m*; frozen ~s petits pois surgelés ❑ ~ soup soupe *f* aux pois; they are as alike as two ~s in a pod ils se ressemblent comme deux gouttes d'eau.

peace [piːs] ◇ *n* -**1.** [not war] paix *f*; the country is at ~ now la paix est maintenant rétablie dans le pays; I come in ~ je viens en ami; to make ~ faire la paix; he made (his) ~ with his father *fig* il a fait la paix OR il s'est réconcilié avec son père ‖ [treaty] (traité *m* de) paix *f*; they wanted to sign a separate ~ with the invaders ils voulaient conclure OR signer une paix séparée avec les envahisseurs. -**2.** [tranquillity] paix *f*, tranquillité *f*; to be at ~ with one's surroundings vivre en paix avec son entourage; ~ be with you! que la paix soit avec vous!; we haven't had a moment's ~ all morning nous n'avons pas eu un moment de tranquillité de toute la matinée; all I want is a bit of ~ and quiet tout ce que je veux, c'est un peu de tranquillité; to have ~ of mind avoir l'esprit tranquille; he'll give you no ~ until you pay him tant que tu ne l'auras pas payé, il ne te laissera pas tranquille; leave us in ~! laissez-nous tranquilles!, laissez-nous en paix! ‖ [silence]: to hold OR to keep one's ~ garder le silence, se taire; hold your ~! silence! -**3.** [law and order] paix *f*, ordre *m* public; to disturb the ~ troubler l'ordre public; to keep the ~ [army, police] maintenir l'ordre.
◇ *comp* [treaty, talks] de paix; [rally, movement] pour la paix.

peaceable ['piːsəbl] *adj* -**1.** [peace-loving – nation, person] pacifique. -**2.** [calm – atmosphere] paisible, tranquille; [– demonstration, methods] pacifique; [– discussion] calme.

peaceably ['piːsəblɪ] *adv* [live] paisiblement, tranquillement; [discuss, listen] calmement, paisiblement; [assemble, disperse] pacifiquement, sans incident.

Peace Corps *pr n organisation américaine de coopération avec les pays en voie de développement.*

peaceful ['piːsfʊl] *adj* -**1.** [calm, serene] paisible, tranquille; it's so ~ in the country! la campagne est si paisible! -**2.** [non-violent] pacifique; we are a ~ nation nous sommes une nation pacifique; a ~ transition to independence une transition pacifique vers l'indépendance; the ~ uses of nuclear energy les utilisations pacifiques de l'énergie nucléaire.

peacefully ['piːsfʊlɪ] *adv* [live, rest] paisiblement, tranquillement; [protest] pacifiquement; the rally went off ~ le meeting s'est déroulé dans le calme OR sans incident.

peacefulness ['piːsfʊlnɪs] *n* paix *f*, calme *m*, tranquillité *f*.

peacekeeper ['piːsˌkiːpəʳ] *n* [soldier] soldat *m* de la paix; [of United Nations] casque *m* bleu.

peacekeeping ['piːsˌkiːpɪŋ] ◇ *n* maintien *m* de la paix.
◇ *adj* de maintien de la paix; a United Nations ~ force des forces des Nations unies pour le maintien de la paix.

peace-loving *adj* pacifique.

peacemaker ['piːsˌmeɪkəʳ] *n* pacificateur *m*, -trice *f*, conciliateur *m*, -trice *f*.

peace offensive *n* offensive *f* de paix.

peace offering *n* offrande *f* de paix.

peace pipe *n* calumet *m* (de la paix).

peace sign *n* signe *m* de la paix.

peacetime ['piːstaɪm] *n* temps *m* de paix; in ~ en temps de paix.

peach [piːtʃ] ◇ *n* -**1.** [fruit] pêche *f*; [tree] pêcher *m*; ~ blossom fleurs *mpl* de pêcher; she has a ~es and cream complexion elle a un teint de pêche. -**2.** [colour] couleur *f* pêche. -**3.** *inf* [expressing approval]: he played a ~ of a shot il a joué un coup superbe; thanks, you're a ~! merci, tu es adorable!
◇ *adj* [colour] pêche *(inv)*.
◇ *vt inf* cafarder, moucharder.
◇ *vi inf* cafarder; to ~ on sb cafarder qqn.

peach melba *n* pêche *f* melba.

peachy ['piːtʃɪ] (*compar* peachier, *superl* peachiest) *adj* -**1.** [taste, flavour] de pêche. -**2.** *inf* [nice] chouette.

peacoat ['piːkəʊt] = **pea jacket**.

peacock ['piːkɒk] (*pl inv* OR peacocks) ◇ *n* -**1.** [bird] paon *m*. -**2.** [colour] = **peacock blue**.
◇ *adj* = **peacock blue**.

peacock blue *n* bleu *m* paon.
◆ **peacock-blue** *adj* bleu paon *(inv)*.

peacock butterfly *n* paon *m* de jour.

peafowl ['piːfaʊl] (*pl inv* OR peafowls) *n* paon *m*.

pea green *n* vert *m* pomme.
◆ **pea-green** *adj* vert pomme *(inv)*.

peahen ['piːhen] *n* paonne *f*.

pea jacket *n* caban *m*.

peak [piːk] ◇ *n* -**1.** [mountain top] pic *m*, sommet *m*; [mountain] pic *m*; snowy ~s pics enneigés. -**2.** [pointed part – of roof] faîte *m*; beat the egg whites until they form ~s battez les blancs d'œufs en neige très ferme. -**3.** [high point – of fame, career] sommet *m*, apogée *m*; [– on graph] sommet *m*; emigration was at its ~ in the 1890s l'émigration a atteint son point culminant OR son sommet dans les années 1890; the gardens are at their ~ in July c'est en juillet que les jardins sont au faîte OR à l'apogée de leur splendeur; the team will be at its ~ in a few weeks l'équipe sera à son top niveau dans quelques semaines; the party was at its ~ la fête battait son plein; sales have reached a new ~ les ventes ont atteint un nouveau record. -**4.** [of cap] visière *f*.
◇ *vi* [production, demand] atteindre un maximum; his popularity ~ed just before the elections sa cote a atteint un OR son maximum juste avant les élections; she ~ed too soon elle s'est donnée à fond trop tôt.
◇ *adj* maximum; ~ demand demande *f* maximum; ~ viewing hours TV heures de grande écoute; the team is in ~ condition l'équipe est à son top niveau; ~ hours OR time [of electricity use] période *f* de pointe; [of traffic] heures *fpl* de pointe OR d'affluence; [in restaurant] coup *m* de feu.

peaked [piːkt] *adj* [roof] pointu; [cap] à visière.

peaky *inf* ['piːkɪ] (*compar* peakier, *superl* peakiest) *adj Br* [unwell] (un peu) malade; [tired] fatigué; I feel a little ~ this morning je ne me sens pas en forme OR je ne me sens pas dans mon assiette ce matin.

peal [piːl] ◇ *n* -**1.** [sound]: the ~ of bells la sonnerie de cloches, le carillon; a ~ of thunder un coup de tonnerre; ~s of laughter came from the garden des éclats de rire se faisaient entendre du jardin; they burst into ~s of laughter ils ont éclaté de rire. -**2.** [set of bells] carillon *m*.
◇ *vi*: to ~ (out) [bells] carillonner; [thunder] gronder.
◇ *vt* [bells] sonner à toute volée.

peanut ['piːnʌt] *n* [nut] ·cacahouète *f*, cacahuète *f*; [plant] arachide *f*.
◆ **peanuts** *inf npl* [small sum] clopinettes *fpl*; to work for ~s travailler pour des clopinettes; it's worth ~s ça ne vaut pas un clou; £100 is ~s for a return ticket 100 livres, ce n'est rien pour un billet aller-retour.

peanut butter *n* beurre *m* de cacahouètes OR de cacahuètes.

peanut oil *n* huile *f* d'arachide.

peapod ['piːpɒd] *n* cosse *f* de pois.

pear [peəʳ] *n* [fruit] poire *f*; [tree, wood] poirier *m*.

pearl [pɜːl] ◇ *n* -**1.** [gem] perle *f*; to cast ~ before swine donner des perles aux cochons OR aux pourceaux. -**2.** [mother-of-pearl] nacre *f*. -**3.** *fig* perle *f*; Hong Kong, ~ of the East Hongkong, perle de l'Orient; ~s of wisdom trésors *mpl* de sagesse.
◇ *adj* -**1.** [made of pearls] de perles; ~ earrings perles montées en boucles d'oreilles; a ~ necklace un collier de perles. -**2.** [made of mother-of-pearl] de OR en nacre; ~ buttons boutons en nacre.
◇ *vi* -**1.** [form drops] perler. -**2.** [search for pearls] pêcher des perles.

pearl barley *n* orge *m* perlé.

pearl diver *n* pêcheur *m*, -euse *f* de perles.

pearl diving *n* pêche *f* aux perles.

pearl grey *n* gris *m* perle.
◆ **pearl-grey** *adj* gris perle *(inv)*.

Pearl Harbor [pɜːl-] *pr n* Pearl Harbor.

PEARL HARBOR:
Importante base navale américaine située à Hawaii et attaquée le 7 décembre 1941 par l'aviation japonaise, qui infligea de lourdes pertes humaines et matérielles aux États-Unis. Le lendemain, l'Amérique, en déclarant la guerre au Japon, fit son entrée dans le conflit mondial.

---

pearlized, -ised ['pɜːlaɪzd] *adj* nacré; ~ nail polish vernis à ongles nacré.

pearl oyster *n* huître *f* perlière.

pearly ['pɜːlɪ] (*compar* pearlier, *superl* pearliest) *adj* -**1.** [pearl-like] nacré; ~ pink nail polish vernis à ongles rose nacré; ~ white teeth dents de perle OR éclatantes. -**2.** [decorated with pearls] perlé; [made of mother-of-pearl] en OR de nacre.

Pearly Gates *inf pr n*: the ~ les portes *fpl* du paradis.

pearly king *n marchand des quatre-saisons cockney dont les vêtements sont ornés d'une profusion de boutons de nacre.*

pearly queen *n marchande des quatre-saisons cockney.*

pear-shaped *adj* en forme de poire, piriforme *lit*.

peasant ['peznt] ◇ *n* -**1.** paysan *m*, -anne *f*; the Peasants' Revolt *Br* HIST la guerre des Gueux. -**2.** *inf pej* [uncouth person] péquenaud *m*, -e *f*, plouc *m*.
◇ *adj* paysan; ~ farmer paysan.

THE PEASANTS' REVOLT:
Première grande révolte populaire de l'histoire d'Angleterre, en 1381, provoquée par la mise en vigueur de la capitation. Son meneur, Wat Tyler, fut assassiné lors de pourparlers avec le roi Richard II et la révolte s'éteignit sans avoir apporté de changements.

---

peasantry ['pezntrɪ] *n* paysannerie *f*, paysans *mpl*.

pease [piːz] (*pl inv*) *n Br arch* OR *dial* (petit) pois *m*.

pease pudding *n purée de pois au jambon.*

peashooter ['piːˌʃuːtəʳ] *n* sarbacane *f*.

pea souper [-'suːpəʳ] *n* -**1.** [fog] purée *f* de pois. -**2.** ▽ *Can terme injurieux désignant un Québécois*

peat [piːt] *n* tourbe *f*.

peat bog *n* tourbière *f*.

peat moss *n* sphaigne *f*.

peaty ['piːtɪ] (*compar* peatier, *superl* peatiest) *adj* tourbeux.

pebble ['pebl] ◇ *n* -**1.** [stone] caillou *m*; [water worn] galet *m*; a ~ beach une plage de galets ❑ he's not the only ~ on the beach un de perdu, dix de retrouvés. -**2.** OPT [lens] lentille *f* en cristal de roche; ~ glasses *inf* lunettes *fpl* à verres très épais.
◇ *vt* -**1.** [road, path] caillouter; a ~d drive une allée de gravillons. -**2.** [leather] greneler.

pebble-dash *Br* ◇ *n* crépi *m (incrusté de cailloux)*.
◇ *vt* crépir.

pebbly ['pebli] (*compar* **pebblier**, *superl* **pebbliest**) *adj* **-1.** [stony - soil, path] caillouteux; a ~ beach une plage de galets. **-2.** [grainy] grené, grenu.

pecan [prɪ'kæn] ◇ *n* [nut] (noix *f* de) pecan *m*, (noix *f* de) pacane *f*; [tree] pacanier *m*.
◇ *adj* [pie, ice cream] à la noix de pecan.

peccadillo [,pekə'dɪləʊ] (*pl* **peccadillos** OR **peccadilloes**) *n* peccadille *f*.

peccary ['pekərɪ] (*pl inv* OR **peccaries**) *n* pécari *m*.

peck [pek] ◇ *vt* **-1.** [pick up] picorer, picoter; [strike with beak] donner un coup de bec à; **chickens were ~ing the ground** des poulets picoraient le sol; **be careful, it'll ~ you!** fais attention, tu vas recevoir un coup de bec! **-2.** [kiss] faire une bise à.
◇ *n* **-1.** [with beak] coup *m* de bec. **-2.** [kiss] bise *f*, (petit) baiser *m*; **she gave me a ~ on the forehead** elle m'a fait une bise sur le front. **-3.** [measure] ≃ boisseau *m*.
◆ **peck at** *vt insep* **-1.** = **peck** *vt* **1. -2. to ~ at one's food** manger du bout des dents.

pecker ['pekə^r] *n* **-1.** *Br* [spirits]: **keep your ~ up** *inf* il faut garder le moral. **-2.** ▽ *Am* [penis] quéquette *f*.

pecking order ['pekɪŋ-] *n* [among birds] ordre *m* hiérarchique; [among people] hiérarchie *f*.

peckish *inf* ['pekɪʃ] *adj esp Br*: **to be** OR **to feel ~** avoir un petit creux; **it made me feel quite ~** ça m'a donné bien faim OR bien ouvert l'appétit.

pectic ['pektɪk] *adj* pectique; **~ acid** acide *m* pectique.

pectin ['pektɪn] *n* pectine *f*.

pectoral ['pektərəl] ◇ *adj* MIL & RELIG pectoral.
◇ *n* ANAT, MIL & RELIG pectoral *m*.

pectoral fin *n* nageoire *f* pectorale.

pectoral muscle *n* muscle *m* pectoral.

peculate ['pekjʊleɪt] *vi fml* détourner les fonds OR deniers publics.

peculation [,pekjʊ'leɪʃn] *n fml* détournement *m* de fonds publics.

peculiar [prɪ'kjuːljə^r] *adj* **-1.** [strange] étrange, bizarre; **what a ~ person!** quelle personne étrange!; **I feel a bit ~** je me sens un peu bizarre. **-2.** [specific, exclusive] particulier; **it has a ~ taste all of its own** ça a un goût spécial; **to be ~ to** être spécifique à; **such phenomena are not ~ to this country** de tels phénomènes ne sont pas spécifiques à ce pays, il n'y a pas que dans ce pays que de tels phénomènes se produisent ‖ [particular] spécial, particulier; **a detail of ~ significance** un détail particulièrement significatif.

peculiarity [pɪ,kjuːlɪ'ærətɪ] (*pl* **peculiarities**) *n* **-1.** [oddness] étrangeté *f*, bizarrerie *f*; **I should explain the ~ of my situation** il faut que je vous explique ce qu'il y a d'étrange dans ma situation; **we all have our little peculiarities** nous avons tous nos petites manies. **-2.** [specific characteristic] particularité *f*; **each region has its own peculiarities** chaque région a son particularisme OR ses particularités.

peculiarly [prɪ'kjuːljəlɪ] *adv* **-1.** [oddly] de manière étrange, bizarrement. **-2.** [especially] particulièrement, singulièrement.

pecuniary [prɪ'kjuːnjərɪ] *adj* pécuniaire.

pedagogic(al) [,pedə'gɒdʒɪk(l)] *adj* pédagogique.

pedagogue ['pedəgɒg] *n arch* OR *fml* pédagogue.

pedagogy ['pedəgɒdʒɪ] *n* pédagogie *f*.

pedal [pedl] (*Br pt & pp* **pedalled**, *cont* **pedalling**, *Am pt & pp* **pedaled**, *cont* **pedaling**) ◇ *n* pédale *f*; **clutch/brake ~** pédale d'embrayage/de frein; **loud/soft ~** [of piano] pédale droite OR forte/gauche OR douce.
◇ *vi* pédaler; **we pedalled along the back roads** nous roulions (à bicyclette) sur les routes de l'arrière-pays; **it's hard pedalling uphill** c'est dur de grimper une côte à bicyclette OR à vélo.
◇ *vt* faire avancer en pédalant.

pedal bin *n Br* poubelle *f* à pédale.

pedal boat *n* pédalo *m*.

pedal car *n* voiture *f* à pédales.

pedalo ['pedələʊ] (*pl* **pedalos** OR **pedaloes**) *n* pédalo *m*.

pedal point *n* MUS pédale *f*.

pedal pushers *npl* (pantalon *m*) corsaire *m*.

pedant ['pedənt] *n* pédant *m*, -e *f*.

pedantic [prɪ'dæntɪk] *adj* pédant.

pedantically [prɪ'dæntɪklɪ] *adv* de manière pédante, avec pédantisme.

pedantry ['pedəntrɪ] (*pl* **pedantries**) *n* **-1.** [behaviour] pédantisme *m*, pédanterie *f*. **-2.** [remark] pédanterie *f*.

peddle ['pedl] ◇ *vt* **-1.** *dated* [wares] colporter; **he didn't want to ~ encyclopedias all his life** il ne voulait pas passer sa vie à faire du porte à porte pour vendre des encyclopédies. **-2.** [drugs] revendre, faire le trafic de; **drug peddling** trafic *m* de drogue. **-3.** *pej* [promote - idea, opinion] propager; [- gossip, scandal] colporter.
◇ *vi* faire du colportage.

peddler ['pedlə^r] *n* **-1.** [seller] colporteur *m*, -euse *f*. **-2.** [drug pusher] trafiquant *m*, -e *f* (de drogue), revendeur *m*, -euse *f*. **-3.** *pej* [promoter - of ideas, opinions] propagateur *m*, -trice *f*; **~s of dreams** marchands *mpl* de rêves.

pederast ['pedəræst] *n* pédéraste *m*.

pederasty ['pedəræstɪ] *n* pédérastie *f*.

pedestal ['pedɪstl] ◇ *n literal* & *fig* piédestal *m*; **to place** OR **to put sb on a ~** mettre qqn sur un piédestal; **that knocked him off his ~** cela l'a fait tomber de son piédestal.
◇ *comp*: **~ basin** lavabo *m* à pied; **~ desk** bureau *m* ministre; **~ table** guéridon *m*.

pedestrian [prɪ'destrɪən] ◇ *n* piéton *m*; **'~s only'** 'réservé aux piétons'.
◇ *adj* **-1.** [prosaic] prosaïque; [commonplace] banal; **a ~ style** un style prosaïque. **-2.** [done on foot - exercise, outing] pédestre, à pied.
◇ *comp* [street, area] piéton, piétonnier; **~ overpass** passerelle *f*.

pedestrian crossing *n Br* passage *m* clouté OR pour piétons.

pedestrianization [pə,destrɪənaɪ'zeɪʃn] *n* transformation *f* en zone piétonne OR piétonnière.

pedestrianize, -ise [pə'destrɪənaɪz] *vt* transformer en zone piétonne OR piétonnière; **~d streets** rues *fpl* piétonnes OR piétonnières.

pedestrian precinct *Br*, **pedestrian zone** *Am n* zone *f* piétonnière.

pediatric [,piːdɪ'ætrɪk] *adj* pédiatrique.

pediatrician [,piːdɪə'trɪʃn] *n* pédiatre.

pediatrics [,piːdɪ'ætrɪks] *n* pédiatrie.

pedicab ['pedɪkæb] *n* cyclo-pousse *m inv*.

pedicure ['pedɪ,kjʊə^r] *n* [treatment] pédicurie *f*.

pedigree ['pedɪgriː] ◇ *n* **-1.** [descent - of animal] pedigree *m*; [- of person] ascendance *f*, lignée *f*; *fig* [background - of person] origine *f*; **his solid middle-class ~** ses origines bourgeoises. **-2.** [document for animal] pedigree *m*. **-3.** [genealogical table] arbre *m* généalogique.
◇ *adj* [horse, cat, dog] de race.

pediment ['pedɪmənt] *n* **-1.** ARCHIT fronton *m*. **-2.** GEOL pédiment *m*.

pedlar ['pedlə^r] = **peddler**.

pedology [prɪ'dɒlədʒɪ] *n* **-1.** MED pédologie *f*. **-2.** GEOL pédologie *f*.

pedometer [prɪ'dɒmɪtə^r] *n* pédomètre *m*, podomètre *m*.

pedophile ['piːdəʊ,faɪl] *n* pédophile *m*.

pedophilia [,piːdəʊ'fɪlɪə] *n* pédophilie *f*.

peduncle [prɪ'dʌŋkl] *n* pédoncule *m*.

pee *inf* [piː] ◇ *n* pipi *m*; **to have** OR **to take a ~** faire pipi.
◇ *vi* faire pipi.

peek [piːk] ◇ *vi* [glance] jeter un coup d'œil; [look furtively] regarder furtivement; **to ~ at sthg** jeter un coup d'œil à OR sur qqch; **someone was ~ing through the keyhole** quelqu'un regardait par le trou de la serrure; **turn around and no ~ing!** retourne-toi et n'essaie pas de voir ce que je fais!
◇ *n* coup *m* d'œil; **to have** OR **to take a ~ at sthg** jeter un coup d'œil à OR sur qqch.

peekaboo *inf* ['piːkəbuː] ◇ *interj*: **~!** coucou!
◇ *n*: **to play ~** jouer à faire coucou.
◇ *adj* [see-through] transparent.

peel [piːl] ◇ *n* **-1.** [of banana] peau *f*; [of orange, lemon] écorce *f*; [of apple, onion, potato] pelure *f*. **-2.** *(U)* [peeling] épluchures *fpl*; **add a twist of lemon ~** ajouter un zeste de citron.
◇ *vt* [fruit, vegetable] peler, éplucher; [boiled egg] écaler, éplucher; [shrimp] décortiquer; [twig] écorcer; [skin, bark] enlever.
◇ *vi* **-1.** [fruit, vegetable] se peler. **-2.** [plaster on wall, ceiling etc] s'écailler, se craqueler; [paint, varnish] s'écailler; [wallpaper] se décoller. **-3.** [skin on back, face etc] peler; **I'm ~ing all over** je pèle de partout.
◆ **peel away** ◇ *vi insep* = **peel** *vi* **2**.
◇ *vt sep* [label, wallpaper] détacher, décoller; [bandage] enlever, ôter.
◆ **peel back** *vt sep* [label, wallpaper] détacher, décoller; **~ back the plastic backing** décoller la pellicule de protection en plastique.
◆ **peel off** ◇ *vi insep* **-1.** = **peel** *vi* **2. -2.** [turn away] se détacher; **two aircraft ~ed off from the main group** deux avions se détachèrent du gros de l'escadre.
◇ *vt sep* **-1.** = **peel away**. **-2.** [item of clothing] enlever; **to ~ off one's clothes** se déshabiller.

peeler ['piːlə^r] *n* **-1.** [device] éplucheur *m*; [electric] éplucheuse *f*; **potato ~** couteau-éplucheur *m*, économe *m*. **-2.** *inf Am* [stripper] effeuilleuse *f*. **-3.** *inf Br dated* flic *m*.

peelings ['piːlɪŋz] *npl* épluchures *fpl*, pelures *fpl*.

peep [piːp] ◇ *vi* **-1.** [glance] jeter un coup d'œil; **to ~ at/over/under sthg** jeter un coup d'œil (furtif) à/par-dessus/sous qqch; **the children were ~ing through the keyhole** les enfants épiaient à travers le trou de la serrure; **shut your eyes and don't ~!** ferme les yeux et n'essaie pas de voir ce que je fais! **-2.** [emerge] se montrer; **the moon ~ed out through the clouds** la lune a percé OR est apparue à travers les nuages; **snowdrops were beginning to ~ through** des perce-neiges commençaient à pointer; **a handkerchief ~ed out from his pocket** la pointe d'un mouchoir dépassait de sa poche; **her nose ~ed out over her scarf** le bout de son nez pointait OR apparaissait par-dessus son écharpe. **-3.** [bird] pépier.
◇ *n* **-1.** [glance] coup *m* d'œil; **to have a ~ at sthg** jeter un coup d'œil à qqch; **I got a ~ at the file before he came in** j'ai réussi à jeter un coup d'œil sur le dossier avant qu'il arrive. **-2.** [of bird] pépiement *m*; *fig*: **any news from Sam? — not a ~!** *inf* tu as eu des nouvelles de Sam? — pas un mot OR que dalle!; **one more ~ out of you and you've had it!** *inf* encore un mot et ton compte est bon!

peepbo *inf* ['piːp,bəʊ] ◇ *interj*: **~!** coucou!
◇ *n*: **to play ~** jouer à faire coucou.

peeper *inf* ['piːpə^r] *n Am* [detective] privé *m*.
◆ **peepers** *inf npl* [eyes] mirettes *fpl*.

peephole ['piːphəʊl] *n* trou *m*; [in house door, cell] judas *m*.

peeping Tom [,piːpɪŋ'tɒm] *n* voyeur *m*.

peepshow ['piːpʃəʊ] *n* [device] stéréoscope *m* *(pour images érotiques)*; [form of entertainment] peep-show *m*.

peep-toe(d) shoes *npl* escarpins *mpl* à bout découpé.

peer [pɪə^r] ◇ *n* **-1.** [nobleman] pair *m*, noble *mf*; **he was made a ~** il a été élevé à la pairie; **the Conservative Peers** POL les pairs conservateurs *(en Grande-Bretagne)*; **~ of the realm** pair du royaume. **-2.** [equal] pair *m*; **a jury of one's ~s** un jury formé OR composé de ses pairs; **as a negotiator she has no ~** c'est une négociatrice hors pair.
◇ *vi* [look - intently] regarder attentivement; [- with difficulty] s'efforcer de voir; **she ~ed out into the darkness** elle scruta l'obscurité; **he ~ed at the suspects' faces** il dévisagea les suspects; **she ~ed at the small print** elle lut attentivement ce qui était écrit en petits caractères.

peerage ['pɪərɪdʒ] *n* -**1.** [title] pairie *f*; life ~ pairie à vie; he was given a ~ il a été élevé à la pairie. -**2.** [body of peers] pairs *mpl*, noblesse *f*. -**3.** [book] nobiliaire *m*.

peeress ['pɪərɪs] *n* pairesse *f*.

peer group *n* SOCIOL pairs *mpl*.

peerless ['pɪəlɪs] *adj* sans pareil.

peer pressure *n* influence *f* des pairs OR du groupe.

peeve *inf* [pi:v] *vt* mettre en rogne; it really ~s me that he got the job ça me met en rogne qu'il ait eu le poste.

peeved *inf* [pi:vd] *adj* énervé; to be ~ at sb être en rogne OR en pétard contre qqn; to get ~ se mettre en rogne.

peevish ['pi:vɪʃ] *adj* [person] irritable, grincheux; [report, expression] irrité; in a ~ mood de mauvaise humeur; he's a ~ child c'est un enfant grognon.

peevishly ['pi:vɪʃlɪ] *adv* [say, refuse] d'un ton irrité; [behave] de façon désagréable; to complain ~ ronchonner.

peevishness ['pi:vɪʃnɪs] *n* mauvaise humeur *f*, irritabilité *f*.

peewit ['pi:wɪt] *n* vanneau *m*.

peg [peg] (*pt* & *pp* pegged, *cont* pegging) ◇ *n* -**1.** [for hat, coat] patère *f*; a ~ to hang an argument on *fig* un prétexte de dispute, une excuse pour se disputer. -**2.** *Br* [clothespeg] pince *f* à linge. -**3.** [dowel - wooden] cheville *f*; [- metal] fiche *f*. -**4.** [for tent] piquet *m*. -**5.** [in mountaineering] piton *m*. -**6.** [in croquet] piquet *m*. -**7.** MUS [on string instrument] cheville *f*. -**8.** *fig* [degree, notch] degré *m*, cran *m*; she's gone down a ~ (or two) in my estimation elle a baissé d'un cran dans mon estime ❑ to bring OR to take sb down a ~ or two rabattre le caquet à qqn. -**9.** *inf Br* [of spirits] petit verre *m*.
◇ *vt* -**1.** [fasten - gen] attacher; [- with dowels] cheviller; [insert - stake] enfoncer, planter; [in mountaineering] pitonner; he was pegging the washing on the line il étendait le linge; to ~ a tent fixer une tente avec des piquets. -**2.** [set - price, increase] fixer; oil was pegged at $20 a barrel le prix du pétrole était fixé à 20 dollars le baril; export earnings are pegged to the exchange rate le revenu des exportations varie en fonction du taux de change. -**3.** *inf* [throw] lancer. -**4.** *inf Am* [classify] classer.
◆ **peg away** *inf vi insep Br* travailler sans relâche; he pegged away at his job for years il a galéré dans son boulot pendant des années; we're pegging away at the backlog petit à petit, nous rattrapons notre retard; she pegged away at her Latin elle bûchait son latin.
◆ **peg down** *vt sep* [fasten down] fixer OR attacher (avec des piquets); he pegged the tarpaulin down il fixa la bâche au sol avec des piquets.
◆ **peg out** ◇ *vt sep* -**1.** [hang out - washing] étendre. -**2.** [mark out with pegs] piqueter.
◇ *vi insep inf* -**1.** [die] crever, claquer. -**2.** [give up] laisser tomber, abandonner.

Pegasus ['pegəsəs] *pr n* Pégase.

pegboard ['pegbɔ:d] *n* plaquette *f* perforée *(utilisée dans certains jeux)*.

peg leg *inf n* jambe *f* artificielle.

peg-top trousers *npl* (pantalon *m*) fuseau *m*.

PEI *written abbr of* Prince Edward Island.

pejoration [,pi:dʒə'reɪʃn] *n* LING péjoration *f*.

pejorative [pɪ'dʒɒrətɪv] ◇ *adj* péjoratif.
◇ *n* péjoratif *m*.

pejoratively [pɪ'dʒɒrətɪvlɪ] *adv* péjorativement.

peke *inf* [pi:k] *n* pékinois *m (chien)*.

Pekinese [,pi:kə'ni:z], **Pekingese** [,pi:kɪŋ'i:z] ◇ *n* -**1.** [person] Pékinois *m*, -e *f*. -**2.** LING pékinois *m*. -**3.** [dog] pékinois *m*.
◇ *adj* pékinois.

Peking [,pi:'kɪŋ] *pr n* Pékin.

pekoe ['pi:kəʊ] *n* pekoe *m*.

pelagic [pe'lædʒɪk] *adj* -**1.** [fauna, sediment] pélagique. -**2.** [not coastal] hauturier, de haute mer.

pelargonium [,pelə'gəʊnjəm] *n* pélargonium *m*.

pelf [pelf] *n pej* lucre *m*.

pelican ['pelɪkən] *n* pélican *m*.

pelican crossing *n Br passage piétons à commande manuelle*.

pellagra [pə'lægrə] *n* pellagre *f*.

pellet ['pelɪt] *n* -**1.** [small ball] boulette *f*; wax/paper ~s boulettes de cire/de papier; ~s of rabbit dung crottes *fpl* de lapin. -**2.** [for gun] (grain *m* de) plomb *m*; ~ gun fusil *m* à plombs. -**3.** [pill] pilule *f*. -**4.** ORNITH pelote *f* de régurgitation.

pell-mell [,pel'mel] *adv Br* [pile, throw] pêle-mêle; the crowd ran ~ into the square la foule s'est ruée sur la place dans une cohue indescriptible.

pellucid [pe'lu:sɪd] *adj* [membrane, zone] pellucide; [water] limpide; *fig* [prose] clair, limpide.

pelmanism ['pelmənɪzm] *n* [card game] paires *fpl*.

pelmet ['pelmɪt] *n* [for curtains] cantonnière *f*; [wood, board] lambrequin *m*.

Peloponnese [,peləpə'ni:z] *pr n*: the ~ le Péloponnèse.

Pelops ['pi:lɒps] *pr n* Pélops.

pelota [pə'lɒtə] *n* pelote *f* basque.

pelt [pelt] ◇ *vt* [person, target] bombarder; they were ~ing each other with snowballs ils se lançaient des boules de neige; the speaker was ~ed with eggs l'orateur a été bombardé d'œufs.
◇ *vi inf* -**1.** [rain]: it was ~ing OR ~ing down with rain il pleuvait à verse, il tombait des cordes; the hail ~ed down la grêle tombait dru; I changed the tyre in the ~ing rain j'ai changé le pneu sous la pluie battante. -**2.** [run] courir à fond de train OR à toute allure; she came ~ing up the stairs elle grimpa l'escalier quatre à quatre; she came ~ing down the stairs elle dévala l'escalier.
◇ *n* -**1.** [skin] peau *f*; [fur] fourrure *f*. -**2.** *Br phr*: at full ~ à fond de train.

pelvic ['pelvɪk] *adj* pelvien.

pelvic girdle *n* ceinture *f* pelvienne.

pelvic inflammatory disease *n* métrite *f*.

pelvis ['pelvɪs] (*pl* pelvises OR pelves [-vi:z]) *n* bassin *m*, pelvis *m*.

pen [pen] (*pt* & *pp sense 1* penned, *pt* & *pp sense 2* penned OR pent [pent], *cont* penning) ◇ *n* -**1.** [for writing] stylo *m*; another novel from the ~ of Hilary Ratcliff un nouveau roman sous la plume de Hilary Ratcliff; she lives by her ~ elle vit de sa plume; to put ~ to paper écrire, prendre sa plume ❑ ball point ~ stylo à bille; fountain ~ stylo à plume; a slip of the ~ un lapsus; the ~ is mightier than the sword *prov* un coup de langue est pire qu'un coup de lance *prov*. -**2.** [of squid] plume *f*. -**3.** [female swan] cygne *m* femelle. -**4.** [for animals] enclos *m*, parc *m*; sheep ~ parc à moutons. -**5.** (submarine) ~ bassin *m* protégé. -**6.** *inf Am* (*abbr of* penitentiary) taule *f*, tôle *f*; he spent ten years in the ~ il a passé dix ans en taule, il a fait dix ans de taule.
◇ *vt* -**1.** [write] écrire; a letter penned in a childish hand une lettre d'une écriture enfantine. -**2.** [enclose]: to ~ in OR up [livestock] parquer, enfermer dans un enclos; [dog] enfermer; [person] enfermer, cloîtrer, claquemurer.

penal ['pi:nl] *adj* -**1.** [law] pénal; [establishment] pénitentiaire; ~ offence infraction *f* pénale. -**2.** [severe - taxation, fine] écrasant.

penal code *n* code *m* pénal.

penal colony *n* colonie *f* pénitentiaire, bagne *m*.

penalization [,pi:nəlaɪ'zeɪʃn] *n* pénalisation *f*, sanction *f*.

penalize, -ise ['pi:nəlaɪz] *vt* -**1.** [punish] pénaliser, sanctionner. -**2.** [disadvantage] pénaliser, défavoriser, désavantager; the new tax ~s large families le nouvel impôt pénalise les familles nombreuses.

penal servitude *n* travaux *mpl* forcés, bagne *m*.

penal settlement = **penal colony**.

penalty ['penltɪ] (*pl* penalties) *n* -**1.** JUR peine *f*; on ~ of sous peine de; under ~ of death sous peine de mort; they advocate stiffer penalties for drunk driving ils préconisent des peines plus lourdes pour conduite en état d'ivresse; the ~ for that offence is six months' imprisonment la peine encourue pour ce délit est de six mois d'emprisonnement; '~ for improper use: £25' 'tout abus est passible d'une amende de 25 livres'. -**2.** ADMIN & COMM [for breaking contract] pénalité *f*, sanction *f*. -**3.** *fig* [unpleasant consequence]: to pay the ~ (for sthg) subir les conséquences (de qqch); that's the ~ for being famous c'est la rançon de la gloire. -**4.** SPORT [gen] pénalisation *f*; [kick - in football] penalty *m*; [- in rubgy] pénalité *f*; to score (from) a ~ [in football] marquer sur (un) penalty; a two-minute (time) ~ [in ice hockey] une pénalité de deux minutes.

penalty area *n* FTBL surface *f* de réparation.

penalty box *n* -**1.** [in football] = **penalty area**. -**2.** [in ice hockey] banc *m* de pénalité.

penalty clause *n* JUR clause *f* pénale.

penalty double *n* [in bridge] contre *m* de pénalité.

penalty goal *n* [in rugby] pénalité *f*.

penalty kick *n* [in football] penalty *m*; [in rugby] (coup *m* de pied de) pénalité *f*.

penalty points *npl* [in quiz, game] gage *m*; [for drivers] points *mpl* de pénalité *(dans le système du permis à points)*.

penalty spot *n* [in football] point *m* de penalty OR de réparation.

penalty try *n* [in rugby] essai *m* de pénalisation.

penance ['penəns] *n* pénitence *f*; to do ~ for one's sins faire pénitence.

pen-and-ink drawing *n* dessin *m* à la plume.

pence [pens] *n* (*pl of* penny) pence *mpl*.

penchant [*Br* pɑ̃ʃɑ̃, *Am* 'pentʃənt] *n* penchant *m*, goût *m*; to have a ~ for sthg avoir un faible pour qqch.

pencil ['pensl] (*Br pt* & *pp* pencilled, *cont* pencilling, *Am pt* & *pp* penciled, *cont* penciling) ◇ *n* -**1.** [for writing, makeup] crayon *m*; a box of coloured ~s une boîte de crayons de couleur; the corrections are in ~ les corrections sont (faites) au crayon ❑ ~ box plumier *m*; ~ case trousse *f*; ~ sharpener taille-crayon *m*. -**2.** *fig* [narrow beam]: a ~ of light un pinceau de lumière.
◇ *comp* au crayon; a ~ sketch un croquis au crayon.
◇ *vt* écrire au crayon; [hastily] crayonner; question marks were pencilled in the margin on avait mis des points d'interrogation au crayon dans la marge; to ~ one's eyebrows se dessiner les sourcils (au crayon).
◆ **pencil in** *vt sep* [date, name, address] noter OR inscrire au crayon; *fig* fixer provisoirement; I'll ~ the meeting/you in for June 6th retenons provisoirement la date du 6 juin pour la réunion/notre rendez-vous.

pendant ['pendənt] ◇ *n* -**1.** [necklace] pendentif *m*. -**2.** [piece of jewellery - on necklace] pendentif *m*; [- on earring] pendeloque *f*; ~ earrings pendants *mpl* d'oreille. -**3.** [chandelier] lustre *m*.
◇ *adj* = **pendent**.

pendent ['pendənt] *adj fml* -**1.** [hanging] pendant, qui pend. -**2.** [overhanging] en surplomb, en saillie.

pending ['pendɪŋ] ◇ *adj* -**1.** [waiting to be settled - gen] en attente; JUR en instance, pendant; a ~ court case une affaire en instance OR en cours. -**2.** [imminent] imminent; a merger is ~ une fusion est imminente.
◇ *prep* en attendant.

pending tray *n Br* corbeille *f* des dossiers en attente; mail is piling up in the ~ le courrier en attente s'accumule.

pendulous ['pendjʊləs] *adj lit* -**1.** [sagging - breasts] tombant; [- lips] pendant. -**2.** [swinging] oscillant.

pendulum ['pendjʊləm] *n* pendule *m*; [in clock] balancier *m*; a swing of the ~ sent the president's popularity plummeting *fig* un revirement de l'opinion a fait chuter la cote de popularité du président; the ~ of fashion has swung back to a sixties look la mode des années soixante est revenue au goût du jour.
Penelope [pə'neləpɪ] *pr n* Pénélope.
peneplain, peneplane ['piːnɪpleɪn] *n* pénéplaine *f*.
penetrate ['penɪtreɪt] ◇ *vt* -**1.** [find way into or through - jungle] pénétrer dans; [- blockade, enemy defences] pénétrer; they ~d unknown territory ils ont pénétré en territoire inconnu; it's not easy to ~ Parisian society il n'est pas facile de s'introduire dans la société parisienne. -**2.** [infiltrate - party, movement] s'infiltrer dans, noyauter; ~d by an informer infiltré par un indicateur. -**3.** [pierce - subj: missile] percer, transpercer; the bullet ~d his right lung la balle lui a perforé le poumon droit. -**4.** [pass through - subj: sound, light etc] traverser, transpercer; the child's cries ~d the silence les cris de l'enfant déchiraient le silence; the cold wind ~d her clothing le vent glacial passait à travers ses vêtements; the ship's lights failed to ~ the fog les lumières du bateau ne parvenaient pas à percer le brouillard. -**5.** COMM s'introduire sur; to ~ the market faire une percée sur OR s'introduire sur le marché. -**6.** [see through - darkness, disguise, mystery] percer; to ~ sb's thoughts lire dans les pensées de qqn. -**7.** [sexually] pénétrer.
◇ *vi* -**1.** [break through] pénétrer; the troops ~d deep into enemy territory les troupes ont pénétré très avant en territoire ennemi. -**2.** [sink in]: I heard what you said but it didn't ~ at the time j'ai entendu ce que tu as dit, mais je n'ai pas saisi sur le moment; I had to explain it to him several times before it finally ~d j'ai dû le lui expliquer plusieurs fois avant qu'il (ne) finisse par comprendre.
penetrating ['penɪtreɪtɪŋ] *adj* -**1.** [sound - pleasant] pénétrant; [- unpleasant] perçant. -**2.** [cold] pénétrant, perçant; [rain] pénétrant. -**3.** [look, mind, question] pénétrant; she had ~ eyes elle avait un regard pénétrant.
penetratingly ['penɪtreɪtɪŋlɪ] *adv* -**1.** [loudly]: to scream ~ pousser un cri perçant; to whistle ~ émettre un sifflement strident. -**2.** *fig* avec perspicacité; she looked at him ~ elle lui lança un regard pénétrant OR aigu.
penetration [ˌpenɪ'treɪʃn] *n* -**1.** [gen & COMM] pénétration *f*. -**2.** MIL percée *f*. -**3.** PHOT profondeur *f* de champ.
penetrative ['penɪtrətɪv] *adj* [force] de pénétration; ~ sex pénétration *f*.
pen friend *n Br* correspondant *m*, -e *f (épistolaire)*.
penguin ['peŋgwɪn] *n* manchot *m*.
penholder ['penˌhəʊldəʳ] *n* porte-plume *m inv*.
penicillin [ˌpenɪ'sɪlɪn] *n* pénicilline *f*.
penile ['piːnaɪl] *adj* pénien.
peninsula [pə'nɪnsjʊlə] *n* [large] péninsule *f*; [small] presqu'île *f*.
peninsular [pə'nɪnsjʊləʳ] *adj* péninsulaire.
◆ **Peninsular** *adj*: the Peninsular War la guerre d'Espagne *(1808-1814)*.
penis ['piːnɪs] *(pl* penises OR penes [-ɪz]) *n* pénis *m*.
penis envy *n* envie *f* du pénis.
penitence ['penɪtəns] *n* pénitence *f*.
penitent ['penɪtənt] ◇ *adj* -**1.** [gen] contrit. -**2.** RELIG pénitent.
◇ *n* RELIG pénitent *m*, -e *f*.
penitential [ˌpenɪ'tenʃl] ◇ *adj* pénitentiel.
◇ *n* [book] pénitentiel *m*.
penitentiary [ˌpenɪ'tenʃərɪ] *(pl* penitentiaries) ◇ *n* -**1.** *Am* [prison] prison *f*. -**2.** RELIG [priest] pénitencier *m*.
◇ *adj* -**1.** *Am* [life, conditions] pénitentiaire; [offence] passible d'une peine de prison; ~ guard gardien *m*, -enne *f* de prison. -**2.** = **penitential**.
◆ **Penitentiary** *n* RELIG: the Penitentiary [cardinal] le grand pénitencier; [tribunal] la Sacrée Pénitencerie, la Pénitencerie apostolique.
penitently ['penɪtəntlɪ] *adv* [say] d'un ton contrit; [submit, kneel] avec contrition.
penknife ['pennaɪf] *(pl* penknives [-naɪvz]) *n* canif *m*.
penlight ['penlaɪt] *n* lampe-stylo *f*, minitorche *f*.
penmanship ['penmənʃɪp] *n* calligraphie *f*.
penna ['penə] *(pl* pennae [-niː]) *n* penne *f*.
pen name *n* nom *m* de plume, pseudonyme *m*.
pennant ['penənt] *n* -**1.** [flag - gen] fanion *m*. -**2.** NAUT [for identification] flamme *f*; [for signalling] pavillon *m*. -**3.** *Am* SPORT *drapeau servant de trophée dans certains championnats*; to win the ~ remporter le championnat.
pen nib *n* plume *f (de stylo)*.
penniless ['penɪlɪs] *adj* sans le sou; they're absolutely ~ ils n'ont pas un sou; the stock market crash left him ~ le krach boursier l'a mis sur la paille.
Pennines ['penaɪnz] *pl pr n*: the ~ Les Pennines *fpl*.
Pennine Way ['penaɪn-] *pr n*: the ~ *sentier de grande randonnée qui suit la crête des Pennines*.
pennon ['penən] *n* -**1.** [flag - gen] fanion *m*; [- on lance] pennon *m*. -**2.** NAUT [for identification] flamme *f*; [for signalling] pavillon *m*.
Pennsylvania [ˌpensɪl'veɪnjə] *pr n* Pennsylvanie *f*; in ~ en Pennsylvanie.
Pennsylvania Avenue *pr n*: 1600 ~ *adresse de la Maison Blanche, utilisée par les médias américains pour faire référence au gouvernement*.
penny ['penɪ] *(pl sense 1* pence [pens], *pl sense 2* pennies) *n* -**1.** [unit of currency - in Britain, Ireland] penny *m*; it cost me 44 pence ça m'a coûté 44 pence. -**2.** [coin - in Britain, Ireland] penny *m*, pièce *f* d'un penny; [- in US] cent *m*, pièce *f* d'un cent; it was expensive, but it was worth every ~ c'était cher, mais j'en ai vraiment eu pour mon argent; it won't cost you a ~ ça ne vous coûtera pas un centime OR un sou; every ~ counts un sou est un sou ❑ they haven't got a ~ to their name OR two pennies to rub together ils n'ont pas un sou vaillant; to earn an honest ~ gagner honnêtement sa vie; people like him are two OR ten a ~ *inf Br* des gens comme lui, ce n'est pas ça qui manque; a ~ for your thoughts à quoi penses-tu?; suddenly the ~ dropped *inf Br* d'un seul coup ça a fait tilt; he keeps turning up like a bad ~ *inf Br* c'est un vrai pot de colle; in for a ~ in for a pound *prov* quand le vin est tiré, il faut le boire *prov*; take care of the pennies and the pounds will take care of themselves *prov* les petits ruisseaux font les grandes rivières *prov*.
penny arcade *n Am* galerie *f* de jeux.
Penny Black *n premier timbre-poste britannique*.
penny dreadful *inf n Br dated* [novel] *roman d'amour ou d'aventures à quatre sous*; [magazine] magazine *m* à sensation.
penny-farthing *n Br* bicycle *m*, vélocipède *m*.
penny loafers *npl Am* mocassins *mpl*.
penny-pincher *inf* [-ˌpɪntʃəʳ] *n* pingre *mf*, radin *m*, -e *f*.
penny-pinching *inf* [-ˌpɪntʃɪŋ] ◇ *n* économies *fpl* de bouts de chandelle; government ~ will ruin the education system à force de serrer les cordons de la bourse, le gouvernement finira par étrangler le système éducatif.
◇ *adj* qui fait des économies de bouts de chandelle, pingre, radin.
pennyweight ['penɪweɪt] *n Br* ≃ 1,5 grammes.
penny whistle *n* pipeau *m*.
penny wise *adj phr*: to be ~ and pound foolish chipoter sur les petites dépenses sans regarder aux grandes.
pennyworth ['penɪwɜːθ, 'penəθ] *(pl inv* OR pennyworths) *n* -**1.** *literal & dated*: she asked for a ~ of toffees elle demanda pour un penny de caramels. -**2.** *Br fig* [small quantity]: if he had a ~ of sense s'il avait une once de bon sens.
penology [piː'nɒlədʒɪ] *n* pénologie *f*.
pen pal *inf n* correspondant *m*, -e *f* (épistolaire).
pen pusher *n pej* gratte-papier *m inv*.
pen pushing *n pej* travail *m* de bureau; a ~ job un travail de gratte-papier.
pension ['penʃn, *sense 2 also* 'pɑ̃sjɔ̃] ◇ *n* -**1.** [for retired people] retraite *f*; [for disabled people] pension *f*; to draw a ~ [retired person] toucher une retraite; [disabled person] toucher une pension, être pensionné; to pay sb a ~ verser une pension à qqn ❑ disability ~ pension d'invalidité; widow's ~ [before retiring age] allocation *f* de veuvage; [at retiring age] pension de réversion. -**2.** [small hotel] pension *f* de famille.
◇ *vt* [for retirement] verser une pension de retraite à; [for disability] pensionner, verser une pension à.
◆ **pension off** *vt sep Br* -**1.** [person] mettre à la retraite. -**2.** *hum* [old car, machine] mettre au rancart.
pensionable ['penʃənəbl] *adj* -**1.** [person - gen] qui a droit à une pension; [- for retirement] qui a atteint l'âge de la retraite; teachers of ~ age les enseignants qui ont atteint l'âge de la retraite. -**2.** [job] qui donne droit à une retraite.
pension book *n* ≃ titre *m* de pension *(en Grande-Bretagne, carnet permettant de retirer sa pension de retraite)*.
pensioned ['penʃənd] *adj* retraité.
pensioner ['penʃənəʳ] *n Br*: (old age) ~ retraité *m*, -e *f*; war ~ ancien combattant *m (titulaire d'une pension militaire d'invalidité)*.
pension fund *n* caisse *f* de retraite.
pension plan, pension scheme *n* régime *m* de retraite.
pensive ['pensɪv] *adj* pensif, méditatif, songeur.
pensively ['pensɪvlɪ] *adv* pensivement.
pent [pent] *pt & pp* → **pen**.
pentacle ['pentəkl] *n* pentacle *m*.
pentagon ['pentəgən] *n* GEOM pentagone *m*.
◆ **Pentagon** *pr n* POL: the Pentagon le Pentagone.

PENTAGON:
Le Pentagone, immense bâtiment à cinq façades situé à Arlington, Virginia, abrite le ministère américain de la Défense; plus généralement, le terme désigne le pouvoir militaire américain.

pentagonal [pen'tægənl] *adj* pentagonal.
pentagram ['pentəgræm] *n* -**1.** GEOM pentagone *m* étoilé. -**2.** [in occultism] pentagramme *m*.
pentahedron [ˌpentə'hiːdrən] *(pl* pentahedrons OR pentahedra [-drə]) *n* pentaèdre *m*.
pentameter [pen'tæmɪtəʳ] ◇ *n* pentamètre *m*.
◇ *adj* pentamètre.
pentangle ['pentæŋgl] = **pentacle**.
Pentateuch ['pentətjuːk] *n*: the ~ le Pentateuque.
pentathlete [pen'tæθliːt] *n* pentathlonien *m*, -enne *f*.
pentathlon [pen'tæθln] *n* pentathlon *m*.
pentatonic scale [ˌpentə'tɒnɪk] *n* échelle *f* OR gamme *f* pentatonique.
pentavalent [ˌpentə'veɪlənt] *adj* pentavalent, quintivalent.
Pentecost ['pentɪkɒst] *n* Pentecôte *f*.
Pentecostal [ˌpentɪ'kɒstl] = **pentecostalist**.
Pentecostalism [ˌpentɪ'kɒstəlɪzm] *n* pentecôtisme *m*.
Pentecostalist [ˌpentɪ'kɒstəlɪst] ◇ *adj* pentecôtiste.
◇ *n* pentecôtiste *mf*.
penthouse ['penthaʊs, *pl* -haʊzɪz] *n* -**1.** [flat] *appartement luxueux avec terrasse généralement au dernier étage d'un immeuble*; ~ suite [in hotel] suite *f* avec terrasse. -**2.** [on roof]: elevator ~ machinerie *f* d'ascenseur *(installée sur un toit)*. -**3.** [doorway shelter] auvent *m*; [shed] appentis *m*.
pentode ['pentəʊd] *n* pentode *f*.
Pentonville ['pentənvɪl] *pr n*: ~ (Prison) *grande prison dans le nord de Londres*.

pentose ['pentəʊz] *n* pentose *m*.

pent-up *adj* [emotion] refoulé, réprimé; [force] contenu, réprimé; his anger is a product of ~ frustration sa colère vient de ce qu'il est frustré; to get rid of ~ energy se défouler; the children are full of ~ energy les enfants débordent d'énergie.

penultimate [pe'nʌltɪmət] ◇ *adj* -1. [gen] avant-dernier. -2. LING pénultième.
◇ *n* -1. [gen] avant-dernier *m*, -ère *f*. -2. LING pénultième *f*.

penumbra [pɪ'nʌmbrə] (*pl* penumbras OR penumbrae [-briː]) *n* pénombre *f* ASTRON & PHYS.

penurious [pɪ'njʊərɪəs] *adj fml* -1. [impoverished] indigent, sans ressources. -2. [miserly] parcimonieux, avare.

penury ['penjʊrɪ] *n fml* -1. [poverty] indigence *f*, dénuement *m*. -2. [scarcity] pénurie *f*.

peon ['piːɒn] *n* -1. AGR [in Latin America] péon *m*. -2. MIL [in India, Sri Lanka] fantassin *m*. -3. *inf Am* [worker] prolo *mf*.

peony ['pɪənɪ] (*pl* peonies) *n* pivoine *f*.

people ['piːpl] ◇ *npl* -1. [gen] personnes *fpl*, gens *mpl*; 500 ~ 500 personnes; there were ~ everywhere il y avait des gens OR du monde partout; how many ~ were there? combien de personnes y avait-il?; there were a lot of ~ there il y avait beaucoup de monde; some ~ think it's true certaines personnes OR certains pensent que c'est vrai; a lot of ~ think that... beaucoup de gens pensent que...; some ~ will believe anything! il y a des gens qui croiraient n'importe quoi!; I've talked to several ~ about it j'en ai parlé à plusieurs personnes; many/most ~ disagree beaucoup de gens/la plupart des gens ne sont pas d'accord ❑ really, some ~! il y a des gens, je vous jure!; are you ~ coming or not? et vous (autres), vous venez ou pas?; it's Meg of all ~! ça alors, c'est Meg!; you of all ~ should know that! si quelqu'un doit savoir ça, c'est bien toi! -2. [in indefinite uses] on; ~ won't like it les gens ne vont pas aimer ça; ~ say it's impossible on dit que c'est impossible; I don't want ~ to know about this je ne veux pas qu'on le sache OR que cela se sache. -3. [with qualifier] gens *mpl*; clever/sensitive ~ les gens intelligents/sensibles; rich/poor/blind ~ les riches/pauvres/aveugles; young ~ les jeunes; old ~ les personnes âgées; city/country ~ les citadins/campagnards; ~ who know her ceux qui la connaissent; ~ like you les gens comme toi; ~ of taste les gens de goût; ~ with large cars ceux qui ont de grandes voitures; they are nice ~ ce sont des gens sympathiques; nice ~ don't do that! les gens bien OR comme il faut ne font pas ce genre de chose!; they are theatre/circus ~ ce sont des gens de théâtre/du cirque ‖ [inhabitants, nationals]: Danish ~ les Danois; the ~ of Brazil les Brésiliens; the ~ of Glasgow les habitants de Glasgow; the ~ of Yorkshire les gens du Yorkshire ‖ [employed in a specified job]: I'll call the electricity/gas ~ tomorrow je téléphonerai à la compagnie d'électricité/de gaz demain; the President's financial ~ les conseillers financiers du Président. -4. POL: the ~ le peuple; the ~ are behind her le peuple la soutient OR est avec elle; power to the ~! le pouvoir au peuple!; a ~'s government/democracy un gouvernement/une démocratie populaire. -5. *dated* [family] famille *f*, parents *mpl*; her ~ emigrated in 1801 sa famille a émigré en 1801.
◇ *n* -1. [nation] peuple *m*, nation *f*; a seafaring ~ un peuple de marins. -2. [ethnic group] population *f*; the native ~s of Polynesia les populations indigènes OR autochtones de Polynésie; the French-speaking ~s les populations francophones.
◇ *vt* -1. *(usu passive)* [inhabit] peupler; the region is ~d by aborigines la région est peuplée d'aborigènes. -2. *fig*: the monsters that ~ his dreams les monstres qui hantent ses rêves.

people mover *n* [gen] système *m* de transport automatique; [moving pavement] trottoir *m* roulant.

People's Republic of China *pr n*: the ~ la République populaire de Chine.

pep *inf* [pep] (*pt* & *pp* pepped, *cont* pepping) *n* punch *m*; to have a lot of OR to be full of ~ avoir du punch.
◆ **pep up** *inf vt sep* -1. [person - depressed] remonter le moral à; [- ill, tired] requinquer, retaper; a cup of tea will soon ~ you up une tasse de thé aura vite fait de te ravigoter OR retaper. -2. [business] faire repartir, dynamiser; [party] remettre de l'entrain dans, dynamiser; [conversation] égayer, ranimer, relancer.

PEP [pep] (*abbr of* personal equity plan) *n plan d'investissement en actions bénéficiant de conditions fiscales avantageuses*.

peplum ['pepləm] (*pl* peplums OR pepla [-lə]) *n* -1. [on jacket] basque *f*. -2. [Roman tunic] peplum *m*.

pepper ['pepəʳ] ◇ *n* -1. [condiment] poivre *m*; black/white ~ poivre noir/blanc; ~ steak *Br* steak *m* au poivre. -2. [vegetable - sweet] poivron *m*; [- hot] piment *m*; ~ sauce sauce *f* aux piments; green/red ~ poivron *m* vert/rouge.
◇ *vt* -1. CULIN poivrer. -2. [scatter, sprinkle] émailler, parsemer; her text was ~ed with quotations son texte était émaillé de citations. -3. [pelt]: the walls were ~ed with lead shot les murs étaient criblés d'impacts de balles; they ~ed the houses with machine-gun fire ils ont mitraillé les maisons.

pepper-and-salt *adj* -1. [hair, beard] poivre et sel *(inv)*. -2. TEX marengo *(inv)*; ~ cloth marengo *m*.

pepperbox ['pepəbɒks] *n Am* poivrier *m*.

peppercorn ['pepəkɔːn] *n* grain *m* de poivre.

peppercorn rent *n Br* loyer *m* modique.

pepper mill *n* moulin *m* à poivre.

peppermint ['pepəmɪnt] ◇ *n* -1. BOT menthe *f* poivrée. -2. [sweet] bonbon *m* à la menthe.
◇ *adj* à la menthe; ~ tea thé *m* à la menthe; ~ OR ~-flavoured toothpaste dentifrice *m* au menthol.

pepperpot *n* poivrier *m* CULIN, poivrière *f* CULIN.

peppery ['pepərɪ] *adj* -1. CULIN poivré. -2. [quick-tempered] coléreux, irascible. -3. [incisive] mordant, piquant.

pep pill *inf n* stimulant *m*, excitant *m*.

peppy *inf* ['pepɪ] (*compar* peppier, *superl* peppiest) *adj* [person] qui a du punch.

pepsin(e) ['pepsɪn] *n* pepsine *f*.

pep talk *inf n* discours *m* d'encouragement; their boss gave them a ~ leur patron leur a dit quelques mots pour leur remonter le moral.

peptic ['peptɪk] *adj* peptique.

peptic ulcer *n* ulcère *m* gastro-duodénal.

peptone ['peptəʊn] *n* peptone *f*.

per [pɜːʳ] *prep* [for each] par; ~ person par personne; ~ head par tête; ~ day/week/month/year par jour/semaine/mois/an; we need five litres of water ~ person ~ day il nous faut cinq litres d'eau par personne et par jour; they are paid £6 ~ hour ils sont payés 6 livres de l'heure; 100 miles ~ hour ≃ 160 kilomètres à l'heure; it costs £8 ~ kilo ça coûte 8 livres le kilo; output ~ worker has increased la production individuelle des ouvriers a augmenté.
◆ **as per** *prep phr* suivant, selon; as ~ specifications [on bill] conformément aux spécifications requises; as ~ your letter conformément à votre lettre; the work is going ahead as ~ schedule le travail avance selon le calendrier prévu; as ~ normal OR usual *inf* comme d'habitude.

peradventure [pərəd'ventʃəʳ] *adv arch* par hasard, d'aventure *lit*.

perambulate [pə'ræmbjʊleɪt] ◇ *vi lit* OR *hum* se promener, (se) baguenauder.
◇ *vt* -1. [estate, boundary] inspecter. -2. [sea, region] parcourir.

perambulation [pəˌræmbjʊ'leɪʃn] *n lit* OR *fml* [stroll] promenade *f*.

per annum [pər'ænəm] *adv* par an, annuellement; $5,000 ~ 5 000 dollars par an.

P-E ratio (*abbr of* price-earnings ratio) *n* taux *m* de capitalisation bousière, PER *m*.

percale [pə'keɪl] *n* percale *f*; ~ sheets des draps en percale.

per capita [pə'kæpɪtə] *fml* ◇ *adj* par personne; ~ income is higher in the south le revenu par habitant est plus élevé dans le sud.
◇ *adv* par personne.

perceive [pə'siːv] *vt* -1. [see] distinguer; [hear, smell etc] percevoir; he was unable to ~ colours il était incapable de distinguer les couleurs; verbs of perceiving LING les verbes de perception. -2. [notice] s'apercevoir de, remarquer; few people ~d the differences peu de gens ont remarqué les différences. -3. [conceive, understand] percevoir, comprendre; their presence is ~d as a threat leur présence est perçue comme une menace.

per cent [pə'sent] (*pl inv*) ◇ *adv* pour cent; prices went up (by) 10 ~ les prix ont augmenté de 10 pour cent; it's 50 ~ cotton il y a 50 pour cent de coton, c'est du coton à 50 pour cent; a 9 ~ interest rate un taux d'intérêt à 9 pour cent; I'm a hundred ~ sure j'en suis absolument certain.
◇ *n* [percentage] pourcentage *m*.

percentage [pə'sentɪdʒ] *n* -1. [proportion] pourcentage *m*; a high ~ of the staff une grande partie du personnel. -2. [share of profits, investment] pourcentage *m*; to get a ~ on sthg toucher un pourcentage sur qqch. -3. *inf Br* [advantage] avantage *m*, intérêt *m*; there's no ~ in kicking up a fuss ça ne sert à rien de faire des histoires.

percentile [pə'sentaɪl] *n* centile *m*.

perceptible [pə'septəbl] *adj* perceptible.

perceptibly [pə'septəblɪ] *adv* [diminish, change] sensiblement; [move] de manière perceptible; she was ~ thinner elle avait sensiblement maigri.

perception [pə'sepʃn] *n* -1. [faculty] perception *f*; visual/aural ~ perception visuelle/auditive. -2. [notion, conception] perception *f*, conception *f*; her ~ of the problem is different from mine sa façon de voir le problème diffère de la mienne; the general public's ~ of the police l'image que le grand public a de la police. -3. [insight] perspicacité *f*, intuition *f*; a man of great ~ un homme très perspicace.

perceptive [pə'septɪv] *adj* -1. [observant - person] perspicace; [- remark] judicieux. -2. [sensitive] sensible. -3. [organ] sensoriel.

perceptiveness [pə'septɪvnɪs] *n* perspicacité *f*, pénétration *f*.

perceptual [pə'septjʊəl] *adj* [organ] percepteur.

perch [pɜːtʃ] (*pl sense 4 inv* OR perches) ◇ *n* -1. [for bird - in cage] perchoir *m*; [- on tree] branche *f*; the bird flew from its ~ on the roof l'oiseau s'envola du toit où il était perché. -2. *inf* [for person - seat] perchoir *m*; to be knocked from OR off one's ~ être détrôné, se faire détrôner. -3. [linear or square measure] ≃ perche *f*. -4. [fish] perche *f*.
◇ *vi* [bird, person] se percher; he ~ed on the edge of the table il se percha OR se jucha sur le bord de la table.
◇ *vt* [person, object] percher, jucher; he/the bucket was ~ed on the top of the ladder il/le seau était perché en haut de l'échelle.

perchance [pə'tʃɑːns] *adv arch* OR *lit* -1. [perhaps] peut-être. -2. [by accident] par hasard, fortuitement.

percipient [pə'sɪpɪənt] *adj* -1. *fml* [person] perspicace. -2. ANAT [organ] sensoriel.

percolate ['pɜːkəleɪt] ◇ *vi* -1. [liquid] filtrer, s'infiltrer; [coffee] passer; toxic chemicals had ~d through the soil des produits chimiques toxiques s'étaient infiltrés dans le sol. -2. [ideas, news] se répandre; his ideas ~d through to the rank and file ses idées ont gagné la base. -3. *inf Am* [be excited] être (tout) excité; he is percolating with joy il déborde de joie; she ~s with ideas elle bouillonne d'idées.
◇ *vt* [coffee] préparer *(avec une cafetière à pres-*

sion); I'll just ~ some coffee je vais faire du café; ~d coffee café fait avec une cafetière à pression.

percolator ['pɜːkəleɪtəʳ] *n* cafetière *f* à pression.

percuss [pə'kʌs] *vt* [gen & MED] percuter.

percussion [pə'kʌʃn] *n* -**1.** MUS percussion *f*; Jane Stowell on ~ aux percussions, Jane Stowell; the ~ section les percussions *fpl*. -**2.** [collision, shock] percussion *f*, choc *m*. -**3.** MED & MIL percussion *f*.

percussion cap *n* amorce *f* fulminante.

percussion instrument *n* MUS instrument *m* à percussion.

percussionist [pə'kʌʃənɪst] *n* MUS percussionniste *mf*.

percussion lock *n* percuteur *m*.

percussion tool *n* outil *m* à percussion.

percussive [pə'kʌsɪv] *adj* [instrument] à percussion; [force] de percussion.

per diem [,pɜː'diːem] *adj* & *adv fml* par jour.

perdition [pə'dɪʃn] *n* -**1.** *lit* [spiritual ruin] perdition *f*; [hell] enfer *m*, damnation *f*. -**2.** *arch* [ruin] perte *f*, ruine *f*.

peregrination [,perɪgrɪ'neɪʃn] *n* , **peregrinations** *npl lit* OR *hum* pérégrinations *fpl*.

peregrine falcon ['perɪgrɪn-] *n* faucon *m* pèlerin.

peremptorily [pə'remptrəlɪ] *adv* de façon péremptoire, impérieusement.

peremptory [pə'remptərɪ] *adj* -**1.** [tone, manner] péremptoire; there was a ~ knock at the door on a frappé à la porte de façon péremptoire. -**2.** *Br* JUR: ~ writ assignation *f* à comparaître en personne.

perennial [pə'renjəl] ◇ *adj* -**1.** BOT vivace. -**2.** *fig* [everlasting] éternel; [recurrent, continual] perpétuel, sempiternel; a ~ subject of debate un éternel OR perpétuel sujet de discussion.
◇ *n* BOT plante *f* vivace.

perennially [pə'renjəlɪ] *adv* [everlastingly] éternellement; [recurrently, continually] perpétuellement, continuellement.

perestroika [,perə'strɔɪkə] *n* perestroïka *f*.

perfect [*adj* & *n* 'pɜːfɪkt, *vb* pə'fekt] ◇ *adj* -**1.** [flawless - person, performance etc] parfait; a ~ circle un cercle parfait; the engine is in ~ condition le moteur est en parfait état de marche; in ~ health en parfaite OR excellente santé; her hearing is still ~ elle entend encore parfaitement; try it yourself, since you think you're (so) ~! essaie toi-même, puisque tu te crois OR tu es si fort!; nobody's ~ personne n'est parfait ☐ practice makes ~ *prov* c'est en forgeant qu'on devient forgeron *prov*. -**2.** [complete - agreement, mastery etc] parfait, complet; there was ~ silence il y avait un silence total; you have a ~ right to be here vous avez parfaitement OR tout à fait le droit d'être ici ‖ [as intensifier] véritable, parfait; it was a ~ disaster! ce fut un véritable désastre!; he's a ~ idiot c'est un parfait imbécile. -**3.** [fine, lovely - conditions] parfait, idéal; [- weather] idéal, superbe. -**4.** [fitting, right - gift, example] parfait, approprié; tonight at 7? — that will be ~ ce soir à 7 h? — c'est parfait; Monday is ~ for me lundi me convient parfaitement; the colour is ~ on you cette couleur te va à merveille OR à la perfection. -**5.** [exemplary - gentleman, host] parfait, exemplaire. -**6.** GRAMM [participle] passé; ~ participle participe *m* passé; the ~ tense le parfait.
◇ *n* GRAMM parfait *m*; in the ~ au parfait; the future ~ le futur antérieur; the past ~ le plus-que-parfait; the present ~ le passé composé.
◇ *vt* -**1.** [improve - knowledge, skill] perfectionner, parfaire. -**2.** [bring to final form - plans, method] mettre au point. -**3.** TYPO imprimer en retiration.

perfect competition *n* ECON concurrence *f* parfaite.

perfectible [pə'fektəbl] *adj* perfectible.

perfection [pə'fekʃn] *n* -**1.** [quality] perfection *f*; it's the only way to attain ~ c'est le seul moyen d'atteindre la perfection; this cake is ~! ce gâteau est un vrai délice!; to do sthg to ~ faire qqch à la perfection. -**2.** [perfecting - of skill, knowledge] perfectionnement *m*; [- of plans, method] mise *f* au point.

perfectionism [pə'fekʃənɪzm] *n* perfectionnisme *m*.

perfectionist [pə'fekʃənɪst] ◇ *adj* perfectionniste.
◇ *n* perfectionniste *mf*.

perfective [pə'fektɪv] *adj* GRAMM perfectif.

perfectly ['pɜːfɪktlɪ] *adv* -**1.** [speak, understand] parfaitement; ~ formed d'une forme parfaite. -**2.** [as intensifier]: you are ~ right vous avez parfaitement OR tout à fait raison; it's a ~ good raincoat cet imperméable est tout à fait mettable.

perfect number *n* MATH nombre *m* parfait.

perfect pitch *n* MUS: to have ~ avoir l'oreille absolue.

perfidious [pə'fɪdɪəs] *adj lit* perfide; ~ Albion la perfide Albion.

perfidiously [pə'fɪdɪəslɪ] *adv lit* perfidement.

perfidy ['pɜːfɪdɪ] (*pl* **perfidies**) *n lit* perfidie *f*.

perforate ['pɜːfəreɪt] *vt* -**1.** [pierce] perforer, percer. -**2.** TECH [punch holes in] perforer.

perforated ['pɜːfəreɪtɪd] *adj* perforé, percé; to have a ~ eardrum avoir un tympan perforé OR crevé; tear along the ~ line détacher suivant les pointillés.

perforated tape *n* COMPUT bande *f* perforée.

perforation [,pɜːfə'reɪʃn] *n* perforation *f*.

perforce [pə'fɔːs] *adv lit* forcément, nécessairement.

perform [pə'fɔːm] ◇ *vt* -**1.** [carry out - manœuvre, task] exécuter, accomplir; [- calculation] effectuer, faire; [- miracle] accomplir; [- wedding, ritual] célébrer; the robot can ~ complex movements le robot peut exécuter des mouvements complexes; to ~ an operation MED opérer. -**2.** [fulfil - function, duty] remplir; the agency ~s a vital service l'agence remplit une fonction vitale. -**3.** [stage - play] jouer, donner; [- concert, ballet, opera] interpréter, jouer; [- solo] exécuter; to ~ a part THEAT jouer OR interpréter un rôle; DANCE danser un rôle.
◇ *vi* -**1.** [actor, comedian, musician] jouer; [dancer] danser; [singer] chanter; the Berlin Philharmonic is ~ing tonight l'Orchestre philharmonique de Berlin donne un concert OR joue ce soir; she ~ed superbly in the role of Lady Chichester elle a magnifiquement interprété le rôle de Lady Chichester. -**2.** [in job, situation] se débrouiller; to ~ well/badly [person] bien/ne pas bien s'en tirer; [company] avoir de bons/mauvais résultats; he'd never spoken in public before, but he ~ed well il n'avait jamais parlé en public avant, mais il s'en est bien tiré OR il s'est bien débrouillé; how does she ~ under pressure? comment réagit-elle lorsqu'elle est sous pression?; the Miami branch is not ~ing well les résultats de la succursale de Miami ne sont pas très satisfaisants. -**3.** [function - vehicle, machine] marcher, fonctionner; the car ~s well/badly in wet conditions cette voiture a une bonne/mauvaise tenue de route par temps de pluie.

performance [pə'fɔːməns] *n* -**1.** [show] spectacle *m*, représentation *f*; CIN séance *f*; afternoon ~ matinée *f*; there is no ~ on Mondays il n'y a pas de représentation le lundi, le lundi est jour de relâche. -**2.** [rendition - by actor, musician, dancer] interprétation *f*; [showing - by sportsman, politician etc] performance *f*, prestation *f*; he gave an excellent ~ in the role of Othello son interprétation du rôle d'Othello fut remarquable; the Prime Minister gave the ~ of his career le Premier ministre n'a jamais été aussi bon de toute sa carrière; another poor ~ by the French team encore une contre-performance de l'équipe française; the country's poor economic ~ les mauvais résultats économiques du pays; sterling's ~ on the Stock Exchange le comportement en bourse de la livre sterling; sexual ~ prouesses sexuelles. -**3.** [of machine, computer, car] performance *f*; (high-)~ car voiture *f* performante. -**4.** [carrying out - of task, manœuvre] exécution *f*; [- of miracle] accomplissement *m*; [- of ritual] célébration *f*; she has always been painstaking in the ~ of her duties elle s'est toujours montrée consciencieuse dans l'accomplissement de ses devoirs. -**5.** *inf* [rigmarole] histoire *f*, cirque *m*; it's such a ~ getting a visa! quelle histoire OR quel cirque pour avoir un visa!; what a ~! quel cirque! -**6.** LING performance *f*.

performance appraisal *n* [system] système *m* d'évaluation; [individual] évaluation *f*.

performance art *n* spectacle *m* total.

performance test *n* PSYCH test *m* de performance.

performative [pə'fɔːmətɪv] ◇ *adj* LING & PHILOS performatif.
◇ *n* LING [verb] performatif *m*; [utterance] énoncé *m* performatif.

performer [pə'fɔːməʳ] *n* [singer, dancer, actor] interprète *mf*; nightclub ~ artiste *mf* de cabaret; he's a good stage ~ but awful on camera il est très bon sur la scène mais il ne passe pas du tout à l'écran.

performing [pə'fɔːmɪŋ] *adj* [bear, dog etc] savant.

performing arts *npl* arts *mpl* du spectacle.

performing rights *npl* THEAT droits *mpl* de représentation; MUS droits *mpl* d'exécution.

perfume [*n* 'pɜːfjuːm, *vb* pə'fjuːm] ◇ *n* -**1.** [bottled] parfum *m*; I don't usually wear ~ d'habitude je ne me parfume pas; what ~ does she wear OR use? quel parfum met-elle?, quel est son parfum? ☐ ~ spray atomiseur *m* de parfum. -**2.** [smell] parfum *m*.
◇ *vt* parfumer.

perfumed [*Br* 'pɜːfjuːmd, *Am* pər'fjuːmd] *adj* parfumé.

perfumer [pə'fjuːməʳ] *n* parfumeur *m*, -euse *f*.

perfumery [pə'fjuːmərɪ] (*pl* **perfumeries**) *n* parfumerie *f*.

perfunctorily [pə'fʌŋktrəlɪ] *adv* [wave] négligemment; [explain, apologize, search] sommairement; [read out, announce] sans conviction.

perfunctory [pə'fʌŋktərɪ] *adj* [gesture] négligent; [greeting, kiss] détaché; [explanation, apology, letter] sommaire; [effort] de pure forme; [interrogation, search] fait pour la forme.

Pergamum ['pɜːgəməm] *pr n* Pergame.

pergola ['pɜːgələ] *n* pergola *f*.

perhaps [pə'hæps] *adv* peut-être; ~ they've forgotten ils ont peut-être oublié, peut-être ont-ils oublié; ~ not peut-être que non; there were ~ 200 people there il y avait peut-être 200 personnes ‖ [used in polite requests, offers]: ~ you'd be kind enough... peut-être aurais-tu la gentillesse...; a glass of something, ~? un verre de quelque chose, peut-être?

perianth ['perɪænθ] *n* périanthe *m*.

pericarditis [,perɪkɑː'daɪtɪs] *n* péricardite *f*.

pericardium [,perɪ'kɑːdjəm] *n* péricarde *m*.

pericarp ['perɪkɑːp] *n* péricarpe *m*.

Pericles ['perɪkliːz] *pr n* Périclès.

peridot ['perɪdɒt] *n* péridot *m*.

perigee ['perɪdʒiː] *n* périgée *m*.

periglacial [,perɪ'gleɪʃl] *adj* périglaciaire.

perihelion [,perɪ'hiːljən] *n* périhélie *m*.

peril ['perɪl] *n* péril *m*, danger *m*; the ~s of hard drugs le danger des drogues dures; to be in ~ être en danger; you do it at your ~ *Br* c'est à vos risques et périls.

perilous ['perələs] *adj* périlleux, dangereux.

perilously ['perələslɪ] *adv* périlleusement, dangereusement; he came ~ close to defeat/drowning il s'en est fallu d'un cheveu qu'il ne perde/qu'il ne se noie.

perimeter [pə'rɪmɪtəʳ] *n* périmètre *m*.

perimeter fence *n* grillage *m*.

perinatal [,perɪ'neɪtl] *adj* périnatal.

perineal [,perɪ'niːəl] *adj* périnéal.

perineum [ˌperɪˈniːəm] (*pl* perinea [-ˈniːə]) *n* périnée *m*.

period [ˈpɪərɪəd] ◇ *n* -**1.** [length of time] période *f*; [historical epoch] période *f*, époque *f*; within a ~ of a few months en l'espace de quelques mois; we have a two-month ~ in which to do it nous avons un délai de deux mois pour le faire; he's going through a difficult ~ il traverse une période difficile; a ~ of colonial expansion une période d'expansion coloniale; the Elizabethan ~ l'époque élisabéthaine; at that ~ in her life à cette époque de sa vie; his cubist/jazz ~ sa période cubiste/jazz; there will be a question/discussion ~ after the lecture un moment sera consacré aux questions/au débat après la conférence. -**2.** GEOL période *f*; the Jurassic ~ la période jurassique. -**3.** SCH [lesson] cours *m*; during the Latin ~ pendant le cours de latin; a free ~ [for pupil] une heure de permanence; [for teacher] une heure de battement. -**4.** [in ice hockey] période *f*. -**5.** ASTRON: ~ of rotation période *f* de rotation. -**6.** [menstruation] règles *fpl*; I've got my ~ j'ai mes règles; my ~s have stopped je n'ai plus mes règles. -**7.** *Am* [full stop] point *m*. -**8.** [sentence] période *f*. -**9.** CHEM [in periodic table] période *f*. -**10.** MUS période *f*. -**11.** COMM: accounting ~ exercice *m*.
◇ *adv inf*: you're not going out alone, ~! tu ne sortiras pas tout seul, un point c'est tout!
◇ *comp* [furniture, costume] d'époque; [novel] historique; the play has a definite ~ flavour la pièce nous transporte vraiment dans une autre époque.

periodic [ˌpɪərɪˈɒdɪk] *adj* -**1.** [gen] périodique. -**2.** CHEM & MATH périodique; ~ function fonction *f* périodique.

periodical [ˌpɪərɪˈɒdɪkl] ◇ *n* [publication] périodique *m*.
◇ *adj* périodique.

periodically [ˌpɪərɪˈɒdɪklɪ] *adv* périodiquement; we see them ~ nous les voyons de temps en temps.

periodicity [ˌpɪərɪəˈdɪsətɪ] *n* périodicité *f*.

periodic table *n* tableau *m* périodique (des éléments).

periodontics [ˌperɪəˈdɒntɪks] *n* (*U*) *branche de la stomatologie qui s'occupe du périodonte*.

period pains *npl* règles *fpl* douloureuses.

period piece *n* objet *m* d'époque.

periosteum [ˌperɪˈɒstɪəm] (*pl* periostea [-stɪə]) *n* périoste *m*.

peripatetic [ˌperɪpəˈtetɪk] *adj* -**1.** [itinerant] itinérant. -**2.** *Br* SCH: ~ teacher *professeur qui enseigne dans plusieurs établissements scolaires*.

peripheral [pəˈrɪfərəl] ◇ *adj* périphérique; ~ vision vue *f* périphérique.
◇ *n* COMPUT: ~ (device OR unit) (unité *f*) périphérique *m*.

periphery [pəˈrɪfərɪ] (*pl* peripheries) *n* -**1.** [of circle, vision, city etc] périphérie *f*; on the ~ à la périphérie. -**2.** [of group, movement] frange *f*; on the ~ of society en marge de la société.

periphrasis [pəˈrɪfrəsɪs] (*pl* periphrases [-siːz]) *n* périphrase *f*, circonlocution *f*.

periphrastic [ˌperɪˈfræstɪk] *adj* périphrastique.

periscope [ˈperɪskəʊp] *n* périscope *m*; up ~! sortez le périscope!

perish [ˈperɪʃ] ◇ *vi* -**1.** *Br* [rot - rubber, leather etc] s'abîmer, se détériorer; [- food] se gâter, pourrir. -**2.** *lit* [die] périr; ~ the thought *hum*: you're not pregnant, are you? — ~ the thought! tu n'es pas enceinte au moins? - tu veux rire OR j'espère bien que non!; and that, ~ the thought, would mean giving up your weekends et pour ça, comble de l'horreur, tu devrais renoncer à tes week-ends.
◇ *vt* [rubber, leather] abîmer, détériorer; [food] gâter.

perishable [ˈperɪʃəbl] *adj* périssable.
◆ **perishables** *npl* denrées *fpl* périssables.

perished *inf* [ˈperɪʃt] *adj Br* [cold] frigorifié.

perisher *inf* [ˈperɪʃəʳ] *n Br* galopin *m*.

perishing *inf* [ˈperɪʃɪŋ] *adj Br*. -**1.** [cold - person, hands] frigorifié; it's ~ (cold) il fait un froid de canard OR de loup. -**2.** [as expletive] sacré, fichu, foutu; that ~ telephone ce fichu téléphone; what a ~ nuisance! c'est vraiment casse-pied!

perishingly *inf* [ˈperɪʃɪŋlɪ] *adv Br*: it's ~ cold il fait un froid de canard.

peristalsis [ˌperɪˈstælsɪs] (*pl* peristalses [-siːz]) *n* péristaltisme *m*.

peristaltic [ˌperɪˈstæltɪk] *adj* péristaltique.

peristyle [ˈperɪstaɪl] *n* péristyle *m*.

peritoneum [ˌperɪtəˈniːəm] (*pl* peritoneums OR peritonea [-ˈniːə]) *n* péritoine *m*.

peritonitis [ˌperɪtəˈnaɪtɪs] *n* (*U*) péritonite *f*; to have ~ avoir une péritonite.

periwig [ˈperɪwɪg] *n* perruque *f*.

periwinkle [ˈperɪˌwɪŋkl] *n* -**1.** BOT pervenche *f*. -**2.** ZOOL bigorneau *m*.

perjure [ˈpɜːdʒəʳ] *vt*: to ~ o.s. faire un faux témoignage.

perjured [ˈpɜːdʒəd] *adj*: ~ evidence faux témoignage *m*; his evidence was ~ il a fait un faux témoignage.

perjurer [ˈpɜːdʒərəʳ] *n* faux témoin *m*.

perjury [ˈpɜːdʒərɪ] (*pl* perjuries) *n*: to commit ~ faire un faux témoignage.

perk *inf* [pɜːk] ◇ *n* [from job] avantage *m* en nature; [advantage - gen] avantage *m*; cheap air travel is one of the ~s of his job un des avantages de son boulot, c'est qu'il peut prendre l'avion pour trois fois rien.
◇ *vi* & *vt* [coffee] passer.
◆ **perk up** ◇ *vt sep* [cheer up] remonter, ragaillardir, revigorer; the news really ~ed me up la nouvelle m'a vraiment remonté le moral || [liven up] revigorer; some wine will ~ you up un peu de vin te remontera.
◇ *vi insep* -**1.** [cheer up] se ragaillardir, retrouver le moral; he ~ed up in the afternoon il a retrouvé son entrain l'après-midi. -**2.** [become interested] dresser l'oreille OR la tête; she ~ed up when money was mentioned elle a dressé l'oreille quand on a parlé d'argent. -**3.** [ears, head] se dresser.

perky [ˈpɜːkɪ] (*compar* perkier, *superl* perkiest) *adj* gai, vif.

perm [pɜːm] ◇ *vt* [hair] permanenter; her hair is ~ed elle a les cheveux permanentés; I've had my hair ~ed je me suis fait faire une permanente.
◇ *n* -**1.** permanente *f*; to have a ~ se faire faire une permanente. -**2.** (*abbr of* permutation) *combinaison jouée dans les paris sur les matches de football en Grande-Bretagne*.

permafrost [ˈpɜːməfrɒst] *n* permagel *m*, permafrost *m*, pergélisol *m*.

permanence [ˈpɜːmənəns] *n* permanence *f*, caractère *m* permanent.

permanency [ˈpɜːmənənsɪ] (*pl* permanencies) *n* -**1.** [person, thing]: they predicted that computers would be a ~ in every office ils avaient prévu que les ordinateurs deviendraient indispensables dans tous les bureaux. -**2.** = **permanence**.

permanent [ˈpɜːmənənt] ◇ *adj* permanent; no ~ damage was caused aucun dégât irréparable n'a été occasionné; ~ address domicile *m*; are you here on a ~ basis? êtes-vous ici à titre définitif?; ~ staff [gen] personnel *m* permanent; [in public service] personnel *m* titulaire; a ~ post [gen] un emploi permanent; [in public service] un poste de titulaire ❑ ~ ink encre *f* indélébile; ~ magnet aimant *m* permanent; ~ tooth dent *f* permanente; Permanent Undersecretary *Br* ≃ secrétaire général *m*, -e *f* (*dans la fonction publique*).
◇ *n Am* [in hair] permanente *f*.

permanently [ˈpɜːmənəntlɪ] *adv* -**1.** [constantly] en permanence, constamment; he's ~ drunk il ne dessoûle jamais. -**2.** [definitively] définitivement, à titre définitif; they came to live here ~ ils sont venus s'installer ici définitivement.

permanent-press *adj*: ~ trousers/skirt pantalon *m*/jupe *f* à pli permanent.

permanent wave *n* permanente *f*.

permanent way *n Br* voie *f* ferrée.

permanganate [pɜːˈmæŋgəneɪt] *n* permanganate *m*.

permeability [ˌpɜːmjəˈbɪlətɪ] *n* perméabilité *f*.

permeable [ˈpɜːmjəbl] *adj* perméable.

permeate [ˈpɜːmɪeɪt] ◇ *vt* -**1.** [subj: gas, smell] se répandre dans; a lovely smell ~d the kitchen une merveilleuse odeur emplissait la cuisine. -**2.** [subj: liquid] s'infiltrer dans; damp had ~d the floorboards le plancher était imprégné OR gorgé d'humidité; the sand is ~d with oil le sable est imbibé de pétrole. -**3.** *fig* [subj: ideas] se répandre dans, se propager à travers; [subj: feelings] envahir, emplir; an atmosphere of gloom ~s his novels ses romans sont empreints d'une mélancolie profonde; the optimism that ~d the sixties l'optimisme qui prévalait OR dominait dans les années soixante.
◇ *vi* -**1.** [gas] se répandre, se diffuser; [smell] se répandre. -**2.** [liquid] filtrer; rain water had ~d through the walls les eaux de pluie avaient filtré à travers les murs. -**3.** *fig* [ideas, feelings] se répandre, se propager.

Permian [ˈpɜːmɪən] ◇ *adj* permien.
◇ *n* permien *m*.

permissible [pəˈmɪsəbl] *adj fml* -**1.** [allowed] permis, autorisé; is it ~ for him to take two days off? est-ce qu'il est autorisé à prendre deux jours de congé? -**2.** [tolerable - behaviour] admissible, acceptable; degree of ~ error marge d'erreur admissible OR admise.

permission [pəˈmɪʃn] *n* permission *f*, autorisation *f*; to ask for ~ to do sthg demander la permission OR l'autorisation de faire qqch; to have ~ to do sthg avoir la permission OR l'autorisation de faire qqch; to give sb ~ to do sthg donner à qqn la permission de faire qqch; who gave them ~? qui le leur a permis?; who gave him ~ to go out? qui lui a permis de OR l'a autorisé à sortir?; with your ~ avec votre permission, si vous le permettez; without my/your/her ~ sans ma/votre/sa permission; photos published by kind ~ of Larousse photos publiées avec l'aimable autorisation de Larousse; you need written ~ to work at home il faut une autorisation écrite pour travailler chez soi.

permissive [pəˈmɪsɪv] *adj* -**1.** [tolerant - behaviour, parent etc] permissif; the ~ society la société permissive. -**2.** *arch* [optional] facultatif.

permissively [pəˈmɪsɪvlɪ] *adv* de manière permissive.

permissiveness [pəˈmɪsɪvnɪs] *n* -**1.** [morally] permissivité *f*. -**2.** [of legislation] caractère *m* facultatif.

permit [*vb* pəˈmɪt, *n* ˈpɜːmɪt] (*pt* & *pp* permitted, *cont* permitting) ◇ *vt* -**1.** [allow] permettre, autoriser; to ~ sb to do sthg permettre à qqn de faire qqch, autoriser qqn à faire qqch; she was permitted to take two weeks off on l'a autorisée à prendre deux semaines de congé; ~ me to inform you that... laissez-moi vous apprendre que...; he won't ~ it il ne le permettra pas; you are not permitted to enter the building vous n'avez pas le droit de pénétrer dans l'immeuble; smoking is not permitted upstairs il est interdit de fumer à l'étage; the hotel won't ~ animals in the bedrooms l'hôtel n'autorise pas la présence d'animaux dans les chambres || [tolerate] tolérer; he ~s far too much rudeness from his children il tolère trop de grossièreté chez ses enfants. -**2.** [enable] permettre; the computer ~s her to take more time off l'ordinateur lui laisse plus de temps libre; the statistics ~ the following conclusions les statistiques permettent (de tirer) les conclusions suivantes.
◇ *vi* permettre; weather/your health permitting si le temps/ta santé le permet; to ~ of *fml* permettre; the text ~s of two readings le texte se prête à deux interprétations différentes; w

can ~ of no delay nous ne pouvons tolérer le moindre retard.
◇ *n* [authorization] autorisation *f*, permis *m* ADMIN; [pass] laissez-passer *m inv*; work ~ permis de travail; export/drinks ~ licence *f* d'exportation/pour la vente de boissons alcoolisées.

ermutate ['pɜːmjʊteɪt] = **permute**.

ermutation [ˌpɜːmjuː'teɪʃn] *n* permutation *f* MATH.

ermute [pə'mjuːt] *vt* permuter.

ernicious [pə'nɪʃəs] *adj* -**1.** [harmful] pernicieux. -**2.** [malicious - gossip, lie] malveillant.

ernicious anaemia *n (U)* anémie *f* pernicieuse.

ernickety *inf* [pə'nɪkətɪ] *Br*, **persnickety** *inf* [pə'snɪkɪtɪ] *Am adj* -**1.** *pej* [person - fussy] tatillon, chipoteur; [- hard to please] difficile; she's very ~ about punctuality elle ne plaisante pas avec OR elle est très à cheval sur la ponctualité. -**2.** [job - fiddly] délicat, minutieux.

erorate ['perəreɪt] *vi fml* discourir, pérorer.

eroration [ˌperə'reɪʃn] *n* péroraison *f*.

eroxide [pə'rɒksaɪd] ◇ *n* -**1.** CHEM peroxyde *m*. -**2.** [for hair] eau *f* oxygénée.
◇ *vt* [bleach - hair] décolorer, oxygéner *spec*.

eroxide blonde *n* [woman] blonde *f* décolorée.

erpendicular [ˌpɜːpən'dɪkjʊlə^r] ◇ *adj* -**1.** GEOM perpendiculaire; the line AB is ~ to the line CD la ligne AB est perpendiculaire à la ligne CD. -**2.** [vertical - cliff] escarpé, abrupt, à pic; [- slope] raide, à pic.
◇ *n* perpendiculaire *f*; the tower is out of (the) ~ la tour n'est pas verticale OR est hors d'aplomb *spec*.
◆ **Perpendicular** *adj* ARCHIT perpendiculaire.

erpendicularly [ˌpɜːpən'dɪkjʊləlɪ] *adv* perpendiculairement.

erpetrate ['pɜːpɪtreɪt] *vt fml* [commit - crime] commettre, perpétrer *lit*; she ~d several frauds elle a escroqué plusieurs personnes; to ~ a hoax être l'auteur d'une farce.

erpetration [ˌpɜːpɪ'treɪʃn] *n fml* perpétration *f*.

erpetrator ['pɜːpɪtreɪtə^r] *n fml* auteur *m*.

erpetual [pə'petʃʊəl] *adj* -**1.** [state, noise] perpétuel; her ~ coughing kept me awake all night sa toux incessante m'a gardé éveillé toute la nuit; it's a ~ worry to us c'est pour nous un sujet d'inquiétude OR un souci permanent; ~ snows neiges *fpl* éternelles. -**2.** HORT perpétuel.

erpetual calendar *n* calendrier *m* perpétuel.

erpetual check *n* [in chess] échec *m* perpétuel.

erpetually [pə'petʃʊəlɪ] *adv* perpétuellement, sans cesse; they're ~ complaining ils sont toujours à se plaindre, ils se plaignent sans arrêt.

erpetual motion *n* mouvement *m* perpétuel.

erpetuate [pə'petʃʊeɪt] *vt* perpétuer.

erpetuation [pəˌpetʃʊ'eɪʃn] *n*: this leads to the ~ of this type of situation c'est ce qui permet à ce type de situation de se perpétuer.

erpetuity [ˌpɜːpɪ'tjuːətɪ] (*pl* **perpetuities**) *n* -**1.** [eternity] perpétuité *f lit*; in OR for ~ à perpétuité. -**2.** [annuity] rente *f* perpétuelle.

erplex [pə'pleks] *vt* -**1.** [puzzle] rendre OR laisser perplexe; his questions ~ed us ses questions nous ont laissés perplexes OR nous ont plongés dans la perplexité. -**2.** [complicate] compliquer.

erplexed [pə'plekst] *adj* perplexe; I'm ~ about what to do je ne sais pas trop quoi faire.

erplexedly [pə'pleksɪdlɪ] *adv* avec perplexité; he looked at me ~ il me regarda d'un air perplexe, il me lança un regard perplexe.

erplexing [pə'pleksɪŋ] *adj* inexplicable, incompréhensible; I find their silence rather ~ je me demande bien ce que peut signifier leur silence; he asked us some ~ questions il a posé des questions qui nous ont laissés perplexes.

erplexity [pə'pleksətɪ] *n* -**1.** [confusion] perplexité *f*; you could see the ~ on his face la perplexité se lisait sur son visage. -**2.** [complexity - of problem] complexité *f*.

perquisite ['pɜːkwɪzɪt] *fml* = **perk** *n*.

perry ['perɪ] (*pl* perries) *n* poiré *m*.

per se [pɜː'seɪ] *adv* [as such] en tant que tel; [in itself] en soi.

persecute ['pɜːsɪkjuːt] *vt* -**1.** [oppress] persécuter; they were ~d for their religious beliefs ils ont été persécutés à cause de leurs convictions religieuses. -**2.** [pester] persécuter, harceler; they ~d her with questions ils l'ont harcelée de questions.

persecution [ˌpɜːsɪ'kjuːʃn] *n* persécution *f*.

persecution complex *n* délire *m* de persécution.

persecution mania *n* manie *f* de la persécution.

persecutor ['pɜːsɪkjuːtə^r] *n* persécuteur *m*, -trice *f*.

Persephone [pɜː'sefənɪ] *pr n* Perséphone.

Perseus ['pɜːsjuːs] *pr n* Persée.

perseverance [ˌpɜːsɪ'vɪərəns] *n* persévérance *f*.

persevere [ˌpɜːsɪ'vɪə^r] *vi* persévérer; ~ in your efforts persévérez dans vos efforts; you must ~ with your studies il faut persévérer dans vos études.

persevering [ˌpɜːsɪ'vɪərɪŋ] *adj* persévérant, obstiné.

Persia ['pɜːʃə] *pr n* Perse *f*; in ~ en Perse.

Persian ['pɜːʃn] ◇ *n* -**1.** [person] Persan *m*, -e *f*; ANTIQ Perse *mf*. -**2.** LING [modern] persan *m*; [ancient] perse *m*.
◇ *adj* persan; ANTIQ perse.

Persian blinds *npl* persiennes *fpl*.

Persian carpet *n* tapis *m* persan.

Persian cat *n* chat *m* persan.

Persian Gulf *pr n*: the ~ le golfe Persique.

persian lamb *n* [animal, fur] karakul *m*, caracul *m*.

persimmon [pə'sɪmən] *n* [fruit] kaki *m*, plaquemine *f*; [tree] plaqueminier *m*.

persist [pə'sɪst] *vi* -**1.** [person] persister; to ~ in doing sthg persister OR s'obstiner à faire qqch; he ~s in the belief that... il persiste à croire que... -**2.** [weather, problem etc] persister; rain will ~ in the north la pluie persistera dans le nord; if the fever ~s si la fièvre persiste.

persistence [pə'sɪstəns], **persistency** [pə'sɪstənsɪ] *n* -**1.** [perseverance] persistance *f*, persévérance *f*; [insistence] persistance *f*, insistance *f*; [obstinacy] obstination *f*; his ~ finally paid off sa persévérance a fini par porter ses fruits; his ~ in asking awkward questions son obstination à poser des questions embarrassantes. -**2.** [continuation - of rain, problem etc] persistance *f*.

persistent [pə'sɪstənt] *adj* -**1.** [continual - demands, rain etc] continuel, incessant; ~ offender récidiviste *mf*. -**2.** [lingering - smell, fever etc] persistant, tenace. -**3.** [persevering] persévérant; you must be more ~ in your efforts il faut être plus persévérant. -**4.** BOT persistant.

persistently [pə'sɪstəntlɪ] *adv* -**1.** [continually] continuellement, sans cesse; I've warned you ~ je me suis acharné à vous prévenir; they ~ insult him ils ne cessent de l'insulter. -**2.** [perseveringly] avec persévérance OR persistance, obstinément.

persnickety *inf Am* = **pernickety**.

person ['pɜːsn] (*pl* people ['piːpl] OR *fml* persons) *n* -**1.** personne *f*; he's just the ~ we need c'est exactement la personne qu'il nous faut; a young ~ [female] une jeune personne; [male] un jeune homme; by a ~ or ~s unknown JUR par des personnes inconnues OR non identifiées; he's a good worker, but I don't really like him as a ~ sur le plan du travail il est bien, mais je n'aime pas trop sa personnalité OR mais sur le plan personnel je ne l'aime pas trop; he's not that sort of ~ ce n'est pas du tout son genre; I'm not a great eating-out ~ *inf* je n'aime pas beaucoup manger au restaurant; in the ~ of en la personne de. -**2.** *fml* [body] personne *f*; to have sthg on OR about one's ~ avoir qqch sur soi; she had the wallet concealed about her ~ le portefeuille était caché sur elle. -**3.** GRAMM personne *f*; in the first/second/third ~ plural à la première/deuxième/troisième personne du pluriel. -**4.** RELIG personne *f*.
◆ **in person** *adv phr* en personne; she came in ~ elle est venue en personne; this letter must be delivered to him in ~ cette lettre doit lui être remise en mains propres.

persona [pə'səʊnə] (*pl* personas OR personae [-niː]) *n* LITERAT & PSYCH personnage *m*; to take on a new ~ se créer un personnage.

personable ['pɜːsnəbl] *adj* plaisant, charmant.

personage ['pɜːsənɪdʒ] *n fml* personnage *m (individu)*; an important ~ un personnage important.

persona grata [pə'səʊnə'grɑːtə] (*pl* personae gratae [pə'səʊniː'grɑːtiː]) *n*: to be ~ être persona grata.

personal ['pɜːsənl] ◇ *adj* -**1.** [individual - experience, belief etc] personnel; she tries to give her work a ~ touch elle essaie de donner une touche personnelle à son travail; my ~ opinion is that he drowned personnellement, je crois qu'il s'est noyé; you get more ~ attention in small shops on s'occupe mieux de vous dans les petits magasins; will you do me a ~ favour? pourriez-vous m'accorder une faveur? -**2.** [in person] personnel; under the ~ supervision of the author supervisé personnellement par l'auteur; the boss made a ~ visit to the scene le patron est venu lui-même OR en personne sur les lieux; we were expecting a ~ appearance by the Prime Minister nous pensions que le Premier ministre ferait une apparition en personne. -**3.** [private - message, letter] personnel; ~ and private [on letter] strictement confidentiel. -**4.** [for one's own use] personnel; ~ belongings objets *mpl* personnels, affaires *fpl*; this is for my ~ use ceci est destiné à mon usage personnel; ~ loan prêt *m* personnel; ~ trainer entraîneur *m* personnel; ~ estate OR property biens *mpl* mobiliers personnels. -**5.** [intimate - feelings, reasons, life] personnel; I'd like to see her on a ~ matter je voudrais la voir pour des raisons personnelles; just a few ~ friends rien que quelques amis intimes. -**6.** [offensive] désobligeant; ~ remark remarque *f* désobligeante; there's no need to be so ~! ce n'est pas la peine de t'en prendre à moi!; nothing ~! ne le prenez pas pour vous!, n'y voyez rien de personnel!; the discussion was getting rather ~ la discussion prenait un tour un peu trop personnel. -**7.** [bodily - cleanliness, hygiene] intime. -**8.** GRAMM personnel; ~ pronoun pronom *m* personnel.
◇ *n Am* [advert] petite annonce *f (pour rencontres)*.

personal assistant *n* secrétaire *m* particulier, secrétaire *f* particulière.

personal column *n* petites annonces *fpl* (personnelles); to put an ad in the ~ passer une petite annonce.

personal computer *n* ordinateur *m* individuel OR personnel, PC *m*.

personal foul *n* [in basketball] faute *f* personnelle.

personality [ˌpɜːsə'nælətɪ] (*pl* **personalities**) *n* -**1.** [character] personnalité *f*, caractère *m*; [of thing, animal etc] caractère *m*; a woman with a lot of ~ une femme dotée d'une forte personnalité; he was an interesting ~ il avait une personnalité intéressante. -**2.** [famous person] personnalité *f*; CIN & TV vedette *f*. -**3.** PSYCH personnalité *f*.
◆ **personalities** *npl dated* [offensive remarks] propos *mpl* désobligeants.

personality cult *n* culte *m* de la personnalité.

personality disorder *n* trouble *m* de la personnalité; he has a serious ~ il a de graves problèmes psychologiques.

personality test *n* test *m* de personnalité, test *m* projectif *spec*.

personality type *n* configuration *f* psychologique.

personalize, -ise ['pɜːsənəlaɪz] *vt* -**1.** [make personal - gen] personnaliser; [- luggage, clothes] marquer (à son nom). -**2.** [argument, campaign] donner un tour personnel à. -**3.** [personify] personnifier.

personalized ['pɜːsənəlaɪzd] *adj* [individually tailored] personnalisé; ~ **stationery** papier *m* à lettres à en-tête; **his** ~ **luggage** ses bagages marqués à son nom.

personally ['pɜːsnəlɪ] *adv* -**1.** [speaking for oneself] personnellement, pour ma/sa *etc* part; ~ **(speaking), I think it's a silly idea** pour ma part OR en ce qui me concerne, je trouve que c'est une idée stupide. -**2.** [in person, directly] en personne, personnellement; **I was not** ~ **involved in the project** je n'ai pas participé directement au projet; **I want to speak to him** ~ j'aimerais lui parler personnellement; **deliver the letter to the director** ~ remettez la lettre en mains propres au directeur. -**3.** [not officially] sur le plan personnel. -**4.** [individually] personnellement; **I was talking about the whole team, not you** ~ je parlais de toute l'équipe, pas de toi personnellement OR en particulier; **to take things** ~ prendre les choses trop à cœur; **don't take it** ~**, but...** ne vous sentez pas visé, mais...

personal stereo *n* baladeur *m offic*, Walkman® *m*.

personalty ['pɜːsənəltɪ] (*pl* **personalties**) *n* JUR biens *mpl* mobiliers.

persona non grata [pə'səʊnənɒn'grɑːtə] (*pl* **personae non gratae** [pə'səʊniːnæn'grɑːtiː]) *n*: **to be** ~ être persona non grata; **he's definitely** ~ **in this house** il n'est absolument pas le bienvenu dans cette maison.

personate ['pɜːsəneɪt] *vt* -**1.** JUR se faire passer pour. -**2.** THEAT jouer le rôle de.

personification [pəˌsɒnɪfɪ'keɪʃn] *n* personnification *f*; **he is the** ~ **of evil** c'est le mal personnifié OR en personne.

personify [pə'sɒnɪfaɪ] (*pt* & *pp* **personified**) *vt* personnifier; **he is evil personified** c'est le mal personnifié OR en personne.

personnel [ˌpɜːsə'nel] *n* -**1.** [staff] personnel *m*; ~ **manager** chef *m* du personnel. -**2.** [department] service *m* du personnel; **she works in** ~ elle travaille au service du personnel. -**3.** MIL [troops] troupes *fpl*.

personnel carrier *n* (véhicule *m* de) transport *m* de troupes.

person-to-person ◇ *adv*: **I'd like to speak to her** ~ je voudrais lui parler en particulier OR seule à seul.
◇ *adj* -**1.** [conversation] personnel. -**2.** TELEC: ~ **call** communication *f* avec préavis *(se dit d'un appel téléphonique où la communication n'est établie et facturée que lorsque la personne à qui l'on veut parler répond)*.

perspective [pə'spektɪv] ◇ *n* -**1.** ARCHIT & ART perspective *f*; **to draw sthg in** ~ dessiner qqch en perspective; **the houses are out of** ~ la perspective des maisons est fausse; ~ **made it look smaller** l'effet de perspective le faisait paraître plus petit. -**2.** [opinion, viewpoint] perspective *f*, optique *f*; **it gives you a different** ~ **on the problem** cela vous permet de voir le problème sous un angle OR un jour différent; **from a psychological** ~ d'un point de vue psychologique; **the latest developments put a new** ~ **on the case** les derniers événements éclairent l'affaire d'un jour nouveau. -**3.** [proportion]: **we must try to keep our (sense of)** ~ OR **to keep things in** ~ nous devons nous efforcer de garder notre sens des proportions; **to get things out of** ~ perdre le sens des proportions; **it should help us to get** OR **to put the role she played into** ~ cela devrait nous aider à mesurer le rôle qu'elle a joué; **the figures must be looked at in (their proper)** ~ il faut étudier les chiffres dans leur contexte. -**4.** [view, vista] perspective *f*, panorama *m*, vue *f*. -**5.** [prospect] perspective *f*; **the** ~ **of higher inflation** la perspective d'une hausse du taux d'inflation.
◇ *adj* [drawing] perspectif.

Perspex® ['pɜːspeks] ◇ *n Br* Plexiglas® *m*.
◇ *comp* [window, windscreen etc] en Plexiglas®.

perspicacious [ˌpɜːspɪ'keɪʃəs] *adj fml* [person] perspicace; [remark, judgment] pénétrant, lucide.

perspicacity [ˌpɜːspɪ'kæsətɪ] *n fml* perspicacité *f*.

perspicuity [ˌpɜːspɪ'kjuːətɪ] *n fml* clarté *f*, lucidité *f*.

perspicuous [pə'spɪkjʊəs] *adj fml* clair, lucide.

perspiration [ˌpɜːspə'reɪʃn] *n* transpiration *f*, sueur *f*; **beads of** ~ des perles de sueur.

perspire [pə'spaɪə^r] *vi* transpirer; **his hands were perspiring** il avait les mains moites; **she was perspiring freely** OR **heavily** elle transpirait à grosses gouttes.

persuadable [pə'sweɪdəbl] *adj* facile à persuader.

persuade [pə'sweɪd] *vt* persuader, convaincre; **to** ~ **sb to do sthg** persuader OR convaincre qqn de faire qqch; **to** ~ **sb not to do sthg** persuader qqn de ne pas faire qqch, dissuader qqn de faire qqch; **I managed to** ~ **him (that) I was right** j'ai réussi à le persuader OR convaincre que j'avais raison; **I let myself be** ~**d into coming** je me suis laissé convaincre qu'il fallait venir; **she finally** ~**d the car to start** *fig* elle a réussi à faire démarrer la voiture; **I was** ~**d of her innocence** *fml* j'étais convaincu OR persuadé qu'elle était innocente.

persuasion [pə'sweɪʒn] *n* -**1.** [act of convincing] persuasion *f*; ~ **works better than force** la persuasion est plus efficace que la force; **the art of gentle** ~ l'art de convaincre en douceur; **I used all my powers of** ~ **on him** j'ai fait tout mon possible OR tout ce qui était en mon pouvoir pour le convaincre; **I wouldn't need much** ~ **to give it up** il ne faudrait pas insister beaucoup pour que j'abandonne. -**2.** [belief] RELIG confession *f*, religion *f*; POL tendance *f*; **men and women of many** ~**s** des hommes et des femmes de nombreuses confessions; **people, regardless of their political** ~ les gens, quelles que soient leurs convictions politiques. -**3.** *fml* [conviction] conviction *f*.

persuasive [pə'sweɪsɪv] *adj* [manner, speaker] persuasif, convaincant; [argument] convaincant.

persuasively [pə'sweɪsɪvlɪ] *adv* de façon convaincante OR persuasive; **she argues** ~ elle emploie des arguments convaincants.

persuasiveness [pə'sweɪsɪvnəs] *n* force *f* de persuasion.

pert [pɜːt] *adj* [person, reply] effronté; [hat] coquet; [nose] mutin; [bottom] ferme.

pertain [pə'teɪn] *vi* -**1.** [apply] s'appliquer. -**2.** to ~ to [concern] avoir rapport à, se rapporter à; JUR [subj: land, property] se rattacher à, dépendre de; **evidence** ~**ing to the case** les témoignages se rattachant OR se rapportant à l'affaire; **books** ~**ing to photography** des livres sur la photographie.

Perth [pɜːθ] *pr n* Perth.

pertinacious [ˌpɜːtɪ'neɪʃəs] *adj fml* opiniâtre.

pertinacity [ˌpɜːtɪ'næsətɪ] *n fml* opiniâtreté *f*.

pertinence ['pɜːtɪnəns] *n* pertinence *f*; **I don't see the** ~ **of that remark** cette remarque ne me semble pas pertinente.

pertinent ['pɜːtɪnənt] *adj* pertinent, à propos; **a very** ~ **question** une question très pertinente.

pertinently ['pɜːtɪnəntlɪ] *adv* pertinemment, avec justesse OR à-propos.

pertly ['pɜːtlɪ] *adv* [reply] avec effronterie; [dress] coquettement.

pertness ['pɜːtnɪs] *n* [of reply, manner] effronterie *f*; [of dress] coquetterie *f*.

perturb [pə'tɜːb] *vt* -**1.** [worry] inquiéter, troubler; **they were very** ~**ed by his disappearance** sa disparition les a beaucoup inquiétés. -**2.** ASTRON & ELECTRON perturber.

perturbation [ˌpɜːtə'beɪʃn] *n* -**1.** *fml* [anxiety] trouble *m*, inquiétude *f*. -**2.** ASTRON & ELECTRON perturbation *f*.

perturbed [pə'tɜːbd] *adj* troublé, inquiet; **I was** ~ **to hear that...** ça m'a troublé OR inquiété d'apprendre que...

perturbing [pə'tɜːbɪŋ] *adj* inquiétant, troublant.

Peru [pə'ruː] *pr n* Pérou *m*; **in** ~ au Pérou.

Perugia [pə'ruːdʒə] *pr n* Pérouse.

Perugino [peruː'dʒiːnəʊ] *pr n*: **Il** ~ le Pérugin; **a painting by Il** ~ un tableau du Pérugin.

perusal [pə'ruːzl] *n* [thorough reading] lecture approfondie, examen *m*; [quick reading] lecture sommaire, survol *m*; **he left the document for her** ~ il lui a laissé le document pour information.

peruse [pə'ruːz] *vt* [read thoroughly] lire attentivement, examiner; [read quickly] parcourir, survoler.

Peruvian [pə'ruːvjən] ◇ *n* Péruvien *m*, -enne *f*
◇ *adj* péruvien.

perv *inf* [pɜːv] *n Br* détraqué *m* (sexuel), détraquée *f* (sexuelle).

pervade [pə'veɪd] *vt* -**1.** [subj: gas, smell] se répandre dans. -**2.** [subj: ideas] se répandre dans, se propager à travers; [subj: feelings] envahir; **the fundamental error that** ~**s their philosophy** l'erreur fondamentale qui imprègne leur philosophie; **a feeling of mistrust** ~**ed their relationship** il y avait toujours entre eux une certaine défiance.

pervasive [pə'veɪsɪv] *adj* [feeling] envahissant; [influence] omniprésent; [effect] général; [smell] envahissant, omniprésent; **the** ~ **influence of television** l'omniprésence de la télévision; **a** ~ **atmosphere of pessimism** une atmosphère de pessimisme général.

perverse [pə'vɜːs] *adj* [stubborn - person] têtu, entêté; [- desire] tenace; [contrary, wayward] contrariant; **he felt a** ~ **urge to refuse** il fut pris d'une envie de refuser simplement pour le plaisir; **she takes a** ~ **delight in doing this** elle y prend un malin plaisir; **you're just being** ~ tu fais ça juste pour embêter le monde!

perversely [pə'vɜːslɪ] *adv* [stubbornly] obstinément; [unreasonably, contrarily] par esprit de contradiction.

perverseness [pə'vɜːsnɪs] *n* [stubbornness] entêtement *m*, obstination *f*; [unreasonableness, contrariness] esprit *m* de contradiction.

perversion [*Br* pə'vɜːʃn, *Am* pə'vɜːrʒn] *n* -**1.** [sexual abnormality] perversion *f*. -**2.** [distortion - of truth] déformation *f*.

perversity [pə'vɜːsətɪ] (*pl* **perversities**) -**1.** = **perverseness**. -**2.** [sexual abnormality] perversité *f*.

pervert [*vb* pə'vɜːt, *n* 'pɜːvɜːt] ◇ *vt* -**1.** [corrupt morally - person] pervertir, corrompre; PSYCH pervertir. -**2.** [distort - truth] déformer; [- words] dénaturer; **our old ideals have been** ~**ed** nos vieux idéaux ont été déformés; **to** ~ **the course of justice** JUR entraver le cours de la justice.
◇ *n* pervers *m*, -e *f*; **you** ~**!** *hum* tu es un vrai pervers!

perverted [pə'vɜːtɪd] *adj* PSYCH pervers.

pervious ['pɜːvjəs] *adj* -**1.** GEOL [permeable] perméable. -**2.** *lit* [receptive] ouvert, perméable.

peseta [pə'seɪtə] *n* peseta *f*.

pesky *inf* ['peskɪ] (*compar* **peskier**, *superl* **peskiest**) *adj esp Am* fichu; ~ **weather!** fichu temps!; ~ **flies!** maudites OR satanées mouches!

peso ['peɪsəʊ] (*pl* **pesos**) *n* peso *m*.

pessary ['pesərɪ] (*pl* **pessaries**) *n* MED pessaire *m*.

pessimism ['pesɪmɪzm] *n* pessimisme *m*.

pessimist ['pesɪmɪst] *n* pessimiste *mf*.

pessimistic [ˌpesɪ'mɪstɪk] *adj* pessimiste; **I feel very** ~ **about her chances of getting the job** je doute fort qu'elle obtienne ce poste; **don't be so** ~ **about your future** ne regarde pas l'avenir d'un œil si sombre.

ssimistically [ˌpesɪˈmɪstɪklɪ] *adv* de façon pessimiste; **he viewed the future somewhat ~** l avait une vision de l'avenir plutôt pessimiste.

st [pest] *n* **-1.** [insect] insecte *m* nuisible; [animal] animal *m* nuisible; **~ control** lutte *f* contre les animaux nuisibles; [of insects] lutte *f* contre les insectes nuisibles. **-2.** *inf* [nuisance] plaie *f*; **what a ~ he is!** quelle plaie!, qu'est-ce qu'il est casse-pieds!; **that dog is a real ~** ce chien est une véritable plaie; **look what she's done, the little ~!** regarde un peu ce qu'elle a fait, la petite peste!; **Christmas shopping is a real ~** c'est une vraie corvée de faire les achats de Noël.

ster [ˈpestəʳ] *vt* importuner, harceler; **stop ~ing your mother!** laisse ta mère tranquille!; **they're always ~ing me for money** ils sont toujours à me réclamer de l'argent; **the children ~ed me to tell them a story** les enfants n'ont eu de cesse que je leur raconte une histoire; **he ~ed me into buying him a computer** il m'a harcelé jusqu'à ce que je lui achète un ordinateur.

sticidal [ˈpestɪsaɪdl] *adj* pesticide.

sticide [ˈpestɪsaɪd] *n* pesticide *m*.

stiferous [peˈstɪfərəs] *adj* **-1.** *inf* [annoying] enquiquinant. **-2.** *lit* [unhealthy] pestilentiel.

stilence [ˈpestɪləns] *n lit* peste *f*, pestilence *f lit*.

stilential [ˌpestɪˈlenʃl] *adj* **-1.** [annoying] agaçant. **-2.** MED pestilentiel.

stle [ˈpesl] *n* pilon *m* CULIN.

et [pet] (*pt & pp* **petted**, *cont* **petting**) ◇ *n* **-1.** [animal] animal *m* domestique; **we don't keep ~s** nous n'avons pas d'animaux à la maison; **he keeps a snake as a ~** il a un serpent apprivoisé; **~ food** aliments *mpl* pour animaux (domestiques). **-2.** [favourite] favori *m*, -ite *f*, chouchou *m*, -oute *f pej*; **the teacher's ~** le chouchou du prof. **-3.** *inf* [term of endearment]: **how are you, ~?** comment ça va, mon chou?; **be a ~ and close the door** tu seras un chou de fermer la porte; **she's a real ~** elle est adorable. **4.** *inf* [temper] crise *f* de colère; **to be in a ~** être de mauvais poil OR en rogne.
◇ *adj* **-1.** [hawk, snake etc] apprivoisé; **they have a ~ budgerigar/hamster** ils ont une perruche/un hamster chez eux. **-2.** *inf* [favourite - project, theory] favori; **it's my ~ ambition to write a novel** ma grande ambition, c'est d'écrire un roman; **his ~ subject** OR **topic** son dada; **Anne is the teacher's ~ pupil** Anne est la chouchoute du prof; **~ hate** bête *f* noire.
◇ *vt* **-1.** [pamper] chouchouter. **-2.** [stroke - animal] câliner, caresser. **-3.** *inf* [caress sexually] caresser.
◇ *vi inf* [sexually] se caresser.

etal [ˈpetl] *n* pétale *m*.

etalled *Br*, **-petaled** *Am* [ˈpetld] *in cpds*: **five~** à cinq pétales; **large~** à grands pétales.

etard [pəˈtɑːd] *n* pétard *m*.

ete [piːt] *pr n*: **for ~'s sake!** *inf* mais nom d'un chien OR bon sang!

eter [ˈpiːtəʳ] *n* **-1.** *inf* [safe] coffiot *m*. **-2.** ▽ *Am* [penis] queue *f*.

◆ **peter out** *vi insep* **-1.** [run out - supplies, money] s'épuiser; [come to end - path] se perdre; [- stream] tarir; [- line] s'estomper, s'évanouir; [- conversation] tarir. **-2.** [die away - voice] s'éteindre; [- fire] s'éteindre, mourir. **-3.** [come to nothing - plan] tomber à l'eau.

eter [ˈpiːtəʳ] *pr n* Pierre; **~ the Great** Pierre le Grand; **Saint ~** saint Pierre ☐ **the ~ Principle** le principe de Peter *(théorème humoristique américain selon lequel chacun finit par atteindre son niveau d'incompétence)*; **'~ and the Wolf'** *Prokofiev* 'Pierre et le loup'; **'~ Pan'** *Barrie* 'Peter Pan'.

eter's Pence *n Br* HIST *impôt annuel (originellement d'un penny) payé en Angleterre par certains propriétaires au siège papal jusqu'à la Réforme*.

thidine [ˈpeθɪdiːn] *n* péthidine *f*.

tite [pəˈtiːt] ◇ *adj* menue.
◇ *n* [clothing size] petites tailles *fpl (pour adultes)*.

petition [pɪˈtɪʃn] ◇ *n* **-1.** [with signatures] pétition *f*; **they got up a ~ against the council's plans** ils ont préparé une pétition pour protester contre les projets de la municipalité; **there were 5,000 signatures on the ~ for his release** la pétition demandant sa libération a recueilli 5 000 signatures. **-2.** [request] requête *f*; **the Petition of Right** *Br* HIST la Pétition de droit. **-3.** JUR requête *f*, pétition *f*; **~ for divorce** demande *f* de divorce; **~ in bankruptcy** demande *f* de mise en liquidation judiciaire. **-4.** RELIG prière *f*.
◇ *vt* **-1.** [lobby] adresser une pétition à; **they ~ed the government for the release of** OR **to release the political prisoners** ils ont adressé une pétition au gouvernement pour demander la libération des prisonniers politiques; **we are going to ~ to have the wall demolished** nous allons demander que le mur soit démoli. **-2.** [beg]: **they ~ed the king to save them** ils ont imploré le roi de les sauver. **-3.** JUR: **to ~ the court** déposer une requête auprès du tribunal.
◇ *vi* **-1.** [with signatures] faire signer une pétition; **they ~ed for his release** ils ont fait circuler une pétition demandant sa libération. **-2.** [take measures]: **why don't you ~ against the plan?** pourquoi n'engagez-vous pas un recours contre le projet? **-3.** JUR: **to ~ for divorce** faire une demande de divorce.

THE PETITION OF RIGHT:
Pétition rédigée en 1628 par le Parlement anglais à l'encontre de l'autorité royale et que Charles Ier, pressé par des besoins d'argent, fut forcé d'accepter. Ce document devint un symbole de la limitation du pouvoir monarchique.

---

petitioner [pɪˈtɪʃənəʳ] *n* **-1.** JUR pétitionnaire *mf*; [in divorce] demandeur *m*, -eresse *f* de divorce. **-2.** [on petition] signataire *mf*.

pet name *n* surnom *m*; **her ~ for him was "honeybun"** elle l'appelait «honeybun».

Petra [ˈpetrə] *pr n* Pétra.

Petrarch [ˈpetrɑːk] *pr n* Pétrarque.

petrel [ˈpetrəl] *n* pétrel *m*.

Petri dish [ˈpiːtrɪ-] *n* boîte *f* de Pétri.

petrifaction [ˌpetrɪˈfækʃn] *n* **-1.** [fossilization] pétrification *f*. **-2.** [shock] ébahissement *m*, pétrification *f lit*.

petrify [ˈpetrɪfaɪ] (*pt & pp* **petrified**) *vt* **-1.** [fossilize] pétrifier; **petrified forest** forêt *f* pétrifiée. **-2.** [terrify] terrifier, pétrifier; **the noise petrified me** le bruit me glaça le sang.

petrochemical [ˌpetrəʊˈkemɪkl] *adj* pétrochimique.

petrochemistry [ˌpetrəʊˈkemɪstrɪ] *n* pétrochimie *f*.

petrocurrency [ˌpetrəʊˈkʌrənsɪ] (*pl* **petrocurrencies**) *n* devise *f* pétrolière.

petrodollar [ˈpetrəʊˌdɒləʳ] *n* pétrodollar *m*.

Petrograd [ˈpetrəgræd] *pr n* Petrograd.

petrol [ˈpetrəl] *Br* ◇ *n* essence *f*; **unleaded ~** essence sans plomb; **we ran out of ~** nous sommes tombés en panne d'essence.
◇ *comp* [fumes, rationing, shortage] d'essence.

petrolatum [ˌpetrəˈleɪtəm] *n Am* vaseline *f*.

petrol blue *n* bleu *m* pétrole.
◆ **petrol-blue** *adj* bleu pétrole *(inv)*.

petrol bomb *n* cocktail *m* Molotov.
◆ **petrol-bomb** *vt* attaquer au cocktail Molotov, lancer un cocktail Molotov contre OR sur; **the police station was petrol-bombed during the night** le commissariat a été attaqué à coups de cocktails Molotov pendant la nuit.

petrol bomber *n* lanceur *m*, -euse *f* de cocktail Molotov.

petrol can *n Br* bidon *m* d'essence.

petrol cap *n Br* bouchon *m* d'essence.

petrol-driven *adj Br* [engine] à essence.

petrol engine *n Br* moteur *m* à essence.

petroleum [pɪˈtrəʊljəm] ◇ *n* pétrole *m*.
◇ *comp* [industry] du pétrole; [imports] de pétrole.

petroleum jelly *n Br* vaseline *f*.

petrol gauge *n Br* jauge *f* à essence.

petrology [peˈtrɒlədʒɪ] *n* pétrologie *f*.

petrol pump *n Br* [at service station] pompe *f* à essence; **prices at the ~ have risen** le prix de l'essence à la pompe a augmenté.

petrol station *n Br* station-service *f*.

petrol tank *n Br* AUT réservoir *m* (d'essence).

petrol tanker *n Br* **-1.** [lorry] camion-citerne *m*. **-2.** [ship] pétrolier *m*, tanker *m*.

Petrushka [pəˈtruːʃkə] *pr n* Petrouchka.

pet shop *n* magasin *m* d'animaux domestiques, animalerie *f*.

petticoat [ˈpetɪkəʊt] ◇ *n* [waist slip] jupon *m*; [full-length slip] combinaison *f*.
◇ *comp pej* [government, politics] de femmes.

Petticoat Lane *pr n rue de Londres connue pour son marché du dimanche matin*.

pettifogger [ˈpetɪfɒgəʳ] *n Br* **-1.** [quibbler] chicaneur *m*, -euse *f*, ergoteur *m*, -euse *f*. **-2.** [lawyer] avocat *m* marron.

pettifogging [ˈpetɪfɒgɪŋ] *adj* **-1.** [petty - person] chicanier; [- details] insignifiant. **-2.** [dishonest] louche; **a ~ lawyer** un avocat marron.

pettiness [ˈpetɪnɪs] *n* **-1.** [triviality - of details] insignifiance *f*; [- of rules] caractère *m* pointilleux. **-2.** [small-mindedness] mesquinerie *f*, étroitesse *f* d'esprit.

petting *inf* [ˈpetɪŋ] *n (U)* [sexual] caresses *fpl*; **there was a lot of heavy ~ going on** ça se pelotait dans tous les coins.

petting zoo *n Am partie d'un zoo où les enfants peuvent s'approcher des animaux*.

pettish [ˈpetɪʃ] *adj Br* [person] grincheux, acariâtre; [mood] maussade; [remark] hargneux, désagréable.

pettishly [ˈpetɪʃlɪ] *adv* avec humeur.

petty [ˈpetɪ] (*compar* **pettier**, *superl* **pettiest**) *adj* **-1.** *pej* [trivial - detail] insignifiant, mineur; [- difficulty] mineur; [- question] tatillon; [- regulation] tracassier; [- ambitions] médiocre. **-2.** *pej* [mean - behaviour, mind, spite] mesquin. **-3.** [minor, small-scale] petit; **~ acts of vandalism** de petits actes de vandalisme; **a ~ offence** une infraction mineure; **a ~ thief** un petit délinquant; **~ expenses** menues dépenses *fpl*; **a ~ official** un petit fonctionnaire.

petty bourgeois ◇ *adj* petit-bourgeois.
◇ *n* petit-bourgeois *m*, petite-bourgeoise *f*.

petty bourgeoisie *n* petite-bourgeoisie *f*.

petty cash *n* petite monnaie *f*; **I took the money out of ~** j'ai pris l'argent dans la caisse des dépenses courantes.

petty larceny *n* larcin *m*.

petty-minded *adj* borné, mesquin.

petty officer *n Br* ≃ second maître *m*.

petty sessions *npl en Angleterre, tribunal dépendant de la juridiction d'un juge de paix*.

petulance [ˈpetjʊləns] *n* irritabilité *f*.

petulant [ˈpetjʊlənt] *adj* [bad-tempered - person] irritable, acariâtre; [- remark] acerbe, désagréable; [- behaviour] désagréable, agressif; [sulky] maussade; **in a ~ mood** de mauvaise humeur.

petulantly [ˈpetjʊləntlɪ] *adv* [act, speak - irritably] avec irritation; [- sulkily] avec mauvaise humeur; **"no!", she said ~** «non!», dit-elle avec mauvaise humeur.

petunia [pəˈtjuːnjə] *n* pétunia *m*.

pew [pjuː] *n* banc *m* d'église; **take a ~** *inf Br hum* assieds-toi donc!

pewit [ˈpiːwɪt] = **peewit**.

pewter [ˈpjuːtəʳ] ◇ *n* **-1.** [metal] étain *m*. **-2.** *(U)* [ware] étains *mpl*. **-3.** [colour] gris étain *m*.
◇ *comp* [tableware, tankard] en étain.

peyote [peɪˈəʊtɪ] *n* peyotl *m*.

Pfc, PFC (*abbr of* **private first class**) *n Am* soldat *m* de première classe.

PG *n* **-1.** CIN (*abbr of* **parental guidance**) *désigne un film dont certaines scènes peuvent choquer*, ≃ pour adultes et adolescents. **-2.** *Br* (*abbr of* **paying guest**) pensionnaire *mf*.

PGA *pr n abbr of* **Professional Golfers Association**.

p & h *written abbr of* **postage and handling**.

pH *n* pH *m.*

PH *n abbr of* Purple Heart.

PHA (*abbr of* Public Housing Administration) *pr n services du logement social aux États-Unis.*

Phaedra ['fiːdrə] *pr n* Phèdre.

Phaëthon ['feɪəθən] *pr n* Phaéton.

phaeton ['feɪtn] *n* -**1.** [carriage] phaéton *m.* -**2.** *Am* AUT *dated* limousine *f* décapotable.

phagocyte ['fægəsaɪt] *n* phagocyte *m.*

phagocytosis [ˌfægəsaɪ'təʊsɪs] *n* phagocytose *f.*

phalange ['fælændʒ] *n* ANAT phalange *f.*

Phalangist [fæ'lændʒɪst] ◇ *adj* phalangiste. ◇ *n* phalangiste *mf.*

phalanstery ['fælənstrɪ] (*pl* **phalansteries**) *n* phalanstère *m* SOCIOL.

phalanx ['fælæŋks] (*pl* **phalanxes** OR **phalanges** [-lændʒiːz]) *n* -**1.** ANTIQ & MIL phalange *f.* -**2.** ANAT phalange *f.* -**3.** POL phalange *f.*

phallic ['fælɪk] *adj* phallique; ~ **symbol** symbole *m* phallique.

phallus ['fæləs] *n* phallus *m.*

phantasm ['fæntæzm] *n* fantasme *m.*

phantasmagoria [ˌfæntæzmə'gɔːrɪə] *n* fantasmagorie *f.*

phantasmagoric(al) [ˌfæntæzmə'gɒrɪk(l)] *adj* fantasmagorique.

phantasmal [fæn'tæzml] *adj* fantomatique.

phantasy ['fæntəsɪ] = **fantasy**.

phantom ['fæntəm] ◇ *n* -**1.** [ghost] fantôme *m,* spectre *m;* 'The Phantom of the Opera' *Leroux, Lloyd Webber* 'le Fantôme de l'opéra'. -**2.** [threat, source of dread] spectre *m.* -**3.** *lit* [illusion] illusion *f.*
◇ *adj* -**1.** [gen] imaginaire, fantôme. -**2.** MED: ~ **limb** membre *m* fantôme; ~ **pregnancy** *Br* grossesse *f* nerveuse.

pharaoh ['feərəʊ] *n* pharaon *m.*

pharaoh ant *n* fourmi *f* de Pharaon.

pharisaic [ˌfærɪ'seɪɪk] *adj* pharisaïque.

Pharisee ['færɪsiː] *n* Pharisien *m,* -enne *f.*

pharmaceutical [ˌfɑːmə'sjuːtɪkl] ◇ *adj* pharmaceutique.
◇ *n* médicament *m.*

pharmacist ['fɑːməsɪst] *n* pharmacien *m,* -enne *f.*

pharmacogenetics [ˌfɑːməkədʒɪ'netɪks] *n (U)* pharmacogénétique *f.*

pharmacological [ˌfɑːməkə'lɒdʒɪkl] *adj* pharmacologique.

pharmacologist [ˌfɑːmə'kɒlədʒɪst] *n* pharmacologiste *mf,* pharmacologue *mf.*

pharmacology [ˌfɑːmə'kɒlədʒɪ] ◇ *n* pharmacologie *f.*
◇ *comp* [laboratory, studies] de pharmacologie, pharmacologique.

pharmacopoeia *Br,* **pharmacopeia** *Am* [ˌfɑːməkə'piːə] *n* pharmacopée *f.*

pharmacy ['fɑːməsɪ] (*pl* **pharmacies**) *n* -**1.** [science] pharmacie *f.* -**2.** [dispensary, shop] pharmacie *f.*

pharyngal [fə'rɪŋgl], **pharyngeal** [ˌfærɪn'dʒiːəl] *adj* -**1.** MED [infection] pharyngé; [organ] pharyngien. -**2.** LING pharyngal.

pharyngitis [ˌfærɪn'dʒaɪtɪs] *n (U)* pharyngite *f;* to have ~ avoir une pharyngite.

pharynx ['færɪnks] (*pl* **pharynxes** OR **pharynges** [fæ'rɪndʒiːz]) *n* pharynx *m.*

phase [feɪz] ◇ *n* -**1.** [period - gen] phase *f,* période *f;* [- of illness] phase *f,* stade *m;* [- of career] étape *f;* [- of civilization] période *f;* the project is going through a critical ~ le projet traverse une phase critique; the final ~ of the election campaign la dernière étape de la campagne électorale; ~ two of the government's incomes policy la deuxième étape de la politique salariale du gouvernement; their daughter's going through a difficult ~ leur fille traverse une période difficile; don't worry, it's just a ~ she's going through ne vous inquiétez pas, ça lui passera. -**2.** ASTRON [of moon] phase *f.* -**3.** CHEM, ELEC & PHYS phase *f;* in the solid ~ en phase OR à l'état solide; to be in ~ *literal* & *fig* être en phase; to be out of ~ *literal* & *fig* être déphasé; the government is out of ~ with the mood of the country le gouvernement est en décalage complet avec les sentiments de la population.
◇ *vt* -**1.** [synchronize] synchroniser, faire coïncider; the two operations have to be perfectly ~d les deux opérations doivent être parfaitement synchronisées. -**2.** *Am* [prearrange - delivery, development] planifier, programmer. -**3.** ELEC & TECH mettre en phase.
◆ **phase in** *vt sep* introduire progressivement OR par étapes; the reforms will obviously have to be ~d in il est évident que les réformes devront être introduites progressivement; the increases will be ~d in over five years les augmentations seront échelonnées sur cinq ans.
◆ **phase out** *vt sep* [stop using - machinery, weapon] cesser progressivement d'utiliser; [stop producing - car, model] abandonner progressivement la production de; [do away with - jobs, tax] supprimer progressivement OR par étapes; [- grant] retirer progressivement; when the use of these pesticides has been ~d out quand ces pesticides auront cessé d'être utilisés.

phased [feɪzd] *adj* [withdrawal, development] progressif, par étapes.

phase-out *n* suppression *f* progressive.

phatic ['fætɪk] *adj* phatique.

PhD (*abbr of* Doctor of Philosophy) *n (titulaire d'un) doctorat de 3e cycle;* ~ **students** étudiants *mpl* inscrits en doctorat; her ~ **thesis** sa thèse de doctorat.

pheasant ['feznt] (*pl inv* OR **pheasants**) *n* faisan *m;* [hen] (poule *f*) faisane *f.*

phenix ['fiːnɪks] *Am* = **phoenix**.

phenobarbitone [ˌfiːnəʊ'bɑːbɪtəʊn], **phenobarbital** [ˌfiːnəʊ'bɑːbɪtl] *n* phénobarbital *m.*

phenol ['fiːnɒl] *n* phénol *m.*

phenomena [fɪ'nɒmɪnə] *pl* → **phenomenon**.

phenomenal [fɪ'nɒmɪnl] *adj* phénoménal; a ~ **success** un immense succès.

phenomenally [fɪ'nɒmɪnəlɪ] *adv* phénoménalement; it's ~ **expensive** ça coûte horriblement cher.

phenomenological [fɪˌnɒmɪnə'lɒdʒɪkl] *adj* phénoménologique.

phenomenology [fɪˌnɒmɪ'nɒlədʒɪ] *n* phénoménologie *f.*

phenomenon [fɪ'nɒmɪnən] (*pl* phenomena [-nə]) *n* phénomène *m;* the **credit-card** ~ le phénomène des cartes de crédit.

phenyl ['fiːnl] *n* phényle *m.*

pheromone ['ferəməʊn] *n* phéromone *f,* phérormone *f.*

phew [fjuː] *interj* [in relief] ouf; [from heat] pff; [in disgust] berk, beurk.

phial ['faɪəl] *n* fiole *f.*

Phi Beta Kappa [ˈfaɪˌbeɪtə'kæpə] *pr n aux États-Unis, association universitaire à laquelle ne peuvent appartenir que les étudiants émérites.*

Philadelphia [ˌfɪlə'delfjə] *pr n* Philadelphie; in ~ à Philadelphie.

philander [fɪ'lændəʳ] *vi pej* courir le jupon.

philanderer [fɪ'lændərəʳ] *n pej* coureur *m* (de jupons).

philandering [fɪ'lændərɪŋ] *n* donjuanisme *m.*

philanthropic(al) [ˌfɪlən'θrɒpɪk(l)] *adj* philanthropique.

philanthropist [fɪ'lænθrəpɪst] *n* philanthrope *mf.*

philanthropy [fɪ'lænθrəpɪ] *n* philanthropie *f.*

philatelic [ˌfɪlə'telɪk] *adj* philatélique.

philatelist [fɪ'lætəlɪst] *n* philatéliste *mf.*

philately [fɪ'lætəlɪ] *n* philatélie *f.*

Philemon [fɪ'liːmɒn] *pr n* Philémon.

philharmonic [ˌfɪlɑː'mɒnɪk] ◇ *adj* philharmonique; ~ **orchestra** orchestre *m* philharmonique.
◇ *n* orchestre *m* philharmonique.

Philip ['fɪlɪp] *pr n* Philippe; ~ **Augustus** P[hi]lippe Auguste; ~ **the Fair** Philippe le Bel.

Philippians [fɪ'lɪpɪənz] *pl pr n* BIBLE: the ~ Philippiens; the Epistle of Paul the Apostle the ~ l'Épître de saint Paul aux Philippien[s].

philippic [fɪ'lɪpɪk] *n* philippique *f.*

Philippines ['fɪlɪpiːnz] *pl pr n:* the ~ les P[hi]lippines *fpl;* in the ~ aux Philippines.

Philistine [*Br* 'fɪlɪstaɪn, *Am* 'fɪlɪstiːn] ◇ -**1.** HIST Philistin *m.* -**2.** *fig* philistin *m lit,* b[éo]tien *m,* -enne *f.*
◇ *adj* philistin.

Philistinism ['fɪlɪstɪnɪzm] *n* philistinisme *m*

Phillips® ['fɪlɪps] *comp:* ~ **screw/screw-dri[ver]** vis *f*/tournevis *m* cruciforme.

philodendron [ˌfɪlə'dendrən] (*pl* philod[en]drons OR philodendra [-drə]) *n* philod[en]dron *m.*

philological [ˌfɪlə'lɒdʒɪkl] *adj* philologique.

philologist [fɪ'lɒlədʒɪst] *n* philologue *mf.*

philology [fɪ'lɒlədʒɪ] *n* philologie *f.*

philosopher [fɪ'lɒsəfəʳ] *n* philosophe *mf;* sh[e's] a bit of a ~ elle est portée sur la philosoph[ie]; the ~'s **stone** la pierre philosophale.

philosophic(al) [ˌfɪlə'sɒfɪk(l)] *adj* -**1.** PHI[LOS] philosophique. -**2.** [calm, resigned] philosoph[e]; feel quite ~ about the situation j'envisage situation avec philosophie.

philosophically [ˌfɪlə'sɒfɪklɪ] *adv* -**1.** PHI[LOS] philosophiquement. -**2.** [calmly] philosophiq[ue]ment, avec philosophie.

philosophize, -ise [fɪ'lɒsəfaɪz] *vi* philosoph[er]; to ~ **about sthg** philosopher sur qqch.

philosophy [fɪ'lɒsəfɪ] (*pl* philosophi[es]) *n* philosophie *f;* she's a ~ **student** elle [est] étudiante en philosophie ‖ *fig:* we share [the] same ~ of life nous avons la même concepti[on] de la vie; she accepted the defeat with ~ e[lle] accepta la défaite avec philosophie.

philtre *Br,* **philter** *Am* ['fɪltəʳ] *n lit* philtre *m*

phiz *inf* [fɪz], **phizog** *inf* ['fɪzɒg] *n Br d[ated]* tronche *f,* poire *f.*

phlebitis [flɪ'baɪtɪs] *n (U)* phlébite *f.*

phlebotomy [flɪ'bɒtəmɪ] *n* phlébotomie *f.*

phlegm [flem] *n* -**1.** MED [in respiratory passag[es]] glaire *f.* -**2.** *fig* [composure] flegme *m.* -**3.** *a[rchaic]* [bodily humour] flegme *m.*

phlegmatic [fleg'mætɪk] *adj* flegmatique.

phlegmatically [fleg'mætɪklɪ] *adv* avec flegm[e], flegmatiquement.

phloem ['fləʊəm] *n* phloème *m.*

phlox [flɒks] *n* phlox *m inv.*

Phnom Penh [ˌnɒm'pen] *pr n* Phnom Penh

phobia ['fəʊbjə] *n* phobie *f;* he has a ~ [of] spiders il a la phobie des araignées; she's g[ot a] ~ about work elle est allergique au travail

phobic ['fəʊbɪk] ◇ *adj* phobique.
◇ *n* phobique *mf.*

Phocaea [fəʊ'siːə] *pr n* Phocée.

Phoebe ['fiːbɪ] *pr n* Phébé.

Phoebus ['fiːbəs] *pr n* Phébus.

Phoenicia [fɪ'nɪʃɪə] *pr n* Phénicie *f.*

Phoenician [fɪ'nɪʃɪən] ◇ *n* -**1.** [person] Phé[ni]cien *m,* -enne *f.* -**2.** LING phénicien *m.*
◇ *adj* phénicien.

phoenix ['fiːnɪks] *n* phénix *m.*

phoenix-like *adj* & *adv* tel un phénix; the n[ew] movement was born ~ out of the old nouveau mouvement est né des cendres précédent.

phon [fɒn] *n* phone *m* ACOUST.

phonate [fəʊ'neɪt] *vi* produire des sons.

phonation [fəʊ'neɪʃn] *n* phonation *f.*

phonatory ['fəʊnətrɪ] *adj* phonatoire.

phone [fəʊn] ◇ *n* -**1.** [telephone] téléphone I answered the ~ j'ai répondu au télépho[ne]; just a minute, I'm on the ~ un instant, je s[uis] au téléphone; we're not on the ~ yet n[ous] n'avons pas encore le téléphone; you['re] wanted on the ~ on vous demande au t[élé]phone; she told me the news by ~ elle r[m']a appris la nouvelle au téléphone; I don't wish

discuss it over the ~ je préfère ne pas en parler au téléphone. -**2.** LING phone *m*.
◇ *comp* [bill] de téléphone; [line, message] téléphonique.
◇ *vi Br* téléphoner; to ~ for a plumber/a taxi appeler un plombier/un taxi *(par téléphone)*.
◇ *vt Br* téléphoner à; I'll ~ him when I arrive je lui téléphonerai à mon arrivée; to ~ Paris téléphoner à Paris; can you ~ me the answer? pouvez-vous me donner la réponse par téléphone?
◆ **phone up** ◇ *vi insep* téléphoner.
◇ *vt sep* téléphoner à.

hone book *n* annuaire *m* (téléphonique).
hone booth *n* cabine *f* téléphonique.
hone box *n Br* cabine *f* téléphonique; I'm calling from a ~ j'appelle d'une cabine.
hone call *n* coup *m* de téléphone, appel *m* (téléphonique).
hone card *n* Télécarte® *f*.
hone-in *n* RADIO & TV: ~ (programme) *émission au cours de laquelle les auditeurs ou les téléspectateurs peuvent intervenir par téléphone*.
honeme ['fəuniːm] *n* phonème *m*.
honemic [fə'niːmɪk] *adj* phonémique, phonématique.
honemics [fə'niːmɪks] *n (U)* phonémique *f*, phonématique *f*.
hone number *n* numéro *m* de téléphone.
hone-tapping [-ˌtæpɪŋ] *n (U)* écoute *f* téléphonique, écoutes *fpl* téléphoniques; ~ has become more widespread la pratique de l'écoute téléphonique est de plus en plus répandue.
honetic [fə'netɪk] *adj* phonétique.
honetically [fə'netɪklɪ] *adv* phonétiquement.
honetic alphabet *n* alphabet *m* phonétique.
honetician [ˌfəunɪ'tɪʃn] *n* phonéticien *m*, -enne *f*.
honetics [fə'netɪks] *n (U)* phonétique *f*.
honey *inf* ['fəunɪ] (*compar* phonier, *superl* phoniest, *pl* phonies) ◇ *adj* -**1.** [false - banknote, jewel, name] faux; [- title, company, accent] bidon; [- tears] de crocodile; [- laughter] qui sonne faux; his story sounds ~ son histoire a tout l'air d'être (du) bidon; the ~ war la drôle de guerre. -**2.** [spurious - person] bidon.
◇ *n* -**1.** [impostor] imposteur *m*; [charlatan] charlatan *m*. -**2.** [pretentious person] frimeur *m*, -euse *f*, m'as-tu-vu *mf inv*.
honic ['fəunɪk] *adj* phonique.
honograph ['fəunəgrɑːf] *n* -**1.** [early gramophone] phonographe *m*. -**2.** *Am dated* [record player] tourne-disque *m*, électrophone *m*.
honological [ˌfəunə'lɒdʒɪkl] *adj* phonologique.
honologist [fəu'nɒlədʒɪst] *n* phonologue *mf*.
honology [fəu'nɒlədʒɪ] (*pl* phonologies) *n* phonologie *f*.
hony ['fəunɪ] = **phoney**.
hooey *inf* ['fuːɪ] *interj* [as expletive - expressing irritation] zut, flûte; [- expressing disbelief] mon œil.
hosgene ['fɒsdʒiːn] *n* phosgène *m*.
hosphate ['fɒsfeɪt] *n* AGR & CHEM phosphate *m*; 'contains no ~s' 'sans phosphates'.
hosphene ['fɒsfiːn] *n* phosphène *m*.
hosphide ['fɒsfaɪd] *n* phosphure *m*.
hosphine ['fɒsfiːn] *n* phosphine *f*, hydrogène *m* phosphoré.
hosphor(e) ['fɒsfəʳ] *n* luminophore *m*, phosphore *m (substance phosphorescente)*.
hosphoresce [ˌfɒsfə'res] *vi* être phosphorescent.
hosphorescence [ˌfɒsfə'resns] *n* phosphorescence *f*.
hosphorescent [ˌfɒsfə'resnt] *adj* phosphorescent.
hosphoric [fɒs'fɒrɪk] *adj* phosphorique; ~ acid acide *m* orthophosphorique.
hosphorism ['fɒsfərɪzm] *n* phosphorisme *m*.
hosphorous ['fɒsfərəs] *adj* phosphorique.
hosphorus ['fɒsfərəs] *n* phosphore *m*.

phot [fɒt] *n* phot *m*.
photic ['fəutɪk] *adj* photique.
photo ['fəutəu] (*pl* photos) (*abbr of* photograph) *n* photo *f*.
photoactive [ˌfəutəu'æktɪv] *adj* [organism] sensible à la lumière.
photo album *n* album *m* de photos.
photocall ['fəutəukɔːl] *n* séance *f* photo *(avec des photographes de presse)*.
photocell ['fəutəusel] *n* cellule *f* photoélectrique.
photochemical [ˌfəutəu'kemɪkl] *adj* photochimique.
photochemistry [ˌfəutəu'kemɪstrɪ] *n* photochimie *f*.
photocompose [ˌfəutəukəm'pəuz] *vt* photocomposer.
photocomposition ['fəutəuˌkɒmpə'zɪʃn] *n* photocomposition *f*.
photoconductivity ['fəutəuˌkɒndʌk'tɪvətɪ] *n* photoconduction *f*.
photocopier [ˌfəutəu'kɒpɪəʳ] *n* photocopieur *m*, photocopieuse *f*.
photocopy ['fəutəuˌkɒpɪ] (*pl* photocopies, *pt* & *pp* photocopied) ◇ *n* photocopie *f*.
◇ *vt* photocopier.
photocopying ['fəutəuˌkɒpɪɪŋ] *n (U)* reprographie *f*, photocopie *f*; there's some ~ to do il y a des photocopies à faire.
photodisintegration ['fəutəudɪsˌɪntɪ'greɪʃn] *n* photodésintégration *f*.
photodynamics [ˌfəutəudaɪ'næmɪks] *n (U)* photodynamique *f*.
photoelasticity [ˌfəutəuɪlæ'stɪsətɪ] *n* photoélasticité *f*.
photoelectric [ˌfəutəuɪ'lektrɪk] *adj* photoélectrique; ~ cell cellule *f* photoélectrique.
photoelectricity [ˌfəutəuɪlek'trɪsətɪ] *n* photoélectricité *f*.
photoelectron [ˌfəutəuɪ'lektrɒn] *n* photoélectron *m*.
photoemission [ˌfəutəuɪ'mɪʃn] *n* photoémission *f*.
photoengraving [ˌfəutəuɪn'greɪvɪŋ] *n* photogravure *f*.
photo finish *n* -**1.** SPORT arrivée *f* groupée; the race was a ~ il a fallu départager les vainqueurs de la course avec la photo-finish. -**2.** *fig* partie *f* serrée; the election is going to be a ~ pour les élections, la partie sera serrée.
Photofit® ['fəutəufɪt] *n*: ~ (picture) photo-robot *f*, portrait-robot *m*.
photoflood ['fəutəuflʌd] *n*: ~ (lamp) lampe *f* flood.
photofluorography [ˌfəutəufluə'rɒgrəfɪ] *n* radiophotographie *f*.
photogenic [ˌfəutəu'dʒenɪk] *adj* photogénique.
photogeology [ˌfəutəudʒɪ'ɒlədʒɪ] *n* photogéologie *f*.
photogram ['fəutəgræm] *n* photogramme *m*.
photogrammetry [ˌfəutəu'græmətrɪ] *n* photogrammétrie *f*.
photograph ['fəutəgrɑːf] ◇ *n* photographie *f (image)*, photo *f (image)*; to take a ~ of sb prendre qqn en photo, photographier qqn; they took our ~ ils nous ont pris en photo; to have one's ~ taken se faire photographier; I'm in this ~ je suis sur cette photo; we took a lot of good ~s on holiday nous avons pris OR fait beaucoup de bonnes photos pendant les vacances; she takes a good ~ [is photogenic] elle est photogénique.
◇ *vt* photographier, prendre en photo; she doesn't like being ~ed elle n'aime pas qu'on la prenne en photo.
◇ *vi*: he ~s well [is photogenic] il est photogénique; the trees won't ~ well in this light il n'y a pas assez de lumière pour faire une bonne photo des arbres.
photograph album *n* album *m* de photos.

photographer [fə'tɒgrəfəʳ] *n* photographe *mf*; I'm not much of a ~ je ne suis pas très doué pour la photographie.
photographic [ˌfəutə'græfɪk] *adj* photographique; to have a ~ memory avoir une bonne mémoire visuelle; ~ shop magasin *m* de photo; ~ society club *m* d'amateurs de photo; ~ library photothèque *f*.
photographically [ˌfəutə'græfɪklɪ] *adv* photographiquement.
photography [fə'tɒgrəfɪ] *n* photographie *f (art)*, photo *f (art)*; an exhibition of French ~ une exposition de photographie française.
photogravure [ˌfəutəugrə'vjuəʳ] *n* photogravure *f*.
photojournalism [ˌfəutəu'dʒɜːnəlɪzm] *n* photojournalisme *m*.
photokinesis [ˌfəutəu'kaɪniːsɪs] *n* photocinèse *f*.
photolithograph [ˌfəutəu'lɪθəgrɑːf] *n* photolithographie *f*.
photolithography [ˌfəutəulɪ'θɒgrəfɪ] *n* photolithographie *f*.
photoluminescent ['fəutəuˌluːmɪ'nesnt] *adj* photoluminescent.
photolysis [fəu'tɒlɪsɪs] *n* photolyse *f*.
photomap ['fəutəumæp] (*pt* & *pp* photomapped, *cont* photomapping) ◇ *n* photocarte *f*.
◇ *vt* faire une photocarte de.
photomechanical [ˌfəutəumɪ'kænɪkl] *adj* photomécanique.
photometer [fəu'tɒmɪtəʳ] *n* photomètre *m*.
photometric [ˌfəutə'metrɪk] *adj* photométrique.
photometry [fəu'tɒmɪtrɪ] *n* photométrie *f*.
photomontage [ˌfəutəumɒn'tɑːʒ] *n* photomontage *m*.
photomultiplier [ˌfəutəu'mʌltɪplaɪəʳ] *n* photomultiplicateur *m*.
photon ['fəutɒn] *n* photon *m*.
photonovel ['fəutəˌnɒvl] *n* roman-photo *m*, photo-roman *m*.
photo-offset *n* offset *m*.
photo opportunity *n* séance *f* photoprotocolaire.
photoperiod [ˌfəutəu'pɪərɪəd] *n* photopériode *f*.
photoperiodic ['fəutəuˌpɪərɪ'ɒdɪk] *adj* photopériodique.
photophily [fəu'tɒfɪlɪ] *n* photophilie *f*.
photophobia [ˌfəutəu'fəubɪə] *n* photophobie *f*.
photophobic [ˌfəutəu'fəubɪk] *adj* photophobique.
photophore [ˌfəutəu'fɔːʳ] *n* (organe *m*) photophore *m*.
photopolymer [ˌfəutəu'pɒlɪməʳ] *n* plastique *m* photopolymère.
photorealism [ˌfəutəu'rɪəlɪzm] *n* photoréalisme *m*.
photoreceptor [ˌfəutəurɪ'septəʳ] *n* photorécepteur *m*.
photoreconnaissance [ˌfəutəurɪ'kɒnɪsns] *n* reconnaissance *f* photographique.
photosensitive [ˌfəutəu'sensɪtɪv] *adj* photosensible.
photosensitivity ['fəutəuˌsensɪ'tɪvətɪ] *n* photosensibilité *f*.
photosensitize, -ise [ˌfəutəu'sensɪtaɪz] *vt* rendre photosensible.
photoset ['fəutəuset] (*pt* & *pp* photoset, *cont* photosetting) *vt* photocomposer.
photostat ['fəutəstæt] (*pt* & *pp* photostatted, *cont* photostatting) *vt* photocopier.
Photostat® *n* photostat *m*, photocopie *f*; ~ copy photocopie *f*; ~ machine photocopieuse *f*.
photosynthesis [ˌfəutəu'sɪnθəsɪs] *n* photosynthèse *f*.
photosynthesize, -ise [ˌfəutəu'sɪnθəsaɪz] *vt* fabriquer par photosynthèse.
phototransistor [ˌfəutəutræn'zɪstəʳ] *n* phototransistor *m*.

phototropism [ˌfəʊtəʊˈtrəʊpɪzm] *n* phototropisme *m*.

phototype [ˈfəʊtəʊtaɪp] ◇ *n* -**1.** [process] phototypie *f*. -**2.** [print] phototype *m*.
◇ *vt* faire un phototype de.

phototypesetting [ˌfəʊtəʊˈtaɪpsetɪŋ] *n* photocomposition *f*.

phototypography [ˌfəʊtəʊtaɪˈpɒgrəfɪ] *n* photocomposition *f*.

photovoltaic [ˌfəʊtəʊvɒlˈteɪɪk] *adj* photovoltaïque; ~ **cell** cellule *f* photovoltaïque, photophile *f*.

phrasal [ˈfreɪzl] *adj*: ~ **conjunction/preposition** locution *f* conjonctive/prépositive.

phrasal verb *n* verbe *m* à postposition.

phrase [freɪz] ◇ *n* -**1.** [expression] expression *f*, locution *f*; **I can't find the right** ~ je ne trouve pas l'expression que je cherche; **set** ~ expression figée; **turn of** ~ tournure *f*. -**2.** LING syntagme *m*, groupe *m*; **noun** ~ syntagme OR groupe nominal. -**3.** MUS phrase *f*.
◇ *vt* -**1.** [letter] rédiger, tourner; [idea] exprimer, tourner; **couldn't you** ~ **it differently?** ne pourriez-vous pas trouver une autre formule?; **how shall I** ~ **it?** comment dire ça?; **he** ~**d it very elegantly** il a trouvé une tournure très élégante (pour le dire). -**2.** MUS phraser.

phrase book *n* guide *m* de conversation.

phrase marker *n* LING indicateur *m* syntagmatique.

phraseology [ˌfreɪzɪˈɒlədʒɪ] (*pl* **phraseologies**) *n* phraséologie *f*.

phrase structure *n* LING structure *f* syntagmatique; ~ **grammar** grammaire *f* syntagmatique; ~ **rules** règles *fpl* syntagmatiques.

phrasing [ˈfreɪzɪŋ] *n* -**1.** [expressing] choix *m* des mots; **with careful** ~ en choisissant ses mots avec le plus grand soin OR soigneusement ses mots; **the** ~ **of her refusal was very elegant** son refus était formulé de manière très élégante. -**2.** MUS phrasé *m*.

phreatic [frɪˈætɪk] *adj* phréatique; **the** ~ **layer** la nappe phréatique.

phrenetic [frəˈnetɪk] = **frenetic**.

phrenic [ˈfrenɪk] *adj* phrénique.

phrenologist [frɪˈnɒlədʒɪst] *n* phrénologue *mf*, phrénologiste *mf*.

phrenology [frɪˈnɒlədʒɪ] *n* phrénologie *f*.

Phrygia [ˈfrɪdʒɪə] *pr n* Phrygie *f*.

Phrygian [ˈfrɪdʒɪən] ◇ *n* Phrygien *m*, -enne *f*.
◇ *adj* phrygien; ~ **cap** bonnet phrygien.

phthisis [ˈθaɪsɪs] *n* *(U)* *dated* phtisie *f*.

phut *inf* [fʌt] ◇ *n*: **the engine made a** ~ **and stopped** le moteur eut un hoquet puis s'arrêta.
◇ *adv*: **to go** ~ rendre l'âme, lâcher.

phycology [faɪˈkɒlədʒɪ] *n* phycologie *f*, algologie *f*.

phylactery [fɪˈlæktərɪ] (*pl* **phylacteries**) *n* RELIG phylactère *m*.

phylloxera [fɪˈlɒksərə] *n* phylloxéra *m*, phylloxera *m*.

phylogenesis [ˌfaɪləʊˈdʒenɪsɪs] (*pl* **phylogeneses** [-ˌsiːz]) *n* phylogenèse *f*, phylogénie *f*.

phylogenetic [ˌfaɪləʊdʒəˈnetɪk] *adj* phylogénétique.

phylogeny [faɪˈlɒdʒənɪ] (*pl* **phylogenies**) = **phylogenesis**.

phylum [ˈfaɪləm] (*pl* **phyla** [-lə]) *n* phylum *m*.

physiatrics [ˌfɪzɪˈætrɪks] *n* *(U)* *Am* kinésithérapie *f*.

physiatrist [ˌfɪzɪˈætrɪst] *n* *Am* kinésithérapeute *mf*.

physic [ˈfɪzɪk] *n* *arch* médicament *m*, remède *m*.

physical [ˈfɪzɪkl] ◇ *adj* -**1.** [bodily - fitness, strength, sport] physique; **a** ~ **examination** un examen médical, une visite médicale; **I don't get enough** ~ **exercise** je ne fais pas assez d'exercice (physique); **it was a very** ~ **match** SPORT ce fut un match très physique; ~ **handicap** infirmité *f*. -**2.** [natural, material - forces, property, presence] physique; [- manifestation, universe] physique, matériel; **it's a** ~ **impossibility** c'est physiquement OR matériellement impossible. -**3.** CHEM & PHYS physique. -**4.** GEOG physique; **the** ~ **features of the desert** la topographie du désert.
◇ *n* visite *f* médicale; **to go for a** ~ passer une visite médicale.

physical education *n* éducation *f* physique.

physical geography *n* géographie *f* physique.

physical jerks *inf npl Br*: **to do** ~ faire des mouvements de gym.

physically [ˈfɪzɪklɪ] *adv* physiquement; **to be** ~ **fit** être en bonne forme physique; **she is** ~ **handicapped** elle a un handicap physique.

physical sciences *npl* sciences *fpl* physiques.

physical therapist *n* kinésithérapeute *mf*.

physical therapy *n* kinésithérapie *f*; [after accident or illness] rééducation *f*.

physical training = **physical education**.

physician [fɪˈzɪʃn] *n* médecin *m*.

physicist [ˈfɪzɪsɪst] *n* physicien *m*, -enne *f*.

physics [ˈfɪzɪks] *n* *(U)* physique *f*.

physio *inf* [ˈfɪzɪəʊ] *n* -**1.** (*abbr of* **physiotherapy**) kiné *f*. -**2.** (*abbr of* **physiotherapist**) kiné *mf*.

physiognomist [ˌfɪzɪˈɒnəmɪst] *n* physionomiste *mf*.

physiognomy [ˌfɪzɪˈɒnəmɪ] (*pl* **physiognomies**) *n* -**1.** [facial features] physionomie *f*. -**2.** GEOG topographie *f*, configuration *f*; **the** ~ **of London is changing** la physionomie de Londres est en train de changer.

physiological [ˌfɪzɪəˈlɒdʒɪkl] *adj* physiologique.

physiologist [ˌfɪzɪˈɒlədʒɪst] *n* physiologiste *mf*.

physiology [ˌfɪzɪˈɒlədʒɪ] *n* physiologie *f*.

physiotherapist [ˌfɪzɪəʊˈθerəpɪst] *n* kinésithérapeute *mf*.

physiotherapy [ˌfɪzɪəʊˈθerəpɪ] *n* kinésithérapie *f*; [after accident or illness] rééducation *f*; **to go for** OR **to have** ~ faire des séances de kinésithérapie.

physique [fɪˈziːk] *n* constitution *f* physique, physique *m*; **to have a fine** ~ avoir un beau corps; **to have a poor** ~ être chétif.

phytogenesis [ˌfaɪtəʊˈdʒenɪsɪs] *n* phytogenèse *f*.

phytogeny [faɪˈtɒdʒənɪ] = **phytogenesis**.

phytoplankton [ˌfaɪtəˈplæŋktən] *n* phytoplancton *m*.

pi [paɪ] ◇ *n* MATH pi *m*.
◇ *adj inf Br pej* -**1.** [pious] bigot *pej*. -**2.** [self-satisfied] suffisant.

Piacenza [pjəˈtʃentsə] *pr n* Plaisance.

pianist [ˈpɪənɪst] *n* pianiste *mf*.

piano[1] [pɪˈænəʊ] (*pl* **pianos**) ◇ *n* piano *m*.
◇ *comp* [duet, lesson, stool, teacher, tuner] de piano; [music] pour piano; [lid, leg] du piano; ~ **key** touche *f*; **the** ~ **keys** le clavier (du piano); ~ **organ** piano *m* mécanique; ~ **player** pianiste *mf*.

piano[2] [ˈpjɑːnəʊ] *adj* & *adv* [softly] piano *(inv)*.

piano accordion [pɪˈænəʊ-] *n* accordéon *m* (à touches).

pianoforte [pɪˌænəʊˈfɔːtɪ] *n fml* pianoforte *m*.

Pianola® [ˌpɪəˈnəʊlə] *n* Pianola® *m*.

piano roll [pɪˈænəʊ-] *n* bande *f* perforée *(pour piano mécanique)*.

piazza [pɪˈætsə] *n* -**1.** [square] place *f*, piazza *f*. -**2.** *Br* [gallery] galerie *f*. -**3.** *Am* [veranda] véranda *f*.

pic *inf* [pɪk] (*pl* **pics** OR **pix** [pɪks]) *n* [photograph] photo *f*; [picture] illustration *f*.

pica [ˈpaɪkə] *n* -**1.** TYPO [unit] pica *m*. -**2.** [on typewriter] pica *m*. -**3.** MED pica *m*.

picador [ˈpɪkədɔːʳ] *n* picador *m*.

picaninny *inf* [ˌpɪkəˈnɪnɪ] (*pl* **picaninnies**) = **piccaninny**.

Picardy [ˈpɪkədɪ] *pr n* Picardie *f*; **in** ~ en Picardie.

picaresque [ˌpɪkəˈresk] *adj* picaresque.

picayune *inf* [ˌpɪkəˈjuːn] ◇ *adj Am* [unimportant] insignifiant; [worthless] sans valeur.
◇ *n* pièce *f* de cinq cents; **I don't care a** ~ je m'en fiche royalement.

piccalilli [ˌpɪkəˈlɪlɪ] *n* piccalilli *m* *(sauce piquan à base de pickles et de moutarde)*.

piccaninny *inf* [ˌpɪkəˈnɪnɪ] (*pl* **piccaninnie** *n* négrillon *m*, -onne *f* *(attention: le terme «pic ninny», comme son équivalent français, est considér comme raciste)*.

piccolo [ˈpɪkələʊ] (*pl* **piccolos**) *n* piccolo *m*, p colo *m*.

pick [pɪk] ◇ *vt* -**1.** [select] choisir; **he always** ~ **the most expensive dish** il choisit toujours plat le plus cher; **she's been** ~**ed for th England team** elle a été sélectionnée dar l'équipe d'Angleterre; **to** ~ **a winner** [in racin choisir un cheval gagnant; **you really (kno how to)** ~ **them!** *iron* tu les choisis bien! □ t ~ **one's way**: **they** ~**ed their way along th narrow ridge** ils avancèrent prudemment long de la crête étroite. -**2.** [gather - fruit, flower cueillir; [- mushrooms] ramasser; **to** ~ **che ries/grapes** [for pleasure] cueillir des cerises/d raisin; [as job] faire la cueillette des cerises/l vendanges. -**3.** [remove] enlever; **I had to** ~ **th cat hairs off my dress** il a fallu que j'enlève l poils de chat de ma robe; **he was** ~**ing a spot/ scab** il était en train de gratter un bouton/ur croûte || [remove bits of food, debris etc from **they** ~**ed the bones clean** ils n'ont rien lais sur les os; **to** ~ **one's nose** se mettre les doig dans le nez; **to** ~ **one's teeth** se curer les den □ **to** ~ **sb/sthg to pieces** démolir qqn/qqc -**4.** [provoke]: **to** ~ **a fight** chercher la bagarr **to** ~ **a quarrel with sb** chercher noise c querelle à qqn. -**5.** [lock] crocheter. -**6.** [pluck guitar string] pincer; [- guitar] pincer les cord de.
◇ *vi*: **to** ~ **and choose**: **I like to be able to** ~ **and choose** j'aime bien avoir le choix; h **always has to** ~ **and choose** *pej* il faut toujou qu'il fasse le difficile; **with your qualificatio you can** ~ **and choose** avec vos diplôme toutes les portes vous sont ouvertes.
◇ *n* -**1.** [choice] choix *m*; **take your** ~ fait votre choix; **you can have your** ~ **of the** vous pouvez choisir celui qui vous plaît □ th ~ **of the bunch** *inf* le dessus du panier, le grati -**2.** [tool] pic *m*, pioche *f*.

◆ **pick at** *vt insep* -**1.** [pull at - thread, loose en tirer sur; [- flake of paint, scab] gratter. -**2.** [foo manger du bout des dents; **he only** ~**ed at th fish** il a à peine touché au poisson. -**3.** [critici pettily] être sur le dos de.

◆ **pick off** *vt sep* -**1.** [shoot one by one] abatt (un par un); **marksmen** ~**ed off the leade** des tireurs ont abattu les meneurs. -**2.** [remov - scab, paint] gratter.

◆ **pick on** *vt insep* -**1.** [victimize] harceler, s'e prendre à; ~ **on someone your own size!** t devrais t'en prendre à quelqu'un de ta taill -**2.** [single out] choisir; **why** ~ **on today of a days?** pourquoi choisir ce jour entre tous?

◆ **pick out** *vt sep* -**1.** [choose] choisir. -**2.** [spc identify] repérer, reconnaître; **I tried to** ~ **hi out in the crowd** j'ai essayé de le repérer dar la foule; **she's easy to** ~ **out because of h hair** elle est facile à reconnaître à cause de s cheveux. -**3.** [highlight, accentuate] rehausser; **th stitching is** ~**ed out in bright green** un vert v fait ressortir les coutures. -**4.** [play - tune] jou d'une manière hésitante.

◆ **pick over**, **pick through** *vt insep* [fruit, ve etables etc] trier.

◆ **pick up** ◇ *vt sep* -**1.** [lift] ramasser; ~ **u those books!** ramassez ces livres!; **to** ~ **up th telephone** décrocher le téléphone; **to** ~ **o.s. u** se relever □ **they left me to** ~ **up the bill** OR **the tab** *Am* ils m'ont laissé l'addition; **to** ~ **up the pieces** recoller les morceaux. -**2.** [give l to] prendre; **I never** ~ **up hitchhikers** je prends jamais d'auto-stoppeurs. -**3.** [colle fetch]: **my father** ~**ed me up at the static** mon père est venu me chercher à la gar **helicopters were sent to** ~ **up the wound** on a envoyé des hélicoptères pour ramener l blessés; **I have to** ~ **up a parcel at the po office** je dois passer prendre un colis à la pos -**4.** [acquire - skill] apprendre; **did you** ~ **up ar**

Greek during your stay? avez-vous appris un peu de grec pendant votre séjour?; to ~ up bad habits prendre de mauvaises habitudes || [win - reputation, prize] gagner; our country ~ed up most of the medals notre pays a remporté la plupart des médailles. -5. [glean - idea, information] glaner; I've ~ed up some useful tips since I started work here j'ai glané quelques bons tuyaux depuis que j'ai commencé à travailler ici. -6. *inf* [buy cheaply]: to ~ up a bargain dénicher une bonne affaire; I ~ed it up at the flea market je l'ai trouvé au marché aux puces. -7. [catch - illness, infection] attraper. -8. *inf* [earn] se faire; you can ~ up good money working on the rigs on peut se faire pas mal de fric en travaillant sur les plates-formes pétrolières. -9. *inf* [arrest] pincer. -10. *inf* [start relationship with] draguer; he ~ed her up in a bar il l'a draguée dans un bar. -11. [detect] détecter; he ~ed up the sound of a distant bell il perçut le son d'une cloche dans le lointain; the dogs ~ed up the scent again les chiens ont retrouvé la piste. -12. RADIO & TV [receive] capter. -13. [notice] relever; the proofreaders ~ up most of the mistakes les correcteurs repèrent OR relèvent la plupart des erreurs. -14. [criticize]: nobody ~ed him up on his sexist comments personne n'a relevé ses remarques sexistes. -15. [resume] reprendre; we ~ed up the discussion where we'd left off nous avons repris la discussion là où nous l'avions laissée. -16. [return to] revenir sur, reprendre; I'd like to ~ up a point you made earlier j'aimerais revenir sur une remarque que vous avez faite tout à l'heure. -17. [gather - speed, momentum] prendre. -18. *inf* [revive] remonter, requinquer.

◇ *vi insep* -1. [get better - sick person] se rétablir, se sentir mieux. -2. [improve - business, weather] s'arranger, s'améliorer; [- trade] reprendre; the market is ~ing up after a slow start COMM après avoir démarré doucement le marché commence à prendre. -3. [resume] continuer; they ~ed up where they had left off [in conversation] ils ont repris la conversation là où ils l'avaient laissée; [in game] ils ont repris le jeu là où ils l'avaient laissé.

pickaback ['pɪkəbæk] = **piggyback**.

pickaninny [,pɪkə'nɪnɪ] (*pl* pickaninnies) = **piccaninny**.

pickaxe *Br*, **pickax** *Am* ['pɪkæks] *n* pic *m*, pioche *f*.

picked [pɪkt] *adj* [products, items] sélectionné; [people] d'élite, trié sur le volet.

picker ['pɪkəʳ] *n* [of fruit, cotton etc] cueilleur *m*, -euse *f*, ramasseur *m*, -euse *f*; grape-~ vendangeur *m*, -euse *f*; strawberry-~ cueilleur de fraises; mushroom-~ ramasseur de champignons.

pickerel ['pɪkərəl] (*pl inv* OR **pickerels**) *n* brochet *m*.

picket ['pɪkɪt] ◇ *n* -1. INDUST [group] piquet *m* de grève; there was a ~ outside the factory il y avait un piquet de grève devant l'usine; to be on ~ duty faire partie d'un piquet de grève || [individual] gréviste *mf*, piquet *m* de grève; 20 ~s stood in front of the factory 20 grévistes se tenaient devant l'usine. -2. [outside embassy, ministry - group] groupe *m* de manifestants; [- individual] manifestant *m*, -e *f*. -3. MIL piquet *m*. -4. [stake] piquet *m*.

◇ *vt* -1. INDUST [workplace, embassy]: the strikers ~ed the factory les grévistes ont mis en place un piquet de grève devant l'usine; demonstrators ~ed the consulate at the week-end des manifestants ont bloqué le consulat ce week-end. -2. [fence] palissader. -3. [tie up] attacher, mettre au piquet.

◇ *vi* INDUST mettre en place un piquet de grève.

picket fence *n* clôture *f* de piquets, palissade *f*.

picketing ['pɪkətɪŋ] *n (U)* -1. [of workplace] piquets *mpl* de grève; there is heavy ~ at the factory gates les piquets de grève sont très nombreux aux portes de l'usine. -2. [of ministry, embassy]: there was ~ outside the embassy today aujourd'hui, il y a eu des manifestations devant l'ambassade.

picket line *n* piquet *m* de grève; to be OR to stand on a ~ faire partie d'un piquet de grève; to cross a ~ franchir un piquet de grève.

picking ['pɪkɪŋ] *n* -1. [selection - of object] choix *m*; [- of team] sélection *f*. -2. [of fruit, vegetables] cueillette *f*, ramassage *m*; cherry-/strawberry-~ cueillette des cerises/des fraises; mushroom-/potato-~ ramassage des champignons/des pommes de terre. -3. [of lock] crochetage *m*.

◆ **pickings** *npl* -1. [remains] restes *mpl*; you can have the ~s vous pouvez prendre ce qui reste. -2. *inf* [spoils] grapillage *m*, gratte *f*; there are rich OR easy ~s to be had on pourrait se faire pas mal d'argent, ça pourrait rapporter gros.

pickle ['pɪkl] ◇ *n* -1. *Am* [gherkin] cornichon *m*. -2. [vinegar] vinaigre *m*; [brine] saumure *f*. -3. *inf* [mess, dilemma] pétrin *m*; to be in a (pretty) ~ être dans le pétrin OR dans de beaux draps. -4. *inf Br* [mischievous child] petit diable *m*, fripon *m*, -onne *f*. -5. *(U) Br* [food] pickles *mpl (petits oignons, cornichons, morceaux de choux-fleurs etc, macérés dans du vinaigre)*.

◇ *vt* -1. CULIN [in vinegar] conserver dans le vinaigre; [in brine] conserver dans la saumure. -2. TECH [metal] nettoyer à l'acide OR dans un bain d'acide.

pickled ['pɪkld] *adj* -1. CULIN [in vinegar] au vinaigre; [in brine] conservé dans la saumure; ~ herring rollmops *m inv*. -2. *inf* [drunk] bourré, rond.

picklock ['pɪklɒk] *n* -1. [instrument] crochet *m*, passe-partout *m inv*. -2. [burglar] crocheteur *m* (de serrures).

pick-me-up *inf n* remontant *m*.

pickpocket ['pɪk,pɒkɪt] *n* pickpocket *m*, voleur *m*, -euse *f* à la tire.

pick-up *n* -1. AUT [vehicle]: ~ (truck) pick-up *m inv*, camionnette *f* (découverte). -2. *inf* [casual relationship] partenaire *mf* de rencontre. -3. [act of collecting]: the truck made several ~s on the way le camion s'est arrêté plusieurs fois en route pour charger des marchandises; where will the ~ be made? où est-ce qu'on doit passer prendre les marchandises?; ~ point [for cargo] aire *f* de chargement; [for passengers] point *m* de ramassage, lieu *m* de rendez-vous. -4. [on record player]: ~ (arm) pick-up *m inv dated*, lecteur *m*. -5. *(U) Am* AUT [acceleration] reprises *fpl*; this car has got good ~ cette voiture a de bonnes reprises. -6. [improvement - of business, economy] reprise *f*; we're hoping for a ~ in sales nous espérons une reprise des ventes. -7. *inf* [arrest] arrestation *f*. -8. TECH [detector] détecteur *m*, capteur *m*. -9. RADIO & TV [reception] réception *f*.

picky *inf* ['pɪkɪ] (*compar* pickier, *superl* pickiest) *adj* difficile; she's really ~ about her food elle est très difficile pour la nourriture; don't be so ~! arrête de faire le difficile!

picnic ['pɪknɪk] (*pt & pp* picnicked, *cont* picnicking) ◇ *n* -1. *literal* pique-nique *m*; to go on OR for a ~ faire un pique-nique; let's have a ~ faisons un pique-nique; we took a ~ lunch ce midi nous avons pique-niqué. -2. *inf fig* [easy task]: it's no ~ showing tourists around London ce n'est pas une partie de plaisir que de faire visiter Londres aux touristes; it was no ~ cleaning all the pans ça n'a pas été du gâteau de nettoyer toutes les casseroles.

◇ *vi* pique-niquer.

picnic basket, **picnic hamper** *n* panier *m* à pique-nique.

picnicker ['pɪknɪkəʳ] *n* pique-niqueur *m*, -euse *f*.

picofarad ['piːkə,færəd] *n* picofarad *m*.

picosecond ['piːkə,sekənd] *n* picoseconde *f*.

Pict [pɪkt] *n* Picte *mf*.

Pictish ['pɪktɪʃ] ◇ *n* langue *f* picte.

◇ *adj* picte.

pictogram ['pɪktəgræm], **pictograph** ['pɪktəgrɑːf] *n* -1. LING [symbol] pictogramme *m*, idéogramme *m*. -2. [chart] graphique *m*.

pictorial [pɪk'tɔːrɪəl] ◇ *adj* -1. [in pictures] en images; [magazine, newspaper] illustré. -2. [vivid - style] vivant. -3. ART pictural.

◇ *n* illustré *m*.

picture ['pɪktʃəʳ] ◇ *n* -1. [gen] image *f*; [drawing] dessin *m*; [painting] peinture *f*, tableau *m*; he used ~s to illustrate his talk il a illustré sa conférence à l'aide d'images; a book with ~s in it/no ~s in it un livre avec des/sans illustrations; to draw a ~ dessiner; to paint a ~ peindre; to draw/to paint a ~ of sthg dessiner/peindre qqch; to paint a ~ of sb peindre le portrait de qqn || [photograph] photo *f*, photographie *f*; to take a ~ prendre une photo; to take a ~ of sb, to take sb's ~ prendre une photo de qqn, prendre qqn en photo; to have one's ~ taken se faire prendre en photo; I saw your ~ in the paper j'ai vu votre photo dans le journal || [on television] image *f*; the ~'s blurred l'image est floue ❑ 'Pictures from an Exhibition' *Mussorgsky* 'Tableaux d'une exposition'; 'The Picture of Dorian Gray' *Wilde* 'le Portrait de Dorian Gray'. -2. [film] film *m*; she was in several Hitchcock ~s elle a joué dans plusieurs films de Hitchcock; to go to the ~s *inf* aller au ciné. -3. [description] tableau *m*, portrait *m*; his novels give a vivid ~ of the period l'époque est peinte de façon très vivante dans ses romans, ses romans brossent un portrait très vivant de l'époque; the TV series gives a good ~ of life in a mining town cette série télévisée donne un bon aperçu de la vie dans une ville minière; the ~ he painted was a depressing one il a brossé OR fait un tableau déprimant de la situation. -4. [idea, image] image *f*; I have a strong mental ~ of what war was like je m'imagine très bien ce qu'était la guerre; they have a distorted ~ of the truth ils se font une fausse idée de la vérité; he's the ~ of health il respire la santé, il est resplendissant de santé; she was the ~ of despair elle était l'image vivante du désespoir; he's the ~ of his elder brother c'est (tout) le portrait de son frère aîné. -5. [situation] situation *f*; the economic ~ is bleak la situation économique est inquiétante. -6. *phr*: to be in the ~ *inf* être au courant; she hates being left out of the ~ elle déteste qu'on la laisse dans l'ignorance; to put sb in the ~ *inf* mettre qqn au courant; I get the ~! je comprends!, j'y suis!; doesn't she look a ~! n'est-elle pas adorable OR ravissante!; you're no ~ yourself! tu n'es pas une beauté non plus!; her face was a real ~ when she heard the news! il fallait voir sa tête quand elle a appris la nouvelle!; the big ~ [overview] une vue d'ensemble.

◇ *vt* -1. [imagine] s'imaginer, se représenter; I can't quite ~ him as a teacher j'ai du mal à me l'imaginer comme enseignant; just ~ the scene imaginez un peu la scène. -2. [describe] dépeindre, représenter. -3. [paint, draw etc] représenter; the artist ~d her on horseback l'artiste l'a représentée à cheval; he was ~d with her on the front page of all the papers une photo où il était en sa compagnie s'étalait à la une de tous les journaux.

picture book *n* livre *m* d'images.

picture card *n* [in card games] figure *f*.

picture frame *n* cadre *m* (pour tableaux).

picturegoer ['pɪktʃə,gəʊəʳ] *n Br dated* cinéphile *mf*.

picture hat *n* capeline *f*.

picture house *n Br dated* cinéma *m*.

picture library *n* banque *f* d'images.

picture palace = **picture house**.

picture postcard *n dated* carte *f* postale (illustrée).

◆ **picture-postcard** *adj* [view] qui ressemble à une OR qui fait carte postale.

picture rail *n* cimaise *f*.

picture research *n* documentation *f* iconographique.

picture researcher *n* documentaliste *mf* iconographique.

picturesque [,pɪktʃə'resk] *adj* pittoresque.

picturesquely [ˌpɪktʃəˈresklɪ] *adv* de façon pittoresque; the village is ~ situated le village se trouve dans un site pittoresque.

picture tube *n* TV tube *m* image.

picture window *n* fenêtre *f* OR baie *f* panoramique.

picture writing *n* écriture *f* idéographique.

PID *n abbr of* pelvic inflammatory disease.

piddle *inf* [ˈpɪdl] ◇ *vi* faire pipi.
◇ *n*: to have a ~ faire pipi.

piddling *inf* [ˈpɪdlɪŋ] *adj* [details] insignifiant; [job, pay] minable.

pidgin [ˈpɪdʒɪn] *n* LING pidgin *m*.

pidgin English *n* -**1.** LING pidgin *m*, pidgin english *m*. -**2.** *pej*: to speak ~ parler de façon incorrecte.

pidginization [ˌpɪdʒɪnaɪˈzeɪʃn] *n* pidginisation *f*.

pie [paɪ] *n* -**1.** CULIN [with fruit] tarte *f*; [with meat, fish etc] tourte *f*; apple ~ tarte aux pommes; chicken ~ tourte au poulet; pork/game ~ pâté *m* de porc/de gibier en croûte ❑ it's just ~ in the sky *inf* ce sont des paroles OR promesses en l'air; I want my piece of the ~ je veux ma part du gâteau. -**2.** TYPO pâte *f*.

piebald [ˈpaɪbɔːld] ◇ *adj* pie *(inv)*.
◇ *n* cheval *m* pie.

piece [piːs] *n* -**1.** [bit - of chocolate, paper, wood] morceau *m*, bout *m*; [- of land] parcelle *f*, lopin *m*; [with uncountable nouns]: a ~ of bread un morceau de pain; a ~ of advice un conseil; a ~ of information un renseignement; a ~ of news une nouvelle; ~s of advice/information/news des conseils/renseignements/nouvelles; that was a real ~ of luck cela a vraiment été un coup de chance; it's a superb ~ of craftsmanship OR workmanship c'est du très beau travail; to be in ~s [in parts] être en pièces détachées; [broken] être en pièces OR en morceaux; to be in one ~ [undamaged] être intact; [uninjured] être indemne; [safe] être sain et sauf; to be all of a ~ [in one piece] être tout d'une pièce OR d'un seul tenant; [consistent] être cohérent; [alike] se ressembler; his actions are of a ~ with his opinions ses actes sont conformes à ses opinions; to break sthg into ~s mettre qqch en morceaux OR en pièces; to pull sthg to ~s *literal* [doll, garment, book] mettre qqch en morceaux; [flower] effeuiller qqch; *fig* [argument, suggestion, idea] démolir qqch; to pull sb to ~s *fig* descendre qqn en flammes; to come to ~s [into separate parts] se démonter; [break] se briser; the toy came to ~s in my hands le jouet s'est brisé entre mes mains; to fall to ~s partir en morceaux; to go (all) to ~s *inf* [person] s'effondrer, craquer; [team] se désintégrer; [market] s'effondrer; to take to ~s démonter ❑ it's a ~ of cake *inf* c'est du gâteau; he's a nasty ~ of work *inf Br* c'est un sale type; I gave him a ~ of my mind *inf* [spoke frankly] je lui ai dit son fait OR ce que j'avais sur le cœur; [spoke harshly] je lui ai passé un savon; to say OR to speak one's ~ dire ce qu'on a sur le cœur. -**2.** [item] pièce *f*; a ~ of furniture un meuble; to sell sthg by the ~ vendre qqch à la pièce OR au détail ‖ [amount of work]: to be paid by the ~ être payé à la pièce OR à la tâche. -**3.** [part - of mechanism, set] pièce *f*; [- of jigsaw] pièce *f*, morceau *m*; to put sthg together ~ by ~ assembler qqch pièce par pièce OR morceau par morceau; an 18-~ dinner service un service de table de 18 pièces; an 18-~ band un orchestre de 18 musiciens. -**4.** GAMES [in chess] pièce *f*; [in draughts, checkers] pion *m*. -**5.** [performance] morceau *m*; [musical composition] morceau *m*, pièce *f*; [sculpture] pièce *f* (de sculpture); a piano ~ un morceau pour piano. -**6.** [newspaper article] article *m*; there was a ~ about it in yesterday's paper il y a eu un article à ce sujet OR on en a parlé dans le journal d'hier. -**7.** [coin] pièce *f*; a 50p ~ une pièce de 50 pence. -**8.** *inf* [firearm, cannon] pièce *f*. -**9.** ▽ [girl]: she's a nice OR tasty ~ c'est un beau brin de fille. -**10.** *Am* [time] moment *m*; [distance] bout *m* de chemin; he walked with me a ~ il a fait un bout de chemin avec moi.
◆ **piece together** *vt sep* -**1.** [from parts - broken object] recoller; [- jigsaw] assembler; the collage was ~d together from scraps of material le collage était fait OR constitué de petits bouts de tissu. -**2.** [story, facts] reconstituer.

piecemeal [ˈpiːsmiːl] ◇ *adv* [little by little] peu à peu, petit à petit; he told the story ~ il a raconté l'histoire par bribes; the town was rebuilt ~ after the war la ville a été reconstruite par étapes après la guerre.
◇ *adj* [fragmentary] fragmentaire, parcellaire.

piece rate *n* paiement *m* à la pièce; to be on ~ être payé aux pièces.

piecework [ˈpiːswɜːk] *n* travail *m* à la pièce; to be on ~ travailler à la pièce.

pieceworker [ˈpiːswɜːkəʳ] *n* travailleur *m*, -euse *f* à la pièce.

pie chart *n* graphique *m* circulaire, camembert *m*.

piecrust [ˈpaɪkrʌst] *n* couche *f* de pâte *(pour recouvrir une tourte)*.

pied [paɪd] *adj* [gen] bariolé, bigarré; [animal] pie *(inv)*.

pie dish *n* plat *m* à tarte; [for meat] terrine *f*; [oven-proof] plat *m* allant au four.

Piedmont [ˈpiːdmənt] *pr n* Piémont *m*; in ~ dans le Piémont.

Piedmontese [ˌpiːdmənˈtiːz] ◇ *n* Piémontais *m*, -e *f*.
◇ *adj* piémontais.

Pied Piper (of Hamelin) [-ˈhæmlɪn] *pr n*: the ~ le joueur de flûte de Hamelin.

pied wagtail *n* bergeronnette *f* grise de Yarrell.

pie-eyed *inf adj* bourré.

pie plate *n Am* plat *m* allant au four.

pier [pɪəʳ] *n* -**1.** *Br* [at seaside] jetée *f*. -**2.** [jetty] jetée *f*; [landing stage] embarcadère *m*; [breakwater] digue *f*. -**3.** [pillar] pilier *m*, colonne *f*; [of bridge] pile *f*.

pierce [pɪəs] *vt* -**1.** [make hole in] percer, transpercer; the knife ~d her lung le couteau lui a perforé OR transpercé le poumon; she had her ears ~d elle s'est fait percer les oreilles; his words ~d my heart ses paroles me fendirent le cœur. -**2.** [subj: sound, scream] percer; a cry ~d the silence un cri perça OR déchira le silence ‖ [subj: light] percer; the beam ~d the darkness le faisceau perça l'obscurité ‖ [subj: cold]: we were ~d (through) with cold nous étions transis OR morts de froid; the biting wind ~d his clothing le vent glacial transperçait ses vêtements. -**3.** [penetrate - defence, barrier] percer; the attack ~d enemy lines l'attaque a percé les lignes ennemies.

pierced [pɪəst] *adj* percé; ~ earring boucle *f* d'oreilles pour oreilles percées; to have ~ ears avoir les oreilles percées.

piercing [ˈpɪəsɪŋ] *adj* [scream, eyes, look] perçant; [question] lancinant; [wind] glacial.

piercingly [ˈpɪəsɪŋlɪ] *adv*: the wind is ~ cold il fait un vent glacial; she looked at me ~ elle m'a fixé d'un regard perçant; a ~ loud scream un cri perçant.

pier glass *n* trumeau *m*.

pierhead [ˈpɪəhed] *n* musoir *m*.

Pierrot [ˈpɪərəʊ] *pr n* Pierrot.

pietism [ˈpaɪətɪzm] *n* piétisme *m*.

piety [ˈpaɪətɪ] (*pl* pieties) *n* piété *f*.

piezoelectric [ˌpiːzəʊɪˈlektrɪk] *adj* piézoélectrique.

piezoelectricity [ˌpiːzəʊˌɪlekˈtrɪsətɪ] *n* piézoélectricité *f*.

piezometer [ˌpiːˈzɒmɪtəʳ] *n* piézomètre *m*.

piffle *inf* [ˈpɪfl] *Br* ◇ *n (U)* balivernes *fpl*, niaiseries *fpl*; don't talk ~! ne dis pas de bêtises!
◇ *interj*: (absolute) ~! des sottises tout ça!
◇ *vi* dire des bêtises; what are you piffling on about? qu'est-ce que tu radotes?

piffling *inf* [ˈpɪflɪŋ] *adj Br* [excuse, amount] insignifiant; a ~ little man un moins que rien.

pig [pɪg] (*pt & pp* pigged, *cont* pigging
◇ *n* -**1.** ZOOL cochon *m*, porc *m*; ~s might fly quand les poules auront des dents!; you mad a real ~'s ear of that ça, vous avez fait d beau!; to buy a ~ in a poke acheter chat e poche. -**2.** *inf* [greedy person] goinfre *m*; [dir eater] cochon *m*, -onne *f*; to eat like a ~ manger comme un cochon OR un porc; to mak a ~ of o.s. se goinfrer, s'empiffrer. -**3.** [dir person] cochon *m*, -onne *f*; to live like ~s vivr dans une écurie OR porcherie. -**4.** *inf* [unpleasar person] ordure *f*; (male) chauvinist/fascist ~ sale phallocrate/fasciste!; the dirty ~! l monstre! ‖ [unpleasant task]: it's a real ~ of a jo ce travail est un véritable cauchemar. -**5.** *inf p* [policeman] flic *m*, poulet *m*.
◇ *vt inf* -**1.** [food] bâfrer, se goinfrer de s'empiffrer de; we really pigged ourselves a Christmas on s'en est mis plein la lampe Noël. -**2.** *phr*: to ~ it vivre comme des cochon
◇ *vi* [sow] mettre bas.
◆ **pig out** *inf vi insep* se goinfrer, s'empiffre

pigeon [ˈpɪdʒɪn] *n* -**1.** ORNITH pigeon *m*; ~ fan cier colombophile *mf*; ~ loft pigeonnier *m*; ~ shooting tir *m* OR chasse *f* aux pigeons. -**2.** *inf B* [business]: it's not my ~ ce n'est pas mo problème; that's their ~ c'est leurs affaires o leurs oignons. -**3.** *inf fig* [dupe] pigeon *m*.

pigeon-breasted [-ˌbrestɪd], **pigeon-cheste** [-ˌtʃestɪd] *adj*: to be ~ avoir la poitrine bombé

pigeonhole [ˈpɪdʒɪnhəʊl] ◇ *n* casier *m* (à cou rier); he tends to put people in ~s *fig* il tendance à étiqueter les gens OR à mettre de étiquettes aux gens.
◇ *vt* -**1.** [file] classer. -**2.** [postpone] différe remettre (à plus tard). -**3.** [classify] étiquete cataloguer; they ~d me as a feminist i m'avaient étiquetée comme féministe.

pigeon-toed *adj*: to be ~ avoir les pieds tou nés en dedans.

piggery [ˈpɪgərɪ] (*pl* piggeries) *n* -**1.** [pig farn pigsty] porcherie *f*. -**2.** [greediness] glouto nerie *f*.

piggish [ˈpɪgɪʃ] *adj pej* -**1.** [dirty] sale, cochor [greedy] glouton. -**2.** *inf Br* [stubborn] têtu.

piggy *inf* [ˈpɪgɪ] (*pl* piggies) ◇ *n baby talk* [pig (petit) cochon *m*; [toe] doigt *m* de pied; [finger doigt *m*; ~ in the middle *jeu d'enfants au cou duquel deux enfants se lancent un ballon alors qu'u troisième placé au milieu essaie de l'attraper*; I'r tired of being ~ in the middle j'en ai asse d'être le dindon de la farce.
◇ *adj inf* -**1.** [greedy] glouton, goinfre. -**2.** [fea tures]: ~ eyes de petits yeux porcins.

piggyback [ˈpɪgɪbæk] ◇ *adv*: to ride OR to b carried ~ se faire porter sur le dos de qqn.
◇ *n*: to give sb a ~ porter qqn sur le dos.
◇ *adj* [ride] sur le dos.

piggy bank *n* tirelire *f (en forme de petit cochon*

pig-headed *adj* têtu, obstiné.

pig-headedly [-ˈhedɪdlɪ] *adv* obstinément, ave entêtement.

pig-headedness [-ˈhedɪdnɪs] *n* entêtement *r* obstination *f*.

pig iron *n* fonte *f* brute.

Pig Latin *n* argot *m* codé, ≃ javanais *m*.

piglet [ˈpɪglɪt] *n* cochonnet *m*, porcelet *m*.

pigman [ˈpɪgmən] (*pl* pigmen [-mən]) porcher *m*.

pigmeat [ˈpɪgmiːt] *n* (viande *f* de) porc *m*.

pigment [*n* ˈpɪgmənt, *vb* pɪgˈment] ◇ *n* pi ment *m*.
◇ *vt* pigmenter.

pigmentation [ˌpɪgmənˈteɪʃn] *n* pigmen tation *f*.

Pigmy [ˈpɪgmɪ] = **Pygmy**.

pignut [ˈpɪgnʌt] *n* -**1.** [earthnut] gland *m* c noix *f* de terre. -**2.** *Am* [hickory nut] noix *f* d hickory.

pigpen [ˈpɪgpen] *n Am literal & fig* porcherie

pigskin [ˈpɪgskɪn] ◇ *n* -**1.** [leather] peau *f* d porc; it's made of ~ c'est en (peau de) por -**2.** *Am* [football] ballon *m (de football américain*
◇ *comp* [bag, watchstrap] en (peau de) porc.

igsticking ['pɪg,stɪkɪŋ] *n* chasse *f* au sanglier.
igsty ['pɪgstaɪ] (*pl* **pigsties**) *n literal* & *fig* porcherie *f*.
igswill ['pɪgswɪl] *n* pâtée *f* (pour les cochons); our school meals are ~ *fig* ce qu'on (nous) sert à la cantine de l'école est bon pour les cochons.
igtail ['pɪgteɪl] *n* natte *f*.
ika ['paɪkə] *n* pika *m*, lapin *m*.
ike [paɪk] (*pl inv* OR **pikes**) *n* -**1.** [fish] brochet *m*. -**2.** [spear] pique *f*. -**3.** *Br dial* [hill] pic *m*. -**4.** = **turnpike**.
ikestaff ['paɪkstɑːf] *n* hampe *f* (d'une pique).
ilaf(f) ['pɪlæf] = **pilau**.
ilaster [pɪ'læstəʳ] *n* pilastre *m*.
ilate ['paɪlət] *pr n* Pilate; Pontius ~ Ponce Pilate.
ilau [pɪ'laʊ] *n* pilaf *m*; ~ rice riz *m* pilaf.
ilchard ['pɪltʃəd] *n* pilchard *m*.
ile [paɪl] ◇ *n* -**1.** [stack] pile *f*; [heap] tas *m*; to put books/magazines in a ~ empiler des livres/magazines; she left her clothes/records in a ~ on the floor elle a laissé ses vêtements/disques en tas par terre. -**2.** *inf (usu pl)* [large quantity] tas *m or mpl*, masses *fpl*; to have ~s of money avoir plein d'argent, être plein aux as; I've got ~s of work to do j'ai un tas de boulot OR un boulot dingue. -**3.** *inf* [fortune]: to make one's ~ faire fortune. -**4.** [large building] édifice *m*; she owns a huge Jacobean ~ in the country elle a un immense manoir du XVIIᵉ siècle à la campagne. -**5.** [battery] pile *f*. -**6.** NUCL pile *f*. -**7.** CONSTR pieu *m*; [for bridge] pile *f*; built on ~s sur pilotis. -**8.** *(U)* TEX fibres *fpl*, poil *m*; a deep-~ carpet une moquette épaisse.
◇ *vt* [stack] empiler; she ~d her clothes neatly on the chair elle empila soigneusement ses habits sur la chaise; don't ~ those records on top of one another n'empilez pas ces disques les uns sur les autres; she ~d her clothes into the suitcase elle a mis tous ses habits pêle-mêle dans la valise; we ~d the toys into the car on a entassé les jouets dans la voiture; the table was ~d high with papers il y avait une grosse pile de papiers sur la table; he ~d more coal on the fire il a remis du charbon dans le feu; he ~d spaghetti onto his plate il a rempli son assiette de spaghettis; a plate ~d with mashed potato une assiette remplie OR pleine de purée; she wears her hair ~d high on her head ses cheveux sont ramenés en chignon au sommet de sa tête.
◇ *vi*: they all ~d off/onto the bus ils sont tous descendus du bus/montés dans le bus en se bousculant; we ~d up the stairs nous avons monté l'escalier en nous bousculant.
◆ **pile in** *inf vi insep* [enter] s'entasser; they opened the doors and we all ~d in ils ont ouvert les portes et nous nous sommes tous bousculés pour entrer || [join fight]: once the first punch was thrown we all ~d in après le premier coup de poing, on s'est tous lancés dans la bagarre.
◆ **pile into** *inf vt insep* -**1.** [crash] rentrer dans; the two cars ~d into each other les deux voitures se sont rentrées dedans OR se sont télescopées. -**2.** [attack - physically] rentrer dans, foncer dans; [- verbally] rentrer dans, tomber sur.
◆ **pile off** *vi insep inf* [from bus, train] descendre en se bousculant.
◆ **pile on** *inf* ◇ *vi insep* [onto bus, train] s'entasser, monter en s'entassant.
◇ *vt sep* -**1.** [increase - suspense] faire durer; [- pressure] augmenter; to ~ on the agony forcer la dose, dramatiser (à l'excès). -**2.** *phr*: to ~ it on [exaggerate] exagérer, en rajouter; stop piling it on! n'en rajoutez pas!
◆ **pile out** *inf vi insep* [off bus, train] descendre en se bousculant; [from cinema, lecture hall] sortir en se bousculant.
◆ **pile up** ◇ *vi insep* -**1.** [crash - car] s'écraser. -**2.** [accumulate - work, debts] s'accumuler, s'entasser; [- washing, clouds] s'amonceler.
◇ *vt sep* -**1.** [stack] empiler. -**2.** [accumulate - evidence, examples] accumuler.

pile driver *n* -**1.** CONSTR sonnette *f*. -**2.** *inf fig* [blow] coup *m* violent.
pile dwelling *n* habitation *f* lacustre OR sur pilotis.
piles [paɪlz] *npl* MED hémorroïdes *fpl*.
pile-up *n* carambolage *m*; there was a 50-car ~ in the fog 50 voitures se sont télescopées OR carambolées dans le brouillard.
pilfer ['pɪlfəʳ] *vi* & *vt* voler *(des objets sans valeur)*.
pilferage ['pɪlfərɪdʒ] *n* = **pilfering**.
pilferer ['pɪlfərəʳ] *n* voleur *m*, -euse *f (d'objets sans valeur)*.
pilfering ['pɪlfərɪŋ] *n* vol *m (d'objets sans valeur)*.
pilgrim ['pɪlgrɪm] *n* pèlerin *m*; 'Pilgrim's Progress' *Bunyan* 'le Voyage du pèlerin'.
pilgrimage ['pɪlgrɪmɪdʒ] *n* pèlerinage *m*; they made OR went on a ~ to Lourdes ils sont allés en pèlerinage à Lourdes; I made a ~ to my childhood home *fig* je suis retourné visiter la maison de mon enfance ❑ 'Childe Harold's Pilgrimage' *Byron* 'le Pèlerinage de Childe Harold'.
Pilgrim Fathers *pl pr n*: the ~ les (Pères) Pèlerins *mpl*.

THE PILGRIM FATHERS:
Puritains persécutés en Angleterre, les «Pèlerins» parvinrent en Amérique à bord du «Mayflower» et fondèrent la première colonie permanente du nouveau monde, à Plymouth (dans ce qui devait devenir l'État du Massachusetts), en 1620.

---

pill [pɪl] *n* -**1.** MED pilule *f*, comprimé *m*; to sugar OR to sweeten the ~ (for sb) dorer la pilule (à qqn). -**2.** [contraceptive pill]: the ~ la pilule; to go on the ~ commencer à prendre la pilule; to be on the ~ prendre la pilule.
◆ **Pill** = **pill 2**.
pillage ['pɪlɪdʒ] ◇ *vt* mettre à sac, piller.
◇ *vi* se livrer au pillage.
◇ *n* pillage *m*.
pillar ['pɪləʳ] *n* -**1.** [structural support] pilier *m*; [ornamental] colonne *f*; to go from ~ to post tourner en rond; he was sent from ~ to post on l'a envoyé à droite et à gauche; the Pillars of Hercules GEOG les colonnes d'Hercule. -**2.** [of smoke] colonne *f*; [of water] trombe *f*; a ~ of salt BIBLE une statue de sel || [mainstay] pilier *m*; a ~ of society un pilier de la société; to be a ~ of strength être ferme comme un roc; you've been a real ~ of strength vous avez été un soutien précieux.
pillar box *n Br* boîte *f* à lettres.
pillar-box red *adj Br* rouge vif.
pillared ['pɪləd] *adj* à piliers, à colonnes.
pillbox ['pɪlbɒks] *n* -**1.** MED boîte *f* à pilules. -**2.** MIL blockhaus *m inv*, casemate *f*. -**3.** [hat] toque *f*.
pillion ['pɪljən] ◇ *n* -**1.** [on motorbike]: ~ (seat) siège *m* arrière; ~ passenger OR rider passager *m*, -ère *f (sur une moto)*. -**2.** [on horse] selle *f* de derrière.
◇ *adv*: to ride ~ [on motorbike] voyager sur le siège arrière; [on horse] monter en croupe.
pillock▽ ['pɪlək] *n Br* con *m*, couillon *m*.
pillory ['pɪlərɪ] (*pl* **pillories**, *pt* & *pp* **pilloried**)
◇ *n* pilori *m*.
◇ *vt* HIST & *fig* mettre OR clouer au pilori.
pillow ['pɪləʊ] ◇ *n* -**1.** [on bed] oreiller *m*. -**2.** TEX [for lace] carreau *m* (de dentellière). -**3.** *Am* [on chair, sofa] coussin *m*.
◇ *vt* [rest] reposer; he ~ed his head on his arms il posa sa tête sur ses bras.
pillowcase ['pɪləʊkeɪs] *n* taie *f* d'oreiller.
pillow fight *n* bataille *f* de polochons.
pillowslip ['pɪləʊslɪp] *Br*, **pillow sham** *Am* = **pillowcase**.
pillow talk *n (U)* confidences *fpl* sur l'oreiller.
pilot ['paɪlət] ◇ *n* -**1.** AERON & NAUT pilote *m*; *fig* [guide] guide *m*. -**2.** TECH [on tool] guidage *m*. -**3.** = **pilot light**.
◇ *vt* -**1.** AERON & NAUT piloter. -**2.** [guide] piloter, guider; he's ~ed the company through several crises il a sorti l'entreprise de la crise OR de ses difficultés à plusieurs reprises; she ~ed the bill through parliament POL elle s'est assurée que le projet de loi serait voté. -**3.** [test] tester, expérimenter; the project was ~ed at Harvard University le projet a été testé à l'Université de Harvard.
◇ *adj* [trial - study, programme, scheme] d'essai, pilote, expérimental.
◇ *comp* [error] de pilotage.
pilotage ['paɪlətɪdʒ] *n* pilotage *m*.
pilot boat *n* bateau-pilote *m*.
pilot engine *n* locomotive *f* pilote.
pilot film *n* épisode *m* pilote.
pilot fish *n* (poisson *m*) pilote *m*.
pilot house *n* poste *m* de pilotage.
pilot jet *n* veilleuse *f* (au gaz).
pilot lamp *n* veilleuse *f* (électrique).
pilot light *n* veilleuse *f*.
pilot officer *n* sous-lieutenant *m* AÉRON.
pilot whale *n* globicéphale *m*.
pimento [pɪ'mentəʊ] (*pl* **pimentos**) *n* piment *m*.
pimp *inf* [pɪmp] ◇ *n* maquereau *m*, souteneur *m*.
◇ *vi inf* faire le maquereau.
pimpernel ['pɪmpənel] *n* mouron *m*.
pimple ['pɪmpl] *n* bouton *m* MÉD.
pimply ['pɪmplɪ] (*compar* **pimplier**, *superl* **pimpliest**) *adj* boutonneux.
pin [pɪn] (*pt* & *pp* **pinned**, *cont* **pinning**)
◇ *n* -**1.** [for sewing] épingle *f*; [safety pin] épingle *f*; [drawing pin] punaise *f*; [hairpin] épingle *f*; she took a ~ from her hair elle enleva une épingle de ses cheveux ❑ for two ~s I'd let the whole thing drop il ne faudrait pas beaucoup me pousser pour que je laisse tout tomber, si je ne me retenais pas, je laisserais tout tomber; he doesn't care two ~s about it il s'en moque complètement; you could have heard a ~ drop on aurait entendu voler une mouche. -**2.** *Am* [brooch] broche *f*; [badge] insigne *m*. -**3.** *inf (usu pl)* [leg] quille *f*, guibole *f*, guibolle *f*; he's a bit unsteady on his ~s il ne tient pas bien sur ses guiboles. -**4.** [peg - in piano, violin] cheville *f*; [- in hinge, pulley] goujon *m*; [- in hand grenade] goupille *f*. -**5.** ELEC [on plug] broche *f*; two-~ plug prise *f* à deux broches. -**6.** MED [for broken bone] broche *f*. -**7.** [in skittles, bowling] quille *f*. -**8.** [in wrestling - gen] prise *f*; [- shoulders on floor] tombé *m*. -**9.** [in chess] clouage *m*. -**10.** [in golf] drapeau *m*.
◇ *vt* -**1.** [attach - with pin or pins] épingler; [- with drawing pin or pins] punaiser; she had a brooch pinned to her jacket elle portait une broche épinglée à sa veste; there was a sign pinned to the door un écriteau était punaisé sur la porte || *fig*: to ~ one's hopes on sb/sthg mettre ses espoirs dans qqn/qqch; to ~ one's faith on sb placer sa foi en qqn; the crime was pinned on James c'est James qu'on a accusé du délit, on a mis le délit sur le dos de James; they pinned the blame on the shop assistant ils ont rejeté la responsabilité sur la vendeuse, ils ont mis ça sur le dos de la vendeuse; they can't ~ anything on me il ne peuvent rien prouver contre moi. -**2.** [immobilize] immobiliser, coincer; they pinned his arms behind his back ils lui ont coincé les bras derrière le dos; to ~ sb to the ground/against a wall clouer qqn au sol/contre un mur; she was pinned under a boulder elle était coincée OR bloquée sous un rocher. -**3.** [in chess] clouer.
◆ **pin back** *vt sep hum*: ~ back your ears! *inf* ouvrez vos oreilles!, écoutez bien!; keep your ears pinned back *inf* continuez à bien écouter.
◆ **pin down** *vt sep* -**1.** [with pin or pins] fixer avec une épingle OR des épingles; [with drawing pin or pins] fixer avec une punaise OR des punaises. -**2.** [immobilize, trap] immobiliser, coincer; his legs were pinned down by the fallen tree ses jambes étaient coincées sous l'arbre. -**3.** [define clearly - difference, meaning] mettre le doigt sur, cerner avec précision. -**4.** [commit] amener à se décider; try to ~ her

down to a definite schedule essayez d'obtenir d'elle un planning définitif; **he doesn't want to be pinned down** il veut avoir les coudées franches, il tient à garder sa liberté de manœuvre.

◆ **pin together** *vt sep* épingler, attacher avec une épingle OR des épingles.

◆ **pin up** *vt sep* -**1.** [poster] punaiser; [results, names] afficher. -**2.** [hem] épingler; [hair] relever (avec des épingles); **she wears her hair pinned up** elle porte ses cheveux relevés en chignon.

PIN [pɪn] (*abbr of* **personal identification number**) *n*: **~ (number)** code *m* confidentiel.

pinafore ['pɪnəfɔːʳ] *Br n* -**1.** [apron] tablier *m*. -**2.** = **pinafore dress**.

pinafore dress *n* robe *f* chasuble.

pinball ['pɪnbɔːl] *n* [game] flipper *m*; **to play ~** jouer au flipper; **~ machine** OR **table** flipper.

pincer ['pɪnsəʳ] *n* [of crab] pince *f*.

◆ **pincers** *npl* [tool] tenaille *f*, tenailles *fpl*; **a pair of ~s** une tenaille, des tenailles.

pincer movement *n* MIL manœuvre *f* OR mouvement *m* d'encerclement.

pinch [pɪntʃ] ◇ *vt* -**1.** [squeeze] pincer; **she ~ed her hand in the gate** elle s'est pincé la main dans la barrière; **he ~ed her cheek** il lui a pincé la joue; **I had to ~ myself to make sure I wasn't dreaming** je me suis pincé pour voir si je ne rêvais pas; **these new shoes ~ my feet** ces chaussures neuves me font mal aux pieds. -**2.** *inf Br* [steal] piquer, faucher; **to ~ sthg from sb** piquer qqch à qqn; **I had my stereo ~ed** on m'a piqué ma chaîne stéréo. -**3.** *inf* [arrest] pincer; **they got ~ed for shoplifting** ils se sont fait pincer pour vol à l'étalage. -**4.** HORT pincer.

◇ *vi* -**1.** [shoes] serrer, faire mal (aux pieds). -**2.** [economize]: **to ~ and scrape** économiser sur tout, regarder (de près) à la dépense.

◇ *n* -**1.** [squeeze] pincement *m*; **at a ~** *Br*, **in a ~** *Am* à la rigueur; **if it comes to the ~** s'il le faut vraiment, en cas de nécessité absolue; **we're beginning to feel the ~** nous commençons à devoir nous priver. -**2.** [of salt, snuff] pincée *f*; **you must take what he says with a ~ of salt** il ne faut pas prendre ce qu'il dit pour argent comptant.

◆ **pinch back, pinch off, pinch out** *vt sep* HORT pincer.

pinchbeck ['pɪntʃbek] ◇ *n* -**1.** [alloy] chrysocale *m*. -**2.** *fig* [sham] toc *m*.

◇ *adj* -**1.** *literal* en chrysocale. -**2.** *fig* [sham] en toc.

pinched [pɪntʃt] *adj* -**1.** [features] tiré; **his face looked pale and ~** il était pâle et avait les traits tirés; **~ with cold** transi de froid. -**2.** [lacking]: **I'm a bit ~ for money** je suis à court d'argent; **I'm a bit ~ for time** je n'ai pas beaucoup de temps; **they're ~ for space in their flat** ils sont à l'étroit OR ils n'ont pas beaucoup de place dans leur appartement.

pinch-hit *vi Am* -**1.** SPORT remplacer un joueur. -**2.** [gen] effectuer un remplacement; **he's pinch-hitting for Joe** il remplace Joe.

pinchpenny ['pɪntʃpenɪ] (*pl* **pinchpennies**) ◇ *adj* de bout de chandelle.

◇ *n* grippe-sou *m*.

pincushion ['pɪn,kʊʃn] *n* pelote *f* à épingles.

Pindar ['pɪndəʳ] *pr n* Pindare.

Pindaric [pɪn'dærɪk] *adj* pindarique.

pine [paɪn] ◇ *n* BOT [tree, wood] pin *m*.

◇ *comp* [furniture] en pin.

◇ *vi* -**1.** [long]: **to ~ for sthg** désirer qqch ardemment, soupirer après qqch; **he was pining for home** il avait le mal du pays; **they're pining to be given another chance** ce qu'ils désirent par-dessus tout, c'est qu'on leur accorde une seconde chance. -**2.** [grieve] languir; **she was pining for her lover** elle se languissait de son amant.

◆ **pine away** *vi insep* dépérir.

pineal ['pɪnɪəl] *adj* pinéal, de l'épiphyse.

pineal gland *n* épiphyse *f*.

pineapple ['paɪn,æpl] ◇ *n* ananas *m*.

◇ *comp* [juice, chunks] d'ananas; [ice cream] à l'ananas.

pineapple weed *n* matricaire *f*.

pine cone *n* pomme de pin *f*.

pine grove *n* pinède *f*.

pine kernel *n* pignon *m*, pigne *f* BOT.

pine marten *n* martre *f*.

pine needle *n* aiguille *f* de pin.

pine nut = **pine kernel**.

pinewood ['paɪnwʊd] *n* -**1.** [group of trees] pinède *f*. -**2.** [material] bois *m* de pin, pin *m*.

ping [pɪŋ] ◇ *n & onomat* ding *m*.

◇ *vi* -**1.** faire ding; [timer] sonner. -**2.** *Am* [car engine] cliqueter.

pinger ['pɪŋəʳ] *n* minuteur *m* (de cuisine).

pinging ['pɪŋɪŋ] *Am* = **pinking**.

ping-pong, ping pong ['pɪŋpɒŋ] *n* ping-pong *m*; **~ player** pongiste *mf*; **~ ball** balle *f* de ping-pong.

pinhead ['pɪnhed] *n* -**1.** *literal* tête *f* d'épingle. -**2.** *inf* [fool] andouille *f*, crétin *m*.

pinheaded *inf* [pɪn'hedɪd] *adj* idiot.

pinhole ['pɪnhəʊl] *n* trou *m* d'épingle.

pinhole camera *n* appareil *m* à sténopé.

pinion ['pɪnjən] ◇ *n* -**1.** ORNITH [wing] aileron *m*. -**2.** *lit* [wing] aile *f*. -**3.** MECH pignon *m*; **~ wheel** roue *f* à pignon.

◇ *vt* -**1.** [hold fast] retenir de force; **two policemen ~ed his arms** deux policiers le retenaient par le bras; **we were ~ed against the wall by the crowd** la foule nous coinçait contre le mur. -**2.** ORNITH [bird] rogner les ailes à.

pink [pɪŋk] ◇ *n* -**1.** [colour] rose *m*. -**2.** *fig*: **to be in the ~ (of health)** se porter à merveille; **you're looking in the ~!** *inf* tu as l'air en pleine forme! -**3.** [flower] œillet *m*; **garden ~** mignardise *f*.

◇ *adj* -**1.** [in colour] rose; **to paint a room ~** peindre une pièce en rose; **the sky turned ~** le ciel vira au rose OR rosit; **she went** OR **turned ~ with delight** elle rosit de bonheur; **to go** OR **to turn ~ with anger/embarrassment** rougir de colère/confusion ❑ **to see ~ elephants** *hum* voir des éléphants roses; **'The Pink Panther'** *Edwards* 'la Panthère rose'. -**2.** *inf* POL [left-wing] de gauche, gauchisant.

◇ *vt* -**1.** [wound - subj: marksman] blesser (légèrement); [- subj: bullet] érafler; **he ~ed my shoulder with his sword** il m'a éraflé OR égratigné l'épaule d'un coup d'épée. -**2.** SEW cranter. -**3.** [punch holes in] perforer.

◇ *vi Br* [car engine] cliqueter.

pinkeye ['pɪŋkaɪ] *n* MED conjonctivite *f* aiguë contagieuse; VETER ophtalmie *f* périodique.

pink gin *n* cocktail *m* de gin et d'angustura.

pinkie ['pɪŋkɪ] = **pinky**.

pinking ['pɪŋkɪŋ] *n Br* AUT cliquetis *m*, cliquettement *m*.

pinking shears *npl* SEW ciseaux *mpl* à cranter.

pinkish ['pɪŋkɪʃ] *adj* rosâtre, rosé; POL *inf* gauchisant.

pink noise *n* bruit *m* rose.

pinko *inf* ['pɪŋkəʊ] (*pl* **pinkos** OR **pinkoes**) *n pej* gauchisant *m*, -e *f*.

pink slip *inf n Am* lettre *f* OR avis *m* de licenciement; **to get a ~** se faire renvoyer.

pinky *inf* ['pɪŋkɪ] (*pl* **pinkies**) *n* petit doigt *m*.

pin money *n* argent *m* de poche; **she works at weekends to earn a bit of ~** elle travaille le week-end pour se faire un peu d'argent pour ses menus plaisirs.

pinnace ['pɪnɪs] *n* chaloupe *f*.

pinnacle ['pɪnəkl] *n* -**1.** [mountain peak] pic *m*, cime *f*; [rock formation] piton *m*, gendarme *m*. -**2.** *fig* [of fame, career] apogée *m*, sommet *m*; **it represents the ~ of modern technology** c'est le fin du fin de la technologie moderne. -**3.** ARCHIT pinacle *m*.

pinnate ['pɪneɪt] *adj* penné.

pin number *n* code *m* secret (*de carte bancaire*).

pinny *inf* ['pɪnɪ] (*pl* **pinnies**) *n* tablier *m*.

Pinocchio [pɪ'nəʊkɪəʊ] *pr n* Pinocchio; **'The Adventures of ~'** *Collodi* 'les Aventures de Pinocchio'.

pinoc(h)le ['piːnʌkl] *n jeu de cartes ressemblant à la belote*.

pinpoint ['pɪnpɔɪnt] ◇ *vt* -**1.** [locate - smell, leak] localiser; [- on map] localiser, repérer. -**2.** [identify - difficulty] mettre le doigt sur.

◇ *n* pointe *f* d'épingle; **a ~ of light** un minuscule point lumineux.

◇ *adj* -**1.** [precise] très précis; **with ~ accuracy** avec une précision parfaite. -**2.** [tiny] minuscule.

pinprick ['pɪnprɪk] *n* -**1.** [puncture] piqûre *f* d'épingle; **a ~ of light** un petit point lumineux. -**2.** [irritation] agacement *m*, tracasserie *f*.

pins and needles *inf n* (*U*) fourmillements *mpl*; **I've got ~ in my arm** j'ai des fourmis dans le bras, je ne sens plus mon bras ❑ **to be on ~** *Am* trépigner d'impatience, ronger son frein.

pinstripe ['pɪnstraɪp] ◇ *n* TEX rayure *f* (très fine).

◇ *adj* = **pinstriped**.

pinstriped ['pɪnstraɪpt] *adj* rayé; **~ suit** costume *m* rayé.

pint [paɪnt] *n* -**1.** [measure] pinte *f*, ≃ demi-litre *m*. -**2.** *inf Br* [beer] bière *f*; **I had a few ~s last night** j'ai bu quelques bières hier soir.

pinta *inf* ['paɪntə] *n Br* pinte *f* de lait.

pintable ['pɪnteɪbl] *n Br* flipper *m*.

pintail ['pɪnteɪl] *n* ORNITH pilet *m* à queue pointue.

pinto ['pɪntəʊ] (*pl* **pintos** OR **pintoes**) ◇ *n Am* cheval *m* pie.

◇ *adj Am* [gen] tacheté; [horse] pie (*inv*).

pinto bean *n* coco *m* rose.

pint-sized *inf adj pej* tout petit, minuscule.

pin tuck *n* SEW nervure *f*.

pinup ['pɪnʌp] ◇ *n* pin-up *f inv*.

◇ *adj* [photo] de pin-up; **~ girl** pin-up *f*.

pinwheel ['pɪnwiːl] *n* -**1.** [firework] soleil *m* (*feu d'artifice*). -**2.** [cogwheel] roue *f* dentée. -**3.** *Am* [windmill] moulin *m* à vent (*jouet*).

pinworm ['pɪnwɜːm] *n* oxyure *m*.

pion ['paɪɒn] *n* pion *m* PHYS.

pioneer [,paɪə'nɪəʳ] ◇ *n* -**1.** [explorer, settler] pionnier *m*, -ère *f*. -**2.** [of technique, activity] pionnier *m*, -ère *f*; **she was a ~ in the field of psychoanalysis** elle a été une pionnière de la psychanalyse; **they were ~s in the development of heart surgery** ils ont ouvert la voie en matière de chirurgie cardiaque. -**3.** MIL pionnier *m*, sapeur *m*. -**4.** BOT espèce *f* pionnière.

◇ *comp* [work, research] novateur, original.

◇ *vt*: **to ~ research in nuclear physics** être à l'avant-garde de la recherche en physique nucléaire; **the town is ~ing a job-creation scheme** la municipalité expérimente un nouveau programme de création d'emplois; **the factory ~ed the use of robots** l'usine a été la première à utiliser des robots.

pioneering [,paɪə'nɪərɪŋ] *adj* [work, spirit] novateur, original.

pious ['paɪəs] *adj* -**1.** [person, act, text] pieux. -**2.** [falsely devout] cagot *lit*, hypocrite. -**3.** [unrealistic] irréel; **to have ~ hopes** avoir de vains espoirs, nourrir des espoirs chimériques.

piously ['paɪəslɪ] *adv* pieusement.

pip [pɪp] (*pt & pp* **pipped**, *cont* **pipping**) ◇ *n* -**1.** [in fruit] pépin *m*; **orange ~** pépin d'orange. -**2.** *Br* [sound] bip *m*; [during telephone call] tonalité *f* (*indiquant une unité supplémentaire*); TELEC [time signal]: **the ~s** le signal sonore, le signal horaire. -**3.** [on playing card, domino] point *m*. -**4.** [on radar screen] spot *m*. -**5.** *inf* MIL ficelle *f* (*galon*). -**6.** *inf phr*: **to give sb the ~** *Br dated* courir sur le haricot à qqn. -**7.** VETER pépie *f*.

◇ *vi* -**1.** [chirrup] pépier. -**2.** [hatch out] éclore.

◇ *vt Br* -**1.** [defeat] battre, vaincre; **to ~ sb at the post** coiffer qqn au poteau. -**2.** *inf* [hit with bullet] atteindre; **he got pipped in the leg** il a pris une balle dans la jambe.

THE PIPS:
Cinq tops courts et un long indiquent l'heure juste à la radio en Grande-Bretagne.

pipe [paɪp] ◇ *n* -**1.** [for smoking] pipe *f*; he smokes a ~ il fume la pipe; he smokes four ~s a day il fume quatre pipes par jour ❑ put that in your ~ and smoke it! *inf* mets ça dans ta poche et ton mouchoir par-dessus! -**2.** [for gas, liquid etc] tuyau *m*, conduite *f*; [for stove] tuyau *m*; to lay gas ~s poser des conduites de gaz; the ~s have frozen les canalisations ont gelé. -**3.** MUS [gen] pipeau *m*; [boatswain's whistle] sifflet *m*; [on organ] tuyau *m*; the ~s [bagpipes] la cornemuse; a ~ band un orchestre de cornemuses. -**4.** ANAT & ZOOL tube *m*; respiratory ~ tube respiratoire. -**5.** [birdsong] pépiement *m*, gazouillis *m*. -**6.** *inf Am* [telephone] bigophone *m*; get on the ~ to Roy passe un coup de bigophone à Roy. -**7.** GEOL: volcanic ~ cheminée *f* volcanique.
◇ *comp* [bowl, stem] de pipe; [tobacco] à pipe.
◇ *vt* -**1.** [convey - liquid] acheminer par tuyau; natural gas is ~d to the cities le gaz naturel est acheminé jusqu'aux villes par gazoducs; the irrigation system will ~ water to the fields le système d'irrigation amènera l'eau jusqu'aux champs; untreated sewage is ~d into the lake les égouts se déversent directement dans le lac; to ~ coolant through a system faire circuler un produit refroidissant dans un système. -**2.** MUS [tune] jouer. -**3.** NAUT [order] siffler; to ~ sb aboard rendre à qqn les honneurs du sifflet *(quand il monte à bord)*; to ~ sb in/out saluer l'arrivée/le départ de qqn au sifflet. -**4.** [say] dire d'une voix flûtée. -**5.** SEW passepoiler. -**6.** CULIN: to ~ cream onto a cake décorer un gâteau de crème fouettée *(à l'aide d'une poche à douille)*.
◇ *vi* MUS [on bagpipes] jouer de la cornemuse; [on simple pipe] jouer du pipeau.
◆ **pipe down** *inf vi insep* la mettre en sourdine.
◆ **pipe up** *vi insep* -**1.** [person] se faire entendre; "me too!", he ~d up «moi aussi!», dit-il, sortant de son silence. -**2.** [band] se mettre à jouer.

pipeclay ['paɪpkleɪ] *n* terre *f* de pipe.
pipe cleaner *n* cure-pipe *m*.
piped music [paɪpt-] *n* musique *f* d'ambiance.
pipe dream *n* chimère *f*; you and your ~s! toi et tes châteaux en Espagne!
pipe fitter *n* tuyauteur *m*.
pipeline ['paɪplaɪn] *n* -**1.** [gen] pipeline *m*; [for oil] oléoduc *m*; [for gas] gazoduc *m*. -**2.** *fig*: to have a ~ to sb *inf Am* avoir l'oreille de qqn; they have a new model in the ~ ils sont en train de mettre un nouveau modèle au point; he's got another film/project in the ~ il travaille actuellement sur un autre film/projet; important changes are in the ~ for next year d'importants changements sont prévus pour l'année prochaine.
pipe major *n* cornemuse *f* principale.
pipemma [,pɪp'emə] *adv dated* & TELEC de l'après-midi.
pipe organ *n* grandes orgues *fpl*.
piper ['paɪpə^r] *n* [gen] joueur *m*, -euse *f* de pipeau; [of bagpipes] joueur *m*, -euse *f* de cornemuse, cornemuseur *m*; he who pays the ~ calls the tune *prov* celui qui paie les pipeaux commande la musique *prov*.
pipe rack *n* râtelier *m* à pipes.
pipette *Br*, **pipet** *Am* [pɪ'pet] *n* pipette *f*.
piping ['paɪpɪŋ] ◇ *n* -**1.** [system of pipes] tuyauterie *f*, canalisations *fpl*; a piece of copper ~ un tuyau de cuivre. -**2.** SEW passepoil *m*. -**3.** MUS [gen] son *m* du pipeau OR de la flûte; [of bagpipes] son de la cornemuse. -**4.** CULIN décoration *f* (appliquée à la douille).
◇ *adv* [as intensifier]: ~ hot très chaud, brûlant; a cup of ~ hot tea une tasse de thé bien chaud.
◇ *adj* [voice] flûté.
piping bag *n* CULIN poche *f* à douille.
pipit ['pɪpɪt] *n* pipit *m*.
pipkin ['pɪpkɪn] *n* poêlon *m*.
pippin ['pɪpɪn] *n* -**1.** [apple] (pomme *f*) reinette *f*. -**2.** [seed] pépin *m*.
pip-pip *inf interj Br dated* [goodbye] salut!
pipsqueak *inf* ['pɪpskwi:k] *n pej* demi-portion *f*.
piquancy ['pi:kənsɪ] *n* -**1.** [interest] piquant *m*, piment *m*; it adds ~ to the situation cela corse un peu la situation. -**2.** [taste] goût *m* piquant.
piquant ['pi:kənt] *adj* piquant.
pique [pi:k] ◇ *n* dépit *m*, ressentiment *m*; he resigned in a fit of ~ il a démissionné par pur dépit, il était tellement dépité qu'il a démissionné.
◇ *vt* -**1.** [vex] dépiter, irriter, froisser. -**2.** [arouse] piquer, exciter; my curiosity was ~d cela a piqué ma curiosité. -**3.** [pride]: to ~ o.s. on (doing) sthg se piquer de (faire) qqch.
piqued [pi:kt] *adj* [resentful] vexé, froissé.
piquet [pɪ'ket] *n* piquet *m (jeu de cartes)*.
piracy ['paɪrəsɪ] (*pl* **piracies**) *n* -**1.** [of vessel] piraterie *f*; air ~ piraterie aérienne. -**2.** [of software, book, tape etc] piratage *m*; [of idea] copie *f*, vol *m*.
Piraeus [paɪ'rɪəs] *pr n* Le Pirée.
piranha [pɪ'rɑ:nə] (*pl inv* OR **piranhas**) *n* piranha *m*, piraya *m*.
pirate ['paɪrət] ◇ *n* -**1.** [person] pirate *m*; [ship] navire *m* de pirates. -**2.** [of software, book, tape etc] pirate *m*; [of idea] voleur *m*, -euse *f*.
◇ *comp* [raid, flag] de pirates.
◇ *vt* [software, book, tape etc] pirater; [idea] s'approprier, voler; ~d edition édition *f* pirate.
pirate radio *n* radio *f* pirate.
piratic(al) [paɪ'rætɪk(l)] *adj* de pirate.
pirouette [,pɪrʊ'et] ◇ *n* pirouette *f*.
◇ *vi* pirouetter.
Pisa ['pi:zə] *pr n* Pise; the Leaning Tower of ~ la tour de Pise.
piscatorial [,pɪskə'tɔ:rɪəl], **piscatory** ['pɪskətrɪ] *adj fml* halieutique; [tribe] de pêcheurs.
Pisces ['paɪsi:z] ◇ *pr n* ASTROL & ASTRON Poissons *mpl*.
◇ *n*: she's (a) ~ elle est Poissons.
pisciculture ['pɪsɪkʌltʃə^r] *n* pisciculture *f*.
pish [pɪʃ] *interj dated* peuh!
piss▽ [pɪs] ◇ *vi* -**1.** [urinate] pisser; to ~ in the wind se fatiguer pour rien; ~ on it! *Am* [forget it] laisse béton!; [I'm fed up] j'en ai plein le cul! -**2.** [rain]: it's ~ing with rain il pleut comme vache qui pisse.
◇ *vt* pisser; to ~ one's pants pisser dans sa culotte.
◇ *n* pisse *f*; to have OR to take a ~ pisser (un coup) ❑ to go on the ~ se soûler la gueule; to take the ~ out of sb *Br* [mock] se foutre de la gueule de qqn; *Am* [calm down] calmer qqn; it's a piece of ~ *Br* c'est du gâteau.
◆ **piss about**▽ *Br*, **piss around**▽ ◇ *vi insep* déconner, faire le con; we don't have time to ~ about on n'a pas de temps à perdre en conneries; don't ~ around with my stuff arrête de tripoter mes affaires OR de foutre le bordel dans mes affaires.
◇ *vt sep* emmerder.
◆ **piss down**▽ *vi insep* [rain]: it's ~ing (it) down il pleut comme vache qui pisse.
◆ **piss off**▽ ◇ *vi insep* foutre le camp; ~ off! fous OR fous-moi le camp!
◇ *vt sep* faire chier; to be ~ed off [bored] s'emmerder; [angry] être en rogne; to be ~ed off with sb en avoir plein le cul de qqn.
piss artist▽ *n Br* [drunkard] poivrot *m*, -e *f*, soûlard *m*, -e *f*.
pissed▽ [pɪst] *adj* -**1.** [drunk] beurré, schlass; to get ~ se soûler la gueule ❑ to be ~ as a newt OR out of one's head être soûl comme un cochon OR complètement noir. -**2.** *Am* [angry] en rogne; I was pretty ~ about it ça m'a vraiment foutu en rogne.
pisshead▽ ['pɪshed] *n* -**1.** *Br* [drunkard] poivrot *m*, -e *f*, soûlard *m*, -e *f*. -**2.** *Am* [mean person] salaud *m*, salope *f*; [bore] emmerdeur *m*, -euse *f*.
piss-take▽ *n* [mockery] mise *f* en boîte; [of book, film] parodie *f*.
piss-up▽ *n Br*: to go on OR to have a ~ se biturer, se soûler la gueule ❑ he couldn't organise a ~ in a brewery il n'est pas foutu d'organiser quoi que ce soit.
pistachio [pɪ'stɑ:ʃɪəʊ] (*pl* **pistachios**) ◇ *n* -**1.** [nut] pistache *f*; [tree] pistachier *m*; ~ OR ~-flavoured ice cream glace à la pistache. -**2.** [colour] (vert *m*) pistache *m*.
◇ *adj* (vert) pistache *(inv)*.
piste [pi:st] *n* piste *f* (de ski).
pistil ['pɪstɪl] *n* pistil *m*.
pistol ['pɪstl] *n* pistolet *m*; I heard ~ shots j'ai entendu des coups de feu; he's holding a ~ to her head *fig* il lui met le couteau sur la gorge.
pistol grip *n* [of tool, camera] crosse *f*.
pistol-whip *vt* frapper (au visage) avec un pistolet.
piston ['pɪstən] *n* piston *m* MECH.
piston ring *n* segment *m* (de piston).
piston rod *n* tige *f* de piston, bielle *f*.
pit [pɪt] (*pt* & *pp* pitted, *cont* pitting) ◇ *n* -**1.** [hole in ground] fosse *f*, trou *m*; [pothole in road] nid *m* de poule; to dig a ~ creuser un trou. -**2.** [shallow mark - in metal] marque *f*, piqûre *f*; [- on skin] cicatrice *f*, marque *f*. -**3.** [mine] mine *f*, puits *m*; [mineshaft] puits *m* de mine; to go down the ~ descendre dans la mine; to work down the ~ travailler à la mine. -**4.** [quarry] carrière *f*. -**5.** *Br* THEAT [for orchestra] fosse *f* (d'orchestre); [seating section] parterre *m*. -**6.** *Am* ST. EX parquet *m* (de la Bourse). -**7.** *(usu pl)* AUT [at race track] stand *m* (de ravitaillement); to make a ~ stop s'arrêter au stand. -**8.** [in cockfighting] arène *f*. -**9.** SPORT [for long jump] fosse *f*. -**10.** ANAT creux *m*; the ~ of the stomach le creux de l'estomac. -**11.** *Am* [in fruit] noyau *m*. -**12.** *lit* [hell]: the ~ l'enfer *m*.
◇ *comp* [closure] de mine; [worker] de fond; [accident] minier; ~ pony cheval *m* de mine; ~ prop poteau *m* OR étau *m* de mine, étançon *m*.
◇ *vt* -**1.** [mark] marquer; his face was pitted with acne son visage était criblé d'acné; meteors have pitted the surface of the moon la lune est criblée de cratères laissés par les météores; a road pitted with potholes une route criblée de nids-de-poule; pitted with rust piqué par la rouille. -**2.** [oppose] opposer, dresser; she was pitted against the champion on l'a opposée à la championne; to ~ one's wits against sb se mesurer à OR avec qqn. -**3.** *Am* [fruit] dénoyauter; pitted olives olives dénoyautées.
◆ **pits** *inf npl* [awful thing, place]: it's the ~s! c'est l'horreur!; this town is the ~s cette ville est un vrai trou.
pit-a-pat = **pitter-patter**.
pit bull terrier *n* pit bull *m*.
pitch [pɪtʃ] ◇ *vt* -**1.** [throw] lancer, jeter; she found herself ~ed into the political arena *fig* elle se trouva propulsée dans l'arène politique. -**2.** MUS [note] donner; [tune] donner le ton de; [one's voice] poser; I can't ~ my voice any higher je n'arrive pas à chanter dans un ton OR un registre plus aigu; the music was ~ed too high/low for her la musique était trop forte/basse pour elle. -**3.** [set level of]: we must ~ the price at the right level il faut fixer le prix au bon niveau; our prices are ~ed too high nos prix sont trop élevés; he ~ed his speech at the level of the man in the street son discours était à la portée de l'homme de la rue, il avait rendu son discours accessible à l'homme de la rue. -**4.** [set up - camp] établir; let's ~ camp here établissons notre camp OR dressons nos tentes ici. -**5.** [in cricket] lancer; [in golf] pitcher. -**6.** *inf* [tell] raconter.
◇ *vi* -**1.** [fall over] tomber; to ~ headlong tomber la tête la première; the passengers ~ed forwards/backwards les passagers ont été projetés en avant/en arrière. -**2.** [bounce - ball] rebondir. -**3.** AERON & NAUT tanguer. -**4.** [in baseball] lancer, être lanceur; to be in there ~ing *inf Am fig* y mettre du sien. -**5.** [slope - roof] être incliné; the roof ~es sharply le toit est fortement incliné.
◇ *n* -**1.** [tone] ton *m*; the ~ of his voice grew higher and higher sa voix devint de plus en plus aiguë; to have perfect ~ avoir l'oreille juste,

avoir de l'oreille. -**2.** [particular level or degree] niveau *m*, degré *m*; [highest point] comble *m*; a high ~ of excitement was reached l'excitation était presque à son comble; how did their relationship reach such a ~? comment leurs relations ont-elles pu se détériorer à ce point?; the suspense was at its highest ~ le suspense était à son comble. -**3.** *Br* [sports field] terrain *m*; rugby ~ terrain de rugby. -**4.** [act of throwing] lancer *m*, lancement *m*; the ball went full ~ through the window la balle passa à travers la vitre sans rebondir. -**5.** *inf Br* [street vendor's place] place *f*, emplacement *m*. -**6.** *inf* [spiel] boniment *m*; the salesman's ~ le boniment du vendeur. -**7.** [slope - of roof etc] pente *f*, inclinaison *f*. -**8.** [movement - of boat, aircraft] tangage *m*. -**9.** TECH [of screw, cogwheel, rotor] pas *m*. -**10.** [in golf] pitch *m*. -**11.** [natural tar] poix *f*; [distillation residue] brai *m*. -**12.** *phr*: to make a ~ for sthg *inf Am* jeter son dévolu sur qqch; he made a ~ at her il lui a fait du plat, il a essayé de la draguer.

◆ **pitch in** *vi insep* [start work] s'attaquer au travail; [lend a hand] donner un coup de main; everybody is expected to ~ in on attend de chacun qu'il mette la main à la pâte.

◆ **pitch into** *vt insep* [attack] s'attaquer à; they ~ed into me ils me sont tombés dessus; they ~ed into the meal ils ont attaqué le repas.

◆ **pitch on** *vt insep* choisir, opter pour.

◆ **pitch out** *vt sep* [rubbish] jeter; [person] expulser, mettre à la porte.

pitch-and-putt *n* pitch-and-putt *m* *(forme simplifiée du golf)*.

pitch-and-toss *n jeu d'adresse et de hasard utilisant des pièces de monnaie*.

pitch-black *adj* [water] noir comme de l'encre; [hair] noir ébène *(inv)*; [night] noir; the cave was ~ la caverne était plongée dans l'obscurité totale; it's ~ in here il fait noir comme dans un four ici.

pitchblende ['pɪtʃblend] *n* pechblende *f*.

pitch-dark *adj* [night] noir; it was ~ inside à l'intérieur, il faisait noir comme dans un four.

pitched [pɪtʃt] *adj* [roof] en pente.

pitched battle *n* MIL & *fig* bataille *f* rangée.

pitcher ['pɪtʃəʳ] *n* -**1.** [jug - earthenware] cruche *f*; [- metal, plastic] broc *m*; *Am* [smaller - for milk] pot *m*. -**2.** [in baseball] lanceur *m*.

pitchfork ['pɪtʃfɔːk] ◇ *n* fourche *f* (à foin).
◇ *vt* -**1.** [hay] fourcher. -**2.** *fig* [person] propulser; she was literally ~ed into the job elle a été littéralement parachutée à ce poste.

pitch pine *n* pitchpin *m*.

pitch pipe *n* diapason *m (sifflet)*.

piteous ['pɪtɪəs] *adj* pitoyable.

piteously ['pɪtɪəslɪ] *adv* pitoyablement.

pitfall ['pɪtfɔːl] *n* -**1.** [hazard] embûche *f*, piège *m*. -**2.** HUNT piège *m*, trappe *f*.

pith [pɪθ] *n* -**1.** [in citrus fruit] peau *f* blanche *(sous l'écorce des agrumes)*. -**2.** [crux] substance *f*, moelle *f*; this is the ~ of the matter c'est le cœur OR le fond du problème ‖ [force] vigueur *f*, force *f*; his argument lacks ~ son argument manque de force. -**3.** [in stem, bone] moelle *f*.

pithead ['pɪthed] *n* carreau *m* de mine; ~ ballot vote *m* des mineurs.

pithecanthropus [ˌpɪθɪkæn'θrəʊpəs] (*pl* pithecanthropi [-paɪ]) *n* pithécanthrope *m*.

pith helmet *n* casque *m* colonial.

pithiness ['pɪθɪnɪs] *n* concision *f*.

pithy ['pɪθɪ] (*compar* pithier, *superl* pithiest) *adj* [comment, writing] concis, lapidaire.

pitiable ['pɪtɪəbl] *adj* -**1.** [arousing pity] pitoyable. -**2.** [arousing contempt] piteux, lamentable.

pitiably ['pɪtɪəblɪ] *adv* -**1.** [touchingly] pitoyablement. -**2.** [contemptibly] lamentablement.

pitiful ['pɪtɪfʊl] *adj* -**1.** [arousing pity] pitoyable; it's ~ to see people living on the street cela fait pitié de voir des gens à la rue. -**2.** [arousing contempt] piteux, lamentable; they're paid a ~ wage ils touchent un salaire de misère.

pitifully ['pɪtɪfʊlɪ] *adv* -**1.** [touchingly] pitoyablement; she was ~ thin sa maigreur faisait peine à voir, elle était maigre à faire pitié. -**2.** [contemptibly] lamentablement; a ~ bad performance une prestation lamentable.

pitiless ['pɪtɪlɪs] *adj* [person] impitoyable, sans pitié; [weather] rude, rigoureux.

pitilessly ['pɪtɪlɪslɪ] *adv* impitoyablement, sans pitié.

pitman ['pɪtmən] (*pl* pitmen [-mən]) *n dial* mineur *m*.

piton ['piːtɒn] *n* piton *m* (d'alpiniste).

pitta (bread) ['pɪtə-] *n* pita *m*.

pittance ['pɪtəns] *n* somme *f* misérable OR dérisoire; to work for a ~ travailler pour un salaire de misère; to live on a ~ vivre de presque rien.

pitted ['pɪtɪd] *adj* [olives, cherries] dénoyauté.

pitter-patter ['pɪtəˌpætəʳ] ◇ *n* [of rain, hail] crépitement *m*; [of feet] trottinement *m*; [of heart] battement *m*.
◇ *adv*: to go ~ [feet] trottiner; [heart] palpiter; the rain fell ~ on the leaves la pluie tambourinait doucement sur les feuilles.

Pittsburgh ['pɪtsbɜːg] *pr n* Pittsburgh.

pituitary [pɪ'tjʊɪtrɪ] ◇ *n*: ~ (gland) glande *f* pituitaire, hypophyse *f*.
◇ *adj* pituitaire.

pit viper *n* crotaliné *m*.

pity ['pɪtɪ] (*pl* pities, *pt* & *pp* pitied) ◇ *n* -**1.** [compassion] pitié *f*, compassion *f*; I feel great ~ for them j'ai beaucoup de pitié pour eux, je les plains énormément; the sight moved her to ~ le spectacle l'a apitoyée OR attendrie; out of ~ par pitié; to take OR to have ~ on sb avoir pitié de qqn. -**2.** [mercy] pitié *f*, miséricorde *f*; have ~ on the children! ayez pitié des enfants!; he showed no ~ to the traitors il s'est montré impitoyable envers les traîtres; for ~'s sake! [entreaty] pitié!; [annoyance] par pitié! -**3.** [misfortune, shame] dommage *m*; what a ~! c'est dommage!; it's a ~ (that) she isn't here quel dommage qu'elle ne soit pas là; it seems a ~ not to finish the bottle ce serait dommage de ne pas finir la bouteille; we're leaving tomorrow, more's the ~ nous partons demain, malheureusement.
◇ *vt* avoir pitié de, s'apitoyer sur; he pities himself il s'apitoie sur son sort; they are greatly to be pitied ils sont bien à plaindre.

pitying ['pɪtɪɪŋ] *adj* [look, smile] de pitié, compatissant.

pityingly ['pɪtɪɪŋlɪ] *adv* avec compassion, avec pitié.

Pius ['paɪəs] *pr n* Pie.

pivot ['pɪvət] ◇ *n* MECH, MIL & *fig* pivot *m*.
◇ *vi* -**1.** *literal* pivoter; ~ on your left foot pivotez sur votre pied gauche. -**2.** *fig*: his life ~s around his family toute son existence tourne autour de sa famille.
◇ *vt* faire pivoter.

◆ **pivot on** *vt insep* dépendre de; everything ~s on her decision tout dépend de sa décision.

pivotal ['pɪvətl] *adj* [crucial] crucial, central.

pivot bridge *n* pont *m* tournant.

pix *inf* [pɪks] *npl* [photos] photos *fpl*; [cinema] cinoche *m*.

pixel ['pɪksl] *n* pixel *m*.

pixie ['pɪksɪ] *n* fée *f*, lutin *m*; ~ hat bonnet *m* pointu; ~ boots bottines *fpl*.

pixy ['pɪksɪ] (*pl* pixies) = **pixie**.

pizazz *inf* [pɪ'zæz] = **pizzazz**.

pizza ['piːtsə] *n* pizza *f*.

pizzazz *inf* [pɪ'zæz] *n* [dynamism] tonus *m*, punch *m*; [panache] panache *m*.

pizzeria [ˌpiːtsə'rɪə] *n* pizzeria *f*.

pizzicato [ˌpɪtsɪ'kɑːtəʊ] *n* pizzicato *m*.

pizzle ['pɪzl] *n arch* & *dial* verge *f* (de taureau).

pl *written abbr of* plural.

Pl. *written abbr of* place.

P & L *written abbr of* profit and loss.

placard ['plækɑːd] ◇ *n* [on wall] affiche *f*, placard *m*; [hand-held] pancarte *f*.
◇ *vt* -**1.** [wall, town] placarder. -**2.** [advertisement] placarder, afficher.

placate [plə'keɪt] *vt* apaiser, calmer.

placating [plə'keɪtɪŋ] *adj* apaisant, lénifiant.

placatory [plə'keɪtərɪ] *adj* apaisant, conciliant.

place [pleɪs] ◇ *n* -**1.** [gen - spot, location] endroit *m*, lieu *m*; this is the ~ c'est ici; the ~ where the accident happened l'endroit où a eu lieu l'accident; keep the documents in a safe ~ gardez les documents en lieu sûr; 'store in a cool ~' 'à conserver au frais'; this looks like a good ~ to pitch the tent l'endroit semble parfait pour monter la tente; this is neither the time nor the ~ to discuss it ce n'est ni le moment ni le lieu pour en discuter; I had no particular ~ to go je n'avais nulle part où aller; you can't be in two ~s at once on ne peut pas être en deux endroits à la fois; her leg is fractured in two ~s elle a deux fractures à la jambe; there are still one or two ~s where the text needs changing le texte doit encore être modifié en un ou deux endroits ❑ to go ~s [travel] aller quelque part; that girl will go ~s! *inf* cette fille ira loin!; ~ of birth lieu de naissance; ~ of safety order *ordonnance autorisant une personne ou un organisme à garder des enfants maltraités en lieu sûr*. -**2.** *Am* [in adverbial phrases]: no ~ nulle part; I'm not going any ~ je ne vais nulle part; some ~ quelque part; I've looked every ~ j'ai cherché partout. -**3.** [locality]: do you know the ~ well? est-ce que tu connais bien le coin?; she comes from a ~ called Barton elle vient d'un endroit qui s'appelle Barton; the whole ~ went up in flames [building] tout l'immeuble s'est embrasé; [house] toute la maison s'est embrasée; how long have you been working in this ~? depuis combien de temps travaillez-vous ici?; ~ of work lieu *m* de travail; we had lunch at a little ~ in the country nous avons déjeuné dans un petit restaurant de campagne ❑ to shout OR to scream the ~ down *inf* hurler comme un forcené; another ~ *Br* POL [in the House of Commons] la Chambre des lords; [in the House of Lords] la Chambre des communes. -**4.** [house] maison *f*; [flat] appartement *m*; nice ~ you've got here c'est joli chez vous; your ~ or mine? on va chez toi ou chez moi?; they met up at Ali's ~ ils se sont retrouvés chez Ali. -**5.** [proper or assigned position] place *f*; take your ~s! prenez vos places!; I lost my ~ in the queue j'ai perdu ma place dans la file d'attente; everything is in its ~ tout est à sa place; put it back in its proper ~ remets-le à sa place; push the lever till it clicks into ~ poussez le levier jusqu'au déclic; suddenly everything fell OR clicked into ~ *fig* [I saw the light] tout à coup, ça a fait tilt; [everything went well] tout s'est arrangé; I'll soon put him in his ~ j'aurai vite fait de le remettre à sa place; to know one's ~ savoir se tenir à sa place; it's not really my ~ to say ce n'est pas à moi de le dire. -**6.** [role, function] place *f*; what would you do (if you were) in my ~? que feriez-vous (si vous étiez) à ma place?; try and put yourself in his ~ essaie de te mettre à sa place; it occupies a central ~ in his philosophy cela occupe une place centrale dans sa philosophie; robots took the ~ of human workers des robots ont remplacé les hommes dans l'accomplissement de leur tâche; if she leaves there's nobody to take OR to fill her ~ si elle part, il n'y a personne pour la remplacer; he needs to find his ~ in society il a besoin de trouver sa place dans la société. -**7.** [seat - on train, in theatre etc] place *f*; [- on committee] siège *m*; she gave up her ~ to an old man elle a offert sa place à un vieux monsieur; save me a ~ garde-moi une place; to change ~s with sb *literal* échanger sa place contre celle de qqn; *fig* être à la place de qqn; we changed ~s so that he could sit by the window nous avons échangé nos places pour qu'il puisse s'asseoir près de la fenêtre; I wouldn't change ~s with her for anything pour rien au monde je n'aimerais être à sa place; there are a few ~s left on the next flight il reste quelques places sur le prochain vol; she has a ~ on the new commission elle siège à la nouvelle commission. -**8.** [table setting] couvert *m*; **how many ~s should I set?** combien de couverts dois-je mettre? -**9.** [post, vacancy] place *f*, poste *m*; **to get a ~ at university** être admis à l'université; **there is keen competition for university ~s** il y a une forte compétition pour les places en faculté. -**10.** [ranking - in competition, hierarchy etc] place *f*; **the prize for second ~** le prix pour la deuxième place; **Brenda took third ~ in the race/exam** Brenda a terminé troisième de la course/a été reçue troisième à l'examen; **the team is in fifth ~** l'équipe est en cinquième position; **for me, work takes second ~ to my family** pour moi, la famille passe avant le travail. -**11.** [in book, speech etc] : **I've lost my ~** je ne sais plus où j'en étais. -**12.** MATH: **to 3 decimal ~s, to 3 ~s of decimals** jusqu'à la troisième décimale. -**13.** *phr*: **to take ~** avoir lieu; **the meeting will take ~ in Geneva** la réunion aura lieu à Genève.

◇ *vt* -**1.** [put, set] placer, mettre; **she ~d the vase on the shelf** elle plaça le vase sur l'étagère; **he ~d an ad in the local paper** il a fait passer OR mis une annonce dans le journal local; **the proposals have been ~d before the committee** les propositions ont été soumises au comité. -**2.** [find work or a home for] placer; **to ~ sb in care** placer qqn; **all the refugee children have been ~d** tous les enfants réfugiés ont été placés. -**3.** *(usu passive)* [situate] placer, situer; **you are better ~d to judge than I am** vous êtes mieux placé que moi pour en juger; **we met several people similarly ~d** nous avons rencontré plusieurs personnes qui se trouvaient dans la même situation; **how are you ~d for money at the moment?** quelle est ta situation financière en ce moment? -**4.** *(usu passive)* [rank - in competition, race etc] placer, classer; **she was ~d third** elle était en troisième position; **the runners ~d in the first five go through to the final** les coureurs classés dans les cinq premiers participent à la finale; **the horse we bet on wasn't even ~d** le cheval sur lequel nous avions parié n'est même pas arrivé placé; **I would ~ her amongst the best writers of our time** je la classerais parmi les meilleurs écrivains de notre époque. -**5.** [identify] (se) remettre; **I can't ~ him** je n'arrive pas à (me) le remettre. -**6.** [order] placer, passer; [bet] placer; **~ your bets!** [in casino] faites vos jeux! -**7.** FIN [invest] placer; [sell] écouler.

◇ *vi Am* [in racing] être placé.

◆ **all over the place** *adv phr*: [everywhere] partout; **you always leave your things all over the ~!** tu laisses toujours traîner tes affaires partout! || [in disorder] en désordre; **my hair's all over the ~** je suis complètement décoiffé.

◆ **in place** *adv phr* en place; **hold it in ~ while I nail it in** tiens-le en place pendant que je le cloue.

◆ **in place of** *prep phr* à la place de; **she came in ~ of her sister** elle est venue à la place de sa sœur.

◆ **in places** *adv phr* par endroits.

◆ **in the first place** *adv phr*: **what drew your attention to it in the first ~?** qu'est-ce qui a attiré votre attention à l'origine OR en premier lieu?; **I didn't want to come in the first ~** d'abord, je ne voulais même pas venir; **in the first ~, it's too big, and in the second ~...** premièrement, c'est trop grand, et deuxièmement..., primo, c'est trop grand, et secundo...

◆ **out of place** *adj phr*: **the wardrobe looks out of ~ in such a small room** l'armoire n'a pas l'air à sa place dans une pièce aussi petite; **he felt out of ~ amongst so many young people** il ne se sentait pas à sa place parmi tous les jeunes; **such remarks are out of ~ at a funeral** de telles paroles sont déplacées lors d'un enterrement.

placebo [plə'siːbəʊ] (*pl* **placebos** OR **placeboes**) *n literal & fig* placebo *m*.

placebo effect *n* MED effet *m* placebo.

place card *n carte marquant la place des convives à table.*

place kick *n* SPORT coup *m* de pied placé.

place mat *n* set *m* (de table).

placement ['pleɪsmənt] *n* -**1.** [gen - act of putting, sending] placement *m*; [situation, position] situation *f*, localisation *f*. -**2.** [job-seeking] placement *m*; **~ office** *Am* UNIV centre *m* d'orientation (professionnelle). -**3.** [work experience] stage *m* en entreprise.

place-name *n* nom *m* de lieu; **the study of ~s** la toponymie.

placenta [plə'sentə] (*pl* **placentas** OR **placentae** [-tiː]) *n* placenta *m*.

place setting *n* couvert *m*.

placid ['plæsɪd] *adj* [person, attitude] placide; [lake, town] tranquille, calme.

placidity [plə'sɪdətɪ] *n* [of person, attitude] placidité *f*; [of place] calme *m*, tranquillité *f*.

placidly ['plæsɪdlɪ] *adv* placidement.

placing ['pleɪsɪŋ] *n* [act of putting] placement *m*; [situation, position] situation *f*, localisation *f*; [arrangement] disposition *f*.

placket ['plækɪt] *n* SEW patte *f* (de boutonnage).

plagiarism ['pleɪdʒjərɪzm] *n* plagiat *m*; **it's a crude (piece of) ~** c'est un plagiat grossier.

plagiarist ['pleɪdʒjərɪst] *n* plagiaire *mf*.

plagiarize, -ise ['pleɪdʒjəraɪz] *vt* plagier.

plague [pleɪg] ◇ *n* -**1.** [bubonic] : **the ~** la peste; **to avoid sb like the ~** fuir qqn comme la peste; **he avoids work like the ~** il est allergique au travail *hum*; **a ~ on them!** *arch* qu'ils crèvent! -**2.** [epidemic] épidémie *f*; **there's been a veritable ~ of burglaries** *fig* il y a eu toute une série de cambriolages. -**3.** [scourge] fléau *m*; BIBLE plaie *f*; **a ~ of rats** une invasion de rats. -**4.** *inf* [annoying person] enquiquineur *m*, -euse *f*.

◇ *vt* -**1.** [afflict] tourmenter; **the region is ~d by floods** la région est en proie aux inondations; **we are ~d with tourists in the summer** l'été, nous sommes envahis par les touristes; **we are ~d with mosquitoes in the summer** l'été, nous sommes infestés de moustiques; **it's an old injury that still ~s him** c'est une vieille blessure dont il souffre encore; **the industry has been ~d with strikes this year** l'industrie a beaucoup souffert des grèves cette année. -**2.** [pester] harceler; **to ~ sb with telephone calls** harceler qqn de coups de téléphone.

plaguey *inf*, **plaguy** *inf* ['pleɪgɪ] *adj dated* enquiquinant.

plaice [pleɪs] (*pl inv* OR **plaices**) *n* carrelet *m*, plie *f*.

plaid [plæd] ◇ *n* -**1.** [fabric, design] tartan *m*, tissu *m* écossais. -**2.** [worn over shoulder] plaid *m*.

◇ *adj* (en tissu) écossais.

Plaid Cymru [,plaɪd'kʌmrɪ] *pr n parti nationaliste gallois*.

plain [pleɪn] ◇ *n* -**1.** plaine *f*; **the Great Plains** [of North America] les Grandes Plaines. -**2.** [in knitting] maille *f* à l'endroit.

◇ *adj* -**1.** [not patterned, unmarked] uni; **~ blue wallpaper** papier peint bleu uni; **under ~ cover, in a ~ envelope** sous pli discret; **~ paper** [unheaded] papier sans en-tête; [unruled] papier non réglé. -**2.** [simple, not fancy] simple; **a ~ dress** une robe toute simple; **he's just a ~ soldier** il n'est que simple soldat; **she was just ~ Sarah Ferguson then** elle s'appelait tout simplement Sarah Ferguson à l'époque; **I like good ~ cooking** j'aime la bonne cuisine bourgeoise OR simple || [with nothing added - omelette, rice] nature *(inv)*; **a ~ piece of bread and butter** une simple tartine beurrée. -**3.** [clear, obvious] clair, évident, manifeste; **it's ~ that he's lying** il est clair OR évident qu'il ment; **it soon became ~ that I was lost** j'ai vite réalisé OR je me suis vite rendu compte que j'étais égaré; **his embarrassment was ~ to see** on pouvait voir qu'il était gêné, sa gêne était évidente; **the facts are ~** c'est clair, les choses sont claires; **I want to make our position absolutely ~ to you** je veux que vous compreniez bien notre position; **she made her intentions ~** elle n'a pas caché ses intentions; **he made it ~ to us that he wasn't interested** il nous a bien fait comprendre que cela ne l'intéressait pas; **I thought I'd made myself ~** je croyais avoir été assez clair ❑ **it's as ~ as a pikestaff** OR **as the nose on your face** *inf* c'est clair comme de l'eau de roche, ça saute aux yeux; **it's ~ sailing from now on** maintenant ça va marcher tout seul OR comme sur des roulettes. -**4.** [blunt, unambiguous] franc; **the ~ truth of the matter is I'm bored** la vérité, c'est que je m'ennuie; **let me be ~ with you** je vais être franc avec vous; **I want a ~ yes or no answer** je veux une réponse claire et nette; **the time has come for ~ words** OR **speaking** le moment est venu de parler franchement; **I told him in ~ English what I thought** je lui ai dit ce que je pensais sans mâcher mes mots. -**5.** [unattractive] pas très beau, quelconque; **she's a bit of a ~ Jane** ce n'est pas une beauté OR une Vénus. -**6.** [in knitting] : **~ stitch/row** maille *f*/rang *m* à l'endroit; **~ one, purl two** une maille à l'endroit, deux à l'envers.

◇ *adv* -**1.** [clearly] franchement, carrément; **you couldn't have put it any ~er** tu n'aurais pas pu être plus clair. -**2.** *inf Am* [utterly] complètement, carrément; **he's just ~ crazy** il est complètement cinglé; **I just ~ forgot!** j'ai tout bonnement oublié!

plainchant ['pleɪntʃɑːnt] = **plainsong**.

plain chocolate *n* chocolat *m* noir OR à croquer.

plain clothes *npl*: **to be in** OR **to wear ~** être en civil.

◆ **plain-clothes** *adj* en civil.

plain flour *n* farine *f* (sans levure).

plainly ['pleɪnlɪ] *adv* -**1.** [manifestly] clairement, manifestement; **you ~ weren't listening** manifestement, vous n'écoutiez pas, il est évident que vous n'écoutiez pas; **he was ~ tired** il était visiblement fatigué; **she's ~ his favourite** il est clair qu'elle est sa préférée. -**2.** [distinctly - remember, hear] clairement, distinctement. -**3.** [simply - dress, lunch] simplement. -**4.** [bluntly, unambiguously] franchement, carrément, sans ambages.

plainness ['pleɪnnɪs] *n* -**1.** [of clothes, cooking] simplicité *f*. -**2.** [clarity, obviousness] clarté *f*. -**3.** [unattractiveness] physique *m* quelconque OR ingrat.

plain sailing *n*: **it's ~ from now on** maintenant ça va marcher tout seul OR comme sur des roulettes.

Plains Indian *n* Indien *m*, -enne *f* de la (Grande) Prairie OR des (Grandes) Prairies.

plainsman ['pleɪnzmən] (*pl* **plainsmen** [-mən]) *n* [gen] habitant *m* de la plaine; [of Great Plains] habitant *m* de la (Grande) Prairie.

plainsong ['pleɪnsɒŋ] *n* plain-chant *m*.

plain-spoken *adj* qui a son franc-parler.

plaint [pleɪnt] *n lit* plainte *f*, lamentation *f*.

plaintiff ['pleɪntɪf] *n* JUR demandeur *m*, -eresse *f*, plaignant *m*, -e *f*.

plaintive ['pleɪntɪv] *adj* [voice, sound] plaintif.

plaintively ['pleɪntɪvlɪ] *adv* plaintivement.

plait [plæt] ◇ *n* [of hair] natte *f*, tresse *f*; [of straw] tresse *f*.

◇ *vt* [hair, rope, grass] natter, tresser; [garland] tresser.

plan [plæn] (*pt & pp* **planned**, *cont* **planning**)

◇ *n* -**1.** [strategy] plan *m*, projet *m*; **to draw up** OR **to make a ~** dresser OR établir un plan; **what's your ~ of action** OR **campaign?** qu'est-ce que vous comptez faire?; **to put a ~ into operation** mettre un plan en œuvre; **to go according to ~** se dérouler comme prévu OR selon les prévisions; **five-year ~** ECON plan quinquennal; **flight/career ~** plan de vol/de carrière. -**2.** [intention, idea] projet *m*; **I had to change my holiday ~s** j'ai dû changer mes projets de vacances; **we had made ~s to stay at a hotel** nous avions prévu de descendre à l'hôtel; **what are your ~s for Monday?** qu'est-ce que tu as prévu pour lundi?; **the ~ is to meet up at John's** l'idée, c'est de se retrouver chez John. -**3.** [diagram, map] plan *m*; **I'll draw you a ~ of the office** je vais vous dessiner un plan du bureau. -**4.** [outline - of book, essay, lesson] plan *m*; rough ~ canevas *m*, esquisse *f*. -**5.** ARCHIT plan *m*; drawn in ~ and in elevation dessiné en plan et en élévation.

◇ *vt* -**1.** [organize in advance - project] élaborer; [- concert, conference] organiser, monter; [- crime, holiday, trip] préparer; ECON planifier; ~ your time carefully organisez votre emploi du temps avec soin; they're planning a surprise for you ils te préparent une surprise; they're planning a new venture ils ont en projet une nouvelle entreprise; the Pope's visit is planned for March la visite du pape doit avoir lieu en mars; an industrial estate is planned for this site il est prévu d'aménager un parc industriel sur ce site; everything went as planned tout s'est déroulé comme prévu. -**2.** [intend] projeter; we're planning to go to the States nous projetons d'aller aux États-Unis; ~ to finish it in about four hours comptez environ quatre heures pour le terminer. -**3.** [design - house, garden, town] concevoir, dresser les plans de. -**4.** [make outline of - book, essay] faire le plan de, esquisser; [- lesson] préparer.

◇ *vi* faire des projets; it is important to ~ ahead il est important de faire des projets pour l'avenir.

◆ **plan for** *vt insep* prévoir; we didn't ~ for this many people nous n'avions pas prévu OR nous n'attendions pas autant de monde; you must ~ for everything vous devez tout prévoir OR parer à toute éventualité.

◆ **plan on** *vt insep* -**1.** [intend] projeter; what are you planning on doing? qu'est-ce que vous projetez de faire OR vous avez l'intention de faire? -**2.** [expect] compter sur; we hadn't planned on it raining nous n'avions pas prévu qu'il pleuvrait.

planar ['pleɪnəʳ] *adj* GEOM plan.

plane [pleɪn] ◇ *n* -**1.** [aeroplane] avion *m*; ~ crash accident d'avion. -**2.** ARCHIT, ART & MATH plan *m*; vertical ~ plan vertical. -**3.** [level, degree] plan *m*; she's on a higher intellectual ~ elle est d'un niveau intellectuel plus élevé. -**4.** [tool] rabot *m*. -**5.** BOT: ~ (tree) platane *m*.

◇ *adj* [flat] plan, plat; MATH plan; ~ geometry géométrie *f* plane.

◇ *vi* -**1.** [glide] planer. -**2.** *inf* [travel by plane] voyager par OR en avion; we ~d back on est revenus par avion.

◇ *vt* [in carpentry]: ~ (down) raboter.

planet ['plænɪt] *n* planète *f*.

planetarium [ˌplænɪ'teərɪəm] (*pl* planetariums OR planetaria [-rɪə]) *n* planétarium *m*.

planetary ['plænɪtrɪ] *adj* planétaire.

planetology [ˌplænɪ'tɒlədʒɪ] *n* planétologie *f*.

plangent ['plændʒənt] *adj lit* [loud] sonore, retentissant; [sad] plaintif, mélancolique.

planisphere ['plænɪˌsfɪəʳ] *n* planisphère *m*.

plank [plæŋk] ◇ *n* -**1.** [board] planche *f*; to walk the ~ subir le supplice de la planche. -**2.** *fig* article *m*; the main ~ of their policy la pièce maîtresse de leur politique.

◇ *vt* [floor, room] planchéier.

planking ['plæŋkɪŋ] *n* (*U*) planches *fpl*, planchéiage *m*; the floor consists of rough ~ quelques planches mal dégrossies font office de plancher.

plankton ['plæŋktən] *n* plancton *m*.

planned [plænd] *adj* projeté, en projet; news of the ~ sale was leaked le projet de vente s'est ébruité; a demonstration against the ~ nuclear power station une manifestation contre le projet de centrale nucléaire; Shula was a ~ baby Shula était un bébé désiré OR voulu ❑ ~ economy ECON économie *f* planifiée; ~ obsolescence INDUST obsolescence *f* planifiée, désuétude *f* calculée; ~ parenthood planning *m* familial.

planner ['plænəʳ] *n* -**1.** [ECON & gen] planificateur *m*, -trice *f*; programme ~ RADIO & TV programmateur *m*, -trice *f*; (town) ~ urbaniste *mf*. -**2.** [chart - in diary, on wall] planning *m*.

planning ['plænɪŋ] *n* -**1.** [of concert, conference] organisation *f*; [of lesson, menu] préparation *f*; [of campaign] organisation *f*, préparation *f*; the new product is still in the ~ stage le nouveau produit n'en est encore qu'au stade de projet. -**2.** [of economy, production] planification *f*; demographic ~ planification des naissances. -**3.** [of town, city] urbanisme *m*.

planning blight *n* (*U*) *Br effets négatifs possibles de l'urbanisation*.

planning permission *n* (*U*) permis *m* de construire.

plant [plɑːnt] ◇ *n* -**1.** BOT plante *f*; azaleas make good house ~s l'azalée est une excellente plante d'appartement. -**2.** [factory] usine *f*. -**3.** (*U*) [industrial equipment] équipement *m*, matériel *m*; [buildings and equipment] bâtiments et matériel. -**4.** *inf* [frame-up] coup *m* monté; he claims the heroin was a ~ by the police il prétend que l'héroïne a été mise là par la police (pour le compromettre). -**5.** *inf* [infiltrator] agent *m* infiltré, taupe *f*.

◇ *comp* BOT: ~ food engrais *m* (*pour plantes d'appartement*); ~ life flore *f*.

◇ *vt* -**1.** [flowers, crops, seed] planter; fields ~ed with wheat des champs (plantés) de blé. -**2.** *inf* [firmly place] planter; she ~ed herself in the doorway elle se planta OR se campa dans l'entrée ‖ [offload]: don't try and ~ the blame on me! *Br* n'essaie pas de me faire porter le chapeau!; they ~ed their kids on us for the weekend ils nous ont laissé leurs gosses sur les bras pour le week-end. -**3.** *inf* [give - kick, blow] envoyer, donner; [- kiss] planter; he ~ed a punch on his nose il lui a mis un coup de poing sur le nez. -**4.** [in someone's mind] mettre, introduire; her talk ~ed doubts in their minds son discours a semé le doute dans leur esprit; who ~ed that idea in your head? qui t'a mis cette idée dans la tête? -**5.** [hide - bomb] mettre, placer; [- microphone] cacher; [infiltrate - spy] infiltrer; he says the weapons were ~ed in his flat il prétend que les armes ont été placées dans son appartement pour le compromettre; to ~ evidence on sb cacher un objet compromettant sur qqn pour l'incriminer.

◆ **plant out** *vt sep* [young plants] repiquer.

Plantagenet [plæn'tædʒənɪt] *n* Plantagenêt *mf*.

plantain ['plæntɪn] *n* plantain *m*.

plantar ['plæntəʳ] *adj* plantaire.

plantation [plæn'teɪʃn] *n* plantation *f*; sugar ~ plantation de canne à sucre.

planter ['plɑːntəʳ] *n* -**1.** [person] planteur *m*, -euse *f*; tea ~ planteur de thé. -**2.** [machine] planteuse *f*. -**3.** [flowerpot holder] cache-pot *m inv*.

planter's punch *n* (punch *m*) planteur *m*.

plantigrade ['plæntɪgreɪd] ◇ *adj* plantigrade.

◇ *n* plantigrade *m*.

plant kingdom *n*: the ~ le règne végétal.

plant louse *n* puceron *m*.

plant pot *n* pot *m* (de fleurs).

plaque [plɑːk] *n* -**1.** [on wall, monument] plaque *f*. -**2.** DENT: (dental) ~ plaque *f* dentaire.

plash [plæʃ] *lit* ◇ *n* [of waves, oars] clapotement *m*, clapotis *m*; [of stream, fountain] murmure *m*.

◇ *vi* [waves] clapoter; [oars] frapper l'eau avec un bruit sourd; [stream, fountain] murmurer.

plashy ['plæʃɪ] (*compar* plashier, *superl* plashiest) *adj lit* [marshy] marécageux.

plasma ['plæzmə] *n* MED & PHYS plasma *m*; blood ~ plasma sanguin.

plasma cell *n* plasmocyte *m*.

plaster ['plɑːstəʳ] ◇ *n* -**1.** [for walls, modelling] plâtre *m*; ~ of Paris plâtre de Paris OR à mouler. -**2.** [for broken limbs] plâtre *m*; her arm was in ~ *Br* elle avait le bras dans le plâtre. -**3.** *Br* [for cut]: (sticking) ~ pansement *m* (adhésif); corn ~s pansements coricides.

◇ *comp* [model, statue] de OR en plâtre.

◇ *vt* -**1.** CONSTR & MED plâtrer. -**2.** [smear - ointment, cream] enduire; she had ~ed make-up on her face, her face was ~ed with make-up elle avait une belle couche de maquillage sur la figure; they were ~ed with mud ils étaient couverts de boue. -**3.** [make stick] coller; the rain had ~ed his shirt to his back la pluie lui avait plaqué la chemise sur le dos; he tried to ~ his hair down with oil il mit de l'huile sur ses cheveux pour essayer de les plaquer sur sa tête. -**4.** [cover]: to ~ sthg with couvrir qqch de; to ~ a wall with notices, to ~ notices over a wall couvrir un mur d'affiches; the town was ~ed with election posters les murs de la ville étaient tapissés OR recouverts d'affiches électorales. -**5.** *inf* [defeat heavily] écraser; [beat up] tabasser, passer à tabac.

◆ **plaster over, plaster up** *vt sep* [hole, crack] boucher (avec du plâtre).

plasterboard ['plɑːstəbɔːd] *n* Placoplâtre® *m*.

plaster cast *n* -**1.** MED plâtre *m*. -**2.** ART moule *m* (en plâtre).

plastered *inf* ['plɑːstəd] *adj* [drunk] bourré; to get ~ se soûler.

plasterer ['plɑːstərəʳ] *n* plâtrier *m*.

plastering ['plɑːstərɪŋ] *n* CONSTR plâtrage *m*.

plasterwork ['plɑːstəwɜːk] *n* (*U*) CONSTR plâtre *m*, plâtres *mpl*.

plastic ['plæstɪk] ◇ *n* -**1.** [material] plastique *m*, matière *f* plastique; the ~s industry l'industrie du plastique. -**2.** *inf* (*U*) [credit cards] cartes *fpl* de crédit; she pays for everything with ~ elle règle tous ses achats avec des cartes de crédit; to put sthg on ~ acheter qqch avec une carte de crédit.

◇ *adj* -**1.** [made of plastic] en OR de plastique; ~ cups gobelets *mpl* en plastique. -**2.** [malleable] plastique, malléable; [adaptable] influençable. -**3.** ART plastique; the ~ arts les arts *mpl* plastiques. -**4.** *inf pej* [artificial] synthétique; the ~ rubbish they call bread cette espèce de caoutchouc qu'ils appellent du pain.

plastic bomb *n* charge *f* de plastique, bombe *f* au plastique.

plastic bullet *n* balle *f* en plastique.

plastic explosive *n* plastic *m*; the laboratory was blown up with ~s le laboratoire a été plastiqué.

Plasticine® ['plæstɪsiːn] *n* pâte *f* à modeler.

plasticity [plæs'tɪsətɪ] *n* plasticité *f*.

plastic money *inf n* (*U*) cartes *fpl* de crédit.

plastic surgeon *n* [cosmetic] chirurgien *m*, -enne *f* esthétique; [therapeutic] plasticien *m*, -enne *f*.

plastic surgery *n* [cosmetic] chirurgie *f* esthétique; [therapeutic] chirurgie *f* plastique OR réparatrice; she had ~ on her nose elle s'est fait refaire le nez.

plate [pleɪt] ◇ *n* -**1.** [for eating] assiette *f*; [for serving] plat *m*; he ate a huge ~ of spaghetti il a mangé une énorme assiette de spaghetti ❑ to hand sthg to sb on a ~ servir qqch à qqn sur un plateau d'argent; she was handed the job on a ~ on lui a offert cet emploi sans qu'elle ait à lever le petit doigt; to have a lot on one's ~ avoir du pain sur la planche. -**2.** [piece of metal, glass etc] plaque *f*; [rolled metal] tôle *f*; he has a metal ~ in his thigh il a une plaque en métal dans la cuisse ❑ microscope ~ lamelle *f*. -**3.** [with inscription] plaque *f*; a car with foreign ~s une voiture avec une plaque d'immatriculation étrangère OR immatriculée à l'étranger. -**4.** [on cooker] plaque *f* (de cuisson). -**5.** [dishes, cutlery - silver] vaisselle *f* en argent; [- gold] vaisselle *f* en or; the burglars took all the (silver) ~ les cambrioleurs ont pris toute l'argenterie. -**6.** [coated metal] plaqué *m*; [metal coating] placage *m*; the knives are silver ~ les couteaux sont en plaqué argent. -**7.** TYPO [for printing] cliché *m*; [for engraving] planche *f*; [illustration] planche *f*, hors-texte *m inv*; offset ~ plaque *f* offset. -**8.** PHOT plaque *f* (sensible). -**9.** [for church collection] plateau *m* (de quête). -**10.** ANAT & ZOOL plaque *f*. -**11.** [denture] dentier *m*, appareil *m* OR prothèse *f* dentaire; [for straightening teeth] appareil *m* (orthodontique). -**12.** [in earth's crust] plaque *f*. -**13.** [trophy, race] trophée *m*. -**14.** ELEC & ELECTRON plaque *f*.

◇ *vt* -**1.** [coat with metal] plaquer; a silver-gold-~d watch une montre plaquée argent/or; nickel ~d nickelé. -2. [cover with metal plates] garnir de plaques; [armour plate] blinder. -3. TYPO clicher.

◆ **Plate** *pr n*: the River ~ le Rio de la Plata.

plate armour *n* armure *f (en plaques de fer)*.

plateau ['plætəʊ] (*pl* plateaus OR plateaux [-təʊz]) *n* GEOG & *fig* plateau *m*; to reach a ~ [activity, process] atteindre un palier.

plateful ['pleɪtfʊl] *n* assiettée *f*, assiette *f*.

plate glass *n* verre *m* (à vitres).

◆ **plate-glass** *adj* en verre; ~ window vitrine *f*.

platelayer ['pleɪt,leɪəʳ] *n Br* RAIL poseur *m* de rails.

platelet ['pleɪtlɪt] *n* ANAT plaquette *f* (sanguine).

platen ['plætn] *n* -1. [on typewriter] rouleau *m*, cylindre *m*; ~ knob bouton *m* (d'entraînement) du cylindre. -2. [in printing press] platine *f*. -3. [on machine tool] table *f*, plateau *m*.

plate rack *n* égouttoir *m*.

plate tectonics *n (U)* tectonique *f* des plaques.

platewarmer ['pleɪt,wɔːməʳ] *n* chauffe-plats *m inv*.

platform ['plætfɔːm] *n* -1. [stage] estrade *f*; [for speakers] tribune *f*; she shared the ~ with her rival elle était à la même tribune que son rival; it serves as a ~ for their racist views *fig* cela sert de tribune pour propager leurs opinions racistes. -2. [raised structure] plate-forme *f*; gun ~ plate-forme de tir; loading ~ quai *m* de chargement. -3. [at station] quai *m*. -4. POL [programme] plate-forme *f*; electoral ~ plate-forme électorale. -5. *Br* [on bus] plate-forme *f*. -6. COMPUT plate-forme *f*.

◆ **platforms** = **platform shoes**.

platform scale *n* (balance *f* à) bascule *f*.

platform shoes *npl* chaussures *fpl* à semelles compensées.

platform-soled *adj* à semelles compensées.

platform soles *npl* semelles *fpl* compensées.

platform ticket *n* ticket *m* de quai.

plating ['pleɪtɪŋ] *n* [gen] placage *m*; [in gold] dorage *m*, dorure *f*; [in silver] argentage *m*, argenture *f*; [in nickel] nickelage *m*.

platinum ['plætɪnəm] ◇ *n* platine *m*.

◇ *adj* [colour] platine *(inv)*.

◇ *comp* [jewellery, pen] en platine.

platinum blonde *n* blonde *f* platine.

◆ **platinum-blonde** *adj* (blond) platine *(inv)*.

platinum record *n* MUS disque *m* de platine.

platitude ['plætɪtjuːd] *n* -1. [trite remark] platitude *f*, lieu *m* commun. -2. [triteness] platitude *f*.

platitudinous [,plætɪ'tjuːdɪnəs] *adj fml* banal, d'une grande platitude.

Plato ['pleɪtəʊ] *pr n* Platon.

platonic [plə'tɒnɪk] *adj* [love, relationship] platonique.

◆ **Platonic** *adj* PHILOS platonicien.

Platonism ['pleɪtənɪzm] *n* platonisme *m*.

Platonist ['pleɪtənɪst] *n* platonicien *m*, -enne *f*.

platoon [plə'tuːn] *n* MIL section *f*; [of bodyguards, firemen etc] armée *f*.

platter ['plætəʳ] *n* -1. [for serving] plat *m*; seafood ~ plateau *m* de fruits de mer. -2. *inf Am* [record] disque *m*.

platypus ['plætɪpəs] *n* ornithorynque *m*.

plaudits ['plɔːdɪts] *npl fml* -1. [applause] applaudissements *mpl*. -2. [praise] éloges *mpl*; her poetry won her ~ from the critics ses poésies lui ont valu les éloges de la critique.

plausibility [,plɔːzə'bɪlətɪ] *n* plausibilité *f*.

plausible ['plɔːzəbl] *adj* [excuse, alibi, theory] plausible; [person] crédible; he's a very ~ liar il ment de façon très convaincante.

plausibly ['plɔːzəblɪ] *adv* de façon convaincante; he argued his case very ~ il s'est défendu de façon très convaincante.

Plautus ['plɔːtəs] *pr n* Plaute.

play [pleɪ] ◇ *vt* -1. [games, cards] jouer à; to ~ tennis/poker/dominoes jouer au tennis/au poker/aux dominos; to ~ hide-and-seek jouer à cache-cache; the children were ~ing dolls/soldiers les enfants jouaient à la poupée/aux soldats; how about ~ing some golf after work? si on faisait une partie de golf après le travail?; do you ~ any sports? pratiquez-vous un sport?; squash is ~ed indoors le squash se pratique en salle ❑ to ~ the game SPORT jouer selon les règles; *fig* jouer le jeu; I won't ~ his game je ne vais pas entrer dans son jeu; she's ~ing games with you elle te fait marcher; to ~ it cool *inf* ne pas s'énerver, garder son calme; to ~ favorites *Am* faire du favoritisme; to play sb for a fool rouler qqn; the meeting's next week, how shall we ~ it? *inf* la réunion aura lieu la semaine prochaine, quelle va être notre stratégie?; to ~ (it) safe ne pas prendre de risque, jouer la sécurité. -2. [opposing player or team] jouer contre, rencontrer; Italy ~s Brazil in the finals l'Italie joue contre OR rencontre le Brésil en finale; I ~ed him at chess j'ai joué aux échecs avec lui; he will ~ Karpov il jouera contre Karpov. -3. [match] jouer, disputer; to ~ a match against sb disputer un match avec OR contre qqn; how many tournaments has he ~ed this year? à combien de tournois a-t-il participé cette année?; the next game will be ~ed on Sunday la prochaine partie aura lieu dimanche. -4. [player] faire jouer; the coach didn't ~ her until the second half l'entraîneur ne l'a fait entrer (sur le terrain) qu'à la deuxième mi-temps. -5. [card, chess piece] jouer; to ~ spades/trumps jouer pique/atout; how should I ~ this hand? comment devrais-je jouer cette main? ❑ she ~ed her ace *literal* elle a joué son as; *fig* elle a abattu sa carte maîtresse; he ~s his cards close to his chest il cache son jeu. -6. [position] jouer; he ~s winger/defence il joue ailier/en défense. -7. [shot, stroke] jouer; she ~ed a chip shot to the green elle a fait un coup coché jusque sur le green; try ~ing your backhand more essayez de faire plus de revers; to ~ a six iron [in golf] jouer un fer numéro six; he ~ed the ball to me il m'a envoyé la balle. -8. [gamble on - stock market, slot machine] jouer à; to ~ the horses jouer aux courses; to ~ the property market spéculer sur le marché immobilier; he ~ed the red/the black il a misé sur le rouge/le noir ❑ to ~ the field jouer sur plusieurs tableaux. -9. [joke, trick]: to ~ a trick/joke on sb jouer un tour/faire une farce à qqn; your memory's ~ing tricks on you votre mémoire vous joue des tours. -10. CIN & THEAT [act - role, part] jouer, interpréter; Cressida was ~ed by Joan Dobbs le rôle de Cressida était interprété par Joan Dobbs; who ~ed the godfather in Coppola's film? qui jouait le rôle du parrain dans le film de Coppola? ‖ *fig*: to ~ a part OR role in sthg prendre part OR contribuer à qqch; an affair in which prejudice ~s its part une affaire dans laquelle les préjugés entrent pour beaucoup OR jouent un rôle important. -11. CIN & THEAT [perform at - theatre, club]: they ~ed Broadway last year ils ont joué à Broadway l'année dernière; "Othello" is ~ing the Strand for another week «Othello» est à l'affiche du Strand pendant encore une semaine; he's now ~ing the club circuit il se produit maintenant dans les clubs. -12. [act as]: to ~ the fool faire l'idiot OR l'imbécile; some doctors ~ God il y a des médecins qui se prennent pour Dieu sur terre; to ~ host to sb recevoir qqn; to ~ the hero jouer les héros; one ~ed the heavy while the other asked the questions l'un jouait les méchants tandis que l'autre posait les questions; don't ~ the wise old professor with me! ce n'est pas la peine de jouer les grands savants avec moi! -13. [instrument] jouer de; [note, melody, waltz] jouer; to ~ the violin jouer du violon; to ~ the blues jouer du blues; they're ~ing our song/Strauss ils jouent notre chanson/du Strauss; to ~ scales on the piano faire des gammes au piano. -14. [put on - record, tape] passer, mettre; [- radio] mettre, allumer; [- tapedeck, jukebox] faire marcher; don't ~ the stereo so loud ne mets pas la chaîne si fort; he's in his room ~ing records il écoute des disques dans sa chambre; I'll ~ the first side again *Br* OR over *Am* for you je vous repasse OR je vous fais réécouter la première face. -15. [direct - beam, nozzle] diriger; he ~ed his torch over the cave walls il promena le faisceau de sa lampe sur les murs de la grotte. -16. [fish] fatiguer.

◇ *vi* -1. jouer, s'amuser; [frolic - children, animals] folâtrer, s'ébattre; I like to work hard and ~ hard quand je travaille, je travaille, quand je m'amuse, je m'amuse; he didn't mean to hurt you, he was only ~ing il ne voulait pas te faire de mal, c'était juste pour jouer; don't ~ on the street! ne jouez pas dans la rue!; to ~ with dolls/with guns jouer à la poupée/à la guerre. -2. GAMES & SPORT jouer; to ~ well/badly/regularly jouer bien/mal/régulièrement; it's her (turn) to ~ c'est à elle de jouer, c'est (à) son tour; to ~ in a tournament participer à un tournoi; he ~s in the Italian team il joue dans l'équipe d'Italie; she ~ed into the left corner elle a envoyé la balle dans l'angle gauche; try ~ing to his backhand essayez de jouer son revers; to ~ to win jouer pour gagner ❑ to ~ dirty SPORT ne pas jouer franc jeu; *fig* ne pas jouer le jeu; to ~ fair SPORT jouer franc jeu; *fig* jouer le jeu; to ~ into sb's hands faire le jeu de qqn; you're ~ing right into his hands! tu entres dans son jeu!; to ~ hard to get *inf* se faire désirer; to ~ for time essayer de gagner du temps. -3. [gamble] jouer; to ~ for drinks/for money jouer les consommations/de l'argent. -4. MUS [person, band, instrument] jouer; [record] passer; I heard a guitar ~ing j'entendais le son d'une guitare; music ~ed in the background [recorded] des haut-parleurs diffusaient de la musique d'ambiance; [band] un orchestre jouait en fond sonore; is that Strauss ~ing? est-ce que c'est du Strauss que l'on entend? ‖ [radio, stereo]: a radio was ~ing upstairs on entendait une radio en haut; the stereo was ~ing full blast on avait mis la chaîne à fond. -5. CIN & THEAT [act] jouer; the last film she ~ed in le dernier film dans lequel elle a joué. -6. CIN & THEAT [show, play, film] se jouer; Hamlet is ~ing tonight on joue Hamlet ce soir; the film is ~ing to full houses le film fait salle comble; the same show has been ~ing there for five years cela fait cinq ans que le même spectacle est à l'affiche; now ~ing at all Park Cinemas actuellement dans toutes les salles (de cinéma) Park; what's ~ing at the Rex? qu'est-ce qui passe au Rex? ‖ [give performances]: the company will be ~ing in the provinces la compagnie va faire une tournée en province. -7. [feign] faire semblant; to ~ dead faire le mort; to ~ innocent OR dumb *inf* faire l'innocent, jouer les innocents. -8. [breeze, sprinkler, light]: to ~ (on) jouer (sur); sun ~ed on the water le soleil jouait sur l'eau; a smile ~ed on OR about OR over his lips un sourire jouait sur ses lèvres; lightning ~ed across the sky le ciel était zébré d'éclairs.

◇ *n* -1. [fun, recreation] jeu *m*; I like to watch the children at ~ j'aime regarder les enfants jouer ❑ ~ on words jeu *m* de mots, calembour *m*. -2. SPORT [course, conduct of game] jeu *m*; ~ was interrupted by a shower le match a été interrompu par une averse; ~ on the centre court is starting la partie sur le court central commence; there was some nice ~ from Brooks Brooks a réussi de belles actions OR a bien joué; she managed to keep the ball in ~ elle a réussi à garder la balle en jeu; out of ~ sorti, hors jeu ‖ *Am* [move, manoeuvre] combinaison *f*; she scored off a passing ~ elle a marqué un but après une combinaison de passes; the coach calls the ~s l'entraîneur choisit les combinaisons. -3. [turn] tour *m*; whose ~ is it? c'est à qui de jouer? -4. [manoeuvre] stratagème *m*; it was a ~ to get money/their sympathy c'était un stratagème pour obtenir de l'argent/pour s'attirer leur sympathie; he is making a ~ for the presidency il se lance dans la course à la présidence; she made a ~ for my boyfriend elle a fait des avances à mon copain. -**5.** [gambling] jeu *m*; I lost heavily at last night's ~ j'ai perdu gros au jeu hier soir. -**6.** [activity, interaction] jeu *m*; the result of a complex ~ of forces le résultat d'un jeu de forces complexe; to come into ~ entrer en jeu; to bring sthg into ~ mettre qqch en jeu. -**7.** THEAT pièce *f* (de théâtre); to be in a ~ jouer dans une pièce; it's been ages since I've seen OR gone to see a ~ ça fait des années que je ne suis pas allé au théâtre ❑ radio ~ pièce radiophonique; television ~ dramatique *f*. -**8.** TECH [slack, give] jeu *m*; there's too much ~ in the socket il y a trop de jeu dans la douille; give the rope more ~ donnez plus de mou à la corde; to give OR to allow full ~ to sthg *fig* donner libre cours à qqch. -**9.** [of sun, colours] jeu *m*; I like the ~ of light and shadow in his photographs j'aime les jeux d'ombre et de lumière dans ses photos. -**10.** *inf* [attention, interest] intérêt *m*; the summit meeting is getting a lot of media ~ les médias font beaucoup de tapage OR battage autour de ce sommet; in my opinion she's getting far too much ~ à mon avis, on s'intéresse beaucoup trop à elle; they made a lot of ~ OR a big ~ about his war record ils ont fait tout un plat de son passé militaire.

◆ **play about** *vi insep Br* [have fun - children] jouer, s'amuser; [frolic] s'ébattre, folâtrer.

◆ **play about with** *vt insep* -**1.** [fiddle with, tamper with]: to ~ about with sthg jouer avec OR tripoter qqch; stop ~ing about with the aerial arrête de jouer avec OR de tripoter l'antenne; I don't think we should be ~ing about with genes à mon avis, on ne devrait pas s'amuser à manipuler les gènes. -**2.** [juggle] considérer; I'll ~ about with the figures and see if I can come up with something more reasonable je vais jouer un peu avec les chiffres et voir si je peux suggérer quelque chose de plus raisonnable; she ~ed about with several endings for her novel elle a essayé plusieurs versions pour le dénouement de son roman. -**3.** *inf* [trifle with]: to ~ about with sb faire marcher qqn.

◆ **play along** ◇ *vi insep* [cooperate] coopérer; to ~ along with sb OR with sb's plans entrer dans le jeu de qqn; you'd better ~ along tu as tout intérêt à te montrer coopératif.

◇ *vt sep* [tease, deceive] faire marcher.

◆ **play around** *vi insep* -**1.** = **play about.** -**2.** *inf* [have several lovers] coucher à droite et à gauche.

◆ **play around with** = **play about with.**

◆ **play at** *vt insep* -**1.** [subj: child] jouer à; to ~ at cops and robbers jouer aux gendarmes et aux voleurs; just what do you think you're ~ing at? *fig* à quoi tu joues exactement? -**2.** [dally in - politics, journalism] faire en dilettante; you're just ~ing at being an artist tu joues les artistes; you can't ~ at being a revolutionary tu ne peux pas t'improviser révolutionnaire.

◆ **play back** *vt sep* [cassette, film] repasser; ~ the last ten frames back repassez les dix dernières images.

◆ **play by** *inf vt sep Am*: ~ it by me again reprenez votre histoire depuis le début.

◆ **play down** *vt sep* [role, difficulty, victory] minimiser; we've been asked to ~ down the political aspects of the affair on nous a demandé de ne pas insister sur le côté politique de l'affaire; her book rightly ~s down the conspiracy theory son livre minimise à juste titre la thèse du complot.

◆ **play in** *vt sep* -**1.** [in basketball]: to ~ the ball in remettre la balle en jeu. -**2.** *Br fig*: to ~ o.s. in s'habituer, se faire la main.

◆ **play off** *vi insep* [teams, contestants] jouer les barrages.

◆ **play off against** *vt sep*: he ~ed Bill off against his father il a monté Bill contre son père; he ~ed his enemies off against each other il a monté ses ennemis l'un contre l'autre.

◆ **play on** ◇ *vt insep* [weakness, naivety, trust] jouer sur; his political strength comes from ~ing on people's fears il tire sa force politique de sa capacité à jouer sur la peur des gens; the waiting began to ~ on my nerves l'attente commençait à me porter sur les nerfs.

◇ *vi insep* continuer à jouer; the referee waved them to ~ on l'arbitre leur fit signe de continuer à jouer.

◆ **play out** *vt sep* -**1.** [enact - scene] jouer; to ~ out a fantasy satisfaire un fantasme; the drama was ~ed out between rioters and police les incidents ont eu lieu entre les émeutiers et les forces de police. -**2.** *inf (usu pass)* [exhaust] crever; I'm ~ed out je suis crevé.

◆ **play through** *vi insep* [in golf] dépasser d'autres joueurs; may we ~ through? vous permettez que nous vous dépassions?

◆ **play up** ◇ *vt sep* -**1.** [exaggerate - role, importance] exagérer; [stress] souligner, insister sur; in the interview, ~ up your sales experience pendant l'entretien, mettez en avant OR insistez sur votre expérience de la vente; his speech ~ed up his working-class background son discours mettait l'accent sur ses origines populaires; the press ~ed up her divorce la presse a monté son divorce en épingle. -**2.** *inf Br* [bother] tracasser; my back is ~ing me up mon dos me joue encore des tours; don't let the kids ~ you up ne laissez pas les enfants vous marcher sur les pieds.

◇ *vi insep inf Br* [cause problems]: my back is ~ing up mon dos me joue encore des tours; he ~s up when his mother leaves il pique une crise chaque fois que sa mère s'en va; the car is ~ing up at the moment la voiture fait des siennes en ce moment.

◆ **play up to** *vt insep*: to ~ up to sb [flatter] faire de la lèche à qqn.

◆ **play upon** = **play on** *vt insep.*

◆ **play with** *vt insep* -**1.** [toy with - pencil, hair] jouer avec; he was ~ing with the radio dials il jouait avec les boutons de la radio; he only ~ed with his meat il a à peine touché à sa viande ❑ to ~ with fire jouer avec le feu. -**2.** [manipulate - words] jouer sur; [- rhyme] manier; she ~s with language in bold and startling ways elle manipule la langue avec une audace saisissante. -**3.** [consider - idea] caresser; he ~ed with the idea for weeks before rejecting it il a caressé l'idée pendant des semaines avant de l'abandonner; we're ~ing with the idea of buying a house nous pensons à acheter une maison; here are a few suggestions to ~ with voici quelques suggestions que je soumets à votre réflexion. -**4.** [treat casually - someone's affections] traiter à la légère; don't you see he's just ~ing with you? tu ne vois pas qu'il se moque de toi OR qu'il te fait marcher? -**5.** [have available - money, time] disposer de; how much time have we got to ~ with? de combien de temps disposons-nous?; they've got $2 million to ~ with ils disposent de deux millions de dollars. -**6.** *inf euph*: to ~ with o.s. [masturbate] se toucher.

playable ['pleɪəbl] *adj* jouable.

play-act *vi* -**1.** *fig* [pretend] jouer la comédie; he's not in pain, he's just ~ing! il n'a pas mal, il joue la comédie OR c'est du cinéma!; stop ~ing! arrête ton cinéma OR de jouer la comédie! -**2.** [act in plays] faire du théâtre.

play-acting *n* -**1.** [pretence] (pure) comédie *f fig*, cinéma *m fig*. -**2.** [acting in play] théâtre *m*.

playback ['pleɪbæk] *n* -**1.** [replay] enregistrement *m*; we watched the ~ after the programme nous avons regardé l'enregistrement après l'émission. -**2.** [function] lecture *f*; put it on ~ mettez-le en position lecture ❑ ~ head tête *f* de lecture.

playbill ['pleɪbɪl] *n* -**1.** [poster] affiche *f* (de théâtre). -**2.** [programme] programme *m*.

playboy ['pleɪbɔɪ] *n* playboy *m*; 'The Playboy of the Western World' *Synge* 'le Baladin du monde occidental'.

Play-Doh® ['pleɪˌdəʊ] *n sorte de pâte à modeler.*

player ['pleɪəʳ] *n* -**1.** [of game, sport] joueur *m*, -euse *f*; bridge ~ bridgeur *m*, -euse *f*; are you a poker ~? est-ce que vous jouez au poker? -**2.** [of musical instrument] joueur *m*, -euse *f*; she's a piano/guitar ~ elle joue du piano/de la guitare. -**3.** *arch* [actor] acteur *m*, -trice *f*.

player piano *n* piano *m* mécanique.

playfellow ['pleɪˌfeləʊ] *n Br* camarade *mf* (de jeux).

playful ['pleɪfʊl] *adj* [lively - person] gai, espiègle; [- animal] espiègle; [good-natured - nudge, answer] taquin; to be in a ~ mood être d'humeur enjouée.

playfully ['pleɪfʊlɪ] *adv* [answer, remark] d'un ton taquin; [act] avec espièglerie.

playfulness ['pleɪfʊlnɪs] *n* enjouement *m*, espièglerie *f*.

playgoer ['pleɪˌgəʊəʳ] *n* amateur *m* de théâtre; disappointed ~s were demanding their money back des spectateurs déçus demandaient à être remboursés.

playground ['pleɪgraʊnd] *n* [at school] cour *f* de récréation; [in park] aire *f* de jeu; the islands are a ~ for the rich *fig* les îles sont des lieux de villégiature pour les riches.

playgroup ['pleɪgruːp] *n réunion régulière d'enfants d'âge préscolaire généralement surveillés par une mère.*

playhouse ['pleɪhaʊs, *pl* -haʊzɪz] *n* -**1.** [theatre] théâtre *m*. -**2.** [children's] maison *f* de poupée.

playing ['pleɪɪŋ] *n* MUS: the pianist's ~ was excellent le pianiste jouait merveilleusement bien; guitar ~ is becoming more and more popular de plus en plus de gens jouent de la guitare.

playing card *n* carte *f* à jouer.

playing field *n Br* terrain *m* de sport; to have a level ~ *fig* être sur un pied d'égalité.

playlet ['pleɪlɪt] *n* pièce *f* en un acte.

playlist ['pleɪlɪst] *n* RADIO playlist *f (programme des disques à passer)*.

playmate ['pleɪmeɪt] *n* camarade *mf* (de jeux).

play-off *n* SPORT (match *m* de) barrage *m*.

playpen ['pleɪpen] *n* parc *m (pour bébés)*.

play-reading *n* lecture *f* d'une pièce (de théâtre).

playroom ['pleɪrʊm] *n* [in house] salle *f* de jeux.

playschool ['pleɪskuːl] = **playgroup.**

playsuit ['pleɪsuːt] *n* [for child] barboteuse *f*.

play-the-ball *n* [in rugby league] dégagement *m* au talon *(après un tenu)*.

plaything ['pleɪθɪŋ] *n literal & fig* jouet *m*.

playtime ['pleɪtaɪm] *n* récréation *f*; at ~ pendant la récréation.

playwright ['pleɪraɪt] *n* dramaturge *m*, auteur *m* dramatique.

plaza ['plɑːzə] *n* -**1.** [open square] place *f*. -**2.** *Am* [shopping centre] centre *m* commercial; toll ~ péage *m* (d'autoroute).

plc, PLC (*abbr of* public limited company) *n Br* ≃ SARL.

plea [pliː] *n* -**1.** [appeal] appel *m*, supplication *f*; they ignored his ~ for help ils n'ont pas répondu à son appel au secours; she made a ~ to the nation not to forget the needy elle conjura la nation de ne pas oublier les nécessiteux. -**2.** JUR [argument] argument *m*; [defence] défense *f*; what is your ~? plaidez-vous coupable ou non coupable?; to enter a ~ of guilty/not guilty/insanity plaider coupable/non coupable/la démence. -**3.** [excuse, pretext] excuse *f*, prétexte *m*; his ~ of ill health didn't fool anyone sa prétendue maladie n'a trompé personne.

plea bargaining *n* JUR *possibilité pour un inculpé de se voir notifier un chef d'inculpation moins grave s'il accepte de plaider coupable.*

plead [pliːd] (*Br pt & pp* pleaded, *Am pt & pp* pleaded OR pled [pled]) ◇ *vi* -**1.** [beg] supplier; to ~ for forgiveness implorer le pardon; she ~ed to be given more time elle supplia qu'on lui accorde plus de temps; to ~ with sb supplier OR implorer qqn; I ~ed with her to give me a second chance je la suppliai de me donner une deuxième chance. -**2.** JUR plaider; to ~ in court plaider devant le tribunal; to ~ guilty/not guilty plaider coupable/non coupa ble; to ~ for the defence plaider pour la défense; how does the accused ~? l'accusé plaide-t-il coupable ou non coupable?

◇ *vt* -**1.** [beg] implorer, supplier; **"please let me go" he ~ed** «laissez-moi partir, je vous en prie» implora-t-il; **she ~ed that her son be forgiven** elle supplia que l'on pardonne à son fils. -**2.** [gen & JUR] plaider; **to ~ sb's case** défendre qqn; *fig* plaider la cause de qqn; **who will ~ our cause to the government?** qui plaidera notre cause auprès du gouvernement?; **to ~ self-defence** plaider la légitime défense. -**3.** [put forward as excuse] invoquer, alléguer; [pretend] prétexter; **we could always ~ ignorance** nous pourrions toujours prétendre que nous ne savions pas; **she ~ed a prior engagement** elle a prétendu qu'elle était déjà prise.

pleading ['pliːdɪŋ] ◇ *adj* implorant, suppliant.
◇ *n* -**1.** [entreaty] supplication *f*, prière *f*; **I couldn't resist her ~** OR **~s** je n'ai pas pu résister à ses prières. -**2.** JUR [presentation of case] plaidoyer *m*, plaidoirie *f*.
◆ **pleadings** *npl* JUR [written exchange of allegations] ≃ débats *mpl* préliminaires *(visant à fixer les points de litige)*.

pleadingly ['pliːdɪŋlɪ] *adv* [look] d'un air suppliant OR implorant; [ask] d'un ton suppliant OR implorant.

pleasant ['pleznt] *adj* -**1.** [enjoyable, attractive] agréable, plaisant; **thank you for a most ~ evening** merci pour cette merveilleuse soirée; **it was ~ to be out in the countryside again** c'était agréable de se retrouver de nouveau à la campagne. -**2.** [friendly - person, attitude, smile] aimable, agréable; **she was very ~ to us as a rule** elle était en général très aimable à notre égard.

pleasantly ['plezntlɪ] *adv* -**1.** [attractively] agréablement; **the room was ~ arranged** la pièce était aménagée de façon agréable. -**2.** [enjoyably] agréablement; **~ surprised** agréablement surpris. -**3.** [kindly - speak, smile] aimablement.

pleasantness ['plezntnɪs] *n* -**1.** [attractiveness] attrait *m*, charme *m*. -**2.** [enjoyableness] agrément *m*. -**3.** [friendliness] amabilité *f*, affabilité *f*.

pleasantry ['plezntrɪ] (*pl* **pleasantries**) *n* [agreeable remark] propos *m* aimable; **to exchange pleasantries** échanger des civilités.

please [pliːz] ◇ *adv* -**1.** [requesting or accepting] s'il vous/te plaît; **could you pass the salt, ~?** pouvez-vous me passer le sel, s'il vous plaît?; **another cup of tea? — (yes) ~!** une autre tasse de thé? — oui, s'il vous plaît! OR volontiers!; **may I sit beside you? — ~ do** puis-je m'asseoir près de vous? — mais bien sûr; **~, make yourselves at home** faites comme chez vous, je vous en prie; **~ carry on** continuez, s'il vous plaît OR je vous en prie; **~, Miss!** s'il vous plaît, Mademoiselle!; **'~ ring'** 'sonnez SVP', 'veuillez sonner'; **'quiet ~'** 'silence'. -**2.** [pleading]: **~ don't hurt him** je vous en prie, ne lui faites pas de mal. -**3.** [remonstrating]: **Henry, ~, we've got guests!** Henry, voyons, nous avons des invités! -**4.** [hoping]: **~ let them arrive safely!** faites qu'ils arrivent sains et saufs!
◇ *vt* -**1.** [give enjoyment to] plaire à, faire plaisir à; [satisfy] contenter; **he only did it to ~ his mother** il ne l'a fait que pour faire plaisir à sa mère; **he's always trying to ~ the boss** il passe son temps à essayer de faire plaisir au patron; **you can't ~ everybody** on ne peut pas faire plaisir à tout le monde; **to be easy/hard to ~** être facile/difficile à satisfaire. -**2.** *phr*: **to ~ oneself** faire comme on veut; **~ yourself!** comme tu veux!; **I can ~ myself what I do** je fais ce qui me plaît; **everything will be all right, ~ God!** tout ira bien, plaise à Dieu!
◇ *vi* -**1.** [give pleasure] plaire, faire plaisir; **to be eager to ~** chercher à faire plaisir. -**2.** [choose]: **she does as** OR **what she ~s** elle fait ce qu'elle veut OR ce qui lui plaît; **I'll talk to whoever I ~!** je parlerai avec qui je veux! ❑ **as you ~!** *fml* comme vous voudrez!, comme bon vous semblera!; **if you ~** [requesting] *fml* s'il vous/te plaît; **she told me I was fat, if you ~!** figure-toi qu'elle m'a dit que j'étais gros!

pleased [pliːzd] *adj* content, heureux; **a ~ smile** un sourire satisfait; **to be ~ with sthg/sb** être content de qqch/qqn; **you're looking very ~ with yourself!** tu as l'air très content de toi!; **I am not at all ~ with the results** je ne suis pas du tout satisfait des résultats; **I'm very ~ to be here this evening** je suis très heureux d'être ici ce soir; **Mr & Mrs Adams are ~ to announce...** *fml* M. et Mme Adams sont heureux de OR ont le plaisir de vous faire part de...; **she would be only too ~ to help us** elle ne demanderait pas mieux que de nous aider; **I'm very ~ (that) you could come** je suis ravi que tu aies pu venir; **I'm afraid they were none too ~!** je crains qu'ils n'aient pas été très contents! ❑ **~ to meet you!** enchanté (de faire votre connaissance)!; **as ~ as Punch** heureux comme un roi.

pleasing ['pliːzɪŋ] *adj* agréable, plaisant.

pleasingly ['pliːzɪŋlɪ] *adv* agréablement, plaisamment.

pleasurable ['pleʒərəbl] *adj* agréable, plaisant.

pleasurably ['pleʒərəblɪ] *adv* agréablement, plaisamment.

pleasure ['pleʒə'] ◇ *n* -**1.** [enjoyment, delight] plaisir *m*; **to write/to paint for ~** écrire/peindre pour le plaisir; **are you here on business or for ~?** êtes-vous là pour affaires ou pour le plaisir?; **to take** OR **to find ~ in doing sthg** prendre plaisir OR éprouver du plaisir à faire qqch; **I'd accept your invitation with ~, but...** j'accepterais votre invitation avec plaisir, seulement...; **another beer? — with ~!** une autre bière? — avec plaisir OR volontiers!; **the ~s of country life** les plaisirs de la vie à la campagne; **it's one of my few ~s in life** c'est un de mes rares plaisirs dans la vie; **thank you very much — my ~!** OR **it's a ~!** merci beaucoup — je vous en prie!; **it's a great ~ (to meet you)** ravi de faire votre connaissance; **would you do me the ~ of having lunch with me?** *fml* me feriez-vous le plaisir de déjeuner avec moi?; **may I have the ~ (of this dance)?** *fml* m'accorderez-vous OR voulez-vous m'accorder cette danse?; **Mr and Mrs Evans request the ~ of your company at their son's wedding** *fml* M. et Mme Evans vous prient de leur faire l'honneur d'assister au mariage de leur fils. -**2.** *fml* [desire]: **at your ~** à votre guise; **they are appointed at the chairman's ~** ils sont nommés selon le bon vouloir du président; **detained at His/Her Majesty's ~** *Br* JUR & *euph* emprisonné aussi longtemps qu'il plaira au roi/à la reine. -**3.** *euph* [sexual gratification] plaisir *m*.
◇ *comp* [yacht] de plaisance; [park] de loisirs; [cruise, tour] d'agrément ❑ **~ boat** bateau *m* de plaisance; **~ trip** excursion *f*.
◇ *vt arch* OR *lit* plaire à, faire plaisir à.

pleasure principle *n*: **the ~** le principe de plaisir.

pleasure-seeker *n* hédoniste *mf*.

pleasure-seeking [-ˌsiːkɪŋ] *adj* hédoniste.

pleat [pliːt] ◇ *n* pli *m*.
◇ *vt* plisser; **a ~ed skirt** une jupe plissée.

pleb [pleb] *n* -**1.** *pej* [plebeian] plébéien *m*, -enne *f*; **it's not for the ~s** ce n'est pas pour n'importe qui! -**2.** *inf pej Br* [vulgar person] plouc *m*; **you ~!** espèce de plouc! -**3.** ANTIQ: **the ~s** la plèbe.

plebby *inf* ['plebɪ] *adj Br* commun, vulgaire.

plebeian [plɪ'biːən] ◇ *n* plébéien *m*, -enne *f*.
◇ *adj* -**1.** *pej* [vulgar] plébéien; **his tastes are rather ~** il a des goûts plutôt vulgaires. -**2.** ANTIQ plébéien.

plebiscite ['plebɪsaɪt] *n* plébiscite *m*.

plectrum ['plektrəm] (*pl* **plectrums** OR **plectra** [-trə]) *n* médiator *m*, plectre *m*.

pled [pled] *Am pt & pp* → **plead**.

pledge [pledʒ] ◇ *vt* -**1.** [promise] promettre; **they have ~d £500 to the relief fund** ils ont promis 500 livres à la caisse de secours; **she ~d never to see him again** [to herself] elle s'est promis de ne plus jamais le revoir; [to sb else] elle a promis de ne plus jamais le revoir; **her heart is ~d to another** *fml* son cœur est déjà pris. -**2.** *fml* [commit] engager; **he ~d himself to fight for the cause** il s'engagea à lutter pour la cause; **I am ~d to secrecy** j'ai juré de garder le secret; **to ~ one's word** donner OR engager sa parole. -**3.** [offer as security] donner en garantie; [pawn] mettre en gage, engager. -**4.** *fml* [toast] porter un toast à, boire à la santé de.
◇ *n* -**1.** [promise] promesse *f*; **manifesto ~** promesse électorale; **a £10 ~** un gage de 10 livres; **thousands of people phoned in with ~s of money** des milliers de personnes ont téléphoné en promettant de donner de l'argent; **you have my ~** vous avez ma parole; **I am under a ~ of secrecy** j'ai juré de garder le secret; **she told me under a ~ of secrecy** elle me l'a dit sous le sceau du secret ❑ **to sign** OR **to take the ~** [stop drinking] cesser de boire; **Pledge of Allegiance** *serment de loyauté prononcé à l'occasion du discours d'investiture du président des États-Unis*. -**2.** [security, collateral] gage *m*, garantie *f*; **in ~** en gage. -**3.** [token, symbol] gage *m*; **as a ~ of our sincerity** comme gage de notre sincérité. -**4.** *fml* [toast] toast *m*; **let us drink a ~ to their success** portons un toast OR buvons à leur réussite.

Pleiades ['plaɪədiːz] *npl*: **the ~** les Pléiades *fpl*.

Pleiocene ['plaɪəsiːn] = **Pliocene**.

Pleistocene ['plaɪstəsiːn] ◇ *adj* pléistocène.
◇ *n* pléistocène *m*.

plenary ['pliːnərɪ] ◇ *adj* -**1.** POL: **~ powers** pleins pouvoirs *mpl*. -**2.** [meeting] plénier; **in ~ session** en séance plénière.
◇ *n* [plenary meeting] réunion *f* plénière; [plenary session] séance *f* plénière.

plenipotentiary [ˌplenɪpə'tenʃərɪ] (*pl* **plenipotentiaries**) ◇ *adj* plénipotentiaire; **ambassador ~** ministre *m* plénipotentiaire.
◇ *n* plénipotentiaire *mf*.

plenitude ['plenɪtjuːd] *n lit* plénitude *f*.

plenteous ['plentjəs] *lit* = **plentiful**.

plentiful ['plentɪfʊl] *adj* [gen] abondant; [meal] copieux; **we have a ~ supply of food** nous avons de la nourriture en abondance.

plentifully ['plentɪfʊlɪ] *adv* abondamment, copieusement; **weeds grow ~ there** les mauvaises herbes y poussent en abondance.

plenty ['plentɪ] ◇ *pron* -**1.** [enough] (largement) assez, plus qu'assez; **no thanks, I've got ~** non merci, j'en ai (largement) assez; **£20 should be ~** 20 livres devraient suffire (amplement); **they have ~ to live on** ils ont largement de quoi vivre; **there's no need to hurry, we've got ~ of time** inutile de nous presser, nous avons largement le temps. -**2.** [a great deal] beaucoup; **there's still ~ to be done** il y a encore beaucoup à faire; **there'll be ~ of other opportunities** il y aura beaucoup d'autres occasions; **you've got ~ of explaining to do** tu vas devoir t'expliquer; **we see ~ of Ray and Janet** on voit beaucoup Ray et Janet.
◇ *n lit* [abundance] abondance *f*; **the years of ~** les années d'abondance.
◇ *adv inf* -**1.** [a lot] beaucoup; **there's ~ more food in the fridge** il y encore plein de choses à manger dans le frigo; **he sure talks ~** *Am* c'est un vrai moulin à paroles. -**2.** [easily]: **the room is ~ big enough for two** la pièce est largement assez grande pour deux.
◇ *det inf Am* OR *dial* [a lot of] plein de; **there's ~ work to be done!** ce n'est pas le boulot qui manque!
◆ **in plenty** *adv phr* en abondance.

pleonasm ['pliːənæzm] *n* pléonasme *m*.

pleonastic [plɪə'næstɪk] *adj* pléonastique.

plethora ['pleθərə] *n* pléthore *f*.

pleura ['plʊərə] (*pl* **pleurae** [-riː]) *n* plèvre *f*.

pleurisy ['plʊərəsɪ] *n (U)* pleurésie *f*.

Plexiglas® ['pleksɪglɑːs] *n* Plexiglas® *m*.

plexus ['pleksəs] *n* -**1.** ANAT plexus *m*. -**2.** *fml* [intricate network] enchevêtrement *m*, dédale *m*.

pliability [ˌplaɪə'bɪlətɪ] *n* -**1.** [of material] flexibilité *f*. -**2.** [of person] malléabilité *f*, docilité *f*.

pliable ['plaɪəbl] *adj* -**1.** [material] flexible, pliable. -**2.** [person] malléable, accommodant, docile.

pliancy ['plaɪənsɪ] = **pliability**.
pliant ['plaɪənt] = **pliable**.
pliers ['plaɪəz] *npl* pince *f*; a pair of ~ une pince.
plight [plaɪt] ◇ *n* [bad situation] situation *f* désespérée; the ~ of the young homeless la situation désespérée dans laquelle se trouvent les jeunes sans-abri; to be in a sad OR sorry ~ être dans une situation désespérée; seeing my ~ she stopped to help voyant mon embarras, elle s'est arrêtée pour m'aider.
◇ *vt arch* [pledge] promettre, engager; to ~ one's troth se fiancer; to ~ one's word donner OR engager sa parole.
plimsoll ['plɪmsəl] *n Br* tennis *m*.
Plimsoll line, Plimsoll mark *n* ligne *f* de flottaison.
plink [plɪŋk] ◇ *n* bruit *m* métallique.
◇ *vi* faire un bruit métallique.
plinth [plɪnθ] *n* [of statue] socle *m*; [of column, pedestal] plinthe *f*.
Pliny ['plɪnɪ] *pr n*: ~ the Elder Pline l'Ancien; ~ the Younger Pline le Jeune.
Pliocene ['plaɪəsiːn] ◇ *adj* pliocène.
◇ *n* pliocène *m*.
PLO (*abbr of* Palestine Liberation Organization) *pr n* OLP *f*.
plod [plɒd] (*pt* & *pp* plodded, *cont* plodding)
◇ *vi* -**1**. [walk] marcher lourdement. -**2**. *inf* [carry on]: he'd been plodding along in the same job for years ça faisait des années qu'il faisait le même boulot; she kept plodding on until it was finished elle s'est acharnée jusqu'à ce que ce soit fini; I plodded through the first five chapters il a fallu que je me force pour arriver au bout des cinq premiers chapitres.
◇ *n*: we could hear the ~ of feet on entendait des pas lourds; we maintained a steady ~ nous avons gardé un pas régulier.
plodder ['plɒdə^r] *n pej*: he's a bit of a ~ il est plutôt lent à la tâche.
plodding ['plɒdɪŋ] *adj pej* [walk, rhythm, style] lourd, pesant; [worker] lent.
plonk [plɒŋk] ◇ *n* -**1**. [heavy sound] bruit *m* sourd. -**2**. *inf Br* [cheap wine] pinard *m*.
◇ *vt inf* [put down] poser bruyamment; he ~ed his glass down il posa son verre bruyamment; she ~ed herself down on the sofa elle s'est affalée sur le canapé.
◇ *vi*: to ~ away on the piano jouer du piano *(mal et assez fort)*.
plop [plɒp] (*pt* & *pp* plopped, *cont* plopping)
◇ *n* plouf *m*, floc *m*.
◇ *adv*: the stone landed ~ in the water le caillou a fait plouf en tombant dans l'eau.
◇ *vi* [splash] faire plouf OR floc.
◇ *vt* [put] poser, mettre.
plosion ['pləʊʒn] *n* occlusion *f* LING.
plosive ['pləʊsɪv] ◇ *adj* occlusif.
◇ *n* occlusive *f*.
plot [plɒt] (*pt* & *pp* plotted, *cont* plotting)
◇ *n* -**1**. [conspiracy] complot *m*, conspiration *f*; a ~ to overthrow the government un complot pour renverser le gouvernement. -**2**. [story line - of novel, play] intrigue *f*; the ~ thickens l'affaire se corse. -**3**. [piece of land] terrain *m*; vacant/building ~ terrain vague/à bâtir; the land has been split up into 12 ~s le terrain a été divisé en 12 lotissements; we have a small vegetable ~ nous avons un petit potager OR carré de légumes. -**4**. *Am* [graph] graphique *m*. -**5**. *Am* ARCHIT plan *m*.
◇ *vt* -**1**. [conspire] comploter; they were accused of plotting to overthrow the government ils ont été accusés de complot OR de conspiration contre le gouvernement; I think they're plotting something je crois qu'ils préparent quelque chose. -**2**. [course, position] déterminer; they're trying to ~ the company's development over the next five years *fig* ils essaient de prévoir le développement de la société dans les cinq années à venir. -**3**. [graph] tracer, faire le tracé de; to ~ figures on OR onto a graph reporter des coordonnées sur un graphique. -**4**. [map, plan] lever.
◇ *vi* [conspire] comploter, conspirer; to ~ against conspirer contre.
plotter ['plɒtə^r] *n* -**1**. [conspirator] conspirateur *m*, -trice *f*. -**2**. [device - gen] traceur *m*; COMPUT table *f* traçante, traceur *m* de courbes.
plotting ['plɒtɪŋ] *n (U)* -**1**. [conspiring] complots *mpl*, conspirations *fpl*. -**2**. COMPUT & MATH traçage *m*.
plough *Br*, **plow** *Am* [plaʊ] ◇ *n* charrue *f*; large areas of moorland have gone under the ~ de larges portions de lande ont été labourées ❑ to put one's hand to the ~ s'atteler à la tâche.
◇ *vt* -**1**. [land] labourer; [furrow] creuser. -**2**. *fig* [invest] investir; to ~ huge sums of money into sthg investir d'énormes sommes d'argent dans qqch.
◇ *vi* -**1**. AGR labourer. -**2**. [crash] emboutir, percuter; the truck ~ed into the wall le camion percuta le mur. -**3**. *Br dated* [fail exam] se faire recaler.
◆ **plough back** *vt sep* [profits] réinvestir.
◆ **plough in** *vt sep* [earth, crops, stubble] enfouir (en labourant).
◆ **plough through** *vt insep* [documents, papers] éplucher; the ship ~ed through the waves le navire fendait les flots; she ~ed (her way) through the crowd elle s'est frayé un chemin à travers la foule.
◆ **plough under** = **plough in**.
◆ **plough up** *vt sep* -**1**. AGR [field, footpath] labourer. -**2**. [rip up] labourer; the grass had been ~ed up by the motorbikes le gazon avait été labouré par les motos.
ploughing *Br*, **plowing** *Am* ['plaʊɪŋ] *n* labourage *m*.
ploughland *Br*, **plowland** *Am* ['plaʊlænd] *n (U)* terre *f* de labour, labours *mpl*.
ploughman *Br*, **plowman** *Am* ['plaʊmən] (*Br pl* ploughmen, *Am pl* plowmen [-mən]) *n* laboureur *m*.
ploughman's (lunch) *n assiette de fromage, de pain et de pickles (généralement servie dans un pub)*.
ploughshare *Br*, **plowshare** *Am* ['plaʊʃeə^r] *n* soc *m*; to turn swords into ~s faire la paix, se réconcilier.
plover ['plʌvə^r] *n* pluvier *m*.
plow *etc Am* = **plough**.
ploy [plɔɪ] *n* -**1**. [stratagem, trick] ruse *f*, stratagème *m*; it's just a ~ to get us to leave ce n'est qu'une ruse pour nous faire partir. -**2**. *inf dated* [pastime] passe-temps *m inv*; [job] turbin *m*.
PLP (*abbr of* Parliamentary Labour Party) *pr n Br* députés *mpl* du Parti travailliste.
PLR (*abbr of* Public Lending Right) *pr n droit d'auteur versé pour les ouvrages prêtés par les bibliothèques*.
pluck [plʌk] ◇ *vt* -**1**. [pick - flower, fruit] cueillir. -**2**. [pull] tirer, retirer; he ~ed the cigarette from my mouth il m'a arraché la cigarette de la bouche; the survivors were ~ed from the sea by helicopter les survivants ont été récupérés en mer par un hélicoptère; to be ~ed from the jaws of death être arraché à la mort. -**3**. [chicken] plumer; [feathers] arracher. -**4**. [instrument] pincer les cordes de; [string] pincer. -**5**. [eyebrow] épiler.
◇ *vi*: he ~ed at my sleeve il m'a tiré par la manche; she was ~ing at (the strings of) her guitar elle pinçait les cordes de sa guitare.
◇ *n* -**1**. [courage] courage *m*; it takes ~ to do that il faut du courage pour faire ça. -**2**. [tug] petite secousse *f*. -**3**. CULIN fressure *f*.
◆ **pluck up** *vt sep* -**1**. [uproot] arracher, extirper. -**2**. *fig*: to ~ up (one's) courage prendre son courage à deux mains; to ~ up the courage to do sthg trouver le courage de faire qqch.
pluckily ['plʌkɪlɪ] *adv* courageusement.
pluckiness ['plʌkɪnɪs] *n* courage *m*.
plucky ['plʌkɪ] (*compar* pluckier, *superl* pluckiest) *adj* courageux.
plug [plʌg] (*pt* & *pp* plugged, *cont* plugging)
◇ *n* -**1**. ELEC [on appliance, cable] fiche *f*, prise *f* (mâle); [socket - in wall] prise *f* (de courant). -**2**. [stopper - gen] bouchon *m*; [- in barrel] bonde *f*; [- for nose] tampon *m*. -**3**. [for sink, bath] bonde *f*; to pull the ~ out retirer la bonde ❑ to pull the ~ on sb/sthg *inf*: this will pull the ~ on our competitors cela va couper l'herbe sous le pied de nos concurrents; he pulled the ~ on our plan [stopped it] il a mis le holà à notre projet; this pulls the ~ on the whole operation ça fiche tout par terre. -**4**. AUT: (spark) ~ bougie *f*. -**5**. [for fixing screws] cheville *f*. -**6**. *inf* [advertising] coup *m* de pub; her book got another ~ on TV last night on a encore fait de la pub pour son livre à la télé hier soir. -**7**. [of tobacco] carotte *f*. -**8**. GEOL: (volcanic) ~ culot *m*. -**9**. *Am*: (fire) ~ bouche *f* d'incendie. -**10**. ▽ [blow] beigne *f*, gnon *m*.
◇ *vt* -**1**. [block - hole, gap] boucher; [- leak] colmater; they ~ed (up) the hole in the dam ils ont colmaté la brèche dans le barrage. -**2**. [insert] enficher; ~ the cable into the socket branchez le câble sur la prise. -**3**. *inf* [advertise] faire de la pub à; the radio stations are continually plugging her record les stations de radio passent son disque sans arrêt. -**4**. ▽ *Am* [shoot] flinguer.
◆ **plug away** *vi insep* travailler dur; he keeps plugging away at his work il s'acharne sur son travail.
◆ **plug in** ◇ *vt sep* brancher.
◇ *vi insep Am*: we try to ~ in to people's needs *fig* nous essayons d'être à l'écoute des besoins de la population.
plugboard ['plʌgbɔːd] *n* tableau *m* de raccordement.
plugged [plʌgd] *adj* [blocked - nose, ear] bouché.
plughole ['plʌghəʊl] *n* trou *m* d'écoulement; that's all our work gone down the ~! *inf Br* tout notre travail est fichu!
plug-in *adj* [radio] qui se branche sur le secteur; [accessory for computer, stereo etc] qui se branche sur l'appareil.
plug-ugly *inf* ◇ *adj* très moche, laid comme un pou.
◇ *n Am* [ruffian] voyou *m*, loubard *m*.
plum [plʌm] ◇ *n* -**1**. [fruit] prune *f*. -**2**. ~ (tree) prunier *m*. -**3**. [colour] couleur *f* lie-de-vin.
◇ *comp* [tart] aux prunes.
◇ *adj* -**1**. [colour] lie-de-vin *(inv)*, prune *(inv)*. -**2**. *inf* [desirable]: it's a ~ job c'est un boulot en or.
plumage ['pluːmɪdʒ] *n* plumage *m*.
plumb [plʌm] ◇ *n* -**1**. [weight] plomb *m*; ~ bob plomb *m*. -**2**. [verticality] aplomb *m*; the wall is out of ~ le mur n'est pas d'aplomb OR à l'aplomb.
◇ *adj* -**1**. [vertical] vertical, à l'aplomb. -**2**. *inf Am* [utter, complete] complet, absolu; it's a ~ nuisance! c'est la barbe!
◇ *adv* -**1**. [in a vertical position] à l'aplomb, d'aplomb; ~ with d'aplomb avec. -**2**. *inf* [exactly, right] exactement, en plein; ~ in the middle of the first act en plein OR au beau milieu du premier acte. -**3**. *inf Am* [utterly, completely] complètement, tout à fait; I'm ~ exhausted! je suis complètement crevé!; she's ~ crazy! elle est complètement dingue!
◇ *vt* sonder; to ~ the depths toucher le fond; his films ~ the depths of bad taste ses films sont d'un mauvais goût inimaginable.
◆ **plumb in** *vt sep* effectuer le raccordement de; [washing machine] raccorder.
plumbago [plʌm'beɪgəʊ] (*pl* plumbagos) *n* -**1**. [plant] plumbago *m*. -**2**. [graphite] plombagine *f*.
plumber ['plʌmə^r] *n* -**1**. [workman] plombier *m*. -**2**. *inf* [secret agent] plombier *m*.
plumber's friend, plumber's helper *n Am* [tool] ventouse *f (pour déboucher)*.
plumbic ['plʌmbɪk] *adj* plombique.
plumbing ['plʌmɪŋ] *n* -**1**. [job] plomberie *f*. -**2**. [pipes] plomberie *f*, tuyauterie *f*.
plumb line *n* CONSTR fil *m* à plomb; NAUT sonde *f*.

plum cake *n* cake *m*.

plum duff *Br* = **plum pudding**.

plume [pluːm] ◇ *n* -**1.** [feather] plume *f*; ostrich ~ plume d'autruche. -**2.** [on helmet] plumet *m*, panache *m*; [on hat] plumet *m*; [on woman's hat] plume *f*. -**3.** [of smoke] volute *f*; [of water] jet *m*.
◇ *vt* -**1.** [preen] lisser; the swan ~d itself OR its feathers le cygne se lissait les plumes. -**2.** *fig* & *lit* [pride]: to ~ o.s. on sthg se glorifier de qqch.

plumed [pluːmd] *adj* -**1.** [hat, helmet] emplumé, empanaché. -**2.** [bird]: brightly ~ peacocks des paons au plumage éclatant.

plummet ['plʌmɪt] ◇ *vi* -**1.** [plunge, dive] tomber, plonger, piquer; he ~ed from the roof il est tombé du toit; the plane ~ed towards the earth l'avion piqua vers le sol. -**2.** [drop, go down - price, rate, amount] chuter, dégringoler; his popularity has ~ed sa cote de popularité a beaucoup baissé; the value of the pound ~ed la livre a chuté; educational standards have ~ed le niveau d'instruction a considérablement baissé.
◇ *n* [weight] plomb *m*; [plumb line] fil *m* à plomb.

plummy ['plʌmɪ] (*compar* plummier, *superl* plummiest) *adj* -**1.** *Br pej* [voice, accent] snob. -**2.** [colour] prune *(inv)*.

plump [plʌmp] ◇ *adj* [person] rondelet, dodu; [arms, legs] dodu, potelé; [fowl] dodu, bien gras; [fruit] charnu.
◇ *adv* [heavily] lourdement; [directly] exactement, en plein; he ran ~ into me il m'a heurté de plein fouet; it landed ~ in the middle ça a atterri en plein milieu.
◇ *vt* -**1.** [pillow, cushion] retaper. -**2.** [fowl] engraisser.
◆ **plump down** ◇ *vt sep*: to ~ sthg down laisser tomber qqch (lourdement); she ~ed herself/her bag down next to me elle s'est affalée/a laissé tomber son sac à côté de moi.
◇ *vi insep* se laisser tomber (lourdement), s'affaler.
◆ **plump for** *inf vt insep* arrêter son choix sur, opter en faveur de.
◆ **plump out** *vi insep* s'arrondir, engraisser.
◆ **plump up** *vt sep* = **plump** *vt* **1**.

plumpness ['plʌmpnɪs] *n* rondeur *f*, embonpoint *m*.

plum pudding *n* plum-pudding *m*.

plunder ['plʌndəʳ] ◇ *vt* piller.
◇ *n* -**1.** [booty] butin *m*. -**2.** [act of pillaging] pillage *m*.

plunderer ['plʌndərəʳ] *n* pillard *m*, -e *f*.

plundering ['plʌndərɪŋ] ◇ *n* pillage *m*.
◇ *adj* pillard.

plunge [plʌndʒ] ◇ *vi* -**1.** [dive] plonger. -**2.** [throw o.s.] se jeter, se précipiter; [fall, drop] tomber, chuter; the bus ~d into the river le bus est tombé dans la rivière; the helicopter ~d to the ground l'hélicoptère piqua vers le sol; to ~ to one's death faire une chute mortelle; I slipped and ~d forward j'ai glissé et je suis tombé la tête la première OR la tête en avant. -**3.** *fig*: sales have ~d by 30% les ventes ont chuté de 30 %; he ~d into a long and complicated story il s'est lancé dans une histoire longue et compliquée; she ~d bravely into the discussion elle se lança courageusement dans la discussion; the neckline ~s deeply at the front le devant est très décolleté. -**4.** *inf* [gamble] flamber.
◇ *vt* -**1.** [immerse] plonger; ~ the tomatoes in the boiling water plonger les tomates dans l'eau bouillante. -**2.** *fig* plonger; he ~d his hands into his pockets il enfonça les mains dans ses poches; he was ~d into despair by the news la nouvelle l'a plongé dans le désespoir; the office was ~d into darkness le bureau fut plongé dans l'obscurité.
◇ *n* -**1.** [dive] plongeon *m*; to take the ~ se jeter à l'eau. -**2.** [fall, drop] chute *f*; a ten-metre ~ une chute de dix mètres; prices have taken a ~ les prix ont chuté OR se sont effondrés.

plunger ['plʌndʒəʳ] *n* -**1.** [for sinks, drains] ventouse *f*, déboucheur *m*. -**2.** [piston] piston *m*. -**3.** *inf Br* [gambler] flambeur *m*, -euse *f*.

plunging ['plʌndʒɪŋ] *adj* plongeant; a ~ neckline un décolleté plongeant.

plunk [plʌŋk] ◇ *n* -**1.** *inf* [sound] bruit *m* sourd; I could hear the ~ of a guitar j'entendais quelqu'un gratter sa guitare. -**2.** ▽ *Am* [blow] beigne *f*, gnon *m*.
◇ *vt* -**1.** *inf* [put down] poser lourdement. -**2.** *inf* [guitar, banjo] gratter. -**3.** ▽ *Am* [hit] flanquer une beigne à; [shoot] flinguer.
◆ **plunk down** *inf* ◇ *vt sep* = **plunk** *vt* **1**.
◇ *vi insep* se laisser tomber (lourdement), s'affaler.

pluperfect [,pluː'pɜːfɪkt] ◇ *adj* plus-que-parfait; the ~ tense le plus-que-parfait.
◇ *n* plus-que-parfait *m*; in the ~ au plus-que-parfait.

plural ['plʊərəl] ◇ *adj* -**1.** GRAMM [form, ending] pluriel, du pluriel; [noun] au pluriel. -**2.** [multiple] multiple; [heterogeneous] hétérogène, pluriel; a ~ system of education un système d'éducation diversifié; a ~ society une société plurielle.
◇ *n* GRAMM pluriel *m*; in the ~ au pluriel.

pluralism ['plʊərəlɪzm] *n* -**1.** [gen & PHILOS] pluralisme *m*. -**2.** [holding of several offices] cumul *m*.

pluralist ['plʊərəlɪst] *n* [gen & PHILOS] pluraliste *mf*.

pluralistic [,plʊərə'lɪstɪk] *adj* pluraliste.

plurality [plʊə'rælətɪ] (*pl* pluralities) *n* -**1.** [multiplicity] pluralité *f*. -**2.** *Am* POL majorité *f* relative. -**3.** = **pluralism 2**.

pluralize, -ise ['plʊərəlaɪz] *vi* prendre le pluriel.

plus [plʌs] (*pl* pluses OR plusses) ◇ *prep* -**1.** MATH plus; two ~ two is OR are OR makes four deux plus deux OR deux et deux font quatre; the result is ~ six le résultat est plus six. -**2.** [as well as] plus; there were six of us, ~ the children nous étions six, sans compter les enfants; £97 ~ VAT 97 livres plus la TVA.
◇ *adj* -**1.** ELEC & MATH positif. -**2.** [good, positive] positif; a ~ factor un facteur positif, un plus; on the ~ side, it's near the shops un des avantages, c'est que c'est près des magasins; it certainly is a big ~ point c'est incontestablement un gros avantage. -**3.** *(after noun)* [over, more than]: children of twelve ~ les enfants de douze ans et plus; we're looking for somebody with talent ~ *inf* notre candidat devra avoir plus que du talent; B ~ [in school marks] B plus.
◇ *n* -**1.** MATH plus *m*; two minuses make a ~ deux moins font un plus. -**2.** [bonus, advantage] plus *m*, avantage *m*; there are a number of ~es to the new plan le nouveau projet comporte un certain nombre d'avantages.
◇ *conj inf* (et) en plus; he's stupid, ~ he's ugly il est bête, et en plus il est laid.

plus-fours *npl* pantalon *m* de golf.

plush [plʌʃ] ◇ *adj* -**1.** *inf* [luxurious] luxueux. -**2.** [made of plush] en peluche.
◇ *n* peluche *f*.

plushy *inf* ['plʌʃɪ] (*compar* plushier, *superl* plushiest) = **plush 1**.

plus sign *n* signe *m* plus.

Plutarch ['pluːtɑːk] *pr n* Plutarque.

Pluto ['pluːtəʊ] *pr n* Pluton.

plutocracy [pluː'tɒkrəsɪ] (*pl* plutocracies) *n* ploutocratie *f*.

plutocrat ['pluːtəkræt] *n* ploutocrate *mf*.

plutocratic [,pluːtə'krætɪk] *adj* ploutocratique.

plutonium [pluː'təʊnɪəm] *n* plutonium *m*; ~ radiation radiation *f* de plutonium.

pluvial ['pluːvjəl] *adj* pluvial.

pluviometer [,pluːvɪ'ɒmɪtəʳ] *n* pluviomètre *m*.

ply [plaɪ] (*pl* plies, *pt* & *pp* plied) ◇ *n* -**1.** [thickness - gen] épaisseur *f*; [layer - of plywood] pli *m*; [strand - of rope, wool] brin *m*. -**2.** *inf* = **plywood**.
◇ *vt* -**1.** [supply insistently]: to ~ sb with sthg: she plied us with food all evening elle nous a gavés toute la soirée; he plied us with drinks il nous versait sans arrêt à boire; we plied her with questions nous l'avons assaillie de questions. -**2.** *lit* [perform, practise] exercer; to ~ one's trade exercer son métier. -**3.** *lit* [use, operate - tool] manier. -**4.** *lit* [travel - river, ocean] naviguer sur; the barges that ~ the Thames les péniches qui descendent et remontent le cours de la Tamise.
◇ *vi* -**1.** [seek work]: to ~ for hire [taxi] prendre des clients. -**2.** [travel - ship, boat]: to ~ between faire la navette entre.

-ply *in cpds*: two/three~ toilet tissue papier *m* hygiénique double/triple épaisseur; five~ wood contreplaqué *m* en cinq épaisseurs; three~ wool laine *f* à trois fils.

Plymouth Brethren ['plɪməθ-] *npl* darbystes *mpl*.

plywood ['plaɪwʊd] *n* contreplaqué *m*.

p.m. (*abbr of* post meridiem) *adv*: 3 ~ 3 h de l'après-midi, 15 h; 11 ~ 11 h du soir, 23 h.

PM *n* -**1.** *abbr of* Prime Minister. -**2.** *abbr of* post mortem.

PMG *n* -**1.** *abbr of* Paymaster General. -**2.** *abbr of* Postmaster General.

PMS (*abbr of* premenstrual syndrome) = **PMT**.

PMT (*abbr of* premenstrual tension) *n* syndrome *m* prémenstruel.

pneumatic [njuː'mætɪk] *adj* pneumatique; ~ brakes freins *mpl* à air comprimé.

pneumatically [njuː'mætɪklɪ] *adv* pneumatiquement.

pneumatic drill *n* marteau-piqueur *m*.

pneumatics [njuː'mætɪks] *n (U)* pneumatique *f*.

pneumatic tyre *n* pneu *m*.

pneumoconiosis [,njuːməʊkəʊnɪ'əʊsɪs] *n* pneumoconiose *f*.

pneumonia [njuː'məʊnjə] *n (U)* pneumonie *f*; you'll catch OR get ~! tu vas attraper une pneumonie!

pneumonologist [,njuːmə'nɒlədʒɪst] *n* pneumologue *mf*.

pneumonology [,njuːmə'nɒlədʒɪ] *n* pneumologie *f*.

pneumothorax [,njuːməʊ'θɔːræks] *n* pneumothorax *m*.

po *inf* [pəʊ] (*pl* pos) *n Br* pot *m* (de chambre).

Po [pəʊ] *pr n*: the (River) Po le Pô.

PO -**1.** *written abbr of* post office. -**2.** *written abbr of* petty officer. -**3.** *abbr of* postal order.

POA (*abbr of* Prison Officers' Association) *pr n syndicat des agents pénitentiaires en Grande-Bretagne*.

poach [pəʊtʃ] ◇ *vt* -**1.** [hunt illegally] prendre en braconnant; all the game has been ~ed les braconniers ont tué tout le gibier. -**2.** *fig* [steal - idea] voler; [- employee] débaucher; several of our staff have been ~ed by a rival company plusieurs de nos employés ont été débauchés par un de nos concurrents; to ~ sb's shots [in tennis] piquer les balles de qqn. -**3.** CULIN pocher; ~ed egg œuf *m* poché.
◇ *vi* braconner; to ~ for hare chasser le lièvre sur une propriété privée; to ~ for salmon prendre du saumon en braconnant; to ~ on sb's territory OR preserves *fig* braconner sur les terres de qqn, empiéter sur le territoire de qqn.

poacher ['pəʊtʃəʳ] *n* -**1.** [person] braconnier *m*. -**2.** CULIN pocheuse *f*; egg ~ pocheuse.

poaching ['pəʊtʃɪŋ] *n* braconnage *m*.

POB, PO Box (*abbr of* post office box) *n* boîte *f* postale, BP *f*.

pock [pɒk] = **pockmark**.

pocked [pɒkt] = **pockmarked**.

pocket ['pɒkɪt] ◇ *n* -**1.** [on clothing] poche *f*; [on car door] compartiment *m*; it's in your coat ~ c'est dans la poche de ton manteau; take your hands out of your ~s! enlève tes mains de tes poches!; I went through his ~s j'ai fouillé OR regardé dans ses poches; he tried to pick her ~ il a essayé de lui faire les poches; the maps are in the ~ of the car door les cartes sont dans (le compartiment de) la portière de la voiture ❑ to have sb in one's ~s avoir qqn dans sa

poche; we had the deal in our ~ le marché était dans la poche; they live in each other's ~s ils vivent entassés les uns sur les autres; to line one's ~s se remplir les poches, s'en mettre plein les poches; he doesn't like putting his hand in his ~ il est du genre radin; to be out of ~ en être de sa poche. -2. *fig* [financial resources] portefeuille *m*, porte-monnaie *m*; we have prices to suit all ~s nous avons des prix pour toutes les bourses. -3. [small area] poche *f*; ~s of water/unemployment poches d'eau/de chômage; ~ of air trou *m* d'air. -4. [on billiard or pool table] blouse *f*.
◇ *comp* [diary, camera, revolver etc] de poche.
◇ *vt* -1. [put in one's pocket] mettre dans sa poche, empocher; I paid up and ~ed the change j'ai payé et j'ai mis la monnaie dans ma poche ‖ *fig*: to ~ one's pride mettre son amour-propre dans sa poche; to ~ an insult encaisser une insulte sans rien dire. -2. [steal]: somebody must have ~ed the money quelqu'un a dû mettre l'argent dans sa poche. -3. [in billiards, pool] mettre dans le trou OR la blouse *spec*. -4. SPORT [another runner] bloquer. -5. *Am* POL: to ~ a bill *garder un projet de loi sous le coude pour l'empêcher d'être adopté*.

pocket battleship *n* cuirassé *m* de poche.

pocket billiards *n* billard *m* américain.

pocketbook ['pɒkɪtbʊk] *n* -1. [notebook] calepin *m*, carnet *m*. -2. *Am* [handbag] pochette *f*.

pocket calculator *n* calculatrice *f* de poche.

pocketful ['pɒkɪtfʊl] *n* poche *f* pleine; I've got ~s of small change j'ai les poches pleines de petite monnaie.

pocket-handkerchief *n* mouchoir *m* de poche.

pocketknife ['pɒkɪtnaɪf] (*pl* pocketknives [-naɪvz]) *n* canif *m*.

pocket money *n Br* argent *m* de poche.

pocket-size(d) *adj* -1. [book, revolver etc] de poche. -2. [tiny] tout petit, minuscule.

pocket veto *n Am refus par le Président de signer une proposition de loi, pour l'empêcher d'être adoptée*.

pockmark ['pɒkmɑːk] *n* [on surface] marque *f*, petit trou *m*; [from smallpox] cicatrice *f* de variole; his face is covered with ~s il a le visage grêlé OR variolé.

pockmarked ['pɒkmɑːkt] *adj* [face] grêlé; [surface] criblé de petits trous; ~ with rust piqué par la rouille.

pod [pɒd] (*pt* & *pp* podded, *cont* podding)
◇ *n* -1. BOT cosse *f*; bean ~ cosse de haricot. -2. ENTOM oothèque *f*. -3. AERON nacelle *f*; ASTRONAUT capsule *f*.
◇ *vt Br* écosser.
◇ *vi* BOT produire des cosses.

podgy ['pɒdʒɪ] (*compar* podgier, *superl* podgiest) *adj Br* dodu, replet.

podiatrist [pə'daɪətrɪst] *n Am* pédicure *mf*.

podiatry [pə'daɪətrɪ] *n Am* pédicurie *f*.

podium ['pəʊdɪəm] (*pl* podiums OR podia [-dɪə]) *n* podium *m*.

POE *n* -1. *abbr of* port of embarkation. -2. *abbr of* port of entry.

poem ['pəʊɪm] *n* poème *m*.

poesy ['pəʊɪzɪ] *n arch* OR *lit* poésie *f*.

poet ['pəʊɪt] *n* poète *m*.

poetaster [,pəʊɪ'tæstə^r] *n pej* rimailleur *m*, -euse *f*.

poetess ['pəʊɪtɪs] *n* poétesse *f*.

poetic(al) [pəʊ'etɪk(l)] *adj* poétique.

poetically [pəʊ'etɪklɪ] *adv* poétiquement.

poeticize, -ise [pəʊ'etɪsaɪz] *vt* poétiser.

poetic justice *n* justice *f* immanente; it's ~ that they ended up losing ce n'est que justice qu'ils aient fini par perdre.

poetic licence *n* licence *f* poétique.

poetics [pəʊ'etɪks] *n (U)* poétique *f*.

poet laureate (*pl* poets laureate OR poet laureates) *n* poète *m* lauréat.

poetry ['pəʊɪtrɪ] *n* poésie *f*.

poetry reading *n* lecture *f* de poèmes.

po-faced *inf* ['pəʊfeɪst] *adj Br* à l'air pincé.

pogo ['pəʊgəʊ] ◇ *n* [dance] pogo *m (danse punk)*.
◇ *vi* danser le pogo.

pogo stick *n* bâton *m* sauteur *(jeu)*.

pogrom ['pɒgrəm] *n* pogrom *m*.

poignancy ['pɔɪnjənsɪ] *n* caractère *m* poignant; a moment of great ~ un moment d'intense émotion.

poignant ['pɔɪnjənt] *adj* poignant.

poignantly ['pɔɪnjəntlɪ] *adv* de façon poignante.

poinsettia [pɔɪn'setɪə] *n* poinsettia *m*.

point [pɔɪnt] ◇ *n* -1. [tip - of sword, nail, pencil etc] pointe *f*; trim one end of the stick into a ~ taillez un des bouts de la branche en pointe; his beard ended in a neat ~ sa barbe était soigneusement taillée en pointe; draw a star with five ~s dessinez une étoile à cinq branches; a dog with white ~s un chien aux pattes et aux oreilles blanches; an eight-~ stag un cerf huit cors. -2. [small dot] point *m*; a tiny ~ of light un minuscule point de lumière. -3. [specific place] point *m*, endroit *m*; ~ of intersection, intersection ~ point d'intersection; 'meeting ~' 'point rencontre'; the runners have passed the halfway ~ les coureurs ont dépassé la mi-parcours; we're back to our ~ of departure OR our starting ~ nous sommes revenus au OR à notre point de départ; to pass/to reach the ~ of no return passer/atteindre le point de non-retour; the ~ where the accident occurred l'endroit où l'accident a eu lieu; at that ~ you'll see a church on the left à ce moment-là, vous verrez une église sur votre gauche; the terrorists claim they can strike at any ~ in the country les terroristes prétendent qu'ils peuvent frapper n'importe où dans le pays; the bus service to Dayton and ~s west le service de bus à destination de Dayton et des villes situées plus à l'ouest; ~s south of here get little rainfall les régions situées au sud d'ici n'ont pas une grande pluviosité. -4. [particular moment] moment *m*; [particular period] période *f*; the country is at a critical ~ in its development le pays traverse une période OR phase critique de son développement; we are at a critical ~ nous voici à un point critique; there comes a ~ when a decision has to be made il arrive un moment où il faut prendre une décision; when it comes to the ~ of actually doing it quand vient le moment de passer à l'acte; at one ~ in the discussion à un moment de la discussion; at one ~ in my travels au cours de mes voyages; at one ~, I thought the roof was going to cave in à un moment (donné), j'ai cru que le toit allait s'effondrer; at one ~ in the book à un moment donné dans le livre; at that ~, I was still undecided à ce moment-là, je n'avais pas encore pris de décision; at that ~ in China's history à ce moment précis de l'histoire de la Chine; it's too late by this ~ il est déjà trop tard à l'heure qu'il est; by that ~, I was too tired to move j'étais alors tellement fatigué que je ne pouvais plus bouger. -5. [stage in development or process] point *m*; she had reached the ~ of wanting a divorce elle en était (arrivée) au point de vouloir divorcer; thank God we haven't reached that ~! Dieu merci, nous n'en sommes pas (encore arrivés) là!; to be at the ~ of death être sur le point de mourir; the conflict has gone beyond the ~ where negotiations are possible le conflit a atteint le stade où toute négociation est impossible; to be on the ~ of sthg: the regime is on the ~ of collapse le régime est au bord de l'effondrement; I was on the ~ of admitting everything j'étais sur le point de tout avouer; she had worked to the ~ of exhaustion elle avait travaillé jusqu'à l'épuisement; he was jealous to the ~ of madness sa jalousie confinait à la folie; he stuffed himself to the ~ of being sick *inf* il s'est gavé à en être malade. -6. [for discussion or debate] point *m*; a seven-~ memorandum un mémorandum en sept points; let's go on to the next ~ passons à la question suivante OR au point suivant; on this ~ we disagree sur ce point nous ne sommes pas d'accord; I want to emphasize this ~ je voudrais insister sur ce point; are there any ~s I haven't covered? y a-t-il des questions que je n'ai pas abordées?; to make OR to raise a ~ faire une remarque; to make the ~ that... faire remarquer que...; all right, you've made your ~! d'accord, on a compris!; the ~s raised in her article les points qu'elle soulève dans son article; the main ~s to keep in mind les principaux points à garder à l'esprit; let me illustrate my ~ laissez-moi illustrer mon propos; to prove his ~ he showed us a photo pour prouver ses affirmations, il nous a montré une photo; I see OR take your ~ je vois ce que vous voulez dire OR où vous voulez en venir; ~ taken! c'est juste!; he may not be home – you've got a ~ there! il n'est peut-être pas chez lui – ça c'est vrai!; the fact that he went to the police is a ~ in his favour/a ~ against him le fait qu'il soit allé à la police est un bon/mauvais point pour lui ‖ [precise detail]: I corrected her on a ~ of grammar je l'ai corrigée sur un point de grammaire; he rose on a ~ of order il a demandé la parole pour soulever un point de procédure; she was disqualified on a technical ~ elle a été disqualifiée pour OR sur une faute technique; to make a ~ of doing sthg tenir à faire qqch; he made a ~ of speaking to her il a tenu à lui adresser la parole; kindly make a ~ of remembering next time faites-moi le plaisir de ne pas oublier la prochaine fois. -7. [essential part, heart - of argument, explanation] essentiel *m*; [conclusion - of joke] chute *f*; I get the ~ je comprends, je vois; the ~ is (that) we're overloaded with work le fait est que nous sommes débordés de travail; we're getting off OR away from the ~ nous nous éloignons OR écartons du sujet; that's the (whole) ~! [that's the problem] c'est là (tout) le problème!; [that's the aim] c'est ça, le but!; that's not the ~! là n'est pas la question! ❑ to be beside the ~: the money is/your feelings are beside the ~ l'argent n'a/vos sentiments n'ont rien à voir là-dedans; get OR come to the ~! dites ce que vous avez à dire!, ne tournez pas autour du pot!; I'll come straight to the ~ je serai bref; to keep to the ~ ne pas s'écarter du sujet. -8. [purpose] but *m*; [meaning, use] sens *m*, intérêt *m*; the ~ of the game is to get rid of all your cards le but du jeu est de se débarrasser de toutes ses cartes; there's no ~ in asking him now ça ne sert à rien OR ce n'est pas la peine de le lui demander maintenant; what's the ~ of all this? à quoi ça sert tout ça?; I don't see the ~ of re-doing it je ne vois pas l'intérêt de le refaire; oh, what's the ~ anyway! oh, et puis à quoi bon, après tout! -9. [feature, characteristic] point *m*; the boss has his good ~s le patron a ses bons côtés; it's my weak ~ c'est mon point faible; her strong ~ is her sense of humour son point fort, c'est son sens de l'humour. -10. [unit - in scoring, measuring] point *m*; the Dow Jones index is up/down two ~s l'indice Dow Jones a augmenté/baissé de deux points; who scored the winning ~? qui a marqué le point gagnant?; an ace is worth 4 ~s un as vaut 4 points; to win/to lead on ~s [in boxing] gagner/mener aux points ❑ game/match ~ [in tennis] balle *f* de jeu/de match; merit ~s SCH bons points *mpl*. -11. [on compass] point *m*; the 32 ~s of the compass les 32 points de la rose des vents; our people were scattered to all ~s of the compass *fig* notre peuple s'est retrouvé éparpillé aux quatre coins du monde. -12. GEOM point *m*; a straight line between two ~s une droite reliant deux points. -13. [in decimals] virgule *f*; five ~ one cinq virgule un. -14. [punctuation mark] point *m*; three OR ellipsis ~s points *mpl* de suspension; vowel ~ point-voyelle *m*. -15. TYPO point *m*; 6 ~ type caractères *mpl* de 6 points. -16. GEOG [promontory] pointe *f*, promontoire *m*. -17. AUT vis *f* platinée. -18. *Br* ELEC [socket]: (power) ~ prise *f* (de courant). -19. HERALD point *m*.

◇ *vi* -**1.** [person] tendre le doigt; to ~ at OR to OR towards sthg montrer qqch du doigt; she ~ed left elle fit un signe vers la gauche; he ~ed back down the corridor il fit un signe vers le fond du couloir; he ~ed at OR to me with his pencil il pointa son crayon vers moi; he was ~ing at me son doigt était pointé vers moi; it's rude to ~ ce n'est pas poli de montrer du doigt. -**2.** [roadsign, needle on dial]: the signpost ~s up the hill le panneau est tourné vers le haut de la colline; a compass needle always ~s north l'aiguille d'une boussole indique toujours le nord; the weather vane is ~ing north la girouette est orientée au nord; when the big hand ~s to twelve quand la grande aiguille est sur le douze. -**3.** [be directed, face - gun, camera] être braqué; [- vehicle] être dirigé, être tourné; hold the gun with the barrel ~ing downwards tenez le canon de l'arme pointé vers le bas; the rifle/the camera was ~ing straight at me la carabine/la caméra était braquée sur moi; ~ your flashlight over there éclaire là-bas; insert the disk with the arrow ~ing right insérez la disquette, la flèche pointée OR pointant vers la droite; the aerial should be ~ing in the direction of the transmitter l'antenne devrait être tournée dans la direction de OR tournée vers l'émetteur; he walks with his feet ~ing outwards il marche les pieds en dehors. -**4.** [dog] tomber en arrêt.

◇ *vt* -**1.** [direct, aim - vehicle] diriger; [- flashlight, hose] pointer, braquer; [- finger] pointer, tendre; to ~ one's finger at sb/sthg montrer qqn/qqch du doigt; he ~ed his finger accusingly at Gus il pointa un doigt accusateur vers Gus, il montra OR désigna Gus d'un doigt accusateur; to ~ a gun at sb braquer une arme sur qqn; he ~ed the rifle at my head il a braqué le fusil sur ma tête; she ~ed the camera at me elle braqua son appareil photo sur moi; she ~ed the truck towards the garage elle tourna le camion vers le garage; he ~ed the boat out to sea il a mis le cap vers le large || [send - person]: if anybody shows up, just ~ them in my direction si quelqu'un arrive, tu n'as qu'à me l'envoyer; just ~ him to the nearest bar tu n'as qu'à lui indiquer le chemin du bar le plus proche ❑ to ~ the finger at sb/sthg montrer qqn/qqch du doigt. -**2.** DANCE: to ~ one's toes faire des pointes. -**3.** CONSTR [wall, building] jointoyer. -**4.** *lit* [moral, necessity] souligner, faire ressortir. -**5.** [sharpen - stick, pencil] tailler. -**6.** LING mettre des points-voyelles à. -**7.** *phr*: to ~ the way [subj: arrow, signpost] indiquer la direction OR le chemin; *fig* [subj: person] montrer le chemin; he ~ed the way to future success il a montré le chemin de la réussite; her research ~s the way to a new understanding of the phenomenon ses recherches vont permettre d'appréhender le phénomène sous un angle différent; they ~ the way (in) which reform must go ils indiquent la direction dans laquelle les réformes doivent aller.

◆ **points** *npl* -**1.** *Br* RAIL aiguilles *fpl*. -**2.** DANCE (chaussons *mpl* à) pointes *fpl*; she's already (dancing) on ~s elle fait déjà des pointes.

◆ **at this point in time** *adv phr* pour l'instant; no more details are available at this ~ in time pour l'instant, nous ne disposons pas d'autres détails.

◆ **in point of fact** *adv phr* en fait, à vrai dire.

◆ **to the point** *adj phr* pertinent.

◆ **up to a point** *adv phr* jusqu'à un certain point; did the strategy succeed? – up to a ~ est-ce que la stratégie a réussi? – dans une certaine mesure; productivity can be increased up to a ~ la productivité peut être augmentée jusqu'à un certain point; she can be persuaded, but only up to a ~ il est possible de la convaincre, mais seulement jusqu'à un certain point.

◆ **point out** *vt sep* -**1.** [indicate] indiquer, montrer; I'll ~ the church out to you as we go by je vous montrerai OR vous indiquerai l'église quand nous passerons devant. -**2.** [mention, call attention to] signaler; she ~ed out several mistakes to us elle nous a signalé plusieurs erreurs, elle a attiré notre attention sur plusieurs erreurs; I'd like to ~ out that it was my idea in the first place je vous ferai remarquer que l'idée est de moi; he ~ed out that two people were missing il fit remarquer qu'il manquait deux personnes.

◆ **point to** *vt insep* -**1.** [signify, denote] signifier, indiquer; [foreshadow] indiquer, annoncer; the facts ~ to only one conclusion les faits ne permettent qu'une seule conclusion; all the evidence ~s to him toutes les preuves indiquent que c'est lui; everything ~s to CIA involvement tout indique que la CIA est impliquée. -**2.** [call attention to] attirer l'attention sur; ecologists ~ to the destruction of forest land les écologistes attirent notre attention sur la destruction des forêts; they proudly ~ to the government's record ils invoquent avec fierté le bilan du gouvernement.

◆ **point up** *vt sep* [subj: person, report] souligner, mettre l'accent sur; his account ~s up the irony of the defeat son exposé met l'accent sur l'ironie de la défaite || [subj: event] faire ressortir; the accident ~s up the need for closer cooperation l'accident fait ressortir le besoin d'une coopération plus étroite.

point-blank ◇ *adj* -**1.** [shot] (tiré) à bout portant; he was shot at ~ range on lui a tiré dessus à bout portant. -**2.** [refusal, denial] catégorique; [question] (posé) de but en blanc, (posé) à brûle-pourpoint.

◇ *adv* -**1.** [shoot] à bout portant. -**2.** [refuse, deny] catégoriquement; [ask] de but en blanc, à brûle-pourpoint.

point-by-point *adj* méthodique.

point duty *n Br*: to be on ~ diriger la circulation.

pointed ['pɔɪntɪd] *adj* -**1.** [sharp] pointu; ~ arch ARCHIT arche *f* en ogive; ~ style ARCHIT style *m* gothique. -**2.** [meaningful - look, comment] insistant; [- reference] peu équivoque. -**3.** [marked] ostentatoire; with ~ indifference avec une indifférence ostentatoire.

-pointed *in cpds*: five/six~ [gen] à cinq/six pointes; [star] à cinq/six branches.

pointedly ['pɔɪntɪdlɪ] *adv* -**1.** [meaningfully - look, comment] de façon insistante; she looked at me ~ elle m'a lancé un regard qui en disait long. -**2.** [markedly] de façon marquée OR prononcée; she ~ ignored me all evening elle m'a ostensiblement ignoré pendant toute la soirée.

pointer ['pɔɪntə^r] *n* -**1.** [for pointing - stick] baguette *f*; [- arrow] flèche *f*. -**2.** [on dial] aiguille *f*. -**3.** [indication, sign] indice *m*, signe *m*; there are several ~s as to what really happened plusieurs indices nous permettent de deviner ce qui s'est réellement passé; all the ~s indicate an impending economic recovery tout indique que la reprise économique est imminente; a ~ to the future une idée de ce que l'avenir nous réserve. -**4.** COMPUT pointeur *m*. -**5.** [dog] pointer *m*.

pointillism ['pɔɪntɪlɪzm] *n* pointillisme *m*.

pointillist ['pɔɪntɪlɪst] ◇ *adj* pointilliste.

◇ *n* pointilliste *mf*.

pointing ['pɔɪntɪŋ] *n (U)* CONSTR [act, job] jointoiement *m*; [cement work] joints *mpl*.

pointless ['pɔɪntlɪs] *adj* [gen] inutile, vain; [crime, violence, vandalism] gratuit; all my efforts seemed ~ tous mes efforts semblaient inutiles OR vains; it's ~ trying to convince him ça ne sert à rien OR il est inutile d'essayer de le convaincre.

pointlessly ['pɔɪntlɪslɪ] *adv* [gen] inutilement, vainement; [hurt, murder, vandalize] gratuitement.

pointlessness ['pɔɪntlɪsnɪs] *n* [gen] inutilité *f*; [of remark] manque *m* d'à-propos; [of crime, violence, vandalism] gratuité *f*.

point of order *n* point *m* de procédure; he rose on a ~ il a demandé la parole pour soulever un point de procédure.

point of reference *n* point *m* de référence.

point-of-sale *adj* sur le point OR sur le lieu de vente; ~ advertising publicité *f* sur le lieu de vente, PLV *f*.

point of view *n* point *m* de vue, opinion *f*.

point shoes *npl* DANCE (chaussons *mpl* à) pointes *fpl*.

pointsman ['pɔɪntsmən] (*pl* **pointsmen** [-mən]) *n Br* RAIL aiguilleur *m*.

point-to-point *n Br rallye hippique pour cavaliers amateurs*.

poise [pɔɪz] ◇ *n* -**1.** [composure, coolness] calme *m*, aisance *f*, assurance *f*. -**2.** [physical bearing] port *m*, maintien *m*; [gracefulness] grâce *f*.

◇ *vt* [balance] mettre en équilibre; [hold suspended] tenir suspendu; she ~d herself on the arm of my chair elle s'est assise gracieusement sur le bras de mon fauteuil.

poised [pɔɪzd] *adj* -**1.** [balanced] en équilibre; [suspended] suspendu; she held her glass ~ near her lips elle tenait son verre près de ses lèvres; he was ~ between life and death il était entre la vie et la mort. -**2.** [ready, prepared] prêt; ~ for action prêt à agir. -**3.** [composed, self-assured] calme, assuré.

poison ['pɔɪzn] ◇ *n* -**1.** poison *m*; [of reptile] venin *m*. -**2.** *fig* poison *m*, venin *m*; the ~ spreading through our society le mal qui se propage dans notre société; they hate each other like ~ ils se détestent cordialement; he's absolute ~! *inf* c'est un vrai poison! ❑ what's your ~? *hum* qu'est-ce que tu bois?, qu'est-ce que je t'offre?

◇ *comp* [mushroom, plant] vénéneux; [gas] toxique; ~ gland ZOOL glande *f* à venin.

◇ *vt* -**1.** *literal* empoisonner; to ~ sb with sthg empoisonner qqn à qqch; a ~ed arrow/drink une flèche/boisson empoisonnée; all these pesticides are ~ing the air tous ces pesticides empoisonnent l'atmosphère. -**2.** *fig* envenimer, gâcher; his arrival ~ed the atmosphere son arrivée rendit l'atmosphère insupportable; they are ~ing his mind ils sont en train de le corrompre; he ~ed our minds against her il nous a montés contre elle.

poisoner ['pɔɪznə^r] *n* empoisonneur *m*, -euse *f*.

poison gas *n* gaz *m* toxique.

poisoning ['pɔɪznɪŋ] *n* empoisonnement *m*; lead ~ saturnisme *m*; mercury ~ empoisonnement au mercure.

poison ivy *n* sumac *m* vénéneux.

poisonous ['pɔɪznəs] *adj* -**1.** [mushroom, plant] vénéneux; [snake, lizard] venimeux; [gas, chemical] toxique; mercury is highly ~ le mercure est très toxique. -**2.** *fig* [person] malveillant, venimeux; [remark, allegation] venimeux; he's got a ~ tongue il a une langue de vipère.

poison-pen letter *n* lettre *f* anonyme.

poke [pəʊk] ◇ *vt* -**1.** [push, prod - gen] pousser; [- with elbow] donner un coup de coude à; somebody ~d me in the back quelqu'un m'a donné un coup dans le dos. -**2.** [stick, thrust] enfoncer; she ~d her finger/knife into the tart elle enfonça son doigt/son couteau dans la tarte; to ~ a hole in sthg faire un trou dans qqch; he ~d his stick at me il fit un mouvement avec son bâton dans ma direction; she opened the door and ~d her head in/out elle ouvrit la porte et passa sa tête à l'intérieur/à l'extérieur; he's always poking his nose into other people's business *fig* il se mêle toujours de ce qui ne le regarde pas. -**3.** [fire] tisonner. -**4.** *inf* [punch] flanquer un coup de poing à; I ~d him in the nose je lui ai flanqué un coup de poing sur le nez. -**5.** ▽ [have sex with] tirer un coup avec.

◇ *n* -**1.** [push, prod] poussée *f*, (petit) coup *m*; he gave me a ~ in the back il m'a donné un (petit) coup dans le dos; give the fire a ~ donne un coup de tisonnier dans le feu. -**2.** *inf Am* [punch] gnon *m*, marron *m*; he's asking for a ~ in the nose! il va prendre un marron s'il continue! -**3.** *dial* [pocket] poche *f*; [bag] pochette *f*.

◆ **poke about, poke around** *vi insep* fouiller, fourrager; she ~d around in her bag for her purse elle a fouillé dans son sac pour trouver son porte-monnaie.
◆ **poke along** *vi insep Am* avancer lentement.
◆ **poke out** ◇ *vi insep* [stick out] dépasser; the new shoots were just poking out of the ground les nouvelles pousses commençaient tout juste à sortir de terre.
◇ *vt sep* [remove] déloger; to ~ sb's eye out crever un œil à qqn.

poker ['pəʊkəʳ] *n* -**1.** [card game] poker *m*. -**2.** [for fire] tisonnier *m*.

poker dice ◇ *n* [game] poker *m* d'as.
◇ *npl* [set of dice] dés *mpl* pour le poker d'as.

poker face *n* visage *m* impassible OR impénétrable; she kept a ~ son visage n'a pas trahi la moindre émotion OR est resté totalement impassible.

poker-faced *adj* (au visage) impassible.

pokerwork ['pəʊkəwɜːk] *n (U)* [art] pyrogravure *f*; [objects] pyrogravures *fpl*.

pokey ['pəʊkɪ] ◇ *n* ▽*Am* [prison] tôle *f*; in ~ en tôle.
◇ *adj inf* = **poky**.

poky *inf* ['pəʊkɪ] (*compar* pokier, *superl* pokiest) *adj* -**1.** *Br* [house, room - cramped] exigu. -**2.** *Am* [slow] lambin.

Polack ▽ ['pəʊlæk] *n offensive* Polaque *mf*.

Poland ['pəʊlənd] *pr n* Pologne *f*; in ~ en Pologne.

polar ['pəʊləʳ] *adj* -**1.** CHEM, ELEC, GEOG & MATH polaire; the Polar Circle le cercle polaire; ~ coordinates coordonnées *fpl* polaires; the ~ lights l'aurore *f* polaire; ~ regions les régions *fpl* polaires. -**2.** *fig* [totally opposite - opinions, attitudes] diamétralement opposé.

polar bear *n* ours *m* polaire OR blanc.

polarimeter [,pəʊlə'rɪmɪtəʳ] *n* polarimètre *m*.

polarity [pəʊ'lærətɪ] (*pl* polarities) *n* polarité *f*.

polarization [,pəʊlərаɪ'zeɪʃn] *n* polarisation *f*.

polarize, -ise ['pəʊləraɪz] ◇ *vt* polariser.
◇ *vi* se polariser.

Polaroid® ['pəʊlərɔɪd] ◇ *adj* [camera] Polaroid®; [film] pour Polaroid®; [glasses] à verre polarisé.
◇ *n* [camera] Polaroid®; [photo] photo *f* OR cliché *m* Polaroid®.
◆ **Polaroids**® *npl* [sunglasses] lunettes *fpl* de soleil à verre polarisé.

pole [pəʊl] ◇ *n* -**1.** ELEC & GEOG pôle *m*; to travel from ~ to ~ parcourir la terre entière ❑ they are ~s apart ils n'ont absolument rien en commun; their positions on disarmament are ~s apart leurs positions sur le désarmement sont diamétralement opposées. -**2.** [rod] bâton *m*, perche *f*; [for tent] montant *m*; [in fence, construction] poteau *m*, pieu *m*; [for gardening] tuteur *m*; [for climbing plants] rame *f*; [for polevaulting, punting] perche *f*; [for skier] bâton *m*. -**3.** [mast - for phonelines] poteau *m*; [- for flags] mât *m*; barber's ~ enseigne *f* de coiffeur. -**4.** [for climbing] mât *m*; [in fire-station] perche *f*; you're up the ~! *inf Br* [mistaken] tu te gourres!; [mad] tu es fou OR cinglé!; the kids are driving me up the ~! *Br* les gosses me rendent dingue! -**5.** *Am* [on racecourse] corde *f*. -**6.** [unit of measure] ≃ perche *f*.
◇ *vt* -**1.** [punt] faire avancer (avec une perche). -**2.** [plants] ramer.

Pole [pəʊl] *n* Polonais *m*, -e *f*.

poleaxe *Br*, **poleax** *Am* ['pəʊlæks] ◇ *n* -**1.** [weapon] hache *f* d'armes. -**2.** [for slaughter] merlin *m*.
◇ *vt literal* abattre; *fig* terrasser.

poleaxed *inf* ['pəʊlækst] *adj* -**1.** [surprised] baba, épaté. -**2.** [drunk] bourré, beurré.

polecat ['pəʊlkæt] (*pl inv* OR polecats) *n* -**1.** [European, African] putois *m*. -**2.** *Am* [skunk] mouffette *f*, moufette *f*.

pole jump = **pole vault**.

polemic [pə'lemɪk] ◇ *adj* polémique.
◇ *n* [argument] polémique *f*.
◆ **polemics** *n (U)* [skill, practice] art *m* de la polémique.

polemical [pə'lemɪkl] *adj* polémique.

polemicist [pə'lemɪsɪst] *n* polémiste *mf*.

pole position *n* [in motor racing] pole position *f*; to be in ~ être en pole position.

Pole Star *n* (étoile *f*) Polaire *f*.

pole vault *n* saut *m* à la perche.
◆ **pole-vault** *vi* [as activity] faire du saut à la perche; [on specific jump] faire un saut à la perche.

pole-vaulter [-,vɔːltəʳ] *n* perchiste *mf*.

police [pə'liːs] ◇ *npl* police *f*; the ~ are on their way la police arrive, les gendarmes arrivent; he's in the ~ il est dans la police, c'est un policier; a man is helping ~ with their enquiries un homme est entendu par les policiers dans le cadre de leur enquête; 18 ~ were injured 18 policiers ont été blessés.
◇ *comp* [vehicle, patrol, spy] de police; [protection, work] de la police, policier; [harassment] policier; ~ complaints procedure procédure *f* pour porter plainte contre la police; he was taken into ~ custody il a été emmené en garde à vue; a ~ escort une escorte policière; all ~ leave was cancelled les permissions des policiers ont été annulées; ~ powers were extended les pouvoirs de la police ont été étendus; there was a heavy ~ presence d'importantes forces de police se trouvaient sur place ❑ Police Complaints Board ≃ Inspection *f* générale des services; the Police Federation *le syndicat de la police britannique*.
◇ *vt* -**1.** [subj: policemen] surveiller, maintenir l'ordre dans; the streets are being ~d 24 hours a day les rues sont surveillées par la police 24 heures sur 24; the May Day parade/the match was heavily ~d d'importantes forces de police étaient présentes lors du défilé du 1er mai/du match ‖ [subj: guards, vigilantes] surveiller; the factory is ~d by security guards l'usine est surveillée par des vigiles; vigilante groups ~ the neighbourhood des groupes d'autodéfense maintiennent l'ordre dans le quartier ‖ [subj: army, international organization] surveiller, contrôler; the area is ~d by army patrols des patrouilles militaires veillent au maintien de l'ordre dans la région. -**2.** [regulate - prices] contrôler; [- agreement] veiller à l'application OR au respect de; prices are ~d by consumer associations les associations de consommateurs contrôlent les prix. -**3.** *Am* [clean - military camp] nettoyer.

police academy *n Am* école *f* de police.

police cell *n* cellule *f* d'un poste de police.

police chief *n* ≃ préfet *m* de police.

police commissioner *n Am* commissaire *m* de police.

police constable *n Br* ≃ gardien *m* de la paix, ≃ agent *m* (de police).

police court *n* tribunal *m* de police.

police dog *n* chien *m* policier.

police force *n* police *f*; the local ~ la police locale; to join the ~ entrer dans la police.

police inspector *n* inspecteur *m*, -trice *f* de police.

policeman [pə'liːsmən] (*pl* policemen [-mən]) *n* agent *m* (de police), policier *m*.

police officer *n* policier *m*, agent *m* de police.

police record *n* casier *m* judiciaire; she has no ~ elle n'a pas de casier judiciaire, son casier judiciaire est vierge.

police sergeant *n* ≃ brigadier *m* (de police).

police state *n* État *m* OR régime *m* policier.

police station *n* [urban] poste *m* de police, commissariat *m* (de police); [rural] gendarmerie *f*.

police wagon *n Am* fourgon *m* cellulaire.

policewoman [pə'liːs,wʊmən] (*pl* policewomen [-,wɪmɪn]) *n* femme *f* policier.

policy ['pɒləsɪ] (*pl* policies) ◇ *n* -**1.** POL politique *f*; the government's economic policies la politique économique du gouvernement. -**2.** COMM [of company, organization] politique *f*, orientation *f*; they don't know what ~ to adopt ils ne savent pas quelle politique adopter; this is in line with company ~ ça va dans le sens de la politique de l'entreprise; our ~ is to hire professionals only nous avons pour politique de n'engager que des professionnels. -**3.** [personal principle, rule of action] principe *m*, règle *f*; her ~ has been always to tell the truth elle a toujours eu pour principe de dire la vérité; it's bad ~ to reveal your objectives early on c'est une mauvaise tactique de dévoiler vos objectifs à l'avance. -**4.** [for insurance] police *f*; to take out an insurance ~ souscrire une police d'assurance.
◇ *comp* [decision, statement] de principe; [debate] de politique générale.

policyholder ['pɒləsɪ,həʊldəʳ] *n* assuré *m*, -e *f*.

policymaker ['pɒləsɪ,meɪkəʳ] *n* POL responsable *mf* politique; COMM décideur *m*.

polio ['pəʊlɪəʊ] *n (U)* polio *f*.

poliomyelitis [,pəʊlɪəʊmaɪə'laɪtɪs] *n (U)* poliomyélite *f*.

polish ['pɒlɪʃ] ◇ *vt* -**1.** [furniture] cirer, encaustiquer; [brass, car] astiquer; [mirror] astiquer; [shoes] cirer, brosser; [gemstone] polir. -**2.** *fig* [perfect] polir, perfectionner; to ~ one's prose/style polir sa prose/son style. -**3.** [person] parfaire l'éducation de; his manners could do with ~ing ses manières laissent à désirer.
◇ *n* -**1.** [for wood, furniture] encaustique *f*, cire *f*; [for shoes] cirage *m*; [for brass, car, silverware] *produit d'entretien pour le cuivre, la voiture, l'argenterie etc*; [for fingernails] vernis *m*. -**2.** [act of polishing]: to give sthg a ~ astiquer qqch; give your shoes a quick ~ donne un petit coup de brosse à tes chaussures; the brass could do with a ~ les cuivres auraient besoin d'être astiqués. -**3.** [shine, lustre] brillant *m*, éclat *m*; the silver has a lovely ~ l'argent a un bel éclat; his shoes have lost their ~ ses chaussures ont perdu leur lustre; to put a ~ on sthg faire briller qqch. -**4.** *fig* raffinement *m*, élégance *f*; she has a lot of ~ elle est très raffinée.
◆ **polish off** *inf vt sep* -**1.** [finish - meal] finir, avaler; they ~ed off half a loaf between them ils ont avalé la moitié d'un pain à eux seuls; they soon ~ed off the rest of the beer ils ont eu vite fait de finir ce qui restait de bière. -**2.** [complete - job] expédier; [- book, essay] en finir avec. -**3.** [beat - competition] se débarrasser de, écraser; [kill] liquider, descendre.
◆ **polish up** ◇ *vi insep*: brass ~es up well le cuivre est facile à faire briller.
◇ *vt sep* -**1.** [furniture, shoes] faire briller; [diamond] polir. -**2.** *fig* [perfect - maths, language] perfectionner, travailler; [- technique] parfaire, améliorer.

Polish ['pəʊlɪʃ] ◇ *n* LING polonais *m*.
◇ *npl* [people]: the ~ les Polonais.
◇ *adj* polonais.

polished ['pɒlɪʃt] *adj* -**1.** [surface] brillant, poli. -**2.** CULIN [rice] décortiqué. -**3.** [person] qui a du savoir-vivre, raffiné; [manners] raffiné. -**4.** [performer] accompli; [performance] parfait, impeccable; [style] raffiné, élégant.

polisher ['pɒlɪʃəʳ] *n* [person] cireur *m*, -euse *f*; [machine] polissoir *m*; [for floors] cireuse *f*.

Politburo ['pɒlɪt,bjʊərəʊ] (*pl* Politburos) *n* Politburo *m*.

polite [pə'laɪt] *adj* -**1.** [person] poli, courtois; [remark, conversation] poli, aimable; to be ~ to sb être poli envers OR avec qqn; it is ~ to ask first quand on est poli, on demande d'abord; to make ~ conversation faire la conversation; she was very ~ about my poems elle s'est montrée très diplomate dans ses commentaires sur mes poèmes. -**2.** [refined - manners] raffiné, élégant; ~ society la bonne société, le beau monde.

politely [pə'laɪtlɪ] *adv* poliment, de manière courtoise.

politeness [pə'laɪtnɪs] *n* politesse *f*, courtoisie *f*; out of ~ par politesse.

politic ['pɒlətɪk] *adj fml* [shrewd] habile, avisé; [wise] judicieux, sage; it would not be ~ to refuse ce ne serait pas prudent de refuser.

political [pə'lɪtɪkl] *adj* -**1.** politique; man is a ~ animal l'homme est un animal politique. -**2.** [interested in politics]: he's always been very ~ il s'est toujours intéressé à la politique.

politically [pə'lɪtɪklɪ] *adv* politiquement.

politically correct *adj caractéristique d'un mouvement intellectuel américain qui vise à établir une nouvelle éthique, notamment en bannissant de la langue certains termes jugés discriminants.*

POLITICALLY CORRECT:
Le mouvement «PC» remplace par exemple: «American Indian» par «Native American», «Black» par «African American», «disabled» par «differently abled», «blind» par «visually challenged».

political science *n (U)* sciences *fpl* politiques.

political scientist *n* spécialiste *mf* en sciences politiques.

politician [,pɒlɪ'tɪʃn] *n* -**1.** [gen] homme *m* politique, femme *f* politique. -**2.** *Am pej* politicien *m*, -enne *f*.

politicization [pə,lɪtɪsaɪ'zeɪʃn] *n* politisation *f*.

politicize, -ise [pə'lɪtɪsaɪz] ◇ *vt* politiser; the whole issue has become highly ~d on a beaucoup politisé toute cette question.
◇ *vi* faire de la politique.

politicking ['pɒlətɪkɪŋ] *n pej activité politique visant uniquement à obtenir des suffrages.*

politico *inf* [pə'lɪtɪkəʊ] (*pl* politicos OR politicoes) *n pej* politicard *m*, -e *f*.

politico- *in cpds* politico-.

politics ['pɒlətɪks] ◇ *n (U)* -**1.** [as a profession]: to go into ~ faire de la politique; local ~ politique locale; ~ has never attracted her la politique ne l'a jamais intéressée. -**2.** [art or science] politique *f*; she studied ~ at university elle a étudié les sciences politiques à l'université. -**3.** [activity] politique *f*; I tried not to be drawn into office ~ j'ai essayé de ne pas me laisser entraîner dans les intrigues de bureau ❑ sexual ~ *ensemble des idées et des problèmes touchant aux droits des femmes, des homosexuels etc.*
◇ *npl* [opinions] idées *fpl* OR opinions *fpl* politiques; what exactly are her ~? quelles sont ses opinions politiques au juste?

polity ['pɒlətɪ] (*pl* polities) *n fml* [state] État *m*; [administration] organisation *f* politique OR administrative; [political unit] entité *f* politique.

polka ['pɒlkə] ◇ *n* polka *f*.
◇ *vi* danser la polka.

polka dot *n* pois *m* TEXT.
◆ **polka-dot** *adj* à pois.

poll [pəʊl] ◇ *n* -**1.** POL [elections] élection *f*, élections *fpl*, scrutin *m*; the ~ took place in June les élections ont eu lieu en juin; to go to the ~s voter, se rendre aux urnes; the country will go to the ~s in September la population se rendra aux urnes en septembre, le pays votera en septembre; eve of ~ voting intentions les intentions de vote à la veille du scrutin; the party is likely to be defeated at the ~s le parti sera probablement battu aux élections ‖ [vote] vote *m*; [votes cast] suffrages *mpl* (exprimés), nombre *m* de voix; there was an unexpectedly heavy ~ contrairement aux prévisions, il y a eu un fort taux de participation au scrutin; the ecology candidate got 3% of the ~ le candidat écologiste a obtenu OR recueilli 3% des suffrages OR des voix. -**2.** [survey - of opinion, intentions] sondage *m*; to conduct a ~ on OR about sthg faire un sondage d'opinion sur qqch, effectuer un sondage auprès de la population concernant qqch; the latest ~ puts the Socialists in the lead le dernier sondage donne les socialistes en tête. -**3.** [count, census] recensement *m*. -**4.** [list - of taxpayers] rôle *m* nominatif; [- of electors] liste *f* électorale.
◇ *vt* -**1.** POL [votes] recueillir, obtenir; the Greens ~ed 14 % of the vote les verts ont obtenu 14 % des voix. -**2.** [person] sonder, recueillir l'opinion de; most of those ~ed were in favour of the plan la plupart des personnes interrogées OR sondées étaient favorables au projet. -**3.** *Am* [assembly] inscrire le vote de. -**4.** COMPUT [terminal] appeler; [data] recueillir. -**5.** [tree] étêter; [cattle] décorner.
◇ *vi* [voter] voter.

pollard ['pɒləd] ◇ *n* -**1.** BOT têtard *m (arbre)*. -**2.** ZOOL animal *m* sans cornes.
◇ *vt* -**1.** BOT étêter. -**2.** ZOOL décorner.

pollen ['pɒlən] *n* pollen *m*; ~ analysis analyse *f* pollinique.

pollen count *n* indice *m* pollinique (de l'air).

pollinate ['pɒləneɪt] *vt* polliniser.

pollination [,pɒlɪ'neɪʃn] *n* pollinisation *f*.

polling ['pəʊlɪŋ] *n (U)* -**1.** POL [voting] vote *m*, suffrage *m*; [elections] élections *fpl*, scrutin *m*; the result of the ~ le résultat du scrutin OR des élections; ~ takes place every five years le scrutin a lieu tous les cinq ans; the first round of ~ le premier tour de scrutin OR des élections; ~ is up on last year la participation au vote est plus élevée que l'année dernière. -**2.** [for opinion poll] sondage *m*.

polling booth *n* isoloir *m*.

polling day *n* jour *m* des élections OR du scrutin.

polling station *n* bureau *m* de vote.

polliwog ['pɒlɪwɒg] *n Am* ZOOL têtard *m*.

pollster *inf* ['pəʊlstəʳ] *n* enquêteur *m*, -euse OR -trice *f*, sondeur *m*, -euse *f*; the ~s are predicting a high turnout les sondages prévoient un fort taux de participation.

poll tax *n* -**1.** [in UK] *impôt local aboli en 1993, basé sur le nombre d'occupants adultes d'un logement.* -**2.** [in US] *impôt, aboli en 1964, donnant droit à être inscrit sur les listes électorales.* -**3.** HIST capitation *f*.

pollutant [pə'luːtnt] *n* polluant *m*.

pollute [pə'luːt] *vt* polluer; the rivers are ~d with toxic waste les cours d'eau sont pollués par les déchets toxiques.

polluter [pə'luːtəʳ] *n* pollueur *m*, -euse *f*.

pollution [pə'luːʃn] *n* -**1.** [of environment] pollution *f*; experts are trying to identify the source of the ~ les experts tentent de localiser la source OR l'origine de la pollution. -**2.** *(U)* [pollutants] polluants *mpl*; volunteers are helping to clear the beach of ~ des volontaires participent aux opérations d'assainissement de la plage. -**3.** *fml* [emission of semen] pollution *f* nocturne.

Pollyanna [,pɒlɪ'ænə] *n individu naïvement optimiste.*

pollywog ['pɒlɪwɒg] = **polliwog**.

polo ['pəʊləʊ] (*pl* polos) ◇ *n* -**1.** SPORT polo *m*. -**2.** *Am* [shirt] = **polo shirt**.
◇ *comp* [match, stick] de polo.

polonaise [,pɒlə'neɪz] *n* MUS & SEW polonaise *f*.

polo neck *n Br* [collar] col *m* roulé; [sweater] (pull *m* à) col *m* roulé.
◆ **polo-neck(ed)** *adj Br* à col roulé.

polonium [pə'ləʊnɪəm] *n* polonium *m*.

polony [pə'ləʊnɪ] (*pl* polonies) *n Br* salami *m*, saucisson *m* de Bologne.

polo shirt *n* polo *m (chemise)*.

poltergeist ['pɒltəgaɪst] *n* esprit *m* frappeur, poltergeist *m*.

poltroon [pɒl'truːn] *n arch* poltron *m*, -onne *f*.

poly *inf* ['pɒlɪ] (*pl* polys) *Br* = **polytechnic**.

polyamide [,pɒlɪ'æmaɪd] *n* polyamide *m*.

polyandrous [,pɒlɪ'ændrəs] *adj* polyandre.

polyandry ['pɒlɪændrɪ] *n* polyandrie *f*.

polyanthus [,pɒlɪ'ænθəs] (*pl* polyanthuses OR polyanthi [-θaɪ]) *n* -**1.** [primrose] primevère *f*. -**2.** [narcissus] narcisse *m* à bouquet.

polyatomic [,pɒlɪə'tɒmɪk] *adj* polyatomique.

polybasic [,pɒlɪ'beɪsɪk] *adj* polybasique.

polychromatic [,pɒlɪkrəʊ'mætɪk] *adj* -**1.** [multicoloured] multicolore, polychrome. -**2.** PHYS [light] polychromatique.

polychrome ['pɒlɪkrəʊm] ◇ *adj* polychrome.
◇ *n* objet *m* polychrome.

polyclinic [,pɒlɪ'klɪnɪk] *n* polyclinique *f*.

polycyclic [,pɒlɪ'saɪklɪk] *adj* polycyclique.

Polydorus [,pɒlɪ'dɔːrəs] *pr n* Polydore.

polyester [,pɒlɪ'estəʳ] ◇ *n* polyester *m*.
◇ *adj* (de OR en) polyester.

polyethylene [,pɒlɪ'eθɪliːn] = **polythene**.

polygamist [pə'lɪgəmɪst] *n* polygame *m*.

polygamous [pə'lɪgəməs] *adj* polygame.

polygamy [pə'lɪgəmɪ] *n* polygamie *f*.

polygenesis [,pɒlɪ'dʒenɪsɪs] *n* -**1.** BIOL polygénie *f*. -**2.** [of man] polygénisme *m*.

polyglot ['pɒlɪglɒt] ◇ *adj* [person] polyglotte; [edition] multilingue.
◇ *n* [person] polyglotte *mf*; [book] édition *f* multilingue.

polyglot(t)ism ['pɒlɪglɒtɪzm] *n* multilinguisme *m*.

polygon ['pɒlɪgɒn] *n* polygone *m*.

polygonal [pɒ'lɪgənl] *adj* polygonal.

polygraph ['pɒlɪgrɑːf] *n* -**1.** [lie detector] détecteur *m* de mensonge. -**2.** [copying device] photocopieuse *f*.

polyhedral [,pɒlɪ'hiːdrəl] *adj* polyèdre, polyédrique.

polyhedron [,pɒlɪ'hiːdrən] (*pl* polyhedrons OR polyhedra [-drə]) *n* polyèdre *m*.

polymath ['pɒlɪmæθ] *n fml* puits *m* de science *fig*, esprit *m* encyclopédique.

polymer ['pɒlɪməʳ] *n* polymère *m*.

polymeric [,pɒlɪ'merɪk] *adj* polymère.

polymerization [,pɒlɪməraɪ'zeɪʃn] *n* polymérisation *f*.

polymerize, -ise ['pɒlɪməraɪz] *vt* & *vi* polymériser.

polymorph ['pɒlɪmɔːf] *n* BIOL espèce *f* polymorphe; CHEM substance *f* polymorphe.

polymorphic [,pɒlɪ'mɔːfɪk] *adj* polymorphe.

polymorphism [,pɒlɪ'mɔːfɪzm] *n* [gen] polymorphisme *m*; CHEM polymorphie *f*.

Polynesia [,pɒlɪ'niːzjə] *pr n* Polynésie *f*; in ~ en Polynésie; French ~ la Polynésie française.

Polynesian [,pɒlɪ'niːzjən] ◇ *n* -**1.** [person] Polynésien *m*, -enne *f*. -**2.** LING polynésien *m*.
◇ *adj* polynésien.

polynomial [,pɒlɪ'nəʊmjəl] ◇ *adj* polynomial.
◇ *n* polynôme *m*.

polyp ['pɒlɪp] *n* polype *m*.

polyphase ['pɒlɪfeɪz] *adj* polyphasé.

Polyphemus [,pɒlɪ'fiːməs] *pr n* Polyphème.

polyphonic [,pɒlɪ'fɒnɪk], **polyphonous** [pə'lɪfənəs] *adj* polyphonique.

polyphony [pə'lɪfənɪ] *n* polyphonie *f*.

polypropylene [,pɒlɪ'prəʊpəliːn] *n* polypropylène *m*.

polysemous [pə'lɪsɪməs] *adj* polysémique.

polysemy [pə'lɪsɪmɪ] *n* polysémie *f*.

polystyrene [,pɒlɪ'staɪriːn] *n* polystyrène *m*; ~ cement colle *f* polystyrène; ~ tiles carreaux *mpl* de polystyrène.

polysyllabic(al) [,pɒlɪsɪ'læbɪk(l)] *adj* polysyllabe, polysyllabique.

polysyllable ['pɒlɪ,sɪləbl] *n* polysyllabe *m*.

polysyndeton [,pɒlɪ'sɪndətən] *n* -**1.** [in rhetoric] polysyndète *f*, syndèse *f*. -**2.** GRAMM *phrase contenant plus de deux propositions coordonnées.*

polysynthetic [,pɒlɪsɪn'θetɪk] *adj* LING polysynthétique.

polytechnic [,pɒlɪ'teknɪk] *n en Grande-Bretagne, avant 1993, établissement d'enseignement supérieur qui appartenait à un système différent de celui des universités. Depuis 1993, les «polytechnics» ont acquis le statut d'universités.*

polytheism ['pɒlɪθiːɪzm] *n* polythéisme *m*.

polythene ['pɒlɪθiːn] ◇ *n* polyéthylène *m*, Polythène® *m*.
◇ *comp* en plastique, en polyéthylène *spec*, en Polythène® *spec*; ~ bag sac *m* (en) plastique.

polyunsaturated [,pɒlɪʌn'sætʃəreɪtɪd] *adj* polyinsaturé.

polyurethane [,pɒlɪ'jʊərəθeɪn] *n* polyuréthane *m*, polyuréthanne *m*; ~ foam mousse *f* de polyuréthane.

polyvalent [ˌpɒlɪˈveɪlənt] *adj* polyvalent CHEM & MED.

polyvinyl [ˌpɒlɪˈvaɪnɪl] *adj* polyvinylique; ~ chloride chlorure *m* de polyvinyle.

pom *inf* [pɒm] *Austr* & *NZ* = **pommie**.

pomade [pəˈmeɪd] ◇ *n* pommade *f (pour les cheveux)*.
◇ *vt* pommader.

pomander [pəˈmændəʳ] *n* [bag] sachet *m* aromatique; [orange stuck with cloves] pomme *f* d'amour.

pome [pəʊm] *n* fruit *m* à pépins.

pomegranate [ˈpɒmɪˌgrænɪt] *n* grenade *f (fruit)*; ~ tree grenadier *m*.

pomelo [ˈpɒmɪləʊ] (*pl* pomelos) *n* pomelo *m*.

Pomerania [ˌpɒməˈreɪnjə] *pr n* Poméranie *f*; in ~ en Poméranie.

Pomeranian [ˌpɒməˈreɪnjən] ◇ *n* -**1.** [person] Poméranien *m*, -enne *f*. -**2.** [dog] loulou *m* (de Poméranie).
◇ *adj* poméranien.

pommel [ˈpɒml] (*Br pt* & *pp* pommelled, *cont* pommelling, *Am pt* & *pp* pommeled, *cont* pommeling) ◇ *n* pommeau *m*.
◇ *vt* = **pummel**.

pommel horse *n* cheval-d'arçons *m inv*.

pommie *inf*, **pommy** *inf* [ˈpɒmɪ] (*pl* pommies) ◇ *n Austr* & *NZ hum* OR *pej* angliche *mf pej*.
◇ *adj* angliche *pej*.

pomology [pɒˈmɒlədʒɪ] *n* AGR pomologie *f*.

pomp [pɒmp] *n* pompe *f*, faste *m*; with great ~ en grande pompe; the ~ of great state occasions le faste des grandes cérémonies nationales.

pompadour [ˈpɒmpəˌdʊəʳ] *n* coiffure *f* style Pompadour.

Pompeii [pɒmˈpeiiː] *pr n* Pompéi.

Pompeiian [pɒmˈpeɪən] ◇ *n* Pompéien *m*, -enne *f*.
◇ *adj* pompéien.

Pompey [ˈpɒmpɪ] *pr n* Pompée.

pompom [ˈpɒmpɒm] *n* -**1.** [flower, bobble] pompon *m*. -**2.** *inf* MIL canon *m* antiaérien.

pomposity [pɒmˈpɒsətɪ] (*pl* pomposities) *n* -**1.** *(U)* [of manner] comportement *m* pompeux, manières *fpl* pompeuses. -**2.** [of ceremony] apparat *m*, pompe *f*; [of style] caractère *m* pompeux.

pompous [ˈpɒmpəs] *adj* [pretentious] pompeux, prétentieux.

pompously [ˈpɒmpəslɪ] *adv* pompeusement; it's rather ~ called a marina on qualifie cela, assez pompeusement, de marina.

ponce *inf* [pɒns] *Br* ◇ *n* -**1.** [pimp] maquereau *m*. -**2.** *pej* [effeminate man] homme *m* efféminé.
◇ *vi* -**1.** [pimp] faire le maquereau. -**2.** *pej* [behave effeminately] faire des simagrées, minauder.
◆ **ponce about** *inf*, **ponce around** *inf vi insep* [mess around] traîner; stop poncing around and get on with it arrête un peu de traîner et dépêche-toi.

poncey *inf*, **poncy** *inf* [ˈpɒnsɪ] *adj Br pej* efféminé.

poncho [ˈpɒntʃəʊ] (*pl* ponchos) *n* poncho *m*.

pond [pɒnd] *n* [small] mare *f*; [large] étang *m*; [in garden] bassin *m*; ~ life la faune des étangs.

ponder [ˈpɒndəʳ] ◇ *vi* [think] réfléchir; [meditate] méditer; he spent hours ~ing over the meaning of it all il passa des heures à méditer sur le sens de tout cela; she had plenty of time to ~ on OR upon the folly of her ways elle a eu tout le temps de réfléchir à la stupidité de ses actes.
◇ *vt* réfléchir à OR sur; I sat down and ~ed what to do next je m'assis et considérai ce que j'allais faire ensuite; she retreated to her own room to ~ her next move elle se retira dans sa chambre pour réfléchir à la décision qu'elle allait prendre.

ponderable [ˈpɒndərəbl] *adj fml* pondérable.
◆ **ponderables** *npl fml* données *fpl* mesurables.

ponderous [ˈpɒndərəs] *adj* [heavy] pesant, lourd; [slow] lent, laborieux; [dull] lourd; with ~ steps d'un pas lourd; a ~ style un style lourd OR laborieux; he has a very ~ way of speaking il s'exprime avec difficulté OR laborieusement.

ponderously [ˈpɒndərəslɪ] *adj* [heavily] lourdement; [laboriously] laborieusement; he walked ~ across the yard il traversa la cour d'un pas pesant; after a long pause, he said ~: "I'm not entirely sure what you mean" au bout d'un long moment, il dit péniblement: «je ne suis pas sûr de bien vous comprendre».

Pondicherry [ˌpɒndɪˈtʃerɪ] *pr n* Pondichéry.

pond lily = **water lily**.

pond skater *n* gerris *m*.

pond snail *n* limnée *f*.

pondweed [ˈpɒndwiːd] *n* potamot *m*.

pone [pəʊn] *n Am*: ~ (bread) pain *m* de maïs.

pong *inf* [pɒŋ] ◇ *n Br* puanteur *f*.
◇ *vi* cocoter.

pontiff [ˈpɒntɪf] *n* souverain pontife *m*, pape *m*.

pontifical [pɒnˈtɪfɪkl] *adj* -**1.** RELIG pontifical. -**2.** [pompous] pompeux.

pontificate [*vb* pɒnˈtɪfɪkeɪt, *n* pɒnˈtɪfɪkɪt] ◇ *vi* [gen & RELIG] pontifier; he's always pontificating about OR on something or other *pej* il faut toujours qu'il pontifie.
◇ *n* pontificat *m*.

Pontius Pilate [ˈpɒntjəs-] *pr n* Ponce Pilate.

pontoon [pɒnˈtuːn] *n* -**1.** [float] ponton *m*; [on seaplane] flotteur *m*. -**2.** [card game] vingt-et-un *m*.

pontoon bridge *n* pont *m* flottant.

pony [ˈpəʊnɪ] (*pl* ponies) *n* -**1.** ZOOL poney *m*; we went for a ~ ride nous avons fait une promenade à dos de poney. -**2.** [glass] verre *m* à liqueur. -**3.** ▽ *Br* [£25] *25 livres*; [bet] *pari de 25 livres*. -**4.** *inf Am* SCH [crib] antisèche *f*.

pony express *n service postal américain à cheval mis en place en 1860 et détrôné par l'apparition du télégraphe*.

ponytail [ˈpəʊnɪteɪl] *n* queue de cheval *f*; she does her hair in a ~ elle a OR se fait une queue de cheval.

pony-trekking *n* randonnée *f* à dos de poney; to go ~ faire une randonnée à dos de poney.

poo *inf* [puː] *n* & *vi* = **pooh**.

pooch *inf* [puːtʃ] *n Am* toutou *m*.

poodle [ˈpuːdl] *n* caniche *m*; I'm not your ~! *fig* je ne suis pas ton chien!

poof [pʊf] ◇ *n* ▽ *Br pej* pédé *m*.
◇ *interj*: and then it was gone, ~, just like that et puis hop! il a disparu d'un coup.

poofter▽ [ˈpʊftəʳ] = **poof** *n*.

poofy▽ [ˈpʊfɪ] (*compar* poofier, *superl* poofiest) *adj Br pej* efféminé; he's a bit ~ il fait un peu pédé.

pooh *inf* [puː] *Br* ◇ *interj* [with disgust] pouah; [with disdain] peuh.
◇ *n baby talk* caca *m*.
◇ *vi baby talk* faire caca.

Pooh-Bah *inf* [ˈpuːˈbɑː] *n Br* cumulard *m*, -e *f*.

pooh-pooh *inf vt Br* rire de, ricaner de.

pool [puːl] ◇ *n* -**1.** [pond - small] mare *f*; [- large] étang *m*; [- ornamental] bassin *m*; rock ~ mare d'eau de mer au milieu des rochers. -**2.** [puddle] flaque *f*; a ~ of blood une flaque OR une mare de sang; a ~ of light un rond de lumière. -**3.** [swimming pool] piscine *f*. -**4.** [in harbour] bassin *m*; [in canal, river] plan *m* d'eau. -**5.** [of money] cagnotte *f*; [in card games] cagnotte *f*, poule *f*. -**6.** [of workmen, babysitters] groupe *m*, groupement *m*; [of experts] équipe *f*; [of typists] pool *m*; [of cars - in firm] parc *m*; [of ideas] réserve *f*; [of talent] pépinière *f*, réserve *f*. -**7.** [consortium] cartel *m*, pool *m*; [group of producers] groupement *m* de producteurs. -**8.** *Am* FIN [group] groupement *m*; [agreement] entente *f*, accord *m*. -**9.** [American billiards] billard *m* américain; to shoot ~ *Am* jouer au billard américain.
◇ *vt* [resources, cars] mettre en commun; [efforts, ideas] unir.

poolroom [ˈpuːlˌruːm] *n* salle *f* de billard.

pools [puːlz] *npl Br*: the (football) ~ les concours de pronostics (au football); to win the (football) ~ gagner aux pronostics (au football); ~ coupon fiche *f* de pari, grille *f* de pronostics *(au football)*.

pool table *n* (table *f* de) billard *m*.

poon▼ [puːn] *n Am* chatte *f*.

Poona [ˈpuːnə] *pr n* Poona, Pune.

poontang▼ [ˈpuːntæŋ] *Am* = **poon**.

poop [puːp] *n*: ~ (deck) poupe *f*.
◆ **poop out** *vi insep Am* [drop out] déclarer forfait.

pooped *inf* [puːpt] *adj Am*: ~ (out) vanné, HS.

pooper-scooper [ˈpuːpəˌskuːpəʳ] *n* ≃ motocrotte *f*.

poor [pʊəʳ] ◇ *adj* -**1.** [financially - person, area, country] pauvre; ~ people les pauvres; ECON les économiquement faibles; they're too ~ to own a car ils n'ont pas les moyens d'avoir une voiture; the oil crisis made these countries considerably ~er la crise du pétrole a considérablement appauvri ces pays ❑ ~ as a church mouse pauvre comme Job. -**2.** [mediocre in quantity - gen] maigre; [- output, sale figures] faible, médiocre; there was an unusually ~ turnout il est venu beaucoup moins de monde que d'habitude; his pay is very ~ il est très mal payé ‖ [mediocre in quality - land, soil] maigre, pauvre; [- effort, excuse] piètre; [- piece of work] médiocre; [- results] médiocre, piètre; [- weather, summer] médiocre; ~ quality goods marchandises de mauvaise qualité; in ~ condition en mauvais état; the match took place in ~ light le match a eu lieu alors qu'on n'y voyait pratiquement rien; the joke was in extremely ~ taste la plaisanterie était du plus mauvais goût; she has very ~ taste in clothes elle s'habille avec un goût douteux; the team put in a ~ performance l'équipe n'a pas très bien joué; our side put up a very ~ show notre équipe a donné un piètre spectacle; don't be such a ~ loser! [in game] ne sois pas si mauvais perdant!; I have only a ~ understanding of economics je ne comprends pas grand-chose à l'économie; ~ work SCH travail insuffisant; our chances of success are very ~ nos chances de réussite sont bien maigres. -**3.** [weak - memory, sight] mauvais; to be in ~ health être en mauvaise santé; I have rather ~ sight j'ai une mauvaise vue; I have rather ~ hearing j'entends mal. -**4.** [in ability] peu doué; I'm a ~ cook je ne suis pas doué pour la cuisine; my spelling/French is ~ je ne suis pas fort en orthographe/en français; she's a ~ sailor elle n'a pas le pied marin; she's a ~ traveller elle supporte mal les voyages; he is very ~ at maths/at making speeches il n'est pas doué en maths/pour les discours. -**5.** [inadequate] faible; their food is ~ in vitamins leur alimentation est pauvre en vitamines. -**6.** [pitiful] pauvre; you ~ thing! mon pauvre!; the ~ girl! la pauvre (fille)!; ~ me! pauvre de moi!; ~ (old) Bill le pauvre Bill.
◇ *npl*: the ~ les pauvres *mpl*; the ~ are always with us il y a toujours des pauvres parmi nous; the new ~ les nouveaux pauvres.

poor box *n* tronc *m* des pauvres.

poorhouse [ˈpʊəhaʊs, *pl* -haʊzɪz] *n dans le passé, hospice pour les indigents*.

poor law *n Br loi qui régissait autrefois l'assistance publique*.

THE POOR LAWS:
Premières lois sociales anglaises, en 1597 et 1601. Motivées autant par la peur et la honte du pauvre que par la charité, et visant à améliorer le sort des plus démunis (construction d'hôpitaux, d'écoles, de logements etc) tout en condamnant les «oisifs» de la société, elles ouvrirent la voie au système d'aide sociale en Angleterre et en Europe.

---

poorly [ˈpʊəlɪ] (*compar* poorlier, *superl* poorliest) ◇ *adj Br* malade, souffrant; his condition is described as ~ MED son état est considéré comme sérieux.

◇ *adv* [badly] mal; ~ lit mal éclairé; ~ dressed pauvrement OR mal vêtu; I did ~ in the maths test je n'ai pas bien réussi à l'interrogation de maths; the school was very ~ maintained l'école était assez mal entretenue; to think ~ of sb avoir une mauvaise opinion de qqn.

poorness ['puənɪs] *n* -**1.** [financially] pauvreté *f*. -**2.** [mediocrity] médiocrité *f*, pauvreté *f*.

poor relation *n Br fig* parent *m* pauvre; we're definitely considered the ~s of the publishing world on nous considère vraiment comme les parents pauvres de l'édition.

poor-spirited *adj* pusillanime; it was rather ~ of him il a fait preuve d'une certaine lâcheté OR d'un certain manque de courage.

poor White *n pej Am personne de race blanche appartenant aux classes défavorisées.*

poove▽ [pu:v] *Br* = **poof** *n*.

pop [pɒp] (*pt* & *pp* popped, *cont* popping) ◇ *onomat* pan; to go ~ [cork] sauter; [balloon] éclater.
◇ *n* -**1.** MUS musique *f* pop. -**2.** [sound] bruit *m* de bouchon qui saute, bruit *m* sec; we heard a ~ on a entendu un bruit sec. -**3.** [drink] boisson *f* gazeuse OR pétillante; ginger ~ boisson gazeuse au gingembre. -**4.** *inf Am* [father] papa *m*.
◇ *written abbr of* population.
◇ *comp* [group, singer, video] pop *(inv)*; ~ magazines des magazines de rock; ~ concert concert *m* rock; ~ music musique *f* pop, pop music *f*.
◇ *vi* -**1.** [cork, buttons] sauter; [bulb, balloon] éclater; to make a popping noise faire un bruit de bouchon qui saute; champagne corks popped and the party began les bouchons de champagne sautèrent et la fête commença; to ~ open [box, bag] s'ouvrir tout d'un coup; [buttons] sauter. -**2.** [ears] se déboucher d'un seul coup; [eyes] s'ouvrir tout grand; his eyes almost popped out of his head in surprise de surprise, les yeux lui sont presque sortis de la tête. -**3.** *inf Br* [go] faire un saut; to ~ into town faire un saut en ville; she popped into the butcher's on her way home elle a fait un saut chez OR elle est passée en vitesse chez le boucher sur le chemin du retour.
◇ *vt* -**1.** [balloon, bag] crever; [button, cork] faire sauter; [corn] faire éclater. -**2.** *inf* [put] mettre, fourrer; she popped her purse into her bag elle a fourré son porte-monnaie dans son sac; just pop the paper through the letterbox glissez juste le journal dans la boîte aux lettres; she kept popping tablets into her mouth elle n'arrêtait pas de se fourrer des comprimés dans la bouche; he popped his head over the wall sa tête surgit en haut du mur; let's ~ open a bottle of beer *Am* ouvrons une bouteille de bière. -**3.** *inf* [hit]: he popped me one on the chin il m'a fichu un coup de poing au menton. -**4.** *drugs sl*: to ~ pills prendre des comprimés *(pour se droguer)*. -**5.** *inf dated* [pawn] mettre au clou. -**6.** *phr*: he's finally popped the question *inf* il a finalement demandé sa main; to ~ one's clogs *inf Br* casser sa pipe.
◆ **pop in** *vi insep Br* faire une petite visite; ~ in on your way home passez chez moi en rentrant (à la maison); to ~ in to see sb passer voir qqn.
◆ **pop off** *inf vi insep* -**1.** [leave] s'en aller, filer; he popped off home to get his tennis things il est allé chez lui chercher ses affaires de tennis. -**2.** [die] casser sa pipe.
◆ **pop out** *inf vi insep* sortir un instant; to ~ out to the tobacconist's faire un saut au bureau de tabac.
◆ **pop over** *inf vi insep Br* passer, faire une petite visite; she popped over to see me elle est passée me voir.
◆ **pop up** *inf vi insep* -**1.** [go upstairs] faire un saut en haut OR à l'étage; ~ up to see me sometime monte donc me voir un de ces jours. -**2.** [crop up] surgir; his name seems to ~ up everywhere on ne parle que de lui.

popadum ['pɒpədəm] *n galette indienne.*

pop art *n* pop art *m*.

popcorn ['pɒpkɔ:n] *n* pop-corn *m inv*.

pope [pəʊp] *n* -**1.** [in Catholic Church] pape *m*. -**2.** [in Eastern Orthodox Church] pope *m*.

popemobile *inf* ['pəʊpməbi:l] *n* papamobile *f*.

popery ['pəʊpərɪ] *n pej* papisme *m*.

pope's nose = **parson's nose**.

pop-eyed *inf adj* ébahi, aux yeux écarquillés; to stare ~ at sthg regarder qqch bouche bée.

popgun ['pɒpgʌn] *n* pistolet *m* (d'enfant) à bouchon.

popinjay ['pɒpɪndʒeɪ] *n arch* & *pej* vaniteux *m*, -euse *f*, prétentieux *m*, -euse *f*.

popish ['pəʊpɪʃ] *adj pej* papiste; the Popish Plot *Br* HIST le complot catholique.

THE POPISH PLOT:
Rumeur lancée en 1678 par Titus Oates et selon laquelle un complot catholique visait à assassiner Charles II, à massacrer les protestants et à incendier Londres. Elle sema la terreur parmi la population et fut responsable de l'assassinat de nombreux catholiques.

---

poplar (tree) ['pɒplə^r-] *n* peuplier *m*.

poplin ['pɒplɪn] ◇ *n* popeline *f*.
◇ *adj* en popeline.

popover ['pɒp,əʊvə^r] *n* -**1.** [garment] débardeur *m*. -**2.** *Am* chausson *m* CULIN; apple ~ chausson *m* aux pommes.

poppa *inf* ['pɒpə] *n Am* papa *m*.

poppadom, poppadum ['pɒpədəm] = **popadum**.

popper ['pɒpə^r] *n* -**1.** *Br* [press-stud] bouton-pression *m*, pression *f*. -**2.** *Am* [for popcorn] appareil *m* à pop-corn. -**3.** *drugs sl* ampoule *f* de nitrite d'amyle.

poppet ['pɒpɪt] *n* -**1.** *inf Br* chéri *m*, -e *f*, mignon *m*, -onne *f*; be a ~ and fetch my bag for me sois mignon et va me chercher mon sac; thanks, ~ [to girl] merci ma mignonne. -**2.** [valve] soupape *f* (à champignon).

poppy ['pɒpɪ] (*pl* poppies) *n* -**1.** [flower] coquelicot *m*; [opium poppy] pavot *m*; [paper flower] coquelicot *m* en papier *(vendu le jour de l'Armistice)*; ~ seed graine *f* de pavot. -**2.** [colour] rouge *m* coquelicot *(inv)*.

poppycock *inf* ['pɒpɪkɒk] *n (U) Br dated* sottises *fpl*, balivernes *fpl*.

Poppy Day *pr n journée de commémoration pendant laquelle on porte un coquelicot en papier en souvenir des soldats britanniques morts lors des guerres mondiales.*

pops *inf* [pɒps] *n Am* [term of address - to father] papa *m*; [- to old man] pépé *m*.

pop shop *inf n dated* mont-de-piété *m*.

Popsicle® ['pɒpsɪkl] *n Am* glace *f* en bâtonnet.

popsy *inf* ['pɒpsɪ] (*pl* popsies) *n Br dated* pépée *f*.

populace ['pɒpjʊləs] *n* -**1.** [population] population *f*; the whole ~ is up in arms *fig* la population entière s'est rebellée. -**2.** [masses] masses *fpl*, peuple *m*.

popular ['pɒpjʊlə^r] *adj* -**1.** [well-liked - person] populaire; she's very ~ with her pupils elle est très populaire auprès de ses élèves, ses élèves l'aiment beaucoup; Britain's most ~ TV personality la personnalité la plus populaire de la télévision britannique; he was a very ~ president ce fut un président très populaire; he isn't very ~ with his men il n'est pas très bien vu de ses hommes, ses hommes ne l'aiment pas beaucoup; I'm not going to be very ~ when they find out it's my fault! je ne vais pas être bien vu quand ils découvriront que c'est de ma faute! -**2.** [appreciated by many - product, colour] populaire; [- restaurant, resort] très couru, très fréquenté; the film was very ~ in Europe le film a été un très grand succès en Europe; the most ~ book of the year le livre le plus vendu OR le best-seller de l'année; videotapes are a ~ present les vidéocassettes sont des cadeaux très appréciés; it's very ~ with the customers les clients l'apprécient beaucoup; a ~ line un article qui se vend bien; it's always been a ~ café with young people ce café a toujours été très populaire auprès des jeunes. -**3.** [common] courant, répandu; a ~ misconception une erreur répandue OR fréquente ‖ [general] populaire; on OR by ~ demand à la demande générale; it's an idea that enjoys great ~ support c'est une idée qui a l'approbation générale OR de tous; ~ unrest mécontentement *m* populaire ❑ ~ front POL front *m* populaire. -**4.** [aimed at ordinary people] populaire; ~ music musique *f* populaire; a book of ~ mechanics un livre de mécanique pour tous OR à la portée de tous; the ~ press la presse à grand tirage et à sensation; quality goods at ~ prices marchandises de qualité à des prix abordables.
◆ **populars** *inf npl Br* presse *f* à grand tirage et à sensation.

popularity [,pɒpjʊ'lærətɪ] *n* popularité *f*; they enjoy a certain ~ with young people ils jouissent d'une certaine popularité auprès des jeunes; sociologists have failed to explain their ~ les sociologues n'ont pas su expliquer leur popularité.

popularization [,pɒpjʊləraɪ'zeɪʃn] *n* -**1.** [of trend, activity] popularisation *f*; [of science, philosophy] vulgarisation *f*. -**2.** [book] œuvre *f* de vulgarisation.

popularize, -ise ['pɒpjʊləraɪz] *vt* -**1.** [make popular] populariser; a sport ~d by television un sport que la télévision a rendu populaire. -**2.** [science, philosophy] vulgariser.

popularizer ['pɒpjʊləraɪzə^r] *n* [of fashion, ideas] promoteur *m*, -trice *f*.

popularly ['pɒpjʊləlɪ] *adv* généralement; [commonly] couramment, communément; antirrhinums are ~ known as snapdragons les antirrhinums sont plus connus sous le nom de gueules-de-loup; once the earth was ~ thought to be flat autrefois tout le monde croyait que la Terre était plate.

populate ['pɒpjʊleɪt] *vt* [inhabit] peupler, habiter; [colonize] peupler, coloniser; a town ~d by miners and their families une ville habitée par des mineurs et leurs familles; a densely ~d country un pays fortement peuplé OR à forte densité de population.

population [,pɒpjʊ'leɪʃn] ◇ *n* population *f*; the whole ~ is in mourning tous les habitants portent OR toute la population porte le deuil; the white ~ of South Africa la population blanche d'Afrique du Sud; Edinburgh has a ~ of about half a million Édimbourg compte environ un demi-million d'habitants; the prison ~ la population carcérale; the beaver ~ is declining la population de castors est en baisse.
◇ *comp* [control, fall, increase] démographique, de la population; ~ explosion explosion *f* démographique.

populism ['pɒpjʊlɪzm] *n* populisme *m*.

populist ['pɒpjʊlɪst] *n* populiste *mf*.

populous ['pɒpjʊləs] *adj* populeux.

pop-up *adj* [book, birthday card] en relief; [toaster] automatique.

porcelain ['pɔ:səlɪn] ◇ *n* porcelaine *f*.
◇ *comp* [dish, vase, lamp] en porcelaine.

porcelain clay *n* kaolin *m*.

porch [pɔ:tʃ] *n* -**1.** [entrance] porche *m*. -**2.** *Am* [veranda] véranda *f*.

porcine ['pɔ:saɪn] *adj* porcin.

porcupine ['pɔ:kjʊpaɪn] *n* porc-épic *m*.

pore [pɔ:^r] ◇ *n* [in skin, plant, fungus, rock] pore *m*.
◇ *vi*: to ~ over [book] être plongé dans OR absorbé par; [picture, details] étudier de près.

pork [pɔ:k] ◇ *n* CULIN porc *m*.
◇ *comp* [chop, sausage] de porc.

pork barrel *inf n Am* POL *projet local entrepris par un parlementaire ou un parti à des fins électorales.*

pork-barrel legislation *n Am* POL *action menée par un parlementaire pour favoriser des intérêts locaux dans sa circonscription.*

pork butcher *n* ≃ charcutier *m*, -ère *f*.
porker [ˈpɔːkəʳ] *n* -**1.** *literal* porcelet *m (engraissé par la boucherie)*. -**2.** *inf fig & hum* petit cochon *m*.
pork pie *n* ≃ pâté *m* en croûte *(à la viande de porc)*.
porkpie hat [ˌpɔːkpaɪ-] *n chapeau de feutre rond et aplati*.
pork scratchings *npl petits morceaux croustillants de couenne de porc mangés comme amuse-gueule*.
porky *inf* [ˈpɔːkɪ] (*compar* **porkier**, *superl* **porkiest**) *adj pej* [fat] gros, gras, adipeux *pej*.
porn *inf* [pɔːn] ◇ *n* porno *m*; **hard** ~ hard-core *m*; **soft** ~ porno *m* soft; ~ **shop** sex-shop *m*.
◇ *adj* porno.
porno *inf* [ˈpɔːnəʊ] *adj* porno.
pornographer [pɔːˈnɒgrəfəʳ] *n* pornographe *mf*.
pornographic [ˌpɔːnəˈgræfɪk] *adj* pornographique.
pornography [pɔːˈnɒgrəfɪ] *n* pornographie *f*; **the customs officers impounded a large consignment of** ~ les douaniers ont saisi une grande quantité de revues pornographiques.
porosity [pɔːˈrɒsɪtɪ] (*pl* **porosities**) *n* porosité *f*.
porous [ˈpɔːrəs] *adj* poreux.
porousness [ˈpɔːrəsnɪs] *n* porosité *f*.
porphyry [ˈpɔːfɪrɪ] (*pl* **porphyries**) *n* porphyre *m*.
porpoise [ˈpɔːpəs] (*pl inv* OR **porpoises**) *n* marsouin *m*.
porridge [ˈpɒrɪdʒ] *n* -**1.** CULIN porridge *m*. -**2.** *Br prison sl* peine *f* de prison; **to do** ~ faire de la tôle.
porridge oats *npl* flocons *mpl* d'avoine.
porringer [ˈpɒrɪndʒəʳ] *n récipient à porridge*.
port [pɔːt] ◇ *n* -**1.** [harbour] port *m*; **to come into** ~ entrer dans le port; **we put into** ~ **at Naples** nous avons relâché dans le port de Naples; **we left** ~ **before dawn** nous avons appareillé avant l'aube; **the country's largest** ~ le plus grand port du pays ❑ ~ **of call** NAUT escale *f*; *fig* course *f*; **her last** ~ **of call was the bank** elle est passée à la banque en dernier; ~ **of entry** port de débarquement; **any** ~ **in a storm** nécessité fait loi *prov*. -**2.** [wine] porto *m*. -**3.** [window - on ship, plane] hublot *m*. -**4.** [for loading] sabord *m* (de charge). -**5.** MIL [in wall] meurtrière *f*; [in tank] fente *f* de visée. -**6.** COMPUT port *m*. -**7.** TECH [in engine] orifice *m*; **inlet/outlet** ~ orifice d'admission/d'échappement. -**8.** NAUT [left side] bâbord *m*; **the ship listed to** ~ le navire donnait de la gîte à bâbord; **ship to** ~**!** navire à bâbord! -**9.** AERON côté *m* gauche, bâbord *m*.
◇ *comp* [authorities, activity, facilities] portuaire; [bow, quarter] de bâbord; **on the** ~ **side** à bâbord.
◇ *vt* -**1.** COMPUT transférer. -**2.** MIL: ~ **arms!** présentez armes! -**3.** NAUT: ~ **the helm!** barre à bâbord!
portability [ˌpɔːtəˈbɪlətɪ] *n* [gen & COMPUT] portabilité *f*.
portable [ˈpɔːtəbl] ◇ *adj* -**1.** portatif, portable; ~ **pension** pension *f* transférable; ~ **TV (set)** télévision *f* portative. -**2.** COMPUT [software, program] compatible.
◇ *n* [typewriter] machine *f* portative; [TV] télévision *f* portative; [computer] ordinateur *m* portatif.
portage [ˈpɔːtɪdʒ] *n* -**1.** [transport] transport *m*; [cost] (frais *mpl* de) port *m*. -**2.** NAUT portage *m*.
Portakabin® [ˈpɔːtəˌkæbɪn] *n* [gen] baraquement *m* préfabriqué.
portal [ˈpɔːtl] *n lit* portail *m*; **she found herself standing at the** ~**s of a new life** *fig* elle se trouvait à l'aube d'une nouvelle vie.
portal vein *n* veine *f* porte.
Port-au-Prince [ˈpɔːtəʊˈprɪns] *pr n* Port-au-Prince.
portcullis [ˌpɔːtˈkʌlɪs] *n* herse *f (de château fort)*.
portend [pɔːˈtend] *vt fml & lit* (laisser) présager, annoncer; **who knows what mysteries these events may** ~? qui sait quels mystères ces événements présagent?
portent [ˈpɔːtənt] *n fml & lit* -**1.** [omen] présage *m*, augure *m*; [bad omen] mauvais présage *m*; **a** ~ **of evil** un très mauvais présage. -**2.** [significance] portée *f*, signification *f*.
portentous [pɔːˈtentəs] *adj lit* -**1.** [ominous - sign] de mauvais présage OR augure. -**2.** [momentous - event] capital, extraordinaire; **I've nothing very** ~ **to announce** je n'ai rien d'extraordinaire OR de très important à annoncer. -**3.** [serious] grave, solennel; **her face took on a** ~ **air** elle prit un air solennel. -**4.** [pompous] pompeux.
portentously [pɔːˈtentəslɪ] *adv lit* -**1.** [ominously] sinistrement. -**2.** [momentously] mémorablement. -**3.** [seriously] solennellement. -**4.** [pompously] pompeusement.
porter [ˈpɔːtəʳ] *n* -**1.** [of luggage] porteur *m*. -**2.** *Br* [door attendant - in hotel] portier *m*; [- in block of flats] concierge *mf*, gardien *m*, -enne *f*; [- on private estate] gardien *m*, -enne *f*; [- in university, college] appariteur *m*. -**3.** *Am* RAIL [on train] employé *m*, -e *f* des wagons-lits. -**4.** [beer] porter *m*, bière *f* brune.
porterage [ˈpɔːtərɪdʒ] *n* [transport] transport *m* (par porteurs); [cost] coût *m* du transport.
porterhouse (steak) [ˈpɔːtəhaʊs-] *n* chateaubriand *m*, châteaubriant *m*.
portfolio [ˌpɔːtˈfəʊljəʊ] (*pl* **portfolios**) *n* -**1.** [briefcase] porte-documents *m inv*. -**2.** [dossier - of artist] dossier *m*. -**3.** POL portefeuille *m*; **minister without** ~ ministre *m* sans portefeuille. -**4.** ST. EX portefeuille *m* (financier OR d'investissements).
porthole [ˈpɔːthəʊl] *n* hublot *m*.
portico [ˈpɔːtɪkəʊ] (*pl* **porticos** OR **porticoes**) *n* ARCHIT portique *m*.
portion [ˈpɔːʃn] *n* -**1.** [part, section] partie *f*; **I've read only a** ~ **of the book** je n'ai lu qu'une partie du livre. -**2.** [share] part *f*; **he cut the cake into five** ~**s** il a coupé le gâteau en cinq (parts); **three** ~**s of flour to one** ~ **of sugar** trois mesures OR doses de farine pour une mesure OR dose de sucre. -**3.** [helping - of food] portion *f*. -**4.** *lit* [fate] sort *m*, destin *m*; **it fell to my** ~ **to break the news to her** c'est à moi qu'échut le devoir de lui annoncer la nouvelle. -**5.** [dowry]: (marriage) ~ *arch* dot *f*.
♦ **portion out** *vt sep* distribuer, répartir.
Portland cement [ˈpɔːtlənd-] *n* portland *m*, ciment *m* Portland.
Portland stone *n* pierre *f* de Portland.
portliness [ˈpɔːtlɪnɪs] *n* corpulence *f*, embonpoint *m*.
portly [ˈpɔːtlɪ] (*compar* **portlier**, *superl* **portliest**) *adj* corpulent, fort; **a** ~ **gentleman** un monsieur corpulent.
portmanteau [ˌpɔːtˈmæntəʊ] (*pl* **portmanteaus** OR **portmanteaux** [-təʊz]) ◇ *n* grande valise *f*.
◇ *adj* qui combine plusieurs éléments OR styles.
portmanteau word *n* mot-valise *m*.
Port of Spain *pr n* Port of Spain.
Porton Down [ˈpɔːtən-] *pr n ville du Wiltshire*.

PORTON DOWN:
Ville célèbre pour son centre de microbiologie. Ce centre a suscité des controverses pour ses recherches sur les armes bactériologiques et chimiques et pour ses expériences sur des animaux vivants.

---

portrait [ˈpɔːtreɪt] ◇ *n* -**1.** [gen & ART] portrait *m*; **he had his** ~ **painted** il a fait faire son portrait; **a** ~ **of 18th century society** un portrait de la société du XVIIIe siècle ❑ **'Portrait of the Artist as a Young Dog'** *Thomas* 'Portrait de l'artiste en jeune chien'; **'A Portrait of the Artist as a Young Man'** *Joyce* 'Portrait de l'artiste jeune par lui-même'; **'The Portrait of a Lady'** *James* 'Un portrait de femme'. -**2.** PRINT: **to print in** ~ imprimer à la française.
◇ *adj* PRINT à la française.
portrait gallery *n* galerie *f* de portraits.
portraitist [ˈpɔːtreɪtɪst] *n* portraitiste *mf*.
portrait painter *n* portraitiste *mf*.
portrait photograph *n* portrait *m* photographique, photo-portrait *f*.
portrait photographer *n* photographe *mf* d'art.
portraiture [ˈpɔːtrɪtʃəʳ] *n* art *m* du portrait.
portray [pɔːˈtreɪ] *vt* -**1.** [represent] représenter; **he** ~**ed John as a scoundrel** il a représenté John sous les traits d'un voyou. -**2.** [act role of] jouer le rôle de; **in the film he** ~**s King Richard** dans le film il joue le rôle du roi Richard. -**3.** [depict in words] dépeindre; **she vividly** ~**s medieval life** elle fait une vivante description de la vie au Moyen Âge. -**4.** [artist] peindre, faire le portrait de.
portrayal [pɔːˈtreɪəl] *n* -**1.** [description] portrait *m*, description *f*; **he disputes the** ~ **of the protesters as extremists** il conteste la façon dont les médias présentent les protestataires comme des extrémistes. -**2.** ART portrait *m*. -**3.** THEAT interprétation *f*.
Port Said [-seɪd] *pr n* Port-Saïd.
Portugal [ˈpɔːtʃʊgl] *pr n* Portugal *m*; **in** ~ au Portugal.
Portuguese [ˌpɔːtʃʊˈgiːz] (*pl inv*) ◇ *n* -**1.** [person] Portugais *m*, -e *f*. -**2.** LING portugais *m*.
◇ *adj* portugais.
Portuguese man-of-war *n* physalie *f*.
pose [pəʊz] ◇ *n* -**1.** [position - gen, ART & PHOT] pose *f*; **to take up** OR **to strike a** ~ prendre une pose. -**2.** [pretence] bluff *m*; **their puritanism is only a** ~ leur puritanisme n'est qu'une façade.
◇ *vi* -**1.** ART & PHOT poser; **to** ~ **for a photograph/for an artist** poser pour une photographie/pour un artiste; **to** ~ **in the nude** poser nu; **she** ~**d as a nymph** elle a posé en nymphe. -**2.** [masquerade]: **he** ~**d as a hero** il s'est posé en héros, il s'est fait passer pour un héros; **a man posing as a policeman** un homme se faisant passer pour un policier.
◇ *vt* [constitute - problem] poser, créer; [- threat] constituer; [set - question] poser; [put forward - claim, idea] formuler.
Poseidon [pɒˈsaɪdn] *pr n* Poséidon; **'The** ~ **Adventure'** *Neame* 'l'Aventure du Poséidon'.
poser *inf* [ˈpəʊzəʳ] *n* -**1.** [question - thorny] question *f* épineuse; [- difficult] colle *f*; **that's a bit of a** ~**!** alors ça, c'est une colle! -**2.** *pej* [show-off] poseur *m*, -euse *f*.
poseur [pəʊˈzɜːʳ] *n pej* poseur *m*, -euse *f*.
posh *inf* [pɒʃ] *Br* ◇ *adj* [clothes] chic; [person] élégant, BCBG ‖ [car] chic; [house] de riches; [restaurant] huppé; **the** ~ **part of town** les quartiers chics de la ville; **to join a** ~ **tennis club** s'inscrire à un club de tennis huppé OR chic; **he moves in some very** ~ **circles** il fréquente des milieux très huppés OR des gens de la haute; ~ **people don't usually come here** généralement les gens de la haute ne viennent pas ici; **he has a** ~ **accent** il a un accent snob.
◇ *adv*: **to talk** ~ parler avec un accent snob.
♦ **posh up** *inf vt sep Br* [person] pomponner; [town, house] embellir; **go and** ~ **yourself up** va te faire beau; **she was all** ~**ed up** elle était sur son trente et un.
posit [ˈpɒzɪt] *vt fml* [idea] avancer; [theory] avancer, postuler.
position [pəˈzɪʃn] ◇ *n* -**1.** [place] position *f*, place *f*, emplacement *m*; **to change** OR **to shift** ~ changer de place; **you've changed the** ~ **of the lamp** vous avez changé la lampe de place; **remember the** ~ **of the cards** souvenez-vous de la position des cartes; **white is now in a strong** ~ [in chess] les blancs sont maintenant très bien placés; **they put the machine guns in** OR **into** ~ ils mirent les mitrailleuses en batterie; **take up your** ~**s!**, **get into** ~**!** [actors, dancers] à vos places!; [soldiers, guards] à vos postes! -**2.** [pose, angle, setting] position *f*; **in a sitting** ~ en position assise; **hold the spray can in an upright** ~ tenez le vaporisateur en position verticale; **the** ~ **of the pointer on the**

dial la position de l'aiguille sur le cadran; the switch/lever should be in the off ~ l'interrupteur/le levier devrait être en position arrêt. -**3.** [circumstances] situation *f*, position *f*; the ~ as I see it is this voici comment je vois la situation OR les choses; to be in a bad/good ~ être en mauvaise/bonne posture; you're in a bad ~ OR in no ~ to judge vous êtes mal placé pour (en) juger; to be in a ~ to do sthg être en mesure de faire qqch; put yourself in my ~ mettez-vous à ma place; it's an awkward ~ to be in c'est une drôle de situation; our financial ~ is improving notre situation financière s'améliore; the present economic ~ la conjoncture économique actuelle. -**4.** [rank - in table, scale] place *f*, position *f*; they're in tenth ~ in the championship ils sont à la dixième place OR ils occupent la dixième place du championnat || [in hierarchy] position *f*, situation *f*; a person in my ~ can't afford a scandal une personne de mon rang ne peut se permettre un scandale; his ~ in the firm is unclear sa situation au sein de l'entreprise n'est pas claire; what exactly is his ~ in the government? quelles sont exactement ses fonctions au sein du gouvernement? || [social standing] position *f*, place *f*; she is concerned about her social ~ elle est préoccupée par sa position sociale. -**5.** [standpoint] position *f*, point *m* de vue; try to see things from my ~ essayez de voir les choses de mon point de vue; could you make your ~ clear on this point? pouvez-vous préciser votre position à ce sujet?; to take up a ~ on sthg adopter une position OR prendre position sur qqch; his ~ on the death penalty is indefensible son point de vue sur la peine de mort est indéfendable. -**6.** [job] poste *m*, situation *f*; there were four candidates for the ~ of manager il y avait quatre candidats au poste de directeur; it is a ~ of great responsibility c'est un poste à haute responsabilité; what was your previous ~? quel était votre poste précédent? ❑ ~ of trust poste *m* de confiance. -**7.** ADMIN [in bank, post office] guichet *m*; '~ closed' 'guichet fermé'. -**8.** SPORT [in team, on field] position *f*; he can play in any ~ il peut jouer à n'importe quelle position OR place; the full back was out of ~ l'arrière était mal placé. -**9.** MIL position *f*; the men took up ~ on the hill les hommes prirent position sur la colline; to defend a ~ défendre une position; to jockey OR to jostle OR to manoeuvre for ~ *literal* chercher à occuper le terrain; *fig* chercher à obtenir la meilleure place.
◇ *vt* -**1.** [put in place - cameras, equipment] mettre en place, placer, disposer; [- precisely] mettre en position; [- guests, officials] placer; the TV cameras were ~ed round the square les caméras de télé ont été disposées autour de la place; he ~ed himself on the roof il a pris position sur le toit. -**2.** *(usu pass)* [situate - house, building] situer, placer; SPORT placer; the school is ~ed near a dangerous crossroads l'école est située OR placée près d'un carrefour dangereux; the flat is well ~ed l'appartement est bien situé. -**3.** [post - guards] placer, poster; they have ~ed their ships in the gulf ils ont envoyé leurs navires dans le golfe. -**4.** COMM [product] positionner.

positional [pəˈzɪʃənl] *adj* [warfare] de position, de positions; LING [variant] contextuel; ~ astronomy astrométrie *f*, astronomie *f* de position; ~ notation MATH numération *f* positionnelle.

positive [ˈpɒzətɪv] ◇ *adj* -**1.** [sure] sûr, certain; are you ~ about that? en êtes-vous sûr?; are you absolutely sure? – yes, ~ en êtes-vous absolument sûr? – sûr et certain; I'm ~ (that) he wasn't there je suis absolument sûr qu'il n'y était pas; it's absolutely ~ c'est sûr et certain. -**2.** [constructive] positif; it's one of my few ~ achievements c'est une des rares choses positives OR constructives que j'aie faites; haven't you got any ~ suggestions? n'avez-vous rien à proposer qui fasse avancer les choses?; she has a very ~ approach to the problem son approche du problème est très positive OR constructive; ~ thinking idées *fpl* constructives. -**3.** [affirmative - reply, response] positif, affirmatif; [- test, result] positif. -**4.** [definite - fact, progress] réel, certain; [clear - change, advantage] réel, effectif; [precise - instructions] formel, clair; we have ~ evidence of his involvement nous avons des preuves irréfutables de son implication; his intervention was a ~ factor in the release of the hostages son intervention a efficacement contribué à la libération des otages; the team needs some ~ support l'équipe a besoin d'un soutien réel OR effectif ❑ proof ~ *Br*, ~ proof preuve *f* formelle. -**5.** [as intensifier - absolute] absolu, véritable, pur; the whole thing was a ~ nightmare tout cela était un véritable cauchemar; a ~ delight un pur délice; a ~ pleasure un véritable plaisir; it's a ~ lie c'est un mensonge, ni plus ni moins. -**6.** [assured] assuré, ferme; she answered in a very ~ tone elle a répondu d'un ton très assuré OR très ferme. -**7.** ELEC, MATH & PHOT positif. -**8.** *Am* POL [progressive] progressiste.
◇ *n* -**1.** GRAMM positif *m*; in the ~ à la forme positive. -**2.** [answer] réponse *f* positive OR affirmative, oui *m*; to reply in the ~ répondre par l'affirmative OR affirmativement. -**3.** PHOT épreuve *f* positive. -**4.** ELEC borne *f* positive.

positive discrimination *n (U)* discrimination *f* positive *(mesures favorisant les membres de groupes minoritaires)*; ~ in favour of people with disabilities mesures en faveur des handicapés.

positive feedback *n* [in electronic circuit] réaction *f* positive; [in mechanical or cybernetic system] feed-back *m inv* positif, rétroaction *f* positive; I didn't get much ~ on my suggestion *fig* il n'y a pas eu beaucoup de réactions positives à la suite de ma proposition.

positively [ˈpɒzətɪvlɪ] *adv* -**1.** [absolutely] absolument, positivement; [definitely] incontestablement, positivement; it's ~ ridiculous c'est absolument ridicule; her behaviour was ~ disgraceful elle s'est comportée de manière absolument scandaleuse. -**2.** [constructively] positivement; it's important to act/think ~ il est important d'agir/de penser de façon positive. -**3.** [affirmatively] affirmativement; [with certainty] avec certitude, positivement; the body has been ~ identified le cadavre a été formellement identifié. -**4.** ELEC positivement; ~ charged chargé positivement.

positive pole *n* -**1.** [magnet] pôle *m* nord. -**2.** [anode] anode *f (pôle positif)*.

positive vetting [ˈvetɪŋ-] *n* contrôle *m* OR enquête *f* de sécurité *(sur un candidat à un poste touchant à la sécurité nationale)*.

positivism [ˈpɒzɪtɪvɪzm] *n* positivisme *m*.

positivist [ˈpɒzɪtɪvɪst] ◇ *n* positiviste *mf*.
◇ *adj* positiviste.

positron [ˈpɒzɪtrɒn] *n* positron *m*, positon *m*.

poss *inf* [pɒs] *adj* possible; as soon as ~ dès que possible.

posse [ˈpɒsɪ] *n Am autrefois, petit groupe d'hommes rassemblés par le shérif en cas d'urgence*; to get up a ~ réunir un groupe d'hommes; a ~ of fans were in hot pursuit *fig* des fans en détachement spécial s'étaient lancés dans une poursuite échevelée.

possess [pəˈzes] *vt* -**1.** [have possession of - permanently] posséder, avoir; [- temporarily] être en possession de, détenir, avoir; I would give all I ~ to be with you je donnerais tout ce que je possède OR j'ai pour être avec toi; what proof do you ~? quelles preuves avez-vous?; she ~es a clear understanding of the subject elle connaît bien son sujet, elle a une bonne connaissance du sujet. -**2.** [obsess] obséder; he was completely ~ed by the idea of going to India il était complètement obsédé par l'idée d'aller en Inde; what on earth ~ed him to do such a thing? qu'est-ce qui lui a pris de faire une chose pareille? -**3.** *fml & lit*: to ~ o.s. of sthg se munir de qqch.

possessed [pəˈzest] *adj* -**1.** [controlled - by an evil spirit] possédé; she/her soul is ~ by the devil elle/son âme est possédée du démon; he was shouting like one ~ il criait comme un possédé || *lit* [filled]: ~ by curiosity dévoré de OR en proie à la curiosité; ~ by hatred en proie à la haine ❑ 'The Possessed' *Dostoevsky* 'les Possédés'. -**2.** *fml & lit*: ~ of: none of her children was ~ of any great talent aucun de ses enfants n'était particulièrement doué.

possession [pəˈzeʃn] *n* -**1.** [gen] possession *f*; to be in ~ of sthg être en possession de qqch; he was found in ~ of a flick-knife, a flick-knife was found in his ~ il a été trouvé en possession d'un couteau à cran d'arrêt; she was charged with ~ of illegal substances elle a été inculpée pour détention de stupéfiants; the file is no longer in my ~ le dossier n'est plus en ma possession, je ne suis plus en possession du dossier; to be in full ~ of one's senses être en pleine possession de ses moyens; to be in OR to have ~ (of the ball) SPORT avoir le ballon; certain documents have come into my ~ certains documents sont tombés en ma possession; she got ~ of the house two weeks ago elle a pris possession de la maison il y a deux semaines; do they have ~ of the necessary documents? ont-ils OR possèdent-ils les documents nécessaires?; to take ~ of sthg [acquire] prendre possession de qqch; [by force] s'emparer de OR s'approprier qqch; [confiscate] confisquer qqch ❑ ~ is nine points OR parts OR tenths of the law *Br* possession vaut titre. -**2.** JUR [of property] possession *f*, jouissance *f*; to take ~ prendre possession ❑ immediate ~ jouissance immédiate. -**3.** [by evil] possession *f*.
◆ **possessions** *npl* -**1.** [belongings] affaires *fpl*, biens *mpl*; the jade vases are our most precious ~s les vases en jade sont ce que nous possédons de plus précieux. -**2.** [colonies] possessions *fpl*; [land] terres *fpl*.

possessive [pəˈzesɪv] ◇ *adj* -**1.** [gen] possessif; he's very ~ about his belongings il a horreur de prêter ses affaires; she's ~ about her children c'est une mère possessive. -**2.** GRAMM possessif; ~ adjective/pronoun adjectif *m*/pronom *m* possessif.
◇ *n* GRAMM [case] (cas *m*) possessif *m*; [word] possessif *m*.

possessively [pəˈzesɪvlɪ] *adv* de manière possessive; she clung ~ to her father's hand elle agrippa jalousement la main de son père.

possessiveness [pəˈzesɪvnɪs] *n* caractère *m* possessif, possessivité *f*.

possessor [pəˈzesəʳ] *n* possesseur *m*, propriétaire *mf*; I found myself the ~ of an old manor house je me suis trouvé propriétaire d'un vieux manoir.

posset [ˈpɒsɪt] *n boisson d'autrefois à base de lait chaud et de bière ou de vin*.

possibility [ˌpɒsəˈbɪlətɪ] (*pl* possibilities) *n* -**1.** [chance] possibilité *f*, éventualité *f*; it's a ~ c'est une possibilité, c'est bien possible; the ~ of a settlement is fading fast la perspective d'un règlement est de moins en moins probable; is there any ~ of you coming up for the weekend? pourriez-vous venir ce week-end?, y a-t-il des chances que vous veniez ce week-end?; if there's any ~ of leaving early, I'll let you know s'il y a moyen de partir de bonne heure, je vous le ferai savoir; there's no ~ of that happening il n'y a aucune chance OR aucun risque que cela se produise; there's little ~ of any changes being made to the budget il est peu probable que le budget soit modifié; there's a strong ~ we'll know the results tomorrow il est fort possible que nous connaissions les résultats demain; they hadn't even considered the ~ that he might leave ils n'avaient même pas envisagé qu'il puisse partir. -**2.** [person - for job] candidat *m*, -e *f* possible; [- as choice] choix *m* possible; she's still a ~ elle conserve toutes ses chances.

◆ **possibilities** *npl* [potential] possibilités *fpl*; the job has a lot of possibilities le poste offre de nombreuses perspectives; job possibilities possibilités d'emploi.

possible [ˈpɒsəbl] ◇ *adj* -**1.** [which can be done] possible; if ~ si possible; I'll be there, if at all ~ j'y serai, dans la mesure du possible; that's ~ c'est possible, ça se peut; it's quite ~ to complete the job in two months il est tout à fait possible de terminer le travail en deux mois; it wasn't ~ to achieve our objectives il ne nous a pas été possible d'atteindre nos objectifs; it isn't ~ for her to come il ne lui est pas possible OR il lui est impossible de venir ‖ *(in comparisons)*: as far as ~ [within one's competence] dans la mesure du possible; [at maximum distance] aussi loin que possible; as long as ~ aussi longtemps que possible; as much OR as many as ~ autant que possible; as soon as ~ dès que OR le plus tôt possible ‖ *(with superl adj)*: the best/the smallest ~ le meilleur/le plus petit possible; I mean that in the nicest ~ way je dis cela sans méchanceté (aucune). -**2.** [conceivable, imaginable] possible, imaginable; the best of all ~ worlds le meilleur des mondes possibles; he tried all ~ means il a essayé tous les moyens possibles (et imaginables); there's no ~ way out il n'y a absolument aucune issue; it seems barely ~ cela semble à peine possible; it doesn't seem ~ that anyone could be so stupid il est difficile d'imaginer que l'on puisse être aussi bête; the doctors did everything ~ to save her les médecins ont fait tout leur possible OR tout ce qu'ils ont pu pour la sauver; what ~ benefit can we get from it? quel bénéfice peut-on bien en tirer?; it's ~ (that) he won't come il se peut qu'il ne vienne pas; it's just ~ she's forgotten il n'est pas impossible qu'elle ait oublié; we chose several ~ candidates on a choisi plusieurs candidats possibles; there is a ~ risk of flooding on low ground il y a des risques d'inondations en contrebas ‖ [feasible] possible, faisable; he comes to see me whenever ~ il vient me voir quand il le peut; the grant made it ~ for me to continue my research la bourse m'a permis de poursuivre mes recherches; it's one ~ answer to the problem c'est une solution possible au problème. -**3.** [potentiel] éventuel; ~ risks des risques éventuels; ~ consequences des conséquences éventuelles.
◇ *n* -**1.** [activity] possible *m*; diplomacy is the art of the ~ la diplomatie est l'art du possible. -**2.** [choice] choix *m* possible; [candidate] candidature *f* susceptible d'être retenue; we looked at ten houses, of which two were ~s nous avons visité dix maisons dont deux nous intéressent OR sont à retenir; she is still a ~ for the prize/job elle garde toutes ses chances d'avoir le prix/d'obtenir le poste ‖ SPORT [player] joueur *m* susceptible d'être choisi; the England ~s *Br* les joueurs susceptibles de faire partie de l'équipe d'Angleterre.
◆ **Possibles** *npl Br*: the Possibles versus the Probables *hum* l'équipe B contre l'équipe A.

possibly [ˈpɒsəblɪ] *adv* -**1.** [perhaps] peut-être; he is ~ the greatest musician of his time c'est peut-être le plus grand musicien de son temps; ~ (so)/~ not, but he had no other choice peut-être (bien)/peut-être pas, mais il n'avait pas le choix; will you be there tomorrow? — ~ vous serez là demain? — c'est possible; could you ~ lend me £5? vous serait-il possible de me prêter 5 livres? -**2.** [conceivably] *(with modal verbs)*: what advantage can we ~ get from it? quel avantage pouvons-nous espérer en tirer?; she can't ~ get here on time elle ne pourra jamais arriver à l'heure; where can they ~ have got to? où peuvent-ils bien être passés?; run as fast as you ~ can cours aussi vite que tu peux; the doctors did all they ~ could to save her les médecins ont fait tout ce qu'ils ont pu OR tout leur possible pour la sauver; I'll come whenever I ~ can je viendrai chaque fois que cela me sera possible; I couldn't ~ accept your offer je ne puis accepter votre proposition; she might ~ still be here il se pourrait qu'elle soit encore ici.

possum [ˈpɒsəm] *n* [American] opossum *m*; [Australian] phalanger *m*; to play ~ *inf* faire le mort.

post [pəʊst] ◇ *n* -**1.** *Br* [letters] courrier *m*; [postal service] poste *f*, courrier *m*; has the ~ come? est-ce que le facteur est passé?; did it come through the ~ OR by ~? est-ce que c'est arrivé par la poste?; I sent it by ~ je l'ai envoyé par la poste; can you put the cheque in the ~? pouvez-vous poster le chèque?; do you want the letters to go first or second class ~? voulez-vous envoyer ces lettres au tarif normal ou au tarif lent? ‖ [delivery] (distribution *f* du) courrier *m*; a parcel came in this morning's ~ un paquet est arrivé au courrier de ce matin ‖ [collection] levée *f* (du courrier); I don't want to miss the ~ je ne veux pas manquer la levée; will we still catch the ~? pourrons-nous poster le courrier à temps OR avant la levée?; I missed the ~ quand je suis arrivé, la levée était déjà faite OR le courrier était déjà parti ‖ [post office] poste *f*; [letterbox] boîte *f* à lettres; can you take the letters to the ~? [post office] pouvez-vous porter les lettres à la poste?; [post them] pouvez-vous poster les lettres OR mettre les lettres à la boîte? -**2.** [station] relais *m* de poste; [rider] courrier *m*. -**3.** [of sign, street lamp, fence] poteau *m*; [of four-poster bed] colonne *f*; [upright - of door] montant *m*. -**4.** [in racing] poteau *m*; his horse was beaten at the ~ son cheval s'est fait coiffer au poteau. -**5.** FTBL poteau *m*, montant *m*; the near/far ~ le premier/deuxième poteau. -**6.** [job] poste *m*, emploi *m*; he got a ~ as an economist il a obtenu un poste d'économiste; a university/diplomatic ~ un poste universitaire/de diplomate; a government ~ un poste au gouvernement. -**7.** [duty station] poste *m*; remain at your ~ restez à votre poste; a sentry ~ un poste de sentinelle. -**8.** *Am* [trading post] comptoir *m*.
◇ *vt* -**1.** [letter - put in box] poster, mettre à la poste; [- send by post] envoyer par la poste; to ~ sthg to sb envoyer qqch à qqn par la poste, poster qqch à qqn ❑ to keep sb ~ed tenir qqn au courant. -**2.** [station] poster; they ~ed men all around the house ils ont posté des hommes tout autour de la maison. -**3.** *Br* [transfer - employee] muter, affecter. -**4.** [publish - banns, names] publier; [- on bulletin board] afficher; he has been ~ed missing il a été porté disparu; '~ no bills' *Am* 'défense d'afficher'. -**5.** BANK & ADMIN inscrire, enregistrer; to ~ an entry passer une écriture; to ~ the ledger tenir le grand-livre à jour. -**6.** *Am* [issue]: to ~ bail déposer une caution.
◆ **post on** *vt sep* [letters] faire suivre; can you ~ my letters on to me? pouvez-vous faire suivre mon courrier?
◆ **post up** *vt sep* -**1.** [notice] afficher. -**2.** [ledger] mettre à jour *(les écritures)*.

postage [ˈpəʊstɪdʒ] ◇ *n (U)* [postal charges] tarifs *mpl* postaux OR d'affranchissement; [cost of posting] frais *mpl* d'expédition OR d'envoi OR de port; what's the ~ on this parcel? c'est combien pour envoyer ce paquet? ❑ ~ and packing *Br* OR handling *Am* frais de port et d'emballage.
◇ *comp* [rates] postal.

postage due stamp *n* timbre *m* taxe.

postage stamp *n* timbre *m*, timbre-poste *m*.

postal [ˈpəʊstl] *adj* [charge, code, district] postal; [administration, service, strike] des postes; [delivery] par la poste; ~ vote *Br* vote *m* par correspondance.

postal order *n Br* mandat *m* postal.

postbag [ˈpəʊstbæg] *n Br* -**1.** [sack] sac *m* postal. -**2.** [correspondence] courrier *m*; we've got a full ~ this morning nous avons reçu énormément de lettres OR une avalanche de courrier ce matin.

postbox [ˈpəʊstbɒks] *n Br* boîte *f* à OR aux lettres.

postbus [ˈpəʊstbʌs] *n Br car transportant (en milieu rural) du courrier et des voyageurs.*

postcard [ˈpəʊstkɑːd] *n* carte *f* postale.

post chaise [-ʃeɪz] *n* chaise *f* de poste.

postcode [ˈpəʊstkəʊd] *n Br* code *m* postal.

postdate [ˌpəʊstˈdeɪt] *vt* -**1.** [letter, cheque] postdater. -**2.** [event] assigner une date postérieure à; historians now ~ the event by several centuries les historiens pensent aujourd'hui que l'événement a eu lieu des siècles plus tard.

postdoctoral [ˌpəʊstˈdɒktərəl], **postdoctorate** [ˌpəʊstˈdɒktərət] *adj* UNIV postdoctoral.

poster [ˈpəʊstəʳ] *n* [informative] affiche *f*; [decorative] poster *m*.

poste restante [ˌpəʊstˈrestɑːnt] *n* poste *f* restante; you can write to me ~ Florence vous pouvez m'écrire poste restante à Florence.

posterior [pɒˈstɪərɪəʳ] ◇ *adj* -**1.** *fml* [in time] postérieur. -**2.** TECH [rear] arrière.
◇ *n inf hum* [of a person] postérieur *m*, arrière-train *m*.

posterity [pɒˈsterətɪ] *n* postérité *f*; for ~ pour la postérité; to go down to ~ entrer dans la postérité OR l'histoire.

postern [ˈpɒstən] *n* poterne *f*.

poster paint *n* gouache *f*.

post exchange *n Am* MIL magasin *m* pour militaires.

post-free ◇ *adj* -**1.** *Br* [prepaid] port payé. -**2.** [free of postal charge] dispensé d'affranchissement.
◇ *adv* -**1.** *Br* [prepaid] en port payé. -**2.** [free of postal charge] en franchise postale.

postgraduate [ˌpəʊstˈgrædʒʊət] ◇ *n* étudiant *m*, -e *f* de troisième cycle.
◇ *adj* [diploma, studies] de troisième cycle.

posthaste [ˌpəʊstˈheɪst] *adv lit* à toute vitesse, en toute hâte.

post horn *n* trompe *f* (de la malle-poste).

post-horse *n* cheval *m* de poste.

post house *n* relais *m* de poste.

posthumous [ˈpɒstjʊməs] *adj* posthume.

posthumously [ˈpɒstjʊməslɪ] *adj* après la mort; the poems were published ~ les poèmes ont été publiés après la mort de l'auteur; the decoration was awarded ~ la décoration a été décernée à titre posthume.

postil(l)ion [pəˈstɪljən] *n* postillon *m*.

postimpressionism [ˌpəʊstɪmˈpreʃnɪzm] *n* postimpressionnisme *m*.

postimpressionist [ˌpəʊstɪmˈpreʃnɪst] ◇ *n* postimpressionniste *mf*.
◇ *adj* postimpressionniste.

postindustrial [ˌpəʊstɪnˈdʌstrɪəl] *adj* postindustriel.

posting [ˈpəʊstɪŋ] *n* -**1.** *Br* [of diplomat] nomination *f*, affectation *f*; [of soldier] affectation *f*; to get an overseas ~ être nommé en poste à l'étranger. -**2.** COMM [in ledger] inscription *f*, enregistrement *m*. -**3.** *Br* [of letter] expédition *f* par la poste.

postman [ˈpəʊstmən] (*pl* postmen [-mən]) *n* facteur *m*, préposé *m* ADMIN.

postman's knock *n jeu d'enfant dans lequel un des joueurs fait semblant de distribuer des lettres, en échange desquelles il reçoit un baiser.*

postmark [ˈpəʊstmɑːk] ◇ *n* [on letter] cachet *m* de la poste; date as ~ le cachet de la poste faisant foi.
◇ *vt* oblitérer; the letter is ~ed Phoenix la lettre vient de OR a été postée à Phoenix.

postmaster [ˈpəʊstˌmɑːstəʳ] *n* receveur *m* des Postes.

Postmaster General (*pl* Postmasters General) *n* ≃ ministre *m* des Postes et Télécommunications.

post meridiem [-məˈrɪdɪəm] *adv fml* [in afternoon] de l'après-midi; [in evening] du soir.

postmistress [ˈpəʊstˌmɪstrɪs] *n* receveuse *f* des Postes.

post-modernism *n* postmodernisme *m*.

post-modernist ◇ *n* postmoderniste *mf*.
◇ *adj* postmoderniste.

postmortem [ˌpəʊstˈmɔːtəm] ◇ *n* -**1.** MED autopsie *f*; to carry out a ~ pratiquer une autopsie. -**2.** *fig* autopsie *f*; they held a ~ on the game ils ont disséqué OR analysé le match après coup.
◇ *adj* après le décès; ~ examination autopsie *f*.

postnatal [ˌpəʊstˈneɪtl] *adj* postnatal; ~ depression dépression *f* postnatale.

post office *n* -**1.** [place] (bureau *m* de) poste *f*; [service] (service *m* des) postes *fpl*, poste *f*; the Post Office la Poste; ~ and general stores *petite épicerie de village faisant office de bureau de poste*. -**2.** *Am* = **postman's knock**.

post office box *n* boîte *f* postale.

post office savings *n* *Br* ≃ Caisse *f* (nationale) d'épargne; we have a little money in ~ nous avons un peu d'argent à la Caisse d'épargne.

postoperative [ˌpəʊstˈɒpərətɪv] *adj* postopératoire.

postpaid [ˌpəʊstˈpeɪd] *adj* & *adv* franco, franc de port.

postpone [ˌpəʊstˈpəʊn] *vt* remettre (à plus tard), reporter; the meeting was ~d for three weeks/until a later date la réunion a été reportée de trois semaines/remise à une date ultérieure; we had to ~ our decision nous avons dû différer notre décision.

postponement [ˌpəʊstˈpəʊnmənt] *n* [of meeting, match] renvoi *m* (à une date ultérieure), report *m*; [of holiday] report *m*.

postposition [ˌpəʊstpəˈzɪʃn] *n* GRAMM postposition *f*.

postprandial [ˌpəʊstˈprændɪəl] *adj fml* postprandial; I like to take a ~ nap/walk j'aime faire une petite sieste/promenade après le déjeuner.

postscript [ˈpəʊsskrɪpt] *n* post-scriptum *m inv*.

post-synch *inf* [ˈpəʊsˌsɪŋk] = **postsynchronization**.

postsynchronization, -isation [ˈpəʊsˌsɪŋkrənaɪˈzeɪʃn] *n* postsynchronisation *f*.

postulant [ˈpɒstjʊlənt] *n* postulant *m*, -e *f* RELIG.

postulate [*vb* ˈpɒstjʊleɪt, *n* ˈpɒstjʊlət] *fml* ◇ *vt* -**1.** [hypothesize] poser comme hypothèse; to ~ the existence of an underground lake soutenir l'hypothèse d'un lac souterrain; we ~ that a cure will soon be found nous sommes sûrs qu'on trouvera bientôt un remède. -**2.** [take as granted] postuler, poser comme principe; the charter ~s that all men are equal la charte part du principe que tous les hommes sont égaux.
◇ *n* postulat *m*.

posture [ˈpɒstʃəʳ] ◇ *n* -**1.** [body position] posture *f*, position *f*; to keep an upright ~ se tenir droit. -**2.** *fig* [attitude] attitude *f*.
◇ *vi* se donner des airs, poser.

postvocalic [ˌpəʊstvəˈkælɪk] *adj* postvocalique.

postwar [ˌpəʊstˈwɔːʳ] *adj* d'après-guerre, après la guerre; the ~ period l'après-guerre *m or f*; in the immediate ~ period au cours des années qui ont immédiatement suivi la guerre, tout de suite après la guerre.

posy [ˈpəʊzɪ] (*pl* posies) *n* petit bouquet *m* (de fleurs).

pot [pɒt] (*pt* & *pp* potted, *cont* potting) ◇ *vt* -**1.** [jam] mettre en pot OR pots; [fruit] mettre en conserve. -**2.** [plant] mettre en pot. -**3.** *Br* [in snooker]: to ~ the ball mettre la bille dans la poche OR la blouse. -**4.** *Br* [shoot] tuer; she potted a partridge elle a abattu une perdrix; he's out potting rabbits il est à la chasse au lapin.
◇ *vi* -**1.** [do pottery] faire de la poterie. -**2.** *Br* [shoot]: to ~ at sthg tirer sur qqch.
◇ *n* -**1.** [container - for paint, plant, jam etc] pot *m*; [teapot] théière *f*; [coffeepot] cafetière *f*; a ~ of paint/mustard un pot de peinture/de moutarde; I drank a whole ~ of tea/coffee j'ai bu une théière/une cafetière entière; I'll make another ~ of tea/coffee je vais refaire du thé/café; a ~ of tea for two du thé pour deux personnes ❑ (chamber) ~ pot *m* de chambre, vase *m* de nuit. -**2.** [saucepan] casserole *f*; ~s and pans batterie *f* de cuisine; (cooking) ~ marmite *f*, fait-tout *m inv*; it's a case of the ~ calling the kettle black *Br prov* c'est la Pitié qui se moque de la Charité *prov*. -**3.** [pottery object] poterie *f*, pot *m*; to throw a ~ tourner une poterie. -**4.** *inf* SPORT [trophy] trophée *m*, coupe *f*. -**5.** *Am* [kitty] cagnotte *f*. -**6.** *inf* [belly] bedaine *f*, brioche *f*. -**7.** *inf Br* [shot]: to take a ~ at sthg tirer sur qqch. -**8.** *drugs sl* marie-jeanne *f*. -**9.** ELEC potentiomètre *m*. -**10.** *phr*: to go to ~ *inf* [country] aller à la dérive; [morals] dégénérer; [plans] tomber à l'eau; [person] se laisser aller; everything has gone to ~ tout est fichu.

◆ **pots** *inf npl Br* [large amount] tas *mpl*, tonnes *fpl*; to have ~s of money avoir plein de fric, être plein aux as.

◆ **pot on** *vt sep* [plant] rempoter.

◆ **pot up** *vt sep* [plant] empoter.

potable [ˈpəʊtəbl] *adj lit* OR *hum* potable, buvable.

potash [ˈpɒtæʃ] *n (U)* potasse *f*.

potassium [pəˈtæsɪəm] *n (U)* potassium *m*; ~ permanganate permanganate *m* de potassium.

potassium-argon dating *n* datation *f* au potassium-argon.

potation [pəʊˈteɪʃn] *n lit* OR *hum* [drink] boisson *f* (alcoolisée); [drinking] libations *fpl*.

potato [pəˈteɪtəʊ] (*pl* potatoes) ◇ *n* pomme *f* de terre; boiled ~es pommes de terre à l'eau; can I have some more ~ OR ~es? est-ce que je peux reprendre des pommes de terre? ❑ the ~ famine *Ir* HIST la disette de la pomme de terre.
◇ *comp* [farming, salad] de pommes de terre.

THE POTATO FAMINE:
Famine qui sévit en Irlande en 1845, provoquée par la maladie de la pomme de terre, aliment de base de la population. Plongeant le pays dans la misère, cette catastrophe poussa plus d'un million de personnes à émigrer aux États-Unis.

---

potato beetle *n* doryphore *m*.

potato blight *n* mildiou *m* de la pomme de terre.

potato bug = **potato beetle**.

potato chip *n* -**1.** *Br* [French fry] (pomme *f*) frite *f*. -**2.** *Am* [crisp] (pomme *f*) chips *f*.

potato crisp *n Br* (pomme *f*) chips *f*.

potato masher *n* presse-purée *m inv*.

potato peeler *n* [implement] éplucheur *m*, épluche-légumes *m*, (couteau *m*) économe *m*; [machine] éplucheuse *f*.

potato soup *n* soupe *f* de pommes de terre.

potbellied [ˈpɒtˌbelɪd] *adj* -**1.** [person] bedonnant; to be ~ avoir du ventre. -**2.** ~ stove poêle *m*.

potbelly [ˈpɒtˌbelɪ] (*pl* potbellies) *n* -**1.** [stomach] ventre *m*, bedon *m*; to have a ~ avoir du ventre. -**2.** *Am* [stove] poêle *m*.

potboiler *inf* [ˈpɒtˌbɔɪləʳ] *n* gagne-pain *m*; he only writes ~s il n'écrit que pour faire bouillir la marmite.

pot-bound *adj* [plant] qui a besoin d'être rempoté.

poteen [pɒˈtiːn] *n Ir whisky fabriqué clandestinement*.

potency [ˈpəʊtənsɪ] (*pl* potencies) *n* -**1.** [strength - of spell, influence, argument] force *f*, puissance *f*; [- of medicine] efficacité *f*; [- of drink] (forte) teneur *f* en alcool. -**2.** [virility] puissance *f*, virilité *f*.

potent [ˈpəʊtənt] *adj* -**1.** [spell, influence] fort, puissant; [argument] convaincant; [medicine, poison, antidote] actif; [drink] fort (en alcool); ~ stuff, this rum! il est fort, ce rhum! -**2.** [virile] viril.

potentate [ˈpəʊtənteɪt] *n* POL potentat *m*; *fig* magnat *m*.

potential [pəˈtenʃl] ◇ *adj* -**1.** [possible] possible, potentiel; that boy is a ~ genius ce garçon est un génie en puissance; they're ~ criminals ce sont des criminels en puissance; we mustn't discourage ~ investors il ne faut pas décourager les investisseurs éventuels OR potentiels. -**2.** LING potentiel. -**3.** ELEC & PHYS potentiel; ~ difference différence *f* de potentiel; ~ energy énergie *f* potentielle.
◇ *n* -**1.** *(U)* [of person] promesse *f*, possibilités *fpl* (d'avenir); your son has ~ votre fils a de l'avenir OR un avenir prometteur; she has the ~ to succeed elle a la capacité de réussir; they don't have much intellectual ~ ils n'ont pas de grandes capacités intellectuelles; she has great ~ as an actress OR great acting ~ elle a toutes les qualités d'une grande actrice; she has ~ as an athlete elle peut devenir une grande athlète; to fulfil one's ~ donner toute sa mesure; he never achieved his full ~ il n'a jamais exploité pleinement ses capacités ‖ [of concept, discovery, situation] possibilités *fpl*; the idea has ~ l'idée a de l'avenir; your latest invention has great ~ for developing countries votre dernière invention ouvre de grandes perspectives dans les pays en voie de développement; the scheme has no ~ le projet n'a aucun avenir; there is little ~ for development in the firm l'entreprise offre peu de possibilités de développement; the country's military ~ le potentiel militaire du pays ‖ [of place] possibilités *fpl*; the area/garden has real ~ le quartier/le jardin offre de nombreuses possibilités. -**2.** ELEC & MATH potentiel *m*.

potentiality [pəˌtenʃɪˈælətɪ] (*pl* potentialities) *n* -**1.** [likelihood] potentialité *f*. -**2.** [potential] possibilités *fpl*, perspective *f* (d'avenir); to have potentialities offrir de nombreuses possibilités.

potentially [pəˈtenʃəlɪ] *adv* potentiellement; she's ~ a great writer elle pourrait être un grand écrivain; ~ lethal poisons des poisons qui peuvent être mortels.

potentiometer [pəˌtenʃɪˈɒmɪtəʳ] *n* potentiomètre *m*.

potful [ˈpɒtfʊl] *n* [volume] (contenu *m* d'un) pot *m*; a ~ of coffee un pot plein de café, une cafetière pleine.

pothead [ˈpɒthed] *n drugs sl* fumeur *m*, -euse *f* de haschisch.

potheen [pɒˈtiːn] = **poteen**.

pother [ˈpɒðəʳ] *n* agitation *f*; to get into a ~ over sthg se mettre dans tous ses états au sujet de qqch.

potherb [ˈpɒthɜːb] *n* [as seasoning] herbe *f* aromatique; [as vegetable] légume *m* vert.

pothole [ˈpɒthəʊl] *n* -**1.** [in road] fondrière *f*, nid-de-poule *m*. -**2.** [underground] caverne *f*, grotte *f*.

potholer [ˈpɒtˌhəʊləʳ] *n Br* spéléologue *mf*.

potholing [ˈpɒtˌhəʊlɪŋ] *n (U) Br* spéléologie *f*; to go ~ faire de la spéléologie.

pothook [ˈpɒthʊk] *n* -**1.** [in fireplace] crémaillère *f* *(crochet en forme de s)*. -**2.** [in writing] boucle *f*.

pothunter [ˈpɒtˌhʌntəʳ] *n pej* -**1.** HUNT chasseur *m*, -euse *f* sans scrupules. -**2.** [archaeologist] archéologue *mf* amateur. -**3.** SPORT chasseur *m*, -euse *f* de médailles.

potion [ˈpəʊʃn] *n* -**1.** MED potion *f*. -**2.** *fig* potion *f*, breuvage *m*; love ~ philtre *m* d'amour; magic ~ potion magique.

potlatch [ˈpɒtlætʃ] *n* -**1.** ANTHR potlatch *m*. -**2.** *inf Am* fête *f* bruyante.

potluck *inf* [ˌpɒtˈlʌk] *n*: to take ~ [for meal] manger à la fortune du pot; [take what one finds] s'en remettre au hasard.

pot plant *n Br* plante *f* d'intérieur.

potpourri [ˌpəʊˈpʊərɪ] *n* pot-pourri *m*.

potroast [ˈpɒtrəʊst] *vt* rôtir à la cocotte.

pot roast *n* rôti *m* à la cocotte.

Potsdam [ˈpɒtsdæm] *pr n* Potsdam.

potshard [ˈpɒtʃɑːd], **potsherd** [ˈpɒtʃɜːd] *n* ARCHEOL tesson *m* de poterie, fragment *m*.

pot shot *n*: to take a ~ at sthg [fire at] tirer à l'aveuglette sur qqch; [attempt] faire qqch à l'aveuglette.

pottage [ˈpɒtɪdʒ] *n* potage *m* épais.

potted ['pɒtɪd] *adj* -**1.** HORT en pot; ~ **palm** palmier *m* en pot; ~ **plant** plante *f* verte. -**2.** CULIN [cooked] (cuit) en terrine; [conserved] (conservé) en terrine OR en pot; ~ **meat** ≃ terrine *f*; ~ **shrimps** crevettes *fpl* en conserve. -**3.** *inf* [condensed - version] condensé, abrégé; **a ~ history of the Second World War** un abrégé d'histoire de la Seconde Guerre mondiale; **she gave me a ~ version of the truth** elle m'a donné une version sommaire des faits.

potter ['pɒtəʳ] ◇ *n* potier *m*, -ère *f*; ~**'s clay** argile *f* de potier, terre *f* glaise; ~**'s wheel** tour *m* de potier; ~**'s field** *Am* cimetière *m* des pauvres.
◇ *vi inf Br* s'occuper de choses et d'autres, bricoler; **after lunch, I'll ~ down to the post office** après le déjeuner, je ferai un saut à la poste; **I spent the evening just ~ing** j'ai passé la soirée à traînasser.
◆ **potter about** *inf Br* ◇ *vi insep* s'occuper, bricoler; **to ~ about in the garden** faire de petits travaux OR bricoler dans le jardin.
◇ *vt insep*: **to ~ about the house/garden** faire de petits travaux OR bricoler dans la maison/le jardin.
◆ **potter along** *inf vi insep Br* aller son petit bonhomme de chemin; **I'd better be ~ing along now** bon, il faudrait que je commence à y aller; **I might ~ along to the library later** j'irai peut-être faire un tour à la bibliothèque tout à l'heure.
◆ **potter around** *inf Br* = **potter about**.

pottery ['pɒtərɪ] (*pl* **potteries**) *n* -**1.** *(U)* [craft] poterie *f*. -**2.** *(U)* [earthenware] poterie *f*, poteries *fpl*; [ceramics] céramiques *fpl*; **a beautiful piece of ~** une très belle poterie. -**3.** [workshop] atelier *m* de poterie.

potting ['pɒtɪŋ] *n* *(U)* -**1.** HORT rempotage *m*; ~ **compost** terreau *m*. -**2.** [pottery] poterie *f*.

potting shed *n* remise *f* OR resserre *f* (de jardin).

pot-trained *Br* = **potty-trained**.

potty ['pɒtɪ] (*pl* **potties**, *compar* **pottier**, *superl* **pottiest**) ◇ *n* [for children] pot *m* (de chambre).
◇ *adj inf Br* fou, cinglé, dingue; **to be ~ about sthg** être toqué de qqch; **he's absolutely ~ about her** il est absolument fou d'elle.

potty-train *vt*: **to ~ a child** apprendre à un enfant à aller sur son pot.

potty-trained *adj* propre.

potty-training *n* apprentissage *m* de la propreté.

pouch [paʊtʃ] *n* -**1.** [bag] (petit) sac *m*; [for tobacco] blague *f*; [for money] sac *m*, bourse *f*; [for ammunition] cartouchière *f*, giberne *f*; [for gunpowder] sacoche *f*, sac *m*; [for mail] sac *m* (postal). -**2.** ZOOL [of marsupial, in cheeks] poche *f*, abajoue *f*; [pocket of skin] poche *f*. -**3.** *Am* [for diplomats] valise *f* diplomatique.

pouf(fe) [puːf] *n* *Br* -**1.** [cushion] pouf *m*. -**2.** ∇ *Br* = **poof** *n*.

poulterer ['pəʊltərəʳ] *n Br* volailler *m*, -ère *f*.

poultice ['pəʊltɪs] ◇ *n* MED cataplasme *m*.
◇ *vt* mettre un cataplasme à.

poultry ['pəʊltrɪ] ◇ *n* *(U)* [meat] volaille *f*.
◇ *npl* [birds] volaille *f*, volailles *fpl*.

poultry farm *n* élevage *m* de volaille OR de volailles.

poultry farmer *n* éleveur *m*, -euse *f* de volaille OR de volailles, aviculteur *m*, -trice *f*.

poultry farming *n* élevage *m* de volaille OR de volailles, aviculture *f*.

poultryman ['pəʊltrɪmən] (*pl* **poultrymen** [-mən]) *n* -**1.** [breeder] éleveur *m* de volaille OR de volailles, aviculteur *m*. -**2.** [dealer] marchand *m* de volaille, volailler *m*.

pounce [paʊns] ◇ *vi* sauter, bondir; **the cat crouched nearby, ready to ~** le chat était tapi là, prêt à bondir; **a man ~d (out) from behind the bush** un homme a surgi de derrière le buisson.
◇ *n* bond *m*; **with a sudden ~** d'un bond.
◆ **pounce on, pounce upon** *vt insep* -**1.** [subj: animal] se jeter sur, bondir sur; [subj: bird] se jeter sur, fondre sur; [subj: police] saisir, arrêter; **the customs ~d on the drug-runners** les douaniers ont arrêté les trafiquants de drogue. -**2.** [in criticism] bondir sur, sauter sur; **they ~ on your slightest mistake** ils sautent OR bondissent sur la moindre de vos erreurs. -**3.** [seize - opportunity] sauter sur, saisir.

pound [paʊnd] ◇ *n* -**1.** [weight] livre *f*; **to sell goods by the ~** vendre des marchandises à la livre; **three ~** OR **~s of apples** trois livres de pommes; **two dollars a ~** deux dollars la livre ❑ **to get one's ~ of flesh** obtenir ce que l'on exigeait; **he wants his pound of flesh** il veut son dû à n'importe quel prix. -**2.** [money] livre *f*; **have you got change for a ~?** avez-vous la monnaie d'une livre?; **two for a ~** deux pour une livre; **the ~ fell yesterday against the deutschmark** la livre est tombée hier face au Deutsche Mark ❑ ~ **coin** pièce *f* d'une livre; **the Lebanese/Maltese ~** la livre libanaise/maltaise; **the ~ sterling** la livre sterling. -**3.** [for dogs, cars] fourrière *f*.
◇ *vt* -**1.** [crush, pulverize - grain] broyer, concasser; [- rocks] concasser, écraser. -**2.** [hammer, hit] cogner sur, marteler; **she ~ed the table with her fist** elle martelait la table du poing; **the soldiers' heavy boots ~ed the earth** les soldats martelaient le sol de leurs lourdes bottes; **the waves ~ed the rocks/boat** les vagues battaient les rochers/venaient s'écraser violemment contre le bateau; **he began ~ing the typewriter keys** il commença à taper sur OR à marteler le clavier de la machine à écrire; **the teacher tried to ~ spelling rules into her pupils** *fig* le professeur s'efforçait de faire rentrer les règles d'orthographe dans la tête de ses élèves. -**3.** [bombard, shell] bombarder, pilonner; **they ~ed the enemy positions with mortar fire** ils ont bombardé les positions ennemies au mortier. -**4.** [walk - corridor] faire les cent pas dans, aller et venir dans; **to ~ the streets** battre le pavé; **to ~ the beat** faire sa ronde.
◇ *vi* -**1.** [hammer - on table, ceiling] cogner, taper; [- on piano, typewriter] taper; **the neighbours started ~ing on the ceiling** les voisins ont commencé à cogner au plafond; **we had to ~ on the door before anyone answered** il a fallu frapper à la porte à coups redoublés avant d'obtenir une réponse; **the waves ~ed against the rocks** les vagues venaient s'écraser sur OR fouettaient les rochers; **the rain was ~ing on the roof** la pluie tambourinait sur le toit. -**2.** [rhythmically - drums] battre; [- heart] battre fort; [- with fear, excitement] battre la chamade; **my head was ~ing from the noise** le bruit me martelait la tête. -**3.** [more heavily]: **he ~ed down the stairs** il descendit l'escalier bruyamment; **the elephants ~ed through the jungle** les éléphants se déplaçaient lourdement à travers la jungle.
◆ **pound away** *vi insep* -**1.** [at task] travailler avec acharnement; **he spent the holidays ~ing away at his thesis** il a passé les vacances à travailler dur à sa thèse. -**2.** [on typewriter, piano, drums] taper; **she's been ~ing away at her typewriter since 8 o'clock** elle s'acharne sur sa machine à écrire depuis 8 h; **every weekend, he ~s away on his drums** il passe ses week-ends à taper sur sa batterie. -**3.** [with artillery]: **to ~ away at the enemy lines** pilonner sans arrêt les lignes ennemies.
◆ **pound down** *vt sep* -**1.** [crush] piler, concasser; **~ the millet down to a fine powder** réduisez le millet en une poudre fine; **~ the mixture down to a pulp** réduisez le mélange en bouillie. -**2.** [flatten - earth] pilonner, tasser.
◆ **pound out** *vt sep Br* -**1.** [rhythm] marteler; **the pianist was ~ing out a tune** le pianiste martelait un air. -**2.** [letter, document] taper (avec fougue); **she ~s out a book a month** elle sort OR écrit un livre par mois.
◆ **pound up** *vt sep* piler, concasser.

poundage ['paʊndɪdʒ] *n* *(U)* -**1.** [on weight] droits *mpl* perçus par livre de poids. -**2.** [on value] droits *mpl* perçus par livre de valeur. -**3.** [weight] poids *m (en livres)*.

pound cake *n* ≃ quatre-quarts *m inv*.

-pounder ['paʊndəʳ] *in cpds*: **a fifteen~** [fish] un poisson de 15 livres; **a two-hundred~** [shell] un obus de 200 livres; **a six~** [gun] un canon qui tire des obus de six livres.

pounding ['paʊndɪŋ] *n* -**1.** [noise] martèlement *m*. -**2.** *(U)* [beating - of heart] battements *mpl*; **I could hear the ~ of her heart** j'entendais son cœur qui battait à tout rompre. -**3.** *inf* [battering] rossée *f*; **he took a real ~ in the first five rounds** il a pris une bonne volée OR il s'est drôlement fait rosser pendant les cinq premières reprises; **the jetty/harbour took a ~ in the storm** la jetée/le port en a pris un coup pendant la tempête; **the dollar took a severe ~ last week** le dollar a été sérieusement malmené la semaine dernière. -**4.** *inf* [severe defeat] déculottée *f*, piquette *f*; **the team took a real ~ last week** l'équipe a subi une lourde défaite OR s'est fait battre à plate couture la semaine dernière.

pour [pɔːʳ] ◇ *vt* -**1.** [liquid] verser; **she ~ed milk into their mugs** elle a versé du lait dans leurs tasses; **we ~ed the water/wine down the sink** nous avons vidé l'eau/jeté le vin dans l'évier; **~ the cider into the jug** versez le cidre dans le pichet; **her jeans were so tight she looked as if she'd been ~ed into them** son jeans était tellement serré qu'elle semblait avoir été coulée dedans; **to ~ scorn on sb** *fig* traiter qqn avec mépris ‖ [serve] servir, verser; **to ~ a drink for sb** servir à boire à qqn; **~ yourself a drink** servez-vous OR versez-vous à boire; **may I ~ you some wine?** je vous sers du vin?; **would you ~ the tea?** voulez-vous servir le thé? ❑ **to ~ cold water on** OR **over sb's plans** *inf* décourager OR refroidir qqn dans ses projets; **to ~ oil on troubled waters** calmer les esprits. -**2.** [invest] investir; **he ~ed all his energy into the project** il a mis toute son énergie dans le projet; **I've already ~ed a fortune into the firm** j'ai déjà investi une fortune dans la société.
◇ *vi* -**1.** [light, liquid, smoke] se déverser, couler à flots; **water ~ed from the gutters** l'eau débordait des gouttières; **tears ~ed down her face** elle pleurait à chaudes larmes; **blood ~ed from the wound** la blessure saignait abondamment; **the sweat was ~ing off his back** son dos ruisselait de sueur; **light ~ed into the church** l'église était inondée de lumière; **smoke ~ed out of the blazing building** des nuages de fumée s'échappaient de l'immeuble en flammes. -**2.** [rain] pleuvoir à verse; **it's ~ing (down), it's ~ing with rain** il pleut à verse OR à torrents; **the rain ~ed down** la pluie tombait à verse. -**3.** [crowd] affluer; **spectators ~ed into/out of the cinema** une foule de spectateurs entrait dans le cinéma/sortait du cinéma; **thousands of cars ~ed out of Paris** des milliers de voitures se pressaient aux portes de Paris; **reporters ~ into Cannes for the festival** les journalistes affluent à Cannes pour le festival. -**4.** [pan, jug]: **to ~ well/badly** verser bien/mal.
◆ **pour away** *vt sep* [empty] vider; [throw out] jeter.
◆ **pour down** *vi insep* = **pour** *vi* **2**.
◆ **pour forth** *vi insep lit* [light, water] se déverser; [people] affluer.
◆ **pour in** *vi insep* -**1.** [rain, light] entrer à flots; **rain ~ed in through a hole in the roof** la pluie entrait à flots par un trou dans le plafond. -**2.** [cars, refugees, spectators] arriver en masse; [information, reports] affluer, arriver en masse; **offers of help ~ed in from all sides** des offres d'aide ont afflué de toutes parts; **money ~ed in for the disaster victims** des milliers de dons ont été envoyés pour les victimes de la catastrophe.
◆ **pour off** *vt sep* [liquid, excess] vider.
◆ **pour on** *vt sep* [cream] verser.
◆ **pour out** ◇ *vt sep* -**1.** [liquid] verser. -**2.** [information, propaganda] répandre, diffuser; [substances]: **the industry ~s out tons of dangerous chemicals** l'industrie déverse des

tonnes de produits chimiques dangereux. -**3.** [emotions] donner libre cours à; she ~ed out all her troubles to me elle m'a raconté tout ce qu'elle avait sur le cœur; to ~ out one's heart to sb parler à qqn à cœur ouvert.
◇ *vi insep* [water] jaillir, couler à flots; [tears] couler abondamment; [light] jaillir.

pouring ['pɔːrɪŋ] *adj* -**1.** [rain] battant, diluvien; we were stranded in the ~ rain nous étions coincés sous une pluie battante. -**2.** [cream] liquide; the sauce should be of ~ consistency il faut que la sauce soit bien liquide.

pout [paʊt] (*pl sense 2 inv* OR pouts) ◇ *vi* faire la moue.
◇ *vt* dire en faisant la moue.
◇ *n* -**1.** [facial expression] moue *f*; with a ~ en faisant la moue. -**2.** [fish - eelpout] lycode *m*, lotte *f*; [- whiting] tacaud *m*.

pouter ['paʊtəʳ] *n* [bird] boulant *m*.

poverty ['pɒvətɪ] *n* -**1.** [financial] pauvreté *f*, misère *f*; to live in ~ vivre dans le besoin. -**2.** [shortage - of resources] manque *m*; [- of ideas, imagination] pauvreté *f*, manque *m*; [weakness - of style, arguments] pauvreté *f*, faiblesse *f*. -**3.** [of soil] pauvreté *f*, aridité *f*.

poverty line *n* seuil *m* de pauvreté; to live on/below the ~ vivre à la limite/en dessous du seuil de pauvreté.

poverty-stricken *adj* [person] dans la misère, dans le plus grand dénuement; [areas] misérable, où sévit la misère.

poverty trap *n situation inextricable de ceux qui dépendent de prestations sociales qu'ils perdent pour peu qu'ils trouvent une activité, même peu rémunérée.*

pow [paʊ] *onomat* [from collision] vlan, v'lan; [from gun] pan.

POW *n abbr of* prisoner of war.

powder ['paʊdəʳ] ◇ *n* -**1.** [gen & MIL] poudre *f*; in ~ form en poudre, sous forme de poudre; to grind sthg to a ~ réduire qqch en poudre, pulvériser qqch ❑ to keep one's ~ dry *Br* se tenir prêt, être aux aguets. -**2.** *dated* & MED: to take a headache ~ prendre un médicament (en sachet) contre le mal de tête ❑ to take a ~ *inf Am* ficher le camp, décamper.
◇ *vt* -**1.** [crush, pulverize] pulvériser, réduire en poudre. -**2.** [make up] poudrer; to ~ one's face se poudrer le visage; to ~ one's nose *euph* [go to the toilet] aller se repoudrer le nez. -**3.** [sprinkle] saupoudrer; the Christmas tree was ~ed with artificial snow le sapin de Noël était saupoudré de neige artificielle.

powder blue *n* bleu *m* pastel.
◆ **powder-blue** *adj* bleu pastel *(inv)*.

powder compact *n* poudrier *m*.

powdered ['paʊdəd] *adj* -**1.** [milk, eggs] en poudre; [coffee] instantané; ~ sugar *Am* sucre *m* glace. -**2.** [hair, face] poudré.

powder horn *n* corne *f*, cartouche *f* à poudre.

powder keg *n* [of gunpowder] baril *m* de poudre; *fig* poudrière *f*.

powder puff *n* houppette *f*.

powder room *n euph* toilettes *fpl* (pour dames).

powdery ['paʊdərɪ] *adj* -**1.** [covered in powder] couvert de poudre. -**2.** [like powder] poudreux; ~ snow (neige *f*) poudreuse *f*. -**3.** [crumbling] friable.

power ['paʊəʳ] ◇ *n* -**1.** [strength, force - gen] puissance *f*, force *f*; they could see the ~ of his muscles ils voyaient travailler ses muscles puissants; I underestimated the ~ of the explosion j'ai sous-estimé la puissance OR la force de l'explosion; we want greater economic and industrial ~ nous voulons renforcer la puissance économique et industrielle ‖ PHYS [of engine, lens, microscope] puissance *f*; at full ~ à plein régime; the vehicle moves under its own ~ le véhicule se déplace par ses propres moyens OR de façon autonome ❑ sea/air ~ puissance *f* maritime/aérienne; more ~ to your elbow! *inf Br* bonne chance!, bon courage! -**2.** [influence] pouvoir *m*, puissance *f*; the ~ of the Church/of student unions le pouvoir de l'Église/des syndicats étudiants; I'll do everything in my ~ to help you je ferai tout mon possible OR tout ce qui est en mon pouvoir pour vous aider; at the height of his ~s à l'apogée de son pouvoir ‖ [control] pouvoir *m*; to have sb in one's ~ avoir qqn en son pouvoir; to fall into sb's ~ tomber au pouvoir de qqn ‖ POL pouvoir *m*; to be in ~ être au pouvoir; to come to/take ~ arriver au/prendre le pouvoir. -**3.** [authority] autorité *f*, pouvoir *m*; [of assembly] pouvoir *m*; to have the ~ to decide/judge avoir le pouvoir de décider/juger, avoir autorité pour décider/juger; the committee doesn't really have much ~ le comité n'a pas grand pouvoir; it's beyond OR outside my ~ cela dépasse ma compétence OR ne relève pas de mon autorité; it's beyond my ~ to do anything je n'ai pas compétence en la matière, je ne suis pas habilité à intervenir; no ~ on earth will persuade me to go rien au monde ne me persuadera d'y aller ‖ [influential group or person] puissance *f*; the President is the real ~ in the land c'est le président qui détient le véritable pouvoir dans le pays; to be a ~ in the land avoir une grande influence OR être très puissant dans un pays ❑ the ~s of darkness les forces OR puissances des ténèbres; the ~ behind the throne [individual] l'éminence *f* grise, celui *m*/celle *f* qui tire les ficelles; [group] ceux qui tirent les ficelles, les véritables acteurs; the ~s that be *fml* OR *hum* les autorités constituées; 'The Power and the Glory' *Greene* 'la Puissance et la gloire'. -**4.** POL [state] puissance *f*; the great Western ~s les grandes puissances occidentales. -**5.** [ability, capacity] capacité *f*, pouvoir *m*; he has great ~s as an orator OR great oratorical ~s il a de grands talents oratoires; it's within her ~ to do it c'est en son pouvoir, elle est capable de le faire; magical/aphrodisiacal ~s pouvoirs magiques/aphrodisiaques; to have great ~s of persuasion/suggestion avoir un grand pouvoir OR une grande force de persuasion/suggestion; the body's ~s of resistance la capacité de résistance du corps; she has great intellectual ~s elle a de grandes capacités intellectuelles ‖ [faculty] faculté *f*, pouvoir *m*; her ~s are failing ses facultés déclinent; the ~ of sight la vue; the ~ of hearing l'ouïe *f*; he lost the ~ of speech il a perdu l'usage de la parole. -**6.** ELEC [current] courant *m*; to turn on/cut off the ~ mettre/couper le courant. -**7.** ELEC & PHYS [energy] énergie *f*; nuclear/solar ~ énergie nucléaire/solaire. -**8.** JUR [proxy] pouvoir *m*. -**9.** MATH puissance *f*; 5 to the ~ (of) 6 5 puissance 6; raised to the 5th ~ élevé à la puissance 5. -**10.** *phr*: a ~ of good *inf*: the holiday did me a ~ of good les vacances m'ont fait énormément de bien.
◇ *comp* [source, consumption] d'énergie; [cable] électrique; [brakes, steering] assisté; ~ breakfast petit déjeuner *m* d'affaires; ~ dressing *façon de s'habiller qu'adoptent certaines femmes cadres dans le but de projeter une image d'autorité.*
◇ *vt* [give power to] faire fonctionner OR marcher; [propel] propulser; the boat is ~ed by gas turbines le bateau est propulsé par des turbines à gaz; ~ed by solar energy fonctionnant à l'énergie solaire.
◇ *vi* avancer à toute vitesse, foncer; he ~ed into his opponent il fonça sur son adversaire; the leading cars ~ed down the home straight les voitures de tête foncèrent dans la dernière ligne.
◆ **power up** *vt sep* [machine] mettre en marche.

power-assisted *adj* assisté.

power base *n* assise *f* politique.

powerboat ['paʊəbəʊt] *n* [outboard] hors-bord *m inv*; [inboard] vedette *f* (rapide); ~ racing courses *fpl* offshore.

power broker *n* décideur *m* politique.

power cut *n* coupure *f* de courant.

power dive *n* AERON (descente *f* en) piqué *m*.

power drill *n* perceuse *f* électrique.

-powered ['paʊəd] *in cpds*: high/low~ de haute/faible puissance; a high~ executive un cadre très haut placé; steam/wind~ mû par la vapeur/le vent; jet~ propulsé par un moteur à réaction.

power failure *n* panne *f* de courant.

powerful ['paʊəfʊl] ◇ *adj* -**1.** [strong] puissant; a ~ swimmer un excellent nageur; she has a very ~ voice elle a une voix très puissante; the engine isn't ~ enough le moteur n'est pas assez puissant; ~ binoculars jumelles puissantes OR à fort grossissement; there was a ~ smell of fish il y avait une forte odeur de poisson; a ~ kick un violent coup de pied; ~ drugs médication *f* puissante OR active; she has a ~ imagination elle a une imagination débordante; he has been a ~ influence in her life il a exercé une influence décisive dans sa vie. -**2.** [influential - person] fort, influent; [- country, firm] puissant.
◇ *adv inf Br* vachement; to try ~ hard faire un effort surhumain.

powerfully ['paʊəfʊlɪ] *adv* puissamment; he's ~ built il est d'une stature imposante.

power game *n* lutte *f* d'influence, course *f* au pouvoir.

powerhouse ['paʊəhaʊs, *pl* -haʊzɪz] *n* -**1.** ELEC centrale *f* électrique. -**2.** *fig* [person] personne *f* énergique, locomotive *f*; she's a ~ of energy elle déborde d'énergie ‖ [place] pépinière *f*; the university became a ~ of new ideas l'université est devenue une vraie pépinière d'idées nouvelles.

powerless ['paʊəlɪs] *adj* impuissant, désarmé; they were ~ to prevent the scandal ils n'ont rien pu faire pour éviter le scandale; our arguments were ~ in the face of such conviction nos arguments sont restés lettre morte devant une telle conviction.

powerlessly ['paʊəlɪslɪ] *adv* sans pouvoir rien faire; I watched ~ as the dogs attacked j'ai regardé, impuissant, les chiens attaquer.

powerlessness ['paʊəlɪsnɪs] *n* impuissance *f*.

power line *n* ligne *f* à haute tension.

power of attorney *n* JUR procuration *f*.

power pack *n* ELEC bloc *m* d'alimentation.

power plant *n* -**1.** [factory] centrale *f* électrique. -**2.** [generator] groupe *m* électrogène. -**3.** [engine] groupe *m* moteur.

power play *n* [in ice hockey] coup *m* de force.

power point *n* prise *f* de courant.

power politics *n (U)* politique *f* du coup de force.

power set *n* MATH ensemble *m* des sous-ensembles.

power sharing [-ʃeərɪŋ] *n* POL partage *m* du pouvoir.

power station *n* centrale *f* (électrique).

power steering *n* direction *f* assistée.

power structure *n* [system] hiérarchie *f*, répartition *f* des pouvoirs; [people with power] *ensemble des personnes qui détiennent le pouvoir.*

power tool *n* outil *m* électrique.

powwow ['paʊwaʊ] ◇ *n* [of American Indians] assemblée *f*; *fig* & *hum* [meeting] réunion *f*; [discussion] discussion *f*, pourparlers *mpl*; to have OR to hold a ~ discuter.
◇ *vi inf* discuter.

pox *inf* [pɒks] *n* vérole *f*; a ~ on him! *arch* qu'il aille au diable!

poxy▽ ['pɒksɪ] (*compar* poxier, *superl* poxiest) *adj* -**1.** MED vérolé. -**2.** *Br* [lousy] merdique.

Poznan ['pɒznən] *pr n* Poznan.

pp (*written abbr of* per procurationem) pp.

p & p *written abbr of* postage and packing.

PPE (*abbr of* philosophy, politics, and economics) *n Br philosophie, science politique et science économique (cours à l'université).*

ppm (*abbr of* parts per million) ppm.

PPS ◇ *n Br abbr of* parliamentary private secretary.
◇ (*written abbr of* post postscriptum) PPS.

ppsi (*abbr of* pounds per square inch) *livres au pouce carré (mesure de pression)*.

PQ *written abbr of* Province of Quebec.

Pr. (*written abbr of* prince) Pce.

PR ◇ *n* -**1.** *abbr of* proportional representation. -**2.** *abbr of* public relations.
◇ *written abbr of* Puerto Rico.

practicability [,præktɪkə'bɪlətɪ] *n* -**1.** [of plan, action] faisabilité *f*, viabilité *f*; **we discussed the ~ of the project** nous avons discuté de la viabilité du projet. -**2.** [of road] praticabilité *f*.

practicable ['præktɪkəbl] *adj* -**1.** [feasible] réalisable, praticable; [possible] possible; **as far as ~** autant que possible, autant que faire se peut. -**2.** [road] praticable.

practical ['præktɪkl] ◇ *adj* -**1.** [convenient, easy to use] pratique, commode; **this electric screwdriver is very ~** ce tournevis électrique est très pratique. -**2.** [sensible, commonsense - person] (qui a le sens) pratique, doué de sens pratique; [- mind, suggestion] pratique; **my sister's the ~ one** s'il y a quelqu'un qui a le sens pratique, c'est bien ma sœur; **now, be ~, we can't afford a new car** allons, un peu de bon sens, nous n'avons pas les moyens de nous offrir une nouvelle voiture; **is white the most ~ colour?** le blanc, c'est ce qu'il y a de plus pratique comme couleur? -**3.** [training, experience, question] pratique, concret; **does it have any ~ application?** est-ce qu'il y a une application pratique?; **for all ~ purposes** à toutes fins utiles; **he has a ~ knowledge of German** il connaît l'allemand usuel ❑ **~ nurse** *Am* aide-soignant *m*, -e *f*. -**4.** [virtual]: **it's a ~ impossibility** c'est pratiquement impossible.
◇ *n Br* SCH & UNIV [class] travaux *mpl* pratiques, TP *mpl*; [exam] épreuve *f* pratique.

practicality [,præktɪ'kælətɪ] (*pl* **practicalities**) *n* [of person] sens *m* pratique; [of ideas] nature *f* pratique; **I'm not too sure about the ~ of his suggestions** je doute que ses propositions puissent trouver une application pratique.
◆ **practicalities** *npl* [details] détails *mpl* pratiques; **let's get down to practicalities** venons-en aux détails pratiques.

practical joke *n* farce *f*; **to play a ~ on sb** faire une farce OR jouer un tour à qqn.

practical joker *n* farceur *m*, -euse *f*.

practically ['præktɪklɪ] *adv* -**1.** [sensibly] de manière pratique; **she very ~ suggested telephoning home** elle a eu la bonne idée de suggérer qu'on téléphone chez elle; **to be ~ dressed** être habillé de façon pratique. -**2.** [based on practice] pratiquement; **the whole course is very much ~ based** le cours est fondé en grande partie sur la pratique. -**3.** [almost] presque, pratiquement; **~ alone/finished** pratiquement seul/terminé. -**4.** [in practice] dans la pratique; **~ speaking** en fait.

practicalness ['præktɪklnɪs] = **practicality**.

practice ['præktɪs] ◇ *n* -**1.** [habit] pratique *f*, habitude *f*; [custom] pratique *f*, coutume *f*, usage *m*; **tribal/religious ~s** pratiques tribales/religieuses; **they make a regular ~ of going jogging on Sundays** ils font régulièrement du jogging le dimanche; **he makes a ~ of voting against** OR **he makes it a ~ to vote against the government** il se fait une règle de voter contre le gouvernement; **they've introduced the ~ of morning prayer** ils ont introduit la prière du matin; **it's not company ~ to refund deposits** il n'est pas dans les habitudes de la société de rembourser les arrhes; **it's normal ~ among most shopkeepers** c'est une pratique courante chez les commerçants; **it's our usual ~** c'est ce que nous faisons habituellement, c'est notre politique habituelle; **it's standard ~ to make a written request** la procédure habituelle veut que l'on fasse une demande par écrit. -**2.** [exercise - of profession, archery, witchcraft] pratique *f*. -**3.** [training] entraînement *m*; [rehearsal] répétition *f*; [study - of instrument] étude *f*, travail *m*; **I've had a lot of ~ at** OR **in dealing with difficult negotiations** j'ai une grande habitude des négociations difficiles; **it's good ~ for your interview** c'est un bon entraînement pour votre entrevue; **to be in ~** être bien entraîné; **to be out of ~** manquer d'entraînement; **I'm getting out of ~** [on piano] je commence à avoir les doigts rouillés; [at sport] je commence à manquer d'entraînement; [at skill] je commence à perdre la main; **it's time for your piano ~** c'est l'heure de travailler ton piano ❑ **fire ~** exercice *m* d'incendie; **~ makes perfect** *prov* c'est en forgeant qu'on devient forgeron *prov*. -**4.** [training session] (séance *f* d') entraînement *m*; [rehearsal - of choir] répétition *f*. -**5.** [practical application] pratique *f*; **to put sthg in** OR **into ~** mettre qqch en pratique; **in ~** dans la pratique. -**6.** [professional activity] exercice *m*; **to be in ~ as a doctor** exercer en tant que médecin; **to go into** OR **to set up in ~ as a doctor** s'installer comme médecin, ouvrir un cabinet de médecin ❑ **medical/legal ~** l'exercice de la médecine/de la profession d'avocat. -**7.** [office, surgery] cabinet *m*; [clientele] clientèle *f*; **he has a country ~** il est médecin de campagne.
◇ *vt* & *vi* *Am* = **practise**.
◇ *comp* [game, run, session] d'entraînement.

practiced *Am* = **practised**.

practicing *Am* = **practising**.

practise *Br*, **practice** *Am* ['præktɪs] ◇ *vt* -**1.** [for improvement - musical instrument] s'exercer à, travailler; [- song] travailler, répéter; [- foreign language] travailler, s'exercer à parler; SPORT [- stroke, shot] travailler; **to ~ one's scales** faire ses gammes; **she was practising a Chopin nocturne** elle travaillait un nocturne de Chopin; **can I ~ my French on you?** est-ce que je peux parler français OR pratiquer mon français avec vous?; **to ~ speaking French** s'entraîner à parler français; **you'll be able to ~ your Spanish in Madrid** à Madrid, vous pourrez en profiter pour pratiquer votre espagnol; **you should ~ your backhand** vous devriez travailler votre revers. -**2.** [put into practice - principle, virtue] pratiquer, mettre en pratique; **in this school, we ~ self-discipline** dans cette école, on pratique l'autodiscipline; **you should ~ what you preach** vous devriez donner l'exemple; **he doesn't ~ what he preaches** il ne met pas en pratique ce qu'il prêche. -**3.** [profession] exercer, pratiquer; **he ~s medicine** il pratique OR exerce la médecine. -**4.** [inflict] infliger; **the cruelty they ~d on their victims** les cruautés qu'ils infligeaient à OR les sévices qu'ils faisaient subir à leurs victimes. -**5.** [customs, beliefs] observer, pratiquer; **pagan rituals are still ~d in the area** on pratique encore certains rites païens dans la région. -**6.** RELIG pratiquer. -**7.** [magic] pratiquer.
◇ *vi* -**1.** [gen & MUS] s'entraîner, s'exercer; SPORT s'entraîner; **I'm just practising** je ne fais que m'entraîner; **she ~s a few hours every day** elle s'entraîne plusieurs heures par jour; **to ~ on the guitar** faire des exercices à la guitare. -**2.** [professionally] exercer; **he ~s in Edinburgh** il exerce à Édimbourg. -**3.** RELIG être pratiquant.

practised *Br*, **practiced** *Am* ['præktɪst] *adj* -**1.** [experienced] expérimenté, chevronné; [skilled] habile. -**2.** [expert - aim, movement] expert; [- ear, eye] exercé. -**3.** [artificial - smile, charm] factice, étudié.

practising *Br*, **practicing** *Am* ['præktɪsɪŋ] *adj* -**1.** RELIG pratiquant; **he's a ~ Jew** c'est un juif pratiquant. -**2.** [professionally - doctor] exerçant; [- lawyer, solicitor] en exercice. -**3.** [homosexual] actif.

practitioner [præk'tɪʃnəʳ] *n* -**1.** MED: **(medical) ~** médecin *m*. -**2.** [gen] praticien *m*, -enne *f*.

praesidium [prɪ'sɪdɪəm] = **presidium**.

praetorian [prɪ'tɔːrɪən] *adj* prétorien; **~ guard** HIST & *fig* garde *f* prétorienne.

pragmatic [præg'mætɪk] *adj* pragmatique; **~ sanction** pragmatique sanction *f*, pragmatique *f*.

pragmatics [præg'mætɪks] *n (U)* LING pragmatique *f*.

pragmatism ['prægmətɪzm] *n* pragmatisme *m*.

pragmatist ['prægmətɪst] *n* pragmatiste *mf*.

Prague [prɑːg] *pr n* Prague.

prairie ['preərɪ] *n* plaine *f* (herbeuse).
◆ **Prairie** *pr n*: **the Prairie** OR **Prairies** [in US] la Grande Prairie; [in Canada] les Prairies *fpl*.

prairie chicken *n* cupidon *m* des prairies.

prairie dog *n* chien *m* de prairie.

prairie oyster *n* *boisson à base d'œuf cru (remède contre les excès d'alcool)*.

Prairie Provinces *pl pr n*: **the ~** les Provinces *fpl* des Prairies *(au Canada)*; **in the ~** dans les Provinces des Prairies.

Prairie State *pr n* Illinois *m*.

prairie wolf *n* coyote *m*.

praise [preɪz] ◇ *n* -**1.** [compliments] éloge *m*, louanges *fpl*; **she was full of ~ for their kindness** elle ne tarissait pas d'éloges sur leur gentillesse; **he was full of our ~** OR **~s** il ne tarissait pas d'éloges sur notre compte; **we have nothing but ~ for the way in which he handled the matter** nous ne pouvons que le féliciter de la façon OR nous n'avons que des éloges à lui faire pour la façon dont il s'est occupé de l'affaire; **her latest film has received high ~ from the critics** son dernier film a été couvert d'éloges par la critique; **it is beyond ~** on ne saurait être trop élogieux. -**2.** RELIG louange *f*, louanges *fpl*, gloire *f*; **to give ~ to the Lord** rendre gloire à Dieu; **~ (be to) the Lord!** Dieu soit loué!; **~ be!** *fig* & *dated* Dieu merci!; **hymn** OR **song of ~** cantique *m*.
◇ *vt* -**1.** louer, faire l'éloge de; **he ~d her for her patience** il la loua de OR pour sa patience; **he ~d her for having been so patient** il la loua d'avoir été si patiente; **to ~ sb to high heaven** OR **to the skies** couvrir qqn d'éloges, porter qqn aux nues. -**2.** RELIG louer, glorifier, rendre gloire à.
◆ **in praise of** *prep phr*: **the director spoke in ~ of his staff** le directeur fit l'éloge de son personnel; **she gave a speech in ~ of the institute's work** elle fit un discours élogieux sur les travaux de l'institut.

praiseworthiness ['preɪz,wɜːðɪnɪs] *n* mérite *m*.

praiseworthy ['preɪz,wɜːðɪ] *adj* [person] digne d'éloges; [action, intention, sentiment] louable, méritoire.

praline ['prɑːliːn] *n* praline *f*.

pram [præm] *n* -**1.** *Br* [for baby] voiture *f* d'enfant, landau *m*. -**2.** NAUT prame *f*.

PRAM [præm] (*abbr of* programmable random access memory) *n* RAM *f* programmable.

prance [prɑːns] ◇ *vi* -**1.** [cavort - horse] caracoler, cabrioler; [- person] caracoler, gambader; **the horses came prancing into the circus ring** les chevaux sont entrés en caracolant sur la piste du cirque. -**2.** [strut] se pavaner, se dandiner; **he came prancing into the room** il entra dans la pièce en se pavanant.
◇ *n* sautillement *m*.

prang *inf* [præŋ] ◇ *vt Br* [car] esquinter; [plane] bousiller.
◇ *n*: **he had a ~** [in car] il a eu un accident (de voiture) OR un accrochage; [in plane] son avion s'est planté.

prank [præŋk] *n* farce *f*, tour *m*; **to play a ~ on sb** jouer un tour OR faire une farce à qqn; **it's only a childish ~** c'est seulement une gaminerie; **they used to get up to all kinds of ~s when they were at school** ils faisaient toutes sortes de farces quand ils étaient à l'école.

prankster ['præŋkstəʳ] *n* farceur *m*, -euse *f*; **he's a little ~** c'est un petit farceur OR polisson.

praseodymium [,preɪzɪəʊ'dɪmɪəm] *n* praséodyme *m*.

prat▽ [præt] *n Br* couillon *m*.

prate [preɪt] *vi dated* & *pej* jacasser, bavarder; **they're always prating on about their holidays** ils n'en finissent pas de raconter leurs vacances.

pratfall *inf* ['prætfɔːl] *n* [fall] gadin *m*, pelle *f*; [blunder] gaffe *f*.

prattle *inf* ['prætl] *Br pej* ◇ *vi* [babble] babiller, jacasser; **she ~s away** OR **on about her chil-**

dren for hours elle radote pendant des heures au sujet de ses enfants || [converse] papoter; they're forever prattling on about politics ils sont toujours à discutailler politique.
◇ *n* [babble] babillage *m*; [conversation] papotage *m*, bavardage *m*.

prawn [prɔːn] *n* crevette *f* (rose), bouquet *m*.

prawn cocktail *n* cocktail *m* de crevettes.

praxis ['præksɪs] (*pl* praxes [-siːz]) *n fml* pratique *f*.

pray [preɪ] ◇ *vi* prier; let us ~ to God for guidance prions Dieu de nous guider; to ~ for sb/for sb's soul prier pour qqn/pour l'âme de qqn; to ~ over sb's grave prier sur la tombe de qqn; she ~ed to God to save her child elle pria Dieu qu'il sauve son enfant; he ~s for release from pain il prie pour que ses souffrances prennent fin; she's past ~ing for [will die] elle est perdue; the country is past ~ing for at this stage il n'y a plus d'espoir pour le pays à ce stade; to ~ for rain prier pour qu'il pleuve; let's just ~ for fine weather espérons qu'il fasse beau.
◇ *vt* -**1.** RELIG: she ~ed God he might live elle pria Dieu pour qu'il vive; we ~ the rain will stop nous prions pour que la pluie cesse; I just ~ he doesn't come back je prie Dieu OR le ciel (pour) qu'il ne revienne pas. -**2.** *arch* OR *fml* [request] prier; to ~ sb to do sthg prier qqn de faire qqch; I ~ you je vous (en) prie.
◇ *interj arch* OR *fml*: ~ be seated asseyez-vous, je vous en prie; ~, do tell me dites-le-moi, je vous (en) prie.

prayer [preəʳ] *n* -**1.** RELIG prière *f*; to be at ~ être en prière, prier; to kneel in ~ prier à genoux, s'agenouiller pour prier; they believe he can be made well through ~ ils croient qu'on peut le guérir par la prière; to say a ~ for sb dire une prière pour qqn; to say one's ~s faire sa prière; remember me in your ~s pensez à moi OR ne m'oubliez pas dans vos prières; her ~ was answered sa prière fut exaucée ☐ he doesn't have a ~ *inf* il n'a pas la moindre chance OR l'ombre d'une chance. -**2.** [wish] souhait *m*; it is my earnest ~ that you will succeed j'espère de tout cœur que vous réussirez, je souhaite sincèrement que vous réussissiez.
◆ **prayers** *npl* [at church] office *m* (divin), prière *f*; *Br* SCH prière *f* du matin.

prayer beads *n* chapelet *m*.

prayer book *n* bréviaire *m*.

prayer mat *n* tapis *m* de prière.

prayer meeting *n* réunion *f* de prière.

prayer rug = **prayer mat**.

prayer shawl *n* talith *m*, tallith *m*.

prayer wheel *n* moulin *m* à prières.

praying mantis ['preɪɪŋ-] *n* mante *f* religieuse.

preach [priːtʃ] ◇ *vi* -**1.** RELIG prêcher; to ~ to sb prêcher qqn; to ~ to the converted prêcher un converti. -**2.** [lecture] prêcher, sermonner; stop ~ing at me! arrête tes sermons OR de me faire la leçon!
◇ *vt* -**1.** RELIG prêcher; to ~ a sermon prêcher, faire un sermon. -**2.** *fig* [recommend] prêcher, prôner.

preacher ['priːtʃəʳ] *n* [gen] prédicateur *m*; *esp Am* [minister] pasteur *m*.

preachify *inf* ['priːtʃɪfaɪ] (*pt* preachified, *pp* preachified) *vi pej* faire la morale.

preaching ['priːtʃɪŋ] *n* (*U*) [sermon] prédication *f*; *pej* [moralizing] sermons *mpl*.

preachy *inf* ['priːtʃɪ] (*compar* preachier, *superl* preachiest) *adj pej* prêcheur, sermonneur.

preamble [priː'æmbl] *n* préambule *m*; Preamble to the Constitution Préambule *m* de la Constitution des États-Unis.

preamplifier [priː'æmplɪfaɪəʳ] *n* préamplificateur *m*.

prearrange [ˌpriːə'reɪndʒ] *vt* fixer OR régler à l'avance; at a ~d time à une heure fixée à l'avance OR au préalable.

prebend ['prebənd] *n* prébende *f*.

prebendary ['prebəndrɪ] (*pl* prebendaries) *n* prébendier *m*.

Precambrian [ˌpriː'kæmbrɪən] ◇ *n* précambrien *m*.
◇ *adj* précambrien.

precancerous [ˌpriː'kænsərəs] *adj* précancéreux.

precarious [prɪ'keərɪəs] *adj* précaire.

precariously [prɪ'keərɪəslɪ] *adv* précairement; ~ balanced en équilibre précaire.

precariousness [prɪ'keərɪəsnɪs] *n* précarité *f*.

precast [ˌpriː'kɑːst] *adj* [concrete element] préfabriqué.

precaution [prɪ'kɔːʃn] *n* précaution *f*; as a ~ par précaution; to take ~s prendre des précautions; she took the ~ of informing her solicitor elle prit la précaution d'avertir son avocat; fire ~s mesures *fpl* de prévention contre l'incendie.

precautionary [prɪ'kɔːʃənərɪ] *adj* de précaution; as a ~ measure par mesure de précaution; to take ~ measures OR steps against sthg prendre des mesures préventives contre qqch.

precede [prɪ'siːd] *vt* -**1.** [in order, time] précéder; during the minutes preceding the operation pendant les minutes précédant l'opération. -**2.** [in importance, rank] avoir la préséance sur, prendre le pas sur. -**3.** [preface] (faire) précéder.

precedence ['presɪdəns], **precedency** ['presɪdənsɪ] *n* (*U*) -**1.** [priority] priorité *f*; to take OR to have ~ over sthg avoir la priorité sur qqch; her health must take ~ over all other considerations sa santé doit passer avant toute autre considération. -**2.** [in rank, status] préséance *f*; to have OR to take ~ over sb avoir la préséance OR prendre le pas sur qqn.

precedent ['presɪdənt] ◇ *n* -**1.** JUR précédent *m*, jurisprudence *f*; to set a ~ faire jurisprudence; there is no ~ il n'y a pas de jurisprudence; to follow a ~ s'appuyer sur un précédent, suivre la jurisprudence. -**2.** [example case] précédent *m*; to create OR to set OR to establish a ~ créer un précédent; without ~ sans précédent. -**3.** [tradition] tradition *f*; the college has broken with ~ by electing a woman president le collège a rompu avec la tradition en élisant une femme à la présidence.
◇ *adj* précédent.

precedented ['presɪdəntɪd] *adj* ayant (un) précédent.

preceding [prɪ'siːdɪŋ] *adj* précédent; the ~ day le jour précédent, la veille; the ~ evening le soir précédent, la veille au soir; on the ~ page à la page précédente; the ~ week/year la semaine/l'année précédente.

precentor [prɪ'sentəʳ] *n* préchantre *m*.

precept ['priːsept] *n* précepte *m*.

preceptor [prɪ'septəʳ] *n* précepteur *m*, -trice *f*.

precession [prɪ'seʃn] *n* précession *f*; ~ of the equinoxes précession des équinoxes.

precinct ['priːsɪŋkt] *n* -**1.** [area - round castle, cathedral] enceinte *f*; [- for pedestrians, shopping] zone *f*, quartier *m*; within the castle ~s dans l'enceinte du château. -**2.** [boundary] pourtour *m*; the question falls within the ~s of philosophy la question est du domaine OR relève de la philosophie. -**3.** *Am* ADMIN arrondissement *m*, circonscription *f* administrative; 7th ~ 7ᵉ arrondissement; ~ police police *f* de quartier OR d'arrondissement; ~ station commissariat *m* de quartier OR d'arrondissement. -**4.** *Am* POL circonscription *f* électorale.
◆ **precincts** *npl* environs *mpl*, alentours *mpl*; somewhere in the ~s quelque part dans les environs OR alentours.

preciosity [ˌpresɪ'ɒsətɪ] *n* préciosité *f*.

precious ['preʃəs] ◇ *adj* -**1.** [jewel, material, object] précieux, de grande valeur; the world's most ~ resources les ressources les plus précieuses de la planète. -**2.** [friend, friendship, moment] précieux; my time is ~ mon temps est précieux; the ambulance lost ~ minutes in a traffic jam l'ambulance a perdu des minutes précieuses dans un embouteillage. -**3.** [affected - style, person] précieux. -**4.** *inf* [expressing irritation]: I don't want your ~ advice je ne veux pas de vos fichus conseils; here's your ~ book! le voilà ton sacré livre!
◇ *adv inf* très; there's ~ little chance of that happening il y a bien peu OR très peu de chances (pour) que cela se produise; ~ few of them turned up il y en a très peu qui sont venus.
◇ *n*: my ~ mon trésor.

precious metal *n* métal *m* précieux.

precious stone *n* pierre *f* précieuse.

precipice ['presɪpɪs] *n literal* précipice *m*; *fig* catastrophe *f*; the car fell over the ~ la voiture est tombée dans le précipice.

precipitance [prɪ'sɪpɪtəns], **precipitancy** [prɪ'sɪpɪtənsɪ] *n* précipitation *f*.

precipitant [prɪ'sɪpɪtənt] ◇ *adj* précipité, hâtif.
◇ *n* précipitant *m*.

precipitate [*vb* & *n* prɪ'sɪpɪteɪt, *adj* prɪ'sɪpɪtət]
◇ *vt* -**1.** [downfall, ruin, crisis] précipiter, hâter. -**2.** [person, vehicle, object] précipiter. -**3.** CHEM précipiter.
◇ *vi* -**1.** CHEM se précipiter. -**2.** METEOR se condenser.
◇ *n* précipité *m*.
◇ *adj* -**1.** [hasty - action] précipité; [- decision, judgment] hâtif; [- remark] irréfléchi. -**2.** [steep] abrupt, à pic.

precipitately [prɪ'sɪpɪtətlɪ] *adv* précipitamment, avec précipitation.

precipitation [prɪˌsɪpɪ'teɪʃn] *n* (*U*) -**1.** [haste] précipitation *f*. -**2.** CHEM précipitation *f*. -**3.** METEOR précipitations *fpl*.

precipitous [prɪ'sɪpɪtəs] *adj* -**1.** [steep - cliff] à pic, escarpé; [- road, stairs] raide; [- fall] à pic. -**2.** [hasty] précipité.

precipitously [prɪ'sɪpɪtəslɪ] *adv* -**1.** [steeply] à pic, abruptement. -**2.** [hastily] précipitamment.

précis [*Br* 'preɪsiː, *Am* 'preɪsiː] (*pl inv* [*Br* -siːz, *Am* pre'siːz]) ◇ *n* précis *m*, résumé *m*; ~ writing compte rendu *m* de lecture.
◇ *vt* faire un résumé de.

precise [prɪ'saɪs] *adj* -**1.** [exact - amount, detail] précis; [- location] exact; [- pronunciation] exact, juste; eleven, to be ~ onze, pour être précis; be more ~! soyez plus précis!; he was very ~ in his description il a donné une description très précise OR détaillée; at that ~ moment à ce moment précis. -**2.** [meticulous - person, manner, mind, movement] précis, méticuleux. -**3.** *pej* [fussy] pointilleux, maniaque.

precisely [prɪ'saɪslɪ] ◇ *adv* [exactly - explain] précisément, exactement; [measure] précisément, avec précision; that describes it ~ c'est exactement cela; that's ~ the reason (why) I'm not going c'est précisément pourquoi je n'y vais pas; she speaks very ~ elle s'exprime avec beaucoup de précision; at 4 o'clock ~ à 4 h précises.
◇ *interj* précisément, exactement; do you think it's too risky? – ~! pensez-vous que ce soit trop risqué? – tout à fait! OR exactement!

preciseness [prɪ'saɪsnɪs] *n* précision *f*.

precision [prɪ'sɪʒn] ◇ *n* précision *f*.
◇ *comp* [instrument, engineering, tool, bombing] de précision.

preclude [prɪ'kluːd] *vt fml* exclure, prévenir; this rule ~s any possibility of a misunderstanding cette règle exclut toute possibilité de malentendu; the crisis ~s her (from) going to Moscow la crise rend impossible son départ pour Moscou OR la met dans l'impossibilité de partir pour Moscou; we were ~d from making any further progress on ne pouvait plus faire de nouveaux progrès.

precocious [prɪ'kəʊʃəs] *adj* précoce.

precociously [prɪ'kəʊʃəslɪ] *adv* précocement, avec précocité.

precociousness [prɪ'kəʊʃəsnɪs], **precocity** [prɪ'kɒsətɪ] *n* précocité *f*.

precognition [ˌpriːkɒg'nɪʃn] *n* [gift] prescience *f*, don *m* de seconde vue; [knowledge] connaissance *f* préalable.

pre-Columbian [ˌpriːkə'lʌmbɪən] *adj* précolombien.

precombustion [ˌpriːkəmˈbʌstʃn] *n* précombustion *f*.

preconceived [ˌpriːkənˈsiːvd] *adj* préconçu; ~ idea idée *f* préconçue.

preconception [ˌpriːkənˈsepʃn] *n* préconception *f*, idée *f* préconçue.

precondition [ˌpriːkənˈdɪʃn] ◇ *n* condition *f* préalable, condition *f* sine qua non; a university degree is a ~ for a diplomatic career il est impossible de faire carrière dans la diplomatie si l'on n'a pas un diplôme universitaire.
◇ *vt* conditionner.

precook [priːˈkʊk] *vt* précuire.

precooked [priːˈkʊkt] *adj* précuit.

precool [priːˈkuːl] *vt* préréfrigérer.

precursor [ˌpriːˈkɜːsəʳ] *n* [person] précurseur *m*; [event] signe *m* avant-coureur; the ~ of the modern computer l'ancêtre de l'ordinateur d'aujourd'hui; the stock exchange crash was a ~ to worldwide recession le krach boursier fut le signe précurseur de la récession à l'échelle mondiale.

precursory [ˌpriːˈkɜːsərɪ] *adj* -**1.** [anticipatory] précurseur, annonciateur. -**2.** [introductory] préliminaire, préalable.

predaceous, predacious [prɪˈdeɪʃəs] *adj* prédateur.

predate [priːˈdeɪt] *vt* -**1.** [give earlier date to - cheque] antidater; [- historical event] attribuer une date antérieure à. -**2.** [precede] être antérieur à.

predator [ˈpredətəʳ] *n* -**1.** [animal, bird] prédateur *m*. -**2.** *fig* [person] rapace *m*.

predatory [ˈpredətrɪ] *adj* -**1.** [animal, bird] prédateur. -**2.** *fig* [gen - person, instinct] rapace; [- attacker] pillard; the ~ world of advertising le milieu rapace de la publicité.

predecease [ˌpriːdɪˈsiːs] *vt* mourir avant.

predecessor [ˈpriːdɪsesəʳ] *n* [person, model] prédécesseur *m*; [event] précédent *m*.

predestination [priːˌdestɪˈneɪʃn] *n* prédestination *f*.

predestine [ˌpriːˈdestɪn] *vt* prédestiner; it was as if they were ~d to lose on aurait dit qu'ils étaient prédestinés à perdre.

predetermination [ˈpriːdɪˌtɜːmɪˈneɪʃn] *n* prédétermination *f*.

predetermine [ˌpriːdɪˈtɜːmɪn] *vt* prédéterminer.

predetermined [ˌpriːdɪˈtɜːmɪnd] *adj* déterminé; at a ~ date à une date déterminée OR arrêtée d'avance.

predeterminer [ˌpriːdɪˈtɜːmɪnəʳ] *n* préarticle *m*, prédéterminant *m*.

predicable [ˈpredɪkəbl] ◇ *adj* prédicable.
◇ *n* prédicable *m*.

predicament [prɪˈdɪkəmənt] *n* situation *f* difficile OR malencontreuse; to be in a ~ être dans une situation difficile; we'll have to find some way out of this ~ il va nous falloir trouver un moyen de nous sortir de ce guêpier.

predicate [*vb* ˈpredɪkeɪt, *n* & *adj* ˈpredɪkət] ◇ *vt fml* -**1.** [state] affirmer. -**2.** [base]: to ~ one's arguments/policy on sthg fonder ses arguments/sa politique sur qqch.
◇ *n* prédicat *m*.
◇ *adj* prédicatif.

predicate calculus *n* calcul *m* fonctionnel.

predicative [prɪˈdɪkətɪv] *adj* prédicatif.

predict [prɪˈdɪkt] *vt* prédire; she ~ed that he would have a long life elle a prédit qu'il vivrait longtemps; the weathermen are ~ing rain les météorologues annoncent de la pluie.

predictability [prɪˌdɪktəˈbɪlətɪ] *n* prévisibilité *f*.

predictable [prɪˈdɪktəbl] *adj* prévisible; the outcome was ~ le résultat était prévisible; you're so ~! *pej* tu es tellement prévisible!

predictably [prɪˈdɪktəblɪ] *adv* [behave] de manière prévisible; ~, she forgot to tell him comme on pouvait le prévoir OR comme on pouvait s'y attendre, elle a oublié de le lui dire.

prediction [prɪˈdɪkʃn] *n* [gen] prévision *f*; [supernatural] prédiction *f*.

predictive [prɪˈdɪktɪv] *adj* prophétique.

predictor [prɪˈdɪktəʳ] *n* -**1.** [prophet] prophète *m*. -**2.** [in statistics] variable *f* indépendante.

predigested [ˌpriːdaɪˈdʒestɪd] *adj* prédigéré.

predilection [ˌpriːdɪˈlekʃn] *n* prédilection *f*; to have a ~ for sthg avoir une prédilection OR un faible pour qqch.

predispose [ˌpriːdɪsˈpəʊz] *vt* prédisposer; to be ~d to do sthg être prédisposé à faire qqch; I was not ~d in his favour je n'étais pas prédisposé en sa faveur.

predisposition [ˈpriːˌdɪspəˈzɪʃn] *n* prédisposition *f*; to have a ~ to OR towards sthg avoir une prédisposition à qqch.

predominance [prɪˈdɒmɪnəns], **predominancy** [prɪˈdɒmɪnənsɪ] *n* prédominance *f*; with a ~ of red shades avec une prédominance de rouges.

predominant [prɪˈdɒmɪnənt] *adj* prédominant.

predominantly [prɪˈdɒmɪnəntlɪ] *adv* principalement; the population is ~ English-speaking la population est majoritairement anglophone.

predominate [prɪˈdɒmɪneɪt] *vi* -**1.** [be greater in number] prédominer; males still ~ over females in industry les hommes continuent à être plus nombreux que les femmes dans l'industrie. -**2.** [prevail] prédominer, prévaloir, l'emporter; a sense of apathy ~d at the meeting lors de la réunion, un sentiment d'apathie a prédominé.

pre-eminence *n* prééminence *f*.

pre-eminent *adj* prééminent.

pre-eminently *adv* de façon prépondérante, avant tout; the reasons are ~ economic les raisons sont avant tout économiques.

pre-empt [ˌpriːˈempt] ◇ *vt* -**1.** [plan, decision] anticiper, devancer; the Prime Minister's decision ~ed their plans for social reform la décision du Premier ministre a devancé leurs projets de réforme sociale. -**2.** [land, property] acquérir par (droit de) préemption.
◇ *vi* [in bridge] faire une enchère de barrage.

pre-emption [ˌpriːˈempʃn] *n* préemption *f*.

pre-emptive [ˌpriːˈemptɪv] *adj* [right] de préemption; [strike] préventif; ~ bid [in bridge] (enchère *f* de) barrage *m*.

preen [priːn] *vt* -**1.** [plumage] lisser; the bird was ~ing its feathers OR was ~ing itself l'oiseau se lissait les plumes; to ~ o.s. *fig* se faire beau, se pomponner. -**2.** [pride]: to ~ o.s. on sthg s'enorgueillir de qqch; he ~ed himself on his success il s'enorgueillissait OR tirait fierté de son succès.

pre-establish *vt* préétablir.

preexist [ˌpriːɪgˈzɪst] *vt* préexister à.

pre-existence *n* préexistence *f*.

pre-existent *adj* préexistant.

prefab *inf* [ˈpriːfæb] *n* (bâtiment *m*) préfabriqué *m*; they live in a ~ ils habitent une maison préfabriquée.

prefabricate [ˌpriːˈfæbrɪkeɪt] *vt* préfabriquer.

prefabricated [ˌpriːˈfæbrɪkeɪtɪd] *adj*: ~ houses maisons *fpl* en préfabriqué.

preface [ˈprefɪs] ◇ *n* -**1.** [to text] préface *f*, avant-propos *m inv*; [to speech] introduction *f*, préambule *m*. -**2.** RELIG préface *f*.
◇ *vt* [book] préfacer; she ~d the book with a reply to her critics la préface de son livre est une réponse à ses critiques ‖ [speech] faire précéder; he usually ~s his speeches with a joke d'habitude, il commence ses discours par une histoire drôle; I'd like to ~ my lecture by posing this question en guise d'introduction à cette conférence, je voudrais vous soumettre la question suivante.

prefaded [priːˈfeɪdɪd] *adj* [fabric] délavé.

prefatory [ˈprefətrɪ] *adj* [remarks] préliminaire, préalable; [note] liminaire; [page] de préface.

prefect [ˈpriːfekt] *n* -**1.** SCH *élève chargé de la discipline*. -**2.** ADMIN [in France, Italy etc] préfet *m*.

prefecture [ˈpriːfekˌtjʊəʳ] *n* préfecture *f*.

prefer [prɪˈfɜːʳ] *vt* -**1.** préférer, aimer mieux; I - Paris to London je préfère Paris à Londre j'aime mieux Paris que Londres; I much - coffee to tea je préfère de beaucoup OR de loi le café au thé; she ~s living OR to live alone el préfère vivre seule; he ~s to walk rather tha take the bus il préfère marcher plutôt que c prendre le bus; many people ~ watching T to going out OR rather than going out bea coup de gens préfèrent regarder la télévisic plutôt que de sortir; do you mind if I smoke – I'd ~ (that) you didn't cela vous dérange je fume? – j'aimerais mieux que vous ne fassiez pas; I'd ~ you not to go je préférera que vous n'y alliez pas. -**2.** JUR: to ~ charge against sb [civil action] porter plainte cont qqn; [police action] ≃ déférer qqn au parque -**3.** [submit - argument, petition] présenter. -**4.** FI [creditor] privilégier.

preferable [ˈprefrəbl] *adj* préférable; it is ~ t book seats il est préférable de OR il vaut mieu retenir des places.

preferably [ˈprefrəblɪ] *adv* de préférence, pr férablement; come tomorrow, ~ in th evening venez demain, de préférence dans soirée.

preference [ˈprefərəns] *n* -**1.** [liking] préf rence *f*; to have OR to show a ~ for sthg avo une préférence pour qqch; his ~ is for Moza il préfère Mozart; he lives in the country by - il a choisi de vivre à la campagne; in order c ~ par ordre de préférence; they chose the fir candidate in ~ to the second ils ont choisi premier candidat plutôt que le second; what your ~? que préférez-vous? -**2.** [priority] pr férence *f*, priorité *f*; to have OR to be given - over avoir la priorité sur.

preference share *n Br* action *f* privilégiée.

preferential [ˌprefəˈrenʃl] *adj* préférentiel, p vilégié; to get ~ treatment bénéficier d'u traitement de faveur.

preferment [prɪˈfɜːmənt] *n* [gen & RELIG] ava cement *m*, promotion *f*.

preferred [prɪˈfɜːd] *adj* -**1.** [best liked] préfér -**2.** COMM: ~ creditor créancier *m* prioritair

preferred stock *n (U) Am* actions *fpl* privil giées.

prefiguration [priːˌfɪgəˈreɪʃn] *n* préfiguration

prefigure [priːˈfɪgəʳ] *vt* -**1.** [foreshadow] pré gurer. -**2.** [foresee] se figurer OR s'imagin (d'avance).

prefix [ˈpriːfɪks] ◇ *n* préfixe *m*.
◇ *vt* préfixer.

preflight [ˈpriːflaɪt] *adj* préalable au décollag ~ checks vérifications avant décollage.

preformation [ˌpriːfɔːˈmeɪʃn] *n* préfo mation *f*.

prefrontal [ˌpriːˈfrʌntl] *adj* préfrontal.

preggers▽ [ˈpregəz] *adj*: she's ~ elle est e cloque.

pregnable [ˈpregnəbl] *adj* prenable.

pregnancy [ˈpregnənsɪ] (*pl* **pregnancies**) *n* [woman] grossesse *f*; [of animal] gestation *f*.

pregnancy test *n* test *m* de grossesse.

pregnant [ˈpregnənt] *adj* -**1.** [woman] enceint [animal] pleine, grosse; to get OR to become - tomber enceinte; to get a woman ~ faire u enfant à une femme; to be six months ~ êt enceinte de six mois; she was ~ with Bria then à cette époque, elle attendait Brian. -**2.** *f* [pause, silence - with meaning] lourd OR chargé d sens; [- with tension] tendu.

preheat [ˌpriːˈhiːt] *vt* préchauffer.

prehensile [prɪˈhensaɪl] *adj* préhensile.

prehistoric [ˌpriːhɪˈstɒrɪk] *adj literal* & *fig* pr historique.

prehistory [ˌpriːˈhɪstərɪ] *n* préhistoire *f*.

pre-ignition *n* préallumage *m*.

pre-industrial *adj* préindustriel.

prejudge [ˌpriːˈdʒʌdʒ] *vt* [issue, topic] préjug (de); [person] porter un jugement prématu sur.

rejudice ['predʒʊdɪs] ◇ *n* -**1.** [bias] préjugé *m*; to have a ~ against sb/sthg avoir un préjugé contre qqn/qqch; to have a ~ in favour of sb/sthg avoir un préjugé en faveur de qqn/qqch; he's full of ~ il est plein de préjugés; racial ~ préjugés raciaux, racisme *m*; I have a certain ~ in favour of the first solution j'ai une petite préférence pour la première solution; he claims to be without ~ il prétend être sans préjugés. -**2.** [detriment] préjudice *m*, tort *m*; to the ~ of sb's rights au préjudice OR au détriment des droits de qqn; without ~ to your guarantee JUR sans préjudice de votre garantie.
◇ *vt* -**1.** [influence] influencer, prévenir; to ~ sb against/in favour of sthg prévenir qqn contre/en faveur de qqch. -**2.** [jeopardize] compromettre, porter préjudice à, nuire à; his political beliefs ~d his chances ses opinions politiques ont compromis ses chances.

rejudiced ['predʒʊdɪst] *adj* [person] qui a des préjugés OR des idées préconçues; to be ~ against sthg avoir des préjugés contre qqch; let's not be ~ about this essayons de ne pas avoir d'idées préconçues là-dessus; he is racially ~ il est raciste || [opinion] partial, préconçu; her politics are ~ ses idées politiques sont fondées sur des préjugés.

rejudicial [,predʒʊ'dɪʃl] *adj* préjudiciable, nuisible; the government's foreign policy is ~ to world peace la politique étrangère du gouvernement risque de compromettre la paix mondiale.

relacy ['preləsɪ] (*pl* prelacies) *n* -**1.** [office] prélature *f*. -**2.** [prelates generally]: the ~ les prélats *mpl*.

relate ['prelɪt] *n* prélat *m*.

relim *inf* ['priːlɪm] (*abbr of* preliminary exam) *n* examen *m* préliminaire.
◆ **prelims** *npl* [in book] préliminaires *mpl*.

reliminary [prɪ'lɪmɪnərɪ] (*pl* preliminaries)
◇ *adj* préliminaire, préalable; after a few ~ remarks après quelques remarques préliminaires; the ~ stages of the inquiry les étapes préliminaires OR les débuts de l'enquête; ~ to departure *fml*, ~ to leaving *fml* avant le départ, avant de partir; ~ hearing JUR première audience *f*; ~ investigation JUR instruction *f* (d'une affaire).
◇ *n* -**1.** [gen] préliminaire *m*; to go through all the preliminaries passer par tous les préliminaires; as a ~ en guise de préliminaire, au préalable. -**2.** [eliminating contest] épreuve *f* éliminatoire.

reliterate [priː'lɪtərɪt] *adj* [society] ne connaissant pas l'écriture.

relude ['preljuːd] ◇ *n* [gen & MUS] prélude *m*.
◇ *vt* préluder à.

remarital [,priː'mærɪtl] *adj* prénuptial, avant le mariage; ~ sex rapports *mpl* sexuels avant le mariage.

remature ['premə,tjʊə^r] *adj* -**1.** [birth, child] prématuré, avant terme; three months ~ né trois mois avant terme. -**2.** [death, decision, judgment] prématuré; don't you think you're being a bit ~? vous ne trouvez pas que c'est un peu prématuré?

rematurely ['premə,tjʊəlɪ] *adv* prématurément; he was born ~ il est né avant terme; he died ~ il est mort prématurément; to be ~ bald/grey être chauve/avoir les cheveux gris avant l'âge.

remed *inf* ['priːmed] ◇ *adj abbr of* premedical.
◇ *n* -**1.** *abbr of* premedication. -**2.** [student] ≃ étudiant *m*, -e *f* en première année de médecine. -**3.** [studies] ≃ études *fpl* de première année de médecine.

remedical [,priː'medɪkl] *adj* [studies] ≃ de première année de médecine; she's a ~ student ≃ elle est en première année de médecine.

remedication [,priːmedɪ'keɪʃn] *n* prémédication *f*.

remeditate [,priː'medɪteɪt] *vt* préméditer.

remeditated [,priː'medɪteɪtɪd] *adj* prémédité.

premeditation [priː,medɪ'teɪʃn] *n* préméditation *f*; without ~ sans préméditation.

premenstrual [priː'menstrʊəl] *adj* prémenstruel.

premenstrual tension *Br*, **premenstrual syndrome** *Am n* syndrome *m* prémenstruel.

premier ['premjə^r] ◇ *adj* premier, primordial.
◇ *n* Premier ministre *m*.

premiere ['premɪeə^r] ◇ *n* CIN & THEAT première *f*; the film's London/television ~ la première londonienne/télévisée du film.
◇ *vt* donner la première de; the opera was ~d in Paris la première de l'opéra a eu lieu à Paris.

Premier League *pr n championnat anglais de football disputé par les plus grands clubs professionnels.*

premiership ['premjəʃɪp] *n* poste *m* de Premier ministre; during her ~ alors qu'elle était Premier ministre; elected to the ~ choisi comme Premier ministre.

premise ['premɪs] ◇ *n* [hypothesis] prémisse *f*; on the ~ that... en partant du principe que...
◇ *vt fml*: to ~ that poser comme hypothèse que; to be ~d on être fondé sur.

premises ['premɪsɪz] *npl* -**1.** [place] locaux *mpl*, lieux *mpl*; business ~ locaux commerciaux; on the ~ sur les lieux, sur place; to vacate the ~ quitter OR libérer les lieux. -**2.** JUR préalable *m*.

premiss ['premɪs] = **premise**.

premium ['priːmjəm] ◇ *n* -**1.** [insurance payment] prime *f* (d'assurance). -**2.** [bonus, extra cost] prime *f*; exchange ~ ST. EX prime de change; fresh fruit is (selling) at a ~ les fruits frais sont très recherchés OR font prime *spec*; honesty is at a ~ these days l'honnêteté se fait rare OR se perd de nos jours; to put OR to place a (high) ~ on sthg attacher beaucoup de valeur à OR faire grand cas de qqch. -**3.** *Am* [fuel] supercarburant *m*.
◇ *comp*: ~ price prix *m* très réduit; ~ quality qualité *f* extra.

premium bond *n* obligation *f* à prime.

premolar [,priː'məʊlə^r] ◇ *adj* prémolaire.
◇ *n* prémolaire *f*.

premonition [,premə'nɪʃn] *n* prémonition *f*, pressentiment *m*; to have a ~ of sthg pressentir qqch, avoir le pressentiment de qqch; I had a ~ he wouldn't come j'avais le pressentiment qu'il ne viendrait pas.

premonitory [prɪ'mɒnɪtrɪ] *adj* prémonitoire.

prenatal [,priː'neɪtl] *adj* prénatal.

prenuptial [,priː'nʌpʃl] *adj* prénuptial.

preoccupation [priː,ɒkjʊ'peɪʃn] *n* préoccupation *f*; I have too many other ~s just now j'ai trop d'autres préoccupations en ce moment; I don't understand his ~ with physical fitness je ne comprends pas qu'il soit si préoccupé par sa forme physique.

preoccupied [priː'ɒkjʊpaɪd] *adj* préoccupé; to be ~ by OR with sthg être préoccupé par OR de *lit* qqch; he seems ~ with the idea il semble que cette idée le préoccupe; she was too ~ with her work to spare a thought for me elle était trop préoccupée par son travail pour penser à moi.

preoccupy [priː'ɒkjʊpaɪ] (*pt* & *pp* preoccupied) *vt* préoccuper.

preop *inf* ['priːɒp] (*abbr of* preoperative) ◇ *adj* préopératoire; ~ medication prémédication *f*, médication *f* préopératoire.
◇ *n*: she's gone for a ~ elle est allée passer un examen préopératoire.

preordain [,priːɔː'deɪn] *vt*: she felt ~ed to be a missionary elle se sentait prédestinée à devenir missionnaire; our defeat was ~ed il était dit que nous perdrions.

prep *inf* [prep] SCH ◇ *n (U) Br* -**1.** [homework] devoirs *mpl*. -**2.** [study period] étude *f (après les cours)*.
◇ *vi Am faire ses études dans un établissement privé.*

prepack [,priː'pæk], **prepackage** [,priː'pækɪdʒ] *vt* préemballer, conditionner; the fruit is all ~ed les fruits sont entièrement conditionnés.

prepackaging [,priː'pækɪdʒɪŋ] *n* préemballage *m*, conditionnement *m*.

prepaid [*pt* & *pp* ,priː'peɪd, *adj* 'priːpeɪd] ◇ *pt* & *pp* → **prepay**.
◇ *adj* payé (d'avance); ~ reply réponse *f* payée.

preparation [,prepə'reɪʃn] *n* -**1.** *(U)* préparation *f*; to be in ~ être en préparation; in ~ for publication en vue d'une publication; in ~ for Christmas pour préparer Noël; the dish requires careful ~ ce plat exige une préparation extrêmement délicate; as a ~ for public life pour préparer à la vie publique. -**2.** *(C)* CHEM & PHARM préparation *f*; to make up a ~ faire une préparation. -**3.** *(U) Br* SCH = **prep**.
◆ **preparations** *npl* [arrangements] préparatifs *mpl*, dispositions *fpl*; ~s for war préparatifs de guerre; she attended to the wedding ~s elle s'est occupée des préparatifs du mariage.

preparatory [prɪ'pærətrɪ] *adj* [work] préparatoire; [measure] préalable, préliminaire; the report is still at the ~ stage le rapport en est encore au stade préliminaire OR préparatoire; ~ to the launch *fml* avant le lancement; ~ to travelling abroad *fml* avant de partir en voyage à l'étranger.

preparatory school *n* -**1.** [in UK] école *f* primaire privée *(pour enfants de sept à treize ans, préparant généralement à entrer dans une «public school»)*. -**2.** [in US] *école privée qui prépare à l'enseignement supérieur.*

prepare [prɪ'peə^r] ◇ *vt* [plan, food, lesson] préparer; to ~ a meal for sb préparer un repas à OR pour qqn; to ~ a surprise for sb préparer une surprise à qqn; to ~ the way/the ground for negotiations ouvrir la voie à/préparer le terrain pour des négociations; we are preparing to leave tomorrow nous nous préparons à partir demain || [person] préparer; she's preparing them for the exam elle les prépare à l'examen; to ~ o.s. for sthg se préparer à qqch; ~ yourself for the worst préparez-vous OR attendez-vous au pire; you'd better ~ yourself for some bad news préparez-vous à recevoir de mauvaises nouvelles.
◇ *vi*: to ~ for sthg faire des préparatifs en vue de OR se préparer à qqch; to ~ to do sthg se préparer OR s'apprêter à faire qqch; to ~ for departure faire des préparatifs en vue d'un départ, se préparer à partir; the country is preparing for war le pays se prépare à la guerre; to ~ for a meeting/an exam préparer une réunion/un examen; ~ for the worst! préparez-vous au pire!

prepared [prɪ'peəd] *adj* [ready - gen] préparé, prêt; [- answer, excuse] tout prêt; I was ~ to leave j'étais préparé OR prêt à partir; he wasn't ~ for what he saw [hadn't expected] il ne s'attendait pas à ce spectacle; [was shocked] il n'était pas préparé à voir cela; you must be ~ for anything il faut s'attendre à tout; the Minister issued a ~ statement le ministre fit une déclaration préparée à l'avance || [willing] prêt, disposé; I am ~ to cooperate je suis prêt OR disposé à coopérer.

preparedness [prɪ'peədnɪs] *n*: ~ for war préparation *f* à la guerre.

prepay [,priː'peɪ] (*pt* & *pp* prepaid [-'peɪd]) *vt* payer d'avance.

prepayment [,priː'peɪmənt] *n* paiement *m* d'avance.

preponderance [prɪ'pɒndərəns] *n* [in importance] prépondérance *f*; [in number] supériorité *f* numérique; there was a ~ of boys in the science subjects les garçons étaient majoritaires dans les disciplines scientifiques.

preponderant [prɪ'pɒndərənt] *adj* prépondérant.

preponderantly [prɪ'pɒndərəntlɪ] *adv* [in importance] de façon prépondérante; [especially] surtout.

preponderate [prɪ'pɒndəreɪt] *vi* être prépondérant, prédominer; to ~ over sthg l'emporter sur qqch.

preposition [ˌprepə'zɪʃn] *n* préposition *f*.

prepositional [ˌprepə'zɪʃnl] *adj* prépositionnel; ~ phrase locution *f* prépositive.

prepositionally [ˌprepə'zɪʃnlɪ] *adv* prépositivement.

prepositive [prɪ'pɒzətɪv] *adj* prépositif.

prepossessing [ˌpriːpə'zesɪŋ] *adj* avenant, engageant; a most ~ young man un jeune homme très présentable; her manners are not very ~ ses manières ne font pas très bon effet OR laissent à désirer.

preposterous [prɪ'pɒstərəs] *adj* absurde, grotesque.

preposterously [prɪ'pɒstərəslɪ] *adv* absurdement, ridiculement.

preppie, preppy *inf* ['prepɪ] (*pl* preppies, *compar* preppier, *superl* preppiest) *Am* ◇ *n*: she's a ~ elle est BCBG.
◇ *adj* BCBG.

preprandial [ˌpriː'prændɪəl] *adj lit* OR *hum* [drink] avant le repas.

preprocessor [ˌpriː'prəʊsesəʳ] *n* préprocesseur *m*.

preprogrammed [ˌpriː'prəʊgræmd] *adj* préprogrammé.

prep school *n abbr of* preparatory school.

prepubescent [ˌpriːpjuː'besənt] *adj* prépubère.

prepuce ['priːpjuːs] *n* prépuce *m*.

prequel *inf* ['priːkwəl] *n film dont l'action est antérieure à celle d'une œuvre existante.*

Pre-Raphaelite [ˌpriː'ræfəlaɪt] ◇ *adj* préraphaélite.
◇ *n* préraphaélite *mf*.

prerecord [ˌpriːrɪ'kɔːd] *vt* préenregistrer; ~ed TV debate débat télévisé préenregistré OR en différé; ~ed cassette cassette *f* enregistrée.

prerelease [ˌpriːrɪ'liːs] ◇ *n* [of film] avant-première *f*; [of record] sortie *f* précommerciale.
◇ *vt* [film, record] faire sortir en avant-première.
◇ *adj*: ~ publicity *publicité qui précède la sortie d'un film, d'un livre, d'un disque*.

prerequisite [ˌpriː'rekwɪzɪt] ◇ *n* (condition *f*) préalable *m*, condition *f* sine qua non; to be a ~ for OR of sthg être une condition préalable à qqch; a knowledge of foreign languages is not a ~ la connaissance de langues étrangères n'est pas indispensable.
◇ *adj*: ~ condition condition *f* préalable.

prerevolutionary ['priːˌrevə'luːʃnərɪ] *adj* prérévolutionnaire.

prerogative [prɪ'rɒgətɪv] *n* prérogative *f*, apanage *m*; to exercise one's ~ exercer ses prérogatives.

Pres. *written abbr of* president.

presage ['presɪdʒ] ◇ *n* présage *m*; to have a ~ of doom pressentir un malheur.
◇ *vt* présager, annoncer.

presbyopia [ˌprezbɪ'əʊpjə] *n* presbytie *f*.

presbyter ['prezbɪtəʳ] *n* membre *m* du conseil presbytéral.

Presbyterian [ˌprezbɪ'tɪərɪən] ◇ *adj* presbytérien.
◇ *n* presbytérien *m*, -enne *f*.

Presbyterianism [ˌprezbɪ'tɪərɪənɪzm] *n* presbytérianisme *m*.

presbytery ['prezbɪtrɪ] *n* -**1.** [house] presbytère *m*. -**2.** [court] presbyterium *m*. -**3.** [part of church] presbyterium *m*.

preschool [ˌpriː'skuːl] ◇ *adj* [playgroup, age] préscolaire; [child] d'âge préscolaire.
◇ *n Am* école *f* maternelle.

preschooler [ˌpriː'skuːləʳ] *n Am* enfant *mf* d'âge préscolaire.

prescience ['presɪəns] *n* prescience *f*.

prescient ['presɪənt] *adj* prescient.

prescribe [prɪ'skraɪb] *vt* -**1.** MED prescrire; to ~ sthg for sb prescrire qqch à qqn; the doctor ~d her a month's rest le médecin lui a prescrit un mois de repos; what can you ~ for migraine? que prescrivez-vous contre la migraine?; 'do not exceed the ~d dose' 'ne pas dépasser la dose prescrite'. -**2.** [advocate] préconiser, recommander; what cure would you ~ for the current economic problems? quelles mesures préconiseriez-vous pour remédier aux problèmes économiques actuels? -**3.** [give, set - punishment] infliger; *Br* SCH [- books] inscrire au programme; ~d form/number *Br* formulaire *m*/nombre *m* prescrit. -**4.** JUR prescrire.

prescription [prɪ'skrɪpʃn] ◇ *n* -**1.** MED ordonnance *f*; the doctor wrote out a ~ for her le médecin lui a rédigé OR fait une ordonnance; to make up a ~ for sb exécuter OR préparer une ordonnance pour qqn; I'll give you a ~ for some antibiotics je vais vous prescrire des antibiotiques; to get sthg on ~ obtenir qqch sur ordonnance; available OR obtainable only on ~ délivré seulement sur ordonnance. -**2.** [recommendation] prescription *f*; what's your ~ for a happy life? quelle est votre recette du bonheur?
◇ *comp*: a ~ drug un médicament délivré seulement sur ordonnance.

prescription charge *n Br* ≃ ticket *m* modérateur.

prescriptive [prɪ'skrɪptɪv] *adj* -**1.** LING [grammar, rule] normatif. -**2.** [dogmatic] dogmatique, strict. -**3.** [customary] consacré par l'usage.

prescriptivism [prɪ'skrɪptɪvɪzm] *n* normativisme *m*.

presence ['prezns] *n* -**1.** présence *f*; in the ~ of sb en présence de qqn; it happened in my ~ cela s'est passé en ma présence; to be aware of sb's ~ sentir la présence de qqn; your ~ is requested at Saturday's meeting vous êtes prié d'assister à la réunion de samedi; to be admitted to the ~ of sb être admis en présence de qqn; ~ of mind présence *f* d'esprit; to show/to have great ~ of mind faire preuve d'une/avoir une grande présence d'esprit. -**2.** [number of people present] présence *f*; there was a large student/police ~ at the demonstration il y avait un nombre important d'étudiants/un important service d'ordre à la manifestation; America has maintained a strong military ~ in the area l'Amérique a maintenu une forte présence militaire dans la région. -**3.** [personality, magnetism] présence *f*; to lack ~ manquer de présence; she has great stage ~ elle a beaucoup de présence sur scène; he certainly knows how to make his ~ felt il sait très bien faire sentir sa présence. -**4.** [entity] présence *f*; I could sense a ~ in the room je sentais comme une présence dans la pièce.

present [*n* & *adj* 'preznt, *vb* prɪ'zent] ◇ *n* -**1.** [gift] cadeau *m*; to give sb a ~ faire un cadeau à qqn; we gave her a pony as a ~ nous lui avons offert un OR fait cadeau d'un poney; to make sb a ~ of sthg faire cadeau de qqch à qqn; it's for a ~ [in shop] c'est pour offrir. -**2.** [in time] présent *m*; at ~ actuellement, à présent; up to the ~ jusqu'à présent, jusqu'à maintenant; as things are OR stand at ~ au point où en sont les choses; that's enough for the ~ ça suffit pour le moment OR pour l'instant; to live only in OR for the ~ vivre pour l'instant présent OR au présent. -**3.** GRAMM présent *m*; in the ~ au présent.
◇ *vt* -**1.** [gift] donner, offrir; [prize] remettre, décerner; to ~ sthg to sb OR sb with sthg donner OR offrir qqch à qqn; they ~ed him with a clock ils lui ont offert une OR fait cadeau d'une pendule; he ~ed his collection to the museum il a fait cadeau de sa collection au musée; the singer was ~ed with a bunch of flowers la chanteuse s'est vu offrir OR remettre un bouquet de fleurs; who is going to ~ the prizes? qui va procéder à la remise des prix?; she was ~ed with first prize on lui a décerné le premier prix; the project ~s us with a formidable challenge le projet constitue pour nous un formidable défi; he ~ed us with a fait accompli il nous a mis devant le fait accompli; she ~ed him with a daughter elle lui a donné une fille. -**2.** *fml* [introduce] présenter; to ~ sb to sb présenter qqn à qqn; allow me to ~ Mr Jones permettez-moi de vous présenter M. Jones; to be ~ed at Court être présenté à la Cour. -**3.** [put on - play, film] donner; [- exhibition] présenter, monter. -**4.** RADIO & TV présenter; the programme was ~ed by Ian King l'émission était présentée par Ian King. -**5.** [offer - entertainment] présenter; we proudly ~ Donna Stewart nous avons le plaisir OR nous sommes heureux de vous présenter Donna Stewart; ~ing Vanessa Brown in the title role avec Vanessa Brown dans le rôle principal; the opera company is ~ing a varied programme la troupe de l'opéra présente un programme varié. -**6.** [put forward - apology, view, report] présenter; [orally] exposer; the essay is well ~ed la dissertation est bien présentée; I wish to ~ my complaint in person je tiens à déposer plainte moi-même; when are you going to ~ your plans? quand allez-vous soumettre vos projets?; to ~ a bill in Parliament présenter ou introduire un projet de loi au parlement. -**7.** [pose, offer - problem, difficulty] présenter, poser; [- chance, view] offrir; the house ~ed a sorry sight la maison offrait un triste spectacle; if the opportunity ~s itself si l'occasion se présente; a strange idea ~ed itself to her une idée étrange lui est venue; the case ~s all the appearances of murder tout semble indiquer qu'il s'agit d'un meurtre. -**8.** [show - passport, ticket] présenter; you must ~ proof of ownership vous devez présenter un certificat de propriété OR prouver que cela vous appartient; ~ arms! MIL présentez armes! -**9.** [arrive, go]: to ~ o.s. se présenter; she ~ed herself at 9 o'clock as instructed elle se présenta, comme convenu, à 9 h. -**10.** MED: the foetus ~ed itself normally la présentation (fœtale) était normale.
◇ *vi* présenter.
◇ *adj* -**1.** [in attendance] présent; to be ~ at a meeting être présent à OR assister à une réunion; how many were ~? combien de personnes étaient là OR étaient présentes?; those ~ were very moved les personnes présentes étaient très émues, l'assistance était très émue; ~ company excepted à l'exception des personnes présentes. -**2.** [current - price, government, job] actuel; in the ~ case dans le cas présent; at the ~ time actuellement, à l'époque actuelle; up to the ~ day jusqu'à présent, jusqu'à aujourd'hui; given the ~ circumstances étant donné les circonstances actuelles, dans l'état actuel des choses; in the ~ writer's opinion de l'avis de l'auteur de ces lignes. -**3.** GRAMM au présent; indicative ~, ~ indicative présent de l'indicatif.

presentable [prɪ'zentəbl] *adj* [person, room] présentable; [clothes] présentable, mettable; do I look ~? est-ce que j'ai l'air présentable? make yourself ~ arrange-toi un peu; I'm afraid the room's not very ~ je crains que la pièce ne soit pas très présentable.

presentation [ˌprezn'teɪʃn] *n* -**1.** [showing] présentation *f*; on ~ of this voucher sur présentation de ce bon; cheque payable on ~ chèque payable à vue || [putting forward - of ideas, facts] présentation *f*, exposition *f*; [- of petition] présentation *f*, soumission *f*; he made a very clear ~ of the case il a très clairement présenté l'affaire. -**2.** COMM [of product, policy] présentation *f*. -**3.** [introduction] présentation *f*; can you make the ~s? pouvez-vous faire les présentations? -**4.** [performance - of play, film] représentation *f*; in a new ~ of "Hamlet" dans une nouvelle mise en scène de «Hamlet». -**5.** [piece of work] présentation *f*; she lost marks for poor ~ elle a perdu des points parce que sa présentation n'était pas assez soignée. -**6.** [award - of prize, diploma] remise *f*; to make sb a ~ of sthg remettre qqch à qqn. -**7.** [award ceremony] = **presentation ceremony**. -**8.** MED [of foetus] présentation *f*.

presentation ceremony *n* cérémonie *f* de remise *(d'un prix)*.

presentation copy *n* [specimen] spécimen *m* (gratuit); [from writer] exemplaire *m* gratuit.

present-day *adj* actuel, contemporain.

presenter [prɪˈzentəʳ] *n* présentateur *m*, -trice *f*.

presentiment [prɪˈzentɪmənt] *n* pressentiment *m*.

presently [ˈprezəntlɪ] *adv* -**1.** [soon] bientôt, tout à l'heure; **he will be here ~** il sera bientôt là; **~, she got up and left** au bout de quelques minutes elle se leva et s'en alla. -**2.** [now] à présent, actuellement; **she's ~ working on a new novel** elle travaille actuellement à un nouveau roman.

presentment [prɪˈzentmənt] *n* -**1.** JUR déclaration *f*. -**2.** COMM [of bill] présentation *f*.

present participle *n* participe *m* présent.

present perfect *n* passé *m* composé; **in the ~** au passé composé.

presents [ˈpreznts] *npl* JUR: **by these ~** par la présente (lettre).

present tense *n* présent *m*; **in the ~** au présent.

preservation [ˌprezəˈveɪʃn] *n* -**1.** [upkeep, maintenance - of tradition] conservation *f*; [- of leather, building, wood] entretien *m*; [- of peace, life] maintien *m*; **the mummy was in a good state of ~** la momie était en bon état de conservation OR était bien conservée. -**2.** [of food] conservation *f*. -**3.** [protection] préservation *f*.

preservation order *n*: **to put a ~ on a building** classer un édifice *(monument historique)*.

preservation society *n association pour la protection des sites et monuments.*

preservative [prɪˈzɜːvətɪv] ◇ *n* agent *m* conservateur OR de conservation, conservateur *m*; **contains no artificial ~s** sans conservateurs artificiels.
◇ *adj* conservateur.

preserve [prɪˈzɜːv] ◇ *vt* -**1.** [maintain - tradition, building] conserver; [- leather] conserver, entretenir; [- silence] garder, observer; [- peace, life] maintenir; **to be well ~d** [building, specimen] être en bon état de conservation; [person] être bien conservé; **she managed to ~ her dignity** elle a réussi à garder OR conserver sa dignité; **they tried to ~ some semblance of normality** ils essayaient de faire comme si de rien n'était. -**2.** [protect] préserver, protéger; **Saints ~ us!** le Ciel OR Dieu nous préserve! -**3.** CULIN mettre en conserve; **~d fruit** fruits *mpl* en conserve.
◇ *n* -**1.** HUNT réserve *f* (de chasse). -**2.** [privilege] privilège *m*, apanage *m*; **it's still very much a male ~** c'est encore un domaine essentiellement réservé aux hommes; **cruises are the ~ of the rich** les croisières sont réservées aux OR sont le privilège des riches.
◆ **preserves** *npl* CULIN [jam] confitures *fpl*; [vegetables, fruit] conserves *fpl*; [pickles] pickles *mpl*.

preserver [prɪˈzɜːvəʳ] *n* sauveur *m*.

preset [ˌpriːˈset] (*pt* & *pp* **preset**) ◇ *vt* prérégler, régler à l'avance.
◇ *adj* préréglé, réglé d'avance.

preshrunk [ˌpriːˈʃrʌŋk] *adj* irrétrécissable.

preside [prɪˈzaɪd] *vi* présider; **to ~ at a meeting/at table** présider une réunion/la table.
◆ **preside over** *vt insep* -**1.** [meeting] présider; [changes] présider à. -**2.** [subj: statue, building] dominer; **the statue ~d over the square** la statue dominait la place.

presidency [ˈprezɪdənsɪ] (*pl* **presidencies**) *n* présidence *f*.

president [ˈprezɪdənt] *n* -**1.** [of state] président *m*, -e *f*; **President Simpson** le président Simpson ❑ **'All the President's Men'** *Pakula* 'les Hommes du Président'. -**2.** [of club, organization] président *m*, -e *f*. -**3.** *Am* [of company, bank] président-directeur général *m*, P-D G *m*.

president-elect *n titre du président des États-Unis nouvellement élu (en novembre) jusqu'à la cérémonie d'investiture présidentielle (le 20 janvier).*

presidential [ˌprezɪˈdenʃl] *adj* [elections, candidate] présidentiel; [aeroplane, suite] présidentiel, du président; **it's a ~ year** c'est l'année des élections présidentielles.

presiding officer [prɪˈzaɪdɪŋ-] *n Br* président *m* (de bureau de vote).

presidium [prɪˈsɪdɪəm] (*pl* **presidiums** OR **presidia** [-dɪə]) *n* praesidium *m*, présidium *m*.

presoak [ˌpriːˈsəʊk] *vt* faire tremper.

press [pres] ◇ *vt* -**1.** [push - button, bell, trigger, accelerator] appuyer sur; **try ~ing it** essayez d'appuyer dessus; **he ~ed the lid shut** il a fermé le couvercle (en appuyant dessus); **to ~ sthg flat** aplatir qqch; **to ~ one's way through a crowd/to the front** se frayer un chemin à travers une foule/jusqu'au premier rang; **he was ~ed (up) against the railings** il s'est trouvé coincé contre le grillage; **I ~ed myself against the wall** je me suis collé contre le mur; **she ~ed a note into my hand** elle m'a glissé un billet dans la main; **he ~ed his nose (up) against the windowpane** il a collé son nez à la vitre; **he ~ed his hat down on his head** il rabattit OR enfonça son chapeau sur sa tête; **she ~ed the papers down into the bin** elle a enfoncé les papiers dans la poubelle. -**2.** [squeeze - hand, arm] presser, serrer; **she ~ed her son to her** elle serra son fils contre elle; [- grapes, olives] presser; **to ~ the flesh** *inf Am* POL prendre un bain de foule. -**3.** [urge] presser, pousser; **to ~ sb for payment/an answer** presser qqn de payer/répondre; **she ~ed me to tell her the truth** elle me pressa de lui dire la vérité ‖ [harass] harceler, talonner; **his creditors were ~ing him hard** ses créanciers le harcelaient OR ne lui laissaient pas le moindre répit. -**4.** [force] forcer, obliger; **I was ~ed into signing the contract** j'ai été obligé de signer le contrat; **don't let yourself be ~ed into going** ne laissez personne vous forcer à y aller. -**5.** [impose, push forward - claim, advantage] appuyer, pousser; [- opinions] insister sur; **can I ~ a cup of tea on you?** *hum* puis-je vous offrir une tasse de thé?; **to ~ (home) an advantage** profiter d'un avantage; **to ~ one's attentions on sb** poursuivre qqn de ses assiduités; **I don't want to ~ the point** je ne veux pas insister; **to ~ charges against sb** JUR engager des poursuites contre qqn. -**6.** [iron - shirt, tablecloth] repasser. -**7.** [manufacture in mould - component] mouler; [- record] presser. -**8.** [preserve by pressing - flower] presser, faire sécher *(dans un livre ou un pressoir)*. -**9.** [in weightlifting] soulever. -**10.** [enlist by force] recruter OR enrôler de force; **to ~ into service** *fig* réquisitionner; **the local mechanic was ~ed into service** le mécanicien du coin fut réquisitionné pour la circonstance.
◇ *vi* -**1.** [push] appuyer; **~ here** appuyez OR pressez ici; **he ~ed (down) on the accelerator** il appuya sur l'accélérateur. -**2.** [be a burden] *literal* faire pression; **the rucksack ~ed on his shoulders** le sac à dos pesait sur ses épaules ‖ *fig* [troubles] peser; **her problems ~ed on her mind** ses problèmes lui pesaient. -**3.** [insist, campaign]: **he ~ed hard to get the grant** il a fait des pieds et des mains pour obtenir la bourse. -**4.** [surge]: **the crowd ~ed against the barriers/round the President** la foule se pressait contre les barrières/autour du président; **they ~ed forward to get a better view** ils poussaient pour essayer de mieux voir; **to ~ through a crowd** se frayer un chemin à travers une foule. -**5.** [iron] se repasser; **some shirts ~ easily** il y a des chemises qui se repassent facilement. -**6.** *phr*: **time ~es!** le temps presse!
◇ *n* -**1.** [newspapers] presse *f*; **the national/local ~** la presse nationale/locale; **they advertised in the ~** ils ont fait passer une annonce dans les journaux; **reports in the ~ were biased** les comptes rendus parus dans la presse étaient tendancieux ❑ **the Press Association** *la principale agence de presse britannique*; **the Press Council** *organisme indépendant veillant au respect de la déontologie dans la presse britannique*. -**2.** [journalists] presse *f*; **the ~ were there** la presse était là; **she's a member of the ~** elle a une carte de presse; **the gentlemen of the ~** *iron* ces messieurs de la presse. -**3.** [report, opinion] presse *f*; **to get (a) good/bad ~** avoir bonne/mauvaise presse; **to give sb (a) good/bad ~** faire l'éloge/la critique de qqn. -**4.** [printing] presse *f*; **to go to ~** [book] être mis sous presse; [newspaper] partir à l'impression; **in** OR **at (the) ~** sous presse; **the proofs were passed for ~** on a donné le bon à tirer; **prices correct at time of going to ~** prix corrects au moment de la mise sous presse. -**5.** [machine]: **(printing) ~** presse *f*; **to set the ~es rolling** *literal* mettre les presses en marche; *fig* mettre la machine en marche. -**6.** [publisher] presses *fpl*. -**7.** [for tennis racket, handicrafts, woodwork, trousers] presse *f*; [for cider, wine] pressoir *m*. -**8.** [push]: **the machine dispenses hot coffee at the ~ of a button** il suffit d'appuyer sur un bouton pour que la machine distribue du café chaud. -**9.** [squeeze] serrement *m*; **he gave my hand a quick ~** il m'a serré la main rapidement. -**10.** [crowd] foule *f*; [rush] bousculade *f*; **in the ~ for the door we became separated** dans la ruée de la foule vers la porte, nous avons été séparés. -**11.** [ironing] coup *m* de fer; **to give sthg a ~** donner un coup de fer à qqch. -**12.** [cupboard] placard *m*. -**13.** [in weightlifting] développé *m*. -**14.** INDUST [forming machine] presse *f*. -**15.** MIL recrutement *m* de force. -**16.** NAUT: **~ of sail** OR **canvas** pleine voilure *f*; **under ~ of sail** toutes voiles dehors.
◇ *comp* [campaign, card, reporter, photographer] de presse; [advertising, coverage] dans la presse; **~ reports of the incident were inaccurate** les articles de presse relatant l'incident étaient inexacts.
◆ **press ahead** = **press on**.
◆ **press for** *vt insep* [demand] exiger, réclamer; **they ~ed for a pay rise** ils ont réclamé OR exigé une augmentation de salaire; **the residents are ~ing for a pedestrian zone** les résidents font pression pour obtenir une zone piétonnière; **the opposition are ~ing for an enquiry** l'opposition exige une enquête OR insiste pour que l'on fasse une enquête.
◆ **press in** *vt sep* enfoncer.
◆ **press on** *vi insep* [on journey] poursuivre OR continuer son chemin; **the travellers ~ed on in the darkness** les voyageurs poursuivirent leur chemin dans la nuit; **we must ~ on to York** OR **as far as York** il faut poursuivre jusqu'à York ‖ [in enterprise, job] poursuivre, persévérer; **we ~ed on regardless** nous avons continué malgré tout.
◆ **press on with** *vt insep* [job, negotiations] continuer, poursuivre; **they ~ed on with the plan in spite of opposition** ils ont poursuivi leur projet malgré l'opposition rencontrée.

press agency *n* agence *f* de presse.

press agent *n* attaché *m*, -e *f* de presse.

press baron *n* magnat *m* de la presse.

press box *n* tribune *f* de (la) presse.

press button *n* bouton-poussoir *m*.
◆ **press-button** *adj* TELEC: **~ dialling** numérotation *f* à touches.

press clipping = **press cutting**.

press conference *n* conférence *f* de presse.

press corps *n* journalistes *mpl*; **the White House ~** les journalistes accrédités à la Maison-Blanche.

press cutting *n* coupure *f* de presse OR de journal; **a collection of ~s** une collection de coupures de journaux, un dossier de presse.

pressed [prest] *adj* -**1.** [flower] pressé, séché. -**2.** [hurried] pressé; [overworked] débordé.
◆ **pressed for** *adj phr* [short of] à court de; **we're ~ for space** nous manquons de place; **we're rather ~ for time** le temps nous est compté.

press gallery *n* tribune *f* de (la) presse *(par exemple au parlement)*.

press-gang ◇ *n* MIL & HIST racoleurs *mpl*, recruteurs *mpl*.
◇ *vt* -**1.** *Br* [force]: **to ~ sb into doing sthg** obliger qqn à faire qqch (contre son gré); **I was ~ed into taking part** on m'a obligé à participer. -**2.** MIL & HIST racoler, recruter de force.

pressing ['presɪŋ] ◇ *adj* -**1.** [urgent - appointment, business, debt] urgent; **the matter is ~** c'est une affaire urgente. -**2.** [insistent - demand, danger, need] pressant; **at her ~ invitation, we agreed to go** devant son insistance, nous avons accepté d'y aller. -**3.** [imminent - danger] imminent.
◇ *n* -**1.** [of fruit, record] pressage *m*. -**2.** [ironing] repassage *m*.
press kit *n* dossier *m* de presse *(distribué aux journalistes)*.
press lord = **press baron**.
pressman ['presmæn] (*pl* **pressmen** [-men]) *n* -**1.** [journalist] journaliste *m*. -**2.** [printer] typographe *m*.
pressmark ['presmɑːk] *n* cote *f (d'un livre)*.
press office *n* bureau *m* de presse.
press officer *n* responsable *mf* des relations avec la presse.
press-on *adj* adhésif.
press release *n* communiqué *m* de presse.
pressroom ['presrʊm] *n* salle *f* de presse.
press run *n* tirage *m*.
press secretary *n* POL ≃ porte-parole *m inv* du gouvernement.
press stud *n Br* bouton-pression *m*, pression *f*.
press-up *n Br* SPORT pompe *f*; **to do ~s** faire des pompes.
pressure ['preʃəʳ] ◇ *n* -**1.** METEOR & PHYS pression *f*; [of blood] tension *f*; **high/low ~ area** [on weather chart] zone *f* de hautes/basses pressions; **a ~ of 20 kilogrammes to the square centimetre** une pression de 20 kilos au centimètre carré; **to work at full ~** *fig* [person] travailler à plein régime; [machine, factory] tourner à plein régime ❑ **oil ~** pression d'huile; **tyre ~** pression des pneus OR de gonflage *spec*. -**2.** [squeezing] pression *f*; **she could feel the ~ of his grip on her arm** elle sentait la pression de sa poigne sur son bras. -**3.** *fig* [force, influence]: **to bring ~ to bear** *fml* OR **to put ~ on sb** faire pression OR exercer une pression sur qqn; **they put ~ on me to come** ils ont fait pression sur moi pour que je vienne; **she did it under ~** elle l'a fait contrainte et forcée; **she came under ~ from her parents** elle est venue parce que ses parents l'y ont obligée; **they're putting too much ~ on him** ils le soumettent à trop de pression. -**4.** *fig* [strain, stress - of circumstances, events] pression *f*; [- of doubts, worries] poids *m*; **the ~s of city life** le stress de la vie en ville; **I can't stand any more of this ~** je ne peux plus supporter cette tension; **he pleaded ~ of work** il s'est excusé en disant qu'il était débordé de travail; **to work under ~** travailler sous pression; **we're under ~ to finish on time** on nous presse de respecter les délais; **the ~ of work is too much for me** la charge de travail est trop lourde pour moi; **there's a lot of ~ on her to succeed** on fait beaucoup pression sur elle pour qu'elle réussisse; **the ~'s on!** il va falloir mettre les bouchées doubles!; **she's under a lot of ~ just now** elle est vraiment sous pression en ce moment.
◇ *vt* faire pression sur; **they ~d him into resigning** ils l'ont contraint à démissionner.
pressure cabin *n* cabine *f* pressurisée.
pressure chamber *n* MECH réservoir *m* d'air comprimé.
pressure-cook *vt* faire cuire à la cocotte-minute OR à l'autocuiseur.
pressure cooker *n* cocotte-minute *f*, autocuiseur *m*.
pressure feed *n* alimentation *f* par pression.
pressure gauge *n* jauge *f* de pression, manomètre *m*.
pressure group *n* groupe *m* de pression.
pressure point *n* point *m* de compression *(sur une artère)*.
pressure suit *n* scaphandre *m* pressurisé.
pressurization [,preʃəraɪ'zeɪʃn] *n* pressurisation *f*.
pressurize, -ise ['preʃəraɪz] *vt* -**1.** [person, government] faire pression sur; **to ~ sb to do sthg** OR **into doing sthg** faire pression sur qqn pour qu'il fasse qqch. -**2.** AERON & ASTRONAUT pressuriser.
pressurized ['preʃəraɪzd] *adj* [container] pressurisé; [liquid, gas] sous pression; **a ~ cabin** une cabine pressurisée OR sous pression.
pressurized-water reactor *n* réacteur *m* à eau sous pression.
Prestel® ['prestel] *pr n service de vidéotexte de la British Telecom*.
prestidigitation ['prestɪ,dɪdʒɪ'teɪʃn] *n fml* OR *hum* prestidigitation *f*.
prestidigitator [,prestɪ'dɪdʒɪteɪtəʳ] *n fml* OR *hum* prestidigitateur *m*.
prestige [pre'stiːʒ] ◇ *n* prestige *m*.
◇ *adj* de prestige.
prestigious [pre'stɪdʒəs] *adj* prestigieux.
presto ['prestəʊ] *adv* presto; **hey ~!** et voilà, le tour est joué!
prestress [,priː'stres] *vt* précontraindre.
prestressed concrete [,priː'strest-] *n* béton *m* précontraint.
presumable [prɪ'zjuːməbl] *adj* présumable.
presumably [prɪ'zjuːməblɪ] *adv* vraisemblablement; **~, he isn't coming** il est probable qu'il ne viendra pas; **~, she married him in the end** elle a vraisemblablement OR sans doute fini par l'épouser.
presume [prɪ'zjuːm] ◇ *vt* -**1.** [suppose] présumer, supposer; **I ~ he isn't coming** je présume OR suppose qu'il ne viendra pas; **I ~d them to be aware** OR **that they were aware of the difficulties** je supposais qu'ils étaient au courant des difficultés; **missing, ~d dead** MIL manque à l'appel OR porté disparu, présumé mort; **every man is ~d innocent until proven guilty** JUR tout homme est présumé innocent tant qu'il n'a pas été déclaré coupable; **I ~ so** je (le) présume OR suppose; **Mr Chalmers, I ~** M. Chalmers, je présume. -**2.** [dare, take liberty] oser, se permettre; **I wouldn't ~ to contradict you** je ne me permettrais pas de vous contredire. -**3.** [presuppose] présupposer; **presuming they agree** à supposer qu'ils soient d'accord.
◇ *vi*: **I don't want to ~** je ne voudrais pas m'imposer; **to ~ on** OR **upon sb** abuser de la gentillesse de qqn.
presumption [prɪ'zʌmpʃn] *n* -**1.** [supposition] présomption *f*, supposition *f*; **the ~ is that he was drowned** on pense OR suppose qu'il s'est noyé; **there is a strong ~ that he is guilty** on croit que c'est lui le coupable; **it's only a ~** ce n'est qu'une hypothèse; **to act on a false ~** agir sur une OR à partir d'une fausse supposition; **we worked on the ~ that she would agree** nous avons agi en supposant qu'elle serait d'accord ❑ **~ of innocence** JUR présomption d'innocence. -**2.** *(U)* [arrogance] présomption *f*, prétention *f*; **she had the ~ to say I was lying** elle a eu l'audace de dire que je mentais; **excuse my ~, but haven't we met somewhere?** excusez mon audace, mais est-ce que nous ne nous sommes pas déjà rencontrés quelque part?
presumptive [prɪ'zʌmptɪv] *adj* [heir] présomptif; **~ proof** preuve *f* par déduction OR par présomption.
presumptuous [prɪ'zʌmptʃʊəs] *adj* présomptueux, arrogant.
presumptuously [prɪ'zʌmptʃʊəslɪ] *adv* présomptueusement, avec arrogance.
presumptuousness [prɪ'zʌmptʃʊəsnɪs] *n* présomption *f*, arrogance *f*.
presuppose [,priːsə'pəʊz] *vt* présupposer.
presupposition [,priːsʌpə'zɪʃn] *n* présupposition *f*.
pre-tax *adj* brut, avant (le prélèvement des) impôts; **~ profits** bénéfices *mpl* bruts OR avant impôts.
pre-teen ◇ *adj* [sizes, fashions] pour préadolescents; [problems] des préadolescents; **~ child** préadolescent *m*, -e *f*.
◇ *n* préadolescent *m*, -e *f*.
pretence *Br*, **pretense** *Am* [prɪ'tens] *n* -**1.** [false display] simulacre *m*; **to make a ~ of doing sthg** faire semblant OR mine de faire qqch; **everyone sees through her ~ of being the devoted wife** elle ne trompe personne en jouant les femmes dévouées; **he's not really ill, it's only** OR **all (a) ~!** il n'est pas vraiment malade, il fait seulement semblant OR c'est (simplement) de la comédie!; **at least SHE made some ~ of sympathy!** elle au moins, elle a fait comme si ça la touchait!; **a ~ of democracy** un simulacre de démocratie. -**2.** [pretext] prétexte *m*; **under** OR **on the ~ of doing sthg** sous prétexte de faire qqch; **he criticizes her on the slightest ~** il la critique pour un rien OR à la moindre occasion. -**3.** [claim] prétention *f*; **a woman without the slightest ~ of culture** une femme qui n'a pas la moindre prétention d'être cultivée; **he has** OR **makes no ~ to musical taste** il ne prétend pas OR il n'a pas la prétention de s'y connaître en musique. -**4.** *(U)* [arrogance] prétention *f*.
pretend [prɪ'tend] ◇ *vt* -**1.** [make believe]: **to ~ to do sthg** faire semblant de faire qqch, feindre de faire qqch; **they ~ to be rich** ils font semblant d'être riches; **they ~ed not to see** OR **to have seen us** ils ont fait semblant OR mine de ne pas nous voir; **she ~ed to be shocked** elle a fait semblant OR mine d'être choquée; **he ~ed not to be interested** il a fait semblant de ne pas être intéressé, il a joué les indifférents; **they ~ed to be ill** ils ont fait semblant d'être malades; **he ~ed to be** OR **that he was their uncle** il s'est fait passer pour leur oncle; **she ~s that everything is all right** elle fait comme si tout allait bien; **it's no use ~ing things will improve** cela ne sert à rien de faire comme si les choses allaient s'améliorer || [in children's play]: **let's ~ you're a princess** on dirait que tu serais une princesse; **you ~ to be Mummy** toi, tu serais une maman. -**2.** [claim] prétendre; **I don't ~ to be an expert** je ne prétends pas être un expert, je n'ai pas la prétention d'être un expert; **I don't ~ to understand** je ne prétends pas comprendre. -**3.** [feign - indifference, ignorance] feindre, simuler.
◇ *vi* -**1.** [feign] faire semblant; **there's no point in ~ing (to me)** inutile de faire semblant (avec moi); **I'm only ~ing!** c'est juste pour rire!; **stop ~ing and admit the truth** arrête de faire semblant et avoue la vérité || [in children's play]: **to play at let's ~** jouer à faire semblant OR comme si; **let's ~** faisons semblant OR comme si. -**2.** [lay claim] prétendre; **to ~ to sthg** prétendre à qqch; **he ~ed to her hand** *arch* il la courtisait.
◇ *adj inf* [child language - money, fight] pour faire semblant, pour jouer; **it was only ~!** c'était pour rire OR pour faire semblant!
pretended [prɪ'tendɪd] *adj* prétendu, soi-disant.
pretender [prɪ'tendəʳ] *n* -**1.** [to throne, title, right] prétendant *m*, -e *f*; **the Young Pretender** HIST le Jeune Prétendant. -**2.** [impostor] imposteur *m*.
pretense *Am* = **pretence**.
pretension [prɪ'tenʃn] *n* -**1.** *(C)* [claim] prétention *f*; **to have ~s to sthg** avoir des prétentions OR prétendre à qqch; **a film with intellectual ~s** un film qui a des prétentions intellectuelles; **I make no ~s to expert knowledge** je n'ai pas la prétention OR je ne me flatte pas d'être expert en la matière; **he has literary ~s** il se prend pour un écrivain. -**2.** *(U)* [pretentiousness] prétention *f*; **a man devoid of ~** un homme dénué de toute prétention.
pretentious [prɪ'tenʃəs] *adj* prétentieux.
pretentiously [prɪ'tenʃəslɪ] *adv* prétentieusement.
pretentiousness [prɪ'tenʃəsnɪs] *n (U)* prétention *f*.
preterit ['pretərət] *Am* = **preterite**.
preterite ['pretərət] ◇ *adj* prétérit; [form] du prétérit; **~ tense** prétérit *m*.
◇ *n* prétérit *m*; **in the ~** au prétérit.

preternatural [ˌpriːtəˈnætʃrəl] ◇ *adj* surnaturel.
◇ *n* surnaturel *m*.

preternaturally [ˌpriːtəˈnætʃrəlɪ] *adv* exceptionnellement.

pretext [ˈpriːtekst] *n* prétexte *m*; **on** OR **under the ~ of doing sthg** sous prétexte de faire qqch; **it's just a ~ for avoiding work** ce n'est qu'un prétexte pour ne pas travailler.

Pretoria [prɪˈtɔːrɪə] *pr n* Pretoria.

prettify [ˈprɪtɪfaɪ] (*pt* & *pp* **prettified**) *vt pej* [room, garden] enjoliver; **to ~ o.s.** se pomponner.

prettily [ˈprɪtɪlɪ] *adv* joliment; **~ dressed** joliment habillé.

prettiness [ˈprɪtɪnɪs] *n* -**1.** [of appearance] beauté *f*; **she had a certain ~** elle avait une certaine beauté. -**2.** *pej* [of style] mièvrerie *f*.

pretty [ˈprɪtɪ] (*compar* **prettier**, *superl* **prettiest**, *pt* & *pp* **prettied**) ◇ *adj* -**1.** [attractive - clothes, girl, place] joli; **she's a ~ little thing** c'est une jolie OR ravissante petite fille; **who's a ~ boy?** [to parrot] le beau perroquet!; **it wasn't a ~ sight** ce n'était pas beau OR joli à voir ❑ **I'm not just a ~ face!** *inf* il y en a, là-dedans!; **to be as ~ as a picture** [person] être joli comme un cœur; [place] être ravissant. -**2.** *iron*: **this is a ~ state of affairs!** c'est du joli OR du propre!; **things have come to a ~ pass!** nous voilà bien!; **to lead sb a ~ dance** donner du fil à retordre à qqn. -**3.** *pej* [dainty - style, expression] précieux; [effeminate - boy] mignon; **it's not enough to make ~ speeches** il ne suffit pas de faire de beaux discours. -**4.** *phr*: **a ~ penny**: **it cost a ~ penny** ça a coûté une jolie petite somme.
◇ *adv inf* -**1.** [quite] assez; **it's ~ good/important** c'est pas mal du tout/assez important; **you did ~ well for a beginner** tu t'en es plutôt bien tiré pour un débutant; **we've got a ~ good idea of what she was like** nous nous imaginons assez bien comment elle était. -**2.** [almost] presque, à peu près, pratiquement; **I'm ~ certain I'm right** je suis presque sûr d'avoir raison; **it's ~ much the same team as last week** c'est à peu près la même équipe que la semaine dernière; **he told her ~ well everything** il lui a raconté pratiquement OR à peu près tout. -**3.** *phr*: **to be sitting ~** avoir la partie belle.
◇ *n inf dated* [girl, animal] mignon *m*, -onne *f*; **come here, my ~** viens ici, mon mignon.
◆ **pretty up** *vt sep* = **prettify**.

pretty-pretty *inf adj pej* [person] gentillet, mignonnet; [dress] cucul la praline *(inv)*; [painting] gentillet; [garden] mignon, gentil.

pretzel [ˈpretsl] *n* bretzel *m*.

prevail [prɪˈveɪl] *vi* -**1.** [triumph] l'emporter, prévaloir *lit*; **to ~ against sb** l'emporter OR prévaloir contre qqn; **to ~ over sb** l'emporter OR prévaloir sur qqn; **luckily, common sense ~ed** heureusement, le bon sens a prévalu OR l'a emporté. -**2.** [exist, be widespread - situation, opinion, belief] régner, avoir cours; **the rumour which is now ~ing** le bruit qui court en ce moment; **the conditions ~ing in the Third World** les conditions que l'on rencontre le plus souvent dans le tiers monde.
◆ **prevail on**, **prevail upon** *vt insep fml* persuader; **he was ~ed upon to accept the post** il s'est laissé persuader d'accepter le poste; **can I ~ on your good nature?** puis-je faire appel à votre bonté?; **he was not to be ~ed on** il fut impossible de le faire changer d'avis.

prevailing [prɪˈveɪlɪŋ] *adj* -**1.** [wind] dominant. -**2.** [belief, opinion] courant, répandu; [fashion] en vogue; **in the ~ conditions** [now] dans les conditions actuelles; [then] à l'époque; **the ~ political climate** le climat politique actuel; **according to ~ opinion** selon l'opinion la plus répandue; **the ~ exchange rate** le taux de change actuel.

prevalence [ˈprevələns] *n* [widespread existence] prédominance *f*; [of disease] prévalence *f*; [frequency] fréquence *f*; **the ~ of rented property surprised him** il fut surpris de constater à quel point les locations étaient répandues; **the ~ of these theories can only do harm** la popularité de ces théories ne peut qu'être nuisible.

prevalent [ˈprevələnt] *adj* -**1.** [widespread] répandu, courant; [frequent] fréquent; **violence is ~ in big cities** la violence est monnaie courante dans les grandes villes; **such behaviour is ~ among certain species** un tel comportement est prédominant chez certaines espèces; **to become ~** se généraliser. -**2.** [current - today] actuel, d'aujourd'hui; [- in past] de OR à l'époque.

prevaricate [prɪˈværɪkeɪt] *vi fml* tergiverser, user de faux-fuyants; **stop prevaricating!** assez de faux-fuyants!

prevarication [prɪˌværɪˈkeɪʃn] *n fml* tergiversation *f*, faux-fuyant *m*, faux-fuyants *mpl*.

prevent [prɪˈvent] *vt* [accident, catastrophe, scandal] éviter; [illness] prévenir; **to ~ sb (from) doing sthg** empêcher qqn de faire qqch; **there is nothing to ~ our going** OR **to ~ us (from) going** rien ne nous empêche d'y aller; **I couldn't ~ her** je n'ai pas pu l'en empêcher; **we were unable to ~ the bomb from exploding** nous n'avons rien pu faire pour empêcher la bombe d'exploser; **they couldn't ~ his departure** ils n'ont pu l'empêcher de partir.

preventable [prɪˈventəbl] *adj* évitable.

preventative [prɪˈventətɪv] *adj* préventif; **to take ~ measures** prendre des mesures préventives.

preventible [prɪˈventəbl] = **preventable**.

prevention [prɪˈvenʃn] *n* prévention *f*; **the ~ of cruelty to animals** la protection des animaux ❑ **crime ~** lutte *f* contre la criminalité; **the Prevention of Terrorism Act** *loi sur la prévention du terrorisme permettant notamment la garde à vue de toute personne suspectée*; **~ is better than cure** *prov* mieux vaut prévenir que guérir *prov*.

preventive [prɪˈventɪv] ◇ *adj* -**1.** [medicine] préventif, prophylactique; [measure] préventif. -**2.** *Br* JUR: **~ detention** *peine de prison allant de 5 à 14 ans*.
◇ *n* -**1.** [measure] mesure *f* préventive; **as a ~** à titre préventif. -**2.** MED médicament *m* préventif OR prophylactique.

preverbal [ˌpriːˈvɜːbl] *adj* -**1.** [infant] qui ne parle pas encore; **~ communication** activité *f* préverbale. -**2.** GRAMM avant le verbe.

preview [ˈpriːvjuː] ◇ *n* [of film, show, exhibition] avant-première *f*; [of art exhibition] vernissage *m*; **and here is a ~ of tomorrow's programmes** et voici un aperçu des programmes de demain; **can you give us a ~ of what to expect?** pouvez-vous nous donner une idée de ce à quoi il faut s'attendre?
◇ *vt*: **to ~ a film** [put on] donner un film en avant-première; [see] voir un film en avant-première; **to ~ the evening's television viewing** passer en revue les programmes télévisés de la soirée.

previous [ˈpriːvjəs] ◇ *adj* -**1.** [prior] précédent; **on a ~ occasion** auparavant; **I have a ~ engagement** j'ai déjà un rendez-vous, je suis déjà pris; **she has had several ~ accidents** elle a déjà eu plusieurs accidents; **have you any ~ experience of this kind of work?** avez-vous déjà une expérience de ce genre de travail?; **the two months ~ to your arrival** les deux mois précédant votre arrivée ‖ JUR: **he has no ~ convictions** il n'a pas de casier judiciaire, il a un casier judiciaire vierge; **he has had several ~ convictions** il a déjà fait l'objet de plusieurs condamnations. -**2.** [former] antérieur; **in a ~ life** dans une vie antérieure; **his ~ marriages ended in divorce** ses autres mariages se sont soldés par des divorces. -**3.** [with days and dates] précédent; **the ~ Monday** le lundi précédent; **the ~ June** au mois de juin précédent; **the ~ day** le jour précédent, la veille; **the ~ evening** le soir précédent, la veille au soir. -**4.** *inf Br* [premature, hasty] prématuré, hâtif; **aren't you being a little ~?** n'êtes-vous pas un peu pressé?, n'allez-vous pas un peu vite?
◇ *adv* antérieurement; **~ to his death** *fml* avant sa mort, avant qu'il ne meure.

previously [ˈpriːvjəslɪ] *adv* -**1.** [in the past] auparavant, précédemment; **six weeks ~** six semaines auparavant OR plus tôt; **~, the country was under British rule** auparavant, le pays était sous autorité britannique. -**2.** [already] déjà; **we've met ~** nous nous sommes déjà rencontrés.

prevocalic [ˌpriːvəˈkælɪk] *adj* prévocalique.

prewar [ˌpriːˈwɔːʳ] *adj* d'avant-guerre; **the ~ years** l'avant-guerre *m ou f*.

prewash [ˈpriːwɒʃ] ◇ *n* prélavage *m*.
◇ *vt* faire un prélavage de.

prey [preɪ] *n (U) literal* & *fig* proie *f*; **a bird/beast of ~** un oiseau/une bête de proie; **hens are often (a) ~ to foxes** les poules sont souvent la proie des renards; **the sheep fell (a) ~ to some marauding beast** les moutons ont été attaqués par un animal maraudeur; **to be (a) ~ to doubts/nightmares** être en proie au doute/à des cauchemars; **she was an easy ~ for** OR **to fast-talking salesmen** elle était une proie facile pour le boniment des vendeurs.
◆ **prey on**, **prey upon** *vt insep* -**1.** [subj: predator] faire sa proie de; **he ~ed on her fears** *fig* il profita de ce qu'elle avait peur; **the thieves ~ed upon old women** *fig* les voleurs s'en prenaient aux OR attaquaient les vieilles dames. -**2.** [subj: fear, doubts] ronger; **the thought continued to ~ on his mind** l'idée continuait à lui ronger l'esprit.

prezzie *inf* [ˈprezɪ] *n* cadeau *m*.

Priam [ˈpraɪəm] *pr n* Priam.

priapic [praɪˈæpɪk] *adj* priapique.

priapism [ˈpraɪəpɪzm] *n* priapisme *m*.

price [praɪs] ◇ *n* -**1.** [cost] prix *m*; **what ~ is the clock?** quel est le prix de cette pendule?; **what is the ~ of petrol?** à quel prix est l'essence?; **the ~ has risen** OR **gone up by 10 %** le prix a augmenté de 10 %; **petrol has gone down in ~** le prix de l'essence a baissé; **~s are rising/falling** les prix sont en hausse/baisse; **I paid a high ~ for it** je l'ai payé cher; **their ~s are a bit expensive** leurs prix sont un peu chers; **they pay top ~s for antique china** ils achètent la porcelaine ancienne au prix fort; **if the ~ is right** si le prix est correct; **to raise the ~ of sthg** augmenter le prix de qqch; **she got a good ~ for her car** elle a obtenu un bon prix de sa voiture; **to sell sthg at a reduced ~** vendre qqch à prix réduit; **I'll let you have the carpet at a reduced ~** je vous ferai un prix d'ami pour le tapis; **I got the chair at a reduced/at half ~** j'ai eu la chaise à prix réduit/à moitié prix; **her jewels fetched huge ~s at auction** ses bijoux ont atteint des sommes folles aux enchères; **that's my ~, take it or leave it** c'est mon dernier prix, à prendre ou à laisser; **name** OR **state your ~!** votre prix sera le mien!; **every man has his ~** tout homme s'achète; **he gave us a ~ for repairing the car** il nous a donné le prix des réparations à faire sur la voiture. -**2.** [value] prix *m*, valeur *f*; **to argue over the ~ of sthg** débattre le prix de qqch; **to put a ~ on sthg** [definite] fixer le prix OR la valeur de qqch; [estimate] évaluer le prix OR estimer la valeur de qqch; **I wouldn't like to put a ~ on that fur coat** je n'ose pas imaginer le prix de ce manteau de fourrure; **to put a ~ on sb's head** mettre la tête de qqn à prix; **there's a ~ on his head** sa tête a été mise à prix; **you can't put a ~ on love** l'amour n'a pas de prix; **what ~ all her hopes now?** que valent tous ses espoirs maintenant?; **he puts a high ~ on loyalty** il attache beaucoup d'importance OR il accorde beaucoup de valeur à la loyauté; **without ~** sans prix. -**3.** ST. EX cours *m*, cote *f*; **today's ~s** les cours du jour; **what is the ~ of gold?** quel est le cours de l'or? -**4.** *fig* [penalty] prix *m*; **it's a small ~ to pay for peace of mind** c'est bien peu de chose pour avoir l'esprit tranquille; **it's a high ~ to pay for independence** c'est bien cher payer l'indépendance; **you've paida high ~ for success** vous avez payé biencher votre réussite; **that's the ~ of fame** c'est la rançon de la gloire. -**5.** [chance, odds] cote *f*; **what ~ are they giving on**

Stardust? quelle est la cote de Stardust?; what ~ he'll keep his word? combien pariez-vous qu'il tiendra parole?; what ~ peace now? quelles sont les chances de paix maintenant? -6. [quotation] devis *m*.
◇ *comp* [bracket, range] de prix; [freeze, drop, rise, level] des prix.
◇ *vt* -1. [set cost of] fixer OR établir OR déterminer le prix de; **the book is ~d at £17** le livre coûte 17 livres; **his paintings are rather highly ~d** le prix de ses tableaux est un peu élevé; **a reasonably ~d hotel** un hôtel aux prix raisonnables || [estimate value of]: **how would you ~ that house?** à combien estimeriez-vous cette maison? -2. [indicate cost of] marquer le prix de; [with label] étiqueter; **this book isn't ~d** le prix de ce livre n'est pas indiqué. -3. [ascertain price of] demander le prix de, s'informer du prix de; **she ~d the stereo in several shops before buying it** elle a comparé le prix de la chaîne dans plusieurs magasins avant de l'acheter.
◆ **at any price** *adv phr*: **she wants a husband at any ~** elle veut un mari à tout prix OR coûte que coûte; **he wouldn't do it at any ~!** il ne voulait le faire à aucun prix OR pour rien au monde!
◆ **at a price** *adv phr* en y mettant le prix; **she'll help you, at a ~** elle vous aidera, à condition que vous y mettiez le prix; **you can get real silk, but only at a ~** vous pouvez avoir de la soie véritable, à condition d'y mettre le prix; **you got what you wanted, but at a ~!** vous avez eu ce que vous souhaitiez, mais à quel prix! OR mais vous l'avez payé cher!
◆ **price down** *vt sep Br* baisser le prix de, démarquer; **everything has been ~d down by 10 % for the sales** tous les articles ont été démarqués de 10 % pour les soldes.
◆ **price out** *vt sep*: **to ~ o.s.** OR **one's goods out of the market** perdre son marché OR sa clientèle en pratiquant des prix trop élevés; **we've been ~d out of the Japanese market** nous avons perdu le marché japonais à cause de nos prix; **cheap charter flights have ~d the major airlines out of the market** les vols charters à prix réduit ont fait perdre des parts de marché aux grandes compagnies aériennes; **imported textiles have ~d ours out** les importations de textiles, en cassant les prix, nous ont fait perdre toute compétitivité; **he ~d himself out of the job** il n'a pas été embauché parce qu'il a demandé un salaire trop élevé.
◆ **price up** *vt sep Br* [raise cost of] augmenter OR majorer le prix de, majorer; [on label] indiquer un prix plus élevé sur.

price control *n* contrôle *m* des prix.

price cut *n* rabais *m*, réduction *f* (de prix); **'huge ~s!'** 'prix sacrifiés!'.

price-cutting *n* *(U)* réductions *fpl* de prix.

-priced [praɪst] *in cpds*: **high~** à prix élevé, (plutôt) cher; **low~** à bas prix, peu cher; **over~** trop cher.

price-fixing [-fɪksɪŋ] *n* [control] contrôle *m* des prix; [rigging] entente *f* sur les prix.

price index *n* indice *m* des prix.

priceless ['praɪslɪs] *adj* -1. [precious - jewels, friendship] d'une valeur inestimable. -2. *inf* [funny - joke] tordant, bidonnant; [- person] impayable.

price list *n* tarif *m*, liste *f* des prix.

price-rigging *n* entente *f* sur les prix.

price-ring *n* cartel *m* des prix.

prices control = **price control**.

prices index = **price index**.

price tag *n* -1. [label] étiquette *f* de prix. -2. [value] prix *m*, valeur *f*; **what's the ~ on a Rolls these days?** combien vaut une Rolls de nos jours?

price war *n* guerre *f* des prix.

pricey *inf* ['praɪsɪ] (*compar* **pricier**, *superl* **priciest**) *adj* chérot.

prick [prɪk] ◇ *vt* -1. [jab, pierce] piquer, percer; **she ~ed her finger/herself with the needle** elle s'est piqué le doigt/elle s'est piquée avec l'aiguille; **to ~ holes in sthg** faire des trous dans qqch; **the kids were ~ing balloons with pins** les gosses crevaient des ballons avec des épingles; **the thorns ~ed their legs** les épines leur piquaient les jambes. -2. [irritate] piquer, picoter; **tears ~ed his eyes** les larmes lui piquaient les yeux; **the smoke was ~ing my eyes/throat** la fumée me piquait les yeux/la gorge; **his conscience was ~ing him** *fig* il n'avait pas la conscience tranquille, il avait mauvaise conscience.
◇ *vi* -1. [pin, cactus, thorn] piquer. -2. [be irritated] picoter; **my eyes are ~ing from the smoke** j'ai les yeux qui me piquent OR brûlent à cause de la fumée; **her conscience was ~ing (at her)** *fig* elle n'avait pas la conscience tranquille, elle avait mauvaise conscience.
◇ *n* -1. [from insect, pin, thorn] piqûre *f*; **he felt a sudden ~ in his finger** soudain il a senti quelque chose lui piquer le doigt; **~s of conscience** *fig* remords *mpl*. -2. ▼ [penis] bite *f*. -3. ▽ [person] con *m*, connard *m*.
◆ **prick out** *vt sep* HORT repiquer.
◆ **prick up** ◇ *vi insep* [ears] se dresser.
◇ *vt sep* dresser; **the dog ~ed up its ears** le chien a dressé les oreilles; **she ~ed up her ears at the sound of her name** elle a dressé OR tendu l'oreille en entendant son nom.

pricking ['prɪkɪŋ] *n* picotement *m*; **she felt a ~ in her fingers** elle avait des picotements dans les doigts; **the ~s of conscience** les remords *mpl*.

prickle ['prɪkl] ◇ *n* -1. [on rose, cactus] épine *f*, piquant *m*; [on hedgehog, porcupine] piquant *m*. -2. [sensation] picotement *m*.
◇ *vt* piquer.
◇ *vi* [skin] picoter, fourmiller; **her skin ~d with excitement** un frisson d'excitation lui parcourut la peau.

prickly ['prɪklɪ] (*compar* **pricklier**, *superl* **prickliest**) *adj* -1. [cactus, plant] épineux; [hedgehog] couvert de piquants; [beard] piquant; [clothes] qui pique; **his fingers felt ~** il avait des fourmillements dans les doigts; **his skin felt ~** sa peau le démangeait; **the surface felt ~** la surface était piquante; **a ~ sensation** une sensation de picotement. -2. *inf* [irritable - person] ombrageux, irritable; [- character] ombrageux; **he's very ~** il se froisse facilement, il est très susceptible; **she's a bit ~ today** elle est plutôt irritable aujourd'hui. -3. [delicate - subject, topic] épineux, délicat; **it's a ~ situation** c'est une situation épineuse OR délicate.

prickly heat *n* *(U)* fièvre *f* miliaire.

prickly pear *n* [fruit] figue *f* de Barbarie; [tree] figuier *m* de Barbarie.

pricy *inf* ['praɪsɪ] = **pricey**.

pride [praɪd] ◇ *n* -1. [satisfaction] fierté *f*; **she takes great ~ in her son** elle est très fière de son fils; **they take ~ in their town** ils sont fiers de leur ville; **to take (a) ~ in one's appearance** prendre soin de sa personne; **he takes no ~ in his work** il ne prend pas du tout son travail à cœur; **to take (a) ~ in doing sthg** mettre de la fierté à faire qqch, s'enorgueillir de faire qqch; **he had ~ in his sister's success** il était fier de la réussite de sa sœur; **she pointed with ~ to her new car** elle montra fièrement du doigt sa nouvelle voiture. -2. [self-respect] fierté *f*, amour-propre *m*; **a sense of ~** un sentiment d'amour-propre; **he has no ~** il n'a pas d'amour-propre; **her ~ was hurt** elle était blessée dans son amour-propre; **they have too much ~ to accept charity** ils sont trop fiers OR ils ont trop d'amour-propre pour accepter la charité. -3. *pej* [arrogance] orgueil *m*; **the sin of ~** le péché d'orgueil; **~ comes** OR **goes before a fall** *prov* plus on est fier, plus dure est la chute; **'Pride and Prejudice'** *Austen* 'Orgueil et préjugé'. -4. [most valuable thing] orgueil *m*, fierté *f*; **she is her parents' ~ and joy** elle fait la fierté de ses parents; **this painting is the ~ of the collection** ce tableau est le joyau de la collection ❑ **~ of place** place *f* d'honneur; **to have** OR **to take ~ of place** occuper la place d'honneur. -5. [of lions] groupe *m*.
◇ *vt*: **to ~ o.s. on** OR **upon sthg** être fier OR s'enorgueillir de qqch; **she ~d herself on being the youngest member of the team** elle s'enorgueillissait OR était fière d'être la plus jeune de l'équipe.

prier ['praɪə'] *n pej* fouineur *m*, -euse *f*.

priest [priːst] *n* prêtre *m*; **a Buddhist ~** un prêtre bouddhiste; **parish ~** curé *m*.

priestcraft ['priːstkrɑːft] *n* -1. [art, skills] sacerdoce *m*; **to learn ~** apprendre à être prêtre. -2. *pej* [influence] pouvoir *m* des curés.

priestess ['priːstɪs] *n* prêtresse *f*.

priest hole *n cachette pour les prêtres à l'époque des persécutions contre les catholiques.*

priesthood ['priːsthʊd] *n* [as vocation] prêtrise *f*; [clergy] clergé *m*; **to enter the ~** être ordonné prêtre.

priestly ['priːstlɪ] (*compar* **priestlier**, *superl* **priestliest**) *adj* sacerdotal, de prêtre.

priest-ridden *adj pej* dominé par l'Église.

prig [prɪg] *n Br*: **he's such a ~!** il fait toujours son petit saint!

priggish ['prɪgɪʃ] *adj Br* pharisaïque.

priggishness ['prɪgɪʃnɪs] *n Br* pharisaïsme *m*.

prim [prɪm] (*compar* **primmer**, *superl* **primmest**) *adj pej* -1. [affectedly proper - person] collet monté *(inv)*; [- attitude, behaviour] guindé, compassé; [- voice] affecté; **she's very ~ and proper** elle est très collet monté. -2. [neat - clothes] (très) comme il faut, (très) classique; [- house, hedge, lawn] impeccable; **it's too ~ for my taste** c'est trop comme il faut à mon goût.

prima ballerina [,priːmə-] *n* danseuse *f* étoile.

primacy ['praɪməsɪ] (*pl* **primacies**) *n* -1. [preeminence] primauté *f*, prééminence *f*; **the ~ of speech** LING la primauté de la parole. -2. RELIG primatie *f*.

prima donna [,priːmə'dɒnə] *n* -1. [opera singer] prima donna *f*. -2. *pej* diva *f*. -3. [star] star *f*.

primaeval [praɪ'miːvəl] = **primeval**.

prima facie [,praɪmə'feɪʃiː] ◇ *adv* à première vue, de prime abord.
◇ *adj* JUR: **a ~ case** une affaire simple a priori; **it's a ~ case of mistaken identity** a priori, il s'agit d'une erreur sur la personne; **there's a ~ case for not acting hastily** a priori, il ne faut pas agir trop hâtivement; **~ evidence** commencement *m* de preuve; **there is no ~ evidence** a priori, il n'y a aucune preuve.

primal ['praɪml] *adj* -1. [original] primitif, premier; **~ scream** PSYCH cri *m* primal. -2. [main] primordial, principal.

primal therapy *n* thérapie *f* primale.

primarily [*Br* 'praɪmərɪlɪ, *Am* praɪ'merəlɪ] *adv* -1. [mainly] principalement, avant tout. -2. [originally] primitivement, à l'origine.

primary ['praɪmərɪ] (*pl* **primaries**) ◇ *adj* -1. [main] principal, premier; [basic] principal, fondamental; **our ~ objective** notre premier objectif, notre objectif principal; **our ~ duty** notre premier devoir; **the ~ meaning of this word** le sens premier de ce mot; **this question is of ~ importance** cette question revêt une importance capitale; **the ~ cause of the accident** la cause principale de l'accident. -2. SCI primaire; **~ circuit** ELEC circuit *m* primaire; **~ feather** ORNITH rémige *f*; **~ tooth** ANAT dent de lait. -3. SCH primaire; **~ education** enseignement *m* primaire. -4. ECON primaire; **the ~ sector** le (secteur) primaire; **the ~ sector industries** les industries du secteur primaire.
◇ *n* -1. POL (élection *f*) primaire *f (aux États-Unis)*. -2. [school] école *f* primaire. -3. [colour] couleur *f* primaire. -4. ORNITH rémige *f*. -5. ELEC (enroulement *m*) primaire *m*.

PRIMARIES:
Les primaires américaines sont des élections (directes ou indirectes selon les États) aboutissant à la sélection des candidats qui seront en lice pour représenter les deux grands partis nationaux à l'élection présidentielle.

primary accent *n* accent *m* principal.

primary cell *n* pile *f* primaire.

primary colour *n* couleur *f* primaire.

primary school *n* école *f* primaire; ~ teacher instituteur *m*, -trice *f*.

primary stress = **primary accent**.

primate ['praɪmeɪt] *n* -**1.** ZOOL primate *m*. -**2.** RELIG primat *m*; the Primate of All England *titre officiel de l'archevêque de Cantorbéry*.

prime [praɪm] ◇ *adj* -**1.** [foremost] premier, primordial; [principal] premier, principal; [fundamental] fondamental; **one of the ~ causes of heart disease** une des principales causes des maladies cardiaques; **our ~ concern is to avoid loss of life** notre préoccupation principale est d'éviter de faire des victimes; **of ~ importance** de la plus haute importance, d'une importance primordiale. -**2.** [perfect] parfait; [excellent] excellent; **in ~ condition** [person] en parfaite santé; [athlete] en parfaite condition; [car] en parfait état; **it's a ~ example of what I mean** c'est un excellent exemple de ce que je veux dire; **~ quality** de première qualité; **~ beef** bœuf *m* de première catégorie; **~ site** emplacement *m* de premier ordre OR privilégié. -**3.** MATH [number] premier; **10 is ~ to 11** 10 et 11 sont premiers entre eux.
◇ *n* -**1.** [best moment]: **to be in one's ~** OR **in the ~ of life** être dans la fleur de l'âge; **I'm past my ~** je ne suis plus dans la fleur de l'âge; **these roses look a bit past their ~** ces roses sont plutôt défraîchies; **these curtains look a bit past their ~** ces rideaux ont vu des jours meilleurs; **when Romantic poetry was in its ~** lorsque la poésie romantique était à son apogée ❑ 'The Prime of Miss Jean Brodie' *Spark* 'le Bel Âge de Miss Brodie'. -**2.** MATH nombre *m* premier.
◇ *vt* -**1.** [gun, machine, pump] amorcer; **to ~ sb with drink** faire boire qqn; **he was well ~d** *inf* il était bien parti; **to ~ the pump** renflouer une entreprise. -**2.** [brief - person] mettre au courant, briefer; **to ~ sb for a meeting** préparer qqn à une réunion; **he is well ~d in local politics** il est bien renseigné sur la politique locale. -**3.** [with paint, varnish] apprêter.

prime cost *n* prix *m* de revient.

prime meridian *n* premier méridien *m*.

prime minister *n* Premier ministre *m*.

prime ministership, prime ministry *n* fonctions *fpl* de Premier ministre; **during her ~** pendant qu'elle était Premier ministre.

prime mover *n* -**1.** PHYS force *f* motrice. -**2.** PHILOS cause *f* première. -**3.** *fig* [person] instigateur *m*, -trice *f*.

prime number *n* nombre *m* premier.

primer ['praɪməʳ] *n* -**1.** [paint] apprêt *m*. -**2.** [for explosives] amorce *f*. -**3.** [book - elementary] manuel *m* (élémentaire); [- for reading] abécédaire *m*; **a Latin ~** un manuel de latin pour débutants.

prime rate *n* taux *m* d'escompte bancaire préférentiel, prime rate *m*.

prime time *n* heure *f* de grande écoute, prime time *m*.
◆ **prime-time** *adj* [TV programme, advertising] diffusé à une heure de grande écoute, de prime time.

primeval [praɪ'miːvl] *adj* -**1.** [prehistoric] primitif, des premiers âges OR temps; **a ~ forest** une forêt préhistorique OR primitive. -**2.** [primordial - fears, emotions] atavique, instinctif.

priming ['praɪmɪŋ] *n* *(U)* -**1.** [of pump] amorçage *m*; [of gun] amorce *f*. -**2.** [paint] première couche *f*.

primitive ['prɪmɪtɪv] ◇ *adj* primitif; **~ art** art *m* primitif.
◇ *n* -**1.** [primitive person] primitif *m*, -ive *f*. -**2.** [artist] primitif *m*. -**3.** COMPUT & MATH primitive *f*.

primitivism ['prɪmɪtɪvɪzm] *n* primitivisme *m*.

primly ['prɪmlɪ] *adv pej* d'une manière guindée OR collet monté; **to be ~ dressed** être habillé très comme il faut; **she sat ~ in the corner** elle se tenait assise très sagement dans le coin; **no thank you, he said ~** non merci, dit-il d'une voix affectée.

primness ['prɪmnɪs] *n pej* [of person] air *m* collet monté OR compassé; [of behaviour] caractère *m* maniéré OR compassé; [of dress] aspect *m* collet monté OR très comme il faut; [of voice] caractère *m* affecté.

primogenitor [,praɪməʊ'dʒenɪtəʳ] *n* (premier) ancêtre *m*.

primogeniture [,praɪməʊ'dʒenɪtʃəʳ] *n* primogéniture *f*.

primordial [praɪ'mɔːdjəl] *adj* primordial; **~ soup** soupe *f* primitive.

primp [prɪmp] ◇ *vi* se faire beau.
◇ *vt*: **to ~ o.s. (up)** se faire beau.

primrose ['prɪmrəʊz] ◇ *n* -**1.** BOT primevère *f*. -**2.** [colour] jaune *m* pâle.
◇ *adj* jaune pâle *(inv)*.

primrose path *n*: **the ~** la voie de la facilité.

primrose yellow *adj* jaune pâle *(inv)*.

primula ['prɪmjʊlə] *(pl* **primulas** OR **primulae** [-liː]) *n* primevère *f*.

Primus® ['praɪməs] *n Br*: **~ (stove)** réchaud *m* (de camping).

prince [prɪns] *n literal & fig* prince *m*; **Prince Rupert** le prince Rupert; **the Prince of Darkness** le prince des ténèbres; **the Prince of Peace** le prince de la paix; **the Prince of Wales** le prince de Galles; **he is a ~ among men** c'est un prince parmi les hommes; **to live like a ~** vivre comme un prince; 'The Prince' *Machiavelli* 'le Prince'; 'The Prince and the Pauper' *Twain* 'le Prince et le pauvre'.

Prince Charming *n* le Prince Charmant.

prince consort *n* prince *m* consort.

princedom ['prɪnsdəm] *n* principauté *f*.

Prince Edward Island *pr n* l'île *f* du Prince-Édouard.

princeling ['prɪnslɪŋ] *n* petit prince *m*.

princely ['prɪnslɪ] *adj* princier; **a ~ sum** une somme princière.

prince regent *n* prince *m* régent.

princess [prɪn'ses] *n* princesse *f*; **Princess Caroline** la princesse Caroline; **the Princess of Wales** la princesse de Galles; **she's like a fairytale ~** c'est une princesse de conte de fées.

princess royal *n*: **the ~** la princesse royale.

principal ['prɪnsəpl] ◇ *adj* [gen] principal; MUS [violin, oboe] premier.
◇ *n* -**1.** [head - of school] directeur *m*, -trice *f*; [- of university] doyen *m*, -enne *f*. -**2.** JUR [employer of agent] mandant *m*, commettant *m*. -**3.** [main character - in play] acteur *m* principal, actrice *f* principale; [- in orchestra] chef *m* de pupitre; [- in crime] auteur *m*. -**4.** FIN [capital - gen] capital *m*; [- of debt] principal *m*. -**5.** CONSTR [rafter] poutre *f* maîtresse.

principal boy *n jeune héros d'une pantomime dont le rôle est traditionnellement joué par une femme*.

principal clause *n* (proposition *f*) principale *f*.

principality [,prɪnsɪ'pælətɪ] *n* principauté *f*; **the Principality** [Wales] le pays de Galles.

principally ['prɪnsəplɪ] *adv* principalement.

principal parts *npl* temps *mpl* primitifs GRAMM.

principle ['prɪnsəpl] *n* -**1.** [for behaviour] principe *m*; **she has high ~s** elle a des principes; **she was a woman of ~** c'était une femme de principes OR qui avait des principes; **he has no ~s** il n'a pas de principes; **it's not the money, it's the ~** ce n'est pas pour l'argent, c'est pour le principe; **on ~, as a matter of ~** par principe; **it's a matter of ~** c'est une question de principe; **it's against my ~s to eat meat** j'ai pour principe de ne pas manger de viande; **she makes it a ~ never to criticize others** elle a pour principe de ne jamais critiquer les autres; **to stick to one's ~s** rester fidèle à ses principes; **he's very strict in matters of ~** il est très à cheval sur les principes. -**2.** [fundamental law] principe *m*; **to go back to first ~s** remonter jusqu'au principe; **the two systems operate on the same ~** les deux systèmes fonctionnent selon le même principe OR selon un principe identique. -**3.** [theory] principe *m*; **in ~** en principe; **basic ~** principe de base; **to be based on false ~s** reposer sur de faux principes OR de fausses prémisses; **we acted on the ~ that everybody knew** nous sommes partis du principe que tout le monde était au courant.

principled ['prɪnsəpld] *adj*: **a ~ man** un homme de principes OR qui a des principes; **to take a ~ stand** adopter une position de principe.

prink [prɪŋk] = **primp**.

print [prɪnt] ◇ *n* -**1.** [of publications]: **to appear in ~** être imprimé OR publié; **to see o.s./one's name in ~** voir ses écrits imprimés/son nom imprimé; **her work will soon be in ~** son œuvre sera bientôt publiée ‖ [of book]: **to be in/out of ~** être disponible/épuisé; **the book is no longer in ~** le livre est épuisé; **his unguarded comments got into ~** ses propos irréfléchis ont été publiés OR imprimés; **he refused to believe the story until he saw it in ~** il a refusé de croire à l'histoire tant qu'il ne l'a pas vue publiée; **the newspapers had already gone to ~ before the news broke** les journaux étaient déjà sous presse lorsque la nouvelle est tombée. -**2.** *(U)* [characters] caractères *mpl*; **in large/small ~** en gros/petits caractères; **in bold ~** en caractères gras. -**3.** *(U)* [text] texte *m* (imprimé); **I had to read through twenty pages of ~** j'ai dû lire vingt pages imprimées ❑ **the small** OR **fine ~ on a contract** les lignes en petits caractères en bas d'un contrat; **don't forget to read the small ~** ne manquez pas de lire ce qui est écrit en petits caractères. -**4.** PHOT épreuve *f*, tirage *m*; **to make a ~ from a negative** tirer une épreuve d'un négatif. -**5.** ART [engraving] gravure *f*, estampe *f*; [reproduction] poster *m*. -**6.** TEX [fabric] imprimé *m*; [dress] robe *f* imprimée; **a floral ~** un imprimé à fleurs. -**7.** [mark - from tyre, foot] empreinte *f*; [fingerprint] empreinte *f* digitale; **the thief left his ~s all over the door handle** le voleur a laissé ses empreintes partout sur la poignée de la porte.
◇ *comp* -**1.** TYPO: **the ~ unions** les syndicats *mpl* des typographes. -**2.** COMPUT: **~ drum** tambour *m* d'impression; **~ head** tête *f* d'impression; **~ menu** menu *m* d'impression; **~ speed** vitesse *f* d'impression.
◇ *adj* [dress] en tissu imprimé.
◇ *vt* -**1.** [book, newspaper, money] imprimer; [publish - story, article] publier; **the novel is being ~ed** le roman est sous presse OR en cours d'impression; **1,000 copies of the book had already been ~ed** on avait déjà tiré le livre à 1 000 exemplaires; **the papers refused to ~ the story** les journaux ont refusé de publier cette histoire; **~ed in Scotland** imprimé en Écosse. -**2.** [write] écrire en caractères d'imprimerie; **~ your name clearly** écrivez votre nom lisiblement. -**3.** PHOT tirer. -**4.** TEX imprimer. -**5.** [mark] imprimer; **the mark of a man's foot was ~ed in the wet sand** la trace d'un pied d'homme était imprimée dans le sable humide ‖ *fig* [in memory] graver, imprimer; **the incident remained ~ed in their memory** l'incident est resté gravé dans leur mémoire.
◇ *vi* -**1.** imprimer; **tomorrow's newspapers haven't started ~ing yet** les journaux de demain ne sont pas encore sous presse OR à l'impression; **the drawing should ~ well** le dessin devrait bien ressortir à l'impression. -**2.** [in handwriting] écrire en caractères d'imprimerie. -**3.** PHOT [negative]: **to ~ well** sortir bien au tirage.
◆ **print off** *vt sep* -**1.** TYPO imprimer, tirer. -**2.** PHOT tirer.
◆ **print out** *vt sep* COMPUT imprimer.
◆ **print up** *vt sep* TYPO imprimer.

printable ['prɪntəbl] *adj* imprimable, publiable; **some of their remarks were hardly ~** certaines de leurs remarques étaient difficilement publiables; **my opinion on the matter is not ~** mon avis sur la question n'est pas très agréable à entendre.

printed ['prɪntɪd] *adj* -**1.** [gen] imprimé; ~ cotton coton *m* imprimé; ~ matter imprimés *mpl*; the ~ word l'écrit *m*. -**2.** [notepaper] à en-tête.

printed circuit *n* circuit *m* imprimé.

printer ['prɪntəʳ] *n* -**1.** [person - gen] imprimeur *m*; [- typographer] typographe *mf*; [- compositor] compositeur *m*, -trice *f*; it's at the ~'s c'est chez l'imprimeur OR à l'impression ❑ ~'s error coquille *f*; ~'s ink encre *f* d'imprimerie; ~'s mark marque *f* d'imprimeur. -**2.** COMPUT imprimante *f*; ~ driver programme *m* de commande d'impression. -**3.** PHOT tireuse *f*.

printer's devil *n* apprenti *m* imprimeur.

printhead ['prɪnthed] *n* tête *f* d'impression.

printing ['prɪntɪŋ] *n* -**1.** [activity] imprimerie *f*; he works in ~ il travaille dans l'imprimerie. -**2.** [copies printed] impression *f*, tirage *m*; fourth ~ quatrième impression. -**3.** PHOT tirage *m*. -**4.** *(U)* [handwriting] (écriture *f* en) caractères *mpl* d'imprimerie.

printing ink *n* encre *f* d'imprimerie.

printing office *n* imprimerie *f*.

printing press *n* presse *f* (d'imprimerie).

printmaker ['prɪnt,meɪkəʳ] *n* -**1.** TYPO typographe *mf*. -**2.** ART graveur *m*.

printout ['prɪntaʊt] *n* [act of printing out] sortie *f* sur imprimante, tirage *m*; to do a ~ sortir un document sur imprimante, imprimer (un document) ‖ [printed version] sortie *f* papier, tirage *m*; [results of calculation] listing *m*; here's the ~ of the results voici le listing des résultats.

print shop *n* imprimerie *f*.

printwheel ['prɪntwiːl] *n* marguerite *f (d'imprimante)*.

prior ['praɪəʳ] ◇ *adj* -**1.** [earlier] antérieur, précédent; she had a ~ engagement elle était déjà prise ‖ [preliminary] préalable; without ~ notice sans préavis; without his ~ agreement sans son accord préalable. -**2.** [more important]: to have a ~ claim to OR on sthg avoir un droit de priorité OR d'antériorité sur qqch; her children had a ~ claim on her attention ses enfants passaient avant tout.
◇ *n* RELIG (père *m*) prieur *m*.
◆ **prior to** *prep phr* avant, antérieurement à, préalablement à; ~ to (his) departure... avant son départ OR avant de partir...; ~ to today avant aujourd'hui; ~ to any discussion préalablement à OR avant toute discussion.

prioress ['praɪərɪs] *n* (mère *f*) prieure *f*.

prioritize, -ise [praɪ'ɒrɪtaɪz] *vt* donner OR accorder la priorité à; if elected, we will ~ health care si nous sommes élus, nous accorderons la priorité aux services de santé; they've ~d those who've been waiting longest ils ont donné la priorité à ceux qui avaient attendu le plus longtemps; it's wrong to ~ any one issue c'est un tort de donner la priorité à une question plutôt qu'à une autre.

priority [praɪ'ɒrətɪ] (*pl* priorities) *n* priorité *f*; to give ~ to donner OR accorder la priorité à; to have OR to take ~ over avoir la priorité sur; to do sthg as a (matter of) ~ faire qqch en priorité; the matter has top ~ l'affaire a la priorité absolue OR est absolument prioritaire; the library came high/low on the list of priorities la bibliothèque venait en tête/venait loin sur la liste des priorités; you should get your priorities right il faudrait que tu apprennes à distinguer ce qui est important de ce qui ne l'est pas; the government has got its priorities all wrong le gouvernement n'accorde pas la priorité aux choses les plus importantes; according to ~ selon l'ordre de priorité.

priority share *n* action *f* privilégiée.

priory ['praɪərɪ] (*pl* priories) *n* prieuré *m*.

prise [praɪz] *vt Br*: to ~ sthg open ouvrir qqch à l'aide d'un levier; he tried to ~ open the door il a essayé de forcer la porte; she managed to ~ her leg free elle a réussi à dégager sa jambe; we ~d the top off with a spoon on a enlevé le couvercle à l'aide d'une cuillère; we managed to ~ the information out of her *fig* on a réussi à lui arracher le renseignement.

prism ['prɪzm] *n* prisme *m*.

prismatic [prɪz'mætɪk] *adj* prismatique.

prison ['prɪzn] ◇ *n* prison *f*; to be in ~ être en prison; he's been in ~ il a fait de la prison; to go to ~ aller en prison, être emprisonné; to send sb to ~, to put sb in ~ envoyer OR mettre qqn en prison; to be sent to OR put in ~ être incarcéré; to sentence sb to three years in ~ condamner qqn à trois ans de prison; marriage had become a ~ *fig* le mariage était devenu une prison.
◇ *comp* [director, warder, cell] de prison; [food, conditions] en prison, dans les prisons; [system, regulations, administration] pénitentiaire, carcéral; ~ sentence peine *f* de prison.

prison camp *n* camp *m* de prisonniers.

prison colony *n* bagne *m*, colonie *f* pénitentiaire.

prisoner ['prɪznəʳ] *n* prisonnier *m*, -ère *f*, détenu *m*, -e *f*; he's a ~ in Wormwood Scrubs il est détenu à la prison de Wormwood Scrubs; to take sb ~ faire qqn prisonnier; to hold sb ~ retenir qqn prisonnier, détenir qqn; to be taken ~ être fait prisonnier; to be held ~ être détenu; she became a ~ of her own fears *fig* elle devint prisonnière de ses propres peurs ❑ political ~ prisonnier OR détenu politique; ~ of conscience prisonnier *m* d'opinion; ~ of war prisonnier de guerre; 'The Prisoner of Zenda' *Hope* 'Le prisonnier de Zenda'.

prison van *n* fourgon *m* cellulaire.

prison visitor *n* visiteur *m*, -euse *f* de prison.

prissy *inf* ['prɪsɪ] *adj* prude, bégueule.

pristine ['prɪstiːn] *adj* -**1.** [immaculate] parfait, immaculé; of ~ cleanliness d'une propreté immaculée; in ~ condition en parfait état. -**2.** [original] primitif, premier.

prithee ['prɪðɪ] *interj arch* je vous prie, s'il vous plaît.

privacy [*Br* 'prɪvəsɪ, *Am* 'praɪvəsɪ] *n* -**1.** [seclusion] solitude *f*; lack of ~ manque *m* d'intimité; I have no ~ here je ne peux jamais être seul ici; can I have some ~ for a few hours? pouvez-vous me laisser seul quelques heures?; she hates having her ~ disturbed elle déteste qu'on la dérange chez elle ‖ [private life] vie *f* privée; I value my ~ je tiens à ma vie privée; you can't have any ~ if you're a star les stars n'ont pas de vie privée; an intrusion on sb's ~ une ingérence dans la vie privée de qqn; in the ~ of one's own home dans l'intimité de son foyer; there's no ~ in this world tout se sait dans ce bas monde. -**2.** [secrecy] intimité *f*, secret *m*; they got married in the strictest ~ ils se sont mariés dans la plus stricte intimité.

private ['praɪvɪt] ◇ *adj* -**1.** [not for the public] privé; ~ land terrain *m* privé; ~ fishing pêche *f* gardée; ~ performance OR showing THEAT représentation *f* privée; ~ road voie *f* privée; 'private' 'privé', 'interdit au public'. -**2.** [independent, not run or controlled by the state] privé; they operate a ~ pension scheme ils ont leur propre caisse de retraite; ~ nursing home foyer *m* privé pour personnes âgées. -**3.** [personal] privé, personnel; for ~ reasons pour des raisons personnelles; don't interfere in my ~ affairs OR business ne vous mêlez pas de mes affaires personnelles; ~ agreement accord *m* à l'amiable; I thought we had a ~ agreement about it je croyais que nous avions réglé ce problème entre nous; it's my ~ opinion c'est mon opinion personnelle; it's a ~ joke c'est une blague que vous ne pouvez pas comprendre; my ~ address mon adresse personnelle, mon domicile; she lives in her own ~ fantasy world elle vit dans un monde imaginaire bien à elle; she keeps her ~ thoughts to herself elle garde pour elle ses opinions personnelles. -**4.** [confidential] privé, confidentiel, personnel; a ~ conversation une conversation privée OR à caractère privé; we had a ~ meeting nous nous sommes vus en privé; I have some ~ information about him j'ai des renseignements confidentiels à son sujet OR le concernant; keep it ~ gardez-le pour vous; can I tell him? – no, it's ~ je peux le lui dire? – non c'est personnel ‖ 'private' [on envelope] 'personnel' ❑ ~ hearing JUR audience *f* à huis clos. -**5.** [individual - bank account] personnel; [- bathroom, lessons, tuition] particulier; she has ~ lessons in French elle prend des cours particuliers de français; ~ pupil élève *mf (à qui l'on donne des cours particuliers)*; he has a lot of ~ pupils il donne beaucoup de cours particuliers; ~ teacher précepteur *m*, -trice *f*; this is a ~ house c'est une maison particulière OR qui appartient à des particuliers; in my ~ capacity à titre personnel; for your ~ use pour votre usage personnel; for your ~ information à titre confidentiel; ~ car voiture *f* personnelle. -**6.** [quiet, intimate] intime, privé; a ~ place un endroit tranquille; he's a very ~ person c'est quelqu'un de très réservé; they want a ~ wedding ils veulent se marier dans l'intimité; it was a ~ funeral les obsèques ont eu lieu dans la plus stricte intimité; do you have a ~ room where we can talk? avez-vous une pièce où l'on puisse parler tranquillement? ❑ ~ bar *salon dans un pub*. -**7.** [ordinary]: a ~ citizen un (simple) citoyen, un particulier; ~ soldier (simple) soldat *m*.
◇ *n* MIL (simple) soldat *m*, soldat *m* de deuxième classe; it belongs to Private Hopkins ça appartient au soldat Hopkins; Private Murdoch! soldat Murdoch!
◆ **privates** *inf npl euph* parties *fpl (génitales)*.
◆ **in private** *adv phr* [confidentially] en privé, en confidence; [in private life] en privé, dans la vie privée; [personally] en privé, personnellement.

private company *n* entreprise *f* OR société *f* privée.

private detective *n* détective *m* privé.

private enterprise *n* libre entreprise *f*.

privateer [,praɪvə'tɪəʳ] *n* corsaire *m*.

private eye *inf n* privé *m*; Private Eye PRESS *magazine satirique britannique*.

private hotel *n* ≃ pension *f* de famille.

private income *n* rentes *fpl*; to live on OR off a ~ vivre de ses rentes.

private investigator = **private detective**.

private life *n* vie *f* privée; in (his) ~ dans sa vie privée, en privé; she has no ~ elle n'a pas de vie privée.

privately ['praɪvɪtlɪ] *adv* -**1.** [not publicly]: a ~ owned company une entreprise privée; she sold her house ~ elle a vendu sa maison de particulier à particulier; they were married ~ leur mariage a eu lieu dans l'intimité; to be ~ educated [at school] faire ses études dans une école privée; [with tutor] avoir un précepteur; the jury's deliberations took place ~ les délibérations du jury se sont déroulées à huis clos. -**2.** [personally] dans mon/son *etc* for intérieur, en moi-même/soi-même *etc*; ~, he didn't agree intérieurement, il n'était pas d'accord; ~, I was disgusted dans mon for intérieur, j'étais dégoûté ‖ [secretly] secrètement; ~, he was plotting to oust his rival il complotait secrètement OR en secret d'évincer son rival ‖ [confidentially] en privé; she informed me ~ that... elle m'a informé en toute confidence que...; we met ~ nous avons eu une entrevue privée; can I see you ~? puis-je vous voir en privé OR en tête-à-tête?; I spoke to her ~ je lui ai parlé en tête-à-tête. -**3.** [as a private individual] à titre personnel; he acted ~ and not in his capacity as mayor il a agi à titre personnel et non en tant que maire.

private means *npl* rentes *fpl*, fortune *f* personnelle; a man of ~ un rentier.

private member's bill *n* proposition *f* de loi.

private parts *inf* = **privates**.

private patient *n patient d'un médecin dont les consultations ne sont pas prises en charge par les services de santé*.

private practice *n* médecine *f* privée OR non conventionnée; she's in ~ elle a un cabinet (médical) privé.

private property *n* propriété *f* privée; '~, keep out!' 'propriété privée', 'défense d'entrer'.

private school *n* ≃ école *f* libre.

private secretary *n* -**1.** COMM secrétaire particulier *m*, secrétaire particulière *f*. -**2.** *Br* POL *haut fonctionnaire dont le rôle est d'assister un ministre*.

private sector *n*: the ~ le secteur privé.

◆ **private-sector** *comp* [business, pay, bosses] privé.

private view *n* ART vernissage *m*.

privation [praɪ'veɪʃn] *n* privation *f*.

privative ['prɪvətɪv] ◇ *adj* privatif.

◇ *n* privatif *m*.

privatization [,praɪvɪtaɪ'zeɪʃn] *n* privatisation *f*.

privatize, -ise ['praɪvɪtaɪz] *vt* privatiser.

privet ['prɪvɪt] *n* troène *m*; ~ **hedge** haie *f* de troènes.

privilege ['prɪvɪlɪdʒ] ◇ *n* -**1.** [right, advantage] privilège *m*; the ~**s of the nobility** les privilèges de la noblesse; **to grant sb the ~ of doing sthg** accorder à qqn le privilège de faire qqch; **the fight for equality is a struggle against ~** le combat pour l'égalité est une lutte contre les privilèges. -**2.** [honour] honneur *m*; **it was a ~ to do business with you** ce fut un honneur de travailler avec vous; **I had the ~ of attending his wedding** j'ai eu le bonheur OR la chance d'assister à son mariage. -**3.** POL: **parliamentary ~** immunité *f* parlementaire.

◇ *vt* privilégier; **these tax changes ~ the rich** ces modifications fiscales privilégient les riches; **I was ~d to meet him after the war** j'ai eu le privilège OR la chance de le rencontrer après la guerre.

privileged ['prɪvɪlɪdʒd] ◇ *adj* -**1.** privilégié; **a ~ position** une position privilégiée; **a ~ minority** une minorité privilégiée, quelques privilégiés *mpl*; **only a ~ few were invited** seuls quelques privilégiés ont été invités; **the ~ few** la minorité privilégiée. -**2.** JUR [document, information] laissé à la discrétion du témoin; **such information is ~** le témoin n'est pas obligé de divulguer une telle information.

◇ *npl*: the ~ les privilégiés *mpl*.

privy ['prɪvɪ] (*pl* **privies**) ◇ *adj* -**1.** *fml* [informed]: **to be ~ to sthg** *fml* être instruit de qqch, être au courant de qqch; **an officer who had been ~ to the plot was arrested** un officier qui était au courant du complot fut arrêté. -**2.** *arch* [secret] secret, caché.

◇ *n arch* OR *hum* [toilet] lieux *mpl* d'aisances.

Privy Council *n*: the ~ *le Conseil privé du souverain en Grande-Bretagne*.

PRIVY COUNCIL:

En font partie tous les ministres du gouvernement ainsi que d'autres personnalités du Commonwealth. Le «Privy Council» compte environ 400 membres, mais ils ne se réunissent en plénière que dans des circonstances exceptionnelles.

Privy Councillor *n membre du Conseil privé*.

Privy Purse *n* cassette *f* royale.

Privy Seal *n*: the~ le Petit Sceau.

PRIVY SEAL:

Sceau apposé sur certains documents royaux qui ne sont pas assez importants pour recevoir le Grand Sceau (the Great Seal).

---

prize [praɪz] ◇ *n* -**1.** [for merit] prix *m*; **to award a ~ to sb** décerner un prix à qqn; **to win (the) first ~ in a contest** remporter le premier prix d'un concours; **she won the ~ for the best pupil** elle s'est vu décerner OR elle a reçu le prix d'excellence; **no ~s for guessing who won** *fig* vous n'aurez aucun mal à deviner le nom du gagnant; **the ~ list** le palmarès. -**2.** [in game] lot *m*; **to win first** OR **top ~ in the National Lottery** gagner le gros lot à la Loterie nationale; **the ~ list** la liste des gagnants; **consolation ~** prix *m* de consolation. -**3.** NAUT prise *f*.

◇ *vt* -**1.** [for value] chérir, attacher une grande valeur à; [for quality] priser; **I ~ his friendship very highly** son amitié m'est très précieuse; **my most ~d possessions** mes biens les plus précieux; **original editions are highly ~d** les éditions originales sont très prisées OR recherchées. -**2.** = **prise**.

◇ *adj* -**1.** [prizewinning] primé, médaillé; ~ **lamb** agneau *m* primé OR médaillé. -**2.** [excellent] parfait, typique; **a ~ specimen of manhood** un superbe mâle; **that's a ~ example of what not to do!** c'est un parfait exemple de ce qu'il ne faut pas faire! || [complete]: **a ~ fool** *inf* un parfait imbécile. -**3.** [valuable] de valeur; [cherished] prisé.

prize day *n Br* SCH (jour *m* de la) distribution *f* des prix.

prize draw *n* tombola *f*, loterie *f*.

prizefight ['praɪzfaɪt] *n* combat *m* professionnel.

prizefighter ['praɪzfaɪtəʳ] *n* boxeur *m* professionnel.

prizefighting ['praɪzfaɪtɪŋ] *n* boxe *f* professionnelle.

prize-giving *n* distribution *f* OR remise *f* des prix.

prize money *n* prix *m* en argent.

prize ring *n* ring *m (pour la boxe professionnelle)*.

prizewinner ['praɪzwɪnəʳ] *n* [of exam, essay contest] lauréat *m*, -e *f*; [of game, lottery] gagnant *m*, -e *f*.

prizewinning ['praɪzwɪnɪŋ] *adj* [novel, entry] primé; [ticket, number, contestant] gagnant.

pro [prəʊ] (*pl* **pros**) ◇ *n inf* -**1.** (*abbr of* professional) pro *mf*; **to turn ~** passer pro. -**2.** *Br* (*abbr of* prostitute) professionnelle *f*.

◇ *prep* [in favour of] pour; **he's very ~ capital punishment** c'est un partisan convaincu de la peine capitale.

◆ **pros** *npl*: the ~**s and cons** le pour et le contre; **the ~s and the antis** ceux qui sont pour et ceux qui sont contre.

pro- *in cpds* [in favour of] pro-; ~**American** proaméricain; **they were ~Stalin** ils étaient pour Staline, c'étaient des partisans de Staline.

PRO *n* -**1.** *abbr of* public relations officer. -**2.** *abbr of* Public Record Office.

proactive [prəʊ'æktɪv] *adj* PSYCH proactif.

pro-am ['prəʊ'æm] *adj* SPORT professionnel et amateur; **a ~ golf tournament** un open de golf.

probabilism ['prɒbəbɪlɪzm] *n* probabilisme *m*.

probability [,prɒbə'bɪlətɪ] (*pl* **probabilities**) *n* -**1.** [likelihood] probabilité *f*; **the ~ is that he won't come** il est probable qu'il ne viendra pas, il y a de fortes chances (pour) qu'il ne vienne pas; **there is little** OR **not much ~ of her changing her mind** il est peu probable qu'elle OR il y a peu de chance (pour) qu'elle change d'avis; **there is a strong ~ of that happening** il y a de fortes chances que cela se produise; **in all ~** selon toute probabilité. -**2.** MATH calcul *m* des probabilités; **what is the ~** OR **what are the probabilities of such a result?** quelle est la probabilité d'un tel résultat?

probable ['prɒbəbl] ◇ *adj* -**1.** [likely] probable, vraisemblable; **a ~ hypothesis** une hypothèse vraisemblable; **her success is more than ~** son succès est plus que probable; **it's highly ~ that we won't arrive before 2 o'clock** il est fort probable OR plus que probable que nous n'arriverons pas avant 14 h; **it's hardly ~ that he will be there** il est peu probable qu'il soit là; **that's quite ~** c'est tout à fait probable. -**2.** [plausible] vraisemblable; **it doesn't sound very ~ to me** ça ne me paraît pas très vraisemblable.

◇ *n*: **he's a ~ for the team next Saturday** il y a de fortes chances pour qu'il joue dans l'équipe samedi prochain; **the Probables and the Possibles** SPORT la sélection A et la sélection B.

probably ['prɒbəblɪ] *adv* probablement, vraisemblablement, selon toute probabilité; **you're ~ right** tu as probablement raison; ~ **not** probablement pas; **will you be able to come? — ~** pourrez-vous venir? — probablement; **will he write to you? — very ~** il t'écrira? — c'est très probable; **she's ~ left already** elle est probablement déjà partie, il est probable qu'elle soit déjà partie.

probate ['prəʊbeɪt] ◇ *n* [authentification] homologation *f*, authentification *f*, validation *f*; **to grant/to take out ~ of a will** homologuer/faire homologuer un testament; **to value sthg for ~** évaluer OR expertiser qqch pour l'homologation d'un testament.

◇ *vt Am* [will] homologuer, faire authentifier.

probate court *n* tribunal *m* des successions et des tutelles.

probation [prə'beɪʃn] *n* -**1.** JUR probation *f*, ≃ condamnation *f* avec sursis et mise à l'épreuve; **to be on ~** ≃ être en sursis avec mise à l'épreuve; **to put sb on ~** ≃ condamner qqn avec mise à l'épreuve. -**2.** [trial employment] essai *m*; **period of ~** période *f* d'essai; **to be on ~** être en période d'essai. -**3.** RELIG probation *f*.

probationary [prə'beɪʃnrɪ] *adj* -**1.** [trial] d'essai; ~ **period** période *f* d'essai; ~ **teacher** professeur *m* stagiaire; ~ **year** *Br* SCH année *f* probatoire. -**2.** JUR de probation. -**3.** RELIG de probation, de noviciat.

probationer [prə'beɪʃnəʳ] *n* -**1.** [employee] employé *m*, -e *f* à l'essai OR en période d'essai; *Br* [teacher] (professeur *m*) stagiaire *mf*; [trainee nurse] élève *m* infirmier, élève *f* infirmière. -**2.** JUR probationnaire *mf*. -**3.** RELIG novice *mf*.

probation officer *n* ≃ agent *m* de probation.

probe [prəʊb] ◇ *n* -**1.** [investigation] enquête *f*, investigation *f*; **there has been a newspaper ~ into corruption** la presse a fait une enquête sur la corruption. -**2.** [question] question *f*, interrogation *f*; **he didn't respond to our ~s into** OR **about his past** il est resté muet lorsque nous avons essayé de l'interroger sur son passé. -**3.** ASTRONAUT, ELECTRON & MED sonde *f*; ZOOL trompe *f*.

◇ *vt* -**1.** [investigate] enquêter sur; **police are probing the company's accounts** la police épluche les comptes OR examine la comptabilité de la société. -**2.** [examine, sound out - person, motive, reasons] sonder; **to ~ sb about sthg** sonder qqn sur qqch. -**3.** [explore, poke around in] explorer, fouiller, sonder; MED sonder; **she ~d the snow with her umbrella** elle fouilla la neige avec la pointe de son parapluie.

◇ *vi* -**1.** [investigate] enquêter, faire une enquête; **the police are probing for clues** les policiers recherchent des indices; **the paper ~d into the allegations** le journal a enquêté sur les accusations; **if you ~ into his past, you'll have some surprises** si vous fouillez dans son passé, vous aurez des surprises. -**2.** MED faire un sondage.

probing ['prəʊbɪŋ] ◇ *adj* [look] inquisiteur, perçant; [mind] pénétrant, clairvoyant; [remark, question] perspicace; **after hours of ~ questioning** après des heures d'un interrogatoire très poussé.

◇ *n* (*U*) -**1.** [investigation] enquête *f*, investigations *fpl*; [questioning] questions *fpl*, interrogatoire *m*; **she didn't react to my ~** je l'ai sondée, mais elle n'a pas réagi. -**2.** MED sondage *m*.

probity ['prəʊbətɪ] *n* probité *f*.

problem ['prɒbləm] ◇ *n* problème *m*; **a mathematical ~** un problème de mathématique; **a technical/financial ~** un problème technique/financier; **to cause ~s for sb** causer des ennuis OR poser des problèmes à qqn; **to solve a ~** résoudre un problème; **he's got ~s with the police** il a des problèmes OR ennuis avec la police; **the oldest one is a real ~ to me** l'aîné me pose de réels problèmes; **that's going to be a bit of a ~** ça va poser un petit problème; **that's no ~!** ça ne pose pas de OR aucun problème!; **can you come on Friday? — no ~!** *inf* pouvez-vous venir vendredi? — pas de problème OR sans problème!; **thanks for doing that for me — no ~!** *inf* merci d'avoir fait ça pour moi — pas de problème!; **I don't see what the ~ is** je ne vois pas où est le problème; **it's a ~ knowing** OR **to know what to get her for Christmas** c'est difficile de savoir quoi lui offrir pour Noël; **what's your ~?** *inf* c'est quoi ton problème?, qu'est-ce qui ne va pas?; **she has a bit of a weight ~** elle a des problèmes de poids.

◇ *comp* [child, family, hair] à problèmes; [play] à thèse; it's a real ~ case c'est un cas qui pose de réels problèmes.

problematic(al) [ˌprɒbləˈmætɪk(l)] *adj* problématique, incertain; staying the night there could be a bit ~ ça paraît compliqué d'y passer la nuit.

problem page *n Br* courrier *m* du cœur.

problem-solving [-ˌsɒlvɪŋ] *n* résolution *f* de problèmes; a ~ test un test par résolution de problèmes.

proboscis [prəʊˈbɒsɪs] (*pl* **proboscises** [-sɪsiːz] OR **proboscides** [-sɪdiːz]) *n* ZOOL trompe *f*; *hum* [nose] appendice *m*.

procaine [ˈprəʊkeɪn] *n* procaïne *f*.

procedural [prəˈsiːdʒərəl] *adj* de procédure, procédural; ~ agreement accord *m* de procédure OR sur la procédure; ~ fault faute *f* de procédure; ~ motion motion *f* d'ordre; the delays were merely ~ les retards étaient dus à de simples questions de procédure.

procedure [prəˈsiːdʒəʳ] *n* -**1.** procédure *f*; you must follow (the) normal ~ vous devez suivre la procédure normale; what's the correct ~? comment doit-on procéder?, quelle est la marche à suivre? ❑ criminal/civil (law) ~ JUR procédure *f* pénale/civile. -**2.** COMPUT procédure *f*, sous-programme *m*.

proceed [prəˈsiːd] *vi* -**1.** [continue] continuer, poursuivre; you may ~ vous pouvez poursuivre OR continuer; before ~ing any further with our investigations... avant de poursuivre nos investigations..., avant de pousser plus avant nos investigations...; just ~ with the announcement as usual faites votre annonce comme à l'accoutumée; before I ~ avant d'aller plus loin. -**2.** [happen] se passer, se dérouler; is the meeting ~ing according to plan? est-ce que la réunion se déroule comme prévu? -**3.** [move on] passer; let's ~ to item 32 passons à la question 32; to ~ to do sthg [start] se mettre à faire qqch; [do next] passer à qqch; he ~ed to tear up my report puis, il a déchiré mon rapport. -**4.** [act] procéder, agir; how should we ~? comment devons-nous procéder?, quelle est la marche à suivre?; I'm not sure how to ~ je ne vois pas très bien comment faire; ~ with caution agissez avec prudence. -**5.** [go, travel] avancer, aller; [car] avancer, rouler; they ~ed at a slow pace ils ont avancé lentement; she ~ed on her way elle a poursuivi son chemin; they are ~ing towards Calais ils se dirigent vers Calais; I then ~ed to the post office je me suis ensuite rendu au bureau de poste; I was ~ing along Henley Road in a westerly direction je longeais Henley Road en me dirigeant vers l'ouest; the road ~s along the coast la route longe la côte. -**6.** JUR: to ~ with charges against sb poursuivre qqn en justice, intenter un procès contre qqn. -**7.** [originate] provenir; problems ~ing from illiteracy difficultés provenant OR découlant de l'analphabétisme; their action ~ed from a desire to do good c'est le désir de bien faire qui les a poussés à agir; smells ~ing from the kitchen des odeurs provenant de la cuisine.

◆ **proceed against** *vt insep* JUR engager des poursuites contre.

proceeding [prəˈsiːdɪŋ] *n* [course of action] manière *f* de procéder OR d'agir; the best way of ~ would be to write to them la meilleure façon de procéder serait de leur écrire, ce qu'il y a de mieux à faire c'est de leur écrire; questionable financial ~s des pratiques financières douteuses.

◆ **proceedings** *npl* -**1.** [happening, event] événement *m*; the ~s passed off peacefully tout s'est déroulé sans incident; we watched the ~s on television nous avons regardé la retransmission télévisée de la cérémonie. -**2.** [meeting] réunion *f*, séance *f*; I missed some of the ~s j'ai manqué une partie de la réunion OR des débats. -**3.** [records - of meeting] compte rendu *m*, procès-verbal *m*; [- of learned society] actes *mpl*. -**4.** JUR [legal action] procès *m*, poursuites *fpl*; to take OR to institute (legal) ~s against sb intenter une action (en justice) contre qqn, engager des poursuites contre qqn ‖ [legal process] procédure *f*; legal ~s are very slow in this country la procédure judiciaire est très lente dans ce pays.

proceeds [ˈprəʊsiːdz] *npl* recette *f*, somme *f* recueillie; all ~ will go to charity tout l'argent recueilli sera versé aux œuvres de charité.

process [*n* & *vt* ˈprəʊses, *vi* prəˈses] ◇ *n* -**1.** [series of events, operation] processus *m*; the ageing ~ le processus de vieillissement; the democratic ~ le processus démocratique; the peace ~ le processus de paix; the ~ of reproduction le processus de reproduction; the whole ~ only takes a few minutes tout le processus OR toute l'opération ne prend que quelques minutes; teaching him French is a slow ~ il en faut du temps pour lui apprendre le français. -**2.** [method] procédé *m*, méthode *f*; to develop a ~ for doing sthg mettre au point un procédé pour faire qqch; a photographic ~ un procédé photographique; a new manufacturing ~ un nouveau procédé de fabrication; by a ~ of elimination par élimination; by a ~ of trial and error en procédant par tâtonnements; to be in ~ être en cours. -**3.** JUR [legal action] procès *m*, action *f* en justice; [writ, summons] citation *f* (en justice), assignation *f* (en justice). -**4.** BIOL [outgrowth] processus *m*.

◇ *vt* -**1.** [transform - raw materials] traiter, transformer; [- cheese, meat, milk] traiter; [- nuclear waste] retraiter; COMPUT [- data] traiter; PHOT développer. -**2.** ADMIN & COMM [deal with - order, information, cheque] traiter; my insurance claim is still being ~ed ma déclaration de sinistre est toujours en cours de règlement; we ~ thousands of applications every week nous traitons des milliers de demandes chaque semaine.

◇ *vi* [march] défiler; RELIG défiler en procession; the bishops ~ed slowly down the aisle la procession des évêques avançait lentement dans l'allée centrale.

◆ **in the process** *adv phr*: I managed to rescue the cat but I twisted my ankle in the ~ j'ai réussi à sauver le chat, mais je me suis tordu la cheville (en le faisant).

◆ **in the process of** *prep phr* en train de; to be in the ~ of doing sthg être en train de faire qqch; it's in the ~ of being discussed/of being carried out c'est en cours de discussion/en voie d'exécution; in the ~ of speaking to him, I found out that his wife was dead c'est en lui parlant que j'ai appris que sa femme était morte; they're in the ~ of getting a divorce ils sont en instance de divorce; in the ~ of time avec le temps, à la longue.

processed [ˈprəʊsest] *adj* [food] traité, industriel *pej*; ~ cheese [for spreading] fromage *m* à tartiner; [in slices] fromage *m* en tranches.

process engineer *n* ingénieur *m* en procédés.

process engineering *n* ingénierie *f* de procédés.

processing [ˈprəʊsesɪŋ] *n* [gen & COMPUT] traitement *m*; ~ plant [for sewage, nuclear waste etc] usine *f* de traitement.

procession [prəˈseʃn] *n* -**1.** [ceremony] procession *f*, cortège *m*; RELIG procession *f*; funeral ~ cortège *m* funèbre. -**2.** [demonstration] défilé *m*, cortège *m*. -**3.** [continous line] procession *f*, défilé *m*; the soldiers marched in ~ through the town les soldats ont défilé à travers la ville; I've had a ~ of people through my office all day toute la journée, ça a été un défilé permanent dans mon bureau.

processional [prəˈseʃənl] ◇ *adj* processionnel; a ~ march une marche processionnelle.

◇ *n* RELIG [hymn] cantique *m* processionnel; [book] processional *m*.

processor [ˈprəʊsesəʳ] *n* -**1.** COMPUT processeur *m*. -**2.** CULIN robot *m* ménager.

process printing *n* impression *f* en couleurs.

pro-choice [ˈprəʊˈtʃɔɪs] *adj* pour l'avortement et l'euthanasie.

proclaim [prəˈkleɪm] *vt* -**1.** [declare] proclamer, déclarer; to ~ independence proclamer l'indépendance; on the day that peace was ~ed le jour de l'armistice; to ~ a state of emergency proclamer l'état d'urgence; a holiday was ~ed for the investiture une journée de congé fut octroyée pour l'investiture; many ~ed that he was mad OR ~ed him to be mad beaucoup de gens ont déclaré qu'il était fou; he ~ed himself emperor il s'est proclamé empereur; she ~ed her innocence elle a clamé son innocence. -**2.** [reveal] révéler, manifester, trahir; his behaviour ~ed his nervousness son comportement trahissait sa nervosité; his expression ~ed his absolute sincerity une sincérité totale se lisait sur son visage.

proclamation [ˌprɒkləˈmeɪʃn] *n* proclamation *f*, déclaration *f*; by public ~ par proclamation publique; to issue OR to make a ~ faire une proclamation.

proclivity [prəˈklɪvətɪ] (*pl* **proclivities**) *n fml* propension *f*, inclination *f*, tendance *f*; to have a ~ to OR towards sthg avoir une propension à qqch; sexual proclivities penchant *m* pour certaines pratiques sexuelles.

proconsul [ˌprəʊˈkɒnsəl] *n* proconsul *m*.

procrastinate [prəˈkræstɪneɪt] *vi* tergiverser, atermoyer, temporiser; he's always procrastinating il remet toujours tout au lendemain, il fait toujours traîner les choses; if you hadn't ~d [wasted time] si vous n'aviez pas fait traîner les choses; [hesitated] si vous n'aviez pas hésité.

procrastination [prəˌkræstɪˈneɪʃn] *n* procrastination *f lit*, tendance *f* à tout remettre au lendemain; ~ is the thief of time *prov* il ne faut jamais remettre au lendemain ce que l'on peut faire le jour même *prov*.

procrastinator [prəʊˈkræstɪneɪtəʳ] *n* indécis *m*, -e *f*, velléitaire *mf*; he's a terrible ~! il a une fâcheuse tendance à toujours tout remettre au lendemain!

procreate [ˈprəʊkrɪeɪt] *fml* ◇ *vi* procréer.

◇ *vt* engendrer.

procreation [ˌprəʊkrɪˈeɪʃn] *n fml* procréation *f*.

Procrustean [prəʊˈkrʌstɪən] *adj* de Procruste.

proctor [ˈprɒktəʳ] ◇ *n* -**1.** JUR [agent] ≃ fondé *m* de pouvoir. -**2.** UNIV [in UK] représentant *m*, -e *f* du conseil de discipline; [in US - invigilator] surveillant *m*, -e *f* (à un examen). -**3.** RELIG procureur *m*.

◇ *vi* & *vt* *Am* surveiller.

procurable [prəˈkjʊərəbl] *adj* que l'on peut se procurer OR obtenir; these goods are ~ only from an overseas supplier on ne peut se procurer ces denrées qu'auprès d'un fournisseur à l'étranger.

procuration [ˌprɒkjʊˈreɪʃn] *n* -**1.** [acquisition] obtention *f*, acquisition *f*. -**2.** JUR procuration *f*. -**3.** [of prostitutes] proxénétisme *m*.

procurator [ˈprɒkjʊreɪtəʳ] *n* -**1.** JUR fondé *m* de pouvoir. -**2.** *Scot* = **procurator fiscal**. -**3.** ANTIQ procurateur *m*.

procurator fiscal *n en Écosse, magistrat qui fait office de procureur et qui remplit les fonctions du «coroner» en Angleterre.*

procure [prəˈkjʊəʳ] ◇ *vt* -**1.** *fml* [obtain] procurer, obtenir; [buy] (se) procurer, acheter; to ~ sthg (for o.s.) se procurer qqch; the defence lawyers ~d his acquittal les avocats de la défense ont obtenu son acquittement; to ~ sthg for sb procurer qqch à qqn. -**2.** JUR [prostitutes] procurer, prostituer. -**3.** *arch* [cause] procurer, causer, provoquer; to ~ sb's death [have killed] faire assassiner qqn; [cause death] provoquer la mort de qqn.

◇ *vi* JUR faire du proxénétisme.

procurement [prəˈkjʊəmənt] *n* -**1.** [acquisition] obtention *f*, acquisition *f*. -**2.** COMM [buying] achat *m*, acquisition *f*; MIL acquisition *f* de matériel.

procurer [prəˈkjʊərəʳ] *n* JUR proxénète *m*.

procuress [prəˈkjʊərɪs] *n* JUR proxénète *f*.

procuring [prəˈkjʊərɪŋ] *n* -**1.** [acquisition] acquisition *f*, obtention *f*. -**2.** JUR proxénétisme *m*.

rod [prɒd] (*pt* & *pp* prodded, *cont* prodding) ◇ *n* -**1.** [with finger] petit coup *m* avec le doigt; [with stick] petit coup *m* de bâton; I gave him a ~ with my walking stick je lui ai donné un petit coup avec ma canne; he gave the sausages a ~ with his fork il a piqué les saucisses avec sa fourchette. -**2.** *fig* [urging]: to give sb a ~ pousser OR aiguillonner qqn; he needs a ~ to make him work il faut le pousser pour qu'il travaille. -**3.** [stick] bâton *m*, pique *f*.
◇ *vt* -**1.** [with finger] donner un coup avec le doigt à, pousser du doigt; [with stick] pousser avec la pointe d'un bâton; he prodded me in the back with his pen il m'a donné un (petit) coup dans le dos avec son stylo; he prodded the mattress with the end of his stick il donna des petits coups dans le matelas avec la pointe de son bâton; to ~ sausages with a fork piquer des saucisses avec une fourchette. -**2.** *fig* [urge] pousser, inciter; to ~ sb into doing sthg pousser OR inciter qqn à faire qqch; to ~ sb into action pousser qqn à agir.
◆ **prod at** *vt insep* pousser, piquer; she prodded at her food distractedly elle piquait dans son assiette d'un air distrait.

rod▽ [prɒd] *n Ir pej* Protestant *m*, -e *f*.

rodigal ['prɒdɪgl] ◇ *adj* prodigue; the ~ son BIBLE le fils prodigue.
◇ *n* prodigue *mf*.

rodigality [,prɒdɪ'gæləti] *n* prodigalité *f*.

rodigally ['prɒdɪgəlɪ] *adv* avec prodigalité.

rodigious [prə'dɪdʒəs] *adj* prodigieux.

rodigiously [prə'dɪdʒəslɪ] *adv* prodigieusement.

rodigy ['prɒdɪdʒɪ] (*pl* prodigies) *n* -**1.** [person] prodige *m*; child OR infant ~ enfant *mf* prodige. -**2.** [marvel] prodige *m*.

rodrome ['prəʊdrəʊm] (*pl* prodromes OR prodromata [prəʊ'drəʊmətə]) *n* prodrome *m*.

roduce [*vb* prə'djuːs, *n* 'prɒdjuːs] ◇ *vt* -**1.** [manufacture, make] produire, fabriquer; we aren't producing enough spare parts nous ne produisons pas assez de pièces détachées; our factory ~s spare parts for washing machines notre usine fabrique des pièces détachées pour machines à laver; Denmark ~s dairy products le Danemark est un pays producteur de produits laitiers; we have ~d three new models this year nous avons sorti trois nouveaux modèles cette année. -**2.** [yield - raw materials, crops] produire; [- interest, profit] rapporter; this mine is producing less and less coal la production de charbon de cette mine est en déclin; this region ~s good wine cette région produit du bon vin; halogen lamps ~ a lot of light les lampes halogènes donnent beaucoup de lumière; my investments ~ a fairly good return mes investissements sont d'un assez bon rapport; this account ~s a high rate of interest ce compte rapporte des intérêts élevés. -**3.** [write, record - book, record] produire, sortir; [publish] publier, éditer; he hasn't ~d a new painting for over a year now cela fait maintenant plus d'un an qu'il n'a rien peint; she has ~d a lot of poetry elle a publié de nombreux poèmes; the publishers ~d a special edition les éditeurs ont publié OR sorti une édition spéciale. -**4.** BIOL [give birth to - subj: woman] donner naissance à; [- subj: animal] produire, donner naissance à; [secrete - saliva, sweat etc] secréter; she ~d many children elle a eu de nombreux enfants. -**5.** [bring about - situation, problem] causer, provoquer, créer; [- illness, death] causer, provoquer; [- anger, pleasure, reaction] susciter, provoquer; [- effect] provoquer, produire; the first candidate ~d a favourable impression on the panel le premier candidat a fait une impression favorable sur le jury; the team has ~d some good results/some surprises this season l'équipe a obtenu quelques bons résultats/provoqué quelques surprises cette saison. -**6.** [present, show - evidence, documents] présenter, produire; he ~d a £5 note from his pocket il a sorti un billet de 5 livres de sa poche; you have to be able to ~ identification vous devez pouvoir présenter une pièce d'identité; the defendant was unable to ~ any proof l'accusé n'a pu fournir OR apporter aucune preuve; to ~ a witness faire comparaître un témoin; they ~d some excellent arguments ils ont avancé d'excellents arguments; she is continually producing new ideas elle ne cesse d'avoir des idées nouvelles; he finally managed to ~ the money il a enfin réussi à trouver l'argent OR réunir la somme nécessaire; the champion ~d some good shots le champion a réussi quelques bons coups; she can ~ a meal from nothing il lui suffit d'un rien pour cuisiner un bon repas. -**7.** [film] produire; [play - organize, finance] produire; [- direct] réaliser, mettre en scène; [radio or TV programme - organize, finance] produire; [- direct] réaliser, mettre en ondes. -**8.** GEOM [line] prolonger, continuer. -**9.** CHEM, ELEC & PHYS [reaction, spark] produire; [discharge] produire, provoquer; [vacuum] faire, créer.
◇ *vi* -**1.** [yield - factory, mine] produire, rendre. -**2.** THEAT assurer la mise en scène; CIN [financer] assurer la production; [director] assurer la réalisation.
◇ *n* (*U*) produits *mpl* (alimentaires); agricultural/dairy ~ produits agricoles/laitiers; farm ~ produits agricoles OR de la ferme; home ~ produits du pays; ~ of Spain produit en Espagne.

producer [prə'djuːsə^r] *n* -**1.** AGR & INDUST producteur *m*, -trice *f*. -**2.** [of film] producteur *m*, -trice *f*; [of play, of TV or radio programme - organizer, financer] producteur *m*, -trice *f*; [- director] réalisateur *m*, -trice *f*.

producer gas *n* gaz *m* de gazogène.

producer goods *npl* biens *mpl* de production.

-producing [prə,djuːsɪŋ] *in cpds* producteur de; oil~ producteur de pétrole; tear/sweat~ glands glandes *f* lacrymales/sudoripares.

product ['prɒdʌkt] *n* -**1.** AGR, CHEM & INDUST produit *m*; finished ~ INDUST produit fini; [piece of work] résultat *m* final; food ~s produits alimentaires, denrées *fpl* alimentaires; ~ of India produit d'Inde. -**2.** [result] produit *m*, résultat *m*; this book is the ~ of many years' hard work ce livre est le fruit de longues années d'un travail acharné; she's the ~ of an unhappy childhood elle est le produit d'une enfance malheureuse; the ~ of our labour le résultat OR le fruit de notre travail; that's the ~ of a lively imagination c'est le produit d'une imagination débordante. -**3.** MATH produit *m*; the ~ of x and y le produit de x par y.

production [prə'dʌkʃn] *n* -**1.** [process of producing - of goods] production *f*, fabrication *f*; [- of crops, electricity, heat] production *f*; the workers have halted ~ les travailleurs ont arrêté la production; the model is now in ~ le modèle est en cours de production; this model went into/out of ~ in 1989 on a commencé la fabrication de ce modèle/ce modèle a été retiré de la production en 1989. -**2.** [amount produced] production *f*; an increase/fall in ~ une hausse/baisse de la production OR du rendement; wine ~ has increased la production viticole a augmenté. -**3.** [of film] production *f*; [of play, of radio or TV programme - organization, financing] production *f*; [- artistic direction] réalisation *f*, mise *f* en scène. -**4.** [show, work of art] CIN & THEAT spectacle *m*; RADIO & TV production *f*; ART & LITERAT œuvre *f*; there's no need to make such a (big) ~ out of it! *inf fig* il n'y a pas de quoi en faire un plat OR toute une histoire! -**5.** [presentation - of document, passport, ticket] présentation *f*; on ~ of this voucher sur présentation de ce bon.

production line *n* chaîne *f* de fabrication; to work on the ~ travailler à la chaîne.

production manager *n* directeur *m*, -trice *f* de la production.

production platform *n* plate-forme *f* de production.

productive [prə'dʌktɪv] *adj* -**1.** [gén & ECON] productif; ~ labour travail *m* productif; the ~ forces les forces productives OR de production. -**2.** [fertile - land] fertile; [- imagination] fertile, fécond; [prolific - writer, artist] prolifique. -**3.** [useful] fructueux, utile; our visit/meeting has been very ~ notre visite/réunion a été très fructueuse. -**4.** [of situation, feeling etc]: to be ~ of engendrer, créer; such methods are ~ of stress de telles méthodes favorisent le stress. -**5.** LING productif.

productively [prə'dʌktɪvlɪ] *adv* -**1.** ECON d'une manière productive. -**2.** [usefully] utilement; [fruitfully] fructueusement, profitablement, avec profit.

productivity [,prɒdʌk'tɪvətɪ] ◇ *n* productivité *f*, rendement *m*.
◇ *comp* [fall, level] de productivité; ~ bonus prime *f* de rendement OR de productivité.

proem ['prəʊem] *n* préface *f*.

prof *inf* [prɒf] (*abbr of* professor) *n* prof *mf*.

Prof. (*written abbr of* professor) Pr.

profanation [,prɒfə'neɪʃn] *n* profanation *f*.

profanatory [prə'fænətrɪ] *adj* profanateur.

profane [prə'feɪn] ◇ *adj* -**1.** [irreligious] sacrilège, impie *lit* OR *dated*. -**2.** [secular] profane, laïque. -**3.** [uninitiated] profane. -**4.** [vulgar - remark, language] vulgaire, grossier.
◇ *vt* profaner.

profanity [prə'fænətɪ] (*pl* profanities) *n* -**1.** [profane nature - of text] nature *f* OR caractère *m* profane; [- of action] impiété *f*; an act of ~ une profanation. -**2.** [oath] grossièreté *f*, juron *m*; to utter profanities proférer des grossièretés.

profess [prə'fes] ◇ *vt* -**1.** [declare] professer *lit*, déclarer, proclamer; to ~ hatred for OR of sb professer sa haine pour qqn; to ~ ignorance avouer son ignorance; to ~ an opinion professer OR proclamer une opinion; to ~ Catholicism/Islam RELIG être catholique/musulman. -**2.** [claim] prétendre, déclarer; she ~es to speak French elle prétend parler le français. -**3.** [profession] exercer; to ~ medicine exercer la profession de médecin.
◇ *vi* RELIG prononcer ses vœux, faire sa profession.

professed [prə'fest] *adj* -**1.** [avowed] déclaré; a ~ marxist un marxiste déclaré; that is my ~ aim c'est mon but avoué. -**2.** [alleged] supposé, prétendu; a ~ friend un soi-disant ami; she's a ~ expert in the field elle se dit experte en la matière. -**3.** RELIG profès; a ~ nun une religieuse professe.

professedly [prə'fesɪdlɪ] *adv* -**1.** [avowedly]: they are ~ anarchists de leur propre aveu, ce sont des anarchistes; she has ~ killed three people d'après elle OR d'après ses dires, elle aurait tué trois personnes. -**2.** [allegedly] soi-disant, prétendument; he came here ~ to help me à l'en croire, il est venu pour m'aider; she's ~ rich c'est une femme prétendument riche.

profession [prə'feʃn] *n* -**1.** [occupation] profession *f*; what's your ~? quelle est votre profession?; she's a lawyer by ~ elle exerce la profession d'avocat, elle est avocate (de profession); I'm not an artist by ~ je ne suis pas un artiste professionnel; the (liberal) ~s les professions libérales; learned ~ profession intellectuelle. -**2.** [body] (membres *mpl* d'une) profession *f*, corps *m*; the teaching ~ le corps enseignant, les enseignants *mpl*. -**3.** [declaration] profession *f*, déclaration *f*; ~ of faith profession de foi; his ~s of love ses déclarations d'amour; the novice made his ~s RELIG le novice a fait sa profession OR a prononcé ses vœux.

professional [prə'feʃənl] ◇ *adj* -**1.** [relating to a profession] professionnel; the surgeon demonstrated his great ~ skill le chirurgien a montré ses grandes compétences professionnelles; a lawyer is a ~ man un avocat exerce une profession libérale; a club for ~ people un club réservé aux membres des professions libérales; it would be against ~ etiquette to tell you vous le dire serait contraire aux usages OR à la déontologie de la profession; his work is not up to ~ standards son travail n'est pas ce

qu'on peut attendre d'un professionnel; **may I give you some ~ advice?** puis-je vous donner l'avis d'un professionnel?; **to take** OR **to get ~ advice** [gen] consulter un professionnel; [from doctor/lawyer] consulter un médecin/un avocat. -**2.** [as career, full-time] professionnel, de profession; **she's a ~ writer/photographer** elle est écrivain professionnel/photographe professionnelle; **he's a ~ painter** il vit de sa peinture; **a ~ soldier/diplomat** un militaire/diplomate de carrière; **some countries have a ~ army** certains pays ont une armée de métier; **he's a ~ drunk** *fig* il passe son temps à boire || SPORT professionnel; **to go** OR **to turn ~** passer professionnel; **~ golf** le golf professionnel. -**3.** [in quality, attitude] professionnel; **a ~ piece of work** un travail de professionnel; **she is very ~ in her approach to the problem** elle aborde le problème de façon très professionnelle; **he works in a very ~ manner** il travaille en professionnel.
◇ *n* professionnel *m*, -elle *f*.

professional association *n* association *f* professionnelle.

professional foul *n* FTBL faute *f* délibérée.

professionalism [prə'feʃnəlɪzm] *n* professionnalisme *m*; **nobody would doubt her ~** personne ne remettrait en question son professionnalisme; **this burglary shows great ~** ce cambriolage est l'œuvre d'un professionnel.

professionally [prə'feʃnəlɪ] *adv* -**1.** [as profession] professionnellement; **he writes ~** il vit de sa plume; **she's a ~ qualified doctor** elle est médecin diplômé; **he plays ~** SPORT c'est un joueur professionnel; **I've only ever met her ~** mes seuls rapports avec elle ont été d'ordre professionnel OR ont été des rapports de travail; **we had the house painted ~** on a fait peindre la maison par un professionnel OR un homme de métier. -**2.** [skilfully, conscientiously] professionnellement, de manière professionnelle; **this work has been done very ~** c'est le travail d'un professionnel; **she works very ~** elle travaille en vraie professionnelle, elle fait un vrai travail de professionnel.

professor [prə'fesəʳ] *n* UNIV [in UK - head of department] titulaire *mf* d'une chaire, professeur *m*; [in US - lecturer] enseignant *m*, -e *f* (de faculté OR d'université); **~ of sociology** *Br* titulaire de la chaire de sociologie, professeur responsable du département de sociologie; *Am* professeur de sociologie; **Professor Colin Appleton** le professeur Colin Appleton; **Dear Professor Appleton** Monsieur le Professeur; [less formally] (Cher) Monsieur.

professorial [,prɒfɪ'sɔːrɪəl] *adj* professoral.

professorship [prə'fesəʃɪp] *n* chaire *f*; **she has a ~ in French at Durham** elle occupe la chaire OR est titulaire de la chaire de français à l'Université de Durham.

proffer ['prɒfəʳ] *vt fml* -**1.** [offer, present - drink, present] offrir, tendre; [- resignation] présenter, offrir, remettre; [- advice] donner; **we all ~ed our excuses to her** nous lui avons tous offert OR présenté nos excuses; **to ~ one's hand to sb** tendre la main à qqn. -**2.** [put forward - idea, opinion] émettre; [- remark, suggestion] émettre, faire.

proficiency [prə'fɪʃənsɪ] *n* compétence *f*, maîtrise *f*; **she attained a high degree of ~ in French** elle a acquis une grande maîtrise du français; **~ in driving is essential** une maîtrise de la conduite (automobile) est indispensable.

proficient [prə'fɪʃənt] *adj* [worker] compétent, expérimenté; [driver] expérimenté, chevronné; **she's a very ~ pianist** c'est une excellente pianiste; **I used to be quite ~ in French** j'étais d'un assez bon niveau OR j'avais un assez bon niveau en français.

proficiently [prə'fɪʃəntlɪ] *adv* de façon (très) compétente, avec (beaucoup de) maîtrise; **she speaks French ~** elle parle couramment le français.

profile ['prəʊfaɪl] ◇ *n* -**1.** ART & ARCHIT profil *m*; **to look at/to draw sb in ~** regarder/dessiner qqn de profil. -**2.** [description - of person] profil *m*, portrait *m*. -**3.** [of candidate, employee] profil *m*; **to have the right ~ for the job** avoir le bon profil pour le poste || [level of prominence]: **to keep a high ~** être très en vue, faire parler de soi; **the President has been keeping a high ~ recently** le président a occupé le devant de la scène ces derniers temps; **to keep a low ~** adopter un profil bas, se montrer discret; **when the boss is in a bad mood I keep a low ~** lorsque le patron est de mauvaise humeur, je me fais tout petit OR je ne me fais pas remarquer. -**4.** [graph] profil *m*. -**5.** GEOG & GEOL profil *m*; **a soil ~** le profil d'un sol.
◇ *vt* -**1.** [show in profile] profiler; **his shadow was ~d against the wall** son ombre se profilait OR se découpait sur le mur. -**2.** [write profile of - person] établir le profil de, brosser le portrait de.

profile drag *n* traînée *f* de profil.

profit ['prɒfɪt] ◇ *n* -**1.** [financial gain] profit *m*, bénéfice *m*; **to make a ~ out of sthg** faire un bénéfice sur qqch; **we made a £200 ~ on the sale** nous avons réalisé un bénéfice de 200 livres sur cette vente; **to move into ~** devenir bénéficiaire; **to make** OR **to turn out a ~** réaliser un bénéfice; **to show a ~** rapporter (un bénéfice OR des bénéfices); **the fair didn't show much of a ~** la foire n'a pas beaucoup rapporté (de bénéfices); **to sell sthg at a ~** vendre qqch à profit, faire un profit sur la vente de qqch; **he only writes for ~** il n'écrit que pour l'argent; **I don't do it for ~** je ne le fais pas dans un but lucratif ❑ **~ and loss account** compte *m* de pertes et profits. -**2.** *fml* [advantage] profit *m*, avantage *m*; **to turn sthg to one's ~**, **to gain ~ from sthg** tirer profit OR avantage de qqch; **to do sthg for ~** faire qqch dans un but intéressé.
◇ *vt* profiter à, bénéficier à; **it won't ~ you to tell lies** cela ne vous servira à rien de mentir.
◇ *vi* profiter, tirer un profit OR avantage; **to ~ from** OR **by sthg** tirer profit OR avantage de qqch, profiter de qqch.

profitability [,prɒfɪtə'bɪlətɪ] *n* FIN rentabilité *f*; [of ideas, action] caractère *m* profitable OR fructueux.

profitable ['prɒfɪtəbl] *adj* -**1.** [lucrative] rentable, lucratif; **this shop is no longer ~** ce magasin n'est plus rentable; **a ~ investment** un investissement rentable OR lucratif; **it wouldn't be very ~ for me to sell** pour moi il ne serait pas très rentable de vendre, cela ne me rapporterait pas grand-chose de vendre. -**2.** [beneficial] profitable, fructueux; **we had a very ~ discussion** nous avons eu une discussion très fructueuse; **this is the most ~ way to do it** c'est la manière la plus avantageuse de le faire.

profitably ['prɒfɪtəblɪ] *adv* -**1.** FIN avec profit, d'une manière rentable; **we sold it very ~** on l'a vendu en faisant un bénéfice confortable. -**2.** [usefully] utilement, avec profit, profitablement; **use your time ~** ne gaspillez pas votre temps.

profit centre *n* centre *m* de profit.

profiteer [,prɒfɪ'tɪəʳ] ◇ *n* profiteur *m*, -euse *f*.
◇ *vi* faire des bénéfices exorbitants.

profiteering [,prɒfɪ'tɪərɪŋ] *n*: **they were accused of ~** on les a accusés de faire des bénéfices excessifs.

profiterole [prə'fɪtərəʊl] *n* profiterole *f*.

profitless ['prɒfɪtlɪs] *adj* [FIN & gen] sans profit; **it would be absolutely ~ to do such a silly thing** il ne servirait à rien de faire quelque chose d'aussi stupide; **we spent a ~ afternoon** nous avons perdu OR gaspillé notre après-midi.

profit-making *adj* -**1.** [aiming to make profit] à but lucratif; **non ~ organization** association *f* à but non lucratif. -**2.** [profitable] rentable.

profit margin *n* marge *f* bénéficiaire.

profit motive *n* recherche *f* du profit, appât *m* du gain *pej*.

profit rate *n* taux *m* de profit OR de bénéfice.

profit-sharing *n* participation *f* OR intéressement *m* aux bénéfices; **we have a ~ agreement/scheme** nous avons un accord/un système de participation (aux bénéfices).

profit squeeze *n* compression *f* des bénéfices, étranglement *m* des marges.

profit-taking *n* prise *f* de bénéfice.

profligacy ['prɒflɪgəsɪ] *n fml* -**1.** [dissoluteness] débauche *f*, licence *f*. -**2.** [extravagance] (extrême) prodigalité *f*.

profligate ['prɒflɪgɪt] *fml* ◇ *adj* -**1.** [dissolute] débauché, dévergondé; **to behave in a ~ manner** se comporter en débauché; **a ~ way of life** une vie dissolue OR de débauche. -**2.** [extravagant] (très) prodigue, dépensier; [wasteful] (très) gaspilleur; **the ~ use of natural resources** le gaspillage des ressources naturelles; **she's ~ with her riches** elle gaspille ses richesses; **he's got ~ tastes** il a des goûts dispendieux *fml*.
◇ *n* -**1.** [dissolute person] débauché *m*, -e *f*, libertin *m*, -e *f*. -**2.** [spendthrift] dépensier *m*, -ère *f*.

pro-form ['prəʊfɔːm] *n* proforme *f*.

pro forma [,prəʊ'fɔːmə] ◇ *adj* pro forma *(inv)*.
◇ *adv* pour la forme.
◇ *n* = **pro forma invoice**.

pro forma invoice *n* facture *f* pro forma.

profound [prə'faʊnd] *adj* profond.

profoundly [prə'faʊndlɪ] *adv* profondément.

profundity [prə'fʌndətɪ] (*pl* **profundities**) *n* profondeur *f*.

profuse [prə'fjuːs] *adj* -**1.** [abundant, copious] abondant, profus *lit*; **~ vegetation** végétation abondante; **~ sweating** transpiration profuse. -**2.** [generous - praise, apologies] prodigue, profus; **to be ~ in one's compliments** se répandre en compliments; **to be ~ in one's apologies** se confondre en excuses.

profusely [prə'fjuːslɪ] *adv* -**1.** [abundantly, copiously] abondamment, en abondance, à profusion; **to sweat ~** transpirer abondamment. -**2.** [generously, extravagantly]: **they thanked her ~** ils la remercièrent avec effusion; **to praise sb ~** se répandre en éloges sur qqn; **she was ~ apologetic** elle s'est confondue en excuses.

profusion [prə'fjuːʒn] *n* profusion *f*, abondance *f*; **in ~** à profusion, en abondance.

prog *inf* [prɒg] *n Br abbr of* **programme**.

progenitor [prəʊ'dʒenɪtəʳ] *n fml* -**1.** [ancestor] ancêtre *m*. -**2.** [originator] auteur *m*; [precursor] précurseur *m*.

progeny ['prɒdʒənɪ] *n fml* [offspring] progéniture *f*; [descendants] descendants *mpl*, lignée *f*.

progesterone [prə'dʒestərəʊn] *n* progestérone *f*.

prognathous [prɒg'neɪθəs] *adj* prognathe.

prognosis [prɒg'nəʊsɪs] (*pl* **prognoses** [-siːz]) *n fml* OR MED pronostic *m*.

prognostic [prɒg'nɒstɪk] ◇ *n* -**1.** MED [symptom] pronostic *m*. -**2.** *fml* [sign] présage *m*; [forecast] pronostic *m*.
◇ *adj* MED pronostique.

prognosticate [prɒg'nɒstɪkeɪt] *vt fml* [foretell] pronostiquer, présager, prédire; [foreshadow] annoncer, présager.

prognostication [prɒg,nɒstɪ'keɪʃn] *n* pronostic *m*.

program ['prəʊgræm] (*pt* & *pp* **programmed** OR **programed**, *cont* **programming** OR **programing**) ◇ *n* -**1.** *Am* = **programme**. -**2.** COMPUT programme *m*.
◇ *vt* -**1.** *Am* = **programme**. -**2.** COMPUT programmer.
◇ *vi* COMPUT programmer.

programable *Am* = **programmable**.

programer *Am* = **programmer**.

programmable *Br*, **programable** *Am* [prəʊ'græməbl] *adj* programmable; **~ function key** touche *f* de fonction programmable.

programme *Br*, **program** *Am* ['prəʊgræm]
◇ *n* -**1.** MUS, POL, THEAT programme *m*; **the ~ of the day's events** le programme des mani

festations de la journée; there's a change in the ~ il y a un changement de programme; the ~ includes three pieces by Debussy il y a trois morceaux de Debussy au programme; an election ~ *esp Am* un programme électoral; a research ~ un programme de recherches; the party has adopted a new ~ le parti a adopté un nouveau programme; what's (on) the ~ for next week? quel est l'emploi du temps prévu pour la semaine prochaine? -**2.** [booklet] programme *m*; [syllabus] programme *m*; [timetable] emploi *m* du temps. -**3.** RADIO & TV [broadcast] émission *f*; there's a good ~ about OR on opera on TV tonight il y a une bonne émission sur l'opéra à la télévision ce soir || [TV station] chaîne *f*; [radio station] station *f*; to change ~ TV changer de chaîne; RADIO changer de station.

◇ *vt* programmer; the heating is ~d to switch itself off at night le chauffage est programmé pour s'arrêter la nuit; the documentary was ~d for 9 o'clock le documentaire était programmé pour 21 h; his arrival wasn't ~d son arrivée n'était pas prévue; all children are ~d to learn language chez les enfants, la capacité d'apprentissage du langage est innée.

programmed learning ['prəʊgræmd-] *n* enseignement *m* programmé.

programme music *n* musique *f* à programme.

programme notes *npl* THEAT notes *fpl* sur le programme; the ~ are very useful les commentaires donnés dans le programme sont très utiles.

programmer *Br*, **programer** *Am* ['prəʊgræmə^r] *n* COMPUT -**1.** [person] programmeur *m*, -euse *f*. -**2.** [device] programmateur *m*.

programming ['prəʊgræmɪŋ] *n* programmation *f*; ~ language langage *m* de programmation.

progress [*n* 'praʊgres, *vb* prəʊ'gres] ◇ *n* *(U)* -**1.** [headway] progrès *mpl*; they have made fast ~ ils ont avancé OR ils ont progressé rapidement; Marie is making ~ in English Marie fait des progrès en anglais; we'll never make any ~ this way nous ne ferons jamais de progrès OR jamais aucun progrès de cette façon; the patient has made excellent ~ l'état du malade s'est nettement amélioré. -**2.** [evolution] progrès *m*; to hinder ~ entraver OR freiner le progrès; she believes in the ~ of mankind elle croit au progrès de l'humanité; you can't stop ~ on ne peut arrêter le progrès. -**3.** [forward movement] progression *f*; we watched the ~ of the boat along the canal nous avons regardé le bateau avancer le long du canal. -**4.** *arch* [journey] voyage *m*.

◇ *vi* -**1.** [make headway - negotiations, research] progresser, avancer; [- situation] progresser, s'améliorer; [- patient] aller mieux; [- student] progresser, faire des progrès; the talks are ~ing well les pourparlers sont en bonne voie. -**2.** [move forward] avancer; to ~ towards a place/an objective se rapprocher d'un lieu/ d'un objectif; as the day ~ed à mesure que la journée avançait.

◆ **in progress** *adj phr*: to be in ~ être en cours; work in ~ travaux *mpl* en cours; while the exam is in ~ pendant l'examen; 'service in ~' [in cathedral] 'office en cours'; the meeting is in ~ la réunion est en cours.

progress chaser *n* responsable *mf* du (suivi d'un) planning.

progression [prə'greʃn] *n* -**1.** [advance - of disease, army] progression *f*. -**2.** MATH & MUS progression *f*; melodic ~ progression mélodique. -**3.** [series, sequence] série *f*, suite *f*; I watched the endless ~ of suburban houses from the taxi du taxi, j'ai regardé la succession sans fin des pavillons de banlieue.

progressive [prə'gresɪv] ◇ *adj* -**1.** [forward-looking - idea, teacher, jazz] progressiste; [- education, method] nouveau, moderne; he has a very ~ outlook sa vision des choses est très moderne. -**2.** [gradual - change] progressif; ~ income tax impôt *m* progressif; to do sthg in ~ steps OR stages faire qqch par étapes successives || MED [disease] progressif; ~ hardening of the arteries artériosclérose *f* progressive. -**3.** GRAMM [aspect] progressif.

◇ *n* -**1.** POL progressiste *mf*. -**2.** GRAMM forme *f* progressive, progressif *m*; in the ~ à la forme progressive.

progressively [prə'gresɪvlɪ] *adv* -**1.** POL & SCH d'une manière progressiste; to think ~ avoir des idées progressistes. -**2.** [gradually] progressivement, graduellement, petit à petit; taxes were ~ increased les impôts ont augmenté progressivement.

progressiveness [prə'gresɪvnɪs] *n* -**1.** [of ideas, teaching] caractère *m* progressiste. -**2.** [gradualness] progressivité *f*.

progress report *n* [gen] compte-rendu *m*; [on work] rapport *m* sur l'avancement des travaux; [on patient] bulletin *m* de santé; [on pupil] bulletin *m* scolaire.

prohibit [prə'hɪbɪt] *vt* -**1.** [forbid] interdire, défendre, prohiber; to ~ sb from doing sthg interdire OR défendre à qqn de faire qqch; drinking alcohol at work is ~ed il est interdit de boire de l'alcool sur le lieu de travail; smoking is strictly ~ed il est formellement interdit de fumer; 'smoking ~ed' 'défense de fumer'; 'parking ~ed' 'stationnement interdit'. -**2.** [prevent] interdire, empêcher; his pacifism ~s him from joining the army son pacifisme lui interdit OR l'empêche de s'engager dans l'armée; my promise to her ~s me from saying more la promesse que je lui ai faite m'interdit OR m'empêche d'en dire plus.

prohibition [,prəʊɪ'bɪʃn] *n* interdiction *f*, prohibition *f*; the ~ of alcohol la prohibition de l'alcool; there should be a ~ on the sale of such goods il devrait y avoir une loi qui interdise la vente de ce genre de marchandises.

◆ **Prohibition** *n Am* HIST la Prohibition.

PROHIBITION:
Le 18e amendement à la Constitution américaine instituant la Prohibition (interdiction de consommer et de vendre de l'alcool) fut voté en 1919 sous la pression de groupes religieux et conservateurs; mais la prolifération de bars clandestins («speakeasies») et l'apparition d'une guerre des gangs (les «bootleggers») pour le monopole de la vente d'alcool incitèrent le Congrès à voter l'annulation de cette mesure en 1933, et les États l'abandonnèrent un à un.

---

prohibitionism [,prəʊɪ'bɪʃənɪzm] *n* prohibitionnisme *m*.

prohibitionist [,prəʊɪ'bɪʃənɪst] ◇ *adj* prohibitionniste.

◇ *n* prohibitionniste *mf*.

prohibitive [prə'hɪbətɪv] *adj* prohibitif.

prohibitively [prə'hɪbətɪvlɪ] *adv*: ~ expensive d'un coût prohibitif.

prohibitory [prə'hɪbɪtrɪ] *adj* prohibitif.

project [*n* 'prɒdʒekt, *vb* prə'dʒekt] ◇ *n* -**1.** [plan] projet *m*; a fund-raising ~ to save OR for saving the shipyard une collecte de fonds pour sauver le chantier naval; they're working on a new building ~ ils travaillent sur un nouveau projet de construction || [enterprise, undertaking] opération *f*, entreprise *f*; the start of the ~ has been delayed le début de l'opération a été retardé. -**2.** SCH travaux *mpl* pratiques, dossier *m*; the class has just finished a nature ~ la classe vient de terminer des travaux pratiques de sciences naturelles; Tina's ~ was the best in the whole class le dossier de Tina était le meilleur de toute la classe. -**3.** [study, research] étude *f*; a mining ~ une étude minière. -**4.** *Am*: (housing) ~ cité *f* HLM.

◇ *vt* -**1.** [plan] prévoir; two new airports are ~ed for the next decade il est prévu de construire deux nouveaux aéroports durant la prochaine décennie. -**2.** [foresee, forecast] prévoir; we have attempted to ~ next year's figures/output nous avons tenté de prévoir les chiffres/la production pour l'année prochaine. -**3.** [send forth - gen] projeter, envoyer; [- film, slide etc] projeter; to ~ one's voice projeter sa voix; the missile was ~ed into space le missile a été envoyé dans l'espace; the explosion ~ed debris high into the air l'explosion a projeté des débris très haut dans les airs; try to ~ yourself forward into the 21st century essayez d'imaginer que vous êtes au 21e siècle. -**4.** [present] présenter, projeter; football hooligans ~ a poor image of our country abroad les hooligans donnent une mauvaise image de notre pays à l'étranger; to ~ one's personality mettre sa personnalité en avant; he tries to ~ himself as a great humanist il essaie de se faire passer pour un grand humaniste. -**5.** PSYCH [transfer] projeter; to ~ one's feelings onto sb projeter ses sentiments sur qqn. -**6.** [cause to jut out] faire dépasser. -**7.** GEOM projeter; to ~ a cylinder on OR onto a plane projeter un cylindre sur un plan.

◇ *vi* -**1.** [protrude, jut out] faire saillie, dépasser; the barrel of his gun ~ed from his overcoat le canon de son revolver dépassait de son pardessus. -**2.** PSYCH se projeter. -**3.** [as personality]: she doesn't ~ well elle présente mal. -**4.** [with voice]: to learn to ~ apprendre à projeter sa voix.

projected [prə'dʒektɪd] *adj* -**1.** [planned - undertaking, visit] prévu; they are opposed to the ~ building scheme ils sont contre le projet de construction. -**2.** [forecast - figures, production] prévu; the ~ growth of the economy la croissance économique prévue, les prévisions de croissance économique.

projectile [prə'dʒektaɪl] *n* projectile *m*.

projecting [prə'dʒektɪŋ] *adj* [roof, balcony etc] saillant, en saillie, qui fait saillie; [teeth] en avant.

projection [prə'dʒekʃn] *n* -**1.** CIN, GEOM & PSYCH projection *f*. -**2.** FIN [estimate] projection *f*, prévision *f*; here are my ~s for the next ten years voici mes prévisions pour les dix années à venir. -**3.** [of missile] lancement *m*, envoi *m*. -**4.** [protrusion] saillie *f*, avancée *f*; [overhang] surplomb *m*.

projectionist [prə'dʒekʃənɪst] *n* projectionniste *mf*.

projective [prə'dʒektɪv] *adj* projectif; ~ psychology psychologie *f* projective.

projective geometry *n* géometrie *f* projective.

projective test *n* test *m* projectif.

project manager *n* [gen] chef *m* de projet; CONSTR maître *m* d'œuvre.

projector [prə'dʒektə^r] *n* projecteur *m*.

Prokofiev [prə'kɒfɪef] *pr n* Prokofiev.

prolactin [prəʊ'læktɪn] *n* prolactine *f*.

prolapse ['prəʊlæps] ◇ *n* MED prolapsus *m*, ptôse *f*; ~ (of the uterus) prolapsus OR descente *f* de l'utérus.

◇ *vi* descendre, tomber.

prole *inf* [prəʊl] *pej* ◇ *adj* prolo.

◇ *n* prolo *mf*.

prolegomenon [,prəʊle'gɒmɪnən] (*pl* **prolegomena** [-nə]) *n* prolégomènes *mpl*.

prolepsis [prəʊ'lepsɪs] (*pl* **prolepses** [-siːz]) *n* prolepse *f*.

proletarian [,prəʊlɪ'teərɪən] ◇ *n* prolétaire *mf*.

◇ *adj* -**1.** ECON, POL & SOCIOL prolétarien. -**2.** *pej* [behaviour, life, attitude] de prolétaire.

proletarianize, -ise [,prəʊlɪ'teərɪənaɪz] *vt* prolétariser.

proletariat [,prəʊlɪ'teərɪət] *n* prolétariat *m*.

pro-life ['prəʊ'laɪf] *adj* contre l'avortement et l'euthanasie.

proliferate [prə'lɪfəreɪt] *vi* proliférer.

proliferation [prəlɪfə'reɪʃn] *n* -**1.** [rapid increase] prolifération *f*. -**2.** [large amount or number] grande quantité *f*.

prolific [prə'lɪfɪk] *adj* prolifique.

prolix ['prəʊlɪks] *adj fml* prolixe.

prolixity [prəʊ'lɪksətɪ] *n fml* prolixité *f*.

prolog ['prəʊlɒg] *Am* = **prologue**.

prologue [ˈprəʊlɒg] *n literal & fig* prologue *m*; her late arrival was the ~ to yet another row son arrivée tardive allait être le prélude d'une OR préluder à une nouvelle querelle.

prolong [prəˈlɒŋ] *vt* prolonger.

prolongation [ˌprəʊlɒŋˈgeɪʃn] *n* [in time] prolongation *f*; [in space] prolongement *m*, extension *f*.

prolonged [prəˈlɒŋd] *adj* long; after a ~ absence après une longue absence.

prom *inf* [prɒm] *n* -**1.** *abbr of* promenade **1,4**. -**2.** *Br abbr of* promenade concert.
◆ **proms** *inf npl festival de concerts-promenades.*

PROM [prɒm] (*abbr of* programmable read only memory) *n* COMPUT PROM *f inv.*

promenade [ˌprɒməˈnɑːd] ◇ *n* -**1.** *Br* [at seaside] front *m* de mer, promenade *f*. -**2.** *Br* MUS = **promenade concert**. -**3.** [walk] promenade *f*. -**4.** *Am* [dance] bal *m (de lycéens ou d'étudiants).*
◇ *comp* THEAT [performance] *où les auditeurs doivent se déplacer pour suivre l'action de la pièce.*
◇ *vi fml* OR *hum* se promener.
◇ *vt fml* OR *hum* promener.

promenade concert *n* concert-promenade *m (où certains auditeurs se tiennent debout dans un promenoir).*

promenade deck *n* pont *m* promenade.

promenader [ˌprɒməˈnɑːdəʳ] *n* MUS auditeur *m*, -trice *f* d'un concert-promenade.

Promethean [prəˈmiːθjən] *adj* prométhéen.

Prometheus [prəˈmiːθɪəs] *pr n* Prométhée.

promethium [prəˈmiːθɪəm] *n* prométhéum *m*.

prominence [ˈprɒmɪnəns] *n* -**1.** [importance] importance *f*; [fame] célébrité *f*; to rise to ~ se hisser au premier rang; to come into OR to ~ [become important] prendre de l'importance; [become famous] devenir célèbre; to bring sb/sthg into ~ attirer l'attention sur qqn/qqch. -**2.** [protuberance] proéminence *f*; the ~ of his ears was very noticeable on ne voyait que ses oreilles décollées; a rocky ~ une saillie rocheuse. -**3.** ASTRON protubérance *f* solaire.

prominent [ˈprɒmɪnənt] *adj* -**1.** [well-known] célèbre; [eminent] éminent; she's a very ~ individual c'est un personnage très en vue; a scandal involving a ~ politician un scandale impliquant un éminent homme politique; he has a ~ position in the government il est très haut placé au gouvernement || [important] important; she played a ~ part OR role in the war elle a joué un rôle important OR de tout premier plan dans la guerre. -**2.** [striking, salient - detail, difference] frappant, remarquable; [- fact, feature] saillant, marquant; put that poster in a ~ position mettez cette affiche (dans un endroit) bien en vue. -**3.** [clearly visible - bones, muscles] saillant; [- land, structure, nose] proéminent; [- teeth] qui avance, proéminent.

prominently [ˈprɒmɪnəntlɪ] *adv* bien en vue; he figures ~ in French politics il occupe une position importante OR de premier plan dans la vie politique française; the medal was ~ displayed la médaille était mise en évidence.

promiscuity [ˌprɒmɪˈskjuːətɪ] *n* promiscuité *f* sexuelle.

promiscuous [prɒˈmɪskjʊəs] *adj* -**1.** [sexually - person]: to be ~ avoir des mœurs sexuelles libres; ~ behaviour promiscuité *f* sexuelle; he's very ~ il couche avec n'importe qui. -**2.** *fig* [disorderly] confus.

promiscuousness [prɒˈmɪskjʊəsnɪs] = **promiscuity**.

promise [ˈprɒmɪs] ◇ *n* -**1.** [pledge] promesse *f*; to make OR to give sb a ~ faire une promesse à qqn, donner sa parole à qqn; to keep a ~ respecter OR tenir une promesse; she always keeps her ~s elle tient toujours ses promesses, elle tient toujours (sa) parole; don't make ~s if you can't keep them on ne fait pas de promesses quand on ne peut pas les tenir; I kept OR held him to his ~ j'ai fait en sorte qu'il tienne parole; to break one's ~ manquer à sa parole, ne pas tenir ses promesses; a ~ of help une promesse d'assistance; he did it under (the) ~ of a Parliamentary seat il l'a fait parce qu'on lui a promis un siège de député; I'm under a ~ of secrecy j'ai promis de garder le secret OR de ne rien dire ❑ a ~ is a ~ chose promise, chose due *prov*; ~s, ~s! toujours des promesses! -**2.** [hope, potential] promesse *f*; she is full of ~ elle est pleine de promesse OR promesses; an artist of ~ un artiste qui promet; to hold out the ~ of sthg to sb promettre qqch à qqn, faire espérer OR miroiter qqch à qqn.
◇ *vt* -**1.** [pledge] promettre; to ~ sthg to sb, to ~ sb sthg promettre qqch à qqn; to ~ sb to do sthg promettre à qqn de faire qqch; I can't ~ (you) anything je ne peux rien vous promettre; he ~d himself a good meal il se promit mentalement de faire un bon repas; she ~d him (that) she would come elle lui a promis de venir OR qu'elle viendrait; you'll get into trouble, I ~ you! tu auras des ennuis, je te le promets OR tu verras ce que je te dis!; the weather forecast ~d us three days of good weather la météo nous a promis OR annoncé trois jours de beau temps ❑ to ~ the moon OR the earth promettre la lune OR monts et merveilles. -**2.** [indicate] promettre, annoncer; the sky ~s fine weather this afternoon le ciel laisse présager un temps agréable pour cet après-midi; next week already ~s to be difficult la semaine prochaine promet déjà d'être difficile OR s'annonce déjà difficile. -**3.** [in marriage]: she was ~d to the king's son at birth dès sa naissance, elle fut promise au fils du roi.
◇ *vi* -**1.** promettre; he wanted to come but he couldn't ~ il espérait pouvoir venir mais ne pouvait rien promettre; OK, I ~! d'accord, c'est promis! -**2.** *fig*: to ~ well [enterprise] promettre, s'annoncer bien; [person] être prometteur OR plein de promesses; [results, harvest, negotiations] s'annoncer bien; his first article ~s well son premier article promet OR est prometteur.

Promised Land *n* BIBLE & *fig* Terre *f* promise.

promising [ˈprɒmɪsɪŋ] *adj* -**1.** [full of potential - person] prometteur, qui promet, plein de promesses; she's a ~ actress c'est une actrice pleine de promesses OR qui promet. -**2.** [encouraging] prometteur, qui promet; these are ~ signs ce sont des signes prometteurs; she got off to a ~ start elle a fait des débuts prometteurs; her work is very ~ son travail est très prometteur; the forecast isn't very ~ for tomorrow les prévisions météo n'annoncent rien de bon pour demain.

promisingly [ˈprɒmɪsɪŋlɪ] *adv* d'une façon prometteuse; he began his acting career ~ il a débuté sa carrière d'acteur de façon prometteuse; France started the match ~ la France a bien débuté la partie.

promissory note [ˈprɒmɪsərɪ-] *n* billet *m* à ordre.

promo *inf* [ˈprəʊməʊ] (*pl* promos) (*abbr of* promotion) *n* clip *m* (promotionnel).

promontory [ˈprɒməntrɪ] (*pl* promontories) *n* promontoire *m*.

promote [prəˈməʊt] *vt* -**1.** [in profession, army] promouvoir; to be OR to get ~d être promu, monter en grade, obtenir de l'avancement; Blyth has been ~d (to) captain OR to the rank of captain Blyth a été promu (au grade de) capitaine; she's been ~d (to) regional manager elle a été promue (au poste de) directrice régionale. -**2.** SPORT: the Rovers were ~d to the second division les Rovers sont montés en deuxième division. -**3.** [foster] promouvoir, favoriser, encourager; to ~ international cooperation promouvoir OR favoriser OR encourager la coopération internationale; cleanliness ~s health la propreté est un facteur de santé; to ~ economic growth promouvoir OR favoriser la croissance économique. -**4.** COMM [advertise, publicize] promouvoir, faire la promotion de; to ~ a new product faire la promotion d'un nouveau produit; she's in England to ~ her new record elle est en Angleterre pour faire la promotion de son nouveau disque.

promoter [prəˈməʊtəʳ] *n* -**1.** COMM promoteur *m*, -trice *f* (des ventes). -**2.** [organizer - of match, concert] organisateur *m*, -trice *f*; [- of scheme] promoteur *m*, -trice *f*, instigateur *m*, -trice *f*. -**3.** [of peace, friendship] promoteur *m*, -trice *f*.

promotion [prəˈməʊʃn] *n* -**1.** [advancement] promotion *f*, avancement *m*; to get ~ être promu, obtenir de l'avancement; there are good prospects of ~ in this company il y a de réelles possibilités de promotion OR d'avancement dans cette société. -**2.** SPORT promotion *f*, the team won ~ to the first division l'équipe a gagné sa place en première division. -**3.** [encouragement, development] promotion *f*, développement *m*; the ~ of good international relations le développement de bonnes relations internationales. -**4.** COMM promotion *f*; sales ~ promotion *f* des ventes; (sales) ~ techniques techniques *fpl* de promotion des ventes; this week's ~ la promotion de la semaine; I helped in the ~ of her new book j'ai contribué à la promotion OR au lancement de son nouveau livre. -**5.** [in chess] promotion *f*.

promotional [prəˈməʊʃənl] *adj* [material] promotionnel, publicitaire.

prompt [prɒmpt] ◇ *adj* -**1.** [quick] rapide, prompt; a ~ answer/decision une réponse/décision rapide; to be ~ to take offence être prompt à s'offenser; Joan was ~ to answer our letter Joan a répondu rapidement OR sans attendre à notre lettre; you should give this matter ~ attention vous devriez vous occuper de cette question sans (plus) attendre OR le plus rapidement possible; to be ~ in paying one's debts être prompt à payer ses dettes; ~ payment COMM paiement *m* dans les délais. -**2.** [punctual] exact, à l'heure.
◇ *adv inf* [exactly]: we begin at 9 o'clock ~ nous commençons à 9 h précises.
◇ *vt* -**1.** [provoke, persuade] pousser, inciter; he's shy and needs to be ~ed to speak up il est timide, il faut l'encourager à s'exprimer; I felt ~ed to intervene je me suis senti obligé d'intervenir; the wave of strikes has ~ed the Government to step up its reform programme la vague de grèves a incité le gouvernement à accélérer son programme de réformes; his letter ~s me to think that he's mad sa lettre m'incite à penser qu'il est fou; what ~ed you to suggest such a thing? qu'est-ce qui vous a incité à proposer une chose pareille?; the scandal ~ed his resignation le scandale a provoqué sa démission. -**2.** THEAT souffler.
◇ *n* -**1.** THEAT: to give an actor a ~ souffler une réplique à un acteur. -**2.** COMPUT message-guide *m (au début de la ligne de commande).*

promptbook [ˈprɒmptbʊk] *n* manuscrit *m* (du souffleur).

prompt box *n* trou *m* (du souffleur).

prompter [ˈprɒmptəʳ] *n* souffleur *m*, -euse *f*; TV téléprompteur *m*.

prompting [ˈprɒmptɪŋ] *n* -**1.** [persuasion] incitation *f*; no amount of ~ will induce me to go there rien ne pourra me décider à y aller; she needed no ~ elle ne s'est pas fait prier, elle l'a fait d'elle-même; at his mother's ~, he wrote a letter of thanks à l'instigation OR sur l'insistance de sa mère, il a écrit une lettre de remerciement. -**2.** THEAT: some actors need frequent ~ certains acteurs ont souvent recours au souffleur; no ~! ne soufflez pas!

promptitude [ˈprɒmptɪtjuːd] *fml* = **promptness**.

promptly [ˈprɒmptlɪ] *adv* -**1.** [quickly] promptement, rapidement; he ~ sent off the telegram il a rapidement envoyé le télégramme; he paid up ~ il a payé immédiatement. -**2.** [punctually] ponctuellement; he always gets up ~ at 7 o'clock il se lève toujours à 7 h précises. -**3.** [immediately] aussitôt, tout de suite; I ~ forgot what I was meant to do j'ai aussitôt oublié ce que j'étais supposé faire.

promptness ['prɒmptnɪs] *n* -**1.** [quickness] promptitude *f*, rapidité *f*. -**2.** [punctuality] ponctualité *f*.

prompt note *n* COMM relance *f*.

prompt side *n* THEAT [in UK] côté *m* cour; [in US] côté *m* jardin.

promulgate ['prɒmlgeɪt] *vt fml* -**1.** [decree, law] promulguer. -**2.** [belief, idea, opinion] répandre, diffuser.

promulgation [,prɒml'geɪʃn] *n fml* -**1.** [of decree, law] promulgation *f*. -**2.** [of belief, idea, opinion] diffusion *f*, dissémination *f*.

prone [prəʊn] *adj* -**1.** [inclined, liable] sujet, enclin; **to be ~ to do sthg** être sujet OR enclin à faire qqch; **to be ~ to accidents/illness** être sujet aux accidents/à la maladie. -**2.** [prostrate] à plat ventre; **in a ~ position** couché sur le ventre.

proneness ['prəʊnnɪs] *n* tendance *f*, prédisposition *f*.

prong [prɒŋ] *n* [of fork] dent *f*; [of tuning fork] branche *f*; [of antler] pointe *f*; [of attack, argument] pointe *f*.

pronged [prɒŋd] *adj* à dents, à pointes.

-pronged *in cpds*: **two~** [fork] à deux dents; MIL [attack] sur deux fronts; [argument] double.

pronominal [prə'nɒmɪnl] *adj* pronominal.

pronominalize, -ise [prə'nɒmɪnəlaɪz] *vt* pronominaliser.

pronoun ['prəʊnaʊn] *n* pronom *m*.

pronounce [prə'naʊns] ◇ *vt* -**1.** [say] prononcer; **his name is hard to ~** son nom est difficile à prononcer; **how's it ~d?** comment est-ce que ça se prononce?; **you don't ~ the "p" in "psalm"** on ne prononce pas le «p» de «psalm», le «p» de «psalm» est muet. -**2.** [declare] déclarer, prononcer; **the doctor ~d him dead** le médecin l'a déclaré mort; **judgment has not yet been ~d** le jugement n'est pas encore prononcé OR rendu.
◇ *vi* -**1.** [articulate] prononcer. -**2.** [declare] se prononcer; **to ~ for/against sthg** [gen] se prononcer pour/contre qqch; JUR prononcer pour/contre qqch; **to ~ on** OR **upon sthg** se prononcer sur qqch.

pronounceable [prə'naʊnsəbl] *adj* prononçable.

pronounced [prə'naʊnst] *adj* prononcé, marqué.

pronouncement [prə'naʊnsmənt] *n* déclaration *f*.

pronto *inf* ['prɒntəʊ] *adv* illico.

pronucleus [prəʊ'nju:klɪəs] (*pl* **pronuclei** [-klɪaɪ]) *n* pronucléus *m*.

pronunciation [prə,nʌnsɪ'eɪʃn] *n* prononciation *f*.

proof [pru:f] ◇ *n* -**1.** *(U)* [evidence] preuve *f*; **to show** OR **to give ~ of sthg** faire OR donner la preuve de qqch; **do you have any ~?** vous en avez la preuve OR des preuves?; **can you produce any ~ for your accusations?** avez-vous des preuves pour justifier vos accusations?; **you need ~ of identity** vous devez fournir une pièce d'identité; **we have written ~ of it** nous en avons la preuve écrite OR par écrit; **that's no ~!** ce n'est pas une preuve!; **by way of ~** comme OR pour preuve; **~ of purchase** reçu *m*; **he cited several other cases in ~ of his argument** il a cité plusieurs autres cas pour défendre sa thèse; **he gave her a locket as ~ of his love** il lui a offert un médaillon comme preuve de son amour pour elle OR en gage d'amour; **they showed ~ of great foresight** ils ont fait preuve d'une grande prévoyance ❑ **the ~ of the pudding is in the eating** *prov* il faut juger sur pièces. -**2.** PHOT & TYPO épreuve *f*; **to correct** OR **to read the ~s** corriger les épreuves. -**3.** [of alcohol] teneur *f* (en alcool); **45 % ~ brandy** ≃ cognac à 45 degrés.
◇ *adj Br*: **to be ~ against** [fire, bullets, acid, rust] être à l'épreuve de; [danger, temptation] être à l'abri de OR insensible à.
◇ *vt* -**1.** [cloth, tent] imperméabiliser. -**2.** TYPO [proofread] corriger les épreuves de; [produce proof of] préparer les épreuves de.

-proof [prʊf, pru:f] *in cpds* à l'épreuve de; **acid~** à l'épreuve des acides; **an idiot~ mechanism** un mécanisme (totalement) indéréglable.

proofread ['pru:fri:d] (*pt* & *pp* **proofread** [-red]) *vt* corriger (les épreuves de).

proofreader ['pru:f,ri:də^r] *n* correcteur *m*, -trice *f* (d'épreuves OR d'imprimerie).

proofreading ['pru:f,ri:dɪŋ] *n* correction *f* (d'épreuves).

proof spirit *n* [in UK] alcool *m* à 57°; [in US] alcool *m* à 50°.

prop [prɒp] (*pt* & *pp* **propped**, *cont* **propping**) ◇ *n* -**1.** [gen] support *m*; CONSTR [for tunnel, wall] étai *m*, étançon *m*; [in pit] étai *m*. -**2.** [pole, stick - for plant, flowers] tuteur *m*; [- for beans, peas] rame *f*; [- for vines] échalas *m*; [- for washing line] perche *f*. -**3.** RUGBY pilier *m*. -**4.** *fig* soutien *m*; **whisky is his ~** le whisky est son réconfort. -**5.** (*abbr of* **property**) THEAT accessoire *m*. -**6.** *inf abbr of* **propeller**.
◇ *vt* -**1.** [lean] appuyer; **she propped her bike (up) against the wall** elle a appuyé son vélo contre le mur; **~ yourself** OR **your back against these cushions** calez-vous contre OR adossez-vous à ces coussins; **he propped his head in his hands** il s'est pris la tête entre les mains. -**2.** *phr*: **to ~ (up)** [wall, tunnel] étayer, étançonner, consolider; [plants] mettre un tuteur à; [peas, beans] ramer; *fig* [regime, family, business] soutenir; **to ~ sthg open: I propped the door open with a chair** j'ai maintenu la porte ouverte avec une chaise; **the government stepped in to ~ up the franc** le gouvernement est intervenu pour soutenir le franc.

prop. *written abbr of* **proprietor**.

propaganda [,prɒpə'gændə] ◇ *n* propagande *f*.
◇ *comp* [film, machine, material, exercise] de propagande.

propagandist [,prɒpə'gændɪst] ◇ *adj* propagandiste.
◇ *n* propagandiste *mf*.

propagandize, -ise [,prɒpə'gændaɪz] ◇ *vi* faire de la propagande.
◇ *vt* [ideas, views] faire de la propagande pour OR en faveur de; [person, masses] faire de la propagande auprès de.

propagate ['prɒpəgeɪt] ◇ *vt* propager.
◇ *vi* se propager.

propagation [,prɒpə'geɪʃn] *n* propagation *f*.

propagator ['prɒpəgeɪtə^r] *n* -**1.** [gen] propagateur *m*, -trice *f*. -**2.** BOT & HORT germoir *m*.

propane ['prəʊpeɪn] *n* propane *m*.

propel [prə'pel] (*pt* & *pp* **propelled**, *cont* **propelling**) *vt* -**1.** [machine, vehicle etc] propulser, faire avancer. -**2.** [person] propulser, pousser; **she was propelled along the road by the crowd** elle fut poussée par la foule sur toute la longueur de la rue; **the sudden stop propelled us all forward** l'arrêt subit nous a tous propulsés vers l'avant; **he was propelled into the position of manager** on l'a bombardé directeur.

propellant, propellent [prə'pelənt] ◇ *n* [for rocket] propergol *m*; [for gun] poudre *f* propulsive; [in aerosol] (agent *m*) propulseur *m*.
◇ *adj* propulsif, propulseur.

propeller [prə'pelə^r] *n* hélice *f*.

propeller shaft *n* AERON arbre *m* porte-hélice; NAUT arbre *m* d'hélice; AUT arbre *m* de transmission.

propelling pencil [prə'pelɪŋ-] *n Br* portemine *m*.

propene ['prəʊpi:n] *n* propène *m*.

propensity [prə'pensətɪ] (*pl* **propensities**) *n fml* propension *f*, tendance *f*, penchant *m*; **he has a ~ for** OR **towards drink** il a tendance à boire (plus que de raison); **my ~ not to trust** OR **for not trusting other people** ma propension OR ma tendance à ne pas faire confiance aux autres.

proper ['prɒpə^r] ◇ *adj* -**1.** [correct] bon, juste, correct; **the ~ answer** la bonne réponse, la réponse correcte; **what is the ~ use of the imperfect?** quand doit-on utiliser l'imparfait?; **John wasn't waiting at the ~ place** John n'attendait pas au bon endroit OR là où il fallait; **she didn't come at the ~ time** elle s'est trompée d'heure; **you're not doing it in the ~ way** vous ne vous y prenez pas comme il faut; **he did the ~ thing by her** *dated* OR *hum* [he married her] il a réparé; **to think it ~ to do sthg** juger bon de faire qqch; **do as you think ~** faites comme bon vous semble. -**2.** [appropriate] convenable, approprié; **that noisy pub isn't a ~ place for a meeting** ce pub bruyant n'est pas un endroit approprié pour tenir une réunion; **that wasn't the ~ thing to say/to do** ce n'était pas ce qu'il fallait dire/faire; **you must go through the ~ channels** il faut suivre la filière officielle; **he wasn't wearing the ~ clothes** il n'était pas vêtu pour la circonstance; **evening dress is the ~ thing to wear for a ball** porter une tenue de soirée est de circonstance pour aller au bal; **I don't have the ~ tools for this engine** je n'ai pas les outils appropriés pour OR qui conviennent pour ce moteur; **put the scissors back in their ~ place** remettez les ciseaux à leur place; **I can't find the ~ word to describe him** je n'arrive pas à trouver le mot juste OR qui convient pour le décrire. -**3.** [real] vrai, véritable; **I haven't had a ~ meal in ages** il y a une éternité que je n'ai pas fait un vrai repas; **we must give the President a ~ welcome** nous devons réserver au président un accueil digne de ce nom; **it's a toy, not a ~ rifle** c'est un jouet, pas un vrai fusil; **they call him Joss but his ~ name's Ross** on l'appelle Joss mais son vrai nom c'est Ross; **he's not a ~ doctor** ce n'est pas un vrai docteur; **putting letters in envelopes isn't a ~ job** mettre des lettres dans des enveloppes n'a rien d'un vrai travail. -**4.** *inf Br* [as intensifier] vrai, véritable, complet; **it's a ~ catastrophe** c'est une vraie OR véritable catastrophe; **you're a ~ idiot** tu es un parfait imbécile OR un imbécile fini; **he made a ~ fool of himself** il s'est couvert de ridicule; **her room was in a ~ mess** il y avait un vrai bazar dans sa chambre; **I gave him a ~ telling-off** *inf* je lui ai passé un bon savon. -**5.** [respectable] correct, convenable, comme il faut; **that's not ~ behaviour** ce n'est pas convenable, cela ne se fait pas; **she's a very ~ young woman** c'est une jeune femme très bien; **may I take my shoes off? — no, that's not the ~ thing to do here** puis-je ôter mes chaussures? — non, ça ne se fait pas OR ce serait déplacé ici. -**6.** [predicative use - specifically] proprement dit; **he lives outside the city ~** il habite en dehors de la ville même OR proprement dite. -**7.** [characteristic]: **~ to** propre à, typique de; **illnesses ~ to tropical climates** maladies propres aux climats tropicaux.
◇ *adv* ▽ -**1.** *Br* [correctly] comme il faut; **I'll learn you how to talk ~!** je vais t'apprendre, moi, à causer comme il faut! -**2.** *Br dial* [very] très, vraiment, complètement; **he was ~ angry with me** il était très OR vraiment en colère contre moi.
◇ *n* RELIG propre *m*.

proper fraction *n* fraction *f* propre.

properly ['prɒpəlɪ] *adv* -**1.** [well, correctly] bien, juste, correctement; **the lid isn't on ~** le couvercle n'est pas bien mis; **the engine isn't working ~** le moteur ne marche pas bien; **for once they pronounced my name ~** pour une fois, ils ont prononcé mon nom correctement OR ils ont bien prononcé mon nom; **I haven't slept ~ in weeks** ça fait des semaines que je n'ai pas bien dormi; **she quite ~ intervened at that point** c'est avec raison OR à juste titre qu'elle est intervenue à ce moment-là. -**2.** [decently] correctement, convenablement, comme il faut; **patrons must be ~ dressed** une tenue vestimentaire correcte est exigée de nos clients; **eat ~!** mange proprement OR comme il faut!; **he didn't behave ~ towards her** il ne s'est pas comporté correctement envers elle; I haven't thanked you ~ je ne vous ai pas remercié comme il faut OR comme il convient. -**3.** [strictly] proprement; he isn't ~ speaking an expert il n'est pas à proprement parler un expert. -**4.** *inf Br* [as intensifier] vraiment, complètement, tout à fait; I'm ~ exhausted je suis complètement crevé; he looks ~ idiotic in those trousers il a l'air complètement OR parfaitement idiot dans ce pantalon; they were ~ told off ils en ont pris pour leur grade.

proper name, proper noun *n* nom *m* propre.

propertied ['prɒpətɪd] *adj fml* possédant; the ~ classes les classes possédantes; a ~ gentleman un homme fortuné.

property ['prɒpətɪ] (*pl* properties) ◇ *n* -**1.** *(U)* [belongings] propriété *f*, biens *mpl*; hands off! that's my ~! n'y touchez pas, c'est à moi OR ça m'appartient!; this book is the ~ of Theresa Lloyd ce livre appartient à Theresa Lloyd; government ~ propriété de l'État ‖ JUR biens *mpl*; she left him all her ~ elle lui a laissé tous ses biens; personal ~ biens meubles OR mobiliers OR personnels ‖ [objects] objets *mpl*; this is stolen ~ ce sont des objets volés; lost ~ objets *mpl* trouvés. -**2.** *(U)* [buildings] propriété *f*; [real estate] biens *mpl* immobiliers, immobilier *m*; [land] terres *fpl*; Smythe is investing his money in ~ Smythe investit son argent dans l'immobilier; they own a lot of ~ in the country [houses] ils ont de nombreuses propriétés à la campagne; [land] ils ont de nombreuses terres à la campagne; private ~ propriété privée; a man of ~ un homme qui possède des biens immobiliers OR une fortune personnelle. -**3.** [plot of land] terrain *m*; [house, building] propriété *f*. -**4.** [quality] propriété *f*; what are the chemical properties of cobalt? quelles sont les propriétés chimiques du cobalt?; healing properties vertus *fpl* thérapeutiques OR curatives. -**5.** THEAT accessoire *m*.
◇ *comp* [speculator] immobilier; [owner, tax] foncier; ~ developer promoteur *m* (immobilier).

property man *n* THEAT accessoiriste *m*.

property mistress *n* THEAT accessoiriste *f*.

prop forward *n* RUGBY pilier *m*.

prophecy ['prɒfɪsɪ] (*pl* prophecies) *n* prophétie *f*.

prophesy ['prɒfɪsaɪ] (*pt* & *pp* prophesied) ◇ *vt* prophétiser, prédire; scaremongers prophesied the end of the world des alarmistes ont annoncé la fin du monde; to ~ that sthg will happen prédire que qqch va arriver.
◇ *vi* faire des prophéties.

prophet ['prɒfɪt] *n* prophète *m*; a ~ of doom un prophète de malheur.
◆ **Prophets** *n* BIBLE: (the Book of) Prophets le livre des Prophètes.

prophetess ['prɒfɪtɪs] *n* prophétesse *f*.

prophetic(al) [prə'fetɪk(l)] *adj* prophétique.

prophetically [prə'fetɪklɪ] *adv* prophétiquement.

prophylactic [,prɒfɪ'læktɪk] ◇ *adj* prophylactique.
◇ *n* -**1.** [drug] médicament *m* prophylactique. -**2.** [condom] préservatif *m*.

prophylaxis [,prɒfɪ'læksɪs] (*pl* prophylaxes [-siːz]) *n* prophylaxie *f*.

propinquity [prə'pɪŋkwətɪ] *n fml* -**1.** [in space, time] proximité *f*. -**2.** [in kinship] consanguinité *f*.

propitiate [prə'pɪʃɪeɪt] *vt fml* apaiser.

propitiation [prə,pɪʃɪ'eɪʃn] *n fml* propitiation *f*.

propitiatory [prə'pɪʃɪətrɪ] *adj fml* propitiatoire.

propitious [prə'pɪʃəs] *adj fml* propice, favorable; ~ for sthg propice à OR favorable à qqch; it wasn't really a ~ moment to ask for a rise le moment était plutôt mal choisi pour demander une augmentation.

proponent [prə'pəʊnənt] *n* avocat *m*, -e *f fig*, partisan *m*, -e *f*.

proportion [prə'pɔːʃn] ◇ *n* -**1.** [gen & MATH - ratio] proportion *f*, rapport *m*; in the ~ of 6 parts water to 1 part shampoo dans la proportion de 6 mesures d'eau pour 1 mesure de shampooing; the sentence is out of all ~ to the crime la peine est disproportionnée par rapport au OR est sans commune mesure avec le délit; the price bears little ~ to its real value le prix n'a guère de rapport avec sa véritable valeur; the ~ of income to OR over expenditure le rapport entre les revenus et les dépenses. -**2.** [perspective] proportion *f*; to have a sense of ~ avoir le sens des proportions; you seem to have got the problem out of (all) ~ vous semblez avoir exagéré OR grossi le problème; you must try to see things in ~ vous devez essayer de ramener les choses à leur juste valeur; the artist has got the tree out of ~ l'artiste n'a pas respecté les proportions de l'arbre. -**3.** [dimension] proportion *f*, dimension *f*; a ship of vast ~s un navire de grande dimension; the affair has assumed worrying ~s l'affaire a pris des proportions alarmantes. -**4.** [share, part] partie *f*, part *f*, pourcentage *m*; she only got a small ~ of the profits elle n'a touché qu'une petite part OR partie des bénéfices; what ~ of your income do you spend on tobacco? quel pourcentage de vos revenus dépensez-vous en tabac?
◇ *vt* proportionner; to ~ one's expenditure to one's resources proportionner ses dépenses à ses ressources, calculer ses dépenses en fonction de ses ressources.
◆ **in proportion to, in proportion with** *prep phr* par rapport à; the office block is huge in ~ to the houses around it l'immeuble de bureaux est énorme par rapport aux maisons qui l'entourent; the job is badly paid in ~ to the effort required cet emploi est mal payé vu le travail exigé; his salary is not in ~ to his experience son salaire ne correspond pas à son expérience; the monthly payments are calculated in ~ to your income les mensualités sont calculées en fonction de OR sont proportionnelles à vos revenus; inflation may increase in ~ with wage rises l'inflation risque d'augmenter proportionnellement aux augmentations de salaire.

proportional [prə'pɔːʃənl] *adj* proportionnel, en proportion; her income is ~ to the work she puts in ses revenus sont proportionnels au travail effectué.

proportionally [prə'pɔːʃnəlɪ] *adv* proportionnellement.

proportional representation *n* représentation *f* proportionnelle.

proportional spacing *n* espacement *m* proportionnel.

proportionate [*adj* prə'pɔːʃnət, *vb* prə'pɔːʃəneɪt] ◇ *adj* proportionné.
◇ *vt* = **proportion.**

proportionately [prə'pɔːʃnətlɪ] *adv* proportionnellement, en proportion.

proposal [prə'pəʊzl] *n* -**1.** [offer] proposition *f*, offre *f*; to make a ~ faire OR formuler une proposition ‖ [of marriage] demande *f* en mariage; she refused his ~ elle a rejeté sa demande en mariage, elle a refusé de l'épouser. -**2.** [suggestion] proposition *f*, suggestion *f*; he accepted her ~ to go on holiday il a accepté de partir en vacances, comme elle l'avait suggéré. -**3.** [plan, scheme] proposition *f*, projet *m*, plan *m*; the ~ for a car park/to build a car park le projet de parking/de construction d'un parking.

propose [prə'pəʊz] ◇ *vt* -**1.** [suggest] proposer, suggérer; to ~ sthg to sb proposer qqch à qqn; to ~ doing sthg proposer de faire qqch; it was ~ed that we might like to stay a few days longer on nous a proposé de rester quelques jours de plus; I ~ (that) we all go for a drink je propose OR suggère que nous allions tous prendre un verre. -**2.** [present - policy, resolution, scheme] proposer, présenter, soumettre; to ~ sb's health, to ~ a toast to sb porter un toast à (la santé de) qqn; I ~ Jones as OR for treasurer je propose Jones comme trésorier ‖ [in marriage]: to ~ marriage to sb demander qqn en mariage, faire une demande en mariage à qqn. -**3.** [intend] se proposer, avoir l'intention, compter; I ~ taking OR to take a few days off work je me propose de prendre quelques jours de congé; they ~ leaving early ils ont l'intention de partir de bonne heure.
◇ *vi* -**1.** [offer marriage] faire une demande en mariage; to ~ to sb demander qqn en mariage. -**2.** *phr*: man ~s, God disposes l'homme propose, Dieu dispose.

proposed [prə'pəʊzd] *adj* projeté; the ~ visit la visite prévue; the building of the ~ car park has been delayed le projet de construction d'un parking a été suspendu.

proposer [prə'pəʊzə^r] *n* -**1.** [of motion] auteur *m* (d'une proposition). -**2.** [of candidate] parrain *m fig*, marraine *f fig*.

proposition [,prɒpə'zɪʃn] ◇ *n* -**1.** [proposal, statement] proposition *f*. -**2.** [task] affaire *f*; that's quite a ~ c'est une tout autre affaire; climbing that mountain will be no easy ~ ce ne sera pas une petite OR mince affaire que de gravir cette montagne; that's a tough ~ you're making ce n'est pas rien, ce que vous demandez là; the boss is a tough ~ *inf* le patron n'est pas quelqu'un de commode OR facile, le patron est du genre coriace. -**3.** [available choice] solution *f*; solar power is not an economic ~ l'énergie solaire n'est pas une solution rentable; the deal wasn't a paying ~ l'affaire n'était pas rentable. -**4.** [offer of sex] proposition *f*; to make sb a ~ faire des propositions (malhonnêtes) OR des avances à qqn. -**5.** MATH proposition *f*.
◇ *vt* faire des propositions (malhonnêtes) OR des avances à.

propound [prə'paʊnd] *vt fml* [argument, theory] avancer, mettre en avant; [opinion, idea] avancer, émettre; [problem] poser.

proprietary [prə'praɪətrɪ] *adj* -**1.** COMM de marque déposée; a ~ process un processus breveté; ~ brand marque *f* déposée. -**2.** [attitude, behaviour, function] de propriétaire; his manner towards her was rather ~ il était plutôt possessif avec elle.

proprietary colony *n* HIST *aux États-Unis, colonie octroyée à un propriétaire par la Couronne anglaise au XVIIe siècle*.

proprietary hospital *n Am* hôpital *m* privé, clinique *f* privée.

proprietary medicine *n* spécialité *f* pharmaceutique.

proprietary name *n* marque *f* déposée.

proprietor [prə'praɪətə^r] *n* propriétaire *mf*.

proprietorial [prə,praɪə'tɔːrɪəl] *adj* de propriétaire.

proprietorship [prə'praɪətəʃɪp] *n* propriété *f*, possession *f*; JUR (droit *m* de) propriété *f*; 'under new ~' 'changement de propriétaire'.

proprietress [prə'praɪətrɪs] *n* propriétaire *f*.

propriety [prə'praɪətɪ] (*pl* proprieties) *n fml* -**1.** [decorum] bienséance *f*, convenance *f*; the rules of ~ require you to write to her les règles de la bienséance vous obligent à lui écrire; his behaviour is lacking in ~ son comportement est tout à fait inconvenant OR déplacé; to have a sense of ~ avoir le sens des convenances; contrary to the proprieties contraire aux bienséances OR convenances. -**2.** [suitability - of action, measure] opportunité *f*; [- of word, remark] justesse *f*, propriété *f*. -**3.** [rectitude] rectitude *f*; to behave with ~ respecter les convenances.

prop shaft *n* arbre *m* de transmission.

propulsion [prə'pʌlʃn] *n* propulsion *f*.

propulsive [prə'pʌlsɪv] *adj* propulseur, propulsif.

propylene ['prɒpɪliːn] *n* propylène *m*.

pro rata [,prəʊ'rɑːtə] *adj* & *adv* au prorata.

prorate ['prəʊreɪt] *vt Am* distribuer au prorata OR de façon proportionnelle.

prorogation [,prəʊrə'geɪʃn] *n* prorogation *f*.

prorogue [prəˈrəʊg] *vt* proroger.
prosaic [prəʊˈzeɪɪk] *adj* prosaïque.
prosaically [prəʊˈzeɪɪklɪ] *adv* prosaïquement.
Pros. Atty *written abbr of* prosecuting attorney.
proscenium [prəˈsiːnjəm] (*pl* prosceniums OR proscenia [-nja]) *n* proscenium *m*.
proscenium arch *n* THEAT ≃ manteau *m* d'Arlequin.
proscribe [prəʊˈskraɪb] *vt* proscrire.
proscription [prəʊˈskrɪpʃn] *n* proscription *f*.
prose [prəʊz] *n* -**1.** LITERAT prose *f*; to write in ~ écrire en prose, faire de la prose. -**2.** *Br* SCH thème *m*.
prosecute [ˈprɒsɪkjuːt] ◇ *vt* -**1.** JUR poursuivre (en justice), engager des poursuites contre; to ~ sb for sthg poursuivre qqn (en justice) pour qqch; he was ~d for disturbing the peace il a été poursuivi pour tapage nocturne. -**2.** *fml* [pursue - war, investigation] poursuivre.
◇ *vi* JUR [lawyer - in civil case] représenter la partie civile; [- in criminal case] représenter le ministère public OR le parquet.
prosecuting attorney [ˈprɒsɪkjuːtɪŋ-] *n Am* ≃ procureur *m* (de la République).
prosecution [ˌprɒsɪˈkjuːʃn] *n* -**1.** JUR [proceedings] poursuites *fpl* (judiciaires); [indictment] accusation *f*; to be liable to ~ s'exposer à des poursuites (judiciaires); to bring a ~ against sb poursuivre qqn en justice; this is her second ~ c'est la deuxième fois qu'elle est poursuivie. -**2.** JUR [lawyer - in civil case] avocat *m* OR avocats *mpl* représentant les plaignants OR la partie plaignante; [- in criminal case] ministère *m* public, accusation *f*; witness for the ~ témoin *m* à charge. -**3.** *fml* [pursuit] poursuite *f*; the ~ of the war la poursuite de la guerre; in the ~ of his duties dans l'exercice OR l'accomplissement de ses fonctions.
prosecutor [ˈprɒsɪkjuːtəʳ] *n* [person bringing case] plaignant *m*, -e *f*; [lawyer]: (public) ~ procureur *m*.
proselyte [ˈprɒsəlaɪt] ◇ *n* prosélyte *mf*.
◇ *vi* & *vt* *esp Am* = **proselytize**.
proselytism [ˈprɒsəlɪtɪzm] *n* prosélytisme *m*.
proselytize, -ise [ˈprɒsəlɪtaɪz] ◇ *vi* faire du prosélytisme.
◇ *vt* faire un prosélyte de.
prose poem *n* poème *m* en prose.
prosodic [prəˈsɒdɪk] *adj* prosodique.
prosody [ˈprɒsədɪ] *n* prosodie *f*.
prospect [*n* ˈprɒspekt, *vb* prəˈspekt] ◇ *n* -**1.** [possibility] chance *f*, perspective *f*; what are his ~s of success? quelles chances a-t-il de réussir?; there's little ~ of their winning the match ils ont peu de chances de remporter OR il y a peu d'espoir (pour) qu'ils remportent le match; we had given up all ~ of hearing from you nous avions renoncé à tout espoir d'avoir OR nous pensions ne jamais plus recevoir de vos nouvelles. -**2.** [impending event, situation] perspective *f*; I don't relish the ~ of working for him la perspective de travailler pour lui ne m'enchante guère; to have sthg in ~ avoir qqch en vue OR en perspective; he has a bright future in ~ il a un bel avenir en perspective OR devant lui; what are the weather ~s for tomorrow? quelles sont les prévisions météorologiques pour demain? -**3.** (*usu pl*) [chance of success] perspectives *fpl* d'avenir; the ~s are not very good les choses se présentent plutôt mal; the ~(s) for the automobile industry les perspectives d'avenir de l'industrie automobile; her ~s are bleak ses perspectives d'avenir sont sombres; she's a woman with good ~s c'est une femme qui a de l'avenir OR une femme d'avenir; this company has good ~s/no ~s cette entreprise a un bel avenir devant elle/n'a pas d'avenir; it's a job without any ~s of promotion c'est un poste qui n'offre aucune perspective d'avancement; good promotion ~s de réelles possibilités d'avancement. -**4.** [person - customer] client *m* potentiel OR éventuel, prospect *m*; [- marriage partner] parti *m dated*; [- candidate] espoir *m*; he's a good ~ for the manager's job c'est un candidat potentiel au poste de directeur; there are two young ~s in the team l'équipe compte deux joueurs prometteurs OR qui ont un bel avenir devant eux; Robbins is a good ~ Robbins a un bel avenir devant lui. -**5.** [view] perspective *f*, vue *f*.
◇ *vi* prospecter; to ~ for oil chercher du pétrole; to ~ for new customers rechercher OR démarcher de nouveaux clients.
◇ *vt* [area, land] prospecter.
prospecting [prəˈspektɪŋ] *n* prospection *f* MIN & PETR.
prospective [prəˈspektɪv] *adj* -**1.** [future] futur; he's our ~ parliamentary candidate il est notre futur candidat parlementaire; Mrs Wilks is my ~ mother-in-law Mme Wilks est ma future belle-mère. -**2.** [possible] potentiel, éventuel; he's a ~ customer c'est un client potentiel. -**3.** [intended, expected] en perspective; my ~ trip to Ireland le voyage que je projette de faire en Irlande.
prospector [prəˈspektəʳ] *n* prospecteur *m*, -trice *f*, chercheur *m*, -euse *f*; gold ~s chercheurs d'or.
prospectus [prəˈspektəs] *n* prospectus *m*.
prosper [ˈprɒspəʳ] *vi* prospérer.
prosperity [prɒˈsperətɪ] *n* prospérité *f*.
prosperous [ˈprɒspərəs] *adj* [business, area, family] prospère; [period] prospère, de prospérité; ~ winds *lit* vents *mpl* favorables.
prosperously [ˈprɒspərəslɪ] *adv* de manière prospère; they live ~ ils vivent dans la prospérité.
prostaglandin [ˌprɒstəˈglændɪn] *n* prostaglandine *f*.
prostate (gland) [ˈprɒsteɪt-] *n* prostate *f*.
prosthesis [prɒsˈθiːsɪs] (*pl* prostheses [-siːz]) *n* -**1.** MED prothèse *f*. -**2.** LING prosthèse *f*.
prosthetic [prɒsˈθetɪk] *adj* -**1.** MED prothétique. -**2.** LING prosthétique.
prostitute [ˈprɒstɪtjuːt] ◇ *n* prostituée *f*; male ~ prostitué *m*.
◇ *vt fig* & *literal* prostituer; to ~ o.s. se prostituer.
prostitution [ˌprɒstɪˈtjuːʃn] *n* prostitution *f*.
prostrate [*adj* ˈprɒstreɪt, *vb* prɒˈstreɪt] ◇ *adj* -**1.** [lying flat] (couché) à plat ventre; [in submission] prosterné; to lie ~ before sb être prosterné devant qqn. -**2.** [exhausted] épuisé, abattu; [overwhelmed] prostré, accablé, atterré; ~ with grief accablé de chagrin.
◇ *vt* -**1.** [flatten] prosterner; to ~ o.s. before sb se prosterner devant qqn. -**2.** [overwhelm] accabler, abattre; to be ~d by illness être accablé OR abattu par la maladie; to be ~d with grief être accablé de chagrin.
prostration [prɒˈstreɪʃn] *n* -**1.** [lying down] prosternement *m*; RELIG prostration *f*. -**2.** [exhaustion] prostration *f*, épuisement *m*; the country was in a state of economic ~ l'économie du pays était en ruine.
prosy [ˈprəʊzɪ] (*compar* prosier, *superl* prosiest) *adj* [dull] ennuyeux, prosaïque; [long-winded] verbeux.
protactinium [ˌprəʊtækˈtɪnɪəm] *n* protactinium *m*.
protagonist [prəˈtægənɪst] *n* protagoniste *mf*.
protean [prəʊˈtiːən] *adj lit* changeant.
protect [prəˈtekt] *vt* protéger; to ~ sb/sthg from OR against sthg protéger qqn/qqch de OR contre qqch; she ~ed her eyes from the sun elle se protégea les yeux du soleil; to ~ o.s. from sthg se protéger de OR contre qqch; ~ed industries industries *fpl* protégées; it is important to ~ your civil rights il est important de veiller à ce que vos droits civiques ne soient pas bafoués.
protected [prəˈtektɪd] *adj* protégé; ~ species espèce *f* protégée.
protection [prəˈtekʃn] *n* -**1.** [safeguard] protection *f*; this drug offers ~ against OR from the virus ce médicament vous protège OR vous immunise contre le virus; cyclists often wear face masks for ~ against car fumes les cyclistes portent souvent des masques pour se protéger des gaz d'échappement des voitures; she travelled under police ~ elle a voyagé sous la protection de la police; environmental ~ protection *f* de l'environnement. -**2.** [insurance] protection *f*; ~ against fire and theft protection contre l'incendie et le vol. -**3.** [run by gangsters]: ~ (money) argent *m* versé aux racketteurs; all the shopkeepers have to pay ~ (money) tous les commerçants sont rackettés; ~ racket racket *m*; to run a ~ (racket) être à la tête d'un racket.
protectionism [prəˈtekʃənɪzm] *n* protectionnisme *m*.
protectionist [prəˈtekʃənɪst] ◇ *adj* protectionniste.
◇ *n* protectionniste *mf*.
protective [prəˈtektɪv] *adj* -**1.** [person] protecteur; [behaviour, attitude] protecteur, de protection; she's too ~ towards her children elle a trop tendance à couver ses enfants; he put a ~ arm around her il l'a entourée d'un bras protecteur. -**2.** [material, clothes] de protection; [cover] protecteur, de protection. -**3.** ECON [duty, measure] protecteur.
protective coloration *n* homochromie *f*.
protective custody *n* détention *f* dans l'intérêt de la personne.
protectively [prəˈtektɪvlɪ] *adv* [behave, act] de façon protectrice; [speak] d'un ton protecteur, d'une voix protectrice; [look] d'un œil protecteur.
protectiveness [prəˈtektɪvnɪs] *n* attitude *f* protectrice.
protector [prəˈtektəʳ] *n* -**1.** [person] protecteur *m*, -trice *f*. -**2.** [on machine] dispositif *m* de protection, protecteur *m*.
◆ **Protector** *n Br* HIST: the Protector le Protecteur.
protectorate [prəˈtektərət] *n* protectorat *m*; the Protectorate *Br* HIST le Protectorat.

THE PROTECTORATE:
En Angleterre, période allant de 1649 à 1660, succédant à la guerre civile, et pendant laquelle Oliver Cromwell, se proclamant «Lord Protector», exerça son autorité sur le pays. Il transmit ensuite cette charge à son fils Richard.

---

protein [ˈprəʊtiːn] *n* protéine *f*; ~ deficiency carence *f* en protéines.
pro tem *inf* [ˌprəʊˈtem], **pro tempore** [ˈprəʊˈtempərɪ] ◇ *adv* temporairement.
◇ *adj* intérimaire, temporaire.
protest [*n* & *comp* ˈprəʊtest, *vb* prəˈtest] ◇ *n* -**1.** [gen] protestation *f*; to make a ~ against OR about sthg élever une protestation contre qqch, protester contre qqch; to register OR to lodge a ~ with sb protester auprès de qqn; in ~ against OR at sthg en signe de protestation contre qqch; they did it without the slightest ~ ils l'ont fait sans élever la moindre protestation OR sans protester le moins du monde; despite their ~s, the children had to go to school malgré leurs protestations, les enfants ont dû aller à l'école; to stage a ~ [complaint] organiser une protestation; [demonstration] organiser une manifestation; to do sthg under ~ faire qqch en protestant. -**2.** COMM & JUR protêt *m*.
◇ *vt* -**1.** [innocence, love etc] protester de; "no one told me", she ~ed «personne ne me l'a dit», protesta-t-elle; she ~ed that it was unfair elle déclara que ce n'était pas juste. -**2.** *Am* [measures, law etc] protester contre.
◇ *vi* protester; to ~ at OR against/about sthg protester contre qqch.
◇ *comp* [letter, meeting] de protestation; ~ demonstration OR march manifestation *f*; ~ marcher manifestant *m*, -e *f*; ~ vote vote *m* de protestation.

Protestant ['prɒtɪstənt] ◇ *adj* protestant; the ~ Church l'Église *f* protestante; the ~ (work) ethic l'éthique *f* protestante (du travail).
◇ *n* Protestant *m*, -e *f*.

Protestantism ['prɒtɪstəntɪzm] *n* protestantisme *m*.

protestation [,prɒte'steɪʃn] *n* protestation *f*.

protester, protestor [prə'testə^r] *n* [demonstrator] manifestant *m*, -e *f*; [complainer] protestataire *mf*.

protium ['prəʊtɪəm] *n* protium *m*.

protocol ['prəʊtəkɒl] *n* [gen & COMPUT] protocole *m*.

Proto-Indo-European [,prəʊtəʊ-] *n* proto-indo-européen *m*.

proton ['prəʊtɒn] *n* proton *m*.

proton microscope *n* microscope *m* protonique.

proton number *n* numéro *m* atomique.

protoplasm ['prəʊtəplæzm] *n* protoplasme *m*, protoplasma *m*.

prototype ['prəʊtətaɪp] *n* prototype *m*.

protozoan [,prəʊtə'zəʊən] (*pl* **protozoans** OR protozoa [-'zəʊə]) *n* protozoaire *m*.

protozoon [,prəʊtə'zəʊən] (*pl* **protozoa** [-'zəʊə]) = **protozoan**.

protract [prə'trækt] *vt* prolonger, faire durer.

protracted [prə'træktɪd] *adj* [stay] prolongé; [argument, negotiations] qui dure, (très) long.

protraction [prə'trækʃn] *n* prolongation *f*.

protractor [prə'træktə^r] *n* -**1.** GEOM rapporteur *m*. -**2.** ANAT protracteur *m*.

protrude [prə'tru:d] ◇ *vi* [rock, ledge] faire saillie; [eyes, chin] saillir; [teeth] avancer; the promontory ~s into the sea le promontoire s'avance dans la mer; his belly ~d over his trousers son ventre débordait de son pantalon; his feet ~d from under the bedclothes ses pieds dépassaient de sous les couvertures.
◇ *vt* avancer, pousser en avant.

protruding [prə'tru:dɪŋ] *adj* [ledge] en saillie; [chin, ribs] saillant; [eyes] globuleux; [teeth] proéminent, protubérant; [belly] protubérant; the ~ end of the nail le bout du clou qui dépasse.

protrusion [prə'tru:ʒn] *n* [ledge, projection] saillie *f*; [bump] bosse *f*.

protrusive [prə'tru:sɪv] = **protruding**.

protuberance [prə'tju:bərəns] *n fml* protubérance *f*.

protuberant [prə'tju:bərənt] *adj fml* protubérant.

proud [praʊd] ◇ *adj* -**1.** [pleased] fier; to be ~ of sb/sthg être fier de qqn/qqch; he was ~ to have won OR of having won il était fier d'avoir gagné; I'm ~ (that) you didn't give up je suis fier que tu n'aies pas abandonné; it's nothing to be ~ of! il n'y a vraiment pas de quoi être fier!; she was too ~ to accept elle était trop fière pour accepter; I'll do anything, I'm not ~ je ferai n'importe quoi, je ne suis pas fier; they are now the ~ parents of a daughter ils sont désormais les heureux parents d'une petite fille; we are ~ to present this concert nous sommes heureux de vous présenter ce concert; it was a ~ moment for me pour moi, ce fut un moment de grande fierté; it was her ~est possession c'était son bien le plus précieux. -**2.** [arrogant] fier, orgueilleux; he's a ~ man c'est un orgueilleux ❑ as ~ as a peacock fier comme un coq. -**3.** *lit* [stately - tree, mountain] majestueux, altier; [- bearing, stallion, eagle] fier, majestueux. -**4.** *Br* [protruding] qui dépasse; it's a few millimetres ~ ça dépasse de quelques millimètres; to stand ~ faire saillie; ~ flesh MED bourgeon *m* conjonctif OR charnu.
◇ *adv inf*: to do sb ~ [entertain lavishly] recevoir qqn comme un roi/une reine; [honour] faire honneur à qqn.

proudly ['praʊdlɪ] *adv* -**1.** [with pride] fièrement, avec fierté; we ~ present... nous sommes fiers de présenter... -**2.** [arrogantly] orgueilleusement. -**3.** [majestically] majestueusement.

Proustian ['pru:stjən] *adj* proustien.

provable ['pru:vəbl] *adj* prouvable, démontrable.

prove [pru:v] (*Br pt & pp* proved, *Am pt* proved, *pp* proved OR proven ['pru:vn]) ◇ *vt* -**1.** [verify, show] prouver; the facts ~ her (to be) guilty les faits prouvent qu'elle est coupable; the autopsy ~d that it was suicide l'autopsie prouva que c'était un suicide; the accused is innocent until ~d OR proven guilty l'accusé est innocent jusqu'à preuve du contraire OR tant que sa culpabilité n'est pas prouvée; to ~ sb right/wrong donner raison/tort à qqn; they can't ~ anything against us ils n'ont aucune preuve contre nous; I think I've ~d my point je crois avoir apporté la preuve de ce que j'avançais; it remains to be ~d whether the decision was correct rien ne prouve que cette décision était la bonne; she quickly ~d herself indispensable elle s'est vite montrée indispensable; he has already ~d his loyalty il a déjà prouvé sa fidélité, sa fidélité n'est plus à prouver. -**2.** LOGIC & MATH [proposition, theorem] démontrer. -**3.** [put to the test] mettre à l'épreuve; the method has not yet been ~d la méthode n'a pas encore fait ses preuves; to ~ o.s. faire ses preuves. -**4.** JUR [will] homologuer. -**5.** *arch* [experience] éprouver.
◇ *vi* -**1.** [turn out] s'avérer, se révéler; your suspicions ~d (to be) well-founded vos soupçons se sont avérés fondés OR légitimes; the arrangement ~d (to be) unworkable cet arrangement s'est révélé impraticable; the hotel ~d to be open l'hôtel s'avéra être ouvert; he may ~ (to be) of help to you il pourrait bien vous être utile; it has ~d impossible to find him il a été impossible de le retrouver; if that ~s to be the case s'il s'avère que tel est le cas. -**2.** CULIN [dough] lever.
◆ **prove out** *Am* ◇ *vt sep* mettre à l'épreuve.
◇ *vi insep* faire ses preuves.

proven ['pru:vn] ◇ *pp* → **prove**.
◇ *adj* -**1.** [tested] éprouvé; a woman of ~ courage une femme qui a fait preuve de courage; a candidate with ~ experience un candidat qui a déjà fait ses preuves; a ~ method une méthode qui a fait ses preuves. -**2.** JUR: a verdict of not ~ ≃ un non-lieu.

provenance ['prɒvənəns] *n* provenance *f*.

Provençal [,prɒvɒn'sɑ:l] ◇ *n* -**1.** [person] Provençal *m*, -e *f*. -**2.** LING provençal *m*.
◇ *adj* provençal.

Provence [prɒ'vɑ:ns] *pr n* Provence *f*; in ~ en Provence.

provender ['prɒvɪndə^r] *n* -**1.** [fodder] fourrage *m*, provende *f*. -**2.** [food] nourriture *f*.

proverb ['prɒvɜ:b] *n* proverbe *m*.
◆ **Proverbs** *n* BIBLE: (the Book of) Proverbs le Livre des Proverbes.

proverbial [prə'vɜ:bjəl] *adj* proverbial, légendaire.

proverbially [prə'vɜ:bjəlɪ] *adv* proverbialement.

provide [prə'vaɪd] ◇ *vt* -**1.** [supply] pourvoir, fournir; to ~ sthg for sb, to ~ sb with sthg fournir qqch à qqn; who ~d them with that information? qui leur a fourni OR transmis ces renseignements?; they ~ a car for her use ils mettent une voiture à sa disposition; the plane is ~d with eight emergency exits l'avion dispose de huit sorties de secours; write the answers in the spaces ~d écrivez les réponses dans les blancs prévus à cet effet. -**2.** [offer, afford] offrir, fournir; a small summerhouse ~s some privacy un petit pavillon dans le jardin offre une certaine intimité; the new plant will ~ 2,000 jobs la nouvelle usine créera 2 000 emplois; I want to ~ my children with a good education je veux pouvoir offrir OR donner une bonne éducation à mes enfants; the book ~s a good introduction to linguistics ce livre est une bonne introduction à la linguistique; milk ~s a good source of protein le lait constitue un bon apport en protéines. -**3.** [stipulate - subj: contract, law] stipuler; the rules ~ that... le règlement stipule que...
◇ *vi*: to ~ against sthg se prémunir contre qqch.
◆ **provide for** *vt insep* -**1.** [support]: to ~ for sb pourvoir OR subvenir aux besoins de qqn; I have a family to ~ for j'ai une famille à nourrir; an insurance policy that will ~ for your children's future une assurance qui subviendra aux besoins de vos enfants; his widow was left well ~d for sa veuve était à l'abri du besoin. -**2.** [prepare]: to ~ for sthg se préparer à qqch; they hadn't ~d for the drop in demand la baisse de la demande les a pris au dépourvu; we try to ~ for all eventualities nous nous efforçons de parer à toute éventualité. -**3.** [contract, law]: to ~ for sthg stipuler OR prévoir qqch; the bill ~s for subsidies to be reduced le projet de loi prévoit une baisse des subventions.

provided [prə'vaɪdɪd] *conj*: ~ (that) pourvu que, à condition que; I'll wait for you ~ (that) it doesn't take too long je t'attendrai à condition que ce ne soit pas trop long; you can leave early ~ (that) you finish your work vous pouvez partir plus tôt à condition d'avoir fini votre travail.

providence ['prɒvɪdəns] *n* -**1.** [fate] providence *f*; Providence smiled on us la Providence nous a souri. -**2.** [foresight] prévoyance *f*; [thrift] économie *f*.

provident ['prɒvɪdənt] *adj* [foresighted] prévoyant; [thrifty] économe.

provident club *n Br système d'achat à tempérament proposé par certains grands magasins*.

providential [,prɒvɪ'denʃl] *adj* providentiel.

providentially [,prɒvɪ'denʃəlɪ] *adv* providentiellement.

providently ['prɒvɪdəntlɪ] *adv* avec prévoyance, prudemment.

provident society *n Br* société *f* de prévoyance.

provider [prə'vaɪdə^r] *n* fournisseur *m*, -euse *f*; she's the family's sole ~ elle subvient seule aux besoins de la famille.

providing [prə'vaɪdɪŋ] = **provided**.

province ['prɒvɪns] *n* -**1.** [region, district] province *f*; the Province of Ontario/Ulster la province d'Ontario/d'Ulster; the Maritime/Prairie Provinces [of Canada] les provinces maritimes/des prairies. -**2.** [field, sphere - of activity] domaine *m*; [- of responsability] compétence *f*; politics was once the sole ~ of men autrefois, la politique était un domaine exclusivement masculin; staff supervision is not within my ~ la gestion du personnel n'est pas de mon ressort. -**3.** RELIG province *f* ecclésiastique.
◆ **provinces** *npl Br* [not the metropolis]: the ~s la province; I couldn't live in the ~s! je ne pourrais pas vivre en province!

provincial [prə'vɪnʃl] ◇ *adj* provincial.
◇ *n* -**1.** [from provinces] provincial *m*, -e *f*. -**2.** RELIG provincial *m*.

provincialism [prə'vɪnʃəlɪzm] *n* provincialisme *m*.

proving ground ['pru:vɪŋ-] *n* terrain *m* d'essai.

provision [prə'vɪʒn] ◇ *vt* approvisionner, ravitailler.
◇ *n* -**1.** [act of supplying] approvisionnement *m*, fourniture *f*, ravitaillement *m*; ~ of supplies in wartime is a major problem le ravitaillement en temps de guerre pose de graves problèmes; one of their functions is the ~ of meals for the homeless un de leurs rôles est de distribuer des repas aux sans-abri; the ~ of new jobs la création d'emplois. -**2.** [stock, supply] provision *f*, réserve *f*; to lay in ~s for the winter faire des provisions pour l'hiver; the US sent medical ~s les États-Unis envoyèrent des stocks de médicaments; I have a week's ~ of firewood left il me reste du bois OR assez de bois pour une semaine. -**3.** [arrangement, prepa-

ration] disposition *f*; they are making ~s for a crisis ils prennent des dispositions en vue d'une crise; no ~ had been made for the influx of refugees aucune disposition n'avait été prise pour faire face à l'afflux de réfugiés; social service ~ has been cut again les services sociaux ont à nouveau connu des compressions budgétaires; to make ~s for one's family pourvoir aux besoins de sa famille; you should think about making ~s for the future vous devriez penser à assurer votre avenir; having a lot of children was a ~ for old age le fait d'avoir de nombreux enfants constituait pour les parents une sorte d'assurance vieillesse. -**4.** [condition, clause] disposition *f*, clause *f*; under the ~s of the UN charter/his will selon les dispositions de la charte de l'ONU/de son testament; a 4% increase is included in the budget's ~s une augmentation de 4 % est prévue dans le budget; notwithstanding any ~ to the contrary JUR nonobstant toute clause contraire.

◆ **provisions** *npl* [food] vivres *mpl*, provisions *fpl*.

provisional [prə'vɪʒənl] *adj* provisoire; ~ (driving) licence *Br* permis *m* de conduire provisoire *(autorisation que l'on doit obtenir avant de prendre des leçons)*.

◆ **Provisional** ◇ *adj* POL: the Provisional IRA l'IRA *f* provisoire.

◇ *n* membre *m* de l'IRA provisoire.

provisionally [prə'vɪʒnəlɪ] *adv* provisoirement.

proviso [prə'vaɪzəʊ] (*pl* provisos OR provisoes) *n* stipulation *f*, condition *f*; with the ~ that the goods be delivered within one month à la condition expresse OR sous réserve que les marchandises soient livrées dans un délai d'un mois; they accept, with one ~ ils acceptent, à une condition.

provisory [prə'vaɪzərɪ] *adj* -**1.** [conditional] conditionnel. -**2.** = **provisional**.

provitamin [prəʊ'vɪtəmɪn, prəʊ'vaɪtəmɪn] *n* provitamine *f*.

Provo *inf* ['prəʊvəʊ] (*pl* Provos) *n Ir* POL membre *m* de l'IRA provisoire.

provocation [,prɒvə'keɪʃn] *n* provocation *f*; he loses his temper at OR given the slightest ~ il se met en colère à la moindre provocation; the crime was committed under ~ ce crime a été commis en réponse à une provocation.

provocative [prə'vɒkətɪv] *adj* -**1.** [challenging] provocateur, provocant; his early films were very ~ ses premiers films étaient très provocants; she doesn't really think that, she was just being ~ elle ne le pense pas vraiment, c'est simplement de la provocation. -**2.** [seductive] provocant. -**3.** [obscene]: a ~ gesture un geste obscène.

provocatively [prə'vɒkətɪvlɪ] *adv* [write, behave, dress] d'une manière provocante; [say] sur un ton provocateur OR provocant.

provoke [prə'vəʊk] *vt* -**1.** [goad] provoquer; to ~ sb into doing sthg pousser qqn à faire qqch; they'll shoot if in any way ~d ils tireront à la moindre provocation; the dog is dangerous when ~d le chien devient méchant si on le provoque OR l'excite ‖ [infuriate] enrager; [vex] exaspérer. -**2.** [cause - accident, quarrel, anger] provoquer; the revelations ~d a public outcry les révélations ont soulevé un tollé général.

provoking [prə'vəʊkɪŋ] *adj* [situation] contrariant; [person, behaviour] exaspérant.

provokingly [prə'vəʊkɪŋlɪ] *adv* par provocation.

provost [*senses 1, 2 and 3* 'prɒvəst, *sense 4* prə'vəʊ] *n* -**1.** UNIV *Br* ≃ recteur *m*, *Am* ≃ doyen *m*. -**2.** RELIG doyen *m*. -**3.** *Scot* maire *m*. -**4.** MIL ≃ gendarme *m*.

provost court ['prɒvəst-] *n* tribunal *m* prévôtal.

provost guard [prə'vəʊ-] *n Am* ≃ prévôté *f*.

provost marshal [prə'vəʊ-] *n* prévôt *m*.

prow [praʊ] *n* proue *f*.

prowess ['praʊɪs] *n (U)* -**1.** [skill] (grande) habileté *f*; her ~ in negotiating son habileté OR son savoir-faire en matière de négociations; he showed great ~ on the sports field il s'est révélé d'une adresse remarquable sur le terrain de sport; sexual ~ prouesses *fpl* sexuelles. -**2.** [bravery] vaillance *f*.

prowl [praʊl] ◇ *vi* rôder.

◇ *vt* [street, jungle] rôder dans; cats ~ed the rooftops des chats rôdaient sur les toits.

◇ *n*: to be on the ~ rôder; the gang was on the ~ for likely victims la bande était à la recherche d'une victime.

◆ **prowl about** *Br*, **prowl around** ◇ *vi insep* rôder.

◇ *vt insep* = **prowl** *vt*.

prowl car *n Am* voiture *f* de police en patrouille.

prowler ['praʊlə^r] *n* rôdeur *m*, -euse *f*.

prowling ['praʊlɪŋ] *adj* rôdeur.

prox *written abbr of* proximo.

proximity [prɒk'sɪmətɪ] *n* proximité *f*; in ~ to, in the ~ of à proximité de.

proximo ['prɒksɪməʊ] *adv* ADMIN du mois prochain; the 4th ~ le 4 du mois prochain.

proxy ['prɒksɪ] (*pl* proxies) *n* [person] mandataire *mf*, fondé *m*, -e *f* de pouvoir; [authorization] procuration *f*, mandat *m*; to vote by ~ voter par procuration.

proxy vote *n* vote *m* par procuration.

prude [pru:d] *n* prude *f*; don't be such a ~! ne sois pas si prude!

prudence ['pru:dns] *n* prudence *f*, circonspection *f*.

prudent ['pru:dnt] *adj* prudent, circonspect.

prudently ['pru:dntlɪ] *adv* prudemment.

prudery ['pru:dərɪ] = **prudishness**.

prudish ['pru:dɪʃ] *adj* prude, pudibond.

prudishness ['pru:dɪʃnɪs] *n* pruderie *f*, pudibonderie *f*.

prune [pru:n] ◇ *n* -**1.** [fruit] pruneau *m*; stewed ~s pruneaux cuits. -**2.** *inf Br* [fool] patate *f*, ballot *m*.

◇ *vt* -**1.** [hedge, tree] tailler; [branch] élaguer. -**2.** *fig* [text, budget] élaguer, faire des coupes sombres dans; to ~ (back OR down) expenditure réduire les dépenses.

pruning ['pru:nɪŋ] *n* [of hedge, tree] taille *f*; [of branches] élagage *m*; *fig* [of budget, staff] élagage *m*; there will have to be some ~ in this department il va falloir faire du nettoyage dans ce service.

pruning hook *n* ébranchoir *m*.

pruning knife *n* serpette *f*.

prurience ['prʊərɪəns] *n* lubricité *f*, lascivité *f lit*.

prurient ['prʊərɪənt] *adj* lubrique, lascif.

pruritus [prʊ'raɪtəs] *n* prurit *m*.

Prussia ['prʌʃə] *pr n* Prusse *f*; in ~ en Prusse.

Prussian ['prʌʃn] ◇ *n* Prussien *m*, -enne *f*.

◇ *adj* prussien.

Prussian blue *n* bleu *m* de Prusse.

prussic acid ['prʌsɪk-] *n* acide *m* prussique.

pry [praɪ] (*pt* & *pp* pried) ◇ *vt Am* = **prise**.

◇ *vi* fouiller, fureter; I didn't mean to ~ je ne voulais pas être indiscret; I told him not to ~ into my affairs je lui ai dit de ne pas venir mettre le nez dans mes affaires; he doesn't like people ~ing into his past il n'aime pas qu'on aille fouiller dans son passé.

prying ['praɪɪŋ] *adj* indiscret; away from ~ eyes à l'abri des regards indiscrets.

PS (*abbr of* postscript) *n* PS *m*.

psalm [sɑ:m] *n* psaume *m*; (the Book of) Psalms (le livre des) Psaumes.

psalmbook ['sɑ:mbʊk] *n* livre *m* de psaumes, psautier *m*.

psalmist ['sɑ:mɪst] *n* psalmiste *m*; the Psalmist le Psalmiste.

psalmody ['sælmədɪ] (*pl* psalmodies) *n* psalmodie *f*.

Psalter ['sɔ:ltə^r] *n* psautier *m*.

PSAT (*abbr of* Preliminary Scholastic Aptitude Test) *n examen blanc préparant au SAT*.

PSBR *n abbr of* public sector borrowing requirement.

psephologist [se'fɒlədʒɪst] *n* spécialiste *mf* des élections.

psephology [se'fɒlədʒɪ] *n étude statistique et sociologique des élections*.

pseud *inf* [sju:d] ◇ *n* poseur *m*, -euse *f*, prétentieux *m*, -euse *f*.

◇ *adj* = **pseudo**.

pseudo *inf* ['sju:dəʊ] *adj* [kindness, interest] prétendu; [person] faux.

pseudo- *in cpds* pseudo-.

pseudonym ['sju:dənɪm] *n* pseudonyme *m*; to write under a ~ écrire sous un pseudonyme OR sous un nom d'emprunt.

pseudonymous [sju:'dɒnɪməs] *adj* pseudonyme.

pseudopodium [,sju:dəʊ'pəʊdɪəm] (*pl* pseudopodia [-dɪə]) *n* pseudopode *m*.

psi (*abbr of* pounds per square inch) *n livres au pouce carré (mesure de pression)*.

psittacosis [,sɪtə'kəʊsɪs] *n (U)* psittacose *f*.

psoriasis [sɒ'raɪəsɪs] *n (U)* psoriasis *m*.

psst [pst] *interj* psitt, pst.

PST *n Am abbr of* Pacific Standard Time.

PSV (*abbr of* public service vehicle) *n* = **PCV**.

psych *inf* [saɪk] *vt* -**1.** [psychoanalyse] psychanalyser. -**2.** *Am* [excite]: I'm really ~ed about my vacation je suis surexcité à l'idée de partir en vacances.

◆ **psych out** *inf vt sep* -**1.** [sense - sb's motives] deviner; [- situation] comprendre, piger. -**2.** [intimidate]: he soon ~ed out his opponent and the game was his très vite il a décontenancé son adversaire et il a gagné.

◆ **psych up** *inf vt sep* [motivate]: to ~ o.s. up for sthg/to do sthg se préparer psychologiquement à qqch/à faire qqch; he had to ~ himself up to tell her il a dû prendre son courage à deux mains pour arriver à le lui dire; she ~ed herself up before the race elle s'est concentrée avant la course; they're all ~ed up and raring to go ils rongent leur frein.

psyche[1] ['saɪkɪ] *n* [mind] psyché *f*, psychisme *m*.

psyche[2] [saɪk] = **psych**.

Psyche ['saɪkɪ] *pr n* Psyché.

psychedelia [,saɪkə'di:lɪə] *npl* [objects] objets *mpl* psychédéliques; [dress, music etc] univers *m* psychédélique.

psychedelic [,saɪkɪ'delɪk] *adj* psychédélique.

psychiatric [,saɪkɪ'ætrɪk] *adj* psychiatrique; he needs ~ help il devrait consulter un psychiatre ❑ ~ nurse infirmier *m*, -ère *f* psychiatrique.

psychiatrist [saɪ'kaɪətrɪst] *n* psychiatre *mf*.

psychiatry [saɪ'kaɪətrɪ] *n* psychiatrie *f*.

psychic ['saɪkɪk] ◇ *adj* -**1.** [supernatural] parapsychique; to be ~, to have ~ powers avoir le don de double vue OR un sixième sens; I'm not ~! *hum* je ne suis pas devin! -**2.** [mental] psychique.

◇ *n* médium *m*.

psychical ['saɪkɪkl] = **psychic** *adj*.

psycho *inf* ['saɪkəʊ] (*pl* psychos) ◇ *n* psychopathe *mf*; 'Psycho' *Hitchcock* 'Psychose'.

◇ *adj* psychopathe.

psychoanalyse *Br*, **-yze** *Am* [,saɪkəʊ'ænəlaɪz] *vt* psychanalyser.

psychoanalysis [,saɪkəʊə'næləsɪs] *n* psychanalyse *f*; to undergo ~ suivre une psychanalyse, se faire psychanalyser; he spent five years in ~ il a été en psychanalyse pendant cinq ans.

psychoanalyst [,saɪkəʊ'ænəlɪst] *n* psychanalyste *mf*.

psychoanalytic(al) ['saɪkəʊ,ænə'lɪtɪk(l)] *adj* psychanalytique.

psychobabble *inf* ['saɪkəʊ,bæbl] *n pej* jargon *m* des psychologues.

psychodrama ['saɪkəʊ,drɑːmə] *n* psychodrame *m*.

psychodynamic [,saɪkəʊdaɪ'næmɪk] *adj* psychodynamique.

psychodynamics [,saɪkəʊdaɪ'næmɪks] *n (U)* psychodynamisme *m*.

psychogenic [,saɪkəʊ'dʒenɪk] *adj* psychogène.

psychogeriatric [,saɪkəʊdʒerɪ'ætrɪk] *adj* psychogériatrique.

psychokinesis [,saɪkəʊkɪ'niːsɪs] *n* psychokinèse *f*, psychokinésie *f*.

psycholinguistic [,saɪkəʊlɪŋ'gwɪstɪk] *adj* psycholinguistique.

psycholinguistics [,saɪkəʊlɪŋ'gwɪstɪks] *n (U)* psycholinguistique *f*.

psychological [,saɪkə'lɒdʒɪkl] *adj* psychologique; the ~ moment le bon moment, le moment favorable OR psychologique.

psychological block *n* blocage *m* psychologique; I have a ~ about driving je fais un blocage quand il s'agit de conduire.

psychologically [,saɪkə'lɒdʒɪklɪ] *adv* psychologiquement.

psychological warfare *n* guerre *f* psychologique.

psychologist [saɪ'kɒlədʒɪst] *n* psychologue *mf*.

psychology [saɪ'kɒlədʒɪ] *n* psychologie *f*; it would be good/bad ~ to tell them ce serait faire preuve de psychologie/d'un manque de psychologie que de le leur dire ❑ child ~ psychologie infantile OR de l'enfant.

psychometric [,saɪkə'metrɪk] *adj* psychométrique.

psychometrics [,saɪkə'metrɪks] *n (U)* psychométrie *f*.

psychometry [saɪ'kɒmɪtrɪ] *n* psychométrie *f*.

psychomotor [,saɪkəʊ'məʊtəʳ] *adj* psychomoteur.

psychoneurosis [,saɪkəʊnjʊə'rəʊsɪs] (*pl* psychoneuroses [-siːz]) *n* psychonévrose *f*.

psychopath ['saɪkəpæθ] *n* psychopathe *mf*.

psychopathic [,saɪkə'pæθɪk] *adj* [person] psychopathe; [disorder, personality] psychopathique.

psychopathology [,saɪkəʊpə'θɒlədʒɪ] *n* psychopathologie *f*.

psychopathy [saɪ'kɒpəθɪ] *n* psychopathie *f*.

psychopharmacology [,saɪkəʊ,fɑːmə'kɒlədʒɪ] *n* psychopharmacologie *f*.

psychophysiology [,saɪkəʊfɪsɪ'ɒlədʒɪ] *n* psychophysiologie *f*.

psychosexual [,saɪkəʊ'sekʃʊəl] *adj* psychosexuel.

psychosis [saɪ'kəʊsɪs] (*pl* psychoses [-siːz]) *n* psychose *f*.

psychosomatic [,saɪkəʊsə'mætɪk] *adj* psychosomatique.

psychotherapist [,saɪkəʊ'θerəpɪst] *n* psychothérapeute *mf*.

psychotherapy [,saɪkəʊ'θerəpɪ] *n* psychothérapie *f*.

psychotic [saɪ'kɒtɪk] ◇ *adj* psychotique.
◇ *n* psychotique *mf*.

psychotropic [,saɪkəʊ'trɒpɪk] *adj* psychotrope.

pt -**1.** *written abbr of* pint. -**2.** *written abbr of* point.

Pt. (*written abbr of* point) [on map] Pte.

PT *n* -**1.** (*abbr of* physical training) EPS *f*; ~ instructor professeur *m* d'éducation physique. -**2.** *Am abbr of* physical therapy.

PTA (*abbr of* parent-teacher association) *n association de parents d'élèves et de professeurs*.

ptarmigan ['tɑːmɪgən] (*pl inv* OR ptarmigans) *n* lagopède *m* des Alpes.

Pte. *Br* MIL *written abbr of* private.

pterodactyl [,terə'dæktɪl] *n* ptérodactyle *m*.

PTO ◇ *Br* (*written abbr of* please turn over) TSVP.
◇ *n Am* (*abbr of* parent-teacher organization) = PTA.

Ptolemaic [,tɒlə'meɪɪk] *adj* -**1.** ANTIQ ptolémaïque. -**2.** ASTRON de Ptolémée; ~ system système *m* de Ptolémée.

Ptolemy ['tɒləmɪ] *pr n* Ptolémée.

ptomaine ['təʊmeɪn] *n* ptomaïne *f*; ~ poisoning intoxication *f* alimentaire.

ptosis ['təʊsɪs] (*pl* ptoses [-siːz]) *n* [of organ] ptôse *f*; [of eyelid] ptôsis *m*, blépharoptôse *f*.

PTV *n* -**1.** (*abbr of* pay television) *télévision à péage*. -**2.** (*abbr of* public television) *programmes télévisés éducatifs*.

pub [pʌb] (*abbr of* public house) *n* pub *m*; we had a ~ lunch nous avons déjeuné dans un pub; ~ grub *inf nourriture (relativement simple) servie dans un pub*.

PUB:

Dans l'ensemble des îles Britanniques, le pub est un des grands foyers de la vie locale, mais son rôle social varie selon les régions (Angleterre, Écosse, Irlande) et selon qu'il se trouve en ville ou dans un village. Ces établissements – interdits aux personnes de moins de 16 ans – étaient soumis à des horaires sévèrement réglementés, qui se sont beaucoup assouplis récemment (voir «licensing hours»). De même, le pub a cessé d'être un simple débit de boissons pour devenir de plus en plus une sorte de brasserie-restaurant servant des repas légers.

---

pub. *written abbr of* published.

pub crawl *inf n Br*: to go on a ~ ≃ faire la tournée des bars.

puberty ['pjuːbətɪ] *n* puberté *f*; to reach ~ atteindre l'âge de la puberté.

pubes ['pjuːbiːz] (*pl inv*) *n* [region] pubis *m*, région *f* pubienne; [hair] poils *mpl* pubiens; [bones] (os *m* du) pubis *m*.

pubescence [pjuː'besns] *n* -**1.** [puberty] (âge *m* de la) puberté *f*. -**2.** [of plant, animal] pubescence *f*.

pubescent [pjuː'besnt] *adj* -**1.** [at puberty] pubère. -**2.** [plant, animal] pubescent.

pubic ['pjuːbɪk] *adj* pubien; ~ hair poils *mpl* pubiens OR du pubis.

pubis ['pjuːbɪs] (*pl* pubes [-biːz]) *n* pubis *m*.

public ['pʌblɪk] ◇ *adj* -**1.** [of, by the state - education, debt] public; built at ~ expense construit avec des fonds publics ❑ ~ bill *Br* POL ≃ projet *m* de loi d'intérêt général; ~ housing *Am* logements *mpl* sociaux, ≃ HLM *f inv*; ~ housing project *Am* ≃ cité *f* HLM; ~ money deniers *mpl* OR fonds *mpl* publics; ~ official fonctionnaire *mf*; ~ ownership nationalisation *f*, étatisation *f*; most airports are under ~ ownership la plupart des aéroports appartiennent à l'État; the ~ purse *Br* le Trésor (public); ~ television *Am* (télévision *f* du) service *m* public. -**2.** [open or accessible to all - place, meeting] public; to hold a ~ inquiry faire une enquête officielle; was it a ~ trial? le public pouvait-il assister au procès?; let's talk somewhere less ~ allons discuter dans un endroit plus tranquille; these gardens are ~ property! ces jardins appartiennent à tout le monde! ❑ ~ baths bains *mpl* publics; ~ library bibliothèque *f* municipale. -**3.** [of, by the people] public; ~ affairs affaires *fpl* publiques; the ~ interest OR good le bien OR l'intérêt *m* public; in the ~ interest dans l'intérêt général; a ~ outcry un tollé général; to restore ~ confidence regagner la confiance de la population; ~ awareness of the problem has increased le public est plus sensible au problème maintenant; the bill has ~ support l'opinion publique est favorable au projet de loi; the increase in crime is generating great ~ concern la montée de la criminalité inquiète sérieusement la population; to be in the ~ eye occuper le devant de la scène (publique); to disappear from the ~ eye tomber dans les oubliettes ❑ ~ access channel *Am* TV *chaîne du réseau câblé à laquelle peuvent avoir accès des particuliers*. -**4.** [publicly known, open] public; to make sthg ~ rendre qqch public; a ~ figure une personnalité très connue; to go into ~ life se lancer dans les affaires publiques; she's active in ~ life elle prend une part active aux affaires publiques; the contrast between his ~ and his private life le contraste entre sa vie publique et sa vie privée; it created a ~ scandal ça a provoqué un scandale retentissant; his first ~ statement sa première déclaration publique; he made a ~ denial of the rumours il a démenti publiquement les rumeurs, il a apporté un démenti public aux rumeurs ❑ ~ spirit sens *m* civique, civisme *m*. -**5.** ST. EX: to go ~ être coté en Bourse; the company is going ~ la société va être cotée en Bourse.
◇ *n* public *m*; the ~ is OR are tired of political scandals la population est lasse des scandales politiques; her books reach a wide ~ ses livres touchent un public très large; the film-going ~ les amateurs de OR les gens qui vont au cinéma; the viewing ~ les téléspectateurs; your ~ awaits OR await you votre public vous attend.
◆ **in public** *adv phr* en public.

public-address system *n* (système *m* de) sonorisation *f*.

publican ['pʌblɪkən] *n* -**1.** *Br* [pub owner] patron *m*, -onne *f* de pub; [manager] tenancier *m*, -ère *f* de pub. -**2.** BIBLE [tax collector] publicain *m*.

public assistance *n Am* aide *f* sociale.

publication [,pʌblɪ'keɪʃn] *n* -**1.** [of book, statistics, banns] publication *f*; [of edict] promulgation *f*; what's the book's ~ date? quelle est la date de publication OR de parution du livre?; her article has been accepted for ~ son article va être publié; this isn't for ~ ceci doit rester entre nous. -**2.** [work] publication *f*, ouvrage *m* publié.

public bar *n Br* salle *f* de bar *(moins confortable et moins cher que le «lounge bar» ou le «saloon bar»)*.

public company *n* ≃ société *f* anonyme *(dont les actions sont négociables en Bourse)*.

public convenience *n Br* toilettes *fpl* publiques.

public corporation *n Br* & *Can* entreprise *f* publique.

public defender *n Am* avocat *m* commis d'office.

public domain *n*: to be in the ~ [publication] être dans le domaine public.

public enemy *n* ennemi *m* public; ~ number one ennemi public numéro un.

public enterprise *n* entreprise *f* publique.

public footpath *n Br* sentier *m* public.

public gallery *n* tribune *f* réservée au public.

public health *n* santé *f* publique; ~ hazard risque *m* pour la santé publique; the ~ authorities *administration régionale des services publics de santé*; ~ clinic centre *m* d'hygiène publique; ~ inspector inspecteur *m* sanitaire.

public holiday *n* jour *m* férié, fête *f* légale.

public house *n Br fml* [pub] pub *m*, bar *m*; *Am* [inn] auberge *f*.

publicist ['pʌblɪsɪst] *n* -**1.** [press agent] (agent *m*) publicitaire *mf*. -**2.** [journalist] journaliste *mf*. -**3.** JUR publiciste *mf*.

publicity [pʌb'lɪsɪtɪ] ◇ *n* publicité *f*; it'll give us free ~ for the product ça fera de la publicité gratuite pour notre produit; she/her film is getting OR attracting a lot of ~ on fait beaucoup de publicité autour d'elle/de son film; the incident will mean bad ~ for us cet incident va être mauvais pour OR va faire du tort à notre image de marque.
◇ *comp* [agent, agency, campaign] publicitaire, de publicité; [manager] de publicité; ~ gimmick astuce *f* publicitaire; ~ stunt coup *m* de pub.

publicity-seeking [-siːkɪŋ] *adj* [person] qui cherche à se faire de la publicité; [operation, manœuvre] publicitaire.

publicize, -ise ['pʌblɪsaɪz] *vt* **-1.** [make known]: he doesn't like to ~ the fact that he's been in prison il n'aime pas qu'on dise qu'il a fait de la prison; his much ~d blunders don't help his image ses célèbres gaffes ne font rien pour arranger son image de marque; the government's environmental reforms have been well ~d in the press la presse a beaucoup parlé des réformes du gouvernement en matière d'environnement. **-2.** [advertise - product, event] faire de la publicité pour; the festival was well ~d le festival a été annoncé à grand renfort de publicité.

public lavatory *n Br* toilettes *fpl* publiques.

public lending right *n droits que touche un auteur ou un éditeur pour le prêt de ses livres en bibliothèque.*

public limited company *n* société *f* à responsabilité limitée.

publicly ['pʌblɪklɪ] *adv* publiquement, en public; his ~ declared intentions les intentions qu'il avait affichées; ~ owned ECON nationalisé; the company is 51% ~ controlled la compagnie est contrôlée à 51% par des capitaux publics.

public nuisance *n* **-1.** [act]: the pub's late opening hours were creating a ~ les heures d'ouverture tardives du pub portaient atteinte à la tranquillité générale. **-2.** [person] fléau *m* public, empoisonneur *m*, -euse *f*.

public opinion *n* opinion *f* publique; ~ poll sondage *m* (d'opinion).

public prosecutor *n* ≃ procureur *m* général, ≃ ministère *m* public.

Public Record Office *n Br* ≃ Archives *fpl* nationales.

public relations ◇ *n (U)* relations *fpl* publiques; giving them a free meal was great ~ en leur offrant le repas, nous avons fait un excellent travail de relations publiques.
◇ *adj*: ~ consultant conseil *m* en relations publiques; ~ exercise opération *f* de relations publiques; ~ officer responsable *mf* des relations publiques.

public school *n* **-1.** [in UK] public school *f*, école *f* privée (prestigieuse). **-2.** [in US] école *f* publique.

PUBLIC SCHOOL:
En Angleterre et au pays de Galles, le terme «public school» désigne une école privée de type traditionnel; certaines de ces écoles (Eton et Harrow, par exemple) sont très réputées et recherchées. La «public school» est censée former l'élite de la nation. Aux États-Unis et parfois en Écosse, le terme désigne une école publique.

---

public schoolboy *n Br* élève *m* d'une «public school».

public schoolgirl *n Br* élève *f* d'une «public school».

public sector *n* secteur *m* public; ~ borrowing requirement emprunts *mpl* d'État.

public servant *n* fonctionnaire *mf*.

public service *n* **-1.** *Br* [civil service] fonction *f* publique; she's in ~ elle est fonctionnaire. **-2.** [amenity] service *m* public OR d'intérêt général; ADMIN: our organization performs a ~ notre association assure un service d'intérêt général.
◆ **public-service** *adj* RADIO & TV: a public-service message OR announcement un communiqué (d'un ministère) ❑ Public-Service Commission *Am commission chargée de la réglementation des sociétés privées assurant des services publics*; public-service corporation *Am société privée assurant un service public et réglementée par une commission d'État*.

public speaker *n* orateur *m*, -trice *f*; he's a very good ~ c'est un excellent orateur.

public speaking *n* art *m* oratoire; unaccustomed as I am to ~ *hum* bien que je n'aie pas l'habitude de prendre la parole en public; ~ contest SCH concours *m* d'éloquence.

public spending *n (U)* dépenses *fpl* publiques OR de l'État.

public-spirited *adj* [gesture] d'esprit civique; [person]: to be ~ faire preuve de civisme.

public transport *n (U)* transports *mpl* en commun; ~ users usagers *mpl* des transports en commun.

public utility *n Am* **-1.** [company] *société privée assurant un service public et réglementée par une commission d'État*. **-2.** [amenity] service *m* public.

public works *npl* travaux *mpl* publics.

publish ['pʌblɪʃ] ◇ *vt* **-1.** [book, journal] publier, éditer; [author] éditer; her latest novel has just been ~ed son dernier roman vient de paraître; he's a ~ed author ses livres sont publiés; it's ~ed by Larousse c'est édité chez Larousse; the magazine is ~ed quarterly la revue paraît tous les trois mois; the newspaper ~ed my letter le journal a publié ma lettre. **-2.** [subj: author]: he's ~ed poems in several magazines ses poèmes ont été publiés dans plusieurs revues. **-3.** [make known - statistics, statement, banns] publier; the price index which was ~ed on Monday l'indice des prix publié lundi.
◇ *vi* **-1.** [newspaper] paraître; the "Sun" didn't ~ yesterday le «Sun» n'est pas paru hier. **-2.** [author] être publié; she ~es regularly in women's magazines ses articles sont régulièrement publiés dans la presse féminine.

publishable ['pʌblɪʃəbl] *adj* publiable; her remarks aren't ~! ses commentaires sont impubliables!, on ne peut pas publier ses commentaires!

publisher ['pʌblɪʃəʳ] *n* [person] éditeur *m*, -trice *f*; [company] maison *f* d'édition.

publishing ['pʌblɪʃɪŋ] ◇ *n* **-1.** [industry] édition *f*; she's OR she works in ~ elle travaille dans l'édition. **-2.** [of book, journal] publication *f*.
◇ *comp*: a ~ giant un géant de l'édition; a ~ empire un des empires de l'édition.

publishing house *n* maison *f* d'édition.

Publius ['pʌblɪəs] *pr n* Publius.

puce [pjuːs] ◇ *n* couleur *f* puce.
◇ *adj* puce *(inv)*.

puck [pʌk] *n* **-1.** [in ice hockey] palet *m*. **-2.** [sprite] lutin *m*, farfadet *m*.

pucker ['pʌkəʳ] ◇ *vi* [face, forehead] se plisser; [fabric, collar] goder, godailler.
◇ *vt* [face, forehead] plisser; [fabric, collar] faire goder, faire godailler; she ~ed her lips at the sour taste elle fit la grimace en sentant le goût acide; the seam/hem is ~ed la couture/l'ourlet fait des plis.
◇ *n* [crease] pli *m*.
◆ **pucker up** ◇ *vi insep* **-1.** = **pucker** *vi*. **-2.** *inf* [for kiss] avancer les lèvres.
◇ *vt sep* = **pucker** *vt*.

puckish ['pʌkɪʃ] *adj* espiègle.

pud [pʊd] *n* **-1.** *inf Br abbr of* pudding. **-2.** ▼ *Am* [penis] bite *f*.

pudding ['pʊdɪŋ] *n* **-1.** [sweet dish]: jam ~ pudding *m* à la confiture; rice/tapioca ~ riz *m*/tapioca *m* au lait. **-2.** *Br* [part of meal] dessert *m*; what are we having for ~? qu'est-ce qu'il y a comme dessert? **-3.** [savoury dish]: steak-and-kidney ~ *viande de bœuf et rognons en croûte*. **-4.** [sausage] boudin *m*; black ~ boudin *m* noir. **-5.** *inf Br* [podgy person] boudin *m*. **-6.** *phr*: to be in the ~ club *inf Br* avoir un polichinelle dans le tiroir.

pudding basin, pudding bowl *n Br jatte dans laquelle on fait cuire le pudding*; ~ haircut coupe *f* au bol.

pudding head *inf n Br* andouille *f*, patate *f*.

pudding stone *n* GEOL poudingue *m*.

puddle ['pʌdl] ◇ *n* flaque *f*.
◇ *vt* [clay] malaxer.
◆ **puddle about** *Br*, **puddle around** *vi insep* **-1.** [wade] patauger, barboter. **-2.** *inf Am* [laze] flemmarder, traîner. **-3.** *inf Am* [tinker, potter] faire des bricoles.

pudendum [pjuː'dendəm] *n*, **pudenda** [pjuː'dendə] *npl* parties *fpl* génitales.

pudgy ['pʌdʒɪ] *(compar* pudgier, *superl* pudgiest*)* = **podgy**.

pueblo ['pwebləʊ] *(pl* pueblos*) n Am* village *m* pueblo.

Pueblo ['pwebləʊ] *(pl inv* OR Pueblos*) n* Pueblo *mf*.

puerile ['pjʊəraɪl] *adj* puéril.

puerility [pjʊə'rɪlətɪ] *n* puérilité *f*.

puerperal [pjuː'ɜːpərəl] *adj* puerpéral; ~ fever fièvre *f* puerpérale.

Puerto Rican [ˌpwɜːtəʊ'riːkən] ◇ *pr n* Portoricain *m*, -e *f*.
◇ *adj* portoricain.

Puerto Rico [ˌpwɜːtəʊ'riːkəʊ] *pr n* Porto Rico, Puerto Rico; in ~ à Porto Rico, à Puerto Rico.

puff[1] [pʌf] ◇ *vt* **-1.** [smoke - cigar, pipe] tirer des bouffées de. **-2.** [emit, expel]: to ~ (out) smoke/steam envoyer des nuages de fumée/des jets de vapeur; he sat opposite me ~ing smoke in my face! il était assis en face de moi et m'envoyait sa fumée en pleine figure! **-3.** [pant]: "I can't go on", he ~ed «je n'en peux plus», haleta-t-il. **-4.** [swell - sail, parachute] gonfler. **-5.** *inf dated* [laud] vanter, faire mousser. **-6.** *phr*: I'm ~ed (out)! *inf* je n'ai plus de souffle!, je suis complètement essoufflé!
◇ *vi* **-1.** [blow - person] souffler; [- wind] souffler en bourrasques. **-2.** [pant] haleter; [breathe heavily] souffler; I was ~ing as I climbed the stairs je haletais en montant l'escalier; he was ~ing and panting il soufflait comme un phoque; I ~ed along beside her je courais, tout essoufflé, à ses côtés. **-3.** [smoke]: to ~ on one's pipe/cigar tirer sur sa pipe/son cigare. **-4.** [issue - smoke, steam] sortir. **-5.** [move - train]: the train ~ed into the station le train entra en gare dans un nuage de fumée.
◇ *n* **-1.** [gust, whiff] bouffée *f*; [gasp] souffle *m*; her breath came in short ~s elle haletait; a ~ of dust/smoke on the horizon un nuage de poussière/fumée à l'horizon; all our plans went up in a ~ of smoke *fig* tous nos projets sont partis en fumée OR se sont évanouis. **-2.** [on cigarette, pipe] bouffée *f*; to have OR to take a ~ tirer une bouffée. **-3.** [sound - of train] teuf-teuf *m*. **-4.** *inf Br* [breath] souffle *m*; to be out of ~ être à bout de souffle OR essoufflé. **-5.** [fluffy mass]: ~s of cloud in the sky des moutons OR des petits nuages dans le ciel. **-6.** [for make-up]: (powder) ~ houppe *f* (à poudrer), houpette *f*. **-7.** [pastry] chou *m*; cream ~ chou à la crème. **-8.** *Am* [eiderdown] édredon *m*. **-9.** *inf dated* [free publicity] publicité *f* gratuite; to give sthg a ~ faire de la réclame pour qqch.
◆ **puff out** ◇ *vt sep* **-1.** [extinguish] souffler, éteindre (en soufflant). **-2.** [inflate, make rounded - cheeks, sail] gonfler; [- cushion, hair] faire bouffer; the pigeon ~ed out its feathers le pigeon fit gonfler ses plumes; he ~ed out his chest il bomba le torse; the wind ~ed out the sails les voiles se gonflèrent. **-3.** [emit]: to ~ out smoke/steam envoyer des nuages de fumée/de vapeur.
◇ *vi insep* **-1.** [parachute, sail] se gonfler. **-2.** [be emitted - smoke] s'échapper.
◆ **puff up** ◇ *vt sep* **-1.** = **puff out 2**. **-2.** *(usu pass)* [swell - lip, ankle, flesh] enfler; her eyes were ~ed up elle avait les yeux bouffis; to be ~ed up with pride *fig* être bouffi d'orgueil.
◇ *vi insep* [lip, ankle, eye] enfler, bouffir.

puff[2] [pʊf] = **poof**.

puff adder [pʌf-] *n* vipère *f* heurtante.

puffball ['pʌfbɔːl] *n* vesse-de-loup *f*; giant ~ vesse-de-loup géante.

puffed [pʌft] *adj* **-1.** [rice, oats] soufflé; ~ wheat cereal céréale *f* de blé soufflé. **-2.** *inf Br* [out of breath] essoufflé, à bout de souffle; we were ~ (out) after the climb la montée nous a essoufflés.

puffed sleeves = **puff sleeves**.

puffed-up *adj* -**1.** [swollen] boursouflé, enflé. -**2.** [conceited] suffisant, content de soi.

puffer ['pʌfəʳ] *n* -**1.** [fish] poisson *m* armé. -**2.** *inf Br* [train] train *m*.

puffin ['pʌfɪn] *n* macareux *m*.

puffiness ['pʌfɪnɪs] *n* boursouflure *f*.

puff pastry [pʌf-] *Br*, **puff paste** [pʌf-] *Am n* [for pies] pâte *f* feuilletée; [for puffs] pâte *f* à choux.

puff-puff *inf* [pʌf-] ◇ *n baby talk* [train] teuf-teuf *m*.
◇ *onomat* teuf-teuf.

puff sleeves [pʌf-] *npl* manches *fpl* ballon.

puffy ['pʌfɪ] (*compar* puffier, *superl* puffiest) *adj* [lip, cheek] enflé; [eye] bouffi; ~ **clouds** moutons *mpl*.

pug [pʌg] *n* -**1.** [dog] carlin *m*. -**2.** ▽ (*abbr of* pugilist) boxeur *m*.

pugilism ['pjuːdʒɪlɪzm] *n lit* pugilat *m lit*, boxe *f*.

pugilist ['pjuːdʒɪlɪst] *n lit* pugiliste *m lit*, boxeur *m*.

pugnacious [pʌg'neɪʃəs] *adj fml* pugnace, agressif.

pugnaciously [pʌg'neɪʃəslɪ] *adv fml* [say] avec pugnacité OR agressivité.

pugnacity [pʌg'næsətɪ] *n fml* pugnacité *f*.

pug nose *n* nez *m* camus.

pug-nosed [-nəʊzd] *adj* [face, person] au nez camus; to be ~ avoir le nez camus.

puke▽ [pjuːk] ◇ *vt* dégueuler, gerber; **you make me ~!** tu me dégoûtes!
◇ *n* dégueulis *m*.

pukka *inf* ['pʌkə] *adj Br dated* OR *hum* -**1.** [genuine] vrai, authentique, véritable; **a ~ sahib** *hum* un vrai gentleman; ~ **information** des renseignements exacts. -**2.** [done well] bien fait, très correct; [excellent] de premier ordre. -**3.** [socially acceptable] (très) comme il faut.

pulchritude ['pʌlkrɪtjuːd] *n lit* beauté *f*, splendeur *f*.

Pulitzer Prize ['pjuːlɪtsəʳ-] *n*: **the ~** le prix Pulitzer.

pull [pʊl] ◇ *vt* -**1.** [object - yank, tug] tirer; [- drag] traîner; **she ~ed my hair** elle m'a tiré les cheveux; **to ~ the blinds** baisser les stores; **to ~ the curtains** *Br* OR **drapes** *Am* tirer OR fermer les rideaux; **we ~ed the heavy log across to the fire** nous avons traîné la lourde bûche jusqu'à la cheminée; ~ **the lamp towards you** tirez la lampe vers vous; **he ~ed his chair closer to the fire** il approcha sa chaise de la cheminée; **she ~ed the hood over her face** elle abaissa le capuchon sur son visage; **he ~ed the steering wheel to the right** il a donné un coup de volant à droite; **to ~ a drawer open** ouvrir un tiroir; **she came in and ~ed the door shut behind her** elle entra et ferma la porte derrière elle; ~ **the rope taut** tendez la corde; ~ **the knot tight** serrez le nœud; ~ **the tablecloth straight** tendez la nappe ‖ [person] tirer, entraîner; **he was ~ing her towards the exit** il l'entraînait vers la sortie; **the current ~ed us into the middle of the river** le courant nous a entraînés au milieu de la rivière; **he ~ed himself onto the riverbank** il se hissa sur la berge; **the sound of the doorbell ~ed him out of his daydream** *fig* le coup de sonnette l'a tiré de OR arraché à ses rêveries; **he was ~ed off the first team** *fig* on l'a écarté OR exclu de la première équipe ‖ [remove forcibly] arracher; **he ~ed the wrapping from the package** il arracha l'emballage du paquet; **he ~ed the sheets off the bed** il enleva les draps du lit; **she ~ed her hand from mine** elle retira (brusquement) sa main de la mienne ❑ ~ **the other one (it's got bells on)!** *inf Br* mon œil!, à d'autres!; **to ~ sthg to bits** OR **pieces** *literal* démonter qqch; *fig* démolir qqch. -**2.** [operate - lever, handle] tirer; ~ **the trigger** appuyez OR pressez sur la détente. -**3.** [tow, draw - load, trailer, carriage, boat] tirer, remorquer; **carts ~ed by mules** des charrettes tirées par des mules; **a suitcase with wheels that you ~ behind you** une valise à roulettes qu'on tire OR traîne derrière soi; **the barges were ~ed along the canals** les péniches étaient halées le long des canaux. -**4.** [take out - tooth] arracher, extraire; [- weapon] tirer, sortir; **he ~ed a dollar bill from his wad/wallet** il a tiré un billet d'un dollar de sa liasse/sorti un billet d'un dollar de son portefeuille; **he ~ed a gun on me** il a braqué un revolver sur moi; **getting him to talk is like ~ing teeth!** *hum* il faut lui arracher les mots de la bouche!; **can you ~ that file for me?** *inf* pourriez-vous me sortir ce dossier? -**5.** [strain - muscle, tendon]: **she ~ed a muscle** elle s'est déchiré un muscle, elle s'est fait un claquage; **my shoulder feels as if I've ~ed something** j'ai l'impression que je me suis froissé un muscle de l'épaule. -**6.** *inf* [bring off] réussir; **she has ~ed several daring financial coups** elle a réussi plusieurs opérations financières audacieuses; **he ~ed a big bank job in Italy** il a réussi un hold-up de première dans une banque italienne; **to ~ a trick on sb** jouer un tour à qqn; **what are you trying to ~?** qu'est-ce que vous êtes en train de combiner OR manigancer?; **don't try and ~ anything!** n'essayez pas de jouer au plus malin! ❑ **I ~ed an all-nighter** *Am* j'ai bossé toute la nuit. -**7.** [hold back]: **to ~ a horse** [in horseracing] retenir un cheval ❑ **to ~ one's punches** *literal* & *fig* retenir ses coups, ménager son adversaire; **she didn't ~ any punches** elle n'y est pas allée de main morte. -**8.** [in golf - ball] puller; **to ~ a shot** puller. -**9.** [in rowing - boat] faire avancer à la rame; **he ~s a good oar** c'est un bon rameur; **the boat ~s eight oars** c'est un bateau à huit avirons. -**10.** TYPO [proof] tirer. -**11.** COMPUT extraire. -**12.** [gut - fowl] vider. -**13.** *inf* [attract - customers, spectators] attirer; **the festival ~ed a big crowd** le festival a attiré beaucoup de monde; **how many votes will he ~?** combien de voix va-t-il récolter? -**14.** *Br* [serve - draught beer] tirer; **he ~s pints at the Crown** *inf* il est barman au Crown. -**15.** ▽ *Br* [seduce] lever.
◇ *vi* -**1.** [exert force, tug] tirer; ~ **harder!** tirez plus fort!; **the bandage may ~ when I take it off** le pansement risque de vous tirer la peau quand je l'enlèverai; **the steering ~s to the right** la direction tire à droite. -**2.** [rope, cord]: **the rope ~ed easily** la corde filait librement. -**3.** [go, move - vehicle, driver]: ~ **into the space next to the Mercedes** mettez-vous OR garez-vous à côté de la Mercedes; **he ~ed into the right-hand lane** il a pris la file de droite; ~ **into the garage** entrez dans le garage; **when the train ~s out of the station** quand le train quitte la gare. -**4.** [strain, labour - vehicle] peiner; [- horse] tirer sur le mors; **the overloaded truck ~ed up the slope** le camion surchargé montait la côte avec difficulté; **the 2-litre model ~s very well** AUT le modèle 2 litres a de bonnes reprises. -**5.** *inf* [exert influence, give support]: **the head of personnel is ~ing for you** OR **on your behalf** vous avez le chef du personnel derrière vous. -**6.** [snag - sweater] filer; **my sweater's ~ed in a couple of places** mon pull a plusieurs mailles filées. -**7.** [row] ramer; **to ~ for shore** ramer vers la côte; **to ~ with a long stroke** ramer à grands coups d'aviron.
◇ *n* -**1.** [tug, act of pulling] coup *m*; **to give sthg a ~, to give a ~ on sthg** tirer (sur) qqch; **we'll need a ~ to get out of the mud** nous aurons besoin que quelqu'un nous remorque OR nous prenne en remorque pour nous désembourber; **with a ~ the dog broke free** le chien tira sur sa laisse et s'échappa; **she felt a ~ at** OR **on her handbag** elle a senti qu'on tirait sur son sac à main; **I felt a ~ on the fishing line** ça mordait. -**2.** [physical force - of machine] traction *f*; [- of sun, moon, magnet] attraction *f*; **the winch applies a steady ~** le treuil exerce une traction continue; **the gravitational ~ is stronger on Earth** la gravitation est plus forte sur Terre; **we fought against the ~ of the current** nous luttions contre le courant qui nous entraînait. -**3.** [resistance - of bowstring] résistance *f*; **adjust the trigger if the ~ is too stiff for you** réglez la détente si elle est trop dure pour vous. -**4.** [psychological, emotional attraction] attrait *m*; **the ~ of city life** l'attrait de la vie en ville; **he resisted the ~ of family tradition and went his own way** il a résisté à l'influence de la tradition familiale pour suivre son propre chemin. -**5.** *inf* [influence, power] influence *f*; **his money gives him a certain political ~** son argent lui confère une certaine influence OR un certain pouvoir politique; **his father's ~ got him in** son père l'a pistonné. -**6.** [climb] montée *f*; **it'll be a long ~ to the summit** la montée sera longue (et difficile) pour atteindre le sommet; **it's going to be a long uphill ~ to make the firm profitable** *fig* ça sera difficile de remettre l'entreprise à flot. -**7.** [in rowing - stroke] coup *m* de rame OR d'aviron; **with another ~ he was clear of the rock** d'un autre coup de rame, il évita le rocher; **it will be a hard ~ upstream** il faudra ramer dur pour remonter le courant. -**8.** [at cigar] bouffée *f*; [at drink, bottle] gorgée *f*; **to take a ~ at** OR **on one's beer** boire OR prendre une gorgée de bière ‖ [on cigarette, pipe]: **to take a ~ at** OR **on** tirer sur. -**9.** (*usu in cpds*) [knob, handle] poignée *f*; [cord] cordon *m*; [strap] sangle *f*. -**10.** [snag - in sweater] accroc *m*. -**11.** TYPO épreuve *f*. -**12.** [in golf] pull *m*.

◆ **pull about** *vt sep* [handle roughly - person] malmener; [- clothes] tirer sur; **stop ~ing me about!** mais lâche-moi donc!

◆ **pull ahead** *vi insep* prendre de l'avance; **to ~ ahead of one's competitors/classmates** prendre de l'avance sur ses concurrents/ses camarades de classe.

◆ **pull along** *vt sep* [load, vehicle] tirer; **he was ~ing the suitcase along by the strap** il tirait la valise derrière lui par la sangle ‖ [person] entraîner; **she ~ed me along by my arm** elle m'entraînait en me tirant par le bras.

◆ **pull apart** ◇ *vt sep* -**1.** [take to pieces - machine, furniture] démonter; **now you've ~ed it all apart, are you sure you can fix it?** maintenant que tu as tout démonté, es-tu sûr de pouvoir le réparer? -**2.** [destroy, break] mettre en morceaux OR en pièces; **the wreck was ~ed apart by the waves** les vagues ont disloqué l'épave; **tell him where it's hidden or he'll ~ the place apart** *inf* dites-lui où c'est (caché) sinon il va tout saccager. -**3.** *fig* [demolish - essay, theory] démolir. -**4.** [separate - fighters, dogs] séparer; [- papers] détacher, séparer. -**5.** [make suffer] déchirer.
◇ *vi insep* [furniture] se démonter, être démontable; **the shelves simply ~ apart** les étagères se démontent sans outils.

◆ **pull around** *vt sep* -**1.** [cart, toy, suitcase] tirer derrière soi. -**2.** [make turn] tourner, faire pivoter; **he tried to ~ the horse around** il essaya de faire faire demi-tour à son cheval.

◆ **pull at** *vt insep* -**1.** [strain at, tug at] tirer sur; **the dog ~ed at the leash** le chien tira sur la laisse; **we ~ed at the rope** nous avons tiré sur la corde; **I ~ed at his sleeve** je l'ai tiré par la manche; **each ~ed at an oar** chacun tirait sur un aviron; **the wind ~ed at her hair** le vent faisait voler ses cheveux. -**2.** [suck - pipe, cigar] tirer sur; [- bottle]: **he ~ed at his bottle of beer** il a bu une gorgée de bière.

◆ **pull away** ◇ *vi insep* -**1.** [withdraw - person] s'écarter, se détourner; **I put out my hand but she ~ed away** j'ai tendu la main vers elle mais elle s'est détournée; **he had me by the arm but I managed to ~ away** il me tenait par le bras mais j'ai réussi à me dégager. -**2.** [move off - vehicle, ship] démarrer; [- train, convoy] s'ébranler; **the boat ~ed away from the bank** le bateau quitta la rive. -**3.** [get ahead - runner, competitor] prendre de l'avance; **she's ~ing away from the pack** elle prend de l'avance sur le peloton, elle se détache du peloton.
◇ *vt sep* [withdraw - covering, hand] retirer; **she ~ed her hand away** elle retira OR ôta sa main; **he ~ed me away from the window** il m'éloigna de la fenêtre ‖ [grab] arracher; **she ~ed the book away from him** elle lui arracha le livre.

◆ **pull back** ◇ *vi insep* **-1.** [withdraw - troops, participant] se retirer; **it's too late to ~ back now** il est trop tard pour se retirer OR pour faire marche arrière maintenant. **-2.** [step backwards] reculer; **to ~ back involuntarily** avoir un mouvement de recul involontaire. **-3.** [jib - horse, person] regimber.
◇ *vt sep* **-1.** [draw backwards or towards one] retirer; **he ~ed his hand back** il retira OR ôta sa main; **she ~ed back the curtains** elle ouvrit les rideaux; **~ the lever back** tirez le levier (vers l'arrière); **he ~ed me back from the railing** il m'a éloigné de la barrière. **-2.** [withdraw - troops] retirer.
◆ **pull down** ◇ *vt sep* **-1.** [lower - lever, handle] tirer (vers le bas); [- trousers, veil] baisser; [- suitcase, book] descendre; **~ the blind/the window down** baissez le store/la vitre; **with his hat ~ed down over his eyes** son chapeau rabattu sur les yeux; **she ~ed her skirt down over her knees** elle ramena sa jupe sur ses genoux; **I ~ed him down onto the chair** je l'ai fait asseoir sur la chaise. **-2.** [demolish - house, wall] démolir, abattre; **they're ~ing down the whole neighbourhood** ils démolissent tout le quartier; **it'll ~ down the government** *fig* ça va renverser le gouvernement. **-3.** *inf* [weaken - subj: illness] affaiblir, abattre; [depress] déprimer, abattre. **-4.** *inf Am* [earn] gagner, se faire.
◇ *vi insep* [blind] descendre.
◆ **pull in** ◇ *vi insep* [vehicle, driver - stop] s'arrêter; [- park] se garer; [- move to side of road] se rabattre; [train] entrer en gare; **I ~ed in for petrol** je me suis arrêté pour prendre de l'essence; **the car in front ~ed in to let me past** la voiture devant moi s'est rabattue pour me laisser passer.
◇ *vt sep* **-1.** [line, fishing net] ramener; **they ~ed the rope in** ils tirèrent la corde à eux; **to ~ sb in** [into building, car] tirer qqn à l'intérieur, faire entrer qqn; [into water] faire tomber qqn à l'eau ‖ [stomach] rentrer. **-2.** [attract - customers, investors, investment] attirer; **her show is really ~ing them in** son spectacle attire les foules. **-3.** *inf* [earn - subj: person] gagner, se faire; [- subj: business] rapporter. **-4.** *inf* [arrest] arrêter, embarquer.
◆ **pull off** ◇ *vi insep* **-1.** [move off] démarrer; [after halt] redémarrer. **-2.** [leave main road] quitter la route; **he ~ed off onto a side road** il bifurqua sur une petite route ‖ [stop] s'arrêter; **there's no place to ~ off** il n'y a pas de place pour s'arrêter.
◇ *vt sep* **-1.** [clothes, boots, ring] enlever, retirer; [cover, bandage, knob] enlever; [page from calendar, sticky backing] détacher; [wrapping, wallpaper] enlever; **I ~ed her hat off** je lui ai enlevé son chapeau; [more violently] je lui ai arraché son chapeau. **-2.** *inf* [accomplish - deal, stratagem, mission, shot] réussir; [- press conference, negotiations] mener à bien; [- plan] réaliser; **the deal will be difficult to ~ off** cette affaire ne sera pas facile à négocier; **will she (manage to) ~ it off?** est-ce qu'elle va y arriver?
◆ **pull on** ◇ *vt sep* [clothes, boots, pillow slip] mettre, enfiler.
◇ *vt insep* **-1.** [tug at - rope, handle etc] tirer sur. **-2.** [draw on - cigarette, pipe] tirer sur.
◆ **pull out** ◇ *vi insep* **-1.** [withdraw - troops, ally, participant] se retirer; **when they ~ed out of Vietnam** quand ils se sont retirés du Viêt-nam; **she's ~ing out of the election** elle retire sa candidature; **they've ~ed out of the deal** ils se sont retirés de l'affaire. **-2.** [move off - vehicle, ship] démarrer; [- train, convoy] s'ébranler; **she was ~ing out of the garage** elle sortait du garage ‖ [move towards centre of road]: **he ~ed out to overtake** il a déboîté pour doubler; **a truck suddenly ~ed out in front of me** soudain, un camion m'a coupé la route; **to ~ out into traffic** s'engager dans la circulation; **to ~ out of a dive** AERON sortir d'un piqué, se rétablir. **-3.** [economy]: **to ~ out of a recession/a crisis** sortir de la récession/d'une crise. **-4.** [slide out]: **the sofa ~s out into a bed** le canapé se transforme en lit; **the shelves ~ out** on peut retirer les étagères; **the table top ~s out** c'est une table à rallonges.
◇ *vt sep* **-1.** [remove - tooth, hair, weeds] arracher; [- splinter, nail] enlever; [- plug, cork] ôter, enlever; [produce - wallet, weapon] sortir, tirer; **she ~ed a map out of her bag** elle a sorti une carte de son sac; **he ~ed a page out of his notebook** il a déchiré une feuille de son carnet; **~ the paper gently out of the printer** retirez doucement le papier de l'imprimante; **the tractor ~ed us out of the mud/ditch** le tracteur nous a sortis de la boue/du fossé; **to ~ the country out of recession** sortir le pays de la récession; **to ~ sb out of a tight spot** tirer qqn d'un mauvais pas. **-2.** [draw towards one - drawer] tirer; [unfold] déplier; **~ the bed out from the wall** écartez le lit du mur; **he ~ed a chair out from under the table** il a écarté une chaise de la table. **-3.** [withdraw - troops, contestant] retirer; **the battalion was ~ed out of the border area** le bataillon a été retiré de la région frontalière; **he threatened to ~ the party out of the coalition** il menaça de retirer le parti de la coalition. **-4.** COMPUT [select, produce - data] sortir.
◆ **pull over** ◇ *vt sep* **-1.** [draw into specified position] tirer, traîner; **~ the chair over to the window** amenez la chaise près de la fenêtre; **she ~ed the dish over and helped herself** elle a tiré le plat vers OR à elle et s'est servie. **-2.** [make fall - pile, person, table] faire tomber, renverser; **watch out you don't ~ that lamp over** fais attention de ne pas faire tomber cette lampe. **-3.** *(usu passive)* [stop - vehicle, driver] arrêter; **I got ~ed over for speeding** je me suis fait arrêter pour excès de vitesse.
◇ *vi insep* [vehicle, driver - stop] s'arrêter; [- move to side of road] se ranger, se rabattre; **~ over and let the fire engine past** rangez-vous OR rabattez-vous sur le côté et laissez passer les pompiers.
◆ **pull round** *Br* ◇ *vt sep* **-1.** = **pull around**. **-2.** [revive] ranimer; **a drop of brandy will ~ her round** un peu de cognac la remettra OR remontera.
◇ *vi insep* [regain consciousness] revenir à soi, reprendre connaissance; [recover] se remettre.
◆ **pull through** ◇ *vi insep* [recover] s'en sortir, s'en tirer.
◇ *vt sep* **-1.** [draw through - rope, thread] faire passer; **~ the needle through to the other side** faites sortir l'aiguille de l'autre côté. **-2.** [help survive or surmount] tirer d'affaire.
◆ **pull to** *vt sep* [shut - door, gate] fermer.
◆ **pull together** ◇ *vi insep* [on rope] tirer ensemble; [on oars] ramer à l'unisson; *fig* [combine efforts] concentrer ses efforts, agir de concert; **we've all got to ~ together on this one** *fig* il faut que nous nous y mettions tous ensemble, il faut que nous nous attelions tous ensemble à la tâche.
◇ *vt sep* **-1.** [place together, join] joindre. **-2.** [organize - demonstration, rescue team] organiser; [prepare] préparer; **I've ~ed together a few suggestions** j'ai préparé OR noté quelques propositions. **-3.** *phr*: **to ~ o.s. together** se reprendre, se ressaisir; **~ yourself together!** ressaisissez-vous!, ne vous laissez pas aller!
◆ **pull up** ◇ *vi insep* **-1.** [stop] s'arrêter; **as I was ~ing up at the red light** alors que j'allais m'arrêter au feu rouge; **~ up at OR outside the main entrance** arrêtez-vous devant l'entrée principale; **to ~ up short** s'arrêter net OR brusquement. **-2.** *inf* [ease up] se détendre, se relâcher. **-3.** [draw even] rattraper; **to ~ up with sb** rattraper qqn; **Sun Boy is ~ing up on the outside!** Sun Boy remonte à l'extérieur! **-4.** [improve - student, athlete, performance] s'améliorer.
◇ *vt sep* **-1.** [draw upwards - trousers, sleeve, blanket, lever] remonter; [hoist] hisser; **they ~ed the boat up onto the beach** ils ont tiré le bateau sur la plage; **she ~ed herself up onto the ledge** elle s'est hissée sur le rebord. **-2.** [move closer - chair] approcher; **I ~ed a chair up to the desk** j'ai approché une chaise du bureau; **why don't you ~ up a chair and join us?** prenez donc une chaise et joignez-vous à nous!; **he ~ed the crate up to the scales** il a traîné la caisse jusqu'à la balance. **-3.** [uproot - weeds] arracher; [- bush, stump, tree] arracher, déraciner; [rip up - floorboards] arracher. **-4.** [stop - person, vehicle, horse] arrêter; [check - person] retenir; **his warning ~ed me up short** je me suis arrêté net lorsqu'il m'a crié de faire attention; **he was about to tell them everything but I ~ed him up (short)** il était sur le point de tout leur dire mais je lui ai coupé la parole. **-5.** *inf* [improve - score, mark] améliorer; [- average] remonter. **-6.** *inf Br* [rebuke] réprimander, enguirlander; **he was ~ed up for being late** il s'est fait enguirlander pour être arrivé en retard; **if your work is sloppy, they'll ~ you up on it** si ton travail est bâclé, tu vas te faire taper sur les doigts.

pullback [ˈpʊlbæk] *n* MIL repli *m*, retraite *f*.

pulldown [ˈpʊldaʊn] *adj* [bench, counter] à abattant; **~ menu** COMPUT menu *m* déroulant; **~ seat** strapontin *m*.

pullet [ˈpʊlɪt] *n* poulette *f*.

pulley [ˈpʊlɪ] *n* [wheel, device] poulie *f*; TECH [set of parallel wheels] molette *f*.

pull-in *n Br* AUT [café] café *m* au bord de la route, ≃ restaurant *m* routier.

Pullman [ˈpʊlmən] (*pl* **Pullmans**) *n* **-1.** [sleeping car]: **~ (carriage** OR **car)** (voiture *f*) pullman *m*. **-2.** [train] rapide *m* de nuit.

pull-on *adj*: **~ boots** bottes *fpl* (sans lacets); **~ skirt** jupe *f* à taille élastique.

pullout [ˈpʊlaʊt] ◇ *n* **-1.** [magazine supplement] supplément *m* détachable. **-2.** [fold-out] hors-texte *m inv (qui se déplie)*. **-3.** [withdrawal - gen & MIL] retrait *m*; [- of candidate] désistement *m*; [evacuation] évacuation *f*; **investment ~** désinvestissement *m*. **-4.** AERON rétablissement *m*.
◇ *adj* [magazine section] détachable; [map, advertising page] hors texte *(inv)*; [legs, shelf] rétractable; **~ bed** canapé-lit *m*.

pullover [ˈpʊlˌəʊvəʳ] *n* pullover *m*, pull *m*.

pull tab *n* [on can] anneau *m*, bague *f*.

pullulate [ˈpʌljʊleɪt] *vi* **-1.** [teem, breed] pulluler. **-2.** BOT [germinate] germer.

pull-up *n* **-1.** SPORT traction *f (sur une barre ou sur des anneaux)*; **to do ~s** faire des tractions. **-2.** *Br* = **pull-in**.

pulmonary [ˈpʌlmənərɪ] *adj* pulmonaire.

pulp [pʌlp] ◇ *n* **-1.** [in fruit] pulpe *f*; [for paper] pâte *f* à papier, pulpe *f*; [in tooth] pulpe *f*; **~ and paper mill** fabrique *f* de papier. **-2.** [mush] bouillie *f*; **to beat** OR **to smash to a ~** réduire en bouillie OR en marmelade. **-3.** MIN pulpe *f*.
◇ *vt* **-1.** [crush - wood] réduire en pâte; [- fruit, vegetables] réduire en pulpe; [- book] mettre au pilon. **-2.** [remove pulp from] ôter la pulpe de.
◇ *comp* **-1.** *pej* [novel, fiction] de hall de gare; **~ magazine** magazine *m* à sensation; **~ writer** romancier *m*, -ère *f* de hall de gare. **-2.** ANAT [cavity, canal] pulpaire.

pulpit [ˈpʊlpɪt] *n* RELIG chaire *f*; *fig* [clergy]: **the ~** le clergé, les ecclésiastiques *mpl*.

pulpwood [ˈpʌlpwʊd] *n* pâte *f* à bois.

pulpy [ˈpʌlpɪ] (*compar* **pulpier**, *superl* **pulpiest**) *adj* **-1.** [fruit, tissue, mass] pulpeux. **-2.** *inf pej* [novel, magazine] à sensation.

pulsar [ˈpʌlsɑːʳ] *n* pulsar *m*.

pulsate [pʌlˈseɪt] *vi* **-1.** [throb - heart] battre fort, pulser MÉD; [- music, room] vibrer; **the pulsating rhythm of jazz** le rythme syncopé du jazz; **the pulsating beat of the drums** le rythme lancinant des tambours. **-2.** PHYS subir des pulsations; ASTRON [variable star] pulser.

pulsation [pʌlˈseɪʃn] *n* [of heart, arteries] battement *m*, pulsation *f*; ASTRON & PHYS pulsation *f*.

pulsatory [ˈpʌlsətərɪ] *adj* [gen] pulsatoire; [insect, organ] pulsatile.

pulse [pʌls] ◇ *n* **-1.** MED pouls *m*; [single throb] pulsation *f*; he took my ~ il a pris mon pouls; her ~ (rate) is a hundred son pouls est à cent (pulsations par minute); my ~ quickens when I see her quand je la vois, j'ai le cœur qui bat plus fort. **-2.** ELECTRON & PHYS [series] série *f* d'impulsions; [single] impulsion *f*. **-3.** [vibration] rythme *m* régulier; I felt the ~ of the ship's motors je sentais le rythme régulier des moteurs du navire. **-4.** [bustle, life] animation *f*. **-5.** BOT [plant] légumineuse *f*; CULIN: (dried) ~s légumes *mpl* secs.
◇ *vi* [blood] battre; [music, room] vibrer; a vein ~d in his temple une veine palpitait sur sa tempe; the whole place ~d with life il y avait partout une animation extraordinaire; the music ~d inside my head la musique résonnait dans ma tête.

pulse modulation *n* ELECTRON [of one parameter] modulation *f* d'impulsions; [by pulse series] modulation *f* par impulsions.

pulverize, -ise ['pʌlvəraɪz] *vt literal & fig* pulvériser.

puma ['pjuːmə] (*pl inv* OR pumas) *n* puma *m*.

pumice ['pʌmɪs] ◇ *n*: ~ (stone) (pierre *f*) ponce *f*.
◇ *vt* poncer, passer à la pierre ponce.

pummel ['pʌml] (*Br pt & pp* pummelled, *cont* pummelling, *Am pt & pp* pummeled, *cont* pummeling) *vt* **-1.** [punch repeatedly] donner des coups de poing à, marteler à coups de poing; she pummelled his chest elle lui martelait la poitrine à coups de poings OR de ses poings. **-2.** [massage] masser, palper. **-3.** [knead - dough] pétrir.

pump [pʌmp] ◇ *n* **-1.** MECH pompe *f*; bicycle/hand/water ~ pompe à vélo/à main/à eau; fuel ~ AUT pompe d'alimentation; ~ attendant pompiste *mf*. **-2.** [shoe - for dancing] ballerine *f*; [- for gym] tennis *m*. **-3.** *inf Am* [heart] cœur *m*, palpitant *m*.
◇ *vt* **-1.** [displace - liquid, gas] pomper; to ~ sthg out of sthg pomper OR aspirer qqch de qqch; the water is ~ed into a tank l'eau est acheminée dans un réservoir au moyen d'une pompe; the factory ~s its waste directly into the river l'usine déverse ses déchets directement dans la rivière; they ~ed air into the football ils ont gonflé le ballon de foot; coolant is ~ed through the system une pompe fait circuler le liquide de refroidissement dans le système; to ~ gas *Am* travailler comme pompiste. **-2.** [empty - stomach] vider; he had to have OR to get his stomach ~ed on a dû lui faire un lavage d'estomac. **-3.** [inflate - tyre, ball etc] gonfler. **-4.** [move back and forth - pedal, handle] appuyer sur OR actionner (plusieurs fois); ~ the brakes or they'll lock freinez progressivement ou les freins se bloqueront; to ~ sb's hand *fig* secouer vigoureusement la main de qqn. **-5.** *inf* [shoot]: to ~ sb full of lead cribler qqn de plomb. **-6.** *inf* [money] investir; he ~ed a fortune into the business il a investi une fortune dans cette affaire; public money is being ~ed into the area la région reçoit des subventions gouvernementales importantes. **-7.** *inf* [interrogate] interroger, tirer les vers du nez à; they ~ed her for information ils l'ont cuisinée. **-8.** *phr*: to ~ iron *inf* faire de la gonflette.
◇ *vi* **-1.** [machine, person] pomper; [heart] battre fort. **-2.** [liquid] couler à flots, jaillir; blood ~ed from the wound du sang coulait de la blessure.

◆ **pump in** *vt sep* **-1.** [liquid, gas] refouler; the village ~s in water from the river l'eau du village est amenée de la rivière à l'aide d'un système de pompage. **-2.** *inf* [funds, capital] investir, injecter.

◆ **pump out** ◇ *vt sep* **-1.** [liquid, gas] pomper; [stomach] vider; it took two hours to ~ the bilge out il a fallu deux heures pour pomper OR écoper l'eau de la cale. **-2.** *inf pej* [mass-produce - music, graduates, products] produire; [- books, essays] produire à la chaîne, pondre en série.
◇ *vi* [liquid, blood] couler à flots.

◆ **pump up** *vt sep* **-1.** [liquid, mixture] pomper. **-2.** [inflate] gonfler.

pumpernickel ['pʌmpənɪkl] *n* ≃ pain *m* noir, pumpernickel *m*.

pump gun *n* fusil *m* à pompe.

pumping station *n* [building] station *f* de pompage; [machinery] installation *f* de pompage.

pumpkin ['pʌmpkɪn] *n* potiron *m*; [smaller] citrouille *f*; ~ fritters beignets *mpl* au potiron; ~ pie tarte *f* au potiron *(dessert achevant traditionnellement le dîner de Thanksgiving)*.

pumpkinseed ['pʌmpkɪnsiːd] *n* **-1.** BOT graine *f* de potiron. **-2.** ZOOL perche-soleil *m*, calicoba *m*.

pump priming *n* ECON *relance de l'économie par injection de fonds publics*.

pump room *n* [at spa - building] pavillon *m*; [- room] buvette *f*.

pun [pʌn] (*pt & pp* punned, *cont* punning)
◇ *n* calembour *m*, jeu *m* de mots.
◇ *vi* faire des calembours.

punch [pʌntʃ] ◇ *n* **-1.** [blow] coup *m* de poing; he gave him a ~ on the chin/in the stomach il lui a donné un coup de poing dans le menton/dans l'estomac; to have OR to pack a powerful ~ avoir du punch. **-2.** *fig* [effectiveness - of person] punch *m*; [of speech, cartoon, play] mordant *m*; find a slogan with a bit more ~ trouvez un slogan un peu plus accrocheur. **-3.** [for holes - in paper] perforateur *m*; [- in metal] poinçonneuse *f*; [for tickets - hand-operated] poinçonneuse *f*; [- machine] composteur *m*; [steel rod, die] poinçon *m*. **-4.** [for stamping design] machine *f* à estamper. **-5.** [for nails, bolts] chasse-clou *m*. **-6.** [drink] punch *m*.
◇ *vt* **-1.** [hit - once] donner un coup de poing à; [- repeatedly] marteler à coups de poing; he ~ed him in OR on the jaw il lui a donné un coup de poing dans les gencives; he ~ed the door il a martelé la porte à coups de poing. **-2.** [key, button] appuyer sur; I ~ed the return key j'ai appuyé sur la touche retour. **-3.** [pierce - ticket] poinçonner; [- in machine] composter; [- paper, computer card] perforer; [- sheet metal] poinçonner; to ~ a hole in sthg faire un trou dans qqch; to ~ the time clock OR one's time card pointer. **-4.** [stamp] estamper.
◇ *vi* [strike] frapper; no ~ing! pas de coups de poing!; they were ~ing away at each other ils se donnaient des coups de poing.

◆ **punch in** ◇ *vt sep* **-1.** [enter - code, number] taper, composer; [- figures, data] introduire. **-2.** [knock in - door] défoncer (à coups de poing); [- nails] enfoncer; I'll ~ your face OR head OR teeth in! *inf* je vais te casser la figure!
◇ *vi insep Am* [on time clock] pointer (en arrivant).

◆ **punch out** ◇ *vt sep* **-1.** [enter - code, number] taper, composer. **-2.** [cut out - form, pattern] découper; the holes are ~ed out by a machine les trous sont faits par une machine. **-3.** [remove - nail, bolt] enlever au chasse-clou. **-4.** [stamp] estamper, emboutir. **-5.** *inf Am* [beat up] tabasser; to get ~ed out se faire tabasser. **-6.** *inf* AERON [subj: pilot] s'éjecter.
◇ *vi insep Am* [on time clock] pointer (en partant).

Punch [pʌntʃ] *pr n* ≃ Polichinelle; ~-and-Judy show ≃ (spectacle *m* de) guignol *m*; as pleased as ~ heureux comme un roi.

PUNCH AND JUDY:
Le «Punch and Judy show» est un spectacle très apprécié des enfants en Grande-Bretagne. Il est souvent présenté dans un jardin public ou sur une plage. On y retrouve Punch le bossu, sa femme Judy avec laquelle il se querelle constamment, et leur chien Toby.

---

punch-bag *n Br* **-1.** SPORT sac *m* de sable, punching-bag *m*. **-2.** *fig* [victim] souffre-douleur *m inv*.

punch ball *n Br* punching-ball *m*.

punch bowl *n* bol *m* à punch.

punch card *Am* = **punched card**.

punch-drunk *adj* [boxer] groggy; *fig* abruti, sonné; I was ~ after seeing four films in a row après avoir vu quatre films d'affilée, j'étais complètement abruti.

punched card ['pʌntʃt-] *n Br* COMPUT carte perforée.

Punchinello [,pʌntʃɪ'neləʊ] *pr n* Polichinelle.

punching bag ['pʌntʃɪŋ-] *Am* = **punch-bag**.

punching ball *Am* = **punch ball**.

punch line *n* fin *f* *(d'une plaisanterie)*; I've forgotten the ~ j'ai oublié la fin OR comment ça finit.

punch-up *inf n* bagarre *f*; they had a ~ ils se sont bagarrés.

punchy *inf* ['pʌntʃɪ] (*compar* punchier, *superl* punchiest) *adj* **-1.** [stimulating, lively] plein de punch; he produced a ~ piece of writing on the election campaign il a écrit un texte plein de punch sur la campagne électorale. **-2.** = **punch-drunk**.

punctilio [pʌŋk'tɪlɪəʊ] (*pl* punctilios) *n* **-1.** [attitude] formalisme *m*. **-2.** [point] formalité *f*.

punctilious [pʌŋk'tɪlɪəs] *adj* pointilleux.

punctiliously [pʌŋk'tɪlɪəslɪ] *adv* pointilleusement, de façon pointilleuse.

punctual ['pʌŋktʃʊəl] *adj* [bus, train] à l'heure; [person] ponctuel; be ~ for the interview soyez à l'heure pour l'entretien.

punctuality [,pʌŋktʃʊ'ælətɪ] *n* ponctualité *f*, exactitude *f*.

punctually ['pʌŋktʃʊəlɪ] *adv* [begin, arrive] à l'heure; [pay] ponctuellement; the flight left ~ at 9/at noon le vol est parti à 9 h pile /à midi juste.

punctuate ['pʌŋktʃʊeɪt] *vt* ponctuer.

punctuation [,pʌŋktʃʊ'eɪʃn] *n* ponctuation *f*.

punctuation mark *n* signe *m* de ponctuation.

puncture ['pʌŋktʃər] ◇ *n* **-1.** [in tyre, ball, balloon] crevaison *f*; one of the front tyres had a ~ un des pneus avant était crevé; I had a ~ on the way to work j'ai crevé en allant travailler; the garage has repaired the ~ le garage a réparé le pneu crevé; ~ repair kit trousse *f* de réparation pour crevaisons. **-2.** [gen - hole] perforation *f*. **-3.** MED ponction *f*.
◇ *vt* **-1.** [gen] perforer; the bullet ~d his lung la balle lui a perforé le poumon. **-2.** [tyre, ball, balloon] crever. **-3.** *fig* [pride, self-esteem] blesser, porter atteinte à.
◇ *vi* crever.

pundit ['pʌndɪt] *n* **-1.** [expert] expert *m* *(qui pontifie)*. **-2.** [Brahmin] pandit *m*.

Pune ['puːnə] = **Poona**.

pungency ['pʌndʒənsɪ] *n* **-1.** [of smell, taste] âcreté *f*; [of food] piquant *m*. **-2.** [of wit, remark] causticité *f*, mordant *m*.

pungent ['pʌndʒənt] *adj* **-1.** [smell, taste - sour] âcre; [- spicy] piquant. **-2.** [wit, remark] caustique, mordant.

Punic ['pjuːnɪk] *adj* punique; the ~ Wars les guerres *fpl* puniques.

punish ['pʌnɪʃ] *vt* **-1.** [person, crime] punir; they will be ~ed for their mistakes ils seront punis pour leurs erreurs; such offences are ~ed by imprisonment ce genre de délit est passible d'une peine de prison. **-2.** *inf* [attack relentlessly - opponent, enemy etc] malmener; they ~ed the French defence ils ont malmené OR mis à mal la défense française; to ~ a bottle of wine/whisky *hum* faire un sort à une bouteille de vin/de whisky.

punishable ['pʌnɪʃəbl] *adj* punissable; a ~ offence un délit; ~ by prison/a £50 fine passible d'emprisonnement/d'une amende de 50 livres.

punishing ['pʌnɪʃɪŋ] ◇ *n* **-1.** [punishment] punition *f*. **-2.** *inf* [relentless attack]: to take a ~ [opponent, team] se faire malmener; *hum* [bottle] en prendre un coup; the car's suspension/the bottle of wine has taken a ~ la suspension de la voiture / cette bouteille de vin OR en a pris un coup.

◇ *adj* [heat, climb, effort] exténuant; [defeat] écrasant; a ~ race une course exténuante.

unishment ['pʌnɪʃmənt] *n* -**1.** [act of punishing] punition *f*, châtiment *m*. -**2.** [means of punishment] punition *f*, châtiment *m*, sanction *f*; JUR peine *f*; **I had to dig the garden as a ~** comme punition, j'ai dû bêcher le jardin; **no ~ is harsh enough for them** aucune peine n'est assez sévère pour eux; **to make the ~ fit the crime** adapter le châtiment au délit. -**3.** *inf* [heavy use]: **the landing gear can take a lot of ~** même soumis à rude épreuve, le train d'atterrissage tiendra le coup.

unitive ['pjuːnətɪv] *adj* -**1.** [expedition] punitif. -**2.** [measures, tax, taxation] écrasant; **to take ~ action** avoir recours à des sanctions; **~ damages** dommages *mpl* et intérêts *mpl* dissuasifs.

unjab [,pʌn'dʒɑːb] *pr n*: **the ~** le Pendjab; **in the ~** au Pendjab.

unjabi [,pʌn'dʒɑːbɪ] ◇ *n* -**1.** [person] Pendjabi *mf*. -**2.** LING pendjabi *m*.
◇ *adj* pendjabi, du Pendjab.

unk [pʌŋk] ◇ *n* -**1.** [music, fashion] punk *m*. -**2.** [punk rocker] punk *mf*. -**3.** ▽ *Am* [worthless person] vaurien *m*, -enne *f*; [hoodlum] voyou *m*.
◇ *adj* -**1.** [music, fashion, hairstyle] punk *(inv)*; **~ rock** punk *m*; **~ rocker** punk *mf*. -**2.** *inf Am* [worthless] nul. -**3.** ▽ *Am* [ill]: **he's feeling kind of ~** il se sent un peu nase.

unky ['pʌŋkɪ] *adj* punk *(inv)*.

unnet ['pʌnɪt] *n Br* barquette *f*.

unster ['pʌnstəʳ] *n* faiseur *m*, -euse *f* de calembours OR de jeux de mots.

unt¹ [pʌnt] ◇ *n* -**1.** [boat] *longue barque à fond plat manœuvrée à la perche*. -**2.** SPORT [kick] coup *m* de pied de volée.
◇ *vt* -**1.** [boat] faire avancer à la perche. -**2.** SPORT [kick] envoyer d'un coup de pied de volée.
◇ *vi* -**1.** [in boat]: **to go ~ing** faire un tour en barque. -**2.** *Br* [gamble] jouer.

unt² [pʊnt] *n* [currency] livre *f* irlandaise.

unter ['pʌntəʳ] *n Br* -**1.** [gambler] parieur *m*, -euse *f*. -**2.** *inf* [customer] client *m*, -e *f*; **the average ~** le client type OR moyen; **the ~s** le public. -**3.** ▽ [prostitute's client] micheton *m*.

uny ['pjuːnɪ] (*compar* **punier**, *superl* **puniest**) *adj* -**1.** [frail - person, animal, plant] malingre, chétif; [- arms, legs] maigre, grêle. -**2.** [feeble - effort] pitoyable.

up [pʌp] (*pt* & *pp* **pupped**, *cont* **pupping**)
◇ *n* -**1.** [young dog] chiot *m*; [young animal] jeune animal *m*; **spaniel ~** jeune OR petit épagneul *m*; **seal ~** jeune OR bébé phoque *m*; **to be in ~** [bitch] être pleine. -**2.** *inf* [youth] blanc-bec *m*; **you cheeky young ~!** espèce de petit blanc-bec!
◇ *vi* mettre bas.

upa ['pjuːpə] (*pl* **pupas** OR **pupae** [-piː]) *n* nymphe *f*, chrysalide *f*, pupe *f*.

upate [pjuː'peɪt] *vi* se métamorphoser (en nymphe OR en chrysalide).

upil ['pjuːpl] ◇ *n* -**1.** [gen] élève *mf*; [of primary school] écolier *m*, -ère *f*; [of lower secondary school] collégien *m*, -enne *f*; [of upper secondary school] lycéen *m*, -enne *f*; [of painter, musician] élève *mf*. -**2.** JUR [minor ward] pupille *mf*. -**3.** ANAT pupille *f*.
◇ *comp* SCH [participation, power] des élèves.

uppet ['pʌpɪt] ◇ *n* -**1.** [gen] marionnette *f*; [string puppet] fantoche *m*, pantin *m*; **glove ~** marionnette *f* à gaine. -**2.** *fig* pantin *m*, fantoche *m*.
◇ *comp* -**1.** [theatre] de marionnettes; **~ show** (spectacle *m* de) marionnettes *fpl*. -**2.** POL [government, president] fantoche.

uppeteer [,pʌpɪ'tɪəʳ] *n* marionnettiste *mf*.

uppetry ['pʌpɪtrɪ] *n* [art - of making] fabrication *f* de marionnettes; [- of manipulating] art *m* du marionnettiste.

uppy ['pʌpɪ] (*pl* **puppies**) *n* chiot *m*.

puppy fat *n Br (U)* rondeurs *fpl* de l'adolescence.

puppy love *n* amourette *f*, amour *m* d'adolescent; **it's only ~** ce n'est qu'une amourette OR qu'un amour de jeunesse.

purblind ['pɜːblaɪnd] *adj* -**1.** [poorly sighted] malvoyant. -**2.** *lit* [obtuse] obtus, borné.

purchase ['pɜːtʃəs] ◇ *vt* acheter; **to ~ sthg from sb** acheter qqch à qqn; **to ~ sthg for sb, to ~ sb sthg** acheter qqch à OR pour qqn.
◇ *n* -**1.** [buy, buying] achat *m*; **to make a ~** faire un achat; **date of ~** date *f* d'achat. -**2.** [grip] prise *f*; **she managed to gain (a) ~ on a small ledge** elle parvint à trouver une prise dans le rocher.

purchase price *n* prix *m* d'achat.

purchaser ['pɜːtʃəsəʳ] *n* acheteur *m*, -euse *f*.

purchase tax *n* taxe *f* à l'achat.

purchasing power ['pɜːtʃəsɪŋ-] *n* pouvoir *m* d'achat.

purdah ['pɜːdə] *n chez certains peuples hindous et musulmans, système qui astreint les femmes à une vie retirée*; **to be in ~** *literal* être reclus; *fig* vivre en reclus.

pure [pjʊəʳ] *adj* -**1.** [unadulterated, untainted] pur; **a ~ silk tie** une cravate (en) pure soie; **~ air** air *m* pur; **~ water** eau *f* pure; **~ thoughts** pensées *fpl* pures; **~ white** blanc *m* immaculé; **the ~ tones of the flute** le son clair OR pur de la flûte ❑ **as ~ as the driven snow** blanc comme neige. -**2.** [science, maths, research] pur. -**3.** [as intensifier] pur; **by ~ chance** par pur hasard; **it's the truth, ~ and simple** c'est la vérité pure et simple.

purebred ['pjʊəbred] *adj* de race (pure).

puree, purée ['pjʊəreɪ] (*pt* & *pp* **pureed** OR **puréed**, *cont* **pureeing** OR **puréeing**) ◇ *n* purée *f*; **tomato ~** [gen] purée de tomates; [in tube] concentré *m* de tomates.
◇ *vt* réduire en purée; **~d carrots** purée *f* de carottes.

purely ['pjʊəlɪ] *adj* purement; **~ and simply** purement et simplement; **ours is a ~ professional relationship** nos rapports sont purement OR strictement professionnels.

pureness ['pjʊənɪs] *n* pureté *f*.

purgation [pɜː'geɪʃn] *n* purgation *f*.

purgative ['pɜːgətɪv] ◇ *n* purgatif *m*.
◇ *adj* purgatif.

purgatory ['pɜːgətrɪ] *n* RELIG purgatoire *m*; **rush hour is absolute ~** *fig* les heures de pointe sont un véritable enfer!

purge [pɜːdʒ] ◇ *vt* -**1.** POL [party, organization] purger, épurer; [undesirable elements] éliminer; **the extreme right was ~d from the party** le parti s'est débarrassé de son extrême droite. -**2.** [free, rid] débarrasser, délivrer; **~ your mind of such morbid ideas** chassez ces idées morbides de votre esprit. -**3.** JUR [clear] disculper, innocenter. -**4.** MED OR *dated* [bowels] purger.
◇ *n* -**1.** [gen & POL] purge *f*, épuration *f*; **he carried out a ~ of the army** il procéda à une purge au sein de l'armée. -**2.** MED purge *f*.

purification [,pjʊərɪfɪ'keɪʃn] *n* -**1.** [of water, oil] épuration *f*. -**2.** RELIG purification *f*; **the Purification (of the Virgin Mary)** la Purification (de la Vierge Marie).

purifier ['pjʊərɪfaɪəʳ] *n* [device - for water, oil] épurateur *m*; [- for air, atmosphere] purificateur *m*.

purify ['pjʊərɪfaɪ] (*pt* & *pp* **purified**) *vt* [water, oil] épurer; [air, soul] purifier.

purism ['pjʊərɪzm] *n* purisme *m*.

purist ['pjʊərɪst] ◇ *adj* puriste.
◇ *n* puriste *mf*.

puritan ['pjʊərɪtən] ◇ *n* puritain *m*, -e *f*.
◇ *adj* puritain.
◆ **Puritan** RELIG ◇ *n* puritain *m*, -e *f*.
◇ *adj* puritain.

THE PURITANS:
Protestants anglais radicaux apparus au XVIᵉ siècle, dont beaucoup se réclamaient du calvinisme, et qui souhaitaient purger l'Église anglicane de tout rite catholique. Soutenus par la Chambre des communes mais rejetés par Elizabeth Ière, ils réussirent à s'imposer pendant la période du Protectorat de Cromwell.

puritanical [,pjʊərɪ'tænɪkl] *adj* puritain.

puritanism ['pjʊərɪtənɪzm] *n* puritanisme *m*.
◆ **Puritanism** *n* RELIG puritanisme *m*.

purity ['pjʊərətɪ] *n* pureté *f*.

purl [pɜːl] ◇ *n* [in knitting]: **~ (stitch)** maille *f* à l'envers.
◇ *vt* tricoter à l'envers; **knit one, ~ one** une maille à l'endroit, une maille à l'envers.

purler *inf* ['pɜːləʳ] *n Br dated*: **to come** OR **to take a ~** se casser la figure.

purlieus ['pɜːljuːz] *npl lit* alentours *mpl*, environs *mpl*; **in the ~ of** aux alentours de, dans les environs de.

purloin [pɜː'lɔɪn] *vt fml* OR *hum* dérober, voler.

purple ['pɜːpl] ◇ *n* -**1.** [colour] violet *m*. -**2.** [dye, cloth] pourpre *f*. -**3.** [high rank]: **the ~** la pourpre.
◇ *adj* -**1.** [in colour] violet, pourpre. -**2.** [prose] emphatique, ampoulé.

purple heart *inf n* [drug] pilule *f* d'amphétamine.
◆ **Purple Heart** *n Am médaille décernée aux blessés de guerre*.

purple patch, purple passage *n* morceau *m* de bravoure.

purplish ['pɜːplɪʃ] *adj* violacé.

purport [*vb* pə'pɔːt, *n* 'pɜːpɔːt] *fml* ◇ *vt* [claim] prétendre; **he ~s to be an expert** il prétend être un expert, il se fait passer pour un expert; **her book ~s to be the definitive work on the French Revolution** son livre se veut la somme de ce qui a été écrit sur la Révolution française.
◇ *n* signification *f*, teneur *f*.

purported [pə'pɔːtɪd] *adj fml* prétendu.

purportedly [pə'pɔːtɪdlɪ] *adv fml* prétendument.

purpose ['pɜːpəs] ◇ *n* -**1.** [objective, reason] but *m*, objet *m*; **what's the ~ of your visit?** quel est le but OR l'objet de votre visite?; **he buys real estate for tax ~s** il investit dans l'immobilier pour des raisons fiscales; **it suits my ~s to stay here** j'ai de bonnes raisons de rester ici; **to do sthg with a ~ in mind** OR **for a ~** faire qqch dans un but précis; **for this ~** dans ce but, à cet effet; **but that's the whole ~ of the exercise!** mais tout l'intérêt de l'exercice est là!; **her remarks were to the ~/not to the ~** ses remarques étaient pertinentes/hors de propos. -**2.** [use, function] usage *m*; [end, result] fin *f*; **what is the ~ of this room/object?** à quoi sert cette pièce/cet objet?; **the hangar wasn't built for that ~** le hangar n'était pas destiné à cet usage; **for our ~s** pour ce que nous voulons faire; **for the ~s of this demonstration** pour les besoins de cette démonstration; **£5,000 will be enough for present ~s** 5 000 livres suffiront à couvrir nos besoins actuels; **the funds are to be used for humanitarian ~s** les fonds seront utilisés à des fins humanitaires; **the money will be put** OR **used to good ~** l'argent sera bien employé; **he will use his knowledge to good ~** there il pourra y mettre à profit ses connaissances; **we are arguing to no ~** nous discutons inutilement; **my efforts had been to no ~** mes efforts étaient restés vains; **the negotiations have been to little ~** les négociations n'ont pas abouti à grand-chose. -**3.** [determination] résolution *f*, détermination *f*; **she has great strength of ~** elle a une volonté de fer, c'est quelqu'un de très déterminé; **to have a sense of ~** avoir un but dans la vie.
◇ *vt lit* avoir l'intention de.

◆ **on purpose** *adv phr* exprès; **I did it on ~** je l'ai fait exprès; **I avoided the subject on ~** j'ai fait exprès d'éviter OR j'ai délibérément évité la question.

purpose-built *adj Br* construit OR conçu pour un usage spécifique; **~ flats for the disabled** appartements *mpl* spécialement adaptés aux besoins des handicapés; **a ~ conference centre** un centre de conférence entièrement conçu pour cet usage.

purposeful ['pɜːpəsfʊl] *adj* [person] résolu; [look, walk] résolu, décidé; [act] réfléchi.

purposefully ['pɜːpəsfʊlɪ] *adv* [for a reason] dans un but précis, délibérément; [determinedly] d'un air résolu; **she walked forward ~** elle avança d'un pas résolu.

purposeless ['pɜːpəslɪs] *adj* [life] sans but, vide de sens; [act, violence] gratuit.

purposely ['pɜːpəslɪ] *adv* exprès, délibérément.

purposive ['pɜːpəsɪv] *adj fml* délibéré.

purr [pɜːʳ] ◇ *vi* [cat, engine] ronronner.
◇ *vt* susurrer; **"do have another drink" she ~ed** «vous prendrez bien encore un verre» susurra-t-elle.
◇ *n* [of cat] ronronnement *m*, ronron *m*; [of engine] ronronnement *m*.

purse [pɜːs] ◇ *n* -**1.** *Br* [for coins] porte-monnaie *m inv*. -**2.** *Am* [handbag] sac *m* à main. -**3.** FIN [wealth, resources] bourse *f*; **to hold** OR **to control the ~ strings** *fig* tenir les cordons de la bourse. -**4.** SPORT [prize money] bourse *f*.
◇ *vt* [lips] pincer.

purser ['pɜːsəʳ] *n* NAUT commissaire *m* de bord.

pursuance [pə'sjʊəns] *n fml* exécution *f*, accomplissement *m*; **in (the) ~ of his duties** dans l'exercice de ses fonctions.

pursuant [pə'sjʊənt]
◆ **pursuant to** *prep phr fml* [following] à la suite de, suivant; [in accordance with] conformément à.

pursue [pə'sjuː] *vt* -**1.** [chase, follow] poursuivre; *fig* suivre, poursuivre; **he was being ~d by dogs** il était poursuivi par des chiens; **she was ~d by ill fortune/ill health** elle était poursuivie par la malchance/la maladie. -**2.** [strive for] poursuivre, rechercher; **we are all pursuing the same goals** nous poursuivons tous les mêmes buts. -**3.** [carry out] exécuter, mettre en œuvre; **the policies ~d by the previous government** la politique menée par le gouvernement précédent ‖ [practise] exercer; **I have no time to ~ any hobbies** je n'ai pas de temps à consacrer à des hobbies. -**4.** [take further] poursuivre; **if I may ~ that line of argument** si je peux me permettre de pousser plus loin OR de développer ce raisonnement; **to ~ a point** insister sur OR revenir sur un point.

pursuer [pə'sjuːəʳ] *n* poursuivant *m*, -e *f*.

pursuit [pə'sjuːt] *n* -**1.** [chasing] poursuite *f*; **they went out in ~ of the vandals** ils se sont lancés à la poursuite des vandales; **with a pack of dogs in hot ~** avec une meute de chiens à leurs trousses. -**2.** [striving after] poursuite *f*, quête *f*, recherche *f*; **the ~ of knowledge/happiness** la quête du savoir/du bonheur. -**3.** [occupation, pastime] occupation *f*; **leisure ~s** loisirs *mpl*, passe-temps *m inv*. -**4.** SPORT [cycle race] poursuite *f*.

pursuit plane *n* avion *m* de chasse.

purulence ['pjʊərʊləns] *n* purulence *f*.

purulent ['pjʊərʊlənt] *adj* purulent.

purvey [pə'veɪ] *vt* -**1.** [sell] vendre, fournir; **to ~ sthg to sb** fournir qqch à qqn, approvisionner qqn en qqch. -**2.** [communicate - information, news] communiquer; [- lies, rumours] colporter.

purveyance [pə'veɪəns] *n* fourniture *f*, approvisionnement *m*.

purveyor [pə'veɪəʳ] *n fml* -**1.** [supplier] fournisseur *m*, -euse *f*; **~s of marmalade to HM the Queen** fournisseurs en confiture de Sa Majesté la Reine. -**2.** [spreader - of gossip, lies] colporteur *m*, -euse *f*.

purview ['pɜːvjuː] *n* -**1.** *fml* [scope] champ *m*, domaine *m*; **the matter falls within/outside the ~ of the committee** la question relève/ne relève pas de la compétence du comité. -**2.** JUR [body of statute] texte *m*.

pus [pʌs] *n* pus *m*.

push [pʊʃ] ◇ *vt* -**1.** [shove, propel] pousser; **she ~ed the door open/shut** elle ouvrit/ferma la porte (en la poussant); **he ~ed her onto the chair** il la poussa sur la chaise; **a man was ~ed out of the window** quelqu'un a poussé un homme par la fenêtre; **he ~ed the branches apart** il a écarté les branches ❑ **to ~ one's way**: **she ~ed her way to the bar** elle se fraya un chemin jusqu'au bar. -**2.** [insert] enfoncer, introduire; **~ one tube into the other** enfoncez un tube dans l'autre ‖ [thrust] enfoncer; **he ~ed a gun into my ribs** il m'enfonça un revolver dans les côtes; **she ~ed the cork into the bottle** elle enfonça le bouchon dans la bouteille; **he ~ed his hands into his pockets** il enfonça ses mains dans ses poches; **~ all that mess under the bed** pousse tout ce bazar sous le lit. -**3.** [press - doorbell, pedal, button] appuyer sur. -**4.** [cause to move in specified direction]: **it will ~ inflation upwards** cela va relancer l'inflation; **the crisis is ~ing the country towards chaos** la crise entraîne le pays vers le chaos; **he is ~ing the party to the right** il fait glisser le parti vers la droite; **buying the car will ~ us even further into debt** en achetant cette voiture, nous allons nous endetter encore plus; **economic conditions have ~ed the peasants off the land** les paysans ont été chassés des campagnes par les conditions économiques. -**5.** [pressurize] pousser; [force] forcer, obliger, contraindre; **to ~ sb to do sthg** pousser qqn à faire qqch; **to ~ sb into doing sthg** forcer OR obliger qqn à faire qqch; **his parents ~ed him to become a doctor** ses parents l'ont poussé à devenir médecin; **her teacher ~ed her in Latin** son professeur l'a poussée à travailler en latin; **their coach doesn't ~ them hard enough** leur entraîneur ne les pousse pas assez; **I like to ~ myself hard** j'aime me donner à fond; **he ~ed the car to its limits** il a poussé la voiture à la limite de ses possibilités; **you're still weak, so don't ~ yourself** tu es encore faible, vas-y doucement; **he won't do it if he's ~ed too hard** il ne le fera pas si l'on insiste trop; **I won't be ~ed!** je ne céderai pas!; **when I ~ed her, she admitted it** quand j'ai insisté, elle a avoué; **he keeps ~ing me for the rent** il me relance sans cesse au sujet du loyer. -**6.** [advocate, argue for - idea, method] prôner, préconiser; [promote - product] promouvoir; **he's trying to ~ his own point of view/his own candidate** il essaie d'imposer son point de vue personnel/son candidat à lui; **the mayor is ~ing his town as the best site for the conference** le maire présente sa ville comme le meilleur endroit pour tenir la conférence; **adverts ~ing beauty products** des publicités pour des produits de beauté. -**7.** [stretch, exaggerate - argument, case] présenter avec insistance, insister sur; **if we ~ the comparison a little further** si on pousse la comparaison un peu plus loin ❑ **I'll try to arrive by 7 p.m., but it's ~ing it a bit** *inf* je tâcherai d'arriver à 19 h, mais ça va être juste; **that's ~ing it a bit!** *inf* c'est un peu fort! -**8.** *inf* [sell - drugs] revendre. -**9.** *inf* [approach] friser; **to be ~ing thirty** friser la trentaine; **the car was ~ing 100 mph** la voiture frisait les 160 (km/h).
◇ *vi* -**1.** [shove] pousser; **no ~ing please!** ne poussez pas, s'il vous plaît!; **'push'** [on door] 'poussez'; **people were ~ing to get in** les gens se bousculaient pour entrer; **he ~ed through the crowd to the bar** il s'est frayé un chemin jusqu'au bar à travers la foule; **somebody ~ed past me** quelqu'un est passé en me bousculant. -**2.** [press - on button, bell, knob] appuyer. -**3.** [advance, move forwards] avancer; **the army ~ed towards the border** l'armée a avancé jusqu'à la frontière ‖ [progress] évoluer; **the country is ~ing towards democracy** le pays évolue vers la démocratie. -**4.** [extend - path, fence] s'étendre; **the road ~ed deep into the hills** la route s'enfonçait dans les collines.
◇ *n* -**1.** [shove] poussée *f*; **to give sb/sthg a ~** pousser qqn/qqch; **would you give me a ~** AUT pourriez-vous me pousser? ❑ **to give sb the ~** *Br inf* [from job] virer qqn; [in relationship] plaquer qqn; **he got the ~** [from boss] il s'est fait virer; [from girlfriend] elle l'a plaqué; **when it comes to the ~** *inf* au moment critique OR crucial; **I can lend you the money if it comes to the ~** *inf* au pire, je pourrai vous prêter l'argent; **I can do it at a ~** *inf* je peux le faire si c'est vraiment nécessaire; **when ~ comes to shove** au moment critique OR crucial. -**2.** [act of pressing]: **the door opens at the ~ of a button** il suffit d'appuyer sur un bouton pour que la porte s'ouvre; **he expects these things to happen at the ~ of a button** *fig* il s'attend à ce que ça se fasse sur commande. -**3.** *fig* [trend]: **the ~ towards protectionism is gathering strength** la tendance au protectionnisme se renforce. -**4.** [encouragement] mot *m* d'encouragement; **he'll do it, but he needs a ~** il le fera, mais il a besoin qu'on le pousse un peu; **the boy's a bit mixed up, but he just needs a ~ in the right direction** il est un peu désorienté, mais il suffit de le mettre sur la bonne voie. -**5.** MIL [advance] poussée *f*; **the platoon made a ~ to capture the airfield** la section a fait une poussée pour s'emparer de l'aérodrome. -**6.** [campaign] campagne *f*; **a sales ~** une campagne de promotion des ventes; **there's a national ~ for improved housing** il y a une campagne à l'échelle nationale pour l'amélioration du logement. -**7.** [drive, dynamism] dynamisme *m*; **he has a lot of ~** il est très dynamique.

◆ **push about** *vt sep Br* -**1.** [physically] malmener; **he didn't hit her but he was ~ing her about** il ne l'a pas frappée mais il la malmenait. -**2.** [bully] donner des ordres à; **I won't be ~ed about!** *fig* je ne vais pas me laisser marcher sur les pieds!

◆ **push ahead** *vi insep* [make progress]: **they decided to ~ ahead with the plans to extend the school** ils ont décidé d'activer les projets d'extension de l'école.

◆ **push along** ◇ *vt sep* [trolley, pram] pousser (devant soi).
◇ *vi insep inf* [leave] filer; **I'll be ~ing along now** bon, il est temps que je file.

◆ **push around** = **push about**.

◆ **push aside** *vt sep* -**1.** [objects] pousser. -**2.** [reject - proposal, idea] écarter, rejeter; [neglect - problem]: **you can't just ~ aside the problem like that** vous ne pouvez pas faire comme si le problème n'existait pas; **issues which have been ~ed aside** des questions qui ont été volontairement écartées; **I ~ed my doubts aside** je n'ai pas tenu compte de mes doutes.

◆ **push away** *vt sep* repousser; **she ~ed my hand away** elle repoussa ma main; **he ~ed his chair away from the fire** il éloigna sa chaise du feu.

◆ **push back** *vt sep* -**1.** [push backwards or away - person] repousser (en arrière); [- bedclothes] rejeter, repousser; **he ~ed me back from the door** il m'a éloigné de la porte. -**2.** [repulse - troops] repousser; **the enemy was ~ed back ten miles/to the river** l'ennemi a été repoussé d'une quinzaine de kilomètres/jusqu'à la rivière. -**3.** [postpone] repousser; **the meeting has been ~ed back to Friday** la réunion a été repoussée à vendredi.

◆ **push down** ◇ *vt sep* -**1.** [lever, handle] abaisser; [pedal] appuyer sur; **she ~ed the clothes down in the bag** elle a tassé les vêtements dans le sac. -**2.** [knock over] renverser, faire tomber.
◇ *vi insep* [on pedal, lever] appuyer (sur la pédale/manette *etc*).

◆ **push for** *vt insep* [argue for] demander; [campaign for] faire campagne pour; [agitate for] militer pour; **some ministers were ~ing for more monetarist policies** certains ministres demandaient une politique plus monétariste; **to ~ for a 35-hour week** demander la semaine de 35 heures; I'm going to ~ for a bigger budget je vais faire tout ce qui est en mon pouvoir pour obtenir un budget plus important.

◆ **push forward** ◇ *vt sep literal* pousser (en avant); to ~ o.s. forward *fig* se mettre en avant, se faire valoir.

◇ *vi insep* -**1.** [advance - person, car] se frayer un chemin; [- crowd, herd] se presser en avant. -**2.** = **push ahead**.

◆ **push in** ◇ *vt sep* -**1.** [drawer] pousser; [electric plug, key, cassette] enfoncer, introduire; [disk] insérer; [knife, stake, spade] enfoncer; [button, switch] appuyer sur; ~ the button right in appuyer à fond sur le bouton. -**2.** [person]: they ~ed me in the water ils m'ont poussé dans l'eau; he opened the cell door and ~ed me in il ouvrit la porte de la cellule et me poussa à l'intérieur. -**3.** [break down - panel, cardboard] enfoncer; the door had been ~ed in la porte avait été enfoncée.

◇ *vi insep* [in queue] se faufiler; he ~ed in next to Sue il s'est faufilé à côté de Sue; no ~ing in! faites la queue!

◆ **push off** ◇ *vi insep* -**1.** *inf* [go away] filer; time for me to ~ off il faut que je file; ~ off! de l'air!, dégage! -**2.** [in boat] pousser au large.

◇ *vt sep* -**1.** [knock off] faire tomber; they ~ed me off the ladder ils m'ont fait tomber de l'échelle; I ~ed him off the chair je l'ai fait tomber de sa chaise. -**2.** [boat] déborder.

◆ **push on** ◇ *vi insep* [on journey - set off again] reprendre la route, se remettre en route; [- continue] poursuivre OR continuer son chemin; let's ~ on to Dundee poussons jusqu'à Dundee || [keep working] continuer, persévérer; they're ~ing on with the reforms ils poursuivent leurs efforts pour faire passer les réformes.

◇ *vt sep* [urge on]: to ~ sb on to do sthg pousser OR inciter qqn à faire qqch.

◆ **push out** ◇ *vt sep* -**1.** [person, object]: they ~ed the car out of the mud ils ont désembourbé la voiture en la poussant; the bed had been ~ed out from the wall le lit avait été écarté du mur ❑ to ~ the boat out *literal* déborder l'embarcation; *fig* faire la fête. -**2.** [stick out - hand, leg] tendre. -**3.** [grow - roots, shoots] faire, produire. -**4.** [oust] évincer; [dismiss from job] mettre à la porte; we've been ~ed out of the Japanese market nous avons été évincés du marché japonais. -**5.** *inf* [churn out - articles, books] produire à la chaîne, pondre en série.

◇ *vi insep* [appear - roots, leaves] pousser; [- snowdrops, tulips] pointer.

◆ **push over** *vt sep* -**1.** [pass - across table, floor] pousser; he ~ed the book over to me il poussa le livre vers moi. -**2.** [knock over] faire tomber, renverser; [from ledge, bridge] pousser, faire tomber; many cars had been ~ed over onto their sides beaucoup de voitures avaient été renversées sur le côté.

◆ **push through** ◇ *vt sep* -**1.** [project, decision] faire accepter; [bill, budget] réussir à faire voter OR passer; he managed to ~ the deal through il a réussi à conclure l'affaire. -**2.** [thrust - needle] passer; she eventually managed to ~ her way through (the crowd) elle réussit finalement à se frayer un chemin (à travers la foule).

◇ *vi insep* [car, person] se frayer un chemin; [troops, army] avancer.

◆ **push to** *vt sep* [door, drawer] fermer.

◆ **push up** *vt sep* -**1.** [push upwards - handle, lever] remonter, relever; [- sleeves] remonter, retrousser; she ~ed herself up onto her feet elle se releva ❑ he's ~ing up (the) daisies *inf* il mange les pissenlits par la racine. -**2.** [increase - taxes, sales, demand] augmenter; [- prices, costs, statistics] faire monter; the effect will be to ~ interest rates up cela aura pour effet de faire grimper les taux d'intérêt.

push-bike *inf n Br* vélo *m*, bécane *f*.

push-broom *n Am* (grand) balai *m*.

push button *n* bouton *m*.

◆ **push-button** *adj* [telephone] à touches; [car window] à commande automatique; push-button controls commandes *fpl* automatiques; push-button warfare guerre *f* presse-bouton.

pushcart ['pʊʃkɑːt] *n Am* charrette *f* à bras.

pushchair ['pʊʃtʃeəʳ] *n Br* poussette *f*.

pushed [pʊʃt] *adj* -**1.** *inf* [lacking - money, time]: to be ~ for sthg manquer de OR être à court de qqch; we're really ~ for time nous n'avons que très peu de temps; I'd like to stay longer, but I'm a bit ~ j'aimerais rester plus longtemps, mais je suis assez pressé. -**2.** [in difficulty]: to be hard ~ to do sthg avoir du mal à faire qqch; a lot of them would be hard ~ to name the President of France beaucoup d'entre eux auraient du mal à dire qui est le président de la République française.

pusher *inf* ['pʊʃəʳ] *n* [drug dealer] trafiquant *m*, -e *f* (de drogue), dealer *m*.

pushiness *inf* ['pʊʃɪnɪs] *n* [ambitiousness] arrivisme *m*; [forwardness] insistance *f*; I can't stand his ~ je ne supporte pas sa façon de s'imposer.

pushing ['pʊʃɪŋ] *n* bousculade *f*; no ~! ne poussez pas!

Pushkin ['pʊʃkɪn] *pr n* Pouchkine.

pushover *inf* ['pʊʃ,əʊvəʳ] *n* -**1.** [easy thing] jeu *m* d'enfant; the exam was a ~ l'examen était un jeu d'enfant; the match will be a ~ le match, c'est du tout cuit OR ça va être du gâteau. -**2.** [sucker] pigeon *m*; when it comes to flattery, I'm a complete ~ la flatterie marche à tous les coups avec moi. -**3.** SPORT [in rugby]: ~ try essai *m* collectif (par les avants).

pushpin ['pʊʃpɪn] *n Am* punaise *f*.

push-pull *adj* ELEC: ~ circuit montage *m* symétrique.

pushrod ['pʊʃrɒd] *n* AUT poussoir *m* de soupape.

push-start ◇ *n* AUT: to give sb a ~ pousser la voiture de qqn pour la faire démarrer.

◇ *vt* faire démarrer en poussant.

push-up *n* pompe *f (exercice physique)*.

pushy *inf* ['pʊʃɪ] (*compar* pushier, *superl* pushiest) *adj pej* [ambitious] arriviste; [attention-seeking] qui cherche à se faire valoir OR mousser; don't be so ~ arrête de te faire mousser.

pusillanimity [,pjuːsɪlə'nɪmətɪ] *n fml* pusillanimité *f*.

pusillanimous [,pjuːsɪ'lænɪməs] *adj fml* pusillanime.

puss [pʊs] *n* -**1.** *inf* [cat] minou *m*; 'Puss in Boots' *Perrault* 'le Chat botté'. -**2.** ▽ [mouth, face] gueule *f*.

pussy ['pʊsɪ] (*pl* pussies) *n* -**1.** *inf* [cat] minou *m*. -**2.** ▼ [female sex organs] chatte *f*.

pussycat *inf* ['pʊsɪkæt] *n* minou *m*.

pussyfoot *inf* ['pʊsɪfʊt] *vi* atermoyer, tergiverser; stop ~ing (about OR around)! assez tergiversé!

pussy willow *n* saule *m* blanc.

pustule ['pʌstjuːl] *n* pustule *f*.

put [pʊt] (*pt* & *pp* put, *cont* putting) ◇ *vt* **A.** -**1.** [into specified place or position] mettre; ~ the saucepan on the shelf mets la casserole sur l'étagère; ~ the chairs nearer the table approche les chaises de la table; she ~ her hand on my shoulder elle a mis sa main sur mon épaule; he ~ his arm around my shoulders il passa son bras autour de mes épaules; to ~ one's head round the door passer la tête par la porte; did you ~ any salt in? as-tu mis du sel (dedans)?; ~ some more water on to boil remettez de l'eau à chauffer; he ~ another brick on the pile il a mis une autre brique sur la pile; she ~ a match to the wood elle a allumé le bois || [send]: to ~ an advert in the paper mettre une annonce dans le journal; they want to ~ me in an old folks' home ils veulent me mettre dans une maison pour les vieux; to ~ a child to bed mettre un enfant au lit, coucher un enfant; to ~ a man on the moon envoyer un homme sur la lune || *fig*: I didn't know where to ~ myself! je ne savais plus où me mettre!; ~ yourself in my place mettez-vous à ma place; we ~ a lot of stress OR emphasis on creativity nous mettons beaucoup l'accent sur la créativité; don't ~ too much trust in what he says ne te fie pas trop à ce qu'il dit ❑ ~ it there! *inf* [shake hands] tope-là! -**2.** [push or send forcefully]: he ~ his fist through the window il a passé son poing à travers la fenêtre; he ~ a bullet through his head il s'est mis une balle dans la tête; she ~ her pen through the whole paragraph elle a rayé tout le paragraphe d'un coup de stylo. -**3.** [impose - responsibility, tax] mettre; it ~s an extra burden on our department c'est un fardeau de plus pour notre service; the new tax will ~ 5p on a packet of cigarettes la nouvelle taxe augmentera de 5 pence le prix d'un paquet de cigarettes. -**4.** [into specified situation or state] mettre; you're putting me in an awkward position vous me mettez dans une situation délicate; I hope I've not ~ you to too much trouble j'espère que je ne vous ai pas trop dérangé; music always ~s him in a good mood la musique le met toujours de bonne humeur; the new rules will be ~ into effect next month le nouveau règlement entrera en vigueur le mois prochain; to ~ sb out of a job mettre qqn au chômage; to ~ a prisoner on bread and water mettre un prisonnier au pain sec et à l'eau; the money will be ~ to good use l'argent sera bien employé; the dog had to be ~ to sleep il a fallu piquer le chien. -**5.** [write down] mettre, écrire; I forgot to ~ my address j'ai oublié de mettre mon adresse; what date shall I ~? quelle date est-ce que je mets? -**6.** [bring about]: to ~ an end OR a stop to sthg mettre fin OR un terme à qqch.

B. -**1.** [say, express] dire, exprimer; to ~ one's thoughts into words exprimer sa pensée, s'exprimer; let me ~ it this way laissez-moi l'exprimer ainsi; it was, how shall I ~ it, rather long c'était, comment dirais-je, un peu long; he ~ it better than that il l'a dit OR formulé mieux que ça; she ~ it politely but firmly elle l'a dit poliment mais clairement; as Churchill once ~ it comme l'a dit Churchill un jour; to ~ it briefly OR simply, they refused bref OR en un mot, ils ont refusé; putting it in terms you'll understand... plus simplement, pour que vous compreniez... -**2.** [present, submit - suggestion, question] soumettre; [- motion] proposer, présenter; to ~ a proposal to the board présenter une proposition au conseil d'administration; he ~ his case very well il a très bien présenté son cas; I have a question to ~ to the Prime Minister j'ai une question à soumettre au Premier ministre; I ~ it to you that you are the real culprit je vous accuse d'être le véritable coupable; I ~ it to the delegates that now is the time to act je tiens à dire aux délégués que c'est maintenant qu'il faut agir.

C. [classify in hierarchy] placer, mettre; I wouldn't ~ them in the same class as the Beatles je ne les mettrais OR placerais pas dans la même catégorie que les Beatles; of course I ~ my family above my job bien sûr que je fais passer ma famille avant mon travail.

D. -**1.** [set to work]: they ~ her on the Jones case ils l'ont mise sur l'affaire Jones. -**2.** [apply, invest - effort] investir, consacrer; to ~ a lot of time/energy into sthg consacrer beaucoup de temps/d'énergie à qqch, investir beaucoup de temps/d'énergie dans qqch; she ~s more into their relationship than he does elle s'investit plus que lui dans leur relation; he ~ everything he had into his first service SPORT il a tout mis dans son premier service. -**3.** [invest - money] placer, investir; she had ~ all her savings into property elle avait investi OR placé toutes ses économies dans l'immobilier. -**4.** [bet] parier, miser; he ~ all his winnings on the red il misa tous ses gains sur le rouge.

E. -**1.** SPORT: to ~ the shot OR the weight lancer le poids. -**2.** NAUT: to ~ a ship into port rentrer un bateau au port.

◇ *vi* NAUT: to ~ to sea lever l'ancre, appareiller; they had to ~ back into harbour ils ont dû rentrer au port; we ~ into port at Bombay nous avons fait escale à Bombay.

◇ *n* -**1.** SPORT lancer *m* (du poids); his third ~ son troisième lancer. -**2.** ST. EX option *f* de vente; ~ and call stellage *m*, double option *f*.

◆ **put about** ◇ *vt sep* -**1.** [spread - gossip, story] faire courir; it is being ~ about that he intends resigning le bruit court qu'il a l'intention de démissionner. -**2.** NAUT: to ~ a boat about faire virer un bateau. -**3.** *inf Br* [sexually]: to ~ o.s. about coucher à droite à gauche.

◇ *vi insep* NAUT virer de bord.

◆ **put across** *vt sep* -**1.** [communicate] faire comprendre; I don't know how to ~ the argument across to them je ne sais pas comment leur faire comprendre cet argument; she's good at putting herself across elle sait se mettre en valeur. -**2.** *inf Br phr*: don't try putting anything across on me! ne me prends pas pour un imbécile!

◆ **put aside** *vt sep* -**1.** [stop - activity, work] mettre de côté, poser. -**2.** [disregard, ignore] écarter, laisser de côté; let's ~ aside our differences of opinion for the moment laissons nos différends de côté pour le moment. -**3.** [save] mettre de côté; we have a little money ~ aside nous avons un peu d'argent de côté.

◆ **put at** *vt sep* [estimate] estimer; they ~ the cost of repairs to the bridge at around $10,000 ils estiment le montant des réparations du pont à environ 10 000 dollars.

◆ **put away** *vt sep* -**1.** [tidy] ranger; ~ your toys away! range tes jouets! -**2.** [lock up - in prison] mettre sous les verrous; [- in mental home] enfermer. -**3.** *inf* [eat] enfourner, s'envoyer; [drink] descendre, écluser. -**4.** [save] mettre de côté; I have a few pounds ~ away j'ai un peu d'argent de côté, j'ai quelques économies.

◆ **put back** ◇ *vt sep* -**1.** [replace, return] remettre; ~ that record back where you found it! remets ce disque où tu l'as trouvé! -**2.** [postpone] remettre; the meeting has been ~ back to Thursday la réunion a été repoussée OR remise à jeudi. -**3.** [slow down, delay] retarder; the strike has ~ our schedule back at least a month la grève nous a fait perdre au moins un mois sur notre planning. -**4.** [turn back - clock] retarder; we ~ the clocks back next weekend le week-end prochain, on passe à l'heure d'hiver. -**5.** *inf* [drink] descendre, écluser.

◇ *vi insep* NAUT: to ~ back (to port) rentrer au port.

◆ **put by** *vt sep* [save] mettre de côté; have you got anything ~ by? avez-vous un peu d'argent de côté?

◆ **put down** ◇ *vt sep* -**1.** [on table, floor etc] poser; ~ that knife down at once! pose ce couteau tout de suite!; to ~ the phone down raccrocher; he ~ the phone down on me il m'a raccroché au nez; it's one of those books you just can't ~ down c'est un de ces livres que tu ne peux pas poser avant de l'avoir fini. -**2.** [drop off - passenger] déposer, laisser. -**3.** [write down] écrire, inscrire; ~ down your name and address écrivez votre nom et votre adresse; she ~ us down as Mr and Mrs Smith elle nous a inscrits sous le nom de M. et Mme Smith; it's never been ~ down in writing ça n'a jamais été mis par écrit; I can ~ it down as expenses je peux le faire passer dans mes notes de frais. -**4.** [place on agenda] inscrire à l'ordre du jour; to ~ down a motion of no confidence déposer une motion de censure. -**5.** [enrol, enlist] inscrire; they've already ~ their son down for public school ils ont déjà inscrit leur fils dans une école privée. -**6.** [quell] réprimer, étouffer; the revolt was ~ down by armed police la révolte a été réprimée par les forces de police. -**7.** [belittle] rabaisser; he's always putting students down il passe son temps à critiquer les étudiants. -**8.** *Br euph* [kill]: to have a cat/dog ~ down faire piquer un chat/chien. -**9.** [pay as deposit] verser; I've already ~ £50 down on the sofa j'ai déjà versé 50 livres pour le canapé. -**10.** [store - wine] mettre en cave. -**11.** [put to bed - baby] coucher. -**12.** [land - plane] poser.

◇ *vi insep* [land - plane, pilot] atterrir, se poser.

◆ **put down as** *vt sep* classer parmi; I think they'd ~ me down as a mere amateur je crois qu'ils me classeraient parmi les simples amateurs.

◆ **put down for** *vt sep* inscrire pour; ~ me down for £20 inscrivez-moi pour 20 livres; I'll ~ you down for Thursday at 3 o'clock je vous mets jeudi à 15 h.

◆ **put down to** *vt sep* mettre sur le compte de; you can't ~ all the country's problems down to inflation vous ne pouvez pas mettre tous les problèmes du pays sur le compte de l'inflation; I ~ it down to her stubbornness je mets ça sur le compte de son entêtement.

◆ **put forth** *vt insep* -**1.** *lit* [sprout - shoots, leaves] produire. -**2.** *fml* [state] avancer.

◆ **put forward** *vt sep* -**1.** [suggest - proposal, idea, hypothesis] avancer; [- candidate] proposer; she ~ her name forward for the post of treasurer elle a posé sa candidature au poste de trésorière. -**2.** [turn forward - clock, hands of clock] avancer; we ~ the clocks forward next weekend le week-end prochain, on passe à l'heure d'été. -**3.** [bring forward] avancer; the meeting has been ~ forward to early next week la réunion a été avancée au début de la semaine prochaine.

◆ **put in** ◇ *vt sep* -**1.** [place inside bag, container, cupboard] mettre dans; he ~ the eggs in the fridge il a mis les œufs dans le réfrigérateur; to ~ the ball in RUGBY remettre la balle en jeu. -**2.** [insert, include] insérer, inclure; have you ~ in the episode about the rabbit? as-tu inclus l'épisode du lapin? -**3.** [interject] placer; her name was Alice, the woman ~ in elle s'appelait Alice, ajouta la femme. -**4.** [install] installer; we're having central heating ~ in nous faisons installer le chauffage central. -**5.** [devote - time] passer; I've ~ in a lot of work on that car j'ai beaucoup travaillé sur cette voiture; I ~ in a few hours' revision before supper j'ai passé quelques heures à réviser avant le dîner; to ~ in a full day at the office passer toute la journée au bureau. -**6.** [appoint] nommer; they've ~ in a new manager at the factory ils ont nommé un nouveau directeur à l'usine. -**7.** [submit - request, demand] déposer, soumettre; they ~ in a claim for a 10% pay rise ils ont déposé une demande d'augmentation de salaire de 10 %; to ~ in an application for a job déposer sa candidature pour OR se présenter pour un emploi.

◇ *vi insep* NAUT faire escale; we ~ in at Wellington nous avons fait escale à Wellington.

◆ **put in for** *vt insep*: to ~ in for sthg [post] poser sa candidature pour qqch; [leave, promotion] faire une demande de qqch, demander qqch; she ~ in for a transfer to Florida elle a demandé à être mutée en Floride.

◆ **put off** *vt sep* -**1.** [drop off - passenger] déposer, laisser; just ~ me off at the corner vous n'avez qu'à me laisser OR me déposer au coin. -**2.** [postpone] renvoyer, remettre; the meeting has been ~ off until tomorrow la réunion a été repoussée OR remise à demain; I kept putting off telling him the truth je continuais à repousser le moment de lui dire la vérité; I can't ~ him off again je ne peux pas encore annuler un rendez-vous avec lui. -**3.** [dissuade]: once he's made up his mind nothing in the world can ~ him off une fois qu'il a pris une décision, rien au monde ne peut le faire changer d'avis. -**4.** [distract] déranger, empêcher de se concentrer; he deliberately tries to ~ his opponent off il fait tout pour empêcher son adversaire de se concentrer; the noise ~ her off her service le bruit l'a gênée OR dérangée pendant son service. -**5.** [repel] dégoûter, rebuter; it's the smell that ~s me off c'est l'odeur qui me rebute; don't be ~ off by his odd sense of humour ne te laisse pas rebuter par son humour un peu particulier; the experience ~ me off skiing for good l'expérience m'a définitivement dégoûté du ski; it ~ me off my dinner ça m'a coupé l'appétit.

◆ **put on** *vt sep* -**1.** [clothes, make-up, ointment] mettre; ~ your hat on mets ton chapeau. -**2.** [present, stage - play, opera] monter; [- poetry reading, whist drive, slide show] organiser. -**3.** [lay on, provide]: they ~ on excellent meals on Sundays ils servent d'excellents repas le dimanche; they have ~ on 20 extra trains ils ont ajouté 20 trains. -**4.** [gain - speed, weight] prendre; I've ~ on a few pounds j'ai pris quelques kilos. -**5.** [turn on, cause to function - light, radio, gas] allumer; [- record, tape] mettre; [- handbrake] mettre, serrer; ~ the heater on mets OR allume le chauffage; to ~ on the brakes freiner. -**6.** [start cooking] mettre (à cuire); I forgot to ~ the peas on j'ai oublié de mettre les petits pois à cuire; I've ~ the kettle on for tea j'ai mis de l'eau à chauffer pour le thé. -**7.** [bet] parier; I ~ £10 on the favourite j'ai parié 10 livres sur le favori. -**8.** [assume] prendre; to ~ on airs prendre des airs; he ~ on a silly voice il a pris une voix ridicule ❑ don't worry, he's just putting it on ne t'inquiète pas, il fait semblant. -**9.** *inf* [tease] faire marcher; you're putting me on! là, tu me fais marcher! -**10.** [apply - pressure] exercer. -**11.** [add] ajouter; the tax increase will ~ another 10p on a gallon of petrol l'augmentation de la taxe va faire monter le prix du gallon d'essence de 10 pence. -**12.** [impose] imposer; new restrictions have been ~ on bringing animals into the country de nouvelles restrictions ont été imposées à l'importation d'animaux dans le pays. -**13.** [attribute]: it's hard to ~ a price on it c'est difficile d'en évaluer OR estimer le prix.

◆ **put onto** *vt sep* [help find] indiquer à; I'll ~ you onto a good solicitor je vous donnerai le nom d'un OR je vous indiquerai un bon avocat; she's ~ me onto quite a few bargains elle m'a indiqué plusieurs bonnes affaires; to ~ the police/taxman onto sb dénoncer qqn à la police/au fisc; what ~ you onto the butler, detective inspector? qu'est-ce qui vous a amené à soupçonner le maître d'hôtel, commissaire?

◆ **put out** ◇ *vt sep* -**1.** [place outside] mettre dehors, sortir; have you ~ the dustbin out? as-tu sorti la poubelle?; I'll ~ the washing out (to dry) je vais mettre le linge (dehors) à sécher. -**2.** [remove]: to ~ sb's eye out éborgner qqn; you almost ~ my eye out! tu as failli m'éborgner! -**3.** [issue, publish - apology, announcement] publier; [- story, rumour] faire circuler; police have ~ out a description of the wanted man la police a publié une description de l'homme qu'elle recherche ‖ [broadcast] émettre; to ~ out an SOS lancer un SOS. -**4.** [extinguish - fire, light, candle] éteindre; [- cigarette] éteindre, écraser; don't forget to ~ the light out when you leave n'oubliez pas d'éteindre (la lumière) en partant. -**5.** [lay out, arrange] sortir; the valet had ~ out a suit for me le valet de chambre m'avait sorti un costume. -**6.** [stick out, stretch out - arm, leg] étendre, allonger; [- hand] tendre; [- tongue] tirer; she walked up to me and ~ out her hand elle s'approcha de moi et me tendit la main. -**7.** [dislocate]: to ~ one's shoulder/ankle out se démettre l'épaule/la cheville; I've ~ my back out je me suis déplacé une vertèbre. -**8.** [annoy, upset]: to be ~ out about sthg être fâché à cause de qqch; he seems quite ~ out about it on dirait que ça l'a vraiment contrarié. -**9.** [inconvenience] déranger; I hope I haven't ~ you out j'espère que je ne vous ai pas dérangé; she's always ready to ~ herself out for other people elle est toujours prête à rendre service. -**10.** [sprout - shoots, leaves] produire. -**11.** [make unconscious - with drug, injection] endormir. -**12.** [subcontract] sous-traiter; we ~ most of our work out nous confions la plus grande partie de notre travail à des sous-traitants. -**13.** HORT [plant out] repiquer.

◇ *vi insep* -**1.** NAUT prendre le large; to ~ out to sea faire appareiller. -**2.** *inf Am* [sexually]:

everyone knows she ~s out tout le monde sait qu'elle est prête à coucher.

◆ **put over** = **put across**.

◆ **put over on** *inf vt sep phr*: to ~ one over on sb avoir OR rouler qqn; he tried to ~ one over on us il a essayé de nous avoir OR rouler.

◆ **put round** *vt sep* [spread - gossip, story] faire courir OR circuler.

◆ **put through** *vt sep* -**1.** TELEC [connect] passer la communication à; hold on, I'll try to ~ you through ne quittez pas, je vais essayer de vous passer la communication; ~ the call through to my office passez-moi la communication dans mon bureau; I'll ~ you through to Mrs Powell je vous passe Mme Powell. -**2.** [carry through, conclude] conclure; we finally ~ through the necessary reforms nous avons fini par faire passer les réformes nécessaires. -**3.** [subject to] soumettre à; he was ~ through a whole battery of tests on l'a soumis à toute une série d'examens; I'm sorry to ~ you through this je suis désolé de vous imposer ça ❑ to ~ sb through it *inf* en faire voir de toutes les couleurs OR des vertes et des pas mûres à qqn; he really ~ me through it il m'en a vraiment fait voir (de toutes les couleurs). -**4.** [pay for]: he ~ himself through college il a payé ses études.

◆ **put together** *vt sep* -**1.** [combine] *(usu passive)* mettre ensemble, réunir; he's more trouble than the rest of them ~ together il nous crée plus de problèmes à lui seul que tous les autres réunis. -**2.** [assemble - kit, furniture, engine] monter, assembler; to ~ sthg (back) together again remonter qqch. -**3.** [compile - dossier] réunir; [- proposal, report] préparer; [- story, facts] reconstituer; we're trying to ~ together enough evidence to convict him nous essayons de réunir assez de preuves pour le faire condamner. -**4.** [organize - show, campaign] organiser, monter.

◆ **put under** *vt sep* [with drug, injection] endormir.

◆ **put up** ◇ *vt sep* -**1.** [raise, hoist - hand] lever; [- flag] hisser; [- hood] relever; [- umbrella] ouvrir; ~ your hands up! haut les mains!; ~ 'em up! *inf* [hands] haut les mains!; [fists] défends-toi! -**2.** [erect, build - tent] dresser, monter; [- house, factory] construire; [- monument, statue] ériger; they ~ up a statue to her ils érigèrent une statue en son honneur. -**3.** [install, put in place] mettre; they've already ~ up the Christmas decorations ils ont déjà installé les décorations de Noël; the shopkeeper ~ up the shutters le commerçant a baissé le rideau de fer. -**4.** [send up - rocket, satellite] lancer. -**5.** [display - sign] mettre; [- poster] afficher; the results will be ~ up tomorrow les résultats seront affichés demain. -**6.** [show - resistance] offrir, opposer; to ~ up a good show bien se défendre; to ~ up a struggle se défendre, se débattre. -**7.** [present - argument, proposal] présenter; he ~s up a good case for abstention il y a des arguments convaincants en faveur de l'abstention. -**8.** [offer for sale]: to ~ sthg up for sale/auction mettre qqch en vente/aux enchères. -**9.** [put forward - candidate] présenter; [- person, name] proposer (comme candidat); we are not putting up any candidates nous ne présentons aucun candidat. -**10.** [provide - capital]: who's putting the money up for the new business? qui finance la nouvelle entreprise?; we ~ up our own money nous sommes auto-financés. -**11.** [increase] faire monter, augmenter; this will ~ up the price of meat ça va faire augmenter OR monter le prix de la viande. -**12.** [give hospitality to] loger; to ~ sb up for the night coucher qqn. -**13.** [urge, incite]: to ~ sb up to (doing) sthg pousser qqn à (faire) qqch. -**14.** *arch* [put away - sword, pistol] rengainer.

◇ *vi insep* -**1.** *Br* [stay - in hotel] descendre; [- with friends] loger; which hotel will you be putting up at? dans quel hôtel descendrez-vous?; I'm putting up at Gary's for the moment je loge chez Gary pour le moment. -**2.** [stand - in election] se présenter, se porter candidat; she ~ up as a Labour candidate elle s'est présentée comme candidate du parti travailliste. -**3.** *Am phr*: ~ up or shut up! *inf* assez parlé, agissez!

◆ **put upon** *vt insep (usu passive)* abuser de; you shouldn't let yourself be ~ upon like that! tu ne devrais pas te laisser marcher sur les pieds comme ça!

◆ **put up with** *vt insep* supporter, tolérer; I refuse to ~ up with this noise any longer! je ne supporterai pas ce bruit une minute de plus!

putative ['pju:tətɪv] *adj fml* putatif.

put-down *inf n* [snub] rebuffade *f*.

put-in *n* RUGBY introduction *f*.

put-off *inf n Am* [evasion] faux-fuyant *m*; [excuse] prétexte *m*.

put-on ◇ *adj* affecté, simulé.
◇ *n inf* -**1.** [pretence] simulacre *m*. -**2.** [hoax] canular *m*. -**3.** *Am* [charlatan] charlatan *m*.

put-put *inf* (*pt* & *pp* **put-putted**, *cont* **put-putting**) *Br* ◇ *n* teuf-teuf *m*.
◇ *vi*: to ~ along avancer en faisant teuf-teuf.

putrefaction [ˌpju:trɪ'fækʃn] *n* putréfaction *f*.

putrefy ['pju:trɪfaɪ] (*pt* & *pp* **putrefied**) ◇ *vi* se putréfier; ~ing corpses des cadavres en état de putréfaction OR de décomposition.
◇ *vt* putréfier.

putrescence [pju:'tresns] *n fml* putrescence *f*.

putrescent [pju:'tresnt] *adj fml* putrescent.

putrid ['pju:trɪd] *adj* -**1.** [decaying] putride; a ~ smell une odeur nauséabonde. -**2.** *inf* [awful] dégueulasse.

putsch [pʊtʃ] *n* putsch *m*, coup *m* d'État.

putt [pʌt] ◇ *n* putt *m*.
◇ *vi* & *vt* putter.

puttee ['pʌtɪ] *n* bande *f* molletière.

putter ['pʌtə^r] ◇ *n* SPORT -**1.** [club] putter *m*. -**2.** [person]: he's a good ~ il putte bien.
◇ *vi* -**1.** [vehicle] avancer en faisant teuf-teuf. -**2.** *Am* = **potter**.

putting ['pʌtɪŋ] *n* SPORT putting *m*.

putting green *n* green *m*.

putty ['pʌtɪ] (*pt* & *pp* **puttied**) ◇ *n* -**1.** [for cracks, holes] mastic *m*; [for walls] enduit *m*; my legs feel like ~ j'ai les jambes en coton ❑ Max is ~ in her hands elle fait de Max (tout) ce qu'elle veut, Max ne sait pas lui résister. -**2.** [colour] (couleur *f*) mastic *m*.
◇ *vt* mastiquer.

putty knife *n* couteau *m* à mastiquer, spatule *f* de vitrier.

put-up *inf adj Br*: ~ job coup *m* monté.

put-upon *adj Br* exploité; he's very ~ tout le monde l'exploite; his poor ~ wife sa pauvre femme qui lui sert de bonne à tout faire.

put-you-up *n Br* canapé-lit *m*.

puzzle ['pʌzl] ◇ *n* -**1.** [game - gen] jeu *m* de patience; [jigsaw] puzzle *m*; [brainteaser] casse-tête *m inv*; [riddle] devinette *f*; crossword ~ mots croisés *mpl*. -**2.** [problem] question *f* (difficile); [enigma, mystery] énigme *f*, mystère *m*; how he escaped remains a ~ la façon dont il s'y est pris pour s'évader reste un mystère OR une énigme. -**3.** [perplexity] perplexité *f*; he was in a ~ about what to do il ne savait pas trop quoi faire.
◇ *vt* laisser perplexe; you ~ me, Mr Cox je ne suis pas sûr de vous suivre, M. Cox; his wife still ~d him sa femme restait un mystère pour lui; I'm still ~d to know how he got out j'essaie toujours de comprendre comment il s'y est pris pour sortir; don't ~ your head over OR about it ne vous tracassez pas pour ça.
◇ *vi* [wonder] se poser des questions; [ponder] réfléchir.

◆ **puzzle out** *vt sep Br* [meaning, solution, route, way] trouver, découvrir; [code, enigma, handwriting] déchiffrer; [problem] résoudre; [behaviour, intentions] comprendre; I was never able to ~ her out je ne suis jamais arrivé OR parvenu à la comprendre; can you ~ out what he meant? avez-vous une idée de ce qu'il voulait dire?

◆ **puzzle over** *vt insep* [answer, explanation] essayer de trouver; [absence, letter, theory] essayer de comprendre; [enigma, crossword] essayer de résoudre; [code, handwriting] essayer de déchiffrer; we're still puzzling over why he did it nous nous demandons toujours ce qui a bien pu le pousser à faire cela; he ~d over the list of figures *Br* la liste des chiffres le laissait perplexe; that'll give you something to ~ over! *Br* cela vous donnera de quoi réfléchir!

puzzle book *n* [gen] livre *m* de jeux; [of crosswords] livre *m* de mots croisés.

puzzled ['pʌzld] *adj* perplexe; you look ~ tu as l'air perplexe; the public are ~ les gens sont perplexes OR ne savent pas quoi penser.

puzzlement ['pʌzlmənt] *n* perplexité *f*.

puzzler ['pʌzlə^r] *n* énigme *f*, casse-tête *m inv*; his statement is a real ~ sa déclaration est des plus ambiguës.

puzzling ['pʌzlɪŋ] *adj* [behaviour, remark] qui laisse perplexe; [symbol, machine] incompréhensible; it's ~ that he hasn't sent word c'est curieux qu'il n'ait pas donné signe de vie; it remains a ~ phenomenon c'est un phénomène encore inexpliqué; it's a ~ affair c'est une affaire difficile à éclaircir.

PVC (*abbr of* polyvinyl chloride) *n* PVC *m*.

Pvt. *written abbr of* private.

pw (*written abbr of* per week) p.sem.

PWA (*abbr of* person with AIDS) *n* sidéen *m*, -enne *f*.

PX (*abbr of* post exchange) *n Am* MIL *économat pour les militaires et leurs familles*.

pye-dog [paɪ-] *n* chien *m* errant *(en Asie)*.

Pygmalion [pɪg'meɪljən] *pr n* Pygmalion.

pygmy ['pɪgmɪ] (*pl* **pygmies**) ◇ *n* -**1.** ZOOL [small animal] nain *m*, -e *f*. -**2.** *fig* [small or insignificant person] nain *m*; he's a political ~ c'est un homme politique sans importance.
◇ *adj* pygmée.

◆ **Pygmy** ◇ *n* Pygmée *mf*.
◇ *adj* pygmée.

pyjama *Br*, **pajama** *Am* [pə'dʒɑ:mə] *comp* [jacket, trousers] de pyjama; ~ party *fête où l'on doit venir en pyjama*.

◆ **pyjamas** *Br*, **pajamas** *Am npl* pyjama *m*; a pair of ~s un pyjama; he was in his ~s il était en pyjama; (lounging) ~s *Br* pyjama *m* d'intérieur *(pour femmes)*.

pylon ['paɪlən] *n* [gen & ARCHEOL] pylône *m*.

PYO *written abbr of* pick your own.

Pyongyang [ˌpjɒŋ'jæŋ] *pr n* Pyongyang.

pyorrhoea *Br*, **pyorrhea** *Am* [ˌpaɪə'rɪə] *n* pyorrhée *f*.

pyramid ['pɪrəmɪd] ◇ *n* pyramide *f*; age OR population ~ pyramide des âges.
◇ *vt* -**1.** [build in pyramid form] ériger en forme de pyramide. -**2.** FIN [companies] structurer en holdings.

pyramidal [pɪ'ræmɪdl] *adj* pyramidal.

pyramid selling *n* vente *f* à la boule de neige.

pyre ['paɪə^r] *n*: (funeral) ~ bûcher *m* funéraire.

Pyrenean [ˌpɪrə'ni:ən] *adj* pyrénéen.

Pyrenean mountain dog *n* chien *m* des Pyrénées, pyrénéen *m*.

Pyrenees [ˌpɪrə'ni:z] *pl pr n*: the ~ les Pyrénées *fpl*.

pyrethrum [paɪ'ri:θrəm] *n* pyrèthre *m*.

pyretic [paɪ'retɪk] *adj* pyrétique.

Pyrex® ['paɪreks] ◇ *n* Pyrex® *m*.
◇ *comp* [dish, bowl] en Pyrex®.

pyrexia [paɪ'reksɪə] *n* pyrexie *f*.

pyrite [paɪ'raɪt], **pyrites** [paɪ'raɪti:z] *n* pyrite *f*.

pyroelectricity [ˈpaɪrəʊɪˌlekˈtrɪsətɪ] *n* pyroélectricité *f.*

pyrography [paɪˈrɒgrəfɪ] *n* pyrogravure *f.*

pyromania [ˌpaɪrəˈmeɪnɪə] *n* pyromanie *f.*

pyromaniac [ˌpaɪrəˈmeɪnɪæk] *n* pyromane *mf.*

pyrostat [ˈpaɪrəʊstæt] *n* pyrostat *m.*

pyrotechnic(al) [ˌpaɪrəʊˈteknɪk(l)] *adj* pyrotechnique.

pyrotechnics [ˌpaɪrəʊˈteknɪks] ◇ *n (U)* [process] pyrotechnie *f.*
◇ *npl* -**1.** [display] feu *m* d'artifice. -**2.** *fig* [display of skill] performance *f* éblouissante.

Pyrrhic victory [ˈpɪrɪk-] *n* victoire *f* à la Pyrrhus.

Pythagoras [paɪˈθægərəs] *pr n* Pythagore.

Pythagoras' theorem *n* théorème *m* de Pythagore.

Pythagorean [paɪˌθægəˈriːən] ◇ *adj* [relating to Pythagoras] pythagoricien; [relating to Pythagoras' theorem] pythagorique; ~ **numbers** nombres *mpl* pythagoriques.
◇ *n* pythagoricien *m,* - enne *f.*

python [ˈpaɪθn] *n* python *m.*
◆ **Python** *pr n* Python.

pyx [pɪks] *n* RELIG ciboire *m.*

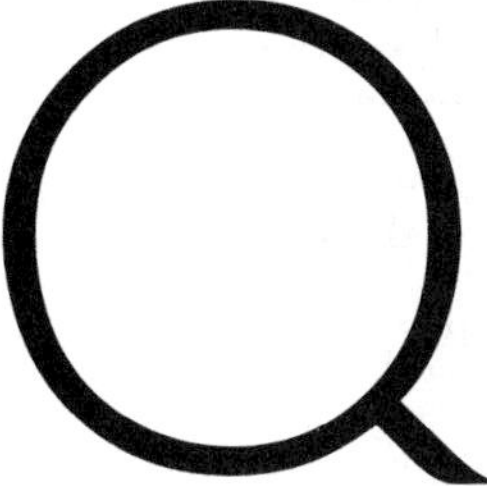

q (*pl* q's OR qs), **Q** (*pl* Q's OR Qs) [kjuː] *n* [letter] q *m*, Q *m*.

q *written abbr of* quart.

Q (*written abbr of* Queen) [in chess] D.

Qatar ['kætɑːʳ] = **Katar**.

QC (*abbr of* Queen's Counsel) *n Br* ≃ bâtonnier *m* de l'ordre.

QED (*abbr of* quod erat demonstrandum) *adv* CQFD.

QE2 (*abbr of* Queen Elizabeth II) *pr n grand paquebot de luxe*.

QM *n abbr of* quartermaster.

Qom [kʊm] *pr n* Qom, Qum.

QSO (*abbr of* quasi-stellar object) *n* objet *m* quasistellaire, QSO *m*.

qt[1] *written abbr of* quart.

qt[2], **QT** (*abbr of* quiet)
◆ **on the qt** *inf adv phr Br* en douce.

qty (*written abbr of* quantity) qté.

qua [kweɪ] *prep fml* en tant que; money ~ money does not interest us l'argent en lui-même ne nous intéresse pas.

quack [kwæk] ◇ *vi* [duck] cancaner, faire coin-coin.
◇ *n* **-1.** [of duck] cancanement *m*, coin-coin *m inv*. **-2.** [charlatan] charlatan *m*. **-3.** *inf Br & Austr hum* [doctor] toubib *m*.
◇ *adj* [medicine, method] de charlatan, charlatanesque; ~ doctor charlatan *m*.
◇ *onomat*: ~ (~)! coin-coin!

quackery ['kwækərɪ] *n* charlatanisme *m*.

quad [kwɒd] *n* **-1.** *abbr of* quadruplet. **-2.** *abbr of* quadrangle. **-3.** *abbr of* quadraphonic. **-4.** TYPO cadrat *m*.

Quadragesima [,kwɒdrə'dʒesɪmə] *n* Quadragésime *f*.

quadrangle ['kwɒdræŋgl] *n* **-1.** GEOM quadrilatère *m*; complete ~ quadrangle *m*. **-2.** [courtyard] cour *f*.

quadrangular [kwɒ'dræŋgjʊləʳ] *adj* quadrangulaire.

quadrant ['kwɒdrənt] *n* **-1.** GEOM quadrant *m*. **-2.** ASTRON & NAUT quart-de-cercle *m*, quadrant *m*.

quadraphonic [,kwɒdrə'fɒnɪk] *adj* quadriphonique; in ~ sound en quadriphonie.

quadratic [kwɒ'drætɪk] ◇ *adj* MATH quadratique; ~ equation équation *f* quadratique OR du second degré.
◇ *n* équation *f* quadratique OR du second degré.

quadrature ['kwɒdrətʃəʳ] *n* quadrature *f*.

quadriceps ['kwɒdrɪseps] (*pl inv* OR quadricepses [-sɪz]) *n* quadriceps *m*.

quadrilateral [,kwɒdrɪ'lætərəl] ◇ *adj* quadrilatère, quadrilatéral.
◇ *n* quadrilatère *m*.

quadrille [kwə'drɪl] *n* quadrille *m*.

quadripartite [,kwɒdrɪ'pɑːtaɪt] *adj* quadripartite.

quadriplegia [,kwɒdrɪ'pliːdʒə] *n* tétraplégie *f*, quadriplégie *f*.

quadriplegic [,kwɒdrɪ'pliːdʒɪk] ◇ *adj* tétraplégique.
◇ *n* tétraplégique *mf*.

quadrisyllable ['kwɒdrɪ,sɪləbl] *n* quadrisyllabe *m*.

quadroon [kwɒ'druːn] *n* quarteron *m*, -onne *f*.

quadrophonic [,kwɒdrə'fɒnɪk] = **quadraphonic**.

quadruped ['kwɒdrʊped] ◇ *adj* quadrupède.
◇ *n* quadrupède *m*.

quadruple [kwɒ'druːpl] ◇ *adj* quadruple.
◇ *n* quadruple *m*.
◇ *vi* & *vt* quadrupler.

quadruplet ['kwɒdrʊplɪt] *n* quadruplé *m*, -e *f*.

quadruplicate [kwɒ'druːplɪkət] ◇ *adj* quadruple.
◇ *n*: in ~ en quatre exemplaires.

quaff [kwɒf] *vt lit* boire.

quagmire ['kwægmaɪəʳ] *n literal & fig* bourbier *m*.

quahog ['kwɑːhɒg] *n Am grand clam (spécialité de la Nouvelle-Angleterre)*.

quail [kweɪl] (*pl inv* OR quails) ◇ *n* [bird] caille *f*.
◇ *vi* [feel afraid] trembler; [give way, lose heart] perdre courage; to ~ before sb/sthg trembler devant qqn/qqch; he ~ed at the thought of having to talk to her il tremblait à l'idée d'avoir à lui parler; I ~ed before the enormity of the task j'ai perdu courage devant l'énormité de la tâche.

quaint [kweɪnt] *adj* **-1.** [picturesque] pittoresque; the ~ narrow streets of the old town les rues étroites et pittoresques de la vieille ville ‖ [old-fashioned] au charme désuet; she made a ~ curtsey elle exécuta une révérence au charme désuet. **-2.** [odd] bizarre, étrange; what a ~ idea! quelle drôle d'idée!

quaintly ['kweɪntlɪ] *adv* **-1.** [picturesquely] de façon pittoresque; the ~ old-fashioned villages les vieux villages pittoresques ‖ [in an old-fashioned way]: they dress very ~ ils s'habillent à l'ancienne (mode). **-2.** [oddly] bizarrement, étrangement.

quaintness ['kweɪntnɪs] *n* **-1.** [picturesqueness] pittoresque *m*; [old-fashioned charm] charme *m* vieillot OR désuet. **-2.** [oddness] bizarrerie *f*, étrangeté *f*.

quake [kweɪk] ◇ *vi* **-1.** [person] trembler, frémir; to ~ with fear trembler de peur; I was quaking at the thought of having to confront her je tremblais à l'idée d'avoir à lui faire face. **-2.** [earth] trembler.
◇ *n inf* tremblement *m* de terre.

Quaker ['kweɪkəʳ] ◇ *n* quaker *m*, -eresse *f*.
◇ *adj* des quakers.

Quakerism ['kweɪkərɪzm] *n* quakerisme *m*.

qualification [,kwɒlɪfɪ'keɪʃn] *n* **-1.** [diploma] diplôme *m*; candidates with formal ~s in translating des candidats possédant un diplôme de traducteur; list your academic ~s indiquez vos diplômes scolaires et universitaires. **-2.** [ability, quality] aptitude *f*, compétence *f*; [for job] qualification *f*; the main ~ we are looking for is a creative mind ce que nous attendons avant tout du candidat, c'est qu'il fasse preuve d'un esprit créatif. **-3.** [restriction] réserve *f*; they accepted the idea with some/without ~ ils acceptèrent l'idée avec quelques réserves/sans réserve. **-4.** [act of qualifying] qualification *f*; her ~ for the semi-final sa qualification pour la demi-finale; most of our students find jobs after ~ la plupart de nos étudiants trouvent du travail dès qu'ils ont obtenu leur diplôme.

qualified ['kwɒlɪfaɪd] *adj* **-1.** [trained] qualifié, diplômé; ~ teachers professeurs *mpl* qualifiés OR diplômés; our staff are highly ~ notre personnel est hautement qualifié. **-2.** [able, competent] compétent, qualifié; I don't feel ~ to discuss such matters ces questions sont hors de ma compétence. **-3.** [limited, conditional] mitigé, nuancé; their efforts met with ~ praise leurs efforts ont recueilli des louanges mitigées OR réservées; ~ acceptance acceptation *f* conditionnelle OR sous condition.

qualifier ['kwɒlɪfaɪəʳ] *n* **-1.** SPORT [person] qualifié *m*, -e *f*; [contest] (épreuve *f*) éliminatoire *f*. **-2.** GRAMM qualificatif *m*.

qualify ['kwɒlɪfaɪ] (*pt* & *pp* qualified) ◇ *vi* **-1.** [pass exams, complete training] obtenir son diplôme; only 10% of the students go on to ~ seuls 10 % des étudiants finissent par obtenir leur diplôme; to ~ as an accountant/a vet obtenir son diplôme de comptable/vétérinaire. **-2.** [be eligible]: in a few years I'll ~ for a pension dans quelques années, j'aurai droit à la retraite; none of the candidates really ~ for the post aucun candidat ne répond véritablement aux conditions requises pour ce poste; it hardly qualifies as a success *fig* c'est loin d'être une réussite. **-3.** [in competition] se qualifier; he qualified for the finals il s'est qualifié pour la finale.
◇ *vt* **-1.** [make able or competent] qualifier, habiliter; her experience qualifies her for the post son expérience lui permet de prétendre à ce poste; this diploma qualifies you to practise acupuncture par ce diplôme, vous êtes habilité à pratiquer l'acupuncture; what qualifies him to talk about French politics? en quoi est-il qualifié pour parler de la politique française? **-2.** [modify - statement, criticism] mitiger, atténuer; [put conditions on] poser des conditions; they qualified their acceptance of the plan ils

ont accepté le projet sous conditions. -**3.** [describe] qualifier; I wouldn't ~ the play as a masterpiece je n'irai pas jusqu'à qualifier cette pièce de chef-d'œuvre. -**4.** GRAMM qualifier.

qualifying ['kwɒlɪfaɪɪŋ] *adj*: ~ examination [at end of course] examen *m* de fin d'études; [to get onto course] examen *m* d'entrée; ~ heat OR round SPORT (épreuve *f*) éliminatoire *f*; ~ mark *Br* SCH moyenne *f*.

qualitative ['kwɒlɪtətɪv] *adj* qualitatif.

qualitative analysis *n* analyse *f* qualitative.

qualitatively ['kwɒlɪtətɪvlɪ] *adv* qualitativement.

quality ['kwɒlətɪ] (*pl* qualities) ◇ *n* -**1.** [standard, nature] qualité *f*; the high/poor ~ of the workmanship la bonne/mauvaise qualité du travail; the ~ of life la qualité de la vie. -**2.** [high standard, excellence] qualité *f*; never mind the price, I'm only interested in ~ peu importe le prix, ce que je recherche, c'est la qualité; we have a reputation for ~ nous sommes réputés pour la qualité de nos produits. -**3.** [feature, attribute] qualité *f*; these are the qualities we are looking for in our candidates voici les qualités que nous recherchons chez nos candidats; he has a lot of good qualities il a de nombreuses qualités; I don't doubt her intellectual qualities je ne doute pas de ses capacités intellectuelles; these tyres have superior road-holding qualities ces pneus offrent une meilleure adhérence au sol. -**4.** *Br* [newspaper]: ~ (paper) *quotidien ou journal du dimanche de qualité (par opposition à la presse populaire)*. -**5.** *arch* [high social status] qualité *f*; a gentleman of ~ un homme de qualité. -**6.** [tone] timbre *m*. -**7.** LING [in phonetics] qualité *f*.
◇ *comp* [goods, work, shop] de qualité.

quality assurance *n Br* garantie *f* de qualité.

quality circle *n Br* cercle *m* de qualité.

quality control *n* contrôle *m* de qualité.

qualm [kwɑːm] *n* -**1.** [scruple] scrupule *m*; [misgiving] appréhension *f*, inquiétude *f*; I occasionally have ~s about the job I do il m'arrive d'avoir des scrupules à faire le travail que je fais; she has no ~s about going out alone elle ne craint pas de sortir seule. -**2.** [pang of nausea] haut-le-cœur *m inv*, nausée *f*.

quandary ['kwɒndərɪ] (*pl* quandaries) *n* dilemme *m*; I'm in a dreadful ~ je suis confronté à un terrible dilemme; she was in a ~ over OR about whether or not to tell him elle ne parvenait pas à décider si elle devait le lui dire.

quango ['kwæŋgəʊ] (*abbr of* quasiautonomous non-governmental organization) *n Br organisme semi-public*.

QUANGO:
Un «quango» est un organisme semi-public surtout financé par l'État mais disposant d'une certaine autonomie; le British Council en est un exemple.

quanta ['kwɒntə] *pl* → **quantum**.

quantifiable ['kwɒntɪfaɪəbl] *adj* quantifiable.

quantifier ['kwɒntɪfaɪə[r]] *n* -**1.** GRAMM quantificateur *m*, quantifieur *m*. -**2.** LOGIC & MATH quantificateur *m*.

quantify ['kwɒntɪfaɪ] (*pt* & *pp* quantified) *vt* -**1.** [estimate] quantifier, évaluer quantitativement; it is hard to ~ the damage il est difficile d'évaluer l'ampleur des dégâts. -**2.** LOGIC quantifier.

quantitative ['kwɒntɪtətɪv], **quantitive** ['kwɒntətɪv] *adj* quantitatif.

quantitative analysis *n* analyse *f* quantitative.

quantity ['kwɒntətɪ] (*pl* quantities) *n* [gen, LING & MATH] quantité *f*; what ~ of sugar do you need for the cake? de quelle quantité de sucre avez-vous besoin pour le gâteau?; in ~ en (grande) quantité; they produce large quantities of cereals OR cereals in large quantities ils produisent de grandes quantités de céréales OR des céréales en grande quantité.

quantity surveying *n* métrage *m*.

quantity surveyor *n* métreur *m*.

quantize, -ise ['kwɒntaɪz] *vt* quantifier PHYS.

quantum ['kwɒntəm] (*pl* quanta [-tə]) *n* quantum *m*.

quantum jump, quantum leap *n* progrès *m* énorme, bond *m* en avant; the new model represents a ~ le nouveau modèle représente un grand bond en avant.

quantum mechanics *n (U)* (mécanique *f*) quantique *f*.

quantum number *n* nombre *m* quantique.

quantum theory *n* théorie *f* des quanta OR quantique.

quarantine ['kwɒrəntiːn] ◇ *n* quarantaine *f* MÉD; our dog is in ~ notre chien est en quarantaine.
◇ *vt* mettre en quarantaine.

quarantine flag *n* pavillon *m* de quarantaine.

quark [kwɑːk] *n* -**1.** PHYS quark *m*. -**2.** [cheese] fromage *m* blanc.

quarrel ['kwɒrəl] (*Br pt* & *pp* quarrelled, *cont* quarrelling, *Am pt* & *pp* quarreled, *cont* quarreling) ◇ *n* -**1.** [dispute] querelle *f*, dispute *f*; they had a ~ over money ils se sont disputés pour des histoires d'argent; are you trying to start a ~? tu cherches la dispute?; to pick a ~ with sb chercher querelle à qqn. -**2.** [cause for complaint]: my only ~ with the plan is its cost la seule chose que je reproche à ce projet, c'est son coût; I have no ~ with her proposal je n'ai rien contre sa proposition.
◇ *vi* -**1.** [argue] se disputer, se quereller; I don't want to ~ with you over OR about this je ne veux pas me disputer avec toi à ce sujet OR à propos de cela; they're always quarrelling over money ils se disputent sans cesse pour des histoires d'argent. -**2.** [take issue]: I can't ~ with your figures je ne peux pas contester vos chiffres; critics might ~ with parts of the introduction les critiques pourraient trouver à redire à certains passages de l'introduction.

quarrelling *Br*, **quarreling** *Am* ['kwɒrəlɪŋ] *n (U)* disputes *fpl*, querelles *fpl*.

quarrelsome ['kwɒrəlsəm] *adj* querelleur.

quarrier ['kwɒrɪə[r]] *n* carrier *m*.

quarry ['kwɒrɪ] (*pl* quarries, *pt* & *pp* quarried) ◇ *n* -**1.** [excavation] carrière *f*; slate ~ carrière d'ardoise, ardoisière *f*. -**2.** [prey] proie *f*.
◇ *vt* -**1.** [sand, slate, marble etc] extraire. -**2.** [land, mountain] exploiter; the hills have been extensively quarried de nombreuses carrières ont été ouvertes dans les collines.
◇ *vi* exploiter; they are ~ing for marble ils exploitent une carrière de marbre.

quarrying ['kwɒrɪɪŋ] *n* -**1.** [of sand, slate, marble etc] extraction *f*. -**2.** [of land, mountain] exploitation *f*; the countryside has been spoilt by ~ les carrières ont défiguré OR massacré le paysage.

quarryman ['kwɒrɪmən] (*pl* quarrymen [-mən]) *n* carrier *m*.

quarry tile *n* carreau *m*.

quart [kwɔːt] *n* ≃ litre *m*; you can't fit a ~ into a pint pot *Br prov* à l'impossible nul n'est tenu *prov*.

quarter ['kwɔːtə[r]] ◇ *adj*: a ~ hour/century/pound un quart d'heure/de siècle/de livre.
◇ *vt* -**1.** [divide into four] diviser en quatre; to ~ a cake couper un gâteau en quatre parts égales. -**2.** [divide by four] diviser par quatre; prices have been ~ed les prix ont été divisés par quatre. -**3.** [lodge] loger; MIL cantonner; the troops are ~ed in the town les soldats sont logés en ville. -**4.** [dismember] écarteler. -**5.** [subj: hunting dog]: to ~ the ground quêter.
◇ *n* -**1.** [one fourth] quart *m*; during the first ~ of the century au cours du premier quart de ce siècle; a ~ of a century/of an hour un quart de siècle/d'heure; a ton and a ~, one and a ~ tons une tonne un quart; he ate a ~/three ~s of the cake il a mangé le quart/les trois quarts du gâteau; it's a ~/three ~s empty c'est au quart/aux trois quarts vide; we've only done (a) ~ of the work nous n'avons fait que le quart du travail. -**2.** [in telling time] quart *m*; (a) ~ to six, (a) ~ of six *Am* six heures moins le quart; (a) ~ past six *Br*, (a) ~ after six *Am* six heures et quart. -**3.** [period of 3 months] trimestre *m*; published every ~ publié tous les trimestres OR tous les trois mois. -**4.** [US and Canadian money] (pièce *f* de) vingt-cinq cents *mpl*. -**5.** [weight - quarter of hundredweight] ≃ 12 kg; [- quarter pound] quart *m* de livre, 113 g. -**6.** [direction] direction *f*, côté *m*; offers of help poured in from all ~s des offres d'aide affluèrent de tous côtés; the decision has been criticized in certain ~s la décision a été critiquée dans certains milieux; in well-informed ~s dans les milieux bien informés, the wind is in the port/starboard ~ NAUT le vent souffle par la hanche de bâbord/tribord. -**7.** [part of town] quartier *m*. -**8.** [phase of moon] quartier *m*; the moon is in the first/last ~ la lune est dans le premier/dernier quartier. -**9.** SPORT [period of play] quart-temps *m inv*. -**10.** [part of butchered animal] quartier *m*. -**11.** *(usu neg) lit* [mercy] quartier *m*; they gave no ~ ils ne firent pas de quartier; there was no ~ given or asked on ne fit pas de quartier.
◆ **quarters** *npl* [accommodation] domicile *m*, résidence *f*; she took up ~s in central London elle a élu domicile OR s'est installée dans le centre de Londres; many families live in very cramped ~s de nombreuses familles vivent dans des conditions de surpeuplement; the servants' ~s les appartements des domestiques ❑ married ~s logement *m* pour couples mariés.

quarterback ['kwɔːtəbæk] ◇ *n* SPORT quarterback *m*, quart-arrière *m Can*.
◇ *vt Am* -**1.** SPORT [team] jouer quarterback dans. -**2.** *fig* être le stratège de, diriger la stratégie de.

quarter day *n Br* (jour *m* du) terme *m*.

quarterdeck ['kwɔːtədek] *n* -**1.** [part of ship] plage *f* arrière NAUT. -**2.** [personnel]: the ~ les officiers.

quarterfinal [,kwɔːtə'faɪnl] *n* quart *m* de finale; they were knocked out in the ~s ils ont été éliminés en quart de finale.

quarter-hourly *adj* & *adv* tous les quarts d'heure.

quartering ['kwɔːtərɪŋ] *n* -**1.** [dividing up] division *f* en quatre. -**2.** MIL [billeting] cantonnement *m*.

quarterlight ['kwɔːtəlaɪt] *n* [in UK] déflecteur *m* AUT.

quarterly ['kwɔːtəlɪ] ◇ *adj* trimestriel.
◇ *n* publication *f* trimestrielle.
◇ *adv* trimestriellement, tous les trois mois.

quartermaster ['kwɔːtə,mɑːstə[r]] *n* -**1.** [in army] commissaire *m*; HIST intendant *m*. -**2.** [in navy] officier *m* de manœuvre.

quarter note *n Am* noire *f* MUS.

quarter rest *n Am* soupir *m* MUS.

quarter sessions *npl* -**1.** [in England and Wales] ≃ cour *f* d'assises *(remplacée en 1972 par la Crown Court)*. -**2.** [in US] *dans certains États, tribunal local à compétence criminelle, pouvant avoir des fonctions administratives*.

quarterstaff ['kwɔːtəstɑːf] *n* bâton *m (utilisé comme arme)*.

quarter tone *n* MUS quart *m* de ton.

quartet(te) [kwɔː'tet] *n* -**1.** [players - classical] quatuor *m*; [- jazz] quartette *m*; [group of four people] quatuor *m*. -**2.** [piece of music] quatuor *m*.

quarto ['kwɔːtəʊ] (*pl* quartos) ◇ *n* in-quarto *m inv*.
◇ *adj* in quarto *(inv)*.

quartz [kwɔːts] ◇ *n* quartz *m*.
◇ *comp* [clock, watch] à quartz.

quartz crystal *n* cristal *m* de quartz.

quartz-iodine lamp *n* lampe *f* à iode.

quartzite ['kwɔːtsaɪt] *n* quartzite *m*.

quasar ['kweɪzɑː[r]] *n* quasar *m*.

quash [kwɒʃ] *vt Br* -**1.** [annul - sentence, verdict] casser; [- decision] annuler. -**2.** [suppress - revolt] étouffer, écraser; [- emotion] réprimer, refouler; [- suggestion] rejeter, repousser; **their creativity is ~ed at an early age** leur créativité est étouffée dès leur jeune âge.

quasi- ['kweɪzaɪ] *in cpds* quasi; **a ~official organization** une organisation quasi officielle.

quasi-stellar *adj* quasistellaire.

quasi-stellar object *n* objet *m* quasistellaire.

quatercentenary [,kwætəsen'tiːnərɪ] (*pl* **quatercentenaries**) *n* quatrième centenaire *m*.

quaternary [kwə'tɜːnərɪ] ◇ *adj* CHEM & MATH quaternaire.
◇ *n* [set of four] ensemble *m* de quatre (éléments).
◆ **Quaternary** GEOL ◇ *adj* quaternaire.
◇ *n*: **the Quaternary** le quaternaire.

quatrain ['kwɒtreɪn] *n* quatrain *m*.

quaver ['kweɪvəʳ] ◇ *vi* [voice] trembloter, chevroter; [person] parler d'une voix tremblotante OR chevrotante.
◇ *n* -**1.** [of sound, in voice] chevrotement *m*, tremblement *m*. -**2.** *Br* MUS croche *f*.

quavering ['kweɪvərɪŋ] ◇ *adj* tremblotant, chevrotant.
◇ *n* tremblement *m*, chevrotement *m*.

quaveringly ['kweɪvərɪŋlɪ] *adv* d'une voix tremblotante OR chevrotante, avec des trémolos dans la voix.

quaver rest *n Br* demi-soupir *m* MUS.

quavery ['kweɪvərɪ] = **quavering** *adj*.

quay [kiː] *n* quai *m*.

quayside ['kiːsaɪd] *n* quai *m*; **we walked along the ~** nous nous sommes promenés le long du quai; **she was waiting at the ~** elle attendait sur le quai.

queasiness ['kwiːzɪnɪs] *n (U)* -**1.** [nausea] nausée *f*. -**2.** [uneasiness] scrupules *mpl*.

queasy ['kwiːzɪ] (*compar* **queasier**, *superl* **queasiest**) *adj* -**1.** [nauseous] nauséeux; **I OR my stomach felt a little ~** j'avais un peu mal au cœur. -**2.** [uneasy] mal à l'aise, gêné.

Quebec [kwɪ'bek] *pr n* -**1.** [province] Québec *m*; **in ~** au Québec. -**2.** [city] Québec.

Quebecker, Quebecer [kwɪ'bekəʳ] *n* Québécois *m*, -e *f*.

Quebecois, Québécois [kebe'kwɑː] (*pl inv*) *n* Québécois *m*, -e *f*.

queen [kwiːn] ◇ *n* -**1.** [sovereign, king's wife] reine *f*; **the Queen of England/Spain/Belgium** la reine d'Angleterre/d'Espagne/de Belgique; **Queen Elizabeth II** la reine Élisabeth II; **she was ~ to Charles II** elle fut la reine OR l'épouse de Charles II. -**2.** [woman considered best] reine *f*; **the ~ of the blues** la reine du blues. -**3.** [in cards, chess] dame *f*, reine *f*; **he played his ~ of clubs** il joua sa dame de trèfle. -**4.** [of bees, ants] reine *f*. -**5.** ▽ *pej* [homosexual] tante *f*, pédale *f*.
◇ *vt* -**1.** *Br phr*: **to ~ it** *inf* prendre des airs de (grande) marquise; **she thinks she can ~ it over us!** elle s'imagine qu'elle est supérieure à nous! -**2.** [in chess]: **to ~ a pawn** aller à dame.

queen bee *n* reine *f* des abeilles; **she's the ~ round here** *inf fig* c'est elle la patronne ici.

queen consort *n* reine *f* (*épouse du roi*).

queenly ['kwiːnlɪ] *adj* royal, majestueux.

queen mother *n* reine *f* mère.

queen regent *n* reine *f* régente.

Queens [kwiːnz] *pr n* Queens (*quartier de New York*).

Queen's Bench (Division) *n En Angleterre et au Pays de Galles, l'une des trois divisions de la High Court*, ≃ tribunal *m* de grande instance.

Queensberry ['kwiːnzbrɪ] *pr n*: **the ~ Rules** *réglementations régissant les matches de boxe*.

Queen's Counsel *n* ≃ bâtonnier *m* de l'ordre (*en Angleterre*).

Queen's English *n l'anglais britannique correct*; **she speaks the ~** elle s'exprime dans un anglais très soigné.

Queen's evidence *n Br*: **to turn ~** témoigner contre ses complices.

Queen's highway *n Br*: **the ~** la voie publique.

Queensland ['kwiːnzlənd] *pr n* Queensland *m*; **in ~** dans le Queensland.

Queenslander ['kwiːnzləndəʳ] *n* habitant *m*, -e *f* du Queensland, originaire *mf* du Queensland.

Queen's Regulations *npl Br* règlement *m* militaire.

Queen's Speech *n* [in UK]: **the ~** *allocution prononcée par la reine (mais préparée par le gouvernement) lors de la rentrée parlementaire et dans laquelle elle définit les grands axes de la politique gouvernementale*.

queer [kwɪəʳ] ◇ *adj* -**1.** [strange] étrange, bizarre; **he's a ~ fish!** c'est un drôle d'individu! -**2.** [suspicious] suspect, louche; **there've been some ~ goings-on around here** il s'est passé des choses bizarres ici. -**3.** *inf* [queasy] mal fichu, patraque. -**4.** *inf* [crazy] timbré, cinglé; **he's a bit ~ in the head** il lui manque une case. -**5.** ▽ [homosexual] homo; *pej* pédé *m*. -**6.** *inf Am* [counterfeit]: **~ money** fausse monnaie *f*.
◇ *n* ▽ homo *m*; *pej* pédé *m*.
◇ *vt inf* gâter, gâcher; **to ~ sb's pitch** *Br* couper l'herbe sous les pieds de qqn.

queer-bashing▽ [-,bæʃɪŋ] *n Br pej* chasse *f* aux pédés.

queerly ['kwɪəlɪ] *adv* étrangement, bizarrement; **she looked at me ~** elle me regarda d'un drôle d'air.

queerness ['kwɪənɪs] *n* -**1.** [strangeness] étrangeté *f*, bizarrerie *f*. -**2.** [queasiness] nausée *f*.

queer street *n Br*: **to be in ~** *inf dated* être dans une mauvaise passe.

quell [kwel] *vt* -**1.** [quash - revolt, opposition] réprimer, étouffer. -**2.** [overcome - emotion, passion] dompter, maîtriser. -**3.** [allay - pain] apaiser, soulager; [- doubts, fears] dissiper.

quench [kwentʃ] *vt* -**1.** *literal*: **to ~ one's thirst** étancher sa soif, se désaltérer. -**2.** [fire, flames] éteindre. -**3.** METALL tremper.

quern [kwɜːn] *n* moulin *m* à céréales (*à meules de pierre*).

querulous ['kwerʊləs] *adj* [person] pleurnicheur; [voice, tone] plaintif, gémissant.

querulously ['kwerʊləslɪ] *adv* d'un ton plaintif.

query ['kwɪərɪ] (*pl* **queries**, *pt* & *pp* **queried**) ◇ *n* -**1.** [question] question *f*; [doubt] doute *m*; **she accepted my explanation without a ~** elle a accepté mon explication sans poser de questions; **the latest facts to come to light raise a ~ about his honesty** les derniers faits qui ont été mis au jour jettent un doute sur son honnêteté. -**2.** *Br* [question mark] point *m* d'interrogation.
◇ *vt* -**1.** [express doubt about] mettre en doute; **it is not for me to ~ their motives** ce n'est pas à moi de mettre en doute leurs mobiles; **the accountant queried the figures** le comptable posa des questions sur les chiffres. -**2.** [ask] demander; **"how much is it?", she queried** «combien est-ce?», demanda-t-elle. -**3.** *Am* [interrogate] interroger; **he queried me about my trip** il m'a posé des questions sur mon voyage.

query language *n* COMPUT langage *m* d'interrogation.

quest [kwest] ◇ *n* quête *f*; **in ~ of truth** en quête de OR à la recherche de la vérité.
◇ *vi lit*: **to ~ for OR after sthg** se mettre en quête de qqch.

question ['kwestʃn] ◇ *n* -**1.** [query] question *f*; **to ask sb a ~** poser une question à qqn; **I wish to put a ~ to the chairman** j'aimerais poser une question au président; **you haven't answered my ~** vous n'avez pas répondu à ma question; **they obeyed without ~** ils ont obéi sans poser de questions ❑ **(Prime Minister's) Question Time** *session bi-hebdomadaire du Parlement britannique réservée aux questions des députés au Premier ministre*. -**2.** [matter, issue] question *f*; [problem] problème *m*; **her article raises some important ~s** son article soulève d'importantes questions OR d'importants problèmes; **it raises the ~ of what teachers should do in such cases** cela nous conduit à nous demander ce que les enseignants devraient faire dans des cas comme celui-là; **the place/time in ~** le lieu/l'heure en question; **the person in ~ is away at the moment** la personne en question est absente en ce moment; **the Jewish ~** la question juive; **the ~ is, will he do it?** toute la question est de savoir s'il le fera; **that is the ~** voilà la question; **but that's not the ~** mais là n'est pas la question; **it's a ~ of how much you want to spend** tout dépend de la somme que vous voulez mettre; **it's only a ~ of money/time** c'est seulement une question d'argent/de temps. -**3.** *(U)* [doubt] doute *m*; **there's no ~ about it, he was murdered** il a été assassiné, cela ne fait aucun doute; **his honesty was never in ~** son honnêteté n'a jamais été mise en doute OR remise en question; **to bring OR to call sthg into ~** remettre qqch en question; **she is without OR beyond ~ the best** elle est incontestablement la meilleure; **they know beyond ~ where their interests lie** ils savent parfaitement (bien) où est leur intérêt; **whether they are happier now is open to ~** sont-ils plus heureux maintenant? on peut se le demander. -**4.** [possibility]: **there's no ~ of our making the same mistake again** nous ne sommes pas près de refaire la même erreur; **there's no ~ of his coming with us, it's out of the ~ that he should come with us** il est hors de question qu'il vienne avec nous; **I'm sorry, you can't go, it's out of the ~!** je regrette, vous ne pouvez pas y aller, c'est hors de question!
◇ *vt* -**1.** [interrogate] interroger, poser des questions à; [subj: police] interroger; SCH interroger. -**2.** [doubt - motives, honesty] mettre en doute, remettre en question; [- statement, claim] mettre en doute, contester; **I ~ed whether it was wise to continue** je me suis demandé s'il était bien sage de continuer.

questionable ['kwestʃənəbl] *adj* -**1.** [doubtful] contestable, douteux; **his involvement in the affair is ~** sa participation dans cette affaire reste à démontrer OR à prouver; **it is ~ whether she knew** rien ne prouve qu'elle était au courant. -**2.** [suspicious - motives] douteux, louche; [- behaviour] louche. -**3.** [strange - taste, style] douteux.

questioner ['kwestʃənəʳ] *n* [gen, in quiz show] animateur *m*, -trice *f*; JUR interrogateur *m*, -trice *f*; **she sent her ~s away** elle renvoya ceux qui l'interrogeaient; **our next ~ is from Belfast** RADIO & TV la question suivante nous vient de Belfast.

question form *n* GRAMM forme *f* interrogative.

questioning ['kwestʃənɪŋ] ◇ *adj* interrogateur.
◇ *n* interrogation *f*; **he was taken in for ~** JUR il a été interpellé pour être interrogé.

questioningly ['kwestʃənɪŋlɪ] *adv* de manière interrogative.

question mark *n* point *m* d'interrogation; *fig*: **a large ~ hangs over the future of this country** il est impossible de prédire quel sort attend ce pays OR sera réservé à ce pays; **there is a ~ over her reasons for leaving** on ignore les raisons qui l'ont poussée à partir.

question master *n* meneur *m* de jeu; RADIO & TV animateur *m*, -trice *f* (*d'un jeu*).

questionnaire [,kwestʃə'neəʳ] *n* questionnaire *m*.

question tag *n tournure en fin de phrase changeant celle-ci en question*.

queue [kjuː] ◇ *n Br* queue *f*, file *f* d'attente; **they were standing in a ~** ils faisaient la queue; **to form a ~** former une queue; **a long ~ of cars** une longue file de voitures; **I was first in the ~** j'étais le premier de la file; **we joined the ~ for foreign exchange** nous avons fait la queue devant le bureau de change.
◇ *vi Br* faire la queue; **'~ here for tickets'** file d'attente pour les billets.
◆ **queue up** *vi insep Br* faire la queue.

queue-jump *vi Br* essayer de passer avant son tour, resquiller.

queue-jumper *n Br* resquilleur *m*, -euse *f (qui n'attend pas son tour)*.

quibble ['kwɪbl] ◇ *vi* chicaner; to ~ over details chicaner sur des détails.
◇ *n* chicane *f*; I have one small ~ il y a juste une petite chose qui me gêne.

quibbler ['kwɪbləʳ] *n* chicaneur *m*, -euse *f*, chicanier *m*, -ère *f*.

quibbling ['kwɪblɪŋ] ◇ *adj* chicaneur, chicanier.
◇ *n* chicanerie *f*.

Quiberon [ki:brɔ̃] *pr n*: the ~ peninsula la presqu'île de Quiberon.

quiche [ki:ʃ] *n* quiche *f*.

quick [kwɪk] ◇ *adj* -**1.** [rapid] rapide; [easy - profits] rapide, facile; he's a ~ worker *literal* il travaille vite; *fig* il ne perd pas de temps; be ~ (about it)! faites vite!, dépêchez-vous!; I need a ~ answer j'ai besoin d'une réponse rapide; to have a ~ look jeter un rapide coup d'œil; can I have a ~ word? est-ce que je peux vous parler un instant?; she did the job in double ~ time elle a fait le travail en deux temps, trois mouvements OR en un rien de temps; we had a ~ lunch nous avons déjeuné sur le pouce; let's have a ~ one *inf* OR a ~ drink prenons un verre en vitesse; the questions came in ~ succession les questions se sont succédé à un rythme très rapide ❑ ~ march! en avant, marche!; (as) ~ as lightning OR as a flash rapide OR vif comme l'éclair. -**2.** [sharp] alerte, éveillé, vif; he is ~ to learn il apprend vite; she has a ~ ear elle a l'oreille fine; she has a ~ eye for detail aucun détail ne lui échappe; thanks to his ~ eye for bargains grâce au chic qu'il a pour dénicher OR faire les bonnes affaires; I was ~ to notice the difference j'ai tout de suite remarqué la différence; she's too ~ for me elle est trop rapide pour moi ❑ she's ~ on the uptake elle comprend vite; they were very ~ off the mark *Br* ils n'ont pas perdu de temps. -**3.** [hasty - judgment] hâtif, rapide; he has a ~ temper il s'emporte facilement; he is ~ to take offence il est prompt à s'offenser, il se vexe pour un rien.
◇ *adv* rapidement; come ~! venez vite!; to get rich ~ s'enrichir rapidement.
◇ *n Br* [of fingernail] vif *m*; his nails were bitten to the ~ il s'était rongé les ongles jusqu'au sang ❑ her remark cut him to the ~ sa remarque l'a piqué au vif.
◇ *npl arch* [living]: the ~ and the dead les vivants *mpl* et les morts *mpl*.

quick- *in cpds*: ~dry OR ~drying paint peinture à séchage rapide; ~setting cement ciment à prise rapide.

quick assets *npl* liquidités *fpl*, avoirs *mpl* liquides.

quick-change artist *n* spécialiste *mf* des transformations rapides.

quicken ['kwɪkn] ◇ *vt* -**1.** [hasten] accélérer, hâter; MUS [tempo] presser; to ~ one's pace OR step hâter OR presser le pas. -**2.** [stir - imagination] stimuler; [- hatred, desire] exciter; [- appetite, interest] stimuler; [- resolve] hâter; the incident ~ed his sense of injustice l'incident a aiguisé son sentiment d'injustice.
◇ *vi* -**1.** [step, pulse] s'accélérer; my heart OR pulse ~ed mon cœur se mit à battre plus vite. -**2.** [hopes, fire] se ranimer. -**3.** [foetus] commencer à bouger.

quickening ['kwɪknɪŋ] *n* accélération *f*; a ~ of the pulse une accélération du pouls.

quickfire ['kwɪkfaɪəʳ] *adj*: he directed ~ questions at me il m'a mitraillé de questions; a series of ~ questions un feu roulant de questions.

quick-freeze (*pt* quick-froze, *pp* quick-frozen) *vt* surgeler.

quickie *inf* ['kwɪkɪ] *n* -**1.** [gen] truc *m* vite fait; [question] question *f* rapide. -**2.** [sex] coup *m* en vitesse OR entre deux portes. -**3.** [drink] pot *m* rapide; we stopped at a pub for a ~ on s'est arrêtés dans un bar pour prendre un pot en vitesse.

quicklime ['kwɪklaɪm] *n* chaux *f* vive.

quickly ['kwɪklɪ] *adv* rapidement, vite; come as ~ as possible venez aussi vite que possible; he ~ telephoned the doctor il se dépêcha d'appeler le médecin.

quickness ['kwɪknɪs] *n* -**1.** [rapidity - of movement, pulse] rapidité *f*; [- of mind, reaction] rapidité, vivacité *f*. -**2.** [acuteness - of sight, wit] vivacité *f*; [- of hearing] finesse *f*. -**3.** [hastiness]: his ~ of temper sa promptitude à s'emporter.

quicksand ['kwɪksænd] *n*, **quicksands** ['kwɪksændz] *npl* sables *mpl* mouvants.

quickset ['kwɪkset] *adj Br*: ~ hedge haie *f* vive.

quicksilver ['kwɪk,sɪlvəʳ] ◇ *n* vif-argent *m*, mercure *m*.
◇ *adj* [mind] très vif, comme du vif-argent.

quickstep ['kwɪkstep] *n* quickstep *m*.

quick-tempered *adj*: he is ~ il s'emporte facilement.

quick-witted *adj* à l'esprit vif; she is very ~ [in answers] elle a de la repartie; [in intelligence] elle a l'esprit vif.

quid *inf* [kwɪd] (*pl sense 1 inv*) *n* -**1.** *Br* [pound] livre *f*; could you lend me ten ~? t'as pas dix livres à me prêter? -**2.** [tobacco] chique *f*. -**3.** *phr*: we're ~s in *Br* on est peinards.

quiddity ['kwɪdətɪ] (*pl* quiddities) *n* quiddité *f*.

quid pro quo [,kwɪdprəʊ'kwəʊ] (*pl* quid pro quos) *n* contrepartie *f*, récompense *f*; what did she get as a ~ for her silence? qu'est-ce qu'elle a reçu en contrepartie de son silence?

quiescence [kwaɪ'esns] *n lit* tranquillité *f*, quiétude *f*.

quiescent [kwaɪ'esnt] *adj lit* [passive] passif; [peaceful] tranquille.

quiet ['kwaɪət] ◇ *adj* -**1.** [silent - person] tranquille, silencieux; be OR keep ~! taisez-vous!; could you try to keep them ~? pourriez-vous essayer de les faire taire?; ~ please! silence, s'il vous plaît!; you're very ~ vous ne dites pas grand-chose; keep ~ about what you've seen ne dites rien de ce que vous avez vu || [subdued, soft] tranquille; we were having a ~ conversation nous bavardions tranquillement; can I have a ~ word with you? est-ce que je peux vous dire un mot en particulier?; in a ~ voice d'une voix douce ❑ it was as ~ as the grave il régnait un silence de mort; she was as ~ as a mouse elle ne faisait pas le moindre bruit; 'The Quiet American' *Greene* 'Un Américain bien tranquille'. -**2.** [calm, tranquil] calme, tranquille, paisible; FIN [market, business, dealing] calme; to lead a ~ life mener une vie paisible OR tranquille; the TV keeps the children ~ pendant qu'ils regardent la télé, les enfants se tiennent tranquilles; sit ~ for ten minutes restez assis tranquillement pendant dix minutes; to have a ~ drink boire un verre tranquillement; we had a ~ Christmas nous avons passé un Noël tranquille; she had a ~ night elle a passé une nuit tranquille OR paisible; all is ~ tout va bien, rien à signaler ❑ all ~ on the western front *hum* à l'ouest rien de nouveau; anything for a ~ life tout pour avoir la paix. -**3.** [docile - animal] docile; [easy -baby] calme; [uncommunicative] silencieux, peu communicatif. -**4.** [private - wedding] dans l'intimité; [- party] avec quelques intimes, avec peu d'invités; [secret] secret, dissimulé; keep the news ~ gardez la nouvelle pour vous. -**5.** [subtle, discreet - irony] discret; [- optimism] tranquille; [- anger] sourd; [- despair, resentment] secret; he had a ~ smile on his lips il avait un petit sourire aux lèvres. -**6.** [muted - colour, style] sobre; he's a ~ dresser il s'habille sobrement OR sans ostentation.
◇ *n* silence *m*; to ask for ~ demander le silence; a minute's ~ une minute de silence.
◇ *vt* [calm] calmer; [silence] faire taire.
◆ **on the quiet** *adv phr Br* [in secrecy] en douce, en cachette; [discreetly] discrètement, en douceur; [in confidence] en confiance.
◆ **quiet down** *vi insep Am* se calmer.

quieten ['kwaɪətn] ◇ *vt Br* [child, audience] calmer, apaiser; [conscience] tranquilliser, apaiser; [doubts] dissiper; does that ~ your fears? est-ce que cela dissipe vos craintes?
◇ *vi* [child] se calmer; [music] devenir plus doux.
◆ **quieten down** ◇ *vi insep* -**1.** [become quiet - person] se calmer; [- storm, wind] se calmer, s'apaiser; the meeting gradually ~ed down peu à peu, l'assemblée s'est calmée. -**2.** [become reasonable] s'assagir; he's ~ed down a lot since he got married il s'est beaucoup assagi depuis son mariage.
◇ *vt sep* [calm] calmer, apaiser; [shut up] faire taire.

quietism ['kwaɪətɪzm] *n* quiétisme *m*.

quietist ['kwaɪətɪst] ◇ *adj* quiétiste.
◇ *n* quiétiste *mf*.

quietly ['kwaɪətlɪ] *adv* [silently] silencieusement, sans bruit; [gently, softly] doucement, calmement; [peacefully] tranquillement, paisiblement; sit ~ restez assis tranquillement; a ~ flowing river une rivière au cours paisible; they got married ~ ils se sont mariés dans l'intimité.

quietness ['kwaɪətnɪs] *n* [stillness] tranquillité *f*, calme *m*; [silence] silence *m*.

quietude ['kwaɪətju:d] *n lit* quiétude *f*.

quietus [kwaɪ'i:təs] *n* -**1.** *lit* [death] trépas *m*. -**2.** JUR [settlement of debt] règlement *m*.

quiff [kwɪf] *n* [hairstyle] banane *f*.

quill [kwɪl] *n* -**1.** [feather] penne *f*; [shaft of feather] hampe *f* creuse; [of hedgehog, porcupine] piquant *m*. -**2.** [pen] plume *f* (d'oie).

quill pen *n* plume *f* d'oie.

quilt [kwɪlt] *n* [eiderdown] édredon *m*; [bedspread] dessus-de-lit *m inv*; [duvet] couette *f*.

quilted ['kwɪltɪd] *adj* matelassé.

quilting ['kwɪltɪŋ] *n* -**1.** [fabric] tissu *m* matelassé; [on furniture] capitonnage *m*. -**2.** [of clothing] ouatinage *m*; [of furniture covering] capitonnage *m*. -**3.** [hobby] *réalisation d'ouvrages (vêtements, dessus de lit) en tissu matelassé*.

quin [kwɪn] (*abbr of* quintuplet) *n Br* quintuplé *m*, -e *f*.

quince [kwɪns] ◇ *n* [fruit] coing *m*; [tree] cognassier *m*.
◇ *comp* [jam, jelly] de coing.

quincentenary [,kwɪnsen'ti:nərɪ] *n* cinquentième anniversaire *m*.

quincentennial [,kwɪnsen'tenɪəl] ◇ *n* cinquentième anniversaire *m*.
◇ *adj* cinq-centième.

quinine [kwɪ'ni:n] *n* quinine *f*.

Quinquagesima [,kwɪŋkwə'dʒesɪmə] *n* Quinquagésime *f*.

quinquennial [kwɪŋ'kwenɪəl] *adj* quinquennal.

quinquennium [kwɪŋ'kwenɪəm] (*pl* quinquenniums OR quinquennia [-nɪə]) *n* quinquennat *m*.

quinsy ['kwɪnzɪ] *n dated* amygdalite *f* purulente.

quint [kwɪnt] (*abbr of* quintuplet) *n Am* quintuplé *m*, -e *f*.

quintal ['kwɪntl] *n* quintal *m*.

quintessence [kwɪn'tesns] *n* quintessence *f*.

quintessential [kwɪntə'senʃl] *adj* typique, type; she's the ~ Parisian c'est la Parisienne type; he's the ~ English gentleman c'est le gentleman anglais typique.

quintet(te) [kwɪn'tet] *n* quintette *m*.

quintillion [kwɪn'tɪljən] *n Br* quintillion *m* (10^{30}); *Am* trillion *m* (10^{18}).

quintuple [kwɪn'tju:pl] ◇ *adj* quintuple.
◇ *n* quintuple *m*.
◇ *vi & vt* quintupler.

quintuplet [kwɪn'tju:plɪt] *n* quintuplé *m*, -e *f*.

quintuplicate [kwɪn'tju:plɪkɪt] *n*: in ~ en cinq exemplaires.

quip [kwɪp] (*pt & pp* quipped, *cont* quipping) ◇ *n* [remark - witty] bon mot *m*, mot *m* d'esprit; [- sarcastic] sarcasme *m*; [gibe] quolibet *m*; to make a ~ faire un bon mot OR de l'esprit; he

made a nasty ~ about her humble origins il a fait une remarque désobligeante sur ses origines modestes.
◇ *vt*: "only if I'm asked", he quipped «seulement si on me le demande», lança-t-il d'un air malicieux.
quipster *inf* ['kwɪpstəʳ] *n Br* plaisantin *m*.
quire ['kwaɪəʳ] *n* [in bookbinding] cahier *m*; [of paper] main *f* (de papier).
Quirinal ['kwɪrɪnl] *pr n* mont *m* Quirinal.
quirk [kwɜːk] *n* -**1.** [idiosyncrasy] manie *f*, excentricité *f*. -**2.** [accident] bizarrerie *f*, caprice *m*; by a ~ of fate we met in Sydney par un caprice du destin, nous nous sommes rencontrés à Sydney. -**3.** [flourish] fioriture *f*.
quirky ['kwɜːkɪ] *adj* bizarre, original.
quirt [kwɜːrt] *Am* ◇ *n* cravache *f*.
◇ *vt* cravacher.
quisling ['kwɪzlɪŋ] *n pej* collaborateur *m*, -trice *f*.
quit [kwɪt] (*pt* & *pp* quit OR quitted, *cont* quitting) ◇ *vt* -**1.** [leave] quitter; we have to ~ the premises by the end of the month nous devons quitter les lieux avant la fin du mois. -**2.** *Am* [give up, stop] quitter, cesser; he ~ school at 15 il a quitté l'école à 15 ans; he ~ his job il a quitté son travail; I ~ work at 4 o'clock je quitte le travail à 16 h; I've ~ smoking j'ai arrêté OR cessé de fumer; ~ it! arrête!, ça suffit!
◇ *vi* -**1.** [give up] renoncer, abandonner; [resign] démissionner; I ~! *inf* j'abandonne!; I want to ~ j'ai envie de tout laisser tomber; you shouldn't ~ so easily vous ne devriez pas abandonner la partie si facilement. -**2.** *Am* [leave] partir.
◇ *adj*: to be ~ of sb/sthg être débarrassé de qqn/qqch.
quite [kwaɪt] ◇ *adv* & *predet* -**1.** [moderately] assez; the film is ~ good le film est assez bon; it's ~ cold today il fait assez froid aujourd'hui; I'd ~ like to go ça me plairait assez d'y aller; ~ a difficult job un travail assez difficile; ~ a good job un assez bon emploi; ~ a lot of people seem to believe it un bon nombre de gens semblent le croire; there were ~ a few good paintings il y avait un assez grand nombre de bons tableaux; there was ~ a crowd il y avait pas mal de monde; I've been here for ~ some time je suis ici depuis un bon moment OR depuis assez longtemps; he was in France for ~ some time il a passé pas mal de temps en France. -**2.** [completely, absolutely] parfaitement, tout à fait; she's ~ right elle a tout à fait OR parfaitement raison; the story isn't ~ true l'histoire n'est pas tout à fait OR entièrement vraie; I ~ understand je comprends tout à fait OR parfaitement; she's ~ brilliant elle est vraiment très brillante; we've always been ~ happy together nous avons toujours été parfaitement heureux ensemble; if you've ~ finished si vous avez terminé; that's ~ another matter! ça, c'est autre chose!; not ~ a month ago il y a un peu moins d'un mois; you've had ~ enough vous en avez eu largement assez; that's ~ enough! ça suffit comme ça!; it's ~ the thing c'est très à la mode; he's ~ the young gentleman c'est le parfait jeune homme. -**3.** [exactly] exactement, tout à fait; that wasn't ~ what I had in mind ce n'est pas exactement ce que j'avais en tête; I'm not ~ sure what you mean je ne vois pas très bien ce que vous voulez dire. -**4.** [expressing approval, appreciation]: that was ~ a OR ~ some party! *inf* ça a été une sacrée soirée!; she's ~ a girl! c'est une sacrée nana! ❑ his speech was ~ something son discours était tout à fait remarquable.
◇ *interj*: ~ (so)! tout à fait!, parfaitement!
Quito ['kiːtəʊ] *pr n* Quito.
quits [kwɪts] *adj* quitte; I'm ~ with her now maintenant, je suis quitte envers elle; now we're ~ maintenant nous sommes quittes; let's call it ~ [financially] disons que nous sommes quittes; [in fight, argument] restons-en là.
quittance ['kwɪtəns] *n* FIN & JUR quittance *f*.
quitter *inf* ['kwɪtəʳ] *n* dégonflé *m*, -e *f*.
quiver ['kwɪvəʳ] ◇ *vi* -**1.** [tremble - person] frémir, trembler; [- lips, hands, voice] trembler; to ~ with fear/rage trembler de peur/rage; to ~ with emotion frissonner d'émotion; the ~ing tones of the violin les trémolos du violon. -**2.** [flutter - heart] trembler, frémir; [leaves] frémir, frissonner; [- flame] trembler, vaciller.
◇ *n* -**1.** [tremble] tremblement *m*; [of violin] trémolo *m*, frémissement *m*; a ~ of fear went down my spine un frisson de peur me parcourut le dos; he had a ~ in his voice sa voix tremblait d'émotion; her heart gave a ~ son cœur fit un bond dans sa poitrine. -**2.** [for arrows] carquois *m*.
qui vive [kiː'viːv] *n Br*: on the ~ sur le qui-vive.
Quixote ['kwɪksət] *pr n*: Don ~ don Quichotte.
quixotic [kwɪk'sɒtɪk] *adj* [idealistic] idéaliste, chimérique; [chivalrous] généreux, chevaleresque.
quixotically [kwɪk'sɒtɪklɪ] *adv* à la (manière de) don Quichotte.
quiz [kwɪz] (*pl* quizzes, *pt* & *pp* quizzed, *cont* quizzing) ◇ *n* -**1.** [game - on TV] jeu *m* télévisé; [- on radio] jeu *m* radiophonique; [- in newspaper] questionnaire *m*; ~ programmes OR shows les jeux télévisés; general knowledge ~ test *m* de culture générale. -**2.** *Am* SCH [test] interrogation *f*.
◇ *vt* -**1.** [question] interroger, questionner; to ~ sb about sthg interroger qqn au sujet de qqch. -**2.** *Am* SCH [test] interroger.
quizmaster ['kwɪz,mɑːstəʳ] *n* RADIO & TV animateur *m*, -trice *f* *(d'un jeu)*.
quizzical ['kwɪzɪkl] *adj* [questioning] interrogateur; [ironic] ironique, narquois; to give sb a ~ look lancer un regard narquois à qqn.
quizzically ['kwɪzɪklɪ] *adv* [questioningly] d'un air interrogateur; [ironically] d'un air ironique OR narquois.
Qum [kʊm] = **Qom**.
quod *inf* [kwɒd] *n Br* [jail] tôle *f*; he's in ~ il est en tôle.
quoin [kɔɪn] *n* [cornerstone] pierre *f* d'angle; [keystone] clef *f* de voûte.
quoit [kɔɪt] *n* [in game] anneau *m*; to play ~s jouer aux anneaux.
quondam ['kwɒndæm] *adj lit* ancien; her ~ suitor son ancien prétendant.
Quonset hut ®['kwɒnsɪt-] *n Am* abri *m* préfabriqué *(en tôle ondulée)*.
quorate ['kwɔːreɪt] *adj Br* où le quorum est atteint.
quorum ['kwɔːrəm] *n* quorum *m*; we don't have a ~ le quorum n'est pas atteint.
quota ['kwəʊtə] *n* -**1.** [limited quantity] quota *m*, contingent *m*; they are admitted on a ~ system il y a un numerus clausus OR un quota pour les admissions. -**2.** [share] part *f*, quota *m*.
quotable ['kwəʊtəbl] *adj* -**1.** [worth quoting] digne d'être cité; an eminently ~ phrase une phrase tout à fait digne d'être citée. -**2.** [on the record] que l'on peut citer; are these figures ~? peut-on citer ces chiffres?; what he said is not ~ ce qu'il a dit ne peut être répété. -**3.** ST. EX cotable.
quotation [kwəʊ'teɪʃn] *n* -**1.** [remark, sentence] citation *f*. -**2.** ST. EX cours *m*, cotation *f*. -**3.** COMM [estimate] devis *m*; [for insurance] cotation *f*.
quotation marks *npl* guillemets *mpl*.
quote [kwəʊt] ◇ *vt* -**1.** [cite - words, example, statistics] citer; can I ~ you on that? me permettez-vous de citer ce que vous venez de dire?; don't ~ me on that [don't repeat it] ne le répétez pas; [don't say it was me who told you] ne dites pas que c'est moi qui vous l'ai dit; she ~d several passages from the book elle cita plusieurs passages du livre; he said, ~, get lost, unquote il a dit, je cite, allez vous faire voir; their leader was ~d as denying the allegation leur leader aurait rejeté l'accusation; you are ~d as saying he's mad vous auriez dit qu'il était fou. -**2.** ADMIN & COMM: please ~ this reference (number) prière de mentionner cette référence. -**3.** [specify - price] indiquer, annoncer; ST. EX coter; gold prices were ~d at £500 l'or a été coté à 500 livres; can you ~ me a price? pouvez-vous me donner OR m'indiquer un prix?
◇ *vi* -**1.** [cite] faire des citations; to ~ from Yeats citer Yeats. -**2.** COMM: to ~ for a job faire un devis pour un travail.
◇ *n* -**1.** [quotation] citation *f*; [statement] déclaration *f*. -**2.** [estimate] devis *m*. -**3.** [quotation mark] guillemet *m*; in ~s entre guillemets.
quoth [kwəʊθ] *vt arch*: "nay", ~ the King «non», fit OR dit le roi.
quotidian [kwɒ'tɪdɪən] *adj fml* quotidien.
quotient ['kwəʊʃnt] *n* quotient *m*.
Qur'an *etc* [kɒ'rɑːn] = **Koran**.
qv (*written abbr of* quod vide) *expression renvoyant le lecteur à une autre entrée dans une encyclopédie*.
qwerty, **Qwerty** ['kwɜːtɪ] *n*: ~ keyboard clavier *m* qwerty.

R

r (*pl* r's OR rs), **R** (*pl* R's OR Rs) [ɑːʳ] *n* [letter] r *m*, R *m*; the three Rs la lecture, l'écriture et l'arithmétique *(qui constituent les fondements de l'enseignement primaire)*.

R ◇ -**1.** (*written abbr of* right) dr. -**2.** *written abbr of* river. -**3.** (*written abbr of* Réaumur) R. -**4.** *Am written abbr of* Republican. -**5.** *Br* (*written abbr of* Rex) *suit le nom d'un roi*. -**6.** *Br* (*written abbr of* Regina) *suit le nom d'une reine*. -**7.** *written abbr of* radius. -**8.** *written abbr of* road. -**9.** *written abbr of* registered (trademark).
◇ *adj Am* (*abbr of* restricted) *indique qu'un film est interdit aux moins de 17 ans*.

RA ◇ *n* -**1.** *abbr of* rear admiral. -**2.** (*abbr of* Royal Academician) *membre de la Royal Academy*.
◇ *pr n abbr of* Royal Academy.

RAAF [ræf] (*abbr of* Royal Australian Air Force) *pr n armée de l'air australienne*.

Rabat [rəˈbɑːt] *pr n* Rabat.

rabbet [ˈræbɪt] ◇ *n* [groove] feuillure *f*.
◇ *vt* feuiller.

rabbet plane *n* feuilleret *m*.

rabbi [ˈræbaɪ] *n* rabbin *m*; chief ~ grand rabbin.

rabbinic [rəˈbɪnɪk] *adj* rabbinique.
◆ **Rabbinic** *n* hébreu *m* rabbinique.

rabbinical [rəˈbɪnɪkl] *adj* rabbinique.

rabbit [ˈræbɪt] ◇ *n* -**1.** [animal] lapin *m*, -e *f*; doe ~ lapine *f*; young ~ lapereau *m*; wild ~ lapin de garenne. -**2.** *inf Br* [poor player]: I'm a bit of a ~ at chess je ne suis pas très bon aux échecs.
◇ *comp* [coat, stole] en (peau de) lapin.
◇ *vi*: to go ~ing chasser le lapin.
◆ **rabbit on** *inf vi insep* [talk] jacasser; he's been ~ing on about his money problems il me rebat les oreilles de ses problèmes d'argent; he's always ~ing on at me about it il me serine cette histoire à longueur de journée; what's she ~ing on about? de quoi elle cause?

rabbit burrow, **rabbit hole** *n* terrier *m* (de lapin).

rabbit hutch *n* clapier *m*, cage *f* OR cabane *f* à lapins; *fig* [housing] cage *f* à lapins.

rabbit punch *n* coup *m* du lapin.

rabbit warren *n* -**1.** *literal* garenne *f*. -**2.** *fig* labyrinthe *m*, dédale *m*.

rabble [ˈræbl] *n* -**1.** [mob]: the ~ *pej* la populace, la racaille. -**2.** TECH [in foundry] râble *m*.

rabble-rouser *n* agitateur *m*, -trice *f*, démagogue *mf*.

rabble-rousing ◇ *n* démagogie *f*.
◇ *adj* démagogique.

Rabelaisian [ˌræbəˈleɪzɪən] *adj* rabelaisien.

rabid [ˈræbɪd, ˈreɪbɪd] *adj* -**1.** MED [animal] enragé; [person] atteint de la rage. -**2.** *fig* [extremist, revolutionary] enragé; [hatred] farouche; [anger] féroce.

rabidly [ˈræbɪdlɪ, ˈreɪbɪdlɪ] *adv* férocement, farouchement.

rabies [ˈreɪbiːz] *n* (*U*) rage *f* MÉD.

RAC (*abbr of* Royal Automobile Club) *pr n*: the ~ *un des deux grands clubs automobiles de Grande-Bretagne*.

raccoon [rəˈkuːn] ◇ *n* raton *m* laveur.
◇ *comp* [coat, stole] en (fourrure de) raton laveur.

race [reɪs] ◇ *n* -**1.** [competition] course *f*; an 800 metre ~ une course de OR sur 800 mètres; a horse ~ une course de chevaux; to have OR to run a ~ courir, participer à une course; a day at the ~s une journée aux courses; a ~ against time une course contre la montre; it'll be a ~ to finish on time il faudra se dépêcher pour finir à temps; the ~ for the Presidency la course à la présidence. -**2.** [ethnic group] race *f*; [in anthropology] ethnie *f*; he belongs to the ~ of poets *fig* il est de la race des poètes; the French ~ *dated* la nation française; the human ~ la race OR l'espèce humaine. -**3.** *lit* [passing - of sun, moon] course *f*; [- of life] cours *m*. -**4.** [current] fort courant *m*; [in sea channel] raz *m* (de courant). -**5.** AERON [slipstream] sillage *m*; [turbulence] turbulence *f*. -**6.** TECH [for ball bearings] voie *f* de roulement.
◇ *comp* [discrimination, hatred, prejudice] racial.
◇ *vi* -**1.** [compete] faire la course; the cars/drivers were racing against each other les voitures/conducteurs faisaient la course; his horse will be racing at Ascot son cheval courra à Ascot. -**2.** [go fast, rush] aller à toute allure OR vitesse; to ~ in/out/past entrer/sortir/passer à toute allure; they ~d out of the café ils se précipitèrent hors du café; to ~ for a bus courir pour attraper un bus; she ~d downstairs elle a dévalé l'escalier; you'll have to ~ to catch your train tu vas devoir te dépêcher si tu veux avoir ton train; my pulse began to ~ mon cœur se mit à battre plus fort OR plus vite; a thousand ideas ~d through her mind mille idées lui sont passées par la tête; the competition is racing ahead of us nous sommes en train de nous faire dépasser par la concurrence. -**3.** [of engine] s'emballer.
◇ *vt* -**1.** [compete against] faire la course avec; (I'll) ~ you there! à qui y arrivera le premier! -**2.** [rush]: the casualties were ~d to hospital les blessés ont été transportés d'urgence à l'hôpital; to ~ a bill through Parliament faire adopter un projet de loi en toute hâte. -**3.** [put into a race]: to ~ a horse faire courir un cheval; this colt hasn't yet been ~d ce poulain n'a pas encore couru; to ~ pigeons faire des courses de pigeons. -**4.** AUT: to ~ the engine accélérer; [excessively] faire s'emballer le moteur.

race card *n* programme *m* (des courses).

racecourse [ˈreɪskɔːs] *n* -**1.** champ *m* de courses, hippodrome *m*. -**2.** *Am* [for cars, motorbikes] circuit *m*; [for runners, cycles] piste *f*.

racegoer [ˈreɪsˌgəʊəʳ] *n* turfiste *mf*.

racehorse [ˈreɪshɔːs] *n* cheval *m* de course.

raceme [ˈræsiːm] *n* grappe *f* *(inflorescence)*.

race meeting *n* courses *fpl*.

racer [ˈreɪsəʳ] *n* [runner] coureur *m*, -euse *f*; [horse] cheval *m* de course; [car] voiture *f* de course; [cycle] vélo *m* de course.

race relations *npl* relations *fpl* interraciales; ~ body OR board organisme *m* luttant contre la discrimination raciale.

race riot *n* émeute *f* raciale.

racetrack [ˈreɪstræk] *n* [gen] piste *f*; [for horses] champ *m* de courses, hippodrome *m*.

raceway [ˈreɪsweɪ] *n Am* -**1.** = **racetrack**. -**2.** [millrace] bief *m*.

Rachel [ˈreɪtʃl] *pr n* BIBLE Rachel.

rachitic [rəˈkɪtɪk] *adj* MED rachitique.

rachitis [rəˈkaɪtɪs] *n* MED rachitisme *m*.

Rachmaninoff [rækˈmænɪnɒf] *pr n* Rachmaninov.

Rachmanism [ˈrækmənɪzm] *n pressions exercées par un propriétaire sur ses locataires pour obtenir leur éviction*.

racial [ˈreɪʃl] *adj* -**1.** [concerning a race] racial, ethnique. -**2.** [between races] racial; ~ discrimination discrimination *f* raciale; ~ harmony harmonie *f* OR entente *f* raciale; ~ violence violence *f* raciale.

racialism [ˈreɪʃəlɪzm] *n* racisme *m*.

racialist [ˈreɪʃəlɪst] ◇ *adj* raciste.
◇ *n* raciste *mf*.

racially [ˈreɪʃəlɪ] *adv* du point de vue racial; the characteristic is not ~ determined cette caractéristique n'est pas déterminée par l'appartenance à une race; ~ prejudiced raciste.

raciness [ˈreɪsɪnɪs] *n* verve *f*, brio *m*.

racing [ˈreɪsɪŋ] ◇ *n*: (horse) ~ courses *fpl* de chevaux; motor ~ courses *fpl* automobiles; cycle ~ courses *fpl* cyclistes.
◇ *comp* [bicycle, yacht] de course.

racing car *n* voiture *f* de course.

racing cyclist *n* coureur *m*, -euse *f* cycliste.

racing driver *n* coureur *m*, -euse *f* automobile, pilote *mf* (de course).

racing pigeon *n* pigeon *m* voyageur *(de compétition)*.

racism [ˈreɪsɪzm] *n* racisme *m*.

racist [ˈreɪsɪst] ◇ *adj* raciste.
◇ *n* raciste *mf*.

rack [ræk] ◇ *n* -**1.** [shelf] étagère *f*; [for cooling drying] grille *f*, claie *f*; [for fodder, bicycles, test tubes, pipes] râtelier *m*; [for bottles] casier *m*; (dish) ~ égouttoir *m*; (luggage) ~ [in train, bus] filet *m* (à bagages); [on cycle] porte-bagages *m inv*; (stereo) ~ meuble *m* pour chaîne hi-fi; (tool) ~ porte-outils *m inv* ‖ [in shop] présentoir *m*; (clothes) ~ triangle *m* (à vêtements); to buy a suit off the ~ acheter un costume en prêt-à-porter. -**2.** HIST chevalet *m*; to put sb on the ~ *literal* faire subir à qqn le supplice du chevalet; *fig* mettre qqn au supplice; **that question put him on the ~** cette question l'a mis dans une position très difficile. -**3.** MECH crémaillère *f*. -**4.** CULIN: ~ **of lamb** carré *m* d'agneau. -**5.** *phr*: **to go to ~ and ruin** [house] tomber en ruine; [garden] être à l'abandon; [person] dépérir; [company] péricliter; [country, institution] aller à vau-l'eau.

◇ *vt* -**1.** [torture] faire subir le supplice du chevalet à; *fig* tenailler, ronger; **~ed by guilt** tenaillé par un sentiment de culpabilité; **to ~ one's brains** se creuser la tête. -**2.** [wine] soutirer.

◆ **rack up** *vt sep Am* [points] marquer.

rack and pinion *n* crémaillère *f*; ~ **railway** = **rack railway**.

racket ['rækɪt] ◇ *n* -**1.** SPORT [bat] raquette *f*; **tennis ~** raquette de tennis. -**2.** [snowshoe] raquette *f*. -**3.** *inf* [din] boucan *m*; **the neighbours are making a terrible ~** les voisins font un boucan épouvantable. -**4.** [extortion] racket *m*; [fraud] escroquerie *f*; [traffic] trafic *m*; **this lottery is such a ~** cette loterie, c'est de l'arnaque. -**5.** *inf* [job] boulot *m*; **what's your ~?** vous travaillez dans quoi?; **is she still in the teaching/publishing ~?** est-ce qu'elle est encore dans l'enseignement/l'édition?

◇ *vi* [be noisy] faire du boucan.

◆ **rackets** *n (U)* [game] racket-ball *m*.

◆ **racket about** *inf Br*, **racket around** *inf vi insep dated* [enjoy oneself] faire la bombe.

racketeer [,rækə'tɪə^r] ◇ *n* racketteur *m*.

◇ *vi* racketter.

racketeering [,rækə'tɪərɪŋ] *n* racket *m*.

racket press *n* presse-raquette *m*.

racking ['rækɪŋ] *adj* [pain] atroce, déchirant.

rack railway *n* chemin *m* de fer à crémaillère.

rack rent *n Br* loyer *m* exorbitant.

raconteur [,rækɒn'tɜː^r] *n* raconteur *m*, -euse *f*.

racoon [rə'kuːn] = **raccoon**.

racquet ['rækɪt] = **racket** *n* **1**.

racquetball ['rækɪtbɔːl] *n* racquetball *m*.

racy ['reɪsɪ] (*compar* racier, *superl* raciest) *adj* -**1.** [lively] plein de verve OR de brio. -**2.** [suggestive] osé. -**3.** [wine] racé.

rad [ræd] *n* rad *m*.

RADA ['rɑːdə] (*abbr of* Royal Academy of Dramatic Art) *pr n conservatoire britannique d'art dramatique*.

radar ['reɪdɑː^r] ◇ *n* radar *m*; **to navigate by ~** naviguer au radar.

◇ *comp* [image, screen, station] radar; ~ **blip** top *m* d'écho (radar); ~ **operator** radariste *mf*; ~ **scanner** antenne *f* radar.

radar beacon *n* radiophare *m*.

radar trap *n* contrôle *m* radar.

raddle ['rædl] ◇ *n* ocre *f* rouge.

◇ *vt* [face] maquiller avec du rouge; [sheep] marquer à l'ocre.

raddled ['rædld] *adj* ravagé.

radial ['reɪdjəl] ◇ *adj* radial; ~ **roads** routes *fpl* en étoile.

◇ *n* -**1.** [tyre] pneu *m* radial OR à carcasse radiale. -**2.** [line] rayon *m*.

radial engine *n* moteur *m* en étoile.

radial-ply *adj* AUT à carcasse radiale.

radial tyre *n* pneu *m* radial OR à carcasse radiale.

radian ['reɪdjən] *n* radian *m*.

radiance ['reɪdjəns] *n* -**1.** [of light, sun] éclat *m*, rayonnement *m*; *fig* [beauty, happiness] éclat *m*. -**2.** PHYS exitance *f*.

radiancy ['reɪdjənsɪ] = **radiance**.

radiant ['reɪdjənt] ◇ *adj* -**1.** *lit* [bright] radieux; **her ~ beauty** *fig* sa beauté éclatante. -**2.** [happy] radieux, rayonnant; **the bride was ~** la mariée était radieuse; **he was ~ with joy** il rayonnait de joie. -**3.** PHYS radiant, rayonnant. -**4.** BOT rayonnant.

◇ *n* -**1.** PHYS point *m* radiant. -**2.** ASTRON radiant *m*.

radiant flux *n* flux *m* de rayonnement.

radiant heat *n* chaleur *f* rayonnante.

radiant heating *n* chauffage *m* par rayonnement.

radiantly ['reɪdjəntlɪ] *adv* [shine, glow] avec éclat; [smile] d'un air radieux; ~ **beautiful** d'une beauté éclatante.

radiate ['reɪdɪeɪt] ◇ *vi* -**1.** [emit energy] émettre de l'énergie; [be emitted] rayonner, irradier; **heat ~s from the centre** le centre dégage de la chaleur. -**2.** [spread] rayonner; **the roads which ~ from Chicago** les routes qui partent de Chicago.

◇ *vt* -**1.** [heat] émettre, dégager; [light] émettre. -**2.** *fig*: **to ~ health** être rayonnant OR rayonner de santé; **the children ~ happiness** les enfants rayonnent de bonheur; **his manner ~d confidence** il semblait très sûr de lui.

radiation [,reɪdɪ'eɪʃn] *n* -**1.** [energy radiated] rayonnement *m*, rayonnements *mpl*; NUCL rayons *mpl*; **atomic ~** radiation *f* OR rayonnement atomique; **low-level ~** radiation de faible intensité; **~ therapy** radiothérapie *f*. -**2.** [act of radiating] rayonnement *m*, radiation *f*.

radiation sickness *n* mal *m* des rayons.

radiator ['reɪdɪeɪtə^r] *n* [gen & AUT] radiateur *m*; ~ **grille** calandre *f*.

radical ['rædɪkl] ◇ *adj* radical.

◇ *n* -**1.** POL radical *m*, -e *f*. -**2.** LING, MATH & CHEM radical *m*.

radicalism ['rædɪkəlɪzm] *n* radicalisme *m*.

radically ['rædɪklɪ] *adv* radicalement.

radicand ['rædɪkænd] *n* MATH quantité *f* radicale.

radices ['reɪdɪsiːz] *pl* → **radix**.

radicle ['rædɪkl] *n* -**1.** BOT [part of plant embryo] radicule *f*; [rootlet] radicelle *f*. -**2.** CHEM radical *m*.

radii ['reɪdɪaɪ] *pl* → **radius**.

radio ['reɪdɪəʊ] (*pl* radios) ◇ *n* -**1.** [apparatus] radio *f*; **to turn the ~ on/off** allumer/éteindre la radio. -**2.** [system] radio *f*; **they talk to base by ~** ils communiquent avec la base par radio || [industry, activity] radio; **I heard it on the ~** je l'ai entendu à la radio; **to be on the ~** passer à la radio; **Radio Birmingham** Radio Birmingham.

◇ *comp* [broadcast, play, programme] radiophonique; [contact, link, silence] radio *(inv)*; [announcer, technician] à la radio.

◇ *vt* -**1.** [person] appeler OR contacter par radio. -**2.** [message, information] envoyer par radio; [position, movement] signaler par radio.

◇ *vi* envoyer un message radio; **to ~ for a doctor** demander un médecin par radio; **she ~ed for help/instructions** elle demanda de l'aide/des instructions par radio.

RADIO:

Les principales stations de radio de la BBC sont: Radio 1 (bulletins d'information, musique pop et rock); Radio 2 (variétés, sports); Radio 3 (musique classique); Radio 4 (actualités, reportages, théâtre, programmes éducatifs); Radio 5 (sports, programmes éducatifs). La BBC comprend également 39 stations locales. Il existe d'autre part plus de 100 stations indépendantes, dont deux diffusent à l'échelle nationale (Classic FM et Independent Music Radio).

---

radioactive [,reɪdɪəʊ'æktɪv] *adj* radioactif; ~ **fallout** retombées *fpl* radioactives; ~ **waste** déchets *mpl* radioactifs OR nucléaires.

radioactivity [,reɪdɪəʊæk'tɪvətɪ] *n* radioactivité *f*.

radio alarm (clock) *n* radioréveil *m*.

radio astronomy *n* radioastronomie *f*.

radio beacon *n* radiobalise *f*.

radio beam *n* faisceau *m* radio.

radiobiology [,reɪdɪəʊbaɪ'ɒlədʒɪ] *n* radiobiologie *f*.

radio car *n* voiture *f* radio.

radiocarbon [,reɪdɪəʊ'kɑːbən] *n* radiocarbone *m*, carbone 14 *m*.

radiocarbon dating *n* datation *f* au carbone 14.

radio cassette *n* radiocassette *m*.

radiocast ['reɪdɪəʊkɑːst] *vt Am* radiodiffuser.

radiochemistry [,reɪdɪəʊ'kemɪstrɪ] *n* radiochimie *f*.

radiocommunication ['reɪdɪəʊkə,mjuːnɪ'keɪʃn] *n* radiocommunication *f*.

radio compass *n* radiocompas *m*.

radio control *n* télécommande *f* (par) radio, radiocommande *f*.

radio-controlled *adj* radioguidé.

radioelement [,reɪdɪəʊ'elɪmənt] *n* radioélément *m*.

radio frequency *n* fréquence *f* radioélectrique, radiofréquence *f*.

radiogram ['reɪdɪəʊ,græm] *n* -**1.** *dated* [radio and record player] radio *f* avec pick-up. -**2.** [message] radiogramme *m*. -**3.** = **radiograph**.

radiograph ['reɪdɪəʊgrɑːf] *n* radiographie *f*.

radiographer [,reɪdɪ'ɒgrəfə^r] *n* radiologue *mf*, radiologiste *mf*.

radiography [,reɪdɪ'ɒgrəfɪ] *n* radiographie *f*.

radio ham *n* radioamateur *m*.

radioisotope [,reɪdɪəʊ'aɪsətəʊp] *n* radioisotope *m*, isotope *m* radioactif.

radiological [,reɪdɪə'lɒdʒɪkl] *adj* radiologique.

radiologist [,reɪdɪ'ɒlədʒɪst] *n* radiologue *mf*, radiologiste *mf*.

radiology [,reɪdɪ'ɒlədʒɪ] *n* radiologie *f*.

radiometer [,reɪdɪ'ɒmɪtə^r] *n* radiomètre *m*.

radio microphone *n* microphone *m* sans fil.

radionuclide [,reɪdɪəʊ'njuːklaɪd] *n* nucléide *m* radioactif.

radiopager ['reɪdɪəʊ,peɪdʒə^r] *n* récepteur *m* d'appel OR de poche.

radiophone ['reɪdɪəʊfəʊn] = **radiotelephone**.

radioscopic [,reɪdɪəʊ'skɒpɪk] *adj*: ~ **image** radiophotographie *f*.

radioscopy [,reɪdɪ'ɒskəpɪ] *n* radioscopie *f*.

radiosonde ['reɪdɪəʊsɒnd] *n* radiosonde *f*.

radio star *n* radiosource *f*.

radio station *n* station *f* de radio.

radio taxi *n* radio-taxi *m*.

radiotelegraph [,reɪdɪəʊ'telɪgrɑːf] ◇ *n* radiotélégraphie *f*.

◇ *vt* envoyer par radiotélégraphie.

radiotelegraphy [,reɪdɪəʊtɪ'legrəfɪ] *n* radiotélégraphie *f*.

radiotelephone [,reɪdɪəʊ'telɪfəʊn] *n* radiotéléphone *m*.

radiotelephony [,reɪdɪəʊtɪ'lefənɪ] *n* radiotéléphonie *f*.

radio telescope *n* radiotélescope *m*.

radiotherapist [,reɪdɪəʊ'θerəpɪst] *n* radiothérapeute *mf*.

radiotherapy [,reɪdɪəʊ'θerəpɪ] *n* radiothérapie *f*.

radio wave *n* onde *f* hertzienne OR radioélectrique.

radish ['rædɪʃ] *n* radis *m*.

radium ['reɪdɪəm] *n* radium *m*; ~ **therapy** OR **treatment** curiethérapie *f*.

radius ['reɪdɪəs] (*pl* radiuses OR radii [-dɪaɪ]) *n* -**1.** [gen & MATH] rayon *m*; **within** OR **in a ~ of 20 km** dans un rayon de 20 km; ~ **of action** MIL rayon d'action. -**2.** ANAT radius *m*.

radix ['reɪdɪks] (*pl* radices [-dɪsiːz]) *n* -**1.** MATH base *f*. -**2.** LING radical *m*.

radon (gas) ['reɪdɒn-] *n* radon *m*.

RAF (*abbr of* Royal Air Force) *pr n armée de l'air britannique*.

raffia ['ræfɪə] *n* raphia *m*.

raffish ['ræfɪʃ] *adj* dissolu.

raffle ['ræfl] ◇ *n* tombola *f*; ~ **ticket** billet *m* de tombola.

◇ *vt*: **to ~ (off)** mettre en tombola.

raft [rɑːft] ◇ *n* -**1.** [craft - gen] radeau *m*; [- inflatable] matelas *m* pneumatique; SPORT raft *m*. -**2.** [logs] train *m* de flottage. -**3.** *inf* [large

amount] tas *m*, flopée *f*; we've got ~s of OR a ~ of mail nous avons reçu des tas de lettres. -**4.** CONSTR radier *m*.
◇ *vt*: they ~ wood down the river ils envoient le bois en aval dans des trains de flottage.
◇ *vi* voyager en radeau; to go ~ing SPORT faire du rafting.

rafter ['rɑːftəʳ] *n* CONSTR chevron *m*.

rag [ræg] (*pt* & *pp* ragged, *cont* ragging) ◇ *n* -**1.** [cloth] chiffon *m*; he wiped his hands on a ~ il s'essuya les mains avec un chiffon; a piece of ~ un bout de chiffon ❑ to chew the ~ *inf* discuter le bout de gras; to feel like a wet ~ *inf* [physically] être crevé; [emotionally] être vidé; to lose one's ~ *inf* se mettre en boule; to be a red ~ to a bull: when he said that to her it was like a red ~ to a bull elle a vu rouge après ce qu'il lui a dit. -**2.** [worn-out garment] loque *f*; this old dress is an absolute ~ cette vieille robe est une vraie loque. -**3.** [shred, scrap] lambeau *m*; torn to ~s mis en lambeaux. -**4.** *inf pej* [newspaper] feuille *f* de chou; the local ~ la feuille de chou du coin. -**5.** ▽ *Am* [sanitary towel] serviette *f* hygiénique; to be on the ~ avoir ses ragnagnas. -**6.** *Br* UNIV: ~ mag *magazine humoristique publié pendant 'rag week'*; ~ (week) *semaine pendant laquelle les étudiants préparent des divertissements, surtout au profit des œuvres charitables*. -**7.** *Br* [joke] farce *f*, canular *m*. -**8.** MUS ragtime *m*.
◇ *vt* [tease] taquiner; they ragged her about her accent ils la taquinaient au sujet de son accent.
◆ **rags** *npl* [worn-out clothes] guenilles *fpl*, haillons *mpl*, loques *fpl*; a tramp dressed in ~s un clochard vêtu de haillons; in ~s and tatters en loques ❑ to go from ~s to riches passer de la misère à la richesse; a ~s-to-riches story un véritable conte de fées.

raga ['rɑːgə] *n* raga *m inv*.

ragamuffin ['rægəˌmʌfɪn] *n* [vagrant] va-nu-pieds *m inv*, gueux *m*, gueuse *f*; [urchin] galopin *m*, polisson *m*, -onne *f*.

rag-and-bone man *n Br* chiffonnier *m*.

ragbag ['rægbæg] *n Br fig* ramassis *m*, bric-à-brac *m inv*, fouillis *m*; a ~ of ideas un fouillis d'idées (confuses).

rag doll *n* poupée *f* de chiffon.

rage [reɪdʒ] ◇ *n* -**1.** [anger] rage *f*, fureur *f*; the boss was in a ~ le patron était furieux; to fly into a ~ entrer dans une rage folle; a fit of ~ un accès OR une crise de rage. -**2.** *inf* [fashion] mode *f*; to be all the ~ faire fureur. -**3.** [of sea, elements] furie *f*.
◇ *vi* -**1.** [person] être furieux, s'emporter; he was raging against the Government il pestait contre le gouvernement. -**2.** [sea] se déchaîner; [storm, war] faire rage; a gun battle was raging in the valley une fusillade faisait rage dans la vallée; the plague was raging throughout Europe la peste ravageait l'Europe; the argument still ~s la question est toujours très controversée.

ragged ['rægɪd] *adj* -**1.** [tattered - clothes] en lambeaux, en loques, en haillons; [- person] loqueteux, vêtu de loques OR de haillons. -**2.** [uneven] irrégulier; the ~ coastline la côte accidentée; a ~ edge un bord irrégulier; they formed a ~ line ils se mirent en file irrégulière. -**3.** [erratic - performance] inégal, décousu. -**4.** *phr*: to run sb ~ *inf* éreinter OR crever qqn; I've been running myself ~ for you! je me suis vraiment décarcassé pour toi!

ragged robin *n* fleur *f* de coucou *(lychnis)*.

raggedy *inf* ['rægɪdɪ] *adj* en loques.

raggle-taggle *inf* ['rægl̩ˌtægl] *adj Br* débraillé, négligé.

raging ['reɪdʒɪŋ] *adj* -**1.** [intense - pain] insupportable, atroce; [- fever] violent; I had ~ toothache j'avais une rage de dents; I've got a ~ thirst je meurs de soif; ~ anticlericalism un anticléricalisme virulent. -**2.** [storm, blizzard] déchaîné, violent; [sea] démonté; [torrent] furieux. -**3.** [person] furieux.

raglan ['ræglən] ◇ *n* raglan *m*.
◇ *adj* raglan *(inv)*.

ragman ['rægmən] (*pl* ragmen [-mən]) = **rag-and-bone man**.

ragout ['rægu:] *n* ragoût *m*.

rag-rolling *n* CONSTR *technique qui consiste à appliquer la peinture à l'aide d'un chiffon*.

ragtag ['rægtæg] *Br* ◇ *adj* de bric et de broc.
◇ *n*: the ~ and bobtail la racaille, la populace.

ragtime ['rægtaɪm] *n* ragtime *m*.

rag trade *inf n* confection *f*; he's in the ~ il est OR travaille dans les fringues.

ragweed ['rægwi:d] *n* ambroisie *f* BOT, ambrosia *f*.

rag week = **rag** *n* **6**.

ragworm ['rægwɜːm] *n* néréide *f*, néréis *m*.

ragwort ['rægwɜːt] *n* jacobée *f*, herbe *f* de Saint-Jacques.

rah [rɑː] *interj Am* hourra.

raid [reɪd] ◇ *n* -**1.** MIL raid *m*, incursion *f*; they made a ~ over the border ils ont fait une incursion de l'autre côté de la frontière; the bombing ~s on the capital les raids aériens sur la capitale; they fear a terrorist ~ on the palace ils craignent une attaque terroriste contre le palais. -**2.** [by police] descente *f*, rafle *f*; a police ~ une descente de police; a drugs ~ une descente de police (pour saisir de la drogue). -**3.** [robbery] hold-up *m*, braquage *m*; a ~ on a bank un hold-up dans une banque; a ~ on the fridge *hum* une razzia dans le frigo. -**4.** ST. EX raid *m*.
◇ *vt* -**1.** MIL [subj: army] faire un raid OR une incursion dans; [subj: airforce] bombarder. -**2.** [subj: police] faire une descente OR une rafle dans. -**3.** [subj: thieves]: to ~ a bank dévaliser une banque; somebody's ~ed my locker quelqu'un a fouillé dans mon casier; to ~ the fridge *hum* dévaliser le frigo.

raider ['reɪdəʳ] *n* -**1.** MIL membre *m* d'un commando; the ~s were repelled le commando a été repoussé ❑ 'Raiders of the Lost Ark' *Spielberg* 'les Aventuriers de l'arche perdue'. -**2.** [thief] voleur *m*, -euse *f*; the bank ~s have all been arrested les auteurs du hold-up (de la banque) ont tous été arrêtés. -**3.** ST. EX: (corporate) ~ raider *m*.

raiding party ['reɪdɪŋ-] *n* commando *m*.

rail [reɪl] ◇ *n* -**1.** [bar - gen] barre *f*; [- in window, on bridge] garde-fou *m*; [- on ship] bastingage *m*; [- on balcony] balustrade *f*; [- on stairway] rampe *f*; [- for carpet] tringle *f*; towel ~ porte-serviettes *m inv*. -**2.** [for train, tram] rail *m*; the live ~ le rail sous tension || [mode of transport]: to travel by ~ voyager en train; it's quicker by ~! c'est plus rapide en train! ❑ to go off the ~s [train] dérailler; *fig* [person] perdre la tête OR le nord. -**3.** ORNITH râle *m*.
◇ *comp* [traffic, transport, link, tunnel] ferroviaire; [ticket, fare] de train; [journey, travel] en train; [employee, union] des chemins de fer; [strike] des chemins de fer, des cheminots; the ~ strike has affected the whole of France la grève SNCF a touché la France entière.
◇ *vt* [enclose] clôturer.◇
◇ *vi* [complain bitterly]: to ~ against OR at pester contre; she ~ed against her fate elle fulminait contre son sort.
◆ **rails** *npl* [fencing] grille *f*; [in horseracing] corde *f*.
◆ **rail in** *vt sep* clôturer.
◆ **rail off** *vt sep* fermer (au moyen d'une barrière); the end of the hall was ~ed off une barrière interdisait l'accès au fond de la salle.

railcar ['reɪlkɑːʳ] *n* autorail *m*.

railcard ['reɪlkɑːd] *n Br carte pour jeunes ou retraités permettant de bénéficier de tarifs avantageux sur les chemins de fer britanniques*; student ~ carte *f* de réduction pour étudiant.

railhead ['reɪlhed] *n* tête *f* de ligne.

railing ['reɪlɪŋ] *n* -**1.** [barrier - gen] barrière *f*; [- on bridge] garde-fou *m*; [- on balcony] balustrade *f*. -**2.** [upright bar] barreau *m*. -**3.** = **railings**.
◆ **railings** *npl* [fence] grille *f*; she squeezed through the ~s elle se glissa entre les barreaux de la grille.

raillery ['reɪlərɪ] *n* raillerie *f*.

railroad ['reɪlrəʊd] *Am* = **railway**.

railway ['reɪlweɪ] *Br* ◇ *n* -**1.** [system, organization] chemin *m* de fer; I'd never travelled by Russian ~ OR on the Russian ~s je n'avais jamais pris le train en Russie; he works on the ~s il est cheminot. -**2.** [track] voie *f* ferrée.
◇ *comp* [bridge, traffic, travel, tunnel] ferroviaire; [company] ferroviaire, de chemin de fer; [journey] en train; [employee, union] des chemins de fer; ~ worker cheminot *m*.

railway carriage *n Br* wagon *m*, voiture *f*.

railway crossing *n Br* passage *m* à niveau.

railway embankment *n Br* remblai *m*.

railway engine *n Br* locomotive *f*.

railway line *n Br* -**1.** [route] ligne *f* de chemin de fer. -**2.** [track] voie *f* ferrée; [rail] rail *m*.

railwayman ['reɪlweɪmən] (*pl* railwaymen [-mən]) *n Br* cheminot *m*.

railway station *n Br* [gen] gare *f* (de chemin de fer); [in France] gare *f* SNCF.

railway track *n Br* voie *f* ferrée.

railway yard *n Br* dépôt *m*.

raiment ['reɪmənt] *n (U) lit* atours *mpl*.

rain [reɪn] ◇ *n* -**1.** *literal* pluie *f*; it was pouring with ~ il pleuvait à verse; the ~ was heavy il pleuvait beaucoup; a light ~ was falling il tombait une pluie fine; come in out of the ~ rentre, ne reste pas sous la pluie; it looks like ~ on dirait qu'il va pleuvoir; Venice in the ~ Venise sous la pluie; the ~s la saison des pluies ❑ come ~ or shine quoi qu'il arrive; don't worry, you'll be as right as ~ in a minute *inf* ne t'inquiète pas, ça va passer. -**2.** *fig* [of projectiles, blows] pluie *f*.
◇ *vi* pleuvoir; it's ~ing il pleut; arrows ~ed from the sky des flèches pleuvaient du ciel ❑ it's ~ing cats and dogs *inf* il pleut des cordes, il tombe des hallebardes; it never ~s but it pours *Br prov*, when it rains, it pours *Am prov* un malheur n'arrive jamais seul *prov*.
◇ *vt* faire pleuvoir; they ~ed blows on his head ils firent pleuvoir des coups sur sa tête.
◆ **rain down** ◇ *vi insep* [projectiles, blows etc] pleuvoir.
◇ *vt sep* [projectiles, blows etc] faire pleuvoir.
◆ **rain off** *vt sep Br*: the game was ~ed off [cancelled] la partie a été annulée à cause de la pluie; [abandoned] la partie a été abandonnée à cause de la pluie.
◆ **rain out** *vt sep* -**1.** [campers]: to be ~ed out être chassé par la pluie. -**2.** *Am* = **rain off**.

rainbelt ['reɪnbelt] *n* zone *f* des pluies.

rainbow ['reɪnbəʊ] ◇ *n* arc-en-ciel *m*; all the colours of the ~ toutes les couleurs de l'arc-en-ciel ❑ it's at the end of the ~ c'est un mirage; to chase ~s se bercer d'illusions.
◇ *comp*: ~ coalition *coalition représentant un large éventail de tendances*.

rainbow-coloured *adj* arc-en-ciel *(inv)*, multicolore.

rainbow trout *n* truite *f* arc-en-ciel.

rain check *n Am bon pour un autre match (ou spectacle) donné par suite d'une annulation à cause de la pluie*; I'll take a ~ on that *inf fig* ça sera pour une autre fois.

rain cloud *n* nuage *m* de pluie.

raincoat ['reɪnkəʊt] *n* imperméable *m*.

rain dance *n* danse *f* de la pluie.

raindrop ['reɪndrɒp] *n* goutte *f* de pluie.

rainfall ['reɪnfɔːl] *n* [amount of rain] pluviosité *f*.

rainforest ['reɪnˌfɒrɪst] *n* forêt *f* pluviale.

rain gauge *n* pluviomètre *m*.

rainless ['reɪnlɪs] *adj* sans pluie.

rainmaker ['reɪnˌmeɪkəʳ] *n* faiseur *m* de pluie.

rainout ['reɪnaʊt] *n* -**1.** *(U)* [pollution] *retombées entraînées par la pluie*. -**2.** *Am* SPORT *match annulé à cause du mauvais temps*.

rainproof ['reɪnpruːf] ◇ *adj* imperméable.
◇ *vt* imperméabiliser.

rainstorm ['reɪnstɔːm] *n* pluie *f* torrentielle.

rainwater ['reɪn,wɔːtəʳ] *n* eau *f* de pluie OR pluviale.

rainwear ['reɪnweəʳ] *n* (U) vêtements *mpl* de pluie.

rainy ['reɪnɪ] (*compar* rainier, *superl* rainiest) *adj* pluvieux; the ~ season la saison des pluies; to save sthg for a ~ day garder qqch pour les mauvais jours.

raise [reɪz] ◇ *vt* -**1.** [lift, move upwards - gen] lever; [- burden, lid] soulever; to ~ one's head lever la tête; she didn't ~ her eyes from her book elle n'a pas levé les yeux de son livre; he tried to ~ himself from the sofa il essaya de se lever du canapé; she ~d herself to her full height elle se dressa de toute sa hauteur. -**2.** [increase - offer, price, tax] augmenter; [- interest rates] relever; [- temperature, tension] faire monter; the speed limit has been ~d to 150 km/h la limitation de vitesse est passée à 150 km/h; the age limit has been ~d to 18 la limite d'âge a été repoussée à 18 ans. -**3.** [boost, improve] remonter, élever; our aim is to ~ overall standards notre but est d'élever le niveau global; to ~ sb's spirits remonter le moral à qqn; to ~ sb's hopes donner des espoirs à qqn. -**4.** [promote] élever, promouvoir; ~d to the rank of colonel élevé au rang de colonel; the Queen ~d him to the peerage la reine l'éleva à la pairie. -**5.** [collect together - support] réunir; [- army] lever; we have ~d over a million signatures nous avons réuni plus d'un million de signatures. -**6.** [obtain - money] trouver, obtenir; [- taxes] lever; we have to ~ $10,000 by Friday il faut que nous trouvions 10 000 dollars d'ici vendredi; they're raising funds for a new church roof ils collectent des fonds pour construire un nouveau toit à l'église. -**7.** [make, produce]: they ~d a cheer when she came in ils ont poussé des bravos quand elle est entrée; to ~ the alarm donner l'alarme; he managed to ~ a smile when he saw us il a réussi à sourire en nous voyant ❑ to ~ hell *inf* OR Cain *inf* OR the roof *inf* [make a noise] faire un boucan de tous les diables; [cause a fuss] faire un scandale. -**8.** [cause as reaction - laugh, welt, blister] provoquer; his jokes didn't even ~ a smile ses plaisanteries n'ont même pas fait sourire. -**9.** *esp Am* [rear - children, family] élever. -**10.** *esp Am* [breed - livestock] élever; [grow - crops] cultiver. -**11.** [introduce, bring up - point, subject, question] soulever; she ~d several objections elle souleva plusieurs objections; this might ~ doubts as to his competence ça pourrait soulever OR susciter des doutes quant à ses compétences. -**12.** [erect] élever, ériger; to ~ a statue to sb ériger une statue en l'honneur de qqn. -**13.** [resuscitate] ressusciter; [evoke - spirit] évoquer; they were making enough noise to ~ the dead ils faisaient un bruit à réveiller les morts. -**14.** [end - ban, siege] lever. -**15.** [contact] contacter; the radio officer was trying to ~ Boston le radio essayait de contacter Boston. -**16.** [in bridge] monter sur; [in poker] relancer; I'll ~ you 5 pounds je relance de 5 livres. -**17.** CULIN [dough, bread] faire lever. -**18.** MATH élever; to ~ a number to the power of n élever un nombre à la puissance n. -**19.** NAUT: to ~ land arriver en vue de terre.
◇ *vi* [in bridge] monter, enchérir; [in poker] relancer.
◇ *n* -**1.** *Am* [pay increase] augmentation *f* de salaire. -**2.** [in bridge] enchère *f*; [in poker] relance *f*.
◆ **raise up** *vt sep*: to ~ o.s. up se soulever; she ~d herself up onto the chair elle se hissa sur la chaise.

raised [reɪzd] *adj* -**1.** [ground, platform, jetty etc] surélevé; [pattern] en relief. -**2.** CULIN levé, à la levure. -**3.** LING [vowel] haut. -**4.** TEX cardé, gratté.

raised beach *n* GEOG plage *f* soulevée.

raiser ['reɪzəʳ] *n* [of livestock] éleveur *m*, -euse *f*; [of crops] cultivateur *m*, -trice *f*.

raisin ['reɪzn] *n* raisin *m* sec.

raising agent ['reɪzɪŋ-] *n* (C) levure *f*.

Raj [rɑːdʒ] *n*: the ~ l'empire *m* britannique (en Inde).

rajah ['rɑːdʒə] *n* raja *m*, rajah *m*, radjah *m*.

rake [reɪk] ◇ *n* -**1.** [in garden, casino] râteau *m*. -**2.** [libertine] roué *m*, libertin *m*; 'The Rake's Progress' *Hogarth* 'la Carrière du roué'; *Stravinsky* 'le Libertin'. -**3.** THEAT pente *f*; NAUT [of mast, funnel] quête *f*.
◇ *vt* -**1.** [soil, lawn, path] ratisser, râteler; she ~d the leaves into a pile elle ratissa les feuilles en tas. -**2.** [search] fouiller (dans); to ~ one's memory fouiller dans ses souvenirs. -**3.** [scan] balayer; his eyes ~d the audience son regard parcourut l'assistance; a searchlight ~d the darkness un projecteur fouilla l'obscurité. -**4.** [strafe] balayer; machine-gun fire ~d the trench le feu d'une mitrailleuse balaya la tranchée.
◇ *vi* -**1.** [search]: to ~ among OR through fouiller dans. -**2.** [slope] être en pente, être incliné.
◆ **rake in** *inf vt sep* [money] ramasser; to be racking it in toucher un joli paquet.
◆ **rake off** *inf vt sep* [share of profits] empocher, ramasser; he was raking off 10% of the profits il empochait OR ramassait 10 % des bénéfices.
◆ **rake out** *vt sep* -**1.** [fire] enlever les cendres de; [ashes] enlever. -**2.** [search out] dénicher.
◆ **rake over** *vt sep* -**1.** [soil, lawn, path] ratisser. -**2.** *fig* remuer; why ~ over the past? pourquoi remuer le passé?
◆ **rake up** *vt sep* -**1.** [collect together - leaves, weeds] ratisser; [- people] réunir, rassembler. -**2.** [dredge up] déterrer; to ~ up sb's past fouiller dans le passé de qqn.

raked [reɪkt] *adj* [inclined] incliné.

rake-off *inf n* petit profit *m*.

rakish ['reɪkɪʃ] *adj* -**1.** [jaunty] désinvolte, insouciant; he wore his hat at a ~ angle il portait son chapeau avec désinvolture. -**2.** [boat] à la forme élancée, allongé.

rale [rɑːl] *n* MED râle *m*.

rally ['rælɪ] (*pl* rallies, *pt* & *pp* rallied) ◇ *n* -**1.** [gathering - gen] rassemblement *m*; MIL [during battle] ralliement *m*; POL rassemblement *m*, (grand) meeting *m*. -**2.** [recovery - gen] amélioration *f*; ST. EX reprise *f*; the England team staged a ~ in the second half l'équipe anglaise s'est reprise au cours de la deuxième mi-temps. -**3.** AUT rallye *m*; the Monte Carlo ~ le rallye de Monte-Carlo; ~ driver pilote *m* de rallye. -**4.** SPORT (long) échange *m*.
◇ *vi* -**1.** [assemble, gather - gen] se rassembler; [- troops, supporters] se rallier; they rallied to the party/to the defence of their leader ils se sont ralliés au parti/pour défendre leur chef. -**2.** [recover - gen] s'améliorer; [- sick person] aller mieux, reprendre des forces; [- stock market, share prices] se reprendre; the pound rallied in the afternoon la livre est remontée dans l'après-midi. -**3.** AUT faire des rallyes; to go ~ing faire un rallye.
◇ *vt* -**1.** [gather] rallier, rassembler; she's trying to ~ support for her project elle essaie de rallier des gens pour soutenir son projet. -**2.** [summon up] reprendre; to ~ one's spirits reprendre ses esprits. -**3.** [boost] ranimer; the news rallied their morale la nouvelle leur a remonté le moral. -**4.** *arch* [tease] taquiner.
◆ **rally round** ◇ *vi insep*: all her family rallied round toute sa famille est venue lui apporter son soutien.
◇ *vt insep*: they rallied round her ils lui ont apporté leur soutien.

rallycross ['rælɪkrɒs] *n Br* rallye-cross *m*.

rallying ['rælɪɪŋ] *adj*: ~ cry/point cri *m*/point *m* de ralliement.

ram [ræm] (*pt* & *pp* rammed, *cont* ramming) ◇ *n* -**1.** ZOOL bélier *m*. -**2.** HIST: (battering) ~ bélier *m*. -**3.** TECH [piston] piston *m*; [flattening tool] hie *f*, dame *f*; [pile driver] mouton *m*; [lifting pump] bélier *m* hydraulique.
◇ *vt* -**1.** [bang into] percuter; NAUT aborder; [in battle] éperonner; the police car rammed them twice la voiture de police les a percutés deux fois. -**2.** [push] pousser (violemment); a table had been rammed up against the door une table avait été poussée contre la porte; she rammed the bolt home elle repoussa le verrou (violemment); she rammed the papers into her bag elle fourra les papiers dans son sac; he rammed his pipe with tobacco il bourra sa pipe; in order to ~ home the point *fig* pour enfoncer le clou.
◇ *vi*: to ~ into sthg entrer dans OR percuter qqch.

RAM [ræm] (*abbr of* random access memory) *n* RAM *f*.

Ramadan [,ræmə'dæn] *n* ramadan *m*.

ramble ['ræmbl] ◇ *n* [hike] randonnée *f* (pédestre); [casual walk] promenade *f*; to go for a ~ aller faire un tour.
◇ *vi* -**1.** [hike] faire une randonnée. -**2.** [wander] se balader. -**3.** [talk] divaguer, radoter; he ~d on and on about nothing il n'arrêtait pas de parler pour ne rien dire. -**4.** [plant] pousser à tort et à travers. -**5.** [path, stream] serpenter.

rambler ['ræmbləʳ] *n* -**1.** [hiker] randonneur *m*, -euse *f*. -**2.** [in speech]: he's a bit of a ~ il est du genre radoteur. -**3.** BOT plante *f* sarmenteuse.

rambling ['ræmblɪŋ] ◇ *adj* -**1.** [building] plein de coins et de recoins. -**2.** [conversation, style] décousu; [ideas, book, thoughts] incohérent, sans suite; [person] qui divague, qui radote. -**3.** [plant] sarmenteux; ~ rose rosier *m* sarmenteux.
◇ *n* [hiking] randonnée *f*; to go ~ aller en randonnée.

rambunctious [ræm'bʌŋkʃəs] *adj* remuant, turbulent.

rambutan ['ræmbuːtn] *n* ramboutan *m*.

RAMC (*abbr of* Royal Army Medical Corps) *pr n service de santé des armées britanniques*.

ramekin, ramequin ['ræmɪkɪn] *n* ramequin *m*.

Rameses ['ræmɪsiːz] = **Ramses**.

ramification [,ræmɪfɪ'keɪʃn] *n* -**1.** [implication] implication *f*; I'm not sure if you understand all the ~s of this decision je ne suis pas sûr que vous compreniez toutes les conséquences qu'aura cette décision. -**2.** [branching] ramification *f*.

ramify ['ræmɪfaɪ] (*pt* & *pp* ramified) ◇ *vt* ramifier.
◇ *vi* se ramifier.

ramjet ['ræmdʒet] *n* [engine] statoréacteur *m*, tuyère *f* thermopropulsive; [aircraft] avion *m* à statoréacteur.

ramp [ræmp] *n* pente *f*, rampe *f*; [in road works] dénivellation *f*.

rampage [ræm'peɪdʒ] ◇ *n* fureur *f*; to be on the ~ être déchaîné; to go on the ~ se livrer à des actes de violence; football fans went on the ~ through the town des supporters de football ont saccagé la ville; the headmaster's on the ~! le directeur est déchaîné!
◇ *vi* se déchaîner; a herd of elephants ~d through the bush un troupeau d'éléphants avançait dans la brousse en balayant tout sur son passage; they ~d through the town ils ont saccagé la ville.

rampant ['ræmpənt] *adj* -**1.** [unrestrained] déchaîné, effréné; they're ~ Marxists ce sont des marxistes purs et durs; corruption is ~ la corruption sévit; the disease is ~ la maladie fait des ravages. -**2.** [exuberant - vegetation] exubérant, foisonnant. -**3.** (*after n*) HERALD rampant.

rampart ['ræmpɑːt] ◇ *n literal* & *fig* rempart *m*.
◇ *vt* fortifier (d'un rempart).

rampion ['ræmpjən] *n* raiponce *f*.

ramraider ['ræm,reɪdəʳ] *n personne qui cambriole les magasins en fracassant les vitrines avec sa voiture*.

ramrod ['ræmrɒd] ◇ *n* baguette *f (d'arme à feu)*; to sit/to stand as stiff as a ~ être assis/se tenir raide comme un piquet.
◇ *adv*: the sentry stood ~ straight la sentinelle se tenait debout, raide comme un piquet.

Ramses ['ræmsiːz] *pr n* Ramsès.

ramshackle ['ræm,ʃækl] *adj* délabré.
ramshorn snail ['ræmz,hɔːn-] *n* planorbe *f*.
ran [ræn] *pt* → **run**.
RAN (*abbr of* Royal Australian Navy) *pr n* *marine de guerre australienne*.
ranch [rɑːntʃ] *Am* ◇ *n* ranch *m*; chicken ~ élevage *m* de poulets.
◇ *comp*: ~ hand ouvrier *m* agricole; ~ house *maison basse faisant partie d'un ranch*.
◇ *vi* exploiter un ranch.◇
◇ *vt*: to ~ cattle élever du bétail (sur un ranch).
rancher ['rɑːntʃər] *n* [owner] propriétaire *mf* de ranch; [manager] exploitant *m*, -e *f* de ranch; [worker] garçon *m* de ranch, cow-boy *m*.
ranching ['rɑːntʃɪŋ] *n* exploitation *f* d'un ranch; cattle/chicken ~ élevage *m* de bétail/de poulets.
rancid ['rænsɪd] *adj* rance; to go OR to turn ~ rancir.
rancor *Am* = **rancour**.
rancorous ['ræŋkərəs] *adj* rancunier.
rancour *Br*, **rancor** *Am* ['ræŋkər] *n* rancœur *f*, rancune *f*.
rand [rænd] (*pl inv*) *n* [money] rand *m*.
R and B *n abbr of* rhythm and blues.
R and D *n abbr of* research and development.
random ['rændəm] *adj* aléatoire, fait OR choisi au hasard; a ~ number un nombre aléatoire; the arrangement of the dots seems completely ~ la disposition des points semble complètement aléatoire; a ~ sample un échantillon pris au hasard; a ~ selection of goods des marchandises prises au hasard, une sélection arbitraire de marchandises; a ~ shot une balle perdue; ~ violence violence *f* aveugle.
◆ **at random** *adv phr* au hasard; chosen at ~ choisi au hasard; to lash out at ~ distribuer des coups à l'aveuglette.
random access *n* COMPUT accès *m* aléatoire OR direct.
◆ **random-access** *adj* COMPUT à accès aléatoire OR direct; random-access memory mémoire *f* vive.
randomize, -ise ['rændəmaɪz] *vt* COMPUT randomiser.
R and R (*abbr of* rest and recreation) *n* permission *f*.
randy *inf* ['rændɪ] (*compar* randier, *superl* randiest) *adj* excité; he's a ~ devil c'est un chaud lapin; a ~ old man un vieux satyre.
ranee ['rɑːnɪ] = **rani**.
rang [ræŋ] *pt* → **ring**.
range [reɪndʒ] ◇ *n* -**1.** [of missile, sound, transmitter etc] portée *f*; [of vehicle, aircraft] autonomie *f*; medium-~ OR intermediate-~ missiles missiles *mpl* à portée intermédiaire; at long/short ~ à longue/courte portée; out of ~ hors de portée; don't fire until they're within OR in ~ ne tirez pas avant qu'ils soient à portée de tir; I called to them as soon as they were in ~ je les ai appelés dès qu'ils ont été à portée de voix; it can kill a man at a ~ of 800 metres ça peut tuer un homme à une distance de 800 mètres; ~ of vision champ *m* visuel; it gives you some idea of the ~ of their powers ça vous donne une petite idée de l'étendue de leurs pouvoirs. -**2.** [bracket] gamme *f*, éventail *m*, fourchette *f*; there is a wide ~ of temperatures in these parts il existe de très grands écarts de température dans ces régions ❑ children in the same age ~ les enfants dans la même tranche d'âge; price ~ gamme OR fourchette de prix; it's within my price ~ c'est dans mes prix. -**3.** [set, selection] gamme *f*; we stock a wide ~ of office materials nous avons en stock une large gamme de matériels de bureaux; the ~ of possibilities is almost infinite l'éventail des possibilités est presque infini; we talked on a wide ~ of topics nous avons discuté de sujets très divers; it provoked a wide ~ of reactions ça a provoqué des réactions très diverses ‖ COMM: the new autumn ~ [of clothes] la nouvelle collection d'automne; this car is the top/bottom of the ~ cette voiture est le modèle haut/bas de gamme. -**4.** *fig* [scope] champ *m*, domaine *m*; that is beyond the ~ of the present inquiry cela ne relève pas de cette enquête; that lies outside the ~ of my responsibility ça dépasse les limites de ma responsabilité. -**5.** [of mountains] chaîne *f*. -**6.** [prairie] prairie *f*. -**7.** [practice area]: (shooting OR firing OR rifle) ~ champ *m* de tir; missile ~ champ *m* de tir de missiles. -**8.** MUS [of instrument] étendue *f*, portée *f*; [of voice] tessiture *f*. -**9.** [cooker] fourneau *m* (de cuisine). -**10.** [row, line] rang *m*, rangée *f*. -**11.** BIOL [habitat] habitat *m*.
◇ *vi* -**1.** [vary] aller, s'étendre; their ages ~ from 5 to 12 OR between 5 and 12 ils ont de 5 à 12 OR entre 5 et 12 ans; the quality ~s from mediocre to excellent la qualité varie de médiocre à excellent. -**2.** [roam]: to ~ over parcourir; they ~ over the countryside ils parcourent la campagne; thugs ~ through the city streets des voyous rôdent dans les rues de la ville. -**3.** [extend]: the survey ~d over the whole country l'enquête couvrait la totalité du pays; our conversation ~d over a large number of topics nous avons discuté d'un grand nombre de sujets. -**4.** [of gun]: to ~ over avoir une portée de.
◇ *vt* -**1.** [roam] parcourir. -**2.** [arrange] ranger; [put in a row or in rows] mettre OR disposer en rang OR rangs; the troops ~d themselves in front of the embassy les troupes se rangèrent devant l'ambassade; the desks are ~d in threes les pupitres sont en rangées de trois. -**3.** [join, ally] ranger, rallier; the forces ~d against me les forces ralliées contre moi. -**4.** [classify] classer, ranger. -**5.** [aim - cannon, telescope] braquer. -**6.** TYPO aligner, justifier.
rangefinder ['reɪndʒ,faɪndər] *n* télémètre *m*.
ranger ['reɪndʒər] *n* -**1.** [in park, forest] garde *m* forestier. -**2.** *Am* [lawman] ≃ gendarme *m*. -**3.** *Am* MIL ranger *m*.
◆ **Ranger (Guide)** *n* guide *m*.
Rangoon [ræŋ'guːn] *pr n* Rangoon.
rangy ['reɪndʒɪ] (*compar* rangier, *superl* rangiest) *adj* -**1.** [tall and thin] grand et élancé. -**2.** [roomy] spacieux.
rani ['rɑːnɪ] *n* rani *f*.
rank [ræŋk] ◇ *n* -**1.** [grade] rang *m*, grade *m*; promoted to the ~ of colonel promu (au rang de OR au grade de) colonel; the ~ of manager le titre de directeur ❑ to pull ~ faire valoir sa supériorité hiérarchique; I don't want to have to pull ~ on you je ne veux pas avoir à user de mon autorité sur vous. -**2.** [quality] rang *m*; we have very few players in the first OR top ~ nous avons très peu de joueurs de premier ordre. -**3.** [social class] rang *m*, condition *f* (sociale); the lower ~s of society les couches inférieures de la société. -**4.** [row, line] rang *m*, rangée *f*; [on chessboard] rangée *f*; a double ~ of policemen une double rangée de policiers ❑ to break ~s MIL rompre les rangs; *fig* se désolidariser; to close ~s MIL & *fig* serrer les rangs. -**5.** *Br*: (taxi) ~ station *f* (de taxis). -**6.** MATH [in matrix] rang *m*.
◇ *vt* -**1.** [rate] classer; she is ~ed among the best contemporary writers elle est classée parmi les meilleurs écrivains contemporains; I ~ this as one of our finest performances je considère que c'est une de nos meilleures représentations; he is ~ed number 3 il est classé numéro 3. -**2.** [arrange] ranger. -**3.** *Am* [outrank] avoir un grade supérieur à; a general ~s a captain un général est au-dessus d'un capitaine.
◇ *vi* -**1.** [rate] se classer; it ~s high/low on our list of priorities c'est/ce n'est pas une de nos priorités; he hardly ~s as an expert on ne peut guère le qualifier d'expert. -**2.** *Am* MIL être l'officier supérieur.
◇ *adj* -**1.** [as intensifier] complet, véritable; it's a ~ injustice c'est une injustice flagrante; he is a ~ outsider in this competition il fait figure d'outsider dans cette compétition. -**2.** [foul-smelling] infect, fétide; [rancid] rance; his shirt was ~ with sweat sa chemise empestait la sueur. -**3.** [coarse - person, language] grossier. -**4.** *lit* [profuse - vegetation] luxuriant; [- weeds] prolifique.
◆ **ranks** *npl* -**1.** [members] rangs *mpl*; to join the ~s of the opposition/unemployed rejoindre les rangs de l'opposition/des chômeurs. -**2.** MIL [rank and file]: the ~s, other ~s les hommes du rang; to come up through OR to rise from the ~s sortir du rang; to reduce an officer to the ~s dégrader un officier.
-rank *in cpds*: top~ grand, majeur; second~ petit, mineur.
rank and file *n*: the ~ MIL les hommes du rang; POL la base; we'll have to consult the ~ il faudra que nous consultions la base.
◆ **rank-and-file** *adj* de la base; to protect rank-and-file interests protéger les intérêts de la base.
ranker ['ræŋkər] *n* MIL [private] homme *m* du rang; [officer] officier *m* sorti du rang.
ranking ['ræŋkɪŋ] ◇ *n* classement *m*.
◇ *adj Am* -**1.** MIL: ~ officer officier *m* responsable. -**2.** [prominent] de premier ordre.
-ranking *in cpds*: high~ de haut rang OR grade; low~ de bas niveau.
rankle ['ræŋkl] *vi*: their decision still ~s with me leur décision m'est restée en travers de la gorge.
rankness ['ræŋknɪs] *n* -**1.** [smell] puanteur *f*; [taste] rance *m*. -**2.** *lit* [luxuriance - of vegetation] luxuriance *f*, profusion *f*.
ransack ['rænsæk] *vt* -**1.** [plunder] saccager, mettre à sac; the burglars had ~ed his flat les cambrioleurs avaient saccagé son appartement. -**2.** [search] fouiller, retourner; he ~ed the wardrobe for his tie il mit l'armoire sens dessus dessous pour trouver sa cravate.
ransom ['rænsəm] ◇ *n* rançon *f*; the family paid the ~ (money) la famille a payé la rançon; they held her to ~ ils l'ont kidnappée pour avoir une rançon; they're holding the country to ~ *fig* ils tiennent le pays en otage ❑ a king's ~ une fortune.
◇ *vt* rançonner.
rant [rænt] *vi* fulminer; they ~ed on and on ils n'arrêtaient pas de fulminer; to ~ at sb fulminer contre qqn; to ~ and rave tempêter, tonitruer.
ranter ['ræntər] *n* énergumène *mf*, exalté *m*, -e *f*.
ranting ['ræntɪŋ] ◇ *n (U)* vociférations *fpl*.
◇ *adj* déclamatoire.
ranunculus [rə'nʌŋkjʊləs] *n* renoncule *f*.
rap [ræp] (*pt* & *pp* rapped, *cont* rapping)
◇ *vt* -**1.** [strike] frapper sur, cogner sur; she rapped the desk elle frappa sur le bureau; to ~ sb's knuckles, to ~ sb over the knuckles *fig* sermonner qqn. -**2.** [in newspaper headlines] réprimander.
◇ *vi* -**1.** [knock] frapper, cogner; somebody rapped on the door quelqu'un a frappé (à la porte). -**2.** *inf Am* [chat] bavarder, discuter le bout de gras. -**3.** MUS jouer du rap.
◇ *n* -**1.** [blow, sound] coup *m* (sec); [rebuke] réprimande *f*; to be given a ~ over OR on the knuckles *fig* se faire taper sur les doigts; to take the ~ for sthg *inf* écoper pour qqch. -**2.** ▽ *Am* [legal charge] accusation *f*; he's up on a murder/drugs ~ il est accusé de meurtre/dans une affaire de drogue; it's a bum ~ c'est un coup monté; to beat the ~ échapper à la justice. -**3.** *inf Am* [chat]: ~ session bavardage *m*; we had a good ~ session on a discuté pendant un bon bout de temps. -**4.** MUS rap *m*. -**5.** *inf Br phr*: I don't care a ~! je m'en fiche (pas mal)!
◆ **rap out** *vt sep* -**1.** [say sharply] lancer, lâcher; she rapped out an order elle lança un ordre. -**2.** [tap out - message] taper.
rapacious [rə'peɪʃəs] *adj* rapace.
rapaciously [rə'peɪʃəslɪ] *adv* avec rapacité OR avidité.
rapaciousness [rə'pəɪʃəsnɪs], **rapacity** [rə'pæsətɪ] *n* rapacité *f*.
rape [reɪp] ◇ *n* -**1.** [sex crime] viol *m*; to commit ~ perpétrer un viol; ~ victim victime *f* d'un

viol; the ~ of the countryside *fig* la dévastation de la campagne □ ~ crisis centre centre d'accueil pour femmes violées. -**2.** *arch* [abduction] rapt *m*; 'The Rape of the Lock' *Pope* 'la Boucle dérobée'; 'The Rape of the Sabine Women' 'l'Enlèvement des Sabines'. -**3.** BOT colza *m*. -**4.** [remains of grapes] marc *m* (de raisin).
◇ *vt* violer.

rape oil *n* huile *f* de colza.

rapeseed ['reɪpsi:d] *n* graine *f* de colza; ~ oil = **rape oil**.

Raphael ['ræfeɪəl] *pr n* Raphaël.

rapid ['ræpɪd] *adj* rapide; in ~ succession en une succession rapide; a ~ pulse un pouls rapide.
◆ **rapids** *npl* rapide *m*, rapides *mpl*; to shoot the ~s franchir le rapide OR les rapides.

rapid eye movement *n mouvement des globes oculaires pendant le sommeil paradoxal*.

rapid-fire *adj* MIL à tir rapide; *fig* [questions, jokes] qui se succèdent à toute allure.

rapidity [rə'pɪdətɪ] *n* rapidité *f*.

rapidly ['ræpɪdlɪ] *adv* rapidement.

rapid transit *n Am* transport *m* urbain rapide.

rapier ['reɪpjə^r] ◇ *n* rapière *f*.
◇ *comp*: ~ thrust coup *m* de rapière; her ~ wit son esprit acerbe.

rapine ['ræpaɪn] *n lit* rapine *f*.

rapist ['reɪpɪst] *n* violeur *m*.

rapper ['ræpə^r] *n* -**1.** [on door] heurtoir *m*. -**2.** MUS musicien *m* rap.

rapport [ræ'pɔ:^r] *n* rapport *m*; I have a good ~ with him j'ai de bons rapports avec lui.

rapscallion [ræp'skæljən] *n arch* fripon *m*, -onne *f arch*, gredin *m*, -e *f*.

rapt [ræpt] *adj* -**1.** [engrossed] absorbé, captivé; the clown held the children ~ le clown fascinait les enfants; with ~ attention complètement absorbé. -**2.** [delighted] ravi; ~ with joy transporté de joie; a ~ smile un sourire ravi.

raptor ['ræptə^r] *n* rapace *m*.

rapture ['ræptʃə^r] *n* ravissement *m*, extase *f*; to go into ~s over OR about sthg s'extasier sur qqch; they were in ~s about their presents leurs cadeaux les ont ravis.

rapturous ['ræptʃərəs] *adj* [feeling] intense, profond; [gaze] ravi, extasié; [praise, applause] enthousiaste; the champions were given a ~ welcome on a réservé un accueil délirant aux champions.

rapturously ['ræptʃərəslɪ] *adv* [watch] d'un air ravi, avec ravissement; [praise, applaud] avec enthousiasme.

rare [reə^r] *adj* -**1.** [uncommon] rare; a ~ stamp un timbre rare; it's ~ to see such marital bliss nowadays un tel bonheur conjugal est rare de nos jours; on ~ occasions en de rares occasions; on the ~ occasions when I've seen him angry les rares fois où je l'ai vu en colère; a ~ opportunity une occasion exceptionnelle □ he's a ~ bird c'est un oiseau rare. -**2.** [exceptional] rare, exceptionnel; she has a ~ gift elle a un don exceptionnel. -**3.** *inf* [extreme] énorme; you gave me a ~ fright! tu m'as fait une peur bleue OR une de ces peurs! || [excellent] fameux, génial; we had a ~ old time on s'est amusés comme des fous. -**4.** [meat] saignant. -**5.** [rarefied - air, atmosphere] raréfié.

rarebit ['reəbɪt] = **Welsh rarebit**.

rare earth *n* CHEM terre *f* rare.

rarefaction [,reərɪ'fækʃn] *n* raréfaction *f*.

rarefied ['reərɪfaɪd] *adj* -**1.** [air, atmosphere] raréfié; to become ~ se raréfier. -**2.** [refined] raffiné; the ~ circles in which she moves les milieux raffinés dans lesquels elle évolue.

rarefy ['reərɪfaɪ] (*pt* & *pp* rarefied) ◇ *vt* raréfier.
◇ *vi* se raréfier.

rarely ['reəlɪ] *adv* rarement.

rareness ['reənɪs] *n* rareté *f*.

raring *inf* ['reərɪŋ] *adj* impatient; to be ~ to go ronger son frein.

rarity ['reərətɪ] (*pl* rarities) *n* -**1.** [uncommon person, thing] rareté *f*; a foreigner's a ~ in these parts les étrangers sont rares par ici. -**2.** [scarcity] rareté *f*.

rascal ['rɑ:skl] *n* -**1.** [naughty child] polisson *m*, -onne *f*. -**2.** *lit* [rogue] vaurien *m*, gredin *m*.

rascally ['rɑ:skəlɪ] *adj lit* [person] coquin; [deed] de coquin.

rash [ræʃ] ◇ *n* -**1.** MED rougeur *f*, éruption *f*; to come out in a ~ avoir une éruption; oysters bring me out in a ~ les huîtres me donnent des éruptions. -**2.** [wave, outbreak] vague *f*; a ~ of strikes une vague de grèves; last summer's ~ of air disasters la série noire de catastrophes aériennes de l'été dernier.
◇ *adj* imprudent; it was ~ of her to walk out c'était imprudent de sa part de partir comme ça; don't be ~ soyez prudent; ~ words des paroles irréfléchies; I bought it in a ~ moment je l'ai acheté dans un moment de folie OR sur un coup de tête.

rasher ['ræʃə^r] *n Br* tranche *f (de bacon)*.

rashly ['ræʃlɪ] *adv* imprudemment; I rather ~ offered to drive her home dans un moment de folie j'ai offert de la reconduire chez elle.

rashness ['ræʃnɪs] *n* imprudence *f*.

rasp [rɑ:sp] ◇ *n* -**1.** [file] râpe *f*. -**2.** [sound] bruit *m* de râpe; the ~ in his voice sa voix rauque.
◇ *vt* -**1.** [scrape, file] râper. -**2.** [say] dire d'une voix rauque.
◇ *vi* [make rasping noise] grincer, crisser.
◆ **rasp out** *vt sep* crier d'une voix rauque.

raspberry ['rɑ:zbərɪ] (*pl* raspberries) ◇ *n* -**1.** [fruit] framboise *f*. -**2.** [noise]: to blow a ~ faire pfft *(en signe de dérision)*; the announcement was greeted with a chorus of raspberries la nouvelle fut accueillie par des sifflements.
◇ *comp* [jam] de framboises; [tart] aux framboises; ~ bush OR cane framboisier *m* BOT.
◇ *adj* [colour] framboise *(inv)*.

rasping ['rɑ:spɪŋ] ◇ *adj* [noise] grinçant, crissant; [voice] grinçant.
◇ *n* [noise] grincement *m*, crissement *m*.

Rasputin [ræ'spju:tɪn] *pr n* Raspoutine.

Rasta ['ræstə] ◇ *n* (*abbr of* Rastafarian) rasta *mf*.
◇ *adj* rasta *(inv)*.

Rastafarian [,ræstə'feərɪən] ◇ *n* rastafari *mf*.
◇ *adj* rastafari *(inv)*.

Rastafarianism [,ræstə'feərɪənɪzm] *n* rastafarisme *m*.

raster ['ræstə^r] *n* PHYS & TV trame *f*.

rat [ræt] (*pt* & *pp* ratted, *cont* ratting) ◇ *n* -**1.** ZOOL rat *m*; female ~, she-~ rate *f*; baby ~ raton *m* □ black ~ rat noir; grey OR sewer ~ rat d'égout, surmulot *m*; to look like a drowned ~ avoir l'air d'un chien mouillé. -**2.** *inf* [as insult - gen] ordure *f*; you dirty ~! espèce d'ordure!
◇ *vi* -**1.** *literal*: to go ratting faire la chasse aux rats. -**2.** *inf fig* retourner sa veste.
◆ **rat on** *inf vt insep* -**1.** [betray] vendre; [inform on] moucharder. -**2.** [go back on] revenir sur.

ratable ['reɪtəbl] = **rateable**.

ratafia [,rætə'fɪə] *n* -**1.** [liqueur] ratafia *m*. -**2.** ~ (biscuit) macaron *m*.

ratal ['reɪtl] *n Br* ADMIN [of building] valeur *f* locative imposable; [of site] évaluation *f* cadastrale (d'impôts locaux).

rat-arsed^▽ ['rætɑ:st] *adj Br* bourré; to get ~ se bourrer la gueule.

rat-a-tat(-tat) ['rætə,tæt('tæt)] *n* toc-toc *m*.

ratbag *inf* ['rætbæg] *n Br* peau *f* de vache; the old ~! la vieille chouette!

ratcatcher ['ræt,kætʃə^r] *n* [gen] chasseur *m*, -euse *f* de rats; [official] agent *m* de la dératisation.

ratchet ['rætʃɪt] *n* rochet *m*; ~ wrench clé *f* à rochet; ~ wheel roue *f* à rochet; this had a ~ effect on prices *fig* cela a entraîné une augmentation irréversible des prix.
◆ **ratchet up** *vt sep* [prices, inflation] faire augmenter de façon irréversible.

rate [reɪt] ◇ *n* -**1.** [ratio, level] taux *m*; the birth/death/divorce ~ le taux de natalité/de mortalité/de divorce; the success ~ is falling le taux de réussite est en baisse; how do you explain the high suicide ~? comment expliquez-vous le nombre élevé de suicides?; the hourly ~ is going to be increased le taux horaire va être augmenté □ ~ of return taux de rendement; ~ of taxation taux d'imposition; interest ~ taux d'intérêt; exchange ~, ~ of exchange taux de change. -**2.** [cost, charge] tarif *m*; his ~s have gone up ses prix ont augmenté; postal OR postage ~ tarifs postaux; standard/reduced ~ tarif normal/réduit □ the going ~ le tarif en vigueur OR normal. -**3.** [speed] vitesse *f*, train *m*; at the ~ we're going OR at this ~ we'll never get there au rythme où nous allons, nous n'y arriverons jamais; she shot past at a terrific ~ elle est passée comme une flèche □ pulse ~ (fréquence *f* du) pouls *m*; at a ~ of knots à toute vitesse OR allure. -**4.** *phr*: any ~ *inf* enfin bref.
◇ *vt* -**1.** [reckon, consider] considérer; she's ~d as one of the best players in the world elle est classée parmi les meilleures joueuses du monde; to ~ sb/sthg highly avoir une haute opinion de qqn/qqch, faire grand cas de qqn/qqch. -**2.** [deserve] mériter; her film ~s better reviews son film mérite de meilleures critiques. -**3.** *inf* [have high opinion of]: I don't ~ him as an actor à mon avis, ce n'est pas un bon acteur; I don't ~ their chances much je ne pense pas qu'ils aient beaucoup de chance. -**4.** *Br* [fix rateable value of] fixer la valeur locative imposable de. -**5.** *lit* [scold] tancer.
◇ *vi* [rank high] se classer; he ~s highly in my estimation je le tiens en très haute estime.
◆ **rates** *npl Br dated* impôts *mpl* locaux.
◆ **at any rate** *adv phr* de toute façon, de toute manière, en tout cas.

-rate *in cpds*: first-~ de premier ordre; second-~ de deuxième ordre.

rateable ['reɪtəbl] *adj*: ~ value *Br* ≃ valeur *f* locative imposable.

rate-cap *vt* [in UK]: the town council was rate-capped le gouvernement a fixé un plafond aux impôts locaux.

rate-capping [-,kæpɪŋ] *n* [in UK] *plafonnement des impôts locaux par le gouvernement*.

ratepayer ['reɪt,peɪə^r] *n* [in UK] contribuable *mf*.

ratfink^▽ ['rætfɪŋk] *n Am* salaud *m*.

rather ['rɑ:ðə^r] ◇ *adv* -**1.** [slightly, a bit] assez, un peu; I was ~ tired j'étais assez fatigué; it's ~ too small for me c'est un peu trop petit pour moi; she cut me ~ a large slice OR a ~ large slice elle m'a coupé une tranche plutôt grande; it tastes ~ like honey ça a un peu le goût du miel; I ~ rashly volunteered j'ai offert mes services un peu rapidement. -**2.** *Br* [as intensifier]: I ~ like this town je trouve cette ville plutôt agréable; she's ~ nice elle est plutôt sympa. -**3.** [expressing preference] plutôt; I'd OR I would ~ go by car je préférerais OR j'aimerais mieux y aller en voiture; I'd ~ not do it today je préférerais OR j'aimerais mieux ne pas le faire aujourd'hui; would you ~ go to Scotland? préféreriez-vous aller en Écosse?; shall we go out tonight? – I'd ~ not si on sortait ce soir? – je n'ai pas très envie □ ~ you than me! je n'aimerais pas être à votre place! -**4.** [more exactly] plutôt, plus exactement; she's English, or ~ Scottish elle est anglaise, ou plutôt écossaise; bring some wine, or ~ some champagne apportez du vin, ou mieux OR plutôt du champagne.
◇ *interj Br dated* et comment; cold, isn't it? – ~! il fait froid, n'est-ce pas? – plutôt!
◆ **rather than** *prep phr*: you should congratulate his wife ~ than him c'est sa femme que tu devrais féliciter, pas lui; it's a melodrama ~ than a tragedy c'est un mélodrame plus qu'une tragédie. *conj phr* plutôt que; ~ than walk I took the bus plutôt que d'y aller à pied, j'ai pris le bus.

ratification [,rætɪfɪ'keɪʃn] *n* ratification *f*.

ratify ['rætɪfaɪ] (*pt* & *pp* ratified) *vt* ratifier.

rating ['reɪtɪŋ] *n* -**1.** [ranking] classement *m*; pop-

ularity ~ cote *f* de popularité || FIN [of bank, company] notation *f*. -**2.** [appraisal, opinion] évaluation *f*, estimation *f*. -**3.** NAUT matelot *m*. -**4.** [scolding] *lit* réprimande *f*, admonestation *f*.
◆ **ratings** *npl* RADIO & TV indice *m* d'écoute; to be high in the ~s avoir un fort indice d'écoute; the ~s battle OR war la course à l'Audimat®.

ratio ['reɪʃɪəʊ] (*pl* ratios) *n* -**1.** [gen] proportion *f*, rapport *m*; in the ~ of six to one dans la proportion de six contre un; the teacher-student ~ is 1 to 10 le rapport enseignants-étudiants est de 1 pour 10. -**2.** MATH raison *f*, proportion *f*. -**3.** ECON ratio.

ratiocinate [,rætɪ'ɒsɪneɪt] *vi fml* raisonner.

ratiocination [,rætɪɒsɪ'neɪʃn] *n fml* raisonnement *m*.

ration ['ræʃn] ◇ *n literal & fig* ration *f*; I've had my ~ of television for today j'ai eu ma dose de télévision pour aujourd'hui.
◇ *comp*: ~ book carnet *m* de tickets de rationnement; ~ card carte *f* de rationnement.
◇ *vt* -**1.** [food] rationner; they are ~ed to one pound of meat a week ils sont rationnés à une livre de viande par semaine; I've ~ed myself to five cigarettes a day je me suis rationné à cinq cigarettes par jour. -**2.** [funds]: arts subsidies are being ~ed because of the recession les subventions à la culture sont limitées du fait de la récession.
◆ **rations** *npl* [food] vivres *mpl*; to be on double/short ~s toucher une ration double/réduite; half ~s demi-rations *fpl*.
◆ **ration out** *vt sep* rationner.

rational ['ræʃənl] ◇ *adj* -**1.** [capable of reason] doué de raison, raisonnable; a ~ being un être doué de raison. -**2.** [reasonable, logical - person] raisonnable; [- behaviour, explanation] rationnel; he seems incapable of ~ thought il semble incapable de raisonner logiquement. -**3.** [of sound mind, sane] lucide. -**4.** MATH rationnel.
◇ *n* rationnel *m*.

rationale [,ræʃə'nɑːl] *n* -**1.** [underlying reason] logique *f*; what is the ~ for OR behind their decision? quelle logique sous-tend leur décision? -**2.** [exposition] exposé *m*.

rationalism ['ræʃənəlɪzm] *n* rationalisme *m*.

rationalist ['ræʃənəlɪst] ◇ *adj* rationaliste.
◇ *n* rationaliste *mf*.

rationalistic [,ræʃənə'lɪstɪk] *adj* rationaliste.

rationality [,ræʃə'nælətɪ] *n* -**1.** [of belief, system etc] rationalité *f*. -**2.** [faculty] raison *f*.

rationalization [,ræʃənəlaɪ'zeɪʃn] *n* rationalisation *f*.

rationalize, -ise ['ræʃənəlaɪz] *vt* -**1.** [gen & COMM] rationaliser. -**2.** MATH rendre rationnel.

rationally ['ræʃənəlɪ] *adv* rationnellement.

rational number *n* nombre *m* rationnel.

rationing ['ræʃənɪŋ] *n* -**1.** [of food] rationnement *m*. -**2.** [of funds]: banks are warning of mortgage ~ les banques annoncent qu'elles vont limiter le nombre de prêts immobiliers.

Ratisbon ['rætɪzbɒn] *pr n* Ratisbonne.

rat kangaroo *n* rat-kangourou *m*.

ratlin(e) ['rætlɪn] *n* enfléchure *f*.

rat poison *n* mort-aux-rats *f inv*.

rat race *n* jungle *f fig*; she dropped out of the ~ to live in the country elle quitta la jungle des affaires pour vivre à la campagne.

rats *inf* [ræts] *interj hum* zut.

rattan [rə'tæn] ◇ *n* [plant] rotang *m*; [substance] rotin *m*.
◇ *comp* [furniture] en rotin.

rat-tat ['ræt,tæt] = **rat-a-tat(-tat)**.

ratter ['rætəʳ] *n* [dog, cat] chasseur *m* de rats.

rattle ['rætl] ◇ *vi* [gen] faire du bruit; [car, engine] faire un bruit de ferraille; [chain, machine, dice] cliqueter; [gunfire, hailstones] crépiter; [door, window] vibrer; the trains make the windows ~ les trains font vibrer les fenêtres; somebody was rattling at the door quelqu'un secouait la porte; an old car came rattling down the hill une vieille voiture descendait la côte dans un bruit de ferraille.
◇ *vt* -**1.** [box] agiter *(en faisant du bruit)*; [key] faire cliqueter; [chain, dice] agiter, secouer; [door, window] faire vibrer. -**2.** [disconcert] ébranler, secouer; I was ~d ça m'a secoué.
◇ *n* -**1.** [noise - of chains] bruit *m*; [- of car, engine] bruit *m* de ferraille; [- of keys] cliquetis *m*; [- of gunfire, hailstones] crépitement *m*; [- of window, door] vibration *f*, vibrations *fpl*. -**2.** [for baby] hochet *m*; [for sports fan] crécelle *f*. -**3.** ZOOL [of rattlesnake] grelot *m*.
◆ **rattle around** *vi insep*: you'll be rattling around in that big old house! tu seras perdu tout seul dans cette grande maison!
◆ **rattle off** *vt sep* [speech, list] débiter, réciter à toute allure; [piece of work] expédier; [letter, essay] écrire en vitesse.
◆ **rattle on** *vi insep* jacasser.
◆ **rattle through** *vt insep* [speech, meeting etc] expédier.

rattlebrain *inf* ['rætlbreɪn] *n dated* écervelé *m*, -e *f*.

rattlebrained *inf* ['rætlbreɪnd] *adj dated* [person] écervelé, qui a un pois chiche à la place du cerveau; [idea] stupide.

rattler *inf* ['rætləʳ] *Am* = **rattlesnake**.

rattlesnake ['rætlsneɪk] *n* serpent *m* à sonnettes, crotale *m*.

rattletrap *inf* ['rætltræp] *n Br dated* [car] tacot *m*.

rattling ['rætlɪŋ] ◇ *n* = **rattle 1**.
◇ *adj* -**1.** [sound]: there was a ~ noise on entendait un cliquetis; her ~ old banger *inf* son vieux tacot bringuebalant. -**2.** [fast] rapide; at a ~ pace à vive allure.
◇ *adv inf dated*: we had a ~ good time on s'est drôlement amusés; this book is a ~ good read ce livre est vraiment formidable.

rat trap *n* -**1.** *literal* piège *m* à rats, ratière *f*. -**2.** *Am* [building] taudis *m*.

ratty *inf* ['rætɪ] (*compar* rattier, *superl* rattiest) *adj* -**1.** [irritable] de mauvais poil. -**2.** *Am* [shabby] miteux.

raucous ['rɔːkəs] *adj* -**1.** [noisy] bruyant. -**2.** [hoarse] rauque.

raucously ['rɔːkəslɪ] *adv* -**1.** [noisily] bruyamment. -**2.** [hoarsely] d'une voix rauque.

raucousness ['rɔːkəsnɪs] *n* -**1.** [noisiness] tapage *m*. -**2.** [hoarseness] ton *m* rauque.

raunchiness ['rɔːntʃɪnɪs] *n* sensualité *f*.

raunchy *inf* ['rɔːntʃɪ] (*compar* raunchier, *superl* raunchiest) *adj* -**1.** [woman] d'une sensualité débordante; [song, film etc] torride. -**2.** *Am* [slovenly] négligé.

ravage ['rævɪdʒ] *vt* ravager, dévaster; the city had been ~d by war la ville avait été ravagée par la guerre.
◆ **ravages** *npl*: the ~s of time les ravages du temps.

ravaged ['rævɪdʒd] *adj* ravagé.

rave [reɪv] ◇ *vi* -**1.** [be delirious] délirer. -**2.** [talk irrationally] divaguer. -**3.** [shout] se déchaîner; she started raving at me elle a commencé à me hurler dessus. -**4.** *inf* [praise] s'extasier; to ~ about sthg/sb s'extasier sur qqch/qqn. -**5.** *inf Br* [at party] faire la bringue OR la fête.
◇ *n inf* -**1.** [praise] critique *f* élogieuse. -**2.** [fashion, craze] mode *f*; the latest ~ la dernière mode, le dernier cri. -**3.** *Br* [party] rave *f (grande fête organisée par des jeunes, généralement dans un bâtiment désaffecté, et où l'on danse sur de la house music, du rap etc, et où l'on prend de la drogue)*.
◇ *adj inf* -**1.** [enthusiastic] élogieux; the play got ~ reviews OR notices les critiques de la pièce furent très élogieuses. -**2.** [trendy] branché.
◆ **rave up** *vt sep Br dated*: to ~ it up *inf* faire la bringue OR la fête.

ravel ['rævl] (*Br pt & pp* ravelled, *cont* ravelling, *Am pt & pp* raveled, *cont* raveling) ◇ *vt* -**1.** [entangle] emmêler, enchevêtrer. -**2.** = **ravel out**.
◇ *vi* -**1.** [tangle up] s'emmêler, s'enchevêtrer. -**2.** [fray] s'effilocher. -**3.** CONSTR [road surface] se détériorer.
◆ **ravel out** ◇ *vt sep* -**1.** [cloth] effilocher; [threads] démêler. -**2.** *lit* [mystery] éclaircir; [difficulty] démêler.
◇ *vi insep* s'effilocher.

raven ['reɪvn] ◇ *n* (grand) corbeau *m*; 'The Raven' *Poe* 'le Corbeau'.
◇ *adj lit* noir comme un corbeau OR comme du jais.

raven-haired *adj lit* aux cheveux de jais.

ravening ['rævənɪŋ] *adj lit* vorace.

Ravenna [rə'venə] *pr n* Ravenne.

ravenous ['rævənəs] *adj* -**1.** [hungry] affamé; I was ~! j'avais une faim de loup! -**2.** [rapacious] *lit* vorace.

ravenously ['rævənəslɪ] *adv* voracement; [as intensifier]: to be ~ hungry avoir une faim de loup.

raver *inf* ['reɪvəʳ] *n Br* [partygoer] fêtard *m*, -e *f*, noceur *m*, -euse *f*; she's a little ~! elle est pas coincée, elle!

rave-up *inf n Br dated* fête *f*; to have a ~ faire une fête.

ravine [rə'viːn] *n* ravin *m*.

raving ['reɪvɪŋ] ◇ *adj* -**1.** [mad] délirant. -**2.** [as intensifier]: she's no ~ beauty elle n'est pas d'une beauté éblouissante; he's a ~ lunatic *inf* c'est un fou furieux, il est fou à lier.
◇ *adv inf*: ~ mad fou à lier.
◆ **ravings** *npl* divagations *fpl*.

ravioli [,rævɪ'əʊlɪ] *n (U)* ravioli *mpl*, raviolis *mpl*.

ravish ['rævɪʃ] *vt* -**1.** [delight] *lit* ravir, transporter de joie. -**2.** *arch* OR *lit* [rape] violer; [abduct] ravir.

ravishing ['rævɪʃɪŋ] *adj* ravissant, éblouissant.

ravishingly ['rævɪʃɪŋlɪ] *adv* de façon ravissante; [as intensifier]: ~ beautiful d'une beauté éblouissante.

ravishment ['rævɪʃmənt] *n* -**1.** *lit* [delight] ravissement *m*. -**2.** *arch* OR *lit* [rape] viol *m*; [abduction] enlèvement *m*.

raw [rɔː] ◇ *adj* -**1.** [uncooked] cru. -**2.** [untreated - sugar, latex, leather] brut; [- milk] cru; [- spirits] pur; [- cotton, linen] écru; [- silk] grège, écru; [- sewage] non traité. -**3.** [data, statistics] brut. -**4.** [sore - gen] sensible, irrité; [- wound, blister] à vif; [- nerves] à fleur de peau; the remark touched a ~ nerve (in him) *fig* la remarque l'a touché OR piqué au vif. -**5.** [emotion, power, energy] brut. -**6.** [inexperienced] inexpérimenté; a ~ recruit un bleu. -**7.** [weather] rigoureux, rude; a ~ February night une froide nuit de février. -**8.** [forthright] franc, direct. -**9.** *Am* [rude, coarse] grossier, cru. -**10.** *phr*: to give sb a ~ deal traiter qqn de manière injuste; he got a ~ deal from his last job il n'était pas gâté dans son dernier emploi; the unemployed get a ~ deal les chômeurs n'ont pas la part belle.
◇ *n phr*: in the ~ *inf* à poil; to touch sb on the ~ *Br* toucher OR piquer qqn au vif.

rawboned ['rɔːbəʊnd] *adj* décharné.

rawhide ['rɔːhaɪd] *n* -**1.** [skin] cuir *m* vert OR brut. -**2.** [whip] fouet *m* (de cuir).

Rawlplug® ['rɔːlplʌg] *n* cheville *f*, fiche *f*.

raw material *n (usu pl)* matière *f* première; her marriage provided her with ~ for her novel son mariage lui a servi de matière première pour son roman.

rawness ['rɔːnɪs] *n* -**1.** [natural state] nature *f* brute. -**2.** [soreness] irritation *f*. -**3.** [inexperience] inexpérience *f*, manque *m* d'expérience. -**4.** [of weather] rigueur *f*, rudesse *f*. -**5.** [frankness] franchise *f*. -**6.** *Am* [coarseness - of person, language] grossièreté *f*.

ray [reɪ] *n* -**1.** [of light] rayon *m*; a ~ of sunlight un rayon de soleil; ultraviolet ~s rayons ultra-violets. -**2.** *fig* lueur *f*; a ~ of comfort une petite consolation; a ~ of hope une lueur d'espoir; he's a little ~ of sunshine *iron* il est de charmante humeur. -**3.** [fish] raie *f*. -**4.** MUS ré *m*.

ray gun *n* pistolet *m* à rayons.

rayon ['reɪɒn] ◇ *n* rayonne *f*.
◇ *adj* en rayonne.

raze [reɪz] *vt* raser; the village was ~d to the ground le village fut entièrement rasé.

razor ['reɪzəʳ] ◇ *n* rasoir *m*; electric/safety ~ rasoir *m* électrique/de sûreté; the company is on a OR the ~'s edge l'entreprise est sur le fil du rasoir; these people are living on the ~'s edge ces gens vivent dans la peur et l'incertitude.
◇ *vt* raser.

razorback ['reɪzəbæk] *n* -**1.** [whale] balénoptère *m*, rorqual *m*. -**2.** *Am* [pig] sanglier *m*.

razorbill ['reɪzəbɪl] *n* pingouin *m*.

razor blade *n* lame *f* de rasoir.

razor clam *Am* = **razor-shell**.

razor cut *n* [hairstyle] coupe *f* au rasoir.
◆ **razor-cut** *vt* [hair] couper au rasoir.

razor-sharp *adj* -**1.** [blade] tranchant comme un rasoir OR comme une lame de rasoir; [nails] acéré. -**2.** [person, mind] vif.

razor-shell *n Br* couteau *m* ZOOL.

razor wire *n (U)* barbelés *mpl* tranchants.

razzle▽ ['ræzl] *n Br*: to be OR to go on the ~ faire la bringue OR la nouba.

razzle-dazzle *inf*, **razzmatazz** *inf* [ræzmə'tæz] *n* clinquant *m*; the ~ of Hollywood le côté tape-à-l'œil de Hollywood.

R & B (*abbr of* rhythm and blues) *n* R & B *m*.

RC *n abbr of* Roman Catholic.

RCA *pr n abbr of* Royal College of Art.

RCAF (*abbr of* Royal Canadian Air Force) *pr n armée de l'air canadienne*.

RCMP (*abbr of* Royal Canadian Mounted Police) *pr n police montée canadienne*.

RCN (*abbr of* Royal Canadian Navy) *pr n marine de guerre canadienne*.

Rd *written abbr of* road.

R & D (*abbr of* research and development) *n* R-D *f*.

RDC *n abbr of* rural district council.

re[1] [reɪ] *n* MUS ré *m*.

re[2] [riː] *prep* -**1.** ADMIN & COMM: ~ your letter of the 6th June en réponse à OR suite à votre lettre du 6 juin ‖ [in letter heading]: Re: job application Objet: demande d'emploi. -**2.** JUR: (in) ~ en l'affaire de.

RE ◇ *n abbr of* religious education.
◇ *written abbr of* Royal Engineers.

reach [riːtʃ] ◇ *vt* -**1.** [arrive at - destination] arriver à; we'll never ~ Las Vegas by nightfall nous n'arriverons jamais à Las Vegas avant la tombée de la nuit; they ~ed port ils arrivèrent au OR gagnèrent le port; I've ~ed the end of chapter one je suis arrivé à la fin du premier chapitre; the letter hasn't ~ed him yet la lettre ne lui est pas encore parvenue; the sound of laughter ~ed their ears des rires parvenaient à leurs oreilles. -**2.** [extend as far as - stage, point, level] arriver à, atteindre; the water ~ed my knees l'eau m'arrivait aux genoux; contributions have ~ed the million-pound mark le montant des contributions a atteint un million de livres; to ~ the age of 80 atteindre l'âge de 80 ans; inflation has ~ed record levels l'inflation a atteint des niveaux record. -**3.** [come to - agreement, decision, conclusion] arriver à, parvenir à; [- compromise] arriver à, aboutir à. -**4.** [be able to touch] atteindre; can you ~ the top shelf? est-ce que tu peux atteindre la dernière étagère?; the ladder doesn't quite ~ the roof l'échelle n'atteint pas tout à fait le toit; his feet don't ~ the floor ses pieds ne touchent pas par terre. -**5.** [pass, hand] passer; could you ~ me that book? pourriez-vous me passer ce livre? -**6.** [contact] joindre; you can always ~ me at this number vous pouvez toujours me joindre à ce numéro. -**7.** *Am* [bribe] soudoyer.
◇ *vi* -**1.** [with hand] tendre la main; she ~ed for her glass elle tendit la main pour prendre son verre; he ~ed across the table for the mustard il allongea le bras par-dessus la table pour prendre la moutarde ☐ ~ for the sky! haut les mains!; to ~ for the stars viser haut. -**2.** [extend] s'étendre; the fields ~ down to the river les champs s'étendent jusqu'au fleuve ‖ [carry - voice] porter. -**3.** [be long enough]: it won't ~ ce n'est pas assez long. -**4.** NAUT faire une bordée.
◇ *n* -**1.** [range] portée *f*, atteinte *f*; within ~ à portée de la main; within ~ of à (la) portée de; the house is within easy ~ of the shops la maison est à proximité des magasins; within everyone's ~ [affordable by all] à la portée de toutes les bourses; out of ~ hors de portée; out of ~ of hors de (la) portée de; 'do not leave within ~ of children' 'ne pas laisser à la portée des enfants'; nuclear physics is beyond my ~ la physique nucléaire, ça me dépasse complètement. -**2.** [in boxing] allonge *f*; a good OR long ~ une bonne allonge. -**3.** NAUT bordée *f*, bord *m*.
◆ **reaches** *npl* étendue *f*; vast ~es of water/moorland de vastes étendues d'eau/de lande; the upper/the lower ~es of a river l'amont/l'aval d'une rivière; the upper ~es of society *fig* les échelons supérieurs de la société.
◆ **reach back** *vi insep* [in time] remonter; a family ~ing back to the 16th century une famille qui remonte au XVIe siècle.
◆ **reach down** ◇ *vt sep* descendre.
◇ *vi insep* -**1.** [person] se baisser. -**2.** [coat, hair] descendre; her skirt ~ed down to her ankles sa jupe lui descendait jusqu'aux chevilles.
◆ **reach out** ◇ *vt sep* [arm, hand] tendre, étendre; he ~ed out his hand and took the money il étendit la main et prit l'argent.
◇ *vi insep* tendre OR étendre le bras; ~ out for Jesus! tendez la main vers le Seigneur!
◆ **reach up** *vi insep* -**1.** [raise arm] lever le bras. -**2.** [rise]: to ~ up to arriver à; the water ~ed up to my waist l'eau m'arrivait à la taille.

reachable ['riːtʃəbl] *adj* -**1.** [town, destination] accessible; is it ~ by boat? peut-on y aller OR accéder par bateau? -**2.** [contactable] joignable; he's ~ at the following number on peut le joindre au numéro suivant.

reach-me-down *inf n Br* vieux vêtement *m (que les aînés passent aux cadets)*.

react [rɪ'ækt] *vi* réagir; to ~ to sthg réagir à qqch; the patient is ~ing well to the treatment le malade réagit bien au traitement; to ~ against sb/sthg réagir contre qqn/qqch; the acid ~s with the metal l'acide réagit avec le métal.

reactance [rɪ'æktəns] *n* réactance *f*.

reactant [rɪ'æktənt] *n* réactif *m*.

reaction [rɪ'ækʃn] *n* -**1.** [gen, CHEM, MED & PHYS] réaction *f*; their ~ to the news was unexpected ils ont réagi à la nouvelle de façon inattendue; her work is a ~ against abstract art son œuvre est une réaction par rapport à l'art abstrait; public ~ to the policy has been mixed la réaction du public face à cette mesure a été mitigée. -**2.** [reflex] réflexe *m*; it slows down your ~s cela ralentit vos réflexes. -**3.** POL réaction *f*; the forces of ~ les forces réactionnaires.

reactionary [rɪ'ækʃənrɪ] ◇ *adj* réactionnaire.
◇ *n* réactionnaire *mf*.

reaction engine *n* moteur *m* à réaction.

reactivate [rɪ'æktɪveɪt] *vt* réactiver.

reactive [rɪ'æktɪv] *adj* [gen, CHEM & PHYS] réactif; PSYCH réactionnel.

reactiveness [rɪ'æktɪvnɪs], **reactivity** [ˌriːæk'tɪvətɪ] *n* réactivité *f*.

reactor [rɪ'æktəʳ] *n* réacteur *m*.

read[1] [riːd] (*pt & pp* read [red]) ◇ *vt* -**1.** [book, magazine etc] lire; ~ me a story lis-moi une histoire; I read it in the paper je l'ai lu dans le journal; everything I've read about the subject tout ce que j'ai lu à ce sujet; she read herself to sleep elle a lu jusqu'à ce qu'elle s'endorme; for "Barry" ~ "Harry" lire «Harry» à la place de «Barry»; can you ~ music/braille/Italian? savez-vous lire la musique/le braille/l'italien? ☐ to ~ sb's lips *literal* lire sur les lèvres de qqn; ~ my lips *fig* faites-moi confiance; to take sthg as read considérer qqch comme allant de soi. -**2.** [interpret] interpréter, lire; I ~ it this way c'est comme ça que je l'interprète. -**3.** [understand - person, mood] comprendre; to ~ sb's thoughts lire dans les pensées de qqn; I can ~ him like a book! je sais comment il fonctionne!; he ~s the game very well SPORT il a un bon sens du jeu. -**4.** [via radio] recevoir; ~ing you loud and clear je vous reçois cinq sur cinq; I ~ you *fig* je vous comprends. -**5.** [at university] étudier; he read history il a étudié l'histoire, il a fait des études d'histoire. -**6.** [gauge, dial, barometer] lire; to ~ the meter relever le compteur. -**7.** [register - subj: gauge, dial, barometer] indiquer; the thermometer is ~ing 40° le thermomètre indique 40°. -**8.** [announce - subj: notice] annoncer; a sign on the door read "staff only" un écriteau sur la porte indiquait «réservé au personnel». -**9.** [proofs] corriger. -**10.** [data, disk] lire.
◇ *vi* -**1.** [person] lire; she's learning to ~ elle apprend à lire; to ~ to sb faire la lecture à qqn; to ~ to o.s. lire; I'd read about it in the papers je l'avais lu dans les journaux; we've all read about OR of such phenomena nous avons tous lu des textes qui traitent de tels phénomènes ☐ to ~ between the lines lire entre les lignes. -**2.** [text]: her article ~s well/badly son article se lit facilement/ne se lit pas facilement; the table ~s from left to right le tableau se lit de gauche à droite; the book ~s like a translation à la lecture, on sent que ce roman est une traduction; article 22 ~s as follows voici ce que dit l'article 22. -**3.** [gauge, meter etc]: the dials ~ differently les cadrans n'indiquent pas le même chiffre. -**4.** [student]: what's he ~ing? qu'est-ce qu'il fait comme études?; to ~ for a degree préparer un diplôme.
◇ *n* -**1.** [act of reading]: to have a ~ lire; can I have a ~ of your paper? est-ce que je peux jeter un coup d'œil sur ton journal? -**2.** [reading matter]: her books are a good ~ ses livres se lisent bien.
◆ **read back** *vt sep* [dictated letter] relire.
◆ **read in** *vt sep* [subj: computer] lire (en mémoire).
◆ **read into** *vt sep*: you shouldn't ~ too much into their silence vous ne devriez pas accorder trop d'importance à leur silence.
◆ **read off** *vt sep* -**1.** [rapidly] lire d'un trait; [aloud] lire (à haute voix). -**2.** [figure on dial, scale etc] relever.
◆ **read on** *vi insep* lire la suite.
◆ **read out** *vt sep* -**1.** [aloud] lire (à haute voix). -**2.** [subj: computer] lire. -**3.** *Am* [expel] expulser.
◆ **read over** *vt sep* relire.
◆ **read through** ◇ *vt insep* [skim through] parcourir.
◇ *vt sep* [carefully] relire (soigneusement).
◆ **read up** *vt sep* étudier.
◆ **read up on** *vt insep* = **read up**.

read[2] [red] ◇ *pt & pp* → **read**.
◇ *adj*: he's widely ~ c'est un homme cultivé.

readability [ˌriːdə'bɪlətɪ] *n* lisibilité *f*.

readable ['riːdəbl] *adj* -**1.** [handwriting] lisible. -**2.** [book] qui se laisse lire.

readdress [ˌriːə'dres] *vt* [mail] faire suivre.

reader ['riːdəʳ] *n* -**1.** [of book] lecteur *m*, -trice *f*; she's an avid ~ c'est une passionnée de lecture; I'm not a fast ~ je ne lis pas vite; he's not a great ~ il ne lit pas beaucoup ☐ publisher's ~ lecteur *m*, -trice *f* de manuscrits *(dans une maison d'édition)*. -**2.** COMPUT lecteur *m*; optical character ~ lecteur *m* optique de caractères. -**3.** [reading book] livre *m* de lecture; [anthology] recueil *m* de textes; German ~ recueil de textes allemands. -**4.** *Br* UNIV ≃ maître-assistant *m*, -e *f*. -**5.** *Am* UNIV ≃ assistant *m*, -e *f*. -**6.** RELIG [Protestant] lecteur *m*, -trice *f*; [Jewish] chantre *m*.

readership ['riːdəʃɪp] *n* -**1.** [of newspaper, magazine] nombre *m* de lecteurs, lectorat *m*; what is their ~ (figure)? combien ont-ils de lecteurs?; this book should attract a wide ~ ce livre devrait intéresser un grand nombre de lecteurs. -**2.** *Br* UNIV ≃ poste *m* de maître-assistant. -**3.** *Am* UNIV ≃ fonction *f* d'assistant.

readily ['redɪlɪ] *adv* -**1.** [willingly] volontiers. -**2.** [with ease] facilement, aisément; ~ understandable ideas des idées qu'on comprend facilement; our products are ~ available nos produits sont en vente partout.

readiness ['redɪnɪs] *n* -**1.** [preparedness]: to be in ~ for sthg être préparé à qqch; to be in a state of ~ être fin prêt. -**2.** [willingness] empressement *m*; their ~ to assist us leur empressement à nous aider.

reading ['riːdɪŋ] ◇ *n* -**1.** [activity] lecture *f*; ~, writing and arithmetic la lecture, l'écriture et le calcul. -**2.** [reading material] lecture *f*; light ~ lecture facile OR distrayante; his autobiography makes fascinating/dull ~ son autobiographie est passionnante/ennuyeuse à lire. -**3.** [recital] lecture *f*; the ~ of the will la lecture du testament. -**4.** [from instrument, gauge] indication *f*; the ~ on the dial was wrong les indications qui apparaissaient sur le cadran étaient fausses; to take a ~ lire les indications données par un compteur. -**5.** POL lecture *f*; to give a bill its first/second ~ examiner un projet de loi en première/deuxième lecture. -**6.** [interpretation] interprétation *f*; my ~ of the situation la manière dont j'interprète la situation; a new ~ of Dante une nouvelle lecture de Dante. -**7.** [variant] variante *f*.
◇ *comp*: take some ~ matter emmenez de quoi lire; the ~ public le public des lecteurs.

reading age *n Br* niveau *m* de lecture; she has a ~ of 11 elle a le niveau de lecture d'un enfant de 11 ans.

reading book *n* livre *m* de lecture.

reading desk *n* pupitre *m*; RELIG lutrin *m*.

reading glass *n* [magnifying glass] loupe *f (pour lire)*.
◆ **reading glasses** *npl* [spectacles] lunettes *fpl* pour lire.

reading lamp *n* lampe *f* de bureau.

reading light *n* liseuse *f*.

reading list *n* [syllabus] liste *f* des ouvrages au programme; [for further reading] liste *f* des ouvrages recommandés.

reading room *n* salle *f* de lecture.

readjust [,riːə'dʒʌst] ◇ *vt* -**1.** [readapt]: to ~ o.s. se réadapter. -**2.** [alter - controls, prices, clothing] rajuster, réajuster.
◇ *vi* se réadapter; to ~ to sthg se réadapter à qqch.

readjustment [,riːə'dʒʌstmənt] *n* -**1.** [readaptation] réadaptation *f*. -**2.** [alteration] rajustement *m*, réajustement *m*.

readmission [,riːəd'mɪʃn] *n* [to political party] réintégration *f*; [to hospital] réadmission *f*; 'no ~' [on ticket] 'ce ticket ne sera accepté qu'une seule fois à l'entrée'.

readmit [,riːəd'mɪt] *vt*: she has been readmitted to hospital elle a été réadmise à l'hôpital; he was readmitted to the concert on l'a relaissé passer à l'entrée du concert.

read-only memory [riːd-] *n* mémoire *f* morte.

readout ['riːdaʊt] *n* COMPUT [gen] lecture *f*; [on screen] affichage *m*; [on paper] sortie *f* papier OR sur imprimante, listing *m*.

readvertise [,riː'ædvətaɪz] ◇ *vt* repasser une annonce de.
◇ *vi* repasser une annonce.

readvertisement [,riːəd'vɜːtɪsmənt] *n* deuxième annonce *f*; 'this is a ~' 'deuxième annonce d'offre d'emploi'.

read-write head [riːd-] *n* tête *f* de lecture-écriture.

read-write memory [riːd-] *n* mémoire *f* vive.

ready ['redɪ] (*compar* readier, *superl* readiest, *pl* readies, *pt* & *pp* readied) ◇ *adj* -**1.** [prepared] prêt; are you ~? êtes-vous prêt?; he's just getting ~ il est en train de se préparer; to be ~ to do sthg être prêt à faire qqch; to be ~ for anything être prêt à tout; he's not ~ for such responsibility il n'est pas prêt pour affronter une telle responsabilité; she's always ~ with an answer, she always has an answer ~ elle a toujours réponse à tout; to get sthg ~ préparer qqch; I'll get the room/the dinner ~ je vais préparer la chambre/le dîner; to get ~ to do sthg se préparer OR s'apprêter à faire qqch; to get ~ for bed s'apprêter à aller au lit; we're ~ when you are nous n'attendons que toi; to make ~ *arch* OR *lit* se préparer; dinner's ~! c'est prêt!; are you ~ to order? vous avez choisi?; the tomatoes are ~ for eating les tomates sont bonnes à manger ❑ ~, steady, go! à vos marques, prêts, partez! -**2.** [willing] prêt, disposé; ~ to do sthg prêt à faire qqch; she's always ~ to lend a hand elle est toujours prête à donner un coup de main; I'm ~ to agree with you on that point je suis entièrement d'accord avec vous sur ce point-là; they are always ~ to find fault ils sont toujours prêts à critiquer; don't be so ~ to believe him ne le crois pas systématiquement; we're ~ to negotiate nous sommes prêts OR disposés à négocier; you know me, I'm ~ for anything tu me connais, je suis toujours partant; I'm ~ for bed! j'ai envie d'aller me coucher! -**3.** [quick] prompt; she has a ~ wit elle a l'esprit d'à-propos; she has a ~ tongue elle n'a pas la langue dans sa poche; he had a ~ smile il souriait facilement. -**4.** [likely]: ~ to do sthg sur le point de faire qqch; she looks ~ to explode on dirait qu'elle est sur le point d'exploser; I'm ~ to collapse! je suis à bout de forces!, je suis épuisé! -**5.** [easily accessible]: a ~ market for our products un marché tout trouvé pour nos produits; ~ to hand [within reach] à portée de main; [available] à disposition; ~ cash OR money (argent *m*) liquide *m*.
◇ *n inf Br* [money]: the ~, the readies le fric, le pognon.
◇ *adv Br*: ~ cut ham jambon *m* prétranché; ~ salted peanuts cacahuètes *fpl* salées.
◇ *vt* préparer; to ~ o.s. for sthg se préparer pour qqch.
◆ **at the ready** *adj phr* (tout) prêt.

ready-cooked *adj* précuit.

ready-made ◇ *adj* -**1.** [clothes] de prêt-à-porter; [food] précuit. -**2.** [excuse, solution, argument] tout prêt.
◇ *n* [garment] vêtement *m* de prêt-à-porter.

ready-mix *adj* [cake] fait à partir d'une préparation; [concrete] prémalaxé.

ready reckoner *n* barème *m*.

ready-to-serve *adj* prêt à l'emploi.

ready-to-wear *adj*: ~ clothing prêt-à-porter *m*.

reaffirm [,riːə'fɜːm] *vt* réaffirmer.

reafforest [,riːə'fɒrɪst] *vt* reboiser.

reafforestation ['riːə,fɒrɪ'steɪʃn] *n* reboisement *m*, reforestation *f*.

reagent [riː'eɪdʒənt] *n* réactif *m*.

real [rɪəl] ◇ *adj* -**1.** [authentic] vrai, véritable; they're ~ silver ils sont en argent véritable; are her pearls ~? ses perles sont-elles vraies?; a ~ man un vrai homme; we'll never know her ~ feelings nous ne saurons jamais quels étaient vraiment ses sentiments; I don't know his ~ name je ne connais pas son vrai nom; my first ~ job mon premier vrai travail; we have no ~ cause for concern nous n'avons aucune raison de nous inquiéter; that's what I call a ~ cup of tea! ça, c'est ce que j'appelle une tasse de thé! ❑ it's the ~ thing [authentic object] c'est du vrai de vrai; [true love] c'est le grand amour. -**2.** [actually existing] réel; the ~ world le monde réel; the threat is a very ~ one la menace est bien réelle; in ~ life dans la réalité. -**3.** [net, overall] réel; salaries have fallen in ~ terms les salaires ont baissé en termes réels. -**4.** [as intensifier] vrai, véritable; it was a ~ surprise ce fut une vraie surprise; she's a ~ pain elle est vraiment rasante. -**5.** COMPUT, MATH, PHILOS & PHYS réel; ~ image image *f* réelle. -**6.** *phr*: get ~![▽] arrête de délirer!
◇ *adv inf Am* vachement.
◇ *n* PHILOS: the ~ le réel.
◆ **for real** *inf adv* & *adj phr* pour de vrai OR de bon; this time it's for ~ cette fois-ci c'est la bonne; is he for ~?[▽] d'où il sort, celui-là?

real ale *n Br* bière *f* artisanale.

real estate *n* (*U*) -**1.** *Am* [property] biens *mpl* immobiliers; he works in ~ il travaille dans l'immobilier. -**2.** *Br* JUR biens *mpl* fonciers.
◆ **real-estate** *comp Am* immobilier; real-estate agent agent *m* immobilier; real-estate office agence *f* immobilière.

realia [,riː'eɪlɪə] *npl* *textes ou objets authentiques utilisés par les enseignants pour animer leurs cours.*

realign [,riːə'laɪn] ◇ *vt* aligner (de nouveau); POL regrouper.
◇ *vi* s'aligner (de nouveau); POL se regrouper.

realignment [,riːə'laɪnmənt] *n* (nouvel) alignement *m*; POL regroupement *m*.

realism ['rɪəlɪzm] *n* réalisme *m*.

realist ['rɪəlɪst] ◇ *adj* réaliste.
◇ *n* réaliste *mf*.

realistic [,rɪə'lɪstɪk] *adj* -**1.** [reasonable] réaliste. -**2.** [lifelike] ressemblant.

realistically [,rɪə'lɪstɪklɪ] *adv* de façon réaliste; they can't ~ expect us to do all this ils ne peuvent pas s'attendre sérieusement à ce que nous fassions tout cela.

reality [rɪ'ælətɪ] (*pl* realities) *n* réalité *f*; the ~ OR realities of living in today's Britain les réalités de la vie dans la Grande-Bretagne d'aujourd'hui; will our dream ever become (a) ~? notre rêve deviendra-t-il un jour réalité?; you have to face ~ il faut que tu regardes la réalité en face.
◆ **in reality** *adv phr* en réalité.

realizable ['rɪəlaɪzəbl] *adj* [gen & FIN] réalisable.

realization [,rɪəlaɪ'zeɪʃn] *n* -**1.** [awareness]: this sudden ~ left us speechless cette découverte nous a laissés sans voix; there has been a growing ~ on the part of the government that... le gouvernement s'est peu à peu rendu compte que...; his ~ that he was gay la prise de conscience de son homosexualité. -**2.** [of aim, dream, project] réalisation *f*. -**3.** FIN [of assets] réalisation *f*.

realize, -ise ['rɪəlaɪz] *vt* -**1.** [be or become aware of] se rendre compte de; I don't think you ~ the work involved je ne crois pas que tu te rendes compte de tout le travail que ça représente; do you ~ what time it is? tu te rends compte de OR tu as vu l'heure qu'il est?; I didn't ~ how late it was je ne m'étais pas rendu compte qu'il était si tard; it made me ~ what a fool I had been cela m'a fait comprendre quel imbécile j'avais été; I ~ you're busy, but... je sais que tu es occupé, mais... -**2.** [achieve] réaliser; will we ever ~ our goal of unity? parviendrons-nous un jour à réaliser notre objectif d'unité?; my worst fears were ~d ce que je craignais le plus s'est produit OR est arrivé; a job where you could ~ your full potential un travail qui te permettrait de te réaliser complètement. -**3.** FIN [yield financially] rapporter; [convert into cash] réaliser.

real-life *adj* vrai; the ~ drama of her battle against illness le drame affreux de sa lutte contre la maladie.

reallocate [,riː'æləkeɪt] *vt* [funds, resources] réaffecter, réattribuer; [task, duties] redistribuer.

really ['rɪəlɪ] ◇ *adv* -**1.** [actually] vraiment, réellement; did you ~ say that? as-tu vraiment dis ça?; what's she ~ like? comment est-elle vraiment?; here's what ~ happened voilà ce qui s'est vraiment passé. -**2.** [as intensifier] vraiment; these cakes are ~ delicious ces gâteaux sont vraiment délicieux; you ~ ought to see it il faut vraiment que vous le voyiez; it ~ doesn't matter ce n'est vraiment pas important; you ~ shouldn't be here vous ne devriez vraiment pas être ici; now you're ~ being silly! tu es vraiment ridicule! -**3.** [reducing force of negative statements]: it doesn't ~ matter ce n'est pas vraiment important; you shouldn't ~ be here vous ne devriez pas vraiment être ici; I don't ~ know je ne sais pas vraiment. -**4.** [tentative use]: he's quite nice, ~ il est plutôt sympa, en fait; do you want to go? — I suppose I do ~ tu veux y aller? — pourquoi pas, après tout. -**5.** [in surprise, interest]: (oh) ~? oh, vraiment?, c'est pas vrai?
◇ *interj* [in irritation]: (well) ~! enfin!

realm [relm] *n* -**1.** [field, domain] domaine *m*; the ~ of the supernatural le domaine du surnaturel; it is within the ~s of possibility c'est du domaine du possible. -**2.** [kingdom] *lit* royaume *m.*

real number *n* nombre *m* réel.

realpolitik [reɪ'ɑːlpɒlitiːk] *n* realpolitik *f.*

real property *n (U)* biens *mpl* immobiliers OR immeubles.

real tennis *n* jeu *m* de paume; to play ~ jouer à la paume.

real time *n* COMPUT temps *m* réel.

◆ **real-time** *adj* [system, control, processing] en temps réel.

realtor ['rɪəltəʳ] *n Am* agent *m* immobilier.

realty ['rɪəltɪ] *n (U) Am* biens *mpl* immobiliers.

ream [riːm] ◇ *n* [of paper] rame *f*; to write ~s *inf fig* écrire des tartines.

◇ *vt* -**1.** TECH fraiser. -**2.** *Am* [lemon] presser. -**3.** *inf Am* [person] rouler.

reamer ['riːməʳ] *n* -**1.** TECH fraise *f.* -**2.** *Am* [lemon squeezer] presse-citron *m inv.*

reanimate [,riː'ænɪmeɪt] *vt* réanimer.

reanimation [,riːænɪ'meɪʃn] *n* réanimation *f.*

reap [riːp] ◇ *vt* -**1.** [crop] moissonner, faucher. -**2.** *fig* récolter, tirer; to ~ the benefit OR the benefits of sthg récolter les bénéfices de qqch; she ~ed a rich reward elle a été bien récompensée.

◇ *vi* moissonner, faire la moisson.

reaper ['riːpəʳ] *n* -**1.** [machine] moissonneuse *f*; ~ and binder moissonneuse-lieuse *f.* -**2.** [person] moissonneur *m*, -euse *f*; the (Grim) Reaper *lit* la Faucheuse.

reaping ['riːpɪŋ] *n* moisson *f*; ~ machine moissonneuse *f.*

reappear [,riːə'pɪəʳ] *vi* [person, figure, sun] réapparaître; [lost object] refaire surface.

reappearance [,riːə'pɪərəns] *n* réapparition *f.*

reapply [,riːə'plaɪ] (*pt* & *pp* reapplied) *vi*: to ~ for a job poser de nouveau sa candidature pour un poste; previous applicants need not ~ les personnes ayant déjà posé leur candidature n'ont pas besoin de le faire à nouveau.

reappoint [,riːə'pɔɪnt] *vt* réengager, rengager.

reappointment [,riːə'pɔɪntmənt] *n*: since her ~ as minister for the arts depuis qu'elle a été nommée à nouveau ministre de la Culture.

reappraisal [,riːə'preɪzl] *n* réexamen *m.*

reappraise [,riːə'preɪz] *vt* réexaminer.

rear [rɪəʳ] ◇ *n* -**1.** [of place] arrière *m*; at the ~ of the bus à l'arrière du bus; the garden at the ~ *Br* OR in the ~ *Am* of the house le jardin qui est derrière la maison; they attacked them from the ~ ils les ont attaqués par derrière. -**2.** MIL arrière *m*, arrières *mpl*; to bring up the ~ MIL & *fig* fermer la marche. -**3.** *inf* [buttocks] arrière-train *m.*

◇ *adj* [door, wheel] arrière *(inv)*, de derrière; [engine] arrière; [carriages] de queue; is there a ~ entrance? est-ce qu'il y a une entrée par derrière? ❑ ~ lamp OR light *Br* AUT feu *m* arrière; ~ window lunette *f* arrière; 'Rear Window' *Hitchcock* 'Fenêtre sur cour'.

◇ *vt* -**1.** [children, animals] élever; [plants] cultiver. -**2.** [head, legs] lever, relever; racism has ~ed its ugly head again *fig* le spectre du racisme a refait son apparition.

◇ *vi* -**1.** [horse]: to ~ (up) se cabrer. -**2.** [mountain, skyscraper]: to ~ (up) se dresser.

rear admiral *n* contre-amiral *m.*

rear-engined *adj* avec moteur à l'arrière.

rearguard ['rɪəgɑːd] *n* arrière-garde *f.*

rearguard action *n* combat *m* d'arrière-garde; to fight a ~ *literal* & *fig* mener un combat d'arrière-garde.

rear gunner *n* mitrailleur *m* arrière.

rearm [riː'ɑːm] ◇ *vt* [nation, ship] réarmer.

◇ *vi* réarmer.

rearmament [rɪ'ɑːməmənt] *n* réarmement *m.*

rearmost ['rɪəməʊst] *adj* dernier.

rear-mounted *adj* monté à l'arrière.

rearrange [,riːə'reɪndʒ] *vt* -**1.** [arrange differently - furniture, objects] réarranger, changer la disposition de; [- flat, room] réaménager. -**2.** [put back in place] réarranger; she ~d her hair elle se recoiffa. -**3.** [reschedule] changer la date/l'heure de; the meeting has been ~d for Monday la réunion a été remise à lundi; we'll have to ~ our schedule il faudra réaménager notre programme.

rearrangement [,riːə'reɪndʒmənt] *n* -**1.** [different arrangement] réarrangement *m*, réaménagement *m.* -**2.** [rescheduling] changement *m* de date/d'heure.

rearrest [,riːə'rest] *vt* arrêter de nouveau.

rearview mirror ['rɪəvjuː-] *n* rétroviseur *m.*

rearward ['rɪəwəd] ◇ *adj* [part, end] arrière *(inv)*; [motion] en arrière, vers l'arrière.

◇ *adv* = **rearwards**.

◇ *n* arrière *m.*

rearwards ['rɪəwədz] *adv* en arrière, vers l'arrière.

rear-wheel drive *n* AUT traction *f* arrière.

reason ['riːzn] ◇ *n* -**1.** [cause, motive] raison *f*; what is the ~ for his absence? quelle est la raison de son absence?; did he give a ~ for being so late? a-t-il donné la raison d'un tel retard?; the ~ (why) they refused la raison de leur refus, la raison pour laquelle ils ont refusé; I (can) see no ~ for disagreeing OR to disagree je ne vois pas pourquoi je ne serais pas d'accord; why do you ask? – oh, no particular ~ pourquoi est-ce que tu me demandes ça? – oh, comme ça; she wouldn't tell me the ~ why elle ne voulait pas me dire pourquoi; you have every ~ OR good ~ to be angry vous avez de bonnes raisons d'être en colère; we have/there is ~ to believe he is lying nous avons de bonnes raisons de croire/il y a lieu de croire qu'il ment; I chose him for the simple ~ I liked him je l'ai choisi pour la simple et bonne raison qu'il me plaisait; but that's the only ~ I came! mais c'est pour ça que je suis venue!; that's no ~ to get annoyed ce n'est pas une raison pour s'énerver; all the more ~ for trying again OR to try again raison de plus pour réessayer; for ~s best known to herself pour des raisons qu'elle est seule à connaître; for some ~ (or other) pour une raison ou pour une autre; give me one good ~ why I should believe you! donne-moi une bonne raison de te croire!; they were upset, and with (good) ~ ils étaient bouleversés, et à juste titre; she's my ~ for living elle est ma raison de vivre. -**2.** [common sense] raison *f*; he won't listen to ~ il refuse d'entendre raison; I can't make her listen to ~ je n'arrive pas à lui faire entendre raison OR à la raisonner; at last he saw ~ il a fini par entendre raison; your demands are beyond all ~ vos exigences dépassent les limites du raisonnable ❑ it stands to ~ c'est logique, ça va de soi. -**3.** [rationality] raison *f*; man has the power of ~ l'homme est doué de raison.

◇ *vi* raisonner; to ~ with sb raisonner qqn; I tried to ~ with them j'ai essayé de les raisonner OR de leur faire entendre raison.

◇ *vt* -**1.** [maintain] maintenir, soutenir; [work out] calculer, déduire; [conclude] conclure; they ~ed that the fault must be in the cooling system ils en ont déduit que la défaillance devait provenir du système de refroidissement. -**2.** [persuade]: I ~ed him out of the idea je l'ai persuadé OR convaincu d'abandonner son idée; she ~ed me into/out of going elle m'a persuadé/dissuadé d'y aller.

◆ **by reason of** *prep phr* en raison de.

◆ **for reasons of** *prep phr*: for ~s of space/national security pour des raisons de place/sécurité nationale.

◆ **within reason** *adv phr* dans la limite du raisonnable; you can do what you like, within ~ vous pouvez faire ce que vous voulez, dans la limite du raisonnable.

◆ **reason out** *vt sep* résoudre *(par la raison)*.

reasonable ['riːznəbl] *adj* -**1.** [sensible - person, behaviour, attitude] raisonnable; [- explanation, decision] raisonnable, sensé; be ~! soyez raisonnable!; you must be ~ in your demands vos revendications doivent être raisonnables. -**2.** [moderate - price] raisonnable, correct; [- restaurant] qui pratique des prix raisonnables. -**3.** [fair, acceptable - offer, suggestion] raisonnable, acceptable; we've had quite a ~ day nous avons passé une journée plutôt agréable; beyond all ~ doubt indubitablement.

reasonableness ['riːznəblnɪs] *n* -**1.** [of person, behaviour] caractère *m* raisonnable. -**2.** [of price] modération *f.*

reasonably ['riːznəblɪ] *adv* -**1.** [behave, argue] raisonnablement; one can ~ expect... on est en droit d'attendre...; ~ priced at $100 au prix raisonnable OR modéré de 100 dollars. -**2.** [quite, rather]: ~ good assez bien, pas mal.

reasoned ['riːznd] *adj* [argument, decision] raisonné.

reasoning ['riːznɪŋ] *n* raisonnement *m.*

reassemble [,riːə'sembl] ◇ *vt* -**1.** [people, arguments] rassembler. -**2.** [machinery] remonter.

◇ *vi* se rassembler; Parliament/school ~s in September la rentrée parlementaire/des classes a lieu en septembre.

reassembly [,riːə'semblɪ] *n* -**1.** [of group] rassemblement *m*; POL rentrée *f.* -**2.** [of machine] remontage *m.*

reassert [,riːə'sɜːt] *vt* [authority] réaffirmer; you'll have to ~ yourself vous devrez imposer à nouveau OR réaffirmer votre autorité.

reassess [,riːə'ses] *vt* -**1.** [position, opinion] réexaminer. -**2.** FIN [damages] réévaluer; [taxation] réviser.

reassessment [,riːə'sesmənt] *n* -**1.** [of position, opinion] réexamen *m.* -**2.** FIN [of damages] réévaluation *f*; [of taxes] révision *f.*

reassign [,riːə'saɪn] *vt* réaffecter.

reassurance [,riːə'ʃɔːrəns] *n* -**1.** [comforting] réconfort *m*; she turned to me for ~ elle s'est tournée vers moi OR est venue à moi pour que je la rassure. -**2.** [guarantee] assurance *f*, confirmation *f*; despite his ~ OR ~s that the contract is still valid bien qu'il affirme que le contrat est toujours valable; the government has given ~s that... le gouvernement a assuré que...

reassure [,riːə'ʃɔːʳ] *vt* -**1.** [comfort] rassurer; I feel ~d now je me sens rassuré maintenant. -**2.** FIN réassurer.

reassuring [,riːə'ʃɔːrɪŋ] *adj* rassurant.

reassuringly [,riːə'ʃɔːrɪŋlɪ] *adv* d'une manière rassurante; he smiled at me ~ il me fit un sourire pour me rassurer || [as intensifier]: ~ simple d'une grande simplicité.

reawake [,riːə'weɪk] (*pt* reawoke [-'wəʊk] OR reawaked, *pp* reawoken [-'wəʊkn] OR reawaked) *vi* se réveiller de nouveau.

reawaken [,riːə'weɪkn] ◇ *vt* [person] réveiller; [concern, interest] réveiller; [feelings] faire renaître, raviver.

◇ *vi* [person] se réveiller de nouveau.

reawakening [,riːə'weɪknɪŋ] *n* [of sleeper] réveil *m*; [of interest, concern] réveil *m*; the ~ of national pride le réveil de l'orgueil national.

rebarbative [rɪ'bɑːbətɪv] *adj fml* rébarbatif.

rebate ['riːbeɪt] *n* -**1.** [reduction - on goods] remise *f*, ristourne *f*; [- on tax] dégrèvement *m*; [refund] remboursement *m.* -**2.** = **rabbet**.

Rebecca [rɪ'bekə] *pr n* Rébecca.

rebel [*n* & *adj* 'rebl, *vb* rɪ'bel] (*pt* & *pp* **rebelled**, *cont* rebelling) ◇ *n* [in revolution] rebelle *mf*, insurgé *m*, -e *f*; *fig* rebelle *mf.*

◇ *adj* [soldier] rebelle; [camp, territory] des rebelles; [attack] de rebelles.

◇ *vi* se rebeller; to ~ against sthg/sb se révolter contre qqch/qqn || [stomach] *hum*: my stomach rebelled mon estomac a protesté.

rebellion [rɪ'beljən] *n* rébellion *f*, révolte *f*; in open ~ en rébellion ouverte; to rise (up) in ~ against sthg/sb se révolter contre qqch/qqn.

rebellious [rɪ'beljəs] *adj* [child, hair] rebelle; [troops] insoumis.

rebelliously [rɪ'beljəslɪ] *adv* [reply] d'un ton de défi; [act] en rebelle.

rebelliousness [rɪ'beljəsnɪs] *n* [of child, politician] esprit *m* de rébellion; [of soldier] insoumission *f*; [of inhabitants] disposition *f* à la rébellion.

rebirth [ˌriːˈbɜːθ] *n* renaissance *f*.

reboot [riːˈbuːt] *vt* [computer] réinitialiser; [programme] relancer.

rebore [ˈriːbɔːʳ] ◇ *vt* réaléser.
◇ *n* réalésage *m*.

reborn [ˌriːˈbɔːn] *adj* réincarné; to be ~ renaître; I feel ~ je me sens renaître.

rebound [*vb* ˌriːˈbaʊnd, *n* ˈriːbaʊnd]
◇ *vi* -**1.** [ball] rebondir; the ball ~ed against the wall/into the road le ballon a rebondi contre le mur/sur la route. -**2.** *fig*: to ~ on sb se retourner contre qqn; the situation ~ed on us la situation s'est retournée contre nous. -**3.** [recover - business] reprendre, repartir; [- prices] remonter.
◇ *n* -**1.** [of ball] rebond *m*; to catch a ball on the ~ attraper une balle au rebond. -**2.** *phr*: to be on the ~ [after relationship] être sous le coup d'une déception sentimentale; [after setback] être sous le coup d'un échec; he married her on the ~ il l'a épousée à la suite d'une déception sentimentale.

rebroadcast [ˌriːˈbrɔːdkɑːst] ◇ *n* retransmission *f*.
◇ *vt* retransmettre.

rebuff [rɪˈbʌf] ◇ *vt* [snub] rabrouer; [reject] repousser.
◇ *n* rebuffade *f*; to meet with OR to suffer a ~ [person] essuyer une rebuffade; [request] être repoussé.

rebuild [ˌriːˈbɪld] (*pt* & *pp* rebuilt [-ˈbɪlt]) *vt* [town, economy] rebâtir, reconstruire; [relationship, life] reconstruire; we must ~ confidence in industry nous devons faire renaître la confiance dans l'industrie.

rebuilding [ˌriːˈbɪldɪŋ] *n* [of town, economy, relationship] reconstruction *f*; ~ work travaux *mpl* de réfection OR de reconstruction.

rebuke [rɪˈbjuːk] ◇ *vt* [reprimand] réprimander; to ~ sb for sthg reprocher qqch à qqn; to ~ sb for doing OR having done sthg reprocher à qqn d'avoir fait qqch.
◇ *n* reproche *m*, réprimande *f*.

rebus [ˈriːbəs] *n* rébus *m*.

rebut [riːˈbʌt] (*pt* & *pp* rebutted, *cont* rebutting) *vt* réfuter.

rebuttal [riːˈbʌtl] *n* réfutation *f*.

rec [rek] *n Br* -**1.** *abbr of* recreation ground. -**2.** *abbr of* recreation room.

recalcitrance [rɪˈkælsɪtrəns] *n fml* caractère *m* OR esprit *m* récalcitrant.

recalcitrant [rɪˈkælsɪtrənt] *adj fml* récalcitrant.

recall [*vb* rɪˈkɔːl, *n* ˈriːkɔːl] ◇ *vt* -**1.** [remember] se rappeler, se souvenir de; I don't ~ seeing OR having seen her je ne me rappelle pas l'avoir vue; as far as I can ~ aussi loin que je m'en souvienne; as I ~ si mes souvenirs sont bons; as you may ~ comme vous vous en souvenez peut-être. -**2.** [evoke - past] rappeler. -**3.** [send for - actor, ambassador] rappeler; [- Parliament] rappeler (en session extraordinaire); [- library book, hire car] demander le retour de; [- faulty goods] rappeler. -**4.** MIL rappeler.
◇ *n* -**1.** [memory] rappel *m*, mémoire *f*; total ~ aptitude à se souvenir des moindres détails; to be beyond OR past ~ être oublié à tout jamais. -**2.** MIL rappel *m*.
◇ *comp*: ~ button [on phone] rappel *m* automatique; ~ slip [for library book] fiche *f* de rappel.

recant [rɪˈkænt] ◇ *vt* [religion] abjurer; [opinion] rétracter.
◇ *vi* [from religion] abjurer; [from opinion] se rétracter .

recantation [ˌriːkænˈteɪʃn] *n* [of religion] abjuration *f*; [of statement] rétractation *f*.

recap [ˈriːkæp] (*pt* & *pp* recapped, *cont* recapping) ◇ *n* -**1.** [summary] récapitulation *f*. -**2.** *Am* [tyre] pneu *m* rechapé.
◇ *vt* -**1.** [summarize] récapituler; so, to ~ donc, pour récapituler OR résumer. -**2.** *Am* [tyre] rechaper.

recapitalize, -ise [ˌriːˈkæpɪtəlaɪz] *vt* changer la structure financière de.

recapitulate [ˌriːkəˈpɪtjʊleɪt] *vt* récapituler; so, to ~ donc, pour récapituler OR résumer.

recapitulation [ˈriːkəˌpɪtjʊˈleɪʃn] *n* récapitulation *f*.

recapture [ˌriːˈkæptʃəʳ] ◇ *vt* -**1.** [prisoner, town] reprendre; [animal] capturer. -**2.** [regain - confidence] reprendre; [- feeling, spirit] retrouver; [evoke - subj: film, book, play] recréer, faire revivre. -**3.** *Am* FIN saisir.
◇ *n* -**1.** [of escapee, animal] capture *f*; [of town] reprise *f*. -**2.** *Am* FIN saisie *f*.

recast [ˌriːˈkɑːst] (*pt* & *pp* recast) ◇ *vt* -**1.** [redraft] réorganiser, restructurer; their policies have been ~ in a more acceptable form ils ont restructuré leur politique de façon plus satisfaisante. -**2.** [play] changer la distribution de; [actor] donner un nouveau rôle à; he was ~ in the role of Prospero on lui a donné un nouveau rôle, celui de Prospero. -**3.** METALL refondre.
◇ *n* METALL refonte *f*.

recce *inf* [ˈrekɪ] (*pt* & *pp* recced OR recceed) MIL
◇ *vt* reconnaître.
◇ *vi* faire une reconnaissance.
◇ *n* reconnaissance *f*; to go on a ~ MIL aller en reconnaissance; [gen] faire la reconnaissance des lieux.

recd, rec'd *written abbr of* received.

recede [riːˈsiːd] ◇ *vi* -**1.** [move away - object] s'éloigner; [- waters] refluer; [- tide] descendre; to ~ into the distance disparaître dans le lointain. -**2.** [fade - hopes] s'évanouir; [- fears] s'estomper; [- danger] s'éloigner. -**3.** [hairline]: his hair has started to ~ son front commence à se dégarnir. -**4.** FIN baisser.
◇ *vt* JUR [right] rétrocéder; [land] recéder.

receding [rɪˈsiːdɪŋ] *adj* -**1.** [hair]: to have a ~ hairline avoir le front qui se dégarnit. -**2.** FIN en baisse.

receipt [rɪˈsiːt] ◇ *n* -**1.** [for purchase] reçu *m*, ticket *m* de caisse; [for bill] acquit *m*; [for rent, insurance] quittance *f*; [for meal, taxi fare] reçu *m*; [from customs] récépissé *m*. -**2.** [reception] réception *f*; to pay on ~ payer à la réception; to acknowledge ~ of sthg COMM accuser réception de qqch; on ~ of your results dès que vous aurez reçu vos résultats; I am in ~ of the goods COMM j'ai bien reçu les marchandises.
◇ *vt Br* acquitter; a ~ed bill une facture acquittée.
◆ **receipts** *npl* [money] recettes *fpl*.

receivable [rɪˈsiːvəbl] *adj* recevable; COMM [outstanding] à recevoir; accounts ~ comptes *mpl* clients, créances *fpl*.
◆ **receivables** *npl* [debts] comptes *mpl* clients, créances *fpl*; [bills] effets *mpl* à recevoir.

receive [rɪˈsiːv] ◇ *vt* -**1.** [gift, letter] recevoir; to ~ sthg from sb recevoir qqch de qqn; we ~d your letter on Monday nous avons reçu votre lettre OR votre lettre nous est parvenue lundi; to ~ a high salary recevoir OR toucher un salaire élevé; '~d with thanks' COMM 'acquitté', 'pour acquit'; to ~ damages JUR obtenir OR recevoir des dommages-intérêts; she ~d ten years JUR elle a été condamnée à dix ans de réclusion. -**2.** [blow] recevoir; [insult, refusal] essuyer; [criticism] être l'objet de; he has ~d dreadful/excellent treatment il a été traité d'une manière épouvantable/avec beaucoup d'égards; she ~d injuries from which she has since died elle est morte des suites de ses blessures. -**3.** [greet, welcome] accueillir, recevoir; the new film was enthusiastically ~d le nouveau film a été accueilli avec enthousiasme; their offer was not well ~d leur proposition n'a pas reçu un accueil favorable; will Madam ~ the doctor now? *fml* Madame recevra-t-elle le médecin maintenant? || [into club, organization] admettre; to be ~d into the Church être reçu OR admis dans le sein de l'Église. -**4.** [signal, broadcast] recevoir, capter; I'm receiving you loud and clear je vous reçois cinq sur cinq. -**5.** SPORT: to ~ service recevoir le service. -**6.** JUR [stolen goods] receler. -**7.** [accommodate] *fml* recevoir, prendre; holes were drilled to ~ the pegs des trous étaient percés pour recevoir les chevilles.
◇ *vi* -**1.** [have guests] *fml* recevoir. -**2.** SPORT recevoir, être le receveur. -**3.** RELIG recevoir la communion. -**4.** JUR [thief] receler; to be accused of receiving être accusé de recel.

received [rɪˈsiːvd] *adj*: ~ idea/opinion idée *f* reçue OR toute faite; ~ wisdom sagesse *f* populaire.

Received Pronunciation *n Br* prononciation *f* standard (de l'anglais).

Received Standard *n Am* prononciation *f* standard (de l'américain).

receiver [rɪˈsiːvəʳ] *n* -**1.** [SPORT & gen] receveur *m*, -euse *f*; [of consignment] destinataire *mf*, consignataire *mf*; [of stolen goods] receleur *m*, -euse *f*. -**2.** [on telephone] combiné *m*, récepteur *m*; to lift/to replace the ~ décrocher/raccrocher (le téléphone); ~ rest berceau *m* (du combiné). -**3.** TV récepteur *m*, poste *m* de télévision; RADIO récepteur *m*, poste *m* de radio. -**4.** FIN administrateur *m* judiciaire; they have been placed in the hands of the ~, the ~ has been called in ils ont été placés sous administration judiciaire. -**5.** CHEM récipient *m*.

receiver general (*pl* receivers general) *n Am* receveur *m* des impôts.

receivership [rɪˈsiːvəʃɪp] *n* FIN: to go into ~ être placé sous administration judiciaire.

receiving [rɪˈsiːvɪŋ] ◇ *adj* [office] de réception; [country] d'accueil.
◇ *n* [of stolen property] recel *m*.

receiving end *n* -**1.** SPORT: to be at the ~ recevoir (le service). -**2.** *phr*: to be on the ~ *inf*: if anything goes wrong, you'll be on the ~ si ça tourne mal, c'est toi qui vas payer les pots cassés; she was on the ~ of their bad mood c'est sur elle qu'ils ont passé leur mauvaise humeur.

receiving order *n Br* JUR ordonnance *f* de mise sous administration judiciaire OR sous séquestre.

recension [rɪˈsenʃn] *n* [revision] révision *f*; [text] texte *m* révisé, texte *m* revu et corrigé.

recent [ˈriːsnt] *adj* [new] récent, nouveau; [modern] récent, moderne; in ~ months ces derniers mois; ~ developments les derniers événements; have you any ~ news of them? avez-vous eu de leurs nouvelles récemment?

recently [ˈriːsntlɪ] *adv* récemment, dernièrement, ces derniers temps; I saw her as ~ as yesterday je l'ai vue pas plus tard qu'hier; until ~ jusqu'à ces derniers temps; I hadn't heard of it until very ~ je n'en ai entendu parler que très récemment.

receptacle [rɪˈseptəkl] *n* -**1.** *fml* [container] récipient *m*. -**2.** *Am* ELEC prise *f* de courant (femelle).

reception [rɪˈsepʃn] *n* -**1.** [welcome] réception *f*, accueil *m*; to get a warm ~ recevoir un accueil chaleureux; to get a cold ~ être reçu froidement; the film got an enthusiastic ~ from the critics les critiques ont réservé un accueil enthousiaste à ce film. -**2.** [formal party] réception *f*; to hold a ~ donner une réception. -**3.** [in hotel] réception *f*; [in office] accueil *m*; at ~ à la réception. -**4.** RADIO & TV réception *f*. -**5.** *Am* SPORT [of ball] réception *f*. -**6.** *Br* SCH ≃ cours *m* préparatoire; ~ class première année *f* de maternelle.

reception centre *n Br* centre *m* d'accueil.

reception clerk *n Am* réceptionniste *mf*.

reception committee *n* comité *m* d'accueil *aussi hum*.

reception desk *n* [in hotel] réception *f*; [in office] accueil *m*.

receptionist [rɪˈsepʃənɪst] *n* [in hotel] réceptionniste *mf*; [in office] hôtesse *f* d'accueil; he's a ~ at Larousse il travaille à l'accueil chez Larousse.

reception room *n* [in hotel] salle *f* de réception; *Br* [in house] salon *m*.

receptive [rɪˈseptɪv] *adj* réceptif; to be ~ to new ideas être ouvert aux idées nouvelles.

receptiveness [rɪˈseptɪvnɪs], **receptivity** [ˌresepˈtɪvətɪ] *n* réceptivité *f*.

receptor [rɪˈseptəʳ] *n* ACOUST & PHYSIOL récepteur *m*.

recess [*Br* rɪ'ses, *Am* 'riːses] ◇ *n* -**1.** [alcove - gen] renfoncement *m*; [- in bedroom] alcôve *f*; [for statue] niche *f*; [in doorway] embrasure *f*. -**2.** [of mind, memory] recoin *m*, tréfonds *m*. -**3.** *Am* JUR suspension *f* d'audience; the court went into ~ l'audience a été suspendue. -**4.** *Am* SCH récréation *f*; during the ~ pendant la récréation; to go ~ aller en récréation. -**5.** [closure - of parliament] vacances *fpl* parlementaires, intersession *f* parlementaire; [- of courts] vacances *fpl* judiciaires, vacations *fpl*; Parliament is in ~ for the summer le Parlement est en vacances pour l'été.
◇ *vi Am* JUR suspendre l'audience; POL suspendre la séance.
◇ *vt* encastrer.

recessed [*Br* rɪ'sest, *Am* 'riːsest] *adj* encastré; ~ bookshelves étagères encastrées; ~ lighting éclairage encastré.

recession [rɪ'seʃn] *n* -**1.** ECON récession *f*; the economy is in ~ l'économie est en récession. -**2.** *fml* [retreat] recul *m*, retraite *f*. -**3.** RELIG sortie *f* en procession du clergé. -**4.** JUR rétrocession *f*.

recessional [rɪ'seʃənl] ◇ *n* RELIG *cantique de sortie en procession du clergé*.
◇ *adj* -**1.** [hymn] de sortie (processionnelle). -**2.** ECON de (la) récession.

recessionary [rɪ'seʃənrɪ] *adj* ECON de crise, de récession.

recessive [rɪ'sesɪv] ◇ *adj* -**1.** [gene] récessif. -**2.** [backward - measure] rétrograde.
◇ *n* [gene] gène *m* récessif; [organism] sujet *m* récessif.

recharge [*vb* ˌriː'tʃɑːdʒ, *n* 'riːtʃɑːdʒ] ◇ *vt* [battery, rifle] recharger; to ~ one's batteries recharger ses batteries.
◇ *n* recharge *f*.

rechargeable [ˌriː'tʃɑːdʒəbl] *adj* rechargeable.

recidivism [rɪ'sɪdɪvɪzm] *n* récidive *f* JUR.

recidivist [rɪ'sɪdɪvɪst] ◇ *adj* récidiviste.
◇ *n* récidiviste *mf*.

Recife [re'siːfə] *pr n* Recife.

recipe ['resɪpɪ] *n* CULIN recette *f*; *fig* recette *f*, secret *m*; a ~ for success/long life le secret de la réussite/la longévité; it's a ~ for disaster c'est le meilleur moyen pour aller droit à la catastrophe.

recipient [rɪ'sɪpɪənt] *n* -**1.** [of letter] destinataire *mf*; [of cheque] bénéficiaire *mf*; [of award, honour] récipiendaire *m*; he was the proud ~ of a gold watch il a eu la chance de se voir remettre une montre en or. -**2.** MED [of transplant] receveur *m*, -euse *f*.

reciprocal [rɪ'sɪprəkl] ◇ *adj* [mutual] réciproque, mutuel; [bilateral] réciproque, bilatéral; GRAMM & MATH réciproque.
◇ *n* MATH réciproque *f*.

reciprocate [rɪ'sɪprəkeɪt] ◇ *vt* -**1.** [favour, invitation, smile] rendre; [love, sentiment] répondre à, rendre. -**2.** MECH actionner d'un mouvement alternatif.
◇ *vi* -**1.** [in congratulations, compliments] retourner le compliment; [in fight] rendre coup pour coup; [in dispute] rendre la pareille; [in argument] répondre du tac au tac. -**2.** MECH avoir un mouvement de va-et-vient.

reciprocating [rɪ'sɪprəkeɪtɪŋ] *adj* MECH alternatif; ~ engine moteur *m* alternatif.

reciprocation [rɪˌsɪprə'keɪʃn] *n*: in ~ for en retour de; his ~ of her feelings was clear il était clair que leurs sentiments étaient réciproques.

reciprocity [ˌresɪ'prɒsətɪ] *n* réciprocité *f*.

recital [rɪ'saɪtl] *n* -**1.** MUS & LITERAT récital *m*; piano/poetry ~ récital de piano/poésie. -**2.** [narrative] narration *f*, relation *f*; [of details] énumération *f*; she bored us with a ~ of all her ills elle nous a assommés avec une énumération de tous ses malheurs.
◆ **recitals** *npl* JUR préambule *m (à un acte notarié)*.

recitation [ˌresɪ'teɪʃn] *n* récitation *f*.

recitative [ˌresɪtə'tiːv] *n* récitatif *m*.

recite [rɪ'saɪt] ◇ *vt* [play, poem] réciter, déclamer; [details, facts] réciter, énumérer.
◇ *vi* réciter; *Am* SCH réciter sa leçon.

reckless ['reklɪs] *adj* -**1.** [rash] imprudent; [thoughtless] irréfléchi; [fearless] téméraire; it was rather a ~ promise c'était une promesse assez hardie; it would be ~ to ignore the consequences/the danger il serait imprudent de ne pas tenir compte des conséquences/du danger. -**2.** ADMIN & JUR: ~ driving conduite *f* imprudente; ~ driver conducteur *m* imprudent, conductrice *f* imprudente.

recklessly ['reklɪslɪ] *adv* [rashly] imprudemment; [thoughtlessly] sans réfléchir; [fearlessly] avec témérité; to spend ~ dépenser sans compter; they rather ~ promised to contribute £500 ils ont promis assez imprudemment OR un peu hâtivement de donner 500 livres; he drives very ~ il conduit dangereusement.

recklessness ['reklɪsnɪs] *n* [rashness] imprudence *f*; [thoughtlessness] insouciance *f*, étourderie *f*; [fearlessness] témérité *f*.

reckon ['rekn] ◇ *vt* -**1.** [estimate]: there were ~ed to be about fifteen hundred demonstrators on a estimé à mille cinq cents le nombre des manifestants; I ~ this building to be about 300 years old je pense que ce bâtiment a environ 300 ans. -**2.** [consider] considérer; I ~ this restaurant to be the best in town je considère ce restaurant comme le meilleur de la ville; I don't ~ her chances much *inf* OR much to her chances *inf* je ne crois pas qu'elle ait beaucoup de chances. -**3.** *inf* [suppose, think] croire, supposer; I ~ you're right je crois bien que tu as raison; I ~ the omelette is ready je crois que l'omelette est prête; how old do you ~ he is? quel âge lui donnez-vous?; it's all over, I ~ je suppose que tout est fini; what do you ~? qu'en pensez-vous? -**4.** [expect] compter, penser; they had ~ed to make more profit from the venture ils comptaient OR pensaient que l'entreprise leur rapporterait de plus gros bénéfices. -**5.** *fml* [calculate] calculer.
◇ *vi* [calculate] calculer, compter.
◆ **reckon in** *vt sep Br* compter, inclure.
◆ **reckon on** *vt insep* -**1.** [rely on] compter sur; you can ~ on him making a mess of it tu peux compter sur lui pour tout gâcher; don't ~ on it n'y comptez pas. -**2.** [expect] s'attendre à, espérer; I was ~ing on more je m'attendais à plus; she had ~ed on going next week elle avait prévu d'y aller la semaine prochaine; I didn't ~ on that extra cost je n'avais pas prévu ces frais supplémentaires.
◆ **reckon up** ◇ *vt sep* [bill, total, cost] calculer.
◇ *vi insep* faire ses comptes; to ~ up with sb régler ses comptes avec qqn.
◆ **reckon with** *vt insep* -**1.** [take into account] tenir compte de, songer à; they didn't ~ with the army/the opposition ils ont compté sans l'armée/l'opposition; she's a force to be ~ed with elle a une influence avec laquelle il faut compter ‖ [as opponent] avoir affaire à; we had to ~ with stiff opposition nous avons eu affaire à une forte opposition; you'll have to ~ with his brother il faudra compter avec son frère. -**2.** [cope with] compter avec; you'll have to ~ with another guest il vous faudra compter avec un invité supplémentaire.
◆ **reckon without** *vt insep Br* -**1.** [do without] se passer de, se débrouiller sans; you'll have to ~ without my help il faudra vous débrouiller sans OR vous passer de moi. -**2.** *inf* [ignore, overlook]: he ~ed without the gold price il n'a pas pris en compte le cours de l'or; she had ~ed without the fact that they had no car elle n'avait pas pris en compte le fait qu'ils n'avaient pas de voiture.

reckoning ['rekənɪŋ] *n* -**1.** *(U)* [calculation] calcul *m*, compte *m*; you are way out in your ~ vous vous êtes complètement trompé dans vos comptes OR calculs; on OR by my ~, you owe us £50 d'après mes calculs, vous nous devez 50 livres; in the final ~ en fin de compte. -**2.** [estimation] estimation *f*; [opinion] avis *m*; to the best of my ~ pour autant que je puisse en juger; by OR on any ~ she's a fine pianist personne ne niera que c'est une excellente pianiste. -**3.** NAUT estime *f*.

reclaim [rɪ'kleɪm] ◇ *vt* -**1.** [land - gen] mettre en valeur; they have ~ed 1,000 hectares of land from the forest/marshes ils ont défriché 1 000 hectares de forêt/asséché 1 000 hectares de marais; they have ~ed 1,000 hectares of land from the sea/the desert ils ont gagné 1 000 hectares de terres sur la mer/le désert. -**2.** [salvage] récupérer; [recycle] recycler. -**3.** [deposit, baggage] récupérer, réclamer; to ~ sthg from sb récupérer qqch auprès de qqn. -**4.** *lit* [sinner, drunkard] ramener dans le droit chemin.
◇ *n*: to be past OR beyond ~ être irrécupérable; baggage ~ livraison *f* des bagages.

reclaimable [rɪ'kleɪməbl] *adj* [land] amendable; [waste - for salvage] récupérable; [- for recycling] recyclable.

reclamation [ˌreklə'meɪʃn] *n* -**1.** [of land - gen] remise *f* en valeur; [- from forest] défrichement *m*; [- from sea, marsh] assèchement *m*, drainage *m*; [- from desert] reconquête *f*. -**2.** [salvage] récupération *f*; [recycling] recyclage *m*.

reclassify [ˌriː'klæsɪfaɪ] (*pt* & *pp* reclassified) *vt* reclasser.

recline [rɪ'klaɪn] ◇ *vt* -**1.** [head] appuyer. -**2.** [seat] baisser, incliner.
◇ *vi* -**1.** [be stretched out] être allongé, être étendu; [lie back] s'allonger; he was reclining on the sofa il était allongé OR étendu sur le canapé. -**2.** [seat] être inclinable, avoir un dossier inclinable.

reclining [rɪ'klaɪnɪŋ] *adj* [seat] inclinable, à dossier inclinable; ~ chair chaise *f* longue.

recluse [rɪ'kluːs] *n* reclus *m*, -e *f*; to live like a ~ vivre en reclus OR en ermite; she's a bit of a ~ elle aime la solitude.

reclusive [rɪ'kluːsɪv] *adj* reclus.

recognition [ˌrekəg'nɪʃn] *n* -**1.** [identification] reconnaissance *f*; she disguised her voice to avoid ~ elle déguisa sa voix pour ne pas être reconnue; the town has changed beyond OR out of all ~ la ville est méconnaissable; she's changed him beyond OR out of all ~ elle l'a changé du tout au tout ❑ optical/speech ~ COMPUT reconnaissance optique/de la parole. -**2.** [acknowledgment, thanks] reconnaissance *f*; in ~ of en reconnaissance de. -**3.** [appreciation]: to win OR to achieve ~ être (enfin) reconnu; to seek ~ (for o.s.) chercher à être reconnu; his play received little ~ sa pièce est passée quasi inaperçue; public ~ la reconnaissance du public. -**4.** [realization - of problem] reconnaissance *f*; the report led to the ~ that there is indeed a problem le rapport nous a amenés à reconnaître qu'il y a effectivement un problème. -**5.** [of state, organization, trade union] reconnaissance *f*.

recognizable ['rekəgnaɪzəbl] *adj* reconnaissable.

recognizably ['rekəgnaɪzəblɪ] *adv* d'une manière OR façon reconnaissable; the car was not ~ Japanese on n'aurait pas dit une voiture japonaise, cette voiture ne ressemblait pas à une voiture japonaise.

recognizance [rɪ'kɒgnɪzəns] *n* JUR [bond] engagement *m*; [monies] caution *f*; to enter into ~s for sb [with money] verser une caution pour qqn; [personally] se porter garant de qqn.

recognize, -ise ['rekəgnaɪz] *vt* -**1.** [identify - person, place, voice] reconnaître; you'll ~ him by his hat vous le reconnaîtrez à son chapeau; they ~d him for what he was ils le reconnurent pour ce qu'il était ‖ COMPUT reconnaître. -**2.** [acknowledge - person] reconnaître les talents de; [- achievement] reconnaître. -**3.** [be aware of, admit] reconnaître; I ~ (that) I made a mistake je reconnais OR j'admets que je me suis trompé; the scale of the disaster has finally been ~d on a fini par se rendre compte de l'étendue du désastre. -**4.** ADMIN & POL [state, diploma] reconnaître. -**5.** *Am* [in debate] donner la parole à.

recognized ['rekəgnaɪzd] *adj* [acknowledged] reconnu, admis; a ~ fact un fait reconnu; she's a ~ authority on medieval history c'est une autorité en histoire médiévale || [identified] reconnu; [official] officiel, attitré; that's not the ~ legal term ce n'est pas le terme juridique officiel.

recoil [*vb* rɪ'kɔɪl, *n* 'riːkɔɪl] ◇ *vi* -**1.** [person] reculer; she ~ed in horror horrifiée, elle recula; to ~ from doing sthg reculer devant l'idée de faire qqch. -**2.** [firearm] reculer; [spring] se détendre; the plan was bound to ~ on him *fig* il était à prévoir que le plan se retournerait contre lui.
◇ *n* -**1.** [of gun] recul *m*; [of spring] détente *f*. -**2.** [of person] mouvement *m* de recul; *fig* répugnance *f*.

recoilless ['riːkɔɪlɪs] *adj* MIL & TECH sans recul.

recollect [,rekə'lekt] *vt* se souvenir de, se rappeler; I don't ~ having asked her je ne me rappelle pas le lui avoir demandé; as far as I (can) ~ autant que je m'en souvienne, autant qu'il m'en souvienne.

recollection [,rekə'lekʃn] *n* [memory] souvenir *m*; I have no ~ of it je n'en ai aucun souvenir; I have a slight ~ of it je n'en ai qu'un vague souvenir; to the best of my ~ (pour) autant que je m'en souvienne.

recombinant [riː'kɒmbɪnənt] *adj*: ~ DNA AND recombinant.

recombination [,riːkɒmbɪ'neɪʃn] BIOL & PHYS recombinaison *f*.

recommence [,riːkə'mens] *vi* & *vt* recommencer.

recommend [,rekə'mend] *vt* -**1.** [speak in favour of] recommander; she ~ed him for the job elle l'a recommandé pour cet emploi; I'll ~ you to the Minister j'appuyerai votre candidature auprès du ministre || [think or speak well of] recommander; the book has been highly ~ed to me le livre m'a été fortement recommandé; it's a restaurant I can thoroughly ~ c'est un restaurant que je recommande vivement; the town has little to ~ it la ville a peu d'attraits. -**2.** [advise] recommander, conseiller; I ~ you (to) see the film je vous recommande OR conseille d'aller voir ce film; not (to be) ~ed à déconseiller. -**3.** *arch* OR *fml* [entrust] recommander; to ~ one's soul to God recommander son âme à Dieu; the orphans were ~ed to the care of their grandmother les orphelins ont été confiés à leur grand-mère.

recommendable [,rekə'mendəbl] *adj* recommandable.

recommendation [,rekəmen'deɪʃn] *n* [personal] recommandation *f*; on your/his ~ sur votre/sa recommandation || [of committee, advisory body] recommandation *f*; to make a ~ faire une recommandation.

recommendatory [,rekə'mendətrɪ] *adj* [letter] de recommandation.

recommit [,riːkə'mɪt] *vt* -**1.** POL [bill] renvoyer devant une commission. -**2.** [prisoner] réincarcérer. -**3.** [crime] commettre une nouvelle fois.

recompense ['rekəmpens] ◇ *n* -**1.** [reward] récompense *f*; in ~ for your trouble en récompense de OR pour vous récompenser de votre peine. -**2.** JUR [compensation] dédommagement *m*, compensation *f*.
◇ *vt* récompenser; to ~ sb for sthg [gen] récompenser qqn de qqch; JUR dédommager qqn de OR pour qqch.

recompose [,riːkəm'pəʊz] *vt* -**1.** [text] réécrire; [print] recomposer. -**2.** [calm]: to ~ o.s. se ressaisir.

reconcilable ['rekənsaɪləbl] *adj* [opinions] conciliable, compatible; [people] compatible.

reconcile ['rekənsaɪl] *vt* -**1.** [people] réconcilier; [ideas, opposing principles] concilier; Peter and Jane are ~d at last Peter et Jane se sont enfin réconciliés; you cannot ~ morality with politics on ne saurait concilier moralité et politique. -**2.** [resign]: to ~ o.s. OR to become ~d to sthg se résigner à qqch; she ~d herself to the idea of going elle s'est faite à l'idée de partir. -**3.** [win over]: to ~ sb to sthg faire accepter qqch à qqn. -**4.** [settle - dispute] régler, arranger.

reconciliation [,rekənsɪlɪ'eɪʃn] *n* [between people] réconciliation *f*; [between ideas] conciliation *f*, compatibilité *f*.

recondite ['rekəndaɪt] *adj fml* [taste] ésotérique; [text, style] abscons, obscur; [writer] obscur.

recondition [,riːkən'dɪʃn] *vt* remettre en état OR à neuf.

reconditioned [,riːkən'dɪʃnd] *adj* remis à neuf; *Br* [tyre] rechapé; ~ engine AUT (moteur *m*) échange *m* standard.

reconfigure [,riːkən'fɪgə^r] *vt* COMPUT reconfigurer.

reconfirm [,riːkən'fɜːm] *vt* [booking] confirmer; [opinion, decision] réaffirmer.

reconnaissance [rɪ'kɒnɪsəns] *n* MIL reconnaissance *f*; aerial ~ reconnaissance aérienne; ~ flight vol *m* de reconnaissance.

reconnect [,riːkə'nekt] *vt* rebrancher; TELEC reconnecter.

reconnoitre *Br*, **reconnoiter** *Am* [,rekə'nɔɪtə^r]
◇ *vt* MIL reconnaître.
◇ *vi* effectuer une reconnaissance.

reconquer [,riː'kɒŋkə^r] *vt* reconquérir.

reconquest [,riː'kɒŋkwest] *n* reconquête *f*.

reconsider [,riːkən'sɪdə^r] ◇ *vt* [decision, problem] réexaminer; [topic] se repencher sur; [judgment] réviser, revoir.
◇ *vi* reconsidérer la question; I advise you to ~ je vous conseille de revoir votre position.

reconsideration ['riːkən,sɪdə'reɪʃn] *n* [reexamination] nouvel examen *m*, nouveau regard *m*; [of judgment] révision *f*.

reconstitute [,riː'kɒnstɪtjuːt] *vt* reconstituer.

reconstituted [,riː'kɒnstɪtjuːtɪd] *adj* reconstitué; ~d vegetable protein protéine *f* végétale reconstituée.

reconstitution ['riː,kɒnstɪ'tjuːʃn] *n* reconstitution *f*.

reconstruct [,riːkən'strʌkt] *vt* [house, bridge] reconstruire, rebâtir; [crime, event] reconstituer; [government, system] reconstituer.

reconstruction [,riːkən'strʌkʃn] *n* [of building] reconstruction *f*; [of shop, façade] réfection *f*; [of crime, event] reconstitution *f*; [of government] reconstitution *f*; the Reconstruction *Am* HIST la Reconstruction.

THE RECONSTRUCTION:
Période allant de 1865 à 1876, succédant à la guerre de Sécession et pendant laquelle les États de l'ex-Confédération (États sudistes) étaient réintégrés dans l'Union à condition d'avoir adopté les trois amendements à la Constitution fédérale précisant les droits des Noirs et stipulant l'élimination des Confédérés de toute activité politique et administrative.

---

reconvene [,riːkən'viːn] *vt* reconvoquer.

record [*vb* rɪ'kɔːd, *n* & *comp* 'rekɔːd]
◇ *vt* -**1.** [take note of - fact, complaint, detail] noter, enregistrer; [- in archives, on computer] enregistrer; your objection has been ~ed nous avons pris acte de votre objection; to ~ the minutes OR the proceedings of a meeting ADMIN faire le procès-verbal OR le compte rendu d'une réunion || [attest, give account of] attester, rapporter; no biography ~s the visit aucune biographie ne fait mention de OR n'atteste la visite; the debate was ~ed in the newsletter le débat a été rapporté dans le bulletin d'informations; their answer was not ~ed leur réponse n'a pas été enregistrée; a photograph was taken to ~ the event une photographie a été prise pour rappeler cet événement; the book ~s life in medieval England le livre dépeint OR évoque la vie en Angleterre au Moyen Âge; how many votes were ~ed? POL combien de voix ont été exprimées? || [explain, tell] raconter, rapporter; history ~s that 30,000 soldiers took part selon les livres d'histoire, 30 000 soldats y ont participé. -**2.** [indicate - measurement] indiquer; [- permanently] enregistrer; temperatures of 50° were ~ed on a relevé des températures de 50°. -**3.** [music, tape, TV programme] enregistrer; the group are in the studio ~ing their new album le groupe est dans le studio en train d'enregistrer son nouveau disque. -**4.** SPORT [score] marquer; he ~ed a time of 10.7 seconds for the 100 metres il a couru le 100 m en 10.7 secondes.
◇ *vi* [on tape, video] enregistrer; don't touch the video, it's ~ing ne touchez pas au magnétoscope, il est en train d'enregistrer; his voice doesn't ~ well sa voix ne se prête pas bien à l'enregistrement.
◇ *n* -**1.** [account, report] rapport *m*; [note] note *f*; [narrative] récit *m*; to make a ~ of sthg noter qqch; to strike sthg from the ~ rayer qqch du procès-verbal; they keep a ~ of all deposits/all comings and goings ils enregistrent tous les versements/toutes les allées et venues; the book provides a ~ of 19th-century Parisian society le livre évoque la société parisienne au XIXe siècle || [testimony] témoignage *m*; [evidence] preuve *f*; there is no ~ of the siege rien ne prouve que le siège ait vraiment eu lieu; do you have any ~ of the transaction? avez-vous gardé une trace de la transaction?; there's no ~ of it at all ce n'est mentionné nulle part; the carvings are a ~ of civilization on the island les sculptures témoignent de l'existence d'une civilisation sur l'île || [from instrument] trace *f*; [graph] courbe *f*; the apparatus gives a permanent ~ of ground movements l'appareil enregistre en permanence les mouvements du sol; to put OR to set the ~ straight mettre les choses au clair; a newspaper of ~ un journal qui fait autorité. -**2.** [past history] passé *m*; [file] dossier *m*; his past ~ with the firm son passé dans l'entreprise; she has an excellent attendance ~ elle a été très assidue, elle n'a presque jamais été absente; the plane has a good safety ~ l'avion est réputé pour sa sécurité || [criminal or police file] casier *m* (judiciaire); to have a ~ avoir un casier judiciaire; a clean ~ un casier judiciaire vierge; he has a ~ of previous convictions il a déjà été condamné || [reputation] réputation *f*; the makers have an excellent ~ for high quality les fabricants sont très réputés pour l'excellente qualité de leurs produits; case ~ MED dossier *m* médical; JUR dossier *m* judiciaire; service OR army ~ MIL états *mpl* de service; school ~ dossier *m* scolaire. -**3.** [disc] disque *m*; [recording] enregistrement *m*; to make OR to cut a ~ faire OR graver un disque. -**4.** [gen & SPORT] record *m*; to set/to break a ~ établir/battre un record; the 200 m ~ le record du 200 m ❑ 'The Guinness Book of Records' *McWhirter* 'le Livre Guinness des records'. -**5.** COMPUT enregistrement *m*.
◇ *comp* -**1.** [company, label, producer, shop] de disques. -**2.** [profits, sales, summer, temperature] record *(inv)*; in ~ time en un temps record; a ~ score un score record; to reach ~ levels atteindre un niveau record; a ~ number of spectators une affluence record.

◆ **records** *npl* [of government, police, hospital] archives *fpl*; [of history] annales *fpl*; [of conference, learned society] actes *mpl*; [register] registre *m*; [of proceedings, debate] procès-verbal *m*, compte rendu *m*; the wettest June since ~s began le mois de juin le plus humide depuis que l'on tient des statistiques ❑ public ~s office archives *fpl* nationales; police accident ~s liste *f* des accidents enregistrés par la police.

◆ **for the record** *adv phr* pour mémoire, pour la petite histoire; just for the ~, you started it! je te signale au passage que c'est toi qui as commencé!

◆ **off the record** ◇ *adj phr* confidentiel; I want these remarks to be off the ~ je veux que ces remarques restent confidentielles; the negotiations were off the ~ [secret] les négociations étaient secrètes; [unofficial] les négociations étaient officieuses; [not reported] les négociations n'ont pas été rapportées (dans la presse); [not recorded] les négociations n'ont pas été enregistrées; all this is strictly off the ~

fig tout ceci doit rester strictement entre nous.
◇ *adv phr*: he admitted off the ~ that he had known il a admis en privé qu'il était au courant.
◆ **on record** *adv phr* enregistré; it's on ~ that you were informed il est établi que vous étiez au courant; we have it on ~ that... il est attesté OR établi que...; it isn't on ~ il n'y en a aucune trace; to put OR to place sthg on ~ [say] dire OR déclarer qqch officiellement; [write] consigner qqch par écrit; I wish to go on ~ as saying that... je voudrais dire officiellement OR publiquement que...; it's the wettest June on ~ c'est le mois de juin le plus humide que l'on ait connu; it's the only example on ~ c'est le seul exemple connu.

record-breaker *n* SPORT nouveau recordman *m*, nouvelle recordwoman *f*; the new product is a ~ *Br fig* le nouveau produit bat tous les records.

record-breaking *adj* **-1.** SPORT: a ~ jump un saut qui a établi un nouveau record. **-2.** [year, temperatures] record *(inv)*.

record cabinet *n* discothèque *f (meuble)*.

record card *n* fiche *f*.

record-changer *n* changeur *m* de disques (automatique).

record deck *n* platine *f* (tourne-disque).

recorded [rɪ'kɔːdɪd] *adj* **-1.** [music, message, tape] enregistré; [programme] préenregistré; [broadcast] transmis en différé. **-2.** [fact] attesté, noté; [history] écrit; [votes] exprimé; throughout ~ history pendant toute la période couverte par les écrits historiques.

recorded delivery *n Br* recommandé *m*; to send (by) ~ envoyer en recommandé avec accusé de réception.

recorder [rɪ'kɔːdəʳ] *n* **-1.** [apparatus] enregistreur *m*; flight ~ enregistreur de vol. **-2.** [musical instrument] flûte *f* à bec. **-3.** [keeper of records] archiviste *mf*; court ~ JUR greffier *m*. **-4.** *Br* JUR *avocat nommé à la fonction de magistrat (à temps partiel)*.

record holder *n* recordman *m*, recordwoman *f*, détenteur *m*, -trice *f* d'un record.

recording [rɪ'kɔːdɪŋ] ◇ *n* [of music, data] enregistrement *m*; this is a very poor ~ cet enregistrement est très mauvais; a mono ~ un enregistrement (en) mono.
◇ *comp* **-1.** MUS & TV *etc* [equipment, session, studio] d'enregistrement; [company] de disques; [star] du disque; she's a ~ artist for Phonolog elle enregistre (des disques) chez Phonolog. **-2.** [indicating - apparatus] enregistreur. **-3.** ADMIN & JUR [official, clerk - in census] chargé du recensement; [- in court of law] qui enregistre les débats.

Recording Angel *n* BIBLE & *fig l'ange qui tient le livre des actes (bons et mauvais) de chacun*.

recording head *n* tête *f* d'enregistrement.

recording studio *n* studio *m* d'enregistrement.

record library *n* discothèque *f (de prêt)*.

record player *n* tourne-disque *m*, platine *f*.

record token *n* chèque-disque *m*.

recork [ˌriː'kɔːk] *vt* reboucher.

recount [rɪ'kaʊnt] *vt* [story, experience] raconter.

re-count [*vb* ˌriː'kaʊnt, *n* 'riːkaʊnt] ◇ *vt* [count again] recompter, compter de nouveau.
◇ *n* POL nouveau décompte *m*; to demand a ~ exiger un nouveau décompte; there were four ~s on a compté le nombre de bulletins de vote à quatre reprises.

recoup [rɪ'kuːp] *vt* **-1.** [get back - losses, cost] récupérer; to ~ one's investments rentrer dans ses fonds; to ~ one's costs rentrer dans OR couvrir ses frais. **-2.** [pay back] rembourser, dédommager. **-3.** [from taxes] défalquer, déduire.

recourse [rɪ'kɔːs] *n* **-1.** [gen] recours *m*; to have ~ to sthg recourir à qqch, avoir recours à qqch. **-2.** FIN recours *m*.

recover [rɪ'kʌvəʳ] ◇ *vt* **-1.** [get back - property] récupérer, retrouver; [- debt, loan, deposit] récupérer, recouvrer; to ~ sthg from sb récupérer qqch de qqn; 50 bodies have been ~ed 50 corps ont été retrouvés ‖ [take back] reprendre; to ~ sthg from sb reprendre qqch à qqn ‖ [regain - territory, ball] regagner; [- composure, control, hearing] retrouver; [- advantage] reprendre; to ~ one's breath/footing reprendre haleine/pied; to ~ one's balance retrouver son équilibre; to ~ one's senses se ressaisir; to ~ consciousness reprendre connaissance; to ~ one's strength reprendre des forces; to ~ lost ground *literal* & *fig* regagner du terrain. **-2.** [salvage - wreck, waste] récupérer; [- from water] récupérer, repêcher. **-3.** JUR: to ~ damages obtenir des dommages-intérêts. **-4.** [extract - from ore] extraire.
◇ *vi* **-1.** [after accident] se remettre; [after illness] se rétablir, guérir; the patient is ~ing in hospital le malade se remet à l'hôpital; to ~ from sthg se remettre de qqch; to be fully ~ed être complètement guéri OR rétabli ‖ [after surprise, setback] se remettre; I still haven't ~ed from the shock je ne me suis pas encore remis du choc. **-2.** [currency, economy] se redresser; [market] reprendre, se redresser; [prices, shares] se redresser, remonter. **-3.** JUR gagner son procès, obtenir gain de cause.

re-cover [ˌriː'kʌvəʳ] *vt* recouvrir.

recoverable [rɪ'kʌvrəbl] *adj* [debt] recouvrable; [losses, mistake] réparable; [by-product] récupérable.

recovery [rɪ'kʌvərɪ] (*pl* recoveries) *n* **-1.** [of lost property, wreck] récupération *f*; [of debt] recouvrement *m*, récupération *f*; the ~ of his sight changed his life le fait de recouvrer la vue a transformé sa vie. **-2.** [from illness] rétablissement *m*, guérison *f*; to make a speedy ~ se remettre vite; she is making a good ~ elle est en bonne voie de guérison. **-3.** [of economy] relance *f*, redressement *m*; [of prices, shares] redressement *m*, remontée *f*; [of currency] redressement *m*; [of market, business] reprise *f*; to stage OR to make a ~ SPORT reprendre le dessus; the country made a slow ~ after the war le pays s'est rétabli lentement après la guerre; to be past OR beyond ~ [situation] être irrémédiable OR sans espoir; [loss] être irrécupérable OR irréparable. **-4.** [of wreck, waste] récupération *f*; [from water] récupération *f*, repêchage *m*. **-5.** COMPUT [of files] récupération *f*. **-6.** JUR [of damages] obtention *f*.

recovery position *n* MED position *f* latérale de sécurité.

recovery room *n* MED salle *f* de réanimation.

recovery vehicle *n Br* dépanneuse *f*.

recreant ['rekrɪənt] *arch* ◇ *adj* [cowardly] lâche; [disloyal] perfide, déloyal.
◇ *n* [coward] lâche *mf*; [turncoat] renégat *m*, -e *f*.

re-create *vt* [past event] reconstituer; [place, scene] recréer.

recreation [ˌrekrɪ'eɪʃn] *n* **-1.** [relaxation] récréation *f*, détente *f*; she only reads for OR as ~ elle ne lit que pour se délasser OR se détendre. **-2.** SCH récréation *f*.

re-creation *n* [of event, scene] recréation *f*, reconstitution *f*.

recreational [ˌrekrɪ'eɪʃənl] *adj* de loisir; ~ drug drogue *f* douce.

recreational vehicle *Am* = **RV**.

recreation ground *n* terrain *m* de jeux.

recreation room *n* [in school, hospital] salle *f* de récréation; [in hotel] salle *f* de jeux; *Am* [at home] salle *f* de jeux.

recriminate [rɪ'krɪmɪneɪt] *vt fml* récriminer; to ~ against sb récriminer contre qqn.

recrimination [rɪˌkrɪmɪ'neɪʃn] *n (usu pl)*: ~s récriminations *fpl*.

recriminatory [rɪ'krɪmɪnətrɪ] *adj* récriminateur.

recrudescence [ˌriːkruː'desns] *n fml* recrudescence *f*.

recrudescent [ˌriːkruː'desnt] *adj fml* recrudescent.

recruit [rɪ'kruːt] ◇ *n* [gen & MIL] recrue *f*.
◇ *vt* [member, army] recruter; [worker] recruter, embaucher.

recruiting [rɪ'kruːtɪŋ] *n* recrutement *m*.

recruiting office *n* bureau *m* de recrutement.

recruiting officer *n* MIL recruteur *m*; HIST racoleur *m*.

recruitment [rɪ'kruːtmənt] *n* recrutement *m*; ~ campaign campagne *f* de recrutement.

rectal ['rektəl] *adj* rectal.

rectangle ['rekˌtæŋgl] *n* rectangle *m*.

rectangular [rek'tæŋgjʊləʳ] *adj* rectangulaire.

rectifiable ['rektɪfaɪəbl] *adj* [gen, CHEM & MATH] rectifiable, qui peut être rectifié; ELEC qui peut être redressé.

rectification [ˌrektɪfɪ'keɪʃn] *n* **-1.** [correction] rectification *f*, correction *f*. **-2.** CHEM & MATH rectification *f*; ELEC redressement *m*.

rectifier ['rektɪfaɪəʳ] *n* **-1.** ELEC redresseur *m*; CHEM rectificateur *m*. **-2.** [person] correcteur *m*, -trice *f*.

rectify ['rektɪfaɪ] (*pt* & *pp* rectified) *vt* **-1.** [mistake] rectifier, corriger; [oversight] réparer; [situation] redresser. **-2.** CHEM & MATH rectifier; ELEC redresser.

rectilinear [ˌrektɪ'lɪnɪəʳ] *adj* rectiligne.

rectitude ['rektɪtjuːd] *n* rectitude *f*; moral ~ droiture *f*.

recto ['rektəʊ] (*pl* rectos) *n* PRINT recto *m*.

rector ['rektəʳ] *n* **-1.** RELIG [Anglican, Presbyterian] pasteur *m*; [Catholic] recteur *m*. **-2.** *Br* SCH proviseur *m*, directeur *m*, -trice *f*. **-3.** *Scot* UNIV président *m*, -e *f* d'honneur.

rectory ['rektərɪ] (*pl* rectories) *n* presbytère *m*.

rectum ['rektəm] (*pl* rectums OR recta [-tə]) *n* rectum *m*.

recumbent [rɪ'kʌmbənt] *adj lit* couché, étendu, allongé; ~ figure ART figure *f* couchée, gisant *m*; ~ effigy [on grave] gisant *m*.

recuperate [rɪ'kuːpəreɪt] ◇ *vi* se remettre, récupérer; to ~ from sthg se remettre de qqch.
◇ *vt* [materials, money] récupérer; [loss] compenser; [strength] reprendre.

recuperation [rɪˌkuːpə'reɪʃn] *n* **-1.** MED rétablissement *m*. **-2.** [of materials] récupération *f*. **-3.** FIN [of market] reprise *f*.

recuperative [rɪ'kuːpərətɪv] *adj* [medicine] régénérateur, reconstituant; [sleep, break] réparateur; [powers] de récupération.

recur [rɪ'kɜːʳ] (*pt* & *pp* recurred, *cont* recurring) *vi* **-1.** [occur again] se reproduire; [reappear] réapparaître, revenir; it's a notion which ~s every now and then c'est une idée qui revient OR qu'on retrouve de temps en temps; come back if the problem ~s revenez si le problème réapparaît OR se représente. **-2.** [to memory] revenir à la mémoire. **-3.** MATH se reproduire, se répéter.

recurrence [rɪ'kʌrəns] *n* [of mistake, notion, event] répétition *f*; [of disease, symptoms] réapparition *f*; [of subject, problem] retour *m*; there must be no ~ of such behaviour ce genre de comportement ne devra jamais se reproduire.

recurrent [rɪ'kʌrənt] *adj* **-1.** [repeated] récurrent; I get ~ headaches/bouts of flu j'ai souvent des maux de tête/la grippe; ~ expenses [gen] dépenses *fpl* courantes; COMM frais *mpl* généraux. **-2.** ANAT & MED récurrent.

recurring [rɪ'kɜːrɪŋ] *adj* **-1.** [persistent - problem] qui revient OR qui se reproduit souvent; [- dream, nightmare] qui revient sans cesse. **-2.** MATH périodique; 2 point 7 ~ 2 virgule 7 périodique.

recurring decimal *n* fraction *f* périodique.

recursion [rɪ'kɜːʃn] *n* récurrence *f*.

recursive [rɪ'kɜːsɪv] *adj* récursif.

recusant ['rekjʊzənt] RELIG ◇ *adj* réfractaire.
◇ *n* rebelle *mf* à l'Église.

recyclable [ˌriː'saɪkləbl] *adj* recyclable.

recycle [ˌriː'saɪkl] *vt* [materials] recycler; [money] réinvestir.

recycled [ˌriː'saɪkld] *adj* [materials] recyclé; ~ paper papier *m* recyclé.

recycling [ˌriːˈsaɪklɪŋ] *n* recyclage *m*.

red [red] (*compar* **redder**, *superl* **reddest**) ◇ *adj* -**1.** [gen] rouge; [hair] roux; to go ~ rougir; ~ **with anger/shame** rouge de colère/honte; **to take a ~ pen to sthg** corriger qqch à l'encre rouge; **to be ~ in the face** [after effort] avoir la figure toute rouge; [with embarrassment] être rouge de confusion ❑ **to go into ~ ink** *Am* [person] être à découvert; [company] être en déficit; **to be as ~ as a beetroot** être rouge comme une pivoine OR une écrevisse; **it's like a ~ rag to a bull** c'est comme le rouge pour les taureaux; **'(Little) Red Riding Hood'** *Perrault* 'le Petit Chaperon rouge'. -**2.** *inf pej* & POL rouge. ◇ *n* -**1.** [colour] rouge *m*; **dressed in ~** habillé en rouge ❑ **to see ~** voir rouge. -**2.** [in roulette] rouge *m*; [in snooker] (bille *f*) rouge *f*. -**3.** [wine] rouge *m*. -**4.** *inf pej* & POL rouge *mf*, coco *mf pej*; **~s under the bed** *expression évoquant la psychose du communisme*. -**5.** [deficit]: **to be in the ~** [accounts, company] être dans le rouge; [person] être à découvert, avoir un découvert (bancaire); **to be £5,000 in the ~** [company] avoir un déficit de 5 000 livres; [person] avoir un découvert de 5 000 livres; **to get out of the ~** [company] sortir du rouge; [person] combler son découvert.

red admiral *n* ENTOM vulcain *m*.

red alert *n* alerte *f* rouge; **to be on ~** être en état d'alerte maximale.

red ant *n* fourmi *f* rouge.

Red Army *pr n* Armée *f* rouge.

red blood cell *n* globule *m* rouge.

red-blooded *inf adj* vigoureux, viril.

redbreast [ˈredbrest] *n* rouge-gorge *m*.

redbrick university [ˈredbrɪk-] *n université britannique fondée à la fin du XIXᵉ siècle*.

redcap [ˈredkæp] *n* -**1.** *inf Br* MIL policier *m* militaire. -**2.** *Am* RAIL porteur *m*.

red card *n* SPORT carton *m* rouge; **to get** OR **to receive the ~** recevoir le carton rouge.

red carpet *n* tapis *m* rouge; **to roll out the ~ for sb** [for VIP] dérouler le tapis rouge en l'honneur de qqn; [for guest] mettre les petits plats dans les grands en l'honneur de qqn; **to give sb the red-carpet treatment** réserver un accueil fastueux OR princier à qqn.

red cent *inf n Am*: **it's not worth a ~** ça ne vaut pas un clou OR un centime.

Red China *inf pr n* Chine *f* communiste OR populaire.

redcoat [ˈredkəʊt] *n Br* -**1.** HIST soldat *m* anglais. -**2.** [in holiday camp] animateur *m*, -trice *f*.

red corpuscle *n* globule *m* rouge.

Red Crescent *pr n* Croissant-Rouge *m*.

Red Cross (Society) *pr n* Croix-Rouge *f*.

redcurrant [ˈredkʌrənt] *n* groseille *f* (rouge); ~ **bush** groseillier *m* rouge; ~ **jelly** gelée *f* de groseille.

red deer *n* cerf *m* commun.

redden [ˈredn] ◇ *vt* rougir, rendre rouge; [hair] teindre en roux.
◇ *vi* [person, face] rougir, devenir (tout) rouge; [leaves] devenir roux, roussir; **to ~ with shame** rougir de honte.

reddish [ˈredɪʃ] *adj* rougeâtre; [fur] roussâtre; [hair] roussâtre, qui tire sur le roux.

red duster *inf Br* = **Red Ensign**.

red dwarf *n* ASTRON naine *f* rouge.

redecorate [ˌriːˈdekəreɪt] ◇ *vt* [repaint] refaire les peintures de; [re-wallpaper] retapisser; **we're redecorating the flat** nous sommes en train de repeindre et de retapisser l'appartement.
◇ *vi* [repaint] refaire les peintures; [re-wallpaper] refaire les papiers peints.

redecoration [riːˌdekəˈreɪʃn] *n* [with paint] remise *f* à neuf des peintures; [with wallpaper] remise *f* à neuf des papiers peints.

redeem [rɪˈdiːm] *vt* -**1.** [from pawn] dégager, retirer. -**2.** [cash - voucher] encaisser; [- bond, share] réaliser; [exchange - coupon, savings stamps] échanger; [- banknote] compenser. -**3.** [pay - debt] rembourser, s'acquitter de; [- bill] honorer; [- loan, mortgage] rembourser. -**4.** [make up for - mistake, failure] racheter, réparer; [- crime, sin] expier; **to ~ o.s.** se racheter. -**5.** [save - situation, position] sauver; [- loss] récupérer, réparer; [- honour] sauver; RELIG [sinner] racheter. -**6.** [fulfil - promise] s'acquitter de, tenir; [- obligation] satisfaire à, s'acquitter de. -**7.** [free - slave] affranchir.

redeemable [rɪˈdiːməbl] *adj* -**1.** [voucher] remboursable; [debt] remboursable, amortissable; **the stamps are not ~ for cash** les timbres ne peuvent être échangés contre des espèces. -**2.** [error] réparable; [sin, crime] expiable, rachetable; [sinner] rachetable.

redeemer [rɪˈdiːməʳ] *n* RELIG & *fig* rédempteur *m*.

redeeming [rɪˈdiːmɪŋ] *adj* [characteristic, feature] qui rachète OR compense les défauts; **his one ~ feature** sa seule qualité, la seule chose qui le rachète.

redefine [ˌriːdɪˈfaɪn] *vt* [restate - objectives, terms] redéfinir; [modify] modifier.

redemption [rɪˈdempʃn] *n* -**1.** [from pawn] dégagement *m*. -**2.** [of debt, loan, mortgage, voucher] remboursement *m*; ST. EX [of shares] liquidation *f*; ~ **yield** rendement *m* à l'échéance. -**3.** [gen & RELIG] rédemption *f*, rachat *m*; **past** OR **beyond ~** [person] perdu à tout jamais, qui ne peut être racheté; [situation, position] irrémédiable, irrécupérable; [book, furniture] irréparable, irrécupérable.

redemptive [rɪˈdemptɪv] *adj* rédempteur.

Red Ensign *n pavillon de la marine marchande britannique*.

redeploy [ˌriːdɪˈplɔɪ] *vt* [troops, forces, resources] redéployer; [workers] reconvertir.

redeployment [ˌriːdɪˈplɔɪmənt] *n* [of troops, resources] redéploiement *m*; [of workers] reconversion *f*.

redevelop [ˌriːdɪˈveləp] *vt* -**1.** [region] réexploiter, revitaliser; [urban area] rénover, reconstruire; [tourism, industry] relancer. -**2.** [argument] réexposer. -**3.** PHOT redévelopper.

redevelopment [ˌriːdɪˈveləpmənt] *n* -**1.** [of region] revitalisation *f*, développement *m*; [of urban area] rénovation *f*; [of tourism, industry] relance *f*; **urban ~** rénovation *f* urbaine. -**2.** PHOT redéveloppement *m*.

redeye [ˈredaɪ] *n Am* -**1.** ▽ [whisky] mauvais whisky *m*, ≃ gnôle *f*. -**2.** *inf* [night flight] vol *m* de nuit.

red eye *n* PHOT *tache rouge dans les yeux des personnes photographiées au flash*.

red-eyed *adj* aux yeux rouges.

red-faced *adj literal* rougeaud; *fig* rouge de confusion OR de honte.

red flag *n* [gen & POL] drapeau *m* rouge.
◆ **Red Flag** *n*: **the Red Flag** *chant socialiste anglais*.

red fox *n* renard *m* roux.

red giant *n* ASTRON géante *f* rouge.

red grouse *n* grouse *f*, coq *m* de bruyère écossais.

Red Guard *pr n* garde *f* rouge.

red-haired *adj* aux cheveux roux, roux; **a ~ girl** une rousse.

red-handed *adv*: **to be caught ~** être pris en flagrant délit OR la main dans le sac.

red hat *n* RELIG barrette *f (de cardinal)*.

redhead [ˈredhed] *n* roux *m*, rousse *f*.

red-headed = **red-haired**.

red heat *n*: **to bring** OR **to raise a metal to ~** chauffer OR porter un métal au rouge.

red herring *n* -**1.** *fig* diversion *f*; **it's just a ~** ce n'est qu'un truc pour nous dépister OR pour brouiller les pistes. -**2.** CULIN hareng *m* saur.

red-hot *adj* -**1.** [metal] chauffé au rouge. -**2.** [very hot] brûlant. -**3.** *fig* [keen] passionné, enthousiaste. -**4.** [recent - news, information] de dernière minute. -**5.** [sure - tip, favourite] certain, sûr. -**6.** [expert] calé; **he's ~ on the best investments** c'est un expert en matière d'investissements. -**7.** [strong - passion] fort, puissant. -**8.** [sensational - scandal, story] croustillant, sensationnel.

red-hot poker *n* BOT tritoma *m*.

redial [ˌriːˈdaɪəl] ◇ *vt*: **to ~ a number** refaire un numéro.
◇ *n*: **automatic ~** système *m* de rappel du dernier numéro.

Red Indian *n* Peau-Rouge *mf*.

redirect [ˌriːdɪˈrekt] *vt* -**1.** [mail] faire suivre, réexpédier; [aeroplane, traffic] dérouter; **the plane was ~ed to Oslo** l'avion a été dérouté sur Oslo. -**2.** *fig* [efforts, attentions] réorienter.

rediscover [ˌriːdɪˈskʌvəʳ] *vt* redécouvrir.

rediscovery [ˌriːdɪˈskʌvrɪ] (*pl* **rediscoveries**) *n* redécouverte *f*.

redistribute [ˌriːdɪˈstrɪbjuːt] *vt* [money, wealth, objects] redistribuer; [tasks] réassigner.

redistribution [ˈriːˌdɪstrɪˈbjuːʃn] *n* redistribution *f*.

red lead *n* minium *m*.

red-letter day *n Br* jour *m* à marquer d'une pierre blanche.

red light *n* AUT feu *m* rouge; **to go through a ~** passer au rouge, brûler le feu rouge.
◆ **red-light** *adj*: **red-light district** quartier *m* chaud.

red-line *vt* discriminer contre *(dans l'attribution de logements ou d'assurances)*.

red meat *n* viande *f* rouge.

red mullet *n* rouget barbet *m*.

redneck *inf* [ˈrednek] *Am pej* ◇ *n Américain d'origine modeste qui a des idées réactionnaires et des préjugés racistes*.
◇ *comp* [attitude] de plouc, borné.

redness [ˈrednɪs] *n (U)* rougeur *f*; [of hair] rousseur *f*; [inflammation] rougeurs *fpl*.

redo [ˌriːˈduː] (*pt* **redid** [-ˈdɪd], *pp* **redone** [-ˈdʌn]) *vt* refaire; [hair] recoiffer; [repaint] refaire, repeindre.

redolence [ˈredələns] *n lit* parfum *m*, odeur *f*.

redolent [ˈredələnt] *adj lit* -**1.** [perfumed]: ~ **of** OR **with lemon** qui sent le citron, qui a une odeur de citron. -**2.** [evocative, reminiscent]: **the style is ~ of James Joyce** le style rappelle celui de James Joyce.

redouble [ˌriːˈdʌbl] ◇ *vt* -**1.** [in intensity] redoubler; **to ~ one's efforts** redoubler ses efforts OR d'efforts. -**2.** CARDS surcontrer.
◇ *vi* CARDS surcontrer.
◇ *n* CARDS surcontre *m*.

redoubt [rɪˈdaʊt] *n* MIL redoute *f*; *fig* forteresse *f*.

redoubtable [rɪˈdaʊtəbl] *adj* [formidable] redoutable, terrifiant; [awe-inspiring] impressionnant.

redound [rɪˈdaʊnd] *vi fml*: **to ~ on** OR **upon sb** [negatively] retomber sur qqn; [positively] rejaillir sur qqn; **to ~ to sb's advantage** être OR rejaillir à l'avantage de qqn; **her behaviour can only ~ to her credit** sa conduite ne peut qu'être portée à son crédit.

red-pencil *vt* [correct] biffer au crayon rouge; [censor] censurer.

red pepper *n* [spice] (poivre *m* de) cayenne *m*; [vegetable] poivron *m* rouge.

redraft [*vb* ˌriːˈdrɑːft, *n* ˈriːdrɑːft] ◇ *vt* [bill, contract] rédiger de nouveau; [demand] reformuler.
◇ *n* [rewriting] nouvelle rédaction *f*; [reformulation] reformulation *f*.

redress [rɪˈdres] ◇ *vt* [grievance, errors] réparer; [wrong] réparer, redresser; [situation] rattraper; **to ~ the balance** rétablir l'équilibre.
◇ *n* [gen & JUR] réparation *f*; **to seek ~ for sthg** demander réparation de qqch.

Red Sea *pr n*: **the ~** la mer Rouge.

red setter *n* setter *m* irlandais.

redshank [ˈredʃæŋk] *n* (chevalier *m*) gambette *m*.

redskin▽ [ˈredskɪn] *n dated* Peau-Rouge *mf (attention: le terme «redskin» est considéré comme raciste)*.

Red Square *pr n* la place Rouge.

red squirrel *n* écureuil *m* commun d'Europe.

redstart ['redstɑːt] *n* rouge-queue *m*, rossignol *m* des murailles.

red tape *n* [bureaucracy] paperasserie *f*; there's too much ~ il y a trop de paperasserie OR de bureaucratie.

red tide *n* marée *f* rouge.

reduce [rɪ'djuːs] ◇ *vt* -**1.** [risk, scale, time, workload] réduire, diminuer; [temperature] abaisser; [speed] réduire, ralentir; [in length] réduire, raccourcir; [in size] réduire, rapetisser, diminuer; [in weight] réduire, alléger; [in height] réduire, abaisser; [in thickness] réduire, amenuiser; [in strength] réduire, affaiblir; the record has been ~d by two seconds le record a été amélioré de deux secondes; I'm trying to ~ my sugar consumption by half j'essaie de réduire ma consommation de sucre de moitié; you must ~ the power il faut réduire la puissance. -**2.** COMM & FIN [price] baisser; [rate, expenses, cost] réduire; [tax] alléger, réduire; [goods] solder, réduire le prix de; the shirt was ~d to £15 la chemise était soldée à 15 livres. -**3.** [render]: to ~ sthg to ashes/to a pulp réduire qqch en cendres/en bouillie; to ~ sb to silence/to tears/to poverty/to submission réduire qqn au silence/aux larmes/à la pauvreté/à l'obéissance; we were ~d to helpless laughter nous riions sans pouvoir nous arrêter; she was ~d to buying her own pencils elle en était réduite à acheter ses crayons elle-même. -**4.** CULIN [sauce] faire réduire. -**5.** CHEM & MATH réduire; to ~ fractions to a common denominator réduire des fractions à un dénominateur commun. -**6.** MED [fracture] réduire; [swelling] résorber, résoudre. -**7.** [dilute] diluer. -**8.** JUR: to ~ sthg to writing consigner qqch par écrit. -**9.** *arch* OR *lit* [subjugate] soumettre. -**10.** MIL dégrader.
◇ *vi* -**1.** CULIN réduire. -**2.** [slim] maigrir.

reduced [rɪ'djuːst] *adj* [price, rate, scale] réduit; [goods] soldé, en solde; at ~ prices à prix réduits; on a ~ scale en plus petit; '~ to clear' 'articles en solde' ☐ to be in ~ circumstances *euph* être dans la gêne.

reducer [rɪ'djuːsəʳ] *n* TECH réducteur *m*; PHOT affaiblisseur *m*; [for slimmer] appareil *m* d'amaigrissement.

reducible [rɪ'djuːsəbl] *adj* réductible.

reducing [rɪ'djuːsɪŋ] *adj* CHEM & TECH réducteur; [diet] amaigrissant.

reducing agent *n* (agent *m*) réducteur *m*.

reducing cream *n* crème *f* amincissante.

reduction [rɪ'dʌkʃn] *n* -**1.** [lessening - gen] réduction *f*, diminution *f*; [- in temperature] baisse *f*, diminution *f*; [- in length] réduction *f*, raccourcissement *m*; [- in weight] réduction *f*, diminution *f*; [- in strength] réduction *f*, affaiblissement *m*; [- in speed] réduction *f*, ralentissement *m*; staff ~s compression *f* de personnel; the ~ of the argument to basic principles la réduction du débat à des principes fondamentaux. -**2.** COMM & FIN [in price, cost] baisse *f*, diminution *f*; [in rate] baisse *f*; [in expenses] réduction *f*, diminution *f*; [in tax] dégrèvement *m*; [on goods] rabais *m*, remise *f*; to make a 5% ~ on an article faire une remise de 5 % sur un article; cash ~ [discount] remise *f* OR escompte *m* au comptant; [refund] remise *f* en espèces. -**3.** CHEM, MATH & PHOT réduction *f*. -**4.** TECH [of gear] démultiplication *f*. -**5.** MED [of fracture] réduction *f*; [of swelling] résorption *f*.

reductionism [rɪ'dʌkʃənɪzm] *n* réductionnisme *m*.

reductive [rɪ'dʌktɪv] *adj* réducteur.

redundancy [rɪ'dʌndənsɪ] (*pl* **redundancies**) ◇ *n* -**1.** *Br* [layoff] licenciement *m*; [unemployment] chômage *m*; voluntary ~ départ *m* volontaire; there is a high level of ~ here il y a un fort taux de chômage ici; 5,000 redundancies have been announced on a annoncé 5 000 licenciements. -**2.** [superfluousness] caractère *m* superflu; [repetition] répétition *f*, redondance *f*; [tautology] tautologie *f*. -**3.** COMPUT, LING & TELEC redondance *f*.
◇ *comp*: ~ notice *Br* lettre *f* de licenciement; ~ payment *Br* indemnité *f* de licenciement.

redundant [rɪ'dʌndənt] *adj* -**1.** INDUST licencié, au chômage; to become OR to be made ~ être licencié OR mis au chômage. -**2.** [superfluous] superflu, surabondant; [repetitive] répétitif, qui fait double emploi; [tautologous] pléonastique; much of what you write is ~ il y a beaucoup de redites OR répétitions dans ce que vous écrivez. -**3.** COMPUT, LING & TELEC redondant.

reduplicate [*vb* rɪ'djuːplɪkeɪt, *adj* rɪ'djuːplɪkɪt]
◇ *vt* redoubler; LING rédupliquer.
◇ *vi* être redoublé; LING être rédupliqué.
◇ *adj* redoublé; LING rédupliqué.

reduplication [rɪˌdjuːplɪ'keɪʃn] *n* redoublement *m*; LING réduplication *f*.

redwing ['redwɪŋ] *n* *Br* mauvis *m*.

redwood ['redwʊd] *n* séquoia *m*.

re-echo ◇ *vt* renvoyer en écho.
◇ *vi* retentir; the wood ~ed with his shouts le bois retentit OR résonna de ses cris.

reed [riːd] ◇ *n* -**1.** BOT roseau *m*. -**2.** MUS anche *f*; the ~s les instruments *mpl* à anche. - *phr*: he's a broken ~ on ne peut pas compter sur lui.
◇ *comp* [chair, mat] en roseau OR roseaux, fait de roseaux.

reed bunting *n* bruant *m* des roseaux.

reeding ['riːdɪŋ] *n* ARCHIT rudenture *f*.

reed instrument *n* instrument *m* à anche.

reedit [ˌriː'edɪt] *vt* rééditer.

reed organ *n* harmonium *m*.

reed pipe *n* pipeau *m*, chalumeau *m*.

reed stop *n* jeu *m* d'anches.

re-educate *vt* rééduquer.

re-education *n* rééducation *f*.

reed warbler *n* fauvette *f* des roseaux, rousserolle *f*.

reedy ['riːdɪ] (*compar* **reedier**, *superl* **reediest**) *adj* -**1.** [place] envahi par les roseaux. -**2.** [sound, voice] flûté, aigu.

reef [riːf] ◇ *n* -**1.** [in sea] récif *m*, écueil *m*; *fig* écueil *m*. -**2.** MIN filon *m*. -**3.** NAUT ris *m*.
◇ *vt* [spar] rentrer; to ~ a sail prendre un ris dans une voile.

reefer ['riːfəʳ] *n* -**1.** [garment]: ~ (jacket) caban *m*. -**2.** *inf dated* [drug] joint *m*. -**3.** *inf Br* [lorry] camion *m* frigorifique.

reef knot *n* nœud *m* plat.

reek [riːk] ◇ *vi* -**1.** [smell] puer, empester; it ~s of tobacco in here ça empeste OR pue le tabac ici; it ~s of hypocrisy *fig* ça pue l'hypocrisie; this place ~s of money *fig* cet endroit pue le fric. -**2.** *Scot* [chimney] fumer.
◇ *n* puanteur *f*.

reel [riːl] ◇ *n* -**1.** [for thread, film, tape] bobine *f*; [for hose] dévidoir *m*, enrouleur *m*; [for cable] enrouleur *m*; [for rope-making] caret *m*; (fishing) ~ moulinet *m* (de pêche). -**2.** [film, tape] bande *f*, bobine *f*. -**3.** [dance] quadrille *m* *(écossais ou irlandais)*; MUS branle *m* *(écossais ou irlandais)*.
◇ *vi* -**1.** [stagger] tituber, chanceler; the blow sent me ~ing across the room le coup m'a envoyé valser à travers la pièce; the force of the shock made us ~ la violence du choc nous a fait chanceler; to ~ back/down/out reculer/descendre/sortir en chancelant; a drunk came ~ing downstairs un ivrogne descendait l'escalier en titubant. -**2.** *fig* [whirl - head, mind] tournoyer; my head is ~ing j'ai la tête qui tourne; he is still ~ing from the shock il ne s'est pas encore remis du choc; the room started ~ing before her la pièce a commencé à vaciller autour d'elle.
◇ *vt* bobiner.
◆ **reel in** *vt sep* [cable, hose] enrouler; [fish] remonter, ramener; [line] enrouler, remonter.
◆ **reel off** *vt sep* [poem, speech, story] débiter.
◆ **reel out** *vt sep* [thread] dévider, dérouler; FISHING [line] laisser filer.
◆ **reel up** *vt sep* enrouler.

re-elect *vt* réélire.

re-election *n* réélection *f*; to stand OR to run for ~ se représenter aux élections.

reel holder *n* porte-bobines *m inv*.

reel-to-reel ◇ *adj* [system, tape recorder] à bobines.
◇ *n* magnétophone *m* à bobines.

re-embark *vi* & *vt* rembarquer.

re-emerge *vi* [new facts] ressortir; [idea, clue] réapparaître; [problem, question] se reposer; [from hiding, tunnel] ressortir, ressurgir.

re-emergence *n* réapparition *f*.

re-emphasize, -ise *vt* insister une fois de plus sur, souligner une nouvelle fois.

re-employ *vt* [materials] réemployer, remployer; [workers] réembaucher, rembaucher.

re-employment *n* [of materials] réemploi *m*, remploi *m*; [of workers] réembauche *f*.

re-enact *vt* -**1.** [scene, crime] reconstituer; we were able to ~ the incident in detail nous avons pu reconstituer l'incident en détail. -**2.** ADMIN & POL [legislation] remettre en vigueur.

re-enactment *n* -**1.** [of scene, crime] reconstitution *f*. -**2.** ADMIN, JUR & POL [of regulation, legislation] remise *f* en vigueur.

re-engage *vt* -**1.** [troops] rengager; [employee] réengager, rengager. -**2.** [mechanism] rengréner; to ~ the clutch rembrayer.

re-engagement *n* -**1.** [of troops, of worker] réengagement *m*, rengagement *m*. -**2.** TECH rengrènement *m*.

re-enlist MIL ◇ *vt* réengager, rengager.
◇ *vi* se réengager, se rengager.

re-enter ◇ *vi* -**1.** [come back in] rentrer, entrer à nouveau; ASTRONAUT rentrer dans l'atmosphère. -**2.** [candidate]: to ~ for an exam se réinscrire à un examen.
◇ *vt* -**1.** [room, country] rentrer dans, entrer à nouveau dans; [atmosphere] rentrer dans. -**2.** COMPUT [data] saisir à nouveau, réintroduire.

re-entry (*pl* re-entries) *n* -**1.** [gen & ASTRONAUT] rentrée *f*. -**2.** MUS [of theme] reprise *f*.

re-entry point *n* ASTRONAUT point *m* de rentrée.

re-equip *vt* ré-équiper.

re-establish *vt* -**1.** [order] rétablir; [practice] restaurer; [law] remettre en vigueur. -**2.** [person] réhabiliter, réintégrer; the team have ~ed themselves as the best in the country l'équipe s'est imposée de nouveau comme la meilleure du pays; to ~ o.s. OR one's position rétablir sa position.

re-establishment *n* -**1.** [of order] rétablissement *m*; [of practice] restauration *f*; [of law] remise *f* en vigueur. -**2.** [of person] réintégration *f*; her ~ as team leader sa réintégration en tant que chef d'équipe.

re-evaluate *vt* réévaluer.

re-evaluation *n* réévaluation *f*.

reeve [riːv] ◇ (*pt* & *pp* **reeved** OR **rove** [rəʊv])
◇ *n* -**1.** *Br* HIST [in town] premier magistrat *m*; [in manor] intendant *m*. -**2.** *Can* président *m* (du conseil municipal).
◇ *vt* NAUT [fasten] capeler.

re-examination *n* [of question] réexamen *m*; JUR nouvel interrogatoire *m*.

re-examine *vt* [question, case] réexaminer, examiner de nouveau; [witness] réinterroger, interroger de nouveau; [candidate] faire repasser un examen à.

re-export [*vb* ˌriːek'spɔːt, *n* ˌriː'ekspɔːt]
◇ *vt* réexporter.
◇ *n* -**1.** [of goods] réexportation *f*. -**2.** [product] marchandise *f* de réexportation.

ref *inf* [ref] *n* *Br abbr of* referee.

ref, ref. (*written abbr of* reference) réf.; your ~ v/réf.

reface [ˌriː'feɪs] *vt* [wall] ravaler.

refashion [ˌriː'fæʃn] *vt* [object] refaçonner; [image] reconstruire.

refectory [rɪ'fektərɪ] (*pl* **refectories**) *n* réfectoire *m*.

refer [rɪ'fɜːʳ] (*pt* & *pp* **referred**, *cont* **referring**) *vt* -**1.** [submit, pass on] soumettre, renvoyer; the dispute has been referred to arbitration le litige a été soumis à arbitrage OR à l'arbitrage d'un médiateur; I ~ the matter to you for a decision je m'en remets à vous pour prendre une décision sur la question; **the question has been referred to Jane** la question a été soumise à Jane; **to ~ a case to a higher court** renvoyer OR déférer une affaire à une instance supérieure; **the contract has been referred to us** le contrat nous a été soumis || [send, direct] renvoyer; **my doctor referred me to the hospital/to a specialist** mon docteur m'a envoyé à l'hôpital/chez un spécialiste || [in writing, reading] renvoyer; **I ~ you to Ludlow's book** je vous renvoie au livre de Ludlow; **here the author ~s us to "Alice in Wonderland"** ici l'auteur nous renvoie à «Alice au pays des merveilles» || BANK: **to ~ a cheque to drawer** refuser d'honorer un chèque; **'referred to drawer'** 'voir le tireur'. -**2.** [attribute] attribuer; **to ~ sthg to an event** attribuer qqch à un événement. -**3.** MED: **the pain may be referred to another part of the body** il peut y avoir irradiation de la douleur dans d'autres parties du corps. -**4.** JUR: **to ~ the accused** déférer l'accusé. -**5.** UNIV [student] refuser, recaler; [thesis] renvoyer pour révision.

◆ **refer back** *vt sep* -**1.** [put off - meeting, decision] ajourner, remettre (à plus tard). -**2.** [redirect -case] renvoyer; **the case was referred back to our office** l'affaire a été renvoyée à notre service.

◆ **refer to** *vt insep* -**1.** [allude to]: **to ~ to sthg** faire allusion OR référence à qqch, parler de qqch; **no-one ~s to it now** personne n'en parle plus maintenant; **I don't know what you are referring to** je ne sais pas à quoi vous faites allusion OR de quoi vous parlez; **he keeps referring to me as Dr Rayburn** il ne cesse de m'appeler Dr Rayburn; **the revolutionaries are referred to as Mantras** ces révolutionnaires sont connus sous le nom de Mantras; **that comment ~s to you** cette remarque s'adresse à vous; **they ~ to themselves as martyrs** ils se qualifient eux-mêmes de martyrs. -**2.** [relate to] correspondre à, faire référence à; **the numbers ~ to footnotes** les chiffres correspondent à OR font référence à des renvois en bas de page || [apply, be connected to] s'appliquer à, s'adresser à; **these measures only ~ to taxpayers** ses mesures ne s'appliquent qu'aux contribuables. -**3.** [consult - notes] consulter; [- instructions] se référer à; [- book, page] se reporter à; [- person]: **I shall have to ~ to my boss** je dois en référer à OR consulter mon patron.

referable [rɪ'fɜːrəbl] *adj*: **~ to** attribuable à, qui relève de.

referee [ˌrefə'riː] ◇ *n* -**1.** SPORT arbitre *m*; TENNIS juge *m* arbitre. -**2.** *Br* [for job] répondant *m*, -e *f*; **I was ~ OR I acted as his ~ for his last job** je lui ai fourni une recommandation pour son dernier emploi; **you can give my name as a ~** vous pouvez me citer comme référence; **please give the names of three ~s** veuillez nous donner le nom de trois personnes susceptibles de fournir une lettre de recommandation. -**3.** JUR conciliateur *m*, médiateur *m*.

◇ *vt* SPORT arbitrer.

◇ *vi* SPORT être arbitre; **who'll ~ for us?** qui va nous servir d'arbitre?

reference ['refrəns] ◇ *n* -**1.** [allusion] allusion *f*; **to make a ~ to sthg** faire allusion à qqch; **it's a biblical ~** c'est une allusion OR une référence biblique; **look up the ~ in the dictionary** cherchez la référence dans le dictionnaire. -**2.** [consultation] consultation *f*; **they refused the application without ~ to me** ils ont refusé la demande sans me consulter. -**3.** [recommendation - for job] recommandation *f*, référence *f*; **could you give me a ~ please?** pouvez-vous me fournir des références, s'il vous plaît?; **I'm often asked for ~s** on me demande souvent de fournir des lettres de recommandation; **banker's ~** références *fpl* bancaires. -**4.** [in code, catalogue] référence *f*; [on map] coordonnées *fpl*; [footnote] renvoi *m*; COMM référence *f*; **quote this ~** rappelez cette référence; **our ~** notre référence. -**5.** [remit - of commission] compétence *f*, pouvoirs *mpl*; **the question is outside the tribunal's ~** la question n'est pas de la compétence du tribunal. -**6.** LING référence *f*. -**7.** JUR [of case] renvoi *m*.

◇ *vt* -**1.** [refer to] faire référence à. -**2.** [thesis] faire OR compiler la liste des citations dans; [quotation] donner la référence de.

◇ *comp* [material, section] de référence; [value, quantity] de référence, étalon.

◆ **with reference to, in reference to** *prep phr* en ce qui concerne.

reference book *n* ouvrage *m* de référence.

reference library *n* bibliothèque *f* d'ouvrages de référence.

reference number *n* numéro *m* de référence.

referendum [ˌrefə'rendəm] (*pl* **referendums** OR **referenda** [-də]) *n* référendum *m*; **to hold a ~** organiser un référendum.

referent ['refərənt] *n* référent *m*.

referential [ˌrefə'renʃl] *adj* référentiel.

referral [rɪ'fɜːrəl] *n* -**1.** [forwarding] renvoi *m*. -**2.** [consultation] consultation *f*. -**3.** UNIV [of thesis] renvoi *m* pour révision. -**4.** [person] patient *m* *(qui a été envoyé par son médecin chez un spécialiste)*.

referred pain [rɪ'fɜːd-] *n* douleur *f* irradiée.

refill [*vb* ˌriː'fɪl, *n* 'riːfɪl] ◇ *vt* [glass] remplir (à nouveau); [lighter, canister] recharger.

◇ *n* [for pen, lighter] (nouvelle) cartouche *f*; [for propelling pencil] mine *f* de rechange; [for notebook] recharge *f*; [drink]: **do you need a ~?** *inf* je vous en ressers un?

◇ *comp* de rechange.

refillable [ˌriː'fɪləbl] *adj* rechargeable.

refinance [ˌriː'faɪnæns] *vt* refinancer.

refine [rɪ'faɪn] *vt* -**1.** [oil, sugar] raffiner; [ore, metal] affiner; [by distillation] épurer. -**2.** [model, manners] améliorer; [judgment, taste] affiner; [lecture, speech] parfaire, peaufiner.

◆ **refine on, refine upon** *vt insep* parfaire, peaufiner.

refined [rɪ'faɪnd] *adj* -**1.** [oil, sugar] raffiné; [ore] affiné; [by distillation] épuré. -**2.** [style, person, taste] raffiné.

refinement [rɪ'faɪnmənt] *n* -**1.** [of oil, sugar] raffinage *m*; [of metals, ore] affinage *m*; [by distillation] épuration *f*. -**2.** [of person] délicatesse *f*, raffinement *m*; [of taste, culture] raffinement *m*; [of morals] pureté *f*; **a man of ~** un homme raffiné. -**3.** [of style, discourse, language] subtilité *f*, raffinement *m*. -**4.** [improvement] perfectionnement *m*, amélioration *f*; **it's a ~ on an old process** c'est un processus ancien qui a été amélioré; **all the latest technical ~s** tous les derniers perfectionnements techniques.

refiner [rɪ'faɪnəʳ] *n* [of oil, sugar] raffineur *m*, -euse *f*; [of metal] affineur *m*, -euse *f*.

refinery [rɪ'faɪnərɪ] (*pl* **refineries**) *n* [for oil, sugar] raffinerie *f*; [for metals] affinerie *f*.

refit [*vb* ˌriː'fɪt, *n* 'riːfɪt] (*pt* & *pp* **refitted**, *cont* **refitting**) ◇ *vt* -**1.** [repair] remettre en état. -**2.** [refurbish] rééquiper, renouveler l'équipement de.

◇ *vi* [ship] être remis en état.

◇ *n* [of plant, factory] rééquipement *m*, nouvel équipement *m*; [of ship] remise *f* en état, réparation *f*.

reflate [ˌriː'fleɪt] *vt* -**1.** [ball, tyre] regonfler. -**2.** ECON relancer.

reflation [ˌriː'fleɪʃn] *n* ECON relance *f*.

reflationary [ˌriː'fleɪʃənrɪ] *adj* ECON [policy] de relance; **~ pressure** pression *f* pour une relance (économique).

reflect [rɪ'flekt] ◇ *vt* -**1.** [image] refléter; [sound, heat] renvoyer; [light] réfléchir; **the mirror ~ed the light from the lamp** le miroir réfléchissait la lumière de la lampe; **her face was ~ed in the mirror/water** son visage se reflétait dans la glace/dans l'eau; **she saw herself ~ed in the window** elle a vu son image dans la vitre; **the plate ~s heat (back) into the room** la plaque renvoie la chaleur dans la pièce; **the sound was ~ed off the rear wall** le son était renvoyé par le mur du fond. -**2.** *fig* [credit] faire jaillir, faire retomber; **the behaviour of a few ~s discredit on us all** le comportement de quelques-uns porte atteinte à l'honneur de tous; **he bathed in the ~ed glory of his wife's achievements** il laissait rejaillir sur lui l'éclat de la réussite de sa femme. -**3.** *fig* [personality, reality] traduire, refléter; **the graph ~s population movements** le graphique traduit les mouvements de population; **many social problems are ~ed in his writing** de nombreux problèmes de société sont évoqués dans ses écrits. -**4.** [think] penser, se dire; [say] dire, réfléchir; **I often ~ that...** je me dis souvent OR je me fais souvent la réflexion que...; **Peter might know, she ~ed** Peter saura peut-être, songeait-elle.

◇ *vi* [think] réfléchir; **to ~ on a question** réfléchir sur une question; **I'll ~ on it** j'y songerai OR réfléchirai; **after ~ing for a while...** après mûre réflexion...

◆ **reflect on, reflect upon** *vt insep* [negatively] porter atteinte à, nuire à; [positively] rejaillir sur; [cast doubt on] mettre en doute, jeter le doute sur; **their behaviour ~s well on them** leur comportement leur fait honneur; **this will ~ badly upon the company** ceci va porter atteinte à l'image de l'entreprise.

reflection [rɪ'flekʃn] *n* -**1.** [of light, sound, heat] réflexion *f*. -**2.** [image] reflet *m*; **a ~ in the mirror/window** un reflet dans la glace/vitre; **can you see your ~?** voyez-vous votre reflet?; **there is some ~ on the screen** il y a des reflets sur l'écran; **the result was not a fair ~ of the game** *fig* le résultat ne reflétait pas la manière dont le match s'était joué; **an accurate ~ of reality** *fig* un reflet exact de la réalité. -**3.** [comment] réflexion *f*, remarque *f*, observation *f*; **to make a ~ on sthg** faire une réflexion sur qqch; **~s on James Joyce/on Communism** réflexions sur James Joyce/sur le communisme || [criticism] critique *f*; **his book was seen as a ~ on the government** son livre a été perçu comme une critique du gouvernement; **it's no ~ on their integrity** leur intégrité n'est pas en cause; **my comment was not meant to be a ~ on you** ce que j'ai dit ne vous visait pas personnellement. -**4.** [deliberation] réflexion *f*; [thought] pensée *f*; **on ~** après OR à la réflexion, en y réfléchissant; **on due ~** après mûre réflexion; **with no ~** sans avoir réfléchi.

reflective [rɪ'flektɪv] *adj* -**1.** OPT [surface] réfléchissant, réflecteur; [power, angle] réflecteur; [light] réfléchi. -**2.** [mind, person] pensif, réfléchi; [faculty] de réflexion.

reflectively [rɪ'flektɪvlɪ] *adv* [speak] d'un ton pensif; [behave] d'un air songeur.

reflector [rɪ'flektəʳ] *n* réflecteur *m*; AUT catadioptre *m*.

reflex ['riːfleks] ◇ *n* -**1.** [gen & PHYSIOL] réflexe *m*. -**2.** PHOT (appareil *m*) reflex *m*.

◇ *adj* -**1.** PHYSIOL réflexe; **~ action** réflexe *m*. -**2.** OPT & PHYS réfléchi. -**3.** PHOT reflex *(inv)*; **~ camera** (appareil *m*) reflex *m*. -**4.** MATH rentrant.

reflexion [rɪ'flekʃn] *Br* = **reflection**.

reflexive [rɪ'fleksɪv] ◇ *adj* -**1.** GRAMM réfléchi. -**2.** PHYSIOL réflexe. -**3.** LOGIC & MATH réflexif.

◇ *n* GRAMM réfléchi *m*.

reflexively [rɪ'fleksɪvlɪ] *adv* GRAMM [in meaning] au sens réfléchi; [in form] à la forme réfléchie.

reflexive pronoun *n* pronom *m* réfléchi.

reflexive verb *n* verbe *m* réfléchi.

reflexology [ˌriːflek'sɒlədʒɪ] *n* réflexothérapie *f*.

refloat [ˌriː'fləʊt] ◇ *vt fig* & NAUT renflouer.

◇ *vi* être renfloué.

refocus [ˌriː'fəʊkəs] (*pt* & *pp* **refocused** OR **refocussed**, *cont* **refocusing** OR **refocussing**)

◇ *vt* [projector, camera] refaire la mise au point de; **it has ~ed attention on the problem** *fig* cela a attiré une nouvelle fois l'attention sur ce problème.

◇ *vi* refaire la mise au point.

reforest [ˌriː'fɒrɪst] = **reafforest**.

reforestation [riːˌfɒrɪ'steɪʃn] = **reafforestation**.

reform [rɪ'fɔːm] ◇ *vt* -**1.** [modify - law, system, institution] réformer. -**2.** [person] faire perdre ses mauvaises habitudes à; [drunkard] faire renon

cer à la boisson; [habits, behaviour] corriger; to ~ o.s. s'amender, se corriger.
◇ *vi* se corriger, s'amender.
◇ *n* réforme *f*.

re-form ◇ *vt* -**1.** MIL [ranks] remettre en rang, reformer; [men] rallier. -**2.** [return to original form] rendre sa forme primitive OR originale à; [in new form] donner une nouvelle forme à; [form again] reformer.
◇ *vi* -**1.** MIL [men] se remettre en rangs; [ranks] se reformer. -**2.** [group, band] se reformer; the band has ~ed for a charity concert le groupe s'est reformé pour donner un concert de bienfaisance.

Reform Act = **Reform Bill**.

reformation [,refə'meɪʃn] *n* -**1.** [of law, institution] réforme *f*. -**2.** [of behaviour] réforme *f*; [of criminal, addict etc] réinsertion *f*.
◆ **Reformation** ◇ *n*: the Reformation la Réforme.
◇ *comp* [music, writer] de la Réforme.

reformative [rɪ'fɔːmətɪv] *adj* [concerning reform] de réforme; [reforming] réformateur.

reformatory [rɪ'fɔːmətrɪ] ◇ *adj* réformateur.
◇ *n Br* ≃ maison *f* de redressement; *Am* ≃ centre *m* d'éducation surveillée.

Reform Bill *n Br* HIST *loi de réforme du système parlementaire*; the great ~s les grandes réformes.

THE GREAT REFORM BILLS:
Série de réformes parlementaires (1832, 1867, 1884-85) concernant le droit de vote et la représentation parlementaire. Elles ouvrirent la voie à l'adoption du suffrage universel en Grande-Bretagne.

---

reformed [rɪ'fɔːmd] *adj* -**1.** [person] qui a perdu ses mauvaises habitudes; [prostitute, drug addict] ancien; he's a ~ character since his marriage il s'est assagi depuis son mariage. -**2.** [institution, system] réformé. -**3.** RELIG [Christian] réformé; [Jewish] non orthodoxe.

reformer [rɪ'fɔːmə^r] *n* réformateur *m*, -trice *f*.

reformism [rɪ'fɔːmɪzm] *n* réformisme *m*.

reformist [rɪ'fɔːmɪst] ◇ *adj* réformiste.
◇ *n* réformiste *mf*.

reform school *n Am* ≃ centre *m* d'éducation surveillée.

refract [rɪ'frækt] ◇ *vt* réfracter.
◇ *vi* se réfracter.

refracting [rɪ'fræktɪŋ] *adj* [material, prism] réfringent; [angle] de réfraction.

refracting telescope *n* télescope *m*, lunette *f* astronomique.

refraction [rɪ'frækʃn] *n* [phenomenon] réfraction *f*; [property] réfringence *f*.

refractive [rɪ'fræktɪv] *adj* réfringent.

refractive index *n* indice *m* de réfraction.

refractor [rɪ'fræktə^r] *n* -**1.** OPT & PHYS [apparatus] appareil *m* de réfraction; [material, medium] milieu *m* réfringent. -**2.** ASTRON réfracteur *m*, lunette *f* astronomique.

refractory [rɪ'fræktərɪ] *adj* -**1.** *fml* [person] réfractaire, rebelle. -**2.** MED & TECH réfractaire.

refrain [rɪ'freɪn] ◇ *vi* [hold back]: to ~ from (doing) sthg s'abstenir de (faire) qqch; she ~ed from making a remark elle s'est retenue OR abstenue de faire une remarque; he couldn't ~ from smiling il n'a pu s'empêcher de sourire; 'please ~ from smoking' 'prière de ne pas fumer'.
◇ *n* MUS, POET & *fig* refrain *m*.

reframe [,riː'freɪm] *vt* [approach, point of view] changer de; [argument] remanier; [question] reformuler.

refreeze [,riː'friːz] (*pt* refroze [-'frəuz], *pp* refrozen [-'frəuzn]) *vt* [ice, ice-cream] remettre au congélateur; [food] recongeler.

refresh [rɪ'freʃ] *vt* -**1.** [revive - subj: drink, shower, ice] rafraîchir; [- subj: exercise, swim] revigorer; [- subj: sleep] reposer, détendre; I feel ~ed [after shower, drink] je me sens rafraîchi; [after exercise] je me sens revigoré; [after rest] je me sens reposé; they returned ~ed [from rest, holiday] ils sont revenus détendus; [from exercise] ils sont revenus revigorés; they woke ~ed ils se sont réveillés frais et dispos. -**2.** [memory, experience] rafraîchir; let me ~ your memory laissez-moi vous rafraîchir la mémoire; she wanted to ~ her German elle voulait se remettre à l'allemand.

refresher [rɪ'freʃə^r] *n* -**1.** [drink] boisson *f* rafraîchissante. -**2.** *Br* JUR honoraires *mpl* supplémentaires.

refresher course *n* stage *m* OR cours *m* de recyclage.

refreshing [rɪ'freʃɪŋ] *adj* -**1.** [physically - drink, rain, breeze] rafraîchissant; [- exercise] tonique, revigorant; [- sleep] réparateur, reposant; [- holiday] reposant. -**2.** [mentally - idea] original, stimulant; [- sight] réconfortant; [- performance] plein de vie; a ~ change un changement agréable OR appréciable.

refreshingly [rɪ'freʃɪŋlɪ] *adv*: it's ~ different c'est un changement agréable.

refreshment [rɪ'freʃmənt] *n* [of body, mind] repos *m*, délassement *m*; would you like some ~? [food] voulez-vous manger un morceau?; [drink] voulez-vous boire quelque chose?
◆ **refreshments** *npl* rafraîchissements *mpl*; '~s available' 'buvette'.

refreshment bar, **refreshment stall** *n* buvette *f*.

refrigerant [rɪ'frɪdʒərənt] ◇ *adj* réfrigérant.
◇ *n* -**1.** [substance] mélange *m* réfrigérant. -**2.** MED réfrigérant *m*.

refrigerate [rɪ'frɪdʒəreɪt] *vt* [in cold store] frigorifier, réfrigérer; [freeze] congeler; [put in fridge] mettre au réfrigérateur.

refrigeration [rɪ,frɪdʒə'reɪʃn] *n* réfrigération *f*; industrial ~ froid *m* industriel.

refrigerator [rɪ'frɪdʒəreɪtə^r] ◇ *n* [in kitchen] réfrigérateur *m*; [storeroom] chambre *f* frigorifique.
◇ *comp* [ship, lorry] frigorifique; ~ unit machine *f* frigorifique.

refrigerator-freezer *n Am* réfrigérateur-congélateur *m*.

refringent [rɪ'frɪndʒənt] *adj* réfringent.

refuel [,riː'fjuəl] (*Br pt* & *pp* refuelled, *cont* refuelling, *Am pt* & *pp* refueled, *cont* refueling) ◇ *vt* ravitailler (en carburant).
◇ *vi* se ravitailler en carburant; *fig* [with food, drink] se restaurer; the aeroplane refuelled in mid-flight l'avion s'est ravitaillé en vol.

refuelling *Br*, **refueling** *Am* [,riː'fjuəlɪŋ] ◇ *n* ravitaillement *m* (en carburant).
◇ *comp* [boom, tanker] de ravitaillement; to make a ~ stop AUT s'arrêter pour prendre de l'essence; AERON faire une escale technique.

refuge ['refjuːdʒ] *n* -**1.** [shelter - gen] refuge *m*, abri *m*; [- in mountains] refuge *m*; [- for crossing road] refuge *m*; women's ~ foyer *m* pour femmes battues. -**2.** [protection - from weather]: to take ~ from the rain s'abriter de la pluie; she took ~ in the tent elle s'est réfugiée sous la tente || [from attack, reality]: to seek ~ chercher refuge; he sought ~ from his persecutors il chercha un asile pour échapper à ses persécuteurs; to seek ~ in drugs chercher refuge dans la drogue; to take ~ in fantasy se réfugier dans l'imagination; place of ~ [from rain] abri *m*; [from pursuit] (lieu *m* d') asile *m*.

refugee [,refju'dʒiː] *n* réfugié *m*, -e *f*.

refugee camp *n* camp *m* de réfugiés.

refulgent [rɪ'fʌldʒənt] *adj lit* [day] resplendissant; [sun] éclatant, radieux.

refund [*vb* riː'fʌnd, *n* 'riːfʌnd] ◇ *vt* -**1.** [expenses, excess, person] rembourser; to ~ sthg to sb rembourser qqch à qqn; they ~ed me the postage ils m'ont remboursé les frais de port. -**2.** FIN & JUR [monies] restituer.
◇ *n* -**1.** COMM remboursement *m*; to get OR to obtain a ~ se faire rembourser. -**2.** FIN & JUR [of monies] restitution *f*. -**3.** *Am* [of tax] bonification *f* de trop-perçu.

refundable [riː'fʌndəbl] *adj* remboursable.

refurbish [,riː'fɜːbɪʃ] *vt* réaménager.

refurbishment [,riː'fɜːbɪʃmənt] *n* remise *f* à neuf.

refurnish [,riː'fɜːnɪʃ] *vt* [house] remeubler.

refusal [rɪ'fjuːzl] *n* -**1.** [of request, suggestion] refus *m*, rejet *m*; to meet with a ~ essuyer OR se heurter à un refus; to receive a ~ recevoir une réponse négative; we don't understand your ~ to compromise nous ne comprenons pas les raisons pour lesquelles vous vous opposez à un compromis. -**2.** EQUIT refus *m*. -**3.** [denial - of justice, truth] refus *m*, déni *m*.

refuse[1] [rɪ'fuːz] ◇ *vt* -**1.** [turn down - invitation, gift] refuser; [- offer] refuser, décliner; [- request, proposition] refuser, rejeter; to ~ to do sthg refuser de OR se refuser à faire qqch; I ~ to accept that all is lost je refuse de croire que tout soit perdu; I ~d to take delivery of the parcel j'ai refusé d'accepter le paquet; he has proposed to her several times but has always been ~d il l'a demandée plusieurs fois en mariage mais a toujours essuyé un refus || EQUIT refuser; to ~ a jump refuser de sauter. -**2.** [deny - permission] refuser (d'accorder); [- help, visa] refuser; he was ~d entry on lui a refusé l'entrée; they were ~d a loan on leur a refusé un prêt; we were ~d permission to see him on nous a refusé la permission de le voir.
◇ *vi* [person] refuser; [horse] refuser l'obstacle.

refuse[2] ['refjuːs] *n Br* [household] ordures *fpl* (ménagères); [garden] détritus *mpl*; [industrial] déchets *mpl*; 'no ~' 'défense de déposer les ordures'.

refuse bin *n Br* poubelle *f*.

refuse chute *n Br* vide-ordures *m inv*.

refuse collection *n Br* ramassage *m* d'ordures.

refuse collector *n Br* éboueur *m*.

refuse disposal *n Br* traitement *m* des ordures; ~ unit broyeur *m* d'ordures.

refuse dump *n Br* [public] décharge *f* (publique), dépotoir *m*.

refus(e)nik [rɪ'fjuːznɪk] *n* refuznik *mf*.

refutable ['refjutəbl] *adj* réfutable.

refutation [,refjuː'teɪʃn] *n* réfutation *f*.

refute [rɪ'fjuːt] *vt* [disprove] réfuter; [deny] nier.

reg (*written abbr of* registered): ~ trademark marque *f* déposée.

regain [rɪ'geɪn] *vt* -**1.** [territory] reconquérir; to ~ possession of sthg rentrer en possession de qqch; to ~ lost time rattraper le temps perdu || [health] recouvrer; [strength] retrouver; [sight, composure] retrouver, recouvrer; [glory] retrouver; to ~ consciousness reprendre connaissance; to ~ one's balance retrouver l'équilibre; to ~ one's footing reprendre pied. -**2.** *fml* [get back to - road, place, shelter] regagner.

regal ['riːgl] ◇ *adj literal* royal; *fig* [person, bearing] majestueux; [banquet, decor] somptueux.
◇ *n* MUS régale *f*.

regale [rɪ'geɪl] *vt*: to ~ sb with sthg régaler qqn de qqch.

regalia [rɪ'geɪljə] *npl* -**1.** [insignia] insignes *mpl*. -**2.** [finery, robes] accoutrement *m*, atours *mpl*; to be in full ~ [judge, general] être en grande tenue; *fig* & *hum* [woman] être paré de tous ses atours.

regally ['riːgəlɪ] *adv* royalement, majestueusement.

regard [rɪ'gɑːd] ◇ *vt* -**1.** [consider] considérer, regarder; [treat] traiter; I ~ him as OR like a brother je le considère comme un frère; I ~ their conclusions as correct OR to be correct je tiens leurs conclusions pour correctes; I prefer to ~ the whole thing as a joke je préfère considérer toute l'affaire comme une plaisanterie; we didn't ~ the problem as deserving attention nous n'avons pas considéré que le problème méritait notre attention; he ~s himself as an expert il se considère comme OR il se prend pour un expert || [esteem] estimer, tenir en estime; to ~ sb highly tenir qqn en grande estime; highly ~ed très estimé. -**2.** *fml* [observe] regarder, observer; they ~ed me with some trepidation ils m'ont regardé avec une certaine inquiétude. -**3.** [heed - advice, wishes] tenir compte de.

◇ *n* -**1.** [notice, attention] considération *f*, attention *f*; to pay ~ to sthg tenir compte de qqch, faire attention à qqch; they paid scant ~ to my explanations ils n'ont guère fait attention à mes explications; having ~ to his age en tenant compte de OR eu égard à son âge; having ~ to paragraph 24 ADMIN vu le paragraphe 24. -**2.** [care, respect] souci *m*, considération *f*, respect *m*; to have ~ for sb avoir de la considération pour qqn; they have no ~ for your feelings ils ne se soucient pas de vos sentiments; Peter has scant ~ for copyright Peter se soucie peu des droits d'auteur; they showed no ~ for our wishes ils n'ont tenu aucun compte de nos souhaits; without ~ for the difficulties sans se soucier des difficultés; with no ~ for his health sans se soucier de sa santé; she did it out of ~ for me elle l'a fait par égard pour moi; with due ~ for your elders avec les égards dus à vos aînés; without due ~ to sans tenir compte de. -**3.** [connection]: in this ~ à cet égard. -**4.** [esteem] estime *f*, considération *f*; I hold them in high ~ je les tiens en grande estime. -**5.** *fml* [eyes, look] regard *m*.

◆ **regards** *npl* [in letters]: ~s, Peter bien cordialement, Peter; kind ~s bien à vous ‖ [in greetings]: give them my ~s transmettez-leur mon bon souvenir; he sends his ~s vous avez le bonjour de sa part.

◆ **as regards** *prep phr* en ce qui concerne, pour ce qui est de; as ~s the cost en ce qui concerne le coût, quant au coût.

◆ **in regard to, with regard to** *prep phr* en ce qui concerne.

regardful [rɪ'gɑːdfʊl] *adj fml*: to be ~ of [needs, wishes, difficulties] être attentif à, faire attention à; [children, interests, image] s'occuper de, soigner.

regarding [rɪ'gɑːdɪŋ] *prep* quant à, en ce qui concerne, pour ce qui est de; what are we going to do ~ Fred? qu'allons-nous faire en ce qui concerne Fred?; questions ~ management des questions relatives à la gestion.

regardless [rɪ'gɑːdlɪs] *adv* [in any case] quand même, en tout cas; [without worrying] sans s'occuper OR se soucier du reste; they carried on ~ ils continuèrent quand même.

◆ **regardless of** *prep phr*: ~ of what you think [without bothering] sans se soucier de ce que vous pensez; [whatever your opinion] quelles que soient vos idées; ~ of the danger sans se soucier du danger; ~ of the expense sans regarder à la dépense.

regatta [rɪ'gætə] *n* régate *f*.

regd = **reg**.

regency ['riːdʒənsɪ] (*pl* regencies) *n* régence *f*.

◆ **Regency** *comp* [style, furniture, period] Regency *(inv)*, de la Régence anglaise.

regenerate [*vb* rɪ'dʒenəreɪt, *adj* rɪ'dʒenərət]
◇ *vt* régénérer; to ~ interest in sthg provoquer un regain d'intérêt pour qqch.
◇ *vi* se régénérer.
◇ *adj* régénéré.

regeneration [rɪ,dʒenə'reɪʃn] *n* [gen] régénération *f*; [of interest] regain *m*; [of urban area] reconstruction *f*, rénovation *f*.

regenerative [rɪ'dʒenərətɪv] *adj* régénérateur.

regent ['riːdʒənt] *n* -**1.** HIST régent *m*, -e *f*. -**2.** *Am membre du conseil d'administration d'une université*.

reggae ['regeɪ] ◇ *n* reggae *m*.
◇ *comp* [music, singer] reggae *(inv)*.

regicide ['redʒɪsaɪd] *n* [person] régicide *mf*; [crime] régicide *m*.

regime, régime [reɪ'ʒiːm] *n* -**1.** POL & SOCIOL régime *m*; under the present ~ sous le régime actuel; military ~ régime militaire. -**2.** = **regimen**.

regimen ['redʒɪmen] *n* régime *m (sous surveillance médicale)*.

regiment [*n* 'redʒɪmənt, *vb* 'redʒɪment]
◇ *n* MIL & *fig* régiment *m*.
◇ *vt* [organize] enrégimenter; [discipline] soumettre à une discipline trop stricte.

regimental [,redʒɪ'mentl] *adj* MIL [mess, dress] régimentaire, du régiment; [band, mascot] du régiment; *fig* [organization] trop discipliné, enrégimenté.

◆ **regimentals** *npl* uniforme *m* OR tenue *f* (militaire); in full ~s en grande tenue.

regimental sergeant major *n* ≃ adjudant-chef *m*.

regimentation [,redʒɪmen'teɪʃn] *n pej* [of business, system] organisation *f* quasi militaire; [in school] discipline *f* étouffante OR trop sévère.

regimented ['redʒɪmentɪd] *adj* strict; a ~ lifestyle un mode de vie strict.

Regina [rɪ'dʒaɪnə] *n Br*: Victoria ~ la reine Victoria; ~ vs Smith JUR le ministère public contre Smith.

region ['riːdʒən] *n* -**1.** GEOG région *f*; in the Liverpool ~ dans la région de Liverpool; the nether OR lower ~s *fig* les Enfers. -**2.** [in body] région *f*; in the ~ of the heart dans la région du cœur; in the lower back ~ dans la région lombaire. -**3.** [realm - of knowledge, sentiments] domaine *m*; now we move into the ~ of mere speculation là, nous entrons dans le domaine de la spéculation pure.

◆ **in the region of** *prep phr* environ; in the ~ of 10 kg dans les 10 kg (environ); in the ~ of £500 aux environs de OR dans les 500 livres.

regional ['riːdʒənl] *adj* régional.

regional development *n* [building, land development] aménagement *m* du territoire; [for jobs] action *f* régionale; ~ corporation *Br organisme pour l'aménagement du territoire*.

regionalism ['riːdʒənəlɪzm] *n* régionalisme *m*.

regionalist ['riːdʒənəlɪst] ◇ *adj* régionaliste.
◇ *n* régionaliste *mf*.

regionalization [,riːdʒənəlaɪ'zeɪʃn] *n* régionalisation *f*.

regionalize, -ise ['riːdʒənəlaɪz] *vt* régionaliser.

regionally ['riːdʒnəlɪ] *adv* à l'échelle régionale.

register ['redʒɪstə^r] ◇ *vt* -**1.** [record - name] (faire) enregistrer, (faire) inscrire; [- birth, death] déclarer; [- vehicle] (faire) immatriculer; [- trademark] déposer; [- on list] inscrire; [- request] enregistrer; [- readings] relever, enregistrer; MIL [recruit] recenser; to ~ a complaint déposer une plainte; to ~ a protest protester; to ~ one's vote exprimer son vote, voter; record wind speeds have been ~ed in the country on a enregistré des vitesses record du vent dans le pays; I'd like officially to ~ my disagreement je voudrais exprimer officiellement mon désaccord. -**2.** [indicate] indiquer; the needle is ~ing 700 kg l'aiguille indique 700 kg ‖ FIN enregistrer; the pound/the stock exchange has ~ed a fall la livre/la Bourse a enregistré une baisse ‖ [subj: person, face] exprimer; her face ~ed disbelief l'incrédulité se lisait sur son visage. -**3.** [obtain - success] remporter; [- defeat] essuyer. -**4.** *inf* [understand] saisir, piger; they don't seem to have ~ed (the fact) that the situation is hopeless ils ne semblent pas se rendre compte que la situation est désespérée. -**5.** [parcel, letter] envoyer en recommandé. -**6.** [at railway station, airport etc - suitcase] (faire) enregistrer. -**7.** TYPO mettre en registre. -**8.** TECH (faire) aligner, faire coïncider.
◇ *vi* -**1.** [enrol] s'inscrire, se faire inscrire; [in hotel] s'inscrire sur OR signer le registre (de l'hôtel); to ~ at night school/for Chinese lessons s'inscrire aux cours du soir/à des cours de chinois; foreign nationals must ~ with the police les ressortissants étrangers doivent se faire enregistrer au commissariat de police; to ~ with a GP/on the electoral roll se faire inscrire auprès d'un médecin traitant/sur les listes électorales. -**2.** [be understood]: maths just doesn't ~ with him il ne comprend absolument rien aux maths; her success didn't really ~ with her elle ne s'était pas vraiment rendu compte de son succès; the truth slowly began to ~ (with me) petit à petit, la vérité m'est apparue ‖ [have effect]: his name doesn't ~ (with me) son nom ne me dit rien. -**3.** [instrument] donner une indication; is the needle/the barometer ~ing? est-ce que l'aiguille/le baromètre indique quelque chose?; the current was too weak to ~ le courant était trop faible pour donner une indication. -**4.** TECH coïncider, être aligné; TYPO être en registre.
◇ *n* -**1.** [book] registre *m*; [list] liste *f*; SCH registre *m* de présences, cahier *m* d'appel; [on ship] livre *m* de bord; to keep a ~ tenir un registre; to call OR to take the ~ SCH faire l'appel ❑ electoral ~ liste *f* électorale; commercial OR trade ~ registre *m* du commerce; ~ of shipping registre *m* maritime; ~ of births, deaths and marriages registre *m* de l'état civil. -**2.** [gauge] enregistreur *m*; [counter] compteur *m*; [cash till] caisse *f* (enregistreuse). -**3.** [pitch - of voice] registre *m*, tessiture *f*; [- of instrument] registre. -**4.** LING registre *m*, niveau *m* de langue. -**5.** TYPO registre *m*; to be in/out of ~ être/ne pas être en registre. -**6.** ART & COMPUT registre *m*.

registered ['redʒɪstəd] *adj* -**1.** [student, elector] inscrit; [charity] *Br* agréé; FIN [bond, securities] nominatif ❑ ~ childminder nourrice *f* agréée; ~ company société *f* inscrite au registre du commerce. -**2.** [letter, parcel] recommandé; send it ~ *Br* envoyez-le en recommandé.

registered disabled *adj Br*: to be ~ avoir une carte d'invalidité.

Registered General Nurse = **RGN**.

Registered Nurse *n* infirmier diplômé *m* OR infirmière diplômée *f* d'État.

registered office *n Br* siège *m* social.

registered post *n Br* envoi *m* recommandé.

registered tonnage *n* NAUT jauge *f*.

Registered Trademark *n* marque *f* déposée.

register office ADMIN = **registry office**.

register ton *n* NAUT tonneau *m* (de jauge).

registrar [,redʒɪ'strɑː^r] *n* -**1.** *Br* ADMIN officier *m* de l'état civil; to inform the ~'s office of a death déclarer un décès au bureau de l'état civil. -**2.** *Br* & *NZ* MED chef *m* de clinique. -**3.** JUR greffier *m*. -**4.** *Am* UNIV chef *m* du service OR du bureau des inscriptions; *Br* UNIV président *m (d'une université)*. -**5.** COMM & FIN: companies' ~ responsable *mf* du registre des sociétés.

registration [,redʒɪ'streɪʃn] *n* -**1.** [of name] enregistrement *m*; [of student] inscription *f*; [of trademark] dépôt *m*; [of vehicle] immatriculation *f*; [of luggage] enregistrement *m*; [of birth, death] déclaration *f*; land ~ inscription au cadastre. -**2.** *Br* SCH appel *m*. -**3.** [of mail] recommandation *f*. -**4.** MUS [on organ] registration *f*.

registration document *n Br* AUT ≃ carte *f* grise.

registration fee *n* frais *mpl* OR droits *mpl* d'inscription.

registration number *n* -**1.** *Br* AUT numéro *m* d'immatriculation; the car has the ~ E 123 SYK la voiture est immatriculée E 123 SYK. -**2.** [of student] numéro *m* d'inscription; [of baggage] numéro *m* d'enregistrement.

registration plate *n Austr* & *NZ* AUT plaque *f* d'immatriculation OR minéralogique.

registry ['redʒɪstrɪ] (*pl* registries) *n* -**1.** [registration] enregistrement *m*; UNIV inscription *f*. -**2.** [office] bureau *m* d'enregistrement. -**3.** NAUT immatriculation *f*; a ship of Japanese ~ un navire battant pavillon japonais; port of ~ port *m* d'attache.

registry office *n Br* bureau *m* de l'état civil; to be married at a ~ ≃ se marier à la mairie.

Regius professor ['riːdʒjəs-] *n Br* UNIV *professeur titulaire d'une chaire de fondation royale*.

regnal ['regnəl] *adj*: ~ year année *f* du règne.

regnant ['regnənt] *adj* -**1.** *(after n)* [queen, prince] régnant. -**2.** *lit* [idea] répandu; [taste] prépondérant.

regrade [,riː'greɪd] *vt* [essay] noter de nouveau; [officer, objects] reclasser.

regress [*vb* rɪ'gres, *n* 'riːgres] ◇ *vi* -**1.** BIOL & PSYCH régresser; to ~ to childhood régresser à un stade infantile; to ~ to an earlier stage

régresser. -**2.** SCH [go back] reculer, revenir en arrière.
◇ *n* = **regression.**

regression [rɪ'greʃn] *n* -**1.** BIOL & PSYCH régression *f.* -**2.** [retreat] recul *m,* régression *f.*

regressive [rɪ'gresɪv] *adj* BIOL, FIN & PSYCH régressif; [movement] de recul.

regret [rɪ'gret] (*pt* & *pp* **regretted**, *cont* **regretting**) ◇ *vt* -**1.** [be sorry about - action, behaviour] regretter; **I ~ to say** [apologize] j'ai le regret de OR je regrette de dire; [unfortunately] hélas, malheureusement; **we ~ to inform you** nous avons le regret de vous informer; **I ~ having agreed** OR **agreeing to go** je regrette d'avoir accepté d'y aller; **I ~ ever mentioning it** je regrette d'en avoir jamais parlé; **I ~ not being able to come** je regrette OR je suis désolé de ne pouvoir venir; **she ~s that she never met Donovan** elle regrette de n'avoir jamais rencontré Donovan; **the accident/error is greatly to be regretted** [gen] l'accident/l'erreur est absolument déplorable; [in diplomatic language] l'accident/l'erreur est infiniment regrettable; **you'll live to ~ this!** vous le regretterez!; **the airline ~s any inconvenience caused to passengers** la compagnie s'excuse pour la gêne occasionnée. -**2.** *lit* [lament] regretter; **she will be much regretted** on la regrettera beaucoup; **he ~s his student days** il regrette l'époque où il était étudiant.
◇ *n* [sorrow, sadness] regret *m;* **with ~** avec regret; **we announce with ~ the death of our chairman** nous avons le regret de vous faire part de la mort de notre directeur; **much to our ~** à notre grand regret; **to express one's ~s at** OR **about sthg** exprimer ses regrets devant qqch; **I have no ~s** je n'ai pas de regrets, je ne regrette rien; **do you have any ~s about** OR **for what you did?** regrettez-vous ce que vous avez fait?; **to send sb one's ~s** [condolences] exprimer ses regrets à qqn; [apologies] s'excuser auprès de qqn.

regretful [rɪ'gretfʊl] *adj* [person] plein de regrets; [expression, attitude] de regret; **to be** OR **to feel ~ about sthg** regretter qqch.

regretfully [rɪ'gretfʊlɪ] *adv* [sadly] avec regret; [unfortunately] malheureusement.

regrettable [rɪ'gretəbl] *adj* [unfortunate] regrettable, malencontreux; [annoying] fâcheux, ennuyeux; **it is most ~ that you were not informed** il est fort regrettable que vous n'ayez pas été informé.

regrettably [rɪ'gretəblɪ] *adv* [unfortunately] malheureusement, malencontreusement; [irritatingly] fâcheusement.

regroup [,riː'gruːp] ◇ *vt* regrouper.
◇ *vi* se regrouper.

regt *written abbr of* **regiment.**

regular ['regjʊlə'] ◇ *adj* -**1.** [rhythmical - footsteps, movement, sound] régulier; [even - breathing, pulse] régulier, égal; **as ~ as clockwork** [punctual] réglé comme une horloge; [frequent] réglé comme du papier à musique. -**2.** [frequent - meetings, service, salary] régulier; **at ~ intervals** à intervalles réguliers; **it's a ~ occurrence** cela arrive régulièrement; **she has ~ treatment** elle suit régulièrement un traitement. -**3.** [usual - brand, dentist, supplier] habituel; [- customer] régulier; [listener, reader] fidèle; **who is your ~ doctor?** qui est votre médecin traitant?; **to be in ~ employment** avoir un emploi régulier; **she's a ~ reader of this paper** elle lit ce journal régulièrement ‖ [normal, ordinary - price, model] courant; [- size] courant, standard; [- procedure] habituel; **to go through the ~ channels** suivre la filière normale OR habituelle; **it's ~ practice to pay by cheque** les paiements par chèque sont pratique courante ‖ [permanent - agent] attitré, permanent; [- police force] permanent, régulier; [- army] de métier; [- soldier] de carrière ❑ **~ (grade) gas** *Am* AUT (essence *f*) ordinaire *m.* -**4.** [even - features, teeth] régulier; [smooth, level] uni, égal. -**5.** [ordered - hours] régulier; [- life] bien réglé. -**6.** GRAMM & MATH régulier; **~ verb** verbe *m* régulier. -**7.** *inf* [as intensifier] vrai, véritable; **a ~ mess** une vraie pagaille. -**8.** *inf Am* [pleasant] sympathique, chouette; **a ~ guy** un type sympa. -**9.** RELIG [clergy] régulier. -**10.** *Am* POL [loyal to party] fidèle au parti.
◇ *n* -**1.** [customer - in bar] habitué *m,* -e *f;* [- in shop] client *m,* -e *f* fidèle. -**2.** [contributor, player]: **she's a ~ on our column** elle contribue régulièrement à notre rubrique; **he's a ~ in the team** il joue régulièrement dans l'équipe. -**3.** [soldier] militaire *m* de carrière. -**4.** RELIG religieux *m* régulier, régulier *m.* -**5.** *Am* [fuel] ordinaire *m.* -**6.** *Am* POL [loyal party member] membre *m* fidèle (du parti).
◇ *adv dial* régulièrement.

regularity [,regjʊ'lærətɪ] (*pl* **regularities**) *n* régularité *f.*

regularization [,regjʊləraɪ'zeɪʃn] *n* régularisation *f.*

regularize, -ise ['regjʊləraɪz] *vt* régulariser.

regularly ['regjʊləlɪ] *adv* régulièrement.

regulate ['regjʊleɪt] *vt* -**1.** [control, adjust - machine, expenditure] régler; [- flow] réguler; **the machine is ~d by a lever** la machine se règle à l'aide d'un levier. -**2.** [organize - habit, life] régler; [- with rules] réglementer; **he followed a well ~d diet** il suivit un régime équilibré.

regulation [,regjʊ'leɪʃn] ◇ *n* -**1.** [ruling] règlement *m;* **it's contrary to** OR **against (the) ~s** c'est contraire au règlement; **it complies with EC ~s** c'est conforme aux dispositions communautaires. -**2.** [adjustment, control - of machine] réglage *m;* [- of flow] régulation *f.*
◇ *comp* [size, haircut, issue, dress] réglementaire; [pistol, helmet] d'ordonnance.

regulator ['regjʊleɪtə'] *n* -**1.** [person] régulateur *m,* -trice *f.* -**2.** [apparatus] régulateur *m.*

regulatory ['regjʊlətrɪ] *adj* réglementaire.

regulo ['regjʊləʊ] *n*: **~ (mark) 4** *Br* thermostat 4.

regurgitate [rɪ'gɜːdʒɪteɪt] ◇ *vt* [food] régurgiter; *fig* [facts] régurgiter, reproduire.
◇ *vi* [bird] dégorger.

regurgitation [rɪ,gɜːdʒɪ'teɪʃn] *n* régurgitation *f.*

rehabilitate [,riːə'bɪlɪteɪt] *vt* -**1.** [convict, drug addict, alcoholic] réhabiliter, réinsérer; [restore to health] rééduquer; [find employment for] réinsérer. -**2.** [reinstate - idea, style] réhabiliter. -**3.** [renovate - aera, building] réhabiliter.

rehabilitation ['riːə,bɪlɪ'teɪʃn] *n* -**1.** [of disgraced person, memory, reputation] réhabilitation *f;* [of convict, alcoholic, drug addict] réhabilitation *f,* réinsertion *f;* [of disabled person] rééducation *f;* [of unemployed] réinsertion. -**2.** [of idea, style] réhabilitation *f.* -**3.** [of area, building] réhabilitation *f.*

rehabilitation centre *n* [for work training] centre *m* de réadaptation; [for drug addicts] centre de réinsertion.

rehash *inf* [*vb* ,riː'hæʃ, *n* 'riːhæʃ] *pej* ◇ *vt* -**1.** *Br* [rearrange] remanier. -**2.** [repeat - argument] ressasser; [- programme] reprendre; [- artistic material] remanier.
◇ *n* réchauffé *m;* **it's just a ~** ce n'est que du réchauffé.

rehear [,riː'hɪə'] (*pt* & *pp* **reheard** [-'hɜːd]) *vt* JUR entendre de nouveau, réviser.

rehearing [,riː'hɪərɪŋ] *n* JUR révision *f* de procès.

rehearsal [rɪ'hɜːsl] *n literal* & *fig* répétition *f;* **when's the ~?** quand est-ce qu'on répète?; **she's in ~** elle est en répétition; **the play is currently in ~** ils sont en train de répéter.

rehearse [rɪ'hɜːs] ◇ *vt* -**1.** MUS, THEAT & *fig* [play, music, speech, coup d'état] répéter; [actors, singers, orchestra] faire répéter; **you'd better ~ your speech** vous feriez bien de répéter votre discours; **well ~d** [play, performance] bien répété, répété avec soin; [actor] qui a bien répété son rôle, qui sait son rôle sur le bout des doigts; [request, coup d'état, applause] bien OR soigneusement préparé. -**2.** [recite - list, facts, complaints] réciter, énumérer; [- old arguments] répéter, ressasser.
◇ *vi* MUS & THEAT répéter.

reheat [,riː'hiːt] *vt* réchauffer.

Rehoboam [,riːə'bəʊəm] *pr n* Roboam.

rehouse [,riː'haʊz] *vt* reloger.

reification [,reɪɪfɪ'keɪʃn] *n* réification *f.*

reify ['reɪɪfaɪ] (*pt* & *pp* **reified**) *vt* réifier.

reign [reɪn] ◇ *n* règne *m;* **in** OR **under the ~ of** sous le règne de; **the ~ of silence** le règne du silence; **~ of terror** règne de terreur.
◇ *vi* -**1.** *literal* régner. -**2.** *fig* [predominate] régner; **silence ~s** le silence règne; **to ~ supreme** régner en maître; **plague/terror ~s over the town** la peste sévit dans/la terreur règne sur la ville.

reigning ['reɪnɪŋ] *adj* -**1.** *literal* [monarch, emperor] régnant. -**2.** [present - champion] en titre. -**3.** [predominant - attitude, idea] régnant, dominant.

reimburse [,riːɪm'bɜːs] *vt* rembourser; **to ~ sb (for) sthg** rembourser qqch à qqn OR qqn de qqch; **I was ~d** je me suis fait rembourser.

reimbursement [,riːɪm'bɜːsmənt] *n* remboursement *m.*

reimport [*vb* ,riːɪm'pɔːt, *n* ,riː'ɪmpɔːt]
◇ *vt* réimporter.
◇ *n* réimportation *f.*

rein [reɪn] *n* -**1.** [for horse] rêne *f.* -**2.** *fig* [control] bride *f;* **to give (a) free ~ to sb** laisser à qqn la bride sur le cou; **to give free ~ to one's emotions/imagination** donner libre cours à ses émotions/son imagination; **to keep a ~ on sthg** tenir qqch en bride, maîtriser qqch; **to keep a tight ~ on sb** tenir la bride haute à qqn.
◆ **reins** *npl* [for horse, child] rêne *f;* **the ~s of government** *fig* les rênes du gouvernement.
◆ **rein back** ◇ *vi insep* tirer sur les rênes, serrer la bride.
◇ *vt sep* faire ralentir, freiner.
◆ **rein in** ◇ *vi insep* ralentir.
◇ *vt sep* -**1.** [horse] serrer la bride à, ramener au pas. -**2.** *fig* [person] ramener au pas; [emotions] maîtriser, refréner.

reincarnate [*vb* riː'ɪnkɑːneɪt, *adj* ,riːɪn'kɑːnɪt]
◇ *vt* réincarner.
◇ *adj* réincarné.

reincarnation [,riːɪnkɑː'neɪʃn] *n* réincarnation *f.*

reindeer ['reɪn,dɪə'] (*pl inv*) *n* renne *m.*

reindeer moss *n* cladonie *f.*

reinfect [,riːɪn'fekt] *vt* réinfecter.

reinfection [,riːɪn'fekʃn] *n* réinfection *f.*

reinforce [,riːɪn'fɔːs] *vt* -**1.** MIL renforcer. -**2.** [gen & CONSTR - wall, heel] renforcer. -**3.** *fig* [demand] appuyer; [argument] renforcer.

reinforced concrete [,riːɪn'fɔːst-] *n* béton *m* armé.

reinforcement [,riːɪn'fɔːsmənt] ◇ *n* -**1.** [gen & MIL] renfort *m;* **~s have arrived** des renforts sont arrivés. -**2.** [gen & CONSTR] armature *f;* **~s were used to prestress the concrete** on a utilisé des armatures pour fabriquer le béton armé. -**3.** *fig* [strengthening] renforcement *m.*
◇ *comp* [troops, ships, supplies] de renfort.

reinsert [,riːɪn'sɜːt] *vt* réinsérer.

reinstate [,riːɪn'steɪt] *vt* [employee] réintégrer, rétablir (dans ses fonctions); [idea, system] rétablir, restaurer.

reinstatement [,riːɪn'steɪtmənt] *n* réintégration *f.*

reinsurance [,riːɪn'ʃɔːrəns] *n* réassurance *f.*

reinsure [,riːɪn'ʃɔː'] *vt* réassurer.

reintegrate [,riː'ɪntɪgreɪt] *vt* réintégrer.

reintegration ['riː,ɪntɪ'greɪʃn] *n* réintégration *f.*

reinterpret [,riːɪn'tɜːprɪt] *vt* réinterpréter.

reintroduce ['riː,ɪntrə'djuːs] *vt* réintroduire.

reinvest [,riːɪn'vest] *vt* réinvestir.

reinvestment [,riːɪn'vestmənt] *n* réinvestissement *m.*

reinvigorate [,riːɪn'vɪgəreɪt] *vt* revigorer.

reissue [riː'ɪʃuː] ◇ *vt* -**1.** [book] rééditer; [film] rediffuser, ressortir. -**2.** ADMIN & FIN [banknote, shares, stamps] réémettre.
◇ *n* -**1.** [of book] réédition *f;* [of film] rediffusion *f.* -**2.** ADMIN & FIN nouvelle émission *f.*

reiterate [riːˈɪtəˌreɪt] *vt* répéter, réaffirmer.
reiteration [riːˌɪtəˈreɪʃn] *n* réitération *f*.
reiterative [riːˈɪtərətɪv] *adj* réitératif.
reject [*vb* rɪˈdʒekt, *n* & *comp* ˈriːdʒekt]
◇ *vt* -**1.** [offer, suggestion, unwanted article] rejeter; [advances, demands] rejeter, repousser; [application, manuscript] rejeter, refuser; [suitor] éconduire, repousser; [belief, system, values] rejeter. -**2.** MED [foreign body, transplant] rejeter. -**3.** COMPUT rejeter.
◇ *n* -**1.** COMM [in factory] article *m* OR pièce *f* de rebut; [in shop] (article *m* de) second choix *m*; *fig* [person] personne *f* marginalisée. -**2.** COMPUT rejet *m*.
◇ *comp* [merchandise] de rebut; [for sale] (de) second choix; [shop] d'articles de second choix.
rejection [rɪˈdʒekʃn] *n* -**1.** [of offer, manuscript, application] refus *m*; [of advances, demands] rejet *m*; **her application met with ~** sa candidature a été rejetée OR n'a pas été retenue; **to be afraid of ~** [emotional] avoir peur d'être rejeté. -**2.** MED rejet *m*.
rejection slip *n* lettre *f* de refus.
rejig [ˌriːˈdʒɪg] (*pt* & *pp* rejigged, *cont* rejigging) *vt Br* -**1.** [reequip] rééquiper, réaménager. -**2.** [reorganize] réarranger, revoir.
rejigger [ˌriːˈdʒɪgəʳ] *Am* = **rejig**.
rejoice [rɪˈdʒɔɪs] ◇ *vi* se réjouir; **they ~d at** OR **over the good news** ils se réjouissaient OR ils étaient ravis de la bonne nouvelle; **he ~s in the name of French-Edwardes** *hum* il a le privilège de porter le nom de French-Edwardes; **the hotel ~s in the title "Imperial Palace"** l'hôtel porte le nom ronflant de «Palais Impérial».
◇ *vt* réjouir, ravir.
rejoicing [rɪˈdʒɔɪsɪŋ] *n* réjouissance *f*; **it was the occasion of much ~** OR **of great ~s** ce fut l'occasion de grandes réjouissances.
rejoin[1] [ˌriːˈdʒɔɪn] *vt* -**1.** [go back to] rejoindre; **to ~ one's regiment** MIL rallier OR rejoindre son régiment; **to ~ ship** NAUT rallier le bord; **we ~ed the main road a few miles later** nous avons rejoint la nationale quelques kilomètres plus loin. -**2.** [join again] rejoindre; [club] se réinscrire à; **to ~ the majority** POL rallier la majorité.
rejoin[2] [rɪˈdʒɔɪn] *vt* & *vi* [reply] répliquer.
rejoinder [rɪˈdʒɔɪndəʳ] *n* réplique *f*.
rejuvenate [rɪˈdʒuːvəneɪt] *vt* rajeunir.
rejuvenating cream [rɪˈdʒuːvəneɪtɪŋ-] *n* crème *f* de beauté rajeunissante.
rejuvenation [rɪˌdʒuːvəˈneɪʃn] *n* rajeunissement *m*.
rekindle [ˌriːˈkɪndl] ◇ *vt* [fire] rallumer, attiser; *fig* [enthusiasm, desire, hatred] raviver, ranimer.
◇ *vi* [fire] se rallumer; *fig* [feelings] se ranimer.
relabel [ˌriːˈleɪbl] *vt* réétiqueter.
relapse [rɪˈlæps] ◇ *n* MED & *fig* rechute *f*; **to have a ~** faire une rechute, rechuter.
◇ *vi* -**1.** MED rechuter, faire une rechute. -**2.** [go back] retomber; **to ~ into silence** redevenir silencieux; **the country has ~d into war** le pays est à nouveau plongé dans la guerre; **to ~ into depression** replonger dans la dépression.
relate [rɪˈleɪt] ◇ *vt* -**1.** [tell - events, story] relater, faire le récit de; [- details, facts] rapporter; **strange to ~, we never met him again** chose curieuse, nous ne l'avons jamais plus revu. -**2.** [connect - ideas, events] rapprocher, établir un rapport OR un lien entre; **we can ~ this episode to a previous scene in the novel** nous pouvons établir un lien entre cet épisode et une scène antérieure du roman; **she always ~s everything to herself** elle ramène toujours tout à elle.
◇ *vi* -**1.** [connect - idea, event] se rapporter, se rattacher; **I don't understand how the two ideas ~** je ne comprends pas la relation entre les deux idées; **this ~s to what I was just saying** ceci est lié à OR en rapport avec ce que je viens de dire. -**2.** [have relationship, interact]: **at school, they learn to ~ to other children** à l'école, ils apprennent à vivre avec d'autres enfants; **I just can't ~ to my parents** je n'arrive pas à communiquer avec mes parents. -**3.** *inf* [appreciate]: **I can't ~ to his music** je n'accroche pas à sa musique.
related [rɪˈleɪtɪd] *adj* -**1.** [in family] parent; **we are ~** nous sommes parents; **she is ~ to the president** elle est parente du président; **they are ~ on his father's side** ils sont parents par son père; **to be ~ by marriage to sb** être parent de qqn par alliance; **they aren't ~** ils n'ont aucun lien de parenté; **they are closely ~** ils sont proches parents ‖ [animal, species] apparenté; [language] de même famille, proche; **an animal ~ to the cat** un animal apparenté au OR de la famille du chat. -**2.** [connected] connexe, lié; [neighbouring] voisin; **psychoanalysis and other ~ areas** la psychanalyse et les domaines qui s'y rattachent; **problems ~ to health** problèmes qui se rattachent OR qui touchent à la santé; **the two topics are closely ~** les deux sujets sont étroitement liés; **the two events are not ~** les deux événements n'ont aucun rapport ‖ ADMIN & JUR afférent; **questions ~ to official procedure** des questions afférentes à la procédure officielle. -**3.** MUS relatif.
-related *in cpds* lié à; **business~ activities** des activités liées OR ayant rapport aux affaires; **performance~ bonus** prime *f* d'encouragement.
relating [rɪˈleɪtɪŋ]
◆ **relating to** *prep phr* ayant rapport à, relatif à, concernant.
relation [rɪˈleɪʃn] *n* -**1.** [member of family] parent *m*, -e *f*; **they have ~s in Paris** ils ont de la famille à Paris; **he's a ~** il est de ma famille; **she is no ~ of mine** il n'y a aucun lien de parenté entre nous; **is she a ~ of yours?** est-elle de votre famille? -**2.** [kinship] parenté *f*; **what ~ is he to you?** quelle est sa parenté avec vous? -**3.** [connection] rapport *m*, relation *f*; **to have** OR **to bear a ~ to sthg** avoir (un) rapport à qqch, être en rapport avec qqch; **your answer bore no ~ to the question** votre réponse n'avait rien à voir avec la question. -**4.** [relationship, contact] rapport *m*, relation *f*; [between people, countries] rapport *m*, rapports *mpl*; **to enter into ~** OR **~s with sb** entrer OR se mettre en rapport avec qqn; **their ~s are somewhat strained** ils ont des rapports assez tendus; **to have (sexual) ~s with sb** *fml* avoir des rapports (sexuels) avec qqn; **to break off diplomatic ~s** interrompre les relations diplomatiques. -**5.** *fml* [narration - of events, story] récit *m*, relation *f*; [- of details] rapport *m*.
◆ **in relation to, with relation to** *prep phr* par rapport à, relativement à.
relational [rɪˈleɪʃənl] *adj* relationnel.
relational database *n* COMPUT base *f* de données relationnelle.
relationship [rɪˈleɪʃnʃɪp] *n* -**1.** [between people, countries] rapport *m*, rapports *mpl*, relation *f*, relations *fpl*; **to have a good/bad ~ with sb** [gen] avoir de bonnes/mauvaises relations avec qqn; **I'd like to talk to you about our ~** j'aimerais qu'on parle un peu de nous deux; **a ~ is something you have to work at** être en couple, ça demande des efforts; **our ~ is purely a business one** nos relations sont simplement des relations d'affaires; **they have a good/bad ~** ils s'entendent bien/mal; **he has a very close ~ with his mother** il est très lié à sa mère; **she has a good ~ with her class** elle a de bons rapports avec sa classe. -**2.** [kinship] lien *m* OR liens *mpl* de parenté; **what is your exact ~ to her?** quels sont vos liens de parenté exacts OR quelle est votre parenté exacte avec elle? -**3.** [connection - between ideas, events, things] rapport *m*, relation *f*, lien *m*.
relative [ˈrelətɪv] ◇ *adj* -**1.** [comparative] relatif; **to live in ~ comfort** vivre dans un confort relatif; **the ~ advantages of electricity as opposed to gas** les avantages relatifs de l'électricité par rapport au gaz ‖ [proportional] relatif; **taxation is ~ to income** l'imposition est proportionnelle au revenu ‖ [respective] respectif; **the ~ qualities of the two candidates** les qualités respectives des deux candidats ❑ **~ atomic mass** poids *m* OR masse *f* atomique. -**2.** [not absolute] relatif. -**3.** MUS relatif; **~ minor/major** ton *m* mineur/majeur relatif. -**4.** GRAMM relatif; **~ clause** (proposition *f*) relative *f*; **~ pronoun** pronom *m* relatif; **~ conjunction** conjonction *f* relative.
◇ *n* -**1.** [person] parent *m*, -e *f*; **she has ~s in Canada** elle a de la famille au Canada; **he's a ~ of mine** il fait partie de ma famille. -**2.** GRAMM relatif *m*.
◆ **relative to** *prep phr* relativement à.
relative density *n* densité *f* relative.
relative humidity *n* humidité *f* relative.
relatively [ˈrelətɪvlɪ] *adv* relativement; **~ difficult** relativement OR assez difficile; **~ speaking** relativement parlant.
relativism [ˈrelətɪvɪzm] *n* relativisme *m*.
relativist [ˈrelətɪvɪst] ◇ *adj* relativiste.
◇ *n* relativiste *mf*.
relativistic [ˌrelətɪˈvɪstɪk] *adj* relativiste.
relativity [ˌreləˈtɪvətɪ] *n* relativité *f*; **theory of ~** théorie *f* de la relativité.
relativization [ˌrelətɪvaɪˈzeɪʃn] *n* relativisation *f*.
relativize, -ise [ˈrelətɪvaɪz] *vt* relativiser.
relax [rɪˈlæks] ◇ *vi* -**1.** [person] se détendre, se délasser; [in comfort, on holiday] se relaxer, se détendre; **you need to ~** vous avez besoin de détente OR de vous détendre ‖ [calm down] se calmer, se détendre; **try and ~ a bit** essayez de vous détendre un peu; **~!** [calm down] du calme!; [don't worry] rassurez-vous! -**2.** [grip] se relâcher, se desserrer; [muscle] se relâcher, se décontracter; TECH [spring] se détendre; **his face ~ed into a smile** son visage s'est détendu et il a souri; **to ~ in one's efforts** relâcher ses efforts.
◇ *vt* -**1.** [mind] détendre, délasser; [muscles] relâcher, décontracter; **the music will ~ you** la musique vous détendra. -**2.** [grip] relâcher, desserrer; MED [bowels] relâcher. -**3.** *fig* [discipline, restriction] assouplir, relâcher; **the government has ~ed the laws on immigration** le gouvernement a assoupli les lois sur l'immigration; **during the holiday period, parking restrictions are ~ed** la réglementation du stationnement est plus souple pendant la période des vacances ‖ [concentration, effort] relâcher.
relaxant [rɪˈlæksənt] ◇ *n* (médicament *m*) relaxant *m*; **muscle ~** myorelaxant *m*, décontracturant *m*.
◇ *adj* relaxant.
relaxation [ˌriːlækˈseɪʃn] *n* -**1.** [rest] détente *f*, relaxation *f*; **she needs a week of ~** elle a besoin d'une semaine de détente OR de repos; **he plays golf for ~** il joue au golf pour se détendre; **she finds ~ in gardening** pour elle, le jardinage est une détente. -**2.** [loosening - of grip] relâchement *m*, desserrement *m*; *fig* [- of authority, law] relâchement *m*, assouplissement *m*.
relaxed [rɪˈlækst] *adj* -**1.** [person, atmosphere] détendu, décontracté; [smile] détendu; **to feel/to look ~** se sentir/avoir l'air détendu; **he's very ~ about the whole business** cette affaire n'a pas l'air de beaucoup le perturber ‖ [attitude] décontracté. -**2.** [muscle] relâché; [discipline] assoupli.
relaxing [rɪˈlæksɪŋ] *adj* [restful - atmosphere, afternoon, holiday] reposant; **she finds gardening ~** elle trouve le jardinage reposant; **you need a nice ~ bath** ce qu'il te faut, c'est un bon bain pour te détendre.
relay [ˈriːleɪ] (*pt* & *pp senses 1 & 2* relayed, *pt* & *pp sense 3* relaid [-ˈleɪd]) ◇ *n* -**1.** [team - of athletes, workers, horses] relais *m*; **to work in ~s** *Br* travailler par relais, se relayer. -**2.** RADIO & TV [transmitter] réémetteur *m*, relais *m*; [broadcast] émission *f* relayée. -**3.** ELEC & TECH relais *m*. -**4.** SPORT: **~ (race)** (course *f* de) relais *m*; **the 4 x 100 m ~** le relais 4 x 100 m.
◇ *vt* -**1.** [pass on - message, news] transmettre. -**2.** RADIO & TV [broadcast] relayer, retransmettre. -**3.** [cable, carpet] reposer.
relay station *n* relais *m*.

relearn [ˌriːˈlɜːn] (*Br pt & pp* relearned OR relearnt [-ˈlɜːnt], *Am pt & pp* relearned) *vt* réapprendre, rapprendre.

release [rɪˈliːs] ◇ *n* -**1.** [from captivity] libération *f*; [from prison] libération *f*, mise *f* en liberté, élargissement *m* ADMIN; [from custody] mise *f* en liberté, relaxe *f*; [from work] congé *m* (spécial); **on his ~ from prison** lors de sa mise en liberté, dès sa sortie de prison; **~ on bail** mise en liberté provisoire (sous caution); **~ on parole** libération *f* conditionnelle || *fig* [from obligation, promise] libération *f*, dispense *f*; [from pain, suffering] délivrance *f*; **death was a ~ for her** pour elle, la mort a été une délivrance ❑ **order of ~** ordre *m* de levée d'écrou. -**2.** COMM [from bond, customs] congé *m*. -**3.** [letting go - of handle, switch] déclenchement *m*; [- of brake] desserrage *m*; **the ~ of the atom bomb** le largage de la bombe atomique. -**4.** [distribution - of film] sortie *f*; [- of book, record] sortie *f*, parution *f*; **the film is on general ~** le film est sorti || [new film, book, record] nouveauté *f*; **her latest ~ is called "Chrissy"** son dernier disque s'appelle «Chrissy»; **it's a new ~** ça vient de sortir. -**5.** MECH [lever] levier *m*; [safety catch] cran *m* de sûreté.
◇ *comp* [button, switch] de déclenchement.
◇ *vt* -**1.** [prisoner] libérer, relâcher, élargir ADMIN; [from custody] remettre en liberté, relâcher, relaxer; [captive person, animal] libérer; [employee, schoolchild] libérer, laisser partir; **to ~ sb from bondage** libérer qqn de ses chaînes; **to be ~d on bail** JUR être libéré sous caution; **the earthquake victims were ~d from the wreckage** les victimes du tremblement de terre ont été dégagées des décombres; **the children were ~d into the care of their grandparents** on a confié les enfants à leurs grands-parents; **death finally ~d her from her suffering** la mort a mis un terme à ses souffrances || [from obligation] libérer, dégager; [from promise] dégager, relever; **he was ~d from his vows** il a été relevé OR dispensé de ses vœux; **to ~ sb from a debt** remettre une dette à qqn. -**2.** [let go - from control, grasp] lâcher; [- feelings] donner OR laisser libre cours à; **he ~d his grip on my hand** il m'a lâché la OR il a lâché ma main || [bomb] larguer, lâcher; [gas, heat] libérer, dégager; **the explosion ~d chemicals into the river** l'explosion a libéré des agents chimiques dans la rivière; **insecticides were ~d over the crops** des pesticides ont été répandus sur les récoltes. -**3.** [issue - film] sortir; [- book, record] sortir, faire paraître. -**4.** [goods, new model] mettre en vente OR sur le marché; [stamps, coins] émettre. -**5.** [make public - statement] publier; [- information, story] dévoiler, annoncer; **the company refuses to ~ details of the contract** la compagnie refuse de divulguer OR de faire connaître les détails du contrat. -**6.** [lever, mechanism] déclencher; [brake] desserrer; **to ~ the clutch** AUT débrayer; **to ~ the shutter** PHOT déclencher (l'obturateur); **~ the catch to open the door** pour ouvrir la porte, soulever le loquet. -**7.** FIN [credits, funds] dégager, débloquer. -**8.** [property, rights] céder.

release print *n* CIN copie *f* d'exploitation.

relegate [ˈrelɪgeɪt] *vt* -**1.** [person, thought, thing] reléguer; **to ~ sb/sthg to sthg** reléguer qqn/qqch à qqch. -**2.** SPORT [team] reléguer, déclasser; **to be ~d** FTBL descendre en OR être relégué à la division inférieure. -**3.** [refer - issue, question] renvoyer.

relegation [ˌrelɪˈgeɪʃn] *n* -**1.** [demotion - of person, team, thing] relégation *f*. -**2.** [referral - of issue, matter] renvoi *m*.

relent [rɪˈlent] *vi* -**1.** [person] se laisser fléchir OR toucher; **they begged him for mercy but he would not ~** ils lui ont demandé grâce mais il est demeuré implacable OR impitoyable; **he finally ~ed and let us go** il a finalement accepté de nous laisser partir. -**2.** [storm] s'apaiser.

relentless [rɪˈlentlɪs] *adj* -**1.** [merciless] implacable, impitoyable. -**2.** [sustained - activity, effort] acharné, opiniâtre; [- noise] ininterrompu; [- rain] incessant.

relentlessly [rɪˈlentlɪslɪ] *adv* -**1.** [mercilessly] impitoyablement, implacablement. -**2.** [persistently] avec acharnement OR opiniâtreté; **he worked ~** il travailla avec acharnement; **the rain beat down ~** il n'a pas cessé de pleuvoir à verse.

relet [ˌriːˈlet] *vt* relouer.

relevance [ˈreləvəns], **relevancy** [ˈreləvənsɪ] *n* pertinence *f*, intérêt *m*; **I don't see the ~ of your remark** la pertinence de votre remarque m'échappe; **what is the ~ of this to the matter under discussion?** quel est le rapport avec ce dont on parle?; **this question has little ~ for us** cette question ne nous concerne pas vraiment.

relevant [ˈreləvənt] *adj* -**1.** [pertinent - information, comment, beliefs, ideas] pertinent; **facts ~ to the case** des faits en rapport avec l'affaire; **such considerations are not ~** de telles considérations sont hors de propos; **confine yourself to the ~ facts** ne vous écartez pas du sujet; **her novels no longer seem ~ to modern life** ses romans ne sont plus d'actualité. -**2.** [appropriate] approprié; **fill in your name in the ~ space** inscrivez votre nom dans la case correspondante; **have you brought the ~ file?** avez-vous apporté le dossier approprié OR le bon dossier?

reliability [rɪˌlaɪəˈbɪlətɪ] *n* -**1.** [of person] sérieux *m*; [of information] sérieux *m*, fiabilité *f*; [of memory, judgment] sûreté *f*, fiabilité *f*. -**2.** [of clock, engine] fiabilité *f*.

reliable [rɪˈlaɪəbl] *adj* -**1.** [trustworthy - friend] sur qui on peut compter, sûr; [- worker] à qui on peut faire confiance, sérieux; [- witness] digne de confiance OR de foi; [- account, information] sérieux, sûr; [- memory, judgment] fiable, auquel on peut se fier; **he's very ~** on peut toujours compter sur lui OR lui faire confiance; **the news came from a ~ source** la nouvelle provenait d'une source sûre. -**2.** [clock, machine, car] fiable; **my watch isn't very ~** ma montre n'est pas très fiable.

reliably [rɪˈlaɪəblɪ] *adv* sérieusement; **we are ~ informed that...** nous avons appris de bonne source OR de source sûre que...

reliance [rɪˈlaɪəns] *n* -**1.** [trust] confiance *f*; **to place ~ on sb/sthg** faire confiance à qqn/qqch. -**2.** [dependence] dépendance *f*; **his ~ on their advice** le fait qu'il ne fasse rien sans les consulter; **her ~ on alcohol** sa dépendance vis-à-vis de l'alcool.

reliant [rɪˈlaɪənt] *adj* -**1.** [dependent] dépendant; **we are heavily ~ on your advice** vos conseils nous sont indispensables; **he is too ~ on tranquillizers** il a trop recours aux tranquillisants. -**2.** [trusting] confiant; **to be ~ on sb** faire confiance à OR avoir confiance en qqn.

relic [ˈrelɪk] *n* -**1.** RELIG relique *f*; [vestige] relique *f*, vestige *m*. -**2.** *inf fig & pej* [old person] croulant *m*, vieux débris *m*.

relict [ˈrelɪkt] *n* -**1.** BIOL & ECOL relique *f*; GEOL forme *f* relique. -**2.** *arch* [widow] veuve *f*.

relief [rɪˈliːf] ◇ *n* -**1.** [from anxiety, discomfort, pain] soulagement *m*; **to bring ~ to sb** soulager qqn, apporter un soulagement à qqn; **the medicine gave OR brought her little ~ from the pain** le médicament ne la soulagea guère; **he finds ~ in writing** ça le soulage d'écrire; **to our great ~, much to our ~** à notre grand soulagement; **it was a great ~ to her when the exams ended** la fin des examens fut un grand soulagement pour elle. -**2.** [aid] secours *m*, aide *f*; **to send ~ to third world countries** apporter de l'aide aux pays du tiers-monde; **famine ~** aide *f* alimentaire. -**3.** *Am* [state benefit] aide *f* sociale; **to be on ~** recevoir des aides sociales OR des allocations. -**4.** [diversion] divertissement *m*, distraction *f*; **he included a few comic scenes in the play for light ~** il a inclus plusieurs scènes comiques dans la pièce pour détendre l'atmosphère; **she reads detective novels for light ~** elle lit des romans policiers pour se distraire. -**5.** [of besieged city] libération *f*, délivrance *f*. -**6.** [of guard, team] relève *f*; **I've been on duty all night with only one hour's ~** j'ai été de garde toute la nuit, sauf une heure pendant laquelle j'ai été relevé; **~s have arrived** [gen] la relève OR l'équipe de relève est arrivée; [troops] les troupes de relève sont arrivées, la relève est arrivée. -**7.** ART relief *m*; **the inscription stood out in ~** l'inscription était en relief || [contrast] relief *m*; **the mountains stood out in bold ~ against the sky** les montagnes se détachaient OR se découpaient nettement sur le ciel; **to bring OR to throw sthg into ~** *fig* mettre qqch en relief OR en valeur. -**8.** GEOG relief *m*. -**9.** JUR [redress] réparation *f*; [exemption] dérogation *f*, exemption *f*; **tax ~** dégrèvement *m* fiscal.
◇ *comp* -**1.** [extra - transport, service] supplémentaire; [replacement - worker, troops, team] de relève; [- bus, machine] de remplacement. -**2.** [for aid - fund, organization] de secours; **~ work** coopération *f*; **~ worker** *membre d'une organisation humanitaire qui travaille sur le terrain.*

relief map *n* carte *f* en relief.

relief printing *n* impression *f* en relief.

relief road *n* itinéraire *m* bis, route *f* de délestage.

relieve [rɪˈliːv] *vt* -**1.** [anxiety, distress, pain] soulager, alléger; [poverty] soulager; **the good news ~d her of her anxiety** la bonne nouvelle a dissipé ses inquiétudes; **to ~ congestion** MED & TRANSP décongestionner. -**2.** [boredom, gloom] dissiper; [monotony] briser; **the darkness of the room was ~d only by the firelight** la pièce n'était éclairée que par la lueur du feu; **they ~d the monotony of the evening by playing cards** pour briser la monotonie de la soirée, ils ont joué aux cartes. -**3.** [unburden]: **to ~ sb of sthg** soulager OR débarrasser qqn de qqch; **he ~d her of her suitcase** il l'a débarrassée de sa valise; **to ~ sb of their wallet** *hum* délester qqn de son portefeuille; **to ~ sb of an obligation** décharger OR dégager qqn d'une obligation; **to ~ sb of his duties OR position** relever qqn de ses fonctions. -**4.** [aid - population, refugees, country] secourir, venir en aide à. -**5.** [replace - worker, team] relayer, prendre la relève de; [- guard, sentry] relever. -**6.** [liberate - fort, city] délivrer, libérer; [from siege] lever le siège de. -**7.** *euph* [urinate]: **to ~ o.s.** se soulager.

relieved [rɪˈliːvd] *adj* soulagé; **to feel ~** se sentir soulagé; **we were greatly ~ at the news** nous avons été très soulagés d'apprendre la nouvelle.

relievo [rɪˈliːvəʊ] (*pl* relievos) *n* ART relief *m*.

relight [ˌriːˈlaɪt] (*pt & pp* relighted OR relit [-ˈlɪt]) *vt* rallumer.

religion [rɪˈlɪdʒn] *n* -**1.** RELIG religion *f*; **the Jewish ~** la religion OR la confession juive; **what is your ~?** à quelle confession appartenez-vous?; **to enter ~** entrer en religion; **a man of ~** un homme de religion OR d'Église; **various ~s were represented at the conference** diverses confessions étaient représentées à la conférence; **it's against my ~ to work on Sundays** *literal & hum* ma religion m'interdit de travailler le dimanche. -**2.** *fig* [obsession] religion *f*, culte *m*; **to make a ~ of sthg** se faire une religion de qqch; **sport is a ~ with him** le sport est son dieu.

religiosity [rɪˌlɪdʒɪˈɒsətɪ] *n* religiosité *f*.

religious [rɪˈlɪdʒəs] ◇ *adj* -**1.** [authority, order, ceremony, art] religieux; [war] de religion; **~ education OR instruction** instruction *f* religieuse. -**2.** [devout] religieux, croyant; **she is very ~** elle est très pieuse OR croyante. -**3.** *fig* [scrupulous] religieux; **to do sthg with ~ care** faire qqch avec un soin religieux.
◇ *n* [monk, nun] religieux *m*, -euse *f*.

religiously [rɪˈlɪdʒəslɪ] *adv literal & fig* religieusement.

reline [ˌriːˈlaɪn] *vt* [garment] mettre une nouvelle doublure à, redoubler; [picture] rentoiler; **to ~ the brakes** AUT changer les garnitures de freins.

relinquish [rɪ'lɪŋkwɪʃ] *vt* -**1.** [give up - claim, hope, power] abandonner, renoncer à; [- property, possessions] se dessaisir de; [- right] renoncer à; she ~ed all hope of ever seeing him again elle abandonna tout espoir de le revoir un jour; he ~ed his voting rights to the chairman il a cédé son droit de vote au président. -**2.** [release - grip, hold] : to ~ one's hold of OR on sthg *literal* lâcher qqch; *fig* relâcher l'étreinte que l'on a sur qqch.

relinquishment [rɪ'lɪŋkwɪʃmənt] *n* abandon *m*, renonciation *f*; the ~ of one's rights l'abandon de OR la renonciation à ses droits.

reliquary ['relɪkwərɪ] (*pl* reliquaries) *n* reliquaire *m*.

relish ['relɪʃ] ◇ *n* -**1.** [pleasure, enthusiasm] goût *m*, plaisir *m*, délectation *f*; to do sthg with ~ faire qqch avec délectation OR grand plaisir, adorer faire qqch; to eat/to drink with ~ adorer manger/boire; he has lost his ~ for reading il a perdu son goût pour la lecture. -**2.** [condiment, sauce] condiment *m*, sauce *f*; horseradish ~ sauce *f* au raifort. -**3.** [flavour] goût *m*, saveur *f*; life had lost its ~ for her *fig* la vie avait perdu toute saveur pour elle.
◇ *vt* -**1.** [enjoy] savourer; to ~ one's triumph savourer son triomphe; I bet he's ~ing this moment je parie qu'il savoure cet instant || [look forward to] : I don't ~ the idea OR prospect OR thought of seeing them again l'idée OR la perspective de les revoir ne m'enchante OR ne me réjouit guère. -**2.** [savour - food, drink] savourer, se délecter de.

relive [,riː'lɪv] *vt* revivre.

reload [,riː'ləʊd] *vt* recharger.

relocate [,riːləʊ'keɪt] ◇ *vt* installer ailleurs, délocaliser; the facilities were ~d to Scotland les services ont été réinstallés OR délocalisés en Écosse.
◇ *vi* s'installer ailleurs, déménager.

relocation [,rɪləʊ'keɪʃn] *n* [of premises, industry] délocalisation *f*, déménagement *m*; [of population] relogement *m*; ~ expenses indemnité *f* de déménagement.

reluctance [rɪ'lʌktəns] *n* -**1.** [unwillingness] répugnance *f*; to do sthg with ~ faire qqch à contrecœur OR de mauvais gré; she expressed some ~ to get involved in the matter elle a dit qu'elle n'avait pas envie de se laisser entraîner dans cette histoire. -**2.** PHYS réluctance *f*.

reluctant [rɪ'lʌktənt] *adj* -**1.** [unwilling] peu enclin OR disposé; to be ~ to do sthg être peu enclin à faire qqch, n'avoir pas envie de faire qqch; she was ~ to admit the truth elle ne voulait pas admettre OR n'avait pas envie d'admettre la vérité. -**2.** [against one's will - commitment, promise, approval] accordé à contrecœur; she gave a ~ smile elle eut un sourire contraint; she was a ~ sex symbol c'est bien malgré elle qu'elle était devenue un sex-symbol.

reluctantly [rɪ'lʌktəntlɪ] *adv* à contrecœur; to do sthg ~ faire qqch à contrecœur; she sat down ~ elle s'est assise à contrecœur.

rely [rɪ'laɪ] (*pt* & *pp* relied)
◆ **rely on, rely upon** *vt insep* -**1.** [depend on] compter sur, faire confiance à; she can always be relied upon to give good advice on peut toujours compter sur elle pour donner de bons conseils; we were ~ing on the weather being good nous comptions sur du beau temps; we relied on you bringing the records on comptait sur vous pour apporter les disques; you can never ~ on them on ne peut jamais compter sur eux; he can never be relied upon to keep a secret on ne peut lui confier aucun secret; you may ~ on OR upon it vous pouvez compter dessus; I ~ on my daughter to drive me to the shops je dépends de ma fille pour me conduire aux magasins; he relies on his family for everything il dépend de sa famille pour tout; she relies too much on luck elle compte trop sur la chance; I'm ~ing on you to find a solution je compte sur vous pour trouver une solution. -**2.** JUR [call on] invoquer; the points of fact and law relied on les arguments de fait et de droit invoqués.

REM (*abbr of* rapid eye movement) *n mouvements oculaires rapides*; ~ sleep sommeil *m* paradoxal.

remain [rɪ'meɪn] *vi* -**1.** [be left] rester; 6 hens ~ il reste 6 poules; very little ~s OR there ~s very little of the original building il ne reste pas grand-chose du bâtiment d'origine; much ~s to be discussed il y a encore beaucoup de choses à discuter; that ~s to be seen cela reste à voir; it ~s to be seen whether he will agree (il) reste à savoir s'il sera d'accord; the fact ~s that we can't afford this house il n'en reste pas moins que OR toujours est-il que nous ne pouvons pas nous offrir cette maison; all that ~ed to be done was to say goodbye il ne restait plus qu'à se dire au revoir; it only ~s for me to thank you il ne me reste plus qu'à vous remercier. -**2.** [stay] rester, demeurer; please ~ seated OR in your seats veuillez rester assis; to ~ faithful to sb rester fidèle à qqn; to ~ silent garder le silence, rester silencieux; for reasons that ~ unknown pour des raisons inconnues; the weather ~ed settled le temps est resté stable; ~ here, please restez-là, je vous prie; he ~ed behind after the meeting il est resté après la réunion; it ~s a mystery whether... on ignore toujours si...; the real reasons were to ~ a secret/mystery les véritables raisons devaient demeurer secrètes/ne furent jamais élucidées; he has ~ed the same despite all that has happened il n'a pas changé malgré tout ce qui s'est passé; let things ~ as they are laissez les choses telles qu'elles sont; I ~, Sir, your most faithful servant *fml* & *dated* veuillez agréer OR je vous prie d'agréer, Monsieur, l'expression de mes sentiments les plus respectueux.

remainder [rɪ'meɪndər] ◇ *n* -**1.** [leftover - food, supplies, time] reste *m*; [- money] solde *m*; [- debt] reliquat *m*; [- people] : the ~ went on a picnic les autres sont allés pique-niquer; for the ~ of his life pour le restant de ses jours; she spent the ~ on sweets elle a dépensé ce qui restait en bonbons. -**2.** MATH reste *m*. -**3.** [unsold book] invendu *m*; [unsold product] fin *f* de série. -**4.** JUR usufruit *m* avec réversibilité.
◇ *vt* COMM solder.

remaining [rɪ'meɪnɪŋ] *adj* qui reste, restant; the only ~ member of her family la seule personne de sa famille (qui soit) encore en vie; the ~ guests le reste des invités; it's our only ~ hope c'est le seul espoir qui nous reste, c'est notre dernier espoir.

remains [rɪ'meɪnz] *npl* -**1.** [of meal, fortune] restes *mpl*; [of building] restes *mpl*, vestiges *mpl*. -**2.** *euph* & *fml* [corpse] restes *mpl*, dépouille *f* mortelle.

remake [*vb* ,riː'meɪk, *n* 'riːmeɪk] (*pt* & *pp* remade [-'meɪd]) ◇ *vt* refaire.
◇ *n* [film] remake *m*.

remand [rɪ'mɑːnd] *Br* ◇ *vt* JUR [case] renvoyer; [defendant] déférer; to ~ sb in custody placer qqn en détention préventive; to ~ sb on bail mettre qqn en liberté OR libérer qqn sous caution; the magistrate ~ed the case for a week le magistrat a renvoyé l'affaire à huitaine.
◇ *n* renvoi *m*; to be on ~ [in custody] être en détention préventive; [on bail] être libéré sous caution.

remand centre *n Br centre de détention préventive*.

remand home *n Br* ≃ centre *m* d'éducation surveillée.

remark [rɪ'mɑːk] ◇ *n* -**1.** [comment] remarque *f*, réflexion *f*; to make OR to pass a ~ faire une remarque; to make OR to pass ~s about sthg/sb faire des réflexions sur qqch/qqn; she made the ~ that no one knew the truth elle fit remarquer OR observer que personne ne savait la vérité; it was a valid ~ c'était une réflexion pertinente; to let sthg pass without ~ laisser passer qqch sans faire de commentaire. -**2.** *fml* [attention] attention *f*, intérêt *m*; worthy of ~ digne d'attention; his behaviour did not escape ~ son comportement n'est pas passé inaperçu.
◇ *vt* -**1.** [comment] (faire) remarquer, (faire) observer; "the days are getting longer", she ~ed «les jours rallongent», fit-elle remarquer. -**2.** *fml* [notice] remarquer.
◆ **remark on, remark upon** *vt insep*: to ~ on OR upon sthg [comment] faire un commentaire OR une observation sur qqch; [criticize] faire des remarques sur qqch; he ~ed on the lateness of the hour il fit remarquer qu'il était tard.

remarkable [rɪ'mɑːkəbl] *adj* [quality, aspect] remarquable; [event, figure] remarquable, marquant; they are ~ for their modesty ils sont d'une rare modestie OR remarquablement modestes.

remarkably [rɪ'mɑːkəblɪ] *adv* remarquablement.

remarriage [,riː'mærɪdʒ] *n* remariage *m*.

remarry [,riː'mærɪ] (*pt* & *pp* remarried) *vi* se remarier.

rematch [*vb* ,riː'mætʃ, *n* 'riːmætʃ] SPORT ◇ *vt* [players, contestants] opposer de nouveau.
◇ *n* [return] match *m* retour; [second] deuxième match *m*.

Rembrandt ['rembrænt] *pr n* Rembrandt.

remediable [rɪ'miːdjəbl] *adj* remédiable.

remedial [rɪ'miːdjəl] *adj* -**1.** [action] réparateur; [measures] de redressement. -**2.** *Br* SCH [classes, education] de rattrapage, de soutien; [pupil, student] qui n'a pas le niveau; she teaches ~ maths elle donne des cours de rattrapage OR de soutien en maths; ~ teaching rattrapage *m* scolaire. -**3.** MED [treatment] correctif, curatif; ~ exercises gymnastique *f* corrective.

remedy ['remədɪ] (*pl* remedies, *pt* & *pp* remedied) ◇ *n* -**1.** *literal* & *fig* remède *m*; it's a good ~ for insomnia/boredom c'est un bon remède contre l'insomnie/l'ennui; to find a ~ for sthg trouver un remède à qqch. -**2.** *Br* JUR recours *m*; to have no ~ at law against sb n'avoir aucun recours légal contre qqn.
◇ *vt* MED remédier à; [failure] rattraper, remédier à; the situation cannot be remedied la situation est sans issue; how can we ~ the loss of our three best players? comment remédier à la perte de nos trois meilleurs joueurs?

remember [rɪ'membər] ◇ *vt* -**1.** [recollect - face, person, past event] se souvenir de, se rappeler; don't you ~ me? [in memory] vous ne vous souvenez pas de moi?; [recognize] vous ne me reconnaissez pas?; I ~ him as a child je me souviens de lui enfant; I ~ locking the door je me rappelle avoir OR je me souviens d'avoir fermé la porte à clé; I don't ~ ever going OR having gone there je ne me rappelle pas y être jamais allé; do you ~ me knocking on your door? vous souvenez-vous que j'ai frappé à votre porte?; I can't ~ anything else c'est tout ce dont je me souviens; I ~ when there was no such thing as a paid holiday je me souviens de l'époque où les congés payés n'existaient pas; I can't ~ her name son nom m'échappe, je ne me souviens pas de son nom; I can never ~ names je n'ai aucune mémoire des noms; we have nothing to ~ him by nous n'avons aucun souvenir de lui; she will always be ~ed as a great poet on se souviendra toujours d'elle comme d'un grand poète; as you will ~, the door is always locked vous savez sans doute que la porte est toujours fermée à clef; nobody could ~ such a thing happening before personne n'avait jamais vu une chose pareille se produire. -**2.** [not forget] penser à, songer à; ~ my advice n'oubliez pas mes conseils; ~ to close the door n'oubliez pas de OR pensez à fermer la porte; we can't be expected to ~ everything nous ne pouvons quand même pas penser à tout; you must ~ that smoking is forbidden n'oubliez pas qu'il est interdit de fumer; that's a date worth ~ing voilà une date qu'il faudrait ne pas oublier; she will ~ you in her prayers elle ne vous oubliera pas OR elle pensera à vous dans ses prières || [be mindful of] :

~ where you are! un peu de tenue, voyons!; ~ who you're talking to! à qui croyez-vous parler?; he ~ed himself just in time il s'est repris juste à temps. -**3.** [give regards to]: ~ me to your parents rappelez-moi au bon souvenir de vos parents; she asked to be ~ed to you elle vous envoie son meilleur souvenir. -**4.** [give tip or present to]: please ~ the driver n'oubliez pas le chauffeur; she always ~s me on my birthday elle n'oublie jamais le jour de mon anniversaire; he ~ed me in his will il a pensé à moi dans son testament. -**5.** [commemorate - war] commémorer; [- victims] se souvenir de.

◇ *vi* se souvenir; I ~ now maintenant, je m'en souviens; as far as I can ~ autant qu'il m'en souvienne; not that I ~ pas que je m'en souvienne; if I ~ rightly si je me OR si je m'en souviens bien, si j'ai bonne mémoire.

remembrance [rɪ'membrəns] *n* -**1.** [recollection] souvenir *m*, mémoire *f*; to the best of my ~ autant qu'il m'en souvienne; I have no ~ of it je n'en ai gardé aucun souvenir. -**2.** [memory] souvenir *m*. -**3.** [keepsake] souvenir *m*; she gave him a ring as a ~ of her elle lui a donné une bague en souvenir d'elle. -**4.** [commemoration] souvenir *m*, commémoration *f*; ~ service, service of ~ cérémonie *f* du souvenir, commémoration *f*.

◆ **in remembrance of** *prep phr*: in ~ of sthg/sb en souvenir OR en mémoire de qqch/qqn.

Remembrance Day, Remembrance Sunday *n Br* (commémoration *f* de l') Armistice *m* *(le dimanche avant ou après le 11 novembre)*.

remind [rɪ'maɪnd] *vt* -**1.** [tell] rappeler à; to ~ sb to do sthg rappeler à qqn de faire qqch, faire penser à qqn qu'il faut faire qqch; to ~ sb about sthg rappeler qqch à qqn; ~ him that we're going out rappelez-lui que nous sortons; can you ~ me about the bills/to pay the bills? pouvez-vous me faire penser aux factures/me rappeler qu'il faut payer les factures?; do I need to ~ you of the necessity for discretion? inutile de vous rappeler que la discrétion s'impose; how many times do they have to be ~ed? combien de fois faut-il le leur rappeler?; I'm glad you ~ed me je suis content que vous me l'ayez rappelé; that ~s me! à propos!, pendant que j'y pense!; passengers are ~ed that the duty-free shop will close in five minutes nous rappelons aux voyageurs que la boutique hors taxe ferme dans cinq minutes. -**2.** [be reminiscent of]: she ~s me of my sister elle me rappelle ma sœur; the music ~ed them of Greece la musique leur rappelait la Grèce.

reminder [rɪ'maɪndə^r] *n* [spoken] rappel *m*; [written] pense-bête *m*; ADMIN & COMM rappel *m*; to give sb a ~ to do sthg rappeler à qqn qu'il doit faire qqch; final ~ dernier rappel; she tied a knot in her handkerchief as a ~ elle a fait un nœud à son mouchoir pour ne pas oublier; the picture was a ~ of her life in Paris cette image lui rappelait sa vie à Paris; their success was a ~ of his own failure leur réussite lui rappelait son propre échec; we gave him a gentle ~ that it's her birthday tomorrow nous lui avons discrètement rappelé que demain c'est son anniversaire.

reminisce [,remɪ'nɪs] *vi* raconter ses souvenirs (avec nostalgie); to ~ about the past évoquer le passé OR parler du passé avec nostalgie.

reminiscence [,remɪ'nɪsns] *n* [memory] réminiscence *f*, souvenir *m*.

◆ **reminiscences** *npl* [memoirs] mémoires *mpl*.

reminiscent [,remɪ'nɪsnt] *adj* -**1.** [suggestive]: ~ of qui rappelle, qui fait penser à; in a voice ~ of that of her mother OR of her mother's d'une voix qui fait penser à OR qui rappelle celle de sa mère; parts of the book are ~ of Proust on trouve des réminiscences de Proust dans certaines parties du livre, certaines parties du livre rappellent Proust. -**2.** [nostalgic - person, smile] nostalgique.

remiss [rɪ'mɪs] *adj fml* négligent; he is ~ in his duties il néglige ses devoirs; it was rather ~ of you to forget her birthday c'était un peu négligent OR léger de votre part d'oublier son anniversaire.

remission [rɪ'mɪʃn] *n* -**1.** *Br* JUR [release - from prison sentence] remise *f* (de peine); [- from debt, claim] remise *f*; he was granted five years' ~ for good behaviour on lui a accordé une remise de peine de cinq ans pour bonne conduite; ~ from a debt remise d'une dette ‖ ADMIN [dispensation] dispense *f*; he asked for the ~ of a deposit il a demandé à être dispensé de verser une caution. -**2.** MED & RELIG rémission *f*.

remit [*vb* rɪ'mɪt, *n* 'riːmɪt] (*pt* & *pp* remitted, *cont* remitting) ◇ *vt* -**1.** [release - from penalty, sins] remettre; his sentence was remitted by five years il a bénéficié d'une remise de peine de cinq ans; to ~ sb's debt remettre la dette de qqn, tenir qqn quitte d'une dette; to ~ sb's sentence accorder une remise de peine à qqn ‖ [dispense, exonerate - fees, tax] remettre; his exam fees were remitted il a été dispensé des droits d'examen. -**2.** [send - money] envoyer; to ~ a sum of money to sb envoyer une somme (d'argent) à qqn. -**3.** JUR [case] renvoyer. -**4.** *fml* [defer] différer, remettre. -**5.** *fml* [relax - attention, activity] relâcher.

◇ *vi* -**1.** [lessen - zeal] diminuer; [- attention, efforts] se relâcher; [- storm] s'apaiser, se calmer. -**2.** MED [fever] tomber, diminuer; [disease] régresser.

◇ *n* attributions *fpl*, pouvoirs *mpl*; that's outside their ~ cela n'entre pas dans (le cadre de) leurs attributions; our ~ is to... il nous incombe de...

remittal [rɪ'mɪtl] *n* -**1.** FIN [of debt] remise *f*. -**2.** JUR renvoi *m*.

remittance [rɪ'mɪtns] *n* -**1.** [payment] versement *m*; [settlement] paiement *m*, règlement *m*; to send a ~ to sb envoyer un versement à qqn. -**2.** [delivery - of papers, documents] remise *f*.

remittee [rɪ,mɪt'iː] *n* ADMIN destinataire *mf (d'un envoi de fonds)*.

remittent [rɪ'mɪtnt] *adj* MED rémittent.

remitter, remittor [rɪ'mɪtə^r] *n* FIN remettant *m*, -e *f*; [of letter, document] porteur *m*.

remix [*vb* ,riː'mɪks, *n* 'riːmɪks] ◇ *vt* [record, recording] remixer, refaire le mixage de.

◇ *n* remix *m*.

remnant ['remnənt] *n* [remains - of meal, material] reste *m*; [vestige - of beauty, culture] vestige *m*; the ~s of the army/his fortune ce qui reste de l'armée/de sa fortune.

◆ **remnants** *npl* COMM [unsold goods] invendus *mpl*; [fabric] coupons *mpl* (de tissus); [oddments] fins *fpl* de série.

remodel [,riː'mɒdl] (*Br pt* & *pp* remodelled, *cont* remodelling, *Am pt* & *pp* remodeled, *cont* remodeling) *vt* remodeler.

remold *Am* = **remould**.

remonstrate ['remənstreɪt] *vi fml* protester; to ~ with sb faire des remontrances à qqn; to ~ against sthg protester contre qqch.

remorse [rɪ'mɔːs] *n* remords *m*; he was filled with ~ at what he had done il était pris de remords en songeant à ce qu'il avait fait; she felt no ~ elle n'éprouvait aucun remords; without ~ [with no regret] sans remords; [pitilessly] sans pitié.

remorseful [rɪ'mɔːsfʊl] *adj* plein de remords.

remorsefully [rɪ'mɔːsfʊlɪ] *adv* avec remords.

remorseless [rɪ'mɔːslɪs] *adj* -**1.** [with no regret] sans remords. -**2.** [relentless] implacable, impitoyable.

remorselessly [rɪ'mɔːslɪslɪ] *adv* -**1.** [with no regret] sans remords. -**2.** [relentlessly] impitoyablement, implacablement.

remorselessness [rɪ'mɔːslɪsnɪs] *n* [lack of regret] absence *f* de remords; [relentlessness] absence *f* de pitié.

remortgage [,riː'mɔːgɪdʒ] *vt* [house, property] hypothéquer de nouveau, prendre une nouvelle hypothèque sur.

remote [rɪ'məʊt] *adj* -**1.** [distant - place] éloigné, lointain; [- time, period] lointain, reculé; [- ancestor] éloigné; in the remotest parts of the continent au fin fond du continent; they live in a very ~ area ils vivent dans un endroit très isolé. -**2.** [aloof - person, manner] distant, froid; [faraway - look] lointain, vague; [- voice] lointain; she seems very ~ elle semble être très distante OR d'un abord difficile. -**3.** [unconnected - idea, comment] éloigné; your comments are rather ~ from the subject vos commentaires n'ont pas grand-chose à voir avec le sujet. -**4.** [slight - chance] petit, faible; [- ressemblance] vague, lointain; our chances of success are rather ~ nos chances de réussite sont assez minces, nous n'avons que peu de chances de réussir; it's a ~ possibility c'est très peu probable; I haven't the remotest idea je n'en ai pas la moindre idée. -**5.** COMPUT [terminal] commandé à distance; ~ job entry lancement *m* de tâches à distance; ~ loading téléchargement *m*; ~ sensing télédétection *f*.

remote control *n* télécommande *f*, commande *f* à distance.

remote-controlled *adj* télécommandé.

remotely [rɪ'məʊtlɪ] *adv* -**1.** [slightly] faiblement, vaguement; the two subjects are only very ~ linked il n'y a qu'un rapport très lointain entre les deux sujets; it is ~ possible that I'm mistaken il n'est pas absolument impossible que je fasse erreur; she's not ~ interested ça ne l'intéresse pas le moins du monde OR absolument pas; I'm not even ~ tired je ne suis pas fatigué du tout OR absolument pas fatigué. -**2.** [distantly]: the house is ~ situated la maison se trouve dans un coin isolé; they are ~ related ils sont parents éloignés. -**3.** [aloofly] de façon distante OR hautaine; [dreamily] vaguement, de façon songeuse.

remoteness [rɪ'məʊtnɪs] *n* -**1.** [distance - in space] éloignement *m*, isolement *m*; [- in time] éloignement *m*. -**2.** [aloofness - of person] distance *f*, froideur *f*.

remould *Br*, **remold** *Am* [*vb* ,riː'məʊld, *n* 'riːməʊld] ◇ *vt* -**1.** ART & TECH remouler, refaçonner. -**2.** AUT [tyre] rechaper. -**3.** *fig* [person, character] changer, remodeler.

◇ *n* [tyre] pneu *m* rechapé.

remount [*vb* ,riː'maʊnt, *n* 'riːmaʊnt] ◇ *vt* -**1.** [horse, bicycle] remonter sur; [hill, steps] remonter, gravir à nouveau; [ladder] remonter à OR sur. -**2.** [picture] rentoiler; [photograph] remplacer le support de; [jewel] remonter.

◇ *vi* [on horse, bicycle] remonter.

◇ *n* EQUIT remonte *f*.

removable [rɪ'muːvəbl] *adj* -**1.** [detachable - lining, cover] amovible, détachable. -**2.** [transportable - furniture, fittings] mobile, transportable.

removal [rɪ'muːvl] ◇ *n* -**1.** [of garment, stain, object] enlèvement *m*; [of abuse, evil, threat] suppression *f*; MED [of organ, tumour] ablation *f*; make-up ~ démaquillage *m*. -**2.** [change of residence] déménagement *m*; their ~ from Dublin leur départ de Dublin; their ~ to Dublin leur départ pour Dublin; we haven't notified them of our ~ nous ne les avons pas avertis de notre changement de domicile ‖ [transfer] transfert *m*; the ~ of the prisoner to a safer place le transfert OR le déplacement du prisonnier dans un endroit plus sûr. -**3.** [dismissal]: ~ from office révocation *f*, renvoi *m*.

◇ *comp* [expenses, firm, van] de déménagement; ~ man *Br* déménageur *m*; ~ van camion *m* de déménagement.

remove [rɪ'muːv] ◇ *vt* -**1.** [take off, out - clothes, object] enlever, retirer, ôter; [- stain] enlever, faire partir; MED [- organ, tumour] enlever, retirer; to ~ one's make-up se démaquiller; to ~ hair from one's legs s'épiler les jambes ‖ [take or send away - object] enlever; [- person] faire sortir; to ~ a picture from the wall enlever un tableau du mur, décrocher un tableau; the chairs were ~d to the attic les chaises ont été mises au grenier; she was ~d to hospital elle a été transportée à l'hôpital OR hospitalisée; the child must be ~d from its mother il faut retirer l'enfant à sa mère; death has ~d her from us

la mort nous l'a enlevée; **the soldiers were ~d to the front** on envoya les soldats au front; **she ~d herself to her room** *fml* elle se retira dans sa chambre; **~ the prisoner!** [in courtroom] qu'on emmène le prisonnier! || [dismiss - employee] renvoyer; [- official] révoquer, destituer; **his opponents had him ~d from office** ses opposants l'ont fait révoquer. -**2.** [suppress - clause, paragraph] supprimer; [- suspicion, doubt, fear] dissiper; **all obstacles have been ~d** tous les obstacles ont été écartés; **does this ~ your objection?** est-ce que cela répond à votre objection?; **his name was ~d from the list** son nom ne figure plus sur la liste || *euph* [kill] faire disparaître, tuer; **I want him ~d** je veux qu'on le fasse disparaître.
◇ *vi fml* -**1.** [firm, premises, family] déménager; **our office ~d to Glasgow** notre service s'est installé à Glasgow. -**2.** [person - go]: **she ~d to her room** elle se retira dans sa chambre.
◇ *n* -**1.** [distance] distance *f*; **this is but one ~ from blackmail** ça frôle le chantage; **it's several ~s** OR **a far ~ from what we need** ce n'est vraiment pas ce qu'il nous faut; **it's only a slight ~ from his usual themes** ça ne diffère pas beaucoup de ses thèmes habituels. -**2.** [degree of kinship] degré *m* de parenté.

removed [rɪ'mu:vd] *adj*: **to be far ~ from** être très éloigné OR loin de; **what you say is not far ~ from the truth** ce que vous dites n'est pas bien éloigné de la vérité; **one stage ~ from insanity** au bord de la folie ❑ **first cousin once/twice ~** cousin *m*, cousine *f* au premier/deuxième degré.

remover [rɪ'mu:vəʳ] *n* -**1.** [of furniture] déménageur *m*. -**2.** [solvent]: **nail-varnish ~** dissolvant *m* (pour vernis à ongles); **paint ~** décapant *m* (pour peinture); **stain ~** détachant *m*.

remunerate [rɪ'mju:nəreɪt] *vt* rémunérer.

remuneration [rɪ,mju:nə'reɪʃn] *n* rémunération *f*; **to receive ~ for sthg** être rémunéré OR payé pour qqch.

remunerative [rɪ'mju:nərətɪv] *adj* rémunérateur.

renaissance [rə'neɪsəns] ◇ *n* renaissance *f*; **the Renaissance** ART & HIST la Renaissance.
◇ *comp* [art, painter] de la Renaissance; [palace, architecture, style] Renaissance *(inv)*.

Renaissance man *n* homme *m* aux talents multiples.

renal ['ri:nl] *adj* rénal.

rename [,ri:'neɪm] *vt* rebaptiser.

renascence [rɪ'næsns] *n* renaissance *f*.

renascent [rɪ'næsnt] *adj* renaissant.

renationalization [ri:,næʃnəlaɪ'zeɪʃn] *n* renationalisation *f*.

renationalize, -ise [ri:'næʃnəlaɪz] *vt* renationaliser.

rend [rend] (*pt* & *pp* **rent** [rent]) *vt lit* -**1.** [tear - fabric] déchirer; [- wood, armour] fendre; *fig* [- silence, air] déchirer; **the country was rent in two by political strife** le pays était profondément divisé par les conflits politiques; **a flash of lightning rent the sky** un éclair déchira le ciel; **to ~ sb's heart** fendre le cœur à qqn. -**2.** [wrench] arracher; **the child was rent from its mother's arms** on a arraché l'enfant des bras de sa mère.

render ['rendəʳ] *vt* -**1.** [deliver - homage, judgment, verdict] rendre; [- assistance] prêter; [- help] fournir; [submit - bill, account] présenter, remettre; **to ~ an account of sthg** [explain] rendre compte de qqch; COMM remettre OR présenter le compte de qqch; **account ~** COMM rappel *m* de facture; **to ~ sb a service** rendre (un) service à qqn; **to ~ an explanation of sthg** fournir une explication à qqch; **to ~ thanks to sb** remercier qqn, faire des remerciements à qqn; **to ~ thanks to God** rendre grâce à Dieu ❑ **~ unto Caesar the things that are Caesar's** BIBLE rendez à César ce qui appartient à César *phr*. -**2.** [cause to become] rendre; **a misprint ~ed the text incomprehensible** une coquille rendait le texte incompréhensible. -**3.** [perform - song, piece of music] interpréter; [convey - atmosphere, spirit] rendre, évoquer. -**4.** [translate] rendre, traduire; **~ed into English** rendu OR traduit en anglais. -**5.** CULIN faire fondre. -**6.** CONSTR crépir, enduire de crépi.
◆ **render down** *vt sep Br* CULIN faire fondre; [reduce] réduire.
◆ **render up** *vt sep lit* [fortress] rendre; [hostage] libérer, rendre; [secret] livrer.

rendering ['rendərɪŋ] *n* -**1.** [performance - of song, play, piece of music] interprétation *f*. -**2.** [evocation - of atmosphere, spirit] évocation *f*. -**3.** [translation] traduction *f*. -**4.** CONSTR crépi *m*.

rendezvous ['rɒndɪvu:] (*pl inv* ['rɒndɪvu:z]) ◇ *n* -**1.** [meeting] rendez-vous *m*. -**2.** [meeting place] lieu *m* de rendez-vous.
◇ *vi* [friends] se retrouver; [group, party] se réunir; **to ~ with sb** rejoindre qqn; **the boats ~ed successfully after the operation** les bateaux se sont retrouvés comme prévu après l'opération.

rendition [ren'dɪʃn] *n* -**1.** [of poem, piece of music] interprétation *f*. -**2.** [translation] traduction *f*. -**3.** *arch* [surrender] reddition *f*.

renegade ['renɪgeɪd] ◇ *n* renégat *m*, -e *f*.
◇ *adj* renégat.

renege [rɪ'ni:g] *vi* [in cards] faire une renonce.
◆ **renege on** *vt insep* [responsibilities] manquer à; [agreement] revenir sur; **to ~ on a promise/contract** revenir sur sa parole/un contrat.

renegotiate [,ri:nɪ'gəʊʃɪeɪt] *vi* & *vt* renégocier.

renegue [rɪ'ni:g] = **renege**.

renew [rɪ'nju:] *vt* -**1.** [extend validity - passport, library book] renouveler; [- contract, lease] renouveler, reconduire; **to ~ one's subscription to sthg** renouveler son abonnement OR se réabonner à qqch. -**2.** [repeat - attack, promise, threat] renouveler; [restart - correspondence, negotiations] reprendre; **to ~ one's acquaintance with sb** renouer avec qqn || [increase - strength] reconstituer, reprendre; **to ~ one's efforts to do sthg** redoubler d'efforts pour faire qqch. -**3.** [replace - supplies] renouveler, remplacer; [- batteries, mechanism] remplacer, changer.

renewable [rɪ'nju:əbl] *adj* renouvelable.

renewal [rɪ'nju:əl] *n* -**1.** [extension - of validity] renouvellement *m*; [restart - of negotiations, hostilities] reprise *f*; [- of acquaintance] fait *m* de renouer; [increase - of energy, enthusiasm, hope] regain *m*; [repetition - of promise, threat] renouvellement *m*. -**2.** [renovation] rénovation *f*. -**3.** RELIG renouveau *m*.

renewed [rɪ'nju:d] *adj* [confidence, hope] renouvelé; [vigour, force] accru; **with ~ enthusiasm** avec un regain d'enthousiasme; **~ outbreaks of fighting** recrudescence *f* des combats.

rennet ['renɪt] *n* -**1.** [for cheese, junket] présure *f*. -**2.** ZOOL caillette *f*.

renounce [rɪ'naʊns] ◇ *vt* [claim, title] abandonner, renoncer à; [faith, principle, habit] renoncer à, renier; [treaty] dénoncer; **to ~ the world** renoncer au monde.
◇ *vi* [in cards] renoncer.

renovate ['renəveɪt] *vt* remettre à neuf, rénover.

renovation [,renə'veɪʃn] *n* remise *f* à neuf, rénovation *f*.

renown [rɪ'naʊn] *n* renommée *f*, renom *f*; **a man of great ~** un homme de grand renom.

renowned [rɪ'naʊnd] *adj* renommé, célèbre, réputé; **to be ~ for sthg** être connu OR célèbre pour qqch.

rent [rent] ◇ *pt* & *pp* → **rend**.
◇ *vt* -**1.** [subj: tenant, hirer] louer, prendre en location; **to ~ sthg from sb** louer qqch à qqn; **they ~ed a car for the holidays** ils ont loué une voiture pour les vacances; **their house must be expensive to ~** le loyer de leur maison doit être élevé. -**2.** [subj: owner] louer, donner en location; **to ~ sthg (out) to sb** louer qqch à qqn.
◇ *n* -**1.** [for apartment, house] loyer *m*; [for farm] loyer *m*, fermage *m*; [for car, television] (prix *m* de) location *f*; **to live in an apartment ~-free** habiter un appartement sans payer de loyer; **for ~** à louer. -**2.** ECON loyer *m*. -**3.** [tear] déchirure *f*. -**4.** [split - in movement, party] rupture *f*, scission *f*.

rent-a-car *n* location *f* de voitures.

rent-a-crowd *inf*, **rent-a-mob** *inf Br n* [protestors] agitateurs *mpl* professionnels; [audience, supporters] claque *f*.

rental ['rentl] ◇ *n* -**1.** [hire agreement - for car, house, TV, telephone] location *f*. -**2.** [payment - for property, land] loyer *m*; [- for TV, car, holiday accommodation] (prix *m* de) location *f*; [- for telephone] abonnement *m*, redevance *f*. -**3.** [income] (revenu *m* des) loyers *mpl*. -**4.** *Am* [apartment] appartement *m* en location; [house] maison *f* en location; [land] terrain *m* en location.
◇ *adj* [agency] de location; **~ agreement** contrat *m* de location; **~ charge** [for telephone] abonnement *m*; [for TV, car] prix *m* de location; **~ library** *Am* bibliothèque *f* de prêt.

rent book *n* carnet *m* de quittances de loyer.

rent boy *n* jeune prostitué *m (pour hommes)*.

rent collector *n* receveur *m*, -euse *f* des loyers.

rent control *n* contrôle *m* des loyers.

rent-controlled *adj* dont le loyer est contrôlé.

rented ['rentɪd] *adj* loué, de location.

rent-free ◇ *adj* exempt de loyer.
◇ *adv* sans payer de loyer, sans avoir de loyer à payer.

rent rebate *n* réduction *f* de loyer.

rent-roll *n Br* [register] registre *m* de l'état des loyers; [income] revenu *m* des loyers.

rent strike *n* grève *f* des loyers.

rent tribunal *n* commission *f* de contrôle des loyers.

renumber [,ri:'nʌmbəʳ] *vt* renuméroter.

renunciation [rɪ,nʌnsɪ'eɪʃn] *n* -**1.** [of authority, claim, title] renonciation *f*, abandon *m*; [of faith, religion] renonciation *f*, abjuration *f*; [of principle] abandon *m*, répudiation *f*; [of treaty] dénonciation *f*. -**2.** JUR répudiation *f*.

reoccupy [,ri:'ɒkjʊpaɪ] (*pt* & *pp* **reoccupied**) *vt* réoccuper.

reopen [,ri:'əʊpn] ◇ *vt* -**1.** [door, border, book, bank account] rouvrir. -**2.** [restart - hostilities] reprendre; [- debate, negotiations] reprendre, rouvrir.
◇ *vi* -**1.** [door, wound] se rouvrir; [shop, theatre] rouvrir; [school - after holiday] reprendre. -**2.** [negotiation] reprendre.

reopening [,ri:'əʊpnɪŋ] *n* [of shop] réouverture *f*; [of negotiations] reprise *f*.

reorder [*vb* ,ri:'ɔ:dəʳ, *n* 'ri:ɔ:dəʳ] ◇ *vt* -**1.** COMM [goods, supplies] commander de nouveau, faire une nouvelle commande de. -**2.** [rearrange - numbers, statistics, objects] reclasser, réorganiser.
◇ *n* COMM nouvelle commande *f*.

reorganization ['ri:,ɔ:gənaɪ'zeɪʃn] *n* réorganisation *f*.

reorganize, -ise [,ri:'ɔ:gənaɪz] ◇ *vt* réorganiser.
◇ *vi* se réorganiser.

rep [rep] *n* -**1.** *inf* COMM (*abbr of* **representative**) VRP *m*. -**2.** *abbr of* **repertory**. -**3.** TEX reps *m*. -**4.** *inf Am abbr of* **reputation**.

Rep *n Am abbr of* **Representative**.

repack [,ri:'pæk] *vt* [goods] remballer, emballer de nouveau; [suitcase] refaire.

repackage [,ri:'pækɪdʒ] *vt* -**1.** [goods] remballer. -**2.** *Am* [public image] redorer *fig*.

repaint [,ri:'peɪnt] *vt* repeindre.

repair [rɪ'peəʳ] ◇ *vt* -**1.** [mend - car, tyre, machine] réparer; [- road, roof] réparer, refaire; [- clothes] raccommoder; [- hull] radouber, caréner; [- tights] repriser; **he ~ed the hole in his trousers** il a raccommodé son pantalon; **she ~ed her tights** elle a reprisé ses bas; **to have one's shoes ~ed** faire réparer ses chaussures. -**2.** [make amends for - error, injustice] réparer, remédier à.
◇ *vi fml* OR *hum* aller, se rendre; **let us ~ to bed** allons nous coucher.
◇ *n* -**1.** [mending - of car, machine, roof] réparation *f*, remise *f* en état; [- of clothes] raccommodage *m*; [- of shoes] réparation *f*; [- of road] réfection *f*, remise *f* en état; NAUT radoub *m*; to

carry out ~s to OR on sthg effectuer des réparations sur qqch; to be under ~ être en réparation; 'road under ~' 'travaux'; 'closed for ~s' 'fermé pour (cause de) travaux'; 'road ~s' réfection de la chaussée; the bridge was damaged beyond ~ le pont avait subi des dégâts irréparables; the ~s to the car cost him a fortune les travaux de réparation OR les réparations sur la voiture lui ont coûté une fortune ❑ ~ kit trousse *f* à outils. -**2.** [condition] état *m*; to be in good/bad ~ être en bon/mauvais état; to keep sthg in good ~ bien entretenir qqch; the road is in a terrible state of ~ la route est très mal entretenue OR en très mauvais état.

repairable [rɪ'peərəbl] *adj* réparable.

repairer [rɪ'peərəʳ] *n* réparateur *m*, -trice *f*.

repairman [rɪ'peəmən] (*pl* repairmen [-mən]) *n* réparateur *m*.

repaper [,riː'peɪpəʳ] *vt* retapisser.

reparable ['repərəbl] *adj* réparable.

reparation [,repə'reɪʃn] *n* -**1.** *fml* [amends] réparation *f*; to make ~s for sthg réparer qqch *fig*. -**2.** *(usu pl)* [damages - after war, invasion etc] réparations *fpl*.

repartee [,repɑː'tiː] *n* -**1.** [witty conversation] esprit *m*, repartie *f*; to be good at ~ avoir la repartie facile, avoir de la repartie. -**2.** [witty comment] repartie *f*, réplique *f*.

repartition [,riːpɑː'tɪʃn] ◇ *n* répartition *f*.
◇ *vt* redistribuer, répartir de nouveau.

repast [rɪ'pɑːst] *n fml* repas *m*.

repatriate [*vb* ,riː'pætrɪeɪt, *n* riː'pætrɪət]
◇ *vt* rapatrier.
◇ *n* rapatrié *m*, -e *f*.

repatriation [,riːpætrɪ'eɪʃn] *n* rapatriement *m*.

repay [riː'peɪ] (*pt* & *pp* repaid [-'peɪd]) *vt* -**1.** [refund - creditor, loan] rembourser; to ~ a debt *literal* rembourser une dette; *fig* s'acquitter d'une dette; he repaid her the money she had lent him il lui a remboursé l'argent qu'elle lui avait prêté. -**2.** [return - visit] rendre; [- hospitality, kindness] rendre, payer de retour; how can I ever ~ you (for your kindness)? comment pourrai-je jamais vous remercier (pour votre gentillesse)?; to ~ good for evil rendre le bien pour le mal ‖ [reward - efforts, help] récompenser; to be repaid for one's efforts/persistence être récompensé de ses efforts/sa persévérance; her generosity was repaid with indifference tout ce qu'elle a obtenu en échange de sa générosité, c'est de l'indifférence.

repayable [riː'peɪəbl] *adj* remboursable; the amount is ~ in five years la somme est remboursable sur cinq ans OR en cinq annuités.

repayment [riː'peɪmənt] *n* -**1.** [of money, loan] remboursement *m*; ~s can be spread over 12 months les remboursements peuvent être échelonnés sur 12 mois; mortgage ~s remboursement *m* de prêt-logement. -**2.** [reward - for kindness, effort] récompense *f*.

repeal [rɪ'piːl] ◇ *vt* [law] abroger, annuler; [prison sentence] annuler; [decree] rapporter, révoquer.
◇ *n* [law] abrogation *f*; [prison sentence] annulation *f*; [decree] révocation *f*.

repeat [rɪ'piːt] ◇ *vt* -**1.** [say again - word, secret, instructions] répéter; [- demand, promise] répéter, réitérer; you're ~ing yourself vous vous répétez; I don't dare ~ what he said je n'ose pas répéter ce qu'il a dit; it doesn't bear ~ing [rude] c'est trop grossier pour être répété; [trivial] ça ne vaut pas la peine d'être répété. -**2.** [redo, reexecute - action, attack, mistake] répéter, renouveler; MUS reprendre; I wouldn't like to ~ the experience je n'aimerais pas renouveler l'expérience; it's history ~ing itself c'est l'histoire qui se répète; the same little ritual is ~ed every morning le même petit rituel se renouvelle chaque matin; the pattern ~s itself le motif se répète. -**3.** RADIO & TV [broadcast] rediffuser. -**4.** COMM [order, offer] renouveler. -**5.** SCH & UNIV [class, year] redoubler.
◇ *vi* -**1.** [say again] répéter; I ~, I have never heard of him je le répète, je n'ai jamais entendu parler de lui; I shall never, ~ never, go there again je n'y retournerai jamais, mais alors ce qui s'appelle jamais; ~ after me SCH répétez après moi. -**2.** [recur] se répéter, se reproduire; MATH se reproduire périodiquement. -**3.** [food] donner des renvois; onions always ~ on me les oignons me donnent toujours des renvois. -**4.** *Am* POL voter plus d'une fois *(à une même élection)*. -**5.** [watch, clock] être à répétition.
◇ *n* -**1.** [gen] répétition *f*; ~ function COMPUT fonction *f* de répétition. -**2.** MUS [passage] reprise *f*; [sign] signe *m* de reprise. -**3.** RADIO & TV [broadcast] rediffusion *f*, reprise *f*.
◇ *comp* [order, visit] renouvelé; ~ offender récidiviste *mf*; ~ prescription ordonnance *f* *(de renouvellement d'un médicament)*; she gave me a ~ prescription elle a renouvelé mon ordonnance.

repeatable [rɪ'piːtəbl] *adj* susceptible d'être répété; what he said is not ~ je n'ose pas répéter ce qu'il a dit.

repeated [rɪ'piːtɪd] *adj* répété.

repeatedly [rɪ'piːtɪdlɪ] *adv* à plusieurs OR maintes reprises; you have been told ~ not to play by the canal on vous a dit cent fois OR on vous a souvent dit de ne pas jouer près du canal; I've ~ said that I can't come on Mondays j'ai répété à maintes reprises OR j'ai bien dit que je ne pouvais (pas) venir le lundi.

repeater [rɪ'piːtəʳ] *n* -**1.** [clock] pendule *f* à répétition; [alarm] réveil *m* à répétition. -**2.** [gun] fusil *m* à répétition. -**3.** ELEC répéteur *m*. -**4.** *Am* SCH redoublant *m*, -e *f*. -**5.** *Am* POL électeur *m*, -trice *f* qui vote plus d'une fois *(à une même élection)*.

repeating [rɪ'piːtɪŋ] *adj* -**1.** MATH périodique. -**2.** [gun] à répétition.

repeating decimal *n* fraction *f* décimale périodique.

repeat performance *n* THEAT deuxième représentation *f*; we don't want a ~ of last year's chaos *fig* nous ne voulons pas que le désordre de l'année dernière se reproduise; to give a ~ *pej* jouer la même comédie.

repechage [,repə'ʃɑːʒ] *n* repêchage *m* SPORT.

repel [rɪ'pel] (*pt* & *pp* repelled, *cont* repelling)
◇ *vt* -**1.** [drive back - attacker, advance, suggestion] repousser. -**2.** [disgust - subj: unpleasant sight, smell etc] rebuter, dégoûter; the sight of blood repelled him la vue du sang lui soulevait le cœur OR le dégoûtait. -**3.** ELEC & PHYS repousser.
◇ *vi* ELEC & PHYS se repousser.

repellent, repellant [rɪ'pelənt] ◇ *adj* repoussant, répugnant; to find sb/sthg ~ éprouver de la répugnance pour qqn/qqch.
◇ *n* -**1.** [for insects] insecticide *m*; [for mosquitoes] anti-moustiques *m inv*. -**2.** [for waterproofing] imperméabilisant *m*.

repent [rɪ'pent] ◇ *vi* se repentir; to ~ of sthg se repentir de qqch.
◇ *vt* se repentir de.

repentance [rɪ'pentəns] *n* repentir *m*.

repentant [rɪ'pentənt] *adj* repentant.

repercussion [,riːpə'kʌʃn] *n* -**1.** [consequence] répercussion *f*, retentissement *m*, contrecoup *m*; to have ~s on avoir des répercussions sur; the scandal has had serious ~s on his family life le scandale a eu de sérieuses répercussions sur sa vie familiale; the ~s of the affair les répercussions OR le contrecoup de l'affaire. -**2.** [echo] répercussion *f*.

repertoire ['repətwɑːʳ] *n literal* & *fig* répertoire *m*.

repertory ['repətrɪ] (*pl* repertories) *n* -**1.** THEAT: to be OR to act in ~ faire partie d'une troupe de répertoire, jouer dans un théâtre de répertoire; ~ (theatre) théâtre *m* de répertoire. -**2.** = **repertoire**.

repertory company *n* compagnie *f* OR troupe *f* de répertoire.

repetition [,repɪ'tɪʃn] *n* -**1.** [of words, orders] répétition *f*. -**2.** [of action, activity] répétition *f*, renouvellement *m*; I don't want any ~ of this disgraceful behaviour je ne veux plus vous voir vous conduire de cette façon scandaleuse. -**3.** MUS reprise *f*.

repetitious [,repɪ'tɪʃəs] *adj* plein de répétitions OR de redites.

repetitive [rɪ'petɪtɪv] *adj* [activity, work, rhythm] répétitif, monotone; [song, speech] plein de répétitions; [person] qui se répète.

rephrase [,riː'freɪz] *vt* reformuler; can you ~ that remark/question? pouvez-vous formuler cette remarque/question autrement?

repine [rɪ'paɪn] *vi lit* [be sad] languir, dépérir; [complain] maugréer.

replace [rɪ'pleɪs] *vt* -**1.** [put back] replacer, remettre (à sa place OR en place); to ~ the receiver [on telephone] reposer le combiné, raccrocher (le téléphone). -**2.** [person] remplacer; [mechanism, tyres] remplacer; you can go if you find someone to ~ you vous pouvez partir si vous vous faites remplacer par quelqu'un; to ~ a worn part by OR with a new one remplacer une pièce usée (par une pièce neuve).

replaceable [rɪ'pleɪsəbl] *adj* remplaçable; he is easily ~ on peut le remplacer facilement.

replacement [rɪ'pleɪsmənt] ◇ *n* -**1.** [putting back] remise *f* en place. -**2.** [substitution] remplacement *m*; the ~ of damaged books le remplacement des livres endommagés. -**3.** [person] remplaçant *m*, -e *f*. -**4.** [engine or machine part] pièce *f* de rechange; [product] produit *m* de remplacement.
◇ *comp* [part] de rechange; [person] remplaçant; ~ teacher (professeur *m*) suppléant *m*, remplaçant *m*, -e *f* SCOL.

replant [,riː'plɑːnt] *vt* replanter.

replay [*n* 'riːpleɪ, *vb* ,riː'pleɪ] ◇ *n* -**1.** TV ralenti *m*; the ~ clearly shows the foul on voit bien la faute au ralenti. -**2.** SPORT match *m* rejoué.
◇ *vt* [match] rejouer; [record, piece of film, video] repasser.

replenish [rɪ'plenɪʃ] *vt fml* -**1.** [restock - cellar, stock] réapprovisionner; to ~ one's supplies of sthg se réapprovisionner en qqch. -**2.** [refill - glass] remplir de nouveau; to ~ one's glass se resservir à boire.

replenishment [rɪ'plenɪʃmənt] *n fml* [of stock, supplies] réapprovisionnement *m*; [of glass] remplissage *m*.

replete [rɪ'pliːt] *adj fml* [full] rempli, plein; [person - full up] rassasié; to be ~ with [food] être repu OR rassasié de; [fuel, supplies] être (bien) ravitaillé en.

repletion [rɪ'pliːʃn] *n fml* satiété *f*; to eat to ~ se rassasier, manger à satiété.

replica ['replɪkə] *n* [of painting, model, sculpture] réplique *f*, copie *f*; [of document] copie *f* (exacte); she is the exact ~ of her mother c'est la réplique vivante OR exacte de sa mère.

replicate ['replɪkeɪt] ◇ *vt* [reproduce] reproduire; certain cells ~ themselves BIOL certaines cellules se reproduisent par mitose.
◇ *vi* BIOL se reproduire par mitose.

replication [,replɪ'keɪʃn] *n* [gen] reproduction *f*; BIOL reproduction *f* par mitose.

reply [rɪ'plaɪ] (*pl* replies, *pt* & *pp* replied)
◇ *n* -**1.** [answer] réponse *f*; [retort] réplique *f*; he made no ~ il n'a pas répondu. -**2.** JUR réplique *f*.
◇ *vt* [answer] répondre; [retort] répliquer, rétorquer; "I don't know", she replied «je ne sais pas», répondit-elle; what did you ~? qu'avez-vous répondu?
◇ *vi* répondre; to ~ to sb répondre à qqn; have you replied to their offer/letter? avez-vous répondu à leur offre/lettre?
◆ **in reply to** *prep phr* en réponse à; to say sthg in ~ to sb/sthg dire qqch en réponse à qqn/qqch; in ~ to your letter en réponse à votre lettre.

reply coupon *n* coupon-réponse *m*.

reply-paid *adj Br* avec réponse payée; ~ letter lettre *f* avec réponse payée.

repoint [,riː'pɔɪnt] *vt* CONSTR rejointoyer.

report [rɪ'pɔːt] ◇ *vt* -**1.** [announce] annoncer, déclarer, signaler; the discovery of a new vaccine is ~ed on annonce la découverte d'un nouveau vaccin; it is ~ed from Delhi that a ten-year contract has been signed on annonce à Delhi qu'un contrat de dix ans a été signé; to ~ the position of a ship signaler la position d'un navire; the company ~s a profit for the first time in five years l'entreprise annonce un bénéfice pour la première fois depuis cinq ans; the doctors ~ his condition as comfortable les médecins déclarent son état satisfaisant. -**2.** [subj: press, media - event, match] faire un reportage sur; [- winner] annoncer; [- debate] faire le compte rendu de; the newspapers ~ heavy casualties les journaux font état de nombreuses victimes; our correspondent ~s that troops have left the city notre correspondant nous signale que des troupes ont quitté la ville; her resignation is ~ed in several papers sa démission est annoncée dans plusieurs journaux; the speech was ~ed in the 8 o'clock news bulletin il y avait un compte rendu du discours dans le bulletin d'informations de 20 h; ~ing restrictions were not lifted JUR l'interdiction faite aux journalistes de rapporter les débats n'a pas été levée || [unconfirmed news]: it is ~ed that a woman drowned une femme se serait noyée; the plane is ~ed to have crashed in the jungle l'avion se serait écrasé dans la jungle; he is ~ed to have left OR as having left the country il aurait quitté le pays. -**3.** [give account of] faire état de, rendre compte de; the police have ~ed some progress in the fight against crime la police a annoncé des progrès dans la lutte contre la criminalité; to ~ one's findings [in research] rendre compte des résultats de ses recherches; [in inquiry, commission] présenter ses conclusions. -**4.** [burglary, disappearance, murder] signaler; [wrongdoer] dénoncer, porter plainte contre; I'd like to ~ an accident je voudrais signaler un accident; to ~ sb missing (to the police) signaler la disparition de qqn (à la police); to be ~ed missing/dead être porté disparu/au nombre des morts; nothing to ~ rien à signaler; they were ~ed to the police for vandalism on les a dénoncés à la police pour vandalisme; the school ~ed the boy's rudeness to his parents l'école a signalé l'insolence du garçon à ses parents. -**5.** *fml* [present]: to ~ o.s. for duty se présenter au travail.

◇ *vi* -**1.** [make a report - committee] faire son rapport, présenter ses conclusions; [- police] faire un rapport; [- journalist] faire un reportage; to ~ on sthg ADMIN faire un rapport sur qqch; PRESS faire un reportage sur qqch; to ~ on a murder case faire un rapport sur un meurtre; to ~ on an aircraft hijacking faire un reportage sur un détournement d'avion; she's ~ing on the train crash elle fait un reportage sur l'accident de train; he ~s for the BBC il est reporter OR journaliste à la BBC; this is Keith Owen, ~ing from Moscow for CBS de Moscou, pour la CBS, Keith Owen. -**2.** [in hierarchy]: to ~ to sb être sous les ordres de qqn; I ~ directly to the sales manager je dépends directement du chef des ventes. -**3.** [present o.s.] se présenter; ~ to my office présentez-vous à mon bureau; to ~ for duty prendre son service, se présenter au travail; ~ to the sergeant when you arrive [go and see] présentez-vous au sergent à votre arrivée; [give account] faites votre rapport au sergent quand vous arriverez; to ~ to base MIL [go] se présenter à la base; [contact] contacter la base; to ~ to barracks OR to one's unit MIL rallier son unité; to ~ sick se faire porter malade.

◇ *n* -**1.** [account, review] rapport *m*; to draw up OR to make a ~ on sthg faire un rapport sur qqch; he gave an accurate ~ of the situation il a fait un rapport précis sur la situation; official/police ~ rapport officiel/de police || [summary - of speech, meeting] compte rendu *m*; [official record] procès-verbal *m*; his ~ on the meeting son compte rendu de la réunion || COMM & FIN [review] rapport *m*; [balance sheet] bilan *m*; sales ~ rapport *m* OR bilan *m* commercial. -**2.** [in media] reportage *m*; [investigation] enquête *f*; [bulletin] bulletin *m*; to do a ~ on sthg faire un reportage OR une enquête sur qqch; here is a ~ from Keith Owen RADIO & TV voici le reportage de Keith Owen; according to newspaper/intelligence ~s selon les journaux/les services de renseignements || [allegation] allégation *f*, rumeur *f*; [news] nouvelle *f*; we have had ~s of several burglaries in city stores on nous a signalé plusieurs cambriolages dans les magasins du centre-ville; there are ~s of civil disturbances in the North il y aurait des troubles dans le Nord; ~s are coming in of an earthquake on parle d'un tremblement de terre; I only know it by ~ je ne le sais que par ouï-dire, j'en ai seulement entendu parler; news/weather ~ bulletin d'informations/météorologique. -**3.** *Br* SCH: (school) ~ bulletin *m* (scolaire); end of term ~ bulletin *m* trimestriel. -**4.** JUR [of court proceedings] procès-verbal *m*; law ~s recueil *m* de jurisprudence. -**5.** *fml* [repute] renom *m*, réputation *f*; a man of good/evil ~ un homme de bonne/mauvaise réputation. -**6.** [sound - of explosion, shot] détonation *f*.

◆ **report back** ◇ *vi insep* -**1.** [return - soldier] regagner ses quartiers, rallier son régiment; [- journalist, salesman] rentrer; to ~ back to headquarters MIL rentrer au quartier général; [salesman, clerk] rentrer au siège; I have to ~ back to the office il faut que je repasse au bureau; what time did he ~ back? à quelle heure est-il rentré OR était-il de retour? -**2.** [present report] présenter son rapport; the commission must first ~ back to the minister la commission doit d'abord présenter son rapport au ministre; can you ~ back on what was discussed? pouvez-vous rapporter ce qui a été dit?; please ~ back to me before you decide anything veuillez vous en référer à moi avant de prendre une décision.

◇ *vt sep* [results, decision] rapporter, rendre compte de.

◆ **report out** *vt sep Am* POL [bill, legislation] renvoyer après examen.

reportage [ˌrepɔːˈtɑːʒ] *n* reportage *m*.

report card *n* SCH bulletin *m* OR carnet *m* scolaire.

reported [rɪˈpɔːtɪd] *adj*: there have been ~ sightings of dolphins off the coast on aurait vu des dauphins près des côtes; the last ~ sighting of the aircraft la dernière fois que l'on a vu l'avion; what was their last ~ position? où ont-ils été signalés pour la dernière fois?

reportedly [rɪˈpɔːtɪdlɪ] *adv*: he is ~ about to resign il serait sur le point de démissionner; 300 people have ~ been killed 300 personnes auraient été tuées.

reported speech *n* GRAMM style *m* OR discours *m* indirect; in ~ en style indirect.

reporter [rɪˈpɔːtəʳ] *n* -**1.** [for newspaper] journaliste *mf*, reporter *m*; RADIO & TV reporter *m*. -**2.** [scribe - in court] greffier *m*, -ère *f*; [- in parliament] sténographe *mf*.

report stage *n Br* POL *examen d'un projet de loi avant la troisième lecture*; the bill has reached ~ ≃ le projet de loi vient de passer en commission.

repose [rɪˈpəʊz] ◇ *vt fml* -**1.** [rest] reposer; to ~ o.s. se reposer. -**2.** [place - confidence, trust] mettre, placer.

◇ *vi* -**1.** [rest - person] se reposer; [- the dead] reposer. -**2.** [be founded - belief, theory] reposer; to ~ on firm evidence reposer sur des preuves solides.

◇ *n fml* repos *m*; in ~ au OR en repos; to pray for the ~ of a soul prier pour le repos d'une âme.

reposition [ˌriːpəˈzɪʃn] *vt* repositionner.

repository [rɪˈpɒzɪtrɪ] (*pl* repositories) *n* -**1.** [storehouse - large] entrepôt *m*; [- smaller] dépôt *m*. -**2.** [of knowledge, secret] dépositaire *mf*.

repossess [ˌriːpəˈzes] *vt* reprendre possession de; JUR saisir; they have OR their house has been ~ed leur maison a été mise en saisie immobilière.

repossession [ˌriːpəˈzeʃn] *n* reprise *f* de possession; JUR saisie *f*.

repossession order *n* ordre *m* de saisie.

repot [ˌriːˈpɒt] (*pt* & *pp* repotted, *cont* repotting) *vt* [plant] rempoter.

repp [rep] = **rep 3**.

reprehend [ˌreprɪˈhend] *vt* [person] réprimander; [conduct, action] condamner, désavouer.

reprehensible [ˌreprɪˈhensəbl] *adj* répréhensible.

reprehensibly [ˌreprɪˈhensəblɪ] *adv* de façon répréhensible.

reprehension [ˌreprɪˈhenʃn] *n fml* [rebuke] réprimande *f*; [criticism] condamnation *f*.

represent [ˌreprɪˈzent] *vt* -**1.** [symbolize - subj: diagram, picture, symbol] représenter; the statue ~s peace la statue représente OR symbolise la paix; what does the scene ~? que représente la scène? -**2.** [depict] représenter, dépeindre; [describe] décrire; he ~ed her as a queen il l'a peinte sous les traits d'une reine. -**3.** [constitute - achievement, change] représenter, constituer; this new development ~s a danger to world peace ce fait nouveau représente un danger pour la paix mondiale; the book ~s five years' work le livre représente cinq années de travail. -**4.** POL [voters, members] représenter; she ~s Tooting elle est député de OR elle représente la circonscription de Tooting || [be delegate for - subj: person] représenter; the President was ~ed by the ambassador le Président était représenté par l'ambassadeur; I ~ the agency je viens de la part de l'agence; the best lawyers are ~ing the victims les victimes sont représentées par les meilleurs avocats || [opinion] représenter; the voice of women is not ~ed on the committee les femmes ne sont pas représentées au comité || [in numbers] représenter; foreign students are well ~ed in the university il y a une forte proportion d'étudiants étrangers à l'université. -**5.** [express, explain - advantages, prospect, theory] présenter; they ~ed their grievances to the director ils ont fait part de OR présenté leurs griefs au directeur. -**6.** THEAT [subj: actor] jouer, interpréter.

re-present [ˌriːprɪˈzent] *vt* présenter de nouveau.

representation [ˌreprɪzenˈteɪʃn] *n* -**1.** POL représentation *f*. -**2.** [description, presentation] représentation *f*.

◆ **representations** *npl* [complaints] plaintes *fpl*, protestations *fpl*; [intervention] démarche *f*, intervention *f*; to make ~s to sb [complain] se plaindre auprès de qqn; [intervene] faire des démarches auprès de qqn.

representational [ˌreprɪzenˈteɪʃənl] *adj* [gen] représentatif; ART figuratif.

representationalism [ˌreprɪsenˈteɪʃənəlɪzm] *n* ART art *m* figuratif.

representationalist [ˌreprɪzenˈteɪʃənəlɪst] ◇ *adj* ART (du genre) figuratif.

◇ *n* ART figuratif *m*.

representative [ˌreprɪˈzentətɪv] ◇ *adj* -**1.** [typical] typique, représentatif; to be ~ of sthg être représentatif de qqch; the high rate of abstention is ~ of the lack of interest in politics le fort taux d'abstention est représentatif du manque d'intérêt pour la politique; is this a ~ sample of your results? est-ce un échantillon représentatif de vos résultats? -**2.** POL représentatif.

◇ *n* -**1.** [gen] représentant *m*, -e *f*; he is our country's ~ abroad il représente notre pays à l'étranger. -**2.** COMM: (sales) ~ représentant *m*, -e *f* (de commerce). -**3.** *Am* POL → **House of Representatives**.

repress [rɪˈpres] *vt* [rebellion] réprimer; PSYCH refouler.

repressed [rɪˈprest] *adj* [gen] réprimé; PSYCH refoulé.

repression [rɪˈpreʃn] *n* [gen] répression *f*; PSYCH refoulement *m*.

repressive [rɪ'presɪv] *adj* [authority, system] répressif; [measures] de répression, répressif.

repressiveness [rɪ'presɪvnɪs] *n* [of legislation, régime] caractère *m* répressif.

reprieve [rɪ'priːv] ◇ *vt* -**1.** JUR [prisoner - remit] gracier; [- postpone] accorder un sursis à. -**2.** *fig* [give respite to - patient] accorder un répit OR un sursis à; [- company] accorder un sursis à.
◇ *n* -**1.** JUR remise *f* de peine, grâce *f*; **the condemned man was given a ~** le condamné a été gracié. -**2.** *fig* [respite - from danger, illness] sursis *m*, répit *m*; [extra time] délai *m*.

reprimand ['reprɪmɑːnd] ◇ *vt* réprimander; **the children were severely ~ed** les enfants ont été sévèrement réprimandés; **he was ~ed for being late** [worker] il a reçu un blâme pour son retard; [schoolchild] on lui a donné un avertissement pour son retard.
◇ *n* [rebuke] réprimande *f*; [professional] blâme *m*.

reprint [*vb* ˌriː'prɪnt, *n* 'riːprɪnt] ◇ *vt* réimprimer; **the book is being ~ed** le livre est en réimpression.
◇ *n* réimpression *f*; **her novel is on its tenth ~** son roman en est à sa dixième réimpression.

reprisal [rɪ'praɪzl] *n* représailles *fpl*; **to take ~s (against sb)** user de représailles OR exercer des représailles (contre qqn); **by way of** OR **in ~, as a ~** par représailles; **he was shot as a ~ for yesterday's killing** on l'a fusillé en représailles de l'assassinat d'hier.

repro *inf* ['riːprəʊ] (*abbr of* **reproduction**) (*pl* repros) *n* (épreuve *f*) repro *f*.

reproach [rɪ'prəʊtʃ] ◇ *n* -**1.** [criticism] reproche *m*; **in a tone of ~** sur un ton réprobateur OR de reproche; **to heap ~es on sb** accabler qqn de reproches; **above** OR **beyond ~** au-dessus de tout reproche, irréprochable. -**2.** [source of shame] honte *f*; **to be a ~ to** être la honte de.
◇ *vt* faire des reproches à; **to ~ sb with sthg** reprocher qqch à qqn; **she ~ed him for** OR **with having broken his promise** elle lui reprochait d'avoir manqué à sa parole; **I ~ myself for failing to warn them** je m'en veux de ne pas les avoir prévenus; **I have nothing to ~ myself for** OR **with** je n'ai rien à me reprocher; **he was ~ed for his insensitivity** on lui a reproché son manque de sensibilité.

reproachful [rɪ'prəʊtʃfʊl] *adj* [voice, look, attitude] réprobateur; [tone, words] de reproche, réprobateur.

reproachfully [rɪ'prəʊtʃfʊlɪ] *adv* avec reproche; **"why not?", she said ~** «pourquoi pas?», dit-elle d'un ton de reproche; **to look at sb ~** lancer des regards réprobateurs à qqn.

reprobate ['reprəbeɪt] ◇ *adj* dépravé.
◇ *n* dépravé *m*, -e *f*.
◇ *vt* réprouver.

reprobation [ˌreprə'beɪʃn] *n* réprobation *f*.

reprocess [ˌriː'prəʊses] *vt* retraiter.

reprocessing [ˌriː'prəʊsesɪŋ] *n* retraitement *m*; **nuclear ~** retraitement des déchets nucléaires.

reproduce [ˌriːprə'djuːs] ◇ *vt* reproduire.
◇ *vi* se reproduire.

reproduction [ˌriːprə'dʌkʃn] ◇ *n* -**1.** BIOL reproduction *f*. -**2.** [of painting, document] reproduction *f*, copie *f*.
◇ *comp*: **~ furniture** reproduction *f* OR copie *f* de meubles d'époque; **a ~ Regency armchair** une reproduction OR copie d'un fauteuil Régence.

reproductive [ˌriːprə'dʌktɪv] *adj* [organs, cells, process] reproducteur, de reproduction.

reprogram [ˌriː'prəʊgræm] *vt* reprogrammer, programmer de nouveau.

REPROM [ˌriː'prɒm] *n* COMPUT mémoire *f* morte reprogrammable.

reproof [rɪ'pruːf] *n* réprimande *f*, reproche *m*.

reproval [rɪ'pruːvl] *n* reproche *m*; **a look of ~** un regard chargé de reproche.

reprove [rɪ'pruːv] *vt* [person] réprimander; [action, behaviour] réprouver; **he was ~d for his conduct** on lui a reproché sa conduite.

reproving [rɪ'pruːvɪŋ] *adj* réprobateur.

reprovingly [rɪ'pruːvɪŋlɪ] *adv* [look] d'un air réprobateur OR de reproche; [say] d'un ton réprobateur OR de reproche.

reptile ['reptaɪl] ◇ *adj* reptile.
◇ *n* reptile *m*.

reptile house *n* vivarium *m*.

reptilian [rep'tɪlɪən] ◇ *adj* -**1.** ZOOL reptilien. -**2.** *fig* & *pej* reptile.
◇ *n* reptile *m*.

republic [rɪ'pʌblɪk] *n* POL & *fig* république *f*; **the ~ of letters** la république des lettres ❑ **the Republic of Ireland** la République d'Irlande; **'The Republic'** *Plato* 'la République'.

republican [rɪ'pʌblɪkən] ◇ *adj* républicain.
◇ *n* républicain *m*, -e *f*.

republicanism [rɪ'pʌblɪkənɪzm] *n* républicanisme *m*.

Republican party *pr n*: **the ~** le Parti républicain.

republication [ˌriːˌpʌblɪ'keɪʃn] *n* [of book] réédition *f*, nouvelle édition *f*; [of banns] nouvelle publication *f*.

republish [ˌriː'pʌblɪʃ] *vt* [book] rééditer; [banns] republier, publier de nouveau.

repudiate [rɪ'pjuːdɪeɪt] *vt* [reject - opinion, belief] renier, désavouer; [- evidence] réfuter; [- authority, accusation, charge] rejeter; [- spouse] répudier; [- friend] désavouer; [- gift, offer] refuser, repousser; [go back on - obligation, debt, treaty] refuser d'honorer.

repudiation [rɪˌpjuːdɪ'eɪʃn] *n* -**1.** [of belief, opinion] reniement *m*, désaveu *m*; [of spouse] répudiation *f*; [of friend, accusation] rejet *m*; [of gift, offer] refus *m*, rejet *m*. -**2.** [of obligation, debt] refus *m* d'honorer.

repugnance [rɪ'pʌgnəns] *n* répugnance *f*.

repugnant [rɪ'pʌgnənt] *adj* répugnant; **I find the idea ~** cette idée me répugne.

repulse [rɪ'pʌls] ◇ *vt* [attack, offer] repousser; **their avarice ~s me** je trouve leur avarice choquante.
◇ *n* MIL [defeat] défaite *f*, échec *m*; *fig* [refusal] refus *m*, rebuffade *f*.

repulsion [rɪ'pʌlʃn] *n* répulsion *f*.

repulsive [rɪ'pʌlsɪv] *adj* [idea, sight, appearance] répugnant, repoussant; PHYS répulsif.

repulsively [rɪ'pʌlsɪvlɪ] *adv* de façon repoussante OR répugnante; **~ ugly** d'une laideur repoussante; **~ dirty** d'une saleté répugnante OR repoussante.

repulsiveness [rɪ'pʌlsɪvnɪs] *n* aspect *m* OR caractère *m* repoussant.

repurchase [ˌriː'pɜːtʃɪs] ◇ *n* rachat *m*.
◇ *vt* racheter.

reputable ['repjʊtəbl] *adj* [person, family] qui a bonne réputation, honorable, estimable; [firm, tradesman] qui a bonne réputation; [profession] honorable; [source] sûr; **they're a very ~ firm** c'est une entreprise d'excellente réputation.

reputation [ˌrepjʊ'teɪʃn] *n* réputation *f*; **the firm has a good ~** l'entreprise a une bonne réputation; **she has a ~ as a cook** sa réputation de cuisinière n'est plus à faire; **they have a ~ for good service** ils sont réputés pour la qualité de leur service; **he certainly lives up to his ~ as a big spender** il mérite tout à fait sa réputation de grand dépensier.

repute [rɪ'pjuːt] ◇ *n* réputation *f*, renom *m*; **to be of good ~** avoir (une) bonne réputation; **a firm of some ~** une entreprise d'un certain renom; **a wine of great ~** un vin hautement réputé OR de grand renom; **I only know her by ~** je ne la connais que de réputation; **she is held in high ~ by all her colleagues** elle jouit d'une excellente réputation auprès de ses collègues.
◇ *vt* [only pass]: **she is ~d to be wealthy** elle passe pour riche; **he is ~d to be a genius** il passe pour un génie.

reputed [rɪ'pjuːtɪd] *adj* réputé; **~ father** JUR père *m* putatif.

reputedly [rɪ'pjuːtɪdlɪ] *adv* d'après ce qu'on dit; **he is ~ a millionaire** on le dit milliardaire.

reqd *written abbr of* **required.**

request [rɪ'kwest] ◇ *n* -**1.** [demand] demande *f*, requête *f*; **to make a ~** faire une demande; **to grant** OR **to meet sb's ~** accéder à la demande OR à la requête de qqn; **at sb's ~** à la demande OR requête de qqn; **I did it at** OR **on her ~** je l'ai fait à sa demande OR à sa requête; **to do sthg on ~** faire qqch sur simple demande; **tickets are available on ~** des billets peuvent être obtenus sur simple demande; **by popular ~** à la demande générale. -**2.** [record - on radio] disque *m* demandé par un auditeur; [- at dance] *disque ou chanson demandé par un membre du public*; **to play a ~ for sb** passer un disque à l'intention de qqn; **here is a birthday ~ for Sarah Brown** voici une chanson (qui a été demandée) pour l'anniversaire de Sarah Brown.
◇ *vt* demander; **to ~ sb to do sthg** demander à qqn OR prier qqn de faire qqch; **'visitors are ~ed not to touch the objects on display'** 'les visiteurs sont priés de ne pas toucher aux objets exposés'; **Mr and Mrs Booth ~ the pleasure of your company** M. et Mme Booth vous prient de leur faire l'honneur de votre présence; **I enclose a postal order for £5, as ~ed** selon votre demande, je joins un mandat postal de 5 livres; **to ~ sthg of sb** *fml* demander qqch à qqn.

request programme *n émission où les disques qui passent à l'antenne ont été choisis par les auditeurs.*

request stop *n Br* arrêt *m* facultatif.

requiem ['rekwɪəm] *n* requiem *m*.

requiem mass *n* messe *f* de requiem.

require [rɪ'kwaɪəʳ] *vt* -**1.** [need - attention, care etc] exiger, nécessiter, demander; **extreme caution is ~d** une extrême vigilance s'impose; **is that all you ~?** c'est tout ce qu'il vous faut?, c'est tout ce dont vous avez besoin?; **if ~d** si besoin est, s'il le faut; **when ~d** quand il le faut; **your presence is urgently ~d** on vous réclame d'urgence. -**2.** [demand - qualifications, standard, commitment] exiger, requérir, réclamer; **to ~ sthg of sb** exiger qqch de qqn; **to ~ sb to do sthg** exiger que qqn fasse qqch; **candidates are ~d to provide three photographs** les candidats doivent fournir trois photographies; **the law ~s you to wear seat-belts** la loi exige que vous portiez une ceinture de sécurité; **custom/tradition ~s it** c'est l'usage/la tradition (qui veut cela); **this job ~s skill and experience** ce travail demande OR requiert OR réclame compétence et expérience; **what do you ~ of me?** que voulez-vous OR qu'attendez-vous de moi?; **it is ~d that you begin work at 8 a.m. every morning** on exige de vous que vous commenciez votre travail à 8 h tous les matins; **'formal dress ~d'** [on invitation] 'tenue correcte exigée'.

required [rɪ'kwaɪəd] *adj* [conditions, qualifications, standard] requis, exigé; **in** OR **by the ~ time** dans les délais (prescrits); **to reach the ~ standard** atteindre le niveau requis; **~ reading** SCH & UNIV lectures *fpl* à faire.

requirement [rɪ'kwaɪəmənt] *n* -**1.** [demand] exigence *f*, besoin *m*; **to meet sb's ~s** satisfaire aux exigences OR aux besoins de qqn; **this doesn't meet our ~s** ceci ne répond pas à nos exigences; **according to your ~s** selon vos besoins ‖ [necessity] besoin *m*, nécessité *f*; **energy ~s** besoins énergétiques. -**2.** [condition, prerequisite] condition *f* requise; **she doesn't fulfil the ~s for the job** elle ne remplit pas les conditions requises pour le poste; **dedication is an essential ~** le dévouement est une condition essentielle; **what are the course ~s?** [for enrolment] quelles conditions faut-il remplir pour s'inscrire à ce cours?; [as student] quel niveau doit-on avoir pour suivre ce cours?

requisite ['rekwɪzɪt] ◇ *n fml* objet *m* nécessaire; **toilet ~s** articles *mpl* OR accessoires *mpl* de toilette.
◇ *adj* requis, nécessaire; **he didn't have the ~ amount of money** il n'avait pas assez d'argent OR l'argent qu'il fallait.

requisition [ˌrekwɪˈzɪʃn] ◇ *n* -**1.** MIL réquisition *f*; to make a ~ for supplies réquisitionner des provisions. -**2.** COMM demande *f*; the boss put in a ~ for staplers le patron a fait une demande d'agrafeuses.
◇ *vt* MIL & *fig* réquisitionner; my car was ~ed to take the team to the match *hum* ma voiture a été réquisitionnée pour emmener l'équipe au match.

requital [rɪˈkwaɪtl] *n fml* [repayment] récompense *f*; [retaliation] revanche *f*; in ~ of OR for sthg [as reward] en récompense de OR pour qqch; [in retaliation] pour se venger de qqch.

requite [rɪˈkwaɪt] *vt* -**1.** [return - payment, kindness] récompenser, payer de retour; to ~ sb's love répondre à l'amour de qqn. -**2.** [satisfy - desire] satisfaire. -**3.** [avenge - injury] venger.

reread [ˌriːˈriːd] (*pt* & *pp* reread [-ˈred]) *vt* relire.

reredos [ˈrɪədɒs] *n* retable *m*.

rerelease [ˌriːrɪˈliːs] ◇ *vt* [film, record] ressortir.
◇ *n* [film, record] reprise *f*.

reroute [ˌriːˈruːt] *vt* dérouter, changer l'itinéraire de; the flight was ~d to Shannon le vol a été dérouté sur Shannon; the traffic was ~d through the suburbs la circulation a été déviée vers la banlieue.

rerun [*n* ˈriːrʌn, *vb* ˌriːˈrʌn] (*pt* reran [-ˈræn], *pp* rerun, *cont* rerunning) ◇ *n* [of film] reprise *f*; [of TV serial] rediffusion *f*; it's a ~ of last year's final ils repassent la finale de l'an dernier.
◇ *vt* -**1.** [film] passer de nouveau; [TV series] rediffuser. -**2.** [race] courir de nouveau; the race had to be ~ la course a dû être recourue.

resale [ˈriːseɪl] *n* revente *f*.

resale price maintenance *n* vente *f* au détail à prix imposé.

reschedule [*Br* ˌriːˈʃedjuːl, *Am* ˌriːˈskedʒʊl] *vt* -**1.** [appointment, meeting] modifier l'heure ou la date de; [bus, train, flight] modifier l'horaire de; [plan, order] modifier le programme de; the meeting has been ~d for next week la réunion a été déplacée à la semaine prochaine. -**2.** FIN [debt] rééchelonner.

rescind [rɪˈsɪnd] *vt fml* [judgment] casser, annuler; [agreement] annuler; [law] abroger; [contract] résilier.

rescission [rɪˈsɪʒn] *n* [of judgment] cassation *f*, annulation *f*; [of agreement] annulation *f*; [of law] abrogation *f*; [of contract] résiliation *f*.

rescue [ˈreskjuː] ◇ *vt* [from danger] sauver; [from captivity] délivrer; [in need, difficulty] secourir, venir au secours de; to ~ sb from drowning sauver qqn de la noyade; they were ~d from a potentially dangerous situation on les a tirés d'une situation qui aurait pu être dangereuse; the survivors were waiting to be ~d les survivants attendaient des secours ‖ *fig*: thanks for rescuing me from that boring conversation merci de m'avoir délivré, cette conversation m'assommait; to ~ sb's name from oblivion arracher le nom de qqn à l'oubli.
◇ *n* [from danger, drowning] sauvetage *m*; [from captivity] délivrance *f*; [in need, difficulty] secours *m*; to go/to come to sb's ~ aller/venir au secours OR à la rescousse de qqn; ~ was impossible toute opération de sauvetage était impossible.
◇ *comp* [attempt, mission, operation, party, team] de sauvetage, de secours; ~ worker sauveteur *m*.

rescuer [ˈreskjʊəʳ] *n* sauveteur *m*.

reseal [ˌriːˈsiːl] *vt* [envelope] recacheter; [jar] refermer hermétiquement.

resealable [ˌriːˈsiːləbl] *adj* qui peut être recacheté.

research [rɪˈsɜːtʃ] ◇ *n (U)* recherche *f*, recherches *fpl*; to do ~ into sthg faire des recherches sur qqch; she's engaged in ~ in genetics/into rare viruses elle fait des recherches en génétique/sur les virus rares; what kind of ~ do you do? quel type de recherches faites-vous?; ~ into the problem revealed a worrying trend les recherches sur le problème ont révélé une tendance inquiétante; an excellent piece of ~ un excellent travail de recherche; ~ and development recherche *f* et développement *m*, recherche-développement *f*; scientific ~ la recherche scientifique.
◇ *vt* [article, book, problem, subject] faire des recherches sur; your essay is not very well ~ed votre travail n'est pas très bien documenté.
◇ *vi* faire des recherches OR de la recherche.
◇ *comp* [establishment, work] de recherche; ~ worker chercheur *m*, -euse *f*.

researcher [rɪˈsɜːtʃəʳ] *n* chercheur *m*, -euse *f*.

research student *n* étudiant *m*, -e *f* qui fait de la recherche *(après la licence)*.

reseat [ˌriːˈsiːt] *vt* -**1.** [person - sit again] faire rasseoir; [- change place] assigner une nouvelle place à; to ~ o.s. [sit down] se rasseoir; [change place] changer de place. -**2.** [chair] refaire le fond de; [trousers] remettre un fond à. -**3.** MECH [valve] roder.

resection [riːˈsekʃn] *n* MED résection *f*.

reselect [ˌriːsɪˈlekt] *vt* sélectionner de nouveau.

resell [ˌriːˈsel] (*pt* & *pp* resold [-ˈsəʊld]) *vt* revendre.

resemblance [rɪˈzembləns] *n* ressemblance *f*; to bear a ~ to sb ressembler vaguement à qqn; the brothers show a strong family ~ les frères se ressemblent beaucoup; any ~ to persons living or dead is purely accidental toute ressemblance avec des personnes existantes ou ayant existé ne peut être que fortuite; the newspaper account bears little ~ to the actual interview il n'y a qu'une vague ressemblance entre l'article du journal et l'interview proprement dite.

resemble [rɪˈzembl] *vt* ressembler à; they ~ each other greatly ils se ressemblent beaucoup.

resent [rɪˈzent] *vt* [person] en vouloir à, éprouver de la rancune à l'égard de; [remark, criticism] ne pas apprécier; to ~ sthg bitterly/strongly éprouver un sentiment d'amertume/un vif ressentiment à l'égard de qqch; he ~ed their criticism il n'a pas apprécié leurs critiques; I ~ their presence le fait qu'ils soient là me déplaît; I ~ that remark! voilà une remarque que je n'apprécie guère!; I ~ that! je proteste!; her presence in the country was strongly ~ed sa présence dans le pays a été très mal acceptée; I ~ them taking over OR the fact that they have taken over je leur en veux de prendre tout en charge; they ~ her enjoying herself ils lui en veulent de s'amuser.

resentful [rɪˈzentfʊl] *adj* plein de ressentiment; to feel ~ about OR at sthg éprouver du ressentiment à l'égard de qqch, mal accepter qqch; to be ~ about OR of sb's achievements envier sa réussite à qqn; don't be so ~! ne soyez pas si rancunier!

resentfully [rɪˈzentfʊlɪ] *adv* avec ressentiment.

resentment [rɪˈzentmənt] *n* ressentiment *m*.

reservation [ˌrezəˈveɪʃn] ◇ *n* -**1.** [doubt] réserve *f*, restriction *f*; to have ~s about sthg faire OR émettre des réserves sur qqch; I have ~s about letting them go abroad j'hésite à les laisser partir à l'étranger; without ~ OR ~s sans réserve; to accept sthg without ~ approuver qqch sans réserve; with (some) ~s avec certaines réserves; he expressed some ~s about the plan il a émis quelques doutes à propos OR au sujet du projet. -**2.** [booking] réservation *f*; to make a ~ [on train] réserver une OR sa place; [in hotel] réserver OR retenir une chambre; [in restaurant] réserver une table; the secretary made all the ~s la secrétaire s'est occupée de toutes les réservations; I have a ~ [at hotel] j'ai une réservation, j'ai réservé une chambre. -**3.** [enclosed area] réserve *f*; Indian ~ réserve indienne. -**4.** *Br* AUT [on dual carriageway]: (central) ~ bande *f* médiane. -**5.** RELIG: the Reservation (of the sacrament) la Sainte Réserve.
◇ *comp* [desk] des réservations.

reserve [rɪˈzɜːv] ◇ *vt* -**1.** [keep back] réserver, mettre de côté; to ~ one's strength garder OR ménager ses forces; to ~ the right to do sthg se réserver le droit de faire qqch; to reserve (one's) judgment about sthg ne pas se prononcer sur qqch. -**2.** [book] réserver, retenir; these seats are ~d for VIPs ces places sont réservées aux personnalités.
◇ *n* -**1.** [store - of energy, money, provisions] réserve *f*; to draw on one's ~s puiser dans ses réserves; the body's food ~s les réserves nutritives du corps; the nation's coal ~s les réserves de charbon du pays; he has great ~s of energy il a beaucoup d'énergie en réserve OR de grandes réserves d'énergie; cash ~s réserves de caisse; gold ~s réserves d'or. -**2.** [storage] réserve *f*; to have OR to keep in ~ avoir OR garder en réserve; luckily, they have some money in ~ heureusement, ils ont (mis) un peu d'argent de côté. -**3.** *Br* [doubt, qualification] réserve *f*; without ~ sans réserve, sans restriction; with all proper ~s sous toutes réserves. -**4.** [reticence] réserve *f*, retenue *f*; to break through sb's ~ amener qqn à sortir de sa réserve. -**5.** MIL réserve *f*; to call up the ~ OR ~s faire appel à la réserve OR aux réservistes. -**6.** [area of land] réserve *f*; nature ~ réserve naturelle; Indian ~ réserve indienne. -**7.** SPORT remplaçant *m*, -e *f*; to play for the ~s jouer dans l'équipe de réserve. -**8.** [at auction] prix *m* minimum.
◇ *comp* -**1.** FIN [funds, currency, resources] de réserve. -**2.** SPORT remplaçant; the ~ goalkeeper le gardien de but remplaçant; the ~ team l'équipe *f* de réserve.

reserve bank *n* banque *f* de réserve.

reserve currency *n* fonds *m* de réserve.

reserved [rɪˈzɜːvd] *adj* -**1.** [shy - person] timide, réservé; she is very ~ elle est très réservée. -**2.** [doubtful]: to be ~ in one's opinion about sthg ne pas se prononcer sur qqch; he has always been rather ~ about the scheme il a toujours exprimé des doutes sur ce projet. -**3.** [room, seat] réservé; all rights ~ tous droits réservés.

reservedly [rɪˈzɜːvɪdlɪ] *adv* avec réserve, avec retenue.

reserve price *n* prix *m* minimum.

reserve tank *n* AUT réservoir *m* de secours.

reservist [rɪˈzɜːvɪst] *n* réserviste *m*.

reservoir [ˈrezəvwɑːʳ] *n literal* & *fig* réservoir *m*.

reset [*vb* ˌriːˈset, *n* ˈriːset] (*pt* & *pp* reset, *cont* resetting) ◇ *vt* -**1.** [jewel] remonter. -**2.** [watch, clock] remettre à l'heure; [alarm] réenclencher; [counter] remettre à zéro. -**3.** COMPUT réinitialiser. -**4.** MED [limb] remettre en place; [fracture] réduire. -**5.** TYPO recomposer. -**6.** [lay]: to ~ the table [in restaurant] remettre le couvert; [in home] remettre la table.
◇ *n* COMPUT réinitialisation *f*.

resettle [ˌriːˈsetl] ◇ *vt* [refugees, population] établir OR implanter (dans une nouvelle région); [territory] repeupler.
◇ *vi* se réinstaller.

resettlement [ˌriːˈsetlmənt] *n* [of people] établissement *m* OR implantation *f* (dans une nouvelle région); [of territory] repeuplement *m*.

reshape [ˌriːˈʃeɪp] *vt* [clay, material] refaçonner; [novel, policy] réorganiser, remanier.

reshuffle [ˌriːˈʃʌfl] ◇ *vt* -**1.** POL [cabinet] remanier. -**2.** [cards] rebattre, battre de nouveau.
◇ *n* -**1.** POL remaniement *m*; a Cabinet ~ un remaniement ministériel. -**2.** [in cards]: to have a ~ battre les cartes à nouveau.

reside [rɪˈzaɪd] *vi fml* -**1.** [live] résider; they ~ in New York ils résident OR ils sont domiciliés à New York. -**2.** *fig* [be located]: authority ~s in OR with the Prime Minister c'est le Premier ministre qui est investi de l'autorité; the problem ~s in the fact that there is too much traffic le problème est dû au fait qu'il y a trop de circulation.

residence [ˈrezɪdəns] *n* -**1.** [home] résidence *f*, demeure *f*; town/country ~ résidence en ville/à la campagne; official summer ~ résidence officielle d'été; 'desirable ~ for sale' [in advert] 'belle demeure OR demeure de caractère à vendre'; to take up ~ in a new house s'installer OR s'établir dans une nouvelle maison;

they took up ~ in Oxford ils se sont installés OR ils ont élu domicile à Oxford; Lord Bellamy's ~ *fml* la résidence de Lord Bellamy; the Hancock ~ *hum* la résidence des Hancock ❑ to be in ~ [monarch] être en résidence; writer/artist in ~ écrivain *m*/artiste *mf* en résidence; place of ~ [on form] domicile *m*; I gave London as my place of ~ j'ai mis Londres comme lieu de résidence. -**2.** UNIV: (university) ~ résidence *f* (universitaire). -**3.** [period of stay] résidence *f*, séjour *m*; a short period of ~ in Spain un bref séjour en Espagne; after three years' ~ abroad après avoir résidé pendant trois ans à l'étranger.

residence hall *n Am* résidence *f* (universitaire).

residence permit *n* ≃ permis *m* de séjour.

residency ['rezɪdənsɪ] (*pl* residencies) *n* -**1.** *fml* [home] résidence *f* officielle. -**2.** *Am* MED *période d'études spécialisées après l'internat.*

resident ['rezɪdənt] ◇ *n* -**1.** [of town] habitant *m*, -e *f*; [of street] riverain *m*, -e *f*; [in hotel, hostel] pensionnaire *mf*; [foreigner] résident *m*, -e *f*; (local) ~s association association *f* des habitants (du quartier); are you a ~ of an EC country? ADMIN êtes-vous ressortissant d'un pays membre de la communauté européenne?; '~s only' 'interdit sauf aux riverains'. -**2.** *Am* MED interne *mf*. -**3.** ZOOL résident *m*.
◇ *adj* -**1.** [as inhabitant] résidant; the ~ population la population résidante OR fixe; to be ~ in a country résider dans un pays; to have permanent ~ status avoir le statut de résident permanent; the swallow is ~ to the area l'hirondelle réside dans la région. -**2.** [teacher, staff] qui habite sur place, à demeure; our ~ interpreter notre interprète; our ~ pianist notre pianiste attitré. -**3.** COMPUT résident.

residential [,rezɪ'denʃl] *adj* [district, accommodation] résidentiel; [status] de résident; [course, job] sur place.

residual [rɪ'zɪdjʊəl] ◇ *adj* [gen] restant; CHEM & GEOL résiduel; PHYS [magnetism] rémanent.
◇ *n* MATH reste *m*; CHEM & GEOL résidu *m*.

residuary [rɪ'zɪdjʊərɪ] *adj* [gen] restant; CHEM résiduaire; GEOL résiduel; ~ legatee JUR légataire *m* universel.

residue ['rezɪdju:] *n* [leftovers] reste *m*, restes *mpl*; [of money, estate] reliquat *m*; CHEM & PHYS résidu *m*; MATH reste *m*, reliquat *m*.

resign [rɪ'zaɪn] ◇ *vi* -**1.** [from post] démissionner, donner sa démission; she ~ed from her job/from the committee elle a démissionné de son emploi/du comité. -**2.** CHESS abandonner.
◇ *vt* -**1.** [give up - advantage] renoncer à; [- job] démissionner de; [- function] se démettre de, démissionner de; she was forced to ~ the party leadership elle a dû démissionner de la tête du parti. -**2.** [give away] céder; to ~ sthg to sb céder qqch à qqn; I ~ed my voting rights to the chairman j'ai cédé mon droit de vote au président. -**3.** [reconcile]: to ~ o.s. to one's fate se résigner à son sort; I had ~ed myself to going alone je m'étais résigné à y aller seul.

re-sign [,ri:'saɪn] *vt* [document] signer une nouvelle fois.

resignation [,rezɪg'neɪʃn] *n* -**1.** [from job] démission *f*; to hand in OR to tender *fml* one's ~ donner sa démission. -**2.** [acceptance - of fact, situation] résignation *f*.

resigned [rɪ'zaɪnd] *adj* résigné; to become ~ to (doing) sthg se résigner à (faire) qqch; she is ~ to her fate elle s'est résignée à son sort; she gave me a ~ look/smile elle m'a regardé/souri avec résignation.

resignedly [rɪ'zaɪnɪdlɪ] *adv* avec résignation.

resilience [rɪ'zɪlɪəns] *n* -**1.** [of rubber, metal - springiness] élasticité *f*; [- toughness] résistance *f*. -**2.** [of character, person] énergie *f*, ressort *m*; [of institution] résistance *f*.

resilient [rɪ'zɪlɪənt] *adj* -**1.** [rubber, metal - springy] élastique; [- tough] résistant. -**2.** [person - in character] qui a du ressort, qui ne se laisse pas abattre OR décourager; [- in health, condition] très résistant.

resin ['rezɪn] *n* résine *f*.

resiniferous [,rezɪ'nɪfərəs] *adj* résinifère.

resinous ['rezɪnəs] *adj* résineux.

resist [rɪ'zɪst] ◇ *vt* [temptation, attack, change, pressure] résister à; [reform] s'opposer à; I can't ~ chocolates je ne peux pas résister aux chocolats; he couldn't ~ having just one more drink il n'a pas pu résister à l'envie de prendre un dernier verre; nobody can ~ her personne ne peut lui résister; I can't ~ it! c'est plus fort que moi!; he was charged with ~ing arrest *fml* il a été inculpé de résistance aux forces de l'ordre.
◇ *vi* résister, offrir de la résistance.

resistance [rɪ'zɪstəns] ◇ *n* [gen, ELEC, MED, PHYS & PSYCH] résistance *f*; their ~ to all reform leur opposition (systématique) à toute réforme; they offered no ~ to the new measures ils ne se sont pas opposés aux nouvelles mesures; they put up fierce ~ to their attackers ils opposèrent une vive résistance à leurs agresseurs; her ~ to infection is low elle offre peu de résistance à l'infection ❑ air/wind ~ résistance de l'air/du vent; the French/Dutch Resistance HIST la Résistance française/hollandaise.
◇ *comp* [movement] de résistance; [group] de résistants; ~ fighter résistant *m*, -e *f*.

resistant [rɪ'zɪstənt] ◇ *adj* [gen, ELEC, MED & PHYS] résistant; she is very ~ to change elle est très hostile au changement; ~ to antibiotics résistant aux antibiotiques.
◇ *n* résistant *m*, -e *f*.

-resistant *in cpds*: heat~ qui résiste à la chaleur; water~ résistant à l'eau; flame~ ignifugé.

resistor [rɪ'zɪstə^r] *n* ELEC résistance *f (objet)*.

resit [*vb* ,ri:'sɪt, *n* 'ri:sɪt] (*pt* & *pp* resat [-'sæt], *cont* resitting) ◇ *vt* [exam] repasser.
◇ *n* examen *m* de rattrapage.

resole [,ri:'səʊl] *vt* ressemeler.

resolute ['rezəlu:t] *adj* [determined - person, expression, jaw] résolu; [steadfast - faith, courage, refusal] inébranlable; he is ~ in his decision il est inébranlable dans sa décision; to be ~ in one's efforts être déterminé dans ses efforts.

resolutely ['rezəlu:tlɪ] *adv* [oppose, struggle, believe] résolument; [refuse] fermement; she marched forward ~ elle avança d'un pas résolu.

resoluteness ['rezəlu:tnɪs] *n* résolution *f*, détermination *f*.

resolution [,rezə'lu:ʃn] *n* -**1.** [decision] résolution *f*, décision *f*; to be full of good ~s être plein de bonnes résolutions; she made a ~ to stop smoking elle a pris la résolution d'arrêter de fumer. -**2.** [formal motion] résolution *f*; they passed/adopted/rejected a ~ to limit the budget ils ont voté/adopté/rejeté une résolution pour limiter le budget; the statutes can only be changed by ~ les statuts ne peuvent être modifiés que par l'adoption d'une résolution. -**3.** [determination] résolution *f*; to say/to act with ~ dire/agir avec fermeté; a note of ~ entered her voice sa voix a pris un ton résolu; he always showed ~ il a toujours fait preuve de résolution. -**4.** [settling, solving] résolution *f*; in Act V we see the ~ of the tragedy au cinquième acte, nous assistons au dénouement de la tragédie. -**5.** COMPUT, OPT & TV résolution *f*; high ~ screen écran *m* à haute résolution. -**6.** MED & MUS résolution *f*.

resolvable [rɪ'zɒlvəbl] *adj* résoluble, soluble.

resolve [rɪ'zɒlv] ◇ *vt* -**1.** [work out - quarrel, difficulty, dilemma] résoudre; [- doubt] dissiper; MATH [- equation] résoudre; there are a few points left to ~ il nous reste encore quelques petits problèmes à résoudre; have you ~d your difficulties yet? avez-vous résolu vos difficultés? -**2.** [decide] (se) résoudre; to ~ to do sthg décider de OR se résoudre à faire qqch; I ~d to resign j'ai pris la décision de démissionner; she had ~d that he would have to leave elle avait décidé qu'il devrait partir; it was ~d that... il a été résolu OR on a décidé que... -**3.** [break down, separate] résoudre, réduire; the problem can be ~d into three simple questions le problème peut se résoudre en OR être ramené à trois questions simples. -**4.** OPT & PHYS [parts, peaks] distinguer; [image] résoudre. -**5.** MED résoudre, faire disparaître. -**6.** MUS résoudre.
◇ *vi* -**1.** [separate, break down] se résoudre. -**2.** MUS [chord] être résolu.
◇ *n* -**1.** [determination] résolution *f*; it only strengthened our ~ ça n'a fait que renforcer notre détermination. -**2.** [decision] résolution *f*, décision *f*; to make a ~ to do sthg prendre la résolution de faire qqch.

resolved [rɪ'zɒlvd] *adj* résolu, décidé, déterminé; I was firmly ~ to go j'étais fermement décidé à partir.

resonance ['rezənəns] *n* résonance *f*.

resonant ['rezənənt] *adj* -**1.** [loud, echoing] retentissant, sonore. -**2.** ACOUST, MUS & PHYS résonant, résonnant; ~ cavity cavité *f* résonante.

resonantly ['rezənəntlɪ] *adv* d'une voix retentissante.

resonate ['rezəneɪt] *vi* [noise, voice, laughter, place] résonner, retentir; the valley ~d with their cries la vallée retentissait de leurs cris.

resonator ['rezəneɪtə^r] *n* résonateur *m*.

resorb [rɪ'sɔ:b] ◇ *vt* -**1.** MED résorber. -**2.** [absorb again] réabsorber.
◇ *vi* MED se résorber.

resorption [rɪ'sɔ:pʃn] *n* MED résorption *f*.

resort [rɪ'zɔ:t] *n* -**1.** [recourse] recours *m*; without ~ to threats sans avoir recours aux menaces; the doctor is our last ~ le médecin est notre dernier recours; as a last ~ en dernier ressort; call me only as a last OR in the last ~ ne m'appelez qu'en dernier ressort; flight was the only ~ left to me OR my only ~ il ne me restait plus qu'à fuir. -**2.** [holiday place] station *f*; seaside/ski ~ station balnéaire/de sports d'hiver; ~ development aménagement *m* touristique; luxury ~ hotel hôtel *m* de tourisme de luxe. -**3.** [haunt, hang-out] repaire *m*.
◆ **resort to** *vt insep* -**1.** [violence, sarcasm etc] avoir recours à, recourir à; you ~ed to lying to your wife vous en êtes venu à mentir à votre femme. -**2.** *arch* OR *lit* [town] se rendre à.

resound [rɪ'zaʊnd] *vi* -**1.** [noise, words, explosion] retentir, résonner; the trumpet ~ed through the barracks le son de la trompette retentissait dans toute la caserne. -**2.** [hall, cave, hills, room] retentir; the woods ~ed with birdsong les bois étaient pleins de chants d'oiseaux. -**3.** *fml* OR *lit* [spread - rumour] se propager; the declaration ~ed throughout the country la déclaration a eu un retentissement national.

resounding [rɪ'zaʊndɪŋ] *adj* -**1.** [loud - noise, blow, wail] retentissant; [- voice] sonore, claironnant; [explosion] violent; with a ~ splash avec un grand plouf; greeted with ~ applause accueilli par des applaudissements retentissants. -**2.** [unequivocal] retentissant, éclatant; it was a ~ failure ce fut un échec retentissant; he was met with a ~ refusal on lui a opposé un refus catégorique.

resoundingly [rɪ'zaʊndɪŋlɪ] *adv* -**1.** [loudly] bruyamment. -**2.** [unequivocally - win] d'une manière retentissante OR décisive; [- criticize, condemn] sévèrement; the measure was ~ unpopular cette mesure fut extrêmement impopulaire; the team was ~ beaten l'équipe a été battue à plate couture.

resource [rɪ'sɔ:s] ◇ *n* -**1.** [asset] ressource *f*; there's a limit to the ~s we can invest il y a une limite à la somme que nous pouvons investir; your health is a precious ~ ta santé est un précieux capital; natural/energy ~s ressources naturelles/énergétiques. -**2.** [human capacity] ressource *f*; the task called for all my ~s of tact cette tâche a demandé toute ma diplomatie ❑ after lunch I'll leave you to your own ~s après le déjeuner je vous abandonnerai à votre sort *hum*; left to their own ~s, they're likely to mess everything up livrés à eux-mêmes, ils risquent de tout gâcher. -**3.** [ingenuity] ressource *f*; a man of ~ un homme plein de ressource OR ressources.

◇ *comp* SCH & UNIV: ~ OR ~s centre/room centre *m*/salle *f* de documentation; ~ materials [written] documentation *f*; [audio-visual] aides *fpl* pédagogiques; ~ person [in career centre] conseiller *m*, -ère *f* d'orientation; [in library] bibliothécaire *mf* *(chargé d'orienter les usagers et d'entreprendre certaines recherches bibliographiques)*.

resourceful [rɪ'sɔːsfʊl] *adj* ingénieux, plein de ressource OR ressources.

resourcefully [rɪ'sɔːsfʊlɪ] *adv* ingénieusement; he acted ~ in a difficult situation dans cette situation difficile il s'est montré très ingénieux.

resourcefulness [rɪ'sɔːsfʊlnɪs] *n* ressource *f*, ingéniosité *f*.

respect [rɪ'spekt] ◇ *vt* -**1.** [esteem - person, judgment, right, authority] respecter; I ~ him for his efficiency je le respecte pour son efficacité; if you don't ~ yourself, no one else will si vous ne vous respectez pas vous-même, personne ne vous respectera. -**2.** [comply with - rules, customs] respecter; to ~ sb's wishes respecter les volontés de qqn; we don't have to ~ his wishes nous ne sommes pas tenu de faire ce qu'il veut; you should ~ the laws of any country you visit il faut respecter les lois des pays dans lesquels on va.

◇ *n* -**1.** [esteem] respect *m*, estime *f*; I have (an) enormous ~ for her competence je respecte infiniment sa compétence; I don't have much ~ for his methods je n'ai pas beaucoup de respect pour ses méthodes; she is held in great ~ by her colleagues elle est très respectée OR elle est tenue en haute estime par ses collègues; you have to get OR to gain the children's ~ il faut savoir se faire respecter par les enfants; you have lost all my ~ je n'ai plus aucun respect pour toi; he has no ~ for authority/money il méprise l'autorité/l'argent. -**2.** [care, politeness] respect *m*, égard *m*; show a little ~! un peu de respect!; he should show more ~ for local customs il devrait se montrer plus respectueux des coutumes locales; they have no ~ for public property ils n'ont aucun respect pour le bien public; to do sthg out of ~ for sthg/sb faire qqch par respect pour qqch/qqn; I stood up in ~ je me suis levé respectueusement; guns should be treated with ~ les armes à feu doivent être maniées avec précaution; with (all due) ~, Mr Clark... avec tout le respect que je vous dois, M. Clark...; with the utmost ~ to Boyd, his figures aren't conclusive malgré tout le respect que je dois à Boyd, ses chiffres ne sont guère concluants. -**3.** [regard, aspect] égard *m*; in every ~ à tous les égards; in some/other ~s à certains/d'autres égards; in many ~s à bien des égards. -**4.** [compliance, observance] respect *m*, observation *f*; his strict ~ of the letter of the law son strict respect de la loi.

◆ **respects** *npl* [salutations] respects *mpl*, hommages *mpl*; give my ~s to your father présentez mes respects à votre père; to pay one's ~s to sb présenter ses respects OR ses hommages à qqn; I went to the funeral to pay my last ~s je suis allé à l'enterrement pour lui rendre un dernier hommage.

◆ **with respect to** *prep phr* quant à, en ce qui concerne.

respectability [rɪ,spektə'bɪlətɪ] *n* respectabilité *f*.

respectable [rɪ'spektəbl] *adj* -**1.** [socially proper, worthy] respectable, convenable, comme il faut; a thoroughly ~ part of town un quartier tout à fait comme il faut; I'm a ~ married woman! je suis une femme mariée et respectable!; that's not done in ~ society ça ne se fait pas dans la bonne société; to be outwardly ~ avoir l'apparence de la respectabilité; I'm sure he had a very ~ reason je suis sûr qu'il avait une raison tout à fait respectable OR honorable; to make o.s. (look) ~ se préparer. -**2.** [fair - speech, athlete] assez bon; [- amount, wage, distance] respectable, correct; a ~ actor un acteur qui n'est pas dénué de talent; a ~ first novel un premier roman qui n'est pas dénué d'intérêt; I play a ~ game of golf je joue passablement bien au golf; he left a ~ tip il a laissé un pourboire correct.

respectably [rɪ'spektəblɪ] *adv* [properly] convenablement, comme il faut; he's ~ married il est convenablement marié; she has to dress ~ for work elle doit s'habiller correctement pour son travail.

respected [rɪ'spektɪd] *adj* respecté; she's a highly ~ researcher c'est une chercheuse très respectée.

respecter [rɪ'spektə^r] *n*: she is no ~ of tradition elle ne fait pas partie de ceux qui respectent la tradition; disease is no ~ of class nous sommes tous égaux devant la maladie.

respectful [rɪ'spektfʊl] *adj* respectueux.

respectfully [rɪ'spektfʊlɪ] *adv* respectueusement.

respecting [rɪ'spektɪŋ] *prep* concernant, en ce qui concerne.

respective [rɪ'spektɪv] *adj* respectif.

respectively [rɪ'spektɪvlɪ] *adv* respectivement.

respiration [,respə'reɪʃn] *n* respiration *f*.

respirator ['respəreɪtə^r] *n* [mask, machine] respirateur *m*.

respiratory [*Br* rɪ'spɪrətrɪ, *Am* 'respərətɔːrɪ] *adj* respiratoire; ~ system système *m* respiratoire; ~ problem OR problems troubles *mpl* respiratoires.

respire [rɪ'spaɪə^r] *vi* & *vt lit* respirer.

respite ['respaɪt] ◇ *n* -**1.** [pause, rest] répit *m*; without ~ sans répit OR relâche; there wasn't a moment's ~ from the noise il y avait un bruit ininterrompu; he never has any ~ from the pain la douleur ne lui laisse aucun répit. -**2.** [delay] répit *m*, délai *m*; [stay of execution] sursis *m*; we've been given a week's ~ before we need to pay on nous a accordé un délai d'une semaine pour payer.

◇ *vt fml* accorder un sursis à.

resplendence [rɪ'splendəns] *n lit* [splendour] splendeur *f*; [brightness] resplendissement *m lit*.

resplendent [rɪ'splendənt] *adj* [splendid] magnifique, splendide; [shining] resplendissant; Joe, ~ in his new suit Joe, resplendissant OR magnifique dans son nouveau costume; her face was ~ with joy/health son visage resplendissait de joie/de santé.

resplendently [rɪ'splendəntlɪ] *adv* [dress, decorate] somptueusement; [shine] avec éclat.

respond [rɪ'spɒnd] ◇ *vi* -**1.** [answer - person, guns] répondre; to ~ to a request répondre à une demande; she ~ed with a smile elle a répondu par un sourire. -**2.** [react] répondre, réagir; the steering is slow to ~ la direction ne répond pas bien; the cells ~ by producing enzymes les cellules réagissent en produisant des enzymes; the patient is ~ing le malade réagit positivement; her condition/tumour isn't ~ing to treatment le traitement ne semble pas agir sur sa maladie/tumeur; syphilis ~s to antibiotics les antibiotiques sont efficaces contre la syphilis ‖ [person]: they'll ~ to the crisis by raising taxes ils répondront à la crise en augmentant les impôts; are people ~ing to the candidate's message? l'opinion publique réagit-elle favorablement au message du candidat?; he doesn't ~ well to criticism il réagit mal à la critique; to ~ to flattery être sensible à la flatterie.

◇ *vt* répondre; "who cares?", he ~ed angrily «qu'est-ce que ça peut bien faire?», répondit-il avec colère.

◇ *n* -**1.** ARCHIT [for arch] pilier *m* butant; [ending colonnade] colonne *f* engagée. -**2.** RELIG répons *m*.

respondent [rɪ'spɒndənt] ◇ *n* -**1.** JUR défendeur *m*, -eresse *f*. -**2.** [in opinion poll] sondé *m*, -e *f*; 10% of the ~s 10 % des personnes interrogées. -**3.** PSYCH [reflex] répondant *m*.

◇ *adj* PSYCH répondant.

response [rɪ'spɒns] *n* -**1.** [answer] réponse *f*; have you had any ~ to your request yet? avez-vous obtenu une réponse à votre demande?; when asked, she gave OR made no ~ quand on lui a posé la question, elle n'a pas répondu; he smiled in ~ il a répondu par un sourire. -**2.** [reaction] réponse *f*, réaction *f*; their ~ to the rioting was harsh ils ont sévèrement réprimé les émeutes; their proposals met with a favourable/lukewarm ~ leurs propositions ont été accueillies favorablement/ont reçu un accueil mitigé; ~ from the public was disappointing la réponse du public a été décevante. -**3.** [in bridge] réponse *f*. -**4.** RELIG répons *m*. -**5.** MED réaction *f*.

◆ **in response to** *prep phr* en réponse à; he resigned in ~ to the party's urging/to the pressure il a démissionné, cédant à l'insistance du parti/à la pression.

response time *n* COMPUT temps *m* de réponse; MED & PSYCH temps *m* de réaction.

responsibility [rɪ,spɒnsə'bɪlətɪ] (*pl* responsibilities) *n* -**1.** [control, authority] responsabilité *f*; ~ for the campaign has been transferred to her c'est à elle qu'incombe désormais la responsabilité de la campagne; to have ~ for sthg avoir la charge OR la responsabilité de qqch; the project is their joint ~ le projet relève de leur responsabilité à tous les deux; a position of great ~ un poste à haute responsabilité; how much ~ for the operation did the president really have? jusqu'à quel point le président était-il responsable de l'opération?; can he handle all that ~? est-il capable d'assumer toutes ces responsabilités?; he authorized it on his own ~ il l'a autorisé de son propre chef, il a pris sur lui de l'autoriser. -**2.** [accountability] responsabilité *f*; he has no sense of ~ il n'a aucun sens des responsabilités; to accept OR to assume ~ for one's mistakes assumer la responsabilité de ses erreurs; I take full ~ for the defeat je prends (sur moi) l'entière responsabilité de la défaite. -**3.** [task, duty] responsabilité *f*; responsibilities include product development vous assurerez entre autres le développement des nouveaux produits; it's his ~! ça le regarde!; they have a ~ to the shareholders/the electors ils ont une responsabilité envers les actionnaires/les électeurs; to shirk one's responsibilities fuir ses responsabilités; children are a big ~ c'est une lourde responsabilité que d'avoir des enfants.

responsible [rɪ'spɒnsəbl] *adj* -**1.** [in charge, in authority] responsable; who's ~ for research? qui est chargé de la recherche?; he was ~ for putting the children to bed c'était lui qui couchait les enfants; a ~ position un poste à responsabilité. -**2.** [accountable] responsable; ~ for sthg responsable de qqch; he's not ~ for her behaviour il n'est pas responsable de ses actes; human error/a malfunction was ~ for the disaster la catastrophe était due à une erreur humaine/à une défaillance technique; who's ~ for this mess? qui est l'auteur OR le responsable de cette pagaille?; he can be held legally ~ for the accident il peut être tenu légalement responsable de l'accident; I hold you personally ~ je vous tiens personnellement responsable; he is ~ only to the managing director il n'est responsable que devant le directeur général. -**3.** [serious, trustworthy] sérieux, responsable; it wasn't very ~ of him ce n'était pas très sérieux de sa part; ~ newspapers won't print the story les journaux sérieux ne publieront pas cet article; the chemical industry has become more environmentally ~ l'industrie chimique se préoccupe davantage de l'environnement; they aren't ~ parents ce ne sont pas des parents dignes de ce nom; our bank makes ~ investments notre banque a une politique d'investissement responsable.

responsibly [rɪ'spɒnsəblɪ] *adv* de manière responsable; to behave ~ avoir un comportement responsable.

responsive [rɪ'spɒnsɪv] *adj* -**1.** [person - sensitive] sensible; [- receptive] ouvert; [- enthusiastic] enthousiaste; [- affectionate] affectueux; I asked him for advice, but h wasn't very ~ je lui ai demandé des conseils mais il semblait peu disposé à me répondre; to be ~ to praise être sensible aux compliments; management should be ~ to suggestions la direction devrait être ouverte aux suggestions; the play opened to a ~ audience la première a eu lieu devant un public enthousiaste. -2. [brakes, controls, keyboard] sensible; the patient isn't proving ~ to treatment le malade ne réagit pas au traitement; the industry is not ~ to market signals l'industrie ne réagit OR ne répond pas aux sollicitations du marché. -3. [answering - glance, smile, nod] en réponse.

responsiveness [rɪ'spɒnsɪvnɪs] *n* -1. [of person - sensitivity] sensibilité *f*; [- receptiveness] ouverture *f*; [- enthusiasm] enthousiasme *m*; [- affection] affection *f*, tendresse *f*. -2. [of brakes, controls, keyboard] sensibilité *f*.

respray [*vb* ˌriː'spreɪ, *n* 'riːspreɪ] ◇ *vt* [car] repeindre.

◇ *n*: I took the car in for a ~ j'ai donné la voiture à repeindre.

rest [rest] ◇ *n* -1. [remainder]: take the ~ of the cake prenez le reste OR ce qui reste du gâteau; take the ~ of the cakes prenez les autres gâteaux OR les gâteaux qui restent; the ~ of the time they watch television le reste du temps, ils regardent la télévision; he's the only amateur, the ~ of them are professionals c'est le seul amateur, les autres sont des professionnels; the ~ of the group disagreed le reste du groupe n'était pas d'accord ❑ and all the ~ (of it) *inf*, and the ~ *inf* et tout le reste OR tout le tralala. -2. [relaxation] repos *m*; [pause] repos *m*, pause *f*; (a) ~ will do him good un peu de repos lui fera du bien; try to get some ~ essayez de vous reposer (un peu); I had OR I took a ten-minute ~ je me suis reposé pendant dix minutes, j'ai fait une pause de dix minutes; you need a week's ~/a good night's ~ vous avez besoin d'une semaine de repos/d'une bonne nuit de sommeil; after a moment's ~ après s'être reposé quelques instants; after her afternoon ~ après sa sieste; day of ~ journée *f* de repos; she had to take several ~s while climbing the stairs en montant l'escalier elle a été obligée de s'arrêter à plusieurs reprises; he needs a ~ from the pressure/the children il a besoin de se détendre/d'un peu de temps sans les enfants; he gave her no ~ until she consented il ne lui a pas laissé une minute de répit jusqu'à ce qu'elle accepte; you'd better give the skiing a ~ vous feriez mieux de ne pas faire de ski pendant un certain temps ❑ ~ and recuperation *Am* MIL permission *f*; *hum* vacances *fpl*; to put OR to set sb's mind at ~ tranquilliser OR rassurer qqn; give it a ~! *inf* arrête, tu veux? -3. [motionlessness] repos *m*; the machines are at ~ les machines sont au repos; her hands were rarely at ~ ses mains restaient rarement inactives; to come to ~ [vehicle, pendulum, ball] s'immobiliser, s'arrêter; [bird, falling object] se poser. -4. *euph* [death] paix *f*; eternal ~ repos *m* éternel; he's finally at ~ il a finalement trouvé la paix; to lay sb to ~ porter qqn en terre; to lay OR to put to ~ [rumour] dissiper; [allegation, notion] abandonner. -5. [support] support *m*, appui *m*; [in snooker] repose-queue *m*; she used it as a ~ for her camera elle s'en est servie comme appui pour son appareil photo. -6. MUS silence *m*; semibreve ~ *Br*, whole ~ *Am* pause *f*; minim ~ *Br*, half ~ *Am* demi-pause *f*; crotchet ~ *Br*, quarter ~ *Am* soupir *m*; quaver ~ *Br*, eighth ~ *Am* demi-soupir *m*. -7. [in poetry] césure *f*.

◇ *vi* -1. [relax, stop working] se reposer; they set off again after ~ing for an hour ils se sont remis en route après s'être reposés pendant une heure; horses ~ing in the shade des chevaux qui se reposent à l'ombre; we shall not ~ until the fight is won nous n'aurons de cesse que la lutte ne soit gagnée. -2. [be held up or supported] reposer; the buildings ~ on solid foundations les bâtiments reposent sur des fondations solides; his arm ~ed on the back of the sofa son bras reposait sur le dossier du canapé ‖ [lean - person] s'appuyer; [- bicycle, ladder] être appuyé; she was ~ing on her broom elle était appuyée sur son balai; the skis were ~ing against the wall les skis étaient appuyés contre le mur. -3. [depend, be based - argument, hope] reposer; the theory ~s on a false assumption la théorie repose sur une hypothèse fausse; the whole problem ~s on a misunderstanding tout le problème repose sur un malentendu. -4. [be, remain] être; ~ assured we're doing our best soyez certain que nous faisons de notre mieux; their fate ~s in your hands leur sort est entre vos mains; that's how things ~ between us voilà où en sont les choses entre nous; can't you let the matter ~? ne pouvez-vous pas abandonner cette idée?; he just won't let it ~ il y revient sans cesse. -5. [reside, belong] résider; power ~s with the committee c'est le comité qui détient le pouvoir; the choice ~s with you c'est à vous de choisir; the decision doesn't ~ with me la décision ne dépend pas de moi. -6. [alight - eyes, gaze] se poser. -7. *euph* [lie dead] reposer; '~ in peace' 'repose en paix'. -8. JUR: the defence ~s la défense conclut sa plaidoirie. -9. AGR [lie fallow] être en repos OR en jachère; to let a field ~ laisser un champ en repos OR en jachère.

◇ *vt* -1. [allow to relax] laisser reposer; they had to stop to ~ the camels ils ont dû s'arrêter pour laisser se reposer les chameaux; sit down and ~ your legs assieds-toi et repose-toi les jambes. -2. [support, lean] appuyer; she ~ed her bicycle against a lamp post elle appuya sa bicyclette contre un réverbère; I ~ed my suitcase on the step j'ai posé ma valise sur la marche; he ~ed his arm on the back of the sofa son bras reposait sur le dossier du canapé. -3. *phr*: I ~ my case JUR j'ai conclu mon plaidoyer; *fig* je n'ai rien d'autre à ajouter.

◆ **for the rest** *adv phr* pour le reste, quant au reste.

◆ **rest up** *inf vi insep* se reposer (un peu), prendre un peu de repos.

restage [ˌriː'steɪdʒ] *vt* remettre en scène.

rest area *n* AUT aire *f* de repos.

restart [*vb* ˌriː'stɑːt, *n* 'riːstɑːt] ◇ *vt* -1. [activity] reprendre, recommencer; [engine, mechanism] remettre en marche. -2. COMPUT [system] relancer, redémarrer; [program] relancer.

◇ *vi* -1. [job, project] reprendre, recommencer; [engine, mechanism] redémarrer. -2. COMPUT [system] redémarrer; [program] reprendre.

◇ *n* -1. [of engine, mechanism] remise *f* en marche. -2. COMPUT [of system] redémarrage *m*; warm/cold ~ redémarrage à chaud/à froid ‖ [of program] reprise *f*; ~ point point *m* de reprise.

restate [ˌriː'steɪt] *vt* -1. [reiterate - argument, case, objection] répéter, réitérer; [- one's intentions, innocence, faith] réaffirmer; the unions ~d their position les syndicats ont réaffirmé leur position. -2. [formulate differently] reformuler.

restatement [ˌriː'steɪtmənt] *n* -1. [repetition - of argument, case, objection] répétition *f*, réitération *f*; [- of one's intentions, innocence, faith] réaffirmation *f*. -2. [different formulation] reformulation *f*; a ~ of our objectives is perhaps necessary at this stage à ce stade, nous devrions peut-être reformuler nos objectifs.

restaurant ['restərɒnt] *n* restaurant *m*.

restaurant car *n Br* wagon-restaurant *m*, voiture-restaurant *f*.

restaurateur [ˌrestɒrə'tɜːʳ] *n* restaurateur *m*, -trice *f (en alimentation)*.

rest cure *n* cure *f* de repos.

rest day *n* jour *m* de repos.

rested ['restɪd] *adj* reposé.

restful ['restfʊl] *adj* reposant, délassant, paisible.

restfully ['restfʊlɪ] *adv* paisiblement.

rest home *n* maison *f* de retraite.

resting place ['restɪŋ-] *n* -1. *literal* lieu *m* de repos. -2. *fig* & *lit* [grave] dernière demeure *f*.

restitution [ˌrestɪ'tjuːʃn] *n* restitution *f*; the company was ordered to make full ~ of the monies la société a été sommée de restituer l'intégralité de la somme.

restive ['restɪv] *adj* -1. [nervous, fidgety] nerveux, agité. -2. [unmanageable] rétif, difficile.

restively ['restɪvlɪ] *adv* nerveusement.

restiveness ['restɪvnɪs] *n* -1. [of person] nervosité *f*, agitation *f*. -2. [of horse] caractère *m* rétif.

restless ['restlɪs] *adj* -1. [fidgety] nerveux, agité; [impatient] impatient; I get ~ after a few days in the country après quelques jours à la campagne, je ne tiens plus en place; the audience was beginning to grow ~ le public commençait à s'impatienter. -2. [constantly moving] agité; her ~ mind son esprit en ébullition. -3. [giving no rest]: a ~ night une nuit agitée.

restlessly ['restlɪslɪ] *adv* -1. [nervously] nerveusement; [impatiently] impatiemment, avec impatience; to pace ~ up and down faire les cent pas. -2. [sleeplessly]: she tossed ~ all night elle a eu une nuit très agitée.

restlessness ['restlɪsnɪs] *n* [fidgeting, nervousness] nervosité *f*, agitation *f*; [impatience] impatience *f*; the audience began showing signs of ~ le public a commencé à montrer des signes d'impatience.

restock [ˌriː'stɒk] *vt* -1. [with food, supplies] réapprovisionner; to ~ a freezer regarnir un congélateur. -2. [with fish] empoissonner; [with game] réapprovisionner en gibier.

restoration [ˌrestə'reɪʃn] *n* -1. [giving back] restitution *f*. -2. [re-establishment, bringing back] restauration *f*, rétablissement *m*; the ~ of law and order la restauration de l'ordre public; the ~ of the monarchy la restauration de la monarchie. -3. [repairing, cleaning - of work of art, building] restauration *f*.

◆ **Restoration** HIST ◇ *n*: the Restoration la Restauration anglaise.

◇ *comp* [literature, drama] de (l'époque de) la Restauration (anglaise).

THE RESTORATION:
La restauration, en 1660, de la monarchie britannique par l'avènement de Charles II mit fin à la période d'austérité du Protectorat de Cromwell.

---

restorative [rɪ'stɒrətɪv] ◇ *adj* fortifiant, remontant.

◇ *n* fortifiant *m*, remontant *m*.

restore [rɪ'stɔːʳ] *vt* -1. [give back] rendre, restituer; the jewels have been ~d to their rightful owners les bijoux ont été rendus OR restitués à leurs propriétaires légitimes. -2. [re-establish, bring back - peace, confidence, order, right] restaurer, rétablir; [- monarchy] restaurer; [- monarch] remettre sur le trône; ~d to his former post rétabli OR réintégré dans ses anciennes fonctions; if the left-wing government is ~d to power si le gouvernement de gauche revient au pouvoir; it ~d my faith in human nature cela m'a redonné confiance en la nature humaine; the treatment should soon ~ his health OR him to health le traitement devrait très vite le remettre sur pied; she managed to ~ the company to profitability grâce à elle, l'entreprise fait de nouveau des profits. -3. [repair, clean - work of art, building] restaurer.

restorer [rɪ'stɔːrəʳ] *n* ART restaurateur *m*, -trice *f (de tableaux)*.

restrain [rɪ'streɪn] *vt* -1. [hold back, prevent] retenir, empêcher; ~ him from spending so much money empêchez-le de dépenser tant d'argent; I couldn't ~ myself from making a remark je n'ai pas pu m'empêcher de faire une remarque. -2. [overpower, bring under control - person] maîtriser; it took four policemen to ~ him il a fallu quatre policiers pour le maîtriser. -3. [repress - emotion, anger, laughter] contenir, réprimer. -4. [imprison] interner, emprisonner.

restrained [rɪ'streɪnd] *adj* -1. [person] retenu, réservé; [emotion] contenu, maîtrisé; they sat in ~ silence ils étaient assis ensemble et se retenaient de parler. -2. [colour, style] sobre, discret.

restraint [rɪ'streɪnt] *n* -1. [self-control] retenue *f*; with remarkable ~ avec une retenue remarquable. -**2.** [restriction] restriction *f*, contrainte *f*; certain **~s should be put on the committee's powers** il faudrait restreindre les pouvoirs du comité; **the right to travel without ~** le droit de se déplacer en toute liberté OR librement; **to place** OR **to keep sb under ~** JUR interner qqn. -**3.** [control] contrôle *m*; **a policy of price ~** une politique de contrôle des prix.

restrict [rɪ'strɪkt] *vt* restreindre, limiter; **I try to ~ myself to ten cigarettes a day** j'essaie de me limiter à dix cigarettes par jour; **airlines ~ the amount of luggage you can take** les lignes aériennes limitent la quantité de bagages qu'on peut emporter.

restricted [rɪ'strɪktɪd] *adj* -**1.** [limited] limité, restreint; **the choice is too ~** le choix est trop restreint ❑ **~ area** [out of bounds] zone *f* interdite; *Br* AUT [with parking restrictions] zone *f* à stationnement réglementé; [with speed limit] zone *f* à vitesse limitée. -**2.** ADMIN [secret - document, information] secret, confidentiel. -**3.** [narrow - ideas, outlook] étroit, borné.

restricted users group *n* COMPUT *nombre restreint d'utilisateurs ayant accès à des informations confidentielles*.

restriction [rɪ'strɪkʃn] *n* -**1.** [limitation] restriction *f*, limitation *f*; **they'll accept no ~ of their liberty** ils n'accepteront pas qu'on restreigne leur liberté; **to put** OR **to place** OR **to impose ~s on sthg** imposer des restrictions sur qqch ❑ **speed ~** limitation de vitesse. -**2.** LOGIC & MATH condition *f*.

restrictive [rɪ'strɪktɪv] *adj* -**1.** [clause, list] restrictif, limitatif; [interpretation] strict. -**2.** LING [clause] déterminatif.

restrictive practice *n* [by union] pratique *f* syndicale restrictive; [by traders] atteinte *f* à la libre concurrence.

restring [ˌriː'strɪŋ] (*pt* & *pp* **restrung** [-'strʌŋ]) *vt* [bow] remplacer la corde de; [musical instrument] remplacer les cordes de; [tennis racket] recorder; [beads] renfiler.

rest room *n Am* toilettes *fpl*.

restructure [ˌriː'strʌktʃəʳ] *vt* restructurer.

rest stop *n Am* AUT aire *f* de stationnement OR de repos.

restyle [ˌriː'staɪl] *vt* [car] changer le design de; [hair, clothes] changer de style de; [magazine] changer la présentation de.

result [rɪ'zʌlt] ◇ *n* -**1.** [consequence] résultat *m*, conséquence *f*; **with disastrous ~s** avec des conséquences désastreuses; **the net ~** le résultat final; **the problems we're having are the ~ of a misunderstanding** les problèmes que nous connaissons actuellement sont dus à un malentendu; **I overslept, with the ~ that I was late for work** je ne me suis pas réveillé à temps, et du coup, je suis arrivé à mon travail en retard. -**2.** [success] résultat *m*; **our policy is beginning to get** OR **show ~s** notre politique commence à porter ses fruits; **they're looking for sales staff who can get ~s** ils cherchent des vendeurs capables d'obtenir de bons résultats. -**3.** [of match, exam, election] résultat *m*; **the football ~s** les résultats des matches de football; **she got good A-level ~s** *Br* ≃ elle a obtenu de bons résultats au baccalauréat; **our team needs a ~ next week** SPORT [win] notre équipe a besoin d'une victoire OR de gagner la semaine prochaine; **the company's ~s are down on last year** FIN les résultats financiers de l'entreprise sont moins bons que (ceux de) l'année dernière. -**4.** MATH [of sum, equation] résultat *m*.
◇ *vi* résulter; **who knows what will ~ from such a step?** qui sait ce qui résultera d'une telle démarche?; **the fire ~ed from a short circuit** c'est un court-circuit qui a provoqué l'incendie; **a price rise would inevitably ~** il en résulterait OR il s'ensuivrait inévitablement une augmentation des prix; **to ~ in** avoir pour résultat; **the dispute ~ed in her resigning** la dispute a entraîné sa démission; **the attack ~ed in heavy losses on both sides** l'attaque s'est soldée par d'importantes pertes des deux côtés.
◆ **as a result** *adv phr*: **as a ~, I missed my flight** à cause de cela, j'ai manqué mon avion.
◆ **as a result of** *prep phr* à cause de; **I was late as a ~ of the strike** j'ai été en retard en raison de la grève.

resultant [rɪ'zʌltənt] ◇ *adj* [gen, MATH & MUS] résultant.
◇ *n* MATH & PHYS résultante *f*.

resultant tone *n* son *m* résultant.

resume [rɪ'zjuːm] ◇ *vt* -**1.** [seat, activity, duties] reprendre; **after he left, we ~d our discussion** après son départ, nous avons repris notre discussion; **kindly ~ your seats** *fml* veuillez reprendre vos places OR vous rasseoir. -**2.** *arch* [sum up] résumer.
◇ *vi* reprendre, continuer; **when everyone's ready, we can ~** quand tout le monde sera prêt nous pourrons continuer OR poursuivre.

résumé ['rezjuːmeɪ] *n* -**1.** [summary] résumé *m*. -**2.** *Am* [curriculum vitae] curriculum vitae *m inv*.

resumption [rɪ'zʌmpʃn] *n* reprise *f*.

resurface [ˌriː'sɜːfɪs] ◇ *vi literal* & *fig* refaire surface; **the stolen jewels ~d in Australia** les bijoux volés ont refait surface en Australie.
◇ *vt* [road] refaire.

resurgence [rɪ'sɜːdʒəns] *n* réapparition *f*, renaissance *f*.

resurgent [rɪ'sɜːdʒənt] *adj* renaissant; **the threat of ~ nationalism** la menace du nationalisme renaissant.

resurrect [ˌrezə'rekt] *vt literal* & *fig* ressusciter; **~ed from the dead** ressuscité des OR d'entre les morts; **they've ~ed this old tradition** ils ont ressuscité cette vieille tradition; **the minister succeeded in ~ing his career** le ministre réussit à faire redémarrer sa carrière OR à donner une nouvelle impulsion à sa carrière.

resurrection [ˌrezə'rekʃn] *n* résurrection *f*; **the Resurrection (of Christ)** la résurrection (du Christ), la Résurrection.

resuscitate [rɪ'sʌsɪteɪt] *vt* ranimer, réanimer.

resuscitation [rɪˌsʌsɪ'teɪʃn] *n* réanimation *f*.

resuscitator [rɪ'sʌsɪteɪtəʳ] *n* [apparatus] respirateur *m*; [person] réanimateur *m*, -trice *f*.

retable [rɪ'teɪbl] *n* retable *m*.

retail ['riːteɪl] ◇ *n* (vente *f* au) détail *m*.
◇ *adj* de détail; **they run a ~ hifi business** ils ont un magasin de matériel hi-fi ❑ **~ goods** marchandises *fpl* vendues au détail; **~ outlet** point *m* de vente (au détail); **the ~ price** le prix de OR au détail; **~ shop** magasin *m* de détail.
◇ *adv* au détail.
◇ *vt* -**1.** COMM vendre au détail. -**2.** *fml* [story, event, experience] raconter; [gossip, scandal] répandre, colporter *pej*.
◇ *vi* [goods] se vendre (au détail); **they ~ at £10 each** ils se vendent à 10 livres la pièce.

retailer ['riːteɪləʳ] *n* détaillant *m*, -e *f*.

retail price index *n Br* indice *m* des prix de détail.

retain [rɪ'teɪn] *vt* -**1.** [keep] garder; **the village has ~ed its charm** le village a conservé son charme. -**2.** [hold, keep in place] retenir; **to ~ heat** retenir la chaleur. -**3.** [remember] retenir, garder en mémoire; **I just can't ~ dates** je suis tout à fait incapable de retenir les dates. -**4.** [reserve - place, hotel room] retenir, réserver. -**5.** [engage - solicitor] engager; **~ing fee** provision *f*.

retainer [rɪ'teɪnəʳ] *n* -**1.** [servant] domestique *mf*, serviteur *m arch*. -**2.** [retaining fee] provision *f*. -**3.** [nominal rent] loyer *m* nominal.

retaining wall [rɪ'teɪnɪŋ-] *n* mur *m* de soutènement.

retake [*vb* ˌriː'teɪk, *n* 'riːteɪk] (*pt* **retook** [-'tʊk], *pp* **retaken** [-'teɪkn]) ◇ *vt* -**1.** [town, fortress] reprendre. -**2.** [exam] repasser. -**3.** CIN [shot] reprendre, refaire; [scene] refaire une prise (de vues) de.
◇ *n* -**1.** [of exam] nouvelle session *f*. -**2.** CIN nouvelle prise *f* (de vues).

retaliate [rɪ'tælɪeɪt] *vi* se venger, riposter; **the government ~d by banning all foreign coal imports** le gouvernement a riposté en interdisant toutes les importations de charbon; **the goalkeeper was sent off for retaliating** le gardien de but a été expulsé pour avoir riposté à l'agression; **she ~d against her critics** elle a riposté à l'attaque de ses critiques.

retaliation [rɪˌtælɪ'eɪʃn] *n (U)* représailles *fpl*, vengeance *f*; **in ~ (for sthg)** en OR par représailles (contre qqch).

retaliatory [rɪ'tælɪətrɪ] *adj* de représailles, de rétorsion; **a ~ attack** une riposte; **to take ~ measures** exercer des représailles, riposter.

retard [rɪ'tɑːd] ◇ *vt fml* OR SCI retarder.
◇ *n Am offensive* retardé *m*, -e *f*.

retardant [rɪ'tɑːdnt] ◇ *n* SCI retardateur *m*.
◇ *adj fml* OR SCI retardateur.

retardation [ˌriːtɑː'deɪʃn] *n* -**1.** [mental] arriération *f*. -**2.** [delaying] retardement *m*.

retarded [rɪ'tɑːdɪd] ◇ *adj* -**1.** [mentally] arriéré. -**2.** [delayed] retardé.
◇ *npl dated*: **the (mentally) ~** les arriérés *mpl* mentaux; **a school for the ~** une école pour enfants arriérés.

retch [retʃ] ◇ *vi* avoir un OR des haut-le-cœur; **the smell made me ~** l'odeur m'a donné des haut-le-cœur OR m'a soulevé l'estomac.
◇ *n* haut-le-cœur *m inv*.

retching ['retʃɪŋ] *n* haut-le-cœur *m inv*.

retd *written abbr of* retired.

retell [ˌriː'tel] (*pt* & *pp* **retold** [-'təʊld]) *vt* raconter de nouveau.

retelling [ˌriː'telɪŋ] *n* nouvelle version *f*; **the story gained in the ~** l'histoire gagnait à être racontée de nouveau.

retention [rɪ'tenʃn] *n* -**1.** [keeping] conservation *f*. -**2.** MED [holding] rétention *f*; **fluid ~** rétention d'eau; **urine ~** rétention d'urine. -**3.** [memory] rétention *f*.

retentive [rɪ'tentɪv] *adj* [memory] qui retient bien; **she's a very ~ pupil** c'est une élève qui a une très bonne mémoire.

retentiveness [rɪ'tentɪvnɪs] *n* mémoire *f*.

retexture [ˌriː'tekstʃəʳ] *vt* apprêter de nouveau.

rethink [*vb* ˌriː'θɪŋk, *n* 'riːθɪŋk] (*pt* & *pp* **rethought** [-'θɔːt]) ◇ *vt* repenser; **we'll have to ~ our strategy** il faudra repenser OR revoir notre stratégie.
◇ *n*: **a ~ of the whole project is necessary** il faut repenser le projet dans son ensemble; **to have a ~ about sthg** réfléchir de nouveau à qqch.

reticence ['retɪsəns] *n* réticence *f*.

reticent ['retɪsənt] *adj* réticent; **he's ~ about explaining his reasons** il hésite OR est peu disposé à expliquer ses raisons.

reticently ['retɪsəntlɪ] *adv* avec réticence.

reticle ['retɪkl] *n* réticule *m*.

reticulate(d) [rɪ'tɪkjʊleɪt(ɪd)] *adj* réticulé.

reticule ['retɪkjuːl] *n* -**1.** [bag] réticule *m*. -**2.** OPT = **reticle**.

reticulum [rɪ'tɪkjʊləm] (*pl* **reticula** [-lə]) *n* réticulum *m*.

retina ['retɪnə] (*pl* **retinas** OR **retinae** [-niː]) *n* rétine *f*.

retinal ['retɪnl] *adj* rétinien.

retinue ['retɪnjuː] *n* suite *f*, cortège *m*.

retire [rɪ'taɪəʳ] ◇ *vi* -**1.** [from job] prendre sa retraite; [from business, politics] se retirer; **to ~ at 65** prendre sa retraite à 65 ans; **to ~ from the political scene** se retirer de la scène politique. -**2.** *fml* OR *hum* [go to bed] aller se coucher. -**3.** [leave] se retirer; **the jury ~d to consider its verdict** les jurés se sont retirés pour délibérer; **shall we ~ to the lounge?** si nous passions au salon?; **to ~ to a monastery** se retirer dans un monastère; **to ~ hurt** SPORT abandonner à la suite d'une blessure. -**4.** MIL [pull back] se replier.
◇ *vt* -**1.** [employee] mettre à la retraite. -**2.** MIL [troops] retirer. -**3.** FIN [coins, bonds, shares] retirer de la circulation.

retired [rɪ'taɪəd] *adj* -**1.** [from job] retraité, à la retraite. -**2.** [secluded] retiré; **to live a ~ life** mener une vie retirée; **a ~ spot** un endroit retiré OR isolé.

retiree [ˌrɪtaɪə'riː] *n Am* retraité *m*, -e *f*.

etirement [rɪ'taɪəmənt] *n* -**1.** [from job] retraite *f*; how do you plan to spend your ~? comment comptez-vous passer votre retraite?; to take early ~ partir en préretraite. -**2.** [seclusion] isolement *m*, solitude *f*. -**3.** MIL [pulling back] repli *m*.

etirement age *n* âge *m* de la retraite.

RETIREMENT AGE:
L'âge de la retraite est actuellement de 65 ans pour les hommes et 60 ans pour les femmes en Grande-Bretagne; aux États-Unis, il est fixé à 65 ans pour les hommes et les femmes.

etirement benefit *n* indemnité *f* de départ en retraite, prime *f* de mise à la retraite.

etirement pay *n* retraite *f*.

etirement pension *n* (pension *f* de) retraite *f*.

etiring [rɪ'taɪərɪŋ] *adj* -**1.** [reserved] réservé. -**2.** [leaving - official, chairman, MP] sortant. -**3.** [employee] qui part à la retraite; to reach ~ age atteindre l'âge de la retraite.

etold [ˌriː'təʊld] *pt* & *pp* → **retell**.

etool [ˌriː'tuːl] ◇ *vt* -**1.** INDUST rééquiper. -**2.** *inf Am* [reorganize] réorganiser.
◇ *vi* -**1.** INDUST se rééquiper. -**2.** *inf Am* [reorganize] se réorganiser.

etort [rɪ'tɔːt] ◇ *vi* & *vt* rétorquer, riposter.
◇ *n* -**1.** [reply] riposte *f*, réplique *f*. -**2.** CHEM cornue *f*.

etouch [ˌriː'tʌtʃ] *vt* [gen & PHOT] retoucher.

etrace [rɪ'treɪs] *vt* -**1.** [go back over - route] refaire; to ~ one's steps rebrousser chemin, revenir sur ses pas. -**2.** [reconstitute - past events, sb's movements] reconstituer.

etract [rɪ'trækt] ◇ *vt* -**1.** [withdraw - statement, confession] retirer, rétracter *lit*; [go back on - promise, agreement] revenir sur. -**2.** [draw in - claws, horns] rétracter, rentrer; AERON [- wheels] rentrer, escamoter.
◇ *vi* -**1.** [recant] se rétracter, se désavouer. -**2.** [be drawn in - claws, horns] se rétracter; AERON [- wheels] rentrer; the undercarriage ~s le train d'atterrissage est escamotable.

etractable [rɪ'træktəbl] *adj* -**1.** [aerial, undercarriage] escamotable. -**2.** [statement] que l'on peut rétracter OR désavouer.

etractile [rɪ'træktaɪl] *adj* rétractile.

etraction [rɪ'trækʃn] *n* [withdrawal of false information] démenti *m*.

etrain [ˌriː'treɪn] ◇ *vt* recycler.
◇ *vi* se recycler.

etraining [ˌriː'treɪnɪŋ] *n* recyclage *m*; a ~ programme un programme de recyclage.

etread [*vb* ˌriː'tred, *n* 'riːtred] (*pt* retrod [-'trɒd], *pp* retrodden [-'trɒdn] OR retrod [-'trɒd])
◇ *vt* AUT rechaper.
◇ *n* pneu *m* rechapé.

etreat [rɪ'triːt] ◇ *vi* -**1.** MIL battre en retraite, se replier; the management was forced to ~ on this point *fig* la direction a été obligée de céder sur ce point. -**2.** [gen] se retirer; we ~ed towards the back of the room nous nous sommes retirés au fond de la salle; to ~ to the country se retirer à la campagne.
◇ *n* -**1.** [MIL & gen - withdrawal] retraite *f*, repli *m*; to beat/to sound the ~ battre/sonner la retraite; this is a considerable ~ from the unions' original position les syndicats ont fait là des concessions importantes par rapport à leur position initiale ❑ to beat a hasty ~ prendre ses jambes à son cou. -**2.** [refuge] refuge *m*, asile *m*; a mountain ~ un refuge de montagne. -**3.** RELIG retraite *f*; to go on a ~ faire une retraite.

retrench [rɪ'trentʃ] ◇ *vt* [costs, expenses] réduire, restreindre.
◇ *vi* faire des économies, se restreindre.

retrenchment [riː'trentʃmənt] *n* [of costs, expenses] réduction *f*, compression *f*.

retrial [ˌriː'traɪəl] *n* nouveau procès *m*.

retribution [ˌretrɪ'bjuːʃn] *n* punition *f*, châtiment *m*; it is divine ~ c'est le châtiment de Dieu.

retributive [rɪ'trɪbjʊtɪv] *adj* [involving punishment] de punition, de châtiment; [avenging] vengeur; they have no ~ powers ils n'ont pas le pouvoir de punir; ~ measures will be taken against the culprits les coupables seront punis.

retrievable [rɪ'triːvəbl] *adj* [object] récupérable; [fortune, health] recouvrable; [error, loss] réparable; [situation] rattrapable.

retrieval [rɪ'triːvl] *n* -**1.** [getting back - of object] récupération *f*; [- of fortune, health] recouvrement *m*. -**2.** COMPUT récupération *f*, extraction *f*; data ~ recherche *f* de données. -**3.** [making good - of mistake] réparation *f*; the situation is beyond ~ il n'y a plus rien à faire (pour sauver la situation).

retrieve [rɪ'triːv] ◇ *vt* -**1.** [get back - lost object] récupérer; [- health, fortune] recouvrer, retrouver; I ~d my bag from the lost property office j'ai récupéré mon sac au bureau des objets trouvés. -**2.** [save] sauver; she managed to ~ her coat from the fire elle réussit à sauver son manteau du feu. -**3.** COMPUT [data] récupérer, extraire. -**4.** [make good - mistake] réparer; [- situation] rattraper, sauver. -**5.** HUNT rapporter.
◇ *vi* HUNT rapporter le gibier.

retriever [rɪ'triːvə^r] *n* [dog] retriever *m*; golden ~ golden retriever *m*.

retro ['retrəʊ] *adj* retro *(inv)*; ~ fashions la mode rétro.

retroact [ˌretrəʊ'ækt] *vi* -**1.** [have retroactive effect] avoir un effet rétroactif, rétroagir *lit*. -**2.** [act in opposition] réagir.

retroaction [ˌretrəʊ'ækʃn] *n* rétroaction *f*.

retroactive [ˌretrəʊ'æktɪv] *adj* rétroactif.

retroactively [ˌretrəʊ'æktɪvlɪ] *adv* rétroactivement.

retrofit ['retrəʊfɪt] (*pt* & *pp* **retrofitted**) *vt* équiper après fabrication.

retroflexed ['retrəʊflekst] *adj* -**1.** LING rétroflexe. -**2.** ANAT rétrofléchi.

retroflexion [ˌretrəʊ'flekʃn] *n* rétroflexion *f*.

retrograde ['retrəgreɪd] ◇ *adj* rétrograde.
◇ *vi* -**1.** [gen] rétrograder. -**2.** *Am* MIL [retreat] battre en retraite.

retrogress ['retrəgres] *vi fml* -**1.** [degenerate] régresser. -**2.** [move backwards] rétrograder.

retrogression [ˌretrə'greʃn] *n* rétrogression *f*, régression *f*.

retrogressive [ˌretrə'gresɪv] *adj* rétrogressif, régressif.

retropack ['retrəʊpæk] *n* système *m* de rétrofusées.

retrorocket ['retrəʊˌrɒkɪt] *n* rétrofusée *f*.

retrospect ['retrəspekt]
◆ **in retrospect** *adv phr* rétrospectivement, avec le recul.

retrospection [ˌretrə'spekʃn] *n* rétrospection *f*.

retrospective [ˌretrə'spektɪv] ◇ *adj* rétrospectif.
◇ *n* ART rétrospective *f*.

retrospectively [ˌretrə'spektɪvlɪ] *adv* rétrospectivement.

retrovirus ['retrəʊˌvaɪrəs] *n* rétrovirus *m*.

retry [ˌriː'traɪ] (*pt* & *pp* **retried**) *vt* JUR refaire le procès de, juger à nouveau.

retsina [ret'siːnə] *n* retsina *m*.

retune [ˌriː'tjuːn] ◇ *vt* -**1.** MUS réaccorder. -**2.** RADIO régler.
◇ *vi* RADIO: listeners in Europe are invited to ~ to medium wave les auditeurs en Europe sont invités à se mettre à l'écoute OR prendre l'écoute sur ondes moyennes; don't forget to ~ tomorrow to the same wavelength n'oubliez pas de reprendre l'écoute demain sur la même longueur d'ondes.

return [rɪ'tɜːn] ◇ *vi* -**1.** [go back] retourner; [come back] revenir; they've ~ed to Australia [speaker is in Australia] ils sont revenus en Australie; [speaker is elsewhere] ils sont retournés OR repartis en Australie; as soon as she ~s dès son retour; to ~ home rentrer (à la maison OR chez soi). -**2.** [to subject, activity, former state] revenir; let's ~ to your question revenons à votre question; when I ~ed to consciousness quand j'ai repris connaissance, quand je suis revenu à moi; to ~ to work reprendre le travail; she ~ed to her reading elle reprit sa lecture; he soon ~ed to his old ways il est vite retombé dans OR il a vite repris ses anciennes habitudes; the situation should ~ to normal next week la situation devrait redevenir normale la semaine prochaine. -**3.** [reappear - fever, pain, good weather, fears] réapparaître.
◇ *vt* -**1.** [give back] rendre; [take back] rapporter; [send back] renvoyer, retourner; the jewels have been ~ed to their rightful owners les bijoux ont été rendus à leurs propriétaires légitimes; I have to ~ the library books today il faut que je rapporte les livres à la bibliothèque aujourd'hui; ~ this coupon for your fabulous free gift renvoyez ce bon pour obtenir votre magnifique cadeau; '~ to sender' 'retour à l'expéditeur'; she ~ed my look elle me regarda à son tour; the soldiers ~ed our fire les soldats répondirent à notre tir. -**2.** [replace, put back] remettre; she ~ed the file to the drawer elle remit le dossier dans le tiroir. -**3.** [repay - greeting, kindness, compliment] rendre (en retour); how can I ~ your favour? comment vous remercier?; they ~ed our visit the following year ils sont venus nous voir à leur tour l'année suivante || [reciprocate - affection] rendre; she did not ~ his love l'amour qu'il éprouvait pour elle n'était pas partagé. -**4.** SPORT [hit or throw back] renvoyer. -**5.** *Br* [elect] élire; she was ~ed as member for Tottenham elle a été élue député de Tottenham. -**6.** [reply] répondre. -**7.** JUR [pronounce - verdict] rendre, prononcer; to ~ a verdict of guilty rendre un verdict de culpabilité. -**8.** FIN [yield - profit, interest] rapporter. -**9.** [in bridge] rejouer; East ~s clubs for dummy's ace Est rejoue pique pour l'as du mort.
◇ *adj* [fare] aller (et) retour; [trip, flight] de retour; the ~ journey le (voyage du) retour.
◇ *n* -**1.** [going or coming back] retour *m*; on her ~ à son retour ❑ the point of no ~ le point de non-retour; 'The Return of the Native' *Hardy* 'le Retour au pays natal'. -**2.** [giving or taking back] retour *m*; [sending back] renvoi *m*, retour *m*; by ~ (of post) *Br* par retour du courrier; on ~ of this coupon sur renvoi de ce bon. -**3.** *Br* [round trip] aller et retour *m*; two ~s to Edinburgh, please deux allers et retours pour Édimbourg, s'il vous plaît; a weekend ~ un billet aller et retour valable du vendredi au dimanche soir. -**4.** [to subject, activity, earlier state] retour *m*; a ~ to normal un retour à la normale; a ~ to traditional methods un retour aux méthodes traditionnelles; the strikers' ~ to work la reprise du travail par les grévistes. -**5.** [reappearance - of fever, pain, good weather] réapparition *f*, retour *m*. -**6.** FIN [yield] rapport *m*; a 10% ~ on investment un rendement de 10 % sur la somme investie. -**7.** [for income tax] (formulaire *m* de) déclaration *f* d'impôts. -**8.** SPORT [esp in tennis] retour *m*. -**9.** ARCHIT retour *m*.
◆ **returns** *npl* -**1.** [results] résultats *mpl*; [statistics] statistiques *fpl*, chiffres *mpl*; the election ~s les résultats des élections; first ~s indicate a swing to the left les premiers résultats du scrutin indiquent un glissement à gauche. -**2.** [birthday greetings]: many happy ~s (of the day)! bon OR joyeux anniversaire!
◆ **in return** *adv phr* en retour, en échange; in ~, he's letting me use his car en retour OR en échange, il me laisse utiliser sa voiture.
◆ **in return for** *prep phr* en échange de.

returnable [rɪ'tɜːnəbl] *adj* -**1.** [container, bottle] consigné. -**2.** [document] à retourner; ~ by July 1st à renvoyer avant le 1er juillet.

returner [rɪ'tɜːnə^r] *n* [person returning to work] *personne réintégrant la vie professionnelle après une période d'inactivité volontaire*.

returning officer [rɪ'tɜːnɪŋ-] *n* président *m*, -e *f* du bureau de vote.

return match *n* match *m* retour.

return ticket *n Br* (billet *m* d') aller (et) retour *m*.
retype [ˌriːˈtaɪp] *vt* [document, text] retaper.
reuben [ˈruːbɪn] *n Am* CULIN *sandwich chaud au pastrami, corned beef et fromage*.
reunification [ˌriːjuːnɪfɪˈkeɪʃn] *n* réunification *f*.
reunify [ˌriːˈjuːnɪfaɪ] (*pt* & *pp* **reunified**) *vt* réunifier.
reunion [ˌriːˈjuːnjən] *n* réunion *f*; a family ~ une réunion familiale.
Reunion [riːˈjuːnjən] *pr n*: ~ **(Island)** (l'île *f* de) la Réunion; in ~ à la Réunion.
reunite [ˌriːjuːˈnaɪt] ◇ *vt* réunir; **when the hostages were ~d with their families** quand les otages ont retrouvé leur famille.
◇ *vi* se réunir.
reupholster [ˌriːʌpˈhəʊlstəʳ] *vt* rembourrer (de nouveau).
reusable [riːˈjuːzəbl] *adj* réutilisable, recyclable.
re-use [*vb* ˌriːˈjuːz, *n* ˌriːˈjuːs] ◇ *vt* réutiliser, remployer, recycler.
◇ *n* réutilisation *f*, remploi *m*, recyclage *m*.
rev *inf* [rev] (*pt* & *pp* **revved**, *cont* **revving**) ◇ *n* (*abbr of* **revolution**) AUT tour *m*; **3,000 ~s per minute** 3000 tours par minute.
◇ *vt* & *vi* = **rev up**.
◆ **rev up** *inf* ◇ *vt sep* [engine] emballer.
◇ *vi insep* [driver] appuyer sur l'accélérateur; [engine] s'accélérer.
revaccinate [ˌriːˈvæksɪneɪt] *vt* revacciner.
revaluate [ˌriːˈvæljʊeɪt] *Am* = **revalue**.
revaluation [ˌriːvæljʊˈeɪʃn] *n* [of currency, property etc] réévaluation *f*.
revalue [ˌriːˈvæljuː] *vt* -**1.** [currency] réévaluer. -**2.** [property] réévaluer, estimer à nouveau la valeur de.
revamp *inf* [ˌriːˈvæmp] *vt* rafistoler, retaper.
revanchism [rɪˈvæntʃɪzm] *n* revanchisme *m*.
revanchist [rɪˈvæntʃɪst] ◇ *adj* revanchiste.
◇ *n* revanchiste *mf*.
rev counter *inf n* compte-tours *m inv*.
Revd *written abbr of* **reverend**.
reveal [rɪˈviːl] *vt* -**1.** [disclose, divulge] révéler; **the press ~ed he had accepted bribes** la presse révéla qu'il avait accepté des pots-de-vin; **to ~ a secret** révéler OR divulguer un secret. -**2.** [show] révéler, découvrir, laisser voir; **she removed the veil to ~ her face** elle enleva son voile pour découvrir son visage; **he tried hard not to ~ his true feelings** il s'efforça de ne pas révéler ses vrais sentiments; **the undertaking ~ed itself to be impossible** l'entreprise s'est révélée impossible.
revealing [rɪˈviːlɪŋ] *adj* -**1.** [experience, action, remark] révélateur. -**2.** [dress] décolleté, qui ne cache rien; [neckline] décolleté.
revealingly [rɪˈviːlɪŋlɪ] *adv* -**1.** [significantly]: **~, not one of them speaks a foreign language** il est révélateur qu'aucun d'entre eux ne parle une langue étrangère. -**2.** [exposing the body]: **a ~ short dress** une robe courte qui laisse tout voir OR qui montre tout.
reveille [*Br* rɪˈvælɪ, *Am* ˈrevəlɪ] *n* MIL réveil *m*; **sound the ~!** sonnez le réveil!
revel [ˈrevl] (*Br pt* & *pp* **revelled**, *cont* **revelling**, *Am pt* & *pp* **reveled**, *cont* **reveling**) *vi* -**1.** [bask, wallow] se délecter; **to ~ in sthg** se délecter de OR à qqch. -**2.** [make merry] s'amuser.
◆ **revels** *npl* festivités *fpl*.
revelation [ˌrevəˈleɪʃn] *n* révélation *f*; **divine ~** révélation divine; **her talent was a ~ to me** son talent a été une révélation pour moi ❑ **the Revelation (of Saint John the Divine), Revelations** l'Apocalypse *f* (de saint Jean l'Évangéliste).
revelatory [ˌrevəˈleɪtərɪ] *adj* révélateur.
reveller *Br*, **reveler** *Am* [ˈrevələʳ] *n* fêtard *m*, -e *f*, noceur *m*, -euse *f*.
revelry [ˈrevəlrɪ] *n* , **revelries** *npl* festivités *fpl*.
revenge [rɪˈvendʒ] ◇ *n* -**1.** [vengeance] vengeance *f*, revanche *f*; **I'll get** OR **I'll take my ~ on him for this!** il va me le payer!; **she did it out of ~** elle l'a fait pour se venger OR par vengeance. -**2.** SPORT revanche *f*.
◇ *vt* venger; **how can I ~ myself on them for this insult?** comment leur faire payer cette insulte?
revengeful [rɪˈvendʒfʊl] *adj* vengeur, vindicatif.
revengefully [rɪˈvendʒfʊlɪ] *adv* vindicativement, par vengeance.
revenger [rɪˈvendʒəʳ] *n* vengeur *m*, -eresse *f*.
revenue [ˈrevənjuː] ◇ *n* revenu *m*; **state ~** OR **~s** les revenus publics OR de l'État.
◇ *comp* [department, official] du fisc.
revenue bond *n* obligation *f* d'État *(remboursable par le revenu du projet qu'elle finance)*.
revenue cutter *n* vedette *f* des garde-côtes.
revenue man *n* agent *m* du fisc.
revenue stamp *n* timbre *m* fiscal.
revenue tariff *n* tarif *m* douanier fiscal.
reverberate [rɪˈvɜːbəreɪt] ◇ *vi* -**1.** [sound] résonner, retentir; **the building ~d with their cries** l'immeuble retentissait de leurs cris. -**2.** [light] se réverbérer. -**3.** *fig* [spread] retentir; **the scandal ~d through the country** ce scandale a secoué tout le pays.
◇ *vt* -**1.** [sound] renvoyer, répercuter. -**2.** [light] réverbérer.
reverberation [rɪˌvɜːbəˈreɪʃn] *n* -**1.** [of sound] retentissement *m*, résonnement *m*. -**2.** [of light] réverbération *f*. -**3.** *fig* [repercussion] retentissement *m*, répercussion *f*; **the crisis had ~s in neighbouring countries** la crise a eu des répercussions dans les pays voisins.
reverberator [rɪˈvɜːbəreɪtəʳ] *n* réflecteur *m*.
revere [rɪˈvɪəʳ] *vt* révérer, vénérer; **she was a much ~d figure** c'était une personnalité très respectée.
reverence [ˈrevərəns] ◇ *n* -**1.** [respect] révérence *f*, vénération *f*; **they hold her in ~** ils la révèrent OR vénèrent. -**2.** [term of address]: **Your Reverence** mon révérend (Père); **His Reverence the Archbishop** Son Excellence l'archevêque.
◇ *vt* révérer, vénérer.
reverend [ˈrevərənd] ◇ *adj* -**1.** RELIG: **a ~ gentleman** un révérend père; **the Reverend Paul James** le révérend Paul James. -**2.** [gen - respected] vénérable, révéré.
◇ *n* [Protestant] pasteur *m*; [Catholic] curé *m*; **yes, ~** [Protestant] oui, Monsieur le pasteur; [Catholic] oui, Monsieur le curé.
Reverend Mother *n* Révérende Mère *f*.
reverent [ˈrevərənt] *adj* respectueux, révérencieux *lit*.
reverential [ˌrevəˈrenʃl] *adj* révérenciel.
reverently [ˈrevərəntlɪ] *adv* avec révérence, révérencieusement *lit*.
reverie [ˈrevərɪ] *n lit* [gen & MUS] rêverie *f*.
revers [rɪˈvɪəʳ] (*pl inv* [rɪˈvɪəz]) *n* revers *m*.
reversal [rɪˈvɜːsl] *n* -**1.** [change - of situation, tendency] retournement *m*; [- of opinion] revirement *m*; [- of order, roles] interversion *f*, inversion *f*; **a complete ~ of policy** un changement total de politique. -**2.** [setback] revers *m*; **~ of fortune** revers de fortune; **the patient has suffered a ~** le malade a fait une rechute. -**3.** JUR [annulment] annulation *f*. -**4.** PHOT inversion *f*.
reversal film *n* film *m* inversible.
reverse [rɪˈvɜːs] ◇ *vt* -**1.** [change - process, trend] renverser; [- situation] retourner; [- order, roles, decline] inverser; **this could ~ the effects of all our policies** ceci pourrait annuler les effets de toute notre politique; **the unions have ~d their policy** les syndicats ont fait volte-face; **I had to ~ my opinion of him** j'ai dû réviser complètement l'opinion que j'avais de lui; **it ~d all our plans** cela a bouleversé tous nos projets. -**2.** [turn round - garment] retourner; [- photo] inverser. -**3.** [annul - decision] annuler; JUR casser, annuler. -**4.** [cause to go backwards - car] mettre en marche arrière; [- machine] renverser la marche de; **this lever ~s the belt** ce levier permet d'inverser la marche de la courroie; **she ~d the car up the street** elle remonta la rue en marche arrière; **he ~d the truck into a lamp-post** en faisant marche arrière avec le camion il est rentré dans un réverbère. -**5.** TELEC **to ~ the charges** appeler en PCV; **she always ~s the charges when she phones her parents** elle appelle toujours ses parents en PCV.
◇ *vi* AUT [car, driver] faire marche arrière; **she ~d up the street** elle remonta la rue en marche arrière; **the driver in front ~d into me** la voiture qui était devant moi m'est rentrée dedans en marche arrière.
◇ *n* -**1.** AUT marche *f* arrière; **in ~** en marche arrière; **he put the bus into ~** le conducteur de l'autobus passa en marche arrière; **the company's fortunes are going into ~** *fig* l'entreprise connaît actuellement un revers de fortune. -**2.** [contrary] contraire *m*, inverse *m*, opposé *m*; **unfortunately, the ~ is true** malheureusement, c'est le contraire qui est vrai; **did you enjoy it? — quite the ~** cela vous a-t-il plu? — pas du tout; **she is the ~ of shy** elle est tout sauf timide; **try to do the same thing in ~** essayez de faire la même chose dans l'ordre inverse. -**3.** [other side - of cloth, leaf] envers *m*; [- of sheet of paper] verso *m*; [- of coin, medal] revers *m*. -**4.** [setback] revers *m*, échec *m*; [defeat] défaite *f*; **his condition has suffered a ~** il a rechuté. -**5.** TYPO noir *m* au blanc; **in ~** en réserve.
◇ *adj* -**1.** [opposite, contrary] inverse, contraire, opposé; **we are now experiencing the ~ trend** actuellement, c'est l'inverse qui se produit; **in ~ order** en ordre inverse; **in the ~ direction** en sens inverse. -**2.** [back]: **the ~ side** [of cloth, leaf] l'envers; [of sheet of paper] le verso; [of coin, medal] le revers. -**3.** [turned around] inversé; **a ~ image** une image inversée. -**4.** AUT: **~ gear** marche *f* arrière.
reverse-charge call *n Br* appel *m* en PCV.
reverser [rɪˈvɜːsəʳ] *n* TECH inverseur *m*; **thrust ~** inverseur de poussée.
reverse video *n* vidéo *f* inverse.
reversi [rɪˈvɜːsɪ] *n* reversi *m* (sur échiquier).
reversible [rɪˈvɜːsəbl] *adj* [coat, process] réversible; [decision] révocable.
reversing light [rɪˈvɜːsɪŋ-] *n* feu *m* de recul.
reversion [rɪˈvɜːʃn] *n* -**1.** [to former condition, practice] retour *m*; **a ~ to anarchy** un retour à l'anarchie. -**2.** BIOL & JUR réversion *f*.
revert [rɪˈvɜːt] *vi* retourner, revenir; **they ~ed to barbarism** ils ont à nouveau sombré dans la barbarie; **he soon ~ed to his old ways** il est vite retombé dans OR il a vite repris ses anciennes habitudes; **to ~ to childhood** retomber en enfance; **the field has ~ed to a wild meadow** le champ est retourné à l'état de prairie; **the property ~s to the spouse** JUR les biens reviennent à l'époux; **to ~ to type** retrouver sa vraie nature.
revetment [rɪˈvetmənt] *n* mur *m* de soutènement.
review [rɪˈvjuː] ◇ *n* -**1.** [critical article] critique *f*; **the play got good/bad ~s** la pièce a eu de bonnes/mauvaises critiques. -**2.** [magazine] revue *f*; [radio or TV programme] magazine *m*. -**3.** [assessment - of situation, conditions] étude *f*, examen *m*, bilan *m*; **the annual ~ of expenditure** le bilan annuel des dépenses; **she first gave us a brief ~ of the situation** elle nous a d'abord présenté un court bilan de la situation; **pollution controls are under ~** on est en train d'examiner la réglementation en matière de pollution; **~ board** commission *f* d'étude. -**4.** [reassessment - of salary, prices, case] révision *f*; **all our prices are subject to ~** tous nos prix sont susceptibles d'être révisés; **my salary comes** OR **is up for ~ next month** mon salaire doit être révisé le mois prochain; **he asked for a ~ of his case** JUR il a demandé la révision de son procès. -**5.** MIL [inspection] revue *f*. -**6.** *Am* SCH & UNIV [revision] révision *f*. -**7.** = **revue**.
◇ *vt* -**1.** [write critical article on] faire la critique de; **she ~s books for an Australian paper** elle

est critique littéraire pour un journal australien. -**2.** [assess] examiner, étudier, faire le bilan de; [reassess] réviser, revoir; JUR [case] réviser; **they should ~ their security arrangements** ils devraient revoir leurs dispositifs de sécurité; **to ~ a decision** reconsidérer une décision. -**3.** [go back over, look back on] passer en revue; **we shall be ~ing the events of the past year** nous passerons en revue les événements qui se sont produits au cours de l'année passée. -**4.** MIL [troops] passer en revue. -**5.** [revise] réviser; **she quickly ~ed her notes before the speech** elle jeta un dernier coup d'œil sur ses notes avant le discours; **he's ~ing his French** *Am* il révise son français.

eview copy *n* exemplaire *m* de service de presse.

eviewer [rɪ'vjuːəʳ] *n* PRESS critique *m*; **book ~** critique littéraire.

evile [rɪ'vaɪl] *vt lit* vilipender, injurier; **our much ~d education system** notre système scolaire tellement décrié OR dont on dit tant de mal.

evise [rɪ'vaɪz] ◇ *vt* -**1.** [alter - policy, belief, offer, price] réviser. -**2.** [read through - text, manuscript] revoir, corriger. -**3.** [update] mettre à jour, corriger; **our dictionaries are ~d regularly** nos dictionnaires sont régulièrement mis à jour. -**4.** *Br* SCH & UNIV réviser; **have you ~d your geography?** as-tu révisé ta géographie?
◇ *vi Br* SCH & UNIV réviser; **she's revising for her end-of-year exams** elle révise pour ses examens de fin d'année.
◇ *n* TYPO deuxième épreuve *f*.

revised [rɪ'vaɪzd] *adj* -**1.** [figures, estimate] révisé. -**2.** [edition] revu et corrigé.

Revised Version *n*: **the ~** *traduction anglaise de la Bible faite en 1885*.

reviser [rɪ'vaɪzəʳ] *n* [gen] réviseur *m*, -euse *f*; TYPO correcteur *m*, -trice *f*.

revision [rɪ'vɪʒn] *n* -**1.** [alteration etc] révision *f*; **the book has undergone several ~s** ce livre a été révisé OR remanié plusieurs fois. -**2.** *Br* SCH & UNIV révision *f*.

revisionism [rɪ'vɪʒnɪzm] *n* révisionnisme *m*.

revisionist [rɪ'vɪʒnɪst] ◇ *adj* révisionniste.
◇ *n* révisionniste *mf*.

revisit [ˌriː'vɪzɪt] *vt* [place] revisiter; [person] retourner voir; **Dickens ~ed** *fig* un réexamen de Dickens ❑ **'Brideshead Revisited'** *Waugh* 'le Retour au château'.

revitalize, -ise [ˌriː'vaɪtəlaɪz] *vt* revitaliser.

revival [rɪ'vaɪvl] *n* -**1.** [resurgence] renouveau *m*, renaissance *f*; **a ~ of interest in Latin poets** un regain d'intérêt pour les poètes latins; **a Catholic ~** un renouveau du catholicisme. -**2.** [bringing back - of custom, language] rétablissement *m*; **they would like to see a ~ of Victorian values** ils souhaitent le retour aux valeurs de l'époque victorienne. -**3.** [of play, TV series] reprise *f*. -**4.** [from a faint] reprise *f* de connaissance; [from illness] récupération *f*.

revivalism [rɪ'vaɪvəlɪzm] *n* -**1.** RELIG revivalisme *m*. -**2.** [of past] passéisme *m*.

revivalist [rɪ'vaɪvəlɪst] ◇ *n* -**1.** RELIG revivaliste *mf*; **Hindu ~s** des revivalistes hindous. -**2.** [of past] traditionaliste *mf*.
◇ *adj* RELIG revivaliste; **a ~ meeting** une réunion revivaliste.

revive [rɪ'vaɪv] ◇ *vi* -**1.** [regain consciousness] reprendre connaissance, revenir à soi; [regain strength or form] récupérer. -**2.** [flourish again - business, the economy] reprendre; [- movement, group] renaître, ressusciter; [- custom, expression] réapparaître; **their interest ~d when the clowns came on** ils ont recommencé à trouver le spectacle intéressant quand les clowns sont entrés en scène; **interest in her work is beginning to ~** on assiste à un renouveau OR regain d'intérêt pour son œuvre.
◇ *vt* -**1.** [restore to consciousness] ranimer; MED réanimer; [restore strength to] remonter. -**2.** [make flourish again - discussion, faith, memory] ranimer, raviver; [- business, the economy] relancer, faire redémarrer; [- interest, hope, fear] raviver, faire renaître; **a plan to ~ the city centre** un projet destiné à dynamiser le centre-ville; **~d interest in the art of this period** un renouveau OR regain d'intérêt pour l'art de cette époque. -**3.** [bring back - law] remettre en vigueur; [- fashion] relancer; [- style, look] remettre en vogue; [- custom, language, movement] raviver, ressusciter; **prewar fashions have been ~d** on est revenu à la mode de l'avant-guerre. -**4.** [play, TV series] reprendre.

revivify [riː'vɪvɪfaɪ] *vt* revivifier.

revocation [ˌrevə'keɪʃn] *n* [of decision] annulation *f*; [of measure, law] abrogation *f*, annulation *f*, révocation *f*; [of will] révocation *f*, annulation *f*; [of title, diploma, permit, right] retrait *m*.

revoke [rɪ'vəʊk] *vt* [decision] annuler; [measure, law] abroger, annuler, révoquer; [will] révoquer, annuler; [title, diploma, permit, right] retirer.

revolt [rɪ'vəʊlt] ◇ *vi* [rise up] se révolter, se rebeller, se soulever; **they ~ed against the tyrant** ils se soulevèrent contre le tyran.
◇ *vt* dégoûter; **she is ~ed by the idea** l'idée la dégoûte OR la révolte; **the sight of food ~s me at the moment** la vue de la nourriture m'écœure OR me dégoûte en ce moment.
◇ *n* -**1.** [uprising] révolte *f*, rébellion *f*; **the peasants rose up in ~** les paysans se sont révoltés OR soulevés; **they are in ~ against the system** ils se rebellent contre le système. -**2.** [disgust] dégoût *m*; [indignation] indignation *f*.

revolting [rɪ'vəʊltɪŋ] *adj* -**1.** [disgusting - story, scene] dégoûtant; [- person, act] ignoble; [- food, mess] écœurant, immonde. -**2.** *inf* [nasty] affreux.

revoltingly [rɪ'vəʊltɪŋlɪ] *adv* de façon dégoûtante; **he's ~ ugly/dirty** il est d'une laideur/d'une saleté repoussante ‖ [as intensifier]: **she's so ~ clever!** ça m'écœure qu'on puisse être aussi intelligent!

revolution [ˌrevə'luːʃn] *n* -**1.** POL & *fig* révolution *f*; **a ~ in computer technology** une révolution dans le domaine de l'informatique. -**2.** [turn] révolution *f*, tour *m*; [turning] révolution *f*; **100 ~s per minute** TECH 100 tours OR révolutions par minute.

revolutionary [ˌrevə'luːʃnərɪ] (*pl* **revolutionaries**) ◇ *adj* révolutionnaire.
◇ *n* révolutionnaire *mf*.

revolutionist [ˌrevə'luːʃənɪst] = **revolutionary**.

revolutionize, -ise [ˌrevə'luːʃənaɪz] *vt* -**1.** [change radically] révolutionner. -**2.** POL [country] faire une révolution dans; [people] insuffler des idées révolutionnaires à.

revolve [rɪ'vɒlv] ◇ *vi* -**1.** [rotate] tourner; **the moon ~s around** OR **round the earth** la Lune tourne autour de la Terre; **couples ~d slowly on the dance floor** des couples évoluaient OR tournaient lentement sur la piste de danse. -**2.** [centre, focus] tourner; **their conversation ~d around** OR **round two main points** leur conversation tournait autour de deux points principaux; **everything ~s around your decision**; tout dépend de votre décision; **his whole life ~s around his work** sa vie tout entière est centrée OR axée sur son travail. -**3.** [recur] revenir; **the seasons ~** les saisons se succèdent; **ideas ~d in her mind** elle tournait et retournait des idées dans sa tête.
◇ *vt* -**1.** [rotate] faire tourner. -**2.** *fml* [ponder] considérer, ruminer; **he ~d the arguments in his mind** il passait mentalement les différents arguments en revue.

revolver [rɪ'vɒlvəʳ] *n* revolver *m*.

revolving [rɪ'vɒlvɪŋ] *adj* [gen] tournant; [chair] pivotant; TECH rotatif; ASTRON en rotation; **~ light** [on ambulance, police car] gyrophare *m*.

revolving credit *n* crédit *m* documentaire renouvelable, crédit *m* revolving.

revolving door *n* tambour *m (porte)*.

revolving fund *n* fonds *m* renouvelable.

revue [rɪ'vjuː] *n* revue *f* THÉÂT.

revulsion [rɪ'vʌlʃn] *n* -**1.** [disgust] répulsion *f*, dégoût *m*; **she turned away in ~** elle s'est détournée, dégoûtée. -**2.** [recoiling] (mouvement *m* de) recul *m*. -**3.** MED révulsion *f*.

reward [rɪ'wɔːd] ◇ *n* récompense *f*; **they're offering a $500 ~** ils offrent 500 dollars de récompense OR une récompense de 500 dollars; **as a ~ for his efforts** en récompense de ses efforts; **I do everything for him, and what do I get in ~?** je fais tout pour lui, et tu vois comment il me remercie?; **she gave it to me as a ~ for helping her** elle me l'a donnée pour me remercier de l'avoir aidée.
◇ *vt* récompenser; **he was handsomely ~ed with a cheque for £1,000** on l'a généreusement récompensé par un chèque de 1 000 livres; **our patience has finally been ~ed** notre patience est enfin récompensée; **I'm sure the book will ~ your attention** je suis sûr que la lecture de ce livre vous sera profitable; **his alibi might ~ investigation** ça vaut peut-être la peine d'enquêter sur son alibi.

rewarding [rɪ'wɔːdɪŋ] *adj* gratifiant; **a very ~ experience/career** une expérience/carrière très gratifiante; **the conference was most ~** le colloque était très enrichissant; **financially ~** rémunérateur, lucratif.

rewind [*vb* ˌriː'waɪnd, *n* 'riːwaɪnd] (*pt* & *pp* **rewound** [-'waʊnd]) ◇ *vt* rembobiner.
◇ *vi* se rembobiner.
◇ *n* rembobinage *m*; **it has automatic ~** ça se rembobine automatiquement; **~ button** bouton *m* de rembobinage.

rewire [ˌriː'waɪəʳ] *vt* [house] refaire l'électricité dans; [machine] refaire les circuits électriques de; **we had to get the place ~d** nous avons dû faire refaire l'électricité.

reword [ˌriː'wɜːd] *vt* reformuler.

rework [ˌriː'wɜːk] *vt* -**1.** [speech, text] retravailler; **his last novel ~s the same theme** son dernier roman reprend le même thème. -**2.** INDUST retraiter.

reworking [ˌriː'wɜːkɪŋ] *n* reprise *f*; **the film is a ~ of the "doppelgänger" theme** le film reprend le thème du double.

rewound [ˌriː'waʊnd] *pt* & *pp* → **rewind**.

rewrap [ˌriː'ræp] (*pt* & *pp* **rewrapped**, *cont* **rewrapping**) *vt* remballer.

rewrite [*vb* ˌriː'raɪt, *n* 'riːraɪt] (*pt* **rewrote** [-'rəʊt], *pp* **rewritten** [-'rɪtn]) ◇ *vt* récrire, réécrire; [for publication] récrire, rewriter.
◇ *n* -**1.** *inf* [act] réécriture *f*, rewriting *m*; **can you do a ~ job on this?** pouvez-vous me récrire OR rewriter ça? -**2.** [text] nouvelle version *f*; **it's a modern ~ of Romeo and Juliet** c'est une version moderne de Roméo et Juliette.

rewrite rule *n* règle *f* de réécriture.

rewritten [ˌriː'rɪtn] *pp* → **rewrite**.

rewrote [ˌriː'rəʊt] *pt* → **rewrite**.

Rex [reks] *n Br*: **Edward/George ~** le roi Édouard/Georges, Édouard/Georges Roi; **~ v Gibson** JUR la Couronne contre Gibson.

REX (*abbr of* **real-time executive routine**) *n superviseur en temps réel*.

Reykjavik ['rekjəvɪk] *pr n* Reykjavik.

RF *n abbr of* **radio frequency**.

RFC (*written abbr of* **Rugby Football Club**) *n club de rugby*.

RGN (*abbr of* **registered general nurse**) *n Br* infirmier *m* diplômé, infirmière *f* diplômée d'État *(remplacé en 1992 par RN)*.

Rh (*written abbr of* **rhesus**) Rh.

rhapsodic [ræp'sɒdɪk] *adj* -**1.** [ecstatic] extatique; [full of praise] dithyrambique. -**2.** MUS rhapsodique, rapsodique.

rhapsodize, -ise ['ræpsədaɪz] *vi* s'extasier; **to ~ about sthg** s'extasier sur qqch.

rhapsody ['ræpsədɪ] (*pl* **rhapsodies**) *n* -**1.** [ecstasy] extase *f*; **to go into rhapsodies about sthg** s'extasier sur qqch. -**2.** MUS & LITERAT rhapsodie *f*, rapsodie *f*.

rhea ['riːə] *n* nandou *m*.

Rheims [riːmz] *pr n* Reims.

rheme [riːm] *n* commentaire *m*; LING rhème *m*.

Rhenish ['riːnɪʃ] ◇ *adj* rhénan, du Rhin; ~ wine vin *m* du Rhin.
◇ *n* vin *m* du Rhin.
rhenium ['riːnɪəm] *n* rhénium *m*.
rheostat ['riːəstæt] *n* rhéostat *m*.
rhesus baby ['riːsəs-] *n* bébé *m* Rhésus.
rhesus factor *n* facteur *m* Rhésus.
rhesus monkey *n* rhésus *m* ZOOL.
rhesus negative *adj* Rhésus négatif.
rhesus positive *adj* Rhésus positif.
rhetoric ['retərɪk] *n* rhétorique *f*.
rhetorical [rɪ'tɒrɪkl] *adj* rhétorique; **his question was purely ~** sa question était purement rhétorique.
rhetorically [rɪ'tɒrɪklɪ] *adv* en rhétoricien; **"who knows?", she asked ~** «qui sait?», demanda-t-elle sans vraiment attendre de réponse; **I was only asking ~** je demandais ça simplement pour la forme.
rhetorical question *n* question *f* posée pour la forme.
rhetorician [,retə'rɪʃn] *n* [speaker] rhétoricien *m*, -enne *f*, rhéteur *m pej*; [teacher of rhetoric] rhéteur *m*.
rheum [ruːm] *n* chassie *f*.
rheumatic [ruː'mætɪk] ◇ *adj* [symptom] rhumatismal; [person] rhumatisant; [limbs] atteint de rhumatismes; **his ~ fingers** ses doigts déformés par les rhumatismes.
◇ *n* rhumatisant *m*, -e *f*.
rheumatic fever *n* rhumatisme *m* articulaire aigu.
rheumaticky *inf* [ruː'mætɪkɪ] *adj* [person] rhumatisant; [limbs] atteint de rhumatismes.
rheumatics *inf* [ruː'mætɪks] *npl* rhumatismes *mpl*.
rheumatism ['ruːmətɪzm] *n* rhumatisme *m*.
rheumatoid ['ruːmətɔɪd] *adj* rhumatoïde.
rheumatoid arthritis *n* polyarthrite *f* rhumatoïde.
rheumatologist [,ruːmə'tɒlədʒɪst] *n* rhumatologue *mf*.
rheumatology [,ruːmə'tɒlədʒɪ] *n* rhumatologie *f*.
rheumy ['ruːmɪ] (*compar* rheumier, *superl* rheumiest) *adj* chassieux.
Rh factor = **rhesus factor**.
Rhine [raɪn] *pr n*: **the (River) ~** le Rhin.
Rhineland ['raɪnlænd] *pr n* Rhénanie *f*.
Rhineland-Palatinate *pr n* Rhénanie-Palatinat *f*.
rhinestone ['raɪnstəʊn] *n* caillou *m* du Rhin.
Rhine wine *n* vin *m* du Rhin.
rhino ['raɪnəʊ] (*pl inv* OR **rhinos**) *n* rhinocéros *m*.
rhinoceros [raɪ'nɒsərəs] (*pl inv* OR **rhinoceroses** OR **rhinoceri** [-raɪ]) *n* rhinocéros *m*.
rhinoplasty ['raɪnəʊ,plæstɪ] *n* rhinoplastie *f*.
rhizome ['raɪzəʊm] *n* rhizome *m*.
Rh-negative = **rhesus negative**.
Rhode Island [rəʊd-] *pr n* Rhode Island *m*; **in ~** dans le Rhode Island.
Rhode Island Red *n* poule *f* Rhode-Island.
Rhodes [rəʊdz] *pr n* Rhodes; **in ~** à Rhodes; **the Colossus of ~** le colosse de Rhodes.
Rhodesia [rəʊ'diːʃə] *pr n* Rhodésie *f*; **in ~** en Rhodésie; **Northern/Southern ~** Rhodésie du Nord/du Sud.
Rhodesian [rəʊ'diːʃn] ◇ *n* Rhodésien *m*, -enne *f*.
◇ *adj* rhodésien.
Rhodesian man *n* l'homme *m* de Rhodésie.
rhodium ['rəʊdɪəm] *n* rhodium.
rhododendron [,rəʊdə'dendrən] *n* rhododendron *m*.
rhomb [rɒm] = **rhombus**.
rhombic ['rɒmbɪk] *adj* **-1.** GEOM rhombique. **-2.** MINER [crystal] orthorhombique.
rhombic aerial *n* antenne *f* rhombique.
rhomboid ['rɒmbɔɪd] ◇ *n* parallélogramme *m* *(dont les côtés adjacents sont inégaux)*.
◇ *adj* rhomboïdal, rhombiforme.

rhombus ['rɒmbəs] (*pl* rhombuses OR rhombi [-baɪ]) *n* losange *m*.
Rhône [rəʊn] *pr n*: **the (River) ~** le Rhône; **the ~ glacier** le glacier du Rhône.
Rh-positive = **rhesus positive**.
rhubarb ['ruːbɑːb] *n* **-1.** BOT rhubarbe *f*. **-2.** THEAT brouhaha *m*, murmures *mpl*. **-3.** ▽ *Am* [squabble] chamailleries *fpl*, engueulade *f*.
rhyme [raɪm] ◇ *n* **-1.** [sound] rime *f*; **the use of ~** l'emploi de la rime; **give me a ~ for "mash"** trouve-moi un mot qui rime avec «mash» ❑ **without ~ or reason** sans rime ni raison; **their demands have neither ~ nor reason** leurs revendications ne riment à rien. **-2.** *(U)* [poetry] vers *mpl*; **in ~** en vers. **-3.** [poem] poème *m*; **I've made up a ~ about you** j'ai composé un petit poème sur toi.
◇ *vi* **-1.** [word, lines] rimer; **what ~s with "orange"?** qu'est-ce qui rime avec «orange»? **-2.** [write verse] écrire OR composer des poèmes.
◇ *vt* faire rimer; **you can't ~ "lost" with "host"** on ne peut pas faire rimer «lost» avec «host».
rhymed [raɪmd] *adj* rimé; **~ verse** vers *mpl* rimés.
rhymer ['raɪmə^r] = **rhymester**.
rhyme royal *n* septain *m (dont le schéma des rimes est ABABBCC)*.
rhyme scheme *n* combinaison *f* de rimes.
rhymester ['raɪmstə^r] *n pej* rimeur *m*, -euse *f*, rimailleur *m*, -euse *f*.
rhyming dictionary ['raɪmɪŋ-] *n* dictionnaire *m* de rimes.
rhyming slang *n sorte d'argot qui consiste à remplacer un mot par un groupe de mots choisis pour la rime.*

RHYMING SLANG:
Ce type d'argot est traditionnellement employé par les «Cockneys», mais certaines expressions sont passées dans la langue courante. Exemples: «pork pie» (lie); «brown bread» (dead).

---

rhythm ['rɪðm] *n* rythme *m*; **she's got ~** elle a le sens du rythme.
rhythm and blues *n* rhythm and blues *m*.
rhythm guitar *n* guitare *f* rythmique.
rhythmic(al) ['rɪðmɪk(l)] *adj* rythmique; **~ structure/movement** structure *f*/mouvement *m* rythmique; **the ~ rattling of the train** le bruit régulier du train; **Greek music is less ~** la musique grecque est moins rythmée.
rhythmically ['rɪðmɪklɪ] *adv* rythmiquement; **they swayed ~ with the music** ils se balançaient au rythme de la musique.
rhythm method *n* méthode *f* des températures.
rhythm section *n* section *f* rythmique.
RI ◇ *n abbr of* religious instruction.
◇ *written abbr of* Rhode Island.
rial [rɪ'ɑːl] *n* rial *m*.
rib [rɪb] (*pt & pp* **ribbed**, *cont* **ribbing**) ◇ *n* **-1.** ANAT côte *f*; **he dug** OR **he poked her in the ~s** il lui a donné un petit coup de coude ❑ **floating ~** côte flottante; **true/false ~** vraie/fausse côte. **-2.** CULIN côte *f*; **~ of beef** côte de bœuf; **barbecued spare ~s** travers *mpl* de porc grillés sauce barbecue. **-3.** [of vault, leaf, aircraft or insect wing] nervure *f*; [of ship's hull] couple *m*, membre *m*; [of umbrella] baleine *f*. **-4.** [in knitting] côte *f*. **-5.** [on mountain - spur] éperon *m*; [- crest] arête *f*. **-6.** [vein of ore] veine *f*, filon *m*.
◇ *vt inf* [tease] taquiner, mettre en boîte.
RIBA *pr n abbr of* Royal Institute of British Architects.
ribald ['rɪbəld] *adj lit* [joke, language] grivois, paillard; [laughter] égrillard.
ribaldry ['rɪbəldrɪ] *n lit* paillardises *fpl*, grivoiserie *f*.
riband, ribband ['rɪbənd] *n* **-1.** [award] ruban *m*, décoration *f*. **-2.** *arch* [in hair] ruban *m*.
ribbed [rɪbd] *adj* **-1.** [leaf, vault] à nervures. **-2.** [sweater, fabric] à côtes.

ribbing ['rɪbɪŋ] *n* **-1.** *(U)* TEX côtes *fpl*. **-2.** [teasing] taquinerie *f*, mise *f* en boîte; **to get a ~ from sb** être mis en boîte par qqn.
ribbon ['rɪbən] ◇ *vt* **-1.** [adorn with ribbon] enrubanner. **-2.** *fig* [streak] sillonner, zébrer. **-3.** [cut] couper en rubans; [shred] mettre en lambeaux.
◇ *n* **-1.** [in hair, for typewriter, medal, parcel] ruban *m*. **-2.** *fig* [of road] ruban *m*; [of land] bande *f*; [of cloud] traînée *f*; **her dress hung in ~s** sa robe était en lambeaux OR en loques.
ribbon development *n Br* croissance *f* urbaine linéaire *(le long des grands axes routiers)*.
ribcage ['rɪbkeɪdʒ] *n* cage *f* thoracique.
riboflavin(e) [,raɪbəʊ'fleɪvɪn] *n* riboflavine *f*.
ribonucleic acid [,raɪbəʊnjuː'kliːɪk-] *n* acide ribonucléique.
rib-tickler *inf n hum* plaisanterie *f*.
rice [raɪs] ◇ *n* riz *m*; **~ paddy** rizière *f*.
◇ *vt Am* [potatoes] faire une purée de.
rice bowl *n* **-1.** *literal* bol *m* à riz. **-2.** *fig* [region] région *f* productrice de riz; **this province was the ~ of Burma** cette province était le grenier à riz de la Birmanie.
riced [raɪst] *adj Am*: **~ potatoes** purée *f* (de pommes de terre).
ricefield ['raɪsfiːld] *n* rizière *f*.
rice paper *n* papier *m* de riz.
rice pudding *n* riz *m* au lait.
ricer ['raɪsə^r] *n Am* presse-purée *m inv*.
rice wine *n* alcool *m* de riz, saké *m*.
rich [rɪtʃ] ◇ *adj* **-1.** [wealthy, affluent] riche; **it doesn't affect ~ people** ça ne touche pas les riches; **they want to get ~ quick** ils veulent s'enrichir très vite; **the ~ part of town** les quartiers riches, les beaux quartiers. **-2.** [elegant luxurious] riche, luxueux, somptueux; **~ tapestries** des tapisseries somptueuses. **-3.** [abundant prolific] riche, abondant; **~ in vitamins/proteins** riche en vitamines/protéines; **~ vegetation** végétation luxuriante; **there are ~ pickings to be had** *literal & fig* ça peut rapporter gros. **-4.** [fertile] riche, fertile; **~ soil** sol *m* fertile OR riche; **a ~ imagination** une imagination fertile. **-5.** [full, eventful] riche; **she led a very ~ life** elle a eu une vie bien remplie; **their culture was extremely ~** ils avaient une culture extrêmement riche. **-6.** [strong, intense - colour] riche, chaud, vif; [- voice, sound] chaud, riche; [- smell] fort. **-7.** CULIN [food] riche; [meal] lourd; **your diet is too ~** vous mangez trop d'aliments riches. **-8.** [funny] drôle; **~ humour** humour *m* très drôle; **I say, that's a bit ~!** *inf* c'est un peu fort (de café)!, ça, c'est le comble!
◇ *npl*: **the ~** les riches *mpl*.
◆ **riches** *npl* richesses *fpl*.
-rich *in cpds* riche en...; **vitamin~ foods** aliments *mpl* riches en vitamines.
Richard ['rɪtʃəd] *pr n*: **~ the Lionheart** Richard Cœur de Lion.
richly ['rɪtʃlɪ] *adv* **-1.** [handsomely, generously] largement, richement; **they will be ~ rewarded** ils seront largement OR généreusement récompensés. **-2.** [thoroughly] largement, pleinement; **the punishment she so ~ deserved** le châtiment qu'elle méritait amplement. **-3.** [abundantly] abondamment, richement; **the region is ~ provided with arable land** la région est riche en terres arables; **~ illustrated** richement illustré. **-4.** [elegantly, luxuriously] somptueusement, luxueusement; **~ dressed/furnished** somptueusement habillé/meublé. **-5.** [vividly]: **~ coloured** aux couleurs riches OR vives.
richness ['rɪtʃnɪs] *n* **-1.** [wealth, affluence] richesse *f*. **-2.** [elegance, luxury] luxe *m*, richesse *f*. **-3.** [abundance] abondance *f*, richesse *f*; **an amazing ~ of detail** une étonnante abondance de détails. **-4.** [fertility] richesse *f*, fertilité *f*; **the ~ of the soil/of her imagination** la richesse du sol/de son imagination. **-5.** [fullness, eventfulness] richesse *f*; **the ~ of his experience** la richesse de son expérience. **-6.** [strength, intensity - of colour, voice, sound] richesse *f*; [- of smell] intensité *f*.

ichter scale ['rɪktə^{r}-] *n* échelle *f* de Richter.

ck [rɪk] ◇ *n* -**1.** AGR meule *f (de foin etc)*. -**2.** [in ankle, wrist] entorse *f*; [in neck] torticolis *m*.
◇ *vt* -**1.** AGR mettre en meules. -**2.** *Br* [sprain] faire une entorse à; to ~ one's neck attraper un torticolis.

ckets ['rɪkɪts] *n (U)* rachitisme *m*; to have ~ souffrir de rachitisme, être rachitique.

ckety ['rɪkətɪ] *adj* -**1.** [shaky - structure] branlant; [- chair] bancal; [- vehicle] (tout) bringuebalant. -**2.** [feeble - person] frêle, chancelant. -**3.** MED rachitique.

ickrack ['rɪkræk] *n (U)* feston *m*.

ickshaw ['rɪkʃɔː] *n* [pulled] pousse *m inv*, pousse-pousse *m inv*; [pedalled] cyclo-pousse *m inv*.

icochet ['rɪkəʃeɪ] (*pt* & *pp* **ricocheted** [-ʃeɪd] OR **ricochetted** [-ʃetɪd], *cont* **ricocheting** [-eɪɪŋ] OR **ricochetting** [-ʃetɪŋ]) ◇ *n* ricochet *m*; **he was injured by a ~** il a été blessé par une balle qui a ricoché.
◇ *vi* ricocher; **to ~ off sthg** ricocher sur qqch.

icrac ['rɪkræk] = **rickrack**.

ictus ['rɪktəs] *n* rictus *m*.

id [rɪd] (*pt* & *pp* **rid** OR **ridded**, *cont* **ridding**)
◇ *vt* débarrasser; **to ~ a house of rats** débarrasser une maison de ses rats, dératiser une maison; **we must ~ the country of corruption** il faut débarrasser le pays de la corruption; **you should ~ yourself of such illusions!** arrêtez de vous bercer d'illusions!
◇ *adj*: **to get ~ of** se débarrasser de; **how can we get ~ of all this rubbish?** comment nous débarrasser de tout ce bazar?; **to be ~ of** être débarrassé de; **I was glad to be ~ of them** j'étais content d'être débarrassé d'eux.

riddance ['rɪdəns] *n* débarras *m*; **good ~ (to bad rubbish)!** *inf* bon débarras!

ridden ['rɪdn] ◇ *pp* → **ride**.
◇ *adj* affligé, atteint.

-ridden *in cpds*: **flea~** infesté de puces; **disease~** infesté de maladies; **debt~** criblé de dettes.

riddle ['rɪdl] ◇ *n* -**1.** [poser] devinette *f*; **to ask sb a ~** poser une devinette à qqn. -**2.** [mystery] énigme *f*; **to talk** OR **to speak in ~s** parler par énigmes. -**3.** [sieve] crible *m*, tamis *m*.
◇ *vt* -**1.** [pierce] cribler; **they ~d the car with bullets** ils criblèrent la voiture de balles. -**2.** [sift] passer au crible, cribler.

riddled ['rɪdld] *adj* plein; **a wall ~ with holes** un mur plein de trous; **his letter is ~ with spelling mistakes** sa lettre est pleine de fautes d'orthographe.

ride [raɪd] (*pt* **rode** [rəʊd], *pp* **ridden** ['rɪdn])
◇ *vt* -**1.** [horse] monter à; [camel, donkey, elephant] monter à dos de; **I don't know how to ~ a horse/a camel** je ne sais pas monter à cheval/à dos de chameau; **they were riding horses/donkeys/camels** ils étaient à cheval/à dos d'âne/à dos de chameau; **she rode her mare in the park each day** elle montait sa jument chaque jour dans le parc; **Razzle, ridden by Jo Burns** Razzle, monté par Jo Burns; **he rode Prince into town** il a pris Prince pour aller en ville; **she rode her horse back** elle est revenue à cheval; **they rode their horses across the river** ils ont traversé la rivière sur leurs chevaux; **he rode his horse down the lane** il descendit le chemin à cheval. -**2.** [bicycle, motorcycle] monter sur; **he won't let me ~ his bike** il ne veut pas que je monte sur OR que je me serve de son vélo; **I don't know how to ~ a bike/a motorbike** je ne sais pas faire du vélo/conduire une moto; **she was riding a motorbike** elle était à OR en moto; **she ~s her bicycle everywhere** elle se déplace toujours à bicyclette; **he ~s his bike to work** il va travailler à vélo, il va au travail à vélo; **a gang of youths riding racers** une bande de jeunes (montés) sur des vélos de course; **he's riding his tricycle in the yard** il fait du tricycle dans la cour. -**3.** [go about - fields, valleys] parcourir; **when the Sioux rode the prairies** à l'époque où les Sioux parcouraient OR sillonnaient la prairie; **you can ~ this highway to Tucson** *Am* vous pouvez prendre OR suivre cette route jusqu'à Tucson. -**4.** [participate in - race] faire; **she's ridden four races this year** elle a fait quatre courses cette année; **he rode a good race** [jockey, horse] il a fait une bonne course. -**5.** *Am* [have a go on - roundabout, fairground attraction] faire un tour de; [lift, ski lift] prendre; **do you want to ~ the roller coaster?** veux-tu faire un tour sur les montagnes russes?; **he rode the chairlift to the top of the slope** il a pris le télésiège jusqu'au sommet de la piste; **she wanted to ~ the miniature train** elle voulait monter dans le petit train. -**6.** *Am* [travel on - bus, subway, train, ferry] prendre; **do you ~ this line often?** est-ce que vous prenez souvent cette ligne?; **she ~s a bus to work** elle prend le bus pour aller travailler, elle va travailler en bus; **he spent three hours riding the subway** il a passé trois heures dans le métro. -**7.** [move with - sea, waves] se laisser porter par; **to ~ the rapids** descendre les rapides; **surfers were riding the waves** des surfeurs glissaient sur les vagues; **hang gliders were riding the updrafts** des deltaplanes se laissaient porter par les courants ascendants; **the candidate is riding a surge of popularity** *fig* le candidat est porté par une vague de popularité ❑ **to ~ one's luck** compter sur sa chance; **to ~ the storm** NAUT étaler la tempête; *fig* surmonter la crise. -**8.** [take, recoil with - punch, blow] encaisser. -**9.** *Am* [nag] harceler; **stop riding her!** laisse-la tranquille!; **you ~ the kids too hard** tu es trop dur avec les gosses; **you're always riding me about being late** tu me reproches sans arrêt d'être en retard. -**10.** *inf Am* [tease] taquiner, mettre en boîte; **we were riding him about his accent** nous le taquinions au sujet de son accent; **my colleagues are really going to ~ me!** je vais être la risée de mes collègues! -**11.** [copulate with - subj: animal] monter; [- subj: person] ▽grimper. -**12.** *Am* [give a lift to] amener; **hop in and I'll ~ you home** monte, je te ramène chez toi. -**13.** *Am phr*: **to ~ sb out of town** [drive out] chasser qqn de la ville; [ridicule] tourner qqn en ridicule OR en dérision; **the sheriff was ridden out of town** ils ont chassé le shérif de la ville.
◇ *vi* -**1.** [ride a horse] monter (à cheval), faire du cheval; **she learnt to ~ very young** elle a appris à faire du cheval OR à monter à cheval très jeune; **I wish I could ~ like you!** j'aimerais bien être aussi bon cavalier que OR monter à cheval aussi bien que vous!; **I like to ~ on the beach in the morning** j'aime faire du cheval le matin sur la plage; **I was stiff after riding all day** j'avais des courbatures après avoir chevauché toute la journée OR après une journée entière à cheval ❑ **Zorro/Nixon ~s again!** *hum* Zorro/Nixon est de retour! -**2.** [go - on horseback] aller (à cheval); [- by bicycle] aller (à bicyclette); [- by car] aller (en voiture); **we rode along the canal and over the bridge** nous avons longé le canal et traversé le pont; **he rode by on a bicycle/on a white horse/on a donkey** il passa à bicyclette/sur un cheval blanc/monté sur un âne; **they ~ to work on the bus/train** ils vont travailler en autobus/train; **I want to ~ in the front seat/in the first carriage** je veux monter à l'avant/dans la voiture de tête; **she was riding in the back seat** elle était assise à l'arrière; **have you ever ridden in a rickshaw?** avez-vous jamais pris un pousse-pousse?; **I'll ~ up/down in the lift** je monterai/descendrai en ascenseur; **they rode to the top in the cable car** ils ont pris la télécabine pour aller au sommet; **you can ~ on the handlebars/my shoulders** tu peux monter sur le guidon/mes épaules; **to ~ off** [leave] partir; [move away] s'éloigner; **he rode off into the sunset** il s'éloigna vers le soleil couchant ❑ **to be riding for a fall** courir à l'échec; **to ~ roughshod over** passer outre à. -**3.** [float, sail] voguer; **to ~ with the current** voguer au fil de l'eau; **the raft will ~ over the reef** le radeau franchira le récif; **to ~ at anchor** être ancré; **the buoy rode with the swell** la bouée se balançait au gré de la houle; **the moon was riding high** la lune était haut dans le ciel ❑ **we'll have to ~ with it** *inf* il faudra faire avec; **to ~ with the punches** *inf Am* encaisser (les coups). -**4.** [be sustained - person] être porté; **she was riding on a wave of popularity** elle était portée par une vague de popularité; **he rode to victory on a policy of reform** il a obtenu la victoire grâce à son programme de réformes; **the team is riding high** l'équipe a le vent en poupe; **he's riding on his reputation** il vit sur sa réputation. -**5.** [depend] dépendre; **everything ~s on whether the meeting is successful** tout dépend de la réussite de la réunion; **my reputation is riding on the outcome** ma réputation est en jeu. -**6.** [money in bet] miser; **I've $5 riding on the favourite** j'ai misé 5 dollars sur le favori; **they have a fortune riding on this project** ils ont investi une fortune dans ce projet. -**7.** [continue undisturbed]: **he decided to let the matter ~** il a décidé de laisser courir; **let it ~!** laisse tomber!
◇ *n* -**1.** [trip - for pleasure] promenade *f*, tour *m*; **to go for a car/motorcycle ~** (aller) faire un tour OR une promenade en voiture/en moto; **we went on long bicycle/horse ~s** nous avons fait de longues promenades à bicyclette/à cheval; **a donkey ~** une promenade à dos d'âne; **he saddled up and went for his morning ~** il sella son cheval et partit faire sa promenade matinale; **he's got a ~ in the 3:00 at Sandown** [jockey] il monte dans la course de 15 h à Sandown; **how about a ~ in my new car?** et si on faisait un tour dans ma nouvelle voiture?; **give Tom a ~** OR **let Tom have a ~ on your tricycle** laisse Tom monter sur ton tricycle; **give me a ~ on your back** porte-moi sur ton dos; **his sister came along for the ~** sa sœur est venue faire un tour avec nous || [when talking about distance] parcours *m*, trajet *m*; **she has a long car/bus ~ to work** elle doit faire un long trajet en voiture/en bus pour aller travailler; **allow an hour for the bus ~** comptez une heure de trajet en bus; **it's a long bus ~ to Mexico** c'est long d'aller en car au Mexique; **it's a 30-minute ~ by bus/train/car** il faut 30 minutes en bus/train/voiture; **how much will the ~ cost?** combien le voyage va-t-il coûter? -**2.** [quality of travel]: **this type of suspension gives a smoother ~** ce type de suspension est plus confortable ❑ **the journalists gave her a rough ~** les journalistes ne l'ont pas ménagée; **it looks as if we're in for a bumpy ~** *fig* ça promet! -**3.** *Am* [lift - in car]: **can you give me a ~ to the station?** peux-tu me conduire à la gare?; **I have a ~ coming** on vient me chercher; **get a ~ to the party with Bill** demande à Bill s'il peut t'emmener à la fête; **don't accept ~s from strangers** ne montez pas dans la voiture de quelqu'un que vous ne connaissez pas; **we got from New York to Chicago in one ~** nous sommes allés de New York jusqu'à Chicago dans la même voiture. -**4.** [in fairground - attraction] manège *m*; [- turn] tour *m*; **it's 50p a ~** c'est 50 pence le tour; **he wanted to go on all the ~s** il a voulu faire un tour sur chaque manège; **to have a ~ on the big wheel** faire un tour sur la grande roue. -**5.** [bridle path] piste *f* cavalière; [wider] allée *f* cavalière. -**6.** *inf phr*: **to take sb for a ~** [deceive] faire marcher qqn; [cheat] arnaquer OR rouler qqn; *Am* [kill] descendre OR liquider qqn; **take a ~!** *Am* fous-moi la paix!

◆ **ride about** *Br*, **ride around** *vi insep*: **she ~s about** OR **around in a limousine** elle se déplace en limousine; **I saw him riding about in a brand new sports car** je l'ai vu passer dans une voiture de sport toute neuve.

◆ **ride down** *vt sep* -**1.** [knock over] renverser; [trample] piétiner. -**2.** [catch up with] rattraper; **they rode the wounded doe down** ils ont poursuivi la biche blessée jusqu'à ce qu'ils la rattrapent.

◆ **ride in** *vt sep* [horse] préparer *(pour un concours)*.

◆ **ride out** ◇ *vt insep* [difficulty, crisis] surmonter; [recession] survivre à; **if we can ~ out the**

next few months si nous pouvons tenir OR nous maintenir à flot encore quelques mois; **they managed to ~ out a bad stretch** ils ont réussi à se tirer d'une mauvaise passe ❑ **to ~ out the storm** NAUT étaler la tempête; *fig* surmonter la crise, tenir.
◇ *vi insep* sortir *(à cheval, à bicyclette etc)*.
◆ **ride up** *vi insep* [garment] remonter.

rider ['raɪdəʳ] *n* -**1.** [of horse, donkey] cavalier *m*, -ère *f*; [of bicycle] cycliste *mf*; [of motorcycle] motocycliste *mf*. -**2.** [proviso] condition *f*, stipulation *f*; **he agrees, with the ~ that he won't have to pay for it** il est d'accord à condition que ce ne soit pas lui qui paie; **I'd like to add one small ~ to what my colleague said** j'aimerais apporter une petite précision à ce qu'a dit mon collègue. -**3.** [annexe - to contract] annexe *f*; *Br* JUR [jury recommendation] recommandation *f*. -**4.** [on scales] curseur *m*.

ridership ['raɪdəʃɪp] *n Am* nombre *m* de voyageurs.

ridge [rɪdʒ] ◇ *n* -**1.** [of mountains] crête *f*, ligne *f* de faîte; [leading to summit] crête *f*, arête *f*. -**2.** [raised strip or part] arête *f*, crête *f*; AGR [in ploughed field] crête *f*; **the wet sand formed ~s** le sable mouillé était couvert de petites rides; **a ~ of high pressure** METEOR une crête de haute pression, une dorsale barométrique *spec*. -**3.** [of roof] faîte *m*.
◇ *vt* [crease] sillonner, rider; **you should ~ the roof with new tiles** vous devriez poser de nouvelles faîtières sur votre toit.

ridged [rɪdʒd] *adj* ridé; **her brow was ~ with worry** l'inquiétude se lisait sur son visage.

ridgepiece ['rɪdʒpiːs] *n* ARCHIT panne *f* faîtière.

ridgepole ['rɪdʒpəʊl] *n* -**1.** [for tent] faîtière *f*. -**2.** = **ridgepiece**.

ridge tent *n* tente *f* à faîtière.

ridge tile *n* (tuile *f*) faîtière *f*.

ridgeway ['rɪdʒweɪ] *n chemin de randonnée qui suit une ligne de faîte*.

ridicule ['rɪdɪkjuːl] ◇ *n* ridicule *m*; **to pour ~ on sthg, to hold sthg up to ~** tourner qqch en ridicule; **to lay o.s. open to ~** s'exposer au ridicule.
◇ *vt* ridiculiser, tourner en ridicule.

ridiculous [rɪ'dɪkjʊləs] ◇ *adj* ridicule; **you look ~ in that hat** tu as l'air ridicule avec ce chapeau; **£500? don't be ~!** 500 livres? vous plaisantez!; **to make o.s. look ~** se ridiculiser, se couvrir de ridicule.
◇ *n*: **the ~** le ridicule.

ridiculously [rɪ'dɪkjʊləslɪ] *adv* ridiculement; **it's ~ expensive** [price] c'est un prix exorbitant; [article, shop] c'est beaucoup trop cher; **it's ~ cheap** [price] c'est un prix dérisoire; [article, shop] c'est très bon marché.

ridiculousness [rɪ'dɪkjʊləsnɪs] *n* ridicule *m*; **the ~ of the situation** le (côté) ridicule de la situation.

riding ['raɪdɪŋ] ◇ *n* -**1.** EQUIT: **(horse) ~** équitation *f*; **to go ~** faire de l'équitation OR du cheval; **do you like ~?** aimez-vous l'équitation OR monter à cheval? -**2.** [in Yorkshire] division *f* administrative. -**3.** [in Canada, New Zealand] circonscription *f* électorale.
◇ *comp* [boots, jacket] de cheval; [techniques] d'équitation.

riding breeches *npl* culotte *f* de cheval.

riding crop *n* cravache *f*.

riding habit *n* tenue *f* d'amazone.

riding school *n* école *f* d'équitation.

rife [raɪf] *adj* -**1.** [widespread] répandu; **corruption is ~** la corruption est chose commune. -**2.** [full]: **~ with** abondant en; **the garden is ~ with caterpillars** le jardin est envahi par les chenilles; **the office is ~ with rumour** les langues vont bon train au bureau.

riff [rɪf] *n* riff *m*.

riffle ['rɪfl] ◇ *vt* -**1.** [magazine, pages] feuilleter. -**2.** [cards] battre, mélanger. -**3.** *Am* = **ripple**.
◇ *n Am* -**1.** [rapids] rapide *m*, rapides *mpl*. -**2.** = **ripple**.
◆ **riffle through** *vt insep* feuilleter.

riffraff ['rɪfræf] *n* racaille *f*.

rifle ['raɪfl] ◇ *vt* -**1.** [search] fouiller (dans); **I caught him rifling my desk** je l'ai surpris en train de fouiller dans mon bureau. -**2.** [rob] dévaliser; **they ~d the safe** ils ont dévalisé le coffre-fort. -**3.** [steal] voler; **all the money had been ~d** tout l'argent avait été volé. -**4.** [gun barrel] rayer.
◇ *vi*: **to ~ through sthg** fouiller dans qqch.
◇ *n* [gun] fusil *m*.
◇ *comp* [bullet, butt, shot] de fusil.
◆ **rifles** *npl* MIL [unit] fusiliers *mpl*.

rifle grenade *n* grenade *f* à fusil.

rifleman ['raɪflmən] (*pl* **riflemen** [-mən]) *n* fusilier *m*.

rifle range *n* -**1.** [for practice] champ *m* de tir. -**2.** [distance]: **within ~** à portée de tir OR de fusil.

rifling ['raɪflɪŋ] *n (U)* [in gun barrel] rayures *fpl*.

rift [rɪft] ◇ *n* -**1.** [gap, cleavage] fissure *f*, crevasse *f*; GEOL [fault] faille *f*; **a ~ in the clouds** une trouée dans les nuages. -**2.** *fig* [split] cassure *f*, faille *f*; POL scission *f*; [quarrel] désaccord *m*, querelle *f*; **in order to prevent a ~ in our relationship** pour éviter une rupture; **there is a deep ~ between them** un abîme les sépare; **she hasn't seen her family since that ~** elle n'a pas vu sa famille depuis cette dispute; **a ~ in the opposition** une scission au sein de l'opposition.
◇ *vt* scinder.
◇ *vi* se scinder.

rift valley *n* fossé *m* d'effondrement.

Rift Valley *pr n*: **the ~** la Rift Valley.

rig [rɪg] (*pt* & *pp* **rigged**, *cont* **rigging**) ◇ *vt* -**1.** [fiddle] truquer; **they were accused of rigging the match/the elections** on les a accusés d'avoir truqué le match/les élections; **the dice were rigged** les dés étaient truqués OR pipés; **the whole affair was rigged!** c'était un coup monté du début jusqu'à la fin!; **to ~ a jury** manipuler un jury. -**2.** NAUT gréer. -**3.** [install] monter, bricoler.
◇ *n* -**1.** [gen - equipment] matériel *m*. -**2.** NAUT gréement *m*. -**3.** PETR [on land] derrick *m*; [offshore] plate-forme *f*; **drilling ~** tour *f* de forage, derrick *m*. -**4.** *inf* [clothes] tenue *f*, fringues *fpl*. -**5.** *Am* [truck] semi-remorque *m*.
◆ **rig down** *vt sep* & *vi insep* dégréer.
◆ **rig out** *vt sep* -**1.** *inf* [clothe] habiller; **he was rigged out in a cowboy costume** il était habillé OR déguisé en cowboy; **look at the way she's rigged out!** *pej* regarde comme elle est fagotée! -**2.** [equip] équiper.
◆ **rig up** *vt sep* [install] monter, installer.

Riga ['riːgə] *pr n* Riga.

-rigged [rɪgd] *in cpds* gréé.

rigger ['rɪgəʳ] *n* -**1.** NAUT gréeur *m*. -**2.** PETR *personne qui travaille sur un chantier de forage*.

rigging ['rɪgɪŋ] *n* -**1.** NAUT gréement *m*. -**2.** THEAT machinerie *f*. -**3.** [fiddling] trucage *m*.

rigging loft *n* -**1.** NAUT (atelier *m* de) garniture *f*. -**2.** THEAT cintre *m*.

right [raɪt] ◇ *adj* -**1.** [indicating location, direction] droit; **raise your ~ hand** levez la main droite; **the ~ side of the stage** le côté droit de OR la droite de la scène; **take the next ~ (turn)** prenez la prochaine à droite; **would you like to try the ~ shoe?** [in shop] vous voulez essayer le pied droit? -**2.** [accurate, correct - prediction] juste, exact; [- answer, address] bon; **the weather forecasts are never ~** les prévisions météo ne sont jamais exactes; **he didn't give me the ~ change** il ne m'a pas rendu la monnaie exacte; **the station clock is ~** l'horloge de la gare est juste OR à l'heure; **have you got the ~ time?** est-ce que vous avez l'heure exacte?; **the sentence doesn't sound/look quite ~** la phrase sonne/a l'air un peu bizarre; **there's something not quite ~ in what he says** il y a quelque chose qui cloche dans ce qu'il dit ‖ [person]: **to be ~** avoir raison; **the customer is always ~** le client a toujours raison; **you were ~ about the bus schedules/about him/about what she would say** vous aviez raison au sujet des horaires de bus/à son sujet/sur ce qu'ell[e] dirait; **I was ~ in thinking he was an acto[r]** j'avais raison de penser que c'était un acteur; **am I ~ in thinking you're German?** vous ête[s] bien allemand, ou est-ce que je me trompe?; **you're the eldest, am I ~** OR **is that ~?** c'es[t] (bien) toi l'aîné, ou est-ce que je me trompe?; **I owe you $5, ~?** je te dois 5 dollars, c'es[t] (bien) ça?; **and I'm telling you you still ow[e] me £10, ~!** et moi je te dis que tu me doi[s] encore 10 livres, vu?; **he's sick today, ~?** il es[t] malade aujourd'hui, non?; **that's ~** c'est juste oui; **he got the pronunciation/spelling ~** il l'a bien prononcé/épelé; **she got the answer ~** elle a donné la bonne réponse; **I never get those quadratic equations ~** je me trompe toujours avec ces équations quadratiques; **he got the time ~ but the date wrong** il ne s'est pas trompé d'heure mais de date; **make sure you get your figures/her name ~** faites attention de ne pas vous tromper dans vos calculs/sur son nom; **get your facts ~!** vérifiez vos renseignements!; **he got it ~ this time** il ne s'est pas trompé cette fois-ci; **let's get this ~** mettons les choses au clair; **time proved her ~** le temps lui a donné raison ❑ **how ~ you are!** vous avez cent fois raison!; **to put sb ~ (about sthg/sb)** détromper qqn (au sujet de qqch/qqn); **he thought he could get away with it, but I soon put him ~** il croyait qu'il pourrait s'en tirer comme ça mais je l'ai vite détrompé; **to put** OR **set ~** [fallen or squint object] redresser, remettre d'aplomb; [clock] remettre à l'heure; [machine, mechanism] réparer; [text, record] corriger; [oversight, injustice] réparer; **to put things** OR **matters ~** [politically, financially etc] redresser OR rétablir la situation; [in relationships] arranger les choses; **he made a mess of it and I had to put things ~** il a raté son coup et j'ai dû réparer les dégâts. -**3.** [appropriate - diploma, tool, sequence, moment] bon; [best - choice, decision] meilleur; **are we going in the ~ direction?** est-ce que nous allons dans le bon sens?; **I think it's the ~ strategy** je crois que c'est la bonne stratégie; **when the time is ~** au bon moment, au moment voulu; **you'll know when the time is ~** tu sauras quand ce sera le bon moment; **to be in the ~ place at the ~ time** être là où il faut quand il faut; **I can't find the ~ word** je ne trouve pas le mot juste; **if the price is ~** si le prix est intéressant; **the colour is just ~** la couleur est parfaite; **the magazine has just the ~ mix of news and commentary** la revue a juste ce qu'il faut d'informations et de commentaires; **she's the ~ woman for the job** c'est la femme qu'il faut pour ce travail; **the ~ holiday for your budget** les vacances qui conviennent le mieux à votre budget; **the frame is ~ for the picture** le cadre convient tout à fait au tableau; **her hairdo isn't ~ for her** sa coiffure ne lui va pas; **teaching isn't ~ for you** l'enseignement n'est pas ce qu'il vous faut; **she's the ~ person to talk to** c'est à elle qu'il faut s'adresser; **is this the ~ sort of outfit to wear?** est-ce la bonne tenue?; **place the document ~ side down/up** placez le document face en bas/vers le haut; **turn the socks ~ side in/out** mettez les chaussettes à l'envers/à l'endroit; **it wasn't the ~ thing to say** ce n'était pas la chose à dire; **you've done the ~ thing to tell us about it** vous avez bien fait de nous en parler; **he did the ~ thing, but for the wrong reasons** il a fait le bon choix, mais pour de mauvaises raisons; **you're not doing it the ~ way!** ce n'est pas comme ça qu'il faut faire OR s'y prendre!; **there's no one ~ way to go about it** il n'y a pas qu'une façon de s'y prendre; **that's the ~ way to approach the problem** c'est comme ça qu'il faut aborder la question ❑ **Mr Right** *inf* l'homme idéal. -**4.** [fair, just] juste, équitable; [morally good] bien *(inv)*; [socially correct] correct; **it's not ~ to separate the children** ce n'est pas bien de séparer les enfants; **I don't think capital punishment is ~** je ne crois pas que la peine de mort soit juste; **it is only ~ and proper for the**

father to be present il est tout à fait naturel que le père soit présent; **do you think it's ~ for them to sell arms?** est-ce que vous croyez qu'ils ont raison de vendre des armes?; **I thought it ~ to ask you first** j'ai cru bon de vous demander d'abord; **I don't feel ~ leaving you alone** ça me gêne de te laisser tout seul; **it's only ~ that you should know** il est juste que vous le sachiez; **I only want to do what is ~** je ne cherche qu'à bien faire ❑ **to do the ~ thing (by sb)** bien agir (avec qqn). -**5.** [functioning properly]: **the window is still not ~** la fenêtre ne marche pas bien encore; **there's something not quite ~ with the motor** le moteur ne marche pas très bien. -**6.** [healthy] bien *(inv)*; **I don't feel ~** je ne me sens pas très bien, je ne suis pas dans mon assiette; **my knee doesn't feel ~** j'ai quelque chose au genou; **a rest will put** OR **set you ~ again** un peu de repos te remettra; **to be ~ in the head** *inf*: **he's not quite ~ in the head** *inf* ça ne va pas très bien dans sa tête; **to be in one's ~ mind** avoir toute sa raison; **nobody in their ~ mind would refuse such an offer!** aucune personne sensée ne refuserait une telle offre! -**7.** [satisfactory] bien *(inv)*; **things aren't ~ between them** ça ne va pas très bien entre eux; **does the hat look ~ to you?** le chapeau, ça va?; **I can't get this hem ~** je n'arrive pas à faire un bel ourlet ❑ **to come ~** *inf* s'arranger. -**8.** [indicating social status] bien *(inv)*, comme il faut; **she took care to be seen in all the ~ places** elle a fait en sorte d'être vue partout où il fallait; **you'll only meet her if you move in the ~ circles** vous ne la rencontrerez que si vous fréquentez le beau monde; **to know the ~ people** connaître des gens bien placés; **he went to the ~ school and belonged to the ~ clubs** il a fréquenté une très bonne école et a appartenu aux meilleurs clubs. -**9.** GEOM [angle, line, prism, cone] droit; **~ triangle** *Am* triangle *m* rectangle. -**10.** *inf Br* [as intensifier] vrai, complet; **I felt like a ~ idiot** je me sentais vraiment bête; **the government made a ~ mess of it** le gouvernement a fait un beau gâchis ❑ **there was a ~ one in here this morning!** *inf* on a eu un vrai cinglé ce matin! -**11.** *inf dial* [ready] prêt.

◇ *adv* -**1.** [in directions] à droite; **turn ~ at the traffic lights** tournez à droite au feu (rouge); **look ~** regardez à droite; **the party is moving further ~** le parti est en train de virer plus à droite ❑ **they're giving out gifts ~ and left** OR **~, left and centre** *inf* ils distribuent des cadeaux à tour de bras; **they're accepting offers ~ and left** OR **~, left and centre** *inf* ils acceptent des offres de tous les côtés. -**2.** [accurately, correctly - hear] bien; [- guess] juste; [- answer, spell] bien, correctement; **if I remember ~** si je me rappelle bien; **he predicted the election results ~** il a vu juste en ce qui concernait les résultats des élections. -**3.** [properly] bien, comme il faut; **the door doesn't shut ~** la porte ne ferme pas bien; **nothing works ~ in this house!** rien ne marche comme il faut dans cette maison!; **you're not holding the saw ~** tu ne tiens pas la scie comme il faut; **the top isn't on ~** le couvercle n'est pas bien mis; **if we organize things ~, there'll be enough time** si nous organisons bien les choses, il y aura assez de temps; **I hope things go ~ for you** j'espère que tout ira bien pour toi; **nothing is going ~ today** tout va de travers aujourd'hui; **he can't do anything ~** il ne peut rien faire correctement OR comme il faut; **do it ~ the next time!** ne vous trompez pas la prochaine fois!; **the roast is done just ~** le rôti est cuit à la perfection. -**4.** [emphasizing precise location]: **the lamp's shining ~ in my eyes** j'ai la lumière de la lampe en plein dans les yeux OR en pleine figure; **it's ~ opposite the post office** c'est juste en face de la poste; **it's ~ in front of/behind you** c'est droit devant vous/juste derrière vous; **I'm ~ behind you there** *fig* je suis entièrement d'accord avec vous là-dessus; **I stepped ~ in it** j'ai marché en plein dedans; **he shot him ~ in the forehead** il lui a tiré une balle en plein front; **the hotel was ~ on the beach** l'hôtel donnait directement sur la plage; **it broke ~ in the middle** ça a cassé juste au milieu; **I left it ~ here** je l'ai laissé juste ici; **stay ~ there** ne bougez pas. -**5.** [emphasizing precise time] juste, exactement; **I arrived ~ at that moment** je suis arrivé juste à ce moment-là; **~ in the middle of the fight** au beau milieu de la bagarre. -**6.** [all the way]: **it's ~ at the back of the drawer/at the front of the book** c'est tout au fond du tiroir/juste au début du livre; **~ down to the bottom** jusqu'au fond; **~ from the start** dès le début; **move ~ over** allez jusqu'au fond; **his shoes were worn ~ through** ses chaussures étaient usées jusqu'à la corde; **the car drove ~ through the road-block** la voiture est passée à travers le barrage; **the path leads ~ to the lake** le sentier va jusqu'au lac; **that girl is going ~ to the top** *fig* cette fille ira loin; **the water came ~ up to the window** l'eau est montée jusqu'à la fenêtre; **we worked ~ up until the last minute** nous avons travaillé jusqu'à la toute dernière minute. -**7.** [immediately] tout de suite; **I'll be ~ over** je viens tout de suite; **I'll be ~ with you** je suis à vous tout de suite; **let's talk ~ after the meeting** parlons-en juste après la réunion. -**8.** [justly, fairly] bien; [properly, fittingly] correctement; **you did ~** tu as bien fait; **to do ~ by sb** agir correctement envers qqn. -**9.** ▽ *Br dial* [very] bien; **she was ~ nice** elle était bien aimable.

◇ *n* -**1.** [in directions] droite *f*; **look to the** OR **your ~** regardez à droite OR sur votre droite; **keep to the** OR **your ~** restez à droite; **he was seated on your ~** il était assis à ta droite; **from ~ to left** de droite à gauche. -**2.** POL droite *f*; **the ~ is** OR **are divided** la droite est divisée; **he's to the ~ of the party leadership** il est plus à droite que les dirigeants du parti. -**3.** [in boxing - fist, punch] droit *m*, droite *f*. -**4.** [entitlement] droit *m*; **the ~ to vote/of asylum** le droit de vote/d'asile; **to have a ~ to sthg** avoir droit à qqch; **she has a ~ to half the profits** elle a droit à la moitié des bénéfices; **to have a** OR **the ~ to do sthg** avoir le droit de faire qqch; **you've no ~ to talk to me like that!** tu n'as pas le droit de me parler ainsi!; **you have every ~ to be angry** tu as toutes les raisons d'être en colère; **by what ~?** de quel droit? ❑ **as of ~** *fml* de (plein) droit; **he's American by ~ of birth** il est américain de naissance; **in one's own ~**: **she's rich in her own ~** elle a une grande fortune personnelle; **he became a leader in his own ~** il est lui-même devenu leader. -**5.** [what is good, moral] bien *m*; **he's old enough to know ~ from wrong** il est assez grand pour distinguer ce qui est bien de ce qui est mal; **to be in the ~** être dans le vrai, avoir raison; **he put himself in the ~ by apologizing** il s'est racheté en s'excusant.

◇ *interj*: **come tomorrow — ~ (you are)!** venez demain — d'accord!; **~, let's get to work!** bon OR bien, au travail!; **~ (you are) then, see you later** bon alors, à plus tard.

◇ *vt* -**1.** [set upright again - chair, ship] redresser; **the crane ~ed the derailed carriage** la grue a redressé le wagon qui avait déraillé; **the raft will ~ itself** le radeau se redressera (tout seul). -**2.** [redress - situation] redresser, rétablir; [- damage] réparer; [- injustice] réparer; **to ~ a wrong** redresser un tort; **to ~ the balance** rétablir l'équilibre; **the problem won't just ~ itself** ce problème ne va pas se résoudre de lui-même OR s'arranger tout seul.

◇ *vi* [car, ship] se redresser.

◆ **rights** *npl* -**1.** [political, social] droits *mpl*; **I know my ~s** je connais mes droits; **you'd be within your ~s to demand a refund** vous seriez dans votre (bon) droit si vous réclamiez un remboursement; **read him his ~s** *Am* [on arresting a suspect] prévenez-le de ses droits; **human/gay ~s** les droits de l'homme/des homosexuels. -**2.** COMM droits *mpl*; **who has the mineral/film/distribution ~s?** qui détient les droits miniers/d'adaptation cinématographique/de distribution? -**3.** FIN: **(application) ~** OR **~s** droits *mpl* OR privilège *m* de souscription; **~s issue** émission *f* prioritaire. -**4.** *phr*: **to put** OR **to set to ~s** [room] mettre en ordre; [firm, country] redresser; [situation] arranger; **they've been going on for hours, setting the world to ~s** *hum* ça fait des heures qu'ils parlent, ils sont en train de refaire le monde.

◆ **by right(s)** *adv phr* en principe; **she ought, by ~s, to get compensation** en principe, elle devrait toucher une compensation.

◆ **right away** *adv phr* [at once] tout de suite, aussitôt; [from the start] dès le début; [first go] du premier coup; **~ away, sir!** tout de suite, monsieur!; **I knew ~ away there'd be trouble** j'ai su tout de suite OR dès le début qu'il y aurait des problèmes.

◆ **right now** *adv phr* -**1.** [at once] tout de suite. -**2.** [at the moment] pour le moment.

◆ **right off** *Am* = **right away**.

right-about turn *n* demi-tour *m*.

right angle *n* angle *m* droit; **the corridors are at ~s** les couloirs sont perpendiculaires; **a line at ~s to the base** une ligne perpendiculaire à la base; **the path made a ~** le sentier formait un coude.

right-angled *adj* [hook, turn] à angle droit.

right-angled triangle *n Br* triangle *m* rectangle.

righten ['raɪtn] *vt* redresser.

righteous ['raɪtʃəs] *adj* -**1.** [just] juste; [virtuous] vertueux. -**2.** *pej* [self-righteous] suffisant; **~ indignation** colère indignée.

righteously ['raɪtʃəslɪ] *adv* -**1.** [virtuously] vertueusement. -**2.** *pej* [self-righteously] avec suffisance.

righteousness ['raɪtʃəsnɪs] *n* vertu *f*, rectitude *f*.

right-footed [-'fʊtɪd] *adj* qui se sert de son pied droit.

right-footer [-'fʊtə^r] *n* -**1.** SPORT joueur *m*, -euse *f* qui joue du pied droit. -**2.** *Ir pej* [Protestant] protestant *m*, -e *f*.

rightful ['raɪtfʊl] *adj* légitime.

rightfully ['raɪtfʊlɪ] *adv* légitimement.

right-hand *adj* droit; **the ~ side of the road** le côté droit de la route; **it's in the ~ drawer** c'est dans le tiroir de droite; **a ~ bend** un virage à droite; **my ~ glove** mon gant droit.

right-hand drive *n* AUT conduite *f* à droite; **a ~ vehicle** un véhicule avec la conduite à droite.

right-handed *adj* -**1.** [person] droitier. -**2.** [punch] du droit. -**3.** [scissors, golf club] pour droitiers; [screw] fileté à droite.

right-hander [-'hændə^r] *n* -**1.** [person] droitier *m*, -ère *f*. -**2.** [blow] coup *m* du droit.

right-hand man *n* bras *m* droit.

right-ho *inf* = **righto**.

Right Honourable *adj Br titre utilisé pour s'adresser à certains hauts fonctionnaires ou à quelqu'un ayant un titre de noblesse.*

rightism ['raɪtɪzm] *n* idées *fpl* de droite.

rightist ['raɪtɪst] ◇ *n* homme *m*, femme *f* de droite; **they're ~s** ils sont de droite.
◇ *adj* de droite.

rightly ['raɪtlɪ] *adv* -**1.** [correctly] correctement, bien; **~ dressed for the occasion** habillé pour la circonstance; **I don't ~ know** *inf* je ne sais pas bien. -**2.** [with justification] à juste titre, avec raison; **he was ~ angry, he was angry and ~ so** il était en colère à juste titre.

right-minded *adj* honnête, probe; **every ~ citizen/Christian** tout citoyen/chrétien honnête.

rightness ['raɪtnɪs] *n* -**1.** [accuracy - of answer] exactitude *f*, justesse *f*; [- of guess] justesse *f*. -**2.** [justness - of decision, judgment] équité *f*; [- of claim] légitimité *f*. -**3.** [appropriateness - of tone, dress] justesse *f*, caractère *m* approprié.

righto *inf* ['raɪtəʊ] *interj Br* OK, d'ac.

right-of-centre *adj* centre droit.

right of way (*pl* **rights of way**) *n* -**1.** AUT priorité *f*; **it's your ~** vous avez (la) priorité; **to have (the) ~** avoir (la) priorité. -**2.** [right to cross land] droit *m* de passage. -**3.** [path, road] chemin *m*; *Am* [for power line, railroad etc] voie *f*.

right-on *inf adj* intello de gauche.

Right Reverend *adj Br*: the ~ James Brown [Protestant] le très révérend James Brown; [Catholic] monseigneur Brown.

rights issue *n* droit *m* préférentiel de souscription.

right-thinking *adj* raisonnable, sensé.

right-to-work movement *n syndicat s'opposant à la pratique du «syndicat unique» aux États-Unis.*

right wing *n* -**1.** POL droite *f*; the ~ of the party l'aile droite du parti. -**2.** SPORT [position] aile *f* droite; [player] ailier *m* droit.

◆ **right-wing** *adj* POL de droite; she's more right-wing than the others elle est plus à droite que les autres.

right-winger *n* -**1.** POL homme *m*, femme *f* de droite; he's a ~ il est de droite; measures unpopular with ~s mesures peu appréciées par la droite. -**2.** SPORT ailier *m* droit.

righty-oh *inf* [ˌraɪtɪ'əʊ] = **righto**.

rigid ['rɪdʒɪd] *adj* -**1.** [structure, material] rigide; [body, muscle] raide; he was ~ with fear il était paralysé par la peur; it shook me ~! *inf* ça m'a fait un de ces coups! -**2.** [person, ideas, policy] rigide, inflexible; [discipline] strict, sévère.

rigid disk *n* disque *m* dur.

rigidity [rɪ'dʒɪdətɪ] *n* -**1.** [of structure, material] rigidité *f*; [of body, muscle] raideur *f*. -**2.** [of person, ideas, policy] rigidité *f*, inflexibilité *f*; [of discipline] sévérité *f*.

rigidly ['rɪdʒɪdlɪ] *adv* rigidement, avec raideur; the rules are ~ applied le règlement est rigoureusement appliqué.

rigmarole *inf* ['rɪgmərəʊl] *n* -**1.** [procedure] cirque *m*; I don't want to go through all the ~ of applying for a licence je ne veux pas m'embêter à déposer une demande de permis. -**2.** [talk] charabia *m*, galimatias *m*.

rigor ['rɪgəʳ] *n* -**1.** *Am* = **rigour**. -**2.** *(U)* MED [before fever] frissons *mpl*; [in muscle] crampe *f*.

rigor mortis [ˌrɪgə'mɔːtɪs] *n* rigidité *f* cadavérique.

rigorous ['rɪgərəs] *adj* rigoureux; ~ proof LOGIC & MATH preuve *f* rigoureuse.

rigorously ['rɪgərəslɪ] *adv* rigoureusement, avec rigueur.

rigour *Br*, **rigor** *Am* ['rɪgəʳ] *n* rigueur *f*.

rigout *inf* ['rɪgaʊt] *n* accoutrement *m*.

rile [raɪl] *vt* -**1.** [person] agacer, énerver. -**2.** *Am* [water] troubler.

Riley ['raɪlɪ] *pr n*: to live the life of ~ *inf* mener une vie de pacha.

rill [rɪl] *n* -**1.** *lit* [brook] ruisselet *m*. -**2.** [on moon] vallée *f*. -**3.** [from erosion] ravine *f*.

rim [rɪm] (*pt & pp* rimmed, *cont* rimming)

◇ *n* -**1.** [of bowl, cup] bord *m*; [of eye, lake] bord *m*, pourtour *m*; [of well] margelle *f*. -**2.** [of spectacles] monture *f*. -**3.** [of wheel] jante *f*. -**4.** [of dirt] marque *f*; a ~ of coffee left in the cup des traces de café à l'intérieur de la tasse; there was a black ~ around the bath il y avait une trace de crasse tout autour de la baignoire.

◇ *vt* border; trees ~ the lake le lac est bordé OR entouré d'arbres.

rime [raɪm] ◇ *n* -**1.** *lit* [frost] givre *m*, gelée *f* blanche. -**2.** *arch* = **rhyme**.

◇ *vt lit* givrer.

Rimini ['rɪmɪnɪ] *pr n* Rimini.

rimless ['rɪmlɪs] *adj* [spectacles] sans monture.

-rimmed [rɪmd] *in cpds*: gold/steel~ spectacles lunettes *fpl* à monture en or/d'acier.

Rimsky-Korsakov [ˌrɪmskɪ'kɔːsəkɒf] *pr n* Rimski-Korsakov.

rimy ['raɪmɪ] (*compar* rimier, *superl* rimiest) *adj lit* givré.

rind [raɪnd] *n* [on bacon] couenne *f*; [on cheese] croûte *f*; [on fruit] écorce *f*; [of bark] couche *f* extérieure.

ring [rɪŋ] (*senses 1 & 2 pt* rang [ræŋ], *pp* rung [rʌŋ], *senses 3, 4, 5 & 6 pt & pp* ringed) ◇ *n* -**1.** [sound of bell] sonnerie *f*; there was a ~ at the door on a sonné (à la porte); she answered the phone after just one ~ le téléphone n'avait sonné qu'une fois quand elle a décroché; give two long ~s and one short one sonnez trois fois, deux coups longs et un coup bref; the ~ of the church bells le carillonnement des cloches de l'église. -**2.** [sound] son *m*; [resounding] retentissement *m*; the ~ of their voices in the empty warehouse leurs voix qui résonnaient dans l'entrepôt vide ‖ *fig* [note] note *f*, accent *m*; his words had a ~ of truth il y avait un accent de vérité dans ses paroles; the name has a familiar ~ ce nom me dit quelque chose; that excuse has got a familiar ~! j'ai déjà entendu ça quelque part! -**3.** [telephone call] coup *m* de téléphone; give me a ~ tomorrow passez-moi un coup de téléphone OR appelez-moi demain. -**4.** [set of bells] jeu *m* de cloches. -**5.** [on finger] anneau *m*, bague *f*; [in nose, ear] anneau *m* ❑ 'The Ring of the Nibelung' *Wagner* 'l'Anneau du Nibelung'. -**6.** [round object] anneau *m*; [for serviette] rond *m*; [for swimmer] bouée *f*; [for identifying bird] bague *f*; [of piston] segment *m*; moor the boat to that ~ amarrez le bateau à cet anneau; the ~s [in gym] les anneaux *mpl*; curtain ~ anneau de rideau. -**7.** [circle] cercle *m*, rond *m*; [of smoke] rond *m*; [in or around tree trunk] anneau *m*; all stand in a ~ mettez-vous tous en cercle; she looked round the ~ of faces elle regarda les visages tout autour d'elle; the glasses left ~s on the piano les verres ont laissé des ronds OR marques sur le piano; the ~s of Saturn les anneaux de Saturne; there's a ~ around the moon la lune est cernée d'un halo; he has ~s round his eyes il a les yeux cernés ❑ to run OR to make ~s round sb *inf* éclipser OR écraser qqn. -**8.** [for boxing, wrestling] ring *m*; [in circus] piste *f*. -**9.** *Br* [for cooking - electric] plaque *f*; [- gas] feu *m*, brûleur *m*. -**10.** [group of people] cercle *m*, clique *f pej*; price-fixing ~ cartel *m*; spy/drug ~ réseau *m* d'espions/de trafiquants de drogue. -**11.** CHEM [of atoms] chaîne *f* fermée.

◇ *vt* -**1.** [bell, alarm] sonner; I rang the doorbell j'ai sonné à la porte; the church clock ~s the hours l'horloge de l'église sonne les heures ❑ the name/title ~s a bell ce nom/titre me dit quelque chose; to ~ the bell *inf* [succeed] décrocher le pompon; to ~ the changes [on church bells] carillonner; *fig* changer; to ~ the changes on sthg apporter des changements à qqch. -**2.** *Br* [phone] téléphoner à, appeler; don't ~ us, we'll ~ you *hum* laissez-nous votre adresse, on vous écrira. -**3.** [surround] entourer, encercler; a lake ~ed with trees un lac entouré OR bordé d'arbres. -**4.** [draw circle round] entourer d'un cercle; ~ the right answer entourez la bonne réponse. -**5.** [bird] baguer; [bull, pig] anneler. -**6.** [in quoits, hoopla - throw ring round] lancer un anneau sur.

◇ *vi* -**1.** [chime, peal - bell, telephone, alarm] sonner; [with high pitch] tinter; [long and loud] carillonner; the doorbell rang on a sonné (à la porte). -**2.** [resound] résonner, retentir; their laughter rang through the house leurs rires résonnaient dans toute la maison; the theatre rang with applause la salle retentissait d'applaudissements; my ears are ~ing j'ai les oreilles qui bourdonnent; my ears are still ~ing with their laughter, their laughter still ~s in my ears leurs rires retentissent encore à mes oreilles; to ~ true/false/hollow sonner vrai/faux/creux. -**3.** [summon] sonner; to ~ for the maid sonner la bonne; I rang for a glass of water j'ai sonné pour qu'on m'apporte un verre d'eau; you rang, Sir? Monsieur a sonné? -**4.** *Br* [phone] téléphoner.

◆ **ring around** = **ring round**.

◆ **ring back** *vi insep & vt sep Br* [phone back] rappeler.

◆ **ring down** *vt sep*: to ~ down the curtain THEAT baisser le rideau; to ~ down the curtain on sthg *fig* mettre un terme à qqch.

◆ **ring in** ◇ *vi insep Br* téléphoner; listeners are encouraged to ~ in on encourage les auditeurs à téléphoner (au studio).

◇ *vt sep* -**1.** *Austr & NZ* [rope in] enrôler. -**2.** *phr*: to ~ the New Year in sonner les cloches pour annoncer la nouvelle année.

◆ **ring off** *vi insep Br* raccrocher.

◆ **ring out** ◇ *vi insep* retentir.

◇ *vt sep*: to ~ out the old year sonner le cloches pour annoncer la fin de l'année.

◆ **ring round** *vt insep* téléphoner à, appeler; if you ~ round everybody, I'm sure you'll find someone to help si tu appelles tout le monde tu trouveras bien quelqu'un pour t'aider.

◆ **ring up** *vt sep Br* -**1.** [phone] téléphoner à, appeler. -**2.** [on cash register - sale, sum] enregistrer. -**3.** *phr*: to ~ up the curtain THEAT lever le rideau; to ~ up the curtain on sthg *fig* inaugurer qqch, marquer le début de qqch.

ring-a-ring-a-roses *n chanson que chantent les enfants en faisant la ronde.*

ring binder *n* classeur *m* (à anneaux).

ringbolt ['rɪŋbəʊlt] *n* boulon *m* à anneau de levage.

ring circuit *n* circuit *m* de bouclage.

ringdove ['rɪŋdʌv] *n* (pigeon *m*) ramier *m*.

ringed plover [rɪŋd-] *n* pluvier *m* à collier.

ringer ['rɪŋəʳ] *n* -**1.** [of bells] sonneur *m*, carillonneur *m*, -euse *f*. -**2.** *inf* [double] sosie *m*; he's a (dead) ~ for you vous vous ressemblez comme deux gouttes d'eau. -**3.** ▽ *Am* SPORT [horse] *cheval qui participe frauduleusement à une course*; [player] *joueur participant frauduleusement à un match*. -**4.** *inf Austr* [expert] as *m*, crack *m*.

ring finger *n* annulaire *m*.

ringing ['rɪŋɪŋ] ◇ *adj* sonore, retentissant.

◇ *n* -**1.** [of doorbell, phone, alarm] sonnerie *f*; [of cowbell] tintement *m*; [of church bells] carillonnement *m*. -**2.** [of cries, laughter] retentissement *m*; [in ears] bourdonnement *m*.

ringing tone *n* sonnerie *f*, signal *m* d'appel.

ringleader ['rɪŋˌliːdəʳ] *n* meneur *m*, -euse *f*.

ringlet ['rɪŋlɪt] *n* boucle *f* (de cheveux).

ring main *n* conducteur *m* de bouclage.

ringmaster ['rɪŋˌmɑːstəʳ] *n* ≃ Monsieur Loyal *m*.

ring-pull *n Br* anneau *m*, bague *f (sur une boîte de boisson)*; ~ can cannette *f*, boîte *f (qu'on ouvre en tirant sur une bague)*.

ring road *n* rocade *f*.

ringside ['rɪŋsaɪd] *n (U)* SPORT premiers rangs *mpl*; to have a ~ seat *fig* être aux premières loges.

ring spanner *n Br* clé *f* polygonale.

ringway ['rɪŋweɪ] *Br* = **ring road**.

ringworm ['rɪŋwɜːm] *n* teigne *f*.

rink [rɪŋk] *n* [for ice-skating] patinoire *f*; [for roller-skating] piste *f (pour patins à roulettes)*.

rinky-dink *inf* ['rɪŋkɪdɪŋk] *adj Am* ringard.

rinse [rɪns] ◇ *vt* rincer; she ~d her hands/her mouth elle se rinça les mains/la bouche; ~ the soap out of the clothes rincez les vêtements.

◇ *n* -**1.** [gen] rinçage *m*; I gave the shirt a good ~ j'ai bien rincé la chemise; put the washing machine on ~ mettez le lave-linge sur rinçage. -**2.** [for hair] rinçage *m*; blue ~ rinçage bleu.

◆ **rinse out** *vt sep* rincer.

Rio ['riːəʊ], **Rio de Janeiro** [ˌriːəʊdədʒə'nɪərəʊ] *pr n* Rio de Janeiro.

Rio Grande [ˌriːəʊ'grændɪ] *pr n*: the ~ le Rio Grande.

Rio Negro [ˌriːəʊ'neɪgrəʊ] *pr n*: the ~ le Rio Negro.

riot ['raɪət] ◇ *n* -**1.** [civil disturbance] émeute *f*; race ~s émeutes raciales. -**2.** *inf* [funny occasion]: the party was a ~ on s'est éclatés à la fête ‖ [funny person]: Jim's a ~ Jim est désopilant OR impayable. -**3.** [profusion] profusion *f*; the garden is a ~ of colour le jardin offre une véritable débauche de couleurs.

◇ *vi* participer à OR faire une émeute; they are afraid the people will ~ ils craignent des émeutes populaires.

◇ *adv*: to run ~: a group of youths ran ~ un groupe de jeunes a provoqué une émeute; the team ran ~ in the second half l'équipe s'est déchaînée au cours de la seconde mi-temps; her imagination ran ~ son imagination s'est déchaînée; the vegetation is running ~ la végétation est foisonnante.

riot act *n* loi *f* antiémeutes; to read the ~ *inf* faire acte d'autorité; I decided to read them the ~ j'ai décidé de les rappeler à l'ordre.

rioter [ˈraɪətəʳ] *n* émeutier *m*, -ère *f*.

rioting [ˈraɪətɪŋ] *n (U)* émeutes *fpl*.

riotous [ˈraɪətəs] *adj* -**1.** [mob] déchaîné; [behaviour] séditieux; ~ assembly JUR attroupement *m* séditieux. -**2.** [debauched] débauché; to lead a ~ life mener une vie déréglée OR dissolue || [exuberant, noisy] tapageur, bruyant; a ~ party was going on upstairs à l'étage au-dessus, des fêtards s'en donnaient à cœur joie; bursts of ~ laughter des éclats de rire bruyants. -**3.** [funny] désopilant, tordant.

riotously [ˈraɪətəslɪ] *adv* -**1.** [seditiously] de façon séditieuse. -**2.** [noisily] bruyamment. -**3.** [as intensifier]: it's ~ funny *inf* c'est à mourir OR à hurler de rire.

riot police *npl* police *f* OR forces *fpl* antiémeutes.

riot shield *n* bouclier *m* antiémeutes.

riot squad *n* brigade *f* antiémeutes.

rip [rɪp] (*pt* & *pp* ripped, *cont* ripping)
◇ *vt* -**1.** [tear] déchirer *(violemment)*; he ripped the envelope open il déchira l'enveloppe; to ~ sthg to shreds OR pieces mettre qqch en morceaux OR en lambeaux. -**2.** [snatch] arracher; she ripped the book from my hands elle m'arracha le livre des mains. -**3.** *inf Am* [rob] voler; she ripped him for all he had elle lui a piqué tout ce qu'il avait.
◇ *vi* -**1.** [tear] se déchirer. -**2.** *inf* [go fast] aller à fond de train OR à fond la caisse; a motorbike ripped past une moto est passée à toute allure ❑ let it ~! [go ahead] vas-y!; [accelerate] appuie sur le champignon!; now they're gone we can really let ~ maintenant qu'ils sont partis, on va pouvoir s'éclater; to let ~ at sb enguirlander qqn.
◇ *n* déchirure *f*.
◆ **rip off** *vt sep* -**1.** [tear off] arracher; the binding had been ripped off the book la reliure du livre avait été arrachée. -**2.** *inf* [cheat, overcharge] arnaquer; they ~ off tourists ils arnaquent les touristes. -**3.** *inf* [rob] dévaliser; they ripped off a bank ils ont braqué une banque || [steal] faucher, piquer; my wallet was ripped off je me suis fait faucher mon portefeuille; he ripped off our idea il nous a piqué notre idée.
◆ **rip out** *vt sep* arracher.
◆ **rip through** *vt insep* [subj: explosion, noise] déchirer; we ripped through the work in no time *fig* on a expédié le travail en un rien de temps.
◆ **rip up** *vt sep* [paper, cloth] déchirer *(violemment)*, mettre en pièces; [road surface, street] éventrer.

RIP (*written abbr of* rest in peace) RIP.

riparian [rɪˈpeərɪən] *fml* ◇ *adj* [person, property] riverain; [rights] des riverains.
◇ *n* riverain *m*, -e *f*.

ripcord [ˈrɪpkɔːd] *n* poignée *f* d'ouverture *(de parachute)*.

ripe [raɪp] *adj* -**1.** [fruit, vegetable] mûr; [cheese] fait, à point. -**2.** [age]: to live to a ~ old age vivre jusqu'à un âge avancé; he married at the ~ old age of 80 il s'est marié au bel âge de 80 ans. -**3.** [ready] prêt, mûr; the country is ~ for a change of regime le pays est mûr pour un changement de régime; this land is ~ for development ce terrain ne demande qu'à être aménagé; the time is ~ to sell c'est le moment de vendre. -**4.** [full - lips] sensuel, charnu; [breasts] plantureux. -**5.** [pungent - smell] âcre. -**6.** *inf* [vulgar] égrillard.

ripen [ˈraɪpn] ◇ *vi* [gen] mûrir; [cheese] se faire; her feelings for him had ~ed over the years *fig* ses sentiments pour lui avaient mûri avec le temps.
◇ *vt* [subj: sun] mûrir; [subj: farmer] (faire) mûrir; sun-~ed oranges oranges mûries au soleil.

ripeness [ˈraɪpnɪs] *n* maturité *f*.

rip-off *inf n* -**1.** [swindle] escroquerie *f*, arnaque *f*; that restaurant's a ~ ce restaurant est une arnaque. -**2.** [theft] vol *m*, fauche *f*; it's a ~ from an Osborne play ils ont pompé l'idée dans une pièce d'Osborne.

riposte [*Br* rɪˈpɒst, *Am* rɪˈpəʊst] ◇ *n* -**1.** [retort] riposte *f*, réplique *f*. -**2.** FENCING riposte *f*.
◇ *vi* riposter.

ripper [ˈrɪpəʳ] *n* -**1.** [criminal] éventreur *m*; Jack the Ripper Jack l'Éventreur. -**2.** [machine] scarificateur *m*.

ripping *inf* [ˈrɪpɪŋ] *adj Br dated* épatant, sensass.

ripple [ˈrɪpl] ◇ *n* -**1.** [on water] ride *f*, ondulation *f*; [on wheatfield, hair, sand] ondulation *f*. -**2.** [sound - of waves] clapotis *m*; [- of brook] gazouillis *m*; [- of conversation] murmure *m*; a ~ of excitement ran through the crowd *fig* un murmure d'excitation parcourut la foule; a ~ of laughter ran through the audience des rires discrets parcoururent l'assistance. -**3.** [repercussion] répercussion *f*, vague *f*; her resignation hardly caused a ~ sa démission a fait très peu de bruit; ~ effect effet *m* de vague. -**4.** CULIN: strawberry/chocolate ~ (ice cream) glace *f* marbrée à la fraise/au chocolat. -**5.** ELECTRON oscillation *f*.
◇ *vi* -**1.** [undulate - water] se rider; [- wheatfield, hair] onduler; moonlight ~d on the surface of the lake le clair de lune scintillait sur la surface du lac; the muscles ~d in his back ses muscles se dessinaient sous la peau de son dos; rippling muscles muscles saillants OR puissants. -**2.** [murmur - water, waves] clapoter. -**3.** [resound, have repercussions] se répercuter; the scandal ~d through the whole department le scandale s'est répercuté à travers OR a fait des vagues dans tout le service.
◇ *vt* [water, lake] rider.

rip-roaring *inf adj* [noisy] bruyant, tapageur; [great, fantastic] génial, super; we had a ~ time on s'est amusés comme des fous; a ~ success un succès monstre.

ripsaw [ˈrɪpsɔː] *n* scie *f* à refendre.

ripsnorter *inf* [ˈrɪpˌsnɔːtəʳ] *n* petite merveille *f*; his new film's a ~ son nouveau film est vraiment génial.

riptide [ˈrɪptaɪd] *n* contre-courant *m*, turbulence *f*.

rise [raɪz] (*pt* rose [rəʊz], *pp* risen [ˈrɪzn])
◇ *vi* -**1.** [get up - from chair, bed] se lever; [- from knees, after fall] se relever; he rose (from his chair) to greet me il s'est levé (de sa chaise) pour me saluer; to ~ to one's feet se lever, se mettre debout; he ~s late every morning il se lève tard tous les matins; the horse rose on its hind legs le cheval s'est cabré ❑ ~ and shine! debout! -**2.** [sun, moon, fog] se lever; [smoke, balloon] s'élever, monter; [tide, river level] monter; [river] prendre sa source; [land] s'élever; [fish] mordre; THEAT [curtain] se lever; CULIN [dough] lever; [soufflé] monter; to ~ into the air [bird, balloon] s'élever (dans les airs); [plane] monter OR s'élever (dans les airs); the birds rose above our heads les oiseaux se sont envolés au-dessus de nos têtes; to ~ to the surface [swimmer, whale] remonter à la surface; the colour rose in OR to her cheeks le rouge lui est monté aux joues; his eyebrows rose in surprise il leva les sourcils de surprise; laughter/cheers rose from the crowd des rires/des hourras montèrent de la foule; disturbing images rose into my mind des images troublantes me vinrent à l'esprit; to ~ from the dead RELIG ressusciter d'entre les morts; to ~ into heaven RELIG monter au ciel; to ~ to the occasion se montrer à la hauteur de la situation ❑ to ~ to the bait *literal* & *fig* mordre à l'hameçon; he looked as if he'd risen from the grave il avait une mine de déterré. -**3.** [increase - value] augmenter; [- number, amount] augmenter, monter; [- prices, costs] monter, augmenter, être en hausse; [- temperature, pressure] monter; [- barometer] monter, remonter; [- wind] se lever; [- tension, tone, voice] monter; [- feeling, anger, panic] monter, grandir; gold has risen in value by 10% la valeur de l'or a augmenté de 10 %; to ~ by 10 dollars/by 10% augmenter de 10 dollars/de 10 %; to make prices ~ faire monter les prix; rents are rising fast les loyers augmentent rapidement; his spirits rose when he heard the news il a été soulagé OR heureux d'apprendre la nouvelle. -**4.** [mountains, buildings] se dresser, s'élever; the trees rose above our heads les arbres se dressaient au-dessus de nos têtes; the mountain ~s to 2,500 m la montagne a une altitude de OR culmine à OR s'élève à 2 500 m; the steeple ~s 200 feet into the air le clocher a OR fait 60 mètres de haut; many new apartment blocks have risen in the past ten years de nombreux immeubles neufs ont été construits au cours des dix dernières années ❑ to ~ from the ashes renaître de ses cendres. -**5.** [socially, professionally] monter, réussir; to ~ in society réussir socialement; to ~ in the world faire son chemin dans le monde; to ~ to fame devenir célèbre; to ~ in sb's esteem monter dans l'estime de qqn; to ~ from the ranks sortir du rang; she rose to the position of personnel manager elle a réussi à devenir chef du personnel. -**6.** [revolt] se soulever, se révolter; to ~ in revolt (against sb/sthg) se révolter (contre qqn/qqch); to ~ in protest against sthg se soulever contre qqch. -**7.** [adjourn - assembly, meeting] lever la séance; [- Parliament, court] clore la session; Parliament rose for the summer recess la session parlementaire est close pour les vacances d'été.
◇ *n* -**1.** [high ground] hauteur *f*, éminence *f*; [slope] pente *f*; we reached the top of a steep ~ nous sommes arrivés au sommet d'une côte raide. -**2.** [of moon, sun, curtain] lever *m*; [to power, influence] montée *f*, ascension *f*; INDUST [development] essor *m*; the ~ and fall of the tide le flux et le reflux de la marée; the ~ and fall of the Roman Empire la croissance et la chute OR la grandeur et la décadence de l'Empire romain; the ~ and fall of the fascist movement la montée et la chute du mouvement fasciste; the actor's ~ to fame was both rapid and spectacular cet acteur a connu un succès à la fois rapide et spectaculaire. -**3.** [increase - of price, crime, accidents] hausse *f*, augmentation *f*; [- in bank rate, interest] relèvement *m*, hausse *f*; [- of temperature, pressure] hausse *f*; [- of affluence, wealth] augmentation *f*; to be on the ~ être en hausse; there has been a steep ~ in house prices les prix de l'immobilier ont beaucoup augmenté; there was a 10% ~ in the number of visitors le nombre de visiteurs a augmenté de 10 %; there has been a steady ~ in the number of accidents les accidents sont en augmentation régulière; ~ in value appréciation *f*; to speculate on a ~ ST. EX miser sur la hausse || *Br* [in salary] augmentation *f* (de salaire); to be given a ~ être augmenté. -**4.** [of river] source *f*. -**5.** *phr*: to give ~ to sthg donner lieu à qqch, entraîner qqch; it gave ~ to a lot of hostility/difficulties cela a provoqué une forte hostilité/beaucoup de difficultés; their disappearance gave ~ to great scandal/suspicion leur disparition a provoqué un énorme scandale/éveillé de nombreux soupçons; to get OR to take a ~ out of sb *inf Br* faire réagir qqn, faire marcher qqn.
◆ **rise above** *vt insep* [obstacle, fear] surmonter; [figure] dépasser; politics should ~ above the level of personal attacks le débat politique ne devrait pas se situer au niveau des attaques personnelles.
◆ **rise up** *vi insep* -**1.** [get up] se lever; to ~ up from one's chair se lever de sa chaise || [go up] monter, s'élever; the smoke/the balloon rose up into the sky la fumée/le ballon s'élevait dans le ciel. -**2.** [revolt] se soulever, se révolter; to ~ up against an oppressor se soulever contre un oppresseur. -**3.** RELIG ressusciter; to ~ up from the dead ressusciter d'entre les

morts. -**4.** [appear] apparaître; **a strange sight rose up before his eyes** un spectacle étrange s'offrit alors à son regard; **a shadowy figure rose up out of the mist** une ombre surgit de la brume.

risen [ˈrɪzn] ◇ *pp* → **rise**.
◇ *adj* ressuscité; **Christ is ~** le Christ est ressuscité.

riser [ˈraɪzəʳ] *n* -**1.** [person]: **to be an early/late ~** être un lève-tôt *(inv)* /lève-tard *(inv)*. -**2.** [of step] contremarche *f*. -**3.** [in plumbing] conduite *f* montante.

risibility [ˌrɪzəˈbɪlətɪ] (*pl* **risibilities**) *n fml* faculté *f* de rire, propension *f* à rire.

risible [ˈrɪzəbl] *adj fml* risible, ridicule.

rising [ˈraɪzɪŋ] ◇ *n* -**1.** [revolt] insurrection *f*, soulèvement *m*. -**2.** [of sun, moon, of theatre curtain] lever *m*. -**3.** [of prices] augmentation *f*, hausse *f*. -**4.** [of river] crue *f*; [of ground] élévation *f*. -**5.** [from dead] résurrection *f*. -**6.** [of Parliament, an assembly] ajournement *m*, clôture *f* de séance.
◇ *adj* -**1.** [sun] levant; **they were up early to see the ~ sun** ils se levèrent de bonne heure pour voir le soleil se lever OR le soleil levant. -**2.** [tide] montant; [water level] ascendant. -**3.** [ground, road] qui monte. -**4.** [temperature, prices] en hausse; FIN [market] orienté à la hausse. -**5.** [up-and-coming]: **the ~ generation** la nouvelle génération, la génération montante; **he's a ~ celebrity** c'est une étoile montante. -**6.** [emotion] croissant.
◇ *adv inf Br*: **she's ~ 40** elle va sur ses 40 ans.

rising damp *n* humidité *f* ascensionnelle OR par capillarité.

rising trot *n* trot *m* enlevé OR à l'anglaise.

risk [rɪsk] ◇ *n* -**1.** [gen] risque *m*; **to take a ~** prendre un risque; **to run the ~** courir le risque; **the government runs the ~ of losing support** le gouvernement (court le) risque de ne plus être soutenu; **if you don't leave now there's a ~ of you not arriving on time** si vous ne partez pas maintenant, vous risquez de ne pas arriver à temps; **is there any ~ of him making another blunder?** est-ce qu'il risque de commettre un nouvel impair?; **it's not worth the ~** c'est trop risqué; **that's a ~ we'll have to take** c'est un risque à courir; **do it at your own ~** faites-le à vos risques et périls; **'cars may be parked here at the owner's ~'** les automobilistes peuvent stationner ici à leurs risques (et périls); **at the ~ of one's life** au péril de sa vie; **at the ~ of sounding ignorant, how does one open this box?** au risque de passer pour un idiot, j'aimerais savoir comment on ouvre cette boîte? -**2.** [in insurance] risque *m*; **fire ~** risque d'incendie; **he's a bad ~** c'est un client à risques.
◇ *vt* risquer, hasarder *fml*; **don't ~ your career/reputation on a shady deal** ne risquez pas votre carrière/réputation sur une affaire louche; **you're ~ing an accident when you drive so fast** vous risquez un accident en conduisant si vite; **to ~ defeat** risquer d'être battu ❑ **to ~ one's neck** OR **skin, to ~ life and limb** risquer sa peau.
◆ **at risk** *adj phr*: **there's too much at ~** les risques OR les enjeux sont trop importants; **our children are at ~ from all kinds of violence** nos enfants ont toutes sortes de violences à craindre; **all our jobs are at ~** tous nos emplois sont menacés; **to be at ~** MED & SOCIOL être vulnérable, être une personne à risque.

risk capital *n (U) Br* capitaux *mpl* à risques.

riskiness [ˈrɪskɪnɪs] *n (U)* risques *mpl*, hasards *mpl*, aléas *mpl*.

risk-taking *n (U) fait m de prendre des risques*; **we knew there would be some ~ involved** nous savions que ce ne serait pas sans risques.

risky [ˈrɪskɪ] (*compar* **riskier**, *superl* **riskiest**) *adj* [hazardous] risqué, hasardeux; **~ business** entreprise hasardeuse.

risotto [rɪˈzɒtəʊ] (*pl* **risottos**) *n* risotto *m*.

risqué [ˈriːskeɪ] *adj* [story, joke] risqué, osé, scabreux.

rissole [ˈrɪsəʊl] *n* rissole *f* CULIN.

rite [raɪt] *n* rite *m*; **initiation/fertility ~s** rites d'initiation/de fertilité; **~ of passage** cérémonie *f* d'initiation; **'The Rite of Spring'** *Stravinsky* 'le Sacre du printemps'.

ritual [ˈrɪtʃʊəl] ◇ *n* rituel *m*; **everyone has to go through the ~ of official receptions** nul ne peut échapper au cérémonial des réceptions officielles.
◇ *adj* rituel; **we all had to sit down to the ~ Sunday lunch** *fig* dimanche, nous avons tous dû prendre part au déjeuner rituel.

ritualism [ˈrɪtʃʊəlɪzm] *n* ritualisme *m*.

ritualist [ˈrɪtʃʊəlɪst] *n* ritualiste *mf*.

ritualistic [ˌrɪtʃʊəˈlɪstɪk] *adj* ritualiste.

ritualize, ise [ˈrɪtʃʊəlaɪz] *vt* ritualiser.

ritually [ˈrɪtʃʊəlɪ] *adv* rituellement.

ritzy *inf* [ˈrɪtsɪ] (*compar* **ritzier**, *superl* **ritziest**) *adj* classe, très chic, luxueux.

rival [ˈraɪvl] (*Br pt* & *pp* **rivalled**, *cont* **rivalling**, *Am pt* & *pp* **rivaled**, *cont* **rivaling**) ◇ *n* [gen] rival *m*, -e *f*; COMM rival *m*, -e *f*, concurrent *m*, -e *f*; **'The Rivals'** *Sheridan* 'les Rivaux'.
◇ *adj* [gen] rival; COMM concurrent, rival.
◇ *vt* [gen] rivaliser avec; COMM être en concurrence avec; **his talent doesn't ~ hers** il n'est pas aussi doué qu'elle; **no-one can ~ her when it comes to business acumen** son sens des affaires n'a pas d'égal; **your stubbornness is rivalled only by your narrow-mindedness** votre entêtement n'a d'égal que votre étroitesse d'esprit.

rivalry [ˈraɪvlrɪ] (*pl* **rivalries**) *n* rivalité *f*; **there's a lot of ~ between the two brothers** il y a une forte rivalité entre les deux frères; **in ~ with sb** en concurrence OR rivalité avec qqn.

riven [ˈrɪvn] *adj* déchiré, divisé; **the party was ~ by deep ideological divisions** le parti était déchiré par de profondes divergences idéologiques.

river [ˈrɪvəʳ] ◇ *n* -**1.** [as tributary] rivière *f*; [flowing to sea] fleuve *m*; **we sailed up/down the ~** nous avons remonté/descendu la rivière ❑ **to be up the ~** *inf Am* [in prison] être en taule. -**2.** *fig* [of mud, lava] coulée *f*; **a ~ of blood** un fleuve de sang.
◇ *comp* [port, system, traffic] fluvial; [fish] d'eau douce.

riverbank [ˈrɪvəbæŋk] *n* rive *f*, berge *f*; **on the ~** sur la rive (de la rivière OR du fleuve).

river basin *n* bassin *m* fluvial.

riverbed [ˈrɪvəbed] *n* lit *m* de rivière OR de fleuve.

river blindness *n* cécité *f* des rivières, onchocercose *f spec*.

riverine [ˈrɪvəraɪn] *adj* [fluvial] fluvial; [riverside] riverain.

riverside [ˈrɪvəsaɪd] ◇ *n* bord *m* d'une rivière OR d'un fleuve, rive *f*; **we walked along the ~** nous nous sommes promenés le long de la rivière.
◇ *adj* au bord d'une rivière OR d'un fleuve; **a ~ park** un parc situé au bord de l'eau OR d'une rivière.

rivet [ˈrɪvɪt] ◇ *n* rivet *m*.
◇ *vt* -**1.** TECH riveter, river. -**2.** *fig*: **to be ~ed to the spot** rester cloué OR rivé sur place; **the children were ~ed to the television set** les enfants étaient rivés au poste de télévision. -**3.** [fascinate] fasciner.

riveter [ˈrɪvɪtəʳ] *n* [person] riveur *m*; [machine] riveteuse *f*.

riveting [ˈrɪvɪtɪŋ] *adj* fascinant, passionnant, captivant.

Riviera [ˌrɪvɪˈeərə] *pr n*: **the French ~** la Côte d'Azur; **on the French ~** sur la Côte d'Azur; **the Italian ~** la Riviera italienne; **on the Italian ~** sur la Riviera italienne.

rivulet [ˈrɪvjʊlɪt] *n* (petit) ruisseau *m*, ru *m lit*.

Riyadh [riːˈæd] *pr n* Riyad, Riad.

RMT (*abbr of* **National Union of Rail, Maritime and Transport Workers**) *pr n syndicat britannique des cheminots et des gens de mer*.

RN ◇ *pr n abbr of* **Royal Navy**.
◇ *n Br* (*abbr of* **registered nurse**) -**1.** [nurse] infirmier *m* diplômé (d'État); infirmière *f* diplômée (d'État). -**2.** [qualification] diplôme *m* (d'État) d'infirmier.

RNA (*abbr of* **ribonucleic acid**) *n* ARN *m*.

RNLI (*abbr of* **Royal National Lifeboat Institution**) *pr n société britannique de sauvetage en mer*.

RNZAF (*abbr of* **Royal New Zealand Air Force**) *pr n armée de l'air néo-zélandaise*.

RNZN (*abbr of* **Royal New Zealand Navy**) *pr n marine de guerre néo-zélandaise*.

roach [rəʊtʃ] (*pl sense 1 inv* OR **roaches**) *n* -**1.** [fish] gardon *m*. -**2.** *inf* [cockroach] cafard *m*, cancrelat *m*. -**3.** *drugs sl* [of marijuana cigarette] filtre *m*.

road [rəʊd] ◇ *n* -**1.** *literal* route *f*; [small] chemin *m*; **main** OR **major ~** route principale (route) nationale *f*; **minor ~** route secondaire; **by ~** par la route; **the Liverpool ~** la route de Liverpool; **is this the (right) ~ for** OR **to Liverpool?** est-ce la (bonne) route pour Liverpool?; **are we on the right ~?** sommes-nous sur la bonne route?; **on the ~ to Liverpool, the car broke down** en allant à Liverpool, la voiture est tombée en panne; **we took the ~ from Manchester to Liverpool** on a pris la route qui va de Manchester à Liverpool OR qui relie Manchester à Liverpool; **to take to the ~** [driver] prendre la route OR le volant; [tramp] partir sur les routes; **to be on the ~** [pop star, troupe] être en tournée; **we've been on the ~ since 6 o'clock this morning** nous roulons depuis 6 h ce matin; **his car shouldn't be on the ~** sa voiture devrait être retirée de la circulation; **someone of his age shouldn't be on the ~** une personne de son âge ne devrait pas prendre le volant; **the price on the ~ excludes numberplates and delivery** *Br* le prix clés en mains ne comprend pas les frais de livraison et d'immatriculation; **my car is off the ~ at the moment** ma voiture est en panne OR chez le garagiste || [street] rue *f*; **a ~ of shops/of houses** une rue de magasins/de maisons, une artère commerçante/résidentielle; **he lives just down the ~** il habite un peu plus loin dans la même rue; **Mr. James from across the ~** M. James qui habite en face; **he lives across the ~ from us** il habite en face de chez nous || [roadway] route *f*, chaussée *f*; **to stand in the middle of the ~** se tenir au milieu de la route OR de la chaussée ❑ **one for the ~** *inf* un petit coup avant de partir; **the ~ to hell is paved with good intentions** *prov* l'enfer est pavé de bonnes intentions *prov*; **'On the Road'** *Kerouac* 'Sur la route'. -**2.** *fig* [path] chemin *m*, voie *f*; **to be on the right ~** être sur la bonne voie; **to be on the ~ to success/recovery** être sur le chemin de la réussite/en voie de guérison; **he is on the ~ to an early death** il est (bien) parti pour mourir jeune; **you're in my ~!** *inf Br* [I can't pass] vous me bouchez le passage!; [I can't see] vous me bouchez la vue!; **get out of my ~!** *inf Br* poussez-vous!, dégagez! -**3.** *Am* [railway] chemin de fer *m*, voie *f* ferrée. -**4.** *(usu pl)* NAUT rade *f*. -**5.** [in mine] galerie *f*. -**6.** *inf Br dial phr*: **any ~ (up)** de toute façon; **it's too late any ~** de toute façon, c'est trop tard.
◇ *comp* [traffic, transport, bridge] routier; [accident] de la route; [conditions, construction, repairs] des routes.

roadbed [ˈrəʊdbed] *n* CONSTR empierrement *m*; RAIL ballast *m*.

roadblock [ˈrəʊdblɒk] *n* barrage *m* routier.

road book *n* guide *m* routier.

road-fund licence *n Br* vignette *f* (automobile).

road hog *inf n* chauffard *m*.

roadholding [ˈrəʊdˌhəʊldɪŋ] *n* tenue *f* de route.

roadhouse [ˈrəʊdhaʊs, *pl* -haʊzɪz] *n* relais *m* routier.

roadie *inf* [ˈrəʊdɪ] *n technicien qui accompagne les groupes de rock en tournée*.

roadman [ˈrəʊdmən] (*pl* **roadmen** [-mən]) *n* cantonnier *m*.

road manager *n* responsable *m* de tournée *(d'un chanteur ou d'un groupe pop)*.
roadmap ['rəʊdmæp] *n* carte *f* routière.
road metal *n* ballast *m*.
road racing *n* compétition *f* automobile *(sur route)*.
road roller *n* rouleau *m* compresseur.
roadrunner ['rəʊd,rʌnəʳ] *n* coucou *m* terrestre de Californie.
road safety *n* sécurité *f* routière.
road sense *n* [for driver] sens *m* de la conduite; [for pedestrian]: **children have to be taught ~** on doit apprendre aux enfants à faire attention à la circulation.
roadshow ['rəʊdʃəʊ] *n* [gen] tournée *f*; [radio show] *animation en direct proposée par une station de radio en tournée*.
roadside ['rəʊdsaɪd] ◇ *n* bord *m* de la route, bas-côté *m*; **we stopped the car by the ~** nous avons arrêté la voiture au bord OR sur le bord de la route.
◇ *adj* au bord de la route; **~ inn** auberge située au bord de la route.
road sign *n* panneau *m* de signalisation.
roadstead ['rəʊdsted] *n* rade *f*.
roadster ['rəʊdstəʳ] *n* -**1.** [car] roadster *m*. -**2.** [bicycle] bicyclette *f* (de tourisme).
roadsweeper ['rəʊd,swiːpəʳ] *n* [person] balayeur *m*, -euse *f*; [vehicle] balayeuse *f*.
road tax *n Br* taxe *f* sur les automobiles; **~ disc** vignette *f* (automobile).
road test *n* essai *m* sur route.
◆ **road-test** *vt* essayer sur route.
road-user *n* usager *m*, -ère *f* de la route.
roadway ['rəʊdweɪ] *n* chaussée *f*.
road works *npl* travaux *mpl* (d'entretien des routes).
roadworthiness ['rəʊd,wɜːðɪnɪs] *n* état *m* général *(d'un véhicule)*.
roadworthy ['rəʊd,wɜːðɪ] *adj* [vehicle] en état de rouler.
roam [rəʊm] ◇ *vt* -**1.** [travel - world] parcourir; [- streets] errer dans; **to ~ the seven seas** aller aux quatre coins du monde. -**2.** [hang about - streets] traîner dans.
◇ *vi* [wander] errer, voyager sans but; **he allowed his imagination/his thoughts to ~** *fig* il a laissé vagabonder son imagination/ses pensées.
◆ **roam about** *Br*, **roam around** *vi insep* -**1.** [travel] vagabonder, bourlinguer. -**2.** [aimlessly] errer, traîner.
roamer ['rəʊməʳ] *n* vagabond *m*, -e *f*.
roaming ['rəʊmɪŋ] ◇ *adj* vagabond, errant.
◇ *n* vagabondage *m*.
roan [rəʊn] ◇ *adj* rouan.
◇ *n* rouan *m*.
roar [rɔːʳ] ◇ *vi* [lion] rugir; [bull] beugler, mugir; [elephant] barrir; [person] hurler, crier; [crowd] hurler; [radio, music] beugler, hurler; [sea, wind] mugir; [storm, thunder] gronder; [fire] ronfler; [cannon] tonner; [car, motorcycle, engine] vrombir; **to ~ with anger** rugir OR hurler de colère; **to ~ with laughter** se tordre de rire; **to ~ with pain** hurler de douleur; **it made everyone ~ (with laughter)** ça a déclenché un tonnerre d'hilarité OR l'hilarité générale; **the car ~ed past** [noisily] la voiture est passée en vrombissant; [fast] la voiture est passée à toute allure; **the leading car ~ed into the pits** la voiture de tête est arrivée à toute allure à son stand; **he ~ed up to us on his motorbike** il est venu vers nous à toute allure en faisant vrombir sa moto.
◇ *vt* [feelings, order] hurler; **the sergeant ~ed (out) an order to the men** le sergent a hurlé un ordre aux hommes; **he ~ed something at me** il m'a hurlé quelque chose; **the crowd ~ed their delight** la foule hurlait de joie.
◇ *n* [of lion] rugissement *m*; [of bull] mugissement *m*, beuglement *m*; [of elephant] barrissement *m*; [of sea, wind] mugissement *m*; [of thunder, storm] grondement *m*; [of fire] ronflement *m*; [of cannons] grondement *m*; [of crowd] hurlements *mpl*; [of engine] vrombissement *m*; **~s of laughter** gros OR grands éclats de rire; **the ~ of the traffic outside my window is awful** le vacarme de la circulation sous ma fenêtre est épouvantable.
roaring ['rɔːrɪŋ] ◇ *adj* -**1.** [lion] rugissant; [bull] mugissant, beuglant; [elephant] qui barrit; [person, crowd] hurlant; [sea, wind] mugissant; [thunder, storm] qui gronde; [engine] vrombissant; **a ~ fire** une bonne flambée. -**2.** *fig* [excellent]: **a ~ success** un succès fou; **to do a ~ trade** *Br* faire des affaires en or; **they did a ~ trade in pancakes** ils ont vendu énormément de crêpes.
◇ *adv inf*: **~ drunk** ivre mort, complètement bourré.
Roaring Forties *npl* NAUT quarantièmes *mpl* rugissants.
Roaring Twenties *npl*: **the ~** les Années *fpl* folles.
roast [rəʊst] ◇ *vt* -**1.** [meat] rôtir; [peanuts, chestnuts] griller; [coffee] griller, torréfier; **I decided to ~ a chicken for dinner** j'ai décidé de faire un poulet rôti pour le dîner. -**2.** [minerals] calciner. -**3.** *fig* [by sun, fire] griller, rôtir; **I sat ~ing my toes by the fire** j'étais assis devant le feu pour me réchauffer les pieds.
◇ *vi* -**1.** [meat] rôtir. -**2.** *fig* [person] avoir très chaud; **we spent a week ~ing in the sun** nous avons passé une semaine à nous rôtir au soleil.
◇ *adj* rôti; **~ beef** rôti *m* de bœuf, rosbif *m*; **~ chicken** poulet *m* rôti; **~ veal/pork** rôti *m* de veau/de porc; **~ potatoes** pommes de terre *fpl* rôties au four.
◇ *n* -**1.** [joint of meat] rôti *m*; **the Sunday ~** le rôti du dimanche. -**2.** *Am* [barbecue] barbecue *m*; **to have a ~** faire un barbecue.
roaster ['rəʊstəʳ] *n* [bird] volaille *f* à rôtir.
roasting ['rəʊstɪŋ] ◇ *n* -**1.** [of meat] rôtissage *m*; [of coffee] torréfaction *f*; **~ spit** tournebroche *m*; **~ tin** plat *m* à rôtir. -**2.** *inf Br fig* [harsh criticism] savon *m*; **to give sb a ~** *inf* passer un savon à qqn.
◇ *adj inf* [weather] torride; **it was ~ in her office** il faisait une chaleur à crever dans son bureau; **I'm ~!** je crève de chaud!
rob [rɒb] *(pt & pp* **robbed**, *cont* **robbing)** *vt* -**1.** [person] voler; [bank] dévaliser; [house] cambrioler; **to ~ sb of sthg** voler OR dérober qqch à qqn; **I've been robbed!** au voleur!; **someone has robbed the till!** on a volé l'argent de la caisse! -**2.** *fig* [deprive] priver; **to ~ sb of sthg** priver qqn de qqch; **the immigrants were robbed of their rights** les immigrés ont été privés de leurs droits; **the team was robbed of its victory** l'équipe s'est vue ravir la victoire; **we were robbed!** [after match] on nous a volés!
❑ **to ~ Peter to pay Paul** déshabiller Pierre pour habiller Paul.
robber ['rɒbəʳ] *n* [of property] voleur *m*, -euse *f*.
robbery ['rɒbərɪ] *(pl* **robberies)** *n* -**1.** [of property] vol *m*; [of bank] hold-up *m*; [of house] cambriolage *m*; **~ with violence** vol *m* avec coups et blessures, vol *m* qualifié *spec*. -**2.** *inf* [overcharging] vol *m*; **it's just plain ~!** c'est de l'escroquerie OR du vol manifeste!
robe [rəʊb] ◇ *n* -**1.** [dressing gown] peignoir *m*, robe *f* de chambre. -**2.** [long garment - gen] robe *f*; [- for judge, academic] robe *f*, toge *f*.
◇ *vt* [dress - gen] habiller, vêtir; [- in robe] vêtir d'une robe; **~d in red** vêtu de rouge; **to ~ o.s.** se vêtir.
◇ *vi* [judge] revêtir sa robe.
Robert the Bruce [,rɒbətðə'bruːs] *pr n* Robert Bruce.
robin ['rɒbɪn] *n* -**1.** [European]: **~ (redbreast)** rouge-gorge *m*. -**2.** [American] merle *m* américain.
Robin Hood *pr n* Robin des Bois.
Robinson Crusoe ['rɒbɪnsən'kruːsəʊ] *pr n* Robinson Crusoé.
robot ['rəʊbɒt] ◇ *n* -**1.** *literal & fig* [automaton] robot *m*, automate *m*. -**2.** *SAfr* [traffic lights] feux *mpl* de circulation.
◇ *comp* [pilot, vehicle, system] automatique.
robot bomb *n* bombe *f* volante.
robot dancing *n danse des années 80 caractérisée par des mouvements saccadés*.
robotic [rəʊ'bɒtɪk] *adj* robotique.
robotics [rəʊ'bɒtɪks] *n (U)* robotique *f*.
robotize, -ise ['rəʊbətaɪz] *vt* robotiser.
robust [rəʊ'bʌst] *adj* [person] robuste, vigoureux, solide; [health] solide; [appetite] robuste, solide; [wine] robuste, corsé; [structure] solide; [economy, style, car] robuste; [response, defence] vigoureux, énergique.
robustly [rəʊ'bʌstlɪ] *adv* solidement, avec robustesse.
robustness [rəʊ'bʌstnɪs] *n* [of person] robustesse *f*, vigueur *f*; [of appetite] robustesse *f*, solidité *f*; [of furniture, health] solidité *f*; [of economy, style, car] robustesse *f*; [of response, defence] vigueur *f*.
roc [rɒk] *n* rock *m*.
rock [rɒk] ◇ *n* -**1.** [substance] roche *f*, roc *m*; **the lighthouse is built on ~** le phare est construit sur le roc. -**2.** [boulder] rocher *m*; **the boat struck the ~s** le bateau a été jeté sur les rochers
❑ **to see the ~s ahead** *fig* anticiper les difficultés futures; **to be on the ~s** *inf* [person] être dans la dèche; [firm] être en faillite; [enterprise, marriage] mal tourner, tourner à la catastrophe; **this time last year the firm seemed to be on the ~s** l'an dernier à cette époque, l'entreprise semblait être au bord de la faillite; **to go on the ~s** [firm] faire faillite; [enterprise, marriage] mal tourner; **on the ~s** [drink] avec des glaçons; **'Brighton Rock'** *Greene* 'le Rocher de Brighton'. -**3.** [music, dance] rock *m*. -**4.** [in place names] rocher *m*, roche *f*; **the Rock (of Gibraltar)** (le rocher de) Gibraltar. -**5.** *Am* [stone, pebble] pierre *f*. -**6.** *Br* [sweet] ≃ sucre *m* d'orge. -**7.** RELIG [stronghold] rocher *m*, roc *m*; **Rock of Ages** Jésus-Christ. -**8.** ▽ [diamond] diam *m*. -**9.** ▽ *(usu pl)* [testicle] couille *f*.
◇ *comp* [film] rock; [band, record] (de) rock; [radio station] de rock; **a ~ guitarist** un guitariste rock.
◇ *vt* -**1.** [swing to and fro - baby] bercer; [- chair] balancer; [- lever] basculer; [- boat] ballotter, tanguer; **to ~ a baby to sleep** bercer un bébé pour l'endormir; **he ~ed himself in the rocking chair** il se balançait dans le fauteuil à bascule; **the boat was ~ed by the waves** [gently] le bateau était bercé par les flots; [violently] le bateau était ballotté par les vagues
❑ **to ~ the boat** jouer les trouble-fête, semer le trouble; **now you've settled in, you must be careful not to ~ the boat** maintenant que tu es bien adapté, essaie de ne pas nous causer d'ennuis. -**2.** [shake] secouer, ébranler; **the village was ~ed by an explosion/an earthquake** le village fut ébranlé par une explosion/un tremblement de terre; **the stock market crash ~ed the financial world to its core** le krach boursier a ébranlé en profondeur le monde de la finance; **she was ~ed by the news** elle a été bouleversée par les nouvelles.
◇ *vi* -**1.** [sway] se balancer; **to ~ on a chair** se balancer sur une chaise. -**2.** [quake] trembler; **to ~ with laughter** se tordre de rire. -**3.** [jive] danser le rock.
rockabilly ['rɒkə,bɪlɪ] *n* rockabilly *m*.
rock and roll *n* rock *m* (and roll); **to do the ~** danser le rock.
rock bass *n* achigan *m* de roche.
rock bottom *n fig*: **to hit ~** [person] avoir le moral à zéro, toucher le fond; [firm, finances] atteindre le niveau le plus bas.
◆ **rock-bottom** *adj* [price] défiant toute concurrence, le plus bas.
rock bun, rock cake *n* rocher *m (gâteau)*.
rock candy *n Am* sucre *m* d'orge.
rock climber *n* varappeur *m*, -euse *f*.
rock climbing *n* escalade *f* (de rochers), varappe *f*; **to go ~** faire de l'escalade OR de la varappe.
rock crystal *n* cristal *m* de roche.
rock dash *n Am* [pebbledash] crépi *m*.
rocker ['rɒkəʳ] *n* -**1.** [of cradle, chair] bascule *f*; **to be off one's ~** *inf* être cinglé, débloquer.

-**2.** [rocking chair] fauteuil *m* à bascule. -**3.** *Br* [youth] rocker *m*; the Rockers *jeunes motards aux cheveux longs qui rivalisaient avec les «Mods» dans les années 60*.

rocker arm *n* culbuteur *m*.

rockery ['rɒkərɪ] (*pl* rockeries) *n* (jardin *m* de) rocaille *f*.

rocket ['rɒkɪt] ◇ *n* -**1.** AERON & ASTRONAUT fusée *f*; to fire OR to send up a ~ lancer une fusée ❑ to go off like a ~ partir comme une fusée; to get a ~ (from sb) *inf Br* se faire enguirlander (par qqn); to give sb a ~ *inf Br* enguirlander qqn. -**2.** MIL [missile] roquette *f*; to fire a ~ lancer une roquette. -**3.** [signal, flare] fusée *f*. -**4.** [firework] fusée *f*.
◇ *vt* -**1.** [missile, astronaut] lancer (dans l'espace); the spacecraft was ~ed to the moon le vaisseau spatial a été lancé en direction de la lune. -**2.** [record, singer] faire monter en flèche; the record ~ed the group into the top 10 grâce à ce disque, le groupe est monté en flèche jusqu'au top 10.
◇ *vi* [price, sales] monter en flèche; to ~ to fame devenir célèbre du jour au lendemain; the group ~ed up the charts le groupe est monté dans le hit-parade comme une flèche; the car ~ed down the road/round the track la voiture a descendu la rue/fait le tour de la piste à une vitesse incroyable.
◇ *comp* [propulsion] par fusée; [engine] de fusée.

rocket bomb *n* roquette *f*.

rocket gun *n* fusil *m* lance-roquettes.

rocket launcher *n* AERON & ASTRONAUT lance-fusées *m inv*; MIL lance-roquettes *m inv*.

rocket range *n* base *f* de lancement de missiles.

rocketry ['rɒkɪtrɪ] *n* -**1.** [science] fuséologie *f*. -**2.** [rockets collectively] arsenal *m* de fusées.

rock face *n* paroi *f* rocheuse.

rockfall ['rɒkfɔːl] *n* chute *f* de pierres OR de rochers.

rockfish ['rɒkfɪʃ] (*pl inv* OR **rockfishes**) *n* gobie *m*, rascasse *f*.

rock garden *n* jardin *m* de rocaille.

rock-hard *adj* dur comme le roc.

Rockies ['rɒkɪz] *pl pr n*: the ~ les Rocheuses *fpl*.

rocking ['rɒkɪŋ] *n* -**1.** [of chair, boat] balancement *m*; [of baby] bercement *m*; [of head - to rhythm] balancement *m*. -**2.** MECH oscillation *f*.

rocking chair *n* fauteuil *m* à bascule, rocking-chair *m*.

rocking horse *n* cheval *m* à bascule.

rock-like *adj* comme un OR le roc.

rock melon *n Am, Austr* & *NZ* cantaloup *m*.

rock music *n* rock *m*.

rock'n'roll = **rock and roll**.

rock oil *n* pétrole *m*.

rock plant *n* plante *f* de rocaille.

rock pool *n* mare *f* d'eau de mer dans les rochers.

rock salmon *n* roussette *f*.

rock salt *n* sel *m* gemme.

rocky ['rɒkɪ] (*compar* **rockier**, *superl* **rockiest**) *adj* -**1.** [seabed, mountain] rocheux; [path, track] rocailleux. -**2.** [unstable - situation] précaire, instable; [- government] peu stable.

Rocky Mountains *pl pr n*: the ~ les montagnes *fpl* Rocheuses.

rococo [rə'kəʊkəʊ] ◇ *adj* rococo.
◇ *n* rococo *m*.

rod [rɒd] *n* -**1.** [stick, bar - of iron] barre *f*; [- of wood] baguette *f*; [- for curtains, carpet] tringle *f*; [- for fishing] canne *f*; [- for punishment] baguette *f*; [- flexible] verge *f*; SCH [pointer] baguette *f*; to be beaten with a ~ recevoir des coups de baguette ❑ ~ and line FISHING canne à pêche; ~ fishing pêche *f* à la ligne; ~ of office (symbole *m* de) pouvoir *m*; to rule with a ~ of iron gouverner d'une main OR poigne de fer; to make a ~ for one's own back donner des bâtons pour se faire battre. -**2.** [of uranium] barre *f*. -**3.** MECH [in engine] tige *f*; [mechanism]: ~s tringlerie *f*, timonerie *f*. -**4.** [for surveying] mire *f*. -**5.** ANAT [in eye] bâtonnet *m*. -**6.** [linear or square measure] ≃ perche *f*. -**7.** ▽ *Am* [gun] flingue *m*. -**8.** ▽ [car] voiture *f* gonflée. -**9.** ▼ [penis] bite *f*.

rode [rəʊd] *pt* → **ride**.

rodent ['rəʊdənt] ◇ *adj* rongeur.
◇ *n* rongeur *m*.

rodent operative *n Br* ADMIN spécialiste *mf* de la dératisation.

rodeo ['rəʊdɪəʊ] (*pl* rodeos) *n* rodéo *m*.

Rodeo Drive *pr n luxueuse rue commerçante à Hollywood, aux États-Unis*.

roe [rəʊ] (*pl sense 2 inv* OR roes) *n* *(U)* -**1.** [eggs] œufs *mpl* de poisson; [sperm] laitance *f*; cod ~ œufs de cabillaud. -**2.** ZOOL: ~ (deer) chevreuil *m*.

roebuck ['rəʊbʌk] *n* chevreuil *m* mâle.

Roedean ['rəʊdiːn] *pr n*: ~ (School) *célèbre école privée pour jeunes filles en Angleterre*.

roentgen ['rɒntjən] ◇ *n* röntgen *m*, rœntgen *m*.
◇ *adj*: ~ rays rayons *mpl* X.

roentgenotherapy [,rɒntjənəʊ'θerəpɪ] *n* radiothérapie *f*.

rogation [rəʊ'geɪʃn] *n* (*usu pl*) rogations *fpl*.

Rogation Days *npl* rogations *fpl*.

Rogation Sunday *n* dimanche *m* des rogations.

roger ['rɒdʒəʳ] ◇ *interj* TELEC reçu et compris, d'accord; ~ and out message reçu, terminé.
◇ *vt* ▽ *Br* baiser.

rogue [rəʊg] ◇ *n* -**1.** [scoundrel] escroc *m*, filou *m*; [mischievous child] polisson *m*, -onne *f*, coquin *m*, -e *f*. -**2.** [animal] solitaire *m*.
◇ *adj* -**1.** [animal] solitaire; a ~ elephant un éléphant solitaire. -**2.** *Am* [delinquent] dévoyé.

roguery ['rəʊgərɪ] (*pl* rogueries) *n* [dishonesty] malhonnêteté *f*; [evil] méchanceté *f*.

rogues' gallery *n* [in police files] photographies *fpl* de repris de justice; they're a real ~! ils ont des mines patibulaires!

roguish ['rəʊgɪʃ] *adj* [mischievous] espiègle, malicieux, coquin.

roister ['rɔɪstəʳ] *vi* faire la fête.

roisterer ['rɔɪstərəʳ] *n* noceur *m*, -euse *f*.

roisterous ['rɔɪstərəs] *adj* [behaviour] tapageur; [crowd] bruyant.

role, rôle [rəʊl] *n* rôle *m*; to have OR to play the leading ~ jouer le rôle principal; she had OR she played an important ~ in this project elle a joué un rôle important dans ce projet ❑ ~ model modèle *m*; ~ play SCH & PSYCH jeu *m* de rôles; ~ playing *(U)* jeux *mpl* de rôles.

roll [rəʊl] ◇ *vt* -**1.** [ball] (faire) rouler; [dice] jeter, lancer; [cigarette, umbrella] rouler; [coil] enrouler; to ~ yarn into a ball faire des pelotes de laine; she ~ed the child in a blanket elle a enroulé OR enveloppé l'enfant dans une couverture; the hedgehog ~ed itself into a tight ball le hérisson s'est mis en boule; the dog ~ed itself in the mud le chien s'est roulé dans la boue; to ~ sthg in OR between one's fingers rouler qqch entre ses doigts; the boy ~ed the modelling clay into a long snake le garçon roula la pâte à modeler pour en faire un long serpent; he ~ed his sleeves above his elbows il a roulé OR retroussé ses manches au-dessus du coude; to ~ the presses faire tourner les presses; to ~ dice jouer aux dés; to ~ one's r's rouler les r; to ~ one's hips/shoulders rouler les hanches/épaules; to ~ one's eyes in fright rouler les yeux de frayeur; she's a company executive, wife and housekeeper all ~ed into one *fig* elle cumule les rôles de cadre dans sa société, d'épouse et de ménagère; to ~ one's own *Br* [cigarettes] rouler ses cigarettes. -**2.** [flatten - grass] rouler; [- pastry, dough] étendre; [- gold, metal] laminer; [- road] cylindrer. -**3.** *inf Am* [rob] dévaliser.
◇ *vi* -**1.** [ball] rouler; to ~ in the mud [gen] se rouler dans la boue; [wallow] se vautrer dans la boue; his eyes ~ed in horror il roulait des yeux horrifiés; the ball ~ed under the car/down the stairs la balle roula sous la voiture/en bas de l'escalier; the boulders ~ed down the mountainside les rochers dévalaient la montagne; the car ~ed down the hill/the slope la voiture dévalait la colline/la pente; the ball ~ed along the floor la balle roulait sur le sol; the parade ~ed slowly past the window le défilé passait lentement devant la fenêtre; the bus ~ed into the yard le bus est entré dans la cour; the car ~ed to a halt la voiture s'est arrêtée lentement ‖ [sweat] dégouliner; [tears] rouler; tears ~ed down her face des larmes roulaient sur ses joues; sweat ~ed off his back la sueur lui dégoulinait dans le dos ❑ to be ~ing in money OR ~ing in it *inf* rouler sur l'or, être plein aux as; he had them ~ing in the aisles il les faisait mourir de rire; heads will ~ des têtes vont tomber. -**2.** [ship] avoir du roulis; [plane - with turbulence] avoir du roulis; [- in aerobatics] faire un tonneau OR des tonneaux; ASTRONAUT tourner sur soi-même. -**3.** [machine, camera] tourner; to keep the cameras/the presses ~ing laisser tourner les caméras/les presses; the credits started to ~ [of film] le générique commença à défiler; the wheels never stop ~ing les roues ne s'arrêtent jamais de tourner ❑ to get OR to start things ~ing mettre les choses en marche; to keep the ball OR the show ~ing COMM faire tourner la boutique; THEAT faire en sorte que le spectacle continue; let the good times ~ que la fête continue. -**4.** [drums] rouler; [thunder] gronder; [voice] retentir; [music] retentir, résonner; [organ] résonner, sonner.
◇ *n* -**1.** [of carpet, paper] rouleau *m*; [of banknotes] liasse *f*; [of tobacco] carotte *f*; [of butter] coquille *f*; [of fat, flesh] bourrelet *m*; [of film] rouleau *m*, bobine *f*; [of tools, equipment] trousse *f*. -**2.** (bread) ~ petit pain *m*. -**3.** [of ball] roulement *m*; [of dice] lancement *m*; [of car, ship] roulis *m*; [of plane - in turbulence] roulis *m*; [- in aerobatics] tonneau *m*; [of hips, shoulders] balancement *m*; [of sea] houle *f*; [somersault] galipette *f*; to have a ~ in the hay *inf* [make love] se rouler dans le foin. -**4.** [list - of members] liste *f*, tableau *m*; ADMIN & NAUT rôle *m*; SCH liste *f* des élèves; to call the ~ faire l'appel; to be on the ~ [of club] être membre; *Br* SCH faire partie des élèves; falling ~s baisse *f* d'effectifs; nominal ~ liste nominative ❑ ~ of honour MIL liste des combattants morts pour la patrie, SCH tableau *m* d'honneur. -**5.** [of drum] roulement *m*; [of thunder] grondement *m*; I can hear the ~s of thunder/the far-off ~ of a drum j'entends gronder le tonnerre/le roulement lointain d'un tambour.

◆ **roll about** *vi insep Br* rouler çà et là; to ~ about on the floor/grass se rouler par terre/dans l'herbe; to ~ about with laughter *fig* se tordre de rire, se tenir les côtes.

◆ **roll along** ◇ *vi insep* -**1.** [river] couler; [car] rouler; the car was ~ing along at 140 km/h la voiture roulait à 140. -**2.** *fig* [project] avancer. -**3.** *inf* [go] passer, se pointer, s'amener; let's ~ along to Jake's place si on se pointait chez Jake?, si on débarquait chez Jake?
◇ *vt sep* [hoop, ball] faire rouler; [car, wheelbarrow] pousser.

◆ **roll around** = **roll about**.

◆ **roll away** ◇ *vi insep* [car, clouds] s'éloigner, [terrain] s'étendre; the hills ~ed away into the distance les collines disparaissaient au loin; the ball ~ed away into the street la balle a roulé jusque dans la rue; suddenly all my troubles simply ~ed away *fig* subitement tous mes ennuis s'éloignèrent.
◇ *vt sep* [take away] emmener; [put away] ranger.

◆ **roll back** ◇ *vt sep* -**1.** [push back - carpet] rouler, enrouler; [- blankets] replier; [- enemy difficulties] faire reculer; the doctor ~ed the wheelchair back against the wall le médecin recula la chaise roulante contre le mur. -**2.** [bring back] ramener. -**3.** [prices] casser. -**4.** [time] faire reculer; it would be nice to ~ back the years

ce serait bien de revenir des années en arrière.
◇ *vi insep* [waves] se retirer; [memories, time] revenir.
◆ **roll by** *vi insep* -**1.** [time] s'écouler, passer. -**2.** [car] passer.
◆ **roll down** ◇ *vi insep* rouler en bas, descendre en roulant; [tears, sweat] couler.
◇ *vt sep* [blind] baisser; [sleeves] redescendre; [blanket] replier; [hoop, ball] faire rouler.
◆ **roll in** ◇ *vi insep* -**1.** [arrive] arriver; [come back] rentrer; **they finally ~ed in at 3 o'clock in the morning** ils sont finalement rentrés à 3 h du matin. -**2.** [car] entrer; [waves] déferler. -**3.** *inf* [money] rentrer; [crowds] affluer.
◇ *vt sep* [bring in] faire entrer; [barrel, car] faire entrer en roulant.
◆ **roll off** ◇ *vi insep* [fall] tomber en roulant; [on floor] rouler par terre; **the top ~ed off into the bath** le bouchon a roulé dans la baignoire.
◇ *vt sep* [print] imprimer.
◇ *vt insep* TYPO: **to ~ off the presses** sortir des presses.
◆ **roll on** ◇ *vi insep* -**1.** [ball] continuer à rouler. -**2.** [time] s'écouler. -**3.** *phr Br*: **~ on Christmas!** vivement (qu'on soit à) Noël!; **~ on the day when I'm my own boss!** vivement que je sois mon propre patron!
◇ *vt sep* -**1.** [paint] appliquer au rouleau; [deodorant] appliquer. -**2.** [stockings] enfiler.
◆ **roll out** ◇ *vi insep* sortir; **to ~ out of bed** [person] sortir du lit; **the ball ~ed out from under the sofa** la balle est sortie de sous le canapé.
◇ *vt sep* -**1.** [ball] rouler (dehors); [car, barrel] rouler OR pousser dehors; [map] dérouler; [pastry] étendre (au rouleau); **we ~ed the lawn mower out into the garden** nous avons sorti la tondeuse dans le jardin ❑ **to ~ out the red carpet** dérouler le tapis rouge. -**2.** [produce - goods, speech] débiter.
◆ **roll over** ◇ *vi insep* [person, animal] se retourner; [car] faire un tonneau; **to ~ over and over** [in bed] se retourner plusieurs fois; [car] faire une série de tonneaux.
◇ *vt sep* retourner.
◇ *vt insep* rouler sur; [subj: car] écraser.
◆ **roll past** ◇ *vt insep* passer devant.
◇ *vi insep* passer.
◆ **roll up** ◇ *vt sep* [map, carpet] rouler; [sleeves] retrousser; [trousers] remonter, retrousser; *Am* [window] remonter; **to ~ sthg up in a blanket** enrouler OR envelopper qqch dans une couverture.
◇ *vi insep* -**1.** [carpet] se rouler; **the map keeps ~ing up on its own** impossible de faire tenir cette carte à plat; **to ~ up into a ball** se rouler en boule. -**2.** *inf* [arrive] se pointer, s'amener.
◇ *interj*: **~ up! ~ up!** approchez!
rollaway ['rəʊləweɪ] *adj* à roulettes.
rollback ['rəʊlbæk] *n Am* réduction *f*, baisse *f*.
roll bar *n* arceau *m* de sécurité.
roll call *n* appel *m*; **to take (the) ~** faire l'appel.
roll collar *n* col *m* roulé.
rolled [rəʊld] *adj* -**1.** [paper] en rouleau; [carpet] roulé. -**2.** [iron] laminé. -**3.** [tobacco] en carotte; **~ oats** flocons *mpl* d'avoine.
rolled gold *n* plaqué *m* or; **a ~ bracelet** un bracelet en plaqué or.
rolled-up *adj* roulé, enroulé.
roller ['rəʊləʳ] *n* -**1.** [cylinder - for paint, pastry, garden, hair] rouleau *m*; [- for blind] enrouleur *m*; [- of typewriter] rouleau *m*, cylindre *m*; TEX calandre *f*; METALL laminoir *m*; **she had her hair in ~s** elle s'était mis des bigoudis. -**2.** [wheel - for marking, furniture] roulette *f*; [- in machine] galet *m*; **the piano is on ~s** le piano est sur roulettes. -**3.** [of sea] rouleau *m*.
roller bearing *n* roulement *m* à rouleaux.
roller blades *npl* patins *mpl* en ligne.
roller blind *n* store *m* à enrouleur.
roller coaster *n* montagnes *fpl* russes, grand huit *m*.
roller skate *n* patin *m* à roulettes.
◆ **roller-skate** *vi* faire du patin à roulettes.
roller-skater *n* patineur *m*, -euse *f (à roulettes)*.
roller-skating *n* patinage *m* à roulettes.
roller towel *n* essuie-mains *m (monté sur un rouleau)*.
roll film *n* pellicule *f* en bobine.
rollick *inf* ['rɒlɪk] ◇ *vi* [romp] s'ébattre; [celebrate] faire la noce.
◇ *n* ébats *mpl*.
◆ **rollick about** *vi insep Br* s'ébattre, faire le fou.
rollicking *inf* ['rɒlɪkɪŋ] ◇ *adj* [joyful] joyeux; [noisy] bruyant; **to lead a ~ life** mener une vie de patachon; **we had a ~ (good) time** on s'est amusés comme des fous.
◇ *n Br*: **to get a ~** se faire enguirlander.
rolling ['rəʊlɪŋ] ◇ *adj* -**1.** [object] roulant, qui roule. -**2.** [countryside, hills] ondulant; **to have a ~ gait** rouler les hanches. -**3.** [sea] houleux; [boat] qui a du roulis. -**4.** [fog] enveloppant; [thunder] grondant. -**5.** [mobile - target] mobile, mouvant; **a ~ plan for development** un plan de développement constamment remis à jour. -**6.** [strikes] tournant.
◇ *n* -**1.** [of ball, marble] roulement *m*; [of dice] lancement *m*. -**2.** [of boat] roulis *m*. -**3.** [of drum] roulement *m*; [of thunder] grondement *m*. -**4.** [of shoulders] roulement *m*. -**5.** METALL laminage *m*.
◇ *adv inf Br*: **to be ~ drunk** être complètement soûl.
rolling mill *n* [factory] usine *f* de laminage; [equipment] laminoir *m*.
rolling pin *n* rouleau *m* à pâtisserie.
rolling stock *n* matériel *m* roulant.
rolling stone *n* [person] vadrouilleur *m*, -euse *f*; **to be a ~** rouler sa bosse, avoir une âme de vagabond; **a ~ gathers no moss** *prov* pierre qui roule n'amasse pas mousse *prov*.
rollmop ['rəʊlmɒp] *n* rollmops *m*.
roll neck *n* col *m* roulé.
◆ **roll-neck** = **roll-necked**.
roll-necked *adj* à col roulé.
roll-on ◇ *n* -**1.** [deodorant] déodorant *m* à bille. -**2.** [corset] gaine *f*, corset *m*.
◇ *adj*: **~ deodorant** déodorant *m* à bille; **~ lip-gloss** brillant *m* à lèvres.
roll-on/roll-off ◇ *n* [ship] (navire *m*) transbordeur *m*, ferry-boat *m*; [system] roll on-roll off *m inv*, manutention *f* par roulage.
◇ *adj* [ferry] transbordeur, ro-ro *(inv)*.
rolltop ['rəʊltɒp] *n*: **~ (desk)** bureau *m* à cylindre.
roll-up ◇ *adj* [map] qui s'enroule.
◇ *n inf Br* cigarette *f* roulée; **she smokes ~s** elle roule elle-même ses cigarettes.
roll-your-own *inf* = **roll-up** *n*.
roly-poly [ˌrəʊlɪ'pəʊlɪ] (*pl* roly-polies) ◇ *adj inf* grassouillet, rondelet.
◇ *n* -**1.** *inf* [plump person]: **she's a real ~** elle est vraiment grassouillette. -**2.** CULIN: **~ (pudding)** gâteau *m* roulé à la confiture.
ROM [rɒm] (*abbr of* **read only memory**) *n* ROM *f*.
romaine [rəʊ'meɪn] *n Am*: **~ (lettuce)** (laitue *f*) romaine *f*.
Roman ['rəʊmən] ◇ *n* Romain *m*, -e *f*; TYPO romain *m*; **the Epistle of Paul to the ~s** l'Épître de saint Paul aux Romains.
◇ *adj* -**1.** [gen & RELIG] romain; **~ Britain** *période de domination romaine en Grande-Bretagne allant du Ier siècle av. J.C. au IVe siècle ap. J.C.*; **~ road** voie *f* romaine. -**2.** [nose] aquilin.
Roman alphabet *n* alphabet *m* romain.
Roman calendar *n* calendrier *m* romain.
Roman candle *n* chandelle *f* romaine.
Roman Catholic ◇ *adj* catholique.
◇ *n* catholique *mf*.
Roman Catholicism *n* catholicisme *m*.
romance [rəʊ'mæns] ◇ *n* -**1.** [love affair] liaison *f* (amoureuse); **to have a ~ with sb** [affair] avoir une liaison avec qqn; [idyll] vivre un roman d'amour avec qqn; **a holiday ~** un amour de vacances. -**2.** [love] amour *m* (romantique); **everyone dreams of ~** tout le monde rêve d'un grand amour. -**3.** [romantic novel] roman *m* d'amour, roman *m* à l'eau de rose *pej*; [film] film *m* romantique, film *m* à l'eau de rose *pej*; **historical ~** *roman d'amour situé à une époque ancienne*. -**4.** [attraction, charm] charme *m*, poésie *f*; [excitement] attrait *m*; **after a while the ~ wore off** après quelque temps, le charme s'estompa. -**5.** [fantasy] fantaisie *f*; [invention] invention *f*; **most of what he says is just ~** il invente presque tout ce qu'il raconte. -**6.** LITERAT roman *m*. -**7.** MUS romance *f*.
◇ *comp*: **~ writer** romancier *m*, -ère *f*, auteur *m* d'histoires romanesques.
◇ *vi* laisser vagabonder son imagination, fabuler; **to ~ on** OR **about sthg** fabuler OR broder sur qqch.
◆ **Romance** ◇ *n* LING roman *m*.
◇ *adj*: **the Romance languages** les langues *fpl* romanes.
romancer [rəʊ'mænsəʳ] *n* -**1.** [writer] *auteur d'œuvres romanesques*. -**2.** [fantasizer] fabulateur *m*, -trice *f*.
Roman Empire *n*: **the ~** l'Empire *m* romain.
Romanesque [ˌrəʊmə'nesk] ◇ *adj* roman ARCHIT.
◇ *n* roman *m* ARCHIT.
Romani ['rəʊmənɪ] = **Romany** *n*.
Romania [ruː'meɪnjə] *pr n* Roumanie *f*; **in ~** en Roumanie.
Romanian [ruː'meɪnjən] ◇ *n* -**1.** [person] Roumain *m*, e *f*. -**2.** LING roumain *m*.
◇ *adj* roumain.
Romanic [rəʊ'mænɪk] ◇ *adj* romain, des Romains.
◇ *n* LING roman *m*.
romanize, -ise ['rəʊmənaɪz] *vt* romaniser.
Roman law *n* droit *m* romain.
Roman numeral *n* chiffre *m* romain.
Romans(c)h [rəʊ'mænʃ] ◇ *n* romanche *m*.
◇ *adj* romanche.
romantic [rəʊ'mæntɪk] ◇ *adj* -**1.** romantique; **~ love** l'amour romantique; **they had a ~ attachment** ils ont eu une liaison amoureuse. -**2.** [unrealistic] romanesque; **she still has some ~ ideas about life** elle a encore des idées romanesques sur l'existence.
◇ *n* romantique *mf*; **he's an incurable ~** c'est un éternel romantique.
◆ **Romantic** *adj* ART, LITERAT & MUS romantique; **the French Romantic poets** les poètes romantiques français.
romantically [rəʊ'mæntɪklɪ] *adv* de manière romantique, romantiquement *lit*; **we're ~ involved** nous avons une liaison amoureuse; **a hotel set ~ by the side of a lake** un hôtel situé dans un cadre romantique tout près d'un lac.
romanticism [rəʊ'mæntɪsɪzm] *n* romantisme *m*.
◆ **Romanticism** *n* ART, LITERAT & MUS romantisme *m*.
romanticist [rəʊ'mæntɪsɪst] *n* romantique *mf*.
romanticize, -ise [rəʊ'mæntɪsaɪz] *vt* [idea, event] idéaliser; **they have a ~d view of life in Britain** ils ont une vision très romantique de la vie en Grande-Bretagne.
Romany ['rəʊmənɪ] (*pl* **Romanies**) ◇ *n* -**1.** [person] Bohémien *m*, -enne *f*, Rom *mf*. -**2.** LING rom *m*.
◇ *adj* bohémien, rom.
Rome [rəʊm] *pr n* Rome; **when in ~, do as the Romans do** *prov* quand tu seras à Rome, fais comme les Romains *prov*; **~ wasn't built in a day** Rome ne s'est pas faite OR Paris ne s'est pas fait en un jour; **all roads lead to ~** tous les chemins mènent à Rome.
Romeo ['rəʊmɪəʊ] ◇ *pr n* Roméo; **'~ and Juliet'** *Shakespeare, Berlioz* 'Roméo et Juliette'.
◇ *n*: **he's a real ~** *fig* c'est un vrai Roméo.
Romish ['rəʊmɪʃ] *adj pej* papiste.
romp [rɒmp] ◇ *vi* s'ébattre (bruyamment); **the children were ~ing gleefully in the garden** les enfants s'ébattaient joyeusement dans le jardin; **the favourite ~ed home ten lengths ahead** le favori est arrivé avec dix bonnes longueurs d'avance.

◇ *n* -**1.** [frolic] ébats *mpl*, gambades *fpl*. -**2.** [film, play] farce *f*, comédie *f*. -**3.** *inf Br* [easy win]: it was a ~ c'était du gâteau.

◆ **romp through** *vt insep*: to ~ through one's work expédier son travail sans difficulté; she ~ed through the test elle a réussi le test haut la main.

rompers ['rɒmpəz] *npl* , **romper suit** *n* barboteuse *f*.

Romulus ['rɒmjʊləs] *pr n*: ~ and Remus Romulus et Rémus.

rondeau ['rɒndəʊ] (*pl* **rondeaux**) *n* rondeau *m*.

rondo ['rɒndəʊ] (*pl* **rondos**) *n* rondo *m*.

Roneo® ['rəʊnɪəʊ] ◇ *n* Ronéo® *f*.
◇ *vt* ronéotyper, ronéoter.

röntgen *etc* ['rɒntjən] = **roentgen**.

rood [ru:d] ◇ *n* -**1.** [cross] crucifix *m*, croix *f (qui surplombe le jubé)*; the Holy Rood la Sainte Croix. -**2.** *Br* [square measure] ≃ 1000 m².
◇ *comp* [arch, beam] du jubé.

rood screen *n* jubé *m*.

roof [ru:f] (*pl* **roofs** OR **rooves** [ru:vz]) ◇ *n* -**1.** [of building] toit *m*; [of cave, tunnel] plafond *m*; [of branches, trees] voûte *f*; [of car] toit *m*, pavillon *m*; to live under the same ~ vivre sous le même toit; I won't have this sort of behaviour under my ~ je ne tolérerai pas ce genre de comportement sous mon toit OR chez moi; to be without a ~ over one's head être à la rue; the Celestial ~ *fig* la voûte céleste ❑ to go through OR to hit the ~ *inf* [person] piquer une crise, sortir de ses gonds; [prices] flamber. -**2.** [roof covering] toiture *f*. -**3.** ANAT: ~ of the mouth voûte *f* du palais.
◇ *vt* couvrir d'un toit; ~ed with corrugated iron avec un toit en tôle ondulée.

◆ **roof over** *vt sep* recouvrir.

-roofed [ru:ft] *in cpds*: flat~ warehouses des entrepôts à toits plats OR en terrasse.

roof garden *n* jardin *m* sur le toit.

roofing ['ru:fɪŋ] *n* toiture *f*, couverture *f*; ~ materials matériaux *mpl* pour toitures.

roofing felt *n* carton *m* bitumé OR goudronné.

roofless ['ru:flɪs] *adj* sans toit, à ciel ouvert.

roof light *n* AUT plafonnier *m*; [window] lucarne *f*.

roof rack *n* galerie *f* AUT.

rooftop ['ru:ftɒp] ◇ *n* toit *m*; a chase over the ~s une poursuite sur les toits; to shout OR to proclaim sthg from the ~s *fig* crier qqch sur les toits.
◇ *comp*: police marksmen have taken up ~ positions des tireurs d'élite ont pris position sur le toit.

rook [rʊk] ◇ *n* -**1.** [bird] freux *m*, corbeau *m*. -**2.** [in chess] tour *f*. -**3.** *dated* [swindler] escroc *m*, filou *m*.
◇ *vt inf* rouler, escroquer.

rookery ['rʊkərɪ] (*pl* **rookeries**) *n* [of rooks] colonie *f* de freux; a ~ of seals/penguins une colonie de phoques/manchots.

rookie *inf* ['rʊkɪ] *n Am* [recruit] bleu *m*.

room [ru:m, rʊm] ◇ *n* -**1.** [in building, public place] salle *f*; [in house] pièce *f*; [in hotel] chambre *f*; the house has ten ~s la maison comporte dix pièces; '~ to let OR to rent' 'chambre à louer'; his ~s are in Bayswater il habite à Bayswater ❑ dining/living ~ salle à manger/de séjour; sitting ~ salon *m*; ~ and board chambre avec pension; the smallest ~ *Br euph* [toilet] le petit coin; 'Room at the Top' *Braine* 'Une pièce en haut'; 'A Room of One's Own' *Woolf* 'Une chambre à soi'; 'A Room with a View' *Forster* 'Avec vue sur l'Arno'; *Ivory* 'Chambre avec vue'. -**2.** [space, place] place *f*; is there enough ~ for everybody? y a-t-il assez de place pour tout le monde?; there's plenty of ~ il y a beaucoup de place; it takes up too much ~ ça prend trop de place; to make ~ for sb faire une place OR de la place pour qqn; it's time to make ~ for young people with fresh ideas *fig* il est temps de laisser la place à des gens jeunes avec des idées neuves; ~ to OR for manoeuvre *literal* place pour manœuvrer; *fig* marge de manœuvre; the new legislation leaves little ~ for manoeuvre la nouvelle loi laisse une faible marge de manœuvre; there's ~ for improvement [make better] il y a des progrès à faire; [below standard] ça laisse à désirer; there's still ~ for discussion/hope on peut encore discuter/espérer; there's no ~ for doubt il n'y a plus aucun doute possible ❑ there's no ~ to swing a cat in here *Br* il n'y a pas la place de se retourner ici. -**3.** [people in room] salle *f*; the whole ~ protested toute la salle a protesté.
◇ *vi Am* loger; to ~ with sb [share flat] partager un appartement avec qqn; [in hotel] partager une chambre avec qqn.

-roomed [ru:md] *in cpds*: a five~ flat un appartement de cinq pièces, un cinq-pièces.

roomer ['ru:mə^r] *n Am* pensionnaire *mf*.

roomette [ru:m'et] *n Am petit wagon-lit à une place*.

roomful ['ru:mfʊl] *n* pleine salle *f* OR pièce *f*; a ~ of furniture une pièce pleine de meubles; a ~ of people une salle pleine de monde.

roominess ['ru:mɪnɪs] *n* grandes dimensions *fpl*, dimensions *fpl* généreuses.

rooming house ['ru:mɪŋ-] *n Am* immeuble *m (avec chambres à louer)*.

roommate ['ru:mmeɪt] *n* [in boarding school, college] camarade *mf* de chambre; *Am* [in flat] *personne avec qui l'on partage un logement*.

room service *n* service *m* dans les chambres *(dans un hôtel)*.

room temperature *n* température *f* ambiante; this plant must be kept at ~ cette plante doit être placée dans une pièce chauffée; 'to be served at ~' [wine] 'servir chambré'.

roomy ['ru:mɪ] (*compar* **roomier**, *superl* **roomiest**) *adj* [house, office] spacieux; [suitcase, bag] grand; [coat] ample.

roorback ['rʊəbæk] *n Am* POL pamphlet *m* diffamatoire.

roost [ru:st] ◇ *n* perchoir *m*, juchoir *m*.
◇ *vi* [bird] se percher, (se) jucher; his misdeeds came home to ~ ses méfaits se sont retournés contre lui.

rooster ['ru:stə^r] *n Am* coq *m*.

root [ru:t] ◇ *n* -**1.** BOT & *fig* racine *f*; to pull up a plant by its ~s déraciner une plante; to take ~ BOT & *fig* prendre racine; to put down ~s BOT & *fig* prendre racine, s'enraciner. -**2.** ANAT [of tooth, hair, nail, tongue] racine *f*. -**3.** [source] source *f*; [cause] cause *f*; [bottom] fond *m*; the ~ of all evil la source de tout mal; to get at OR to the ~ of the problem aller au fond du problème; poor housing is at the ~ of much delinquency la mauvaise qualité des logements est souvent à l'origine de la délinquance. -**4.** LING [in etymology] racine *f*; [baseform] radical *m*, base *f*. -**5.** MATH racine *f*; the cube ~ of 27 la racine cubique de 27. -**6.** MUS fondamentale *f*.
◇ *comp* [cause, problem] fondamental, de base.
◇ *vt* enraciner; he stood ~ed to the spot *fig* il est resté cloué sur place.
◇ *vi* -**1.** [plant] s'enraciner, prendre racine. -**2.** [pigs] fouiller *(avec le groin)*; to ~ for truffles chercher des truffes.

◆ **roots** *npl* [of person - origin] racines *fpl*, origines *fpl*; he has no real ~s il n'a pas de véritables racines; she is in search of her ~s elle est à la recherche de ses origines; their actual ~s are in Virginia en fait, ils sont originaires de Virginie.

◆ **root about** *Br*, **root around** *vi insep* [animal] fouiller *(avec le museau)*; [person] fouiller; to ~ about for sthg fouiller pour trouver qqch.

◆ **root for** *vt insep* [team] encourager, soutenir.

◆ **root out** *vt sep* -**1.** [from earth] déterrer; [from hiding place] dénicher. -**2.** [suppress] supprimer, extirper.

◆ **root through** *vt insep* [search through] fouiller.

◆ **root up** *vt sep* [plant] déraciner; [subj: pigs] déterrer.

root-and-branch *adj* [reform] complet.

◆ **root and branch** *adv*: corruption must be eliminated root and branch il faut éradiquer la corruption.

root beer *n boisson gazeuse à base d'extraits végétaux*.

root canal *n* canal *m* dentaire; ~ treatment traitement *m* canalaire.

root crop *n* racine *f* comestible.

rooted ['ru:tɪd] *adj* [prejudice, belief, habits] enraciné; deeply ~ superstitions des superstitions bien enracinées OR profondément ancrées.

rootle ['ru:tl] *vi Br* [pigs] fouiller *(avec le groin)*.

rootless ['ru:tlɪs] *adj* sans racine OR racines.

rootlet ['ru:tlɪt] *n* radicelle *f*.

root mean square *n* moyenne *f* quadratique.

rootstock ['ru:tstɒk] *n* rhizome *m*.

rope [rəʊp] ◇ *n* -**1.** [gen] corde *f*; [collectively] cordage *m*; [of steel, wire] filin *m*; [cable] câble *m*; [for bell, curtains] cordon *m*; a piece OR length of ~ un bout de corde, une corde ❑ to come to the end of one's ~ être au bout du rouleau; to give sb more ~ laisser à qqn une plus grande liberté d'action, lâcher la bride à qqn; she gave him plenty of ~ elle lui a donné une grande liberté d'action OR marge de manœuvre; give him enough ~ and he'll hang himself si on le laisse faire, il creusera sa propre tombe; 'Rope' *Hitchcock* 'la Corde'. -**2.** [in mountaineering] cordée *f*. -**3.** [of pearls] collier *m*; [of onions] chapelet *m*.
◇ *vt* -**1.** [package] attacher avec une corde, corder; the climbers were ~d together les alpinistes étaient encordés; he was ~d to a post il a été attaché à un poteau. -**2.** *Am* [cattle, horses] prendre au lasso.

◆ **ropes** *npl* -**1.** BOXING cordes *fpl*; to be on the ~s [boxer] être dans les cordes; *fig* être aux abois; to be up against the ~s être le dos au mur. -**2.** [know-how]: to know the ~s connaître les ficelles OR son affaire; to show OR to teach sb the ~s montrer les ficelles du métier à qqn; to learn the ~s se mettre au courant, apprendre à se débrouiller.

◆ **rope in** *vt sep* -**1.** [land] entourer de cordes, délimiter par des cordes. -**2.** [cattle] mettre dans un enclos. -**3.** *fig*: to ~ sb in to do sthg enrôler qqn pour faire qqch; he got himself ~d in as chairman il a été forcé d'accepter la présidence.

◆ **rope off** *vt sep* [part of hall, of church] délimiter par une corde; [street, building] interdire l'accès de.

◆ **rope up** ◇ *vi insep* s'encorder.
◇ *vt sep* -**1.** [parcel] attacher avec une corde, corder. -**2.** [climbers] encorder.

ropedancer ['rəʊp,dɑ:nsə^r] *n* funambule *mf*, danseur *m*, -euse *f* de corde.

rope ladder *n* échelle *f* de corde.

rope sandals *npl* espadrilles *fpl*.

rope trick *n tour de prestidigitation réalisé avec une cordelette*.

ropewalker ['rəʊp,wɔ:kə^r] *n* funambule *mf*.

rop(e)y ['rəʊpɪ] (*compar* **ropier**, *superl* **ropiest**) *adj Br* -**1.** *inf* [mediocre] médiocre, pas fameux; [ill] mal fichu. -**2.** [substance] visqueux.

ro-ro ['rəʊrəʊ] = **roll-on/roll-off**.

Rorschach test ['rɔ:ʃɑ:k-] *n* test *m* de Rorschach.

rosary ['rəʊzərɪ] (*pl* **rosaries**) *n* -**1.** RELIG [beads] chapelet *m*, rosaire *m*; [prayers] rosaire *m*; to tell OR to say the ~ dire son rosaire. -**2.** [rose garden] roseraie *f*.

rose [rəʊz] ◇ *pt* → **rise**.
◇ *n* -**1.** BOT [flower] rose *f*; [bush] rosier *m*; life isn't just a bed of ~s, life isn't all ~s tout n'est pas rose dans la vie; her life isn't exactly a bed of ~s sa vie n'est pas vraiment rose; there's no ~ without a thorn il n'y a pas de roses sans épines, chaque médaille a son revers; to come up ~s [enterprise] marcher comme sur des roulettes; [person] réussir, avoir le vent en

poupe; under the ~ *lit* en cachette, en confidence; that'll put the ~s back into your cheeks ça va te redonner des couleurs. -**2.** [rose shape - on hat, dress] rosette *f*; [- on ceiling] rosace *f*. -**3.** [colour] rose *m*. -**4.** [on hosepipe, watering can] pomme *f*.
◇ *adj* rose, de couleur rose.

rosé ['rəʊzeɪ] *n* (vin *m*) rosé *m*.

roseate ['rəʊzɪət] *adj lit* rose.

rosebay ['rəʊzbeɪ] *n* laurier-rose *m*.

rosebed ['rəʊzbed] *n* parterre *m* OR massif *m* de roses.

Rose Bowl [rəʊz-] *pr n*: the ~ *match de football universitaire organisé le Jour de l'An à Pasadena, en Californie*.

rosebud ['rəʊzbʌd] *n* bouton *m* de rose.

rosebush ['rəʊzbʊʃ] *n* rosier *m*.

rose-coloured *adj* rose, rosé; to see life through ~ spectacles voir la vie en rose.

rose garden *n* roseraie *f*.

rose hip *n* gratte-cul *m*, cynorhodon *m spec*; ~ syrup sirop *m* d'églantine.

rosemary ['rəʊzmərɪ] (*pl* rosemaries) *n* romarin *m*.

Rosenberg ['rəʊzənbɜːg] *pr n* Rosenberg; the ~ case l'affaire *f* Rosenberg.

THE ROSENBERG CASE:
Procès aboutissant à l'exécution, en 1953, des époux Rosenberg, scientifiques américains accusés d'avoir livré à l'URSS des informations sur la bombe atomique. Premiers civils à être condamnés à mort pour espionnage, leur exécution souleva des protestations dans le monde entier de la part de ceux qui y voyaient l'œuvre du maccarthysme.

---

roseola [rəʊ'ziːələ] *n (U)* roséole *f*.

rose quartz *n* quartz *m* rose.

rose-red *adj* vermeil.

rose-tinted *adj* teinté en rose.

rose tree *n* rosier *m*.

Rosetta [rə'zetə] *pr n* Rosette; the ~ Stone la pierre de Rosette.

rosette [rəʊ'zet] *n* -**1.** [made of ribbons] rosette *f*; SPORT cocarde *f*. -**2.** ARCHIT rosace *f*. -**3.** BOT rosette *f*.

rosewater ['rəʊz,wɔːtəʳ] *n* eau *f* de rose.

rose window *n* rosace *f*.

rosewood ['rəʊzwʊd] ◇ *n* bois *m* de rose.
◇ *comp* en bois de rose.

Rosicrucian [,rəʊzɪ'kruːʃn] ◇ *n* rosicrucien *m*, -enne *f*, rose-croix *m inv*.
◇ *adj* rosicrucien.

Rosicrucianism [,rəʊzɪ'kruːʃənɪzm] *n* philosophie *f* de l'ordre de la Rose-Croix.

rosin ['rɒzɪn] ◇ *n* colophane *f*, arcanson *m*.
◇ *vt* traiter à la colophane, enduire de colophane.

ROSPA ['rɒspə] (*abbr of* Royal Society for the Prevention of Accidents) *pr n association britannique pour la prévention des accidents*.

roster ['rɒstəʳ] ◇ *n* [list] liste *f*; [for duty] tableau *m* de service; by ~ à tour de rôle; promotion ~ tableau d'avancement.
◇ *vt* inscrire au tableau de service OR au planning; I'm ~ed on Sunday je suis de service dimanche.

rostrum ['rɒstrəm] (*pl* rostrums OR rostra [-trə]) -**1.** [platform - for speaker] estrade *f*, tribune *f*; [- for conductor] estrade *f*; SPORT podium *m*; to take the ~ monter sur l'estrade OR à la tribune. -**2.** HIST & NAUT rostres *mpl*.

rosy ['rəʊzɪ] (*compar* rosier, *superl* rosiest) *adj* [in colour] rose, rosé; to have ~ cheeks avoir les joues roses ‖ *fig* [future, situation] brillant, qui se présente bien; to paint a ~ picture of a situation peindre une situation en rose; to have a ~ view of life voir la vie en rose.

rot [rɒt] (*pt* & *pp* rotted, *cont* rotting) ◇ *vi* -**1.** [fruit, vegetable] pourrir, se gâter; [teeth] se carier. -**2.** *fig* [person] pourrir; to ~ in prison pourrir OR croupir en prison; let them ~! *inf* qu'ils crèvent!
◇ *vt* [vegetable, fibres] (faire) pourrir; [tooth] carier, gâter.
◇ *n* -**1.** [of fruit, vegetable] pourriture *f*; [of tooth] carie *f*. -**2.** *fig* [in society] pourriture *f*; the ~ has set in ça commence à se gâter; to stop the ~ redresser la situation. -**3.** *(U)* [nonsense - spoken] bêtises *fpl*, sottises *fpl*; [- written] bêtises *fpl*; [- on TV] émission *f* idiote, émissions *fpl* idiotes; don't talk ~! ne dis pas de sottises!; that's utter ~! c'est vraiment n'importe quoi!
◆ **rot away** *vi insep* tomber en pourriture.

rota ['rəʊtə] *n* roulement *m*; [for duty] tableau *m* de service, planning *m*; on a ~ basis à tour de rôle, par roulement.
◆ **Rota** *n* RELIG rote *f*.

Rotarian [rəʊ'teərɪən] ◇ *adj* rotarien.
◇ *n* rotarien *m*.

rotary ['rəʊtərɪ] (*pl* rotaries) ◇ *adj* rotatif.
◇ *n Am* rond-point *m*.

Rotary Club *pr n* Rotary Club *m*; ~ member rotarien *m*.

rotary cultivator *n* motoculteur *m*.

rotary engine *n* moteur *m* rotatif.

rotary press *n* rotative *f*.

rotary tiller *n Am* motoculteur *m*.

rotate [*vb* rəʊ'teɪt, *adj* 'rəʊteɪt] ◇ *vt* -**1.** [turn] faire tourner; [on pivot] faire pivoter. -**2.** AGR [crops] alterner. -**3.** [staff] faire un roulement de; [jobs] faire à tour de rôle OR par roulement.
◇ *vi* -**1.** [turn] tourner; [on pivot] pivoter. -**2.** [staff] changer de poste par roulement.
◇ *adj* BOT rotacé.

rotating [rəʊ'teɪtɪŋ] *adj* -**1.** *literal* tournant, rotatif; ~ body corps *m* en rotation. -**2.** AGR: ~ crops cultures *fpl* alternantes OR en rotation.

rotation [rəʊ'teɪʃn] *n* -**1.** [of machinery, planets] rotation *f*; ~s per minute tours *mpl* par minute. -**2.** [of staff, jobs] roulement *m*; in OR by ~ par roulement, à tour de rôle. -**3.** [of crops] rotation *f*.

rotator [rəʊ'teɪtəʳ] *n* -**1.** [spindle] axe *m* rotatif; [machine] appareil *m* rotateur; [propeller] hélice *f*. -**2.** ANAT rotateur *m*.

rotatory ['rəʊtətrɪ] *adj* rotatoire.

rotavate ['rəʊtəveɪt] = **rotovate**.

Rotavator® ['rəʊtəveɪtəʳ] = **Rotovator**.

rote [rəʊt] ◇ *n* routine *f*; to learn sthg by ~ apprendre qqch par cœur.
◇ *adj*: ~ learning apprentissage *m* par cœur.

rotgut▽ ['rɒtgʌt] *n (U)* [spirits] tord-boyaux *m inv*; [wine] piquette *f*.

rotisserie [rəʊ'tɪːsərɪ] *n* [spit] rôtissoire *f*.

rotogravure [,rəʊtəgrə'vjʊəʳ] *n* rotogravure *f*.

rotor ['rəʊtəʳ] *n* rotor *m*.

rotor arm *n* [of helicopter] rotor *m*; [of engine] rotor *m*, balai *m*.

rotor blade *n* pale *f* de rotor.

rotovate ['rəʊtəveɪt] *vt* labourer avec un motoculteur.

Rotovator® ['rəʊtəveɪtəʳ] *n Br* motoculteur *m*.

rotten ['rɒtn] *adj* -**1.** [fruit, egg, wood] pourri; [tooth] carié, gâté. -**2.** [corrupt] pourri, corrompu; ~ through and through OR to the core complètement pourri, corrompu jusqu'à la moelle. -**3.** *inf* [person - unfriendly] rosse, peu aimable; to be ~ to sb être dur avec qqn; what a ~ thing to say! c'est moche de dire des choses pareilles!; I feel ~ about what happened je ne suis pas très fier de ce qui est arrivé; what a ~ trick! quel sale tour!; you ~ so-and-so! *inf* tu es vraiment dur! -**4.** *inf* [ill] mal en point; I feel ~ je ne me sens pas du tout dans mon assiette; you look ~ vous n'avez pas l'air en forme. -**5.** *inf* [bad] lamentable, nul; [weather] pourri; [performer] mauvais, nul; he's a ~ goalkeeper il est nul OR il ne vaut rien comme gardien de but; what ~ luck! quelle poisse!; I always get the ~ jobs! on me refile toujours les sales besognes!; I've had a ~ time recently j'ai traversé une sale période récemment ‖ [in indignation] fichu; keep your ~ (old) sweets! tes bonbons pourris, tu peux te les garder!

rotten borough *n* HIST *circonscription électorale britannique dont les électeurs, bien que peu nombreux, pouvaient élire un député (avant 1832)*.

rottenly ['rɒtnlɪ] *adv* abominablement; to behave ~ to sb se conduire d'une manière inqualifiable avec qqn.

rotter *inf* ['rɒtəʳ] *n Br dated* crapule *f*.

Rotterdam ['rɒtədæm] *pr n* Rotterdam.

rotting ['rɒtɪŋ] *adj* qui pourrit, pourri.

rotund [rəʊ'tʌnd] *adj* -**1.** [shape] rond, arrondi; [person] rondelet. -**2.** [style, speech] grandiloquent.

rotunda [rəʊ'tʌndə] *n* rotonde *f*.

rotundity [rəʊ'tʌndətɪ] *n* -**1.** [of person] embonpoint *m*. -**2.** [of style, speech] grandiloquence *f*.

rouble ['ruːbl] *n* rouble *m*.

roué ['ruːeɪ] *n arch* OR *hum* roué *m*, débauché *m*.

rouge [ruːʒ] ◇ *n* rouge *m* (à joues).
◇ *vt*: she had ~d cheeks elle s'était mis du rouge aux joues.

rough [rʌf] ◇ *adj* -**1.** [uneven - surface, skin, hands] rugueux, rêche; [- road] accidenté, rocailleux; [- coast] accidenté; [- cloth] rêche; [- edge] rugueux; ~ linen gros lin *m*; ~ ground [bumpy] terrain *m* rocailleux OR raboteux; [waste] terrain *m* vague. -**2.** [violent, coarse - behaviour] brutal; [- manners] rude, fruste; [- neighbourhood] dur, mal fréquenté; they came in for some ~ treatment ils ont été malmenés; the parcels got some ~ handling les paquets ont été traités sans ménagement OR malmenés; they're ~ kids ce sont des petites brutes OR des petits voyous; he's a ~ customer c'est un dur; ~ play SPORT jeu *m* brutal; rugby can be a ~ game le rugby peut être un jeu brutal; you see some ~ behaviour at football matches *inf* on voit des violences OR des brutalités aux matches de foot; they were ~ with OR on the new recruits ils n'ont pas été tendres avec les nouvelles recrues ❑ he has a ~ tongue il ne mâche pas ses mots; to give sb the ~ edge of one's tongue réprimander qqn, ne pas ménager ses reproches à qqn. -**3.** [unpleasant, harsh] rude, dur; to have a ~ life avoir une vie dure; she's had a ~ time of it elle en a vu des dures OR de toutes les couleurs; they gave him a ~ time OR ride ils lui ont mené la vie dure; we got a ~ deal on n'a pas eu de veine; to make things ~ for sb mener la vie dure à qqn; he was ~ on us il n'a pas été tendre avec nous; it's ~ on her [unlucky] c'est dur pour elle; [unjust] c'est injuste pour elle; ~ luck! pas de veine!; ~ justice justice *f* sommaire. -**4.** [not finalized]: ~ draft OR work brouillon *m*; ~ sketch croquis *m*, ébauche *f*; just give me a ~ sketch OR outline of your plans donnez-moi juste un aperçu de vos projets; ~ paper papier *m* brouillon ‖ [approximate] approximatif; at a ~ guess grosso modo, approximativement; I only need a ~ estimate je n'ai pas besoin d'une réponse précise; to have a ~ idea of sthg avoir une idée approximative de qqch; it gives you a ~ guide cela vous donne une indication approximative ‖ [crude - equipment] grossier, rudimentaire; they built a ~ canoe from a log ils ont construit un canoë de fortune avec un tronc d'arbre. -**5.** [sea] agité, houleux; [climate] rude; we had a ~ crossing on a eu une traversée agitée; ~ weather gros temps *m*; ~ passage *literal* traversée *f* difficile; the bill had a ~ passage through the House *fig* le projet de loi a eu des difficultés à passer à la Chambre. -**6.** [sound, voice] rauque; [tone] brusque; [speech, accent] rude, grossier. -**7.** [taste] âcre; ~ wine gros vin *m*. -**8.** [ill] mal en point; I'm feeling a bit ~ je ne suis pas dans mon assiette.
◇ *n* -**1.** [ground] terrain *m* rocailleux; GOLF rough *m*; to take the ~ with the smooth prendre les choses comme elles viennent. -**2.** [draft] brouillon *m*; in ~ à l'état de brouillon OR d'ébauche; he drafted the proposal in ~ il rédigea un brouillon de la proposition. -**3.** *inf* [hoodlum] dur *m*, voyou *m*.
◇ *adv* [play] brutalement; [speak] avec rudesse; to treat sb ~ malmener qqn; to live ~ vivre à

la dure; to sleep ~ *Br* coucher à la dure OR dans la rue.

◇ *vt phr*: to ~ it *inf Br* vivre à la dure.

◆ **rough out** *vt sep Br* [drawing, plan] ébaucher, esquisser.

◆ **rough up** *vt sep* **-1.** [hair] ébouriffer; [clothes] mettre en désordre. **-2.** *inf* [person] tabasser, passer à tabac.

roughage ['rʌfɪdʒ] *n (U)* fibres *fpl* (alimentaires).

rough-and-ready *adj* **-1.** [makeshift - equipment, apparatus] rudimentaire, de fortune; [careless - work] grossier, fait à la hâte; [- methods] grossier, expéditif. **-2.** [unrefined - person] sans façons, rustre; [- living conditions] dur.

rough-and-tumble ◇ *adj* [life - hectic] mouvementé; [- disorderly] désordonné.

◇ *n* [fight] bagarre *f*; [hurly-burly] tohu-bohu *m inv*; the ~ of politics le bouillonnement de la politique; I enjoyed the ~ of circus life la vie mouvementée du cirque me plaisait.

roughcast ['rʌfkɑːst] ◇ *adj* crépi.

◇ *n* crépi *m*.

◇ *vt* crépir.

rough diamond *n literal* diamant *m* brut; he's a ~ *Br fig* il est bourru mais il a un cœur d'or.

rough-dry (*pt* & *pp* rough-dried) ◇ *vt* sécher sans repasser OR repassage.

◇ *adj* séché sans repassage.

roughen ['rʌfn] ◇ *vt* [surface] rendre rugueux; [hands] rendre rugueux OR rêche.

◇ *vi* devenir rugueux.

rough-hewn *adj* taillé grossièrement; his ~ features *fig* son visage taillé à coups de serpe.

roughhouse *inf* ['rʌfhaʊs] *n* bagarre *f*.

roughly ['rʌflɪ] *adv* **-1.** [brutally] avec brutalité, brutalement; they treated us very ~ ils nous ont traités avec brutalité; he answered her very ~ il lui a répondu sur un ton très sec. **-2.** [sketchily - draw] grossièrement; [crudely - make] grossièrement, sans soin; the dress is ~ stitched la robe est grossièrement cousue. **-3.** [approximately] approximativement, à peu près; ~ 500 à peu près OR environ 500; it was ~ five o'clock il était environ 17 h; ~ speaking en gros, approximativement; she told me ~ how to get there elle m'a expliqué en gros comment y aller.

roughneck ['rʌfnek] *n* **-1.** *inf* [thug] voyou *m*, dur *m*. **-2.** [oil-rig worker] *ouvrier travaillant sur une plate-forme pétrolière*.

roughness ['rʌfnɪs] *n* **-1.** [of surface, hands] rugosité *f*; [of road, ground] inégalités *fpl*. **-2.** [of manner, behaviour] rudesse *f*; [of reply, speech] brusquerie *f*; [of person] rudesse *f*, brutalité *f*; [of living conditions] rudesse *f*, dureté *f*. **-3.** [of sea] agitation *f*.

roughrider ['rʌf,raɪdəʳ] *n* dresseur *m*, -euse *f* de chevaux.

roughshod ['rʌfʃɒd] ◇ *adj Br* [horse] ferré à glace.

◇ *adv Br phr*: to ride ~ over faire peu de cas de.

rough sleeper *n* [homeless person] SDF *mf*.

rough-spoken *adj* [vulgar] au langage grossier.

roulette [ruː'let] *n* roulette *f*.

Roumania *etc* [ruː'meɪnjə] = **Romania**.

round [raʊnd] ◇ *adj* **-1.** [circular] rond, circulaire; [spherical] rond, sphérique; to have a ~ face avoir la figure ronde; she looked up, her eyes ~ with surprise elle leva des yeux écarquillés de surprise; the earth is ~ la terre est ronde. **-2.** [in circumference]: the tree is 5 metres ~ l'arbre fait 5 mètres de circonférence. **-3.** [curved - belly, cheeks] rond; to have ~ shoulders avoir le dos rond OR voûté ❑ ~ arch arc *m* en plein cintre. **-4.** [figures] rond; 500, in ~ numbers 500 tout rond; a ~ dozen une douzaine tout rond. **-5.** *lit* [candid] net, franc; they gave a ~ denial ils ont nié tout net. **-6.** LING [vowel] arrondi.

◇ *prep* **-1.** [on all sides of] autour de; to sit ~ the fire/table s'asseoir autour du feu/de la table; the village is built ~ a green le village est construit autour d'un jardin public; they were all grouped ~ the teacher ils étaient tous rassemblés autour du professeur; the story centres ~ one particular family l'histoire est surtout centrée autour d'une famille. **-2.** [measuring the circumference of]: the pillar is three feet ~ the base la base du pilier fait trois pieds de circonférence. **-3.** [in the vicinity of, near] autour de; the countryside ~ Bath is lovely la campagne autour de Bath est très belle; they live somewhere ~ here ils habitent quelque part par ici. **-4.** [to the other side of]: the nearest garage is just ~ the corner le garage le plus proche est juste au coin de la rue; she disappeared ~ the back of the house elle a disparu derrière la maison; the orchard is ~ the back le verger est derrière; to go ~ the corner passer le coin, tourner au coin; there must be a way ~ the problem *fig* il doit y avoir un moyen de contourner ce problème. **-5.** [so as to cover]: he put a blanket ~ her legs il lui enveloppa les jambes d'une couverture. **-6.** [so as to encircle] autour de; he put his arm ~ her shoulders/waist il a passé son bras autour de ses épaules/de sa taille; she wears a scarf ~ her neck elle porte une écharpe autour du cou; the shark swam ~ the boat le requin faisait des cercles autour du bateau; Drake sailed ~ the world Drake a fait le tour du monde en bateau; the earth goes OR moves ~ the sun la terre tourne autour du soleil; they were dancing ~ a fire ils dansaient autour d'un feu. **-7.** [all over, everywhere in]: all ~ the world dans le monde entier, partout dans le monde; to travel ~ the world/country faire le tour du monde/du pays; she looked ~ the room elle a promené son regard autour de la pièce; to walk ~ the town faire le tour de la ville (à pied); we went for a stroll ~ the garden nous avons fait une balade dans le jardin; there's a rumour going ~ the school une rumeur circule dans l'école. **-8.** [approximately] environ, aux environs de; ~ 6 o'clock aux environs de OR vers les 6 h; ~ Christmas aux environs de Noël.

◇ *adv* **-1.** [on all sides] autour; there's a fence all ~ il y a une clôture tout autour; there are trees all the way ~ il y a des arbres tout autour ❑ taking things all ~ à tout prendre, tout compte fait. **-2.** [to other side]: you'll have to go ~, the door's locked il faudra faire le tour, la porte est fermée à clé; we drove ~ to the back nous avons fait le tour (par derrière). **-3.** [in a circle or cycle]: turn the wheel right ~ OR all the way ~ faites faire un tour complet à la roue; the shark swam ~ in circles le requin tournait en rond; all year ~ tout au long de OR toute l'année; summer will soon be OR come ~ again l'été reviendra vite. **-4.** [in the opposite direction]: turn ~ and look at me retournez-vous et regardez-moi; she looked ~ at us elle se retourna pour nous regarder; we'll have to turn the car ~ on va devoir faire demi-tour; try it the other way ~ essayez dans l'autre sens; is it the right way ~? est-ce qu'il est à l'endroit?; it's the wrong way ~ c'est dans le mauvais sens; no, it was the other way ~, HE invited ME non, c'est le contraire, c'est lui qui m'a invité. **-5.** [to various parts]: we spent the summer just travelling ~ on a passé l'été à voyager; can I have a look ~? je peux jeter un coup d'œil? **-6.** [from one person to another]: hand the sweets ~, hand ~ the sweets faites passer les bonbons; there's a rumour going ~ il y a une rumeur qui court; there wasn't enough to go ~ il n'y en avait pas assez pour tout le monde. **-7.** [to a particular place]: she came ~ to see me elle est passée me voir; let's invite some friends ~ et si on invitait des amis?; come ~ for supper some time viens dîner un soir; take these cakes ~ to her house apportez-lui ces gâteaux. **-8.** [to a different place, position]: she's always moving the furniture ~ elle passe son temps à changer les meubles de place; try shifting the aerial ~ a bit essaie de bouger un peu l'antenne. **-9.** [by indirect route]: we had to take the long way ~ on a dû faire le grand tour OR un grand détour; she went ~ by the stream elle fit un détour par le ruisseau.

◇ *n* **-1.** [circle] rond *m*, cercle *m*. **-2.** [slice - of ham, cheese, bread, toast] tranche *f*; [sandwich] sandwich *m*. **-3.** [one in a series - of discussions, negotiations] série *f*; [- of elections] tour *m*; [- of increases] série *f*, train *m*; the next ~ of arms talks will be held in Moscow les prochains pourparlers sur le désarmement auront lieu à Moscou; his life is one long ~ of parties il passe sa vie à faire la fête. **-4.** [delivery] ronde *f*; a paper/milk ~ une distribution de journaux/de lait; to do OR make the ~s circuler; she's doing OR making the ~s of literary agents elle fait le tour des agents littéraires; to go on one's ~s [paperboy, milkman] faire sa tournée; [doctor] faire ses visites ❑ to go the ~s circuler; there's a joke/rumour/virus going the ~s in the office il y a une blague/une rumeur/un virus qui circule au bureau; there are several theories going the ~s at the moment il y a plusieurs théories qui circulent en ce moment. **-5.** [routine]: the daily ~ le train-train quotidien, la routine quotidienne. **-6.** [in golf] partie *f*. **-7.** [in boxing, wrestling] round *m*, reprise *f*. **-8.** [in cards] partie *f*. **-9.** [in showjumping]: there were six clear ~s six chevaux avaient fait un sans-faute. **-10.** [stage of competition] tour *m*, manche *f*; she's through to the final ~ elle participera à la finale. **-11.** [of drinks] tournée *f*; it's my ~ c'est ma tournée; let's have another ~ prenons encore un verre. **-12.** [of cheering] salve *f*; a ~ of applause des applaudissements *mpl*; give her a ~ of applause on peut l'applaudir; they got a ~ of applause ils se sont fait applaudir. **-13.** [of ammunition] cartouche *f*; how many ~s have we got left? combien de cartouches nous reste-t-il? **-14.** [song] canon *m*. **-15.** THEAT: theatre in the ~ théâtre *m* en rond.

◇ *vt* **-1.** [lips, vowel] arrondir. **-2.** [corner] tourner; NAUT [cape] doubler, franchir.

◆ **round about** ◇ *prep phr* environ; we need ~ about 6,000 posters il nous faut environ 6 000 affiches; ~ about midnight vers minuit.

◇ *adv phr* alentour OR des alentours; the villages ~ about les villages alentour OR des alentours.

◆ **round and round** ◇ *adv phr*: to go ~ and ~ tourner; we drove ~ and ~ for hours on a tourné en rond pendant des heures; my head was spinning ~ and ~ j'avais la tête qui tournait.

◇ *prep phr*: we drove ~ and ~ the field on a fait plusieurs tours dans le champ; the helicopter flew ~ and ~ the lighthouse l'hélicoptère a tourné plusieurs fois autour du phare.

◆ **round down** *vt sep* arrondir au chiffre inférieur; their prices were ~ed down to the nearest £10 ils ont arrondi leurs prix aux 10 livres inférieures.

◆ **round off** *vt sep* **-1.** [finish, complete] terminer, clore; he ~ed off his meal with a glass of brandy il a terminé son repas par un verre de cognac. **-2.** [figures - round down] arrondir au chiffre inférieur; [- round up] arrondir au chiffre supérieur.

◆ **round on** *vt insep* attaquer, s'en prendre à.

◆ **round out** ◇ *vi insep* prendre des rondeurs.

◇ *vt sep* [complete] compléter; [deepen] approfondir.

◆ **round up** *vt sep* **-1.** [cattle, people] rassembler; [criminals] ramasser. **-2.** MATH [figures] arrondir au chiffre supérieur.

roundabout ['raʊndəbaʊt] ◇ *n Br* **-1.** [at fair] manège *m*. **-2.** AUT rond-point *m*.

◇ *adj* détourné, indirect; to take a ~ route prendre un chemin détourné; he has a ~ way of doing things il a une façon détournée de faire les choses; by ~ means par des moyens détournés.

round dance *n* ronde *f*.

rounded ['raʊndɪd] *adj* **-1.** [shape] arrondi; [cheeks] rond, rebondi; [vowel] arrondi. **-2.** [number] arrondi. **-3.** [style] harmonieux.

roundel ['raʊndl] *n* **-1.** LITERAT rondeau *m*. **-2.** AERON cocarde *f*. **-3.** [window] œil-de-bœuf *m*; [panel, medal] médaillon *m*.

roundelay ['raʊndɪleɪ] *n* [dance] ronde *f*; [song] rondeau *m*.

rounders ['raʊndəz] *n (U) Br sport proche du baseball*.

round-eyed *adj literal* aux yeux ronds; *fig* [surprised] avec des yeux ronds.

round-faced *adj* au visage rond.

Roundhead ['raʊndhed] *n Br* HIST: the **~s** les têtes rondes *(partisans du Parlement pendant la guerre civile anglaise, de 1642 à 1646)*.

roundhouse ['raʊndhaʊs, *pl* -haʊzɪz] *n* rotonde *f*.

rounding ['raʊndɪŋ] *n* COMPUT & MATH arrondi *m*, arrondissage *m*; **~ error** erreur *f* d'arrondi.

roundish ['raʊndɪʃ] *adj* plutôt rond; **she has a ~ figure** elle est plutôt rondelette.

roundly ['raʊndlɪ] *adv fig* [severely] vivement, sévèrement; **the film was ~ attacked for its racist content** le film fut vivement critiqué pour son caractère raciste || *Br* [plainly] carrément; **he told her ~ what he thought** il lui a dit carrément ce qu'il pensait.

roundness ['raʊndnɪs] *n* **-1.** [shape] rondeur *f*. **-2.** [frankness] franchise *f*. **-3.** [of sound, voice] richesse *f*, ampleur *f*.

round robin *n* **-1.** [letter] pétition *f (où les signatures sont disposées en rond)*. **-2.** *Am* [contest] poule *f*.

round-shouldered *adj*: **to be ~** avoir le dos rond, être voûté.

roundsman ['raʊndzmən] (*pl* roundsmen [-mən]) *n Br* livreur *m*.

round table *n* table *f* ronde.

◆ **round-table** *adj*: **round-table discussions** OR **negotiations** table *f* ronde.

◆ **Round Table** *pr n*: **the Round Table** la Table ronde.

round-the-clock *adj* 24 heures sur 24; **a ~ vigil** une permanence nuit et jour.

round trip *n* (voyage *m*) aller et retour *m*; **I did the ~ in 6 hours** j'ai fait l'aller-retour en 6 heures.

round-trip ticket *n Am* (billet *m*) aller-retour *m*.

roundup ['raʊndʌp] *n* **-1.** [of cattle, people] rassemblement *m*; [of criminals] rafle *f*. **-2.** [of news, sports] résumé *m* de l'actualité.

roundworm ['raʊndwɜːm] *n* ascaride *m*.

rouse [raʊz] *vt* **-1.** [wake - person] réveiller; **the burglar ~d them (from their sleep)** le cambrioleur les a réveillés OR les a tirés de leur sommeil; **he was ~d from his thoughts by the doorbell** la sonnette l'a arraché à ses pensées; **she did everything to ~ him from his apathy** elle a tout fait pour le faire sortir de son apathie; **it's time you ~d yourself and did some work** il est temps de vous secouer et de vous mettre au travail. **-2.** [provoke - interest, passion] éveiller, exciter; [- hope] éveiller; [- suspicion] éveiller, susciter; [- admiration, anger, indignation] susciter, provoquer; **to ~ a crowd** exciter une foule; **to ~ sb to action** pousser OR inciter qqn à agir; **to ~ sb to anger, to ~ sb's anger** susciter la colère de qqn, mettre qqn en colère; **to be ~d to anger** se mettre en colère; **now she's ~d, sparks will fly** maintenant qu'elle s'est mise en colère, ça va barder. **-3.** HUNT [game] lever.

rousing ['raʊzɪŋ] *adj* [speech] vibrant, passionné; [march, music] entraînant; [applause] enthousiaste.

roust [raʊst] *vt*: **to ~ sb (out) from bed** faire sortir qqn du lit.

roustabout ['raʊstəbaʊt] *n Am* ouvrier *m*, manœuvre *m*.

rout [raʊt] ◇ *n* **-1.** MIL déroute *f*, débâcle *f*; **to put an enemy/army to ~** mettre un ennemi/une armée en déroute. **-2.** JUR attroupement *m* illégal.

◇ *vt* MIL mettre en déroute OR en fuite; *fig* [team, opponent] battre à plate couture, écraser.

◇ *vi* fouiller; **the pigs were ~ing in the soil for worms** les porcs fouillaient le sol pour y trouver des vers.

◆ **rout about** *vi insep* fouiller.

◆ **rout out** *vt sep* **-1.** [find] dénicher. **-2.** [remove, force out] déloger, expulser; **they ~ed us out of our hiding-place** ils nous ont délogés de notre cachette.

route [*Br* ruːt, *Am* raʊt] ◇ *n* **-1.** [way - gen] itinéraire *m*, route *f*; **what is the best ~ to Manchester?** quel est le meilleur itinéraire pour aller à Manchester?; **the climbers took the easy ~ up the south face** les alpinistes ont emprunté l'itinéraire OR la voie la plus facile, par la face sud; **a large crowd lined the ~** il y avait une foule nombreuse sur tout le parcours; **giving up one's studies is hardly the best ~ to success** *fig* le meilleur moyen de réussir ce n'est pas d'abandonner ses études; **sea/air ~** voie maritime/aérienne; **trade ~** route commerciale. **-2.** [for buses] trajet *m*, parcours *m*; **we need a map of the bus ~s** il nous faut un plan des lignes d'autobus; **are they on a bus ~?** sont-ils desservis par les autobus? **-3.** MED voie *f*; **by oral ~** par voie orale. **-4.** *Am* [for deliveries] tournée *f*; **he's got a paper ~** il livre des journaux à domicile. **-5.** *Am* [highway] ≃ route *f* (nationale), ≃ nationale *f*; **Route 66** ≃ la nationale 66.

◇ *vt* **-1.** [procession, motorist] fixer l'itinéraire de, diriger; [train, bus] fixer l'itinéraire de; **the police ~d the marchers via Post Street** la police a fait passer les manifestants par Post Street; **during the building work, the buses are ~d along the sidestreets** pendant les travaux, les bus passent par les petites rues. **-2.** [luggage, parcel] expédier, acheminer; **our bags have been ~d to Hong Kong** nos bagages ont été expédiés sur OR à Hongkong.

◆ **en route** *adv phr* en route; **we were en ~ for the park when it started to hail** nous nous dirigions vers le parc quand il a commencé à grêler; **we stopped en ~ for a meal** nous nous sommes arrêtés en route pour manger.

route map *n* [for roads] carte *f* routière; [for buses] plan *m* du réseau; [for trains] carte *f* du réseau.

route march *n* marche *f* d'entraînement.

router ['raʊtəʳ] *n* détoureuse *f*.

routine [ruː'tiːn] ◇ *n* **-1.** [habit] routine *f*, habitude *f*; **our Sunday morning walk has become a regular ~** notre promenade du dimanche matin est devenue une habitude. **-2.** *pej* routine *f*; **daily ~** la routine quotidienne, le train-train quotidien. **-3.** [formality] formalité *f*; **it's just ~** c'est une simple formalité. **-4.** [dance, play] numéro *m*, séquence *f*; **they taught us some new dance ~s** ils nous ont appris de nouveaux enchaînements de danse. **-5.** [insincere act]: **don't give me that old ~!** ne me ressors pas cette vieille rengaine!, mets un autre disque! **-6.** COMPUT sous-programme *m*, routine *f*.

◇ *adj* **-1.** [ordinary, regular - flight, visit] de routine; [- investigation] de routine, d'usage; **can I ask you some ~ questions?** puis-je vous poser quelques questions de routine?; **she comes in once a year for a ~ check-up** elle vient une fois par an pour un examen de routine. **-2.** [everyday] de routine. **-3.** [monotonous] routinier, monotone.

routinely [ruː'tiːnlɪ] *adv* systématiquement.

roux [ruː] (*pl inv* [ruːz]) *n* roux *m* CULIN.

rove [rəʊv] ◇ *vi* **-1.** [person] errer, vagabonder. **-2.** [eyes] errer; **her eyes ~d over the page/the crowd** son regard errait sur la page/parmi la foule.

◇ *vt* [country] parcourir, errer dans; [streets] errer dans.

rover ['rəʊvəʳ] *n* vagabond *m*, -e *f*.

◆ **Rover** *pr n nom typique donné aux chiens*, ≃ Médor.

roving ['rəʊvɪŋ] ◇ *adj* vagabond, nomade; **to lead a ~ life** mener une vie de nomade; **~ reporter** reporter *m*; **he has a ~ commission** il a toute liberté de manœuvre; **he has a ~ eye (for the girls)** *fig* il aime bien lorgner les filles.

◇ *n* vagabondage *m*.

row¹ [rəʊ] ◇ *n* **-1.** [of chairs, trees] rangée *f*; [of seeds, vegetables] rang *m*; [of people - next to one another] rangée *f*; [- behind one another] file *f*, queue *f*; [of cars] file *f*; [in knitting] rang *m*; **for the third time in a ~** pour la troisième fois de suite; **she put the boxes in a ~** elle aligna les boîtes; **they sat/stood in a ~** ils étaient assis/debout en rang. **-2.** [in cinema, hall] rang *m*; **in the third ~** au troisième rang. **-3.** RUGBY ligne *f*; **the front/second/back ~** la première/deuxième/troisième ligne (de mêlée). **-4.** *Br* [in street names] rue *f*; **56 Charrington Row** 56 rue Charrington. **-5.** COMPUT ligne *f*. **-6.** [in boat] promenade *f* (en bateau à rames); **to go for a ~** faire une promenade en canot à rames; **to have a ~ round the island** faire le tour de l'île à la rame; **it was a hard ~** il a fallu ramer dur.

◇ *vi* [in boat] ramer; **to ~ across a lake** traverser un lac à la rame || SPORT faire de l'aviron; **the Cambridge team ~ed round the canal bend in the lead** l'équipe d'aviron de Cambridge arriva en tête au virage du canal.

◇ *vt* [boat] faire avancer à la rame OR à l'aviron; [passengers] transporter en canot; **Morgan ~ed the boat across the lake** Morgan traversa le lac à la rame; **Morgan ~ed the tourists across the lake** Morgan fit traverser le lac aux touristes dans un bateau à rames; **to ~ a race** faire une course d'aviron.

row² [raʊ] ◇ *n Br* **-1.** [quarrel] dispute *f*, querelle *f*; **to have a ~ with sb** se disputer avec qqn; **to get into a ~** se faire gronder; **a ~ broke out as a result of the new legislation** la nouvelle loi a fait beaucoup de raffut. **-2.** [din] tapage *m*, vacarme *m*; **to make a ~** faire du tapage OR du vacarme; **stop that ~!** arrêtez ce boucan!; **what's all the ~ about?** qu'est-ce que c'est que tout ce raffut? ❑ **shut your ~!** *inf* la ferme!

◇ *vi* se disputer; **to ~ with sb** se disputer avec qqn.

rowan ['raʊən, 'rəʊən] *n* [tree] sorbier *m*; [fruit] sorbe *f*.

rowboat ['rəʊbəʊt] *n Am* bateau *m* à rames.

rowdiness ['raʊdɪnɪs] *n* tapage *m*, chahut *m*.

rowdy ['raʊdɪ] (*compar* rowdier, *superl* rowdiest, *pl* rowdies) ◇ *adj* [person] chahuteur, bagarreur; [behaviour] chahuteur; **what a ~ bunch!** quelle bande de chahuteurs!

◇ *n* bagarreur *m*, voyou *m*; [at football matches] hooligan *m*.

rowdyism ['raʊdɪɪzm] *Br* = **rowdiness**.

rower ['rəʊəʳ] *n* rameur *m*, -euse *f*.

row house [rəʊ-] *n Am maison attenante aux maisons voisines*.

rowing ['rəʊɪŋ] *n* [gen] canotage *m*; SPORT aviron *m*; **to go ~** faire du canotage OR de l'aviron.

rowing boat *n Br* bateau *m* à rames.

rowing machine *n* rameur *m*.

rowlock ['rɒlək] *n* dame *f* de nage.

royal ['rɔɪəl] ◇ *adj* **-1.** *literal* [family, residence] royal; [horse, household, vehicle] royal, du roi, de la reine; **by ~ charter** par acte du souverain ❑ **~ assent** *signature royale qui officialise une loi*; **the Royal Enclosure** *la tribune royale à Ascot*; **the Royal Family** la famille royale; **the Royal Show** *le salon annuel de l'agriculture en Grande-Bretagne*; **the Royal Variety Show** *spectacle de variétés organisé à Londres en faveur de la Fédération des artistes de variétés*. **-2.** *fig* & *fml* [splendid] royal, princier; **they gave us a (right) ~ welcome** ils nous ont accueillis comme des rois; **we had a ~ time** nous nous sommes amusés comme des fous; **to be in ~ spirits** être d'excellente humeur. **-3.** *fig* [perfect]: **the ~ road to fame/success** la voie royale vers la renommée/la réussite. **-4.** [paper] (format) grand raisin; **~ octavo/quarto** in-huit *m*/in-quarto *m* raisin.

◇ *n inf membre de la famille royale*; **the Royals** la famille royale.

Royal Academy (of Arts) *pr n* Académie *f* royale britannique.

Royal Air Force *pr n* armée *f* de l'air britannique.

royal blue *n* bleu roi *m*.
◆ **royal-blue** *adj* bleu roi *(inv)*.

Royal Engineers *pl pr n* génie *m* militaire britannique.

royal flush *n* flush *m* royal.

Royal Highness *n*: Your ~ Votre Altesse Royale; His ~, the Prince of Wales Son Altesse Royale, le prince de Galles.

royal icing *n Br* CULIN *glaçage à base de sucre glace et de blancs d'œufs (utilisé pour les cakes)*.

Royal Institution *pr n* Académie *f* des sciences britannique.

royalism ['rɔɪəlɪzm] *n* royalisme *m*.

royalist ['rɔɪəlɪst] ◇ *adj* royaliste.
◇ *n* royaliste *mf*.

royal jelly *n* gelée *f* royale.

royally ['rɔɪəlɪ] *adv literal* & *fig* royalement; [like a king] en roi; [like a queen] en reine.

Royal Mail *pr n*: the ~ *la Poste britannique*.

Royal Marines *pl pr n* Marines *mpl* (britanniques).

Royal Navy *pr n* marine *f* nationale britannique.

Royal Society *pr n* Académie *f* des sciences britannique.

THE ROYAL SOCIETY:
Société à vocation scientifique fondée par Charles II en 1660. Elle contribua à renforcer la crédibilité des hommes de science, qui jouirent également d'une plus grande liberté. En firent notamment partie Isaac Newton et Robert Boyle.

---

royalty ['rɔɪəltɪ] ◇ *comp*: ~ payments [for writer] (paiement *m* des) droits *mpl* d'auteur; [for patent] (paiement *m* des) royalties *fpl*.
◇ *n* -**1.** [royal family] famille *f* royale. -**2.** [rank] royauté *f*.
◆ **royalties** *npl* [for writer, musician] droits *mpl* d'auteur; [for patent] royalties *fpl*, redevance *f*.

Royal Ulster Constabulary *pr n*: the ~ *corps de police d'Irlande du Nord*.

rozzer▽ ['rɒzəʳ] *n Br dated* flic *m*, poulet *m*.

RP (*abbr of* received pronunciation) *n prononciation standard de l'anglais britannique*.

RPI (*abbr of* retail price index) *n Br* indice *m* des prix à la consommation.

rpm (*written abbr of* revolutions per minute) tr/min.

RR *Am written abbr of* railroad.

RSA (*abbr of* Royal Society of Arts) *pr n* société *f* royale des arts.

RSC (*abbr of* Royal Shakespeare Company) *pr n célèbre troupe de théâtre basée à Stratford-on-Avon et à Londres*.

RSFSR (*abbr of* Russian Soviet Federal Socialist Republic) *pr n* RSFSR *f*; in the ~ en RSFSR.

RSI (*abbr of* repetitive strain/stress injury) *n douleur dans le bras due à certains mouvements de tête que font les violonistes, les pianistes ou les opérateurs de saisie*.

RSJ (*abbr of* rolled-steel joist) *n* solive *f* en I.

RSM ◇ *n* (*abbr of* regimental sergeant major) ≃ adjudant-chef *m*.
◇ *pr n* (*abbr of* Royal Society of Music) ≃ Académie *f* de musique.

RSPB (*abbr of* Royal Society for the Protection of Birds) *pr n ligue britannique pour la protection des oiseaux*.

RSPCA (*abbr of* Royal Society for the Prevention of Cruelty to Animals) *pr n société britannique protectrice des animaux*, ≃ SPA *f*.

RST (*abbr of* Royal Shakespeare Theatre) *pr n célèbre théâtre à Stratford-upon-Avon*.

RSVP (*written abbr of* répondez s'il vous plaît) RSVP.

RTE (*abbr of* Radio Télefis Éireann) *pr n* office *m* de radio et de télévision irlandais.

Rt Hon *written abbr of* Right Honourable.

Rt Rev *written abbr of* Right Reverend.

RU (*abbr of* Rugby Union) ◇ *n* SPORT rugby *m* (à quinze).
◇ *pr n* [authority] fédération *f* de rugby.

rub [rʌb] (*pt* & *pp* rubbed, *cont* rubbing) ◇ *vt* -**1.** [gen] frotter; to ~ sthg with a pad/cloth frotter qqch avec un tampon/chiffon; she was rubbing her leg against the chair elle se frottait la jambe contre la chaise; these shoes ~ my heels ces chaussures me blessent aux talons; to ~ one's eyes se frotter les yeux; to ~ one's hands (in delight) se frotter les mains (de joie); we rubbed ourselves dry with a towel nous nous sommes séchés OR essuyés avec une serviette; ~ it clean with meths nettoyez-le en le frottant avec de l'alcool à brûler; ~ it better! [to child] frotte! ❑ to ~ shoulders with sb côtoyer OR coudoyer qqn; she really rubbed his nose in it elle a retourné le couteau dans la plaie. -**2.** [ointment, lotion]: ~ the ointment into the skin faire pénétrer la pommade; ~ your chest with the ointment frottez-vous la poitrine avec la pommade ❑ to ~ salt into the wound remuer le couteau dans la plaie. -**3.** [polish] astiquer, frotter.
◇ *vi* frotter; the cat rubbed against my leg le chat s'est frotté contre ma jambe; her leg rubbed against mine sa jambe a effleuré la mienne; my shoe is rubbing ma chaussure me fait mal.
◇ *n* -**1.** [rubbing] frottement *m*; [massage] friction *f*, massage *m*; give yourself a ~ with the towel frictionnez-vous avec la serviette; can you give my back a ~? pouvez-vous me frotter le dos?; give it a ~! [after injury] frotte! -**2.** [with rag, duster] coup *m* de chiffon; [with brush] coup *m* de brosse; [with teatowel] coup *m* de torchon; give the table/glasses a ~ passez un coup de chiffon sur la table/les verres; give your shoes a ~ [with cloth] donne un coup de chiffon à tes chaussures; [with brush] donne un coup de brosse à tes chaussures. -**3.** SPORT [unevenness] inégalité *f* (du terrain). -**4.** *Br phr*: there's the ~! voilà le nœud du problème!, c'est là que le bât blesse!; what's the ~? où est le problème?
◆ **rub along** *inf vi insep Br* -**1.** [manage] se débrouiller; she ~s along in tennis elle se débrouille au tennis; we don't have much money, but we ~ along on n'a pas beaucoup d'argent mais on se débrouille. -**2.** [get on - people] s'entendre; they ~ along (together) ils s'entendent tant bien que mal.
◆ **rub away** ◇ *vt sep* -**1.** [stain, writing] faire disparaître en frottant; the inscription has been rubbed away l'inscription a été effacée. -**2.** [wipe - tears, sweat] essuyer; she rubbed away the sweat with a towel elle s'épongea avec une serviette.
◇ *vi insep* disparaître en frottant; these stains won't ~ away on a beau frotter, ces taches ne partent pas.
◆ **rub down** *vt sep* -**1.** [horse] bouchonner; [dog] frotter *(pour sécher)*; to ~ o.s. down se sécher. -**2.** [clean - wall] frotter, nettoyer en frottant; [with sandpaper] frotter, poncer.
◆ **rub in** *vt sep* [lotion, oil] faire pénétrer (en frottant); ~ the butter into the mixture CULIN travailler la pâte (du bout des doigts) pour incorporer le beurre ❑ to ~ it in remuer le couteau dans la plaie, insister lourdement; there's no need to ~ it in inutile de remuer le couteau dans la plaie; he is always rubbing it in that he was right all along il ne manque jamais de rappeler qu'il avait raison depuis le début.
◆ **rub off** ◇ *vt sep* [erase - writing] effacer; [- mark, dirt] enlever en frottant.
◇ *vi insep* -**1.** [mark] s'en aller, partir; the red dye has rubbed off on my shirt/hands la teinture rouge a déteint sur ma chemise/m'a déteint sur les mains; the newspaper ink rubbed off on the cushions l'encre du journal a noirci les coussins. -**2.** *fig* [quality] déteindre; with a bit of luck, her common sense will ~ off on the twins avec un peu de chance, son bon sens déteindra sur les jumeaux.
◆ **rub on** *vt sep* [spread] étaler (en frottant); [apply] appliquer (en frottant).
◆ **rub out** ◇ *vt sep* -**1.** [erase - stain, writing] effacer. -**2.** ▽ *Am* [kill] liquider, descendre.
◇ *vi insep* [mark, stain] partir, s'en aller (en frottant).
◆ **rub together** *vt sep* frotter l'un contre l'autre; I rubbed my hands together to try to keep warm je me suis frotté les mains pour essayer de me réchauffer.
◆ **rub up** ◇ *vi insep* -**1.** [animal] se frotter; the cat rubbed up against my leg le chat s'est frotté contre ma jambe; to ~ up against sb *fig* côtoyer qqn, coudoyer qqn. -**2.** *inf Br* [revise]: to ~ up on sthg revoir qqch, réviser qqch.
◇ *vt sep* -**1.** [polish] frotter, astiquer. -**2.** *inf* [revise] potasser; it's time you rubbed up your Greek il est temps que tu potasses ton grec. -**3.** *phr*: to ~ sb up the wrong way prendre qqn à rebrousse-poil.

rubber ['rʌbəʳ] ◇ *adj* [ball, gloves, hose] en OR de caoutchouc; [bullet] en caoutchouc; ~ boots *Am* bottes *fpl* en caoutchouc; ~ dinghy canot *m* pneumatique; ~ ring bouée *f* (de natation).
◇ *n* -**1.** [material] caoutchouc *m*; to lay ~ ▽ *Am* démarrer en trombe OR sur les chapeaux de roue. -**2.** *Br* [eraser - for pencil] gomme *f*; (board) ~ tampon *m (pour essuyer le tableau)*. -**3.** *inf Am* [condom] préservatif *m*, capote *f*. -**4.** [in bridge, whist] robre *m*, rob *m*; to play a ~ faire un robre.
◆ **rubbers** *npl Am* [boots] caoutchoucs *mpl*, bottes *fpl* en caoutchouc.

rubber band *n* élastique *m*.

rubber cement *n* dissolution *f* de caoutchouc.

rubber cheque *inf n fig* chèque *m* sans provision, chèque *m* en bois.

rubberize, -ise ['rʌbəraɪz] *vt* caoutchouter.

rubberneck *inf* ['rʌbənek] ◇ *n* -**1.** [onlooker] badaud *m*, -e *f*. -**2.** [tourist] touriste *mf*.
◇ *vi* faire le badaud.

rubber plant *n* caoutchouc *m*, ficus *m*.

rubber stamp *n* tampon *m* OR timbre *m* en caoutchouc.
◆ **rubber-stamp** *vt* -**1.** *literal* tamponner. -**2.** *fig* [decision] approuver sans discussion.

rubber tree *n* hévéa *m*.

rubbery ['rʌbərɪ] *adj* caoutchouteux.

rubbing ['rʌbɪŋ] *n* -**1.** [gen] frottement *m* -**2.** ART décalque *m*; to take a ~ of an inscription décalquer une inscription *(en frottant)*.

rubbing alcohol *n* alcool *m* à 90 (degrés).

rubbish ['rʌbɪʃ] ◇ *n (U)* -**1.** [from household] ordures *fpl* (ménagères); [from garden] détritus *mpl*; [from factory] déchets *mpl*; [from building site] gravats *mpl*; ~ van *Br* camion *m* d'éboueurs. -**2.** *inf* [worthless goods] camelote *f*, pacotille *f*; this book is ~ ce livre ne vaut rien. -**3.** *inf* [nonsense] bêtises *fpl*, sottises *fpl*; don't talk ~! ne dis pas de bêtises!; ~! mon œil!, et puis quoi encore!; this film is absolute ~! ce film est complètement nul!
◇ *vt inf* débiner; he always ~es my ideas il faut toujours qu'il débine mes idées.

rubbish bin *n Br* poubelle *f*.

rubbish chute *n Br* [in building] vide-ordures *m inv*; [at building site] gaine *f* d'évacuation des gravats.

rubbish dump *n Br* décharge *f* (publique), dépotoir *m*.

rubbish heap *n Br* [household] tas *m* d'ordures [garden] tas *m* de détritus; [public] décharge *f* dépotoir *m*.

rubbishy *inf* ['rʌbɪʃɪ] *adj Br* [poor quality - goods] de pacotille; [stupid - idea, book] débile; what a ~ programme! quelle émission débile!

rubble ['rʌbl] *n (U)* -**1.** [ruins] décombres *mpl* [debris] débris *mpl*; [stones] gravats *mpl*; the building was reduced to (a heap of) ~ l'immeuble n'était plus qu'un amas de décombres

-**2.** [for roadmaking, building] blocage *m*, blocaille *f*.

rubblework ['rʌblwɜːk] *n* maçonnerie *f* en moellons bruts.

rubdown ['rʌbdaʊn] *n* friction *f*; to give sb a ~ frictionner qqn; to give a horse a ~ bouchonner un cheval.

rube *inf* [ruːb] *n Am* plouc *m*, péquenot *m*.

rubella [ruː'belə] *n (U)* MED rubéole *f*.

Rubicon ['ruːbɪkən] *pr n* Rubicon *m*; to cross OR to pass the ~ franchir le Rubicon.

rubicund ['ruːbɪkənd] *adj* rubicond.

rubidium [ruː'bɪdɪəm] *n* rubidium *m*.

ruble ['ruːbl] = **rouble**.

rubric ['ruːbrɪk] *n* rubrique *f*.

ruby ['ruːbɪ] (*pl* **rubies**) ◇ *n* -**1.** [jewel] rubis *m*. -**2.** [colour] couleur *f* (de) rubis, couleur *f* vermeille.
◇ *adj* -**1.** [in colour] vermeil, rubis *(inv)*; ~ (red) lips des lèvres vermeilles; ~ port porto *m* rouge. -**2.** [made of rubies] de rubis. -**3.** [anniversary]: ~ wedding (anniversary) noces *fpl* de vermeil.

RUC *pr n abbr of* Royal Ulster Constabulary.

ruche [ruːʃ] ◇ *vt* rucher.
◇ *n* ruché *m*.

ruck [rʌk] ◇ *n* -**1.** SPORT [in rugby] mêlée *f* ouverte; [in race] peloton *m*. -**2.** [fight] bagarre *f*; there was a bit of a ~ last night il y a eu de la bagarre hier soir. -**3.** [crease] faux pli *m*, godet *m*. -**4.** [masses]: the (common) ~ les masses *fpl*, la foule.
◇ *vi* -**1.** SPORT former une mêlée ouverte; the Welsh forwards ~ed well les avants gallois étaient bons dans les mêlées ouvertes. -**2.** [crease] se froisser, se chiffonner.
◇ *vt* [crease] froisser, chiffonner.
◆ **ruck up** *vi insep* se froisser.

rucksack ['rʌksæk] *n* sac *m* à dos.

ruckus *inf* ['rʌkəs] *n Am* boucan *m*.

ructions *inf* ['rʌkʃnz] *npl* grabuge *m*; there'll be ~ if they find out il va y avoir du grabuge OR ça va barder s'ils l'apprennent.

rudd [rʌd] *n* rotengle *m*, gardon *m* rouge.

rudder ['rʌdə^r] *n* [of boat, plane] gouvernail *m*.

rudderless ['rʌdəlɪs] *adj* [boat] sans gouvernail; *fig* à la dérive.

ruddiness ['rʌdɪnɪs] *n* teint *m* rouge.

ruddy ['rʌdɪ] (*compar* **ruddier**, *superl* **ruddiest**)
◇ *adj* -**1.** [red - gen] rougeâtre, rougeoyant; [- face] rougeaud, rubicond; to have a ~ complexion avoir le teint rouge, être rougeaud. -**2.** *inf Br dated* [as intensifier] fichu, sacré; he's eaten the ~ lot! il a tout mangé, ce sale goinfre!
◇ *adv inf Br dated* [as intensifier] sacrément, vachement; he was ~ marvellous! il a été super chouette!

rude [ruːd] *adj* -**1.** [ill-mannered] impoli, mal élevé; [stronger] grossier; [insolent] insolent; to be ~ to sb être impoli envers qqn; it's ~ to talk with your mouth full c'est mal élevé de parler la bouche pleine; he was very ~ about my new hairstyle il a fait des commentaires très désagréables sur ma nouvelle coiffure. -**2.** [indecent, obscene] indécent, obscène, grossier; to make a ~ gesture faire un geste obscène; a ~ joke une histoire grivoise OR scabreuse; ~ words gros mots *mpl*. -**3.** [sudden] rude, violent, brutal; a ~ shock un choc brutal; it was a ~ awakening for us nous avons été rappelés brutalement à la réalité. -**4.** *lit* [rudimentary, rough - tool, hut] rudimentaire, grossier. -**5.** *lit* [primitive - tribesman, lifestyle] primitif, rude. -**6.** *lit* [vigorous] vigoureux; to be in ~ health être en pleine santé.

rudely ['ruːdlɪ] *adv* -**1.** [impolitely] impoliment, de façon mal élevée; [stronger] grossièrement; [insolently] insolemment. -**2.** [indecently, obscenely] indécemment, d'une manière obscène; to gesture ~ faire un geste obscène. -**3.** [suddenly] violemment, brutalement. -**4.** [in a rudimentary way] grossièrement; ~ made tools des outils rudimentaires.

rudeness ['ruːdnɪs] *n* -**1.** [impoliteness] impolitesse *f*; [stronger] grossièreté *f*; [insolence] insolence *f*. -**2.** [indecency, obscenity] indécence *f*, obscénité *f*. -**3.** [suddenness] violence *f*, brutalité *f*. -**4.** [rudimentary nature] caractère *m* rudimentaire; [primitive nature] caractère *m* primitif.

rudiment ['ruːdɪmənt] *n* ANAT rudiment *m*.
◆ **rudiments** *npl* [of a language, a skill] rudiments *mpl*, notions *fpl* élémentaires.

rudimentary [,ruːdɪ'mentərɪ] *adj* [gen & ANAT] rudimentaire.

rue [ruː] ◇ *vt lit* OR *hum* regretter; I lived to ~ my words toute ma vie, j'ai regretté mes propos; I ~ the day I met him je maudis le jour où je l'ai rencontré.
◇ *n* BOT rue *f*.

rueful ['ruːfʊl] *adj* [sad] triste, chagrin *lit*.

ruefully ['ruːfʊlɪ] *adv* [sadly] tristement; [regretfully] avec regret.

ruff [rʌf] ◇ *n* -**1.** [collar] fraise *f*; ZOOL [on bird] collier *m*. -**2.** ORNITH [sandpiper] combattant *m*. -**3.** [in cards] action *f* de couper; I was expecting a ~ je m'attendais à ce que la carte soit coupée.
◇ *vt* [in cards] couper.

ruffian ['rʌfjən] *n* voyou *m*; *hum* [naughty child] petit vaurien *m*.

ruffianly ['rʌfjənlɪ] *adj* [person] brutal; [appearance, behaviour] de voyou.

ruffle ['rʌfl] ◇ *vt* -**1.** [hair, fur, feathers] ébouriffer; [clothes] friper, froisser, chiffonner; the wind ~d her hair le vent ébouriffait ses cheveux; the parrot ~d its feathers le perroquet hérissa ses plumes. -**2.** [lake, sea, grass] agiter. -**3.** [upset - person] troubler, décontenancer.
◇ *n* -**1.** [frill - on dress] ruche *f*. -**2.** [ripple - on lake, sea] ride *f*.

ruffled ['rʌfld] *adj* -**1.** [flustered] décontenancé. -**2.** [rumpled - sheets] froissé; [- hair] ébouriffé. -**3.** [decorated with frill] ruché, plissé.

rug [rʌg] *n* -**1.** [for floor] carpette *f*, (petit) tapis *m*; to pull the ~ from under sb's feet couper l'herbe sous le pied à qqn; to sweep sthg under the ~ *Am fig* enterrer qqch . -**2.** *Br* [blanket] couverture *f*; tartan ~ plaid *m*.

rugby ['rʌgbɪ] ◇ *n*: ~ (football) rugby *m*.
◇ *comp* [ball, match, team] de rugby; ~ player joueur *m*, -euse *f* de rugby, rugbyman *m*.

rugby league *n* rugby *m* OR jeu *m* à treize.

rugby tackle *n* plaquage *m*.
◆ **rugby-tackle** *vt* plaquer; the policeman rugby-tackled him le policier l'a plaqué.

rugby union *n* rugby *m* à quinze.

rugged ['rʌgɪd] *adj* -**1.** [countryside, region] accidenté; [road, path - bumpy] cahoteux, défoncé; [- rocky] rocailleux; [coastline] échancré, découpé. -**2.** [face, features] rude; he had ~ good looks il était d'une beauté sauvage. -**3.** [unrefined - person, character, manners] rude, mal dégrossi; [- lifestyle] rude, fruste; [determined - resistance] acharné. -**4.** [healthy] vigoureux, robuste; [tough - clothing, equipment, vehicle] solide, robuste.

ruggedness ['rʌgɪdnɪs] *n (U)* -**1.** [of countryside, region] caractère *m* accidenté; [of road, path] inégalités *fpl*; [of coastline] échancrures *fpl*; the ~ of the terrain les inégalités du terrain. -**2.** [of face, features] irrégularité *f*. -**3.** [of person, manners, lifestyle] rudesse *f*. -**4.** [toughness - of clothing, equipment, vehicle] solidité *f*, robustesse *f*.

rugger *inf* ['rʌgə^r] *n Br* rugby *m*.

ruin ['ruːɪn] ◇ *n* -**1.** *(usu pl)* [remains] ruine *f*; the monastery is now a ~ le monastère n'est plus qu'une ruine; the ~s of an old castle les ruines d'un vieux château; the economy/town is in ~s l'économie/la ville est en ruine. -**2.** [destruction] ruine *f*; this spelt the ~ of our hopes c'était la fin de nos espoirs; to fall into ~ tomber en ruine; you will be my ~ OR the ~ of me tu me perdras. -**3.** [bankruptcy] ruine *f*; the business was on the brink of (financial) ~ l'affaire était au bord de la ruine.
◇ *vt* -**1.** [destroy] ruiner, détruire, abîmer; [spoil] gâter, gâcher; that's ~ed our chances ça nous a fait perdre toutes nos chances; you're ~ing your eyesight tu es en train de t'abîmer la vue OR les yeux; the rain ~ed our trip la pluie a gâché notre voyage; you've ~ed my best dress tu as abîmé ma plus jolie robe. -**2.** [bankrupt] ruiner.

ruination [ruːɪ'neɪʃn] *n* ruine *f*, perte *f*; you'll be the ~ of me! tu me perdras!; the ~ of the countryside la destruction de la campagne.

ruined ['ruːɪnd] *adj* -**1.** [house, reputation, health] en ruine, ruiné; [clothes] abîmé. -**2.** [person - financially] ruiné.

ruinous ['ruːɪnəs] *adj* -**1.** [expensive] ruineux; maintaining such a large house proved ~ l'entretien d'une aussi grande maison s'est avéré ruineux. -**2.** [disastrous] désastreux.

ruinously ['ruːɪnəslɪ] *adv* de façon ruineuse; ~ expensive ruineux.

rule [ruːl] ◇ *n* -**1.** [law, tenet] règle *f*; [regulation] règlement *m*; the ~s of chess/grammar les règles du jeu d'échecs/de la grammaire; to break the ~s ne pas respecter les règles; to play according to the ~s OR by the ~s (of the game) jouer suivant les règles (du jeu); the ~s and regulations le règlement; the club ~s are very strict on this point le règlement du club est très strict sur ce point; smoking is against the ~s, it's against the ~s to smoke le règlement interdit de fumer; that contravenes ~ 5b c'est contraire à la règle 5b; to stretch OR to bend the ~s (for sb) faire une entorse au règlement (pour qqn) ❑ ~ of thumb point *m* de repère. -**2.** [convention, guideline] règle *f*; ~s of conduct règles de conduite; the ~s for a happy marriage comment réussir son mariage; he makes it a ~ not to trust anyone il a comme OR pour règle de ne faire confiance à personne. -**3.** [normal state of affairs] règle *f*; tipping is the ~ here les pourboires sont de règle ici; it's often the case, but there's no hard and fast ~ c'est souvent le cas, mais il n'y a pas de règle absolue; politeness seems to be the exception rather than the ~ on dirait que la politesse est l'exception plutôt que la règle; long hair was the ~ in those days tout le monde avait les cheveux longs à cette époque. -**4.** [government] gouvernement *m*, autorité *f*; [reign] règne *m*; a return to majority/mob ~ un retour à la démocratie/à l'anarchie; the territories under French ~ les territoires sous autorité française; in the days of British ~ à l'époque de la domination britannique; the ~ of law (l'autorité de) la loi. -**5.** [for measuring] règle *f*; folding ~ mètre *m* pliant; metre ~ mètre *m*.
◇ *vt* -**1.** [govern - country] gouverner; if I ~d the world si j'étais maître du monde. -**2.** [dominate - person] dominer; [- emotion] maîtriser; their lives are ~d by fear leur vie est dominée par la peur; don't be ~d by what he says ce n'est pas à lui de vous dire ce que vous avez à faire ❑ to ~ the roost faire la loi. -**3.** [judge, decide] juger, décider; the referee ~d the ball out OR that the ball was out l'arbitre a déclaré OR jugé que la balle était hors jeu; the strike was ~d illegal la grève a été jugée illégale; the court ~d that he should have custody of the children c'est à lui que la cour a accordé la garde des enfants. -**4.** [draw - line, margin] tirer à la règle; [draw lines on - paper] régler.
◇ *vi* -**1.** [govern - monarch, dictator] régner; [- elected government] gouverner; he ~d over a vast kingdom il régna sur un vaste royaume; Chelsea ~ OK! *inf* vive l'équipe de Chelsea! -**2.** [prevail] régner; chaos ~d le désordre régnait; the philosophy currently ruling in the party la philosophie actuellement en vigueur au parti. -**3.** JUR [decide] statuer; to ~ on a dispute statuer sur un litige; to ~ against/in favour of sb décider OR prononcer contre/en faveur de qqn.
◆ **as a (general) rule** *adv phr* en règle générale.
◆ **rule off** *vt sep* tirer une ligne sous.
◆ **rule out** *vt sep* [possibility, suggestion, suspect] exclure, écarter; we cannot ~ out that possibility on ne saurait exclure cette éventualité; she cannot be ~d out of the inquiry elle n'a

pas encore été mise hors de cause; the injury ~s him out of Saturday's game sa blessure ne lui permettra pas de jouer samedi.

rulebook ['ruːlbʊk] *n* règlement *m*; the ~ le règlement, les règles *fpl*; to do sthg by the ~ faire qqch strictement selon les règles; to go by the ~ suivre scrupuleusement le règlement.

ruled [ruːld] *adj* [paper, block] réglé.

ruler ['ruːləʳ] *n* -**1.** [sovereign] souverain *m*, -e *f*; [president, prime minister etc] homme *m* d'État, dirigeant *m*. -**2.** [for measuring] règle *f*.

ruling ['ruːlɪŋ] ◇ *adj* -**1.** [governing - monarch] régnant; [- party] au pouvoir; [- class] dirigeant; football's ~ body les instances dirigeantes du football. -**2.** [dominant - feeling, passion, factor] dominant.
◇ *n* JUR [finding] décision *f*, jugement *m*.

rum [rʌm] (*compar* rummer, *superl* rummest)
◇ *n* [drink] rhum *m*.
◇ *comp* [ice cream, toddy] au rhum.
◇ *adj* *inf Br dated* [odd] bizarre; he's a ~ old chap c'est un drôle de bonhomme; I was feeling a bit ~ je n'étais pas dans mon assiette.

Rumania *etc* [ruː'meɪnjə] = **Romania**.

rumba ['rʌmbə] ◇ *n* rumba *f*.
◇ *vi* danser la rumba.

rum baba *n* baba *m* au rhum.

rumble ['rʌmbl] ◇ *n* -**1.** [of thunder, traffic, cannons] grondement *m*; [of conversation] murmure *m*, bourdonnement *m*; [in stomach] borborygme *m*, gargouillis *m*, gargouillement *m*. -**2.** *inf Am* [street fight] bagarre *f*, castagne *f (entre gangs)*.
◇ *vi* -**1.** [thunder, traffic, cannons] gronder; [stomach] gargouiller; trucks were rumbling past all night toute la nuit, on entendait le grondement des camions. -**2.** *inf Am* [fight] se bagarrer.
◇ *vt* -**1.** *inf Br* [discover - plan] découvrir; [understand - person, trick] piger; I soon ~d their little game j'ai tout de suite pigé leur petit jeu. -**2.** [mutter - comment, remark] grommeler, bougonner.
◆ **rumble on** *vi insep* [person] palabrer; [conversation, debate] ne pas en finir; he ~d on about India for a good hour il a palabré sur l'Inde pendant une bonne heure; the dispute's been rumbling on for weeks now le conflit dure depuis des semaines.

rumble seat *n Am* strapontin *m*.

rumbling ['rʌmblɪŋ] *n* [of thunder, traffic, cannons] grondement *m*; [of stomach] borborygmes *mpl*, gargouillis *mpl*, gargouillements *mpl*.
◆ **rumblings** *npl* [of discontent] grondement *m*, grondements *mpl*; [omens] présages *mpl*; I've heard ~s to that effect j'ai entendu des bruits qui semblent le confirmer.

rumbustious *inf* [rʌm'bʌstʃəs] *adj Br* [boisterous] exubérant, tapageur, bruyant; [unruly] turbulent, indiscipliné.

rumen ['ruːmen] (*pl* rumens OR rumina [-mɪnə]) *n* ZOOL panse *f (de ruminant)*, rumen *m*.

ruminant ['ruːmɪnənt] ◇ *adj* -**1.** ZOOL ruminant. -**2.** *lit* = **ruminative**.
◇ *n* ZOOL ruminant *m*.

ruminate ['ruːmɪneɪt] ◇ *vi* -**1.** ZOOL ruminer. -**2.** *fml* [person] ruminer; I've been ruminating over OR about OR on your suggestion j'ai longuement réfléchi à votre proposition.
◇ *vt* -**1.** ZOOL ruminer. -**2.** *fml* [person] ruminer.

rumination [ˌruːmɪ'neɪʃn] *n* rumination *f*.

ruminative ['ruːmɪnətɪv] *adj* [person] pensif, méditatif; [look, mood] pensif.

ruminatively ['ruːmɪnətɪvlɪ] *adv* pensivement.

rummage ['rʌmɪdʒ] ◇ *n* -**1.** [search]: to have a ~ through OR around in sthg fouiller (dans) qqch. -**2.** *Am* [jumble] bric-à-brac *m*.
◇ *vi* fouiller; he ~d in OR through his pockets il fouilla dans ses poches.
◆ **rummage about** *Br*, **rummage around** = **rummage** *vi*.
◆ **rummage out, rummage up** *vt sep* dénicher.

rummage sale *n Am* vente *f* de charité.

rummer ['rʌməʳ] *n* grand verre *m* à pied.

rummy ['rʌmɪ] (*pl* rummies, *compar* rummier, *superl* rummiest) ◇ *n* -**1.** [card game] rami *m*. -**2.** *inf Am* [drunk] alcolo *mf*, poivrot *m*, -e *f*.
◇ *adj* = **rum**.

rumour *Br*, **rumor** *Am* ['ruːməʳ] ◇ *n* rumeur *f*, bruit *m* (qui court); there's a ~ going round OR ~ has it that he's going to resign le bruit court qu'il va démissionner; the ~ that she's left the country is untrue la rumeur selon laquelle elle aurait quitté le pays n'est pas fondée.
◇ *vt*: it is ~ed that... le bruit court que...; she is ~ed to be extremely rich on la dit extrêmement riche; he is ~ed to have killed a man on dit OR le bruit court qu'il a tué un homme.

rumourmonger *Br*, **rumormonger** *Am* ['ruːməˌmʌŋgəʳ] *n* commère *f*.

rump [rʌmp] *n* -**1.** [of mammal] croupe *f*; CULIN culotte *f*; [of bird] croupion *m*; *hum* [of person] postérieur *m*, derrière *m*. -**2.** [remnant]: the organization was reduced to a ~ il ne restait pas grand-chose de l'organisation.

rumple ['rʌmpl] *vt* [clothes] friper, froisser, chiffonner; [banknote, letter] froisser; [hair, fur] ébouriffer; the wind had ~d my hair le vent m'avait décoiffé; pages ~d at the edges des pages cornées.

Rump Parliament *pr n*: the ~ le Parlement croupion *(nom du Parlement anglais pendant la période du Protectorat de Cromwell, de 1649 à 1660)*.

rump steak *n* romsteck *m*, rumsteck *m*.

rumpus *inf* ['rʌmpəs] *n* raffut *m*, boucan *m*; the announcement caused a ~ la nouvelle fit l'effet d'une bombe; to kick up a ~ faire du chahut OR des histoires.

rumpus room *n esp Am* salle *f* de jeu *(souvent située au sous-sol et également utilisée pour des fêtes)*.

rumpy-pumpy *inf* ['rʌmpɪˌpʌmpɪ] *n Br hum* partie *f* de jambes en l'air.

run [rʌn] (*pt* ran [ræn], *pp* run, *cont* running)
◇ *vi* **A.** -**1.** [gen] courir; I ~ every morning in the park je cours tous les matins dans le parc; they ran out of the house ils sont sortis de la maison en courant; to ~ upstairs/downstairs monter/descendre l'escalier en courant; I had to ~ for the train j'ai dû courir pour attraper le train; ~ and fetch me a glass of water cours me chercher un verre d'eau; I've been running all over the place looking for you j'ai couru partout à ta recherche; to ~ to meet sb courir OR se précipiter à la rencontre de qqn ‖ *fig*: I didn't expect her to go running to the press with the story je ne m'attendais pas à ce qu'elle coure raconter l'histoire à la presse; don't come running to me with your problems ne viens pas m'embêter avec tes problèmes. -**2.** [compete in race] courir; there are twenty horses running in the race vingt chevaux participent à la course; she ran for her country in the Olympics elle a couru pour son pays aux jeux Olympiques ‖ [be positioned in race] arriver; [in cricket, baseball] marquer; Smith is running second Smith est en seconde position. -**3.** [flee] se sauver, fuir; if the night watchman sees you, ~ (for it *inf*)! si le veilleur de nuit te voit, tire-toi OR file!; he turned and ran il prit ses jambes à son cou; ~ for your lives! sauve qui peut!; you can't just keep running from your past *fig* vous ne pouvez pas continuer à fuir votre passé.
B. -**1.** [road, railway, boundary] passer; a tunnel ~s under the mountain un tunnel passe sous la montagne; the railway line ~s through a valley/over a viaduct le chemin de fer passe dans une vallée/sur un viaduc; the pipes ~ under the road les tuyaux passent sous la route; the road ~s alongside the river/parallel to the coast la route longe la rivière/la côte; hedgerows ~ between the fields des haies séparent les champs; the road ~s due north la route va droit vers le nord; a canal running from London to Birmingham un canal qui va de Londres à Birmingham; a high fence ~s around the building une grande barrière fait le tour du bâtiment; the lizard has red markings running down its back le dos du lézard est zébré de rouge; the line of print ran off the page la ligne a débordé de la feuille; our lives seem to be running in different directions *fig* il semble que nos vies prennent des chemins différents. -**2.** [hand, fingers]: his fingers ran over the controls ses doigts se promenèrent sur les boutons de commande; her eyes ran down the list elle parcourut la liste des yeux. -**3.** [travel - thoughts, sensation]: a shiver ran down my spine un frisson me parcourut le dos; his thoughts ran to that hot August day in Paris cette chaude journée d'août à Paris lui revint à l'esprit. -**4.** [describing song, poem, theory etc]: their argument OR reasoning ~s something like this voici plus ou moins leur raisonnement. -**5.** [occur - inherited trait, illness]: twins ~ in our family les jumeaux sont courants dans la famille; heart disease ~s in the family les maladies cardiaques sont fréquentes dans notre famille. -**6.** [spread - rumour, news] se répandre. -**7.** [move or travel freely - ball, vehicle] rouler; the pram ran down the hill out of control le landau a dévalé la côte; the crane ~s on rails la grue se déplace sur des rails; the piano ~s on casters le piano est monté sur (des) roulettes; the truck ran off the road le camion a quitté la route ‖ [slip, slide - rope, cable] filer; let the cord ~ through your hands laissez la corde filer entre vos mains. -**8.** [drive] faire un tour OR une promenade; why don't we ~ down to the coast/up to London? si on faisait un tour jusqu'à la mer/jusqu'à Londres? -**9.** NAUT [boat]: to ~ (before the wind) filer vent arrière.
C. -**1.** [flow - water, tap, nose] couler; [paint] goutter; let the water ~ until it's hot laisse couler l'eau jusqu'à ce qu'elle soit chaude; you've let the water ~ cold tu as laissé couler l'eau trop longtemps, elle est devenue froide; your bath is running ton bain est en train de couler; your nose is running tu as le nez qui coule; the cold made our eyes ~ le froid nous piquait les yeux; her mascara had ~ son mascara avait coulé; the hot water ~s along/down this pipe l'eau chaude passe/descend dans ce tuyau; their faces were running with sweat *Br* leurs visages ruisselaient de transpiration; tears ran down her face des larmes coulaient sur son visage ☐ my blood ran cold mon sang se figea. -**2.** [river, stream] couler; the river ran red with blood les eaux de la rivière étaient rouges de sang; the Jari ~s into the Amazon le Jari se jette dans l'Amazone. -**3.** [butter, ice cream, wax] fondre; [cheese] couler. -**4.** [in wash - colour, fabric] déteindre; wash that dress separately, the colour might ~ lave cette robe à part, elle pourrait déteindre. -**5.** [tide] monter.
D. -**1.** [operate - engine, machine, business] marcher, fonctionner; to ~ on OR off electricity/gas/diesel fonctionner à l'électricité/au gaz/au diesel; the tape recorder was still running le magnétophone était encore en marche; leave the engine running laissez tourner le moteur; the new assembly line is up and running la nouvelle chaîne de montage est en service; do not interrupt the program while it is running COMPUT ne pas interrompre le programme en cours d'exécution; this software ~s on DOS ce logiciel tourne sous DOS; everything is running smoothly *fig* tout marche très bien. -**2.** [public transport] circuler; this train doesn't ~/only ~s on Sundays ce train ne circule pas/ne circule que le dimanche; some bus lines ~ all night certaines lignes d'autobus sont en service toute la nuit; trains running to Calais are cancelled les trains pour OR en direction de Calais sont annulés; he took the tube that ~s through Clapham il prit la ligne de métro qui passe par Clapham.
E. -**1.** [last] durer; the sales ~ from the beginning to the end of January les soldes durent du début à la fin janvier; the sales have only another two days to ~ il ne reste que deux

jours de soldes; **the meeting ran for an hour longer than expected** la réunion a duré une heure de plus que prévu; **I'd like the ad to ~ for a week** je voudrais que l'annonce passe pendant une semaine. -**2.** [be performed - play, film] tenir l'affiche; **his new musical should ~ and ~!** sa nouvelle comédie musicale devrait tenir l'affiche pendant des mois!; **this soap opera has been running for 20 years** ça fait 20 ans que ce feuilleton est diffusé; **America's longest-running TV series** la plus longue série télévisée américaine. -**3.** [be valid, remain in force - contract] être OR rester valide; [- agreement] être OR rester en vigueur; **the lease has another year to ~** le bail n'expire pas avant un an; **your subscription will ~ for two years** votre abonnement sera valable deux ans. -**4.** FIN [be paid, accumulate - interest] courir; **interest ~s from January 1st** les intérêts courent à partir du 1er janvier. -**5.** [range] aller; **the colours ~ from dark blue to bright green** les couleurs vont du bleu foncé au vert vif.

F. -**1.** [indicating current state or condition]: **feelings were running high** les passions étaient exacerbées; **their ammunition was running low** ils commençaient à manquer de munitions; **to ~ late** être en retard, avoir du retard; **programmes are running ten minutes late** les émissions ont toutes dix minutes de retard; **sorry I can't stop, I'm running a bit late** désolé, je ne peux pas rester, je suis un peu en retard; **events are running in our favour** les événements tournent en notre faveur. -**2.** [reach]: **inflation was running at 18%** le taux d'inflation était de 18 %.

G. -**1.** *Am* [be candidate, stand] se présenter; **to ~ for president** OR **the presidency** être candidat aux élections présidentielles OR à la présidence; **she's running on a law-and-order ticket** elle se présente aux élections avec un programme basé sur la lutte contre l'insécurité; **he ran against Reagan in 1984** il s'est présenté contre Reagan en 1984. -**2.** [ladder - stocking, tights] filer.

◇ *vt* **A.** -**1.** [manage - company, office] diriger, gérer; [- shop, restaurant, club] tenir, diriger; [- theatre] diriger; [- house] tenir; [- country] gouverner, diriger; **she ~s the bar while her parents are away** elle tient le bar pendant l'absence de ses parents; **a badly ~ organization** une organisation mal gérée; **the library is ~ by volunteer workers** la bibliothèque est tenue par des bénévoles; **the farm was too big for him to ~ alone** la ferme était trop grande pour qu'il puisse s'en occuper seul; **who's running this outfit?** *inf* qui est le patron ici?; **I wish she'd stop trying to ~ my life!** j'aimerais bien qu'elle arrête de me dire comment vivre ma vie! -**2.** [organize, lay on - service, course, contest] organiser; **to ~ a bridge tournament/a raffle** organiser un tournoi de bridge/une tombola; **they ~ evening classes in computing** ils organisent des cours du soir en informatique || [train, bus] mettre en service; **they ~ extra trains in the summer** l'été ils mettent (en service) des trains supplémentaires; **several private companies ~ buses to the airport** plusieurs sociétés privées assurent un service d'autobus pour l'aéroport. -**3.** [operate, work - piece of equipment] faire marcher, faire fonctionner; **you can ~ it off solar energy/the mains** vous pouvez le faire fonctionner à l'énergie solaire/sur secteur || [vehicle]: **I can't afford to ~ a car any more** *Br* je n'ai plus les moyens d'avoir une voiture; **she ~s a Porsche** elle roule en Porsche. -**4.** [conduct - experiment, test] effectuer. -**5.** COMPUT [program] exécuter.

B. -**1.** [do or cover at a run - race, distance] courir; **to ~ the marathon** courir le marathon; **I can still ~ 2 km in under 7 minutes** j'arrive encore à courir OR à couvrir 2 km en moins de 7 minutes; **the children were running races** les enfants faisaient la course; **the race will be ~ in Paris next year** la course aura lieu à Paris l'année prochaine; **to ~ messages** OR **errands** faire des commissions OR des courses ❑ **he'd ~ a mile if he saw it** il prendrait ses jambes à son cou s'il voyait ça; **it looks as if his race is ~** on dirait qu'il a fait son temps. -**2.** [cause to run]: **you're running the poor boy off his feet!** le pauvre, tu es en train de l'épuiser!; **to be ~ off one's feet** être débordé; **to ~ o.s. to a standstill** courir jusqu'à l'épuisement. -**3.** [enter for race - horse, greyhound] faire courir. -**4.** [chase] chasser; **the outlaws were ~ out of town** les hors-la-loi furent chassés de la ville. -**5.** [hunt] chasser; **to ~ deer** chasser le cerf.

C. -**1.** [transport - goods] transporter; [give lift to - person] accompagner; **I'll ~ you to the bus stop** je vais te conduire à l'arrêt de bus; **I've got to ~ these boxes over to my new house** je dois emporter ces boîtes dans ma nouvelle maison. -**2.** [smuggle] faire le trafic de; **he's suspected of running drugs/guns** il est soupçonné de trafic de drogue/d'armes. -**3.** [drive - vehicle] conduire; **I ran the car into the driveway** j'ai mis la voiture dans l'allée; **could you ~ your car back a bit?** pourriez-vous reculer un peu votre voiture?; **I ran my car into a lamppost** je suis rentré dans un réverbère (avec ma voiture); **he tried to ~ me off the road!** il a essayé de me faire sortir de la route!

D. -**1.** [pass, quickly or lightly] passer; **she ran her hands over the controls** elle promena ses mains sur les boutons de commande; **he ran his hand/a comb through his hair** il passa sa main/un peigne dans ses cheveux; **I'll ~ a duster over the furniture** je passerai un coup de chiffon sur les meubles; **she ran her finger down the list/her eye over the text** elle parcourut la liste du doigt/le texte des yeux. -**2.** [send via specified route]: **we could ~ a cable from the house** nous pourrions amener un câble de la maison; **it would be better to ~ the wires under the floorboards** ce serait mieux de faire passer les fils sous le plancher; **~ the other end of the rope through the loop** passez l'autre bout de la corde dans la boucle.

E. -**1.** [go through or past - blockade] forcer; [- rapids] franchir; *Am* [- red light] brûler. -**2.** [cause to flow] faire couler; **~ the water into the basin** faites couler l'eau dans la cuvette; **to ~ a bath** faire couler un bain. -**3.** [publish] publier; **the local paper is running a series of articles on the scandal** le journal local publie une série d'articles sur le scandale; **to ~ an ad (in the newspaper)** passer OR faire passer une annonce (dans le journal). -**4.** [enter for election] présenter; **they're running a candidate in every constituency** ils présentent un candidat dans chaque circonscription. -**5.** MED: **to ~ a temperature** OR **fever** avoir de la fièvre. -**6.** [expose o.s. to]: **to ~ the danger** OR **risk of doing sthg** courir le risque de faire qqch; **you ~ the risk of a heavy fine** vous risquez une grosse amende; **do you realize the risks you're running?** est-ce que vous réalisez les risques que vous prenez?

◇ *n* -**1.** [action] course *f*; **to go for a ~** aller faire du jogging; **to go for a five-mile ~** courir huit kilomètres; **I took the dog for a ~ in the park** j'ai emmené le chien courir dans le parc; **two policemen arrived at a ~** deux policiers sont arrivés au pas de course; **to break into a ~** se mettre à courir; **to make a ~ for it** prendre la fuite, se sauver ❑ **we have the ~ of the house while the owners are away** nous disposons de toute la maison pendant l'absence des propriétaires; **we give the au pair the ~ of the place** nous laissons à la jeune fille au pair la libre disposition de la maison; **to be on the ~**: **the murderer is on the ~** le meurtrier est en cavale; **she was on the ~ from her creditors/the police** elle essayait d'échapper à ses créanciers/à la police; **we've got them on the ~!** MIL & SPORT nous les avons mis en déroute!; **you've had a good ~ (for your money), it's time to step down** tu en as bien profité, maintenant il faut laisser la place à un autre; **they gave the Russian team a good ~ for their money** ils ont donné du fil à retordre à l'équipe soviétique. -**2.** [race] course *f*; **a charity ~** une course de charité. -**3.** [drive] excursion *f*, promenade *f*; **we went for a ~ down to the coast** nous sommes allés nous promener au bord de la mer; **she took me for a ~ in her new car** elle m'a emmené faire un tour dans sa nouvelle voiture; **there was very little traffic on the ~ down** nous avons rencontré très peu de circulation; **shall I make** OR **do a beer ~?** *inf hum* je vais chercher de la bière? || [for smuggling] passage *m*; **the gang used to make ~s across the border** le gang passait régulièrement la frontière. -**4.** [route, itinerary] trajet *m*, parcours *m*; **the buses on the London to Glasgow ~** les cars qui font le trajet OR qui assurent le service Londres-Glasgow; **it's only a short ~ into town** le trajet jusqu'au centre-ville n'est pas long. -**5.** AERON [flight] vol *m*, mission *f*; **bombing ~** mission de bombardement. -**6.** SPORT [in cricket, baseball] point *m*. -**7.** [track - for skiing, bobsleighing] piste *f*. -**8.** [series, continuous period] série *f*, succession *f*, suite *f*; **they've had a ~ of ten defeats** ils ont connu dix défaites consécutives; **you seem to be having a ~ of good/bad luck** on dirait que la chance est/n'est pas de ton côté en ce moment || [series of performances]: **the play had a triumphant ~ on Broadway** la pièce a connu un succès triomphal à Broadway; **the play had a ~ of nearly two years** la pièce a tenu l'affiche (pendant) presque deux ans ❑ **in the long/short ~** à long/court terme. -**9.** [in card games] suite *f*. -**10.** INDUST [production] lot *m*, série *f*; **a ~ of less than 500 would be uneconomical** fabriquer une série de moins de 500 unités ne serait pas rentable ❑ **print ~** TYPO tirage *m*. -**11.** [general tendency, trend] tendance *f*; **to score against the ~ of play** marquer contre le jeu; **I was lucky and got the ~ of the cards** j'avais de la chance, les cartes m'étaient favorables; **the usual ~ of colds and upset stomachs** les rhumes et les maux de ventre habituels; **she's well above the average** OR **ordinary ~ of students** elle est bien au-dessus de la moyenne des étudiants; **the ordinary ~ of mankind** le commun des mortels; **in the ordinary ~ of things,...** normalement,... -**12.** [great demand] ruée *f*; **the heatwave caused a ~ on suntan cream** la vague de chaleur provoqua une ruée sur les crèmes solaires; **a ~ on the banks** une panique bancaire || ST. EX: **there was a ~ on the dollar** il y a eu une ruée sur le dollar. -**13.** [operation - of machine] opération *f*; **computer ~** passage *m* machine. -**14.** [bid - in election] candidature *f*; **his ~ for the presidency** sa candidature à la présidence. -**15.** [ladder - in stocking, tights] échelle *f*, maille *f* filée; **I've got a ~ in my tights** mon collant est filé. -**16.** [enclosure - for animals] enclos *m*; **chicken ~** poulailler *m*. -**17.** MUS roulade *f*.

◆ **runs** *inf npl* [diarrhoea] courante *f*; **to have the ~s** avoir la courante.

◆ **run about** *vi insep* courir (çà et là); **I've been running about all day looking for you!** j'ai passé ma journée à te chercher partout!

◆ **run across** ◇ *vi insep* traverser en courant. ◇ *vt insep* [meet - acquaintance] rencontrer par hasard, tomber sur; [find - book, reference] trouver par hasard, tomber sur.

◆ **run after** *vt insep literal & fig* courir après; **it's not like her to ~ after a man** ce n'est pas son genre de courir après un homme.

◆ **run along** *vi insep* [go away] s'en aller, partir; **it's getting late, I must be running along** il se fait tard, il faut que j'y aille; **~ along to bed now, children!** allez les enfants, au lit maintenant!

◆ **run around** *vi insep* -**1.** = **run about**. -**2.** [husband] courir après les femmes; [wife] courir après les hommes; **he's always running around with other women** il est toujours en train de courir après d'autres femmes.

◆ **run away** *vi insep* -**1.** [flee] se sauver, s'enfuir; **their son has ~ away from home** leur fils a fait une fugue; **I'll be with you in a minute, don't ~ away** je serai à toi dans un instant, ne te sauve pas; **~ away and play now, children** allez jouer ailleurs, les enfants; to ~ away from one's responsibilities *fig* fuir ses responsabilités. -**2.** [elope] partir.

◆ **run away with** *vt insep* -**1.** [secretly or illegally] partir avec; **he ran away with his best friend's wife** il est parti avec la femme de son meilleur ami; **he ran away with the takings** il est parti avec la caisse. -**2.** [overwhelm]: **don't let your excitement ~ away with you** gardez votre calme; **she tends to let her imagination ~ away with her** elle a tendance à se laisser emporter par son imagination. -**3.** [get - idea]: **don't go running away with the idea** OR **the notion that it will be easy** n'allez pas vous imaginer que ce sera facile. -**4.** [win - race, match] emporter haut la main; [- prize] remporter; **they ran away with nearly all the medals** ils ont remporté presque toutes les médailles.

◆ **run back** ◇ *vi insep* -**1.** *literal* retourner OR revenir en courant. -**2.** [review]: to ~ **back over sthg** passer qqch en revue.
◇ *vt sep* -**1.** [drive back] raccompagner (en voiture); **she ran me back home** elle m'a ramené OR raccompagné chez moi; **he ran me back on his motorbike** il m'a raccompagné en moto. -**2.** [rewind - tape, film] rembobiner.

◆ **run by** *vt sep*: to ~ **sthg by sb** [submit] soumettre qqch à qqn; **you'd better ~ that by the committee** vous feriez mieux de demander l'avis du comité; ~ **that by me again** répétez-moi ça.

◆ **run down** ◇ *vi insep* -**1.** *literal* descendre en courant. -**2.** [clock, machine] s'arrêter; [battery - through use] s'user; [- through a fault] se décharger; **the batteries in the radio are beginning to ~ down** les piles de la radio commencent à être usées.
◇ *vt sep* -**1.** [reduce, diminish] réduire; **they are running down their military presence in Africa** ils réduisent leur présence militaire en Afrique; **the government was accused of running down the steel industry** le gouvernement a été accusé de laisser dépérir la sidérurgie. -**2.** *inf* [criticize, denigrate] rabaisser; **they're always running her friends down** ils passent leur temps à dire du mal de OR à dénigrer ses amis; **stop running yourself down all the time** cesse de te rabaisser constamment. -**3.** AUT [pedestrian, animal] renverser, écraser; **he was ~ down by a bus** il s'est fait renverser par un bus. -**4.** [track down - animal, criminal] (traquer et) capturer; [- object] dénicher; **I finally ran down the reference in the library** j'ai fini par dénicher la référence à la bibliothèque.

◆ **run in** ◇ *vi insep* -**1.** *literal* entrer en courant. -**2.** *Br* [car, engine]: **'running in'** 'en rodage'.
◇ *vt sep* -**1.** *Br* [car, engine] roder. -**2.** *inf* [arrest] pincer.

◆ **run into** *vt insep* -**1.** [encounter - problem, difficulty] rencontrer. -**2.** [meet - acquaintance] rencontrer (par hasard), tomber sur. -**3.** [collide with - subj: car, driver] percuter, rentrer dans; **I ran into a lamppost** je suis rentrée dans un réverbère. -**4.** [amount to] s'élever à; **debts running into millions of dollars** des dettes qui s'élèvent à des millions de dollars. -**5.** [merge into] se fondre dans, se confondre avec; **the red ~s into orange** le rouge devient orange; **the words began to ~ into each other before my eyes** les mots commençaient à se confondre devant mes yeux.

◆ **run off** ◇ *vi insep* -**1.** = **run away**. -**2.** [liquid] s'écouler.
◇ *vt sep* -**1.** [print] tirer, imprimer; [photocopy] photocopier; ~ **me off five copies of this report** faites-moi cinq copies de ce rapport. -**2.** SPORT [race] disputer; **the heats will be ~ off tomorrow** les éliminatoires se disputeront demain. -**3.** [lose - excess weight, fat] perdre en courant. -**4.** [liquid] laisser s'écouler.

◆ **run on** ◇ *vi insep* -**1.** [continue] continuer, durer; [drag on] s'éterniser; **the play ran on for hours** la pièce a duré des heures; **the discussion ran on for an extra hour** la discussion a duré une heure de plus que prévu. -**2.** *inf* [talk nonstop] parler sans cesse; **he does ~ on rather** il ne cesse pas de parler. -**3.** [line of text] suivre sans alinéa; [verse] enjamber.
◇ *vt sep* [lines of writing] ne pas découper en paragraphes; [letters, words] ne pas séparer, lier.

◆ **run out** ◇ *vi insep* -**1.** *literal* [person, animal] sortir en courant; [liquid] s'écouler. -**2.** [be used up - supplies, money, ammunition] s'épuiser, (venir à) manquer; [- time] filer; **hurry up, time is running out!** dépêchez-vous, il ne reste plus beaucoup de temps!; **their luck finally ran out** la chance a fini par tourner, leur chance n'a pas duré. -**3.** [expire - contract, passport, agreement] expirer, venir à expiration.
◇ *vt sep* -**1.** [cable, rope] laisser filer. -**2.** [in cricket]: to ~ **a batsman out** mettre un batteur hors jeu.

◆ **run out of** *vt insep* manquer de; **we're running out of ammunition** nous commençons à manquer de munitions; to ~ **out of patience** être à bout de patience; **he's ~ out of money** il n'a plus d'argent; to ~ **out of petrol** tomber en panne d'essence.

◆ **run out on** *vt insep* [spouse, colleague] laisser tomber, abandonner; **she ran out on her husband** elle a quitté son mari; **his assistants all ran out on him** ses assistants l'ont tous abandonné OR laissé tomber.

◆ **run over** ◇ *vt sep* [pedestrian, animal] écraser, renverser; **I nearly got ~ over** j'ai failli me faire écraser OR renverser.
◇ *vt insep* [review] revoir; [rehearse] répéter; [recap] récapituler; **let's ~ over the arguments one more time before the meeting** reprenons les arguments une dernière fois avant la réunion; **could you ~ over the main points for us?** pourriez-vous nous récapituler les principaux points?
◇ *vi insep* -**1.** [overflow] déborder; **my cup runneth over** *lit* je nage dans le bonheur. -**2.** [run late] dépasser l'heure; RADIO & TV dépasser le temps d'antenne; **the programme ran over by 20 minutes** l'émission a dépassé son temps d'antenne de 20 minutes.

◆ **run past** ◇ *vi insep* *literal* passer en courant.
◇ *vt sep* = **run by**.

◆ **run through** ◇ *vt insep* -**1.** *literal* traverser en courant. -**2.** [pervade - thought, feeling]: **a strange idea ran through my mind** une idée étrange m'a traversé l'esprit; **a thrill of excitement ran through her** un frisson d'émotion la parcourut; **an angry murmur ran through the crowd** des murmures de colère parcoururent la foule; **his words kept running through my head** ses paroles ne cessaient de retentir dans ma tête; **an air of melancholy ~s through the whole film** une atmosphère de mélancolie imprègne tout le film. -**3.** [review] revoir; [rehearse] répéter; [recap] récapituler; **she ran through the arguments in her mind** elle repassa les arguments dans sa tête. -**4.** [read quickly] parcourir (des yeux), jeter un coup d'œil sur. -**5.** [squander - fortune] gaspiller.
◇ *vt sep*: to ~ **sb through (with a sword)** transpercer qqn (d'un coup d'épée).

◆ **run to** *vt insep* -**1.** [amount to] se chiffrer à; **her essay ran to 20 pages** sa dissertation faisait 20 pages. -**2.** [afford, be enough for]: **your salary should ~ to a new computer** ton salaire devrait te permettre d'acheter un nouvel ordinateur; **the budget won't ~ to champagne** le budget ne nous permet pas d'acheter du champagne. -**3.** [become]: to ~ **to fat** devenir gros.

◆ **run up** ◇ *vi insep* [climb rapidly] monter en courant; [approach] approcher en courant; **a young man ran up to me** un jeune homme s'approcha de moi en courant.
◇ *vt sep* -**1.** [debt, bill] laisser s'accumuler; **I've ~ up a huge overdraft** j'ai un découvert énorme. -**2.** [flag] hisser. -**3.** [sew quickly] coudre (rapidement OR à la hâte).

◆ **run up against** *vt insep* [encounter] se heurter à; **we've ~ up against some problems** nous nous sommes heurtés à quelques problèmes.

runabout *inf* ['rʌnəbaʊt] *n* [car] petite voiture *f*, voiture *f* de ville; [boat] runabout *m*; [plane] petit avion *m*.

runaround *inf* ['rʌnəraʊnd] *n*: **to give sb the ~** raconter des salades à qqn; [husband, wife] tromper qqn.

runaway ['rʌnəweɪ] ◇ *n* [gen] fugitif *m*, -ive *f*; [child - from home, school etc] fugueur *m*, -euse *f*.
◇ *adj* -**1.** [convict] fugitif; [child] fugueur; [horse] emballé; [train, car] fou; a ~ **marriage** un mariage clandestin. -**2.** [rampant, extreme - inflation] galopant; [- success] fou; **her book was this year's ~ bestseller** son livre a été le best-seller de l'année; a ~ **victory** une victoire remportée haut la main.

rundown ['rʌndaʊn] *n* -**1.** [reduction] réduction *f*, déclin *m*; **the ~ of the coal industry** le déclin de l'industrie houillère. -**2.** *inf* [report] compte rendu *m*; **to give sb a ~ of** OR **on sthg** mettre qqn au courant de qqch.

run-down *inf adj* -**1.** [tired] vanné, crevé; **I think you're just a bit ~** je pense que c'est juste un peu de surmenage; **I'm feeling very ~** je me sens complètement à plat. -**2.** [dilapidated] délabré.

rune [ruːn] *n* rune *f*.

rung [rʌŋ] ◇ *pp* → **ring** (*bell*).
◇ *n* [of ladder] barreau *m*, échelon *m*; [of chair] barreau *m*; *fig* [in hierarchy] échelon *m*; **he's on the top ~ of his profession** il a atteint l'échelon le plus élevé dans sa profession.

runic ['ruːnɪk] *adj* runique.

run-in *inf n* -**1.** *inf* [quarrel] engueulade *f*, prise de bec; **I had a bit of a ~ with the police last week** j'ai eu un petit accrochage avec la police la semaine dernière. -**2.** = **run-up 1,2**.

runnel ['rʌnl] *n lit* ruisselet *m*, ru *m lit*.

runner ['rʌnə^r] *n* -**1.** [in race - person] coureur *m*, -euse *f*; [- horse] partant *m*; **he's a good/fast ~** il court bien/vite. -**2.** [messenger] coursier *m*, -ère *f*. -**3.** (*usu in cpds*) [smuggler] contrebandier *m*, -ère *f*, trafiquant *m*, -e *f*; **drug ~** trafiquant *m* de drogue. -**4.** [slide - for door, drawer etc] glissière *f*; [- on sledge] patin *m*; [- on skate] lame *f*. -**5.** BOT coulant *m*, stolon *m*. -**6.** [stair carpet] tapis *m* d'escalier.

runner bean *n Br* haricot *m* d'Espagne.

runner-up (*pl* runners-up) *n* second *m*, -e *f*; **her novel was ~ for the Prix Goncourt** son roman était le second favori pour le prix Goncourt; **there will be 50 consolation prizes for the runners-up** il y aura 50 lots de consolation pour les autres gagnants.

running ['rʌnɪŋ] ◇ *n* -**1.** SPORT course *f* (à pied); ~ **is forbidden in the corridors** il est interdit de courir dans les couloirs ❑ **to make the ~** SPORT mener le train; *fig* prendre l'initiative; **to be in the ~ for sthg** être sur les rangs pour obtenir qqch; **to be out of the ~** ne plus être dans la course. -**2.** [management] gestion *f*, direction *f*; [organization] organisation *f*; **she leaves the day-to-day ~ of the department to her assistant** elle laisse son assistant s'occuper de la gestion quotidienne du service. -**3.** [working, functioning] marche *f*, fonctionnement *m*. -**4.** [operating] conduite *f*, maniement *m*. -**5.** [smuggling] contrebande *f*; **drug ~** trafic *m* de drogue.
◇ *adj* -**1.** [at a run - person, animal] courant, qui court; **to take a ~ kick at sthg** prendre son élan pour donner un coup de pied dans qqch ❑ ~ **jump** *literal* saut *m* avec élan; **(go) take a ~ jump!** *inf* va te faire voir (ailleurs)! -**2.** (*after n*) [consecutive] de suite; **three times/weeks/years ~** trois fois/semaines/années de suite. -**3.** [continuous] continu, ininterrompu; ~ **account** FIN compte *m* courant; ~ **battle** lutte continuelle; ~ **total** montant *m* à reporter. -**4.** [flowing]: **the sound of ~ water** le bruit de l'eau qui coule; **to wash sthg under ~ water** laver qqch à l'eau courante; **all the rooms have ~ water** toutes les chambres ont l'eau courante; a ~ **tap** un robinet qui coule; a ~ **sore** une plaie suppurante. -**5.** [working, operating]: **in ~ order** en état de marche ❑ ~ **costs** frais *mpl* d'exploitation; [of car] frais *mpl* d'entretien; ~

repairs réparations *fpl* courantes. -**6.** [cursive - handwriting] cursif.
◇ *comp* [shoe, shorts, track] de course (à pied).
running board *n* marchepied *m*.
running commentary *n* RADIO & TV commentaire *m* en direct; she gave us a ~ on what the neighbours were doing *fig* elle nous a expliqué en détail ce que les voisins étaient en train de faire.
running head *n* TYPO titre *m* courant.
running mate *n Am* POL *personne choisie par un candidat à la présidence des États-Unis pour être son vice-président s'il est élu*.
running stitch *n* SEW point *m* droit.
running title *n* TYPO titre *m* courant.
runny ['rʌnɪ] (*compar* runnier, *superl* runniest) *adj* -**1.** [sauce, honey] liquide; [liquid] (très) fluide; a ~ egg un œuf dont le jaune coule; a ~ omelette une omelette baveuse. -**2.** [nose] qui coule; [eye] qui pleure; I've got a ~ nose j'ai le nez qui coule.
run-off *n* -**1.** SPORT [final] finale *f*; [after tie] belle *f*. -**2.** [water] trop-plein *m*.
run-of-the-mill *adj* ordinaire, banal.
run-on *n* -**1.** [in printed matter] texte *m* composé à la suite *(sans alinéa)*. -**2.** [in dictionary] sous-entrée *f*.
runt [rʌnt] *n* -**1.** [animal] avorton *m*. -**2.** *inf* [person] avorton *m*.
run-through *n* [review] révision *f*; [rehearsal] répétition *f*; [recap] récapitulation *f*.
run-up *n* -**1.** SPORT élan *m*; she only takes a short ~ elle ne prend pas beaucoup d'élan. -**2.** [period before] période *f* préparatoire; the ~ to the elections la période qui précède les élections OR pré-électorale. -**3.** *Am* [increase] augmentation *f*, hausse *f*.
runway ['rʌnweɪ] *n* AERON piste *f* (d'atterrissage OR d'envol); ~ lights feux *mpl* de piste.
rupee [ruː'piː] *n* roupie *f*.
rupture ['rʌptʃəʳ] ◇ *n* -**1.** [split] rupture *f*. -**2.** [hernia] hernie *f*.
◇ *vt* -**1.** [split] rompre. -**2.** MED: to ~ o.s. se faire une hernie.
rural ['rʊərəl] *adj* [life, country, scenery] rural.
rural dean *n Br* doyen *m*.
rural district *n Br* ≃ canton *m*.
Ruritania [ˌrʊərɪ'teɪnjə] *pr n nom d'un petit pays imaginaire d'Europe centrale, théâtre par excellence d'intrigues et d'aventures romanesques*.
ruse [ruːz] *n* ruse *f*; it's just a ~ to get us to agree ce n'est qu'une ruse pour obtenir notre accord.
rush [rʌʃ] ◇ *vi* -**1.** [hurry, dash - individual] se précipiter; [- crowd] se ruer, se précipiter; [- vehicle] foncer; I ~ed home after work je me suis précipité chez moi après le travail; people ~ed out of the blazing house les gens se ruèrent hors de la maison en flammes; there's no need to ~ pas besoin de se presser; passers-by ~ed to help the injured man des passants se sont précipités au secours du blessé; the dog ~ed at me le chien s'est précipité OR jeté sur moi; a group of demonstrators ~ed at the speaker un groupe de manifestants se rua sur l'orateur; he ~ed in/out/past il est entré précipitamment/sorti précipitamment/passé à toute allure. -**2.** [act overhastily]: to ~ into a decision prendre une décision à la hâte; now don't ~ into anything ne va pas foncer tête baissée. -**3.** [surge - air] s'engouffrer; [- liquid] jaillir; the cold water ~ed over her bare feet l'eau froide déferla sur ses pieds nus; I could hear the wind ~ing through the trees j'entendais le vent s'engouffrer dans les branches; the blood ~ed to her head le sang lui est monté à la tête; I felt the blood ~ to my face j'ai senti le sang me monter au visage.
◇ *vt* -**1.** [do quickly] expédier; [do overhastily] faire à la hâte OR à la va-vite; I don't like having to ~ my work je n'aime pas devoir expédier mon travail; I'll ~ it off on the computer l'ordinateur me fera ça en deux minutes; don't ~ your food ne mange pas trop vite. -**2.** [cause to hurry] bousculer, presser; [pressurize] faire pression sur, forcer la main à; don't ~ me! ne me bouscule pas!; she was too ~ed to stay and talk elle était trop pressée pour rester bavarder; to ~ sb into sthg OR doing sthg forcer qqn à faire qqch à la hâte; don't be ~ed into signing ne signez pas sous la pression □ to be ~ed off one's feet être complètement débordé. -**3.** [attack - person] attaquer, agresser; [- place] attaquer, prendre d'assaut; a group of prisoners ~ed the guards un groupe de prisonniers s'attaqua aux gardiens. -**4.** [transport quickly] transporter d'urgence; [send quickly] envoyer OR expédier d'urgence; the injured were ~ed to hospital les blessés ont été transportés d'urgence à l'hôpital; they ~ed a first aid team to the site ils ont envoyé en toute hâte une équipe de premiers secours sur les lieux; please ~ me your new catalogue veuillez me faire parvenir au plus vite votre nouveau catalogue. -**5.** *inf Am* [court] courtiser.
◇ *n* -**1.** [hurry] précipitation *f*, hâte *f*; to do sthg in a ~ faire qqch à la hâte; to be in a ~ être (très) pressé; what's the ~? pourquoi tant de précipitation?; there's no (great) ~ rien ne presse; it'll be a bit of a ~, but we should make it il faudra se dépêcher mais on devrait y arriver; your essay was written in too much of a ~ vous avez fait votre dissertation à la va-vite. -**2.** [stampede] ruée *f*, bousculade *f*; there was a ~ for the door tout le monde s'est rué vers la porte; I lost a shoe in the ~ j'ai perdu une chaussure dans la bousculade ‖ [great demand] ruée; they're expecting a ~ to get tickets, they're expecting a ~ on OR for tickets ils s'attendent à ce que les gens se ruent sur les billets; there's a ~ on that particular model ce modèle est très demandé. -**3.** [busy period] heure *f* de pointe OR d'affluence; the six o'clock ~ la foule de six heures ‖ [in shops, post office etc]: I try to avoid the lunchtime ~ j'essaie d'éviter la foule de l'heure du déjeuner; the holiday ~ [leaving] les grands départs en vacances; [returning] les embouteillages des retours de vacances. -**4.** [attack] attaque *f*, assaut *m*; to make a ~ at OR for sb se jeter sur qqn. -**5.** [surge - of water] jaillissement *m*; [- of air] bouffée *f*; [- of emotion, nausea] accès *m*, montée *f*; I could hear nothing above the ~ of water le bruit de l'eau (qui bouillonnait) m'empêchait d'entendre quoi que ce soit; she had a ~ of blood to the head le sang lui est monté à la tête. -**6.** BOT jonc *m*; [for seats] paille *f*; ~ mat natte *f* (de jonc); the floor is covered with ~ matting des nattes (de jonc) recouvrent le sol. -**7.** *drugs sl* [from drugs] flash *m*.
◇ *adj* -**1.** [urgent] urgent; it's a ~ job for Japan c'est un travail urgent pour le Japon; ~ order commande *f* urgente. -**2.** [hurried] fait à la hâte OR à la va-vite; I'm afraid it's a bit of a ~ job je suis désolé, le travail a été fait un peu vite OR a été un peu bâclé. -**3.** [busy - period] de pointe, d'affluence.
◆ **rushes** *npl* CIN rushes *mpl*, épreuves *fpl* de tournage.
◆ **rush about** *Br*, **rush around** *vi insep* courir çà et là; stop ~ing about! arrête de courir dans tous les sens!
◆ **rush in** *vi insep* -**1.** *literal* entrer précipitamment OR à toute allure. -**2.** [decide overhastily]: you always ~ in without thinking first tu fonces toujours tête baissée sans réfléchir.
◆ **rush out** ◇ *vi insep* sortir précipitamment OR à toute allure.
◇ *vt sep* [book, new product] sortir rapidement.
◆ **rush through** *vt sep* [job] expédier; [goods ordered] envoyer d'urgence; [order, application] traiter d'urgence; [bill, legislation] faire voter à la hâte.
◆ **rush up** ◇ *vi insep* accourir.
◇ *vt sep* envoyer d'urgence; troops were ~ed up as reinforcements on envoya d'urgence des troupes en renfort.
rush candle = **rush light**.
rush hour *n* heure *f* de pointe OR d'affluence; I never travel at ~ je ne me déplace jamais aux heures de pointe.
◆ **rush-hour** *comp* [crowds, traffic] des heures de pointe OR d'affluence.
rush light *n* chandelle *f* à mèche de jonc.
rusk [rʌsk] *n* biscotte *f*.
russet ['rʌsɪt] ◇ *n* -**1.** [colour] brun roux *m inv*. -**2.** [apple] reinette *f*.
◇ *adj* [colour] brun roux *(inv)*.
Russia ['rʌʃə] *pr n* Russie *f*; in ~ en Russie.
Russian ['rʌʃn] ◇ *n* -**1.** [person] Russe *mf*. -**2.** LING russe *m*.
◇ *adj* russe.
Russian dressing *n* sauce *f* (de salade) relevée au piment.
Russian roulette *n* roulette *f* russe.
Russian salad *n* salade *f* russe.
Russian wolfhound *n* lévrier *m* russe.
russification [ˌrʌsɪfɪ'keɪʃn] *n* russification *f*.
Russky *inf* ['rʌskɪ] (*pl* **Russkies**) *n* Ruskof *m*, Ruski *mf*.
Russo- ['rʌsəʊ] *in cpds* russo-.
rust [rʌst] ◇ *n* -**1.** [on metal & BOT] rouille *f*. -**2.** [colour] couleur *f* rouille.
◇ *adj* rouille *(inv)*.
◇ *vi* rouiller, se rouiller; it's completely ~ed through il est complètement mangé par la rouille; the car was left to ~ away la voiture fut abandonnée à la rouille.
◇ *vt* rouiller.
◆ **rust up** *vi insep* rouiller, se rouiller; the hinges have ~ed up les gonds sont bloqués par la rouille.
rusted ['rʌstɪd] *adj esp Am* rouillé.
rustic ['rʌstɪk] ◇ *adj* rustique.
◇ *n* paysan *m*, -anne *f*, campagnard *m*, -e *f*.
rusticate ['rʌstɪkeɪt] *fml* ◇ *vt Br* UNIV [student] renvoyer OR expulser temporairement.
◇ *vi* [retire to country] se retirer à la campagne; [live in country] vivre à la campagne.
rustiness ['rʌstɪnɪs] *n* rouille *f*.
rustle ['rʌsl] ◇ *vi* -**1.** [make sound - gen] produire un froissement OR bruissement; [- leaves] bruire; [- dress, silk] froufrouter; something was rustling against the window quelque chose frottait contre la fenêtre; the leaves ~d in the wind les feuilles bruissaient dans le vent. -**2.** [steal cattle] voler du bétail.
◇ *vt* -**1.** [leaves] faire bruire; [papers] froisser; [dress, silk] faire froufrouter. -**2.** [cattle] voler.
◇ *n* [sound - gen] froissement *m*, bruissement *m*; [- of dress, silk] froufrou *m*, froufroutement *m*.
◆ **rustle up** *inf vt sep* [meal] faire en vitesse; I could ~ up an omelette for you je pourrais te faire une omelette en vitesse.
rustler ['rʌsləʳ] *n* -**1.** [of cattle] voleur *m*, -euse *f* de bétail; horse ~ voleur de chevaux. -**2.** *inf Am* [dynamic person] homme *m* dynamique, femme *f* dynamique.
rustling ['rʌslɪŋ] *n* -**1.** [sound - gen] froissement *m*, bruissement *m*; [- of leaves] bruissement *m*; [- of dress, silk] froufrou *m*, froufroutement *m*. -**2.** [of cattle] vol *m* de bétail; horse ~ vol *m* de chevaux.
rustproof ['rʌstpruːf] ◇ *adj* [metal, blade] inoxydable; [paint] antirouille *(inv)*.
◇ *vt* traiter contre la rouille.
rustproofing ['rʌstpruːfɪŋ] *n* traitement *m* antirouille.
rust-resistant = **rustproof** *adj*.
rusty ['rʌstɪ] (*compar* rustier, *superl* rustiest) *adj literal & fig* rouillé; a ~ old car une vieille voiture rouillée; my German is a bit ~ mon allemand est un peu rouillé; a ~ brown dress une robe brun rouille.
rut [rʌt] (*pt & pp* rutted, *cont* rutting) ◇ *n* -**1.** [in ground] ornière *f*. -**2.** *fig* routine *f*; to be (stuck) in a ~ s'encroûter; to get out of the ~ sortir de l'ornière. -**3.** ZOOL rut *m*; in ~ en rut.
◇ *vt* [ground] sillonner; the track had been deeply rutted by tractors des tracteurs avaient creusé de profondes ornières dans le chemin.
◇ *vi* ZOOL être en rut.
rutabaga [ˌruːtə'beɪgə] *n Am* rutabaga *m*, chou-navet *m*.

Ruth [ruːθ] *pr n* Ruth.

Ruthenia [ruːˈθiːnjə] *pr n* Ruthénie *f*; in ~ en Ruthénie.

Ruthenian [ruːˈθiːnjən] ◇ *n* Ruthénien *m*, -enne *f*.
◇ *adj* ruthénien.

ruthenium [ruːˈθiːnɪəm] *n* ruthénium *m*.

rutherford [ˈrʌðəfəd] *n* rutherford *m*.

rutherfordium [ˌrʌðəˈfɔːdɪəm] *n* rutherfordium *m*.

ruthless [ˈruːθlɪs] *adj* [person, behaviour - unpitying] impitoyable, cruel; [- determined] résolu, acharné; [criticism] impitoyable, implacable.

ruthlessly [ˈruːθlɪslɪ] *adv* [pitilessly] impitoyablement, sans pitié; [relentlessly] implacablement.

ruthlessness [ˈruːθlɪsnɪs] *n* [of person, behaviour - pitilessness] caractère *m* impitoyable, dureté *f*; [- determination] acharnement *m*; [of criticism] dureté *f*.

rutted [ˈrʌtɪd] *adj* sillonné; a badly ~ road une route complètement défoncée.

ruttish [ˈrʌtɪʃ] *adj* -**1.** [animal] en rut. -**2.** *pej* [person] libidineux, salace.

RV *n* -**1.** *abbr of* revised version. -**2.** *Am* (*abbr of* recreational vehicle) camping-car *m*.

Rwanda [rʊˈændə] ◇ *pr n* GEOG Ruanda *m*, Rwanda *m*; in ~ au Ruanda.
◇ *n* LING ruanda *m*.

Rwandan [rʊˈændən] ◇ *n* Ruandais *m*, -e *f*.
◇ *adj* ruandais.

rye [raɪ] *n* -**1.** [cereal] seigle *m*; 'The Catcher in the Rye' *Salinger* 'l'Attrape-cœur'. -**2.** [drink] = **rye whiskey**.

rye bread *n* pain *m* de seigle.

ryegrass [ˈraɪgrɑːs] *n* ray-grass *m inv*.

rye whiskey *n* whisky *m* (de seigle).

S

s (*pl* **s's** OR **ss**), **S** (*pl* **S's** OR **Ss**) [es] *n* [letter] s *m*, S *m*.
S (*written abbr of* south) S.
SA ◇ -**1.** *written abbr of* South Africa. -**2.** *written abbr of* South America.
◇ *pr n abbr of* Salvation Army.
Saar [sɑːʳ] *pr n*: the ~ la Sarre.
Saarbrücken [,sɑːˈbrʊkən] *pr n* Sarrebruck.
Saarland [ˈsɑːlænd] *pr n* Sarre *f*; in ~ dans la Sarre.
Sabbath [ˈsæbəθ] *n* RELIG [Christian] dimanche *m*, jour *m* du Seigneur; [Jewish] sabbat *m*; to observe/to break the ~ [Christian] observer/violer le repos du dimanche; [Jew] observer/violer le sabbat.
◆ **sabbath** *n*: (witches') sabbath sabbat *m (de sorcières)*.
sabbatical [səˈbætɪkl] ◇ *adj* [gen & RELIG] sabbatique; to take a ~ year prendre une année sabbatique.
◇ *n* congé *m* sabbatique.
saber *Am* = **sabre**.
sable [ˈseɪbl] ◇ *n* [animal, fur] zibeline *f*.
◇ *adj* [colour] noir; HERALD sable *(inv)*.
◇ *comp* [coat] de OR en zibeline; [paintbrush] en poil de martre.
sable antelope *n* hippotrague *m* noir.
sabot [ˈsæbəʊ] *n* -**1.** [shoe] sabot *m*. -**2.** MIL sabot *m*.
sabotage [ˈsæbətɑːʒ] ◇ *n* sabotage *m*.
◇ *vt* saboter.
saboteur [,sæbəˈtɜːʳ] *n* saboteur *m*, -euse *f*.
sabra *inf* [ˈsæbrə] *n Am* sabra *mf*.
sabre *Br*, **saber** *Am* [ˈseɪbəʳ] *n* sabre *m*.
sabre-rattling ◇ *n* *(U)* bruits *mpl* de sabre.
◇ *adj* belliqueux.
sabre-toothed tiger *n* machairodonte *m*.
sac [sæk] *n* ANAT & BOT sac *m*.
saccharide [ˈsækəraɪd] *n* saccharide *m*, glucide *m*.
saccharin [ˈsækərɪn] *n* saccharine *f*.
saccharine [ˈsækərɪn] ◇ *adj* -**1.** CHEM saccharin. -**2.** *fig* & *pej* [exaggeratedly sweet - smile] mielleux; [- politeness] onctueux; [- sentimentality] écœurant, sirupeux.
◇ *n* = **saccharin**.
saccharose [ˈsækərəʊz] *n* saccharose *m*.
sacerdotal [,sæsəˈdəʊtl] *adj* sacerdotal.
sachet [ˈsæʃeɪ] *n* sachet *m*.
sack [sæk] ◇ *n* -**1.** [bag] (grand) sac *m*; two ~s of potatoes deux sacs de pommes de terre; grocery ~ *Am* sac *m* à provisions. -**2.** *inf Br* [dismissal] licenciement *m*; to give sb the ~ virer qqn; to get the ~ se faire virer; you'll get me the ~ tu vas me faire perdre mon boulot. -**3.** [pillage] sac *m*, pillage *m*. -**4.** *inf* [bed] pieu *m*, plumard *m*; to hit the ~ se pieuter. -**5.** *arch* [wine] vin *m* blanc sec.
◇ *vt* -**1.** *inf* [dismiss] mettre à la porte, virer. -**2.** [pillage] mettre à sac, piller.
◆ **sack out** *inf vi insep Am* s'endormir.
sackbut [ˈsækbʌt] *n* saqueboute *f*.
sackcloth [ˈsækklɒθ] *n* toile *f* à sac OR d'emballage; to wear ~ and ashes RELIG faire pénitence avec le sac et la cendre; to be in ~ and ashes *fig* être contrit.
sackful [ˈsækfʊl] *n* sac *m*; (whole) ~s of flour des sacs entiers de farine; we've been getting letters by the ~ nous avons reçu des sacs entiers de lettres.
sacking [ˈsækɪŋ] *n* -**1.** TEX toile *f* à sac OR d'emballage. -**2.** *inf* [dismissal] licenciement *m*. -**3.** [pillaging] sac *m*, pillage *m*.
sackload [ˈsækləʊd] = **sackful**.
sack race *n* course *f* en sac.
sacrament [ˈsækrəmənt] *n* sacrement *m*.
◆ **Sacrament** *n*: the Blessed OR holy Sacrament le saint sacrement.
sacramental [,sækrəˈmentl] ◇ *adj* [rite] sacramentel; [theology] sacramentaire.
◇ *n* sacramental *m*.
sacred [ˈseɪkrɪd] *adj* -**1.** [holy] sacré, saint; a ~ place un lieu saint; ~ to their gods consacré à leurs dieux; ~ to his memory voué OR dédié à sa mémoire; ~ music musique *f* sacrée OR religieuse. -**2.** [solemn, important - task, duty] sacré, solennel; [- promise, right] inviolable, sacré; [revered, respected] sacré; nothing was ~ in his eyes il n'y avait rien de sacré pour lui; is nothing ~ any more? on ne respecte donc plus rien aujourd'hui?
sacred cow *n fig* vache *f* sacrée.
Sacred Heart *n* RELIG Sacré-Cœur *m*.
sacredness [ˈseɪkrɪdnɪs] *n* -**1.** [holiness] caractère *m* sacré. -**2.** [solemness, importance] inviolabilité *f*.
sacrifice [ˈsækrɪfaɪs] ◇ *n* RELIG & *fig* sacrifice *m*; to offer sthg (up) as a ~ to the gods offrir qqch en sacrifice aux dieux; I've made a lot of ~s for you j'ai fait beaucoup de sacrifices pour vous.
◇ *vt* RELIG & *fig* sacrifier; to ~ sthg to God sacrifier qqch à Dieu; she ~d herself for her children elle s'est sacrifiée pour ses enfants.
sacrificial [,sækrɪˈfɪʃl] *adj* [rite, dagger] sacrificiel; [lamb, victim] du sacrifice.
sacrilege [ˈsækrɪlɪdʒ] *n literal* & *fig* sacrilège *m*; to commit ~ commettre un sacrilège.
sacrilegious [,sækrɪˈlɪdʒəs] *adj literal* & *fig* sacrilège.
sacristan [ˈsækrɪstn] *n* sacristain *m*.
sacristy [ˈsækrɪstɪ] (*pl* **sacristies**) *n* sacristie *f*.
sacrosanct [ˈsækrəʊsæŋkt] *adj literal* & *fig* sacro-saint.
sacrum [ˈseɪkrəm] (*pl* **sacra** [-krə]) *n* sacrum *m*.
sad [sæd] (*compar* **sadder**, *superl* **saddest**) *adj* -**1.** [unhappy, melancholy] triste; [stronger] affligé; it makes me ~ to see what's become of them ça me rend triste OR m'attriste de voir ce qu'ils sont devenus; I shall be ~ to see you leave je serai désolé de vous voir partir; to be ~ at heart avoir le cœur gros; the flowers look OR are a bit ~ les fleurs ont triste mine. -**2.** [depressing - news, day, story] triste; [- sight, occasion] triste, attristant; [- painting, music, landscape] lugubre, triste; [- loss] cruel, douloureux; but ~ to say it didn't last long mais, malheureusement, cela n'a pas duré; she came to a ~ end elle a eu une triste fin; the ~ fact is that he's incompetent c'est malheureux à dire, mais c'est un incapable. -**3.** [regrettable, unsatisfactory] triste, regrettable; it's a ~ state of affairs when this sort of thing can go unpunished il est vraiment regrettable que de tels actes restent impunis; it's a ~ reflection on modern society ça n'est pas flatteur pour la société moderne.
SAD *n abbr of* seasonal affective disorder.
sadden [ˈsædn] *vt* rendre triste, attrister; [stronger] affliger.
saddle [ˈsædl] ◇ *n* -**1.** [on horse, bicycle] selle *f*; to be in the ~ *literal* & *fig* être en selle; you'll soon be back in the ~ again vous allez bientôt pouvoir vous remettre en selle. -**2.** CULIN [of lamb, mutton] selle *f*; [of hare] râble *m*. -**3.** GEOG col *m*.
◇ *vt* -**1.** [horse] seller. -**2.** *inf* [lumber]: to ~ sb with sthg refiler qqch à qqn; I always get ~d with doing the nasty jobs c'est toujours moi qui fais le sale boulot; she was ~d with the children elle s'est retrouvée avec les enfants sur les bras; I don't want to ~ myself with any more work je ne veux pas me taper du travail supplémentaire.
◆ **saddle up** *vi insep* seller sa monture.
saddlebacked [ˈsædlbækt] *adj* [horse] ensellé.
saddlebag [ˈsædlbæg] *n* [for bicycle, motorcycle] sacoche *f*; [for horse] sacoche *f* de selle.
saddlebill [ˈsædlbɪl] *n* jabiru *m*.
saddlebow [ˈsædlbəʊ] *n* [pommel] pommeau *m* (de selle); [front] arçon *m*.
saddlecloth [ˈsædlklɒθ] *n* tapis *m* de selle.
saddle horse *n* cheval *m* de selle.
saddler [ˈsædləʳ] *n* sellier *m*.
saddlery [ˈsædlərɪ] (*pl* **saddleries**) *n* [trade, shop, goods] sellerie *f*.
saddle soap *n* cirage *m* pour selles.
saddle sore *n* [on rider] *meurtrissures provoquées par de longues heures en selle*; [on horse] écorchure *f* OR excoriation *f* sous la selle.
◆ **saddle-sore** *adj*: he was saddle-sore il avait les fesses meurtries par de longues heures à cheval.
Sadducee [ˈsædjʊsiː] *n* Saducéen *m*, -enne *f*, Sadducéen *m*, -enne *f*.

sadism ['seɪdɪzm] *n* sadisme *m.*
sadist ['seɪdɪst] *n* sadique *mf.*
sadistic [sə'dɪstɪk] *adj* sadique.
sadly ['sædlɪ] *adv* -**1.** [unhappily] tristement; **she looked at me ~** elle m'a regardé tristement OR d'un air triste. -**2.** [unfortunately] malheureusement; **~, I won't be able to come** malheureusement, je ne pourrai pas venir. -**3.** [regrettably] déplorablement; **you are ~ mistaken** vous vous trompez du tout au tout; **the house had been ~ neglected** la maison était dans un état déplorable.
sadness ['sædnɪs] *n* tristesse *f.*
sadomasochism [,seɪdəʊ'mæsəkɪzm] *n* sadomasochisme *m.*
sadomasochist [,seɪdəʊ'mæsəkɪst] *n* sadomasochiste *mf.*
sadomasochistic ['seɪdəʊ,mæsə'kɪstɪk] *adj* sadomasochiste.
Saducee ['sædjʊsiː] = **Sadhucee**.
s.a.e., sae *n Br abbr of* **stamped addressed envelope**.
safari [sə'fɑːrɪ] *n* safari *m*; **they've gone on** OR **they're on ~** ils font un safari.
safari jacket *n* saharienne *f.*
safari park *n* safari park *m.*
safari suit *n* saharienne *f.*
safe [seɪf] ◇ *adj* -**1.** [harmless, not dangerous - car, machine] sûr; [- structure, building, fastening] solide; [- beach] pas dangereux; **the staircase doesn't look very ~** l'escalier n'a pas l'air très sûr; **they claim nuclear power is perfectly ~** ils prétendent que l'énergie nucléaire n'est pas du tout dangereuse; **this part of town is/isn't ~ at night** ce quartier est/n'est pas sûr la nuit; **this medicine is/isn't ~ for young children** ce médicament convient/ne convient pas aux enfants en bas âge; **is it ~ to come out now?** est-ce qu'on peut sortir (sans danger OR sans crainte) maintenant?; **is it ~ to swim here?** est-ce qu'on peut OR est-ce dangereux de nager ici?; **it isn't ~ to play in the street** il est dangereux de jouer dans la rue; **the bomb has been made ~** la bombe a été désamorcée; **the police kept the crowd at a ~ distance** les policiers ont empêché la foule d'approcher de trop près ❑ **the ~ period** *inf* MED *période du cycle pendant laquelle la femme est censée ne pas être féconde*; **~ sex** le sexe sans risque; **safer sex** le sexe à moindre risque. -**2.** [not risky, certain - course of action] sans risque OR risques, sans danger; [- investment] sûr; [- guess] certain; [- estimate] raisonnable; **to play ~** ne pas prendre de risques; **I played it ~ and arrived an hour early** pour ne pas prendre de risques, je suis arrivé une heure en avance; **you're always ~ ordering a steak** on ne prend jamais de risques en commandant un steak; **a ~ winner** un gagnant certain; **it's a ~ bet that he'll be late** on peut être sûr qu'il arrivera en retard; **the safest option** l'option la moins risquée; **I think it's ~ to say that everybody enjoyed themselves** je pense que l'on peut dire avec certitude que ça a plu à tout le monde; **it is a ~ assumption that...** on peut présumer sans risque que...; **take an umbrella (just) to be on the ~ side** prends un parapluie, c'est plus sûr OR au cas où ❑ **~ seat** *Br* POL *siège de député qui traditionnellement va toujours au même parti*; **it's as ~ as houses** cela ne présente pas le moindre risque; **better ~ than sorry** *prov* deux précautions valent mieux qu'une *prov.* -**3.** [secure - place] sûr; **keep it in a ~ place** gardez-le en lieu sûr; **is there anywhere ~ to leave my handbag?** y a-t-il un lieu sûr où je puisse laisser mon sac à main?; **in ~ hands** en mains sûres; **in ~ custody** [child] sous bonne garde; [securities, assets etc] en dépôt ❑ **~ haven zone** *f* protégée; **~ house** [for spies, wanted man] lieu *m* sûr. -**4.** [reliable]: **is he ~ with the money/the children?** est-ce qu'on peut lui confier l'argent/les enfants (sans crainte)?; **she's a very ~ driver** c'est une conductrice très sûre, elle ne prend pas de risques au volant. -**5.** [protected, out of danger] en sécurité, hors de danger; **I don't feel ~ alone at night** je ne me sens pas en sécurité tout seul la nuit; **the money's ~ in the bank** l'argent est en sécurité à la banque; **keep ~!** *Am* prends bien soin de toi!; **the secret will be ~ with her** elle ne risque pas d'ébruiter le secret; **~ from attack** à l'abri d'une attaque; **nobody is ~ from suspicion** personne n'est à l'abri des soupçons; **no woman is ~ with him** c'est un coureur invétéré; **you don't look very ~ standing on that chair** tu as l'air d'être en équilibre instable debout sur cette chaise; **(have a) ~ journey!** bon voyage! -**6.** [unharmed, undamaged] sain et sauf; **we shall pay upon ~ delivery of the goods** nous payerons après réception des marchandises; **he arrived ~ (and sound)** il est arrivé sain et sauf.
◇ *n* -**1.** [for money, valuables etc] coffre-fort *m.* -**2.** [for food] garde-manger *m inv.*
safeblower ['seɪf,bləʊəʳ] *n* perceur *m*, -euse *f* de coffres-forts *(qui emploie des explosifs).*
safebreaker ['seɪf,breɪkəʳ] *n* perceur *m*, -euse *f* de coffres-forts.
safe-conduct [-'kɒndʌkt] *n* sauf-conduit *m.*
safecracker ['seɪf,krækəʳ] *Am* = **safebreaker**.
safe-deposit box *n* coffre *m (dans une banque).*
safeguard ['seɪfgɑːd] ◇ *vt* sauvegarder; **to ~ sb/sthg against sthg** protéger qqn/qqch contre qqch.
◇ *n* sauvegarde *f*; **as a ~ against theft** comme précaution contre le vol.
safekeeping [,seɪf'kiːpɪŋ] *n* (bonne) garde *f*; **she was given the documents for ~** on lui a confié les documents; **the money is in your ~** je vous confie l'argent.
safelight ['seɪflaɪt] *n* PHOT lampe *f* inactinique.
safely ['seɪflɪ] *adv* -**1.** [without taking risks] sûrement; **drive ~!** soyez prudent sur la route!; **an area where women can ~ go out at night** un quartier où les femmes peuvent sortir la nuit en toute tranquillité; **you can ~ invest with them** vous pouvez investir chez eux en toute tranquillité. -**2.** [confidently, certainly] avec confiance OR certitude; **we can ~ predict that...** nous pouvons prédire avec certitude que... -**3.** [securely] en sécurité, à l'abri; **I've put the money away ~** j'ai mis l'argent en sécurité; **all the doors and windows are ~ locked** toutes les portes et les fenêtres sont bien fermées. -**4.** [without incident] sans incident; **I'm just phoning to say I've arrived ~** je téléphone juste pour dire que je suis bien arrivé; **the bill was seen ~ through Parliament** le projet de loi fut voté sans problème par le Parlement.
safety ['seɪftɪ] ◇ *n* [absence of danger] sécurité *f*; **the injured were helped to ~** on a aidé les blessés à se mettre à l'abri; **there are fears for the ~ of the hostages** on craint pour la vie des otages; **we are concerned about the ~ of imported toys** nous craignons que les jouets importés présentent certains dangers; **he ran for ~** il a couru se mettre à l'abri; **he reached ~** il arriva en lieu sûr; **in a place of ~** en lieu sûr; **there's ~ in numbers** plus on est nombreux, plus on est en sécurité; **~ first!** ne prenez pas de risques! ❑ **road ~** sécurité *f* routière.
◇ *comp* [device, feature, measures etc] de sécurité; **~ regulations** consignes *fpl* de sécurité.
safety belt *n* ceinture *f* de sécurité.
safety catch *n* -**1.** [on gun] cran *m* de sécurité. -**2.** [on window, door] cran *m* de sûreté.
safety chain *n* [on door] chaîne *f* de sûreté; [on bracelet] chaînette *f* de sûreté.
safety curtain *n* THEAT rideau *m* de fer.
safety-deposit box = **safe-deposit box**.
safety film *n* film *m* de protection.
safety-first *adj* [campaign, measures] de sécurité; [investment, shares] de toute sécurité.
safety glass *n* verre *m* de sécurité.
safety helmet *n* casque *m* (de protection).
safety island *n Am* refuge *m (sur une route).*
safety lamp *n* lampe *f* de mineur.
safety match *n* allumette *f* de sûreté.
safety net *n literal* & *fig* filet *m*; **without a ~** sans filet.
safety officer *n* responsable *mf* de la sécurité
safety pin *n* -**1.** [fastener] épingle *f* de nourrice OR de sûreté. -**2.** [of grenade, bomb] goupille *f* de sûreté.
safety razor *n* rasoir *m* de sûreté.
safety valve *n literal* & *fig* soupape *f* de sûreté.
saffron ['sæfrən] ◇ *n* -**1.** BOT & CULIN safran *m* -**2.** [colour] jaune *m* safran.
◇ *adj* (jaune) safran *(inv).*
sag [sæg] (*pt* & *pp* **sagged**, *cont* **sagging**)
◇ *vi* -**1.** [rope] être détendu; [roof, beam, shelf bridge] s'affaisser; [branch] ployer; [jowls, cheeks hemline] pendre; [breasts] tomber; **the bed ~s in the middle** le lit s'affaisse au milieu. -**2.** [prices, stocks, demand] fléchir, baisser; [conversation] traîner; **the novel ~s a bit in the middle** le roman perd un peu de son intérêt au milieu; **their spirits sagged** ils perdirent courage.
◇ *n* -**1.** [in rope] relâchement *m*; [of structure] affaissement *m.* -**2.** [in prices, stocks, demand] fléchissement *m*, baisse *f.*
saga ['sɑːgə] *n* -**1.** [legend, long novel, film] saga *f* -**2.** [complicated story]: **I heard the whole ~ of her trip to France** elle m'a raconté son voyage en France en long et en large; **it's a ~ of bad management and wrong decisions** c'est une longue histoire de mauvaise gestion et de mauvaises décisions.
sagacious [sə'geɪʃəs] *adj lit* [person] sagace, perspicace, avisé; [remark] judicieux.
sagaciously [sə'geɪʃəslɪ] *adv lit* avec sagacité judicieusement.
sagaciousness [sə'geɪʃəsnɪs], **sagacity** [sə'gæsətɪ] *n lit* sagacité *f.*
sage [seɪdʒ] ◇ *n* -**1.** *lit* [wise person] sage *m* -**2.** BOT & CULIN sauge *f*; **~ and onion stuffing** farce *f* à la sauge et à l'oignon.
◇ *adj lit* [wise] sage, judicieux.
sagebrush ['seɪdʒbrʌʃ] *n* armoise *f.*
sage green *n* vert cendré *m.*
◆ **sage-green** *adj* vert cendré *(inv).*
sagely ['seɪdʒlɪ] *adv* avec sagesse, avec sagacité
sagging ['sægɪŋ] *adj* -**1.** [rope] détendu; [bed roof, bridge] affaissé; [shelf, beam] qui ploie [hemline] qui pend; [jowls, cheeks] pendant [breasts] tombant. -**2.** [prices, demand] en baisse [spirits] abattu, découragé.
Sagittarius [,sædʒɪ'teərɪəs] ◇ *pr n* ASTROL & ASTRON Sagittaire *m.*
◇ *n*: **he's a ~** il est (du signe du) Sagittaire
sago ['seɪgəʊ] *n* sagou *m*; **~ pudding** sagou au lait.
sago palm *n* sagoutier *m.*
Sahara [sə'hɑːrə] *pr n*: **the ~ (Desert)** le (désert du) Sahara.
Saharan [sə'hɑːrən] ◇ *n* LING saharien *m.*
◇ *adj* saharien; **sub-~ Africa** Afrique *f* subsaharienne.
sahib ['sɑːɪb] *n* sahib *m.*
said [sed] ◇ *pt* & *pp* → **say**.
◇ *adj*: **the ~ Howard Riley** le dit OR dénommé Howard Riley; **the ~ Anne Smith** la dite OR dénommée Anne Smith; **the ~ article** les dits articles.
Saida ['saɪdə] *pr n* Saida, Sayda.
sail [seɪl] ◇ *n* -**1.** [on boat] voile *f*; **in full ~** toutes voiles dehors; **the boat was under ~** le bateau était sous voiles; **they rounded the cape under ~** ils doublèrent le cap à la voile; **under 300 m² of ~** avec une voilure de 300 m²; **to set ~** [boat] prendre la mer, appareiller; [person] partir (en bateau); **to make ~** [hoist sails] hisser les voiles; [leave] prendre la mer, appareiller. -**2.** [journey] voyage *m* en bateau; [pleasure trip] promenade *f* en bateau; **to go for a ~** faire un tour en bateau; **it's a few hours' ~ from here** c'est à quelques heures d'ici en bateau. -**3.** [of windmill] aile *f.*
◇ *vi* -**1.** [move over water - boat, ship] naviguer; **the trawler was ~ing north** le chalutier se dirigeait OR cinglait vers le nord; **the boat ~s**

up/down the river le bateau remonta/descendit le fleuve; the ferry ~ed into Dover le ferry-boat entra dans le port de Douvres ❑ to ~ close to the wind naviguer au (plus) près; *fig* jouer un jeu dangereux. -**2.** [set off - boat, passenger] partir, prendre la mer, appareiller; the Britannica ~s at noon le Britannica appareille à midi. -**3.** [travel by boat] voyager (en bateau); are you flying or ~ing? est-ce que vous y allez en avion ou en bateau?; they ~ed from Liverpool to Boston ils ont fait le voyage de Liverpool à Boston en bateau. -**4.** [as sport or hobby]: to ~, to go ~ing faire de la voile. -**5.** *fig*: swans ~ed by on the lake des cygnes glissaient sur le lac; birds ~ed across the sky des oiseaux passaient dans le ciel; a sports car ~ed past me une voiture de sport m'a doublé à toute vitesse; the balloons ~ed into the air les ballons se sont envolés; the ball ~ed over the wall la balle est passée par-dessus le mur; my hat ~ed off my head and into the water un coup de vent m'a arraché mon chapeau qui s'est retrouvé dans l'eau; she ~ed across the room to greet me elle traversa la pièce d'un pas majestueux pour venir à ma rencontre.

◇ *vt* -**1.** [boat - subj: captain] commander; [- subj: helmsman, yachtsman] barrer; have you ever ~ed a catamaran before? est-ce que vous avez déjà barré un catamaran?; to ~ a boat through a channel manœuvrer un bateau dans un chenal; she ~ed the boat into port elle a manœuvré OR piloté le bateau jusque dans le port. -**2.** [cross - sea, lake] traverser; to ~ the Atlantic single-handed traverser l'Atlantique en solitaire; to ~ the seas parcourir les mers.

◆ **sail into** *inf vt insep* [attack] tomber à bras raccourcis sur.

◆ **sail through** *vt insep* & *vi insep* [succeed] réussir haut la main.

sailboard ['seɪlbɔːd] *n* planche *f* à voile.

sailboarder ['seɪl,bɔːdəʳ] *n* véliplanchiste *mf*.

sailboarding ['seɪl,bɔːdɪŋ] *n* planche *f* à voile *(activité)*.

sailboat ['seɪlbəʊt] *n Am* voilier *m*, bateau *m* à voile.

sailcloth ['seɪlklɒθ] *n* toile *f* à voile OR à voiles.

sailing ['seɪlɪŋ] *n* -**1.** [activity] navigation *f*; [hobby] voile *f*, navigation *f* de plaisance; [sport] voile *f*. -**2.** [departure] départ *m*; there are three ~s a day for Cherbourg il y a trois départs par jour pour Cherbourg.

sailing boat *n* voilier *m*, bateau *m* (à voiles).

sailing dinghy *n* canot *m* à voile.

sailing ship *n* (grand) voilier *m*, navire *m* à voile OR à voiles.

sailmaker ['seɪl,meɪkəʳ] *n* voilier *m (personne)*.

sailor ['seɪləʳ] *n* -**1.** [gen] marin *m*, navigateur *m*, -trice *f*; I'm a good/bad ~ j'ai/je n'ai pas le pied marin. -**2.** [as rank] matelot *m*.

sailor collar *n* col *m* marin.

sailor hat *n* béret *m* de marin.

sailor suit *n* costume *m* marin.

sailplane ['seɪlpleɪn] *n* planeur *m*.

sainfoin ['sænfɔɪn] *n* sainfoin *m*.

saint [seɪnt] *n* saint *m*, -e *f*; Saint David saint David; Saint David's day la Saint-David; Saint David's (Church) (l'église *f*) Saint-David; All Saints' (Day) la Toussaint.

Saint Bernard [*Br* -'bɜːnəd, *Am* -bəʳ'nɑːrd] *n* [dog] saint-bernard *m inv*.

sainted ['seɪntɪd] *adj* [person] sanctifié; [place] sacré, consacré; my ~ aunt! *inf dated* vingt dieux!

Saint Elmo's fire [-'elməʊ-] *n* feu *m* Saint-Elme.

Saint Gotthard Pass [-'gɒtəd-] *pr n*: the ~ le col du Saint-Gothard.

Saint Helena [-ɪ'liːnə] *pr n* Sainte-Hélène; on ~ à Sainte-Hélène.

sainthood ['seɪnthʊd] *n* sainteté *f*.

Saint John's wort [-wɜːt] *n* millepertuis *m*.

Saint Lawrence [-'lɒrəns] *pr n*: the ~ (River) le Saint-Laurent.

Saint Lawrence Seaway *pr n* GEOG voie *f* maritime du Saint-Laurent.

saintlike ['seɪntlaɪk] = **saintly**.

saintliness ['seɪntlɪnɪs] *n* sainteté *f*.

Saint Lucia [-'luːʃə] *pr n* Sainte-Lucie.

saintly ['seɪntlɪ] (*compar* **saintlier**, *superl* **saintliest**) *adj* [life, behaviour, humility, virtue] de saint; she was a ~ woman c'était une vraie sainte.

Saint Mark's Square *pr n* la place Saint-Marc.

Saint Peter *pr n*: ~'s Basilica la basilique Saint-Pierre.

Saint Petersburg [-'piːtəzbɜːg] *pr n* Saint-Pétersbourg.

Saint Pierre and Miquelon [-,pjɜːrən'mɪkəlɒn] *pr n* Saint-Pierre-et-Miquelon; in ~ à Saint-Pierre-et-Miquelon.

saint's day *n* fête *f (d'un saint)*.

Saint Vitus' dance [-'vaɪtəs] *n* MED danse *f* de Saint-Guy, chorée *f*.

saith [seθ] *arch* OR BIBLE *pres sg* → **say**.

saithe [seɪθ] *n Br* colin *m*, lieu *m* noir.

sake[1] [seɪk] *n*: for sb's ~ [for their good] pour (le bien de) qqn; [out of respect for] par égard pour qqn; [out of love for] pour l'amour de qqn; do it for my ~/for your own ~ fais-le pour moi/pour toi; I only came for your ~ je ne suis venu qu'à cause de toi OR que pour toi; please come, for both our ~s viens s'il te plaît, fais-le pour nous deux; they decided not to divorce for the ~ of the children ils ont décidé de ne pas divorcer à cause des enfants; I walk to work for its own ~, not to save money je vais travailler à pied pour le plaisir, pas par esprit d'économie; they're just talking for the ~ of talking OR of it ils parlent pour ne rien dire; art for art's ~ l'art pour l'art; for the ~ of higher profits pour réaliser de plus gros bénéfices; all that for the ~ of a few dollars tout ça pour quelques malheureux dollars; for old times' ~ en souvenir du passé; for the ~ of argument, let's assume it costs £100 (pour les besoins de la discussion,) admettons que ça coûte 100 livres; for goodness OR God's OR Christ's OR pity's OR heaven's ~! pour l'amour du ciel OR de Dieu!

sake[2] ['sɑːkɪ] *n* [drink] saké *m*.

Sakhalin ['sækəliːn] *pr n* Sakhaline.

sal [sæl] *n* CHEM sel *m*.

salaam [sə'lɑːm] ◇ *n* salutation *f* à l'orientale.
◇ *vi* saluer à l'orientale.
◇ *interj* salam.

salable ['seɪləbl] *adj* vendable.

salacious [sə'leɪʃəs] *adj fml* [joke, book, look] salace, grivois, obscène.

salaciousness [sə'leɪʃəsnɪs], **salacity** [sə'læsətɪ] *n fml* salacité *f*, grivoiserie *f*, obscénité *f*.

salad ['sæləd] *n* salade *f*; chicken ~ poulet *m* en salade; tomato/fruit/mixed ~ salade de tomates/de fruits/mixte.

salad bar *n* [restaurant] *restaurant où l'on mange des salades*; *Br* [area] salad bar *m*.

salad bowl *n* saladier *m*.

salad cream *n Br sorte de mayonnaise (vendue en bouteille)*.

salad days *npl fig* & *lit* années *fpl* de jeunesse.

salad dressing *n* [gen] sauce *f (pour salade)*; [French dressing] vinaigrette *f*.

salad oil *n* huile *f* pour assaisonnement.

salad servers *npl* couverts *mpl* à salade.

Salamanca [,sælə'mæŋkə] *pr n* Salamanque.

salamander ['sælə,mændəʳ] *n* salamandre *f*.

salami [sə'lɑːmɪ] *n* salami *m*, saucisson *m* sec.

salaried ['sælərɪd] *adj* salarié; a ~ job [gen] un emploi salarié; [as opposed to wage-earning] *emploi dont le salaire est mensuel et non hebdomadaire*.

salary ['sælərɪ] (*pl* **salaries**) ◇ *n* salaire *m*; I have to bring up a family on a teacher's ~ je dois faire vivre ma famille avec un salaire d'enseignant.
◇ *comp* [bracket, level, scale] des salaires; ~ earner salarié *m*, -e *f*.

sale [seɪl] ◇ *n* -**1.** [gen] vente *f*; to make a ~ conclure une vente; the ~ of alcohol is forbidden la vente d'alcool est interdite; ~s of satellite TV dishes are growing les ventes d'antennes paraboliques sont en hausse; the branch with the highest ~s la succursale avec le chiffre de vente le plus élevé; 'for ~' 'à vendre'; I'm afraid that article is not for ~ je regrette, cet article n'est pas à vendre; our house is up for ~ nous avons mis notre maison en vente; to put sthg up for ~ mettre qqch en vente; on ~ en vente; on ~ at a supermarket near you en vente dans tous les supermarchés; we bought the goods on a ~ or return basis nous avons acheté la marchandise à condition ❑ ~ of work vente *f* de charité. -**2.** [event] soldes *mpl*; the January ~s attract huge crowds les soldes de janvier attirent les foules; the ~s are on in London les soldes ont commencé à Londres; I got it in a ~ je l'ai acheté en solde ❑ closing-down ~ liquidation *f*; ~ price prix *m* soldé. -**3.** [auction] vente *f* (aux enchères).
◇ *comp* [goods] soldé.

◆ **sales** *comp* [department, executive] des ventes, commercial; [promotion, forecasts, figures] des ventes.

saleable ['seɪləbl] = **salable**.

Salem ['seɪləm] *pr n* Salem; the ~ witch trials *Am* HIST la chasse aux sorcières de Salem.

THE SALEM WITCH TRIALS:
Série de procès qui se déroulèrent dans une atmosphère d'hystérie collective, aboutissant à la pendaison d'une vingtaine de personnes accusées de sorcellerie, dans la ville américaine de Salem (Massachusetts) en 1692.

saleratus [,sælə'reɪtəs] *n Am* CULIN bicarbonate *m* de soude.

Salerno [sə'lɜːnəʊ] *pr n* Salerne.

saleroom ['seɪlrʊm] *n Br* salle *f* des ventes.

salesclerk [*Br* 'seɪlzklɑːk, *Am* 'seɪlzklɜːrk] *n Am* vendeur *m*, -euse *f*.

sales force *n* force *f* de vente.

salesgirl ['seɪlzgɜːl] *n* vendeuse *f*.

salesman ['seɪlzmən] (*pl* **salesmen** [-mən]) *n* [in shop] vendeur *m*; [rep] représentant *m* (de commerce); an insurance/encyclopedia ~ un représentant en assurances/encyclopédies.

sales manager *n* directeur *m* commercial, directrice *f* commerciale.

salesmanship ['seɪlzmənʃɪp] *n* art *m* de la vente, technique *f* de vente; high-pressure OR aggressive ~ techniques de vente agressives.

salesperson ['seɪlz,pɜːsn] (*pl* **salespeople** [-,piːpl]) *n* [in shop] vendeur *m*, -euse *f*; [rep] représentant *m*, -e *f* (de commerce).

sales pitch = **sales talk**.

sales rep, sales representative *n* représentant *m*, -e *f* (de commerce).

sales resistance *n* réticence *f* de la part du consommateur; our product met with some initial ~ le public n'a pas accepté notre produit tout de suite.

salesroom ['seɪlzrʊm] *Am* = **saleroom**.

sales slip *n Am* ticket *m* de caisse.

sales talk *n* boniment *m*.

sales tax *n Am* taxe *f* à la vente.

saleswoman ['seɪlz,wʊmən] (*pl* **saleswomen** [-,wɪmɪn]) *n* [in shop] vendeuse *f*; [rep] représentante *f* (de commerce).

Salic law ['sælɪk-] *n* HIST loi *f* salique.

salient ['seɪljənt] ◇ *adj* saillant.
◇ *n* ARCHIT & MIL saillant *m*.

salify ['sælɪfaɪ] (*pt* & *pp* **salified**) *vt* salifier.

salina [sə'laɪnə] *n* [marsh] marais *m* salant; [spring] source *f* saline; [lake] lac *m* salé.

saline ['seɪlaɪn] *adj* salin; ~ drip MED perfusion *f* saline.

salinity [sə'lɪnətɪ] *n* salinité *f*.

salinometer [,sælɪ'nɒmɪtəʳ] *n* salinomètre *m*.

saliva [sə'laɪvə] *n* salive *f*.

salivary gland ['sælɪvərɪ-] *n* glande *f* salivaire.

salivate ['sælɪveɪt] *vi* saliver.
salivation [ˌsælɪ'veɪʃn] *n* salivation *f*.
sallow ['sæləʊ] ◇ *adj* [gen] jaunâtre; [face, complexion] jaunâtre, cireux.
◇ *n* BOT saule *m*.
sallowness ['sæləʊnɪs] *n* teint *m* cireux.
sally ['sælɪ] (*pl* sallies, *pt* & *pp* sallied) *n* -**1.** [gen & MIL] sortie *f*; a successful ~ into the world of cinema *fig* une entrée réussie dans le monde du cinéma. -**2.** *fml* [quip] saillie *f lit*.
◆ **sally forth, sally out** *vi insep lit* sortir; we all sallied forth OR out into the snow nous sommes tous partis gaillardement sous la neige.
Sally Army *inf n Br abbr of* Salvation Army.
salmon ['sæmən] (*pl inv* OR salmons) *n* saumon *m*; smoked ~ saumon fumé; young ~ tacon *m*.
salmonella [ˌsælmə'nelə] (*pl* salmonellae [-liː]) *n* salmonella *f inv*, salmonelle *f*; ~ poisoning salmonellose *f*.
salmonellosis [ˌsælməne'ləʊsɪs] *n* salmonellose *f*.
salmon pink *n* (rose *m*) saumon *m*.
◆ **salmon-pink** *adj* (rose) saumon *(inv)*.
salmon trout *n* truite *f* saumonée.
Salome [sə'ləʊmɪ] *pr n* Salomé.
salon ['sælɒn] *n* salon *m*; hairdressing/beauty ~ salon *m* de coiffure/beauté.
Salonica, Salonika [sə'lɒnɪkə] *pr n* Salonique, Thessalonique.
saloon [sə'luːn] *n* -**1.** *Br* = **saloon car**. -**2.** [public room] salle *f*, salon *m*; [on ship] salon *m*. -**3.** *Am* [bar] bar *m*; [in Wild West] saloon *m*. -**4.** *Br* = **saloon bar**.
saloon bar *n Br* salon *m (dans un pub)*.
saloon car *n Br* conduite *f* intérieure, berline *f*.
salpingitis [ˌsælpɪn'dʒaɪtɪs] *n* salpingite *f*.
salsa ['sælsə] *n* MUS salsa *f*.
salsify ['sælsɪfaɪ] (*pl* salsifies) *n* salsifis *m*.
salt [sɔːlt, sɒlt] ◇ *n* -**1.** CHEM & CULIN sel *m*; there's too much ~ in the soup la soupe est trop salée; the ~ of the earth le sel de la terre ❑ table ~ sel de table; I should take everything he says with a grain OR pinch of ~ je ne devrais pas prendre tout ce qu'il dit au pied de la lettre; to rub ~ into sb's wounds remuer le couteau dans la plaie. -**2.** *inf* [sailor]: old ~ (vieux) loup *m* de mer.
◇ *vt* -**1.** [food] saler. -**2.** [roads] saler, répandre du sel sur.
◇ *adj* salé; ~ pork porc *m* salé, petit salé *m*.
◆ **salts** *npl* PHARM sels *mpl*; like a dose of ~s rapidement.
◆ **salt away** *inf vt sep fig* [money] mettre de côté.
◆ **salt down** *vt sep* saler, conserver dans du sel.
SALT [sɔːlt, sɒlt] (*abbr of* Strategic Arms Limitation Talks/Treaty) *n* SALT *m*; ~ talks négociations *fpl* SALT.
saltcellar ['sɔːltˌselə'] *n* salière *f*.
salted ['sɔːltɪd] *adj* salé.
salt flat *n* salant *m*.
salt-free *adj* sans sel.
saltiness ['sɔːltɪnɪs] *n* [quality of salt] salinité *f*; [taste] goût *m* salé.
salt lake *n* lac *m* salé.
Salt Lake City *pr n* Salt Lake City.
saltlick ['sɔːltlɪk] *n* -**1.** [block] pierre *f* à lécher. -**2.** [place] salant *m*.
salt marsh *n* marais *m* salant.
salt mine *n* mine *f* de sel.
saltpan ['sɔːltpæn] *n* marais *m* salant.
saltpetre *Br*, **saltpeter** *Am* [ˌsɔːlt'piːtə'] *n* salpêtre *m*.
salt shaker *n Am* salière *f*.
salt tax *n* HIST gabelle *f*.
salt water *n* eau *f* salée.
◆ **saltwater** *adj* [fish, plant] de mer.
saltworks ['sɔːltwɜːks] *n* saline *f*, salines *fpl*.
salty ['sɔːltɪ] (*compar* saltier, *superl* saltiest) *adj* [food, taste] salé; [deposit] saumâtre.

salubrious [sə'luːbrɪəs] *adj* -**1.** [respectable] respectable, bien; it's not the most ~ of bars c'est un bar plutôt mal famé. -**2.** [healthy] salubre, sain.
salubrity [sə'luːbrətɪ] *n* salubrité *f*.
saluki [sə'luːkɪ] *n* saluki *m*.
salutary ['sæljʊtrɪ] *adj* salutaire; a ~ lesson une leçon salutaire.
salutation [ˌsæljʊ'teɪʃn] *n* -**1.** [greeting] salut *m*, salutation *f*. -**2.** [on letter] formule *f* de début de lettre.
salute [sə'luːt] ◇ *n* -**1.** MIL [with hand] salut *m*; to give (sb) a ~ faire un salut (à qqn); the lieutenant returned his ~ le lieutenant lui a rendu son salut; to stand at ~ garder le salut; to take the ~ passer les troupes en revue || [with guns] salve *f*; a twenty-one gun ~ une salve de vingt et un coups de canon. -**2.** [greeting] salut *m*, salutation *f*. -**3.** [tribute] hommage *m*; a ~ to British artists un hommage aux artistes britanniques.
◇ *vt* -**1.** MIL [with hand] saluer; [with guns] tirer une salve en l'honneur de; to ~ the flag saluer le drapeau. -**2.** [greet] saluer; she ~d me with a wave elle m'a salué d'un geste de la main. -**3.** [acknowledge, praise] saluer, acclamer; the press today ~s a new world champion la presse salue aujourd'hui un nouveau champion du monde.
◇ *vi* MIL faire un salut.
Salvador ['sælvədɔː'] *pr n* Salvador *(port)*.
Salvadorean, Salvadorian [ˌsælvə'dɔːrɪən] ◇ *n* Salvadorien *m*, -enne *f*.
◇ *adj* salvadorien.
salvage ['sælvɪdʒ] ◇ *vt* -**1.** [vessel, cargo, belongings] sauver; [old newspapers, scrap metal] récupérer; they managed to ~ some furniture from the fire ils ont réussi à sauver quelques meubles de l'incendie; a counter ~d from an old butcher's shop un comptoir récupéré dans une ancienne boucherie. -**2.** *fig* [mistake, meal] rattraper; [situation] rattraper, sauver; to ~ one's reputation sauver sa réputation.
◇ *n* -**1.** [recovery - of vessel, cargo, belongings, furniture] sauvetage *m*; [- of old newspapers, scrap metal] récupération *f*. -**2.** *(U)* [things recovered - from shipwreck, disaster] objets *mpl* sauvés; [- for re-use, recycling] objets *mpl* récupérés. -**3.** [payment] indemnité *f* OR prime *f* de sauvetage.
◇ *comp* [company, operation, vessel] de sauvetage.
salvation [sæl'veɪʃn] *n* -**1.** RELIG salut *m*. -**2.** *fig*: writing has always been my ~ écrire m'a toujours sauvé; the country's ~ does not lie in rearmament le pays ne va pas trouver son salut dans le réarmement, ce n'est pas le réarmement qui va sauver le pays.
Salvation Army *pr n*: the ~ l'Armée *f* du salut.
salvationist [sæl'veɪʃənɪst] *n* -**1.** [member of evangelical sect] salutiste *mf*. -**2.** [member of Salvation Army] salutiste *mf*.
salve [sælv] ◇ *n* -**1.** [ointment] baume *m*, pommade *f*; lip ~ pommade pour les lèvres. -**2.** *fig* [relief] baume *m lit*, apaisement *m*.
◇ *vt* -**1.** [relieve] calmer, soulager; I did it to ~ my conscience je l'ai fait par acquit de conscience. -**2.** [salvage] sauver.
salver ['sælvə'] *n* plateau *m* (de service); a silver ~ un plateau en argent.
salvia ['sælvɪə] *n* BOT salvia *f*, sauge *f*.
salvo ['sælvəʊ] (*pl* salvos OR salvoes) *n* -**1.** MIL salve *f*. -**2.** *fig* [of applause] salve *f*; [of laughter] éclat *m*; [of insults] torrent *m*.
sal volatile [ˌsælvə'lætəlɪ] *n (U)* sel *m* volatile, sels *mpl* (anglais).
salvor ['sælvə'] *n* sauveteur *m* (en mer).
Salzburg ['sæltsbɜːg] *pr n* Salzbourg.
SAM [sæm] (*abbr of* surface-to-air missile) *n* missile *m* sol-air.
Samaria [sə'meərɪə] *pr n* Samarie *f*; in ~ en Samarie.

Samaritan [sə'mærɪtn] ◇ *n* RELIG Sama tain *m*, -e *f*; the Good ~ le bon Samaritai she's a real good ~ elle est très secourable.
◇ *adj* samaritain.
◆ **Samaritans** *pl pr n*: the ~s *association pr posant un soutien moral par téléphone aux personn déprimées*, ≃ SOS Amitié.
samarium [sə'meərɪəm] *n* samarium *m*.
samba ['sæmbə] ◇ *n* samba *f*.
◇ *vi* danser la samba.
sambo▼ ['sæmbəʊ] (*pl* sambos) *n terme racis et vieilli désignant un Noir*, ≃ nègre *m*.
same [seɪm] ◇ *adj* même; she's wearing the glasses as you elle porte les mêmes lunettes qu toi; you saw the ~ film I did tu as vu le mêm film que moi; their son is the ~ age as ou leur fils a le même âge que le nôtre; are you st at the ~ address? êtes-vous toujours à la mêm adresse?; the two suitcases are exactly the colour/shape les deux valises sont exacteme de la même couleur/ont exactement la mêm forme; it always seems to be the ~ peop who suffer on dirait que ce sont toujours l mêmes qui souffrent; they are one and the thing c'est une seule et même chose; they a one and the ~ person ils ne font qu'un; it a boils down to the ~ thing cela revient a même; see you ~ time, ~ place je te retrou à la même heure, au même endroit ❑ difference! *inf* c'est du pareil au même!
◇ *pron* -**1.** the ~ [unchanged] le même *m*, même *f*, les mêmes *mfpl*; it's the ~ as befo c'est comme avant; life's just not the ~ no they're gone les choses ont changé depu qu'ils sont partis; the city centre is still the le centre ville n'a pas changé; it's not spelt th ~ ça ne s'écrit pas de la même façon; she exactly the ~ elle n'a pas changé du tout [identical] identique; the two vases are exact the ~ les deux vases sont identiques. -**2.** [use in comparisons]: the ~ la même chose; it's th ~ in Italy c'est la même chose OR c'est pare en Italie; it's always the ~ c'est toujours même chose OR toujours pareil; it's not a bit th ~ ce n'est pas du tout la même chose OR pa du tout pareil; it's the ~ here as in France c'e la même chose ici qu'en France ❑ aren't yo Freddie Fortescue? — the very ~ vous n'ête pas Freddie Fortescue? — lui-même; (the) again, please la même chose (, s'il vous plaît if it's all the ~ to you, I'll go now si cela r vous fait rien, je vais partir maintenant; it's a OR just the ~ to me what you do tu peux fai ce que tu veux, ça m'est bien égal; I was reall cross — ~ here! *inf* j'étais vraiment fâché — moi donc!; Happy Christmas — (and the) to you! Joyeux Noël — à vous aussi OR c même!; stupid idiot — and the ~ to you! *i* espèce d'imbécile! — imbécile toi-même -**3.** JUR: the ~ [aforementioned] le susdit *m*, susdite *f*. -**4.** COMM: and for delivery of ~ pour livraison de ces (mêmes) articles.
◆ **all the same, just the same** *adv phr* quan même; all OR just the ~, I would like to kno what happened quand même, j'aimerais bie savoir ce qui s'est passé; all the ~, I still lik her je l'aime bien quand même; thanks all th ~ merci quand même.
same-day *adj* COMM [processing, delivery] dans journée.
sameness ['seɪmnɪs] *n* -**1.** [similarity] simi tude *f*, ressemblance *f*. -**2.** [tedium] monot nie *f*, uniformité *f*.
samey *inf* ['seɪmɪ] *adj Br pej* monotone, e nuyeux.
samizdat ['sæmɪzdæt] *n* samizdat *m*.
Samoa [sə'məʊə] *pr n* Samoa *m*; in ~ à Samo
Samoan [sə'məʊən] ◇ *n* -**1.** [person] S moan *m*, -e *f*. -**2.** LING samoan *m*.
◇ *adj* samoan.
samosa [sə'məʊsə] (*pl inv* OR samosas) *n pet pâté indien à la viande ou aux légumes*.
samovar ['sæməˌvɑː'] *n* samovar *m*.

amoyed [sə'mɔɪəd] (*pl inv* OR Samoyeds) ◇ *npl* [people]: the ~ les Samoyèdes *mpl*.
◇ *n* LING samoyède *m*.

ampan ['sæmpæn] *n* sampan *m*, sampang *m*.

amphire ['sæmfaɪəʳ] *n*: (rock) ~ criste-marine *f*, crithme *m*; golden ~ inule *f*; marsh ~ salicorne *f*.

ample ['sɑːmpl] ◇ *n* -**1.** [gen, COMM & SOCIOL] échantillon *m*; a free ~ un échantillon gratuit; a representative ~ of the population un échantillon représentatif de la population; please bring a ~ of your work veuillez apporter un échantillon de votre travail; up to ~ COMM conforme à l'échantillon. -**2.** GEOL, MED & SCI échantillon *m*, prélèvement *m*; [of blood] prélèvement *m*; [of urine] échantillon *m*; water/rock ~s prélèvements *mpl* d'eau/de roche; to take a ~ prélever un échantillon, faire un prélèvement; to take a blood ~ faire une prise de sang.
◇ *comp*: a ~ bottle/pack *etc* un échantillon; we'll send you a ~ bottle of our shampoo nous vous enverrons un échantillon de notre shampooing; do the ~ exercise first faites d'abord l'exercice donné à titre d'exemple; a ~ question from last year's exam paper un exemple de question tiré de l'examen de l'année dernière.
◇ *vt* -**1.** [food, drink] goûter (à), déguster; [new experience, way of life] goûter à. -**2.** MUS échantillonner.

ampler ['sɑːmpləʳ] *n* -**1.** SEW modèle *m* de broderie. -**2.** [collection of samples] échantillonnage *m*, sélection *f*. -**3.** MUS échantillonneur *m*.

ampling ['sɑːmplɪŋ] *n* [gen & COMPUT] échantillonnage *m*.

amson ['sæmsn] *pr n*: ~ and Delilah Samson et Dalila; he's a real ~ il est fort comme un Turc.

amuel ['sæmjʊəl] *pr n* BIBLE Samuel; the Books of ~ les livres *mpl* de Samuel.

amurai ['sæmʊraɪ] (*pl inv*) *n* samouraï *m*, samourai *m inv*.

ana'a [sɑː'nɑː] *pr n* Sana'a.

anatorium [ˌsænə'tɔːrɪəm] (*pl* sanatoriums OR sanatoria [-rɪə]) *n* [nursing home] sanatorium *m*; [sick bay] infirmerie *f*.

ancta ['sæŋktə] *pl* → **sanctum**.

anctification [ˌsæŋktɪfɪ'keɪʃn] *n* sanctification *f*.

anctify ['sæŋktɪfaɪ] (*pt* & *pp* sanctified) *vt* sanctifier.

anctimonious [ˌsæŋktɪ'məʊnjəs] *adj* moralisateur; I hate his ~ manner je ne supporte pas ses airs de petit saint.

anctimoniously [ˌsæŋktɪ'məʊnjəslɪ] *adv* [look] d'un air de petit saint; [speak] d'un ton bigot OR moralisateur.

anctimoniousness [ˌsæŋktɪ'məʊnjəsnɪs] *n* airs *mpl* de petit saint, pharisaïsme *m*.

anction ['sæŋkʃn] ◇ *n* -**1.** [approval] sanction *f*, accord *m*, consentement *m*; with the ~ of the government avec l'accord du gouvernement; it hasn't yet been given official ~ ceci n'a pas encore été officiellement approuvé OR sanctionné, ceci n'a pas encore eu l'approbation OR sanction officielle; it has the ~ of long usage c'est consacré par l'usage. -**2.** [punitive measure] sanction *f*; the firm was accused of ~s busting la société a été accusée d'avoir contourné les sanctions; to impose (economic) ~s on a country prendre des sanctions (économiques) à l'encontre d'un pays.
◇ *vt* sanctionner, entériner; [behaviour] approuver; tradition has long ~ed this error la tradition a entériné OR consacré cette erreur depuis longtemps.

anctity ['sæŋktətɪ] *n* [of person, life] sainteté *f*; [of marriage, property, place - holiness] caractère *m* sacré; [- inviolability] inviolabilité *f*.

anctuary ['sæŋktʃʊərɪ] (*pl* sanctuaries) *n* -**1.** [holy place] sanctuaire *m*. -**2.** [refuge] refuge *m*, asile *m*; to seek ~ chercher asile OR refuge ❑ wildlife ~ réserve *f* animale.

sanctum ['sæŋktəm] (*pl* sanctums OR sancta [-tə]) *n* -**1.** [holy place] sanctuaire *m*. -**2.** *hum* [private place] refuge *m*, retraite *f*, tanière *f*; he's in his inner ~ il s'est retiré dans sa tanière.

sand [sænd] ◇ *n* -**1.** [substance] sable *m*; miles of golden ~s des kilomètres de sable doré; shifting ~ sables mouvants; the ~s of time le temps qui passe; to build on ~ *fig* bâtir sur le sable. -**2.** ▽ *Am* [courage] cran *m*.
◇ *comp* [dune] de sable.
◇ *vt* -**1.** [polish, smooth] poncer. -**2.** [spread sand on] sabler.
◆ **sand down** *vt sep* [wood, metal] poncer au papier de verre, décaper.

sandal ['sændl] *n* -**1.** [footwear] sandale *f*. -**2.** = **sandalwood**.

sandalwood ['sændlwʊd] *n* bois *m* de santal; ~ oil essence *f* de bois de santal.

sandbag ['sændbæg] (*pt* & *pp* sandbagged) ◇ *n* sac *m* de sable OR de terre.
◇ *vt* -**1.** [shore up] renforcer avec des sacs de sable; [protect] protéger avec des sacs de sable. -**2.** *inf* [hit] assommer. -**3.** *inf Am* [coerce]: to ~ sb into doing sthg forcer qqn à faire qqch.

sandbank ['sændbæŋk] *n* banc *m* de sable.

sandbar ['sændbɑːʳ] *n* barre *f (dans la mer, dans un estuaire)*.

sandblast ['sændblɑːst] ◇ *vt* décaper à la sableuse, sabler.
◇ *n* jet *m* de sable.

sandblaster ['sændˌblɑːstəʳ] *n* sableuse *f*.

sandblasting ['sændˌblɑːstɪŋ] *n* décapage *m* à la sableuse, sablage *m*.

sand-blind *adj* mal voyant.

sandbox ['sændbɒks] *n* -**1.** RAIL sablière *f*. -**2.** [for children] bac *m* à sable.

sandboy ['sændbɔɪ] *n phr*: (as) happy as a ~ heureux comme un poisson dans l'eau.

sand-cast *vt* couler en sable.

sandcastle ['sændˌkɑːsl] *n* château *m* de sable.

sand dollar *n* clypéastéroïde *m*.

sand eel *n* lançon *m*, équille *f*.

sander ['sændəʳ] *n* [tool] ponceuse *f*; finishing ~ ponceuse *f* à bande; orbital ~ ponceuse *f* orbitale.

sand flea *n* [sandhopper] puce *f* de mer, talitre *m*; [chigoe] chique *f*.

sand fly *n* phlébotome *m*, mouche *f* des sables.

sandglass ['sændglɑːs] *n* sablier *m*.

sandhopper ['sændˌhɒpəʳ] *n* puce *f* de mer.

Sandhurst ['sændhɜːst] *pr n centre de formation militaire britannique établi à Sandhurst, dans le Berkshire*.

sanding ['sændɪŋ] *n* -**1.** [of wood, plaster] ponçage *m*. -**2.** [of roads] sablage *m*.

Sandinista [ˌsændɪ'niːstə] ◇ *adj* sandiniste.
◇ *n* sandiniste *mf*.

sand lance = **sand eel**.

sand lot *n Am* terrain *m* vague.

sandman ['sændmæn] *n* marchand *m* de sable *fig*.

sand martin *n* hirondelle *f* de rivage.

Sandown Park ['sændaʊn-] *pr n champ de courses dans le Surrey (Angleterre)*.

sandpaper ['sændˌpeɪpəʳ] ◇ *n* papier *m* de verre.
◇ *vt* poncer (au papier de verre).

sandpie ['sændpaɪ] *n* pâté *m* de sable.

sandpiper ['sændˌpaɪpəʳ] *n* bécasseau *m*, chevalier *m*.

sandpit ['sændpɪt] *n Br* -**1.** [for children] bac *m* à sable. -**2.** [quarry] sablonnière *f*.

Sandringham ['sændrɪŋəm] *pr n village du Norfolk où la famille royale possède une résidence de campagne*.

sandshoe ['sændʃuː] *n Br* (chaussure *f* de) tennis *m*.

sandstone ['sændstəʊn] *n* grès *m*.

sandstorm ['sændstɔːm] *n* tempête *f* de sable.

sand trap *n Am* bunker *m* (de sable).

sand wedge *n* sand-wedge *m*.

sandwich ['sænwɪdʒ] ◇ *n* -**1.** [bread] sandwich *m*; a ham ~ un sandwich au jambon. -**2.** = **sandwich cake**.
◇ *vt* -**1.** *inf* [place] intercaler; I'll try to ~ you (in) between appointments j'essaierai de vous caser entre deux rendez-vous. -**2.** *inf* [trap] prendre en sandwich, coincer; I was ~ed (in) between two large Russians j'étais coincé entre deux gros Russes. -**3.** [join] joindre, coller; we ~ed the boards together with glue nous avons collé les planches.

sandwich bar *n Br* ≃ snack *m (où on vend des sandwiches)*.

sandwich board *n* panneau *m* publicitaire *(porté par un homme-sandwich)*.

sandwich cake *n Br* gâteau *m* fourré.

sandwich course *n Br formation en alternance*.

sandwich loaf *n* ≃ pain *m* de mie.

sandwich man *n* homme-sandwich *m*.

sandy ['sændɪ] (*compar* sandier, *superl* sandiest) *adj* -**1.** [beach, desert] de sable; [soil, road] sablonneux; [water, alluvium] sableux; [floor, clothes] couvert de sable. -**2.** [in colour] (couleur) sable *(inv)*; he has ~ OR ~-coloured hair il a les cheveux blond roux.

sand yacht *n* char *m* à voile.

sand-yachting *n* char *m* à voile; to go ~ faire du char à voile.

sane [seɪn] *adj* -**1.** [person] sain d'esprit; to be of ~ mind être sain d'esprit; how do you manage to stay ~ in this environment? comment fais-tu pour ne pas devenir fou dans une ambiance pareille? -**2.** [action] sensé; [attitude, approach, policy] raisonnable, sensé.

sanely ['seɪnlɪ] *adv* raisonnablement.

Sanforize® ['sænfəraɪz] *vt* sanforiser.

San Francisco [ˌsænfrən'sɪskəʊ] *pr n* San Francisco; the ~ earthquake le tremblement de terre de San Francisco.

THE SAN FRANCISCO EARTHQUAKE:
La plus importante catastrophe naturelle qu'aient connue les États-Unis (avril 1906). L'incendie provoqué par le séisme dura trois jours et détruisit les trois quarts de la ville, jetant 225 000 personnes à la rue et faisant 400 millions de dollars de dégâts. La ville fut reconstruite très rapidement avec l'aide de pays tout entier.

---

sang [sæŋ] *pt* → **sing**.

sangfroid [ˌsɒŋ'frwɑː] *n* sang-froid *m*.

sangria [sæŋ'grɪə] *n* sangria *f*.

sanguinary ['sæŋgwɪnərɪ] *adj lit* [murderer, tyrant] sanguinaire; [battle] sanglant.

sanguine ['sæŋgwɪn] ◇ *adj* -**1.** [optimistic - person, temperament] optimiste, confiant; [- attitude, prospect]: he was ~ about the company's prospects il voyait l'avenir de l'entreprise avec optimisme. -**2.** *lit* [ruddy - complexion] sanguin, rubicond.
◇ *n* ART sanguine *f*.

sanguinely ['sæŋgwɪnlɪ] *adv* avec optimisme OR confiance.

sanguineous [sæŋ'gwɪnɪəs] = **sanguine** *adj*.

sanies ['seɪnɪiːz] *n* pus *m*.

sanitarium [ˌsænɪ'teərɪəm] *Am* = **sanatorium**.

sanitary ['sænɪtrɪ] *adj* -**1.** [hygienic] hygiénique; the kitchen didn't look very ~ la cuisine n'avait pas l'air très propre. -**2.** [arrangements, conditions, measures, equipment] sanitaire.

sanitary engineer *n* technicien *m* du service sanitaire.

sanitary inspector *n* inspecteur *m* de la santé publique.

sanitary towel *Br*, **sanitary napkin** *Am* *n* serviette *f* hygiénique.

sanitation [ˌsænɪ'teɪʃn] *n* [public health] hygiène *f* publique; [sewers] système *m* sanitaire; [plumbing] sanitaires *mpl*; the shanty towns have no ~ whatsoever les bidonvilles n'ont absolument aucun système sanitaire.

sanitation worker *n Am* éboueur *m*.

sanitize, ise ['sænɪtaɪz] *vt* -**1.** [disinfect] désinfecter. -**2.** *fig* [expurgate] expurger; the original tapes had been ~d les bandes originales avaient été expurgées; this is the ~d image he would like to project c'est l'image proprette OR aseptisée qu'il voudrait présenter.

sanity ['sænətɪ] *n* -**1.** [mental health] santé *f* mentale; to lose one's ~ perdre la raison. -**2.** [reasonableness] bon sens *m*, rationalité *f*.

sank [sæŋk] *pt* → **sink**.

San Marino [,sænmə'riːnəʊ] *pr n* Saint-Marin; in ~ à Saint-Marin.

sans [sænz] *prep arch* sans.

San Salvador [,sæn'sælvədɔːʳ] *pr n* San Salvador.

San Sebastian [,sænsə'bæstɪən] *pr n* Saint-Sébastien.

Sanskrit ['sænskrɪt] ◇ *adj* sanskrit.
◇ *n* sanskrit *m*.

sansserif [,sæn'serɪf] *n (U)* TYPO caractères *mpl* bâton OR sans empattement.

Santa *inf* ['sæntə], **Santa Claus** ['sæntə,klɔːz] *pr n* le père Noël.

Santa Fe [,sæntə'feɪ] *pr n* Santa Fe.

Santiago [,sæntɪ'ɑːgəʊ] *pr n* Santiago.

Santiago de Compostela [-dəkɒmpɒ'stelə] *pr n* Saint-Jacques-de-Compostelle.

Santorini [,sæntə'riːnɪ] *pr n* Santorin.

Sao Paulo [,saʊ'paʊləʊ] *pr n* -**1.** [city] Sao Paulo. -**2.** [state]: ~ (State) Sao Paulo *m*, l'État *m* de Sao Paulo; in ~ dans le Sao Paulo.

sap [sæp] (*pt* & *pp* sapped, *cont* sapping) ◇ *n* -**1.** BOT sève *f*. -**2.** *inf Am* [fool] bêta *m*, -asse *f*, andouille *f*; [gullible person] nigaud *m*, -e *f*. -**3.** *inf Am* [cosh] matraque *f*, gourdin *m*. -**4.** MIL sape *f*.
◇ *vt* -**1.** *fig* [strength, courage] saper, miner. -**2.** *Am* [cosh] assommer (d'un coup de gourdin). -**3.** MIL saper.

saphead *inf* ['sæphed] *n Am* bêta *m*, -asse *f*, andouille *f*.

sapient ['seɪpjənt] *adj fml* sage.

sapling ['sæplɪŋ] *n* -**1.** BOT jeune arbre *m*. -**2.** *lit* [youth] jouvenceau *m*.

saponaceous [,sæpə'neɪʃəs] *adj* saponacé.

sapper ['sæpəʳ] *n Br* MIL soldat *m* du génie, sapeur *m*.

Sapphic ['sæfɪk] ◇ *adj* -**1.** [relating to Sappho] saphique. -**2.** LITERAT: ~ metre vers *m* saphique. -**3.** *dated* [lesbian] saphique.
◇ *n* LITERAT [verse, line] saphique *m*.

sapphire ['sæfaɪəʳ] ◇ *n* [gem, colour] saphir *m*.
◇ *adj* [in colour] saphir *(inv)*.
◇ *comp* [ring, pendant] de saphir.

sapphism ['sæfɪzm] *n* saphisme *m*.

Sappho ['sæfəʊ] *pr n* Sapho, Sappho.

sappy ['sæpɪ] (*compar* sappier, *superl* sappiest) *adj* -**1.** [tree, leaves] plein de sève; [wood] vert. -**2.** *inf Am* [stupid] cloche. -**3.** *inf Am* [corny] nunuche.

sapwood ['sæpwʊd] *n* aubier *m*.

saraband(e) ['særəbænd] *n* sarabande *f*.

Saracen ['særəsn] ◇ *n* Sarrasin *m*, -e *f*.
◇ *adj* sarrasin.

Saragossa [,særə'gɒsə] *pr n* Saragosse.

Sarah ['seərə] *pr n* Sarah, Sara.

Sarajevo [,særə'jeɪvəʊ] *pr n* Sarajevo.

Saratoga [,særə'təʊgə] *pr n* Saratoga; the battle of ~ la bataille de Saratoga.

THE BATTLE OF SARATOGA:
Bataille décisive, en 1777, de la guerre d'Indépendance américaine, à l'issue de laquelle les Anglais durent se rendre. Cette victoire décida la France à apporter son aide aux États-Unis.

Sarawak [sə'rɑːwək] *pr n* Sarawak; in ~ à Sarawak.

sarcasm ['sɑːkæzm] *n (U)* sarcasme *m*; enough of your ~! ça suffit, les sarcasmes!

sarcastic [sɑː'kæstɪk] *adj* sarcastique.

sarcastically [sɑː'kæstɪklɪ] *adv* d'un ton sarcastique.

sarcoma [sɑː'kəʊmə] (*pl* sarcomas OR sarcomata [-mətə]) *n* sarcome *m*.

sarcophagus [sɑː'kɒfəgəs] (*pl* sarcophaguses OR sarcophagi [-gaɪ]) *n* sarcophage *m*.

sardine [sɑː'diːn] *n* sardine *f*; we were packed OR crammed in like ~s nous étions serrés comme des sardines.

Sardinia [sɑː'dɪnjə] *pr n* Sardaigne *f*; in ~ en Sardaigne.

Sardinian [sɑː'dɪnjən] ◇ *n* -**1.** [person] Sarde *mf*. -**2.** LING sarde *m*.
◇ *adj* sarde.

sardonic [sɑː'dɒnɪk] *adj* sardonique.

sardonically [sɑː'dɒnɪklɪ] *adv* sardoniquement.

sargasso [sɑː'gæsəʊ] (*pl* sargassos) *n* sargasse *f*.

Sargasso Sea *pr n*: the ~ la mer des Sargasses.

sarge *inf* [sɑːdʒ] (*abbr of* sergeant) *n* sergent *m*.

sari ['sɑːrɪ] *n* sari *m*.

Sark [sɑːk] *pr n* Sercq.

sarky *inf* ['sɑːkɪ] (*compar* sarkier, *superl* sarkiest) *adj Br* sarcastique; don't you get ~ with me! ne sois pas sarcastique avec moi!

sarnie▽ ['sɑːnɪ] (*abbr of* sandwich) *n Br* sandwich *m*.

sarong [sə'rɒŋ] *n* sarong *m*.

sarsaparilla [,sɑːspə'rɪlə] *n* [plant] salsepareille *f*; [drink] boisson *f* à la salsepareille.

sartorial [sɑː'tɔːrɪəl] *adj* vestimentaire; his ~ elegance son élégance vestimentaire, l'élégance de sa mise.

Sartrean, Sartrian ['sɑːtrɪən] *adj* sartrien.

SAS (*abbr of* Special Air Service) *pr n commando d'intervention spéciale de l'armée britannique*.

SASE *n Am abbr of* self-addressed stamped envelope.

sash [sæʃ] *n* -**1.** [belt] ceinture *f* (en étoffe); [sign of office] écharpe *f*. -**2.** [frame of window, door] châssis *m*, cadre *m*.

sashay *inf* ['sæʃeɪ] *vi Am* [saunter] flâner; [strut] parader, se pavaner; he ~ed in and said hello [casually] il entra d'un pas nonchalant et dit bonjour; [ostentatiously] il entra en se pavanant et dit bonjour.

sash cord *n* corde *f (d'une fenêtre à guillotine)*.

sash window *n* fenêtre *f* à guillotine.

Saskatchewan [sæs'kætʃɪwən] *pr n* Saskatchewan *m*; in ~ dans le Saskatchwan.

sasquatch ['sæskwætʃ] *n animal légendaire (sorte de yéti) du Canada et du nord des États-Unis*.

sass *inf* [sæs] *Am* ◇ *n* culot *m*, toupet *m*.
◇ *vt* répondre (avec impertinence) à; don't you ~ me! ne me réponds pas sur ce ton!

sassafras ['sæsəfræs] *n* sassafras *m*; ~ oil essence *f* de sassafras.

Sassenach ['sæsənæk] *n Scot pej terme péjoratif par lequel les Écossais désignent les Anglais*.

sassy *inf* ['sæsɪ] (*compar* sassier, *superl* sassiest) *adj Am* culotté, gonflé.

sat [sæt] *pt* & *pp* → **sit**.

Sat. (*written abbr of* Saturday) sam.

SAT [sæt] (*abbr of* Scholastic Aptitude Test) *n examen d'entrée à l'université aux États-Unis*.

Satan ['seɪtn] *pr n* Satan.

satanic [sə'tænɪk] *adj* satanique; 'The Satanic Verses' *Rushdie* 'les Versets sataniques'.

satanically [sə'tænɪklɪ] *adv* sataniquement, d'une manière satanique.

satanism ['seɪtənɪzm] *n* satanisme *m*.

satanist ['seɪtənɪst] ◇ *adj* sataniste.
◇ *n* sataniste *mf*.

satchel ['sætʃəl] *n* cartable *m*.

sate [seɪt] *vt* [satisfy - person] rassasier; [- hunger] assouvir; [- thirst] étancher; to feel ~d se sentir rassasié OR repu.

sateen [sæ'tiːn] *n* satinette *f*.

satellite ['sætəlaɪt] ◇ *n* -**1.** ASTRON & TELEC satellite *m*; broadcast live by ~ transmis en direct par satellite; communications ~ satellite de télécommunications. -**2.** [country] pays *m* satellite; the country is a ~ of the United States c'est un pays satellite des États-Un[is]. -**3.** [in airport] satellite *m*.
◇ *comp* -**1.** [broadcast, broadcasting, netwo[rk], relay] par satellite; ~ dish antenne *f* de télé[vi]sion par satellite; ~ television télévision *f* p[ar] satellite; ten ~ channels dix chaînes (de té[lé]vision) par satellite. -**2.** [country] satellite; state état *m* satellite; ~ town ville *f* satellit[e].

satiate ['seɪʃɪeɪt] *vt lit* -**1.** [satisfy - hunger, desi[re]] assouvir; [- thirst] étancher. -**2.** [gorge] rassasie[r]; ~d with pleasure repu de plaisir.

satiation [,seɪʃɪ'eɪʃn] *n* satiété *f*; to the point ~ à satiété, jusqu'à satiété.

satiety [sə'taɪətɪ] = **satiation**.

satin ['sætɪn] ◇ *n* satin *m*.
◇ *comp* -**1.** [dress, shirt] en OR de satin. -**2.** [finis[h]] satiné.

satinet(te) [,sætɪ'net] *n* satinette *f*.

satin stitch *n* plumetis *m*.

satin weave *n* armure *f* satin.

satinwood ['sætɪnwʊd] *n* (bois *m* de) satin satiné *m*.

satire ['sætaɪəʳ] *n* satire *f*; it's a ~ on t[he] English c'est une satire contre les Anglais; h[is] novels are full of wit and ~ ses romans so[nt] pleins de traits d'esprit et d'observations sa[ti]riques.

satiric(al) [sə'tɪrɪk(l)] *adj* satirique.

satirically [sə'tɪrɪklɪ] *adv* satiriquement.

satirist ['sætərɪst] *n* satiriste *mf*.

satirize, ise ['sætəraɪz] *vt* faire la satire de; [in] her book, she ~s English manners son liv[re] est une satire OR fait la satire des mœu[rs] anglaises.

satisfaction [,sætɪs'fækʃn] *n* -**1.** [fulfilment - curiosity, hunger, demand, conditions] satisfa[c]tion *f*; [- of contract] exécution *f*, réalisation [- of debt] acquittement *m*, remboursement *m*; the ~ of the union's demands la satisfactio[n] des revendications syndicales. -**2.** [pleasure] s[a]tisfaction *f*, contentement *m*; to our (great) ~ they left early à notre (grande) satisfaction, i[ls] sont partis tôt; is everything to your ~? est-[ce] que tout est à votre convenance?; the plan w[as] agreed to everyone's ~ le projet fut accepté à satisfaction générale; to the ~ of the cou[rt] d'une manière qui a convaincu le tribunal; don't get much job ~ je ne tire pas beaucoup d[e] satisfaction de mon travail. -**3.** [pleasing thin[g]] satisfaction *f*; life's little ~s les petites satisfa[c]tions de la vie. -**4.** [redress - of a wrong] répar[a]tion *f*; [- of damage] dédommagement *m*; [- of a[n] insult] réparation *f*; to demand ~ [gen] exig[er] réparation; [in a duel] demander satisfaction.

satisfactorily [,sætɪs'fæktərəlɪ] *adv* de faço[n] satisfaisante; the trip went off most ~ voyage s'est déroulé de manière tout à fa[it] satisfaisante.

satisfactory [,sætɪs'fæktərɪ] *adj* satisfaisan[t]; we're looking for a solution ~ to both side[s] nous recherchons une solution satisfaisan[te] pour les deux parties; their progress is only ~ leurs progrès sont satisfaisants, sans plus; hope she has a ~ excuse j'espère qu'elle a un[e] excuse valable; the patient's condition is ~ l'état du malade n'est pas inquiétant.

satisfied ['sætɪsfaɪd] *adj* -**1.** [happy] satisfai[t], content; a ~ customer un client satisfait; a ~ sigh un soupir de satisfaction; the teacher isn['t] ~ with their work le professeur n'est pa[s] satisfait de leur travail; are you ~ now you'v[e] made her cry? tu es content de l'avoir fa[it] pleurer?; they'll have to be ~ with wha[t] they've got ils devront se contenter de ce qu'i[ls] ont. -**2.** [convinced] convaincu, persuadé; I'[m] not entirely ~ with the truth of his story je n[e] suis pas tout à fait convaincu que son histoi[re] soit vraie.

satisfy ['sætɪsfaɪ] (*pt* & *pp* satisfied) ◇ -**1.** [please] satisfaire, contenter; nothing sati[s]fies him il n'est jamais content; Richard Fo[x] has satisfied the examiners in the followin[g] subjects SCH Richard Fox a été reçu dans le[s] matières suivantes. -**2.** [fulfil - curiosity, desir[e]

hunger] satisfaire; [- thirst] étancher; [- demand, need, requirements] satisfaire à, répondre à; [- conditions, terms of contract] remplir; [- debt] s'acquitter de. -**3.** [prove to] persuader, convaincre; you have to ~ the authorities that you have been resident here for three years vous devez prouver aux autorités que vous résidez ici depuis trois ans; I satisfied myself that all the windows were closed je me suis assuré que toutes les fenêtres étaient fermées.
◇ *vi* donner satisfaction; the drink that satisfies la boisson qui étanche la soif.

satisfying ['sætɪsfaɪɪŋ] *adj* [job, outcome, evening] satisfaisant; [meal] substantiel.

satisfyingly ['sætɪsfaɪɪŋlɪ] *adv* de façon satisfaisante.

satrap ['sætrəp] *n* satrape *m*.

satsuma [ˌsæt'suːmə] *n Br* mandarine *f*.

saturate ['sætʃəreɪt] *vt* -**1.** *fig* [swamp] saturer; to ~ sb with sthg saturer qqn de qqch; the market is ~d le marché est saturé. -**2.** [drench] tremper; my clothes were ~d mes vêtements étaient complètement trempés. -**3.** CHEM saturer.

saturated ['sætʃəreɪtɪd] *adj* -**1.** CHEM saturé; ~ fats graisses *fpl* saturées; ~ solution solution *f* saturée. -**2.** [very wet] trempé.

saturation [ˌsætʃə'reɪʃn] *n* saturation *f*.

saturation bombing *n* bombardement *m* intensif.

saturation point *n* point *m* de saturation; we've reached ~ nous sommes arrivés à saturation; the market is at OR has reached ~ le marché est saturé.

Saturday ['sætədɪ] *n* samedi *m*; ~ night special▽ *Am* revolver *m* de poche; '~ Night Fever' *Badham* 'la Fièvre du samedi soir'.

Saturn ['sætən] *pr n* ASTRON & MYTH Saturne.

saturnalia [ˌsætə'neɪljə] *n* saturnales *fpl*.

saturnine ['sætənaɪn] *adj* saturnien.

satyr ['sætəʳ] *n* satyre *m*.

satyriasis [ˌsætə'raɪəsɪs] *n* satyriasis *m*.

sauce [sɔːs] *n* -**1.** CULIN sauce *f*; apple ~ compote *f* de pommes; tomato/mint ~ sauce tomate/à la menthe; what's ~ for the goose is ~ for the gander *prov* ce qui est bon pour l'un est bon pour l'autre. -**2.** *inf* [insolence] culot *m*, toupet *m*; what a ~! quel culot OR toupet!

sauce boat *n* saucière *f*.

saucebox *inf* ['sɔːsbɒks] *n* petit effronté *m*, petite effrontée *f*.

saucepan ['sɔːspən] *n* casserole *f*.

saucer ['sɔːsəʳ] *n* soucoupe *f*.

saucily *inf* ['sɔːsɪlɪ] *adv* -**1.** [cheekily] avec effronterie. -**2.** [provocatively] de manière provocante.

sauciness *inf* ['sɔːsɪnɪs] *n* -**1.** [cheekiness] effronterie *f*. -**2.** [provocativeness] provocation *f*, aspect *m* provocant.

saucy *inf* ['sɔːsɪ] (*compar* saucier, *superl* sauciest) *adj* -**1.** [cheeky] effronté. -**2.** [provocative - action] provocant; [- postcard, joke] grivois.

Saudi (Arabian) ['saʊdɪ-] ◇ *n* Saoudien *m*, -enne *f*.
◇ *adj* saoudien.

Saudi Arabia *pr n* Arabie Saoudite *f*; in ~ en Arabie Saoudite.

sauerkraut ['saʊəkraʊt] *n* choucroute *f*.

Saul [sɔːl] *pr n* Saül.

sauna ['sɔːnə] *n* sauna *m*.

saunter ['sɔːntəʳ] ◇ *vi* se promener d'un pas nonchalant, flâner; to ~ in/out/across entrer/sortir/traverser d'un pas nonchalant; to ~ down the street descendre la rue d'un pas nonchalant; I think I'll ~ down to the library je pense que je vais aller faire un petit tour jusqu'à la bibliothèque.
◇ *n* petite promenade *f*; to go for a ~ (aller) faire une petite balade OR un petit tour.

saurian ['sɔːrɪən] ◇ *adj* saurien.
◇ *n* saurien *m*.

sausage ['sɒsɪdʒ] *n* saucisse *f*; [of pre-cooked meats] saucisson *m*; she rolled her napkin into a ~ elle a fait un boudin de sa serviette ❑ garlic ~ saucisson *m* à l'ail; pork ~s saucisses *fpl* de porc; not a ~! *inf Br* que dalle!, des clous!

sausage dog *n Br hum* teckel *m*.

sausage machine *n* machine *f* à saucisses.

sausage meat *n* chair *f* à saucisse.

sausage roll *n sorte de friand à la saucisse*.

sauté [*Br* 'səʊteɪ, *Am* səʊ'teɪ] (*pt* & *pp* sautéed, *cont* sautéing) ◇ *vt* faire sauter; ~ the potatoes in a little butter faire sauter les pommes de terre dans un peu de beurre.
◇ *adj*: ~ potatoes pommes de terre sautées.
◇ *n* sauté *m*.

savage ['sævɪdʒ] ◇ *adj* -**1.** [ferocious - person] féroce, brutal; [- dog] méchant; [- fighting, tiger] féroce; [reply, attack] violent, féroce; he came in for some ~ criticism from the press il a été violemment critiqué dans la presse; the new policy deals a ~ blow to the country's farmers la nouvelle politique porte un coup très dur OR fatal aux agriculteurs. -**2.** [primitive - tribe] primitif; [- customs] barbare, primitif.
◇ *n* sauvage *mf*; they behaved like ~s ils se sont comportés comme des sauvages; they're little better than ~s ce sont de vrais sauvages.
◇ *vt* -**1.** [subj: animal] attaquer; she was ~d by a tiger elle a été attaquée par un tigre. -**2.** [subj: critics, press] attaquer violemment; the opposition leader ~d the government's latest proposals le chef de l'opposition a violemment attaqué les dernières propositions du gouvernement.

savagely ['sævɪdʒlɪ] *adv* sauvagement, brutalement.

savagery ['sævɪdʒrɪ] *n* -**1.** [brutality] sauvagerie *f*, férocité *f*, brutalité *f*; the ~ of the assault la brutalité de l'agression. -**2.** [primitive state]: the tribe still lives in ~ la tribu vit toujours à l'état sauvage.

savanna(h) [sə'vænə] *n* savane *f*.

save [seɪv] ◇ *vt* -**1.** [rescue] sauver; she ~d my life elle m'a sauvé la vie; to ~ sb from a fire/from drowning sauver qqn d'un incendie/de la noyade; the doctors managed to ~ her eyesight les médecins ont pu lui sauver la vue; he ~d me from making a terrible mistake il m'a empêché de faire une erreur monstrueuse; they had only the belongings they had ~d from the flood ils n'avaient que les affaires qu'ils avaient sauvées de l'inondation; nothing can ~ their marriage now rien ne peut plus sauver leur mariage; to ~ a species from extinction sauver une espèce en voie de disparition; ~d by the bell! sauvé par le gong! ❑ to ~ one's neck *inf* OR skin *inf* OR hide *inf* OR bacon *inf* sauver sa peau; I couldn't climb up there to ~ my life *inf* je serais bien incapable de grimper là-haut; he can't play baseball/sing to ~ his life *inf* il joue au baseball/chante comme un pied; to ~ face sauver la face; to ~ the day sauver la mise. -**2.** [put by - money] économiser, épargner, mettre de côté; I ~ £100 a month in a special account j'économise 100 livres par mois sur un compte spécial; how much money have you got ~d? à combien se montent vos économies?, combien d'argent avez-vous mis de côté?; I'm saving money to buy a car je fais des économies pour acheter une voiture || [collect] collectionner; do you still ~ stamps? est-ce que tu collectionnes toujours les timbres? -**3.** [economize on - fuel, electricity] économiser, faire des économies de; [- money] économiser; [- effort] économiser; [- time, space] gagner; [- strength] ménager, économiser; buy now and ~ £15! achetez dès maintenant et économisez 15 livres!; their advice ~d me a fortune leurs conseils m'ont fait économiser une fortune; you'd ~ a lot of time if you used a computer vous gagneriez beaucoup de temps si vous utilisiez un ordinateur; a computer would ~ you a lot of time un ordinateur vous ferait gagner beaucoup de temps. -**4.** [spare - trouble, effort] éviter, épargner; [- expense] éviter; it'll ~ you getting up early/going into town ça t'évitera de te lever tôt/d'aller en ville; thanks, you've ~d me a trip/having to go myself merci, vous m'avez évité un trajet/d'y aller moi-même. -**5.** [protect - eyes, shoes] ménager. -**6.** [reserve] garder, mettre de côté; I'll ~ you a place je te garderai une place; I always ~ the best part till last je garde toujours le meilleur pour la fin. -**7.** FTBL [shot, penalty] arrêter; to ~ a goal arrêter OR bloquer un tir. -**8.** RELIG [sinner, mankind] sauver, délivrer; [soul] sauver. -**9.** COMPUT sauvegarder.
◇ *vi* -**1.** [spend less] faire des économies, économiser; you ~ if you buy in bulk on fait des économies en achetant en gros; to ~ on fuel économiser sur le carburant. -**2.** [put money aside] faire des économies, épargner; I'm saving for a new car je fais des économies pour acheter une nouvelle voiture.
◇ *n* -**1.** FTBL arrêt *m*; great ~! superbe arrêt! -**2.** COMPUT sauvegarde *f*.
◇ *prep fml* sauf, hormis; we'd thought of every possibility ~ one nous avions pensé à tout sauf à ça.
◆ **save for** *prep phr* à part; ~ for the fact we lost, it was a great match à part le fait qu'on a perdu, c'était un très bon match; she was utterly alone, ~ for one good friend à part une seule amie, elle n'avait personne.
◆ **save up** ◇ *vt sep* = **save** *vt* **2**.
◇ *vi insep* = **save** *vi* **2**.

save as you earn *n Br* plan *m* d'épargne *(avec prélèvements automatiques sur le salaire)*.

saveloy ['sævəlɔɪ] *n* cervelas *m*.

saver ['seɪvəʳ] *n* -**1.** [person] épargnant *m*, -e *f*; small ~s les petits épargnants. -**2.** [product] bonne affaire *f*; super ~ (ticket) billet *m* à tarif réduit.

-saver *in cpds*: it's a real money~ ça permet d'économiser de l'argent OR de faire des économies.

Save the Children Fund *pr n organisme international d'assistance à l'enfance*.

Savile Row [ˌsævɪl'rəʊ] *pr n rue de Londres célèbre pour ses tailleurs de luxe*.

saving ['seɪvɪŋ] ◇ *n* -**1.** [thrift] épargne *f*; measures to encourage ~ des mesures pour encourager l'épargne. -**2.** [money saved] économie *f*; we made a ~ of £20 on the usual price nous avons fait une économie de 20 livres sur le prix habituel; he drew all his ~s out of the bank il a retiré toutes ses économies de la banque.
◇ *prep fml* sauf, hormis; ~ Your Grace *fml* sauf le respect que je dois à Votre Excellence.

-saving *in cpds*: energy~ qui économise de l'énergie; time~ qui fait gagner du temps.

saving grace *n bon côté qui rachète des défauts*; her sense of humour is her ~ elle rachète ses défauts OR elle se rachète par son sens de l'humour; the film has one ~ une seule chose sauve le film.

savings account *n* compte *m* sur livret.

savings and loan association *n Am* caisse *f* d'épargne logement.

savings bank *n* caisse *f* d'épargne.

savings bond *n Am* bon *m* d'épargne.

savings book *n Br* livret *m* (de caisse) d'épargne.

savings certificate *n Br* bon *m* d'épargne.

savings stamp *n Br* timbre-épargne *m*.

saviour *Br*, **savior** *Am* ['seɪvjəʳ] *n* sauveur *m*; the Saviour le Sauveur.

savoir-faire [ˌsævwɑː'feəʳ] *n* [know-how] savoir-faire *m*; [social skills] savoir-vivre *m*.

savor *etc Am* = **savour**.

savory ['seɪvərɪ] *n* BOT sarriette *f*.

savour *Br*, **savor** *Am* ['seɪvəʳ] ◇ *n* -**1.** [taste] goût *m*, saveur *f*; it has a ~ of garlic il y a un petit goût d'ail. -**2.** [interest, charm] saveur *f*; life had lost its ~ for him il avait perdu toute joie de vivre.
◇ *vt* [taste] goûter (à), déguster; [enjoy - food, experience, one's freedom] savourer; he ~ed the memory of his triumph il savourait le souvenir de son succès triomphal.

◇ *vi*: to ~ of sthg sentir qqch; it ~s of heresy cela sent l'hérésie.

savouriness *Br*, **savoriness** *Am* ['seɪvərɪnɪs] *n* saveur *f*.

savoury *Br*, **savory** *Am* ['seɪvərɪ] ◇ *adj* -**1.** [salty] salé; [spicy] épicé; ~ **biscuits** biscuits salés. -**2.** [appetizing] savoureux; a ~ **meal** un repas savoureux. -**3.** *fml* [wholesome]: **it's not a very ~ subject** c'est un sujet peu ragoûtant; **he's not a very ~ individual** c'est un individu peu recommandable.
◇ *n petit plat salé servi soit comme hors d'œuvre, soit en fin de repas après le dessert.*

Savoy [sə'vɔɪ] ◇ *pr n* Savoie *f*; **in ~** en Savoie.
◇ *adj* savoyard.

savoy cabbage *n* chou *m* frisé de Milan.

savvy *inf* ['sævɪ] ◇ *n* [know-how] savoir-faire *m*; [shrewdness] jugeote *f*, perspicacité *f*.
◇ *vi dated*: **no ~** j'sais pas.
◇ *adj Am* [well-informed] bien informé, calé; [shrewd] perspicace, astucieux.

saw [sɔː] (*Br pt* sawed, *pp* sawed OR sawn [sɔːn], *Am pt* & *pp* sawed) ◇ *pt* → **see**.
◇ *n* -**1.** [tool] scie *f*; **to cut sthg up with a ~** couper OR débiter qqch à la scie; **metal ~** scie à métaux. -**2.** [saying] dicton *m*.
◇ *vt*: **to ~ a tree into logs** débiter un arbre en rondins; **he ~ed the table in half** il a scié la table en deux; **his arms ~ed the air** *fig* il battait l'air de ses bras.
◇ *vi* scier; **she ~ed through the branch** elle a scié la branche; **he was ~ing away at the cello** *fig* il raclait le violoncelle.
◆ **saw down** *vt sep* [tree] abattre.
◆ **saw off** *vt sep* scier, enlever à la scie.
◆ **saw up** *vt sep* scier en morceaux, débiter à la scie.

sawbones *inf* ['sɔːbəʊnz] *n Am* chirurgien *m*.

sawbuck ['sɔːbʌk] *n Am* -**1.** = **sawhorse**. -**2.** *inf* [$10] (billet *m* de) dix dollars *mpl*.

sawdust ['sɔːdʌst] *n* sciure *f* (de bois).

sawed-off *Am* = **sawn-off**.

sawfly ['sɔːflaɪ] (*pl* sawflies) *n* mouche *f* à scie, tenthrède *f*.

sawhorse ['sɔːhɔːs] *n* chevalet *m* (pour scier du bois), chèvre *f*.

sawmill ['sɔːmɪl] *n* scierie *f*.

sawn [sɔːn] *pp* → **saw**.

sawn-off *adj* -**1.** [truncated] scié, coupé (à la scie); ~ **shotgun** carabine *f* à canon scié. -**2.** *inf Br* [short - person] court sur pattes.

sawtooth ['sɔːtuːθ] ◇ *n* dent *f* de scie.
◇ *adj* = **sawtoothed**.

sawtoothed ['sɔːtuːθt] *adj* en dents de scie.

sawyer ['sɔːjəʳ] *n* scieur *m*.

sax *inf* [sæks] (*abbr of* saxophone) *n* saxo *m*.

saxifrage ['sæksɪfrɪdʒ] *n* saxifrage *f*.

Saxon ['sæksn] ◇ *n* -**1.** [person] Saxon *m*, -onne *f*. -**2.** LING saxon *m*.
◇ *adj* saxon.

Saxony ['sæksənɪ] *pr n* Saxe *f*; **in ~** en Saxe; **Lower ~** Basse-Saxe *f*.

saxophone ['sæksəfəʊn] *n* saxophone *m*.

saxophonist [*Br* sæk'sɒfənɪst, *Am* 'sæksəfəʊnɪst] *n* saxophoniste *mf*.

say [seɪ] (*pt* & *pp* said [sed], *3rd pers pres sing* says [sez]) ◇ *vt* **A.** -**1.** [put into words] dire; **to ~ sthg (to sb)** dire qqch (à qqn); **to ~ hello/goodbye to sb** dire bonjour/au revoir à qqn; **~ hello to them for me** dites-leur bonjour de ma part; **I think you can ~ goodbye to your money** *fig* je crois que vous pouvez dire adieu à votre argent; **to ~ yes/no** dire oui/non; **did you ~ yes or no to his offer?** tu as répondu oui ou non à sa proposition?; **I wouldn't ~ no!** je ne dis pas non!, ce n'est pas de refus!; **I wouldn't ~ no to a cold drink** je prendrais volontiers une boisson fraîche; **to ~ please/thank you** dire s'il vous plaît/merci; **I said to myself "let's wait a bit"** je me suis dit «attendons un peu»; **to ~ a prayer (for)** dire une prière (pour); **to ~ one's prayers** faire sa prière; **I can't ~ Russian names properly** je n'arrive pas à bien prononcer les noms russes ‖ [expressing fact, idea, comment]: **to ~ sthg about sthg: what did he ~ about his plans?** qu'a-t-il dit de ses projets?; **don't ~ too much about our visit** ne parlez pas trop de notre visite; **what did you ~ in reply?** qu'avez-vous répondu?; **well, ~ something then!** eh bien, dites quelque chose!; **I can't think of anything to ~** je ne trouve rien à dire; **I have nothing to ~** [gen] je n'ai rien à dire; [no comment] je n'ai aucune déclaration à faire; **I have nothing more to ~ on the matter** je n'ai rien à ajouter là-dessus; **nothing was said about going to Moscow** on n'a pas parlé d'aller OR il n'a pas été question d'aller à Moscou; **let's ~ no more about it** n'en parlons plus; **can you ~ that again?** pouvez-vous répéter ce que vous venez de dire?; **~ what you think** dites ce que vous pensez; **~ what you mean** dites ce que vous avez à dire; **the chairman would like to ~ a few words** le président voudrait dire quelques mots; **he didn't have a good word to ~ about the plan** il n'a dit que du mal du projet; **he doesn't have a good word to ~ about anybody** il n'a jamais rien de positif à dire sur personne; **he didn't have much to ~ for himself** [spoke little] il n'avait pas grand-chose à dire; [no excuses] il n'avait pas de véritable excuse à donner; **he certainly has a lot to ~ for himself** il n'a pas la langue dans la poche; **as you might ~** pour ainsi dire; **so ~ing, he walked out** sur ces mots, il est parti; **to ~ nothing of the overheads** sans parler des frais; **just ~ the word, you only have to ~ (the word)** *Br* vous n'avez qu'un mot à dire ❑ **to ~ one's piece** dire ce qu'on a à dire; **it goes without ~ing that we shall travel together** il va sans dire OR il va de soi que nous voyagerons ensemble; **you can ~ that again!** c'est le cas de le dire!, je ne vous le fais pas dire!; **you said it!** *inf* tu l'as dit!; **~ no more** n'en dis pas plus; **enough said** [I understand] je vois; **well said!** bien dit!; **~ when** dis-moi stop. -**2.** [with direct or indirect speech] dire; **"not at all", she said** «pas du tout», dit-elle; **she ~s (that) the water's too cold** elle dit que l'eau est trop froide; **she said (we were) to come** elle a dit qu'on devait venir; **she said to get back early** elle a dit qu'on devait rentrer tôt; **they said on the news that...** on a dit OR annoncé aux informations que...; **they said it was going to rain** ils ont annoncé de la pluie. -**3.** [claim, allege] dire; **they ~ ghosts really do exist** ils disent que les fantômes existent vraiment; **you know what they ~, no smoke without fire** tu sais ce qu'on dit, il n'y a pas de fumée sans feu; **it is said that no one will ever know the real story** on dit que personne ne saura jamais ce qui s'est vraiment passé; **these fans are said to be very efficient** ces ventilateurs sont très efficaces, d'après ce qu'on dit; **he is said to have emigrated** on dit qu'il a émigré; **that's what she ~s** c'est ce qu'elle dit; **don't ~ you've forgotten!** ne (me) dites pas que vous avez oublié!; **who can ~?** qui sait?; **who can ~ when he'll come?** qui peut dire quand il viendra? -**4.** [expressing personal opinion] dire; **as you ~, he is the best candidate** comme tu dis, c'est lui le meilleur candidat; **so he ~s** c'est ce qu'il dit; **I really can't ~ which I prefer** je ne peux vraiment pas dire lequel je préfère; **(you can) ~ what you like, but I'm going** vous pouvez dire ce que vous voulez, moi je m'en vais; **I can't ~ how long it will last** je ne peux pas dire combien de temps cela va durer; **I must ~ she's been very helpful** je dois dire qu'elle nous a beaucoup aidés; **well this is a fine time to arrive, I must ~!** *iron* en voilà une heure pour arriver!; **I'll ~ this much for them, they don't give up easily** au moins, on peut dire qu'ils n'abandonnent pas facilement; **I'll ~ this for him, he certainly tries hard** je dois reconnaître qu'il fait tout son possible; **you might as well ~ we're all mad!** autant dire qu'on est tous fous!; **I should ~ so** bien sûr que oui, je pense bien; **as they ~** comme ils disent OR on dit; **and so ~ all of us** et nous sommes tous d'accord OR de cet avis ❑ **there's no ~ing what will happen** impossible de prédire ce qui va arriver; **to ~ the least** c'est le moins qu'on puisse dire; **it's rather dangerous, to ~ the least** c'est plutôt dangereux, c'est le moins qu'on puisse dire; **I was surprised, not to ~ astounded** j'étais surpris, pour ne pas dire stupéfait; **there's something to be said for the idea** l'idée a du bon; **there's not much to be said for the idea** l'idée ne vaut pas grand-chose; **there's a lot to be said for doing sport** il y a beaucoup d'avantages à faire du sport; **that's not ~ing much** ça ne veut pas dire grand-chose; **it doesn't ~ much for his powers of observation** cela en dit long sur son sens de l'observation; **that isn't ~ing much for him** ce n'est pas à son honneur; **it ~s a lot for his courage/about his real motives** cela en dit long sur son courage/ses intentions réelles.

B. -**1.** [think] dire, penser; **I ~ you should leave** je pense que vous devriez partir; **what do you ~ we drive over OR to driving over to see them?** que diriez-vous de prendre la voiture et d'aller les voir?; **what do you ~?** [do you agree?] qu'en dites-vous?; **what will people ~?** que vont dire les gens?; **what did they ~ to your offer?** qu'ont-ils dit de votre proposition?; **what would you ~ to a picnic?** que diriez-vous d'un pique-nique?, si on faisait un pique-nique?; **when would you ~ would be the best time for us to leave?** quel serait le meilleur moment pour partir, à votre avis?; **to look at them, you wouldn't ~ they were a day over forty** à les voir, on ne leur donnerait pas plus de quarante ans. -**2.** [suppose, assume]: **(let's) ~ your plan doesn't work, what then?** admettons que votre plan ne marche pas, qu'est-ce qui se passe?; **~ he doesn't arrive, who will take his place?** si jamais il n'arrive pas, qui prendra sa place?; **look at, ~, Jane Austen or George Eliot...** prends Jane Austen ou George Eliot, par exemple...; **come tomorrow, ~ after lunch** venez demain, disons OR mettons après le déjeuner; **shall we ~ Sunday?** disons dimanche, d'accord? -**3.** [indicate, register] indiquer, marquer; **the clock ~s 10.40** la pendule indique 10 h 40; **the sign ~s 50 km** le panneau indique 50 km; **the gauge ~s 3.4** la jauge indique OR marque 3,4; **it ~s "shake well"** c'est marqué «bien agiter»; **the instructions ~ (to) open it out of doors** dans le mode d'emploi, on dit qu'il faut l'ouvrir dehors. -**4.** [express - subj: intonation, eyes] exprimer, marquer; **his expression said everything** son expression était très éloquente OR en disait long; **that look ~s a lot** ce regard en dit long. -**5.** [mean]: **it's short, that's to ~, about 20 pages** c'est court, ça fait 20 pages; **that's not to ~ I don't like it** cela ne veut pas dire que je ne l'aime pas.
◇ *vi* [tell] dire; **he won't ~** il ne veut pas le dire; **I'd rather not ~** je préfère ne rien dire; **I can't ~ exactly** je ne sais pas au juste; **it's not for me to ~** [speak] ce n'est pas à moi de le dire [decide] ce n'est pas à moi de décider; **I can't ~ fairer than that** je ne peux pas mieux dire ❑ **so to ~** pour ainsi dire; **I ~!** [expressing surprise] eh bien!; [to attract attention] dites!; **you don't ~!** *inf* sans blague!, ça alors!
◇ *n*: **to have a ~ in sthg** avoir son mot à dire dans qqch; **I had no ~ in choosing the wallpaper** on ne m'a pas demandé mon avis pour le choix du papier peint; **we had little ~ in the matter** on ne nous a pas vraiment demandé notre avis; **to have one's ~** dire ce qu'on a à dire; **now you've had your ~, let me have mine** maintenant que vous avez dit ce que vous aviez à dire, laissez-moi parler.
◇ *interj Am* dites donc!; **~, aren't you June Naylor, the novelist?** dites donc, vous ne seriez pas June Naylor, la romancière?
◆ **when all's said and done** *adv phr* tout compte fait, au bout du compte.

SAYE *n abbr of* save as you earn.

saying ['seɪɪŋ] *n* dicton *m*, proverbe *m*; as the ~ goes [proverb] comme dit le proverbe; [people in general] comme on dit.

say-so *n Br* -**1.** [authorization]: I'm not going without her ~ je n'irai pas sans qu'elle m'y autorise OR sans son accord; he refused to do it without the boss's ~ il a refusé de le faire sans avoir l'aval du patron; you may open the box only on my ~ n'ouvrez OR vous ne pourrez ouvrir la boîte que lorsque je vous le dirai, n'ouvrez pas la boîte avant que je vous le dise. -**2.** [assertion]: I won't believe it just on his ~ ce n'est pas parce qu'il l'a dit que j'y crois.

SBA (*abbr of* Small Business Administration) *pr n organisme fédéral américain d'aide aux petites entreprises.*

SBS *n abbr of* sick building syndrome.

SC ◇ *n abbr of* supreme court.
◇ *written abbr of* South Carolina.

S/C *written abbr of* self contained.

scab [skæb] (*pt & pp* scabbed, *cont* scabbing) ◇ *n* -**1.** MED [from cut, blister] croûte *f*. -**2.** BOT & ZOOL gale *f*. -**3.** *inf pej* [strikebreaker] jaune *mf*. -**4.** *inf* [cad] crapule *f*, sale type *m*.
◇ *vi* -**1.** MED former une croûte. -**2.** *inf Br pej* briser une grève, refuser de faire grève.

scabbard ['skæbəd] *n* [for sword] fourreau *m*; [for dagger, knife] gaine *f*, étui *m*.

scabbard-fish *n* sabre *m*.

scabby ['skæbɪ] (*compar* scabbier, *superl* scabbiest) *adj* -**1.** MED [skin] croûteux, recouvert d'une croûte. -**2.** *inf pej* [mean - person] mesquin; [- attitude] moche.

scabies ['skeɪbiːz] *n* (*U*) gale *f*.

scabious ['skeɪbjəs] ◇ *adj* MED scabieux.
◇ *n* BOT scabieuse *f*.

scabrous ['skeɪbrəs] *adj lit* -**1.** [joke, story] scabreux, osé; [subject] scabreux, risqué. -**2.** [skin] rugueux, rêche.

scad [skæd] (*pl sense 1 inv* OR scads) *n* -**1.** [fish] carangue *f*, chinchard *m*. -**2.** *inf (usu pl)* [lots] tas *m*, floppée *f*; ~s of apples des tas de pommes.

scaffold ['skæfəʊld] *n* -**1.** CONSTR échafaudage *m*. -**2.** [for execution] échafaud *m*; to go to the ~ monter à l'échafaud.

scaffolder ['skæfəldə^r] *n* monteur *m* d'échafaudages.

scaffolding ['skæfəldɪŋ] *n* [framework] échafaudage *m*.

scag [skæg] *n drugs sl* héroïne *f*.

scalar ['skeɪlə^r] ◇ *adj* scalaire.
◇ *n* scalaire *m*.

scalawag ['skæləwæg] *n Am* = **scallywag**.

scald [skɔːld] ◇ *vt* -**1.** [hands, skin] ébouillanter; I ~ed myself with the milk je me suis ébouillanté avec le lait; the hot tea ~ed my tongue le thé bouillant m'a brûlé la langue. -**2.** CULIN [tomatoes] ébouillanter; [milk] porter presque à ébullition. -**3.** [sterilize] stériliser.
◇ *vi* brûler.
◇ *n* brûlure *f (causée par un liquide, de la vapeur)*; I got a nasty ~ je me suis bien ébouillanté.

scalding ['skɔːldɪŋ] ◇ *adj* -**1.** [water] bouillant; [metal, tea, soup, tears] brûlant. -**2.** [sun] brûlant; [heat] suffocant, torride; [weather] très chaud, torride. -**3.** [criticism] cinglant, acerbe.
◇ *adv*: ~ hot [coffee] brûlant; [weather] torride.

scale [skeɪl] ◇ *n* -**1.** [of model, drawing] échelle *f*; the sketch was drawn to ~ l'esquisse était à l'échelle; the map is on a ~ of 1 cm to 1 km l'échelle de la carte est de 1 cm pour 1 km; the ~ of the map is 1 to 50,000 la carte est au 50 millième; the drawing is out of ~ OR is not to ~ le croquis n'est pas à l'échelle. -**2.** [for measurement, evaluation] échelle *f*; [of salaries, taxes] échelle *f*, barème *m*; the social ~ l'échelle sociale; at the top of the ~ en haut de l'échelle; it all depends on your ~ of values tout dépend de votre échelle de valeurs || [graduation] échelle *f* (graduée), graduation *f*. -**3.** [extent] échelle *f*, étendue *f*; [size] importance *f*; the ~ of the devastation l'étendue des dégâts; the sheer ~ of the problem l'ampleur même du problème; we've started to produce fruit on a large ~ nous avons commencé à produire des fruits sur une grande échelle; on an industrial ~ à l'échelle industrielle. -**4.** MUS gamme *f*; to practise OR to do one's ~s faire ses gammes; the ~ of D major la gamme de ré majeur. -**5.** [of fish, reptile] écaille *f*; [of epidermis] squame *f*; the ~s fell from her eyes *fig* les écailles lui sont tombées des yeux. -**6.** [in kettle, pipes] tartre *m*, (dépôt *m*) calcaire *m*; [on teeth] tartre *m*. -**7.** [of paint, plaster, rust] écaille *f*, écaillure *f*. -**8.** [scale pan] plateau *m* (de balance). -**9.** *Am* [for weighing] pèse-personne *m*, balance *f*.
◇ *vt* -**1.** [climb over - wall, fence] escalader. -**2.** [drawing] dessiner à l'échelle. -**3.** [test] graduer, pondérer. -**4.** [fish, paint] écailler; [teeth, pipes] détartrer.
◇ *vi* [paint, rust] s'écailler; [skin] peler.
◆ **scales** *npl* [for food] balance *f*; [for letters] pèse-lettre *m*; [for babies] pèse-bébé *m*; [public] bascule *f*; (a pair of) kitchen ~s une balance de cuisine; (a pair of) bathroom ~s un pèse-personne.
◆ **scale down** *vt sep* -**1.** [drawing] réduire l'échelle de. -**2.** [figures, demands] réduire, baisser, diminuer; production is being ~d down on a entrepris de réduire la production.
◆ **scale off** ◇ *vi insep* [paint, rust] s'écailler.
◇ *vt sep* écailler.
◆ **scale up** *vt sep* -**1.** [drawing] augmenter l'échelle de. -**2.** [figures, demands] réviser à la hausse, augmenter; allowances were ~d up by 10% les allocations ont été augmentées de 10 %.

scaled [skeɪld] *adj* [pipe, kettle, tooth] entartré.

scale drawing *n* dessin *m* à l'échelle.

scale model *n* [of car, plane] modèle *m* réduit; [of buildings, town centre] maquette *f*.

scalene ['skeɪliːn] *adj* scalène.

scalepan ['skeɪlpæn] *n* plateau *m* de balance.

scallion ['skæljən] *n Am* CULIN [spring onion] oignon *m* blanc; [leek] poireau *m*; [shallot] échalote *f*.

scallop ['skɒləp] ◇ *vt* -**1.** CULIN [fish, vegetable] gratiner; ~ed potatoes gratin *m* de pommes de terre. -**2.** SEW [edge, hem] festonner.
◇ *n* CULIN & ZOOL coquille Saint-Jacques *f*.
◆ **scallops** *npl* SEW festons *mpl*.

scalloped ['skɒləpt] *adj* -**1.** CULIN: ~ potatoes gratin *m* de pommes de terre. -**2.** SEW [edge, hem] festonné.

scallywag ['skælɪwæg] *n* -**1.** *inf* [rascal] voyou *m*, coquin *m*. -**2.** *Am* HIST *sudiste favorable à l'émancipation des Noirs (et par conséquent considéré comme un traître par les siens)*.

scalp [skælp] ◇ *n* -**1.** [top of head] cuir *m* chevelu. -**2.** [Indian trophy] scalp *m*. -**3.** *fig* [trophy] trophée *m*; HUNT trophée *m* de chasse. -**4.** *inf Am* [profit] petit profit *m*.
◇ *vt* -**1.** [person, animal] scalper. -**2.** *inf* [tickets] vendre en réalisant un bénéfice substantiel; to ~ shares OR securities *Am* boursicoter. -**3.** *inf* [cheat] arnaquer; to get ~ed se faire avoir OR arnaquer.

scalpel ['skælpəl] *n* scalpel *m*.

scalper ['skælpər] *n Am* revendeur *m*, -euse *f* de tickets à la sauvette *(pour un concert, un match etc)*.

scaly ['skeɪlɪ] (*compar* scalier, *superl* scaliest) *adj* [creature] écailleux; [paint] écaillé; [skin] squameux; [pipe] entartré.

scam[▽] [skæm] *n* escroquerie *f*, arnaque *f*.

scamp *inf* [skæmp] ◇ *n* [child] garnement *m*, coquin *m*, -e *f*; [rogue] voyou *m*.
◇ *vt* [work] bâcler.

scamper ['skæmpə^r] ◇ *vi* -**1.** [small animal] trottiner; we could hear mice ~ing around in the attic on entendait des souris trottiner OR qui trottinaient dans le grenier || [children] gambader, galoper; the kids ~ed into the house/up the stairs les gosses sont entrés dans la maison/ont monté l'escalier en courant. -**2.** *inf* [work quickly]: I positively ~ed through the book j'ai lu le livre à toute vitesse.
◇ *n* trottinement *m*.
◆ **scamper about** *vi insep* [animal] courir OR trottiner çà et là; [children] gambader.
◆ **scamper away, scamper off** *vi insep* détaler, se sauver.

scampi ['skæmpɪ] *n (U)* scampi *mpl*.

scan [skæn] (*pt & pp* scanned, *cont* scanning) ◇ *vt* -**1.** [look carefully at] scruter, fouiller du regard; [read carefully] lire attentivement; we scanned the horizon nous avons scruté l'horizon; the troops scanned the sky for enemy planes les soldats scrutaient OR observaient le ciel à la recherche d'avions ennemis; I scanned her face for some reaction j'ai scruté son visage pour y déceler quelque réaction. -**2.** [consult quickly - report, notes] lire en diagonale, parcourir rapidement; [- magazine] feuilleter; [- screen, image] balayer; [- tape, memory] lire; he ~s the local papers for bargains il parcourt le journal local à la recherche de bonnes affaires. -**3.** PHYS [spectrum] balayer, parcourir; [subj: radar, searchlight] balayer. -**4.** MED examiner au scanner, faire une scanographie de. -**5.** ELECTRON & TV balayer. -**6.** LITERAT scander.
◇ *vi* LITERAT se scander; this line doesn't ~ ce vers est faux.
◇ *n* -**1.** MED scanographie *f*, examen *m* au scanner. -**2.** LITERAT scansion *f*. -**3.** ELECTRON & TV balayage *m*.

scandal ['skændl] *n* -**1.** [disgrace] scandale *m*; the whole business is an absolute ~! toute cette affaire est absolument scandaleuse OR est un véritable scandale!; it would cause a dreadful ~ if the newspapers found out cela provoquerait un horrible scandale si les journaux en entendaient parler; it's a ~ that people like them should be let free c'est scandaleux de laisser des gens pareils en liberté; it's a national ~ c'est une honte nationale OR un scandale public. -**2.** *(U)* [gossip] ragots *mpl*; [evil] médisance *f*, médisances *fpl*, calomnie *f*; to spread ~ about sb répandre des ragots sur le compte de qqn; this newspaper specializes in ~ c'est un journal à scandale; the latest society ~ les derniers potins mondains; a juicy bit of ~ des ragots savoureux OR croustillants.

scandalize, -ise ['skændəlaɪz] *vt* scandaliser, choquer; he was ~d by what she said il a été scandalisé par ses propos; she's easily ~d elle se scandalise OR s'indigne vite.

scandalmonger ['skændl,mʌŋgə^r] *n* mauvaise langue *f*, colporteur *m*, -euse *f* de ragots.

scandalmongering ['skændl,mʌŋgərɪŋ] *n (U)* commérage *m*, médisance *f*.

scandalous ['skændələs] *adj* -**1.** [conduct] scandaleux, choquant; [news, price] scandaleux; it's absolutely ~ that they should expect you to work late! vous forcer à travailler tard, c'est un véritable scandale! -**2.** [gossip] calomnieux.

scandalously ['skændələslɪ] *adv* -**1.** [act] scandaleusement. -**2.** [speak, write] de manière diffamatoire; she gave a ~ explicit account of their affair elle a raconté leur liaison en termes si explicites que c'en était choquant.

Scandinavia [,skændɪ'neɪvjə] *pr n* Scandinavie *f*; in ~ en Scandinavie.

Scandinavian [,skændɪ'neɪvjən] ◇ *n* -**1.** [person] Scandinave *mf*. -**2.** LING scandinave *m*.
◇ *adj* scandinave.

scandium ['skændɪəm] *n* scandium *m*.

scanner ['skænə^r] *n* -**1.** MED & ELECTRON scanner *m*. -**2.** [for radar] antenne *f*. -**3.** COMPUT: (optical) ~ scanner *m*.

scanning electron microscope ['skænɪŋ-] *n* microscope *m* électronique à balayage.

scansion ['skænʃn] *n* LITERAT scansion *f*.

scant [skænt] ◇ *adj* maigre; to pay ~ attention to sb/sthg ne prêter que peu d'attention à qqn/qqch; she received ~ praise elle n'a reçu que de maigres louanges; they showed ~ regard for our feelings ils ne se sont pas beaucoup souciés OR ils se sont peu souciés de ce que nous pouvions ressentir; a ~ teaspoonful une cuillerée à café rase.

◇ *vt* -**1.** [skimp on] lésiner sur; [restrict] restreindre. -**2.** [treat superficially] traiter de manière superficielle.

scantily ['skæntɪlɪ] *adv* [furnished] pauvrement, chichement; [dressed] légèrement; ~ **clad bathing beauties** de belles baigneuses légèrement vêtues.

scantiness ['skæntɪnɪs] *n* [of meal] frugalité *f*; [of crops] maigreur *f*; [of knowledge] insuffisance *f*; [of dress] légèreté *f*.

scanty ['skæntɪ] (*compar* scantier, *superl* scantiest) *adj* -**1.** [small in number, quantity - meal, crops] maigre, peu abondant; [- income, payment] maigre, modeste; [- information, knowledge] maigre, limité; [- applause] maigre, peu fourni; [- audience] clairsemé; [- praise, aid] limité. -**2.** [brief - clothing] léger; **she was wearing only a ~ negligee** elle ne portait qu'un négligé qui ne cachait pas grand-chose *hum*.

scapegoat ['skeɪpgəʊt] *n* bouc *m* émissaire.

scapegrace ['skeɪpgreɪs] *n Br* voyou *m*, vaurien *m*.

scapolite ['skæpə,laɪt] *n* scapolite *f*, wernérite *f*.

scapula ['skæpjʊlə] (*pl* scapulas OR scapulae [-liː]) *n* omoplate *f*.

scapular ['skæpjʊlə^r] ◇ *adj* scapulaire.
◇ *n* scapulaire *m*.

scar [skɑː^r] (*pt* & *pp* scarred, *cont* scarring) ◇ *n* -**1.** [from wound, surgery] cicatrice *f*; [from deep cut on face] balafre *f*. -**2.** *fig* [on land, painted surface, tree] cicatrice *f*, marque *f*; [emotional] cicatrice *f*; **the ~s of battle** les traces de la bataille; **the mine was like an ugly ~ on the landscape** la mine déparait terriblement le paysage. -**3.** [rock] rocher *m* escarpé; [in river] écueil *m*.
◇ *vt* -**1.** [skin, face] laisser une cicatrice sur; **his hands were badly scarred** il avait sur les mains de profondes cicatrices; **smallpox had scarred his face** il avait le visage grêlé par la variole. -**2.** *fig* [surface] marquer; **the paintwork was badly scarred** la peinture était tout éraflée; **bullet holes scarred the walls** les murs portaient des traces de balles ‖ [emotionally] marquer; **she was permanently scarred by the experience** cette expérience l'avait marquée pour la vie.
◇ *vi* [form scar] se cicatriser; [leave scar] laisser une cicatrice.
◆ **scar over** *vi insep* [form scar] former une cicatrice; [close up] se cicatriser.

scarab ['skærəb] *n* scarabée *m*.

Scaramouche [,skærə'muːʃ] *pr n* Scaramouche.

scarce ['skeəs] ◇ *adj* [rare] rare; [infrequent] peu fréquent; [in short supply] peu abondant; **sugar is ~ at the moment** il y a une pénurie de sucre en ce moment; **to become ~** se faire rare; **water is becoming ~** l'eau commence à manquer; **rain is ~ in this region** il ne pleut pas souvent dans cette région ❑ **to make o.s. ~** *inf* [run away] se sauver, décamper; [get out] débarrasser le plancher; **can you make yourself ~ for half an hour?** peux-tu disparaître pendant une demi-heure?
◇ *adv lit* à peine; **I could ~ believe my eyes** j'en croyais à peine mes yeux.

scarcely ['skeəslɪ] *adv* -**1.** [no sooner] à peine; **we had ~ begun** OR **~ had we begun when the bell rang** nous avions tout juste commencé quand OR à peine avions-nous commencé que la cloche a sonné. -**2.** [barely]: **he ~ spoke to me** c'est tout juste s'il m'a adressé la parole; **we ~ saw her** nous l'avons à peine vue; **she's ~ more than a child** elle n'est encore qu'une enfant; **~ any** presque pas de; **~ anybody** presque personne; **~ anything** presque rien; **I know ~ any of those people** je ne connais pratiquement personne parmi ces gens OR pratiquement aucune de ces personnes; **he has ~ any hair left** il n'a presque plus de cheveux; **they were ~ ever together** ils n'étaient presque jamais ensemble. -**3.** [indicating difficulty] à peine, tout juste; **I could ~ tell his mother, now could I!** je ne pouvais quand même pas le dire à sa mère, non?; **I ~ know where to begin** je ne sais pas trop par où commencer; **I can ~ wait** je bous d'impatience; **I can ~ wait to meet her** j'ai hâte de la rencontrer; **I can ~ believe what you're saying** j'ai du mal à croire ce que vous dites.

scarceness ['skeəsnɪs] = **scarcity**.

scarcity ['skeəsətɪ] (*pl* scarcities) *n* [rarity] rareté *f*; [lack] manque *m*; [shortage] manque *m*, pénurie *f*; **there is a ~ of new talent today** les nouveaux talents se font rares; **the ~ of food** le manque de vivres, la disette.

scarcity value *n* valeur *f* de rareté; **the book has a high ~** ce livre vaut cher parce qu'il est pratiquement introuvable OR parce qu'il n'en existe que très peu d'exemplaires.

scare [skeə^r] ◇ *vt* effrayer, faire peur à; **thunder really ~s me** le tonnerre me fait vraiment très peur; **you'll ~ her** vous allez lui faire peur OR l'effrayer ❑ **the film ~d me stiff!** *inf* le film m'a flanqué une de ces frousses!; **to ~ the wits** OR **the living daylights** OR **the life out of sb** *inf* flanquer une peur bleue OR une trouille pas possible à qqn; **he ~d the shit**▼ OR **the hell** *inf* **out of me** il m'a foutu les jetons.
◇ *vi* s'effrayer, prendre peur; **he ~s easily** il a peur de tout, un rien l'effraie; **I don't ~ easily** je ne suis pas peureux.
◇ *n* -**1.** [fright] peur *f*, frayeur *f*; **to give sb a ~** effrayer qqn, faire peur à qqn. -**2.** [alert] alerte *f*; [rumour] bruit *m* alarmiste, rumeur *f*; **there was another war ~ last year** l'an dernier on a craint une autre guerre; **a takeover ~** des rumeurs concernant une possible OPA; **a bomb/fire ~** une alerte à la bombe/au feu.
◇ *comp* [sensational - headlines] alarmiste; [frightening - story] effrayant, qui fait peur.
◆ **scare away, scare off** *vt sep* [bird, customer] faire fuir.
◆ **scare up** *inf vt sep Am* dénicher.

scarecrow ['skeəkrəʊ] *n* [for birds] épouvantail *m*; *fig* [person - thin] squelette *m*; [- badly dressed] épouvantail *m*.

scared ['skeəd] *adj* [frightened] effrayé; [nervous] craintif, peureux; **to be ~ (of sthg)** avoir peur (de qqch); **he was ~ to ask** il avait peur de demander; **he's ~ of being told off/that she might tell him off** il craint de se faire gronder/qu'elle ne le gronde; **to be ~ stiff** OR **to death** avoir une peur bleue; **I was ~ out of my wits!** j'étais mort de peur!; **to run like a ~ rabbit** courir comme un dératé.

scaredy cat *inf* ['skeədɪ-] *n* froussard *m*, -e *f*.

scaremonger ['skeə,mʌŋgə^r] *n* alarmiste *mf*.

scaremongering ['skeə,mʌŋgrɪŋ] *n* alarmisme *m*.

scarf [skɑːf] (*pl sense 1* scarfs OR scarves [skɑːvz], *pl senses 2 & 3* scarfs) ◇ *n* -**1.** [long] écharpe *f*; [headscarf, cravat] foulard *m*. -**2.** ~ (join) enture *f*, assemblage *m* à mi-bois. -**3.** CONSTR [cut] entaille *f*.
◇ *vt* CONSTR -**1.** [join] joindre par enture. -**2.** [cut] entailler.

Scarface ['skɑːfeɪs] *pr n* le Balafré.

scarify ['skeərɪfaɪ] (*pt* & *pp* scarified) *vt* -**1.** AGR & MED scarifier. -**2.** *inf* [frighten] donner la frousse à.

scarlatina [,skɑːlə'tiːnə] *n* (*U*) MED scarlatine *f*.

scarlet ['skɑːlət] ◇ *adj* [gen] écarlate; [face - from illness, effort] cramoisi; [- from shame] écarlate, cramoisi.
◇ *n* écarlate *f*.

scarlet fever *n* (*U*) scarlatine *f*.

scarlet pimpernel *n* BOT mouron *m* rouge; 'The Scarlet Pimpernel' *Orczy* 'le Mouron rouge'.

scarlet runner *n Br* haricot *m* (à rames).

scarlet woman *n Br hum* femme *f* de mauvaise vie.

scarp [skɑːp] *n* escarpement *m*.

scarped [skɑːpt] *adj* escarpé, abrupt.

scarper *inf* ['skɑːpə^r] *vi Br* déguerpir, se barrer; ~! fichez le camp!

scar tissue *n* tissu *m* cicatriciel.

scarves [skɑːvz] *pl* → **scarf 1**.

scary *inf* ['skeərɪ] (*compar* scarier, *superl* scariest) *adj* -**1.** [frightening - place, person] effrayant; [- story] qui donne le frisson. -**2.** [fearful] peureux.

scat [skæt] (*pt* & *pp* scatted, *cont* scatting) ◇ *vi inf* [go away] se sauver, ficher le camp; ~! allez, ouste!
◇ *n* MUS scat *m*.

scathing ['skeɪðɪŋ] *adj* [criticism, remark] caustique, cinglant; **to give sb a ~ look** foudroyer qqn du regard; **he can be very ~** il sait se montrer acerbe OR cinglant.

scathingly ['skeɪðɪŋlɪ] *adv* [retort, criticize] de manière cinglante; **she refers to him ~ as "the toad"** elle l'appelle méchamment «le crapaud».

scatological [,skætə'lɒdʒɪkl] *adj* scatologique.

scatology [skæ'tɒlədʒɪ] *n* scatologie *f*.

scatter ['skætə^r] ◇ *vt* -**1.** [strew] éparpiller, disperser; **don't ~ your toys all over the room** n'éparpille pas tes jouets partout dans la pièce; **papers had been ~ed all over the desk** le bureau était jonché OR couvert de papiers. -**2.** [spread] répandre; [sprinkle] saupoudrer; **she ~ed crumbs for the birds** elle a jeté des miettes de pain aux oiseaux; **we ~ed the floor with sawdust** nous avons répandu de la sciure sur le sol; **to ~ seeds** semer des graines à la volée. -**3.** [disperse - crowd, mob] disperser; [- enemy] mettre en fuite; [- clouds] dissiper, disperser; **my friends are ~ed all over the world** mes amis sont dispersés aux quatre vents OR un peu partout dans le monde. -**4.** PHYS [light] disperser.
◇ *vi* -**1.** [people, clouds] se disperser; **they told us to ~** ils nous ont dit de partir. -**2.** [beads, papers] s'éparpiller.
◇ *n* -**1.** [of rice, bullets] pluie *f*; **a ~ of farms on the hillside** quelques fermes éparpillées à flanc de coteau. -**2.** [in statistics] dispersion *f*.
◆ **scatter about, scatter around** *vt sep* éparpiller.

scatter bomb *n* obus *m* à mitraille, shrapnel *m*, shrapnell *m*.

scatterbrain ['skætəbreɪn] *n* tête *f* de linotte, étourdi *m*, -e *f*.

scatterbrained ['skætəbreɪnd] *adj* écervelé, étourdi.

scatter cushion *n* petit coussin *m*.

scattered ['skætəd] *adj* -**1.** [strewn] éparpillé; **papers/toys lying ~ all over the floor** des papiers/des jouets éparpillés par terre; **the table was ~ with empty cups** il y avait des tasses vides éparpillées sur la table. -**2.** [sprinkled] parsemé; **the tablecloth was ~ with crumbs** la nappe était parsemée de miettes. -**3.** [dispersed population] dispersé, disséminé; [- clouds] épars; [- villages, houses] épars; [- light] diffus; **his ~ fortune** sa fortune dissipée; **she tried to collect her ~ thoughts** elle essaya de mettre de l'ordre dans ses idées; **~ showers** averses *fpl* intermittentes.

scatter-gun *n* fusil *m* de chasse.

scattering ['skætərɪŋ] *n* -**1.** [small number]: **a ~ of followers** une poignée d'adeptes; **there was a ~ of farms** il y avait quelques fermes çà et là. -**2.** [dispersion] dispersion *f*.

scatter rug *n* petit tapis *m*, carpette *f*.

scattiness *inf* ['skætɪnɪs] *n* [forgetfulness] étourderie *f*; [silliness] sottise *f*.

scatty *inf* ['skætɪ] (*compar* scattier, *superl* scattiest) *adj* [forgetful] étourdi, écervelé; [silly] bêta.

scavenge ['skævɪndʒ] ◇ *vi* -**1.** [bird, animal]: **to ~ (for food)** chercher sa nourriture. -**2.** [person]: **if you haven't got any tools, you'll have to ~** si vous n'avez pas d'outils, il va falloir en récupérer à droite et à gauche; **he was scavenging among the dustbins** il fouillait dans OR faisait les poubelles.
◇ *vt* -**1.** [material, metals] récupérer; **he managed to ~ a meal** il a finalement trouvé quelque chose à se mettre sous la dent. -**2.** [streets] nettoyer.

scavenger ['skævɪndʒə^r] *n* -**1.** ZOOL charognard *m*. -**2.** [salvager] ramasseur *m* d'épaves.

[in rubbish] pilleur *m* de poubelles. -**3.** *Br* [street cleaner] éboueur *m*.

cavenger hunt *n* ≃ chasse *f* au trésor.

CE (*abbr of* Scottish Certificate of Education) *n certificat de fin d'études secondaires en Écosse*.

cenario [sɪˈnɑːrɪəʊ] (*pl* scenarios) *n* scénario *m*.

cenarist [*Br* ˈsiːnərɪst, *Am* sɪˈnɑːrɪst] *n* scénariste *mf*.

cene [siːn] *n* -**1.** [sphere of activity, milieu] scène *f*, situation *f*; the world political ~ la scène politique internationale; she's a newcomer on OR to the sports ~ c'est une nouvelle venue sur la scène sportive OR dans le monde du sport; the drug ~ le monde de la drogue; she came on the ~ just when we needed her elle est arrivée juste au moment où nous avions besoin d'elle; he disappeared from the ~ for a few years il a disparu de la circulation OR de la scène pendant quelques années. -**2.** CIN & THEAT [in film] scène *f*, séquence *f*; [in play] scène *f*; the murder/love ~ la scène du meurtre/d'amour; Act IV – 2 Acte IV scène 2; to set the ~ planter le décor; the ~ is set OR takes place in Bombay la scène se passe OR l'action se déroule à Bombay; the ~ was set for the arms negotiations *fig* tout était prêt pour les négociations sur les armements. -**3.** [place, spot] lieu *m*, lieux *mpl*, endroit *m*; the ~ of the disaster l'endroit où s'est produit la catastrophe; the ~ of the crime le lieu du crime; the police were soon on the ~ la police est rapidement arrivée sur les lieux OR sur place; I was first on the ~ j'étais le premier présent OR le premier sur les lieux; to arrive on the ~ arriver sur place; ~ of operations MIL théâtre *m* des opérations. -**4.** [image] scène *f*, spectacle *m*; [incident] scène *f*, incident *m*; ~s of horror/violence scènes d'horreur/de violence; ~s from OR of village life scènes de la vie villageoise; just picture the ~ essayez de vous représenter la scène; there were some nasty ~s at the match il y a eu des incidents violents lors du match; a ~ of married bliss une scène de bonheur conjugal || [view] spectacle *m*, perspective *f*, vue *f*; a ~ of calm beauty lay before us nous avions devant nous un paysage d'une beauté paisible; a change of ~ will do you good un changement d'air OR de décor vous fera du bien || ART tableau *m*, scène *f*; city/country ~s scènes de ville/champêtres. -**5.** [fuss, row] scène *f*; to make a ~ faire une scène; to have a ~ with sb se disputer avec qqn; he made an awful ~ about it il en a fait toute une histoire. -**6.** *inf* [favourite activity]: jazz isn't really my ~ le jazz, ça n'est pas vraiment mon truc.

scene change *n* changement *m* de décors.

scene designer *n* décorateur *m*, -trice *f* de théâtre.

scene dock *n* case *f* à décor OR décors.

scenery [ˈsiːnərɪ] *n* -**1.** [natural setting] paysage *m*; mountain ~ paysage de montagne; I was admiring the ~ j'admirais le paysage; the ~ round here is lovely les paysages sont très beaux par ici; we drove through picturesque ~ nous avons traversé des paysages très pittoresques; she needs a change of ~ *fig* elle a besoin de changer de décor OR d'air. -**2.** THEAT décor *m*, décors *mpl*.

sceneshifter [ˈsiːnˌʃɪftəʳ] *n* machiniste *m* THÉÂT.

scenic [ˈsiːnɪk] *adj* -**1.** [of surroundings] pittoresque; let's take the ~ route prenons la route touristique. -**2.** ART & THEAT scénique.

scenic railway *n* -**1.** [for tourists] petit train *m* (touristique). -**2.** [in fairground] montagnes *fpl* russes.

scent [sent] ◇ *n* -**1.** [smell] parfum *m*, odeur *f*; the ~ of new-mown hay l'odeur du foin fraîchement fauché; the ~ of polished wood le parfum OR l'odeur de bois ciré. -**2.** HUNT [track -of animal] fumet *m*; [- of person] odeur *f*; [track] trace *f*, piste *f*; the hounds are on the ~ OR have picked up the ~ of a fox les chiens sont sur la trace d'un renard OR ont dépisté un renard; they've lost the ~ ils ont perdu la piste; to put OR to throw sb off the ~ semer qqn; we're on the ~ of a major scandal nous flairons un gros scandale. -**3.** *Br* [perfume] parfum *m*.

◇ *vt* -**1.** [smell - prey] flairer; [detect - danger, treachery] flairer, subodorer. -**2.** [perfume] parfumer; ~ed notepaper papier *m* à lettres parfumé.

scentless [ˈsentlɪs] *adj* -**1.** [odourless - substance] inodore; [- flower] sans parfum. -**2.** [unable to smell] sans odorat.

scepter *Am* = **sceptre**.

sceptic *Br*, **skeptic** *Am* [ˈskeptɪk] ◇ *adj* sceptique.

◇ *n* sceptique *mf*.

sceptical *Br*, **skeptical** *Am* [ˈskeptɪkl] *adj* sceptique.

sceptically *Br*, **skeptically** *Am* [ˈskeptɪklɪ] *adv* avec scepticisme.

scepticism *Br*, **skepticism** *Am* [ˈskeptɪsɪzm] *n* scepticisme *m*.

sceptre *Br*, **scepter** *Am* [ˈseptəʳ] *n* sceptre *m*.

SCF *pr n abbr of* Save the Children Fund.

schedule [*Br* ˈʃedjuːl, *Am* ˈskedʒʊl] ◇ *n* -**1.** [programme] programme *m*; [calendar] programme *m*, calendrier *m*; [timetable] programme *m*, emploi *m* du temps; [plan] prévisions *fpl*, plan *m*; I have a busy ~ [for visit] j'ai un programme chargé; [in general] j'ai un emploi du temps chargé; [over period] j'ai un calendrier chargé; everything went according to ~ tout s'est déroulé comme prévu; the work was carried out according to ~ le travail a été effectué selon les prévisions; we are on ~ OR up to ~ nous sommes dans les temps; our work is ahead of/behind ~ nous sommes en avance/en retard dans notre travail; the bridge was opened on/ahead of ~ le pont a été ouvert à la date prévue/en avance sur la date prévue; the doors opened on ~ les portes se sont ouvertes à l'heure prévue; a ~ was agreed for the work on s'est mis d'accord sur un programme de travail OR un planning pour le travail; to fall behind ~ prendre du retard sur les prévisions de travail. -**2.** [timetable - for transport] horaire *m*; the train is on ~ le train est à l'heure; the trains were running behind ~ les trains avaient du retard. -**3.** [list - of prices] barème *m*; [- of contents] inventaire *m*; [- of payments] échéancier *m*; [for taxes] rôle *m*; ~ of charges tarifs *mpl*. -**4.** JUR [annexe] annexe *f*, avenant *m*.

◇ *vt* -**1.** [plan - event] fixer la date OR l'heure de; [- appointment] fixer; the meeting was ~d for 3 o'clock/Wednesday la réunion était prévue pour 15 heures/mercredi; the plane was ~d to touch down at 18.45 il était prévu que l'avion arrive OR l'arrivée de l'avion était prévue à 18 h 45; the building is ~d for demolition il est prévu que le bâtiment soit démoli; she wasn't ~d to arrive until Sunday elle ne devait pas arriver OR il n'était pas prévu qu'elle arrive avant dimanche; which day is the film ~d for? quel jour a été retenu pour le film?; it's ~d for Saturday il est programmé pour samedi; you aren't ~d to sing until later d'après le programme, vous devez chanter plus tard (dans la soirée). -**2.** [period, work, series] organiser; to ~ one's time aménager OR organiser son temps; to ~ a morning établir l'emploi du temps d'une matinée; our whole week is ~d notre programme OR emploi du temps pour cette semaine est déjà établi; that lunch hour is already ~d ce déjeuner est déjà réservé; to ~ one's reading se faire un plan de lecture. -**3.** [topic, item] inscrire; it's ~d as a topic for the next meeting c'est inscrit à l'ordre du jour de la prochaine réunion. -**4.** *Br* ADMIN [monument] classer.

scheduled [*Br* ˈʃedjuːld, *Am* ˈskedʒʊld] *adj* -**1.** [planned] prévu; at the ~ time à l'heure prévue; he didn't make his ~ speech il n'a pas prononcé le discours qu'il avait prévu; we announce a change to our ~ programmes TV nous annonçons une modification de nos programmes. -**2.** [regular - flight] régulier; [- stop, change] habituel. -**3.** [official - prices] tarifé. -**4.** *Br* ADMIN: ~ building bâtiment *m* classé (monument historique); the ~ territories la zone sterling. -**5.** [privileged]: ~ castes castes qui ont droit à certains privilèges *(en Inde)*.

scheelite [ˈʃiːlaɪt] *n* scheelite *f*.

Scheherazade [ʃəˌherəˈzɑːd] *pr n* Shéhérazade.

schema [ˈskiːmə] (*pl* schemata [-mətə]) *n* -**1.** [diagram] schéma *m*. -**2.** PHILOS & PSYCH schème *m*.

schematic [skɪˈmætɪk] ◇ *adj* schématique.

◇ *n* schéma *m*.

scheme [skiːm] ◇ *n* -**1.** [plan] plan *m*, projet *m*; a ~ for helping the homeless un projet pour aider les sans-abri; a ~ for new investment un plan OR projet pour de nouveaux investissements; a ~ to get rich quick un procédé pour s'enrichir rapidement; he's always dreaming up mad ~s for entertaining the children il a toujours des idées lumineuses pour distraire les enfants; the ~ of things l'ordre des choses; where does he fit into the ~ of things? quel rôle joue-t-il dans cette affaire?; it just doesn't fit into her ~ of things cela n'entre pas dans sa conception des choses. -**2.** [plot] intrigue *f*, complot *m*; [unscrupulous] procédé *m* malhonnête; their little ~ didn't work leur petit complot a échoué. -**3.** *Br* ADMIN plan *m*, système *m*; the firm has a profit-sharing/a pension ~ l'entreprise a un système de participation aux bénéfices/un régime de retraites complémentaires; the unions would not agree to the new productivity ~ les syndicats ont refusé d'accepter OR ont rejeté le nouveau plan de productivité; government unemployment ~s plans antichômage du gouvernement ❑ housing ~ lotissement *m*; National Savings Scheme ≃ Caisse *f* nationale d'épargne. -**4.** [arrangement] disposition *f*, schéma *m*.

◇ *vi* intriguer; to ~ to do sthg projeter de faire qqch; they ~d against the general ils ont comploté contre le général.

◇ *vt* combiner, manigancer.

schemer [ˈskiːməʳ] *n* intrigant *m*, -e *f*; [in conspiracy] conspirateur *m*, -trice *f*.

scheming [ˈskiːmɪŋ] ◇ *n (U)* intrigues *fpl*, machinations *fpl*.

◇ *adj* intrigant, conspirateur.

schism [ˈsɪzm, ˈskɪzm] *n* schisme *m*.

schismatic [sɪzˈmætɪk, skɪzˈmætɪk] ◇ *adj* schismatique.

◇ *n* schismatique *mf*.

schist [ʃɪst] *n* schiste *m*.

schist oil *n* huile *f* de schiste.

schizo▽ [ˈskɪtsəʊ] (*pl* schizos) ◇ *adj* schizophrène, schizo.

◇ *n* schizophrène *mf*, schizo *mf*.

schizoid [ˈskɪtsɔɪd] ◇ *adj* schizoïde.

◇ *n* schizoïde *mf*.

schizophrenia [ˌskɪtsəˈfriːnjə] *n* schizophrénie *f*; to suffer from ~ être atteint de schizophrénie, être schizophrène.

schizophrenic [ˌskɪtsəˈfrenɪk] ◇ *adj* schizophrène.

◇ *n* schizophrène *mf*.

schlemiel▽, **schlemihl**▽ [ʃləˈmiːl] *n esp Am* pauvre type *m* OR mec *m*.

schlep(p)▽ [ʃlep] (*pt* & *pp* schlepped, *cont* schlepping) *esp Am* ◇ *vt* trimbaler; I've got to ~ all this stuff over to the office il faut que je trimballe OR transbahute tous ces trucs au bureau.

◇ *vi*: to ~ (around) se trimbaler.

◇ *n* crétin *m*, -e *f*.

Schleswig-Holstein [ˈʃlezvɪgˈhɒlstaɪn] *pr n* Schleswig-Holstein *m*; in ~ dans le Schleswig-Holstein.

schlock▽ [ʃlɒk] ◇ *n* -**1.** [worthless objects] camelote *f*. -**2.** *esp Am* [lazy person] flemmard *m*, -e *f*.

◇ *adj* en toc.

schlong▼ [ʃlɒŋ] *n Am* pine *f*.

schmal(t)z *inf* [ʃmɔːlts] *n* sentimentalité *f.*
schmal(t)zy *inf* [ˈʃmɔːltsɪ] *adj* à l'eau de rose.
schmuck▽ [ʃmʌk] *n* connard *m.*
schnap(p)s [ʃnæps] (*pl inv*) *n* schnaps *m.*
schnorkel [ˈsnɔːkl] *Br* = **snorkel**.
scholar [ˈskɒləʳ] *n* -**1.** [academic] érudit *m,* -e *f,* savant *m;* [specialist] spécialiste *mf;* [intellectual] intellectuel *m,* -elle *f;* an Egyptian ~ un spécialiste de l'Égypte; I'm not much of a ~ je ne suis pas très savant. -**2.** [holder of grant] boursier *m,* -ère *f.* -**3.** *dated* [pupil] élève *mf;* she's a poor/good ~ c'est une mauvaise/bonne élève.
scholarly [ˈskɒləlɪ] *adj* -**1.** [person] érudit, cultivé. -**2.** [article, work] savant. -**3.** [approach] rigoureux, scientifique. -**4.** [circle] universitaire.
scholarship [ˈskɒləʃɪp] *n* -**1.** SCH & UNIV [grant] bourse *f;* to win a ~ to Stanford obtenir une bourse pour Stanford *(sur concours)*; ~ student OR holder boursier *m,* -ère *f.* -**2.** [knowledge] savoir *m,* érudition *f.*
scholastic [skəˈlæstɪk] ◇ *adj* -**1.** [ability, record, supplier] scolaire; [profession] d'enseignant; [competition] inter-écoles; ~ agency agence *f* de placement (pour enseignants). -**2.** [philosophy, approach, argument] scolastique.
◇ *n* scolastique *m.*
scholasticism [skəˈlæstɪsɪzm] *n* scolastique *f.*
school [skuːl] ◇ *n* -**1.** [educational establishment] école *f,* établissement *m* scolaire; [secondary school - to age 15] collège *m;* [- 15 to 18] lycée *m;* to go to ~ aller à l'école OR au collège OR au lycée; to be at OR in ~ être à l'école OR en classe; to go back to ~ [after illness] reprendre l'école; [after holidays] rentrer; parents have a duty to send their children to ~ les parents ont le devoir d'envoyer leurs enfants à l'école OR de scolariser leurs enfants; what are you going to do when you leave ~? qu'est-ce que tu comptes faire quand tu auras quitté l'école OR fini ta scolarité?; I was at ~ with him j'étais en classe avec lui, c'était un de mes camarades de classe; to go skiing/sailing with the ~ ≃ aller en classe de neige/de mer; television for ~s télévision *f* scolaire ‖ [classes] école *f,* classe *f,* classes *fpl,* cours *mpl;* there's no ~ today il n'y a pas (d') école OR il n'y a pas classe aujourd'hui; ~ starts at nine l'école commence OR les cours commencent à 9 h; ~ starts back next week c'est la rentrée (scolaire OR des classes) la semaine prochaine; see you after ~ on se voit après l'école OR la classe ‖ [pupils] école *f;* the whole ~ is OR are invited toute l'école est invitée ‖ *fig* école *f;* the ~ of life l'école de la vie ❑ ~s broadcasting émissions *fpl* scolaires; 'The School for Scandal' *Sheridan* 'l'École de la médisance'. -**2.** [institute] école *f,* académie *f;* ~ of dance, dancing ~ académie OR école de danse; ~ of music [gen] école de musique; [superior level] conservatoire *m;* driving ~, ~ of motoring auto-école *f,* école *f* de conduite. -**3.** UNIV [department] département *m,* institut *m;* [faculty] faculté *f;* [college] collège *m; Am* [university] université *f;* ~ of medicine faculté de médecine; London School of Economics institut d'études économiques de l'université de Londres; she's at law ~ elle fait des études de droit, elle fait son droit ‖ [at Oxbridge] salle *f* d'examens; history ~s examens finals OR finaux d'histoire. -**4.** [of art, literature] école *f;* a doctor of the old ~ *fig* un médecin de la vieille école OR de la vieille garde; the Florentine/classical ~ l'école florentine/classique ❑ ~ of thought *literal* école *f* de pensée; *fig* théorie *f.* -**5.** [training session] stage *m;* a two-day ~ for doctors un stage de deux jours pour les médecins. -**6.** HIST: the Schools l'École *f,* la scolastique. -**7.** [of fish, porpoise] banc *m.*
◇ *comp* [doctor, report] scolaire; ~ day journée *f* scolaire OR d'école; ~ dinners repas *mpl* servis à la cantine (de l'école); ~ fees frais *mpl* de scolarité; ~ governor *Br* membre *m* du conseil de gestion de l'école; ~ milk *lait offert aux élèves dans le primaire*.
◇ *vt* -**1.** [send to school] envoyer à l'école, scolariser. -**2.** [train - person] entraîner; [- animal] dresser; to be ~ed in monetary/military matters être rompu aux questions monétaires/militaires; she ~ed herself to listen to what others said elle a appris à écouter (ce que disent) les autres; she is well ~ed in diplomacy elle a une bonne formation diplomatique.
school age *n* âge *m* scolaire.
schoolbag [ˈskuːlbæg] *n* cartable *m.*
schoolbook [ˈskuːlbʊk] *n* livre *m* OR manuel *m* scolaire.
schoolboy [ˈskuːlbɔɪ] *n* écolier *m;* ~ slang argot *m* scolaire.
school bus *n* car *m* de ramassage scolaire.
schoolchild [ˈskuːltʃaɪld] (*pl* schoolchildren [-tʃɪldrən]) *n* écolier *m,* -ère *f.*
schooldays [ˈskuːldeɪz] *npl* années *fpl* d'école.
school district *n aux États-Unis, autorité locale décisionnaire dans le domaine de l'enseignement primaire et secondaire*.
schoolfellow [ˈskuːlˌfeləʊ] *n* camarade *m* OR copain *m* de classe.
schoolgirl [ˈskuːlgɜːl] ◇ *n* écolière *f.*
◇ *comp*: ~ complexion teint *m* de jeune fille; she had the usual ~ crush on the gym teacher comme toutes les filles de son âge, elle était tombée amoureuse de son prof de gym.
school holiday *n* jour *m* de congé scolaire; tomorrow is a ~ il n'y a pas école OR classe OR cours demain; during the ~s pendant les vacances OR congés scolaires.
school hours *npl* heures *fpl* de classe OR d'école; in ~ pendant les heures de classe; out of ~ en dehors des heures de classe.
schoolhouse [ˈskuːlhaʊs, *pl* -haʊzɪz] *n* école *f* (du village).
schooling [ˈskuːlɪŋ] *n* -**1.** [education] instruction *f,* éducation *f;* [enrolment at school] scolarité *f;* I haven't had much ~ je ne suis pas allé longtemps à l'école, je ne suis pas très instruit; ~ is compulsory la scolarité est obligatoire. -**2.** [of horse] dressage *m.*
schoolkid *inf* [ˈskuːlkɪd] *n* écolier *m,* -ère *f;* he's only a ~ ce n'est qu'un gosse.
school-leaver *n Br jeune qui entre dans la vie active à la fin de sa scolarité*.
school-leaving age *n* fin *f* de la scolarité obligatoire; the ~ was raised to 16 l'âge légal de fin de scolarité a été porté à 16 ans.
schoolma'am *inf,* **schoolmarm** *inf* [ˈskuːlmɑːm] *n* -**1.** *hum* [teacher] maîtresse *f* d'école. -**2.** *Br pej* [prim woman] bégueule *f.*
schoolman [ˈskuːlmən] (*pl* schoolmen [-mən]) *n* HIST & PHILOS scolastique *m.*
schoolmarmish *inf* [ˈskuːlmɑːmɪʃ] *adj Br pej:* she's very ~ elle fait très maîtresse d'école.
schoolmaster [ˈskuːlˌmɑːstəʳ] *n Br* [at primary school] maître *m,* instituteur *m;* [at secondary school] professeur *m.*
schoolmate [ˈskuːlmeɪt] *n* camarade *mf* d'école.
schoolmistress [ˈskuːlˌmɪstrɪs] *n Br* [primary school] maîtresse *f,* institutrice *f;* [secondary school] professeur *m.*
schoolroom [ˈskuːlrʊm] *n* (salle *f* de) classe *f.*
schoolteacher [ˈskuːlˌtiːtʃəʳ] *n* [at any level] enseignant *m,* -e *f;* [at primary school] instituteur *m,* -trice *f;* [at secondary school] professeur *m.*
schoolteaching [ˈskuːlˌtiːtʃɪŋ] *n* enseignement *m.*
school tie *n cravate propre à une école et faisant partie de l'uniforme*.
schooltime [ˈskuːltaɪm] *n* [school hours] heures *fpl* d'école; [outside holidays] année *f* scolaire.
school uniform *n* uniforme *m* scolaire.
schoolwork [ˈskuːlwɜːk] *n (U)* travail *m* scolaire; [at home] devoirs *mpl,* travail *m* à la maison.
school year *n* année *f* scolaire; my ~s ma scolarité, mes années d'école; the ~ runs from September to July l'année scolaire dure de septembre à juillet.
schooner [ˈskuːnəʳ] *n* -**1.** NAUT schooner *m* -**2.** [for sherry, beer] grand verre *m;* a ~ of sherr un verre de xérès.
schuss [ʃʊs] ◇ *n* schuss *m.*
◇ *vi* descendre tout schuss.
schwa [ʃwɑː] *n* [in phonetics] schwa *m.*
sciatic [saɪˈætɪk] *adj* sciatique; ~ nerve nerf *n* sciatique.
sciatica [saɪˈætɪkə] *n* sciatique *f.*
science [ˈsaɪəns] ◇ *n (U)* [gen] science *f,* scien ces *fpl;* modern ~ la science moderne; sh studied ~ elle a fait des études de science OR scientifiques; I've always been interested in ~ j'ai toujours été intéressé par les sciences ‖ [branch] science *f;* farming is becoming more and more of a ~ l'agriculture devient de plus en plus scientifique.
◇ *comp* [exam] de science; [teacher] de science, de sciences; [student] en sciences; [lab, subject] scientifique.
science fiction *n* science-fiction *f.*
science park *n* parc *m* scientifique.
scientific [ˌsaɪənˈtɪfɪk] *adj* -**1.** [research, expedition] scientifique; on ~ principles selon des principes scientifiques. -**2.** [precise, strict] scientifique, rigoureux.
scientifically [ˌsaɪənˈtɪfɪklɪ] *adv* scientifiquement, de manière scientifique; ~ speaking d'un OR du point de vue scientifique.
scientism [ˈsaɪəntɪzm] *n* PHILOS scientisme *m.*
scientist [ˈsaɪəntɪst] *n* [worker] scientifique *m;* [academic] scientifique *mf,* savant *m.*
Scientology® [ˌsaɪənˈtɒlədʒɪ] *n* RELIG scientologie *f.*
sci-fi *inf* [ˌsaɪˈfaɪ] *n abbr of* science fiction.
scilicet [ˈsaɪlɪset] *adv fml* à savoir, c'est-à-dire.
Scilly Isles [ˈsɪlɪ-], **Scillies** [ˈsɪlɪz] *pl pr n*: the ~ les îles *fpl* Sorlingues; in the ~ aux îles Sorlingues.
scimitar [ˈsɪmɪtəʳ] *n* cimeterre *m.*
scintilla [sɪnˈtɪlə] *n*: there is not a ~ of doubt that... il n'y a pas le moindre doute OR il ne fait pas l'ombre d'un doute que...
scintillate [ˈsɪntɪleɪt] *vi* [stars] scintiller, briller; *fig* [person - in conversation] briller, être brillant; to ~ with wit briller par son esprit, pétiller d'esprit.
scintillating [ˈsɪntɪleɪtɪŋ] *adj* [conversation, wit] brillant, pétillant, étincelant; [person, personality] brillant.
scintillation [ˌsɪntɪˈleɪʃn] *n* scintillation *f.*
scion [ˈsaɪən] *n* -**1.** *lit* [descendant] descendant *m,* -e *f.* -**2.** BOT scion *m.*
Scipio [ˈskɪpɪəʊ] *pr n* Scipion.
scission [ˈsɪʃn] *n* scission *f.*
scissor [ˈsɪzəʳ] *vt* couper avec des ciseaux.
◆ **scissors** *npl*: (a pair of) ~s (une paire de) ciseaux *mpl.*
scissors hold *n* SPORT ciseau *m.*
scissors jump *n* SPORT saut *m* en ciseaux, ciseau *m.*
scissors kick *n* SPORT ciseau *m.*
sclerosis [skləˈrəʊsɪs] *n (U)* BOT, MED & *fig* sclérose *f.*
sclerotic [skləˈrɒtɪk] *adj* -**1.** MED sclérosé. -**2.** BOT scléreux, sclérosé.
scoff [skɒf] ◇ *vi* -**1.** [mock] se moquer, être méprisant; they ~ed at my efforts/ideas ils se sont moqués de mes efforts/idées; don't ~, I'm serious ne te moque pas de moi, je parle sérieusement. -**2.** *inf* [eat] s'empiffrer.
◇ *vt inf Br* [eat] bouffer, s'empiffrer de; he ~ed the whole packet il s'est enfilé tout le paquet; don't ~ your food like that ne t'empiffre pas comme ça.
scoffer [ˈskɒfəʳ] *n* railleur *m,* -euse *f.*
scoffing [ˈskɒfɪŋ] ◇ *n* moquerie *f,* sarcasme *m.*
◇ *adj* railleur, sarcastique.
scold [skəʊld] ◇ *vt* gronder, réprimander; we were ~ed OR we got ~ed for giggling in class on s'est fait gronder pour avoir pouffé de rire OR parce qu'on avait pouffé de rire en classe.

◇ *vi* rouspéter.
◇ *n arch* chipie *f*, mégère *f*.

scolding ['skəʊldɪŋ] *n* gronderie *f*, gronderies *fpl*, réprimande *f*, réprimandes *fpl*; to give sb a ~ for doing sthg gronder qqn pour avoir fait qqch; **he got a good ~ from his mother for lying** il s'est fait attraper par sa mère pour avoir menti.

scollop ['skɒləp] = **scallop**.

scone [skɒn] *n* scone *m (petit pain rond)*; cheese ~ scone au fromage.

scoop [sku:p] ◇ *n* -**1.** PRESS scoop *m*, exclusivité *f*; to get OR to make a ~ faire un scoop; **the paper got a ~ on the story** le journal a publié la nouvelle en exclusivité. -**2.** [utensil, ladle - for ice-cream, potatoes] cuillère *f* à boule; [- for flour, grain] pelle *f*; [- for water] écope *f*; [on crane, dredger] pelle *f*; [on bulldozer] lame *f*. -**3.** [amount scooped - of ice-cream, potatoes] boule *f*; [- of flour, grain] pelletée *f*; [- of earth, rocks] pelletée *f*. -**4.** *inf Br* FIN [profit] bénéfice *m* (important); to make a ~ faire un gros bénéfice.
◇ *vt* -**1.** [take, measure, put] prendre (avec une mesure); to ~ **flour/grain from a bin** prendre de la farine/du grain dans un tonneau; **the ice-cream was ~ed into a dish** on a mis la glace dans un plat (à l'aide d'une cuillère); she ~**ed the papers into her case** elle a ramassé les journaux dans sa mallette; **we had to ~ the water out of the barrel** nous avons dû vider le tonneau avec un récipient; **she ~ed the grain out of the bucket** elle a pris le grain dans le seau à l'aide d'une mesure || [serve] servir (avec une cuillère); **he ~ed the potatoes onto my plate** il m'a servi des pommes de terre. -**2.** FIN [market] s'emparer de; [competitor] devancer; **they ~ed a big profit** ils ont ramassé un gros bénéfice; **to ~ the field** OR **the pool** *fig* tout rafler. -**3.** PRESS [story] publier en exclusivité; [competitor] publier avant, devancer.
◆ **scoop out** *vt sep* -**1.** [take - with scoop] prendre (avec une cuillère); [- with hands] prendre (avec les mains). -**2.** [hollow - wood, earth] creuser; [empty, remove] vider; ~ **out the tomatoes** épépinez OR égrenez les tomates; ~ **out the flesh from the grapefruit** évidez le pamplemousse.
◆ **scoop up** *vt sep* -**1.** [take, pick up - in scoop] prendre OR ramasser à l'aide d'une pelle OR d'un récipient; [- in hands] prendre OR ramasser dans les mains; **the gangsters ~ed the money up and jumped into the car** les gangsters ont ramassé l'argent et ont sauté dans la voiture; **she ~ed the papers up in her arms** elle a ramassé une brassée de journaux. -**2.** [gather together] entasser; **can you ~ up the spilt beans?** pouvez-vous faire un tas avec les haricots qui ont été renversés?

scoopful ['sku:pfʊl] *n* pelletée *f*.

scoop neck *n* décolleté *m*.

scoot *inf* [sku:t] ◇ *vi* filer; **the children ~ed across the fields/up the stairs** les enfants ont filé à travers champs/ont monté les escaliers à toute vitesse; ~! fichez le camp!, allez, ouste!
◇ *n*: **to make a ~ for it** *Br* prendre ses jambes à son cou.
◆ **scoot away** *inf*, **scoot off** *inf vi insep* filer.

scooter ['sku:tə^r] *n* -**1.** [child's] trottinette *f*. -**2.** [moped]: (**motor**) ~ scooter *m*. -**3.** *Am* [ice yacht] yacht *m* à glace.

scope [skəʊp] *n* -**1.** [range] étendue *f*, portée *f*; [limits] limites *fpl*; **what is the ~ of the enquiry?** jusqu'où portent OR vont les ramifications de l'enquête?; **does the matter fall within the ~ of the law?** est-ce que l'affaire tombe sous le coup de la loi?; **it is beyond the ~ of this study/of my powers** cela dépasse le cadre de cette étude/de mes compétences; **to extend the ~ of one's activities/of an enquiry** élargir le champ de ses activités/le cadre d'une enquête; **the book is too narrow in ~** le livre est d'une portée trop limitée || [size, extent - of change] étendue *f*; [- of undertaking] étendue *f*, envergure *f*; **it's a venture of unusual ~** c'est une entreprise d'une envergure exceptionnelle. -**2.** [opportunity, room] occasion *f*, possibilité *f*; **there's plenty of ~ for development/for improvement** les possibilités de développement/d'amélioration ne manquent pas; **the job gave him full/little ~ to demonstrate his talents** son travail lui fournissait de nombreuses/peu d'occasions de montrer ses talents; **I'd like a job with more ~** j'aimerais un poste qui me donne plus de perspectives d'évolution. -**3.** *inf* [telescope] télescope *m*; [microscope] microscope *m*; [periscope] périscope *m*.

scorbutic [skɔ:'bju:tɪk] *adj* scorbutique.

scorch [skɔ:tʃ] ◇ *vt* -**1.** [with iron - clothing, linen] roussir, brûler légèrement; [with heat - skin] brûler; [- meat] brûler, carboniser; [- woodwork] brûler, marquer. -**2.** [grass, vegetation - with sun] roussir, dessécher; [- with fire] brûler. -**3.** *inf* [criticize] éreinter.
◇ *vi* -**1.** [linen] roussir. -**2.** *inf Br* [in car] filer à toute allure; [on bike] pédaler comme un fou OR à fond de train; **we were soon ~ing along at over 100 mph** nous filions bientôt à plus de 160 à l'heure.
◇ *n* [on linen] marque *f* de roussi; [on hand, furniture] brûlure *f*; **there's a ~ (mark) on my shirt** ma chemise a été roussie; **the cigarette has left a ~ (mark) on the table** la cigarette a fait une marque de brûlure sur la table.

scorched-earth policy *n* politique *f* de la terre brûlée.

scorcher *inf* ['skɔ:tʃə^r] *n* -**1.** [hot day] journée *f* torride; **yesterday was a real ~** hier c'était une vrai fournaise. -**2.** [something exciting, fast etc]: **this film is a ~** ce film est absolument génial; **she's a real ~** c'est une fille superbe.

scorching ['skɔ:tʃɪŋ] ◇ *adj* -**1.** [weather, tea, surface] brûlant; **the sun is ~** il fait un soleil de plomb. -**2.** [criticism] cinglant. -**3.** [of speed]: **the car does a ~ 120 mph** la voiture file à 190 à l'heure.
◇ *adv*: **a ~ hot day** une journée torride.

score [skɔ:^r] ◇ *n* -**1.** SPORT score *m*; CARDS points *mpl*; **the ~ was five-nil** le score était de cinq à zéro; **there was still no ~ at half-time** à la mi-temps, aucun but n'avait encore été marqué; **to make a high ~** FTBL marquer de nombreux buts; CARDS & GAMES faire beaucoup de points; **to keep the ~** GAMES compter OR marquer les points; SPORT tenir le score; [on scorecard] tenir la marque || [in exam, test - mark] note *f*; [- result] résultat *m*; **to get a good ~** obtenir une bonne note; **the final ~** FTBL le score final; [gen & CARDS] le résultat final; **what's the ~?** FTBL quel est le score?; [gen & CARDS] on a marqué combien de points?; [in tennis] où en est le jeu?; *fig* on en est où? ☐ **to know the ~** *inf* connaître le topo. -**2.** *fig* [advantage - in debate] avantage *m*, points *mpl*; **to make a ~ off an opponent** marquer des points sur son adversaire. -**3.** [debt] compte *m*; **I prefer to forget old ~s** je préfère oublier les vieilles histoires. -**4.** [subject, cause] sujet *m*, titre *m*; **don't worry on that ~** ne vous inquiétez pas à ce sujet; **he deserved to be rejected on more than one ~** il méritait d'être refusé à plus d'un titre; **on what ~ was I turned down?** à quel titre OR sous quel prétexte ai-je été refusé? -**5.** [twenty] vingtaine *f*; **three ~ and ten** *arch* soixante-dix || [many]: **~s of people** beaucoup de gens; **I've told you ~s of times** je vous l'ai dit des centaines de fois; **motorbikes by the ~** des motos par dizaines. -**6.** MUS partition *f*; CIN & THEAT musique *f*; **Cleo wrote the (film) ~** Cleo est l'auteur de la musique (du film); **to follow the ~** suivre (sur) la partition. -**7.** [mark - on furniture] rayure *f*; [notch, deep cut] entaille *f*; [in leather] entaille *f*, incision *f*; GEOL strie *f*.
◇ *vt* -**1.** SPORT [goal, point] marquer; **to ~ 5 goals/50 points for one's team** marquer 5 buts/50 points pour son équipe; **to ~ a hit** [with bullet, arrow, bomb] atteindre la cible; [in fencing] toucher; *fig* réussir; **the bomber ~d a direct hit** le bombardier a visé en plein sur la cible; **to ~ a success** remporter un succès || [in test, exam - marks] obtenir; **she ~d the highest mark** elle a obtenu OR eu la note la plus élevée; **he's always trying to ~ points off me** *fig* il essaie toujours d'avoir le dessus avec moi. -**2.** [scratch] érafler; [make shallow cut in - paper] marquer; [- rock] strier; [- pastry, meat] inciser, faire des incisions dans. -**3.** MUS [symphony, opera] orchestrer; **the piece is ~d for six trombones/treble voices** le morceau est écrit pour six trombones/pour soprano || CIN & THEAT composer la musique de. -**4.** *Am* [grade, mark - test] noter.
◇ *vi* -**1.** SPORT [team, player] marquer un point OR des points; FTBL marquer un but OR des buts; [scorekeeper] marquer les points; **the team didn't ~** l'équipe n'a pas marqué; **would you mind scoring for us?** vous voulez bien marquer les points pour nous? || [in test]: **to ~ high/low** obtenir un bon/mauvais score. -**2.** [succeed] avoir du succès, réussir; **he certainly ~s with the girls** il a du succès auprès des filles, c'est sûr; **that's where we ~** c'est là que nous l'emportons, c'est là que nous avons l'avantage. -**3.** ▽ [sexually] avoir une touche; **did you ~?** tu as réussi à tomber une fille? -**4.** *drugs sl* [get drugs] se procurer de la drogue.
◆ **score off** ◇ *vt insep* prendre l'avantage sur, marquer des points sur.
◇ *vt sep* rayer, barrer.
◆ **score over** *vt insep* -**1.** = **score off** *vt insep*. -**2.** [be more successful than] avoir l'avantage sur.
◆ **score out**, **score through** *vt sep* biffer, barrer.
◆ **score up** *vt sep* -**1.** [subj: team, player] marquer. -**2.** [debt] marquer, noter.

scoreboard ['skɔ:bɔ:d] *n* tableau *m* d'affichage *(du score)*.

scorecard ['skɔ:kɑ:d] *n* -**1.** [for score - in game] fiche *f* de marque OR de score; [- in golf] carte *f* de parcours. -**2.** [list of players] liste *f* des joueurs.

score draw *n* FTBL match *m* nul *(où chaque équipe a marqué)*.

scorekeeper ['skɔ:,ki:pə^r] *n* marqueur *m*, -euse *f*.

scoreline ['skɔ:laɪn] *n* score *m*.

scorer ['skɔ:rə^r] *n* -**1.** FTBL [regularly] buteur *m*; [of goal] marqueur *m*; **Watkins was the ~** c'est Watkins qui a marqué le but. -**2.** [scorekeeper] marqueur *m*, -euse *f*. -**3.** [in test, exam]: **the highest ~** le candidat qui obtient le meilleur score.

scoresheet ['skɔ:ʃi:t] *n* feuille *f* de match.

scoria ['skɔ:rɪə] (*pl* scoriae [-rɪi:]) *n* scorie *f*.

scoring ['skɔ:rɪŋ] *n (U)* -**1.** FTBL [of goals] marquage *m* d'un but; [number scored] buts *mpl* (marqués); **the ~ was fairly slow** il nous a fallu assez longtemps pour marquer. -**2.** CARDS & GAMES [scorekeeping] marquage *m* des points, marque *f*; [points scored] points *mpl* marqués; **I'm not sure about the ~** je ne suis pas sûr de la manière dont on marque les points. -**3.** [scratching] rayures *fpl*, éraflures *fpl*; [notching] entaille *f*, entailles *fpl*; GEOL striage *m*. -**4.** MUS [orchestration] orchestration *f*; [arrangement] arrangement *m*; [composition] écriture *f*.

scorn [skɔ:n] ◇ *n* -**1.** [contempt] mépris *m*, dédain *m*; **I feel nothing but ~ for them** ils ne m'inspirent que du mépris. -**2.** [object of derision] (objet *m* de) risée *f*; **she was the ~ of the whole school** elle était la risée de toute l'école.
◇ *vt* -**1.** [be contemptful of] mépriser. -**2.** [reject - advice, warning] rejeter, refuser d'écouter; [- idea] rejeter; [- help] refuser, dédaigner; **she ~ed to answer** *lit* elle n'a pas daigné répondre.

scornful ['skɔ:nfʊl] *adj* dédaigneux, méprisant; **she's rather ~ about** OR **of my ideas** elle manifeste un certain mépris envers mes idées.

scornfully ['skɔ:nfʊlɪ] *adv* avec mépris, dédaigneusement; **they looked at us ~** ils nous ont regardés avec dédain OR d'un air méprisant; **"of course not", he said ~** «bien sûr que non», dit-il d'un ton méprisant.

Scorpio ['skɔ:pɪəʊ] ◇ *pr n* ASTROL & ASTRON Scorpion *m*.
◇ *n*: **he's a ~** il est Scorpion.

scorpion ['skɔːpjən] *n* ZOOL scorpion *m*.
scorpion fish *n* rascasse *f*, scorpène *f spec*.
Scot [skɒt] *n* Écossais *m*, -e *f*; the ~s les Écossais.
scotch [skɒtʃ] *vt* -**1.** [suppress - revolt, strike] mettre fin à, réprimer, étouffer; [- rumour] étouffer; **we'll have to ~ that idea** il faudra abandonner cette idée. -**2.** [hamper - plans] entraver, contrecarrer. -**3.** [block - wheel] caler.
Scotch [skɒtʃ] ◇ *n* [whisky] scotch *m*; **a glass of ~** un verre de scotch.
◇ *npl* [people]: **the ~** les Écossais *mpl*.
◇ *adj* écossais.
Scotch broth *n soupe écossaise à base de légumes et d'orge perlée*.
Scotch egg *n œuf dur entouré de chair à saucisse et enrobé de chapelure*.
Scotch mist *n* bruine *f*.
Scotch pancake *n crêpe épaisse*.
Scotch pine *n* pin *m* sylvestre.
Scotch tape® *n Am* Scotch® *m*.
◆ **scotch-tape**® *vt* scotcher.
Scotch terrier = **Scottish terrier**.
Scotch whisky *n* scotch *m*, whisky *m* écossais.
scot-free *adj* impuni; **they were let off ~** on les a relâchés sans les punir.
Scotland ['skɒtlənd] *pr n* Écosse *f*; **in ~** en Écosse.
Scotland Yard *pr n ancien nom du siège de la police à Londres (aujourd'hui New Scotland Yard)*, ≃ Quai *m* des Orfèvres.
Scots [skɒts] ◇ *n* [language - Gaelic] écossais *m*, erse *m*; [- Lallans] anglais *m* d'Écosse.
◇ *adj* [accent, law, name] écossais; **do you know the ~ language?** connaissez-vous l'écossais?
Scotsman ['skɒtsmən] (*pl* Scotsmen [-mən]) *n* Écossais *m*; **the ~** PRESS *un des grands quotidiens écossais*.
Scots pine *n* pin *m* sylvestre.
Scotswoman ['skɒtswʊmən] (*pl* Scotswomen [-ˌwɪmɪn]) *n* Écossaise *f*.
Scotticism ['skɒtɪsɪzm] *n* expression *f* propre à l'anglais d'Écosse.
scottie ['skɒtɪ] = **Scottish terrier**.
Scottish ['skɒtɪʃ] ◇ *n* LING écossais *m*.
◇ *npl*: **the ~** les Écossais *mpl*.
◇ *adj* écossais.
Scottish Gaelic *n* LING gaélique *m* d'Écosse, erse *m*.
Scottish National Party *pr n parti indépendantiste écossais fondé en 1934*.
Scottish terrier *n* scottish-terrier *m*, Scotch-terrier *m*.
scotty ['skɒtɪ] (*pl* scotties) = **Scottish terrier**.
scoundrel ['skaʊndrəl] *n* bandit *m*, vaurien *m*; [child] vilain *m*, -e *f*, coquin *m*, -e *f*; **come here you little ~!** viens ici, petit coquin OR vaurien!
scour ['skaʊəʳ] ◇ *vt* -**1.** [clean - pan] récurer; [- metal surface] décaper; [- floor] lessiver, frotter; [- tank] vidanger, purger. -**2.** [scratch] rayer. -**3.** [subj: water, erosion] creuser; **the rain water had ~ed a deep channel in the hillside** l'eau de pluie avait creusé une profonde rigole sur le flanc de la colline. -**4.** [search - area] ratisser, fouiller; **the surrounding countryside was ~ed for the missing girl** on a ratissé OR fouillé la campagne environnante pour retrouver la jeune fille disparue; **the police spent the weekend ~ing the woods** la police a passé le week-end à battre les bois; **I've ~ed the whole library looking for her** j'ai fouillé toute la bibliothèque pour la trouver.
◇ *n*: **give the pans a good ~** récurez bien les casseroles; **the sink could do with a ~** l'évier aurait bien besoin d'être récuré.
◆ **scour about** *vi insep Br* battre la campagne; **they ~ed about after** OR **for a red car** ils ont parcouru toute la région à la recherche d'une voiture rouge.
◆ **scour away** *vt sep* éroder, emporter par érosion.
◆ **scour off** *vt sep* enlever (à l'aide d'un tampon à récurer).

scourer ['skaʊrəʳ] *n* tampon *m* à récurer.
scourge [skɜːdʒ] ◇ *n* -**1.** [bane] fléau *m*; **the ~ of war/of disease** le fléau de la guerre/de la maladie; **pollution is the ~ of the century** la pollution est le fléau de ce siècle. -**2.** [person] peste *f*. -**3.** [whip] fouet *m*.
◇ *vt* -**1.** [afflict] ravager. -**2.** [whip] fouetter.
scouring pad ['skaʊərɪŋ-] *n* tampon *m* à récurer.
scouring powder *n* poudre *f* à récurer.
scourings ['skaʊərɪŋz] *npl* résidu *m* (de récurage).
Scouse *inf* [skaʊs] *Br* ◇ *n* -**1.** [person] *surnom donné aux habitants de Liverpool*. -**2.** [dialect] *dialecte de la région de Liverpool*.
◇ *adj* de Liverpool.
scout [skaʊt] ◇ *n* -**1.** [boy] scout *m*, éclaireur *m*; [girl] scoute *f*, éclaireuse *f*; **he's a good ~** *Am* c'est un chouette OR brave type. -**2.** MIL [searcher] éclaireur *m*; [watchman] sentinelle *f*, guetteur *m*; [ship] vedette *f*; [aircraft] avion *m* de reconnaissance. -**3.** [for players, models, dancers] dénicheur *m* de vedettes. -**4.** [exploration] tour *m*; **to have** OR **to take a ~ around** (aller) reconnaître le terrain. -**5.** *Br* AUT [patrolman] dépanneur *m*.
◇ *comp* [knife, uniform] (de) scout, d'éclaireur; **~ camp** camp *m* scout; **the ~ movement** le mouvement scout, le scoutisme.
◇ *vt* [area] explorer; MIL reconnaître; **to ~ (out) a trail** reconnaître une piste.
◇ *vi* partir en reconnaissance; **he used to ~ for the cavalry** il était éclaireur dans OR il effectuait des missions de reconnaissance pour la cavalerie.
◆ **scout about** *Br*, **scout around** *vi insep* explorer les lieux; MIL partir en reconnaissance; **to ~ about for an excuse** chercher un prétexte.
◆ **Scout** = **scout 1**.
scout car *n* scout-car *m*.
scouting ['skaʊtɪŋ] *n* -**1.** [movement]: **~, Scouting** scoutisme *m*. -**2.** MIL reconnaissance *f*.
scoutmaster ['skaʊtˌmɑːstəʳ] *n* chef *m* scout.
scow [skaʊ] *n* NAUT chaland *m*.
scowl [skaʊl] ◇ *n* [angry] mine *f* renfrognée OR hargneuse, air *m* renfrogné; [threatening] air *m* menaçant; **judging from his ~, I gathered he had lost** à (en juger par) son air renfrogné, j'ai compris qu'il avait perdu; **she had an angry ~ on her face** la colère se lisait sur son visage; **of course not, she said with a ~** bien sûr que non, dit-elle d'un air renfrogné.
◇ *vi* [angrily] se renfrogner, faire la grimace; [threateningly] prendre un air menaçant; **to ~ at sb** jeter un regard mauvais à qqn.
scowling ['skaʊlɪŋ] *adj* [face] renfrogné, hargneux; **he fell silent, a ~ look on his face** il s'est tu, l'air renfrogné.
SCR (*abbr of* **senior common room**) *n Br salle des étudiants de 3ᵉ cycle*.
scrabble ['skræbl] ◇ *vi* -**1.** [search]: **she was scrabbling in the grass for the keys** elle cherchait les clés à tâtons dans l'herbe; **the man was scrabbling for a handhold on the cliff face** l'homme cherchait désespérément une prise sur la paroi de la falaise. -**2.** [scrape] gratter. -**3.** [scuffle]: **to ~ with sb for sthg** lutter avec qqn pour s'emparer de qqch.
◇ *n* [scramble]: **there was a wild ~ for the food** les gens se ruèrent sur la nourriture.
◆ **scrabble about** *Br*, **scrabble around** *vi insep* [grope] fouiller, tâtonner; **I had to ~ about in the drawer for a bit of string** j'ai dû fouiller dans le tiroir pour trouver un bout de ficelle; **she was scrabbling about on all fours looking for her contact lens** à quatre pattes, elle cherchait à tâtons son verre de contact.
Scrabble® ['skræbl] *n* Scrabble® *m*; **do you fancy a game of ~?** tu veux faire un Scrabble?
scrag [skræg] (*pt & pp* scragged, *cont* scragging) ◇ *n* -**1.** [person] personne *f* très maigre; [horse] haridelle *f*. -**2.** [neck] cou *m*. -**3.** = **scrag end**.
◇ *vt inf* tordre le cou à.
scrag end *n Br* CULIN collet *m (de mouton ou de veau)*.

scraggy ['skrægɪ] (*compar* scraggier, *superl* scraggiest) *adj* -**1.** [thin - neck, person] efflanqué, maigre, décharné; [- horse, cat] efflanqué, étique *lit*. -**2.** [jagged] déchiqueté.
scram [skræm] (*pt & pp* scrammed, *cont* scramming) ◇ *vi* -**1.** [get out] déguerpir, ficher le camp; **~, all of you!** fichez-moi tous le camp! -**2.** [reactor] être arrêté d'urgence.
◇ *vt* [reactor] arrêter d'urgence.
◇ *n* [of reactor] arrêt *m* d'urgence.
scramble ['skræmbl] ◇ *vi* -**1.** [verb of movement - hurriedly or with difficulty]: **they ~d for shelter** ils se sont précipités pour se mettre à l'abri; **he ~d into a diving suit** il a enfilé à la hâte une combinaison de plongée; **he ~d to his feet** il s'est levé précipitamment; **to ~ away** s'enfuir à toutes jambes; **to ~ down** dégringoler; **to ~ up** grimper avec difficulté; **she ~d out of the path of the bus** elle a tout juste eu le temps de s'écarter pour ne pas être renversée par le bus; **I had to ~ over three rows of seats** j'ai dû escalader trois rangées de sièges; **to ~ over rocks** escalader des rochers en s'aidant des mains; **the soldiers ~d up the hill** les soldats ont escaladé la colline tant bien que mal. -**2.** [scrabble, fight]: **to ~ for seats** se bousculer pour trouver une place assise, se ruer sur les places assises; **everyone was scrambling to get to the telephones** tout le monde se ruait vers les téléphones; **as happens every summer, young people are having to ~ for jobs** comme tous les étés, les jeunes doivent se battre OR se démener pour trouver un boulot. -**3.** AERON & MIL décoller sur-le-champ. -**4.** SPORT: **to go scrambling** faire du trial.
◇ *vt* -**1.** RADIO & TELEC brouiller. -**2.** [jumble] mélanger. -**3.** AERON & MIL ordonner le décollage immédiat de. -**4.** CULIN [eggs] brouiller; **I'll ~ some eggs** je vais faire des œufs brouillés.
◇ *n* -**1.** [rush] bousculade *f*, ruée *f*; **my glasses were broken in the ~ to get out** mes lunettes ont été cassées dans la ruée vers la sortie; **there was a ~ for seats** *literal* on s'est bousculé pour avoir une place assise, on s'est rué sur les places assises; [for tickets] on s'est arraché les places; **there was a ~ for the door** nous nous sommes rués vers la porte; **a ~ for profits/for jobs** une course effrénée au profit/à l'emploi. -**2.** SPORT [on motorbikes] course *f* de trial. -**3.** AERON & MIL décollage *m* immédiat. -**4.** [in rock climbing] grimpée *f* à quatre pattes.
scrambled egg ['skræmbld-] *n*, **scrambled eggs** *npl* œufs *mpl* brouillés.
scrambler ['skræmbləʳ] *n* RADIO & TELEC brouilleur *m*.
scrambling ['skræmblɪŋ] *n* -**1.** *Br* SPORT trial *m*. -**2.** [in rock climbing] grimpée *f* à quatre pattes.
scrap [skræp] (*pt & pp* scrapped, *cont* scrapping) ◇ *n* -**1.** [small piece - of paper, cloth] bout *m*; [- of bread, cheese] petit bout *m*; [- of conversation] bribe *f*; **he left a few ~s of poetry** il a laissé quelques vers; **~s of news/of information** des bribes de nouvelles/d'informations; **there isn't a ~ of truth in the story** il n'y a pas une parcelle de vérité OR il n'y a absolument rien de vrai dans cette histoire; **it didn't do me a ~ of good** [action] cela ne m'a servi absolument à rien; [medicine] cela ne m'a fait aucun bien; **what I say won't make a ~ of difference** ce que je dirai ne changera rien du tout. -**2.** [waste]: **we sold the car for ~** on a vendu la voiture à la ferraille OR à la casse; **it has no value even as ~** même à la casse, ça ne vaut rien; **~ (metal)** ferraille *f*. -**3.** *inf* [fight] bagarre *f*; **to get into** OR **to have a ~ with** se bagarrer avec qqn.
◇ *vt* -**1.** [discard - shoes, furniture] jeter; [- idea, plans] renoncer à, abandonner; [- system] abandonner, mettre au rancart; [- machinery] mettre au rebut OR au rancart; **you can ~ the whole idea** vous pouvez laisser tomber OR abandonner cette idée. -**2.** [send for scrap - car, ship] envoyer OR mettre à la ferraille OR à la casse.
◇ *vi inf* [fight] se bagarrer.
◇ *comp* [value] de ferraille; **~ lead** plomb *m* de récupération; **~ iron** OR **metal** ferraille *f*; **~ merchant** *Br* ferrailleur *m*; **~ (metal) dealer**

ferrailleur *m*; ~ **yard** chantier *m* de ferraille, casse *f*; **I found it in a ~ yard** je l'ai trouvé à la ferraille OR à la casse.

◆ **scraps** *npl* [food] restes *mpl*; [fragments] débris *mpl*.

scrapbook ['skræpbʊk] *n* album *m (de coupures de journaux, de photos etc)*.

scrape [skreɪp] ◇ *vt* -**1.** [rasp, rub - boots, saucepan, earth] gratter, racler; [- tools] gratter, décaper; [- vegetables, windows] gratter; ~ **the mud off your shoes** enlève OR gratte la boue de tes chaussures; **I spent the afternoon scraping the paint off the door** j'ai passé l'après-midi à gratter la peinture de la porte; **to ~ sthg clean/smooth** gratter qqch pour qu'il soit propre/lisse; **I ~d (at) the ground with a stick** j'ai gratté le sol avec un bâton; **the boat ~d the bottom** [ran aground] le bateau a touché le fond; [on beach] le bateau s'est échoué sur le sable || [drag] traîner; **don't ~ the chair across the floor like that** ne traîne pas la chaise par terre comme ça ❑ **to ~ the bottom of the barrel** racler les fonds de tiroir; **you took him on? you must really be scraping the bottom of the barrel!** tu as embauché ce type-là? tu devais vraiment être coincé! -**2.** [touch lightly] effleurer, frôler; [scratch - paint, table, wood] rayer; **the plane just ~d the surface of the water** l'avion frôla OR rasa la surface de l'eau; **I just ~d the garage door as I drove in** j'ai seulement frôlé OR effleuré la porte du garage en rentrant la voiture. -**3.** [skin, knee] érafler; **I ~d my knee** je me suis éraflé le genou. -**4.** [with difficulty]: **to ~ a living** arriver tout juste à survivre, vivoter; **to ~ acquaintance with sb** *Br* se débrouiller pour faire la connaissance de qqn.

◇ *vi* -**1.** [rub] frotter; [rasp] gratter; **the door ~d shut** la porte s'est refermée en grinçant; **the gardener ~d at the ground with a stick** le jardinier grattait la terre avec un bâton; **I heard the noise of his pen scraping across the paper** j'entendais le grattement de son stylo sur le papier. -**2.** *fig* [avoid with difficulty]: **she just ~d clear of the bus in time** elle a évité le bus de justesse; **the ambulance just ~d past** l'ambulance est passée de justesse. -**3.** [economize] faire des petites économies. -**4.** [be humble] faire des courbettes OR des ronds de jambes.

◇ *n* -**1.** [rub, scratch]: **he had a nasty ~ on his knee** il avait une méchante éraflure au genou, il s'était bien éraflé le genou; **don't worry if it won't come clean, just give it a quick ~** ne t'inquiète pas si ça ne part pas, frotte-le OR gratte-le un peu. -**2.** *inf* [dilemma, trouble] pétrin *m*; **to get into a ~** se mettre dans le pétrin; **now you've really got yourself into a ~!** vous voilà dans de beaux draps OR dans un sacré pétrin!; **you got me into this ~, now get me out of it!** c'est vous qui m'avez mis dans ce pétrin, maintenant il faut me tirer de là! -**3.** [scraping] grattement *m*, grincement *m*. -**4.** = **scraping 2**.

◆ **scrape along** *vi insep* [financially] se débrouiller, vivre tant bien que mal; **she had to ~ along on a small pension** elle devait se débrouiller avec une petite retraite; **we'll ~ along somehow** on va se débrouiller avec ce qu'on a.

◆ **scrape away** ◇ *vt sep* enlever en grattant.
◇ *vi insep* gratter; **to ~ away at a violin** racler du violon; **the gardener was scraping away at the dry earth** le jardinier grattait la terre sèche.

◆ **scrape by** *vi insep* [financially] se débrouiller; **I have just enough to ~ by (on)** j'ai juste assez d'argent pour me débrouiller.

◆ **scrape down** *vt sep* [paintwork] décaper; [woodwork, door] gratter.

◆ **scrape in** *vi insep* [in election] être élu de justesse; **I just ~d in as the doors were closing** j'ai réussi à entrer juste au moment où les portes se fermaient.

◆ **scrape into** *vt insep*: **he just ~d into university/parliament** il est entré à l'université/au parlement d'extrême justesse.

◆ **scrape off** ◇ *vt sep* [mud, paint] enlever au grattoir OR en grattant; [skin] érafler
◇ *vi insep* s'enlever au grattoir; **this paint ~s off easily** pour enlever cette peinture, il suffit de la gratter.

◆ **scrape out** *vt sep* -**1.** [saucepan] récurer, racler; [residue] enlever en grattant OR raclant; **to ~ out a mixing bowl** [with spatula] racler un bol avec une spatule; [with finger] racler un bol avec le doigt. -**2.** [hollow] creuser.

◆ **scrape through** ◇ *vt insep* [exam] réussir de justesse; [doorway, gap] passer (de justesse); **the government will probably just ~ through the next election** le gouvernement va probablement réussir tout juste à l'emporter OR va probablement l'emporter de justesse aux prochaines élections.
◇ *vi insep* [in exam] réussir de justesse; [in election] être élu OR l'emporter de justesse; [financially] se débrouiller tout juste; [through gap] passer de justesse.

◆ **scrape together** *vt sep* -**1.** [two objects] frotter l'un contre l'autre. -**2.** [into pile] mettre en tas. -**3.** [collect - supporters, signatures] réunir OR rassembler à grand-peine; [- money for o.s.] réunir en raclant les fonds de tiroirs; [- money for event] réunir avec beaucoup de mal.

◆ **scrape up** = **scrape together 3**.

scraper ['skreɪpəʳ] *n* grattoir *m*; [for muddy shoes] décrottoir *m*.

scraperboard ['skreɪpəbɔːd] *n* carte *f* à gratter.

scrapheap ['skræphiːp] *n* -**1.** *literal* décharge *f*. -**2.** *fig* rebut *m*; **to be thrown on** OR **consigned to the ~** être mis au rebut.

scraping ['skreɪpɪŋ] ◇ *adj* [sound] de grattement.
◇ *n* -**1.** [sound] grattement *m*; **I could hear the sound of ~** j'ai entendu un grattement OR un bruit de grattement; **the ~ of chalk on the blackboard** le crissement OR le grincement de la craie sur le tableau. -**2.** [thin layer] mince couche *f*; **toast with a ~ of butter** du pain grillé recouvert d'une mince couche de beurre.

◆ **scrapings** *npl* [food] déchets *mpl*, restes *mpl*; [from paint, wood] raclures *fpl*; **give the ~s to the dogs** donnez les restes aux chiens.

scrap paper *n Br* (papier *m*) brouillon *m*.

scrapper *inf* ['skræpəʳ] *n Br* bagarreur *m*, -euse *f*.

scrappy ['skræpɪ] (*compar* **scrappier**, *superl* **scrappiest**) *adj* -**1.** [disconnected] décousu; **I had rather a ~ education** je n'ai pas bénéficié d'une instruction très suivie. -**2.** *inf Am* [quarrelsome] bagarreur, chamailleur.

scratch [skrætʃ] ◇ *vt* -**1.** [itch, rash] gratter; **to ~ one's head** se gratter la tête || [earth, surface] gratter; **he was ~ing the ground with a stick** il grattait le sol avec un bâton; **you've barely ~ed the surface** *fig* vous avez fait un travail très superficiel, vous avez seulement effleuré la question; **they ~ a living selling secondhand books** *Br fig* ils gagnent péniblement leur vie en vendant des livres d'occasion ❑ **you ~ my back, and I'll ~ yours** si vous me rendez ce service, je vous le revaudrai OR je vous renverrai l'ascenseur. -**2.** [subj: cat] griffer; [subj: thorn, nail] égratigner, écorcher; **the cat ~ed my hand** le chat m'a griffé la main; **she ~ed her hand on the brambles** elle s'est écorché OR égratigné la main dans les ronces || [mark - woodwork, marble] rayer, érafler; [- glass, record] rayer; **the car's hardly ~ed** la voiture n'a presque rien OR n'a pratiquement aucune éraflure; **the paintwork's badly ~ed** la peinture est sérieusement éraflée; **someone has ~ed their initials on the tree** quelqu'un a gravé ses initiales sur l'arbre. -**3.** [irritate] gratter; **this wool ~es my skin** cette laine me gratte la peau. -**4.** SPORT [cancel - match] annuler. -**5.** *Am* POL rayer de la liste.
◇ *vi* -**1.** [person, monkey] se gratter; **stop ~ing** arrête de te gratter. -**2.** [hen] gratter (le sol); [pen] gratter; **I could hear something ~ing at the door** j'entendais quelque chose gratter à la porte, j'entendais un grattement à la porte. -**3.** [cat] griffer; [brambles, nail] griffer, écorcher.
◇ *n* -**1.** [for itch] grattement *m*; **to have a ~** se gratter; **the dog was having a good ~** le chien se grattait un bon coup. -**2.** [from cat] coup *m* de griffe; [from fingernails] coup *m* d'ongle; [from thorns, nail] égratignure *f*, écorchure *f*; **how did you get that ~?** comment est-ce que tu t'es égratigné?; **I've got a ~ on my hand** je me suis égratigné la main; **her hands were covered in ~es** elle avait les mains tout écorchées OR couvertes d'égratignures; **it's only a ~** ce n'est qu'une égratignure; **we escaped without a ~** on s'en est sorti sans une égratignure. -**3.** [mark - on furniture] rayure *f*, éraflure *f*; [- on glass, record] rayure *f*. -**4.** *phr*: **to be up to ~** [in quality] avoir la qualité voulue; [in level] avoir le niveau voulu; **her work still isn't up to ~** son travail n'est toujours pas satisfaisant; **their performance wasn't up to** OR **didn't come up to ~** leur performance n'était pas suffisante OR à la hauteur; **we must get the team up to ~ before April** il faut mettre l'équipe à niveau avant avril.
◇ *adj* [team, meal] improvisé; [player] scratch *(inv)*, sans handicap; [shot] au hasard.

◆ **from scratch** *adv phr* à partir de rien OR de zéro; **I learnt Italian from ~ in six months** j'ai appris l'italien en six mois en ayant commencé à zéro.

◆ **scratch off** *vt sep* enlever en grattant.

◆ **scratch out** *vt sep* [name] raturer; **to ~ sb's eyes out** arracher les yeux à qqn; **I'll ~ your eyes out!** *fig* je vais t'écorcher vif!

◆ **scratch together** *vt sep Br* [team] réunir (difficilement); [sum of money] réunir OR rassembler (en raclant les fonds de tiroir).

◆ **scratch up** *vt sep* -**1.** [dig up - bone, plant] déterrer. -**2.** *Br* [money] réunir (en raclant les fonds de tiroir).

scratch mark *n* [on hand] égratignure *f*; [on leather, furniture] rayure *f*, éraflure *f*.

scratch pad *n Am* bloc-notes *m*; ~ **memory** COMPUT mémoire *f* bloc-notes.

scratch paper *Am* = **scrap paper**.

scratch sheet *n Am* [for horse races] journal *m* des courses.

scratch test *n* test *m* cutané.

scratchy ['skrætʃɪ] (*compar* **scratchier**, *superl* **scratchiest**) *adj* -**1.** [prickly - jumper, blanket] rêche, qui gratte; [- bush] piquant. -**2.** [pen] qui gratte. -**3.** [drawing, writing] griffonné. -**4.** [record] rayé.

scrawl [skrɔːl] ◇ *n* griffonnage *m*, gribouillage *m*; **I can't read this ~** je ne peux pas déchiffrer ce gribouillage; **I thought I recognized his ~** je pensais bien avoir reconnu ses gribouillis; **her signature is just a ~** sa signature est totalement illisible.
◇ *vt* griffonner, gribouiller; **she left me a ~ed note** elle m'a laissé quelques mots griffonnés; **he ~ed her a note** il lui a griffonné un mot; **someone has ~ed anti-war slogans on the walls** quelqu'un a gribouillé des slogans pacifistes sur le mur.
◇ *vi* gribouiller.

scrawny ['skrɔːnɪ] (*compar* **scrawnier**, *superl* **scrawniest**) *adj* -**1.** [person, neck] efflanqué, décharné; [cat, chicken] efflanqué, étique *lit*. -**2.** [vegetation] maigre.

scream [skriːm] ◇ *vi* -**1.** [shout] crier, pousser des cris, hurler; [baby] crier, hurler; [birds, animals] crier; **to ~ at sb** crier après qqn; **to ~ in anger/with pain** hurler de colère/de douleur; **to ~ in delight** crier OR hurler de plaisir; **she ~ed for help** elle cria à l'aide OR au secours; **they were ~ing with laughter** ils se tordaient de rire, ils riaient aux éclats. -**2.** [tyres] crisser; [engine, siren] hurler; **bombers ~ed over the rooftops** les bombardiers hurlèrent en survolant les toits.
◇ *vt* -**1.** [shout] hurler; **she just stood there ~ing insults at me** elle est restée plantée là à me couvrir d'insultes; **she ~ed her anger** *lit* elle hurlait sa colère; **she ~ed herself hoarse** elle cria jusqu'à en perdre la voix ❑ **to ~ one's head off** crier à tue-tête; **to ~ blue murder** crier comme un putois OR un perdu. -**2.** [order, answer] hurler; **"come here at once!", she ~ed** «viens ici tout de suite!», hurla-t-elle. -**3.** [newspaper] étaler; **headlines ~ed the news of his defeat** la nouvelle de sa défaite s'étalait en gros titres.

◇ *n* -**1.** [cry] cri *m* perçant, hurlement *m*; **she gave a loud ~** elle a poussé un hurlement; **I heard terrible ~s coming from next door** j'ai entendu des hurlements atroces qui venaient d'à côté; **~s of laughter** des éclats de rire ❑ **'The Scream'** *Munch* 'le Cri'. -**2.** [of tyres] crissement *m*; [of sirens, engines] hurlement *m*. -**3.** [person]: **he's an absolute ~** il est vraiment désopilant OR impayable; **you do look a ~ in that hat!** vous êtes à mourir de rire avec ce chapeau! || [situation, event]: **the party was a ~** on s'est amusés comme des fous à la soirée; **it's a ~ the way they clamber up the bars** c'est vraiment tordant de les voir grimper aux barreaux.

◆ **scream out** ◇ *vi insep* pousser de grands cris; **to ~ out in pain** hurler de douleur; **she ~ed out in her sleep** elle a poussé un grand cri pendant qu'elle dormait.
◇ *vt sep* hurler.

screamer [ˈskriːməʳ] *n* -**1.** [shouter] personne *f* qui crie (beaucoup). -**2.** *inf* [funny person] personne *f* désopilante; [film] film *m* désopilant; [joke] blague *f* désopilante. -**3.** *inf Am* PRESS & TYPO point *m* d'exclamation.

screaming [ˈskriːmɪŋ] *adj* [fans] qui crie, qui hurle; [tyres] qui crisse; [sirens, jets] qui hurle; [need] criant; **~ headlines** grandes manchettes *fpl*; **he tends to dress in ~ reds and greens** il s'habille souvent de rouges et de verts criards.

screamingly *inf* [ˈskriːmɪŋlɪ] *adv*: **~ funny** on ne peut plus drôle, à se tordre OR à mourir de rire.

scree [skriː] *n* (U) éboulis *m*, pierraille *f*.

screech [skriːtʃ] ◇ *vi* -**1.** [owl] ululer, hululer, huer; [gull] crier, piailler; [parrot] crier; [monkey] hurler. -**2.** [person - in high voice] pousser des cris stridents OR perçants; [- loudly] hurler; [singer] crier, chanter d'une voie stridente. -**3.** [tyres] crisser; [brakes, machinery] grincer (bruyamment); [siren, jets] hurler; **the car ~ed to a halt** la voiture s'est arrêtée dans un crissement de pneus; **the machine ~ed to a stop** la machine s'est arrêtée en grinçant; **the car came ~ing round the corner** la voiture a pris le virage dans un crissement de pneus.
◇ *vt* [order] hurler, crier à tue-tête; **"never", she ~ed** «jamais», dit-elle d'une voix stridente.
◇ *n* -**1.** [of owl] ululement *m*, hululement *m*; [of gull] cri *m*, piaillement *m*; [of parrot] cri *m*; [of monkey] hurlement *m*; **the parrot gave a loud ~** le perroquet a poussé un grand cri. -**2.** [of person] cri *m* strident OR perçant; [with pain, rage] hurlement *m*; **we heard ~es of laughter coming from next door** on entendait des rires perçants qui venaient d'à côté; **"never", she said with a ~** «jamais», dit-elle d'une voix stridente. -**3.** [of tyres] crissement *m*; [of brakes] grincement *m*; [of sirens, jets] hurlement *m*; **we stopped with a ~ of brakes/tyres** on s'arrêta dans un grincement de freins/dans un crissement de pneus.

screech owl *n* chat-huant *m*, hulotte *f*.

screed [skriːd] *n* -**1.** [essay, story] longue dissertation *f*; [letter] longue lettre *f*; [speech] laïus *m*; **he wrote ~s and ~s on the French Revolution** il écrivit des pages et des pages OR des volumes sur la Révolution française. -**2.** CONSTR [level] règle *f* à araser le béton; [depth guide] guide *m*; [plaster] plâtre *m* de ragrément OR de ragréage.

screen [skriːn] ◇ *n* -**1.** CIN, PHOT & TV écran *m*; **stars of stage and ~** des vedettes de théâtre et de cinéma; **the book was adapted for the ~** le livre a été porté à l'écran. -**2.** [for protection - in front of fire] pare-étincelles *m inv*; [- over window] moustiquaire *f*. -**3.** [for privacy] paravent *m*; **the girls formed a ~ round her while she changed** les filles ont fait écran autour d'elle pendant qu'elle se changeait; **a ~ of trees** un rideau d'arbres; **the rooms are divided by sliding ~s** les pièces sont séparées par des cloisons coulissantes. -**4.** *fig* [mask] écran *m*, masque *m*; **it's only a ~ to hide his embarassment** ce n'est qu'un masque pour cacher sa gêne. -**5.** [sieve] tamis *m*, crible *m*; [filter - for employees, candidates] filtre *m*, crible *m*. -**6.** SPORT écran *m*.
◇ *vt* -**1.** CIN & TV [film] projeter, passer. -**2.** [shelter, protect] protéger; **he ~ed his eyes from the sun with his hand** il a mis sa main devant ses yeux pour se protéger du soleil; **they've tried to ~ her from the harsh realities of life** ils ont essayé de la protéger des dures réalités de la vie || [hide] cacher, masquer; **to ~ sthg from sight** cacher OR masquer qqch aux regards; **a line of trees ~ed the entrance** une rangée d'arbres cachait l'entrée. -**3.** [filter, check - employees, applications, suspects] passer au crible; **we ~ all our security staff** nous faisons une enquête préalable sur tous les candidats aux postes d'agent de sécurité; **all airlines now ~ passengers systematically** les compagnies aériennes font maintenant passer systématiquement tous les passagers par un détecteur; **the hospital ~s thousands of women a year for breast cancer** MED l'hôpital fait passer un test de dépistage du cancer du sein à des milliers de femmes tous les ans. -**4.** [sieve - coal, dirt] cribler, passer au crible.
◇ *comp* [actor, star] de cinéma.

◆ **screen off** *vt sep* -**1.** [put screens round - patient] abriter derrière un paravent; [- bed] entourer de paravents; **the police had ~ed off the garden** la police avait mis des bâches autour du jardin. -**2.** [divide, separate - with partition] séparer par une cloison; [- with curtain] séparer par un rideau; [- with folding screen] séparer par un paravent; **the manager's office is ~ed off from the typing pool by a glass partition** le bureau du directeur est séparé du pool des dactylos par une cloison vitrée. -**3.** [hide - with folding screen] cacher derrière un paravent; [- with curtain] cacher derrière un rideau; [- behind trees, wall] cacher; **the house was ~ed off from the road by tall trees** de grands arbres empêchaient de voir la maison depuis la route.

◆ **screen out** *vt sep* filtrer, éliminer; **this cream ~s out UV rays** cette crème protège des UV, cette crème absorbe OR filtre les UV; **unsuitable blood donors are ~ed out** les donneurs dont le sang est inutilisable sont exclus OR éliminés.

screen door *n Am* porte *f* avec moustiquaire.

screening [ˈskriːnɪŋ] *n* -**1.** CIN projection *f* (en salle); TV passage *m* (à l'écran), diffusion *f*. -**2.** [of applications, candidates] tri *m*, sélection *f*; [for security] contrôle *m*; MED [for cancer, tuberculosis] test *m* OR tests *mpl* de dépistage; **she went for cancer ~** elle est allée passer un test de dépistage du cancer. -**3.** [mesh] grillage *m*. -**4.** [of coal] criblage *m*; **coal ~s** [waste] déchets *mpl* de charbon.

screen memory *n* souvenir écran *m*.

screenplay [ˈskriːnpleɪ] *n* scénario *m*.

screen printing *n* sérigraphie *f*.

screen process *n* sérigraphie *f*.

screen test *n* CIN bout *m* d'essai.

◆ **screen-test** *vt* faire faire un bout d'essai à; **she was screen-tested for the part** on lui a fait faire un bout d'essai pour le rôle.

screenwriter [ˈskriːnˌraɪtəʳ] *n* scénariste *mf*.

screw [skruː] ◇ *n* -**1.** [for wood] vis *f*; [bolt] boulon *m*; [in vice] vis *f*; **to turn the ~** OR **~s** *fig* serrer la vis ❑ **to put the ~s on sb** *inf* faire pression sur qqn; **the Mafia put the ~s on him** la mafia lui a forcé la main; **to have a ~ loose** *inf* avoir la tête fêlée, être fêlé. -**2.** [turn] tour *m* de vis; **give it a couple more ~s** donnez-lui encore un ou deux tours de vis. -**3.** [thread] pas *m* de vis. -**4.** [propeller] hélice *f*. -**5.** *Br* [of salt, tobacco] cornet *m*; **a ~ of paper** un cornet en papier. -**6.** *prison sl* maton *m*. -**7.** ▽ *Br* [salary] salaire *m*, paye *f*; **he's on a good ~** il gagne plein de fric. -**8.** ▼ [sexual]: **to have a ~** *Br* baiser, s'envoyer en l'air; **she's a good ~** elle baise bien.
◇ *vt* -**1.** [bolt, screw] visser; [handle, parts] fixer avec des vis; [lid on bottle] visser; **to ~ sthg shut** fermer qqch (en vissant); **to ~ the lid on a bottle** visser le bouchon d'une bouteille; **~ it tight** vissez-le bien. -**2.** [crumple] froisser, chiffonner; **I ~ed the letter/my handkerchief into a ball** j'ai fait une boule de la lettre/de mo mouchoir. -**3.** [wrinkle - face]: **he ~ed his fac into a grimace** une grimace lui tordit le visage **he ~ed his face into a forced smile** il grimaç un sourire. -**4.** *inf* [obtain] arracher; **to ~ promise/an agreement out of sb** arracher un promesse/un accord à qqn; **he managed to ~ the money/the answer out of her** il a réussi lui soutirer l'argent/la réponse. -**5.** ▽[con] a naquer, baiser; **we've been ~ed!** on s'est fa arnaquer OR baiser! -**6.**▼ [sexually] baiser. -**7.**▽ [a invective]: **~ you all!** allez tous vous fair foutre!; **~ the expense!** et merde, je peux bie m'offrir ça!
◇ *vi* -**1.** [bolt, lid] se visser. -**2.** ▽ [sexually] baise

◆ **screw around** *vi insep* -**1.** ▽ *Am* [waste time glander; [fool about] déconner. -**2.** ▼ [slee around] baiser avec n'importe qui, coucher droite à gauche.

◆ **screw down** ◇ *vt sep* visser.
◇ *vi insep* se visser.

◆ **screw off** ◇ *vt sep* dévisser.
◇ *vi insep* se dévisser.

◆ **screw on** ◇ *vt sep* visser; **the cupboard wa ~ed on to the wall** le placard était vissé a mur.
◇ *vi insep* se visser; **it ~s on to the wall** ça s visse dans le mur.

◆ **screw round** *vt sep Br* visser, tourner; **h ~ed his head round to see** il a brusquemen tourné la tête pour voir.

◆ **screw up** *vt sep* -**1.** [tighten, fasten] visse -**2.** [crumple - handkerchief, paper] chiffonne faire une boule de. -**3.** *Br* [eyes] plisser; **she ~e up her eyes** elle plissa les yeux; **he ~ed up hi face in concentration** la concentration fit s plisser les traits de son visage; **to ~ up one' courage** prendre son courage à deux mains -**4.** *inf* [mess up - plans, chances] bousiller, foutr en l'air; [- person] faire perdre ses moyens à angoisser, mettre dans tous ses états; **he's ~e up any chance of promotion** il a foutu en l'ai toute chance de promotion; **the divorce reall ~ed her up** le divorce l'a complètement per turbée OR déboussolée.

screwball *inf* [ˈskruːbɔːl] *Am* ◇ *n* -**1.** [crazy cinglé *m*, -e *f*, dingue *mf*. -**2.** [in baseball] *balle qu dévie de sa trajectoire*.
◇ *adj* cinglé, dingue.

screwdriver [ˈskruːˌdraɪvəʳ] *n* -**1.** [tool] tourne vis *m*. -**2.** [drink] vodka-orange *f*.

screwed▽ [skruːd] *adj Br* beurré.

screwed-up *adj* -**1.** [crumpled] froissé, chif fonné. -**2.** *inf* [confused] paumé; [neurotic] per turbé, angoissé; **I just feel very ~ about the whole thing** tout cela m'angoisse terriblement **he's very ~** il est complètement paumé.

screw jack *n* cric *m* à vis.

screw propeller *n* NAUT hélice *f*.

screw thread *n* pas *m* OR filet *m* de vis.

screw top *n* couvercle *m* qui se visse; **the jar has a ~** le couvercle du pot se visse.

◆ **screwtop** *adj* dont le couvercle se visse.

screwy *inf* [ˈskruːɪ] (*compar* **screwier**, *super* **screwiest**) *adj* timbré, cinglé.

scribble [ˈskrɪbl] ◇ *vt* -**1.** [note, drawing] gribouiller, griffonner; **she left me a hastily ~d note** elle m'a laissé un mot gribouillé à la hâte; **she ~d a few lines to her sister** elle griffonna quelques lignes à l'intention de sa sœur. -**2.** [wool] carder.
◇ *vi* gribouiller.
◇ *n* gribouillis *m*, gribouillage *m*, griffonnage *m*; **the last word was an illegible ~** le dernier mot n'était qu'un illisible gribouillis; **I can't read this ~** je n'arrive pas à déchiffrer ce gribouillage; **what are all these ~s?** qu'est-ce que c'est que tous ces gribouillis?

◆ **scribble down** *vt sep* [address, number] griffonner, noter (rapidement).

◆ **scribble out** *vt sep* -**1.** [cross out] biffer, raturer. -**2.** [write] griffonner.

scribbler [ˈskrɪbləʳ] *n Br pej* [author] écrivaillon *m*.

scribbling ['skrɪblɪŋ] *n* gribouillis *m*, gribouillage *m*.
scribbling pad *n* bloc-notes *m*.
scribe [skraɪb] ◇ *n* scribe *m*.
◇ *vt* graver.
scriber ['skraɪbəʳ] *n* traçoir *m*, traceret *m*.
scrimmage ['skrɪmɪdʒ] ◇ *n* -**1.** SPORT mêlée *f*. -**2.** [brawl] mêlée *f*, bagarre *f*.
◇ *vi* SPORT faire une mêlée.
◇ *vt* SPORT [ball] mettre dans la mêlée.
scrimp [skrɪmp] ◇ *vi* lésiner; she ~s on food elle lésine sur la nourriture; to ~ and save économiser sur tout, se serrer la ceinture.
◇ *vt* [children, family] se montrer pingre avec; [food] lésiner sur.
scrimshank *inf* ['skrɪmʃæŋk] *vi Br* MIL tirer au flanc.
scrimshanker *inf* ['skrɪmʃæŋkəʳ] *n Br* MIL tire-au-flanc *m inv*.
scrip [skrɪp] *n* -**1.** ST. EX titre *m* provisoire. -**2.** [of paper] morceau *m*.
scrip issue *n* ST. EX émission *f* d'actions gratuites.
script [skrɪpt] ◇ *n* -**1.** [text] script *m*, texte *m*; CIN script *m*. -**2.** *(U)* [handwriting] script *m*, écriture *f* script; the letter is written in beautiful ~ la lettre est superbement calligraphiée; to write in ~ écrire en script || [lettering, characters] écriture *f*, caractères *mpl*, lettres *fpl*; Arabic ~ caractères arabes, écriture arabe; in italic ~ en italique. -**3.** [copy] JUR original *m*; UNIV copie *f* (d'examen).
◇ *vt* CIN écrire le script de.
scripted ['skrɪptɪd] *adj* [speech, interview etc] (dont le texte a été) écrit d'avance.
script girl *n* scripte *mf*, script girl *f*.
scriptural ['skrɪptʃərəl] *adj* biblique.
Scripture ['skrɪptʃəʳ] *n* -**1.** [Christian] Écriture *f* (sainte); a reading from the ~s une lecture biblique OR de la Bible; a ~ lesson une leçon d'études bibliques. -**2.** [non-Christian]: the ~s les textes *mpl* sacrés.
scriptwriter ['skrɪpt,raɪtəʳ] *n* scénariste *mf*.
scrivener ['skrɪvnəʳ] *n arch* écrivain *m* public.
scrod [skrɒd] *n Am* CULIN moruette *f*.
scrofula ['skrɒfjʊlə] *n (U)* scrofule *f*.
scrofulous ['skrɒfjʊləs] *adj* scrofuleux.
scroll [skrəʊl] ◇ *n* -**1.** [of parchment] rouleau *m*. -**2.** [manuscript] manuscrit *m* (ancien). -**3.** [on column, violin, woodwork] volute *f*.
◇ *vt* COMPUT faire défiler.
◇ *vi* COMPUT défiler.
◆ **scroll through** *vt insep* COMPUT faire défiler d'un bout à l'autre.
scrolling ['skrəʊlɪŋ] *n* COMPUT défilement *m*.
scroll saw *n* scie *f* à chantourner.
scrooge [skru:dʒ] *n* grippe-sou *m*, harpagon *m*.
◆ **Scrooge** *pr n personnage de Dickens incarnant l'avarice*.
scrotum ['skrəʊtəm] (*pl* scrotums OR scrota [-tə]) *n* scrotum *m*.
scrounge *inf* [skraʊndʒ] ◇ *vt* [sugar, pencil] emprunter, piquer; [meal] se faire offrir; [money] se faire prêter; he tried to ~ $10 off me il a essayé de me taper de 10 dollars; can I ~ a lift? pouvez-vous m'emmener en voiture?
◇ *vi*: he came scrounging round *Br* OR around *Am* to see what he could find il est venu faire un tour pour voir s'il n'y avait pas quelque chose à récolter; to ~ on OR off sb [habitually] vivre aux crochets de qqn; he's always scrounging off his friends il fait toujours le pique-assiette chez ses amis, il tape toujours ses amis; I'm sorry to be always scrounging je suis désolé d'être toujours à quémander.
◇ *n*: to be on the ~ [for food] venir quémander de quoi manger; [for cigarette] venir quémander une cigarette; she's on the ~ for a meal elle veut se faire inviter à manger; he's always on the ~ il vit toujours aux crochets des autres.
scrounger *inf* ['skraʊndʒəʳ] *n* pique-assiette *mf*, parasite *m*.
scrub [skrʌb] (*pt* & *pp* scrubbed, *cont* scrubbing)
◇ *vt* -**1.** [clean, wash] brosser *(avec de l'eau et du savon)*; [floor, carpet] nettoyer à la brosse, frotter avec une brosse; [saucepan, sink] frotter, récurer; [clothes, face, back] frotter; [fingernails] brosser; to ~ sthg clean nettoyer qqch à fond, récurer qqch; ~ yourself all over frotte-toi bien partout; have you scrubbed your hands clean? est-ce que tu t'es bien nettoyé les mains? -**2.** [cancel - order] annuler; [- plans, holiday] annuler, laisser tomber; we'll have to ~ dinner il faudra qu'on se passe de dîner || [recording, tape] effacer; I'd prefer to ~ that remark j'aimerais mieux que cette remarque soit effacée. -**3.** TECH [gas] laver.
◇ *vi*: I spent the morning scrubbing j'ai passé la matinée à frotter les planchers OR les sols.
◇ *n* -**1.** [with brush] coup *m* de brosse; give the floor a good ~ frotte bien le plancher; can you give my back a ~? peux-tu me frotter le dos? -**2.** [vegetation] broussailles *fpl*. -**3.** *Am* SPORT [team] équipe *f* de seconde zone; [player] joueur *m*, -euse *f* de second ordre. -**4.** *inf Austr* [wilderness] cambrousse *f*.
◆ **scrub away** ◇ *vt sep* [mark, mud] faire partir en brossant.
◇ *vi insep* partir à la brosse.
◆ **scrub down** *vt sep* [wall, paintwork] lessiver; [horse] bouchonner.
◆ **scrub out** ◇ *vt sep* -**1.** [dirt, stain] faire partir à la brosse; [bucket, tub] nettoyer à la brosse; [pan] récurer; [ears] nettoyer, bien laver. -**2.** [erase - graffiti, comment] effacer; [- name] barrer, biffer.
◇ *vi insep* partir à la brosse.
◆ **scrub up** *vi insep* MED [before operation] se laver les mains.
scrubber ['skrʌbəʳ] *n* -**1.** [for saucepans] tampon *m* à récurer. -**2.** ▽ *Br pej* [whore] pute *f*.
scrubbing brush *Br* ['skrʌbɪŋ-], **scrub brush** *Am n* brosse *f* à récurer.
scrubby ['skrʌbɪ] (*compar* scrubbier, *superl* scrubbiest) *adj* -**1.** [land] broussailleux. -**2.** [tree, vegetation] rabougri. -**3.** *inf Br* [messy] en désordre.
scrubland ['skrʌblænd] *n* maquis *m*, garrigue *f*.
scrubwoman ['skrʌb,wʊmən] (*pl* scrubwomen [-,wɪmɪn]) *n Am* femme *f* de ménage.
scruff [skrʌf] *n* -**1.** *inf Br* [untidy person] individu *m* débraillé OR dépenaillé OR peu soigné; [ruffian] voyou *m*; you look a real ~ tu es ficelé comme l'as de pique. -**2.** *phr*: by the ~ of the neck par la peau du cou.
scruffily ['skrʌfɪlɪ] *adv*: ~ dressed dépenaillé, mal habillé.
scruffy ['skrʌfɪ] (*compar* scruffier, *superl* scruffiest) *adj* [appearance, clothes] dépenaillé, crasseux; [hair] ébouriffé; [building, area] délabré, miteux; he's a ~ dresser il s'habille mal.
scrum [skrʌm] (*pt* & *pp* scrummed, *cont* scrumming) ◇ *n* -**1.** RUGBY mêlée *f*. -**2.** [brawl] mêlée *f*, bousculade *f*; there was a ~ for tickets les gens se sont bousculés pour obtenir des billets.
◇ *vi* former une mêlée.
◆ **scrum down** *vi insep* former une mêlée; ~ down! [as instruction] mêlée!
scrum-cap *n* casquette *f (de joueur de rugby)*.
scrumhalf [,skrʌm'hɑ:f] *n* demi *m* de mêlée.
scrummage ['skrʌmɪdʒ] ◇ *n* -**1.** RUGBY mêlée *f*. -**2.** [brawl] mêlée *f*, bousculade *f*; there was a ~ for the best bargains les gens se sont arrachés les soldes les plus intéressants.
◇ *vi* RUGBY former une mêlée.
scrump *inf* [skrʌmp] *Br* ◇ *vi*: to go ~ing (for apples) aller chaparder (des pommes).
◇ *vt* [apples] chaparder.
scrumptious *inf* ['skrʌmpʃəs] *adj* délicieux, succulent.
scrumpy ['skrʌmpɪ] *n cidre brut et sec fabriqué dans le sud-ouest de l'Angleterre*.
scrunch [skrʌntʃ] ◇ *vt* [biscuit, apple] croquer; [snow, gravel] faire craquer OR crisser; [paper - noisily] froisser (bruyamment).
◇ *vi* [footsteps - on gravel, snow] craquer, faire un bruit de craquement; [gravel, snow - underfoot] craquer, crisser.
◇ *n* [of gravel, snow, paper] craquement *m*, bruit *m* de craquement.
◇ *onomat* crac! crac!
◆ **scrunch up** *vt sep* -**1.** [crumple - paper] froisser; he ~ed up his face in disgust il a fait une grimace de dégoût. -**2.** *Am* [hunch]: she was sitting with her shoulders ~ed up elle était assise, les épaules rentrées.
scruple ['skru:pl] ◇ *n* scrupule *m*; he has no ~s il n'a aucun scrupule; he had ~s about accepting payment il avait des scrupules à accepter qu'on le paie; to act without ~ agir sans scrupule.
◇ *vi (only in negative uses)*: they don't ~ to cheat ils n'ont aucun scrupule OR ils n'hésitent pas à tricher.
scrupulous ['skru:pjʊləs] *adj* -**1.** [meticulous] scrupuleux, méticuleux; she's very ~ about her dress elle prête une attention scrupuleuse à la façon dont elle s'habille; they're rather ~ about punctuality ils tiennent beaucoup à la ponctualité; the papers were all in ~ order les papiers avaient été rangés avec un soin méticuleux; he acted with ~ honesty il a agi avec une honnêteté irréprochable. -**2.** [conscientious] scrupuleux.
scrupulously ['skru:pjʊləslɪ] *adv* [meticulously] scrupuleusement, parfaitement; [honestly] scrupuleusement, avec scrupule; ~ clean d'une propreté impeccable; ~ honest d'une honnêteté irréprochable; ~ punctual parfaitement à l'heure.
scrutineer [,skru:tɪ'nɪəʳ] *n Br* POL scrutateur *m*, -trice *f*.
scrutinize, -ise ['skru:tɪnaɪz] *vt* scruter, examiner attentivement.
scrutiny ['skru:tɪnɪ] (*pl* scrutinies) *n* -**1.** [examination] examen *m* approfondi; [watch] surveillance *f*; [gaze] regard *m* insistant; to be under ~ [prisoners] être sous surveillance; [accounts, staff] faire l'objet d'un contrôle; to come under ~ être contrôlé; everything we do is under close ~ tous nos actes sont surveillés de près; her work does not stand up to close ~ son travail ne résiste pas à un examen minutieux. -**2.** *Br* POL deuxième pointage *m* (des suffrages).
scuba ['skju:bə] *n* scaphandre *m* autonome.
scuba dive *vi* faire de la plongée sous-marine.
scuba diver *n* plongeur *m* sous-marin, plongeuse *f* sous-marine.
scuba diving *n* plongée *f* sous-marine.
scud [skʌd] (*pt* & *pp* scudded, *cont* scudding) *vi* glisser, filer; clouds scudded across the sky des nuages filaient dans le ciel; two boats scudded across the lake deux voiliers filaient sur le lac; she sent the pebble scudding over the waves elle envoya le galet voler au-dessus des vagues.
scuff [skʌf] ◇ *vt* -**1.** [shoe, leather] érafler, râper; her shoes were all ~ed (up) ses chaussures étaient toutes éraflées OR râpées. -**2.** [drag]: to ~ one's feet marcher en traînant les pieds, traîner les pieds.
◇ *vi* marcher en traînant les pieds.
◇ *n*: ~ (mark) éraflure *f*.
scuffle ['skʌfl] ◇ *n* -**1.** [fight] bagarre *f*, échauffourée *f*; after a brief ~, he was marched away by the police après une courte bagarre, il fut emmené par les policiers. -**2.** [of feet] piétinement.
◇ *vi* -**1.** [fight] se bagarrer, se battre; demonstrators ~d with the police des manifestants se sont battus avec la police, il y a eu des bagarres entre manifestants et policiers. -**2.** [with feet] marcher en traînant les pieds; they ~d along the corridor ils avançaient dans le couloir en traînant les pieds.
◇ *vt*: they stood at the door, scuffling their feet ils piétinaient devant la porte.
scuffling ['skʌflɪŋ] *n* bruit *m* étouffé.
scull [skʌl] ◇ *n* -**1.** [double paddle] godille *f*; [single oar] aviron *m*. -**2.** [boat] yole *f*.

◇ *vt* [with double paddle] godiller; [with oars] ramer.
◇ *vi* ramer en couple; to go ~ing faire de l'aviron.

scullery ['skʌlərɪ] (*pl* sculleries) *n Br* arrière-cuisine *f*.

scullery maid *n Br* fille *f* de cuisine.

sculpt [skʌlpt] ◇ *vt* sculpter.
◇ *vi* faire de la sculpture.

sculptor ['skʌlptəʳ] *n* sculpteur *m*.

sculptress ['skʌlptrɪs] *n* (femme *f*) sculpteur *m*.

sculptural ['skʌlptʃərəl] *adj* sculptural.

sculpture ['skʌlptʃəʳ] ◇ *n* -**1.** [art] sculpture *f*. -**2.** [object] sculpture *f*; it's a beautiful (piece of) ~ c'est une très belle sculpture.
◇ *vt* sculpter.
◇ *vi* sculpter; to ~ in bronze sculpter dans le bronze.

scum [skʌm] ◇ *n* [on liquid, sea] écume *f*; [in bath] (traînées *fpl* de) crasse *f*; METALL écume *f*, scories *fpl*; to take the ~ off [liquid] écumer; [bath] nettoyer.
◇ *npl inf* [people] rebut *m*, lie *f*; they're just ~ ce sont des minables; the ~ of the earth le rebut de l'humanité; they treated us like ~ on nous a traités comme des moins que rien OR des chiens.

scumbag▽ ['skʌmbæg] *n* salaud *m*, ordure *f*.

scummy ['skʌmɪ] (*compar* scummier, *superl* scummiest) *adj* -**1.** [liquid] écumeux. -**2.** ▽ [person] salaud.

scuncheon ['skʌntʃən] *n* ARCHIT battée *f*.

scunner ['skʌnəʳ] ◇ *n Scot* [dislike]: to take a ~ to sb/sthg prendre qqn/qqch en grippe.
◇ *vt Scot* détester, avoir horreur de.

scupper ['skʌpəʳ] ◇ *vt Br* -**1.** [ship] saborder. -**2.** [plans, attempt] saborder, faire capoter; we're completely ~ed unless we can find the cash on est finis si on ne trouve pas l'argent.
◇ *n* NAUT dalot *m*.

scurf [skɜːf] *n (U)* [dandruff] pellicules *fpl*; [on skin] squames *fpl*; [on plant] lamelles *fpl*.

scurfy ['skɜːfɪ] (*compar* scurfier, *superl* scurfiest) *adj* [scalp] couvert de pellicules; [skin] squameux.

scurrility [skʌ'rɪlətɪ] (*pl* scurrilities) *n* -**1.** [of remarks] caractère *m* calomnieux OR outrageant; [of action] bassesse *f*. -**2.** [vulgarity] grossièreté *f*.

scurrilous ['skʌrələs] *adj* [lying] calomnieux, mensonger; [insulting] outrageant, ignoble; [bitter] fielleux; [vulgar] grossier, vulgaire.

scurry ['skʌrɪ] (*pt* & *pp* scurried, *pl* scurries)
◇ *vi* se précipiter, courir; all the animals were ~ing for shelter tous les animaux couraient pour se mettre à l'abri; they scurried for the trees ils se précipitèrent vers les arbres; the sound of ~ing feet le bruit de pas précipités.
◇ *n* -**1.** [rush] course *f* (précipitée), débandade *f*; there was a ~ for the door tout le monde s'est rué vers la porte. -**2.** [sound - of feet] bruit *m* de pas précipités.
◆ **scurry away, scurry off** *vi insep* [animal] détaler; [person] décamper, prendre ses jambes à son cou.
◆ **scurry out** *vi insep* [animal] détaler; [person] sortir à toute vitesse.

scurvy ['skɜːvɪ] (*compar* scurvier, *superl* scurviest) ◇ *n (U)* scorbut *m*.
◇ *adj* [trick] honteux, ignoble; you ~ knave! *arch* OR *hum* (espèce de) misérable fripon!

scutcheon ['skʌtʃn] = **escutcheon**.

scuttle ['skʌtl] ◇ *vi insep* [run] courir à pas précipités, se précipiter.
◇ *vt* -**1.** NAUT saborder; the whole fleet was ~d tout la flotte a été sabordée. -**2.** [hopes] ruiner; [plans] saborder, faire échouer.
◇ *n* -**1.** [run] course *f* précipitée, débandade *f*. -**2.** (coal) ~ seau *m* à charbon. -**3.** NAUT écoutille *f*. -**4.** *Am* [in ceiling, floor] trappe *f*.
◆ **scuttle away, scuttle off** *vi insep* [animal] détaler; [person] déguerpir, se sauver.
◆ **scuttle out** *vi insep* sortir précipitamment.

scuttlebutt ['skʌtlbʌt] *n* [for drinking] fontaine *f*; NAUT tonneau *m* d'eau douce.

scuzzy▽ ['skʌzɪ] *adj Am* dégueulasse.

Scylla ['sɪlə] *pr n* → **Charybdis**.

scythe [saɪð] ◇ *n* faux *f*.
◇ *vt* faucher.

SD *written abbr of* South Dakota.

SDI (*abbr of* Strategic Defense Initiative) *pr n* IDS *f*.

SDLP *pr n abbr of* Social Democratic and Labour Party.

SDP *pr n abbr of* Social Democratic Party.

SDRs (*abbr of* special drawing rights) *npl* DTS *mpl*.

SE (*written abbr of* south-east) S-E.

sea [siː] ◇ *n* -**1.** GEOG mer *f*; by land and ~ par terre et par mer; to travel by ~ voyager par mer OR par bateau; the goods were sent by ~ les marchandises ont été expédiées par bateau; he's spent all his life on the ~ il a passé toute sa vie en mer; at ~ [boat, storm] en mer; [as sailor] de OR comme marin; we spent six months at ~ on a passé six mois en mer; life at ~ la vie en mer OR de marin; to swim in the ~ nager OR se baigner dans la mer; to put (out) to ~ prendre la mer; to go to ~ [boat] prendre la mer; [sailor] se faire marin; to run away to ~ partir se faire marin; to look out to ~ regarder vers le large; the little boat was swept OR washed out to ~ le petit bateau a été emporté vers le large; across OR over the ~ OR ~s outre-mer; a heavy ~, heavy ~s une grosse mer ☐ the Sea of Tranquillity la mer de la Tranquillité; ~ and air search recherches *fpl* maritimes et aériennes; to be at ~ *inf Br* [be lost] nager; [be mixed-up] être déboussolé OR désorienté; when it comes to computers, I'm all at ~ je ne connais strictement rien aux ordinateurs; he's been all at ~ since his wife left him il est complètement déboussolé OR il a complètement perdu le nord depuis que sa femme l'a quitté; the resignation of our secretary has left the reference department all at ~ la démission de notre secrétaire a totalement perturbé notre service des archives. -**2.** [seaside] bord *m* de la mer; they live by OR beside the ~ ils habitent au bord de la mer; the town is by the ~ la ville est au bord de la mer. -**3.** [large quantity - of blood, mud] mer *f*; [- of problems, faces] multitude *f*.
◇ *comp* [fish] de mer; ~ bathing bains *mpl* de mer; ~ battle bataille *f* navale; ~ breeze brise *f* marine; ~ view vue *f* sur la mer.

sea air *n* air *m* marin OR de la mer.

sea anemone *n* anémone *f* de mer.

sea bass *n* bar *m*, loup *m*.

seabed ['siːbed] *n* fond *m* de la mer OR marin.

seabird ['siːbɜːd] *n* oiseau *m* de mer.

seaboard ['siːbɔːd] *n* littoral *m*, côte *f*; on the Atlantic ~ sur la côte atlantique.

seaborne ['siːbɔːn] *adj* [trade] maritime; [goods, troops] transporté par mer OR par bateau.

sea bream *n* daurade *f*, dorade *f*.

sea captain *n* capitaine *m* de la marine marchande.

sea change *n* changement *m* radical, profond changement.

seacoast [ˌsiː'kəʊst] *n* côte *f*, littoral *m*.

sea cow *n* vache *f* marine, sirénien *m*.

sea cucumber *n* concombre *m* de mer, holothurie *f*.

sea dog *n* -**1.** [fish] roussette *f*, chien *m* de mer; [seal] phoque *m*. -**2.** *lit* OR *hum* [sailor] (vieux) loup *m* de mer. -**3.** [in fog] arc-en-ciel *m* *(aperçu dans le brouillard)*.

seafarer ['siːˌfeərəʳ] *n* marin *m*.

seafaring ['siːˌfeərɪŋ] ◇ *adj* [nation] maritime, de marins; [life] de marin.
◇ *n* vie *f* de marin.

seafloor ['siːflɔːʳ] *n* fond *m* de (la) mer OR marin.

sea fog *n* brouillard *m* *(en mer)*.

seafood ['siːfuːd] *n (U)* (poissons *mpl* et) fruits *mpl* de mer.

seafront ['siːfrʌnt] *n* bord *m* de mer, front *m* de mer.

sea god *n* dieu *m* marin OR de la mer.

seagoing ['siːˌgəʊɪŋ] *adj* [trade, nation] maritime; [life] de marin; a ~ man un marin, un homme de mer; a ~ ship un navire de haute mer, un (navire) long-courrier.

sea green *n* vert *m* glauque.
◆ **sea-green** *adj* glauque.

seagull ['siːgʌl] *n* mouette *f*; 'The Seagull' *Chekhov* 'la Mouette'.

seahorse ['siːhɔːs] *n* hippocampe *m*.

seakale ['siːkeɪl] *n* chou *m* marin, crambe *m*.

seal [siːl] ◇ *n* -**1.** ZOOL phoque *m*. -**2.** [tool] sceau *m*, cachet *m*; [on document, letter] sceau *m*; [on crate] plombage *m*; [on battery, gas cylinder] bande *f* de garantie; [on meter] plomb *m*; given under my hand and ~ *Br* ADMIN & JUR signé et scellé par moi; to put one's ~ to a document apposer son sceau à un document; does the project have her ~ of approval? est-ce qu'elle a approuvé le projet?; to put OR to set the ~ on sthg [confirm] sceller qqch; [bring to end] mettre fin à qqch. -**3.** *(U)* JUR [on door] scellé *m*, scellés *mpl*; under ~ sous scellés; under (the) ~ of secrecy/of silence *fig* sous le sceau du secret/du silence; under the ~ of confession RELIG dans le secret de la confession. -**4.** COMM label *m*; ~ of quality label de qualité. -**5.** [joint - for engine, jar, sink] joint *m* d'étanchéité; [putty] mastic *m*. -**6.** [stamp]: Christmas ~ timbre *m* de Noël.
◇ *vt* -**1.** [document] apposer son sceau à, sceller; ~ed with a kiss scellé d'un baiser; her fate is ~ed *fig* son sort est réglé; they finally ~ed the deal *fig* ils ont enfin conclu l'affaire. -**2.** [close - envelope] cacheter, fermer; [- with sticky tape] coller, fermer; [- jar] sceller, fermer hermétiquement; [- can] souder; [- tube, mineshaft] sceller; [window, door - for insulation] isoler; ~ed orders des ordres scellés sous pli; my lips are ~ed *fig* mes lèvres sont scellées. -**3.** JUR [door] apposer des scellés sur; [evidence] mettre sous scellés; [at customs - goods] (faire) sceller. -**4.** CULIN [meat] saisir.
◇ *vi* ZOOL: to go ~ing aller à la chasse au phoque.
◆ **seal in** *vt sep* enfermer hermétiquement; the flavour is ~ed in by freeze-drying le produit garde toute sa saveur grâce à la lyophilisation.
◆ **seal off** *vt sep* [passage, road] interdire l'accès de; [entrance] condamner; the street had been ~ed off la rue avait été fermée (à la circulation).
◆ **seal up** *vt sep* = **seal** *vt* **2**.

sea lane *n* couloir *m* de navigation.

sealant ['siːlənt] *n* -**1.** [paste, putty] produit *m* d'étanchéité; [paint] enduit *m* étanche; [for radiator] anti-fuite *m*. -**2.** [joint] joint *m* d'étanchéité.

sealed [siːld] *adj* scellé; [document] scellé; [envelope] cacheté; [jar] fermé hermétiquement; [mineshaft] obturé, bouché; [joint] étanche.

sealed-beam *adj*: ~ headlight phare *m* type sealed-beam.

sea legs *npl*: to find OR to get one's ~ s'amariner, s'habituer à la mer.

sealer ['siːləʳ] *n* -**1.** [hunter] chasseur *m* de phoques; [ship] navire *m* équipé pour la chasse aux phoques. -**2.** [paint, varnish] enduit *m*, première couche *f*.

sea level *n* niveau *m* de la mer; above/below ~ au-dessus/au-dessous du niveau de la mer.

sealing ['siːlɪŋ] *n* -**1.** [hunting] chasse *f* aux phoques. -**2.** [of document] cachetage *m*; [of crate] plombage *m*; [of door] scellage *m*; [of shaft, mine] fermeture *f*, obturation *f*.

sealing wax *n* cire *f* à cacheter.

sea lion *n* otarie *f*.

sea-lord *n Br* NAUT amiral *m* de l'état-major de la marine.

seal-point *n* seal-point *m*.

seal ring *n* chevalière *f*.

sealskin ['siːlskɪn] ◇ *n* peau *f* de phoque.
◇ *adj* en peau de phoque.

seam [siːm] ◇ *n* -**1.** [on garment, stocking] couture *f*; [in airbed, bag] couture *f*, joint *m*; [weld] soudure *f*; [between planks] joint *m*; **your coat is coming** OR **falling apart at the ~s** votre manteau se découd; **my suitcase was bulging** OR **bursting at the ~s** ma valise était pleine à craquer; **their marriage is coming** OR **falling apart at the ~s** *fig* leur mariage craque. -**2.** [of coal, ore] filon *m*, veine *f*; [in rocks] couche *f*.
◇ *comp* [in cricket]: **a ~ bowler** *un lanceur qui utilise les coutures de la balle pour la faire dévier*.
◇ *vt* [garment] faire une couture dans, coudre; [plastic, metal, wood] faire un joint à.

seaman ['siːmən] (*pl* **seamen** [-mən]) *n* -**1.** [sailor] marin *m*. -**2.** [in US Navy] quartier-maître *m* de 2ᵉ classe; **~ apprentice** matelot *m* en formation; **~ recruit** matelot *m*.

seamanship ['siːmənʃɪp] *n (U)* qualités *fpl* de marin.

seamark ['siːmɑːk] *n* NAUT amer *m*, repère *m*.

seamed [siːmd] *adj* [furrowed] ridé, sillonné; **the rock was ~ with quartz** la roche était veinée de quartz; **his face was ~ by deep wrinkles** son visage était marqué de profondes rides.

seamen ['siːmən] *pl* → **seaman**.

sea mile *n* mille *m* marin.

seamless ['siːmlɪs] *adj* sans couture; *fig* homogène, cohérent.

seamlessly ['siːmlɪslɪ] *adv* d'une façon cohérente OR homogène.

seamstress ['semstrɪs] *n* couturière *f*.

seamy ['siːmɪ] (*compar* **seamier**, *superl* **seamiest**) *adj* sordide, louche; **the ~ side of life** le côté sordide de la vie.

séance ['seɪɑːns] *n* -**1.** [for raising spirits] séance *f* de spiritisme. -**2.** [meeting] séance *f*, réunion *f*.

sea otter *n* loutre *f* de mer.

seaplane ['siːpleɪn] *n* hydravion *m*.

seaport ['siːpɔːt] *n* port *m* maritime.

sear [sɪəʳ] ◇ *vt* -**1.** [burn] brûler; [brand] marquer au fer rouge; MED cautériser; **the scene ~ed itself on my memory** la scène est restée gravée OR marquée dans ma mémoire. -**2.** [wither] dessécher, flétrir. -**3.** *arch* [harden - heart, feelings] endurcir.
◇ *n* [burn] (marque *f* de) brûlure *f*.
◇ *adj lit* desséché, flétri.
◆ **sear through** *vt insep* [metal, wall] traverser, percer; **the pain ~ed through me** la douleur me transperça.

search [sɜːtʃ] ◇ *vt* -**1.** [look in - room] chercher (partout) dans; [- pockets, drawers] fouiller (dans), chercher dans; **we've ~ed the whole house for the keys** nous avons cherché dans toute la maison pour retrouver les clés; **she ~ed her bag for a comb** elle fouilla dans son sac à la recherche d'une peigne. -**2.** [subj: police, customs] fouiller; [with warrant] perquisitionner, faire une perquisition dans; **the flat was ~ed for drugs** on a fouillé l'appartement pour trouver de la drogue; **the spectators were ~ed before they were let in** les spectateurs ont été fouillés à l'entrée; **they ~ed the undergrowth for the murder weapon** on a fouillé le sous-bois OR on a passé le sous-bois au peigne fin pour retrouver l'arme du crime; **customs ~ed our luggage/our car** les douaniers ont fouillé nos bagages/notre voiture ❑ **~ me!** *inf* je n'en ai pas la moindre idée! -**3.** [examine, consult - records] chercher dans; [- memory] chercher dans, fouiller; [- conscience] sonder; COMPUT [file] consulter; **I ~ed her face for some sign of emotion** j'ai cherché sur son visage des signes d'émotion.
◇ *vi* chercher; **to ~ for sthg** chercher qqch, rechercher qqch; **to ~ after the truth** rechercher la vérité ‖ COMPUT: **to ~ for a file** rechercher un fichier; **'searching'** 'recherche'.
◇ *n* -**1.** [gen] recherche *f*, recherches *fpl*; **in the ~ for** OR **in my ~ for ancestors, I had to travel to Canada** au cours des recherches OR de mes recherches pour retrouver mes ancêtres, j'ai dû me rendre au Canada; **at first light, the ~ for the missing climbers was resumed** dès l'aube, les recherches ont repris pour retrouver les alpinistes disparus; **helicopters made a ~ for survivors** des hélicoptères ont fait OR effectué des recherches pour retrouver des survivants; **to make a ~ through one's pockets/the drawers** fouiller (dans) ses poches/les tiroirs ❑ **~ and rescue operation** opération *f* de recherche et secours. -**2.** [by police, customs - of house, person, bags] fouille *f*; [- with warrant] perquisition *f*; **the police made a thorough ~ of the premises** la police a fouillé les locaux de fond en comble; **customs carried out a ~ of the van** les douaniers ont procédé à la fouille de la camionnette; **the ~ unearthed a stockpile of arms** la fouille a permis de mettre à jour une cache d'armes. -**3.** COMPUT recherche *f*.
◆ **in search of** *prep phr* à la recherche de; **in ~ of the truth** à la recherche de la vérité; **I went in ~ of a restaurant** je suis parti à la recherche d'un restaurant.
◆ **search out** *vt sep* [look for] rechercher; [find] trouver, dénicher.
◆ **search through** *vt insep* [drawer, pockets] fouiller (dans); [case, documents] fouiller; [records] consulter, faire des recherches dans; [memory] fouiller, chercher dans.

searcher ['sɜːtʃəʳ] *n* chercheur *m*, -euse *f*; **300 ~s combed the woods** 300 personnes ont passé les bois au peigne fin; **~s after truth** ceux qui sont à la recherche de la vérité.

searching ['sɜːtʃɪŋ] *adj* -**1.** [look, eyes] pénétrant; **he gave me a ~ look** il m'a lancé un regard pénétrant. -**2.** [examination] rigoureux, minutieux; **he asked me some ~ questions** il m'a posé des questions inquisitrices.

searchingly ['sɜːtʃɪŋlɪ] *adv* [look] de façon pénétrante; [examine] rigoureusement; [question] minutieusement.

searchlight ['sɜːtʃlaɪt] *n* projecteur *m*; **in the ~** à la lumière des projecteurs.

search party *n* équipe *f* de secours.

search warrant *n* mandat *m* de perquisition.

searing ['sɪərɪŋ] *adj* -**1.** [pain] fulgurant; [light] éclatant, fulgurant. -**2.** [attack, criticism] sévère, impitoyable.

Sears Roebuck® [,sɪəz'rəʊbʌk] *pr n grande chaîne de magasins américaine*.

seascape ['siːskeɪp] *n* -**1.** [view] paysage *m* marin. -**2.** ART marine *f*.

sea scout *n* scout *m* marin.

sea serpent *n* serpent *m* de mer.

sea shanty *n* chanson *f* de marins.

seashell ['siːʃel] *n* coquillage *m*.

seashore ['siːʃɔːʳ] *n* [edge of sea] rivage *m*, bord *m* de (la) mer; [beach] plage *f*.

seasick ['siːsɪk] *adj*: **to be ~** avoir le mal de mer.

seasickness ['siːsɪknɪs] *n* mal *m* de mer.

seaside ['siːsaɪd] ◇ *n* bord *m* de (la) mer; **we spent the afternoon at the ~** nous avons passé l'après-midi au bord de la mer OR à la mer; **we live by** OR **at the ~** nous habitons au bord de la mer.
◇ *comp* [holiday, vacation] au bord de la mer, à la mer; [town, hotel] au bord de la mer, de bord de mer; **~ landlady** *Br propriétaire d'une pension de famille au bord de la mer*; **~ resort** station *f* balnéaire.

sea slug *n* nudibranche *m*.

sea snake *n* serpent *m* de mer.

season ['siːzn] ◇ *n* -**1.** [summer, winter etc] saison *f*; **in the rainy ~** pendant la saison des pluies ❑ **'The Four Seasons'** *Vivaldi* 'les Quatre Saisons'. -**2.** [for trade] saison *f*; **the start of the tourist/of the holiday ~** le début de la saison touristique/des vacances; **at the height of the Christmas ~** en pleine période de Noël; **it's a busy ~ for tour operators** c'est une époque très chargée pour les voyagistes; **the low/high ~** la basse/haute saison; **in ~** en saison; **off ~** hors saison. -**3.** [for fruit, vegetables] saison *f*; **strawberries are in/out of ~** les fraises sont/ne sont pas de saison, c'est/ce n'est pas la saison des fraises. -**4.** [for breeding] époque *f*, période *f*; **the breeding ~** la période de la reproduction, la saison des amours; **to be in ~** [animal] être en chaleur. -**5.** [for sport, entertainment] saison *f*; **the football ~** la saison de football; **next ~, he's playing for Liverpool** la saison prochaine, il joue dans l'équipe de Liverpool ‖ [for show, actor] saison *f*; **the summer ~** la saison d'été; **he did a ~ at Brighton** il a fait la saison de Brighton; **a new ~ of French drama** RADIO & TV un nouveau cycle de pièces de théâtre français ‖ [for hunting] saison *f*, période *f*; **the hunting/fishing ~** la saison de la chasse/de la pêche; **the grouse ~** la saison de (la chasse à) la grouse; **the start of the ~** HUNT l'ouverture de la chasse; FISHING l'ouverture de la pêche ‖ [for socializing] saison *f*; **the social ~** la saison mondaine; **the London/New York ~** la saison londonienne/new-yorkaise. -**6.** [Christmas]: **'Season's Greetings'** 'Joyeux Noël et Bonne Année'. -**7.** *lit* [suitable moment] moment *m* opportun; **in due ~** en temps voulu, au moment opportun.
◇ *vt* -**1.** [food - with seasoning] assaisonner; [- with spice] épicer; **his speech was ~ed with witty remarks** *fig* son discours était parsemé OR agrémenté de remarques spirituelles. -**2.** [timber] (faire) sécher, laisser sécher; [cask] abreuver. -**3.** *fml* [moderate] modérer, tempérer.

seasonable ['siːznəbl] *adj* -**1.** [weather] de saison. -**2.** [opportune] à propos, opportun.

seasonal ['siːzənl] *adj* saisonnier; **~ worker** saisonnier *m*; **~ affective disorder** troubles *mpl* de l'humeur saisonniers.

seasonally ['siːznəlɪ] *adv* de façon saisonnière; **~ adjusted statistics** statistiques corrigées des variations saisonnières, statistiques désaisonnalisées.

seasoned ['siːznd] *adj* -**1.** [food] assaisonné, épicé; **highly ~** bien épicé OR relevé. -**2.** [wood] desséché, séché. -**3.** [experienced] expérimenté, chevronné, éprouvé; **a ~ traveller** un voyageur expérimenté.

seasoning ['siːznɪŋ] *n* -**1.** [for food] assaisonnement *m*; **there isn't enough ~** ce n'est pas assez assaisonné. -**2.** [of wood] séchage *m*; [of cask] abreuvage *m*.

season ticket *n* (carte *f* d') abonnement *m*; **to take out a ~** prendre un abonnement; **~ holder** abonné *m*, -e *f*.

seat [siːt] ◇ *n* -**1.** [chair, stool] siège *m*; [on bicycle] selle *f*; [in car - single] siège *m*; [- bench] banquette *f*; [on train, at table] place *f*; **take a ~** asseyez-vous, prenez un siège; **please stay in your ~s** restez assis s'il vous plaît; **keep a ~ for me** gardez-moi une place. -**2.** [accommodation, place - in theatre, cinema, train] place *f*; [space to sit] place *f* assise; **I'd like to book two ~s for tomorrow** je voudrais réserver deux places pour demain; **please take your ~s** veuillez prendre OR gagner vos places; **I couldn't find a ~ on the train** je n'ai pas pu trouver de place (assise) dans le train. -**3.** [of trousers] fond *m*; [of chair] siège *m*; [buttocks] derrière *m* ❑ **they grabbed him by the ~ of his pants** ils l'ont attrapé par le fond du pantalon; **by the ~ of one's pants** *inf* de justesse. -**4.** POL siège *m*; **he kept/lost his ~** il a été/il n'a pas été réélu; **she has a ~ in Parliament** elle est députée; **he was elected to a ~ on the council** [municipal] il a été élu conseiller municipal; [commercial] il a été élu au conseil; **the government has a 30-~ majority** le gouvernement a une majorité de 30 sièges. -**5.** [centre - of commerce] centre *m*; ADMIN siège *m*; MED [- of infection] foyer *m*; **the ~ of government/of learning** le siège du gouvernement/du savoir. -**6.** [manor]: **(country) ~** manoir *m*. -**7.** EQUIT: **to have a good ~** se tenir bien en selle, avoir une bonne assiette; **to lose one's ~** être désarçonné. -**8.** TECH [of valve] siège *m*; [of machine] embase *f*, surface *f* d'appui.
◇ *vt* -**1.** [passengers, children] faire asseoir; [guests - at table] placer; **please be ~ed** veuillez vous asseoir; **please remain ~ed** restez OR veuillez rester assis. -**2.** [accommodate] avoir des places assises pour; **the plane can ~ 400** l'avion a une capacité de 400 personnes; **how**

many does the bus ~? combien y a-t-il de places assises dans le bus?; how many does the table ~? combien de personnes peut-on asseoir autour de la table?; we can only ~ 40 people nous n'avons de place que pour 40 personnes. -**3.** [chair] mettre un fond à; [with straw] rempailler; [with cane] canner. -**4.** TECH [valve] ajuster le siège de.
◇ *vi* [skirt, trousers] se déformer (à l'arrière).

seat belt *n* ceinture *f* de sécurité.

-seater ['siːtəʳ] *in cpds*: two/four~ (car) voiture *f* à deux/quatre places.

seating ['siːtɪŋ] ◇ *n (U)* -**1.** [seats] sièges *mpl*; [benches, pews] bancs *mpl*; the ~ isn't very comfortable les sièges ne sont pas très confortables. -**2.** [sitting accommodation] places *fpl* (assises); there's additional ~ at the back il y a des places (assises) supplémentaires au fond; there's ~ for 300 in the hall il y a 300 places dans la salle; there's ~ for eight round this table on peut asseoir huit personnes autour de cette table. -**3.** [plan] affectation *f* des places; who's in charge of the ~? qui est chargé de placer les gens? -**4.** [material - cloth, canvas] (tissu *m* du) siège *m*; [- wicker] cannage *m*. -**5.** TECH [of bearing] logement *m*; [of valve] siège *m*.
◇ *comp*: ~ accommodation OR capacity nombre *m* de places assises; the hall has ~ accommodation for 800 people la salle a une capacité de 800 places (assises); the ~ arrangements le placement *m* OR la disposition *f* des gens; ~ plan [in theatre] plan *m* de la disposition des places; [at table] plan *m* de table.

SEATO ['siːtəʊ] (*abbr of* Southeast Asia Treaty Organization) *pr n* OTASE *f*.

sea trout *n* truite *f* de mer.

sea urchin *n* oursin *m*.

sea wall *n* digue *f*.

seaward ['siːwəd] ◇ *adj* de (la) mer; ~ breeze brise *f* de mer; on the ~ side du côté de la mer.
◇ *adv* = **seawards**.

seawards ['siːwədz] *adv* vers la mer OR le large; to sail ~ mettre le cap au large.

seawater ['siːˌwɔːtəʳ] *n* eau *f* de mer.

seaway ['siːweɪ] *n* route *f* maritime.

seaweed ['siːwiːd] *n (U)* algues *fpl*.

seaworthiness ['siːˌwɜːðɪnɪs] *n* navigabilité *f*.

seaworthy ['siːˌwɜːðɪ] *adj* [boat] en état de naviguer.

sebaceous [sɪ'beɪʃəs] *adj* sébacé.

Sebastian [sɪ'bæstjən] *pr n*: Saint ~ saint Sébastien.

Sebastopol [sɪ'bæstəpəl] *pr n* Sébastopol.

seborrhoea *Br*, **seborrhea** *Am* [ˌsebə'riːə] *n* séborrhée *f*.

sebum ['siːbəm] *n* sébum *m*.

sec *inf* [sek] (*abbr of* second) *n* seconde *f*, instant *m*; in a ~! une seconde!; I'll only be a ~ j'en ai pour une seconde.

Sec. *written abbr of* second.

SEC (*abbr of* Securities and Exchange Commission) *pr n* commission *f* américaine des opérations de Bourse, ≃ COB *f*.

SECAM ['siːkæm] (*abbr of* séquentiel couleur à mémoire) *n* secam *m*.

secant ['siːkənt] *n* secante *f*.

secateurs [ˌsekə'tɜːz] *npl Br*: (pair of) ~ sécateur *m*.

secede [sɪ'siːd] *vi* faire sécession, se séparer; they voted to ~ from the federation ils ont voté en faveur de leur sécession de la fédération.

secession [sɪ'seʃn] *n* sécession *f*, scission *f*.

secessionist [sɪ'seʃnɪst] ◇ *adj* sécessionniste.
◇ *n* sécessionniste *mf*.

seclude [sɪ'kluːd] *vt* éloigner du monde, isoler; they are ~d from the world ils sont retirés du monde; she ~s herself from contact with society elle se coupe de tout contact avec autrui.

secluded [sɪ'kluːdɪd] *adj* [village] retiré, à l'écart; [garden] tranquille; to live a ~ life mener une vie solitaire, vivre en reclus; I tried to find a ~ corner to read j'ai essayé de trouver un coin tranquille pour lire.

seclusion [sɪ'kluːʒn] *n* -**1.** [isolation - chosen] solitude *f*, isolement *m*; he lives a life of total ~ il vit en solitaire OR retiré du monde. -**2.** [isolation - imposed] isolement *m*; the ~ of women l'isolement des femmes.

second[1] ['sekənd] ◇ *n* -**1.** [unit of time] seconde *f*; the ambulance arrived within ~s l'ambulance est arrivée en quelques secondes. -**2.** [instant] seconde *f*, instant *m*; I'll be with you in a ~ je serai à vous dans un instant; I'll only be a ~ j'en ai seulement pour deux secondes; just a OR half a ~! une seconde! -**3.** MATH seconde *f*. -**4.** [in order] second *m*, -e *f*, deuxième *mf*; I was the ~ to arrive je suis arrivé deuxième OR le deuxième; to come a close ~ [in race] être battu de justesse. -**5.** [in duel] témoin *m*, second *m*; [in boxing] soigneur *m*; ~s out! soigneurs hors du ring! -**6.** AUT seconde *f*; in ~ en seconde. -**7.** *Br* UNIV: an upper/lower ~ une licence avec mention bien/assez bien. -**8.** MUS seconde *f*.
◇ *adj* -**1.** [in series] deuxième; [of two] second; he's ~ only to his teacher as a violinist en tant que violoniste, il n'y a que son professeur qui le surpasse OR qui lui soit supérieur; every ~ person une personne sur deux; to be ~ in command [in hierarchy] être deuxième dans la hiérarchie; MIL commander en second; he's ~ in line for promotion il sera le second à bénéficier d'une promotion; he's ~ in line for the throne c'est le deuxième dans l'ordre de succession au trône; ~ floor *Br* deuxième étage *m*; *Am* premier étage; in the ~ person singular/plural GRAMM à la deuxième personne du singulier/pluriel; to take ~ place [in race] prendre la deuxième place; [in exam] être deuxième; his wife took ~ place to his career sa femme venait après sa carrière; and in the ~ place... [in demonstration, argument] et en deuxième lieu...; ~ showing deuxième représentation; for the ~ time pour la deuxième fois ❑ it's ~ nature to her c'est une deuxième nature chez elle; ~ reading POL seconde lecture *f*; ~ teeth deuxième dentition *f*, dentition *f* définitive; ~ violin MUS deuxième violon *m*; as a goalkeeper, he's ~ to none comme gardien de but, il n'a pas son pareil; her short stories are ~ to none ses nouvelles sont inégalées OR sans pareil; 'The Second Sex' *Beauvoir* 'le Deuxième Sexe'. -**2.** [additional, extra] deuxième, second, autre; he was given a ~ chance (in life) on lui a accordé une seconde chance (dans la vie); you are unlikely to get a ~ chance to join the team il est peu probable que l'on vous propose à nouveau de faire partie de l'équipe; to take a ~ helping se resservir; would you like a ~ helping/a ~ cup? en reprendrez-vous (un peu/une goutte)?; can I have a ~ helping of meat? est-ce que je peux reprendre de la viande?; they have a ~ home in France ils ont une résidence secondaire en France; I'd like a ~ opinion [doctor] je voudrais prendre l'avis d'un confrère; [patient] je voudrais consulter un autre médecin; I need a ~ opinion on these results j'aimerais avoir l'avis d'un tiers sur ces résultats.
◇ *adv* -**1.** [in order] en seconde place; to come ~ [in race] arriver en seconde position; she arrived ~ [at party, meeting] elle est arrivée la deuxième; the horse came ~ to Juniper's Lad le cheval s'est classé deuxième derrière Juniper's Lad. -**2.** [with superl adj]: the ~ oldest le cadet; the ~ largest le deuxième par ordre de grandeur. -**3.** [secondly] en second lieu, deuxièmement.
◇ *vt* [motion] appuyer; [speaker] appuyer la motion de; I'll ~ that! je suis d'accord!
◆ **seconds** *npl* -**1.** [goods] marchandises *fpl* de second choix; [crockery] vaisselle *f* de second choix. -**2.** *inf* [of food] rab *m*; are there any ~s? il y a du rab?

second[2] [sɪ'kɒnd] *vt Br fml* [employee] affecter (provisoirement), envoyer en détachement; MIL détacher; she was ~ed to the UN elle a été détachée à l'ONU; Peter was ~ed for service abroad Peter a été envoyé en détachement à l'étranger.

secondary ['sekəndrɪ] (*pl* secondaries) ◇ *adj* -**1.** [gen & MED] secondaire; the word has a ~ meaning le mot a un sens secondaire ‖ [minor] secondaire, de peu d'importance; this issue is of ~ importance cette question est d'une importance secondaire; it's only a ~ problem c'est un problème secondaire OR qui a peu d'importance; any other considerations are ~ to her well being son bien-être prime sur toute autre considération ❑ ~ accent accent *m* secondaire; ~ cause PHILOS cause *f* seconde; ~ cell ELEC élément *m* d'accumulateur; ~ colour couleur *f* secondaire OR binaire; ~ era GEOL (ère *f*) secondaire *m*; ~ product sous-produit *m*. -**2.** SCH secondaire *m*; ~ education enseignement *m* secondaire OR du second degré.
◇ *n* -**1.** [deputy] subordonné *m*, -e *f*, adjoint *m*, -e *f*. -**2.** ASTRON satellite *m*. -**3.** MED [tumour] tumeur *f* secondaire, métastase *f*.

secondary modern (school) *n Br établissement secondaire d'enseignement général et technique, aujourd'hui remplacé par la «comprehensive school»*.

secondary picketing *n (U) Br* INDUST piquets *mpl* de grève de solidarité.

secondary school *n établissement secondaire*; ~ teacher professeur *m* du secondaire.

secondary stress *n* accent *m* secondaire.

second ballot *n* deuxième tour *m*.

second best ◇ *n* pis-aller *m inv*; I refuse to make do with ~ je refuse de me contenter d'un pis-aller.
◇ *adv*: to come off ~ être battu, se faire battre.
◆ **second-best** *adj* [clothes, objects] de tous les jours.

second chamber *n* [gen] deuxième chambre *f*; [in UK] Chambre *f* des lords; [in US] Sénat *m*.

second childhood *n* gâtisme *m*, seconde enfance *f*; he's in his ~ il est retombé en enfance.

second class *n* RAIL seconde *f* (classe *f*).
◆ **second-class** ◇ *adj* -**1.** RAIL de seconde (classe); a ~ season ticket un abonnement de seconde; two ~ returns to Glasgow deux allers (et) retours pour Glasgow en seconde (classe). -**2.** [hotel] de seconde catégorie. -**3.** [mail] à tarif réduit OR lent. -**4.** *Br* UNIV: a ~ honours degree ≃ une licence avec mention (assez) bien. -**5.** [inferior] de qualité inférieure.
◇ *adv* -**1.** RAIL en seconde (classe); to travel ~ voyager en seconde. -**2.** [for mail]: to send a parcel ~ expédier un paquet en tarif réduit.

SECOND-CLASS MAIL:
Le tarif postal réduit est utilisé en Grande-Bretagne pour les lettres et les paquets non urgents. Aux États-Unis, il est réservé aux magazines et aux journaux.

second-class citizen *n* citoyen *m*, -enne *f* de seconde zone; to be treated like a ~ être traité comme un citoyen de seconde zone.

Second Coming *n* RELIG: the ~ le deuxième avènement du Messie.

second cousin *n* cousin *m*, -e *f* au second degré, cousin *m* issu OR cousine *f* issue de germains.

second-degree burn *n* brûlure *f* au deuxième degré.

seconder ['sekəndəʳ] *n* -**1.** [in debate - of motion] personne *f* qui appuie une motion. -**2.** [of candidate] deuxième parrain *m*.

second-generation *adj* [immigrant, computer] de la seconde génération.

second-guess *inf vt* -**1.** [after event] comprendre après coup. -**2.** [before event] essayer de prévoir OR d'anticiper.

second hand *n* [of watch, clock] aiguille *f* des secondes, trotteuse *f*.
◆ **second-hand** ◇ *adj* -**1.** [car, clothes, books] d'occasion; second-hand shop magasin *m* d'occasions. -**2.** [information] de seconde main; to hear OR to discover sthg at second-hand apprendre OR découvrir qqch de seconde main.

◇ *adv* -**1.** [buy] d'occasion. -**2.** [indirectly]: I heard the news second-hand j'ai appris la nouvelle indirectement.

second-in-command *n* MIL commandant *m* en second; NAUT second *m*, officier *m* en second; [in hierarchy] second *m*, adjoint *m*.

second language *n* langue *f* seconde.

second lieutenant *n* sous-lieutenant *m*.

secondly ['sekəndlı] *adv* deuxièmement, en deuxième lieu.

secondment [sı'kɒndmənt] *n Br fml* détachement *m*, affectation *f* provisoire; to be on ~ [teacher] être en détachement; [diplomat] être en mission.

second name *n* nom *m* de famille.

second officer *n* NAUT (officier *m* en) second *m*.

second-rate *adj* [goods, equipment] de qualité inférieure; [film, book] médiocre; [politician, player] médiocre, de second ordre.

second sight *n* seconde OR double vue *f*; to have ~ avoir un don de double vue.

second-strike *adj* [weapons] de deuxième frappe.

second-string *adj Am* SPORT remplaçant.

second thought *n*: to have ~s avoir des doutes; he left his family without a ~ il a quitté sa famille sans réfléchir OR sans se poser de questions; on ~s *Br* OR on ~ *Am* I'd better go myself toute réflexion faite, il vaut mieux que j'y aille moi-même.

secrecy ['si:krəsı] *n (U)* secret *m*; the negotiations were carried out in the strictest ~ les négociations ont été menées dans le plus grand secret; absolute ~ is vital to the success of the mission le secret absolu est essentiel pour le succès de la mission ‖ [mystery] mystère *m*; there's no ~ about their financial dealings ils ne font aucun mystère de leurs affaires financières.

secret ['si:krıt] ◇ *n* -**1.** [information kept hidden] secret *m*; it's a ~ between you and me c'est un secret entre nous; I have no ~s from her je ne lui cache rien; can you keep a ~? pouvez-vous garder un secret?; shall we let them into the ~? est-ce qu'on va les mettre dans le secret OR dans la confidence?; I'll tell you OR I'll let you into a ~ je vais vous dire OR révéler un secret; not many people were in on the ~ il n'y avait pas beaucoup de gens qui étaient dans la confidence OR au courant; I make no ~ of OR about my humble origins je ne cache pas mes origines modestes. -**2.** [explanation] secret *m*; the ~ of his success le secret de sa réussite; the ~ is to warm the dish first le secret consiste à chauffer le plat d'abord; the ~ of making pastry le secret pour réussir une pâte. -**3.** [mystery] secret *m*, mystère *m*; the ~s of nature les secrets OR les mystères de la nature; these locks have OR hold no ~ for me ces serrures n'ont pas de secret pour moi.

◇ *adj* -**1.** [meeting, plan] secret; ~ funds caisse *f* noire, fonds *mpl* secrets; the news was kept ~ la nouvelle a été gardée OR tenue secrète, on n'a pas révélé la nouvelle; they managed to keep their plans ~ ils ont réussi à tenir leurs projets secrets ‖ [personal] secret; it's my ~ belief that he doesn't really love her je crois secrètement OR en mon for intérieur qu'il ne l'aime pas vraiment ☐ ~ ballot vote *m* à bulletin secret. -**2.** [hidden - door] caché, dérobé; [- compartment, safe] caché; a ~ hiding place une cachette secrète. -**3.** [identity] inconnu; the flowers were from a ~ admirer of hers les fleurs venaient d'un admirateur inconnu. -**4.** [secluded - beach, garden] retiré, secret.

◆ **in secret** *adv phr* en secret, secrètement.

secret agent *n* agent *m* secret; 'The Secret Agent' *Conrad* 'l'Agent secret'.

secretaire [,sekrı'teəʳ] *n* secrétaire *m (meuble)*.

secretarial [,sekrə'teərıəl] *adj* [tasks] de secrétaire, de secrétariat; I have a part-time ~ job j'ai un travail de secrétaire à mi-temps; she does ~ work elle fait un travail de secrétariat OR de secrétaire; I followed a ~ course j'ai pris des cours de secrétariat; ~ skills notions *fpl* de secrétariat; ~ college OR school école *f* de secrétariat.

secretariat [,sekrə'teərıət] *n* secrétariat *m*.

secretary [*Br* 'sekrətrı, *Am* 'sekrə,terı] (*pl* secretaries) *n* -**1.** [COMM & gen] secrétaire *mf*. -**2.** POL [minister] secrétaire *m* d'État, ministre *m*; Secretary of Defense secrétaire *m* d'État à la Défense *(équivalent américain du ministre de la Défense)*; ~ of state *Br* ministre; *Am* secrétaire *m* d'État, ministre des Affaires étrangères; Secretary (of State) for Education *Br* ministre de l'Éducation; Treasury Secretary *Am* ministre des Finances; parliamentary private ~ *Br député à la Chambre des Communes travaillant en liaison avec un ministre*. -**3.** [diplomat] secrétaire *m* d'ambassade.

secretary bird *n* ORNITH serpentaire *m*, secrétaire *m*.

secretary-general *n* secrétaire *m* général, secrétaire *f* générale.

secrete [sı'kri:t] *vt* -**1.** ANAT & MED sécréter. -**2.** *fml* [hide] cacher.

secretion [sı'kri:ʃn] *n* -**1.** ANAT & MED sécrétion *f*. -**2.** *fml* [act of hiding] action *f* de cacher.

secretive ['si:krətıv] *adj* [nature] secret; [behaviour] cachottier; she's very ~ about her new job elle ne dit pas grand-chose de son nouveau travail; she's quite a ~ person c'est une personne assez secrète.

secretively ['si:krətıvlı] *adv* en se cachant, discrètement.

secretiveness ['si:krətıvnıs] *n (U)* [of character] réserve *f*; [keeping secrets] cachotteries *fpl*.

secretly ['si:krıtlı] *adv* [do, act] en secret, secrètement; [believe, think] en son for intérieur, secrètement.

secret police *n* police *f* secrète.

secret service *n* services *mpl* secrets.

◆ **Secret Service** *n* [in US]: the ~ *service de protection du président, du vice-président des États-Unis et de leurs familles*.

sect [sekt] *n* secte *f*.

sectarian [sek'teərıən] *adj* sectaire; ~ violence violence *f* d'origine religieuse.

sectarianism [sek'teərıənızm] *n* sectarisme *m*.

section ['sekʃn] ◇ *n* -**1.** [sector] section *f*, partie *f*; the business ~ of the community les commerçants et les hommes d'affaires de notre communauté; there has been snow over large ~s of Southern England il a neigé sur une grande partie du sud de l'Angleterre; the residential ~ of the town les quartiers résidentiels de la ville ‖ [division - of staff, services] section *f*; [- in army] groupe *m* de combat; [- in orchestra] section *f*; the brass/percussion ~ les cuivres/percussions. -**2.** [component part - of furniture] élément *m*; [- of tube] section *f*; [- of track, road] section *f*, tronçon *m*; RAIL section *f*; the kitchen units/the shelves come in easy-to-assemble ~s les éléments de cuisine/les étagères se vendent en kit. -**3.** [subdivision - of law] article *m*; [- of book, exam, text] section *f*, partie *f*; [- of library] section *f*; the children's ~ la section pour enfants ‖ [of newspaper - page] page *f*; [- pages] pages *fpl*; the sports/women's ~ les pages des sports/réservées aux femmes ‖ [in department store] rayon *m*; furniture/children's ~ rayon meubles/enfants. -**4.** *Am* RAIL [train] train *m* supplémentaire; [sleeper] compartiment-lits *m*. -**5.** [cut, cross-section - drawing] coupe *f*, section *f*; GEOM section *f*; [for microscope] coupe *f*, lamelle *f*; [in metal] profilé *m*. -**6.** MED sectionnement *m*. -**7.** *Am* [land] *division (administrative) d'un mille carré*.

◇ *vt* sectionner.

◆ **section off** *vt sep* séparer; part of the church was ~ed off l'accès à une partie de l'église était interdit.

sectional ['sekʃənl] *adj* -**1.** [furniture] en kit. -**2.** [interests] d'un groupe. -**3.** [drawing] en coupe.

sectionalism ['sekʃənəlızm] *n* défense *f* des intérêts régionaux OR d'un groupe.

section gang *n Am* RAIL (équipe *f* de) terrassiers *mpl*.

section hand *n Am* RAIL terrassier *m*.

section mark *n* signe *m* de paragraphe.

sector ['sektəʳ] ◇ *n* -**1.** [area, realm] secteur *m*, domaine *m*; ECON secteur *m*; [part, subdivision] secteur *m*, partie *f*; COMPUT [of screen] secteur *m*; the banking ~ le secteur bancaire; whole ~s of society live below the poverty line des catégories sociales entières vivent en dessous du seuil de pauvreté. -**2.** MIL secteur *m*, zone *f*. -**3.** GEOM secteur *m*. -**4.** [for measuring] compas *m* de proportion.

◇ *vt* diviser en secteurs; ADMIN & GEOG sectoriser.

secular ['sekjʊləʳ] *adj* -**1.** [life, clergy] séculier. -**2.** [education, school] laïque. -**3.** [music, art] profane. -**4.** [ancient] séculaire. -**5.** ASTRON séculaire.

secularism ['sekjʊlərızm] *n* laïcisme *m*.

secularization [,sekjʊləraı'zeıʃn] *n* sécularisation *f*.

secularize, -ise ['sekjʊləraız] *vt* séculariser; [education] laïciser.

secure [sı'kjʊəʳ] ◇ *adj* -**1.** [protected] sûr, en sécurité, en sûreté; put the papers in a ~ place mettez les papiers en lieu sûr; I feel ~ from OR against attack je me sens à l'abri des attaques. -**2.** [guaranteed - job] sûr; [- victory, future] assuré; a country must ensure its borders are ~ un pays doit assurer ses frontières OR faire en sorte que ses frontières soient sûres. -**3.** [calm, confident] tranquille, sécurisé; now she's married, she feels more ~ maintenant qu'elle est mariée, elle se sent plus sécurisée; I was ~ in the belief that all danger was past j'étais intimement persuadé que tout danger était écarté. -**4.** [solid - investment, base] sûr; [- foothold, grasp] sûr, ferme; [solidly fastened - bolt, window] bien fermé; [- scaffolding, aerial] solide, qui tient bien; [- knot] solide; can you make the door/the rope ~? pouvez-vous vous assurer que la porte est bien fermée/la corde est bien attachée?

◇ *vt* -**1.** *fml* [obtain] se procurer, obtenir; [agreement] obtenir; [loan] obtenir, se voir accorder; to ~ a majority [gen] obtenir une majorité; POL emporter la majorité; to ~ the release of sb obtenir la libération de qqn; will it be possible to ~ a hall for the debate? serait-il possible de réserver une salle pour le débat? -**2.** [fasten, fix - rope] attacher; [- parcel] ficeler; [- ladder, aerial] bien fixer; [- window, lock] bien fermer; the rope was ~d around a rock la corde était solidement attachée à un rocher; ~ the ladder against the wall first assurez-vous d'abord que l'échelle est bien appuyée contre le mur. -**3.** [guarantee - future] assurer; [- debt] garantir. -**4.** [from danger] préserver; we did everything we could to ~ the boat against OR from the storm nous avons tout fait pour protéger le bateau contre la tempête.

secured [sı'kjʊəd] *adj* FIN [debt, loan] garanti.

securely [sı'kjʊəlı] *adv* -**1.** [firmly] fermement, solidement; the door was ~ fastened la porte était bien fermée OR verrouillée. -**2.** [safely] en sécurité, en sûreté; put the jewels ~ away mettez les bijoux en lieu sûr.

secure tenancy *n* location *f* assurée OR garantie.

security [sı'kjʊərətı] (*pl* securities) ◇ *n* -**1.** [safety] sécurité *f*; terrorism is a threat to national ~ le terrorisme menace la sécurité nationale; the President's national ~ advisers les conseillers du président en matière de sécurité nationale; they slipped through the ~ net ils sont passés au travers des mailles du filet des services de sécurité ‖ [police measures, protection etc] sécurité *f*; for reasons of ~ par mesure de OR pour des raisons de sécurité; there was maximum ~ for the President's visit des mesures de sécurité exceptionnelles ont été prises pour la visite du président; maximum ~ wing [in prison] quartier *m* de haute surveillance. -**2.** *(U)* [assurance] sécurité *f*; job ~ sécurité de l'emploi; to have ~ of tenure [in job] être titulaire, avoir la sécurité de l'emploi; [as tenant] avoir un bail qui ne peut être résilié; what she really needs is emotional ~ ce qu'il lui faut vraiment c'est une sécurité affective; financial ~ sécurité matérielle OR financière. -**3.** [guarantee] garantie *f*, caution *f*; what ~ do you have for the loan? quelle garantie avez-vous pour couvrir ce prêt?; have you anything to put up as ~? qu'est-ce que vous pouvez fournir comme garantie?; she gave her diamonds as ~ for the loan elle a donné ses diamants comme garantie pour le prêt; loans without ~ prêts *mpl* sans garantie || [guarantor] garant *m*, -e *f*; to stand ~ for sb *Br* se porter garant de qqn; to stand ~ for a loan avaliser un prêt. -**4.** [department] sécurité *f*; please call ~ appelez la sécurité s'il vous plaît. -**5.** COMPUT sécurité *f*.

◇ *comp* [measures] de sécurité; ~ device sécurité *f*.

◆ **securities** *npl* FIN titres *mpl*, actions *fpl*, valeurs *fpl*; government securities titres *mpl* d'État; the securities market le marché des valeurs.

security blanket *n morceau de tissu que certains jeunes enfants ont toujours avec eux pour se rassurer.*

Security Council *n* Conseil *m* de Sécurité.

security guard *n* garde *m* (chargé de la sécurité); [for armoured van] convoyeur *m* de fonds.

security leak *n* fuite *f* de documents OR d'informations concernant la sécurité.

security officer *n* [on ship] officier *m* chargé de la sécurité; [in firm] employé *m* chargé de la sécurité; [inspector] inspecteur *m* de la sécurité.

security police *n* (services *mpl* de la) sûreté *f*.

security risk *n*: she's considered to be a ~ on considère qu'elle représente un risque pour la sécurité.

secy (*written abbr of* secretary) secr.

sedan [sɪ'dæn] *n* -**1.** *Am* [car] berline *f*. -**2.** [chair]: ~ (chair) chaise *f* à porteurs.

sedate [sɪ'deɪt] ◇ *adj* [person, manner] calme, posé; [behaviour] calme, pondéré; we strolled home at a ~ pace nous sommes rentrés chez nous sans hâte OR en flânant; we live a very ~ existence nous menons une existence très calme.

◇ *vt* donner des sédatifs à; he's heavily ~d il prend de fortes doses de calmants.

sedately [sɪ'deɪtlɪ] *adv* posément, calmement; she walked ~ back to her house elle est revenue chez elle d'un pas lent OR tranquille.

sedation [sɪ'deɪʃn] *n* sédation *f*; under ~ sous calmants.

sedative ['sedətɪv] ◇ *adj* calmant.

◇ *n* calmant *m*.

sedentary ['sedntrɪ] *adj* sédentaire.

sedge [sedʒ] *n* laîche *f*, carex *m*.

sedge warbler *n* phragmite *m* des joncs.

sedilia [se'dɪlɪə] *npl* stalles *fpl*.

sediment ['sedɪmənt] ◇ *n* -**1.** GEOL sédiment *m*. -**2.** [in liquid] sédiment *m*, dépôt *m*; [in wine] dépôt *m*, lie *f*.

◇ *vt* déposer.

◇ *vi* se déposer.

sedimentary [,sedɪ'mentərɪ] *adj* sédimentaire; ~ rock roche *f* sédimentaire.

sedimentation [,sedɪmen'teɪʃn] *n* sédimentation *f*.

sedition [sɪ'dɪʃn] *n* sédition *f*.

seditious [sɪ'dɪʃəs] *adj* séditieux.

seduce [sɪ'djuːs] *vt* -**1.** [sexually] séduire. -**2.** [attract] séduire, attirer; [draw] entraîner; she was ~d away from the company by an offer of more money on l'a persuadée de OR incitée à quitter la société en lui offrant plus d'argent.

seducer [sɪ'djuːsəʳ] *n* séducteur *m*, -trice *f*.

seduction [sɪ'dʌkʃn] *n* séduction *f*.

seductive [sɪ'dʌktɪv] *adj* [person] séduisant; [personality] séduisant, attrayant; [voice, smile] aguichant, séducteur; they made me a very ~ offer ils m'ont fait une offre très séduisante OR alléchante; she was wearing a rather ~ dress elle était plutôt séduisante dans cette robe.

seductively [sɪ'dʌktɪvlɪ] *adv* [dress] d'une manière séduisante; [smile] d'une manière enjôleuse.

seductiveness [sɪ'dʌktɪvnɪs] *n* caractère *m* séduisant.

sedulous ['sedjʊləs] *adj fml* diligent, persévérant.

sedulously ['sedjʊləslɪ] *adv fml* assidûment, avec persévérance.

sedum ['siːdəm] *n* sédum *m*.

see [siː] (*pt* saw [sɔː], *pp* seen [siːn]) ◇ *vt* **A.** -**1.** [perceive with eyes] voir; can you ~ me? est-ce que tu me vois?; I can't ~ a thing je ne vois rien; she could ~ a light in the distance elle voyait une lumière au loin; he saw her talk OR talking to the policeman il l'a vue parler OR qui parlait au policier; did anyone ~ you take it? est-ce que quelqu'un t'a vu le prendre?; did you ~ what happened? avez-vous vu ce qui s'est passé?; let me ~ your hands fais-moi voir OR montre-moi tes mains; can I ~ your newspaper a minute? puis-je voir votre journal OR jeter un coup d'œil sur votre journal un instant?; we've never actually spoken, but I ~ her around a lot nous ne nous sommes jamais vraiment parlé, mais je la croise assez souvent; I could ~ she'd been crying je voyais qu'elle avait pleuré; I don't want to be seen with him je ne veux pas être vu OR qu'on me voie avec lui; there wasn't a car to be seen il n'y avait pas une seule voiture en vue; nothing more was ever seen of her on ne l'a plus jamais revue || [imagine]: she began to ~ spies everywhere elle s'est mise à voir des espions partout; there's nothing there, you're ~ing things! il n'y a rien, tu as des hallucinations!; I could ~ what was going to happen (a mile off *inf*) *fig* je le voyais venir (gros comme une maison) ❑ could you ~ your way (clear) to lending me £20? est-ce que vous pourriez me prêter 20 livres?; to ~ the back OR last of sthg en avoir fini avec qqch; I'll be glad to ~ the back OR last of her je serai content d'être débarrassé d'elle; ~ing is believing *prov* il faut le voir pour le croire. -**2.** [watch - film, play, programme] voir; I saw it on the news je l'ai vu au journal télévisé; did you ~ the match last night? as-tu vu le match hier soir? -**3.** [refer to - page, chapter] voir; ~ page 317 voir page 317.

B. -**1.** [meet by arrangement, consult] voir; you should ~ a doctor tu devrais voir OR consulter un médecin; I'll be ~ing my lawyer about this je vais consulter mon avocat à ce sujet; I'll be ~ing the candidates next week je verrai les candidats la semaine prochaine. -**2.** [meet by chance] voir, rencontrer; guess who I saw at the supermarket! devine qui j'ai vu OR qui j'ai rencontré au supermarché! -**3.** [visit - person, place] voir; come round and ~ me some time passe me voir un de ces jours; they came to ~ me in hospital ils sont venus me voir à l'hôpital; I've always wanted to ~ China j'ai toujours voulu voir la Chine; to ~ the world voir le monde. -**4.** [receive a visit from] recevoir, voir; he's too ill to ~ anyone il est trop malade pour voir qui que ce soit; she can't ~ you right now, she's busy elle ne peut pas vous voir maintenant, elle est trop occupée. -**5.** [spend time with socially] voir; do you still ~ the Browns? est-ce que vous voyez toujours les Brown?; we've seen quite a lot of them recently nous les avons beaucoup vus dernièrement; we ~ less of them these days nous les voyons moins en ce moment; is he ~ing anyone at the moment? [going out with] est-ce qu'il a quelqu'un en ce moment? -**6.** *phr*: ~ you! *inf*, (I'll) be ~ing you! *inf* salut!; ~ you later! *inf* à tout à l'heure!; ~ you around! *inf* à un de ces jours!; ~ you tomorrow/this evening/next week! *inf* à demain/ce soir/la semaine prochaine!; ~ you in London! *inf* on se verra à Londres!

C. -**1.** [understand] voir, comprendre; I ~ what you mean je vois OR comprends ce que vous voulez dire; I don't ~ what's so funny! je ne vois pas ce qu'il y a de si drôle!; I could ~ his point je voyais ce qu'il voulait dire; I don't ~ any point in going back now je ne vois pas du tout l'intérêt qu'il y aurait à y retourner maintenant; I can ~ why you were worried je vois pourquoi vous étiez inquiet; I can't ~ that it matters je ne vois pas quelle importance ça a. -**2.** [consider, view] voir; try to ~ things from my point of view essayez de voir les choses de mon point de vue; we ~ things differently nous ne voyons pas les choses de la même façon; you'll ~ things differently in the morning demain tu verras les choses d'un autre œil; he doesn't ~ his drinking as a problem il ne se considère pas comme un alcoolique; how do you ~ the current situation? que pensez-vous de la situation actuelle?; as I ~ it, it's the parents who are to blame à mon avis, ce sont les parents qui sont responsables. -**3.** [imagine, picture] voir, s'imaginer; I can't ~ him getting married je ne le vois pas OR je ne me l'imagine pas se mariant; she just couldn't ~ herself as a wife and mother elle ne s'imaginait pas se mariant et ayant des enfants; I can't ~ it myself moi, je n'arrive pas à imaginer ça.

D. -**1.** [try to find to] voir; I'll ~ if I can fix it je vais voir si je peux le réparer; I'll ~ what I can do je vais voir ce que je peux faire; go and ~ if he's still asleep va voir s'il dort encore; she called by to ~ what had happened elle est venue pour savoir ce qui s'était passé. -**2.** [notice, become aware of] voir; I can't ~ any improvement je ne vois pas d'amélioration; they must have seen how worried I was ils ont dû voir combien j'étais inquiet. -**3.** [discover, learn] voir; I'm pleased to ~ you're enjoying life je suis heureux de voir que tu profites de la vie; I'll be interested to ~ how he gets on je serais curieux de voir comment il se débrouillera; I ~ (that) he's getting married j'ai appris qu'il allait se marier; I saw it in the paper this morning je l'ai vu OR lu ce matin dans le journal; as we shall ~ in a later chapter comme nous le verrons dans un chapitre ultérieur; I ~ she's in the new Scorsese film je vois qu'elle est dans le nouveau film de Scorsese. -**4.** [make sure] s'assurer, veiller à; ~ that all the lights are out before you leave assurez-vous que OR veillez à ce que toutes les lumières soient éteintes avant de partir; ~ (that) everything's ready for when they arrive veillez à ce que tout soit prêt pour leur arrivée ❑ she'll ~ you right *inf* elle veillera à ce que tu ne manques de rien, elle prendra bien soin de toi. -**5.** [inspect - file, passport, ticket] voir; can I ~ your ticket, sir? puis-je voir votre ticket, Monsieur?

E. -**1.** [experience] voir, connaître; he thinks he's seen it all il croit tout savoir; most recruits never ~ active service la plupart des recrues ne voient jamais la guerre de près; our car has seen better days notre voiture a connu des jours meilleurs. -**2.** [witness] voir; they have seen their purchasing power halved ils ont vu leur pouvoir d'achat diminuer de moitié; last year saw an increase in profits l'année dernière a vu une augmentation des bénéfices; the next decade will ~ enormous changes la prochaine décennie verra se produire des changements considérables; this old house has seen some changes cette vieille maison a subi quelques transformations; I never thought I'd ~ the day when he'd admit he was wrong je n'aurais jamais cru qu'un jour il admettrait avoir tort; you don't ~ athletes like her any more! il n'y a plus beaucoup d'athlètes comme elle!

F. -**1.** [accompany] accompagner; I'll ~ you to the bus stop je t'accompagne à l'arrêt du bus; I'll ~ you home je te raccompagne chez toi; ~ Mr Smith to the door, please veuillez raccompagner M. Smith jusqu'à la porte; he saw her into a taxi/onto the train il l'a mise dans un taxi/le train. -**2.** [in poker] voir; I'll ~ you je vous vois; I'll ~ your ten dollars and raise you twenty je vois vos dix dollars et je relance de vingt.

◇ *vi* -**1.** [perceive with eyes] voir; I can't ~

without (my) glasses je ne vois rien sans mes lunettes; he may never ~ again il se peut qu'il ne voie plus jamais; on a clear day you can ~ as far as the coast par temps clair on voit jusqu'à la mer; cats can ~ in the dark les chats voient dans l'obscurité; to ~ into the future voir OR lire dans l'avenir; she can't ~ any further than the end of her nose elle ne voit pas plus loin que le bout de son nez; for all to ~ au vu et au su de tous. -**2.** [find out] voir; is that the baby crying? – I'll go and ~ c'est le bébé qu'on entend pleurer? – je vais voir; you'll ~! tu verras! -**3.** [understand] voir, comprendre; it makes no difference as far as I can ~ autant que je puisse en juger, ça ne change rien; you ~, there's something else you should know tu vois, il y a quelque chose d'autre que tu devrais savoir; I was tired, you ~, and... j'étais fatigué, voyez-vous, et...; now ~ here, young man! écoutez-moi, jeune homme!; I haven't quite finished – so I ~ je n'ai pas tout à fait terminé – c'est ce que je vois; I ~ [expressing understanding or disapproval] je vois; I don't want any trouble, ~? *inf* je ne veux pas d'histoires, OK? -**4.** [indicating a pause or delay]: let me OR let's ~ voyons voir; Mum said you'd take us to the fair – we'll ~ Maman a dit que tu nous amènerais à la foire – on verra (ça).

◇ *n* RELIG [of bishop] siège *m* épiscopal, évêché *m*; [of archbishop] archevêché *m*.

◆ **see about** *vt insep* s'occuper de; I'll ~ about making the reservations je m'occuperai des réservations; they're sending someone to ~ about the gas ils envoient quelqu'un pour vérifier le gaz; they won't let us in – we'll (soon) ~ about that! *inf* ils ne veulent pas nous laisser entrer – c'est ce qu'on va voir!

◆ **see around** *vt insep* = **see round**.

◆ **see in** ◇ *vt sep* -**1.** [escort] faire entrer. -**2.** [celebrate]: to ~ in the New Year fêter le Nouvel An.

◇ *vt insep* trouver; what can she possibly ~ in him? qu'est-ce qu'elle peut bien lui trouver?

◇ *vi insep literal* voir à l'intérieur.

◆ **see off** *vt sep* -**1.** [say goodbye to] dire au revoir à; she came to ~ me off at the station elle est venue à la gare me dire au revoir. -**2.** [chase away] chasser; ~ him off! [to dog] chasse-le! -**3.** [repel - attack] repousser.

◆ **see out** *vt sep* -**1.** [accompany to the door] reconduire OR raccompagner à la porte; can you ~ yourself out? pouvez-vous trouver la sortie tout seul?; goodbye, I'll ~ myself out au revoir, ce n'est pas la peine de me raccompagner. -**2.** [last]: we've got enough food to ~ the week out nous avons assez à manger pour tenir jusqu'à la fin de la semaine. -**3.** [celebrate]: to ~ out the Old Year fêter le Nouvel An.

◆ **see over** *vt insep* = **see round**.

◆ **see round** *vt insep* visiter; they came to ~ round the house ils sont venus pour visiter la maison.

◆ **see through** ◇ *vt insep* -**1.** [window, fabric] voir à travers. -**2.** [be wise to - person] ne pas être dupe de, voir dans le jeu de; [- trick, scheme, behaviour] ne pas se laisser tromper par; she saw through his apparent cheerfulness elle ne s'est pas laissée tromper OR abuser par OR elle n'a pas été dupe de son apparente bonne humeur.

◇ *vt sep* -**1.** [bring to a successful end] mener à bonne fin; we can count on her to ~ the job through on peut compter sur elle pour mener l'affaire à bien. -**2.** [support, sustain]: I've got enough money to ~ me through the week j'ai assez d'argent pour tenir jusqu'à la fin de la semaine; their love has seen them through many a crisis leur amour les a aidés à surmonter de nombreuses crises; her good humour will always ~ her through any difficulties sa bonne humeur lui permettra toujours de traverser les moments difficiles.

◆ **see to** *vt insep* -**1.** [look after] s'occuper de; I'll ~ to the dinner je m'occuperai du dîner; ~ to it that everything's ready by 5 p.m. veillez à ce que tout soit prêt pour 17 h; she saw to it that our picnic was ruined [thanks to her] elle a fait en sorte de gâcher notre pique-nique. -**2.** [repair] réparer; you should get the brakes seen to tu devrais faire réparer les freins.

seed [siːd] ◇ *n* -**1.** BOT & HORT *(C)* graine *f*; *(U)* graines *fpl*, semence *f*; sunflower ~s graines de tournesol; grass ~ semence pour gazon ❑ to go OR to run to ~ HORT monter en graine; *fig* [physically] se laisser aller, se décatir; [mentally] perdre ses facultés; his mother has really gone to ~ during the past year sa mère a bien baissé OR s'est bien décatie au cours de l'année passée. -**2.** [in fruit, tomatoes] pépin *m*. -**3.** [source] germe *m*; the ~s of doubt/of suspicion les germes du doute/de la suspicion. -**4.** BIBLE & *lit* [offspring] progéniture *f*; [sperm] semence *f*. -**5.** SPORT tête *f* de série; the top ~s les meilleurs joueurs classés.

◇ *vt* -**1.** BOT & HORT [garden, field] ensemencer; [plants] planter; ~ed borders bordures *fpl* ensemencées; to ~ clouds ensemencer les nuages. -**2.** [take seeds from - raspberries, grapes] épépiner. -**3.** SPORT: ~ed player tête *f* de série; he's ~ed number 5 il est tête de série numéro 5.

◇ *vi* [lettuce] monter en graine; [corn] grener.

seedbed ['siːdbed] *n* semis *m*, couche *f* à semis; a ~ of revolution *fig* les germes d'une révolution.

seedbox ['siːdbɒks] *n* germoir *m*.

seedcake ['siːdkeɪk] *n* gâteau *m* aux graines de carvi.

seedcorn ['siːdkɔːn] *n* blé *m* de semence; ~ investments investissements *mpl* pour l'avenir.

seedily ['siːdɪlɪ] *adv* minablement, de façon miteuse.

seediness ['siːdɪnɪs] *n* -**1.** [appearance] aspect *m* miteux OR minable. -**2.** *inf dated* [of health] mauvais état *m*.

seeding machine ['siːdɪŋ-] *n* semoir *m*.

seedless ['siːdlɪs] *adj* sans pépins.

seedling ['siːdlɪŋ] *n* [plant] semis *m*, jeune plant *m*; [tree] jeune plant *m*.

seed merchant *n* grainetier *m*, -ère *f*.

seed money *n* capital *m* initial OR de départ, mise *f* de fonds.

seed pearl *n* semence *f* de perles.

seedpod ['siːdpɒd] *n* BOT cosse *f*.

seed potato *n* pomme *f* de terre de semence.

seedsman ['siːdzmən] (*pl* **seedsmen** [-mən]) *n* grainetier *m*.

seedy ['siːdɪ] (*compar* **seedier**, *superl* **seediest**) *adj* -**1.** [person, hotel, clothes] miteux, minable; a ~-looking drunk approached her un ivrogne d'aspect minable OR miteux s'avança vers elle; the hotel was in the seediest part of town l'hôtel était dans le quartier le plus délabré de la ville. -**2.** *inf dated* [unwell] patraque, mal fichu. -**3.** [fruit] plein de pépins.

seeing[1] ['siːɪŋ] *n* [vision] vue *f*, vision *f*; ~ is believing *prov* il faut le voir pour le croire.

seeing[2] ['siːɪŋ] *conj* vu que; ~ (that OR as how *inf*) no-one came, we decided to leave vu que OR étant donné que personne n'est venu, nous avons décidé de partir; I decided not to encourage him, ~ as how he was married *inf* je décidai de ne pas l'encourager, puisqu'il était OR vu qu'il était marié.

seeing eye (dog) *n Am* chien *m* d'aveugle.

seek [siːk] (*pt* & *pp* **sought** [sɔːt]) ◇ *vt* -**1.** [search for - job, person, solution] chercher, rechercher; he constantly sought her approval il cherchait constamment à obtenir son approbation; he sought revenge on them il a cherché à se venger d'eux; they sought (for) an answer to their problems ils ont cherché une réponse à leurs problèmes; we'd better ~ help il vaut mieux aller chercher de l'aide; they sought shelter from the rain ils ont cherché à se mettre à l'abri de la pluie; we sought shelter in a shop doorway nous avons cherché refuge OR à nous réfugier dans l'entrée d'un magasin; to ~ one's fortune chercher fortune; to ~ re-election chercher à se faire réélire; to ~ after sthg rechercher qqch. -**2.** [ask for - advice, help] demander, chercher; I sought professional advice j'ai demandé conseil à un professionnel, j'ai cherché conseil auprès d'un professionnel; he sought my help il m'a demandé de l'aide OR de l'aider. -**3.** [attempt]: to ~ to do sthg chercher à faire qqch, tenter de faire qqch; we are ~ing to improve housing conditions nous nous efforçons d'améliorer OR nous cherchons à améliorer les conditions de logement. -**4.** [move towards] chercher; water ~s its own level l'eau atteint spontanément son niveau; heat-seeking missile missile *m* thermoguidé.

◇ *vi* chercher; ~ and you shall find BIBLE cherchez et vous trouverez.

◆ **seek out** *vt sep* -**1.** [go to see] aller voir. -**2.** [search for] chercher, rechercher; [dig out] dénicher.

seeker ['siːkə^r] *n* chercheur *m*, -euse *f*; a ~ after pleasure/truth une personne qui recherche le plaisir/la vérité.

-seeker *in cpds*: pleasure/peace~ personne qui recherche le plaisir/la paix.

seem [siːm] *vi* **A.** -**1.** [with adjective] sembler, paraître, avoir l'air; he ~s very nice il a l'air très gentil; you don't ~ very pleased with the result vous n'avez pas l'air ravi du résultat; you ~ (to be) lost vous semblez (être) OR vous avez l'air (d'être) perdu; things aren't always what they ~ (to be) les apparences sont parfois trompeuses; just do whatever ~s right fais ce que tu jugeras bon de faire; the wind makes it ~ colder than it is on dirait qu'il fait plus froid à cause du vent; her behaviour ~ed perfectly normal to me son comportement m'a semblé tout à fait normal; how does the situation ~ to you? – it ~s hopeless que pensez-vous de la situation? – elle me semble désespérée; how did grandfather ~ to you? – he ~ed much older comment as-tu trouvé grand-père? – j'ai trouvé qu'il avait beaucoup vieilli. -**2.** [with infinitive] sembler, avoir l'air; the door ~ed to open by itself la porte sembla s'ouvrir toute seule; she ~s to have recovered completely elle a l'air d'être tout à fait remise; he didn't ~ to know, he ~ed not to know il n'avait pas l'air de savoir; you ~ to think you can do as you like here vous avez l'air de croire que vous pouvez faire ce que vous voulez ici; I ~ to sleep better with the window open je crois que je dors mieux avec la fenêtre ouverte ‖ [used to soften a statement, question etc]: I ~ to remember (that)... je crois bien me souvenir que...; I'm sorry, I ~ to have forgotten your name excusez-moi, je crois que j'ai oublié votre nom; now, what ~s to be the problem? alors, quel est le problème d'après vous? ‖ [with 'can't', 'couldn't']: I can't ~ to do it je n'y arrive pas; I can't ~ to remember je n'arrive pas à me souvenir; I couldn't ~ to get any answer impossible d'obtenir une réponse. -**3.** [with noun, often with 'like'] sembler, paraître; he ~s (like) a nice boy il a l'air très sympathique OR d'un garçon charmant; it ~s (like) an excellent idea cela me semble (être) une excellente idée; after what ~ed (like) ages, the doctor arrived après une attente qui parut interminable, le médecin arriva; it ~s like only yesterday il me semble que c'était hier.

B. -**1.** [impersonal use]: it ~ed that OR as if nothing could make her change her mind il semblait que rien ne pourrait la faire changer d'avis; it ~ed as though we'd known each other for years nous avions l'impression de nous connaître depuis des années; it ~s to me there's no solution j'ai l'impression qu'il n'y a pas de solution; there ~s to be some mistake on dirait qu'il y a une erreur; there ~ to be many opponents of the bill il semble y avoir OR qu'il y ait beaucoup de gens qui s'opposent au projet de loi; there doesn't ~ (to be) much point in going on je ne crois pas qu'il y ait grand intérêt à continuer; we've been having a spot of bother – so it ~s OR would ~! nous avons eu un petit problème – on dirait bien! -**2.** [indicating that information is hearsay or second-hand] paraître; it ~s OR it would ~ (that) he already knew il semble OR il semblerait qu'il était déjà au courant; he doesn't ~ to have known about the operation apparemment, il n'était pas au courant de l'opération; it ~s over 200 people were killed il paraît que plus de 200 personnes ont été tuées; it would ~ so il paraît que oui; it would ~ not il paraît que non, apparemment pas.

seeming ['si:mɪŋ] *adj* apparent; I don't trust him, for all his ~ concern over our welfare je n'ai aucune confiance en lui bien qu'il semble se préoccuper de notre bien-être; her explanation soon resolved any ~ contradictions in her story ses précisions ne tardèrent pas à lever les apparentes contradictions de son récit.

seemingly ['si:mɪŋlɪ] *adv* -**1.** [judging by appearances] apparemment, en apparence; she has ~ limitless amounts of money les sommes d'argent dont elle dispose semblent être illimitées. -**2.** [from reports] à ce qu'il paraît; ~ so/not il paraît que oui/non; he ~ never received the letter à ce qu'il paraît, il n'a jamais reçu la lettre.

seemly ['si:mlɪ] (*compar* seemlier, *superl* seemliest) *adj lit* -**1.** [of behaviour] convenable, bienséant; it is not ~ to ask so many personal questions cela ne se fait pas de poser tant de questions personnelles. -**2.** [of dress] décent; it was hardly the most ~ attire for a supper party ce n'était certainement pas la tenue la plus indiquée pour un dîner.

seen [si:n] *pp* → **see**.

seep [si:p] *vi* filtrer, s'infiltrer; water was ~ing through the cracks in the floor l'eau s'infiltrait par OR filtrait à travers les fissures du sol.

◆ **seep away** *vi insep* s'écouler goutte à goutte.

◆ **seep in** *vi insep* -**1.** [liquid] s'infiltrer. -**2.** *fig* faire son effet.

◆ **seep out** *vi insep* -**1.** [blood, liquid] suinter; [gas, smoke] se répandre. -**2.** [information, secret] filtrer.

seepage ['si:pɪdʒ] *n* [gradual - process] suintement *m*, infiltration *f*; [- leak] fuite *f*.

seer ['sɪə^r] *n lit* prophète *m*, prophétesse *f*.

seersucker ['sɪə,sʌkə^r] *n* crépon *m* de coton, seersucker *m*.

seesaw ['si:sɔ:] ◇ *n* balançoire *f* (à bascule).
◇ *comp* [motion] de bascule.
◇ *vi* osciller.

seethe [si:ð] *vi* -**1.** [liquid, lava] bouillir, bouillonner; [sea] bouillonner. -**2.** [with anger, indignation] bouillir; he was seething with anger il bouillait de rage; the country is currently seething with unrest le mécontentement gronde en ce moment dans le pays. -**3.** [teem] grouiller; the streets seethed with shoppers les rues grouillaient de gens qui faisaient leurs courses.

seething ['si:ðɪŋ] *adj* -**1.** [liquid, sea] bouillonnant. -**2.** [furious] furieux. -**3.** [teeming] grouillant; a ~ mass of people une masse fourmillante de gens.

see-through *adj* transparent.

segment [*n* 'segmənt, *vb* seg'ment] ◇ *n* -**1.** [piece - gen, ANAT & GEOM] segment *m*; [- of fruit] quartier *m*; in ~s par segments. -**2.** [part - of book, film, programme] partie *f*. -**3.** LING segment *m*.
◇ *vt* segmenter, diviser OR partager en segments.
◇ *vi* se segmenter.

segmentation [,segmen'teɪʃn] *n* segmentation *f*.

segmented [seg'mentɪd] *adj* segmentaire.

Segovia [sɪ'gəʊvɪə] *pr n* Ségovie.

segregate ['segrɪgeɪt] ◇ *vt* [separate] séparer; [isolate] isoler; he went to a school where the sexes were ~d l'école qu'il a fréquentée n'était pas mixte; the children were ~d into racial groups les enfants ont été regroupés en fonction de leur race; the sick were ~d from the other villagers les malades étaient tenus à l'écart des autres habitants du village.
◇ *vi* [in genetics] se diviser.

segregated ['segrɪgeɪtɪd] *adj* POL *où la ségrégation raciale est pratiquée*.

segregation [,segrɪ'geɪʃn] *n* -**1.** POL ségrégation *f*. -**2.** [separation - of sexes, patients] séparation *f*. -**3.** [in genetics] division *f*.

segregationist [,segrɪ'geɪʃnɪst] ◇ *adj* ségrégationniste.
◇ *n* ségrégationniste *mf*.

seine [seɪn] *n*: ~ (net) senne *f*.

Seine [seɪn] *pr n*: the (River) ~ la Seine.

seise [si:z] *vt* JUR mettre en possession de; to be OR to stand ~d of a property posséder une propriété de droit.

seismic ['saɪzmɪk] *adj* sismique, séismique.

seismograph ['saɪzməgrɑ:f] *n* sismographe *m*, séismographe *m*.

seismography [saɪz'mɒgrəfɪ] *n* sismographie *f*, séismographie *f*.

seismologist [saɪz'mɒlədʒɪst] *n* sismologue *mf*, séismologue *mf*.

seismology [saɪz'mɒlədʒɪ] *n* sismologie *f*, séismologie *f*.

seize [si:z] ◇ *vt* -**1.** [grasp] attraper, saisir; [in fist] saisir, empoigner; my mother ~d me by the arm/the collar ma mère m'a attrapé par le bras/le col; she ~d the rail to steady herself elle s'agrippa à la rampe pour ne pas tomber; he ~d a knife and held it to my throat il s'empara d'un couteau OR il saisit un couteau et l'appuya sur ma gorge; to ~ hold of sthg saisir OR attraper qqch; someone ~d hold of my arm quelqu'un m'a empoigné par le bras. -**2.** [by force] s'emparer de, saisir; to ~ power s'emparer du pouvoir; the rebels have ~d control of the radio station les rebelles se sont emparés de la station de radio; pirates ~d the ship des pirates se sont rendus maîtres du navire; five hostages were ~d during the hold-up les auteurs du hold-up ont pris cinq otages. -**3.** [arrest - terrorist, smuggler] se saisir de, appréhender, capturer; [capture, confiscate - contraband, arms] se saisir de, saisir; JUR [property] saisir; all copies of the book were ~d tous les exemplaires du livre ont été saisis. -**4.** [opportunity] saisir, sauter sur; ~ any opportunity that comes your way saute sur la moindre occasion qui se présentera. -**5.** [understand - meaning] saisir; he is quick to ~ the implications il saisit vite les implications. -**6.** [overcome] saisir; to be ~d with fright être saisi d'effroi; to be ~d with rage avoir un accès de rage; she was ~d with a desire to travel elle fut prise d'une envie irrésistible de voyager; the story never really ~s your imagination l'histoire ne parvient jamais à vraiment frapper l'imagination; I was ~d with a sudden sneezing fit j'ai soudain été pris d'éternuements. -**7.** *Am* = **seise**.
◇ *vi* [mechanism] se gripper.

◆ **seize on** *vt insep* [opportunity] saisir, sauter sur; [excuse] saisir; [idea] saisir, adopter.

◆ **seize up** *vi insep* -**1.** [machinery] se gripper; the brakes ~d up les freins se sont grippés OR bloqués. -**2.** [system] se bloquer; traffic in the centre has ~d up completely la circulation dans le centre est complètement bloquée. -**3.** [leg] s'ankyloser; [back] se bloquer; [heart] s'arrêter.

◆ **seize upon** = **seize on**.

seizure ['si:ʒə^r] *n* -**1.** *(U)* [of goods, property] saisie *f*; [of city, fortress] prise *f*; [of ship] capture *f*; [arrest] arrestation *f*; ~ of power prise de pouvoir; the police made a big arms ~ la police a saisi un important stock d'armes. -**2.** MED crise *f*, attaque *f*; to have a ~ *literal* & *fig* avoir une attaque; heart ~ crise cardiaque.

seldom ['seldəm] *adv* rarement; I ~ see her je la vois rarement, je la vois peu; he ~ comes il ne vient que OR il vient rarement; he ~, if ever, visits his mother il rend rarement, pour ne pas dire jamais, visite à sa mère.

select [sɪ'lekt] ◇ *vt* [gen] choisir; [team] sélectionner; you have been ~ed from among our many customers vous avez été choisie parmi nos nombreux clients; she hopes to be ~ed to play for Ireland elle espère faire partie de la sélection qui jouera pour l'Irlande.
◇ *adj* -**1.** [elite - restaurant, neighbourhood] chic, sélect; [- club] fermé, sélect; the membership is very ~ les membres appartiennent à la haute société; she invited a few ~ friends elle a invité quelques amis choisis; only a ~ few were informed seuls quelques privilégiés furent informés. -**2.** [in quality - goods] de (premier) choix.

select committee *n* POL commission *f* d'enquête parlementaire.

selected [sɪ'lektɪd] *adj* [friends, poems] choisi; [customers] privilégié; [fruit, cuts of meat] de (premier) choix; before a ~ audience devant un public choisi.

selection [sɪ'lekʃn] ◇ *n* -**1.** [choice] choix *m*, sélection *f*; [of team] sélection *f*; no one thought he stood a chance of ~ personne ne pensait qu'il serait sélectionné; make your ~ from among the books on the bottom shelf faites votre choix parmi les livres de l'étagère du bas; the restaurant offers an excellent ~ of wines ce restaurant propose un excellent choix de vins OR dispose d'une excellente carte des vins. -**2.** [of stories, music] choix *m*, sélection *f*; a ~ of poems [in book] poèmes *mpl* choisis; [for recital] un choix de poèmes; ~s from Balzac morceaux *mpl* choisis de Balzac.
◇ *comp* [committee, criteria] de sélection.

selective [sɪ'lektɪv] *adj* -**1.** [gen] sélectif; we can't take them all, we have to be ~ on ne peut pas les emmener tous, il faut faire un choix; you should be more ~ in your choice of friends/in your reading vous devriez choisir vos amis/vos lectures avec plus de discernement; there was a wave of ~ strikes il y eut une série de grèves tournantes ❑ ~ breeding élevage *m* sélectif; ~ entry SCH sélection *f*; ~ service *Am* service *m* militaire obligatoire, conscription *f*; ~ weedkiller herbicide *m* sélectif; ~ welfare allocations *fpl* sociales sélectives. -**2.** ELECTRON sélectif.

selectively [sɪ'lektɪvlɪ] *adv* sélectivement, de manière sélective.

selectivity [,sɪlek'tɪvətɪ] *n* -**1.** [choice] discernement *m*. -**2.** ELECTRON sélectivité *f*.

selector [sɪ'lektə^r] *n* -**1.** [gen & SPORT] sélectionneur *m*. -**2.** TELEC & TV sélecteur *m*.

selenium [sɪ'li:nɪəm] *n* sélénium *m*.

selenography [,si:lə'nɒgrəfɪ] *n* sélénographie *f*.

self [self] (*pl* selves [selvz]) ◇ *n* -**1.** [individual]: she's back to her old OR usual ~ elle est redevenue elle-même OR comme avant; she's only a shadow of her former ~ elle n'est plus que l'ombre d'elle-même; he was his usual tactless ~ il a fait preuve de son manque de tact habituel; they began to reveal their true selves ils ont commencé à se montrer sous leur véritable jour. -**2.** PSYCH moi *m*; the conscious ~ le moi conscient. -**3.** [self-interest]: all she thinks of is ~, ~, ~ elle ne pense qu'à sa petite personne. -**4.** [on cheque]: pay ~ payez à l'ordre de soi-même.
◇ *adj* [matching] assorti.
◇ *in cpds* -**1.** [of o.s.] de soi-même, auto-; ~-actualization épanouissement *m* de la personnalité; ~-accusation autoaccusation *f*; ~-admiration narcissisme *m*. -**2.** [by o.s.] auto-, par soi-même; ~-financing qui s'autofinance. -**3.** [automatic] auto-, automatique; ~-checking à contrôle automatique; ~-lubricating autolubrifiant; ~-opening à ouverture automatique.

self-absorbed *adj* égocentrique.

self-absorption *n* égocentrisme *m*.

self-abuse *n pej* onanisme *m*, masturbation *f*.

self-addressed *adj*: send three ~ envelopes envoyez trois enveloppes portant vos nom et adresse.

self-adhesive *adj* autocollant, autoadhésif.

self-analysis *n* autoanalyse *f*.

self-appointed *adj* qui s'est nommé OR proclamé lui-même; she is our ~ guide elle a assumé d'elle-même le rôle de guide au sein de notre groupe.

self-assembly *adj* [furniture] en kit.

self-assertive *adj* sûr de soi, impérieux.
self-assurance *n* confiance *f* en soi, aplomb *m*; she has plenty of ~ elle ne manque pas de confiance en elle.
self-assured *adj*: he's very ~ il est très sûr de lui.
self-aware *adj* conscient de soi-même.
self-awareness *n* conscience *f* de soi.
self-catering *adj Br* [flat, accommodation] indépendant *(avec cuisine)*; [holiday] dans un appartement OR un logement indépendant.
self-centred *Br*, **self-centered** *Am adj* égocentrique.
self-certification *n* certificat *m* de maladie *(rédigé par un employé)*.
self-cleaning *adj* autonettoyant.
self-closing *adj* à fermeture automatique.
self-coloured *Br*, **self-colored** *Am adj* uni.
self-complacent *adj* satisfait de soi, suffisant.
self-composure *n* calme *m*, sang-froid *m*; to keep/to lose one's ~ garder/perdre son sang-froid.
self-conceited *adj* vaniteux, suffisant.
self-confessed *adj* [murderer, rapist] qui reconnaît sa culpabilité; he's a ~ drug addict il avoue lui-même qu'il se drogue.
self-confidence *n* confiance *f* en soi, assurance *f*; she is full of/she lacks ~ elle a une grande/elle manque de confiance en elle.
self-confident *adj* sûr de soi, plein d'assurance.
self-confidently *adv* avec assurance OR aplomb.
self-congratulation *n* autosatisfaction *f*.
self-congratulatory *adj* satisfait de soi.
self-conscious *adj* -**1.** [embarrassed] timide, gêné; to make sb feel ~ intimider qqn; he's very ~ about his red hair il fait un complexe de ses cheveux roux; I feel very ~ in front of all these people je me sens très mal à l'aise devant tous ces gens. -**2.** [style] appuyé; I find her writing too ~ je trouve son style un peu trop appuyé.
self-consciously *adv* timidement.
self-consciousness *n* timidité *f*, gêne *f*.
self-contained *adj* -**1.** [device] autonome. -**2.** [flat] indépendant. -**3.** [person] réservé.
self-contradictory *adj* qui se contredit; your arguments are ~ vos arguments se contredisent.
self-control *n* sang-froid *m*, maîtrise *f* de soi; at that point I lost all ~ à ce moment-là, j'ai perdu tout mon sang-froid.
self-controlled *adj* maître de soi.
self-critical *adj* qui fait son autocritique.
self-criticism *n* autocritique *f*.
self-defeating [-dɪ'fi:tɪŋ] *adj* contraire au but recherché.
self-defence *n* -**1.** [physical] autodéfense *f*; the art of ~ l'art de l'autodéfense. -**2.** JUR légitime défense *f*; it was ~ j'étais en état de légitime défense; to plead ~ plaider la légitime défense; to act in ~ agir en état de légitime défense; I shot him in ~ j'ai tiré sur lui en état de légitime défense.
self-denial *n* abnégation *f*, sacrifice *m* de soi.
self-deprecating *adj*: to be ~ se déprécier.
self-destruct ◇ *vi* s'autodétruire.
◇ *adj* [mechanism] autodestructeur.
self-destruction *n* -**1.** [of spacecraft, missile] autodestruction *f*. -**2.** PSYCH [of personality] autodestruction *f*. -**3.** [suicide] suicide *m*.
self-destructive *adj* autodestructeur.
self-determination *n* POL autodétermination *f*.
self-determined *adj* POL autodéterminé.
self-discipline *n* [self-control] maîtrise *f* de soi; [good behaviour] autodiscipline *f*.
self-disciplined *adj* [self-controlled] maître de soi; [well-behaved] qui fait preuve d'autodiscipline.
self-doubt *n* doute *m* de soi-même.
self-drive *adj*: ~ car voiture *f* sans chauffeur; ~ car hire location *f* de voitures sans chauffeur.
self-educated *adj* autodidacte.
self-effacing *adj* modeste, effacé.
self-employed ◇ *adj* indépendant, qui travaille à son compte.
◇ *npl*: the ~ les travailleurs *mpl* indépendants.
self-esteem *n* respect *m* de soi, amour-propre *m*.
self-evident *adj* évident, qui va de soi, qui saute aux yeux; the truth is ~ la vérité saute aux yeux; it's ~ that neither side can win il est évident qu'aucune des deux parties ne peut gagner.
self-evidently *adv* bien évidemment.
self-examination *n* examen *m* de conscience.
self-explanatory *adj* qui se passe d'explications, évident.
self-expression *n* expression *f* libre.
self-financing [-faɪ'nænsɪŋ] *adj* autofinancé.
self-fulfilling *adj*: ~ prophecy *prophétie défaitiste qui se réalise*.
self-governing *adj* autonome POL.
self-government *n* autonomie *f* POL.
self-help ◇ *n* autonomie *f*; [in welfare] entraide *f*.
◇ *comp*: ~ group groupe *m* d'entraide; ~ guide guide *m* pratique.
selfhood ['selfhʊd] *n* PSYCH le soi.
self-hypnosis *n* autohypnose *f*.
self-image *n* image *f* de soi-même.
self-importance *n* suffisance *f*.
self-important *adj* vaniteux, suffisant.
self-imposed [-ɪm'pəʊzd] *adj* que l'on s'impose à soi-même; ~ exile exil *m* volontaire.
self-improvement *n* perfectionnement *m* des connaissances personnelles.
self-induced *adj* que l'on provoque soi-même.
self-indulgence *n* complaisance *f* envers soi-même, habitude *f* de ne rien se refuser.
self-indulgent *adj* qui ne se refuse rien; I find the book terribly ~ je trouve le livre terriblement complaisant.
self-inflicted [-ɪn'flɪktɪd] *adj*: his wounds were ~ il s'était auto-infligé ses blessures.
self-interest *n* intérêt *m* personnel; to act out of ~ agir par intérêt personnel.
self-interested *adj* intéressé, qui agit par intérêt personnel.
selfish ['selfɪʃ] *adj* égoïste; you're acting out of purely ~ motives vous agissez par pur égoïsme.
selfishly ['selfɪʃlɪ] *adv* égoïstement.
selfishness ['selfɪʃnɪs] *n* égoïsme *m*.
self-justification *n* autojustification *f*.
self-knowledge *n* connaissance *f* de soi.
selfless ['selflɪs] *adj* altruiste, désintéressé.
selflessly ['selflɪslɪ] *adv* de façon désintéressée, avec désintéressement.
selflessness ['selflɪsnɪs] *n* altruisme *m*, désintéressement *m*.
self-loading *adj* [gun] automatique.
self-locking *adj* à verrouillage automatique.
self-love *n* narcissisme *m*, amour *m* de soi-même.
self-made *adj* qui a réussi tout seul OR par ses propres moyens; a ~ man un self-made man.
self-mockery *n* autodérision *f*.
self-opinionated *adj* sûr de soi.
self-perpetuating [-pə'petʃʊeɪtɪŋ] *adj* qui se perpétue.
self-pity *n* apitoiement *m* sur soi-même OR sur son sort; she's full of ~ elle s'apitoie beaucoup sur son sort.
self-pitying *adj* qui s'apitoie sur son (propre) sort; don't be so ~ cesse de t'apitoyer sur ton sort.
self-portrait *n* [in painting] autoportrait *m*; [in book] portrait *m* de l'auteur par lui-même.
self-possessed *adj* maître de soi, qui garde son sang-froid.
self-possession *n* sang-froid *m*.
self-preservation *n* instinct *m* de conservation.
self-proclaimed *adj*: he is the ~ king of the ring il s'est proclamé lui-même roi du ring; she's a ~ art critic elle se proclame critique d'art.
self-propelled *adj* autopropulsé.
self-raising *Br*, **self-rising** *Am adj*: ~ flour farine *f* avec levure incorporée.
self-regard *n* égoïsme *m*.
self-regulating [-'regjʊleɪtɪŋ] *adj* autorégulateur.
self-reliant *adj* indépendant; you must learn to be more ~ tu dois apprendre à moins compter sur les autres.
self-respect *n* respect *m* de soi, amour-propre *m*.
self-respecting [-rɪ'spektɪŋ] *adj* qui se respecte; no ~ girl would be seen dead going out with him une fille qui se respecte ne sortirait pour rien au monde avec lui.
self-restraint *n* retenue *f*; to exercise ~ se retenir; with great ~ avec beaucoup de retenue.
self-righteous *adj* suffisant.
self-righteousness *n* suffisance *f*, pharisaïsme *m*.
self-righting [-'raɪtɪŋ] *adj* inchavirable.
self-rising *Am* = **self-raising**.
self-rule *n* autonomie *f* POL.
self-sacrifice *n* abnégation *f*; there's no need for ~ vous n'avez pas besoin de vous sacrifier (pour les autres).
self-sacrificing [-'sækrɪfaɪsɪŋ] *adj* qui se sacrifie, qui a l'esprit de sacrifice.
selfsame ['selfseɪm] *adj* même, identique; the ~ day I got the sack *inf* le jour même j'ai été viré.
self-satisfied *adj* suffisant, content de soi; she gave a ~ smile elle esquissa un sourire empreint de suffisance.
self-sealing *adj* [envelope] autocollant, autoadhésif; [tank] à obturation automatique.
self-seeking [-'si:kɪŋ] *adj* égoïste.
self-service ◇ *adj* en self-service, en libre service; ~ restaurant self-service *m*; ~ shop libre-service *m*.
◇ *n* [restaurant] self-service *m*; [garage, shop] libre-service *m*.
self-serving *adj* intéressé.
self-starter *n* starter *m* automatique.
self-styled [-'staɪld] *adj* prétendu, soi-disant; he's a ~ expert on the matter il se prétend OR c'est un soi-disant expert en la matière.
self-sufficiency *n* -**1.** [of person - independence] indépendance *f*; [- self-assurance] suffisance *f*. -**2.** ECON [of nation, resources] autosuffisance *f*; ECON & POL: (economic) ~ autarcie *f*.
self-sufficient *adj* -**1.** [person - independent] indépendant; [- self-assured] plein de confiance en soi, suffisant. -**2.** ECON [nation, resources] autosuffisant; ~ in copper autosuffisant en cuivre ‖ ECON & POL autarcique.
self-supporting *adj* -**1.** [financially] indépendant. -**2.** [framework] autoporteur, autoportant.
self-tapping [-'tæpɪŋ] *adj*: ~ screw vis *f* autotaraudeuse.
self-taught *adj* autodidacte.
self-test *n* COMPUT test *m* imprimante.
self-willed *adj* têtu, obstiné.
self-winding [-'waɪndɪŋ] *adj* [watch] qui n'a pas besoin d'être remonté, (à remontage) automatique.
sell [sel] (*pt* & *pp* sold [səʊld]) ◇ *vt* -**1.** [goods] vendre; to ~ sb sthg OR sthg to sb vendre qqch à qqn; he sold me his car for $1,000 il m'a vendu sa voiture (pour) 1 000 dollars; stamps are now also sold in some shops les timbres sont maintenant vendus aussi dans certains

magasins; he ~s computers for a living il gagne sa vie en vendant des ordinateurs; the book sold 50,000 copies, 50,000 copies of the book were sold le livre s'est vendu à 50 000 exemplaires; to ~ sthg for cash vendre qqch au comptant; to ~ sthg cheap vendre qqch à bas prix; they ~ the cassettes at £3 each or £30 a dozen ils vendent les cassettes 3 livres pièce ou 30 livres la douzaine; what really ~s newspapers is scandal ce sont les scandales qui font vraiment vendre les journaux; he'd ~ his own grandmother for a pint of beer il vendrait son âme pour une bière; she was sold into slavery/prostitution on l'a vendue comme esclave/prostituée; she sold her body OR herself to buy food elle s'est prostituée pour acheter à manger; they sold classified information to our competitors ils ont vendu des renseignements confidentiels à nos concurrents; he sold state secrets to the enemy il a vendu des secrets d'État à l'ennemi; to ~ one's soul (to the devil) vendre son âme (au diable); we'd ~ our souls for a holiday in the Caribbean *hum* nous ferions n'importe quoi pour passer des vacances aux Caraïbes ❑ we were sold a pup *inf dated* OR a dud *inf* [cheated] on nous a roulés; [sold rubbish] on nous a vendu de la camelote. -**2.** [promote - idea] faire accepter; she sold the idea to the whole council elle a fait accepter l'idée à tout le conseil; as a politician, it is important to be able to ~ yourself les hommes politiques doivent savoir se mettre en valeur. -**3.** *phr*: to ~ sb short *inf* [cheat] rouler qqn; [disparage] débiner qqn; don't ~ yourself short il faut vous mettre en valeur; I'm often accused of ~ing the country short on m'accuse souvent de donner une mauvaise image du pays; to ~ sb down the river trahir qqn. -**4.** [make enthusiastic about] convaincre; I'm completely sold on the idea je suis emballé par l'idée. -**5.** *inf* [cheat, deceive] rouler; we've been sold! on s'est fait avoir OR posséder!

◇ *vi* se vendre; the record is ~ing well le disque se vend bien; the cakes ~ for OR at 70 pence each les gâteaux se vendent (à) OR valent 70 pence pièce; sorry, I'm not interested in ~ing (my car/house) désolé, je ne cherche pas à vendre (ma voiture/maison) ❑ to ~ short FIN vendre à découvert; they sold like hot cakes ils se sont vendus comme des petits pains.

◇ *n* -**1.** COMM vente *f*. -**2.** *inf* [disappointment] déception *f*; [hoax] attrape-nigaud *m*.

◆ **sell back** *vt sep* revendre.

◆ **sell off** *vt sep* [at reduced price] solder; [clear] liquider; [get cash] vendre; the house was sold off to pay debts la maison a été vendue pour régler des créances; they're ~ing the plates off at bargain prices ils liquident les assiettes à des prix défiant toute concurrence.

◆ **sell on** *vt sep* revendre *(en faisant du bénéfice)*.

◆ **sell out** ◇ *vt sep* -**1.** [concert, match]: the match was sold out le match s'est joué à guichets fermés. -**2.** [betray] trahir. -**3.** ST. EX vendre, réaliser.

◇ *vi insep* -**1.** COMM [sell business] vendre son commerce; [sell stock] liquider (son stock); [run out] vendre tout le stock; my father sold out and retired mon père a vendu son affaire et a pris sa retraite; he sold out to some Japanese investors il a vendu à des investisseurs japonais; we've sold out of sugar nous n'avons plus de sucre, nous avons écoulé tout notre stock de sucre. -**2.** [be traitor] trahir; to ~ out to the enemy passer à l'ennemi; the government were accused of ~ing out to terrorism le gouvernement fut accusé d'avoir traité avec les terroristes; critics accuse her of ~ing out as a writer les critiques l'accusent d'être un écrivain vendu OR sans principes.

◆ **sell up** ◇ *vt sep* -**1.** FIN & JUR [goods] opérer la vente forcée de, procéder à la liquidation de. -**2.** COMM [business] vendre, liquider.

◇ *vi insep* [shopkeeper] vendre son fonds de commerce OR son affaire; [businessman] vendre son affaire.

sell-by date *n* date *f* limite de vente.

seller ['selə^r] *n* -**1.** [person - gen] vendeur *m*, -euse *f*; [- merchant] vendeur *m*, -euse *f*, marchand *m*, -e *f*; it's a ~'s market le marché est à la hausse OR favorable aux vendeurs. -**2.** [goods]: these shoes are good/poor ~s ces chaussures se vendent bien/mal; it's one of our biggest ~s c'est un des articles qui se vend le mieux.

selling ['selɪŋ] *n (U)* vente *f*.

selling point *n* avantage *m*, atout *m*, point *m* fort.

selling price *n* prix *m* de vente.

selloff ['selɒf] *n* [gen] vente *f*; [of shares] dégagement *m*.

Sellotape® ['seləteɪp] *n Br* Scotch® *m*, ruban *m* adhésif.

◆ **sellotape** *vt Br* scotcher, coller avec du ruban adhésif.

sell-out *n* -**1.** COMM liquidation *f*. -**2.** [betrayal] trahison *f*; [capitulation] capitulation *f*. -**3.** [of play, concert etc]: it was a ~ on a vendu tous les billets; the match was a ~ le match s'est joué à guichets fermés.

seltzer ['seltsə^r] *n*: ~ (water) eau *f* de Seltz.

selvage, selvedge ['selvɪdʒ] *n* lisière *f (d'un tissu)*.

selves [selvz] *pl* → **self**.

semanteme [sɪ'mæntiːm] *n* sémantème *m*.

semantic [sɪ'mæntɪk] *adj* sémantique.

semantically [sɪ'mæntɪklɪ] *adv* du point de vue sémantique.

semanticist [sɪ'mæntɪsɪst] *n* sémanticien *m*, -enne *f*.

semantics [sɪ'mæntɪks] *n (U)* sémantique *f*.

semaphore ['seməfɔː^r] ◇ *n* -**1.** *(U)* [signals] signaux *mpl* à bras; in OR by ~ par signaux à bras. -**2.** RAIL & NAUT sémaphore *m*.

◇ *vt* transmettre par signaux à bras.

semblance ['sembləns] *n* semblant *m*, apparence *f*; a ~ of order un semblant d'ordre; we need to show at least some ~ of unity nous devons au moins montrer un semblant d'unité.

semeiology *etc* [,semɪ'ɒlədʒɪ] = **semiology**.

sememe ['siːmiːm] *n* sémème *m*.

semen ['siːmen] *n (U)* sperme *m*, semence *f*.

semester [sɪ'mestə^r] *n* semestre *m*.

semi *inf* ['semɪ] *n* -**1.** *Br abbr of* semi-detached house. -**2.** *abbr of* semifinal. -**3.** *Am, Austr* & *NZ (abbr of* semitrailer) semi *m*.

semi- *in cpds* -**1.** [partly] semi-, demi-; ~arid semi-aride; in ~darkness dans la pénombre OR la semi-obscurité; he's ~retired OR in ~retirement il est en semi-retraite. -**2.** [twice]: ~annual semestriel.

semi-automatic ◇ *adj* semi-automatique.

◇ *n* arme *f* semi-automatique.

semibreve ['semɪbriːv] *n* ronde *f* MUS.

semicircle ['semɪ,sɜːkl] *n* demi-cercle *m*.

semicircular [,semɪ'sɜːkjʊlə^r] *adj* demi-circulaire, semi-circulaire.

semicolon [,semɪ'kəʊlən] *n* point-virgule *m*.

semiconduction [,semɪkən'dʌkʃn] *n* semi-conduction *f*.

semiconductor [,semɪkən'dʌktə^r] *n* semi-conducteur *m*.

semiconscious [,semɪ'kɒnʃəs] *adj* à demi OR moitié conscient; she was only ~ [losing] elle avait pratiquement perdu connaissance; [regaining] elle n'avait pas encore tout à fait repris connaissance.

semiconsciousness [,semɪ'kɒnʃəsnɪs] *n*: in a state of ~ à demi conscient.

semiconsonant [,semɪ'kɒnsənənt] *n* semi-consonne *f*.

semidarkness [,semɪ'dɑːknɪs] *n* pénombre *f*.

semi-detached *adj*: ~ house maison *f* jumelée.

semifinal [,semɪ'faɪnl] *n* demi-finale *f*; she lost in the ~s elle a perdu en demi-finale.

semifinalist [,semɪ'faɪnəlɪst] *n* demi-finaliste *mf*.

semifluid [,semɪ'fluːɪd] ◇ *adj* semi-liquide, semi-fluide.

◇ *n* semi-fluide *m*.

semi-invalid *n*: he is a ~ il n'est pas très valide.

semiliterate [,semɪ'lɪtərət] *adj* quasi analphabète.

seminal ['semɪnl] *adj* -**1.** ANAT & BOT séminal; ~ duct voie *f* séminale; ~ fluid liquide *m* séminal. -**2.** [important] majeur, qui fait école; she was a ~ influence on his art elle eut une influence majeure sur son art.

seminar ['semɪnɑː^r] *n* -**1.** [conference] séminaire *m*, colloque *m*. -**2.** UNIV [class] séminaire *m*, travaux *mpl* dirigés.

seminarian [,semɪ'neərɪən] *n* séminariste *mf*.

seminary ['semɪnərɪ] (*pl* **seminaries**) *n* RELIG & SCH [for boys, priests] séminaire *m*; [for girls] pensionnat *m* de jeunes filles.

seminiferous [,semɪ'nɪfərəs] *adj* séminifère.

semiologist [,semɪ'ɒlədʒɪst] *n* sémioticien *m*, -enne *f*, sémiologue *mf*.

semiology [,semɪ'ɒlədʒɪ] *n* sémiologie *f*.

semiotic [,semɪ'ɒtɪk] *adj* sémiotique.

semiotics [,semɪ'ɒtɪks] *n (U)* sémiotique *f*.

semiprecious ['semɪ,preʃəs] *adj* semi-précieux.

semiprofessional [,semɪprə'feʃənl] ◇ *adj* semi-professionnel.

◇ *n* semi-professionnel *m*, -elle *f*.

semiquaver ['semɪ,kweɪvə^r] *n* double croche *f*.

semiretired [,semɪrɪ'taɪəd] *adj* en semi-retraite.

semiskilled [,semɪ'skɪld] *adj* [worker] spécialisé.

semisubmersible [,semɪsəb'mɜːsəbl] ◇ *adj* semi-submersible.

◇ *n* plateforme *f* semi-submersible.

Semite ['siːmaɪt] *n* Sémite *mf*.

Semitic [sɪ'mɪtɪk] ◇ *n* LING langue *f* sémitique, sémitique *m*.

◇ *adj* sémite, sémitique.

semitone ['semɪtəʊn] *n* demi-ton *m*.

semitrailer [,semɪ'treɪlə^r] *n* semi-remorque *m*.

semitropical [,semɪ'trɒpɪkl] *adj* semi-tropical.

semivowel ['semɪ,vaʊəl] *n* semi-voyelle *f*.

semolina [,semə'liːnə] *n* semoule *f*; ~ pudding gâteau *m* de semoule.

sempiternal [,sempɪ'tɜːnl] *adj lit* sempiternel, éternel.

sempstress ['sempstrɪs] = **seamstress**.

sen. *written abbr of* senior.

Sen. *written abbr of* Senator.

SEN (*abbr of* State Enrolled Nurse) *n* *infirmier ou infirmière diplômé(e) d'État*.

senate ['senɪt] *n* -**1.** POL sénat *m*; the United States Senate le Sénat américain. -**2.** UNIV Conseil *m* d'Université.

SENATE:

Le Sénat constitue, avec la Chambre des Représentants, l'organe législatif américain; composé de 100 membres (deux par État), il détient l'exclusivité du droit d'impeachment.

senator ['senətə^r] *n* sénateur *m*.

senatorial [,senə'tɔːrɪəl] *adj* sénatorial.

send [send] (*pt* & *pp* sent [sent]) ◇ *vt* -**1.** [letter, parcel, money] envoyer, expédier; to ~ sb a letter, to ~ a letter to sb envoyer une lettre à qqn; he sent (us) word that he would be delayed il (nous) a fait savoir qu'il aurait du retard; he sent word to say he would be late il a fait dire OR savoir qu'il serait en retard; she ~s her love OR regards elle vous envoie ses amitiés; ~ them our love embrassez-les pour nous; ~ them our best wishes faites-leur nos amitiés; I sent my luggage by train j'ai fait expédier OR envoyer mes bagages par le train; it's like manna sent from heaven c'est une véritable aubaine; what will the future ~ us? que nous réserve l'avenir?; we sent help to the refugees nous avons envoyé des secours aux réfugiés; they sent a car to fetch us ils ont envoyé une voiture nous chercher || [to carry out task] envoyer; she sent her daughter for the meat OR to get the meat elle a envoyé sa fille chercher la viande; she sent her brother on an errand/with a message elle a envoyé son frère faire une course/porter un message; the children were sent to say goodnight on envoya les enfants dire bonsoir; the dogs were sent after him on lança les chiens à sa poursuite OR à ses trousses ❑ to ~ sb packing *inf* OR about his business envoyer promener qqn, envoyer qqn sur les roses. -**2.** [to a specific place] envoyer; the government sent an ambassador to Mexico le gouvernement envoya un ambassadeur au Mexique; ~ the children indoors faites rentrer les enfants; ~ him to me envoyez-le moi; ~ him to my office dites-lui de venir dans mon bureau, envoyez-le moi; he sent the ball over the heads of the spectators il envoya le ballon par-dessus la tête des spectateurs; the collision sent showers of sparks/clouds of smoke into the sky la collision fit jaillir une gerbe d'étincelles/provoqua des nuages de fumée; the sound sent shivers down my spine le bruit m'a fait froid dans le dos; the news sent a murmur of excitement through the hall la nouvelle provoqua un murmure d'agitation dans la salle; heavy smoking sent him to an early grave il est mort prématurément parce qu'il fumait trop || [order]: I was sent to bed/to my room on m'a envoyé me coucher/dans ma chambre; to ~ sb home [from school] renvoyer qqn chez lui; [from abroad] rapatrier qqn; INDUST [lay off] mettre qqn en chômage technique; to ~ sb to prison envoyer qqn en prison; to ~ sb to school envoyer qqn à l'école. -**3.** *(with present participle)* [propel] envoyer, expédier; a gust of wind sent the papers flying across the table un coup de vent balaya les papiers qui se trouvaient sur la table; I sent the cup flying j'ai envoyé voler la tasse; the blow sent me flying le coup m'a envoyé rouler par terre; a sudden storm sent us all running for shelter un orage soudain nous força à courir nous mettre à l'abri; the boy sent the marbles rolling across the floor le garçon envoya les billes rouler par terre. -**4.** [into a specific state] rendre; the noise is ~ing me mad OR out of my mind le bruit me rend fou; the news sent them into a panic les nouvelles les ont fait paniquer; to ~ sb to sleep *literal* & *fig* endormir qqn. -**5.** *inf dated* [into raptures] emballer; his voice really ~s me sa voix me fait vraiment craquer.

◇ *vi* -**1.** [send word]: he sent to say he couldn't come il nous a fait savoir qu'il ne pouvait pas venir. -**2.** [for information, equipment]: we sent to Paris for a copy nous avons demandé une copie à Paris.

◆ **send away** ◇ *vt sep* -**1.** [letter, parcel] expédier, mettre à la poste. -**2.** [person] renvoyer, faire partir; the children were sent away to school les enfants furent mis en pension.

◇ *vi insep*: to ~ away for sthg se faire envoyer qqch; [by mail order] commander qqch par correspondance; [from catalogue] commander qqch sur catalogue.

◆ **send back** *vt sep* -**1.** [return - books, goods] renvoyer; ~ the chocolates back to the shop renvoyez les chocolats au magasin. -**2.** [order - person]: we sent her back to fetch a coat OR for a coat nous l'avons envoyée prendre un manteau.

◆ **send down** ◇ *vt sep* -**1.** [person, lift] faire descendre, envoyer en bas; they sent me down to the cellar ils m'ont fait descendre à la cave; she was sent down to ask if they wanted coffee on l'a envoyée en bas pour demander s'ils voulaient du café. -**2.** [prices, temperature] faire baisser, provoquer la baisse de. -**3.** *Br* UNIV [student] expulser, renvoyer. -**4.** *inf* [to prison] envoyer en prison; he was sent down for twenty years il a écopé de vingt ans (de prison), il en a pris pour vingt ans.

◇ *vi insep* [by message or messenger]: to ~ down for sthg (se) faire monter qqch.

◆ **send for** *vt insep* -**1.** [doctor, taxi] faire venir, appeler; [mother, luggage] faire venir; [police] appeler; [help] envoyer chercher; we sent for another bottle on a demandé une autre bouteille. -**2.** [by post, from catalogue] se faire envoyer, commander; [catalogue, price list] demander.

◆ **send forth** *vt insep lit* -**1.** [army, messenger] envoyer. -**2.** [produce - leaves] produire; [- light] produire, émettre; [- smell] répandre; [- cry] pousser.

◆ **send in** *vt sep* -**1.** [visitor] faire entrer; [troops, police] envoyer. -**2.** [submit - report, form] envoyer; [- suggestions, resignation] envoyer, soumettre; why don't you ~ your name in for the competition? pourquoi ne pas vous inscrire au concours?; to ~ in a request faire une demande; please ~ in a written application veuillez envoyer une demande écrite; [for job] veuillez poser votre candidature par écrit.

◆ **send off** ◇ *vt sep* -**1.** [by post] expédier, mettre à la poste. -**2.** [person] envoyer; I sent him off home/upstairs je l'ai envoyé chez lui/en haut; they sent us off to bed/to get washed ils nous ont envoyés nous coucher/nous laver; they are sent off to school every morning on les envoie à l'école tous les matins. -**3.** SPORT expulser. -**4.** [to sleep]: to ~ sb off (to sleep) *literal* & *fig* endormir qqn.

◇ *vi insep*: to ~ off for sthg [by catalogue] commander qqch par correspondance OR sur catalogue; [by post] se faire envoyer qqch.

◆ **send on** *vt sep* -**1.** [mail] faire suivre; to ~ a message on to sb faire suivre un message à qqn; my luggage was sent on to New York [in advance] on a expédié mes bagages à New York; [by mistake] mes bagages ont été expédiés à New York par erreur; if you've forgotten anything, we'll ~ it on si vous avez oublié quelque chose, nous vous le renverrons. -**2.** [person]: they sent us on ahead OR in front ils nous ont envoyés en éclaireurs; we sent them on to find a hotel nous les avons envoyés en éclaireurs pour trouver un hôtel; they sent me on to Dundee [further] ils m'ont envoyé jusqu'à Dundee. -**3.** SPORT [player] faire entrer (sur le terrain).

◆ **send out** ◇ *vt sep* -**1.** [by post - invitations] expédier, poster. -**2.** [messengers, search party] envoyer, dépêcher; [patrol] envoyer; they sent out a car for us ils ont envoyé une voiture nous chercher || [transmit - message, signal] envoyer; a call was sent out for Dr Bramley on a fait appeler le Dr Bramley. -**3.** [outside] envoyer dehors; we sent them all out into the garden on les a tous envoyés dans le jardin; ~ the children out to play envoyez les enfants jouer dehors || [on errand, mission] envoyer; we sent her out for coffee nous l'avons envoyée chercher du café; they sent me out to Burma ils m'ont envoyé en Birmanie. -**4.** [produce, give out - leaves] produire; [- light, heat] émettre, répandre, diffuser; [- fumes, smoke, smell] répandre.

◇ *vi insep*: to ~ out for coffee/sandwiches [to shop] envoyer quelqu'un commander du café/des sandwiches.

◆ **send round** *vt sep* -**1.** [circulate - petition] faire circuler; to ~ round the hat faire la quête. -**2.** [dispatch - messenger, repairman] envoyer; [- message] faire parvenir; they sent a car round ils ont envoyé une voiture; her mother sent her round to our house for some sugar sa mère l'a envoyée chez nous demander du sucre.

◆ **send up** *vt sep* -**1.** [messenger, luggage, drinks] faire monter; [rocket, flare] lancer; [plane] faire décoller; [smoke] répandre. -**2.** [raise - price, pressure, temperature] faire monter. -**3.** *inf* [ridicule] mettre en boîte, se moquer de. -**4.** *inf Am* [to prison] envoyer en prison, coffrer.

sender ['sendəʳ] *n* expéditeur *m*, -trice *f*; return to ~ retour à l'expéditeur.

send-off *n*: to give sb a ~ dire au revoir à qqn, souhaiter bon voyage à qqn; he was given a warm ~ by all his colleagues tous les collègues sont venus lui faire des adieux chaleureux.

send-up *inf n* parodie *f*.

Seneca ['senɪkə] *pr n* Sénèque *m*.

Senegal [ˌsenɪ'gɔːl] *pr n* Sénégal *m*; in ~ au Sénégal.

Senegalese [ˌsenɪgə'liːz] (*pl inv*) ◇ *n* Sénégalais *m*, -e *f*.

◇ *adj* sénégalais.

Senegambia [ˌsenɪ'gæmbɪə] *pr n* Sénégambie *f*.

Senegambian [ˌsenɪ'gæmbɪən] ◇ *n* Sénégambien *m*, -enne *f*.

◇ *adj* sénégambien.

senescence [sɪ'nesns] *n* sénescence *f*.

senescent [sɪ'nesnt] *adj* sénescent.

senile ['siːnaɪl] *adj* sénile; ~ decay dégénérescence *f* sénile; ~ dementia démence *f* sénile.

senility [sɪ'nɪlətɪ] *n* sénilité *f*.

senior ['siːnjəʳ] ◇ *adj* -**1.** [in age] plus âgé, aîné; [in rank] (de grade) supérieur; I am ~ to them [higher position] je suis leur supérieur; [longer service] j'ai plus d'ancienneté qu'eux; ~ airport officials refused to comment la direction de l'aéroport s'est refusée à toute déclaration; ~ clerk commis *m* principal, chef *m* de bureau; ~ executive cadre *m* supérieur; ~ government official haut fonctionnaire *m*; ~ officer officier *m* supérieur; George is the ~ partner in our firm Georges est l'associé principal de notre société. -**2.** SCH: ~ master *Br* professeur *m* principal || *Am*: ~ high school lycée *m*; ~ year terminale *f*, dernière année *f* d'études secondaires.

◇ *n* -**1.** [older person] aîné *m*, -e *f*; he is my ~ by six months, he is six months my ~ il a six mois de plus que moi, il est de six mois mon aîné. -**2.** *Am* SCH élève *mf* de terminale; UNIV étudiant *m*, -e *f* de licence. -**3.** *Br* SCH: the ~s ≃ les grands *mpl*, les grandes *fpl*. -**4.** [in hierarchy] supérieur *m*, -e *f*.

◆ **Senior** *adj* [in age]: John Brown ~ John Brown père.

senior citizen *n* personne *f* âgée OR du troisième âge; ~s' club club *m* du troisième âge; ~s' rail pass ≃ Carte *f* Vermeil.

Senior Common Room *n Br* UNIV salle *f* des professeurs.

seniority [ˌsiːnɪ'ɒrətɪ] *n* -**1.** [in age] priorité *f* d'âge; he became chairman by virtue of ~ il est devenu président parce qu'il était le plus âgé OR le doyen. -**2.** [in rank] supériorité *f*; to have ~ over sb être le supérieur de qqn || [length of service] ancienneté *f*; according to OR by ~ en fonction de OR à l'ancienneté.

Senior Service *n Br* marine *f*.

senna ['senə] *n* séné *m*; ~ tea infusion *f* OR tisane *f* de séné.

sensate ['senseɪt] *adj* perçu par les sens.

sensation [sen'seɪʃn] *n* -**1.** *(U)* [sensitivity] sensation *f*; the cold made me lose all ~ in my hands le froid m'a complètement engourdi les mains. -**2.** [impression] impression *f*, sensation *f*; I had a strange ~ in my leg j'avais une drôle de sensation dans la jambe; I had the ~ of falling j'avais la sensation OR l'impression de tomber. -**3.** [excitement, success] sensation *f*; to cause a ~ faire sensation; the film was a ~ le film a fait sensation.

sensational [sen'seɪʃənl] *adj* -**1.** [causing a sensation] sensationnel, qui fait sensation; a ~ story une histoire sensationnelle; a ~ crime un crime qui fait sensation; it was the most ~ event of the year ce fut l'événement le plus sensationnel de l'année. -**2.** [press] à sensation. -**3.** [wonderful] formidable, sensationnel; you look ~ tu es superbe; that's ~ news c'est une nouvelle formidable OR sensationnelle.

sensationalism [sen'seɪʃnəlɪzm] *n* -**1.** [in press, novels etc] sensationnalisme *m*. -**2.** PHILOS sensationnisme *m*. -**3.** PSYCH sensualisme *m*.

sensationalist [sen'seɪʃnəlɪst] ◇ *n* [writer] auteur *m* à sensation; [journalist] journaliste *mf* à sensation.

◇ *adj* à sensation.

sensationally [sen'seɪʃnəlɪ] *adv* d'une manière sensationnelle; [as intensifier]: **we found this ~ good restaurant** *inf* on a découvert un restaurant vraiment génial.

sense [sens] ◇ *n* -**1.** [faculty] sens *m*; **to be in possession of all one's ~s** jouir de toutes ses facultés; **to excite the ~s** exciter les sens; **some sixth ~ warned me of danger** une sorte de sixième sens m'avertit du danger. -**2.** [sensation] sensation *f*; [feeling] sentiment *m*; **I felt a certain ~ of pleasure** j'ai ressenti un certain plaisir; **I felt a ~ of shame** je me suis senti honteux; **children need a ~ of security** les enfants ont besoin de se sentir en sécurité; **there's a new ~ of foreboding in her writing** ses écrits sont maintenant empreints d'un sentiment d'angoisse devant l'avenir ‖ [notion] sens *m*, notion *f*; **she seems to have lost all ~ of reality** elle semble avoir perdu le sens des réalités; **I lost all ~ of time** j'ai perdu toute notion de l'heure; **to have a (good) ~ of direction** avoir le sens de l'orientation; **she lost her ~ of direction when her husband died** *fig* elle a perdu le nord après la mort de son mari; **he has a good ~ of humour** il a le sens de l'humour; **I try to teach them a ~ of right and wrong** j'essaie de leur inculquer la notion du bien et du mal; **she acted out of a ~ of duty/of responsibility** elle a agi par sens du devoir/des responsabilités; **they have no business ~ at all** ils n'ont aucun sens des affaires; **he has an overdeveloped ~ of his own importance** il est trop imbu de lui-même. -**3.** [practicality, reasonableness] bon sens *m*; **to show good ~** faire preuve de bon sens; **to see ~** entendre raison; **oh, come on, talk ~!** voyons, ne dis pas n'importe quoi!; **there's no ~ in all of us going** cela ne sert à rien OR c'est inutile d'y aller tous; **there's a lot of ~ in what she says** il y beaucoup de bon sens dans ce qu'elle dit, ce qu'elle dit est tout à fait sensé; **they didn't even have enough ~ to telephone** ils n'ont même pas eu l'idée de téléphoner ❑ **'Sense and Sensibility'** *Austen* 'Bon sens et sensibilité'. -**4.** [meaning - of word, expression] sens *m*, signification *f*; [- of text] sens *m*; **don't take what I say in its literal ~** ne prenez pas ce que je dis au sens propre OR au pied de la lettre; **in every ~ of the word** dans tous les sens du terme; **I think we have, in a very real ~, grasped the problem** je crois que nous avons parfaitement saisi le problème; **I got the general ~** j'ai saisi le sens général. -**5.** [coherent message] sens *m*; **to make ~** [words] avoir un sens; [be logical] tenir debout, être sensé; **can you make (any) ~ of this message?** est-ce que vous arrivez à comprendre ce message?; **it makes no ~** ça n'a pas de sens; **it makes ~ to wait** c'est une bonne idée d'attendre; **it doesn't make ~ to wait** c'est idiot d'attendre; **to talk ~** dire des choses sensées. -**6.** [way]: **in a ~** dans un sens; **in no ~** en aucune manière; **in more ~s than one** dans tous les sens.
◇ *vt* -**1.** [feel - presence] sentir; [- danger, catastrophe] pressentir; **I ~d something was wrong** j'ai senti que quelque chose n'allait pas; **I ~d as much** c'est bien l'impression OR le sentiment que j'avais; **I ~d her meaning** j'ai compris ce qu'elle voulait dire. -**2.** ELECTRON détecter; COMPUT lire.
◆ **senses** *npl* [sanity, reason] raison *f*; **to come to one's ~s** [become conscious] reprendre connaissance; [be reasonable] revenir à la raison; **you've taken leave of your ~s!** vous avez perdu la raison OR la tête!; **to bring sb to his/her ~s** ramener qqn à la raison.

senseless ['senslɪs] *adj* -**1.** [futile] insensé, absurde; **it's ~ trying to persuade her** inutile d'essayer OR on perd son temps à essayer de la persuader; **there has been a lot of ~ killing in this war** cette guerre a fait beaucoup de morts inutiles; **what a ~ waste of time!** quelle perte de temps stupide! -**2.** [unconscious] sans connaissance; **to knock sb ~** assommer qqn; **he fell ~ to the deck** il est tombé sans connaissance sur le pont (du navire).

senselessly ['senslɪslɪ] *adv* stupidement, de façon absurde.

senselessness ['senslɪsnɪs] *n* [silliness] manque *m* de bon sens, stupidité *f*; [absurdity] absurdité *f*.

sense organ *n* organe *m* sensoriel OR des sens.

sensibility [,sensɪ'bɪlətɪ] (*pl* **sensibilities**) *n* [physical or emotional] sensibilité *f*; **he's a man of great ~** c'est un homme d'une grande sensibilité; **~ to pain** sensibilité à la douleur.
◆ **sensibilities** *npl* susceptibilité *f*, susceptibilités *fpl*; **we must avoid offending our viewers' sensibilities** nous devons éviter de heurter la sensibilité de nos spectateurs.

sensible ['sensəbl] *adj* -**1.** [reasonable - choice] judicieux, sensé; [- reaction] sensé, qui fait preuve de bon sens; [- person] sensé, doué de bon sens; **it's a very ~ idea** c'est une très bonne idée; **the most ~ thing to do is to phone** la meilleure chose à faire, c'est de téléphoner. -**2.** [practical - clothes, shoes] pratique; **you need ~ walking shoes** il vous faut de bonnes chaussures de marche; **it's not a very ~ swimsuit** ce maillot de bain n'est pas très pratique. -**3.** *fml* [notable - change] sensible, appréciable. -**4.** *fml* & *lit* [aware]: **I am ~ of the fact that things have changed between us** j'ai conscience du fait que les choses ont changé entre nous.

sensibly ['sensəblɪ] *adv* -**1.** [reasonably] raisonnablement; **they very ~ decided to give up before someone got hurt** ils ont pris la décision raisonnable de renoncer avant que quelqu'un ne soit blessé; **to be ~ dressed** porter des vêtements pratiques. -**2.** *fml* [perceptibly] sensiblement, perceptiblement.

sensing ['sensɪŋ] *n* *(U)* ELECTRON exploration *f*, sondage *m*.

sensitive ['sensɪtɪv] *adj* -**1.** [eyes, skin] sensible; **my eyes are very ~ to bright light** j'ai les yeux très sensibles à la lumière vive; **special soaps for ~ skin** savons spéciaux pour peaux sensibles OR délicates. -**2.** [emotionally] sensible; **we are all ~ to kindness** nous sommes tous sensibles à la gentillesse. -**3.** [aware] sensibilisé; **the seminar made us more ~ to the problem** le séminaire nous a sensibilisés au problème. -**4.** [touchy - person] susceptible; [- age] où l'on est susceptible; [- public opinion] sensible; **she's very ~ about her height/looks** elle n'aime pas beaucoup qu'on lui parle de sa taille/de son apparence ‖ [difficult - issue, topic] délicat, épineux; **you're touching on a ~ area** vous abordez un sujet délicat OR épineux ‖ [information] confidentiel; **avoid such politically ~ issues** évitez des questions politiques aussi délicates. -**5.** [instrument] sensible; PHOT [film] sensible; [paper] sensibilisé. -**6.** ST. EX [market] instable.

-sensitive *in cpds* sensible; **heat~** sensible à la chaleur, thermosensible; **price~** sensible aux fluctuations des prix; **voice~** sensible à la voix.

sensitively ['sensɪtɪvlɪ] *adv* avec sensibilité.

sensitivity [,sensɪ'tɪvətɪ] *n* -**1.** [physical] sensibilité *f*. -**2.** [emotional] sensibilité *f*; [touchiness] susceptibilité *f*. -**3.** [of equipment] sensibilité *f*. -**4.** ST. EX instabilité *f*.

sensitize, -ise ['sensɪtaɪz] *vt* sensibiliser, rendre sensible.

sensor ['sensəʳ] *n* détecteur *m*, capteur *m*.

sensorium [sen'sɔːrɪəm] (*pl* **sensoriums** OR sensoria [-rɪə]) *n* sensorium *m*.

sensory ['sensərɪ] *adj* [nerve, system] sensoriel; **~ perception** perception *f* sensorielle.

sensual ['sensjʊəl] *adj* sensuel.

sensualism ['sensjʊəlɪzm] *n* [gen] sensualité *f*; PHILOS sensualisme *m*.

sensualist ['sensjʊəlɪst] *n* [gen] personne *f* sensuelle; PHILOS sensualiste *mf*.

sensuality [,sensjʊ'ælətɪ] *n* sensualité *f*.

sensuous ['sensjʊəs] *adj* [music, arts] qui affecte les sens; [lips, person] sensuel.

sensuously ['sensjʊəslɪ] *adv* voluptueusement, sensuellement.

sensuousness ['sensjʊəsnɪs] *n* volupté *f*.

sent [sent] *pt* & *pp* → **send**.

sentence ['sentəns] ◇ *n* -**1.** GRAMM phrase *f*; **~ structure** structure *f* de phrase. -**2.** JUR condamnation *f*, peine *f*, sentence *f*; **to pass ~ on sb** prononcer une condamnation contre qqn; **to pronounce ~** prononcer la sentence; **life/death ~** condamnation à perpétuité/à mort; **under ~ of death** condamné à mort; **he got a 5-year ~ for burglary** il a été condamné à 5 ans de prison OR à une peine de 5 ans pour cambriolage.
◇ *vt* JUR condamner; **to ~ sb to life imprisonment** condamner qqn à la prison à perpétuité.

sententious [sen'tenʃəs] *adj* sententieux, pompeux.

sententiously [sen'tenʃəslɪ] *adv* sententieusement.

sententiousness [sen'tenʃəsnɪs] *n* [personality] caractère *m* sententieux; [in speech] ton *m* sententieux.

sentient ['sentɪənt] *adj fml* doué de sensation.

sentiment ['sentɪmənt] *n* -**1.** [feeling] sentiment *m*; **your ~s towards my sister** vos sentiments envers ma soeur, les sentiments que vous éprouvez pour ma sœur ‖ [opinion] sentiment *m*, avis *m*, opinion *f*; **my ~s exactly** c'est exactement ce que je pense, voilà mon sentiment. -**2.** [sentimentality] sentimentalité *f*; **there's no place for ~ in business matters** il n'y a pas de place pour les sentiments en affaires.

sentimental [,sentɪ'mentl] *adj* sentimental; **the photos have great ~ value** ces photos ont une grande valeur sentimentale.

sentimentalism [,sentɪ'mentəlɪzm] *n* sentimentalisme *m*.

sentimentalist [,sentɪ'mentəlɪst] *n* sentimental *m*, -e *f*.

sentimentality [,sentɪmen'tælətɪ] (*pl* **sentimentalities**) *n* sentimentalité *f*, sensiblerie *f pej*.

sentimentalize, -ise [,sentɪ'mentəlaɪz] ◇ *vt* [to others] présenter de façon sentimentale; [to o.s.] percevoir de façon sentimentale.
◇ *vi* faire du sentiment.

sentimentally [,sentɪ'mentəlɪ] *adv* sentimentalement, de manière sentimentale; **he spoke ~ about his past** il a évoqué son passé avec émotion.

sentinel ['sentɪnl] *n* sentinelle *f*, factionnaire *m*.

sentry ['sentrɪ] (*pl* **sentries**) *n* sentinelle *f*, factionnaire *m*.

sentry box *n* guérite *f*.

sentry duty *n* MIL faction *f*; **to be on ~** être en OR de faction.

Seoul [səʊl] *pr n* Séoul.

sepal ['sepəl] *n* sépale *m*.

separable ['seprəbl] *adj* séparable.

separate [*adj* & *n* 'seprət, *vb* 'sepəreɪt] ◇ *adj* [different, distinct - category, meaning, issue] distinct, à part; [- incident] différent; **that's quite a ~ matter** ça, c'est une toute autre affaire; **they sleep in ~ rooms** [children] ils ont chacun leur chambre; [couple] ils font chambre à part; **administration and finance are in ~ departments** l'administration et les finances relèvent de services différents; **the canteen is ~ from the main building** la cantine se trouve à l'extérieur du bâtiment principal; **begin each chapter on a ~ page** commencez chaque chapitre sur une nouvelle page; **I'd prefer them to come on ~ days** je préférerais qu'ils viennent à des jours différents; **it happened on four ~ occasions** cela s'est produit à quatre reprises; **she likes to keep her home life ~ from the office** elle tient à ce que son travail n'empiète pas sur sa vie privée; **the peaches must be kept ~ from the lemons** les pêches et les citrons ne doivent pas être mélangés; **he was kept ~ from the other children** on le tenait à l'écart OR on l'isolait des autres enfants ‖ [independent - entrance, living quarters] indépendant, particulier; [- existence, organization] indépendant;

they lead very ~ lives ils mènent chacun leur vie ❑ ~ school *Can* ≃ école *f* libre; they went their ~ ways *literal* [after meeting] ils sont partis chacun de leur côté; *fig* [in life] chacun a suivi sa route.
◇ *n* -**1.** [in stereo] élément *m* séparé. -**2.** *Am* [offprint] tiré *m* à part.
◇ *vt* -**1.** [divide, set apart] séparer; he stepped in to ~ the fighting dogs il est intervenu pour séparer les chiens qui se battaient; her parents are ~d ses parents sont séparés; the Bosphorus ~s Europe from Asia le Bosphore sépare l'Europe de l'Asie; the seriously ill were ~d from the other patients les malades gravement atteints étaient isolés des autres patients; the records can be ~d into four categories les disques peuvent être divisés OR classés en quatre catégories ‖ [detach - parts, pieces] séparer, détacher; the last three coaches will be separated from the rest of the train les trois derniers wagons seront détachés du reste du train. -**2.** [keep distinct] séparer, distinguer; to ~ reality from myth distinguer le mythe de la réalité, faire la distinction entre le mythe et la réalité. -**3.** CULIN [milk] écrémer; [egg] séparer; ~ the whites from the yolks séparez les blancs des jaunes.
◇ *vi* -**1.** [go different ways] se quitter, se séparer; they ~d after the meeting ils se sont quittés après la réunion. -**2.** [split up - couple] se séparer, rompre; [- in boxing, duel] rompre; POL [party] se scinder; they ~d on good terms ils se sont séparés à l'amiable; the party ~d into various factions le parti s'est scindé en diverses factions. -**3.** [come apart, divide - liquid] se séparer; [- parts] se séparer, se détacher, se diviser; the boosters ~ from the shuttle les propulseurs auxiliaires se détachent de la navette; the model ~s into four parts la maquette se divise en quatre parties.
◆ **separates** *npl* [clothes] coordonnés *mpl*.
◆ **separate out** ◇ *vt sep* séparer, trier.
◇ *vi insep* se séparer.
◆ **separate up** *vt sep* séparer, diviser; to ~ sthg up into equal shares diviser OR partager qqch en parts égales.

separately ['seprətlɪ] *adv* -**1.** [apart] séparément, à part; woollens must be washed ~ les lainages doivent être lavés séparément. -**2.** [individually] séparément; can we pay ~? pouvons-nous payer séparément OR avoir des additions séparées?; they don't sell yogurts ~ ils ne vendent pas les yaourts à l'unité.

separateness ['seprətnɪs] *n* séparation *f*.

separation [ˌsepə'reɪʃn] *n* -**1.** [division] séparation *f*; the ~ of Church and State la séparation de l'Église et de l'État; her ~ from her family caused her great heartache sa séparation d'avec sa famille l'a beaucoup chagrinée. -**2.** [of couple] séparation *f*; trial ~ séparation à l'essai; legal OR judicial ~ séparation de corps.

separation allowance *n* -**1.** MIL allocation *f* mensuelle *(versée par l'armée à la femme d'un soldat)*. -**2.** [alimony] pension *f* alimentaire.

separatism ['seprətɪzm] *n* séparatisme *m*.

separatist ['seprətɪst] ◇ *adj* séparatiste.
◇ *n* séparatiste *mf*.

separator ['sepəreɪtəʳ] *n* [gen] séparateur *m*; CULIN [for milk] écrémeuse *f*.

Sephardi [se'fɑːdiː] (*pl* Sephardim [-dɪm]) *n* Séfarade *mf*.

Sephardic [se'fɑːdɪk] *adj* séfarade.

sepia ['siːpjə] ◇ *n* -**1.** [pigment, print] sépia *f*. -**2.** [fish] seiche *f*.
◇ *adj* sépia *(inv)*.

sepoy ['siːpɔɪ] *n* cipaye *m*.

sepsis ['sepsɪs] *n* septicité *f*.

Sept. (*written abbr of* September) sept.

September [sep'tembəʳ] ◇ *n* septembre *m*.
◇ *comp* [weather, weekend] (du mois) de septembre.

Septembrist [sep'tembrɪst] *n* septembriseur *m*.

septenary ['septɪnərɪ] *adj* septénaire.

septennial [sep'tenjəl] *adj* septennal.

septet [sep'tet] *n* septuor *m*.

septic ['septɪk] *adj* septique; [wound] infecté; to go OR to become ~ s'infecter; I have a ~ finger j'ai une blessure infectée au doigt; ~ poisoning septicémie *f*.

septicaemia, **septicemia** [ˌseptɪ'siːmɪə] *n (U)* septicémie *f*.

septic tank *n* fosse *f* septique.

septuagenarian [ˌseptjʊədʒɪ'neərɪən] ◇ *adj* septuagénaire.
◇ *n* septuagénaire *mf*.

Septuagesima [ˌseptjʊə'dʒesɪmə] *n* septuagésime *f*.

Septuagint ['septjʊədʒɪnt] *n*: the~ la version des Septante.

septum ['septəm] *n* ANAT septum *m*.

septuplet [sep'tjuːplɪt] *n* -**1.** [baby] septuplé *m*, -e *f*; ~s des septuplés. -**2.** MUS septolet *m*.

sepulcher *Am* = **sepulchre**.

sepulchral [sɪ'pʌlkrəl] *adj* [figure, voice] sépulcral; [atmosphere] funèbre, lugubre.

sepulchre *Br*, **sepulcher** *Am* ['sepʌlkəʳ] *n* sépulcre *m*.

sequel ['siːkwəl] *n* -**1.** [result, aftermath] conséquence *f*, suites *fpl*, conséquences *fpl*; [to illness, war] séquelles *fpl*; as a ~ to this event à la suite de cet événement; there was a disastrous ~ to the race la course a eu des suites OR des conséquences désastreuses. -**2.** [to novel, film etc] suite *f*.

sequence ['siːkwəns] ◇ *n* -**1.** [order] suite *f*, ordre *m*; in ~ [in order] par ordre, en série; [one after another] l'un après l'autre; numbered in ~ numérotés dans l'ordre; in historical ~ par ordre chronologique; logical ~ suite logique; ~ of tenses GRAMM concordance *f* des temps. -**2.** [series] série *f*; [in cards] séquence *f*; the ~ of events le déroulement OR l'enchaînement des événements. -**3.** CIN & MUS séquence *f*; dance ~ numéro *m* de danse; film ~ séquence de film. -**4.** LING & MATH séquence *f*. -**5.** BIOL & CHEM séquençage *m*.
◇ *vt* -**1.** [order] classer, ordonner. -**2.** BIOL & CHEM faire le séquençage de.

sequencer ['siːkwənsəʳ] *n* séquenceur *m*.

sequential [sɪ'kwenʃl] *adj* -**1.** COMPUT séquentiel; ~ access accès *m* séquentiel. -**2.** *fml* [following] subséquent; a lower income is ~ upon retirement la retraite entraîne une baisse de revenus.

sequentially [sɪ'kwenʃəlɪ] *adv* [follow, happen] séquentiellement.

sequester [sɪ'kwestəʳ] *vt* -**1.** *fml* [set apart] isoler, mettre à part. -**2.** *fml* [shut away] séquestrer; he was ~ed in his office il a été séquestré dans son bureau. -**3.** JUR [goods, property] séquestrer, placer sous séquestre.

sequestered [sɪ'kwestəd] *adj lit* [place] retiré, isolé; to lead a ~ life vivre à l'écart, mener une vie de reclus.

sequestrate [sɪ'kwestreɪt] *vt* -**1.** JUR séquestrer, placer sous séquestre. -**2.** *fml* [confiscate] saisir.

sequestration [ˌsiːkwe'streɪʃn] *n* JUR mise *f* sous séquestre; *fml* [confiscation] saisie *f*.

sequin ['siːkwɪn] *n* paillette *f*.

sequin(n)ed ['siːkwɪnd] *adj* pailleté.

sequoia [sɪ'kwɔɪə] *n* séquoia *m*.

serac [seræk] *n* sérac *m*.

seraglio [se'rɑːlɪəʊ] (*pl* seraglios) *n* sérail *m*.

seraph ['serəf] (*pl* seraphs OR seraphim [-fɪm]) *n* séraphin *m*.

seraphic [se'ræfɪk] *adj lit* séraphique.

seraphim ['serəfɪm] *pl* → **seraph**.

Serb [sɜːb] ◇ *n* Serbe *mf*.
◇ *adj* serbe.

Serbia ['sɜːbjə] *pr n* Serbie *f*; in ~ en Serbie.

Serbian ['sɜːbjən] ◇ *n* -**1.** [person] Serbe *mf*. -**2.** LING serbe *m*.
◇ *adj* serbe.

Serbo-Croat [ˌsɜːbəʊ'krəʊæt], **Serbo-Croatian** [ˌsɜːbəʊkrəʊ'eɪʃn] ◇ *n* LING serbo-croate *m*.
◇ *adj* serbo-croate.

sere [sɪəʳ] *adj lit* flétri, desséché.

serenade [ˌserə'neɪd] ◇ *n* sérénade *f*.
◇ *vt* [sing] chanter une sérénade à; [play] jouer une sérénade à; she ~d me to sleep elle m'a chanté une sérénade pour m'endormir.

serendipity [ˌserən'dɪpətɪ] *n lit don de faire des découvertes (accidentelles)*; you don't find such things by ~ ces choses-là ne tombent pas du ciel.

serene [sɪ'riːn] *adj* [person, existence, sky] serein; [sea, lake] calme; His/Her Serene Highness *fml* Son Altesse Sérénissime.

serenely [sɪ'riːnlɪ] *adv* sereinement, avec sérénité; she was ~ unaware of what was going on elle vivait dans la douce inconscience de ce qui se passait autour d'elle; "of course not", she answered ~ «bien sûr que non», répondit-elle tranquillement.

serenity [sɪ'renətɪ] *n* sérénité *f*.

serf [sɜːf] *n* serf *m*, serve *f*.

serfdom ['sɜːfdəm] *n* servage *m*.

serge [sɜːdʒ] ◇ *n* serge *f*.
◇ *comp* [cloth, trousers] de OR en serge; a blue ~ suit un costume de OR en serge bleue.

sergeant ['sɑːdʒənt] *n* -**1.** MIL [in army] sergent *m*; [in air force] *Br* sergent-chef *m*; *Am* caporal-chef *m*. -**2.** [in police] brigadier *m*.

sergeant-at-arms *n* huissier *m* d'armes.

sergeant major *n* sergent-chef *m*.

serial ['sɪərɪəl] ◇ *n* -**1.** RADIO & TV feuilleton *m*; TV ~ feuilleton télévisé ‖ [in magazine] feuilleton *m*; published in ~ form publié sous forme de feuilleton. -**2.** [periodical] périodique *m*.
◇ *adj* -**1.** [in series] en série; [from series] d'une série; [forming series] formant une série; in ~ order en ordre sériel. -**2.** [music] sériel. -**3.** COMPUT [processing, transmission] série *(inv)*; ~ access accès *m* séquentiel; ~ port port *m* série.

serialization, **-isation** [ˌsɪərɪəlaɪ'zeɪʃn] *n* [of book] publication *f* en feuilleton; [of play, film] adaptation *f* en feuilleton.

serialize, **-ise** ['sɪərɪəlaɪz] *vt* [book] publier en feuilleton; [play, film] adapter en feuilleton; [in newspaper] publier OR faire paraître en feuilleton.

serial killer *n* tueur *m* fou *(qui commet des meurtres en série)*.

serially ['sɪərɪəlɪ] *adv* -**1.** MATH en série. -**2.** PRESS [as series] en feuilleton, sous forme de feuilleton; [periodically] périodiquement, sous forme de périodique.

serial number *n* [of car, publication] numéro *m* de série; [of cheque, voucher] numéro *m*; [of soldier] (numéro *m*) matricule *m*.

serial rights *npl* droits *mpl* de reproduction en feuilleton.

sericulture [ˌsɪərɪ'kʌltʃəʳ] *n* sériciculture *f*.

series ['sɪəriːz] (*pl inv*) *n* -**1.** [set, group - gen, CHEM & GEOL] série *f*; [sequence - gen & MATH] séquence *f*, suite *f*. -**2.** LING & MUS série *f*, séquence *f*; we drove through a ~ of mining villages on a traversé en voiture une série de villages miniers; a whole ~ of catastrophes toute une série de catastrophes. -**3.** [of cars, clothes] série *f*; ~ IV computer ordinateur série IV. -**4.** RADIO & TV série *f*; an American detective ~ une série policière américaine; TV ~ série télévisée ‖ [in magazine, newspaper] série *f* d'articles; there's a ~ on OR about the life of the stars il y a une série d'articles sur la vie des stars. -**5.** [collection - of stamps, coins, books] collection *f*, série *f*; a new detective ~ une nouvelle série OR collection de romans policiers. -**6.** ELEC série *f*; wired in ~ branché en série. -**7.** SPORT série *f* de matches; a Test ~ between the West Indies and Australia une série de matches entre les Antilles et l'Australie.

series connection *n* ELEC montage *m* en série.

serif ['serɪf] *n* TYPO empattement *m*.

serious ['sɪərɪəs] *adj* -**1.** [not frivolous - suggestion, subject, worker, publication, writer, theatre] sérieux; is that a ~ offer? c'est une offre sérieuse?; the book is meant for the ~ student of astronomy le livre est destiné aux personnes qui possèdent déjà de solides connaissances en astronomie; **life is a ~ business** la vie est une affaire sérieuse; **it's a ~ occasion** c'est un moment solennel; **can I have a ~ conversation with you?** est-ce qu'on peut parler sérieusement?; **she's a ~ actress** [cinema] elle fait des films sérieux; [theatre] elle joue dans des pièces sérieuses; **the ~ cinemagoer** le cinéphile averti. -**2.** [in speech, behaviour] sérieux; **you can't be ~!** vous n'êtes pas sérieux!; **I'm quite ~** je suis tout à fait sérieux, je ne plaisante absolument pas; **is she ~ about Peter?** est-ce que c'est sérieux avec Peter? -**3.** [thoughtful - person, expression] sérieux, plein de sérieux; [- voice, tone] sérieux, grave; **don't look so ~** ne prends pas cet air sérieux || [careful - examination] sérieux, approfondi; [- consideration] sérieux, sincère; **he's giving ~ thought** OR **consideration to emigrating** il songe sérieusement à émigrer. -**4.** [grave - mistake, problem, illness] sérieux, grave; **the situation is ~** la situation est préoccupante; **~ crime** crime *m*; **those are ~ allegations** ce sont de graves accusations; **it poses a ~ threat to airport security** cela constitue une menace sérieuse pour la sécurité des aéroports; **there have been several ~ border clashes** il y a eu plusieurs affrontements graves à la frontière; **his condition is described as ~** MED son état est jugé préoccupant || [considerable - damage] important, sérieux; [- loss] lourd; [- doubt] sérieux; **the fire caused ~ damage to the hotel** l'incendie a causé d'importants dégâts à l'hôtel. -**5.** *inf* [as intensifier]: **we're talking ~ money here** il s'agit de grosses sommes d'argent; **they go in for some really ~ drinking at the weekends** le week-end, qu'est-ce qu'ils descendent!

seriously ['sɪərɪəslɪ] *adv* -**1.** [earnestly] sérieusement, avec sérieux; **to take sb/sthg ~** prendre qqn/qqch au sérieux; **he takes himself too ~** il se prend trop au sérieux; **are you ~ suggesting we sell it?** pensez-vous sérieusement que nous devrions vendre?; **she is ~ thinking of leaving him** elle pense OR songe sérieusement à le quitter; **think about it ~ before you do anything** réfléchissez-y bien avant de faire quoi que ce soit; **~ though, what are you going to do?** sérieusement, qu'est-ce que vous allez faire?; **you can't ~ expect me to believe that!** vous plaisantez, j'espère? -**2.** [severely - damage] sérieusement, gravement; [- ill] gravement; [- injured, wounded] grièvement; **she is ~ worried about him** elle se fait énormément de souci à son sujet.

serious-minded *adj* sérieux.

seriousness ['sɪərɪəsnɪs] *n* -**1.** [of person, expression] sérieux *m*; [of voice, manner] (air *m*) sérieux *m*; [of intentions, occasion, writing] sérieux *m*; **in all ~** sérieusement, en toute sincérité. -**2.** [of illness, situation, loss] gravité *f*; [of allegation] sérieux *m*; [of damage] importance *f*, étendue *f*; **it is a matter of some ~** c'est une affaire assez sérieuse; **it will take some weeks to assess the ~ of the damage** on ne pourra pas évaluer l'étendue OR l'ampleur des dégâts avant plusieurs semaines; **you don't seem aware of the ~ of the problem** vous ne semblez pas avoir conscience de la gravité du problème.

serjeant ['sɑːdʒənt] = **sergeant**.

sermon ['sɜːmən] *n* -**1.** RELIG sermon *m*; **to give** OR **to preach a ~** faire un sermon; **the Sermon on the Mount** BIBLE le Sermon sur la Montagne. -**2.** *fig* & *pej* sermon *m*, laïus *m*; **he gave me a ~ on the evils of drink** il m'a fait un sermon sur les effets néfastes de l'alcool.

sermonize, -ise ['sɜːmənaɪz] ◇ *vt* sermonner.
◇ *vi* faire des sermons, prêcher.

serology [sɪə'rɒlədʒɪ] *n* sérologie *f*.

serous ['sɪərəs] *adj* séreux.

serpent ['sɜːpənt] *n* serpent *m*.

serpentine ['sɜːpəntaɪn] ◇ *adj lit* [winding] sinueux, qui serpente.
◇ *n* MINER serpentine *f*.

SERPS [sɜːps] (*abbr of* State Earnings-Related Pension Scheme) *n régime de retraite minimal en Grande-Bretagne*.

serrated [sɪ'reɪtɪd] *adj* [edge] en dents de scie, dentelé; [knife, scissors, instrument] cranté, en dents de scie.

serration [sɪ'reɪʃn] *n* dentelure *f*.

serried ['serɪd] *adj* serré; **in ~ ranks** en rangs serrés.

serum ['sɪərəm] (*pl* serums OR sera [-rə]) *n* sérum *m*.

servant ['sɜːvənt] *n* -**1.** [in household] domestique *mf*; [maid] bonne *f*, servante *f*; **I'm not your ~!** je ne suis pas ta bonne!; **~s' quarters** appartements *mpl* des domestiques. -**2.** [of God, people] serviteur *m*; **politicians are the ~s of the community** les hommes politiques sont au service de la communauté. -**3.** *fml* & *dated* [in correspondence]: **your most obedient ~** votre très humble OR dévoué serviteur, veuillez agréer l'expression de mes sentiments les plus dévoués.

servant girl *n* servante *f*, bonne *f*.

serve [sɜːv] ◇ *vt* -**1.** [employer, monarch, country, God] servir; **she has ~d the company well over the years** elle a bien servi la société pendant des années ❑ **you cannot ~ two masters** *prov* nul ne peut servir deux maîtres *prov*. -**2.** [in shop, restaurant - customer] servir; **to ~ sb with sthg** servir qqch à qqn; **are you being ~d?** est-ce qu'on s'occupe de vous? -**3.** [provide - with electricity, gas, water] alimenter; [- with transport service] desservir; **the village is ~d with water from the Roxford reservoir** le village est alimenté en eau depuis le réservoir de Roxford; **the town is well ~d with transport facilities** la ville est bien desservie par les transports en commun; **this train ~s all stations south of Roxborough** ce train dessert toutes les gares au sud de Roxborough. -**4.** [food, drink] servir; **dinner is ~d** le dîner est servi; **coffee is now being ~d in the lounge** le café est servi au salon; **they ~d me (with) some soup** ils m'ont servi de la soupe; **melon is often ~d with port** on sert souvent le melon avec du porto; **the wine should be ~d at room temperature** le vin doit être servi chambré; **this recipe ~s four** cette recette est prévue pour quatre personnes; **to ~ mass** RELIG servir la messe. -**5.** [be suitable for] servir; **the plank ~d him as a rudimentary desk** la planche lui servait de bureau rudimentaire; **this box will ~ my purpose** cette boîte fera l'affaire; **when the box had ~d its purpose, he threw it away** quand il n'eut plus besoin de la boîte, il la jeta; **it must ~ some purpose** cela doit bien servir à quelque chose; **it ~s no useful purpose** cela ne sert à rien de spécial. -**6.** [term, apprenticeship] faire; **he has ~d two terms (of office) as president** il a rempli deux mandats présidentiels; **to ~ one's apprenticeship as an electrician** faire son apprentissage d'électricien; **to ~ one's time** MIL faire son service || [prison sentence] faire; **to ~ time** faire de la prison; **he has ~d his time** il a purgé sa peine; **she ~d four years for armed robbery** elle a fait quatre ans (de prison) pour vol à main armée. -**7.** JUR [summons, warrant, writ] notifier, remettre; **to ~ sb with a summons, to ~ a summons on sb** remettre une assignation à qqn; **to ~ sb with a writ, to ~ a writ on sb** assigner qqn en justice. -**8.** SPORT servir; **she ~d the ball into the net** son service a échoué dans le filet. -**9.** AGR servir. -**10.** *phr*: **it ~s you right** c'est bien fait pour toi; **it ~s them right for being so selfish!** ça leur apprendra à être si égoïstes!
◇ *vi* -**1.** [in shop or restaurant, at table] servir; **to ~ at table** servir à table; **Violet ~s in the dining-room in the evenings** Violet s'occupe du service dans la salle à manger le soir; **could you ~, please?** pourriez-vous faire le service, s'il vous plaît? || [be in service - maid, servant] servir; **she ~d as Lady Greenmount's maid** elle était au service de Lady Greenmount. -**2.** [as soldier] servir; **to ~ in the army** servir dans l'armée; **he ~d as a corporal during the war** il a servi comme caporal pendant la guerre; **her grandfather ~d under General Adams** son grand-père a servi sous les ordres du général Adams || [in profession]: **he ~d as treasurer for several years** il a exercé les fonctions de trésorier pendant plusieurs années || [on committee]: **she ~s on the housing committee** elle est membre de la commission au logement. -**3.** [function, act - as example, warning] servir; **let that ~ as a lesson to you!** que cela vous serve de leçon!; **it only ~s to show that you shouldn't listen to gossip** cela prouve qu'il ne faut pas écouter les commérages; **the tragedy should ~ as a reminder of the threat posed by nuclear power** cette tragédie devrait rappeler à tous la menace que représente l'énergie nucléaire || [be used as]: **this stone will ~ to keep the door open** cette pierre servira à maintenir la porte ouverte; **their bedroom had to ~ as a cloakroom for their guests** leur chambre a dû servir OR faire office de vestiaire pour leurs invités. -**4.** SPORT servir, être au service; **whose turn is it to ~?** c'est à qui de servir?; **Smith to ~** au service, Smith; **he ~d into the net** son service a échoué dans le filet. -**5.** RELIG servir la messe.
◇ *n* SPORT service *m*; **it's your ~** c'est à vous de servir; **to have a good ~** avoir un bon service.

◆ **serve out** ◇ *vt sep* -**1.** [food] servir; [provisions] distribuer. -**2.** [period of time] faire; **the president retired before he had ~d his term out** le président a pris sa retraite avant d'arriver à OR d'atteindre la fin de son mandat; **to ~ out a prison sentence** purger une peine (de prison).
◇ *vi insep* SPORT sortir son service.

◆ **serve up** *vt sep* [meal, food] servir; *fig* [facts, information] servir, débiter; **she ~s up the same old excuse every time** elle ressort chaque fois la même excuse.

server ['sɜːvəʳ] *n* -**1.** [at table] serveur *m*, -euse *f*. -**2.** SPORT serveur *m*, -euse *f*. -**3.** RELIG servant *m*. -**4.** [utensil] couvert *m* de service. -**5.** COMPUT serveur *m*.

servery ['sɜːvərɪ] (*pl* serveries) *n* [hatch] guichet *m*, passe-plat *m*; [counter] comptoir *m*.

service ['sɜːvɪs] ◇ *n* -**1.** [to friend, community, country, God] service *m*; **in the ~ of one's country** au service de sa patrie; **he was rewarded for ~s rendered to industry/to his country** il a été récompensé pour services rendus à l'industrie/à son pays; **to require the ~s of a priest/of a doctor** avoir recours aux services d'un prêtre/d'un médecin; **many people gave their ~s free** beaucoup de gens donnaient des prestations bénévoles; **at your ~** à votre service, à votre disposition; **to be of ~ to sb** rendre service à qqn, être utile à qqn; **may I be of ~ (to you)?** *fml* puis-je vous aider OR vous être utile?; [in shop] qu'y a-t-il pour votre service?; **she's always ready to be of ~** elle est très serviable, elle est toujours prête à rendre service; **the jug had to do ~ as a teapot** le pichet a dû faire office de OR servir de théière; **to do sb a ~** rendre (un) service à qqn; **he did me a great ~ by not telling them** il m'a rendu un grand service en ne leur disant rien; **the car has given us/has seen good ~** la voiture nous a bien servi/a fait long usage. -**2.** [employment - in firm] service *m*; **20 years' ~ with the same company** 20 ans de service dans la même entreprise; **bonuses depend on length of ~** les primes sont versées en fonction de l'ancienneté || [as domestic servant] service; **to be in ~** être domestique; **to go into** OR **to enter sb's ~** entrer au service de qqn; **he's in Lord Bellamy's ~** il est au service de Lord Bellamy. -**3.** [in shop, hotel, restaurant] service *m*; **the food was good but the ~ was poor** on a bien mangé mais le service n'était pas à la hauteur; **you get fast ~ in a supermarket** on est servi rapidement dans un supermarché; **'10% ~ included/not included'** 'service 10 % compris/non compris'; **10% is added for ~** service 10 % non compris; **~ with a smile** [slogan] servi avec le sourire. -**4.** MIL service *m*; **he saw active ~ in Korea** il

a servi en Corée, il a fait la campagne de Corée; the ~s les (différentes branches des) forces armées; their son is in the ~s leur fils est dans les forces armées. -5. ADMIN [department, scheme] service *m*; bus/train ~ service d'autobus/de trains; a new 24-hour banking ~ un nouveau service bancaire fonctionnant 24 heures sur 24; a bus provides a ~ between the two stations un autobus assure la navette entre les deux gares ❑ the diplomatic ~ le service diplomatique; health/social ~s services de santé/sociaux. -6. RELIG [Catholic] service *m*, office *m*; [Protestant] service *m*, culte *m*; to attend (a) ~ assister à l'office OR au culte. -7. [of car, machine - upkeep] entretien *m*; [- overhaul] révision *f*; the car is due for its 20,000 mile ~ la voiture arrive à la révision des 32 000 km. -8. [working order - esp of machine] service *m*; to bring a machine into ~ mettre une machine en service; to come into ~ [system, bridge] entrer en service; the cash dispenser isn't in ~ at the moment le distributeur automatique de billets est hors service OR n'est pas en service en ce moment. -9. [set of tableware] service *m*; tea/dinner ~ service à thé/de table. -10. SPORT service *m*; Smith broke his opponent's ~ Smith a pris le service de son adversaire OR a fait le break. -11. JUR [of summons, writ] signification *f*, notification *f*; ~ of documents signification d'actes. -12. [tree] sorbier *m*, cormier *m*.
◇ *vt* -1. [overhaul - central heating, car] réviser; to have one's car ~d faire réviser sa voiture; the car has been regularly ~d la voiture a été régulièrement entretenue. -2. FIN [debt] assurer le service de. -3. AGR [subj: bull, stallion] servir.
◇ *comp* -1. [entrance, hatch, lift, stairs] de service. -2. AUT & MECH [manual, record] d'entretien. -3. MIL [family, pay] de militaire; [conditions] dans les forces armées.
◆ **services** *npl* -1. *Br* [on motorway] aire *f* de service. -2. COMM & ECON services *mpl*; goods and ~s biens et services; more and more people will be working in ~s de plus en plus de gens travailleront dans le tertiaire.

serviceable ['sɜːvɪsəbl] *adj* -1. [durable - clothes, material] qui fait de l'usage, qui résiste à l'usure; [- machine, construction] durable, solide. -2. [useful - clothing, tool] commode, pratique. -3. [usable] utilisable, qui peut servir; this coat is still ~ ce manteau peut encore servir. -4. [ready for use] prêt à servir.

service academy *n Am* école *f* militaire.

service area *n* -1. AUT [on motorway] aire *f* de service. -2. RADIO zone *f* desservie OR de réception.

serviceberry ['sɜːvɪsˌberɪ] (*pl* serviceberries) *n* sorbe *f*, corme *f*.

service ceiling *n* AERON plafond *m* de fonctionnement normal.

service charge *n* service *m*; they've forgotten to include the ~ on the bill ils ont oublié de facturer le service.

service flat *n Br appartement avec services ménagers et de restauration.*

service game *n* TENNIS jeu *m* de service.

service industry *n* industrie *f* de services.

service line *n* SPORT ligne *f* de service.

serviceman ['sɜːvɪsmən] (*pl* servicemen [-mən]) *n* -1. MIL militaire *m*. -2. *Am* [mechanic] dépanneur *m*.

service module *n* ASTRONAUT module *m* de service.

service plaza *n Am* relais *m*.

service road *n* [behind shops, factory] *voie d'accès réservée aux livreurs*; [on motorway] *voie d'accès réservée à l'entretien et aux services d'urgence*.

service station *n* station-service *f*.

servicewoman ['sɜːvɪsˌwʊmən] (*pl* servicewomen [-ˌwɪmɪn]) *n* femme *f* soldat.

servicing ['sɜːvɪsɪŋ] *n* -1. [of heating, car] entretien *m*. -2. [by transport] desserte *f*; the ~ of an area by rail la desserte d'une région par chemin de fer.

serviette [ˌsɜːvɪ'et] *n Br* serviette *f* (de table); ~ ring rond *m* de serviette.

servile ['sɜːvaɪl] *adj* [person, behaviour] servile, obséquieux; [admiration, praise] servile; [condition, task] servile, d'esclave.

servility [sɜː'vɪlətɪ] *n* servilité *f*.

serving ['sɜːvɪŋ] ◇ *n* -1. [of drinks, meal] service *m*. -2. [helping] portion *f*, part *f*.
◇ *adj* ADMIN [member, chairman] actuel, en exercice.

servitude ['sɜːvɪtjuːd] *n* servitude *f*; in a state of ~ en esclavage.

servo ['sɜːvəʊ] (*pl* servos) ◇ *adj* servo-.
◇ *n* [mechanism] servomécanisme *m*; [motor] servomoteur *m*.

servo-assisted [-ə'sɪstɪd] *adj* TECH assisté; ~ brakes freinage *m* assisté, servofreins *mpl*.

servomechanism ['sɜːvəʊˌmekənɪzm] *n* servomécanisme *m*.

servomotor ['sɜːvəʊˌməʊtə^r] *n* servomoteur *m*.

sesame ['sesəmɪ] *n* sésame *m*; open ~! sésame, ouvre-toi!

sesame oil *n* huile *f* de sésame.

sesame seed *n* graine *f* de sésame.

sessile ['sesaɪl] *adj* sessile.

session ['seʃn] *n* -1. ADMIN, JUR & POL séance *f*, session *f*; this court is now in ~ l'audience est ouverte; the House is not in ~ during the summer months la Chambre ne siège pas pendant les mois d'été; to go into secret ~ siéger à huis clos. -2. [interview, meeting, sitting] séance *f*; [for painter, photographer] séance *f* de pose; he had a long ~ with his psychiatrist il a eu une longue séance chez son psychiatre; we're having another ~ tomorrow [working] nous avons encore une séance de travail OR nous allons retravailler demain; [negotiation, discussion] nous avons encore une séance (de négociations OR d'entretiens) demain; a drinking ~ une beuverie. -3. SCH [classes] cours *mpl*. -4. *Am* & *Scot* UNIV [term] trimestre *m*; [year] année *f* universitaire; school is in ~ *Am* on est en période scolaire. -5. RELIG conseil *m* presbytéral.

sessional ['seʃənl] *adj* de séance.

session musician *n* musicien *m*, -enne *f* de studio.

sestet [ses'tet] *n* sizain *m*.

set [set] (*pt* & *pp* set, *cont* setting) ◇ *vt* **A.** -1. [put in specified place or position] mettre, poser; he ~ his cases down on the platform il posa ses valises sur le quai; she ~ the steaming bowl before him elle plaça le bol fumant devant lui; to ~ sb ashore débarquer qqn. -2. (*usu passive*) [locate, situate - building, story] situer; the house is ~ in large grounds la maison est située dans un grand parc; his eyes are ~ too close together ses yeux sont trop rapprochés; the story is ~ in Tokyo l'histoire se passe OR se déroule à Tokyo; her novels are ~ in the 18th century ses romans se passent au XVIIIe siècle. -3. [adjust - gen] régler; [- mechanism] mettre; I've ~ the alarm for six j'ai mis le réveil à (sonner pour) six heures; how do I ~ the margins? comment est-ce que je fais pour placer les marges?; ~ the timer for one hour mettez le minuteur sur une heure; first ~ the control knob to the desired temperature mettez tout d'abord le bouton de réglage sur la température voulue; the lever was ~ in the off position le levier était sur «arrêt»; ~ your watches an hour ahead avancez vos montres d'une heure; I ~ my watch to New York time j'ai réglé ma montre à l'heure de New York; he's so punctual you can ~ your watch by him! il est si ponctuel qu'on peut régler sa montre sur lui! -4. [fix into position] mettre, fixer; [jewel, diamond] sertir, monter; to ~ a bone réduire une fracture; the brooch was ~ with pearls la broche était sertie de perles; the ruby was ~ in a simple ring le rubis était monté sur un simple anneau; the handles are ~ into the drawers les poignées sont encastrées dans les tiroirs; there was a peephole ~ in the door il y avait un judas dans la porte; metal bars had been ~ in the concrete des barres en métal avaient été fixées dans le béton. -5. [lay, prepare in advance - table] mettre; [- trap] poser, tendre; ~ an extra place at table rajoutez un couvert. -6. [place - in hierarchy] placer; they ~ a high value on creativity ils accordent une grande valeur à la créativité. -7. [establish - date, schedule, price, terms] fixer, déterminer; [- rule, guideline, objective] établir; [- mood, precedent] créer; they still haven't ~ a date for the party ils n'ont toujours pas fixé de date pour la réception; you've ~ yourself a tough deadline OR a tough deadline for yourself vous vous êtes fixé un délai très court; it's up to them to ~ their own production targets c'est à eux d'établir OR de fixer leurs propres objectifs de production; a deficit ceiling has been ~ un plafonnement du déficit a été imposé OR fixé OR décidé; the price was ~ at £500 le prix a été fixé à 500 livres; the judge ~ bail at $1,000 le juge a fixé la caution à 1 000 dollars; how are exchange rates ~? comment les taux de change sont-ils déterminés?; to ~ a new fashion OR trend lancer une nouvelle mode; to ~ a new world record établir un nouveau record mondial; to ~ the tone for OR of sthg donner le ton de qqch.
B. -1. [indicating change of state or activity]: to ~ sthg alight OR on fire mettre le feu à qqch; it ~s my nerves on edge ça me crispe; she ~ me in the right direction *literal* & *fig* elle m'a mis sur la bonne voie; he/the incident ~ the taxman on my trail il/l'incident a mis le fisc sur ma piste; to ~ the dogs on sb lâcher les chiens sur qqn; the incident ~ the family against him l'incident a monté la famille contre lui; it will ~ the country on the road to economic recovery cela va mettre le pays sur la voie de la reprise économique; his failure ~ him thinking son échec lui a donné à réfléchir; the scandal will ~ the whole town talking le scandale va faire jaser toute la ville; the wind ~ the leaves dancing le vent a fait frissonner les feuilles; to ~ a machine going mettre une machine en marche. -2. [solidify - yoghurt, jelly, concrete] faire prendre; pectin will help to ~ the jam la pectine aidera à épaissir la confiture. -3. [make firm, rigid]: his face was ~ in a frown son visage était figé dans une grimace renfrognée; she ~ her jaw and refused to budge elle serra les dents et refusa de bouger; we had ~ ourselves to resist nous étions déterminés à résister. -4. [pose - problem] poser; [assign - task] fixer; the strikers' demands ~ the management a difficult problem les exigences des grévistes posent un problème difficile à la direction; I ~ them to work tidying the garden je les ai mis au désherbage du jardin; I've ~ myself the task of writing to them regularly je me suis fixé la tâche de leur écrire régulièrement. -5. *Br* SCH [exam] composer, choisir les questions de; [books, texts] mettre au programme; she ~ the class a maths exercise, she ~ a maths exercise for the class elle a donné un exercice de maths à la classe; who ~s the test questions? qui choisit les questions de l'épreuve? -6. [hair]: to ~ sb's hair faire une mise en plis à qqn; and I've just had my hair ~! et je viens de me faire faire une mise en plis!; I ~ my own hair je me fais moi-même mes mises en plis. -7. HORT [plant] planter. -8. TYPO [text, page] composer. -9. MUS [poem, words]: to ~ sthg to music mettre qqch en musique.
◇ *vi* -1. [sun, stars] se coucher. -2. [become firm - glue, cement, plaster, jelly, yoghurt] prendre. -3. [bone] se ressouder. -4. (*with infinitive*) [start] se mettre; he ~ to work il s'est mis au travail. -5. [plant, tree] prendre racine. -6. [hen] couver. -7. [wind]: the wind looks ~ fair to the east on dirait un vent d'ouest.
◇ *n* -1. [of facts, conditions, characteristics] ensemble *m*; [of people] groupe *m*; [of events, decisions, questions] série *f*, suite *f*; [of numbers, names, instructions, stamps, weights] série *f*; [of tools, keys, golf clubs, sails] jeu *m*; [of books] collection *f*; [of furniture] ensemble *m*; [of dishes] service *m*; [of tyres] train *m*; PRINT [of proofs, characters] jeu *m*; they make a ~ ils vont

ensemble; **they've detected two ~s of fingerprints** ils ont relevé deux séries d'empreintes digitales OR les empreintes digitales de deux personnes; **given another ~ of circumstances, things might have turned out differently** dans d'autres circonstances, les choses auraient pu se passer différemment; **he made me a duplicate ~** [keys] il m'a fait un double des clés; [contact lenses] il m'en a fait une autre paire; **the first ~ of reforms** la première série OR le premier train de réformes; **a full ~ of the encyclopedia** une encyclopédie complète; **a full ~ of Tolstoy's works** une collection complète des œuvres de Tolstoï; **they ran a whole ~ of tests on me** ils m'ont fait subir toute une série d'examens; **the cups/the chairs are sold in ~s of six** les tasses/les chaises sont vendues par six; **I can't break up the ~** je ne peux pas les dépareiller; **a ~ of matching luggage** un ensemble de valises assorties; **a ~ of table/bed linen** une parure de table/de lit ❑ **badminton/chess ~** jeu de badminton/d'échecs; **they're playing with Damian's train ~** ils jouent avec le train électrique de Damian. -**2.** [social group] cercle *m*, milieu *m*; **he's not in our ~** il n'appartient pas à notre cercle; **we don't go around in the same ~** nous ne fréquentons pas le même milieu OR monde; **the riding/yachting ~** le monde de l'équitation/du yachting; **the Markham ~** Markham et ses amis. -**3.** MATH ensemble *m*; **null ~** ensemble vide. -**4.** [electrical device] appareil *m*; RADIO & TV poste *m*; **a colour TV ~** un poste de télévision OR un téléviseur couleur. -**5.** SPORT set *m*, manche *f*. -**6.** CIN, THEAT & TV [scenery] décor *m*; [place] CIN & TV plateau *m*; THEAT scène *f*; **on (the) ~** CIN & TV sur le plateau; THEAT sur scène ❑ **~ designer** CIN & TV chef décorateur *m*. -**7.** [part of performance - by singer, group]: **he'll be playing two ~s tonight** il va jouer à deux reprises ce soir; **her second ~ was livelier** la deuxième partie de son spectacle a été plus animée. -**8.** [for hair] mise *f* en plis; **to have a ~** se faire faire une mise en plis. -**9.** [posture - of shoulders, body] position *f*, attitude *f*; [- of head] port *m*; **I could tell he was angry by the ~ of his jaw** rien qu'à la façon dont il serrait les mâchoires, j'ai compris qu'il était en colère. -**10.** [direction - of wind, current] direction *f*; **suddenly the ~ of the wind changed** le vent a tourné soudainement. -**11.** PSYCH [tendency] tendance *f*. -**12.** HORT [seedling] semis *m*; [cutting] bouture *f*; **tomato/tulip ~s** tomates/tulipes à repiquer. -**13.** [clutch of eggs] couvée *f*.

◇ *adj* -**1.** [specified, prescribed - rule, quantity, sum, wage] fixe; **meals are at ~ times** les repas sont servis à heures fixes; **there are no ~ rules for raising children** il n'y a pas de règles toutes faites pour l'éducation des enfants; **the tasks must be done in the ~ order** les tâches doivent être accomplies dans l'ordre prescrit ❑ **~ figures** [in skating] figures *fpl* imposées; **~ menu** OR **meal** *Br* menu *m*. -**2.** [fixed, rigid - ideas, views] arrêté; [- smile, frown] figé; **her day followed a ~ routine** sa journée se déroulait selon un rituel immuable; **to become ~ in one's ways/one's views** devenir rigide dans ses habitudes/ses opinions; **~ expression** OR **phrase** GRAMM expression *f* figée. -**3.** [intent, resolute] résolu, déterminé; **to be ~ on** OR **upon sthg** vouloir qqch à tout prix; **I'm (dead) ~ on finishing it tonight** je suis (absolument) déterminé à le finir ce soir; **he's dead ~ against it** il s'y oppose formellement. -**4.** [ready, in position] prêt; **are you (all) ~ to go?** êtes-vous prêt à partir? -**5.** [likely] probablement; **he seems well ~ to win** il semble être sur la bonne voie OR être bien parti pour gagner; **house prices are ~ to rise steeply** les prix de l'immobilier vont vraisemblablement monter en flèche. -**6.** *Br* SCH [book, subject] au programme.

◆ **set about** *vt insep* -**1.** [start - task] se mettre à; **she ~ about changing the tyre** elle s'est mise à changer le pneu; **I didn't know how to ~ about it** je ne savais pas comment m'y prendre; **how does one ~ about getting a visa?** comment fait-on pour obtenir un visa? -**2.** [attack] attaquer, s'en prendre à; **he ~ about the mugger with his umbrella** il s'en est pris à son agresseur à coups de parapluie.

◆ **set against** *vt sep* -**1.** FIN [offset]: **some of these expenses can be ~ against tax** certaines de ces dépenses peuvent être déduites des impôts. -**2.** [friends, family] monter contre; **religious differences have ~ family against family** les différences religieuses ont monté les familles les unes contre les autres.

◆ **set ahead** *vt sep Am*: **to ~ the clock ahead** avancer l'horloge; **we're setting the clocks ahead tonight** on change d'heure cette nuit.

◆ **set apart** *vt sep* -**1.** *(usu passive)* [place separately] mettre à part OR de côté; **there was one deck chair ~ slightly apart from the others** il y avait une chaise longue un peu à l'écart des autres. -**2.** [distinguish] distinguer; **her talent ~s her apart from the other students** son talent la distingue des autres étudiants.

◆ **set aside** *vt sep* -**1.** [put down - knitting, book] poser. -**2.** [reserve, keep - time, place] réserver; [- money] mettre de côté; [arable land] mettre en friche; **I've ~ tomorrow aside for house hunting** j'ai réservé la journée de demain pour chercher une maison; **the room is ~ aside for meetings** la pièce est réservée aux réunions; **can you ~ the book aside for me?** pourriez-vous me mettre ce livre de côté?; **chop the onions and ~ them aside** coupez les oignons et réservez-les. -**3.** [overlook, disregard] mettre de côté, oublier, passer sur; **they ~ their differences aside in order to work together** ils ont mis de côté leurs différences pour travailler ensemble. -**4.** [reject - dogma, proposal, offer] rejeter; [annul - contract, will] annuler; JUR [verdict, judgment] casser.

◆ **set back** *vt sep* -**1.** [towards the rear]: **the building is ~ back slightly from the road** l'immeuble est un peu en retrait par rapport à la route. -**2.** [delay - plans, progress] retarder; **his illness ~ him back a month in his work** sa maladie l'a retardé d'un mois dans son travail. -**3.** *inf* [cost] coûter; **the trip will ~ her back a good bit** le voyage va lui coûter cher.

◆ **set down** *vt sep* -**1.** [tray, bag etc] poser. -**2.** *Br* [passenger] déposer; **the bus ~s you down in front of the station** le bus vous dépose devant la gare. -**3.** [note, record] noter, inscrire; **try and ~ your thoughts down on paper** essayez de mettre vos pensées par écrit. -**4.** [establish - rule, condition] établir; **the government has ~ down a margin for pay increases** le gouvernement a fixé une fourchette pour les augmentations de salaire; **it is clearly ~ down that drivers must be insured** il est clairement signalé OR indiqué que tout conducteur doit être assuré.

◆ **set forth** ◇ *vi insep lit* = **set off**.

◇ *vt insep fml* [expound - plan, objections] exposer, présenter; **the recommendations are ~ forth in the last chapter** les recommandations sont détaillées OR énumérées dans le dernier chapitre.

◆ **set in** ◇ *vi insep* [problems] survenir, surgir; [disease] se déclarer; [winter] commencer; [night] tomber; **if infection ~s in** si la plaie s'infecte; **the bad weather has ~ in for the winter** le mauvais temps s'est installé pour tout l'hiver; **panic ~ in** [began] la panique éclata; [lasted] la panique s'installa.

◇ *vt sep* SEW [sleeve] rapporter.

◆ **set off** ◇ *vi insep* partir, se mettre en route; **he ~ off at a run** il est parti en courant; **I ~ off to explore the town** je suis parti explorer la ville; **after lunch, we ~ off again** après le déjeuner, nous avons repris la route.

◇ *vt sep* -**1.** [alarm] déclencher; [bomb] faire exploser; [fireworks] faire partir. -**2.** [reaction, process, war] déclencher, provoquer; **their offer ~ off another round of talks** leur proposition a déclenché une autre série de négociations; **to ~ sb off laughing** faire rire qqn; **it ~ her off on a long tirade against bureaucracy** cela eut pour effet de la lancer dans une longue tirade contre la bureaucratie. -**3.** [enhance] mettre en valeur; **the vase ~s off the flowers beautifully** le vase met vraiment les fleurs en valeur. -**4.** FIN [offset]: **some of these expenses can be ~ off against tax** certaines de ces dépenses peuvent être déduites des impôts.

◆ **set on** = **set upon**.

◆ **set out** ◇ *vi insep* -**1.** = **set off**. -**2.** [undertake course of action] entreprendre; **he has trouble finishing what he ~s out to do** il a du mal à terminer ce qu'il entreprend; **I can't remember now what I ~ out to do** je ne me souviens plus de ce que je voulais faire à l'origine; **they all ~ out with the intention of changing the world** au début, ils veulent tous changer le monde; **she didn't deliberately ~ out to annoy you** il n'était pas dans ses intentions de vous froisser.

◇ *vt sep* -**1.** [arrange - chairs, game pieces] disposer; [spread out - merchandise] étaler. -**2.** [design] concevoir; **the shopping centre is very well ~ out** le centre commercial est très bien conçu. -**3.** [present] exposer, présenter; **the information is ~ out in the table below** ces données sont présentées dans le tableau ci-dessous.

◆ **set to** *vi insep* [begin work] commencer, s'y mettre; **we ~ to with a will** nous nous y sommes mis avec ardeur.

◆ **set up** ◇ *vt sep* -**1.** [install - equipment, computer] installer; [put in place - roadblock] installer, disposer; [- experiment] préparer; **everything's ~ up for the show** tout est préparé OR prêt pour le spectacle; **~ the chairs up in a circle** mettez OR disposez les chaises en cercle; **he ~ the chessboard up** il a disposé les pièces sur l'échiquier ‖ *fig*: **to ~ up a meeting** organiser une réunion; **the equation ~s up a relation between the two variables** l'équation établit un rapport entre les deux variables; **the system wasn't ~ up to handle so many users** le système n'était pas conçu pour gérer autant d'usagers; **he ~ the situation up so she couldn't refuse** il a arrangé la situation de telle manière qu'elle ne pouvait pas refuser. -**2.** [erect, build - tent, furniture kit, crane, flagpole] monter; [- shed, shelter] construire; [- monument, statue] ériger; **to ~ up camp** installer OR dresser le camp. -**3.** [start up, institute - business, scholarship] créer; [- hospital, school] fonder; [- committee, task force] constituer; [- system of government, republic] instaurer; [- programme, review process, system] mettre en place; [- inquiry] ouvrir; **to ~ up house** OR **home** s'installer; **they ~ up house together** ils se sont mis en ménage; **to ~ up a dialogue** entamer le dialogue; **you'll be in charge of setting up training programmes** vous serez responsable de la mise en place des programmes de formation; **the medical system ~ up after the war** le système médical mis en place après la guerre. -**4.** [financially, in business] installer, établir; **he ~ his son up in a dry-cleaning business** il a acheté à son fils une entreprise de nettoyage à sec; **she could finally ~ herself up as an accountant** elle pourrait enfin s'installer comme comptable; **the money would ~ him up for life** l'argent le mettrait à l'abri du besoin pour le restant de ses jours; **the army ~ him up as a dictator** l'armée l'installa comme dictateur. -**5.** [provide]: **we're well ~ up with supplies** nous sommes bien approvisionnés; **she can ~ you up with a guide/the necessary papers** elle peut vous procurer un guide/les papiers qu'il vous faut; **I can ~ you up with a girlfriend of mine** je peux te présenter à OR te faire rencontrer une de mes copines. -**6.** [restore energy to] remonter, remettre sur pied; **have a brandy, that'll ~ you up** prends un cognac, ça va te remonter. -**7.** *inf* [frame] monter un coup contre; **she claims she was ~ up** elle prétend qu'elle est victime d'un coup monté; **he was ~ up as the fall guy** on a fait de lui le bouc émissaire, il a joué le rôle de bouc émissaire.

◇ *vi insep* s'installer, s'établir; **he's setting up in the fast-food business** il se lance dans la restauration rapide; to ~ up on one's own [business] s'installer à son compte; [home] prendre son propre appartement.

◆ **set upon** *vt insep* [physically or verbally] attaquer, s'en prendre à.

setaside ['setəsaɪd] *n* mise *f* en jachère.

setback ['setbæk] *n* revers *m*, échec *m*; [minor] contretemps *m*.

set-in *adj* [sleeve] rapporté.

set piece *n* -**1.** ART, LITERAT & MUS morceau *m* de bravoure. -**2.** [fireworks] pièce *f* (de feu) d'artifice. -**3.** [of scenery] élément *m* de décor.

set point *n* TENNIS balle *f* de set.

set scrum *n* RUGBY mêlée *f* fermée.

setsquare ['setskweəʳ] *n* équerre *f (à dessiner)*.

sett [set] *n* -**1.** [for paving] pavé *m*. -**2.** [of badger] terrier *m* (de blaireau).

settee [se'ti:] *n* canapé *m*.

setter ['setəʳ] *n* -**1.** [dog] setter *m*. -**2.** [of jewels] sertisseur *m*.

set theory *n* théorie *f* des ensembles.

setting ['setɪŋ] *n* -**1.** [of sun, moon] coucher *m*. -**2.** [situation, surroundings] cadre *m*, décor *m*; THEAT décor *m*; **the house is in a lovely country ~** la maison est située dans un très beau cadre campagnard; **they photographed the foxes in their natural ~** ils ont photographié les renards dans leur milieu naturel; **the film has Connemara as its ~** le film a pour cadre le Connemara. -**3.** [position, level - of machine, instrument] réglage *m*. -**4.** [for jewels] monture *f*; [of jewels] sertissage *m*. -**5.** [at table] set *m* de table. -**6.** MUS [of poem, play] mise *f* en musique; [for instruments] arrangement *m*, adaptation *f*; **~ for male voice** arrangement pour voix d'homme. -**7.** [of fracture] réduction *f*; [in plaster] plâtrage *m*. -**8.** [of jam] prise *f*; [of cement] prise *f*, durcissement *m*. -**9.** TYPO composition *f*.

setting lotion *n* lotion *f* pour mise en plis.

setting-up *n* -**1.** [of company, organization] lancement *m*, création *f*; [of enquiry] ouverture *f*. -**2.** TYPO composition *f*.

settle ['setl] ◇ *vt* -**1.** [solve - question, issue] régler; [- dispute, quarrel] régler, trancher; **to ~ differences** régler OR trancher des différends; **the case was ~d out of court** l'affaire a été réglée à l'amiable; **to ~ old scores** régler des comptes ❑ **that's ~d him** OR **his hash!** *inf* ça l'a remis à sa place! -**2.** [determine, agree on - date, price] fixer; **have you ~d where to go for the picnic?** avez-vous décidé d'un endroit pour le pique-nique?; **it was ~d that I would go to boarding school** il fut convenu OR décidé que j'irais en pension; **you must ~ that among yourselves** il va falloir que vous arrangiez cela entre vous; **nothing is ~d yet** rien n'est encore décidé OR arrêté; **that's one point ~d** voilà déjà un point d'acquis; **that's that ~d then!** voilà une affaire réglée!; **that's ~d then, I'll meet you at 8 o'clock** alors c'est entendu OR convenu, on se retrouve à 8 h; **that ~s it, the party's tomorrow!** c'est décidé, la fête aura lieu demain!; **that ~s it, he's fired** trop c'est trop, il est renvoyé! -**3.** [pay - debt] régler; **to ~ one's affairs** mettre ses affaires en ordre, régler ses affaires; **to ~ an account/a bill** régler une note/une facture; **to ~ a claim** [insurance] régler un litige. -**4.** [install] installer; **when I'm ~d, I'll write to you** quand je serai installé, je vous écrirai; **to ~ o.s. comfortably in an armchair** s'installer confortablement dans un fauteuil; **he ~d the children for the night** il a mis les enfants au lit, il est allé coucher les enfants; **to get ~d** s'installer (confortablement) ‖ [arrange, place - on table, surface] installer, poser (soigneusement); **she ~d the rug over her knees** elle enroula la couverture autour de ses genoux. -**5.** [colonize] coloniser; **Peru was ~d by the Spanish** le Pérou a été colonisé par les Espagnols, les Espagnols se sont établis au Pérou. -**6.** [calm - nerves, stomach] calmer, apaiser; **this brandy will ~ your nerves** ce cognac te calmera les nerfs; **the rain ~d the dust** la pluie a fait retomber la poussière. -**7.** JUR [money, allowance, estate] constituer; **to ~ an annuity on sb** constituer une rente à qqn; **she ~d all her money on her nephew** elle a légué toute sa fortune à son neveu; **how are you ~d for money at the moment?** *fig* est-ce que tu as suffisamment d'argent en ce moment?

◇ *vi* -**1.** [go to live - gen] s'installer, s'établir; [- colonist] s'établir; **she finally ~d abroad** elle s'est finalement installée à l'étranger. -**2.** [become calm - nerves, stomach, storm] s'apaiser, se calmer; [- situation] s'arranger; **wait for things to ~ before you do anything** attends que les choses se calment OR s'arrangent avant de faire quoi que ce soit. -**3.** [install o.s. - in new flat, bed] s'installer; **to ~ for the night** s'installer pour la nuit; **it took me a long time to ~** mon installation a pris du temps ‖ [adapt - to circumstances] s'habituer; **I just can't ~ to my work somehow** je ne sais pas pourquoi, mais je suis incapable de me concentrer sur mon travail. -**4.** [come to rest - dust, snow] retomber; [- sediment] se déposer; [- bird, insect, eyes] se poser; **the snow began to ~ (on the ground)** la neige commençait à tenir; **let your dinner ~ before you go out** prends le temps de digérer avant de sortir; **a fly ~d on the butter** une mouche s'est posée sur le beurre; **her gaze ~ed on the book** son regard se posa sur le livre. -**5.** [spread]: **a look of utter contentment ~d on his face** son visage prit une expression de profonde satisfaction; **an eerie calm ~d over the village** un calme inquiétant retomba sur le village; **the cold ~d on his chest** le rhume lui est tombé sur la poitrine. -**6.** CONSTR [road, wall, foundations] se tasser; **contents may ~ during transport** le contenu risque de se tasser pendant le transport; **cracks appeared in the walls as the house ~d** des fissures apparaissaient dans les murs au fur et à mesure que la maison se tassait OR s'affaissait. -**7.** [financially]: **to ~ with sb for sthg** régler le prix de qqch à qqn; **can I ~ with you tomorrow?** est-ce que je peux vous régler demain?; **to ~ out of court** régler une affaire à l'amiable. -**8.** [decide] se décider; **they've ~d on a Volkswagen** ils se sont décidés pour une Volkswagen; **they've ~d on Rome for their honeymoon** ils ont décidé d'aller passer leur lune de miel à Rome; **they ~d on a compromise solution** ils ont finalement choisi le compromis.

◇ *n* [seat] banquette *f* à haut dossier.

◆ **settle down** ◇ *vi insep* -**1.** [in armchair, at desk] s'installer; [in new home] s'installer, se fixer; [at school, in job] s'habituer, s'adapter; **they ~d down by the fire for the evening** ils se sont installés près du feu pour la soirée; **to ~ down to watch television** s'installer (confortablement) devant la télévision; **it took the children some weeks to ~ down in their new school** il a fallu plusieurs semaines aux enfants pour s'habituer à leur nouvelle école; **Susan is finding it hard to ~ down to life in Paris** Susan a du mal à s'habituer OR à s'adapter à la vie parisienne; **to ~ down to work** se mettre au travail. -**2.** *fig* [become stable - people] se ranger, s'assagir; **it's about time Tom got married and ~d down** il est temps que Tom se marie et s'installe dans la vie; **they never ~ down anywhere for long** ils ne se fixent jamais nulle part bien longtemps. -**3.** [concentrate, apply o.s.]: **to ~ down to do sthg** se mettre à faire qqch; **I can't seem to ~ down to anything these days** je n'arrive pas à me concentrer sur quoi que ce soit ces jours-ci. -**4.** [become calm - excitement] s'apaiser; [- situation] s'arranger.

◇ *vt sep* [person] installer; **to ~ o.s. down in an armchair** s'installer (confortablement) dans un fauteuil; **she ~d the patient down for the night** elle a installé le malade pour la nuit.

◆ **settle for** *vt insep* accepter, se contenter de; **I won't ~ for less than £200** 200 livres, c'est mon dernier prix, je ne descendrai pas au-dessous de 200 livres; **there was no wine left so they had to ~ for beer** comme il ne restait plus de vin, ils durent se contenter de bière; **they ~d for a compromise** ils ont choisi une solution de compromis.

◆ **settle in** *vi insep* [at new house] s'installer; [at new school, job] s'habituer, s'adapter; **once we're ~d in, we'll invite you round** une fois que nous serons installés, nous t'inviterons; **it took him a while to ~ in at his new school** il a mis un certain temps à s'habituer à sa nouvelle école.

◆ **settle into** ◇ *vt insep* [job, routine] s'habituer à, s'adapter à; **she soon ~d into her new post** elle s'est vite adaptée à son nouveau poste; **life soon ~d into the usual dull routine** la vie reprit bientôt son rythme monotone.

◇ *vt sep* installer dans; **she's busy settling her daughter into her new flat** elle est occupée à installer sa fille dans son nouvel appartement.

◆ **settle up** ◇ *vi insep* régler (la note); **I must ~ up with the plumber** il faut que je règle le plombier; **can we ~ up?** est-ce qu'on peut faire les comptes?

◇ *vt sep* régler.

settled ['setld] *adj* -**1.** [stable, unchanging - person] rangé, établi; [- life] stable, régulier; [- habits] régulier; **he's very ~ in his ways** il est très routinier, il a ses petites habitudes. -**2.** METEOR [calm] beau; **the weather will remain ~** le temps demeurera au beau fixe. -**3.** [inhabited] peuplé; [colonized] colonisé. -**4.** [fixed - population] fixe, établi. -**5.** [account, bill] réglé.

settlement ['setlmənt] *n* -**1.** [resolution - of question, dispute] règlement *m*, solution *f*; [of problem] solution *f*. -**2.** [payment] règlement *m*; **I enclose a cheque in ~ of your account** veuillez trouver ci-joint un chèque en règlement de votre facture; **out-of-court ~** règlement à l'amiable. -**3.** [agreement] accord *m*; **to reach a ~** parvenir à OR conclure un accord; **wage ~** accord salarial. -**4.** [decision - on details, date] décision *f*; **~ of the final details will take some time** il faudra un certain temps pour régler les derniers détails. -**5.** JUR [financial] donation *f*; [dowry] dot *f*; [of annuity] constitution *f*; **to make a ~ on sb** faire une donation à OR en faveur de qqn. -**6.** [colony] colonie *f*; [village] village *m*; [dwellings] habitations *fpl*. -**7.** [colonization] colonisation *f*, peuplement *m*; **signs of human ~** des traces d'une présence humaine. -**8.** [of contents, road] tassement *m*; [of sediment] dépôt *m*.

settler ['setləʳ] *n* colonisateur *m*, -trice *f*, colon *m*.

settling ['setlɪŋ] *n* -**1.** [of question, problem, dispute] règlement *m*. -**2.** [of account, debt] règlement *m*. -**3.** [of contents] tassement *m*. -**4.** [of country] colonisation *f*.

◆ **settlings** *npl* [sediment] dépôt *m*, sédiment *m*.

set-to *inf* (*pl* set-tos) *n* [fight] bagarre *f*; [argument] prise *f* de bec.

set-up *n* -**1.** [arrangement, system] organisation *f*, système *m*; **the project manager explained the ~ to me** le chef de projet m'a expliqué comment les choses fonctionnaient OR étaient organisées; **this is the ~** voici comment ça se passe; **what's the economic ~ in these countries?** quel est le système économique de ces pays? -**2.** *inf* [frame-up] coup *m* monté.

seven ['sevn] ◇ *adj* sept; 'The Seven Samurai' *Kurosawa* 'les Sept Samouraïs'.

◇ *n* sept *m inv*.

sevenfold ['sevnfəʊld] ◇ *adj* septuple.

◇ *adv* au septuple; **profits have increased ~** les bénéfices ont été multipliés par sept.

seven-league boots *npl* bottes *fpl* de sept lieux.

seven seas *npl*: **the ~** toutes les mers (du monde); **to sail the ~** parcourir les mers.

seventeen [ˌsevn'ti:n] ◇ *adj* dix-sept.

◇ *n* dix-sept *m inv*.

seventeenth [ˌsevn'ti:nθ] ◇ *adj* dix-septième.

◇ *n* [ordinal] dix-septième *mf*; [fraction] dix-septième *m*.

seventh ['sevnθ] ◇ *adj* septième.

◇ *n* [ordinal] septième *mf*; [fraction] septième *m*; MUS septième *f*.

Seventh Day Adventist *n* adventiste *mf* du septième jour.

seventh heaven *n* le septième ciel; to be in (one's) ~ être au septième ciel.

seventieth ['sevntjəθ] ◇ *adj* soixante-dixième.
◇ *n* [ordinal] soixante-dixième *mf*; [fraction] soixante-dixième *m*.

seventy ['sevntɪ] (*pl* seventies) ◇ *adj* soixante-dix.
◇ *n* soixante-dix *m inv*.

seventy-eight *n* [record] 78 tours *m inv*; a collection of old 78s une collection de vieux 78 tours.

seven-year itch *n hum* tentation *f* d'infidélité *(après sept ans de mariage)*.

sever ['sevəʳ] ◇ *vt* -**1.** [cut off - rope, limb] couper, trancher; his hand was ~ed (at the wrist) il a eu la main coupée (au poignet); the roadworks ~ed a watermain les travaux ont crevé une canalisation d'eau; communications with outlying villages have been ~ed les communications avec les villages isolés ont été rompues. -**2.** [cease - relationship, contact] cesser, rompre; they ~ed all connections with the organization ils ont cessé toute relation avec l'organisation; she ~ed all ties with her family elle a rompu tous les liens avec sa famille.
◇ *vi* se rompre, casser, céder; the rope ~ed under the strain la corde a cédé sous la tension.

several ['sevrəl] ◇ *det* plusieurs; on ~ occasions à plusieurs occasions OR reprises; ~ thousand dollars plusieurs milliers de dollars.
◇ *pron* plusieurs; ~ of my colleagues have left plusieurs de mes collègues sont partis; ~ of us plusieurs d'entre nous; there are ~ of them ils sont plusieurs; ~ of us got together to organize a party nous nous sommes mis à plusieurs pour organiser une soirée.
◇ *adj* JUR [separate] distinct.

severally ['sevrəlɪ] *adv fml* séparément, individuellement.

severance ['sevrəns] *n* [of relations] rupture *f*, cessation *f*; [of communications, contact] interruption *f*, rupture *f*.

severance pay *n (U)* indemnité *f* OR indemnités *fpl* de licenciement.

severe [sɪ'vɪəʳ] *adj* -**1.** [harsh - criticism, punishment, regulations] sévère, dur; [- conditions] difficile, rigoureux; [- storm] violent; [- winter, climate] rude, rigoureux; [- frost] intense; [- competition] rude, serré; ~ weather conditions conditions *fpl* météorologiques très rudes ‖ [strict - tone, person] sévère; she's too ~ with her children elle est trop dure avec ses enfants; I gave them a ~ telling-off je les ai sévèrement grondés. -**2.** [serious - illness, handicap] grave, sérieux; [- defeat] grave; [- pain] vif, aigu; I've got ~ backache/toothache j'ai très mal au dos/une rage de dents; to suffer ~ losses subir de lourdes pertes; his death was a ~ blow to them/to their chances sa mort les a sérieusement ébranlés/a sérieusement compromis leurs chances; it will be a ~ test of our capabilities cela mettra nos aptitudes à rude épreuve. -**3.** [austere - style, dress, haircut] sévère, strict; the building has a certain ~ beauty l'édifice a une certaine beauté austère.

severely [sɪ'vɪəlɪ] *adv* -**1.** [harshly - punish, treat, criticize] sévèrement, durement; don't judge them too ~ ne les jugez pas trop sévèrement OR avec trop de sévérité ‖ [strictly] strictement, sévèrement; he spoke ~ to them il leur parla d'un ton sec. -**2.** [seriously - ill, injured, disabled] gravement, sérieusement; to be ~ handicapped être gravement handicapé. -**3.** [austerely] d'une manière austère, sévèrement; she dresses very ~ elle s'habille de manière très austère.

severity [sɪ'verətɪ] *n* -**1.** [harshness - of judgment, treatment, punishment, criticism] sévérité *f*, dureté *f*; [- of climate, weather] rigueur *f*, dureté *f*; [- of frost, cold] intensité *f*. -**2.** [seriousness - of illness, injury, handicap] gravité *f*, sévérité *f*. -**3.** [austerity] austérité *f*, sévérité *f*.

Seville [sə'vɪl] *pr n* Séville.

Seville orange *n* orange *f* amère, bigarade *f*.

sew [səʊ] (*pt* sewed, *pp* sewn [səʊn] OR sewed) ◇ *vt* coudre; to ~ a button on(to) a shirt coudre OR recoudre un bouton sur une chemise; she can't even ~ a button on elle ne sait même pas coudre un bouton; could you ~ this armband on for me? pouvez-vous me coudre ce brassard?; he ~ed the money into the lining il a cousu l'argent dans la doublure; you'll have to ~ the pieces together again il va falloir recoudre les pièces ensemble.
◇ *vi* coudre, faire de la couture.
◆ **sew up** *vt sep* -**1.** [tear, slit] coudre, recoudre; [seam] faire; MED [wound] coudre, recoudre, suturer; I must ~ up this hole il faut que je raccommode ce trou. -**2.** *inf fig* [arrange, settle - contract] régler; [- details] régler, mettre au point; the deal is all sewn up l'affaire est dans le sac ‖ [control] contrôler, monopoliser; multinationals have sewn up the economy les multinationales contrôlent l'économie; they've got the election all sewn up l'élection est gagnée d'avance.

sewage ['su:ɪdʒ] *n (U)* vidanges *fpl*, eaux *fpl* d'égout, eaux-vannes *fpl*; the ~ system les égouts *mpl*; ~ disposal évacuation *f* des eaux usées.

sewage farm, sewage works *n* station *f* d'épuration.

sewer ['sʊəʳ] *n* [drain] égout *m*.

sewerage ['sʊərɪdʒ] *n (U)* -**1.** [disposal] évacuation *f* des eaux usées. -**2.** [system] égouts *mpl*, réseau *m* d'égouts. -**3.** [sewage] eaux *fpl* d'égout.

sewer rat *n* rat *m* d'égout.

sewing ['səʊɪŋ] ◇ *n* -**1.** [activity] couture *f*; she likes ~ elle aime coudre OR la couture. -**2.** [piece of work] couture *f*, ouvrage *m*; what have I done with my ~? où ai-je posé ma couture?
◇ *comp* [basket, kit] à couture; [cotton] à coudre; [class] de couture.

sewing machine *n* machine *f* à coudre.

sewn [səʊn] *pp* → **sew**.

sex [seks] ◇ *n* -**1.** [gender] sexe *m*; the club is open to both ~es le club est ouvert aux personnes des deux sexes; single ~ school établissement *m* scolaire non mixte. -**2.** *(U)* [sexual intercourse] relations *fpl* sexuelles, rapports *mpl* (sexuels); to have ~ with sb avoir des rapports (sexuels) OR faire l'amour avec qqn; extramarital ~ relations extraconjugales. -**3.** [sexual activity] sexe *m*; that film is just full of ~ il n'y a que du sexe dans ce film; all he ever thinks about is ~ c'est un obsédé (sexuel); there is too much ~ and violence on TV il y a trop de sexe et de violence à la télévision.
◇ *comp* sexuel; ~ drive pulsion *f* sexuelle, pulsions *fpl* sexuelles, libido *f*; ~ life vie *f* sexuelle.
◇ *vt* [animal] déterminer le sexe de.

sexadecimal [,seksə'desɪml] *adj* sexadécimal.

sexagenarian [,seksədʒɪ'neərɪən] ◇ *adj* sexagénaire.
◇ *n* sexagénaire *mf*.

sex appeal *n* sex-appeal *m*.

sex change *n* changement *m* de sexe; to have a ~ changer de sexe.

sex chromosome *n* chromosome *m* sexuel.

sexed [sekst] *adj* BIOL & ZOOL sexué; to be highly ~ [person] avoir des pulsions sexuelles très fortes, avoir une forte libido.

sex education *n* éducation *f* sexuelle.

sex hormone *n* hormone *f* sexuelle.

sexily ['seksɪlɪ] *adv* sensuellement; he dances very ~ il danse de façon très sensuelle.

sexism ['seksɪzm] *n* sexisme *m*.

sexist ['seksɪst] ◇ *adj* sexiste.
◇ *n* sexiste *mf*.

sex kitten *inf n* bombe *f* sexuelle.

sexless ['sekslɪs] *adj* -**1.** BIOL asexué. -**2.** [person - asexual] asexué; [- frigid] frigide; [marriage] blanc.

sex-mad *inf adj*: he's/she's ~ il/elle ne pense qu'à ça.

sex maniac *n* obsédé *m* sexuel, obsédée *f* sexuelle.

sex object *n* objet *m* sexuel.

sex offender *n* auteur *m* d'un délit sexuel.

sexologist [sek'sɒlədʒɪst] *n* sexologue *mf*.

sexology [sek'sɒlədʒɪ] *n* sexologie *f*.

sex organ *n* organe *m* sexuel.

sexpot *inf* ['sekspɒt] *n hum* homme *m* très sexy, femme *f* très sexy.

sex shop *n* sex-shop *m*.

sex-starved *adj hum* (sexuellement) frustré.

sex symbol *n* sex-symbol *m*.

sextant ['sekstənt] *n* sextant *m*.

sextet [seks'tet] *n* sextuor *m*.

sex therapist *n* sexologue *mf*.

sex therapy *n* sexothérapie *f*.

sexton ['sekstən] *n* sacristain *m*, bedeau *m*.

sextuple ['sekstjʊpl] ◇ *adj* sextuple.
◇ *n* sextuple *m*.
◇ *vi* & *vt* sextupler.

sextuplet ['sekstjʊplɪt] *n* sextuplé *m*, -e *f*.

sextuplicate [seks'tju:plɪkɪt] ◇ *n* sextuple *m*; in ~ en six exemplaires.
◇ *adj* sextuple.

Sextus ['sekstəs] *pr n* Sextus.

sexual ['sekʃʊəl] *adj* sexuel.

sexual abuse *n* sévices *mpl* sexuels.

sexual harassment *n* harcèlement *m* sexuel.

sexual intercourse *n (U)* rapports *mpl* sexuels.

sexuality [,sekʃʊ'ælətɪ] *n* sexualité *f*.

sexually ['sekʃʊəlɪ] *adv* sexuellement; to be ~ assaulted être victime d'une agression sexuelle; ~ transmitted disease maladie *f* sexuellement transmissible, MST *f*.

sexy *inf* ['seksɪ] (*compar* sexier, *superl* sexiest) *adj literal* sexy *(inv)*; *fig* branché.

Seychelles [seɪ'ʃelz] *pl pr n*: the ~ les Seychelles *fpl*; in the ~ aux Seychelles.

sez▽ [sez] = **says**.

SF (*abbr of* science fiction) *n* SF *f*.

SG *n abbr of* Surgeon General.

sh [ʃ] *interj* chut!

shabbily ['ʃæbɪlɪ] *adv* -**1.** [dressed, furnished] pauvrement. -**2.** [behave, treat] mesquinement, petitement; I think she's been very ~ treated je trouve qu'on l'a traitée avec beaucoup de mesquinerie OR de manière très mesquine.

shabbiness ['ʃæbɪnɪs] *n* -**1.** [poor condition - of dress, person] pauvreté *f*; [- of house, street] délabrement *m*; [- of carpet] mauvais état *m*. -**2.** [meanness - of behaviour, treatment, trick] mesquinerie *f*, petitesse *f*. -**3.** [mediocrity - of excuse, reasoning] médiocrité *f*.

shabby ['ʃæbɪ] (*compar* shabbier, *superl* shabbiest) *adj* -**1.** [clothes] râpé, élimé; [carpet, curtains] usé, élimé; [person] pauvrement vêtu; [hotel, house] miteux, minable; [furniture] pauvre, minable; [street, area] misérable, miteux. -**2.** [mean - behaviour, treatment] mesquin, vil, bas; that was a ~ trick c'était vraiment mesquin. -**3.** [mediocre - excuse] piètre; [- reasoning] médiocre.

shabby-genteel *adj* pauvre mais digne.

shack [ʃæk] *n* cabane *f*, case *f*, hutte *f*.
◆ **shack up** *inf vi insep*: to ~ up with sb s'installer avec qqn; they've ~ed up together ils vivent ensemble OR se sont mis à la colle.

shackle ['ʃækl] *vt literal* enchaîner, mettre aux fers; *fig* entraver; he was ~d to the post on l'a enchaîné au poteau.
◆ **shackles** *n pl literal* chaînes *fpl*, fers *mpl*; *fig* chaînes *fpl*, entraves *fpl*.

shad [ʃæd] *n* alose *f*.

shaddock ['ʃædək] *n sorte de pamplemousse*.

shade [ʃeɪd] ◇ *n* -**1.** [shadow] ombre *f*; to sit in the ~ s'asseoir à l'ombre; 45 degrees in the ~ 45 degrés à l'ombre; in the ~ of a tree à l'ombre d'un arbre; these trees give plenty of ~ ces arbres font beaucoup d'ombre ‖ ART ombre *f*, ombres *fpl*; the use of light and ~ in the painting l'utilisation des ombres et des lumières OR du clair-obscur dans le tableau

❑ to put sb in the ~ éclipser qqn; his achievements really put mine in the ~ ses réalisations éclipsent vraiment les miennes. -**2.** [variety - of colour] nuance *f*, ton *m*; **a different ~ of green** un ton de vert différent, une autre nuance de vert || [nuance - of meaning, opinion] nuance *f*; **all ~s of political opinion were represented** toutes les nuances politiques étaient représentées, tous les courants politiques étaient représentés. -**3.** [for lamp] abat-jour *m inv*; [for eyes] visière *f*; *Am* [blind - on window] store *m*; **to pull the ~s (down)** baisser les stores. -**4.** *lit* [spirit] ombre *f*; **the Shades** MYTH les Enfers *mpl*, le royaume des ombres.

◇ *vt* -**1.** [screen - eyes, face] abriter; [- place] ombrager, donner de l'ombre à; **he ~d his eyes (from the sun) with his hand** il a mis sa main devant ses yeux pour se protéger du soleil. -**2.** [cover - light, lightbulb] masquer, voiler. -**3.** ART [painting] ombrer; [by hatching] hachurer; **I've ~d the background green** j'ai coloré l'arrière-plan en vert.

◇ *vi* [merge] se dégrader, se fondre; **the blue ~s into purple** le bleu se fond en violet; **questions of right and wrong tend to ~ into each other** les questions du bien et du mal ont tendance à se rejoindre.

◆ **shades** *npl* -**1.** *lit* [growing darkness]: **the ~s of evening** les ombres du soir. -**2.** *inf* [sunglasses] lunettes *fpl* de soleil. -**3.** [reminder, echo] échos *mpl*; **~s of Proust** des échos proustiens.

◆ **a shade** *adv phr*: **she's a ~ better today** elle va un tout petit peu mieux aujourd'hui; **his books are just a ~ too sentimental for me** ses livres sont un peu trop sentimentaux pour moi.

◆ **shade in** *vt sep* [background] hachurer, tramer; [with colour] colorer.

shadiness ['ʃeɪdɪnɪs] *n* -**1.** [of place] ombre *f*. -**2.** [of behaviour, dealings] caractère *m* louche OR suspect.

shading ['ʃeɪdɪŋ] *n (U)* ART [in painting] ombres *fpl*; [hatching] hachure *f*, tramage *m*, hachures *fpl*; *fig* [difference] nuance *f*.

shadow ['ʃædəʊ] ◇ *n* -**1.** [of figure, building] ombre *f*; **to see a ~ on a wall** voir une ombre sur un mur; **the ~ of suspicion fell on them** on a commencé à les soupçonner; **she's a ~ of her former self** elle n'est plus que l'ombre d'elle-même ❑ **he's afraid of his own ~** il a peur de son ombre; **to live in sb's ~** vivre dans l'ombre de qqn; **to cast a ~ on** OR **over sthg** *literal* & *fig* projeter OR jeter une ombre sur qqch. -**2.** [under eyes] cerne *m*. -**3.** [shade] ombre *f*, ombrage *m*; **in the ~ of the trees** à l'ombre des arbres; **in the ~ of the doorway** dans l'ombre de la porte; **she was standing in (the) ~** elle se tenait dans l'ombre; **the gardens lie in ~ now** les jardins sont maintenant à l'ombre. -**4.** [slightest bit] ombre *f*; **without a** OR **the ~ of a doubt** sans l'ombre d'un doute. -**5.** [detective]: **I want a ~ put on him** je veux qu'on le fasse suivre; **he managed to lose his ~** il a réussi à semer la personne qui l'avait pris en filature. -**6.** [companion] ombre *f*; **he follows me everywhere like a ~** il me suit comme mon ombre, il ne me lâche pas d'une semelle.

◇ *vt* -**1.** [follow secretly] filer, prendre en filature; **our job was to ~ enemy submarines** nous étions chargés de suivre les sous-marins ennemis. -**2.** [screen from light] *lit* ombrager; **tall trees ~ed the pathway** de grands arbres ombrageaient le chemin.

◇ *adj Br* POL: **~ cabinet** cabinet *m* fantôme; **the Shadow Education Secretary/Defence Secretary** le porte-parole de l'opposition pour l'éducation/pour la défense nationale.

◆ **shadows** *npl lit* [darkness] ombre *f*, ombres *fpl*, obscurité *f*; **the ~s of the evening** les ombres du soir.

SHADOW MINISTERS:
Les «ministres fantômes» sont les parlementaires de l'opposition qui deviendraient ministres si l'opposition prenait le pouvoir.

shadow-box *vi* SPORT faire de la boxe à vide.

shadow-boxing *n* SPORT boxe *f* à vide; **let's stop all this ~ and get down to business** arrêtons de tourner autour du pot et parlons sérieusement.

shadowy ['ʃædəʊɪ] *adj* -**1.** [shady - woods, path] ombragé; **he looked into the ~ depths** il scruta les profondeurs insondables. -**2.** [vague - figure, outline] vague, indistinct; [- plan] vague, imprécis.

shady ['ʃeɪdɪ] (*compar* shadier, *superl* shadiest) *adj* -**1.** [place] ombragé. -**2.** *inf* [person, behaviour] louche, suspect; [dealings] louche.

shaft [ʃɑːft] ◇ *n* -**1.** [of spear] hampe *f*; [of feather] tuyau *m*; ARCHIT [of column] fût *m*; ANAT [of bone] diaphyse *f*. -**2.** [of axe, tool, golf club] manche *m*. -**3.** [of cart, carriage] brancard *m*, limon *m*; **to put a horse between the ~s** atteler un cheval. -**4.** MECH [for propeller, in machine] arbre *m*. -**5.** [in mine] puits *m*; [of ventilator, chimney] puits *m*, cheminée *f*; [of lift] cage *f*. -**6.** [of light] rai *m*; **a ~ of wit** *fig* un trait d'esprit. -**7.** *lit* [arrow] flèche *f*. -**8.** ▽ *Am phr*: **he got the ~** qu'est-ce qu'il s'est pris!

◇ *vt* -**1.** ▽ [cheat]: **he got ~ed** il s'est fait rouler! -**2.** ▼ [have sex with] baiser.

shag [ʃæg] (*pt* & *pp* shagged) ◇ *n* -**1.** [of hair, wool] toison *f*; **~ (pile) carpet** moquette *f* à poils longs. -**2.** **~ (tobacco)** tabac *m* (très fort). -**3.** ORNITH cormoran *m* huppé. -**4.** ▼ [sex]: **to have a ~** baiser. -**5.** *Am* [dance] shag *m*. -**6.** *Am* [ballboy] ramasseur *m* de balles.

◇ *vt* -**1.** ▽ [tire] crever; **to be shagged (out)** être complètement crevé OR HS. -**2.** ▼ [have sex with] baiser. -**3.** *Am* [follow] poursuivre. -**4.** *Am* [fetch] aller chercher.

◇ *vi* -**1.** ▼ [have sex] baiser. -**2.** *Am* [dance] danser le shag.

shaggy ['ʃægɪ] (*compar* shaggier, *superl* shaggiest) *adj* [hair, beard] hirsute, touffu; [eyebrows] hérissé, broussailleux; [dog, pony] à longs poils (rudes); [carpet, rug] à longs poils; **a ~-looking man** un homme hirsute.

shaggy dog story *n* histoire *f* sans queue ni tête.

shagreen [ʃæ'griːn] *n* chagrin *m (cuir)*.

shah [ʃɑː] *n* chah *m*, shah *m*; **the Shah of Persia** le chah de Perse.

shake [ʃeɪk] (*pt* shook [ʃʊk], *pp* shaken ['ʃeɪkn]) ◇ *vt* -**1.** [rug, tablecloth, person] secouer; [bottle, cocktail, dice] agiter; [subj: earthquake, explosion] ébranler, faire trembler; **he had to be shaken awake** on a dû le secouer pour le réveiller; **she shook me by the shoulders** elle m'a secoué par les épaules; **the wind shook the branches** le vent agitait les branches; **they shook the apples from the tree** ils secouèrent l'arbre pour (en) faire tomber les pommes; **he shook the gravel into the bag** il secouait le gravier pour le faire tomber dans le sac; **to ~ sugar onto sthg** saupoudrer qqch de sucre; **to ~ vinegar onto sthg** asperger qqch de vinaigre; **to ~ salt/pepper onto sthg** saler/poivrer qqch; **'~ well before use'** 'bien agiter avant l'emploi'; **the dog shook itself (dry)** le chien s'est ébroué (pour se sécher); **they shook themselves free** ils se sont libérés d'une secousse; **he needs to be shaken out of his apathy** il a besoin qu'on le secoue (pour le tirer de son apathie); **he shook his head** [in refusal] il a dit OR fait non de la tête; [in resignation, sympathy] il a hoché la tête ❑ **~ a leg!** *inf* secoue-toi!, remue-toi!; **to ~ the dust from one's feet** partir le cœur léger. -**2.** [brandish] brandir; **to ~ one's finger at sb** [in warning] avertir qqn en lui faisant signe du doigt; [threateningly] menacer qqn du doigt; **he shook his fist at him** il l'a menacé du poing; **the farmer shook his stick at the boys** le fermier menaçait les garçons de son bâton ❑ **he's made more films than you can ~ a stick at** *inf* il a réalisé un nombre incroyable de films. -**3.** [hand] serrer; **to ~ hands with sb, to ~ sb's hand** serrer la main à qqn; **they shook hands** ils se sont serré la main; **let me ~ you by the hand** permettez-moi de vous serrer la main; **let's ~ hands on the deal** serrons-nous la main pour sceller cet accord. -**4.** [upset - faith, confidence, health, reputation] ébranler; **they were rather shaken by the news** ils ont été plutôt secoués par la nouvelle; **the whole world was shaken by the news** le monde entier a été ébranlé par la nouvelle; **his beliefs would not be that easily shaken** ses convictions ne sauraient être ébranlées pour si peu. -**5.** [amaze] bouleverser, ébranler; **she shook everyone with her revelations** tout le monde a été bouleversé par ses révélations; **10 days that shook the world** 10 jours qui ébranlèrent le monde; **I bet that shook him!** voilà qui a dû le secouer!

◇ *vi* -**1.** [ground, floor, house] trembler, être ébranlé; [leaves, branches] trembler, être agité; **the whole house shook with the sound** la maison entière a été ébranlée par le bruit; **the child shook free of his captor** l'enfant a échappé à son ravisseur. -**2.** [with emotion - voice] trembler, frémir; [- body, knees] trembler; **her whole frame shook** elle tremblait de tous ses membres; **to ~ with laughter** se tordre de rire; **to ~ with fear** trembler de peur; **to ~ with cold** trembler de froid, grelotter; **to ~ like a jelly** OR **leaf** trembler comme une feuille; **to ~ in one's shoes** avoir une peur bleue, être mort de peur; **his hands were shaking uncontrollably** il ne pouvait empêcher ses mains de trembler. -**3.** [in agreement]: **let's ~ on it!** tope-là!; **they shook on the deal** ils ont scellé leur accord par une poignée de main.

◇ *n* -**1.** secousse *f*, ébranlement *m*; **to give sthg a ~** secouer qqch; **she gave the thermometer a few ~s** elle secoua un peu le thermomètre; **with a ~ of his head** [in refusal, in resignation, sympathy] avec un hochement de tête; **give him a ~** [to waken] secouez-le; **I feel like giving him a good ~** [to stimulate] j'ai une furieuse envie de le secouer; **to be all of a ~** *inf Br* être tout tremblant. -**2.** *inf* [moment] instant *m*; **you go, I'll be there in a ~** OR **a couple of ~s** vas-y, j'arrive dans un instant OR dans une seconde; **in two ~s (of a lamb's tail)** en un clin d'œil. -**3.** *inf Am* [earthquake] tremblement *m* de terre. -**4.** *inf Am* milk-shake *m*; **a banana ~** un milk-shake à la banane. -**5.** *inf Am* [deal]: **he'll give you a fair ~** il ne te roulera pas. -**6.** MUS trille *m*.

◆ **shake down** ◇ *vi insep* -**1.** *inf* [go to bed] coucher; **they had to ~ down on the floor for the night** ils ont dû dormir OR coucher par terre. -**2.** *inf* [adapt - to new situation, job] s'habituer; **she's new to the job but she'll ~ down soon enough** elle débute dans le métier mais elle s'y fera rapidement. -**3.** [contents of packet, bottle] se tasser.

◇ *vt sep* -**1.** [from tree] faire tomber en secouant; **to ~ cherries down from a tree** secouer un arbre pour en faire tomber les cerises. -**2.** [after fall]: **to ~ o.s. down** s'ébrouer, se secouer. -**3.** *inf Am*: **to ~ sb down** [rob] racketter qqn; [search] fouiller qqn. -**4.** *inf Am* [test] essayer, tester.

◆ **shake off** *vt sep* -**1.** [physically] secouer; **to ~ the sand/water off sthg** secouer le sable/l'eau de qqch. -**2.** [get rid of - cold, pursuer, depression] se débarrasser de; [- habit] se défaire de, se débarrasser de.

◆ **shake out** ◇ *vt sep* -**1.** [tablecloth, rug] (bien) secouer; [sail, flag] déferler, déployer; [bag] vider en secouant; **he shook the coins out of the bag** il a fait tomber les pièces en secouant le sac. -**2.** [rouse - person]: **I can't seem to ~ him out of his apathy** je n'arrive pas à le tirer de son apathie.

◇ *vi insep* MIL se disperser, se disséminer.

◆ **shake up** *vt sep* -**1.** [physically - cushion, pillow] secouer, taper; [- bottle] agiter. -**2.** *fig* [upset - person] secouer, bouleverser; **they were badly shaken up after the accident** ils ont été très secoués après l'accident. -**3.** [rouse - person] secouer; **he needs shaking up a bit** il a besoin qu'on le secoue un peu. -**4.** *inf* [overhaul - organization, company] remanier, réorganiser de fond en comble.

◆ **shakes** *npl* -**1.** to have the ~s avoir la tremblote. -**2.** *phr*: no great ~s pas grand-chose; I'm no great ~s at painting OR as a painter je ne casse rien OR pas des briques comme peintre.

shakedown [ˈʃeɪkdaʊn] ◇ *n* -**1.** [bed] lit *m* improvisé OR de fortune. -**2.** *inf* [of ship, plane - test] essai *m*; [flight, voyage] voyage *m* OR vol *m* d'essai. -**3.** ▽ *Am* [search] fouille *f*. -**4.** ▽ *Am* [extortion] racket *m*.
◇ *adj* [test, flight, voyage] d'essai.

shaken [ˈʃeɪkn] *pp* → **shake**.

shakeout [ˈʃeɪkaʊt] *n* ECON dégraissage *m*.

shaker [ˈʃeɪkəʳ] *n* [for cocktails] shaker *m*; [for salad] panier *m* à salade; [for dice] cornet *m*; sugar/flour ~ saupoudreuse *f* à sucre/farine.

Shakers [ˈʃeɪkəz] *npl* Shakers *mpl (secte religieuse)*.

Shakespearean [ʃeɪkˈspɪərɪən] *adj* shakespearien.

Shakespeareana [ˈʃeɪk,spɪərɪˈɑːnə] *npl* [by Shakespeare] écrits *mpl* de Shakespeare; [about Shakespeare] articles *mpl* et livres *mpl* sur Shakespeare.

Shakespearian [ʃeɪkˈspɪərɪən] = **Shakespearean**.

shake-up *inf n* -**1.** [of company, organization] remaniement *m*, restructuration *f*. -**2.** [emotional] bouleversement *m*.

shakily [ˈʃeɪkɪlɪ] *adv* -**1.** [unsteadily - walk] d'un pas chancelant OR mal assuré; [- write] d'une main tremblante; [- speak] d'une voix tremblante OR chevrotante. -**2.** [uncertainly] d'une manière hésitante OR peu assurée; she started ~ then went on to win the game au début, elle n'était pas très sûre d'elle, mais elle a fini par gagner la partie.

shakiness [ˈʃeɪkɪnɪs] *n* -**1.** [unsteadiness - of chair, table] manque *m* de stabilité; [- of foundations, building] manque *m* de solidité; [- of hand] tremblement *m*; [- of voice] chevrotement *m*, tremblement *m*. -**2.** [weakness, uncertainty - of health, memory, argument, faith] faiblesse *f*; [- of knowledge] insuffisance *f*; [- of position, authority] fragilité *f*, faiblesse *f*; [- of future] incertitude *f*.

shaky [ˈʃeɪkɪ] (*compar* shakier, *superl* shakiest) *adj* -**1.** [unsteady - chair, table] branlant, peu solide; [- ladder] branlant, peu stable; [- hand] tremblant, tremblotant; [- writing] tremblé; [- voice] tremblotant, chevrotant; [- steps] chancelant; he's a bit ~ on his legs il ne tient pas bien sur ses jambes; I'm still ~ after my accident je ne me suis pas encore complètement remis de mon accident; to be based OR built on ~ foundations avoir des bases chancelantes. -**2.** [uncertain, weak - health, faith] précaire, vacillant; [- authority, regime] incertain, chancelant; [- future, finances] incertain, précaire; [- business] incertain; her memory is a bit ~ sa mémoire n'est pas très sûre; my memories of the war are rather ~ mes souvenirs de la guerre sont assez vagues; things got off to a ~ start les choses ont plutôt mal commencé; my knowledge of German is a bit ~ mes notions d'allemand sont plutôt vagues; he came up with some very ~ arguments ses arguments étaient très peu convaincants.

shale [ʃeɪl] *n* argile *f* schisteuse, schiste *m* argileux.

shale oil *n* huile *f* de schiste.

shall [*weak form* ʃəl, *strong form* ʃæl] *modal vb* -**1.** [as future auxiliary]: I ~ OR I'll come tomorrow je viendrai demain; I ~ not OR I shan't be able to come je ne pourrai pas venir; we ~ have finished by tomorrow nous aurons fini demain; I ~ now attempt a triple somersault je vais à présent essayer d'exécuter un triple saut périlleux. -**2.** [in suggestions, questions]: ~ I open the window? voulez-vous que j'ouvre la fenêtre?; I'll shut that window, ~ I? je peux fermer cette fenêtre, si vous voulez; we'll all go then, ~ we? dans ce cas, pourquoi n'y allons-nous pas tous?; what ~ we buy? qu'est-ce qu'on va acheter?; where ~ we go? où est-ce qu'on va aller? -**3.** *fml* [emphatic use]: you ~ go to the ball! vous irez au bal!; it ~ be done ce sera fait; thou shalt not kill BIBLE tu ne tueras point.

shallot [ʃəˈlɒt] *n* échalote *f*.

shallow [ˈʃæləʊ] ◇ *adj* -**1.** [water, soil, dish] peu profond; the ~ end [of swimming pool] le petit bain. -**2.** [superficial - person, mind, character] superficiel, qui manque de profondeur; [- conversation] superficiel, futile; [- argument] superficiel. -**3.** [breathing] superficiel.
◇ *vi fml* devenir moins profond.
◆ **shallows** *npl* bas-fond *m*, bas-fonds *mpl*, haut-fond *m*, hauts-fonds *mpl*.

shallow-minded *adj*: to be ~ être superficiel OR futile.

shallowness [ˈʃæləʊnɪs] *n* -**1.** [of water, soil, dish] faible profondeur *f*. -**2.** [of mind, character, sentiments] manque *m* de profondeur; [of person] esprit *m* superficiel, manque *m* de profondeur; [of talk, ideas] futilité *f*. -**3.** [of breathing] respiration *f* restreinte.

shalt [ʃælt] *arch 2nd person sg* → **shall**.

sham [ʃæm] (*pt* & *pp* shammed, *cont* shamming) ◇ *n* -**1.** [pretence - of sentiment, behaviour] comédie *f*, faux-semblant *m*; what he says is all ~ il n'y a rien de vrai dans ce qu'il dit; her illness/grief is a ~ sa maladie/son chagrin n'est qu'une mascarade; their marriage is a complete ~ leur mariage est une véritable farce. -**2.** [impostor - person] imposteur *m*; [- organization] imposture *f*.
◇ *adj* -**1.** [pretended - sentiment, illness] faux, feint, simulé; [- battle] simulé. -**2.** [mock - jewellery] imitation *(adj)*, faux; a ~ election un simulacre d'élections.
◇ *vt* feindre, simuler; to ~ illness faire semblant d'être malade.
◇ *vi* faire semblant, jouer la comédie; he's not really ill, he's only shamming il n'est pas vraiment malade, il fait semblant.

shaman [ˈʃæmən] *n* chaman *m*.

shamanism [ˈʃæmənɪzm] *n* chamanisme *m*.

shamateur *inf* [ˈʃæmətɜːʳ] ◇ *n* SPORT faux amateur *m*.
◇ *adj* [competition, game, race] *auquel participent de faux amateurs*.

shamble [ˈʃæmbl] *vi*: to ~ (along) marcher en traînant les pieds; to ~ in/out/past entrer/sortir/passer en traînant les pieds; he ~d up to them il s'approcha d'eux d'un pas traînant; a shambling gait une démarche traînante.

shambles [ˈʃæmblz] *n* -**1.** [place] désordre *m*; your room is a total ~! ta chambre est dans un état!; the house was in a ~ la maison était sens dessus dessous. -**2.** [situation, event] désastre *m*; his life is (in) a real ~ sa vie est un véritable désastre; the evening was a ~ la soirée fut un vrai désastre; to make a ~ of a job saboter un travail.

shambolic [ʃæmˈbɒlɪk] *adj Br* désordonné.

shame [ʃeɪm] ◇ *n* -**1.** [feeling] honte *f*, confusion *f*; to my great ~ à ma grande honte; he has no sense of ~ il n'a aucune honte; to lose all sense of ~ perdre toute honte; have you no ~? vous n'avez pas honte? -**2.** [disgrace, dishonour] honte *f*; to bring ~ on one's family/country déshonorer sa famille/sa patrie, couvrir sa famille/sa patrie de honte; to put sb to ~ faire honte à qqn; she works so hard, she puts you to ~ elle vous ferait honte, tellement elle travaille; the ~ of it! quelle honte!; ~ on him! c'est honteux!, quelle honte! ‖ *Br* [in Parliament]: her speech brought cries of "~!" son discours provoqua des huées. -**3.** [pity] dommage *m*; it's a ~! c'est dommage!; what a ~! quel dommage!; it's a ~ he can't come/you missed it c'est dommage qu'il ne puisse pas venir/que vous l'ayez manqué; it would be a great ~ if she missed it ce serait vraiment dommage qu'elle ne le voie pas; what a ~ he forgot to tell you! quel dommage qu'il ait oublié de vous le dire!
◇ *vt* [disgrace - family, country] être la honte de, faire honte à, déshonorer; [put to shame] faire honte à, humilier; their record on staff training ~s other firms ce qu'ils réalisent en matière de formation du personnel devrait faire honte aux autres entreprises; it ~s me to admit it j'ai honte de l'avouer; to ~ sb into doing sthg obliger qqn à faire qqch en lui faisant honte; she was ~d into admitting the truth elle avait tellement honte qu'elle a dû avouer la vérité.

shamefaced [ʃeɪmˈfeɪst] *adj* honteux, penaud; he was a bit ~ about it il en avait un peu honte.

shamefacedly [ʃeɪmˈfeɪstlɪ] *adv* d'un air honteux OR penaud; he admitted, rather ~, that it was his fault il a reconnu, d'un air plutôt penaud, que c'était (de) sa faute.

shameful [ˈʃeɪmfʊl] *adj* honteux, indigne; it's ~ to spread such rumours! c'est honteux OR une honte de faire courir de telles rumeurs!; it's a ~ waste of talent c'est un gaspillage de talent honteux OR scandaleux.

shamefully [ˈʃeɪmfʊlɪ] *adv* honteusement, indignement; she has been treated ~ elle a été traitée de façon honteuse; they've been ~ neglected ils ont été honteusement négligés; he was ~ ignorant about the issue son ignorance sur la question était honteuse.

shameless [ˈʃeɪmlɪs] *adj* effronté, sans vergogne; that's a ~ lie! c'est un mensonge éhonté!; they are quite ~ about it! ils ne s'en cachent pas!; she's a ~ hussy! *hum* c'est une dévergondée!

shamelessly [ˈʃeɪmlɪslɪ] *adv* sans honte, sans vergogne, sans pudeur; to lie ~ mentir effrontément; they were walking about quite ~ with nothing on ils se promenaient tout nus sans la moindre gêne OR sans que ça ait l'air de les gêner.

shamelessness [ˈʃeɪmlɪsnɪs] *n* effronterie *f*, impudence *f*.

shaming [ˈʃeɪmɪŋ] *adj* mortifiant, humiliant; how ~! quelle humiliation!

shammy [ˈʃæmɪ] *n*: ~ (leather) peau *f* de chamois.

shampoo [ʃæmˈpuː] ◇ *n* shampooing *m*; ~ and set shampooing *m* (et) mise en plis *f*.
◇ *vt* [person, animal] faire un shampooing à; [carpet] shampouiner; to ~ one's hair se faire un shampooing, se laver les cheveux; to have one's hair ~ed se faire faire un shampooing.

shamrock [ˈʃæmrɒk] *n* trèfle *m*.

shamus▽ [ˈʃeɪməs] *n Am dated* [policeman] flic *m*, poulet *m*; [detective] privé *m*.

shandy [ˈʃændɪ] (*pl* shandies) *n Br* panaché *m*.

shanghai [,ʃæŋˈhaɪ] *vt* -**1.** NAUT embarquer de force *(comme matelot)*. -**2.** *inf fig*: to ~ sb into doing sthg forcer qqn à faire qqch; I was ~ed into it on m'a forcé la main.

Shanghai [ʃæŋˈhaɪ] *pr n* Shanghai.

Shangri-La [,ʃæŋgrɪˈlɑː] *n* paradis *m* terrestre.

shank [ʃæŋk] *n* -**1.** ANAT jambe *f*; [of horse] canon *m*; CULIN jarret *m*. -**2.** [stem - of screw, anchor] manche *m*; [- of glass] pied *m*.

shanks's pony *inf* [ˈʃæŋksɪz-] *n hum*: to go on ~ *inf* aller pedibus OR à pattes.

shan't [ʃɑːnt] = **shall not**.

shantung [,ʃænˈtʌŋ] *n* shantung *m*, chantoung *m*.

shanty [ˈʃæntɪ] (*pl* shanties) *n* -**1.** [shack] baraque *f*, cabane *f*. -**2.** [song] chanson *f* de marins.

shantytown [ˈʃæntɪtaʊn] *n* bidonville *m*.

shape [ʃeɪp] ◇ *n* -**1.** [outer form] forme *f*; the room was triangular in ~ la pièce était de forme triangulaire OR avait la forme d'un triangle; a sweet in the ~ of a heart un bonbon en forme de cœur; the house/garden is an odd ~ la maison/le jardin a une drôle de forme; all the pebbles are different ~s OR a different ~ chaque caillou a une forme différente; they come in all ~s and sizes il y en a de toutes les formes et de toutes les tailles; she moulded the clay into ~ elle façonna l'argile; he bent/beat the copper into ~ il plia/martela le cuivre; my pullover lost its ~ in the wash mon pull s'est déformé au lavage. -**2.** [figure, silhouette] forme *f*, silhouette *f*; vague ~s could be seen in the mist on distinguait des formes vagues dans la brume. -**3.** [abstract form or structure] forme *f*; the ~ of our society la structure de notre société; to take ~ prendre forme OR tournure; her plan was beginning to take ~ son projet commençait à se concrétiser OR à prendre forme; to give ~ to sthg donner forme à qqch; she plans to change the whole ~ of the company elle a l'intention de modifier complètement la structure de l'entreprise. -**4.** [guise] forme *f*; help eventually arrived in the ~ of her parents ce sont ses parents qui finirent par arriver pour lui prêter secours; he can't take alcohol in any ~ or form il ne supporte l'alcool sous aucune forme; the ~ of things to come ce qui nous attend, ce que l'avenir nous réserve. -**5.** [proper condition, fitness, effectiveness etc] forme *f*; to be in good/bad ~ [person] être en bonne/mauvaise forme, être/ne pas être en forme; [business, economy] marcher bien/mal; I'm rather out of ~ je ne suis pas très en forme; I need to get (back) into ~ j'ai besoin de me remettre en forme; the economy is in poor ~ at the moment l'économie est mal en point OR dans une mauvaise passe actuellement; to keep o.s. OR to stay in ~ garder la OR rester en forme; what sort of ~ was he in? dans quel état était-il?, comment allait-il? ❑ to knock OR to lick sthg into ~ *inf* arranger qqch, mettre qqch au point; I'll soon knock OR lick them into ~! *inf* [soldiers] j'aurai vite fait de les dresser, moi!; [team] j'aurai vite fait de les remettre en forme, moi! -**6.** [apparition, ghost] apparition *f*, fantôme *m*. -**7.** [mould - gen] moule *m*; [- for hats] forme *f*.

◇ *vt* -**1.** [mould - clay] façonner, modeler; [- wood, stone] façonner, tailler; she ~d the clay into rectangular blocks elle a façonné l'argile en blocs rectangulaires; he ~d a pot from the wet clay il a façonné un pot dans l'argile; the paper had been ~d into a cone le papier avait été plié en forme de cône. -**2.** [influence - events, life, future] influencer, déterminer; to ~ sb's character former OR pétrir le caractère de qqn. -**3.** [plan - essay] faire le plan de; [- excuse, explanation, statement] formuler. -**4.** SEW ajuster; the jacket is ~d at the waist la veste est ajustée à la taille.

◇ *vi* [develop - plan] prendre forme OR tournure; things are shaping well les choses se présentent bien OR prennent une bonne tournure ‖ [person] se débrouiller; how is he shaping as a teacher? comment se débrouille-t-il dans l'enseignement?

◆ **shape up** *vi insep* -**1.** [improve] se secouer; you'd better ~ up, young man! il est temps que tu te secoues, jeune homme!; ~ up and look smart! *inf* grouille-toi! -**2.** *Am* [get fit again] retrouver la forme. -**3.** [progress, develop] prendre (une bonne) tournure; the business is beginning to ~ up les affaires commencent à bien marcher; our plans are shaping up nicely nos projets prennent une bonne tournure; the new team is shaping up well la nouvelle équipe commence à bien fonctionner; they are shaping up into a good orchestra ils commencent à former un bon orchestre; how is she shaping up as a translator? comment se débrouille-t-elle OR comment s'en sort-elle en tant que traductrice?; she isn't shaping up too badly elle ne se débrouille OR ne s'en sort pas trop mal.

SHAPE [ʃeɪp] (*abbr of* Supreme Headquarters Allied Powers Europe) *pr n* SHAPE *m*.

shaped [ʃeɪpt] *adj* -**1.** [garment] ajusté; [wooden or metal object] travaillé. -**2.** [in descriptions]: ~ like a triangle en forme de triangle; a rock ~ like a man's head un rocher qui a la forme d'une tête d'homme.

-shaped *in cpds* en forme de; egg/crescent~ en forme d'œuf/de croissant; pear~ en forme de poire, piriforme *spec*.

shapeless [ˈʃeɪplɪs] *adj* [mass, garment, heap] informe; to become ~ se déformer.

shapelessness [ˈʃeɪplɪsnɪs] *n* absence *f* de forme, aspect *m* informe.

shapeliness [ˈʃeɪplɪnɪs] *n* [of legs] galbe *m*; [of figure] beauté *f*, belles proportions *fpl*.

shapely [ˈʃeɪplɪ] (*compar* shapelier, *superl* shapeliest) *adj* [legs] bien galbé, bien tourné; [figure, woman] bien fait; a ~ pair of legs une belle paire de jambes.

shard [ʃɑːd] *n* -**1.** [of glass] éclat *m*; [of pottery] tesson *m*. -**2.** ZOOL élytre *m*.

share [ʃeəʳ] ◇ *vt* -**1.** [divide - money, property, food, chores] partager; he ~d the chocolate with his sister il a partagé le chocolat avec sa sœur; I ~d the chocolate among the children j'ai partagé le chocolat entre les enfants; responsibility is ~d between the manager and his assistant la responsabilité est partagée entre le directeur et son assistant; they must ~ the blame for the accident ils doivent se partager la responsabilité de l'accident; they ~d the work between them ils se sont partagé le travail. -**2.** [use jointly - tools, flat, bed] partager; we ~d a taxi home nous avons partagé un taxi pour rentrer; ~d line TELEC ligne *f* partagée, raccordement *m* collectif. -**3.** [have in common - interest, opinion] partager; [- characteristic] avoir en commun; [- worry, sorrow] partager, prendre part à, compatir à; I ~ your hope that war may be avoided j'espère comme vous qu'on pourra éviter la guerre; we ~ the same name nous avons le même nom; we ~ a common heritage nous avons un patrimoine commun; ~d experience expérience *f* partagée.

◇ *vi* partager; to ~ in [cost, work] participer à, partager; [profits] avoir part à; [credit, responsibility] partager; [joy, sorrow] prendre part à, partager; we all ~ in your grief nous compatissons tous à votre douleur; he doesn't like sharing il n'aime pas partager; some children will have to ~ certains enfants devront partager ❑ ~ and ~ alike *prov* à chacun sa part.

◇ *n* -**1.** [portion - of property, cost, food, credit, blame] part *f*; divided into equal ~s divisé en parts OR portions égales; there's your ~ voici votre part OR ce qui vous revient; they've had their ~ of misfortune ils ont eu leur part de malheurs; he's come in for his full ~ of criticism il a été beaucoup critiqué; they have their ~ of responsibility in this matter ils ont leur part de responsabilité dans cette affaire; we've had more than our (fair) ~ of rain this summer nous avons eu plus que notre compte de pluie cet été; he got his (fair) ~ of the profits il a eu sa part des bénéfices; they all had a ~ in the profits ils ont tous eu une part des bénéfices; to pay one's ~ payer sa part OR quote-part OR son écot; they went ~s in the cost of the present ils ont tous participé à l'achat du cadeau; I went half ~s with her on a payé la moitié chacun; to have a ~ in a business être l'un des associés dans une affaire. -**2.** [part, role - in activity, work] part *f*; what was his ~ in the robbery? quelle part a-t-il prise au vol?; what was her ~ in it all? quel rôle a-t-elle joué dans tout cela?; to do one's ~ (of the work) faire sa part du travail; he hasn't done his ~ il n'a pas fait sa part du travail; to have a ~ in doing sthg contribuer à faire qqch; she must have had a ~ in his downfall elle doit être pour quelque chose dans sa chute. -**3.** ST. EX action *f*; ~ prices have fallen le prix des actions est tombé. -**4.** AGR soc *m* (de charrue).

◆ **share out** *vt sep* partager, répartir; the profits were ~d out among them ils se sont partagé les bénéfices.

share capital *n* capital *m* social.

share certificate *n* certificat *m* OR titre *m* d'actions.

sharecrop [ˈʃeəkrɒp] (*pt* & *pp* sharecropped) ◇ *vt Am* cultiver (en tant que métayer).

◇ *vi* travailler comme métayer, avoir une ferme en métayage.

sharecropper [ˈʃeəˌkrɒpəʳ] *n* métayer *m*, -ère *f*.

sharecropping [ˈʃeəˌkrɒpɪŋ] *n Am système de métayage en usage dans le sud des États-Unis après la guerre de Sécession*.

sharefarmer [ˈʃeəˌfɑːməʳ] *n Austr fermier qui partage ses bénéfices avec ses ouvriers*.

shareholder [ˈʃeəˌhəʊldəʳ] *n* actionnaire *mf*.

shareholding [ˈʃeəˌhəʊldɪŋ] *n* actionnariat *m*.

share index *n* indice *m* boursier.

share-out *n* partage *m*, répartition *f*.

shareware [ˈʃeəweəʳ] *n* *(U)* shareware *m*.

sharing [ˈʃeərɪŋ] ◇ *adj* [person] partageur.

◇ *n* [of money, power] partage *m*.

shark [ʃɑːk] *n* -**1.** ZOOL requin *m*. -**2.** *inf fig* [swindler] escroc *m*, filou *m*; [predator - in business] requin *m*; he's a real ~ c'est un véritable escroc; the ~s are out les requins ont flairé un bon coup. -**3.** *inf Am* [genius] génie *m*; to be a ~ at sthg être calé en qqch. -**4.** *Am* [at match] revendeur *m* de billets à la sauvette.

sharkskin [ˈʃɑːkskɪn] ◇ *n* peau *f* de requin.

◇ *comp* en peau de requin.

sharp [ʃɑːp] ◇ *adj* -**1.** [blade, scissors, razor] affûté, bien aiguisé; [edge] tranchant, coupant; [point] aigu, acéré; [teeth, thorn] pointu; [claw] acéré; [needle, pin - for sewing] pointu; [- for pricking] qui pique; [pencil] pointu, bien taillé; these scissors are ~ ces ciseaux coupent bien; give me a ~ knife donnez-moi un couteau qui coupe ‖ [nose] pointu; she has ~ features elle a des traits anguleux ❑ the ~ end la première ligne; the men and women at the ~ end les hommes et les femmes en première ligne. -**2.** [clear - photo, line, TV picture] net; [- contrast, distinction] net, marqué. -**3.** [abrupt, sudden - blow, bend, turn] brusque; [- rise, fall, change] brusque, soudain; the car made a ~ turn la voiture a tourné brusquement; a ~ rise/fall in prices une forte hausse/baisse des prix. -**4.** [piercing - wind, cold] vif, fort. -**5.** [intense - pain, disappointment] vif. -**6.** [sour, bitter - taste, food] âpre, piquant. -**7.** [harsh - words, criticism] mordant, cinglant; [- reprimand] sévère; [- voice, tone] âpre, acerbe; [- temper] vif; some ~ words were exchanged on échangea quelques propos acerbes; he can be very ~ with customers il lui arrive d'être très brusque avec les clients; she has a ~ tongue elle a la langue bien affilée. -**8.** [keen - eyesight] perçant; [- hearing, senses] fin; she is ~ of hearing elle a l'oreille OR l'ouïe fine; he has a ~ eye il a le coup d'œil; to have a ~ eye for a bargain savoir repérer une bonne affaire; to keep a ~ lookout for sb guetter qqn; keep a ~ lookout! restez à l'affût! ‖ [in intellect, wit - person] vif, malin; [- child] vif, éveillé; [- judgment] vif; she has a very ~ mind elle a l'esprit très vif; she was too ~ for them elle était trop maligne pour eux ❑ he's as ~ as a needle [intelligent] il est malin comme un singe; [shrewd] il est très perspicace, rien ne lui échappe. -**9.** [quick, brisk - reflex, pace]: be ~ (about it)! dépêche-toi!; that was a ~ piece of work! ça a été vite fait!, ça n'a pas traîné! -**10.** [shrill - sound, cry] aigu, perçant. -**11.** MUS: C ~ minor do dièse mineur; to be ~ [singer] chanter trop haut; [violinist] jouer trop haut. -**12.** *pej* [unscrupulous - trading, lawyer] peu scrupuleux, malhonnête; accused of ~ practice accusé de procédés indélicats OR malhonnêtes. -**13.** *inf* [smart] classe *(adj)*; he's always been a ~ dresser il s'est toujours habillé très classe.

◇ *adv* -**1.** [precisely]: at 6 o'clock ~ à 6 h pile OR précises. -**2.** [in direction]: turn ~ left tournez tout de suite à gauche; the road turns ~ left la route tourne brusquement à gauche. -**3.** MUS [sing, play] trop haut *(adv)*, faux *(adv)*. -**4.** *inf phr*: look ~ (about it)! dépêche-toi!, grouille-toi!

◇ *n* MUS dièse *m*.

sharpen [ˈʃɑːpn] ◇ *vt* -**1.** [blade, knife, razor] affiler, aiguiser, affûter; [pencil] tailler; [stick] tailler en pointe; the cat ~ed its claws on the wood le chat aiguisait ses griffes OR se faisait les griffes sur le bois. -**2.** [appetite, pain] aviver, aiguiser; [intelligence] affiner; the events ~ed my desire to travel les événements ont accru mon désir de voyager; you'll need to ~ your wits il va falloir te secouer. -**3.** [outline, image] mettre au point, rendre plus net; [contrast] accentuer, rendre plus marqué. -**4.** *Br* MUS diéser.

◇ *vi* [tone, voice] devenir plus vif OR âpre; [pain] s'aviver, devenir plus vif; [appetite] s'aiguiser; [wind, cold] devenir plus vif.

sharpener ['ʃɑːpnəʳ] *n*: (knife) ~ [machine] aiguisoir *m* (à couteaux); [steel] fusil *m* (à aiguiser); (pencil) ~ taille-crayon *m inv*.

sharpening ['ʃɑːpnɪŋ] *n* affilage *m*, aiguisage *m*, affûtage *m*.

sharpening stone *n* pierre *f* à affûter.

sharp-eyed *adj* [with good eyes] qui a l'œil vif; [with insight] à qui rien n'échappe.

sharpish *inf* ['ʃɑːpɪʃ] *adv Br* [quickly] en vitesse, sans tarder; you'd better get over there ~! tu ferais mieux d'y aller en vitesse!; look ~! grouille-toi!

sharply ['ʃɑːplɪ] *adv* -**1.** ~ pointed [knife] pointu; [pencil] à pointe fine, taillé fin; [nose, chin, shoes] pointu. -**2.** [contrast, stand out] nettement; [differ] nettement, clairement; this contrasts ~ with her usual behaviour voilà qui change beaucoup de son comportement habituel; the bare trees stood out ~ against the snow les arbres dénudés se détachaient nettement sur la neige. -**3.** [abruptly, suddenly - curve, turn] brusquement; [- rise, fall, change] brusquement, soudainement; the car took the bend too ~ la voiture a pris le virage trop vite; the road rises/drops ~ la route monte/descend en pente raide; inflation has risen ~ since last year l'inflation est montée en flèche depuis l'année dernière. -**4.** [harshly - speak] vivement, sèchement, de façon brusque; [- criticize] vivement, sévèrement; [- reply, retort] vertement, vivement; she reprimanded him ~ for being late elle lui a fait de vifs reproches pour son retard; I had to speak to her ~ about her persistent lateness j'ai dû lui faire des observations sévères au sujet de ses retards répétés. -**5.** [alertly - listen] attentivement.

sharpness ['ʃɑːpnɪs] *n* -**1.** [of blade, scissors, razor] tranchant *m*; [of needle, pencil, thorn] pointe *f* aiguë; [of features] aspect *m* anguleux. -**2.** [of outline, image, contrast] netteté *f*. -**3.** [of bend, turn] angle *m* brusque; [of rise, fall, change] soudaineté *f*. -**4.** [of wind, cold, frost] âpreté *f*. -**5.** [of taste, smell] piquant *m*, aigreur *f*. -**6.** [of word, criticism, reprimand] sévérité *f*; [of tone, voice] brusquerie *f*, aigreur *f*; there was a certain ~ in the way he spoke to me il m'a parlé sur un ton plutôt sec. -**7.** [of eyesight, hearing, senses] finesse *f*, acuité *f*; [of appetite, pain] acuité *f*; [of mind, intelligence] finesse *f*, vivacité *f*; [of irony, wit] mordant *m*; ~ of vision acuité *f* visuelle.

sharpshooter ['ʃɑːp,ʃuːtəʳ] *n* tireur *m* d'élite.

sharp-sighted *adj* [with good eyes] qui a l'œil vif; [perspicacious] perspicace; [observant] observateur, à qui rien n'échappe.

sharpster *inf* ['ʃɑːpstəʳ] *n* escroc *m*, tricheur *m*, -euse *f*.

sharp-tempered *adj* coléreux, soupe au lait (*inv*).

sharp-tongued [-tʌŋd] *adj* caustique.

sharp-witted *adj* à l'esprit vif OR fin.

shat▼ [ʃæt] *pt* & *pp* → **shit**.

shatter ['ʃætəʳ] ◇ *vt* -**1.** [break - glass, window] briser, fracasser; [- door] fracasser; a stone ~ed the windscreen un caillou a fait éclater le pare-brise; the noise ~ed my eardrums le bruit m'a assourdi. -**2.** *fig* [destroy - career, health] briser, ruiner; [- nerves] démolir, détraquer; [- confidence, faith, hope] démolir, détruire; they were ~ed by the news, the news ~ed them ils ont été complètement bouleversés par la nouvelle, la nouvelle les a complètement bouleversés.
◇ *vi* [glass, vase, windscreen] voler en éclats; her whole world ~ed son univers tout entier s'est écroulé OR a été anéanti.

shattered ['ʃætəd] *adj* -**1.** [upset] bouleversé; ~ dreams des rêves brisés. -**2.** *inf Br* [exhausted] crevé. -**3.** ▽ *Am* [drunk] bourré.

shattering ['ʃætərɪŋ] *adj* -**1.** [emotionally - news, experience] bouleversant; [disappointment] fort, cruel. -**2.** [extreme - defeat] écrasant; a ~ blow *literal* un coup violent; *fig* un grand coup. -**3.** *inf Br* [tiring] crevant.

-shattering *in cpds*: earth~ extraordinaire, époustouflant; an ear~ noise un bruit à vous déchirer les tympans.

shatterproof ['ʃætəpruːf] *adj*: ~ glass verre *m* sans éclats OR Securit®.

shave [ʃeɪv] ◇ *vt* -**1.** raser; the barber ~d him OR his face le barbier l'a rasé; to ~ one's legs/one's head se raser les jambes/la tête. -**2.** [wood] raboter; can you ~ a few millimetres off the bottom of the door? pouvez-vous raboter le bas de la porte de quelques millimètres? -**3.** [graze] raser, frôler; the car just ~d the garage door la voiture n'a fait que frôler la porte du garage. -**4.** [reduce] réduire; to ~ a few pence off the price faire un rabais de quelques centimes; a few percentage points have been ~d off their lead ils ont perdu un peu de leur avantage.
◇ *vi* se raser.
◇ *n*: to have a ~ se raser; you need a ~ tu as besoin de te raser; to give sb a ~ raser qqn.
◆ **shave off** *vt sep* -**1.** to ~ off one's beard/moustache se raser la barbe/la moustache; to ~ off one's hair se raser les cheveux OR la tête. -**2.** = **shave** *vt* **2**.

shaven ['ʃeɪvn] *adj* [face, head] rasé.

shaver ['ʃeɪvəʳ] *n* -**1.** [razor] rasoir *m* (électrique). -**2.** *inf dated* [youngster] gosse *m*, gamin *m*.

Shavian ['ʃeɪvjən] ◇ *adj* [writings] de George Bernard Shaw; [style] à la Shaw; [society] consacré à Shaw.
◇ *n* partisan *m* OR disciple *mf* de George Bernard Shaw.

shaving ['ʃeɪvɪŋ] ◇ *n* -**1.** [of wood] copeau *m*; [of metal] copeau *m*, rognure *f*; [of paper] rognure *f*. -**2.** [act] rasage *m*.
◇ *comp* [cream, foam] à raser; ~ brush blaireau *m*; ~ soap savon *m* à barbe; ~ stick (bâton *m* de) savon *m* à barbe.

shawl [ʃɔːl] *n* châle *m*.

shawl collar *n* col *m* châle.

shawm [ʃɔːm] *n* chalumeau *m* MUS.

she [ʃiː] ◇ *pron* -**1.** [referring to woman, girl] elle; ~'s tall elle est grande; ~'s a teacher/an engineer elle est enseignante/ingénieur; ~'s a very interesting woman c'est une femme très intéressante; SHE can't do it elle? elle ne peut pas le faire; if I were ~ *fml* si j'étais elle, si j'étais à sa place; ~ who OR whom he loves *fml* celle qu'il aime || [referring to boat, car, country]: ~'s a fine ship c'est un bateau magnifique; ~ can do over 120 mph elle fait plus de 150 km à l'heure. -**2.** [referring to female animal]: ~'s a lovely dog/cat c'est une chienne/chatte adorable.
◇ *n* [referring to animal, baby]: it's a ~ [animal] c'est une femelle; [baby] c'est une fille.

she- *in cpds*: ~elephant éléphant *m* femelle; ~bear ourse *f*; ~dog chienne *f*; ~wolf louve *f*.

s/he (*written abbr of* she/he) *pers pron* il ou elle.

sheaf [ʃiːf] (*pl* sheaves [ʃiːvz]) ◇ *n* -**1.** [of papers, letters] liasse *f*. -**2.** [of barley, corn] gerbe *f*; [of arrows] faisceau *m*.
◇ *vt* gerber, engerber.

shear [ʃɪəʳ] (*pt* sheared, *pp* sheared OR shorn [ʃɔːn]) ◇ *vt* -**1.** [sheep, wool] tondre; her blonde locks had been shorn on avait tondu ses boucles blondes; to be shorn of sthg *fig* être dépouillé de qqch; he was shorn of all real power il s'est vu dépouiller de tout pouvoir véritable. -**2.** [metal] couper (net), cisailler; the girder had been shorn in two la poutre métallique avait été coupée en deux.
◇ *vi* céder.
◆ **shears** *npl* [for gardening] cisaille *f*; [for sewing] grands ciseaux *mpl*; [for sheep] tondeuse *f*; a pair of ~s HORT une paire de cisailles; SEW une paire de grands ciseaux.
◆ **shear off** ◇ *vt sep* [wool, hair] tondre; [branch] couper, élaguer; [something projecting] couper, enlever; the tail section of the car had been ~ed off on impact la partie arrière de la voiture avait été arrachée par le choc.
◇ *vi insep* [part, branch] se détacher; the wing ~ed right off l'aile a été complètement arrachée.

shearer ['ʃɪərəʳ] *n* [machine] tondeuse *f* (à moutons); [person] tondeur *m*, -euse *f*.

shearing ['ʃɪərɪŋ] *n* [process] tonte *f*.
◆ **shearings** *npl*: ~s (of wool) laine *f* tondue.

shearwater ['ʃɪə,wɔːtəʳ] *n* puffin *m*.

sheath [ʃiːθ] (*pl* sheaths [ʃiːðz]) *n* -**1.** [scabbard, case - for sword] fourreau *m*; [- for dagger] gaine *f*; [- for scissors, tool] étui *m*. -**2.** [covering - for cable] gaine *f*; [- for water pipe] gaine *f*, manchon *m*; BOT, ANAT & ZOOL gaine *f*. -**3.** *Br* [condom] préservatif *m*. -**4.** = **sheath dress**.

sheath dress *n* (robe *f*) fourreau *m*.

sheathe [ʃiːð] *vt* -**1.** [sword, dagger] rengainer; the cat ~d her claws la chatte a rentré ses griffes. -**2.** [cable] gainer; [water pipe] gainer, mettre dans un manchon protecteur; she was ~d from head to foot in black satin *fig* elle était moulée dans du satin noir de la tête aux pieds.

sheathing ['ʃiːðɪŋ] *n* [gen] revêtement *m*; [of cable] gaine *f*.

sheath knife *n* couteau *m* à gaine.

sheave [ʃiːv] *vt* gerber, engerber.

sheaves [ʃiːvz] *pl* → **sheaf**.

Sheba ['ʃiːbə] *pr n* Saba; the Queen of ~ la reine de Saba.

shebang *inf* [ʃɪ'bæŋ] *n*: the whole ~ tout le tremblement.

shebeen [ʃɪ'biːn] *n Ir, Scot* & *SAfr* débit *m* de boissons clandestin.

she-cat *n literal* chatte *f*; *fig* furie *f*.

shed [ʃed] (*pt* & *pp* shed, *cont* shedding) ◇ *n* -**1.** [in garden] abri *m*, remise *f*, resserre *f*; [lean-to] appentis *m*. -**2.** [barn] grange *f*, hangar *m*; [for trains, aircraft, vehicles] hangar *m*; cattle ~ étable *f*. -**3.** [in factory] atelier *m*.
◇ *vt* -**1.** [cast off - leaves, petals] perdre; [- skin, shell] se dépouiller de; [- water] ne pas absorber; the snake regularly ~s its skin le serpent mue; the dog has ~ her hairs all over the carpet la chienne a laissé des poils partout sur la moquette; the trees are beginning to ~ their leaves les arbres commencent à perdre leurs feuilles || [take off - garments] enlever; with the heat, he ~ first his tie, then his jacket avec la chaleur, il a enlevé d'abord sa cravate, puis sa veste. -**2.** [get rid of - inhibitions, beliefs] se débarrasser de, se défaire de; [- staff] congédier. -**3.** [tears, blood] verser, répandre; [weight] perdre; to ~ bitter tears over sthg verser des larmes amères sur qqch; they came to power without shedding civilian blood ils ont pris le pouvoir sans faire couler le sang des civils. -**4.** [eject, lose] déverser; ASTRONAUT larguer; the truck ~ its load on the by-pass le camion a perdu son chargement sur la rocade; the plane needs to ~ 10 tons of fuel l'avion doit larguer 10 tonnes de carburant. -**5.** *phr*: to ~ light on *literal* éclairer; *fig* éclairer, éclaircir; perhaps this will ~ some new light on the situation ça éclairera peut-être la situation d'un jour nouveau.

she'd [*weak form* ʃɪd, *strong form* ʃiːd] -**1.** = **she had**. -**2.** = **she would**.

she-devil *n* furie *f*.

sheen [ʃiːn] *n* [on satin, wood, hair, silk] lustre *m*; [on apple] poli *m*; his hair has lost its ~ ses cheveux ont perdu leur éclat; the cello had a beautiful red ~ le violoncelle avait de magnifiques reflets rouges.

sheep [ʃiːp] (*pl inv*) ◇ *n* mouton *m*; [ewe] brebis *f*; they're just a load of ~ *pej* ils se comportent comme des moutons (de Panurge) OR un troupeau de moutons ❑ to separate OR to sort out the ~ from the goats séparer le bon grain de l'ivraie.
◇ *comp* [farm, farming] de moutons.

sheep-dip *n* bain *m* parasiticide (pour moutons).

sheepdog ['ʃiːpdɒg] *n* chien *m* de berger.

sheepdog trial *n* concours *m* de chiens de berger.
sheepfold ['ʃi:pfəʊld] *n* parc *m* à moutons, bergerie *f*.
sheepish ['ʃi:pɪʃ] *adj* penaud.
sheepishly ['ʃi:pɪʃlɪ] *adv* d'un air penaud.
sheepishness ['ʃi:pɪʃnɪs] *n* air *m* penaud.
sheep's eyes *inf npl*: to cast OR to make ~ at sb *dated* faire les yeux doux à qqn.
sheepshank ['ʃi:pʃæŋk] *n* (nœud *m* de) jambe *f* de chien.
sheepshearer ['ʃi:pˌʃɪərəʳ] *n* [person] tondeur *m*, -euse *f* (de moutons); [machine] tondeuse *f* (à moutons).
sheepshearing ['ʃi:pˌʃɪərɪŋ] *n* tonte *f* (des moutons).
sheepskin ['ʃi:pskɪn] ◇ *n* -**1.** TEX peau *f* de mouton. -**2.** *inf Am* UNIV [diploma] parchemin *m*. ◇ *comp* [coat, rug] en peau de mouton.
sheep tick *n* mélophage *m*.
sheer [ʃɪəʳ] ◇ *adj* -**1.** [as intensifier] pur; it was ~ coincidence c'était une pure coïncidence; the ~ scale of the project was intimidating l'envergure même du projet était impressionnante; the ~ boredom of her job drove her mad elle s'ennuyait tellement dans son travail que ça la rendait folle; by ~ accident OR chance tout à fait par hasard, par pur hasard; out of OR in ~ boredom par pur ennui; in ~ desperation en désespoir de cause; that's ~ nonsense! c'est complètement absurde!; it's ~ folly! c'est de la folie pure! -**2.** [steep - cliff] à pic, abrupt; it's a ~ 50 metre drop cela descend à pic sur 50 mètres; a ~ drop to the sea un à-pic jusqu'à la mer; we came up against a ~ wall of water nous nous sommes trouvés devant un véritable mur d'eau. -**3.** TEX [stockings] extra fin, 15 deniers.
◇ *adv* à pic, abruptement.
◇ *vi* NAUT [ship] faire une embardée.
◆ **sheer away** *vi insep* -**1.** [ship] larguer les amarres, prendre le large. -**2.** [animal, shy person] filer, détaler; to ~ away from éviter.
◆ **sheer off** *vi insep* -**1.** [ship] faire une embardée. -**2.** *fig* [person] changer de chemin OR de direction; when he saw us, he ~ed off in the opposite direction il a fait demi-tour en nous apercevant.
sheet [ʃi:t] ◇ *n* -**1.** [for bed] drap *m*; [for furniture] housse *f*; [shroud] linceul *m*; [tarpaulin] bâche *f*; to change the ~s (on a bed) changer les draps (d'un lit). -**2.** [of paper] feuille *f*; [of glass, metal] feuille *f*, plaque *f*; [of cardboard, plastic] feuille *f*; [of iron, steel] tôle *f*, plaque *f*; a ~ of newspaper une feuille de journal; the book is still in ~s le livre n'a pas encore été relié ❑ attendance ~ feuille de présence; order ~ bulletin *m* de commande. -**3.** [newspaper] feuille *f*, journal *m*; it's a weekly union ~ c'est une feuille syndicale hebdomadaire. -**4.** [of water, snow] nappe *f*, étendue *f*; [of rain] rideau *m*, torrent *m*; [of flame] rideau *m*; a ~ of ice une plaque de glace; [on road] une plaque de verglas; the rain came down in ~s il pleuvait des hallebardes OR à torrents. -**5.** CULIN: baking ~ plaque *f* de four OR à gâteaux. -**6.** NAUT écoute *f*; to be three ~s to the wind *inf fig* en tenir une bonne.
◇ *vt* [figure, face] draper, couvrir d'un drap; [furniture] couvrir de housses; ~ed (over) in snow *fig* couvert de neige.
◆ **sheet down** *vi insep* [rain, snow] tomber à torrents.
sheet anchor *n* NAUT ancre *f* de veille; *fig* ancre *f* de salut.
sheet bend *n* nœud *m* d'écoute.
sheet-fed *adj* [printer] feuille à feuille.
sheet feed *n* avancement *m* du papier.
sheet ice *n* plaque *f* de glace; [on road] (plaque *f* de) verglas *m*.
sheeting ['ʃi:tɪŋ] *n* -**1.** [cloth] toile *f* pour draps. -**2.** [plastic, polythene] feuillet *m*; [metal] feuille *f*, plaque *f*.
sheet lightning *n* éclair *m* en nappe OR en nappes.
sheet metal *n* tôle *f*.
sheet music *n* *(U)* partitions *fpl*.
sheet steel *n* tôle *f* d'acier.
sheik(h) [ʃeɪk] *n* cheikh *m*.
sheik(h)dom ['ʃeɪkdəm] *n* territoire *m* sous l'autorité d'un cheikh.
sheila(h) *inf* ['ʃi:lə] *n* *Austr* & *NZ* nana *f*.
shekel ['ʃekl] *n* [Israeli coin] shekel *m*; BIBLE sicle *m*.
◆ **shekels** *inf npl esp Am* [money] fric *m*, sous *mpl*.
sheldrake ['ʃeldreɪk] *n* tadorne *m*.
shelduck ['ʃeldʌk] *n* tadorne *m*, harle *m*.
shelf [ʃelf] (*pl* shelves [ʃelvz]) *n* -**1.** [individual] planche *f*, étagère *f*; [as part of set, in fridge] étagère *f*; [short] tablette *f*; [in oven] plaque *f*; [in shop] étagère *f*, rayon *m*; to put up shelves/a ~ monter des étagères/une étagère; to buy sthg off the ~ acheter qqch tout fait; I bought the cakes off the ~ j'ai acheté les gâteaux tout faits; you can't buy alcohol off the ~ in that shop l'alcool n'est pas en vente libre dans ce magasin; to stay on the shelves [goods] se vendre difficilement ❑ to be left on the ~ [woman] devenir vieille fille; [man] devenir vieux garçon. -**2.** GEOL banc *m*, rebord *m*, saillie *f*; [under sea] écueil *m*, plate-forme *f*.
shelf life *n* COMM durée *f* de conservation avant vente; bread has a short ~ le pain ne se conserve pas très longtemps.
shelf mark *n* [of book] cote *f*.
shelf space *n* espace *m* disponible *(sur un rayonnage)*.
shell [ʃel] ◇ *n* -**1.** BIOL [gen - of egg, mollusc, nut] coquille *f*; [- of peas] cosse *f*; [- of crab, lobster, tortoise] carapace *f*; [empty - on seashore] coquillage *m*; to come out of one's ~ *literal* & *fig* sortir de sa coquille; to go back OR to retire into one's ~ *inf literal* & *fig* rentrer dans sa coquille; defeated, he crawled back into his ~ vaincu, il rentra dans sa coquille. -**2.** [of building] carcasse *f*; [of car, ship, machine] coque *f*; he's just an empty ~ il n'est plus que l'ombre de lui-même. -**3.** CULIN fond *m* (de tarte). -**4.** MIL obus *m*; *Am* [cartridge] cartouche *f*. -**5.** [boat] outrigger *m*.
◇ *comp* [ornament, jewellery] de OR en coquillages.
◇ *vt* -**1.** [peas] écosser, égrener; [nut] décortiquer, écaler; [oyster] ouvrir; [prawn, crab] décortiquer. -**2.** MIL bombarder (d'obus).
◆ **shell out** *inf* ◇ *vi insep* casquer; to ~ out for sthg casquer pour qqch, payer qqch; I'm always shelling out je suis toujours en train de casquer; she had to ~ out for new school uniforms elle a dû casquer pour acheter de nouveaux uniformes scolaires.
◇ *vt insep* payer, sortir; I had to ~ out £500 j'ai dû sortir 500 livres.
she'll [ʃi:l] = **she will**.
shellac [ʃə'læk] (*pt* & *pp* shellacked) ◇ *n* gomme-laque *f*.
◇ *vt* -**1.** [varnish] laquer. -**2.** *inf Am* [defeat] battre à plate couture OR à plates coutures.
shellacking *inf* [ʃə'lækɪŋ] *n Am* râclée *f*; to get a ~ prendre une râclée.
shelled [ʃeld] *adj* [peas] écossé, égrené; [nut, shellfish] décortiqué.
shellfire ['ʃelfaɪəʳ] *n (U)* tirs *mpl* d'obus; we heard a lot of ~ on a entendu beaucoup de tirs d'obus.
shellfish ['ʃelfɪʃ] (*pl inv*) *n* -**1.** ZOOL [crab, lobster, shrimp] crustacé *m*; [mollusc] coquillage *m*. -**2.** *(U)* CULIN fruits *mpl* de mer.
shelling ['ʃelɪŋ] *n* MIL pilonnage *m*.
shellproof ['ʃelpru:f] *adj* MIL blindé, à l'épreuve des obus.
shell shock *n* *(U)* psychose *f* traumatique *(due à une explosion)*.
shell-shocked *adj* commotionné *(après une explosion)*; a ~ soldier un commotionné (de guerre); I'm still feeling pretty ~ by it all *fig* je suis encore sous le choc après toute cette histoire.
shell suit *n* survêtement *m (en polyamide froissé et doublé)*.
shelter ['ʃeltəʳ] ◇ *n* -**1.** [cover, protection] abri *m*; to take OR to get under ~ se mettre à l'abri OR à couvert; they took ~ from the rain under a tree ils se sont abrités de la pluie sous un arbre; where can we find ~? où peut-on trouver un abri?; we ran for ~ nous avons couru nous mettre à l'abri; under the ~ of the mountain à l'abri de la montagne ‖ [accommodation] asile *m*, abri *m*; to give ~ to sb [hide] donner asile à OR cacher qqn; [accommodate] héberger qqn; they gave us food and ~ il nous ont offert le gîte et le couvert. -**2.** [enclosure - gen] abri *m*; [- for sentry] guérite *f*; (bus) ~ Abribus® *m*.
◇ *vt* [protect - from rain, sun, bombs] abriter; [- from blame, suspicion] protéger; to ~ sb from sthg protéger qqn de qqch; the trees ~ed us from the wind les arbres nous abritaient du vent; her reputation ~ed her from any scandal sa réputation lui évita le scandale; we were ~ed from the rain/from danger nous étions à l'abri de la pluie/du danger ‖ [give asylum to - fugitive, refugee] donner asile à, abriter; the police suspected them of ~ing a murderer la police les soupçonnait d'abriter un assassin.
◇ *vi* s'abriter, se mettre à l'abri; [from bullets] se mettre à couvert; he ~ed from the rain in a shop doorway il s'est abrité de la pluie OR il s'est mis à l'abri de la pluie dans l'entrée d'un magasin.
shelterbelt ['ʃeltəbelt] *n* ceinture *f* de protection.
sheltered ['ʃeltəd] *adj* -**1.** [place] abrité. -**2.** [protected - industry] protégé *(de la concurrence)*; [- work] dans un centre pour handicapés; to lead a ~ life vivre à l'abri des soucis; she led a very ~ life as a child elle a eu une enfance très protégée.
sheltered accommodation, **sheltered housing** *n logement dans une résidence pour personnes âgées ou handicapées*.
shelve [ʃelv] ◇ *vt* -**1.** [put aside, suspend] laisser en suspens; the project was ~d for two years le projet a été abandonné pendant deux ans; the problem has been ~d le problème reste en suspens; all discussion on the question has been ~d toute discussion sur la question a été ajournée OR suspendue. -**2.** [books - in shop] mettre sur les rayons; [- at home] mettre sur les étagères. -**3.** [wall, room - in shop] garnir de rayons; [- at home] garnir d'étagères.
◇ *vi* [ground] être en pente douce; the beach ~s steeply la plage descend en pente raide.
shelves [ʃelvz] *pl* → **shelf**.
shelving ['ʃelvɪŋ] *n (U)* -**1.** [in shop] rayonnage *m*, rayonnages *mpl*, étagères *fpl*; [at home] étagères *fpl*. -**2.** [suspension - of plan, question etc] mise *f* en attente OR en suspens. -**3.** GEOL plateau *m*.
Shem [ʃem] *pr n* Sem.
shemozzle▽ [ʃɪ'mɒzl] *n esp Am* -**1.** [confusion] bazar *m*, pagaille *f*. -**2.** [fight] chamaillerie *f*, bagarre *f*.
shenanigans *inf* [ʃɪ'nænɪgənz] *npl* -**1.** [mischief] malice *f*, espièglerie *f*. -**2.** [scheming, tricks] manigances *fpl*, combines *fpl*; there have been some ~ going on here il s'est passé des choses pas très claires ici.
shepherd ['ʃepəd] ◇ *n* -**1.** berger *m*, pâtre *m lit*; ~'s crook bâton *m* de berger, houlette *f*. -**2.** RELIG & *lit* pasteur *m*, berger *m*; the Good Shepherd le bon pasteur OR berger; the Lord is my Shepherd BIBLE l'Éternel est mon berger.
◇ *vt* -**1.** [tourists, children] guider, conduire; the boys were ~ed onto the coach on a fait entrer les garçons dans le car; to ~ sb out of a room escorter qqn jusqu'à la porte; to ~ sb into a room faire entrer OR introduire qqn dans une pièce. -**2.** [sheep] garder, surveiller; he ~ed all the ewes into the fold il a conduit toutes les brebis dans la bergerie.
shepherd boy *n* jeune berger *m* OR pâtre *m lit*.
shepherd dog *n* (chien *m* de) berger *m*.
shepherdess [ˌʃepə'des] *n* bergère *f*.

shepherd's pie *n* hachis *m* Parmentier.
shepherd's purse *n* BOT bourse-à-pasteur *f*.
sherbet [ˈʃɜːbət] *n* -**1**. *Br* [powder] poudre *f* acidulée. -**2**. *Am* [ice] sorbet *m*.
sheriff [ˈʃerɪf] *n* -**1**. *Am* [in Wild West and today] shérif *m*. -**2**. *Br* [crown officer] shérif *m*, officier *m* de la Couronne. -**3**. *Scot* JUR ≃ juge *m* au tribunal de grande instance.
Sheriff Court *n Scot* JUR ≃ tribunal *m* de grande instance.
Sherlock Holmes [ˈʃɜːlɒkˈhəʊmz] *pr n*: 'The Adventures of ~' *Conan Doyle* 'les Aventures de Sherlock Holmes'.
Sherpa [ˈʃɜːpə] *n* Sherpa *m*.
sherry [ˈʃerɪ] (*pl* sherries) *n* sherry *m*, xérès *m*, vin *m* de Xérès.
she's [ʃiːz] -**1**. = **she has**. -**2**. = **she is**.
Shetland [ˈʃetlənd] ◇ *pr n* GEOG: the ~s, the ~ Isles, the ~ Islands les (îles *fpl*) Shetland *fpl*; in the ~s OR the ~ Isles OR the ~ Islands dans les Shetland.
◇ *adj* -**1**. GEOG shetlandais. -**2**. TEX [pullover] en shetland; ~ wool laine *f* d'Écosse OR de Shetland.
Shetlander [ˈʃetləndəʳ] *n* Shetlandais *m*, -e *f*.
Shetland pony *n* poney *m*.
Shetland sheepdog *n* berger *m* des Shetland.
shew [ʃəʊ] (*pt* shewed, *pp* shewn [ʃəʊn] OR shewed) *arch* = **show** *vt* & *vi*.
shh [ʃ] *interj* chut.
Shia(h) [ˈʃiːə] ◇ *n* -**1**. [religion] chiisme *m*. -**2**. [Shiite]: ~ (Muslim) chiite *mf*.
◇ *adj* chiite.
shibboleth [ˈʃɪbəleθ] *n* -**1**. [custom, tradition] vieille coutume *f*, vieille tradition *f*; [idea, principle] vieille idée *f*, vieux principe *m*. -**2**. [catchword] mot *m* d'ordre.
shield [ʃiːld] ◇ *n* -**1**. [carried on arm] bouclier *m*, écu *m* HÉRALD; riot ~ bouclier antiémeutes. -**2**. *fig* bouclier *m*, paravent *m*; to provide a ~ against sthg protéger contre qqch; to use sthg/sb as a ~ se servir de qqch/qqn comme bouclier. -**3**. TECH [on machine] écran *m* de protection OR de sécurité; [on nuclear reactor, spacecraft] bouclier *m*; nuclear ~ bouclier atomique; sun ~ pare-soleil *m inv*. -**4**. [trophy] trophée *m*.
◇ *vt* protéger; to ~ sb from sthg protéger qqn de OR contre qqch; we need a shelter to ~ us from the wind/sun il nous faut un abri contre le vent/soleil; the police think he's trying to ~ somebody la police pense qu'il essaie de protéger quelqu'un; she ~ed him with her own body elle lui a fait un rempart de son corps.
shieling [ˈʃiːlɪŋ] *n Scot* -**1**. [pasture] pâturage *m* (d'été). -**2**. [hut] abri *m* OR cabane *f* (de berger).
shift [ʃɪft] ◇ *vt* -**1**. [move, put elsewhere] déplacer, bouger; it took three strong men to ~ the wardrobe il a fallu trois hommes forts pour déplacer l'armoire; help me ~ the bed nearer the window aide-moi à rapprocher le lit de OR pousser le lit vers la fenêtre; they're trying to ~ the blame onto me ils essaient de rejeter la responsabilité sur moi ‖ [part of body] bouger, remuer; she kept ~ing from one foot to the other elle n'arrêtait pas de se balancer d'un pied sur l'autre; ~ yourself! *inf* [move] pousse-toi!, bouge-toi!; [hurry] remue-toi!, grouille-toi! ‖ [employee – to new job or place of work] muter; [– to new department] affecter; THEAT [scenery] changer; he's got a job ~ing scenery il a trouvé du travail comme machiniste. -**2**. [change] changer de; they won't be ~ed from their opinion impossible de les faire changer d'avis; we're trying to ~ the balance towards exports nous essayons de mettre l'accent sur les exportations; the latest developments have ~ed attention away from this area les événements récents ont détourné l'attention de cette région; to ~ gears *Am* changer de vitesse. -**3**. [remove – stain] enlever, faire partir. -**4**. *inf* COMM [sell] écouler; how can we ~ this old stock? comment écouler OR nous débarrasser de ces vieilles marchandises?
◇ *vi* -**1**. [move] se déplacer, bouger; the cargo has ~ed in the hold la cargaison s'est déplacée dans la cale; the table won't ~, it's bolted to the floor la table ne bougera pas, elle est fixée au sol; the anticyclone is expected to ~ eastwards l'anticyclone devrait se déplacer vers l'est; could you ~ up OR along OR down a bit, please? pourrais-tu te pousser un peu, s'il te plaît? -**2**. [change, switch – gen] changer; [– wind] tourner; their policy has ~ed over the last week leur politique a changé OR s'est modifiée au cours de la semaine; in the second act the scene ~s to Venice dans le deuxième acte, l'action se déroule à Venise; to ~ into third/fourth (gear) *Am* AUT passer en troisième/quatrième (vitesse). -**3**. *inf* [travel fast] filer; he was really ~ing il fonçait carrément. -**4**. [manage]: to ~ for o.s. se débrouiller tout seul; he's had to learn to ~ for himself since his wife left il a dû apprendre à se débrouiller tout seul depuis le départ de sa femme. -**5**. [stain] partir, s'enlever. -**6**. *inf Br* COMM [sell] se vendre; those TVs just aren't ~ing at all ces télévisions ne se vendent pas du tout.
◇ *n* -**1**. [change] changement *m*; a ~ in position/opinion un changement de position/d'avis; there was a sudden ~ in public opinion/the situation il y a eu un revirement d'opinion/de situation; there was a light ~ in the wind le vent a légèrement tourné; a ~ in meaning LING un glissement de sens ❑ (gear) ~ *Am* AUT changement *m* de vitesse; vowel/consonant ~ mutation *f* vocalique/consonantique. -**2**. [move] déplacement *m*; there's been a ~ of population towards the towns on a assisté à un déplacement de la population vers les villes; get a ~ on! *inf* grouille-toi!, magne-toi! -**3**. [turn, relay] relais *m*; to do sthg in ~s se relayer; there was a lot of work so they did it in ~s comme il y avait beaucoup de travail, ils se sont relayés (pour le faire); I'm exhausted, can you take a ~ at the wheel? je suis épuisé, peux-tu me relayer au volant? -**4**. INDUST [period of time] poste *m*, équipe *f*; what ~ are you on this week? à quel poste avez-vous été affecté cette semaine?; I'm on the night/morning ~ je suis dans l'équipe de nuit/du matin; she works long ~s elle fait de longues journées; he's on eight-hour ~s il fait les trois-huit; to work ~s, to be on ~s travailler en équipe, faire les trois-huit ‖ [group of workers] équipe *f*, brigade *f*; when does OR do the morning ~ arrive? à quelle heure arrive l'équipe du matin? -**5**. *dated* [expedient] expédient *m*; to make ~ with sthg se contenter de qqch. -**6**. *Br dated* OR *Am* [woman's slip] combinaison *f*; [dress] (robe *f*) fourreau *m*. -**7**. COMPUT [in arithmetical operation] décalage *m*; [in word processing, telegraphy etc] touche *f* de majuscule; press ~ appuyer sur la touche majuscule. -**8**. *Am* AUTO = **shift stick**.
◆ **shift over** *inf*, **shift up** *inf vi insep* se pousser, se déplacer; can you ~ over OR up a bit? tu peux te pousser un peu?
shifter [ˈʃɪftəʳ] *n Am* AUT levier *m* de changement de vitesse.
shiftily [ˈʃɪftɪlɪ] *adv* sournoisement.
shiftiness [ˈʃɪftɪnɪs] *n* sournoiserie *f*.
shifting [ˈʃɪftɪŋ] *adj* [ideas, opinions] changeant; [alliances] instable; [ground, sand] mouvant.
shift key *n* touche *f* de majuscule.
shiftless [ˈʃɪftlɪs] *adj* [lazy] paresseux, fainéant; [apathetic] apathique, mou; [helpless] sans ressource, perdu.
shiftlessness [ˈʃɪftlɪsnɪs] *n* [laziness] paresse *f*, fainéantise *f*; [apathy] apathie *f*, mollesse *f*; [helplessness] absence *f* de ressources.
shift lock *n* touche *f* de blocage des majuscules.
shift stick *n Am* AUTO levier *m* de (changement de) vitesse.
shift work *n* travail *m* en équipe; she does ~ elle fait les trois-huit.
shift worker *n personne qui fait les trois-huit*.
shifty *inf* [ˈʃɪftɪ] (*compar* shiftier, *superl* shiftiest) *adj* [look] sournois, furtif, fuyant; he looks a ~ customer *inf* il a l'air louche.
Shiism [ˈʃiːɪzm] *n* chiisme *m*.
Shiite [ˈʃiːaɪt] ◇ *n*: ~ (Muslim) chiite *mf*.
◇ *adj* chiite.
shillelagh [ʃɪˈleɪlɪ] *n* gourdin *m*.
shilling [ˈʃɪlɪŋ] *n* -**1**. *Br* shilling *m (ancienne pièce valant 12 pence, soit un vingtième de livre)*. -**2**. [in Kenya, Tanzania etc] shilling *m*.
shilly-shally *inf* [ˈʃɪlɪˌʃælɪ] (*pt* & *pp* shilly-shallied) *vi pej* hésiter; stop ~ing (around) décide-toi enfin!
shilly-shallying *inf* [ˈʃɪlɪˌʃælɪɪŋ] *n (U) pej* hésitations *fpl*, valse-hésitation *f*; after a lot of ~ they eventually came to an agreement après une longue valse-hésitation ils ont fini par se mettre d'accord.
shim [ʃɪm] *n* TECH rondelle *f* de calage, cale *f*.
shimmer [ˈʃɪməʳ] ◇ *vi* [sequins, jewellery, silk] chatoyer, scintiller; [water] miroiter; the sea ~ed in the moonlight, the moonlight ~ed on the sea la mer miroitait au clair de lune; the pavements ~ed in the heat l'air tremblait au-dessus des trottoirs brûlants.
◇ *n* [of sequins, jewellery, silk] chatoiement *m*, scintillement *m*; [of water] miroitement *m*.
shimmering [ˈʃɪmərɪŋ] *adj* [light] scintillant; [jewellery, silk] chatoyant; [water] miroitant.
shimmy [ˈʃɪmɪ] (*pl* shimmies, *pt* & *pp* shimmied) ◇ *n* -**1**. [dance] shimmy *m*; to do the ~ danser le shimmy. -**2**. *Am* AUT shimmy *m*, flottement *m* des roues directrices.
◇ *vi* -**1**. [dance] danser le shimmy. -**2**. *Am* AUT avoir du shimmy; at speed it tends to ~ la direction a tendance à flotter à grande vitesse.
shin [ʃɪn] (*pt* & *pp* shinned) ◇ *n* -**1**. ANAT tibia *m*; she kicked him in the ~s elle lui a donné un coup de pied dans les tibias. -**2**. CULIN [of beef] gîte *m* OR gîte-gîte *m* (de bœuf); [of veal] jarret *m* (de veau).
◇ *vi* grimper; to ~ (up) a lamp post grimper à un réverbère; he shinned to the top of the mast il a grimpé au sommet du mât; I shinned down the drainpipe je suis descendu le long de la gouttière.
shinbone [ˈʃɪnbəʊn] *n* tibia *m*.
shindig *inf* [ˈʃɪndɪg] *n* -**1**. [party] (grande) fête *f*; we had a real ~ last night on a fait une sacrée java hier soir. -**2**. [fuss] tapage *m*; he kicked up a real ~ il a fait un sacré tapage.
shine [ʃaɪn] (*pt* & *pp all senses of vi, sense 1 of vt* shone [ʃɒn], *sense 2 of vt* shined) ◇ *vi* -**1**. [sun, moon, lamp, candle] briller; [surface, glass, hair] briller, luire; the sun was shining le soleil brillait, il y avait du soleil; the sun was shining in my eyes j'avais le soleil dans les yeux, le soleil m'éblouissait; there was a light shining in the window une lumière brillait à la fenêtre; bright light shone from the window une lumière vive brillait à la fenêtre; a small desk lamp shone on the table une petite lampe de bureau éclairait la table; his eyes shone with excitement ses yeux brillaient OR son regard brillait d'émotion; her face shone with joy son visage rayonnait de joie. -**2**. [excel] briller; John ~s at sports John est très bon en sport.
◇ *vt* -**1**. [focus] braquer, diriger; the guard shone his torch on the prisoner le gardien a braqué sa lampe sur le prisonnier; don't ~ that lamp in my eyes ne m'éblouis pas avec cette lampe. -**2**. [polish] faire briller, faire reluire, astiquer.
◇ *n* -**1**. [polished appearance] éclat *m*, brillant *m*, lustre *m*; to put a ~ on sthg, to give sthg a ~ faire reluire OR briller qqch; to take the ~ off sthg faire perdre son éclat à qqch, ternir qqch ❑ to take a ~ to sb *inf* [take a liking to] se prendre d'amitié pour qqn; [get a crush on] s'enticher de qqn. -**2**. [polish] polissage *m*; your shoes need a ~ tes chaussures ont besoin d'un coup de brosse OR chiffon.
◆ **shine down** *vi insep* briller; the hot sun shone down on us le soleil tapait dur.
◆ **shine out, shine through** *vi insep* [light] jaillir; *fig* [courage, skill, generosity] rayonner,

briller; she ~s out from the others in the class elle dépasse tous ses camarades de classe de la tête et des épaules.

◆ **shine up to** *inf vt insep Am* faire de la lèche à.

shiner *inf* ['ʃaɪnəʳ] *n* [black eye] coquart *m*, œil *m* au beurre noir.

shingle ['ʃɪŋgl] ◇ *n* -**1.** *(U)* [pebbles] galets *mpl*; ~ beach plage *f* de galets. -**2.** CONSTR [for roofing] bardeau *m*, aisseau *m*; ~ roof toit *m* en bardeaux. -**3.** *Am* [nameplate] plaque *f*. -**4.** [haircut] coupe *f* à la garçonne.

◇ *vt* -**1.** [roof] couvrir de bardeaux OR d'aisseaux. -**2.** [hair] couper à la garçonne.

shingles ['ʃɪŋglz] *n (U)* MED zona *m*.

shingly ['ʃɪŋglɪ] *adj* [ground] couvert de galets; [beach] de galets.

shinguard ['ʃɪngɑːd] = **shinpad**.

shininess ['ʃaɪnɪnɪs] *n* éclat *m*, brillant *m*.

shining ['ʃaɪnɪŋ] ◇ *adj* -**1.** [gleaming - glass, metal, shoes] luisant, reluisant; [- eyes] brillant; [- face] rayonnant. -**2.** [outstanding] éclatant, remarquable; a ~ example of bravery un modèle de courage; John is a ~ example to us all John est un modèle pour nous tous.

◇ *n*: 'The Shining' *Kubrick* 'Shining'.

shinny ['ʃɪnɪ] *(pt & pp* shinnied) *Am* = **shin** *vi*.

shinpad ['ʃɪnpæd] *n* jambière *f*.

Shinto ['ʃɪntəʊ] ◇ *n* shinto *m*.

◇ *adj* shintoïste.

Shintoism ['ʃɪntəʊɪzm] *n* shintoïsme *m*.

Shintoist ['ʃɪntəʊɪst] ◇ *adj* shintoïste.

◇ *n* shintoïste *mf*.

shinty ['ʃɪntɪ] *n sorte de hockey sur gazon d'origine écossaise*.

shiny ['ʃaɪnɪ] *(compar* shinier, *superl* shiniest) *adj* -**1.** [gleaming - glass, metal, shoes] luisant, reluisant; my nose is ~ j'ai le nez qui brille. -**2.** [clothing - with wear] lustré; ~ at the elbows lustré aux coudes.

ship [ʃɪp] *(pt & pp* shipped) ◇ *n* -**1.** NAUT navire *m*, vaisseau *m*, bateau *m*; on board OR aboard ~ à bord; the ~'s company l'équipage *m*; the ~'s papers les papiers *mpl* de bord ❑ merchant ~ navire *m* marchand OR de commerce; sailing ~ bateau *m* à voiles, voilier *m*; the ~ of the desert le vaisseau du désert; the ~ of State le char de l'État; when my ~ comes in OR home *inf* [money] quand je serai riche, quand j'aurai fait fortune; [success] quand j'aurai réussi dans la vie. -**2.** [airship] dirigeable *m*; [spaceship] vaisseau *m* (spatial).

◇ *vt* -**1.** [send by ship] expédier (par bateau OR par mer); [carry by ship] transporter (par bateau OR par mer); we're having most of our luggage shipped nous expédions la plupart de nos bagages par bateau. -**2.** [send by any means] expédier; [carry by any means] transporter; the goods will be shipped by train [sent] les marchandises seront expédiées par le train; [transported] les marchandises seront transportées par chemin de fer. -**3.** [embark - passengers, cargo] embarquer. -**4.** [take into boat - gangplank, oars] rentrer; [- water] embarquer.

◇ *vi* [passengers, crew] embarquer, s'embarquer.

◆ **ship off** *inf vt sep* expédier; we've shipped the kids off to their grandparents' nous avons expédié les gosses chez leurs grands-parents.

shipboard ['ʃɪpbɔːd] ◇ *n*: on ~ à bord (d'un navire).

◇ *adj* [romance, drama] qui a lieu à bord d'un navire.

ship broker *n* courtier *m* maritime.

shipbuilder ['ʃɪp,bɪldəʳ] *n* constructeur *m*, -trice *f* de navires.

shipbuilding ['ʃɪp,bɪldɪŋ] *n* construction *f* navale; the ~ industry (l'industrie *f* de) la construction navale.

ship canal *n* canal *m* maritime.

shipload ['ʃɪpləʊd] *n* cargaison *f*, fret *m*.

shipmaster ['ʃɪp,mɑːstəʳ] *n* capitaine *m*, commandant *m*.

shipmate ['ʃɪpmeɪt] *n* compagnon *m* de bord.

shipment ['ʃɪpmənt] *n* -**1.** [cargo, goods sent] cargaison *f*; arms ~ cargaison d'armes. -**2.** [sending of goods] expédition *f*.

shipowner ['ʃɪp,əʊnəʳ] *n* armateur *m*.

shipper ['ʃɪpəʳ] *n* [charterer] affréteur *m*, chargeur *m*; [transporter] transporteur *m*; [sender] expéditeur *m*, -trice *f*.

shipping ['ʃɪpɪŋ] ◇ *n (U)* -**1.** [ships] navires *mpl*; [traffic] navigation *f*; dangerous to ~ dangereux pour la navigation; ~ has been warned to steer clear of the area on a prévenu les navires qu'il fallait éviter le secteur; the decline of British merchant ~ le déclin de la marine marchande britannique. -**2.** [transport - gen] transport *m*; [- by sea] transport *m* maritime; cost includes ~ le coût du transport est compris. -**3.** [loading] chargement *m*, embarquement *m*.

◇ *comp* [company, line] maritime, de navigation; [sport, trade, intelligence] maritime; ~ forecast météo *f* OR météorologie *f* marine.

shipping agent *n* agent *m* maritime.

shipping clerk *n* expéditionnaire *mf*.

shipping lane *n* voie *f* de navigation.

ship's biscuit *n* biscuit *m* de mer.

ship's chandler *n* shipchandler *m*, marchand *m*, -e *f* d'articles de marine.

shipshape ['ʃɪpʃeɪp] *adj* en ordre, rangé; let's try to get this place ~ essayons de mettre un peu d'ordre ici ❑ all ~ and Bristol fashion! *inf hum* tout est impeccable!

shipwreck ['ʃɪprek] ◇ *n* -**1.** [disaster at sea] naufrage *m*; they died in a ~ ils ont péri dans un naufrage. -**2.** [wrecked ship] épave *f*.

◇ *vt* -**1.** to be ~ed [boat] faire naufrage; [passenger, crew] être naufragé; they were ~ed on a desert island ils ont échoué sur une île déserte; a ~ed sailor un marin naufragé. -**2.** *fig & literal* [ruin, spoil] ruiner.

shipwright ['ʃɪpraɪt] *n* [company] constructeur *m* de navires; [worker] ouvrier *m*, -ère *f* de chantier naval.

shipyard ['ʃɪpjɑːd] *n* chantier *m* naval; hundreds of ~ workers were sacked des centaines d'ouvriers des chantiers navals ont été licenciés.

shire ['ʃaɪəʳ] *n Br* -**1.** [county] comté *m*. -**2.** = **shire horse**.

◆ **Shires** *pl pr n*: the Shires *les comtés (ruraux) du centre de l'Angleterre*.

shire horse *n* shire *m*.

shirk [ʃɜːk] ◇ *vt* [work, job, task] éviter de faire, échapper à; [duty] se dérober à; [problem, difficulty, question] esquiver, éviter; he always ~s doing the washing-up il s'arrange toujours pour éviter de OR ne pas faire la vaisselle; she doesn't ~ her responsibilities elle n'essaie pas de se dérober à ses responsabilités.

◇ *vi* tirer au flanc.

shirker ['ʃɜːkəʳ] *n* tire-au-flanc *mf inv*.

shirr [ʃɜːʳ] *vt* -**1.** SEW froncer. -**2.** *Am* CULIN: ~ed eggs œufs *mpl* en ramequin.

shirring ['ʃɜːrɪŋ] *n* SEW fronces *fpl*.

shirt [ʃɜːt] *n* [gen] chemise *f*; [footballer's etc] maillot *m*; ~ collar/cuff col *m*/manchette *f* de chemise ❑ keep your ~ on! *inf* ne vous énervez pas!; to lose one's ~ *inf* y laisser sa chemise, perdre tout ce qu'on a; to put one's ~ on sthg miser toute sa fortune sur qqch.

shirtfront ['ʃɜːtfrʌnt] *n* plastron *m*.

shirting ['ʃɜːtɪŋ] *n* shirting *m*, tissu *m* pour chemises.

shirtless ['ʃɜːtlɪs] *adj* sans chemise.

shirt-sleeved *adj* en manches OR bras de chemise.

shirtsleeves ['ʃɜːtsliːvz] *npl*: to be in (one's) ~ être en manches OR bras de chemise.

shirttail ['ʃɜːtteɪl] *n* pan *m* de chemise.

shirtwaister ['ʃɜːt,weɪstəʳ] *Br*, **shirtwaist** ['ʃɜːtweɪst] *Am n* robe *f* chemisier.

shirty *inf* ['ʃɜːtɪ] *(compar* shirtier, *superl* shirtiest) *adj Br* désagréable; don't get ~ with me ne te mets pas en rogne contre moi.

shish kebab ['ʃɪʃkə,bæb] *n* chiche-kebab *m*.

shit▼ [ʃɪt] *(pt & pp* shat [ʃæt], *cont* shitting) ◇ *n* -**1.** [excrement] merde *f*; to have a ~ (aller) chier; to have the ~s avoir la chiasse ❑ dog ~ merde de chien; tough ~! tant pis pour ma/ta/sa *etc* gueule!; to kick OR to beat OR to knock the ~ out of sb casser la gueule à qqn; to scare the ~ out of sb foutre la trouille à qqn; I don't give a ~ je m'en fous, j'en ai rien à foutre; to give sb a lot of ~ faire chier qqn; to be in the ~ être dans la merde; no ~? *Am* sans blague?; when the ~ hits the fan quand nous serons dans la merde (jusqu'au cou). -**2.** *(U)* [nonsense, rubbish] conneries *fpl*; that's a load of ~! c'est des conneries, tout ça!; don't give me that ~! arrête tes conneries! -**3.** [disliked person] salaud *m*, salope *f*, connard *m*, connasse *f*. -**4.** *drugs sl* [hashish] shit *m*, hasch *m*. -**5.** *Am* [anything]: I can't see ~ j'y vois que dalle; that doesn't mean ~ ça veut rien dire.

◇ *vi* chier.

◇ *vt*: to ~ oneself chier dans son froc.

◇ *interj* merde.

shite▼ [ʃaɪt] = **shit**.

shithead▼ ['ʃɪthed] *n* [disliked person] salaud *m*, salope *f*.

shit-hot▼ *adj Am* vachement bon; he's ~ as an actor il est vachement bon comme acteur.

shithouse▼ ['ʃɪthaʊs, *pl* -haʊzɪz] *n* chiottes *fpl*.

shitless▼ ['ʃɪtlɪs] *adj*: to be scared ~ avoir une trouille bleue; to be bored ~ se faire chier à mort.

shit-scared▼ *adj*: to be ~ chier dans son froc.

shitty▼ ['ʃɪtɪ] *(compar* shittier, *superl* shittiest) *adj* -**1.** [worthless] merdique; we stayed in a really ~ hotel nous sommes descendus dans un hôtel vraiment merdique. -**2.** [mean] dégueulasse; what a ~ thing to do! c'est dégueulasse de faire ça!

shiv▽ [ʃɪv] *n crime sl* surin *m*.

shiver ['ʃɪvəʳ] ◇ *vi* -**1.** [with cold, fever, fear] grelotter, trembler; [with excitement] frissonner, trembler. -**2.** NAUT [sail] faseyer. -**3.** [splinter] se fracasser, voler en éclats.

◇ *n* -**1.** [from cold, fever, fear] frisson *m*, tremblement *m*; [from excitement] frisson *m*; it gives me the ~s *inf* ça me donne le frisson OR des frissons. -**2.** [fragment] éclat *m*.

shivery ['ʃɪvərɪ] *adj* [cold] frissonnant; [frightened] frissonnant, tremblant; [feverish] fiévreux, grelottant de fièvre.

shoal [ʃəʊl] ◇ *n* -**1.** [of fish] banc *m*. -**2.** *fig* [large numbers] foule *f*; ~s of tourists une foule de touristes. -**3.** [shallows] haut-fond *m*. -**4.** [sandbar] barre *f*; [sandbank] banc *m* de sable.

◇ *vi* [fish] se mettre OR se rassembler en bancs.

shock [ʃɒk] ◇ *n* -**1.** [surprise] choc *m*, surprise *f*; she got a ~ when she saw me again ça lui a fait un choc de me revoir; what a ~ you gave me! qu'est-ce que tu m'as fait peur! -**2.** [upset] choc *m*; that comes as no ~ to me ça ne m'étonne pas; it's all been a bit of a ~ for us tous ces événements nous ont bouleversés; the news of his death came as a terrible ~ to me la nouvelle de sa mort a été un grand choc pour moi. -**3.** ELEC décharge *f* (électrique); to get a ~ recevoir OR prendre une décharge (électrique); I got a nasty ~ from the toaster j'ai pris une sacrée décharge en touchant le grille-pain. -**4.** [impact - of vehicles, armies] choc *m*, heurt *m*; [vibration - from explosion, earthquake] secousse *f*. -**5.** MED choc *m*; to be in a state of ~, to be suffering from ~ être en état de choc; post-operative ~ choc postopératoire. -**6.** [bushy mass]: a ~ of hair une crinière *fig*.

◇ *comp* [measures, argument, headline] choc *(inv)*; [attack] surprise *(inv)*; [tactics] de choc; [result, defeat] inattendu.

◇ *vt* -**1.** [stun] stupéfier, bouleverser, secouer; I was ~ed to hear that she had left j'ai été stupéfait d'apprendre qu'elle était partie; she was deeply ~ed by her daughter's death elle a été profondément bouleversée par la mort de sa fille. -**2.** [offend, scandalize] choquer, scandaliser; his behaviour ~ed them son comportement les a choqués OR scandalisés; I'm not easily ~ed, but that book... il en faut beaucoup pour me choquer, mais ce livre... -**3.** [incite, force]: to ~ sb out of sthg secouer qqn pour le sortir de qqch; to ~ sb into action pousser qqn à agir; to ~ sb into doing sthg secouer qqn jusqu'à ce qu'il fasse qqch. -**4.** ELEC donner une secousse OR un choc électrique à.

shock absorber *n* amortisseur *m*.

shocked [ʃɒkt] *adj* -**1.** [stunned] bouleversé, stupéfait; a ~ meeting was told of the takeover c'est avec stupéfaction que l'assemblée a appris le rachat de l'entreprise; they all listened in ~ silence ils ont tous écouté, muets de stupéfaction. -**2.** [offended, scandalized] choqué, scandalisé; I tried to look suitably ~ je me suis efforcée de prendre un air scandalisé; she spoke in ~ tones elle parlait d'un ton scandalisé.

shocker *inf* ['ʃɒkəʳ] *n* -**1.** [book] livre *m* à sensation; [film] film *m* à sensation; [news] nouvelle *f* sensationnelle; [play] pièce *f* à sensation; [story] histoire *f* sensationnelle; that's a real ~ of a story cette histoire est vraiment choquante. -**2.** *hum* [atrocious person]: you little ~! petit monstre!

shockheaded ['ʃɒkhedɪd] *adj* hirsute.

shocking ['ʃɒkɪŋ] ◇ *adj* -**1.** [scandalous] scandaleux, choquant; a ~ price un prix scandaleux; it's ~ the way he behaves son comportement est scandaleux, sa conduite est scandaleuse; a ~ new film un nouveau film scandaleux. -**2.** [horrifying] atroce, épouvantable; a ~ crime un crime affreux OR atroce. -**3.** *inf* [very bad] affreux, épouvantable; you look ~ today tu as une mine affreuse aujourd'hui; his room is in a ~ state sa chambre est dans un état épouvantable; ~ weather, isn't it? quel temps affreux OR épouvantable!; he's a ~ actor il est nul comme acteur; I'm ~ at football je suis nul au football.
◇ *adv inf*: it was raining something ~! il fallait voir ce qu'il OR comme ça tombait!

shockingly ['ʃɒkɪŋlɪ] *adv* -**1.** [as intensifier] affreusement, atrocement; this whisky is ~ expensive ce whisky est affreusement cher; the weather has been ~ bad lately la météo est vraiment affreuse depuis quelque temps. -**2.** [extremely badly] très mal, lamentablement; he played ~ on Saturday il a très mal joué samedi.

shocking pink ◇ *n* rose *m* bonbon.
◇ *adj* rose bonbon *(inv)*.

shockproof ['ʃɒkpru:f] *adj* résistant aux chocs.

shock therapy, shock treatment *n* MED (traitement *m* par) électrochoc *m*, sismothérapie *f*.

shock troops *npl* troupes *fpl* de choc.

shock wave *n* onde *f* de choc; *fig* répercussion *f*.

shod [ʃɒd] *pt* & *pp* → **shoe**.

shoddily ['ʃɒdɪlɪ] *adv* -**1.** [built, made] mal. -**2.** [meanly, pettily] de façon mesquine; they've treated you ~ ils ont été mesquins avec vous.

shoddiness ['ʃɒdɪnɪs] *n* -**1.** [poor quality] mauvaise qualité *f*. -**2.** [meanness, pettiness] mesquinerie *f*.

shoddy ['ʃɒdɪ] (*compar* shoddier, *superl* shoddiest) ◇ *adj* -**1.** [of inferior quality] de mauvaise qualité; ~ workmanship du travail mal fait; a ~ imitation une piètre OR médiocre imitation. -**2.** [mean, petty] sale; that's a ~ trick to play on her! on lui a joué un sale tour!; I want no part in that ~ affair je ne veux pas être mêlé à cette sale affaire.
◇ *n* tissu *m* shoddy OR de renaissance.

shoe [ʃu:] (*pt* & *pp* shod [ʃɒd]) ◇ *n* -**1.** [gen] chaussure *f*; a pair of ~s une paire de chaussures; a man's/woman's ~ une chaussure d'homme/de femme; to take off one's ~s enlever ses chaussures, se déchausser; to put on one's ~s mettre ses chaussures, se chausser ❑ ~ size pointure *f*; I wouldn't like to be in his ~s je n'aimerais pas être à sa place; put yourself in my ~s mettez-vous à ma place; to step into OR to fill sb's ~s prendre la place de qqn, succéder à qqn; if the ~ fits (, wear it) qui se sent morveux (qu'il) se mouche *prov*. -**2.** (horse) ~ fer *m* (à cheval). -**3.** AUT: (brake) ~ sabot *m* (de frein). -**4.** [in casino - for baccarat etc] sabot *m*. -**5.** [on electric train] frotteur *m*.
◇ *comp* [cream, leather] pour chaussures.
◇ *vt* -**1.** [horse] ferrer. -**2.** *(usu pass) lit* [person] chausser; John was shod in sandals John était chaussé de OR portait des sandales.

shoeblack ['ʃu:blæk] *n dated* cireur *m*, -euse *f* (de chaussures).

shoe box *n* boîte *f* à chaussures.

shoebrush ['ʃu:brʌʃ] *n* brosse *f* à chaussures.

shoehorn ['ʃu:hɔ:n] *n* chausse-pied *m*.

shoelace ['ʃu:leɪs] *n* lacet *m* (de chaussures); your ~ is undone ton lacet est défait.

shoe leather *n* cuir *m* pour chaussures; save your ~ and take the bus prenez l'autobus au lieu d'user vos souliers.

shoemaker ['ʃu:,meɪkəʳ] *n* [cobbler] cordonnier *m*; [manufacturer] fabricant *m*, -e *f* de chaussures, chausseur *m*.

shoe polish *n* cirage *m*.

shoeshine ['ʃu:ʃaɪn] *n* -**1.** cirage *m*; to get a ~ se faire cirer les chaussures. -**2.** *inf* = **shoeshine boy**.

shoeshine boy *n* (petit) cireur *m* (de chaussures).

shoeshop ['ʃu:ʃɒp] *n* magasin *m* de chaussures; I was in the ~ j'étais chez le marchand de chaussures.

shoestring ['ʃu:strɪŋ] ◇ *n* -**1.** *Am* [shoelace] lacet *m* (de chaussure). -**2.** *inf phr*: on a ~ avec trois fois rien; the film was made on a ~ c'est un film à très petit budget; cookery on a ~ la cuisine économique OR bon marché.
◇ *comp*: ~ budget petit budget *m*.

shoetree ['ʃu:tri:] *n* embauchoir *m*.

shone [ʃɒn] *pt* & *pp* → **shine**.

shoo [ʃu:] (*pt* & *pp* shooed) ◇ *interj* oust, ouste.
◇ *vt* chasser; to ~ sb/sthg away chasser qqn/qqch.

shoo-in *inf n Am*: he's/she's a ~ il/elle gagnera à coup sûr; it's a ~ *inf* c'est couru d'avance.

shook [ʃʊk] ◇ *pt* → **shake**.
◇ *n* AGR gerbe *f*, botte *f*.

shook-up *inf adj* bouleversé.

shoot [ʃu:t] (*pt* & *pp* shot [ʃɒt]) ◇ *vi* -**1.** [with gun] tirer; ~! tirez!, feu!; don't ~! ne tirez pas!; ~ first and ask questions later tirez d'abord et posez des questions ensuite; to ~ at sb/sthg tirer sur qqn/qqch; to ~ on sight tirer à vue; to ~ to kill tirer pour tuer; to ~ into the air tirer en l'air; to ~ back (at sb) retourner le feu (à qqn). -**2.** [hunt] chasser; to go ~ing aller à la chasse; do you ~? est-ce que vous chassez? -**3.** [go fast]: she shot across the road elle a traversé la rue comme une flèche; I shot out after her j'ai couru après elle; he shot ahead of the other runners il a rapidement distancé les autres coureurs; she shot along the corridor elle a couru à toutes jambes le long du couloir; the bus was ~ing along le bus filait à toute vitesse; ~ along to the baker's and get a loaf, will you? est-ce que tu peux filer à la boulangerie acheter du pain?; the rabbit shot into its burrow le lapin s'est précipité dans son terrier; the car shot out in front of us [changed lanes] la voiture a déboîté tout d'un coup devant nous; [from another street] la voiture a débouché devant nous; the water shot out of the hose l'eau a jailli du tuyau d'arrosage; debris shot into the air des débris ont été projetés en l'air; Paul has shot ahead at school recently Paul a fait d'énormes progrès à l'école ces derniers temps; a violent pain shot up my leg j'ai senti une violente douleur dans la jambe. -**4.** CIN tourner; ~! moteur!, on tourne!; we'll begin ~ing next week nous commencerons à tourner la semaine prochaine. -**5.** SPORT tirer, shooter. -**6.** *inf* [go ahead, speak]: may I ask you something? — ~! puis-je vous poser une question? — allez-y! -**7.** BOT [sprout] pousser; [bud] bourgeonner. -**8.** *Am*: to ~ for OR at [aim for] viser.
◇ *vt* -**1.** [hit] atteindre; [injure] blesser; he's been badly shot il a été grièvement blessé par balle OR balles; she was shot in the arm/leg elle a reçu une balle dans le bras/la jambe ‖ [kill] abattre, descendre, tuer (d'un coup de pistolet OR de fusil); to ~ o.s. se tuer, se tirer une balle; they shot him (dead) ils l'ont tué OR abattu; don't ~ the pianist ne tirez pas sur le pianiste ‖ [execute by firing squad] fusiller; spies will be shot les espions seront fusillés ❑ you'll get me shot *inf hum* je vais me faire incendier à cause de toi; to ~ o.s. in the foot *inf* ramasser une pelle; 'They Shoot Horses, Don't They?' *Pollack* 'On achève bien les chevaux'. -**2.** [fire - gun] tirer un coup de; [- bullet] tirer; [- arrow] tirer, lancer, décocher; [- rocket, dart, missile] lancer; they were ~ing their rifles in the air ils tiraient des coups de feu en l'air; to ~ it out with sb *inf* s'expliquer avec qqn à coups de revolver OR de fusil; to ~ questions at sb *fig* bombarder OR mitrailler qqn de questions; she shot a shy smile at him *fig* elle lui jeta un petit sourire timide. -**3.** [hunt] chasser, tirer; to ~ grouse chasser la grouse. -**4.** CIN tourner; the film was shot in Rome le film a été tourné à Rome ‖ PHOT prendre (en photo); the photos were all shot on location in Paris les photos ont toutes été prises à Paris. -**5.** GAMES & SPORT [play] jouer; to ~ pool jouer au billard américain; to ~ dice jouer aux dés ‖ [score] marquer; to ~ a goal/basket marquer un but/panier; he shot 71 in the first round GOLF il a fait 71 au premier tour. -**6.** [send] envoyer; the explosion shot debris high into the air l'explosion a projeté des débris dans les airs; she shot out a hand elle a étendu le bras d'un geste vif. -**7.** [go through - rapids] franchir; [- traffic lights]: the car shot the lights la voiture a brûlé le feu rouge. -**8.** [bolt - close] fermer; [- open] ouvrir, tirer. -**9.** *drugs sl* [drugs] se shooter à; to ~ heroin se shooter à l'héroïne. -**10.** *Am phr*: to ~ the breeze OR (the) bull *inf* tailler une bavette, discuter le bout de gras; to ~ one's wad▽ tirer son coup.
◇ *n* -**1.** BOT pousse *f*; bamboo ~s pousses de bambou. -**2.** HUNT [party] partie *f* de chasse; he went on a pheasant ~ il est allé chasser le faisan ‖ [land] (terrain *m* de) chasse *f*; to rent a ~ louer une chasse; '~ private ~' 'chasse gardée'. -**3.** *Am* [chute - for coal, rubbish etc] glissière *f*. -**4.** MIL tir *m*. -**5.** *Am* ASTRONAUT tir *m*, lancement *m*. -**6.** CIN tournage *m*. -**7.** *Am* [rapid] rapide *m*. -**8.** *inf phr*: the whole (bang) ~ *inf* tout le tremblement.
◇ *interj inf Am* zut, mince.

◆ **shoot down** *vt sep* [person, plane, helicopter] abattre; my proposal was shot down by the chairman *inf* ma proposition a été démolie par le président ❑ to ~ sb/sthg down in flames *literal* & *fig* descendre qqn/qqch en flammes; well, ~ me down! if it isn't Willy Power! *inf Am* ça alors! mais c'est Willy Power!

◆ **shoot off** ◇ *vi insep* s'enfuir à toutes jambes; he shot off down the alley il s'est enfui à toutes jambes dans la ruelle.
◇ *vt sep* -**1.** [weapon] tirer, décharger; they shot off their rifles to celebrate their victory ils ont tiré des coups de feu en l'air pour fêter la victoire. -**2.** [limb] emporter, arracher. -**3.** *phr*: to ~ one's mouth off *inf* ouvrir le bec; don't go ~ing your mouth off about it ne va pas le crier sur les toits; they killed him to stop him ~ing his mouth off to the police ils l'ont tué pour l'empêcher d'aller tout raconter à la police.

◆ **shoot up** ◇ *vi insep* -**1.** [move skywards - flame, geyser, lava] jaillir; [- rocket] monter en flèche. -**2.** [increase - inflation, price] monter en flèche. -**3.** [grow] pousser rapidement OR vite; you've really shot up since I last saw you! qu'est-ce que tu as grandi depuis que je t'ai vu la dernière fois! -**4.** *drugs sl* [with drug] se shooter.
◇ *vt sep* -**1.** *inf Am* [with weapon - saloon, town] terroriser en tirant des coups de feu. -**2.** *drugs sl* [drug] se shooter à.

shooter▽ ['ʃu:təʳ] *n* [gun] flingue *m*.

shooting ['ʃu:tɪŋ] ◇ *n* -**1.** *(U)* [firing] coups *mpl* de feu, fusillade *f*; we heard a lot of ~ in the night nous avons entendu de nombreux coups de feu dans la nuit. -**2.** [incident] fusillade *f*; four people died in the ~ quatre personnes ont

trouvé la mort au cours de la fusillade || [killing] meurtre *m*; there have been several ~s in the area plusieurs personnes ont été tuées OR abattues dans le secteur. -**3.** [ability to shoot] tir *m*; he's useless at ~ il tire mal. -**4.** *Br* HUNT chasse *f*; I've done a lot of ~ j'ai beaucoup chassé. -**5.** CIN tournage *m*.
◇ *comp* -**1.** [with weapon]: ~ incident fusillade *f*; ~ practice entraînement *m* au tir. -**2.** HUNT de chasse; ~ lodge/party pavillon *m*/partie *f* de chasse; the ~ season la saison de la chasse; he's not a ~ man ce n'est pas un chasseur.
◇ *adj* [pain] lancinant.

shooting brake *n Br* AUT break *m*.

shooting gallery *n* stand *m* de tir.

shooting iron *inf n Am dated* pétoire *f*.

shooting script *n* découpage *m* CIN.

shooting star *n* étoile *f* filante.

shoot-out *inf n* fusillade *f*; there was a ~ at the saloon il y a eu une fusillade OR un règlement de comptes au bar.

shop [ʃɒp] (*pt* & *pp* shopped, *cont* shopping)
◇ *n* -**1.** *Br* [store] magasin *m*; [smaller] boutique *f*; she's gone out to the ~s elle est sortie faire des courses; to have OR to keep a ~ être propriétaire d'un magasin, tenir un magasin; would you mind the ~ for me for a few hours? est-ce que vous voulez bien me tenir le magasin pendant quelques heures? ❑ at the chemist's ~ chez le pharmacien, à la pharmacie; at the fruit ~ chez le marchand de fruits, chez le fruitier, à la fruiterie; shoe ~ marchand *m*, -e *f* de chaussures; to set up ~ *literal* ouvrir un magasin; *fig* s'établir, s'installer; he's set up ~ as a freelance translator il s'est installé comme traducteur indépendant; to shut up ~ *literal* & *fig* fermer boutique; all over the ~ *inf* [everywhere] partout; [in disorder] en pagaille; to talk ~ parler métier OR boutique. -**2.** [shopping trip]: to do one's weekly ~ faire les courses OR les achats de la semaine. -**3.** *Br* [workshop] atelier *m*; the repair/paint/assembly ~ l'atelier de réparations/de peinture/de montage.
◇ *vi* [for food, necessities] faire les OR ses courses; [for clothes, gifts etc] faire les magasins, faire du shopping; he usually ~s on Mondays d'habitude, il fait ses courses le lundi; I always ~ at the local supermarket je fais toujours mes courses OR mes achats au supermarché du coin; to go shopping faire des courses, courir les magasins; I went shopping for a new dress je suis allée faire les magasins pour m'acheter une nouvelle robe.
◇ *vt inf Br* [to the police] donner, balancer.
◆ **shop around** *vi insep* comparer les prix; prices vary a lot, so ~ around les prix varient énormément, il vaut mieux faire plusieurs magasins avant d'acheter; I shopped around before opening a bank account j'ai comparé plusieurs banques OR je me suis renseigné auprès de plusieurs banques avant d'ouvrir un compte; our company is shopping around for new premises notre société est à la recherche de nouveaux locaux.

shop assistant *n Br* vendeur *m*, -euse *f*.

shopfitter ['ʃɒp,fɪtəʳ] *n Br* décorateur *m*, -trice *f* de magasin.

shop floor *n* [place] atelier *m*; [workers]: the ~ les ouvriers *mpl*; he was on the ~ for 22 years before becoming personnel manager il a passé 22 ans comme ouvrier avant de devenir directeur du personnel.
◆ **shop-floor** *comp*: ~ worker ouvrier *m*, -ère *f*; the decision was taken at ~ level la décision a été prise par la base.

shopfront ['ʃɒpfrʌnt] *n Br* devanture *f* (de magasin).

shopgirl ['ʃɒpgɜːl] *n Br* vendeuse *f*.

shopkeeper ['ʃɒp,kiːpəʳ] *n Br* commerçant *m*, -e *f*; small ~ petit commerçant.

shoplift ['ʃɒplɪft] *vt* voler à l'étalage.

shoplifter ['ʃɒp,lɪftəʳ] *n* voleur *m*, -euse *f* à l'étalage.

shoplifting ['ʃɒp,lɪftɪŋ] *n* vol *m* à l'étalage.

shopper ['ʃɒpəʳ] *n* -**1.** [person] personne *f* qui fait ses courses; the streets were crowded with Christmas ~s les rues étaient bondées de gens qui faisaient leurs courses pour Noël. -**2.** [shopping bag] cabas *m*.

shopping ['ʃɒpɪŋ] ◇ *n* (*U*) -**1.** [for food, necessities] courses *fpl*; [for clothes, gifts etc] courses *fpl*, shopping *m*; I do all the ~ c'est moi qui fais toutes les courses; we're going into town to do some ~ nous allons en ville pour faire des courses OR pour faire le tour des magasins; this area is good for ~ ce quartier est bon pour faire les courses; to do a bit of ~ faire quelques (petites) courses OR emplettes. -**2.** [goods bought] achats *mpl*, courses *fpl*, emplettes *fpl*; there were bags of ~ everywhere il y avait des cabas remplis de provisions partout.
◇ *comp* [street, area] commerçant.

shopping bag *n* sac *m* OR filet *m* à provisions, cabas *m*.

shopping basket *n* panier *m* (à provisions).

shopping centre *n* centre *m* commercial.

shopping list *n* liste *f* des courses.

shopping mall *n Am* centre *m* commercial.

shopping trolley *n* chariot *m*.

shopsoiled ['ʃɒpsɔɪld] *adj Br literal* & *fig* défraîchi.

shoptalk ['ʃɒptɔːk] *n*: all I ever hear from you is ~ tu ne fais que parler boutique OR travail.

shopwalker ['ʃɒp,wɔːkəʳ] *n Br* chef *m* de rayon.

shop window *n* vitrine *f* (de magasin); a ~ for British exports *fig* une vitrine pour les exportations britanniques.

shopworn ['ʃɒpwɔːn] *Am* = **shopsoiled**.

shore [ʃɔːʳ] ◇ *n* -**1.** [edge, side - of sea] rivage *m*, bord *m*; [- of lake, river] rive *f*, rivage *m*, bord *m*; [coast] côte *f*, littoral *m*; the ~s of the Mediterranean les rivages de la Méditerranée; can you see the houses on the other ~? vois-tu les maisons sur l'autre rive? || [dry land] terre *f*; all the crew members are on ~ tous les membres de l'équipage sont à terre; to go on ~ débarquer. -**2.** [prop] étai *m*, étançon *m*.
◇ *vt* étayer, étançonner.
◆ **shores** *npl lit* [country] rives *fpl*; he was one of the first Europeans to set foot on these ~s il fut l'un des premiers Européens à poser le pied sur ces rives.
◆ **shore up** *vt sep Br*. -**1.** *literal* étayer, étançonner. -**2.** *fig* étayer, appuyer, consolider; the army ~d up the crumbling dictatorship l'armée a maintenu au pouvoir la dictature qui s'effondrait; the government must act to ~ up the pound le gouvernement doit prendre des mesures visant à renforcer la livre.

shorebird ['ʃɔːbɜːd] *n* oiseau *m* des rivages.

shore crab *n* crabe *m* vert OR enragé.

shore leave *n* permission *f* à terre.

shoreline ['ʃɔːlaɪn] *n* littoral *m*.

shore patrol *n Am* police *f* militaire (de la Marine).

shoreward ['ʃɔːwəd] ◇ *adj* [near the shore] près du rivage OR de la côte; [facing the shore] face au rivage OR à la côte.
◇ *adv* = **shorewards**.

shorewards ['ʃɔːwədz] *adv* vers le rivage OR la côte.

shorn [ʃɔːn] ◇ *pp* → **shear**.
◇ *adj* -**1.** [head, hair] tondu. -**2.** *fig*: ~ of dépouillé de.

short [ʃɔːt] ◇ *adj* -**1.** [in length] court; her dress is too ~/~er than yours sa robe est trop courte/plus courte que la tienne; to have ~ hair avoir les cheveux courts; to be ~ in the leg [trousers] être court; skirts are getting ~er and ~er les jupes raccourcissent de plus en plus OR sont de plus en plus courtes; the editor made the article ~er by a few hundred words le rédacteur a raccourci l'article de quelques centaines de mots; to win/to lose by a ~ head SPORT gagner/perdre d'une courte tête; she made a ~ speech elle a fait un court OR petit discours; he read out a ~ statement il a lu une courte OR brève déclaration; I'd just like to say a few ~ words j'aimerais dire quelques mots très brefs; ~ and to the point bref et précis ❑ ~ and sweet *inf* court mais bien; to be in ~ trousers être en culottes courtes. -**2.** [in distance] court, petit; a straight line is the ~est distance between two points la ligne droite est le chemin le plus court entre deux points; what's the ~est way home? quel est le chemin le plus court pour rentrer?; it's ~er this way c'est plus court par ici; we took the ~est route nous avons pris le chemin le plus court; to go for a ~ walk faire une petite promenade; a few ~ miles away à quelques kilomètres de là à peine; at ~ range à courte portée; how could he have missed at such ~ range? comment a-t-il pu rater de si près?; it's only a ~ distance from here ce n'est pas très loin (d'ici); she lives a ~ distance from the church elle n'habite pas très loin de l'église; they continued for a ~ distance ils ont poursuivi un peu leur chemin. -**3.** [in height] petit, de petite taille; he's ~ and stocky il est petit et râblé. -**4.** [period, interval] court, bref; a ~ stay un court séjour; you should take a ~ holiday vous devriez prendre quelques jours de vacances; after a ~ time après un court intervalle OR un petit moment; to have a ~ memory avoir la mémoire courte; for a ~ time I thought of becoming an actress pendant quelque temps, j'ai pensé devenir actrice; she was in London for a ~ time elle a passé quelque temps à Londres; I met him a ~ time OR while later je l'ai rencontré peu (de temps) après; it's rather ~ notice to invite them for tonight c'est un peu juste pour les inviter ce soir; time's getting ~ il ne reste plus beaucoup de temps; a few ~ hours/years ago il y a à peine quelques heures/années; the days are getting ~er les jours raccourcissent; to demand ~er hours/a ~er working week exiger une réduction des heures de travail/une réduction du temps de travail hebdomadaire ❑ in the ~ run à court terme; to be on ~ time *Br* faire des journées réduites. -**5.** FIN: ~ loan/investment prêt *m*/investissement *m* à court terme. -**6.** [abbreviated]: HF is ~ for high frequency HF est l'abréviation de haute fréquence; Bill is ~ for William Bill est un diminutif de William. -**7.** [gruff] brusque, sec; she tends to be a bit ~ with people elle a tendance à être un peu brusque avec les gens; Mary was very ~ with me on the telephone Mary a été très sèche avec moi au téléphone; to have a ~ temper être irascible. -**8.** [sudden - sound, action] brusque; her breath came in ~ gasps elle avait le souffle court; he gave a ~ laugh il eut un rire bref; ~, sharp shock *punition sévère mais de courte durée*. -**9.** [lacking, insufficient]: to give sb ~ weight ne pas donner le bon poids à qqn; money is ~ on manque d'argent, l'argent manque; whisky is in ~ supply on manque OR on est à court de whisky; to be ~ of breath [in general] avoir le souffle court; [at the moment] être hors d'haleine; to be ~ of staff manquer de personnel; to be ~ of sleep n'avoir pas assez dormi; I'm a bit ~ (of money) at the moment je suis un peu à court (d'argent) en ce moment; he's a bit ~ on imagination *fig* il manque un peu d'imagination. -**10.** *Br* [drink]: a ~ drink un petit verre. -**11.** LING bref; ~ syllable/vowel syllabe/voyelle brève. -**12.** CULIN [pastry] ≃ brisé. -**13.** ST. EX [sale] à découvert. -**14.** [in betting - odds] faible.
◇ *adv* -**1.** [suddenly]: to stop ~ s'arrêter net; the driver stopped ~ just in front of the child le conducteur s'arrêta net juste devant l'enfant ❑ to pull OR to bring sb up ~ interrompre qqn; to be taken OR caught ~ *inf Br* être pris d'un besoin pressant. -**2.** *phr*: to fall ~ of [objective, target] ne pas atteindre; [expectations] ne pas répondre à; his winnings fell far ~ of what he had expected ses gains ont été bien moindres que ce à quoi il s'attendait; to go ~ (of sthg) manquer (de qqch); my children never went ~ of anything mes enfants n'ont jamais manqué de rien; to run ~ (of sthg) être

à court (de qqch); we're running ~ of fuel/money/sugar nous commençons à manquer de carburant/d'argent/de sucre; time is running ~ le temps commence à manquer.

◇ *vt* ELEC court-circuiter.

◇ *vi* ELEC se mettre en court-circuit.

◇ *n* -1. *inf* ELEC court-circuit *m*. -2. *Br* [drink] *alcool servi dans de petits verres*. -3. CIN court-métrage *m*.

◆ **shorts** *npl* [short trousers] short *m*; a pair of khaki ~s un short kaki ‖ [underpants] caleçon *m*.

◆ **for short** *adv phr*: they call him Ben for ~ on l'appelle Ben pour faire plus court; trinitrotoluene, or TNT for ~ le trinitrotoluène ou TNT en abrégé.

◆ **in short** *adv phr* (en) bref.

◆ **short of** *prep phr* sauf; he would do anything ~ of stealing il ferait tout sauf voler; nothing ~ of a miracle can save him now seul un miracle pourrait le sauver maintenant; ~ of resigning, what can I do? à part démissionner, que puis-je faire?

shortage [ˈʃɔːtɪdʒ] *n* [of labour, resources, materials] manque *m*, pénurie *f*; [of food] disette *f*, pénurie *f*; [of money] manque *m*; a petrol ~, a ~ of petrol une pénurie d'essence; the housing/energy ~ la crise du logement/de l'énergie; there's no ~ of good restaurants in this part of town les bons restaurants ne manquent pas dans ce quartier.

short-arse▽ *n*: he's a ~ il est court sur pattes.

short back and sides *n* coupe *f* courte OR dégagée sur la nuque et derrière les oreilles.

shortbread [ˈʃɔːtbred] *n* sablé *m*; ~ biscuit *Br* sablé *m*.

shortcake [ˈʃɔːtkeɪk] *n* -1. *Br* CULIN [biscuit] = **shortbread**. -2. [cake] tarte *f* sablée.

short-change *vt* -1. *literal*: to ~ sb ne pas rendre assez (de monnaie) à qqn. -2. *inf* [swindle] rouler, escroquer.

short circuit *n* court-circuit *m*.

◆ **short-circuit** ◇ *vt* ELEC & *fig* court-circuiter.

◇ *vi* se mettre en court-circuit.

shortcoming [ˈʃɔːtˌkʌmɪŋ] *n* défaut *m*.

shortcrust pastry [ˈʃɔːtkrʌst-] *n* pâte *f* brisée.

short cut *n literal* & *fig* raccourci *m*; to take a ~ prendre un raccourci.

short-cycle *adj* SCH à cycle court.

short-dated *adj* FIN à courte échéance.

short division *n* MATH division *f* à un ou deux chiffres.

shorten [ˈʃɔːtn] ◇ *vt* -1. [in length - garment, string] raccourcir; [- text, article, speech] raccourcir, abréger; the name James is often ~ed to Jim on utilise souvent Jim comme diminutif du prénom James. -2. [in time] écourter; we had to ~ our trip nous avons dû écourter notre voyage; the new railway line will ~ the journey time to London la nouvelle ligne de chemin de fer réduira le temps de trajet jusqu'à Londres.

◇ *vi* -1. [gen] (se) raccourcir. -2. [in betting - odds] devenir moins favorable.

shortening [ˈʃɔːtnɪŋ] *n* -1. CULIN matière *f* grasse. -2. [of garment, string] raccourcissement *m*; [of text, article, speech] raccourcissement *m*, abrègement *m*; [of time, distance] réduction *f*.

shortfall [ˈʃɔːtfɔːl] *n* insuffisance *f*, manque *m*; there's a ~ of $100 il manque 100 dollars; a ~ in coal supplies was expected on prévoyait que les réserves de charbon seraient insuffisantes.

short-haired *adj* [person] à cheveux courts; [animal] à poil ras.

shorthand [ˈʃɔːthænd] *n* sténographie *f*, sténo *f*; to take notes in ~ prendre des notes en sténo.

shorthanded [ˌʃɔːtˈhændɪd] *adj* à court de personnel; we're very ~ at the moment nous sommes vraiment à court OR nous manquons vraiment de personnel en ce moment.

shorthand typist *n* sténodactylo *mf*.

short-haul *adj* [transport] à courte distance; ~ aircraft court-courrier *m*.

shorthorn [ˈʃɔːthɔːn] *n* shorthorn *m (race de bovins)*.

shortie [ˈʃɔːtɪ] *n* -1. *inf* = **shorty**. -2. [nightdress] chemise *f* de nuit courte, nuisette *f*.

shortish [ˈʃɔːtɪʃ] *adj* [in length] plutôt court; [in height] plutôt petit; [in time] plutôt court OR bref.

short list *n Br* liste *f* de candidats présélectionnés.

◆ **short-list** *vt Br*: five candidates have been ~ed cinq candidats ont été présélectionnés.

short-lived [-lɪvd] *adj* [gen] de courte durée, éphémère, bref; [animal, species] à la vie éphémère.

shortly [ˈʃɔːtlɪ] *adv* -1. [soon] bientôt, sous peu, avant peu; I'll join you ~ je vous rejoindrai bientôt; ~ afterwards peu (de temps) après. -2. [gruffly] sèchement, brusquement. -3. [briefly] brièvement, en peu de mots.

shortness [ˈʃɔːtnɪs] *n* [in length] manque *m* de longueur; [in height] petite taille *f*; [in time] brièveté *f*; [of speech, essay] brièveté.

short-order cook *n* cuisinier *m*, -ère *f* dans un snack-bar.

short-range *adj* -1. [weapon] de courte portée; [vehicle, aircraft] à rayon d'action limité. -2. [prediction, outlook] à court terme.

shortsighted [ˌʃɔːtˈsaɪtɪd] *adj* -1. *literal* myope. -2. *fig* myope, qui manque de perspicacité OR de prévoyance; I find their attitude extremely ~ je trouve qu'ils font preuve d'un manque total de prévoyance.

shortsightedly [ˌʃɔːtˈsaɪtɪdlɪ] *adv* -1. *literal*: he peered ~ at the book il scruta le livre de ses yeux myopes. -2. *fig*: to act ~ agir sans prévoyance.

shortsightedness [ˌʃɔːtˈsaɪtɪdnɪs] *n* -1. *literal* myopie *f*. -2. *fig* myopie *f*, manque *m* de perspicacité OR de prévoyance.

short-sleeved *adj* à manches courtes.

short-staffed [-stɑːft] *adj* à court de personnel; we're a bit ~ nous sommes un peu à court de OR nous manquons un peu de personnel.

short-stay *adj*: ~ car park parking *m* courte durée; ~ patient patient *m* hospitalisé pour une courte durée.

short story *n* nouvelle *f*.

short-tempered *adj* irascible, irritable.

short tennis *n* tennis *m* pour enfants.

short-term *adj* à court terme; ~ loan prêt *m* à court terme.

short-time *adj Br*: to be on ~ working être en chômage partiel.

short ton *n* tonne *f* (américaine), short ton *f*.

short wave *n* onde *f* courte; on ~ sur ondes courtes.

◆ **short-wave** *comp* [radio] à ondes courtes; [programme, broadcasting] sur ondes courtes.

shorty *inf* [ˈʃɔːtɪ] (*pl* shorties) *n* petit *m*, -e *f*, minus *m*, nabot *m*.

Shostakovich [ˌʃɒstəˈkəʊvɪtʃ] *pr n* Chostakovitch.

shot [ʃɒt] ◇ *pt* & *pp* → **shoot**.

◇ *n* -1. [instance of firing] coup *m* (de feu); he fired four ~s il a tiré quatre coups de feu; to have OR to fire OR to take a ~ at sthg tirer sur qqch; he hit it with his first ~ il l'a atteint du premier coup ❑ a ~ across the bows *literal* & *fig* un coup de semonce; it was a ~ in the dark j'ai/il a *etc* dit ça au hasard; the dog was off like a ~ *inf* le chien est parti comme une flèche; would you marry him? – like a ~! *inf* est-ce que tu l'épouserais? – sans hésiter OR et comment!; I'd accept the offer like a ~ *inf* j'accepterais l'offre sans la moindre hésitation; the ~ heard around the world *expression évoquant le début de la guerre d'Indépendance américaine*. -2. [sound of gun] coup *m* de feu; I was woken by a ~ j'ai été réveillé par un coup de feu. -3. *(U)* [shotgun pellets] plomb *m*, plombs *mpl*. -4. [marksman] tireur *m*, -euse *f*, fusil *m*; she's a good ~ c'est une excellente tireuse, elle tire bien; she's a poor ~ elle tire mal. -5. SPORT [at goal - in football, hockey etc] tir *m*; [stroke - in tennis, cricket, billiards etc] coup *m*; [throw - in darts] lancer *m*; his first ~ at goal hit the post son premier tir a touché le poteau; each player has three ~s chaque joueur joue trois fois; good ~! bien joué! ❑ to call the ~s mener le jeu; to call one's ~ *inf Am* annoncer la couleur. -6. SPORT: to put the ~ lancer le poids. -7. ASTRONAUT [launch] tir *m*; moon ~ lancement *m* d'un vaisseau lunaire. -8. PHOT photo *f*; CIN plan *m*, prise *f* de vue; the opening ~s of the film les premières images du film. -9. *inf* [try] tentative *f*, essai *m*; I'd like to have a ~ at it j'aimerais tenter le coup; it's a bit of a long ~ il y a peu de chances pour que cela réussisse. -10. [injection] piqûre *f*; tetanus ~ piqûre antitétanique; a ~ in the arm *fig* un coup de fouet *fig*. -11. [drink] (petit) verre *m*; have a ~ of vodka prenez un petit verre de vodka.

◇ *adj* -1. *Br* [rid]: to get ~ of sthg/sb *inf* se débarrasser de qqch/qqn; I'll be glad to be ~ of them je serai content d'en être débarrassé. -2. [streaked] strié; ~ silk soie *f* changeante; the book is ~ through with subtle irony *fig* le livre est plein d'une ironie subtile. -3. *inf esp Am* [exhausted] épuisé, crevé; [broken, spoilt] fichu, bousillé; my nerves are ~ je suis à bout de nerfs.

THE SHOT HEARD AROUND THE WORLD: Titre d'un poème de Ralph Waldo Emerson, en hommage au premier coup de feu échangé entre les «Minutemen» américains et les forces anglaises, en avril 1775, à Lexington. L'écrivain y loue la détermination des colons et salue l'avènement d'une nouvelle nation.

---

shotgun [ˈʃɒtgʌn] ◇ *n* fusil *m* de chasse.

◇ *adj* forcé; a ~ merger une fusion imposée.

◇ *adv Am*: to ride ~ voyager comme passager.

shotgun wedding *n* mariage *m* forcé.

shot put *n* lancer *m* du poids.

shot putter *n* lanceur *m*, -euse *f* de poids.

shot putting [-ˈpʊtɪŋ] *n* (lancer *m* du) poids *m*.

should [ʃʊd] *modal vb* -1. [indicating duty, necessity]: I ~ be working, not talking to you je devrais être en train de travailler au lieu de parler avec vous; you really ~ call her, you know tu devrais l'appeler, tu sais; they ~ be severely punished ils devraient être sévèrement punis; [indicating likelihood]: they ~ have arrived by now ils devraient être arrivés maintenant; I ~ have finished the work yesterday j'aurais dû finir ce travail hier; the election results ~ be out soon on devrait bientôt connaître les résultats des élections ‖ [indicating what is acceptable, desirable etc]: I ~ never have married him je n'aurais jamais dû l'épouser; you shouldn't have done that! tu n'aurais pas dû faire ça!; you ~ have seen the state of the house! si tu avais vu dans quel état était la maison!; you ~ hear the way he talks! il faut voir comment il s'exprime!; ~ he tell her? – yes he ~ est-ce qu'il devrait le lui dire? – oui, sans aucun doute; I'm very sorry – and so you ~ be! je suis vraiment désolé – il y a de quoi!; why shouldn't I enjoy myself now and then? pourquoi est-ce que je n'aurais pas le droit de m'amuser de temps en temps? ‖ [prefacing an important remark]: I ~ perhaps say, at this point, that... à ce stade, je devrais peut-être dire que... -2. *(forming conditional tense)* [would]: I ~ like to meet your parents j'aimerais rencontrer vos parents; if I were you I ~ apologize si j'étais à votre place, je présenterais mes excuses; I shouldn't be surprised if they got married cela ne m'étonnerait pas qu'ils se marient; I ~ say OR think it costs about £50 je dirais que ça coûte dans les 50 livres; I ~ have thought the answer was obvious j'aurais pensé que la réponse était évidente; ~ you be interested, I know a good hotel there si cela vous intéresse, je connais un bon hôtel là-bas; how ~ I know? comment voulez-vous que je le sache?; I ~

think so/not! j'espère bien/bien que non! -**3.** [were to - indicating hypothesis, speculation]: if I ~ forget si (jamais) j'oublie; I'll be upstairs ~ you need me je serai en haut si (jamais) vous avez besoin de moi; suppose nobody ~ come? et si personne ne venait? -**4.** [after 'that' and in expressions of feeling, opinion etc]: it's strange (that) she ~ do that c'est bizarre qu'elle fasse cela; I'm anxious that she ~ come je tiens à ce qu'elle vienne; we decided we ~ meet at the station nous avons décidé de nous retrouver à la gare; lest it ~ rain *lit* de crainte OR de peur qu'il ne pleuve. -**5.** *(after 'who' or 'what')* [expressing surprise]: and who ~ I meet but Betty! et sur qui je tombe? Betty! -**6.** *inf iron* [needn't]: he ~ worry (about money), he owns half of Manhattan! tu parles qu'il a des soucis d'argent, la moitié de Manhattan lui appartient!

shoulda *inf* ['ʃʊdə] = **should have**.

shoulder ['ʃəʊldəʳ] ◇ *n* -**1.** [part of body, of garment] épaule *f*; he's got broad ~s il est large d'épaules OR de carrure; it's a bit big on the ~s c'est un peu large aux épaules OR de carrure; she put an arm around my ~ elle mit son bras autour de mon épaule; you can carry it over your ~ tu peux le porter en bandoulière; put a jacket over your ~s mets une veste sur tes épaules; I looked over my ~ j'ai jeté un coup d'œil derrière moi; it's a heavy burden to place on his ~s c'est une lourde charge à mettre sur ses épaules ❑ to cry on sb's ~ pleurer sur l'épaule de qqn; we all need a ~ to cry on nous avons tous besoin d'une épaule pour pleurer; to put one's ~ to the wheel s'atteler à la tâche; to stand ~ to ~ être coude à coude. -**2.** CULIN épaule *f*; ~ of lamb épaule d'agneau. -**3.** [along road] accotement *m*, bas-côté *m*; 'soft ~' 'accotement non stabilisé'; hard ~ bande *f* d'arrêt d'urgence. -**4.** [on hill, mountain] replat *m*; [of bottle] renflement *m*.

◇ *vt* -**1.** [pick up] charger sur son épaule; she ~ed the heavy load elle chargea le lourd fardeau sur son épaule; to ~ arms MIL se mettre au port d'armes; ~ arms! MIL portez armes! -**2.** *fig* [take on - responsibility, blame] assumer; [cost] faire face à. -**3.** [push] pousser (de l'épaule); he ~ed me aside il m'écarta d'un coup d'épaule; I ~ed my way through the crowd je me suis frayé un chemin à travers la foule (en jouant des épaules).

shoulder bag *n* sac *m* à bandoulière.

shoulder blade *n* omoplate *f*.

shoulder charge *n* charge *f* épaule contre épaule.

◆ **shoulder-charge** *vt* charger épaule contre épaule.

shoulder-high ◇ *adj* qui arrive (jusqu') à l'épaule; we pushed through the ~ grass nous nous frayâmes un chemin dans l'herbe qui nous arrivait (jusqu') à l'épaule.

◇ *adv*: to carry sb ~ porter qqn en triomphe.

shoulder holster *n* holster *m*.

shoulder-length *adj* [hair] mi-long, qui arrive (jusqu') aux épaules.

shoulder pad *n* [in garment] épaulette *f (coussinet de rembourrage)*; SPORT protège-épaule *m*.

shoulder strap *n* [on dress, bra, accordion] bretelle *f*; [on bag] bandoulière *f*.

shouldn't ['ʃʊdnt] = **should not**.

should've ['ʃʊdəv] = **should have**.

shout [ʃaʊt] ◇ *n* -**1.** [cry] cri *m*, hurlement *m*; I heard a ~ of joy j'ai entendu un cri de joie; give me a ~ if you need a hand appelle-moi si tu as besoin d'un coup de main. -**2.** *inf Br & Austr* [round of drinks] tournée *f*; whose ~ is it? c'est à qui de payer la tournée?

◇ *vi* crier, hurler; there's no need to ~, I can hear you pas besoin de crier comme ça, je ne suis pas sourd; to ~ at the top of one's voice crier à tue-tête; to ~ (out) for help appeler au secours; he ~ed (out) to her to be careful il lui a crié de faire attention; he ~ed at me for being late il a crié parce que j'étais en retard ❑ my new job is nothing to ~ about *inf* mon nouveau travail n'a rien de bien passionnant.

◇ *vt* crier; the sergeant ~ed (out) an order le sergent hurla un ordre; they ~ed themselves hoarse ils crièrent jusqu'à en perdre la voix ❑ to ~ sthg from the rooftops crier qqch sur les toits.

◆ **shout down** *vt sep* [speaker] empêcher de parler en criant; [speech] couvrir par des cris; she was ~ed down les gens ont hurlé tellement fort qu'elle n'a pas pu parler.

shouting ['ʃaʊtɪŋ] *n (U)* cris *mpl*, vociférations *fpl*; within ~ distance à deux pas, tout près ❑ it's all over bar the ~ c'est pour ainsi dire terminé.

shove [ʃʌv] ◇ *vt* -**1.** [push] pousser; [push roughly] pousser sans ménagement; we ~d all the furniture up against the walls nous avons poussé tous les meubles contre les murs; he ~d me out of the way il m'a écarté sans ménagement; she ~d him down the stairs elle l'a poussé dans les escaliers || [insert, stick] enfoncer; he ~d an elbow into my ribs il m'enfonça son coude dans les côtes. -**2.** *inf* [put hurriedly or carelessly] mettre, flanquer, ficher; ~ it in the drawer fiche-le dans le tiroir; ~ a few good quotes in and it'll be fine tu y ajoutes quelques citations bien choisies et ce sera parfait.

◇ *vi* -**1.** [push] pousser; [jostle] se bousculer; people kept pushing and shoving les gens n'arrêtaient pas de se bousculer; stop shoving! arrêtez de pousser! -**2.** *inf Br* [move up] se pousser; ~ up OR over OR along a bit pousse-toi un peu.

◇ *n* -**1.** [push] poussée *f*; to give sb/sthg a ~ pousser qqn/qqch. -**2.** *inf phr*: to give sb the ~ sacquer qqn; to get the ~ se faire sacquer.

◆ **shove about** *Br*, **shove around** *vt sep* [jostle] bousculer; [mistreat] malmener; don't let him ~ you about! ne le laisse pas te marcher sur les pieds!

◆ **shove off** ◇ *vi insep* -**1.** *inf* [go away] se casser, se tirer; ~ off, I'm busy! casse-toi, je suis occupé! -**2.** [boat] pousser au large.

◇ *vt sep* [boat] pousser au large, déborder.

shove-halfpenny *n* jeu *m* de palet de table.

shovel ['ʃʌvl] (*Br pt & pp* shovelled, *cont* shovelling, *Am pt & pp* shoveled, *cont* shoveling)

◇ *n* pelle *f*; [on excavating machine] pelle *f*, godet *m*; coal ~ pelle mécanique.

◇ *vt* [coal, earth, sand] pelleter; [snow] déblayer (à la pelle); they shovelled the gravel onto the drive avec une pelle, ils ont répandu les gravillons sur l'allée; ~ all that rubble into a corner prenez une pelle et mettez tous ces gravats dans un coin; to ~ food into one's mouth *inf* enfourner de la nourriture; he shovelled his meal down *inf* il a englouti son repas.

shovelful ['ʃʌvlfʊl] *n* pelletée *f*.

show [ʃəʊ] (*pt* showed, *pp* shown [ʃəʊn])

◇ *vt* -**1.** [display, present] montrer, faire voir; to ~ sthg to sb, to ~ sb sthg montrer qqch à qqn; ~ me your presents fais-moi voir OR montre-moi tes cadeaux; you have to ~ your pass/your ticket on the way in il faut présenter son laissez-passer/son billet à l'entrée; you're ~ing a lot of leg this evening! tu es habillée bien court ce soir!; a TV screen ~s what's happening in the next room un écran de télévision permet de voir ce qui se passe dans la pièce d'à côté; I had very little to ~ for my efforts mes efforts n'avaient donné que peu de résultats; three months' work, and what have we got to ~ for it? trois mois de travail, et qu'est-ce que cela nous a rapporté?; this jacket/colour really ~s the dirt cette veste/couleur est vraiment salissante; come out from behind there and ~ yourself! sortez de là-derrière et montrez-vous!; if he ever ~s himself round here again, I'll kill him! si jamais il se montre encore par ici, je le tue!; she ~ed herself more than willing to join in elle s'est montrée plus que prête à participer; to ~ one's age faire son âge || [reveal - talent, affection, readiness, reluctance] montrer, faire preuve de; she never ~s any emotion elle ne laisse jamais paraître OR ne montre jamais ses sentiments; to ~ a preference for sthg manifester une préférence pour qqch; they will be shown no mercy ils seront traités sans merci; the audience began to ~ signs of restlessness le public a commencé à s'agiter; the situation is ~ing signs of improvement la situation semble être en voie d'amélioration. -**2.** [prove] montrer, démontrer, prouver; first I shall ~ that Greenham's theory cannot be correct je démontrerai d'abord que la théorie de Greenham ne peut être juste; it just ~s the strength of public opposition to the plan cela montre à quel point le public est opposé à ce projet; it just goes to ~ that nothing's impossible c'est la preuve que rien n'est impossible; it just goes to ~ what you can do if you work hard cela montre OR c'est la preuve de ce que l'on peut faire en travaillant dur. -**3.** [register - subj: instrument, dial, clock] marquer, indiquer; the thermometer ~s a temperature of 20° C le thermomètre indique 20° C. -**4.** [represent, depict] montrer, représenter; this photo ~s him at the age of 17 cette photo le montre à l'âge de 17 ans. -**5.** [point out, demonstrate] montrer, indiquer; ~ me how to do it montrez-moi comment faire; to ~ (sb) the way montrer le chemin (à qqn); the government has very much shown the way with its green policies *fig* le gouvernement a bien donné l'exemple avec sa politique écologique ❑ I'll ~ you! *inf* tu vas voir! -**6.** [escort, accompany]: let me ~ you to your room je vais vous montrer votre chambre; will you ~ this gentleman to the door? veuillez reconduire Monsieur à la porte; an usherette ~ed us to our seats une ouvreuse nous a conduits à nos places. -**7.** [profit, loss] faire; prices ~ a 10% increase on last year les prix sont en hausse OR ont augmenté de 10 % par rapport à l'an dernier. -**8.** [put on - film, TV programme] passer; the film has never been shown on television le film n'est jamais passé à la télévision; 'as shown on TV' 'vu à la télé'. -**9.** [exhibit - work of art, prize, produce] exposer; some of the drawings have never been shown in Europe before quelques-uns des dessins n'ont jamais été exposés en Europe auparavant.

◇ *vi* -**1.** [be visible - gen] se voir; [- petticoat] dépasser; fear ~ed in his eyes la peur se lisait dans ses yeux; she doesn't like him, and it ~s elle ne l'aime pas, et ça se voit; a patch of sky ~ed through a hole in the roof on voyait un pan de ciel à travers un trou dans le toit; their tiredness is beginning to ~ ils commencent à donner des signes de fatigue. -**2.** [be on - film, TV programme] passer. -**3.** *Br* [in a vote] lever la main; all those in favour please ~ que tous ceux qui sont pour lèvent la main. -**4.** *inf Am* [turn up] arriver, se pointer.

◇ *n* -**1.** [demonstration, display] démonstration *f*, manifestation *f*; [pretence] semblant *m*, simulacre *m*; she put on a ~ of indifference elle a fait semblant d'être indifférente || [ostentation] ostentation *f*, parade *f*; he always makes such a ~ of his knowledge il faut toujours qu'il fasse étalage de ses connaissances; the metal strips are just for ~ les bandes métalliques ont une fonction purement décorative ❑ a ~ of strength une démonstration de force; a ~ of hands un vote à main levée. -**2.** THEAT spectacle *m*; TV émission *f*; we went to a restaurant after the ~ nous sommes allés au restaurant après le spectacle ❑ variety ~ émission de variétés; the ~ must go on THEAT & *fig* le spectacle continue. -**3.** [exhibition] exposition *f*; [trade fair] foire *f*, salon *m*; have you been to the Picasso ~? avez-vous visité l'exposition Picasso?; I dislike most of the paintings on ~ je n'aime pas la plupart des tableaux exposés; the agricultural/motor ~ le salon de l'agriculture/de l'auto. -**4.** *inf* [business, affair] affaire *f*; she planned and ran the whole ~ c'est elle qui a tout organisé et qui s'est occupée de tout; it's up to you, it's your ~ c'est à toi de décider, c'est toi le chef ❑ let's get this ~ on the road! il faut y aller maintenant! -**5.** [achievement, performance] performance *f*, prestation *f*; the team put up a pretty good ~ l'équipe s'est bien défendue; it's a pretty poor ~ when your own mother forgets your birthday c'est un peu triste que ta propre mère oublie ton anniversaire ❑ (jolly) good ~, Henry! *dated* bravo, Henry!

◆ **show around** *vt sep* faire visiter; my secretary will ~ you around (the factory) ma secrétaire va vous faire visiter (l'usine).

◆ **show in** *vt sep* faire entrer.

◆ **show off** ◇ *vi insep* crâner, frimer, se faire remarquer; stop ~ing off! arrête de te faire remarquer!

◇ *vt sep* -**1.** [parade] faire étalage de; to ~ off one's skill faire étalage de son savoir-faire; he only came to ~ off his new girlfriend il n'est venu que pour exhiber sa nouvelle petite amie. -**2.** [set off] mettre en valeur; the black background ~s off the colours nicely le fond noir fait bien ressortir les couleurs.

◆ **show out** *vt sep* reconduire OR raccompagner (à la porte).

◆ **show over** *Br* = **show around**.

◆ **show round** = **show around**.

◆ **show through** *vi insep* se voir (à travers), transparaître; the old paint still ~s through l'ancienne peinture se voit encore à travers.

◆ **show up** ◇ *vi insep* -**1.** *inf* [turn up, arrive] arriver; only two of our guests have shown up seuls deux de nos invités sont arrivés. -**2.** [be visible] se voir, être visible; the difference is so slight it hardly ~s up at all la différence est tellement minime qu'elle se remarque à peine.

◇ *vt sep Br* -**1.** [unmask] démasquer; the investigation ~ed him up for the coward he is l'enquête a révélé sa lâcheté. -**2.** [draw attention to - deficiency, defect] faire apparaître, faire ressortir; the poor results ~ up the deficiencies in the training programme les mauvais résultats font apparaître les défauts du programme de formation. -**3.** [embarrass] faire honte à; you're always ~ing me up in public il faut toujours que tu me fasses honte en public.

showbiz *inf* [ˈʃəʊbɪz] *n* show-biz *m*, monde *m* du spectacle; she wants to get into ~ elle veut entrer dans le show-biz.

showboat [ˈʃəʊbəʊt] *n Am* -**1.** [boat] bateau-théâtre *m*. -**2.** *inf* [person] cabotin *m*, -e *f*, m'as-tu-vu *mf inv*.

show business *n* show-business *m*, monde *m* du spectacle; a show-business personality une personnalité du monde du spectacle.

showcase [ˈʃəʊkeɪs] ◇ *n* vitrine *f*; a ~ for British exports *fig* une vitrine pour les exportations britanniques.

◇ *adj* [role] prestigieux; [operation] de prestige.

◇ *vt* servir de vitrine à *fig*.

showdown [ˈʃəʊdaʊn] *n* -**1.** [confrontation] confrontation *f*, épreuve *f* de force. -**2.** [in poker] étalement *m* du jeu.

shower [ʃaʊəʳ] ◇ *n* -**1.** [for washing] douche *f*; to have OR to take a ~ prendre une douche. -**2.** METEOR averse *f*; scattered ~s averses intermittentes; a snow ~ une chute de neige. -**3.** [stream - of confetti, sparks, gravel] pluie *f*; [- of praise, abuse] avalanche *f*; [- of blows] pluie *f*, volée *f*, grêle *f*. -**4.** *Am* [party] *fête au cours de laquelle les invités offrent des cadeaux*; they're having a baby ~ ils font une fête où les invités apporteront des cadeaux pour leur bébé. -**5.** *inf Br pej* [group] bande *f*; what a ~! quelle bande de crétins!

◇ *vi* -**1.** [have a shower] prendre une douche, se doucher. -**2.** [rain] pleuvoir par averses; it's started to ~ une averse a commencé. -**3.** *fig* [rain down] pleuvoir.

◇ *vt*: passers-by were ~ed with broken glass des passants ont été atteints par des éclats de verre; they ~ed him with gifts, they ~ed gifts on him ils l'ont comblé de cadeaux; to ~ sb with kisses couvrir qqn de baisers.

shower cap *n* bonnet *m* de douche.

showerproof [ˈʃaʊəpruːf] *adj* imperméable.

showery [ˈʃaʊərɪ] *adj*: the weather was ~ il pleuvait de façon intermittente; it will be rather a ~ day tomorrow il y aura des averses demain.

showgirl [ˈʃəʊgɜːl] *n* girl *f*.

showground [ˈʃəʊgraʊnd] *n* parc *m* d'expositions.

show house *n* maison *f* témoin.

showily [ˈʃəʊɪlɪ] *adv* de façon voyante OR ostentatoire.

showing [ˈʃəʊɪŋ] *n* -**1.** [of paintings, sculpture] exposition *f*; [of film] projection *f*, séance *f*; a private ~ of her new film une projection privée de son nouveau film; a special midnight ~ une séance spéciale à minuit. -**2.** [performance] performance *f*, prestation *f*; on its present ~ our party should win hands down à en juger par ses performances actuelles, notre parti devrait gagner haut la main.

showing off *n*: I've had enough of his ~ j'en ai assez de sa vantardise.

show jumper *n* [rider] cavalier, -ère *m (participant à des concours de saut d'obstacle)*; [horse] sauteur *m*.

show jumping *n* jumping *m*, concours *m* de saut d'obstacles.

showman [ˈʃəʊmən] (*pl* showmen [-mən]) *n* THEAT metteur *m* en scène; [in fairground] forain *m*; [circus manager] propriétaire *m* de cirque; he's a real ~ *fig* il a vraiment le sens de la mise en scène.

showmanship [ˈʃəʊmənʃɪp] *n* sens *m* de la mise en scène.

shown [ʃəʊn] *pp* → **show**.

show-off *inf n* frimeur *m*, -euse *f*.

showpiece [ˈʃəʊpiːs] *n*: that carpet is a real ~ ce tapis est une pièce remarquable; the ~ of his collection le joyau de sa collection; the school had become a ~ of educational excellence l'école est devenue un modèle quant à la qualité de l'enseignement.

showplace [ˈʃəʊpleɪs] *n* endroit *m* pittoresque, site *m* touristique.

showroom [ˈʃəʊrʊm] *n* salle *f* OR salon *m* d'exposition; the new model will be in the ~s soon le nouveau modèle sera bientôt chez votre concessionnaire; a car in ~ condition une voiture à l'état neuf.

showstopper [ˈʃəʊˌstɒpəʳ] *n* numéro *m* sensationnel; her song was a real ~ sa chanson a eu OR remporté un succès fou.

show trial *n* procès *m* à grand spectacle.

showy [ˈʃəʊɪ] (*compar* showier, *superl* showiest) *adj* voyant, ostentatoire.

shrank [ʃræŋk] *pt* → **shrink**.

shrapnel [ˈʃræpnl] *n* -**1.** *(U)* [fragments] éclats *mpl* d'obus; a piece of ~ un éclat d'obus. -**2.** [shell] shrapnel *m*.

shred [ʃred] ◇ *n* -**1.** [of paper, fabric etc] lambeau *m*; in ~s en lambeaux; to tear sthg to ~s *literal* déchirer qqch en petits morceaux; *fig* démolir qqch. -**2.** [of truth, evidence] parcelle *f*.

◇ *vt* -**1.** [tear up - paper, fabric] déchiqueter; ~ this document as soon as you have read it détruisez ce document dès que vous l'aurez lu. -**2.** CULIN râper; shredded cabbage chou râpé.

shredder [ˈʃredəʳ] *n* -**1.** CULIN [manual] râpe *f*; [in food processor] disque-râpeur *m*. -**2.** [for documents] destructeur *m* de documents.

shrew [ʃruː] *n* -**1.** ZOOL musaraigne *f*. -**2.** *pej* [woman] mégère *f*, harpie *f*.

shrewd [ʃruːd] *adj* [person - astute] perspicace; [- crafty] astucieux, rusé, habile; [judgment] perspicace; I had a ~ suspicion that they were up to something je les soupçonnais fortement de manigancer quelque chose; to make a ~ guess deviner juste; a ~ investment un placement judicieux.

shrewdly [ˈʃruːdlɪ] *adv* [act] avec perspicacité OR sagacité; [answer, guess] astucieusement.

shrewdness [ˈʃruːdnɪs] *n* [astuteness] perspicacité *f*; [craftiness] habileté *f*, ruse *f*.

shrewish [ˈʃruːɪʃ] *adj* [woman, character] acariâtre, hargneux.

shriek [ʃriːk] ◇ *vi* hurler, crier; to ~ with pain pousser un cri de douleur; to ~ with laughter hurler de rire.

◇ *vt* hurler, crier; "stop!", he ~ed «arrêtez!», hurla-t-il.

shrift [ʃrɪft] *n* -**1.** *arch* [confession] confession *f*; [absolution] absolution *f*. -**2.** *phr*: to give sb short ~ envoyer promener qqn.

shrike [ʃraɪk] *n* pie-grièche *f*.

shrill [ʃrɪl] ◇ *adj* perçant, aigu, strident.

◇ *vi* [siren, whistle] retentir.

◇ *vt* crier d'une voix perçante; "cooee!", she ~ed «coucou!», cria-t-elle d'une voix perçante.

shrillness [ˈʃrɪlnɪs] *n* [of voice] ton *m* perçant OR aigu; [of note, whistle] stridence *f lit*.

shrilly [ˈʃrɪlɪ] *adv* [say, sing] d'une voix perçante OR aiguë; [whistle] d'une manière stridente.

shrimp [ʃrɪmp] ◇ *n* -**1.** ZOOL crevette *f*; ~ cocktail cocktail *m* de crevettes; ~ crackers chips *fpl* à la crevette. -**2.** *inf pej* [small person] minus *m*, avorton *m*.

◇ *vi*: to go ~ing aller aux crevettes.

shrine [ʃraɪn] *n* -**1.** [place of worship] lieu *m* saint. -**2.** [container for relics] reliquaire *m*. -**3.** [tomb] tombe *f*, mausolée *m*. -**4.** *fig* haut lieu *m*; a ~ of learning un haut lieu du savoir.

shrink [ʃrɪŋk] (*pt* shrank [ʃræŋk], *pp* shrunk [ʃrʌŋk]) ◇ *vi* -**1.** [garment, cloth] rétrécir. -**2.** [grow smaller - gen] rétrécir, rapetisser; [- economy] se contracter; [- meat] réduire; [- person] rapetisser; [- numbers, profits, savings] diminuer, baisser; [- business, trade] se réduire; the wood has shrunk le bois a dégonflé; the village seems to have shrunk le village semble plus petit; the number of candidates has shrunk alarmingly le nombre de candidats a diminué de façon inquiétante; the size of computers has shrunk dramatically les ordinateurs sont devenus nettement plus compacts; my savings have shrunk (away) to nothing mes économies ont complètement fondu. -**3.** [move backwards] reculer; they shrank (away OR back) in horror ils reculèrent, horrifiés; to ~ into o.s. se refermer OR se replier sur soi-même. -**4.** [shy away] se dérober; [hesitate] répugner; he ~s from any responsibility il se dérobe devant n'importe quelle responsabilité; she shrank from the thought of meeting him again l'idée de le revoir lui faisait peur.

◇ *vt* (faire) rétrécir; old age had shrunk him il s'était tassé avec l'âge.

◇ *n inf pej* [psychiatrist, psychoanalyst] psy *mf*.

shrinkage [ˈʃrɪŋkɪdʒ] *n (U)* -**1.** [gen] rétrécissement *m*, contraction *f*; allow for ~ tenir compte du rétrécissement; they forecast a further ~ in output ils prévoient une nouvelle diminution de la production. -**2.** COMM [of goods in transit] pertes *fpl*; [of goods stolen] vol *m* (des stocks).

shrinking [ˈʃrɪŋkɪŋ] *adj* [fearful] craintif; [shy] timide.

shrinking violet *n* personne *f* sensible et timide.

shrink-wrap (*pt* & *pp* shrink-wrapped, *cont* shrink-wrapping) *vt* emballer sous film plastique.

shrive [ʃraɪv] (*pt* shrived OR shrove [ʃrəʊv], *pp* shrived OR shriven [ˈʃrɪvn]) *arch* ◇ *vt* confesser, absoudre.

◇ *vi* se confesser.

shrivel [ˈʃrɪvl] (*Br pt* & *pp* shrivelled, *cont* shrivelling, *Am pt* & *pp* shriveled, *cont* shriveling) ◇ *vi* [fruit, vegetable] se dessécher, se ratatiner; [leaf] se recroqueviller; [flower, crops] se flétrir; [face, skin] se flétrir; [meat, leather] se racornir; I almost shrivelled up with shame j'ai failli mourir de honte.

◇ *vt* [fruit, vegetable] dessécher, ratatiner; [leaf] dessécher; [flower, crops] flétrir; [face, skin] flétrir, rider, parcheminer; [meat, leather] racornir; a shrivelled old woman une vieille femme toute ratatinée.

◆ **shrivel up** *vi insep* & *vt sep* = **shrivel**.

shriven [ˈʃrɪvn] *pp* → **shrive**.

shroud [ʃraʊd] ◇ *n* -**1.** [burial sheet] linceul *m*, suaire *m*. -**2.** *fig* [covering] voile *m*, linceul *m*; a ~ of mist/mystery un voile de brume/mystère.

-**3.** [shield - for spacecraft] coiffe *f*. -**4.** [rope, cord - for aerial, mast etc] hauban *m*; [- on parachute] suspente *f*.
◇ *vt* -**1.** [body] envelopper dans un linceul OR suaire; she always ~s herself in voluminous black clothes elle se drape toujours dans de grands vêtements noirs. -**2.** [obscure] voiler, envelopper; the town was ~ed in mist/darkness la ville était noyée dans la brume/plongée dans l'obscurité; its origins are ~ed in mystery ses origines sont entourées de mystère.

shrove [ʃrəʊv] *pt* → **shrive**.

Shrovetide [ˈʃrəʊvtaɪd] *n* les jours *mpl* gras *(précédant le Carême)*.

Shrove Tuesday [ʃrəʊv-] *pr n* Mardi gras.

shrub [ʃrʌb] *n* arbrisseau *m*, arbuste *m*.

shrubbery [ˈʃrʌbərɪ] (*pl* **shrubberies**) *n* [shrub garden] jardin *m* d'arbustes; [scrubland] maquis *m*.

shrubby [ˈʃrʌbɪ] (*compar* **shrubbier**, *superl* **shrubbiest**) *adj* arbustif.

shrug [ʃrʌg] (*pt* & *pp* **shrugged**, *cont* **shrugging**)
◇ *vt*: to ~ one's shoulders hausser les épaules.
◇ *vi* hausser les épaules.
◇ *n* haussement *m* d'épaules.
◆ **shrug off** *vt sep* [disregard] dédaigner; to ~ off one's problems faire abstraction de ses problèmes; she just shrugged off her failure elle ne s'est pas laissé abattre par son échec; it's not a problem you can simply ~ off on ne peut pas faire simplement comme si le problème n'existait pas.

shrunk [ʃrʌŋk] *pp* → **shrink**.

shrunken [ˈʃrʌŋkn] *adj* [garment, fabric] rétréci; [person, body] ratatiné, rapetissé; [head] réduit.

shuck [ʃʌk] *Am* ◇ *n* [pod] cosse *f*; [of nut] écale *f*; [of chestnut] bogue *f*; [of maize] spathe *f*; [of oyster] coquille *f*.
◇ *vt* -**1.** [beans, peas] écosser; [nuts] écaler; [chestnuts, maize] éplucher; [oysters] écailler. -**2.** *inf* [discard] se débarrasser de; to ~ (off) one's clothes se déshabiller. -**3.** *inf* [tease] faire marcher, mener en bateau.

shucks *inf* [ʃʌks] *interj* (ah) zut.

shudder [ˈʃʌdəʳ] *vi* -**1.** [person] frissonner, frémir, trembler; I ~ to think how much it must have cost! je frémis rien que de penser au prix que ça a dû coûter!; I wonder what they're doing now? — I ~ to think! je me demande ce qu'ils sont en train de faire — je préfère ne pas savoir! -**2.** [vehicle, machine] vibrer; [stronger] trépider; the train ~ed to a halt le train s'arrêta dans une secousse.

shuffle [ˈʃʌfl] ◇ *vi* -**1.** [walk] traîner les pieds; don't ~! ne traîne pas les pieds!; she ~s round the house in her slippers elle traîne dans la maison en pantoufles; he ~d shamefacedly into the room il est entré tout penaud dans la pièce. -**2.** [fidget] remuer, s'agiter. -**3.** [in card games] battre les cartes.
◇ *vt* -**1.** [walk]: to ~ one's feet traîner les pieds; he'll have trouble shuffling his way out of this one! *fig* cette fois-ci, il ne va pas s'en tirer comme ça! -**2.** [move round - belongings, papers] remuer; she was shuffling the papers on her desk elle déplaçait les papiers qui se trouvaient sur son bureau. -**3.** [cards] battre, brasser; [dominoes] mélanger, brasser.
◇ *n* -**1.** [walk] pas *m* traînant. -**2.** [of cards] battage *m*; let's give the cards a ~ battons les cartes; it's your ~ c'est à toi de battre (les cartes).
◆ **shuffle off** ◇ *vi sep* partir en traînant les pieds; to ~ off this mortal coil *lit* OR *hum* quitter cette vie.
◇ *vt sep* [responsibility] se dérober à; he ~d the responsibility off on to me il s'est déchargé de la responsabilité sur moi.

shuffleboard [ˈʃʌflbɔːd] *n* jeu *m* de palet.

shufti *inf* [ˈʃʌftɪ] *n Br dated* coup *m* d'œil; have a ~ at this! jette un coup d'œil là-dessus!

shun [ʃʌn] (*pt* & *pp* **shunned**, *cont* **shunning**) *vt* fuir, éviter; she ~s all publicity elle fuit toute publicité.

'shun [ʃʌn] *interj* MIL garde-à-vous.

shunt [ʃʌnt] ◇ *vt* -**1.** [move] déplacer; the neighbours upstairs were ~ing furniture around les voisins du dessus déplaçaient des meubles; they ~ed him off to the Fresno office ils l'ont muté à Fresno. -**2.** *Br* RAIL [move about] manœuvrer; [direct] aiguiller; [marshal] trier; the carriages had been ~ed into a siding les wagons avaient été mis sur une voie de garage. -**3.** ELEC [circuit] shunter, monter en dérivation; [current] dériver.
◇ *vi* -**1.** RAIL manœuvrer. -**2.** [travel back and forth] faire la navette.
◇ *n* -**1.** RAIL manœuvre *f* (de triage). -**2.** ELEC shunt *m*, dérivation *f*. -**3.** MED shunt *m*. -**4.** *inf Br* [car crash] collision *f*.

shunter [ˈʃʌntəʳ] *n* locomotive *f* de manœuvre.

shunting [ˈʃʌntɪŋ] ◇ *n* -**1.** RAIL manœuvres *fpl* (de triage). -**2.** ELEC shuntage *m*, dérivation *f*.
◇ *comp* [engine, track] de manœuvre.

shunting yard *n* gare *f* de triage.

shush [ʃʊʃ] ◇ *interj* chut.
◇ *vt*: he kept ~ing us il n'arrêtait pas de nous dire de nous taire.

shut [ʃʌt] (*pt* & *pp* **shut**, *cont* **shutting**)
◇ *vt* -**1.** [close] fermer; ~ your eyes! fermez les yeux!; you shouldn't ~ your eyes to the problem *fig* vous ne devriez pas fermer les yeux sur le problème; ~ your books refermez OR fermez vos livres; please ~ the door after you veuillez fermer OR refermer la porte derrière vous ❑ ~ your mouth *inf* OR your face *inf*! boucle-la!, la ferme! -**2.** [trap]: her skirt got ~ in the door sa robe est restée coincée dans la porte; I ~ my finger in the door je me suis pris le doigt dans la porte.
◇ *vi* -**1.** [door, window, container, cabinet etc] (se) fermer; the door won't ~ la porte ne ferme pas; the lid ~s very tightly le couvercle ferme hermétiquement. -**2.** [shop, gallery etc] fermer; the post office ~s at 6 pm la poste ferme à 18 h.
◇ *adj* fermé; keep your mouth OR trap ~! *inf* ferme-la!, boucle-la!
◆ **shut away** *vt sep* [criminal, animal] enfermer; [precious objects] mettre sous clé; I ~ myself away for two months to finish my novel je me suis enfermé pendant deux mois pour terminer d'écrire mon roman.
◆ **shut down** ◇ *vt sep* [store, factory, cinema] fermer; [machine, engine] arrêter.
◇ *vi insep* [store, factory, cinema] fermer.
◆ **shut in** *vt sep* enfermer; he went to the bathroom and ~ himself in il est allé à la salle de bains et s'y est enfermé.
◆ **shut off** ◇ *vt sep* -**1.** [cut off - supplies, water, electricity] couper; [- radio, machine] éteindre, arrêter. -**2.** [isolate] couper, isoler; the village was ~ off from the rest of the world le village a été coupé du reste du monde. -**3.** [block] boucher; that new building ~s off all our sunlight ce nouvel immeuble nous cache la lumière du jour.
◇ *vi insep* se couper, s'arrêter; it ~s off automatically ça s'arrête automatiquement.
◆ **shut out** *vt sep* -**1.** [of building, room]: she ~ us out elle nous a enfermés dehors; we got ~ out nous ne pouvions plus rentrer. -**2.** [exclude] exclure; he drew the curtains to ~ out the light il tira les rideaux pour empêcher la lumière d'entrer; she felt ~ out from all decision-making elle avait l'impression que toutes les décisions étaient prises sans qu'elle soit consultée. -**3.** [block out - thought, feeling] chasser (de son esprit). -**4.** SPORT [opponent] empêcher de marquer.
◆ **shut up** ◇ *vi insep* -**1.** *inf* [be quiet] se taire; ~ up! tais-toi!; ~ up and do your work tais-toi et fais ton travail. -**2.** [close] fermer; we decided to ~ up early nous avons décidé de fermer tôt.
◇ *vt sep* -**1.** [close - shop, factory] fermer; to ~ up shop *Br literal* & *fig* fermer boutique. -**2.** [lock up, confine] enfermer. -**3.** *inf* [silence] faire taire.

shutdown [ˈʃʌtdaʊn] *n* fermeture *f* définitive.

shut-eye *inf n*: to get a bit of ~ faire un somme, piquer un roupillon.

shut-in ◇ *adj* confiné, enfermé.
◇ *n Am* malade *m* qui reste confiné, malade *f* qui reste confinée.

shutoff [ˈʃʌtɒf] *n* -**1.** [device]: the automatic ~ didn't work le dispositif d'arrêt automatique n'a pas fonctionné. -**2.** [action] arrêt *m*.

shutout [ˈʃʌtaʊt] *n* -**1.** INDUST lock-out *m*. -**2.** SPORT *Am* victoire écrasante *(remportée sans que l'adversaire marque un seul point)*.

shutter [ˈʃʌtəʳ] *n* -**1.** [on window] volet *m*; to put up the ~s [gen] mettre les volets; [on shop] fermer boutique. -**2.** PHOT obturateur *m*.

shuttered [ˈʃʌtəd] *adj*: ~ windows [with shutters fitted] fenêtres *fpl* à volets; [with shutters closed] fenêtres *fpl* aux volets fermés; all the windows were tightly ~ les volets de toutes les fenêtres étaient bien fermés.

shutter priority *n* priorité *f* à l'obturation.

shutter release *n* déclencheur *m* d'obturateur.

shutter speed *n* vitesse *f* d'obturation.

shuttle [ˈʃʌtl] ◇ *n* -**1.** [vehicle, service] navette *f*; there is a ~ bus service from the station to the stadium il y a une navette d'autobus entre la gare et le stade; the 8 o'clock ~ to Glasgow la navette de 8 h pour Glasgow. -**2.** [on weaving loom, sewing machine] navette *f*. -**3.** = **shuttlecock**.
◇ *vi* faire la navette; he ~s between New York and Chicago il fait la navette entre New York et Chicago.
◇ *vt*: a helicopter ~d the injured to hospital un hélicoptère a fait la navette pour transporter les blessés à l'hôpital; passengers are ~d to the airport by bus les passagers sont transportés en bus à l'aéroport.

shuttlecock [ˈʃʌtlkɒk] *n* volant *m* *(au badminton)*.

shuttle diplomacy *n* navette *f* diplomatique.

shwa [ʃwɑː] = **schwa**.

shy [ʃaɪ] (*compar* **shyer**, *superl* **shyest**, *pt* & *pp* **shied**) ◇ *adj* -**1.** [person - timid] timide; [- ill at ease] gêné, mal à l'aise; [- unsociable] sauvage; she gave a ~ smile elle sourit timidement; he's ~ of adults il est timide avec les adultes; she's camera ~ elle n'aime pas être prise en photo; to make sb ~ intimider qqn; most people are ~ of speaking in public la plupart des gens ont peur de parler en public; don't be ~ of asking for more n'hésitez pas à en redemander. -**2.** [animal, bird] peureux. -**3.** *Am* [short, lacking]: to be ~ of manquer de, être à court de; we're $600 ~ of making our goal il nous manque 600 dollars pour atteindre notre objectif.
◇ *n Br* -**1.** [throw] lancer *m*, jet *m*; he took a ~ at the pigeon with a stone il a lancé une pierre sur le pigeon. -**2.** [attempt] essai *m*, tentative *f*; she decided to have OR to take a ~ at skiing elle a décidé d'essayer le ski.
◇ *vi* [horse] broncher; his horse shied at the last fence son cheval a bronché devant le dernier obstacle.
◇ *vt* lancer, jeter.
◆ **shy away from** *vt insep* éviter de; she shied away from talking to him elle a évité de lui parler.

Shylock [ˈʃaɪlɒk] *n pej* usurier *m*, -ère *f*.

shyly [ˈʃaɪlɪ] *adv* timidement.

shyness [ˈʃaɪnɪs] *n* timidité *f*.

shyster *inf* [ˈʃaɪstəʳ] *n esp Am* [crook] escroc *m*, filou *m*; [corrupt lawyer] avocat *m* marron.

si [siː] *n* MUS si *m inv*.

SI (*abbr of* Système International) *n* SI *m*; ~ unit unité *f* SI.

Siam [ˌsaɪˈæm] *pr n* Siam *m*; in ~ au Siam.

Siamese [ˌsaɪəˈmiːz] (*pl inv*) ◇ *n* -**1.** [person] Siamois *m*, -e *f*. -**2.** LING siamois *m*. -**3.** = **Siamese cat**.
◇ *adj* siamois.

Siamese cat *n* chat *m* siamois.

Siamese twins *npl* [male] frères *mpl* siamois; [female] sœurs *fpl* siamoises.

sib *inf* [sɪb] = **sibling**.

SIB *pr n* (*abbr of* Securities and Investments Board) *organisme mis en place en 1986 pour superviser le marché financier londonien*.

Siberia [saɪˈbɪərɪə] *pr n* Sibérie *f*; in ~ en Sibérie.

Siberian [saɪˈbɪərɪən] ◇ *n* Sibérien *m*, -enne *f*. ◇ *adj* sibérien.

sibilance [ˈsɪbɪləns] *n* sifflement *m*.

sibilant [ˈsɪbɪlənt] *adj* sifflant.

sibilate [ˈsɪbɪleɪt] ◇ *vt* prononcer en sifflant. ◇ *vi* siffler.

sibling [ˈsɪblɪŋ] ◇ *n* [brother] frère *m*; [sister] sœur *f*; all his ~s tous ses frères et sœurs; Bob and Sue are ~s Bob et Sue sont frère et sœur. ◇ *adj*: ~ rivalry rivalité *f* entre frères et sœurs.

sibyl [ˈsɪbl] *n* sibylle *f*.

sibylline [ˈsɪbəlaɪn] *adj* sibyllin.

sic [sɪk] *adv* sic.

siccative [ˈsɪkətɪv] *n* siccatif *m*.

Sicilian [sɪˈsɪljən] ◇ *n* -**1.** [person] Sicilien *m*, -enne *f*. -**2.** LING sicilien *m*. ◇ *adj* sicilien.

Sicily [ˈsɪsɪlɪ] *pr n* Sicile *f*; in ~ en Sicile.

sick [sɪk] ◇ *adj* -**1.** [unwell - person, plant, animal] malade; [- state] maladif; to fall ~, to get OR to take ~ *Am* tomber malade; to look ~ *Am* avoir l'air malade; my secretary is off ~ ma secrétaire est absente, elle est malade; they care for ~ people ils soignent les malades; to report OR to go *inf* ~ MIL se faire porter malade OR pâle; are you ~ in the head or something? *inf* tu n'es pas un peu malade?; to be ~ with fear/worry être malade de peur/d'inquiétude; you're so good at it you make me look ~! *inf Am* tu le fais si bien que j'ai l'air complètement nul! -**2.** [nauseous]: to be ~ vomir; to feel ~ avoir envie de vomir OR mal au coeur; I get ~ at the sight of blood la vue du sang me rend malade OR me soulève le cœur; oysters make me ~ les huîtres me rendent malade; you'll make yourself ~ if you eat too fast tu vas te rendre malade si tu manges trop vite; the very idea gives me a ~ feeling in my stomach rien que d'y penser j'ai mal au cœur; I felt ~ to my stomach j'avais mal au cœur ☐ to be ~ as a dog *inf* être malade comme un chien. -**3.** [fed up, disgusted] écœuré, dégoûté; I'm ~ (and tired) of telling you! j'en ai assez de te le répéter!; it made him ~ to think of all that waste ça l'écœurait de penser à tout ce gâchis; you make me ~! tu m'écœures OR me dégoûtes!; he was ~ of living alone il en avait assez de vivre seul ☐ to be ~ to death of sb/sthg *inf* en avoir vraiment assez OR ras le bol de qqn/qqch; I was as ~ as a parrot! *Br hum* j'en étais malade!; to be ~ at heart *lit* avoir la mort dans l'âme. -**4.** *inf* [unwholesome] malsain, pervers; [morbid - humour] malsain; [- joke] macabre; I find their relationship really ~ je trouve leurs rapports vraiment malsains; that's the ~est thing I ever heard! je n'ai jamais entendu quelque chose d'aussi écœurant! -**5.** *lit* [longing]: to be ~ for sb/sthg languir après qqn/qqch. ◇ *npl*: the ~ les malades *mpl*. ◇ *n inf Br* [vomit] vomi *m*.
◆ **sick up** *inf vt sep Br* vomir, rendre.

sick-bag *n sachet mis à la disposition des passagers malades dans les avions*.

sickbay [ˈsɪkbeɪ] *n* infirmerie *f*.

sickbed [ˈsɪkbed] *n* lit *m* de malade.

sick building syndrome *n effets néfastes du séjour dans un environnement muni de l'air conditionné*.

sick call *n* -**1.** [visit - by doctor] visite *f* à domicile; [- by priest] visite *f* aux malades. -**2.** *Am* = **sick parade**.

sicken [ˈsɪkn] ◇ *vt* -**1.** [disgust, distress] écœurer, dégoûter; it ~ed him to see them together ça l'écœurait de les voir ensemble. -**2.** [make nauseous] donner mal au cœur à, écœurer; [make vomit] faire vomir; the smell ~s me cette odeur me soulève le cœur OR me donne des hauts-le-cœur. ◇ *vi* -**1.** [fall ill - person, animal] tomber malade; [- plant] dépérir; he's ~ing for something *Br* il couve quelque chose. -**2.** *lit* [become weary] se lasser; she ~ed of her idle life elle se lassa de mener une vie désœuvrée.

sickening [ˈsɪknɪŋ] *adj* -**1.** [nauseating - smell, mess] nauséabond, écœurant; [- sight] écœurant. -**2.** *fig* écœurant, répugnant; it's ~ the way the refugees are treated c'est écœurant, la façon dont on traite les réfugiés; he fell with a ~ thud il est tombé avec un bruit qui laissait présager le pire; she's so talented it's ~! *hum* elle est si douée que c'en est écœurant!

sickeningly [ˈsɪknɪŋlɪ] *adv*: he's ~ pious il est d'une piété écœurante; she's ~ successful *hum* elle réussit si bien que c'en est écœurant.

sick headache *n Br* migraine *f*.

sickle [ˈsɪkl] *n* faucille *f*; a ~ moon un mince croissant de lune.

sick leave *n* congé *m* (de) maladie; to be (away) on ~ être en congé (de) maladie.

sickle-cell anaemia *n* drépanocytose *f*, anémie *f* à hématies falciformes.

sickliness [ˈsɪklɪnɪs] *n* -**1.** [of person] faiblesse *f*, fragilité *f*; [of complexion] pâleur *f* maladive. -**2.** [of food] goût *m* écœurant.

sick list *n* liste *f* des malades; to be on the ~ se faire porter malade.

sickly [ˈsɪklɪ] (*compar* sicklier, *superl* sickliest) *adj* -**1.** [person] chétif, maladif; [complexion, pallor] maladif; [plant] chétif; [dawn, light, glare] blafard; [smile] pâle. -**2.** [nauseating] écœurant; [sentimentality] mièvre; a ~ sweet smell une odeur écœurante OR douceâtre. -**3.** *arch* [unwholesome - vapour, climate] insalubre, malsain.

sick-making *inf adj* dégueulasse.

sickness [ˈsɪknɪs] *n* -**1.** [nausea] nausée *f*. -**2.** [illness] maladie *f*; radiation ~ mal *m* des rayons.

sickness benefit *n* (*U*) *Br* prestations *fpl* de l'assurance maladie, ≃ indemnités *fpl* journalières.

sick note *n* mot d'absence *(pour cause de maladie)*.

sicko [ˈsɪkəʊ] *adj Am* dérangé, malade.

sick parade *n Br* MIL: to go on ~ se faire porter malade.

sick pay *n* indemnité *f* de maladie *(versée par l'employeur)*.

sickroom [ˈsɪkrʊm] *n* [sickbay] infirmerie *f*; [in home] chambre *f* de malade.

side [saɪd] ◇ *n* -**1.** [part of body - human] côté *m*; [- animal] flanc *m*; lie on your ~ couchez-vous sur le côté; I've got a pain in my right ~ j'ai mal au côté droit; her fists were clenched at her ~s ses poings étaient serrés le long de son corps; I sat down at OR by his ~ je me suis assis à ses côtés OR à côté de lui; the child remained at her mother's ~ l'enfant restait à côté de sa mère; she was called to the president's ~ elle a été appelée auprès du président; to get on sb's good/bad ~ s'attirer la sympathie/l'antipathie de qqn. -**2.** [as opposed to top, bottom, front, back] côté *m*; the bottle was on its ~ la bouteille était couchée; lay the barrel on its ~ mettez le fût sur le côté; her hair is cut short at the ~s ses cheveux sont coupés court sur les côtés; there's a door at the ~ il y a une porte sur le côté; the car was hit from the ~ la voiture a subi un choc latéral. -**3.** [outer surface - of cube, pyramid] côté *m*, face *f*; [flat surface - of biscuit, sheet of paper, cloth] côté *m*; [- of coin, record, tape] côté *m*, face *f*; write on both ~s of the paper écrivez recto verso; grill for three minutes on each ~ passez au grill trois minutes de chaque côté; 'this ~ up' 'haut'; the right/wrong ~ of the cloth l'endroit *m*/l'envers *m* du tissu; the other ~ of the tape is blank l'autre face de la cassette est vierge ‖ [inner surface - of bathtub, cave, stomach] paroi *f*; the ~s of the crate are lined with newspaper l'intérieur de la caisse est recouvert de papier journal ☐ to know which ~ one's bread is buttered on ne pas perdre le nord; the other ~ of the coin le revers de la médaille. -**4.** [edge - of triangle, lawn] côté *m*; [- of road, pond, river] bord *m*; there's a wall on three ~s of the property il y a un mur sur trois côtés du terrain; she held on to the ~ of the pool elle s'accrochait au rebord de la piscine; a wave washed him over the ~ une vague l'emporta par-dessus bord; I sat on the ~ of the bed je me suis assis sur le bord du lit; I sat on OR at the ~ of the road je me suis assis au bord de la route; she was kneeling by the ~ of the bed elle était agenouillée à côté du lit. -**5.** [slope - of mountain, hill, valley] flanc *m*, versant *m*; the village is set on the ~ of a mountain le village est situé sur le flanc d'une montagne. -**6.** [opposing part] côté *m*; on the other ~ of the room/wall de l'autre côté de la pièce/du mur; on OR to one ~ of the door d'un côté de la porte; you're driving on the wrong ~! vous conduisez du mauvais côté!; which ~ of the bed do you sleep on? de quel côté du lit dors-tu?; she got in on the driver's ~ elle est montée côté conducteur; the sunny ~ of the stadium le côté ensoleillé du stade; the dark ~ of the moon la face cachée de la lune; the Mexican ~ of the border le côté mexicain de la frontière; the lamppost leaned to one ~ le réverbère penchait d'un côté; he wore his hat on one ~ il portait son chapeau de côté; move the bags to one ~ écartez OR poussez les sacs; to jump to one ~ faire un bond de côté; to take sb to one ~ prendre qqn à part; leaving that on one ~ for the moment... en laissant cela de côté pour l'instant...; Manhattan's Lower East Side le quartier sud-est de Manhattan; it's way on the other ~ of town c'est à l'autre bout de la ville; on every ~, on all ~s de tous côtés, de toutes parts; they were attacked on OR from all ~s ils ont été attaqués de tous côtés OR de toutes parts; there were flames on every ~ il y avait des flammes de tous (les) côtés; the ship rolled from ~ to ~ le bateau roulait; he's on the right/wrong ~ of forty il n'a pas encore/il a dépassé la quarantaine; stay on the right ~ of the law restez dans la légalité; he operates on the wrong ~ of the law il fait des affaires en marge de la loi; there's no other hotel this ~ of Reno il n'y a pas d'autre hôtel entre ici et Reno; these are the best beaches this ~ of Hawaii ce sont les meilleures plages après celles de Hawaii; I can't see myself finishing the work this ~ of Easter je ne me vois pas finir ce travail d'ici Pâques; it's a bit on the pricey/small ~ c'est un peu cher/petit ☐ to live on the right/wrong ~ of the tracks *Am* habiter un bon/mauvais quartier. -**7.** [facet, aspect - of problem] aspect *m*, côté *m*; [- of person] côté *m*; to examine all ~s of an issue examiner un problème sous tous ses aspects; there are many ~s to this issue c'est une question complexe; he stressed the positive/humanitarian ~ il a souligné le côté positif/humanitaire; she's very good at the practical ~ of things elle est excellente sur le plan pratique; she has her good ~ elle a ses bons côtés; I've seen his cruel ~ je sais qu'il peut être cruel; she showed an unexpected ~ of herself elle a révélé une facette inattendue de sa personnalité; I've kept my ~ of the deal j'ai tenu mes engagements dans cette affaire. -**8.** [group, faction] côté *m*, camp *m*; [team] équipe *f*; [party] POL parti *m*; the winning ~ le camp des vainqueurs; to pick OR to choose ~s former des équipes; whose ~ is he on? de quel côté est-il?; which ~ won the war? qui a gagné la guerre?; the rebel ~ les rebelles *mpl*; there is mistrust on both ~s il y a de la méfiance dans les deux camps; there's still no concrete proposal on OR from their ~ il n'y a toujours pas de proposition concrète de leur part; to go over to the other ~, to change ~s changer de camp; luck is on our ~ la chance est avec nous; time is on their ~ le temps joue en leur faveur; he has youth on his ~ il a l'avantage de la jeunesse; he really let the ~ down il nous/leur *etc* a fait faux bond; don't let the ~ down! nous comptons sur vous!; she tried to get the committee on her ~ elle a essayé de mettre le comité de son côté; to take ~s prendre parti; he took Tom's ~ against me il a pris le parti de Tom contre moi; to be on the ~ of peace être pour la paix. -**9.** [position, point of view] point *m* de vue; there are two ~s to every argument dans toute discussion il y a deux points de vue; he's told me his ~ of the story il m'a donné sa version de l'affaire. -**10.** [line of descent]: she's a Smith on her mother's ~ c'est une Smith par sa mère; he's Polish on both ~s ses parents sont tous les deux polonais; my grandmother on my mother's/father's ~ ma grand-mère maternelle/paternelle; she gets her love for music from her mother's ~ of the family elle tient son goût pour la musique du côté maternel de sa famille; they are all blond on her father's ~ of the family ils sont tous blonds du côté de OR dans la famille de son père. -**11.** CULIN: ~ of pork demi-porc *m*; ~ of beef/lamb quartier *m* de bœuf/d'agneau. -**12.** *Br* [page of text] page *f*; I wrote ten ~s j'ai écrit dix pages. -**13.** *inf Br* [TV channel] chaîne *f*; what's on the other ~? qu'est-ce qu'il y a sur l'autre chaîne? -**14.** *Br* [in snooker, billiards etc] effet *m*. -**15.** *inf Br* [cheek] culot *m*; [arrogance] fierté *f*; there's no ~ to him il est très simple, ce n'est pas un frimeur.

◇ *vi*: to ~ with sb se ranger OR se mettre du côté de qqn, prendre parti pour qqn; it's in our interest to ~ with the majority nous avons intérêt à nous ranger du côté de la majorité; they all ~d against her ils ont fait cause commune contre elle.

◇ *adj* -**1.** [situated on one side - panel, window] latéral, de côté; ~ aisle [in church] bas-côté *m*; THEAT allée *f* latérale; ~ door porte *f* latérale; ~ entrance entrée *f* latérale; ~ pocket poche *f* extérieure; ~ rail [on bridge] garde-fou *m*; NAUT rambarde *f*. -**2.** [directional - view] de côté, de profil; [- elevation, kick] latéral; to do a ~ split DANCE faire un grand écart latéral; to put ~ spin on a ball SPORT donner de l'effet à une balle. -**3.** [additional] en plus; a ~ order of toast une portion de toast en plus OR en supplément.

◆ **on the side** *adv phr*: to make a bit of money on the ~ [gen] se faire un peu d'argent en plus OR supplémentaire; [dishonestly] remplir ses poches; she's an artist but works as a taxi driver on the ~ elle est artiste mais elle fait le chauffeur de taxi pour arrondir ses fins de mois; a hamburger with salad on the ~ un hamburger avec une salade; anything on the ~, sir? [in restaurant] *Am* et avec cela, Monsieur?

◆ **side by side** *adv phr* côte à côte; they were walking ~ by ~ ils marchaient côte à côte; the tribes lived peacefully ~ by ~ les tribus vivaient paisiblement côte à côte; the road and the river run ~ by ~ la route longe la rivière; we'll be working ~ by ~ with the Swiss on this project nous travaillerons en étroite collaboration avec les Suisses sur ce projet.

sidearm ['saɪdɑːm] *n* arme *f* de poing.

sideband ['saɪdbænd] *n* RADIO bande *f* latérale.

sideboard ['saɪdbɔːd] *n* [for dishes] buffet *m* bas.

◆ **sideboards** *Br* = **sideburns**.

sideburns ['saɪdbɜːnz] *npl* pattes *fpl*.

sidecar ['saɪdkɑːʳ] *n* -**1.** [on motorbike] side-car *m*. -**2.** [drink] side-car *m* (*cocktail composé de cognac, de cointreau et de jus de citron*).

side chain *n* CHEM chaîne *f* latérale.

-sided ['saɪdɪd] *in cpds*: three/five~ à trois/cinq côtés; a many~ figure une figure polygonale; a glass~ box une boîte à parois de verre; elastic~ boots bottes avec de l'élastique sur les côtés; a steep~ valley une vallée encaissée.

side dish *n* plat *m* d'accompagnement; [of vegetables] garniture *f*; with a ~ of spinach avec une garniture d'épinards.

side drum *n* caisse *f* claire.

side effect *n* effet *m* secondaire; the drug was found to have harmful ~s on a découvert que la drogue avait des effets secondaires nocifs; consumers suffered the ~s of inflation les consommateurs ont subi les effets secondaires OR indésirables de l'inflation.

side glance *n literal* regard *m* oblique OR de côté; *fig* [allusion] allusion *f*.

side issue *n* question *f* secondaire.

sidekick *inf* ['saɪdkɪk] *n* acolyte *m*.

sidelight ['saɪdlaɪt] *n* -**1.** *Br* AUT feu *m* de position. -**2.** NAUT feu *m* de position. -**3.** [information]: to give (sb) a ~ on sthg donner à qqn un aperçu de qqch.

sideline ['saɪdlaɪn] ◇ *n* -**1.** SPORT [gen] ligne *f* de côté; [touchline] (ligne *f* de) touche *f*, ligne *f* de jeu; to wait on the ~s SPORT attendre sur la touche; *fig* attendre dans les coulisses; her injury kept her on the ~s all season sa blessure l'a laissée sur la touche pendant toute la saison; I prefer to stand on the ~s *fig* je préfère ne pas m'en mêler. -**2.** [job] activité *f* OR occupation *f* secondaire; as a ~ he takes wedding photos il fait des photos de mariage pour arrondir ses fins de mois. -**3.** COMM [product line] ligne *f* de produits secondaires; they've made recycling a profitable ~ ils ont fait du recyclage une activité secondaire rentable; it's only a ~ for us ce n'est pas notre spécialité.

◇ *vt* SPORT & *fig* mettre sur la touche.

sidelong ['saɪdlɒŋ] ◇ *adj* oblique, de côté; they exchanged ~ glances ils ont échangé un regard complice.

◇ *adv* en oblique, de côté.

sideman ['saɪdmən] (*pl* sidemen [-mən]) *n* MUS membre *m* de l'orchestre; he was one of Count Basie's sidemen in Chicago il a joué avec Count Basie à Chicago.

side meat *inf n Am* poitrine *f* fumée.

side-on ◇ *adv* de profil; ~, she looks very like you de profil, elle te ressemble beaucoup; the car was hit ~ la voiture a subi un choc latéral.

◇ *adj* [photo] de profil; [collision] latéral.

side order *n esp Am* portion *f*; I'd like a ~ of fries je voudrais aussi des frites.

side plate *n* petite assiette *f* (*que l'on met à gauche de chaque convive*).

sidereal [saɪ'dɪərɪəl] *adj* sidéral.

side road *n* [minor road - in country] route *f* secondaire; [- in town] petite rue *f*; [road at right angles] rue *f* transversale; the car was coming out of a ~ la voiture débouchait d'une route transversale.

sidesaddle ['saɪd,sædl] ◇ *n* selle *f* de femme.

◇ *adv*: to ride ~ monter en amazone.

side salad *n* salade *f* (*pour accompagner un plat*).

sideshow ['saɪdʃəʊ] *n* -**1.** [in fair - booth] stand *m*, baraque *f* foraine; [- show] attraction *f*. -**2.** [minor event] détail *m*.

sideslip ['saɪdslɪp] (*pt* & *pp* sideslipped, *cont* sideslipping) ◇ *n* -**1.** AERON glissade *f*. -**2.** AUT dérapage *m*; to go into ~ déraper.

◇ *vi* AERON glisser sur l'aile.

sidesman ['saɪdzmən] (*pl* sidesmen [-mən]) *n Br* RELIG ≃ bedeau *m*.

sidesplitting *inf* ['saɪd,splɪtɪŋ] *adj* [story, joke] tordant, bidonnant.

sidestep ['saɪdstep] (*pt* & *pp* sidestepped, *cont* sidestepping) ◇ *n* crochet *m*; SPORT esquive *f*.

◇ *vt* -**1.** [opponent, tackle - in football, rugby] crocheter; [- in boxing] esquiver. -**2.** [issue, question] éluder, éviter; [difficulty] esquiver; he'll ~ making any decision il évitera de prendre quelque décision que ce soit; they'll ~ the regulations/the law ils contourneront le règlement/la loi.

◇ *vi* -**1.** [dodge] esquiver. -**2.** [in skiing]: to ~ up a slope monter une pente en escalier. -**3.** [be evasive] rester évasif.

side street *n* [minor street] petite rue *f*; [at right angles] rue *f* transversale.

sidestroke ['saɪdstrəʊk] *n* nage *f* indienne; to swim ~ nager à l'indienne.

sideswipe ['saɪdswaɪp] ◇ *n* -**1.** [blow - glancing] coup *m* oblique; [- severe] choc *m* latéral. -**2.** [remark] allusion *f* désobligeante; he took a few ~s at the project il a fait quelques allusions désobligeantes sur le projet.

◇ *vt Am* faucher.

side table *n* petite table *f*; [for dishes] desserte *f*; [beside bed] table *f* de chevet.

sidetrack ['saɪdtræk] ◇ *vt* [person - in talk] faire dévier de son sujet; [- in activity] distraire; [enquiry, investigation] détourner; the speaker kept getting ~ed le conférencier s'écartait sans cesse de son sujet; sorry, I got ~ed for a moment pardon, je m'égare.

◇ *n* -**1.** [digression] digression *f*; he went off on a ~ [topic] il s'est écarté de son sujet; [activity] il s'est laissé distraire. -**2.** *Am* RAIL [in yard] voie *f* de garage; [off main line] voie *f* d'évitement.

sidewalk ['saɪdwɔːk] *n Am* trottoir *m*; to hit the ~s *inf* chercher du boulot.

sidewalk artist *n Am* artiste *mf* de rue (*qui dessine à la craie sur le trottoir*).

sidewalk café *n Am* café *m* avec terrasse.

sidewalk furniture *n Am* mobilier *m* urbain.

sideways ['saɪdweɪz] ◇ *adv* [lean] d'un côté; [glance] obliquement, de côté; [walk] en crabe; to step ~ faire un pas de côté; I was thrown ~ j'ai été projeté sur le côté; the cup slid ~ la tasse glissa de côté; now turn ~ maintenant mettez-vous de profil; the pieces can move forwards and backwards but not ~ les pièces peuvent se déplacer en avant ou en arrière, mais pas latéralement ❑ the news really knocked him ~ *inf* [astounded him] la nouvelle l'a vraiment époustouflé; [upset him] la nouvelle l'a vraiment mis dans tous ses états.

◇ *adj* [step] de côté; [look] oblique, de côté; the job is a ~ move c'est une mutation et non pas une promotion.

side-wheeler *n Am* bateau *m* à aubes.

side-whiskers *npl* favoris *mpl*.

sidewinder ['saɪd,waɪndəʳ] *n Am* -**1.** [blow] grand coup *m* de poing. -**2.** [snake] crotale *m*, serpent *m* à sonnettes.

siding ['saɪdɪŋ] *n* -**1.** RAIL [in yard] voie *f* de garage; [off main track] voie *f* d'évitement. -**2.** *Am* CONSTR revêtement *m*.

sidle ['saɪdl] *vi* se faufiler; to ~ up OR over to sb se glisser vers OR jusqu'à qqn; to ~ in/out entrer/sortir furtivement; to ~ along marcher de côté, avancer de biais.

Sidon ['saɪdn] *pr n* Sidon.

SIDS *n abbr of* sudden infant death syndrome.

siege [siːdʒ] ◇ *n* MIL & *fig* siège *m*; to lay ~ to sthg assiéger qqch; to be under ~ être assiégé; to raise a ~ lever le siège; a state of ~ has been declared l'état de siège a été déclaré.

◇ *comp* [machine, warfare] de siège; to have a ~ mentality être toujours sur la défensive.

siege economy *n* économie *f* protectionniste.

Siegfried ['siːgfriːd] *pr n* Siegfried.

siemens ['siːmənz] (*pl inv*) *n* siemens *m*.

Siena [sɪ'enə] *pr n* Sienne.

sienna [sɪ'enə] ◇ *n* -**1.** [earth] terre *f* de Sienne; raw/burnt ~ terre de Sienne naturelle/brûlée. -**2.** [colour] ocre *m* brun.

◇ *adj* ocre brun (*inv*).

sierra [sɪ'erə] *n* sierra *f*.

Sierra Leone [sɪ'erəlɪəʊn] *pr n* Sierra Leone *f*; in ~ en Sierra Leone.

Sierra Leonean [sɪ'erəlɪ'əʊnjən] ◇ *n habitant de la Sierra Leone*.

◇ *adj* de la Sierra Leone.

Sierra Madre [sɪ,erə'mɑːdreɪ] *pr n*: the ~ la Sierra Madre.

Sierra Nevada [sɪ,erənə'vɑːdə] *pr n*: the ~ la Sierra Nevada.

siesta [sɪ'estə] *n* sieste *f*; to have OR to take a ~ faire la sieste.

sieve [sɪv] ◇ *n* [gen] tamis *m*; [kitchen utensil] passoire *f*; [for gravel, ore] crible *m*; I've got a memory OR mind like a ~! ma mémoire est une vraie passoire!

◇ *vt* [flour, sand, powder] tamiser, passer au tamis; [purée, soup] passer; [gravel, ore] cribler, passer au crible.

sievert ['siːvət] *n* sievert *m*.

sift [sɪft] ◇ *vt* -**1.** [ingredients, soil] tamiser, passer au tamis; [gravel, seed, ore] cribler, passer au crible; ~ a little sugar onto the cakes saupoudrez un peu de sucre sur les gâteaux. -**2.** [scrutinize - evidence, proposal] passer au crible *fig*; the experts are ~ing the facts les experts passent les faits au crible. -**3.** = **sift out**.
◇ *vi* -**1.** [search] fouiller; they ~ed through the garbage/the ruins ils fouillaient (dans) les ordures/les ruines; he was ~ing through some old correspondence il était en train de fouiller dans une vieille correspondance. -**2.** [pass, filter] filtrer; dust had ~ed in through the cracks la poussière s'était infiltrée par les fentes; I let the sand ~ through my fingers j'ai laissé le sable couler entre mes doigts.
◆ **sift out** *vt sep* -**1.** [remove - lumps, debris] enlever (à l'aide d'un tamis OR d'un crible); he ~ed out the lumps from the flour il a tamisé la farine pour enlever les grumeaux. -**2.** [distinguish] dégager, distinguer; they ~ed out the relevant information ils n'ont retenu que les éléments intéressants.

sifter ['sɪftəʳ] *n* [sieve - for flour, powder, soil] tamis *m*; [- for gravel, seed, ore] crible *m*; [shaker] saupoudreuse *f*.

sifting ['sɪftɪŋ] *n* [of flour, powder, soil] tamisage *m*; [of seed, gravel, ore] criblage *m*.
◆ **siftings** *npl* [residue] résidu *m*; AGR criblure *f*.

sigh [saɪ] ◇ *vi* -**1.** [gen] soupirer, pousser un soupir; to ~ with relief pousser un soupir de soulagement. -**2.** *lit* [lament] se lamenter; to ~ over sthg se lamenter sur qqch || [grieve] soupirer; to ~ for OR over sb/sthg soupirer pour qqn/qqch. -**3.** [wind] murmurer; [tree, reed] bruire.
◇ *vt*: "it's so lovely here", she ~ed «c'est tellement joli ici», soupira-t-elle.
◇ *n* soupir *m*; to give OR to heave a ~ of relief pousser un soupir de soulagement.

sighing ['saɪɪŋ] *n (U)* [of person] soupirs *mpl*; [of wind] murmure *m*; [of trees] bruissement *m*.

sight [saɪt] ◇ *n* -**1.** [faculty, sense] vue *f*; her ~ is failing sa vue baisse; to lose/to recover one's ~ perdre/recouvrer la vue. -**2.** [act, instance of seeing] vue *f*; it was my first ~ of the Pacific c'était la première fois que je voyais le Pacifique; he fainted at the ~ of the blood il s'est évanoui à la vue du sang; to catch ~ of sb/sthg apercevoir OR entrevoir qqn/qqch; to lose ~ of sb/sthg perdre qqn/qqch de vue; at first ~ the place seemed abandoned à première vue, l'endroit avait l'air abandonné; it was love at first ~ ce fut le coup de foudre; do you believe in love at first ~? est-ce que tu crois au coup de foudre?; I can't stand OR bear the ~ of him! je ne le supporte pas!; to know sb by ~ connaître qqn de vue; to buy sthg ~ unseen acheter qqch sans l'avoir vu; he can play music at OR *Am* by ~ il sait déchiffrer une partition; to shoot at OR on ~ tirer à vue; payable at OR *Am* on ~ payable à vue. -**3.** [range of vision] (portée *f* de) vue *f*; the plane was still in ~ l'avion était encore en vue; there wasn't a taxi in ~ il n'y avait pas un (seul) taxi en vue; I heard her voice but she was nowhere in ~ j'entendais sa voix mais je ne la voyais nulle part; is the end in ~? est-ce que tu en vois la fin?; there's still no end in ~ je n'en vois pas la fin; keep that car/your goal in ~ ne perdez pas cette voiture/votre but de vue; the mountains came into ~ les montagnes sont apparues; the runners came into ~ les coureurs sont apparus; out of ~ hors de vue; I watched her until she was out of ~ je l'ai regardée jusqu'à ce qu'elle disparaisse de ma vue; keep out of ~! ne vous montrez pas!, cachez-vous!; keep it out of ~ ne le montrez pas, cachez-le; she never lets him out of her ~ elle ne le perd jamais de vue; get out of my ~! disparais de ma vue!; get that dog out of my ~! faites disparaître ce chien!; a peace settlement now seems within ~ un accord de paix semble maintenant possible; it was impossible to get within ~ of the accident il était impossible de s'approcher du lieu de l'accident pour voir ce qui se passait; he had to give up within ~ of the summit il a dû renoncer à quelques mètres du sommet ❑ out of ~, out of mind *prov* loin des yeux, loin du cœur *prov*. -**4.** [spectacle] spectacle *m*; the cliffs were an impressive ~ les falaises étaient impressionnantes à voir; beggars are a common ~ on the streets on voit beaucoup de mendiants dans les rues; it was not a pretty ~ ça n'était pas beau à voir; the waterfalls are a ~ worth seeing les cascades valent la peine d'être vues ❑ you're a ~ for sore eyes! Dieu merci te voilà! -**5.** [tourist attraction] attraction *f*; one of the ~s of Rome une des choses à voir à Rome; I'll show you OR take you round the ~s tomorrow je vous ferai visiter OR voir la ville demain. -**6.** *lit* [opinion, judgment] avis *m*, opinion *f*; in my father's ~ she could do no wrong aux yeux de mon père, elle était incapable de faire du mal; we are all equal in the ~ of God nous sommes tous égaux devant Dieu. -**7.** *inf* [mess] pagaille *f*; [ridiculously dressed person] tableau *m fig*; the kitchen was a ~! quelle pagaille dans la cuisine!; your hair is a ~! tu as vu tes cheveux?; you look a ~ in that outfit! tu as vu de quoi tu as l'air dans cette tenue?; I must look a ~! je ne dois pas être beau à voir! -**8.** [aiming device] viseur *m*; [on mortar] appareil *m* de pointage ❑ wait till the target crosses your line of ~ attendez que la cible traverse votre ligne de mire; to take a ~ on sthg viser qqch; front ~ guidon *m*; notch ~ cran *m* de mire; telescopic ~ lunette *f* de visée; to have sthg in one's ~s *literal* avoir qqch dans sa ligne de tir; *fig* avoir qqch en vue; to lower one's ~s viser moins haut; to set one's ~s on sthg décider d'obtenir qqch; he's set his ~s on becoming a doctor son ambition est de devenir médecin; she has her ~s set on the presidency/a diplomatic career elle vise la présidence/une carrière de diplomate.
◇ *vt* -**1.** [see] voir, apercevoir; [spot] repérer; the clouds parted and we ~ed the summit les nuages se déchirèrent et nous aperçûmes le sommet; a submarine was ~ed un sous-marin a été repéré. -**2.** [aim - gun] pointer; he carefully ~ed his pistol at the target il visa soigneusement la cible avec son pistolet.
◆ **a sight** *inf adv phr Br* beaucoup; you'd earn a ~ more money working in industry votre salaire serait beaucoup plus important si vous travailliez dans l'industrie; it's a (far) ~ worse than before c'est bien pire qu'avant; he's a ~ too modest il est bien OR beaucoup trop modeste; not by a long ~ loin de là, bien au contraire.

sighted ['saɪtɪd] *adj* voyant; the school also accepts ~ students l'école reçoit aussi des étudiants voyants; partially ~ mal voyant.

sighting ['saɪtɪŋ] *n*: UFO ~s have increased un nombre croissant de personnes déclarent avoir vu des ovnis.

sightless ['saɪtlɪs] *adj* [blind] aveugle.

sightline ['saɪtlaɪn] *n*: to block sb's ~ boucher la vue de qqn; drivers need an unobstructed ~ at intersections les conducteurs doivent avoir un champ de vision dégagé aux croisements.

sightly ['saɪtlɪ] (*compar* sightlier, *superl* sightliest) *adj* agréable à regarder.

sight-read [-riːd] (*pt* & *pp* sight-read [-red]) *vi* & *vt* MUS déchiffrer.

sight-reading *n* MUS déchiffrage *m*.

sightsee ['saɪtsiː] *vi*: to go ~ing faire du tourisme.

sightseeing ['saɪt,siːɪŋ] ◇ *n* tourisme *m*; to do some ~ faire du tourisme; [in town] visiter la ville.
◇ *comp*: ~ bus car *m* de touristes; I went on a ~ tour of Rome j'ai fait une visite guidée de Rome.

sightseer ['saɪt,siːəʳ] *n* touriste *mf*.

sigma ['sɪgmə] *n* sigma *m*.

sign [saɪn] ◇ *n* -**1.** [gen, LING, MATH & MUS] signe *m*; this ~ means "real leather" ce symbole signifie «cuir véritable»; minus ~ signe *m* moins. -**2.** [gesture, motion] signe *m*, geste *m*; to make a ~ to sb faire signe à qqn; she made a ~ for me to enter elle m'a fait signe d'entrer; the chief made ~s for me to follow him le chef m'a fait signe de le suivre; to make the ~ of the cross faire le signe de croix; wait until the policeman gives the ~ to cross attendez que le policier vous fasse signe de traverser; the victory ~ le signe de la victoire. -**3.** [arranged signal] signal *m*; a lighted lamp in the window is the ~ that it's safe une lampe allumée à la fenêtre signifie qu'il n'y a pas de danger; when I give the ~, run à mon signal, courez. -**4.** [written notice - gen & AUT] panneau *m*; [- hand-written] écriteau *m*; [- on shop, bar, cinema etc] enseigne *f*; the ~s are all in Arabic tous les panneaux sont en arabe; neon ~ enseigne *f* au néon; I didn't see the stop ~ je n'ai pas vu le stop; obey traffic ~s respectez les panneaux de signalisation. -**5.** [evidence, indication] signe *m*, indice *m*; MED signe *m*; the speech was interpreted as a ~ of goodwill on a interprété son discours comme un signe de bonne volonté; as a ~ of respect en témoignage OR en signe de respect; they wear red as a ~ of mourning ils portent le rouge en signe de deuil; a distended belly is a ~ of malnutrition un ventre dilaté est un signe de sous-alimentation; a red sunset is a ~ of fair weather un coucher de soleil rouge est signe qu'il fera beau; it's a ~ of the times c'est un signe des temps; if he's making jokes it's a good ~ c'est bon signe s'il fait des plaisanteries; at the first ~ of trouble, he goes to pieces *inf* au premier petit problème, il craque; were there any ~s of a struggle? y avait-il des traces de lutte?; all the ~s are that the economy is improving tout laisse à penser que l'économie s'améliore; there's no ~ of her changing her mind rien n'indique qu'elle va changer d'avis; there's no ~ of the file anywhere on ne trouve trace du dossier nulle part; he gave no ~ of having heard me il n'a pas eu l'air de m'avoir entendu; is there any ~ of Amy yet? – not a ~ est-ce qu'on a eu des nouvelles de Amy? – pas la moindre nouvelle; since then, he's given no ~ of life depuis lors, il n'a pas donné signe de vie. -**6.** ASTROL signe *m*; what ~ are you? de quel signe êtes-vous? -**7.** RELIG [manifestation] signe *m*; a ~ from God un signe divin.
◇ *vt* -**1.** [document, book] signer; ~ your name here signez ici; here are the letters to be ~ed voici les lettres à signer; a ~ed Picasso lithograph une lithographie signée (par Picasso); he gave me a ~ed photo of himself il m'a donné une photo dédicacée; she ~s herself A.M. Hall elle signe A.M. Hall; the deal will be ~ed and sealed tomorrow l'affaire sera définitivement conclue demain; you're ~ing your own death warrant *fig* vous signez votre arrêt de mort. -**2.** SPORT [contract] signer; [player] engager; he's been ~ed for next season il a été engagé pour la saison prochaine. -**3.** [provide with signs] signaliser; the museum is not very well ~ed la signalisation du musée n'est pas très bonne.
◇ *vi* -**1.** [write name] signer; he ~ed with an X il a signé d'une croix; to ~ on the dotted line *literal* signer à l'endroit indiqué; *fig* s'engager. -**2.** [signal]: to ~ to sb to do sthg faire signe à qqn de faire qqch. -**3.** [use sign language] communiquer par signes; they were ~ing to each other ils se parlaient par signes.
◆ **sign away** *vt sep* [right, land, inheritance] se désister de; [independence] renoncer à; [power, control] abandonner; I felt I was ~ing away my freedom j'avais l'impression qu'en signant, je renonçais à ma liberté.
◆ **sign in** ◇ *vi insep* -**1.** [at hotel] remplir sa fiche (d'hôtel); [in club] signer le registre. -**2.** [worker] pointer (en arrivant).
◇ *vt sep* -**1.** [guest] faire signer en arrivant;

guests must be ~ed in les visiteurs doivent être inscrits sur le registre en arrivant. -**2.** [file, book] rendre, retourner.

◆ **sign for** *vt insep* -**1.** [accept] signer; to ~ for a delivery/a registered letter signer un bon de livraison/le récépissé d'une lettre recommandée; the files have to be ~ed for il faut signer pour retirer les dossiers. -**2.** [undertake work] signer (un contrat d'engagement); she's ~ed for another series elle a signé pour un autre feuilleton.

◆ **sign off** *vi insep* -**1.** RADIO & TV terminer l'émission; it's time to ~ off for today il est l'heure de vous quitter pour aujourd'hui. -**2.** [in letter]: I'll ~ off now je vais conclure ici.

◆ **sign on** *Br* ◇ *vi insep* -**1.** = **sign up 3.** -**2.** [register as unemployed] s'inscrire au chômage; you have to ~ on every two weeks il faut pointer (au chômage) toutes les deux semaines.
◇ *vt sep* = **sign up 2.**

◆ **sign out** ◇ *vi insep* [gen] signer le registre (en partant); [worker] pointer (en partant).
◇ *vt sep* -**1.** [file, car] retirer (contre décharge); [library book] emprunter; the keys are ~ed out to Mr Hill c'est M. Hill qui a signé pour retirer les clés. -**2.** [hospital patient] autoriser le départ de; he ~ed himself out il est parti sous sa propre responsabilité.

◆ **sign over** *vt sep* transférer; she ~ed the property over to her son elle a transféré la propriété au nom de son fils; the house is being ~ed over to its new owners tomorrow les nouveaux propriétaires entrent en possession de la maison demain.

◆ **sign up** ◇ *vi insep* -**1.** [for job] se faire embaucher; he ~ed up as a crew member il s'est fait embaucher comme membre d'équipage. -**2.** MIL [enlist] s'engager; to ~ up for the Marines s'engager dans les marines. -**3.** [enrol] s'inscrire; she ~ed up for an evening class elle s'est inscrite à des cours du soir.
◇ *vt sep* -**1.** [employee] embaucher; MIL [recruit] engager. -**2.** [student, participant] inscrire.

signal ['sɪgnl] (*Br pt & pp* signalled, *cont* signalling, *Am pt & pp* signaled, *cont* signaling) ◇ *n* -**1.** [indication] signal *m*; to give sb the ~ to do sthg donner à qqn le signal de faire qqch; he'll give the ~ to attack il donnera le signal de l'attaque; she gave the ~ for us to leave elle nous a donné le signal de départ; it was the first ~ (that) the regime was weakening c'était le premier signe de l'affaiblissement du régime; they are sending the government a clear signal that... ils indiquent clairement au gouvernement que... ❑ to send smoke ~s envoyer des signaux de fumée. -**2.** RAIL sémaphore *m*. -**3.** RADIO, TELEC & TV signal *m*; radio ~ signal radiophonique; station ~ RADIO indicatif *m* (de l'émetteur).
◇ *comp* -**1.** NAUT: ~ book code *m* international des signaux; ~ beacon OR light AERON & NAUT balise *f*. -**2.** RADIO & TELEC [strength, frequency] de signal.
◇ *adj fml* insigne; you showed a ~ lack of tact vous avez fait preuve d'une maladresse insigne.
◇ *vt* -**1.** [send signal to] envoyer un signal à; he signalled the plane forward il a fait signe au pilote d'avancer; the brain ~s the muscles to contract le cerveau envoie aux muscles le signal de se contracter; to ~ sb *Am* faire signe à qqn. -**2.** [indicate - refusal] indiquer, signaler; [- malfunction] signaler, avertir de; the parachutist signalled his readiness to jump le parachutiste fit signe qu'il était prêt à sauter; the linesman signalled the ball out le juge de ligne a signalé que le ballon était sorti; the cyclist signalled a left turn le cycliste a indiqué qu'il tournait à gauche. -**3.** [announce, mark - beginning, end, change] marquer; the speech signalled a radical change in policy le discours a marqué une modification radicale de la politique.
◇ *vi* -**1.** [gesture] faire des signes; to ~ to sb to do sthg faire signe à qqn de faire qqch; he signalled for the bill il a fait signe qu'il voulait l'addition; she was signalling for us to stop elle nous faisait signe de nous arrêter. -**2.** [send signal] envoyer un signal; the satellite is still signalling le satellite émet OR envoie toujours des signaux. -**3.** AUT [with indicator] mettre son clignotant; [with arm] indiquer de la main un changement de direction.

signal box *n* RAIL poste *m* de signalisation.

signaling *Am* = **signalling**.

signalize, -ise ['sɪgnəlaɪz] *vt* -**1.** *Am* [call attention to] signaler, faire remarquer. -**2.** *fml* [distinguish, mark] marquer; his term of office was ~d by numerous scandals son mandat a été marqué par de nombreux scandales.

signalling *Br*, **signaling** *Am* ['sɪgnəlɪŋ] ◇ *n* -**1.** AERON, AUT, NAUT & RAIL signalisation *f*. -**2.** [warning] avertissement *m*; the ~ of any malfunction is automatic toute défaillance est signalée par un dispositif automatique. -**3.** [of electronic message] transmission *f*; the satellite ~ was interrupted le satellite a cessé d'émettre des signaux.
◇ *comp* [error, equipment] de signalisation; ~ flag NAUT pavillon *m* de signalisation; MIL drapeau *m* de signalisation.

signally ['sɪgnəlɪ] *adv fml*: they have ~ failed to achieve their goal ils n'ont manifestement pas pu atteindre leur but.

signalman ['sɪgnlmən] (*pl* **signalmen** [-mən]) *n* RAIL aiguilleur *m*; MIL & NAUT signaleur *m*.

signal-to-noise ratio *n* rapport *m* signal-bruit.

signal tower *n Am* poste *m* d'aiguillage.

signatory ['sɪgnətrɪ] (*pl* **signatories**) ◇ *n* signataire *mf*; Namibia is a ~ to OR of the treaty la Namibie a ratifié le traité.
◇ *adj* signataire; the ~ nations les nations signataires.

signature ['sɪgnətʃə^r] ◇ *n* -**1.** [name] signature *f*; to put one's ~ to sthg apposer sa signature sur qqch. -**2.** [signing] signature *f*; to witness a ~ signer comme témoin; the bill is awaiting ~ *Am* POL le projet de loi attend la signature du président. -**3.** MUS: (key) ~ armature *f*. -**4.** *Am* PHARM [instructions] posologie *f*. -**5.** TYPO [section of book] cahier *m*; [mark] signature *f*.
◇ *comp*: Chanel and her ~ two-piece suit Chanel et le tailleur (deux-pièces) qui lui est si caractéristique.

signature tune *n Br* RADIO & TV indicatif *m* (musical); the song became their ~ *fig* cette chanson est devenue leur indicatif.

signboard ['saɪnbɔːd] *n* [gen] panneau *m*; [for notices] panneau *m* d'affichage; [for ads] panneau publicitaire; [on shop, bar, cinema etc] enseigne *f*.

signer ['saɪnə^r] *n* signataire *mf*.

signet ['sɪgnɪt] *n* sceau *m*, cachet *m*.

signet ring *n* chevalière *f*.

significance [sɪg'nɪfɪkəns] *n* -**1.** [importance, impact] importance *f*, portée *f*; what happened? — nothing of any ~ qu'est-ce qui s'est passé? — rien d'important OR de spécial; his decision is of no ~ to our plans sa décision n'aura aucune incidence sur nos projets. -**2.** [meaning] signification *f*, sens *m*; sounds take on a new ~ at night la nuit, les bruits se chargent d'un autre sens OR acquièrent une autre signification; the ~ of her words escaped me at the time la signification de ses paroles m'a échappé sur le coup; the stones have religious ~ for the tribe les pierres ont une signification religieuse pour la tribu.

significant [sɪg'nɪfɪkənt] *adj* -**1.** [notable - change, amount, damage] important, considérable; [- discovery, idea, event] de grande portée; no ~ progress has been made on n'a guère fait de progrès; was anything ~ decided at the meeting? s'est-il décidé quelque chose d'important à la réunion? ❑ ~ other partenaire *mf* (*dans une relation affective*). -**2.** [meaningful, indicative - look, pause] significatif; the government has made a small but ~ gesture le gouvernement a fait un geste petit mais significatif.

significant digits, **significant figures** *Am npl* chiffres *mpl* significatifs.

significantly [sɪg'nɪfɪkəntlɪ] *adv* -**1.** [differ, change, increase] considérablement; his health has improved ~ sa santé s'est considérablement améliorée; taxes have been ~ reduced les impôts ont été considérablement réduits; unemployment figures are not ~ lower le nombre de chômeurs n'a pas considérablement baissé. -**2.** [nod, frown, wink] de façon significative; she smiled ~ elle a eu un sourire lourd de signification OR qui en disait long; ~, she arrived early fait révélateur, elle est arrivée en avance.

signification [ˌsɪgnɪfɪ'keɪʃn] *n* signification *f*.

significative [sɪg'nɪfɪkətɪv] *adj* significatif.

signified ['sɪgnɪfaɪd] *n* LING signifié *m*.

signifier ['sɪgnɪfaɪə^r] *n* LING signifiant *m*.

signify ['sɪgnɪfaɪ] (*pt & pp* **signified**) ◇ *vt* -**1.** [indicate, show] signifier, indiquer; she stood up, ~ing that the interview was over elle se leva, signifiant ainsi que l'entrevue était terminée; the riots ~ an urgent need for reform les émeutes indiquent un besoin pressant de réforme. -**2.** [mean] signifier, vouloir dire; for him, socialism signified chaos pour lui, le socialisme était synonyme de chaos.
◇ *vi inf* être important; it doesn't ~! c'est sans importance!

signing ['saɪnɪŋ] *n traduction simultanée en langage par signes.*

sign language *n* (*U*) langage *m* des signes; to speak in ~ parler par signes; using ~, he managed to ask for food (en s'exprimant) par signes, il s'est débrouillé pour demander à manger.

signpost ['saɪnpəʊst] ◇ *n* -**1.** *literal* poteau *m* indicateur. -**2.** *fig* [guide] repère *m*; [omen] présage *m*.
◇ *vt literal & fig* [indicate] indiquer; [provide with signs] signaliser; the village is clearly ~ed le chemin du village est bien indiqué.

signposting ['saɪnˌpəʊstɪŋ] *n* signalisation *f*.

signwriter ['saɪnˌraɪtə^r] *n* peintre *m* en lettres.

Sikh [siːk] ◇ *n* Sikh *mf*.
◇ *adj* sikh.

silage ['saɪlɪdʒ] *n* ensilage *m*.

silence ['saɪləns] ◇ *n* silence *m*; an embarrassed/a shocked ~ un silence gêné/scandalisé; an explosion shattered the ~ of the night une explosion déchira le silence de la nuit; a ~ fell between them un silence s'installa entre eux; to suffer in ~ souffrir en silence; to pass sthg over in ~ passer qqch sous silence; his ~ on the issue/about his past intrigues me le silence qu'il garde à ce sujet/sur son passé m'intrigue; what's my ~ worth to you? combien êtes-vous disposé à payer pour acheter mon silence?; to observe a minute's ~ observer une minute de silence ❑ ~ is golden *prov* le silence est d'or *prov*.
◇ *vt* -**1.** [person] réduire au silence, faire taire; [sound] étouffer; [guns] faire taire; she ~d the child with a look d'un regard elle fit taire l'enfant; dissidents cannot be ~d forever on ne peut pas réduire les dissidents au silence OR faire taire les dissidents très longtemps. -**2.** [stifle - opposition] réduire au silence; [- conscience, rumours, complaints] faire taire.

silencer ['saɪlənsə^r] *n* -**1.** [on gun] silencieux *m*. -**2.** *Br* AUT pot *m* d'échappement, silencieux *m*.

silent ['saɪlənt] ◇ *adj* -**1.** [saying nothing] silencieux; he was ~ for a moment il resta silencieux un moment; to fall ~ se taire; to keep OR to be ~ garder le silence, rester silencieux; history remains OR is ~ on this point l'histoire ne dit rien sur ce point ❑ to give sb the ~ treatment *inf* rester silencieux pour mettre qqn mal à l'aise. -**2.** [taciturn] silencieux, taciturne; Hal's the strong, ~ type Hal est du genre fort et taciturne. -**3.** [unspoken - prayer, emotion, reproach] muet; his mouth twisted in ~ agony sa bouche se tordit dans un cri de douleur muette. -**4.** [soundless - room, forest] silencieux, tranquille; [- tread] silencieux; [- film] muet; the machines/the wind fell ~ le bruit des machines/du vent cessa ❑ as ~ as the grave

muet comme la tombe. -**5.** LING muet; the "g" is ~ le «g» est muet.
◇ *n* CIN film *m* muet; the ~s le (cinéma) muet.
silently ['saɪləntlɪ] *adv* silencieusement.
silent majority *n* majorité *f* silencieuse.
silent partner *n Am* COMM (associé *m*) commanditaire *m*, bailleur *m* de fonds.
Silesia [saɪ'liːzjə] *pr n* Silésie *f*; in ~ en Silésie; Lower ~ la basse Silésie; Upper ~ la haute Silésie.
silex ['saɪleks] *n* silex *m*.
silhouette [ˌsɪluː'et] ◇ *n* silhouette *f*; I saw her ~ at the window j'ai aperçu sa silhouette à la fenêtre; he could just see the church in ~ against the sky il ne voyait que la silhouette de l'église qui se découpait contre le ciel.
◇ *vt (usu pass)*: to be ~d against sthg se découper contre qqch; the tower was ~d against the sky la tour se découpait sur le ciel; she stood at the window, ~d against the light elle se tenait à la fenêtre, sa silhouette se détachant à contre-jour.
silica ['sɪlɪkə] *n* silice *f*; ~ gel/glass gel *m*/verre *m* de silice.
silicate ['sɪlɪkɪt] *n* silicate *m*.
siliceous, silicious [sɪ'lɪʃəs] *adj* siliceux.
silicon ['sɪlɪkən] *n* silicium *m*.
silicon chip *n* puce *f*.
silicone ['sɪlɪkəʊn] *n* silicone *f*; she's had a ~ implant elle s'est fait poser des implants en silicone.
Silicon Valley *pr n* Silicon Valley *f (centre de l'industrie électronique américaine, situé en Californie)*.
silicosis [ˌsɪlɪ'kəʊsɪs] *n (U)* silicose *f*.
silk [sɪlk] ◇ *n* -**1.** [fabric] soie *f*; [thread] fil *m* de soie; fine ladies in their ~s and satins de belles dames dans leurs plus beaux atours. -**2.** [filament - from insect, on maize] soie *f*. -**3.** *Br* JUR: to take ~ être nommé avocat de la couronne.
◇ *comp* [scarf, blouse etc] de OR en soie; the ~ industry l'industrie *f* de la soie; ~ merchant OR trader marchand *m*, -e *f* de soierie, soyeux *m spec*; ~ finish paint peinture *f* satinée.
◆ **silks** *npl* [jockey's jacket] casaque *f*; Jo Burns, in the Graham (Stable) ~s Jo Burns, portant les couleurs (de l'Écurie) Graham.
silk cotton *n* kapok *m*; silk-cotton tree fromager *m*.
silken ['sɪlkn] *adj lit.* -**1.** [made of silk] de OR en soie. -**2.** [like silk - hair, cheek etc] soyeux; [- voice, tone] doux.
silk hat *n* haut-de-forme *m*, chapeau *m* haut de forme.
silk screen *n*: ~ (printing OR process) sérigraphie *f*.
◆ **silk-screen** *vt* sérigraphier, imprimer en sérigraphie.
silkworm ['sɪlkwɜːm] *n* ver *m* à soie; ~ breeder séricicultеur *m*; ~ breeding sériciculture *f*.
silkworm moth *n* bombyx *m* du mûrier.
silky ['sɪlkɪ] (*compar* silkier, *superl* silkiest) *adj* -**1.** [like silk - hair, cheek] soyeux. -**2.** [suave - tone, manner] doux. -**3.** [made of silk] de OR en soie.
sill [sɪl] *n* -**1.** [ledge - gen] rebord *m*; [- of window] rebord *m*, appui *m*; [- of door] seuil *m*. -**2.** AUT marchepied *m*. -**3.** MIN [deposit] filon *m*, gisement *m*.
silliness ['sɪlɪnɪs] *n* bêtise *f*, stupidité *f*; I want no more ~ from you! arrête de faire l'idiot!
silly ['sɪlɪ] (*compar* sillier, *superl* silliest) ◇ *adj* -**1.** [foolish - person] bête, stupide; [- quarrel, book, grin, question] bête, stupide, idiot; [infantile] bébête; I'm sorry, it was a ~ thing to say excusez-moi, c'était bête de dire ça; don't do anything ~ ne fais pas de bêtises; how ~ of me! que je suis bête!; it's ~ to worry c'est idiot de s'inquiéter; you ~ idiot! espèce d'idiot OR d'imbécile!; you look ~ in that tie tu as l'air ridicule avec cette cravate; I couldn't get the ~ door open *inf* je n'arrivais pas à ouvrir cette fichue OR satanée porte. -**2.** [comical - mask, costume, voice] comique, drôle; we all wore ~ hats nous portions tous des chapeaux marrants.
◇ *adv inf* [senseless]: the blow knocked me ~ le coup m'a étourdi; I was bored ~ je m'ennuyais à mourir; I was scared ~ j'avais une peur bleue; he drank himself ~ il s'est complètement soûlé.
silly-billy *inf* (*pl* silly-billies) *n* gros bêta *m*, grosse bêtasse *f*.
silly season *n Br* PRESS: the ~ la période creuse *(pour les journalistes)*.
silly-willy *inf* (*pl* silly-willies) *Am* = **silly-billy**.
silo ['saɪləʊ] (*pl* silos) *n* AGR & MIL silo *m*.
silt [sɪlt] *n* GEOL limon *m*; [mud] vase *f*.
◆ **silt up** ◇ *vi insep* [with mud] s'envaser; [with sand] s'ensabler.
◇ *vt sep* [subj: mud] envaser; [subj: sand] ensabler; the old harbour is now completely ~ed up le vieux port est maintenant complètement ensablé.
Silurian [saɪ'lʊərɪən] ◇ *adj* silurien.
◇ *n* silurien *m*.
silver ['sɪlvəʳ] ◇ *n* -**1.** [metal] argent *m*; ~ mine mine *f* d'argent; ~ ore minerai *m* argentifère. -**2.** *(U)* [coins] pièces *fpl* (d'argent); I'd like two £10 notes and the rest in ~ je voudrais deux billets de 10 livres et le reste en pièces (de monnaie); ~ collection quête *f*. -**3.** *(U)* [dishes] argenterie *f*; [cutlery - gen] couverts *mpl*; [- made of silver] argenterie *f*, couverts *mpl* en argent; to clean the ~ nettoyer OR faire l'argenterie. -**4.** [colour] (couleur *f*) argent *m*. -**5.** SPORT [medal] médaille *f* d'argent; he's hoping to win the ~ il espère remporter la médaille d'argent.
◇ *adj* -**1.** [of silver] d'argent, en argent; is your ring ~? est-ce que votre bague est en argent? ❑ to be born with a ~ spoon in one's mouth être né riche; ~ lining bon côté *m*; every cloud has a ~ lining *prov* à quelque chose malheur est bon *prov*. -**2.** [in colour] argenté, argent *(inv)*; ~ hair des cheveux argentés. -**3.** [sound] argentin; she has a ~ tongue elle sait parler.
◇ *vt literal & fig* argenter; the moon ~ed the lake la lune donnait au lac des reflets d'argent.
silver birch *n* bouleau *m* blanc.
silver bromide *n* bromure *m* d'argent.
silver chloride *n* chlorure *m* d'argent.
silvered ['sɪlvəd] *adj lit* argenté.
silver fir *n* [gen] sapin *m* blanc OR pectiné; [ornamental] sapin *m* argenté.
silverfish ['sɪlvəfɪʃ] (*pl inv* OR silverfishes) *n* [insect] poisson *m* d'argent, lépisme *m*.
silver foil *n* papier *m* d'aluminium.
silver fox *n* renard *m* argenté.
silver-gilt ◇ *n* vermeil *m*.
◇ *comp* en vermeil.
silver grey *n* gris *m* argenté.
◆ **silver-grey** *adj* gris argenté *(inv)*.
silver-haired *adj* aux cheveux argentés.
silver iodide *n* iodure *m* d'argent.
silver jubilee *n* (fête *f* du) vingt-cinquième anniversaire *m*; the Queen's ~ le vingt-cinquième anniversaire de l'accession au trône de la reine.
silver maple *n* érable *m* à sucre OR du Canada.
silver medal *n* SPORT médaille *f* d'argent.
silver nitrate *n* nitrate *m* d'argent.
silver paper *n* papier *m* d'aluminium.
silver plate *n* -**1.** [coating] plaquage *m* d'argent; the cutlery is ~ les couverts sont en plaqué argent. -**2.** [tableware] argenterie *f*.
◆ **silver-plate** *vt* argenter.
silver-plated *adj* argenté, plaqué argent; ~ tableware argenterie *f*.
silver plating *n* argentage *m*; [layer] argenture *f*.
silver screen *n dated*: the ~ le grand écran, le cinéma.
silverside ['sɪlvəsaɪd] *n Br* CULIN ≃ gîte *m* à la noix.
silversides ['sɪlvəsaɪdz] (*pl inv*) *n* ZOOL prêtre *m*.
silversmith ['sɪlvəsmɪθ] *n* orfèvre *m*.
silver standard *n* étalon *m* argent.
silverware ['sɪlvəweəʳ] *n* -**1.** [gen] argenterie *f*. -**2.** *Am* [cutlery] couverts *mpl*.
silver wedding *n*: ~ (anniversary) noces *fpl* d'argent.
silvery ['sɪlvərɪ] *adj* [hair, fabric] argenté; [voice, sound] argentin.
silviculture ['sɪlvɪˌkʌltʃəʳ] *n* sylviculture *f*.
Simeon ['sɪmɪən] *pr n* Siméon.
simian ['sɪmɪən] ◇ *adj* simien; [resembling ape] simiesque.
◇ *n* simien *m*.
similar ['sɪmɪləʳ] *adj* -**1.** [showing resemblance] similaire, semblable; they're very ~ ils se ressemblent beaucoup; other customers have had ~ problems d'autres clients ont eu des problèmes similaires OR analogues OR du même ordre; they are very ~ in content leurs contenus sont pratiquement identiques; the print is ~ in quality to that of a typewriter la qualité de l'impression est proche de celle d'une machine à écrire; it's an assembly ~ to the US Senate c'est une assemblée comparable au Sénat américain; a fruit ~ to the orange un fruit voisin de l'orange. -**2.** GEOM [triangles] semblable.
similarity [ˌsɪmɪ'lærətɪ] *n* [resemblance] ressemblance *f*, similarité *f*; there is a certain ~ to her last novel ça ressemble un peu à son dernier roman; there are points of ~ in their strategies leurs stratégies ont des points communs OR présentent des similitudes.
◆ **similarities** *npl* [features in common] ressemblances *fpl*, points *mpl* communs; the molecules show similarities in structure les molécules présentent des analogies de structure; our similarities are more important than our differences nos points communs sont plus importants que nos différends.
similarly ['sɪmɪləlɪ] *adv* -**1.** [in a similar way] d'une façon similaire; the houses are ~ constructed les maisons sont construites sur le même modèle; other people were ~ treated d'autres personnes ont été traitées de la même manière. -**2.** [likewise] de même; ~, it is obvious that... de même, il est évident que...
simile ['sɪmɪlɪ] *n* LITERAT comparaison *f*.
similitude [sɪ'mɪlɪtjuːd] *n* similitude *f*.
simmer ['sɪməʳ] ◇ *vi* -**1.** [water, milk, sauce] frémir; [soup, stew] mijoter, mitonner; [vegetables] cuire à petit feu. -**2.** [smoulder - violence, quarrel, discontent] couver, fermenter; [seethe - with anger, excitement] être en ébullition; unrest is ~ing in the big cities des troubles couvent dans les grandes villes; the audience ~ed with excitement les spectateurs étaient en ébullition; tempers are ~ing les passions s'échauffent; his anger ~ed just below the surface il bouillait de colère. -**3.** [be hot] rôtir; [when humid] mijoter; the city ~ed in the heat la ville était accablée par la canicule.
◇ *vt* [milk, sauce] laisser frémir; [soup, stew] mijoter, mitonner; [vegetables] faire cuire à petit feu.
◇ *n* faible ébullition *f*; bring the mixture to a ~ portez le mélange à ébullition.
◆ **simmer down** *inf vi insep* [person] se calmer; ~ down! calme-toi!, du calme!
simnel cake ['sɪmnl-] *n Br gâteau aux fruits confits, recouvert de pâte d'amandes ou fourré à la pâte d'amandes (mangé traditionnellement à Pâques)*.
Simon ['saɪmən] *pr n* Simon.
simony ['saɪmənɪ] *n* simonie *f*.
simoom [sɪ'muːm], **simoon** [sɪ'muːn] *n* simoun *m*.
simp *inf* [sɪmp] *n Am* bêta *m*, -asse *f*, nigaud *m*, -e *f*.
simper ['sɪmpəʳ] ◇ *vi* minauder.
◇ *vt*: "of course, madam", he ~ed «bien sûr, chère Madame», dit-il en minaudant.
◇ *n* sourire *m* affecté; "may I help you?", she said with a ~ «vous désirez?», dit-elle en minaudant.
simpering ['sɪmpərɪŋ] *n (U)* minauderies *fpl*.

simple ['sɪmpl] *adj* -**1.** [easy] simple, facile; [uncomplicated] simple; **his reasons are never ~** ses raisons ne sont jamais simples; **it's a ~ operation** c'est une opération simple; **getting there was the ~ part** ce n'est pas d'y aller qui était difficile; **it's a ~ meal to prepare** c'est un repas facile à préparer; **it would be ~r to do it myself** ce serait plus simple que je le fasse OR si je le faisais moi-même; **it should be a ~ matter to change your ticket** tu ne devrais avoir aucun mal à changer ton billet; **let's hear your story, then, but keep it ~** bon, racontez votre histoire, mais passez-moi les détails. -**2.** [plain - tastes, ceremony, life, style] simple; **she wore a ~ black dress** elle portait une robe noire toute simple; **I want a ~ "yes" or "no"** répondez-moi simplement par «oui» ou par «non»; **let me explain in ~ terms** OR **language** laissez-moi vous expliquer ça en termes simples; **I did it for the ~ reason that I had no choice** je l'ai fait pour la simple raison que je n'avais pas le choix. -**3.** [unassuming] simple, sans façons; **despite her success, she remains ~ and unaffected** malgré sa réussite, elle est restée simple et naturelle. -**4.** [naive] simple, naïf; [feeble-minded] simple, niais; **he's a bit ~** il est un peu simplet. -**5.** [basic, not compound - substance, fracture, sentence] simple; BIOL [eye] simple; **~ equation** MATH équation *f* du premier degré.

simple fraction *n* fraction *f* ordinaire.

simple fracture *n* fracture *f* simple.

simple-hearted *adj* [person] candide, ouvert; [wisdom, gesture] simple, naturel.

simple interest *n (U)* intérêts *mpl* simples.

simple-minded *adj* [naive] naïf, simplet; [feeble-minded] simple d'esprit; **it's a very ~ view of society** c'est une vision très simpliste de la société.

simple-mindedness [-'maɪndɪdnɪs] *n* [naivety] naïveté *f*; [feeble-mindedness] simplicité *f* d'esprit.

Simple Simon *n* naïf *m*, nigaud *m*.

simple tense *n* temps *m* simple.

simpleton ['sɪmpltən] *n dated* nigaud *m*, -e *f*.

simplex ['sɪmpleks] ◇ *adj* COMPUT & TELEC simplex *(inv)*, unidirectionnel.
◇ *n* COMPUT & TELEC simplex *m*, transmission *f* unidirectionnelle; GEOM simplexe *m*; LING [sentence] unité *f* proportionnelle; [word] mot *m* simple.

simplicity [sɪm'plɪsətɪ] (*pl* **simplicities**) *n* simplicité *f*; **the instructions are ~ itself** les instructions sont simples comme bonjour OR tout ce qu'il y a de plus simple.

simplification [,sɪmplɪfɪ'keɪʃn] *n* simplification *f*.

simplify ['sɪmplɪfaɪ] (*pt* & *pp* **simplified**) *vt* simplifier.

simplistic [sɪm'plɪstɪk] *adj* simpliste.

simplistically [sɪm'plɪstɪklɪ] *adv* de manière simpliste.

simply ['sɪmplɪ] *adv* -**1.** [in a simple way] simplement, avec simplicité; **put quite ~, it's a disaster** c'est tout simplement une catastrophe. -**2.** [just, only] simplement, seulement; **it's not ~ a matter of money** ce n'est pas une simple question d'argent; **I ~ told her the truth** je lui ai tout simplement dit la vérité. -**3.** [as intensifier] absolument; **it's ~ perfect!** c'est absolument parfait!; **I ~ don't understand you** je ne vous comprends vraiment pas; **we ~ must go now** il faut absolument que nous partions maintenant.

simulacrum [,sɪmjʊ'leɪkrəm] (*pl* **simulacra** [-krə]) *n fml* OR *lit* simulacre *m*, semblant *m*.

simulate ['sɪmjʊleɪt] *vt* -**1.** [imitate - blood, battle, sound] simuler, imiter; **the insect ~s a piece of bark** l'insecte prend l'apparence d'un morceau d'écorce. -**2.** [feign - pain, pleasure] simuler, feindre. -**3.** COMPUT & TECH simuler.

simulated ['sɪmjʊleɪtɪd] *adj* simulé; **a ~ nuclear disaster** une catastrophe nucléaire simulée.

simulation [,sɪmjʊ'leɪʃn] *n* simulation *f*; **~ model** COMPUT modèle *m* de simulation.

simulator ['sɪmjʊleɪtə^r] *n* simulateur *m*; **flight ~** simulateur de vol.

simulcast [*Br* 'sɪməlkɑːst, *Am* 'saɪməlkæst] ◇ *vt* diffuser simultanément à la télévision et à la radio.
◇ *adj* radiotélévisé.
◇ *n* émission *f* radiotélévisée.

simultaneity [,sɪməltə'nɪətɪ] *n* simultanéité *f*.

simultaneous [*Br* ,sɪməl'teɪnjəs, *Am* ,saɪməl'teɪnjəs] *adj* simultané; **~ translation** traduction *f* simultanée.

simultaneous equations *npl* système *m* d'équations différentielles.

simultaneously [*Br* ,sɪməl'teɪnjəslɪ, *Am* ,saɪməl'teɪnjəslɪ] *adv* simultanément, en même temps.

sin [sɪn] (*pt* & *pp* **sinned**, *cont* **sinning**) ◇ *n* péché *m*; **to commit a ~** pécher, commettre un péché; **the ~ of pride** le péché d'orgueil; **it's a ~ to tell a lie** mentir OR le mensonge est un péché; **it would be a ~ to sell it** ce serait un crime de le vendre ❑ **for my ~s, I'm the person in charge of all this** *hum* malheureusement pour moi, c'est moi le responsable de tout ça; **to live in ~** RELIG OR *hum* vivre dans le péché.
◇ *vi* pécher; **to ~ against sthg** pécher contre qqch; **to be more sinned against than sinning** être plus victime que coupable.

Sinai ['saɪnaɪ] *pr n* [region] Sinaï *m*; **the ~ (Desert)** le (désert du) Sinaï; **the ~ Peninsula** la presqu'île de Sinaï.

Sinbad ['sɪnbæd] *pr n*: **~ the Sailor** Sinbad le marin.

sin bin *inf n* -**1.** *Am* [brothel] lupanar *m*, bordel *m*. -**2.** SPORT banc *m* des pénalités, prison *f*.

since [sɪns] ◇ *prep* depuis; **he has been talking about it ~ yesterday/~ before Christmas** il en parle depuis hier/depuis avant Noël; **the fair has been held annually ever ~ 1950** la foire a lieu chaque année depuis 1950; **she's the best soul singer ~ Aretha Franklin** c'est la meilleure chanteuse de soul depuis Aretha Franklin; **how long is it ~ their divorce?** ça fait combien de temps qu'ils ont divorcé?; **~ then** depuis lors; **that was in 1966, ~ when the law has been altered** c'était en 1966; depuis, la loi a été modifiée; **~ when have you been married?** depuis quand êtes-vous marié?; **they really have changed – oh yes, ~ when?** ils ont vraiment changé – ah oui, depuis quand?
◇ *conj* -**1.** [in time] depuis que; **I've worn glasses ~ I was six** je porte des lunettes depuis que j'ai six ans OR depuis l'âge de six ans; **how long has it been ~ you last saw Hal?** ça fait combien de temps que tu n'as pas vu Hal?; **it's been ages ~ we've gone to a play** ça fait une éternité que nous ne sommes pas allés au théâtre; **~ leaving New York/changing jobs, I...** depuis que j'ai quitté New York/changé de travail, je...; **it had been ten years ~ I had seen him** cela faisait dix ans que je ne l'avais pas revu. -**2.** [expressing cause] puisque, comme; **~ you don't want to go, I'll go by myself** puisque OR comme tu ne veux pas y aller, j'irai tout seul.
◇ *adv* depuis; **she used to be his assistant, but she's ~ been promoted** elle était son assistante, mais depuis elle a été promue; **I've never seen it/her ~** je ne l'ai jamais revu/revue depuis.
◆ **ever since** ◇ *conj phr* depuis que; **ever ~ she resigned, things have been getting worse** depuis qu'elle a démissionné OR depuis sa démission, les choses ont empiré.
◇ *prep phr* depuis; **ever ~ that day he's been afraid of dogs** depuis ce jour-là, il a peur des chiens.
◇ *adv phr* depuis; **he arrived at 9 o'clock and he's been sitting there ever ~** il est arrivé à 9 h et il est assis là depuis.
◆ **long since** *adv phr*: **I've long ~ forgotten why** il y a longtemps que j'ai oublié pourquoi; **I've long ~ got used to it** il y a longtemps que j'y suis habitué.

sincere [sɪn'sɪə^r] *adj* sincère; **please accept my ~ apologies** veuillez accepter mes sincères excuses; **it is my ~ belief that war can be avoided** je crois sincèrement qu'on peut éviter la guerre.

sincerely [sɪn'sɪəlɪ] *adv* sincèrement; **~ held views** des opinions auxquelles on croit sincèrement; **I ~ hope we can be friends** j'espère sincèrement que nous serons amis; **Yours ~** [formally] je vous prie d'agréer, Monsieur (OR Madame), mes sentiments les meilleurs; [less formally] bien à vous.

sincerity [sɪn'serətɪ] *n* sincérité *f*; **to doubt sb's ~** douter de la sincérité OR bonne foi de qqn; **in all ~, I must admit that...** en toute sincérité, je dois admettre que...

sine [saɪn] *n* MATH sinus *m*.

sinecure ['saɪnɪ,kjʊə^r] *n* sinécure *f*.

sine die [,saɪnɪ'daɪiː] *adv* sine die.

sine qua non [,saɪnɪkweɪ'nɒn] *n* condition *f* sine qua non.

sinew ['sɪnjuː] *n* [tendon] tendon *m*; [muscle] muscle *m*; *lit* [strength] force *f*, forces *fpl*; **I will resist with every ~ of my body** je résisterai de toutes mes forces.
◆ **sinews** *npl lit* [source of strength] nerf *m*, vigueur *f*; **coal and steel were the ~s of our economy** le charbon et la sidérurgie étaient le nerf de notre économie.

sinewy ['sɪnjuːɪ] *adj* -**1.** [muscular - person, body, arm] musclé; [- neck, hands] nerveux. -**2.** [with tendons - tissue] tendineux; **~ meat** viande *f* nerveuse OR tendineuse. -**3.** *lit* [forceful - style] vigoureux, nerveux.

sinful ['sɪnfʊl] *adj* [deed, urge, thought] coupable, honteux; [world] plein de péchés, souillé par le péché; **his ~ ways** sa vie de pécheur; **~ man** pécheur *m*; **~ woman** pécheresse *f*; **how could such pleasure be ~?** comment un tel plaisir pourrait-il être coupable?; **she thought alcohol was ~** pour elle, boire de l'alcool était un péché; **it's downright ~!** c'est un vrai scandale!

sinfully ['sɪnfʊlɪ] *adv* d'une façon coupable OR scandaleuse.

sing [sɪŋ] (*pt* **sang** [sæŋ], *pp* **sung** [sʌŋ]) ◇ *vi* -**1.** [person] chanter; **to ~ like a lark** chanter comme un rossignol; **she ~s of a faraway land** elle chante une terre lointaine ❑ **'Singin' in the Rain'** *Kelly, Donen* 'Chantons sous la pluie'. -**2.** [bird, kettle] chanter; [wind, arrow] siffler; [ears] bourdonner, siffler; **bullets sang past his ears** des balles sifflaient à ses oreilles; **the noise made my ears ~** ce bruit m'a fait bourdonner les oreilles. -**3.** *inf Am* [act as informer] parler; **he sang like a songbird at the trial** il a tout dit au procès; **somebody's been ~ing to our competitors** quelqu'un a vendu la mèche à OR tuyauté nos concurrents.
◇ *vt* -**1.** [song, note, mass] chanter; **to ~ opera/jazz** chanter de l'opéra/du jazz; **who ~s tenor?** qui est ténor?; **to ~ sb to sleep** chanter pour endormir qqn ❑ **now they're ~ing another** OR **a different tune** ils ont changé de ton. -**2.** [laud] célébrer, chanter; **to ~ sb's praises** chanter les louanges de qqn.
◆ **sing along** *vi insep* chanter (tous) ensemble; **they sang along with her in the chorus** ils ont repris le refrain avec elle; **to ~ along to** OR **with the radio** chanter en même temps que la radio.
◆ **sing out** *vi insep* -**1.** [sing loudly] chanter fort. -**2.** *inf* [shout] crier; **when you're ready, ~ out** quand tu seras prêt, fais-moi signe.
◆ **sing up** *vi insep* chanter plus fort; **~ up!** plus fort!

sing-along *n* chants *mpl* en chœur; **let's have a ~** chantons tous en chœur OR tous ensemble.

Singapore [,sɪŋə'pɔː^r] ◇ *pr n* Singapour.
◇ *comp*: **~ dollar** dollar *m* de Singapour.

Singaporean [ˌsɪŋəˈpɔːrɪən] ◇ *n* Singapourien *m*, -enne *f*.
◇ *adj* singapourien.

singe [sɪndʒ] (*cont* singeing) ◇ *vt* -**1.** [gen] brûler légèrement; [shirt, fabric, paper] roussir; **the lighter ~d his moustache** il s'est brûlé la moustache avec le briquet. -**2.** CULIN [carcass, chicken] flamber, passer à la flamme.
◇ *vi* [fabric] roussir.
◇ *n* [burn] brûlure *f* (légère); ~ **(mark)** marque *f* de brûlure.

singer [ˈsɪŋəʳ] *n* chanteur *m*, -euse *f*; **she's a jazz ~** elle est chanteuse de jazz; **I'm a terrible ~** je chante affreusement mal.

Singhalese [ˌsɪŋhəˈliːz] = **Sinhalese**.

singing [ˈsɪŋɪŋ] ◇ *n* -**1.** [of person, bird] chant *m*; [of kettle, wind] sifflement *m*; [in ears] bourdonnement *m*, sifflement *m*; **the ~ went on until dawn** on a chanté OR les chants ont continué jusqu'à l'aube; **we left after the ~ of the national anthem** nous sommes partis après l'hymne national. -**2.** [art] chant *m*; **to study ~** étudier le chant; **her ~ has improved** elle chante mieux.
◇ *adj* [lesson, teacher, contest] de chant; **she's got a fine ~ voice** elle a une belle voix; **it's a ~ role** c'est un rôle qui comporte des passages chantés.

singing telegram *n* *vœux présentés sous forme chantée, généralement à l'occasion d'un anniversaire*.

single [ˈsɪŋgl] ◇ *adj* -**1.** [sole] seul, unique; **the room was lit by a ~ lamp** la pièce était éclairée par une seule lampe; **the report comes in a ~ volume** le rapport est publié en un (seul) volume; **I can't think of one ~ reason why I should do it** je n'ai aucune raison de le faire; **there wasn't a ~ person in the street** il n'y avait pas un chat dans la rue; **not a ~ one of her friends came** pas un seul de ses amis OR aucun de ses amis n'est venu; **I couldn't think of a ~ thing to say** je ne trouvais absolument rien à dire ❑ **the Single Market** le Marché unique (européen). -**2.** [individual, considered discretely] individuel, particulier; **he gave her a ~ red rose** il lui a donné une rose rouge; **our ~ most important resource is oil** notre principale ressource est le pétrole; **what would my ~ best investment be?** quel serait le meilleur placement?; **we sell ~ items at a higher price per unit** le prix unitaire est plus élevé; **~ copies cost more** un exemplaire seul coûte plus cher; **in any ~ year, average sales are ten million** sur une seule année, les ventes sont en moyenne de dix millions; **every ~ apple** OR **every ~ one of the apples was rotten** toutes les pommes sans exception étaient pourries; **every ~ time I take the plane, there's some problem** chaque fois que je prends l'avion, il y a un problème. -**3.** [not double - flower, thickness] simple; [- combat] singulier; **five years ago we had ~ figure inflation** il y a cinq ans nous avions un taux d'inflation inférieur à 10 %; **the score is still in ~ figures** le score est toujours inférieur à dix; **~ yellow line** ligne *f* jaune. -**4.** [for one person - room] pour une personne; [- bed] d'une personne; **a ~ sheet** un drap pour un lit d'une personne. -**5.** [unmarried] célibataire; **the ~ life seems to agree with you** la vie de célibataire a l'air de te convenir; **he's a ~ parent** c'est un père célibataire. -**6.** *Br* [one way]: **a ~ ticket to Oxford** un aller (simple) pour Oxford; **the ~ fare is £12** un aller simple coûte 12 livres.
◇ *n* -**1.** [hotel room] chambre *f* pour une personne OR individuelle; **I've reserved a ~ with bath** j'ai réservé une chambre pour une personne avec bain. -**2.** [record] 45 tours *m inv*, single *m*. -**3.** *Br* [ticket] billet *m*, aller *m* simple; **we only have ~s left** THEAT il ne nous reste que des places séparées. -**4.** (*usu pl*) [money] *Br* pièce *f* d'une livre; *Am* billet *m* d'un dollar; **she gave me the change in ~s** *Br* elle m'a rendu la monnaie en pièces d'une livre; *Am* elle m'a rendu la monnaie en billets d'un dollar. -**5.** [in cricket] point *m*.
◆ **single out** *vt sep* [for attention, honour] sélectionner, distinguer; **a few candidates were ~d out for special praise** quelques candidats ont eu droit à des félicitations supplémentaires; **they were all guilty, so why ~ anyone out?** ils étaient tous coupables, alors pourquoi accuser quelqu'un en particulier?

single-action *adj* [firearm] que l'on doit réarmer après chaque coup.

single-breasted [-ˈbrestɪd] *adj* [jacket, coat] droit.

single-celled [-seld] *adj* BIOL unicellulaire.

single cream *n* *Br* crème *f* (fraîche) liquide.

single-decker *n*: ~ **(bus)** autobus *m* sans impériale.

single-density *adj* COMPUT: ~ **disk** disquette *f* simple densité.

single-engined *adj* [plane] monomoteur.

single entry bookkeeping *n* comptabilité *f* en partie simple.

single file *n* file *f* indienne; **to walk in ~** marcher en file indienne OR à la queue leu leu.

single-handed ◇ *adv* [on one's own] tout seul, sans aucune aide; **she's tripled our sales ~** elle a triplé nos ventes à elle toute seule.
◇ *adj* -**1.** [unaided - voyage] en solitaire; **to be ~** être tout seul, n'avoir aucune aide. -**2.** [using one hand] à une main; ~ **backhand shot** revers *m* à une main; ~ **saw** (scie *f*) égoïne *f*.

single-handedly [-ˈhændɪdlɪ] *adv* -**1.** [on one's own] tout seul. -**2.** [with one hand] d'une seule main.

single-lens reflex *n* reflex *m* (mono-objectif).

single-masted [-ˈmɑːstɪd] *adj* à un (seul) mât.

single-minded *adj* résolu, acharné; **the ~ pursuit of money** la poursuite acharnée de l'argent; **to be ~ about sthg** s'acharner sur qqch; **he is ~ in his efforts to block the project** il fait tout ce qu'il peut pour bloquer le projet.

single-mindedly [-ˈmaɪndɪdlɪ] *adv* avec acharnement OR ténacité.

single-mindedness [-ˈmaɪndɪdnɪs] *n* résolution *f*, acharnement *m*.

single-parent family *n* famille *f* monoparentale.

single-party *adj* à parti unique.

singles [ˈsɪŋglz] (*pl inv*) ◇ *n* SPORT simple *m*; **the men's ~ champion** le champion du simple messieurs.
◇ *comp* [club, magazine] pour célibataires; **~ bar** bar *m* pour célibataires; **Tuesday is ~ night** mardi, c'est la soirée pour célibataires.

single-seater *n* AERON (avion *m*) monoplace *m*.

single-sex *adj* SCH non mixte.

single-space *vt* [on typewriter] taper avec un interligne simple; [on printer] imprimer avec un interligne simple; **the typescript should be ~d** le texte dactylographié devra être en interligne simple.

singlet [ˈsɪŋglɪt] *n* *Br* [undergarment] maillot *m* de corps; SPORT maillot *m*.

singleton [ˈsɪŋgltən] *n* CARDS & MATH singleton *m*.

single track *n* RAIL voie *f* unique.
◆ **single-track** *adj* à voie unique.

singly [ˈsɪŋglɪ] *adv* -**1.** [one at a time] séparément; **I'd rather see them ~** je préférerais les voir séparément. -**2.** [alone] seul; **they arrived either in couples or ~** ils sont arrivés en couples ou seuls. -**3.** [individually - packaged] individuellement; **you can't buy them ~** vous ne pouvez pas les acheter à la pièce.

singsong [ˈsɪŋsɒŋ] ◇ *n* -**1.** [melodious voice, tone]: **to speak in a ~** parler d'une voix chantante. -**2.** *Br* [singing] chants *mpl* (en chœur); **let's have a ~** chantons tous ensemble OR en chœur.
◇ *adj* [voice, accent] chantant; **in a ~ voice** d'une voix chantante.

singular [ˈsɪŋgjʊləʳ] ◇ *adj* -**1.** [remarkable] singulier; [odd] singulier, bizarre. -**2.** GRAMM singulier.
◇ *n* GRAMM singulier *m*; **in the third person ~** à la troisième personne du singulier.

singularity [ˌsɪŋgjʊˈlærətɪ] (*pl* singularities) *n* singularité *f*.

singularize, **-ise** [ˈsɪŋgjʊləraɪz] *vt* -**1.** [distinguish] singulariser. -**2.** GRAMM mettre au singulier.

singularly [ˈsɪŋgjʊləlɪ] *adv* singulièrement.

Sinhalese [ˌsɪŋhəˈliːz] ◇ *n* -**1.** [person] Cinghalais *m*, -e *f*. -**2.** LING cinghalais *m*.
◇ *adj* cinghalais.

sinister [ˈsɪnɪstəʳ] *adj* -**1.** [ominous, evil] sinistre; **he looks very ~ in black** le noir lui donne un air sinistre. -**2.** HERALD senestre, sénestre.

sink [sɪŋk] (*pt* sank [sæŋk], *pp* sunk [sʌŋk])
◇ *n* -**1.** [for dishes] évier *m*; [for hands] lavabo *m*; **double ~** évier à deux bacs; **~ board** *Am* égouttoir *m*. -**2.** [cesspool] puisard *m*; **a ~ of sin and corruption** un cloaque du vice. -**3.** GEOL doline *f*.
◇ *vi* -**1.** [below surface - boat] couler, sombrer; [- person, stone, log] couler; **to ~ like a stone** couler à pic; **the bottle sank slowly to the bottom of the pool** la bouteille a coulé lentement jusqu'au fond de la piscine; **the prow had not yet sunk beneath the surface** la proue n'était pas encore submergée; **Atlantis sank beneath the seas** l'Atlantide a été engloutie par les mers; **the sun/moon is ~ing** le soleil/la lune disparaît à l'horizon; **the moon sank behind the mountains** la lune a disparu derrière les montagnes; **as I climbed, the valley sank out of sight** au fur et à mesure que je grimpais, la vallée disparaissait; **to ~ without (a) trace** [whereabouts unknown] disparaître sans laisser de trace; *fig* [no longer famous] tomber dans l'oubli ❑ **it was a case of ~ or swim** il a bien fallu se débrouiller; **now it's up to them to ~ or swim by themselves** à eux maintenant de se débrouiller comme ils peuvent. -**2.** [in mud, snow etc] s'enfoncer; **at each step, I sank up to my knees in water** à chaque pas, je m'enfonçais dans l'eau jusqu'aux genoux; **the wheels sank deeper and deeper into the mud** les roues s'enfonçaient de plus en plus profondément dans la boue. -**3.** [subside - level, water, flames] baisser; [- building, ground] s'affaisser; **Venice is ~ing** Venise est en train de s'affaisser. -**4.** [sag, slump - person] s'affaler, s'écrouler; [- hopes] s'écrouler; **I sank back in my seat** je me suis enfoncé dans mon fauteuil; **her head sank back on the pillow** sa tête retomba sur l'oreiller; **he sank onto the bed** il s'est affalé OR il s'est laissé tomber sur le lit; **to ~ to the ground** s'effondrer; **to ~ to one's knees** tomber à genoux; **she sank down on her knees** elle tomba à genoux; **my heart** OR **spirits sank when I saw I was too late** j'ai perdu courage en voyant que j'arrivais trop tard; **his heart ~s every time he gets a letter from her** il a un serrement de cœur chaque fois qu'il reçoit une lettre d'elle. -**5.** [decrease, diminish - wages, rates, temperature] baisser; [more dramatically] plonger, chuter; **you have sunk in my estimation** tu as baissé dans mon estime; **the dollar has sunk to half its former value** le dollar a perdu la moitié de sa valeur; **profits have sunk to an all-time low** les bénéfices sont au plus bas ‖ [voice] se faire plus bas; **her voice had sunk to a whisper** [purposefully] elle s'était mise à chuchoter; [weakly] sa voix n'était plus qu'un murmure. -**6.** [slip, decline] sombrer, s'enfoncer; **to ~ into apathy/depression** sombrer dans l'apathie/dans la dépression; **he sank deeper into crime** il s'enfonça dans la délinquance; **the house sank into decay and ruin** la maison est tombée en ruines; **how could you ~ to this?** comment as-tu pu tomber si bas?; **to ~ to new depths** tomber plus bas; **the patient is ~ing fast** le malade décline rapidement; **he has sunk into a coma** il est tombé dans le coma; **I sank into a deep sleep** j'ai sombré dans un sommeil profond. -**7.** [penetrate - blade, arrow] s'enfoncer; **I felt the dog's teeth ~ into my arm** j'ai senti les crocs du chien s'enfoncer dans mon bras.
◇ *vt* -**1.** [boat, submarine] couler, envoyer par le fond; **to be sunk in thought** *fig* être plongé dans ses pensées. -**2.** [ruin - plans] faire échouer; **their bid has sunk any chance of us getting the contract** leur offre a réduit à néant nos chances

de décrocher le contrat; **this latest scandal looks certain to ~ him** ce dernier scandale va sûrement le couler; **if they don't come we're sunk!** *inf* s'ils ne viennent pas, nous sommes fichus! -**3.** [forget] oublier; **he sank his troubles in drink** il noya ses soucis dans l'alcool; **they'll have to learn to ~ their differences** il faudra qu'ils apprennent à oublier leurs différends. -**4.** [plunge, drive - knife, spear] enfoncer; **they're ~ing the piles for the jetty** ils sont en train de mettre en place les pilotis de la jetée; **the fishpond was a metal basin sunk in the ground** l'étang à poissons était un bassin en métal enfoncé dans le sol; **I sank my teeth into the peach** j'ai mordu dans la pêche; **the dog sank its teeth into my leg** le chien m'enfonça OR me planta ses crocs dans la jambe. -**5.** [dig, bore - well, mine shaft] creuser, forer. -**6.** [invest - money] mettre, investir; [- extravagantly] engloutir; **we sank a fortune into this company** nous avons englouti une fortune dans cette société. -**7.** SPORT [score - basket] marquer; [- putt] réussir; **to ~ a shot** [in snooker] couler une bille; [in basketball] réussir un tir OR un panier. -**8.** [debt] s'acquitter de, payer; FIN amortir. -**9.** *inf Br* [drink down] s'envoyer, siffler.

◆ **sink in** *vi insep* -**1.** [nail, blade] s'enfoncer. -**2.** [soak - varnish, cream] pénétrer. -**3.** [register - news] être compris OR assimilé; [- allusion] faire son effet; **I heard what you said, but it didn't ~ in at the time** je vous ai entendu, mais je n'ai pas vraiment saisi sur le moment; **the implications of the epidemic have not yet sunk in** on ne se rend pas encore vraiment compte OR on ne réalise pas encore quelles seront les conséquences de cette épidémie; **I paused to let my words ~ in** j'ai marqué une pause pour que mes paroles fassent leur effet.

sinker ['sɪŋkəʳ] *n* -**1.** [weight] plomb *m (pour la pêche)*. -**2.** *inf Am* [doughnut] beignet *m*; **~s and suds**▽ des beignets et du café.

sinking ['sɪŋkɪŋ] ◇ *n* -**1.** [of ship - accidental] naufrage *m*; [- deliberate] torpillage *m*. -**2.** [of building, ground] affaissement *m*. -**3.** [of money] engloutissement *m*.

◇ *adj*: **~ feeling**: to get that ~ feeling se sentir accablé; **it was that ~ feeling you get when you realize you've made a dreadful mistake** c'était l'accablement que l'on ressent quand on se rend compte qu'on a commis une erreur irréparable.

sinking fund *n* FIN caisse *f* OR fonds *mpl* d'amortissement.

sink tidy (*pl* sink tidies) *n rangement pour ustensiles sur un évier*.

sink unit *n* bloc-évier *m*.

sinner ['sɪnəʳ] *n* pécheur *m*, -eresse *f*.

Sinn Féin [ʃɪn'feɪn] *pr n* le Sinn Fein *(faction politique de l'IRA)*.

SINN FEIN:
Mouvement nationaliste et républicain irlandais fondé en 1902, qui se consacre à la lutte pour l'indépendance et la renaissance de la culture gaélique. Force politique vitale en Irlande à partir de 1916, il devient, après la seconde guerre mondiale, la branche politique de l'IRA (Irish Republican Army). Tourné vers le socialisme, il remporte cinq sièges aux élections de 1982, mais se divise quelques années plus tard, donnant naissance au «Sinn Fein républicain».

Sino- ['saɪnəʊ] *in cpds* sino-; **the ~Japanese War** la guerre sino-japonaise.

sinologist [saɪ'nɒlədʒɪst] *n* sinologue *mf*.

sinology [saɪ'nɒlədʒɪ] *n* sinologie *f*.

sinophile ['saɪnəfaɪl] *n* sinophile *mf*.

sinuosity [,sɪnjʊ'ɒsətɪ] *n* sinuosité *f*.

sinuous ['sɪnjʊəs] *adj* [road, neck, movement, reasoning] sinueux; **he danced with ~ grace** lorsqu'il dansait, son corps ondulait avec grâce.

sinus ['saɪnəs] *n* sinus *m*; **for fast ~ relief** pour dégager rapidement les sinus.

sinusitis [,saɪnə'saɪtɪs] *n (U)* sinusite *f*.

Sioux [suː] (*pl inv* [suː, suːz]) ◇ *n* -**1.** [person] Sioux *mf inv*. -**2.** LING sioux *m*.

◇ *adj* sioux *(inv)*; **the ~ Indians** les Sioux *mpl*.

sip [sɪp] (*pt & pp* **sipped**, *cont* **sipping**) ◇ *vt* [drink slowly] boire à petites gorgées OR à petits coups; [savour] siroter.

◇ *vi*: **he was at the bar, sipping at a cognac** il était au comptoir, sirotant un cognac.

◇ *n* petite gorgée *f*; **can I have a ~?** je peux goûter OR en boire un peu?; **she took a ~ of wine** elle a bu une petite gorgée de vin.

siphon ['saɪfn] ◇ *n* siphon *m*.

◇ *vt* -**1.** [liquid, petrol] siphonner. -**2.** [money, resources] transférer; [illicitly] détourner; **the money is ~ed from one account into another** l'argent est transféré d'un compte à un autre; **huge sums were ~ed into public housing** des sommes énormes ont été injectées dans les logements sociaux.

◆ **siphon off** *vt sep* -**1.** [liquid, petrol] siphonner. -**2.** [remove - money] absorber, éponger; [divert illegally] détourner; **the private sector is ~ing off the best graduates** le secteur privé absorbe les meilleurs diplômés; **the road will ~ traffic off from the city centre** la route va détourner une bonne partie de la circulation du centre-ville.

sir [sɜːʳ] *n* -**1.** [term of address] monsieur *m*; **no, ~** [gen & SCH] non, Monsieur; MIL [to officer] non, mon général/mon colonel *etc*; **(Dear) Sir** [in letter] (Cher) Monsieur ❑ **not for me, no ~!** *inf* [emphatic] pas pour moi, ça non OR pas question! -**2.** [title of knight, baronet]: **Sir Ian Hall** sir Ian Hall; **to be made a ~** être anobli. -**3.** *Br inf* [male teacher]: **Sir's coming!** le maître arrive!

sire ['saɪəʳ] ◇ *n* -**1.** [animal] père *m*. -**2.** *arch* [father] père *m*. -**3.** [term of address]: **no, ~** [to king] non, sire; *arch* [to lord] non, seigneur.

◇ *vt* engendrer; **Buttons, ~d by Goldfly** Buttons, issu de Goldfly.

siree *inf* [sɜː'riː] = **sirree**.

siren ['saɪərən] *n* -**1.** [device] sirène *f*; **ambulance/police ~** sirène d'ambulance/de voiture de police. -**2.** MYTH sirène *f*; *fig* [temptress] sirène *f*, femme *f* fatale.

siren call, siren song *n literal* chant *m* des sirènes; *fig* attrait *m*, appât *m*; **who can resist the ~ of fame and wealth?** qui peut résister à l'attrait de la gloire et de la fortune?

Sirius ['sɪrɪəs] *pr n* Sirius *m*.

sirloin ['sɜːlɔɪn] *n* aloyau *m*; **a ~ steak** un bifteck dans l'aloyau.

sirocco [sɪ'rɒkəʊ] (*pl* **siroccos**) *n* sirocco *m*, siroco *m*.

sirree *inf* [sɜː'riː] *interj Am*: **yes/no ~!** ça oui/non!

sis *inf* [sɪs] *n* [sister] frangine *f*, sœurette *f*.

sisal ['saɪsl] ◇ *n* sisal *m*.

◇ *adj* en OR de sisal.

sissy ['sɪsɪ] (*pl* **sissies**) ◇ *n* [coward] peureux *m*, -euse *f*; [effeminate person]: **he's a real ~** c'est une vraie mauviette.

◇ *adj* [cowardly] peureux; [effeminate]: **don't be so ~!** t'es une mauviette, ou quoi?

sister ['sɪstəʳ] ◇ *n* -**1.** sœur *f*; **they're ~s** elles sont sœurs; **my big/little ~** ma grande/petite sœur. -**2.** [nun] religieuse *f*, (bonne) sœur *f*; **no, Sister** non, ma sœur; **Sister Pauline** sœur Pauline. -**3.** *Br* [nurse] infirmière *f* en chef; **I'll have to ask Sister** il faudra que je demande à l'infirmière en chef. -**4.** POL [comrade] sœur *f*; **our ~s in Africa** nos sœurs d'Afrique. -**5.** *Am inf* [black woman] *nom donné par les Noirs américains à une femme noire*.

◇ *adj (esp with feminine nouns)* sœur; *(esp with masculine nouns)* frère; **~ countries** pays *mpl* frères, nations *fpl* sœurs; **~ ship** [belonging to same company] navire *m* de la même ligne; [identical] navire-jumeau *m*, sister-ship *m*.

sisterhood ['sɪstəhʊd] *n* -**1.** [group of women - gen & RELIG] communauté *f* de femmes. -**2.** [solidarity] solidarité *f* entre femmes.

sister-in-law (*pl* **sisters-in-law**) *n* belle-sœur *f*.

sisterly ['sɪstəlɪ] *adj* [kiss, hug] sororal *lit*, fraternel; [advice] de sœur; **~ devotion** dévouement *m* de sœur.

Sistine Chapel ['sɪstiːn-] *pr n*: **the ~** la chapelle Sixtine.

Sisyphus ['sɪsɪfəs] *pr n* Sisyphe; **the myth of ~** le mythe de Sisyphe.

sit [sɪt] (*pt & pp* **sat** [sæt], *cont* **sitting**) ◇ *vi* -**1.** [take a seat] s'asseoir; [be seated] être assis; **she came and sat next to me** elle est venue s'asseoir à côté de moi; **she sat by me all evening** elle était assise à côté de moi toute la soirée; **~ in the back of the car** mettez-vous à l'arrière (de la voiture); **~ still!** tiens-toi OR reste tranquille!; **~!** [to dog] assis!; **they sat over the meal for hours** ils sont restés à table pendant des heures; **don't think I'm just going to ~ and wait for you!** ne t'imagine pas que je vais rester là à t'attendre!; **he ~s in front of the television all day** il passe toute la journée devant la télévision ❑ **~ tight, I'll be back in a moment** *inf* ne bouge pas, je reviens tout de suite; **we just have to ~ tight and wait for things to get better** on ne peut qu'attendre patiemment que les choses s'arrangent. -**2.** ART & PHOT [pose] poser; **she sat for Modigliani** elle a posé pour Modigliani. -**3.** [be a member]: **to ~ on a board** faire partie OR être membre d'un conseil d'administration; **he sat for Swansea** *Br* POL il était député de Swansea. -**4.** [be in session] être en séance, siéger; **the council was still sitting at midnight** à minuit, le conseil siégeait toujours OR était toujours en séance; **the House ~s for another two months** la session de la Chambre doit durer encore deux mois. -**5.** [baby-sit]: **I'll ask Amy to ~ for us** je demanderai à Amy de garder les enfants; **she's sitting for the neighbours** elle garde les enfants des voisins. -**6.** *Br* SCH & UNIV [be a candidate]: **to ~ for an exam** se présenter à OR passer un examen. -**7.** [be situated - building] être, se trouver; [- vase] être posé; **the houses ~ nestled in a beautiful valley** les maisons sont nichées OR blotties dans une belle vallée; **a clock sat on the mantlepiece** une horloge était posée sur la cheminée; **your keys are sitting right in front of you** tes clés sont là, devant ton nez; **her mail sat in a pile on her desk** son courrier était empilé sur son bureau; **a tank sat in the middle of the road** un char d'assaut était planté au milieu de la route; **the wind ~s in the east** *lit* le vent vient de l'est. -**8.** [remain inactive or unused] rester; **the plane sat waiting on the runway** l'avion attendait sur la piste; **the letter sat unopened** la lettre n'avait pas été ouverte. -**9.** [fit - coat, dress] tomber; **the jacket ~s well on you** la veste vous va parfaitement; **the collar should ~ flat** le col devrait rester à plat || *fig*: **age ~s well on him** la maturité lui va bien; **the thought sat uneasily on my conscience** cette pensée me pesait sur la conscience. -**10.** [bird - perch] se percher, se poser; [- brood] couver; **they take turns sitting on the eggs** ils couvent les œufs à tour de rôle.

◇ *vt* -**1.** [place] asseoir, installer; **he sat the child in the pram** il a assis l'enfant dans le landau. -**2.** [invite to be seated] faire asseoir; **she sat me in the waiting room** elle m'a fait asseoir dans la salle d'attente. -**3.** *Br* [examination] se présenter à, passer. -**4.** EQUIT: **to ~ a horse badly/well** monter (un cheval) mal/bien, avoir une mauvaise/bonne assiette.

◆ **sit about** *Br*, **sit around** *vi insep* rester à ne rien faire, traîner; **she just ~s around (the house) all day** elle reste toute la journée à la maison à ne rien faire; **I'm not going to ~ around waiting for you** je ne vais pas passer mon temps à t'attendre.

◆ **sit back** *vi insep* -**1.** [relax] s'installer confortablement; **I sat back against the cushions** je me suis calé contre les coussins; **just ~ back and close your eyes** installe-toi bien et ferme les yeux; **~ back and enjoy it** détends-toi et profites-en. -**2.** [refrain from intervening]: **I can't just ~ back and watch!** je ne peux pas rester là à regarder sans rien faire!; **he just ~s back** and lets the others do the work il regarde les autres travailler sans lever le petit doigt; we can't just ~ back and ignore the danger nous ne pouvons tout de même pas faire comme s'il n'y avait pas de danger.

◆ **sit by** *vi insep* rester sans rien faire; how can you ~ by while others suffer? comment peux-tu rester sans rien faire quand d'autres souffrent?

◆ **sit down** ◇ *vi insep* s'asseoir; please ~ down asseyez-vous, je vous en prie; I was just sitting down to work when the phone rang j'étais sur le point de me mettre au travail quand le téléphone a sonné; to ~ down to table se mettre à table, s'attabler; the two sides have decided to ~ down together at the negotiating table les deux camps ont décidé de s'asseoir à la table des négociations.

◇ *vt sep* [place - person] asseoir, installer; he sat himself down beside me il s'est assis à côté de moi; ~ yourself down and have a drink asseyez-vous et prenez un verre.

◆ **sit in** *vi insep* -**1.** [attend]: to ~ in on a meeting/a class assister à une réunion/un cours. -**2.** [replace]: to ~ in for sb remplacer qqn. -**3.** [hold a sit-in] faire un sit-in.

◆ **sit on** *inf vt insep* -**1.** [suppress, quash - file, report] garder le silence sur; [- suggestion, proposal] repousser, rejeter; any new initiative is promptly sat on on décourage rapidement toute nouvelle initiative. -**2.** [take no action on] ne pas s'occuper de; his office has been sitting on those recommendations for months now ça fait des mois que son bureau a ces recommandations sous le coude. -**3.** [silence - person] faire taire; [rebuff] rabrouer.

◆ **sit out** ◇ *vi insep* [sit outside] s'asseoir OR se mettre dehors.

◇ *vt sep* -**1.** [endure] attendre la fin de; it was very boring but I sat it out c'était très ennuyeux, mais je suis restée jusqu'au bout. -**2.** [not take part in]: I think I'll ~ the next one out [dance] je crois que je ne vais pas danser la prochaine danse; [in cards] je crois que je ne jouerai pas la prochaine main.

◆ **sit through** *vt insep* attendre la fin de; I can't bear to ~ through another of his speeches je ne supporterai pas un autre de ses discours; we sat through dinner in silence nous avons passé tout le dîner sans rien dire.

◆ **sit up** ◇ *vi insep* -**1.** [raise o.s. to sitting position] s'asseoir; [sit straight] se redresser; she was sitting up in bed reading elle lisait, assise dans son lit; the baby can ~ up now le bébé peut se tenir assis maintenant; ~ up straight! redresse-toi!, tiens-toi droit! -**2.** [not go to bed] rester debout, ne pas se coucher; don't bother sitting up for me ne m'attendez pas; I sat up watching TV until 3 a.m. j'ai regardé la télé jusqu'à 3 h du matin; I'll ~ up with her until the fever passes je vais rester avec elle jusqu'à ce que sa fièvre tombe. -**3.** *inf* [look lively]: to make sb ~ up secouer qqn, secouer les puces à qqn; the public began to ~ up and take notice le public a commencé à montrer un certain intérêt.

◇ *vt sep* [child, patient] asseoir, redresser.

sitar [sɪ'tɑːʳ] *n* sitar *m*.

sitcom ['sɪtkɒm] *n* comédie *f* de situation, sitcom *m*.

sit-down ◇ *n* -**1.** ~ (strike) *Br* grève *f* sur le tas. -**2.** *inf* [rest] pause *f*; I could do with a bit of a ~ j'aimerais bien faire une pause OR m'asseoir un peu.

◇ *adj*: ~ dinner dîner pris à table; there are too many guests for a ~ meal il y a trop d'invités pour que tout le monde puisse s'asseoir à table.

site [saɪt] ◇ *n* -**1.** [piece of land] terrain *m*; the development project includes ~s for small businesses le projet immobilier prévoit des terrains pour de petites entreprises; caravan ~ terrain de camping pour caravanes. -**2.** [place, location] emplacement *m*, site *m*; there's been a church on this ~ for centuries cela fait des siècles qu'il y a une église à cet endroit OR ici; this forest has been the ~ of several battles cette forêt a été le théâtre de plusieurs batailles ❑ ~ of special scientific interest *site protégé présentant un intérêt particulier du point de vue de la faune, de la flore ou de la géologie*. -**3.** CONSTR: helmets must be worn on the ~ le port du casque est obligatoire sur le chantier; (building) ~ chantier *m*; demolition ~ chantier de démolition. -**4.** ARCHEOL site *m*. -**5.** *phr*: on ~ sur place.

◇ *comp* CONSTR [office, inspection, visit] de chantier.

◇ *vt* placer, situer; the argument continues over where the new airport should be ~d les discussions continuent pour décider de l'emplacement du nouvel aéroport.

sit-in *n* -**1.** [demonstration] sit-in *m inv*; to stage OR to hold a ~ faire un sit-in. -**2.** [strike] grève *f* sur le tas.

siting ['saɪtɪŋ] *n*: the ~ of the nuclear plant is highly controversial le choix de l'emplacement de la centrale nucléaire provoque une vive controverse; access is important in the ~ of the stadium l'accessibilité est un facteur important dans le choix du site pour le stade.

sitter ['sɪtəʳ] *n* -**1.** [babysitter] baby-sitter *mf*. -**2.** ART [model] modèle *m*. -**3.** [hen] couveuse *f*. -**4.** *inf Br* SPORT [easy chance] coup *m* facile; to miss a ~ rater un coup facile.

sitting ['sɪtɪŋ] ◇ *n* [for meal] service *m*; ART [for portrait] séance *f* de pose; [of assembly, committee] séance *f*; I read the book at OR in one ~ j'ai lu le livre d'une traite.

◇ *adj* -**1.** [seated] assis; he propped up the body in a ~ position il a calé le corps en position assise. -**2.** [in office] en exercice; the ~ member for Leeds le député actuel de Leeds.

sitting duck *inf n* [target] cible *m* facile; [victim] proie *f* facile, pigeon *m*; old people are ~s for all sorts of confidence tricksters les personnes âgées sont des proies faciles pour les escrocs en tous genres.

sitting room *n Br* salon *m*, salle *f* de séjour.

sitting target *n Br* cible *f* facile.

sitting tenant *n Br* locataire *mf* en place.

sitting trot *n* trot *m* assis.

situate ['sɪtjʊeɪt] *vt fml* [in place] situer, implanter; they plan to ~ the new hospital near the town centre ils envisagent d'implanter le nouvel hôpital près du centre-ville ‖ [in context] resituer.

situated ['sɪtjʊeɪtɪd] *adj* -**1.** [physically] situé; the house is conveniently ~ for shops and public transport la maison est située à proximité des commerces et des transports en commun; the town is well/badly ~ for tourist development la situation de la ville est/n'est pas favorable à son développement touristique; the island is strategically ~ l'île occupe une position stratégique. -**2.** [circumstantially]: how are we ~ as regards the competition? comment est-ce qu'on est situés par rapport à la concurrence?

situation [ˌsɪtjʊ'eɪʃn] *n* -**1.** [state of affairs] situation *f*; the ~ at work/in China is getting worse la situation au travail/en Chine ne s'arrange pas; I've got myself into a ridiculous ~ je me suis mis dans une situation ridicule; what would you do in my ~? qu'est-ce que tu ferais à ma place OR dans ma situation?; can't you do something about the ~? ne pouvez-vous pas faire quelque chose?; the firm's financial ~ isn't good la situation financière de la société n'est pas bonne; a crisis ~ une situation de crise; it won't work in a classroom ~ ça ne marchera pas dans une salle de classe; the skills needed in an interview ~ les compétences dont on a besoin pour faire face à un entretien. -**2.** [job] situation *f*, emploi *m*; ~s vacant/wanted offres *fpl*/demandes *fpl* d'emploi. -**3.** [location] situation *f*, emplacement *m*.

situational [ˌsɪtjʊ'eɪʃnl] *adj* situationnel.

situation comedy *n* comédie *f* de situation.

situationism [ˌsɪtjʊ'eɪʃnɪzm] *n* situationnisme *m*.

situationist [ˌsɪtjʊ'eɪʃnɪst] ◇ *adj* situationniste.

◇ *n* situationniste *mf*.

sit-up *n* SPORT redressement *m* assis.

six [sɪks] ◇ *n* -**1.** [number] six *m*; to be at ~es and sevens *Br* être sens dessus dessous; I'm at ~es and sevens as to what to do je ne sais absolument pas quoi faire; it's ~ of one and half a dozen of the other *inf* c'est blanc bonnet et bonnet blanc, c'est kif-kif; to get ~ of the best *inf Br* SCH *dated* se faire fouetter. -**2.** [ice hockey team] équipe *f*; [cub or brownie patrol] patrouille *f*. -**3.** [in cricket] six points *mpl*; he scored five ~es il a marqué cinq fois six points.

◇ *adj* six; to be ~ feet under *inf* être six pieds sous terre, manger les pissenlits par la racine; 'Six Characters in Search of an Author' *Pirandello* 'Six personnages en quête d'auteur'.

◆ **Six** *npl*: the ~ [Common Market pre-1973] les Six *mpl*.

Six Counties *pl pr n*: the ~ (les six comtés *mpl* de) l'Irlande *f* du Nord.

Six Day War *n*: the ~ la guerre des six jours.

sixer ['sɪksəʳ] *n Br* [in cubs, brownies] chef *m* de patrouille.

sixfold ['sɪksfəʊld] ◇ *adj* sextuple.

◇ *adv* au sextuple; the population has increased ~ la population a sextuplé OR s'est multipliée par six; profits are up ~ on last year les bénéfices sont six fois plus importants que OR se sont multipliés par six depuis l'année dernière.

six-footer *inf* [-'fʊtəʳ] *n* [person]: both her sons are ~s ses deux fils mesurent plus de 1,80 m.

six-gun = **six-shooter**.

six-pack *n* pack *m* de six; he polishes off a couple of ~s every night il s'envoie une bonne douzaine de bières chaque soir.

sixpence ['sɪkspəns] *n* [coin] (ancienne) pièce *f* de six pence; it costs ~ ça coûte six pence.

six-shooter *inf n Am* pistolet *m* à six coups, six-coups *m inv*.

sixteen [sɪks'tiːn] ◇ *adj* seize; she was sweet ~ c'était une jolie jeune fille de seize ans.

◇ *n* seize *m*.

sixteenmo [sɪks'tiːnməʊ] (*pl* **sixteenmos**) ◇ *adj* in-seize.

◇ *n* in-seize *m inv*.

sixteenth [sɪks'tiːnθ] ◇ *adj* seizième.

◇ *n* -**1.** [ordinal] seizième *m*. -**2.** [fraction] seizième *m*.

sixteenth note *n Am* MUS double croche *f*.

sixth [sɪksθ] ◇ *adj* sixième.

◇ *n* -**1.** [ordinal] sixième *mf*. -**2.** [fraction] sixième *m*. -**3.** MUS sixte *f*. -**4.** *Br* SCH: to be in the lower/upper ~ ≃ être en première/en terminale.

◇ *adv* -**1.** [in contest] en sixième position, à la sixième place. -**2.** = **sixthly**.

sixth form *n Br* SCH *classe terminale de l'enseignement secondaire en Grande-Bretagne, préparant aux A-levels*, ≃ classes *fpl* de première et de terminale.

◆ **sixth-form** *adj* [student, teacher, subject] de première OR terminale; sixth-form college *établissement préparant aux A-levels*.

sixth former *n Br* SCH élève *mf* de première OR de terminale; all the ~s tous les élèves de première et de terminale.

sixthly ['sɪksθlɪ] *adv* sixièmement.

sixth sense *n* sixième sens *m*; some ~ told me she wouldn't come j'avais l'intuition qu'elle ne viendrait pas.

sixtieth ['sɪkstɪəθ] ◇ *adj* soixantième.

◇ *n* -**1.** [ordinal] soixantième *m*. -**2.** [fraction] soixantième *m*.

Sixtus ['sɪkstəs] *pr n* Sixte.

sixty ['sɪkstɪ] (*pl* **sixties**) ◇ *adj* soixante; about ~ cars une soixantaine de voitures; he must be close to OR getting on for ~ il doit approcher de la soixantaine.

◇ *n* soixante *m*; she's in her sixties elle a entre soixante et soixante-dix ans; sixties pop music la musique pop des années soixante; daytime temperatures will be in the sixties pendant la journée, les températures seront comprises entre 15°C et 20°C ❑ that's the ~-four thousand dollar question! *inf* ça c'est la grande question!

sizable *etc* ['saɪzəbl] = **sizeable**.

size [saɪz] ◇ *n* -**1.** [gen] taille *f*; [of ball, tumour] taille *f*, grosseur *f*; [of region, desert, forest] étendue *f*, superficie *f*; [of difficulty, operation, protest movement] importance *f*, ampleur *f*; [of debt, bill, sum] montant *m*, importance *f*; **to buy a house of comparable ~ in London would be impossible** on ne pourrait pas acheter une maison de cette taille à Londres; **the two rooms are the same ~** les deux pièces sont de la même taille OR ont les mêmes dimensions; **it's about the ~ of a dinner plate** c'est à peu près de la taille d'une assiette; **the kitchen is the ~ of a cupboard** la cuisine est grande comme un placard; **my garden is half the ~ of hers** mon jardin fait la moitié du sien; **average family ~ is four persons** la famille moyenne est composée de quatre personnes; **you should have seen the ~ of the truck!** si tu avais vu la taille du camion!; **it's a city of some ~** c'est une ville assez importante; **the town has no hotels of any ~** la ville n'a pas d'hôtel important; **we weren't expecting a crowd of this ~** nous ne nous attendions pas à une foule aussi nombreuse; **the crowd was steadily growing in ~** la foule grossissait à vue d'œil; **the tumour is increasing in ~** la tumeur grossit; **the budget will have to double in ~** le budget devra être multiplié par deux; **the army has doubled in ~** les effectifs de l'armée ont doublé; **a block of marble one cubic metre in ~** un bloc de marbre d'un mètre cube; **the cupboards can be built to ~** les placards peuvent être construits sur mesure ❑ **that's about the ~ of it!** *inf* en gros, c'est ça! -**2.** [of clothes - gen] taille *f*; [of shoes, gloves, hat] pointure *f*, taille *f*; **what ~ are you?, what ~ do you take?** quelle taille faites-vous?; **I take (a) ~ 40** je fais du 40; **I take a ~ 7 shoe** ≃ je chausse du 37; **I need a ~ larger/smaller** il me faut la taille au-dessus/au-dessous; **we've nothing in your ~** nous n'avons rien dans votre taille; **try this jacket on for ~** essayez cette veste pour voir si c'est votre taille ❑ **collar ~** encolure *f*. -**3.** [for paper, textiles, leather] apprêt *m*; [for plaster] enduit *m*.
◇ *vt* -**1.** [sort] trier selon la taille. -**2.** [make] fabriquer aux dimensions voulues; **the clothing is ~d for the American market** les vêtements sont faits pour le marché américain. -**3.** [paper, textiles, leather] apprêter; [plaster] enduire.
◆ **size up** *vt sep* [stranger, rival] jauger; [problem, chances] mesurer; **we all waited outside, sizing each other up** nous attendions tous dehors, nous observant les uns les autres; **she ~d up the situation immediately** elle a tout de suite compris ce qui se passait.

-size = **-sized**.

sizeable ['saɪzəbl] *adj* [piece, box, car] assez grand; [apple, egg, tumour] assez gros; [sum, income, quantity, crowd] important; [town] assez important; [error] de taille; **they were elected by a ~ majority** ils ont été élus à une assez large majorité.

sizeably ['saɪzəblɪ] *adv* considérablement.

-sized [saɪzd] *in cpds*: **medium~** de taille moyenne; **small and medium~ businesses** petites et moyennes entreprises *fpl*, PME *fpl*; **a fair~ crowd** une foule assez nombreuse; **a man~ portion** une grosse portion.

sizing ['saɪzɪŋ] *n* [process] apprêtage *m*; [substance] colle *f*.

sizzle ['sɪzl] ◇ *vt* -**1.** [sputter] grésiller. -**2.** *inf* [be hot]: **the city ~d in the heat** la ville étouffait sous la chaleur.
◇ *n* grésillement *m*.

sizzler *inf* ['sɪzlə^r] *n* journée *f* torride; **it's going to be a ~!** il va faire une chaleur torride aujourd'hui!

sizzling ['sɪzlɪŋ] ◇ *adj* -**1.** [sputtering] grésillant. -**2.** *inf* [hot] brûlant.
◇ *adv inf*: **~ hot** brûlant.

SK *written abbr of* Saskatchewan.

ska [skɑː] *n* ska *m*.

skat [skæt] *n jeu de cartes à 3 personnes, comprenant 32 cartes.*

skate [skeɪt] (*pl sense 2 inv* OR **skates**) ◇ *n* -**1.** [ice] patin *m* à glace; [roller] patin *m* à roulettes; **to get** OR **to put one's ~s on** *inf* se dépêcher, se grouiller. -**2.** [fish] raie *f*.
◇ *vi* -**1.** [gen] patiner; **to go skating** [ice] faire du patin OR du patinage; [roller] faire du patin à roulettes; **we used to ~ to school** nous allions à l'école en patins à roulettes; **couples ~d around the rink** des couples patinaient autour de la piste ❑ **to ~ on thin ice** être sur un terrain dangereux, avancer en terrain miné. -**2.** [slide - pen, plate] glisser. -**3.** [person] glisser; **his legs ~d out from under him** ses jambes se sont dérobées sous lui.
◆ **skate around, skate over** *vt insep* [problem, issue] esquiver, éviter; **the book ~s around** OR **over his two divorces** le livre passe sous silence ses deux divorces.

skateboard ['skeɪtbɔːd] ◇ *n* skateboard *m*, planche *f* à roulettes.
◇ *vi* faire du skateboard OR de la planche à roulettes.

skateboarding ['skeɪtbɔːdɪŋ] *n*: **to go ~** faire de la planche à roulettes OR du skateboard.

skater ['skeɪtə^r] *n* [on ice] patineur *m*, -euse *f*; [on roller skates] patineur *m*, -euse *f* à roulettes.

skating ['skeɪtɪŋ] ◇ *n* [on ice] patin *m* (à glace); [on roller skates] patin *m* (à roulettes).
◇ *adj* de patinage.

skating rink *n* [for ice skating] patinoire *f*; [for roller skating] piste *f* pour patin à roulettes.

skedaddle *inf* [skɪ'dædl] *vi* mettre les voiles, se tirer, déguerpir; **I'd better ~** il faut que je me sauve OR que je file.

skein [skeɪn] *n* -**1.** [of wool, silk] écheveau *m*. -**2.** [flight - of geese] vol *m*.

skeletal ['skelɪtl] *adj* squelettique.

skeleton ['skelɪtn] ◇ *n* -**1.** ANAT squelette *m*; **he was little more than a ~** il n'avait plus que la peau sur les os ❑ **to have a ~ in the cupboard** *Br* OR **closet** *Am* avoir quelque chose à cacher. -**2.** CONSTR & CHEM [structure] squelette *m*. -**3.** [outline - of book, report] ébauche *f*, esquisse *f*; [- of project, strategy, speech] schéma *m*, grandes lignes *fpl*.
◇ *comp* [crew, team] (réduit au) minimum, squelettique *pej*; **a ~ staff** *Br* OR **crew** *Am* des effectifs réduits au minimum; **they're running a ~ train service** ils assurent un service minimum de trains.

skeleton key *n* passe-partout *m inv*, passe *m*.

skeptic *etc Am* = **sceptic**.

sketch [sketʃ] ◇ *n* -**1.** [drawing] croquis *m*, esquisse *f*; **the map is only a ~** la carte n'est qu'un croquis. -**2.** [brief description] résumé *m*; **historical ~** résumé historique; **a biographical ~ of the author** une biographie succincte de l'auteur; [on book jacket] une notice bibliographique sur l'auteur ‖ [preliminary outline - of book] ébauche *f*; [- of proposal, speech, campaign] grandes lignes *fpl*; **give us a rough ~ of your plan** donnez-nous un aperçu de ce que vous proposez ❑ **character ~** portrait *m* OR description *f* rapide. -**3.** THEAT sketch *m*.
◇ *vt* -**1.** [person, scene] faire un croquis OR une esquisse de, croquer, esquisser; [line, composition, form] esquisser, croquer; [portrait, illustration] faire (rapidement); **he began by ~ing the foreground** il a commencé par esquisser OR croquer le premier plan. -**2.** [book] ébaucher, esquisser; [proposal, campaign, speech] ébaucher, préparer dans les grandes lignes.
◆ **sketch in** *vt sep* -**1.** [provide - background, main points] indiquer; **Harry will ~ a few more details in for you** Harry va vous donner encore quelques précisions. -**2.** [draw] ajouter, dessiner.
◆ **sketch out** *vt sep* -**1.** [book] ébaucher, esquisser; [campaign, plan, speech] ébaucher, préparer dans les grandes lignes; [details, main points] indiquer. -**2.** [draw] ébaucher.

sketchblock ['sketʃblɒk] *n* bloc *m* à dessins.

sketchbook ['sketʃbʊk] *n* carnet *m* à dessins; **Picasso's ~s** les carnets (de dessins) de Picasso.

sketchily ['sketʃɪlɪ] *adv* [describe, report] sommairement; **his article is very ~ researched** son article repose sur des recherches très superficielles.

sketchpad ['sketʃpæd] *n* carnet *m* à dessins.

sketchy ['sketʃɪ] (*compar* **sketchier**, *superl* **sketchiest**) *adj* [description, account] sommaire; [research, work, knowledge] superficiel; [idea, notion] vague; [plan] peu détaillé; **my memory of that day is very ~** mes souvenirs de cette journée sont très flous.

skew [skjuː] ◇ *vt* [distort - facts, results] fausser; [- idea, truth] dénaturer; [- statistics]: **it will ~ the sample** ça va fausser l'échantillonnage.
◇ *vi* obliquer, dévier de sa trajectoire; **the truck ~ed across the intersection** le camion a traversé le carrefour en biais; **he ~ed off the road** il a quitté la route.
◇ *adj Br* -**1.** [crooked - picture] de travers; [- pole] penché. -**2.** [distorted - notion, view] partial; **~ distribution** [in statistics] distribution *f* asymétrique. -**3.** [angled, slanting] oblique, en biais.
◇ *n Br*: **to be on the ~** être de travers.

skewbald ['skjuːbɔːld] ◇ *adj* fauve et blanc, pie-rouge *(inv)*.
◇ *n* cheval *m* fauve et blanc OR pie-rouge.

skewed [skjuːd] = **skew** *adj*.

skewer ['skjʊə^r] ◇ *n* CULIN brochette *f*; [larger] broche *f*.
◇ *vt* CULIN [roast, duck] embrocher; [meat, mushrooms, tomatoes] mettre en brochette; *fig* [person] transpercer.

skew-whiff *inf* [ˌskjuː'wɪf] *adj* & *adv* *Br* de traviole, de travers.

skewy *inf* ['skjuːɪ] (*compar* **skewier**, *superl* **skewiest**) *adj* -**1.** [crooked - picture, hat] de traviole, de travers; **the shelf is ~** l'étagère est de traviole OR de travers; **the steering is ~** la direction est faussée, il y a du jeu dans la direction. -**2.** [weird, odd] farfelu.

ski [skiː] ◇ *n* -**1.** SPORT ski *m (equipment)*; **(a pair of) ~s** (une paire de) skis. -**2.** AERON patin *m*, ski *m*.
◇ *vi* faire du ski, skier; **to go ~ing** [activity] faire du ski; [on holiday] partir aux sports d'hiver OR faire du ski; **they ~ed down the slope** ils descendirent la pente à ski.
◇ *vt*: **I've never ~ed the red run** je n'ai jamais descendu la piste rouge.
◇ *comp* [clothes, boots, lessons] de ski; [resort] de ski, de sports d'hiver; **~ instructor** moniteur *m*, -trice *f* de ski; **~ pole** OR **stick** bâton *m* de ski; **~ wax** fart *m* (pour skis).

skibob ['skiːbɒb] *n* ski-bob *m*, véloski *m*.

skid [skɪd] (*pt* & *pp* **skidded**, *cont* **skidding**) ◇ *vi* -**1.** [on road - driver, car, tyre] déraper; **the car skidded across the junction** la voiture a traversé le carrefour en dérapant; **I skidded into the truck** j'ai dérapé et percuté le camion; **to ~ to a halt** s'arrêter en dérapant. -**2.** [slide - person, object] déraper, glisser; **I skidded on the wet floor** j'ai dérapé OR glissé sur le sol mouillé; **the plates skidded off the tray** les assiettes ont glissé du plateau.
◇ *vt* [vehicle]: **he skidded the truck into the ditch** il a perdu le contrôle du camion qui est parti dans le fossé.
◇ *n* -**1.** AUT dérapage *m*; **to go into a ~** partir en dérapage, déraper; **to get out of** OR **to correct a ~** redresser OR contrôler un dérapage. -**2.** [wedge] cale *f*. -**3.** *Am* [log] rondin *m*; [dragging platform] traîneau *m*, ≃ schlitte *f* ❑ **to put the ~s on** OR **under sb** mettre des bâtons dans les roues à qqn; **to hit the ~s** *inf* devenir clochard.

skiddoo *inf* [skɪ'duː] *vi Am dated* mettre les voiles, déguerpir; **twenty-two ~!** [get out] foutez-le camp, et plus vite que ça!; [let's go] barrons-nous!, tirons-nous!

skid-lid *inf n Br* casque *m* (de moto).

skid mark *n* trace *f* de pneus *(après un dérapage)*.

skidoo *inf* [skɪ'duː] = **skiddoo**.

skidpan ['skɪdpæn] *n Br* piste *f* d'entraînement au dérapage.

skidproof ['skɪdpruːf] *adj* antidérapant.

skid road *n Am* - **1.** [for logs] voie *f* faite de troncs d'arbres, ≃ chemin *m* de schlitte. - **2.** = **skid row**.

skid row *inf n Am* quartier *m* des clochards; you'll end up on ~! tu es sur une mauvaise pente!

skier ['skiːəʳ] *n* skieur *m*, -euse *f*.

skiff [skɪf] *n* skiff *m*, yole *f*.

skiffle ['skɪfl] *n* skiffle *m (type de musique pop des années 50 jouée avec des guitares et des instruments à percussion improvisés)*.

skiing ['skiːɪŋ] ◇ *n* ski *m (activité)*.

◇ *comp* [lessons, accident, clothes] de ski; to go on a ~ holiday partir aux sports d'hiver; ~ instructor moniteur *m*, -trice *f* de ski.

ski jump ◇ *n* [ramp] tremplin *m* de ski; [event, activity] saut *m* à skis.

◇ *vi* faire du saut à skis.

skilful *Br*, **skillful** *Am* ['skɪlfʊl] *adj* habile, adroit; a ~ carpenter un menuisier habile; a ~ pianist un pianiste accompli; she's very ~ with the scissors elle sait se servir d'une paire de ciseaux; a ~ move une démarche habile.

skilfully *Br*, **skillfully** *Am* ['skɪlfʊlɪ] *adv* habilement, avec habileté, adroitement.

skilfulness *Br*, **skillfulness** *Am* ['skɪlfʊlnɪs] *n* habileté *f*, adresse *f*.

ski lift *n* [gen] remontée *f* mécanique; [chair lift] télésiège *m*.

skill [skɪl] *n* - **1.** [ability] compétence *f*, aptitude *f*; [dexterity] habileté *f*, adresse *f*; [expertise] savoir-faire *m inv*; you don't need any special ~ ça ne demande aucune compétence précise; it involves a lot of ~ ça demande beaucoup d'habileté; with great ~ [in manoeuvre] avec une grande habileté; [diplomacy] avec un grand savoir-faire; [dexterity] avec beaucoup d'adresse; his work shows ~ and imagination son travail est plein de talent et d'imagination. - **2.** [learned technique] aptitude *f*, technique *f*; [knowledge] connaissances *fpl*; management ~s techniques de gestion; poor reading ~s de faibles aptitudes pour la lecture; language ~s aptitudes linguistiques; computer technology requires us to learn new ~s l'informatique nous oblige à acquérir de nouvelles compétences.

Skillcentre ['skɪlˌsentəʳ] *n centre de formation professionnelle relevant du ministère de l'Emploi en Grande-Bretagne*.

skilled [skɪld] *adj* - **1.** INDUST [engineer, worker] qualifié; [task] de spécialiste; ~ labour main-d'œuvre *f* qualifiée. - **2.** [experienced - driver, negotiator] habile, expérimenté; [expert] habile, expert; [manually] adroit; [clever - gesture] habile, adroit; ~ in the art of public speaking versé dans l'art oratoire, rompu aux techniques oratoires; he's ~ at mending bicycles il est doué pour réparer les bicyclettes.

skillet ['skɪlɪt] *n Am* poêle *f* (à frire).

skillful *etc Am* = **skilful**.

skim [skɪm] (*pt* & *pp* skimmed, *cont* skimming) ◇ *vt* - **1.** [milk] écrémer; [jam] écumer; [floating matter - with skimmer] écumer, enlever avec une écumoire; [- with spatula] enlever avec une spatule; to ~ the froth from OR off a glass of beer enlever la mousse d'un verre de bière; to ~ the fat from the gravy dégraisser la sauce; to ~ the cream from the milk écrémer le lait. - **2.** [glide over - surface] effleurer, frôler; the seagull skimmed the waves la mouette volait au ras de l'eau OR rasait les vagues; the glider skimmed the tops of the trees le planeur frôlait OR rasait la cime des arbres; the stone skimmed the lake la pierre a ricoché à la surface du lac; the book only ~s the surface *fig* le livre ne fait qu'effleurer OR que survoler la question. - **3.** [stone] faire ricocher; the children were skimming stones over the lake les enfants faisaient des ricochets sur le lac. - **4.** [read quickly - letter, book] parcourir, lire en diagonale; [- magazine] parcourir, feuilleter.

◇ *vi*: to ~ over the ground/across the waves [bird] raser le sol/les vagues; to ~ over OR across the lake [stone] faire des ricochets sur le lac.

◆ **skim off** *vt sep* [cream, froth] enlever (avec une écumoire); the book dealers skimmed off the best bargains *fig* les marchands de livres ont fait les meilleures affaires.

◆ **skim over** *vt insep* [letter, report] parcourir, lire en diagonale; [difficult passage] lire superficiellement, parcourir rapidement.

◆ **skim through** *vt insep* [letter, page] parcourir, lire en diagonale; [magazine] feuilleter; I only had time to ~ through the report je n'ai eu que le temps de lire le rapport en vitesse.

skimmed milk *n* lait *m* écrémé.

skimmer ['skɪməʳ] *n* - **1.** ORNITH bec-en-ciseaux *m*. - **2.** CULIN écumoire *f*.

skim milk = **skimmed milk**.

skimming *inf* ['skɪmɪŋ] *n Am* [tax fraud] fraude *f* fiscale.

skimp [skɪmp] ◇ *vi* lésiner; the builders ~ed on materials les constructeurs ont lésiné sur les matériaux.

◇ *vt* [resources, food] économiser sur, lésiner sur; [job] faire à la va-vite.

skimpily ['skɪmpɪlɪ] *adv* [scantily]: ~ dressed légèrement vêtu.

skimpy ['skɪmpɪ] (*compar* skimpier, *superl* skimpiest) *adj* - **1.** [mean - meal, offering] maigre, chiche; [- praise, thanks] maigre, chiche. - **2.** [clothes, dress - too small] trop juste; [- light] léger; a ~ skirt une jupe étriquée.

skin [skɪn] (*pt* & *pp* skinned, *cont* skinning) ◇ *n* - **1.** [of person] peau *f*; to have dark/fair ~ avoir la peau brune/claire; to have bad/good ~ avoir une vilaine/jolie peau; you're nothing but ~ and bone tu n'as que la peau et les os; we're all human under the ~ au fond, nous sommes tous humains ❑ she escaped by the ~ of her teeth elle l'a échappé belle, elle s'en est tirée de justesse; he got into office by the ~ of his teeth il a été élu de justesse; she nearly jumped out of her ~ elle a sauté au plafond; it's no ~ off my nose *inf* ça ne me coûte rien *fig*, ça ne me gêne pas; he really gets under my ~ *inf* il me tape sur les nerfs, celui-là; to save one's ~ sauver sa peau; to be soaked to the ~ être trempé jusqu'aux os. - **2.** [from animal] peau *f*; a crocodile-~ handbag un sac en crocodile. - **3.** [on fruit, vegetable, sausage] peau *f*; [on onion] pelure *f*; potatoes cooked in their ~s des pommes de terre en robe des champs. - **4.** [on milk, pudding] peau *f*; take the ~ off the custard enlevez la peau de la crème anglaise. - **5.** [of plane] revêtement *m*; [of building] revêtement *m* extérieur; [of drum] peau *f*. - **6.** [for wine] outre *f*. - **7.** *inf* [skinhead] skin *m*. - **8.** ▽ *Br* [cigarette paper] papier *m* à cigarette.

◇ *vt* - **1.** [animal] dépouiller, écorcher; [vegetable] éplucher; if I find him I'll ~ him alive *fig* si je le trouve, je l'écorche vif ❑ there's more than one way to ~ a cat *prov* il y a bien des moyens d'arriver à ses fins. - **2.** [graze - limb] écorcher; I skinned my knee je me suis écorché le genou. - **3.** *inf Br* [rob] plumer; he got skinned at cards il s'est laissé plumer aux cartes; you've been skinned tu t'es fait avoir OR arnaquer.

◇ *comp* [cancer, disease, tone] de la peau.

◆ **skins** ▽ *npl* [drums] batterie *f*.

skin-deep ◇ *adj* superficiel.

◇ *adv* superficiellement.

skin diver *n* plongeur *m*, -euse *f*.

skin diving *n* plongée *f* sous-marine.

skin flick ▽ *n* film *m* porno.

skinflint ['skɪnflɪnt] *n* avare *mf*.

skin food *n (U)* crème *f* nourrissante (pour la peau).

skinful *inf* ['skɪnfʊl] *n Br*: he's had a ~ il est beurré.

skin game ▽ *n* arnaque *f*.

skin graft *n* greffe *f* de la peau; to have a ~ subir une greffe de la peau.

skin grafting [-ˌgrɑːftɪŋ] *n* greffage *m* de la peau.

skinhead ['skɪnhed] *n* skinhead *m*.

skinless ['skɪnlɪs] *adj* [sausages] sans peau.

skin mag ▽ *n Am* revue *f* porno.

-skinned [skɪnd] *in cpds* à la peau...; she's dark~ elle a la peau foncée.

skinny ['skɪnɪ] (*compar* skinnier, *superl* skinniest) *adj* très mince; the ~ look is in fashion c'est à la mode d'être très mince; she's a ~ little thing elle est petite et menue.

skinny-dip *inf* (*pt* & *pp* skinny-dipped, *cont* skinny-dipping) *vi* se baigner à poil.

skinny-dipping *inf* [-ˌdɪpɪŋ] *n* baignade *f* à poil; to go ~ se baigner à poil.

skint *inf* [skɪnt] *adj Br* fauché, raide.

skin test *n* MED cuti-réaction *f*.

skin-tight *adj* moulant.

skip [skɪp] (*pt* & *pp* skipped, *cont* skipping) ◇ *vi* - **1.** [with skipping rope] sauter à la corde. - **2.** [jump] sautiller; he skipped out of the way il s'est écarté d'un bond; the children were skipping around in the garden les enfants gambadaient dans le jardin; the book keeps skipping from one subject to another *fig* le livre passe sans arrêt d'un sujet à l'autre. - **3.** *inf* [go] faire un saut, aller; we skipped across to Paris for the weekend on a fait un saut à Paris pour le week-end.

◇ *vt* - **1.** [omit] sauter, passer; ~ the details passez les détails, épargnez-nous les détails; let's ~ the next chapter sautons le chapitre suivant ‖ [miss - meeting, meal] sauter; SCH [- class] sécher; we decided to ~ lunch nous avons décidé de sauter le déjeuner OR de ne pas déjeuner; my heart skipped a beat *fig* mon cœur s'est arrêté de battre pendant une seconde ❑ ~ it! *inf* laisse tomber! - **2.** *inf* [leave] fuir, quitter; the thieves have probably skipped the country by now à l'heure qu'il est, les voleurs ont probablement quitté le pays.

◇ *n* - **1.** *inf* = **skipper**. - **2.** [jump] (petit) saut *m*; with a little ~, she jumped over the rope d'un bond léger, elle sauta par-dessus la corde. - **3.** [on lorry, for rubbish] benne *f*.

◆ **skip off** *inf vi insep* - **1.** [disappear] décamper; they skipped off without doing the washing up ils ont décampé sans faire la vaisselle. - **2.** [go] faire un saut; we skipped off to Greece for a holiday on est allés passer quelques jours de vacances en Grèce.

◆ **skip over** *vt insep* [omit] sauter, passer.

ski pants *npl* fuseau *m*, pantalon *m* de ski.

ski plane *n* avion *m* à skis.

skipper ['skɪpəʳ] ◇ *n* - **1.** NAUT [gen] capitaine *m*; [of yacht] skipper *m*. - **2.** SPORT capitaine *m*, chef *m* d'équipe. - **3.** *inf* [boss] patron *m*.

◇ *vt* - **1.** [ship, plane] commander, être le capitaine de; [yacht] skipper. - **2.** SPORT [team] être le capitaine de.

skipping ['skɪpɪŋ] *n* saut *m* à la corde.

skipping rope *n Br* corde *f* à sauter.

skirl [skɜːl] ◇ *vi* [emit a sound] sonner; [player] jouer de la cornemuse.

◇ *n* son *m* (de la cornemuse).

skirmish ['skɜːmɪʃ] ◇ *n fig* & MIL escarmouche *f*, accrochage *m*; I had a bit of a ~ with the authorities j'ai eu un différend avec les autorités.

◇ *vi* MIL s'engager dans une escarmouche; to ~ with sb over sthg *fig* avoir un accrochage OR s'accrocher avec qqn au sujet de qqch.

skirt [skɜːt] ◇ *n* - **1.** [garment] jupe *f*; [part of coat] pan *m*, basque *f*. - **2.** MECH jupe *f*. - **3.** *Br* [cut of meat] ≃ flanchet *m*. - **4.** ▽ *(U) Br* [woman]: a bit of ~ une belle nana.

◇ *vt* - **1.** [go around] contourner; the road ~s the mountain la route contourne la montagne. - **2.** [avoid - issue, problem] éluder, esquiver.

◆ **skirt round** *vt insep* = **skirt** *vt*.

skirting (board) ['skɜːtɪŋ-] *n Br* plinthe *f*.

ski run *n* piste *f* de ski.

skit [skɪt] *n* parodie *f*, satire *f*; to do a ~ on sthg parodier qqch; it's a ~ on football commentators c'est une parodie des commentateurs de football.

ski tow *n* téléski *m*.

skitter ['skɪtəʳ] *vi* -**1.** [small animal] trottiner; [bird] voleter; **the bird ~ed over the ground** l'oiseau volait en rase-mottes. -**2.** [ricochet] faire des ricochets; **the stone ~ed across the lake** la pierre a fait des ricochets sur le lac.

skittish ['skɪtɪʃ] *adj* -**1.** [person - playful] espiègle; [- frivolous] frivole. -**2.** [horse] ombrageux, difficile.

skittishly ['skɪtɪʃlɪ] *adv* -**1.** [of person - playfully] avec espièglerie; [- frivolously] avec frivolité. -**2.** [of horse] d'une manière ombrageuse.

skittle ['skɪtl] *n* quille *f*.

◆ **skittles** *n* (jeu *m* de) quilles *fpl*; **to play ~s** jouer aux quilles, faire une partie de quilles.

skittle alley *n* piste *f* de jeu de quilles.

skive *inf* [skaɪv] *vi Br* [avoid work] tirer au flanc; SCH sécher les cours.

◆ **skive off** *inf Br* ◇ *vi insep* se défiler.

◇ *vt insep* [work, class] sécher; **to ~ off school** sécher les cours.

skiver *inf* ['skaɪvəʳ] *n Br* tire-au-flanc *m inv*.

skivvy *inf* ['skɪvɪ] (*pl* **skivvies**) ◇ *vi Br* faire la boniche; **I won't ~ for you** je ne vais pas vous servir de boniche.

◇ *n Br pej* bonne *f* à tout faire; **I'm not your ~** je ne suis pas ta boniche.

◆ **skivvies** *inf npl Am* sous-vêtements *mpl* (masculins).

skua ['skjuːə] *n* skua *m*.

skulduggery [skʌl'dʌgərɪ] *n (U)* combines *fpl* OR manœuvres *fpl* douteuses.

skulk [skʌlk] *vi* rôder; **there's somebody ~ing (about) in the garden/bushes** il y a quelqu'un qui rôde dans le jardin/qui se cache dans les buissons; **to ~ away** OR **off** s'éclipser.

skull [skʌl] *n* crâne *m*; **can't you get it into your thick ~ that she doesn't like you!** *fig* tu n'as toujours pas compris qu'elle ne t'aime pas!

skull and crossbones *n* [motif] tête *f* de mort; [flag] pavillon *m* à tête de mort.

skullcap ['skʌlkæp] *n* -**1.** [headgear] calotte *f*. -**2.** BOT scutellaire *f*.

skullduggery [skʌl'dʌgərɪ] = **skulduggery**.

skunk [skʌŋk] (*pl sense 1 inv* OR **skunks**, *pl sense 2* **skunks**) ◇ *n* -**1.** [animal] moufette *f*, mouffette *f*, sconse *m*; [fur] sconse *m*. -**2.** *inf* [person] canaille *f*, ordure *f*.

◇ *vt inf Am* [opponent] battre à plate couture, flanquer une déculottée à.

sky [skaɪ] (*pl* **skies**, *pt & pp* **skied** OR **skyed**) ◇ *n* [gen] ciel *m*; **the ~ went dark** le ciel s'est assombri; **smoke rose into the ~** de la fumée s'élevait dans le ciel; **the ~ at night** le ciel nocturne; **to sleep under the open ~** dormir à la belle étoile ☐ **the ~'s the limit** *inf* tout est possible.

◇ *vt* -**1.** FTBL [ball] envoyer au ciel. -**2.** [in rowing]: **to ~ the oars** lever les avirons trop haut.

◆ **skies** *npl* [climate] cieux *mpl*; [descriptive] ciels *mpl*; **we spend the winter under sunnier skies** nous passons l'hiver sous des cieux plus cléments; **Turner is famous for his skies** Turner est renommé pour ses ciels.

sky blue *n* bleu ciel *m*.

◆ **sky-blue** *adj* bleu ciel *(inv)*.

skycap *n* ['skaɪkæp] *Am* porteur *m (dans un aéroport)*.

skydiver ['skaɪˌdaɪvəʳ] *n* parachutiste *mf*.

skydiving ['skaɪˌdaɪvɪŋ] *n* parachutisme *m*.

sky-high ◇ *adj literal* très haut dans le ciel; *fig* [prices] inabordable, exorbitant.

◇ *adv* -**1.** *literal* très haut dans le ciel. -**2.** *fig* [very high]: **prices soared** OR **went ~** les prix ont grimpé en flèche; **the explosion blew the building ~** l'explosion a complètement soufflé le bâtiment; **our plans were blown ~** nos projets sont complètement tombés à l'eau.

skyjack ['skaɪdʒæk] *vt* [plane] détourner.

skyjacker ['skaɪˌdʒækəʳ] *n* pirate *m* de l'air.

skylark ['skaɪlɑːk] ◇ *n* alouette *f* des champs.

◇ *vi inf dated* faire le fou, chahuter.

skylarking *inf* ['skaɪlɑːkɪŋ] *n dated* chahut *m*.

skylight ['skaɪlaɪt] *n* lucarne *f*.

skyline ['skaɪlaɪn] *n* [horizon] horizon *m*; [urban]: **the New York ~** la silhouette (des immeubles) de New York.

sky pilot *n mil sl* aumônier *m (dans l'armée)*.

skyrocket ['skaɪˌrɒkɪt] ◇ *n* fusée *f*.

◇ *vi inf* [prices] grimper en flèche.

skyscape ['skaɪskeɪp] *n* ART & PHOT ciel *m*.

skyscraper ['skaɪˌskreɪpəʳ] *n* gratte-ciel *m inv*.

skyward(s) ['skaɪwəd(z)] *adj & adv* vers le ciel.

skyway ['skaɪweɪ] *n* -**1.** AERON couloir *m* aérien. -**2.** *Am* AUT route *f* surélevée.

skywriting ['skaɪˌraɪtɪŋ] *n* publicité *f* aérienne *(tracée dans le ciel par un avion)*.

slab [slæb] (*pt & pp* **slabbed**, *cont* **slabbing**) ◇ *n* -**1.** [block - of stone, wood] bloc *m*; [flat] plaque *f*, dalle *f*; [for path] pavé *m*; **the path was made of stone ~s** le chemin était pavé de pierres; **a wooden ~** un bloc de bois; **a concrete ~** une dalle de béton. -**2.** [piece - of cake] grosse tranche *f*; [- of chocolate] tablette *f*; [- of meat] pavé *m*. -**3.** [table, bench - of butcher] étal *m*; **on the ~** [in mortuary] sur la table d'autopsie; [for operation] *inf* sur la table d'opération.

◇ *vt* [cut - stone] tailler en blocs; [- log] débiter.

slack [slæk] ◇ *adj* -**1.** [loose - rope, wire] lâche, insuffisamment tendu; [- knot] mal serré, desserré; [- chain] lâche; [- grip] faible; **the rope is very ~** la corde a du mou; **the chain is very ~** la chaîne n'est pas assez tendue. -**2.** [careless - work] négligé; [- worker, student] peu sérieux, peu consciencieux; **he's becoming very ~ about his appearance/his work** il commence à négliger son apparence/son travail; **her work has become rather ~ lately** il y a eu un certain laisser-aller dans son travail dernièrement; **she's very ~ about** OR **at getting orders ready on time** elle n'est pas très sérieuse pour ce qui est de préparer les commandes en temps voulu. -**3.** [slow, weak - demand] faible; [- business] calme; **the ~ season for tourists** la période creuse pour le tourisme; **after lunch is my ~ period** après le déjeuner, c'est mon heure creuse; **business is ~ at the moment** les affaires marchent au ralenti en ce moment. -**4.** [lax - discipline, laws, control] mou, relâché; [- parents] négligent; **they're rather ~ about discipline** ils sont plutôt laxistes. -**5.** NAUT: **~ water, ~ tide** mer *f* étale.

◇ *n* -**1.** [in rope] mou *m*; [in cable joint] jeu *m*; NAUT [in cable] battant *m*; **to take up the ~ in a rope** tendre une corde; **leave a bit of ~** laissez un peu de mou. -**2.** *fig* [in economy] secteurs *mpl* affaiblis; **to take up the ~ in the economy** relancer les secteurs faibles de l'économie. -**3.** [still water] eau *f* morte; [tide] mer *f* étale. -**4.** [coal] poussier *m*.

◇ *vi* se laisser aller.

◆ **slack up** *inf vi insep* [slow down] se laisser aller.

slacken ['slækn] ◇ *vt* -**1.** [loosen - cable, rope] détendre, relâcher; [- reins] relâcher; [- grip, hold] desserrer. -**2.** [reduce - pressure, speed] réduire, diminuer; [- pace] ralentir; **the train ~ed speed** le train a ralenti.

◇ *vi* -**1.** [rope, cable] se relâcher; [grip, hold] se desserrer. -**2.** [lessen - speed, demand, interest] diminuer; [- business] ralentir; [- wind] diminuer de force; [- standards] baisser.

◆ **slacken off** ◇ *vt sep* -**1.** [rope] relâcher, donner du mou à. -**2.** [speed, pressure] diminuer; [efforts] relâcher.

◇ *vi insep* -**1.** [rope] se relâcher. -**2.** [speed, demand] diminuer.

◆ **slacken up** *vi insep* [speed] diminuer; [person] se relâcher.

slackening ['slæknɪŋ] *n* [in speed] diminution *f*, réduction *f*; [in interest] diminution *f*; [in demand] affaiblissement *m*; [in knot] desserrement *m*; [in rope] relâchement *m*; [in standards] abaissement *m*; **a ~ of speed** un ralentissement.

slacker *inf* ['slækəʳ] *n* fainéant *m*, -e *f*; **she's no ~** elle n'est pas fainéante.

slackly ['slæklɪ] *adv* [work] négligemment, sans soin; [hang] mollement.

slackness ['slæknɪs] *n* -**1.** [in rope] mou *m*. -**2.** [in business] ralentissement *m*. -**3.** [negligence] négligence *f*, paresse *f*.

slacks [slæks] *npl*: **(a pair of) ~** un pantalon.

slag [slæg] (*pt & pp* **slagged**, *cont* **slagging**) *n* -**1.** *(U)* [waste - from mine] stériles *mpl*; [- from foundry] scories *fpl*, crasses *fpl*; [- from volcano] scories *fpl* volcaniques. -**2.** ▽ *Br pej* [woman] garce *f*, salope *f*.

◆ **slag off** *inf vt sep Br* dénigrer, débiner.

slag heap *n* terril *m*, crassier *m*.

slain [sleɪn] ◇ *pp* → **slay**.

◇ *npl lit*: **the ~** les soldats tombés au champ d'honneur.

slake [sleɪk] *vt* -**1.** *lit* [thirst] étancher; [desire] assouvir. -**2.** CHEM éteindre.

slaked lime [sleɪkt-] *n* chaux *f* éteinte.

slalom ['slɑːləm] ◇ *n* [gen & SPORT] slalom *m*.

◇ *vi* slalomer, faire du slalom.

slam [slæm] (*pt & pp* **slammed**, *cont* **slamming**) ◇ *vt* -**1.** [close - window, door] claquer; [- drawer] fermer violemment; **to ~ the door shut** claquer la porte; **I tried to explain but she slammed the door in my face** j'ai essayé de lui expliquer mais elle m'a claqué la porte au nez ‖ [bang]: **he slammed the books on the desk** il a posé bruyamment les livres sur le bureau; **he slammed the ball into the net** il a envoyé le ballon dans le filet d'un grand coup de pied. -**2.** *inf* [defeat] écraser; **our team got slammed** notre équipe a été battue à plate couture. -**3.** *inf* [criticize] descendre; **her latest novel was slammed by the critics** son dernier roman à été descendu par les critiques.

◇ *vi* [door, window] claquer; **the door slammed shut** la porte a claqué.

◇ *n* -**1.** [of door, window] claquement *m*; **the door swung shut with a ~** la porte s'est refermée en claquant; **give the door a good ~** claque la porte un bon coup; **I heard a loud ~** j'ai entendu un grand claquement. -**2.** CARDS chelem *m*.

◆ **slam down** *vt sep* [lid] refermer en claquant; [books, keys] poser bruyamment; **she slammed the money down on the table** elle a jeté l'argent sur la table.

◆ **slam on** *vt sep*: **to ~ on the brakes** freiner brutalement; **he slammed on a hat and stormed out** il enfonça un chapeau sur sa tête et sortit comme un ouragan.

◆ **slam to** *vt sep* refermer en claquant; **she slammed the gate to** elle a refermé la porte en la claquant.

slam-bang *inf adv Am* -**1.** [directly]: **she ran ~ into me** elle m'est rentrée (en plein) dedans. -**2.** [recklessly] sans faire attention, n'importe comment.

slammer▽ ['slæməʳ] *n* [jail] tôle *f*.

slander ['slɑːndəʳ] ◇ *vt* [gen] calomnier, dire du mal de; JUR diffamer.

◇ *n* [gen] calomnie *f*; JUR diffamation *f*.

slanderer ['slɑːndərəʳ] *n* [gen] calomniateur *m*, -trice *f*; JUR diffamateur *m*, -trice *f*.

slanderous ['slɑːndrəs] *adj* [gen] calomniateur; JUR diffamatoire; **~ gossip** calomnies *fpl*.

slanderously ['slɑːndrəslɪ] *adv* [gen] calomnieusement; JUR de façon diffamatoire.

slang [slæŋ] ◇ *n* [gen & LING] argot *m*; **he uses a lot of ~** il emploie beaucoup de mots d'argot; **prison ~** argot carcéral OR de prison.

◇ *adj* argotique, d'argot.

◇ *vt inf Br* traiter de tous les noms; **they started ~ing each other in the street** ils commencèrent à se traiter de tous les noms dans la rue.

slanging match *inf* ['slæŋɪŋ-] *n Br* échange *m* d'insultes; **to have a ~ with sb** échanger des insultes avec qqn.

slangy ['slæŋɪ] (*compar* slangier, *superl* slangiest) *adj* argotique.

slant [slɑːnt] ◇ *n* -**1.** [line] ligne *f* oblique; [slope] inclinaison *f*; **the table has a ~** OR **is on a ~** la table penche OR n'est pas d'aplomb. -**2.** [point of view] perspective *f*, point *m* de vue; **his articles usually have an anti-government ~** il a tendance à critiquer le gouvernement dans ses articles; **the book gives a different ~ on the whole business** le livre offre un point de vue différent sur toute cette affaire OR présente toute l'affaire sous un jour différent.
◇ *vt* -**1.** [news, evidence] présenter avec parti pris OR de manière peu objective. -**2.** [line, perspective] incliner, faire pencher.
◇ *vi* [line, handwriting] pencher; [ray of light] passer obliquement.

slant-eyed *adj* aux yeux bridés, qui a les yeux bridés.

slanting ['slɑːntɪŋ] *adj* [floor, table] en pente, incliné; [writing] penché; [line] oblique, penché.

slantwise ['slɑːntwaɪz] *adv* [hang, fall] en oblique, obliquement; [write] d'une écriture penchée.

slap [slæp] (*pt* & *pp* slapped, *cont* slapping)
◇ *vt* -**1.** [hit] donner une claque à; **she slapped his face, she slapped him across the face** elle l'a giflé, elle lui a donné une gifle; **to ~ sb on the back** [for hiccups, in greeting] donner à qqn une tape dans le dos; [in praise] féliciter qqn en lui donnant une tape dans le dos ❑ **to ~ sb's wrist** OR **wrists, to ~ sb on the wrist** OR **wrists** taper sur les doigts de qqn. -**2.** [put]: **just ~ some paint over it** passe un coup de pinceau dessus; **~ some Sellotape across it** mets juste un bout de Scotch dessus.
◇ *vi*: **the waves slapped against the harbour wall** les vagues battaient contre la digue; **the flag was slapping against the mast** le drapeau claquait contre le mât.
◇ *n* -**1.** [smack] claque *f*; [on face] gifle *f*; [on back] tape *f* dans le dos; [on wrist] tape *f*; **they gave him a ~ on the back** [in praise] ils lui ont donné une tape dans le dos pour le féliciter ❑ **I got a ~ in the face** *literal* j'ai reçu une gifle; **it was a real ~ in the face** *fig* ça m'a fait l'effet d'une gifle; **I got away with just a ~ on the wrist** j'en ai été quitte pour une tape sur les doigts. -**2.** [noise]: **the ~ of bare feet on the floor** le bruit de pieds nus sur le plancher; **the ~ of the waves against the side of the boat** le clapotis des vagues contre la coque.
◇ *adv inf* en plein; **she rode ~ into me** elle m'est rentrée en plein dedans; **I ran ~ into a tree** je suis rentré en plein OR tout droit dans un arbre; **~ in the middle of the meeting** en plein OR au beau milieu de la réunion.
◆ **slap down** *vt sep* -**1.** [book, money] poser avec violence; **she slapped £1,000 down on the table** elle a jeté 1 000 livres sur la table. -**2.** *inf* [suggestion] rejeter; [person] rembarrer, envoyer promener OR paître.
◆ **slap on** *vt sep* -**1.** [paint] appliquer n'importe comment OR à la va-vite; [jam, butter] étaler généreusement; **~ some paint on the door** donne un coup de pinceau sur la porte; **the whitewash only needs to be slapped on** le blanc de chaux n'a pas besoin d'être étalé soigneusement; **hang on, I'll just ~ some make-up on** attends, je vais juste me maquiller vite fait. -**2.** [tax, increase]: **they slapped on a 3% surcharge** ils ont mis une surtaxe de 3 %; **10% was slapped on the price** ils ont augmenté le prix de 10 %.

slap and tickle *inf n Br* pelotage *m*; **a bit of ~** une partie de pelotage.

slap-bang *inf adv* en plein, tout droit; **she went ~(-wallop) into a tree** elle est rentrée en plein OR tout droit dans un arbre; **he walked ~ into his boss** *fig* il s'est trouvé nez à nez avec son patron.

slapdash ['slæpdæʃ] ◇ *adv* à la va-vite, sans soin, n'importe comment.
◇ *adj* [work] fait n'importe comment OR à la va-vite; [person] négligent; **he's very ~ in everything he does** il fait tout un peu n'importe comment OR à la va-vite.

slaphappy *inf* ['slæp,hæpɪ] *adj* relax.

slapjack ['slæpdʒæk] *n Am* CULIN crêpe *f*.

slapstick ['slæpstɪk] ◇ *n* grosse farce *f*, bouffonnerie *f*.
◇ *adj* [humour] bouffon; **~ comedy** comédie *f* bouffonne.

slap-up *inf adj Br*: **a ~ meal** un repas de derrière les fagots; **he invited me out for a ~ lunch** il m'a invité à déjeuner dans un restaurant chic.

slash [slæʃ] ◇ *vt* -**1.** [cut - gen] taillader; [- face] balafrer; **he ~ed my arm with a knife** il m'a tailladé le bras avec un couteau; **the bus seats had been ~ed by vandals** les sièges du bus avaient été lacérés par des vandales; **he ~ed his way through the jungle** il s'est taillé OR frayé un chemin à travers la jungle à coups de couteau. -**2.** [hit - with whip] frapper, cingler; [- with stick] battre; **the rider ~ed the horse with his whip** le cavalier frappait OR cinglait le cheval de son fouet; **she ~ed the bushes with a stick** elle donnait des coups de bâton dans les buissons. -**3.** *Am* [verbally] critiquer violemment; **she ~ed the government in her speech** elle a violemment critiqué le gouvernement dans son discours. -**4.** [prices] casser; [cost, taxes] réduire considérablement; **'prices ~ed!'** 'prix cassés!'; **prices have been ~ed by 40%** les prix ont été réduits de 40 %. -**5.** SEW: **a green jacket ~ed with blue** une veste verte avec des crevés laissant apercevoir du bleu.
◇ *vi*: **to ~ at sb with a knife/stick** donner des coups de couteau/de bâton en direction de qqn; **he ~ed at the bushes with a stick** il donna des coups de bâton dans les buissons.
◇ *n* -**1.** [with knife] coup *m* de couteau; [with sword] coup *m* d'épée; [with whip] coup *m* de fouet; [with stick] coup *m* de bâton. -**2.** [cut] entaille *f*; [on face] balafre *f*. -**3.** SEW crevé *m*. -**4.** TYPO (barre *f*) oblique *f*. -**5.** *Br phr*: **to have a ~** ▽ pisser un coup.

slash-and-burn *adj* par abattage et brûlage des arbres.

slashing ['slæʃɪŋ] *adj* [attack] cinglant.

slat [slæt] *n* [in blinds, louvre] lamelle *f*; [wooden] latte *f*; AERON aileron *m*.

slate [sleɪt] ◇ *n* -**1.** CONSTR & SCH ardoise *f*; **put it on the ~** *inf Br fig* mettez-le sur mon compte. -**2.** *Am* POL liste *f* provisoire de candidats; **the Republicans have a full ~** les Républicains présentent des candidats dans toutes les circonscriptions.
◇ *vt* -**1.** [cover - roof] couvrir d'ardoises. -**2.** *Am* POL proposer *(un candidat)*; **Magee is ~d for President** Magee a été choisi comme candidat aux élections présidentielles. -**3.** *Am* [destine]: **she was ~d for a gold medal/for victory** elle devait remporter une médaille d'or/la victoire || [expect] prévoir; **we're slating a full house** nous comptons faire salle comble. -**4.** *inf Br* [criticize - film, actor] descendre; **his latest novel was ~d by the critics** les critiques ont descendu son dernier roman.
◇ *comp* [mine] d'ardoise; [roof] en ardoise OR ardoises, d'ardoise; [industry] ardoisier; **~ quarry** carrière *f* d'ardoise, ardoisière *f*.

slate blue *n* bleu ardoise *m inv*.
◆ **slate-blue** *adj* bleu ardoise *(inv)*.

slate-coloured *adj* ardoise *(inv)*.

slate-grey *adj* gris ardoise *(inv)*.

slate quarry *n* carrière *f* d'ardoise, ardoisière *f*.

slater ['sleɪtəʳ] *n* -**1.** [roofer] couvreur *m*. -**2.** *Ir, Scot, Austr* & *NZ* [woodlouse] cloporte *m*.

slather ['slæðəʳ] ◇ *n inf Br*: **~s of cream** des masses OR des tonnes de crème.
◇ *vt* ▽*Am* -**1.** [waste] gaspiller. -**2.** [butter] étaler généreusement.

slating ['sleɪtɪŋ] *n* -**1.** *(U)* CONSTR [of roof] couverture *f*; [material] ardoises *fpl*. -**2.** *inf Br phr*: **to get a ~** [criticism] se faire descendre *(par la critique)*; [scolding] se faire enguirlander.

slatted ['slætɪd] *adj* à lattes.

slattern ['slætən] *n* souillon *f*.

slaty ['sleɪtɪ] *adj* [in colour] ardoise *(inv)*; [in appearance, texture] qui ressemble à l'ardoise.

slaughter ['slɔːtəʳ] ◇ *vt* -**1.** [kill - animal] abattre, tuer; [- people] massacrer, tuer (sauvagement). -**2.** *inf fig* [defeat - team, opponent] massacrer.
◇ *n* [of animal] abattage *m*; [of people] massacre *m*, tuerie *f*.

slaughterer ['slɔːtərəʳ] *n* [in abattoir] tueur *m* *(dans un abattoir)*; [murderer] meurtrier *m*, -ère *f* [in massacre] massacreur *m*, -euse *f*.

slaughterhouse ['slɔːtəhaus, *pl* -hauzɪz] *n* abattoir *m*.

Slav [slɑːv] ◇ *adj* slave.
◇ *n* Slave *mf*.

slave [sleɪv] ◇ *n literal* & *fig* esclave *mf*; **to be a ~ to fashion/habit** être esclave de la mode/de ses habitudes; **he's a ~ to drink** il est prisonnier de l'alcool.
◇ *vi* travailler comme un esclave OR un forçat, trimer; **I've been slaving over a hot stove all morning** j'ai travaillé comme un forçat à la cuisine toute la matinée; **he ~d over his books all day long** il était plongé dans ses livres à longueur de journée; **they ~d (away) to get their house finished in time** ils ont travaillé comme des forçats pour terminer leur maison à temps.

slave cylinder *n* cylindre *m* récepteur.

slave driver *n literal* meneur *m* d'esclaves; *fig* négrier *m*.

slaveholder ['sleɪv,həuldəʳ] *n* propriétaire *m* d'esclaves.

slave labour *n* [work] travail *m* fait par des esclaves; **the Great Wall was built by ~** la grande Muraille a été construite par des esclaves || *fig* travail *m* de forçat; **I'm not working there any more, it's ~** je ne travaillerai plus pour eux, c'est le OR un vrai bagne.

slaver[1] ['sleɪvəʳ] *n* -**1.** [trader] marchand *m* d'esclaves. -**2.** [ship] (vaisseau *m*) négrier *m*.

slaver[2] ['slævəʳ] ◇ *vi* [dribble] baver; **the dog was ~ing at the mouth** le chien bavait.
◇ *n* [saliva] bave *f*.
◆ **slaver over** *vt insep* [person] s'extasier devant; [possession] convoiter; [event] se délecter de.

slavery ['sleɪvərɪ] *n* esclavage *m*; **to be sold into ~** être vendu comme esclave.

slave ship *n* négrier *m (bateau)*.

slave state *n Am* HIST État *m* esclavagiste.

slave trade *n* commerce *m* des esclaves; [of Africans] traite *f* des Noirs.

slave trader *n* marchand *m* d'esclaves, négrier *m*.

slavey *inf* ['sleɪvɪ] *n Br* boniche *f*.

Slavic ['slɑːvɪk] = **Slavonic**.

slavish ['sleɪvɪʃ] *adj* [mentality, habits] d'esclave; [devotion] servile; [imitation] sans aucune originalité, servile.

slavishly ['sleɪvɪʃlɪ] *adv* [work] comme un forçat; [copy, worship] servilement.

Slavonic [slə'vɒnɪk] ◇ *n* LING slave *m*; HIST slavon *m*.
◇ *adj* slave.

slaw [slɔː] *n Am* salade *f* de chou cru.

slay [sleɪ] (*pt* slew [sluː], *pp* slain [sleɪn]) *vt* -**1.** [kill] tuer. -**2.** *inf Br* [impress] impressionner. -**3.** *inf Br* [amuse] faire crever de rire.

slayer ['sleɪəʳ] *n lit* tueur *m*, -euse *f*.

sleaze *inf* [sliːz] *n* [squalidness] aspect *m* miteux, caractère *m* sordide; [pornography] porno *m*.

sleazy *inf* ['sliːzɪ] (*compar* sleazier, *superl* sleaziest) *adj* [squalid] miteux, sordide; [disreputable] mal famé; **a ~ bar** un bar miteux OR mal famé.

sled [sled] ◇ *n Br* = **sledge 1, 2**; *Am* = **sledge 1**.
◇ *vi Br* = **sledge 1, 2**; *Am* = **sledge 1**.
◇ *vt Am* transporter en luge.

sledge [sledʒ] ◇ *n* -**1.** [for fun or sport] luge *f*. -**2.** [pulled by animals] traîneau *m*.
◇ *vi* -**1.** *Br* [for fun or sport] faire de la luge; **to go sledging** faire de la luge; **children were sledging down the slope** des enfants descen

daient la pente sur une OR en luge. -**2.** [pulled by animals] faire du traîneau.
◇ *vt Am* transporter en traîneau.

sledgehammer ['sledʒˌhæməʳ] *n* masse *f (outil)*; a ~ blow *fig* un coup très violent.

sleek [sliːk] *adj* -**1.** [fur, hair] luisant, lustré, lisse; [feathers] brillant, luisant; [bird] aux plumes luisantes; [cat] au poil soyeux OR brillant. -**2.** [person - in appearance] soigné, tiré à quatre épingles; [- in manner] onctueux, doucereux. -**3.** [vehicle, plane] aux lignes pures; the car has very ~ lines cette voiture a une très belle ligne.
◆ **sleek back, sleek down** *vt sep*: to ~ one's hair back OR down se lisser les cheveux.

sleekly ['sliːklɪ] *adv* -**1.** [glossily]: its fur shone ~ il avait le poil luisant. -**2.** [elegantly - dress] élégamment, avec chic. -**3.** [unctuously - behave] onctueusement, doucereusement.

sleekness ['sliːknɪs] *n* -**1.** [of fur, hair] brillant *m*, luisant *m*. -**2.** [of person - in appearance] chic *m*, élégance *f*; [- in manner] onctuosité *f*. -**3.** [of vehicle, plane] pureté *f* de lignes, ligne *f* aérodynamique.

sleep [sliːp] (*pt* & *pp* **slept** [slept]) ◇ *vi* -**1.** [rest] dormir; ~ well OR tight! bonne nuit!; did you ~ well? avez-vous bien dormi?; to ~ soundly dormir profondément OR à poings fermés; to ~ rough coucher sur la dure; I'm not ~ing well at the moment je ne dors pas bien en ce moment; she slept through the storm la tempête ne l'a pas réveillée || [spend night] coucher, passer la nuit; can I ~ at your place? est-ce que je peux coucher OR dormir chez vous?; you can ~ on the sofa tu peux dormir OR coucher sur le canapé; where did you ~ last night? où est-ce que tu as passé la nuit? ☐ to ~ like a log dormir comme une souche OR comme un loir OR du sommeil du juste; 'The Sleeping Beauty' *Perrault, Tchaikovsky* 'la Belle au bois dormant'. -**2.** [daydream] rêvasser, rêver; Walsh is ~ing at the back of the class as usual Walsh rêvasse au fond de la classe, comme d'habitude. -**3.** *euph* & *lit* [be dead] dormir du dernier sommeil.
◇ *vt* -**1.** [accommodate]: the sofa bed ~s two deux personnes peuvent coucher dans le canapé-lit; the house ~s four on peut loger quatre personnes dans cette maison. -**2.** *phr*: I didn't ~ a wink all night je n'ai pas fermé l'œil de la nuit.
◇ *n* -**1.** [rest] sommeil *m*; to turn over in one's ~ se retourner dans son sommeil; to talk in one's ~ parler en dormant OR dans son sommeil; to walk in one's ~ être somnambule; to be in a deep ~ dormir profondément; to have a good ~ bien dormir; I only had two hours' ~ je n'ai dormi que deux heures; you need (to get) a good night's ~ il te faut une bonne nuit de sommeil; I couldn't get to ~ je n'arrivais pas à m'endormir; to go to ~ s'endormir; my legs have gone to ~ *fig* [numb] j'ai les jambes engourdies; [tingling] j'ai des fourmis dans les jambes; you're not going to lose ~ over it! tu ne vas pas en perdre le sommeil!; to put to ~ [patient] endormir; [horse, dog] *euph* piquer; the horse had to be put to ~ on a dû faire piquer le cheval; I was put to ~ before the operation on m'a endormi avant l'opération; to send sb to ~ *literal* endormir qqn; *fig* [bore] endormir qqn, assommer qqn. -**2.** *Br* [nap]: the children usually have a ~ in the afternoon en général les enfants font la sieste l'après-midi; I could do with a ~ je ferais bien un petit somme. -**3.** [substance in eyes] chassie *f*; to rub the ~ out of one's eyes se frotter les yeux *(au réveil)*. -**4.** *lit* [death] la mort.
◆ **sleep around** *inf vi insep* coucher à droite et à gauche.
◆ **sleep away** *vt sep*: he slept the night away il a dormi toute la nuit; he ~s the day away il passe toute la journée à dormir.
◆ **sleep in** *vi insep* -**1.** [lie in - voluntarily] faire la grasse matinée; [- involuntarily] se lever en retard. -**2.** [sleep at home] coucher à la maison; [staff] être logé sur place.
◆ **sleep off** *vt sep* [hangover, fatigue] dormir pour faire passer; he's ~ing off the effects of the journey il dort pour se remettre de la fatigue du voyage; he's ~ing it off *inf* il cuve son vin.
◆ **sleep on** ◇ *vi insep* continuer à dormir; let her ~ on a bit laisse-la dormir encore un peu; she slept on until lunchtime elle a dormi jusqu'à l'heure du déjeuner.
◇ *vt insep phr*: ~ on it la nuit porte conseil *prov*.
◆ **sleep out** *vi insep* [away from home] découcher; [in the open air] coucher à la belle étoile; [in tent] coucher sous la tente; some of the nurses ~ out les infirmières ne sont pas toutes logées sur place.
◆ **sleep through** ◇ *vi insep*: he slept through till five o'clock il a dormi jusqu'à cinq heures.
◇ *vt insep*: I slept through the last act j'ai dormi pendant tout le dernier acte; she slept through her alarm elle n'a pas entendu son réveil; they slept through my speech ils ont dormi pendant mon discours.
◆ **sleep together** *vi insep euph* coucher ensemble.
◆ **sleep with** *vt insep euph* coucher avec.

sleeper ['sliːpəʳ] *n* -**1.** [sleeping person] dormeur *m*, -euse *f*; to be a light/heavy ~ avoir le sommeil léger/lourd. -**2.** [train] train-couchettes *m*; [sleeping car] wagon-lit *m*, voiture-lit *f*; [berth] couchette *f*; I took the ~ to Rome je suis allé à Rome en train-couchettes. -**3.** RAIL *Br* [track support] traverse *f*. -**4.** [spy] agent *m* dormant. -**5.** *Br* [earring] clou *m*. -**6.** *inf* [unexpected success] révélation *f*.

sleepily ['sliːpɪlɪ] *adv* [look] d'un air endormi; [speak] d'un ton endormi; she wandered ~ into the kitchen elle est arrivée à moitié endormie dans la cuisine.

sleepiness ['sliːpɪnɪs] *n* [of person] envie *f* de dormir; [of town] torpeur *f*.

sleeping ['sliːpɪŋ] *adj* qui dort, endormi; let ~ dogs lie *prov* ne réveillez pas le chat qui dort *prov*.

sleeping bag *n* sac *m* de couchage.

sleeping berth *n* RAIL & NAUT couchette *f*.

sleeping car *n* wagon-lit *m*.

sleeping draught *n Br* soporifique *m*.

sleeping partner *n Br* COMM (associé *m*) commanditaire *m*, bailleur *m* de fonds.

sleeping pill *n* somnifère *m*.

sleeping policeman *n Br* casse-vitesse *m inv*, ralentisseur *m*.

sleeping quarters *npl* chambres *fpl* à coucher; MIL chambrées *fpl*; SCH dortoir *m*.

sleeping sickness *n* maladie *f* du sommeil.

sleeping tablet = **sleeping pill**.

sleep-learning *n* apprentissage *m* en dormant, hypnopédie *f*.

sleepless ['sliːplɪs] *adj* -**1.** [without sleep] sans sommeil; I had OR spent a ~ night j'ai passé une nuit blanche, je n'ai pas fermé l'œil de la nuit. -**2.** *lit* [person] qui ne peut trouver le sommeil.

sleeplessly ['sliːplɪslɪ] *adv* sans pouvoir dormir.

sleeplessness ['sliːplɪsnɪs] *n (U)* insomnie *f*, insomnies *fpl*.

sleepwalk ['sliːpwɔːk] *vi*: he was ~ing last night il a eu une crise de somnambulisme hier soir.

sleepwalker ['sliːpˌwɔːkəʳ] *n* somnambule *mf*.

sleepwalking ['sliːpˌwɔːkɪŋ] *n* somnambulisme *m*.

sleepwear ['sliːpweəʳ] *n (U)* vêtements *mpl* de nuit.

sleepy ['sliːpɪ] (*compar* **sleepier**, *superl* **sleepiest**) *adj* -**1.** [person] qui a envie de dormir, somnolent; I'm OR I feel ~ j'ai sommeil, j'ai envie de dormir. -**2.** [town] plongé dans la torpeur.

sleepyhead *inf* ['sliːpɪhed] *n*: come on, ~, it's time for bed! allez, va au lit, tu dors debout!

sleet [sliːt] ◇ *n* neige *f* fondue *(tombant du ciel)*.
◇ *vi*: it's ~ing il tombe de la neige fondue.

sleeve [sliːv] *n* -**1.** [on garment] manche *f*; to have OR to keep something up one's ~ avoir plus d'un tour dans son sac; I wonder what else she's got up her ~ je me demande ce qu'elle nous réserve encore comme surprise; I've still got a few ideas up my ~ j'ai encore quelques idées en réserve. -**2.** TECH [tube] manchon *m*; [lining] chemise *f*. -**3.** *Br* [for record] pochette *f*.

sleeve board *n* jeannette *f*.

-sleeved [sliːvd] *in cpds* à manches...; short~ à manches courtes.

sleeveless ['sliːvlɪs] *adj* sans manches.

sleeve notes *npl Br texte figurant au dos des pochettes de disques*.

sleeving ['sliːvɪŋ] *n Br* ELEC gaine *f* isolante.

sleigh [sleɪ] ◇ *n* traîneau *m*; ~ ride promenade *f* en traîneau.
◇ *vi* se promener en traîneau, aller en traîneau.

sleigh bell *n* grelot *m* (de traîneau).

sleight of hand [slaɪt-] *n* [skill] dextérité *f*; [trick] tour *m* de passe-passe; by ~ par un tour de passe-passe.

slender ['slendəʳ] *adj* -**1.** [slim, narrow - figure] mince, svelte; [- fingers, neck, stem] fin; Peter is tall and ~ Peter est grand et élancé; [- margin, beam] étroit. -**2.** [limited - resources] faible, maigre, limité; [- majority] étroit, faible; [- hope, chance] maigre, faible; [- knowledge] faible, limité; he's a person of ~ means *euph* il ne roule pas sur l'or.

slenderize *inf* ['slendəraɪz] *Am* ◇ *vi* maigrir, mincir.
◇ *vt* mincir, amincir.

slenderizing *inf* ['slendəraɪzɪŋ] *Am* ◇ *n* amaigrissement *m*.
◇ *adj* [diet] amaigrissant; [cream, product] amincissant; [exercises] pour maigrir; [lunch] qui ne fait pas grossir.

slenderly ['slendəlɪ] *adv*: ~ built svelte, mince.

slenderness ['slendənɪs] *n* -**1.** [of figure] minceur *f*, sveltesse *f*; [of neck, fingers] finesse *f*. -**2.** [of resources] insuffisance *f*; [of hope, majority] faiblesse *f*.

slept [slept] *pt* & *pp* → **sleep**.

sleuth *inf* [sluːθ] *hum* ◇ *n* (fin) limier *m*, détective *m*.
◇ *vi* enquêter.
◇ *vt* enquêter sur.

sleuthhound ['sluːθhaʊnd] *n* -**1.** *inf* = **sleuth**. -**2.** [dog] limier *m (chien)*.

sleuthing *inf* ['sluːθɪŋ] *n hum* travail *m* de détective; I decided to do a bit of ~ of my own j'ai décidé de mener ma propre petite enquête.

slew [sluː] ◇ *pt* → **slay**.
◇ *vi* -**1.** [pivot - person] pivoter, se retourner; he ~ed round in his chair il a pivoté sur sa chaise. -**2.** [vehicle - skid] déraper; [- swerve] faire une embardée; [- turn] virer; the car ~ed into the ditch la voiture a dérapé et a fini dans le fossé.
◇ *vt* -**1.** [turn, twist] faire tourner OR pivoter; NAUT [mast] virer, dévirer. -**2.** [vehicle] faire déraper; he ~ed the car around il a fait un tête-à-queue.
◇ *n inf*: a ~ of, ~s of un tas de; a whole ~ of photographers un tas de photographes; ~s of people des OR un tas de gens.

slewed *inf* [sluːd] *adj Br* rond, ivre; to get ~ prendre une cuite.

slice [slaɪs] ◇ *n* -**1.** [of bread, meat, cheese] tranche *f*; [of pizza] part *f*; [round] rondelle *f*, tranche *f*. -**2.** *fig* [share, percentage] part *f*, partie *f*; a large ~ of my income goes on rent une bonne partie de mes revenus est absorbée par le loyer; employees receive a ~ of the profits les employés reçoivent une part des bénéfices; they were all very keen to get a ~ of the action *inf* tout le monde voulait participer. -**3.** [utensil] pelle *f*, spatule *f*; cake ~ pelle *f* à gâteau. -**4.** SPORT slice *m*; to give a ball a ~ slicer une balle; she puts a lot of ~ in her serve elle slice beaucoup ses balles au service.
◇ *vt* -**1.** [cut into pieces - cake, bread] couper (en tranches); [- sausage, banana] couper (en rondelles); any way you ~ it *inf Am* il n'y a pas à tortiller. -**2.** [cut] couper, trancher. -**3.** SPORT couper, slicer.

◇ *vi* [knife] couper; [bread] se couper; **this bread doesn't ~ very easily** ce pain n'est pas très facile à couper.

◆ **slice away** *vt sep* [branch] couper (avec une machette).

◆ **slice off** *vt sep* [branch] couper; **his finger was ~d off** il a eu le doigt coupé; **~ me off some ham/cheese** coupe-moi une tranche de jambon/fromage.

◆ **slice through** *vt insep* -**1.** [cut - rope, cable] couper (net), trancher; **she just ~d straight through all the red tape** *fig* elle a réussi à éviter toute la paperasserie. -**2.** [go, move] traverser (rapidement), fendre; **the boat ~d through the water** le bateau fendait l'eau; **the arrow ~d through the air** la flèche fendit l'air.

◆ **slice up** *vt sep* [loaf, cake] couper (en tranches); [banana] couper (en rondelles).

sliced bread [slaɪst-] *n* pain *m* (coupé) en tranches; **it's the best thing since ~** *inf* on n'a rien fait de mieux depuis le fil à couper le beurre.

slice of life *n* THEAT tranche *f* de vie; [novel] description *f* réaliste.

slicer ['slaɪsəʳ] *n* [gen] machine *f* à trancher; [for bread] machine *f* à couper le pain; [for meat] machine *f* à couper la viande; [for salami, ham] coupe-jambon *m inv*.

slick [slɪk] ◇ *adj* -**1.** *pej* [glib] qui a du bagout; [in speech] enjôleur; [in manner] doucereux; [in content] superficiel; **she always has a ~ excuse** elle a toujours une bonne excuse; **he always has a ~ answer** il a toujours réponse à tout; **the explanation was rather too ~** l'explication était trop bonne (pour être vraie). -**2.** [smoothly efficient] habile; **she made a ~ gear change** elle effectua un changement de vitesse en souplesse; **a ~ campaign** une campagne astucieuse; **a ~ sale** une vente rondement menée; **a ~ take-over** un rachat rondement mené. -**3.** [style, magazine] beau. -**4.** [smart, chic] chic, tiré à quatre épingles; **you're looking very ~** tu fais très chic. -**5.** [hair] lisse, lissé, luisant; [road surface] glissant, gras; [tyre] lisse. -**6.** *Am* [slippery] glissant; [greasy] gras; **the road was ~ with ice/mud** le verglas/la boue avait rendu la chaussée glissante. -**7.** *Am* [cunning] malin, rusé.

◇ *n* -**1.** [oil spill]: **(oil) ~** [on sea] nappe *f* de pétrole; [on beach] marée *f* noire. -**2.** [tyre] pneu *m* lisse. -**3.** *Am* [glossy magazine] *magazine en papier glacé contenant surtout des articles et des photos sur la vie privée des stars.*

◆ **slick back, slick down** *vt sep*: **to ~ one's hair back** OR **down** se lisser les cheveux.

◆ **slick up** *vt sep Am* [appearance] mettre en valeur; [house, room] astiquer, faire reluire; **to ~ o.s. up** se pomponner.

slicker ['slɪkəʳ] *n* -**1.** *inf* [sly person] combinard *m*, -e *f*. -**2.** *Am* [raincoat] imperméable *m*, ciré *m*.

slickly ['slɪklɪ] *adv* [answer] habilement; [perform] brillamment; **his hair shone ~** il avait les cheveux luisants; **the deal went through ~ enough** l'affaire fut assez rondement menée.

slickness ['slɪknɪs] *n* -**1.** [of hair] brillant *m*, luisant *m*. -**2.** *pej* [in speech] bagout *m*; [in manner] caractère *m* doucereux; [in style] brillance *f* (apparente). -**3.** [of deal, sale] rapidité *f*, efficacité *f*.

slide [slaɪd] (*pt* & *pp* **slid** [slɪd]) ◇ *vi* -**1.** [on ice, slippery surface] glisser; **he slid on the ice** il a glissé sur la glace; **he slid down the bannisters** il a descendu l'escalier en glissant sur la rampe; **tears slid down her face** des larmes roulèrent sur son visage. -**2.** [move quietly]: **the car slid away into the dark** la voiture s'enfonça dans l'obscurité; **she slid into/out of the room** elle s'est glissée dans la pièce/hors de la pièce; **the door slid open/shut** la porte s'est ouverte/fermée en glissant; **her eyes slid over the familiar objects in the room** elle promena son regard sur les objets familiers de la pièce. -**3.** [go gradually] glisser; **the sheet music slid (down) behind the piano** la partition a glissé derrière le piano; **she slid slowly into debt** elle a fini par s'endetter; **he's sliding into bad habits** il est en train de prendre de mauvaises habitudes; **to let things ~** laisser les choses aller à la dérive. -**4.** [prices, value] baisser.

◇ *vt* faire glisser, glisser; **I slid the book into my pocket** j'ai glissé le livre dans ma poche; **he slid the door open/shut** il a ouvert/fermé la porte en la faisant coulisser; **~ the lid into place** faites glisser le couvercle à sa place; **she slid the money across the table** elle fit glisser l'argent sur la table.

◇ *n* -**1.** [in playground] toboggan *m*; [on ice, snow] glissoire *f*; [for logs] glissoire *f*. -**2.** [act of sliding] glissade *f*; **to go into a ~** faire une glissade. -**3.** [fall - in prices] baisse *f*; **the stock exchange is on a downward ~** la Bourse est en baisse; **the ~ in standards** la dégradation des valeurs. -**4.** PHOT diapositive *f*, diapo *f*; [for microscope] porte-objet *m*; **I illustrated my lecture with ~s** j'ai illustré mon cours avec des diapositives. -**5.** *Br* [in hair] barrette *f*. -**6.** [runner - in machine, trombone] coulisse *f*. -**7.** MUS coulé *m*.

◆ **slide off** *vi insep* -**1.** [lid] s'enlever en glissant; **this part ~s off easily** il suffit de faire coulisser cette pièce pour l'enlever. -**2.** [fall] glisser; **the book keeps sliding off** le livre n'arrête pas de glisser. -**3.** [go away - visitor] s'en aller discrètement, s'éclipser; **where are you sliding off to?** où est-ce que tu te sauves comme ça?; **she slid off to the bar in the interval** elle s'est éclipsée à l'entracte pour aller au bar.

◆ **slide over** ◇ *vt insep* [evade - issue] éviter de parler de, esquiver.

◇ *vi insep* se glisser; **she slid over to me in the interval** elle m'a rejoint pendant l'entracte; **~ over and let me drive** pousse-toi et laisse-moi le volant.

slide fastener *n Am* fermeture *f* à glissière, fermeture *f* Éclair®.

slide guitar *n* slide guitar *f*.

slide projector *n* projecteur *m* de diapositives.

slide rule *n* règle *f* à calcul.

slide show *n* diaporama *m*.

slide valve *n* (soupape *f* à) clapet *m*.

sliding ['slaɪdɪŋ] ◇ *adj* [part] qui glisse; [movement] glissant; [door] coulissant; **the safe was hidden behind a ~ panel** le coffre était caché derrière un panneau mobile.

◇ *n* glissement *m*.

sliding roof *n* AUT toit *m* ouvrant.

sliding scale *n* [for salaries] échelle *f* mobile; [for prices] barème *m* des prix; [for tax] barème *m* des impôts.

slight [slaɪt] ◇ *adj* -**1.** [person - slender] menu, mince; [- frail] frêle; [structure] fragile, frêle; **she is of ~ build** elle est fluette. -**2.** [minor, insignificant - error, increase, movement] faible, léger, petit; [- cut, graze] léger; **there's a ~ drizzle/wind** il y a un peu de crachin/de vent; **the difference is only very ~, there's only a very ~ difference** la différence est minime, il n'y a qu'une très légère différence; **he has a ~ accent** il a un léger accent; **she has a ~ temperature** elle a un peu de température; **she has a ~ cold** elle est un peu enrhumée; **a ~ piece of work** un ouvrage insignifiant ‖ [in superl form]: **it makes not the ~est bit of difference** ça ne change absolument rien; **I haven't the ~est idea** je n'en ai pas la moindre idée; **he gets angry at the ~est thing** il se fâche pour un rien; **they haven't the ~est chance of winning** ils n'ont pas la moindre chance OR la plus petite chance de l'emporter; **not in the ~est** pas le moins du monde, pas du tout.

◇ *vt* [snub] manquer d'égards envers; [insult] insulter; [offend] froisser, blesser; **she felt ~ed** elle a été blessée OR froissée; **to ~ sb's memory** faire affront à la mémoire de qqn.

◇ *n* [snub, insult] manque *m* d'égards, vexation *f*, affront *m*; **it's a ~ on her reputation** c'est une offense à sa réputation.

slighting ['slaɪtɪŋ] *adj* offensant, désobligeant.

slightingly ['slaɪtɪŋlɪ] *adv* [behave] d'une manière désobligeante; **to speak ~ of sb** faire des remarques désobligeantes sur qqn.

slightly ['slaɪtlɪ] *adv* -**1.** [a little] un peu, légèrement; **I know him only ~** je le connais très peu; **~ better** légèrement mieux, un peu mieux; **a ~ higher number** un chiffre un peu plus élevé; **I felt ever so ~ ridiculous** *Br* je me suis senti légèrement ridicule. -**2.** [slenderly]: **~ built** fluet, frêle.

slightness ['slaɪtnɪs] *n* -**1.** [of number, increase] caractère *m* insignifiant OR négligeable. -**2.** [of build] minceur *f*; [frailty] fragilité *f*.

slily ['slaɪlɪ] = **slyly**.

slim [slɪm] (*compar* **slimmer**, *superl* **slimmest**, *pt* & *pp* **slimmed**) ◇ *adj* -**1.** [person, waist, figure] mince, svelte; [wrist] mince, fin, délicat; **a ~-hipped young man** un jeune homme aux hanches étroites; **to keep ~** rester mince. -**2.** [volume, wallet, diary] mince. -**3.** [faint, feeble - hope, chance] faible, minime; [- pretext] mince, piètre, dérisoire; **they have only a ~ chance of winning the next election** ils n'ont que de faibles chances de gagner les prochaines élections.

◇ *vi* [get thin] maigrir, mincir; [diet] faire OR suivre un régime.

◇ *vt* [subj: diet, exercise] faire maigrir.

◆ **slim down** ◇ *vt sep* -**1.** [subj: diet] faire maigrir; [subj: clothes] amincir. -**2.** *fig* [industry] dégraisser; [workforce] réduire; [ambitions, plans] limiter, réduire; [design, car] épurer, alléger; **a slimmed-down version of the old model** une version épurée de l'ancien modèle.

◇ *vi insep* -**1.** [person] maigrir, suivre un régime. -**2.** [industry] être dégraissé.

slime [slaɪm] *n* [sticky substance] substance *f* gluante OR poisseuse; [from snail] bave *f*; [mud] vase *f*.

slimline ['slɪmlaɪn] *adj* -**1.** [butter] allégé; [milk, cheese] sans matière grasse, minceur *(inv)*; [soft drink] light *(inv)*. -**2.** *fig*: **clothes for the new ~ you** des vêtements pour votre nouvelle silhouette allégée; **the ~ version of the 1990 model** la version épurée du modèle 90.

slimmer ['slɪməʳ] *n* personne *f* qui suit un régime (amaigrissant); **good news for ~s** une bonne nouvelle pour ceux qui veulent maigrir OR perdre du poids.

slimming ['slɪmɪŋ] ◇ *n* amaigrissement *m*; **~ can be bad for you** les régimes amaigrissants ne sont pas toujours bons pour la santé.

◇ *adj* -**1.** [diet] amaigrissant; [cream, product] amincissant; [exercises] pour maigrir; [meal] à faible teneur en calories. -**2.** [flattering - dress, suit, colour] amincissant.

slimness ['slɪmnɪs] *n* -**1.** [of person, waist, figure] minceur *f*, sveltesse *f*; [of wrist, ankle] minceur *f*, finesse *f*, délicatesse *f*. -**2.** [weakness - of chance, hope] faiblesse *f*.

slimy ['slaɪmɪ] (*compar* **slimier**, *superl* **slimiest**) *adj* -**1.** [with mud] vaseux, boueux; [with oil, secretion] gluant, visqueux; [wall] suintant; **~ stones** des pierres glissantes; **the slug left a ~ trail** la limace laissa une traînée visqueuse. -**2.** *Br* [obsequious - person] mielleux; [- manners] doucereux, obséquieux; **I can't stand him, he's so ~** je ne le supporte pas, il est tellement mielleux.

sling [slɪŋ] (*pt* & *pp* **slung** [slʌŋ]) ◇ *vt* -**1.** [fling] jeter, lancer; **the children were ~ing stones at the statue** les enfants lançaient des pierres sur la statue; **can you ~ the ball back to me?** pouvez-vous me relancer le ballon?; **she slung the case into the back of the car** elle a jeté la valise à l'arrière de la voiture; **can you ~ me (over) the salt?** *inf* tu peux me balancer le sel?; **if he's not careful, he'll get slung off the course** *inf* s'il ne fait pas attention, il se fera virer du cours ❑ **to ~ mud (at sb)** couvrir (qqn) de boue; **to ~ one's hook** *inf* mettre les bouts, ficher le camp. -**2.** [lift, hang - load] hisser; NAUT élinguer; **the hammock was slung between two trees** le hamac était suspendu OR accroché entre deux arbres; **the soldiers wore rifles slung across** OR **over their shoulders** les soldats portaient des fusils en bandoulière; **the jacket was slung over the back of the chair** la veste était négligemment jetée sur le dossier de la chaise; **he slung his jacket over his shoulder** il

a jeté sa veste par-dessus son épaule; I slung the towel over the washing line j'ai jeté la serviette par-dessus la corde à linge.
◇ *n* -**1.** [for broken arm] écharpe *f*; she had her arm in a ~ elle avait le bras en écharpe. -**2.** [for baby] porte-bébé *m*. -**3.** [for loads - NAUT & CONSTR] élingue *f*; [belt] courroie *f*; [rope] corde *f*, cordage *m*; [for removal men] corde *f*, courroie *f*; [for rifle] bretelle *f*; [for mast] cravate *f*. -**4.** [weapon] fronde *f*; [toy] lance-pierres *m inv*. -**5.** [for climber] baudrier *m*. -**6.** [cocktail] sling *m* *(cocktail à base de spiritueux et de jus de citron, allongé d'eau plate ou gazeuse)*; gin ~ gin-fizz *m*.
◆ **sling away** *inf vt sep Br* bazarder, balancer, ficher en l'air.
◆ **sling out** *inf vt sep Br* [person] flanquer OR ficher à la porte; [rubbish, magazines etc] bazarder, ficher en l'air; he was slung out on his ear il a été fichu à la porte, on l'a fichu dehors.
◆ **sling over** *inf vt sep Br* lancer, envoyer; can you ~ the paper over? tu peux me lancer le journal?
◆ **sling up** *inf vt sep* suspendre, accrocher.

slingback ['slɪŋbæk] *n Br* chaussure *f* à talon découvert.

slingshot ['slɪŋʃɒt] *n Am* lance-pierres *m inv*.

slink [slɪŋk] (*pt* & *pp* slunk [slʌŋk]) *vi*: to ~ in/out entrer/sortir furtivement; she slunk into the room elle s'est glissée discrètement dans la pièce; to ~ away s'éclipser.

slinkily *inf* ['slɪŋkɪlɪ] *adv* [walk] d'une démarche ondoyante; [dress] d'une manière sexy.

slinky *inf* ['slɪŋkɪ] (*compar* slinkier, *superl* slinkiest) *adj* [manner] aguichant; [dress] sexy *(inv)*; [walk] ondoyant, chaloupé.

slip [slɪp] (*pt* & *pp* slipped, *cont* slipping)
◇ *vi* -**1.** [lose balance, slide] glisser; I slipped on some loose shale/on the ice j'ai glissé sur de la terre glaise/sur une plaque de verglas; he slipped and fell il glissa et tomba || [move unexpectedly] glisser; the knife slipped and cut my finger le couteau a glissé et je me suis coupé le doigt; my hand slipped ma main a glissé; the cup slipped out of my hands la tasse m'a glissé des mains; she let the sand ~ through her fingers elle laissa le sable glisser entre ses doigts; the prize slipped from her grasp OR from her fingers *fig* le prix lui a échappé; somehow, the kidnappers slipped through our fingers *fig* je ne sais comment les ravisseurs nous ont filé entre les doigts. -**2.** [go gradually] glisser; the patient slipped into a coma le patient a glissé OR s'est enfoncé peu à peu dans le coma; she slipped into the habit of visiting him every day petit à petit elle a pris l'habitude d'aller le voir tous les jours. -**3.** [go down] baisser; prices have slipped (by) 10% les prix ont baissé de 10 %. -**4.** [go discreetly or unnoticed] se glisser, se faufiler; to ~ into bed se glisser dans son lit; she slipped quietly into the room elle s'est glissée discrètement dans la pièce; the thieves managed to ~ through the road blocks les voleurs ont réussi à passer à travers les barrages routiers; why don't you ~ through the kitchen/round the back? pourquoi ne passez-vous pas par la cuisine/par derrière?; some misprints have slipped into the text des coquilles se sont glissées dans le texte || [go quickly] se faufiler; we slipped through the rush hour traffic on s'est faufilés dans les embouteillages des heures de pointe || [into clothes]: I'll ~ into something cooler je vais enfiler OR mettre quelque chose de plus léger; he slipped into a dressing gown il a passé OR mis une robe de chambre. -**5.** [slide - runners, drawer] glisser; the back should just ~ into place l'arrière devrait glisser à sa place. -**6.** *inf* [be less efficient]: you're slipping! tu n'es plus ce que tu étais! -**7.** AUT [clutch] patiner. -**8.** *phr*: to let ~ [opportunity] laisser passer OR échapper; [word] lâcher, laisser échapper; you shouldn't let this chance ~ *Br* tu ne devrais pas laisser passer cette chance; she let (it) ~ that she was selling her house elle a laissé échapper qu'elle vendait sa maison.
◇ *vt* -**1.** [give or put discreetly] glisser; to ~ sb a note glisser un mot à qqn; to ~ a letter into sb's hand/pocket glisser une lettre dans la main/la poche de qqn; I slipped the pen into my pocket j'ai glissé le stylo dans ma poche; ~ the car into gear mettez la voiture en prise; ~ the key under the door glissez la clé sous la porte; I slipped the photo between the pages of the book j'ai glissé la photo entre les pages du livre; she slipped the jigsaw piece into place elle a fait glisser le morceau de puzzle à sa place. -**2.** [escape]: it slipped my mind ça m'est sorti de la tête; her name has completely slipped my memory j'ai complètement oublié son nom. -**3.** [release]: he slipped the dog's lead *Br* il a lâché la laisse du chien; the dog slipped its lead *Br* le chien s'est dégagé de sa laisse; to ~ anchor/a cable filer l'ancre/un câble; to ~ a stitch glisser une maille; to ~ a disc, to have a slipped disc MED avoir une hernie discale. -**4.** AUT [clutch] faire patiner.
◇ *n* -**1.** [piece of paper]: ~ (of paper) feuille *f* OR bout *m* de papier; withdrawal ~ [in bank] bordereau *m* de retrait; delivery ~ COMM bordereau *m* de livraison. -**2.** [on ice, banana skin] glissade *f*. -**3.** [mistake] erreur *f*; [blunder] bévue *f*; [careless oversight] étourderie *f*; [moral] écart *m*, faute *f* légère; ~ of the tongue OR pen lapsus *m*; there's many a ~ twixt cup and lip *Br prov* il y a loin de la coupe aux lèvres *prov*. -**4.** [landslide] éboulis *m*, éboulement *m*. -**5.** [petticoat - full length] combinaison *f*, fond *m* de robe; [- skirt] jupon *m*. -**6.** BOT bouture *f*. -**7.** NAUT *(usu pl)* cale *f*; the Queen Helen is still on the ~s le Queen Helen est toujours en cale sèche. -**8.** TECH [glaze] engobe *m*. -**9.** *phr*: a ~ of a girl *Br* une petite jeune; a ~ of a boy *Br* un petit jeune; to give sb the ~ semer qqn.
◆ **slips** *npl* -**1.** THEAT coulisses *fpl*. -**2.** SPORT [in cricket] station *f* à droite du guichet.
◆ **slip along** *vi insep* -**1.** [go quickly] faire un saut; I'll just ~ along to the chemist's je fais juste un saut à la pharmacie. -**2.** [discreetly] aller en cachette.
◆ **slip away** *vi insep* [person] s'éclipser, partir discrètement; [moment] passer; [boat] s'éloigner doucement; her children gradually slipped away from her *fig* ses enfants se sont peu à peu éloignés d'elle; I felt my life slipping away j'avais l'impression que ma vie me glissait entre les doigts.
◆ **slip back** *vi insep* [car] glisser (en arrière); [person] revenir discrètement; he slipped back into a coma il est retombé dans le coma; she slipped back for a sweater elle est retournée chercher un pull-over; he slipped back into his old habits il est retombé dans ses vieilles habitudes.
◆ **slip by** *vi insep* [time] passer; [person] se faufiler; I slipped by without being noticed je me suis faufilé sans qu'on me remarque.
◆ **slip down** *vi insep* -**1.** [fall - picture, car, socks, skirt] glisser. -**2.** [go or come down] descendre; can you ~ down to the shops for me? *inf Br* peux-tu aller me faire quelques courses?
◆ **slip in** ◇ *vi insep* [person] entrer discrètement OR sans se faire remarquer; [boat] entrer lentement; I just slipped in for five minutes je n'ai fait qu'entrer cinq minutes, je suis juste passé; a blank page has slipped in by mistake une page blanche s'y est glissée par erreur; some misprints have slipped in somehow des fautes de frappe se sont glissées dans le texte.
◇ *vt sep* [moving part] faire glisser à sa place; [quotation, word] glisser, placer; to ~ the clutch in AUT embrayer.
◆ **slip off** ◇ *vi insep* -**1.** [go away] s'éclipser. -**2.** [fall - bottle, hat, book] glisser (et tomber).
◇ *vt sep* [remove - coat, hat] enlever, ôter; [- shoe, ring, sock] enlever; [- top, lid] faire glisser pour ouvrir.
◆ **slip on** *vt sep* [dress, ring, coat] mettre, enfiler; [lid] mettre OR remettre (en faisant glisser).
◆ **slip out** ◇ *vi insep* -**1.** [leave - person] sortir discrètement, s'esquiver. -**2.** [escape - animal, child] s'échapper; the word slipped out before he could stop himself le mot lui a échappé; the story slipped out l'affaire s'est ébruitée. -**3.** [go out] sortir (un instant); I'll just ~ out into the garden je sors un instant dans le jardin; I'll ~ out and buy some milk je sors juste acheter du lait.
◇ *vt sep* sortir.
◆ **slip over** ◇ *vi insep* aller; we slipped over to Blackpool to see them nous sommes allés à Blackpool pour les voir.
◇ *vt sep phr*: to ~ one over on sb *inf* rouler qqn.
◆ **slip past** *vi insep* [time] passer; [person] se faufiler; I managed to ~ past unseen j'ai réussi à passer discrètement.
◆ **slip round** *vi insep* -**1.** *Br* [go] passer; can you ~ round after supper? peux-tu passer (chez moi) après souper? -**2.** [saddle] se retourner; [skirt] tourner.
◆ **slip through** *vi insep* [person] passer sans se faire remarquer; [mistake] passer inaperçu.
◆ **slip up** *inf vi insep* faire une gaffe; you've slipped up badly here tu t'es bien planté.

slipcase ['slɪpkeɪs] *n* [for single volume] étui *m*; [for several volumes, for records] coffret *m*.

slipcover ['slɪpkʌvəʳ] *n Am* -**1.** [for furniture] housse *f*. -**2.** = **slipcase**.

slipknot ['slɪpnɒt] *n* nœud *m* coulant.

slip-on ◇ *adj* [shoe] sans lacets.
◇ *n* chaussure *f* sans lacets.

slipover ['slɪp,əʊvəʳ] ◇ *adj* [garment] qui s'enfile par la tête.
◇ *n* débardeur *m (vêtement)*.

slippage ['slɪpɪdʒ] *n* -**1.** MECH patinage *m*. -**2.** [in targeting] retard *m (par rapport aux prévisions)*; [in standards] baisse *f*.

slipped disc [slɪpt-] *n* hernie *f* discale.

slipper ['slɪpəʳ] ◇ *n* [soft footwear] chausson *m*, pantoufle *f*; [mule] mule *f*; [for dancing] escarpin *m*.
◇ *vt Br* [hit]: to ~ sb donner une fessée à qqn *(avec une pantoufle)*.

slipper bath *n* [in bathroom] (baignoire *f*) sabot *m*.
◆ **slipper baths** *npl* [public] bains *mpl* publics.

slipperiness ['slɪpərɪnɪs] *n* -**1.** [of surface, soap]: the ~ of the road l'état glissant de la route. -**2.** [of person - evasiveness] caractère *m* insaisissable OR fuyant; [- unreliability] nature *f* peu fiable.

slippery ['slɪpərɪ] *adj* -**1.** [surface, soap] glissant; the path is ~ le chemin est glissant; we're on the ~ slope to bankruptcy *fig* nous allons droit à la faillite. -**2.** *inf* [person - evasive] fuyant; [unreliable] sur qui on ne peut pas compter; he's a ~ customer c'est le genre de type à qui on ne peut pas se fier ❑ he's (as) ~ as an eel il est fuyant comme une anguille.

slippy ['slɪpɪ] (*compar* slippier, *superl* slippiest) *adj* -**1.** [slippery] glissant. -**2.** *inf Br* [fast]: look ~! grouille-toi!

slip road *n Br* bretelle *f* d'accès.

slip sheet *n* TYPO feuille *f* intercalaire.

slipshod ['slɪpʃɒd] *adj* [appearance] négligé, débraillé; [habits, behaviour] négligent; [style] peu soigné, négligé; [work] négligé, mal fait.

slip stitch *n* SEW point *m* perdu.

slipstream ['slɪpstriːm] ◇ *n* AUT sillage *m*.
◇ *vt* [driver] rester dans le sillage de.

slip-up *inf n* bévue *f*, gaffe *f*; there must have been a ~ quelqu'un a dû faire une gaffe; there mustn't be any ~s pas de gaffe.

slipway ['slɪpweɪ] *n* NAUT [for repairs] cale *f* de halage; [for launching] cale *f* de lancement.

slit [slɪt] (*pt* & *pp* slit, *cont* slitting) ◇ *n* [narrow opening] fente *f*; [cut] incision *f*; the skirt has a ~ at the back la jupe a une fente OR est fendue dans le dos; make a ~ in the surface faire une incision superficielle.
◇ *vt* -**1.** [split] fendre; [cut] inciser, couper; the skirt was ~ up the side la jupe était fendue sur le côté; the mattress had been ~ open le matelas avait été éventré; to ~ sb's throat égorger qqn; she ~ her wrists elle s'est ouvert les veines. -**2.** [open - parcel, envelope] ouvrir

(avec un couteau OR un coupe-papier); she ~ the packet open with a knife elle a ouvert le paquet avec un couteau.

◇ *adj* [skirt] fendu; [eyes] bridé.

slither ['slɪðəʳ] *vi* -**1.** [snake] ramper, onduler. -**2.** [car, person - slide] glisser, patiner; [- skid] déraper; the car ~ed on a patch of oil la voiture a dérapé sur une flaque d'huile; I ~ed down the tree/drainpipe je me suis laissé glisser le long de l'arbre/de la gouttière.

slithery ['slɪðərɪ] *adj* [surface] glissant; [snake] ondulant.

slit pocket *n* poche *f* fendue.

slit trench *n* MIL tranchée *f* étroite.

sliver ['slɪvəʳ] *n* -**1.** [of glass] éclat *m*. -**2.** [small slice - of cheese, cake] tranche *f* fine.

slivovitz ['slɪvəvɪts] *n* slivovitz *m*.

Sloane [sləʊn] *n*: ~ (Ranger) *personne de la haute bourgeoisie (généralement une jeune femme) portant des vêtements sports mais chics et parlant de façon affectée*, ≃ NAP *f*.

Sloaney *inf* ['sləʊnɪ] *adj* ≃ NAP.

slob *inf* [slɒb] *n* [dirty] souillon *mf*; [uncouth] plouc *m*; [lazy] flemmard *m*, -e *f*.

◆ **slob about** *inf Br*, **slob around** *inf*

◇ *vi insep* traînasser.

◇ *vt insep* traînasser.

slobber ['slɒbəʳ] ◇ *vi* -**1.** [dribble - baby, dog] baver; to ~ over baver sur; the baby has ~ed all over the book le bébé a bavé partout sur le livre; the dog came and ~ed all over me le chien est venu baver sur moi. -**2.** *fig*: to ~ over [possession, pet] s'extasier sur OR devant; [person] faire des ronds de jambe à.

◇ *n* -**1.** [dribble] bave *f*. -**2.** *pej* [behaviour] sensiblerie *f*.

slobbery ['slɒbərɪ] *adj* [kiss] baveux.

sloe [sləʊ] *n* [berry] prunelle *f*; [tree] prunellier *m*.

sloe-eyed *adj* aux yeux de biche.

sloe gin *n* gin *m* à la prunelle.

slog *inf* [slɒg] (*pt* & *pp* slogged, *cont* slogging)

◇ *n* -**1.** [hard task] travail *m* d'Hercule; [chore] corvée *f*, travail *m* pénible; [effort] (gros) effort *m*; it was a real ~ to finish in time on a dû bosser comme des malades pour finir à temps; what a ~! quelle corvée!; it was a ~ teaching them history leur enseigner l'histoire n'était pas une mince affaire; it's been a long hard ~ for her to get where she is elle en a bavé pour arriver là où elle est; it was quite a ~ getting up that hill on en a bavé pour monter cette côte. -**2.** *Br* [hit] grand coup *m*; he gave the ball an almighty ~ il a frappé la balle de toutes ses forces.

◇ *vi* -**1.** [work hard] trimer, bosser; she spent all weekend slogging away at that report elle a passé tout le week-end à trimer sur ce rapport; she slogged on until ten o'clock elle est restée bosser jusqu'à 10h; do we really have to ~ through all this paperwork? est-ce qu'il est indispensable de se farcir toute cette paperasse? -**2.** [walk, go] avancer péniblement; he slogged (along) through the snow il avançait péniblement dans la neige; we slogged slowly up the hill nous avons gravi la côte à pas lents; I had to ~ back home again j'ai dû refaire tout le trajet pour rentrer à la maison.

◇ *vt* -**1.** [move]: we slogged our way through the snow/across the fields nous nous sommes péniblement frayé un chemin dans la neige/avons péniblement traversé les champs. -**2.** *Br* [hit - ball] donner un grand coup dans; [- person] cogner sur; to ~ it out *inf* [fight] se tabasser; [argue] s'enguirlander.

slogan ['sləʊgən] *n* slogan *m*.

slogger *inf* ['slɒgəʳ] *n Br* bosseur *m*, -euse *f*.

sloop [sluːp] *n* sloop *m*.

slop [slɒp] (*pt* & *pp* slopped, *cont* slopping)

◇ *vi* [spill] renverser; the tea slopped into the saucer/onto the tablecloth le thé s'est renversé dans la soucoupe/sur la nappe ‖ [overflow - liquid] déborder; the soup slopped onto the cooker la soupe a débordé sur la cuisinière.

◇ *vt* renverser; he slopped soup onto the tablecloth il a renversé OR répandu de la soupe sur la nappe; don't ~ water all over the floor ne renverse pas d'eau par terre.

◇ *n* (*U*) [liquid waste - for pigs] pâtée *f*; [- from tea, coffee] fond *m* de tasse; [tasteless food] mixture *f pej*.

◆ **slop about** *Br*, **slop around** ◇ *vi insep* -**1.** [liquid] clapoter. -**2.** [paddle] patauger; the children were slopping about in the puddles les enfants pataugeaient dans les flaques d'eau. -**3.** *inf* [be lazy] traînasser; I just slopped around all morning j'ai traînassé OR flemmardé toute la matinée.

◇ *vt sep* [paint] éclabousser; [tea] renverser.

◇ *vt insep inf*: he ~s about the house doing nothing il traîne à la maison à ne rien faire.

◆ **slop out** *vi insep* [prisoner] vider les seaux hygiéniques.

◆ **slop over** ◇ *vi insep* [spill] se renverser; [overflow] déborder; the water slopped over onto the floor l'eau s'est renversée OR a débordé sur le sol.

◇ *vt sep* renverser, répandre.

slop basin *n Br* vide-tasses *m inv*.

slop bucket = **slop pail**.

slope [sləʊp] ◇ *n* -**1.** [incline - of roof] inclinaison *f*, pente *f*; [- of ground] pente *f*; a steep/gentle ~ une pente raide/douce; the house is built on a ~ la maison a été construite sur une pente; rifle at the ~ MIL fusil sur l'épaule. -**2.** [hill - up] côte *f*, montée *f*; [- down] pente *f*, descente *f*; [mountainside] versant *m*, flanc *m*; tea is grown on the higher ~s on cultive le thé plus haut sur les versants de la montagne; on the ~s of Mount Fuji sur les versants du mont Fuji. -**3.** [for skiing] piste *f*.

◇ *vi* [roof] être en pente OR incliné; [writing] pencher; the beach ~d gently to the sea la plage descendait en pente douce vers la mer; the table ~s la table penche OR n'est pas droite.

◇ *vt* MIL: ~ arms! portez arme!

◆ **slope off** *inf vi insep* filer.

sloping ['sləʊpɪŋ] *adj* [table, roof] en pente, incliné; [writing] penché; [shoulders] tombant.

slop pail *n* [for pigs] seau *m* à pâtée; [in kitchen] seau *m* à ordures; [for cleaning] seau *m*.

sloppily ['slɒpɪlɪ] *adv* -**1.** [work] sans soin; [dress] de façon négligée. -**2.** *inf Br* [sentimentally] avec sensiblerie OR mièvrerie.

sloppiness ['slɒpɪnɪs] *n* -**1.** [of work] manque *m* de soin OR de sérieux; [in dress] négligence *f*, manque *m* de soin; [of thought] flou *m*, manque *m* de précision. -**2.** *inf* [of emotions] sensiblerie *f*, mièvrerie *f*.

sloppy ['slɒpɪ] (*compar* sloppier, *superl* sloppiest) *adj* -**1.** [untidy - appearance] négligé, débraillé; [careless - work] bâclé, négligé; [- writing] peu soigné; [- thinking] flou, vague, imprécis; he has a very ~ way of speaking il s'exprime d'une manière peu élégante. -**2.** *inf* [loose - garment] large, lâche. -**3.** *inf* [sentimental - person, letter] sentimental; [- book, film] à l'eau de rose; stop all that ~ talk! arrête de faire du sentiment!

sloppy joe *inf n* -**1.** *Br* [sweater] gros pull *m*. -**2.** *Am* [hamburger] hamburger *m*.

slosh [slɒʃ] ◇ *vt* -**1.** *inf* [spill] renverser, répandre; [pour - onto floor] répandre; [- into glass, bucket] verser; she ~ed some bleach into the bucket elle a versé de l'eau de Javel dans le seau ‖ [apply - paint, glue] flanquer; she ~ed whitewash on OR over the wall elle a barbouillé le mur de blanc de chaux. -**2.** ▽ *Br* [hit] mettre une beigne à.

◇ *vi* -**1.** *inf* [liquid] se répandre; the juice ~ed all over the cloth le jus s'est renversé partout sur la nappe; water ~ed over the edge l'eau a débordé. -**2.** *inf* [move - in liquid, mud] patauger; we ~ed through the mud on a pataugé dans la boue.

◇ *onomat* plouf!

◆ **slosh about** *Br*, **slosh around** *inf vi insep* [liquid] clapoter; [person] patauger; the water ~ed about in the bucket l'eau clapotait dans le seau; the children were ~ing about in puddles les enfants pataugeaient dans des flaques d'eau.

sloshed *inf* [slɒʃt] *adj* rond, soûl; to get ~ prendre une cuite.

slot [slɒt] (*pt* & *pp* slotted, *cont* slotting)

◇ *n* -**1.** [opening - for coins, papers] fente *f* [groove] rainure *f*; put the coin in the ~ mettez la pièce dans la fente; there's a ~ in the door for letters il y a une fente dans la porte pour le courrier. -**2.** [in schedule, timetable] tranche *f* OR plage *f* horaire, créneau *m*; RADIO & TV créneau *m*; we could put the new series in the 7:30 ~ on pourrait caser OR placer le nouveau feuilleton dans le créneau de 19 h 30; what shall we put in the ~ before the news? qu'est-ce qu'on va mettre dans la tranche OR le créneau qui précède les informations? ‖ [opening] créneau *m*; there's a ~ for someone with marketing skills il y a un créneau pour quelqu'un qui s'y connaît en marketing. -**3.** AERON fente *f*.

◇ *vt* -**1.** [insert] emboîter; ~ this bit in here [in machine, model] introduisez cette pièce ici; [in jigsaw] posez OR mettez cette pièce ici. -**2.** [find time for, fit] insérer, faire rentrer; she managed to ~ me into her timetable elle a réussi à me réserver un moment OR à me caser dans son emploi du temps.

◇ *vi* -**1.** [fit - part] rentrer, s'encastrer, s'emboîter; the tape ~s into the recorder here c'est ici qu'on introduit la cassette dans le magnétophone; the blade ~s into the handle la lame rentre dans le manche. -**2.** [in timetable, schedule] rentrer, s'insérer; our programme ~s into the space after the news notre émission s'insère dans le créneau qui suit les informations; where do we ~ into the scheme? où intervenons-nous dans le projet?

◆ **slot in** ◇ *vt sep* [into schedule] faire rentrer; she just ~s me in when it suits her elle n'est disponible pour moi que quand ça l'arrange; when can you ~ me in? quand pouvez-vous me caser OR trouver un moment pour moi?

◇ *vi insep* [part] s'emboîter, s'encastrer; [programme] s'insérer.

◆ **slot together** ◇ *vt sep* emboîter, encastrer; ~ these two parts together emboîtez ces deux pièces l'une dans l'autre.

◇ *vi insep* s'emboîter, s'encastrer; the two parts ~ together les deux pièces s'emboîtent l'une dans l'autre.

sloth [sləʊθ] *n* -**1.** [laziness] paresse *f*. -**2.** ZOOL paresseux *m*.

slothful ['sləʊθfʊl] *adj* paresseux.

slothfully ['sləʊθfʊlɪ] *adv* paresseusement, avec indolence.

slot machine *n* [for vending] distributeur *m* (automatique); [for gambling] machine *f* à sous.

slotted spatula ['slɒtɪd-] *n Am* pelle *f* à poisson.

slotted spoon *n* écumoire *f*.

slouch [slaʊtʃ] ◇ *vi*: she was ~ing against the wall elle était nonchalamment adossée au mur; stop ~ing! redresse-toi!; to ~ in/out entrer/sortir en traînant les pieds.

◇ *vt*: to ~ one's shoulders rentrer les épaules.

◇ *n* -**1.** [in posture]: to have a ~ avoir le dos voûté. -**2.** *inf* [person]: he's no ~ when it comes to housework ce n'est pas un empoté pour ce qui est du ménage.

◆ **slouch about** *Br*, **slouch around** *vi insep* se traîner.

slouch hat *n* chapeau *m* à larges bords.

slough[1] [slaʊ] *n* [mud pool] bourbier *m*; [swamp] marécage *m*; a ~ of gloom/of despair *fig* un accès de mélancolie/de désespoir ❑ the Slough of Despond le tréfonds du désespoir.

slough[2] [slʌf] ◇ *n* -**1.** [skin - of snake] dépouille *f*, mue *f*; MED escarre *f*. -**2.** CARDS carte *f* défaussée.

◇ *vt*: the snake ~s its skin le serpent mue.

◆ **slough off** *vt sep* [skin] se dépouiller de; the snake ~s off its skin le serpent mue ‖ *fig* [worries] se débarrasser de; [habit] perdre, se débarrasser de.

Slovak ['slәʊvæk] ◇ *n* -**1.** [person] Slovaque *mf.* -**2.** LING slovaque *m.*
◇ *adj* slovaque.

Slovakia [slә'vækɪә] *pr n* Slovaquie *f;* in ~ en Slovaquie.

Slovakian [slә'vækɪәn] ◇ *n* Slovaque *mf.*
◇ *adj* slovaque.

sloven ['slʌvn] *n lit* souillon *mf.*

Slovene ['slәʊvi:n] ◇ *n* -**1.** [person] Slovène *mf.* -**2.** LING slovène *m.*
◇ *adj* slovène.

Slovenia [slә'vi:njә] *pr n* Slovénie *f;* in ~ en Slovénie.

Slovenian [slә'vi:njәn] ◇ *n* Slovène *mf.*
◇ *adj* slovène.

slovenliness ['slʌvnlɪnɪs] *n* [of dress] négligé *m,* débraillé *m;* [of habits] laisser-aller *m;* [of work] manque *m* de soin.

slovenly ['slʌvnlɪ] *adj* [appearance] négligé, débraillé; [habits] relâché; [work] peu soigné; [style, expression] relâché, négligé; **he's often ~ in appearance** il fait souvent négligé.

slow [slәʊ] ◇ *adj* -**1.** [not fast - movements, speed, service, traffic] lent; **he's a ~ worker** il travaille lentement; **it's ~ work** c'est un travail qui n'avance pas vite OR de longue haleine; **~ growth** ANAT, BOT & ECON croissance *f* lente; **to make ~ progress** [in work, on foot] avancer lentement; **~ movement** MUS mouvement *m* lent; **a ~ dance** un slow; **it was ~ going, the going was ~** ça n'avançait pas; **with ~ steps** d'un pas lent; **we had a painfully ~ journey** le voyage a duré un temps fou; **the pace of life is ~** on vit au ralenti; **the fog was/the clouds were ~ to clear** le brouillard a mis/les nuages ont mis longtemps à se dissiper || [in reactions] lent; **he was rather ~ to make up** OR **in making up his mind** il a mis assez longtemps à se décider; **she wasn't ~ to offer her help/in accepting the cheque** elle ne se fit pas prier pour proposer son aide/pour accepter le chèque; **I was rather ~ to understand** OR **in understanding** il m'a fallu assez longtemps pour comprendre; **you were a bit ~ there** là, tu t'es laissé prendre de vitesse; **she's very ~ to anger** il lui en faut beaucoup pour se mettre en colère || [in progress] lent; **the company was ~ to get off the ground** la société a été lente à démarrer || [intellectually] lent; **he's a ~ learner/reader** il apprend/lit lentement; **they're rather ~ in that class** les élèves de cette classe sont assez lents ❑ **the ~ lane** AUT [when driving on left] la file de gauche; [when driving on right] la file de droite; **~ train** omnibus *m;* **to be ~ off the mark** *Br literal* être lent à démarrer; *fig* avoir l'esprit lent. -**2.** [slack - business, market] calme; **business is ~** les affaires ne marchent pas fort; **~ economic growth** une faible croissance économique. -**3.** [dull - evening, film, party] ennuyeux. -**4.** [clock] qui retarde; **your watch is (half an hour) ~** ta montre retarde (d'une demi-heure). -**5.** CULIN: **~ burner** feu *m* doux; **bake in a ~ oven** faire cuire à four doux.
◇ *adv* lentement; **go a bit ~er** ralentissez un peu; **the clock is going** OR **running ~** l'horloge prend du retard; **'slow'** [road marking] 'ralentir'; **~ astern!** NAUT arrière doucement! ❑ **to go ~** faire une grève perlée.
◇ *vt* ralentir; **I ~ed the horse to a trot** j'ai mis le cheval au trot; **these drugs ~ the heart rate** ces médicaments ralentissent le rythme cardiaque; **the mud ~ed our progress** la boue nous a ralentis.
◆ **slow down** ◇ *vt sep* -**1.** [in speed - bus, machine, progress] ralentir; [- person] (faire) ralentir; [in achievement, activity] ralentir; **having to write the addresses by hand ~ed the work down** le fait de devoir écrire les adresses à la main a ralenti le travail; **production is ~ed down during the winter** pendant l'hiver, la production tourne au ralenti. -**2.** [delay] retarder.
◇ *vi insep* [driver, train, speed] ralentir; *fig* [person] ralentir; **if he doesn't ~ down he'll have a heart attack** s'il ne ralentit pas le rythme il va faire une crise cardiaque; **~ down!** moins vite!; **growth ~ed down in the second quarter** il y a eu une diminution OR un ralentissement de la croissance au cours du deuxième trimestre.
◆ **slow up** = **slow down**.

slow burn *n Am*: **to do a ~** sentir la colère monter.

slowcoach *inf* ['slәʊkәʊtʃ] *n Br* [in moving] lambin *m,* -e *f,* traînard *m,* -e *f;* [in thought] balourd *m,* -e *f,* lourdaud *m,* -e *f;* **come on ~!** allez, du nerf!

slowdown ['slәʊdaʊn] *n* -**1.** *Am* [go-slow] grève *f* perlée. -**2.** [slackening] ralentissement *m.*

slow handclap *n Br* applaudissements *mpl* rythmés *(pour montrer sa désapprobation)*; **they gave him the ~** ≃ ils l'ont sifflé.

slowly ['slәʊlɪ] *adv* -**1.** [not fast] lentement; **the bus came ~ down the hill** le bus a descendu la côte lentement; **could you walk/speak more ~?** pouvez-vous marcher/parler moins vite?; **~ but surely** lentement mais sûrement. -**2.** [gradually] peu à peu.

slow match *n* mèche *f* à combustion lente.

slow motion *n* CIN & TV ralenti *m;* **in ~** au ralenti.
◆ **slow-motion** *adj* (tourné) au ralenti; **slow-motion replay** TV ralenti *m.*

slow-moving *adj* [person, car] lent; [film, plot] dont l'action est lente; [market] stagnant; **~ target** cible *f* qui bouge lentement.

slowness ['slәʊnɪs] *n* -**1.** [of progress, reaction, service, traffic] lenteur *f;* [of plot, play] lenteur *f,* manque *m* d'action. -**2.** [of intellect] lenteur *f* (d'esprit). -**3.** [of trading, market] stagnation *f.* -**4.** [of watch] retard *m.*

slowpoke *inf* ['slәʊpәʊk] *Am* = **slowcoach**.

slow-witted [-'wɪtɪd] *adj* (intellectuellement) lent.

slowworm ['slәʊwɜ:m] *n* orvet *m.*

SLR (*abbr of* **single-lens reflex**) *n* reflex *m* (monoobjectif).

sludge [slʌdʒ] *n (U)* -**1.** [mud] boue *f,* vase *f;* [snow] neige *f* fondue. -**2.** [sediment] dépôt *m,* boue *f.* -**3.** [sewage] vidanges *fpl.*

slue [slu:] *Am* = **slew** *vi* & *vt.*

sluff [slʌf] = **slough** CARDS.

slug [slʌg] (*pt* & *pp* **slugged**, *cont* **slugging**)
◇ *n* -**1.** ZOOL limace *f.* -**2.** *inf fig* [lazy person] mollusque *m.* -**3.** PRINT [of metal] lingot *m.* -**4.** *Am* [token] jeton *m.* -**5.** *inf* [hit] beigne *f.* -**6.** *inf* [drink] coup *m;* [mouthful] lampée *f;* **to take a ~ of whisky** boire une gorgée de whisky. -**7.** *inf* [bullet] balle *f.*
◇ *vt inf* -**1.** [hit] frapper (fort), cogner; **he was slugged over the head with a rubber cosh** il a reçu un coup de matraque en caoutchouc sur la tête. -**2.** *phr*: **to ~ it out** *inf* [fight] se taper dessus; [argue] s'enguirlander; **I left them to ~ it out** [fight] je les ai laissés régler leurs comptes à coups de poing.

sluggard ['slʌgәd] *n lit* paresseux *m,* -euse *f,* fainéant *m,* -e *f.*

slugger *inf* ['slʌgә^r] *n* SPORT [boxer] cogneur *m,* puncheur *m;* [in ball games] joueur *m,* -euse *f* qui frappe très fort.

sluggish ['slʌgɪʃ] *adj* -**1.** [lethargic] mou, apathique. -**2.** [slow - traffic, growth, reaction] lent; [- digestion] lent, paresseux; [- market, business] calme, stagnant; **trading is always rather ~ on Mondays** les affaires ne marchent jamais très bien OR très fort le lundi. -**3.** [engine] qui manque de reprise OR de nervosité; **the engine is very ~ in the mornings** le moteur est très lent à démarrer le matin.

sluggishly ['slʌgɪʃlɪ] *adv* [slowly] lentement; [lethargically] mollement; **trading began ~** les affaires ont démarré lentement; **the market reacted ~** la bourse a réagi faiblement; **the car started ~** la voiture a démarré avec difficulté.

sluggishness ['slʌgɪʃnɪs] *n* [lethargy] mollesse *f;* [of reaction, pulse, market] lenteur *f;* [of growth] faiblesse *f,* lenteur *f;* [of engine] manque *m* de nervosité.

sluice [slu:s] ◇ *n* -**1.** [lock] écluse *f;* [gate] porte *f* OR vanne *f* d'écluse; [channel] canal *m* à vannes; *(U)* [lock water] eaux *fpl* retenues par la vanne. -**2.** [wash]: **to give sthg a ~ (down)** laver qqch à grande eau; **to give sb a ~ (down)** asperger qqn d'eau.
◇ *vt* -**1.** [drain] drainer; [irrigate] irriguer. -**2.** [wash] laver à grande eau; MIN [ore] laver; **to ~ sthg (down)** laver qqch à grande eau; **they ~d out the stable** ils ont lavé l'écurie à grande eau; **we ~d down the meal with cheap red wine** on a arrosé le repas d'un petit rouge.

sluice gate, sluice valve *n* porte *f* OR vanne *f* d'écluse.

sluiceway ['slu:sweɪ] *n* canal *m* à vannes.

slum [slʌm] (*pt* & *pp* **slummed**, *cont* **slumming**)
◇ *n literal* & *fig* taudis *m;* [district] quartier *m* pauvre, bas quartiers *mpl;* **~ dwelling** taudis *m.*
◇ *vt Br*: **to ~ it** *inf* s'encanailler.
◇ *vi inf hum*: **we're slumming tonight** on va s'encanailler ce soir *hum.*

slumber ['slʌmbә^r] ◇ *n lit* sommeil *m* (profond); **deep in ~** plongé dans un sommeil profond.
◇ *vi* dormir.

slumber party *n Am* soirée *f* entre copines *(au cours de laquelle on regarde des films, on discute et on dort toutes ensemble)*.

slumberwear ['slʌmbәweә^r] *n (U)* vêtements *mpl* de nuit.

slum clearance *n Br* rénovation *f* OR aménagement *m* des quartiers insalubres.

slummy ['slʌmɪ] (*compar* **slummier**, *superl* **slummiest**) *adj* [area, house, lifestyle] sordide, misérable.

slump [slʌmp] ◇ *n* -**1.** [in attendance, figures, popularity] chute *f,* forte baisse *f,* baisse *f* soudaine; **there has been a ~ in investment** les investissements sont en forte baisse; **a ~ in prices/demand** une forte baisse des prix/de la demande. -**2.** ECON [depression] crise *f* économique; [recession] récession *f;* ST. EX effondrement *m* (des cours), krach *m* (boursier). -**3.** *Am* SPORT passage *m* à vide.
◇ *vi* -**1.** [flop - with fatigue, illness] s'écrouler, s'effondrer; **she ~ed (down) in an armchair** elle s'est effondrée dans un fauteuil. -**2.** [shoulders] avoir le dos voûté. -**3.** [collapse - business, prices, market] s'effondrer; [morale, attendance] baisser soudainement.
◇ *vt (usu pass)*: **to be ~ed in an armchair** être affalé OR affaissé dans un fauteuil; **he was ~ed over the wheel** [in car] il était affaissé sur le volant.
◆ **slump back** *vi insep* retomber en arrière.

slung [slʌŋ] *pt* & *pp* → **sling**.

slunk [slʌŋk] *pt* & *pp* → **slink**.

slur [slɜ:^r] (*pt* & *pp* **slurred**, *cont* **slurring**)
◇ *n* -**1.** [insult] insulte *f,* affront *m;* **a racial ~** une insulte raciste || [blot, stain] tache *f;* **it's a ~ on his character** c'est une tache à sa réputation; **to cast a ~ on sb** porter atteinte à la réputation de qqn. -**2.** [confused sound] articulation *f* confuse. -**3.** MUS liaison *f.*
◇ *vt* -**1.** [speech] mal articuler; **his speech was slurred** il articulait mal. -**2.** [denigrate] dénigrer. -**3.** MUS lier.
◇ *vi* [speech, words] devenir indistinct; **his speech slurred** ses paroles étaient indistinctes.

slurp *inf* [slɜ:p] ◇ *vt* & *vi* boire bruyamment.
◇ *n*: **a loud ~** un lapement bruyant; **can I have a quick ~ of your tea?** je peux boire une gorgée de ton thé?

slurry ['slʌrɪ] *n* [cement, clay] barbotine *f;* [manure] purin *m.*

slush [slʌʃ] *n* -**1.** [snow] neige *f* fondue; [mud] gadoue *f.* -**2.** *inf* [sentimentality] sensiblerie *f.*

slush fund *n* caisse *f* noire *(servant généralement au paiment des pots-de-vin)*.

slushy ['slʌʃɪ] (*compar* **slushier**, *superl* **slushiest**) *adj* -**1.** [snow] fondu; [ground] détrempé; [path] couvert de neige fondue. -**2.** [film, book] à l'eau de rose.

slut [slʌt] *n pej* [slovenly woman] souillon *f*; [immoral woman] fille *f* facile.

sluttish ['slʌtɪʃ] *adj pej* [appearance] de souillon, sale; [morals] dépravé; [behaviour] débauché, dépravé.

sly [slaɪ] (*compar* slyer OR slier, *superl* slyest OR sliest) ◇ *adj* -**1.** [cunning, knowing] rusé; he's a ~ (old) devil OR dog c'est une fine mouche; he gave me a ~ look/smile il m'a regardé/souri d'un air rusé. -**2.** [deceitful - person] sournois; [- behaviour] déloyal; that was a ~ trick c'était un tour plutôt malhonnête. -**3.** [mischievous] malin, espiègle. -**4.** [secretive] dissimulé; he's a ~ one! c'est un petit cachottier!
◇ *n phr*: on the ~ *inf* en douce.

slyboots *inf* ['slaɪbuːts] *n Br* (petit) malin *m*, (petite) maligne *f*.

slyly ['slaɪlɪ] *adv* -**1.** [cunningly] de façon rusée, avec ruse. -**2.** [deceitfully] sournoisement. -**3.** [mischievously] avec espièglerie, de façon espiègle. -**4.** [secretly] discrètement.

slyness ['slaɪnɪs] *n* -**1.** [cunning] ruse *f*. -**2.** [deceitfulness] fausseté *f*. -**3.** [mischief] espièglerie *f*. -**4.** [secrecy] dissimulation *f*.

SM *n abbr of* sergeant major.

s/m *n abbr of* sadomasochism.

S & M (*abbr of* sadism and masochism) *n* S-M *m*.

smack [smæk] ◇ *n* -**1.** [slap] grande tape *f*, claque *f*; [on face] gifle *f*; [on bottom] fessée *f*; to give sb a ~ in the face gifler qqn; to give sb a ~ on the bottom donner une tape sur les fesses à qqn; a ~ in the face OR eye *fig* une gifle, une rebuffade; take a good ~ at the ball donne un grand coup dans le ballon. -**2.** [sound] bruit *m* sec; [of whip] claquement *m*; there was a resounding ~ as the bat hit the ball la batte heurta la balle avec un claquement sonore. -**3.** [taste] léger OR petit goût *m*; CULIN soupçon *m*. -**4.** [boat] smack *m*, sémaque *m*. -**5.** [kiss] gros baiser *m*; to give sb a ~ on the lips faire un gros baiser à qqn. -**6.** *inf Br* [try]: to have a ~ at doing sthg essayer de faire qqch; I'll have a ~ at it je vais essayer. -**7.** *drugs sl* [heroin] poudre *f*, blanche *f*.
◇ *vt* donner une grande tape à, donner une claque à; [in face] donner une gifle à, gifler; [on bottom] donner une fessée à; to ~ sb's face OR sb in the face gifler qqn, donner une gifle à qqn; to ~ sb's bottom [in punishment] donner la fessée à qqn; [in play] donner une tape sur les fesses à qqn; she ~ed the book down on the table elle posa le livre sur la table avec un claquement sonore; to ~ one's lips se lécher les babines.
◇ *vi*: to ~ of sthg *literal* & *fig* sentir qqch; the whole thing ~s of corruption tout ça, ça sent la corruption.
◇ *adv* -**1.** [forcefully] en plein; she went ~ into a wall elle est rentrée en plein dans un mur; she kissed him ~ on the lips elle l'a embrassé en plein sur la bouche. -**2.** [exactly] en plein; we arrived ~ in the middle of the meeting nous sommes arrivés au beau milieu de la réunion.

smack-dab *esp Am*, **smack-bang** = **smack** *adv* **2**.

smacker *inf* ['smækəʳ] *n* -**1.** [kiss] grosse bise *f*. -**2.** [banknote] *Am* dollar *m*; *Br* [pound] livre *f*; ten lovely ~s dix beaux billets.
◆ **smackers** *inf npl* [lips] lèvres *fpl*.

smacking ['smækɪŋ] ◇ *n* fessée *f*; I gave the child a good ~ j'ai donné une bonne fessée à l'enfant.
◇ *adj inf Br*: at a ~ pace à vive allure, à toute vitesse.

small [smɔːl] ◇ *adj* -**1.** [in size - person, town, garden] petit; ~ children les jeunes enfants; in ~ letters en (lettres) minuscules; ~ sizes les petites tailles; to get OR to grow ~er devenir plus petit, diminuer; to make ~er [garment] diminuer; [hole] réduire; the new wallpaper makes the room look ~er le nouveau papier peint rapetisse la pièce; to make o.s. ~ se faire tout petit ❑ the ~est room *euph* le petit coin; to feel ~ se trouver OR se sentir bête; to make sb look OR feel ~ humilier qqn. -**2.** [in number - crowd] peu nombreux; [- family] petit; [in quantity - amount, percentage, resources] petit, faible; [- supply] petit; [- salary, sum] petit, modeste; [- helping] petit, peu copieux; [- meal] léger; the audience was very ~ l'assistance était très peu nombreuse, il y avait très peu de monde; a country with a ~ population un pays à faible population; the ~est possible number of guests le moins d'invités possible; to get OR to grow ~er diminuer, décroître; the problems don't get any ~er les problèmes ne vont pas (en) s'amenuisant; to make ~er [income] diminuer; [staff] réduire. -**3.** [in scale, range] petit; [minor] petit, mineur; down to the ~est details jusqu'aux moindres détails; it's no ~ achievement c'est une réussite non négligeable; there's the ~ matter of the £150 you still owe me il reste ce petit problème des 150 livres que tu me dois; a ~ voice une petite voix; I like to be able to help in a ~ way j'aime me sentir utile; he felt responsible in his own ~ way il se sentait responsable à sa façon ‖ COMM: a ~ farmer un petit cultivateur; ~ businessmen les petits entrepreneurs *mpl* OR patrons *mpl*; ~ businesses [firms] les petites et moyennes entreprises *fpl*, les PME *fpl*; [shops] les petits commerçants *mpl*. -**4.** [mean, narrow] petit, mesquin; they've got ~ minds ce sont des esprits mesquins.
◇ *adv*: to cut sthg up ~ couper qqch en tout petits morceaux; to roll sthg up ~ [long] rouler qqch bien serré; [ball] rouler qqch en petite boule; the cat curled itself up ~ le chat s'est roulé en boule.
◇ *n*: he took her by the ~ of the waist il l'a prise par la taille; I have a pain in the ~ of my back j'ai mal aux reins OR au creux des reins.
◆ **smalls** *inf npl hum* sous-vêtements *mpl*.

small ad *n* petite annonce *f*.

small arms *npl* armes *fpl* portatives.

small beer *inf n Br*: it's ~ c'est de la petite bière; we're very ~ in the advertising world nous sommes très peu de chose OR nous ne représentons pas grand-chose dans le monde de la publicité.

small-bore *adj* de petit calibre.

small change *n* petite monnaie *f*.

small-claims court *n* JUR tribunal *m* d'instance.

small fry *n* menu fretin *m*; he's ~ *Br* OR a ~ *Am* il ne compte pas.

smallholder ['smɔːl,həʊldəʳ] *n Br* petit propriétaire *m*.

smallholding ['smɔːl,həʊldɪŋ] *n Br* petite propriété *f*.

small hours *npl* petit matin *m*; in the ~ au petit matin.

small intestine *n* intestin *m* grêle.

smallish ['smɔːlɪʃ] *adj* [room, child] assez petit; [income] assez modeste; [family] assez peu nombreux; [meal] assez léger.

small letter *n* (lettre *f*) minuscule *f*; in ~s en (lettres) minuscules.

small-minded *adj* [attitude, person] mesquin.

small-mindedness [-'maɪndɪdnɪs] *n* mesquinerie *f*, petitesse *f*.

smallness ['smɔːlnɪs] *n* -**1.** [of child] petite taille *f*; [of hand, room] petitesse *f*; [of salary, fee] modicité *f*; [of extent] caractère *m* limité. -**2.** [of mind] mesquinerie *f*.

small potatoes *inf npl Am* = **small beer**.

smallpox ['smɔːlpɒks] *n* variole *f*.

small print *n*: in ~ en petits caractères, écrit petit; make sure you read the ~ before you sign lisez bien ce qui est écrit en petits caractères avant de signer.

small scale *n* petite échelle *f*; on a ~ sur une petite échelle.
◆ **small-scale** *adj* [replica, model] à taille réduite, réduit; [operation] à petite échelle; a small-scale event un événement de peu d'importance.

small screen *n*: the ~ le petit écran.

small talk *n (U)* papotage *m*, menus propos *mpl*; to make ~ échanger des banalités; I'm no good at ~ je ne sais pas faire la conversation.

small-time *adj* peu important, de petite envergure; a ~ thief/crook un petit voleur/escroc.

small-timer *inf n* minable *mf*.

small-town *adj* provincial; ~ rivalries rivalités *fpl* de clocher; ~ gossip commérages *mpl* de quartier.

smalt [smɔːlt] *n* smalt *m*.

smarm *inf* [smɑːm] ◇ *vt Br pej* faire du plat OR lécher les bottes à; you won't ~ your way out of this one! tu ne t'en tireras pas avec des flatteries, cette fois-ci!
◇ *vi*: to ~ up to sb passer de la pommade à OR lécher les bottes à qqn.
◇ *n* obséquiosité *f*; full of ~ très obséquieux.

smarmily *inf* ['smɑːmɪlɪ] *adv Br pej* avec onctuosité, mielleusement.

smarmy *inf* ['smɑːmɪ] (*compar* smarmier, *superl* smarmiest) *adj Br pej* [toadying] lèche-bottes *(inv)*; [obsequious] obséquieux.

smart [smɑːt] ◇ *adj* -**1.** *Br* [elegant - person, clothes] chic, élégant; she's a ~ dresser elle s'habille avec beaucoup de chic; you look very ~ in your new suit vous avez beaucoup d'allure avec votre nouveau costume ‖ [fashionable - hotel, district] élégant, chic; the ~ set les gens chics, le beau monde. -**2.** [clever - person] malin, habile; [- reply] habile, adroit; [- shrewd person] habile, astucieux; [witty - person, remark] spirituel; he's a ~ lad il n'est pas bête; he's trying to be ~ il essaie de faire le malin; he thinks he's so ~ il se croit très malin; it was ~ of her to think of it c'était futé de sa part d'y penser; she was too ~ for them elle était trop maligne OR futée pour eux. -**3.** [impertinent] impertinent, audacieux; don't get ~ with me! n'essaie pas de jouer au plus malin avec moi! -**4.** [quick - pace, rhythm] vif, prompt; that was ~ work! voilà du travail rapide!, voilà qui a été vite fait!; look ~! *inf* grouille-toi! -**5.** [sharp - reprimand] bon, bien envoyé; a ~ slap across the face une bonne gifle; give the top a ~ tap donnez une bonne tape sur le dessus; give the top a ~ pull tirez fort sur le dessus. -**6.** COMPUT intelligent.
◇ *vi* -**1.** [eyes, wound] cuire, picoter, brûler; her eyes were ~ing elle avait les yeux qui piquaient; the onion made her eyes ~ les oignons lui piquaient les yeux OR la faisaient pleurer; my face was still ~ing from the blow le visage me cuisait encore du coup que j'avais reçu. -**2.** [person] être piqué au vif; he's still ~ing from the insult il n'a toujours pas digéré l'insulte.
◇ *adv* [quickly - walk] vivement, à vive allure; [- act] vivement, promptement.
◇ *n* -**1.** [pain] douleur *f* cuisante; *fig* effet *m* cinglant. -**2.** *inf Am* [useful hint] tuyau *m*, combine *f*.

smart aleck *inf n* je-sais-tout *mf inv*.
◆ **smart-aleck** *inf adj* gonflé.

smartarse▽ *Br*, **smartass**▽ *Am* ['smɑːtɑːs] = **smart aleck**.

smart card *n* carte *f* à puce.

smarten ['smɑːtn] *vt* -**1.** [improve appearance]: to ~ o.s. se faire beau. -**2.** *Br* [speed up]: to ~ one's pace accélérer l'allure.
◆ **smarten up** ◇ *vi insep* -**1.** [person] se faire beau; [restaurant] devenir plus chic, être retapé; [town, street] devenir plus pimpant; I went upstairs to ~ up je suis monté me faire beau. -**2.** *Br* [output, speed] s'accélérer.
◇ *vt sep* -**1.** [person] pomponner; [room, house] arranger, rendre plus élégant; the town has been ~ed up for the president's visit on a décoré la ville pour la visite du président; a coat of paint would help ~ up the restaurant/the car une couche de peinture et le restaurant/la voiture aurait déjà meilleure allure; to ~ o.s. up se faire beau, soigner son apparence. -**2.** [production] accélérer.

smartly ['smɑːtlɪ] *adv* -**1.** [elegantly] avec beaucoup d'allure OR de chic, élégamment. -**2.** [cleverly] habilement, adroitement. -**3.** [briskly - move] vivement; [- act, work] rapidement, promptement. -**4.** [sharply - reprimand] vertement; [- reply] du tac au tac, sèchement.

smart money *inf n*: all the ~ is on him to win the presidency il est donné pour favori aux élections présidentielles.

smartness ['smɑːtnɪs] *n* -**1.** *Br* [elegance - of appearance, dress, style] allure *f*, chic *m*, élégance *f*. -**2.** [cleverness] intelligence *f*, habileté *f*; [shrewdness] astuce *f*, vivacité *f* (d'esprit); [ingenuity] débrouillardise *f*. -**3.** [impertinence] impertinence *f*. -**4.** [briskness - of pace] rapidité *f*; [- of action, behaviour] promptitude *f*, rapidité *f*.

smarty *inf* ['smɑːtɪ] (*pl* smarties) *n* (Monsieur OR Madame OR Mademoiselle) je-sais-tout *mf inv*.

smarty-pants *inf* (*pl inv*) *n*: you're a real ~ aren't you? tu crois vraiment tout savoir!

smash [smæʃ] ◇ *n* -**1.** [noise - of breaking] fracas *m*; with a loud ~ avec un grand fracas; the vase fell with a ~ le vase s'est fracassé en tombant; there was a tremendous ~ as the two cars collided il y eut un très violent fracas quand les deux voitures entrèrent en collision. -**2.** [blow] coup *m* OR choc *m* violent; a ~ on the head un coup violent sur la tête. -**3.** *inf* [collision] collision *f*; [accident] accident *m*; [pile-up] carambolage *m*; a five-car ~ un carambolage de cinq voitures. -**4.** ECON & FIN [collapse - of business, market] débâcle *f* (financière), effondrement *m* (financier); ST. EX krach *m*, effondrement *m* des cours; [bankruptcy] faillite *f*. -**5.** SPORT smash *m*. -**6.** *inf* [success] succès *m* bœuf; it was a ~ ça a fait un tabac.
◇ *onomat* patatras.
◇ *adv*: to go OR to run ~ into a wall heurter un mur avec violence, rentrer en plein dans un mur.
◇ *vt* -**1.** [break - cup, window] fracasser, briser; to ~ sthg to pieces briser qqch en morceaux; I've ~ed my glasses j'ai cassé mes lunettes; to ~ sthg open ouvrir qqch d'un grand coup ‖ PHYS [atom] désintégrer. -**2.** [crash, hit] écraser; he ~ed his fist (down) on the table il écrasa son poing sur la table; they ~ed their way in ils sont entrés par effraction *(en enfonçant la porte ou la fenêtre)*; the raft was ~ed against the rocks le radeau s'est fracassé contre OR sur les rochers. -**3.** SPORT: to ~ the ball faire un smash, smasher; he ~ed the ball into the net il a envoyé son smash dans le filet. -**4.** [destroy - conspiracy, organization] briser, démolir; [- resistance, opposition] briser, écraser; [- chances, hopes, career] ruiner, briser; [- opponent, record] pulvériser.
◇ *vi* [break, crash] se briser, se fracasser; to ~ into bits se briser en mille morceaux; the car ~ed into the lamppost la voiture s'est écrasée contre le réverbère.
◆ **smash down** *vt sep* [door] fracasser, écraser.
◆ **smash in** *vt sep* [door, window] enfoncer; to ~ sb's face OR head in *inf* démolir le portrait à qqn.
◆ **smash up** *vt sep* [furniture] casser, démolir; [room, shop] tout casser OR démolir dans; [car] démolir.

smash-and-grab (raid) *n cambriolage commis en brisant une devanture*; the jewels were stolen in a ~ des cambrioleurs ont brisé la vitrine et se sont enfuis avec les bijoux.

smashed *inf* [smæʃt] *adj* [on alcohol] rond; [on drugs] défoncé.

smasher *inf* ['smæʃəʳ] *n Br* -**1.** [person]: she's a real ~ [in appearance] c'est un vrai canon; [in character] elle est vraiment sensass. -**2.** [object]: it's a real ~! c'est sensass!

smash hit *n* [song, record] gros succès *m*; this record is a ~ in America ce disque fait fureur OR connaît un succès fou en Amérique.

smashing *inf* ['smæʃɪŋ] *adj Br* super, terrible; it was a ~ party! ça a été une soirée du tonnerre!; we had a ~ time! on s'est super bien amusés!; she's a ~ girl c'est une fille super.

smash-up *n* [accident] accident *m*; [pile-up] carambolage *m*, télescopage *m*; five cars were involved in the ~ cinq voitures se sont télescopées.

smattering ['smætərɪŋ] *n (U)* [of knowledge] notions *fpl* vagues; [of people, things] poignée *f*, petit nombre *m*; they only have a ~ of grammar ils n'ont que quelques vagues notions de grammaire; she has a ~ of Italian elle a quelques notions d'italien, elle sait un peu d'italien; there was the usual ~ of artists at the party comme toujours, il y avait un petit groupe d'artistes à la réception.

smaze *inf* [smeɪz] *n Am* brume *f*, smog *m*.

smear [smɪəʳ] ◇ *n* -**1.** [mark - on glass, mirror, wall] trace *f*, tache *f*; [longer] traînée *f*; [of ink] pâté *m*, bavure *f*; ~s of blood/paint des traînées de sang/de peinture. -**2.** [slander] diffamation *f*; a ~ on sb's integrity/reputation une atteinte à l'honneur/à la réputation de qqn; to use ~ tactics avoir recours à la calomnie. -**3.** MED frottis *m*, prélèvement *m*.
◇ *vt* -**1.** [spread - butter, oil] étaler; [coat] barbouiller; she ~ed the dish with butter elle a beurré le plat; to ~ paint/chocolate on one's face se barbouiller le visage de peinture/de chocolat; they ~ed red paint everywhere ils ont tout barbouillé de peinture rouge. -**2.** [smudge]: the ink on the page was ~ed l'encre a coulé sur la page; don't ~ the wet paint/varnish ne faites pas de taches de peinture/de vernis; the mirror was ~ed with fingermarks il y avait des traces de doigts sur la glace. -**3.** [slander]: to ~ sb salir la réputation de qqn, calomnier qqn. -**4.** *inf Am* [thrash] battre à plates coutures.
◇ *vi* [wet paint, ink] se salir, se maculer.

smear campaign *n* campagne *f* de diffamation OR dénigrement.

smear test *n* MED frottis *m*.

smegma ['smegmə] *n* smegma *m*.

smell [smel] (*Br pt* & *pp* smelled OR smelt [smelt], *Am pt* & *pp* smelled) ◇ *vt* -**1.** [notice an odour of] sentir; to ~ gas sentir le gaz; I can ~ (something) burning (je trouve que) ça sent le brûlé; she smelt OR she could ~ alcohol on his breath elle s'aperçut que son haleine sentait l'alcool. -**2.** *fig* [sense - trouble, danger] flairer, pressentir; to ~ a rat flairer quelque chose de louche. -**3.** [sniff at - food] sentir, renifler; [- flower] sentir, humer; she smelt the cream to see if it was fresh elle a senti la crème pour voir si elle était fraîche.
◇ *vi* -**1.** [have odour] sentir; to ~ good OR sweet sentir bon; to ~ bad sentir mauvais; it ~s awful! ça pue!; it ~s musty ça sent le renfermé; that soup ~s delicious! cette soupe sent délicieusement bon!; what does it ~ of OR like? qu'est-ce que ça sent?; it ~s of lavender ça sent la lavande; it ~s like lavender on dirait de la lavande; to ~ of treachery/hypocrisy *fig* sentir latrahison/l'hypocrisie ❑ to ~ fishy sembler louche. -**2.** [have bad odour] sentir (mauvais); his breath ~s il a mauvaise haleine; the dog ~s le chien sent mauvais OR pue. -**3.** [perceive odour]: he can't ~ il n'a pas d'odorat; you ~ with your nose le nez sert à sentir.
◇ *n* -**1.** [sense - of person] odorat *m*; [- of animal] odorat *m*, flair *m*; he has no sense of ~ il n'a pas d'odorat; to have a keen sense of ~ avoir le nez fin. -**2.** [odour] odeur *f*; [bad odour] mauvaise odeur *f*, relent *m*; [stench] puanteur *f*; there's a strong ~ of gas in here il y a une forte odeur de gaz ici; there was a ~ of burning in the kitchen il y avait une odeur de brûlé dans la cuisine; a ~ of onions cooking une odeur d'oignons qui cuisent; there was a lovely ~ of lavender ça sentait bon la lavande; does it have a ~? est-ce que ça sent quelque chose?, est-ce que ça a une odeur?; natural gas has no ~ le gaz naturel n'a pas d'odeur OR est inodore; what an awful ~! qu'est-ce que ça sent mauvais!; the ~ of defeat/fear *fig* l'odeur de la défaite/de la peur. -**3.** [sniff]: have a ~ of this sentez-moi ça.
◆ **smell out** *vt sep* [subj: dog] dénicher en flairant; *fig* [subj: person] découvrir, dépister; [secret, conspiracy] découvrir.

smelliness ['smelɪnɪs] *n* mauvaise odeur *f*; [stench] puanteur *f*.

smelling salts ['smelɪŋ-] *npl* sels *mpl*.

smelly ['smelɪ] (*compar* smellier, *superl* smelliest) *adj* [person, socks etc] qui sent mauvais, qui pue; it's awfully ~ in here ça sent horriblement mauvais OR ça pue ici; to have ~ feet sentir des pieds.

smelt [smelt] (*pl inv* OR smelts) ◇ *pt* & *pp* → **smell**.
◇ *n* [fish] éperlan *m*.
◇ *vt* METALL [ore] fondre; [metal] extraire par fusion.

smidgen *inf*, **smidgin** *inf* ['smɪdʒɪn] *n*: a ~ of un tout petit peu de; there isn't a ~ of truth in what he says il n'y a pas une ombre de vérité dans ce qu'il dit.

smile [smaɪl] ◇ *n* sourire *m*; with a ~ on her lips (avec) le sourire aux lèvres; "of course" he said with a ~ «bien sûr» dit-il en souriant; he has a nice ~ il a un joli sourire; come on, give us a ~! allez, fais-nous un sourire!; she gave me a friendly little ~ elle m'a adressé un petit sourire amical; to have a ~ on one's face avoir le sourire; take that ~ off your face! arrête de sourire comme ça!; to knock OR to wipe the ~ off sb's face *inf fig* faire passer à qqn l'envie de sourire; service with a ~ servi avec le sourire; to be all ~s être tout souriant OR tout sourire.
◇ *vi* sourire; to ~ at sb sourire à qqn; to ~ to o.s. sourire pour soi; she ~d at his awkwardness sa maladresse l'a fait sourire; he ~d to think of it il a souri en y pensant, y penser le faisait sourire; keep smiling! gardez le sourire!; she sat smiling through it all elle a gardé le sourire du début à la fin; heaven ~d on them *fig* le ciel leur sourit.
◇ *vt*: to ~ one's approval exprimer son approbation par un sourire; to ~ one's thanks remercier d'un sourire; she ~d a sad smile elle eut un sourire triste.

smiling ['smaɪlɪŋ] *adj* souriant.

smilingly ['smaɪlɪŋlɪ] *adv* en souriant, avec un sourire.

smirch [smɜːtʃ] *vt lit* -**1.** [stain] salir, souiller. -**2.** *fig* [name, reputation] salir, ternir.

smirk [smɜːk] ◇ *vi* [smugly] sourire d'un air suffisant OR avec suffisance; [foolishly] sourire bêtement.
◇ *n* [smug] petit sourire *m* satisfait OR suffisant; [foolish] sourire *m* bête.

smite [smaɪt] (*pt* smote [sməʊt], *pp* smitten ['smɪtn]) *vt* -**1.** *lit* OR *arch* [strike - object] frapper; [- enemy] abattre. -**2.** *(usu pass)* [afflict]: to be smitten with remorse être accablé de remords; they were smitten with blindness/fear ils ont été frappés de cécité/frayeur. -**3.** BIBLE [punish] châtier.

smith [smɪθ] *n* [blacksmith - gen] forgeron *m*; EQUIT maréchal-ferrant *m*.

smithereens [ˌsmɪðəˈriːnz] *npl* morceaux *mpl*; to smash sthg to ~ briser qqch en mille morceaux; the house was blown to ~ in the explosion la maison a été complètement soufflée par l'explosion.

Smithfield Market ['smɪθfiːld-] *pr n marché de gros de la viande à Londres*.

Smith Square *pr n place à Londres où se trouve le siège du parti conservateur*.

smithy ['smɪðɪ] (*pl* smithies) *n* forge *f*.

smitten ['smɪtn] ◇ *pp* → **smite**.
◇ *adj*: he was ~ with OR by her beauty il a été ébloui par sa beauté; he's really ~ (with that girl) il est vraiment très épris (de cette fille).

smock [smɒk] ◇ *n* [loose garment] blouse *f*; [maternity wear - blouse] tunique *f* de grossesse; [- dress] robe *f* de grossesse.
◇ *vt* faire des smocks à.

smocking ['smɒkɪŋ] *n (U)* smocks *mpl*.

smog [smɒg] *n* smog *m*.

smoggy ['smɒgɪ] (*compar* smoggier, *superl* smoggiest) *adj*: a ~ day une journée de smog; it's ~ il y a du smog.

smoke [sməʊk] ◇ *n* -**1.** [from fire, cigarette] fumée *f*; to go up in ~ [building] brûler; [plans] partir OR s'en aller en fumée; there's no ~ without fire *prov* il n'y a pas de fumée sans feu *prov*. -**2.** [act of smoking]: to have a ~ fumer; I went outside for a ~ je suis sorti fumer une cigarette. -**3.** *inf dated* [cigarette] clope *m or f*. -**4.** *Br drugs sl* [hashish] shit *m*. -**5.** *inf Br* [city]: the Smoke [any city] la grande métropole; [London] Londres.
◇ *vi* -**1.** [fireplace, chimney, lamp] fumer. -**2.** [person] fumer; do you mind if I ~? ça vous gêne si je fume? ❑ to ~ like a chimney *inf* fumer comme un pompier OR un sapeur.
◇ *vt* -**1.** [cigarette, pipe, opium etc] fumer; to ~ a pipe fumer la pipe. -**2.** CULIN & INDUST [fish, meat, glass] fumer. -**3.** [fumigate - plants, greenhouse, room] soumettre à des fumigations.
◆ **smoke out** *vt sep* -**1.** [from den, hiding place - fugitive, animal] enfumer; *fig* [discover - traitor] débusquer, dénicher; [- conspiracy, plot] découvrir. -**2.** [room] enfumer.
◆ **smoke up** *vt sep Am* [room] enfumer.

smoke bomb *n* bombe *f* fumigène.

smoked [sməʊkt] *adj* fumé; ~ salmon saumon *m* fumé; ~ glass verre *m* fumé.

smoke-dried *adj* fumé.

smoke-filled [-fɪld] *adj* enfumé.

smokehouse ['sməʊkhaʊs, *pl* -haʊzɪz] *n* fumoir *m (pour aliments)*.

smokeless fuel ['sməʊklɪs-] *n* combustible *m* non polluant.

smokeless zone *n zone dans laquelle seul l'usage de combustibles non polluants est autorisé*.

smoker ['sməʊkəʳ] *n* -**1.** [person] fumeur *m*, -euse *f*; to have a ~'s cough avoir une toux de fumeur. -**2.** [on train] compartiment *m* fumeurs.

smokescreen ['sməʊkskriːn] *n* MIL écran *m* OR rideau *m* de fumée; *fig* paravent *m*, couverture *f*.

smoke shop *n Am* tabac *m*.

smoke signal *n* signal *m* de fumée.

smokestack ['sməʊkstæk] *n* cheminée *f*.

smokestack industry *n* industrie *f* lourde.

smoking ['sməʊkɪŋ] *n*: I've given up ~ j'ai arrêté de fumer; 'no ~' 'défense de fumer'; ~ can cause cancer le tabac peut provoquer le cancer.

smoking compartment *n* compartiment *m* fumeurs.

smoking jacket *n* veste *f* d'intérieur.

smoking room *n* fumoir *m (pour fumeurs)*.

smoky ['sməʊkɪ] (*compar* smokier, *superl* smokiest) *adj* -**1.** [atmosphere, room] enfumé. -**2.** [chimney, lamp, fire] qui fume. -**3.** [in flavour - food] qui sent le fumé, qui a un goût de fumé. -**4.** [in colour] gris cendré *(inv)*.

smolder *etc Am* = **smoulder**.

smolt [sməʊlt] *n* tacon *m (poisson)*.

smooch *inf* [smuːtʃ] ◇ *n*: to have a ~ [kiss] se bécoter; [pet] se peloter.
◇ *vi* -**1.** [kiss] se bécoter. -**2.** *Br* [dance] danser joue contre joue.

smoochy *inf* [-smuːtʃɪ] (*compar* smoochier, *superl* smoochiest) *adj* [music] sentimental, tendre.

smooth [smuːð] ◇ *adj* -**1.** [surface] lisse; [pebble, stone] lisse, poli; [skin] lisse, doux; [chin - close-shaven] rasé de près; [- beardless] glabre, lisse; [hair, fabric, road] lisse; [sea, water] calme; this razor gives a ~ shave ce rasoir vous rase de près; the stone has been washed OR worn ~ by the sea la pierre avait été polie par la mer. -**2.** [ride, flight] confortable; [takeoff, landing] en douceur; they had a ~ crossing la traversée a été calme. -**3.** [steady, regular - flow, breathing, working, supply] régulier; [- organization] qui marche bien; [- rhythm, style] coulant; the ~ running of the service la bonne marche du service; the ~ running of the operation le bon déroulement de l'opération. -**4.** [trouble-free - life, course of events] paisible, calme; to get off to a ~ start démarrer en douceur; to make the way ~ for sb aplanir les difficultés pour qqn; the way is now ~ for further reforms il n'y a plus d'obstacles maintenant aux nouvelles réformes; the bill had a ~ passage through Parliament le projet de loi a été voté sans problèmes au Parlement. -**5.** CULIN [in texture] onctueux, homogène; [in taste] moelleux. -**6.** *pej* [slick, suave] doucereux, onctueux, suave; he's a ~ operator *inf* il sait y faire; he's a ~ talker c'est un beau parleur.
◇ *vt* -**1.** [tablecloth, skirt] défroisser; [hair, feathers] lisser; [wood] rendre lisse, planer; to ~ the way for sb, to ~ sb's path aplanir les difficultés pour qqn. -**2.** [rub - oil, cream] masser; to ~ oil into one's skin mettre de l'huile sur sa peau *(en massant doucement)*. -**3.** [polish] lisser, polir.
◇ *n* -**1.** to give one's hair a ~ lisser ses cheveux, se lisser les cheveux. -**2.** [smooth part] partie *f* lisse; [smooth surface] surface *f* unie.
◆ **smooth back** *vt sep* [hair] lisser en arrière; [sheet] rabattre en lissant.
◆ **smooth down** *vt sep* [hair] lisser; [sheets, dress] lisser, défroisser; [wood] planer, aplanir; *fig* [person] apaiser, calmer.
◆ **smooth out** *vt sep* [skirt, sheet, curtains] lisser, défroisser; [crease, pleat, wrinkle] faire disparaître (en lissant); *fig* [difficulties, obstacles] aplanir, faire disparaître.
◆ **smooth over** *vt sep* -**1.** [gravel, sand] rendre lisse (en ratissant); [soil] aplanir, égaliser. -**2.** *fig* [difficulties, obstacles] aplanir; [embarrassing situation]: to ~ things over arranger les choses.

smoothbore ['smuːðbɔːʳ] ◇ *adj* à canon lisse.
◇ *n* fusil *m* non rayé.

smooth-faced *adj literal* au visage lisse; [after shaving] rasé de près; *fig* & *pej* trop suave OR poli, onctueux.

smoothie *inf* ['smuːðɪ] *n pej*: he's a real ~ [in manner] il roule des mécaniques; [in speech] c'est vraiment un beau parleur.

smoothing iron ['smuːðɪŋ-] *n* fer *m* à repasser *(non électrique)*.

smoothly ['smuːðlɪ] *adv* -**1.** [easily, steadily - operate, drive, move] sans à-coups, en douceur; to run ~ [engine] tourner bien; [operation] marcher comme sur des roulettes; things are not going very ~ between them ça ne va pas très bien entre eux; the meeting went off quite ~ la réunion s'est déroulée sans heurt OR accroc. -**2.** [gently - rise, fall] doucement, en douceur; the plane took off ~ l'avion a décollé en douceur. -**3.** *pej* [talk] doucereusement; [behave] (trop) suavement.

smoothness ['smuːðnɪs] *n* -**1.** [of surface] égalité *f*, aspect *m* uni OR lisse; [of fabric, of skin, of hair] douceur *f*; [of road] surface *f* lisse; [of sea] calme *m*; [of stone] aspect *m* lisse OR poli; [of tyre] aspect *m* lisse; she has a wonderful ~ of touch on the piano elle a un merveilleux doigté au piano. -**2.** [of flow, breathing, pace, supply] régularité *f*; [of engine, machine] bon fonctionnement *m*; [of life, course of events] caractère *m* paisible OR serein; *fig* [of temperament] calme *m*, sérénité *f*; the operation was carried out with great ~ l'opération s'est déroulée sans accroc OR heurt. -**3.** CULIN [of texture] onctuosité *f*; [of taste] moelleux *m*. -**4.** [of voice] douceur *f*. -**5.** *pej* [suaveness] caractère *m* doucereux OR mielleux, onctuosité *f*.

smooth-running *adj* [machine] qui fonctionne bien OR sans à-coups; [engine] qui tourne bien; [car] confortable *(qui roule sans secousses)*; [business, organization] qui marche bien; [plan, operation] qui se déroule bien.

smooth-shaven *adj* rasé de près.

smooth-spoken *adj* qui sait parler.

smooth-talk *vt*: don't let him ~ you ne te laisse pas enjôler par lui; she was ~ed into accepting the job ils l'ont convaincu d'accepter le travail à force de belles paroles.

smooth-tongued = **smooth-spoken**.

smoothy *inf* ['smuːðɪ] = **smoothie**.

smorgasbord ['smɔːgəsbɔːd] *n* CULIN smorgasbord *m*, buffet *m* scandinave.

smote [sməʊt] *pt* → **smite**.

smother ['smʌðəʳ] ◇ *vt* -**1.** [suppress - fire, flames] étouffer; [- sound] étouffer, amortir; [- emotions, laughter, yawn] réprimer; [suppress - scandal, opposition] étouffer. -**2.** [suffocate - person] étouffer. -**3.** [cover] couvrir, recouvrir; strawberries ~ed in OR with cream des fraises couvertes de crème; she was ~ed in furs elle était emmitouflée dans des fourrures. -**4.** [overwhelm - with kindness, love] combler; to ~ sb with kisses couvrir OR dévorer qqn de baisers; to ~ sb with attention être aux petits soins pour qqn.
◇ *vi* [person] étouffer.

smoulder *Br*, **smolder** *Am* ['sməʊldəʳ] *vi* -**1.** [fire - before flames] couver; [- after burning] fumer. -**2.** [feeling, rebellion] couver; her eyes ~ed with passion son regard était plein de désir.

smouldering *Br*, **smoldering** *Am* ['sməʊldərɪŋ] *adj* [fire, anger, passion] qui couve; [embers, ruins] fumant; [eyes] de braise.

smudge [smʌdʒ] ◇ *n* -**1.** [on face, clothes, surface] (petite) tache *f*; [of make-up] traînée *f*; [on page of print] bavure *f*; you've got a ~ on your chin tu as du noir sur le menton ‖ [blur]: the ship was just a ~ on the horizon le navire n'était plus qu'une tache à l'horizon. -**2.** *Am* [fire] feu *m* (de jardin).
◇ *vt* [face, hands] salir; [clothes, surface] tacher, salir; [ink] répandre; [writing] étaler; you've made me ~ my lipstick à cause de toi je me suis mis du rouge à lèvres partout.
◇ *vi* [ink, make-up] faire des taches; [print] être maculé; [wet paint] s'étaler.

smudgy ['smʌdʒɪ] (*compar* smudgier, *superl* smudgiest) *adj* [make-up, ink] étalé; [print, page] maculé; [writing] à demi effacé; [face] sali, taché; [outline] estompé, brouillé.

smug [smʌg] (*compar* smugger, *superl* smuggest) *adj pej* [person] content de soi, suffisant; [attitude, manner, voice] suffisant; he's so ~! ce qu'il peut être suffisant OR content de sa petite personne!; you sound awfully ~ about the whole thing tu as l'air content OR fier de toi.

smuggle ['smʌgl] ◇ *vt* [contraband] passer en contrebande; [into prison - mail, arms] introduire clandestinement; to ~ sthg through customs passer qqch en fraude à la douane; the terrorists were ~d over the border les terroristes ont passé la frontière clandestinement; they are suspected of smuggling arms/heroin on les soupçonne de trafic d'armes/d'héroïne ‖ *fig* [into classroom, meeting etc] introduire subrepticement.
◇ *vi* faire de la contrebande.
◆ **smuggle in** *vt sep* [on a large scale - drugs, arms] faire entrer OR passer en contrebande; [as tourist - cigarettes, alcohol] introduire en fraude; [move secretly - books, mail etc] introduire clandestinement; to ~ goods/mercenaries into a country introduire des marchandises/des mercenaires clandestinement dans un pays; he managed to ~ a knife into the prison il a réussi à faire entrer OR passer clandestinement un couteau dans la prison.
◆ **smuggle out** *vt sep* [goods] faire sortir en fraude OR en contrebande; he was ~d out of the country il a quitté le pays clandestinement OR en secret.

smuggled ['smʌgld] *adj* [arms, drugs] passé en contrebande; [excised goods] de contrebande; ~ goods contrebande *f*.

smuggler ['smʌgləʳ] *n* contrebandier *m*, -ère *f*; drug ~ trafiquant *m*, -e *f* de drogue.

smuggling ['smʌglɪŋ] *n* contrebande *f*.

smugly ['smʌglɪ] *adv* [say] d'un ton suffisant, avec suffisance; [look, smile] d'un air suffisant, avec suffisance.

smut [smʌt] (*pt* & *pp* smutted, *cont* smutting)
◇ *n* -**1.** *inf (U)* [obscenity] cochonneries *fpl*;

[pornography] porno *m*; that bookshop sells nothing but ~ cette librairie ne vend que du porno. -**2.** *Br* [speck of dirt] poussière *f*; [smudge of soot] tache *f* de suie; you've got a ~ on your cheek tu as de la suie sur la joue; I've got a ~ in my eye j'ai une poussière dans l'œil. -**3.** AGR charbon *m* OR nielle *f* du blé.
◇ *vt* [smudge, stain] salir, noircir.

smuttiness *inf* ['smʌtɪnɪs] *n* obscénité *f*.

smutty ['smʌtɪ] (*compar* smuttier, *superl* smuttiest) *adj* -**1.** *inf* [obscene] cochon; [pornographic] porno; a book full of ~ stories un livre plein d'histoires cochonnes. -**2.** [dirty - hands, face, surface] sali, noirci.

Smyrna ['smɜːnə] *pr n* Smyrne.

snack [snæk] ◇ *n* -**1.** [light meal] casse-croûte *m inv*, en-cas *m inv*; to have a ~ casser la croûte, manger un morceau; to have a ~ lunch déjeuner sur le pouce. -**2.** (*usu pl*) [appetizer - esp at party] amuse-gueule *m*.
◇ *vi Am* grignoter.

snack bar *n* snack *m*, snack-bar *m*.

snaffle ['snæfl] ◇ *vt* -**1.** *inf Br* [get] se procurer; [steal] piquer, faucher; they ~d (up) all the prizes ils ont raflé tous les prix. -**2.** EQUIT mettre un bridon à.
◇ *n*: ~ (bit) mors *m* brisé, bridon *m*.

snafu▽ [snæ'fuː] ◇ *adj* MIL en pagaille, bordélique.
◇ *vt Am* mettre la pagaille OR le bordel dans.
◇ *n* pagaille *f*, bordel *m fig*.

snag [snæg] (*pt* & *pp* snagged, *cont* snagging)
◇ *n* -**1.** [problem] problème *m*, difficulté *f*, hic *m*; to come across OR to run into a ~ tomber sur un hic OR sur un os; there are several ~s in your plan il y a plusieurs choses qui clochent dans ton projet; the only ~ is that you have to pay first le seul problème, c'est qu'il faut payer d'abord. -**2.** [tear - in garment] accroc *m*; [- in stocking] fil *m* tiré. -**3.** [sharp protuberance] aspérité *f*; [tree stump] chicot *m*; I caught my dress on a ~ j'ai fait un accroc à ma robe.
◇ *vt* -**1.** [tear - cloth, garment] faire un accroc à, déchirer; she snagged her stocking on the brambles elle a accroché son bas OR fait un accroc à son bas dans les ronces. -**2.** *inf Am* [obtain] s'emparer de.
◇ *vi* s'accrocher; the rope snagged on the ledge la corde s'est trouvée coincée sur le rebord.

snail [sneɪl] *n* escargot *m*; at a ~'s pace [move, walk] comme un escargot, à une allure d'escargot; [change, progress] très lentement.

snake [sneɪk] ◇ *n* -**1.** ZOOL serpent *m*; ~s alive! *Br dated* ciel! -**2.** [person] vipère *f*; he's a real ~ c'est un faux jeton ❑ a ~ in the grass un faux frère. -**3.** ECON serpent *m* (monétaire).
◇ *vi* serpenter, sinuer *lit*; the smoke ~d upwards une volute de fumée s'élevait vers le ciel; the path ~d between the trees le chemin serpentait entre les arbres.
◇ *vt*: the river/road ~s its way down to the sea le fleuve serpente/la route descend en lacets jusqu'à la mer.

snakebird ['sneɪkbɜːd] *n* oiseau-serpent *m*.

snakebite ['sneɪkbaɪt] *n* morsure *f* de serpent.

snake charmer *n* charmeur *m*, -euse *f* de serpent.

snakes and ladders *n* (*U*) *jeu d'enfants ressemblant au jeu de l'oie*.

snakeskin ['sneɪkskɪn] ◇ *n* peau *f* de serpent.
◇ *comp* [shoes, handbag] en (peau de) serpent.

snaky ['sneɪkɪ] (*compar* snakier, *superl* snakiest) *adj* -**1.** [sinuous - river, road, movement] sinueux. -**2.** [person] insidieux, perfide; [cunning, acts] perfide.

snap [snæp] (*pt* & *pp* snapped, *cont* snapping)
◇ *vt* -**1.** [break - sharply] casser net; [- with a crack] casser avec un bruit sec; to ~ sthg in two OR in half casser qqch en deux d'un coup sec. -**2.** [make cracking sound] faire claquer; she snapped her case shut elle ferma sa valise d'un coup sec; she only needs to ~ her fingers and he comes running il lui suffit de claquer des doigts pour qu'il arrive en courant; to ~ one's fingers at sb faire claquer ses doigts pour attirer l'attention de qqn; [mockingly] faire la nique à qqn; they snapped their fingers at the idea ils ont rejeté l'idée avec mépris. -**3.** [say brusquely] dire d'un ton sec OR brusque; "no", he snapped «non», dit-il d'un ton sec. -**4.** [seize - gen] saisir; [- subj: dog] happer; she snapped the letter out of my hand elle m'a arraché la lettre des mains. -**5.** *inf* PHOT prendre une photo de.
◇ *vi* -**1.** [break - branch] se casser net OR avec un bruit sec, craquer; [- elastic band] claquer; [- rope] se casser, rompre; to ~ in two se casser net. -**2.** [make cracking sound - whip, fingers] claquer; to ~ open/shut s'ouvrir/se fermer avec un bruit sec OR avec un claquement ❑ ~ to it! *inf* grouille-toi!, magne-toi! -**3.** *fig* [person, nerves] craquer; after his divorce he just snapped après son divorce, il a craqué. -**4.** [speak brusquely]: to ~ at sb parler à qqn d'un ton sec; there's no need to ~! tu n'as pas besoin de parler sur ce ton-là! -**5.** [try to bite]: to ~ at chercher à OR essayer de mordre; the dog snapped at his ankles le chien essayait de lui mordre les chevilles; the fish snapped at the bait les poissons cherchaient à happer l'appât; the taxmen were beginning to ~ at his heels *fig* les impôts commençaient à le talonner.
◇ *n* -**1.** [of whip] claquement *m*; [of sthg breaking, opening, closing] bruit *m* sec; with a ~ of his fingers en claquant des doigts; to open/to close sthg with a ~ ouvrir/refermer qqch d'un coup sec; the branch broke with a ~ la branche a cassé avec un bruit sec. -**2.** [of jaws]: to make a ~ at sb/sthg essayer de mordre qqn/qqch; the puppy made a ~ at my ankles le chiot a essayé de me mordiller les chevilles; the dog made a ~ at the bone le chien a essayé de happer l'os. -**3.** *inf* PHOT photo *f*, instantané *m*; to take a ~ of sb prendre qqn en photo; holiday ~s photos de vacances. -**4.** *Br* CARDS ≃ bataille *f*; to play ~ ≃ jouer à la bataille. -**5.** METEOR: a cold ~, a ~ of cold weather une vague de froid. -**6.** *inf* [effort] effort *m*; [energy] énergie *f*; put some ~ into it! allez, mettez-y un peu de nerf! -**7.** *inf Am* [easy task]: it's a ~! c'est simple comme bonjour! -**8.** CULIN biscuit *m*, petit gâteau *m* sec. -**9.** [clasp, fastener] fermoir *m*. -**10.** *inf Br dial* [food] bouffe *f*.
◇ *adj* -**1.** [vote] éclair; [reaction] immédiat; [judgment] irréfléchi, hâtif; she made a ~ decision to go to Paris elle décida tout à coup d'aller à Paris; the President made a ~ decision to send troops le Président décida immédiatement d'envoyer des troupes; to call a ~ election procéder à une élection surprise. -**2.** *inf Am* [easy] facile.
◇ *adv*: to go ~ casser net.
◇ *interj Br* -**1.** CARDS: ~! ≃ bataille! -**2.** *inf* [in identical situation]: ~! tiens!, quelle coïncidence!; my mother's a teacher — ~, so's mine! ma mère est prof — tiens! la mienne aussi!

◆ **snap off** ◇ *vt sep* casser; he snapped off a piece of chocolate il a cassé un morceau de chocolat ❑ to ~ sb's head off *inf* envoyer promener qqn.
◇ *vi insep* casser net.

◆ **snap on** *vt sep Am*: to ~ a light on allumer une lampe.

◆ **snap out** ◇ *vi insep*: to ~ out of [depression, mood, trance] se sortir de, se tirer de; [temper] dominer, maîtriser; ~ out of it! [depression] ne te laisse pas aller comme ça!; [bad temper] ne t'énerve pas comme ça!; he can't seem to ~ out of this mood he's in il n'a pas l'air de vouloir changer d'humeur.
◇ *vt sep* [question] poser d'un ton sec; [order, warning] lancer brutalement; "stop!" he snapped out «arrête!» lança-t-il brutalement.

◆ **snap up** *vt sep* -**1.** [subj: dog, fish] happer, attraper. -**2.** *fig* [bargain, offer, opportunity] sauter sur, se jeter sur; the records were snapped up in no time les disques sont partis OR se sont vendus en un rien de temps; the cakes/the best bargains were soon snapped up les gâteaux sont partis/les meilleures affaires sont parties très vite. -**3.** *inf Am phr*: ~ it up! dépêchons!

snap bean *n Am* haricot *m* vert.

snapdragon ['snæpˌdrægən] *n* muflier *m*, gueule-de-loup *f*.

snap fastener *n* [press stud] bouton-pression *m*, pression *f*; [clasp - on handbag, necklace] fermoir *m* (à pression).

snap-on *adj* [collar, cuffs, hood] détachable, amovible (à pressions).

snapper ['snæpəʳ] (*pl inv* OR snappers) *n* [fish] lutjanidé *m*; red ~ vivaneau *m*.

snappily *inf* ['snæpɪlɪ] *adv* -**1.** [dress] avec chic. -**2.** [act, converse] vivement; [work] vite, sans traîner; [reply] du tac-au-tac.

snappish ['snæpɪʃ] *adj* [dog] hargneux, toujours prêt à mordre; [person] hargneux; [voice] mordant, cassant; [reply] brusque, cassant, sec; she's in a very ~ mood today elle n'est pas à prendre avec des pincettes aujourd'hui.

snappy *inf* ['snæpɪ] (*compar* snappier, *superl* snappiest) *adj* -**1.** [fashionable]: she's a ~ dresser elle sait s'habiller. -**2.** [lively - pace, rhythm] vif, entraînant; [- dialogue, debate] plein d'entrain, vivant; [- style, slogan] qui a du punch; [- reply] bien envoyé; look ~! *inf* grouille-toi!, active!; make it ~! *inf* et que ça saute! -**3.** [unfriendly - person] hargneux; [- answer] brusque; [- voice] cassant; you're a bit ~ today! tu es de mauvais poil aujourd'hui!; a ~ little dog un petit roquet.

snapshot ['snæpʃɒt] *n* instantané *m*.

snare [sneəʳ] ◇ *n* -**1.** [trap - gen] piège *m*; [- made of rope, wire] lacet *m*, collet *m*, lacs *m*; *fig* piège *m*, traquenard *m*; to set a ~ tendre un piège; to be caught in a ~ [animal] être pris dans un piège; *fig* [person] être pris au piège; the ~s of love *lit* les pièges de l'amour. -**2.** MUS: ~ (drum) caisse *f* claire.
◇ *vt* [animal - gen] piéger; [- in wire or rope trap] prendre au lacet OR au collet; *fig* [person] prendre au piège, piéger.

snarl [snɑːl] ◇ *vi* -**1.** [dog] gronder, grogner; [person] gronder; the dog ~ed at me as I walked past le chien a grogné quand je suis passé; the lions ~ed at their tamer les lions rugissaient contre leur dompteur; there's no need to ~ at me! tu n'as pas besoin de prendre ce ton hargneux pour me parler! -**2.** [thread, rope, hair] s'emmêler; [traffic] se bloquer; [plan, programme] cafouiller.
◇ *vt* -**1.** [person] lancer d'une voix rageuse, rugir; to ~ a reply répondre d'une voix rageuse; "shut up", she ~ed «tais-toi», lança-t-elle d'un ton hargneux. -**2.** [thread, rope, hair] enchevêtrer, emmêler; you hair is all ~ed tu as les cheveux tout emmêlés; the wool is all ~ed la laine est tout enchevêtrée.
◇ *n* -**1.** [sound] grognement *m*, grondement *m*; to give a ~ [subj: dog] pousser un grognement; [subj: tiger] feuler; [subj: person] gronder; she answered him with a ~ elle lui a répondu d'un ton hargneux. -**2.** [tangle - in thread, wool, hair] nœud *m*, nœuds *mpl*; caught in a ~ of traffic pris dans un embouteillage OR un bouchon.

◆ **snarl up** ◇ *vi insep* = **snarl** *vi* **2**.
◇ *vt sep* (*usu pass*) -**1.** [thread, rope, hair] emmêler, enchevêtrer; to get ~ed up s'emmêler, s'enchevêtrer. -**2.** [traffic] bloquer, coincer; [plans] faire cafouiller; the postal service is completely ~ed up le service des postes est complètement bloqué.

snarl-up *n* [of traffic] bouchon *m*, embouteillage *m*; [of plans] cafouillage *m*.

snatch [snætʃ] ◇ *vt* -**1.** [seize - bag, money] saisir; [- opportunity] saisir, sauter sur; to ~ sthg from sb OR from sb's hands arracher qqch des mains de qqn; a boy on a motorbike ~ed her bag un garçon en moto lui a arraché son sac; his mother ~ed him out of the path of the bus sa mère l'a attrapé par le bras pour l'empêcher d'être renversé par le bus. -**2.** [manage to get - meal, drink] avaler à la hâte; [- holiday, rest] réussir à avoir; to ~ some sleep réussir à dormir un peu; I was only able to ~ a sandwich j'ai juste eu le temps d'avaler un sandwich; to ~ a glance at sb lancer un coup d'œil furtif à qqn. -**3.** [steal] voler; [kiss] voler, dérober; [victory] décrocher. -**4.** [kidnap] kidnapper.

◇ *vi* [to child]: don't ~! [from hand] prends-le doucement!; [from plate] prends ton temps!; to ~ at sthg essayer de saisir OR d'attraper qqch; she ~es at the slightest hope/opportunity *fig* elle s'accroche au moindre espoir/saute sur la moindre occasion.

◇ *n* -**1.** [grab] geste *m* vif de la main *(pour attraper qqch)*; to make a ~ at sthg essayer de saisir OR d'attraper qqch; to make a ~ at victory *fig* essayer de s'emparer de la victoire. -**2.** *inf Br* [robbery] vol *m* à l'arraché; bag ~ vol (de sac) à l'arraché. -**3.** *inf* [kidnapping] kidnapping *m*. -**4.** [fragment - of conversation] fragment *m*, bribes *fpl*; [- of song, music] fragment *m*, mesure *f*; [- of poetry] fragment *m*, vers *m*; she could only catch a few ~es of their conversation/the song elle ne put saisir que quelques bribes de leur conversation/quelques mesures de la chanson. -**5.** [short spell] courte période *f*; to sleep in ~es dormir par intervalles OR de façon intermittente; to work in ~es travailler par à-coups. -**6.** [in weightlifting] arraché *m*. -**7.** ▼ [vagina] con *m*, chatte *f*.

◆ **snatch away** *vt sep* [letter, plate etc] arracher, enlever d'un geste vif; [hope] ôter, enlever; to ~ sthg away from sb arracher qqch à qqn; she ~ed her hand away from the hot stove elle a vite enlevé sa main du fourneau brûlant; victory was ~ed from them in the last minute la victoire leur a été soufflée à la dernière minute.

◆ **snatch up** *vt sep* ramasser vite OR vivement OR d'un seul coup; she ~ed up her child elle a saisi OR empoigné son enfant.

-snatcher ['snætʃəʳ] *in cpds* arracheur *m*, -euse *f*; bag~ voleur *m*, -euse *f* (de sac) à l'arraché.

snatch squad *n Br groupe de policiers chargé d'arrêter les meneurs (lors d'une manifestation)*.

snatchy *inf* ['snætʃɪ] (*compar* snatchier, *superl* snatchiest) *adj* [sleep] intermittent; [work] fait par à-coups OR de façon intermittente; [conversation] à bâtons rompus.

snazzily *inf* ['snæzɪlɪ] *adv* [dress] avec chic.

snazzy *inf* ['snæzɪ] (*compar* snazzier, *superl* snazziest) *adj* [garment] chic, qui a de l'allure; [car, house] chouette; she's a ~ dresser elle s'habille avec chic, elle est toujours bien sapée; he's got a ~ new suit il s'est acheté un nouveau costume drôlement chic.

sneak [sniːk] (*Br pt & pp* sneaked, *Am pt & pp* sneaked OR snuck [snʌk]) ◇ *vi* -**1.** [verb of movement] se glisser, se faufiler; [furtively] se glisser furtivement; [quietly] se glisser à pas feutrés OR sans faire de bruit; [secretly] se glisser sans se faire remarquer; to ~ up/down the stairs monter/descendre l'escalier furtivement; to ~ into/out of a room entrer dans une pièce/sortir d'une pièce à pas feutrés; he ~ed into her bedroom il s'est glissé OR faufilé dans sa chambre; we ~ed in at the back nous nous sommes glissés dans le fond discrètement OR sans nous faire remarquer; they ~ed into the cinema without paying ils se sont introduits dans le cinéma sans payer; we managed to ~ past the guards/window nous avons réussi à passer devant les gardes/la fenêtre sans nous faire remarquer; I ~ed round to the back door je me suis glissé sans bruit jusqu'à la porte de derrière. -**2.** *inf Br* SCH moucharder, cafter; to ~ on sb moucharder qqn.

◇ *vt* -**1.** [give - letter, message] glisser en douce OR sans se faire remarquer; they ~ed the money to her ils lui ont glissé l'argent en douce; the visitor managed to ~ him a knife le visiteur réussit à lui glisser un couteau sans se faire remarquer. -**2.** [take] enlever, prendre; he ~ed the keys from her pocket il a pris les clés dans sa poche sans qu'elle s'en aperçoive; to ~ a look at sthg lancer OR jeter un coup d'œil furtif à qqch. -**3.** *inf* [steal] chiper, piquer, faucher.

◇ *n inf* -**1.** [devious person] faux jeton *m*. -**2.** *Br* SCH cafardeur *m*, -euse *f*, mouchard *m*, -e *f*.

◇ *adj* [attack] furtif.

◆ **sneak away**, **sneak off** *vi insep* se défiler, s'esquiver.

◆ **sneak up** *vi insep* s'approcher à pas feutrés OR furtivement; to ~ up on OR behind sb s'approcher de qqn à pas feutrés.

sneaker ['sniːkəʳ] *n Am* (chaussure *f* de) tennis *m or f*, basket *m or f*.

sneaking ['sniːkɪŋ] *adj* [feeling, respect] inavoué, secret; she had a ~ suspicion that he was guilty elle ne pouvait (pas) s'empêcher de penser qu'il était coupable; she felt a ~ admiration for him elle ne pouvait (pas) s'empêcher de l'admirer; I had a ~ feeling that he was right quelque chose me disait qu'il avait raison.

sneak preview *n* avant-première *f* privée; I was given a ~ of the new film j'ai pu voir le nouveau film en avant-première.

sneak thief *n Br* chapardeur *m*, -euse *f*.

sneaky ['sniːkɪ] (*compar* sneakier, *superl* sneakiest) *adj* [person] sournois; [action] faite en cachette, faite à la dérobée; I caught him having a ~ cigarette je l'ai surpris en train de fumer une cigarette en cachette.

sneer [snɪəʳ] ◇ *vi* ricaner, sourire avec mépris OR d'un air méprisant; don't ~ ne sois pas si méprisant; to ~ at sb/sthg se moquer de qqn/qqch; an achievement not to be ~ed at un exploit qu'il ne faudrait pas minimiser.

◇ *n* [facial expression] ricanement *m*, rictus *m*; [remark] raillerie *f*, sarcasme *m*; "who do you think you are?", he said with a ~ «pour qui est-ce que tu te prends?», dit-il en ricanant OR ricana-t-il.

sneering ['snɪərɪŋ] ◇ *adj* ricaneur, méprisant.

◇ *n (U)* ricanement *m*, ricanements *mpl*.

sneeringly ['snɪərɪŋlɪ] *adv* [look] d'un air ricaneur, méprisant; [say] d'un ton ricaneur, en ricanant.

sneeze [sniːz] ◇ *n* éternuement *m*.

◇ *vi* éternuer; an offer not to be ~d at *inf fig* une proposition qui n'est pas à dédaigner OR sur laquelle il ne faut pas cracher.

snick [snɪk] ◇ *n* -**1.** [notch] petite entaille *f*, encoche *f*; to make a ~ in sthg faire une entaille OR une encoche à qqch. -**2.** [in cricket] *coup (de batte) qui fait dévier la balle*.

◇ *vt* -**1.** [cloth, wood] faire une petite entaille OR une encoche dans. -**2.** [in cricket] couper la balle.

snicker ['snɪkəʳ] ◇ *n* -**1.** [snigger] ricanement *m*. -**2.** [of horse] (petit) hennissement *m*.

◇ *vi* -**1.** [snigger] ricaner. -**2.** [horse] hennir doucement.

snide [snaɪd] *adj* [sarcastic] narquois, railleur; [unfriendly] inamical, insidieux; I've had enough of your ~ remarks! j'en ai assez de tes sarcasmes!; a ~ dig at his colleagues une remarque inamicale destinée à ses collègues.

snidely ['snaɪdlɪ] *adv* [sarcastically] railleusement; [in unfriendly manner] insidieusement.

sniff [snɪf] ◇ *vi* -**1.** [from cold, crying etc] renifler. -**2.** [scornfully] faire la grimace OR la moue.

◇ *vt* -**1.** [smell - food, soap] renifler, sentir l'odeur de; [- rose, perfume] humer, sentir l'odeur de; [subj: dog] renifler, flairer; the dog was ~ing the bone suspiciously le chien flairait l'os d'un air soupçonneux. -**2.** [inhale - air] humer, respirer; [- smelling salts] respirer; [- cocaine] sniffer, priser; [- snuff] priser; [- glue] respirer, sniffer. -**3.** [say scornfully] dire d'un air méprisant OR dédaigneux; "it's not my cup", she ~ed «ce n'est pas ma tasse», fit-elle d'un air méprisant.

◇ *n* [gen] reniflement *m*; to give a ~ *literal* renifler; [scornfully] faire la grimace OR la moue; "I've no idea", she said with a scornful ~ «je n'en ai aucune idée», dit-elle d'un air dédaigneux; to have OR to take a ~ of sthg renifler OR flairer qqch; take a ~ of this meat/this perfume renifle-moi cette viande/ce parfum; one ~ of that stuff is enough to knock you out *inf* une bouffée de ce truc et tu tombes raide; I didn't even get a ~ of a cup of coffee *fig* ils ne m'ont même pas offert une tasse de café.

◆ **sniff at** *vt insep* -**1.** *literal*: to ~ at sthg [subj: person] renifler qqch; [subj: dog] renifler OR flairer qqch. -**2.** *fig* faire la grimace OR la moue devant; to ~ at an idea/a une suggestion faire la grimace devant une idée/suggestion; their offer is not to be ~ed at leur offre n'est pas à dédaigner.

◆ **sniff out** *vt sep* [subj: dog] découvrir en reniflant OR en flairant; [criminal] découvrir, dépister; [secret] découvrir.

sniffer dog ['snɪfəʳ-] *n* chien *m* policier *(dressé pour le dépistage de la drogue, des explosifs)*.

sniffle ['snɪfl] ◇ *vi* [sniff] renifler; [have runny nose] avoir le nez qui coule.

◇ *n* [sniff] (léger) reniflement *m*; [cold] petit rhume *m* de cerveau; to have the ~s *inf* avoir le nez qui coule.

sniffy *inf* ['snɪfɪ] (*compar* sniffier, *superl* sniffiest) *adj* méprisant, dédaigneux; to be ~ about sthg faire le dédaigneux devant qqch.

snifter ['snɪftəʳ] *n* -**1.** *inf Br* [drink] petit verre *m* (d'alcool); fancy a ~? tu prends un petit verre? -**2.** *Am* [glass] verre *m* à dégustation.

snigger ['snɪgəʳ] ◇ *vi* ricaner, rire dans sa barbe; to ~ at [suggestion, remark] ricaner en entendant; [appearance] se moquer de, ricaner à la vue de.

◇ *n* rire *m* en dessous; [sarcastic] ricanement *m*; to give a ~ ricaner.

sniggering ['snɪgərɪŋ] ◇ *n (U)* rires *mpl* en dessous; [sarcastic] ricanements *mpl*.

◇ *adj* ricaneur.

snip [snɪp] (*pt & pp* snipped, *cont* snipping) ◇ *n* -**1.** [cut] petit coup *m* de ciseaux, petite entaille *f* OR incision *f*. -**2.** [sound] clic *m*; he could hear the ~ of scissors il entendait le clic-clac de ciseaux. -**3.** [small piece - of cloth, paper] petit bout *m*; [- of hair] mèche *f* (coupée). -**4.** *inf Br* [bargain] (bonne) affaire *f*; [horse] tuyau *m* sûr. -**5.** *inf Br* [cinch]: it's a ~! c'est du gâteau!, c'est simple comme bonjour!

◇ *vt* couper *(en donnant de petits coups de ciseaux)*.

◇ *vi*: he was snipping at the hedge il coupait la haie.

◆ **snip off** *vt sep* couper OR enlever (à petits coups de ciseaux); the rose heads had been snipped off les roses avaient été décapitées.

snipe [snaɪp] (*pl inv*) ◇ *n* bécassine *f*.

◇ *vi* -**1.** [shoot] tirer (d'une position cachée); to ~ at sb *literal* tirer sur qqn; *fig* [criticize] critiquer qqn par en-dessous; sniping criticism critiques insidieuses. -**2.** HUNT aller à la chasse aux bécassines.

sniper ['snaɪpəʳ] *n* tireur *m* embusqué OR isolé; killed by a ~'s bullet abattu par un tireur (embusqué).

snippet ['snɪpɪt] *n* [of material, paper] petit bout *m*; [of conversation, information] bribe *f*; a ~ of news une petite nouvelle.

snippy ['snɪpɪ] (*compar* snippier, *superl* snippiest) *adj Am* brusque, vif.

snitch *inf* [snɪtʃ] ◇ *n* -**1.** [person] cafardeur *m*, -euse *f*, mouchard *m*, -e *f*. -**2.** *Br hum* [nose] pif *m*. -**3.** *Br phr*: it's a ~ [easy] c'est simple comme bonjour; [bargain] c'est une (bonne) occase.

◇ *vi* [tell tales] moucharder; to ~ on sb moucharder OR cafarder qqn.

◇ *vt* [steal] chiper, piquer, faucher.

snivel ['snɪvl] (*Br pt & pp* snivelled, *cont* snivelling, *Am pt & pp* sniveled, *cont* sniveling) ◇ *vi* [whine] pleurnicher; [because of cold] renifler (continuellement); [with runny nose] avoir le nez qui coule; stop snivelling! [crying] arrête de pleurnicher comme ça!; [sniffing] arrête de renifler comme ça!

◇ *vt*: "it wasn't my fault", he snivelled «ce n'était pas de ma faute», fit-il en pleurnichant.

◇ *n* [sniffing] reniflement *m*, reniflements *mpl*; [tears] pleurnichements *mpl*; to have a ~ pleurnicher.

sniveller *Br*, **sniveler** *Am* ['snɪvlə^r] pleurnicheur *m*, -euse *f*, pleurnichard *m*, -e *f*.

snivelling *Br*, **sniveling** *Am* ['snɪvlɪŋ] ◇ *adj* pleurnicheur, larmoyant; shut up, you ~ little wretch! tais-toi, espèce de pleurnicheur!
◇ *n (U)* [crying] pleurnichements *mpl*; [because of cold] reniflement *m*, reniflements *mpl*; stop your ~! [tears] arrête de pleurnicher comme ça!; [sniffing] arrête de renifler comme ça!

snob [snɒb] *n* snob *mf*; she's an awful ~/a bit of a ~ elle est terriblement/un peu snob; to be an intellectual/a literary ~ être un snob intellectuel/en matière de littérature; inverted *Br* OR reverse ~ *personne d'origine modeste qui affiche un mépris pour les valeurs bourgeoises*.

snobbery ['snɒbərɪ] *n* snobisme *m*.

snobbish ['snɒbɪʃ] *adj* snob.

snobbishness ['snɒbɪʃnɪs] *n* snobisme *m*.

snobby *inf* ['snɒbɪ] (*compar* snobbier, *superl* snobbiest) = **snobbish**.

Sno-Cat® ['snəʊkæt] = **snowcat**.

snog *inf* [snɒg] (*pt* & *pp* snogged, *cont* snogging) *Br* ◇ *vi* se rouler une pelle.
◇ *vt* rouler une pelle à.
◇ *n*: to have a ~ se rouler une pelle.

snogging *inf* ['snɒgɪŋ] *n Br*: there was a lot of ~ going on ça s'embrassait dans tous les coins.

snood [snu:d] *n* résille *f (pour les cheveux)*.

snook [snu:k] *n* -1. ZOOL brochet *m* de mer. -2. → **cock**.

snooker ['snu:kə^r] ◇ *n* snooker *m (sorte de billard joué avec 22 boules)*.
◇ *vt* -1. *inf Br* [thwart] mettre dans l'embarras, mettre dans une situation impossible; [trick] arnaquer, avoir; we're ~ed! [stuck] on est coincé!; [tricked] on s'est fait avoir!; they've got us ~ed! ils nous ont eus! -2. GAMES laisser dans une position difficile.

snoop *inf* [snu:p] ◇ *vi* fourrer son nez dans les affaires des autres; someone has been ~ing about in my room quelqu'un est venu fouiner dans ma chambre; to ~ on sb espionner qqn; he's always ~ing around il est toujours à se mêler des affaires des autres OR de ce qui ne le regarde pas.
◇ *n* -1. [search]: to have a ~ around fouiller, fouiner; she had a good ~ around the house elle a fouillé OR fureté partout dans la maison. -2. = **snooper**.

snooper ['snu:pə^r] *n* fouineur *m*, -euse *f*; she's a born ~ c'est une vraie fouineuse.

snoot *inf* [snu:t] *n Br* pif *m*.

snooty *inf* ['snu:tɪ] (*compar* snootier, *superl* snootiest) *adj* [person] snobinard; [restaurant] snob; she's very ~ c'est une vraie pimbêche.

snooze *inf* [snu:z] ◇ *n* petit somme *m*, roupillon *m*; to have a ~ faire un petit somme, piquer un roupillon; he always has a ~ in the afternoon il fait toujours la sieste l'après-midi; ~ (position) [on alarm clock] (position *f*) sommeil *m*.
◇ *vi* sommeiller, piquer un roupillon; [in afternoon] faire la sieste.

snore [snɔ:^r] ◇ *vi* ronfler.
◇ *n* ronflement *m*.

snorer ['snɔ:rə^r] *n* ronfleur *m*, -euse *f*.

snoring ['snɔ:rɪŋ] *n (U)* ronflement *m*, ronflements *mpl*.

snorkel ['snɔ:kl] (*Br pt* & *pp* snorkelled, *cont* snorkelling, *Am pt* & *pp* snorkeled, *cont* snorkeling) ◇ *n* [of swimmer] tuba *m*; [on submarine] schnorchel *m*, schnorkel *m*.
◇ *vi* nager sous l'eau *(avec un tuba)*.

snort [snɔ:t] ◇ *vi* -1. [horse] s'ébrouer; [pig] grogner; [bull] renâcler. -2. [person - in anger] grogner, ronchonner; to ~ with laughter s'étouffer OR pouffer de rire; he ~ed in disbelief il eut un petit grognement incrédule.
◇ *vt* -1. [angrily] grogner; [laughingly] dire en pouffant de rire; "nonsense!", he ~ed «c'est absurde!», grommela-t-il. -2. ▽ [cocaine] sniffer.
◇ *n* -1. [of bull, horse] ébrouement *m*; [of person] grognement *m*; the horse gave a loud ~ le cheval s'ébroua bruyamment; he gave a ~ of contempt il poussa un grognement de mépris; he gave a ~ of laughter il pouffa de rire. -2. *inf* [drink] petit verre *m* (d'alcool).

snorter *inf* ['snɔ:tə^r] *n Br* -1. [as intensifier]: her second serve was a ~ son deuxième service a été terrible; a ~ of a performance une interprétation époustouflante; a ~ of a problem un vrai casse-tête, un sacré problème; he wrote them a real ~ of a letter il leur a écrit une vraie lettre d'engueulade. -2. [drink] petit verre *m* (d'alcool); to have a ~ prendre un petit verre.

snot *inf* [snɒt] *n* -1. [in nose] morve *f*; ~ rag▽ tire-jus *m*. -2. [person] morveu *m*, -euse *f*; you pathetic little ~! pauvre petit morveux!

snotty *inf* ['snɒtɪ] (*compar* snottier, *superl* snottiest, *pl* snotties) ◇ *adj* -1. [nose] qui coule; [face, child] morveux. -2. [uppity] crâneur, snobinard; a ~ letter une lettre agressive.
◇ *n* NAUT aspirant *m*.

snotty-faced *inf adj* morveux, qui a le nez qui coule.

snotty-nosed *inf adj literal* & *fig* morveux.

snout [snaʊt] *n* -1. [of pig] groin *m*, museau *m*; [of other animal] museau *m*. -2. [projection] saillie *f*; the ~ of a gun le canon d'un fusil. -3. *inf hum* [nose] pif *m*. -4. ▽ *Br* [cigarette] sèche *f*, clope *f*; [tobacco] tabac *m*, foin *m*. -5. *inf Br* [informer] mouchard *m*, -e *f*, indic *m*.

snow [snəʊ] ◇ *n* -1. *literal* neige *f*; heavy ~ is forecast la météo prévoit d'abondantes chutes de neige; the ~s of yesteryear les neiges d'antan; the roads are covered with ~ les routes sont enneigées ❑ 'Snow White and the Seven Dwarfs' *Grimm, Disney* 'Blanche-Neige et les sept nains'; 'The Snow Maiden' *Rimsky-Korsakov* 'Fleur de neige'; 'The Snow Queen' *Andersen* 'la Reine des glaces'. -2. *fig* [on screen] neige *f*. -3. *drugs sl* [cocaine] neige *f sl*.
◇ *vi* neiger; it's ~ing il neige.
◇ *vt inf Am* [sweet-talk] baratiner; she ~ed him into giving her the money elle l'a embobiné pour qu'il lui donne l'argent.
◆ **snow in** *vt sep*: to be ~ed in être bloqué par la neige.
◆ **snow under** *vt sep fig*: to be ~ed under with work être débordé OR complètement submergé de travail; they're ~ed under with applications/offers ils ont reçu une avalanche de demandes/d'offres.
◆ **snow up** *vt sep*: to be ~ed up [house, village, family] être bloqué par la neige; [road] être complètement enneigé.

snowball ['snəʊbɔ:l] ◇ *n* -1. boule *f* de neige; they had a ~ fight ils ont fait une bataille de boules de neige ❑ he hasn't a ~'s chance in hell *inf* il n'a pas l'ombre d'une chance. -2. [cocktail] snowball *m (advokaat allongé de limonade)*.
◇ *comp*: ~ effect effet *m* boule de neige.
◇ *vt* bombarder de boules de neige, lancer des boules de neige à.
◇ *vi fig* faire boule de neige.

snowbank ['snəʊbæŋk] *n* congère *f*.

snowberry ['snəʊbərɪ] (*pl* snowberries) *n* boule-de-neige *f* BOT.

snow-blind *adj*: to be ~ être atteint de OR souffrir de la cécité des neiges.

snow blindness *n* cécité *f* des neiges.

snow blower *n* chasse-neige *m* à soufflerie.

snow-boot *n* après-ski *m*.

snowbound ['snəʊbaʊnd] *adj* [person, house, village] bloqué par la neige; [road] enneigé.

snowcap ['snəʊkæp] *n* sommet *m* couronné de neige.

snow-capped *adj* couronné de neige.

snowcat ['snəʊkæt] *n* autoneige *f*, motoneige *f*.

snow-clad *adj* couvert de neige, enneigé.

snowdrift ['snəʊdrɪft] *n* congère *f*.

snowdrop ['snəʊdrɒp] *n* perce-neige *m or f inv*.

snowfall ['snəʊfɔ:l] *n* -1. [snow shower] chute *f* de neige. -2. [amount] enneigement *m*.

snow fence *n* pare-neige *m inv*.

snowfield ['snəʊfi:ld] *n* champ *m* de neige.

snowflake ['snəʊfleɪk] *n* flocon *m* de neige.

snow goose *n* oie *f* des neiges.

snow job *inf n Am*: to give sb a ~ baratiner qqn; it's a ~ c'est du baratin.

snow leopard *n* léopard *m* des neiges, once *f*.

snowline ['snəʊlaɪn] *n* limite *f* des neiges éternelles.

snowman ['snəʊmæn] (*pl* snowmen [-men]) *n* bonhomme *m* de neige.

snowmobile ['snəʊməbi:l] = **snowcat**.

snowplough *Br*, **snowplow** *Am* ['snəʊplaʊ] ◇ *n* -1. [vehicle] chasse-neige *m inv*. -2. [in skiing] chasse-neige *m inv*.
◇ *vi* [in skiing] faire du chasse-neige.

snowshoe ['snəʊʃu:] *n* raquette *f (pour marcher sur la neige)*.

snowslide ['snəʊslaɪd], **snowslip** ['snəʊslɪp] *n* avalanche *f*.

snowstorm ['snəʊstɔ:m] *n* tempête *f* de neige.

snowsuit ['snəʊsu:t] *n* combinaison *f* de ski.

snow tyre *n* pneu *m* neige.

snow-white *adj* blanc comme neige.

snowy ['snəʊɪ] (*compar* snowier, *superl* snowiest) *adj* -1. [weather, region etc] neigeux; [countryside, roads etc] enneigé, couvert OR recouvert de neige; [day] de neige; a ~ Christmas un Noël enneigé. -2. *fig* [hair, beard] de neige; [sheets, tablecloth] blanc comme neige.

snowy owl *n* chouette *f* blanche, harfang *m*.

SNP *pr n abbr of* Scottish National Party.

Snr (*written abbr of* Senior) *utilisé après le nom de quelqu'un pour le distinguer d'un autre membre de la famille, plus jeune et portant le même nom*.

snub [snʌb] (*pt* & *pp* snubbed, *cont* snubbing) ◇ *n* rebuffade *f*.
◇ *vt* [person] remettre à sa place, rabrouer; [offer, suggestion] repousser (dédaigneusement); to be snubbed essuyer une rebuffade; I felt snubbed je me suis senti rabroué.
◇ *adj* [nose] retroussé.

snub-nosed *adj* au nez retroussé.

snuck [snʌk] *pt* & *pp* → **sneak**.

snuff [snʌf] ◇ *n* tabac *m* à priser; to take ~ priser; a pinch of ~ une prise (de tabac) ❑ to be up to ~ *inf dated* [in good health] être en forme; [of sufficient quality] être à la hauteur.
◇ *vi* [sniff] priser.
◇ *vt* -1. [candle] moucher. -2. *phr*: to ~ it *inf hum* casser sa pipe. -3. [sniff] renifler, flairer.
◆ **snuff out** *vt sep* [candle] éteindre, moucher; *fig* [hope] ôter, supprimer; [rebellion] étouffer; [enthusiasm] briser.

snuffbox ['snʌfbɒks] *n* tabatière *f (pour tabac à priser)*.

snuffer ['snʌfə^r] *n*: (candle) ~ éteignoir *m*.
◆ **snuffers** *npl* mouchettes *fpl*.

snuffle ['snʌfl] ◇ *vi* -1. [sniffle] renifler. -2. [in speech] parler du nez, nasiller.
◇ *vt* dire OR prononcer d'une voix nasillarde.
◇ *n* -1. [sniffle] reniflement *m*; to have the ~s être un peu enrhumé. -2. [in speech] voix *f* nasillarde; to speak in a ~ parler d'une voix nasillarde.

snuff movie *inf n film pornographique comportant une scène de meurtre filmée en direct*.

snug [snʌg] ◇ *adj* -1. [warm and cosy - bed, room] douillet, (bien) confortable; [- sleeping bag, jacket] douillet, bien chaud; a ~ little house une petite maison confortable; it's very ~ in this room on est bien OR il fait bon dans cette pièce; I wish I was home and ~ in bed j'aimerais être bien au chaud dans mon lit ❑ to be (as) ~ as a bug in a rug *inf* être bien au chaud. -2. [fit] bien ajusté; my skirt is a ~ fit ma jupe me va comme un gant. -3. [harbour] bien abrité; [hideout] sûr.
◇ *n Br* [in pub] petite arrière-salle *f*.

snuggery ['snʌgərɪ] (*pl* snuggeries) *n Br* petite pièce *f* douillette; [in pub] petite arrière-salle *f*.

snuggle ['snʌgl] ◇ *vi* se blottir, se pelotonner; to ~ into a corner se blottir OR se pelotonner dans un coin.
◇ *vt* [child, kitten] serrer contre soi, câliner.
◇ *n* câlin *m*; to have a ~ (se) faire un câlin.

◆ **snuggle down** *vi insep* se blottir, se pelotonner; to ~ down under the blankets s'enfouir sous les couvertures; she ~d down to sleep elle se pelotonna pour dormir; she ~d down beside her mum elle s'est blottie contre sa maman.

◆ **snuggle up** *vi insep*: to ~ up to sb se blottir OR se serrer contre qqn.

snugly ['snʌglɪ] *adv* -**1.** [cosily] douillettement, confortablement; soon they were settled ~ by the fire ils se retrouvèrent bientôt réunis autour d'un bon feu. -**2.** [in fit]: the skirt fits ~ la jupe est très ajustée; the two parts fit together ~ les deux pièces s'emboîtent parfaitement.

so[1] [səʊ] ◇ *adv* -**1.** *(before adj, adv)* [to such an extent] si, tellement; I'm so glad to see you ça me fait tellement plaisir OR je suis si content de te voir; he can be so irritating at times il est tellement énervant par moments; she makes me so angry elle a le don de me mettre en colère; I've never been so surprised in all my life jamais de ma vie je n'avais eu une surprise pareille OR une telle surprise; it was so beautiful a sight *fml* c'était un si beau spectacle; she was so shocked (that) she couldn't speak [result] elle était tellement choquée qu'elle ne pouvait pas parler; so complex was the problem that it baffled even the experts le problème était si OR tellement complexe que même les experts ne comprenaient pas; his handwriting's so bad (that) it's illegible OR so bad as to be illegible il écrit si mal que c'est impossible à lire; would you be so kind as to carry my case? auriez-vous l'amabilité OR la gentillesse de porter ma valise?; is it so very hard to say you're sorry? est-ce si difficile de demander pardon? || *(after verb)* comme ça, ainsi; you mustn't worry so il ne faut pas te faire du souci comme ça; I wish he wouldn't go on so j'aimerais qu'il arrête de radoter || *(with 'that' clause)*: she so detests him OR she detests him so that she won't even speak to him elle le hait au point de refuser OR elle le déteste tellement qu'elle refuse de lui parler; he was upset, so much so that he cried il était bouleversé, à tel point qu'il en a pleuré || *(in negative comparisons)* si, aussi; I'm not so sure je n'en suis pas si sûr; it's not so bad, there's only a small stain ça n'est pas si grave que ça, il n'y a qu'une petite tache; the young and the not so young les jeunes et les moins jeunes; he's not so handsome as his father/as all that il n'est pas aussi beau que son père/si beau que ça; he was not so ill (that) he couldn't go out il n'était pas malade au point de ne pas pouvoir sortir. -**2.** [indicating a particular size, length etc]: the table is about so high/wide la table est haute/large comme ça à peu près. -**3.** [referring to previous statement, question, word etc]: I believe/think/suppose so je crois/pense/suppose; I don't believe/think so je ne crois/pense pas; I don't suppose so je suppose que non; I hope so [answering question] j'espère que oui; [agreeing] j'espère bien, je l'espère; who says so? qui dit ça?; I told you so! je vous l'avais bien dit!; if so si oui; perhaps so peut-être bien; quite so tout à fait, exactement; so I believe/see c'est ce que je crois/vois; so I've been told/he said c'est ce qu'on m'a dit/qu'il a dit; isn't that Jane over there? – why, so it is! ce ne serait pas Jane là-bas? – mais si (c'est elle)!; he was told to leave the room and did so immediately on lui a ordonné de quitter la pièce et il l'a fait immédiatement; she was furious and understandably/and justifiably so elle était furieuse et ça se comprend/et c'est normal; the same only more so tout autant sinon plus; he's very sorry – so he should be! il est désolé – c'est la moindre des choses OR j'espère bien! || [used mainly by children]: I can so! *inf* si, je peux!; I didn't say that! – you did so! *inf* je n'ai pas dit ça! – si, tu l'as dit! ❑ so be it! *arch* OR *hum* soit!, qu'il en soit ainsi!; so help me God! *fml* que Dieu me vienne en aide! -**4.** [likewise] aussi; I had brought food, and so had they j'avais apporté de quoi manger et eux aussi; we arrived early and so did he nous sommes arrivés tôt et lui aussi; if he can do it, then so can I s'il peut OR est capable de le faire, alors moi aussi; my shoes are Italian and so is my shirt mes chaussures sont italiennes et ma chemise aussi. -**5.** [like this, in this way] ainsi; hold the pen (like) so tenez le stylo ainsi OR comme ceci; any product so labelled is guaranteed lead-free tous les produits portant cette étiquette sont garantis sans plomb; the laptop computer is so called because... l'ordinateur lap-top tient son nom de... || [in such a way]: the helmet is so constructed as to absorb OR that it absorbs most of the impact le casque est conçu de façon à amortir le choc ❑ it (just) so happens that... il se trouve (justement) que...; she likes everything (to be) just so elle aime que tout soit parfait; it has to be positioned just so or it won't go in il faut le mettre comme ça sinon ça n'entre pas. -**6.** [introducing the next event in a sequence]: and so to bed! et maintenant au lit!; and so we come to the next question et maintenant nous en venons à la question suivante; so then she left alors elle est partie || [requesting more information]: so what's the problem? alors, qu'est-ce qui ne va pas? || [summarizing, inferring]: so we can't go after all donc nous ne pouvons plus y aller || [in exclamations] alors; so you're Anna's brother! alors (comme ça) vous êtes le frère d'Anna?; so that's why she didn't phone! alors c'est pour ça qu'elle n'a pas téléphoné!; so publish it! eh bien OR alors allez-y, publiez-le! || [introducing a concession] et alors; so I'm late, who cares? je suis en retard, et alors, qu'est-ce que ça peut faire?; so it costs a lot of money, we can afford it ça coûte cher, et alors? on peut se le permettre; so? et alors?, et après? ❑ he'll be angry – so what? il va se fâcher! – qu'est-ce que ça peut (me) faire OR et alors?; so what if she does find out! qu'est-ce que ça peut faire si elle s'en rend compte?

◇ *conj* -**1.** [indicating result] donc, alors; the door was open, so I went in la porte était ouverte, alors je suis entré. -**2.** [indicating purpose] pour que, afin que; give me some money so I can buy some sweets donne-moi de l'argent pour que je puisse acheter des bonbons. -**3.** [in the same way] de même; as 3 is to 6, so 6 is to 12 le rapport entre 6 et 12 est le même qu'entre 3 et 6; as he has lived so will he die il mourra comme il a vécu.

◇ *adj* ainsi, vrai; is that so? c'est vrai?; *iron* vraiment?; that is so c'est vrai, c'est exact; if that is so si c'est le cas, s'il en est ainsi.

◆ **or so** *adv phr* environ, à peu près; it costs £5 or so ça coûte environ 5 livres; there were thirty or so people il y avait trente personnes environ OR à peu près, il y avait une trentaine de personnes.

◆ **so as** *inf conj phr* pour que, afin que.

◆ **so as to** *conj phr* pour, afin de; she went to bed early so as not to be tired next day elle s'est couchée tôt afin de OR pour ne pas être fatiguée le lendemain.

◆ **so that** *conj phr* -**1.** [in order that] pour que, afin que; they tied him up so that he couldn't escape ils l'ont attaché afin qu'il OR pour qu'il ne s'échappe pas; I took a taxi so that I wouldn't be late j'ai pris un taxi pour ne pas être en retard. -**2.** [with the result that] si bien que, de façon à ce que; she didn't eat enough, so that in the end she fell ill elle ne mangeait pas assez, de telle sorte OR si bien qu'elle a fini par tomber malade.

◆ **so to speak, so to say** *adv phr* pour ainsi dire.

so[2] [səʊ] *n* MUS sol *m*.

SO *n abbr of* standing order.

soak [səʊk] ◇ *vt* -**1.** [washing, food] faire OR laisser tremper; he ~ed the shirts in warm water il a fait tremper les chemises dans de l'eau chaude; ~ the prunes overnight laisser tremper les pruneaux toute la nuit; to ~ o.s. (in the bath) faire trempette dans la baignoire. -**2.** [drench – person, dog etc] tremper; to be ~ed through OR to the skin être trempé jusqu'aux os; I got ~ed waiting in the rain je me suis fait tremper en attendant sous la pluie; his shirt was ~ed in blood/in sweat sa chemise était maculée de sang/trempée de sueur. -**3.** *fig* [immerse] imprégner; to ~ o.s. in the history of a period se plonger dans OR s'imprégner de l'histoire d'une époque. -**4.** *inf* [exploit – by swindling] rouler, arnaquer; [– through taxation] faire casquer; to ~ the rich faire casquer les riches.

◇ *vi* [washing] tremper; he put the washing (in) to ~ il a mis le linge à tremper; to ~ in the bath faire trempette dans la baignoire.

◇ *n* -**1.** [in water] trempage *m*; the shirts are in ~ les chemises sont en train de tremper; these shirts need a good ~ il faut laisser OR bien faire tremper ces chemises; I had a nice long ~ in the bath je suis resté longtemps plongé dans un bon bain. -**2.** *inf* [heavy drinker] soûlard *m*, -e *f*, pochard *m*, -e *f*. -**3.** *inf Br* [rain shower] saucée *f*, rincée *f*.

◆ **soak in** *vi insep* -**1.** [water] pénétrer, s'infiltrer. -**2.** *inf fig* [comment, news] faire son effet; she told me what happened, but it hasn't ~ed in yet elle m'a dit ce qui s'est passé, mais je n'ai pas encore vraiment bien compris.

◆ **soak out** ◇ *vi insep* [dirt, stains] partir (au trempage).

◇ *vt sep* [dirt, stains] faire disparaître OR partir (en faisant tremper).

◆ **soak through** *vi insep* [liquid] filtrer au travers, s'infiltrer.

◆ **soak up** *vt sep* -**1.** [absorb] absorber; we spent a week ~ing up the sun nous avons passé une semaine à lézarder OR à nous faire dorer au soleil; they come to Europe to ~ up the culture ils viennent en Europe pour s'imbiber de culture. -**2.** *inf hum* [drink]: he can really ~ it up il peut vraiment boire comme un trou.

soaked [səʊkt] *adj fig* [immersed] imprégné; the place is ~ in history l'endroit est imprégné d'histoire.

soaking ['səʊkɪŋ] ◇ *adj* trempé; take off your shirt, it's ~ enlève ta chemise, elle est trempée; I'm ~ (wet)! je suis trempé jusqu'aux os!

◇ *n* -**1.** [gen] trempage *m*; these clothes need a good ~ il faut laisser tremper ces vêtements || [in rain] *inf*: to get a ~ se faire tremper OR saucer. -**2.** *inf* [financial loss] perte *f* financière; we got a real ~ on the stock market on a vraiment beaucoup perdu à la bourse.

so-and-so *inf n* -**1.** [referring to stranger] untel *m*, unetelle *f*; Mr ~ Monsieur Untel; Mrs ~ Madame Unetelle. -**2.** [annoying person]: you little ~! espèce de petit minable!

soap [səʊp] ◇ *n (U)* -**1.** savon *m*; a bar of ~ un savon, une savonnette; ~ bubble bulle *f* de savon. -**2.** *inf* = **soft soap**. -**3.** *inf phr Am*: no ~! des clous!, des nèfles! -**4.** *inf* = **soap opera**.

◇ *vt* savonner.

◆ **soap down** *vt sep* savonner; to ~ o.s. down se savonner.

◆ **soap up** *inf vt sep* -**1.** [flatter] passer de la pommade à. -**2.** *Am* [bribe] soudoyer.

soapbox ['səʊpbɒks] ◇ *n* -**1.** *literal* caisse *f* à savon; *fig* [for speaker] tribune *f* improvisée OR de fortune; get off your ~! ne monte pas sur tes grands chevaux! -**2.** [go-kart] chariot *m*, ≃ kart *m (sans moteur)*.

◇ *comp* [orator] de carrefour; [oratory] de démagogue; he's just a ~ orator ce n'est qu'un orateur de carrefour.

soapdish ['səʊpdɪʃ] *n* porte-savon *m*.

soapflakes ['səʊpfleɪks] *npl* paillettes *fpl* de savon, savon *m* en paillettes.

soap opera *n* RADIO & TV soap-opera *m*.

soap powder *n* lessive *f* (en poudre), poudre *f* à laver.

soapstone ['səʊpstəʊn] *n* stéatite *f*.

soapsuds ['səʊpsʌdz] *npl* [foam] mousse *f* de savon; [soapy water] eau *f* savonneuse.

soapy ['səʊpɪ] *(compar* soapier, *superl* soapiest) *adj* -**1.** [water, hands, surface] savonneux; [taste] de savon. -**2.** *inf fig & pej* [person, manner, voice] onctueux, mielleux.

soar [sɔːʳ] *vi* -**1.** [bird, plane] monter en flèche; [flames] jaillir; to ~ into the sky OR the air [bird, balloon etc] s'élever dans les airs; the ball ~ed over the fence/our heads le ballon s'est envolé au-dessus de la clôture/de nos têtes; the jet ~ed above us l'avion est monté en flèche au-dessus de nous. -**2.** [spire] se dresser vers le ciel; [mountain] s'élever vers le ciel; the mountain seemed to ~ into the clouds la montagne paraissait s'élancer dans les nuages. -**3.** [temperature, profits, prices] monter OR grimper en flèche; [suddenly] faire un bond; sales have ~ed since the TV adverts les ventes ont grimpé en flèche depuis les publicités à la télé. -**4.** [spirits] remonter en flèche; [hopes, imagination] grandir démesurément; [reputation] monter en flèche. -**5.** [sound, music] s'élever.

soaring [ˈsɔːrɪŋ] ◇ *adj* -**1.** [bird, glider] qui s'élève dans le ciel; [spire, tower] qui s'élance vers le ciel; [mountain] qui s'élève vers le ciel; the ~ spire of the cathedral la flèche de la cathédrale qui s'élance vers le ciel. -**2.** [prices, inflation] qui monte OR qui grimpe en flèche; [imagination] débordant; [hopes, reputation] grandissant.
◇ *n* [of bird] essor *m*, élan *m*; [of plane] envol *m*; [of prices] envolée *f*, explosion *f*.

SOAS [ˈsəʊæs] (*abbr of* School of Oriental and African Studies) *pr n école des études orientales et africaines de Londres*.

sob[1] [sɒb] (*pt* & *pp* sobbed, *cont* sobbing)
◇ *n* sanglot *m*; she answered him with a ~ elle lui répondit dans un sanglot; it wasn't me, he said with a ~ ce n'est pas moi, dit-il en sanglotant; with a ~ in her voice la voix étouffée par un sanglot.
◇ *vi* sangloter.
◇ *vt*: to ~ o.s. to sleep s'endormir à force de sangloter OR en sanglotant; "I can't remember!", he sobbed «je ne me rappelle pas», dit-il en sanglotant OR dans un sanglot.
◆ **sob out** *vt sep* raconter en sanglotant; she sobbed out her grief son chagrin se traduisait par des sanglots; to ~ one's heart out sangloter de tout son corps, pleurer à gros sanglots.

sob[2] *inf*, **SOB** *inf* [ˈesəʊbiː] *n Am abbr of* son of a bitch.

sobbing [ˈsɒbɪŋ] ◇ *n (U)* sanglots *mpl*; stop your ~ arrête de sangloter.
◇ *adj* sanglotant.

sober [ˈsəʊbəʳ] ◇ *adj* -**1.** [not drunk] sobre; he's always ~ il ne boit jamais; he's never ~ il est toujours ivre ‖ [sobered up] dessoûlé; wait until he's ~ again attends qu'il dessoûle ❑ to be as ~ as a judge [serious] être sérieux comme un pape; [temperate] être sobre comme un chameau. -**2.** [moderate - person] sérieux, posé, sensé; [- attitude, account, opinion] modéré, mesuré; [- manner] sérieux, posé. -**3.** [serious, solemn - atmosphere, occasion] solennel, plein de solennité; [- expression] grave, plein de gravité; [- voice] grave, empreint de gravité; [- reminder] solennel; you're in (a) ~ mood vous êtes d'humeur bien solennelle. -**4.** [subdued - colour, clothing] discret, sobre; he was wearing a ~ blue tie il portait une cravate d'un bleu sobre; of ~ appearance d'aspect sobre. -**5.** [plain - fact, reality] (tout) simple; [- truth] simple, tout nu; the ~ fact is... le fait est que...; a man of ~ tastes un homme aux goûts simples OR sobres.
◇ *vt* [calm] calmer, assagir.
◆ **sober down** ◇ *vi insep* [calm down] se calmer, s'assagir.
◇ *vt sep* [calm] calmer, assagir.
◆ **sober up** *vi insep* & *vt sep* dessoûler.

sobering [ˈsəʊbərɪŋ] *adj*: it's a ~ thought cela donne à réfléchir; what she said had a ~ effect on everyone ce qu'elle a dit donnait à réfléchir à tous.

soberly [ˈsəʊbəlɪ] *adv* [act, speak] avec sobriété OR modération OR mesure; [dress] sobrement, discrètement; he said ~ [calmly] dit-il d'un ton posé OR mesuré; [solemnly] dit-il d'un ton grave; the soldiers filed ~ past les soldats défilèrent solennellement.

soberness [ˈsəʊbənɪs] = **sobriety**.

sobersides *inf* [ˈsəʊbəsaɪdz] *n Br*: he's a real ~ c'est un vrai bonnet de nuit.

sobriety [səʊˈbraɪətɪ] *n* -**1.** [non-drunkenness] sobriété *f*; his ~ cannot be guaranteed rien ne garantit qu'il ne sera pas ivre. -**2.** [moderation - of person] sobriété *f*, sérieux *m*; [- of opinion, judgement] mesure *f*, modération *f*; [- of manner, style, tastes] sobriété *f*. -**3.** [solemnity - of occasion] solennité *f*; [- of voice] ton *m* solennel OR grave; [- of mood] sobriété *f*. -**4.** [of colour, dress] sobriété *f*.

sobriquet [ˈsəʊbrɪkeɪ] *n lit* sobriquet *m*.

sob story *inf n pej* histoire *f* larmoyante, histoire *f* à vous fendre le cœur; she's always full of sob stories elle cherche toujours à vous apitoyer OR à vous fendre le cœur avec ses histoires; he told us some ~ about his deprived childhood il nous a parlé de son enfance malheureuse, à faire pleurer dans les chaumières.

Soc [sɒk] (*abbr of* Society) *n* ≃ club *m (abréviation utilisée dans la langue parlée notamment par les étudiants pour désigner les différents clubs universitaires)*.

so-called [-kɔːld] *adj* soi-disant *(inv)*, prétendu; his ~ aunt sa soi-disant tante; ~ social workers des soi-disant assistants sociaux; her ~ boudoir son boudoir, comme elle l'appelle.

soccer [ˈsɒkəʳ] ◇ *n* football *m*, foot *m*.
◇ *comp* [pitch, match, team] de football, de foot; [supporter] d'une équipe de foot; ~ hooligans hooligans *mpl (lors de matches de football)*; ~ player footballeur *m*, -euse *f*.

sociability [ˌsəʊʃəˈbɪlətɪ] *n* sociabilité *f*.

sociable [ˈsəʊʃəbl] ◇ *adj* -**1.** [enjoying company] sociable, qui aime la compagnie (des gens); [friendly] sociable, amical; [evening] amical, convivial; try to be more ~ [go out more] essaie de sortir un peu et de rencontrer des gens; [mix more] essaie d'être un peu plus sociable; I'm not in a ~ mood je ne suis pas d'humeur sociable, je n'ai pas envie de voir de monde. -**2.** SOCIOL & ZOOL sociable.
◇ *n Am* fête *f*.

sociably [ˈsəʊʃəblɪ] *adv* [behave] de manière sociable, amicalement; [say] amicalement.

social [ˈsəʊʃl] ◇ *adj* -**1.** [background, behaviour, conditions, reform, tradition] social; [phenomenon] social, de société; to bow to ~ pressures se plier aux pressions sociales; they are our ~ equals ils sont de même condition sociale que nous; they move in high ~ circles ils évoluent dans les hautes sphères de la société; ~ benefits prestations *fpl* sociales; ~ class classe *f* sociale; it's ~ death to wear such clothes there *hum* plus personne ne te connaît si tu t'habilles comme ça pour y aller ❑ ~ conscience conscience *f* sociale; ~ order ordre *m* social; ~ outcast paria *m*. -**2.** [in society - activities] mondain; [leisure] de loisir OR loisirs; his life is one mad ~ whirl il mène une vie mondaine insensée. -**3.** [evening, function] amical. -**4.** ZOOL social; ants are ~ insects les fourmis sont une espèce sociale; man is a ~ animal l'homme est un animal social.
◇ *n* soirée *f* (dansante).

social climber *n* arriviste *mf*.

social climbing *n* arrivisme *m*.

social contract *n* contrat *m* social.

social democracy *n* -**1.** [system] social-démocratie *f*. -**2.** [country] démocratie *f* socialiste; we live in a ~ nous vivons dans une démocratie socialiste.

social democrat *n* social-démocrate *mf*.

social democratic *adj* social-démocrate.

Social Democratic and Labour Party *pr n parti travailliste d'Irlande du Nord*.

Social Democratic Party *pr n* Parti *m* social-démocrate.

social disease *n* [gen] maladie *f* provoquée par des facteurs socio-économiques; *euph* [venereal] maladie *f* vénérienne.

social drinker *n*: he's purely a ~ il ne boit pas seul, il boit seulement en société OR en compagnie.

social drinking *n* alcoolisme *m* mondain.

social engineering *n* manipulation *f* des structures sociales.

social fund *n caisse d'aide sociale*.

social insurance *n (U)* prestations *fpl* sociales.

socialism [ˈsəʊʃəlɪzm] *n* socialisme *m*.

socialist [ˈsəʊʃəlɪst] ◇ *adj* socialiste.
◇ *n* socialiste *mf*.

socialistic [ˌsəʊʃəˈlɪstɪk] *adj* socialiste, de nature socialiste.

socialite [ˈsəʊʃəlaɪt] *n* mondain *m*, -e *f*, personne *f* qui fréquente la haute société; she's a famous ~ elle est connue pour fréquenter beaucoup la haute société.

sociality [ˌsəʊʃɪˈælətɪ] *n* socialité *f*.

socialization [ˌsəʊʃəlaɪˈzeɪʃn] *n* POL & PSYCH socialisation *f*.

socialize, -ise [ˈsəʊʃəlaɪz] ◇ *vi* [go out] sortir, fréquenter des gens; [make friends] se faire des amis; to ~ with sb frayer avec qqn; she used to ~ a lot when she was at college elle sortait beaucoup quand elle était étudiante; he finds it difficult to ~ il a du mal à lier connaissance, il est très peu sociable.
◇ *vt* POL & PSYCH socialiser.

socialized medicine [ˈsəʊʃəlaɪzd-] *n esp Am système de sécurité sociale*.

socializing [ˈsəʊʃəlaɪzɪŋ] *n* fait *m* de fréquenter des gens; ~ between teachers and pupils is discouraged les relations entre élèves et professeurs ne sont pas encouragées.

social life *n* vie *f* mondaine; to have a busy ~ [be fashionable] mener une vie très mondaine; [go out often] sortir beaucoup; he doesn't have much of a ~ il ne sort pas beaucoup; there isn't much of a ~ in this town les gens ne sortent pas beaucoup dans cette ville, il ne se passe rien dans cette ville; what's the ~ like here? est-ce que vous sortez beaucoup ici?

socially [ˈsəʊʃəlɪ] *adv* socialement; ~ acceptable behaviour comportement socialement acceptable; we've never met ~ on ne s'est jamais rencontrés en société.

social science *n* sciences *fpl* humaines.

social scientist *n* spécialiste *mf* des sciences humaines.

social security *n* -**1.** [gen] prestations *fpl* sociales; to be on ~ toucher une aide sociale. -**2.** *Br* [money paid to unemployed] ≃ allocations *fpl* de chômage.

social services *npl* services *mpl* sociaux.

social studies *npl* sciences *fpl* sociales.

social work *n* assistance *f* sociale, travail *m* social.

social worker *n* assistant social *m*, assistante sociale *f*, travailleur social *m*, travailleuse sociale *f*.

society [səˈsaɪətɪ] (*pl* societies) ◇ *n* -**1.** [social community] société *f*; it is a danger to ~ cela constitue un danger pour la société; for the good of ~ dans l'intérêt de la société; woman's place in ~ la place de la femme dans la société. -**2.** [nation, group] société *f*; primitive/industrial societies des sociétés primitives/industrielles; Western ~ la société occidentale. -**3.** [fashionable circles]: (high) ~ la haute société, le (beau OR grand) monde; to make one's debut in ~ faire ses débuts dans le monde. -**4.** *lit* [company] société *f*, compagnie *f*; to avoid the ~ of sb éviter la société de qqn; I do not care for their ~ je ne me plais pas en leur compagnie OR en leur société; in polite ~ dans la bonne société OR le (beau) monde. -**5.** [association, club] société *f*, association *f*; [for sports] club *m*, association *f*; SCH & UNIV [for debating, study etc] société *f*; charitable ~ œuvre *f* de charité, association *f* caritative; the Society of Friends la Société des Amis *(les Quakers)*; the Society of Jesus la Société de Jésus.
◇ *comp* [gossip, news, wedding] mondain; the ~

column PRESS la chronique mondaine; a ~ man/woman un homme/une femme du monde.

sociobiology [ˌsəʊsɪəʊbaɪˈɒlədʒɪ] *n* sociobiologie *f.*

sociocultural [ˌsəʊsɪəʊˈkʌltʃərəl] *adj* socioculturel.

socioeconomic [ˈsəʊsɪəʊˌiːkəˈnɒmɪk] *adj* socio-économique.

sociolinguistic [ˌsəʊsɪəʊlɪŋˈgwɪstɪk] *adj* sociolinguistique.

sociolinguistics [ˌsəʊsɪəʊlɪŋˈgwɪstɪks] *n (U)* sociolinguistique *f.*

sociological [ˌsəʊsjəˈlɒdʒɪkl] *adj* sociologique.

sociologist [ˌsəʊsɪˈɒlədʒɪst] *n* sociologue *mf.*

sociology [ˌsəʊsɪˈɒlədʒɪ] *n* sociologie *f.*

sociometric [ˌsəʊsɪəʊˈmetrɪk] *adj* sociométrique.

sociometry [ˌsəʊsɪˈɒmɪtrɪ] *n* sociométrie *f.*

sociopath [ˌsəʊsɪəʊˈpæθ] *n* sociopathe *mf.*

sociopathic [ˌsəʊsɪəʊˈpæθɪk] *adj* sociopathe, sociopathique.

sociopolitical [ˌsəʊsɪəʊpəˈlɪtɪkl] *adj* sociopolitique.

sock [sɒk] ◇ *n* -**1.** [garment] chaussette *f*; (ankle) ~ socquette *f*; to pull one's ~s up *inf* se secouer (les puces); put a ~ in it! *inf Br* la ferme! -**2.** [insole] semelle *f* (intérieure). -**3.** [of horse] paturon *m.* -**4.** AERON & METEOR: (wind) ~ manche *f* à air. -**5.** *inf* [blow] gnon *m*, beigne *f*; I got a ~ on the jaw j'ai pris une beigne.
◇ *adv inf*: the blow caught him ~ in the face il a pris le coup en pleine poire.
◇ *vt inf* [hit] flanquer une beigne à; he ~ed him on the jaw il lui a flanqué un coup de poing à la mâchoire; they ~ed me over the head with a cosh ils m'ont flanqué un coup de matraque sur la tête ❑ ~ it to him!, ~ him one! fous-lui une beigne!, cogne-le!; ~ it to them! [in performance] allez, montrez-leur un peu de quoi vous êtes capables!; ~ it to me then! allez, accouche!
◆ **sock away** *inf vt sep Am* [money] mettre de côté, économiser; to ~ it away remplir son bas de laine.
◆ **sock in** *inf vt sep Am* [airport] fermer *(à cause de mauvaises conditions météorologiques).*

sockdolager *inf*, **sockdologer** *inf* [sɒkˈdɒlədʒəʳ] *n Am* -**1.** [decisive blow] coup *m* décisif. -**2.** [remarkable person] personne *f* extraordinaire; [phenomenon] chose *f* extraordinaire; that was a ~ of a thunderstorm/film! quel orage incroyable/film génial!

socket [ˈsɒkɪt] *n* -**1.** ELEC [for bulb] douille *f*; *Br* [in wall] prise *f* (de courant). -**2.** ESP TECH cavité *f*; [in carpentry] mortaise *f*; it fits into a ~ ça s'emboîte dans un support prévu à cet effet. -**3.** ANAT [of arm, hipbone] cavité *f* articulaire; [of tooth] alvéole *f*; [of eye] orbite *f*; her arm was pulled out of its ~ elle a eu l'épaule luxée; her eyes almost popped OR jumped out of their ~s *fig* les yeux lui en sont presque sortis de la tête.

socket joint *n* -**1.** [in carpentry] joint *m* à rotule. -**2.** ANAT énarthrose *f.*

socket set *n* coffret *m* de douilles.

socket wrench *n* clef *f* à douille.

sockeye [ˈsɒkaɪ] *n* ZOOL saumon *m* rouge.

socking *inf* [ˈsɒkɪŋ] *adv Br* [as intensifier] vachement; he had a ~ great bruise! il avait un de ces bleus!

Socrates [ˈsɒkrətiːz] *pr n* Socrate.

Socratic [sɒˈkrætɪk] *adj* socratique *(inv).*

sod [sɒd] (*pt* & *pp* sodded, *cont* sodding) ◇ *n* -**1.**▽ *Br* [obnoxious person] enfoiré *m*, con *m*; the stupid ~! tu parles d'un enfoiré!; you (rotten) ~! espèce de saligaud!; he's a real ~! c'est un salopard! -**2.** ▽ *Br* [fellow] bougre *m*, con *m*; poor ~ le pauvre con; he's not such a bad old ~ ce n'est pas un mauvais bougre. -**3.** ▽ *Br* [difficult or unpleasant thing] corvée *f*; it's a ~ of a job c'est vraiment chiant comme boulot; these screws are real ~s to get out ces vis sont vraiment emmerdantes OR chiantes à enlever ❑ that's ~'s law c'est la poisse. -**4.** [of turf] motte *f* (de gazon); [earth and grass] terre *f*; [lawn] gazon *m*; the ~ of old Ireland la bonne vieille terre d'Irlande.
◇ *vt* ▽ *Br*: ~ it! merde!; ~ him! qu'il aille se faire foutre!
◇ *interj* ▽ *Br*: ~! merde!
◆ **sod off**▽ *vi insep Br* foutre le camp; ~ off! va te faire foutre!

soda [ˈsəʊdə] *n* -**1.** CHEM soude *f*; caustic ~ soude caustique; washing ~ cristaux *mpl* de soude. -**2.** [sparkling water] eau *f* de Seltz; a whisky and ~ un whisky soda. -**3.** *Am* [soft drink] soda *m.*

soda ash *n* soude *f* du commerce.

soda biscuit *n Br biscuit sec à la levure chimique.*

soda bread *n* pain *m* à la levure chimique.

soda fountain *n Am* -**1.** [café] ≃ café *m*; [counter] buvette *f (où sont servis des sodas).* -**2.** [apparatus] siphon *m* d'eau de Seltz.

soda jerk *inf n Am* serveur *m*, -euse *f (de soda).*

soda lime *n* chaux *f* sodée.

sodality [səˈdælətɪ] (*pl* sodalities) *n* -**1.** *fml* [fellowship] fraternité *f*, camaraderie *f.* -**2.** RELIG [association] confrérie *f.*

sod all▽ *n Br*: he does ~ around the house il n'en fout pas une dans la maison; I'll tell you what you'll get out of him: ~! tu sais ce qu'il te donnera: que dalle!

soda siphon *n* siphon *m* (d'eau de Seltz).

soda water *n* eau *f* de Seltz.

sodden [ˈsɒdn] *adj* [ground] détrempé; [clothes] trempé; to be ~ with drink *fig* être abruti par l'alcool.

sodding▽ [ˈsɒdɪŋ] *Br* ◇ *adj* foutu; I lost my ~ umbrella j'ai perdu ce foutu parapluie.
◇ *adv* vachement; you can ~ well do it yourself! tu n'as qu'à le faire toi-même, merde!

sodium [ˈsəʊdɪəm] *n* sodium *m.*

sodium bicarbonate *n* bicarbonate *m* de soude.

sodium carbonate *n* carbonate *m* de sodium, soude *f.*

sodium chloride *n* chlorure *m* de sodium.

sodium lamp *n* lampe *f* à vapeur de sodium.

sodium sulphate *n* sulfate *m* de sodium.

sodium-vapour lamp = **sodium lamp**.

Sodom [ˈsɒdəm] *pr n*: ~ and Gomorrah Sodome et Gomorrhe.

sodomite [ˈsɒdəmaɪt] *n* sodomite *m.*

sodomize, -ise [ˈsɒdəmaɪz] *vt* sodomiser.

sodomy [ˈsɒdəmɪ] *n* sodomie *f.*

sofa [ˈsəʊfə] *n* sofa *m*, canapé *m.*

sofa bed *n* canapé-lit *m.*

Sofia [ˈsəʊfjə] *pr n* Sofia.

soft [sɒft] ◇ *adj* -**1.** [to touch - skin, hands] doux; [- wool, fur, pillow] doux, moelleux; [- leather] souple; [- material, hair] doux, soyeux; as ~ as velvet/as a baby's bottom doux comme du velours/comme une peau de bébé; to become ~ OR ~er, to get ~ OR ~er [skin] s'adoucir; [leather] s'assouplir; the cream will make your hands/the leather ~ la crème t'adoucira les mains/assouplira le cuir. -**2.** [yielding to pressure - bed, mattress] moelleux; [- collar, ground, snow] mou; [- butter] mou, ramolli; [- muscles, body] ramolli, avachi, flasque; [too yielding - bed, mattress] mou; the butter has gone ~ le beurre s'est ramolli; the mattress will get ~er with wear le matelas deviendra plus moelleux à l'usage; mix to a ~ paste mélanger jusqu'à obtention d'une pâte molle; these chocolates have ~ centres ces chocolats sont mous à l'intérieur; the brakes are ~ *fig* il y a du mou dans les freins; the brakes have gone ~ *fig* il y a du mou dans la pédale de frein; the going is ~ [in horseracing] le terrain est mou ❑ ~ cheese fromage *m* à pâte molle. -**3.** [malleable - metal, wood, stone] tendre; [- pencil] gras, tendre; ~ contact lenses lentilles *fpl* souples. -**4.** [gentle - breeze, rain, words] doux; [- expression, eyes] doux, tendre; [- curve, shadow] doux; [- climate, weather] doux, clément; she suits a ~er hairstyle ce qui lui va bien, c'est une coiffure plus souple; it's a ~ day *Br* il bruine aujourd'hui. -**5.** [quiet, not harsh - voice, music] doux; [- sound, accent] doux, léger; [- tap, cough] petit, léger; [- step] feutré; yes, he said in a ~ whisper/voice oui, murmura-t-il doucement/dit-il d'une voix douce; she gave a ~ laugh elle rit doucement. -**6.** [not bright - colour, glow] doux; [- shade] doux, pastel *(inv)*; [- light] doux, tamisé. -**7.** [blurred - outline] estompé, flou. -**8.** [kind, gentle - person] doux, tendre; [- reply] gentil, aimable; [- glance] doux, gentil; to have a ~ heart avoir le cœur tendre; to have a ~ nature être doux de nature || [lenient] indulgent; you're too ~ with the boy vous êtes trop indulgent avec le garçon; to be ~ on sb se montrer indulgent envers qqn, faire preuve d'indulgence envers qqn; to be ~ on terrorism faire preuve de laxisme envers le terrorisme. -**9.** [weak - physically] mou; the boy's too ~ ce garçon n'a pas de caractère; you're getting ~ tu te ramollis; city life has made you ~ la vie citadine t'a ramolli. -**10.** *inf* [mentally]: he's going ~ in his old age il devient gâteux en vieillissant; you must be ~ in the head! ça va pas, non?; don't be ~ [stop crying] arrête de pleurer; [silly] arrête de dire des bêtises. -**11.** [fond]: to be ~ on sb *inf* avoir le béguin pour qqn; to have a ~ spot for sb avoir un faible pour qqn. -**12.** [easy - life] doux, tranquille, facile; [- job] facile; to have a ~ time of it *inf* se la couler douce; it's the ~ option c'est la solution de facilité; to take the ~ option opter pour la solution de facilité. -**13.** [moderate] modéré; the ~ left POL la gauche modérée; to take a ~ line on sthg adopter une ligne modérée sur qqch; [compromise] adopter une politique de compromis sur qqch. -**14.** ECON & FIN [currency] faible; [market] faible, lourd; ~ terms conditions *fpl* favorables; ~ loan prêt *m* avantageux OR à des conditions avantageuses. -**15.** [water] doux. -**16.** LING [consonant] doux. -**17.** [drug] doux.
◇ *adv* doucement.

softball [ˈsɒftbɔːl] *n Am* -**1.** [game] *sorte de base-ball joué sur un terrain plus petit et avec une balle moins dure.* -**2.** [ball] *balle utilisée au softball (plus grande et plus molle qu'une balle de base-ball).*

soft-boiled [-bɔɪld] *adj*: ~ egg œuf *m* (à la) coque.

softbound [ˈsɒftbaʊnd] = **soft-cover**.

soft-centred *adj* [chocolate, sweet] mou.

soft coal *n* houille *f* grasse.

soft-core *adj* [pornography] soft *(inv).*

soft-cover *adj* broché.

soft drink *n* boisson *f* non alcoolisée.

soften [ˈsɒfn] ◇ *vt* -**1.** [butter, ground] ramollir; [skin, water] adoucir; [fabric, wool, leather] assouplir; a cream to ~ chapped skin une crème pour adoucir les peaux gercées; ~ the paste by kneading it between your fingers ramollir la pâte en la malaxant avec les doigts; centuries of erosion had ~ed the stone des siècles d'érosion avaient rendu la pierre tendre. -**2.** [voice, tone] adoucir, radoucir; [colour, light, sound] adoucir, atténuer; to ~ one's voice [less strident] parler d'une voix plus douce; [quieter] parler moins fort. -**3.** [make less strict] assouplir; he has ~ed his stance on vegetarianism son attitude envers le végétarisme est plus modérée qu'avant. -**4.** [lessen - pain, emotion] soulager, adoucir, atténuer; [- shock, effect, impact] adoucir, amoindrir; [- opposition, resistance] réduire, amoindrir; to ~ the blow *literal* & *fig* amortir le choc.
◇ *vi* -**1.** [butter, ground etc] se ramollir; [skin] s'adoucir; [cloth, wool, leather] s'assouplir. -**2.** [become gentler - eyes, expression, voice] s'adoucir; [- breeze, rain] s'atténuer; [- lighting, colour] s'atténuer, s'adoucir; [- angle, outline] s'adoucir, s'estomper. -**3.** [become friendlier, more receptive]: to ~ towards sb se montrer plus indulgent envers qqn; their attitude towards immigration has ~ed noticeably leur position par rapport à l'immigration est nettement plus tolérante; his face ~ed son expres-

sion se radoucit; her heart ~ed at the sound of his voice elle s'attendrit en entendant sa voix.

◆ **soften up** ◇ *vt sep* -**1.** *inf* [make amenable - gen] attendrir, rendre plus souple; [- by persuasion] amadouer; [- aggressively] intimider; **they tried to ~ us up with champagne lunches** ils ont essayé de nous amadouer à coups de déjeuners au champagne; **they sent in bully boys to ~ the shopkeepers up** ils ont envoyé des gros bras pour intimider les commerçants. -**2.** MIL affaiblir. -**3.** [make softer - butter, ground] ramollir; [- skin] adoucir; [- leather] assouplir.
◇ *vi insep* -**1.** [ground] devenir mou, se ramollir; [butter] se ramollir; [leather] s'assouplir; [skin] s'adoucir. -**2.** [become gentler - person, voice] s'adoucir; **to ~ up on sb** faire preuve de plus d'indulgence envers qqn.

softener ['sɒfnəʳ] *n* -**1.** (water) ~ adoucisseur *m* (d'eau); (fabric) ~ assouplissant *m* (textile). -**2.** *inf* [bribe] pot-de-vin *m*.

softening ['sɒfnɪŋ] *n* [of substance, ground] ramollissement *m*; [of fabric, material] assouplissement *m*, adoucissement *m*; [of attitude, expression, voice] adoucissement *m*; [of colours, contrasts] atténuation *f*; **there has been no ~ of attitude on the part of the management** la direction n'a pas modéré son attitude ❑ **~ of the brain** MED ramollissement *m* cérébral.

soft focus *n* PHOT flou *m* artistique.

soft fruit *n* (*U*) ≃ fruits *mpl* rouges.

soft furnishings *npl Br* tissus *mpl* d'ameublement.

soft goods *npl Br* tissus *mpl*, textiles *mpl*.

soft-headed *inf adj* [weak-minded] faible d'esprit; [silly] bête, idiot.

softhearted [,sɒft'hɑːtɪd] *adj* (au cœur) tendre.

softie *inf* ['sɒftɪ] (*pl* softies) *n* -**1.** [weak] mauviette *f*, mollasson *m*, -onne *f*; [coward] poule *f* mouillée, dégonflé *m*, -e *f*. -**2.** [softhearted] sentimental *m*, -e *f*; **he's just a big ~ really** au fond, c'est un grand sentimental.

soft landing *n* atterrissage *m* en douceur.

softly ['sɒftlɪ] *adv* -**1.** [quietly - breathe, say, sing, whisper] doucement; [- move, walk] à pas feutrés, (tout) doucement. -**2.** [gently - blow, touch] doucement, légèrement. -**3.** [fondly - smile, look] tendrement, avec tendresse.

softly-softly *Br* ◇ *adv* tout doucement, avec prudence.
◇ *adj* prudent; **try a ~ approach** allez-y doucement.

softness ['sɒftnɪs] *n* -**1.** [to touch - of skin, hands, hair] douceur *f*; [- of fabric, wool, fur, pillow] douceur *f*, moelleux *m*; [- of leather] souplesse *f*. -**2.** [to pressure - of bed, ground, snow, butter] mollesse *f*; [- of collar] souplesse *f*; [- of wood] tendreté *f*. -**3.** [gentleness - of breeze, weather, voice, music] douceur *f*; [- of expression, manner] douceur *f*, gentillesse *f*; [- of eyes, light, colour] douceur *f*; [- of outline, curve] flou *m*, douceur *f*. -**4.** [kindness - of person] douceur *f*; [- of heart] tendresse *f*; [indulgence] indulgence *f*. -**5.** [weakness - of character, person] mollesse *f*. -**6.** [easiness - of life] douceur *f*; [- of job] facilité *f*. -**7.** *inf* [silliness] niaiserie *f*, stupidité *f*.

soft palate *n* voile *m* du palais.

soft pedal (*Br pt & pp* **soft-pedalled**, *cont* **soft-pedalling**, *Am pt & pp* **soft-pedaled**, *cont* **soft-pedaling**) *n* [on piano] pédale *f* douce, sourdine *f*.
◆ **soft-pedal** ◇ *vi* -**1.** MUS mettre la sourdine. -**2.** *fig*: **to ~ on reforms/negotiations** ralentir le rythme des réformes/négociations.
◇ *vt fig* glisser sur, atténuer.

soft porn *n* porno *m* soft.

soft science *n*: **the ~s** ≃ les sciences *fpl* humaines.

soft sell *n* COMM *méthodes de vente non agressives*; **she has a flair for the ~** elle a le don de OR pour circonvenir ses clients.

soft-shell crab *n* crabe *m* à carapace molle.

soft-shelled turtle *n* tortue *f* à carapace molle.

soft shoulder = **soft verge**.

soft soap *n* -**1.** MED savon *m* vert. -**2.** (*U*) *inf* [flattery] flagornerie *f*, flatterie *f*, flatteries *fpl*.
◆ **soft-soap** *vt* passer de la pommade à.

soft-spoken *adj* à la voix douce.

soft top *inf n* AUT (voiture *f*) décapotable *f*.

soft touch *inf n Br* pigeon *m*; **he's a real ~** [easily fooled] il se laisse berner facilement; [for money] il se laisse avoir OR rouler facilement.

soft toy *n* (jouet *m* en) peluche *f*.

soft verge *n* [on road] accotement *m* non stabilisé.

software ['sɒftweəʳ] ◇ *n* COMPUT logiciel *m*, software *m*.
◇ *comp*: **~ house** société *f* de services et de conseils en informatique; **~ package** progiciel *m*.

softwood ['sɒftwʊd] *n* bois *m* tendre.

softy *inf* ['sɒftɪ] = **softie**.

soggy ['sɒgɪ] (*compar* **soggier**, *superl* **soggiest**) *adj* [ground] détrempé, imbibé d'eau; [clothes] trempé; [bread, cake] mou; [rice] trop cuit, collant; **the ground is ~ underfoot** on s'enfonce dans le sol détrempé; **my shoes are all ~** mes chaussures sont trempées.

soh [səʊ] *n* MUS sol *m*.

Soho ['səʊhəʊ] *pr n quartier chaud de Londres connu pour ses restaurants*.

soil [sɔɪl] ◇ *n* -**1.** [earth] terre *f*; **to work the ~** travailler la terre. -**2.** [type of earth] terre *f*, sol *m*; **good farming ~** de la bonne terre agricole; **sandy/clay ~s** sols sablonneux/argileux, terres sablonneuses/argileuses. -**3.** *fig* [land] terre *f*, sol *m*; **his native ~** sa terre natale; **on Irish ~** sur le sol irlandais. -**4.** (*U*) [excrement] excréments *mpl*, ordures *fpl*; [sewage] vidange *f*.
◇ *vt* -**1.** [dirty - clothes, linen, paper] salir; *fig & lit* souiller; **she refused to ~ her hands with such work** elle a refusé de se salir les mains avec ce genre de travail. -**2.** *fig* [reputation] salir, souiller, entacher.
◇ *vi* [clothes, material] se salir; **these covers ~ easily** ces housses sont salissantes.

soiled [sɔɪld] *adj* [dressings] usagé; [bedlinen] souillé; [goods] défraîchi.

soil pipe *n* tuyau *m* de vidange.

sojourn ['sɒdʒɜːn] *lit* ◇ *n* séjour *m*.
◇ *vi* séjourner.

solace ['sɒləs] *lit* ◇ *n* consolation *f*, réconfort *m*; **he found ~ in religion** il a trouvé un réconfort dans la religion.
◇ *vt* [person] consoler, réconforter; [pain, suffering] soulager.

solar ['səʊləʳ] *adj* -**1.** [of, concerning the sun - heat, radiation] solaire, du soleil; [- cycle, year] solaire; **~ eclipse** éclipse *f* solaire. -**2.** [operated by the sun, using the sun's power - energy, heating] solaire; **~ battery** batterie *f* solaire.

solar cell *n* pile *f* solaire, photopile *f*.

solar flare *n* éruption *f* solaire.

solar furnace *n* four *m* solaire.

solarium [sə'leərɪəm] *n* solarium *m*.

solar panel *n* panneau *m* solaire.

solar plexus *n* plexus *m* solaire.

solar power *n* énergie *f* solaire.

solar-powered [-'paʊəd] *adj* à énergie solaire.

solar system *n* système *m* solaire.

sold [səʊld] ◇ *pt & pp* → **sell**.
◇ *adj* -**1.** COMM vendu. -**2.** *inf fig*: **to be ~ on sb/sthg** être emballé par qqn/qqch; **he's really ~ on her** il est vraiment entiché OR toqué d'elle; **she's ~ on the new plan** elle est complètement emballée par le nouveau projet.
◆ **sold out** *adj phr* -**1.** [goods] épuisé; '**~ out**' [for play, concert] 'complet'; **the concert was completely ~ out** tous les billets pour le concert ont été vendus. -**2.** [stockist]: **we're ~ out of bread** nous avons vendu tout le pain, il ne reste plus de pain.

solder ['sɒldəʳ] ◇ *vt* souder; **to ~ a wire to a contact** souder un fil à un plot.
◇ *n* soudure *f*, métal *m* d'apport; **brazing ~** soudure au laiton, brasure *f*; **soft ~** soudure à l'étain, brasure *f* tendre.

soldering iron ['sɒldərɪŋ-] *n* fer *m* à souder.

soldier ['səʊldʒəʳ] ◇ *n* -**1.** soldat *m*, militaire *m*; **to become a ~** se faire soldat, entrer dans l'armée; **to play (at) ~s** [children] jouer aux soldats OR à la guerre; *pej* [country, adults] jouer à la guerre OR à la guéguerre ❑ **~ of Christ** soldat du Christ; **~ of fortune** soldat de fortune; **old ~** MIL vétéran *m*; **don't play** OR **come** *inf* **the old ~ with me** ne prenez pas de grands airs avec moi. -**2.** ENTOM soldat *m*.
◇ *vi* être soldat, servir dans l'armée.
◆ **soldier on** *vi insep Br* continuer OR persévérer (malgré tout); **despite the freezing conditions they ~ed on** ils ont persévéré en dépit d'un froid glacial.

soldier ant *n* (fourmi *f*) soldat *m*.

soldiering ['səʊldʒərɪŋ] *n* carrière *f* OR vie *f* (de) militaire; **to go ~** partir à l'armée OR à la guerre; **their love of ~** leur amour de la vie militaire; **after many years' ~** après avoir servi pendant de nombreuses années dans l'armée.

soldierly ['səʊldʒəlɪ] *adj* [act, behaviour] de soldat; [appearance, manner, bearing] militaire.

soldiery ['səʊldʒərɪ] *n* -**1.** [soldiers collectively] soldats *mpl*, militaires *mpl*. -**2.** [profession] métier *m* de soldat.

sole [səʊl] (*pl sense 3 inv* OR **soles**) ◇ *adj* -**1.** [only] seul, unique; **the ~ survivor** le seul survivant. -**2.** [exclusive] exclusif; **to have ~ rights on sthg** avoir l'exclusivité des droits sur qqch; **to have ~ responsibility for sthg** être entièrement responsable de qqch ❑ **~ agent** COMM concessionnaire *mf*; **~ legatee** JUR légataire *m* universel , légataire *f* universelle .
◇ *n* -**1.** [of foot] plante *f*. -**2.** [of shoe, sock] semelle *f*. -**3.** [fish] sole *f*.
◇ *vt* ressemeler; **to have one's shoes ~d** faire ressemeler ses chaussures.

solecism ['sɒlɪsɪzm] *n* -**1.** GRAMM solécisme *m*. -**2.** *fml* [violation of good manners] manque *m* de savoir-vivre.

-soled [səʊld] *in cpds* à semelle de; **rubber~ shoes** chaussures *fpl* à semelles de caoutchouc.

solely ['səʊllɪ] *adv* -**1.** [only] seulement, uniquement. -**2.** [entirely] entièrement; **to be ~ responsible for sthg** être entièrement responsable de qqch.

solemn ['sɒləm] *adj* -**1.** [grave, serious] sérieux, grave, solennel; **a ~ face** un visage grave OR solennel ‖ [sombre] sobre; **a ~ grey suit** un costume gris sobre. -**2.** [formal - agreement, promise] solennel; **a ~ oath** un serment solennel. -**3.** [grand - occasion, music] solennel; **~ mass** grand-messe *f*, messe *f* solennelle.

solemnify [sə'lemnɪfaɪ] (*pt & pp* **solemnified**) *vt* rendre solennel OR sérieux.

solemnity [sə'lemnətɪ] (*pl* **solemnities**) *n* -**1.** [serious nature] sérieux *m*, gravité *f*. -**2.** [formality] solennité *f*; **she was received with great ~** elle fut accueillie en grande solennité OR très solennellement. -**3.** (*usu pl*) *lit* [solemn event] solennité *f*; **the Easter solemnities** les solennités de Pâques.

solemnization [,sɒləmnaɪ'zeɪʃn] *n lit* [gen] solennisation *f lit*; [of marriage] célébration *f*.

solemnize, -ise ['sɒləmnaɪz] *vt lit* [gen] solenniser *lit*; [marriage] célébrer.

solemnly ['sɒləmlɪ] *adv* -**1.** [seriously, gravely] gravement, solennellement; **"it's time I left", he said ~** «il est temps que je parte», dit-il d'un ton grave; **she ~ believes that what she did was right** elle croit fermement que ce qu'elle a fait était juste. -**2.** [formally] solennellement; **they ~ swore to avenge their brother's death** ils jurèrent solennellement de venger la mort de leur frère. -**3.** [grandly] solennellement, avec solennité.

solenoid ['səʊlɪnɔɪd] *n* solénoïde *m*.

sol-fa [,sɒl'fɑː] *n* solfège *m*.

solfeggio [sɒl'fedʒɪəʊ] (*pl* **solfeggios** OR **solfeggi** [-dʒɪ]) *n* solfège *m*.

solicit [sə'lɪsɪt] ◇ *vt* -**1.** [business, support, information] solliciter; [opinion] demander. -**2.** [subj: prostitute] racoler.
◇ *vi* [prostitute] racoler.

solicitation [səˌlɪsɪ'teɪʃn] *n* sollicitation *f*.

soliciting [sə'lɪsɪtɪŋ] *n* [by prostitute] racolage *m*.

solicitor [sə'lɪsɪtə[r]] *n* -**1.** *Br* JUR ≃ avocat *m*, -e *f*, ≃ conseil *m* juridique. -**2.** *Am* ADMIN conseil *m* juridique d'une municipalité. -**3.** [person who solicits] solliciteur *m*, -euse *f*; 'caution, unofficial **~s**' *Am* attention aux démarcheurs non autorisés.

solicitor general (*pl* solicitors general OR solicitor generals) *n* -**1.** [in UK] conseil *m* (juridique de la Couronne). -**2.** [in US] représentant *m* du gouvernement *(auprès de la Cour suprême)*.

solicitous [sə'lɪsɪtəs] *adj* [showing consideration, concern] plein de sollicitude; [eager, attentive] empressé; [anxious] soucieux; **he was most ~ about your future happiness** il était extrêmement soucieux de votre avenir et de votre bonheur.

solicitously [sə'lɪsɪtəslɪ] *adv* [with consideration, concern] avec sollicitude; [eagerly, attentively] avec empressement; [anxiously] avec inquiétude.

solicitude [sə'lɪsɪtjuːd] *n* [consideration, concern] sollicitude *f*; [eagerness, attentiveness] empressement *m*; [anxiety] souci *m*, préoccupation *f*.

solid ['sɒlɪd] ◇ *adj* -**1.** [not liquid or gas] solide; **a ~ body** un corps solide; **frozen ~** complètement gelé; **the fat had set ~** la graisse était complètement figée; **she can't eat ~ food** elle ne peut pas absorber d'aliments solides. -**2.** [of one substance] massif; **her necklace is ~ gold** son collier est en or massif; **~ oak furniture** meubles *mpl* en chêne massif; **they dug until they reached ~ rock** ils ont creusé jusqu'à ce qu'ils atteignent la roche compacte; **caves hollowed out of ~ rock** des grottes creusées à même la roche. -**3.** [not hollow] plein; **~ tyres** pneus pleins. -**4.** [unbroken, continuous] continu; **a ~ yellow line** une ligne jaune continue; **I worked for eight ~ hours** OR **eight hours ~** j'ai travaillé sans arrêt pendant huit heures, j'ai travaillé huit heures d'affilée; **we had two ~ weeks of rain** nous avons eu deux semaines de pluie ininterrompue; **~ compound** GRAMM composé *m* écrit en un seul mot. -**5.** *Am* [of one colour] uni; **the walls were painted a ~ green** les murs étaient peints en vert uni. -**6.** [dense, compact] dense, compact; **knead it until it forms a ~ mass** travailler jusqu'à ce que cela forme une masse compacte; **the streets were a ~ mass of people** les rues étaient noires de monde; **the concert hall was packed ~** la salle de concert était bondée. -**7.** [powerful - blow] puissant; **I gave him a ~ punch to the jaw** je lui ai assené un violent coup de poing sur la mâchoire. -**8.** [sturdy, sound - structure, understanding, relationship] solide; [- evidence, argument] solide, irréfutable; [- advice] valable, sûr; **a man of ~ build** un homme bien charpenté; **their marriage was never ~** leur mariage n'a jamais été très solide; **I have very ~ reasons for believing the opposite** j'ai de solides raisons de croire le contraire; **we need somebody with some ~ experience in the field** nous avons besoin de quelqu'un qui possède une solide expérience de travail sur le terrain; **he's a good ~ worker** c'est un bon travailleur ❑ **to be on ~ ground** *literal* être sur la terre ferme; *fig* être en terrain sûr. -**9.** [respectable, worthy] respectable, honorable; **the ~ citizens of this town** les respectables citoyens de cette ville. -**10.** POL [firm] massif; [unanimous] unanime; **we have the ~ support of the electorate** nous avons le soutien massif des électeurs; **the south is ~ for the Christian Democrats** le sud soutient massivement les démocrates-chrétiens; **the strike was 100% ~** la grève était totale; **the committee was ~ against the proposal** le comité a rejeté la proposition à l'unanimité. -**11.** MATH: **~ figure** solide *m*.
◇ *n* GEOM & PHYS solide *m*.
◆ **solids** *npl* -**1.** [solid food] aliments *mpl* solides; **I can't eat ~s** je ne peux pas absorber d'aliments solides. -**2.** CHEM particules *fpl* solides; **milk ~s** extrait *m* du lait.

solid angle *n* MATH angle *m* solide.

solidarity [ˌsɒlɪ'dærətɪ] ◇ *n* solidarité *f*; **they went on strike in ~ with the miners** ils ont fait grève par solidarité avec les mineurs.
◇ *comp* [strike] de solidarité.

solid fuel *n* combustible *m* solide.
◆ **solid-fuel** *adj* à combustible solide; **a solid-fuel heating system** un chauffage à combustibles solides.

solid geometry *n* MATH géométrie *f* des solides.

solidification [səˌlɪdɪfɪ'keɪʃn] *n* solidification *f*.

solidify [sə'lɪdɪfaɪ] (*pt* & *pp* **solidified**)
◇ *vi* -**1.** [liquid, gas] se solidifier. -**2.** [system, opinion] se consolider.
◇ *vt* -**1.** [liquid, gas] solidifier. -**2.** [system, opinion] consolider.

solidity [sə'lɪdətɪ] *n* solidité *f*.

solidly ['sɒlɪdlɪ] *adv* -**1.** [sturdily] solidement; **the town hall stands ~ in the middle of the square** la mairie est solidement plantée au milieu de la place ‖ [person]: **to be ~ built** avoir une forte carrure. -**2.** [thoroughly] très, tout à fait; **a ~ established reputation** une réputation solidement établie. -**3.** [massively] massivement, en masse; **Massachusetts voted ~ for the Democrats** l'État du Massachussetts a voté massivement OR en masse pour les démocrates. -**4.** [continuously] sans arrêt; **I worked ~ for five hours** j'ai travaillé sans interruption pendant cinq heures.

solid-state *adj* -**1.** PHYS des solides. -**2.** ELECTRON à semi-conducteurs.

solidus ['sɒlɪdəs] (*pl* **solidi** [-daɪ]) *n* TYPO barre *f* oblique.

soliloquize, -ise [sə'lɪləkwaɪz] *vi* soliloquer, monologuer.

soliloquy [sə'lɪləkwɪ] (*pl* **soliloquies**) *n* soliloque *m*, monologue *m*.

solipsism ['sɒlɪpsɪzm] *n* solipsisme *m*.

solipsistic [ˌsɒlɪp'sɪstɪk] *adj* solipsiste.

solitaire [ˌsɒlɪ'teə[r]] *n* -**1.** [pegboard] solitaire *m*. -**2.** *Am* [card game] réussite *f*, patience *f*; **to play ~** faire des réussites OR des patiences. -**3.** [gem] solitaire *m*.

solitary ['sɒlɪtrɪ] (*pl* **solitaries**) ◇ *adj* -**1.** [alone - person, life, activity] solitaire; **she had a ~ childhood** elle a eu une enfance solitaire. -**2.** [single] seul, unique; **a ~ tree on the horizon** un seul arbre à l'horizon; **can you give me one ~ reason why I should go?** peux-tu me donner une seule raison d'y aller? -**3.** [remote - place] retiré, isolé. -**4.** [empty of people] vide, désert; **the ~ streets of the suburbs** les rues désertes de la banlieue.
◇ *n* -**1.** *inf* = **solitary confinement**. -**2.** [person] solitaire *mf*.

solitary confinement *n* isolement *m (d'un prisonnier)*.

solitude ['sɒlɪtjuːd] *n* solitude *f*; **to live in ~** vivre dans la solitude.

solo ['səʊləʊ] (*pl* **solos**) ◇ *n* -**1.** MUS solo *m*; **he played a violin/drum ~** il a joué un solo de violon/de batterie. -**2.** [flight] vol *m* solo. -**3.** = **solo whist**.
◇ *adj* -**1.** MUS solo; **she plays ~ violin** elle est soliste de violon, elle est violon solo. -**2.** [gen] en solitaire; **the first ~ attempt on the north face** la première tentative d'escalade de la face nord en solitaire; **her first ~ flight** son premier vol en solo.
◇ *adv* -**1.** MUS en solo; **to play/to sing ~** jouer/chanter en solo. -**2.** [gen] seul, en solitaire, en solo; **to fly ~** voler en solo.

soloist ['səʊləʊɪst] *n* soliste *mf*.

Solomon ['sɒləmən] *pr n* Salomon.

Solomon Islander *n* Salomonien *m*, -enne *f*.

Solomon Islands *pl pr n*: **the ~** les îles *fpl* Salomon; **in the ~** dans les îles Salomon.

Solothurn ['sɒləˌθɜːn] *pr n* Soleure; **in ~** en Soleure.

solo whist *n* solo *m (variante du whist)*.

solstice ['sɒlstɪs] *n* solstice *m*; **the summer/winter ~** le solstice d'été/d'hiver.

solubility [ˌsɒljʊ'bɪlətɪ] *n* solubilité *f*.

solubilize, -ise ['sɒljʊbɪlaɪz] *vt* solubiliser.

soluble ['sɒljʊbl] *adj* -**1.** [substance] soluble. -**2.** [problem] soluble.

solute ['sɒljuːt] *n* soluté *m*, corps *m* dissous.

solution [sə'luːʃn] *n* -**1.** [answer - to problem, equation, mystery] solution *f*; **a political ~ to the conflict** une solution politique au conflit. -**2.** [act of solving - of problem, equation, mystery] résolution *f*; **our main aim should be the rapid ~ of the problem** notre principal objectif devrait être de résoudre rapidement le problème. -**3.** CHEM & PHARM solution *f*; **salt in ~** sel en solution.

solvable ['sɒlvəbl] *adj* soluble.

solve [sɒlv] *vt* [equation] résoudre; [problem] résoudre, trouver la solution de; [crime, mystery] élucider; **I couldn't ~ a single clue in the Times crossword** je n'ai pas réussi à trouver une seule définition dans les mots croisés du Times.

solvency ['sɒlvənsɪ] *n* solvabilité *f*.

solvent ['sɒlvənt] ◇ *adj* -**1.** [financially] solvable. -**2.** [substance, liquid] dissolvant.
◇ *n* solvant *m*, dissolvant *m*.

solvent abuse *n fml* usage *m* de solvants hallucinogènes.

Solzhenitsyn [ˌsɒlʒə'nɪtsɪn] *pr n* Soljenitsyne.

Som. *written abbr of* Somerset.

soma ['səʊmə] (*pl* **somas** OR **somata** [-mətə]) *n* soma *m*.

Somali [sə'mɑːlɪ] ◇ *n* -**1.** [person] Somalien *m*, -enne *f*. -**2.** LING somali *m*.
◇ *adj* somalien.

Somalia [sə'mɑːlɪə] *pr n* Somalie *f*; **in ~** en Somalie.

Somalian [sə'mɑːlɪən] = **Somali**.

Somali Democratic Republic *pr n*: **the ~** la République démocratique de Somalie.

Somaliland [sə'mɑːlɪlænd] *pr n* Somalie *f*; **British/Italian ~** Somalie britannique/italienne.

somatic [sə'mætɪk] *adj* somatique.

somatology [ˌsəʊmə'tɒlədʒɪ] *n* somatologie *f*.

somber *etc Am* = **sombre**.

sombre *Br*, **somber** *Am* ['sɒmbə[r]] *adj* -**1.** [dark - colour, place] sombre. -**2.** [grave, grim - outlook, person, day] sombre, morne; **what are you looking so ~ about?** pourquoi cet air si sombre?; **a ~ episode in the history of Europe** un épisode sombre dans l'histoire de l'Europe.

sombrely *Br*, **somberly** *Am* ['sɒmbəlɪ] *adv* sombrement.

sombreness *Br*, **somberness** *Am* ['sɒmbənɪs] *n* -**1.** [darkness] obscurité *f*; **the ~ of the colours** les couleurs sombres. -**2.** [graveness, grimness] gravité *f*, caractère *m* sombre; **the news was announced with great ~** on annonça la nouvelle avec beaucoup de gravité.

sombrero [sɒm'breərəʊ] (*pl* **sombreros**) *n* sombrero *m*.

some [sʌm] ◇ *det* -**1.** [a quantity of] *(before uncountable nouns)*: **don't forget to buy ~ cheese/beer/garlic** n'oublie pas d'acheter du fromage/de la bière/de l'ail; **let me give you ~ advice** laissez-moi vous donner un conseil ‖ [a number of] *(before plural nouns)* des; **we've invited ~ friends round** nous avons invité des amis à la maison; **I met ~ old friends last night** j'ai rencontré de vieux amis hier soir. -**2.** [not all] *(before uncountable nouns)*: **~ wine/software is very expensive** certains vins/logiciels coûtent très cher; **~ petrol still contains lead** il existe encore de l'essence avec plomb ‖ *(before plural nouns)* certains *mpl*, certaines *fpl*; **~ English people like frogs' legs** certains Anglais aiment les cuisses de grenouille; **~ cars shouldn't be allowed on the road** il y a des voitures qu'on ne devrait pas laisser circuler; **~ employees like the new system, others don't** certains employés aiment le nouveau système, d'autres pas. -**3.** [a fairly large amount of] *(before uncountable nouns)* un certain *m*, une certaine *f*; **I haven't been abroad for ~ time** ça fait un certain temps que je ne suis pas allé à l'étranger; it happened (quite) ~ time ago ça s'est passé il y a (bien) longtemps; it's ~ distance from here c'est assez loin d'ici; the money should go ~ way towards compensating them l'argent devrait les dédommager dans une certaine mesure; not without ~ opposition non sans rencontrer une certaine opposition || [a fairly large number of] *(before plural nouns)* certains *mpl*, certaines *fpl*, quelques *mfpl*; it happened ~ years ago ça s'est passé il y a quelques années. -**4.** [a fairly small amount of] *(before uncountable nouns)* un peu de; you might have shown ~ gratitude! tu aurais pu faire preuve d'un peu de gratitude (,quand même)!; you must have ~ idea of how much it will cost vous devez avoir une petite idée de combien ça va coûter; I hope I've been of ~ help to you j'espère que je vous ai un peu aidé || [a fairly small number of] *(before plural nouns)*: I'm glad ~ people understand me! je suis content qu'il y ait quand même des gens qui me comprennent! -**5.** [not known or specified]: we must find ~ alternative il faut que nous trouvions une autre solution; he's gone to ~ town in the north il est parti dans une ville quelque part dans le nord; she works for ~ publishing company elle travaille pour je ne sais quelle maison d'édition; I'll get even with them ~ day! je me vengerai d'eux un de ces jours OR un jour ou l'autre!; come back ~ other time revenez un autre jour. -**6.** *inf* [expressing scorn]: did you go to the party? – ~ party! est-ce que tu es allé à la fête? – tu parles d'une fête!; ~ hope we've got of winning! comme si on avait la moindre chance de gagner! || [expressing irritation, impatience]: ~ people! il y a des gens, je vous assure! -**7.** *inf* [expressing admiration, approval]: that was ~ party! ça c'était une fête!; he's ~ tennis player! c'est un sacré tennisman!

◇ *pron* -**1.** [an unspecified number or amount - as subject] quelques-uns *mpl*, quelques-unes *fpl*, certains *mpl*, certaines *fpl*; ~ are plain and ~ OR others are patterned certains sont unis et certains OR d'autres ont des motifs; ~ say it wasn't an accident certains disent OR il y a des gens qui disent que ce n'était pas un accident || [as object] en; I've got too much cake, do you want ~? j'ai trop de gâteau, en voulez-vous un peu?; can I have ~ more? est-ce que je peux en reprendre?; where are the envelopes? – there are ~ in my drawer où sont les enveloppes? – il y en a dans mon tiroir ❑ he wants the lot and then ~ il veut tout et puis le reste. -**2.** [not all]: ~ of the snow had melted une partie de la neige avait fondu; I only believe ~ of what I read in the papers je ne crois pas tout ce que je lis dans les journaux; ~ of the most beautiful scenery in the world is in Australia quelques-uns des plus beaux paysages du monde se trouvent en Australie; I've seen ~ of her films j'ai vu quelques-uns OR certains de ses films; ~ of us/them certains d'entre nous/eux; if you need pencils, take ~ of these/mine si vous avez besoin de crayons à papier, prenez quelques-uns de ceux-ci/des miens; do you want ~ or all of them? en voulez-vous quelques-uns ou les voulez-vous tous?

◇ *adv* -**1.** [approximately] quelque, environ; it's ~ fifty kilometres from London c'est à environ cinquante kilomètres OR c'est à une cinquantaine de kilomètres de Londres; ~ 500 people quelque 500 personnes. -**2.** *inf Am* [a little] un peu; [a lot] beaucoup, pas mal; I need to rest up ~ j'ai besoin de me reposer un peu; admit it, you like her ~! avoue-le, tu l'aimes bien!

somebody ['sʌmbədɪ] *pron* -**1.** [an unspecified person] quelqu'un; I'm busy, ask ~ else je suis occupé, demande à quelqu'un d'autre; ~ big/small quelqu'un de grand/de petit; they're looking for ~ with a lot of experience ils cherchent quelqu'un qui ait beaucoup d'expérience; there's ~ on the phone for you on vous demande au téléphone; ~'s at the door, there's ~ at the door on a frappé; ~ in the crowd/from head office quelqu'un dans la foule/à la direction; ~ has left their OR his OR her umbrella behind quelqu'un a oublié son parapluie; ~ or other quelqu'un, je ne sais qui. -**2.** [an important person]: you really think you're ~, don't you? tu te crois vraiment quelqu'un, n'est-ce pas?

someday ['sʌmdeɪ] *adv* un jour (ou l'autre), un de ces jours; ~ we'll go to the Bahamas un jour (ou l'autre), nous irons aux Bahamas.

somehow ['sʌmhaʊ] *adv* -**1.** [in some way or another] d'une manière ou d'une autre, d'une façon ou d'une autre; don't worry, we'll manage ~ (or other) ne t'inquiète pas, nous nous débrouillerons d'une façon ou d'une autre; she'd ~ (or other) managed to lock himself in elle avait trouvé moyen de s'enfermer. -**2.** [for some reason] pour une raison ou pour une autre, je ne sais pas trop pourquoi; ~ I'm not surprised he didn't come je ne sais pas trop pourquoi, mais cela ne m'étonne pas qu'il ne soit pas venu; it ~ doesn't look right je ne sais pas pourquoi mais il me semble qu'il y a quelque chose qui ne va pas.

someone ['sʌmwʌn] = **somebody**.

someplace ['sʌmpleɪs] *Am* = **somewhere 1**.

somersault ['sʌməsɔːlt] ◇ *n* [roll] culbute *f*; [by car] tonneau *m*; [acrobatic feat - in air] saut *m* périlleux; to do OR to turn ~s faire des culbutes.

◇ *vi* faire la culbute OR un saut périlleux OR des sauts périlleux; [car] faire un tonneau OR des tonneaux.

Somerset House ['sʌməset-] *pr n édifice sur le Strand à Londres.*

SOMERSET HOUSE:
Dans cet édifice du XVIIIe siècle se trouvaient autrefois l'état civil, les impôts et d'autres administrations.

---

something ['sʌmθɪŋ] ◇ *pron* -**1.** [an unspecified object, event, action etc] quelque chose; there must be ~ going on il doit se passer quelque chose; I've got ~ in my eye j'ai quelque chose dans l'œil; ~ flashed past the window une lumière est passée devant la fenêtre; I've thought of ~ j'ai eu une idée; don't just stand there, do ~! ne reste pas là, fais quelque chose!; ~ else quelque chose d'autre, autre chose; ~ or other quelque chose; ~ big/small quelque chose de grand/de petit; I've done/said ~ stupid j'ai fait/dit une bêtise; I've got a feeling there's ~ wrong j'ai le sentiment que quelque chose ne va pas; there's ~ wrong with the ship's computer l'ordinateur de bord ne marche pas bien; take ~ to read on the train prenez quelque chose à lire OR prenez de quoi lire dans le train; he gave them ~ to eat/drink il leur a donné à manger/boire; would you like ~ to eat? voulez-vous manger quelque chose?; a film with ~ for everybody un film qui peut plaire à tout le monde; they all want ~ for nothing ils veulent tous avoir tout pour rien; you can't get ~ for nothing on n'a rien pour rien; there's ~ about him/in the way he talks that reminds me of Gary il y a quelque chose chez lui/dans sa façon de parler qui me rappelle Gary; there must be ~ in OR to all these rumours il doit y avoir quelque chose de vrai dans toutes ces rumeurs; she's ~ in the City/in insurance elle travaille dans la finance/dans les assurances ❑ would you like a little ~ to drink? voulez-vous un petit quelque chose à boire?; she slipped the head waiter a little ~ elle a glissé un petit pourboire au maître d'hôtel; that new singer has got ~ ce nouveau chanteur n'est pas mal; he's got a certain ~ il a un petit quelque chose; I'm sure she's got ~ going with him *inf* je suis sûr qu'il y a quelque chose entre elle et lui; I think you've got ~ there! je crois que vous avez un début d'idée, là!; at least they've replied to my letter, that's ~ au moins, ils ont répondu à ma lettre, c'est mieux que rien OR c'est toujours ça; wow, that's ~ else! *inf* ça, c'est génial!; well, isn't that ~? *inf* et bien, ça alors!; it was really ~ to see those kids dancing! c'était quelque chose de voir ces gosses danser!; the new model is really ~ *inf* le nouveau modèle est sensationnel. -**2.** *inf* [in approximations]: the battle took place in 1840 ~ la bataille a eu lieu dans les années 1840; he's forty ~ il a dans les quarante ans; it cost £7 ~ ça a coûté 7 livres et quelques || [replacing forgotten word, name etc]: her friend, Maisie ~ (or other) son amie, Maisie quelque chose. -**3.** *phr*: ~ of: he's ~ of an expert in the field c'est en quelque sorte un expert dans ce domaine; she became ~ of a legend elle est devenue une sorte de légende; how they do it remains ~ of a mystery comment ils s'y prennent, ça c'est un mystère; to be OR have ~ to do with avoir un rapport avec; her job is OR has ~ to do with the Stock Exchange son travail a un rapport avec la Bourse; I don't know what it means, I think it's got ~ to do with nuclear physics je ne sais pas ce que ça veut dire, je crois que ça a (quelque chose) à voir avec la physique nucléaire; I'm sure the weather has ~ to do with it je suis sûre que le temps y est pour quelque chose OR que ça a un rapport avec le temps.

◇ *adv* -**1.** [a little] un peu; ~ over a month's salary un peu plus d'un mois de salaire; temperatures were ~ under what we expected les températures étaient un peu en-dessous de ce que nous attendions || [somewhere]: ~ in the region of $10,000 quelque chose comme 10 000 dollars; an increase of ~ between 10 and 15 per cent une augmentation de 10 à 15 pour cent. -**2.** *inf* [as intensifier] vraiment, vachement; it hurts ~ awful *inf* ça fait vachement mal.

◆ **or something** *inf adv phr*: would you like a cup of tea or ~? veux-tu une tasse de thé, ou autre chose?; she must be ill or ~ elle doit être malade ou quelque chose dans ce genre-là; I thought they were engaged or ~ je croyais qu'ils étaient fiancés ou quelque chose comme ça; are you deaf or ~? tu es sourd ou quoi?

◆ **something like** *prep phr* -**1.** [rather similar to]: it looks ~ like a grapefruit ça ressemble un peu à un pamplemousse ❑ now that's ~ like it! c'est déjà mieux! -**2.** [roughly] environ; it's ~ like 5 metres long/wide ça fait quelque chose comme 5 mètres de long/large; it costs ~ like £500 ça coûte quelque chose comme OR dans les 500 livres.

sometime ['sʌmtaɪm] ◇ *adv* -**1.** [in future] un jour (ou l'autre), un de ces jours; you must come and see us ~ il faut que vous veniez nous voir un de ces jours; I hope we'll meet again ~ soon j'espère que nous nous reverrons bientôt; you'll have to face up to it ~ or other un jour ou l'autre il faudra bien voir les choses en face; her baby is due ~ in May elle attend son bébé pour le mois de mai; ~ before/after next April après le mois/d'ici au mois d'avril; ~ next year dans le courant de l'année prochaine. -**2.** [in past]: she phoned ~ last week elle a téléphoné (dans le courant de) la semaine dernière; it happened ~ before/after the Second World War ça s'est passé avant/après la Seconde Guerre mondiale; ~ around 1920 vers 1920.

◇ *adj* -**1.** [former] ancien; Mrs Evans, the club's ~ president l'ancienne présidente du club, Mme Evans. -**2.** *Am* [occasional] intermittent; he was a baseball player and ~ golfer il jouait au base-ball et parfois au golf; it's very much a ~ thing *inf* c'est très épisodique.

sometimes ['sʌmtaɪmz] *adv* quelquefois, parfois; I ~ think that it's a waste of time parfois je me dis que c'est une perte de temps; you can be so irritating ~! qu'est-ce que tu peux être agaçant quelquefois!; ~ (they're) friendly, ~ they're not tantôt ils sont aimables, tantôt (ils ne le sont) pas.

someway *inf* ['sʌmweɪ] *Am* = **somehow 1**.

somewhat ['sʌmwɒt] quelque peu, un peu; I was ~ disappointed j'ai été quelque peu déçu; everybody came, ~ to my surprise tout le monde est venu, ce qui n'a pas été sans me surprendre ❑ I was in ~ of a hurry to get home j'étais quelque peu pressé de rentrer chez moi; it was ~ of a failure c'était plutôt un échec.

somewhere ['sʌmweəʳ] *adv* -**1.** [indicating an unspecified place] quelque part; ~ in the drawer/on the desk quelque part dans le tiroir/sur le bureau; she's ~ around elle est quelque part par là, elle n'est pas loin; let's go ~ else allons ailleurs OR autre part; but it's got to be ~ or other! mais il doit bien être quelque part!; I read ~ that it can be fatal j'ai lu quelque part que ça peut être mortel; I'm looking for ~ to stay je cherche un endroit où loger; she's found ~ more comfortable to sit elle a trouvé un siège plus confortable ❑ now we're getting ~! nous arrivons enfin à quelque chose! -**2.** [approximately] environ; she earns ~ around $2,000 a month elle gagne quelque chose comme 2 000 dollars par mois; ~ between five and six hundred people were there il y avait entre cinq et six cents personnes; he must be ~ in his forties il doit avoir entre 40 et 50 ans.

somnambulism [sɒm'næmbjʊlɪzm] *n* somnambulisme *m*.

somnambulist [sɒm'næmbjʊlɪst] *n* somnambule *mf*.

somniferous [sɒm'nɪfərəs] *adj* soporifique, somnifère.

somnolence ['sɒmnələns] *n* somnolence *f*.

somnolent ['sɒmnələnt] *adj* somnolent.

son [sʌn] *n* -**1.** fils *m*; she's got two ~s elle a deux fils OR garçons; the ~s of Ireland *fig* les fils de l'Irlande ❑ ~ and heir héritier *m*; 'All my Sons' *Miller* 'Tous mes fils'; 'Dombey and Son' *Dickens* 'Dombey et fils'; 'Sons and Lovers' *Lawrence* 'Amants et fils'. -**2.** *inf* [term of address] fiston *m*.

◆ **Son** *n* RELIG Fils *m*; the Father, the Son and the Holy Ghost le Père, le Fils et le Saint-Esprit ❑ the Son of God le Fils de Dieu; the Son of Man le Fils de l'Homme.

sonant ['səʊnənt] ◇ *adj* LING sonore.
◇ *n* sonore *f*.

sonar ['səʊnɑːʳ] *n* sonar *m*.

sonata [sə'nɑːtə] *n* sonate *f*; piano/violin ~ sonate pour piano/violon.

sonatina [,sɒnə'tiːnə] *n* sonatine *f*.

sonde [sɒnd] *n* sonde *f* ASTRONAUT & MÉTÉO.

sone [səʊn] *n* sone *m*.

song [sɒŋ] *n* -**1.** chanson *f*; I'll sing you a ~ je vais vous chanter une chanson ❑ a ~ and dance act un numéro de comédie musicale; the Song of Songs, the Song of Solomon BIBLE le Cantique des cantiques; I bought it/it was going for a ~ je l'ai acheté/ça se vendait pour une bouchée de pain OR trois fois rien; to make a ~ and dance about sthg *inf Br* faire toute une histoire pour qqch; she gave me that old ~ and dance about being broke *inf* elle m'a ressorti son couplet habituel, comme quoi elle était fauchée; to be on ~ *inf Br* être en super forme. -**2.** [songs collectively, act of singing] chanson *f*; an anthology of British ~ une anthologie de la chanson britannique; they all burst into ~ ils se sont tous mis à chanter; we raised our voice in ~ nous avons entonné une chanson à pleins poumons. -**3.** [of birds, insects] chant *m*.

songbird ['sɒŋbɜːd] *n* oiseau *m* chanteur.

songbook ['sɒŋbʊk] *n* recueil *m* de chansons.

song cycle *n* cycle *m* de chansons.

songfest ['sɒŋfest] *n Am* festival *m* de chant.

songster ['sɒŋstəʳ] *n* -**1.** [person] chanteur *m*, -euse *f*. -**2.** *lit* [bird] oiseau *m* chanteur.

songstress ['sɒŋstrɪs] *n lit* chanteuse *f*.

song thrush *n* grive *f* musicienne.

songwriter ['sɒŋ,raɪtəʳ] *n* [of lyrics] parolier *m*, -ère *f*; [of music] compositeur *m*, -trice *f*; [of lyrics and music] auteur-compositeur *m*.

sonic ['sɒnɪk] *adj* -**1.** [involving, producing sound] acoustique; ~ frequency fréquence *f* acoustique. -**2.** [concerning speed of sound] sonique.

sonic barrier = **sound barrier**.

sonic boom *n* bang *m*.

son-in-law (*pl* sons-in-law) *n* gendre *m*, beau-fils *m*.

sonnet ['sɒnɪt] *n* sonnet *m*.

sonny *inf* ['sʌnɪ] *n* fiston *m*; come here, ~ (boy OR Jim) viens-là, fiston.

sonobuoy ['səʊnə,bɔɪ] *n* bouée *f* acoustique.

son-of-a-bitch▽ (*pl* sons-of-bitches) *n Am* salaud *m*, fils *m* de pute.

son-of-a-gun *inf* (*pl* sons-of-guns) *n Am*: you old ~! sacré bonhomme!

sonority [sə'nɒrətɪ] *n* sonorité *f*.

sonorous ['sɒnərəs] *adj* -**1.** [resonant] sonore. -**2.** [grandiloquent] grandiloquent.

sonorously ['sɒnərəslɪ] *adv* [speak, sing] d'une voix sonore; [echo, crash] avec un bruit retentissant.

soon [suːn] *adv* -**1.** [in a short time] bientôt, sous peu; (I'll) see you OR speak to you ~! à bientôt!; write ~! écris-moi vite!; I'll be back ~ je serai vite de retour; a burglar can ~ open a lock like that un cambrioleur a vite fait d'ouvrir une serrure comme celle-ci; she phoned ~ after you'd left elle a téléphoné peu après ton départ. -**2.** [early] tôt; oh dear, I spoke too ~! mince, j'ai parlé trop tôt!; it's too ~ to make any predictions il est trop tôt pour se prononcer; how ~ can you finish it? pour quand pouvez-vous le terminer?; the police have arrived, and not a moment too ~ les policiers sont arrivés, et ce n'est pas trop tôt.

◆ **as soon as** *conj phr* dès que, aussitôt que; as ~ as possible dès OR aussitôt que possible; phone me as ~ as you hear anything téléphonez-moi dès que vous aurez des nouvelles; he came as ~ as he could il est venu dès OR aussitôt qu'il a pu.

◆ **(just) as soon** *adv phr*: I'd (just) as ~ go by boat as by plane j'aimerais autant OR mieux y aller en bateau qu'en avion; do you want to come with us? – I'd just as ~ not, if you don't mind veux-tu venir avec nous? – j'aimerais autant OR mieux pas, si ça ne t'ennuie pas; I'd just as ~ he came tomorrow j'aimerais autant OR mieux qu'il vienne demain; I'd as ~ die as do that! plutôt mourir que de faire ça!

sooner ['suːnəʳ] ◇ *adv* (*compar of* soon) -**1.** [earlier] plus tôt; the ~ the better le plus tôt sera le mieux; the ~ it's over the ~ we can leave plus tôt ce sera fini, plus tôt nous pourrons partir; no ~ said than done! aussitôt dit, aussitôt fait!; no ~ had I sat down than the phone rang again je venais juste de m'asseoir quand le téléphone a de nouveau sonné; it was bound to happen ~ or later cela devait arriver tôt ou tard. -**2.** [indicating preference]: would you ~ I called back tomorrow? préférez-vous que je rappelle demain?; shall we go out tonight? – I'd ~ not si on sortait ce soir? – j'aimerais mieux pas; I'd ~ die than go through that again! plutôt mourir que de revivre ça!
◇ *n Am* [pioneer] pionnier *m*, -ère *f* du Far West *(se dit surtout de ceux qui s'installaient sans posséder de titre légal de propriété)*.

Sooner ['suːnəʳ] *n habitant ou natif de l'Oklahoma*; the ~ State l'Oklahoma *m*.

soonish ['suːnɪʃ] *adv* assez rapidement.

soot [sʊt] *n* suie *f*.

◆ **soot up** *vt sep* [dirty] couvrir OR recouvrir de suie; [clog] encrasser.

sooth [suːθ] *n arch*: in ~ en vérité.

soothe [suːð] *vt* -**1.** [calm, placate - person, anger, fears] calmer, apaiser. -**2.** [relieve - pain] calmer, soulager; this will ~ your sore throat ça va soulager votre mal de gorge.

soothing ['suːðɪŋ] *adj* -**1.** [music, words, voice] apaisant; [atmosphere, presence] rassurant; the music had a ~ effect on them la musique les a calmés; the chairman made the usual ~ noises *inf* le président a fait son laïus habituel pour calmer les esprits. -**2.** [lotion, ointment] lénitif, calmant.

soothingly ['suːðɪŋlɪ] *adv* [gen] d'une manière apaisante OR rassurante; [say, speak] d'un ton apaisant OR tranquillisant.

soothsayer ['suːθ,seɪəʳ] *n* devin *m*, devineresse *f*.

soothsaying ['suːθ,seɪɪŋ] *n* divination *f*.

sooty ['sʊtɪ] (*compar* sootier, *superl* sootiest) *adj* -**1.** [dirty] couvert de suie, noir de suie. -**2.** [dark] noir comme de la suie.

sop [sɒp] (*pt* & *pp* sopped, *cont* sopping) *n* [concession, appeasement]: they threw in the measure as a ~ to the ecologists ils ont ajouté cette mesure pour amadouer les écologistes; she said it as a ~ to their pride/feelings elle l'a dit pour flatter leur amour-propre/pour ménager leur sensibilité.

◆ **sops** *npl* CULIN pain *m* trempé.

◆ **sop up** *vt sep* absorber.

SOP (*abbr of* standard operating procedure) *n marche à suivre normale*.

sophism ['sɒfɪzm] *n* sophisme *m*.

sophist ['sɒfɪst] *n* [false reasoner] sophiste *mf*.

◆ **Sophist** *n* PHILOS sophiste *m*.

sophistic(al) [sə'fɪstɪk(l)] *adj* sophistique.

sophisticate [sə'fɪstɪkeɪt] *n* personne *f* raffinée; he thinks he's a ~ il se croit raffiné.

sophisticated [sə'fɪstɪkeɪtɪd] *adj* -**1.** [person, manner, tastes - refined] raffiné; [- chic] chic, élégant; [- well-informed] bien informé; [- mature] mûr; they used to think it was ~ to smoke ils croyaient que ça faisait chic de fumer; a ~ restaurant un restaurant chic; the electorate has become too ~ to believe that promise l'électorat est désormais trop bien informé OR trop averti pour croire à cette promesse. -**2.** [argument, novel, film - subtle] subtil; [- complicated] complexe. -**3.** [machine, system, technology - advanced] sophistiqué, perfectionné.

sophistication [sə,fɪstɪ'keɪʃn] *n* -**1.** [of person, manners, tastes - refinement] raffinement *m*; [- chic] chic *m*, élégance *f*; [- maturity] maturité *f*; the growing ~ of cinema audiences la maturité croissante du public de cinéma. -**2.** [of argument, novel, film - subtlety] subtilité *f*; [- complexity] complexité *f*. -**3.** [of machine, system, technology] sophistication *f*, perfectionnement *m*.

sophistry ['sɒfɪstrɪ] (*pl* sophistries) *n* -**1.** [argumentation] sophistique *f*. -**2.** [argument] sophisme *m*.

Sophocles ['sɒfəkliːz] *pr n* Sophocle.

sophomore ['sɒfəmɔːʳ] *n Am* étudiant *m*, -e *f* de seconde année.

soporific [,sɒpə'rɪfɪk] ◇ *adj* soporifique.
◇ *n* soporifique *m*, somnifère *m*.

sopping *inf* ['sɒpɪŋ] *adj* & *adv*: ~ (wet) [person] trempé (jusqu'aux os); [shirt, cloth] détrempé.

soppy *inf* ['sɒpɪ] (*compar* soppier, *superl* soppiest) *adj Br* -**1.** [sentimental - person] sentimental, fleur bleue *(inv)*; [- story, picture] sentimental, à l'eau de rose. -**2.** [silly] nigaud, bébête. -**3.** [in love]: to be ~ about sb avoir le béguin pour qqn.

soprano [sə'prɑːnəʊ] (*pl* sopranos OR soprani [-niː]) ◇ *n* [singer] soprano *mf*; [voice, part, instrument] soprano *m*; to sing ~ avoir une voix de soprano.
◇ *adj* [voice, part] de soprano; [music] pour soprano; ~ saxophone saxophone *m* soprano.

sorb [sɔːb] *n* [fruit] sorbe *f*; [tree] sorbier *m*.

sorbet ['sɔːbeɪ] *n* -**1.** *Br* sorbet *m*. -**2.** *Am pulpe de fruit glacée*.

sorbic acid ['sɔːbɪk-] *n* acide *m* sorbique.

sorbitol ['sɔːbɪtɒl] *n* sorbitol *m*.

sorcerer ['sɔːsərəʳ] *n* sorcier *m*; 'The Sorcerer's Apprentice' *Dukas* 'l'Apprenti sorcier'.

sorceress ['sɔːsərɪs] *n* sorcière *f*.

sorcery ['sɔːsərɪ] *n* sorcellerie *f*.

sordid ['sɔːdɪd] *adj* -**1.** [dirty, wretched] sordide, misérable; they live in extremely ~ conditions ils vivent dans des conditions vraiment sordides. -**2.** [base, loathsome] sordide, infâme, vil; they've got ~ little minds ce sont des esprits mesquins et sordides; a ~ affair une affaire sordide; I'll spare you the ~ details je vous épargnerai les détails sordides.

sordino [sɔː'diːnəʊ] (*pl* sordini [-niː]) *n* sourdine *f* MUS.

sore [sɔː^r] ◇ *adj* -**1.** [aching] douloureux; **we stopped to rest our ~ feet** nous nous sommes arrêtés pour reposer nos pieds endoloris; **I'm ~ all over** j'ai mal partout; **I've a ~ throat** j'ai mal à la gorge; **my arms/legs are ~** j'ai mal aux bras/jambes, mes bras/jambes me font mal; **don't touch me there, it's ~** ne me touche pas là, ça fait mal; **where is it ~?** où as-tu mal?; **it's a ~ point with her** *fig* elle est très sensible sur ce point OR là-dessus. -**2.** *inf Am* [angry] en boule; **are you still ~ at me?** est-ce que tu es toujours en boule contre moi?; **he got ~** il s'est mis en boule || [resentful] vexé, amer; **he's ~ because they left him out of the team** il est vexé parce qu'ils l'ont laissé en dehors de l'équipe. -**3.** *lit* [great] grand; **in ~ distress** dans une grande détresse; **to be in ~ need of sthg** avoir grand besoin de qqch.
◇ *n* plaie *f*; **open ~s** des plaies ouvertes.
◇ *adv arch* grandement; **they were ~ afraid** ils éprouvèrent une grande frayeur.

sorehead *inf* ['sɔːhed] *n Am* râleur *m*, -euse *f*; **don't be such a ~!** ne râle pas comme ça!, quel râleur tu fais!

sorely ['sɔːlɪ] *adv* -**1.** [as intensifier] grandement; **the house is ~ in need of a new coat of paint** la maison a grandement OR bien besoin d'être repeinte; **we are ~ pressed for time** nous manquons cruellement de temps; **she will be ~ missed** elle nous manquera cruellement; **I was ~ tempted to accept her offer** j'ai été très tenté d'accepter sa proposition. -**2.** *lit* [painfully]: **~ wounded** grièvement blessé.

sorghum ['sɔːgəm] *n* sorgho *m*.

sorority [sə'rɒrətɪ] (*pl* sororities) *n Am* UNIV [association] club *m* d'étudiantes; [residence] résidence *f* (universitaire) pour femmes.

sorrel ['sɒrəl] ◇ *n* -**1.** BOT & CULIN oseille *f*. -**2.** [colour] roux *m*, brun rouge *m*. -**3.** [horse] alezan *m* clair.
◇ *adj* [gen] roux; [horse] alezan clair *(inv)*.

sorrow ['sɒrəʊ] ◇ *n* chagrin *m*, peine *f*, tristesse *f*; [stronger] affliction *f*, douleur *f*; **I am writing to express my ~ at your sad loss** je vous écris pour vous faire part de la tristesse que j'ai éprouvée en apprenant votre deuil; **her ~ at OR over losing the match was short-lived** le chagrin qu'elle a éprouvé OR la tristesse qu'elle a éprouvée d'avoir perdu le match n'a pas duré; **to our great ~** à notre grand regret; **more in ~ than in anger** avec plus de tristesse que de colère; **his son's failure was a great ~ to him** l'échec de son fils lui a fait OR causé beaucoup de peine; **life is full of joys and ~s** la vie est faite de joies et de peines ❑ **'The Sorrows of Young Werther'** *Goethe* 'les Souffrances du jeune Werther'.
◇ *vi lit* éprouver du chagrin OR de la peine; **he is still ~ing over his son's death** il pleure encore la mort de son fils.

sorrowful ['sɒrəʊfʊl] *adj* [person] triste; [look, smile] affligé.

sorrowfully ['sɒrəʊflɪ] *adv* tristement.

sorrowing ['sɒrəʊɪŋ] *adj* attristé, affligé.

sorry ['sɒrɪ] (*compar* sorrier, *superl* sorriest) *adj* -**1.** [in apologies] désolé; **I'm ~ we won't be able to fetch you** je regrette que OR je suis désolé que nous ne puissions venir vous chercher; **(I'm) ~ to have bothered you** (je suis) désolé de vous avoir dérangé; **I'm ~ to say there's little we can do** malheureusement, nous ne pouvons pas faire grand-chose; **I'm so OR very OR terribly ~** je suis vraiment navré; **ouch, that's my foot! – (I'm) ~!** aïe! mon pied! – je suis désolé OR excusez-moi!; **(I'm) ~ about the mess** excusez le désordre; **I'm ~ about the mix-up** excusez-moi pour la confusion; **~ to interrupt you but you're wanted on the phone** excusez-moi de vous interrompre mais on vous demande au téléphone; **~ about forgetting your birthday** désolé d'avoir oublié ton anniversaire; **he said he was ~** il a présenté ses excuses; **say (you're) ~ to the lady** demande pardon à la dame; **what's the time? – ~?** quelle heure est-il? – pardon? OR comment?; **they're coming on Tuesday, ~, Thursday** ils viennent mardi, pardon, jeudi. -**2.** [regretful]: **to be ~** regretter; **I'm ~ I ever came here!** je regrette d'être venu ici!; **you'll be ~ for this** tu le regretteras. -**3.** [expressing sympathy] désolé, navré, peiné; **I was ~ to hear about your father's death** j'ai été désolé OR peiné OR navré d'apprendre la mort de votre père. -**4.** [pity]: **to be OR to feel ~ for sb** plaindre qqn; **it's the children I feel ~ for** ce sont les enfants que je plains; **there's no need to feel ~ for them** ils ne sont pas à plaindre; **she felt ~ for him and gave him a pound** elle eut pitié de lui et lui donna une livre; **to be OR to feel ~ for o.s.** s'apitoyer sur soi-même OR sur son propre sort; **stop feeling ~ for yourself!** arrête un peu de t'apitoyer sur ton propre sort!; **he's just feeling a bit ~ for himself** il est juste un peu déprimé. -**5.** [pitiable, wretched] triste, piteux; **to cut a ~ figure** faire triste OR piètre figure; **they were a ~ sight after the match** ils étaient dans un triste état après le match; **the garden was in a ~ state** le jardin était en piteux état OR dans un triste état; **it's a ~ state of affairs** c'est bien triste.

sort [sɔːt] ◇ *n* -**1.** [kind, type] sorte *f*, espèce *f*, genre *m*; [brand] marque *f*; **a hat with a ~ of veil** un chapeau avec une sorte OR une espèce OR un genre de voile; **it's a strange ~ of film** c'est un drôle de film; **it's a different ~ of problem** c'est un autre type de problème; **I've got a ~ of feeling about what the result will be** j'ai comme un pressentiment sur ce que sera le résultat; **I think that he's some ~ of specialist OR that he's a specialist of some ~** je crois que c'est un genre de spécialiste; **she's not the ~ (of woman) to let you down** elle n'est pas du genre à vous laisser tomber; **I love this OR these** *inf* **~ of biscuits** j'adore ces biscuits-là; **there's too much of this ~ of thing going on** il se passe trop de choses de ce genre; **they're not our ~ (of people)** nous ne sommes pas du même monde; **I know your ~!** les gens de ton espèce, je les connais!; **what ~ of fish are we having?** qu'est-ce qu'on mange comme poisson?; **what ~ of washing machine have you got?** qu'est-ce que vous avez comme (marque de) machine à laver?; **what ~ of dog is that?** qu'est-ce que c'est comme chien OR comme race de chien?; **what ~ of woman is she?** quel genre de femme est-ce?; **what ~ of girl do you take me for?** pour qui me prenez-vous?; **what ~ of way is that to speak to your grandmother?** en voilà une façon de parler à ta grand-mère!; **good luck, and all that ~ of thing!** bonne chance, et tout et tout!; **there are all ~s of materials to choose from** on peut choisir parmi toutes sortes de matériaux; **I've heard all ~s of good things about you** j'ai entendu dire beaucoup de bien de vous ❑ **I said nothing of the ~!** je n'ai rien dit de pareil OR de tel!; **you were drunk last night – I was nothing of the ~!** tu étais ivre hier soir – absolument pas! OR mais pas du tout!; **I feel out of ~s** je ne suis pas dans mon assiette; **it takes all ~s (to make a world)** *prov* il faut de tout pour faire un monde *prov*. -**2.** *inf* [person]: **she's a good ~** [young woman] c'est une brave fille; [older woman] c'est une brave femme. -**3.** [gen & COMPUT - act of sorting] tri *m*; **the program will do an alphabetical ~** le programme exécutera un tri alphabétique; **I've had a ~ through all the winter clothes** *inf* j'ai trié tous les vêtements d'hiver ❑ **~ routine** routine *f* de tri.
◇ *vt* -**1.** [classify] classer, trier; [divide up] répartir; [separate] séparer; COMPUT trier; **to ~ mail** trier le courrier; **I've ~ed the index cards into alphabetical order** j'ai classé OR trié les fiches par ordre alphabétique; **they were ~ing the shirts according to colour** ils triaient les chemises selon leur couleur; **~ the cards into two piles** répartissez les cartes en deux piles; **~ the letters into urgent and less urgent** répartissez les lettres entre celles qui sont urgentes et celles qui le sont moins; **help me ~ the good fruit from the bad** aidez-moi à séparer les bons fruits des mauvais. -**2.** [organize] = **sort out 2**.

◆ **of a sort, of sorts** *adj phr*: **they served us champagne of a ~ OR of ~s** ils nous ont servi une espèce de champagne.

◆ **sort of** *inf adv phr*: **I ~ of expected it to rain** je m'attendais un peu à ce qu'il pleuve; **I'm ~ of glad that I missed them** je suis plutôt content de les avoir ratés; **it's ~ of big and round** c'est du genre grand et rond; **did you hit him? – well, ~ of** tu l'as frappé? – en quelque sorte, oui.

◆ **sort out** *vt sep* -**1.** [classify] = **sort** *vt* **1**. -**2.** [select and set aside] trier; **I've been ~ing out some books for you to take** j'ai trié quelques livres pour que tu les emportes; **we've already ~ed out the likely candidates from the rest** nous avons déjà trié les candidats intéressants (et les autres). -**3.** [tidy up - papers, clothes, room, cupboard] ranger; [put in order - finances, ideas] mettre en ordre; **she needs to get her personal life ~ed out** il faut qu'elle règle ses problèmes personnels. -**4.** [settle, resolve - problem, dispute] régler, résoudre; **I'm glad that bit of bother has been ~ed out** je suis content que ce petit problème ait été réglé; **they still haven't ~ed out the mistake in my tax demand** ils n'ont toujours pas réglé cette erreur dans ma feuille d'impôts; **everything's ~ed out now** tout est arrangé maintenant; **once the initial confusion had ~ed itself out** une fois que la confusion du début se fut dissipée; **things will ~ themselves out in the end** les choses finiront par s'arranger. -**5.** [work out]: **have you ~ed out how to do it?** est-ce que tu as trouvé le moyen de le faire?; **she couldn't ~ out what they wanted** elle n'arrivait pas à savoir au juste ce qu'ils voulaient; **I'm trying to ~ out what's been going on** j'essaie de savoir OR de comprendre ce qui s'est passé || [arrange] arranger, fixer; **we still have to ~ out a date for the next meeting** il nous faut encore arranger OR choisir une date pour la prochaine réunion. -**6.** *inf Br* [solve the problems of - person]: **he's very depressed, you should try to ~ him out** il est très déprimé, tu devrais essayer de l'aider à s'en sortir; **she needs time to ~ herself out** il lui faut du temps pour régler ses problèmes. -**7.** *inf Br* [punish] régler son compte à; **just wait till he gets home, I'll ~ him out!** attends un peu qu'il rentre à la maison, je vais lui régler son compte!

◆ **sort through** *vt insep* trier; **I've been ~ing through the old magazines** j'ai trié les vieux magazines.

sorta *inf* ['sɔːtə] = **sort of**.

sort code *n* BANK code *m* guichet.

sorter ['sɔːtə^r] *n* -**1.** [person] trieur *m*, -euse *f*; **letter ~** employé *m*, -e *f* au tri postal. -**2.** [machine - gen] trieur *m*; [- for punched cards] trieuse *f*.

sortie ['sɔːtiː] *n* MIL sortie *f*; **I sometimes make the odd ~ to the pub** *hum* de temps en temps je fais une petite sortie au pub.

sorting ['sɔːtɪŋ] *n* tri *m*; **~ routine** COMPUT routine *f* de tri.

sorting code = **sort code**.

sorting office *n* centre *m* de tri.

sort-out *inf n Br* [tidying] rangement *m*; **the attic needs a good ~** il faudrait ranger le grenier.

SOS (*abbr of* save our souls) *n* SOS *m*; **to send out an ~** lancer un SOS; **we received an ~ message** nous avons reçu un SOS.

so-so *inf adj* pas fameux; [in health] comme ci comme ça, couci-couça; **the film was only ~** le film n'était pas fameux.

sot [sɒt] *n lit* ivrogne *m*, -esse *f*.

Sotheby's ['sʌðəbiːz] *pr n société londonienne de vente aux enchères*.

sottish ['sɒtɪʃ] *adj lit* sot, stupide, abruti.

sotto voce [ˌsɒtəʊ'vəʊtʃɪ] *adv* -**1.** [gen] à voix basse. -**2.** MUS sotto voce.

sou [suː] *n* sou *m*.

soufflé ['suːfleɪ] *n* soufflé *m*; cheese/chocolate ~ soufflé au fromage/au chocolat; ~ dish moule *m* à soufflé.

sough [saʊ] *lit* ◇ *vi* murmurer, susurrer.
◇ *n* murmure *m*, susurrement *m (du vent)*.

sought [sɔːt] *pt* & *pp* → **seek**.

sought-after *adj* recherché; furniture of this period is much ~ les meubles de cette époque sont très recherchés (actuellement).

soul [səʊl] ◇ *n* -**1.** RELIG âme *f*; God rest his ~! que Dieu ait son âme!; All Soul's Day le jour des Morts, la Toussaint; upon my ~! *dated* grands dieux!; you've got no ~! tu n'as pas de cœur! ‖ [emotional depth] profondeur *f*; it was a polished performance, but it lacked ~ c'était une performance très accomplie, mais sans profondeur ☐ I can't call my ~ my own these days je ne m'appartiens plus ces jours-ci. -**2.** [leading figure] âme *f*; she was the ~ of the early feminist movement elle était l'âme du mouvement féministe à ses débuts. -**3.** [perfect example] modèle *m*; the ~ of discretion la discrétion même OR personnifiée. -**4.** [person] personne *f*, âme *f*; poor old ~! le pauvre!, la pauvre!; there wasn't a ~ in the streets il n'y avait pas âme qui vive dans les rues; I didn't know a ~ at the party je ne connaissais personne à la réception; I won't tell a ~ je ne le dirai à personne ‖ *lit*: a town of 20,000 ~s une ville de 20 000 âmes; the ship went down with all ~s le navire a sombré corps et biens. -**5.** [music] (musique *f*) soul *f*, soul music *f*; a ~ singer un chanteur de soul.
◇ *adj Am dated caractéristique de la culture des Noirs américains*.

soul brother *inf n Am dated* frère *m* de race.

soul-destroying [-dɪˌstrɔɪɪŋ] *adj* [job] abrutissant; [situation, place] déprimant.

soul food *inf n cuisine traditionnelle des Noirs américains*.

soulful ['səʊlfʊl] *adj* [song, performance, sigh] émouvant, attendrissant; [look, eyes] expressif.

soulfully ['səʊlfʊlɪ] *adv* [sing, perform, sigh] de façon émouvante OR attendrissante; [look] de façon expressive.

soulless ['səʊllɪs] *adj* -**1.** [inhuman - place] inhumain, sans âme; [- work] abrutissant. -**2.** [heartless] sans cœur, insensible.

soul mate *n* âme *f* sœur.

soul music *n* musique *f* soul, soul music *f*.

soul-searching *n* introspection *f*; after much ~ she decided to hand in her resignation après mûre réflexion OR après avoir mûrement réfléchi, elle décida de donner sa démission.

soul sister *inf n Am dated nom que les Noirs américains donnaient aux femmes noires*.

soul-stirring *adj* (profondément) émouvant.

sound [saʊnd] ◇ *n* -**1.** [noise - of footsteps, thunder, conversation] bruit *m*; [- of voice, musical instrument] son *m*; I was woken by the ~ of voices/laughter/breaking glass j'ai été réveillé par un bruit de voix/par des éclats de rires/par un bruit de verre cassé; I love the ~ of her voice j'adore le son de sa voix; don't make a ~! surtout ne faites pas de bruit!; they tiptoed out without (making) a ~ ils sont sortis sur la pointe des pieds sans faire de bruit; the plaintive ~ of the bagpipes le son plaintif de la cornemuse ☐ 'The Sound and the Fury' *Faulkner* 'le Bruit et la fureur'; 'The Sound of Music' *Wise* 'la Mélodie du bonheur'. -**2.** PHYS son *m*; light travels faster than ~ la lumière se déplace plus vite que le son; the speed of ~ la vitesse du son. -**3.** LING son *m*; it's a similar ~ to the Scots "ch" c'est un son qui ressemble au «ch» écossais; the English vowel ~s les sons vocaliques de l'anglais ☐ speech ~ phonème *m*. -**4.** RADIO & TV son *m*; the ~ is very poor le son est mauvais; to turn the ~ up/down monter/baisser le son OR volume. -**5.** [type of music] style *m* de musique, musique *f*; the Liverpool ~ la musique de Liverpool; a brand new ~ has hit the charts un son complètement nouveau a fait son entrée au hit-parade. -**6.** [impression, idea]: I don't like the ~ of these new measures ces nouvelles mesures ne me disent rien qui vaille; it's pretty easy by the ~ of it ça a l'air assez facile. -**7.** [earshot]: within the ~ of the church bells à portée du son des cloches de l'église. -**8.** MED [probe] sonde *f*. -**9.** NAUT [sounding line] (ligne *f* de) sonde *f*. -**10.** GEOG [channel] détroit *m*, bras *m* de mer. -**11.** ZOOL [air bladder] vessie *f* natatoire.
◇ *comp* [level, recording] sonore; [broadcasting] radiophonique; LING [change] phonologique; ~ crew équipe *f* du son.
◇ *adj* -**1.** [structure, building, wall - sturdy] solide; [- in good condition] en bon état; built on ~ foundations construit sur des fondations solides; the house is structurally ~ le gros œuvre de la maison est en bon état. -**2.** [healthy - person] en bonne santé; [- body, mind, limbs] sain; to be of ~ mind être sain d'esprit ☐ to be as ~ as a bell être en parfaite santé; to be ~ of wind and limb avoir bon pied bon œil. -**3.** [sensible, well-founded - advice, idea, strategy] sensé, judicieux; [- argument, claim] valable, fondé, solide; to show ~ judgment faire preuve de jugement; do you think that was a ~ move? croyez-vous que c'était un acte judicieux? -**4.** [reliable, solid] solide, compétent; we need somebody with a ~ grasp of the subject il nous faut quelqu'un avec de solides connaissances en la matière; my knowledge of German history isn't too ~ mes connaissances en ce qui concerne l'histoire de l'Allemagne laissent à désirer; Crawford seems a ~ enough chap Crawford semble être quelqu'un en qui on peut avoir confiance; is she politically ~? ses convictions politiques sont-elles solides? -**5.** [safe - investment] sûr; [- company, business] solide. -**6.** [severe - defeat] total; [- hiding] bon; he needs a ~ thrashing il a besoin d'une bonne correction. -**7.** [deep - sleep] profond; I'm a very ~ sleeper j'ai le sommeil profond.
◇ *adv*: to be ~ asleep dormir profondément OR à poings fermés.
◇ *vi* -**1.** [make a sound] sonner, résonner, retentir; it ~s hollow if you tap it ça sonne creux lorsqu'on tape dessus; their voices ~ed very loud in the empty house leurs voix résonnaient bruyamment dans la maison vide; sirens ~ed in the streets des sirènes retentissaient dans les rues; if the alarm ~s, run si vous entendez l'alarme, enfuyez-vous. -**2.** *Br* [be pronounced] se prononcer; in English words are rarely spelt as they ~ en anglais, les mots s'écrivent rarement comme ils se prononcent. -**3.** [seem] sembler, paraître; he ~ed sad il semblait triste; he ~ed bored il semblait s'ennuyer; it doesn't ~ very interesting to me ça ne m'a pas l'air très intéressant; (that) ~s like a good idea ça semble être une bonne idée; two weeks in Crete, that ~s nice! deux semaines en Crète, pas mal du tout!; the name ~ed French le nom avait l'air d'être français; you ~ as though OR you ~ as if OR you ~ like you've got a cold on dirait que tu es enrhumé; it ~s to me as though they don't want to do it j'ai l'impression qu'ils ne veulent pas le faire; it doesn't ~ to me as though they want to do it je n'ai pas l'impression qu'ils veuillent le faire; you ~ just like your brother on the phone tu as la même voix que ton frère OR on dirait vraiment ton frère au téléphone; it's an instrument which ~s rather like a recorder c'est un instrument dont le son ressemble assez à OR est assez proche de la flûte à bec; that ~s like the postman now je crois entendre le facteur.
◇ *vt* -**1.** [bell, alarm] sonner; [wind instrument] sonner de; the huntsman ~ed his horn le chasseur sonna du cor; the driver behind me ~ed his horn le conducteur derrière moi a klaxonné; they ~ed the church bells ils sonnèrent les cloches; the bugler ~ed the reveille le clairon sonna le réveil; to ~ a warning lancer un avertissement. -**2.** [pronounce] prononcer; the "p" isn't ~ed le «p» ne se prononce pas; he doesn't ~ his aitches il ne prononce pas ses «h». -**3.** MED [chest, lungs] ausculter; [cavity, passage] sonder. -**4.** NAUT sonder. -**5.** [person] sonder; I'll try to ~ their feelings on the matter j'essaierai de connaître leur sentiment à cet égard.
◆ **sound off** *inf vi insep* -**1.** [declare one's opinions] crier son opinion sur tous les toits; [complain] râler; he's always ~ing off about the management il est toujours à râler contre la direction; to ~ off at sb [angrily] passer un savon à qqn. -**2.** [boast] se vanter.
◆ **sound out** *vt sep fig* sonder; the company is ~ing out potential buyers la compagnie sonde les acheteurs potentiels.

sound archives *npl* phonothèque *f*; a recording from the BBC ~ un enregistrement qui vient des archives de la BBC.

sound barrier *n* mur *m* du son; to break the ~ franchir le mur du son.

soundbite ['saʊndbaɪt] *n* petite phrase *(prononcée par un homme politique à la radio ou à la télévision pour frapper les esprits)*.

soundboard ['saʊndbɔːd] *n* -**1.** [over pulpit, rostrum] abat-voix *m inv*. -**2.** MUS table *f* d'harmonie.

sound box *n* caisse *f* de résonance.

sound effects *npl* bruitage *m*.

sound engineer *n* ingénieur *m* du son.

sounder ['saʊndəʳ] *n* NAUT sondeur *m*.

sound hole *n* [of violin, viola etc] ouïe *f*, esse *f*; [of guitar, lute etc] rosace *f*, rose *f*.

sounding ['saʊndɪŋ] *n* -**1.** AERON, METEOR & NAUT [measuring] sondage *m*. -**2.** [of bell, horn] son *m*; wait for the ~ of the alarm attendez le signal d'alarme OR que le signal d'alarme retentisse.
◆ **soundings** *npl* [investigations] sondages *mpl*; to take ~s faire des sondages.

-sounding *in cpds*: a foreign~ name un nom à consonance étrangère; high~ phrases des phrases ronflantes OR grandiloquentes.

sounding board *n* -**1.** *fig* [person]: she uses her assistants as a ~ for any new ideas elle essaie toutes ses nouvelles idées sur ses assistants. -**2.** = **soundboard**.

sounding line *n* (ligne *f* de) sonde *f*.

soundless ['saʊndlɪs] *adj* -**1.** [silent] silencieux. -**2.** *lit* [deep] insondable.

soundlessly ['saʊndlɪslɪ] *adv* [silently] silencieusement, sans bruit.

soundly ['saʊndlɪ] *adv* -**1.** [deeply - sleep] profondément. -**2.** [sensibly - advise, argue] judicieusement, avec bon sens. -**3.** [safely - invest] de façon sûre, sans risque OR risques. -**4.** [competently - work, run] avec compétence. -**5.** [thoroughly - defeat] à plate couture OR plates coutures; he deserves to be ~ thrashed il mérite une bonne correction.

soundness ['saʊndnɪs] *n* -**1.** [of body, mind] santé *f*, équilibre *m*; [of health] robustesse *f*. -**2.** [of building, structure] solidité *f*; [of business, financial situation] solvabilité *f*; [of decision, advice] bon sens *m*; [of argument, reasoning] justesse *f*. -**3.** [of sleep] profondeur *f*.

soundproof ['saʊndpruːf] ◇ *adj* insonorisé.
◇ *vt* insonoriser.

soundproofing ['saʊndpruːfɪŋ] *n* insonorisation *f*.

sound shift *n* mutation *f* phonologique.

sound system *n* [hi-fi] chaîne *f* hifi; [PA system] sonorisation *f*.

soundtrack ['saʊndtræk] *n* bande *f* sonore.

sound wave *n* onde *f* sonore.

soup [suːp] *n* -**1.** CULIN soupe *f*; [thin or blended] soupe *f*, potage *m*; [smooth and creamy] velouté *m*; onion/fish/leek ~ soupe à l'oignon/de poisson/aux poireaux; cream of mushroom ~ velouté de champignons ☐ ~ ladle louche *f*; to be in the ~ *inf* être dans le pétrin; from ~ to nuts *Am inf* du début à la fin. -**2.** ▽ [nitroglycerine] nitroglycérine *f*, nitro *f*.
◆ **soup up** *inf vt sep* [engine] gonfler; [car] gonfler le moteur de; [machine, computer program] perfectionner.

soupçon ['suːpsɒn] *n fml* OR *hum* soupçon *m*, pointe *f*.

souped-up *inf* [suːpt-] *adj* [engine] gonflé, poussé; [car] au moteur gonflé OR poussé; [machine, computer program] perfectionné.

soup kitchen *n* soupe *f* populaire.

soup plate *n* assiette *f* creuse OR à soupe.

soup spoon *n* cuillère *f* OR cuiller *f* à soupe.

soup tureen *n* soupière *f*.

soupy ['suːpɪ] (*compar* soupier, *superl* soupiest) *adj* -**1.** [thick] épais, dense. -**2.** *inf Am* [sentimental] à l'eau de rose.

sour [saʊəʳ] ◇ *adj* -**1.** [flavour, taste] aigre, sur. -**2.** [rancid - milk] tourné, aigre; [- breath] fétide; **the milk has gone** OR **turned ~** le lait a tourné. -**3.** [disagreeable - person, character, mood] aigre, revêche, hargneux; [- look] hargneux; [- comment, tone] aigre, acerbe. -**4.** [wrong, awry]: **to go** OR **to turn ~** mal tourner; **everything suddenly went ~ on us** tout a soudainement mal tourné pour nous; **their marriage went ~** leur mariage a tourné au vinaigre. -**5.** [too acidic - soil] trop acide.

◇ *vi* -**1.** [wine] surir, s'aigrir; [milk] tourner, aigrir. -**2.** [person, character] aigrir; [relationship] se dégrader, tourner au vinaigre; [situation] mal tourner.

◇ *vt* -**1.** [milk, wine] aigrir. -**2.** [person, character] aigrir; [relationship] gâter, empoisonner; [situation] gâter; **the experience ~ed his view of life** cette expérience l'a aigri.

◇ *n*: **whisky ~** whisky sour *m* *(cocktail à base de whisky et de jus de citron)*.

source [sɔːs] ◇ *n* -**1.** [gen] source *f*; **they have traced the ~ of the power cut** ils ont découvert l'origine de la panne de courant; **energy ~s** sources d'énergie; **at ~** à la source; **~ of infection** MED foyer *m* d'infection. -**2.** [of information] source *f*; **the journalist refused to name his ~s** le journaliste a refusé de nommer ses sources; **according to reliable ~s war is imminent** selon des sources sûres, la guerre est imminente. -**3.** [of river] source *f*.

◇ *comp*: **~ material** OR **materials** [documents] documentation *f*.

◇ *vt*: **the quotations are ~d in footnotes** la source des citations figure dans les notes en bas de page.

source language *n* -**1.** LING langue *f* source. -**2.** COMPUT langage *m* source.

source program *n* COMPUT programme *m* source.

sour cream *n* crème *f* aigre.

sourdough ['saʊədəʊ] *n* -**1.** *dial* & CULIN levain *m*; **~ bread** pain *m* au levain. -**2.** [pioneer] pionnier *m*, -ère *f* *(de l'Alaska ou de l'Ouest du Canada)*.

sour-faced *adj* à la mine revêche; **what are you looking so ~ about?** pourquoi cet air maussade OR cette mine revêche?

sour grapes *n* jalousie *f*, envie *f*; **it's a simple case of ~** c'est tout simplement du dépit.

sourly ['saʊəlɪ] *adj* aigrement, avec aigreur.

sour mash *n* *pâte spéciale utilisée dans la fabrication de certains whiskies américains*.

sourness ['saʊənɪs] *n* -**1.** [of flavour, taste] aigreur *f*, acidité *f*; [of milk] aigreur *f*. -**2.** [of person, character, mood] aigreur *f*; [of speech, comment] ton *m* aigre.

sourpuss *inf* ['saʊəpʊs] *n* grincheux *m*, -euse *f*.

soursop ['saʊəsɒp] *n* corossol *m*, cachiman *m* épineux.

sousaphone ['suːzəfəʊn] *n* sousaphone *m*.

souse [saʊs] ◇ *vt* -**1.** CULIN [in vinegar] (faire) mariner dans du vinaigre; [in brine] (faire) mariner dans de la saumure; **~d herrings** harengs au vinaigre. -**2.** [immerse] immerger, plonger; [drench] tremper; **he ~d himself with cold water** il s'aspergea abondamment d'eau froide. -**3.** *inf* [make drunk] soûler; **he comes home ~d every night** il rentre soûl tous les soirs.

◇ *n* CULIN [vinegar] marinade *f* de vinaigre; [brine] saumure *f*.

soutane [suː'tɑːn] *n* soutane *f*.

south [saʊθ] ◇ *n* -**1.** GEOG sud *m*; **the region to the ~ of Birmingham** la région qui est au sud de Birmingham; **I was born in the ~** je suis né dans le Sud; **in the South of France** dans le Midi (de la France); **the wind is in the ~** le vent vient du sud ‖ [in US]: **the South** le Sud, les États du Sud; **the Deep South** le Sud profond. -**2.** CARDS sud *m*.

◇ *adj* -**1.** GEOG sud *(inv)*, du sud, méridional; **the ~ coast** la côte sud; **in ~ London** dans le sud de Londres; **in ~ India** dans le sud de l'Inde ❑ **the South Atlantic/Pacific** l'Atlantique *m*/le Pacifique Sud. -**2.** [wind] du sud.

◇ *adv* au sud, vers le sud; **the village lies ~ of York** le village est situé au sud de York; **the living room faces ~** la salle de séjour est exposée au sud; **the path heads (due) ~** le chemin va OR mène (droit) vers le sud; **walk ~ until you come to a main road** marchez vers le sud jusqu'à ce que vous arriviez à une route principale; **we're going ~ for our holidays** nous allons passer nos vacances dans le Sud; **I travelled ~** je suis allée vers le sud; **they live down ~** ils habitent dans le Sud.

South Africa *pr n* Afrique *f* du Sud; **in ~** en Afrique du Sud; **the Republic of ~** la République d'Afrique du Sud.

South African ◇ *n* Sud-Africain *m*, -e *f*.

◇ *adj* sud-africain, d'Afrique du Sud.

South America *pr n* Amérique *f* du Sud; **in ~** en Amérique du Sud.

South American ◇ *n* Sud-Américain *m*, -e *f*.

◇ *adj* sud-américain, d'Amérique du Sud.

South Australia *pr n* Australie-Méridionale *f*; **in ~** en Australie-Méridionale.

South Bank *pr n*: **the ~** *complexe sur la rive sud de la Tamise réunissant des salles de concert, des théâtres et des musées*.

southbound ['saʊθbaʊnd] *adj* en direction du sud; **the ~ carriageway of the motorway is closed** l'axe sud de l'autoroute est fermé (à la circulation).

South Carolina *pr n* Caroline *f* du Sud; **in ~** en Caroline du Sud.

South Dakota *pr n* Dakota *m* du Sud; **in ~** dans le Dakota du Sud.

southeast [,saʊθ'iːst] ◇ *n* sud-est *m*; **in the ~ of England** dans le sud-est de l'Angleterre.

◇ *adj* -**1.** GEOG sud-est *(inv)*, du sud-est; **in ~ England** dans le sud-est de l'Angleterre. -**2.** [wind] de sud-est.

◇ *adv* au sud-est, vers le sud-est; **it's 50 miles ~ of Liverpool** c'est à 80 kilomètres au sud-est de Liverpool.

Southeast Asia *pr n* Asie *f* du Sud-Est; **in ~** en Asie du Sud-Est.

southeaster [,saʊθ'iːstəʳ] *n* vent *m* de sud-est.

southeasterly [,saʊθ'iːstəlɪ] (*pl* southeasterlies) ◇ *adj* -**1.** GEOG sud-est *(inv)*, du sud-est; **to travel in a ~ direction** aller vers le sud-est. -**2.** [wind] de sud-est.

◇ *adv* au sud-est, vers le sud-est.

◇ *n* = **southeaster**.

southeastern [,saʊθ'iːstən] *adj* sud-est *(inv)*, du sud-est; **the ~ suburbs** la banlieue sud-est.

southeastwards [,saʊθ'iːstwədz] *adv* vers le sud-est, en direction du sud-est.

souther ['saʊðəʳ] *n* NAUT fort vent *m* du sud.

southerly ['sʌðəlɪ] (*pl* southerlies) ◇ *adj* -**1.** GEOG sud *(inv)*, du sud; **in a ~ direction** vers le sud; **a room with a ~ aspect** une pièce exposée au sud OR au midi. -**2.** [wind] du sud.

◇ *adv* vers le sud.

◇ *n* vent *m* du sud.

southern ['sʌðən] *adj* -**1.** GEOG sud *(inv)*, du sud, méridional; **he has a ~ accent** il a un accent du sud; **~ Africa** l'Afrique *f* australe; **~ Europe** l'Europe *f* méridionale; **in ~ India** dans le sud de l'Inde ❑ **the ~ hemisphere** l'hémisphère *m* sud OR austral; **Southern Baptists** *membres de la Southern Baptist convention fondée en 1845 à Augusta en Géorgie*. -**2.** [wind] du sud.

Southern Cross *n*: **the ~** la Croix du Sud.

southerner ['sʌðənəʳ] *n* [gen] homme *m*, femme *f* du sud; [in continental Europe] méridional *m*, -e *f*; **she's a ~** elle vient du sud.

Southern Ireland *pr n* Irlande *f* du Sud; **in ~** en Irlande du Sud.

southernmost ['sʌðənməʊst] *adj* le plus au sud; **the ~ town in Chile** la ville la plus au sud du Chili; **the ~ limits of the Sahara** les limites méridionales du Sahara.

Southern Rhodesia *pr n* Rhodésie *f* du Sud.

south-facing *adj* [house, wall] (exposé) au sud OR au midi.

South Island *pr n* l'île *f* du Sud.

South Korea *pr n* Corée *f* du Sud; **in ~** en Corée du Sud.

South Korean ◇ *n* Sud-Coréen *m*, -enne *f*, Coréen *m*, -enne *f* du Sud.

◇ *adj* sud-coréen.

South Pacific *pr n*: **the ~** le Pacifique Sud.

southpaw *inf* ['saʊθpɔː] ◇ *n Am* gaucher *m*, -ère *f*.

◇ *adj* gaucher.

South Pole *pr n* pôle *m* Sud; **at the ~** au pôle Sud.

South Sea Bubble *pr n*: **the ~** *krach financier de 1720 en Angleterre*.

THE SOUTH SEA BUBBLE:
Krach financier qui eut lieu en 1720, après que la «South Sea Company» eut repris à son compte la dette nationale britannique en échange du monopole du commerce sur les mers du sud; cette nouvelle provoqua une ruée sur les actions de la compagnie et une spéculation avide, qui entraîna la chute des cours et la ruine de nombreux investisseurs.

South Seas *pl pr n*: **the ~** les mers *fpl* du Sud.

south-southeast ◇ *n* sud-sud-est *m*.

◇ *adj* sud-sud-est *(inv)*, du sud-sud-est.

◇ *adv* au sud-sud-est, vers le sud-sud-est.

south-southwest ◇ *n* sud-sud-ouest *m*.

◇ *adj* sud-sud-ouest *(inv)*, du sud-sud-ouest.

◇ *adv* au sud-sud-ouest, vers le sud-sud-ouest.

South Vietnam *pr n* Sud Viêt-Nam *m*; **in ~** au Sud Viêt-Nam.

South Vietnamese ◇ *n* Sud-Vietnamien *m*, -enne *f*; **the ~** les Sud-Vietnamiens.

◇ *adj* sud-vietnamien.

southward ['saʊθwəd] ◇ *adj* au sud.

◇ *adv* vers le sud, en direction du sud.

southwards ['saʊθwədz] = **southward** *adv*.

southwest [,saʊθ'west] ◇ *n* sud-ouest *m*; **in the ~ of the United States** dans le sud-ouest des États-Unis.

◇ *adj* -**1.** GEOG sud-ouest *(inv)*, du sud-ouest; **in ~ Scotland** dans le sud-ouest de l'Écosse. -**2.** [wind] de sud-ouest.

◇ *adv* au sud-ouest, vers le sud-ouest; **it's ~ of London** c'est au sud-ouest de Londres.

southwester [,saʊθ'westəʳ] *n* vent *m* de sud-ouest, suroît *m*.

southwesterly [,saʊθ'westəlɪ] (*pl* southwesterlies) ◇ *adj* -**1.** GEOG sud-ouest *(inv)*, du sud-ouest; **in a ~ direction** vers le sud-ouest. -**2.** [wind] de sud-ouest.

◇ *adv* au sud-ouest, vers le sud-ouest.

◇ *n* = **southwester**.

southwestern [,saʊθ'westən] *adj* sud-ouest *(inv)*, du sud-ouest; **the ~ States** les États du sud-ouest.

southwestwards [,saʊθ'westwədz] *adv* vers le sud-ouest, en direction du sud-ouest.

South Yemen *pr n* Yémen *m* du Sud; **in ~** au Yémen du Sud.

souvenir [,suːvə'nɪəʳ] *n* souvenir *m* *(objet)*.

sou'wester [saʊ'westəʳ] *n* -**1.** [headgear] suroît *m*. -**2.** [wind] = **southwester**.

sovereign ['sɒvrɪn] ◇ *n* -**1.** [monarch] souverain *m*, -e *f*. -**2.** [coin] souverain *m* *(ancienne pièce de monnaie britannique en or)*.

◇ *adj* -**1.** POL [state, territory] souverain; [powers] souverain, suprême; [rights] de souveraineté; **Parliament remains ~** le parlement reste souverain. -**2.** *lit* [excellent - remedy] souverain; [utmost - scorn, indifference] souverain, absolu.

sovereignty ['sɒvrɪntɪ] (*pl* **sovereignties**) *n* souveraineté *f*; with no loss of ~ sans perte de souveraineté.

soviet ['səʊvɪət] *n* [council] soviet *m*; the Supreme Soviet le Soviet suprême.
◆ **Soviet** ◇ *n* [inhabitant] Soviétique *mf*.
◇ *adj* soviétique; Soviet Russia la Russie soviétique; the Union of Soviet Socialist Republics l'Union *f* des Républiques Socialistes Soviétiques.

sovietize, -ise ['səʊvɪətaɪz] *vt* soviétiser.

Soviet Union *pr n*: the ~ l'Union *f* soviétique; in the ~ en Union soviétique.

sow[1] [səʊ] (*pt* sowed, *pp* sowed OR sown [səʊn], *cont* sowing) ◇ *vt* -**1.** [seed, crop] semer; [field] ensemencer. -**2.** *fig* semer; to ~ discord/terror semer la discorde/la terreur; he ~ed (the seeds of) doubt in their minds il a semé le doute dans leur esprit; it was at this time that the seeds of the Industrial Revolution were sown c'est à cette époque que remontent les origines de la révolution industrielle ❑ ~ the wind and reap the whirlwind *prov* qui sème le vent récolte la tempête *prov*.
◇ *vi* semer; as you ~ so shall you reap BIBLE comme tu auras semé tu moissonneras.

sow[2] [saʊ] *n* [pig] truie *f*.

sow bug [saʊ-] *n Am* cloporte *m*.

sower ['səʊə^r] *n* [person] semeur *m*, -euse *f*; [machine] semoir *m*.

sowing ['səʊɪŋ] *n* -**1.** [act] ensemencement *m*. -**2.** *(U)* [work, period, seed] semailles *fpl*.

sown [səʊn] *pp* → **sow**.

sow thistle [saʊ-] *n* laiteron *m (potager)*.

sox *inf* [sɒks] *n pl Am* chaussettes *fpl*.

soy [sɔɪ] = **soy sauce**.

soya ['sɔɪə] *n* soja *m*; ~ flour/milk farine *f*/lait *m* de soja.

soya bean *Br*, **soybean** ['sɔɪbiːn] *Am n* graine *f* de soja.

soy sauce *n* sauce *f* de soja.

sozzled *inf* ['sɒzld] *adj Br* soûl, paf.

spa [spɑː] *n* -**1.** [resort] ville *f* d'eau. -**2.** [spring] source *f* minérale.

space [speɪs] ◇ *n* -**1.** ASTRON & PHYS espace *m*; the first man in ~ le premier homme dans l'espace; a particular point in ~ and time un point particulier dans l'espace et le temps; she sat staring into ~ elle était assise, le regard perdu dans le vide. -**2.** [room] espace *m*, place *f*; there's too much wasted ~ in this kitchen il y a trop de place perdue OR d'espace inutilisé dans cette cuisine; your books take up an awful lot of ~ tes livres prennent énormément de place; the large windows give an impression of ~ les grandes fenêtres donnent une impression d'espace; he cleared a OR some ~ on his desk for the tray il a fait un peu de place sur son bureau pour le plateau; can you make ~ for one more? pouvez-vous faire de la place pour une personne de plus?; the author devotes a lot of ~ to philosophical speculations l'auteur fait une large part aux spéculations philosophiques. -**3.** [volume, area, distance] espace *m*; an enclosed ~ un espace clos; there are at least five pubs in the ~ of a few hundred yards il y a au moins cinq pubs sur quelques centaines de mètres ❑ living ~ espace *m* vital; a work ~ un coin pour travailler, un coin-travail; advertising ~ espace *m* publicitaire. -**4.** [gap] espace *m*, place *f*; there's barely any ~ between the houses il n'y a pratiquement pas d'espace entre les maisons ‖ [on page, official form] espace *m*, case *f*; leave a ~ for the teacher's comments laissez un espace pour les remarques du professeur; please add any further details in the ~ provided veuillez ajouter tout détail supplémentaire dans la case prévue à cet effet ❑ parking ~ place de parking. -**5.** TYPO [gap between words] espace *m*, blanc *m*; [blank type] espace *m*. -**6.** [period of time, interval] intervalle *m*, espace *m* (de temps), période *f*; in OR within the ~ of six months en (l'espace de) six mois; over a ~ of several years sur une période de plusieurs années; it'll all be over in a very short ~ of time tout sera fini dans très peu de temps OR d'ici peu. -**7.** [seat, place] place *f*.
◇ *comp* [programme, research, travel, flight] spatial.
◇ *vt* = **space out**.
◆ **space out** *vt sep* -**1.** [in space] espacer; the buoys are well ~d out les bouées sont largement espacées; ~ yourselves out a bit more écartez-vous un peu plus les uns des autres. -**2.** [in time] échelonner, espacer; ~d out over a period of ten years échelonné sur une période de dix ans.

space age *n*: the ~ l'ère *f* spatiale.
◆ **space-age** *adj* -**1.** SCI de l'ère spatiale. -**2.** [futuristic] futuriste.

space bar *n* [on typewriter] barre *f* d'espacement.

space blanket *n* couverture *f* de survie.

space capsule *n* capsule *f* spatiale.

spacecraft ['speɪskrɑːft] *n* vaisseau *m* OR engin *m* spatial.

-spaced [speɪst] *in cpds* -**1.** [gen]: the buildings are closely/widely~ les bâtiments sont proches les uns des autres/largement espacés; widely~ eyes des yeux très écartés. -**2.** TYPO: single/double~ à interligne simple/double.

spaced-out[▽] *adj* shooté; they were ~ on acid ils étaient shootés à l'acide.

space heater *n* radiateur *m*.

Space Invaders® *npl jeu vidéo dont le but est de détruire des envahisseurs venant de l'espace*.

spacelab ['speɪslæb] *n* laboratoire *m* spatial.

spaceman ['speɪsmæn] (*pl* **spacemen** [-men]) *n* [gen] spationaute *m*; [American] astronaute *m*; [Russian] cosmonaute *m*.

space platform = **space station**.

spaceport ['speɪspɔːt] *n* base *f* de lancement.

space probe *n* sonde *f* spatiale.

space race *n* course *f* pour la suprématie dans l'espace.

space rocket *n* fusée *f* spatiale OR interplanétaire.

space-saving *adj* qui fait gagner de la place.

spaceship ['speɪsʃɪp] *n* vaisseau *m* OR engin *m* spatial habité.

space shot *n* lancement *m* spatial.

space shuttle *n* navette *f* spatiale.

space-sick *adj*: to be ~ avoir le mal de l'espace.

space sickness *n* mal *m* de l'espace.

space station *n* station *f* spatiale OR orbitale.

spacesuit ['speɪssuːt] *n* combinaison *f* spatiale.

space-time continuum *n* continuum *m* spatio-temporel.

space travel *n* voyages *mpl* dans l'espace, astronautique *f spec*.

space walk ◇ *n* marche *f* dans l'espace.
◇ *vi* marcher dans l'espace.

spacewoman ['speɪsˌwʊmən] (*pl* **spacewomen** [-ˌwɪmɪn]) *n* [gen] spationaute *f*, astronaute *f*; [Russian] cosmonaute *f*.

spacey[▽] ['speɪsɪ] (*compar* **spacier**, *superl* **spaciest**) *adj* -**1.** [music] planant. -**2.** [person]: to feel ~ être dans les vapes.

spacial ['speɪʃl] = **spatial**.

spacing ['speɪsɪŋ] *n* -**1.** [of text on page - horizontal] espacement *m*; [- vertical] interligne *m*; typed in single/double ~ tapé avec interligne simple/double. -**2.** [between trees, columns, buildings etc] espacement *m*, écart *m*.

spacious ['speɪʃəs] *adj* [house, room, office] spacieux, grand; [park, property] étendu, grand.

spaciousness ['speɪʃəsnɪs] *n* grandeur *f*, dimensions *fpl* spacieuses.

spade [speɪd] *n* -**1.** [tool] bêche *f*; to call a ~ a ~ appeler un chat un chat; to have sthg in ~s *inf Am* avoir des tonnes de qqch; and you've got it in ~s et tu en as à revendre. -**2.** [in cards] pique *m*; my partner played a ~ mon partenaire a joué pique; the ace/ten of ~s l'as/le dix de pique. -**3.** ▼*terme raciste désignant un Noir*, ≃ nègre *m*, ≃ négresse *f*.

spadeful ['speɪdfʊl] *n* pelletée *f*.

spadework ['speɪdwɜːk] *n* travail *m* de préparation OR de déblayage.

spaghetti [spə'getɪ] *n (U)* spaghetti *mpl*, spaghettis *mpl*.

Spaghetti Junction *pr n surnom d'un échangeur sur l'autoroute M6 au nord de Birmingham*.

spaghetti western *n* western-spaghetti *m*.

Spain [speɪn] *pr n* Espagne *f*; in ~ en Espagne.

spake [speɪk] *arch pt* → **speak**.

Spam® [spæm] *n pâté de jambon en conserve*.

span [spæn] (*pt* & *pp* **spanned**, *cont* **spanning**)
◇ *n* -**1.** [duration] durée *f*, laps *m* de temps; memory ~ capacité *f* de mémorisation *(de courte durée)*; a short attention ~ une capacité d'attention limitée; man's ~ on earth le séjour terrestre de l'homme ‖ [intervening period, interval] intervalle *m*; his work covers a ~ of twenty-odd years son œuvre s'étend sur une vingtaine d'années. -**2.** [range] gamme *f*; we cover only a limited ~ of subjects nous ne couvrons qu'un nombre restreint de sujets. -**3.** [of hands, arms, wings] envergure *f*. -**4.** [of bridge] travée *f*; [of arch, dome, girder] portée *f*. -**5.** [unit of measurement] empan *m*. -**6.** [matched pair - of horses, oxen] paire *f*.
◇ *vt* -**1.** [encompass, stretch over - in time, extent] couvrir, embrasser; her career spanned more than 50 years sa carrière s'étend sur plus de 50 ans. -**2.** [cross - river, ditch etc] enjamber, traverser; a modern bridge now ~s the valley un pont moderne enjambe maintenant la vallée. -**3.** [build bridge over] jeter un pont sur.
◇ *arch pt* → **spin**.

spang *inf* [spæŋ] *adv Am* directement, pile; ~ on target en plein dans le mille.

spangle ['spæŋgl] ◇ *n* paillette *f*.
◇ *vt* pailleter, décorer de paillettes; ~d with gold pailleté d'or; stars ~d the night sky le ciel était semé d'étoiles.

Spaniard ['spænjəd] *n* Espagnol *m*, -e *f*.

spaniel ['spænjəl] *n* épagneul *m*.

Spanish ['spænɪʃ] ◇ *adj* espagnol; ~ guitar guitare *f* classique.
◇ *n* LING espagnol *m*.
◇ *npl*: the ~ les Espagnols *mpl*.

Spanish America *pr n* Amérique *f* hispanophone.

Spanish-American ◇ *n* -**1.** [in the US] Hispanique *mf*. -**2.** [in Latin America] Hispano-Américain *m*, -e *f*.
◇ *adj* -**1.** [in the US] hispanique. -**2.** [in Latin America] hispano-américain. -**3.** *Am* HIST: the ~ War la guerre hispano-américaine.

THE SPANISH-AMERICAN WAR:
Conflit qui opposa, en 1898, les États-Unis à l'Espagne dans les Caraïbes. Se posant en défenseurs des Cubains opprimés par les Espagnols, les Américains eurent la victoire facile. Elle leur permit d'étendre leur influence sur le Pacifique et les Caraïbes tout en conférant à leur pays le statut de puissance mondiale.

Spanish Armada *pr n*: the ~ l'Invincible Armada *f*.

THE SPANISH ARMADA:
Flotte envoyée par Philippe II d'Espagne en 1588 dans le but d'envahir l'Angleterre et d'y rétablir le catholicisme. Malgré une supériorité numérique et une longue préparation, une série de contretemps et la maniabilité de la flotte britannique firent échouer le projet.

Spanish fly *n* -**1.** [insect] cantharide *f*. -**2.** [product] poudre *f* de cantharide.

Spanish Inquisition *n*: the ~ l'Inquisition *f* espagnole.

Spanish Main *pr n*: the ~ la mer des Caraïbes.

Spanish omelette *n* omelette *f* à l'espagnole.

Spanish onion *n* oignon *m* d'Espagne.

spank [spæŋk] ◇ *vt* donner une fessée à, fesser.
◇ *vi* [go at a lively pace]: to be OR to go ~ing along aller bon train OR à bonne allure.
◇ *n* tape *f* sur les fesses; to give a child a ~ donner une tape sur les fesses à un enfant.

spanking ['spæŋkɪŋ] ◇ *n* fessée *f*; to give sb a ~ donner une fessée à qqn.
◇ *adj* *inf* -**1.** [excellent] excellent; in ~ condition en excellent état. -**2.** [brisk] vif; a ~ breeze une bonne brise; to go at a ~ pace aller bon train OR à bonne allure.
◇ *adv* *inf*: ~ new flambant neuf; ~ clean propre comme un sou neuf.

spanner ['spænəʳ] *n* clé *f*, clef *f (outil)*; adjustable ~ clé à molette; to throw OR to put a ~ in the works poser des problèmes; if they both arrived together that would really put a ~ in the works s'ils arrivaient tous les deux ensemble ça poserait quelques problèmes.

spar [spɑːʳ] (*pt* & *pp* sparred, *cont* sparring)
◇ *vi* -**1.** [in boxing - train] s'entraîner (avec un sparring-partner); [- test out opponent] faire des feintes *(pour tester son adversaire)*; they sparred with each other for a few rounds ils boxèrent amicalement durant quelques rounds. -**2.** [argue] se disputer.
◇ *n* -**1.** [pole - gen] poteau *m*, mât *m*; NAUT espar *m*. -**2.** AERON longeron *m*. -**3.** MINER spath *m*.

spare [speəʳ] ◇ *adj* -**1.** [not in use] dont on ne se sert pas, disponible; [kept in reserve] de réserve, de rechange; [extra, surplus] de trop, en trop; take a ~ pullover prenez un pull de rechange; have you got a ~ piece of paper? est-ce que tu as une feuille de papier à me prêter?; have you got any ~ cash on you? est-ce que tu peux me prêter de l'argent?; we had no ~ cash left to buy souvenirs nous n'avions plus assez d'argent pour acheter des souvenirs; I've got two ~ tickets for the match j'ai deux billets en plus pour le match; I'll have some more cake if there's any going ~ *inf* je vais reprendre du gâteau s'il en reste; you can stay here if you want, we have a ~ bed tu peux rester ici si tu veux, nous avons un lit pour toi. -**2.** [free] libre, disponible; there are plenty of ~ seats at the back il y a de nombreuses places libres au fond; call in next time you have a ~ moment passez la prochaine fois que vous aurez un moment de libre. -**3.** [lean] maigre, sec. -**4.** [austere - style, decor] austère; [frugal - meal] frugal. -**5.** *inf Br* [mad]: to go ~ devenir dingue; to drive sb ~ rendre qqn fou.
◇ *n* -**1.** [spare part] pièce *f* de rechange; [wheel] roue *f* de secours; [tyre] pneu *m* de rechange. -**2.** [in ten-pin bowling] honneur *m* simple; to get OR to score a ~ réussir un honneur simple.
◇ *vt* -**1.** [make available, give] accorder, consacrer; Mr Austen can ~ you a few minutes this afternoon M. Austen peut vous consacrer quelques minutes cet après-midi; come and see us if you can ~ the time venez nous voir si vous avez le temps; ~ a thought for their poor parents! pensez un peu à leurs pauvres parents!; less money can be ~d for research these days on ne peut plus consacrer autant d'argent à la recherche aujourd'hui; can you ~ (me) a few pounds? vous n'auriez pas quelques livres (à me passer)?|| [do without] se passer de; I'm afraid we can't ~ anyone at the moment je regrette mais nous ne pouvons nous passer de personne OR nous avons besoin de tout le monde en ce moment; I need £50, if you think you can ~ it j'aurais besoin de 50 livres si c'est possible. -**2.** [refrain from harming, punishing, destroying] épargner; a few villages were miraculously ~d par miracle, quelques villages furent épargnés; to ~ sb's life épargner la vie de qqn; to ~ sb's feelings ménager les sentiments de qqn; to ~ sb's blushes épargner qqn; ~ my blushes! ne me faites pas rougir! -**3.** [save - trouble, suffering] épargner, éviter; I could have ~d myself the bother j'aurais pu m'épargner le dérangement; she was ~d further distress by the judge's intervention l'intervention du juge mit fin à ses tortures; he was ~d the shame of a public trial la honte d'un procès public lui a été épargnée; ~ us the sordid details! épargnez-nous les détails (sordides)! -**4.** [economize] ménager; they ~d no expense on the celebrations ils n'ont reculé devant aucune dépense pour les fêtes; the first prize is a real luxury trip, with no expense ~d le premier prix est un voyage de rêve pour lequel on n'a pas regardé à la dépense; we shall ~ no effort to push the plan through nous ne reculerons devant aucun effort pour faire accepter le projet ❑ ~ the rod and spoil the child *prov* qui aime bien châtie bien *prov*.
◆ **to spare** *adj phr*: young people with money to ~ des jeunes qui ont de l'argent à dépenser; he's got enough money and to ~ il a plus d'argent qu'il ne lui en faut; do you have a few minutes to ~? avez-vous quelques minutes de libres OR devant vous?; we got to the airport with over an hour to ~ nous sommes arrivés à l'aéroport avec plus d'une heure d'avance; I caught the train with just a few seconds to ~ à quelques secondes près je ratais le train.

spare part *n* pièce *f* de rechange, pièce *f* détachée.

spare-part surgery *inf n* chirurgie *f* des greffes.

sparerib [speə'rɪb] *n* travers *m* de porc.

spare room *n* chambre *f* d'amis.

spare time *n* temps *m* libre; what do you do in your ~? que faites-vous pendant votre temps libre OR pendant vos moments de loisirs?
◆ **spare-time** *adj* (fait) pendant ses moments de loisirs OR, à ses moments perdus; spare-time activities loisirs *mpl*.

spare tyre *n* -**1.** AUT pneu *m* de secours OR de rechange. -**2.** *inf* [roll of fat] bourrelet *m (à la taille)*.

spare wheel *n* roue *f* de secours.

sparing ['speərɪŋ] *adj* -**1.** [economical - person] économe; she's very ~ with her compliments elle est très avare de compliments; they were ~ in their efforts to help us ils ne se sont pas donnés beaucoup de mal pour nous aider. -**2.** [meagre - quantity] limité, modéré; [- use] modéré, économe; the author makes ~ use of metaphors l'auteur utilise la métaphore avec parcimonie OR modération.

sparingly ['speərɪŋlɪ] *adv* [eat] frugalement; [drink, use] avec modération; [praise] chichement, avec parcimonie; they should be watered often but ~ il faudrait les arroser souvent mais avec modération; use your strength ~ ménagez vos forces.

spark [spɑːk] ◇ *vt* [trigger - interest, argument] susciter, provoquer; the incident was the catalyst that ~ed the revolution c'est l'incident qui a déclenché la révolution; the news ~ed (off) an intense debate la nouvelle déclencha un débat animé.
◇ *vi* -**1.** [produce sparks - gen] jeter des étincelles. -**2.** AUT [spark plug, ignition system] allumer *(par étincelle)*.
◇ *n* -**1.** [from flame, electricity] étincelle *f*; *fig*: whenever they meet the ~s fly chaque fois qu'ils se rencontrent, ça fait des étincelles; they strike ~s off each other ils se stimulent mutuellement. -**2.** [flash, trace - of excitement, wit] étincelle *f*, lueur *f*; [- of interest, enthusiasm, understanding]: she hasn't a ~ of common sense elle n'a pas le moindre bon sens.
◆ **sparks**▽ *n Br* [electrician] électricien *m*, -enne *f*; [radio operator] radio *m*.
◆ **spark off** *vt sep* = **spark**.

spark chamber *n* chambre *f* à étincelles.

spark gap *n* AUT écartement *m* des électrodes.

sparking plug ['spɑːkɪŋ-] *Br* = **spark plug**.

sparkle ['spɑːkl] ◇ *vi* -**1.** [jewel, frost, glass, star] étinceler, briller, scintiller; [sea, lake] étinceler, miroiter; [eyes] étinceler, pétiller. -**2.** [person] briller; [conversation] être brillant. -**3.** [wine, cider, mineral water] pétiller.
◇ *n* -**1.** [of jewel, frost, glass, star] étincellement *m*, scintillement *m*; [of sea, lake] étincellement *m*, miroitement *m*; [of eyes] éclat *m*; she has a ~ in her eye elle a des yeux pétillants. -**2.** [of person, conversation, wit, performance] éclat *m*.

sparkler ['spɑːkləʳ] *n* -**1.** [firework] cierge *m* magique. -**2.** ▽ *Br* [diamond] diam *m*.

sparkling ['spɑːklɪŋ] ◇ *adj* -**1.** [jewel, frost, glass, star] étincelant, scintillant; [sea, lake] étincelant, miroitant; [eyes] étincelant, pétillant. -**2.** [person, conversation, wit, performance] brillant. -**3.** [soft drink, mineral water] gazeux, pétillant.
◇ *adv*: ~ clean/white d'une propreté/blancheur éclatante.

sparkling wine *n* vin *m* mousseux.

spark plug *n* bougie *f* AUT.

sparring match ['spɑːrɪŋ-] *n* -**1.** [in boxing] combat *m* d'entraînement. -**2.** [argument] discussion *f* animée.

sparring partner *n* -**1.** [in boxing] sparring-partner *m*. -**2.** *fig* adversaire *m*.

sparrow ['spærəʊ] *n* moineau *m*.

sparrowhawk ['spærəʊhɔːk] *n*: (Eurasian) ~ épervier *m*; American ~ faucon *m* des moineaux.

sparse [spɑːs] *adj* clairsemé, rare.

sparsely ['spɑːslɪ] *adv* [wooded, populated] peu; the room was ~ furnished la pièce contenait peu de meubles; it grows only ~ in the north ça ne pousse pas beaucoup dans le nord.

sparseness ['spɑːsnɪs] *n* [of population] faible densité *f*; [of hair, vegetation] manque *m*.

Sparta ['spɑːtə] *pr n* Sparte.

Spartacist ['spɑːtəsɪst] ◇ *adj* spartakiste.
◇ *n* spartakiste *mf*.

Spartacus ['spɑːtəkəs] *pr n* Spartacus.

spartan ['spɑːtn] *adj fig* spartiate; ~ living conditions des conditions de vie spartiates; a ~ room une chambre austère OR sans aucun confort.
◆ **Spartan** HIST ◇ *n* Spartiate *mf*.
◇ *adj* spartiate.

spasm ['spæzm] *n* -**1.** [muscular contraction] spasme *m*. -**2.** [fit] accès *m*; a ~ of anger/pain un accès de colère/de douleur; he had a ~ of coughing il a eu une quinte de toux; she went into ~s of laughter elle a été prise d'une crise de fou rire; I tend to work in ~s *Br* j'ai tendance à travailler de façon irrégulière.

spasmodic [spæz'mɒdɪk] *adj* -**1.** [intermittent] intermittent, irrégulier. -**2.** MED [pain, contraction] spasmodique.

spasmodically [spæz'mɒdɪklɪ] *adv* de façon intermittente, par à-coups.

spastic ['spæstɪk] ◇ *n* -**1.** MED [gen] handicapé *m*, -e *f* (moteur); [person affected by spasms] spasmophilique *mf*. -**2.** ▽ *offensive* [clumsy person] maladroit *m*, -e *f*, lourdaud *m*, -e *f*.
◇ *adj* -**1.** MED [gen] handicapé (moteur); [affected by spasms] spasmophilique; ~ paralysis tétanie *f*. -**2.** ▽ *offensive* [clumsy] empoté, gourde.

spat [spæt] ◇ *n* -**1.** [gaiter] guêtre *f*. -**2.** *inf* [quarrel] prise *f* de bec. -**3.** [shellfish] naissain *m*.
◇ *pt* & *pp* → **spit**.

spate [speɪt] *n* -**1.** [of letters, visitors] avalanche *f*; [of abuse, insults] torrent *m*; a ~ of murders/burglaries une série de meurtres/cambriolages. -**2.** *Br* [flood] crue *f*; the river was in ~ le fleuve était en crue; sorry for interrupting you in full ~ *fig* je suis désolé de vous interrompre en plein discours.

spatial ['speɪʃl] *adj* spatial.

spatiotemporal [,speɪʃɪəʊ'temprəl] *adj* spatiotemporel.

spatter ['spætəʳ] ◇ *vt* [splash] éclabousser; he ~ed ink on OR over the table il a fait des éclaboussures d'encre sur la table; the car ~ed me with mud, the car ~ed mud over me l'auto m'a éclaboussé OR aspergé de boue.
◇ *vi* [liquid] gicler; [oil] crépiter; rain ~ed on the windowpane la pluie crépitait sur la vitre.
◇ *n* [on garment] éclaboussure *f*, éclaboussures *fpl*; [sound - of rain, oil, applause] crépitement *m*.

spatterdash ['spætədæʃ] *n Am* [roughcast] crépi *m.*

spatula ['spætjʊlə] *n* -**1.** CULIN spatule *f.* -**2.** MED abaisse-langue *m inv*, spatule *f.*

spavin ['spævɪn] *n* éparvin *m*, épervin *m.*

spawn [spɔːn] ◇ *n (U)* -**1.** ZOOL [of frogs, fish] œufs *mpl*, frai *m.* -**2.** BOT [of mushrooms] mycélium *m.* -**3.** *fig* & *pej* [offspring] progéniture *f.*
◇ *vt* -**1.** ZOOL pondre. -**2.** *fig* [produce] engendrer.
◇ *vi* ZOOL frayer.

spay [speɪ] *vt* enlever les ovaires de.

SPCA (*abbr of* Society for the Prevention of Cruelty to Animals) *pr n société américaine protectrice des animaux*, ≃ SPA.

SPCC (*abbr of* Society for the Prevention of Cruelty to Children) *pr n société américaine pour la protection de l'enfance.*

speak [spiːk] (*pt* spoke [spəʊk], *pp* spoken ['spəʊkn]) ◇ *vi* -**1.** [talk] parler; to ~ to/with *esp Am* sb parler à/avec qqn; to ~ about OR of sthg parler de qqch; to ~ to sb about sthg parler à qqn de qqch; I'll ~ to her about it je lui en parlerai; to ~ in a whisper chuchoter; ~ to me! dites (-moi) quelque chose!; don't ~ to your mother like that! ne parle pas à ta mère sur ce ton!; ~ when you're spoken to! ne parlez que lorsque l'on s'adresse à vous!; don't ~ with your mouth full ne parle pas la bouche pleine; it seems I spoke too soon on dirait que j'ai parlé un peu vite; his plays are hugely popular, not to ~ of his many novels ses pièces sont extrêmement populaires, sans parler de ses nombreux romans ‖ [on telephone] parler; who's ~ing? [gen] qui est à l'appareil?; [switchboard] c'est de la part de qui?; Kate Smith ~ing Kate Smith à l'appareil, c'est Kate Smith; may I ~ to Kate? – ~ing puis-je parler à Kate? – c'est moi ❑ ~ now or forever hold your peace parlez maintenant ou gardez le silence pour toujours. -**2.** [in debate, meeting etc – make a speech] faire un discours, parler; [– intervene] prendre la parole, parler; he began to ~ il a pris la parole; she got up to ~ elle s'est levée pour parler; the chair called upon Mrs Fox to ~ le président a demandé à Mme Fox de prendre la parole; he was invited to ~ to us on OR about Chile il a été invité à venir nous parler du Chili; she spoke for an hour on imperialism elle a parlé de l'impérialisme pendant une heure; to ~ to OR on a motion soutenir une motion; to ~ from the floor intervenir dans un débat. -**3.** [be on friendly terms with]: she isn't ~ing to me elle ne me parle plus; I don't know them to ~ to je ne les connais que de vue; to be on ~ing terms with sb connaître qqn *(assez pour lui parler)*; we're no longer on ~ing terms nous ne nous parlons plus. -**4.** [as spokesperson]: to ~ for sb [on their behalf] parler au nom de qqn; [in their favour] parler en faveur de qqn; let her ~ for herself! laisse-la s'exprimer!; ~ for yourself! *hum* parle pour toi!; the facts ~ for themselves *fig* les faits parlent d'eux-mêmes; the title ~s for itself *fig* le titre se passe de commentaire. -**5.** [in giving an opinion]: generally ~ing en général; personally ~ing en ce qui me concerne, quant à moi; ~ing of which justement, à ce propos; financially ~ing financièrement parlant, du point de vue financier; ~ing as a politician en tant qu'homme politique; you shouldn't ~ ill of the dead tu ne devrais pas dire du mal des morts; he always ~s well/highly of you il dit toujours du bien/beaucoup de bien de vous; the gift ~s well of her concern for old people son don témoigne de l'intérêt qu'elle porte aux personnes âgées. -**6.** *fig* [give an impression]: everything he saw seemed to ~ to him of Greece tout ce qu'il voyait lui semblait évoquer la Grèce; his paintings ~ of terrible loneliness ses peintures expriment une immense solitude. -**7.** *lit* [sound – trumpet] sonner, retentir; [– organ pipe] parler; [– gun] retentir.
◇ *vt* -**1.** [say, pronounce] dire, prononcer; the baby spoke his first words le bébé a dit ses premiers mots; I only had three lines to ~ in the play je n'avais que trois lignes à dire dans la pièce; to ~ one's mind dire sa pensée OR façon de penser; she spoke my name in her sleep elle a prononcé mon nom dans son sommeil; he didn't ~ a word il n'a pas dit un mot; without a word being spoken sans qu'un mot ne soit prononcé; to ~ the truth dire la vérité; their behaviour ~s volumes for their generosity leur comportement en dit long sur leur générosité OR montre à quel point ils sont généreux; his silence ~s volumes son silence en dit long. -**2.** [language] parler; he doesn't ~ a word of Greek il ne parle pas un mot de grec; 'English spoken' 'ici on parle anglais'; we just don't ~ the same language *fig* nous ne parlons pas le même langage, c'est tout.
◆ **so to speak** *adv phr* pour ainsi dire.
◆ **to speak of** *adv phr*: there's no wind/mail to ~ of il n'y a presque pas de vent/de courrier.
◆ **speak for** *vt insep (usu pass)*: these goods are already spoken for ces articles sont déjà réservés OR retenus; she's already spoken for elle est déjà prise.
◆ **speak out** *vi insep* parler franchement, ne pas mâcher ses mots; don't be afraid to ~ out n'aie pas peur de parler franchement OR de dire ce que tu penses; to ~ out for sthg parler en faveur de qqch; to ~ out against sthg s'élever contre qqch; she spoke out strongly against the scheme elle a condamné le projet avec véhémence.
◆ **speak up** *vi insep* -**1.** [louder] parler plus fort; [more clearly] parler plus clairement. -**2.** [be frank] parler franchement; to ~ up for sb parler en faveur de qqn, défendre les intérêts de qqn; why didn't you ~ up? pourquoi n'avez-vous rien dit?

-speak *in cpds pej*: psycho~ jargon *m* psychologique OR des psychologues; computer~ langage *m* OR jargon *m* de l'informatique.

speakeasy ['spiːkˌiːzɪ] (*pl* speakeasies) *n* bar *m* clandestin *(pendant la prohibition).*

speaker ['spiːkə^r] *n* -**1.** [gen] celui *m*, celle *f* qui parle; [in discussion] interlocuteur *m*, -trice *f*; [in public] orateur *m*, -trice *f*; [in lecture] conférencier *m*, -ère *f*; she's a good ~ elle sait parler OR s'exprimer en public; the chairman called the next ~ le président a appelé l'orateur suivant. -**2.** LING locuteur *m*, -trice *f*; native ~s of English ceux dont la langue maternelle est l'anglais; Spanish ~ hispanophone *mf*; she's a Polish ~ sa langue maternelle est le polonais; my parents are Welsh ~s mes parents sont gallois ants OR parlent (le) gallois. -**3.** POL speaker *m*, président *m*, -e *f* de l'assemblée ❑ the Speaker (of the House of Commons) le président de la Chambre des communes; the Speaker of the House *le président de la Chambre des représentants américaine.* -**4.** [loudspeaker] haut-parleur *m*; [in stereo system] enceinte *f*, baffle *m.*

THE SPEAKER OF THE HOUSE:
Le président de la Chambre des représentants est l'une des personnalités politiques les plus influentes à la Maison-Blanche, et vient en deuxième position pour remplacer le président des États-Unis en cas de force majeure.

Speakers' Corner *pr n angle nord-est de Hyde Park où chacun peut venir le week-end haranguer la foule sur des tribunes improvisées.*

speaking ['spiːkɪŋ] ◇ *adj* -**1.** [involving speech]: do you have a ~ part in the play? est-ce que vous avez du texte?; she has a good ~ voice elle a une belle voix. -**2.** [which speaks – robot, machine, doll] parlant.
◇ *n* art *m* de parler; unaccustomed as I am to public ~... *hum* bien que je sois peu habitué à parler OR à prendre la parole en public...

-speaking *in cpds* -**1.** [person] parlant, qui parle; they're both German/Spanish~ ils sont tous deux germanophones/hispanophones; a child of Polish~ parents un enfant dont les parents sont de langue OR d'origine polonaise. -**2.** [country]: French/English~ countries les pays francophones/anglophones; the Arab~ world le monde arabophone.

speaking clock *n Br* horloge *f* parlante.

speaking tube *n* tuyau *m* acoustique.

spear [spɪə^r] ◇ *n* -**1.** [weapon] lance *f*; [harpoon] harpon *m.* -**2.** [of asparagus, broccoli etc] pointe *f.*
◇ *vt* -**1.** [enemy] transpercer d'un coup de lance; [fish] harponner. -**2.** [food] piquer; he ~ed a piece of meat with his fork/on a skewer il a piqué un morceau de viande avec sa fourchette/enfilé un morceau de viande sur une brochette.

spearfish ['spɪəfɪʃ] (*pl inv* OR spearfishes)
◇ *n* marlin *m.*
◇ *vi Am* pratiquer la pêche sous-marine.

speargun ['spɪəgʌn] *n* fusil *m* (de pêche sous-marine).

spearhead ['spɪəhed] ◇ *n literal* & *fig* fer *m* de lance.
◇ *vt* [attack] être le fer de lance de; [campaign, movement] mener, être à la tête de.

spearmint ['spɪəmɪnt] ◇ *n* -**1.** [plant] menthe *f* verte; [flavour] menthe *f.* -**2.** [sweet] bonbon *m* à la menthe.
◇ *adj* [flavour] de menthe; [toothpaste, chewing gum] à la menthe.

spearwort ['spɪəwɜːt] *n* renoncule *f.*

spec [spek] *n* -**1.** *phr*: on ~ *inf Br* au hasard; I called by on ~ je suis passé au hasard; he bought the car on ~ il a risqué le coup en achetant la voiture; he bought the books on ~ il a acheté les livres dans l'espoir de faire une affaire. -**2.** *abbr of* specification.

special ['speʃl] ◇ *adj* -**1.** [exceptional, particular – offer, friend, occasion, ability] spécial; [– reason, effort, pleasure] particulier; [– powers] extraordinaire; pay ~ attention to the details faites particulièrement attention aux détails; this is a very ~ moment for me c'est un moment particulièrement important pour moi; as a ~ treat [present] comme cadeau; [outing] pour vous faire plaisir; can you do me a ~ favour? pouvez-vous me rendre un grand service?; I'll do it as a ~ favour to you je le ferai, mais c'est bien pour toi OR parce que c'est toi; it's a ~ case c'est un cas particulier OR à part; a ~ feature [in paper] un article spécial; [on TV] une émission spéciale; they put on a ~ train for the match ils ont prévu un train supplémentaire pour le match; what did you do last night? – nothing ~ qu'as-tu fait hier soir? – rien de spécial; I'm going to cook something ~ for dinner tonight ce soir, je vais cuisiner quelque chose qui sorte de l'ordinaire ❑ ~ interest holidays vacances *fpl* à thème. -**2.** [specific – need, problem] spécial, particulier; [– equipment] spécial; [– adviser] particulier; you need ~ permission il vous faut une autorisation spéciale; by ~ permission of the Lyme museum avec l'aimable autorisation du musée Lyme; she has a ~ interest in Italian art elle s'intéresse beaucoup à OR porte un intérêt tout particulier à l'art italien. -**3.** [peculiar] particulier; it has a ~ taste ça a un goût particulier OR assez spécial. -**4.** [valued] cher; this house is very ~ to me cette maison m'est très chère; you're very ~ to me je tiens beaucoup à toi; a ~ relationship des rapports privilégiés; a present for a ~ person un cadeau pour un être cher.
◇ *n* -**1.** [train] train *m* supplémentaire; [bus] car *m* supplémentaire; they put on a football/holiday ~ ils ont mis un train supplémentaire pour le match de football/les départs en vacances. -**2.** [in restaurant] spécialité *f*; the chef's/the house ~ la spécialité du chef/de la maison; today's ~ le plat du jour. -**3.** TV émission *f* spéciale; PRESS [issue] numéro *m* spécial; [feature] article *m* spécial; they brought out a ~ on the war ils ont sorti un numéro spécial sur la guerre. -**4.** *Br* [police officer] = **special constable**. -**5.** *Am* COMM offre *f* spéciale; sugar is on ~ today le sucre est en promotion aujourd'hui.

Special Air Service *pr n commando d'intervention spéciale de l'armée britannique.*

Special Branch *pr n renseignements généraux britanniques*.

special constable *n Br* auxiliaire *mf* de police.

special correspondent *n* PRESS envoyé *m* spécial.

special delivery *n service postal britannique garantissant la distribution du courrier sous 24 heures*.

special effects *npl* CIN & TV effets *mpl* spéciaux.

specialism ['speʃəlɪzm] *n* spécialisation *f*; **my ~ is maths** je me spécialise dans les maths.

specialist ['speʃəlɪst] ◇ *n* -**1.** [gen & MED] spécialiste *mf*; **she's a heart ~** elle est cardiologue; **he's a ~ in rare books** c'est un spécialiste en livres rares. -**2.** *Am* MIL officier *m* technicien.
◇ *adj* [skills, vocabulary] spécialisé, de spécialiste; [writing, publication] pour spécialistes; **it's a ~ job** c'est un travail de spécialiste; **to seek ~ advice** demander conseil à OR consulter un spécialiste; **~ teacher** professeur *m* spécialisé; **she's a ~ maths teacher** elle n'enseigne que OR enseigne uniquement les maths.

speciality [ˌspeʃɪ'ælətɪ] *Br* (*pl* **specialities**), **specialty** ['speʃltɪ] *Am* (*pl* **specialties**) *n* -**1.** [service, product] spécialité *f*; **a local ~** une spécialité de la région; **he made a ~ of croissants** il s'est spécialisé dans les croissants; **our ~ is electronic components** nous nous spécialisons OR nous sommes spécialisés dans les composants électroniques. -**2.** [area of study] spécialité *f*; **her ~ is Chinese** elle est spécialisée en chinois.

specialization [ˌspeʃəlaɪ'zeɪʃn] *n* spécialisation *f*; **his ~ is computers** il est spécialisé en informatique.

specialize, -ise ['speʃəlaɪz] *vi* [company, restaurant, student] se spécialiser; **we ~ in Provençal cuisine/electronics** nous nous spécialisons dans la cuisine provençale/l'électronique.

specialized ['speʃəlaɪzd] *adj* spécialisé; **a hospital with highly ~ equipment** un hôpital avec des installations hautement spécialisées; **we need somebody with ~ knowledge** il nous faut un spécialiste.

special licence *n Br* dispense *f* de bans; **to be married by ~** se marier avec dispense de bans.

specially ['speʃəlɪ] *adv* -**1.** [above all] spécialement, particulièrement, surtout; **she was ~ interested in old cars** elle s'intéressait particulièrement OR surtout aux vieilles voitures; **I would ~ like to hear that song** j'aimerais beaucoup écouter cette chanson. -**2.** [on purpose, specifically] exprès, spécialement; **I made your favourite meal ~** j'ai fait exprès ton repas préféré; **the coat was ~ made for him** le manteau a été fait tout spécialement pour lui; **we've driven 500 miles ~ to see you** nous avons fait 800 kilomètres spécialement pour venir te voir. -**3.** [particularly] spécialement; **the chocolate mousse is ~ good here** la mousse au chocolat est particulièrement bonne ici; **do you want to come? — not ~** (est-ce que) tu veux venir? — pas spécialement.

special school *n Br* [for the physically handicapped] établissement *m* d'enseignement spécialisé *(pour enfants handicapés)*; [for the mentally handicapped] établissement *m* d'enseignement spécialisé *(pour enfants inadaptés)*.

special sort *n* TYPO caractère *m* spécial.

specialty ['speʃltɪ] (*pl* **specialties**) *n* -**1.** *Am* = **speciality**. -**2.** JUR contrat *m* sous seing privé.

speciate ['spiːʃɪeɪt] *vi* BIOL subir la spéciation.

specie ['spiːʃiː] *n (U)* [coins] espèces *fpl*, numéraire *m*; **in ~** *literal* en espèces, en numéraire; *fig* de manière identique.

species ['spiːʃiːz] (*pl inv*) *n* -**1.** BIOL espèce *f*; **a rare ~ of butterfly** une espèce rare de papillon. -**2.** *fig* espèce *f*; **an unusual ~ of politician** un homme politique d'une espèce rare.

specific [spə'sɪfɪk] ◇ *adj* -**1.** [explicit] explicite; [precise] précis; [clear] clair; [particular] particulier; **I gave him ~ instructions** je lui ai donné des instructions précises; **give me a ~ example** donnez-moi un exemple précis; **she was quite ~ about it** elle s'est montrée très claire OR précise à ce sujet; **what did he say? — nothing ~** qu'a-t-il dit? — rien de précis OR de particulier. -**2.** BIOL & BOT: **~ name** nom *m* spécifique OR d'espèce.
◇ *n* MED (remède *m*) spécifique *m*; **insulin is a ~ for diabetes** l'insuline est le médicament spécifique pour le diabète.
◆ **specifics** *npl* détails *mpl*; **let's not bother with the ~s of the case** inutile d'entrer dans les détails de l'affaire.

specifically [spə'sɪfɪklɪ] *adv* -**1.** [explicitly] explicitement; [precisely] précisément, de façon précise; [clearly] clairement, expressément; **his book does not ~ say what happened** son livre ne dit pas clairement ce qui s'est passé; **I ~ asked to speak to Mr Hawkins** j'avais bien spécifié OR précisé que je voulais parler à M. Hawkins; **I ~ told you to telephone** je t'avais bien dit de téléphoner. -**2.** [particularly] particulièrement; [specially] spécialement; [purposely] exprès, expressément; **our kitchens are ~ designed for the modern family** nos cuisines sont (tout) spécialement conçues pour la famille moderne; **it's not a ~ British problem** ce n'est pas un problème spécifiquement britannique.

specification [ˌspesɪfɪ'keɪʃn] *n* -**1.** *(often pl)* [in contract, of machine, building materials etc] spécifications *fpl*; **made (according) to ~** construit en fonction de spécifications techniques; **the builder didn't follow the architect's ~s** le constructeur n'a pas respecté le cahier des charges rédigé par l'architecte. -**2.** [stipulation] spécification *f*, précision *f*; **there was no ~ as to age** l'âge n'était pas précisé.

specific gravity *n* densité *f*.

specific heat *n* chaleur *f* spécifique.

specificity [ˌspesɪ'fɪsətɪ] (*pl* **specificities**) *n* spécificité *f*.

specify ['spesɪfaɪ] (*pt* & *pp* **specified**) *vt* spécifier, préciser; **the rules ~ a 5-minute break** le règlement spécifie une pause de 5 minutes; **unless otherwise specified** sauf indication contraire; **the person previously specified** la personne précitée OR déjà nommée; **on a specified date** à une date précise.

specimen ['spesɪmən] ◇ *n* -**1.** [sample – of work, handwriting] spécimen *m*; [– of blood] prélèvement *m*; [– of urine] échantillon *m*. -**2.** [single example] spécimen *m*; **this butterfly is a superb ~** ce papillon est un superbe spécimen; **a fine ~ of Gothic architecture** un bel exemple d'architecture gothique. -**3.** *inf fig* & *pej* [person] spécimen *m*; **he's a peculiar ~** c'est un drôle de spécimen; **that pathetic ~ is her husband** ce triste spécimen est son mari.
◇ *comp* [page, letter, reply] spécimen; **they will ask you for a ~ signature** ils vous demanderont un exemplaire de votre signature; **~ copy** spécimen *m (livre, magazine)*.

specious ['spiːʃəs] *adj* [argument, reasoning] spécieux; [appearance] trompeur.

speck [spek] ◇ *n* -**1.** [of dust, dirt] grain *m*; [in eye] poussière *f*; **there wasn't a ~ of dust anywhere** il n'y avait pas le moindre grain de poussière. -**2.** [stain, mark – gen] petite tache *f*; [– on skin, fruit] tache *f*, tavelure *f*; [– of blood] petite tache *f*; **I keep seeing black ~s in front of my eyes** j'ai souvent des taches noires devant les yeux. -**3.** [dot – on horizon, from height] point *m* noir; **from the top of the tower, the people looked like mere ~s** vus du haut de la tour, les gens avaient l'air de minuscules points noirs. -**4.** [tiny amount] tout petit peu *m*; **there isn't a ~ of truth in the rumour** il n'y a pas la moindre vérité OR un atome de vérité dans cette rumeur.
◇ *vt (usu pass)* tacheter.

speckle ['spekl] ◇ *n* moucheture *f*.
◇ *vt* tacheter, moucheter; **~d with yellow** tacheté OR moucheté de jaune.

speckled ['spekld] *adj* tacheté, moucheté.

specs *inf* [speks] (*abbr of* **spectacles**) *npl* lunettes *fpl*, binocles *mpl*.

spectacle ['spektəkl] *n* -**1.** [sight] spectacle *m*; **he was a sorry** OR **sad ~** il était triste à voir; **to make a ~ of o.s.** se donner en spectacle. -**2.** CIN, THEAT & TV superproduction *f*.

spectacled ['spektəkld] *adj* [gen & ZOOL] à lunettes.

spectacles ['spektəklz] *npl* lunettes *fpl*; **a pair of ~** une paire de lunettes.

spectacular [spek'tækjʊlə^r] ◇ *adj* [event, defeat, result, view] spectaculaire; **it was the most ~ success of the decade** ce fut la réussite la plus spectaculaire de la décennie; **there has been a ~ rise in house prices** le prix des maisons a fait un bond spectaculaire.
◇ *n* CIN, THEAT & TV superproduction *f*.

spectacularly [spek'tækjʊləlɪ] *adv* [big, beautiful] spectaculairement; **it went ~ wrong** ça s'est vraiment très mal passé.

spectate [spek'teɪt] *vi* assister à.

spectator [spek'teɪtə^r] *n* spectateur *m*, -trice *f*.

spectator sport *n* sport *m* grand public.

specter *Am* = **spectre**.

spectra ['spektrə] *pl* → **spectrum**.

spectral ['spektrəl] *adj* [gen & PHYS] spectral.

spectre *Br*, **specter** *Am* ['spektə^r] *n* spectre *m*.

spectrogram ['spektrəgræm] *n* spectrogramme *m*.

spectrograph ['spektrəgrɑːf] *n* spectrographe *m*.

spectroscope ['spektrəskəʊp] *n* spectroscope *m*.

spectroscopy [spek'trɒskəpɪ] *n* spectroscopie *f*.

spectrum ['spektrəm] (*pl* **spectrums** OR **spectra** [-trə]) *n* -**1.** PHYS spectre *m*. -**2.** *fig* [range] gamme *f*; **right across the ~** sur toute la gamme; **we've covered the whole ~ of opinion** nous avons couvert tous les secteurs d'opinion; **the political ~** l'éventail *m* politique.

spectrum analysis *n* analyse *f* spectrale.

speculate ['spekjʊleɪt] *vi* -**1.** [wonder] s'interroger, se poser des questions; [make suppositions] faire des suppositions; PHILOS spéculer; **we can only ~** nous ne pouvons que spéculer OR faire des suppositions; **the press is speculating about the future of the present government** la presse s'interroge sur l'avenir du gouvernement actuel. -**2.** COMM & FIN spéculer; **to ~ on the stock market** spéculer OR jouer en Bourse.

speculation [ˌspekjʊ'leɪʃn] *n* -**1.** *(U)* [supposition, conjecture] conjecture *f*, conjectures *fpl*, supposition *f*, suppositions *fpl*; PHILOS spéculation *f*; **it's pure ~** ce n'est qu'une hypothèse; **there's been a lot of ~ about her motives** tout le monde s'est demandé quels étaient ses motifs. -**2.** [guess] supposition *f*, conjecture *f*. -**3.** COMM & FIN spéculation *f*; **~ in oil** spéculation sur le pétrole.

speculative ['spekjʊlətɪv] *adj* spéculatif.

speculator ['spekjʊleɪtə^r] *n* COMM & ST. EX spéculateur *m*, -trice *f*.

speculum ['spekjʊləm] (*pl* **speculums** OR **specula** [-lə]) *n* MED spéculum *m*; OPT miroir *m*, réflecteur *m*.

sped [sped] *pt* & *pp* → **speed**.

speech [spiːtʃ] *n* -**1.** [ability to speak] parole *f*; [spoken language] parole *f*, langage *m* parlé; **to lose the power of ~** perdre (l'usage de) la parole; **their poetry is based on ~ rather than writing** leur poésie relève de la tradition orale plus que de l'écriture; **to express o.s. in ~** s'exprimer oralement OR par la parole ❑ **freedom of ~** liberté *f* d'expression; **~ is silver but silence is golden** *prov* la parole est d'argent, mais le silence est d'or *prov*. -**2.** [manner of speaking] façon *f* de parler, langage *m*; [elocution] élocution *f*, articulation *f*; **his ~ was slurred** il bafouillait; **her ~ grew hesitant** son élocution devenait hésitante. -**3.** [dialect, language] parler *m*, langage *m*; **the ~ of the islanders/local fishermen** le parler des habitants de l'île/des pêcheurs du coin. -**4.** [talk] discours *m*, allocution *f fml*; [shorter, more informal] speech *m*; **to make a ~ on** OR **about sthg** faire un discours sur qqch; **~! ~!** un discours!, un discours! ❑ the Queen's Speech POL le discours du Trône. -5. THEAT monologue *m*.

speech act *n* LING acte *m* de parole.

speech community *n* LING communauté *f* linguistique.

speech day *n Br* SCH distribution *f* des prix; on ~ le jour de la distribution des prix.

SPEECH DAY:
À la fin de l'année scolaire en Grande-Bretagne, certaines écoles invitent une personnalité à prononcer un discours et à distribuer des prix.

---

speech defect *n* défaut *m* de prononciation; ~s troubles *mpl* du langage.

speechify ['spiːtʃɪfaɪ] (*pt* & *pp* speechified) *vi pej* discourir, faire de beaux discours.

speech impediment *n* défaut *m* d'élocution OR de prononciation.

speechless ['spiːtʃlɪs] *adj* -1. [with amazement, disbelief] muet, interloqué; [with rage, joy] muet; she was ~ with admiration elle était muette d'admiration; to leave sb ~ laisser qqn sans voix; I'm ~! *inf* je ne sais pas quoi dire!, les bras m'en tombent! -2. [inexpressible – rage, fear] muet.

speechmaker ['spiːtʃˌmeɪkəʳ] *n* orateur *m*, -trice *f*.

speechmaking ['spiːtʃˌmeɪkɪŋ] *n (U)* discours *mpl*; *pej* beaux discours *mpl*.

speech pattern *n* schéma *m* linguistique.

speech processing *n* compréhension *f* du langage parlé.

speech recognition *n* COMPUT reconnaissance *f* de la parole.

speech sound *n* LING phone *m*, son *m* linguistique.

speech therapist *n* orthophoniste *mf*.

speech therapy *n* orthophonie *f*.

speechwriter ['spiːtʃˌraɪtəʳ] *n* personne *f* qui écrit des discours; she's the mayor's ~ c'est elle qui écrit les discours du maire.

speed [spiːd] (*pt* & *pp vi sense 1* sped [sped], *vi sense 2* speeded, *vt* sped [sped] OR speeded) ◇ *n* -1. [rate, pace – of car, progress, reaction, work] vitesse *f*; I was driving OR going at a ~ of 65 mph je roulais à 100 km/h; to do a ~ of 100 km/h faire du 100 km/h; at (a) great OR high ~ à toute vitesse, à grande vitesse; at top OR full ~ [drive] à toute vitesse OR allure; [work] très vite, en quatrième vitesse; at the ~ of light/sound à la vitesse de la lumière/du son ❑ reading ~ vitesse *f* de lecture; typing/shorthand ~ nombre *m* de mots-minute en dactylo/en sténo; wind/air ~ vitesse *f* du vent/de vol. -2. [rapid rate] vitesse *f*, rapidité *f*; he replied with ~ [quickly] il a répondu rapidement; [promptly] il a répondu avec promptitude; I hate having to work at ~ *Br* j'ai horreur de devoir travailler vite; the actress delivered her lines at ~ *Br* l'actrice a débité son texte à toute allure; to pick up/to lose ~ prendre/perdre de la vitesse. -3. [gear – of car, bicycle] vitesse *f*; a 10-~ racer un vélo de course à 10 vitesses. -4. PHOT [of film] rapidité *f*, sensibilité *f*; [of shutter] vitesse *f*; [of lens] luminosité *f*. -5. *drugs sl* speed *m*, amphétamines *fpl*.
◇ *vi* -1. [go fast] aller à toute allure; we sped across the field nous avons traversé le champ à toute allure; I saw her ~ing down the street je l'ai vue descendre la rue à toute allure; he sped away il est parti à toute vitesse, il a pris ses jambes à son cou; time seems to ~ by le temps passe comme un éclair; the jetplane sped through the sky le jet traversa le ciel comme un éclair; the torpedo sped through the water la torpille se déplaçait dans l'eau à toute vitesse. -2. AUT [exceed speed limit] faire des excès de vitesse, rouler trop vite; I was stopped for ~ing j'ai été arrêté pour excès de vitesse. -3. *drugs sl* [on amphetamines] être parti.
◇ *vt* [person]: to ~ sb on his way souhaiter bon voyage à qqn; I gave him a drink to ~ him on his way je lui ai offert quelque chose pour la route; God ~ (you)! *arch* (que) Dieu vous garde!

◆ **speed up** ◇ *vi insep* [gen] aller plus vite; [driver] rouler plus vite; [worker] travailler plus vite; [machine, film] accélérer; can't you get him to ~ up? [work harder] vous ne pouvez pas le faire travailler plus vite?; [hurry] vous ne pouvez pas le faire se dépêcher?
◇ *vt sep* [worker] faire travailler plus vite; [person] faire aller plus vite; [work] activer, accélérer; [pace] presser; [production] accélérer, augmenter; [reaction, film] accélérer.

speedboat ['spiːdbəʊt] *n* vedette *f* (rapide); [with outboard engine] hors-bord *m inv*.

speed bump *n* casse-vitesse *m*.

speed cop *inf n Am* motard *m* (de la police).

speeder ['spiːdəʳ] *n* [fast driver] *personne qui conduit vite*; [convicted driver] *automobiliste condamné pour excès de vitesse*.

speedily ['spiːdɪlɪ] *adv* [quickly] vite, rapidement; [promptly] promptement, sans tarder; [soon] bientôt.

speeding ['spiːdɪŋ] ◇ *n* AUT excès *m* de vitesse.
◇ *comp*: a ~ conviction une condamnation pour excès de vitesse; a ~ ticket un P-V pour excès de vitesse.

speed limit *n* limitation *f* de vitesse; the ~ is 60 la vitesse est limitée à 60.

speed merchant *inf n* mordu *m*, -e *f* de vitesse.

speedo *inf* ['spiːdəʊ] (*pl* speedos) *Br* = **speedometer**.

speedometer [spɪ'dɒmɪtəʳ] *n* compteur *m* de vitesse.

speed-read *vi* & *vt* lire selon la méthode de lecture rapide.

speed-reading *n* lecture *f* rapide.

speed trap *n* contrôle *m* de vitesse; radar ~ contrôle radar.

speed-up *n* accélération *f*.

speedway ['spiːdweɪ] *n* -1. [racing] speedway *m*. -2. *Am* [track] piste *f* de vitesse pour motos. -3. *Am* [expressway] voie *f* express OR rapide.

speedwell ['spiːdwel] *n* BOT véronique *f*.

Speedwriting® ['spiːdˌraɪtɪŋ] *n* sténo *f* alphabétique.

speedy ['spiːdɪ] (*compar* speedier, *superl* speediest) *adj* -1. [rapid] rapide; [prompt] prompt; her help brought a ~ end to the dispute son aide a permis de mettre rapidement fin au différend. -2. [car] rapide, nerveux.

speleologist [ˌspiːlɪ'ɒlədʒɪst] *n* spéléologue *mf*.

speleology [ˌspiːlɪ'ɒlədʒɪ] *n* spéléologie *f*.

spell [spel] (*Br pt* & *pp vi* & *vt senses 1, 2* & *3* spelt [spelt] OR spelled, *pt* & *pp vt sense 4* spelled, *Am pt* & *pp* spelled) ◇ *vt* -1. [write] écrire, orthographier; they've spelt my name wrong ils ont mal écrit mon nom; his name is spelt J-O-N son nom s'écrit J-O-N; how do you ~ it? comment est-ce que ça s'écrit?; he ~s Martin with a "y" il écrit Martin avec un «y» ‖ [aloud] épeler; shall I ~ my name for you? voulez-vous que j'épelle mon nom? -2. [subj: letters] former, donner; C-O-U-G-H ~s "cough" C-O-U-G-H donnent «cough». -3. *fig* [mean] signifier; the floods ~ disaster for our region les inondations signifient le désastre pour notre région; her discovery could ~ success for the business sa découverte pourrait être très profitable à notre entreprise. -4. [worker, colleague] relayer; can I ~ you at the wheel? est-ce que je peux vous relayer au volant?
◇ *vi*: to learn to ~ apprendre l'orthographe; he ~s badly il est mauvais en orthographe.
◇ *n* -1. [period] (courte) période *f*; we had a ~ of cold weather nous avons eu une période de (temps) froid; scattered showers and sunny ~s des averses locales et des éclaircies; she did OR had a ~ as a reporter elle a été journaliste pendant un certain temps; he had a dizzy ~ il a été pris de vertige. -2. [of duty] tour *m*; do you want me to take OR to do a ~ at the wheel? voulez-vous que je vous relaie au volant OR que je conduise un peu? -3. [magic words] formule *f* magique, incantation *f*; she muttered a ~ elle marmonna une incantation. -4. [enchantment] charme *m*, sort *m*, sortilège *m*; to cast OR to put a ~ on sb jeter un sort OR un charme à qqn, ensorceler OR envoûter qqn; she was put under an evil ~ on lui a jeté un maléfice OR mauvais sort; to break the ~ rompre le charme ❑ to be under sb's ~ *literal* & *fig* être sous le charme de qqn.

◆ **spell out** *vt sep* -1. [read out letter by letter] épeler; [decipher] déchiffrer. -2. [make explicit] expliquer bien clairement; let me ~ out the implications of his study laissez-moi expliquer en détail la portée de son étude; she spelt out in detail what the scheme would cost elle a expliqué en détail quel serait le coût du projet; do I have to ~ it out for you? est-ce qu'il faut que je mette les points sur les i?

spellbinder ['spelˌbaɪndəʳ] *n* -1. [speaker] orateur *m* fascinant, oratrice *f* fascinante. -2. [fascinating thing]: her latest novel is a ~ son dernier roman est un enchantement; the match was a ~ le match a tenu tout le monde en haleine.

spellbinding ['spelˌbaɪndɪŋ] *adj* ensorcelant, envoûtant.

spellbound ['spelbaʊnd] *adj* [spectator, audience] captivé, envoûté; the children listened ~ les enfants écoutaient, captivés; the film held me ~ from start to finish le film m'a tenu en haleine OR m'a captivé du début jusqu'à la fin.

spell-check ◇ *n* vérification *f* orthographique; to do OR run a ~ on a document effectuer la vérification orthographique d'un document.
◇ *vt* faire la vérification orthographique de.

spell-checker *n* correcteur *m* OR vérificateur *m* orthographique.

speller ['speləʳ] *n* -1. [person]: he is a good/bad ~ il est bon/mauvais en orthographe. -2. [book] livre *m* d'orthographe.

spelling ['spelɪŋ] ◇ *n* -1. [word formation] orthographe *f*; what is the ~ of this word? quelle est l'orthographe de OR comment s'écrit ce mot? -2. [ability to spell]: he is good at ~ il est fort en orthographe.
◇ *comp* [error, test, book] d'orthographe; [pronunciation] orthographique; ~ bee *Am* concours *m* d'orthographe; ~ mistake faute *f* d'orthographe.

spelling checker = **spell-checker**.

spelt [spelt] ◇ *pt* & *pp* → **spell** *vi* & *vt* **1, 2, 3**.
◇ *n* BOT épeautre *m*.

spelunker [spɪ'lʌŋkəʳ] *n Am* spéléologue *mf*.

spelunking [spɪ'lʌŋkɪŋ] *n Am* spéléologie *f*.

spencer ['spensəʳ] *n* [jacket] spencer *m*.

spend [spend] (*pt* & *pp* spent [spent]) ◇ *vt* -1. [money, fortune] dépenser; to ~ money on [food, clothes] dépenser de l'argent en; [house, car] dépenser de l'argent pour, consacrer de l'argent à; how much do you ~ on the children's clothes? combien (d'argent) dépensez-vous pour habiller vos enfants?; he ~s all his money (on) gambling il dépense tout son argent au jeu; he ~s most of his pocket money on (buying) records la plus grande partie de son argent de poche passe dans l'achat de disques; I consider it money well spent je considère que c'est un bon investissement; without ~ing a penny sans dépenser un centime, sans bourse délier ❑ to ~ a penny *inf Br euph* aller au petit coin. -2. [time – pass] passer; [– devote] consacrer; to ~ time on sthg/on doing sthg passer du temps sur qqch/à faire qqch; she spent the whole afternoon knitting elle a passé tout l'après-midi à tricoter; I spent three hours on the job le travail m'a pris OR demandé trois heures; what a way to ~ Easter! quelle façon de passer les vacances de Pâques!; I spent a lot of time and effort on this j'y ai consacré beaucoup de temps et d'efforts; she spent her life helping the underprivileged elle a consacré sa vie à aider les défavorisés. -3. [exhaust, use up] épuiser; the gale had spent itself le vent avait fini par tomber; she has at

last spent her indignation son indignation s'est enfin calmée.
◇ *vi* dépenser, faire des dépenses.
◇ *n Br* [allocated money] allocation *f*; **we must increase our marketing ~** nous devons augmenter le budget marketing.

pender ['spendəʳ] *n* dépensier *m*, -ère *f*; **she's a big ~** elle est très dépensière.

pending ['spendɪŋ] *n (U)* dépenses *fpl*; **public** OR **government ~** dépenses publiques; **a cut in defence ~** une réduction du budget de la défense.

pending money *n* argent *m* de poche.

pending power *n* pouvoir *m* d'achat.

pending spree *n*: **we went on a ~** nous avons fait des folies, nous avons dépensé des sommes folles.

pendthrift ['spendθrɪft] ◇ *n* dépensier *m*, -ère *f*; **she's a terrible ~** elle est terriblement dépensière, elle jette l'argent par les fenêtres.
◇ *adj* dépensier.

penserian [spen'sɪərɪən] *adj* [in style] à la manière de Spenser; [of Spenser] de Spenser.

pent [spent] ◇ *pt* & *pp* → **spend**.
◇ *adj* -**1.** [used up - fuel, bullet, match] utilisé; **~ cartridges** cartouches *fpl* brûlées; **he's a ~ force in the firm** il n'a plus rien à apporter à l'entreprise; **the party is a ~ force in politics** le parti n'a plus l'influence qu'il avait en politique; **her courage was ~** elle n'avait plus de courage. -**2.** [tired out] épuisé; **he was completely ~** il était épuisé OR à bout.

perm [spɜːm] (*pl inv* OR **sperms**) *n* -**1.** [cell] spermatozoïde *m*. -**2.** [liquid] sperme *m*.

permaceti [,spɜːmə'setɪ] *n* spermaceti *m*.

permatic [spɜː'mætɪk] *adj* spermatique; **~ cord** cordon *m* spermatique; **~ fluid** sperme *m*.

permatocyte ['spɜːmətəʊsaɪt] *n* spermatocyte *m*.

permatozoon [,spɜːmətəʊ'zəʊɒn] (*pl* **spermatozoa** [-'zəʊə]) *n* spermatozoïde *m*.

perm bank *n* banque *f* de sperme.

permicidal [,spɜːmɪ'saɪdl] *adj* spermicide; **~ cream/jelly** crème *f*/gelée *f* spermicide.

permicide ['spɜːmɪsaɪd] *n* spermicide *m*.

perm whale *n* cachalot *m*.

pew [spjuː] ◇ *vt* -**1.** ▽ *literal* dégueuler. -**2.** *fig* vomir.
◇ *vi* -**1.** ▽ *literal* dégueuler. -**2.** *fig* [pour out] gicler; **the acid ~ed everywhere** l'acide a giclé partout.
◇ *n* ▽ vomi *m*, dégueulis *m*.
◆ **spew forth, spew out** *vi insep* & *vt sep lit* vomir.
◆ **spew up**▽ *vi insep* & *vt sep* vomir.

sphagnum ['sfægnəm] *n* sphaigne *f*.

sphere [sfɪəʳ] *n* -**1.** [globe] sphère *f*; *lit* [sky] cieux *mpl*; **the heavenly ~** la sphère céleste. -**2.** *fig* [of interest, activity] sphère *f*, domaine *m*; **her ~ of activity** [professional] son domaine d'activité; [personal] sa sphère d'activité; **it's not my ~** ce n'est pas de mon domaine, cela ne relève pas de mes compétences; **the question is outside the committee's ~** la question ne relève pas des compétences du comité; **the guests came from various social and professional ~s** les invités venaient de divers horizons sociaux et professionnels; **~ of influence** sphère d'influence; **in the public ~** [industry] dans le domaine public; [politics] dans la vie politique.

spherical ['sferɪkl] *adj* sphérique; **~ triangle** triangle *m* sphérique; **~ trigonometry/geometry** trigonométrie *f*/géométrie *f* sphérique.

spheroid ['sfɪərɔɪd] *n* sphéroïde *m*.

spheroidal [,sfɪə'rɔɪdl] *adj* sphéroïdal.

sphincter ['sfɪŋktəʳ] *n* sphincter *m*.

Sphinx [sfɪŋks] *pr n*: **the ~** le sphinx.

sphygmomanometer [,sfɪgməʊmə'nɒmɪtəʳ] *n* sphygmomanomètre *m*.

spic▼ [spɪk] *n Am terme injurieux désignant les Américains hispanophones, en particulier les Portoricains.*

spice [spaɪs] ◇ *n* -**1.** CULIN épice *f*; **mixed ~** épices mélangées; **kitchen ~s** épices de cuisine; **it needs more ~** ce n'est pas assez épicé OR relevé ❑ **~ cake** gâteau *m* aux épices; **~ rack** étagère *f* OR présentoir *m* à épices. -**2.** *fig* piquant *m*, sel *m*; **the story lacks ~** l'histoire manque de sel OR de piquant; **it added a bit of ~ to our routine** ça a ajouté un peu de piquant à notre train-train quotidien.
◇ *vt* -**1.** CULIN épicer, parfumer; **~d with nutmeg** parfumé à la muscade. -**2.** *fig* pimenter, corser; **the story is ~d with political anecdotes** l'histoire est pimentée d'anecdotes politiques.
◆ **spice up** *vt sep* = **spice 2**.

spiciness ['spaɪsɪnɪs] *n* -**1.** [of food] goût *m* épicé OR relevé. -**2.** *fig* [of story, adventure] piquant *m*.

spick-and-span [,spɪkən'spæn] *adj* [room] impeccable, reluisant de propreté; [appearance] tiré à quatre épingles.

spicy ['spaɪsɪ] (*compar* **spicier**, *superl* **spiciest**) *adj* -**1.** [food] épicé. -**2.** *fig* [book, story] piquant, corsé.

spider ['spaɪdəʳ] *n* -**1.** ZOOL araignée *f*; **~'s web** toile *f* d'araignée. -**2.** *Br* [for luggage] araignée *f* (à bagages). -**3.** *Am* CULIN poêle *f* (à trépied).

spider crab *n* araignée *f* (de mer).

spiderman *inf* ['spaɪdəmæn] (*pl* **spidermen** [-men]) *n Br ouvrier travaillant sur de hautes constructions.*
◆ **Spiderman** *pr n* [cartoon hero] l'Araignée *m*.

spider monkey *n* singe *m* araignée, atèle *m*.

spider plant *n* chlorophytum *m*.

spiderweb ['spaɪdəweb] *n Am* toile *f* d'araignée.

spidery ['spaɪdərɪ] *adj* [in shape] en forme d'araignée; [finger] long et mince; **~ writing** pattes *fpl* de mouches.

spiel *inf* [ʃpiːl] ◇ *n* -**1.** [speech] laïus *m*, baratin *m*; **he gave his usual ~ about the need to work hard** il a ressorti son laïus habituel sur la nécessité de travailler dur. -**2.** [sales talk] baratin *m*.
◇ *vi* baratiner.

spiffing *inf* ['spɪfɪŋ] *adj Br dated* épatant.

spiffy ['spɪfɪ] (*compar* **spiffier**, *superl* **spiffiest**) *adj Am* chic.

spif(f)licate *inf* ['spɪflɪkeɪt] *vt Br dated* écrabouiller.

spigot ['spɪgət] *n* -**1.** [in cask] fausset *m*. -**2.** [part of tap] clé *f*. -**3.** *Am* [tap] robinet *m* (extérieur).

spike [spaɪk] ◇ *vt* -**1.** [shoes, railings] garnir de pointes. -**2.** [impale] transpercer. -**3.** *fig* [thwart] contrarier; **to ~ sb's guns** *Br* mettre des bâtons dans les roues à qqn. -**4.** *inf* [drink] corser; **my coffee was ~d with brandy** mon café était arrosé de cognac. -**5.** PRESS [story] rejeter.
◇ *vi* [in volleyball] smasher.
◇ *n* -**1.** [on railings, shoe] pointe *f*; [on cactus] épine *f*; [on tyre] clou *m*; [for paper] pique-notes *m inv*; **her hair was standing up in ~s** elle avait les cheveux coiffés en épis; **the story was put on the ~** PRESS l'article a été rejeté. -**2.** [peak - on graph] pointe *f*. -**3.** [nail] gros clou *m*. -**4.** [antler] dague *f*. -**5.** [in volleyball] smash *m*.
◆ **spikes** *inf npl* [shoes] chaussures *fpl* à pointes.

spiked [spaɪkt] *adj* [railings] à pointes de fer; [shoes] à pointes; [tyre] clouté, à clous.

spikenard ['spaɪknɑːd] *n* BOT nard *m* (indien).

spiky ['spaɪkɪ] (*compar* **spikier**, *superl* **spikiest**) *adj* -**1.** [branch, railings] garni OR hérissé de pointes; [hair] en épis; [writing] pointu. -**2.** *inf Br* [bad-tempered] chatouilleux, ombrageux.

spill [spɪl] (*Br pt* & *pp* **spilt** [spɪlt] OR **spilled**, *Am pt* & *pp* **spilled**) ◇ *vt* -**1.** [liquid, salt etc] renverser, répandre; **she spilt coffee down** OR **over her dress** elle a renversé du café sur sa robe; **try to carry the bucket upstairs without ~ing any water** essaie de monter le seau sans renverser d'eau; **she spilt the contents of her handbag onto the bed** elle vida (le contenu de) son sac à main sur le lit. -**2.** *fig* [secret] dévoiler; **to ~ the beans** *inf* vendre la mèche. -**3.** [blood] verser, faire couler; **not a drop of blood was ~ed** pas une goutte de sang n'a été versée. -**4.** [person]: **he was ~ed from his motorbike** il est tombé de sa moto; **the rider was ~ed into the stream** le cavalier a été projeté dans le ruisseau. -**5.** NAUT: **to ~ (wind from) a sail** étouffer une voile OR la toile.
◇ *vi* -**1.** [liquid, salt etc] se renverser, se répandre. -**2.** [crowd] se déverser; **the huge crowd ~ed into the square** l'immense foule se répandit sur OR envahit la place.
◇ *n* -**1.** [spillage - of liquid] renversement *m*. -**2.** [fall - from horse, bike] chute *f*, culbute *f*; *dated* [accident] accident *m*; **to take a ~** faire la culbute. -**3.** [channel] déversoir *m*. -**4.** *Austr* POL remaniement *m*. -**5.** [for fire] longue allumette *f*.
◆ **spill out** ◇ *vt sep* -**1.** [contents, liquid] renverser, répandre. -**2.** *fig* [secret] dévoiler, révéler; **he got drunk and ~ed out all his problems** il a bu et s'est mis à parler de tous ses problèmes.
◇ *vi insep* -**1.** [contents, liquid] se renverser, se répandre; **the water spilt out onto the floor** l'eau s'est renversée par terre. -**2.** *fig* [crowd] se déverser, s'échapper; **the commuters ~ed out of the train** un flot de banlieusards s'est échappé du train.
◆ **spill over** *vi insep* -**1.** [liquid] déborder, se répandre; **the tea ~ed over into the saucer** le thé a débordé dans la soucoupe. -**2.** *fig* [overflow] se déverser, déborder; **the city's population has ~ed over into the surrounding villages** les habitants de la ville ont envahi les villages environnants; **her work ~s over into her family life** son travail empiète sur sa vie familiale.

spillage ['spɪlɪdʒ] *n* [act of spilling] renversement *m*, fait *m* de renverser; [liquid spilt] liquide *m* renversé; **we managed to avoid too much ~** nous avons réussi à ne pas trop en renverser.

spillikin ['spɪlɪkɪn] *n* jonchet *m*; **to play ~s** jouer aux jonchets.

spillover ['spɪl,əʊvəʳ] *n* -**1.** [act of spilling] renversement *m*; [quantity spilt] quantité *f* renversée. -**2.** [excess] excédent *m*. -**3.** ECON retombées *fpl* (économiques).

spillway ['spɪlweɪ] *n* déversoir *m*.

spilt [spɪlt] *Br pt* & *pp* → **spill**.

spin [spɪn] (*pt* & *pp* **spun** [spʌn], *cont* **spinning**) ◇ *vt* -**1.** [cause to rotate - wheel, chair] faire tourner; [- top] lancer, faire tournoyer; SPORT [- ball] donner de l'effet à; **to ~ the wheel** [in casino] faire tourner la roue; [in car] braquer. -**2.** [yarn, glass] filer; [thread] fabriquer; **he spun the glass into the shape of a swan** il a filé le verre en forme de cygne. -**3.** [subj: spider, silkworm] tisser. -**4.** [invent - tale] inventer, débiter; **she spun some yarn about the buses being on strike** elle a prétexté que les bus étaient en grève; **he ~s a good yarn** il raconte bien les histoires. -**5.** [in spin-dryer] essorer.
◇ *vi* -**1.** [rotate] tourner, tournoyer; SPORT [ball] tournoyer; **it ~s on its axis** il tourne sur son axe OR sur lui-même; **the skater/ballerina spun on one foot** le patineur/la ballerine virevolta sur un pied; **the room seemed to be spinning (around me)** la pièce semblait tourner autour de moi; **a strange shape was spinning across the sky** une forme étrange traversait le ciel en tournoyant sur elle-même; **the wheels were spinning in the mud** les roues patinaient dans la boue; **to ~ out of control** [plane] tomber en vrille; [car] faire un tête-à-queue. -**2.** *fig* [grow dizzy] tourner; **my head is spinning** j'ai la tête qui (me) tourne; **these figures make your head ~** ces chiffres vous donnent le tournis OR le vertige; **his mind was spinning from the recent events** les derniers événements lui donnaient le vertige. -**3.** [spinner] filer; [spider] tisser sa toile. -**4.** [in spin-dryer] essorer; **put the clothes in to ~** mets le linge à essorer. -**5.** [travel fast]: **we were spinning along at a hundred** on filait à cent à l'heure. -**6.** FISHING: **to ~ for pike** pêcher le brochet à la cuiller.
◇ *n* -**1.** [rotation] tournoiement *m*; **give the wheel a ~** faites tourner la roue; **give the top**

a ~ lancez la toupie; **the plane went into a ~** [accidentally] l'avion a fait une chute en vrille; [in aerobatics] l'avion a effectué une descente en vrille; **the car went into a ~** la voiture a fait un tête-à-queue; **my head is in a ~** *fig* j'ai la tête qui tourne. -**2.** *inf* [panic] : **to be in a (flat) ~** être dans tous ses états; **the office was thrown into a (flat) ~ by the arrival of the boss** les employés se sont affolés en voyant arriver le patron. -**3.** SPORT [on ball] effet *m*; **to put ~ on a ball** donner de l'effet à une balle. -**4.** [in spin-dryer] essorage *m*; **long/short ~** essorage complet/court; **to give sthg a ~** essorer qqch. -**5.** *inf* [ride - in car] tour *m*, balade *f*; **to go for a ~** faire une (petite) balade en voiture. -**6.** *inf* [try] : **to give sthg a ~** essayer OR tenter qqch; **would you like to give the car a ~?** voulez-vous essayer la voiture?

◆ **spin off** *vt sep* [hive off] : **they spun off their own company** ils ont monté leur propre affaire.

◆ **spin out** *vt sep* [story, idea] faire durer, délayer; [supplies, money] faire durer, économiser.

◆ **spin round** *Br*, **spin around** ◇ *vi insep* [planet, wheel] tourner (sur soi-même); [skater, top] tournoyer, tourner; [person] se retourner; **he suddenly spun round** il pivota sur ses talons OR se retourna brusquement; **she spun round and faced me** elle se retourna vivement vers moi.

◇ *vt sep* faire tourner.

spina bifida [ˌspaɪnəˈbɪfɪdə] *n* spina-bifida *m inv*.

spinach [ˈspɪnɪdʒ] *n (U)* épinards *mpl*.

spinal [ˈspaɪnl] *adj* [nerve, muscle] spinal; [ligament, disc] vertébral; **a ~ injury** une blessure à la colonne vertébrale.

spinal column *n* colonne *f* vertébrale.

spinal cord *n* moelle *f* épinière.

spin bowler *n* bôleur *m*.

spindle [ˈspɪndl] *n* -**1.** [for spinning - by hand] fuseau *m*; [- by machine] broche *f*. -**2.** TECH broche *f*, axe *m*; [in motor, lathe] arbre *m*; [of valve] tige *f*.

spindleshanks [ˈspɪndlˌʃæŋks] *n* [person] grand gringalet *m*.

spindle tree *n* fusain *m*.

spindling [ˈspɪndlɪŋ] *adj* filiforme.

spindly [ˈspɪndlɪ] (*compar* **spindlier**, *superl* **spindliest**) *adj* [legs] grêle, comme des allumettes; [body] chétif, maigrichon; [tree] grêle; [plant] étiolé.

spin doctor *n pej expression désignant une personne chargée des relations avec la presse qui manipule et filtre les informations fournies à celle-ci*.

spindrift [ˈspɪndrɪft] *n (U)* embruns *mpl*.

spin-dry *vi* & *vt* essorer.

spin-dryer *n* essoreuse *f*.

spine [spaɪn] *n* -**1.** ANAT colonne *f* vertébrale; ZOOL épine *f* dorsale. -**2.** [prickle - of hedgehog] piquant *m*; [- of plant, rose] épine *f*. -**3.** [of book] dos *m*. -**4.** [of hill] crête *f*. -**5.** *Am* [courage] résolution *f*, volonté *f*.

spine-chiller *n* [book] livre *m* d'horreur; [film] film *m* d'épouvante; **that story is a real ~** c'est une histoire à vous glacer le sang.

spine-chilling *adj* à vous glacer le sang, terrifiant.

spinel [spɪˈnel] *n* spinelle *m*.

spineless [ˈspaɪnlɪs] *adj* -**1.** [weak] mou; [cowardly] lâche. -**2.** ZOOL invertébré. -**3.** BOT sans épines.

spinet [spɪˈnet] *n* épinette *f*.

spinnaker [ˈspɪnəkəʳ] *n* spinnaker *m*, spi *m*.

spinner [ˈspɪnəʳ] *n* -**1.** TEX [person] fileur *m*, -euse *f*. -**2.** [in fishing] cuiller *f*. -**3.** [spin-dryer] essoreuse *f (à linge)*. -**4.** *Br* SPORT [bowler in cricket] lanceur *m*; [ball] balle *f* qui a de l'effet; **to bowl a ~** lancer une balle avec de l'effet.

spinneret [ˈspɪnəret] *n* ENTOM & TEX filière *f*.

spinney [ˈspɪnɪ] *n Br* bosquet *m*, boqueteau *m*, petit bois *m*.

spinning [ˈspɪnɪŋ] ◇ *n* -**1.** TEX [by hand] filage *m*; [by machine] filature *f*. -**2.** [in fishing] pêche *f* à la cuiller.

◇ *adj* tournant, qui tourne.

spinning jenny *n* jenny *f*.

spinning top *n* toupie *f*.

spinning wheel *n* rouet *m*.

spin-off *n* -**1.** [by-product] retombée *f*, produit *m* dérivé; **the ~s from research into nuclear physics** les retombées des recherches en physique nucléaire. -**2.** [work derived from another] : **the book is a ~ from the TV series** le roman est tiré de la série télévisée; **the TV series gave rise to a number of ~s** la série télévisée a donné lieu à plusieurs produits dérivés.

spinster [ˈspɪnstəʳ] *n* ADMIN & JUR célibataire *f*; *pej* vieille fille *f*.

spinsterhood [ˈspɪnstəhʊd] *n* célibat *m (pour une femme)*.

spiny [ˈspaɪnɪ] (*compar* **spinier**, *superl* **spiniest**) *adj* épineux, couvert d'épines.

spiny lobster *n* langouste *f*.

spiracle [ˈspaɪrəkl] *n* -**1.** ZOOL [in insect] stigmate *m*; [in whale] évent *m*, spiracle *m*; [in fish] ouïe *f*. -**2.** GEOL fissure *f*.

spiral [ˈspaɪərəl] (*Br pt* & *pp* **spiralled**, *cont* **spiralling**, *Am pt* & *pp* **spiraled**, *cont* **spiraling**) ◇ *n* -**1.** [gen, ECON & GEOM] spirale *f*; **in a ~** en spirale; **a ~ of smoke rose into the sky** une volute de fumée s'éleva dans le ciel; **the wage-price ~** la spirale des prix et des salaires; **an inflationary ~** une spirale inflationniste. -**2.** AERON vrille *f*.

◇ *adj* [motif, shell, curve] en (forme de) spirale; [descent, spring] en spirale; **the plane went into a ~ descent** l'avion commença une descente en vrille; **~ binding** reliure *f* spirale.

◇ *vi* -**1.** [in flight - plane] vriller; [- bird] voler en spirale; [in shape - smoke, stairs] former une spirale. -**2.** [prices, inflation] s'envoler, monter en flèche; **to ~ downwards** chuter.

◆ **spiral down** *vi insep* [plane] descendre en vrille; [leaf, feather] tomber en tourbillonnant.

◆ **spiral up** *vi insep* [plane, smoke] monter en spirale; [prices] monter en flèche.

spiral galaxy *n* galaxie *f* spirale.

spirally [ˈspaɪərəlɪ] *adv* [gen] en spirale; AERON en vrille.

spiral staircase *n* escalier *m* en colimaçon.

spire [ˈspaɪəʳ] *n* -**1.** ARCHIT flèche *f*. -**2.** [of blade of grass] tige *f*; [of mountain, tree] cime *f*.

spirit [ˈspɪrɪt] ◇ *n* -**1.** [non-physical part of being, soul] esprit *m*; **the poor in ~** les pauvres d'esprit; **the ~ is willing but the flesh is weak** l'esprit est prompt mais la chair est faible; **he is with us in ~** il est avec nous en esprit OR par l'esprit. -**2.** [supernatural being] esprit *m*; **I don't believe in ghosts or ~s** je ne crois ni aux fantômes ni aux esprits; **she is possessed by ~s** elle est possédée par des esprits; **to call up the ~s of the dead** évoquer les âmes des morts ❑ **evil ~s** esprits malins; **the ~ world** le monde des esprits. -**3.** [person] esprit *m*, âme *f*; **he is one of the great ~s of modern philosophy** c'est un des grands esprits de la philosophie moderne. -**4.** [attitude, mood] esprit *m*, attitude *f*; **the ~ of the age** l'esprit OR le génie de l'époque; **to do sthg in a ~ of fun** faire qqch pour s'amuser; **you mustn't do it in a ~ of vengeance** il ne faut pas le faire par esprit de vengeance; **she took my remarks in the wrong ~** elle a mal pris mes remarques; **he went about the job entirely in the wrong ~** il n'a pas compris dans quel esprit il devait travailler; **where's your fighting ~?** où est ton esprit combatif? ❑ **to enter into the ~ of things** [at party] se mettre au diapason; [in work] participer de bon cœur; **have you no team ~?** n'avez-vous aucun esprit d'équipe?; **that's the ~!** voilà comment il faut réagir!, à la bonne heure! -**5.** [loyalty] : **there is a strong community ~** il y a un fort esprit de groupe. -**6.** [deep meaning] esprit *m*, génie *m*; **the ~ of the law** l'esprit de la loi; **you haven't understood the ~ of the poem** vous n'avez pas saisi l'esprit du poème. -**7.** [energy] énergie *f*, entrain *m*; [courage] courage *m*; [character] caractère *m*; **to do sthg with ~** faire quelque chose avec entrain; **he replied with ~** il a répondu énergiquement; **they sang with ~** ils ont chanté avec entrain; **a man of ~** un homme de caractère; **he is entirely lacking in ~** il est complètement amorphe; **his ~ was broken** il avait perdu courage. -**8.** (*usu pl*) *Br* [alcoholic drink] alcool *m*, spiritueux *m*; **I prefer beer to ~s** je préfère la bière aux spiritueux; **brandy is my favourite ~** le cognac est mon alcool préféré; **taxes on ~s have increased** les taxes sur les spiritueux ont augmenté. -**9.** CHEM essence *f*, sel *m*; **~ OR ~s of ammonia** ammoniaque *m* liquide; **~ of turpentine** (essence de) térébenthine *f*.

◇ *vt* [move secretly] : **they ~ed her in/out by a side door** ils l'ont fait entrer/sortir discrètement par une porte dérobée; **he seems to have been ~ed into thin air** il semble avoir disparu comme par enchantement.

◆ **spirits** *npl* [mood, mental state] humeur *f*, état *m* d'esprit; [morale] moral *m*; **to be in good ~s** être de bonne humeur, avoir le moral; **to feel out of ~s** avoir le cafard; **to be in high ~s** être de très bonne humeur; **to be in low ~s** être déprimé; **you must keep your ~s up** il faut garder le moral, il ne faut pas vous laisser abattre; **my ~s rose at the thought** mon moral est remonté rien que d'y penser; **to raise sb's ~s** remonter le moral à qqn.

◆ **spirit away**, **spirit off** *vt sep* [carry off secretly] faire disparaître (comme par enchantement); [steal] escamoter, subtiliser.

spirited [ˈspɪrɪtɪd] *adj* -**1.** [lively - person] vif, plein d'entrain; [- horse] fougueux; [- manner] vif; [- reply, argument] vif; [- music, rhythm, dance] entraînant. -**2.** [courageous - person, action, decision, defence] courageux; **to put up a ~ resistance** résister courageusement, opposer une résistance courageuse; **he's a ~ young fellow** il ne manque pas de courage, ce petit

spirit gum *n* colle *f* gomme.

spirit lamp *n* lampe *f* à alcool.

spiritless [ˈspɪrɪtlɪs] *adj* [lifeless] sans vie, sans entrain, apathique; [depressed] démoralisé, déprimé; [cowardly] lâche.

spirit level *n* niveau *m* à bulle.

Spirit of Saint Louis *pr n*: **the ~** *avion spécialement conçu pour l'aviateur américain Charles Lindbergh, avec lequel il effectua, en 1927, la première traversée de l'Atlantique sans escale, de New York à Paris.*

spirit stove *n* réchaud *m* à alcool.

spiritual [ˈspɪrɪtʃʊəl] ◇ *adj* -**1.** [relating to the spirit] spirituel; **a very ~ man** un homme d'une grande spiritualité; **the ~ death of the people** la mort spirituelle du peuple; **a ~ heir** un successeur spirituel; **China is her ~ home** la Chine est sa patrie d'adoption. -**2.** [religious, sacred] religieux, sacré; **~ adviser** conseiller *m* spirituel.

◇ *n*: **(Negro) ~** (negro) spiritual *m*.

spiritualism [ˈspɪrɪtʃʊəlɪzm] *n* RELIG spiritisme *m*; PHILOS spiritualisme *m*.

spiritualist [ˈspɪrɪtʃʊəlɪst] ◇ *adj* RELIG spirite; PHILOS spiritualiste.

◇ *n* RELIG spirite *mf*; PHILOS spiritualiste *mf*.

spirituality [ˌspɪrɪtʃʊˈælətɪ] *n* spiritualité *f*.

◆ **spiritualities** *npl* biens *mpl* ecclésiastiques.

spiritually [ˈspɪrɪtʃʊəlɪ] *adv* spirituellement, en esprit.

spirit varnish *n* vernis *m* à alcool.

spirogyra [ˌspaɪrəʊˈdʒaɪrə] *n* spirogyre *f*.

spirt [spɜːt] = **spurt**.

spit [spɪt] (*pt* & *pp* **spit** OR **spat** [spæt], *cont* **spitting**) ◇ *vi* -**1.** [in anger, contempt] cracher; **to ~ at sb** cracher sur qqn; **to ~ in sb's face** cracher à la figure de qqn; **she spat at him** elle lui a craché dessus. -**2.** [while talking] postillonner, envoyer des postillons. -**3.** [hot fat] sauter, grésiller; **the oil spat onto my hand** l'huile m'a éclaboussé la main. -**4.** *phr*: **it's spitting (with rain)** il bruine, il pleut légèrement.

◇ *vt literal* & *fig* cracher.

◇ *n* -**1.** *(U)* [spittle - in mouth] salive *f*; [- spat out] crachat *m*; [- ejected while speaking] postillon *m*; [act of spitting] crachement *m*; ~ and polish MIL astiquage *m*; ~ and sawdust *expression évoquant un pub miteux*. -**2.** *inf Br* [likeness]: he's the ~ of his dad c'est son père tout craché. -**3.** [of insects] écume *f* printanière, crachat *m* de coucou. -**4.** *phr*: there was just a ~ of rain il n'est tombé que quelques gouttes de pluie. -**5.** CULIN broche *f*. -**6.** GEOG pointe *f*, langue *f* de terre. -**7.** HORT [spade's depth]: to dig the ground three ~s deep creuser la terre à une profondeur de trois fers de bêche.

◆ **spit out** *vt sep* [food, medicine, words, invective] cracher; come on, ~ it out! *inf* allez, accouche!

◆ **spit up** *vt sep* [blood, food] cracher.

spit curl *n Am* accroche-cœur *m*.

spite [spaɪt] ◇ *n* [malice] dépit *m*, malveillance *f*; to do sthg out of ~ faire qqch par dépit; out of pure ~ par pur dépit, par pure méchanceté.

◇ *vt* contrarier, vexer.

◆ **in spite of** *prep phr* en dépit de, malgré; he went out in ~ of my advice il est sorti en dépit de mes conseils; in ~ of myself malgré moi; in ~ of the fact that we have every chance of winning bien que nous ayons toutes les chances de gagner.

spiteful ['spaɪtfʊl] *adj* [person, remark, character] malveillant; that was a ~ thing to say c'était méchant de dire ça; to have a ~ tongue avoir une langue de vipère.

spitefully ['spaɪtfʊlɪ] *adv* par dépit, par méchanceté, méchamment.

spitefulness ['spaɪtfʊlnɪs] *n* méchanceté *f*.

spitfire *inf* ['spɪtfaɪəʳ] *n*: she's a real ~ elle est très soupe au lait.

spit roast *n* rôti *m* à la broche.

◆ **spit-roast** *vt* faire rôtir à la broche.

Spitsbergen ['spɪts,bɜːgən] *pr n* Spitsberg, Spitzberg.

spitting ['spɪtɪŋ] *n*: 'no ~' 'défense de cracher' ❑ to be within ~ distance of: he was within ~ distance of me *inf* il était à deux pas de moi.

spitting image *inf n*: to be the ~ of sb: he's the ~ of his father c'est son père tout craché.

spittle ['spɪtl] *n* [saliva - of person] salive *f*; [- of dog] bave *f*; [- on floor] crachat *m*.

spittoon [spɪ'tuːn] *n* crachoir *m*.

Spitzbergen ['spɪts,bɜːgən] = **Spitsbergen**.

spiv *inf* [spɪv] *n Br* filou *m*.

splash [splæʃ] ◇ *vt* -**1.** [with water, mud] éclabousser; the bus ~ed us with mud OR ~ed mud over us le bus nous a éclaboussés de boue; she ~ed wine on OR over her dress elle a fait des taches de vin sur sa robe; paint was ~ed on his trousers il y avait des éclaboussures de peinture sur son pantalon; I ~ed my face with cold water OR cold water onto my face je me suis aspergé le visage d'eau froide OR avec de l'eau froide; he ~ed his way across the river il a traversé la rivière en pataugeant. -**2.** [pour carelessly] répandre; he ~ed bleach on the tiles il a répandu de l'eau de Javel sur le carrelage; I ~ed disinfectant round the sink j'ai aspergé le tour de l'évier de désinfectant. -**3.** [daub] barbouiller; he ~ed whitewash on the wall il a barbouillé le mur au blanc de chaux. -**4.** PRESS étaler; the story was ~ed across the front page l'affaire était étalée à la une des journaux.

◇ *vi* -**1.** [rain, liquid] faire des éclaboussures; the tea ~ed onto the floor/over the book le thé éclaboussa le sol/le livre; the paint ~ed on my trousers la peinture a éclaboussé mon pantalon; heavy drops of rain ~ed on the ground de grosses gouttes de pluie s'écrasaient sur le sol. -**2.** [walk, run etc] patauger, barboter; we ~ed across the stream nous avons traversé le ruisseau en pataugeant; he ~ed through the mud/puddles il a traversé la boue/les flaques d'eau en pataugeant.

◇ *n* -**1.** [noise] floc *m*, plouf *m*; the ball made a loud ~ le ballon a fait un grand floc; he fell/jumped in with a ~ il est tombé/il a sauté dedans avec un grand plouf. -**2.** [of mud, paint] éclaboussure *f*; [of colour, light] tache *f*; to give sthg a ~ of colour donner une touche de couleur à qqch; ~es of white des taches blanches; there was a bright ~ of light on the wall il y avait une tache de lumière vive sur le mur. -**3.** [small quantity - of whisky] goutte *f*; [- of soda, tonic]: would you like a ~ of soda in your whisky? voulez-vous un peu de soda dans votre whisky?; just a ~ of lemonade, please juste une goutte de limonade, s'il vous plaît. -**4.** *inf fig* [sensation] sensation *f*; to make a ~ faire sensation; his arrival caused a bit of a ~ son arrivée n'est pas passée inaperçue.

◇ *adv*: to go/to fall ~ into the water entrer/tomber dans l'eau en faisant plouf.

◆ **splash about** *Br*, **splash around** ◇ *vi insep* [duck, swimmer] barboter; he was ~ing about in the bath/swimming pool il barbotait dans son bain/la piscine.

◇ *vt sep* [liquid] faire des éclaboussures de; [money] dépenser sans compter.

◆ **splash down** *vi insep* [spaceship] amerrir.

◆ **splash out** *inf* ◇ *vi insep* [spend] faire des folies; to ~ out on sthg se payer qqch.

◇ *vt insep* [money] claquer; she ~ed out a lot of money on a camera elle a claqué un argent fou pour s'acheter un appareil photo.

splashback ['splæʃbæk] *n* revêtement *m (derrière un évier, un lavabo)*.

splashboard ['splæʃbɔːd] *n* [on car] garde-boue *m inv*.

splashdown ['splæʃdaʊn] *n* [of spaceship] amerrissage *m*.

splashguard ['splæʃgɑːd] *n Am* garde-boue *m inv*.

splashy *inf* ['splæʃɪ] *adj Am* tape-à-l'œil.

splat [splæt] ◇ *n* floc *m*.

◇ *adv*: to go ~ faire floc.

splatter ['splætəʳ] ◇ *vt* éclabousser; ~ed with mud/blood éclaboussé de boue/sang.

◇ *vi* [rain] crépiter; [mud] éclabousser.

◇ *n* -**1.** [mark - of mud, ink] éclaboussure *f*. -**2.** [sound - of rain] crépitement *m*.

splay [spleɪ] ◇ *vt* [fingers, legs] écarter; [feet] tourner en dehors.

◇ *vi* [fingers, legs] s'écarter; [feet] se tourner en dehors.

◆ **splay out** *vt sep* & *vi insep* = **splay**.

splayfooted [,spleɪ'fʊtɪd] *adj* [person] aux pieds plats; [horse] panard.

spleen [spliːn] *n* -**1.** ANAT rate *f*. -**2.** [bad temper] humeur *f* noire, mauvaise humeur *f*; to vent one's ~ on sthg/sb décharger sa bile sur qqch/qqn.

splendid ['splendɪd] ◇ *adj* -**1.** [beautiful, imposing - dress, setting, decor] splendide, superbe, magnifique. -**2.** [very good - idea, meal] excellent, magnifique; [- work] excellent, superbe; I think he's a ~ cook je trouve que c'est un excellent cuisinier; ~ isolation splendide isolement; we had a ~ time on holiday nous avons passé d'excellentes vacances; how ~ for you! mais c'est formidable pour vous!

◇ *interj* excellent!, parfait!

splendidly ['splendɪdlɪ] *adv* -**1.** [dress, decorate, furnish] magnifiquement, superbement; [entertain] somptueusement; he was ~ turned out in military uniform il était vraiment superbe en uniforme militaire. -**2.** [perform] superbement; you acted ~! tu as été merveilleux!; the children behaved ~ les enfants ont été des anges; my work is going ~ mon travail avance à merveille.

splendiferous *inf* [,splen'dɪfərəs] *adj hum* épatant, mirobolant.

splendour *Br*, **splendor** *Am* ['splendəʳ] *n* splendeur *f*.

splenetic [splɪ'netɪk] *adj lit* [ill-humoured] atrabilaire.

splice [splaɪs] ◇ *vt* -**1.** to ~ (together) [film, tape] coller; [rope] épisser; [pieces of wood] enter; to ~ one piece of tape onto another coller un morceau de bande sur un autre ❑ to ~ the mainbrace *inf* NAUT ≃ distribuer une ration de rhum; [gen] boire un coup. -**2.** *inf Br hum* [marry]: to get ~d convoler (en justes noces).

◇ *n* [in tape, film] collure *f*; [in rope] épissure *f*; [in wood] enture *f*.

splint [splɪnt] ◇ *n* MED éclisse *f*, attelle *f*; her arm was in a ~ OR in ~s elle avait le bras dans une attelle.

◇ *vt* éclisser, mettre dans une attelle.

splinter ['splɪntəʳ] ◇ *n* [of glass, wood] éclat *m*; [of bone] esquille *f*; [in foot, finger] écharde *f*.

◇ *vt* [glass, bone] briser en éclats; [wood] fendre en éclats.

◇ *vi* [glass, bone] se briser en éclats; [marble, wood] se fendre en éclats; [political party] se scinder, se fractionner.

splinter group *n* groupe *m* dissident OR scissionniste.

split [splɪt] (*pt* & *pp* split, *cont* splitting) ◇ *vt* -**1.** [cleave - stone] fendre, casser; [- slate] cliver; [- wood] fendre; he was splitting wood for the fire il fendait du bois pour faire du feu; the lightning ~ the oak right down the middle la foudre a fendu le chêne en plein milieu; karate experts can ~ bricks with their bare hands les karatékas sont capables de casser des briques à main nue; to ~ sthg in two OR in half casser OR fendre qqch en deux; to ~ sthg open ouvrir qqch *(en le coupant en deux ou en le fendant)*; the customs ~ the boxes open les douaniers ont ouvert les cartons d'un coup de canif; he ~ his head open on the concrete il s'est fendu le crâne sur le béton; they ~ open the mattress in their search for drugs ils ont éventré le matelas à la recherche de stupéfiants; to ~ the atom PHYS fissionner l'atome ❑ to ~ hairs couper les cheveux en quatre; to ~ one's sides (laughing) se tordre de rire. -**2.** [tear] déchirer; the plastic sheet had been ~ right down the middle la bâche en plastique avait été fendue en plein milieu; I've ~ my trousers j'ai déchiré mon pantalon. -**3.** [divide - family] diviser; POL [- party] diviser, créer OR provoquer une scission dans; we were ~ into two groups on nous a divisés en deux groupes; you can't ~ it in three on ne peut pas le diviser en trois; the committee is ~ on this issue le comité est divisé sur cette question; the vote was ~ down the middle les deux camps avaient obtenu exactement le même nombre de voix; we were ~ 30-70 on était 30% d'un côté et 70% de l'autre. -**4.** [share - profits] (se) partager, (se) répartir; [- bill] (se) partager; FIN [- stocks] faire une redistribution de; they decided to ~ the work/visits between them ils ont décidé de se partager le travail/les visites; to ~ the profits four ways diviser les bénéfices en quatre; to ~ the difference [share out] partager la différence; [compromise] couper la poire en deux. -**5.** GRAMM: to ~ an infinitive *intercaler un adverbe ou une expression adverbiale entre «to» et le verbe*. -**6.** ▽ [leave] quitter; we ~ town nous avons quitté la ville; I'm going to ~ this scene je me tire OR barre.

◇ *vi* -**1.** [break - wood, slate] se fendre, éclater; the ship ~ in two le navire s'est brisé (en deux); my head is splitting *fig* j'ai un mal de tête atroce. -**2.** [tear - fabric] se déchirer; [- seam] craquer; the bag ~ open le sac s'est déchiré; her dress ~ right down the back le dos de sa robe s'est déchiré de haut en bas. -**3.** [divide - gen] se diviser, se fractionner; [- political party] se scinder; [- cell] se diviser; [- road, railway] se diviser, bifurquer; the hikers ~ into three groups les randonneurs se sont divisés en trois groupes; the party ~ over the question of pollution le parti s'est scindé OR divisé sur la question de la pollution; the committee ~ down the middle on the issue le comité s'est divisé en deux clans sur la question. -**4.** [separate - couple] se séparer; [- family, group] s'éparpiller, se disperser; she has ~ with her old school friends elle ne voit plus ses anciennes camarades de classe. -**5.** ▽ [leave] se casser, mettre les bouts; let's ~! on se casse!; they ~ for San Francisco ils sont partis à San Fransisco.

◇ *n* -**1.** [crack - in wood, rock] fissure *f*; **there is a long ~ in the wood** le bois est fendu sur une bonne longueur. -**2.** [tear] déchirure *f*. -**3.** [division] division *f*; [separation] séparation *f*; [quarrel] rupture *f*; POL scission *f*, schisme *m*; RELIG schisme *m*; [gap] fossé *m*, écart *m*; **the ~ between rich and poor nations** l'écart entre les pays riches et les pays pauvres; **a ~ in the ranks** une division dans les rangs; **there was a three-way ~ in the voting** les votes étaient répartis en trois groupes. -**4.** [share] part *f*; **he asked to be given his ~ of the booty** il a demandé qu'on lui donne sa part du butin. -**5.** [dessert]: **banana ~** banana split *m*. -**6.** *Am* [bottle]: **soda ~** petite bouteille *f* de soda.
◇ *adj* [lip, skirt] fendu.
◆ **splits** *npl*: **to do the ~s** *Br*, **to do ~s** *Am* faire le grand écart.
◆ **split off** ◇ *vi insep* -**1.** [branch, splinter] se détacher; **a large rock ~ off from the cliff** un gros rocher s'est détaché de la falaise. -**2.** [separate - person, group] se séparer; **we ~ off (from the others) to visit the museum** nous avons quitté les autres pour visiter le musée; **a radical movement ~ off from the main party** un mouvement radical s'est détaché du gros du parti.
◇ *vt sep* -**1.** [break, cut - branch, piece] enlever (en fendant). -**2.** [person, group] séparer; **our branch was ~ off from the parent company** notre succursale a été séparée de la maison mère.
◆ **split on** *inf vt insep Br* [inform] vendre, moucharder; **he ~ on his friend to the police** il a donné son ami à la police; **don't ~ on him!** ne le vends pas!
◆ **split up** ◇ *vi insep* -**1.** [wood, marble] se fendre; [ship] se briser. -**2.** [couple] se séparer, rompre; [friends] rompre, se brouiller; [meeting, members] se disperser; POL se diviser, se scinder; **to ~ up with sb** rompre avec qqn; **the search party ~ up into three groups** l'équipe de secours s'est divisée en trois groupes.
◇ *vt sep* -**1.** [wood] fendre; [cake] couper en morceaux; **he ~ the wood up into small pieces** il a fendu le bois en petits morceaux. -**2.** [divide - profits] partager; [- work] répartir; **let's ~ the work up between us** répartissons-nous le travail; **the teaching syllabus is ~ up into several chapters** le programme d'enseignement est divisé en plusieurs chapitres. -**3.** [separate] séparer; **the teacher ~ the boys up** le professeur a séparé les garçons; **the police ~ up the meeting/crowd** la police a mis fin à la réunion/dispersé la foule.
split cane *n* osier *m*.
◆ **split-cane** *adj* en osier.
split decision *n* SPORT [in boxing] victoire *f*, décision *f* aux points.
split end *n* fourche *f*.
split infinitive *n* GRAMM *infinitif où un adverbe ou une expression adverbiale est intercalé entre «to» et le verbe*.
split-level *adj* -**1.** [house, flat] à deux niveaux. -**2.** **~ cooker** cuisinière *f* à éléments de cuisson séparés.
split pea *n* pois *m* cassé.
split personality *n* double personnalité *f*, dédoublement *m* de la personnalité.
split pin *n Br* goupille *f* fendue.
split ring *n* bague *f* à fente.
split screen *n* CIN écran *m* divisé.
split second *n*: **in a ~** en une fraction de seconde; **it only took a ~** cela n'a demandé qu'une fraction de seconde.
◆ **split-second** *adj* [timing, reaction] au quart de seconde.
split shift *n*: **he works a ~** sa journée de travail est divisée en deux tranches horaires.
split ticket *n Am* POL panachage *m*.
splitting ['splɪtɪŋ] ◇ *n* -**1.** [of wood, marble] fendage *m*; **the ~ of the atom** PHYS la fission de l'atome. -**2.** [of fabric, seams] déchirure *f*. -**3.** [division] division *f*. -**4.** [sharing] partage *m*.
◇ *adj*: **I have a ~ headache** j'ai un mal de tête atroce.
split-up *n* [gen] rupture *f*, séparation *f*; POL scission *f*.
splodge *inf* ['splɒdʒ] ◇ *n* -**1.** [splash - of paint, ink] éclaboussure *f*, tache *f*; [- of colour] tache *f*. -**2.** [dollop - of cream, of jam] bonne cuillerée *f*.
◇ *vt* éclabousser, barbouiller.
◇ *vi* s'étaler, faire des pâtés.
splosh *inf* [splɒʃ] ◇ *vi* -**1.** [splash - liquid] faire des éclaboussures; **the water ~ed on the floor** l'eau a éclaboussé le sol. -**2.** [as verb of movement]: **we ~ed through the mud/puddles** nous avons traversé la boue/les flaques d'eau en pataugeant.
◇ *vt* [pour - water, disinfectant] verser, mettre; [daub - paint] barbouiller.
◇ *n* éclaboussure *f*.
splotch [splɒtʃ] *Am* = **splodge**.
splurge *inf* [splɜːdʒ] ◇ *n* -**1.** [spending spree] folie *f*, folles dépenses *fpl*; **I went on** OR **I had a ~ and bought a fur coat** j'ai fait une folie, je me suis acheté un manteau de fourrure. -**2.** [display] fla-fla *m*, tralala *m*; **the book came out in a ~ of publicity** le livre est sorti avec un grand battage publicitaire; **a great ~ of colour** une débauche de couleur.
◇ *vt* [spend] dépenser; [waste] dissiper; **she ~d her savings on a set of encyclopedias** toutes ses économies ont été englouties par l'achat d'une encyclopédie.
◆ **splurge out** *vi insep* faire une folie OR des folies; **to ~ out on sthg** se payer qqch.
splutter ['splʌtəʳ] ◇ *vi* -**1.** [spit - speaker] postillonner; [- flames, fat] crépiter, grésiller; [- pen, ink] cracher. -**2.** [stutter - speaker] bredouiller; [- engine] tousser, avoir des ratés; **she was ~ing with rage** elle bredouillait de rage; **the engine ~ed and died** le moteur toussa et s'arrêta.
◇ *vt* [protest, apology, thanks] bredouiller, balbutier.
◇ *n* -**1.** [spitting - in speech] crachotement *m*; [- of fat, flames] crépitement *m*, grésillement *m*. -**2.** [stutter - in speech] bredouillement *m*, balbutiement *m*; [- of engine] toussotement *m*.
Spode [spəʊd] *n*: **~ (china)** *porcelaine fabriquée par la manufacture Spode*.
spoil [spɔɪl] (*pt* & *pp* **spoilt** [spɔɪlt] OR **spoiled**)
◇ *vt* -**1.** [make less attractive or enjoyable] gâter, gâcher; **the tall chimneys ~ the view** les hautes cheminées gâchent OR gâtent la vue; **our holiday was spoilt by the wet weather/the news** le temps pluvieux/la nouvelle a gâché nos vacances; **you've spoilt everything by your foolish behaviour** tu as tout gâché avec ton comportement stupide; **the ending spoilt the film for me** la fin m'a gâché le film; **don't ~ the ending for me** ne me raconte pas la fin, ça va tout gâcher. -**2.** [damage] abîmer, endommager; **I spoilt my eyesight by reading in the dark** je me suis abîmé la vue OR les yeux en lisant dans la pénombre; **if you eat those chocolates, you'll ~ your appetite for dinner** si tu manges ces chocolats, tu n'auras plus faim OR plus d'appétit à l'heure du dîner; **the dinner was spoilt because they were late** le dîner a été gâché par leur retard ❑ **to ~ the ship for a hap'orth of tar** faire des économies de bouts de chandelle. -**3.** [pamper] gâter; **she's spoilt rotten** *inf* elle est super gâtée, c'est une enfant pourrie; **we like to ~ our clients** nous aimons gâter nos clients; **to ~ o.s.** s'offrir une petite folie. -**4.** POL [ballot paper] rendre nul.
◇ *vi* -**1.** [fruit, food] se gâter, s'abîmer; [in store, hold of ship] s'avarier, devenir avarié. -**2.** *phr*: **to be ~ing for a fight** être impatient d'en découdre.
◇ *n* (*U*) -**1.** = **spoils 1.** -**2.** [earth, diggings] déblai *m*, déblais *mpl*.
◆ **spoils** *npl* -**1.** [loot] butin *m*, dépouilles *fpl*; [profit] bénéfices *mpl*, profits *mpl*; [prize] prix *m*; **he made off with the ~s** il s'est enfui avec le butin; **the ~s of war** les dépouilles de la guerre. -**2.** *Am* POL assiette *f* au beurre.
◆ **spoil for** *vt insep*: **to be ~ing for a fight/an argument** chercher la bagarre/la dispute.
spoilage ['spɔɪlɪdʒ] *n* (*U*) [damage] détérioration *f*; [spoilt matter] déchets *mpl*.
spoiler ['spɔɪləʳ] *n* AUT becquet *m*; AERON aérofrein *m*.
spoilsman ['spɔɪlsmən] (*pl* **spoilsmen** [-mən]) *n Am* POL *personne qui bénéficie d'un piston politique*.
spoilsport ['spɔɪlspɔːt] *n* trouble-fête *mf inv*, rabat-joie *m inv*, empêcheur *m*, -euse *f* de tourner en rond.
spoils system *n Am* POL assiette *f* au beurre *pej*, système *m* des dépouilles.
spoilt [spɔɪlt] ◇ *pt* & *pp* → **spoil**.
◇ *adj* -**1.** [child] gâté; [behaviour] d'enfant gâté; **we were ~ for choice** nous n'avions que l'embarras du choix. -**2.** [harvest] abîmé; [food, dinner] gâché, gâté. -**3.** POL [ballot paper] nul.
spoke [spəʊk] ◇ *pt* → **speak**.
◇ *n* [in wheel] rayon *m*; [in ladder] barreau *m*, échelon *m*; [on ship's wheel] manette *f*; **to put a ~ in sb's wheel** *Br* mettre des bâtons dans les roues à qqn.
spoken ['spəʊkn] ◇ *pp* → **speak**.
◇ *adj* -**1.** [language, dialogue] parlé, oral; **the ~ word** la langue parlée, la parole; **she's better at the ~ language** elle se débrouille mieux lorsqu'il s'agit de parler. -**2.** *phr*: **to be ~ for** être pris; **she's already ~ for** elle est déjà prise.
-spoken *in cpds*: **soft~** à la voix douce; **well~** qui s'exprime bien.
spokeshave ['spəʊkʃeɪv] *n* vastringue *f*.
spokesman ['spəʊksmən] (*pl* **spokesmen** [-mən]) *n* porte-parole *m inv*; **a government ~, a ~ for the government** un porte-parole du gouvernement.
spokesperson ['spəʊks,pɜːsn] *n* porte-parole *m inv*.
spokeswoman ['spəʊks,wʊmən] (*pl* **spokeswomen** [-,wɪmɪn]) *n* porte-parole *m inv* *(femme)*.
spoliation [,spəʊlɪ'eɪʃn] *n* -**1.** [plundering] spoliation *f*, pillage *m*. -**2.** JUR [of document] altération *f*.
spondee ['spɒndiː] *n* spondée *m*.
sponge [spʌndʒ] ◇ *n* -**1.** ZOOL [in sea] éponge *f*. -**2.** [for cleaning, washing] éponge *f*; **I gave the table a ~** j'ai passé un coup d'éponge sur la table ❑ **to throw in the ~** jeter l'éponge. -**3.** *inf pej* [scrounger] parasite *m*. -**4.** *Br* [cake] gâteau *m* de Savoie; **jam/cream ~** gâteau de Savoie fourré à la confiture/à la crème.
◇ *vt* -**1.** [wipe - table, window] donner un coup d'éponge sur; [- body] éponger; **she ~d his face** elle lui a épongé le visage. -**2.** [soak up] éponger; **can you ~ the milk off the table?** peux-tu éponger le lait renversé sur la table? -**3.** *inf* [cadge - food, money] taper; **I ~d £20 off** OR **from him** je l'ai tapé de 20 livres; **can I ~ a cigarette off you?** est-ce que je peux te taper une cigarette?; **she ~d a meal off her friends** elle s'est fait inviter à manger par ses amis.
◇ *vi inf* [cadge]: **to ~ on** OR **from sb** vivre aux crochets de qqn; **she's always sponging** c'est un vrai parasite; **too many people ~ off the state** trop de gens vivent aux crochets de l'État.
◆ **sponge down** *vt sep* éponger, laver à l'éponge; **he ~d himself down** il s'est lavé avec une éponge.
◆ **sponge up** *vt sep* [liquid] éponger.
sponge bag *n Br* trousse *f* OR sac *m* de toilette.
sponge bath *n* toilette *f* à l'éponge.
sponge cake *n* gâteau *m* de Savoie.
sponge-down *n* coup *m* d'éponge.
sponge finger *n* boudoir *m* *(biscuit)*.
sponge pudding *n dessert chaud fait avec une pâte de gâteau de Savoie*.
sponger *inf* ['spʌndʒəʳ] *n pej* parasite *m*.
sponge rubber *n* mousse *f*, caoutchouc *m* Mousse®.
spongy ['spʌndʒɪ] (*compar* **spongier**, *superl* **spongiest**) *adj* spongieux.

sponsor ['spɒnsəʳ] ◇ *n* -**1.** COMM & SPORT [of sportsman, team, tournament] sponsor *m*; [of film, TV programme] sponsor *m*, commanditaire *m*; [of artist, musician] commanditaire *m*, mécène *m*; [of student, studies] parrain *m*; [for charity] donateur *m*, -trice *f*; **he's looking for ~s for his Channel swim** [for finance] il cherche des sponsors pour financer sa traversée de la Manche à la nage; [for charity] il cherche des gens qui accepteront de faire une donation aux bonnes œuvres s'il réussit sa traversée de la Manche à la nage; **to act as ~ for sb** sponsoriser qqn. -**2.** [of proposal, appeal] personne *f* qui lance; [of would-be club member] parrain *m*, marraine *f*; [guarantor - for loan] répondant *m*, -e *f*, garant *m*, -e *f*; [backer - for business] parrain *m*, bailleur *m* de fonds; **her uncle stood (as) ~ to her** [for loan] son oncle a été son répondant; [for business] son oncle l'a parrainée.
◇ *vt* -**1.** COMM & SPORT sponsoriser; RADIO & TV [programme] sponsoriser, parrainer; [concert, exhibition] parrainer, commanditer; [studies, student] parrainer; **the rally is ~ed by the milk industry** le rallye est sponsorisé par l'industrie laitière; **our firm ~ed her to the tune of £10,000** notre firme l'a sponsorisée pour un montant de 10 000 livres. -**2.** [for charity]: **I ~ed him to swim 10 miles** je me suis engagé à lui donner de l'argent (pour des œuvres charitables) s'il faisait OR parcourait 10 milles à la nage. -**3.** [appeal, proposal] présenter; [would-be club member] parrainer; [loan, borrower] se porter garant de; [firm] patronner; **to ~ a bill** POL présenter un projet de loi. -**4.** [godchild] être le parrain OR la marraine de.

sponsored walk ['spɒnsəd-] *n marche parrainée.*

SPONSORED WALK:
Les «sponsored walks» sont destinées à rassembler des fonds, chaque marcheur établissant une liste de personnes ayant accepté de donner une certaine somme d'argent par kilomètre parcouru. Le terme «sponsored» s'applique également à d'autres activités, sportives ou non: «sponsored swim», «sponsored parachute jump» etc.

---

sponsorship ['spɒnsəʃɪp] *n* -**1.** COMM & SPORT sponsoring *m*. -**2.** [of appeal, proposal] présentation *f*; POL [of bill] proposition *f*, présentation *f*; [of would-be club member, godchild] parrainage *m*; [of loan, borrower] cautionnement *m*.

spontaneity [ˌspɒntə'neɪətɪ] *n* spontanéité *f*.

spontaneous [spɒn'teɪnjəs] *adj* spontané.

spontaneous combustion *n* combustion *f* spontanée.

spontaneously [spɒn'teɪnjəslɪ] *adv* spontanément.

spoof *inf* [spuːf] ◇ *n* -**1.** [mockery] satire *f*, parodie *f*; **it's a ~ on horror films** c'est une parodie des films d'horreur. -**2.** [trick] blague *f*, canular *m*; **the whole thing was just a ~** c'était un simple canular du début à la fin.
◇ *adj* prétendu, fait par plaisanterie; **a ~ phone call** un canular téléphonique.
◇ *vi* raconter des blagues.
◇ *vt* [book, style] parodier; [person] faire marcher.

spook *inf* [spuːk] ◇ *n* -**1.** [ghost] fantôme *m*. -**2.** *Am* [spy] barbouze *mf*.
◇ *vt Am* -**1.** [frighten] faire peur à, effrayer. -**2.** [haunt] hanter.

spooky *inf* ['spuːkɪ] (*compar* **spookier**, *superl* **spookiest**) *adj* -**1.** [atmosphere] qui donne la chair de poule, qui fait froid dans le dos. -**2.** *Am* [skittish] peureux; [odd] bizarre.

spool [spuːl] ◇ *n* [of film, tape, thread] bobine *f*; [for fishing] tambour *m*; [of wire] rouleau *m*; SEW & TEX cannette *f*.
◇ *vt* bobiner.

spoon [spuːn] ◇ *n* -**1.** [utensil] cuiller *f*, cuillère *f*. -**2.** [quantity] cuillerée *f*; **add two ~s of sugar** ajoutez deux cuillerées de sucre. -**3.** FISHING cuiller *f*, cuillère *f*. -**4.** [in golf] spoon *m*.
◇ *vt* [food - serve] servir; [- transfer] verser; **to ~ the cream from** OR **off the milk** enlever la crème du lait avec une cuiller; **to ~ the fat from** OR **off the gravy** dégraisser la sauce à l'aide d'une cuiller; **he ~ed the ice cream into a bowl** il a servi la glace dans un bol (avec une cuiller); **she ~ed the porridge into his mouth** elle lui a fait manger la bouillie avec une cuiller.
◇ *vi inf dated* se faire des mamours.
◆ **spoon out** *vt sep* [serve] servir à l'aide d'une cuiller; [transfer] verser à l'aide d'une cuillère.
◆ **spoon up** *vt sep* [eat] manger avec une cuiller; [clear up] ramasser avec une cuiller.

spoonbill ['spuːnbɪl] *n* ORNITH spatule *f*.

spoonerism ['spuːnərɪzm] *n* contrepèterie *f*.

spoon-feed *vt* -**1.** *literal* [child, sick person] nourrir à la cuiller. -**2.** *fig*: **to ~ sb** mâcher le travail à qqn.

spoonful ['spuːnfʊl] *n* cuillerée *f*.

spoor [spɔːʳ] *n* trace *f*, traces *fpl*, empreintes *fpl*.

Sporades ['spɒrədiːz] *pl pr n*: **the ~** les Sporades *fpl*; **in the ~** aux Sporades.

sporadic [spə'rædɪk] *adj* sporadique; **~ outbreaks of gunfire** des coups de feu isolés OR sporadiques.

sporadically [spə'rædɪklɪ] *adv* sporadiquement.

spore [spɔːʳ] *n* spore *f*.

sporran ['spɒrən] *n Scot* escarcelle *f (portée avec le kilt)*.

sport [spɔːt] ◇ *n* -**1.** [physical exercise] sport *m*; **she does** OR **plays a lot of ~** elle fait beaucoup de sport, elle est très sportive; **you shouldn't mix ~ and politics** tu ne devrais pas mélanger sport et politique; **minority ~s** les sports minoritaires; **I hated ~** OR **~s at school** je détestais le sport OR les sports à l'école ☐ **the ~ of kings** [horse racing] les courses de chevaux. -**2.** *lit* [hunting] chasse *f*; [fishing] pêche *f*. -**3.** *dated* [fun] amusement *m*, divertissement *m*; **to say sthg in ~** dire qqch pour rire OR en plaisantant; **it's great ~ flying these remote-controlled planes** c'est très amusant de faire voler ces avions radio-guidés; **to make ~ of sb/sthg** se moquer de qqn/qqch, tourner qqn/qqch en ridicule. -**4.** *inf* [friendly person] chic type *m*, chic fille *f*; **he's a real ~** c'est vraiment un chic type; **go on, be a ~!** allez, sois sympa! -**5.** [good loser]: **to be a (good) ~** être beau joueur; **they're not very good ~s** ils sont plutôt mauvais joueurs. -**6.** [gambler] joueur *m*, -euse *f*; [high flyer] bon vivant *m*. -**7.** *inf Austr* & *NZ* [fellow] pote *m*, vieux *m*. -**8.** BIOL variété *f* anormale.
◇ *vt* [wear] porter, arborer; **he was ~ing a tartan jacket/a yellow carnation** il portait une veste tartan/arborait un œillet jaune.
◇ *vi lit* batifoler, s'ébattre.
◆ **sports** ◇ *npl* [athletics meeting] meeting *m* d'athlétisme; [competition] compétition *f* sportive; **this weekend is the inter-regional ~s** ce week-end ont lieu les compétitions sportives inter-régionales; **the school ~s** la compétition sportive scolaire.
◇ *comp* [equipment, programme, reporter] sportif; [fan] de sport.

sporting ['spɔːtɪŋ] *adj* -**1.** SPORT [fixtures, interests] sportif. -**2.** [friendly, generous - behaviour] chic *(inv)*; **it's very ~ of you** c'est très chic de votre part. -**3.** [fairly good - chance] assez bon; **we're in with a ~ chance** on a une assez bonne chance de gagner; **there's a ~ chance he'll come** il y a de fortes chances (pour) qu'il vienne.

sportingly ['spɔːtɪŋlɪ] *adv* (très) sportivement.

sportive ['spɔːtɪv] *adj lit* folâtre, badin.

sport jacket *Am* = **sports jacket**.

sports car *n* voiture *f* de sport.

sportscast ['spɔːtskɑːst] *n Am* émission *f* sportive.

sportscaster ['spɔːtsˌkɑːstəʳ] *n Am* reporter *m* sportif.

sports coat *Am* = **sports jacket**.

sports day *n Br* SCH *réunion sportive annuelle où les parents sont invités.*

sports jacket *n* veste *f* sport.

sportsman ['spɔːtsmən] (*pl* **sportsmen** [-mən]) *n* -**1.** [player of sport] sportif *m*. -**2.** [person who plays fair]: **he's a real ~** il est très sport OR très fair-play OR beau joueur.

sportsmanlike ['spɔːtsmənlaɪk] *adj* sportif.

sportsmanship ['spɔːtsmənʃɪp] *n* sportivité *f*, sens *m* sportif.

sportsperson ['spɔːtsˌpɜːsn] (*pl* **sportspeople** [-ˌpiːpl]) *n* sportif *m*, sportive *f*.

sportswear ['spɔːtsweəʳ] *n (U)* vêtements *mpl* de sport.

sportswoman ['spɔːtsˌwʊmən] (*pl* **sportswomen** [-ˌwɪmɪn]) *n* sportive *f*.

sporty ['spɔːtɪ] (*compar* **sportier**, *superl* **sportiest**) *adj* [person] sportif; [garment] de sport; **he's got a very ~ image** il a un look très sport.

spot [spɒt] (*pt* & *pp* **spotted**, *cont* **spotting**) ◇ *n* -**1.** [dot - on material, clothes] pois *m*; [- on leopard, giraffe] tache *f*, moucheture *f*; [- on dice, playing card] point *m*; **a tie with red ~s** une cravate à pois rouges; **I've got ~s before my eyes** j'ai des points lumineux OR des taches devant les yeux; **the carnations brought a ~ of colour into the church** les œillets apportaient une tache de couleur dans l'église. -**2.** [stain, unwanted mark] tache *f*; [on fruit] tache *f*, tavelure *f*; [splash] éclaboussure *f*; **a dirty ~** une tache, une salissure; **there are some ~s of mould on the jam** il y a des taches de moisissure sur la confiture; **how did you get these ~s of blood on your shirt?** d'où viennent ces taches de sang sur ta chemise? -**3.** *Br* [pimple] bouton *m*; [freckle] tache *f* de son OR de rousseur; **I've got a ~ on my chin** j'ai un bouton sur le menton; **to come out in ~s** avoir une éruption de boutons; **to suffer from ~s** souffrir d'acné. -**4.** [blemish - on character] tache *f*, souillure *f*; **there isn't a ~ on his reputation** sa réputation est sans tache. -**5.** [small amount - of liquid] goutte *f*; [- of salt] pincée *f*; [- of irony, humour] pointe *f*, soupçon *m*; **there were a few ~s of rain** il est tombé quelques gouttes (de pluie); **would you like cream in your coffee? — just a ~** voulez-vous de la crème dans votre café? — juste un soupçon; **I've got a ~ of bad news** *inf* j'ai une mauvaise nouvelle; **she hardly did a ~ of work** *inf* elle n'a quasiment rien fait; **I'm having a ~ of bother with the neighbours** *inf* j'ai quelques ennuis OR problèmes avec les voisins; **I could do with a ~ of sleep** *inf* un petit somme me ferait du bien; **do you want a ~ of supper?** *inf* veux-tu manger un morceau? -**6.** [place] endroit *m*, coin *m*; [site] site *m*; [on body] endroit *m*, point *m*; **a tender** OR **sore ~** un point sensible; **this is a peaceful ~** c'est un endroit très tranquille; **this is the exact ~ where the market cross was situated** c'est l'endroit exact où se trouvait la croix du marché ☐ **TV cameras are sent to all the trouble/hot ~s** des caméras de télévision sont envoyées dans tous les points du conflit/les points chauds; **night ~** *inf* boîte *f* de nuit; **that hits the ~!** *Am* ça fait du bien! -**7.** [aspect, feature, moment]: **the high ~ of our holiday in France** le meilleur moment de nos vacances en France; **the only bright ~ of the week** le seul bon moment de la semaine. -**8.** [position, job] poste *m*, position *f*. -**9.** *inf* [difficult situation] embarras *m*; **to be in a ~** être dans l'embarras; **we're in a bit of a (tight) ~** nous sommes dans le pétrin OR dans de beaux draps; **you're putting us in a ~** vous nous mettez dans l'embarras; **to put sb on the ~** prendre qqn au dépourvu, coincer qqn. -**10.** RADIO & TV [for artist, interviewee] numéro *m*; [news item] brève *f*; **he got a ~ on the Margie Warner show** [as singer, comedian] il a fait un numéro dans le show de Margie Warner; [interview] il s'est fait interviewer OR il est passé dans le show de Margie Warner ☐ **advertising ~** message *m* OR spot *m* publicitaire. -**11.** [spotlight] spot *m*, projecteur *m*. -**12.** [in billiards] mouche *f*. -**13.** *inf Am* [dollar]: **it'll cost you a ten-~** ça te coûtera dix dollars.
◇ *vt* -**1.** [notice - friend, object] repérer, aperce-

voir; [- talent, mistake] trouver, déceler; I could ~ him a mile off je pourrais le repérer à des kilomètres; well spotted! bien vu! -2. [stain] tacher; [mark with spots] tacheter; the wall is spotted with mildew le mur est taché OR piqué d'humidité; the rain spotted the pavement des gouttes de pluie formaient des taches sur le trottoir. -3. *Am* [opponent] accorder un avantage à; he spotted his opponent ten points il a cédé OR concédé dix points à son adversaire. -4. *Am* [stain] enlever; a chemical for spotting clothes/stains un produit pour détacher les vêtements/enlever les taches.

◇ *vi* -1. [garment, carpet] se tacher, se salir. -2. [rain]: it's spotting with rain il tombe quelques gouttes de pluie. -3. MIL servir d'observateur.

◇ *comp* -1. COMM [price] comptant; [transaction, goods] payé comptant. -2. [random - count, test] fait à l'improviste. -3. TV: ~ advertisement spot *m* publicitaire; ~ announcement flash *m*.

◆ **on the spot** *adv phr* [at once] sur-le-champ; [at the scene] sur les lieux, sur place; he was killed on the ~ il a été tué sur le coup; the man on the ~ [employee, diplomat] l'homme qui est sur place OR sur le terrain; [journalist] l'envoyé spécial; the doctor arrived on the ~ in five minutes le docteur est arrivé sur les lieux en cinq minutes; to run on the ~ courir sur place.

◆ **on-the-spot** *adj phr*: an on-the-~ fine une amende immédiate; an on-the-~ report un reportage sur place OR sur le terrain.

spot cash *n Br* argent *m* liquide.

spot check *n* [investigation] contrôle *m* surprise; [for quality] sondage *m*; [by customs] fouille *f* au hasard.

◆ **spot-check** *vt* contrôler au hasard; [for quality] sonder.

spotless ['spɒtlɪs] *adj* [room, appearance] impeccable; [character] sans tache.

spotlessly ['spɒtlɪslɪ] *adv*: ~ clean reluisant de propreté, d'une propreté impeccable.

spotlight ['spɒtlaɪt] (*pt* & *pp* spotlit [-lɪt])

◇ *n* -1. [in theatre] spot *m*, projecteur *m*; in the ~ *literal* & *fig* sous le feu OR la lumière des projecteurs; to turn the ~ on sb *literal* braquer les projecteurs sur qqn; *fig* mettre qqn en vedette; the ~ was on her *literal* les projecteurs étaient braqués sur elle; *fig* elle était en vedette; the political ~ was on Mrs Warner this week les feux de l'actualité étaient braqués sur Mme Warner cette semaine. -2. [lamp - in home, on car] spot *m*.

◇ *vt* -1. THEAT diriger les projecteurs sur. -2. *fig* [personality, talent] mettre en vedette; [pinpoint - flaws, changes] mettre en lumière, mettre le doigt sur.

spotlit ['spɒtlɪt] *adj* éclairé par des projecteurs.

spot market *n* marché *m* au comptant.

spot-on *inf* ◇ *adj Br* -1. [correct - remark, guess] en plein dans le mille; [- measurement] pile, très précis. -2. [perfect] parfait.

◇ *adv* [guess] en plein dans le mille; he timed it ~ il a calculé son coup à la seconde près.

spotted ['spɒtɪd] ◇ *pt* & *pp* → **spot**.

◇ *adj* -1. [leopard, bird] tacheté, moucheté; [apple, pear] tavelé. -2. [tie, dress] à pois. -3. [stained - carpet, wall] taché.

spotted dick *n Br* pudding *m* aux raisins.

spotted fever *n* fièvre *f* éruptive.

spotted flycatcher *n* gobe-mouches *m inv* gris.

spotter ['spɒtəʳ] ◇ *n* -1. [observer] observateur *m*, -trice *f*; [lookout] dénicheur *m*. -2. *Br* [enthusiast]: train/plane ~ passionné *m*, -e *f* de trains/d'avions. -3. *inf Am* COMM surveillant *m*, -e *f* du personnel.

◇ *comp* [plane] de recherche OR recherches.

spotty ['spɒtɪ] (*compar* spottier, *superl* spottiest) *adj* -1. [covered with spots - skin, person] boutonneux; [- wallpaper] piqué OR taché d'humidité; [- mirror] piqueté, piqué; [stained] taché. -2. [patterned - fabric, tie] à pois. -3. [patchy] irrégulier; a ~ performance une représentation inégale.

spot-weld ◇ *vt* souder par points.

◇ *n* soudure *f* par points.

spouse [spaʊs] *n fml* époux *m*, épouse *f*; ADMIN & JUR conjoint *m*, -e *f*.

spout [spaʊt] ◇ *n* -1. [of teapot, kettle, tap, watering can] bec *m*; [of carton] bec *m* verseur; [of pump, gutter] dégorgeoir *m*; [of pipe] embout *m*. -2. [of water - from fountain, geyser] jet *m*; [- from whale] jet *m*, souffle *m* d'eau; [of flame] colonne *f*; [of lava] jet *m*; a ~ of boiling water un jet d'eau bouillante. -3. *Br phr*: to be up the ~ *inf* [ruined] être fichu OR foutu; [pregnant] être enceinte; our plans are up the ~ nos projets sont tombés à l'eau; now we're really up the ~ maintenant nous sommes vraiment dans de beaux draps OR dans le pétrin.

◇ *vi* -1. [water, oil] jaillir, sortir en jet; [whale] souffler; water ~ed out of the pipe de l'eau jaillit du tuyau. -2. *inf pej* [talk] dégoiser; he's always ~ing (on) about politics il est toujours à dégoiser sur la politique.

◇ *vt* -1. [water, oil] faire jaillir un jet de; [fire, smoke] vomir, émettre un jet de. -2. *inf pej* [words, poetry] débiter, sortir; she's always ~ing Latin quotations elle est toujours en train de débiter OR sortir des citations latines.

sprain [spreɪn] ◇ *vt* [joint] fouler, faire une entorse à; [muscle] étirer; she has ~ed her ankle OR has a ~ed ankle elle s'est fait une entorse à la cheville OR s'est foulé la cheville.

◇ *n* entorse *f*, foulure *f*.

sprang [spræŋ] *pt* → **spring**.

sprat [spræt] *n* sprat *m*.

sprawl [sprɔːl] ◇ *vi* -1. [be sitting, lying] être affalé OR vautré; [sit down, lie down] s'affaler, se laisser tomber; she was ~ing in the armchair/on the bed elle était avachie dans le fauteuil/vautrée sur le lit; the blow sent him ~ing le coup l'a fait tomber de tout son long. -2. [spread] s'étaler, s'étendre; the new industrial estate is beginning to ~ into the countryside la nouvelle zone industrielle commence à grignoter OR envahir la campagne; her signature ~ed across half the page sa signature s'étalait sur la moitié de la page.

◇ *vt* (*usu pass*): she was ~ed in the armchair/on the pavement elle était vautrée dans le fauteuil/étendue de tout son long sur le trottoir.

◇ *n* -1. [position] position *f* affalée; she lay in an ungainly ~ elle était étendue de tout son long de façon peu élégante. -2. [of city] étendue *f*; the urban ~ still hasn't reached us l'expansion urbaine n'est pas encore arrivée jusqu'ici.

sprawling ['sprɔːlɪŋ] *adj* [body] affalé; [suburbs, metropolis] tentaculaire; [handwriting] informe.

spray [spreɪ] ◇ *vt* -1. [treat - crops, garden] faire des pulvérisations sur, traiter; [- field] pulvériser; [- hair, house plant] vaporiser; [sprinkle - road] asperger; to ~ a plant with insecticide, to ~ insecticide on a plant pulvériser de l'insecticide sur une plante; she ~ed her hairstyle in place elle s'est mis de la laque pour faire tenir sa coiffure; I got ~ed with cold water je me suis fait arroser OR asperger d'eau froide; they ~ed the bar with bullets/with machine-gun fire *fig* ils arrosèrent le bar de balles/de rafales de mitrailleuses. -2. [apply - water, perfume] vaporiser; [- paint, insecticide] pulvériser; [- coat of paint, fixer] mettre, appliquer; [- graffiti, slogan] écrire, tracer (à la bombe); she ~ed perfume behind her ears elle se vaporisa du parfum derrière les oreilles; they ~ed water on the flames ils vaporisèrent de l'eau sur les flammes; she ~ed air freshener around the room elle vaporisa du désodorisant dans la pièce.

◇ *vi* -1. [liquid] jaillir; the water ~ed (out) over OR onto the road l'eau a jailli sur la route. -2. [against crop disease] pulvériser, faire des pulvérisations.

◇ *n* -1. [droplets] gouttelettes *fpl* fines; [from sea] embruns *mpl*; the liquid comes out in a fine ~ le liquide est pulvérisé. -2. [container - for aerosol] bombe *f*, aérosol *m*; [- for perfume] atomiseur *m*; [- for cleaning fluids, water, lotion] vaporisateur *m*; this deodorant is a ~ ce déodorant est un aérosol; throat ~ vaporisateur pour la gorge. -3. [act of spraying - of crops] pulvérisation *f*; [- against infestation] traitement *m* (par pulvérisation); [- of aerosol product] coup *m* de bombe; I'll give your hair a light ~ je vais donner un petit coup de laque sur vos cheveux. -4. *fig* [of bullets] grêle *f*; the welding sent up ~s OR a ~ of bright sparks la soudure faisait voler des gerbes d'étincelles. -5. [cut branch] branche *f*; forsythia ~s branches de forsythia; a single ~ of orchids in a vase une simple branche d'orchidées dans un vase. -6. [bouquet] (petit) bouquet *m*. -7. [brooch] aigrette *f*.

◇ *comp* [insecticide, deodorant] en aérosol; he took the car in for a ~ job *inf Br* il a amené la voiture au garage pour la faire repeindre.

◆ **spray on** ◇ *vt sep* appliquer (à la bombe); he ~ed on some deodorant il s'est mis un peu de déodorant; ~ the paint on evenly vaporisez la peinture de façon uniforme.

◇ *vi insep* [paint, polish, cleaner] s'appliquer (par pulvérisation); the product ~s on le produit est présenté sous forme d'aérosol.

spray can *n* [for aerosol] bombe *f*, aérosol *m*; [refillable] vaporisateur *m*.

sprayer ['spreɪəʳ] *n* -1. [container - for perfume] atomiseur *m*; [spray gun] pistolet *m* (à peinture); [nozzle] buse *f*. -2. AGR [machine] pulvérisateur *m*; [plane] avion-pulvérisateur *m*. -3. [person] arroseur *m*, -euse *f*.

spray gun *n* [for paint] pistolet *m* (à peinture).

spray-on *adj* en bombe, en aérosol; ~ deodorant déodorant *m* en bombe OR en spray.

spray paint *n* peinture *f* en bombe; a can of ~ une bombe de peinture.

◆ **spray-paint** *vt* [with can] peindre à la bombe; [with spray gun] peindre au pistolet.

spread [spred] (*pt* & *pp* spread) ◇ *vt* -1. [apply - jam, icing, plaster, glue] étaler; [- asphalt] répandre; [- manure] épandre; I ~ mustard on the ham, I ~ the ham with mustard j'ai étalé de la moutarde sur le jambon; he ~ butter on a slice of toast OR a slice of toast with butter il a tartiné de beurre une tranche de pain grillé. -2. [open out, unfold, stretch - wings, sails] étendre, déployer; [- arms, legs, fingers] écarter; [- map, napkin, blanket] étaler; [- rug] étendre; [- fan] ouvrir; he ~ his handkerchief over his face il étala son mouchoir sur son visage; she lay on her back, her arms ~ (out) elle était allongée sur le dos, les bras écartés ❑ it's time you ~ your wings il est temps que vous voliez de vos propres ailes. -3. [lay out, arrange - photos, cards, possessions] étaler; he ~ his papers on the desk il étala ses papiers sur le bureau; her hair was ~ over the pillow ses cheveux s'étalaient sur l'oreiller; we ~ the contents of the bag over the floor nous étalâmes le contenu du sac sur le sol. -4. [diffuse, disseminate - disease, fire] propager, répandre; [- news, idea, faith] propager; [- rumour] répandre, faire courir; [- terror, joy, panic] répandre; the disease is ~ by rats la maladie est propagée par les rats; the wind will ~ the fire to the fields le vent va propager l'incendie jusque dans les champs; trade helped to ~ the new technology to Asia le commerce a facilité la diffusion OR la dissémination de cette nouvelle technologie en Asie; the attack is at noon, ~ the word! l'attaque est pour midi, faites passer OR passez le mot!; to ~ the gospel prêcher OR répandre l'Évangile. -5. [strew, scatter - over an area] répandre; [- over a period of time] échelonner, étaler; the floor was ~ with straw le sol était recouvert de paille; take your shoes off, you're ~ing dirt everywhere! enlève tes chaussures, tu salis tout!; the explosion had ~ debris over a large area l'explosion avait dispersé des débris sur une grande superficie; their troops are ~ (out) too thinly to be effective leurs troupes sont trop dispersées pour être efficaces; to ~ o.s too thinly disperser ses efforts; the tourist season is now ~ over six months la saison touristique s'étale maintenant sur six mois; to ~ (out) the losses over five years répartir les pertes sur cinq ans. -**6.** [divide up - tax burden, work load] répartir; a policy designed to ~ wealth more evenly une mesure qui vise à distribuer plus équitablement les richesses. -**7.** MUS [chord] arpéger.

◇ *vi* -**1.** [stain] s'élargir; [disease, suburb] s'étendre; [fire, desert, flood] gagner du terrain, s'étendre; [rumour, ideas, faith, terror, crime, suspicion] se répandre; the news ~ like wildfire la nouvelle s'est répandue comme une traînée de poudre; panic ~ through the crowd la panique a envahi OR gagné la foule; the epidemic is ~ing to other regions l'épidémie gagne de nouvelles régions; the cancer had ~ through her whole body le cancer s'était généralisé; the suburbs are ~ing further everyday les banlieues s'étendent chaque jour un peu plus; the flood waters have ~ across OR over the whole plain l'inondation a gagné toute la plaine; the species ~ throughout Africa l'espèce s'est répandue à travers toute l'Afrique; a ~ing waistline une taille qui s'épaissit. -**2.** [extend - over a period of time, a range of subjects] s'étendre; their correspondence ~s over 20 years leur correspondance s'étend sur 20 ans. -**3.** [butter, glue] s'étaler; the icing should ~ easily le glaçage devrait s'étaler facilement.

◇ *n* -**1.** [diffusion, growth - of epidemic, fire] propagation *f*, progression *f*; [- of technology, idea] diffusion *f*, dissémination *f*; [- of religion] propagation *f*; they are trying to prevent the ~ of unrest to other cities ils essaient d'empêcher les troubles d'atteindre OR de gagner d'autres villes. -**2.** [range - of products, ages, interests] gamme *f*, éventail *m*; the commission represented a broad ~ of opinion la commission représentait un large éventail d'opinions; maximum May temperatures show a ten-point ~ les températures maximales du mois de mai montrent une variation de dix degrés. -**3.** [wingspan] envergure *f*. -**4.** [period] période *f*; growth occurred over a ~ of several years la croissance s'étala sur une période de plusieurs années. -**5.** [expanse] étendue *f*; a ~ of land une étendue de terre. -**6.** [cover - for bed] couvre-lit *m*; [tablecloth] nappe *f*; [dustcover] housse *f*. -**7.** CULIN [paste] pâte *f* à tartiner; [jam] confiture *f*; salmon ~ beurre *m* de saumon; chocolate ~ chocolat *m* à tartiner. -**8.** PRESS & TYPO [two pages] double page *f*; [advertisement] double page *f* publicitaire; the event was given a good ~ l'événement a été largement couvert par la presse. -**9.** *inf* [meal] gueuleton *m*; the hotel lays on a decent ~ l'hôtel propose des repas tout à fait convenables. -**10.** *inf Am* [farm] ferme *f*; [ranch] ranch *m*; nice ~ you've got here! belle propriété que vous avez là! -**11.** ST. EX spread *m*. -**12.** *Am* [bedspread] couvre-lit *m*.

◇ *adj* -**1.** [arms, fingers, legs] écarté.-**2.** LING [vowel] non arrondi.

◆ **spread out** ◇ *vi insep* -**1.** [town, forest] s'étendre. -**2.** [disperse] se disperser; [in formation] se déployer; the search party had ~ out through the woods l'équipe de secours s'était déployée à travers les bois. -**3.** [open out - sail] se déployer, se gonfler. -**4.** [make o.s. at ease] s'installer confortablement; I need an office where I can ~ out j'ai besoin d'un bureau où je puisse étaler mes affaires.

◇ *vt sep* -**1.** *(usu pass)* [disperse] disperser, éparpiller; the buildings are ~ out among the trees les bâtiments sont dispersés parmi les arbres; the runners are now ~ out (along the course) les coureurs sont maintenant éparpillés le long du parcours; the population is very ~ out la population est très dispersée; in a city as ~ out as Los Angeles dans une ville aussi étendue que Los Angeles. -**2.** = **spread** *vt* **2, 3**.

spread eagle *n* -**1.** HERALD aigle *f* éployée. -**2.** [in skating] grand aigle *m*; to do a ~ faire un grand aigle.

◆ **spread-eagle** ◇ *vt* -**1.** [lay flat]: he ~d himself against the wall il se plaqua contre le mur, bras et jambes écartés. -**2.** [knock flat] envoyer par terre; he was ~d by the blow le coup l'a fait tomber à la renverse.

◇ *adj* -**1.** = **spread-eagled**. -**2.** *inf Am* chauvin.

spread-eagled [-iːgld] *adj* bras et jambes écartés; the police had him ~ against the wall les policiers l'ont plaqué contre le mur, bras et jambes écartés; sunbathers lay ~ on the sand les baigneurs étaient étalés sur le sable.

spreader ['spredəʳ] *n* AGR & TECH [for fertilizer, manure, asphalt] épandeur *m*, épandeuse *f*.

spreadsheet ['spredʃiːt] *n* tableur *m*.

spree [spriː] *n* fête *f*; to go OR to be on a ~ faire la fête; her drinking/gambling ~s les périodes où elle boit/joue; to go on a shopping ~ faire des folies dans les magasins.

sprig [sprɪg] *n* brin *m*.

sprightliness ['spraɪtlɪnɪs] *n* [of person] vivacité *f*, vitalité *f*; [of tune] gaieté *f*.

sprightly ['spraɪtlɪ] (*compar* sprightlier, *superl* sprightliest) *adj* [person] alerte, guilleret; [step] vif; [tune, whistle] gai; he's a ~ 80-year-old c'est un alerte octogénaire.

spring [sprɪŋ] (*pt* sprang [spræŋ] OR sprung [sprʌŋ], *pp* sprung) ◇ *n* -**1.** [season] printemps *m*; in (the) ~ au printemps; ~ is here! c'est le printemps!; the Spring Bank Holiday *Br le dernier lundi de mai, jour férié en Grande-Bretagne*. -**2.** [device, coil] ressort *m*; the ~s AUT la suspension. -**3.** [natural source] source *f*; volcanic ~s sources volcaniques. -**4.** [leap] bond *m*, saut *m*; he made a sudden ~ for the knife tout à coup, il bondit pour s'emparer du couteau. -**5.** [resilience] élasticité *f*; the diving board has plenty of ~ le plongeoir est très élastique; the mattress has no ~ left le matelas n'a plus de ressort; the news put a ~ in her step la nouvelle l'a rendue toute guillerette; he set out with a ~ in his step il est parti d'un pas alerte.

◇ *comp* -**1.** [flowers, weather, colours] printanier, de printemps; his new ~ collection sa nouvelle collection de printemps; ~ term SCH & UNIV ≃ dernier trimestre *m*. -**2.** [mattress] à ressorts; ~ binding reliure *f* à ressort. -**3.** [water] de source.

◇ *vi* -**1.** [leap] bondir, sauter; to ~ at bondir OR se jeter sur; the cat sprang at the bird le chat bondit sur l'oiseau; he saw the blow coming and sprang away in time il a vu le coup arriver et l'a esquivé de justesse; the couple sprang apart le couple se sépara hâtivement; the bus stopped and she sprang off le bus s'arrêta et elle descendit d'un bond; he sprang ashore/on board il sauta à terre/à bord; the car sprang forward la voiture fit un bond en avant; ~ing out of the armchair bondissant du fauteuil; I sprang to my feet je me suis levé d'un bond; to ~ to attention bondir au garde-à-vous. -**2.** [be released]: to ~ shut/open se fermer/s'ouvrir brusquement; the branch sprang back la branche s'est redressée d'un coup. -**3.** *fig*: the police sprang into action les forces de l'ordre passèrent rapidement à l'action; the engine sprang to OR into life le moteur s'est mis soudain en marche OR a brusquement démarré; she sprang to my defence elle a vivement pris ma défense; the issue has made the town ~ to life l'affaire a galvanisé la ville; to ~ to the rescue se précipiter pour porter secours; tears sprang to his eyes les larmes lui sont montées OR venues aux yeux; a protest sprang to her lips elle eut envie de protester; just say the first thing which ~s to mind dites simplement la première chose qui vous vient à l'esprit; you didn't notice anything strange? — nothing that ~s to mind vous n'avez rien remarqué d'anormal? — rien qui me frappe particulièrement; where did you ~ from? *inf* d'où est-ce que tu sors? -**4.** [originate] venir, provenir; the problem ~s from a misunderstanding le problème provient OR vient d'un malentendu; their conservatism ~s from fear leur conservatisme vient de ce qu'ils ont peur. -**5.** [plank - warp] gauchir, se gondoler; [- crack] se fendre. -**6.** *inf Am* [pay]: to ~ for sthg casquer pour qqch.

◇ *vt* -**1.** [trap] déclencher; [mine] faire sauter; [bolt] fermer; the mouse-trap had been sprung but it was empty la souricière OR tapette avait fonctionné, mais elle était vide. -**2.** [make known - decision, news] annoncer de but en blanc OR à brûle-pourpoint; I hate to have to ~ it on you like this cela m'embête d'avoir à vous l'annoncer de but en blanc comme ça; he doesn't like people ~ing surprises on him il n'aime pas les surprises OR qu'on lui réserve des surprises; to ~ a question on sb poser une question à qqn de but en blanc. -**3.** [develop]: to ~ a leak [boat] commencer à prendre l'eau; [tank, pipe] commencer à fuir; the radiator has sprung a leak il y a une fuite dans le radiateur. -**4.** [jump over - hedge, brook] sauter. -**5.** [plank - warp] gauchir, gondoler; [- crack] fendre. -**6.** HUNT [game] lever. -**7.** *inf* [prisoner] faire sortir; the gang sprung him from prison with a helicopter le gang l'a fait évader de prison en hélicoptère.

◆ **spring up** *vi insep* -**1.** [get up] se lever d'un bond. -**2.** [move upwards] bondir, rebondir; the lid sprang up le couvercle s'est ouvert brusquement; several hands sprang up plusieurs mains se sont levées. -**3.** [grow in size, height] pousser; hasn't Lisa sprung up this year! comme Lisa a grandi cette année! -**4.** [appear - towns, factories] surgir, pousser comme des champignons; [- doubt, suspicion, rumour, friendship] naître; [- difficulty, threat] surgir; [- breeze] se lever brusquement; new companies are ~ing up every day de nouvelles entreprises apparaissent chaque jour; an argument sprang up between them une querelle éclata entre eux.

spring balance *n* peson *m* à ressort.

springboard ['sprɪŋbɔːd] *n* SPORT & *fig* tremplin *m*; the job is a ~ for ministerial office ce poste est un tremplin pour un portefeuille ministériel.

springbok ['sprɪŋbɒk] (*pl inv* OR springboks) *n* springbok.

◆ **Springbok** *pr n*: the Springboks [rugby team] les Springboks.

spring chicken *n Am* poulet *m (à rôtir)*; he's no ~ il n'est plus tout jeune.

spring-clean ◇ *vi* faire un nettoyage de printemps.

◇ *vt* nettoyer de fond en comble.

◇ *n Br* nettoyage *m* de printemps; to give the house a ~ nettoyer la maison de fond en comble; the accounting department needs a ~ *fig* le service de comptabilité a besoin d'un bon coup de balai.

spring-cleaning *n* nettoyage *m* de printemps.

springe [sprɪndʒ] *n* [snare] collet *m*.

springer ['sprɪŋəʳ] *n* -**1.** = **springer spaniel**. -**2.** ARCHIT [stone] sommier *m*; [impost] imposte *f*.

springer spaniel *n* springer *m*.

spring fever *n* agitation *f* printanière.

spring greens *npl* choux *mpl* précoces.

spring lock *n* serrure *f* à fermeture automatique.

spring onion *n* petit oignon *m* blanc.

spring roll *n* rouleau *m* de printemps.

springtide ['sprɪŋtaɪd] *n lit* printemps *m*.

spring tide *n* grande marée *f*; [at equinox] marée *f* d'équinoxe (de printemps).

springtime ['sprɪŋtaɪm] *n* printemps *m*.

springy ['sprɪŋɪ] (*compar* springier, *superl* springiest) *adj* [mattress, diving board] élastique; [step] souple, élastique; [floor] souple; [moss, carpet] moelleux; [hair] dru.

sprinkle ['sprɪŋkl] ◇ *vt* -**1.** [salt, sugar, spices, breadcrumbs, talc] saupoudrer; [parsley, raisins] parsemer; I ~d sugar on OR over my cereal, I ~d my cereal with sugar j'ai saupoudré mes céréales de sucre; ~ with grated cheese recouvrez de fromage râpé; he ~d sawdust on the floor il a répandu de la sciure par terre || [liquid]: to ~ water on sthg OR sthg with water asperger qqch d'eau; he ~d vinegar on OR over his chips il mit un peu de vinaigre sur ses frites. -**2.** *(usu pass)* [strew, dot] parsemer, semer; the

sky was ~d with stars le ciel était parsemé d'étoiles; the fields were ~d with snow les champs étaient tachetés de neige; his hair was ~d with grey ses cheveux étaient légèrement grisonnants; a speech ~d with metaphors un discours émaillé de métaphores; a few policemen were ~d among the crowd quelques policiers étaient disséminés dans la foule.
◇ *vi* [rain] tomber des gouttes.
◇ *n* -1. [rain] petite pluie *f*; I felt a ~ (of rain) j'ai senti quelques gouttes (de pluie). -2. = **sprinkling**.

sprinkler ['sprɪŋklə^r] *n* -1. AGR & HORT arroseur *m* (automatique); ~ truck arroseuse *f*. -2. [fire-extinguishing device] sprinkler *m*; ~ system installation *f* d'extinction automatique d'incendie. -3. [for holy water] goupillon *m*, aspersoir *m*.

sprinkling ['sprɪŋklɪŋ] *n* [small quantity] petite quantité *f*; [pinch] pincée *f*; a ~ of paprika makes all the difference une pincée de paprika fait toute la différence; it was a male audience with a ~ of women c'était une assistance masculine avec quelques rares femmes; a ~ of freckles gave his face a youthful look quelques taches de rousseur donnaient à son visage un air de jeunesse; there was a ~ of grey in her hair elle avait quelques cheveux gris.

sprint [sprɪnt] ◇ *n* SPORT [dash] sprint *m*; [race] course *f* de vitesse, sprint *m*; he was beaten in the finishing ~ il a été battu au sprint final; the 60 metre ~ le 60 mètres; to break into OR to put on a ~ [gen] piquer un sprint.
◇ *vi* sprinter; she ~ed to OR for her car elle sprinta jusqu'à sa voiture.

sprinter ['sprɪntə^r] *n* sprinter *m*.

sprit [sprɪt] *n* livarde *f*, baleston *f*, balestron *m*.

sprite [spraɪt] *n* MYTH [male] lutin *m*; [female] nymphe *f*; water ~ naïade *f* MYTH.

spritzer ['sprɪtsə^r] *n mélange de vin blanc et de soda*.

sprocket ['sprɒkɪt] *n* [wheel] pignon *m*; film transport ~ PHOT pignon d'entraînement de la pellicule.

sprog *inf* [sprɒg] *n Br* -1. [child] gosse *mf*, môme *mf*. -2. MIL [novice] bleu *m*, nouvelle recrue *f*.

sprout [spraʊt] ◇ *n* -1. [on plant, from ground] pousse *f*; [from bean, potato] germe *m*; alfalfa ~s germes de luzerne. -2. (Brussels) ~s choux *mpl* de Bruxelles. -3. *inf Am* [child] gosse *mf*, môme *mf*.
◇ *vi* -1. [germinate - bean, seed, onion] germer. -2. [grow - leaves, hair] pousser; he had hair ~ing from his ears des touffes de poils lui sortaient des oreilles. -3. [appear] apparaître, surgir; satellite TV receivers have ~ed on all the rooftops des antennes paraboliques ont surgi sur tous les toits.
◇ *vt* -1. [grow - leaves] pousser, produire; [- beard] faire pousser; some lizards can ~ new tails la queue de certains lézards repousse. -2. [germinate - seeds, beans, lentils] faire germer.
◆ **sprout up** *vi insep* -1. [grow - grass, wheat, plant] pousser, pointer; [- person] pousser; hasn't she ~ed up! comme elle a poussé! -2. [appear - towns, factories] pousser comme des champignons, surgir; a tented city had ~ed up overnight une ville de toile avait poussé OR surgi pendant la nuit.

spruce [spru:s] (*pl inv*) ◇ *n* BOT épicéa *m*; [timber] épinette *f*.
◇ *adj* [person, car, building, town] pimpant; [haircut] net; [garment] impeccable; ~ white curtains des rideaux blancs impeccables; she looked very ~ in her uniform elle était toute pimpante dans son uniforme.
◆ **spruce up** *vt sep* [car, building, town] donner un coup de neuf à; [paintwork] refaire; [child] faire beau; a coat of paint will ~ the room up une couche de peinture rafraîchira la pièce; his image needs sprucing up son image de marque a besoin d'être rafraîchie; to ~ o.s. up, to get ~d up se faire beau; he was all ~d up il était tiré à quatre épingles.

sprucely ['spru:slɪ] *adv* [painted, polished, starched] impeccablement; ~ dressed tiré à quatre épingles.

sprung [sprʌŋ] ◇ *pt* & *pp* → **spring**.
◇ *adj* [mattress] à ressorts.

spry [spraɪ] (*compar* sprier OR spryer, *superl* spriest OR spryest) *adj* [person] alerte, leste.

spryly ['spraɪlɪ] *adv* agilement, lestement; she leapt ~ out of bed elle sauta lestement hors du lit.

SPUC [spʌk] (*abbr of* Society for the Protection of the Unborn Child) *pr n ligue contre l'avortement*.

spud [spʌd] (*pt* & *pp* spudded, *cont* spudding) ◇ *n* -1. *inf* [potato] patate *f*. -2. [gardening tool] sarcloir *m*.
◇ *vt* PETR: to ~ a well (in) amorcer un puits.

spud-bashing *inf n Br* MIL corvée *f* de patates.

spume [spju:m] *n lit* écume *f*.

spun [spʌn] ◇ *pt* & *pp* → **spin**.
◇ *adj* filé; her hair was like ~ gold elle avait des cheveux d'or.

spun glass *n* verre *m* filé.

spunk [spʌŋk] *n* -1. *inf* [pluck] cran *m*, nerf *m*; show some ~! un peu de nerf, voyons! -2. ▼ *Br* [semen] foutre *m*.

spunky *inf* ['spʌŋkɪ] (*compar* spunkier, *superl* spunkiest) *adj* [person] plein de cran, qui a du cran; [retort, fight] courageux.

spun silk *n* schappe *f*.

spun sugar *n Am* barbe *f* à papa.

spun yarn *n* bitord *m*.

spur [spɜ:^r] (*pt* & *pp* spurred, *cont* spurring) ◇ *n* -1. EQUIT éperon *m*; to win one's ~s HIST gagner son épée de chevalier; *fig* faire ses preuves. -2. *fig* [stimulation] aiguillon *m*; the ~ of competition l'aiguillon de la concurrence; easy credit is a ~ to consumption le crédit facile pousse OR incite à la consommation; on the ~ of the moment sur le coup, sans réfléchir. -3. GEOG [ridge] éperon *m*, saillie *f*. -4. RAIL [siding] voie *f* latérale OR de garage; [branch line] embranchement *m*; the warehouse is served by a ~ line l'entrepôt est desservi par un embranchement. -5. [on motorway] bretelle *f*. -6. [breakwater] brise-lames *m inv*, digue *f*. -7. BOT & ZOOL éperon *m*; [on gamecock] ergot *m*.
◇ *vt* -1. [horse] éperonner. -2. *fig* inciter; her words spurred me into action ses paroles m'ont incité à agir.
◆ **spur on** *vt sep* -1. [horse] éperonner. -2. *fig* éperonner, aiguillonner; their shouts spurred us on leurs cris nous aiguillonnaient OR encourageaient; to ~ sb on to do sthg inciter OR pousser qqn à faire qqch; the move towards rearmament was spurred on by the Cold War la tendance au réarmement a été encouragée par la guerre froide.

spurge [spɜ:dʒ] *n* euphorbe *f*.

spurge laurel *n* daphné *m*.

spurious ['spʊərɪəs] *adj* -1. [false - gen] faux; [- comparison, argument, reason, objection] spécieux; your claim is a ~ one votre revendication est sans fondement. -2. [pretended - enthusiasm, sympathy] simulé; [- flattery, compliment] hypocrite. -3. [of doubtful origin - text] apocryphe, inauthentique.

spuriously ['spjʊərɪəslɪ] *adv* faussement.

spurn [spɜ:n] *vt* [gen] dédaigner, mépriser; [suitor] éconduire, rejeter; those who ~ tradition ceux qui dédaignent les traditions; a ~ed lover un amoureux éconduit.

spur-of-the-moment *adj* [purchase, phone call] fait sur le coup OR sans réfléchir; [excuse, tactics, invitation] improvisé; I made a ~ decision je me suis décidé sur le moment.

spurred [spɜ:d] *adj* [boots] à éperons.

spurt [spɜ:t] ◇ *vi* -1. [water, blood] jaillir, gicler; [flames, steam] jaillir; beer ~ed (out) from the can la bière a giclé de la boîte; the milk ~ed into the pail le lait gicla dans le seau; some lemon juice ~ed into my eye j'ai reçu une giclée de jus de citron dans l'œil. -2. [dash - runner, cyclist] sprinter, piquer un sprint; he ~ed past us il nous a dépassés comme une flèche; the car ~ed through the maze of streets la voiture fila à travers le dédale de rues.
◇ *vt* [gush - subj: pierced container] laisser jaillir; [spit - subj: gun, chimney] cracher; his wound ~ed blood le sang gicla OR jaillit de sa blessure; we ~ed each other with water nous nous sommes mutuellement aspergés d'eau.
◇ *n* -1. [of steam, water, flame] jaillissement *m*; [of blood, juice] giclée *f*; the water came out of the tap in ~s l'eau jaillit du robinet par à-coups; a ~ of machine gun fire une rafale de mitrailleuse. -2. [dash] accélération *f*; [at work] coup *m* de collier; [revival] regain *m*; [flash - of temper, jealousy, sympathy] sursaut *m*; to put on a ~ [while running, cycling] piquer un sprint; [while working] donner un coup de collier; after a brief ~ of economic growth après un bref regain de croissance économique; a ~ in prices une poussée OR flambée des prix; her inspiration came in ~s l'inspiration lui venait par à-coups.
◆ **spurt out** *vi insep* = **spurt** *vi* 1.

Sputnik ['spʊtnɪk] *n* Spoutnik *m*.

sputter ['spʌtə^r] ◇ *vi* -1. [motor] toussoter, crachoter; [fire, candle] crépiter; the engine ~ed to a halt le moteur s'arrêta dans un toussotement. -2. [stutter] bredouiller, bafouiller; he ~ed angrily il bredouillait de colère. -3. [spit - gen] crachoter; [- when talking] postillonner.
◇ *vt* [curses, apology] bredouiller, bafouiller.
◇ *n* -1. [of motor] toussotement *m*, hoquet *m*; [of fire, candle] crépitement *m*; the engine gave a final ~ le moteur toussa une dernière fois. -2. [stuttering] bredouillement *m*; "go away!", he said with a ~ «va-t'en!», bredouilla-t-il.
◆ **sputter out** *vi insep* [candle, enthusiasm, anger] s'éteindre.

sputum ['spju:təm] (*pl* sputa [-tə]) *n* MED crachat *m*, expectoration *f*.

spy [spaɪ] (*pl* spies, *pt* & *pp* spied) ◇ *n* espion *m*, -onne *f*; 'The Spy Who Came in From the Cold' *Le Carré, Ritt* 'l'Espion qui venait du froid'.
◇ *comp* [novel, film, scandal] d'espionnage; [network] d'espions; ~ ring réseau *m* d'espions; ~ satellite satellite *m* espion.
◇ *vi* [engage in espionage] faire de l'espionnage; accused of ~ing for the enemy accusé d'espionnage au profit de l'ennemi.
◇ *vt lit* [notice] apercevoir; [make out] discerner; he spied someone running away il a aperçu quelqu'un qui se sauvait.
◆ **spy on** *vt insep* espionner; they now ~ on each other using satellites maintenant ils s'espionnent à l'aide de satellites; you've been ~ing on me! tu m'as espionné!
◆ **spy out** *vt sep* [sb's methods, designs] chercher à découvrir (subrepticement); [landing sites] repérer; to ~ out the land *literal* & *fi* reconnaître le terrain.

spycatcher ['spaɪˌkætʃə^r] *n* chasseur *m* d'espions.

spyglass ['spaɪglɑ:s] *n* longue-vue *f*.

spyhole ['spaɪhəʊl] *n* judas *m*.

spying ['spaɪɪŋ] *n* [gen & INDUST] espionnage *m*

spymaster ['spaɪˌmɑ:stə^r] *n* chef *m* des services secrets.

sq., Sq. *written abbr of* square.

squab [skwɒb] (*pl inv* OR squabs, *compa* squabber, *superl* squabbest) ◇ *n* -1. ORNITH pigeonneau *m*. -2. [person] homme *m* rond OI rondelet, femme *f* ronde OR rondelette -3. [cushion] coussin *m* bien rembourré; [sofa sofa *m*; AUT [of car seat] dossier *m*.
◇ *adj* -1. [tubby] rond, enrobé. -2. ORNITH SAN plumes.

squabble ['skwɒbl] ◇ *vi* se disputer, se quereller.
◇ *n* dispute *f*, querelle *f*.

squabbling ['skwɒblɪŋ] *n (U)* chamailleries *fpl*, disputes *fpl*.

squad [skwɒd] *n* -**1.** [group - gen] équipe *f*, escouade *f*; the England football ~ SPORT l'équipe anglaise de football. -**2.** MIL escouade *f*, section *f*. -**3.** [of police detachment] brigade *f*; the drug ~ la brigade des stupéfiants.

squad car *n* voiture *f* de patrouille de police.

squaddy *inf* ['skwɒdɪ] (*pl* squaddies) *n Br* MIL bidasse *m*, troufion *m*.

squadron ['skwɒdrən] *n* [in air force] escadron *m*; [in navy - small] escadrille *f*; [- large] escadre *f*; [in armoured regiment, cavalry] escadron *m*.

squadron leader *n* [in air force] commandant *m*.

squalid ['skwɒlɪd] *adj* sordide.

squall [skwɔːl] ◇ *n* -**1.** METEOR [storm] bourrasque *f*, rafale *f*, grain *m* NAUT; [rain shower] grain *m*; snow ~s bourrasques de neige. -**2.** [argument] dispute *f*; the treaty ratification caused a ~ in Parliament la ratification du traité a soulevé une tempête au Parlement. -**3.** [bawling] braillement *m*.

◇ *vi* -**1.** [bawl] brailler; he could hear ~ing children il entendait brailler des enfants. -**2.** NAUT: it was ~ing on a pris un grain.

◇ *vt*: "no!", he ~ed «non!», brailla-t-il.

squally ['skwɔːlɪ] (*compar* squallier, *superl* squalliest) *adj* [wind] qui souffle par OR en rafales; [rain] qui tombe par rafales; the weather will be ~ il y aura des bourrasques.

squalor ['skwɒlə^r] *n (U)* [degrading conditions] conditions *fpl* sordides; [filth] saleté *f* repoussante; to live in ~ vivre dans des conditions sordides OR dans une misère noire; the ~ of OR in the stairwell la saleté repoussante de la cage d'escalier.

squamate ['skweɪmeɪt] *adj* [reptile] squamifère.

squamous ['skweɪməs] *adj* -**1.** [scaly] écailleux; [flaky] squameux. -**2.** BIOL: ~ cell cellule *f* épithéliale; ~ epithelium épithélium *m* simple.

squander ['skwɒndə^r] *vt* [resources, time, money] gaspiller; [inheritance] dissiper; [opportunity] gâcher, passer à côté de; huge sums were ~ed on unworkable schemes des sommes énormes ont été dépensées en pure perte pour des projets irréalisables.

square [skweə^r] ◇ *n* -**1.** [shape - gen & GEOM] carré *m*; she arranged the pebbles in a ~ elle a disposé les cailloux en carré; he folded the napkin into a neat ~ il a plié la serviette en un carré bien net; cut the cake into ~s coupez le gâteau en carrés; the drawer is out of ~ le tiroir n'est pas d'équerre ❑ to be on the ~ *inf* être réglo; I'm telling you this on the ~ *inf* je vous le dis carrément. -**2.** [square object - gen] carré *m*; [- tile] carreau *m*; a silk ~ un carré de soie; a ~ of chocolate un carré OR morceau de chocolat; a bathroom in grey and white ~s une salle de bains avec un carrelage gris et blanc. -**3.** [square space - in matrix, crossword, board game] case *f*; locate ~ D4 on the map trouvez la case D4 sur la carte ❑ back to ~ one! retour à la case départ!; we're back at OR to ~ one nous voilà revenus à la case départ; I had to start from ~ one again j'ai dû repartir à zéro. -**4.** [open area - with streets] place *f*; [- with gardens] square *m*; MIL [parade ground] place *f* d'armes; barrack ~ cour *f* de caserne; the town ~ la place, la grand-place. -**5.** MATH [multiple] carré *m*; nine is the ~ of three neuf est le carré de trois. -**6.** [instrument] équerre *f*. -**7.** *inf pej* [person] ringard *m*, -e *f*; he's such a ~! qu'est-ce qu'il est ringard!

◇ *adj* -**1.** [in shape - field, box, building, face] carré; a tall man with ~ shoulders un homme grand aux épaules carrées ❑ to be a ~ peg in a round hole être comme un chien dans un jeu de quilles. -**2.** [mile, inch etc] carré; 10 ~ kilometres 10 kilomètres carrés; the room is 15 feet ~ la pièce fait 5 mètres sur 5. -**3.** [at right angles] à angle droit; a ~ corner un angle droit; the shelves aren't ~ les étagères ne sont pas droites ❑ ~ pass SPORT passe *f* latérale; ~ leg [cricket] *chasseur situé derrière le batteur*. -**4.** [fair, honest] honnête; to give sb a ~ deal agir correctement avec qqn; I got a ~ deal on the car rental je n'ai rien à redire au prix de location de la voiture; the farmers aren't getting a ~ deal les perdants dans l'affaire, ce sont les agriculteurs. -**5.** [substantial - meal] consistant. -**6.** [frank, blunt - person] franc; [- denial] clair, net, catégorique; he won't give me a ~ answer il refuse de me donner une réponse claire et nette. -**7.** [even, equal]: we're all ~ [in money] nous sommes quittes; they were (all) ~ at two games each SPORT ils étaient à égalité deux parties chacun; did you get things ~ with Julia? est-ce que tu as pu arranger les choses avec Julia?

◇ *adv* -**1.** = **squarely**. -**2.** [at right angles]: she set the box ~ with OR to the edge of the paper elle a aligné la boîte sur les bords de la feuille de papier; the house stands ~ to the street la maison est parallèle à la rue. -**3.** [directly]: he hit the ball ~ in the middle of the racket il frappa la balle avec le milieu de sa raquette; she looked him ~ in the face elle le regarda bien en face.

◇ *vt* -**1.** [make square - pile of paper] mettre droit, aligner; [- stone] carrer; [- log] équarrir; [- shoulders] redresser; it's like trying to ~ the circle c'est la quadrature du cercle. -**2.** MATH carrer, élever au carré; three ~d is nine trois au carré égale neuf. -**3.** [reconcile] concilier; how do you ~ your wealth with being a socialist? comment arrivez-vous à concilier votre richesse avec vos idées socialistes?; I couldn't ~ the story with the image I had of him je n'arrivais pas à faire coïncider cette histoire avec l'image que j'avais de lui. -**4.** [settle - account, bill] régler; [- debt] acquitter; [- books] balancer, mettre en ordre; to ~ accounts with sb *fig* régler son compte à qqn. -**5.** SPORT: his goal ~d the match son but a mis les équipes à égalité. -**6.** *inf* [arrange] arranger; can you ~ it with the committee? pourriez-vous arranger cela avec le comité?; we shouldn't do it unless we ~ it with them first nous ne devrions pas le faire avant d'avoir arrangé ça avec eux. -**7.** *(usu pass)* [rule into squares] quadriller; ~d paper papier *m* quadrillé. -**8.** *inf* [bribe] soudoyer.

◇ *vi* cadrer, coïncider; his story doesn't ~ with the facts son histoire ne cadre OR ne coïncide pas avec les faits; her figures/results don't ~ with mine ses chiffres/résultats ne cadrent pas avec les miens; does their offer ~ with your asking price? leur offre correspond-elle au prix que vous demandez?

◆ **square away** *inf vt sep (usu pass) Am* régler, mettre en ordre; did you get everything ~d away? est-ce que tu as pu tout régler?

◆ **square off** ◇ *vi insep* [opponents, boxers] se mettre en garde.

◇ *vt sep* -**1.** [piece of paper, terrain] quadriller. -**2.** [stick, log] carrer, équarrir.

◆ **square up** *vi insep* -**1.** [settle debt] régler les comptes; I'll ~ up with you when you have finished all the work je réglerai mes comptes avec toi dès que tu auras fini tout le travail. -**2.** = **square off**.

◆ **square up to** *vt insep* [confront - situation, criticism] faire face OR front à; [- in physical fight] se mettre en position de combat contre; he ~d up to me il se mit en garde devant moi; the unions are squaring up to the management les syndicats cherchent la confrontation avec la direction.

square-bashing *inf n Br (U)* MIL exercice *m*.

square bracket *n* crochet *m* IMPR; in ~s entre crochets.

square-cut *adj* [gem, rock] coupé à angle droit OR d'équerre; [log] équarri; *fig* [jaw] carré.

square dance *n* quadrille *m* américain.

◆ **square-dance** *vi* danser le quadrille américain.

square dancing *n (U)* quadrille *m* américain; there'll be ~ at the saloon tonight on va danser au saloon ce soir.

square knot *n Am* [reef knot] nœud *m* plat.

squarely ['skweəlɪ] *adv* -**1.** [firmly] fermement, carrément; [directly] en plein; they are ~ opposed to the bill ils sont fermement opposés au projet de loi; we must confront the dilemma ~ nous devons affronter ce dilemme avec fermeté; to look sb ~ in the eye regarder qqn droit dans les yeux; ~ in the middle en plein milieu; the blow landed ~ on his nose il a reçu le coup en plein sur le nez. -**2.** [honestly] honnêtement; to deal ~ with sb agir avec qqn de façon honnête.

Square Mile *pr n*: the ~ *la City de Londres, dont la superficie fait environ un mile carré*.

square number *n* carré *m*.

square-rigged *adj* NAUT [boat] gréé en carré.

square root *n* racine *f* carrée.

squash [skwɒʃ] ◇ *vt* -**1.** [crush] écraser; he sat on my hat and ~ed it en s'asseyant il a écrasé mon chapeau; you're ~ing me! tu m'écrases!; I was ~ed between two large ladies j'étais serré OR coincé entre deux grosses dames; we were ~ed in like sardines nous étions serrés comme des sardines. -**2.** [cram, stuff] fourrer; she ~ed the laundry down in the bag elle a tassé le linge dans le sac; I ~ed another sweater into my rucksack j'ai pu faire entrer un pull supplémentaire dans mon sac à dos. -**3.** [silence, repress - person] remettre à sa place; [- objection] écarter; [- suggestion] repousser; [- argument] réfuter; [- hopes] réduire à néant; [- rumour] mettre fin à; [- rebellion] réprimer; she ~ed him with a look elle l'a foudroyé du regard.

◇ *vi* -**1.** [push - people] s'entasser; all seven of us managed to ~ into her car on a réussi à s'entasser à sept dans sa voiture. -**2.** [fruit, package] s'écraser; be careful, the fruit ~es easily faites attention, ces fruits s'écrasent facilement.

◇ *n* -**1.** [crush of people] cohue *f*; with five of us it'll be a bit of a ~ à cinq, nous serons un peu serrés. -**2.** SPORT squash *m*. -**3.** *Br* [drink]: lemon/orange ~ sirop *m* de citron/d'orange. -**4.** *Am* [vegetable] courge *f*.

◇ *comp* [ball, court, champion, racket] de squash; ~ court terrain *m* de squash; ~ rackets *Br* [game] squash *m*.

◆ **squash in** *vi insep* [people] s'entasser; the lift arrived and everybody ~ed in l'ascenseur arriva et tout le monde s'entassa dedans; I ~ed in between two very fat men je me suis fait une petite place entre deux hommes énormes.

◆ **squash together** ◇ *vi insep* [people] se serrer (les uns contre les autres), s'entasser.

◇ *vt sep* serrer, tasser.

squashy ['skwɒʃɪ] (*compar* squashier, *superl* squashiest) *adj* [fruit, package] mou; [cushion, sofa] moelleux; [ground] spongieux.

squat [skwɒt] (*pt & pp* squatted, *cont* squatting, *compar* squatter, *superl* squattest) ◇ *vi* -**1.** [crouch - person] s'accroupir; [- animal] se tapir; we ate squatting (down) on our haunches nous avons mangé accroupis. -**2.** [live] vivre dans un squat; they're allowed to ~ in abandoned buildings on leur permet de squatter dans des immeubles abandonnés.

◇ *vt* [building] squatter, squattériser.

◇ *n* -**1.** [building] squat *m*; [action] squat *m*, occupation *f* de logements vides; the ~ held out for two years le squat a duré deux ans. -**2.** [crouch] accroupissement *m*; she rested in an easy ~ elle était confortablement assise sur ses talons.

◇ *adj* [person, figure] courtaud, ramassé; [building] trapu; he had short, ~ legs il avait des petites jambes trapues.

squatter ['skwɒtə^r] *n* squatter *m*; *Austr* [rancher] squatter *m*, éleveur *m*; there are ~ settlements all round the town il y a des squats un peu partout dans la ville.

squaw [skwɔː] *n* -**1.** [American Indian] squaw *f*. -**2.** *inf pej* OR *hum* [woman] femme *f*, gonzesse *f*; [wife] épouse *f*; my ~ la patronne, ma bourgeoise.

squawk [skwɔːk] ◇ *vi* -**1.** [bird] criailler; [person] brailler. -**2.** *inf* [complain] criailler, râler. -**3.** *inf* [inform] moucharder, vendre la mèche.
◇ *vt*: "let go of me!", she ~ed «lâchez-moi!», brailla-t-elle.
◇ *n* [of bird] criaillement *m*, cri *m*; [of person] cri *m* rauque; to let out OR to give a ~ pousser un cri rauque; the measure raised ~s of protest from the oil industry *fig* cette mesure a suscité de vives protestations au sein de l'industrie pétrolière.

squawk box *inf n Am* [loudspeaker] haut-parleur *m*; [intercom] interphone *m*; [telephone] bigophone *m*.

squeak [skwiːk] ◇ *vi* -**1.** [floorboard, chalk, wheel] grincer; [animal] piauler, piailler; [person] glapir; she ~ed with delight elle poussa un cri de joie. -**2.** *inf* [succeed narrowly]: the team ~ed into the finals l'équipe s'est qualifiée de justesse pour la finale; they ~ed past Canada to become the biggest wheat producer ils ont dépassé le Canada de justesse pour devenir le plus grand producteur de blé.
◇ *vt*: "who, me?", he ~ed «qui? moi?», glapit-il.
◇ *n* -**1.** [of floorboard, hinge, chalk etc] grincement *m*; [of animal] piaillement *m*; [of person] petit cri *m* aigu, glapissement *m*; [of soft toy] couinement *m*; to let out OR to give a ~ of pleasure pousser un petit cri de plaisir; don't let me hear one more ~ out of you! et que je ne t'entende plus! -**2.** *phr*: that was a narrow ~! on l'a échappé belle!
◆ **squeak by** *inf*, **squeak through** *inf vi insep* -**1.** [pass through] se faufiler; there was just enough room to ~ by il y avait juste assez de place pour se faufiler. -**2.** [succeed narrowly] réussir de justesse; [in exam] être reçu de justesse; [in election] l'emporter de justesse.

squeaky ['skwiːkɪ] (*compar* squeakier, *superl* squeakiest) *adj* [floorboard, bed, hinge] grinçant; [voice] aigu.

squeaky clean *inf adj* -**1.** [hands, hair] extrêmement propre; a shampoo that leaves your hair ~ un shampooing qui donne à vos cheveux une propreté impeccable. -**2.** [reputation] sans tache.

squeal [skwiːl] ◇ *vi* -**1.** [person] pousser un cri perçant; [tyres, brakes] crisser; [pig] couiner; to ~ with pain pousser un cri de douleur; to ~ with laughter hurler de rire; the car ~ed around the corner la voiture prit le virage dans un crissement de pneus ❑ he was ~ing like a stuck pig il criait comme un cochon qu'on égorge. -**2.** ▽ [inform] moucharder; to ~ on sb balancer qqn.
◇ *vt*: "ouch", she ~ed «aïe!», cria-t-elle.
◇ *n* [of person] cri *m* perçant; [of tyres, brakes] crissement *m*; he gave a ~ of delight il poussa un cri de joie.

squeamish ['skwiːmɪʃ] *adj* hypersensible; I'm very ~ about the sight of blood je ne supporte pas la vue du sang; she's ~ about physical violence elle ne supporte pas les scènes de violence; he was too ~ even to taste it il n'a même pas eu le courage d'y goûter; this film is not for the ~ ce film n'est pas conseillé aux âmes sensibles.

squeamishness ['skwiːmɪʃnɪs] *n* hypersensibilité *f*; her ~ really annoys me [about blood] ça m'énerve qu'elle supporte aussi mal la vue du sang; [about food] ça m'énerve qu'elle soit aussi difficile sur la nourriture; [about violence] ça m'énerve qu'elle supporte aussi mal les scènes de violence.

squeegee ['skwiːdʒiː] ◇ *n* [with rubber blade] raclette *f*; [sponge mop] balai-éponge *m*; PHOT [roller] rouleau *m (en caoutchouc)*.
◇ *vt* [window] passer une raclette sur, laver avec une raclette.

squeeze [skwiːz] ◇ *vt* -**1.** [press - tube, sponge, pimple] presser; [- trigger] presser sur, appuyer sur; [- package] palper; [- hand, shoulder] serrer; I ~d as hard as I could j'ai serré aussi fort que j'ai pu; she ~d her knees together elle serra les genoux; I kept my eyes ~d tight shut j'ai gardé les yeux bien fermés. -**2.** [extract, press out - liquid] exprimer; [- paste, glue] faire sortir; I ~d a dab of cream onto my nose je me suis mis un peu de crème sur le nez; a glass of freshly ~d orange juice une orange pressée; to ~ the air out of OR from sthg faire sortir l'air de qqch en appuyant dessus. -**3.** *fig* [money, information] soutirer; it won't be easy to ~ the results out of him il ne sera pas facile de lui soutirer les résultats; you won't ~ another penny out of me! tu n'auras pas un sou de plus!; they want to ~ more concessions from the EC ils veulent forcer la CEE à faire de nouvelles concessions; she's squeezing a lot of publicity out of the issue elle exploite le sujet au maximum pour se faire de la publicité. -**4.** [cram, force] faire entrer (avec difficulté); I can't ~ another thing into my suitcase je ne peux plus rien faire entrer dans ma valise; they're squeezing more and more circuits onto microchips ils réussissent à mettre de plus en plus de circuits sur les puces; she ~d the ring onto her finger elle enfila la bague avec difficulté; he ~d his huge bulk behind the steering wheel il parvint à glisser son corps volumineux derrière le volant; 20 men were ~d into one small cell 20 hommes étaient entassés dans une petite cellule; the airport is ~d between the sea and the mountains l'aéroport est coincé entre la mer et les montagnes. -**5.** [constrain - profits, budget] réduire; [- taxpayer, workers] pressurer; universities are being ~d by the cuts les réductions (de budget) mettent les universités en difficulté; I'm a bit ~d for time/money *inf* question temps/argent, je suis un peu juste. -**6.** [in bridge] squeezer.
◇ *vi*: the lorry managed to ~ between the posts le camion a réussi à passer de justesse entre les poteaux; I ~d into the crowded room j'ai réussi à me glisser dans la salle bondée; they all ~d onto the bus ils se sont tous entassés dans le bus; can you ~ into that parking space? y a-t-il assez de place pour te garer là?; try and ~ into these trousers essayez de rentrer dans ce pantalon; it was possible just to ~ under the wire il était tout juste possible de se glisser sous le fil de fer.
◇ *n* -**1.** [amount - of liquid, paste] quelques gouttes *fpl*; a ~ of toothpaste un peu de dentifrice. -**2.** [crush of people] cohue *f*; it was a tight ~ [in vehicle, room] on était très serré; [through opening] on est passé de justesse. -**3.** [pressure, grip] pression *f*; [handshake] poignée *f* de main; [hug] étreinte *f*; he gave my hand a reassuring ~ il a serré ma main pour me rassurer ❑ to put the ~ on sb *inf* faire pression sur qqn. -**4.** *inf* [difficult situation] situation *f* difficile; in a ~ you can always borrow my car en cas de problème, tu peux toujours emprunter ma voiture. -**5.** ECON: (credit) ~ resserrement *m* du crédit. -**6.** [in bridge] squeeze *m*. -**7.** *inf Am* [friend] copain *m*, copine *f*.
◆ **squeeze in** ◇ *vi insep* [get in] se faire une petite place; I had to ~ in past six people to reach my seat j'ai dû me glisser devant six personnes pour atteindre mon siège.
◇ *vt sep* [in schedule] réussir à faire entrer; she's hoping to ~ in a trip to Rome too elle espère avoir aussi le temps de faire un saut à Rome; the dentist says he can ~ you in le dentiste dit qu'il peut vous prendre entre deux rendez-vous; can you ~ in a lunch with me next week? vous n'aurez pas une petite heure disponible pour déjeuner avec moi la semaine prochaine?
◆ **squeeze out** *vt sep* -**1.** [sponge, wet clothes] essorer. -**2.** [liquid] exprimer; TECH [plastic] extruder; I ~d out the last of the glue j'ai fini le tube de colle; she gently ~d the splinter out en pressant doucement, elle a fait sortir l'écharde. -**3.** [replace - candidate, competitor] l'emporter sur; we were ~d out by a German firm une société allemande nous a devancés d'une courte tête; the Japanese are squeezing them out of the market ils sont en train de se faire évincer du marché par les Japonais.
◆ **squeeze up** *vi insep* se serrer, se pousser.

squeezebox *inf* ['skwiːzbɒks] *n* [accordion] accordéon *m*, piano *m* à bretelles; [concertina] concertina *m*.

squeezer ['skwiːzə^r] *n* CULIN presse-agrumes *m inv*; lemon ~ presse-citron *m inv*.

squelch [skweltʃ] ◇ *vi* -**1.** [walk - in wet terrain] patauger; [- with wet shoes] marcher les pieds trempés; I ~ed across the field j'ai traversé le champ en pataugeant; he ~ed into the kitchen il entra dans la cuisine avec les pieds trempés. -**2.** [make noise - mud] clapoter; I heard something soft ~ beneath my foot j'ai entendu quelque chose de mou s'écraser sous mon pied.
◇ *vt* -**1.** [crush] écraser. -**2.** *inf* [rumour] étouffer; [person] clouer le bec à.
◇ *n* [noise] clapotement; I heard the ~ of tyres in mud j'ai entendu le bruit des pneus dans la boue.

squib [skwɪb] *n* -**1.** [firecracker] pétard *m*. -**2.** [piece of satire] pamphlet *m*.

squid [skwɪd] (*pl inv* OR squids) *n* calmar *m*, calamar *m*, encornet *m*.

squidgy *inf* ['skwɪdʒɪ] (*compar* squidgier, *superl* squidgiest) *adj Br* mou, spongieux.

squiffy *inf* ['skwɪfɪ] (*compar* squiffier, *superl* squiffiest) *adj Br dated* éméché, pompette.

squiggle ['skwɪgl] ◇ *n* -**1.** [scrawl, doodle] gribouillis *m*. -**2.** [wavy line, mark] ligne *f* ondulée; something had left ~s in the sand quelque chose avait laissé des traces sinueuses sur le sable.
◇ *vi* -**1.** [scrawl, doodle] gribouiller, faire des gribouillages. -**2.** [twist - road, lines] sinuer, serpenter; [- worm] se tortiller.

squiggly *inf* ['skwɪglɪ] *adj* pas droit, ondulé.

squinch *inf* [skwɪntʃ] *vt Am*: to ~ one's eyes plisser les yeux.

squint [skwɪnt] ◇ *n* -**1.** MED strabisme *m*; to have a ~ loucher. -**2.** *inf* [glimpse] coup *m* d'œil; have OR take a ~ at this! vise-moi un peu ça!
◇ *vi* -**1.** MED loucher. -**2.** [half-close one's eyes] plisser les yeux; he ~ed at the photo [with difficulty] il regarda la photo en plissant les yeux; [quickly] il jeta un coup d'œil à la photo; [sidelong] il regarda la photo du coin de l'œil.

squint-eyed *adj* -**1.** *inf* [cross-eyed] qui louche, bigleux. -**2.** [sidelong] de côté.

squirarchy ['skwaɪərɑːkɪ] = **squirearchy**.

squire ['skwaɪə^r] ◇ *n* -**1.** [landowner] *propriétaire d'un domaine en Grande-Bretagne*; he's the village ~ c'est le propriétaire du plus grand domaine du coin; Squire Greaves le squire Greaves. -**2.** [for knight] écuyer *m*. -**3.** *dated* [escort] cavalier *m*; her ~ for the evening son cavalier pour la soirée. -**4.** *inf Br* [term of address]: evening, ~! bonsoir, chef!
◇ *vt dated* [woman] escorter, accompagner.

squirearchy ['skwaɪərɑːkɪ] (*pl* squirearchies) *n* propriétaires *mpl* terriens; the island's planters form a ~ les planteurs de l'île forment une petite noblesse terrienne.

squirm [skwɜːm] ◇ *vi* -**1.** [wriggle] se tortiller; he ~ed out of my grasp il a échappé à mon étreinte en se tortillant; she ~ed with impatience elle était tellement impatiente qu'elle ne tenait plus en place. -**2.** [be ill-at-ease] être gêné, être très mal à l'aise; [be ashamed] avoir honte; to ~ with embarrassment être mort de honte; the reporters are going to make him ~! devant la presse, il ne saura pas où se mettre!; I still ~ when I remember how I treated her j'ai encore honte quand je pense à la manière dont je l'ai traitée; his speech was so bad it made me ~ son discours était si mauvais que j'en ai eu honte pour lui.
◇ *n*: she gave a ~ of embarrassment elle ne put cacher sa gêne.

squirrel [*Br* 'skwɪrəl, *Am* 'skwɜːrəl] (*Br pt* & *pp* squirrelled, *cont* squirrelling, *Am pt* & *pp* squirreled, *cont* squirreling) *n* -**1.** ZOOL écureuil *m*; red ~ écureuil; grey/flying ~ écureuil gris/

volant. -2. *fig* [hoarder]: she's a real ~ c'est une vraie fourmi.

◆ **squirrel away** *vt sep* [hoard, store] engranger *fig*; [hide] cacher; he's got a fortune squirrelled away in various Swiss banks il a amassé une fortune dans plusieurs banques suisses.

squirt [skwɜːt] ◇ *vt* [liquid] faire gicler; [mustard, ketchup, washing-up liquid] faire jaillir; ~ some oil on the hinges mettez quelques gouttes d'huile sur les gonds; they were ~ing each other with water, they were ~ing water at each other ils s'aspergeaient d'eau mutuellement; he ~ed some soda water into his whisky il versa une rasade d'eau de Seltz dans son whisky; she ~ed perfume on her wrists elle se vaporisa du parfum sur les poignets.
◇ *vi* [juice, blood, ink] gicler; [water] jaillir; juice ~ed onto my shirt le jus a giclé sur ma chemise; the milk ~ed (out) into the pail le lait giclait dans le seau.
◇ *n* -1. [of juice, ink] giclée *f*; [of water] jet *m*; [of mustard, ketchup, washing-up liquid] dose *f*; [of oil, perfume] quelques gouttes *fpl*. -2. *inf pej* [person] minus *m*; [short person] avorton *m*; [child] mioche *mf*; get lost, you little ~! va donc, eh minus!

squirt gun *n Am* pistolet *m* à eau.

squish *inf* [skwɪʃ] ◇ *vt Am* [crush] écrabouiller; he ~ed his nose against the glass il a écrasé son nez contre la vitre; the cake got all ~ed le gâteau était complètement écrabouillé.
◇ *vi* -1. *Am* [squash - insect, fruit] s'écrabouiller. -2. [squelch] clapoter; the mud ~ed between my toes la boue s'infiltrait entre mes orteils.

squishy *inf* ['skwɪʃɪ] (*compar* squishier, *superl* squishiest) *adj* [fruit, wax] mou; [chocolate] ramolli; [ground] boueux; a ~ blob of dough un petit tas de pâte molle.

squit *inf* [skwɪt] *n Br* -1. [person] minus *m*. -2. *(U)* [nonsense] bêtises *fpl*.

Sr -1. (*written abbr of* senior): Ralph Todd ~ Ralph Todd père. -2. *written abbr of* sister.

SRC ◇ *n Br* (*abbr of* students' representative council) *comité étudiant*.
◇ *pr n* (*abbr of* Science Research Council) *conseil de la recherche scientifique*.

Sri Lanka [ˌsriː'læŋkə] *pr n* Sri Lanka *m*; in ~ au Sri Lanka.

Sri Lankan [ˌsriː'læŋkn] ◇ *n* Sri Lankais *m*, -e *f*.
◇ *adj* sri lankais.

SRN *n abbr of* State Registered Nurse.

SRO *abbr of* standing room only.

SRV *n abbr of* space rescue vehicle.

SS ◇ (*abbr of* steamship) *initiales précédant le nom des navires de la marine marchande*; the ~ "Norfolk" le «Norfolk».
◇ *pr n* (*abbr of* Schutzstaffel): the ~ les SS; an ~ officer un officier SS.

SSA *pr n Am abbr of* Social Security Administration.

SSP *n abbr of* statutory sick pay.

SST *n abbr of* supersonic transport.

st *written abbr of* stone.

St -1. (*written abbr of* saint) St, Ste. -2. *written abbr of* street.

ST *n abbr of* Standard Time.

stab [stæb] (*pt* & *pp* stabbed, *cont* stabbing) ◇ *vt* -1. [injure - with knife] donner un coup de couteau à, poignarder; [- with bayonet] blesser d'un coup de baïonnette; [- with spear] blesser avec une lance; he stabbed me in the arm il me donna un coup de couteau dans le bras; they were stabbed to death ils ont été tués à coups de couteau; he was stabbed to death with a kitchen knife il a été tué avec un couteau de cuisine ❑ to ~ sb in the back *literal* & *fig* poignarder qqn dans le dos. -2. [thrust, jab] planter; she stabbed the needle into my arm elle planta l'aiguille dans mon bras; I stabbed myself in the thumb with a pin je me suis enfoncé une épingle dans le pouce; I stabbed my finger in his eye je lui ai enfoncé mon doigt dans l'œil; I stabbed a turnip with my fork j'ai piqué un navet avec ma fourchette.
◇ *vi*: he stabbed at the map with his finger il frappa la carte du doigt; she stabbed frantically at the different control buttons elle poussa frénétiquement les différents boutons de contrôle; he stabbed at the dead leaves with his walking stick il piquait les feuilles mortes de la pointe de sa canne.
◇ *n* -1. [thrust] coup *m* (de couteau OR de poignard); he made a vicious ~ at me with the broken bottle il fit un mouvement agressif vers moi avec la bouteille cassée; she felt the ~ of the needle in her finger elle a senti la piqûre de l'aiguille dans son doigt ❑ ~ wound blessure *f* par arme blanche; a man was rushed to hospital with ~ wounds un homme blessé à coups de couteau a été transporté d'urgence à l'hôpital; it was a ~ in the back c'était un véritable coup de poignard dans le dos. -2. *lit* [of neon, colour] éclat *m*; a ~ of lightning un éclair. -3. [of pain] élancement *m*; [of doubt, guilt] remords *m*; I felt a ~ of envy je sentis un pincement de jalousie. -4. *inf* [try]: to have OR to make OR to take a ~ at (doing) sthg s'essayer à (faire) qqch; why don't you take a ~ at it? pourquoi n'essayez-vous pas?

stabbing ['stæbɪŋ] ◇ *n* [knife attack] agression *f* (à l'arme blanche); there were two fatal ~s at the football match deux personnes ont été tuées à coups de couteau au match de football.
◇ *adj* [pain] lancinant.

stability [stə'bɪlətɪ] *n* stabilité *f*; a period of political ~ une période de stabilité politique; it will undermine the ~ of their marriage cela va ébranler leur mariage; his mental ~ son équilibre mental.

stabilization [ˌsteɪbəlaɪ'zeɪʃn] *n* stabilisation *f*.

stabilize, -ise ['steɪbəlaɪz] ◇ *vt* stabiliser.
◇ *vi* se stabiliser; the political situation has ~d la situation politique s'est stabilisée.

stabilizer ['steɪbəlaɪzəʳ] *n* -1. AERON, AUT & ELEC [device] stabilisateur *m*; NAUT stabilisateur *m*; [on bicycle] stabilisateur *m*; the measure is intended to act as an economic ~ *fig* cette mesure a pour but de stabiliser l'économie. -2. CHEM [in food] stabilisateur *m*, stabilisant *m*.

stable ['steɪbl] ◇ *adj* -1. [steady, permanent - gen] stable; [- marriage] solide; the patient's condition is ~ l'état du malade est stationnaire; he never had a ~ family life il n'a jamais eu de vie de famille stable. -2. [person, personality] stable, équilibré. -3. CHEM & PHYS stable.
◇ *n* -1. [building] écurie *f*; riding ~ OR ~s centre *m* d'équitation. -2. [group - of racehorses, racing drivers etc] écurie *f*.
◇ *vt* [take to stable] mettre à l'écurie; her horse is ~d at Dixon's son cheval est en pension chez Dixon.

stable boy *n* valet *m* d'écurie.

stable door *n* porte *f* d'écurie, porte *f* à deux vantaux OR battants; to shut OR to close the ~ after the horse has bolted envoyer les pompiers après l'incendie.

stable girl *n* valet *m* d'écurie *(fille)*.

stable lad *n* -1. = **stable boy**. -2. [in racing stable] lad *m*.

stablemate ['steɪblmeɪt] *n* -1. [horse] compagnon *m* d'écurie. -2. *fig* [person - at work] collègue *mf* de travail; [- from same school] camarade *mf* d'études.

stabling ['steɪblɪŋ] *n (U)* écuries *fpl*; we supply ~ for 40 horses nous pouvons accueillir 40 chevaux.

staccato [stə'kɑːtəʊ] ◇ *adj* -1. MUS [note] piqué; [passage] joué en staccato; ~ mark trait *m* vertical. -2. [noise, rhythm] saccadé; in a ~ voice d'une voix saccadée.
◇ *adv* MUS staccato.

stack [stæk] ◇ *n* -1. [pile] tas *m*, pile *f*; a huge ~ of books une pile énorme de livres. -2. *inf* [large quantity] tas *m*; I've written a ~ of OR ~s of postcards j'ai écrit un tas de cartes postales; she has ~s of money elle est bourrée de fric. -3. AGR [of hay, straw] meule *f*. -4. [chimney] cheminée *f*. -5. AERON avions *mpl* en attente, empilage *m*; the ~ is twenty planes high il y a vingt avions qui attendent le feu vert de la tour de contrôle pour atterrir. -6. COMPUT [file] pile *f*. -7. MIL [of rifles] faisceau *m*. -8. [in library]: the ~ OR ~s les rayons *mpl*. -9. *Br* [measure of firewood] ≃ 3 stères *mpl (3,06 mètres cubes)*.
◇ *vt* -1. [pile - chairs, boxes etc] empiler; ~ the glasses in the cupboard empilez les verres dans l'armoire; oil cans were ~ed in pyramids des bidons d'huile étaient empilés en pyramide. -2. AGR [hay] mettre en meule OR meules. -3. [fill - room, shelf] remplir; his desk was ~ed high with files des piles de dossiers s'entassaient sur son bureau. -4. COMPUT empiler. -5. AERON [planes] mettre en attente (à altitudes échelonnées). -6. [fix, rig - committee] remplir de ses partisans; [- cards, odds etc]: to ~ the cards OR the deck truquer les cartes; he's playing with a ~ed deck *fig* [in his favour] les dés sont pipés en sa faveur; [against him] les dés sont pipés contre lui; the cards OR the odds are ~ed against us nous sommes dans une mauvaise situation; a woman lawyer starts with the cards ~ed against her une femme avocat part avec un handicap; the elections are heavily ~ed against the smaller parties ce mode de scrutin défavorise fortement les petits partis.
◇ *vi* s'empiler.

◆ **stacks** *inf adv Br* vachement; it's ~s easier c'est vachement plus facile.

◆ **stack up** ◇ *vt sep* [pile up] empiler.
◇ *vi insep* -1. *inf Am* [add up, work out]: I don't like the way things are ~ing up je n'aime pas la tournure que prennent les événements; I wanted someone honest and dynamic and that's how Jan ~s up je voulais quelqu'un d'honnête et de dynamique et Jan fait parfaitement l'affaire. -2. [compare] se comparer; our product ~s up well against theirs notre produit soutient bien la comparaison avec le leur; how does he ~ up against OR with the other candidates? que vaut-il comparé aux autres candidats?

stacked [stækt] *adj* -1. ~ heel talon *m* compensé. -2. ▽ [woman]: she's (well) ~ il y a du monde au balcon.

stacker ['stækəʳ] *n* [worker] manutentionnaire *mf*; [pallet truck] transpalette *m*.

stadium ['steɪdjəm] (*pl* stadiums OR stadia [-djə]) *n* stade *m*.

staff [stɑːf] (*pl senses 3 & 4* staffs OR staves [stɑːvz]) ◇ *n* -1. [work force] personnel *m*; [teachers] professeurs *mpl*, personnel *m* enseignant; the company has a ~ of fifty l'effectif de la société est de cinquante personnes; we have ten lawyers on the ~ notre personnel comprend dix avocats; reductions in the clerical ~ une réduction du personnel administratif; is he ~ OR a member of ~? est-ce qu'il fait partie du personnel?; ~/student ratio taux *m* d'encadrement des étudiants. -2. MIL & POL état-major *m*; she was asked to join the President's campaign ~ on lui a demandé de faire partie de l'état-major de campagne du Président. -3. [rod] bâton *m*; [flagpole] mât *m*; [for shepherd] houlette *f*; [for bishop] crosse *f*, bâton *m* pastoral; *Br* [in surveying] jalon *m* TECH; *fig* [support] soutien *m*; the ~ of life [bread] l'aliment de base; *fig* le pain et le sel de la vie. -4. MUS portée *f*; treble ~ portée à la clé de sol.
◇ *comp* [canteen, outing etc] du personnel.
◇ *vt (usu pass)* pourvoir en personnel; the branch is ~ed by OR with competent people le personnel de la succursale est compétent; the committee is completely ~ed by volunteers le comité est entièrement composé de bénévoles.

staff association *n* ≃ comité *m* d'entreprise.

staff college *n* MIL école *f* supérieure de guerre.

staff corporal *n* MIL ≃ sergent-major *m*.

staffer ['stɑːfəʳ] *n* PRESS rédacteur *m*, -trice *f*, membre *m* de la rédaction.

staffing ['stɑːfɪŋ] *n* [recruiting] recrutement *m*; the delay is due to ~ difficulties le retard est dû à des problèmes de recrutement.

staff nurse *n* infirmier *m*, -ère *f*.

staff officer *n* MIL officier *m* d'état-major.

staffroom ['stɑːfrʊm] *n* SCH salle *f* des enseignants OR des professeurs.

Staffs *written abbr of* Staffordshire.

staff sergeant *n* MIL *Br* ≃ sergent-chef *m*, *Am* ≃ sergent *m*.

stag [stæg] (*pl inv* OR stags) ◇ *n* -**1.** ZOOL cerf *m*. -**2.** *Br* ST. EX spéculateur *m*, -trice *f* sur un titre nouveau.
◇ *adj* -**1.** [event for men] entre hommes; **Thursday night is ~ night** le jeudi soir est réservé aux hommes. -**2.** *inf* [pornographic] porno; **~ films** films *mpl* pornos.

stag beetle *n* cerf-volant *m* ENTOM, lucane *m*.

stage [steɪdʒ] ◇ *n* -**1.** [period, phase - of development, project etc] stade *m*; [- of illness] stade *m*, phase *f*; **larval ~** stade larvaire; **the bill is at the committee ~** le projet de loi va maintenant être examiné par un comité; **we'll deal with that at a later ~** nous nous en occuperons plus tard; **the details can wait for a later ~** nous nous occuperons des détails plus tard; **at this ~ of the negotiations, I won't venture to comment** à ce stade des négociations, je m'interdirai tout commentaire; **the conflict is still in its early ~s** le conflit n'en est encore qu'à ses débuts; **the next ~ in computer technology** le stade suivant OR l'étape suivante du développement de l'informatique; **by** OR **in ~s** par paliers; **the changes were instituted in ~s** les changements ont été introduits progressivement; **to do sthg ~ by ~** faire qqch par étapes OR progressivement. -**2.** [stopping place, part of journey] étape *f*; **we travelled to Lisbon in easy ~s** nous avons voyagé jusqu'à Lisbonne par petites étapes; (fare) **~** *Br* section *f*. -**3.** THEAT [place] scène *f*; **the ~** [profession, activity] le théâtre; **on ~** sur scène; **~ right/left** côté jardin/cour; **to go on ~** monter sur (la) scène; **to go on the ~** [as career] monter sur les planches, faire du théâtre; **he first appeared on the ~ in 1920** il a commencé à faire du théâtre en 1920; **to write for the ~** écrire pour la scène; **she was the first to bring the play to the London ~** elle a été la première à monter cette pièce sur la scène londonienne ‖ *fig*: **the political ~** la scène politique; **on the ~ of world events** sur la scène internationale; **his concerns always take centre ~** ses soucis à lui doivent toujours passer avant tout; **to set the ~ for sthg** préparer le terrain pour qqch. -**4.** ASTRONAUT étage *m*; **a three-~ satellite launcher** un lanceur spatial à trois étages. -**5.** [platform - gen] plate-forme *f*; [- on microscope] platine *f*; [scaffolding] échafaudage *m*; (landing) **~** débarcadère *m*. -**6.** = **stagecoach**. -**7.** ELECTRON [circuit part] étage *m*.
◇ *comp* [design] scénique; [version] pour le théâtre; **a ~ Irishman** une caricature d'Irlandais; **she has great ~ presence** elle a énormément de présence sur scène.
◇ *vt* -**1.** THEAT [put on - play] monter, mettre en scène; [set] situer; **it's the first time the play has been ~d** c'est la première fois qu'on monte cette pièce; **Macbeth was very well ~d** la mise en scène de Macbeth était très réussie; **the company is staging plays in parks this summer** la troupe joue dans les parcs cet été; **the play was ~d in Paris in the 20s** la pièce avait pour cadre le Paris des années 20. -**2.** [organize - ceremony, festival] organiser; [carry out - robbery] organiser; **to ~ a hijacking** détourner un avion; **to ~ a diversion** créer une OR faire diversion; **she ~d her entrance for maximum effect** elle prépara son entrée de façon à faire le plus d'effet possible; **the historic handshake was ~d for the TV cameras** la poignée de main historique était une mise en scène destinée aux caméras de télévision. -**3.** [fake - accident] monter, manigancer; **they ~d an argument for your benefit** ils ont fait semblant de se disputer parce que vous étiez là; **the murder was ~d to look like a suicide** le meurtre a été maquillé en suicide.

stagecoach ['steɪdʒkəʊtʃ] *n* diligence *f*; 'Stagecoach' *Ford* 'la Chevauchée fantastique'.

stagecraft ['steɪdʒkrɑːft] *n* [of playwright] maîtrise *f* de l'écriture théâtrale; [of director] maîtrise *f* de la mise en scène; [of actor] maîtrise *f* du jeu.

stage designer *n* décorateur *m* de théâtre.

stage direction *n* indication *f* scénique.

stage door *n* entrée *f* des artistes.

stage effect *n* effet *m* scénique.

stage fright *n* trac *m*; **to have ~** avoir le trac, être pris de trac.

stagehand ['steɪdʒhænd] *n* THEAT machiniste *mf*.

stage-manage *vt* -**1.** THEAT [play, production] s'occuper de la régie de. -**2.** [press conference, appearance] mettre en scène; **her arrival at the airport was ~d to generate publicity** son arrivée à l'aéroport a été une vraie mise en scène publicitaire; **the unrest was ~d to coincide with the summit meeting** les troubles ont été orchestrés de manière à coïncider avec le sommet.

stage manager *n* THEAT régisseur *m*.

stage name *n* nom *m* de scène.

stager ['steɪdʒəʳ] *n* -**1.** [veteran]: **old ~** vieux routier *m*, vétéran *m*. -**2.** *arch* [actor] acteur *m*.

stage set *n* THEAT décor *m*.

stagestruck ['steɪdʒstrʌk] *adj* possédé par le démon du théâtre, qui rêve de faire du théâtre.

stage whisper *n* aparté *m*; **"it's midnight", he announced in a loud ~** «il est minuit», chuchota-t-il, suffisamment fort pour que tout le monde l'entende.

stagey ['steɪdʒɪ] *Am* = **stagy**.

stagflation [stæg'fleɪʃn] *n* stagflation *f*.

stagger ['stægəʳ] ◇ *vi* [totter - person, horse] chanceler, tituber; **to ~ with tiredness** chanceler de fatigue; **to ~ out** sortir en chancelant OR titubant; **I ~ed over to the chair** je me suis dirigé vers la chaise d'un pas chancelant; **I ~ed under the weight** je titubais sous le poids; **we ~ed into bed at 3 o'clock in the morning** nous nous sommes écroulés sur nos lits à 3 h du matin.
◇ *vt* -**1.** (*usu pass*) [payments] échelonner; [holidays] étaler; **they plan to bring in ~ed working hours** ils ont l'intention de mettre en place un système d'échelonnement des heures de travail; **employees' vacation times are ~ed over the summer months** les vacances du personnel sont étalées sur tout l'été; **lampposts were ~ed along the street** la rue était jalonnée de réverbères; **~ed start** SPORT [on oval track] départ *m* décalé; **~ed wings** AERON ailes *fpl* décalées. -**2.** (*usu pass*) [astound]: **to be ~ed** être atterré, être stupéfait; **I was ~ed to learn of his decision** j'ai été stupéfait d'apprendre sa décision.
◇ *n* [totter] pas *m* chancelant; **he got up with a ~** il s'est levé en chancelant.
◆ **staggers** *n* [in diver] ivresse *f* des profondeurs; (blind) **~s** [in sheep] tournis *m*, cœnurose *f*; [in horses] vertigo *m*.

staggering ['stægərɪŋ] ◇ *adj* [news, amount] stupéfiant, ahurissant; [problems] énorme; **it was a ~ blow** *literal* & *fig* ce fut un sacré coup; **the price tag is a ~ $500,000** c'est au prix astronomique de 500 000 dollars.
◇ *n* -**1.** [of vacations] étalement *m*; [of payments] échelonnement *m*. -**2.** [unsteady gait] démarche *f* chancelante.

staghound ['stæghaʊnd] *n* chien *m* d'équipage.

staging ['steɪdʒɪŋ] ◇ *n* -**1.** THEAT [of play] mise *f* en scène. -**2.** [scaffolding] échafaudage *m*; [shelving] rayonnage *f*. -**3.** ASTRONAUT largage *m* (*d'un étage de fusée*).
◇ *comp* MIL: **~ area** OR **point** lieu *m* de rassemblement.

staging post *n* lieu *m* OR point *m* de ravitaillement.

stagnancy ['stægnənsɪ] *n* stagnation *f*.

stagnant ['stægnənt] *adj* -**1.** [water, pond - still] stagnant; [- stale] croupissant; [air - still] confiné; [- stale] qui sent le renfermé. -**2.** [trade, career] stagnant; [society] statique, en stagnation.

stagnate [stæg'neɪt] *vi* -**1.** [water - be still] stagner; [- be stale] croupir. -**2.** [economy, career] stagner; **he ~d in the same job for years** il a croupi dans le même emploi pendant des années.

stagnation [stæg'neɪʃn] *n* stagnation *f*.

stag night, **stag party** *n* [gen] soirée *f* entre hommes; [before wedding day]: **we're having** OR **holding a ~ for Bob** nous enterrons la vie de garçon de Bob.

stagy ['steɪdʒɪ] (*compar* **stagier**, *superl* **stagiest**) *adj* théâtral; **she's very ~** elle a des manières très théâtrales.

staid [steɪd] *adj* [person] rangé, collet monté (*inv*) *pej*; [colours] sobre, discret; [job] très ordinaire; **a man of ~ habits** un homme rangé; **a ~ and simple life** une vie simple et rangée; **the party was all very ~** la soirée fut sans surprises OR très banale.

staidly ['steɪdlɪ] *adv* [sit, watch] calmement; [walk, dance] dignement; [dress] sobrement.

staidness ['steɪdnɪs] *n* sobriété *f*.

stain [steɪn] ◇ *n* -**1.** [mark, spot] tache *f*; **coffee/ink ~s** taches de café/d'encre; **to leave a ~** laisser une tache; **I couldn't get the ~ out** je n'ai pas réussi à enlever OR faire disparaître la tache. -**2.** *fig* [on character] tache *f*; **it was a ~ on his reputation** cela a entaché sa réputation. -**3.** [colour, dye] teinte *f*, teinture *f*; **a wood ~** une teinture pour bois; **oak/mahogany ~** teinte chêne/acajou.
◇ *vt* -**1.** [soil, mark] tacher; **the sink was ~ed with rust** l'évier était taché de rouille; **smoking ~s your teeth** le tabac jaunit les dents; **his hands are ~ed with blood** *literal* & *fig* il a du sang sur les mains. -**2.** [honour, reputation] tacher, entacher, ternir. -**3.** [colour, dye - wood] teindre; [- glass, cell specimen] colorer; **the lake was ~ed pink by the dawn** la lumière rosée de l'aube se reflétait dans le lac.
◇ *vi* -**1.** [mark - wine, oil etc] tacher; **white wine doesn't ~** le vin blanc ne tache pas. -**2.** [become marked - cloth] se tacher; **silk ~s easily** la soie se tache facilement OR est salissante.

stained [steɪnd] *adj* -**1.** [soiled - collar, sheet] taché; [- teeth] jauni. -**2.** [coloured - gen] coloré; [- wood] teint.

-stained *in cpds* taché; **rust/ink~** taché de rouille/d'encre; **his sweat~ shirt** sa chemise tachée de transpiration; **nicotine~** jauni par la nicotine.

stained glass *n* vitrail *m*; **she works in ~** elle fabrique des vitraux.
◆ **stained-glass** *adj*: **stained-glass window** vitrail *m*.

stainless ['steɪnlɪs] *adj* -**1.** [rust-resistant] inoxydable. -**2.** *fig* sans tache, pur; **a ~ reputation** une réputation sans tache.

stainless steel ◇ *n* acier *m* inoxydable, Inox® *m*.
◇ *comp* en acier inoxydable, en Inox®.

stain remover *n* détachant *m*.

stair [steəʳ] *n* -**1.** [step] marche *f*; **the bottom ~** la première marche. -**2.** *lit* [staircase] escalier *m*.
◆ **stairs** *npl* [stairway] escalier *m*, escaliers *mpl*; **I slipped on the ~s** j'ai glissé dans l'escalier; **to run up/down the ~s** monter/descendre les escaliers en courant; **at the top of the ~s** en haut de l'escalier; **at the bottom** OR **the foot of the ~s** en bas OR au pied de l'escalier; **we passed on the ~s** on s'est croisés dans les escaliers ❑ **above/below ~s** *Br* chez les patrons/les domestiques.

staircase ['steəkeɪs] *n* escalier *m*.

stair-rod *n* tringle *f* d'escalier.

stairway ['steəweɪ] = **staircase**.

stairwell ['steəwel] *n* cage *f* d'escalier.

stake [steɪk] ◇ *n* -**1.** [post, pole] pieu *m*; [for plant] tuteur *m*; [in surveying] piquet *m*, jalon *m*; [for tent] piquet *m*; [for execution] poteau *m*; **to die** OR **to be burned at the ~** mourir sur le bûcher; **it's an important principle but I'm not**

about to go to the ~ for it *fig* c'est un principe important mais je ne me sacrifierais pas OR je ne mourrais pas pour le défendre ❑ to (pull) up ~s *Am* [leave place, job] faire ses valises; [continue journey] se remettre en route. -**2.** [in gambling] enjeu *m*, mise *f*; **to play for high ~s** jouer gros jeu; **the ~s are too high for me** l'enjeu est trop important pour moi; **to lose one's ~** perdre sa mise. -**3.** [interest, share] intérêt *m*, part *f*; [investment] investissement *m*, investissements *mpl*; [shareholding] participation *f*; **she has a 10% ~ in the company** elle a une participation de 10 % dans la société, elle détient 10 % du capital de la société; **the company has a big ~ in nuclear energy** la société a misé gros sur OR a fait de gros investissements dans le nucléaire; **we all have a ~ in the education of the young** l'éducation des jeunes nous concerne tous. -**4.** *Am* [savings] (petit) pécule *m*, bas *m* de laine.

◇ *vt* -**1.** [bet - sum of money, valuables] jouer, miser; *fig* [- reputation] jouer, risquer; **he ~d $10 on Birdy** il a joué OR misé OR mis 10 dollars sur Birdy; **she had ~d her reputation on the outcome of the negotiations** elle avait risqué OR joué sa réputation sur le résultat des négociations; **he had ~d everything** OR **his all on getting the job** il avait tout misé sur l'acceptation de sa candidature; **I'd ~ my all** OR **my life on it** j'en mettrais ma main au feu. -**2.** *Am* [aid financially] financer; **they are staking the newspaper for half a million dollars** ils investissent un demi-million de dollars dans le journal; **can you ~ me for a new suit?** *inf* est-ce que tu peux m'avancer de quoi m'acheter un nouveau costume? -**3.** [fasten - boat, animal] attacher (à un pieu OR un piquet); [- tent] attacher avec des piquets; [- plant] tuteurer. -**4.** [put forward]: **to ~ a** OR **one's claim to sthg** revendiquer qqch; **to ~ one's claim to a territory** *literal* revendiquer un territoire *(en le délimitant avec des piquets)*; **each gang has ~d its claim to a piece of the territory** chaque gang a délimité sa part de territoire; **she has ~d her claim to a place in the history of our country** elle mérite une place d'honneur dans l'histoire de notre pays. -**5.** *phr*: **to be at ~** être en jeu; **what** OR **how much is at ~?** quels sont les enjeux?, qu'est-ce qui est en jeu?; **basic issues of public health are at ~** les bases mêmes de la santé publique sont en jeu; **there are lives at ~!** il y a des vies en jeu!; **she has a lot at ~** elle joue gros jeu, elle risque gros.

◆ **stakes** *npl* [horse race] course *f* de chevaux; [money prize] prix *m*; **the Bingham Stakes** EQUIT le Prix de Bingham; **the promotion ~s** *fig* la course à l'avancement.

◆ **stake off** *vt sep* = **stake out 1**.

◆ **stake out** *vt sep* -**1.** [delimit - area, piece of land] délimiter (avec des piquets); [- boundary, line] marquer, jalonner; *fig* [- sphere of influence] définir; [- market] se tailler; [- job, research field] s'approprier. -**2.** *Am* [keep watch on] mettre sous surveillance, surveiller; **they've got the house ~d out** ils surveillent la maison.

stakeholder ['steɪk,həʊldəʳ] *n* [for bets] dépositaire *mf* des enjeux; [for property] dépositaire *mf* d'enjeux.

stakeout ['steɪkaʊt] *n Am* [activity] surveillance *f*; [place] locaux *mpl* sous surveillance; **to be on ~ duty** effectuer une surveillance.

Stakhanovism [stə'kænəvɪzm] *n* stakhanovisme *m*.

Stakhanovite [stə'kænəvaɪt] *n* stakhanoviste *mf*.

stalactite ['stæləktaɪt] *n* stalactite *f*.

stalag ['stælæg] *n* stalag *m*.

stalagmite ['stæləgmaɪt] *n* stalagmite *f*.

stale [steɪl] ◇ *adj* -**1.** [bread, cake] rassis, sec; [chocolate, cigarette] vieux; [cheese - hard] desséché; [- mouldy] moisi; [fizzy drink] éventé, plat; [air - foul] vicié; [- confined] confiné; **the car smelt of ~ cigarette smoke** la voiture sentait le tabac froid; **~ breath** haleine *f* fétide; **to go ~** [bread] (se) rassir; [chocolate, cigarette] perdre son goût; [cheese] se dessécher; [beer] s'éventer. -**2.** [idea, plot, joke] éculé, rebattu; [discovery, news] éventé, dépassé; [pleasure] émoussé, qui n'a plus de goût; [beauty] fané, défraîchi; **his arguments were ~ and unconvincing** ses arguments étaient éculés et peu convaincants; **her marriage had gone ~** son bonheur conjugal s'était fané, elle s'était lassée de son mariage; **he's getting ~ in that job** il sèche sur pied dans ce poste. -**3.** JUR [warrant] périmé; [debt] impayable; **~ cheque** FIN chèque *m* prescrit.

◇ *vi lit* [novelty, place, activity] perdre son charme.

stalemate ['steɪlmeɪt] ◇ *n* -**1.** [in chess] pat *m*; **the game ended in ~** la partie s'est terminée par un pat. -**2.** [deadlock] impasse *f*; **the nuclear arms ~** l'impasse de la course aux armements nucléaires; **the argument ended in (a) ~** la discussion s'est terminée dans une impasse; **the announcement broke the ~ in the negotiations** l'annonce a fait sortir les négociations de l'impasse.

◇ *vt (usu pass)* [in chess - opponent] faire pat à; **the negotiations were ~d** *fig* les négociations étaient dans l'impasse.

staleness ['steɪlnɪs] *n* [of food, air] manque *m* de fraîcheur; [of information, joke etc] manque *m* de nouveauté.

Stalin ['stɑːlɪn] *pr n* Staline.

Stalingrad ['stɑːlɪngræd] *pr n* Stalingrad.

Stalinism ['stɑːlɪnɪzm] *n* stalinisme *m*.

Stalinist ['stɑːlɪnɪst] ◇ *adj* stalinien.

◇ *n* stalinien *m*, - enne *f*.

stalk [stɔːk] ◇ *n* -**1.** BOT [of flower, plant] tige *f*; [of cabbage, cauliflower] trognon *m*; **(grape) ~s** râpe *f*, rafle *f*. -**2.** ZOOL pédoncule *m*; **his eyes stood out on ~s** *inf* il avait les yeux qui lui sortaient de la tête. -**3.** [gen - long object] tige *f*.

◇ *vt* -**1.** [game, fugitive etc] traquer. -**2.** [subj: wolf, ghost] rôder dans; **to ~ the woods/the bush on foot** [gen] battre les bois/la brousse à pied; HUNT faire une battue dans les bois/la brousse; **enemy patrols ~ed the hills** des patrouilles ennemies rôdaient dans les collines. -**3.** *lit* [subj: disease, terror] régner dans, rôder dans; **hunger ~ed the countryside** la faim régnait dans les campagnes; **evil ~s the night** les forces du mal rôdent dans la nuit.

◇ *vi* -**1.** [person]: **she ~ed out angrily/proudly/in disgust** elle sortit d'un air furieux/hautain/dégoûté; **he was ~ing up and down the deck** il arpentait le pont. -**2.** [prowl - tiger, animal] rôder; [hunt] chasser; **a ~ing lion** un lion en chasse; **famine ~ed through the land** *lit* la famine régnait dans le pays.

stalking horse ['stɔːkɪŋ-] *n* -**1.** *literal* cheval *m* d'abri. -**2.** *fig* stratagème *m*.

stall [stɔːl] ◇ *n* -**1.** [at market] étal *m*, éventaire *m*; [at fair, exhibition] stand *m*; **I bought some peaches at a fruit ~** j'ai acheté des pêches chez un marchand de fruits; **flower ~** *Br* [on street] kiosque *m* de fleuriste. -**2.** [for animal] stalle *f*; **(starting) ~s** EQUIT stalles de départ. -**3.** [cubicle] cabine *f*. -**4.** [in church] stalle *f*. -**5.** *Br* CIN & THEAT orchestre *m*, fauteuil *m* d'orchestre; **the ~s** l'orchestre; **a seat in the ~s** un fauteuil d'orchestre. -**6.** *Am* [in parking lot] emplacement *m (de parking)*. -**7.** [for finger] doigtier *m*. -**8.** AERON décrochage *m*; AUT calage *m (du moteur)*; **the aircraft went into a ~** l'avion a décroché. -**9.** [delaying tactic] manœuvre *f* dilatoire; [pretext] prétexte *m*.

◇ *vi* -**1.** [motor, vehicle, driver] caler; [plane] décrocher; [pilot] faire décrocher son avion. -**2.** [delay]: **to ~ for time** essayer de gagner du temps; **I can ~ for another month** je peux essayer de gagner du temps pendant encore un mois; **I think they're ~ing on the loan until we make more concessions** je crois qu'ils vont retarder le prêt jusqu'à ce que nous leur fassions davantage de concessions.

◇ *vt* -**1.** [motor, vehicle] caler; [plane] faire décrocher. -**2.** [delay - sale, decision] retarder; [- person] faire attendre; **try to ~ him (off)!** essayez de gagner du temps!; **I'll ~ her in the lobby while you grab a taxi** je la retiendrai dans le hall le temps que tu sautes dans un taxi; **I can't ~ them (off) for much longer** je ne peux guère les faire attendre plus longtemps; **the project/his career is ~ed** le projet/sa carrière en est au point mort; **we managed to ~ the enemy's advance** on a réussi à retarder la progression de l'ennemi. -**3.** [animal] mettre à l'étable.

stall-fed *adj* AGR engraissé à l'étable.

stallholder ['stɔːl,həʊldəʳ] *n* [in market] marchand *m*, -e *f* de OR des quatre-saisons; [in fair] forain *m*, -e *f*; [in exhibition] exposant *m*, -e *f*.

stalling ['stɔːlɪŋ] ◇ *n (U)* atermoiements *mpl*, manœuvres *fpl* dilatoires.

◇ *adj*: **~ tactic** manœuvre *f* dilatoire.

stallion ['stæljən] *n* étalon *m (cheval)*.

stalwart ['stɔːlwət] ◇ *adj* [person] robuste; [citizen, fighter] vaillant, brave; [work, worker] exemplaire; **he was a ~ supporter of the England team** c'était un supporter inconditionnel de l'équipe d'Angleterre.

◇ *n* fidèle *mf*; **the party ~s** les fidèles du parti.

stamen ['steɪmən] (*pl* **stamens** OR **stamina** ['stæmɪnə]) *n* BOT étamine *f*.

stamina ['stæmɪnə] *n* [physical] résistance *f*, endurance *f*; [mental] force *f* intérieure, résistance *f*; **to build up one's ~** SPORT développer son endurance; **she has more ~ than he does** elle est plus résistante que lui.

stammer ['stæməʳ] ◇ *vi* [through fear, excitement] balbutier, bégayer; [through speech defect] bégayer, être bègue.

◇ *vt* bredouiller, bégayer; **I managed to ~ (out) an apology** j'ai réussi à bredouiller des excuses.

◇ *n* [through fear, excitement] balbutiement *m*, bégaiement *m*; [through speech defect] bégaiement *m*; **to have a ~** bégayer, être bègue; **he has a bad ~** il est affligé d'un bégaiement prononcé.

stammerer ['stæmərəʳ] *n* bègue *mf*.

stammering ['stæmərɪŋ] *n* [through fear, excitement] bégaiement *m*, balbutiement *m*; [speech defect] bégaiement *m*.

stammeringly ['stæmərɪŋlɪ] *adv* en bégayant, en bredouillant.

stamp [stæmp] ◇ *n* -**1.** [sticker, token] timbre *m*; **fiscal** OR **revenue ~** timbre fiscal; **UNESCO ~s** timbres de l'Unesco; **television (licence) ~** timbre pour la redevance ❑ **(national insurance) ~** *Br* cotisation *f* de sécurité sociale; **(postage) ~** timbre, timbre-poste *m*; **the Stamp Act** *Am* HIST le Stamp Act; **trading ~** COMM vignette-épargne *f*, timbre-prime *m*. -**2.** [instrument - rubber stamp] tampon *m*, timbre *m*; [- for metal] poinçon *m*; [- for leather] fer *m*; **date ~** tampon dateur. -**3.** [mark, impression - in passport, library book etc] cachet *m*, tampon *m*; [- on metal] poinçon *m*; [- on leather] motif *m*; [- on antique] estampille *f*; [postmark] cachet *m* (d'oblitération de la poste); **he has an Israeli ~ in his passport** il a un visa israélien sur son passeport; **silversmith's ~** poinçon d'orfèvre; **~ of approval** *fig* approbation *f*, aval *m*. -**4.** [distinctive trait] marque *f*, empreinte *f*; **a work which bears the ~ of originality** une œuvre qui porte l'empreinte de l'originalité; **his story had the ~ of authenticity** son histoire semblait authentique; **poverty has left its ~ on him** la pauvreté a laissé son empreinte sur lui OR l'a marqué de son sceau; **their faces bore the ~ of despair** le désespoir se lisait sur leur visage. -**5.** [type, ilk, class] genre *m*, acabit *m pej*; [calibre] trempe *f*; **we need more teachers of his ~** nous avons besoin de plus d'enseignants de sa trempe; **of the old ~** [servant, worker] comme on n'en fait plus; [doctor, disciplinarian] de la vieille école. -**6.** [noise - of boots] bruit *m* (de bottes); [- of audience] trépignement *m*; **"no!", he cried with an angry ~ of his foot** «non!», cria-t-il rageusement en tapant du pied.

◇ *comp* [album, collection] de timbres, de timbres-poste.

◇ *vt* -**1.** [envelope, letter] timbrer, affranchir. -**2.** [mark - document] tamponner; [- leather, metal] estamper; he ~ed the firm's name on each document il a tamponné le nom de la société sur chaque document; incoming mail is ~ed with the date received le courrier qui arrive est tamponné à la date de réception; the machine ~s the time on your ticket la machine marque OR poinçonne l'heure sur votre ticket; it's ~ed "fragile" c'est marqué «fragile»; the belt has a ~ed design la ceinture porte un motif estampé. -**3.** [affect, mark - society, person] marquer; as editor she ~ed her personality on the magazine comme rédactrice en chef, elle a marqué la revue du sceau de sa personnalité. -**4.** [characterise, brand] étiqueter; recent events have ~ed the president as indecisive le président a été taxé d'indécision au vu des derniers événements; her actions ~ed her as a pacifist in the eyes of the public son action lui a valu une réputation de pacifiste. -**5.** [foot]: she ~ed her foot in anger furieuse, elle tapa du pied; the audience were ~ing their feet and booing la salle trépignait et sifflait; they were ~ing their feet to keep warm ils sautillaient sur place pour se réchauffer; he ~ed the snow off his boots il a tapé du pied pour enlever la neige de ses bottes.

◇ *vi* -**1.** [in one place - person] taper du pied; [- audience] trépigner; [- horse] piaffer; I ~ed on his fingers je lui ai marché sur les doigts; he ~ed on the rotten plank and it broke il a tapé du pied sur la planche pourrie et elle s'est cassée. -**2.** [walk]: to ~ in/out [noisily] entrer/sortir bruyamment; [angrily] entrer/sortir en colère; he ~ed up the stairs il monta l'escalier d'un pas lourd; they were ~ing about OR around to keep warm ils sautillaient sur place pour se réchauffer.

◆ **stamp down** *vt sep* [loose earth, snow] tasser avec les pieds; [peg] enfoncer du pied.

◆ **stamp on** *vt insep* [rebellion] écraser; [dissent, protest] étouffer; [proposal] repousser.

◆ **stamp out** *vt sep* -**1.** [fire] éteindre avec les pieds OR en piétinant. -**2.** [end - disease, crime] éradiquer; [- strike, movement] supprimer; [- dissent, protest] étouffer; [- ideas, corruption] extirper. -**3.** [hole] découper (à l'emporte-pièce); [medal] frapper; [pattern] estamper.

THE STAMP ACT:
Impôt britannique auquel furent soumises les colonies américaines à partir de 1765. Portant sur un certain nombre de publications, dont les actes juridiques et les journaux, il doit son nom au timbre justifiant de son acquittement. Premier impôt direct levé par la Couronne, il souleva une violente opposition chez les colons, qui obtinrent sa suppression un an plus tard.

---

stamp book *n* -**1.** [of postage stamps] carnet *m* de timbres OR de timbres-poste. -**2.** [for trading stamps] carnet *m* pour coller les vignettes-épargnes; I got the toaster for ten ~s j'ai eu le grille-pain avec dix carnets de vignettes.

stamp collecting *n* philatélie *f*.

stamp collector *n* collectionneur *m*, -euse *f* de timbres OR de timbres-poste, philatéliste *mf*.

stamped [stæmpt] *adj* [letter, envelope] timbré; send a ~ addressed envelope envoyez une enveloppe timbrée portant vos nom et adresse.

stampede [stæm'pi:d] ◇ *n* -**1.** [of animals] fuite *f*, débandade *f*; what started the ~? qu'est-ce qui a provoqué cette débandade? -**2.** [of people - flight] sauve-qui-peut *m inv*, débandade *f*; [- rush] ruée *f*; there was a ~ for seats il y a eu une ruée vers OR sur les sièges; there's been a ~ to buy up the share issue les acheteurs se sont précipités OR se sont jetés sur la souscription.

◇ *vi* [flee] s'enfuir (pris d'affolement); [rush] se ruer, se précipiter; the cattle ~d across the river pris d'affolement, le bétail a traversé la rivière; shoppers ~d for the sales counters les clients se sont rués OR se sont précipités vers les rayons des soldes; the children came stampeding along the corridor les enfants se sont rués dans le couloir.

◇ *vt* -**1.** [animals] faire fuir; [crowd] semer la panique dans. -**2.** [pressurize] forcer la main à; don't let yourself be ~d into anything ne vous laissez pas forcer la main.

stamping ground *inf* ['stæmpɪŋ-] *n* lieu *m* favori.

stance [stæns] *n* -**1.** [physical posture] posture *f*; she altered her ~ slightly elle changea légèrement de position; he took up a boxer's ~ il adopta la position d'un boxeur; he took up his usual ~ in front of the fire il s'est planté devant le feu à sa place habituelle; widen your ~ SPORT écartez les jambes. -**2.** [attitude] position *f*; to adopt OR to take a tough ~ on sthg adopter OR prendre une position ferme sur qqch.

stanch [stɑ:ntʃ] *Am* = **staunch** *vt*.

stanchion ['stænʃn] *n* -**1.** [post] étai *m*, étançon *m*; [in window] montant *m*. -**2.** [for cow] attache *f*.

stand [stænd] (*pt* & *pp* stood [stʊd]) ◇ *vi*
A. -**1.** [rise to one's feet] se lever, se mettre debout; he refused to ~ for the national anthem il a refusé de se lever pendant l'hymne national. -**2.** [be on one's feet] être OR se tenir debout; I've been ~ing all day je suis resté debout toute la journée; I had to ~ all the way j'ai dû voyager debout pendant tout le trajet; she was so tired she could hardly ~ elle était si fatiguée qu'elle avait du mal à tenir debout OR sur ses jambes; wear flat shoes if you have to ~ a lot portez des chaussures à talons plats si vous devez rester debout pendant des heures; I don't mind ~ing ça ne me gêne pas de rester debout ‖ [in a specified location] être (debout), rester (debout); don't ~ near the edge ne restez pas près du bord; don't just ~ there, do something! ne restez pas là à ne rien faire!; ~ clear! écartez-vous!; I saw her ~ing at the window je l'ai vue (debout) à la fenêtre; do you see that man ~ing over there? vous voyez cet homme là-bas?; where should I ~? – beside Yvonne où devrais-je me mettre? – à côté d'Yvonne; I'll be ~ing outside the theatre j'attendrai devant le théâtre; small groups of men stood talking at street corners des hommes discutaient par petits groupes au coin des rues; he was ~ing at the bar il était debout au comptoir; is there a chair I can ~ on? y a-t-il une chaise sur laquelle je puisse monter?; they were ~ing a little way off/in the wings ils se tenaient un peu à l'écart/dans les coulisses; excuse me, you're ~ing on my foot excusez-moi, vous me marchez sur le pied; to ~ in line *Am* faire la queue; ~ in the corner! SCH au coin! ‖ [in a specified posture] se tenir; to ~ upright OR erect se tenir droit; he was so nervous he couldn't ~ still il était si nerveux qu'il ne tenait pas en place; I stood perfectly still, hoping they wouldn't see me je me suis figé sur place en espérant qu'ils ne me verraient pas; ~ still! ne bougez pas!, ne bougez plus!; ~ with your feet apart écartez les pieds; the heron was ~ing on one leg le héron se tenait debout sur une patte; to ~ on tiptoe se tenir sur la pointe des pieds ❑ ~ and deliver! la bourse ou la vie! -**3.** [be upright - post, target etc] être debout; not a stone was left ~ing il ne restait plus une seule pierre debout; the aqueduct has stood for centuries l'aqueduc est là depuis des siècles; the wheat stood high les blés étaient hauts. -**4.** [be supported, be mounted] reposer; the coffin stood on trestles le cercueil reposait sur des tréteaux; the house ~s on solid foundations la maison repose OR est bâtie sur des fondations solides; this argument ~s on three simple facts *fig* ce raisonnement repose sur trois simples faits. -**5.** [be located - building, tree, statue] se trouver; [- clock, vase, lamp] être, être posé; the fort ~s on a hill la forteresse se trouve en haut d'une colline; this is where the city gates once stood c'est ici qu'autrefois se dressaient les portes de la ville; the piano stood in the centre of the room le piano était au centre OR occupait le centre de la pièce; the bottles stood in rows of five les bouteilles étaient disposées en rangées de cinq; do you see the lorry ~ing next to my car? vous voyez le camion qui est à côté de ma voiture?; a wardrobe stood against one wall il y avait une armoire contre un mur.

B. -**1.** [indicating current state of affairs, situation] être; how do things ~? où en est la situation?; I'd like to know where I ~ with you j'aimerais savoir où en sont les choses entre nous; as things ~ telles que les choses se présentent; he's dissatisfied with the contract as it ~s il n'est pas satisfait du contrat tel qu'il a été rédigé; just print the text as it ~s faites imprimer le texte tel quel; he ~s accused of rape il est accusé de viol; she ~s alone in advocating this approach elle est la seule à préconiser cette approche; I ~ corrected je reconnais m'être trompé OR mon erreur; the doors stood wide open les portes étaient grandes ouvertes; I've got a taxi ~ing ready j'ai un taxi qui attend; the police are ~ing ready to intervene la police se tient prête à intervenir; the party ~s united behind him le parti est uni derrière lui; no-one ~s above the law personne n'est au-dessus des lois; to ~ at [gauge, barometer] indiquer; [score] être de; [unemployment] avoir atteint; their turnover now ~s at three million pounds leur chiffre d'affaires atteint désormais les trois millions de livres; the exchange rate ~s at 5 francs to the dollar le taux de change est de 5 francs pour un dollar; nothing stood between her and victory rien ne pouvait désormais l'empêcher de remporter la victoire; it's the only thing ~ing between us and financial disaster c'est la seule chose qui nous empêche de sombrer dans un désastre financier; he ~s in danger of losing his job il risque de perdre son emploi; I stood lost in admiration j'en suis resté béat d'admiration ❑ to ~ in sb's way *literal* être sur le chemin de qqn; *fig* gêner qqn; don't ~ in my way! ne reste pas sur mon chemin!; nothing ~s in our way now maintenant, la voie est libre; if you want to leave school I'm not going to ~ in your way si tu veux quitter l'école, je ne m'y opposerai pas; it's his lack of experience that ~s in his way c'est son manque d'expérience qui le handicape; their foreign debt ~s in the way of economic recovery leur dette extérieure constitue un obstacle à la reprise économique; her pride is the only thing ~ing in the way of their reconciliation son orgueil est le seul obstacle à leur réconciliation. -**2.** [remain] rester; [be left undisturbed - marinade, dough] reposer; [- tea] infuser; the machines stood idle les machines étaient arrêtées; the houses stood empty awaiting demolition les maisons, vidées de leurs occupants, attendaient d'être démolies; time stood still le temps semblait s'être arrêté; the car has been ~ing in the garage for a year ça fait un an que la voiture n'a pas bougé du garage; the champion ~s unbeaten le champion reste invaincu; his theory stood unchallenged for a decade pendant dix ans, personne n'a remis en cause sa théorie; I've decided to let my flight reservation ~ j'ai décidé de ne pas changer ma réservation d'avion; let the mixture ~ until the liquid is clear laissez reposer le mélange jusqu'à ce que le liquide se clarifie. -**3.** [be valid, effective - offer, law] rester valable; [- decision] rester inchangé; my invitation still ~s vous êtes toujours le bienvenu; the verdict ~s unless there's an appeal le jugement reste valable à moins que l'on ne fasse appel; even with this new plan, our objection still ~s ce nouveau projet ne remet pas en cause notre objection première.

C. -**1.** [measure - person, tree] mesurer; she ~s 5 feet in her stocking feet elle mesure moins de 1,50 m pieds nus; the building ~s ten storeys high l'immeuble compte dix étages. -**2.** [rank] se classer, compter; this hotel ~s among the best in the world cet hôtel figure parmi les meilleurs du monde; she ~s first/last in her class *Am* elle est la première/la dernière de sa classe; I know she ~s high in your opinion je sais que tu as une très bonne opinion d'elle; for price and quality, it ~s high on my list en ce qui concerne le prix et la qualité, je le range OR le compte parmi les meilleurs. -**3.** [on issue]: how OR where does he ~ on the nuclear issue? quelle est sa position OR son point de vue sur la question nucléaire?; you ought to tell them where you ~ vous devriez leur faire part de votre position. -**4.** [succeed]: the government will ~ or fall on the outcome of this vote le maintien ou la chute du gouvernement dépend du résultat de ce vote ❑ united we ~, divided we fall l'union fait la force. -**5.** [be likely]: to ~ to lose risquer de perdre; to ~ to win avoir des chances de gagner; they ~ to make a huge profit on the deal ils ont des chances de faire un bénéfice énorme dans cette affaire. -**6.** *Br* [run in election] se présenter, être candidat; she stood for Waltham elle a été candidate à la circonscription de Waltham; will he ~ for re-election? va-t-il se représenter aux élections?; she's ~ing as an independent elle se présente en tant que candidate indépendante. -**7.** *Am* [stop] se garer *(pour un court instant)*; 'no ~ing' 'arrêt interdit'. -**8.** *Am* [pay] payer la tournée; you're ~ing c'est ta tournée.

◇ *vt* -**1.** [set, place] mettre, poser; he stood the boy on a chair il a mis le garçon debout sur une chaise; she stood her umbrella in the corner elle a mis son parapluie dans le coin; to ~ sthg on (its) end faire tenir qqch debout; help me ~ the bedstead against the wall aide-moi à dresser le sommier contre le mur. -**2.** [endure, withstand] supporter; his heart couldn't ~ the shock son cœur n'a pas résisté au OR n'a pas supporté le choc; it will ~ high temperatures without cracking cela peut résister à OR supporter des températures élevées sans se fissurer; how much weight can the bridge ~? quel poids le pont peut-il supporter?; the motor wasn't built to ~ intensive use le moteur n'a pas été conçu pour supporter un usage intensif; wool carpeting can ~ a lot of hard wear une moquette en laine est beaucoup plus solide; she's not strong enough to ~ another operation elle n'est pas assez forte pour supporter une nouvelle opération ‖ *fig*: he certainly doesn't ~ comparison with Bogart il n'est absolument pas possible de le comparer avec Bogart; their figures don't ~ close inspection leurs chiffres ne résistent pas à un examen sérieux. -**3.** [put up with, bear - toothache, cold] supporter; [- behaviour] supporter, tolérer; I can't ~ it any longer! je n'en peux plus!; how can you ~ working with him? comment est-ce que vous faites pour OR comment arrivez-vous à travailler avec lui?; I've had as much as I can ~ of your griping! j'en ai assez de tes jérémiades!; I can't ~ (the sight of) him! je ne peux pas le supporter!, je ne peux pas le voir en peinture!; she can't ~ Wagner/smokers/flying elle déteste Wagner/les fumeurs/prendre l'avion. -**4.** *inf* [do with, need] supporter, avoir besoin de; oil company profits could certainly ~ a cut une diminution de leurs bénéfices ne ferait aucun mal aux compagnies pétrolières; he could ~ a bath! un bain ne lui ferait pas de mal!; could I ~ a drink! *Am* je ne dirais pas non à un verre! -**5.** [perform duty of] remplir la fonction de; to ~ witness for sb [at marriage] être le témoin de qqn. -**6.** *inf* [treat to]: to ~ sb a meal payer un repas à qqn; I'll ~ you a drink *Br*, I'll ~ you to a drink *Am* je t'offre un verre. -**7.** *phr*: to ~ a chance (of doing sthg) avoir de bonnes chances (de faire qqch); you don't ~ a chance! vous n'avez pas la moindre chance!; the plans ~ little chance of being approved les projets ont peu de chances d'être approuvés.

◇ *n* -**1.** [stall, booth - gen] stand *m*; [- in exhibition] stand *m*; [- in market] étal *m*, éventaire *m*; [- for newspapers] kiosque *m*; a shooting ~ un stand de tir. -**2.** [frame, support - gen] support *m*; [- for lamp, sink] pied *m*; [- on bicycle, motorbike] béquille *f*; [- for pipes, guns] râtelier *m*; COMM [- for magazines, sunglasses] présentoir *m*; [lectern] lutrin *m*; bicycle ~ [in street] râtelier à bicyclettes; plant ~ sellette *f*; plate ~ support à assiette, présentoir; revolving ~ COMM tourniquet *m*, présentoir rotatif; umbrella ~ porte-parapluies *m inv*. -**3.** [platform - gen] plate-forme *f*; [- for speaker] tribune *f*; [pulpit] chaire *f*. -**4.** [in sports ground] tribune *f*; the ~s roared un rugissement s'éleva des tribunes OR des gradins. -**5.** [for taxis]: (taxi) ~ station *f* de taxis. -**6.** *Am* [in courtroom] barre *f*; the first witness took the ~ le premier témoin est venu à la barre. -**7.** *literal* & *fig* [position] position *f*; to take a ~ on sthg prendre position à propos de qqch; what's your ~ on the issue? quelle est votre position sur la question?; he refuses to take a ~ il refuse de prendre position. -**8.** MIL & *fig* [defensive effort] résistance *f*, opposition *f*; they made a ~ at the foot of the hill ils ont résisté au pied de la colline; Custer's last ~ HIST la dernière bataille de Custer. -**9.** [of trees] bosquet *m*, futaie *f*; [of crop] récolte *f* sur pied; a fine ~ of corn un beau champ de blé; a ~ of bamboo un massif de bambous.

◆ **stand about** *Br*, **stand around** *vi insep* rester là, traîner *pej*; we stood about OR around waiting for the flight announcement nous restions là à attendre que le vol soit annoncé; the prisoners stood about OR around in small groups les prisonniers se tenaient par petits groupes; after Mass, the men ~ about OR around in the square après la messe, les hommes s'attardent sur la place; I'm not just going to ~ about waiting for you to make up your mind! je n'ai pas l'intention de poireauter là en attendant que tu te décides!

◆ **stand aside** *vi insep* [move aside] s'écarter; ~ aside, someone's fainted! écartez-vous, quelqu'un s'est évanoui!; he politely stood aside to let us pass il s'écarta OR s'effaça poliment pour nous laisser passer; to ~ aside in favour of sb [gen] laisser la voie libre à qqn; POL se désister en faveur de qqn.

◆ **stand back** *vi insep* -**1.** [move back] reculer, s'écarter; ~ back from the doors! écartez-vous des portes!; she stood back to look at herself in the mirror elle recula pour se regarder dans la glace; the painting is better if you ~ back from it le tableau est mieux si vous prenez du recul. -**2.** [be set back] être en retrait OR à l'écart; the house ~s back from the road la maison est en retrait de la route. -**3.** [take mental distance] prendre du recul; I need to ~ back and take stock j'ai besoin de prendre du recul et de faire le point.

◆ **stand by** ◇ *vi insep* -**1.** [not intervene] rester là (sans rien faire); how could you just ~ by and watch them mistreat that poor dog? comment as-tu pu rester là à les regarder maltraiter ce pauvre chien sans intervenir?; I stood by helplessly while they searched the room je restais là, impuissant, pendant qu'ils fouillaient la pièce. -**2.** [be ready - person] être OR se tenir prêt; [- vehicle] être prêt; [- army, embassy] être en état d'alerte; the riot squad was ~ing by to disperse the crowd la brigade antiémeutes se tenait prête à disperser la foule; we have an oxygen machine ~ing by nous avons une machine à oxygène prête en cas d'urgence; ~ by! attention!; ~ by for takeoff préparez-vous pour le décollage; ~ by to receive RADIO prenez l'écoute; ~ing by for orders! MIL à vos ordres!

◇ *vt insep* -**1.** [support - person] soutenir; I'll ~ by you through thick and thin je te soutiendrai OR je resterai à tes côtés quoi qu'il arrive. -**2.** [adhere to - promise, word] tenir; [- decision, offer] s'en tenir à; to ~ by an agreement respecter un accord; I ~ by my original analysis of the situation je m'en tiens à ma première analyse de la situation.

◆ **stand down** ◇ *vi insep* -**1.** *Br* POL [withdraw] se désister; [resign] démissionner; will he ~ down in favour of a younger candidate? va-t-il se désister en faveur d'un candidat plus jeune? -**2.** [leave witness box] quitter la barre; you may ~ down, Mr Simms vous pouvez quitter la barre, M. Simms. -**3.** MIL [troops] être déconsigné *(en fin d'alerte)*; ~ down! [after drill] rompez (les rangs)!

◇ *vt sep* [workers] licencier.

◆ **stand for** *vt insep* -**1.** [represent] représenter; what does DNA ~ for? que veut dire l'abréviation ADN?; the R ~s for Ryan le R signifie Ryan; the dove ~s for peace la colombe symbolise OR signifie la paix; we want our name to ~ for quality and efficiency nous voulons que notre nom soit synonyme de qualité et d'efficacité; she supports the values and ideas the party once stood for elle soutient les valeurs et les idées qui furent autrefois celles du parti; I detest everything that they ~ for! je déteste tout ce qu'ils représentent! -**2.** [tolerate] tolérer, supporter; [allow] permettre; I'm not going to ~ for it! je ne le tolérerai OR permettrai pas!

◆ **stand in** *vi insep* assurer le remplacement; to ~ in for sb remplacer qqn.

◆ **stand off** ◇ *vi insep* -**1.** [move away] s'écarter. -**2.** NAUT [take up position] croiser; [sail away] mettre le cap au large.

◇ *vt sep Br* [workers] mettre en chômage technique.

◇ *vt insep* NAUT [coast, island] croiser au large de; they have an aircraft carrier ~ing off Aden ils ont un porte-avions qui croise au large d'Aden.

◆ **stand out** *vi insep* -**1.** [protrude - vein] saillir; [- ledge] faire saillie, avancer; the veins in his neck stood out les veines de son cou saillaient OR étaient gonflées. -**2.** [be clearly visible - colour, typeface] ressortir, se détacher; [- in silhouette] se découper; the pink ~s out against the green background le rose ressort OR se détache sur le fond vert; the masts stood out against the sky les mâts se découpaient OR se dessinaient contre le ciel; the name on the truck stood out clearly le nom sur le camion était bien visible. -**3.** [be distinctive] ressortir, se détacher; this one book ~s out from all his others ce livre-ci surclasse tous les autres livres qu'il a écrits; there is no one issue which ~s out as being more important than the others il n'y a pas une question qui soit plus importante que les autres; she ~s out above all the rest elle surpasse OR surclasse tous les autres; I don't like to ~ out in a crowd je n'aime pas me singulariser; the day ~s out in my memory cette journée est marquée d'une pierre blanche dans ma mémoire. -**4.** [resist, hold out] tenir bon, tenir; they won't be able to ~ out for long ils ne pourront pas tenir OR résister longtemps; to ~ out against [attack, enemy] résister à; [change, tax increase] s'opposer avec détermination à; to ~ out for sthg revendiquer qqch; they are ~ing out for a pay increase/for better working conditions ils réclament une augmentation de salaire/de meilleures conditions de travail.

◆ **stand over** ◇ *vt insep* [watch over] surveiller; I can't work with someone ~ing over me je ne peux pas travailler quand quelqu'un regarde par-dessus mon épaule; she stood over him until he'd eaten every last bit elle ne l'a pas lâché avant qu'il ait mangé la dernière miette.

◇ *vt sep Br* [postpone] remettre (à plus tard); I'd prefer to ~ this discussion over until we have more information je préférerais remettre cette discussion jusqu'à ce que nous disposions de plus amples renseignements.

◇ *vi insep Br* être remis (à plus tard); we have two items ~ing over from the last meeting il nous reste deux points à régler depuis la dernière réunion.

◆ **stand to** *vi insep* MIL se mettre en état d'alerte; ~ to! à vos postes!

◆ **stand up** ◇ *vi insep* -**1.** [rise to one's feet] se lever, se mettre debout; she stood up to offer me her seat elle se leva pour m'offrir sa place ❑ to ~ up and be counted avoir le courage de ses opinions. -**2.** [be upright] être debout; I can't get the candle to ~ up straight je n'arrive pas à faire tenir la bougie droite. -**3.** [last] tenir, résister; how is that repair job ~ing up? est-ce que cette réparation tient toujours? -**4.** [be valid - argument, claim] être valable, tenir debout; his evidence won't ~ up in court son témoignage ne sera pas valable en justice.

◇ *vt sep* -**1.** [set upright - chair, bottle] mettre debout; they stood the prisoner up against a tree ils ont adossé le prisonnier à un arbre; ~ the ladder up against the wall mettez OR appuyez l'échelle contre le mur. -**2.** *inf* [fail to meet] poser un lapin à, faire faux bond à; I was stood up twice in a row on m'a posé un lapin deux fois de suite.

◆ **stand up for** *vt insep* défendre; to ~ up for o.s. se défendre.

◆ **stand up to** *vt insep*: to ~ up to sthg résister à qqch; to ~ up to sb tenir tête à OR faire face à qqn; he's too weak to ~ up to her il est trop faible pour lui tenir tête; she had a hard time ~ing up to their criticism ça ne lui a pas été facile de faire face à leurs critiques; her hypothesis doesn't ~ up to empirical testing son hypothèse ne résiste pas à la vérification expérimentale.

stand-alone *adj* COMPUT [system] autonome; it has ~ capability ça peut fonctionner de façon autonome.

standard ['stændəd] ◇ *n* -**1.** [norm] norme *f*; [level] niveau *m*; [criterion] critère *m*; most of the goods are OR come up to ~ la plupart des marchandises sont de qualité satisfaisante; your work isn't up to ~ OR is below ~ votre travail laisse à désirer; he sets high ~s for himself il est très exigeant avec lui-même; to set quality ~s for a product fixer des normes de qualité pour un produit; it's an airline with high safety ~s cette compagnie aérienne a des règles de sécurité très strictes; their salaries are low by European ~s leurs salaires sont bas par rapport aux salaires européens; she's an Olympic ~ swimmer c'est une nageuse de niveau olympique; it's a difficult task by any ~ OR by anybody's ~s c'est indiscutablement une tâche difficile; we apply the same ~s to all candidates nous jugeons tous les candidats selon les mêmes critères; their only ~ of success is money leur unique critère de réussite, c'est l'argent; we don't have the same aesthetic ~s nous n'avons pas les mêmes valeurs esthétiques ❑ ~ of living niveau de vie. -**2.** [moral principle] principe *m*; I won't do it! I have my ~s! je ne le ferai pas! j'ai des principes!; to have high moral ~s avoir de grands principes moraux. -**3.** [for measures, currency - model] étalon *m*; [in coins - proportion] titre *m*. -**4.** [established item] standard *m*; [tune] standard *m*; a jazz ~ un classique du jazz. -**5.** *Am* [car]: I can't drive a ~ je ne sais conduire que les voitures à boîte de vitesse automatique. -**6.** [flag] étendard *m*; [of sovereign, noble] bannière *f*; under the ~ of Liberty *fig* sous l'étendard de la liberté. -**7.** [support - pole] poteau *m*; [- for flag] mât *m*; [- for lamp] pied *m*; [- for power-line] pylône *m*. -**8.** *Br* [lamp] lampadaire *m* (de salon). -**9.** AGR & HORT [fruit tree] haute-tige *f*. -**10.** BOT [petal] étendard *m*. -**11.** *Br dated* SCH [class] classe *f*.

◇ *adj* -**1.** [ordinary, regular - gen] normal; [- model, size] standard; they come in three ~ sizes ils existent en trois tailles standard; catalytic converters are now ~ features les pots catalytiques sont désormais la norme; the ~ return fare is $500 l'aller-retour au tarif normal coûte 500 dollars; what's the ~ tip? que laisse-t-on normalement comme pourboire?; there's a ~ procedure for reporting accidents il y a une procédure bien établie pour signaler les accidents; any ~ detergent will do n'importe quel détergent usuel fera l'affaire; an apartment with all the ~ amenities un appartement doté de tout le confort moderne; it was just a ~ hotel room c'était une chambre d'hôtel ordinaire; she has a ~ speech for such occasions elle a un discours tout prêt pour ces occasions; ~ gear shift *Am* AUT changement *m* de vitesse manuel. -**2.** [measure - metre, kilogramme etc] étalon *(inv)*. -**3.** [text, work] classique, de base; the ~ works in English poetry les ouvrages classiques de la poésie anglaise; it's the ~ work on the Reformation c'est l'ouvrage de base sur la Réforme. -**4.** LING [pronunciation, spelling etc] standard; ~ English l'anglais correct. -**5.** AGR & HORT [fruit tree, shrub] à haute tige; ~ rose rose *f* tige.

standard bearer *n* -**1.** [of cause] porte-drapeau *m*; [of political party] chef *m* de file. -**2.** [of flag] porte-étendard *m*.

standard deviation *n* [in statistics] écart-type *m*.

standard gauge RAIL *n* voie *f* normale, écartement *m* normal.

◆ **standard-gauge** *adj* [line] à voie normale; [carriage, engine] pour voie normale.

standardization [ˌstændədaɪ'zeɪʃn] *n* -**1.** [gen] standardisation *f*; [of dimensions, terms etc] normalisation *f*. -**2.** TECH [verification] étalonnage *m*.

standardize, -ise ['stændədaɪz] *vt* -**1.** [gen] standardiser; [dimensions, products, terms] normaliser; ~d parts pièces *fpl* standardisées OR standard. -**2.** TECH [verify] étalonner.

standard lamp *n Br* lampadaire *m* (de salon).

standard time *n* heure *f* légale.

standaway ['stændəweɪ] *adj* [skirt, sleeve] bouffant; ~ collar *col qui dégage le cou ou les épaules*.

standby ['stændbaɪ] (*pl* standbys) ◇ *adj* -**1.** [equipment, provisions etc] de réserve; [generator] de secours; to be on ~ duty [doctor] être de garde OR d'astreinte; [flight personnel, emergency repairman] être d'astreinte; [troops, police, firemen] être prêt à intervenir; the ~ team can take over operations within an hour l'équipe de secours est prête à prendre le contrôle des opérations en moins d'une heure; the shortages meant some factories were put on a ~ basis à cause de la pénurie, certaines usines ont dû ralentir leur rythme de production; in ~ position RADIO en écoute. -**2.** AERON [ticket, fare] stand-by *(inv)*; [passenger] stand-by *(inv)*, en attente; ~ list liste *f* d'attente. -**3.** FIN: ~ credit crédit *m* stand-by OR de soutien; ~ loan prêt *m* conditionnel.

◇ *n* -**1.** [substitute - person] remplaçant *m*, -e *f*; THEAT [understudy] doublure *f*; to be on ~ [doctor] être de garde OR d'astreinte; [flight personnel, emergency repairman] être d'astreinte; [troops, police, firemen] être prêt à intervenir; we have a repair crew on ~ nous avons une équipe de réparateurs prête à intervenir en cas de besoin; make sure you have a ~ [equipment] vérifiez que vous en avez un OR une de secours; [person] assurez-vous que vous pouvez vous faire remplacer; I'll keep the old typewriter as a ~ je garderai la vieille machine à écrire en cas de besoin OR au cas où; eggs are a great ~ in the kitchen des œufs sont toujours bons à avoir dans une cuisine; that story is an old ~ of his cette histoire lui a beaucoup servi. -**2.** AERON [system] stand-by *m inv*; [passenger] (passager *m*, -ère *f*) stand-by *m inv*; to be on ~ [passenger] être en stand-by OR sur la liste d'attente.

◇ *adv* [travel] en stand-by.

standee [stæn'diː] *n Am* [in theatre] *spectateur qui n'a pas de place assise*; [in public transport] passager *m*, -ère *f* (qui reste) debout.

stand-in ◇ *n* [gen] remplaçant *m*, -e *f*; CIN [for lighting check] doublure *f*; [stunt person] cascadeur *m*, -euse *f*; THEAT [understudy] doublure *f*; she asked him to go as her ~ elle lui a demandé de la remplacer.

◇ *adj* [gen] remplaçant; [office worker] intérimaire; [teacher] suppléant, qui fait des remplacements; we'll need ~ staff during the summer nous aurons besoin d'intérimaires pendant l'été; I can't find a ~ speaker for tomorrow's session je ne trouve personne qui puisse remplacer le conférencier prévu pour demain.

standing ['stændɪŋ] ◇ *adj* -**1.** [upright - position, person, object] debout *(inv)*; ~ room OR places places *fpl* debout; it was ~ room only at the meeting il n'y avait plus de places assises OR la salle était pleine à craquer lors de la réunion ❑ ~ lamp *Am* lampadaire *m* (de salon); ~ ovation ovation *f*; to get a ~ ovation se faire ovationner; ~ stone menhir *m*. -**2.** [stationary]: ~ jump SPORT saut *m* à pieds joints; ~ start SPORT départ *m* debout; AUT départ *m* arrêté; it reaches 100 mph in 40 seconds from a ~ start elle va de 0 à 160 km/h en 40 secondes; ~ wave PHYS onde *f* stationnaire. -**3.** [grain, timber] sur pied; ~ crop AGR récolte *f* sur pied; BIOL [of plankton] biomasse *f*. -**4.** [stagnant - water] stagnant. -**5.** [permanent - army, offer etc] permanent; [- claim] de longue date; it's a ~ joke with us c'est une vieille plaisanterie entre nous ❑ to pay by ~ order *Br* payer par prélèvement (bancaire) automatique; I get paid by ~ order je reçois mon salaire par virement bancaire; ~ orders *Br* POL règlement *m* intérieur *(d'une assemblée délibérative)*.

◇ *n* -**1.** [reputation] réputation *f*; [status] standing *m*; a man of your ~ needs to be more careful un homme de votre standing se doit d'être plus prudent; an economist of considerable ~ un économiste de grand renom OR très réputé; people of lower/higher social ~ des gens d'une position sociale moins/plus élevée; they are a family of some ~ in the community c'est une famille qui jouit d'une certaine position dans la communauté; enquiries were made into his financial ~ on a enquêté sur sa situation financière; Mr Pym is a client in good ~ with our bank M. Pym est un client très estimé de notre banque; the scandal has damaged the company's ~ in the eyes of the public le scandale a nui à la réputation de la société auprès du public. -**2.** [ranking] rang *m*, place *f*; SCH & SPORT [ordered list] classement *m*; her ~ in the opinion polls is at its lowest yet sa cote de popularité dans les sondages est au plus bas; the ~s in the Senate are Liberals 62 seats and Conservatives 30 la répartition des sièges au Sénat est de 62 sièges pour les libéraux et 30 pour les conservateurs; what's their ~ in the league table? quel est leur classement dans le championnat? -**3.** [duration] durée *f*; of long ~ de longue date; of 15 years' ~ [collaboration, feud] qui dure depuis 15 ans; [treaty, account] qui existe depuis 15 ans; [friend, member] depuis 15 ans; an employee of 10 years' ~ un salarié qui a 10 ans d'ancienneté dans l'entreprise. -**4.** *Am* AUT: 'no ~' 'arrêt interdit'. -**5.** *Am* JUR position *f* en droit; homosexuals have no ~ to collect alimony payments aucune disposition légale n'autorise les homosexuels à toucher une pension alimentaire.

standoff ['stændɒf] *n* -**1.** POL [inconclusive clash] affrontement *m* indécis; [deadlock] impasse *f*; their debate ended in a ~ leur débat n'a rien donné; the ~ over the budget is making Wall Street nervous l'impasse dans laquelle se trouve le budget inquiète Wall Street. -**2.** *Am* SPORT [tie] match *m* nul. -**3.** *Br* [in rugby]: ~ (half) demi *m* d'ouverture.

standoffish [ˌstænd'ɒfɪʃ] *adj* distant, froid; there's no need to be ~ ce n'est pas la peine de prendre cet air supérieur.

standoff missile *n* missile *m* tiré à distance de sécurité.

standpipe ['stændpaɪp] *n* -**1.** [in street - for fire brigade] bouche *f* d'incendie; [- for public] point *m* d'alimentation en eau de secours. -**2.** [in pumping system] tuyau *m* ascendant, colonne *f* d'alimentation.

standpoint ['stændpɔɪnt] *n* point *m* de vue; try to see the situation from her ~ essayez de voir la situation de son point de vue à elle.

standstill ['stændstɪl] *n* arrêt *m*; to come to a ~ [vehicle, person] s'immobiliser; [talks, work etc] piétiner; to bring to a ~ [vehicle, person] arrêter; [talks, traffic] paralyser; to be at a ~ [talks, career] être au point mort; [traffic] être paralysé; [economy] piétiner, stagner.

stand-up *adj* [collar] droit; [meal] (pris) debout; a ~ fight [physical] une bagarre en règle; [verbal] une discussion violente ❑ ~ comic OR comedian comique *mf (qui se produit seul en scène)*; ~ counter OR diner *Am* buvette *f*.

stank [stæŋk] *pt* → **stink**.

Stanley knife® ['stænlɪ-] *n* cutter *m*.

stannic ['stænɪk] *adj* stannique.

stanza ['stænzə] *n* -**1.** [in poetry] strophe *f*. -**2.** *Am* SPORT période *f*.

staphylococcus [ˌstæfɪləʊ'kɒkəs] (*pl* staphylococci [-'kɒksaɪ]) *n* staphylocoque *m*.

staple ['steɪpl] ◇ *n* -**1.** [for paper] agrafe *f*. -**2.** [for wire] cavalier *m*, crampillon *m*. -**3.** [foodstuff] aliment *m* OR denrée *f* de base; kitchen OR household ~s provisions *fpl* de base; ~s are being rationed en ce moment, les produits de première nécessité sont rationnés. -**4.** COMM & ECON [item] article *m* de base; [raw material] matière *f* première. -**5.** [constituent] partie *f* intégrale; divorce cases are a ~ of his law practice son cabinet s'occupe essentiellement de divorces. -**6.** TEX fibre *f* artificielle à filer.
◇ *vt* [paper, upholstery etc] agrafer; ~ the sheets together agrafez les feuilles; posters were ~d on OR onto OR to the walls des posters étaient agrafés aux murs.
◇ *adj* -**1.** [food, products] de base; [export, crop] principal; a ~ diet of rice and beans un régime à base de riz et de haricots; for young children, milk is the ~ diet pour de jeunes enfants, le lait est l'aliment de base; the ~ diet of these TV channels consists of quiz shows and soap operas *fig* les programmes de ces chaînes de télévision sont essentiellement constitués de jeux et de feuilletons; their ~ commodity is cotton le coton est leur produit de base; tanks are a ~ feature of conventional warfare les tanks sont un des éléments de base de la guerre conventionnelle. -**2.** TEX: ~ fibre fibre *f* artificielle à filer.

staple gun *n* agrafeuse *f* (professionnelle).

stapler ['steɪplə^r] *n* agrafeuse *f* (de bureau).

staple remover *n* ôte-agrafes *m inv*.

star [stɑː^r] (*pt* & *pp* starred, *cont* starring) ◇ *n* -**1.** [in sky] étoile *f*; to sleep (out) under the ~s dormir OR coucher à la belle étoile ❑ the morning/evening star l'étoile du matin/du soir; falling OR shooting ~ étoile filante; to see ~s voir trente-six chandelles; The Star PRESS *nom abrégé du Daily Star*. -**2.** [symbol of fate, luck] étoile *f*; ASTROL astre *m*, étoile *f*; his ~ is rising son étoile brille chaque jour davantage; his ~ is on the wane son étoile pâlit; to be born under a lucky ~ être né sous une bonne étoile; I thanked my (lucky) ~s I wasn't chosen j'ai remercié le ciel de ne pas avoir été choisi; the influence of the ~s l'influence des astres; what do my ~s say today? *inf* que dit mon horoscope aujourd'hui?; it's written in the ~s c'est le destin. -**3.** [figure, emblem] étoile *f*; SCH bon point *m*; the restaurant has gained another ~ le restaurant s'est vu décerner une étoile supplémentaire ❑ the Star of David l'étoile de David; the Stars and Bars le drapeau des États Confédérés; the Stars and Stripes *le drapeau américain*. -**4.** [asterisk] astérisque *m*. -**5.** [celebrity] vedette *f*, star *f*; one film won't make him a ~ un seul film ne fera pas de lui une vedette OR une star; she was an up-and-coming rock ~ elle était en train de devenir une grande star du rock; he's a rising ~ in the ecologist movement il est en train de devenir un personnage important du mouvement écologiste; to be the ~ of the class être la vedette de la classe ❑ 'A Star Is Born' *Wellman* 'Une étoile est née'. -**6.** [blaze - on animal] étoile *f*.
◇ *vt* -**1.** CIN & THEAT avoir comme OR pour vedette; the play starred David Caffrey la pièce avait pour vedette David Caffrey; "Casablanca", starring Humphrey Bogart and Ingrid Bergman «Casablanca», avec Humphrey Bogart et Ingrid Bergman (dans les rôles principaux). -**2.** [mark with asterisk] marquer d'un astérisque. -**3.** *lit* [adorn with stars] étoiler; candles starred the darkness des bougies étoilaient l'obscurité; the bay was starred with sail boats la baie était parsemée de voiliers.
◇ *vi* CIN & THEAT être la vedette; who starred with Redford in "The Sting"? qui jouait avec Redford dans «l'Arnaque»?; "Othello", with Laurence Olivier starring in the title role «Othello», avec Laurence Olivier dans le rôle principal; he's starring in a new TV serial il est la vedette d'un nouveau feuilleton télévisé.
◇ *comp* -**1.** CIN & THEAT: the ~ attraction of tonight's show la principale attraction du spectacle de ce soir; the ~ turn la vedette; to get ~ billing être en tête d'affiche; to give sb ~ billing mettre qqn en tête d'affiche; the hotel gives all its clients ~ treatment cet hôtel offre à sa clientèle un service de première classe. -**2.** [salesman, pupil etc] meilleur; he's our ~ witness c'est notre témoin-vedette OR notre témoin principal. -**3.** ELEC: ~ connection couplage *m* en étoile; ~ point point *m* neutre.

-star *in cpds*: a two~ hotel un hôtel deux étoiles; a four~ general un général à quatre étoiles; two~ petrol *Br* (essence *f*) ordinaire *m*; four~ petrol *Br* super *m*.

star apple *n* pomme *f* étoilée.

starboard ['stɑːbəd] ◇ *n* NAUT tribord *m*; AERON tribord *m*, droite *f*; to ~ à tribord; vessel to ~! navire par tribord!
◇ *adj* NAUT [rail, lights] de tribord; AERON [door, wing] droit, de tribord.
◇ *vt* NAUT: to ~ the helm OR rudder mettre la barre à tribord.

starch [stɑːtʃ] ◇ *n* -**1.** [for laundry] amidon *m*, empois *m*. -**2.** [in cereals] amidon *m*; [in root vegetables] fécule *f*; try and avoid ~ OR ~es essayez d'éviter les féculents. -**3.** *inf (U)* [formality] manières *fpl* guindées. -**4.** *Am phr*: to take the ~ out of sb [critic, bully] rabattre le caquet à qqn.
◇ *vt* empeser, amidonner.

Star Chamber *n Br* HIST tribunal *m* correctionnel; *fig* & *pej* tribunal *m* arbitraire OR inquisitorial; Court of ~ *tribunal anglais de 1487*.
◆ **star-chamber** *adj pej* [decision] arbitraire; [trial, procedure] arbitraire, inquisitorial; star-chamber sessions of the town council des réunions secrètes OR à huis clos du conseil municipal.

COURT OF STAR CHAMBER:
Organe judiciaire anglais mis en place par Henri VII en 1487 dans le but de renforcer l'autorité de son gouvernement. Ce tribunal jouissait d'une grande popularité de par son impartialité et le fait qu'il échappait à la corruption des nobles, les obligeant à se plier à la justice royale.

---

starch-reduced *adj* [bread] de régime; [diet] pauvre en féculents.

starchy ['stɑːtʃɪ] (*compar* starchier, *superl* starchiest) *adj* -**1.** [diet] riche en féculents; [taste] farineux; ~ foods féculents *mpl*. -**2.** *pej* [person] guindé, compassé; he's so ~! on dirait qu'il a avalé son parapluie!

star-crossed *adj lit* maudit par le sort.

stardom ['stɑːdəm] *n* célébrité *f*, vedettariat *m*; to rise to ~ devenir célèbre, devenir une vedette; he never actively sought ~ il n'a jamais vraiment couru après la célébrité; she has been groomed for ~ on l'a façonnée pour en faire une vedette.

stardust ['stɑːdʌst] *n (U)* [illusions] chimères *fpl*, illusions *fpl*; [sentimentality] sentimentalité *f*; to have ~ in one's eyes [be deluded] être en proie aux chimères; [be a romantic] être très fleur bleue.

stare [steə^r] ◇ *vi* regarder (fixement); to ~ at sb/sthg regarder qqn/qqch fixement; it's rude to ~! ça ne se fait pas de regarder les gens comme ça!; stop it, people are staring! arrête, les gens nous regardent!; I ~d into his eyes je l'ai regardé dans le blanc des yeux; she ~d at me in disbelief elle m'a regardé avec des yeux incrédules; to ~ in amazement regarder d'un air ébahi; he ~d straight ahead il regardait fixement devant lui; she sat staring into the distance elle était assise, le regard perdu (au loin); I ~d out of the train window j'ai regardé longuement par la fenêtre du train; doesn't being ~d at in the street bother you? ça ne vous gêne pas d'attirer les regards des gens dans la rue?
◇ *vt* -**1.** [intimidate]: to ~ sb into silence faire taire qqn en le fixant du regard; her steely eyes ~d him into submission son regard d'acier l'a réduit à l'obéissance. -**2.** *phr*: the answer is staring you in the face! mais la réponse saute aux yeux!; I'd looked everywhere for my keys and there they were staring me in the face j'avais cherché mes clefs partout alors qu'elles étaient là sous mon nez; failure was staring us in the face nous courions à l'échec.
◇ *n* regard *m* (fixe); to give sb a hostile/an incredulous ~ fixer qqn d'un regard hostile/incrédule.
◆ **stare out** *Br*, **stare down** *Am vt sep* faire baisser les yeux à.

starfish ['stɑːfɪʃ] (*pl inv* OR starfishes) *n* étoile *f* de mer.

stargaze ['stɑːgeɪz] *vi* -**1.** [watch] observer les étoiles. -**2.** [daydream] rêvasser.

stargazer ['stɑːˌgeɪzə^r] *n* -**1.** [astronomer] astronome *mf*; [astrologer] astrologue *mf*. -**2.** [daydreamer] rêveur *m*, -euse *f*, rêvasseur *m*, -euse *f*. -**3.** [fish] uranoscope *m*.

stargazing ['stɑːˌgeɪzɪŋ] *n* -**1.** [astronomy] observation *f* des étoiles; [astrology] astrologie *f*; economists are often accused of indulging in ~ *fig* on accuse souvent les économistes de tirer des plans sur la comète. -**2.** *(U)* [daydreaming] rêveries *fpl*, rêvasseries *fpl*.

staring ['steərɪŋ] ◇ *adj* [bystanders] curieux; with ~ eyes [fixedly] aux yeux fixes; [wide-open] aux yeux écarquillés; [blank] aux yeux vides.
◇ *adv* → **stark**.

stark [stɑːk] ◇ *adj* -**1.** [bare, grim - landscape] désolé; [- branches, hills] nu; [- crag, rock] âpre, abrupt; [- room, façade] austère; [- silhouette] net; in the ~ light of day à la lumière crue du jour; the chimneys rose in ~ relief against the sky les cheminées se découpaient nettement contre le ciel; the ~ simplicity of the shapes l'austère dépouillement des formes. -**2.** [blunt - description, statement] cru, sans ambages; [- refusal, denial] catégorique; [harsh - words] dur; the ~ realities of war les dures réalités de la guerre; those are the ~ facts ce sont les faits tels qu'ils sont; the ~ realism of her book le réalisme cru de son livre. -**3.** [utter - brutality, terror] absolu; [- madness] pur; in ~ poverty dans la misère absolue OR la plus noire; in ~ violation of the ceasefire en violation flagrante du cessez-le-feu; their foreign policy success is in ~ contrast to the failure of their domestic policies la réussite de leur politique étrangère contraste nettement avec l'échec de leur politique intérieure.
◇ *adv* complètement; ~ raving OR staring mad *inf* complètement fou OR dingue; ~ naked tout nu.

starkers *inf* ['stɑːkəz] *adj* & *adv Br* à poil.

starkly ['stɑːklɪ] *adv* [describe] crûment; [tell] carrément, sans ambages; [stand out] nettement; the room was ~ lit la pièce était éclairée par une lumière crue; in ~ realistic terms en termes d'un réalisme cru.

starkness ['stɑːknɪs] *n* [of landscape, scene] désolation *f*; [of room, façade] austérité *f*; [of branches] nudité *f*; [of light] crudité *f*; [of life, reality] dureté *f*; the ~ of the author's style le style dépouillé de l'auteur; a mirror offset the ~ of the bare walls une glace adoucissait l'austérité des murs nus.

starless ['stɑːlɪs] *adj* sans étoile.

starlet ['stɑːlɪt] *n* starlette *f*.

starlight ['stɑːlaɪt] *n* lumière *f* des étoiles; by ~ à OR sous la lumière des étoiles.

starling ['stɑːlɪŋ] *n* étourneau *m*, sansonnet *m*.

starlit ['stɑːlɪt] *adj* [night] étoilé; [landscape] illuminé par les étoiles; [beach, sea] baigné par la lumière des étoiles.

starry ['stɑːrɪ] (*compar* starrier, *superl* starriest) *adj* -**1.** [adorned with stars] étoilé; a ~ **night** une nuit étoilée; the ~ **light** la lumière des étoiles. -**2.** [sparkling] étincelant, brillant; a ~ **diadem** un diadème étincelant. -**3.** *lit* & *fig* [lofty] élevé; the ~ **heights of Mount Olympus** les hauteurs infinies de l'Olympe.

starry-eyed *adj* [idealistic] idéaliste; [naive] naïf, ingénu; [dreamy] rêveur, dans la lune; **there's nothing** ~ **about her** elle a vraiment les pieds sur terre.

star sapphire *n* saphir *m* en forme d'étoile.

star shell *n* MIL obus *m* éclairant.

starship ['stɑːʃɪp] *n* vaisseau *m* spatial.

star sign *n* signe *m* (du zodiaque).

star-spangled [-'spæŋgld] *adj* [flag] étoilé; [sky] parsemé d'étoiles.

Star-Spangled Banner *n*: the ~ la bannière étoilée.

star-studded *adj* -**1.** [show, film] à vedettes; a ~ **cast** une distribution où figurent de nombreuses vedettes OR qui réunit une brochette de stars. -**2.** = **star-spangled**.

star system *n* -**1.** CIN & THEAT star-system *m*. -**2.** ASTRON système *m* stellaire.

start [stɑːt] ◇ *vt* -**1.** [begin - gen] commencer; [- climb, descent] amorcer; **I've** ~**ed the first chapter** [write] j'ai commencé (à écrire) le premier chapitre; [read] j'ai commencé (à lire) le premier chapitre; **to** ~ **doing** OR **to do sthg** commencer à OR se mettre à faire qqch; **it's** ~**ing to rain** il commence à pleuvoir; **it had just** ~**ed raining** OR **to rain when I left** il venait juste de commencer à pleuvoir quand je suis parti; **she** ~**ed driving** OR **to drive again a month after her accident** elle a recommencé à conduire OR elle s'est remise à conduire un mois après son accident; **to** ~ **school** [for the first time] commencer l'école; [after holidays] rentrer à OR reprendre l'école; **she** ~**ed her speech with a quotation from the Bible** elle a commencé son discours par une citation de la Bible; **I** ~**ed my investigation with a visit to Carl** j'ai commencé mon enquête par une visite chez Carl; **they** ~**ed the year with a deficit** ils ont commencé l'année avec un déficit; **he** ~**ed work at sixteen** il a commencé à travailler à seize ans; **he** ~**ed life as a delivery boy** il débuta dans la vie comme garçon livreur; **frogs** ~ **life as tadpoles** les grenouilles commencent par être des têtards; **go ahead and** ~ **lunch without me** allez-y, vous pouvez commencer (à déjeuner) sans moi; **I like to finish anything I** ~ j'aime aller au bout de tout ce que j'entreprends; **I think I'm** ~**ing a cold** je crois que j'ai attrapé un rhume; **to get** ~**ed**: **I got** ~**ed on the dishes** je me suis mis à la vaisselle; **let's get** ~**ed!** allons-y!; **once he gets** ~**ed there's no stopping him** une fois lancé, il n'y a pas moyen de l'arrêter; **I need a coffee to get me** ~**ed in the morning** j'ai besoin d'un café pour commencer la journée. -**2.** [initiate, instigate - reaction, revolution, process] déclencher; [- fashion] lancer; [- violence] déclencher, provoquer; [- conversation, discussion] engager, amorcer; [- rumour] faire naître; **her article** ~**ed the controversy** son article a été à l'origine de la controverse; **which side** ~**ed the war?** quel camp a déclenché la guerre?; **the referee blew his whistle to** ~ **the match** l'arbitre siffla pour signaler le début du match; **it wasn't me who** ~**ed the quarrel/the fight!** ce n'est pas moi qui ai commencé la dispute/la bagarre!; **the breakup of the empire** ~**ed the process of decline** le démantèlement de l'empire a déclenché le processus de déclin; **to** ~ **a fire** [in fireplace] allumer le feu; [campfire] faire du feu; [by accident, bomb] mettre le feu; **the fire was** ~**ed by arsonists** l'incendie a été allumé par des pyromanes ❑ **are you trying to** ~ **something?** *inf*, **just what are you trying to** ~**?** *inf* tu cherches la bagarre, ou quoi? -**3.** [cause to behave in specified way] faire; **it** ~**ed her (off) crying/laughing** cela l'a fait pleurer/rire; **I'll** ~ **a team working on it right away** je vais mettre une équipe là-dessus tout de suite; **the news is going to** ~ **tongues wagging** la nouvelle va faire jaser. -**4.** [set in motion - motor, car] (faire) démarrer, mettre en marche; [- machine, device] mettre en marche; [- meal] mettre en route; **how do I** ~ **the tape (going)?** comment est-ce que je dois faire pour mettre le magnétophone en marche?; **I couldn't get the car** ~**ed** je n'ai pas réussi à faire démarrer la voiture; **to** ~ **the printer again, press this key** pour remettre en marche l'imprimante, appuyez sur cette touche. -**5.** [begin using - bottle, pack] entamer. -**6.** [establish, found - business, school, political party] créer, fonder; [- restaurant, shop] ouvrir; [- social programme] créer, instaurer; **to** ~ **a newspaper** créer OR fonder un journal; **to** ~ **a family** fonder un foyer. -**7.** [person - in business, work] installer, établir; **he** ~**ed his son in the family business** il a fait entrer son fils dans l'entreprise familiale; **his election success** ~**ed him on his political career** son succès aux élections l'a lancé dans sa carrière d'homme politique; **they** ~ **new pilots on domestic flights** ils font débuter les nouveaux pilotes sur les vols intérieurs; **I** ~ **on $500 a week** je débute à 500 dollars par semaine. -**8.** SPORT: **to** ~ **the race** donner le signal du départ. -**9.** HUNT [flush out] lever.

◇ *vi* -**1.** [in time] commencer; **the film** ~**s at 8 o'clock** le film commence à 20 h; **when did the contractions** ~**?** quand les contractions ont-elles commencé?; **our problems are just** ~**ing** nos ennuis ne font que commencer; **before the New Year/the rainy season** ~**s** avant le début de l'année prochaine/de la saison des pluies; **before the cold weather** ~**s** avant qu'il ne commence à faire froid; ~**ing (from) next week** à partir de la semaine prochaine; **to** ~ **again** OR **afresh** recommencer; **to** ~ **all over again, to** ~ **again from scratch** recommencer à zéro; **school** ~**s on September 5th** la rentrée a lieu OR les cours reprennent le 5 septembre || [story, speech]: **calm down and** ~ **at the beginning** calmez-vous et commencez par le commencement; **I didn't know where to** ~ je ne savais pas par quel bout commencer; **she** ~**ed with a joke/by introducing everyone** elle a commencé par une plaisanterie/par faire les présentations; **I'd like to** ~ **by saying how pleased I am to be here tonight** j'aimerais commencer par vous dire à quel point je suis heureux d'être parmi vous ce soir; **the book** ~**s with a quotation** le livre commence par une citation || [in career, job] débuter; **she** ~**ed in personnel/as an assistant** elle a débuté au service du personnel/comme assistante; **have you been working here long? – no, I've just** ~**ed** vous travaillez ici depuis longtemps? – non, je viens de commencer OR je débute; **gymnasts have to** ~ **young** les gymnastes doivent commencer jeunes ❑ **I'll have the soup to** ~ **(with)** pour commencer, je prendrai du potage; **she was an architect to** ~ **with, then a journalist** elle a d'abord été architecte, puis journaliste; **isn't it time you got a job? – don't YOU** ~**!** il serait peut-être temps que tu trouves du travail – tu ne vas pas t'y mettre, toi aussi! -**2.** [in space - desert, fields, slope, street] commencer; [- river] prendre sa source; **the neutral zone** ~**s at the river** la zone neutre commence à la rivière; **there's an arrow where the path** ~**s** il y a une flèche qui indique le début du sentier; **the bus route** ~**s at the station** la ligne de bus commence à la gare; **where does the tunnel** ~**?** où est l'entrée du tunnel? -**3.** [car, motor] démarrer, se mettre en marche; **the engines** ~**ed with a roar** les moteurs ont démarré en vrombissant; **why won't the car** ~**?** pourquoi la voiture ne veut-elle pas démarrer? -**4.** [set off - person, convoy] partir, se mettre en route; [- train] s'ébranler; **the tour** ~**s at** OR **from the town hall** la visite part de la mairie; **I'll have to** ~ **for the airport soon** il va bientôt falloir que je parte pour l'aéroport; **the train was** ~**ing across** OR **over the bridge** le train commençait à traverser le pont OR abordait le pont; **she** ~**ed along the path** elle s'engagea sur le sentier; **only four horses** ~**ed** SPORT quatre chevaux seulement ont pris le départ. -**5.** [range - prices] commencer; **houses here** ~ **at $100,000** ici, le prix des maisons démarre à 100 000 dollars; **return fares** ~ **from £299** on trouve des billets aller retour à partir de 299 livres. -**6.** [jump involuntarily - person] sursauter; [- horse] tressaillir, faire un soubresaut; [jump up] bondir; **he** ~**ed in surprise** il a tressailli de surprise; **she** ~**ed from her chair** elle bondit de sa chaise. -**7.** [gush] jaillir, gicler; **tears** ~**ed to his eyes** les larmes lui sont montées aux yeux.

◇ *n* -**1.** [beginning - gen] commencement *m*, début *m*; [- of inquiry] ouverture *f*; **it's the** ~ **of a new era** c'est le début OR le commencement d'une ère nouvelle; **the** ~ **of the school year** la rentrée scolaire; **the** ~ **of the footpath is marked by an arrow** le début du sentier est signalé par une flèche; **it was an inauspicious** ~ **to his presidency** c'était un début peu prometteur pour sa présidence; **things are off to a bad/good** ~ ça commence mal/bien, on est mal/bien partis; **my new boss and I didn't get off to a very good** ~ au début, mes rapports avec mon nouveau patron n'ont pas été des meilleurs; **to get a good** ~ **in life** prendre un bon départ dans la vie OR l'existence; **we want an education that will give our children a good** ~ nous voulons une éducation qui donne à nos enfants des bases solides; **a second honeymoon will give us a fresh** ~ une deuxième lune de miel nous fera repartir d'un bon pied; **the program will give ex-prisoners a fresh** OR **new** ~ **(in life)** le programme va donner aux anciens détenus une seconde chance (dans la vie); **to make a** ~ **(on sthg)** commencer (qqch); **to make** OR **to get an early** ~ [gen] commencer de bonne heure; [on journey] partir de bonne heure; **I've made a good** ~ **on my Christmas shopping** j'ai déjà fait une bonne partie de mes achats de Noël; **I was lonely at the** ~ au début je me sentais seule; **at the** ~ **of the war no one thought it would last very long** au début de la guerre, personne ne pensait qu'elle durerait très longtemps ❑ **from the** ~ dès le début OR commencement; **the trip was a disaster from** ~ **to finish** le voyage a été un désastre d'un bout à l'autre; **I laughed from** ~ **to finish** j'ai ri du début à la fin; **the project was ill-conceived from** ~ **to finish** le projet était mal conçu de bout en bout. -**2.** SPORT [place] (ligne *f* de) départ *m*; [signal] signal *m* de départ; **they are lined up for** OR **at the** ~ ils sont sur la ligne de départ; **where's the** ~ **of the rally?** où est le départ du rallye? -**3.** [lead, advance] avance *f*; **she has two hours'** ~ OR **a two-hour** ~ **on us** elle a une avance de deux heures sur nous; **he gave him 20 metres'** ~ OR **a 20-metre** ~ il lui a accordé une avance de 20 mètres; **our research gives us a** ~ **over our competitors** nos recherches nous donnent de l'avance sur nos concurrents. -**4.** [jump] sursaut *m*; **she woke up with a** ~ elle s'est réveillée en sursaut; **with a** ~**, I recognized my own handwriting** j'ai eu un sursaut quand j'ai reconnu ma propre écriture; **to give a** ~ sursauter, tressaillir; **to give sb a** ~ faire sursauter OR tressaillir qqn.

◆ **for a start** *adv phr* d'abord, pour commencer.

◆ **for starts** *inf Am* = **for a start**.

◆ **to start with** *adv phr* pour commencer, d'abord; **to** ~ **(off) with, my name isn't Jo** pour commencer OR d'abord, je ne m'appelle pas Jo.

◆ **start back** *vi insep* -**1.** [turn back] rebrousser chemin. -**2.** [start again] recommencer; **the children** ~ **back at school tomorrow** c'est la rentrée scolaire demain.

◆ **start in on** *vt insep* s'attaquer à; **I** ~**ed in on the pile of mail** je me suis attaqué à la pile de courrier; once he ~s in on liberty and democracy, there's no stopping him une fois qu'il est lancé sur le sujet de la liberté et de la démocratie, il n'y a plus moyen de l'arrêter; to ~ in on sb *inf* s'en prendre à qqn, tomber à bras raccourcis sur qqn.

◆ **start off** ◇ *vi insep* -**1.** [leave] partir, se mettre en route; **he ~ed off at a run** il est parti en courant; **when do you ~ off on your trip?** quand est-ce que vous partez en voyage? -**2.** [begin - book, speech, film] commencer; **it ~s off with a description of the town** ça commence par une description de la ville; **~ off with a summary of the problem** commencez par un résumé du problème; **the interview ~ed off badly/well** l'entrevue a mal/bien commencé; **I ~ed off agreeing with him** au début, j'étais d'accord avec lui. -**3.** [in life, career] débuter; **he ~ed off as a cashier** il a débuté comme caissier; **she ~ed off as a Catholic** elle était catholique à l'origine; **you're ~ing off with all the advantages** vous partez avec tous les avantages.

◇ *vt sep* -**1.** [book, campaign, show] commencer; **she ~ed the meeting off with introductions** elle a commencé la réunion en faisant les présentations. -**2.** [person - on new task]: **here's some wool to ~ you off** voici de la laine pour commencer. -**3.** [set off] déclencher; **what ~ed the alarm off?** qu'est-ce qui a déclenché l'alarme?; **if you mention it it'll only ~ her off again** n'en parle pas, sinon elle va recommencer; **to ~ sb off laughing/crying** faire rire/pleurer qqn.

◆ **start on** *vt insep* -**1.** [begin - essay, meal] commencer; [- task, dishes] se mettre à; [- new bottle, pack] entamer; **they had already ~ed on their dessert** ils avaient déjà commencé à manger OR entamé leur dessert; **after they'd searched the car they ~ed on the luggage** après avoir fouillé la voiture, ils sont passés aux bagages. -**2.** [attack, berate] s'en prendre à; **don't ~ on me, I'm not to blame!** ne t'en prends pas à moi, ce n'est pas de ma faute!

◆ **start out** *vi insep* -**1.** = **start off**. -**2.** [begin career] se lancer, s'installer, s'établir; **he ~ed out in business with his wife's money** il s'est lancé dans les affaires avec l'argent de sa femme; **when she ~ed out there were only a few women lawyers** quand elle a commencé sa carrière, il y avait très peu de femmes avocats.

◆ **start over** *vi insep* & *vt sep Am* recommencer (depuis le début).

◆ **start up** ◇ *vt sep* -**1.** [establish, found - business, school, political party] créer, fonder; [- restaurant, shop] ouvrir. -**2.** [set in motion - car, motor] faire démarrer; [- machine] mettre en marche.

◇ *vi insep* -**1.** [guns, music, noise, band] commencer; [wind] se lever; **the applause ~ed up again** les applaudissements ont repris. -**2.** [car, motor] démarrer, se mettre en marche; [machine] se mettre en marche. -**3.** [set up business] se lancer, s'installer, s'établir.

starter [ˈstɑːtəʳ] *n* -**1.** AUT [motor, button] démarreur *m*; [on motorbike] kick *m*, kick-starter *m*, démarreur *m* au pied; **~ switch** bouton *m* de démarrage; **~ handle** *Am* AUT manivelle *f*. -**2.** [runner, horse] partant *m*; [in relay race] premier coureur *m*, première coureuse *f*; **to be a slow ~** [gen & SPORT] être lent à démarrer, avoir du retard à l'allumage. -**3.** SPORT [official] starter *m*, juge *m* de départ; **~'s pistol** OR **gun** pistolet *m* du starter; **to be under ~'s orders** [in horseracing] être sous les ordres du starter. -**4.** [fermenting agent] ferment *m*; **yoghurt ~** ferment lactique pour yaourt. -**5.** *Br* [hors d'œuvre] hors-d'œuvre *m inv*; **for ~s** [in meal] comme hors-d'œuvre; *fig inf* pour commencer; **the sock on the jaw was just for ~s** ce coup de poing dans les gencives n'était qu'un hors-d'œuvre. -**6.** *inf Am* = **starter home**.

starter home *n* première maison *f (achetée par un individu ou un couple)*.

starter motor *n* moteur *m* auxiliaire de démarrage.

starter pack *n* kit *m* de base.

starter set *n Am* [dishes] service *m* pour six.

starting [ˈstɑːtɪŋ] ◇ *n* commencement *m*; **who wants to be responsible for the ~ of a nuclear war?** qui veut assumer la responsabilité du déclenchement d'une guerre nucléaire?

◇ *adj* initial; **the ~ line-up** la composition initiale de l'équipe; **~ salary** salaire *m* d'embauche.

starting block *n* starting-block *m*.

starting gate *n* SPORT [for horse] starting-gate *f*; [for skier] porte *f* de départ.

starting grid *n* [in motor racing] grille *f* de départ.

starting handle *n Br* AUT manivelle *f*.

starting line = **starting post**.

starting pistol *n* pistolet *m* du starter.

starting point *n* point *m* de départ.

starting post *n* SPORT ligne *f* de départ.

starting price *n* [gen] prix *m* initial; [in horseracing] cote *f* au départ; [at auction] mise *f* à prix, prix *m* d'appel.

startle [ˈstɑːtl] ◇ *vt* [person - surprise] surprendre, étonner; [- frighten, alarm] faire peur à, alarmer; [- cause to jump] faire sursauter; [animal, bird, fish] effaroucher; **I didn't mean to ~ you** je ne voulais pas vous faire peur; **it ~d me** OR **I was ~d to see how much he had aged** j'ai été surpris OR ça a été un choc pour moi de voir à quel point il avait vieilli; **the noise ~d him out of his reverie** le bruit l'a brusquement tiré de ses rêveries.

◇ *vi* s'effaroucher.

startled [ˈstɑːtld] *adj* [person] étonné; [expression, shout, glance] de surprise; [animal] effarouché; **there was a ~ silence** il y a eu un silence étonné; **the ~ waiter dropped the tray** le serveur, surpris, a laissé tomber son plateau; **the ~ guests didn't move** les invités, ahuris, restaient sans bouger.

startling [ˈstɑːtlɪŋ] *adj* étonnant, surprenant; [contrast, resemblance] saisissant; **~ green eyes** des yeux d'un vert saisissant.

start-up *adj* [costs] de démarrage; **~ loan** prêt *m* initial.

starvation [stɑːˈveɪʃn] *n* faim *f*; **to die of** OR **from ~** mourir de faim; **~ had decimated the troops** la famine avait décimé les troupes.

starvation diet *n literal* ration *f* de famine; *fig* régime *m* draconien; **the prisoners subsisted on a ~ of rice and water** les prisonniers devaient se contenter de riz et d'eau.

starvation wages *npl* salaire *m* de famine; **they pay ~** ce sont des affameurs.

starve [stɑːv] ◇ *vi* [suffer] souffrir de la faim, être affamé; **to ~ (to death)** [die] mourir de faim; **I'm starving!** *inf* je meurs de faim!

◇ *vt* -**1.** [cause to suffer] affamer; **he ~d himself to feed his child** il s'est privé de nourriture pour donner à manger à son enfant; **I'm ~d!** *inf* je meurs de faim!; **the garrison was ~d into surrender** la garnison affamée a fini par se rendre. -**2.** [cause to die] laisser mourir de faim. -**3.** [deprive] priver; **the libraries have been ~d of funds** les bibliothèques manquent cruellement de subventions; **to be ~d of affection** être privé d'affection; **the inhabitants were ~d of news** les habitants étaient privés d'informations.

◆ **starve out** *vt sep* [rebels, inmates] affamer, réduire par la faim; [animal] obliger à sortir en l'affamant.

starveling [ˈstɑːvlɪŋ] *n lit* [person] crève-la-faim *m inv*; [animal] animal *m* famélique.

starving [ˈstɑːvɪŋ] *adj* affamé; **I've got four ~ kids to feed!** *inf* j'ai quatre gosses affamés à nourrir!; **think of all the ~ people in the world** pense à tous ces gens qui meurent de faim dans le monde.

Star Wars ◇ *pr n* la guerre des étoiles *(nom donné à l'Initiative de Défense Stratégique, programme militaire spatial mis en place dans les années 80 par le président Reagan)*.

◇ *comp* [policy, advocate, weapon] de la Guerre des Étoiles; **~ research** la recherche sur la défense stratégique.

stash *inf* [stæʃ] ◇ *vt* -**1.** [hide] planquer, cacher; **it was ~ed under the bed** c'était planqué OR caché sous le lit; **he's probably got it ~ed (away) here somewhere** il l'a certainement planqué OR caché ici quelque part; **he's got a lot of money ~ed (away) somewhere** il a plein de fric planqué quelque part. -**2.** [put away] ranger; **let me ~ my things** attends que je ramasse mon bazar.

◇ *n* -**1.** [reserve] réserve *f*; **a ~ of money** un magot; **the police found a big ~ of guns/of cocaine** la police a découvert une importante cache d'armes/un important stock de cocaïne. -**2.** *inf* [hiding place] planque *f*, cachette *f*. -**3.** *drugs sl* cache *f*.

◆ **stash away** *inf vt sep* = **stash** *vt*.

stasis [ˈsteɪsɪs] (*pl* **stases** [-siːz]) *n* -**1.** MED stase *f*. -**2.** [equilibrium] équilibre *m*, repos *m*; [stagnation] stagnation *f*.

state [steɪt] ◇ *n* -**1.** [condition] état *m*; **the country is in a ~ of war/shock** le pays est en état de guerre/choc; **a ~ of confusion prevailed** la confusion régnait; **chlorine in its gaseous/liquid ~** le chlore à l'état gazeux/liquide; **to be in a good/bad ~** [road, carpet, car] être en bon/mauvais état; [person, economy, friendship] aller bien/mal; **the house was in a good/poor ~ of repair** la maison était en bon/mauvais état; **he was in a ~ of confusion** il ne savait plus où il en était; **she was in no (fit) ~ to make a decision** elle était hors d'état de OR elle n'était pas en état de prendre une décision; **the car's not in a ~ to be driven** la voiture n'est pas en état d'être conduite; **to get into a ~** *inf* se mettre dans tous ses états; **he gets into an awful ~ if I don't phone** si je ne lui téléphone pas, il se met dans tous ses états; **there's no need to get into such a ~ about it** ce n'est pas la peine de te mettre dans un état pareil OR de t'affoler comme ça ❑ **a ~ of emergency has been declared** l'état d'urgence a été déclaré; **~ of mind** état d'esprit; **in your present ~ of mind** dans l'état d'esprit dans lequel vous êtes; **success is just a ~ of mind** la réussite n'est qu'un état d'esprit; **is he in a better ~ of mind?** est-ce qu'il est dans de meilleures dispositions? -**2.** POL [nation, body politic] État *m*; **a ~ within a ~** un État dans l'État; **the member ~s** les États membres; **the head of ~** le chef de l'État; **heads of ~** chefs d'État; **the separation of (the) Church and (the) State** la séparation de l'Église et de l'État ❑ **~ lottery** *Am loterie d'État dont les gros lots sont soumis à l'impôt et sont versés au gagnant sur une période de 10 ou 20 ans*; **the State Opening of Parliament** *ouverture officielle du Parlement britannique en présence de la reine*. -**3.** [in US, Australia, India etc - political division] État *m*; **the States** *inf* les États-Unis, les US; **the State of Ohio** l'État de l'Ohio. -**4.** *Am* [department]: **State** le Département d'État. -**5.** [pomp] apparat *m*, pompe *f*; **the carriages are used only on ~ occasions** les carrosses sont uniquement réservés aux cérémonies de grande pompe. -**6.** *arch* [social position, estate] état *m*.

◇ *comp* -**1.** [secret] d'État; [subsidy, intervention] de l'État; ECON [sector] public; **~ buildings** bâtiments *mpl* publics; **the ~ airline** la compagnie d'aviation nationale; **a ~ funeral** des funérailles nationales. -**2.** *Br* SCH [education system] public. -**3.** *Am* [not federal - legislature, policy, law] de l'État; **the ~ capital** la capitale de l'État; **a ~ university** une université d'État OR publique; **the Michigan State team** l'équipe de l'État du Michigan; **a ~ park** un parc régional. -**4.** [official, ceremonious] officiel; **~ dinner** dîner *m* officiel OR d'apparat.

◇ *vt* [utter, say] déclarer; [express, formulate - intentions] déclarer; [- demand] formuler; [- proposition, problem, conclusions, views] énoncer, formuler; [- conditions] poser; **the president ~d emphatically that the rumours were untrue** le président a démenti catégoriquement les rumeurs; I have already ~d my position on that issue j'ai déjà fait connaître ma position à ce sujet; we ~ the current figures on page five les chiffres actuels sont donnés en page cinq; the regulations clearly ~ that daily checks must be made le règlement dit OR indique clairement que des vérifications quotidiennes doivent être effectuées; please ~ salary expectations veuillez indiquer le salaire souhaité; ~ your name and address donnez vos nom, prénoms et adresse; the man refused to ~ his business l'homme a refusé d'expliquer ce qu'il faisait; as ~d above ainsi qu'il est dit OR indiqué plus haut; ~ the figure as a percentage exprimez OR indiquez le chiffre en pourcentage; to ~ one's case présenter ses arguments; to ~ the case for the defence/the prosecution JUR présenter le dossier de la défense/de l'accusation.

◆ **in state** *adv phr* en grand apparat, en grande pompe; to lie in ~ être exposé solennellement; to live in ~ mener grand train.

state apartments *npl* appartements *mpl* de parade.

state bank *n Am* banque *f* de dépôts *(agréée par un État)*.

state capitalism *n* capitalisme *m* d'État.

state control *n* contrôle *m* étatique; [doctrine] étatisme *m*; to be put OR placed under ~ être nationalisé; ~ of the means of communication la nationalisation des moyens de communication.

state-controlled *adj* [industry] nationalisé; [economy] étatisé; [activities] soumis au contrôle de l'État; the oil company is 51% ~ l'État détient 51 % des actions de la compagnie pétrolière.

statecraft ['steɪtkrɑːft] *n* [skill - in politics] habileté *f* politique; [- in diplomacy] (art *m* de la) diplomatie *f*; he is a master of ~ c'est un maître confirmé de la diplomatie.

stated ['steɪtɪd] *adj* [amount, date] fixé; [limit] prescrit; [aim] déclaré; it will be finished within the ~ time cela va être terminé dans les délais prescrits OR prévus; at the ~ price au prix fixé OR convenu.

State Department *n Am* ministère *m* des Affaires étrangères.

State Enrolled Nurse *n Br* aide-soignant *m* diplômé, aide-soignante *f* diplômée.

statehood ['steɪthʊd] *n*: the struggle for ~ la lutte pour l'indépendance; to achieve ~ devenir un État.

Statehouse ['steɪthaʊs, *pl* -haʊzɪz] *n siège de l'assemblée législative d'un État aux États-Unis*.

stateless ['steɪtlɪs] *adj* apatride; ~ person apatride *mf*.

state line *n Am* frontière *f* entre États.

stateliness ['steɪtlɪnɪs] *n* [of ceremony, building, monument] majesté *f*, grandeur *f*; [of person, bearing] dignité *f*.

stately ['steɪtlɪ] (*compar* statelier, *superl* stateliest) *adj* [ceremony, building] majestueux, imposant; [person, bearing] noble, plein de dignité.

stately home *n château ou manoir à la campagne, généralement ouvert au public*.

statement ['steɪtmənt] *n* -**1.** [declaration - gen] déclaration *f*, affirmation *f*; [- to the press] communiqué *m*; a written/policy ~ une déclaration écrite/de principe; can you back that ~ up? pouvez-vous confirmer cette déclaration?; to put out OR to issue OR to make a ~ about sthg émettre un communiqué concernant qqch; the chairman was asked to withdraw his ~ le président a été prié de retirer sa déclaration; a ~ to the effect that... une déclaration selon laquelle...; to make a fashion ~ s'habiller à la dernière mode. -**2.** [act of stating - of theory, opinions, policy, aims] exposition *f*; [- of problem] exposé *m*, formulation *f*; [- of facts, details] exposé *m*, compte-rendu *m*. -**3.** JUR déposition *f*; to make a ~ to the police faire une déposition dans un commissariat de police; a sworn ~ une déposition faite sous serment ☐ ~ of claim demande *f* introductive d'instance. -**4.** COMM & FIN relevé *m*; bank ~ relevé de compte. -**5.** LING affirmation *f*. -**6.** COMPUT instruction *f*.

Staten Island ['stætn-] *pr n* Staten Island *(quartier de New York)*.

state of affairs *n* affaires *fpl*, circonstances *fpl* actuelles; nothing can be done in the present ~ vu les circonstances actuelles, on ne peut rien faire; this is an appalling ~ c'est une situation épouvantable.

state of the art *n* [of procedures, systems] pointe *f* du progrès; the ~ in linguistics l'état actuel des connaissances en linguistique.

◆ **state-of-the-art** *adj* [design, device] de pointe; the method incorporates ~ technology la méthode utilise des techniques de pointe; it's ~ *inf* c'est ce qui se fait de mieux, c'est du dernier cri.

State of the Union address *n*: the ~ le discours sur l'état de l'Union.

STATE OF THE UNION ADDRESS:
Ce discours radiotélévisé, dans lequel le président des États-Unis dresse le bilan de son programme et en définit les orientations, est prononcé devant le Congrès.

state-owned *adj* nationalisé.

state prison *n Am* prison *f* d'État *(pour les longues peines)*.

State Registered Nurse *n Br* infirmier *m* diplômé, infirmière *f* diplômée *(remplacé en 1992 par «Registered Nurse»)*.

stateroom ['steɪtrʊm] *n* -**1.** [in ship] cabine *f* de grand luxe; *Am* [in railway coach] compartiment *m* privé. -**2.** [in public building] salon *m* (de réception).

state school *n Br* école *f* publique.

state's evidence *n Am*: to turn ~ *témoigner contre ses complices en échange d'une remise de peine*.

States General *n pl* États généraux *mpl*.

stateside *inf* ['steɪtsaɪd] *adj* & *adv Am* aux États-Unis, ≃ au pays; he has a wife ~ il a une épouse au pays.

statesman ['steɪtsmən] (*pl* statesmen [-mən]) *n* homme *m* d'État.

statesmanlike ['steɪtsmənlaɪk] *adj* [protest, reply] diplomatique; [solution] de grande envergure; [caution] pondéré.

statesmanship ['steɪtsmənʃɪp] *n* qualités *fpl* d'homme d'État; he showed great ~ in dealing with the problem il a traité ce problème avec toute l'habileté d'un grand chef d'État.

state socialism *n* socialisme *m* d'État.

stateswoman ['steɪts,wʊmən] (*pl* stateswomen [-,wɪmɪn]) *n* femme *f* politique.

state trooper *n Am* ≃ gendarme *m*.

state visit *n* POL visite *f* officielle; he's on a ~ to Japan il est en voyage officiel au Japon.

state-wide ◇ *adj Am* [support, protest, celebration] dans tout l'État; the epidemic/our distribution is ~ l'épidémie/notre réseau de distribution s'étend à tout l'État.

◇ *adv* dans tout l'État; better schools are needed ~ on a besoin de meilleures écoles dans tout l'État.

static ['stætɪk] ◇ *adj* -**1.** [stationary, unchanging] stationnaire, stable; prices are fairly ~ just now les prix sont relativement stables en ce moment. -**2.** ELEC statique; ~ electricity électricité *f* statique.

◇ *n (U)* -**1.** RADIO & TELEC parasites *mpl*. -**2.** ELEC électricité *f* statique; you get a lot of ~ from nylon carpets les moquettes en nylon produisent beaucoup d'électricité statique. -**3.** *inf Am* [aggravation, criticism]: to give sb ~ about OR over sthg passer un savon à qqn à propos de qqch; to get a lot of ~ (about OR over sthg) se faire enguirlander (pour qqch).

statics ['stætɪks] *n (U)* SCI statique *f*.

station ['steɪʃn] ◇ *n* -**1.** TRANSP gare *f*; [underground] station *f* (de métro); I'll meet you at Brighton ~ je vous retrouverai à la gare de Brighton; railway ~ *Br*, train ~ gare (de chemin de fer); bus OR coach ~ gare routière. -**2.** [establishment, building] station *f*, poste *m*; police ~ poste de police, commissariat *m*; I must ask you to accompany me to the ~ je dois vous demander de m'accompagner au commissariat; polling ~ *Br* bureau *m* de vote; weather ~ station météorologique. -**3.** [MIL & gen - position] poste *m*; to take up one's ~ prendre position; action OR battle ~s! à vos postes! -**4.** MIL [base] poste *m*, base *f*; airforce ~ *Br* base aérienne. -**5.** RADIO & TV station *f*; [smaller] poste *m* émetteur; commercial radio ~ station de radio commerciale, radio *f* commerciale; relay ~ station relais. -**6.** [social rank] rang *m*, condition *f*, situation *f*; they tend to forget their true ~ in life ils ont tendance à oublier leur véritable position sociale; to marry below one's ~ faire une mésalliance; to marry above one's ~ se marier au-dessus de sa condition sociale. -**7.** COMPUT station *f*. -**8.** RELIG: the Stations of the Cross le chemin de la Croix.

◇ *comp* [buffet, platform etc] de gare.

◇ *vt* -**1.** [position] placer, poster; police were ~ed at all the exits des policiers étaient postés à toutes les issues. -**2.** MIL [garrison]: British troops ~ed in Germany les troupes britanniques stationnées en Allemagne.

stationary ['steɪʃnərɪ] *adj* -**1.** [not moving] stationnaire; he hit a ~ vehicle il a heurté un véhicule à l'arrêt OR en stationnement; ~ front METEOR front *m* stationnaire. -**2.** [fixed] fixe; ~ engine/shaft MECH moteur *m*/arbre *m* fixe.

station break *n Am* pause *f* OR page *f* de publicité.

stationer ['steɪʃnəʳ] *n Br* papetier *m*, -ère *f*; ~'s (shop) papeterie *f*; at the ~'s à la papeterie.

stationery ['steɪʃnərɪ] *n* [in general] papeterie *f*; [writing paper] papier *m* à lettres; a letter written on hotel ~ une lettre écrite sur le papier à en-tête d'un hôtel; school/office ~ fournitures *fpl* scolaires/de bureau.

station house *n Am* [police station] poste *m* de police, commissariat *m*; [fire station] caserne *f* de pompiers.

stationmaster ['steɪʃn,mɑːstəʳ] *n* chef *m* de gare.

station wagon *n Am* break *m*.

statistic [stə'tɪstɪk] *n* chiffre *m*, statistique *f*; that particular ~ is certain to embarrass the government ces chiffres OR statistiques vont sûrement embarrasser le gouvernement; he may be just another ~ to the police, but he was my brother ce n'est peut-être qu'une statistique de plus pour la police, mais il s'agissait de mon frère.

statistical [stə'tɪstɪkl] *adj* [analysis, technique] statistique; [error] de statistique; it's a ~ certainty c'est statistiquement certain; ~ mechanism mécanique *f* statistique.

statistically [stə'tɪstɪklɪ] *adv* statistiquement.

statistician [,stætɪ'stɪʃn] *n* statisticien *m*, -enne *f*.

statistics [stə'tɪstɪks] ◇ *n (U)* [science] statistique *f*.

◇ *npl* -**1.** [figures] statistiques *fpl*, chiffres *mpl*. -**2.** *inf* [of woman]: (vital) ~ mensurations *fpl*.

stative ['steɪtɪv] *adj*: ~ verb verbe *m* d'état.

stator ['steɪtəʳ] *n* stator *m*.

stats *inf* [stæts] = **statistics**.

statuary ['stætʃʊərɪ] ◇ *n (U) fml* [statues collectively] statues *fpl*; [art] statuaire *f*.

◇ *adj* statuaire; ~ marble marbre *m* statuaire.

statue ['stætʃuː] *n* statue *f*; the Statue of Liberty la statue de la Liberté.

statuesque [,stætjʊ'esk] *adj*: a ~ woman une femme d'une beauté sculpturale.

statuette [,stætjʊ'et] *n* statuette *f*.

stature ['stætʃəʳ] *n* -**1.** [height] stature *f*, taille *f*; he is rather short in OR of ~ il est plutôt petit. -**2.** [greatness] envergure *f*, calibre *m*; he doesn't have the ~ to be prime minister il n'a pas l'envergure d'un premier ministre; a mathematician of considerable ~ un mathématicien d'une très grande envergure.

status ['steɪtəs] ◇ *n* -**1.** [position - in society, hierarchy etc] rang *m*, position *f*, situation *f*; **what's your ~ in the company?** quelle est votre position dans l'entreprise?; **she quickly achieved celebrity ~** elle est vite devenue une célébrité. -**2.** [prestige] prestige *m*, standing *m*; **living here definitely confers a certain ~** le fait de vivre ici confère indéniablement un certain standing OR prestige. -**3.** [legal or official standing] statut *m*; **legal ~** statut légal; **marital ~** situation *f* de famille. -**4.** [general state or situation] état *m*, situation *f*, condition *f*; **to make a ~ report on sthg** faire le point sur qqch; **their financial ~ is under investigation** on enquête sur leur situation financière.
◇ *comp* [car, club] de prestige, prestigieux.

status line *n* COMPUT ligne *f* d'état.

status quo [ˌsteɪtəs'kwəʊ] *n* statu quo *m*; **to maintain** OR **to preserve the ~** maintenir le statu quo.

status symbol *n* marque *f* de prestige.

statute ['stætjuːt] *n* -**1.** JUR loi *f*; **~ of limitations** loi *f* de prescription, prescription *f* légale. -**2.** [of club, company, university] règle *f*; **the ~s** le règlement, les statuts *mpl*.

statute book *n Br* code *m* (des lois), recueil *m* de lois; **the new law is not yet on the ~** la nouvelle loi n'est pas encore entrée en vigueur.

statute law *n* droit *m* écrit.

statutorily ['stætjʊtərɪlɪ] *adv* statutairement.

statutory ['stætjʊtrɪ] *adj* -**1.** [regulations] statutaire; [rights, duties, penalty] statutaire, juridique; [holiday] légal; [offence] prévu par la loi; [price controls, income policy] obligatoire; **~ rape** *Am* détournement *m* de mineur; **~ sick pay** *indemnité de maladie versée par l'employeur*; **~ tenant** locataire *mf* en place. -**2.** *Br* [token]: **the ~ woman** la femme-alibi *(présente pour que soit respectée la réglementation sur l'égalité des sexes)*.

staunch [stɔːntʃ] ◇ *adj* [loyal] loyal, dévoué; [unswerving] constant, inébranlable; **he's my ~est ally** c'est mon allié le plus sûr.
◇ *vt* [liquid, blood] étancher; [flow] arrêter, endiguer.

staunchly ['stɔːntʃlɪ] *adv* [loyally] loyalement, avec dévouement; [unswervingly] avec constance, fermement; **their house is in a ~ Republican area** ils habitent un quartier résolument républicain.

staunchness ['stɔːntʃnɪs] *n* [loyalty] loyauté *f*, dévouement *m*; [firmness] constance *f*, fermeté *f*.

stave [steɪv] (*pt* & *pp* **staved** OR **stove** [stəʊv]) *n* -**1.** MUS portée *f*. -**2.** [stanza] stance *f*, strophe *f*. -**3.** [part of barrel] douve *f*, douelle *f*.
◆ **stave in** *vt sep* enfoncer, défoncer.
◆ **stave off** *vt sep* [defeat] retarder; [worry, danger] écarter; [disaster, threat] conjurer; [misery, hunger, thirst] tromper; **his lawyer tried to ~ off any awkward questions** son avocat a essayé d'éluder toute question gênante.

staves [steɪvz] *pl* → **staff, stave.**

stay [steɪ] ◇ *vi* -**1.** [remain] rester; **~ here** OR **~ put until I come back** restez ici OR ne bougez pas jusqu'à ce que je revienne; **I can't ~ long, I've got a train to catch** je ne peux pas rester longtemps, j'ai un train à prendre; **would you like to ~ for** OR **to dinner?** voulez-vous rester dîner?; **I don't want to ~ in the same job all my life** je ne veux pas faire le même travail toute ma vie; **to ~ awake all night** rester éveillé toute la nuit, ne pas dormir de la nuit; **it ~s dark here until at least 10 o'clock in the morning** ici, il ne fait pas jour avant 10 h du matin; **let's try and ~ calm** essayons de rester calmes; **she managed to ~ ahead of the others** elle a réussi à conserver son avance sur les autres; **~ tuned for the news** restez à l'écoute pour les informations; **personal computers have come to ~** OR **are here to ~** l'ordinateur personnel est devenu indispensable. -**2.** [reside temporarily]: **how long are you ~ing in New York?** combien de temps restez-vous à New York?; **we decided to ~ an extra week** nous avons décidé de rester une semaine de plus OR de prolonger notre séjour d'une semaine; **I always ~ at the same hotel** je descends toujours au même hôtel; **we met a couple ~ing at the same hotel as us** nous avons rencontré un couple qui séjournait au même hôtel que nous; **she's ~ing with friends** elle séjourne chez des amis; **to look for a place to ~** chercher un endroit où loger; **you can ~ here for the night, you can ~ the night here** tu peux coucher ici cette nuit OR passer la nuit ici. -**3.** *lit* [stop, pause] s'arrêter.
◇ *vt* -**1.** [last out] aller jusqu'au bout de, tenir jusqu'à la fin de; **to ~ the course** *literal* finir la course; *fig* tenir jusqu'au bout. -**2.** [stop] arrêter, enrayer; [delay] retarder; **to ~ sb's hand** retenir qqn; **to ~ one's hand** se retenir. -**3.** [prop up - wall] étayer; [secure with cables - mast] haubaner.
◇ *n* -**1.** [visit] séjour *m*; **hope you enjoy your ~!** je vous souhaite un bon séjour!; **an overnight ~ in hospital** une nuit d'hospitalisation. -**2.** JUR [suspension] suspension *f*; **~ of execution** ordonnance *f* à surseoir (à un jugement). -**3.** [support, prop] étai *m*, support *m*, soutien *m*. -**4.** [in corset] baleine *f*. -**5.** [cable, wire - for mast, flagpole etc] étai *m*, hauban *m*.
◆ **stays** *npl dated* corset *m*.
◆ **stay away** *vi insep* ne pas aller, s'abstenir d'aller; **she ~ed away from school last week** elle n'est pas allée à l'école la semaine dernière; **people are ~ing away from the beaches** les plages sont désertées en ce moment; **~ away from my sister!** ne t'approche pas de ma sœur!
◆ **stay behind** *vi insep* rester; **I'll ~ behind to clear up** je vais rester pour ranger; **a few pupils ~ed behind to talk to the teacher** quelques élèves sont restés (après le cours) pour parler au professeur.
◆ **stay down** *vi insep* -**1.** [gen] rester en bas. -**2.** *Br* SCH redoubler; **she had to ~ down a year** elle a dû redoubler. -**3.** [food]: **I do eat, but nothing will ~ down** je mange, mais je ne peux rien garder.
◆ **stay in** *vi insep* -**1.** [stay at home] rester à la maison, ne pas sortir; [stay indoors] rester à l'intérieur, ne pas sortir. -**2.** [be kept in after school] être consigné, être en retenue. -**3.** [not fall out] rester en place, tenir; **I can't get this nail to ~ in** je n'arrive pas à faire tenir ce clou.
◆ **stay on** *vi insep* rester; **more pupils are ~ing on at school after the age of 16** aujourd'hui, davantage d'élèves poursuivent leur scolarité au-delà de l'âge de 16 ans.
◆ **stay out** *vi insep* -**1.** [not come home] ne pas rentrer; **she ~ed out all night** elle n'est pas rentrée de la nuit. -**2.** [remain outside] rester dehors; **don't ~ out there in the rain!** ne reste pas dehors sous la pluie! -**3.** [remain on strike] rester en grève; **the miners ~ed out for nearly a year** la grève des mineurs a duré près d'un an. -**4.** [not get involved] ne pas se mêler; **~ out of this!** ne te mêle pas de ça!
◆ **stay over** *vi insep* -**1.** [not leave] s'arrêter un certain temps; **we decided to ~ over until the weekend** nous avons décidé de prolonger notre séjour jusqu'au week-end. -**2.** [stay the night] passer la nuit; **do you want to ~ over?** veux-tu passer la nuit ici?
◆ **stay up** *vi insep* -**1.** [not go to bed] veiller, ne pas se coucher; **don't ~ up too late** ne veillez pas OR ne vous couchez pas trop tard. -**2.** [not fall - building, mast] rester debout; [- socks, trousers] tenir; [remain in place - pictures, decorations] rester en place.
◆ **stay with** *inf vt insep*: **just ~ with it, you can do it** accroche-toi, tu peux y arriver.

stay-at-home *inf pej* ◇ *n* pantouflard *m*, -e *f*.
◇ *adj* pantouflard, popote *(inv)*.

stayer *inf* ['steɪəʳ] *n*: **he's a real ~** il est drôlement résistant.

staying power ['steɪɪŋ-] *n* résistance *f*, endurance *f*.

staysail ['steɪseɪl] *n* voile *f* d'étai.

stay stitch *n* point *m* d'arrêt.

STD *n* -**1.** *Br* TELEC (*abbr of* **subscriber trunk dialling**) automatique *m* (interurbain); **~ code** indicatif *m* de zone. -**2.** (*abbr of* **sexually transmitted disease**) MST *f*.

stead [sted] *n Br*: **in sb's ~** *fml* à la place de qqn; **he asked me to go in his ~** il m'a demandé d'y aller à sa place ❑ **to stand sb in good ~** rendre grand service OR être très utile à qqn.

steadfast ['stedfɑːst] *adj* -**1.** [unswerving] constant, inébranlable; [loyal] loyal, dévoué; **to be ~ in one's support of sb** apporter un soutien inconditionnel à qqn. -**2.** [steady - stare, gaze] fixe.

steadfastly ['stedfɑːstlɪ] *adv* avec constance, fermement.

steadfastness ['stedfɑːstnɪs] *n* constance *f*, fermeté *f*; **they showed great ~ of purpose** ils ont fait preuve d'une grande ténacité OR persévérance.

steadily ['stedɪlɪ] *adv* -**1.** [regularly - increase, decline] régulièrement, progressivement; [- breathe] régulièrement; [non-stop - rain] sans interruption, sans cesse; **her health grew ~ worse** sa santé s'est progressivement détériorée. -**2.** [firmly - stand] planté OR campé sur ses jambes; [- walk] d'un pas ferme; [- gaze] fixement, sans détourner les yeux.

steadiness ['stedɪnɪs] *n* -**1.** [regularity - of increase, speed, pulse etc] régularité *f*. -**2.** [stability - of ladder, relationship, market etc] stabilité *f*; [firmness - of voice] fermeté *f*; [- of hand] sûreté *f*; **the ~ of her gaze** la fixité de son regard. -**3.** [reliability - of person] sérieux *m*.

steady ['stedɪ] (*compar* **steadier**, *superl* **steadiest**, *pl* **steadies**, *pt* & *pp* **steadied**) ◇ *adj* -**1.** [regular, constant - growth, increase, decline] régulier, progressif; [- speed, pace] régulier, constant; [- pulse] régulier, égal; [- work] stable; [- income] régulier; **inflation remains at a ~ 5%** l'inflation s'est stabilisée à 5 %; **he's never been able to hold down a ~ job** il n'a jamais pu garder un emploi stable; **~ boyfriend** petit ami *m* régulier OR attitré; **~ girlfriend** petite amie *f* régulière OR attitrée; **I've got several boyfriends but no one ~** j'ai des flirts, mais pas de petit ami attitré. -**2.** [firm, stable - ladder, boat, relationship] stable; [- structure, desk, chair] solide, stable; **hold the ladder ~ for me** tiens-moi l'échelle; **to have a ~ hand** avoir la main sûre ‖ [calm - voice] ferme; [- gaze] fixe; [- nerves] solide ❑ **ready, ~, go!** *Br* à vos marques, prêts, partez! -**3.** [reliable - person] sérieux.
◇ *adv*: **to go ~ with sb** sortir avec qqn; **are Diana and Paul going ~?** c'est sérieux entre Diana et Paul?
◇ *n inf Am* petit ami *m*, petite amie *f*.
◇ *interj*: **~ (on)!** [be careful] attention!; [calm down] du calme!; **~! you almost knocked me over!** eh! doucement! tu as failli me faire tomber!
◇ *vt* -**1.** [stabilize] stabiliser; [hold in place] maintenir, retenir; **I reached out to ~ the vase** j'ai tendu le bras pour retenir le vase; **he almost fell off, but he managed to ~ himself** il a failli tomber, mais il a réussi à se rattraper; **she rested her elbows on the wall to ~ the camera** elle appuya ses coudes sur le mur pour que l'appareil photo ne bouge pas; **we were trying to ~ the boat** nous essayions de stabiliser le bateau. -**2.** [calm] calmer; **drink this, it'll ~ your nerves** bois ça, ça te calmera (les nerfs); **living with Edith has had a ~ing influence on him** il s'est assagi OR calmé depuis qu'il vit avec Edith.
◇ *vi* [boat, prices, stock market] se stabiliser; [pulse, breathing] devenir régulier; [person - regain balance] retrouver son équilibre; [- calm down] se calmer.

steady state theory *n* PHYS théorie *f* de l'état OR de l'univers stationnaire.

steak [steɪk] *n* -**1.** [beefsteak - for frying, grilling] steak *m*, bifteck *m*; **~ and chips** steak frites *m*. -**2.** [beef - for stews, casseroles] bœuf *m* à braiser; **~ and kidney pie** *tourte à la viande et aux rognons cuite au four*; **~ and kidney pudding** *tourte à la viande et aux rognons cuite à la vapeur*. -**3.** [cut - of veal, turkey] escalope *f*; [- of horse meat] steak *m*, bifteck *m*; [- of other meat] tranche *f*; [- of fish] tranche *f*, darne *f*.

steakhouse ['steɪkhaʊs, *pl* haʊzɪz] *n* grill *m*, grill-room *m*.

steak knife *n* couteau *m* à steak OR à viande.

steak tartare [-tɑː'tɑːʳ] *n* steak *m* tartare.

steal [stiːl] (*pt* stole [stəʊl], *pp* stolen ['stəʊln]) ◇ *vt* -**1.** [money, property] voler; to ~ sthg from sb voler qqch à qqn; he stole money from her purse il a volé de l'argent dans son porte-monnaie; several paintings have been stolen from the museum plusieurs tableaux ont été volés au musée; they've stolen my idea! ils ont volé mon idée! -**2.** *fig* [time] voler, prendre; [attention, affection] détourner; to ~ sb's heart séduire qqn; to ~ all the credit for sthg s'attribuer tout le mérite de qqch; may I ~ a few moments of your precious time? pouvez-vous m'accorder quelques instants de votre temps si précieux?; to ~ a glance at sb jeter un regard furtif à qqn ❑ to ~ a march on sb *Br* prendre qqn de vitesse, couper l'herbe sous le pied de qqn; to ~ the show from sb ravir la vedette à qqn; he really stole the show with that act of his! son numéro a été le clou du spectacle!; to ~ sb's thunder éclipser qqn.
◇ *vi* -**1.** [commit theft] voler; he was caught ~ing il a été pris en train de voler; thou shalt not ~ BIBLE tu ne voleras point. -**2.** [move secretively]: to ~ in/out entrer/sortir à pas furtifs OR feutrés; to ~ into a room se glisser OR se faufiler dans une pièce; she stole up on me from behind elle s'est approchée de moi par derrière sans faire de bruit || *fig*: shadows began to ~ across the courtyard *lit* des ombres commencèrent à envahir la cour; a strange sadness stole over me *lit* une étrange tristesse m'envahit.
◇ *n inf Am* [bargain] affaire *f*; it was a ~ c'était une bonne affaire.
◆ **steal away** *vi insep* partir furtivement, s'esquiver.

stealing ['stiːlɪŋ] *n* vol *m*.

stealth [stelθ] *n* -**1.** [of animal] ruse *f*. -**2.** *(U)* [underhandedness] moyens *mpl* détournés; the documents were obtained by ~ nous nous sommes procuré les documents en cachette OR par des moyens détournés.

stealthily ['stelθɪlɪ] *adv* furtivement, subrepticement, en catimini.

stealthy ['stelθɪ] (*compar* stealthier, *superl* stealthiest) *adj* furtif.

steam [stiːm] ◇ *n* -**1.** [vapour] vapeur *f*; [condensation] buée *f*; she wiped the ~ from the mirror elle essuya la buée sur la glace. -**2.** MECH & RAIL [as power] vapeur *f*; the trains used to run on OR to work by ~ autrefois, les trains marchaient à la vapeur ❑ at full ~ à toute vapeur, à pleine vitesse; full ~ ahead! en avant toute!; to do sthg under one's own ~ faire qqch par ses propres moyens; to get up OR to pick up ~ [vehicle] prendre de la vitesse; [campaign, project] être lancé; the battle against drugs is finally picking up ~ la lutte contre la drogue est enfin bien lancée; to let off ~ se défouler; to run out of ~ s'essouffler, s'épuiser.
◇ *comp* [boiler, ferry, locomotive etc] à vapeur.
◇ *vt* -**1.** [unstick with steam]: ~ the stamps off the envelope passez l'enveloppe à la vapeur pour décoller les timbres; to ~ open an envelope décacheter une enveloppe à la vapeur. -**2.** CULIN (faire) cuire à la vapeur; ~ed vegetables légumes *mpl* (cuits) à la vapeur.
◇ *vi* -**1.** [soup, kettle, wet clothes] fumer. -**2.** [go - train, ship]: the train ~ed into/out of the station le train entra en gare/quitta la gare; the liner ~ed into the harbour le paquebot entra dans le port; cargo boats regularly ~ed across the Atlantic des cargos à vapeur traversaient régulièrement l'Atlantique; my brother ~ed on ahead *fig* mon frère filait devant; she ~ed into/out of the room *fig* elle est entrée dans/sortie de la pièce comme une furie.
◆ **steam up** ◇ *vi insep* [window, glasses] s'embuer, se couvrir de buée.
◇ *vt sep* [window, glasses] embuer.

steam bath *n* bain *m* de vapeur.

steamboat ['stiːmbəʊt] *n* bateau *m* à vapeur, vapeur *m*.

steam coal *n* charbon *m* à vapeur, houille *f* de chaudière.

steam-driven *adj* à vapeur.

steamed-up *inf* [stiːmd-] *adj* [angry] énervé, dans tous ses états; what's he all ~ about? pourquoi est-il dans tous ses états OR dans un état pareil?; she got very ~ about the whole business (toute) cette histoire l'a mise dans tous ses états OR l'a beaucoup énervée.

steam engine *n* MECH moteur *m* à vapeur; RAIL locomotive *f* à vapeur.

steamer ['stiːməʳ] *n* -**1.** NAUT bateau *m* à vapeur, vapeur *m*. -**2.** CULIN [pan] marmite *f* à vapeur; [basket inside pan] panier *m* de cuisson à la vapeur.

steam heat *n* chaleur *f* fournie par la vapeur.

steaming ['stiːmɪŋ] ◇ *adj* -**1.** [very hot] fumant. -**2.** *inf* [angry] furibard, furax.
◇ *adv*: ~ hot fumant.

steam iron *n* fer *m* (à repasser) à vapeur.

steam point *n* point *m* d'ébullition.

steam radio *inf n Br dated & hum* -**1.** [broadcasting] ≃ la bonne vieille radio *(par opposition à la télévision)*. -**2.** [set] poste *m* de radio antédiluvien.

steamroll ['stiːmrəʊl] *vt* [road] cylindrer.

steamroller ['stiːm,rəʊləʳ] ◇ *n literal & fig* rouleau *m* compresseur; to use ~ tactics *fig* employer la technique du rouleau compresseur.
◇ *vt* -**1.** [crush - opposition, obstacle] écraser. -**2.** [force]: to ~ a bill through Parliament *faire passer une loi à la Chambre sans tenir compte de l'opposition*; to ~ sb into doing sthg forcer qqn à faire qqch. -**3.** = **steamroll**.

steamship ['stiːmʃɪp] *n* navire *m* à vapeur, vapeur *m*.

steam shovel *n Am* bulldozer *m*.

steamy ['stiːmɪ] (*compar* steamier, *superl* steamiest) *adj* -**1.** [room] plein de vapeur; [window, mirror] embué. -**2.** *inf* [erotic] érotique, d'un érotisme torride.

stearic [stɪ'ærɪk] *adj* stéarique; ~ acid acide *m* stéarique.

steatite ['stɪə,taɪt] *n* stéatite *f*.

steed [stiːd] *n lit* coursier *m*.

steel [stiːl] ◇ *n* -**1.** [iron alloy] acier *m*; rolled/cast/stainless ~ acier laminé/moulé/inoxydable; to have nerves of ~ avoir des nerfs d'acier. -**2.** [steel industry] industrie *f* sidérurgique, sidérurgie *f*; the nationalization of ~ la nationalisation de l'industrie sidérurgique. -**3.** [for sharpening knives] aiguisoir *m*. -**4.** *lit* [sword] fer *m*.
◇ *adj* [helmet, cutlery etc] en acier.
◇ *comp* [industry, plant] sidérurgique; [strike] des sidérurgistes; ~ manufacturer sidérurgiste *mf*.
◇ *vt* -**1.** *Br* [harden]: to ~ o.s. against sthg se cuirasser contre qqch; he ~ed himself against any further hurt il s'est cuirassé contre toute nouvelle blessure sentimentale; ~ yourself for a terrible ordeal préparez-vous à affronter une rude épreuve; I had ~ed myself for the worst je m'étais préparé au pire. -**2.** METALL aciérer.

steel band *n* MUS steel band *m*.

steel blue *n* bleu *m* acier.
◆ **steel-blue** *adj* bleu acier *(inv)*.

steel grey *n* gris *m* acier.
◆ **steel-grey** *adj* gris acier *(inv)*.

steel guitar *n* guitare *f* à cordes d'acier.

steel wool *n* paille *f* de fer.

steelworker ['stiːl,wɜːkəʳ] *n* sidérurgiste *mf*.

steelworks ['stiːlwɜːks] (*pl inv*) *n* aciérie *f*, usine *f* sidérurgique.

steely ['stiːlɪ] *adj* -**1.** [in colour] d'acier, gris acier *(inv)*. -**2.** [strong - determination, will] de fer; [- look] d'acier.

steelyard ['stiːljɑːd] *n* balance *f* romaine.

steep [stiːp] ◇ *adj* -**1.** [hill] raide, abrupt, escarpé; [slope] fort, raide; [cliff] abrupt; [road, path] raide, escarpé; [staircase] raide; it's a ~ climb to the village la montée est raide pour arriver au village; the plane went into a ~ dive l'avion se mit à piquer du nez. -**2.** [increase, fall] fort; a ~ drop in share prices une forte chute du prix des actions. -**3.** *inf* [fee, price] excessif, élevé; the prices are a bit ~ l'addition est plutôt salée. -**4.** *inf* [unreasonable]: it's a bit ~ asking us to do all that work by Friday c'est un peu fort OR un peu raide de nous demander de faire tout ce travail pour vendredi.
◇ *vt* [soak] (faire) tremper; CULIN (faire) macérer, (faire) mariner; ~ the onions in vinegar faites macérer les oignons dans du vinaigre; I want to ~ myself in the atmosphere of the place *fig* je veux m'imprégner de l'atmosphère de l'endroit.
◇ *vi* [gen] tremper; CULIN macérer, mariner.

steeped [stiːpt] *adj* imprégné; ~ in tradition/mystery imprégné de tradition/mystère.

steepen ['stiːpn] *vi* -**1.** [slope, road, path] devenir plus raide OR escarpé; the climb ~ed as we neared the top la pente devenait de plus en plus raide à mesure que nous approchions du sommet. -**2.** [increase - inflation, rate] croître.

steeple ['stiːpl] *n* clocher *m*, flèche *f*.

steeplechase ['stiːpltʃeɪs] *n* [in horse racing, athletics] steeple *m*, steeple-chase *m*.

steeplechaser ['stiːpl,tʃeɪsəʳ] *n* -**1.** [jockey] jockey *m* de steeple OR steeple-chase. -**2.** [runner] coureur *m*, -euse *f* de steeple OR steeple-chase.

steeplejack ['stiːpldʒæk] *n Br réparateur de clochers et de cheminées*.

steeply ['stiːplɪ] *adv* en pente raide, à pic; the path climbs ~ le chemin monte en pente raide; a ~ sloping field leads down to the lake un champ descend en pente raide jusqu'au lac; costs are rising ~ les coûts montent en flèche.

steepness ['stiːpnɪs] *n* -**1.** [of climb, road, staircase] raideur *f*. -**2.** [of price rise] importance *f*.

steer [stɪəʳ] ◇ *vt* -**1.** [car] conduire; the lorry was surprisingly easy to ~ le camion était étonnamment facile à conduire; she ~ed the car into the garage/out onto the main road elle a rentré la voiture au garage/conduit la voiture jusqu'à la route principale || NAUT [boat] gouverner, barrer; to ~ a course for mettre le cap sur; the management has decided to ~ a radically different course *fig* la direction a décidé de changer radicalement de cap; it's a dangerous course you're ~ing *fig* vous vous engagez sur un terrain dangereux ❑ ~ed course route *f* au compas OR apparente. -**2.** [person] guider, diriger; she ~ed me over to a sofa elle m'a guidé vers un canapé; try to ~ him away from the bar essayez de l'éloigner du bar. -**3.** [conversation, project etc] diriger; I tried to ~ the conversation round to/away from the subject j'ai essayé d'amener la conversation sur le sujet/de détourner la conversation du sujet; she successfully ~ed the company through the crisis elle a réussi à sortir la société de la crise; to ~ a bill through Parliament réussir à faire voter un projet de loi par le Parlement.
◇ *vi* -**1.** [driver] conduire; I'd feel safer if you ~ed with both hands! je me sentirais mieux si tu conduisais des deux mains!; I ~ed carefully into the garage j'ai manœuvré avec soin pour entrer dans le garage; she ~ed smoothly round the bend elle prit le virage en douceur || NAUT [helmsman] gouverner, barrer; ~ for that buoy mettez le cap sur cette bouée ❑ to ~ clear of sthg/sb éviter qqch/qqn; ~ clear of her husband, he's a real bore évite son mari, c'est un vrai raseur. -**2.** [car]: this car ~s very well/badly cette voiture a une excellente/très mauvaise direction; a taxi ~ed out of a side street un taxi a débouché d'une rue latérale || NAUT [boat] se diriger; the ferry was ~ing for Dover le ferry se dirigeait vers Douvres.
◇ *n* -**1.** AGR bœuf *m*. -**2.** *inf Am* [piece of advice] conseil *m*; [tip] tuyau *m*.

steerage ['stɪərɪdʒ] *n* NAUT -**1.** *dated* [accommodation] entrepont *m*; ~ passengers passagers *mpl* d'entrepont. -**2.** [steering] conduite *f*, pilotage *m*.

steerageway ['stɪərɪdʒweɪ] *n* NAUT vitesse *f* acquise, erre *f spec*; to get up/to lose ~ augmenter/diminuer l'erre.

steering ['stɪərɪŋ] ◇ *n* -**1.** AUT [apparatus, mechanism] direction *f*; [manner of driving] conduite *f*; power ~ direction assistée. -**2.** NAUT conduite *f*, pilotage *m*.
◇ *comp* AUT [arm, column, lever] de direction.

steering committee *n Br* comité *m* directeur.

steering gear *n* AERON & AUT mécanisme *m* de direction; NAUT appareil *m* à gouverner.

steering lock *n* AUT -**1.** [turning circle] rayon *m* de braquage. -**2.** [antitheft device] antivol *m* de direction.

steering wheel *n* -**1.** AUT volant *m*. -**2.** NAUT roue *f* du gouvernail, barre *f*.

steersman ['stɪəzmən] (*pl* **steersmen** [-mən]) *n* timonier *m*, barreur *m*.

stegosaurus [,stegə'sɔːrəs] *n* stégosaure *m*.

stein [staɪn] *n* chope *f*.

stellar ['stelə^r] *adj* -**1.** ASTRON stellaire. -**2.** *inf* CIN & THEAT: the play boasts a ~ cast cette pièce a une distribution éblouissante.

stem [stem] (*pt* & *pp* **stemmed**, *cont* **stemming**)
◇ *n* -**1.** BOT [of plant, tree] tige *f*; [of fruit, leaf] queue *f*. -**2.** [of glass] pied *m*. -**3.** [of tobacco pipe] tuyau *m*. -**4.** LING [of word] radical *m*. -**5.** TECH [in lock, watch] tige *f*; winding ~ tige de remontoir. -**6.** [vertical stroke - of letter] hampe *f*; [- of musical note] queue *f*. -**7.** NAUT [timber, structure] étrave *f*; [forward section] proue *f*; from ~ to stern de l'étrave à l'étambot. -**8.** BIBLE [family, stock] souche *f*.
◇ *vt* -**1.** [check, stop - flow, spread, bleeding] arrêter, endiguer; [- blood] étancher; [- river, flood] endiguer, contenir; the government has taken new measures to ~ the flow of capital abroad le gouvernement a pris de nouvelles mesures pour arrêter la fuite des capitaux à l'étranger; they are trying to ~ the tide of protest ils essaient d'endiguer le nombre croissant de protestations. -**2.** SPORT: to ~ one's skis faire un stem OR stemm.
◇ *vi* -**1.** [derive]: to ~ from avoir pour cause, être le résultat de; all her difficulties ~ from her insecure childhood tous ses problèmes ont pour cause une enfance difficile. -**2.** SPORT faire du stem OR stemm.

stem glass *n* verre *m* à pied.

-stemmed [stemd] *in cpds* -**1.** BOT à tige...; a long/short/thin~ plant une plante à tige longue/courte/mince. -**2.** [gen]: a long/short~ glass un verre à pied haut/bas; a long/short~ pipe une pipe à tuyau long/court.

stem turn *n* SPORT (virage *m* de) stem *m*.

stem-winder *n* montre *f* à remontoir.

Sten [sten] = **Sten gun**.

stench [stentʃ] *n* puanteur *f*, odeur *f* nauséabonde.

stencil ['stensl] (*Br pt* & *pp* **stencilled**, *cont* **stencilling**, *Am pt* & *pp* **stenciled**, *cont* **stenciling**) ◇ *n* -**1.** [for typing] stencil *m*. -**2.** [template] pochoir *m*. -**3.** [pattern] dessin *m* au pochoir.
◇ *vt* dessiner au pochoir.

Sten gun [sten-] *n* mitraillette *f* légère.

steno *inf* ['stenəʊ] (*pl* **stenos**) *n Am* -**1.** [stenographer] sténo *mf*. -**2.** [stenography] sténo *f*.

stenographer [stə'nɒgrəfə^r] *n Am* sténographe *mf*.

stenography [stə'nɒgrəfɪ] *n* sténographie *f*.

Stenotype® ['stenəʊtaɪp] *n* sténotype *f*.

stenotypist ['stenəʊ,taɪpɪst] *n* sténotypiste *mf*.

stentorian [sten'tɔːrɪən] *adj lit* [voice] de stentor.

step [step] (*pt* & *pp* **stepped**, *cont* **stepping**)
◇ *n* -**1.** [pace] pas *m*; take two ~s forwards/backwards faites deux pas en avant/en arrière; I grew wearier with every ~ I took je m'épuisais un peu plus à chaque pas (que je faisais); I heard her ~ OR ~s on the stairs j'ai entendu (le bruit de) ses pas dans l'escalier; that's certainly put a spring in her ~ ça a dû lui donner un peu de ressort; he was following a few ~s behind me il me suivait à quelques pas; it's only a (short) ~ to the shops les magasins sont à deux pas d'ici ❑ watch your ~! *literal* faites attention où vous mettez les pieds!; *fig* faites attention! -**2.** [move, action] pas *m*; [measure] mesure *f*, disposition *f*; it's a great ~ forward for mankind c'est un grand pas en avant pour l'humanité; our first ~ will be to cut costs notre première mesure sera de réduire les coûts; to take ~s to do sthg: the government should take ~s to ban the book le gouvernement devrait prendre des mesures pour interdire le livre; what ~s have you taken? quelles mesures avez-vous prises?; it's only a short ~ from what you are suggesting to an outright ban entre ce que vous suggérez et une interdiction absolue, il n'y a qu'un pas; it's a ~ in the right direction c'est un pas dans la bonne direction. -**3.** [stage] étape *f*; the different ~s in the manufacturing process les différentes étapes du processus de fabrication; this promotion is a big ~ up for me cette promotion est un grand pas en avant pour moi; we are still one ~ ahead of our competitors nous conservons une petite avance sur nos concurrents; if I may take your argument one ~ further si je peux pousser votre raisonnement un peu plus loin; we'll support you every ~ of the way nous vous soutiendrons à fond OR sur toute la ligne. -**4.** [stair - gen] marche *f*; [- into bus, train etc] marche-pied *m*; a flight of ~s un escalier; the church ~s le perron de l'église; 'mind the ~' 'attention à la marche'. -**5.** DANCE pas *m*; a minuet ~ un pas de menuet; do try and keep ~! essaie donc de danser en mesure! -**6.** [in marching] pas *m*; in ~ au pas; to march in ~ marcher au pas; to be out of ~ ne pas être en cadence; they were walking out of ~ ils ne marchaient pas en cadence; to break ~ rompre le pas; to change ~ changer de pas; to fall into ~ se mettre au pas; he fell into ~ beside me arrivé à ma hauteur, il régla son pas sur le mien; to keep ~ marcher au pas ❑ to be in ~ with the times/with public opinion être au diapason de son temps/de l'opinion publique; to be out of ~ with the times/with public opinion être déphasé par rapport à son époque/à l'opinion publique. -**7.** *Am* MUS [interval] seconde *f*.
◇ *vi* -**1.** [take a single step] faire un pas; [walk, go] marcher, aller; ~ this way, please par ici, je vous prie; ~ inside! entrez!; he carefully stepped round the sleeping dog il contourna prudemment le chien endormi; I stepped onto/off the train je suis monté dans le/descendu du train; she stepped lightly over the ditch elle enjamba le fossé lestement. -**2.** [put one's foot down, tread] marcher; I stepped on a banana skin/in a puddle j'ai marché sur une peau de banane/dans une flaque d'eau ❑ ~ on the gas!, ~ on it! *inf* appuie sur le champignon!; to ~ out of line s'écarter du droit chemin.
◇ *vt* -**1.** [measure out] mesurer. -**2.** [space out] échelonner.

◆ **steps** *npl Br* [stepladder]: (pair of) ~s escabeau *m*.

◆ **step aside** *vi insep* -**1.** [move to one side] s'écarter, s'effacer. -**2.** = **step down 2**.

◆ **step back** *vi insep* -**1.** *literal* reculer, faire un pas en arrière. -**2.** *fig* prendre du recul; we don't have time to ~ back and figure out what it all means nous n'avons pas le temps de prendre du recul pour essayer de comprendre tout cela.

◆ **step down** ◇ *vi insep* -**1.** [descend] descendre. -**2.** [quit position, job] se retirer, se désister; he stepped down in favour of a younger person il a cédé la place à quelqu'un de plus jeune.
◇ *vt sep* ELEC [voltage] abaisser.

◆ **step forward** *vi insep* -**1.** *literal* faire un pas en avant. -**2.** *fig* [volunteer] se présenter, être volontaire.

◆ **step in** *vi insep* -**1.** [enter] entrer. -**2.** [intervene] intervenir.

◆ **step out** *vi insep* -**1.** [go out of doors] sortir. -**2.** [walk faster] presser le pas.

◆ **step out on** *vt insep Am*: to ~ out on sb laisser tomber qqn.

◆ **step up** ◇ *vi insep* s'approcher; to ~ up to sb s'approcher de qqn.
◇ *vt sep* -**1.** [increase - output, pace] augmenter, accroître; [- activity, efforts] intensifier. -**2.** ELEC [voltage] augmenter.

step aerobics *n* step *m*.

stepbrother ['step,brʌðə^r] *n* demi-frère *m*.

step-by-step ◇ *adv* [gradually] pas à pas, petit à petit.
◇ *adj* [point by point]: a ~ guide to buying your own house un guide détaillé pour l'achat de votre maison.

stepchild ['step,tʃaɪld] (*pl* **stepchildren** [-,tʃɪldrən]) *n* beau-fils *m*, belle-fille *f*.

stepdaughter ['step,dɔːtə^r] *n* belle-fille *f*.

step-down *n*: ~ transformer transformateur *m* dévolteur.

stepfather ['step,fɑːðə^r] *n* beau-père *m*.

Stephen ['stiːvn] *pr n*: Saint ~ saint Etienne.

step-in *adj* [skirt] à enfiler *(sans boutons ni fermeture Éclair)*.

stepladder ['step,lædə^r] *n* escabeau *m*.

stepmother ['step,mʌðə^r] *n* belle-mère *f*.

stepparent ['step,peərənt] *n* beau-père *m*, belle-mère *f*; relations between children and their ~s are often difficult les rapports entre un enfant et son beau-père ou sa belle-mère sont souvent difficiles.

steppe [step] *n* steppe *f*.

stepped-up [stept-] *adj* [output] accru, augmenté; [pace] plus rapide; [activity, efforts, war] intensifié.

stepping-stone ['stepɪŋ-] *n* -**1.** *literal* pierre *f* de gué. -**2.** *fig* tremplin *m*; a ~ to a new career un tremplin pour (se lancer dans) une nouvelle carrière.

stepsister ['step,sɪstə^r] *n* demi-sœur *f*.

stepson ['stepsʌn] *n* beau-fils *m (fils du conjoint d'un précédent mariage)*.

stere [stɪə^r] *n* stère *m*.

stereo ['sterɪəʊ] (*pl* **stereos**) ◇ *n* -**1.** [stereo sound] stéréo *f*; broadcast in ~ retransmis en stéréo. -**2.** [hifi system] chaîne *f* (stéréo); I need a new ~ il me faudrait une nouvelle chaîne.
◇ *adj* [cassette, record, record player] stéréo *(inv)*; [recording, broadcast] en stéréo.

stereogram ['sterɪəgræm] *n* -**1.** = **stereograph**. -**2.** *Br dated* chaîne *f* stéréo.

stereograph ['sterɪəgrɑːf] *n* stéréogramme *m*.

stereography [,sterɪ'ɒgrəfɪ] *n* stéréographie *f*.

stereometry [,sterɪ'ɒmɪtrɪ] *n* stéréométrie *f*.

stereophonic [,sterɪə'fɒnɪk] *adj* stéréophonique.

stereoscope ['sterɪəʊskəʊp] *n* stéréoscope *m*.

stereoscopic [,sterɪə'skɒpɪk] *adj* stéréoscopique.

stereoscopy [,sterɪ'ɒskəpɪ] *n* stéréoscopie *f*.

stereotype ['sterɪətaɪp] ◇ *n* -**1.** [idea, trait, convention] stéréotype *m*; they don't really conform to our ~ of what Americans are like ils ne correspondent pas vraiment au stéréotype que nous avons des Américains. -**2.** TYPO cliché *m*.
◇ *vt* -**1.** [person, role] stéréotyper. -**2.** TYPO clicher.

stereotyped ['sterɪəʊtaɪpt] *adj* stéréotypé; the film is full of very ~ images of women dans ce film, les personnages de femmes sont très stéréotypés OR les femmes ont des rôles très stéréotypés.

stereotypical [,sterɪəʊ'tɪpɪkl] *adj* stéréotypé.

stereotyping ['sterɪəʊ,taɪpɪŋ] *n*: we want to avoid sexual ~ nous voulons éviter les stéréotypes sexuels.

sterile ['steraɪl] *adj* stérile.

sterility [ste'rɪlətɪ] *n* stérilité *f*.

sterilization [,sterəlaɪ'zeɪʃn] *n* stérilisation *f*.

sterilize, -ise ['sterəlaɪz] *vt* stériliser; ~d milk lait *m* stérilisé.

sterilizer ['sterəlaɪzəʳ] *n* stérilisateur *m*.

sterling ['stɜːlɪŋ] ◇ *n* -**1.** [currency] sterling *m inv*; twenty thousand pounds ~ vingt mille livres sterling; ~ area zone *f* sterling. -**2.** [standard] titre *m*. -**3.** [silverware] argenterie *f (fine)*.
◇ *adj* -**1.** [gold, silver] fin. -**2.** *fml* [first-class] excellent, de premier ordre.
◇ *comp* [reserves, balances] en sterling; [traveller's cheques] en livres sterling.

stern [stɜːn] ◇ *adj* -**1.** [strict, harsh - person, measure] sévère, strict; [- appearance] sévère, austère; [- discipline, punishment] sévère, rigoureux; [- look, rebuke] sévère, dur; [- warning] solennel, grave. -**2.** [robust] solide, robuste; his wife is made of ~er stuff sa femme est d'une autre trempe.
◇ *n* -**1.** NAUT arrière *m*, poupe *f*. -**2.** [of horse] croupe *f*.

sterna ['stɜːnə] *pl* → **sternum**.

sternforemost [stɜːn'fɔːməʊst] *adv* NAUT par l'arrière.

sternly ['stɜːnlɪ] *adv* sévèrement.

sternness ['stɜːnnɪs] *n* sévérité *f*.

Sterno can® ['stɜːnəʊ-] *n Am boîte contenant une substance inflammable et que l'on transporte pour cuisiner*.

sternum ['stɜːnəm] (*pl* sternums OR sterna [-nə]) *n* sternum *m*.

sternward(s) ['stɜːnwəd(z)] *adv* vers l'arrière.

steroid ['stɪərɔɪd] *n* stéroïde *m*; the doctor put him on a course of ~s le médecin lui a prescrit OR donné un traitement stéroïdien.

sterol ['stɪərɒl] *n* stérol *m*.

stertorous ['stɜːtərəs] *adj lit* stertoreux, ronflant.

stet [stet] *interj* TYPO bon, à maintenir.

stethoscope ['steθəskəʊp] *n* stéthoscope *m*.

Stetson® ['stetsn] *n* Stetson® *m*, chapeau *m* de cow-boy.

stevedore ['stiːvədɔːʳ] ◇ *n Am* docker *m*, débardeur *m*.
◇ *vi* travailler comme docker OR débardeur.

stew [stjuː] ◇ *n* CULIN ragoût *m*; lamb/vegetable ~ ragoût d'agneau/de légumes (mijotés); to be in a ~ *inf Br* [bothered] être dans tous ses états; [in a mess] être dans de beaux draps OR dans le pétrin.
◇ *vt* [meat] préparer en ragoût, cuire (en ragoût); [fruit] (faire) cuire en compote.
◇ *vi* CULIN [meat] cuire en ragoût, mijoter; [fruit] cuire; leave the meat to ~ for at least two hours laissez mijoter la viande pendant deux bonnes heures || [tea] infuser trop longtemps ❑ to let sb ~ (in their own juice) *inf Br* laisser cuire OR mijoter qqn dans son jus.

steward ['stjʊəd] *n* -**1.** [on aeroplane, ship] steward *m*. -**2.** [at race, sports event] commissaire *m*; ~'s enquiry *Br* enquête *f* des commissaires. -**3.** [at dance, social event] organisateur *m*, -trice *f*; [at meeting, demonstration] membre *m* du service d'ordre. -**4.** [of property] intendant *m*, -e *f*; [estate, finances] régisseur *m*, -euse *f*; [in college] économe *mf*.

stewardess ['stjʊədɪs] *n* hôtesse *f*.

stewardship ['stjʊədʃɪp] *n* intendance *f*, économat *m*.

stewed [stjuːd] *adj* -**1.** CULIN: ~ meat ragoût *m*; we had ~ lamb for supper au dîner, nous avons mangé un ragoût d'agneau; ~ fruit compote *f* de fruits. -**2.** [tea] trop infusé. -**3.** *inf* [drunk] bourré, cuité; to get ~ se cuiter.

St. Ex. *written abbr of* stock exchange.

stg *written abbr of* sterling.

stick [stɪk] (*pt* & *pp* stuck [stʌk]) ◇ *n* -**1.** [piece of wood] bout *m* de bois; [branch] branche *f*; [twig] petite branche *f*, brindille *f*; gather some ~s, we'll make a fire ramassez du bois, on fera du feu. -**2.** [wooden rod - as weapon] bâton *m*; [walking stick] canne *f*, bâton *m*; [drumstick] baguette *f*; [for plants] rame *f*, tuteur *m*; [for lollipop] bâton *m*; she had legs like ~s elle avait des jambes comme des allumettes; to give sb the ~ *Br* donner la bastonnade à qqn; I'm going to take a ~ to that boy one day! un jour je vais mettre une raclée à ce garçon!; the threat of redundancy has become a ~ with which industry beats the unions *fig* pour le patronat, la menace du licenciement est devenue une arme contre les syndicats; a few ~s (of furniture) *inf Br* quelques vagues meubles; we don't have one ~ of decent furniture nous n'avons pas un seul meuble convenable ❑ to get (hold of) the wrong end of the ~ mal comprendre, comprendre de travers; you've got (hold of) the wrong end of the ~ about this business vous avez tout compris de travers dans cette histoire; to get the short OR dirty end of the ~ être mal loti; she got the short OR dirty end of the ~ as usual c'est tombé sur elle comme d'habitude; ~s and stones may break my bones but words will never hurt me *prov* la bave du crapaud n'atteint pas la blanche colombe *prov*. -**3.** [piece - of chalk] bâton *m*, morceau *m*; [- of cinnamon, incense, liquorice, dynamite] bâton *m*; [- of charcoal] morceau *m*; [- of chewing gum] tablette *f*; [- of glue, deodorant] bâton *m*, stick *m*; [- of celery] branche *f*; [- of rhubarb] tige *f*; French ~ baguette *f* (de pain). -**4.** GAMES & SPORT [in hockey, lacrosse] crosse *f*; [ski pole] bâton *m* (de ski); [baseball bat] batte *f*; [billiard cue] queue *f* de billard; [in pick-up-sticks] bâton *m*, bâtonnet *m*, jonchet *m*. -**5.** *inf (U) Br* [criticism] critiques *fpl* (désobligeantes); to get OR to come in for a lot of ~: the police got a lot of ~ from the press la police s'est fait éreinter OR démolir par la presse; he got a lot of ~ from his friends about his new hairstyle ses amis l'ont bien charrié avec sa nouvelle coupe. -**6.** *inf* [control lever] AERON manche *m* à balai; AUT levier *m* de vitesse. -**7.** MIL [cluster - of bombs] chapelet *m*; [- of parachutists] stick *m*. -**8.** *inf Br dated* [person] type *m*; he's a dull OR dry old ~ il est rasoir; she's not a bad old ~, she's a nice old ~ elle est plutôt sympa. -**9.** *inf* [glue] colle *f*; [stickiness] pouvoir *m* adhésif. -**10.** *Am dated drugs sl* [cannabis cigarette] joint *m*.
◇ *vt* -**1.** [jab, stab - spear, nail, knife] planter, enfoncer; [- needle] piquer, planter; [- pole, shovel] planter; [- elbow, gun] enfoncer; he stuck his fork into a potato il a planté sa fourchette dans une pomme de terre; don't ~ drawing pins in the wall ne plantez pas de punaises dans le mur; there were maps with coloured pins stuck in them il y avait des cartes avec des épingles de couleur; a ham stuck with cloves un jambon piqué de clous de girofle; watch out! you almost stuck your umbrella in my eye! fais attention! tu as failli m'enfoncer ton parapluie dans l'œil!; he stuck his elbow in my ribs il m'a enfoncé son coude dans les côtes; she stuck the revolver in his back elle lui a enfoncé le revolver dans le dos; he pulled out his gun and stuck it in my face *inf* il a sorti son arme et l'a brandie sous mon nez; ~ the skewer through the chicken enfilez le poulet sur la broche, embrochez le poulet. -**2.** [insert] insérer, mettre, ficher; [put] mettre; ~ the candles in the holders mettez les bougies dans les bougeoirs; he stuck a rose in his lapel il s'est mis une rose à la boutonnière; she stuck the cork in the bottle elle a enfoncé le bouchon dans le goulot de la bouteille; to ~ a flower in one's hair piquer une fleur dans ses cheveux; here, ~ this under the chair leg tenez, calez la chaise avec ça; the door was closing but he managed to ~ his foot in it la porte se refermait mais il réussit à glisser son pied dans l'entrebâillement OR à la bloquer du pied; he stood there with a cigar stuck in his mouth/with his hands stuck in his pockets il était planté là, un cigare entre les dents/les mains enfoncées dans les poches; he stuck the card back in the pack il a remis la carte dans le jeu; she stuck her head into the office/out of the window elle a passé la tête dans le bureau/par la fenêtre; I had to ~ my fingers down my throat il a fallu que je me mette les doigts dans la bouche || [put casually] *inf* mettre, ficher; mix it all together and ~ it in the oven mélangez bien (le tout) et mettez au four; can you ~ my name on the list? tu peux ajouter mon nom sur la liste? ❑ he can ~ the job!▽ *Br* il sait où il peut se le mettre, son boulot!; ~ it!▽ tu peux te le mettre où je pense OR quelque part! -**3.** [fasten] fixer; [pin up] punaiser; she stuck the broom head on the handle elle a fixé la brosse à balai au manche; it was stuck on the noticeboard with tacks c'était punaisé au tableau d'affichage. -**4.** [with adhesive] coller; help me ~ this vase together aide-moi à recoller le vase; to ~ a stamp on an envelope coller un timbre sur une enveloppe; he had posters stuck to the walls with Sellotape il avait scotché des posters aux murs; '~ no bills' 'défense d'afficher'. -**5.** [kill - pig] égorger; to squeal like a stuck pig crier comme un cochon qu'on égorge. -**6.** *inf Br* [bear - person, situation] supporter; I don't know how you've stuck it for so long je ne sais pas comment tu as fait pour supporter ça si longtemps; I can't ~ him je ne peux pas le sentir; what I can't ~ is her telling me how to run my life ce que je ne supporte pas c'est qu'elle me dise comment je dois vivre; I'm amazed she stuck a term, let alone three years je suis étonné qu'elle ait tenu (le coup) un trimestre, et à plus forte raison trois ans. -**7.** *inf* [with chore, burden]: to ~ sb with a fine/the blame coller une amende/faire endosser la responsabilité à qqn; I always get stuck with the dishes je me retrouve toujours avec la vaisselle sur les bras, c'est toujours moi qui dois me taper la vaisselle. -**8.** *inf Am* [give injection to] faire une piqûre à, piquer.
◇ *vi* -**1.** [arrow, dart, spear] se planter; I've got a splinter stuck in my finger je me suis planté une écharde dans le doigt; you'll find some tacks already ~ing in the notice-board vous trouverez quelques punaises déjà plantées dans le tableau d'affichage. -**2.** [attach, adhere - wet clothes, bandage, chewing gum] coller; [- gummed label, stamp] tenir, coller; [- burr] s'accrocher; the dough stuck to my fingers la pâte collait à mes doigts; the damp has made the stamps ~ together l'humidité a collé les timbres les uns aux autres; the dust will ~ to the wet varnish la poussière va coller sur le vernis frais; a butterfly had got stuck to the flypaper un papillon était venu se coller au papier tue-mouches; these badges ~ to any surface ces autocollants adhèrent sur toutes les surfaces; food won't ~ to these pans ces casseroles n'attachent pas; they had straw ~ing in their hair ils avaient des brins de paille dans les cheveux; the noodles had got all stuck together les nouilles avaient collé OR étaient toutes collées; have some porridge! that'll ~ to your ribs! *inf Br* prends du porridge, ça tient au corps! -**3.** [become jammed, wedged - mechanism, drawer, key] se coincer, se bloquer; the lorry stuck fast in the mud le camion s'est complètement enlisé dans la boue; he tried to wriggle out but his shoulders got stuck il a essayé de se libérer en se tortillant mais ses épaules sont restées bloquées; I have a fishbone stuck in my throat j'ai une arête (de poisson) coincée dans la gorge ❑ it ~s in my throat *inf* OR *Br* gullet *inf* ça me reste sur l'estomac OR en travers de la gorge; having to ask him for a loan really ~s in my throat ça me coûte vraiment d'avoir à lui demander un prêt. -**4.** [remain, keep] rester; they called him Boney as a child and the name stuck quand il était petit, on le surnommait Boney et le nom lui est resté; she has the kind of face that ~s in your memory elle a un visage qu'on n'oublie pas OR dont on se souvient; dates just never ~ in my head je n'ai vraiment pas la mémoire des dates; ~ close to the house restez près de la maison; his bodyguards ~ close to him at all times ses gardes du corps l'accompagnent

partout OR ne le quittent jamais d'une semelle; ~ to the main road suivez la route principale. -**5.** *inf* [be upheld]: **we know he's guilty, but will the charge ~?** nous savons qu'il est coupable, mais est-ce qu'un tribunal le condamnera?; **to make the charge** OR **charges ~** prouver la culpabilité de qqn; **the important thing now is to make the agreement ~** ce qui compte maintenant, c'est de faire respecter l'accord. -**6.** [extend, project]: **the antenna was ~ing straight up** l'antenne se dressait toute droite; **his ticket was ~ing out of his pocket** son billet sortait OR dépassait de sa poche; **one leg was ~ing out of the sheets** une jambe dépassait de sous les draps; **only her head was ~ing out of the water** seule sa tête sortait OR émergeait de l'eau. -**7.** [in card games]: (I) ~ j'arrête, je ne veux pas d'autre carte; **the dealer must ~ on** OR **with seventeen** le donneur doit s'arrêter à dix-sept.

◆ **sticks** *inf npl* [backwoods] cambrousse *f*; **they live way out in the ~s** ils habitent en pleine cambrousse.

◆ **stick around** *inf vi insep* [stay] rester (dans les parages); [wait] attendre; **~ around if you want, she'll be back in a little while** tu peux rester si tu veux, elle ne va pas tarder à rentrer; **I'm not ~ing around a moment longer!** je n'attendrai pas une minute de plus!

◆ **stick at** *vt insep* -**1.** to ~ at it *Br* [persevere] persévérer. -**2.** [stop]: **to ~ at nothing** ne reculer OR n'hésiter devant rien; **she'll ~ at nothing to get her way** elle ne reculera devant rien pour parvenir à ses fins.

◆ **stick away** *inf vt sep* -**1.** [put away] ranger. -**2.** [hide] planquer.

◆ **stick by** *vt insep* -**1.** [person] soutenir; **don't worry, I'll always ~ by you** sois tranquille, je serai toujours là pour te soutenir. -**2.** [one's decision] s'en tenir à; **I ~ by what I said** je maintiens ce que j'ai dit.

◆ **stick down** ◇ *vt sep* -**1.** [flap, envelope] coller. -**2.** *inf Br* [note down] noter; [scribble] griffonner. -**3.** *inf* [place] poser; **~ the box down in the corner** posez le carton dans le coin; **he stuck the plate down in front of me** il flanqua l'assiette devant moi.

◇ *vi insep* [flap, envelope] (se) coller.

◆ **stick in** ◇ *vt sep* -**1.** [nail, knife, spear] planter, enfoncer; [needle] piquer, enfoncer; [pole, shovel] enfoncer, planter; **he stuck the knife all the way in** il a enfoncé le couteau jusqu'au bout OR jusqu'à la garde; **she stuck the knife in again and again** elle donna plusieurs coups de couteau. -**2.** [insert - coin, bank card] insérer; [- electric plug] brancher; [- cork, sink plug] enfoncer; [- word, sentence] ajouter; **it's simple, just ~ the key in and turn** c'est très simple, il suffit d'insérer la clé et de tourner; **I stuck my hand in to test the water temperature** j'y ai plongé la main pour vérifier la température de l'eau; **he stuck his head in through the door** il passa la tête par la porte; **she's stuck in a lot of footnotes to give weight to her thesis** elle a ajouté un tas de notes pour donner du poids à sa thèse. -**3.** [glue in] coller; **there's not enough space to ~ in all these stamps/photos** il ne reste pas assez de place pour coller tous ces timbres/toutes ces photos.

◇ *vi insep* [dart, arrow, spear] se planter; **if the javelin doesn't ~ in the throw doesn't count** si le javelot ne se plante pas, le jet ne compte pas; **the last dart failed to ~ in** la dernière fléchette n'est pas restée plantée.

◆ **stick on** ◇ *vt sep* -**1.** [fasten on - gummed badge, label, stamp] coller; [- china handle] recoller; [- broom head] fixer. -**2.** *inf* [jacket, boots] enfiler; **he hurriedly stuck a hat on** il s'est collé en vitesse un chapeau sur la tête.

◇ *vi insep* coller, se coller; **the stamp won't ~ on** le timbre ne colle pas; **the patch ~s on when ironed** la pièce se colle au tissu quand on la repasse.

◆ **stick out** ◇ *vt sep* -**1.** [extend - hand, leg] tendre, allonger; [- feelers, head] sortir; **to ~ one's tongue out (at sb)** tirer la langue (à qqn); **he stuck his foot out to trip me up** il a allongé la jambe pour me faire un croche-pied; **I opened the window and stuck my head out** j'ai ouvert la fenêtre et j'ai passé la tête au dehors; **to ~ one's chest out** bomber le torse; **to ~ out one's lower lip** faire la moue. -**2.** *phr*: **to ~ it out** *inf* tenir le coup jusqu'au bout.

◇ *vi insep* -**1.** [protrude - nail, splinter] sortir; [- teeth] avancer; [- plant, shoot] pointer; [- ledge, balcony] être en saillie; **his belly stuck out over his belt** son ventre débordait au-dessus de sa ceinture; **her ears ~ out** elle a les oreilles décollées; **my feet stuck out over the end of the bed** mes pieds dépassaient du lit; **the front of the car stuck out of the garage** l'avant de la voiture dépassait du garage. -**2.** [be noticeable - colour] ressortir; **the red Mercedes really ~s out** on ne voit que la Mercedes rouge; **I don't like to ~ out in a crowd** je n'aime pas me singulariser OR me faire remarquer; **it's her accent that makes her ~ out** c'est à cause de son accent qu'on la remarque.

◆ **stick out for** *vt insep* s'obstiner à vouloir, exiger; **the union is ~ing out for a five per cent rise** le syndicat continue à revendiquer une augmentation de cinq pour cent; **after ~ing out for higher quotas, they had to settle for last year's levels** après s'être battus pour obtenir une augmentation des quotas, ils ont dû se contenter de ceux de l'année dernière.

◆ **stick to** *vt insep*: **it won't be easy to ~ to this schedule** ce ne sera pas facile de tenir OR respecter ce planning; **I can never ~ to diets** je n'arrive jamais à suivre un régime longtemps; **we must ~ to our plan** nous devons continuer à suivre notre plan; **once I make a decision I ~ to it** une fois que j'ai pris une décision, je m'y tiens OR je n'en démords pas; **to ~ to one's word** OR **promises** tenir (sa) parole; **to ~ to one's principles** rester fidèle à ses principes; **~ as close to the truth as possible** restez aussi près que possible de la vérité; **she's still ~ing to her story** elle maintient ce qu'elle a dit; **~ to the point!** ne vous éloignez pas du sujet!; **~ to the facts!** tenez-vous-en aux faits!; **can we ~ to the business in hand?** peut-être pourrions-nous en finir avec les digressions?; **the author would be better off ~ing to journalism** l'auteur ferait mieux de se cantonner au journalisme.

◆ **stick together** *inf vi insep* [people] rester ensemble; **we'd better ~ together** il vaut mieux que nous restions ensemble, il vaut mieux ne pas nous séparer; **we'll get through the bad time if we ~ together** *fig* on sortira de cette mauvaise passe si on se serre les coudes.

◆ **stick up** ◇ *vt sep* -**1.** [sign, notice, poster] afficher; [postcard] coller; [with drawing pins] punaiser. -**2.** [raise - pole] dresser; **~ the target back up** redressez la cible; **to ~ one's hand up** lever la main ▫ **~ 'em up!** *inf* haut les mains! -**3.** *inf Am* [rob - person, bank, supermarket] braquer.

◇ *vi insep* [point upwards - tower, antenna] s'élever; [- plant shoots] pointer; **I saw a chimney ~ing up in the distance** j'ai vu une cheminée qui s'élevait au loin; **a branch was ~ing up out of the water** une branche sortait de l'eau.

◆ **stick up for** *vt insep*: **to ~ up for sb** prendre la défense OR le parti de qqn; **~ up for yourself!** ne te laisse pas faire!; **he has trouble ~ing up for himself/his rights** il a du mal à défendre ses intérêts/à faire valoir ses droits.

◆ **stick with** *vt insep* -**1.** [activity, subject] s'en tenir à, persister dans; **now I've started the job, I'm going to ~ with it** maintenant que j'ai commencé ce travail, je ne le lâche pas. -**2.** [person]: **~ with me, kid, and you'll be all right** *inf* reste auprès de moi, petit, et tout ira bien.

sticker ['stɪkəʳ] *n* -**1.** [adhesive label] autocollant *m*. -**2.** *inf* [determined person]: **she's a ~** elle est persévérante, elle va au bout de ce qu'elle entreprend.

stick figure *n personnage dessiné à l'aide de bâtonnets.*

stickiness ['stɪkɪnɪs] *n* -**1.** [of hands, substance, surface, jamjar] caractère *m* gluant OR poisseux. -**2.** [of weather, climate] moiteur *f*, humidité *f*.

sticking plaster ['stɪkɪŋ-] *n Br* pansement *m*, sparadrap *m*.

sticking point *n fig* point *m* de friction.

stick insect *n* phasme *m*.

stick-in-the-mud *inf n* [fogey] vieux croûton *m*; [killjoy] rabat-joie *m inv*; **don't be such a ~!** ne sois pas rabat-joie!

stickleback ['stɪklbæk] *n* épinoche *f (de rivière)*.

stickler ['stɪkləʳ] *n*: **to be a ~ for** [regulations, discipline, good manners] être à cheval sur; [tradition, routine] insister sur.

stickman ['stɪkmæn] (*pl* **stickmen** [-men]) *n Am* -**1.** [croupier] croupier *m*. -**2.** SPORT [hockey player] hockeyeur *m*, joueur *m* de hockey; [lacrosse player] joueur *m* de lacrosse; [billiard player] joueur *m* de billard. -**3.** = **stick figure**.

stick-on *adj* autocollant.

stickpin ['stɪkpɪn] *n Am* épingle *f* de cravate.

stick shift *n Am* AUT levier *m* de vitesse; **I don't know how to drive a ~** je ne sais pas conduire une voiture à vitesses manuelles.

stick-up *inf n Am* braquage *m*, hold-up *m*; **this is a ~!** c'est un hold-up!

sticky ['stɪkɪ] (*compar* **stickier**, *superl* **stickiest**) *adj* -**1.** [adhesive] adhésif, gommé; **~ tape** ruban *m* adhésif. -**2.** [tacky, gluey - hands, fingers] collant, poisseux; [- substance, surface, jamjar] gluant, poisseux; **his mouth was all ~ with jam** il avait la bouche poisseuse de confiture; **to have ~ fingers** *literal* avoir les doigts collants OR poisseux; *fig inf* être porté sur la fauche. -**3.** [sweaty] moite. -**4.** [humid - weather] moite, humide; **it was a hot, ~ afternoon** c'était un après-midi chaud et moite. -**5.** *inf* [awkward - situation] difficile, délicat; **to be (batting) on a ~ wicket** *Br* être dans une situation difficile; **to come to a ~ end** *Br* mal finir.

sticky-fingered *inf adj*: **to be ~** être porté sur la fauche.

stiff [stɪf] ◇ *adj* -**1.** [rigid] raide, rigide; **~ paper/cardboard** papier/carton rigide; **a ~ brush** une brosse à poils durs; **to be ~ with terror** être glacé de terreur ▫ **as ~ as a poker** raide comme un piquet; **to keep a ~ upper lip** garder son flegme. -**2.** [thick, difficult to stir] ferme, consistant; **beat the mixture until it is ~** battez jusqu'à obtention d'une pâte consistante; **beat the eggwhites until ~** battre les blancs en neige jusqu'à ce qu'ils soient (bien) fermes. -**3.** [difficult to move] dur; **this door handle is very ~** cette poignée de porte est très dure; **the drawers have got a bit ~** les tiroirs sont devenus un peu durs à ouvrir. -**4.** [aching] courbaturé, raide; **I'm still ~ after playing squash the other day** j'ai encore des courbatures d'avoir joué au squash l'autre jour; **to have a ~ back** avoir mal au dos; **to have a ~ neck** avoir un OR le torticolis. -**5.** [over-formal - smile, welcome] froid; [- person, manners, behaviour] froid, guindé; [- style] guindé. -**6.** [difficult] dur, ardu; **to face ~ competition** avoir affaire à forte concurrence; **it will be a ~ match** la partie sera dure; **competition for university places is getting ~er** la compétition pour les places à l'université devient de plus en plus acharnée. -**7.** [severe] sévère; **a ~ sentence** une condamnation sévère, une lourde condamnation; **I sent them a ~ letter** je leur ai envoyé une lettre bien sentie. -**8.** [strong - breeze, drink] fort; **she poured herself a ~ whisky** elle s'est versé un whisky bien tassé. -**9.** [high - price, bill] élevé. -**10.** [determined - resistance, opposition] tenace, acharné; [- resolve] ferme, inébranlable. -**11.** *inf Br* [full] plein (à craquer); **the place was ~ with men in suits** l'endroit était plein de messieurs en costume.

◇ *adv inf*: **to be bored ~** mourir d'ennui; **to be worried/scared ~** être mort d'inquiétude/de peur.

◇ *n* ▽ [corpse] macchabée *m*.

stiffen ['stɪfn] ◇ *vt* -**1.** [paper, fabric] raidir, renforcer. -**2.** [thicken - batter, dough, concrete]

donner de la consistance à; [- sauce] lier. -**3.** [make painful - arm, leg, muscle] courbaturer; **his joints had become ~ed by arthritis** ses articulations s'étaient raidies à cause de l'arthrite. -**4.** [strengthen - resistance, resolve] renforcer.
◇ *vi* -**1.** [harden - paper, fabric] devenir raide OR rigide. -**2.** [tense, stop moving] se raidir; **everybody in the room suddenly ~ed** tout à coup, tout le monde dans la pièce retint son souffle OR s'immobilisa. -**3.** [thicken - batter, dough, concrete] épaissir, devenir ferme; [- sauce] se lier. -**4.** [become hard to move - hinge, handle, door] se coincer. -**5.** [start to ache] s'ankyloser. -**6.** [strengthen - resistance, resolve] se renforcer; [- breeze] forcir.

stiffener ['stɪfnəʳ] *n* -**1.** [in collar] baleine *f*. -**2.** *inf Br* [drink] remontant *m*.

stiffening ['stɪfnɪŋ] *n* renforcement *m*.

stiffly ['stɪflɪ] *adv* -**1.** [rigidly]: **~ starched** très empesé OR amidonné; **they stood ~ to attention** ils se tenaient raides au garde-à-vous. -**2.** [painfully - walk, bend] avec raideur. -**3.** [coldly - smile, greet] froidement, d'un air distant.

stiff-necked *adj* opiniâtre, entêté, intraitable.

stiffness ['stɪfnɪs] *n* -**1.** [of paper, fabric] raideur *f*, rigidité *f*. -**2.** [of batter, dough, concrete] consistance *f*, fermeté *f*. -**3.** [of hinge, handle, door] dureté *f*. -**4.** [of joints, limbs] raideur *f*, courbatures *fpl*. -**5.** [of manners, smile, welcome] froideur *f*, distance *f*; [of style] caractère *m* guindé. -**6.** [difficulty - of exam, competition] difficulté *f*, dureté *f*. -**7.** [severity - of sentence, warning] sévérité *f*. -**8.** [determination - of resistance] ténacité *f*, acharnement *m*; [- of resolve] fermeté *f*.

stifle ['staɪfl] ◇ *vt* -**1.** [suppress - resistance, creativity, progress] réprimer, étouffer; [- tears, anger, emotion] réprimer; **to ~ a cough** réprimer une envie de tousser; **I tried to ~ my laughter/a yawn** j'ai essayé de ne pas rire/bailler. -**2.** [suffocate] étouffer, suffoquer.
◇ *vi* étouffer, suffoquer.

stifling ['staɪflɪŋ] *adj* suffocant, étouffant; **open the window, it's ~ in here!** ouvre la fenêtre, on étouffe ici!; **it was a ~ hot day** ce fut une journée étouffante de chaleur.

stigma ['stɪgmə] *n* -**1.** [social disgrace] honte *f*; **the ~ attached to having been in prison** l'opprobe qui ne quitte pas ceux qui ont fait de la prison. -**2.** BOT, MED & ZOOL stigmate *m*.

stigmata [stɪg'mɑːtə] *npl* RELIG stigmates *mpl*.

stigmatism ['stɪgmətɪzm] *n* OPT stigmatisme *m*.

stigmatize, -ise ['stɪgmətaɪz] *vt* stigmatiser.

stile [staɪl] *n* -**1.** [over fence] échalier *m*. -**2.** [turnstile] tourniquet *m*. -**3.** CONSTR [upright] montant *m*.

stiletto [stɪ'letəʊ] (*pl* **stilettos**) *n* -**1.** [heel] talon *m* aiguille. -**2.** [knife] stylet *m*.
◆ **stilettos** *npl* (chaussures *fpl* à) talons *mpl* aiguilles.

stiletto heel *n* talon *m* aiguille.

still[1] [stɪl] *adv* -**1.** [as of this moment] encore, toujours; **is it ~ raining?** est-ce qu'il pleut encore OR toujours?; **we're ~ waiting for the repairman to come** nous attendons toujours que le réparateur vienne; **there's ~ a bit of cake left** il reste encore un morceau de gâteau; **the worst was ~ to come** le pire n'était pas encore arrivé. -**2.** [all the same] quand même; **it's certainly difficult, but it's ~ better than my last job** c'est difficile, c'est sûr, mais c'est quand même mieux que mon dernier emploi; **whatever she's done, she's ~ your mother** quoi qu'elle ait fait, c'est quand même ta mère; **it's a shame we lost — ~, it was a good game** (c'est) dommage que nous ayons perdu — quand même, c'était un bon match; **~ and all** *inf* quand même. -**3.** *(with comparatives)* [even, yet] encore; **~ more/less** encore plus/moins; **~ further, further ~** encore plus loin; **the sea was getting ~ rougher** la mer était de plus en plus agitée.

still[2] [stɪl] ◇ *adj* -**1.** [motionless - person, object, air, surface] immobile; **her eyes were never ~** ses yeux ne restaient jamais immobiles; **be ~!** arrête de remuer! ❑ **~ waters run deep** *prov* méfie-toi de l'eau qui dort *prov*. -**2.** [calm] calme, tranquille; [quiet] silencieux; **a ~ night** une nuit calme. -**3.** [not fizzy] plat; **~ mineral water** eau *f* minérale non gazeuse OR plate.
◇ *adv* sans bouger; **stand ~!** ne bougez pas!; **my heart stood ~** mon cœur a cessé de battre; **they're so excited they can't sit ~** ils sont tellement excités qu'ils ne peuvent pas rester en place; **try to hold the camera ~** essaie de ne pas bouger l'appareil photo.
◇ *vt lit* -**1.** [silence] faire taire; **the voices of protest had been ~ed** on avait fait taire les contestataires. -**2.** [allay - doubts, fears] apaiser, calmer.
◇ *n* -**1.** *lit* [silence] silence *m*; **in the ~ of the night** dans le silence de la nuit. -**2.** CIN photo *f* (de plateau); **~ photographer** photographe *mf* de plateau. -**3.** [apparatus] alambic *m*.

stillbirth ['stɪlbɜːθ] *n* [birth] mort *f* à la naissance; [fœtus] enfant *m* mort-né, enfant *f* mort-née.

stillborn ['stɪlbɔːn] *adj* -**1.** MED mort-né. -**2.** *fig* [idea, plan] avorté.

still life (*pl* **still lifes**) *n* nature *f* morte.

stillness ['stɪlnɪs] *n* -**1.** [motionlessness] immobilité *f*. -**2.** [calm] tranquillité *f*, paix *f*.

stilt [stɪlt] *n* -**1.** [for walking] échasse *f*; **to walk on ~s** marcher sur des échasses. -**2.** ARCHIT pilotis *m*.

stilted ['stɪltɪd] *adj* [speech, writing, person] guindé, emprunté; [discussion] qui manque de naturel.

Stilton® ['stɪltn] *n* stilton *m*, fromage *m* de Stilton.

stimulant ['stɪmjʊlənt] ◇ *n* stimulant *m*; **devaluation acts as a ~ to exports** la dévaluation stimule les exportations.
◇ *adj* stimulant.

stimulate ['stɪmjʊleɪt] *vt* stimuler; **the bracing sea air ~d me** l'air de la mer m'a revigoré; **to ~ sb to do sthg** inciter OR encourager qqn à faire qqch; **sexually ~d** excité (sexuellement).

stimulating ['stɪmjʊleɪtɪŋ] *adj* -**1.** [medicine, drug] stimulant. -**2.** [work, conversation, experience] stimulant, enrichissant; **intellectually ~** intellectuellement stimulant.

stimulation [,stɪmjʊ'leɪʃn] *n* -**1.** [of person] stimulation *f*. -**2.** [stimulus] stimulant *m*.

stimulus ['stɪmjʊləs] (*pl* **stimuli** [-laɪ, -liː]) *n* -**1.** [incentive] stimulant *m*, incitation *f*; **her example will be a powerful ~ to others** son exemple sera un stimulant extrêmement efficace pour d'autres. -**2.** PHYSIOL stimulus *m*.

sting [stɪŋ] (*pt* & *pp* **stung** [stʌŋ]) ◇ *vt* -**1.** [subj: insect, nettle, scorpion] piquer; [subj: smoke] piquer, brûler; [subj: vinegar, acid, disinfectant] brûler; [subj: whip, rain] cingler; **the smoke stung my eyes** la fumée me brûlait OR me piquait les yeux. -**2.** [subj: remark, joke, criticism] piquer (au vif), blesser; **she was stung by their sharp criticisms** leurs critiques acérées l'ont piquée au vif; **our comments might ~ them into doing something** nos remarques les inciteront peut-être à faire quelque chose. -**3.** *inf* [cheat] arnaquer; **they stung me for £20** ils m'ont arnaqué de 20 livres.
◇ *vi* -**1.** [insect, nettle, scorpion] piquer; [vinegar, acid, disinfectant] brûler, piquer; [whip, rain] cingler. -**2.** [eyes, skin] piquer, brûler; **my eyes are ~ing** j'ai les yeux qui piquent.
◇ *n* -**1.** [organ - of bee, wasp, scorpion] aiguillon *m*, dard *m*; [- of nettle] poil *m* (urticant); **there's a ~ in the tail** *Br* il y a une mauvaise surprise à la fin; **his remarks often have a ~ in the tail** ses remarques sont rarement innocentes; **to take the ~ out of sthg** rendre qqch moins douloureux, adoucir qqch. -**2.** [wound, pain, mark - from insect, nettle, scorpion] piqûre *f*; [- from vinegar, acid, disinfectant] brûlure *f*; [- from whip] douleur *f* cinglante. -**3.** *inf* [trick] arnaque *f*; **'The Sting'** *Hill* 'l'Arnaque'.

stingily ['stɪndʒɪlɪ] *adv* [give, serve out, behave] chichement.

stinginess ['stɪndʒɪnɪs] *n* [of person, behaviour] avarice *f*, pingrerie *f*; [of amount, helping] insuffisance *f*.

stinging ['stɪŋɪŋ] *adj* -**1.** [wound, pain] cuisant; [bite, eyes] qui pique; [lash, rain] cinglant. -**2.** [remark, joke, criticism] cinglant, mordant.

stinging nettle *n* ortie *f*.

stingray ['stɪŋreɪ] *n* pastenague *f*.

stingy ['stɪndʒɪ] *adj* [person] chiche; [amount, helping] misérable; **he's too ~ with his money** il est trop avare; **they're never ~ about food** ils ne lésinent jamais sur la nourriture.

stink [stɪŋk] (*pt* **stank** [stæŋk], *pp* **stunk** [stʌŋk])
◇ *vi* -**1.** [smell] puer, empester; **the room stank of cigarette smoke** la pièce puait OR empestait la fumée de cigarette. -**2.** *inf* [be bad]: **I think your idea ~s!** je trouve ton idée nulle!; **this town ~s!** cette ville est pourrie!
◇ *n* -**1.** [stench] puanteur *f*, odeur *f* nauséabonde; **what a ~!** qu'est-ce que ça pue! -**2.** *inf* [fuss] esclandre *m*; **to kick up** OR **to make** OR **to raise a ~ about sthg** faire un esclandre OR un scandale à propos de qqch.
◆ **stink out** *inf vt sep* -**1.** [drive away] chasser par la mauvaise odeur. -**2.** [fill with a bad smell] empester; **your cigar's ~ing the whole house out!** ton cigare empeste toute la maison!

stink-bomb *n* boule *f* puante.

stinker *inf* ['stɪŋkəʳ] *n* -**1.** [person] peau *f* de vache. -**2.** [unpleasant thing]: **the exam was a real ~!** cet examen était vraiment vache!; **today's crossword's a ~** les mots croisés d'aujourd'hui sont vraiment coriaces; **I've got a ~ of a cold** j'ai un rhume carabiné.

stinkhorn ['stɪŋkhɔːn] *n* BOT phallus *m* impudique, satyre *m* puant.

stinking ['stɪŋkɪŋ] ◇ *adj* -**1.** [smelly] puant, nauséabond. -**2.** *inf* [as intensifier]: **I'm tired of seeing this ~ mess all the time!** j'en ai assez de voir tout le temps cette pagaille OR ce bazar!; **I've got a ~ cold** j'ai un rhume carabiné.
◇ *adv inf* vachement; **to be ~ drunk** être soûl comme un cochon; **to be ~ rich** être plein de fric OR plein aux as.

stint [stɪnt] ◇ *n* -**1.** [period of work] période *f* de travail; [share of work] part *f* de travail; **she did a ~ in Africa/as a teacher** elle a travaillé pendant un certain temps en Afrique/comme professeur; **we expect everybody to do their ~** nous attendons de chacun qu'il fournisse sa part du travail; **I'll take** OR **I'll do another ~ at the wheel** je vais reprendre le volant. -**2.** *fml* [limitation]: **without ~** [spend] sans compter; [give] généreusement; [work] inlassablement.
◇ *vt Br* -**1.** [skimp on] lésiner sur; **don't ~ the cream** ne lésine pas sur la crème. -**2.** [deprive] priver; **he's incapable of ~ing himself of anything** il est incapable de se priver de quoi que ce soit.
◇ *vi Br*: **to ~ on sthg** lésiner sur qqch.

stipend ['staɪpend] *n* traitement *m*, appointements *mpl*.

stipendiary [staɪ'pendjərɪ] (*pl* **stipendiaries**)
◇ *adj* [work, person] rémunéré.
◇ *n* [clergyman] *prêtre percevant un traitement*; [magistrate] *juge d'un tribunal de police correctionnelle*.

stipple ['stɪpl] *vt* -**1.** [apply - paint] pointiller. -**2.** [mark - cement, wet paint] granuler.

stippled ['stɪpld] *adj* tacheté, moucheté; **~ with yellow** tacheté OR moucheté de jaune.

stipulate ['stɪpjʊleɪt] ◇ *vt* stipuler; **please ~ the quantity on your order form** veuillez stipuler la quantité sur votre commande; **the contract ~s that the work must be finished by March** le contrat stipule que le travail doit être terminé d'ici le mois de mars.
◇ *vi fml*: **to ~ for sthg** stipuler qqch; **the sum of money ~d for** la somme stipulée.

stipulation [,stɪpjʊ'leɪʃn] *n* stipulation *f*; **they accepted, but with the ~ that the time limit be extended** ils ont accepté sous réserve que les délais soient prolongés.

stir [stɜːʳ] (*pt* & *pp* **stirred**, *cont* **stirring**)
◇ *vt* -**1.** [mix] remuer, tourner; **your tea is**

sugared but not stirred ton thé est sucré mais il faut le remuer; ~ the flour into the sauce incorporez la farine à la sauce en remuant. -**2.** [move] agiter, remuer; **a light breeze stirred the leaves** une brise légère agitait les feuilles ❑ **~ yourself** OR **your stumps** *inf*, **it's time to go!** *Br* grouille-toi, il est l'heure de partir! -**3.** [touch] émouvoir; **his story has stirred us deeply** son histoire nous a profondément émus. -**4.** [rouse, excite] éveiller, exciter; **to ~ sb's curiosity/sympathy** éveiller la curiosité/ sympathie de qqn; **to ~ sb to do sthg** inciter OR pousser qqn à faire qqch; **to ~ sb into action** pousser qqn à agir.
◇ *vi* -**1.** [move - person] bouger, remuer; [- leaves] remuer; **I shan't ~ from my bed until midday** je ne bougerai pas de mon lit avant midi. -**2.** [awaken, be roused - feeling, anger] s'éveiller; **a mood of nationalism was stirring in the country** un sentiment nationaliste s'éveillait dans le pays. -**3.** *inf* [cause trouble] faire de la provocation OR des histoires.
◇ *n* -**1.** [act of mixing]: **to give sthg a ~** remuer qqch; **the sauce needs a ~** il faudrait remuer la sauce. -**2.** [commotion] émoi *m*, agitation *f*; **to cause** OR **to create** OR **to make quite a ~** soulever un vif émoi, faire grand bruit; **there was a big ~ about** OR **over the unemployment figures** les chiffres du chômage ont soulevé un vif émoi. -**3.** [movement] mouvement *m*; **a ~ of excitement** un frisson d'excitation. -**4.** *prison sl* [prison] taule *f*.
◆ **stir in** *vt sep* CULIN ajouter OR incorporer en remuant.
◆ **stir up** *vt sep* -**1.** [disturb - dust, mud] soulever. -**2.** [incite, provoke - trouble] provoquer; [- emotions] exciter, attiser; [- dissent] fomenter; [- memories] réveiller; [- crowd, followers] ameuter; **he likes stirring it** OR **things up** il aime provoquer. -**3.** *lit* [fire] attiser, tisonner.

stir-fry ◇ *vt* CULIN faire sauter à feu vif *(tout en remuant)*.
◇ *adj* sauté; **~ pork** porc sauté.

stirrer ['stɜːrəʳ] *n* -**1.** *inf* [troublemaker] provocateur *m*, -trice *f*. -**2.** [implement] fouet *m* CULIN.

stirring ['stɜːrɪŋ] ◇ *adj* [music, song] entraînant; [story] excitant, passionnant; [speech] vibrant.
◇ *n*: **he felt vague ~s of guilt** il éprouva un vague sentiment de culpabilité; **the first ~s of what was to become the Romantic movement** les premières manifestations de ce qui allait devenir le mouvement romantique.

stirrup ['stɪrəp] *n* EQUIT étrier *m*; **to put one's feet in the ~s** chausser les étriers.
◆ **stirrups** *npl* MED étriers *mpl*.

stirrup cup *n* coup *m* de l'étrier.

stirrup leather *n* étrivière *f*.

stirrup pump *n* seau-pompe *m*.

stitch [stɪtʃ] ◇ *n* -**1.** SEW point *m*; [in knitting] maille *f*; **to drop a ~** sauter une maille; **to pick up a ~** reprendre une maille ❑ **I didn't have a ~ (of clothing) on** *inf* j'étais nu comme un ver, j'étais dans le plus simple appareil; **a ~ in time saves nine** *prov* un point à temps en vaut cent *prov*. -**2.** MED point *m* de suture; **she had to have ten ~es in her face** il a fallu lui faire dix points de suture au visage; **I'm having my ~es taken out tomorrow** on m'ôte les fils demain. -**3.** [pain] point *m* de côté; **to get a ~** attraper un point de côté. -**4.** *phr*: **to be in ~es** *inf* se tordre OR être écroulé de rire; **his story had us in ~es** son histoire nous a fait pleurer de rire.
◇ *vt* -**1.** [material, shirt, hem] coudre; **he ~ed the button back on his shirt** il a recousu son bouton de chemise. -**2.** MED suturer. -**3.** [in bookbinding] brocher.
◆ **stitch down** *vt sep* rabattre.
◆ **stitch up** *vt sep* -**1.** [material, shirt, hem] coudre. -**2.** MED suturer. -**3.** *inf* [deal] conclure, sceller. -**4.** *inf* [frame - person]: **he reckons the police ~ed him up** il pense que la police a monté un coup contre lui.

stitching ['stɪtʃɪŋ] *n* -**1.** [gen] couture *f*; **the ~'s coming undone** la couture se défait. -**2.** [in bookbinding] brochage *m*.

stoat [stəʊt] *n* hermine *f*.

stochastic [stɒ'kæstɪk] *adj* stochastique.

stock [stɒk] ◇ *n* -**1.** [supply] réserve *f*, provision *f*, stock *m*; COMM & INDUST stock *m*; **we got in a ~ of food** nous avons fait tout un stock de nourriture; **huge ~s of nuclear weapons** d'énormes stocks d'armes nucléaires; **she always has a wonderful ~ of funny stories** elle a toujours un tas d'histoires drôles en réserve; **in ~** en stock, en magasin; **out of ~** épuisé; **I'm afraid we're out of ~** je regrette, nous n'en avons plus en stock ❑ **to take ~** *literal* faire l'inventaire; *fig* faire le point; **we took ~ of the situation** nous avons fait le point de la situation. -**2.** [total amount] parc *m*; **the housing ~** le parc de logements. -**3.** *(usu pl)* ST. EX [gen] valeur *f* mobilière; [share] action *f*; [bond] obligation *f*; **mining ~s are falling** les actions minières sont en baisse; **to invest in ~s and shares** investir dans des actions et obligations OR en portefeuille; **government ~s** obligations *fpl* OR titres *mpl* d'État. -**4.** FIN [equity] capital *m*; **he already owns 27% of the company's ~** il possède déjà 27 % du capital de la société. -**5.** *fig* [value, credit] cote *f*; **the Prime Minister's ~ is rising/falling** la cote du Premier ministre est en hausse/en baisse; **to put ~ in sthg** faire (grand) cas de qqch; **I don't put much ~ in this new system** je ne suis pas très convaincu par ce nouveau système. -**6.** [descent, ancestry] souche *f*, lignée *f*; **of peasant/noble ~** de souche paysanne/noble. -**7.** AGR [animals] cheptel *m*. -**8.** CULIN bouillon *m*; **vegetable ~** bouillon de légumes. -**9.** [handle, butt - of gun, plough] fût *m*; [- of whip] manche *m*; [- of fishing rod] gaule *f*. -**10.** BOT giroflée *f*. -**11.** [tree trunk] tronc *m*; [tree stump] souche *f*. -**12.** HORT [stem receiving graft] porte-greffe *m*, sujet *m*; [plant from which graft is taken] plante *f* mère *(sur laquelle on prélève un greffon)*. -**13.** [in card games, dominoes] talon *m*, pioche *f*. -**14.** THEAT répertoire *m*. -**15.** [neckcloth] lavallière *f*, foulard *m*; **riding ~** col-cravate *m*.
◇ *vt* -**1.** COMM [have in stock] avoir (en stock), vendre; **I'm afraid we don't ~ that item any more** je regrette, mais nous ne vendons plus OR nous ne faisons plus cet article. -**2.** [supply] approvisionner; [fill] remplir; **they have a well ~ed cellar** ils ont une cave bien approvisionnée; **we ~ed the fridge with food** nous avons rempli le frigo de nourriture. -**3.** [stream, lake] empoissonner; [farm] monter en bétail.
◇ *adj* -**1.** [common, typical - phrase, expression] tout fait; [- question, answer, excuse] classique. -**2.** COMM [kept in stock] en stock; [widely available] courant; **the sale of ~ goods** la liquidation du stock; **available in all ~ sizes** disponible dans toutes les tailles courantes. -**3.** AGR [for breeding] destiné à la reproduction. -**4.** THEAT [play] du répertoire.
◆ **stocks** *npl* -**1.** [instrument of punishment] pilori *m*; **sentenced to the ~s** condamné au pilori. -**2.** NAUT [frame] cale *f*; **on the ~s** en chantier.
◆ **stock up** ◇ *vi insep* s'approvisionner; **to ~ up on** OR **with sthg** s'approvisionner en qqch.
◇ *vt sep* approvisionner, garnir.

stockade [stɒ'keɪd] ◇ *n* -**1.** [enclosure] palissade *f*. -**2.** *Am* MIL [prison] prison *f* (militaire).
◇ *vt* palissader.

stockbreeder ['stɒk,briːdəʳ] *n* éleveur *m*, -euse *f* de bétail.

stockbreeding ['stɒk,briːdɪŋ] *n* élevage *m* de bétail.

stockbroker ['stɒk,brəʊkəʳ] *n* agent *m* de change.

stockbroker belt *n*: **the ~** *partie de la banlieue sud de Londres où habitent les agents de change et autres personnes du même milieu socio-professionnel*.

stockbroking ['stɒk,brəʊkɪŋ] *n* commerce *m* des valeurs en Bourse.

stockbuild ['stɒkbɪld] *vi*: **CWX have been ~ing in Gomez for several months** cela fait plusieurs mois que CWX accumule des actions de Gomez.

stockbuilding ['stɒk,bɪldɪŋ] *n* achat *m* d'actions.

stock car *n* -**1.** AUT stock-car *m*; **~ racing** (courses *fpl* de) stock-car *m*. -**2.** *Am* RAIL wagon *m* à bestiaux.

stock certificate *n Am* titre *m* FIN.

stock company *n Am* -**1.** FIN société *f* anonyme par actions. -**2.** THEAT troupe *f* de répertoire.

stock cube *n* bouillon *m* Kub®.

stock exchange *n* Bourse *f*; **he lost a fortune on the ~** il a perdu une fortune à la Bourse.
◆ **stock-exchange** *comp* boursier, de la Bourse; **~ prices** cours *m* des actions.

stock farm *n* élevage *m* (de bétail).

stock farming *n* élevage *m* (de bétail) *(activité)*.

stockfish ['stɒkfɪʃ] *n* stockfisch *m*, poisson *m* séché.

stockholder ['stɒk,həʊldəʳ] *n* actionnaire *mf*.

Stockholm ['stɒkhəʊm] *pr n* Stockholm.

stockily ['stɒkɪlɪ] *adv*: **~ built** trapu, râblé.

stockiness ['stɒkɪnɪs] *n* aspect *m* trapu OR râblé; **he inherited his ~ from his father** il a hérité de la silhouette trapue OR râblée de son père.

stockinet(te) [,stɒkɪ'net] *n* [fabric] jersey *m*; [stitch] point *m* de jersey.

stocking ['stɒkɪŋ] *n* -**1.** [for women] bas *m*; **silk ~s** bas *mpl* de soie; **~ mask** bas *m (utilisé par un bandit masqué)*. -**2.** *dated* [sock] bas *m* de laine; **in one's ~ feet** sans chaussures, en chaussettes.

stockinged ['stɒkɪŋd] *adj*: **in one's ~ feet** sans chaussures, en chaussettes.

stocking filler *n petit cadeau destiné à remplir le bas de laine à Noël*.

stocking stitch *n* point *m* de jersey.

stock-in-trade *n* -**1.** COMM marchandises *fpl* en stock OR en magasin. -**2.** *fig*: **charm is part of an actor's ~** le charme est l'un des outils du comédien.

stockist ['stɒkɪst] *n* stockiste *mf*.

stockjobber ['stɒk,dʒɒbəʳ] *n* -**1.** *Br* [wholesale dealer in stocks] *intermédiaire en Bourse qui traite directement avec les agents de change et non avec le public (cette fonction n'existe plus depuis 1987)*. -**2.** *Am pej* agent *m* de change.

stockkeeper ['stɒk,kiːpəʳ] *n* -**1.** [cowherd] vacher *m*, -ère *f*, bouvier *m*, -ère *f*. -**2.** *Am* [storekeeper] magasinier *m*, -ère *f*.

stockman ['stɒkmən] (*pl* **stockmen** [-mən]) *n* [cowherd] vacher *m*, -ère *f*, bouvier *m*, -ère *f*; [breeder] éleveur *m*, -euse *f* (de bétail).

stock market *n* Bourse *f* (des valeurs), marché *m* financier; **he lost a fortune on the ~** il a perdu une fortune à la Bourse; **the London ~ is rising** la Bourse de Londres est en hausse.
◆ **stock-market** *comp* boursier, de la Bourse; **the ~ crash** le krach boursier; **~ prices** cours *m* des actions.

stockpile ['stɒkpaɪl] ◇ *n* stock *m*, réserve *f*.
◇ *vt* [goods] stocker, constituer un stock de; [weapons] amasser, accumuler.
◇ *vi* faire des stocks.

stockpiling ['stɒkpaɪlɪŋ] *n*: **to accuse sb of ~** [food] accuser qqn de faire des réserves de nourriture; [weapon] accuser qqn de faire des réserves d'armes.

stockpot ['stɒkpɒt] *n* marmite *f (pour le bouillon)*.

stockroom ['stɒkrʊm] *n* magasin *m*, réserve *f*.

stock saddle *n Am* selle *f* de cow-boy.

stock-still *adv* (complètement) immobile; **she was standing ~ in the middle of the road** elle se tenait complètement immobile au milieu de la route.

stocktaking ['stɒk,teɪkɪŋ] *n* -**1.** COMM inventaire *m*; **'closed for ~'** 'fermé pour inventaire'. -**2.** *fig*: **the time has come for some long overdue ~** assez attendu! le moment est venu de faire le point.

stocky ['stɒkɪ] (*compar* **stockier**, *superl* **stockiest**) *adj* trapu, râblé.

stockyard ['stɒkjɑːd] *n* parc *m* à bestiaux.

stodge *inf* [stɒdʒ] *n Br (U)* -**1.** [food] aliments *mpl* bourratifs, étouffe-chrétien *m inv*; **the canteen food is pure ~** ce qu'on mange à la cantine est vraiment bourratif. -**2.** [writing] littérature *f* indigeste.

stodgy *inf* ['stɒdʒɪ] (*compar* **stodgier**, *superl* **stodgiest**) *adj* -**1.** [food, meal] bourratif, lourd. -**2.** [style] lourd, indigeste. -**3.** [person, manners, ideas] guindé.

stogie *inf*, **stogy** *inf* ['stəʊgɪ] (*pl* **stogies**) *n Am* cigare *m* bon marché.

stoic ['stəʊɪk] ◇ *adj* stoïque.
◇ *n* stoïque *mf*.
◆ **Stoic** *n* PHILOS stoïcien *m*, -enne *f*.

stoical ['stəʊɪkl] *adj* stoïque.

stoically ['stəʊɪklɪ] *adv* stoïquement, avec stoïcisme.

stoicism ['stəʊɪsɪzm] *n* stoïcisme *m*.
◆ **Stoicism** *n* PHILOS stoïcisme *m*.

stoke [stəʊk] *vt* -**1.** [fire, furnace] alimenter, entretenir; [locomotive, boiler] chauffer. -**2.** *fig* [emotions, feelings, anger] entretenir, alimenter.
◆ **stoke up** ◇ *vi insep* -**1.** [put fuel on - fire] alimenter le feu; [- furnace] alimenter la chaudière. -**2.** *inf Br* [fill one's stomach] s'empiffrer.
◇ *vt sep* = **stoke**.

stokehold ['stəʊkhəʊld] *n* NAUT chambre *f* de chauffe, chaufferie *f*.

stokehole ['stəʊkhəʊl] *n* -**1.** [in boiler, furnace] porte *f* de chauffe. -**2.** = **stokehold**.

stoker ['stəʊkəʳ] *n* chauffeur *m* OR chargeur *m* *(d'un four, d'une chaudière etc)*.

STOL [stɒl] (*abbr of* **short takeoff and landing**) *n* ADAC *m*.

stole [stəʊl] ◇ *pt* → **steal**.
◇ *n* -**1.** étole *f*, écharpe *f*; **mink ~** étole de OR en vison. -**2.** RELIG étole *f*.

stolen ['stəʊln] *pp* → **steal**.

stolid ['stɒlɪd] *adj* flegmatique, impassible.

stolidity [stɒ'lɪdətɪ] *n* flegme *m*, impassibilité *f*.

stolidly ['stɒlɪdlɪ] *adv* flegmatiquement, avec flegme, de manière impassible.

stoma ['stəʊmə] (*pl* **stomata** [-mətə]) *n* stomate *m*.

stomach ['stʌmək] ◇ *n* -**1.** [organ] estomac *m*; **to have an upset ~** avoir l'estomac barbouillé; **I can't work on an empty ~** je ne peux pas travailler l'estomac vide; **he has a cast-iron ~** il a l'estomac solide; **to have a pain in one's ~** avoir mal à l'estomac; [lower] avoir mal au ventre; **the sight was enough to turn your ~** le spectacle avait de quoi vous soulever le cœur ❑ **an army marches on its ~** une armée ne peut pas se battre l'estomac vide. -**2.** [region of body] ventre *m*; **he has a fat ~** il a du ventre; **lie on your ~** couchez-vous sur le ventre. -**3.** *(usu neg)* [desire, appetite] envie *f*, goût *m*; **she has no ~ for spicy food** elle supporte mal la cuisine épicée; **I've no ~ for his vulgar jokes this evening** je n'ai aucune envie d'écouter ses plaisanteries vulgaires ce soir.
◇ *vt* -**1.** [tolerate] supporter, tolérer; **I just can't ~ the thought of him being my boss** je ne supporte simplement pas l'idée qu'il soit mon patron. -**2.** [digest] digérer; **I can't ~ too much rich food** je ne digère pas bien la cuisine riche.
◇ *comp* [infection] de l'estomac, gastrique; [ulcer, operation] à l'estomac; [pain] à l'estomac, au ventre.

stomachache ['stʌməkeɪk] *n* mal *m* de ventre; **to have (a) ~** avoir mal au ventre; **don't eat so much, you'll get (a) ~** ne mange pas tant, ça va te donner mal au ventre.

stomachic [stə'mækɪk] *adj* stomachique, stomacal.

stomach pump *n* pompe *f* stomacale.

stomatitis [,stəʊmə'taɪtɪs] *n (U)* stomatite *f*.

stomatologist [,stəʊmə'tɒlədʒɪst] *n* stomatologiste *mf*, stomatologue *mf*.

stomatology [,stəʊmə'tɒlədʒɪ] *n* stomatologie *f*.

stomp *inf* [stɒmp] ◇ *vi* marcher d'un pas lourd; **he ~ed out of the room** il est sorti de la pièce d'un pas lourd.
◇ *n* -**1.** [tread] pas *m* lourd. -**2.** [dance] *jazz que l'on danse en frappant du pied pour marquer le rythme*.

stone [stəʊn] (*pl senses 1-6* **stones**, *pl sense 7 inv* OR **stones**) ◇ *n* -**1.** [material] pierre *f*; **the houses are built of ~** les maisons sont en pierre; **are you made of ~?** *fig* n'as-tu donc pas de cœur?; **a heart of ~** *fig* un cœur de pierre. -**2.** [piece of rock] pierre *f*, caillou *m*; [on beach] galet *m*; **they threw ~s at me** ils m'ont lancé des pierres; **to fall like a ~** tomber comme une pierre ❑ **to leave no ~ unturned** remuer ciel et terre; **we will leave no ~ unturned to find the culprits** nous remuerons ciel et terre pour retrouver les coupables; **it's within a ~'s throw of the countryside** c'est à deux pas de la campagne. -**3.** [memorial] stèle *f*, pierre *f*; **standing ~** menhir *m*. -**4.** [gem] pierre *f*; **precious ~** pierre précieuse. -**5.** MED calcul *m*; **he has a ~ in his kidney** il a un calcul rénal. -**6.** [in fruit] noyau *m*. -**7.** [unit of weight] ≃ 6 kg; **she weighs about 8 ~** OR **~s** elle pèse dans les 50 kilos.
◇ *adj* de OR en pierre; **a ~ jar** un pot de grès.
◇ *vt* -**1.** [fruit, olive] dénoyauter. -**2.** [person, car] jeter des pierres sur, bombarder de pierres; [as punishment] lapider. -**3.** *Br phr*: **~ the crows!** *inf*, **~ me!** *inf* mince alors!

Stone Age *n*: **the ~** l'âge *m* de (la) pierre.
◆ **Stone-Age** *comp* [man, dwelling, weapon] de l'âge de (la) pierre.

stone-blind *adj* complètement aveugle.

stonebreaker ['stəʊn,breɪkəʳ] *n* [person] casseur *m* de pierres; [machine] concasseur *m*.

stone-broke *inf* = **stony broke**.

stonechat ['stəʊntʃæt] *n* traquet *m* (pâtre).

stone-cold ◇ *adj* complètement froid.
◇ *adv inf*: **~ sober** pas du tout soûl.

stonecrop ['stəʊnkrɒp] *n* orpin *m*.

stonecutter ['stəʊn,kʌtəʳ] *n* -**1.** [person - of stone] tailleur *m* de pierre; [- of precious stones] lapidaire *m*. -**2.** [machine] lapidaire *m*.

stoned▽ [stəʊnd] *adj* [drunk] bourré, schlass; [drugged] défoncé.

stone-dead *adj* raide mort.

stone-deaf *adj* complètement sourd.

stone fruit *n Br* fruit *m* à noyau.

stone-ground *adj* moulu à la pierre.

stonemason ['stəʊn,meɪsn] *n* tailleur *m* de pierre.

stonewall [,stəʊn'wɔːl] *vi* -**1.** [filibuster] monopoliser la parole *(pour empêcher les autres de parler)*; [avoid questions] donner des réponses évasives. -**2.** SPORT jouer très prudemment, bétonner.

Stonewall [,stəʊn'wɔːl] *pr n Am* HIST Stonewall.

STONEWALL:
Terme faisant référence à un bar new-yorkais fréquenté par des homosexuels où, en 1969, les incessantes descentes de police provoquèrent des émeutes préludant à la naissance du mouvement pour l'égalité des droits des homosexuels.

---

stoneware ['stəʊnweəʳ] *n* (poterie *f* en) grès *m*.

stonewashed ['stəʊnwɒʃt] *adj* [jeans, denim] délavé *(avant l'achat)*.

stonework ['stəʊnwɜːk] *n* maçonnerie *f*, ouvrage *m* en pierre.

stonily ['stəʊnɪlɪ] *adv* froidement; **to look at sb ~** regarder qqn froidement.

stonker *inf* ['stɒŋkəʳ] *n*: **what a ~ of a goal!** quel but génial!

stony ['stəʊnɪ] (*compar* **stonier**, *superl* **stoniest**) *adj* -**1.** [covered with stones - ground, soil, road, land] pierreux, caillouteux, rocailleux; [- beach] de galets; **his requests fell on ~ ground** *fig* ses démarches n'ont rien donné. -**2.** [stone-like - texture, feel] pierreux. -**3.** [unfeeling] insensible; [look, silence] glacial; **a ~ heart** un cœur de pierre.

stony-broke *inf adj Br* fauché (comme les blés), à sec.

stony-faced *adj* au visage impassible.

stony-hearted *adj* au cœur de pierre.

stood [stʊd] *pt & pp* → **stand**.

stooge [stuːdʒ] *n* -**1.** *inf pej* larbin *m*, laquais *m*. -**2.** THEAT [straight man] faire-valoir *m inv*.

stook [stʊk] ◇ *n* moyette *f*.
◇ *vt* moyetter.

stool [stuːl] *n* -**1.** [seat] tabouret *m*; **bar/piano ~** tabouret de bar/de piano; **prayer ~** prie-Dieu *m inv*; **to fall between two ~s** *Br* être assis entre deux chaises. -**2.** MED selle *f*. -**3.** HORT [tree stump] souche *f*; [shoot] rejet *m* de souche; [base of plant] pied *m* de plante. -**4.** *Am* [windowsill] rebord *m* de fenêtre.

stoolie▽ ['stuːlɪ] *Am* indic *mf*.

stoolpigeon *inf* ['stuːl,pɪdʒɪn] *n* indicateur *m*, -trice *f*, indic *mf*, mouchard *m*, -e *f*.

stoop [stuːp] ◇ *vi* -**1.** [bend down] se baisser, se pencher; **she ~ed to pick up her pen** elle se baissa OR se pencha pour ramasser son stylo. -**2.** [stand, walk with a stoop] avoir le dos voûté. -**3.** [abase o.s.] s'abaisser; **I can't believe he ~ed to lying** je n'arrive pas à croire qu'il se soit abaissé à mentir; **she would ~ to anything** elle est prête à toutes les bassesses ❑ **'She Stoops to Conquer'** *Goldsmith* 'Elle s'abaisse pour triompher'. -**4.** [condescend] daigner; **she wouldn't ~ to doing the dirty work herself** elle ne s'abaisserait pas à faire elle-même le sale travail. -**5.** [bird of prey] fondre, plonger.
◇ *vt* baisser, pencher, incliner; **he ~ed his head to go through the door** il a baissé la tête pour passer la porte.
◇ *n* -**1.** [of person]: **to walk with** OR **to have a ~** avoir le dos voûté. -**2.** [by bird of prey] attaque *f* en piqué. -**3.** *Am* [veranda] véranda *f*, porche *m*.

stooping ['stuːpɪŋ] *adj* [back, shoulders, figure] voûté.

stop [stɒp] (*pt & pp* **stopped**, *cont* **stopping**)
◇ *vt* -**1.** [cease, finish] arrêter, cesser; **it hasn't stopped raining all day** il n'a pas arrêté de pleuvoir toute la journée; **you should ~ smoking** tu devrais arrêter de fumer; **I wish they'd ~ that noise!** j'aimerais qu'ils arrêtent ce bruit!; **she stopped work when she got married** elle a arrêté de travailler quand elle s'est mariée; **~ it, that hurts!** arrête, ça fait mal! -**2.** [prevent] empêcher; **to ~ sb (from) doing sthg** empêcher qqn de faire qqch; **it's too late to ~ the meeting from taking place** il est trop tard pour empêcher la réunion d'avoir lieu; **she's made up her mind and there's nothing we can do to ~ her** elle a pris sa décision et nous ne pouvons rien faire pour l'arrêter. -**3.** [cause to halt] arrêter; **this lever ~s the motor** ce levier arrête le moteur; **I managed to ~ the car** j'ai réussi à arrêter la voiture; **a policeman stopped the traffic** un agent arrêta la circulation; **we could do nothing to ~ the bleeding** nous ne pouvions rien faire pour arrêter l'hémorragie; **a woman stopped me to ask the way to the station** une femme m'a arrêté pour me demander le chemin de la gare; **the sound of voices stopped him short** OR **stopped him in his tracks** un bruit de voix le fit s'arrêter net ❑ **to ~ a bullet** *inf* se prendre une balle; **~ thief!** au voleur! -**4.** [arrest] arrêter. -**5.** *Br* [withhold - sum of money, salary] retenir; **the money will be stopped out of your wages** la somme sera retenue sur votre salaire; **taxes are stopped at source** les impôts sont retenus à la source. -**6.** [interrupt] interrompre, arrêter; [suspend] suspendre, arrêter; [cut off] couper; **once he starts talking about the war there's no stopping him** une fois qu'il commence à parler de la guerre, on ne peut plus l'arrêter; **the referee stopped the fight in the third round** l'arbitre a arrêté le combat à la troisième reprise; **his father threatened to ~ his allowance** son père menaça de lui couper les vivres; **I forgot to ~ the newspaper** j'ai oublié de faire suspendre mon abonnement au journal; **to ~ a cheque** faire opposition à un chèque. -**7.** [block - hole, gap] boucher; **to ~ one's ears** se boucher les oreilles. -**8.** [fill - tooth] plomber.

-**9.** MUS [string] presser; [wind instrument] boucher.
◇ *vi* -**1.** [halt, pause - person, vehicle, machine] arrêter, s'arrêter; go on, don't ~ continue, ne t'arrête pas; **my watch has stopped** ma montre s'est OR est arrêtée; **does the bus ~ near the church?** le bus s'arrête-t-il près de l'église?; **we can ~ for tea on the way** nous pouvons nous arrêter en chemin pour prendre le thé; **we drove from London to Edinburgh without stopping** nous avons roulé de Londres à Édimbourg d'une traite; **to ~ dead in one's tracks** s'arrêter net || *fig*: **she doesn't know where** OR **when to ~** elle ne sait pas s'arrêter; **they'll ~ at nothing to get what they want** ils ne reculeront devant rien pour obtenir ce qu'ils veulent; **we don't have time to ~ and think** nous n'avons pas le temps de nous arrêter pour réfléchir; **if you stopped to consider, you'd never do anything** si on prenait le temps de réfléchir, on ne ferait jamais rien; **they stopped short of actually harming him** ils ne lui ont pas fait de mal, mais il s'en est fallu de peu; **she began talking then stopped short** elle commença à parler puis s'arrêta net OR brusquement. -**2.** [come to an end] cesser, s'arrêter, se terminer; **the rain has stopped** la pluie s'est arrêtée; **wait for the music to ~** attendez que la musique s'arrête; **the road ~s a few miles east of Alice Springs** la route se termine à quelques kilomètres à l'est d'Alice Springs. -**3.** [stay] rester; [reside] loger; **I'm late, I can't ~** je suis en retard, je ne peux pas rester; **we've got friends stopping with us** nous avons des amis qui séjournent chez nous en ce moment; **which hotel did you ~ at?** dans quel hôtel êtes-vous descendus?
◇ *n* -**1.** [stopping place - for buses] arrêt *m*; [- for trains] station *f*; **we get off at the next ~** nous descendons au prochain arrêt. -**2.** [break - in journey, process] arrêt *m*, halte *f*; [- in work] pause *f*; **we made several ~s to pick up passengers** nous nous sommes arrêtés à plusieurs reprises pour prendre des passagers; **our first ~ was Brussels** nous avons fait une première halte à Bruxelles; **my whole career has been full of ~s and starts** ma carrière entière est faite de hauts et de bas. -**3.** [standstill] arrêt *m*; **to come to a ~** s'arrêter; **she brought the bus to a ~** elle arrêta le bus. -**4.** [end]: **to put a ~ to sthg** mettre fin OR un terme à qqch. -**5.** *Br* [full stop] point *m*; [in telegrams] stop *m*. -**6.** [on organ] jeu *m* (d'orgue); **to pull out all the ~s (to do sthg)** remuer ciel et terre (pour faire qqch). -**7.** [plug, stopper] bouchon *m*. -**8.** [blocking device] arrêt *m*. -**9.** PHOT diaphragme *m*. -**10.** LING occlusive *f*. -**11.** [in bridge] contrôle *m*; **to have a ~ in hearts** avoir un contrôle à cœur.
◇ *comp* [button, mechanism, signal] d'arrêt.
◆ **stop around** *inf Am* = **stop by**.
◆ **stop away** *inf vi insep Br* rester absent.
◆ **stop by** *inf vi insep* passer; **you must ~ by and see us next time you're in London** il faut que vous passiez nous voir la prochaine fois que vous venez à Londres; **I'll ~ by at the chemist's on my way home** je passerai à la pharmacie en rentrant.
◆ **stop down** ◇ *vi insep* -**1.** *Br* [gen] rester en bas; **to ~ down a year** SCH redoubler une année. -**2.** PHOT diaphragmer.
◇ *vt sep* PHOT diaphragmer.
◆ **stop in** *inf vi insep Br* -**1.** [stay at home] ne pas sortir, rester à la maison. -**2.** = **stop by**.
◆ **stop off** *vi insep* s'arrêter, faire une halte.
◆ **stop out** *inf vi insep Br* ne pas rentrer.
◆ **stop over** *vi insep* [gen] s'arrêter, faire une halte; TRANSP [on flight, cruise] faire escale.
◆ **stop round** *inf Am* = **stop by**.
◆ **stop up** *inf vi insep Br* ne pas se coucher, veiller.

stop-and-go *Am* = **stop-go**.
stop bath *n* bain *m* d'arrêt.
stopcock ['stɒpkɒk] *n Br* robinet *m* d'arrêt.
stop consonant *n* (consonne *f*) occlusive *f*.
stope [stəʊp] *n* gradin *m*.
stopgap ['stɒpgæp] ◇ *n Br* bouche-trou *m*.
◇ *adj* de remplacement.
stop-go *adj* ECON: **~ policy** politique *f* économique en dents de scie *(alternant arrêt de la croissance et mesures de relance)*, politique *f* du stop-and-go.
stoplight ['stɒplaɪt] *n* -**1.** [traffic light] feu *m* rouge. -**2.** *Br* [brake-light] stop *m*.
stop-off *n* halte *f*, courte halte *f*.
stop order *n* ordre *m* stop.
stopover ['stɒp,əʊvəʳ] *n* [gen] halte *f*; [on cruise, flight] escale *f*.
stoppage ['stɒpɪdʒ] *n* -**1.** [strike] grève *f*, arrêt *m* de travail. -**2.** *Br* [sum deducted] retenue *f*; **my wages are a lot less after ~s** après les retenues, il ne reste plus grand-chose de mon salaire. -**3.** [halting, stopping] arrêt *m*, interruption *f*; FTBL arrêt *m* de jeu. -**4.** [blockage] obstruction *f*; MED occlusion *f*.
stop payment *n* opposition *f (à un chèque)*.
stopper ['stɒpəʳ] ◇ *n* -**1.** [for bottle, jar] bouchon *m*; [for sink] bouchon *m*, bonde *f*; [for pipe] obturateur *m*; [on syringe] embout *m* de piston; **I can't get the ~ out of the jar/back on the jar** je n'arrive pas à déboucher/à reboucher le bocal. -**2.** FTBL stoppeur *m*. -**3.** [in bridge] arrêt *m*; **to have a ~ in clubs** avoir un arrêt à trèfle.
◇ *vt* boucher, fermer.
stopping ['stɒpɪŋ] ◇ *n* -**1.** [coming or bringing to a halt] arrêt *m*. -**2.** [blocking] obturation *f*; **the ~ (up) of a leak** le colmatage d'une fuite. -**3.** [cancellation - of payment, leave etc] suspension *f*; [- of service] suppression *f*; [- of cheque] opposition *f*.
◇ *adj* [place] où l'on s'arrête.
stopping train *n Br* omnibus *m*.
stop-press ◇ *n* nouvelles *fpl* de dernière minute.
◇ *adj* de dernière heure OR minute.
stop sign *n* (signal *m* de) stop *m*.
stop valve *n* soupape *f* OR robinet *m* d'arrêt.
stopwatch ['stɒpwɒtʃ] *n* chronomètre *m*.
storage ['stɔːrɪdʒ] ◇ *n* -**1.** [putting into store] entreposage *m*, emmagasinage *m*, stockage *m*; [keeping, conservation] stockage *m*; **careful packing should prevent the goods being damaged in ~** un bon emballage devrait empêcher la détérioration des marchandises pendant le stockage; **our furniture is in ~** nos meubles sont au garde-meubles. -**2.** COMPUT (mise *f* en) mémoire *f*.
◇ *comp* -**1.** [charges] de stockage, d'emmagasinage. -**2.** COMPUT de mémoire.
storage battery *n* accumulateur *m*, batterie *f* secondaire.
storage card *n* carte *f* à mémoire.
storage cell = **storage battery**.
storage heater, storage radiator *n* radiateur *m* à accumulation.
storage space *n* espace *m* de rangement.
storage tank *n* [for fuel] réservoir *m* (de stockage); [for rainwater] citerne *f*.
storax ['stɔːræks] *n* [tree, resin] styrax *m*, storax *m*.
store [stɔːʳ] ◇ *n* -**1.** [large shop] grand magasin *m*; *Am* [shop] magasin *m*; **candy ~** *Am* confiserie *f*; **liquor ~** *Am* magasin *m* de vins et spiritueux. -**2.** [stock - of goods] stock *m*, réserve *f*, provision *f*; [- of food] provision *f*; [- of facts, jokes, patience, knowledge] réserve *f*; [- of wisdom] fonds *m*; **we should get in** OR **lay in a ~ of coal** nous devrions faire provision de charbon; **I have my own private ~ of tea** j'ai ma provision personnelle de thé. -**3.** [place - warehouse] entrepôt *m*, dépôt *m*; [- in office, home, shop] réserve *f*; [- in factory] magasin *m*, réserve *f*; **goods in ~** *Br* marchandises *fpl* en entrepôt; **furniture ~** garde-meubles *m inv*. -**4.** COMPUT [memory] mémoire *f*. -**5.** [value]: **to lay** OR **to put** OR **to set great ~ by sthg** faire grand cas de qqch; **I don't set much ~ by his advice** je ne fais pas grand cas de ses conseils.
◇ *comp* -**1.** *Am* [store-bought - gen] de commerce; [- clothes] de confection; **a ~ cake** un gâteau acheté dans une pâtisserie. -**2.** [for storage]: **~ cupboard** placard *m* de rangement.
◇ *vt* -**1.** [put away, put in store - goods, food] emmagasiner, entreposer; [- grain, crop] engranger; [- heat] accumuler, emmagasiner; [- electricity] accumuler; [- files, documents] classer; [- facts, ideas] engranger, enregistrer dans sa mémoire; **we ~d our furniture at my mother's house** nous avons laissé OR mis nos meubles chez ma mère; **they ~d the ship with provisions for the voyage** ils ont rempli le bateau de provisions pour le voyage. -**2.** [keep] conserver, stocker; '**~ in a cool place**' 'à conserver au frais'. -**3.** [fill with provisions] approvisionner. -**4.** COMPUT stocker.
◆ **stores** *npl* [provisions] provisions *fpl*; **the expedition's ~s are running low** l'expédition commence à manquer de provisions.
◆ **in store** *adv phr*: **they had a surprise in ~ for her** ils lui avaient réservé une surprise; **who knows what the future has in ~?** qui sait ce que l'avenir nous réserve?; **if only we'd realised all the problems that were in ~ for us** si seulement nous nous étions rendu compte de tous les problèmes qui nous attendaient.
◆ **store away, store up** *vt sep* garder en réserve; **he ~d (away) the anecdote for future use** il a noté l'anecdote en se disant qu'il la replacerait; **he's just storing up trouble for himself by keeping silent** en ne disant rien, il ne fait que se préparer des ennuis.
store-bought *adj* [gen] de commerce; [clothes] de confection; **a ~ cake** un gâteau de pâtisserie.
store detective *n* vigile *m (dans un magasin)*.
storefront ['stɔːfrʌnt] *n Am* devanture *f* de magasin.
storehouse ['stɔːhaʊs, *pl* -haʊzɪz] *n* -**1.** *literal* magasin *m*, entrepôt *m*, dépôt *m*. -**2.** *fig* [of information, memories] mine *f*.
storekeeper ['stɔː,kiːpəʳ] *n* -**1.** [in warehouse] magasinier *m*, -ère *f*. -**2.** *Am* [shopkeeper] commerçant *m*, -e *f*.
storeman ['stɔːmən] (*pl* **storemen** [-mən]) *n Br* manutentionnaire *m*.
storeroom ['stɔːrʊm] *n* -**1.** [in office, shop] réserve *f*; [in factory] magasin *m*, réserve *f*; [in home] débarras *m*. -**2.** NAUT soute *f*, magasin *m*.
storey *Br* (*pl* **storeys**), **story** *Am* (*pl* **stories**) ['stɔːrɪ] *n* étage *m*.
-storey(ed) *Br*, **-storied** *Am* ['stɔːrɪ(d)] *in cpds*: **a single~/five~ building** un bâtiment à un étage/à cinq étages.
stork [stɔːk] *n* cigogne *f*.
storm [stɔːm] ◇ *n* -**1.** METEOR tempête *f*; [thunderstorm] orage *m*; [on Beaufort scale] tempête *f*; **electric ~** orage *m*; **it was a ~ in a teacup** *Br* ce fut une tempête dans un verre d'eau. -**2.** *fig* [furore] tempête *f*, ouragan *m*; **the arms deal caused a political ~** la vente d'armes a déclenché un véritable scandale politique; **a ~ of protest** une tempête de protestations; **a ~ of criticism** une marée de condamnations || [roar] tempête *f*; **a ~ of applause** une tempête d'applaudissements; **a ~ of abuse** une tornade d'injures. -**3.** MIL: **to take by ~** prendre d'assaut; **the show took Broadway by ~** *fig* le spectacle a connu un succès foudroyant à Broadway.
◇ *vi* -**1.** [go angrily]: **to ~ in/out** entrer/sortir comme un ouragan; **she ~ed off without saying a word** elle est partie furieuse, sans dire un mot. -**2.** [be angry] tempêter, fulminer. -**3.** [thunderstorm]: **it ~ed all night** il y a eu de l'orage toute la nuit. -**4.** MIL donner OR livrer l'assaut; **the enemy ~ed through our defences** l'ennemi donna l'assaut et franchit nos lignes de défense.
◇ *vt* emporter, enlever d'assaut; **the troops ~ed the ramparts** les troupes ont pris d'assaut les remparts.
stormbound ['stɔːmbaʊnd] *adj* bloqué par l'orage OR la tempête.
storm cellar *n Am* abri *m* contre les cyclones.

storm centre *n* -**1.** METEOR œil *m* de la tempête OR du cyclone. -**2.** *fig* centre *m* de l'agitation, point *m* névralgique.

storm cloud *n* -**1.** METEOR nuage *m* d'orage. -**2.** *fig* nuage *m* menaçant; the ~s of war were gathering le danger OR la menace d'une guerre grandissait.

storm cone *n* cône *m* de tempête.

storm door *n Am* porte *f* extérieure *(qui double la porte de la maison pour éviter les courants d'air)*.

storm drain *n* égout *m* pluvial.

storming ['stɔːmɪŋ] *n* [attack] assaut *m*; [capture] prise *f* (d'assaut); the ~ of the Bastille HIST la prise de la Bastille.

storm lantern *n* lampe *f* tempête.

Stormont ['stɔːmənt] *pr n château de la banlieue de Belfast qui a abrité le parlement d'Irlande du Nord entre 1921 et 1972*.

storm petrel *n* pétrel *m*.

stormproof ['stɔːmpruːf] *adj* à l'épreuve de la tempête.

storm trooper *n* membre *m* des troupes d'assaut; the ~s les troupes *fpl* d'assaut.

◆ **stormtrooper** *adj* [tactics] brutal, impitoyable.

storm troops *npl* troupes *fpl* d'assaut.

stormwater ['stɔːm,wɔːtəʳ] *n* eau *f* pluviale.

storm window *n* contre-fenêtre *f*.

stormy ['stɔːmɪ] (*compar* stormier, *superl* stormiest) *adj* -**1.** [weather] orageux, d'orage; [sea] houleux, démonté; it was a ~ day il faisait un temps orageux. -**2.** *fig* [debate, relationship] orageux; [look] furieux; [career, life] tumultueux, mouvementé.

stormy petrel = **storm petrel**.

story ['stɔːrɪ] (*pl* stories) *n* -**1.** [tale, work of fiction - spoken] histoire *f*; [- written] histoire *f*, conte *m*; to tell sb a ~ raconter une histoire à qqn; ghost ~ histoire *f* de fantômes; this is a true ~ c'est une histoire vraie; a collection of her poems and stories un recueil de ses poèmes et nouvelles; it's always the same old ~ *fig* c'est toujours la même histoire. -**2.** [plot - story line] intrigue *f*, scénario *m*; the ~ of the film is very complicated l'intrigue du film est très compliquée; I like a play with a good ~ to it j'aime les pièces qui ont une bonne intrigue. -**3.** [account] histoire *f*; I got the inside ~ from his wife j'ai appris la vérité sur cette histoire par sa femme; let me tell you my side of the ~ laisse-moi te donner ma version de l'histoire; well, that's my ~ and I'm sticking to it *hum* c'est la version officielle; the witness changed his ~ le témoin est revenu sur sa version des faits; but that's another ~ mais ça, c'est une autre histoire; that's not the whole ~, that's only part of the ~ mais ce n'est pas tout; we'll probably never know the whole OR full ~ nous ne saurons peut-être jamais le fin mot de l'histoire; to cut a long ~ short enfin bref. -**4.** [history] histoire *f*; his life ~ l'histoire de sa vie; that's the ~ of my life! *hum* ça m'arrive tout le temps! -**5.** *euph* [lie] histoire *f*; are you telling stories again? est-ce que tu racontes encore des histoires? -**6.** [rumour] rumeur *f*, bruit *m*; there's a ~ going about that they're getting divorced le bruit court qu'ils vont divorcer; or so the ~ goes c'est du moins ce que l'on raconte. -**7.** PRESS [article] article *m*; there's a front-page ~ about OR on the riots il y a un article en première page sur les émeutes; the editor refused to run her ~ le rédacteur en chef a refusé de publier son article; all the papers ran OR carried the ~ tous les journaux en ont parlé ‖ [event, affair] affaire *f*; have you been following this corruption ~? est-ce que vous avez suivi cette affaire de corruption?; the ~ broke just after the morning papers had gone to press on a appris la nouvelle juste après la mise sous presse des journaux du matin. -**8.** *Am* = **storey**.

storyboard ['stɔːrɪbɔːd] *n* story-board *m*, scénarimage *m offic*.

storybook ['stɔːrɪbʊk] ◇ *n* livre *m* de contes.
◇ *adj*: a ~ ending une fin romanesque; a ~ romance une idylle de conte de fées; a ~ castle un château de conte de fées.

story line *n* intrigue *f*, scénario *m*.

storyteller ['stɔːrɪ,teləʳ] *n* -**1.** conteur *m*, -euse *f*. -**2.** *euph* [liar] menteur *m*, -euse *f*.

stoup [stuːp] *n* RELIG bénitier *m*.

stout [staʊt] ◇ *adj* -**1.** [corpulent] gros, corpulent, fort. -**2.** [strong - stick] solide; [- structure, material] solide, robuste; a pair of ~ walking shoes une paire de chaussures de marche solides OR robustes. -**3.** [brave] vaillant, courageux; [firm, resolute - resistance, opposition, enemy] acharné; [- support, supporter] fidèle, loyal; a ~ heart un cœur vaillant.
◇ *n* stout *m*, bière *f* brune forte.

stouthearted [,staʊt'hɑːtɪd] *adj lit* vaillant, courageux.

stoutly ['staʊtlɪ] *adv* -**1.** [solidly] solidement, robustement; ~ built houses des maisons solides. -**2.** [bravely] vaillamment, courageusement; [firmly, resolutely - resist, defend, oppose] avec acharnement; [- support] fidèlement, loyalement; she still ~ maintains she was in the right elle continue à prétendre dur comme fer qu'elle avait raison.

stoutness ['staʊtnɪs] *n* -**1.** [corpulence] corpulence *f*, embonpoint *m*. -**2.** [solidity, strength - of structure, materials] solidité *f*, robustesse *f*. -**3.** [bravery] vaillance *f*, courage *m*; [firmness, resolution - of resistance, defence, opposition] acharnement *m*; [- of support, supporter] fidélité *f*, loyauté *f*; ~ of heart vaillance, courage.

stove [stəʊv] ◇ *pt* & *pp* → **stave**.
◇ *n* -**1.** [for heating] poêle *m*; paraffin ~ poêle à mazout. -**2.** [cooker - gen] cuisinière *f*; [- portable] réchaud *m*; [kitchen range] fourneau *m*; gas ~ cuisinière à gaz. -**3.** INDUST [kiln] four *m*, étuve *f*.

stove enamel *n* laque *f* OR vernis *m* à cuire.

stove-in *adj Am* défoncé, enfoncé.

stovepipe ['stəʊvpaɪp] *n* -**1.** *literal* tuyau *m* de poêle. -**2.** *inf* ~ (hat) tuyau *m* de poêle.

◆ **stovepipes** *npl Br* [trousers] pantalon-cigarette *m*.

stovies ['stəʊvɪz] *npl* CULIN *ragoût écossais de pommes de terre et d'oignons*.

stow [stəʊ] *vt* -**1.** [store] ranger, stocker; [in warehouse] emmagasiner; NAUT [cargo] arrimer; [equipment, sails] ranger; where do you ~ the coffee? où rangez-vous le café?; he ~ed the keys behind the clock [hid] il a caché les clés derrière la pendule; [hurriedly] il a fait disparaître les clés derrière la pendule. -**2.** [pack, fill] remplir. -**3.** ▽ *Br phr*: ~ it! [stop] ça suffit!; [shut up] la ferme!

◆ **stow away** ◇ *vi insep* [on ship, plane] s'embarquer clandestinement, être un passager clandestin; I ~ed away to Brazil je me suis embarqué clandestinement pour le Brésil.
◇ *vt sep* -**1.** = **stow 1**. -**2.** *inf Br* [food] enfourner; he can certainly ~ it away! qu'est-ce qu'il descend!

stowage ['stəʊɪdʒ] *n* -**1.** [of goods - in warehouse] emmagasinage *m*; [- on ship] arrimage *m*. -**2.** [capacity - gen] espace *m* utile OR de rangement; [- in warehouse] espace *m* d'emmagasinage; [- on ship] espace *m* d'arrimage.

stowaway ['stəʊəweɪ] *n* passager *m* clandestin, passagère *f* clandestine.

strabismus [strə'bɪzməs] *n* MED strabisme *m*.

straddle ['strædl] ◇ *vt* -**1.** [sit astride of - horse, bicycle, chair, wall] chevaucher; [mount - horse, bicycle] enfourcher; [step over - ditch, gap, obstacle] enjamber. -**2.** [span, spread over] enjamber; the bridge ~s the river le pont enjambe la rivière; the park ~s the state line le parc est à cheval sur la frontière entre les États. -**3.** MIL [target] encadrer. -**4.** *inf Am*: to ~ the fence [be non committal] ne pas prendre position; you can't ~ the fence vous devez prendre position.
◇ *vi inf Am fig* [sit on the fence] ne pas prendre position.

strafe [strɑːf] *vt* [with machine guns] mitrailler (au sol); [with bombs] bombarder.

straggle ['strægl] ◇ *vi* -**1.** [spread in long line - roots, creeper, branches] pousser de façon désordonnée; [be scattered - trees, houses] être disséminé; vines ~d over the fence la vigne envahissait la clôture; the suburbs ~d on for miles along the railway line la banlieue s'étendait sur des kilomètres le long de la voie ferrée; the excavations ~d down the hillside les fouilles s'étendaient jusqu'en bas de la colline ‖ [hang untidily - hair] pendre (lamentablement); her hair ~d over her forehead des mèches pendaient sur son front. -**2.** [linger] traîner, traînasser; she was straggling behind all the others elle traînassait derrière tous les autres; stop straggling! do try and keep up! ne traînez pas! essayez de rester groupés!; to ~ in/out entrer/sortir de manière dispersée OR par petits groupes; the crowd began to ~ away from the scene la foule commença à se disperser petit à petit.
◇ *n*: there was a constant ~ of visitors il y a eu un défilé ininterrompu de visiteurs; all I saw was a ~ of houses/trees on the hillside je n'ai aperçu que quelques maisons disséminées/quelques arbres disséminés sur la colline; a ~ of islands un long chapelet d'îles.

straggler ['stræglәʳ] *n* -**1.** [lingerer] traînard *m*, -e *f*; [in race] retardataire *mf*. -**2.** BOT gourmand *m*.

straggling ['stræglɪŋ] *adj* [vine, plant] maigre, (qui pousse) tout en longueur; [houses, trees] disséminé; [village, street] tout en longueur; [beard] épars; to have long, ~ hair avoir une chevelure longue et maigre.

straggly ['stræglɪ] *adj* [hair] maigre; [beard] épars, hirsute; [roots] long et mince.

straight [streɪt] ◇ *adj* -**1.** [not curved - line, road, nose] droit; [- hair] raide; a ~ line MATH une (ligne) droite; keep your back ~ tiens-toi droit, redresse-toi. -**2.** [level, upright] droit; the picture isn't ~ le tableau n'est pas droit OR est de travers; is my tie ~? est-ce que ma cravate est droite?; to put OR to set ~ [picture] remettre d'aplomb, redresser; [hat, tie] ajuster; hold OR keep the tray ~ tenez le plateau bien droit. -**3.** [honest, frank] franc, droit; to be ~ with sb être franc avec qqn; to give sb a ~ answer répondre franchement à qqn; to have a ~ talk about sthg parler franchement de qqch; he's always been ~ in his dealings with me il a toujours été honnête avec moi; to do some ~ talking parler franchement; at the meeting he did some ~ talking il n'a pas mâché ses mots à la réunion; it's time we did some ~ talking il faut qu'on parle, tous les deux; are you being ~ with me? est-ce que tu joues franc jeu avec moi? -**4.** [correct, clear] clair; to put OR to set the record ~ mettre les choses au clair; just to set the record ~ pour que ce soit bien clair; I'd like to get things ~ before I leave je voudrais mettre les choses au clair avant de partir; let's get this ~ entendons-nous bien sur ce point; have you put her ~? as-tu mis les choses au point avec elle?; now just you get this ~! mets-toi bien ceci dans la tête!, qu'on se mette bien d'accord sur ce point! -**5.** [tidy, in order - room, desk, accounts] en ordre; to put OR to set ~ [room, house] mettre en ordre, mettre de l'ordre dans; [affairs] mettre de l'ordre dans; put your desk ~ rangez votre bureau; put your things ~ on the desk mettez un peu d'ordre sur le bureau. -**6.** [quits] quitte; here's the £5 I owe you, now we're ~ voilà les 5 livres que je te dois, maintenant nous sommes quittes. -**7.** [direct] droit, direct; he hit him a ~ left il lui a porté un direct du gauche ‖ POL: ~ fight: a ~ fight between Labour and Conservative *une élection où ne se présentent que deux candidats, un travailliste et un conservateur* ❑ to vote a ~ ticket *Am* voter pour une liste sans panachage. -**8.** [pure, utter] pur; it's just ~ prejudice ce sont des préjugés, tout simplement; it's just ~ propaganda c'est de la propagande pure et simple. -**9.** [consecutive] consécutif, de suite; to

have three ~ wins gagner trois fois de suite OR d'affilée; we worked for three ~ days nous avons travaillé trois jours d'affilée; a ~ flush CARDS une quinte flush. -10. [neat - whisky, vodka] sec. -11. [serious] sérieux; to keep a ~ face garder son sérieux; ~ theatre le théâtre traditionnel; it's the first ~ role she's played in years c'est son premier rôle sérieux depuis des années. -12. *inf* [conventional] vieux jeu *(inv)*; [heterosexual] hétéro; [not a drug user] qui ne se drogue pas. -13. AUT [cylinders] en ligne; a ~ eight engine un moteur huit cylindres en ligne. -14. GEOM [angle] plat. -15. *Am* SCH: he got ~ As all term il n'a eu que de très bonnes notes tout le semestre; a ~ A student un étudiant brillant.
◇ *adv* -1. [in a straight line] droit, en ligne droite; try and walk ~! essaie de marcher droit!; the rocket shot ~ up la fusée est montée à la verticale OR en ligne droite; to shoot ~ viser juste || *fig*: I can't see ~ je ne vois pas bien; I can't think ~ je n'ai pas les idées claires ❑ to go ~ *inf* [criminal] revenir dans le droit chemin. -2. [upright - walk, sit, stand] (bien) droit; sit up ~! tiens-toi droit OR redresse-toi (sur ta chaise)! -3. [directly] (tout) droit, directement; he looked me ~ in the eye il me regarda droit dans les yeux; it's ~ across the road c'est juste en face; the car came ~ at me la voiture a foncé droit sur moi; come ~ home after the concert! rentre à la maison tout de suite après le concert!; go ~ to bed! va tout de suite te coucher!; the ball went ~ through the window la balle est passée par la fenêtre; the knife went ~ through my arm le couteau m'a transpercé le bras; they mostly go ~ from school to university pour la plupart, ils passent directement du lycée à l'université; to come ~ to the point aller droit au fait; it went ~ to his heart cela lui est allé droit au cœur; ~ ahead tout droit; where's the crossroads? – it's ~ ahead où se trouve le carrefour? – c'est tout droit devant vous; he looked ~ ahead il regarda droit devant lui; ~ off *inf* sur-le-champ, tout de suite; ~ on tout droit; go ~ on till you come to a roundabout continuez tout droit jusqu'à ce que vous arriviez à un rond-point; at the roundabout go ~ over au rond-point allez tout droit ❑ she gave it me ~ from the shoulder elle me l'a dit sans ambages OR sans prendre de gants. -4. [frankly] franchement, carrément, tout droit; I told him ~ (out) what I thought of him je lui ai dit franchement ce que je pensais de lui; I'm giving it to you ~ *inf* je vous le dis tout net ❑ ~ up *inf Br* [honestly] sans blague. -5. [neat, unmixed]: to drink whisky ~ boire son whisky sec.
◇ *n* -1. [on racecourse, railway track] ligne *f* droite; the final OR home ~ la dernière ligne droite ❑ to keep to the ~ and narrow rester dans le droit chemin. -2. [level]: to be out of ~ *Br* être de biais OR de travers; on the ~ TEX de droit fil. -3. *inf* [person]: he's a ~ [conventional person] il est conventionnel, c'est quelqu'un de conventionnel; [heterosexual] il est hétéro, c'est un hétéro.

straight-arm ◇ *adj* [in American football]: ~ tackle raffût *m*.
◇ *vt* raffûter.

straightaway [,streɪtə'weɪ] ◇ *adv* tout de suite, sur-le-champ.
◇ *adj Am* droit.
◇ *n Am* ligne *f* droite.

straight-cut *adj* [tobacco] *en tranches coupées dans le sens de la longueur des feuilles*.

straightedge ['streɪtedʒ] *n* [gen] règle *f*; [in carpentry] limande *f*.

straighten ['streɪtn] ◇ *vt* -1. [remove bend or twist from - line, wire] redresser; [- nail] redresser, défausser; [- wheel] redresser, dévoiler; [- hair] décrêper. -2. [adjust - picture] redresser, remettre d'aplomb; [- tie, hat] redresser, ajuster; [- hem] arrondir, rectifier; she ~ed her back OR shoulders elle se redressa; he had his nose ~ed il s'est fait redresser le nez. -3. [tidy - room, papers] ranger, mettre de l'ordre dans; [organize - affairs, accounts] mettre en ordre, mettre de l'ordre dans; ~ your desk before you leave rangez votre bureau avant de partir.
◇ *vi* [person] se dresser, se redresser; [plant] pousser droit; [hair] devenir raide; heading into the desert the road ~s à l'entrée du désert, la route devient droite.
◆ **straighten out** ◇ *vt sep* -1. [nail, wire] redresser. -2. [situation] débrouiller, arranger; [problem] résoudre; [mess, confusion] mettre de l'ordre dans, débrouiller; don't worry, things will ~ themselves out ne t'en fais pas, les choses vont s'arranger. -3. to ~ sb out *inf* [help] remettre qqn dans la bonne voie; [punish] remettre qqn à sa place; I'll soon ~ her out! je vais lui apprendre!
◇ *vi insep* [road] devenir droit; [plant] pousser droit; [hair] devenir raide.
◆ **straighten up** ◇ *vi insep* [person] se dresser, se redresser; [plant] pousser droit.
◇ *vt sep* [room, papers] ranger, mettre de l'ordre dans; [affairs] mettre de l'ordre dans, mettre en ordre.

straight-faced *adj* qui garde son sérieux, impassible.

straightforward [,streɪt'fɔːwəd] *adj* -1. [direct - person] direct; [- explanation] franc; [- account] très clair; it's impossible to get a ~ answer out of her il est impossible d'obtenir d'elle une réponse nette et précise. -2. [easy, simple - task, problem] simple, facile; [- instructions] clair; it was all quite ~ ce n'était pas compliqué du tout. -3. [pure, utter] pur; it's ~ elitism ça s'appelle de l'élitisme, c'est de l'élitisme pur et simple.

straightforwardly [,streɪt'fɔːwədlɪ] *adv* -1. [honestly - act, behave] avec franchise; [- answer] franchement, sans détour. -2. [without complications] simplement, sans anicroche; the meeting did not go off quite as ~ as hoped la réunion ne s'est pas passée aussi bien qu'on l'avait espéré.

straightjacket ['streɪt,dʒækɪt] = **straitjacket**.

straightlaced [,streɪt'leɪst] = **straitlaced**.

straight-line *adj* ECON & FIN constant.

straight man *n* faire-valoir *m inv*.

straight-out *inf adj Am* -1. [forthright - answer] net; [- refusal] catégorique; he gave a ~ answer il a répondu franchement. -2. [utter - liar, hypocrite] fieffé; [- lie, dishonesty] pur; [- opponent, supporter] inconditionnel.

straightway ['streɪtweɪ] *adv arch* tout de suite, sur-le-champ.

strain [streɪn] ◇ *n* -1. [on rope, girder - pressure] pression *f*; [- tension] tension *f*; [- pull] traction *f*; [- weight] poids *m*; the rope snapped under the ~ la corde a rompu sous la tension; the weight put too much ~ on the rope le poids a exercé une trop forte tension sur la corde; to collapse under the ~ [bridge, animal] s'effondrer sous le poids; I took most of the ~ c'est moi qui ai fourni le plus gros effort; the buttress takes the ~ off the wall le contrefort réduit la pression qui s'exerce sur le mur; the girder can't take the ~ la poutre ne peut pas supporter cette pression OR sollicitation; the war is putting a great ~ on the country's resources la guerre pèse lourd sur OR grève sérieusement les ressources du pays; the new taxes take the ~ off the budget les nouveaux impôts renflouent le budget. -2. [mental or physical effort] (grand) effort *m*; [overwork] surmenage *m*; [tiredness] (grande) fatigue *f*; he's beginning to feel/show the ~ il commence à sentir la fatigue/à donner des signes de fatigue; I've been under great physical ~ je me suis surmené; it was quite a ~ for me to have to stand j'ai trouvé très fatigant de devoir rester debout; the ~ of making polite conversation l'effort que ça demande de faire la conversation à quelqu'un || [stress] stress *m*, tension *f* OR fatigue *f* nerveuse; the situation has put our family under a great deal of ~ la situation a mis notre famille à rude épreuve; recent events have placed considerable ~ on their relationship les événements récents ont mis leur relation à rude épreuve; he can't take the ~ anymore il ne peut plus supporter cette situation stressante; it's a terrible ~ on her nerves elle trouve ça difficile à supporter nerveusement; they've been under a lot of ~ recently leurs nerfs ont été mis à rude épreuve ces derniers temps; the arrival of a new secretary took the immediate ~ off me avec l'arrivée d'une nouvelle secrétaire, j'ai été immédiatement soulagée d'une partie de mon travail; I couldn't stand the ~ of commuting je trouvais trop épuisant de prendre les transports en commun tous les matins. -3. MED [of muscle] froissement *m*; [sprain - of ankle, wrist] entorse *f*; to give one's back a ~ se donner un tour de reins. -4. [breed, variety - of animals] lignée *f*, race *f*; [of plant, virus etc] souche *f*. -5. [style] genre *m*, style *m*; his other books are all very much in the same ~ ses autres livres sont tout à fait dans le même genre OR dans le même esprit. -6. [streak, touch] fond *m*, tendance *f*; there is a ~ of madness in the family il y a une prédisposition à la folie dans la famille; there's a strong ~ of fantasy in his novels il y a une grande part de rêve dans ses romans.
◇ *vt* -1. [rope, cable, girder] tendre (fortement); he ~ed the canvas over the frame il a tendu la toile sur le cadre; to be ~ed to breaking point être tendu au point de se rompre || [resources, economy, budget] grever; this new expense is ~ing our income to the limit nos revenus nous permettent tout juste cette dépense supplémentaire. -2. [force - voice] forcer; he ~ed his ears to hear what they were saying il tendit l'oreille pour entendre ce qu'ils disaient; to ~ one's eyes to see sthg plisser les yeux pour mieux voir qqch; to ~ every nerve OR sinew to do sthg s'efforcer de faire qqch. -3. [hurt, damage - muscle] froisser; [- eyes] fatiguer; reading small print ~s your eyes ça fatigue les yeux de lire des petits caractères; you'll ~ your eyes tu vas te fatiguer les yeux; I have to be careful not to ~ my heart il faut que je veille à ménager mon cœur; to ~ one's back se donner un tour de reins; I've ~ed my arm je me suis froissé un muscle du bras; to ~ o.s. [by gymnastics, lifting] se froisser un muscle; [by overwork] se surmener; mind you don't ~ yourself lifting that typewriter attention de ne pas te faire mal en soulevant cette machine à écrire || *hum*: don't ~ yourself! surtout ne te fatigue pas!; she lent a hand, but she didn't exactly ~ herself elle a mis la main à la pâte, mais elle ne s'est pas vraiment fatiguée. -4. [force - meaning] forcer; [- word] forcer le sens de; it would be ~ing the truth to call the play a masterpiece dire que cette pièce est un chef-d'œuvre serait exagéré. -5. [test - patience] mettre à l'épreuve, abuser de; [- friendship, relationship] mettre à l'épreuve, mettre à rude épreuve. -6. CULIN [soup, milk] passer; [vegetables] (faire) égoutter. -7. *lit* [press - child, lover] serrer; she ~ed the child to her breast elle serra l'enfant contre sa poitrine.
◇ *vi* -1. [pull] tirer fort; [push] pousser fort; she was ~ing at the door [pull] elle tirait sur la porte de toutes ses forces; [push] elle poussait (sur) la porte de toutes ses forces; the dog ~ed at the leash le chien tirait sur sa laisse; I had to ~ against the wind j'ai dû lutter contre le vent; she ~ed under the weight elle ployait sous la charge. -2. [strive] s'efforcer, faire beaucoup d'efforts; to ~ to do sthg s'efforcer de faire qqch; I ~ed to understand/hear what they were saying je me suis efforcé de comprendre/d'entendre ce qu'ils disaient; he tends to ~ after effect il a tendance à vouloir se faire remarquer. -3. [rope, cable] se tendre.
◆ **strains** *npl* [in music] accents *mpl*, accords *mpl*; [in verse] accents *mpl*; the crowd rose to the ~s of the national anthem le public s'est levé aux accents de l'hymne national.
◆ **strain off** *vt sep* [liquid] vider, égoutter.

strained [streɪnd] *adj* -1. [forced - manner, laugh] forcé, contraint; [- voice] forcé; [- language, style etc] forcé, exagéré; she gave me a ~ smile elle m'adressa un sourire contraint OR forcé.

-**2.** [tense - atmosphere, relations, person] tendu. -**3.** [sprained - ankle, limb] foulé; [- muscle] froissé; **to have a ~ shoulder** s'être froissé un muscle à l'épaule; **to have a ~ neck** avoir un torticolis || [tired - eyes] fatigué; **his eyes looked ~** il avait l'air d'avoir les yeux fatigués. -**4.** CULIN [liquid] filtré; [soup] passé; [vegetables] égoutté; [baby food] en purée.

strainer ['streɪnəʳ] *n* passoire *f*; **tea ~** passoire à thé, passe-thé *m inv*.

strait [streɪt] ◇ *n* GEOG: ~, ~s détroit *m*.
◇ *adj arch* étroit.
◆ **straits** *npl* [difficulties] gêne *f*, situation *f* fâcheuse; **to be in financial ~s** avoir des ennuis financiers OR des problèmes d'argent.

STRAITS:
the Straits of Dover le pas de Calais;
the Strait of Gibraltar le détroit de Gibraltar;
the Strait of Hormuz OR Ormuz le détroit d'Hormuz OR d'Ormuz;
the Strait of Magellan le détroit de Magellan;
the Strait of Malacca le détroit de Malacca.

---

straitened ['streɪtnd] *adj*: **in ~ circumstances** dans le besoin OR la gêne.

straitjacket ['streɪt,dʒækɪt] *n* camisole *f* de force.

straitlaced [,streɪt'leɪst] *adj* collet monté *(inv)*; **he was always very proper and ~** il était toujours très digne et très guindé.

strand [strænd] ◇ *n* -**1.** [of thread, string, wire] brin *m*, toron *m*; **a ~ of hair** une mèche de cheveux. -**2.** [in argument, plot, sequence] fil *m*; **the main ~ of the narrative** le fil conducteur (du récit). -**3.** *lit* [beach] plage *f*; [shore] grève *f*, rivage *m*.
◇ *vt* -**1.** [ship, whale] échouer; **the ship was ~ed on a mudbank** le bateau s'est échoué sur un banc de vase. -**2.** *(usu pass)*: **to be ~ed** [person, vehicle] rester en plan OR coincé; **she was ~ed in Seville with no money** elle s'est retrouvée coincée à Séville sans un sou vaillant; **we were left ~ed with no way of getting home** on est restés en plan sans aucun moyen de rentrer chez nous.

stranded ['strændɪd] *adj* -**1.** [person, car] bloqué; **the ~ holidaymakers camped out in the airport** les vacanciers, ne pouvant pas partir, campèrent à l'aéroport. -**2.** BIOL & CHEM [molecule, sequence] torsadé.

strange [streɪndʒ] *adj* -**1.** [odd] étrange, bizarre; [peculiar] singulier, insolite; **it's ~ that he should be so late** c'est bizarre OR étrange qu'il ait tant de retard; **she has some ~ ideas** elle a des idées bizarres OR de drôles d'idées; **~ to say, I've never been there** chose curieuse OR étrange, je n'y suis jamais allé; **~ as it may seem** aussi étrange que cela paraisse OR puisse paraître; **truth is ~r than fiction** la vérité dépasse la fiction. -**2.** [unfamiliar] inconnu; **to find o.s. in ~ surroundings** se trouver dans un endroit inconnu; **~ faces** des visages inconnus; **I woke up to find a ~ man in my room** lorsque je me suis réveillé il y avait un inconnu dans ma chambre; **a ~ car was seen in the neighbourhood earlier in the week** en début de semaine on avait remarqué la présence dans le voisinage d'une voiture qu'on ne connaissait pas. -**3.** [unaccustomed] inaccoutumé; **he is still ~ to city life** il n'est pas encore accoutumé à OR il n'a pas encore l'habitude de la vie citadine. -**4.** [unwell] bizarre; **to look/to feel ~** avoir l'air/se sentir bizarre. -**5.** PHYS [matter, particle] étrange.

strangely ['streɪndʒlɪ] *adv* étrangement, bizarrement; **~ enough, I never heard of him again** chose curieuse OR chose étrange, je n'ai jamais plus entendu parler de lui; **her face was ~ familiar to him** son visage lui était singulièrement familier; **he spoke in a ~ calm voice** il parla d'une voix étonnamment calme.

strangeness ['streɪndʒnɪs] *n* -**1.** [of person, situation] étrangeté *f*, bizarrerie *f*, singularité *f*. -**2.** PHYS étrangeté *f*.

stranger ['streɪndʒəʳ] *n* -**1.** [unknown person] inconnu *m*, -e *f*; **never talk to ~s** ne parle jamais à des inconnus; **we are complete ~s** nous ne nous sommes jamais rencontrés; **we were ~s until yesterday** nous ne nous connaissons que depuis hier; **a perfect ~** un parfait inconnu; **they greeted each other for all the world like perfect ~s** ils se sont salués comme de parfaits étrangers; **she has become a ~ to her own family** elle est devenue une étrangère pour sa propre famille; **you've become quite a ~ round here** on ne vous voit plus beaucoup par ici OR dans les parages; **hello ~!** *hum* tiens, un revenant! -**2.** [person from elsewhere] étranger *m*, -ère *f*; **~s to the town often get lost** les étrangers se perdent souvent dans cette ville; **I'm a ~ here myself** je ne suis pas d'ici non plus. -**3.** [novice] novice *m*; **I am not exactly a ~ to classical music** je ne suis pas complètement ignorant en matière de musique classique; **he is no ~ to loneliness/misfortune** il sait ce qu'est la solitude/le malheur.

Strangers' Gallery *pr n*: **the ~** *la tribune du public à la Chambre des communes et à la Chambre des lords.*

strangle ['stræŋgl] *vt* -**1.** *literal* étrangler; **I could cheerfully have ~d that child** ce n'est pas l'envie qui me manquait d'étrangler cet enfant. -**2.** *fig* [opposition, growth, originality] étrangler, étouffer.

strangled ['stræŋgld] *adj* [cry, sob] étranglé, étouffé; [voice] étranglé.

stranglehold ['stræŋglhəʊld] *n* [grip around throat] étranglement *m*, étouffement *m*, strangulation *f*; [in wrestling] étranglement *m*; **to have a ~ on sb** *literal & fig* tenir qqn à la gorge; **to have a ~ on sthg** *fig* tenir qqch à la gorge; **they have a ~ on the government** ils tiennent le gouvernement à leur merci; **superstition still retains a ~ on the country** l'emprise des superstitions sur le pays est toujours très forte; **to have a ~ on the market/economy** jouir d'un monopole sur le marché/l'économie.

strangler ['stræŋgləʳ] *n* étrangleur *m*, -euse *f*.

strangling ['stræŋglɪŋ] *n* -**1.** [killing] étranglement *m*, strangulation *f*; *fig* [of opposition, protest, originality] étranglement *m*, étouffement *m*. -**2.** [case]: **there has been yet another ~** une nouvelle victime a été étranglée; **that brings to five the number of ~s** cela porte à cinq le nombre de personnes étranglées.

strangulate ['stræŋgjʊleɪt] *vt* -**1.** MED étrangler; **a ~d hernia** une hernie étranglée. -**2.** = **strangle**.

strangulation [,stræŋgjʊ'leɪʃn] *n* strangulation *f*; **the victim died of ~** la victime est morte étranglée.

strap [stræp] (*pt & pp* **strapped**, *cont* **strapping**)
◇ *n* -**1.** [belt - of leather] courroie *f*, sangle *f*, lanière *f*; [- of cloth, metal] sangle *f*, bande *f*. -**2.** [support - for bag, camera, on harness] sangle *f*; (shoulder) ~ bandoulière *f* || [fastening - for dress, bra] bretelle *f*; [- for hat, bonnet] bride *f*; [- for helmet] attache *f*; [- for sandal] lanière *f*; [- under trouser leg] sous-pied *m*; [- for watch] bracelet *m*. -**3.** [as punishment]: **to give sb/to get the ~** administrer/recevoir une correction (à coups de ceinture). -**4.** [on bus, underground] poignée *f*. -**5.** = **strop**. -**6.** TECH lien *m*.
◇ *vt* sangler, attacher; **she had a knife strapped to her leg** elle portait un couteau fixé à sa jambe.
◆ **strap down** *vt sep* sangler, attacher avec une sangle OR une courroie.
◆ **strap in** *vt sep* [in car] attacher la ceinture (de sécurité) de; [child - in high chair, pram] attacher avec un harnais OR avec une ceinture; **let me ~ you in** laisse-moi attacher ta ceinture; **he strapped himself into the driving seat** il s'est installé au volant et a attaché sa ceinture de sécurité; **are you strapped in?** as-tu mis ta ceinture?
◆ **strap on** *vt sep* [bag, watch] attacher; **the diver strapped his aqualung on** le plongeur mit son scaphandre.
◆ **strap up** *vt sep* [suitcase, parcel] sangler; [limbs, ribs] mettre un bandage à, bander.

straphang *inf* ['stræphæŋ] *vi Br* voyager debout *(dans les transports en commun)*.

straphanger *inf* ['stræphæŋəʳ] *n Br* voyageur *m*, -euse *f* debout *(dans les transports en commun)*.

strapless ['stræplɪs] *adj* [dress, bra etc] sans bretelles.

strapline ['stræplaɪn] *n* PRESS sous-titre *m*.

strapped *inf* [stræpt] *adj*: **to be ~ for cash** être fauché.

strapper *inf* ['stræpəʳ] *n* costaud *m*, -e *f*.

strapping *inf* ['stræpɪŋ] *adj* costaud; **a fine ~ girl** un beau brin de fille.

strata ['strɑːtə] *pl* → **stratum**.

stratagem ['strætədʒəm] *n* stratagème *m*.

strategic(al) [strə'tiːdʒɪk(l)] *adj* stratégique; **we decided on a ~ withdrawal of our troops** nous avons décidé d'opérer un repli stratégique de nos troupes; **a ~ position** une position stratégique.

strategically [strə'tiːdʒɪklɪ] *adv* stratégiquement, du point de vue de la stratégie.

strategics [strə'tiːdʒɪks] *n (U)* MIL (l'art *m* de la) stratégie *f*.

strategist ['strætɪdʒɪst] *n* stratège *m*.

strategy ['strætɪdʒɪ] (*pl* strategies) *n* [gen & MIL] stratégie *f*; **marketing strategies** stratégies de marketing.

strati ['streɪtaɪ] *pl* → **stratus**.

stratification [,strætɪfɪ'keɪʃn] *n* stratification *f*.

stratificational [,strætɪfɪ'keɪʃnl] *adj* LING stratificationnel.

stratified ['strætɪfaɪd] *adj* stratifié, en couches.

stratify ['strætɪfaɪ] (*pt & pp* **stratified**)
◇ *vt* stratifier.
◇ *vi* se stratifier.

stratigraphy [strə'tɪgrəfɪ] *n* stratigraphie *f*.

stratocumulus [,strætəʊ'kjuːmjʊləs] (*pl* stratocumuli [-laɪ]) *n* stratocumulus *m*.

stratosphere ['strætə,sfɪəʳ] *n* stratosphère *f*.

stratum ['strɑːtəm] (*pl* strata [-tə]) *n* -**1.** GEOL strate *f*, couche *f*. -**2.** *fig* couche *f*; **the various strata of society** les différentes couches de la société.

stratus ['streɪtəs] (*pl* strati [-taɪ]) *n* stratus *m*.

Stravinsky [strə'vɪnskɪ] *pr n* Stravinski.

straw [strɔː] ◇ *n* -**1.** AGR paille *f*; **man of ~** *Br*, **~ man** *Am* homme *m* de paille. -**2.** [for drinking] paille *f*; **to drink sthg through a ~** boire qqch avec une paille. -**3.** *phr*: **to catch** OR **to clutch at a ~** OR **at ~s** se raccrocher désespérément à la moindre lueur d'espoir; **you're just grasping at ~s** vous vous raccrochez à de faux espoirs; **to draw** OR **to get the short ~** être tiré au sort, être de corvée; **a ~ in the wind** un aperçu (de ce que l'avenir nous réserve); **that's the last ~** OR **the ~ that breaks the camel's back** c'est la goutte d'eau qui fait déborder le vase; **I don't care a ~** OR **two ~s!** *inf Br* je m'en fiche!; **it's not worth a ~** *inf* ça ne vaut pas un clou.
◇ *comp* [gen] de OR en paille; [roof] en paille, en chaume; **'Straw Dogs'** *Peckinpah* 'les Chiens de paille'.

strawberry ['strɔːbərɪ] (*pl* **strawberries**)
◇ *n* [fruit] fraise *f*; [plant] fraisier *m*.
◇ *comp* [jam] de fraises; [tart] aux fraises; [ice cream] à la fraise.

STRAWBERRIES AND CREAM:
En Grande-Bretagne, les fraises à la crème sont traditionnellement consommées lors de certaines manifestations en plein air, notamment aux tournois de tennis de Wimbledon.

---

strawberry blonde ◇ *adj* blond vénitien *(inv)*.
◇ *n* blonde *f* qui tire sur le roux.

strawberry mark *n* tache *f* de vin, envie *f*.

strawboard ['strɔːbɔːd] *n* carton-paille *m*.

straw-coloured *adj* (couleur) paille *(inv)*.

straw hat *n* chapeau *m* de paille.

straw mattress *n* paillasse *f*.

straw poll *n* [vote] vote *m* blanc; [opinion poll] sondage *m* d'opinion.

straw vote *Am* = **straw poll**.

stray [streɪ] ◇ *vi* -**1.** [child, animal] errer; some sheep had ~ed onto the railway line des moutons s'étaient aventurés sur la ligne de chemin de fer; to ~ away [get lost] s'égarer; [go away] s'en aller; the children ~ed (away) from the rest of the group les enfants se sont écartés du groupe; we ~ed into what must have been the red light area nous nous sommes retrouvés dans ce qui devait être le quartier des prostituées; to ~ from the fold *literal* & *fig* s'écarter du troupeau; to ~ (away) from the right path *literal* & *fig* faire fausse route. -**2.** [speaker, writer] s'éloigner du sujet; but I am ~ing from the point mais je m'écarte du sujet. -**3.** [thoughts] errer, vagabonder; her thoughts ~ed (back) to her days in Japan elle se mit à penser à sa vie au Japon.
◇ *n* [dog] chien *m* errant OR perdu; [cat] chat *m* errant OR perdu; [cow, sheep] animal *m* égaré; [child] enfant *m* perdu OR abandonné; she set up a home for ~s elle a ouvert un centre pour recueillir les chiens et les chats perdus.
◇ *adj* -**1.** [lost - dog, cat] perdu, errant; [- cow, sheep] égaré; [- child] perdu, abandonné. -**2.** [random - bullet] perdu; [- thought] vagabond; [- memory] fugitif; she pushed back a few ~ curls elle repoussa quelques mèches folles OR rebelles. -**3.** [occasional - car, boat] isolé, rare; a few ~ cars drove by quelques rares voitures passaient par là.
◆ **strays** *npl* RADIO & TELEC parasites *mpl*, friture *f*.

streak [striːk] ◇ *n* -**1.** [smear - of blood, dirt] filet *m*; [- of ink, paint] traînée *f*; there were ~s of green ink across the page il y avait des traînées d'encre verte sur la page; there were a few ~s of cloud in an otherwise blue sky il y avait quelques traînées nuageuses dans le ciel bleu; the tears had left grubby ~s down her face les larmes avaient laissé des traînées sales sur ses joues || [line, stripe - of light] trait *m*, rai *m*; [- of ore] filon *m*, veine *f*; [- in marble] veine *f*; black wings with white ~s des ailes noires avec des traînées blanches; the carpet has green ~s la moquette est striée de vert; her hair had grey ~s in it elle avait des cheveux gris; to have blond ~s put in one's hair se faire faire des mèches blondes; ~s of lightning lit up the sky des éclairs zébraient le ciel; they drove past like a ~ of lightning leur voiture est passée comme un éclair. -**2.** [of luck] période *f*; I've had a ~ of (good) luck je viens de traverser une période faste; he's hit a winning ~ [in gambling] la chance lui a souri; [good deal] il tient un bon filon; he's just had a ~ of bad luck lately il vient d'essuyer toute une série de revers. -**3.** [tendency]: he has a mean ~ OR a ~ of meanness in him il est un peu mesquin; there has always been a ~ of madness in the family il y a toujours eu une prédisposition à la folie dans la famille || [trace] trace *f*; there's a ~ of Indian blood in the family il y a un peu de sang indien dans la famille. -**4.** *inf* [naked dash]: to do a ~ *traverser un lieu public nu en courant*.
◇ *vt* [smear] tacher; the wall was ~ed with paint il y avait des traînées de peinture sur le mur; her hands were ~ed with blue ink elle avait des taches d'encre bleue sur les mains; the mirror was ~ed with finger marks il y avait des traces de doigts sur le miroir; the sink was ~ed with coffee stains il y avait des taches de café partout dans l'évier; their cheeks were ~ed with tears leurs joues étaient couvertes de larmes || [stripe] strier, zébrer; the carpet is ~ed with green la moquette est striée de vert; marble ~ed with red du marbre strié de rouge; her hair is ~ed with grey [natural] elle a des cheveux gris; [artificial] elle s'est fait des mèches grises; she's had her hair ~ed elle s'est fait faire des mèches.
◇ *vi* -**1.** [go quickly]: to ~ in/out entrer/sortir comme un éclair; to ~ past passer en courant d'air. -**2.** [run naked] faire du streaking *(traverser un lieu public nu en courant)*; he was arrested for ~ing ≃ il a été arrêté pour exhibitionnisme.

streaker *inf* ['striːkəʳ] *n* streaker *mf (personne nue qui traverse un lieu public en courant)*.

streaky ['striːkɪ] (*compar* streakier, *superl* streakiest) *adj* -**1.** [colour, surface] marbré, jaspé, zébré; [rock, marble] veiné; ~ clouds de longues traînées nuageuses. -**2.** CULIN [meat] entrelardé, persillé; ~ bacon bacon *m* entrelardé.

stream [striːm] ◇ *n* -**1.** [brook] ruisseau *m*. -**2.** [current] courant *m*; to go with the ~ *literal* aller au fil de l'eau; *fig* suivre le courant OR le mouvement; to go against the ~ *literal* & *fig* aller à contre-courant. -**3.** [flow - of liquid] flot *m*, jet *m*; [- of air] courant *m*; [- of blood, lava] ruisseau *m*, flot *m*, cascade *f*, torrent *m*; [- of people, traffic] flot *m*, défilé *m* (continu); [- of tears] ruisseau *m*, torrent *m*; the vent sent out a ~ of hot air du conduit s'échappait un courant d'air chaud; a red hot ~ of lava flowed down the mountain une coulée de lave incandescente descendait le flanc de la montagne; there was a continuous ~ of visitors il y avait un défilé continu OR ininterrompu de visiteurs; ~s of wellwishers have been arriving all day des flots de sympathisants sont arrivés tout au long de la journée; we've received a steady ~ of applications nous avons reçu un flot incessant de candidatures; she unleashed a ~ of insults elle lâcha un torrent d'injures ❑ ~ of consciousness monologue *m* intérieur. -**4.** INDUST & TECH: to be on/off ~ être en service/hors service; to come on ~ être mis en service. -**5.** *Br* SCH classe *f* de niveau; we're in the top ~ nous sommes dans la section forte.
◇ *vi* -**1.** [flow - water, tears] ruisseler, couler à flots; [- blood] ruisseler; the wall was ~ing with condensation, condensation ~ed down the wall la condensation ruisselait le long du mur; tears ~ed down her face des larmes ruisselaient sur son visage; the onions made her eyes ~ les oignons l'ont fait pleurer; sunlight ~ed into the room le soleil entra à flots dans la pièce. -**2.** [flutter] flotter, voleter; flags were ~ing in the wind des drapeaux flottaient au vent; her long hair ~ed (out) behind her ses longs cheveux flottaient derrière elle. -**3.** [people, traffic]: to ~ in/out entrer/sortir à flots; cars ~ed out of the city in their thousands des milliers de voitures sortaient de la ville en un flot ininterrompu; I watched as the demonstrators ~ed past je regardai passer les flots de manifestants.
◇ *vt* -**1.** [flow with]: to ~ blood/tears ruisseler de sang/de larmes. -**2.** *Br* SCH répartir en classes de niveau.

streamer ['striːməʳ] *n* -**1.** [decoration] serpentin *m*. -**2.** [banner] banderole *f*; [pennant] flamme *f*. -**3.** ASTRON flèche *f* lumineuse. -**4.** PRESS manchette *f*.

streaming ['striːmɪŋ] ◇ *n* *Br* SCH répartition *f* en classes de niveau.
◇ *adj* [surface, window, windscreen] ruisselant; I've got a ~ cold *Br* j'ai attrapé un gros rhume.

streamline ['striːmlaɪn] ◇ *vt* -**1.** AUT & AERON donner un profil aérodynamique à, profiler, caréner. -**2.** ECON & INDUST [organization, production] rationaliser; [industry] dégraisser, restructurer.
◇ *n* -**1.** AUT & AERON ligne *f* aérodynamique, forme *f* profilée OR carénée. -**2.** PHYS écoulement *m* non perturbé.

streamlined ['striːmlaɪnd] *adj* -**1.** AUT & AERON aérodynamique, profilé, caréné. -**2.** *fig* [building] aux contours harmonieux; [figure] svelte. -**3.** ECON & INDUST [organization, production] rationalisé; [industry] dégraissé, restructuré.

streamlining ['striːmlaɪnɪŋ] *n* -**1.** AUT & AERON carénage *m*. -**2.** ECON & INDUST [of business, organization] rationalisation *f*; [of industry] dégraissage *m*, restructuration *f*.

street [striːt] ◇ *n* rue *f*; in *Br* OR on *Am* a ~ dans une rue; a ~ of houses une rue résidentielle; the whole ~ knows about it toute la rue est au courant; to put OR to turn sb (out) into the ~ mettre qqn à la rue; to be on the ~ OR ~s [as prostitute] *inf* faire le trottoir; [homeless person] être à la rue OR sur le pavé; to take to the ~s [protestors] descendre dans la rue; to walk the ~s [as prostitute] *inf* faire le trottoir; [from idleness] battre le pavé, flâner dans les rues; [in search] faire les rues; they walked the ~s looking for her ils ont parcouru la ville à pied à sa recherche ❑ that's right up his ~! *inf* [competence] c'est tout à fait son rayon OR dans ses cordes!; [interest] c'est tout à fait son truc!
◇ *comp* [sounds, noises] de la rue; [beggar, musician] des rues.
◆ **streets** *inf adv*: to be ~s ahead of sb dépasser qqn de loin; they're ~s apart in the way they think ils ne partagent pas du tout les mêmes opinions.

street Arab *Br dated & offensive* = **street urchin**.

street café *n Br* café *m* avec terrasse; we had breakfast at a ~ nous avons pris le petit déjeuner à la terrasse d'un café.

streetcar ['striːtkɑːʳ] *n Am* tramway *m*; 'A Streetcar Named Desire' *Williams, Kazan* 'Un tramway nommé Désir'.

street cleaner = **street sweeper**.

street cred *inf* [-kred], **street credibility** *n* ≃ allure *f* cool, ≃ look *m* branché; she reckons the leather jacket gives her more ~ elle trouve que son blouson en cuir fait très branché OR lui donne l'air encore plus cool.

street cry *n* cri *m* de colporteur; the street cries of old Paris le cri des colporteurs du vieux Paris.

street door *n* porte *f* (qui donne) sur la rue, porte *f* d'entrée.

street guide *n* plan *m* de la ville, répertoire *m* des rues.

street hawker *n* colporteur *m*, -euse *f*.

streetlamp ['striːtlæmp], **streetlight** ['striːtlaɪt] *n* réverbère *m*.

street lighting *n* éclairage *m* public; the ~ comes on at sunset on allume la lumière dans les rues au coucher du soleil.

street map *n* plan *m* de la ville.

street market *n* marché *m* en plein air OR à ciel ouvert.

street party *n fête de rue organisée en l'honneur d'un événement national*.

street photographer *n* photostoppeur *m*, -euse *f*.

street sweeper *n* [person] balayeur *m*, -euse *f*; [machine] balayeuse *f*.

street theatre *n* théâtre *m* de rue OR de foire.

street trader *n* marchand *m* ambulant, marchande *f* ambulante.

street trading *n* vente *f* ambulante.

street urchin *n* gamin *m*, -e *f* OR gosse *mf* des rues.

street value *n* [of drugs] valeur *f* marchande.

street vendor *Am* = **street trader**.

streetwalker ['striːtˌwɔːkəʳ] *n dated* fille *f* de joie.

streetwalking ['striːtˌwɔːkɪŋ] *n dated* racolage *m*.

streetwise *inf* ['striːtwaɪz] *adj qui connaît la vie de la rue, ses dangers et ses codes*.

strength [streŋθ] *n* -**1.** *(U)* [physical power - of person, animal, muscle] force *f*, puissance *f*; she doesn't know her own ~ elle ne connaît pas sa force; his ~ failed him ses forces l'ont trahi OR abandonné; I haven't the ~ to lift these boxes je n'ai pas assez de force OR je ne suis pas assez fort pour soulever ces cartons; he has great ~ in his arms/hands il a beaucoup de force dans les bras/les mains; to lose ~ perdre des forces, s'affaiblir; by sheer ~ de force; with all my ~ de toutes mes forces || [health] forces *fpl*; to get one's ~ back reprendre des OR recouvrer ses forces ❑ to go from ~ to ~ *literal* [sick person] aller de mieux en mieux; *fig* [business] être en plein essor. -**2.** [of faith, opinion, resolution] force *f*, fermeté *f*; [of emotion, feeling] force *f*; [of music, art] force *f*; ~ of character force de caractère; ~ of purpose résolution *f*;

they have no ~ of purpose ils n'ont aucune détermination; **they have great ~ of purpose** ils sont très déterminés; **~ of will** volonté *f*; **I haven't the ~ to start again** je n'ai pas le courage de recommencer ❑ **give me ~!** pitié! -**3.** [intensity - of earthquake, wind] force *f*, intensité *f*; [- of current, light] intensité *f*; [- of sound, voice, lens, magnet] force *f*, puissance *f*. -**4.** [strong point, asset] force *f*, point *m* fort; **her ambition is her main ~** son ambition fait l'essentiel de sa force; **the nation's ~ lies in its young people** ce sont les jeunes qui font la force du pays; **it's one of their ~s** c'est un de leurs points forts. -**5.** [solidity] solidité *f*; *fig* [of claim, position, relationship] solidité *f*; [vigour - of argument, protest] force *f*, vigueur *f*; **to argue from a position of ~** être en position de force ‖ FIN [of currency, economy] solidité *f*; **the dollar has gained/fallen in ~** le dollar s'est consolidé/a chuté. -**6.** [of alcohol] teneur *f* en alcool; [of solution] titre *m*; [of coffee, tobacco] force *f*. -**7.** *(U)* [numbers] effectif *m*, effectifs *mpl*; **the office staff is below** OR **under ~** il nous manque du personnel de bureau; **we're at full ~** nos effectifs sont au complet; **the staff must be brought up to ~** il faut engager du personnel; **the protestors turned up in ~** les manifestants sont venus en force OR en grand nombre.

◆ **on the strength of** *prep phr* en vertu de, sur la foi de; **he was accepted on the ~ of his excellent record** il a été accepté grâce à ses excellents antécédents; **I was convicted on the ~ of the flimsiest of evidence** j'ai été condamné sur la foi de preuves bien minces.

strengthen ['streŋθn] ◇ *vt* -**1.** [physically - body, muscle] fortifier, raffermir; [- person] fortifier, tonifier; [- voice] renforcer; [improve - eyesight, hearing] améliorer; **to ~ one's body by exercise** fortifier son corps en faisant de l'exercice; **to ~ one's grip** OR **hold on sthg** *literal & fig* resserrer son emprise sur qqch. -**2.** [reinforce - firm, nation] renforcer; [- fear, emotion, effect] renforcer, intensifier; [- belief, argument] renforcer; [- link, friendship] renforcer, fortifier; **the decision ~ed my resolve** la décision n'a fait que renforcer ma détermination ‖ [morally - person] fortifier; **I felt ~ed by the experience** je suis sorti plus fort de cette expérience. -**3.** [foundation, structure] renforcer, consolider; [material] renforcer. -**4.** FIN [currency, economy] consolider.
◇ *vi* -**1.** [physically - body, muscle] se fortifier, se raffermir; [- voice] devenir plus fort; [- grip] se resserrer. -**2.** [increase - influence, effect, desire] augmenter, s'intensifier; [- wind] forcir; [- current] augmenter, se renforcer; [- friendship, character, resolve] se renforcer, se fortifier. -**3.** FIN [prices, market] se consolider, se raffermir.

strengthening ['streŋθənɪŋ] ◇ *n* -**1.** [physical - of body, muscle] raffermissement *m*; [- of voice] renforcement *m*; [- of hold, grip] resserrement *m*. -**2.** [increase - of emotion, effect, desire] renforcement *m*, augmentation *f*, intensification *f*; [reinforcement - of character, friendship, position] renforcement *m*; [- of wind, current] renforcement *m*. -**3.** [of structure, building] renforcement *m*, consolidation *f*. -**4.** FIN consolidation *f*.
◇ *adj* fortifiant, remontant; MED tonifiant; **to have a ~ effect on sb** fortifier qqn.

strenuous ['strenjʊəs] *adj* -**1.** [physically - activity, exercise, sport] ardu; **it was a long, ~ climb** ce fut une longue et difficile ascension; **I'm not allowed to do anything ~** je ne dois pas me fatiguer; **avoid very ~ games like squash** évitez les sports comme le squash qui demandent une grande dépense d'énergie; **she leads a ~ life** elle mène une vie stressante. -**2.** [vigorous - opposition, support] acharné, énergique; [- protest] vigoureux, énergique; [- opponent, supporter] zélé, très actif; **to make ~ efforts to do sthg** faire des efforts considérables pour faire qqch; **he is a ~ campaigner for civil rights** il milite avec acharnement pour les droits civils.

strenuously ['strenjʊəslɪ] *adv* -**1.** [play, swim, work] en se dépensant beaucoup, en faisant de gros efforts. -**2.** [fight, oppose, resist] avec acharnement, énergiquement.

streptococcal [,streptə'kɒkl], **streptococcic** [,streptə'kɒksɪk] *adj* streptococcique.

streptococcus [,streptə'kɒkəs] (*pl* **streptococci** [-'kɒksaɪ]) *n* streptocoque *m*.

streptomycin [,streptə'maɪsɪn] *n* streptomycine *f*.

stress [stres] ◇ *n* -**1.** [nervous tension] stress *m*, tension *f* nerveuse; **to suffer from ~** être stressé; **to be under ~** [person] être stressé; [relationship] être tendu; **she's been under a lot of ~ lately** elle a été très stressée ces derniers temps; **the ~es and strains of city life** le stress de la vie urbaine; **the ~es and strains of being a parent** les angoisses qu'on éprouve lorsqu'on a des enfants; **she copes well in times of ~** elle sait faire face dans les moments difficiles ‖ [pressure] pression *f*; **I always work better under ~** je travaille toujours mieux quand je suis sous pression. -**2.** CONSTR & TECH contrainte *f*, tension *f*; **tensile ~** force *f* de tension; **to be in ~** [beam, girder] être sous contrainte; **there is too much ~ on the foundations** la contrainte que subissent les fondations est trop forte; **we have measured the ~es produced in the metal plates** nous avons mesuré l'effort que produisent les plaques métalliques; **can the girders take the ~?** est-ce que les poutres peuvent soutenir la charge OR la tension?; **earthquakes are caused by subterranean ~es** les tremblements de terre sont provoqués par des tensions souterraines. -**3.** [emphasis] insistance *f*; **to lay ~ on sthg** [fact, point, detail] insister sur, souligner; [qualities, values, manners] insister sur, mettre l'accent sur; **the ~ has always been on productivity** nous avons toujours mis l'accent sur la productivité. -**4.** LING [gen] accentuation *f*; **the rules of English sentence ~** les règles d'accentuation de la phrase anglaise ‖ [on syllable] accent *m*; **the ~ is** OR **falls on the third syllable** l'accent tombe sur la troisième syllabe ‖ [accented syllable] syllabe *f* accentuée; **there are three ~es in the sentence** il y a trois syllabes accentuées dans la phrase. -**5.** MUS accent *m*.
◇ *vt* -**1.** [emphasize - fact, point, detail] insister sur, faire ressortir, souligner; [- value, qualities] insister sur, mettre l'accent sur; **this point cannot be ~ed enough** on ne saurait trop insister sur ce point. -**2.** [in phonetics, poetry, music] accentuer. -**3.** CONSTR & TECH [structure, foundation] mettre sous tension OR en charge; [concrete, metal] solliciter.

stressed [strest] *adj* -**1.** [person] stressé, tendu; [relationship] tendu. -**2.** [syllable, word] accentué.

stressed-out *inf adj* stressé.

stressful ['stresfʊl] *adj* [lifestyle, job, conditions] stressant; [moments] de stress; **to lead a ~ life** mener une vie très stressante.

stress mark *n* LING marque *f* d'accent.

stress-timed *adj*: **~ language** *langue dont le rythme est fonction des syllabes accentuées.*

stretch [stretʃ] ◇ *vt* -**1.** [pull tight] tendre; **~ the rope tight** tendez bien la corde; **a cable was ~ed across the ravine** on avait tendu un câble à travers le ravin; **they ~ed a net over the pit** ils ont tendu un filet au-dessus de la fosse. -**2.** [pull longer or wider - elastic] étirer; [- garment, shoes] élargir; **to ~ sthg out of shape** déformer qqch; **don't pull your socks like that, you'll ~ them** ne tire pas sur tes chaussettes comme ça, tu vas les déformer. -**3.** [extend, reach to full length] étendre; **~ your arms upwards** tendez les bras vers le haut; **if I ~ up my hand I can reach the ceiling** si je tends la main (vers le haut) je peux toucher le plafond; **to ~ o.s.** s'étirer; **to ~ one's legs** se dégourdir les jambes; **the bird ~ed its wings** l'oiseau déploya ses ailes; **to ~ one's wings** *fig* prendre son envol. -**4.** [force, strain, bend - meaning, truth] forcer, exagérer; [- rules] tourner, contourner, faire une entorse à; [- principle] faire une entorse à; [- imagination] faire un gros effort de; **you're really ~ing my patience** ma patience a des limites; **they have ~ed their authority a bit too far** ils ont un peu abusé de leur autorité; **that's ~ing it a bit (far)!** là vous exagérez!, là vous allez un peu loin!; **it would be ~ing a point to call him a diplomat** dire qu'il est diplomate serait exagérer OR aller un peu loin; **I suppose we could ~ a point and let him stay** je suppose qu'on pourrait faire une entorse au règlement et lui permettre de rester. -**5.** [budget, income, resources, supplies - get the most from] tirer le maximum de; [- overload] surcharger, mettre à rude épreuve; **I can't ~ my income that far** mon salaire ne me permet pas de faire de telles dépenses; **our resources are ~ed to the limit** nos ressources sont exploitées OR utilisées au maximum; **our staff are really ~ed today** le personnel travaille à la limite de ses possibilités aujourd'hui; **to be fully ~ed** [machine, engine] tourner à plein régime; [factory, economy] fonctionner à plein régime; [person, staff] faire son maximum ‖ [person - use one's talents]: **the job won't ~ you enough** le travail ne sera pas assez stimulant pour vous; **she believes young people need to be ~ed** elle pense qu'il faut être exigeant avec les jeunes pour qu'ils donnent le meilleur d'eux-mêmes. -**6.** MED [ligament, muscle] étirer.
◇ *vi* -**1.** [be elastic] s'étirer; [become longer] s'allonger; [become wider] s'élargir; **this fabric tends to ~** ce tissu a tendance à s'étirer; **the shoes will ~ with wear** vos chaussures vont se faire OR s'élargir à l'usage; **my pullover has ~ed out of shape** mon pull s'est déformé. -**2.** [person, animal - from tiredness] s'étirer; [- on ground, bed] s'étendre, s'allonger; [- to reach something] tendre la main; **she ~ed lazily** elle s'étira nonchalamment; **he had to ~ to reach it** [reach out] il a dû tendre le bras pour l'atteindre; [stand on tiptoe] il a dû se mettre sur la pointe des pieds pour l'atteindre; **she ~ed across me to get the salt** elle a passé le bras devant moi pour attraper le sel; **can you ~ over and get me the paper?** pouvez-vous tendre le bras et me passer le journal?; **to ~ up to touch the ceiling** essayer de toucher le plafond *(en se mettant sur la pointe des pieds)*. -**3.** [spread, extend - in space, time] s'étendre; **the forest ~es as far as the eye can see** la forêt s'étend à perte de vue; **the road ~ed across 500 miles of desert** la route parcourait 800 km de désert; **minutes ~ed into hours** les minutes devenaient des heures; **our powers don't ~ as far as you imagine** nos pouvoirs ne sont pas aussi étendus que vous l'imaginez; **my salary won't ~ to a new car** mon salaire ne me permet pas d'acheter une nouvelle voiture.
◇ *n* -**1.** [expanse - of land, water] étendue *f*; **this ~ of the road is particularly dangerous in the winter** cette partie de la route est très dangereuse en hiver; **a new ~ of road/motorway** un nouveau tronçon de route/d'autoroute; **a long straight ~** une longue route en ligne droite; **it's a lovely ~ of river/scenery** cette partie de la rivière/du paysage est magnifique ‖ [on racetrack] ligne *f* droite; **to go into the final** OR **finishing ~** entamer la dernière ligne droite. -**2.** [period of time] laps *m* de temps; **for a long ~ of time** pendant longtemps; **for long ~es at a time there was nothing to do** il n'y avait rien à faire pendant de longues périodes; **to do a ~ of ten years in the army** passer dix ans dans l'armée; **a prison ~ of three years** une peine de prison de trois ans; **he did a ~ in Dartmoor** *inf* il a fait de la taule à Dartmoor. -**3.** [act of stretching] étirement *m*; **he stood up, yawned and had a ~** il se leva, bâilla et s'étira; **to give one's legs a ~** se dégourdir les jambes; **by no ~ of the imagination** même en faisant un gros effort d'imagination ❑ **by a long ~: he's the better writer by a long ~** c'est lui de loin le meilleur écrivain; **not by a long ~!** loin de là! -**4.** [elasticity] élasticité *f*; **there isn't much ~ in these gloves** ces gants ne sont pas très souples; **there's a lot of ~ in these stockings** ces bas

sont très élastiques OR s'étirent facilement. -**5.** SPORT [exercise] étirement *m*; **do a couple of ~es before breakfast** faites quelques exercices d'assouplissement avant le petit déjeuner.

◇ *adj* TEX [material, socks] élastique, stretch (*inv*); [cover] extensible.

◆ **at a stretch** *adv phr* d'affilée; **we worked for five hours at a ~** nous avons travaillé cinq heures d'affilée.

◆ **at full stretch** *adv phr*: **to be at full ~** [factory, machine] fonctionner à plein régime OR à plein rendement; [person] se donner à fond, faire son maximum; **we were working at full ~** nous travaillions d'arrache-pied; **even at full ~, we can't meet the delivery date** même en tournant à plein régime, nous ne pouvons pas respecter les délais de livraison.

◆ **stretch out** ◇ *vt sep* -**1.** [pull tight] tendre; **the sheets had been ~ed out on the line to dry** on avait étendu les draps sur le fil à linge pour qu'ils sèchent; **the plastic sheet was ~ed out on the lawn** la bâche en plastique était étalée sur la pelouse. -**2.** [extend, spread - arms, legs] allonger, étendre; [- hand] tendre; [- wings] déployer; **she ~ed out her hand towards him/for the cup** elle tendit la main vers lui/pour prendre la tasse; **she lay ~ed out in front of the television** elle était allongée par terre devant la télévision. -**3.** [prolong - interview, meeting] prolonger, faire durer; [- account] allonger; **she has to ~ her thesis out a bit for publication** il faut qu'elle étoffe un peu sa thèse pour la publier. -**4.** [make last - supplies, income] faire durer.

◇ *vi insep* -**1.** [person, animal] s'étendre, s'allonger; **they ~ed out on the lawn in the sun** ils se sont allongés au soleil sur la pelouse. -**2.** [forest, countryside] s'étendre; [prospects, season] s'étendre, s'étaler; **a nice long holiday ~ed out before them** ils avaient de longues vacances devant eux.

stretcher ['stretʃəʳ] *n* -**1.** MED brancard *m*, civière *f*. -**2.** [for shoes] tendeur *m*, forme *f*; [for gloves] ouvre-gants *m inv*; [in umbrella] baleine *f*; ART & SEW [for canvas] cadre *m*, châssis *m*. -**3.** CONSTR [brick, stone] panneresse *f*, carreau *m*. -**4.** [crossbar - in structure] traverse *f*, tirant *m*; [- on chair] barreau *m*, bâton *m*.

stretcher-bearer *n* brancardier *m*.

stretcher case *n blessé ou malade ayant besoin d'être porté sur un brancard*; **I was practically a ~ by the time the parents got home** *hum* je ne tenais plus debout OR j'étais bon pour l'hôpital quand les parents sont rentrés.

stretcher party *n* détachement *m* de brancardiers.

stretchmarks ['stretʃmaːks] *npl* vergetures *fpl*.

stretchy ['stretʃɪ] (*compar* **stretchier**, *superl* **stretchiest**) *adj* élastique, extensible.

strew [struː] (*pt* **strewed**, *pp* **strewn** [struːn] OR **strewed**) *vt lit* -**1.** [scatter - seeds, flowers, leaves] répandre, éparpiller; [throw - toys, papers] éparpiller, jeter; [- debris] éparpiller, disséminer; **they ~ed sand on the floor** ils ont répandu du sable sur le sol; **the guests ~ed confetti over the bride** les invités ont lancé des confettis sur la mariée; **wreckage was strewn all over the road** il y avait des débris partout sur la route; **their conversation was strewn with four-letter words** leur conversation était truffée de gros mots. -**2.** [cover - ground, floor, path] joncher, parsemer; [- table] joncher; **the path was strewn with leaves/litter** l'allée était jonchée de feuilles/de détritus.

strewth▽ [struːθ] *interj Br dated*: **~!** mon Dieu!, bon sang!

striated [straɪ'eɪtɪd] *adj* ANAT & GEOL strié.

striation [straɪ'eɪʃn] *n* striation *f*.

stricken ['strɪkn] *adj fml* -**1.** [ill] malade; [wounded] blessé; [damaged, troubled] ravagé, dévasté; **to be ~ in years** être âgé et infirme; **our ~ industry** notre industrie dévastée; **the ~ army retreated** l'armée défaite battit en retraite. -**2.** [afflicted] frappé, atteint; **~ by** OR **with blindness** frappé de cécité; **they were ~ with grief/fear** ils étaient accablés de chagrin/transis de peur.

-stricken *in cpds*: **grief~** accablé de chagrin; **terror~** saisi d'épouvante.

strict [strɪkt] *adj* -**1.** [severe, stern - person, discipline] strict, sévère; **you must be very ~ with them** il faut être très strict avec eux ‖ [inflexible - principles] strict, rigoureux; [- belief, code, rules] strict, rigide; **they belong to a ~ religious sect** ils appartiennent à une secte religieuse très stricte; **she's a ~ vegetarian** c'est une végétarienne pure et dure; **I gave ~ orders not to be disturbed** j'ai formellement ordonné qu'on ne me dérange pas; **I'm on a ~ diet** j'ai un régime très strict. -**2.** [exact, precise - meaning, interpretation] strict; **in the ~ sense of the word** au sens strict du terme; **the ~ truth** la stricte vérité; **it's a ~ translation from the Hebrew** c'est une traduction exacte OR fidèle de l'hébreu ❑ **~ construction** *Am* JUR interprétation *f* stricte de la constitution. -**3.** [absolute - accuracy, hygiene] strict, absolu; **he told me in the ~est confidence** il me l'a dit à titre strictement confidentiel; **in ~ secrecy** dans le plus grand secret.

strictly ['strɪktlɪ] *adv* -**1.** [severely - act, treat] strictement, avec sévérité; **the children were very ~ brought up** les enfants ont reçu une éducation extrêmement stricte. -**2.** [exactly - interpret, translate] fidèlement, exactement; **~ speaking** à strictement OR à proprement parler. -**3.** [absolutely, rigorously] strictement, absolument; **what you say is not ~ accurate** ce que vous dites n'est pas tout à fait exact; **~ confidential** strictement confidentiel; **to adhere ~ to one's principles** adhérer rigoureusement à ses principes; **the rules must be ~ observed** le règlement doit être scrupuleusement observé; **to adhere ~ to one's diet** suivre scrupuleusement son régime; **~ forbidden** OR **prohibited** formellement interdit; **'smoking ~ forbidden'** 'défense absolue de fumer'.

strictness ['strɪktnɪs] *n* -**1.** [severity - of person, rules, diet] sévérité *f*. -**2.** [exactness - of interpretation] exactitude *f*, rigueur *f*.

stricture ['strɪktʃəʳ] *n fml* -**1.** [criticism] critique *f* sévère; **to pass ~ on sb/sthg** critiquer qqn/qqch sévèrement. -**2.** [restriction] restriction *f*. -**3.** MED striction *f*, sténose *f*.

stride [straɪd] (*pt* **strode** [strəʊd], *pp* **stridden** ['strɪdn]) ◇ *n* -**1.** [step] grand pas *m*, enjambée *f*, foulée *f* SPORT; **to take big** OR **long ~s** faire de grandes enjambées; **with giant ~s** à pas de géant; **he crossed the threshold in** OR **with one ~** il a franchi le seuil d'une seule enjambée; **she recognized him by his purposeful ~** elle l'a reconnu à son pas décidé ❑ **to get** OR **to hit** *Am* **into one's ~** trouver son rythme; **to be caught off ~** *Am* être pris au dépourvu; **to take sthg in one's ~** faire qqch avec une facilité déconcertante; **he took all their criticisms in his ~** leurs critiques n'ont pas semblé le déranger; **they've always taken exams in their ~** ils ont toujours réussi leurs examens facilement; **she takes everything in her ~** elle ne se laisse jamais démonter OR abattre; **to put sb off their ~** faire perdre le rythme à qqn. -**2.** *fig* [progress]: **to make great ~s** faire de grands progrès, avancer à pas de géant; **he is making great ~s in German** il fait de grands progrès en allemand; **he is making great ~s with his research** sa recherche avance à grands pas.

◇ *vi* marcher à grands pas OR à grandes enjambées; **to ~ away/in/out** s'éloigner/entrer/sortir à grands pas; **he came striding over** OR **up to them** il avança vers eux à grands pas; **she strode away across the fields** elle s'éloigna à travers les champs à grands pas; **he strode up and down the street** il faisait les cent pas dans la rue; **he strode up and down the room** il arpentait la pièce.

◇ *vt* [streets, fields, deck] arpenter.

◆ **strides** *inf npl Br & Austr* [trousers] pantalon *m*.

stridency ['straɪdənsɪ] *n* stridence *f*.

strident ['straɪdnt] *adj* strident; **~ demands** des revendications véhémentes.

stridently ['straɪdəntlɪ] *adv* [call, cry, sing] d'une voix stridente; [sound, ring] en faisant un bruit strident; [demand] avec véhémence, à grands cris.

stridulate ['strɪdjʊleɪt] *vi* striduler.

strife [straɪf] *n (U) fml* [conflict] dissensions *fpl*; [struggles] luttes *fpl*; [quarrels] querelles *fpl*; **a period of political ~** une période marquée par des dissensions politiques; **industrial ~** conflits sociaux; **sectarian ~** luttes sectaires.

strife-torn *adj* déchiré par les conflits.

strike [straɪk] (*pt & pp* **struck** [strʌk], *cont* **striking**) ◇ *n* -**1.** [by workers] grève *f*; **to go on ~** se mettre en OR faire grève; **to be (out) on ~** être en grève; **the Italian air ~** la grève des transports aériens en Italie; **railway ~** grève des chemins de fer; **teachers' ~** grève des enseignants; **coal** OR **miners' ~** grève des mineurs; **postal** OR **post office ~** grève des postes; **rent ~** grève des loyers ❑ **the General Strike** *Br* HIST la grande grève. -**2.** MIL raid *m*, attaque *f*; **to carry out air ~s against** OR **on enemy bases** lancer des raids aériens contre des bases ennemies; **retaliatory ~** raid de représailles ‖ [nuclear] deuxième frappe *f*; [by bird of prey, snake] attaque *f*. -**3.** AERON & MIL [planes] escadre *f (d'avions participant à un raid)*. -**4.** PETR & MIN [discovery] découverte *f*; **a gold ~** la découverte d'un gisement d'or; **the recent oil ~s in the North Sea** la découverte récente de gisements de pétrole en mer du Nord ❑ **it was a lucky ~** c'était un coup de chance. -**5.** [of clock - chime, mechanism] sonnerie *f*; **life was regulated by the ~ of the church clock** la vie était rythmée par la cloche de l'église. -**6.** [act or instance of hitting] coup *m*; [sound] bruit *m*; **the ~ of iron on iron** le bruit du fer qui frappe le fer; **he adjusted the ~ of the keys on the platen roll** il a réglé la frappe des caractères contre le cylindre. -**7.** [in baseball] strike *m*; *Am fig* [black mark] mauvais point *m*; **he has two ~s against him** *fig* il est mal parti; **being too young was another ~ against her** *fig* le fait d'être trop jeune constituait un handicap supplémentaire pour elle. -**8.** [in bowling] honneur *m* double; **to get** OR **to score a ~** réussir un honneur double. -**9.** FISHING [by fisherman] ferrage *m*; [by fish] touche *f*. -**10.** *arch*: **at the ~ of day** à la pointe OR au point du jour.

◇ *comp* -**1.** [committee, movement] de grève; **to threaten ~ action** menacer de faire OR de se mettre en grève. -**2.** MIL [aircraft, mission] d'intervention, d'attaque.

◇ *vt* -**1.** [hit] frapper; **she raised her hand to ~ him** elle leva la main pour le frapper; **he struck me with his fist** il m'a donné un coup de poing; **the chairman struck the table with his gavel** le président donna un coup de marteau sur la table; **she took the vase and struck him on** OR **over the head** elle saisit le vase et lui donna un coup sur la tête; **she struck him across the face** elle lui a donné une gifle; **a light breeze struck the sails** une légère brise gonfla les voiles; **the phenomenon occurs when warm air ~s cold** ce phénomène se produit lorsque de l'air chaud entre en contact avec de l'air froid; **a wave struck the side of the boat** une vague a heurté le côté du bateau ‖ [inflict, deliver - blow] donner; **he went for them striking blows left and right** il s'est jeté sur eux, distribuant les coups de tous côtés; **who struck the first blow?** qui a porté le premier coup?, qui a frappé le premier?; **he struck the tree a mighty blow with the axe** il a donné un grand coup de hache dans l'arbre; **the trailer struck the post a glancing blow** la remorque a percuté le poteau en passant; **to ~ a blow for democracy/women's rights** *fig* [law, event] faire progresser la démocratie/les droits de la femme; [person, group] marquer des points en faveur de la démocratie/des droits des femmes. -**2.** [bump into, collide with] heurter, cogner; **his foot struck the bar on his first jump** son pied a heurté la barre lors de son premier saut; **she fell and struck her head on** OR **against** the kerb elle s'est cogné la tête contre le bord du trottoir en tombant; the Volvo struck the bus head-on la Volvo a heurté le bus de plein fouet; we've struck ground! NAUT nous avons touché (le fond)! -**3.** [assail, attain - subj: bullet, torpedo, bomb] toucher, atteindre; [- subj: lightning] frapper; the arrow struck the target la flèche a atteint la cible; a hail of bullets struck the car la voiture a été mitraillée; he was struck by a piece of shrapnel il a été touché par OR il a reçu un éclat de grenade; to be struck by lightning être frappé par la foudre, être foudroyé || [afflict - subj: drought, disease, worry, regret] frapper; [- subj: storm, hurricane, disaster, wave of violence] s'abattre sur, frapper; an earthquake struck the city un tremblement de terre a frappé la ville; he was struck by a heart attack il a eu une crise cardiaque; the pain struck her as she tried to get up la douleur l'a saisie au moment où elle essayait de se lever; I was struck by OR with doubts j'ai été pris de doute, le doute s'est emparé de moi. -**4.** [occur to] frapper; only later did it ~ me as unusual ce n'est que plus tard que j'ai trouvé ça OR que cela m'a paru bizarre; it suddenly struck him how little had changed il a soudain pris conscience du fait que peu de choses avaient changé; a terrible thought struck her une idée affreuse lui vint à l'esprit; it ~s me as useless/as the perfect gift ça me semble inutile/être le cadeau idéal; it doesn't ~ me as being the best course of action il ne me semble pas que ce soit la meilleure voie à suivre. -**5.** [impress] frapper, impressionner; the first thing that struck me was his pallor la première chose qui m'a frappé, c'était sa pâleur; what ~s you is the silence ce qui (vous) frappe, c'est le silence; how did she ~ you? quelle impression vous a-t-elle faite?, quel effet vous a-t-elle fait?; how did Tokyo/the film ~ you? comment avez-vous trouvé Tokyo/le film?; we can eat here and meet them later, how does that ~ you? on peut manger ici et les retrouver plus tard, qu'en penses-tu?; I was very struck with *Br* OR by *Am* the flat l'appartement m'a plu énormément; I wasn't very struck with *Br* OR by *Am* his colleague son collègue ne m'a pas fait une grande impression. -**6.** [chime] sonner; the church clock struck five l'horloge de l'église a sonné cinq heures; it was striking midnight as we left minuit sonnait quand nous partîmes. -**7.** [play - note, chord] jouer; she struck a few notes on the piano elle a joué quelques notes sur le piano; when he struck the opening chords the audience applauded quand il a joué OR plaqué les premiers accords le public a applaudi; to ~ a false note MUS faire une fausse note; [speech] sonner faux; his presence/his words struck a gloomy note sa présence a/ses paroles ont mis une note de tristesse; the report ~s an optimistic note/a note of warning for the future le rapport est très optimiste/très alarmant pour l'avenir ❑ to ~ a chord: does it ~ a chord? est-ce que cela te rappelle OR dit quelque chose?; to ~ a chord with the audience faire vibrer la foule; her description of company life will ~ a chord with many managers beaucoup de cadres se reconnaîtront dans sa description de la vie en entreprise. -**8.** [arrive at, reach - deal, treaty, agreement] conclure; to ~ a bargain conclure un marché; I'll ~ a bargain with you je te propose un marché; it's not easy to ~ a balance between too much and too little freedom il n'est pas facile de trouver un équilibre OR de trouver le juste milieu entre trop et pas assez de liberté. -**9.** [cause a feeling of]: to ~ fear OR terror into sb remplir qqn d'effroi. -**10.** [cause to become] rendre; to ~ sb blind/dumb rendre qqn aveugle/muet; the news struck us speechless with horror nous sommes restés muets d'horreur en apprenant la nouvelle; I was struck dumb by the sheer cheek of the man! je suis resté muet devant le culot de cet homme!; a stray bullet struck him dead il a été tué par une balle perdue; she was struck dead by a heart attack elle a été foudroyée par une crise cardiaque; God ~ me dead if I lie! je jure que c'est la vérité! -**11.** [ignite - match] frotter, allumer; [- sparks] faire jaillir; he struck a match OR a light il a frotté une allumette. -**12.** [discover - gold] découvrir; [- oil, water] trouver; to ~ it lucky *inf Br* [material gain] trouver le filon; [be lucky] avoir de la veine; to ~ it rich *inf* trouver le filon, faire fortune. -**13.** [adopt - posture, attitude] adopter; he struck an attitude of wounded righteousness il a pris un air de dignité offensée. -**14.** [mint - coin, medal] frapper. -**15.** [take down - tent] démonter; NAUT [- sail] amener, baisser; to ~ camp lever le camp; to ~ the flag OR the colours NAUT amener les couleurs. -**16.** [delete - name, remark, person] rayer; [- from professional register] radier; the judge ordered the evidence to be struck from the record le juge a ordonné que le témoignage soit rayé du procès-verbal. -**17.** [attack] attaquer. -**18.** *Am* [go on strike at]: the union is striking four of the company's plants le syndicat a déclenché des grèves dans quatre des usines de la société; students are striking their classes les étudiants font la grève des cours; the dockers are striking ships carrying industrial waste les dockers refusent de s'occuper des cargos chargés de déchets industriels. -**19.** BOT: to ~ roots prendre racine; the tree had struck deep roots into the ground l'arbre avait des racines très profondes.

◇ *vi* -**1.** [hit] frapper; she struck at me with her umbrella elle essaya de me frapper avec son parapluie; to ~ home [blow] porter; [missile, remark] faire mouche ❑ to ~ lucky *inf* avoir de la veine; ~ while the iron is hot *prov* il faut battre le fer pendant qu'il est chaud *prov*. -**2.** [stop working] faire grève; they're striking for more pay ils font grève pour obtenir une augmentation de salaire; the nurses struck over the minister's decision to freeze wages les infirmières ont fait grève suite à la décision du ministre de bloquer les salaires. -**3.** [attack - gen] attaquer; [- snake] mordre; [- wild animal] sauter OR bondir sur sa proie; [- bird of prey] fondre OR s'abattre sur sa proie; the bombers struck at dawn les bombardiers attaquèrent à l'aube; the Liverpool murderer has struck again l'assassin de Liverpool a encore frappé; these are measures which ~ at the root/heart of the problem voici des mesures qui attaquent le problème à la racine/qui s'attaquent au cœur du problème; this latest incident ~s right at the heart of government policy ce dernier incident remet complètement en cause la politique gouvernementale. -**4.** [chime] sonner; midnight had already struck minuit avait déjà sonné. -**5.** [happen suddenly - illness, disaster, earthquake] survenir, se produire, arriver; we were travelling quietly along when disaster struck nous roulions tranquillement lorsque la catastrophe s'est produite; the first tremors struck at 3 a.m. les premières secousses sont survenues à 3 h du matin. -**6.** FISHING [fisherman] ferrer; [fish] mordre (à l'hameçon).

◆ **strike back** *vi insep* se venger; MIL contre-attaquer.

◆ **strike down** *vt sep* foudroyer, terrasser.

◆ **strike off** ◇ *vt sep* -**1.** [delete, remove - from list] rayer, barrer; [- from professional register] radier. -**2.** [sever] couper. -**3.** TYPO tirer.

◇ *vi insep* [go] aller; we struck off into the forest nous sommes entrés OR avons pénétré dans la forêt.

◆ **strike on** *vt insep Br* [solution, right answer] trouver (par hasard), tomber sur; [plan] trouver; [idea] avoir.

◆ **strike out** ◇ *vi insep* -**1.** [set up on one's own] s'établir à son compte; [launch out] se lancer; they decided to ~ out into a new field ils ont décidé de se lancer dans un nouveau domaine. -**2.** [go] aller; she struck out across the fields elle prit à travers champs. -**3.** [swim]: we struck out for the shore nous avons commencé à nager en direction de la côte. -**4.** [aim a blow]: he struck out at me il essaya de me frapper; they struck out in all directions with their truncheons ils distribuaient des coups de matraque à droite et à gauche.

◇ *vt sep* [cross out] rayer, barrer.

◆ **strike through** *vt sep Br* [cross out] rayer, barrer.

◆ **strike up** ◇ *vt insep* -**1.** [start]: to ~ up a conversation with sb engager la conversation avec qqn; to ~ up an acquaintance/a friendship with sb lier connaissance/se lier d'amitié avec qqn. -**2.** MUS [start playing] commencer à jouer; the band struck up the national anthem l'orchestre commença à jouer l'hymne national OR entonna les premières mesures de l'hymne national.

◇ *vi insep* [musician, orchestra] commencer à jouer; [music] commencer.

◆ **strike upon** *Br* = **strike on**.

THE GENERAL STRIKE:

La plus grande grève générale qu'ait connue l'Angleterre, en 1926. Elle éclata dans le secteur minier et s'étendit rapidement à tous les secteurs industriels. Elle ne paralysa le pays que 9 jours, mais la grève des mineurs dura 6 mois.

---

strikebound ['straɪkbaʊnd] *adj* [factory, department] bloqué par une OR la grève; [industry, country] bloqué par des grèves.

strikebreaker ['straɪk,breɪkəʳ] *n* briseur *m*, -euse *f* de grève, jaune *m*.

strikebreaking ['straɪk,breɪkɪŋ] *n* refus *m* de faire grève.

strike force *n* -**1.** [nuclear capacity] force *f* de frappe. -**2.** [of police, soldiers - squad] détachement *m* OR brigade *f* d'intervention; [- larger force] force *f* d'intervention.

strikeover ['straɪk,əʊvəʳ] *n* surimpression *f*.

strike pay *n* salaire *m* de gréviste *(versé par le syndicat ou par un fonds de solidarité)*.

striker ['straɪkəʳ] *n* -**1.** INDUST gréviste *mf*. -**2.** FTBL buteur *m*. -**3.** [device - on clock] marteau *m*; [- in gun] percuteur *m*.

striking ['straɪkɪŋ] ◇ *adj* -**1.** [remarkable - contrast, resemblance, beauty] frappant, saisissant. -**2.** [clock] qui sonne les heures; ~ mechanism sonnerie *f* (des heures). -**3.** MIL [force] d'intervention. -**4.** INDUST en grève; ~ workers des travailleurs en grève, des grévistes. -**5.** *phr*: within ~ distance à proximité; they came within ~ distance of finding a solution ils ont failli trouvé OR presque trouvé une solution; she lives within ~ distance of London elle habite tout près de Londres.

◇ *n* -**1.** [of clock] sonnerie *f* (des heures). -**2.** [of coins] frappe *f*.

strikingly ['straɪkɪŋlɪ] *adv* remarquablement; a ~ beautiful woman une femme d'une beauté saisissante; it was ~ obvious to everyone but me c'était une évidence pour tout le monde sauf pour moi.

Strine [straɪn] *n hum* l'anglais *m* australien.

string [strɪŋ] (*pt* & *pp* strung [strʌŋ]) ◇ *n* -**1.** [gen - for parcel] ficelle *f*; [- on apron, pyjamas] cordon *m*; a piece of ~ un bout OR un morceau de ficelle || [for puppet] ficelle *f*, fil *m* ❑ to have sb on a ~ *inf* mener qqn par le bout du nez; he pulls the ~s c'est lui qui tire les ficelles; to pull ~s for sb *inf* [obtain favours] user de son influence OR faire jouer ses relations pour aider qqn; [get job, promotion] pistonner qqn; she needs somebody to pull a few ~s for her elle a besoin d'être pistonnée OR d'un coup de piston; somebody pulled ~s to get him the job il a eu le poste par piston; no ~s attached *inf* sans condition OR conditions; there are no ~s attached cela n'engage à rien. -**2.** [for bow, tennis racket, musical instrument] corde *f*; the ~s MUS les cordes ❑ to have more than one/a second ~ to one's bow avoir plus d'une/une seconde corde à son arc. -**3.** [row, chain - of beads, pearls] rang *m*, collier *m*; [- of onions, sausages] chapelet *m*; [- of visitors, cars] file *f*; a ~ of islands un chapelet d'îles; a ~ of fairy lights une guirlande (électrique); she owns a ~ of shops elle est propriétaire d'une chaîne de magasins; a ~ of race horses une écurie de course. -**4.** [series - of successes, defeats] série *f*; [- of lies, insults] kyrielle *f*, chapelet *m*; **he has a whole ~ of letters after his name** il a toute une kyrielle de diplômes. -**5.** COMPUT & LING chaîne *f*; MATH séquence *f*. -**6.** BOT fil *m*.

◇ *comp* -**1.** MUS [band, instrument, orchestra] à cordes; **~ player** musicien *m*, -enne *f* qui joue d'un instrument à cordes; **the ~ section** les cordes *fpl*; **~ quartet** quatuor *m* à cordes. -**2.** [made of string] de OR en ficelle; **~ bag** filet *m* à provisions; **~ vest** tricot *m* de corps à grosses mailles.

◇ *vt* -**1.** [guitar, violin] monter, mettre des cordes à; [racket] corder; [bow] mettre une corde à. -**2.** [beads, pearls] enfiler. -**3.** [hang] suspendre; [stretch] tendre; **Christmas lights had been strung across the street** des décorations de Noël avaient été suspendues en travers de la rue; **he strung the chain across the gateway** il a tendu OR attaché la chaîne en travers de l'entrée. -**4.** CULIN [beans] enlever les fils de.

◆ **string along** *inf* ◇ *vi insep* -**1.** [tag along] suivre (les autres); **do you mind if I ~ along?** est-ce que ça vous gêne si je viens avec vous OR si je vous accompagne? -**2.** [agree]: **to ~ along with sb** se ranger à l'avis de qqn; **he always ~s along with everybody else** il est toujours d'accord avec tout le monde.

◇ *vt sep* [person] faire marcher.

◆ **string out** *vt sep* [washing, lamps] suspendre (sur une corde); **lights were strung out along the runway** des lumières s'échelonnaient le long de la piste; **armed guards were strung out along the route** des gardes armés avaient été postés tout le long du parcours.

◆ **string together** *vt sep* -**1.** [beads] enfiler; [words, sentences] enchaîner; **she can barely ~ two words together in French** c'est à peine si elle peut faire une phrase en français. -**2.** [improvise - story] monter, improviser; **we managed to ~ together some story about missing the last bus** on a raconté qu'on avait raté le dernier bus.

◆ **string up** *vt sep* -**1.** [lights] suspendre; [washing] étendre. -**2.** *inf* [hang - person] pendre; **I could ~ her up!** *fig* je lui tordrais bien le cou!

string bean *n* -**1.** [vegetable] haricot *m* vert. -**2.** *inf* [person] grande perche *f*.

stringboard ['strɪŋbɔːd] *n* limon *m* (d'escalier).

stringed [strɪŋd] *adj* [instrument] à cordes.

-stringed *in cpds*: **five~** à cinq cordes.

stringency ['strɪndʒənsɪ] *n* -**1.** [severity] rigueur *f*, sévérité *f*. -**2.** ECON & FIN austérité *f*; **there is a need for financial ~** des mesures d'austérité s'imposent.

stringent ['strɪndʒənt] *n* -**1.** [rules] rigoureux, strict, sévère; [measures, conditions] rigoureux, draconien. -**2.** ECON & FIN [market] tendu.

stringently ['strɪndʒəntlɪ] *adv* rigoureusement, strictement.

stringer ['strɪŋəʳ] *n* -**1.** PRESS reporter *m* local. -**2.** CONSTR [timber] poutre *f* de renforcement; [metal] serre *f*. -**3.** MINER filet *m*, veine *f*. -**4.** [stringboard] limon *m* (d'escalier).

string-puller [-ˌpʊləʳ] *n personne qui utilise ses relations*.

string-pulling [-ˌpʊlɪŋ] *n* piston *m*; **he got the job through ~** il a décroché ce poste grâce à ses relations.

string variable *n* COMPUT variable *f* alphanumérique.

stringy ['strɪŋɪ] (*compar* stringier, *superl* stringiest) *adj* -**1.** [meat, vegetable] filandreux, fibreux; [cooked cheese] qui file. -**2.** [long - plant] (qui pousse) tout en longueur; [- build, limbs] filiforme.

strip [strɪp] (*pt* & *pp* **stripped**) ◇ *n* -**1.** [of paper, carpet] bande *f*; [of metal] bande *f*, ruban *m*; [of land] bande *f*, langue *f*; **there was a thin ~ of light under the door** il y avait un mince rai de lumière sous la porte; **each house had a ~ of grass in front of it** il y avait une bande de gazon devant chaque maison; **a narrow ~ of water** [sea] un étroit bras de mer; [river] un étroit ruban de rivière; **can you cut off a ~ of material** pouvez-vous couper une bande de tissu?; **she cut the dough/material into ~s** elle coupa la pâte en lamelles/le tissu en bandes; **to tear sthg into ~s** déchirer qqch en bandes ❑ **the Strip, Sunset Strip** *artère de Las Vegas où se trouvent tous les casinos*. -**2.** AERON piste *f*; **landing ~** piste d'atterrissage. -**3.** [cartoon]: **comic ~** bande *f* dessinée. -**4.** [light]: **neon ~** tube *m* néon. -**5.** SPORT tenue *f*; **the Liverpool ~** la tenue OR les couleurs de l'équipe de Liverpool. -**6.** [striptease] striptease *m*; **to do a ~** faire un strip-tease.

◇ *vt* -**1.** [undress] déshabiller, dévêtir; **they were stripped to the waist** ils étaient torse nu, ils étaient nus jusqu'à la ceinture; **to ~ sb naked** déshabiller qqn (complètement). -**2.** [make bare - tree] dépouiller, dénuder; [- door, furniture] décaper; [- wire] dénuder; **the walls need to be stripped first** [of wallpaper] il faut d'abord enlever OR arracher le papier peint; [of paint] il faut d'abord décaper les murs. -**3.** [remove cover from] découvrir; [take contents from] vider; **to ~ a bed** défaire un lit; **to ~ a room/house** vider une pièce/maison; **the windows had been stripped of their curtains** on avait enlevé les rideaux des fenêtres; **the Christmas tree looks odd stripped of its decorations** le sapin a un drôle d'air une fois qu'on lui a enlevé ses décorations; **the liner is to be completely stripped and refitted** le paquebot doit être refait de fond en comble. -**4.** [remove - gen] enlever; [- paint] décaper; **we stripped the wallpaper from the walls** nous avons arraché le papier peint des murs; **the birds have stripped the cherries from the trees** les oiseaux ont fait des ravages dans les cerisiers; **the storm stripped the leaves off the trees** la tempête a dépouillé les arbres de leurs feuilles; **the years of suffering had stripped away all pretence** les années de souffrance avaient effacé toute trace d'affectation. -**5.** [deprive] dépouiller, démunir; **to ~ sb of his/her privileges/possessions** dépouiller qqn de ses privilèges/biens; **he was stripped of his rank** il a été dégradé; **overcooking ~s vegetables of all their nutritional value** une cuisson prolongée élimine tous les éléments nutritifs des légumes. -**6.** [dismantle - engine, gun] démonter. -**7.** TECH [screw, bolt] arracher le filet de; [gear] arracher les dents de.

◇ *vi* -**1.** [undress] se déshabiller, se dévêtir; **to ~ to the waist** se dévêtir jusqu'à la ceinture, se mettre torse nu. -**2.** [do a striptease] faire un strip-tease.

◆ **strip down** ◇ *vt sep* -**1.** [bed] défaire (complètement); [wallpaper] arracher, enlever; [door, furniture] décaper; **to ~ the walls down** [remove wallpaper] arracher OR enlever le papier peint des murs; [remove paint] décaper les murs; **the text has been stripped down to its bare essentials** *fig* le texte a été réduit à l'essentiel. -**2.** [dismantle - engine, mechanism] démonter.

◇ *vi insep* se déshabiller; **he stripped down to his underpants** il s'est déshabillé, ne gardant que son slip.

◆ **strip off** ◇ *vt sep* [gen] enlever, arracher; [clothes, shirt] enlever; [paint] décaper; **to ~ the leaves off a tree** dépouiller un arbre de ses feuilles; **to ~ the bark off a tree** dénuder un arbre de son écorce.

◇ *vi insep* se déshabiller, se mettre nu.

◆ **strip out** *vt sep* [engine, mechanism] démonter, démanteler.

strip cartoon *n Br* bande *f* dessinée.

strip club *n* boîte *f* de strip-tease.

strip cropping [-ˌkrɒpɪŋ] *n* (U) culture *f* en bande *(pour limiter l'érosion)*.

stripe [straɪp] ◇ *n* -**1.** [on animal] zébrure *f*; [on material, shirt] raie *f*, rayure *f*; [on car] filet *m*; **black with orange ~s** noir avec des rayures orange. -**2.** MIL galon *m*, chevron *m*; **to get/to lose one's ~s** gagner/perdre ses galons. -**3.** [kind] genre *m*; **they are of the same political ~** ils partagent les mêmes idées politiques, ils appartiennent à la même famille politique. -**4.** [lash] coup *m* de fouet; [mark] marque *f* d'un coup de fouet.

◇ *vt* rayer, marquer de rayures.

striped [straɪpt] *adj* [animal] tigré, zébré; [material, shirt, pattern] rayé, à rayures; **~ with blue** avec des rayures bleues.

stripey ['straɪpɪ] = **stripy**.

strip farming *n* -**1.** HIST système *m* des openfields. -**2.** = **strip cropping**.

strip light *n* (tube *m*) néon *m*.

strip lighting *n* éclairage *m* fluorescent OR au néon.

stripling ['strɪplɪŋ] *n lit* OR *hum* tout jeune homme *m*.

strip mining *n esp Am* extraction *f* à ciel ouvert.

strippagram ['strɪpəgræm] *n message qu'on envoie par l'intermédiaire d'une personne qui fait un strip-tease*.

stripped [strɪpt] *adj* [wood] décapé; **~ pine furniture** meubles *mpl* en pin naturel.

stripper ['strɪpəʳ] *n* -**1.** [in strip club] stripteaseuse *f*; **the club had two male ~s** le club avait deux strip-teaseurs. -**2.** [for paint]: **(paint) ~** décapant *m*.

strip poker *n* strip-poker *m*.

strip search *n* fouille *f* corporelle *(la personne fouillée devant se déshabiller)*.

◆ **strip-search** *vt*: **to ~ sb** fouiller qqn après l'avoir fait déshabiller; **he was ~ed by prison warders** des gardiens de prison lui ont fait subir une fouille corporelle OR l'ont fouillé après l'avoir fait déshabiller.

strip show *n* (spectacle *m* de) strip-tease *m*.

striptease ['stripti:z] *n* strip-tease *m*; **~ artist** strip-teaseur *m*, -euse *f*.

stripy ['straɪpɪ] (*compar* stripier, *superl* stripiest) *adj* [material, shirt, pattern] rayé, à rayures; ZOOL tigré, zébré.

strive [straɪv] (*pt* strove [strəʊv], *pp* striven ['strɪvn]) *vt fml* & *lit* -**1.** [attempt]: **to ~ to do sthg** s'évertuer à OR s'acharner à faire qqch; **to ~ after** OR **for sthg** faire tout son possible pour obtenir qqch, s'efforcer d'obtenir qqch; **to ~ for effect** chercher à se faire remarquer à tout prix. -**2.** [struggle] lutter, se battre; **to ~ against misfortune** lutter OR se battre contre la malchance; **all her life she strove for success/recognition** toute sa vie, elle s'est battue pour réussir/être reconnue.

strobe [strəʊb] *n* -**1.** **~ (lighting)** lumière *f* stroboscopique. -**2.** = **stroboscope**.

stroboscope ['strəʊbəskəʊp] *n* stroboscope *m*.

strode [strəʊd] *pt* → **stride**.

stroke [strəʊk] ◇ *n* -**1.** [blow, flick] coup *m*; **with a ~ of the whip** d'un coup de fouet; **with a ~ of the brush** d'un coup de pinceau; **with a ~ of the pen** d'un trait de plume; **a ~ of lightning** un coup de foudre; **they were given 50 ~s** ils ont reçu 50 coups de fouet. -**2.** SPORT [in golf, tennis, cricket, billiards] coup *m*; [in swimming - movement] mouvement *m* des bras; [- style] nage *f*; [in rowing - movement] coup *m* d'aviron; [- technique] nage *f*; **she swam across the river with quick ~s** elle traversa rapidement la rivière à la nage; **the Oxford team rowed at 25 ~s to the minute** l'équipe d'Oxford ramait à une cadence de 25 coups à la minute; **to keep ~** garder la cadence ❑ **to set the ~** *literal* & *fig* donner la cadence; **to put sb off his ~** *literal* [in rowing] faire perdre sa cadence OR son rythme à qqn; [in golf] faire manquer son coup à; *fig* faire perdre tous ses moyens à qqn; **to be off one's ~** ne pas être au mieux de sa forme. -**3.** [mark - from pen, pencil] trait *m*; [from brush] trait *m*, touche *f*; [on letters, figures] barre *f*; **written with thick/thin ~s** écrit d'une écriture appuyée/fine ‖ TYPO [oblique dash] barre *f* oblique; **225 ~ 62** *Br* 225 barre oblique 62. -**4.** [piece, example - of luck] coup *m*; [- of genius] trait *m*; **it was a ~ of brilliance!** c'était un coup de génie!; **she didn't do a ~ (of work) all day** *Br* elle n'a rien fait de la journée. -**5.** [of clock, bell] coup *m*; **on the ~ of midnight** sur le coup de minuit; **on the ~ of 6** à 6 h sonnantes OR tapantes; **he arrived on the ~** il est arrivé à l'heure exacte OR précise; **at the third ~ it will be 6:32 precisely** *Br* TELEC au troisième top, il sera exactement 6 h 32. **-6.** MED attaque *f* (d'apoplexie); **to have a ~** avoir une attaque. **-7.** NAUT [oarsman] chef *m* de nage; **to row ~** être chef de nage, donner la nage. **-8.** TECH [of piston] course *f*; **two-/four-~ engine** un moteur à deux/quatre temps. **-9.** [caress] caresse *f*; **she gave the cat a ~** elle a caressé le chat. **-10.** *inf* [compliment] compliment *m* flatteur.

◇ *vt* **-1.** [caress] caresser; **he ~d the back of her hand** il lui caressait le dos de la main; **she ~d the piano keys with her fingers** elle caressait les touches du piano. **-2.** [in rowing]: **to ~ a boat** être chef de nage, donner la nage. **-3.** SPORT [ball] frapper.

◇ *vi* [in rowing] être chef de nage, donner la nage.

◆ **at a stroke, at one stroke** *adv phr* d'un seul coup.

stroke play *n* [in golf] partie *f* par coups.

stroll [strəʊl] ◇ *vi* se balader, flâner; **to ~ in/out/past** entrer/sortir/passer sans se presser; **we ~ed round the shops** nous avons fait un petit tour dans les magasins.

◇ *vt*: **to ~ the streets** se promener dans les rues.

◇ *n* petit tour *m*, petite promenade *f*; **to go for a ~** aller faire un tour OR une petite promenade.

stroller ['strəʊlə^r] *n* **-1.** [walker] promeneur *m*, -euse *f*. **-2.** *Am* [pushchair] poussette *f*.

strolling ['strəʊlɪŋ] *adj* [player, musician] ambulant; **a troupe of ~ players** une troupe ambulante.

strong [strɒŋ] (*compar* **stronger** ['strɒŋgə^r], *superl* **strongest** ['strɒŋgɪst]) ◇ *adj* **-1.** [sturdy - person, animal, constitution, arms] fort, robuste; [- building] solide; [- cloth, material] solide, résistant; [- shoes, table] solide, robuste; **I'm not very ~** je ne suis pas très fort; **you need a ~ stomach to eat this junk** *inf* il faut avoir un estomac en béton pour manger des cochonneries pareilles; **you'd need a ~ stomach to go and watch that film** il faut avoir l'estomac bien accroché pour aller voir ce film || [in health - person] en bonne santé; [- heart] solide, robuste; [- eyesight] bon; **he'll be able to go out once he's ~ again** il pourra sortir quand il aura repris des forces; **I wasn't very ~ as a child** je n'étais pas un enfant très robuste ❑ **to be as ~ as a horse** [powerful] être fort comme un turc OR un bœuf; [in good health] avoir une santé de fer. **-2.** [in degree, force - sea current, wind, light, lens, voice] fort, puissant; [- magnet] puissant; ELEC [- current] intense; MUS [- beat] fort; **there is a ~ element of suspense in the story** il y a beaucoup de suspense dans cette histoire; **it's my ~ suit** [in cards] c'est ma couleur forte; *fig* c'est mon fort; **tact isn't her ~ suit** OR **point** *fig* le tact n'est pas son (point) fort; **what are his ~ points?** quels sont ses points forts? || [firm - conviction, belief] ferme, fort, profond; [- protest, support] énergique, vigoureux; [- measures] énergique, draconien; **he is a ~ believer in discipline** il est de ceux qui croient fermement à la discipline; **it is my ~ opinion that the men are innocent** je suis convaincu OR persuadé que ces hommes sont innocents; **she is a ~ supporter of the government** elle soutient le gouvernement avec ferveur; **she is a ~ supporter of Sunday trading** c'est une ardente partisane de l'ouverture des commerces le dimanche || [intense, vivid - desire imagination, interest] vif; [- colour] vif, fort; **to exert a ~ influence on sb** exercer beaucoup d'influence OR une forte influence sur qqn || [emotionally, morally - character] fort, bien trempé; [- feelings] intense, fort; [- nerves] solide; **she has a ~ personality** elle a une forte personnalité; **I have ~ feelings on** OR **about the death penalty** [against] je suis absolument contre la peine de mort; [for] je suis tout à fait pour la peine de mort; **I have no ~ feelings** OR **views one way or the other** cela m'est égal; **he had a ~ sense of guilt** il éprouvait un fort sentiment de culpabilité; **to have a ~ will** avoir de la volonté; **you'll have to be ~ now** [when consoling or encouraging] il va falloir être courageux maintenant. **-3.** [striking - contrast, impression] fort, frappant, marquant; [- accent] fort; **to bear a ~ resemblance to sb** ressembler beaucoup OR fortement à qqn; **his speech made a ~ impression on them** son discours les a fortement impressionnés OR a eu un profond effet sur eux; **there is a ~ chance** OR **probability that he will win** il y a de fortes chances pour qu'il gagne. **-4.** [solid - argument, evidence] solide, sérieux; **we have ~ reasons to believe them innocent** nous avons de bonnes OR sérieuses raisons de croire qu'ils sont innocents; **they have a ~ case** ils ont de bons arguments; **we're in a ~ bargaining position** nous sommes bien placés OR en position de force pour négocier. **-5.** [in taste, smell] fort; **I like ~ coffee** j'aime le café fort OR corsé; **this whisky is ~ stuff** ce whisky est fort; **there's a ~ smell of gas in here** il y a une forte odeur de gaz ici. **-6.** [in ability - student, team] fort; [- candidate, contender] sérieux; **he is a ~ contender for the presidency** il a de fortes chances de remporter l'élection présidentielle; **she is particularly ~ in science subjects** elle est particulièrement forte dans les matières scientifiques; **in very ~ form** en très grande forme; **the film was ~ on style but weak on content** le film était très bon du point de vue de la forme mais pas du tout du point de vue du contenu. **-7.** [tough, violent - language] grossier; **to use ~ language** dire des grossièretés, tenir des propos grossiers; **I wrote him a ~ letter** je lui ai écrit une lettre bien sentie; **she gave us her opinion in ~ terms** elle nous a dit ce qu'elle pensait sans mâcher ses mots; **his latest film is ~ stuff** son dernier film est vraiment dur. **-8.** [in number]: **an army 5,000 ~** une armée forte de 5 000 hommes; **the marchers were 400 ~** les manifestants étaient au nombre de 400. **-9.** COMM & ECON [currency, price] solide; [market] ferme; **the dollar has got ~er** le dollar s'est consolidé. **-10.** GRAMM [verb, form] fort.

◇ *adv inf*: **to be going ~** [person] être toujours solide OR toujours d'attaque; [machine, car] fonctionner toujours bien; [business, economy] être florissant, prospérer; **he's 80 years of age and still going ~** il a 80 ans et toujours bon pied bon œil; **the favourite was going ~ as they turned into the home straight** le favori marchait fort quand les chevaux ont entamé la dernière ligne droite; **to come on ~** [insist] insister lourdement; [make a pass] faire des avances; **that's (coming it) a bit ~!** vous y allez un peu fort!, vous exagérez!

strongarm *inf* ['strɒŋɑːm] *adj* [methods] brutal, violent; **to use ~ tactics** employer la manière forte.

◆ **strong-arm** *inf vt* faire violence à; **to strong-arm sb into doing sthg** forcer la main à qqn pour qu'il fasse qqch.

strongbox ['strɒŋbɒks] *n* coffre-fort *m*.

stronghold ['strɒŋhəʊld] *n* **-1.** MIL forteresse *f*, fort *m*. **-2.** *fig* bastion *m*; **a Conservative Party ~** un bastion du parti conservateur.

strong-limbed *adj* aux membres forts OR athlétiques OR vigoureux.

strongly ['strɒŋlɪ] *adv* **-1.** [greatly - regret] vivement, profondément; [- impress, attract] fortement, vivement; **the kitchen smelt ~ of bleach** il y avait une forte odeur de Javel dans la cuisine; **I ~ advise you to accept** je vous conseille vivement d'accepter; **I am ~ tempted to say yes** j'ai très envie de dire oui; **I ~ disagree with you** je ne suis pas du tout d'accord avec vous; **the report was ~ critical of the hospital** le rapport était extrêmement critique à l'égard de l'hôpital; **he ~ resembles his mother** il ressemble beaucoup à sa mère. **-2.** [firmly - believe, support] fermement; [forcefully - attack, defend, protest] énergiquement, vigoureusement, avec force; [- emphasize] fortement; **a ~ worded protest** une violente protestation; **I feel very ~ about the matter** c'est un sujet OR une affaire qui me tient beaucoup à cœur; **the importance of the elections cannot be too ~ stressed** on ne saurait trop insister sur l'importance des élections. **-3.** [sturdily - constructed] solidement; **~ built** [person] costaud, bien bâti; [wall, structure] solide, bien construit.

strongman ['strɒŋmæn] (*pl* **strongmen** [-men]) *n* hercule *m* (de foire).

strong-minded *adj* résolu, déterminé; **she is very ~** elle sait ce qu'elle veut.

strong-mindedness [-'maɪndɪdnɪs] *n* force *f* de caractère, résolution *f*.

strongroom ['strɒŋruːm] *n Br* [in castle, house] chambre *f* forte; [in bank] chambre *f* forte, salle *f* des coffres.

strong-willed *adj* volontaire, résolu, tenace.

strontium ['strɒntɪəm] *n* strontium *m*; **~ 90** strontium 90.

strop [strɒp] (*pt* & *pp* **stropped**, *cont* **stropping**) ◇ *n* cuir *m* (à rasoir).

◇ *vt* [razor] repasser sur le cuir.

strophe ['strəʊfɪ] *n* strophe *f*.

stroppy *inf* ['strɒpɪ] (*compar* **stroppier**, *superl* **stroppiest**) *adj Br*: **there's no need to get ~!** tu n'as pas besoin de monter sur tes grands chevaux!; **he can be a very ~ individual at times** il peut être très embêtant par moments.

strove [strəʊv] *pt* → **strive**.

struck [strʌk] ◇ *pt* & *pp* → **strike**.

◇ *adj Am* [industry] bloqué pour cause de grève; [factory] fermé pour cause de grève.

structural ['strʌktʃərəl] *adj* **-1.** [gen] structural; [change, problem] structurel, de structure; [unemployment] structurel; LING [analysis] structural, structurel; **~ linguistics/psychology** linguistique *f*/psychologie *f* structurale. **-2.** CONSTR [fault, steel] de construction; [damage, alterations] structural; **~ engineering** génie *m* civil.

structuralism ['strʌktʃərəlɪzm] *n* structuralisme *m*.

structuralist ['strʌktʃərəlɪst] ◇ *n* structuraliste *mf*.

◇ *adj* structuraliste.

structurally ['strʌktʃərəlɪ] *adv* **-1.** [gen] du point de vue de la structure; **~ similar** de structure semblable; **the book is ~ well written** le livre est bien structuré OR construit. **-2.** CONSTR du point de vue de la construction; **the building is ~ sound** le bâtiment est solidement construit.

structure ['stʌktʃə^r] ◇ *n* **-1.** [composition, framework] structure *f*; [of building] structure *f*, ossature *f*, armature *f*; **the ~ of the tower enables it to withstand winds of up to 150 mph** la structure de la tour lui permet de résister à des vents pouvant atteindre 249 km/h ❑ **cell ~** structure cellulaire; **sentence ~** structure de la phrase OR syntaxique; **social ~** structure sociale. **-2.** [building] construction *f*, bâtisse *f*; **the scaffolding was a flimsy-looking ~** l'échafaudage était une construction d'apparence fragile.

◇ *vt* structurer.

structured ['strʌktʃəd] *adj* structuré.

struggle ['strʌgl] ◇ *n* [gen] lutte *f*; [physical fight] bagarre *f*, lutte *f*; **armed ~** lutte armée; **power ~** lutte pour le pouvoir; **he got hurt in the ~** il a été blessé dans la bagarre; **there was evidence of a ~** il y avait des traces de lutte; **the rebels put up a fierce ~** les rebelles ont opposé une vive résistance; **they surrendered without a ~** ils se sont rendus sans opposer de résistance; **I finally succeeded but not without a ~** j'y suis finalement parvenu, non sans peine; **it was a ~ to convince him** on a eu du mal à le convaincre; **power ~** lutte pour le pouvoir; **there was a bitter ~ for leadership of the party** les candidats à la direction du parti se sont livrés une lutte acharnée; **bringing up the children on her own was an uphill ~** *Br* élever ses enfants seule n'a pas été facile; **it's a bit of a ~ to manage on one income** ce n'est pas

facile de s'en sortir avec un seul salaire; **it was a ~ for him to climb the ten flights of stairs** il a eu de la peine à monter les dix étages à pied.
◇ *vi* -**1.** [fight] lutter, se battre; **she ~d with her attacker** elle a lutté contre OR s'est battue avec son agresseur; **to ~ with one's conscience** se débattre avec sa conscience; **he ~d violently when they tried to force him into the car** il s'est violemment débattu quand ils ont essayé de le pousser dans la voiture. -**2.** [try hard, strive] lutter, s'efforcer, se démener; **I ~d to open the door** je me suis démené pour ouvrir la porte; **he ~d with the lock** il s'est battu avec la serrure; **she ~d to control her temper** elle avait du mal à garder son calme; **we're struggling to meet their deadlines** nous faisons tout notre possible pour finir dans les délais; **she had to ~ to make ends meet** elle a eu bien du mal à joindre les deux bouts; **I left him struggling through a Latin translation** je l'ai laissé aux prises avec une traduction latine. -**3.** [expressing movement]: **he ~d back up onto the ledge** il remonta avec peine OR avec difficulté sur la corniche; **he ~d into his clothes** il enfila ses habits avec peine; **the dog ~d out of the water** le chien s'est débattu pour sortir de l'eau; **she ~d through the undergrowth** elle s'est péniblement frayé un chemin à travers les broussailles; **to ~ to one's feet** [old person] se leveravec difficulté OR avec peine; [in fight] se relever péniblement; **to ~ up a hill** [person] gravir péniblement une colline; [car] peiner dans une côte.
◆ **struggle along** *vi insep literal* peiner, avancer avec peine; *fig* subsister avec difficulté; **how are you? — oh, struggling along** comment ça va? — oh, on fait aller.
◆ **struggle on** *vi insep* -**1.** = **struggle along**. -**2.** [keep trying] continuer à se battre; **we must ~ on** nous devons continuer à nous battre.
◆ **struggle through** *vi insep* [in difficult situation] subsister OR se débrouiller avec difficulté, se défendre tant bien que mal; **we'll ~ through somehow** on trouvera bien un moyen de se débrouiller.

struggling ['strʌglɪŋ] *adj* [hard up - painter, writer etc] qui tire le diable par la queue, qui a du mal à joindre les deux bouts.

strum [strʌm] (*pt & pp* **strummed**, *cont* **strumming**) ◇ *vt* [guitar] gratter sur; **to ~ a tune on the guitar** jouer un petit air à la guitare.
◇ *vi* [guitarist] gratter; **she started strumming on her guitar** elle commença à gratter sa guitare.
◇ *n* [on guitar] raclement *m*; **he gave the guitar a ~** il a gratté les cordes de la guitare.

strumming ['strʌmɪŋ] *n* [on guitar] raclement *m*.

strumpet ['strʌmpɪt] *n arch* OR *hum* femme *f* de petite vertu *arch*.

strung [strʌŋ] ◇ *pt & pp* → **string**.
◇ *adj* [guitar, piano] muni de cordes, monté; [tennis racket] cordé.

strung-out▽ *adj* -**1.** *drugs sl*: **to be ~** [addicted] être accroché OR accro; [high] être shooté, planer; [suffering withdrawal symptoms] être en état de manque; **to get ~** se défoncer. -**2.** [uptight] crispé, tendu.

strung-up *inf adj* tendu, nerveux; **she's all ~ about her exams** elle est très tendue à la perspective de ses examens; **don't get ~ about it!** ne te mets pas dans tous tes états!

strut [strʌt] (*pt & pp* **strutted**, *cont* **strutting**) ◇ *n* -**1.** [support - for roof, wall] étrésillon *m*, étançon *m*, contrefiche *f*; [- for building] étai *m*, support *m*; [- between uprights] entretoise *f*, traverse *f*; [- for beam] jambe *f* de force; [- in plane wing, model] support *m*; **metal ~** support métallique. -**2.** [crossbar - of chair, ladder] barreau *m*. -**3.** [gait] démarche *f* fière.
◇ *vi*: **to ~ (about OR around)** plastronner, se pavaner; **he strutted about the room** il arpentait la pièce en se pavanant.
◇ *vt Am*: **to ~ one's stuff** *inf* se montrer en spectacle.

strychnine ['strɪkniːn] *n* strychnine *f*.

St Trinian's [-'trɪnɪənz] *pr n école de jeunes filles apparaissant dans des bandes dessinées et des films anglais; le nom évoque des élèves indisciplinées et impertinentes.*

stub [stʌb] (*pt & pp* **stubbed**, *cont* **stubbing**) ◇ *n* -**1.** [stump - of tree] chicot *m*, souche *f*; [- of pencil] bout *m*; [- of tail] moignon *m*; [- of cigarette] mégot *m*; **she was trying to write with a tiny ~ of pencil** elle essayait d'écrire avec un bout de crayon minuscule; **an ashtray full of cigarette ~s** un cendrier plein de mégots. -**2.** [counterfoil - of cheque] souche *f*, talon *m*; [- of ticket] talon *m*.
◇ *vt*: **to ~ one's toe/foot** se cogner le doigt de pied/le pied; **he stubbed his toe against the kerb** il a buté contre le bord du trottoir.
◆ **stub out** *vt sep* [cigarette] écraser.

stub axle *n* essieu *m* à chapes fermées.

stubble ['stʌbl] *n* -**1.** AGR chaume *m*. -**2.** [on chin] barbe *f* de plusieurs jours.

stubble burning *n* action *f* de brûler le chaume.

stubbly ['stʌblɪ] (*compar* stubblier, *superl* stubbliest) *adj* -**1.** [chin, face] mal rasé; [beard] de plusieurs jours; [hair] en brosse. -**2.** [field] couvert de chaume.

stubborn ['stʌbən] *adj* -**1.** [determined - person] têtu, obstiné; [- animal] rétif, récalcitrant; [- opposition] obstiné, acharné; [- refusal, insistence] obstiné; **she maintained a ~ silence** elle garda obstinément le silence OR s'obstina à ne rien dire; **as ~ as a mule** têtu comme une mule. -**2.** [resistant - cold, cough, symptoms] persistant, opiniâtre; [- stain] récalcitrant, rebelle.

stubbornly ['stʌbənlɪ] *adv* obstinément, opiniâtrement; **he ~ insisted on doing it himself** il s'obstina à le faire lui-même.

stubbornness ['stʌbənnɪs] *n* [of person] entêtement *m*, obstination *f*, opiniâtreté *f*; [of opposition, resistance] acharnement *m*.

stubby ['stʌbɪ] (*compar* stubbier, *superl* stubbiest, *pl* **stubbies**) ◇ *adj* [finger] boudiné, court et épais; [tail] très court, tronqué; [person] trapu; **a ~ pencil** un petit bout de crayon.
◇ *n inf Austr* [bottle of beer] canette *f*.

stucco ['stʌkəʊ] (*pl* **stuccos** OR **stuccoes**)
◇ *n* stuc *m*.
◇ *vt* stuquer.
◇ *comp* [ceiling, wall, façade] de OR en stuc, stuqué.

stuccoed ['stʌkəʊd] *adj* décoré de stuc.

stuck [stʌk] ◇ *pt & pp* → **stick**.
◇ *adj* -**1.** [jammed - window, mechanism] coincé, bloqué; [- vehicle, lift] bloqué; **he got his hand ~ inside the jar** il s'est pris OR coincé la main dans le pot; **the window was ~** la fenêtre était coincée; **the wheel is ~ fast** la roue est complètement coincée; **to get ~ in the mud** s'embourber; **to get ~ in the sand** s'enliser; **to be OR to get ~ in traffic** être coincé OR bloqué dans les embouteillages || [stranded] coincé, bloqué; **they were OR they got ~ at the airport overnight** ils sont restés bloqués OR ils ont dû passer toute la nuit à l'aéroport. -**2.** [in difficulty]: **if you get ~ go on to the next question** si tu sèches, passe à la question suivante; **he's never ~ for an answer** il a toujours réponse à tout; **to be ~ for money** être à court d'argent. -**3.** [in an unpleasant situation, trapped] coincé; **to be ~ in a boring/dead-end job** avoir un boulot ennuyeux/sans avenir. -**4.** *inf* [lumbered]: **to get OR to be ~ with sthg** se retrouver avec qqch sur les bras; **as usual I got ~ with (doing) the washing-up** comme d'habitude, c'est moi qui me suis tapé la vaisselle; **he was ~ with the nickname all through school** ce surnom lui est resté pendant toutes ses années d'école; **it's not a very good car but we're ~ with it** ce n'est pas génial comme voiture, mais on n'a pas le choix. -**5.** *inf* [fond, keen]: **to be ~ on sb** en pincer pour qqn; **I'm not exactly ~ on the idea** je ne peux pas dire que l'idée m'emballe vraiment. -**6.** *inf Br phr*: **he got ~ into his work** il s'est mis au travail; **get ~ in!** allez-y!

stuck-up *inf adj* bêcheur, snob; **she's very ~** elle s'y croit vraiment.

stud [stʌd] (*pt & pp* **studded**, *cont* **studding**) ◇ *n* -**1.** [nail, spike] clou *m (à grosse tête)*; [decorative] clou *m (décoratif)*; [on shoe] clou *m (à souliers)*, caboche *f*; [on belt] clou *m*; [on football boots, track shoes] crampon *m*; [on tyre] clou *m*. -**2.** [earring] = **stud earring**. -**3.** [on roadway] catadioptre *m*. -**4.** [on shirt]: **(collar) ~** bouton *m* de col. -**5.** TECH [screw] goujon *m*; [pin, pivot] tourillon *m*; [lug] ergot *m*. -**6.** CONSTR montant *m*. -**7.** [on chain] étai *m*. -**8.** [reproduction] monte *f*; **animals kept for ~** animaux destinés à la monte; **to put a stallion (out) to ~** mener un étalon à la monte; **to be at ~** saillir. -**9.** [stud farm] haras *m*. -**10.** [stallion] étalon *m*. -**11.** ▽ [man - gen] mec *m*; [promiscuous man] tombeur *m*; [lover] jules *m*. -**12.** *Am* = **stud poker**.
◇ *vt* [shoes, belt] clouter; [door, chest] clouter, garnir de clous; **stars studded the night sky** *fig* le ciel était parsemé d'étoiles.

studbook ['stʌdbʊk] *n* stud-book *m*.

studded ['stʌdɪd] *adj* -**1.** [tyre, belt, jacket] clouté. -**2.** [spangled]: **~ with** émaillé OR parsemé de; **a crown ~ with jewels** une couronne émaillée de pierres précieuses; **the sky was ~ with stars** le ciel était parsemé d'étoiles.

-studded *in cpds*: **diamond~** émaillé de diamants; **star~** [sky] parsemé d'étoiles; [show] plein de vedettes.

stud earring *n* clou *m* d'oreille.

student ['stjuːdnt] ◇ *n* UNIV étudiant *m*, -e *f*; SCH élève *mf*, lycéen *m*, -enne *f*; **she's a biology ~ OR a ~ of biology** elle étudie la biologie OR est étudiante en biologie; **a good ~** un bon élève ❑ **mature ~** étudiant de plus de 26 ans; **'The Student Prince'** *Lubitsch* 'le Prince étudiant'.
◇ *comp* [life] d'étudiant, estudiantin; [hall of residence, canteen, club] universitaire; [participation] UNIV étudiant; SCH des élèves; [power] étudiant; [march, protest] UNIV d'étudiants, étudiant; SCH d'élèves, de lycéens; [attitudes] UNIV des étudiants; SCH des élèves.

student adviser *n* conseiller *m*, -ère *f* pédagogique.

student card *n* carte *f* d'étudiant.

student grant *n* bourse *f* (d'études).

student hostel *n* résidence *f* universitaire.

student lamp *n Am* lampe *f* de bureau.

student nurse *n* élève *m* infirmier, élève *f* infirmière.

studentship ['stjuːdntʃɪp] *n Br* bourse *f* (d'études).

students' union *n* -**1.** [trade union] syndicat *m* OR union *f* des étudiants. -**2.** [premises] ≃ foyer *m* des étudiants.

STUDENTS' UNION:
Dans les universités britanniques, on appelle «students' union» à la fois le syndicat et les locaux où il se trouve. Le syndicat est chargé de défendre les intérêts des étudiants et de leur offrir des services.

---

student teacher *n* [in primary school] instituteur *m*, -trice *f* stagiaire; [in secondary school] professeur *m* stagiaire.

stud farm *n* haras *m*.

studhorse ['stʌdhɔːs] *n* étalon *m*.

studied ['stʌdɪd] *adj* [ease, politeness, indifference] étudié; [insult, rudeness, negligence] délibéré; [elegance] recherché; [manner, pose] étudié, affecté; **he wore a look of ~ boredom** il affichait l'ennui.

studio ['stjuːdɪəʊ] (*pl* **studios**) *n* [gen, CIN & RADIO] studio *m*.

studio apartment *n Am* studio *m*.

studio audience *n* public *m (présent lors de la diffusion ou de l'enregistrement d'une émission)*.

studio couch *n* canapé-lit *m*, canapé *m* convertible.

studio flat *n Br* studio *m*.

studio portrait *n* portrait *m* photographique.

studious ['stju:djəs] *adj* -**1.** [diligent - person] studieux, appliqué; [painstaking - attention, effort] soutenu; [- piece of work] soigné, sérieux. -**2.** [deliberate - indifference] délibéré, voulu.

studiously ['stju:djəslɪ] *adv* -**1.** [diligently - prepare, work, examine] minutieusement, soigneusement. -**2.** [deliberately] d'une manière calculée OR délibérée; ~ indifferent d'une indifférence feinte; she ~ ignored him elle s'ingéniait à ignorer sa présence.

studiousness ['stju:djəsnɪs] *n* application *f* (à l'étude), assiduité *f*.

stud poker *n* stud-poker *m (variété de poker où certaines cartes sont exposées)*.

study ['stʌdɪ] (*pt* & *pp* studied, *pl* studies) ◇ *vt* -**1.** [gen, SCH & UNIV] étudier; she's studying medicine/history elle fait des études de médecine/d'histoire, elle est étudiante en médecine/histoire. -**2.** [examine - plan, evidence, situation] étudier, examiner; [observe - expression, reactions] étudier, observer attentivement; [- stars] observer.
◇ *vi* [gen] étudier; SCH & UNIV étudier, faire ses études; she's ~ing to be an architect elle fait des études pour devenir architecte OR des études d'architecture; he's ~ing for a degree in history il étudie dans le but d'obtenir un diplôme d'histoire; where's Brian? — he's upstairs ~ing où est Brian? — il travaille en haut; to ~ for an exam préparer un examen; I studied under her at university j'étais son élève OR je suivais ses cours à l'université.
◇ *n* -**1.** [gen] étude *f*; she devotes most evenings to ~ elle passe la plupart de ses soirées à étudier; he sets aside one day a week for ~ il consacre un jour par semaine à ses études; the plan is under ~ le projet est à l'étude; her thesis is a ~ of multi-racial communities sa thèse est une étudedes communautés OR sur les communautés multiraciales; I've made an extensive ~ of animal behaviour j'ai fait une étude approfondie du comportement animal; scientific studies have shown that... des études OR des recherches scientifiques ont montré que... -**2.** [room] bureau *m*, cabinet *m* de travail. -**3.** ART, MUS & PHOT étude *f*; a ~ in black une étude en noir; her face was a ~ *fig* & *lit* il fallait voir son visage.
◇ *comp* [hour, period, room] d'étude; we have a ~ period on Monday mornings nous avons une heure d'étude le lundi matin; ~ tour voyage *m* d'étude.
◆ **studies** *npl* SCH & UNIV études *fpl*; how are your studies going? comment vont vos études?; the School of Oriental Studies l'Institut des Études orientales.

study group *n* groupe *m* de travail OR d'étude.

stuff [stʌf] ◇ *n (U)* -**1.** *inf* [indefinite sense - things] choses *fpl*, trucs *mpl*; [- substance] substance *f*, matière *f*; he writes some good ~ il écrit de bons trucs; what's that sticky ~ in the sink? qu'est-ce que c'est que ce truc gluant dans l'évier?; his pockets are always full of all kinds of ~ il a toujours un tas de trucs dans les poches; it's made of tomatoes and onions and ~ il y a des tomates, des oignons et des trucs comme ça; they go climbing and sailing and ~ like that ils font de l'escalade, de la voile et des trucs du même genre; this material is good ~ c'est un bon tissu OR du tissu de bonne qualité; I used to drink whisky but now I never touch the ~ avant, je buvais du whisky, mais maintenant je n'y touche plus; no thanks, I can't stand the ~ non merci, j'ai horreur de ça; this whisky is strong ~ il arrache, ce whisky; this mustard is strong ~ cette moutarde est forte; the book is strong ~ [sexually explicit] ce livre n'est pas à mettre entre toutes les mains; [depressing] ce livre est dur; she's a nice bit of ~! c'est un canon! -**2.** *inf pej* [rubbish, nonsense] bêtises *fpl*, sottises *fpl*; ~ and nonsense! *pej* balivernes!; don't give me all that ~ about the British Empire! passe-moi le topo débile sur l'empire britannique!; you don't believe all that ~ about ghosts, do you? vous ne croyez tout de même pas à toutes ces bêtises sur les fantômes?; do you call that ~ art/music? vous appelez ça de l'art/de la musique?; it's no use trying on that sweet and innocent ~ with me! pas la peine de jouer au plus fin avec moi! -**3.** *inf* [possessions] affaires *fpl*; clear all that ~ off the table! enlève tout ce bazar de sur la table!; have you packed all your ~? est-ce que tu as fini de faire tes bagages? || [equipment] affaires *fpl*, matériel *m*; where's my shaving/fishing ~? où est mon matérielde rasage/de pêche? -**4.** *inf phr*: to do one's ~ faire ce qu'on a à faire; get out there and do your ~! allez, fais ce que tu as à faire!; that's the ~! c'est ça!, allez-y!; to know one's ~ connaître son affaire; he certainly knows his ~ il connaît son affaire. -**5.** *lit* [essence] étoffe *f*; he's the ~ that heroes are made of il est de l'étoffe dont sont faits les héros; the very ~ of melodrama ce dont on fait les mélodrames. -**6.** *drugs sl* came *f*. -**7.** *arch* [fabric] étoffe *f* (de laine). -**8.** *Am* SPORT [spin] effet *m*.
◇ *vt* -**1.** *inf* [shove] fourrer; he ~ed the papers into his pocket il a fourré les papiers dans sa poche; when the police came, he ~ed the drugs down the toilet quand la police est arrivée, il a fourré la drogue dans la cuvette des toilettes; just ~ everything under the bed vous n'avez qu'à tout fourrer sous le lit || [expressing anger, rejection etc]: he told me I could ~ my report▽ il m'a dit qu'il se foutait pas mal de mon rapport; you can ~ that idea!▽ tu sais où tu peux te la mettre, ton idée!; ~ it!▽ la ferme!; get ~ed!▽ va te faire foutre!; ~ him!▽ il peut aller se faire foutre! -**2.** *inf* [cram, pack full] bourrer; their house is ~ed with souvenirs from India leur maison est bourrée de souvenirs d'Inde; his teachers ~ed his head with a load of political nonsense ses professeurs lui ont bourré le crâne d'un tas d'idées politiques fausses; her head is ~ed with useless information elle a la tête farcie de renseignements inutiles. -**3.** [plug - gap] boucher; the hole had been ~ed with paper le trou avait été bouché avec du papier. -**4.** [cushion, armchair] rembourrer; ~ed with foam rembourré de mousse. -**5.** CULIN farcir; ~ed with sausagemeat farci de chair à saucisse. -**6.** [in taxidermy - animal, bird] empailler. -**7.** *inf* [with food]: to ~ o.s. OR one's face▽ bâfrer, s'empiffrer; to ~ o.s. with cake s'empiffrer de gâteau; stop ~ing your face with chocolate! arrête de t'empiffrer de chocolat!; I'm ~ed je n'ai plus faim. -**8.** *Am* POL [ballot box] remplir de bulletins de votes truqués.
◆ **stuff away** *inf vt sep* [food] enfourner, s'enfiler.
◆ **stuff up** *vt sep* [block] boucher; my nose is all ~ed up j'ai le nez complètement bouché.

stuffed [stʌft] *adj* -**1.** CULIN farci. -**2.** [chair, cushion] rembourré; [animal] empaillé; [toy] en peluche.

stuffed shirt *n* prétentieux *m*, -euse *f*.

stuffily ['stʌfɪlɪ] *adv* [say, reply] d'un ton désapprobateur.

stuffiness ['stʌfɪnɪs] *n* -**1.** [of room] manque *m* d'air. -**2.** [of person] esprit *m* collet monté OR vieux jeu, pruderie *f*.

stuffing ['stʌfɪŋ] *n* -**1.** [for furniture, toys] rembourrage *m*, bourre *f*; [for clothes] rembourrage *m*; [in taxidermy] paille *f*; he's got no ~! *fig* il n'a rien dans le ventre!; to knock the ~ out of sb *inf* [in fight] casser la figure à qqn; the news of his death really knocked the ~ out of me *inf* ça m'a fait un sacré coup d'apprendre qu'il était mort. -**2.** CULIN farce *f*.

stuffy ['stʌfɪ] (*compar* stuffier, *superl* stuffiest) *adj* -**1.** [room] mal aéré, mal ventilé, qui sent le renfermé; it's terribly ~ in here [stale] ça sent terriblement le renfermé ici; [stifling] on manque d'air OR on étouffeici. -**2.** *pej* [person - prim] collet monté *(inv)*; [- old-fashioned] vieux jeu *(inv)*; [atmosphere, reception] guindé; don't be so ~! [shocked] il n'y a pas de quoi être scandalisé!; [prim] ne sois pas si prude!; [old-fashioned] ne sois pas si vieux jeu! -**3.** [dull - book, subject, lecture] ennuyeux. -**4.** [nose] bouché.

stultify ['stʌltɪfaɪ] (*pt* & *pp* stultified) *vt* [make stupid] abrutir; [stifle - creativity, talent] étouffer.

stultifying ['stʌltɪfaɪɪŋ] *adj* [work] abrutissant, assommant; [atmosphere] abrutissant, débilitant; their policies have had a ~ effect on the country's economy leur politique a paralysé OR étouffé l'économie du pays.

stumble ['stʌmbl] ◇ *vi* -**1.** [person] trébucher, faire un faux pas; [horse] broncher, faire un faux pas; she ~d and fell elle trébucha et tomba; he ~d against me il a trébuché et m'a heurté; he ~d over the toys in the hall il a trébuché sur les jouets dans le couloir; to ~ along/in/out avancer/entrer/sortir en trébuchant; they ~d, exhausted, over the finishing line ils ont franchi la ligne d'arrivée en titubant de fatigue; he was stumbling about in the dark il avançait en trébuchant dans le noir; they ~d out into the bright light ils sortirent en chancelant sous la lumière aveuglante. -**2.** [in speech] trébucher; to ~ over a long word trébucher sur un mot long; he managed to ~ through his lecture c'est d'une voix mal assurée qu'il a finalement prononcé son cours.
◇ *n* -**1.** [in walking] faux pas *m*. -**2.** [in speech]: she read the poem without a ~ elle a lu le poème sans se tromper OR sans se reprendre une seule fois.
◆ **stumble across, stumble on, stumble upon** *vt insep* -**1.** [meet] rencontrer par hasard, tomber sur. -**2.** [discover] trouver par hasard, tomber sur.

stumblebum▽ ['stʌmblbʌm] *n Am* abruti *m*, -e *f*.

stumbling block ['stʌmblɪŋ-] *n* pierre *f* d'achoppement.

stump [stʌmp] ◇ *n* -**1.** [of tree] chicot *m*, souche *f*. -**2.** [of limb, tail] moignon *m*; [of tooth] chicot *m*; [of pencil, blade] (petit) bout *m*. -**3.** *Am* POL estrade *f (d'un orateur politique)*; to be OR to go on the ~ faire une tournée électorale.
◇ *vt* -**1.** *inf* [bewilder] laisser perplexe; [with question] coller; I'm ~ed [don't know answer] je sèche; [don't know what to do] je ne sais pas quoi faire; the question had them ~ed la question les a laissés sans voix; she's ~ed for an answer [in quiz] elle ne connaît pas la réponse; [for solution] elle ne trouve pas de solution; it ~s me how anybody could be so silly! que quelqu'un puisse être aussi bête, ça me dépasse! -**2.** *Am* POL [constituency, state] faire une tournée électorale dans.
◇ *vi* -**1.** [walk heavily] marcher d'un pas lourd; to ~ in/out [heavily] entrer/sortir d'un pas lourd. -**2.** *Am* POL faire une tournée électorale.
◆ **stumps** *inf npl* [legs] quilles *fpl*.
◆ **stump up** *inf Br* ◇ *vi insep* casquer; I had to ~ up for the taxi c'est moi qui ai dû payer le taxi.
◇ *vt sep* [money] cracher, aligner; [deposit] payer.

stumpage ['stʌmpɪdʒ] *n Am* valeur *f* de bois d'œuvre.

stumpy ['stʌmpɪ] (*compar* stumpier, *superl* stumpiest) *adj* [person] boulot, courtaud; [arms, legs] court et épais; [tail] tronqué.

stun [stʌn] (*pt* & *pp* stunned, *cont* stunning) *vt* -**1.** [knock out] assommer. -**2.** *fig* [astonish] abasourdir, stupéfier.

stung [stʌŋ] *pt* & *pp* → **sting**.

stun gun *n* fusil *m* paralysant.

stunk [stʌŋk] *pp* → **stink**.

stunned [stʌnd] *adj* -**1.** [knocked out] assommé. -**2.** *fig* abasourdi, stupéfait; she was ~ by the news la nouvelle l'a abasourdi.

stunner *inf* ['stʌnəʳ] *n* [woman] fille *f* superbe; [car] voiture *f* fantastique.

stunning ['stʌnɪŋ] *adj* -**1.** [blow] étourdissant. -**2.** [astounding - news, event] stupéfiant, renversant; [beautiful - dress, car] fantastique; [- woman, figure] superbe; the film wasn't exactly ~ le film n'avait rien de bien sensationnel.

stunningly ['stʌnɪŋlɪ] *adv* remarquablement, incroyablement; she is ~ beautiful elle est d'une beauté éblouissante.

stunt [stʌnt] ◇ *n* -**1.** [feat] tour *m* de force, exploit *m* spectaculaire; [in plane] acrobatie *f* (aérienne); it was quite a ~! il fallait le faire! -**2.** [by stunt man] cascade *f*; to do a ~ [in plane] faire des acrobaties; [stunt man] faire une cascade. -**3.** [trick] truc *m*; [hoax] farce *f*, canular *m*; to pull a ~ faire un canular OR une farce; publicity ~ coup *m* de pub; it's just a ~ to raise money ce n'est qu'un truc OR une combine pour se faire de l'argent. -**4.** [plant] plante *f* chétive OR rabougrie; [animal] animal *m* dont la croissance a été freinée.
◇ *comp*: ~ driver conducteur *m* cascadeur, conductrice *f* cascadeuse; ~ driving cascades *fpl* automobiles; ~ pilot aviateur *m*, -trice *f* qui fait des cascades, spécialiste *mf* de l'acrobatie aérienne.
◇ *vi* -**1.** AERON faire des acrobaties. -**2.** CIN & TV faire des cascades.
◇ *vt* [impede - growth, development] retarder; [- person] freiner OR retarder la croissance de; [- intelligence] freiner le développement de.

stunted ['stʌntɪd] *adj* [person] chétif; [plant] chétif, rabougri; [growth, intelligence] retardé.

stunt man *n* cascadeur *m*.

stunt woman *n* cascadeuse *f*.

stupa ['stu:pə] *n* stupa *m*, stoupa *m*.

stupefaction [,stju:prˈfækʃn] *n* stupéfaction *f*, stupeur *f*.

stupefied ['stju:pɪfaɪd] *adj* stupéfait.

stupefy ['stju:pɪfaɪ] (*pt* & *pp* **stupefied**) *vt* -**1.** [subj: alcohol, drugs, tiredness] abrutir; [subj: blow] assommer, étourdir. -**2.** [astound] stupéfier, abasourdir.

stupefying ['stju:pɪfaɪɪŋ] *adj* stupéfiant.

stupendous [stju:'pendəs] *adj* [amount, achievement, talent] extraordinaire, prodigieux; [event] prodigieux, extraordinaire; [book, film] extraordinaire.

stupendously [stju:'pendəslɪ] *adv* prodigieusement, formidablement.

stupid ['stju:pɪd] ◇ *adj* -**1.** [foolish] stupide, bête; he's always saying/doing ~ things il dit/fait sans arrêt des bêtises; I was ~ enough to go and apologize j'ai eu la sottise d'aller OR j'ai été assez bête pour aller m'excuser; he's ~ enough to believe you il est assez bête pour vous croire; stop being so ~! arrête de faire l'idiot OR l'imbécile! -**2.** *lit* [from alcohol, drugs, sleep] abruti, hébété; [from blow] étourdi; he was still ~ from OR with sleep il était encore abruti de sommeil; to drink o.s. ~ s'abrutir d'alcool. -**3.** *inf* [wretched, confounded] maudit, fichu; where did I put that ~ hammer? où est-ce que j'ai mis ce maudit marteau?
◇ *n inf* bêta *m*, -asse *f*, idiot *m*, -e *f*; I'm only joking, ~! je plaisante, gros bêta!

stupidity [stju:'pɪdətɪ] (*pl* **stupidities**) *n* stupidité *f*, bêtise *f*, sottise *f*.

stupidly ['stju:pɪdlɪ] *adv* stupidement, bêtement; I ~ forgot to phone them je suis bête, j'ai oublié de leur téléphoner.

stupor ['stju:pəʳ] *n* stupeur *f*, abrutissement *m*; to be in a drunken ~ être abruti par l'alcool.

sturdily ['stɜ:dɪlɪ] *adv* -**1.** [solidly] solidement, robustement; to be ~ built [person] être costaud OR bien bâti; [toys, furniture, equipment] être solide; [house] être de construction solide, être robuste. -**2.** [firmly - deny, refuse, oppose] énergiquement, vigoureusement.

sturdiness ['stɜ:dɪnɪs] *n* -**1.** [solidity] solidité *f*, robustesse *f*. -**2.** [firmness] fermeté *f*; with great ~ of purpose avec une grande résolution.

sturdy ['stɜ:dɪ] (*compar* **sturdier**, *superl* **sturdiest**) *adj* -**1.** [robust - person] robuste, vigoureux; [- limbs] robuste; [- table, tree, shoes] robuste, solide. -**2.** [firm - denial, defence, opposition, support] énergique, vigoureux; [- voice] ferme; with ~ determination avec une ferme résolution.

sturgeon ['stɜ:dʒən] (*pl inv*) *n* esturgeon *m*.

stutter ['stʌtəʳ] ◇ *n* bégaiement *m*; to speak with a OR to have a ~ bégayer, être bègue.
◇ *vi* bégayer.
◇ *vt*: to ~ (out) bégayer, bredouiller; she ~ed (out) an apology elle bredouilla une excuse.

stutterer ['stʌtərəʳ] *n* bègue *mf*.

stuttering ['stʌtərɪŋ] ◇ *n* bégaiement *m*.
◇ *adj* bègue, qui bégaie.

sty [staɪ] (*pl* **sties**) *n* -**1.** [for pigs] porcherie *f*. -**2.** = **stye**.

stye [staɪ] *n* orgelet *m*, compère-loriot *m*.

Stygian ['stɪdʒɪən] *adj lit* ténébreux, sombre; ~ gloom ténèbres *fpl* impénétrables OR insondables.

style [staɪl] ◇ *n* -**1.** [manner] style *m*, manière *f*; ART, LITERAT & MUS style *m*; in the ~ of Vermeer dans le style de Vermeer; February 12th old/new ~ [in calendar] le 12 février vieux/nouveau style; ~ of life mode *m* de vie; I don't like his ~ of dressing je n'aime pas sa façon de s'habiller; they've adopted a new management ~ [approach] ils ont adopté un nouveau style de gestion; they danced the charleston, 1920s ~ ils ont dansé le charleston comme on le dansait dans les années vingt; the meal was prepared in authentic Japanese ~ le repas a été préparé dans la plus pure tradition japonaise. -**2.** [fashion - in clothes] mode *f*; to be dressed in the latest ~ être habillé à la dernière mode ‖ [model, design] modèle *m*; a new ~ of dress un nouveau modèle de robe; all the latest ~s tous les derniers modèles; this winter's ~s les modèles de cet hiver; the boots come in two ~s ces bottes existent en deux modèles. -**3.** [elegance, sophistication - of person] allure *f*, chic *m*; [- of dress, picture, building, film] style *m*; she's got real ~ elle a vraiment de l'allure OR du chic; she does everything with great ~ elle fait tout avec beaucoup de style; to live in ~ mener grand train, vivre dans le luxe; he likes to do things in ~ il aime faire bien les choses; they were dressed in ~ ils étaient habillés avec beaucoup de chic; they made their entrance in great ~ ils ont fait une entrée très remarquée; they drove off in ~ in a fleet of limousines ils sont partis en grande pompe dans un cortège de limousines. -**4.** [type] genre *m*; I wouldn't have thought cheating was your ~ je n'aurais jamais pensé que c'était ton genre de tricher; I don't like his ~ je n'aime pas son genre; that's the ~! c'est ça!, bravo! -**5.** TYPO [in editing] style *m*; house ~ style de la maison. -**6.** *Br fml* [title] titre *m*. -**7.** BOT style *m*. -**8.** = **stile**.
◇ *vt* -**1.** [call] appeler, désigner; she ~s herself "countess" elle se fait appeler «comtesse». -**2.** [design - dress, jewel, house] créer, dessiner; dress ~d by Dior robe créée par Dior; to ~ sb's hair coiffer qqn; ~d for comfort and elegance conçu pour le confort et l'élégance. -**3.** PRESS & TYPO [manuscript] mettre au point *(selon les précisions stylistiques de l'éditeur)*.

-style *in cpds* dans le style de; a sixties'~ haircut une coupe de cheveux (dans le style des) années soixante; baroque~ architecture architecture *f* de style baroque, baroque *m*.

stylebook ['staɪlbʊk] *n* TYPO manuel *m* OR protocole *m* de style.

stylet ['staɪlɪt] *n* stylet *m*.

styli ['staɪlaɪ] *pl* → **stylus**.

styling ['staɪlɪŋ] *n* [of dress] forme *f*, ligne *f*; [of hair] coupe *f*; [of car] ligne *f*; ~ gel gel *m* coiffant; ~ mousse mousse *f* coiffante.

stylish ['staɪlɪʃ] *adj* [person] élégant, chic *(inv)*; [clothes, hotel, neighbourhood] élégant, chic *(inv)*; [book, film] qui a du style.

stylishly ['staɪlɪʃlɪ] *adv* [dress] avec chic, avec allure, élégamment; [live] élégamment; [travel] dans le luxe; [write] avec style OR élégance.

stylishness ['staɪlɪʃnɪs] *n* chic *m*, élégance *f*.

stylist ['staɪlɪst] *n* -**1.** [designer - for clothes] styliste *mf* (de mode), modéliste *mf*; [- for cars, furniture] styliste *mf*; (hair) ~ coiffeur *m*, -euse *f*. -**2.** ART & LITERAT styliste *mf*.

stylistic [staɪ'lɪstɪk] *adj* ART, LITERAT & LING stylistique.

stylistically [staɪ'lɪstɪklɪ] *adv* d'un point de vue stylistique.

stylistics [staɪ'lɪstɪks] *n (U)* stylistique *f*.

stylize, **-ise** ['staɪlaɪz] *vt* styliser.

stylized ['staɪlaɪzd] *adj* stylisé.

stylograph ['staɪləʊgrɑ:f] *n* stylographe *m*.

stylus ['staɪləs] (*pl* **styluses** OR **styli** [-laɪ]) *n* [on record player] saphir *m*; [tool] style *m*, stylet *m*.

stymie ['staɪmɪ] ◇ *vt* -**1.** [in golf] barrer le trou à. -**2.** *inf fig* [person] coincer; [plan] ficher en l'air.
◇ *n* [in golf] trou *m* barré; *fig* obstacle *m*, entrave *f*.

styptic ['stɪptɪk] ◇ *adj* styptique.
◇ *n* styptique *m*.

styptic pencil *n* crayon *m* hémostatique.

Styria ['stɪrɪə] *pr n* Styrie *f*.

Styrofoam® ['staɪrəfəʊm] *n* polystyrène *m* expansé.

Styx [stɪks] *pr n*: the (River) ~ le Styx.

suave [swɑ:v] *adj* -**1.** [polite, charming] poli; *pej* [smooth] doucereux, mielleux, onctueux; he's a bit too ~ for my liking je le trouve un peu trop doucereux. -**2.** [elegant] élégant, chic.

suavely ['swɑ:vlɪ] *adv* -**1.** [politely, charmingly] poliment; *pej* [smoothly] mielleusement. -**2.** [elegantly] avec élégance.

suaveness ['swɑ:vnɪs], **suavity** ['swɑ:vətɪ] *n* -**1.** [politeness, charm] politesse *f*; *pej* manières *fpl* doucereuses. -**2.** [elegance] élégance *f*.

sub [sʌb] (*pt* & *pp* **subbed**, *cont* **subbing**) ◇ *n* -**1.** *abbr of* **submarine**. -**2.** *abbr of* **subeditor**. -**3.** *abbr of* **subscription**. -**4.** *abbr of* **substitute**.
◇ *vi* & *vt* -**1.** *abbr of* **subcontract**. -**2.** *abbr of* **subedit**.

sub- *in cpds* sub-, sous; to run a ~four minute mile courir le mile en moins de quatre minutes.

subagent [,sʌb'eɪdʒənt] *n* sous-agent *m*.

subalpine [,sʌb'ælpaɪn] *adj* subalpin.

subaltern ['sʌbltən] ◇ *n* -**1.** *Br* MIL *officier de l'armée de terre d'un rang inférieur à celui de capitaine*. -**2.** [subordinate - gen] subalterne *mf*, subordonné *m*, -e *f*.
◇ *adj* subalterne.

sub-aqua [-'ækwə] *adj* sous-marin, subaquatique.

subaquatic [,sʌbə'kwætɪk] *adj* subaquatique.

subarctic [,sʌb'ɑ:ktɪk] ◇ *adj* -**1.** GEOG subarctique. -**2.** [very cold - weather, wind] glacial, arctique.
◇ *n* zone *f* subarctique.

subatomic [,sʌbə'tɒmɪk] *adj* subatomique.

subbasement ['sʌb,beɪsmənt] *n* deuxième sous-sol *m*.

subcategory ['sʌb,kætəgərɪ] (*pl* **subcategories**) *n* sous-catégorie *f*.

subclass ['sʌbklɑ:s] *n* sous-classe *f*.

subclinical [,sʌb'klɪnɪkl] *adj* infraclinique.

subcommittee ['sʌbkə,mɪtɪ] *n* sous-comité *m*, sous-commission *f*.

subcompact [,sʌbkəm'pækt] *n Am* (très) petite voiture *f*.

subconscious [,sʌb'kɒnʃəs] ◇ *adj* subconscient; the ~ mind le subconscient.
◇ *n* subconscient *m*.

subconsciously [,sʌb'kɒnʃəslɪ] *adv* d'une manière subconsciente, inconsciemment.

subcontinent [,sʌb'kɒntɪnənt] *n* sous-continent *m*; the (Indian) Subcontinent le sous-continent indien.

subcontract [*vb* ,sʌbkən'trækt, *n* sʌb'kɒntrækt] ◇ *vt* [pass on] (faire) sous-traiter; they ~ some of the work (out) to local firms ils sous-traitent une partie du travail à des entreprises locales.
◇ *vi* travailler en sous-traitance; they have a lot of small companies who ~ for them beaucoup de petites sociétés travaillent pour eux en sous-traitance.
◇ *n* (contrat *m* de) sous-traitance *f*.
◆ **subcontract out** *vt sep* = **subcontract** *vt*.

subcontracting [,sʌbkən'træktɪŋ] *adj* sous-traitant.

subcontractor [ˌsʌbkənˈtræktəʳ] *n* sous-traitant *m*.

subcortex [ˌsʌbˈkɔːteks] *n* zone *f* (cérébrale) sous-corticale.

subcritical [ˌsʌbˈkrɪtɪkl] *adj* sous-critique.

subculture [ˈsʌbˌkʌltʃəʳ] *n* **-1.** [gen & SOCIOL] subculture *f*. **-2.** BIOL culture *f* repiquée OR secondaire.

subcutaneous [ˌsʌbkjuːˈteɪnjəs] *adj* sous-cutané.

subcutaneously [ˌsʌbkjuːˈteɪnjəslɪ] *adv* de manière sous-cutanée; to be injected ~ à administrer par injection sous-cutanée.

subdeacon [ˌsʌbˈdiːkən] *n* sous-diacre *m*.

subdeb *inf* [ˌsʌbˈdeb], **subdebutante** [ˌsʌbˈdebjuːtɑːnt] *n Am* préadolescente *f*.

subdistrict [ˈsʌbˌdɪstrɪkt] *n* subdivision *f* (d'arrondissement).

subdivide [ˌsʌbdɪˈvaɪd] ◇ *vt* subdiviser.
◇ *vi* se subdiviser.

subdivision [ˌsʌbdɪˈvɪʒn] *n* subdivision *f*.

subdominant [ˌsʌbˈdɒmɪnənt] *n* BIOL & MUS sous-dominante *f*.

subdue [səbˈdjuː] *vt* **-1.** [country, tribe] assujettir, soumettre; [rebels] soumettre; [rebellion] réprimer. **-2.** [feelings, passions] refréner, maîtriser; [fears, anxiety] apaiser.

subdued [səbˈdjuːd] *adj* **-1.** [person] silencieux; [mood] sombre; [emotion, feeling] contenu; [audience] peu enthousiaste; you're very ~, what's the matter? vous n'êtes pas très bavard, qu'est-ce qui ne va pas?; it was rather a ~ gathering ce fut un rassemblement plutôt tranquille. **-2.** [voice, sound] bas; [conversation] à voix basse. **-3.** [light, lighting] tamisé, atténué; [colours] sobre.

subedit [ˌsʌbˈedɪt] ◇ *vt* corriger, préparer pour l'impression.
◇ *vi* travailler comme secrétaire de rédaction.

subeditor [ˌsʌbˈedɪtəʳ] *n* secrétaire *mf* de rédaction.

subentry [ˌsʌbˈentrɪ] (*pl* subentries) *n* sous-entrée *f*.

subequatorial [ˈsʌbˌekwəˈtɔːrɪəl] *adj* subéquatorial.

subfamily [ˈsʌbˌfæməlɪ] (*pl* subfamilies) *n* sous-famille *f*.

subframe [ˈsʌbˌfreɪm] *n* AUT faux-chassis *m inv*.

subfusc [ˈsʌbfʌsk] ◇ *n Br* tenue *f* universitaire *(en particulier à Oxford)*.
◇ *adj lit* [dark] sombre; [dusky] bistre *(inv)*.

subgenus [ˌsʌbˈdʒiːnəs] (*pl* subgenuses OR subgenera [-dʒenərə]) *n* sous-genre *m*.

subgroup [ˈsʌbgruːp] *n* sous-groupe *m*.

subharmonic [ˌsʌbhɑːˈmɒnɪk] *adj* sous-harmonique.

subhead [ˈsʌbhed], **subheading** [ˈsʌbˌhedɪŋ] *n* [title] sous-titre *m*; [division] paragraphe *m*.

subhuman [ˌsʌbˈhjuːmən] ◇ *adj* [intelligence] limité; [crime] brutal, bestial; to live in ~ conditions vivre dans des conditions terribles OR inhumaines.
◇ *n* sous-homme *m*.

subject [*n, adj & prep* ˈsʌbdʒekt, *vb* səbˈdʒekt]
◇ *n* **-1.** [topic] sujet *m*; on the ~ of au sujet de, à propos de; let's come OR get back to the ~ revenons à nos moutons; don't try and change the ~ n'essaie pas de changer de conversation OR de sujet; let's drop the ~ parlons d'autre chose; while we're on the ~ à (ce) propos; while we're on the ~ of holidays puisque nous parlons de vacances; that's a touchy ~ c'est un sujet délicat. **-2.** [in letters and memos]: ~: recruitment of new staff objet: recrutement de personnel. **-3.** ART, LITERAT & PHOT sujet *m*; the ~ of her film/novel le sujet de son film/roman; he always photographs his ~s in natural light il photographie toujours ses sujets en lumière naturelle. **-4.** GRAMM & PHILOS sujet *m*. **-5.** SCH & UNIV matière *f*, discipline *f*; [field] domaine *m*; she's taking exams in four ~s elle passe des examens dans quatre matières; I was always better at science ~s j'ai toujours été plus fort en sciences; it's not really my ~ ce n'est pas vraiment mon domaine; that would be a good ~ for a PhD thesis ce serait un bon sujet pour une thèse de doctorat. **-6.** POL sujet *m*, -ette *f*; she is a British ~ c'est une ressortissante britannique; foreign ~s ressortissants *mpl* étrangers. **-7.** MED & PSYCH [of test] sujet *m*; she'd be a good ~ for the new treatment elle serait un bon sujet pour le nouveau traitement; ~s were tested for their reactions on a testé la réaction des sujets. **-8.** [cause] sujet *m*, motif *m*, raison *f*; he was the ~ of much comment il a été l'objet de nombreux commentaires.
◇ *adj* **-1.** [subordinate] dépendant; they are ~ to my authority ils sont placés sous mon autorité, ils dépendent de moi; we are all ~ to the rule of law nous sommes tous soumis à la loi; ~ states États *mpl* dépendants. **-2.** [liable, prone]: ~ to sujet à; he is ~ to frequent lung infections il est sujet à de fréquentes infections pulmonaires; ~ to attack exposé à l'attaque; the terms are ~ to alteration without notice les termes peuvent être modifiés sans préavis; ~ to tax imposable; the price is ~ to a handling charge les frais de manutention sont en sus.
◇ *vt* **-1.** [country, people] soumettre, assujettir. **-2.** [expose]: to ~ to soumettre à; they ~ all applicants to lengthy testing procedures ils font passer de longs examens à tous les candidats; the material was ~ed to intense heat le matériau a été soumis OR exposé à une température très élevée; I refuse to ~ anyone to such indignities je refuse de faire subir de tels affronts à qui que ce soit.
◆ **subject to** *prep phr* [save for] sous réserve de, sauf; [conditional upon] à condition de; these are the rules, ~ to revision voici le règlement, sous réserve de modification; ~ to your passing the exam à condition de réussir OR à condition que vous réussissiez l'examen.

subject catalogue *n* fichier *m* par matières.

subject index *n* [in book] index *m* des matières; [in library] fichier *m* par matières.

subjection [səbˈdʒekʃn] *n* **-1.** [act of subjecting] assujettissement *m*. **-2.** [state of being subjected] sujétion *f*, assujettissement *m*, soumission *f*; they live in (a state of) complete ~ ils vivent dans la soumission la plus totale.

subjective [səbˈdʒektɪv] ◇ *adj* **-1.** [viewpoint, argument, criticism] subjectif. **-2.** GRAMM [pronoun, case] sujet; [genitive] subjectif. **-3.** MED [symptom] subjectif.
◇ *n* GRAMM (cas *m*) sujet *m*, nominatif *m*.

subjectively [səbˈdʒektɪvlɪ] *adv* subjectivement.

subjectivism [səbˈdʒektɪvɪzm] *n* subjectivisme *m*.

subjectivity [ˌsʌbdʒekˈtɪvətɪ] *n* subjectivité *f*.

subject matter *n* [topic] sujet *m*, thème *m*; [substance] substance *f*, contenu *m*.

subjoin [ˌsʌbˈdʒɔɪn] *vt* adjoindre.

sub judice [ˈdʒuːdɪsɪ] *adj* en instance, pendant; I cannot comment on a case which is still ~ je ne peux faire aucun commentaire sur une affaire qui est encore en cours de jugement.

subjugate [ˈsʌbdʒʊgeɪt] *vt* **-1.** [people, tribe, country] assujettir, soumettre; [rebels] soumettre. **-2.** [feelings] dompter; [reaction] réprimer.

subjugation [ˌsʌbdʒʊˈgeɪʃn] *n* soumission *f*, assujettissement *m*.

subjunctive [səbˈdʒʌŋktɪv] ◇ *adj* subjonctif; ~ mood mode *m* subjonctif.
◇ *n* subjonctif *m*; in the ~ au subjonctif; some verbs always take the ~ certains verbes sont toujours suivis du subjonctif.

subkingdom [ˌsʌbˈkɪŋdəm] *n* BIOL embranchement *m*.

sublease [ˌsʌbˈliːs] ◇ *n* sous-location *f*.
◇ *vt* sous-louer.

sublet [ˌsʌbˈlet] (*pt & pp* sublet, *cont* subletting)
◇ *vt* sous-louer.
◇ *n* sous-location *f*.

sublieutenant [ˌsʌblefˈtenənt] *n Br* ≃ enseigne *m* de vaisseau deuxième classe.

sublimate [*vb* ˈsʌblɪmeɪt, *n* ˈsʌblɪmət] ◇ *vt* [gen, CHEM & PSYCH] sublimer.
◇ *n* CHEM sublimé *m*.

sublimation [ˌsʌblɪˈmeɪʃn] *n* sublimation *f*.

sublime [səˈblaɪm] ◇ *adj* **-1.** [noble, inspiring] sublime. **-2.** *inf* [very good] génial, sensationnel; you look ~ tu es superbe. **-3.** [utter – disregard, contempt, ignorance] suprême, souverain.
◇ *n*: the ~ le sublime; from the ~ to the ridiculous du sublime au grotesque.
◇ *vt* sublimer.

sublimely [səˈblaɪmlɪ] *adv* complètement, totalement; they were ~ unaware of the danger ils étaient totalement inconscients du danger.

subliminal [ˌsʌbˈlɪmɪnl] *adj* infraliminaire, subliminaire, subliminal; ~ advertising publicité *f* subliminale OR invisible.

sublimity [səˈblɪmətɪ] *n* sublimité *f*.

submachine gun [ˌsʌbməˈʃiːn-] *n* mitraillette *f*.

submarine [ˌsʌbməˈriːn] ◇ *n* sous-marin *m*.
◇ *adj* sous-marin.

submariner [sʌbˈmærɪnəʳ] *n* sous-marinier *m*.

submaxillary [ˌsʌbmækˈsɪlərɪ] *adj* sous-maxillaire.

submediant [ˌsʌbˈmiːdjənt] *n* sus-dominante *f*, sixte *f*.

submerge [səbˈmɜːdʒ] ◇ *vt* **-1.** [plunge] submerger, immerger; to ~ o.s. in work *fig* se plonger dans le travail. **-2.** [flood] submerger, inonder; the flood waters had ~d the fields les eaux en crue avaient inondé les champs; the rocks were soon ~d by the tide les rochers furent bientôt recouverts par la marée.
◇ *vi* [submarine] plonger.

submerged [səbˈmɜːdʒd] *adj* submergé; a ~ volcano un volcan sous-marin.

submersible [səbˈmɜːsəbl] ◇ *adj* submersible.
◇ *n* submersible *m*.

submersion [səbˈmɜːʃn] *n* **-1.** [in liquid] immersion *f*; [of submarine] plongée *f*. **-2.** [flooding] inondation *f*.

subminiature [ˌsʌbˈmɪnətʃəʳ] *adj* subminiature.

submission [səbˈmɪʃn] *n* **-1.** [yielding] soumission *f*; their total ~ to fate leur fatalisme; to beat sb into ~ réduire qqn par la violence. **-2.** [submissiveness] soumission *f*, docilité *f*. **-3.** [referral – gen] soumission *f*; JUR [of case] renvoi *m*; after ~ of the project to the coordinating committee après soumission du projet au comité de coordination. **-4.** [proposition, argument – gen] thèse *f*; JUR plaidoirie *f*; her ~ is that... elle soutient que...; in my ~, the defendant is lying je soutiens que l'accusé ment. **-5.** [in wrestling] soumission *f*.

submissive [səbˈmɪsɪv] *adj* soumis.

submissively [səbˈmɪsɪvlɪ] *adv* [behave, confess, accept] docilement; [yield, react] avec résignation.

submissiveness [səbˈmɪsɪvnɪs] *n* soumission *f*, docilité *f*.

submit [səbˈmɪt] (*pt & pp* submitted, *cont* submitting) ◇ *vi* **-1.** *literal* se rendre, se soumettre. **-2.** *fig* se soumettre, se plier; we shall never ~ to such demands nous n'accéderons jamais à de telles exigences; to ~ to one's fate accepter son destin.
◇ *vt* **-1.** [propose] soumettre; all proposals must be submitted to the coordinating committee toutes les propositions doivent être soumises au comité de coordination; I ~ that... JUR je soutiens OR je maintiens que... **-2.** [yield]: to ~ o.s. to sb/sthg se soumettre à qqn/qqch.

submultiple [ˌsʌbˈmʌltɪpl] *n* sous-multiple *m*.

subnormal [ˌsʌbˈnɔːml] *adj* **-1.** [person] arriéré; educationally ~ children des enfants arriérés *(du point de vue scolaire)*. **-2.** [temperatures] au-dessous de la normale.

suborder [ˈsʌbˌɔːdəʳ] *n* BIOL sous-ordre *m*.

subordinate [*n* səˈbɔːdɪnət, *vt* səˈbɔːdɪneɪt]
◇ *n* subordonné *m*, -e *f*, subalterne *mf*.

◇ *adj* -**1.** [in rank, hierarchy] subordonné, subalterne; **he is ~ to the duty officer** son grade est inférieur à celui de l'officier de permanence; **of ~ rank** de rang subalterne; **she had a very ~ position in the company** elle occupait un poste tout à fait subalterne dans l'entreprise. -**2.** [secondary] subordonné, accessoire; **but that is ~ to the main problem** mais c'est secondaire par rapport au problème principal. -**3.** GRAMM subordonné.
◇ *vt* subordonner.

subordinate clause [sə'bɔːdɪnət-] *n* GRAMM (proposition *f*) subordonnée *f*.

subordinating conjunction [sə'bɔːdɪneɪtɪŋ-] *n* GRAMM conjonction *f* de subordination.

subordination [sə,bɔːdɪ'neɪʃn] *n* subordination *f*.

suborn [sʌ'bɔːn] *vt* suborner.

subplot ['sʌb,plɒt] *n* intrigue *f* secondaire.

subpoena [səb'piːnə] ◇ *n* citation *f (à comparaître en qualité de témoin)*, assignation *f*.
◇ *vt* citer *(à comparaître en qualité de témoin)*.

subpopulation ['sʌb,pɒpjʊ'leɪʃn] *n* sous-population *f*.

sub-postmaster *n Br* receveur *m (dans un petit bureau de poste local)*.

sub-postmistress *n Br* receveuse *f (dans un petit bureau de poste local)*.

sub-post office *n Br* petit bureau *m* de poste local.

subprogram ['sʌb,prəʊgræm] *n* COMPUT sous-programme *m*.

subrogate ['sʌbrəgeɪt] *vt* subroger.

sub rosa [-'rəʊzə] *adv* confidentiellement, sous le sceau du secret.

subroutine ['sʌbruː,tiːn] *n* COMPUT sous-programme *m*.

sub-Saharan Africa *pr n* Afrique *f* Noire; **in ~** en Afrique Noire.

subscribe [səb'skraɪb] ◇ *vi* -**1.** [to magazine, service] s'abonner, être abonné; **we ~ to several American publications** nous sommes abonnés à plusieurs publications américaines. -**2.** [to loan, fund, campaign, share issue] souscrire; **to ~ to a charity** faire des dons à une œuvre de charité. -**3. to ~ to** [opinion, belief] souscrire à; **I cannot ~ to that view of politics** il m'est impossible de souscrire à cette vision de la politique.
◇ *vt* -**1.** [donate] donner, faire don de; **she ~d £800 to the election fund** elle a donné 800 livres à la caisse électorale. -**2.** *fml* [write - one's name, signature] apposer; [sign - document] signer.

subscriber [səb'skraɪbəʳ] *n* -**1.** [to newspaper, service, telephone system] abonné *m*, -e *f*. -**2.** [to fund, campaign, share issue] souscripteur *m*, -trice *f*; **~s to various charities** les personnes qui ont fait des dons à diverses œuvres de charité. -**3.** [to opinion, belief] partisan *m*, adepte *mf*.

subscriber trunk dialling *n Br* automatique *m*.

subscript ['sʌbskrɪpt] ◇ *n* COMPUT, MATH & TYPO indice *m*.
◇ *adj* en indice.

subscription [səb'skrɪpʃn] *n* -**1.** [to newspaper, magazine] abonnement *m*; **~ charges** tarifs *mpl* d'abonnement; **to cancel a ~** résilier un abonnement; **to take out a ~ to a magazine** s'abonner à un magazine. -**2.** [to fund, campaign, share issue] souscription *f*; [to club, organization] cotisation *f*. -**3.** [to opinion, belief] adhésion *f*.

subsection ['sʌb,sekʃn] *n* [of text, contract etc] article *m*, paragraphe *m*.

subsequent ['sʌbsɪkwənt] *adj* -**1.** [next] suivant, subséquent *fml*; **the ~ days** les jours suivants; **to await ~ events** attendre de connaître la suite des événements; **~ generations** les générations suivantes; **~ to 1880** après 1880; **~ to this** par la suite. -**2.** [consequent] conséquent, consécutif.

subsequently ['sʌbsɪkwəntlɪ] *adv* par la suite, subséquemment *fml*.

subserve [səb'sɜːv] *vt fml* encourager, favoriser.

subservience [səb'sɜːvjəns] *n* -**1.** [servility] servilité *f*. -**2.** [subjugation] asservissement *m*; **~ to a foreign power** asservissement à une puissance étrangère.

subservient [səb'sɜːvjənt] *adj* -**1.** [servile] servile, obséquieux *pej*. -**2.** [subjugated] asservi; **they are totally ~ to the town council** ils sont totalement dépendants de la municipalité. -**3.** [secondary] secondaire, accessoire.

subset ['sʌbset] *n* sous-ensemble *m*.

subside [səb'saɪd] *vi* -**1.** [abate - shooting, laughter] cesser; [- storm, rage, pain] se calmer; [recede - water] se retirer, baisser; [- danger] s'éloigner. -**2.** [sink - house, land] s'abaisser; [- wall, foundations] se tasser; [settle - sediment] se déposer.

subsidence [səb'saɪdns, 'sʌbsɪdns] *n* [of house, land] affaissement *m*; [of wall, foundations] tassement *m*; **'road liable to ~'** ≃ 'chaussée déformée'.

subsidiarity [sʌb,sɪdɪ'ærɪtɪ] *n* subsidiarité *f*.

subsidiary [səb'sɪdjərɪ] (*pl* **subsidiaries**)
◇ *adj* [supplementary] supplémentaire, complémentaire; [secondary - question, reason] subsidiaire; [- idea, action] accessoire; **~ company** filiale *f*.
◇ *n* COMM filiale *f*.

subsidize, -ise ['sʌbsɪdaɪz] *vt* subventionner.

subsidized ['sʌbsɪdaɪzd] *adj* subventionné.

subsidy ['sʌbsɪdɪ] (*pl* **subsidies**) *n* subvention *f*; **government ~** subvention de l'État; **export subsidies** primes *fpl* à l'exportation.

subsist [səb'sɪst] *vi* subsister; **they ~ on fish and rice** ils vivent de poisson et de riz.

subsistence [səb'sɪstəns] ◇ *n* subsistance *f*, existence *f*; **means of ~** moyens *mpl* d'existence.
◇ *comp* [wage] à peine suffisant pour vivre; [economy, farming] d'autoconsommation; **to live at ~ level** avoir tout juste de quoi vivre.

subsistence allowance *n Br* [advance] acompte *m (perçu avant l'engagement définitif)*; [expenses] frais *mpl* (de subsistance).

subsoil ['sʌbsɔɪl] *n* sous-sol *m* GÉOL.

subsonic [,sʌb'sɒnɪk] *adj* subsonique.

subspecies ['sʌb,spiːʃiːz] (*pl inv*) *n* sous-espèce *f*.

substance ['sʌbstəns] *n* -**1.** [matter] substance *f*; **tobacco contains harmful ~s** le tabac contient des substances nocives; **illegal ~s** stupéfiants *mpl*. -**2.** [solidity] solidité *f*; **it seemed to have as little ~ as a ghost** cela semblait aussi immatériel qu'un fantôme. -**3.** [essential part, gist] essentiel *m*, substance *f*; [basis] fond *m*; **that's the ~ of what he said** voilà en substance ce qu'il a dit; **the ~ of the charges** l'essentiel de l'inculpation; **the ~ of the case** le fond de l'affaire. -**4.** [significance, weight] étoffe *f*, poids *m*; **these developments add ~ to our hypothesis** ces développements donnent davantage de poids à notre hypothèse; **I find his stories lack ~** je trouve que ses histoires manquent d'étoffe; **their claim lacks ~** leur revendication est sans fondement OR n'est pas fondée. -**5.** [wealth] richesses *fpl*; [power] pouvoir *m*; [influence] influence *f*; **a woman of ~** [rich] une femme riche OR aisée; [powerful] une femme puissante; [influential] une femme influente.
◆ **in substance** *adv phr* [generally] en gros, en substance; [basically] à la base, au fond; [in brief] en substance, en somme.

substance abuse *n fml* abus *m* de stupéfiants.

substandard [,sʌb'stændəd] *adj* -**1.** [work, output] médiocre, en-dessous des niveaux requis; [meal, merchandise] de qualité inférieure; **they live in ~ housing** ils habitent des logements insalubres. -**2.** LING non conforme à la norme.

substantial [səb'stænʃl] *adj* -**1.** [large] considérable, important; JUR [damages] élevé; **~ differences remain** il reste des divergences importantes; **a ~ number of teachers were there** il y avait de nombreux professeurs. -**2.** [nourishing - food] nourrissant; [- meal] solide, copieux, substantiel. -**3.** [convincing - argument, evidence] solide, convaincant. -**4.** [real, tangible] réel, substantiel; PHILOS substantiel. -**5.** [solidly built] solide; **the town hall is a ~ Victorian building** la mairie est un solide bâtiment de l'époque victorienne. -**6.** [rich] riche, aisé; [powerful] puissant; [influential] influent; [well-established] solide, bien établi; **a ~ company** une société solidement implantée.

substantially [səb'stænʃəlɪ] *adv* -**1.** [considerably] considérablement; **taxes have been cut ~** les impôts ont été considérablement réduits. -**2.** [generally] en gros, en grande partie; [fundamentally] fondamentalement, au fond; **it is ~ correct** c'est en grande partie correct. -**3.** [solidly] solidement; **~ built** solide. -**4.** PHILOS [as for the substance] substantiellement.

substantiate [səb'stænʃɪeɪt] *vt* confirmer, apporter OR fournir des preuves à l'appui de.

substantiation [səb,stænʃɪ'eɪʃn] *n (U)* [proof] preuve *f*; [reason] bien-fondé *m*, justification *f*; **do you have any ~ for your allegations?** pouvez-vous fournir des preuves de ce que vous avancez?

substantival [,sʌbstən'taɪvl] *adj* GRAMM substantif.

substantive [*n* 'sʌbstəntɪv, *adj* sʌb'stæntɪv]
◇ *adj* -**1.** [real, important] substantiel; [permanent - rank] permanent; [independent - means, resources] indépendant. -**2.** GRAMM nominal.
◇ *n* GRAMM substantif *m*.

substation ['sʌb,steɪʃn] *n* sous-station *f*.

substitute ['sʌbstɪtjuːt] ◇ *n* -**1.** [person] remplaçant *m*, -e *f*; **each team is allowed three ~s** chaque équipe a droit à trois remplaçants. -**2.** [thing] produit *m* de remplacement OR de substitution; **we'll have to find a ~ for it** il faut que nous trouvions quelque chose pour le remplacer; **use a low-fat ~ instead of butter** utilisez un produit à faible teneur en matière grasse à la place du beurre; **sugar ~** édulcorant *m* de synthèse; **there's no ~ for real coffee** rien ne vaut le vrai café; **tapes are a poor ~ for live music** les cassettes ne valent pas la musique live. -**3.** GRAMM terme *m* suppléant.
◇ *adj* remplaçant; **a ~ goalkeeper** un gardien de but remplaçant; **it'll do as a ~ cork** ça fera office de bouchon.
◇ *vt* [gen] substituer, remplacer; SPORT remplacer; **to ~ sthg for sthg** substituer qqch à qqch; **margarine may be ~d for butter** on peut remplacer le beurre par de la margarine, on peut utiliser de la margarine au lieu du beurre.
◇ *vi*: **to ~ for sb/sthg** remplacer qqn/qqch.

substitution [,sʌbstɪ'tjuːʃn] *n* [gen] remplacement *m*, substitution *f*; SPORT remplacement *m*; **the ~ of man-made fibres for cotton** le fait d'avoir remplacé le coton par des fibres synthétiques.

substrata [,sʌb'strɑːtə] *pl* → **substratum**.

substrate ['sʌbstreɪt] *n* [gen, CHEM & ELECTRON] substrat *m*.

substratum [,sʌb'strɑːtəm] (*pl* **substrata** [-tə]) *n* -**1.** [infrastructure, base] fond *m*. -**2.** GEOL [underlying formation] substratum *m*; [subsoil] sous-sol *m*. -**3.** LING substrat *m*. -**4.** PHOT substratum *m*.

substructure ['sʌb,strʌktʃəʳ] *n* CONSTR structure *f*; **various ~s make up the organization** l'organisation se compose de plusieurs services distincts.

subsume [səb'sjuːm] *vt* subsumer.

subsystem ['sʌb,sɪstəm] *n* sous-système *m*.

subteen [,sʌb'tiːn] *Am* ◇ *n* préadolescent *m*, -e *f*.
◇ *adj* [fashions, sizes] pour les préadolescents.

subteenage [,sʌb'tiːneɪdʒ] *Am* = **subteen** *adj*.

subteenager [,sʌb'tiːneɪdʒəʳ] *Am* = **subteen** *n*.

subtenancy [,sʌb'tenənsɪ] (*pl* **subtenancies**) *n* sous-location *f*.

subtenant [,sʌb'tenənt] *n* sous-locataire *mf*.

subtend [səb'tend] *vt* sous-tendre.

subterfuge ['sʌbtəfjuːdʒ] *n* subterfuge *m*.

subterranean [ˌsʌbtəˈreɪnjən] *adj* souterrain; ~ **forces were at work** des forces secrètes étaient à l'œuvre.

subtitle [ˈsʌbˌtaɪtl] ◇ *n* CIN, LITERAT & PRESS sous-titre *m*.
◇ *vt* sous-titrer.

subtitled [ˈsʌbˌtaɪtld] *adj* sous-titré, avec sous-titrage.

subtitling [ˈsʌbˌtaɪtlɪŋ] *n* sous-titrage *m*.

subtle [ˈsʌtl] *adj* subtil; **a ~ sense of humour** un sens de l'humour subtil; **there's a very ~ difference between them** il y a une très légère différence entre eux; ~ **shades of green and blue** des nuances subtiles de vert et de bleu; **you're not very ~, are you?** la subtilité n'est vraiment pas ton fort!

subtlety [ˈsʌtltɪ] (*pl* **subtleties**) *n* -**1.** [subtleness] subtilité *f*; ~ **is not one of his strong points** la subtilité n'est pas son fort. -**2.** [detail, distinction] subtilité *f*.

subtly [ˈsʌtlɪ] *adv* subtilement.

subtonic [ˌsʌbˈtɒnɪk] *n* sous-tonique *f*.

subtotal [ˈsʌbˌtəʊtl] *n* total *m* partiel.

subtract [səbˈtrækt] *vt* soustraire, déduire; ~ **52 from 110** ôtez OR retranchez 52 de 110.

subtraction [səbˈtrækʃn] *n* soustraction *f*.

subtropical [ˌsʌbˈtrɒpɪkl] *adj* subtropical.

subtropics [ˌsʌbˈtrɒpɪks] *npl* zones *fpl* subtropicales.

subtype [ˈsʌbtaɪp] *n* sous-classe *f*.

suburb [ˈsʌbɜːb] *n* banlieue *f*, faubourg *m*; **the London ~ of Barking** Barking, dans la banlieue de Londres; **the ~s stretch for miles** la banlieue s'étend sur des kilomètres; **in the ~s** en banlieue; **the outer ~s** la grande banlieue.

suburban [səˈbɜːbn] *adj* -**1.** [street, railway, dweller] de banlieue; [population, growth] de banlieue, suburbain. -**2.** *pej* [mentality, outlook] de petit-bourgeois.

suburbanite [səˈbɜːbənaɪt] *n* banlieusard *m*, -e *f*.

suburbia [səˈbɜːbɪə] *n* la banlieue; **in ~** en banlieue.

subvention [səbˈvenʃn] *n* subvention *f*.

subversion [səbˈvɜːʃn] *n* subversion *f*.

subversive [səbˈvɜːsɪv] ◇ *adj* subversif.
◇ *n* élément *m* subversif.

subvert [səbˈvɜːt] *vt* -**1.** [undermine - society, state, institution] subvertir *lit*, renverser. -**2.** [corrupt - individual] corrompre.

subway [ˈsʌbweɪ] *n* -**1.** *Br* [pedestrian underpass] passage *m* souterrain. -**2.** *Am* [railway] métro *m*; **it's quicker by ~** c'est plus rapide en métro.

sub-zero *adj* au-dessous de zéro.

succeed [səkˈsiːd] ◇ *vi* -**1.** [manage successfully] réussir; **to ~ in doing sthg** réussir OR parvenir OR arriver à faire qqch; **he ~ed only in confusing things further** il n'a réussi qu'à compliquer davantage les choses ❑ **if at first you don't ~, try again** *prov* si vous ne réussissez pas du premier coup, recommencez. -**2.** [work out] réussir; **the first attack did not ~** la première offensive a échoué. -**3.** [do well] réussir, avoir du succès; **we all want to ~ in life** nous voulons tous réussir dans la vie; **to ~ in business/in publishing** réussir dans les affaires/l'édition; **he ~s in everything he does** il réussit tout ce qu'il entreprend, tout lui réussit ❑ **nothing ~s like success** *prov* un succès en entraîne un autre. -**4.** [follow on] succéder; **to ~ to the throne** monter sur le trône.
◇ *vt* [subj: person] succéder à, prendre la suite de; **I ~ed him as editor** je lui ai succédé au poste de rédacteur || [subj: event, thing] succéder à, suivre; **as month ~ed month** au fur et à mesure que les mois passaient OR se succédaient.

succeeding [səkˈsiːdɪŋ] *adj* -**1.** [subsequent] suivant, qui suit; **we met several times during the ~ weeks** nous nous sommes vus plusieurs fois pendant les semaines qui ont suivi; **each ~ year** chaque année qui passe. -**2.** [future] futur, à venir; ~ **generations will right these wrongs** les générations à venir redresseront ces torts.

success [səkˈses] ◇ *n* réussite *f*, succès *m*; **her ~ in the elections** sa victoire aux élections; **his ~ in the exam** son succès à l'examen; **to meet with** OR **to achieve ~** réussir; **I wish you every ~** je vous souhaite beaucoup de succès; **I had no ~ in trying to persuade them** je n'ai pas réussi à les convaincre; **I tried to convince them, but without ~** j'ai essayé de les convaincre,mais sans succès; **to make a ~ of sthg** mener qqch à bien; **he made a ~ of the campaign** il a mené la campagne à bien; **she made a great ~ of her career** elle a bien réussi dans son métier; **I haven't had much ~ in finding work** mes recherches pour un emploi n'ont pas donné grand-chose; **their first record was a great ~** leur premier disque a eu un succès fou; **you were a great ~ at the party** tu as eu beaucoup de succès à la fête; **the evening was a ~** la soirée a été réussie OR a été une réussite.
◇ *comp* [rate] de réussite, de succès.

successful [səkˈsesfʊl] *adj* -**1.** [resulting in success - attempt, effort, plan] qui réussit; [- negotiations] fructueux; [- outcome] heureux; [- performance, mission, partnership] réussi; **his efforts were supremely ~** ses efforts ont été couronnés de succès; **she was not ~ in her application for the post** sa candidature à ce poste n'a pas été retenue; **I was ~ in convincing them** j'ai réussi OR je suis arrivé OR je suis parvenu à les convaincre; **it's not been a very ~ day for me** ma journée n'a pas été très fructueuse; **she brought the project to a ~ conclusion** elle a mené le projet à bien. -**2.** [thriving - singer, record, author, book, play] à succès; [- businessman] qui a réussi; [- life, career] réussi; **their first record was very ~** leur premier disque a eu un succès fou; **she's a ~ businesswoman** elle a réussi dans les affaires; **she's ~ in everything she does** tout lui réussit, elle réussit tout ce qu'elle entreprend.

successfully [səkˈsesfʊlɪ] *adv* avec succès; **to do sthg ~** réussir à faire qqch; **we managed to tackle the problem ~** nous avons trouvé une solution satisfaisante au problème; **he was ~ operated on for a stomach ulcer** il a été opéré avec succès d'un ulcère de l'estomac.

succession [səkˈseʃn] *n* -**1.** [series] succession *f*, suite *f*; **a ~ of visitors** une succession OR une suite de visiteurs; **we won three years in ~** nous avons gagné trois ans de suite; **for five years in ~** pendant cinq années consécutives OR cinq ans de suite; **she made three phone calls in ~** elle a passé trois coups de fil de suite; **they filed into the room in close ~** ils sont entrés dans la pièce les uns derrière les autres; **the fireworks went off in quick** OR **rapid ~** les feux d'artifice sont partis les uns après les autres; **a ~ of gains and losses** une succession de gains et de pertes. -**2.** [ascension to power] succession *f*; **his ~ to the post** sa succession au poste; **she's first in ~ (to the throne)** elle occupe la première place dans l'ordre de succession (au trône); **in ~ to her boss** à la suite de son patron. -**3.** JUR [descendants] descendance *f*; [heirs] héritiers *mpl*.

successive [səkˈsesɪv] *adj* [attempts, generations] successif; [days, years] consécutif.

successively [səkˈsesɪvlɪ] *adv* [in turn] successivement, tour à tour, l'un/l'une après l'autre.

successor [səkˈsesəʳ] *n* -**1.** [replacement] successeur *m*; **I'm her ~ to the position** je suis son successeur à ce poste; **I'm to be his ~** c'est moi qui dois lui succéder; **she's the ~ to the throne** c'est l'héritière de la couronne. -**2.** [heir] héritier *m*, -ère *f*.

success story *n* réussite *f*; **one of the great success stories of the 20th century** une des grandes réussites du XXe siècle.

succinct [səkˈsɪŋkt] *adj* succinct, concis.

succinctly [səkˈsɪŋktlɪ] *adv* succinctement, avec concision.

succinctness [səkˈsɪŋktnɪs] *n* concision *f*.

succor *Am* = **succour**.

succotash [ˈsʌkətæʃ] *n plat américain composé de maïs en grain et de haricots*.

succour *Br*, **succor** *Am* [ˈsʌkəʳ] ◇ *n* secours *m*, aide *f*.
◇ *vt* secourir, aider.

succubus [ˈsʌkjʊbəs] (*pl* **succubi** [-baɪ]) *n* succube *m*.

succulence [ˈsʌkjʊləns] *n* succulence *f*.

succulent [ˈsʌkjʊlənt] ◇ *adj* -**1.** [tasty] succulent. -**2.** BOT succulent.
◇ *n* plante *f* grasse.

succumb [səˈkʌm] *vi* -**1.** [yield] succomber, céder; **don't ~ to temptation!** ne succombez pas à la tentation!; **he ~ed to her charm** il a succombé à son charme. -**2.** [die] succomber, mourir; **he ~ed to cancer** il est mort d'un cancer; **he finally ~ed** il a finalement succombé.

such [sʌtʃ] ◇ *det & predet* -**1.** [of the same specified kind] tel, pareil; **~ a song** une telle chanson, une chanson pareille OR de ce genre; **~ songs** de telles chansons, des chansons pareilles OR de ce genre; **~ weather** un temps pareil OR comme ça; **how can you tell ~ lies?** comment peux-tu raconter de tels mensonges OR des mensonges pareils?; **no ~ place exists** un tel endroit n'existe pas; **on ~ an occasion** en une telle occasion; **we had ~ a case last year** nous avons eu un cas semblable l'année dernière; **have you ever heard ~ a thing?** avez-vous jamais entendu une chose pareille?; **~ a thing is unheard-of** ce genre de chose est sans précédent; **I said no ~ thing!** je n'ai rien dit de tel OR de la sorte!; **you'll do no ~ thing!** il n'en est pas question!; **no ~ thing exists here** il n'existe rien de tel ici; **they called her Jane or some ~ thing** ils l'ont baptisée Jane ou quelque chose de ce genre || [followed by 'as']: **there is no ~ thing as magic** la magie n'existe pas; **we will take ~ steps as are considered necessary** nous prendrons toutes les mesures nécessaires; **I'm not ~ a fool as to believe him!** je ne suis pas assez bête pour le croire!; **he speaks in ~ a way as to be incomprehensible** il parle de telle manière que personne ne le comprend; **~ money as we have** le peu d'argent que nous avons || [followed by 'that']: **their timetable is ~ that we never see them** leur emploi du temps est tel que nous ne les voyons jamais; **she works in ~ a way that we can't keep up** elle travaille de telle façon que nous ne pouvons pas suivre. -**2.** [as intensifier] tel; **my accounts are in ~ a mess!** mes comptes sont dans un de ces états!; **she has ~ courage!** elle a un de ces courages!; **it's ~ a pity you can't come!** c'est tellement dommage que vous ne puissiez pas venir!; **you gave me ~ a scare!** tu m'as fait une de ces peurs!; **~ tall buildings** des immeubles aussi hauts; **~ a handsome man** un si bel homme; **she has ~ a nice voice!** elle a une si jolie voix!; **it's been ~ a long time since I've seen her** ça fait si longtemps que je ne l'ai pas vue; **I didn't realize it was ~ a long way** je ne me rendais pas compte que c'était si loin; **I've never read ~ beautiful poetry** je n'ai jamais lu de si belle poésie || [followed by 'that']: **her grief was ~ that we feared for her sanity** son chagrin était tel que nous craignions pour sa santé mentale; **he was in ~ pain that he fainted** il souffrait tellement qu'il s'est évanoui.
◇ *pron*: **~ is the power of the media** voilà ce que peuvent faire les médias; **~ was the result** voilà quel était le résultat; **~ were my thoughts last night** voilà où j'en étais hier soir; **~ is life!** c'est la vie!
◆ **and such** *adv phr* et d'autres choses de ce genre OR de la sorte; **detective stories, thrillers and ~** des policiers, des romans à suspense et d'autres livres de ce genre OR de la sorte.
◆ **as such** *adv phr* [strictly speaking] en soi; [in that capacity] en tant que tel, à ce titre; **she doesn't get a salary as ~** elle n'a pas de véritable salaire OR pas de salaire à proprement parler; **have they offered you more money? — well, not as ~** vous ont-ils proposé plus d'argent? — pas véritablement; **they are not**

opposed to privatization as ~ ils ne sont pas opposés à la privatisation en soi OR à proprement parler; she's an adult and as ~ she has rights elle est majeure et en tant que telle elle a des droits.

◆ **such and such** *predet phr* tel; on ~ and ~ a date à telle date.

◆ **such as** *prep phr* tel que, comme; a country ~ as Germany un pays tel que OR comme l'Allemagne; films ~ as Fellini's les films tels que ceux de Fellini; I can think of lots of reasons – ~ as? je vois beaucoup de raisons – comme quoi par exemple?

◆ **such as it is, such as they are** *adv phr*: and this is my study, ~ as it is et voici ce que j'appelle mon bureau; I'll give you my opinion, ~ as it is je vais vous donner mon avis, prenez-le pour ce qu'il vaut; you're welcome to use my notes, ~ as they are je te prêterai mes notes avec plaisir, elles valent ce qu'elles valent.

suchlike ['sʌtʃlaɪk] ◇ *adj* semblable, pareil; and other ~ dishes et d'autres plats du même genre.

◇ *pron*: frogs, toads and ~ les grenouilles, les crapauds et autres animaux (du même genre).

suck [sʌk] ◇ *vt* -**1.** [with mouth] sucer; to ~ one's thumb sucer son pouce; he ~ed the end of his pencil thoughtfully il suçait pensivement le bout de son crayon; she was ~ing orange juice through a straw elle sirotait du jus d'orange avec une paille; he was ~ing a sweet il suçait un bonbon; ~ the poison out aspirez le poison ❑ to ~ sb dry prendre jusqu'à son dernier sou à qqn. -**2.** [pull] aspirer; the whirlpool ~ed him to the bottom le tourbillon l'a entraîné au fond; we found ourselves ~ed into an argument *fig* nous nous sommes trouvés entraînés dans une dispute.

◇ *vi* -**1.** [with mouth]: to ~ at OR on sthg sucer OR suçoter qqch; the child was ~ing at her breast l'enfant tétait son sein. -**2.** ▽ *Am* [be disgusting]: this town ~s! cette ville est dégueulasse! -**3.** ▽ *dated phr*: (ya boo) ~s to you! va te faire voir!

◇ *n* -**1.** [act of sucking – gen]: to have a ~ at sthg sucer OR suçoter qqch; he took a long ~ on his cigar il tira longuement sur son cigare ‖ [at breast] tétée *f*; to give ~ donner le sein, allaiter. -**2.** [force] aspiration *f*.

◆ **suck down** *vt sep* [subj: sea, quicksand, whirlpool] engloutir.

◆ **suck off**▼ *vt sep* sucer, tailler une pipe à.

◆ **suck up** ◇ *vt sep* [subj: person] aspirer, sucer; [subj: vacuum cleaner, pump, machine] aspirer; [subj: porous surface] absorber.

◇ *vi insep inf*: to ~ up to sb lécher les bottes à qqn.

sucker ['sʌkəʳ] ◇ *n* -**1.** *inf* [dupe] pigeon *m*, gogo *m*; he's a real ~ c'est un vrai pigeon; I'm a ~ for chocolate je raffole du chocolat; you've been played for a ~ *Am* vous vous êtes fait rouler OR pigeonner; OK, ~, you asked for it OK, mec, tu l'auras voulu. -**2.** *Br* [suction cup or pad] ventouse *f*; there are rubber ~s on the end of the arrows il y a des ventouses au bout des flèches. -**3.** ZOOL [of insect] suçoir *m*; [of octopus, leech] ventouse *f*. -**4.** BOT drageon *m*. -**5.** *Am* [lollipop] sucette *f*.

◇ *vt* -**1.** HORT enlever les drageons de. -**2.** ▽ *Am* [dupe] refaire, pigeonner; she ~ed him out of $300 elle l'a refait de 300 dollars.

◇ *vi* BOT [plant] drageonner.

sucking pig ['sʌkɪŋ-] *n* cochon *m* de lait.

suckle ['sʌkl] ◇ *vt* -**1.** [child] allaiter, donner le sein à; [animal] allaiter. -**2.** *fig* [raise] élever.

◇ *vi* téter.

suckling ['sʌklɪŋ] *n* -**1.** [child] nourrisson *m*, enfant *m* encore au sein; [animal] animal *m* qui tète. -**2.** [act] allaitement *m*.

suckling pig = **sucking pig**.

sucrose ['suːkrəʊz] *n* saccharose *f*.

suction ['sʌkʃn] *n* succion *f*, aspiration *f*; it adheres by ~ ça fait ventouse.

suction pad *n* ventouse *f*.

suction pump *n* pompe *f* aspirante.

suction valve *n* clapet *m* OR soupape *f* d'aspiration.

Sudan [suː'dɑːn] *pr n* Soudan *m*; in ~, in the ~ au Soudan.

Sudanese [ˌsuːdə'niːz] (*pl inv*) ◇ *n* Soudanais *m*, -e *f*.

◇ *adj* soudanais.

Sudanic [suː'dænɪk] ◇ *adj* soudanais.

◇ *n* LING soudanais *m*.

sudden ['sʌdn] *adj* soudain, subit; a ~ twinge of remorse un remords subit; there was a ~ bend in the road il y avait un virage soudain; she had a ~ change of heart elle a soudainement OR subitement changé d'avis; this is all very ~! c'est plutôt inattendu!; ~ death *literal* mort *f* subite; GAMES & SPORT *jeu pour partager les ex aequo (où le premier point perdu, le premier but concédé etc, entraîne l'élimination immédiate)*.

◆ **all of a sudden** *adv phr* soudain, subitement tout d'un coup; I feel very cold all of a ~ j'ai très froid tout d'un coup.

sudden infant death syndrome *n* mort *f* subite du nourrisson.

suddenly ['sʌdnlɪ] *adv* soudainement, subitement, tout à coup; he died ~ in the night il est mort subitement dans la nuit.

suddenness ['sʌdnnɪs] *n* soudaineté *f*, caractère *m* subit OR imprévu; the ~ of the attack surprised us la soudaineté de l'attaque nous a surpris.

sudorific [ˌsuːdə'rɪfɪk] ◇ *adj* sudorifique.

◇ *n* sudorifique *m*.

suds [sʌdz] *npl* -**1.** [foam] mousse *f*; [soapy water] eau *f* savonneuse. -**2.** *inf Am* [beer] bière *f*.

sudsy ['sʌdzɪ] (*compar* **sudsier**, *superl* **sudsiest**) *adj* [foamy] mousseux; [soapy] savonneux.

sue [suː] ◇ *vt* poursuivre en justice, intenter un procès à; to ~ sb for OR over sthg poursuivre qqn en justice pour qqch; he ~d the factory for damages il a poursuivi l'usine pour obtenir des dommages et intérêts; to be ~d for damages/libel être poursuivi en dommages-intérêts/en diffamation; she's suing him for divorce elle a entamé une procédure de divorce.

◇ *vi* -**1.** JUR intenter un procès, engager des poursuites; she threatened to ~ for libel elle a menacé d'intenter un procès en diffamation; he's suing for divorce il a entamé une procédure de divorce. -**2.** *fml* [solicit]: to ~ for solliciter; to ~ for peace solliciter la paix.

suede [sweɪd] ◇ *n* daim *m*, suède *m spec*.

◇ *comp* [jacket, purse, shoes] en OR de daim; [leather] suédé.

suedette [sweɪ'det] *n* suédine *f*.

suet ['suɪt] *n* graisse *f* de rognon.

suet pudding *n sorte de pudding sucré ou salé à base de farine et de graisse de bœuf*.

Suez ['suɪz] *pr n* Suez; the ~ Canal le canal de Suez; the ~ crisis l'affaire du canal de Suez.

suffer ['sʌfəʳ] ◇ *vi* -**1.** [feel pain] souffrir; to ~ in silence souffrir en silence; I'll make you ~ for this! *fig* tu vas me payer ça!, je te revaudrai ça! -**2.** [be ill, afflicted] souffrir; to ~ from [serious disease] souffrir de; [cold, headache] avoir; to ~ from rheumatism souffrir de OR avoir des rhumatismes; to ~ from diabetes être diabétique; he's still ~ing from the effects of the anaesthetic il ne s'est pas encore tout à fait remis des suites de l'anesthésie; to ~ from a speech defect avoir un défaut de prononciation; they're still ~ing from shock ils sont encore sous le choc; she ~s from an inferiority complex elle fait un complexe d'infériorité. -**3.** [be affected]: it's the children who ~ in a marriage break-up ce sont les enfants qui souffrent lors d'une séparation; the low-paid will be the first to ~ les petits salaires seront les premiers touchés; to ~ from subir; the schools ~ from a lack of funding les établissements scolaires manquent de crédits. -**4.** [deteriorate] souffrir, se détériorer; her health is ~ing under all this stress sa santé se ressent de tout ce stress; the business really ~ed when he left l'affaire a beaucoup souffert de son départ; in the wake of government cutbacks, safety standards are beginning to ~ la sécurité commence à se ressentir OR à souffrir des réductions effectuées par le gouvernement.

◇ *vt* -**1.** [experience – pain, thirst] souffrir de; [– hardship] souffrir, subir; she ~ed a lot of pain elle a beaucoup souffert; I ~ed agonies! *inf* j'ai souffert le martyre!; our scheme has ~ed a serious setback notre projet a subi OR essuyé un grave revers; you'll have to ~ the consequences vous devrez en subir les conséquences; his popularity ~ed a decline sa cote de popularité a baissé. -**2.** [stand, put up with] tolérer, supporter; I won't ~ him another minute je ne le supporterai pas une minute de plus; he doesn't ~ fools gladly il ne tolère pas les imbéciles. -**3.** *lit* [allow] permettre, souffrir *lit*; to ~ sb to do sthg souffrir que qqn fasse qqch; ~ the little children to come unto me BIBLE laissez venir à moi les petits enfants.

sufferance ['sʌfrəns] *n* -**1.** [tolerance] tolérance *f*; on ~ par tolérance; remember you are only here on ~ n'oubliez pas que votre présence ici n'est que tolérée OR est tout juste tolérée. -**2.** [endurance] endurance *f*, résistance *f*. -**3.** [suffering] souffrance *f*.

sufferer ['sʌfrəʳ] *n* malade *mf*, victime *f*; ~s from heart disease les personnes cardiaques; a polio ~ un polio; good news for arthritis ~s une bonne nouvelle pour les personnes sujettes à l'arthrite OR qui souffrent d'arthrite.

suffering ['sʌfrɪŋ] ◇ *n* souffrance *f*, souffrances *fpl*; war causes great ~ la guerre est cause de nombreuses souffrances; all their ~s have been unnecessary toutes leurs souffrances ont été inutiles.

◇ *adj* souffrant, qui souffre.

suffice [sə'faɪs] ◇ *vi fml* suffire, être suffisant; will some bread and soup ~? du pain et de la soupe seront-ils suffisants?; ~ it to say (that) she's overjoyed inutile de dire qu'elle est ravie.

◇ *vt* suffire à, satisfaire; empty promises will not ~ him il ne se contentera pas de vaines promesses.

sufficiency [sə'fɪʃnsɪ] (*pl* **sufficiencies**) *n* quantité *f* suffisante; the country already had a ~ of oil le pays avait déjà suffisamment de pétrole OR du pétrole en quantité suffisante.

sufficient [sə'fɪʃnt] *adj* -**1.** [gen] suffisant; there's ~ food for everyone il y a assez OR suffisamment à manger pour tout le monde; have you had ~ to eat? avez-vous mangé à votre faim?; three will be quite ~ for our needs trois nous suffiront amplement; we don't have ~ evidence to convict them nous ne disposons pas d'assez de preuves pour les inculper. -**2.** PHILOS suffisant; a ~ condition une condition suffisante.

sufficiently [sə'fɪʃntlɪ] *adv* suffisamment, assez; it's ~ strong to withstand your weight c'est assez solide pour supporter votre poids; a ~ large quantity une quantité suffisante.

suffix ['sʌfɪks] ◇ *n* suffixe *m*.

◇ *vt* suffixer.

suffocate ['sʌfəkeɪt] ◇ *vi* -**1.** [die] suffoquer, étouffer, s'asphyxier. -**2.** [be hot, lack fresh air] suffoquer, étouffer; open the window, I'm suffocating! ouvre la fenêtre, j'étouffe! -**3.** *fig* [with anger, emotion etc] s'étouffer, suffoquer.

◇ *vt* -**1.** [kill] suffoquer, étouffer, asphyxier. -**2.** *fig* [repress, inhibit] étouffer, suffoquer.

suffocating ['sʌfəkeɪtɪŋ] *adj* -**1.** [heat, room] suffocant, étouffant; [smoke, fumes] asphyxiant, suffocant. -**2.** *fig* étouffant.

suffocation [ˌsʌfə'keɪʃn] *n* suffocation *f*, étouffement *m*, asphyxie *f*; to die from ~ mourir asphyxié.

suffragan ['sʌfrəgən] ◇ *n*: ~ (bishop) (évêque *m*) suffragant *m*.

◇ *adj* suffragant.

suffrage ['sʌfrɪdʒ] *n* -**1.** [right to vote] droit *m* de suffrage OR de vote; universal ~ suffrage *m* universel; women's ~ le droit de vote pour les femmes. -**2.** *fml* [vote] suffrage *m*, vote *m*.

suffragette [ˌsʌfrəˈdʒet] *n* suffragette *f*.

THE SUFFRAGETTES:
Militantes britanniques réclamant le droit de vote pour les femmes au début du XXe siècle. Menées par Emmeline Pankhurst, elles mirent en œuvre des moyens (manifestations, interruptions de meetings, attentats, incendies criminels, grèves de la faim) qui eurent finalement raison du Premier ministre Asquith, lequel fit adopter par le Parlement, en 1917, un projet de loi accordant le droit de vote à certaines catégories de femmes (les femmes mariées, les femmes au foyer et les femmes diplômées âgées d'au moins 30 ans). En 1928, une nouvelle loi étendit ce droit à toutes les femmes.

suffuse [səˈfjuːz] *vt (usu pass)* se répandre sur, baigner; ~d with light inondé de lumière; the sky was ~d with red le ciel était tout empourpré.

Sufi [ˈsuːfɪ] *n* soufi *m*, çoufi *m*.

Sufism [ˈsuːfɪzm] *n* soufisme *m*.

sugar [ˈʃʊgəʳ] ◇ *n* -**1.** [gen & CHEM] sucre *m*; how many ~s? combien de sucres?; I don't take ~ je ne prends pas de sucre; blood ~ glycémie *f*. -**2.** *inf Am* [to a man] mon chéri; [to a woman] ma chérie.
◇ *vt* sucrer.
◇ *interj inf*: oh ~! mince alors!

sugar basin *n Br* sucrier *m*.

sugar beet *n* betterave *f* sucrière OR à sucre.

sugar bowl *n* sucrier *m*; the Sugar Bowl *Am* SPORT *tournoi de football américain de La Nouvelle-Orléans*.

sugar candy *n* sucre *m* candi.

sugarcane [ˈʃʊgəkeɪn] *n* canne *f* à sucre.

sugar-coated *adj* dragéifié; ~ pill comprimé *m* dragéifié; ~ almonds dragées *fpl*.

sugar cube *n* morceau *m* de sucre.

sugar daddy *inf n* vieux protecteur *m*.

sugared [ˈʃʊgəd] *adj* -**1.** *literal* sucré. -**2.** *fig* mielleux, doucereux; he spoke in ~ tones il parlait d'un ton mielleux OR doucereux.

sugared almond *n* dragée *f*.

sugar-free *adj* sans sucre.

sugarless [ˈʃʊgəlɪs] *adj* sans sucre.

sugarloaf [ˈʃʊgələʊf] (*pl* sugarloaves [-ləʊvz]) *n* pain *m* de sucre.

sugar lump *n* morceau *m* de sucre.

sugar maple *n* érable *m* à sucre.

sugar pea *n* mange-tout *m inv*.

sugarplum [ˈʃʊgəplʌm] *n* [candied plum] prune *f* confite; [boiled sweet] bonbon *m*.

sugar shaker *n* saupoudreuse *f* (à sucre).

sugary [ˈʃʊgərɪ] *adj* -**1.** [drink, food] (très) sucré; [taste] sucré. -**2.** [manner, tone] mielleux, doucereux; ~ sentimentality mièvrerie *f*.

suggest [səˈdʒest] *vt* -**1.** [propose, put forward] suggérer, proposer; I ~ (that) we do nothing for the moment je suggère OR je propose que nous ne fassions rien pour l'instant; he ~ed that the meeting be held next Tuesday il a proposé de fixer la réunion à mardi prochain; a new plan ~ed itself un nouveau plan s'est dessiné; this, I ~, is how it happened voici, à mon avis, comment c'est arrivé. -**2.** [recommend] proposer, conseiller, recommander; who do you ~ for the job? qui suggérez-vous pour cette tâche? -**3.** [imply, insinuate] suggérer; just what are you ~ing? que voulez-vous dire par là?, qu'allez-vous insinuer là?; are you ~ing that I might be wrong? suggérez-vous que je pourrais avoir tort? -**4.** [indicate, point to] suggérer, laisser supposer; recent studies ~ that radiation may be the cause des études récentes semblent indiquer que le problème est dû à des radiations. -**5.** [evoke] suggérer, évoquer; what does this picture ~ to you? qu'est-ce que ce tableau évoque pour vous?, à quoi ce tableau vous fait-il penser?

suggestibility [səˌdʒestəˈbɪlətɪ] *n* suggestibilité *f*.

suggestible [səˈdʒestəbl] *adj* suggestible.

suggestion [səˈdʒestʃn] *n* -**1.** [proposal] suggestion *f*, proposition *f*; may I make OR offer a ~? puis-je faire une suggestion?; if nobody has any other ~s, we'll move on si personne n'a rien d'autre à suggérer OR à proposer, nous allons passer à autre chose; we are always open to ~s toute suggestion est la bienvenue; there's never been any ~ before of the rules being changed jusqu'à présent, il n'a jamais été question de modifier le règlement ❑ 'serving ~' 'suggestion de présentation'. -**2.** [recommendation] conseil *m*, recommandation *f*; at her doctor's ~ she stayed in bed suivant le conseil de son médecin, elle est restée au lit; their ~ is that we stop work immediately ils proposent que nous arrêtions le travail immédiatement. -**3.** [indication] indication *f*; her expression gave no ~ of what she was really thinking son expression ne donnait aucune indication sur OR ne laissait rien paraître de ce qu'elle pensait vraiment. -**4.** [trace, hint] soupçon *m*, trace *f*; with just a ~ of irony avec un soupçon d'ironie. -**5.** [implication] suggestion *f*, implication *f*; there is no ~ of negligence on the part of the parents rien ne laisse penser qu'il y ait eu négligence de la part des parents. -**6.** PSYCH suggestion *f*; the power of ~ le pouvoir de suggestion.

suggestive [səˈdʒestɪv] *adj* -**1.** [indicative, evocative] suggestif; his sculptures are ~ of natural forms ses sculptures rappellent OR évoquent des formes naturelles. -**2.** [erotic] suggestif.

suggestively [səˈdʒestɪvlɪ] *adv* de façon suggestive.

suicidal [sʊɪˈsaɪdl] *adj* suicidaire; ~ tendencies des tendances *fpl* suicidaires; I was feeling ~ j'avais envie de me tuer; to stop now would be ~ ce serait un suicide de s'arrêter maintenant.

suicide [ˈsʊɪsaɪd] ◇ *n* [act] suicide *m*; to commit ~ se suicider; an attempted ~ une tentative de suicide; privatization would be financial ~ la privatisation représenterait un véritable suicide financier.
◇ *comp* [mission, plane, squad] suicide; [attempt, bid, pact] de suicide; ~ note lettre *f (que l'on laisse quand on se suicide)*.

suit [suːt] ◇ *n* -**1.** [outfit - for men] costume *m*, complet *m*; [- for women] tailleur *m*; [- for particular activity] combinaison *f*; he came in a ~ and tie il est venu en costume-cravate; the workers wear protective ~s les ouvriers portent des combinaisons de protection; ~ of clothes tenue *f*; ~ of armour armure *f* complète. -**2.** [complete set] jeu *m*; a ~ of sails un jeu de voiles. -**3.** [in card games] couleur *f*; long OR strong ~ couleur forte; generosity is not his strong ~ *fig* la générosité n'est pas vraiment son (point) fort. -**4.** JUR [lawsuit] action *f*, procès *m*; to bring OR to file a ~ against sb intenter un procès à qqn, poursuivre qqn en justice; criminal ~ action au pénal. -**5.** *fml* [appeal] requête *f*, pétition *f*; *lit* [courtship] cour *f*; to pay ~ to sb faire la cour à qqn.
◇ *vt* -**1.** [be becoming to - subj: clothes, colour] aller à; black really ~s her le noir lui va à merveille. -**2.** [be satisfactory or convenient to] convenir à, arranger; Tuesday ~s me best c'est mardi qui me convient OR qui m'arrange le mieux; their relaxed approach ~s me fine leur attitude décontractée me convient tout à fait ❑ that ~s me to a T *inf* OR down to the ground *inf* ça me va au poil; ~ yourself! *inf* faites ce qui vous chante! -**3.** [agree with] convenir à, aller à, réussir à; life in the country obviously ~s her de toute évidence, la vie à la campagne lui convient OR lui réussit. -**4.** [be appropriate] convenir à, aller à, être fait pour; clothes to ~ all tastes des vêtements pour tous les goûts; the role ~s her perfectly le rôle lui va comme un gant. -**5.** [adapt] adapter, approprier; he tries to ~ his act to his audience il essaie d'adapter son numéro à son public; to ~ the action to the word joindre le geste à la parole.
◇ *vi* [be satisfactory] convenir, aller; will that date ~? cette date vous convient-elle OR est-elle à votre convenance?
◆ **suit up** *vi insep* [dress - diver, pilot, astronaut etc] mettre sa combinaison.

suitability [ˌsuːtəˈbɪlətɪ] *n* [of clothing] caractère *m* approprié; [of behaviour, arrangements] caractère *m* convenable; [of act, remark] à-propos *m*, pertinence *f*; [of time, place] opportunité *f*; they doubt his ~ for the post ils ne sont pas sûrs qu'il soit fait pour ce poste; they're worried about the film's ~ for younger audiences ils ont peur que le film ne convienne pas à un public jeune.

suitable [ˈsuːtəbl] *adj* -**1.** [convenient] approprié, adéquat; will that day be ~ for you? cette date-là vous convient-elle?; afternoons aren't ~ ça n'est pas possible l'après-midi. -**2.** [appropriate - gen] qui convient; [- clothing] approprié, adéquat; [- behaviour] convenable; [- act, remark] approprié, pertinent; [- time, place] propice; ~ for all occasions qui convient dans toutes les occasions; 'not ~ for children' 'réservé aux adultes'; this is hardly a ~ time for a heart to heart ce n'est pas vraiment le bon moment pour se parler à cœur ouvert; the most ~ candidate for the post le candidat le plus apte à occuper ce poste; the house is not ~ for a large family la maison ne conviendrait pas à une famille nombreuse; the stage was not considered a ~ career for a woman le théâtre n'était pas considéré comme un métier convenable pour une femme.

suitably [ˈsuːtəblɪ] *adv* [dress] de façon appropriée; [behave] convenablement, comme il faut; he was ~ equipped for his trip il était convenablement équipé pour son voyage; I tried to look ~ surprised j'ai essayé d'adopter une expression de surprise ‖ [as intensifier]: he was ~ impressed il a été plutôt impressionné.

suitcase [ˈsuːtkeɪs] *n* valise *f*; I've been living out of a ~ for the last month ça fait un mois que je n'ai pas défait mes valises.

suite [swiːt] *n* -**1.** [rooms] suite *f*, appartement *m*; a ~ of rooms une enfilade de pièces; the bridal ~ la suite réservée aux jeunes mariés. -**2.** [furniture] mobilier *m*; bedroom ~ chambre *f* à coucher. -**3.** MUS suite *f*; a cello ~ une suite pour violoncelle; 'The Firebird Suite' *Stravinsky* 'l'Oiseau de feu'. -**4.** [staff, followers] suite *f*. -**5.** COMPUT ensemble *m* (de programmes), progiciel *m*.

suited [ˈsuːtɪd] *adj* -**1.** [appropriate] approprié; he's not ~ to teaching il n'est pas fait pour l'enseignement; she's ideally ~ for the job ce travail lui convient tout à fait. -**2.** [matched] assorti; they are well ~ (to each other) ils sont faits l'un pour l'autre, ils sont bien assortis.

suiting [ˈsuːtɪŋ] *n* tissu *m* de confection.

suitor [ˈsuːtəʳ] *n* -**1.** *dated* [wooer] amoureux *m*, soupirant *m*. -**2.** JUR plaignant *m*, -e *f*.

Sulawesi [ˌsuːləˈweɪsɪ] *pr n* Sulawesi; in ~ à Sulawesi.

Suleiman [ˌsuːleɪˈmɑːn] *pr n*: ~ the Magnificent Soliman le Magnifique.

sulfa drug *Am* = **sulpha drug**.

sulfate *Am* = **sulphate**.

sulfide *Am* = **sulphide**.

sulfonamide *Am* = **sulphonamide**.

sulfur *etc Am* = **sulphur**.

sulk [sʌlk] ◇ *vi* bouder, faire la tête; there's no need to ~! (ce n'est) pas la peine de faire la tête!
◇ *n* bouderie *f*; to have a ~ OR (a fit of) the ~s faire la tête.

sulkily [ˈsʌlkɪlɪ] *adv* [act] en boudant, d'un air maussade; [answer] d'un ton maussade.

sulkiness [ˈsʌlkɪnɪs] *n* [mood] bouderie *f*, humeur *f* maussade; [temperament] caractère *m* boudeur OR maussade.

sulky [ˈsʌlkɪ] (*compar* sulkier, *superl* sulkiest, *pl* sulkies) ◇ *adj* [person, mood] boudeur, maussade; now, don't go all ~ on me! allez, pas la peine de me faire la tête!
◇ *n* sulky *m*.

sullen ['sʌlən] *adj* -**1.** [person, behaviour, appearance, remark] maussade, renfrogné. -**2.** [clouds] menaçant.

sullenly ['sʌlənlɪ] *adv* [behave] d'un air maussade OR renfrogné; [answer, say, refuse] d'un ton maussade; [agree, obey] de mauvaise grâce, à contre-cœur.

sullenness ['sʌlənnɪs] *n* [temperament] humeur *f* maussade; [of appearance] air *m* renfrogné.

sully ['sʌlɪ] (*pt* & *pp* sullied) *vt* -**1.** [dirty] souiller. -**2.** *fig* [reputation] ternir.

sulpha drug *Br*, **sulfa drug** *Am* ['sʌlfə-] *n* sulfamide *m*.

sulphate *Br*, **sulfate** *Am* ['sʌlfeɪt] *n* sulfate *m*; copper/zinc ~ sulfate de cuivre/de zinc.

sulphide *Br*, **sulfide** *Am* ['sʌlfaɪd] *n* sulfure *m*; to treat sthg with ~ sulfurer qqch; hydrogen ~ sulfure d'hydrogène, hydrogène *m* sulfuré.

sulphite *Br*, **sulfite** *Am* ['sʌlfaɪt] *n* sulfite *m*.

sulphonamide *Br*, **sulfonamide** *Am* [sʌl'fɒnəmaɪd] *n* sulfonamide *m*, sulfamide *m*.

sulphur *Br*, **sulfur** *Am* ['sʌlfəʳ] *n* soufre *m*.

sulphur dioxide *n* dioxyde *m* de soufre, anhydride *m* sulfureux.

sulphuric *Br*, **sulfuric** *Am* [sʌl'fjʊərɪk] *adj* sulfurique; ~ acid acide *m* sulfurique.

sulphurous *Br*, **sulfurous** *Am* ['sʌlfərəs] *adj literal* & *fig* sulfureux.

sultan ['sʌltən] *n* sultan *m*.

sultana [səl'tɑːnə] *n* -**1.** *Br* [raisin] raisin *m* de Smyrne; ~ cake gâteau *m* aux raisins de Smyrne. -**2.** [woman] sultane *f*.

sultanate ['sʌltənət] *n* sultanat *m*.

sultriness ['sʌltrɪnɪs] *n* -**1.** [of weather] chaleur *f* étouffante. -**2.** [sensuality] sensualité *f*.

sultry ['sʌltrɪ] (*compar* sultrier, *superl* sultriest) *adj* -**1.** [weather] lourd; [heat] étouffant, suffocant. -**2.** [person, look, smile] sensuel; [voice] chaud, sensuel.

sum [sʌm] (*pt* & *pp* summed, *cont* summing) ◇ *n* -**1.** [amount of money] somme *f*; it's going to cost us a considerable ~ (of money) ça va nous coûter beaucoup d'argent OR très cher. -**2.** [total] total *m*, somme *f*; a good orchestra is greater than the ~ of its parts un bon orchestre est plus que la somme de ses membres. -**3.** [arithmetical operation] calcul *m*; to do ~s *Br* faire du calcul; he's very weak at ~s *Br* il est très faible en calcul; I tried to do the ~ in my head j'ai essayé de faire le calcul de tête. -**4.** [gist] somme *f*; in ~ en somme, somme toute; the ~ and substance of her argument les grandes lignes de son raisonnement.
◇ *vt* [add] additionner, faire le total de; [calculate] calculer.
◆ **sum up** ◇ *vt sep* -**1.** [summarize] résumer, récapituler; one word ~s the matter up un mot suffit à résumer la question. -**2.** [size up] jauger; he summed us up immediately il nous a jaugés OR classés sur-le-champ; I summed up the situation at a glance un simple coup d'œil m'a suffi pour jauger la situation.
◇ *vi insep* [gen] récapituler, faire un résumé; JUR [judge] résumer.

sumac(h) ['ʃuːmæk] ◇ *n* sumac *m*.
◇ *adj* sumérien.

Sumatra [sʊ'mɑːtrə] *pr n* Sumatra; in ~ à Sumatra.

Sumatran [sʊ'mɑːtrən] ◇ *n* Sumatranais *m*, -e *f*.
◇ *adj* sumatranais.

Sumer ['suːməʳ] *pr n* Sumer.

Sumerian [suː'mɪərɪən] ◇ *n* -**1.** [person] Sumérien *m*, -enne *f*. -**2.** LING sumérien *m*.
◇ *adj* sumérien.

summa cum laude ['sʌmə,kʊm'laʊdeɪ] *adj* & *adv* *Am* avec les plus grands honneurs; to graduate ~ obtenir un diplôme avec mention très honorable.

summarily ['sʌmərəlɪ] *adv* sommairement; they were ~ dismissed without any explanation on les a sommairement OR tout simplement congédiés sans plus d'explications.

summarize, -ise ['sʌməraɪz] *vt* résumer.

summary ['sʌmərɪ] (*pl* summaries) ◇ *n* -**1.** [synopsis - of argument, situation] résumé *m*, récapitulation *f*; [- of book, film] résumé *m*; he gave us a brief ~ of the situation il nous a donné un bref résumé de la situation; there is a news ~ every hour il y a un court bulletin d'information toutes les heures. -**2.** [written list] sommaire *m*, résumé *m*; FIN [of accounts] relevé *m*.
◇ *adj* [gen & JUR] sommaire.

summary offence *n* infraction *f* mineure, délit *m*.

summat *inf* ['sʌmət] *Br dial* = **something**.

summation [sʌ'meɪʃn] *n* -**1.** [addition] addition *f*; [sum] somme *f*, total *m*. -**2.** [summary] récapitulation *f*, résumé *m*; the book is a ~ of her life's work ce livre constitue une récapitulation de l'œuvre de sa vie.

summer ['sʌməʳ] ◇ *n* -**1.** [season] été *m*; in (the) ~ en été; in the ~ of 1942 pendant OR au cours de l'été 1942; they spend every ~ at the seaside ils passent tous leurs étés au bord de la mer; we've had a good ~ [good weather] on a eu un bel été; [profitable tourist season] la saison était bonne. -**2.** *lit* [year of age] : a youth of 15 ~s un jeune homme de 15 printemps. -**3.** *fig* [high point] apogée *m*.
◇ *comp* [clothes, residence, day, holidays] d'été; [heat, sports] estival.
◇ *vi* passer l'été.
◇ *vt* [cattle, sheep] estiver.

summer camp *n* *Am* colonie *f* de vacances.

summerhouse ['sʌməhaʊs, *pl* -haʊzɪz] *n* *Br* pavillon *m* (de jardin).

summer pudding *n* *Br* *pudding composé d'une compote de fruits rouges enveloppée de pain ou de biscuit.*

summersault ['sʌməsɔːlt] = **somersault**.

summer school *n* stage *m* d'été.

summer solstice *n* solstice *m* d'été.

summer squash *n* *Am* courgette *f* jaune.

summer term *n* troisième trimestre *m*.

summertime ['sʌmətaɪm] *n* [season] été *m*; in the ~ en été.
◆ **summer time** *n* heure *f* d'été; British Summer Time heure d'été britannique.

summerweight ['sʌməweɪt] *adj* léger, d'été.

summery ['sʌmərɪ] *adj* d'été.

summing-up [,sʌmɪŋ-] (*pl* summings-up) *n* [gen] résumé *m*, récapitulation *f*; JUR résumé *m*.

summit ['sʌmɪt] ◇ *n* -**1.** [peak - of mountain] sommet *m*, cime *f*; [- of glory, happiness, power] apogée *m*, summum *m*. -**2.** POL [meeting] sommet *m*.
◇ *comp* [talks, agreement] au sommet.

summit conference *n* (conférence *f* au) sommet *m*.

summon ['sʌmən] *vt* -**1.** [send for - person] appeler, faire venir; [- help] appeler à, requérir; we were ~ed to his presence nous fûmes appelés auprès de lui. -**2.** [convene] convoquer; to ~ a meeting convoquer une réunion. -**3.** JUR citer, assigner; to ~ sb to appear in court citer qqn en justice; the court ~ed her as a witness la cour l'a citée comme témoin. -**4.** [muster - courage, strength] rassembler, faire appel à; he couldn't ~ enough courage to ask her out il n'a pas trouvé le courage nécessaire pour lui demander de sortir avec lui. -**5.** *fml* [order] sommer, ordonner à; she ~ed us in/up elle nous a sommés OR ordonné d'entrer/de monter.
◆ **summon up** *vt sep* -**1.** [courage, strength] rassembler, faire appel à; she ~ed up her courage to ask him elle a pris son courage à deux mains pour lui poser la question; I'll be there if I can ~ up the energy j'y serai si j'arrive à rassembler suffisamment d'énergie. -**2.** [help, support] réunir, faire appel à; I can't ~ up much interest in this plan je n'arrive pas à m'intéresser beaucoup à ce projet. -**3.** [memories, thoughts] évoquer. -**4.** [spirits] rassembler (ses esprits).

summons ['sʌmənz] (*pl* summonses) ◇ *n* -**1.** JUR citation *f*, assignation *f*; he received OR got a ~ for speeding il a reçu une citation à comparaître en justice pour excès de vitesse; to take out a ~ against sb faire assigner qqn en justice. -**2.** [gen] convocation *f*. -**3.** MIL sommation *f*; the town received a ~ to surrender les habitants de la ville furent sommés de se rendre.
◇ *vt* JUR citer OR assigner (à comparaître); she was ~ed to testify elle a été citée à comparaître en tant que témoin.

sumo ['suːməʊ] ◇ *n* sumo *m*.
◇ *comp*: ~ wrestler lutteur *m* de sumo; ~ wrestling sumo *m*.

sump [sʌmp] *n* -**1.** TECH puisard *m*; *Br* AUT carter *m*. -**2.** [cesspool] fosse *f* d'aisances.

sump oil *n* *Br* huile *f* de carter.

sumptuous ['sʌmptʃʊəs] *adj* somptueux.

sumptuously ['sʌmptʃʊəslɪ] *adv* somptueusement.

sumptuousness ['sʌmptʃʊəsnɪs] *n* somptuosité *f*.

sum total *n* totalité *f*, somme *f* totale; the report contains the ~ of research in the field ce rapport contient tous les résultats de la recherche en ce domaine; that is the ~ of our knowledge voilà à quoi se résume tout ce que nous savons.

sun [sʌn] (*pt* & *pp* sunned, *cont* sunning) ◇ *n* soleil *m*; the ~ is shining le soleil brille, il y a du soleil; the ~ is rising/setting le soleil se lève/se couche; the ~ is in my eyes j'ai le soleil dans les yeux; I can't stay in the ~ for very long je ne peux pas rester très longtemps au soleil; she's caught the ~ elle a attrapé un coup de soleil; the living room gets the ~ in the afternoon le salon est ensoleillé l'après-midi; to take a photograph into the ~ prendre une photo à contre-jour ❑ a place in the ~ une place au soleil; under the ~: I've tried everything under the ~ j'ai tout essayé; she called him all the names under the ~ elle l'a traité de tous les noms; there's nothing new under the ~ il n'y a rien de nouveau sous le soleil; 'The Sun Also Rises' *Hemingway* 'le Soleil se lève aussi'; The Sun PRESS *quotidien britannique à sensation*; Sun reader lecteur du Sun *(typique de la droite populaire)*.
◇ *vt*: to ~ o.s. [person] prendre le soleil, se faire bronzer; [animal] se chauffer au soleil.

Sun. (*written abbr of* Sunday) dim.

sunbaked ['sʌnbeɪkt] *adj* desséché par le soleil.

sunbath ['sʌnbɑːθ, *pl* -bɑːðz] *n* bain *m* de soleil.

sunbathe ['sʌnbeɪð] ◇ *vi* prendre un bain de soleil, se faire bronzer.
◇ *n* *Br* bain *m* de soleil.

sunbather ['sʌnbeɪðəʳ] *n personne qui prend un bain de soleil*; hundreds of ~s converged on the beach des centaines de gens se dirigeaient vers la plage pour aller s'étendre au soleil.

sunbathing ['sʌnbeɪðɪŋ] *n (U)* bains *mpl* de soleil.

sunbeam ['sʌnbiːm] *n* rayon *m* de soleil.

sunbed ['sʌnbed] *n* [in garden, on beach] lit *m* pliant; [with tanning lamps] lit *m* à ultra-violets.

sunbelt ['sʌnbelt] *n* *Am*: the ~ OR Sunbelt les États du sud des États-Unis.

sunblind ['sʌnblaɪnd] *n* *Br* store *m*.

sun block *n* écran *m* total.

sunbonnet ['sʌn,bɒnɪt] *n* capeline *f*.

sunburn ['sʌnbɜːn] *n* coup *m* de soleil.

sunburnt ['sʌnbɜːnt], **sunburned** ['sʌnbɜːnd] *adj* brûlé par le soleil; I get ~ easily j'attrape facilement des coups de soleil.

sunburst ['sʌnbɜːst] *n* -**1.** [through clouds] rayon *m* de soleil. -**2.** [pattern] soleil *m*; [brooch] broche *f* en forme de soleil; a ~ clock une pendule soleil.

sun-cured [-kjʊəd] *adj* séché au soleil.

sundae ['sʌndeɪ] *n coupe de glace aux fruits et à la crème chantilly.*

Sunda Islands ['sʌndə-] *pl pr n*: the ~ les îles *fpl* de la Sonde; in the ~ dans les îles de la Sonde.
sun dance *n* danse *f* du soleil.
Sunday ['sʌndɪ] ◇ *n* -**1.** [day] dimanche *m*; 'Sunday, Bloody Sunday' *Schlesinger* 'Un dimanche comme les autres'. -**2.** *Br* [newspaper]: the ~s les journaux *mpl* du dimanche.
◇ *comp* [clothes, newspaper, driver, painter] du dimanche; [peace, rest, mass] dominical; the ~ roast OR joint *plat dominical traditionnellement composé d'un rôti de boeuf chaud, de légumes et de sauce.*

SUNDAY PAPERS:
Les principaux hebdomadaires britanniques paraissant le dimanche sont les suivants:
the Independent on Sunday;
the Mail on Sunday (tendance conservatrice);
the News of the World (à sensation);
the Observer (tendance centre-gauche);
the People (à sensation);
the Sunday Express (tendance conservatrice);
the Sunday Mirror (tendance centre-gauche);
the Sunday Telegraph (tendance conservatrice);
the Sunday Times (tendance conservatrice).

Sunday best *n* vêtements *mpl* du dimanche; they were dressed in their ~ ils étaient tout endimanchés, ils avaient mis leurs vêtements du dimanche.
Sunday school *n* ≃ catéchisme *m*.
sun deck *n* [of house] véranda *f*, terrasse *f*; NAUT pont *m* supérieur OR promenade.
sunder ['sʌndəʳ] *arch* ◇ *vt* séparer, briser.
◇ *n*: in ~ en morceaux.
sundial ['sʌndaɪəl] *n* cadran *m* solaire.
sundown ['sʌndaʊn] *n* coucher *m* du soleil; at ~ au coucher du soleil.
sundowner *inf* ['sʌndaʊnəʳ] *n* [drink] verre *m* *(qu'on prend le soir)*.
sundrenched ['sʌndrentʃt] *adj* inondé de soleil.
sundress ['sʌndres] *n* bain *m* de soleil *(robe)*.
sun-dried *adj* séché au soleil.
sundry ['sʌndrɪ] ◇ *adj* divers, différent.
◇ *pron*: all and ~ were having a good time tout le monde s'amusait bien; she told all and ~ about it elle l'a raconté à qui voulait l'entendre.
◆ **sundries** *npl* articles *mpl* divers.
sunfast ['sʌnfɑːst] *adj* qui ne se décolore pas au soleil.
sunfish ['sʌnfɪʃ] (*pl inv* OR sunfishes) *n* poisson-lune *m*, môle *f*.
sunflower ['sʌn,flaʊəʳ] ◇ *n* tournesol *m*, soleil *m*.
◇ *comp* [oil, seed] de tournesol; the Sunflower State *Am* le Kansas.
sung [sʌŋ] ◇ *pp* → **sing**.
◇ *adj*: ~ mass messe *f* chantée.
sunglasses ['sʌn,glɑːsɪz] *npl* lunettes *fpl* de soleil.
sunglow ['sʌnglәʊ] *n embrasement de l'horizon au moment du coucher ou du lever du soleil.*
sun god *n* dieu *m* solaire, dieu-soleil *m*.
sunhat ['sʌnhæt] *n* chapeau *m* de soleil.
sunk [sʌŋk] ◇ *pp* → **sink**.
◇ *adj inf* fichu; if she catches us, we're ~ si elle nous surprend, on est fichus.
sunken ['sʌŋkən] *adj* -**1.** [boat, rock] submergé; [garden] en contrebas; [bathtub] encastré (au ras du sol). -**2.** [hollow - cheeks] creux, affaissé; [- eyes] creux.
sunk fence *n* saut-de-loup *m*.
Sun King *pr n* HIST: the ~ le Roi-Soleil.
sunlamp ['sʌnlæmp] *n* lampe *f* à rayons ultraviolets OR à bronzer.
sunless ['sʌnlɪs] *adj* sans soleil.
sunlight ['sʌnlaɪt] *n* (lumière *f* du) soleil *m*; in the ~ au soleil.
sunlit ['sʌnlɪt] *adj* ensoleillé.
sun lotion *n* lait *m* solaire.
sun lounge *n Br* solarium *m*.
sunlounger ['sʌn,laʊndʒəʳ] *n Br* chaise *f* longue *(où l'on s'allonge pour bronzer)*.

Sunna ['sʌnə] *n* sunna *f*.
Sunni ['sʌnɪ] *n* -**1.** [religion] sunnisme *m*. -**2.** [person] sunnite *mf*.
Sunnite ['sʌnaɪt] ◇ *adj* sunnite.
◇ *n* sunnite *mf*.
sunny ['sʌnɪ] (*compar* sunnier, *superl* sunniest) *adj* -**1.** [day, place etc] ensoleillé; it's a ~ day, it's ~ il fait (du) soleil OR beau; ~ intervals OR periods METEOR éclaircies *fpl*. -**2.** *fig* [cheerful - disposition] heureux; [- smile] radieux, rayonnant; to look on the ~ side voir le bon côté des choses; he's on the ~ side of sixty *Br* il n'a pas encore la soixantaine.
sunny-side up *adj*: eggs ~ œufs *mpl* sur le plat.
sun parlor, sun porch *n Am* solarium *m*.
sunray lamp ['sʌnreɪ-] = **sunlamp**.
sunray pleats *npl* plissé *m* soleil.
sunray treatment *n* héliothérapie *f*.
sunrise ['sʌnraɪz] *n* lever *m* du soleil; at ~ au lever du soleil; to get up at ~ se lever avec le soleil; ~ is about 6 o'clock le soleil se lève vers 6 h; the ~ was beautiful this morning il y avait un superbe lever de soleil ce matin.
sunrise industry *n* industrie *f* de pointe.
sunroof ['sʌnruːf] *n* toit *m* ouvrant.
sunscreen ['sʌnskriːn] *n* [suntan lotion] écran *m* total.
sunset ['sʌnset] *n* coucher *m* du soleil; at ~ au coucher du soleil; ~ is about 6 o'clock le soleil se couche vers 18 h; it was a beautiful ~ le coucher de soleil était magnifique.
sunshade ['sʌnʃeɪd] *n* [lady's parasol] ombrelle *f*; [for table] parasol *m*; [on cap] visière *f*.
sunshine ['sʌnʃaɪn] *n* -**1.** [sunlight] (lumière *f* du) soleil *m*; in the ~ au soleil; we generally get at least 150 hours of ~ in July en général, nous avons au moins 150 heures d'ensoleillement en juillet; his visit brought a little ~ into our lives *fig* sa visite a apporté un peu de soleil dans notre vie. -**2.** *inf* [term of address]: hello ~! salut ma jolie!, salut mon mignon!
sunshine law *n Am* loi *f* sur la transparence dans l'administration.
sunshine roof = **sunroof**.
sun-soaked *adj* [beach] inondé de soleil.
sunspecs *inf* ['sʌnspeks] *npl* lunettes *fpl* noires.
sunspot ['sʌnspɒt] *n* tache *f* solaire.
sunstroke ['sʌnstrəʊk] *n (U)* insolation *f*; to have/to get ~ avoir/attraper une insolation.
sunsuit ['sʌnsuːt] *n* (costume *m*) bain *m* de soleil.
suntan ['sʌntæn] ◇ *n* bronzage *m*; to have a ~ être bronzé; to get a ~ se faire bronzer, bronzer; where did you get that lovely ~? d'où est-ce que tu viens pour être bronzé comme ça?
◇ *comp* [cream, lotion, oil] solaire, de bronzage.
suntanned ['sʌntænd] *adj* bronzé.
suntrap ['sʌntræp] *n* coin *m* abrité et très ensoleillé; the garden is a real ~ le jardin est toujours très ensoleillé.
sun-up *n* lever *m* du soleil; at ~ au lever du soleil.
sun visor *n* [on cap, for eyes] visière *f*; AUT pare-soleil *m*.
sun-worship *n* culte *m* du Soleil.
sun-worshipper *n* -**1.** RELIG adorateur *m*, -trice *f* du Soleil. -**2.** *fig* adepte *mf* OR fanatique *mf* du bronzage.
sup [sʌp] (*pt & pp* supped, *cont* supping)
◇ *vi arch* [have supper] souper; they supped on OR off some leftovers ils ont soupé de quelques restes.
◇ *vt* boire à petites gorgées.
◇ *n* petite gorgée *f*.
super ['suːpəʳ] ◇ *adj* -**1.** *inf* [wonderful] super *(inv)*, terrible, génial; it was a ~ party! c'était super OR génial comme fête! -**2.** [superior] supérieur, super-; they're developing a new sort of ~ hydrogen bomb ils sont en train de mettre au point une nouvelle superbombe H.
◇ *interj inf* super, formidable.
◇ *n* -**1.** *Am* [petrol] super *m*, supercarburant *m*. -**2.** *inf* [police superintendent] ≃ commissaire *m* (de police).
superable ['suːpərəbl] *adj* surmontable.
superabundance [,suːpərə'bʌndəns] *n* surabondance *f*.
superabundant [,suːpərə'bʌndənt] *adj* surabondant.
superannuate [,suːpə'rænjʊeɪt] *vt* -**1.** [person] mettre à la retraite. -**2.** [object] mettre au rebut.
superannuated [,suːpə'rænjʊeɪtɪd] *adj* -**1.** [person] à la retraite, retraité. -**2.** [object] suranné, désuet.
superannuation ['suːpə,rænjʊ'eɪʃn] *n* -**1.** [act of retiring] mise *f* à la retraite. -**2.** [pension] pension *f* de retraite. -**3.** [contribution] versement *m* OR cotisation *f* pour la retraite; ~ fund caisse *f* de retraite.
superb [suː'pɜːb] *adj* superbe, magnifique.
superblock ['suːpəblɒk] *n Am* zone *f* piétonne OR piétonnière.
superbly [suː'pɜːblɪ] *adv* superbement, magnifiquement; she performed ~ elle a merveilleusement bien joué.
Super Bowl *pr n Am* Superbowl *m (finale du championnat des États-Unis de football américain)*.
supercargo ['suːpə,kɑːgəʊ] (*pl* supercargoes) *n* subrécargue *m*.
supercharge ['suːpətʃɑːdʒ] *vt* -**1.** TECH [engine] surcomprimer, suralimenter. -**2.** *fig* [atmosphere] électriser, galvaniser, survolter.
supercharged ['suːpətʃɑːdʒd] *adj* TECH [engine] surcomprimé.
supercharger ['suːpətʃɑːdʒəʳ] *n* compresseur *m*.
supercilious [,suːpə'sɪlɪəs] *adj* hautain, arrogant, dédaigneux.
superciliously [,suːpə'sɪlɪəslɪ] *adv* [act] d'un air hautain, avec arrogance OR dédain; [speak] d'un ton hautain, avec arrogance OR dédain.
superciliousness [,suːpə'sɪlɪəsnɪs] *n* hauteur *f*, arrogance *f*, dédain *m*.
superclass ['suːpəklɑːs] *n* superclasse *f*.
supercomputer [,suːpəkəm'pjuːtəʳ] *n* supercalculateur *m*, super-ordinateur *m*.
superconductive [,suːpəkən'dʌktɪv] *adj* supraconducteur.
superconductivity ['suːpə,kɒndʌk'tɪvətɪ] *n* supraconductivité *f*.
superconductor [,suːpəkən'dʌktəʳ] *n* supraconducteur *m*.
super-duper *inf* [-'duːpəʳ] *adj* super, superchouette.
superego [,suːpər'iːgəʊ] (*pl* superegos) *n* sur-moi *m*.
supereminent [,suːpər'emɪnənt] *adj* suréminent.
supererogation ['suːpər,erə'geɪʃn] *n* surérogation *f*.
superfamily ['suːpə,fæməlɪ] (*pl* superfamilies) *n* BIOL superfamille *f*.
superficial [,suːpə'fɪʃl] *adj* [knowledge] superficiel; [differences] superficiel, insignifiant; [person] superficiel, frivole, léger; [wound] superficiel, léger.
superficiality ['suːpə,fɪʃɪ'ælətɪ] *n* caractère *m* superficiel, manque *m* de profondeur.
superficially [,suːpə'fɪʃəlɪ] *adv* superficiellement.
superfine ['suːpəfaɪn] *adj* [quality, product] extra-fin, superfin, surfin; [analysis] très fin; [distinction, detail] subtil.
superfluity [,suːpə'fluətɪ] *n* -**1.** [superfluousness] caractère *m* superflu. -**2.** [excess] surabondance *f*; a ~ of details une surabondance de détails.
superfluous [suː'pɜːfluəs] *adj* superflu; it is ~ to say... (il est) inutile de OR il va sans dire...; I felt ~ j'avais l'impression d'être de trop OR d'être la cinquième roue du carrosse.
superfluously [suː'pɜːfluəslɪ] *adv* de manière superflue, inutilement.
supergiant ['suːpə,dʒaɪənt] *n* ASTRON supergéante *f*.

Superglue® ['su:pəglu:] *n* Superglu® *f.*

supergrass ['su:pəgrɑ:s] *n indicateur de police très efficace.*

supergroup ['su:pəgru:p] *n groupe de rock dont chaque membre est déjà célèbre pour avoir appartenu à un autre groupe.*

superheat [ˌsu:pə'hi:t] *vt* surchauffer; ~ed steam vapeur *f* surchauffée.

superhero ['su:pəˌhɪərəʊ] (*pl* superheroes) *n* superman *m*, surhomme *m.*

superhet ['su:pəhet], **superheterodyne receiver** [ˌsu:pə'hetərədaɪn-] *n* superhétérodyne *m.*

superhigh frequency ['su:pəhaɪ-] *n* ondes *fpl* centimétriques.

superhighway ['su:pəˌhaɪweɪ] *n Am* autoroute *f.*

superhuman [ˌsu:pə'hju:mən] *adj* surhumain.

superimpose [ˌsu:pərɪm'pəʊz] *vt* superposer; to ~ sthg on sthg superposer qqch à qqch; ~d photos des photos en surimpression.

superintend [ˌsu:pərɪn'tend] *vt* -**1.** [oversee - activity] surveiller; [- person] surveiller, avoir l'œil sur. -**2.** [run - office, institution] diriger.

superintendent [ˌsu:pərɪn'tendənt] *n* -**1.** [of institution] directeur *m*, -trice *f*; [of department, office] chef *m*. -**2.** [of police] ≃ commissaire *m* (de police). -**3.** *Am* [of apartment building] gardien *m*, -enne *f*, concierge *mf.*

superior [su:'pɪərɪə^r] ◇ *adj* -**1.** [better, greater] supérieur; a ~ wine un vin de qualité supérieure; ~ to supérieur à; the book is vastly ~ to the film le livre est bien meilleur que le film; ~ in number to supérieur en nombre à, numériquement supérieur à; the enemy troops were ~ in numbers les troupes ennemies étaient en plus grand nombre OR supérieures en nombre. -**2.** [senior - officer, position] supérieur; ~ to supérieur à, au-dessus de; the ~ classes les classes *fpl* dirigeantes. -**3.** *pej* [supercilious] suffisant, hautain; with a ~ smile avec un sourire suffisant OR condescendant; in a ~ voice d'un ton suffisant OR supérieur; she feels ~ elle se croit supérieure. -**4.** [upper] supérieur; the ~ limbs les membres *mpl* supérieurs. -**5.** TYPO: ~ letter lettre *f* supérieure OR suscrite. -**6.** BIOL supérieur; the ~ mammals les mammifères *mpl* supérieurs.
◇ *n* supérieur *m*, -e *f.*
◆ **Superior** *pr n*: Lake Superior le lac Supérieur.

superiority [su:ˌpɪərɪ'ɒrətɪ] *n* -**1.** [higher amount, worth] supériorité *f*; their ~ in numbers leur supériorité numérique; the ~ of this brand to OR over all the others la supériorité de cette marque par rapport à toutes les autres. -**2.** *pej* [arrogance] supériorité *f*, arrogance *f.*

superiority complex *n* complexe *m* de supériorité.

superlative [su:'pɜ:lətɪv] ◇ *adj* -**1.** [outstanding - quality, skill, performance] sans pareil; [- performer, athlete] sans pareil, inégalé. -**2.** [overwhelming - indifference, ignorance, joy] suprême. -**3.** GRAMM superlatif.
◇ *n* superlatif *m*; in the ~ au superlatif; she always speaks in ~s elle a tendance à tout exagérer.

superlatively [su:'pɜ:lətɪvlɪ] *adv* au plus haut degré, exceptionnellement; a ~ good candidate un candidat exceptionnel; she is ~ efficient elle est on ne peut plus efficace.

superman ['su:pəmæn] (*pl* supermen [-men]) *n* [PHILOS & gen] surhomme *m*; [gen] superman *m.*
◆ **Superman** *pr n* [comic book hero] Superman *m.*

supermarket ['su:pəˌmɑ:kɪt] *n* supermarché *m.*

supernal [su:'pɜ:nl] *adj lit* céleste, divin.

supernatural [ˌsu:pə'nætʃrəl] ◇ *adj* surnaturel.
◇ *n* surnaturel *m.*

supernormal [ˌsu:pə'nɔ:ml] *adj* -**1.** [above average] au-dessus de la moyenne OR de la normale. -**2.** [paranormal] supranormal, paranormal.

supernova [ˌsu:pə'nəʊvə] (*pl* supernovas OR supernovae [-vi:]) *n* supernova *f.*

supernumerary [ˌsu:pə'nju:mərərɪ] (*pl* supernumeraries) ◇ *adj* [extra] surnuméraire; [superfluous] superflu.
◇ *n* [gen & ADMIN] surnuméraire *m*; CIN & TV figurant *m*, -e *f.*

superorder ['su:pərˌɔ:də^r] *n* superordre *m.*

superphosphate [ˌsu:pə'fɒsfeɪt] *n* superphosphate *m.*

superpose [ˌsu:pə'pəʊz] *vt* superposer; to ~ sthg on sthg superposer qqch à qqch.

superposition [ˌsu:pəpə'zɪʃn] *n* superposition *f.*

superpower ['su:pəˌpaʊə^r] *n* superpuissance *f*, supergrand *m.*

supersaturated [ˌsu:pə'sætʃəreɪtɪd] *adj* sursaturé.

superscript ['su:pəskrɪpt] ◇ *n* exposant *m.*
◇ *adj* en exposant.

supersede [ˌsu:pə'si:d] *vt* succéder à, remplacer; she ~d him as director elle lui a succédé OR elle l'a remplacé à la direction; this price list ~s all previous ones ce tarif remplace et annule les précédents; ~d methods méthodes périmées.

supersonic [ˌsu:pə'sɒnɪk] *adj* supersonique; ~ bang OR boom bang *m* (supersonique).

superstar ['su:pəstɑ:^r] *n* superstar *f.*

superstition [ˌsu:pə'stɪʃn] *n* superstition *f.*

superstitious [ˌsu:pə'stɪʃəs] *adj* superstitieux; they are ~ about death ils sont superstitieux au sujet de la mort.

superstitiously [ˌsu:pə'stɪʃəslɪ] *adv* superstitieusement.

superstore ['su:pəstɔ:^r] *n* hypermarché *m.*

superstratum [ˌsu:pə'strɑ:təm] (*pl* superstratums OR superstrata [-tə]) *n* -**1.** GEOL couche *f* supérieure. -**2.** LING superstrat *m.*

superstructure ['su:pəˌstrʌktʃə^r] *n* superstructure *f.*

supertanker ['su:pəˌtæŋkə^r] *n* supertanker *m*, superpétrolier *m.*

supertax ['su:pətæks] *n* ≃ impôt *m* sur les grandes fortunes.

supertonic [ˌsu:pə'tɒnɪk] *n* sus-tonique *f.*

supervene [ˌsu:pə'vi:n] *vi* survenir.

supervise ['su:pəvaɪz] ◇ *vt* -**1.** [oversee - activity, exam] surveiller; [- child, staff] surveiller, avoir l'œil sur. -**2.** [run - office, workshop] diriger.
◇ *vi* surveiller.

supervision [ˌsu:pə'vɪʒn] *n* -**1.** [of person, activity] surveillance *f*, contrôle *m*; the children must be under the ~ of qualified staff at all times les enfants doivent être sous la surveillance de personnel qualifié à tout moment; translated under the ~ of the author traduit sous la direction de l'auteur; her work needs ~ elle a besoin d'être surveillée dans son travail. -**2.** [of office] direction *f.*

supervision order *n* JUR ordonnance *f* de surveillance.

supervisor ['su:pəvaɪzə^r] *n* [gen] surveillant *m*, -e *f*; COMM [of department] chef *m* de rayon; SCH & UNIV [at exam] surveillant *m*, -e *f*; UNIV [of thesis] directeur *m*, -trice *f* de thèse; [of research] directeur *m*, -trice *f* de recherches.

supervisory ['su:pəvaɪzərɪ] *adj* de surveillance; staff in ~ posts le personnel de surveillance; in a ~ role OR capacity à titre de surveillant.

superwoman ['su:pəˌwʊmən] (*pl* superwomen [-ˌwɪmɪn]) *n* superwoman *f.*
◆ **Superwoman** *pr n* [comic book heroine] Superwoman.

supine ['su:paɪn] *adj* -**1.** *lit* [on one's back] couché OR étendu sur le dos; she was lying ~, she was in a ~ position elle était couchée sur le dos. -**2.** *fig* [passive] indolent, mou, passif.

supper ['sʌpə^r] *n* [evening meal] dîner *m*; [late-night meal] souper *m*; to have OR to eat ~ dîner, souper; we had steak for ~ nous avons mangé du steak au dîner OR au souper ❑ to sing for one's ~: I'll raise his salary but I intend to make him sing for his ~! je vais lui accorder une augmentation, mais c'est donnant donnant!

supper club *n Am boîte de nuit qui fait aussi restaurant.*

suppertime ['sʌpətaɪm] *n* [in evening] heure *f* du OR de dîner; [later at night] heure *f* du OR de souper; at ~ à l'heure du dîner OR du souper.

supplant [sə'plɑ:nt] *vt* [person] supplanter, évincer; [thing] supplanter, remplacer.

supple ['sʌpl] *adj* souple; to become ~ s'assouplir.

supplement [*n* 'sʌplɪmənt, *vb* 'sʌplɪment] ◇ *n* -**1.** [additional amount] supplément *m*; a small ~ to my income un petit supplément à mes revenus; a ~ is charged for occupying a single room il y a un supplément à payer pour les chambres à un lit -**2.** PRESS supplément *m*; they have produced a ~ to the encyclopedia ils ont sorti un supplément à l'encyclopédie -**3.** *Br* ADMIN [allowance] allocation *f.*
◇ *vt* augmenter, compléter; I work nights to ~ my income j'augmente mes revenus en travaillant la nuit; he ~s his diet with vitamins il complète son régime en prenant des vitamines.

supplementary [ˌsʌplɪ'mentərɪ] *adj* -**1.** [gen] supplémentaire, additionnel; ~ to en plus de; may I ask a ~ question? puis-je poser encore une question? ❑ ~ income revenus *mpl* annexes. -**2.** GEOM [angle] supplémentaire.

supplementary benefit *n ancien nom pour «income support».*

suppleness ['sʌplnɪs] *n* souplesse *f.*

suppletion [sə'pli:ʃn] *n* LING suppléance *f.*

suppletive [sə'pli:tɪv] *adj* LING supplétif.

suppliant ['sʌplɪənt] ◇ *adj* suppliant.
◇ *n* = **supplicant**.

supplicant ['sʌplɪkənt] *n* suppliant *m*, -e *f.*

supplicate ['sʌplɪkeɪt] *lit* OR *fml* ◇ *vt* supplier, implorer; he ~d the court to intervene il a prié la cour d'intervenir.
◇ *vi*: to ~ for forgiveness/mercy implorer le pardon/la pitié.

supplication [ˌsʌplɪ'keɪʃn] *n* supplication *f*; he knelt in ~ il supplia à genoux.

supplier [sə'plaɪə^r] *n* COMM fournisseur *m*, -euse *f.*

supply[1] [sə'plaɪ] (*pt* & *pp* supplied, *pl* supplies) ◇ *vt* -**1.** [provide - goods, services] fournir; to ~ sthg to sb fournir qqch à qqn; to ~ electricity/water to a town alimenter une ville en électricité/eau; cows ~ milk les vachent donnent du lait. -**2.** [provide sthg to - person, institution, city] fournir, approvisionner; MIL ravitailler, approvisionner; to ~ sb with sthg fournir qqch à qqn, approvisionner qqn en qqch; they ~ all the local retailers ils fournissent OR approvisionnent tous les détaillants du coin; the farm keeps us supplied with eggs and milk grâce à la ferme nous avons toujours des œufs et du lait; I supplied him with the details/the information je lui ai fourni les détails/les informations. -**3.** [equip] munir; all toys are supplied with batteries des piles sont fournies avec tous les jouets. -**4.** [make good - deficiency] suppléer à; [- omission] réparer, compenser; [satisfy - need] répondre à.
◇ *n* -**1.** [stock] provision *f*, réserve *f*; the nation's ~ of oil les réserves nationales de pétrole; we're getting in OR laying in a ~ of coal nous faisons des provisions de charbon, nous nous approvisionnons en charbon; to get in a fresh ~ of sthg renouveler sa provision de OR se réapprovisionner en qqch; water is in short ~ in the South on manque d'eau dans le Sud. -**2.** [provision - of goods, equipment] fourniture *f*; [- of fuel] alimentation *f*; MIL ravitaillement *m*, approvisionnement *m*; the domestic hot water ~ l'alimentation domestique en eau chaude; they won a contract for the ~ of 10,000 computers to schools ils ont obtenu un contrat pour la fourniture de 10 000 ordinateurs à des établissements scolaires. -**3.** ECON offre *f*; the law of ~ and demand la loi de l'offre et de la demande. -**4.** *Br* [clergyman,

secretary, teacher] remplaçant *m*, -e *f*, suppléant *m*, -e *f*; to be on ~ faire des remplacements OR des suppléances. -**5.** *(usu pl)* POL [money] crédits *mpl*.

◇ *comp* -**1.** [convoy, train, truck, route] de ravitaillement; ~ ship ravitailleur *m*. -**2.** [secretary] intérimaire; [clergyman] suppléant.

◆ **supplies** *npl* [gen] provisions *fpl*; [of food] vivres *mpl*; MIL subsistances *fpl*, approvisionnements *mpl*; **our supplies are running low** nos provisions seront bientôt épuisées, nous commençons à manquer de provisions; **office supplies** fournitures *fpl* de bureau.

supply[2] ['sʌplɪ] *adv* souplement, avec souplesse.

supply-side economics [sə'plaɪ-] *n* économie *f* de l'offre.

supply teacher [sə'plaɪ-] *n Br* remplaçant *m*, -e *f*.

support [sə'pɔːt] ◇ *vt* -**1.** [back - action, campaign, person] soutenir, appuyer; [- cause, idea] être pour, soutenir; **she ~s the Labour Party** elle est pour OR elle soutient le parti travailliste; **to ~ a candidate** appuyer OR soutenir un candidat; **I can't ~ their action** je ne peux pas approuver leur action; **we ~ her in her decision** nous approuvons sa décision; **the Democrats will ~ the bill** les Démocrates seront pour OR appuieront le projet de loi || SPORT être supporter de, supporter; **he ~s Tottenham** c'est un supporter de Tottenham. -**2.** [assist] soutenir, aider; **he made it with only her love to ~ him** il a réussi avec son amour comme seul soutien || CIN & THEAT: **~ed by a superb cast** avec une distribution superbe. -**3.** [hold up] supporter, soutenir; **the pillars that ~ the ceiling** les piliers qui soutiennent le plafond; **her legs were too weak to ~ her** ses jambes étaient trop faibles pour la porter; **will you ~ the shelf while I fix it to the wall?** tu peux tenir l'étagère le temps OR pendant que je la fixe au mur?; **she held on to the table to ~ herself** elle s'agrippa à la table pour ne pas tomber. -**4.** [provide for financially] subvenir aux besoins de; **she has three children to ~** elle a trois enfants à charge; **she earns enough to ~ herself** elle gagne assez pour subvenir à ses propres besoins; **he ~s himself by teaching** il gagne sa vie en enseignant; **the theatre is ~ed by contributions** le théâtre est financé par des contributions. -**5.** [sustain] faire vivre; **the land has ~ed four generations of tribespeople** cette terre a fait vivre la tribu pendant quatre générations. -**6.** [substantiate, give weight to] appuyer, confirmer, donner du poids à; **there is no evidence to ~ his claim** il n'y a aucune preuve pour confirmer ses dires; **a theory ~ed by experience** une théorie confirmée par l'expérience. -**7.** [endure] supporter, tolérer. -**8.** FIN [price, currency] maintenir.

◇ *n* -**1.** [backing] soutien *m*, appui *m*; **~ for the Socialist Party is declining** le nombre de ceux qui soutiennent le parti socialiste est en baisse; **he's trying to drum up** OR **to mobilize ~ for his scheme** il essaie d'obtenir du soutien pour son projet; **to give** OR **to lend one's ~ to sthg** accorder OR prêter son appui à qqch; **she gave us her full ~** elle nous a pleinement appuyés; **to speak in ~ of a motion** appuyer une motion; **they are striking in ~ of the miners** ils font grève par solidarité avec les mineurs; **a collection in ~ of the homeless** une quête au profit des sans-abri. -**2.** [assistance, encouragement] appui *m*, aide *f*; **I couldn't have managed without the ~ of the neighbours** je n'aurais pas pu y arriver sans l'appui des voisins; **a mutual ~ scheme** un système d'entraide; **she gave me the emotional ~ I needed** elle m'a apporté le soutien affectif dont j'avais besoin. -**3.** [person who offers assistance, encouragement] soutien *m*; **she's been a great ~ to me** elle m'a été d'un grand soutien. -**4.** [holding up] soutien *m*; **the upper floors need extra ~** les étages supérieurs ont besoin d'un soutien supplémentaire; **I was holding his arm for ~** je m'appuyais sur son bras; **this bra gives good ~** ce soutien-gorge maintient bien la poitrine. -**5.** [supporting structure, prop] appui *m*; CONSTR & TECH soutien *m*, support *m*; **the steel ~s had buckled** les supports en acier s'étaient déformés. -**6.** [funding] soutien *m*; **they depend on the government for financial ~** ils sont subventionnés par le gouvernement; **he has no visible means of ~** ses sources de revenus sont inconnues; **what are your means of ~?** quelles sont vos sources de revenus?; **she is their only means of ~** ils n'ont qu'elle pour les faire vivre. -**7.** [substantiation, corroboration] corroboration *f*; **in ~ of her theory** à l'appui de OR pour corroborer sa théorie; **the investigation found no ~ for this view** l'enquête n'a rien trouvé pour corroborer ce point de vue. -**8.** *Am* ECON [subsidy] subvention *f*; **farm ~s** subventions agricoles.

◇ *comp* -**1.** [troops, unit] de soutien. -**2.** [hose, stockings] de maintien; [bandage] de soutien. -**3.** CONSTR & TECH [structure, device, frame] de soutien.

supportable [sə'pɔːtəbl] *adj fml* supportable.

supporter [sə'pɔːtə^r] *n* -**1.** CONSTR & TECH [device] soutien *m*, support *m*. -**2.** [advocate, follower - of cause, opinion] adepte *mf*, partisan *m*; [- of political party] partisan *m*; SPORT supporter *m*, supporteur *m*, -trice *f*; **he's a Liverpool ~** c'est un supporter de Liverpool. -**3.** HERALD tenant *m*.

supporting [sə'pɔːtɪŋ] *adj* -**1.** CONSTR & TECH [pillar, structure] d'appui, de soutènement; [wall] porteur, de soutènement; **~ beam** sommier *m* CONSTR. -**2.** CIN & THEAT [role] secondaire, de second plan; [actor] qui a un rôle secondaire OR de second plan; **with a ~ cast of thousands** avec des milliers de figurants; **~ film** OR **programme** *film qui passe en première partie de la séance*. -**3.** [substantiating] qui confirme, qui soutient; **do you have any ~ evidence?** avez-vous des preuves à l'appui?

supportive [sə'pɔːtɪv] *adj* [person] qui est d'un grand soutien; [attitude] de soutien; **my parents have always been very ~** mes parents m'ont toujours été d'un grand soutien; **they need ~ counselling** ils ont besoin d'être soutenus et orientés; **~ therapy** MED thérapie *f* de soutien.

support price *n* prix *m* de soutien.

suppose [sə'pəʊz] ◇ *vt* -**1.** [assume] supposer; **I ~ it's too far to go and see them now** je suppose que c'est trop loin pour qu'on aille les voir maintenant; **if we ~ it is worth £5** si nous supposons que cela vaut cinq livres; **~ x equals y** MATH soit x égal à y; **I ~ you think that's funny!** je suppose que vous trouvez ça drôle! -**2.** [think, believe] penser, croire; **do you ~ he'll do it?** pensez-vous OR croyez-vous qu'il le fera?; **I ~ so** je suppose que oui; **I ~ not, I don't ~ so** je ne (le) pense pas; **I don't ~ he'll agree** ça m'étonnerait qu'il soit d'accord, je ne pense pas qu'il sera d'accord; **I ~ it must be three years since I last saw her** je pense que ça doit faire trois ans que je ne l'ai pas vue; **you don't ~ anything's happened to them, do you?** tu ne penses pas qu'il leur est arrivé quelque chose?; **and who do you ~ I met in the shop?** et devine qui j'ai rencontré dans le magasin! -**3.** [presuppose, imply] supposer; **that theory ~s a balanced budget** cette théorie suppose un budget équilibré.

◇ *vi* supposer, imaginer; **he's gone, I ~?** il est parti, je suppose OR j'imagine?; **there were, I ~, about 50 people there** il y avait, je dirais, une cinquantaine de personnes.

◇ *conj* si; **~ they see you?** et s'ils vous voyaient?; **~ we wait and see** et si on attendait pour voir?; **~ I'm right and she does come?** mettons OR supposons que j'aie raison et qu'elle vienne?

supposed [sə'pəʊzd] *adj* -**1.** [presumed] présumé, supposé; [alleged] prétendu; **the ~ author of this poem** l'auteur présumé de ce poème; **all these ~ experts** *pej* tous ces prétendus experts. -**2.** *phr*: **to be ~ to**: **to be ~ to do sthg** être censé faire qqch; **she was ~ to be at work** elle était censée être à son travail; **what's that switch ~ to do?** à quoi sert cet interrupteur?; **how am I ~ to know?** comment est-ce que je saurais OR suis censé savoir, moi?; **I'm not ~ to know** je ne suis pas censé savoir; **you're not ~ to do that!** tu ne devrais pas faire ça!; **what's that ~ to mean?** qu'est-ce que tu veux dire par là?; **we're not ~ to use dictionaries** nous n'avons pas le droit de nous servir de dictionnaires; **this restaurant is ~ to be very good** il paraît que ce restaurant est excellent.

supposedly [sə'pəʊzɪdlɪ] *adv* soi-disant (*adv*); **she ~ went to get help** elle est soi-disant allée chercher de l'aide; **he's ~ too sick to walk** il est soi-disant trop malade pour marcher.

supposing [sə'pəʊzɪŋ] *conj* si, à supposer que; **~ he still wants to go** et s'il veut encore y aller?; **even ~ she does come** même si elle vient OR venait; **~ you are right** admettons OR mettons que vous ayez raison; **always ~ I can do it** en supposant OR en admettant que je puisse le faire.

supposition [,sʌpə'zɪʃn] *n* supposition *f*, hypothèse *f*; **his theory was pure ~** sa théorie n'était qu'une hypothèse; **on the ~ that your mother agrees** dans l'hypothèse où votre mère serait d'accord, à supposer que votre mère soit d'accord.

suppositional [,sʌpə'zɪʃənl] *adj* hypothétique.

suppositious [,sʌpə'zɪʃəs], **supposititious** [sə,pɒzɪ'tɪʃəs] *adj fml* -**1.** [hypothetical] hypothétique. -**2.** [fraudulent] faux.

suppository [sə'pɒzɪtrɪ] (*pl* **suppositories**) *n* suppositoire *m*.

suppress [sə'pres] *vt* -**1.** [put an end to] supprimer, mettre fin à; **the new régime ~ed all forms of dissent** le nouveau régime a mis fin OR un terme à toute forme de dissidence. -**2.** [withhold] supprimer, faire disparaître; **to ~ evidence** faire disparaître des preuves || [conceal] supprimer, cacher; **to ~ the truth/a scandal** étouffer la vérité/un scandale. -**3.** [withdraw from publication] supprimer, interdire; **all opposition newspapers have been ~ed** tous les journaux d'opposition ont été interdits OR supprimés; **the government has ~ed the report** le gouvernement a interdit la parution du rapport. -**4.** [delete] supprimer, retrancher; **the judge ordered that the controversial passages should be ~ed** le juge ordonna la suppression des passages controversés. -**5.** [inhibit - growth, weeds] supprimer, empêcher. -**6.** [hold back, repress - anger, yawn, smile] réprimer; [- tears] retenir, refouler; [- feelings, desires] étouffer, refouler; **to ~ a cough** réprimer OR retenir son envie de tousser; **to ~ a sneeze** se retenir pour ne pas éternuer; **to ~ a yawn** étouffer OR réprimer un bâillement; **she ~ed a smile** elle réprima un sourire. -**7.** PSYCH refouler. -**8.** ELECTRON & RADIO antiparasiter.

suppression [sə'preʃn] *n* -**1.** [ending - of rebellion, demonstration] suppression *f*, répression *f*; [- of rights] suppression *f*, abolition *f*; [- of a law, decree] abrogation *f*. -**2.** [concealment - of evidence, information] suppression *f*, dissimulation *f*; [- of scandal] étouffement *m*. -**3.** [non-publication - of document, report] suppression *f*, interdiction *f*; [- of part of text] suppression *f*. -**4.** [holding back - of feelings, thoughts] refoulement *m*. -**5.** PSYCH refoulement *m*. -**6.** ELECTRON & RADIO antiparasitage *m*.

suppressive [sə'presɪv] *adj* répressif.

suppressor grid [sə'presə^r-] *n* grille *f* d'arrêt.

suppurate ['sʌpjʊreɪt] *vi* suppurer; **a suppurating wound** une plaie suppurante.

suppuration [,sʌpjʊ'reɪʃn] *n* suppuration *f*.

supra ['suːprə] *adv* supra.

supranational [,suːprə'næʃənl] *adj* supranational.

suprasegmental [,suːprəseg'mentl] *adj* suprasegmental.

supremacist [sʊ'preməsɪst] *n personne qui croit en la suprématie d'un groupe*; **they are white ~s** ils croient en la suprématie de la race blanche.

supremacy [sʊ'preməsɪ] *n* **-1.** [dominance] suprématie *f*, domination *f*; **each nation tried to gain ~ over the other** chaque nation essayait d'avoir la suprématie sur l'autre. **-2.** [superiority] suprématie *f*; **they believe in the ~ of their methods over all others** ils croient leurs méthodes supérieures à OR meilleures que toutes les autres.

supreme [sʊ'priːm] *adj* **-1.** [highest in rank, authority] suprême; **the Supreme Commander of Allied Forces** le commandant suprême OR le commandant en chef des Forces alliées; **the Supreme Court of Judicature** HIST la Cour souveraine de justice. **-2.** [great, outstanding] extrême; **a ~ effort** un effort suprême; **she handles politicians with ~ skill** elle sait parfaitement s'y prendre avec les hommes politiques; **it would be an act of ~ folly to do that now** ce serait de la folie pure de faire ça maintenant; **to make the ~ sacrifice** sacrifier sa vie, faire le sacrifice de sa vie.

Supreme Court *pr n*: **the ~** la Cour suprême *(des États-Unis)*.

SUPREME COURT:
La Cour suprême est l'organe supérieur du pouvoir judiciaire américain, et est composée de membres nommés par le président des États-Unis; elle détient le pouvoir de décision final ainsi que le droit d'interpréter la Constitution.

supremely [sʊ'priːmlɪ] *adv* suprêmement, extrêmement.

Supreme Soviet *pr n* Soviet *m* suprême.

supremo *inf* [sʊ'priːməʊ] (*pl* supremos) *n Br* (grand) chef *m*.

Supt. *written abbr of* superintendent.

sura ['sʊərə] *n* surate *f*.

surcharge ['sɜːtʃɑːdʒ] ◇ *n* **-1.** [extra duty, tax] surtaxe *f*; **a 7% import ~** une surtaxe de 7 % sur les importations. **-2.** [extra cost] supplément *m*; **there is a ~ for the express train** il faut payer un supplément pour le train rapide; **some travel companies guarantee no ~** certains voyagistes s'engagent à ne faire payer aucun supplément. **-3.** [overprinting - on postage stamp] surcharge *f*.
◇ *vt* **-1.** [charge extra duty or tax on] surtaxer. **-2.** [charge a supplement to] faire payer un supplément à. **-3.** [overprint - postage stamp] surcharger.

surd [sɜːd] ◇ *n* **-1.** LING sourde *f*. **-2.** MATH équation *f* irrationnelle.
◇ *adj* **-1.** LING sourd. **-2.** MATH irrationnel.

sure [ʃɔːʳ] ◇ *adj* **-1.** [convinced, positive] sûr, certain; **are you ~ of the facts?** êtes-vous sûr OR certain des faits?; **I'm not ~ you're right** je ne suis pas sûr OR certain que vous ayez raison; **he's not ~ whether he's going to come or not** il n'est pas sûr de venir; **she isn't ~ of** OR **about her feelings for him** elle n'est pas sûre de ses sentiments pour lui; **you seem convinced, but I'm not so ~** tu sembles convaincu, mais moi j'ai des doutes; **he'll win, I'm ~** il gagnera, j'en suis sûr; **I'm ~ I've been here before** je suis sûr d'être déjà venu ici; **she's ~ she didn't receive your letter** elle est sûre de ne pas avoir reçu ta lettre; **what makes you so ~?, how can you be so ~?** qu'est-ce qui te fait dire ça? **-2.** [confident, assured] sûr; **is he someone we can be ~ of?** est-ce quelqu'un de sûr?; **you can be ~ of good service in this restaurant** dans ce restaurant, vous êtes sûr d'être bien servi; **to be ~ of o.s.** être sûr de soi, avoir confiance en soi. **-3.** [certain - to happen] sûr, certain; **one thing is ~, he won't be back in a hurry!** une chose est sûre OR certaine, il ne va pas revenir de sitôt!; **we're ~ to meet again** nous nous reverrons sûrement; **she's ~ to be here soon** elle va sûrement arriver bientôt; **they're ~ to get caught** ils vont sûrement se faire prendre; **the play is ~ to be a success** la pièce va certainement avoir du succès; **it's a ~ bet he'll be late** il y a tout à parier qu'il sera en retard; **~ thing!** *inf* bien sûr (que oui)!, pour sûr!; **be ~ to: be ~ to be on time tomorrow** il faut que vous soyez à l'heure demain; **be ~ to go to bed early** il faut que tu te couches tôt; **to make ~ (that): we made ~ that no one was listening** nous nous sommes assurés OR nous avons vérifié que personne n'écoutait; **it is his job to make ~ that everyone is satisfied** c'est lui qui veille à ce que tout le monde soit satisfait; **make ~ you don't lose your ticket** prends garde à ne pas perdre ton billet; **make ~ you've turned off the gas** vérifie que tu as éteint le gaz. **-4.** [firm, steady] sûr; **with a ~ hand** d'une main sûre; **a ~ grasp of the subject** *fig* des connaissances solides en la matière. **-5.** [reliable, irrefutable] sûr; **work is a ~ remedy for boredom** le travail est un remède sûr contre l'ennui; **insomnia is a ~ sign of depression** l'insomnie est un signe incontestable de dépression.
◇ *adv* **-1.** *inf* [of course] bien sûr, pour sûr; **can I borrow your car? — ~ (you can)!** (est-ce que) je peux emprunter ta voiture? — bien sûr (que oui)! **-2.** *inf Am* [really] drôlement, rudement; **he ~ is ugly** il est drôlement laid; **she ~ can cook!** elle cuisine drôlement bien!; **are you hungry? — I ~ am!** as-tu faim? — plutôt! OR et comment! **-3.** [as intensifier]: **(as) ~ as** aussi sûr que; **as ~ as my name is Jones** aussi sûr que je m'appelle Jones; **as ~ as I'm standing here (today)** aussi sûr que deux et deux font quatre; **I ~ as hell do object!** *inf* et comment que je proteste!
◆ **for sure** *adv phr*: **I'll give it to you tomorrow for ~** je te le donnerai demain sans faute; **one thing is for ~, I'm not staying here!** une chose est sûre, je ne reste pas ici!; **I think he's single but I can't say for ~** je crois qu'il est célibataire, mais je ne peux pas l'affirmer.
◆ **sure enough** *adv phr* effectivement, en effet; **she said she'd ring and ~ enough she did** elle a dit qu'elle appellerait, et c'est ce qu'elle a fait.
◆ **to be sure** *adv phr*: **to be ~, his offer is well-intentioned** on ne peut pas nier que son offre soit bien intentionnée.

surefire *inf* ['ʃɔːfaɪəʳ] *adj* infaillible, sûr; **there's no ~ cure** il n'y a pas de remède infaillible.

surefooted ['ʃɔː,fʊtɪd] *adj* au pied sûr.

surely ['ʃɔːlɪ] *adv* **-1.** [used to express surprise, incredulity, to contradict] quand même, tout de même; **they ~ can't have forgotten** ils n'ont pas pu oublier, quand même; **you're ~ not suggesting it was my fault?** vous ne suggérez pas que c'était de ma faute, j'espère OR quand même?; **~ you must be joking!** vous plaisantez, j'espère?; **~ he didn't say that** il n'a pas pu dire ça; **the real figures are a lot higher, ~?** mais les chiffres sont en fait beaucoup plus élevés, non?; **~ to goodness** OR **to God they must know by now** *Br* ce n'est pas possible qu'ils ne soient pas au courant à l'heure qu'il est. **-2.** [undoubtedly, assuredly] sûrement, sans (aucun) doute; **they will ~ succeed** ils réussiront sûrement. **-3.** [steadily] sûrement; **things are improving slowly but ~** les choses s'améliorent lentement mais sûrement. **-4.** *Am* [of course] bien sûr, certainement; **would you give me a hand? — ~!** peux-tu me donner un coup de main? — bien sûr OR certainement!

sureness ['ʃɔːnɪs] *n* **-1.** [certainty] certitude *f*. **-2.** [assurance] assurance *f*. **-3.** [steadiness] sûreté *f*; [accuracy] justesse *f*, précision *f*; **he handled the problem with great ~ of touch** il a réglé le problème avec beaucoup de doigté.

surety ['ʃɔːrətɪ] (*pl* sureties) *n* **-1.** [guarantor] garant *m*, -e *f*, caution *f*; **to act as** OR **to stand ~ (for sb)** se porter garant (de qqn). **-2.** [collateral] caution *f*, sûreté *f*.

surf [sɜːf] ◇ *n (U)* **-1.** [waves] vagues *fpl* (déferlantes), ressac *m*; **the ~ crashed against the rocks** les vagues venaient s'écraser contre les rochers; **to ride the ~** faire du surf. **-2.** [foam] écume *f*.
◇ *vi* surfer, faire du surf; **he goes ~ing every weekend** il fait du surf tous les week-ends.

surface ['sɜːfɪs] ◇ *n* **-1.** [exterior, top] surface *f*; **the polished ~ of the desk** la surface polie du bureau; **bubbles rose to the ~ of the pond** des bulles montèrent à la surface de la mare; **the submarine/diver came to the ~** le sous-marin/plongeur fit surface; **the miners who work on the ~** les mineurs qui travaillent à la surface; **all the old tensions came** OR **rose to the ~ when they met** *fig* toutes les vieilles discordes ont refait surface quand ils se sont revus. **-2.** [flat area] surface *f*; **roll the dough out on a smooth clean ~** étalez la pâte sur une surface lisse et propre. **-3.** [covering layer] revêtement *m*; **the pan has a non-stick ~** la poêle a une surface anti-adhésive OR qui n'attache pas; **road ~** chaussée *f*. **-4.** [outward appearance] surface *f*, extérieur *m*, dehors *m*; **on the ~ she seems nice enough** au premier abord elle paraît assez sympathique; **there was a feeling of anxiety lying beneath** OR **below the ~** on sentait une angoisse sous-jacente; **the discussion hardly scratched the ~ of the problem** le problème a à peine été abordé dans la discussion. **-5.** GEOM [area] surface *f*, superficie *f*.
◇ *vi* **-1.** [submarine, diver, whale] faire surface, monter à la surface; **to ~ again** refaire surface, remonter à la surface. **-2.** [become manifest] apparaître, se manifester; **he ~d again after many years of obscurity** il a réapparu après être resté dans l'ombre pendant de nombreuses années; **rumours like this tend to ~ every so often** ce type de rumeur a tendance à refaire surface de temps à autre. **-3.** *inf* [get up] se lever, émerger; **he didn't ~ till 11 o'clock** il n'a pas émergé avant 11 h.
◇ *vt* [put a surface on - road] revêtir; [- paper] calandrer; **the track is ~d with cement** la piste est revêtue de ciment.
◇ *adj* **-1.** [superficial] superficiel; **a ~ scratch** une égratignure superficielle, une légère égratignure; **his enthusiasm is purely ~** *fig* son enthousiasme n'est que superficiel. **-2.** [exterior] de surface; **~ finish** [of metal] état *m* de surface, finissage *m*; **~ measurements** superficie *f*. **-3.** MIN [workers] de surface, au jour; [work] à la surface, au jour; MIL [forces] au sol; [fleet] de surface.

surface area *n* surface *f*, superficie *f*.

surface mail *n* courrier *m* par voie de terre; **to send sthg by ~** envoyer qqch par voie de terre.

surface noise *n* grésillement *m*.

surface structure *n* structure *f* superficielle OR de surface.

surface tension *n* tension *f* superficielle.

surface-to-air *adj* sol-air *(inv)*.

surface-to-surface *adj* sol-sol *(inv)*.

surfboard ['sɜːfbɔːd] *n* (planche *f* de) surf *m*.

surfboarder ['sɜːfbɔːdəʳ] *n* surfeur *m*, -euse *f*.

surfboarding ['sɜːfbɔːdɪŋ] *n* surf *m*.

surfcasting ['sɜːfkɑːstɪŋ] *n* pêche *f* à la ligne dans le ressac.

surfeit ['sɜːfɪt] ◇ *n fml* [excess] excès *m*, surabondance *f*; **we had a ~ of pasta while on holiday in Rome** nous nous sommes gavés de pâtes pendant nos vacances à Rome; **there is a ~ of imported goods** il y a trop d'importations.
◇ *vt* rassasier.

surfer ['sɜːfəʳ] *n* surfeur *m*, -euse *f*.

surfing ['sɜːfɪŋ] *n* surf *m*; **~ is forbidden on this beach** le surf est interdit sur cette plage.

surfride ['sɜːfraɪd] *vi* surfer, faire du surf.

surfrider ['sɜːf,raɪdəʳ] *n* surfeur *m*, -euse *f*.

surfriding ['sɜːf,raɪdɪŋ] *n* surf *m*.

surge [sɜːdʒ] ◇ *n* **-1.** [increase - of activity] augmentation *f*, poussée *f*; [- of emotion] vague *f*, accès *m*; ELEC [- of voltage, current] pointe *f*; **a big ~ in demand** une forte augmentation de la demande; **a ~ of pain/pity** un accès de douleur/de pitié; **he felt a ~ of pride at the sight of his son** la fierté l'envahit en regardant son fils; **I felt a ~ of hatred** j'ai senti la haine monter en moi. **-2.** [rush, stampede] ruée *f*; **there was a sudden ~ for the exit** tout à coup les gens se sont rués vers la sortie; **a ~ of spectators carried him forward** il fut emporté par le flot des spectateurs; **the demonstrators made a ~ forward and broke through the police cordon** les manifestants se ruèrent en avant et le cordon de police céda. -**3.** NAUT houle *f*.

◇ *vi* -**1.** [well up - emotion] monter; **I felt anger/hope/despair ~ in me** j'ai senti la colère/l'espoir/le désespoir monter en moi. -**2.** [rush - crowd] se ruer, déferler; [- water] couler à flots OR à torrents; [- waves] déferler; **the demonstrators ~d forward** les manifestants se ruèrent en avant; **the gates of the stadium opened and the fans ~d in/out** les portes du stade s'ouvrirent et des flots de spectateurs s'y engouffrèrent/en sortirent; **the truck ~d forward** le camion a bondi en avant; **water ~d through the breach in the dam** des torrents OR trombes d'eau jaillirent de la brèche dans le barrage; **blood ~d to her cheeks** le sang lui est monté au visage. -**3.** ELEC subir une brusque pointe de tension.

◆ **surge up** *vi insep* = **surge** *vi* **1**.

surgeon ['sɜːdʒən] *n* chirurgien *m*, -enne *f*; **she hopes to become a ~** elle espère devenir chirurgien OR chirurgienne; **a woman ~** une chirurgienne, une femme chirurgien.

surgeon general (*pl* **surgeons general**) *n* -**1.** MIL médecin-général *m*. -**2.** *Am* ADMIN chef *m* des services de santé.

surgery ['sɜːdʒərɪ] (*pl* **surgeries**) *n* -**1.** [field of medicine] chirurgie *f*; **to study ~** étudier la chirurgie. -**2.** *(U)* [surgical treatment] intervention *f* chirurgicale, interventions *fpl* chirurgicales; **minor/major ~ might be necessary** une intervention chirurgicale mineure/importante pourrait s'avérer nécessaire; **to perform ~ on sb** opérer qqn; **to have brain/heart ~** se faire opérer du cerveau/du cœur; **the patient is undergoing ~** le malade est au bloc opératoire. -**3.** *Br* [consulting room] cabinet *m* médical OR de consultation; [building] centre *m* médical; [consultation] consultation *f*; **Doctor Jones doesn't take ~ on Fridays** le docteur Jones ne consulte pas le vendredi; **can I come to the ~ tomorrow?** puis-je venir au cabinet OR à la consultation demain?; **~ hours** heures *fpl* de consultation. -**4.** *Br* POL permanence *f*; **our MP holds a ~ on Saturdays** notre député tient une permanence le samedi.

surgical ['sɜːdʒɪkl] *adj* -**1.** [operation, treatment] chirurgical; [manual, treatise] de chirurgie; [instrument, mask] chirurgical, de chirurgien; [methods, shock] opératoire. -**2.** [appliance, boot, stocking] orthopédique. -**3.** MIL: **~ strike** offensive *f* «chirurgicale».

surgical cotton *n* coton *m* hydrophile.

surgical dressing *n* pansement *m*.

surgically ['sɜːdʒɪklɪ] *adv* par intervention chirurgicale; **the tumour was removed ~** la tumeur fut enlevée par intervention chirurgicale.

surgical spirit *n Br* alcool *m* à 90 (degrés).

surging ['sɜːdʒɪŋ] *adj* [crowd, waves] déferlant; [water] qui coule à flots OR à torrents.

Surinam [ˌsʊərɪ'næm] *pr n* Surinam *m*, Suriname *m*; **in ~** au Surinam.

Surinamese [ˌsʊərɪnæ'miːz] ◇ *n* Surinamien *m*, -enne *f*; **the ~** les Surinamiens.

◇ *adj* surinamien.

surliness ['sɜːlɪnɪs] *n* [character] caractère *m* hargneux OR grincheux; [mood] humeur *f* hargneuse OR grincheuse.

surly ['sɜːlɪ] (*compar* **surlier**, *superl* **surliest**) *adj* [ill-tempered] hargneux, grincheux; [gloomy] maussade, renfrogné.

surmise [sɜː'maɪz] ◇ *vt* conjecturer, présumer; **I can only ~ what the circumstances were** je ne puis que conjecturer quelles étaient les circonstances; **I ~d that he was lying** je me suis douté qu'il mentait.

◇ *n fml* conjecture *f*, supposition *f*; **your conclusion is pure ~** votre conclusion est entièrement hypothétique.

surmount [sɜː'maʊnt] *vt* -**1.** [triumph over] surmonter, vaincre. -**2.** *fml* [cap, top] surmonter; **the building is ~ed by a large dome** le bâtiment est surmonté d'un grand dôme.

surmountable [sɜː'maʊntəbl] *adj* surmontable.

surname ['sɜːneɪm] *n Br* nom *m* (de famille); **~ and Christian name** nom et prénom.

surpass [sə'pɑːs] *vt* -**1.** [outdo, outshine] surpasser; **you have ~ed yourselves** vous vous êtes surpassés. -**2.** [go beyond] surpasser, dépasser; **that kind of behaviour ~es my understanding** ce genre de comportement me dépasse; **the result ~ed all our expectations** le résultat dépassa toutes nos espérances.

surpassing [sə'pɑːsɪŋ] *adj lit* sans égal; **a woman of ~ beauty** une femme d'une beauté sans égale OR inégalable.

surplice ['sɜːplɪs] *n* surplis *m*.

surplus ['sɜːpləs] ◇ *n* -**1.** [overabundance] surplus *m*, excédent *m*; **a labour ~** un surplus de main-d'œuvre; **Japan's trade ~** l'excédent commercial du Japon. -**2.** *(U)* [old military clothes] surplus *mpl*; **an army ~ overcoat** un manteau des surplus de l'armée; **an army ~ store** un magasin de surplus de l'armée. -**3.** FIN [in accounting] boni *m*.

◇ *adj* -**1.** [gen] en surplus, en trop; **pour off any ~ liquid** enlevez tout excédent de liquide; **to be ~ to requirements** excéder les besoins. -**2.** COMM & ECON en surplus, excédentaire; **~ production** production *f* excédentaire; **they export their ~ agricultural produce** ils exportent leur surplus agricole; **~ stock** stocks *mpl* excédentaires, surplus *m*.

surprise [sə'praɪz] ◇ *n* -**1.** [unexpected event, experience etc] surprise *f*; **it was a ~ to me** cela a été une surprise pour moi, cela m'a surpris; **what a lovely ~!** quelle merveilleuse surprise!; **her death came as no ~** sa mort n'a surpris personne; **his resignation came as a ~ to everyone** sa démission a surpris tout le monde; **to give sb a ~** faire une surprise à qqn; **you're in for (a bit of) a ~** tu vas être surpris!, tu vas avoir une (sacrée) surprise! -**2.** [astonishment] surprise *f*, étonnement *m*; **much to my ~, she agreed** à ma grande surprise OR à mon grand étonnement, elle accepta; **her announcement caused some ~** sa déclaration a provoqué un certain étonnement; **he looked at me in ~** il me regarda d'un air surpris OR étonné. -**3.** [catching unawares] surprise *f*; **the element of ~ is on our side** nous avons l'effet de surprise pour nous; **their arrival took me by ~** leur arrivée m'a pris au dépourvu; **the soldiers took the enemy by ~** les soldats ont pris l'ennemi par surprise.

◇ *comp* [attack, present, victory] surprise; [announcement] inattendu; **the Prime Minister made a ~ visit to Ireland** le Premier ministre a fait une visite surprise en Irlande ❑ **~ party** *fête organisée pour quelqu'un sans qu'il ou elle le sache*.

◇ *vt* -**1.** [amaze] surprendre, étonner; **it ~d me that they didn't give her the job** j'ai été surpris OR étonné qu'ils ne l'aient pas embauchée; **shall we ~ her?** si on lui faisait une surprise?; **it wouldn't ~ me if they lost** ça ne m'étonnerait pas OR je ne serais pas surpris qu'ils perdent; **go on, ~ me!** *iron* vas-y, annonce! -**2.** [catch unawares] surprendre; **the burglar was ~d by the police** le cambrioleur fut surpris par la police; **we ~d the enemy at dawn** nous avons surpris l'ennemi à l'aube.

surprised [sə'praɪzd] *adj* surpris, étonné; **she was ~ to learn that she had got the job** elle a été surprise d'apprendre qu'on allait l'embaucher; **don't be ~ if she doesn't come** ne vous étonnez pas si elle ne vient pas; **I wouldn't** OR **I shoudn't be ~ if they'd forgotten** cela ne m'étonnerait pas qu'ils aient oublié; **I'm ~ by** OR **at his reaction** sa réaction me surprend OR m'étonne; **it looks easy but you'd be ~** ça semble facile mais ne vous y fiez pas; **his lack of good manners is nothing to be ~ about** son manque de savoir-vivre n'a rien d'étonnant.

surprising [sə'praɪzɪŋ] *adj* surprenant, étonnant; **it's ~ (that) she left so early** il est surprenant OR étonnant qu'elle soit partie si tôt; **it's not at all** OR **not in the least ~** cela n'a rien d'étonnant.

surprisingly [sə'praɪzɪŋlɪ] *adv* étonnamment; **for a ten-year-old, she's ~ mature** elle est vraiment très mûre pour une fille de dix ans; **~, he managed to win** chose suprenante OR étonnante, il a quand même gagné; **he apologized, ~ enough** chose surprenante OR étonnante, il s'est excusé; **not ~, the play sold out** toutes les places ont été louées, ce qui n'a rien d'étonnant.

surreal [sə'rɪəl] ◇ *adj* -**1.** [strange, dreamlike] étrange, onirique. -**2.** [surrealist] surréaliste.

◇ *n*: **the ~** le surréel.

surrealism [sə'rɪəlɪzm] *n* ART & LITERAT surréalisme *m*.

surrealist [sə'rɪəlɪst] ART & LITERAT ◇ *adj* surréaliste.

◇ *n* surréaliste *mf*.

surrealistic [səˌrɪəl'ɪstɪk] *adj* -**1.** ART & LITERAT surréaliste. -**2.** *fig* surréel, surréaliste.

surrender [sə'rendəʳ] ◇ *vi* -**1.** MIL [capitulate] se rendre, capituler; **they ~ed to the enemy** ils se rendirent à OR ils capitulèrent devant l'ennemi. -**2.** [give o.s. up] se livrer; **after 16 hours the hijackers ~ed to the police** au bout de16 heures, les pirates de l'air se sont livrés à la police; **to ~ to bail** JUR comparaître en jugement (après une libération sous caution). -**3.** *fig* [abandon o.s.] se livrer, s'abandonner; **to ~ to temptation** se livrer OR s'abandonner à la tentation.

◇ *vt* -**1.** [city, position] livrer; [relinquish - possessions, territory] céder, rendre; [- one's seat] céder, laisser; [- arms] rendre, livrer; [- claim, authority, freedom, rights] renoncer à; [- hopes] abandonner; **to ~ o.s to sthg** se livrer OR s'abandonner à qqch. -**2.** [hand in - ticket, coupon] remettre.

◇ *n* -**1.** [capitulation] reddition *f*, capitulation *f*; **the town was starved into ~** la famine a obligé la ville à capituler; **the government's ~ to the unions** la capitulation du gouvernement devant les syndicats; **he laughed at the idea of ~** l'idée de se rendre l'a fait rire. -**2.** [relinquishing - of possessions, territory] cession *f*; [- of arms] remise *f*; [- of claim, authority, freedom, rights] renonciation *f*, abdication *f*; [- of hopes] abandon *m*; **it is tantamount to a ~ of all our rights** cela équivaut à l'abdication de OR renoncer à tous nos droits.

surreptitious [ˌsʌrəp'tɪʃəs] *adj* subreptice *lit*, furtif, clandestin.

surreptitiously [ˌsʌrəp'tɪʃəslɪ] *adv* subrepticement *lit*, furtivement, à la dérobée.

surrey ['sʌrɪ] *n voiture hippomobile à deux places*.

surrogacy ['sʌrəgəsɪ] *n* maternité *f* de remplacement OR de substitution.

surrogate ['sʌrəgeɪt] ◇ *n* -**1.** *fml* [substitute - person] remplaçant *m*, -e *f*, substitut *m*; [- thing] succédané *m*. -**2.** PSYCH substitut *m*. -**3.** *Am* JUR magistrat *m* de droit civil *(juridiction locale)*. -**4.** *Br* RELIG évêque *m* auxiliaire.

◇ *adj* de substitution, de remplacement; **they served as ~ parents to her** ils ont en quelque sorte remplacé ses parents.

surrogate mother *n* PSYCH substitut *m* maternel; MED mère *f* porteuse.

surround [sə'raʊnd] ◇ *vt* -**1.** [gen] entourer; **the garden is ~ed by a brick wall** le jardin est entouré d'un mur en briques; **the president ~ed himself with advisers** le président s'est entouré de conseillers; **there is a great deal of controversy ~ing the budget cuts** il y a une vive controverse autour des réductions budgétaires. -**2.** [subj: troops, police, enemy] encercler, cerner; **~ed by enemy soldiers** encerclé OR cerné par des troupes ennemies.

◇ *n Br* [border, edging] bordure *f*.

surrounding [sə'raʊndɪŋ] *adj* environnant; **there's a lovely view of the ~ countryside** il y a une belle vue sur le paysage alentour.

◆ **surroundings** *npl* -**1.** [of town, city] alentours *mpl*, environs *mpl*. -**2.** [setting] cadre *m*, décor *m*; **it's a pleasure to be in such lovely ~s** c'est un vrai plaisir de se trouver dans un cadre aussi joli. **-3.** [environment] environnement *m*, milieu *m*; **she's indifferent to her ~s** elle est indifférente à son environnement.

surtax ['sɜːtæks] *n impôt supplémentaire qui s'applique au-delà d'une certaine tranche de revenus.*

surveillance [sɜː'veɪləns] *n* surveillance *f*; **to keep sb under constant ~** garder qqn sous surveillance continue; **the house is under police ~** la maison est surveillée par la police.

survey [*vb* sə'veɪ, *n* 'sɜːveɪ] ◇ *vt* **-1.** [contemplate] contempler; [inspect] inspecter, examiner; [review] passer en revue; **we sat ~ing the view** nous étions assis à contempler le paysage; **he stepped back to ~ the painting** il fit un pas en arrière pour contempler le tableau. **-2.** [make a study of] faire une étude de, étudier; **the report ~s the current state of manufacturing industry in Britain** le rapport étudie l'état actuel de l'industrie manufacturière en Grande-Bretagne. **-3.** [poll] sonder; **65% of women ~ed were opposed to the measure** 65 % des femmes interrogées étaient contre cette mesure. **-4.** [land] arpenter, relever, faire un relèvement de; *Br* [house] expertiser, faire une expertise de; **always have a house independently ~ed before buying** il faut toujours faire faire une expertise indépendante avant d'acheter une maison.

◇ *n* **-1.** [study, investigation] étude *f*, enquête *f*; **they carried out a ~ of retail prices** ils ont fait une enquête sur les prix au détail. **-2.** [overview] vue *f* d'ensemble; **the exhibition offers a comprehensive ~ of contemporary British art** l'exposition présente une vision d'ensemble de l'art contemporain britannique. **-3.** [poll] sondage *m*. **-4.** [of land] relèvement *m*, levé *m*; **aerial ~** levé aérien ‖ *Br* [of house] expertise *f*; **to have a ~ done** faire faire une expertise.

surveying [sə'veɪɪŋ] *n* [measuring - of land] arpentage *m*, relèvement *m*; *Br* [examination - of buildings] examen *m*.

surveyor [sə'veɪə^r] *n* **-1.** [of land] arpenteur *m*, géomètre *m*. **-2.** *Br* [of buildings] géomètre-expert *m*; **the council ~ declared the building unsafe** l'expert envoyé par la mairie déclara l'immeuble dangereux.

survival [sə'vaɪvl] ◇ *n* **-1.** [remaining alive] survie *f*; **what are their chances of ~?** quelles sont leurs chances de survie?; **the ~ of the fittest** la survie du plus apte. **-2.** [relic, remnant] survivance *f*, vestige *m*; **the custom is a ~ from the Victorian era** cette coutume remonte à l'époque victorienne.

◇ *comp* [course, kit] de survie.

survivalism [sə'vaɪvəlɪzm] *n entraînement en vue de la survie en cas de catastrophe.*

survivalist [sə'vaɪvəlɪst] *n personne qui s'entraîne à la survie en cas de catastrophe.*

survive [sə'vaɪv] ◇ *vi* **-1.** [remain alive] survivre; **nobody thought she'd ~** personne ne pensait qu'elle survivrait. **-2.** [cope, pull through]: **don't worry, I'll ~!** *inf* ne t'inquiète pas, je n'en mourrai pas!; **how can they ~ on such low wages?** comment font-ils pour vivre OR pour subsister avec des salaires si bas?; **he earned just enough to ~ on** il gagnait tout juste de quoi survivre. **-3.** [remain, be left] subsister; **only a dozen of his letters have ~d** il ne subsiste OR reste qu'une douzaine de ses lettres.

◇ *vt* **-1.** [live through] survivre à, réchapper à OR de; **few of the soldiers ~d the battle** peu de soldats ont survécu à la bataille; **we thought he'd never ~ the shock** nous pensions qu'il ne se remettrait jamais du choc. **-2.** [cope with, get through] supporter; **she ~d the death of her father better than expected** elle a surmonté la mort de son père mieux que prévu; **I never thought I'd ~ the evening!** jamais je n'aurais cru que je tiendrais jusqu'à la fin de la soirée! **-3.** [outlive, outlast] survivre à; **she ~d her husband by 20 years** elle a survécu 20 ans à son mari; **she is ~d by two daughters** elle laisse deux filles. **-4.** [withstand] survivre à, résister à; **the house didn't ~ the storm** la maison n'a pas survécu OR résisté à la tempête; **her beauty has ~d the passage of time** sa beauté a résisté au temps.

surviving [sə'vaɪvɪŋ] *adj* survivant; **his only ~ son** son seul fils encore en vie; **the longest ~ whale in captivity** la baleine ayant survécu le plus longtemps en captivité.

survivor [sə'vaɪvə^r] *n* **-1.** [of an accident, attack] survivant *m*, -e *f*, rescapé *m*, -e *f*; **the ~s of the death camps** les rescapés des camps de la mort; **there are no reports of any ~s** aucun survivant n'a été signalé; **she'll be all right, she's a born ~** elle s'en sortira, elle est solide. **-2.** JUR survivant *m*, -e *f*.

sus *inf* [sʌs] *n Br*: **~ laws** *lois abrogées en 1981, équivalant au système du contrôle d'identité et autorisant l'arrestation de personnes dont le comportement paraît suspect.*

susceptibility [sə,septə'bɪlətɪ] (*pl* susceptibilities) *n* **-1.** [predisposition - to an illness] prédisposition *f*; **she has a ~ to respiratory complaints** elle a une prédisposition aux infections respiratoires. **-2.** [vulnerability] sensibilité *f*; **his ~ to flattery** sa sensibilité à la flatterie. **-3.** [sensitivity] sensibilité *f*, émotivité *f*. **-4.** PHYS susceptibilité *f*.

◆ **susceptibilities** *npl* [feelings] sentiments *mpl*, susceptibilité *f*; **try to spare their susceptibilities** essayez de ménager leur susceptibilité.

susceptible [sə'septəbl] *adj* **-1.** [prone - to illness] prédisposé; **I'm very ~ to colds** je m'enrhume très facilement; **only the more ~ children contracted the disease** seuls les enfants les plus prédisposés ont été contaminés par la maladie. **-2.** [responsive] sensible; **the management is ~ to pressure from the staff** la direction est sensible aux pressions du personnel; **~ to flattery** sensible à la flatterie; **the virus is not ~ to treatment** le virus ne répond pas au traitement. **-3.** [sensitive, emotional] sensible, émotif. **-4.** *fml* [capable] susceptible; **her decisions are ~ of modification** ses décisions sont susceptibles d'être modifiées.

sushi ['suːʃɪ] *n* sushi *m*; **~ bar** sushi-bar *m*.

suspect [*vb* sə'spekt, *n* & *adj* 'sʌspekt] ◇ *vt* **-1.** [presume, imagine] soupçonner, se douter de; **to ~ foul play** soupçonner quelque chose de louche; **I ~ed there would be trouble** je me doutais qu'il y aurait des problèmes; **I ~ed as much!** je m'en doutais!; **what happened, I ~, is that they had an argument** ce qui s'est passé, j'imagine, c'est qu'ils se sont disputés. **-2.** [mistrust] douter de, se méfier de; **to ~ sb's motives** avoir des doutes sur les intentions de qqn. **-3.** [person - of wrongdoing] soupçonner, suspecter; **to be ~ed of sthg** être soupçonné de qqch; **to ~ sb of sthg** OR **of doing sthg** soupçonner qqn de qqch OR d'avoir fait qqch.

◇ *n* suspect *m*, -e *f*.

◇ *adj* suspect; **his views on apartheid are rather ~** ses vues sur l'apartheid sont plutôt douteuses.

suspected [sə'spektɪd] *adj* présumé; **a ~ terrorist** un terroriste présumé; **a ~ case of cholera** un cas présumé de choléra; **he's undergoing tests for a ~ tumour** on est en train de lui faire des analyses pour s'assurer qu'il ne s'agit pas d'une tumeur.

suspend [sə'spend] *vt* **-1.** [hang] suspendre; **~ed from the ceiling** suspendu au plafond; **particles of radioactive dust were ~ed in the atmosphere** des particules radioactives étaient en suspension dans l'atmosphère. **-2.** [discontinue] suspendre; [withdraw - permit, licence] retirer (provisoirement); **bus services have been ~ed** le service des autobus a été suspendu OR interrompu; **the government has ~ed the repayment of foreign debts** le gouvernement a suspendu le remboursement de sa dette extérieure. **-3.** [defer] suspendre, reporter; **to ~ judgment** suspendre son jugement; **the commission decided to ~ its decision** la commission décida de surseoir à sa décision; **to ~ one's disbelief** faire taire son incrédulité. **-4.** [exclude temporarily - official, member, sportsman] suspendre; [- worker] suspendre, mettre à pied; [- pupil, student] exclure provisoirement; **~ed for six months** suspendu pendant six mois; **two pupils have been ~ed from school for smoking** deux élèves surpris à fumer font l'objet d'un renvoi provisoire.

suspended animation [sə'spendɪd-] *n* [natural state] hibernation *f*; [induced state] hibernation *f* artificielle.

suspended sentence *n* JUR condamnation *f* avec sursis; **she got a three-month ~** elle a été condamnée à trois mois de prison avec sursis.

suspender [sə'spendə^r] *n Br* [for stockings] jarretelle *f*; [for socks] fixe-chaussette *m*.

◆ **suspenders** *npl Am* [for trousers] bretelles *fpl*.

suspender belt *n Br* porte-jarretelles *m inv*.

suspense [sə'spens] *n* **-1.** [anticipation] incertitude *f*; **to keep** OR **to leave sb in ~** laisser qqn dans l'incertitude; **to break the ~** mettre fin à l'incertitude; **the ~ is killing me!** *inf* quel suspense! ‖ [in films, literature] suspense *m*; **she manages to maintain the ~ throughout the book** elle réussit à maintenir OR faire durer le suspense jusqu'à la fin du livre. **-2.** ADMIN & JUR: **in ~** en suspens.

suspense account *n* compte *m* d'ordre.

suspension [sə'spenʃn] *n* **-1.** [interruption] suspension *f*; [withdrawal] suspension *f*, retrait *m* (provisoire); **the ~ of hostilities/payments** la suspension des hostilités/des paiements. **-2.** [temporary dismissal - from office, political party, club, team] suspension *f*; [- from job] suspension *f*, mise *f* à pied; [- from school, university] exclusion *f* provisoire. **-3.** AUT & TECH suspension *f*; **independent ~** suspension à roues indépendantes. **-4.** CHEM suspension *f*; **in ~** en suspension.

suspension bridge *n* pont *m* suspendu.

suspension points *npl* points *mpl* de suspension.

suspensor [sə'spensə^r] *n* **-1.** ANAT [ligament] ligament *m* suspenseur; [muscle] muscle *m* suspenseur. **-2.** BOT suspenseur *m*.

suspensory [sə'spensərɪ] (*pl* suspensories) ◇ *n* **-1.** ANAT = **suspensor 1**. **-2.** MED [bandage, sling] suspensoir *m*.

◇ *adj* **-1.** ANAT suspenseur. **-2.** MED [bandage, sling] de soutien.

suspicion [sə'spɪʃn] *n* **-1.** [presumption of guilt, mistrust] soupçon *m*, suspicion *f*; **her neighbours' strange behaviour aroused her ~** OR **~s** le comportement étrange de ses voisins éveilla ses soupçons; **to be above** OR **beyond ~** être au-dessus de tout soupçon; **I have my ~s about this fellow** j'ai des doutes sur cet individu; **the new boss was regarded with ~** on considérait le nouveau patron avec méfiance; **the discovery cast ~ on the maid** la découverte jeta la suspicion sur la bonne; **to be under ~** être soupçonné; **he was arrested on ~ of drug trafficking** JUR il a été arrêté parce qu'on le soupçonnait de trafic de drogue. **-2.** [notion, feeling] soupçon *m*; **I had a growing ~ that he wasn't telling the truth** je soupçonnais de plus en plus qu'il ne disait pas la vérité; **I had a (sneaking) ~ you'd be here** j'avais comme un pressentiment que tu serais là. **-3.** [trace, hint] soupçon *m*, pointe *f*; **there was a ~ of bitterness in her voice** il y avait un soupçon OR une pointe d'amertume dans sa voix.

suspicious [sə'spɪʃəs] *adj* **-1.** [distrustful] méfiant, soupçonneux; **his strange behaviour made us ~** son comportement étrange a éveillé nos soupçons OR notre méfiance; **she became ~ when he refused to give his name** elle a commencé à se méfier quand il a refusé de donner son nom; **I'm ~ of his motives** je me méfie de ses intentions; **she gave him a ~ look** elle lui jeta un regard méfiant. **-2.** [suspect] suspect; **the minister resigned in very ~ circumstances** le ministre démissionna dans des circonstances très suspectes; **there are a lot**

of ~-looking characters in this pub il y a beaucoup d'individus suspects dans ce pub; it is ~ that she didn't phone the police le fait qu'elle n'a pas téléphoné à la police est suspect.

suspiciously [sə'spɪʃəslɪ] *adv* -**1.** [distrustfully] avec méfiance, soupçonneusement. -**2.** [strangely] de façon suspecte; police saw a man acting ~ la police a vu un homme qui se comportait de façon suspecte; she was ~ keen to leave son empressement à partir était suspect; they came ~ close to guessing the truth il est étrange qu'ils aient failli deviner la vérité; it looks ~ like malaria ça ressemble étrangement au paludisme.

suspiciousness [sə'spɪʃəsnɪs] *n* -**1.** [distrust] méfiance *f*. -**2.** [suspect nature] caractère *m* suspect.

suss *inf* [sʌs] ◇ *vt Br* flairer; she ~ed what he was after elle a compris où il voulait en venir.
◇ *n* = **sus**.
◆ **suss out** *inf vt sep Br* -**1.** [device, situation] piger; she ~ed out how it worked in ten minutes elle a pigé comment ça marchait en dix minutes; I can't ~ out this computer program je n'arrive pas à piger (comment marche) ce nouveau logiciel. -**2.** [person] saisir le caractère de; I've got him ~ed out je sais à qui j'ai affaire.

sustain [sə'steɪn] *vt* -**1.** [maintain, keep up - conversation] entretenir; [- effort, attack, pressure] soutenir, maintenir; [- sb's interest] maintenir; if the present level of economic growth is ~ed si le niveau actuel de croissance économique est maintenu. -**2.** [hold up, support physically] soutenir, supporter; steel girders ~ the weight of the bridge le pont est soutenu par des poutres en acier. -**3.** [support morally] soutenir; it was only their belief in God that ~ed them seule leur croyance en Dieu les a soutenus. -**4.** MUS [note] tenir, soutenir. -**5.** [nourish] nourrir; they had only dried fruit and water to ~ them ils n'avaient que des fruits secs et de l'eau pour subsister; one meal a day is not enough to ~ you l'homme a besoin pour vivre de plus d'un repas par jour; a planet capable of ~ing life une planète capable de maintenir la vie. -**6.** [suffer - damage] subir; [- defeat, loss] subir, essuyer; [- injury] recevoir; to ~ an injury recevoir une blessure, être blessé; the man ~ed a serious blow to the head l'homme a été grièvement atteint à la tête || [withstand] supporter; her fragile condition will not ~ another shock étant donné la fragilité de son état, elle ne supportera pas un nouveau choc. -**7.** JUR [accept as valid] admettre; the court refused to ~ the motion le tribunal refusa d'admettre OR d'accorder la requête; objection ~ed objection admise; the court ~ed her claim le tribunal lui accorda gain de cause. -**8.** [corroborate - assertion, theory, charge] corroborer. -**9.** THEAT [role] tenir.

sustainable [səs'teɪnəbl] *adj* [development, agriculture, politics] viable.

sustained [sə'steɪnd] *adj* [effort, attack] soutenu; [discussion] prolongé.

sustaining [sə'steɪnɪŋ] *adj* nourrissant, nutritif.

sustaining pedal *n* pédale *f* forte.

sustaining program *n Am* RADIO & TV émission *f* non sponsorisée.

sustenance ['sʌstɪnəns] *n* -**1.** [nourishment] valeur *f* nutritive; there is little ~ in such foods de tels aliments ont peu de valeur nutritive OR sont peu nourrissants; stale bread provided her only form of ~ elle se nourrissait uniquement de pain rassis; his neighbours provided moral ~ during the crisis *fig* ses voisins l'ont soutenu moralement pendant la crise. -**2.** [means of subsistence] subsistance *f*; they could not derive ~ from the land ils ne pouvaient pas vivre de la terre.

susurration [ˌsjuːsə'reɪʃn] *n lit* susurrement *m*.

suttee ['sʌtiː] *n* [tradition] sati *m inv*; [widow] sati *f inv*.

suture ['suːtʃə^r] ◇ *n* -**1.** MED point *m* de suture. -**2.** ANAT & BOT suture *f*.
◇ *vt* MED suturer.

suzerain ['suːzəreɪn] ◇ *n* -**1.** HIST suzerain *m*, -e *f*. -**2.** POL [state] État *m* dominant.
◇ *adj* -**1.** HIST suzerain; ~ lord suzerain *m*. -**2.** POL [state, power] dominant.

suzerainty ['suːzəreɪntɪ] *n* -**1.** HIST suzeraineté *f*. -**2.** POL dominance *f*.

svelte [svelt] *adj* svelte.

Svengali [ˌsveŋ'gɑːlɪ] *n* manipulateur *m*.

SW -**1.** (*written abbr of* short wave) OC. -**2.** (*written abbr of* south-west) S-O.

swab [swɒb] (*pt & pp* swabbed, *cont* swabbing)
◇ *n* -**1.** MED [cotton] tampon *m*; [specimen] prélèvement *m*. -**2.** [mop] serpillière *f*. -**3.** [brush for firearms] écouvillon *m*.
◇ *vt* -**1.** MED [clean] nettoyer (avec un tampon). -**2.** [mop] laver; to ~ down the decks laver le pont.

Swabia ['sweɪbjə] *pr n* Souabe *f*; in ~ en Souabe.

swaddle ['swɒdl] *vt* -**1.** [wrap] envelopper, emmitoufler; ~d in blankets enveloppé OR emmitouflé dans des couvertures; her head was ~d in bandages elle avait la tête enveloppée de pansements. -**2.** *arch* [baby] emmailloter.

swaddling clothes *npl arch* OR BIBLE maillot *m*, langes *mpl*; the infant was wrapped in ~ le nourrisson était emmailloté.

swag *inf* [swæg] ◇ *n* -**1.** *Br* [booty] butin *m*. -**2.** *Austr & NZ* [bundle] baluchon *m*, balluchon *m*; to go on the ~ *inf* vagabonder. -**3.** *inf Austr & NZ*: ~s of [lots of] un tas de, une flopée de.
◇ *vi Austr & NZ* [roam] vagabonder.

swagger ['swægə^r] ◇ *vi* -**1.** [strut] se pavaner; he ~ed into/out of the room il entra dans/sortit de la pièce en se pavanant. -**2.** [boast] se vanter, fanfaronner, plastronner.
◇ *n* [manner] air *m* arrogant; [walk] démarche *f* arrogante; he entered the room with a ~ il entra dans la pièce en se pavanant.

swagger cane = **swagger stick**.

swaggering ['swægərɪŋ] ◇ *adj* [gait, attitude] arrogant; [person] fanfaron, bravache.
◇ *n* [proud gait] démarche *f* OR allure *f* arrogante; [boasting] vantardise *f*.

swagger stick *n* [gen] badine *f*, canne *f*; MIL bâton *m* (d'officier).

swagman *inf* ['swægmæn] (*pl* swagmen [-men]) *n Austr & NZ* clochard *m*.

Swahili [swɑː'hiːlɪ] ◇ *n* -**1.** LING swahili *m*, souahéli *m*. -**2.** [person] Swahili *m*, -e *f*, Souahéli *m*, -e *f*.
◇ *adj* swahili, souahéli.

swain [sweɪn] *n arch* [young man] jeune homme *m* de la campagne; [lover] soupirant *m*.

SWALK *inf* [swɔːlk] (*abbr of* sealed with a loving kiss) *doux baisers (écrit sur une enveloppe contenant une lettre d'amour)*.

swallow ['swɒləʊ] ◇ *vt* -**1.** [food, drink, medicine] avaler; he almost ~ed his tongue il a failli avaler sa langue. -**2.** *inf* [believe] avaler, croire; she ~ed the story whole elle a avalé OR cru toute l'histoire; he'll ~ anything il avalerait n'importe quoi; I find it hard to ~ j'ai du mal à avaler ça. -**3.** [accept unprotestingly] avaler, accepter; I find it hard to ~ je trouve ça un peu raide; I'm not going to ~ that sort of treatment pas question que j'accepte d'être traité de cette façon. -**4.** [repress] ravaler; to ~ one's anger/disappointment ravaler sa colère/sa déception; he had to ~ his pride il a dû ravaler sa fierté. -**5.** [retract]: to ~ one's words ravaler ses paroles. -**6.** [absorb] engloutir; they were soon ~ed by the crowd la foule eut tôt fait de les engloutir.
◇ *vi* avaler, déglutir; it hurts when I ~ j'ai mal quand j'avale; she ~ed hard and continued her speech elle avala sa salive et poursuivit son discours.
◇ *n* -**1.** [action] gorgée *f*; she took a long ~ of champagne elle prit OR but une grande gorgée de champagne; he finished his drink with one ~ il finit sa boisson d'un trait OR d'un seul coup. -**2.** ORNITH hirondelle *f*; one ~ doesn't make a summer *prov* une hirondelle ne fait pas le printemps *prov*.
◆ **swallow up** *vt sep* engloutir; the Baltic States were ~ed up by the Soviet Union les pays baltes ont été engloutis par l'Union soviétique; I wished the ground would open and ~ me up j'aurais voulu être à six pieds sous terre; they were soon ~ed up in the mist ils furent bientôt noyés dans la brume; they were ~ed up in the crowd ils ont disparu dans la foule.

swallow dive *n Br* SPORT saut *m* de l'ange.

swallow hole *n Br* gouffre *m*, aven *m*.

swallowtail ['swɒləʊteɪl] *n* machaon *m*.

swallow-tailed coat *n* queue-de-pie *f*.

swam [swæm] *pt* → **swim**.

swami ['swɑːmɪ] (*pl* swamis OR swamies) *n* swami *m*.

swamp [swɒmp] ◇ *n* marais *m*, marécage *m*.
◇ *vt* -**1.** [flood] inonder; [cause to sink] submerger. -**2.** [overwhelm] inonder, submerger; she was ~ed with calls elle a été submergée d'appels; we're ~ed (with work) at the office at the moment nous sommes débordés de travail au bureau en ce moment.

swamp buggy *n Am* [boat] hydroglisseur *m*; [tractor] tracteur *m* amphibie.

swamp fever *n Am* [malaria] paludisme *m*, malaria *f*.

swampland ['swɒmplænd] *n (U)* marécages *mpl*, terrain *m* marécageux.

swampy ['swɒmpɪ] (*compar* swampier, *superl* swampiest) *adj* marécageux.

swan [swɒn] (*pt & pp* swanned, *cont* swanning)
◇ *n* cygne *m*; the Swan of Avon Shakespeare; 'Swan Lake' *Tchaikovsky* 'le Lac des cygnes'.
◇ *vi inf Br*: they spent a year swanning round Europe ils ont passé une année à se balader en Europe; they swanned off to the pub ils sont tranquillement allés au pub; he came swanning into the office at 10:30 il est arrivé au bureau comme si de rien n'était à 10 h 30.

swan dive *n Am* SPORT saut *m* de l'ange.

swank *inf* [swæŋk] ◇ *vi* se vanter, frimer.
◇ *n Br* -**1.** [boasting] frime *f*; ignore him, it's all ~ ne fais pas attention à lui, tout ça c'est de la frime. -**2.** [boastful person] frimeur *m*, -euse *f*. -**3.** *Am* [luxury] luxe *m*, chic *m*; it's got lots of ~ ça a une de ces classes!
◇ *adj* = **swanky**.

swanky *inf* ['swæŋkɪ] (*compar* swankier, *superl* swankiest) *adj* [gen] chic; [club, school] chic.

swan neck *n* col-de-cygne *m*.

swan-necked *adj Br* -**1.** [person] au cou de cygne. -**2.** [object] en col-de-cygne.

swannery ['swɒnərɪ] (*pl* swanneries) *n* réserve *f* de cygnes.

swansdown ['swɒnzdaʊn] *n* -**1.** [feathers] duvet *m* de cygne. -**2.** TEX molleton *m*.

swansong ['swɒnsɒŋ] *n* chant *m* du cygne.

swan-upping *n Br recensement et marquage annuels des cygnes de la Tamise appartenant à la Couronne*.

swap [swɒp] (*pt & pp* swapped, *cont* swapping)
◇ *vt* -**1.** [possessions, places] échanger; to ~ sthg for sthg échanger qqch contre qqch; I'll ~ my coat for yours, I'll ~ coats with you échangeons nos manteaux; they've swapped places ils ont échangé leurs places; he swapped places with his sister il a échangé sa place contre celle de sa sœur; I wouldn't ~ places with him for love nor money je ne voudrais être à sa place pour rien au monde; I'd ~ jobs with him any day! j'échangerais mon travail contre le sien sans hésiter!; as soon as the music stops, everybody ~ partners dès que la musique s'arrête, tout le monde change de cavalier. -**2.** [ideas, opinions] échanger; they meet to ~ stories about the war ils se rencontrent pour échanger des histoires de guerre; they swapped insults over the garden fence ils échangèrent des insultes par-dessus la clôture du jardin.

◇ *vi* échanger, faire un échange OR un troc; I'll ~ with you on échangera, on fera un échange.
◇ *n* -**1.** [exchange] troc *m*, échange *m*; to do a ~ faire un troc OR un échange; I gave her my bicycle as a ~ for hers je lui ai donné mon vélo en échange du sien. -**2.** [duplicate - stamp in collection etc] double *m*.
◆ **swap over, swap round** ◇ *vt sep* échanger, intervertir; she swapped their glasses over OR round when he left the room elle échangea leurs verres quand il quitta la pièce.
◇ *vi insep*: do you mind swapping over OR round so I can sit next to Max? est-ce que ça te dérange qu'on échange nos places pour que je puisse m'asseoir à côté de Max?

swap meet *n Am* foire *f* au troc.

SWAPO ['swɑːpəʊ] (*abbr of* South West Africa People's Organization) *pr n* SWAPO *f*.

swap shop *n* foire *f* au troc, magasin *m* de troc.

sward [swɔːd] *n arch* OR *lit* gazon *m*, pelouse *f*.

swarf [swɔːf] *n (U)* ébarbures *fpl*, limaille *f*.

swarm [swɔːm] ◇ *n* -**1.** [of bees] essaim *m*; [of ants] colonie *f*. -**2.** *fig* [of people] essaim *m*, nuée *f*, masse *f*; surrounded by a ~ of admirers entouré d'une foule d'admirateurs.
◇ *vi* -**1.** ENTOM essaimer. -**2.** *fig* [place] fourmiller, grouiller; the streets were ~ing with people les rues grouillaient de monde. -**3.** *fig* [people] affluer; the crowd ~ed in/out la foule s'est engouffrée à l'intérieur/est sortie en masse; bargain-hunters ~ed into the department store les chercheurs d'occasions envahirent le grand magasin; children were ~ing round the ice-cream van les enfants s'agglutinaient autour du camion du marchand de glaces. -**4.** [climb] grimper (lestement); she ~ed up the tree elle grimpa lestement à l'arbre.

swarthiness ['swɔːðɪnɪs] *n* teint *m* basané.

swarthy ['swɔːðɪ] (*compar* swarthier, *superl* swarthiest) *adj* basané; he has a ~ complexion il a le teint basané.

swash [swɒʃ] ◇ *n* [splash] clapotis *m*.
◇ *vi* clapoter.

swashbuckler ['swɒʃ,bʌklə^r] *n* -**1.** [adventurer] aventurier *m*, -ère *f*; [swaggerer] fier-à-bras *m*, matamore *m*. -**2.** [film] film *m* de cape et d'épée; [novel] roman *m* de cape et d'épée.

swashbuckling ['swɒʃ,bʌklɪŋ] *adj* [person] fanfaron; [film, story] de cape et d'épée.

swastika ['swɒstɪkə] *n* ANTIQ svastika *m*; [Nazi] croix *f* gammée.

swat [swɒt] (*pt* & *pp* swatted, *cont* swatting) ◇ *vt* -**1.** [insect] écraser. -**2.** *inf* [slap] frapper.
◇ *n* -**1.** [device] tapette *f*. -**2.** [swipe]: he took a ~ at the mosquito il essaya d'écraser le moustique. -**3.** *inf* = **swot**.

swatch [swɒtʃ] *n* échantillon *m* de tissu.

swath [swɔːθ] = **swathe** *n*.

swathe [sweɪð] ◇ *vt* -**1.** [bind] envelopper, emmailloter; his head was ~d in bandages sa tête était enveloppée de pansements; she lay in bed ~d in blankets elle était dans son lit, enveloppée OR emmitouflée dans des couvertures. -**2.** [envelop] envelopper; ~d in mist enveloppé de brume.
◇ *n* -**1.** AGR andain *m*. -**2.** [strip of land] bande *f* de terre; the army cut a ~ through the town l'armée a tout détruit sur son passage dans la ville; the new motorway cuts a ~ through the countryside la nouvelle autoroute coupe à travers la campagne; she cut a ~ through the opposition elle a fait des ravages dans les rangs de l'opposition. -**3.** [strip of cloth] lanière *f*.

swatter ['swɒtə^r] *n* tapette *f*.

sway [sweɪ] ◇ *vi* -**1.** [pylon, bridge] se balancer, osciller; [tree] s'agiter; [bus, train] pencher; [boat] rouler; [person - deliberately] se balancer; [- from tiredness, drink] chanceler, tituber; the poplars ~ed in the wind les peupliers étaient agités par le vent; they were ~ing to the music ils se balançaient au rythme de la musique; to ~ from side to side/to and fro se balancer de droite à gauche/d'avant en arrière. -**2.** [vacillate] vaciller, hésiter; to ~ between two opinions vaciller OR hésiter entre deux opinions ‖ [incline, tend] pencher; to ~ towards conservatism pencher vers le conservatisme.
◇ *vt* -**1.** [pylon] (faire) balancer, faire osciller; [tree] agiter; [hips] rouler, balancer; they started ~ing their bodies in time to the music ils ont commencé à se balancer au rythme de la musique. -**2.** [influence] influencer; his plea for mercy did not ~ the judge sa demande de clémence n'a pas influencé le juge; don't be ~ed by his charm ne te laisse pas influencer OR impressionner par son charme. -**3.** *arch* [rule] régner sur.
◇ *n* -**1.** [rocking - gen] balancement *m*; [- of a boat] roulis *m*. -**2.** [influence] influence *f*, emprise *f*, empire *m*; to hold ~ over sb/sthg avoir de l'influence OR de l'emprise sur qqn/qqch; the economic theories that hold ~ today les théories économiques qui ont cours aujourd'hui.

Swazi ['swɑːzɪ] *n* Swazi *mf*.

Swaziland ['swɑːzɪlænd] *pr n* Swaziland *m*; in ~ au Swaziland.

swear [sweə^r] (*pt* swore [swɔː^r], *pp* sworn [swɔːn]) ◇ *vi* -**1.** [curse] jurer; to ~ at sb injurier qqn; they started ~ing at each other ils ont commencé à se traiter de tous les noms OR à s'injurier; don't ~ in front of the children ne dis pas de gros mots devant les enfants ❑ to ~ like a trooper jurer comme un charretier. -**2.** [vow, take an oath] jurer; he swore on the Bible il jura sur la Bible; she swore on her honour/on her mother's grave elle jura sur l'honneur/sur la tombe de sa mère; I can't ~ to its authenticity je ne peux pas jurer de son authenticité; I wouldn't ~ to it, but I think it was him je n'en jurerais pas, mais je crois que c'était lui; I ~ I'll never do it again! je jure de ne plus jamais recommencer!; he ~s he's never seen her before il jure qu'il ne l'a jamais vue; did YOU break it? – no, I ~ I didn't c'est toi qui l'as cassé? – je vous jure que non OR que ce n'est pas moi; they swore to defend the family honour ils jurèrent de défendre l'honneur de la famille.
◇ *vt* -**1.** [pledge, vow]: to ~ an oath prêter serment; to ~ allegiance to the Crown jurer allégeance à la couronne; to ~ a charge against sb JUR faire une déposition sous serment contre qqn. -**2.** [make sb pledge]: to ~ sb to secrecy faire jurer à qqn de garder le secret.
◆ **swear by** *vt insep*: she ~s by that old sewing machine of hers elle ne jure que par sa vieille machine à coudre; you should try honey and hot milk for your cold, my mother ~s by it pour ton rhume, tu devrais essayer du miel dans du lait chaud, ma mère ne jure que par ça.
◆ **swear in** *vt sep* [witness, president] faire prêter serment à, assermenter *fml*.
◆ **swear off** *inf vt insep Br* renoncer à; he has sworn off drinking il a renoncé à l'alcool OR arrêté de boire.
◆ **swear out** *vt sep Am* JUR: he swore out a warrant for Baker's arrest il a témoigné sous serment afin de faire arrêter Baker.

swearword ['sweəwɜːd] *n* grossièreté *f*, juron *m*, gros mot *m*.

sweat [swet] (*Br pt* & *pp* sweated, *Am pt* & *pp* sweat OR sweated) ◇ *n* -**1.** [perspiration] sueur *f*, transpiration *f*; ~ was dripping from his forehead son front était ruisselant de sueur; I woke up covered in ~ je me suis réveillé en nage OR couvert de sueur OR tout en sueur; to break into OR to come out in a cold ~ avoir des sueurs froides; she earned it by the ~ of her brow elle l'a gagné à la sueur de son front. -**2.** *inf* [unpleasant task] corvée *f*; picking strawberries is a real ~ *Br* la cueillette des fraises est une vraie corvée ❑ can you give me a hand? – no ~! *inf* peux-tu me donner un coup de main? – pas de problème! -**3.** *inf Br* [anxious state]: there's no need to get into a ~ about it! pas la peine de te mettre dans des états pareils! -**4.** *inf* [person]: (old) ~ *Br* [old soldier] vieux soldat *m*; [experienced worker] vieux routier *m*.
◇ *vi* -**1.** [perspire] suer, transpirer; the effort made him ~ l'effort l'a mis en sueur; she was ~ing profusely elle suait à grosses gouttes ❑ to ~ like a pig *inf* suer comme un bœuf. -**2.** *fig* [work hard, suffer] suer; my mother ~ed over a hot stove from morning till night ma mère suait sur ses fourneaux du matin jusqu'au soir; I'll make them ~ for this! ils vont me le payer!; she's ~ing over her homework elle est en train de suer sur ses devoirs. -**3.** [ooze - walls] suer, suinter; [- cheese] suer.
◇ *vt* -**1.** [cause to perspire] faire suer OR transpirer; the doctor recommended ~ing the patient le médecin recommanda de faire transpirer le malade ‖ [exude]: to ~ blood *fig* suer sang et eau; he ~ed blood over this article il a sué sang et eau sur cet article; to ~ buckets *inf* suer comme un bœuf. -**2.** *inf Am* [extort]: we ~ed the information out of him on lui a fait cracher le morceau. -**3.** *Am phr*: don't ~ it! *inf* pas de panique! -**4.** CULIN cuire à l'étouffée.
◆ **sweat off** *vt sep* éliminer; you should do some exercise to ~ off those excess pounds tu devrais faire un peu d'exercice pour éliminer ces kilos superflus.
◆ **sweat out** *vt sep* -**1.** [illness]: stay in bed and try to ~ out the cold restez au chaud dans votre lit et votre rhume partira. -**2.** *phr*: leave him to ~ it out laissez-le se débrouiller tout seul; to ~ one's guts out *inf* suer sang et eau, se crever.

sweatband ['swetbænd] *n* -**1.** SPORT [headband] bandeau *m*; [wristband] poignet *m*. -**2.** [in a hat] cuir *m* intérieur.

sweated ['swetɪd] *adj*: ~ labour [staff] main-d'œuvre *f* exploitée; [work] exploitation *f*.

sweater ['swetə^r] *n* pull-over *m*, pull *m*.

sweat gland *n* glande *f* sudoripare.

sweating ['swetɪŋ] *n* transpiration *f*, sudation *f spec*; the illness can cause heavy ~ la maladie peut provoquer une transpiration abondante OR des sueurs abondantes.

sweatshirt ['swetʃɜːt] *n* sweat-shirt *m*.

sweatshop ['swetʃɒp] *n* ≃ atelier *m* clandestin.

sweat suit *n* survêtement *m*.

sweaty ['swetɪ] (*compar* sweatier, *superl* sweatiest) *adj* -**1.** [person] (tout) en sueur; [hands] moite; [feet] qui transpire; [clothing] trempé de sueur; he's got ~ feet il transpire des pieds; his uniform smelt ~ son uniforme sentait la sueur. -**2.** [weather, place] d'une chaleur humide OR moite; she went back into the ~ workshop elle replongea dans la chaleur humide de l'atelier. -**3.** [activity] qui fait transpirer; it was a hard, ~ climb l'ascension était rude et donnait chaud.

swede [swiːd] *n Br* rutabaga *m*, chou-navet *m*.

Swede [swiːd] *n* Suédois *m*, -e *f*.

Sweden ['swiːdn] *pr n* Suède *f*; in ~ en Suède.

Swedish ['swiːdɪʃ] ◇ *npl*: the ~ les Suédois *mpl*.
◇ *n* LING suédois *m*.
◇ *adj* suédois.

Sweeney▽ ['swiːnɪ] *n Br*: the ~ la brigade volante de Scotland Yard.

sweep [swiːp] (*pt* & *pp* swept [swept]) ◇ *vt* -**1.** [with a brush - room, street, dust, leaves] balayer; [- chimney] ramoner; to ~ the floor balayer le sol; he swept the room (out) il a balayé la pièce; she swept the leaves from the path into a pile elle balaya les feuilles du chemin et les mit en tas; I swept the broken glass into the dustpan j'ai poussé le verre cassé dans la pelle avec le balai ❑ to ~ sthg under the carpet OR the rug tirer le rideau sur qqch. -**2.** [with hand]: he angrily swept the papers off the desk d'un geste furieux, il balaya les papiers de dessus le bureau; she swept the coins off the table into her handbag elle a fait glisser les pièces de la table dans son sac à main. -**3.** [subj: wind, tide, crowd etc]: the wind swept his hat into the river le vent a fait tomber son chapeau dans la rivière; the small boat was swept out to sea le petit bateau a été emporté vers le large; three fishermen were swept overboard un paquet de mer emporta trois pêcheurs; to ~ everything before one *fig* faire des ravages; the incident swept all other thoughts from her mind l'incident lui fit oublier tout le reste; he was swept to power on a wave of popular discontent il a été porté au pouvoir par une vague de mécontentement populaire ❑ to be swept off one's feet (by sb) [fall in love] tomber fou amoureux (de qqn); [be filled with enthusiam] être enthousiasmé (par qqn). -**4.** [spread through - subj: fire, epidemic, rumour, belief] gagner; a new craze is ~ing America une nouvelle mode fait fureur aux États-Unis; a wave of fear swept the city une vague de peur gagna la ville; the flu epidemic which swept Europe in 1919 l'épidémie de grippe qui sévit en Europe en 1919. -**5.** [scan, survey] parcourir; her eyes swept the horizon/the room elle parcourut l'horizon/la pièce des yeux; searchlights continually ~ the open ground outside the prison camp des projecteurs parcourent OR balayent sans cesse le terrain qui entoure la prison. -**6.** [win easily] gagner OR remporter haut la main; the Popular Democratic Party swept the polls le parti démocratique populaire a fait un raz-de-marée aux élections; she swept the tournament *Am* SPORT elle a gagné le tournoi sans concéder une seule partie ❑ to ~ the board remporter tous les prix; the German athletes swept the board at the Olympics les athlètes allemands ont remporté toutes les médailles aux jeux Olympiques. -**7.** NAUT [mines, sea, channel] draguer; the port has been swept for mines le port a été dragué.

◇ *vi* -**1.** [with a brush] balayer. -**2.** [move quickly, powerfully]: harsh winds swept across the bleak steppes un vent violent balayait les mornes steppes; a hurricane swept through the town un ouragan a dévasté la ville; I watched storm clouds ~ing across the sky je regardais des nuages orageux filer dans le ciel; the Barbarians who swept into the Roman Empire les Barbares qui déferlèrent sur l'Empire romain; nationalism swept through the country une vague de nationalisme a submergé le pays; the planes swept low over the town les avions passèrent en rase-mottes au-dessus de la ville; the fire swept through the forest l'incendie a ravagé la forêt. -**3.** [move confidently, proudly]: he swept into/out of the room il entra/sortit majestueusement de la pièce; she swept past me without even a glance elle passa majestueusement à côté de moi sans même m'adresser un regard. -**4.** [stretch - land] s'étendre; the fields ~ down to the lake les prairies descendent en pente douce jusqu'au lac; the river ~s round in a wide curve le fleuve décrit une large courbe. -**5.** NAUT: to ~ for mines draguer, déminer.

◇ *n* -**1.** [with a brush] coup *m* de balai; the room needs a good ~ la pièce aurait besoin d'un bon coup de balai. -**2.** [movement]: with a ~ of her arm d'un geste large; with a ~ of his sword/scythe d'un grand coup d'épée/de faux; in OR at one ~ d'un seul coup. -**3.** [curved line, area] (grande) courbe *f*, étendue *f*; a vast ~ of woodland une vaste étendue de forêt; from where we stood, we could see the whole ~ of the bay de là où nous étions, nous voyions toute (l'étendue de) la baie. -**4.** [range] gamme *f*; the members of the commission represent a broad ~ of opinion les membres de la commission représentent des opinions variées. -**5.** [scan, survey]: her eyes made a ~ of the room elle parcourut la pièce des yeux; they jumped over the wall between two ~s of the searchlight ils sautèrent par-dessus le mur entre deux mouvements du projecteur. -**6.** ELECTRON [by electron beam] balayage *m*. -**7.** [search] fouille *f*; police made a drugs ~ on the university la police a ratissé l'université à la recherche de drogues. -**8.** [gen & MIL - attack] attaque *f*; [- reconnaissance] reconnaissance *f*; the rescue party made a ~ of the area l'équipe de secours a ratissé les environs. -**9.** [chimney sweep] ramoneur *m*. -**10.** *inf* [sweepstake] sweepstake *m*. -**11.** AERON flèche *f*; to vary the angle of ~ varier la flèche.

◆ **sweep along** *vt sep* [subj: wind, tide, crowd] emporter, entraîner.

◆ **sweep aside** *vt sep* -**1.** [object, person] écarter. -**2.** [advice, objection] repousser, rejeter; [obstacle] écarter.

◆ **sweep away** *vt sep* -**1.** [dust, snow] balayer. -**2.** [subj: wind, tide, crowd] emporter, entraîner; three bathers were swept away by a huge wave trois baigneurs ont été emportés par une énorme vague.

◆ **sweep by** *vi insep* [car] passer à toute vitesse; [person - majestically] passer majestueusement; [- disdainfully] passer dédaigneusement.

◆ **sweep down** *vi insep* [steps] descendre.

◆ **sweep past** = **sweep by**.

◆ **sweep up** ◇ *vt sep* [dust, leaves] balayer; she swept up the pieces of glass elle balaya les morceaux de verre.

◇ *vi* balayer; can you ~ up after the meeting? peux-tu balayer OR peux-tu passer un coup de balai après la réunion?

sweepback ['swi:pbæk] *n* flèche *f* (arrière).

sweeper ['swi:pəʳ] *n* -**1.** [person] balayeur *m*, -euse *f*. -**2.** [device - for streets] balayeuse *f*; [- for carpets] balai *m* mécanique. -**3.** FTBL libero *m*.

sweep hand *n* trotteuse *f*.

sweeping ['swi:pɪŋ] *adj* -**1.** [wide - movement, curve] large; with a ~ gesture d'un geste large, d'un grand geste; a ~ view une vue panoramique. -**2.** [indiscriminate]: a ~ generalization OR statement une généralisation excessive; he makes ~ statements about the European mentality il fait des généralisations excessives sur la mentalité européenne; that's rather a ~ generalization là, vous généralisez un peu trop. -**3.** [significant, large - amount] considérable; ~ budget cuts des coupes sombres dans le budget; the opposition has made ~ gains l'opposition a énormément progressé. -**4.** [far-reaching - measure, change] de grande portée, de grande envergure; ~ reforms des réformes de grande envergure.

◆ **sweepings** *npl* balayures *fpl*.

sweepstake ['swi:psteɪk] *n* sweepstake *m*.

sweet [swi:t] ◇ *adj* -**1.** [tea, coffee, taste] sucré; [fruit, honey] doux, sucré; [wine] moelleux; this tea is too ~ for me ce thé est trop sucré pour moi. -**2.** [fresh, clean - air] doux; [- breath] frais; [- water] pur. -**3.** [fragrant - smell] agréable, suave; the roses smell so ~! les roses sentent si bon! -**4.** [musical - sound, voice] mélodieux; [- words] doux; the ~ song of the lark le chant mélodieux de l'alouette; to whisper ~ nothings in sb's ear murmurer des mots d'amour à l'oreille de qqn, conter fleurette à qqn. -**5.** [pleasant, satisfactory - emotion, feeling, success] doux; revenge is ~ la vengeance est douce. -**6.** [kind, generous] gentil; it was very ~ of you c'était gentil de votre part; how ~ of her to phone! comme elle est gentille d'avoir téléphoné! ❑ to keep sb ~ *inf Br* cultiver les bonnes grâces de qqn. -**7.** [cute] mignon, adorable; what a ~ little baby/hat! quel adorable bébé/chapeau! -**8.** *inf* [in love]: to be ~ on sb *Br* avoir le béguin pour qqn. -**9.** *inf* [as intensifier]: he'll please his own ~ self, he'll go his own ~ way il n'en fera qu'à sa tête; she'll come in her own ~ time elle viendra quand ça lui plaira; you can bet your ~ life that something funny's going on! tu peux être sûr qu'il se passe quelque chose de louche! ❑ ~ FA▽ *Br* rien du tout, que dalle.

◇ *n* -**1.** *Br* [confectionery] bonbon *m*. -**2.** *Br* [dessert] dessert *m*; what's for ~? qu'est-ce qu'il y a comme dessert? -**3.** [term of address]: my ~ mon chéri *m*, ma chérie *f*.

sweet-and-sour *adj* aigre-doux; ~ pork porc *m* à la sauce aigre-douce.

sweetbread ['swi:tbred] *n* [thymus] ris *m*; [pancreas] pancréas *m*.

sweetbrier [ˌswi:t'braɪəʳ] *n* églantier *m* odorant.

sweet chestnut *n* marron *m*.

sweet cider *n* -**1.** *Am* jus *m* de pomme *(non fermenté)*. -**2.** *Br* cidre *m* doux.

sweet corn *n* maïs *m* doux.

sweeten ['swi:tn] *vt* -**1.** [food, drink] sucrer; ~ed with honey sucré avec du miel. -**2.** [mollify]: to ~ (up) amadouer, enjôler; she tried to ~ him (up) by taking him out to dinner elle a essayé de l'amadouer en l'emmenant dîner au restaurant; their remarks did nothing to ~ my temper leurs remarques n'ont rien fait pour apaiser ma colère. -**3.** *inf* [bribe] graisser la patte à; how much would it cost to ~ (up) the committee? combien ça coûterait de graisser la patte au comité? -**4.** [make more attractive - task] adoucir; [- offer] améliorer. -**5.** [improve the odour of] parfumer, embaumer; the scent of roses ~ed the air l'odeur des roses parfumait OR embaumait l'atmosphère.

sweetener ['swi:tnəʳ] *n* -**1.** [for food, drink] édulcorant *m*, sucrette *f*; artificial ~s édulcorants artificiels. -**2.** *inf Br* [present] cadeau *m*; [bribe] pot-de-vin *m*; they gave him a bigger office as a ~ ils lui ont donné un plus grand bureau pour l'amadouer; the government was accused of offering the company ~s on a accusé le gouvernement de donner des pots-de-vin à la compagnie.

sweetening ['swi:tnɪŋ] *n* -**1.** [substance] édulcorant *m*, édulcorants *mpl*. -**2.** [process - of wine] sucrage *m*; [- of water] adoucissement *m*.

sweetheart ['swi:thɑ:t] *n* -**1.** [lover] petit ami *m*, petite amie *f*; they're ~s ils sont amoureux; they were childhood ~s ils s'aimaient OR ils étaient amoureux quand ils étaient enfants. -**2.** [term of address] (mon) chéri *m*, (ma) chérie *f*.

sweetie *inf* ['swi:tɪ] *n* -**1.** [darling] chéri *m*, -e *f*, chou *m*; he's a real ~ il est vraiment adorable; what's the matter, ~? qu'est-ce qu'il y a, mon chou? -**2.** *Br baby talk* [sweet] bonbon *m*.

sweetiepie *inf* ['swi:tɪpaɪ] = **sweetie 1**.

sweetly ['swi:tlɪ] *adv* -**1.** [pleasantly, kindly] gentiment; [cutely] d'un air mignon; she smiled at him ~ elle lui sourit gentiment; the child smiled at them ~ l'enfant leur adressa un joli sourire; he was whispering ~ in her ear il lui chuchotait tendrement à l'oreille. -**2.** [smoothly] sans à-coups; the engine was running ~ le moteur ronronnait ‖ [accurately] avec précision; he's starting to hit the ball more ~ *Br* il commence à frapper la balle avec plus de précision. -**3.** [musically] harmonieusement, mélodieusement; she sings very ~ elle a une voix très mélodieuse.

sweetmeal ['swi:tmi:l] *adj*: ~ biscuit *Br* sablé *m* à la farine complète.

sweetmeat ['swi:tmi:t] *n arch* friandise *f*.

sweetness ['swi:tnɪs] *n* -**1.** [of food, tea, coffee] goût *m* sucré; [of wine] (goût *m*) mœlleux *m*. -**2.** [freshness - of air] douceur *f*; [- of breath] fraîcheur *f*; [- of water] pureté *f*. -**3.** [fragrance] parfum *m*. -**4.** [musicality - of sound] son *m* mélodieux; [- of voice, words] douceur *f*. -**5.** [pleasure, satisfaction] douceur *f*; the ~ of revenge le plaisir (exquis) de la vengeance. -**6.** [kindness, generosity] gentillesse *f*; she's all ~ and light elle est on ne peut plus gentille.

sweet pea *n* pois *m* de senteur.

sweet pepper *n* poivron *m*.

sweet potato *n* patate *f* douce.

sweet-scented *adj* parfumé.

sweet shop *n Br* confiserie *f*.

sweet talk *inf n (U)* flatteries *fpl*, paroles *fpl* mielleuses.

◆ **sweet-talk** *inf vt* amadouer; don't try to sweet-talk me! n'essaie pas de m'embobiner!; she sweet-talked him into doing it elle l'a si bien embobiné qu'il a fini par le faire.

sweet tooth *n*: to have a ~ adorer les OR être friand de sucreries.

sweet william *n* œillet *m* de poète.

swell [swel] (*pt* swelled, *pp* swelled OR swollen ['swəʊln]) ◇ *vi* -**1.** [distend - wood, pulses etc] gonfler; [- part of body] enfler, gonfler; the damp has made the wood ~ l'humidité a fait gonfler le bois; **he felt his lip begin to ~** il sentit sa lèvre enfler OR gonfler; **her heart ~ed with joy/pride** *fig* son cœur s'est gonflé de joie/d'orgueil. -**2.** [increase] augmenter; **the crowd ~ed to nearly two hundred** la foule grossit et il y eut bientôt près de 200 personnes. -**3.** [well up - emotion] monter, surgir; **I felt anger ~ in me** je sentais la colère monter en moi. -**4.** [rise - sea, tide] monter; [- river] se gonfler, grossir. -**5.** [grow louder] s'enfler; **the music ~ed to its climax** la musique atteignit alors son point culminant.

◇ *vt* -**1.** [distend] gonfler; **the wind ~ed the sails** le vent gonfla les voiles; **her eyes were swollen with tears** ses yeux étaient pleins de larmes. -**2.** [increase] augmenter, grossir; **she asked her friends to come along to ~ the numbers** elle a demandé à ses amis de venir pour qu'il y ait plus de monde; **to ~ the ranks of the unemployed** venir grossir les rangs des chômeurs. -**3.** [cause to rise] gonfler, grossir; **the rivers had been swollen by torrential rains** les cours d'eau avaient été gonflés OR grossis par des pluies torrentielles.

◇ *n* -**1.** NAUT houle *f*; **there was a deep** OR **heavy ~** il y avait une forte houle. -**2.** [bulge] gonflement *m*; **the ~ of the sails** le gonflement des voiles. -**3.** [increase] augmentation *f*. -**4.** MUS crescendo *m*. -**5.** *inf Am dated* [big shot] gros bonnet *m*; [dandy] dandy *m*, gandin *m*; [rich person] personne *f* huppée, rupin *m*.

◇ *adj inf Am* [great] super, chouette; **she's a ~ girl** c'est une chic fille; **we had a ~ time** on s'est super bien amusés.

◇ *interj inf Am* super.

◆ **swell out** ◇ *vi insep* (se) gonfler.

◇ *vt sep* gonfler.

◆ **swell up** = **swell** *vi* **1**.

swell-headed *inf adj* suffisant, qui a la grosse tête.

swelling ['swelɪŋ] ◇ *n* -**1.** MED enflure *f*, gonflement *m*; **they gave her something to relieve the ~** ils lui ont donné quelque chose pour que ça désenfle; **there was some ~ around the ankle** la cheville était un peu enflée. -**2.** [increase] augmentation *f*, grossissement *m*.

◇ *adj* [increasing] croissant; **the ~ numbers of the unemployed** le nombre croissant des chômeurs.

swelter ['sweltəʳ] *vi* [feel too hot] étouffer de chaleur; [sweat] suer à grosses gouttes, être en nage.

sweltering ['sweltərɪŋ] *adj* [day, heat] étouffant, oppressant; **it was simply ~ in the kitchen** il faisait une chaleur vraiment étouffante dans la cuisine.

swelteringly ['sweltərɪŋlɪ] *adv*: **it's ~ hot** il fait une chaleur étouffante; **a ~ hot day** une journée étouffante.

swept [swept] *pt* & *pp* → **sweep**.

swept-back *adj* -**1.** AERON [wings] en flèche (arrière). -**2.** [hair] ramené en arrière.

swept-wing *adj* [aircraft] aux ailes en flèche.

swerve [swɜːv] ◇ *vi* -**1.** [car, driver, ship] faire une embardée; [ball] dévier; [aeroplane, bird, runner] virer; **I had to ~ to avoid the cyclist** j'ai dû faire une embardée OR j'ai dû donner un coup de volant pour éviter le cycliste; **the car ~d to the left/towards us/round the corner/off the road** la voiture fit une embardée vers la gauche/vira pour foncer droit vers nous/prit le virage brusquement/fit une embardée et quitta la chaussée. -**2.** *fig* [budge, deviate] dévier; **she'll never ~ from her resolve** rien ne la détournera de sa résolution.

◇ *vt* -**1.** [vehicle] faire virer; [ball] faire dévier; **she ~d the car to the left** elle donna un coup de volant vers la gauche. -**2.** *fig* [person] détourner, faire dévier; **no one can ~ him from his ambition** personne ne peut le détourner de ses ambitions.

◇ *n* [by car, driver, ship] embardée *f*; [by aeroplane, bird, runner, ball] déviation *f*.

swift [swɪft] ◇ *adj* -**1.** [fast] rapide; **she is ~ of foot** *lit* elle est leste; **let's stop here for a ~ half** *inf Br* arrêtons-nous ici pour boire un coup en vitesse. -**2.** [prompt] prompt, rapide; **~ to react** prompt à réagir; **she received a ~ reply** elle reçut une réponse immédiate; **he is ~ in finding fault** il a la critique facile; **the government was ~ to deny the rumours** le gouvernement fut prompt à démentir les rumeurs; **she took ~ revenge** elle n'a pas tardé à se venger; **he has a ~ temper** il est très susceptible, il se fâche facilement.

◇ *adv*: **~-moving** rapide; **~-flowing** [river, stream] au cours rapide.

◇ *n* ORNITH martinet *m*.

swift-footed *adj lit* leste, véloce *lit*.

swiftly ['swɪftlɪ] *adv* -**1.** [quickly] rapidement, vite; **the meeting moved ~ to its conclusion** la réunion se termina rapidement; **moving ~ along!** passons! -**2.** [promptly] promptement, rapidement; **they reacted ~ to the threat** ils réagirent promptement à la menace.

swiftness ['swɪftnɪs] *n* -**1.** [speed] rapidité *f*, célérité *f lit*. -**2.** [promptness] promptitude *f*, rapidité *f*; **the ambulance arrived with remarkable ~** l'ambulance arriva avec une rapidité remarquable.

swig *inf* [swɪg] (*pt* & *pp* swigged, *cont* swigging)

◇ *vt* lamper, siffler.

◇ *n* lampée *f*, coup *m*; **have a ~ of this** bois un coup de ça; **he took a long ~ at his bottle** il porta sa bouteille à sa bouche et but un grand coup.

◆ **swig down** *inf vt sep* vider d'un trait, siffler.

swill [swɪl] ◇ *vt* -**1.** *Br* [wash] laver à grande eau; **he ~ed the floor (down)** il a lavé le sol à grande eau; **go and ~ the glass (out) under the tap** va passer le verre sous le robinet. -**2.** *inf* [drink] écluser.

◇ *n* -**1.** [for pigs] pâtée *f*. -**2.** [wash]: **to give sthg a ~** laver qqch.

swim [swɪm] (*pt* swam [swæm], *pp* swum [swʌm], *cont* swimming) ◇ *vi* -**1.** [fish, animal] nager; [person - gen] nager; [- for amusement] nager, se baigner; [- for sport] nager, faire de la natation; **to go swimming** [gen] (aller) se baigner; [in swimming pool] aller à la piscine; **we went swimming in the lake** nous sommes allés nous baigner dans le lac; **she's learning to ~** elle apprend à nager; **I can't ~!** je ne sais pas nager!; **the lake was too cold to ~ in** le lac était trop froid pour se baigner; **to ~ across a river** traverser une rivière à la nage; **to ~ upstream/downstream** monter/descendre le courant à la nage; **she swam away from/back to the shore** elle quitta/regagna la rive à la nage; **he managed to ~ to safety** il a réussi à se sauver en nageant; **the raft sank and they had to ~ for it** le radeau a coulé et ils ont été obligés de nager ❑ **to ~ against the tide** *literal* & *fig* nager à contre-courant. -**2.** [be soaked] nager, baigner; **the salad was swimming in oil** la salade baignait dans l'huile; **the kitchen floor was swimming with water** le sol de la cuisine était inondé. -**3.** [spin]: **my head is swimming** j'ai la tête qui tourne; **that awful feeling when the room starts to ~** cette impression horrible quand la pièce se met à tourner.

◇ *vt* -**1.** [river, lake etc] traverser à la nage; **she swam the (English) Channel** elle a traversé la Manche à la nage. -**2.** [a stroke] nager; **can you ~ butterfly?** est-ce que tu sais nager le papillon? -**3.** [distance] nager; **she swam ten lengths** elle a fait dix longueurs. -**4.** [animal]: **they swam their horses across the river** ils ont fait traverser la rivière à leurs chevaux (à la nage).

◇ *n*: **to go for a ~** [gen] (aller) se baigner; [in swimming pool] aller à la piscine; **he had his morning ~** il s'est baigné comme tous les matins; **I feel like a ~** j'ai envie d'aller me baigner; **did you have a nice ~?** est-ce que la baignade a été agréable?; **it's a good 20-minute ~ out to the island** il faut 20 bonnes minutes pour atteindre l'île à la nage; **it was a long hard ~ back to the shore** ça a été long et difficile de regagner la rive à la nage.

swimmer ['swɪməʳ] *n* [one who swims] nageur *m*, -euse *f*; [bather] baigneur *m*, -euse *f*; **he's an excellent ~** c'est un excellent nageur, il nage très bien.

swimming ['swɪmɪŋ] ◇ *n* [gen] nage *f*; SPORT natation *f*; **her doctor advised her to take up ~** son médecin lui a conseillé la natation; **'~ forbidden'** 'baignade interdite'.

◇ *comp* [lesson, classes] de natation.

swimming bath *n*, **swimming baths** *npl Br* piscine *f*.

swimming cap *n* bonnet *m* de bain.

swimming costume *n Br* maillot *m* de bain.

swimming instructor *n* maître-nageur *m*.

swimmingly *inf* ['swɪmɪŋlɪ] *adv Br* à merveille; **your mother and I are getting on ~** nous nous entendons à merveille, ta mère et moi; **everything's going ~** tout marche comme sur des roulettes.

swimming pool *n* piscine *f*.

swimming trunks *npl* maillot *m* OR slip *m* de bain.

swimsuit ['swɪmsuːt] *n* maillot *m* de bain.

swimwear ['swɪmweəʳ] *n* (*U*) maillots *mpl* de bain.

swindle ['swɪndl] ◇ *vt* escroquer; **they were ~d out of all their savings** on leur a escroqué toutes leurs économies.

◇ *n* escroquerie *f*, vol *m*; **it's a real ~** c'est une véritable escroquerie.

swindler ['swɪndləʳ] *n* escroc *m*.

swine [swaɪn] (*pl sense 1 inv, pl sense 2 inv* OR swines) *n* -**1.** *lit* [pig] porc *m*, pourceau *m lit*. -**2.** *inf* [unpleasant person] fumier *m*, ordure *f*; **you (filthy) ~!** espèce de fumier!; **it's a ~ of a job** c'est un sale boulot.

swine fever *n* peste *f* porcine.

swineherd ['swaɪnhɜːd] *n* porcher *m*, -ère *f*.

swing [swɪŋ] (*pt* & *pp* swung [swʌŋ]) ◇ *vi* -**1.** [sway, move to and fro - gen] se balancer; [- pendulum] osciller; [hang, be suspended] pendre, être suspendu; **to ~ to and fro** se balancer; **he walked along with his arms ~ing** il marchait en balançant les bras; **a basket swung from her arm** un panier se balançait à son bras; **~ing from a cord** suspendu à une corde; **a long rope swung from the ceiling** une longue corde pendait du plafond ❑ **to ~ both ways** *inf* marcher à voile et à vapeur. -**2.** [move from one place to another]: **to ~ from tree to tree** se balancer d'arbre en arbre; **they came ~ing down the street** ils ont descendu la rue d'un pas rapide; **to ~ into action** *fig* passer à l'action. -**3.** [make a turn] virer; **the car swung left** la voiture vira à gauche; **the lorry swung through the gate** le camion vira pour franchir le portail; **the car in front swung out to overtake** la voiture de devant a déboîté pour doubler; **the road ~s east** la route oblique vers l'est; **the door swung open/shut** la porte s'est ouverte/s'est refermée; **the gate swung back in my face** le portail s'est refermé devant moi. -**4.** *fig* [change direction] virer; **the country has swung to the left** le pays a viré à gauche; **her mood ~s between depression and elation** elle passe de la dépression à l'exultation. -**5.** *inf* [be hanged] être pendu; **he'll ~ for this!** il sera pendu pour ça! -**6.** [hit out, aim a blow] essayer de frapper; **he swung at them with the hammer** il a essayé de les frapper avec le marteau; **I swung at him** je lui ai décoché un coup de poing. -**7.** *inf* [musician] swinguer; [music] swinguer, avoir du swing; **the saxophonist really ~s!** il swingue, ce saxo! -**8.** *inf dated* [be modern, fashionable] être dans le vent OR in; **he was there in the sixties, when London was really ~ing** il était là dans les années soixante, quand ça bougeait à Londres. -**9.** *inf* [be lively] chauffer; **the party was beginning to ~** la fête commençait à être très animée. -**10.** *inf* [try hard]: **he's in there ~ing** il fait ce qu'il peut; **I'm in there ~ing for you** je fais tout ce que je peux pour toi.

◇ *vt* -**1.** [cause to sway] balancer; **she was ~ing her umbrella as she walked** elle marchait en balançant son parapluie; **he walked along ~ing his arms** il marchait en balançant les bras; **to ~ one's hips** balancer les OR rouler des hanches. -**2.** [move from one place to another]: she **swung her bag onto the back seat** elle jeta son sac sur le siège arrière; **he swung a rope over a branch** il lança une corde par-dessus une branche; **the crane swung the cargo onto the wharf** la grue pivota pour déposer la cargaison sur le quai; **he swung his son (up) onto his shoulders** il hissa son fils sur ses épaules; **I swung myself (up) into the saddle** je me suis hissé sur la selle, j'ai sauté en selle. -**3.** [turn - steering wheel] (faire) tourner; [- vehicle] faire virer; **the helmsman swung the wheel to port** le timonier fit tourner la roue à bâbord; **she swung the door shut** elle ferma la porte; **I swung the lorry through 180°** j'ai pris le virage à 180° (avec le camion); **the accident swung public opinion against the company** *fig* l'accident a provoqué un revirement de l'opinion contre la compagnie. -**4.** [aim]: **she swung the bat at the ball** elle essaya de frapper la balle avec sa batte; **I swung the club at him** j'ai essayé de le frapper avec le gourdin. -**5.** *inf* [manage, pull off]: **to ~ sthg** réussir OR arriver à faire qqch; **I swung the deal** l'affaire est dans la poche; **I think I should be able to ~ it** je crois pouvoir me débrouiller. -**6.** *inf* **to ~ it** avoir le swing. -**7.** *inf phr*: **to ~ the lead** tirer au flanc.

◇ *n* -**1.** [to-and-fro movement, sway - gen] balancement *m*; [- of pendulum] oscillation *f*; **with a ~ of his arm** en balançant son bras; **a ~ of the political pendulum has restored him to power** un revirement électoral l'a ramené au pouvoir. -**2.** [arc described] arc *m*, courbe *f*; **the plane came round in a wide ~** l'avion décrivit une grande courbe. -**3.** [swipe, attempt to hit] (grand) coup *m*; **I took a ~ at him** je lui ai décoché un coup de poing; **he took a ~ at the ball** il donna un coup pour frapper la balle. -**4.** [hanging seat] balançoire *f*; **they're playing on the ~s** ils jouent sur les balançoires ❑ **what you lose on the ~s you gain on the roundabouts** ce que l'on perd d'un côté, on le récupère de l'autre; **it's ~s and roundabouts really** en fait, on perd d'un côté ce qu'on gagne de l'autre. -**5.** [change, shift] changement *m*; **his mood ~s are very unpredictable** ses sautes d'humeur sont très imprévisibles; **seasonal ~s** COMM fluctuations *fpl* saisonnières; **the upward/downward ~ of the market** ST. EX la fluctuation du marché vers le haut/le bas || POL revirement *m*; **America experienced a major ~ towards conservatism** les États-Unis ont connu un important revirement vers le conservatisme; **the party needs a 10 % ~ to win the election** le parti a besoin d'un revirement d'opinion de 10 % pour gagner aux élections. -**6.** [in boxing, golf] swing *m*. -**7.** [rhythm - gen] rythme *m*; [jazz rhythm, style of jazz] swing *m*; **a ~ band** un orchestre de swing. -**8.** *Am* POL [tour] tournée *f*; **on his ~ around the circle, the President visited 35 States** pendant sa tournée électorale, le Président a visité 35 États. -**9.** *phr*: **to get into the ~ of things** *inf*: **I'm beginning to get into the ~ of things** je commence à être dans le bain; **it'll be a lot easier once you've got into the ~ of things** ce sera beaucoup plus facile une fois que tu seras dans le bain; **to go with a ~** *inf* [music] être très rythmé OR entraînant; [party] swinguer; [business] marcher très bien.

◆ **in full swing** *adj phr*: **the party was in full ~** la fête battait son plein; **production is in full ~** on produit à plein rendement; **the town's packed when the season's in full ~** en pleine saison, il y a foule en ville; **once it's in full ~, the project will require more people** une fois lancé, il faudra plus de gens sur le projet.

◆ **swing round** ◇ *vt sep* [vehicle] faire virer; [person] faire tourner; **he swung the car round the corner** il a tourné au coin; **he swung her round** il la fit tourner.

◇ *vi insep* [turn round - person] se retourner, pivoter; [- crane] tourner, pivoter; **he swung round to look at me** il se retourna pour me regarder.

◆ **swing to** *vi insep* [door, gate] se refermer.

swingboat ['swɪŋbəʊt] *n* nacelle *f (balançoire de champ de foire)*.

swingbridge ['swɪŋbrɪdʒ] *n* pont *m* tournant.

swing door *n* porte *f* battante.

swingeing ['swɪndʒɪŋ] *adj Br* [increase, drop] énorme; [cuts] draconien; [blow] violent; [criticism, condemnation] sévère; [victory, defeat] écrasant.

swinger *inf* ['swɪŋəʳ] *n dated* -**1.** [fashionable person] branché *m*, -e *f*; [pleasure-seeker] noceur *m*, -euse *f*. -**2.** [promiscuous person] débauché *m*, -e *f*.

swinging ['swɪŋɪŋ] *adj* -**1.** [swaying] balançant; [pivoting] tournant, pivotant. -**2.** [rhythmic - gen] rythmé, cadencé; [- jazz, jazz musician] swinguant. -**3.** *inf dated* [trendy] in; **the ~ sixties** les folles années soixante.

swingometer [swɪŋ'ɒmɪtəʳ] *n* indicateur *m* de tendances *(lors de la diffusion télévisée des résultats d'élections législatives)*.

swing shift *inf n Am* [work period] *poste de 16 h à minuit*; [team] *équipe qui travaille de 16 h à minuit*.

swing-wing ◇ *adj* à géométrie variable.

◇ *n* avion *m* à géométrie variable.

swinish *inf* ['swaɪnɪʃ] *adj* sale, pas sympa; **that was a ~ trick!** c'était pas sympa!

swipe [swaɪp] ◇ *vi*: **to ~ at**: **he ~d at the fly with his newspaper** il donna un grand coup de journal pour frapper la mouche; **she ~d at the ball and missed** elle donna un grand coup pour frapper la balle et la manqua.

◇ *vt* -**1.** [hit] donner un coup à. -**2.** *inf* [steal] piquer, faucher.

◇ *n* (grand) coup *m*; **to take a ~ at sthg** *literal* donner un grand coup pour frapper qqch; *fig* [criticize] tirer à boulets rouges sur qqch.

swirl [swɜːl] ◇ *vi* tourbillonner, tournoyer; **the dead leaves ~ed round our feet** les feuilles mortes tourbillonnaient OR tournoyaient à nos pieds; **the water ~ed beneath us** l'eau tourbillonnait au-dessous de nous.

◇ *vt* faire tourbillonner OR tournoyer; **a sudden wind ~ed the leaves around** une brusque bourrasque fit tournoyer OR tourbillonner les feuilles; **~ a bit of water round the sink** rince un peu le lavabo; **the raft was ~ed downstream** le radeau a été emporté dans le tourbillon du courant; **he ~ed her round the dance floor** il la fit tournoyer autour de la piste (de danse).

◇ *n* tourbillon *m*; **~s of smoke rose from the fire** des tourbillons de fumée s'élevaient du feu.

swish [swɪʃ] ◇ *vi* [whip] siffler; [leaves, wind] chuinter, bruire *lit*; [fabric, skirt] froufrouter; [water] murmurer; **the curtains ~ed open/shut** les rideaux s'ouvrirent/se refermèrent en froufroutant.

◇ *vt*: **the horse ~ed its tail** le cheval donna un coup de queue.

◇ *n* -**1.** [sound - of fabric, skirt] froufroutement *m*, froissement *m*; [- of leaves, wind] bruissement *m*; [- of water] murmure *m*. -**2.** [movement]: **the cow flicked the flies away with a ~ of its tail** la vache chassa les mouches d'un coup de queue.

◇ *adj* -**1.** *inf Br* [smart] chic. -**2.** ▽ *Am* [effeminate] efféminé.

swishy *inf* ['swɪʃɪ] (*compar* swishier, *superl* swishiest) = **swish** *adj*.

Swiss [swɪs] (*pl inv*) ◇ *n* Suisse *m*, Suissesse *f*; **the ~** les Suisses *mpl*.

◇ *adj* [gen] suisse; [confederation, constitution, government] helvétique; **the ~ franc** le franc suisse; **~ bank account** compte *m* en Suisse; **'The ~ Family Robinson'** *Wyss* 'le Robinson suisse'.

Swiss chard *n* bette *f*, blette *f*.

Swiss cheese *n* gruyère *m*; **~ plant** monstera *m*.

Swiss-French ◇ *n* -**1.** LING suisse *m* romand. -**2.** [person] Suisse *m* romand, Suisse *f* romande.

◇ *adj* suisse romand.

Swiss-German ◇ *n* -**1.** LING suisse *m* allemand OR alémanique. -**2.** [person] Suisse *m* allemand, Suisse *f* allemande.

◇ *adj* suisse allemand OR alémanique.

Swiss Guard *n* -**1.** [papal bodyguard] garde *f* (pontificale) suisse. -**2.** HIST [in France] membre *m* des troupes suisses; **the ~** les troupes *fpl* suisses.

swiss roll *n* (gâteau *m*) roulé *m*.

switch [swɪtʃ] ◇ *n* -**1.** ELEC [for light] interrupteur *m*; [on radio, television] bouton *m*; TECH & TELEC commutateur *m*; **is the ~ on/off?** est-ce que c'est allumé/éteint?; **to flick** OR **to throw a ~** actionner un commutateur; **two-way ~** (interrupteur *m*) va-et-vient *m*. -**2.** [change - gen] changement *m*; [- of opinion, attitude] changement *m*, revirement *m*; **the ~ to the new equipment went very smoothly** on s'est très bien adaptés au nouveau matériel; **a sudden ~ in foreign policy** un subit revirement de la politique étrangère. -**3.** [swap, trade] échange *m*. -**4.** *Am* RAIL: **~es** [points] aiguillage *m*. -**5.** [stick] baguette *f*, badine *f*; [riding crop] cravache *f*. -**6.** [hairpiece] postiche *m*. -**7.** ZOOL [hair on tail] fouet *m* de la queue.

◇ *vt* -**1.** [change, exchange] changer de; **he ~ed subjects after two years at university** il a changé de filière après deux ans d'université; **the two employees asked to ~ jobs** les deux employés ont demandé à échanger leurs postes; **to ~ places with sb** échanger sa place avec qqn; **she offered to ~ jobs with me** elle a offert d'échanger son poste contre le mien. -**2.** [transfer - allegiance, attention] transférer; **she ~ed her attention back to the speaker** elle reporta son attention sur le conférencier || [divert - conversation] orienter, détourner; **I tried to ~ the discussion to something less controversial** j'ai essayé d'orienter la discussion vers un sujet moins épineux. -**3.** ELEC, RADIO & TV [circuit] commuter; **to ~ channels/frequencies** changer de chaîne/de fréquence. -**4.** *Am* RAIL aiguiller; **the freight train was ~ed to another track** le train de marchandises fut aiguillé sur une autre voie.

◇ *vi* changer; **she started studying medicine but ~ed to architecture** elle a commencé par étudier la médecine, mais elle a changé pour faire architecture; **I'd like to ~ to another topic** j'aimerais changer de sujet; **can I ~ to another channel?** est-ce que je peux changer de chaîne?; **the committee ~ed to the problem of recruitment** le comité passa au problème du recrutement; **we've ~ed to another brand** nous avons changé de marque; **they've ~ed to American equipment** ils ont adopté du matériel américain; **he ~es effortlessly from one language to another** il passe d'une langue à une autre avec une grande aisance.

◆ **switch around** = **switch round**.

◆ **switch off** ◇ *vt sep* [light] éteindre; [electrical appliance] éteindre, arrêter; **don't forget to ~ the lights off when you leave** n'oublie pas d'éteindre la lumière en partant; **the radio ~es itself off** la radio s'éteint OR s'arrête automatiquement; **they've ~ed off the power** ils ont coupé le courant; **to ~ off the engine** AUT couper le contact, arrêter le moteur.

◇ *vi insep* -**1.** [go off - light] s'éteindre; [- electrical appliance] s'éteindre, s'arrêter; **how do you get the oven to ~ off?** comment tu éteins le four? -**2.** [TV viewer, radio listener] éteindre le poste; **don't ~ off!** restez à l'écoute! -**3.** *inf* [stop paying attention] décrocher; **he ~es off whenever we talk about politics** il décroche chaque fois qu'on parle politique.

◆ **switch on** ◇ *vt sep* -**1.** ELEC [light, heating, oven, TV, radio] allumer; [engine, washing machine, vacuum cleaner] mettre en marche; **could you ~ on the light?** pourrais-tu allumer (la lumière)?; **the power isn't ~ed on** il n'y a pas de courant; **to ~ on the ignition** AUT mettre le contact. -**2.** *fig & pej*: **to ~ on the charm/tears** sourire/pleurer sur commande.

◇ *vi insep* -**1.** ELEC [light, heating, oven, TV, radio] s'allumer; [engine, washing machine, vacuum cleaner] se mettre en marche; **the lights ~ on and off automatically** les lumières s'allument et s'éteignent automatiquement. -**2.** [TV viewer, radio listener] allumer le poste; don't forget to ~ on at the same time tomorrow! soyez à l'écoute demain à la même heure!

◆ **switch over** *vi insep* -**1.** = **switch** *vi*. -**2.** TV changer de chaîne; RADIO changer de station; can we ~ over at 8 p.m.? est-ce que nous pouvons changer de chaîne à 20 h?

◆ **switch round** ◇ *vt sep* changer de place, déplacer; he ~ed the glasses round when she wasn't looking il échangea les verres pendant qu'elle ne regardait pas; the manager has ~ed the team round again l'entraîneur a encore changé l'équipe.
◇ *vi insep* [two people] changer de place; she's ~ed round with her brother elle a changé de place avec son frère.

switchback ['swɪtʃbæk] ◇ *n* -**1.** [road] route *f* accidentée et sinueuse. -**2.** *Br* [roller coaster] montagnes *fpl* russes.
◇ *adj*: a ~ road une route accidentée et sinueuse.

switchblade ['swɪtʃbleɪd] *n Am* (couteau *m* à) cran d'arrêt *m*.

switchboard ['swɪtʃbɔːd] *n* -**1.** TELEC standard *m*. -**2.** ELEC tableau *m*.

switchboard operator *n* standardiste *mf*.

switched-on *inf adj Br dated* [fashionable] dans le vent, in.

switcheroo▽ [,swɪtʃə'ruː] *n Am* changement *m* inattendu; to pull a ~ surprendre tout le monde.

switchgear ['swɪtʃgɪəʳ] *n* appareillage *m* de commutation.

switch-hitter *n Am* -**1.** SPORT batteur *m* ambidextre. -**2.** ▽ [bisexual] bi *mf*; he's a ~ il marche à voile et à vapeur.

switching ['swɪtʃɪŋ] *n* COMPUT, ELEC & TELEC commutation *f*; data/packet ~ COMPUT commutation de données/par paquets.

switchman ['swɪtʃmən] (*pl* switchmen [-mən]) *n Am* aiguilleur *m*.

switchover ['swɪtʃ,əʊvəʳ] *n* [to another method, system] passage *m*, conversion *f*; there's to be a ~ from the British to the continental system il va y avoir un passage du système britannique au système continental.

switchyard ['swɪtʃjɑːd] *n Am* gare *f* de triage.

Switzerland ['swɪtsələnd] *pr n* Suisse *f*; in ~ en Suisse; French-/Italian-speaking ~ la Suisse romande/italienne; German-speaking ~ la Suisse allemande OR alémanique.

swivel ['swɪvl] (*Br pt* & *pp* swivelled, *cont* swivelling, *Am pt* & *pp* swiveled, *cont* swiveling) ◇ *n* [gen] pivot *m*; [for gun] tourillon *m*.
◇ *comp* [lamp, joint etc] pivotant, tournant.
◇ *vi*: to ~ (round) pivoter, tourner; she swivelled round in her chair elle pivota sur sa chaise; his eyes swivelled back to the screen ses yeux se tournèrent à nouveau vers l'écran.
◇ *vt*: to ~ (round) [chair, wheel etc] faire pivoter.

swivel chair *n* chaise *f* pivotante; [with arms] fauteuil *m* pivotant.

swivel pin *n* AUT pivot *m* central.

swiz(z) *inf* [swɪz] *n Br* escroquerie *f*, vol *m*; what a ~! c'est du vol!

swizzle ['swɪzl] *n* -**1.** *inf Br* = **swiz(z)**. -**2.** *Am* [cocktail] cocktail *m (préparé dans un verre mélangeur)*.

swizzle stick *n* fouet *m*.

swollen ['swəʊln] ◇ *pp* → **swell**.
◇ *adj* -**1.** [part of body] enflé, gonflé; her ankle was badly ~ sa cheville était très enflée; his face was ~ il avait le visage enflé OR bouffi; starving children with ~ abdomens des enfants affamés au ventre ballonné; her eyes were red and ~ with crying elle avait les yeux rouges et gonflés à force de pleurer. -**2.** [sails] bombé, gonflé; [lake, river] en crue.

swollen-headed *inf* = **swell-headed**.

swoon [swuːn] ◇ *vi* -**1.** [become ecstatic] se pâmer, tomber en pâmoison; he used to make all the young girls ~ il fut un temps où toutes les jeunes filles se pâmaient devant lui. -**2.** *dated* [faint] s'évanouir, se pâmer *lit*.
◇ *n* pâmoison *f*; to fall to the ground in a ~ tomber par terre en pâmoison; she was (all) in a ~ over meeting her idol elle était tout en émoi après avoir rencontré son idole.

swoop [swuːp] ◇ *vi* -**1.** [dive - bird] s'abattre, fondre; [- aircraft] piquer, descendre en piqué; the gulls ~ed down on the rocks les mouettes s'abattirent sur OR fondirent sur les rochers; the helicopter ~ed low over the battlefield l'hélicoptère descendit en piqué au-dessus du champ de bataille. -**2.** [make a raid - police, troops etc] faire une descente.
◇ *n* -**1.** [dive - by bird, aircraft] descente *f* en piqué. -**2.** [raid - by police, troops etc] descente *f*; a dawn ~ une descente à l'aube; fifteen arrested in drugs ~ quinze personnes arrêtées dans une opération anti-drogue. -**3.** *phr*: in one fell ~ d'un seul coup.

swoosh *inf* [swʊʃ] ◇ *vi* [water] murmurer; [vehicle, tyres] siffler, chuinter; the express train ~ed past le rapide est passé à toute vitesse; the car ~ed through the puddle la voiture a fait gicler l'eau en passant dans la flaque.
◇ *n* bruissement *m*, chuintement *m*, sifflement *m*.

swop [swɒp] (*pt* & *pp* swopped, *cont* swopping) = **swap**.

sword [sɔːd] ◇ *n* épée *f*; they fought with ~s ils se sont battus à l'épée; all the prisoners were put to the ~ tous les prisonniers furent passés au fil de l'épée; the ~ of justice le glaive de la justice; he lived by the ~ and died by the ~ il a vécu par l'épée, il a péri par l'épée.
◇ *comp* [blow, handle, wound] d'épée.

swordbearer ['sɔːd,beərəʳ] *n* [in ceremony] *officier qui porte le glaive*.

sword dance *n* danse *f* du sabre.

sword-fight *n* [between two people] duel *m* (à l'épée); [between several people] bataille *f* à l'épée.

swordfish ['sɔːdfɪʃ] (*pl inv* OR swordfishes) *n* espadon *m*, poisson-épée *m*.

swordplay ['sɔːdpleɪ] *n* [skill] maniement *m* de l'épée; they were taught riding and ~ on leur apprenait à monter à cheval et à manier l'épée ‖ [activity]: the last scene consisted of ~ la dernière scène était une scène de combats à l'épée.

swordsman ['sɔːdzmən] (*pl* swordsmen [-mən]) *n* épéiste *m*, lame *f (personne)*; he's a fine ~ c'est une fine lame.

swordsmanship ['sɔːdzmənʃɪp] *n* maniement *m* de l'épée; we admired her ~ nous admirâmes sa façon de manier l'épée.

swordstick ['sɔːdstɪk] *n* canne-épée *f*, canne *f* armée.

sword-swallower *n* avaleur *m*, -euse *f* de sabres.

swore [swɔːʳ] *pt* → **swear**.

sworn [swɔːn] ◇ *pp* → **swear**.
◇ *adj* -**1.** JUR [declaration] fait sous serment; [evidence] donné sous serment; ~ affidavits des déclarations faites sous serment; a ~ statement une déposition faite sous serment. -**2.** [committed - enemy] juré; [- friend] indéfectible.

swot *inf* [swɒt] (*pt* & *pp* swotted, *cont* swotting) *Br* ◇ *vi* bûcher, potasser; to ~ for an exam bûcher OR potasser un examen.
◇ *n pej* bûcheur *m*, -euse *f*.

◆ **swot up** *inf Br* ◇ *vi insep* bûcher, potasser; to ~ up on sthg bûcher OR potasser qqch.
◇ *vt sep* bûcher, potasser.

swotting *inf* ['swɒtɪŋ] *n Br* bachotage *m*; I'll have to do some ~ to pass my exam il va falloir que je bûche OR que je potasse pour réussir mon examen.

swum [swʌm] *pp* → **swim**.

swung [swʌŋ] *pt* & *pp* → **swing**.

swung dash *n* tilde *m*.

sybarite ['sɪbəraɪt] *n* sybarite *mf*.

sybaritic [,sɪbə'rɪtɪk] *adj* sybarite.

sycamore ['sɪkəmɔːʳ] *n* sycomore *m*, faux platane *m*.

sycophancy ['sɪkəfənsɪ] *n* flagornerie *f*.

sycophant ['sɪkəfænt] *n* flagorneur *m*, -euse *f*.

sycophantic [,sɪkə'fæntɪk] *adj* [person] flatteur, flagorneur; [behaviour] de flagorneur; [approval, praise] obséquieux.

Sydney ['sɪdnɪ] *pr n* Sydney.

syllabary ['sɪləbərɪ] (*pl* syllabaries) *n* syllabaire *m*.

syllabi ['sɪləbaɪ] *pl* → **syllabus**.

syllabic [sɪ'læbɪk] *adj* syllabique.

syllabify [sɪ'læbɪfaɪ] (*pt* & *pp* syllabified) *vt* décomposer en syllabes.

syllable ['sɪləbl] *n* syllabe *f*; I had to explain it to him in words of one ~ j'ai dû le lui expliquer en termes simples.

syllabled ['sɪləbld] *adj* prononcé OR écrit en syllabes.

syllabub ['sɪləbʌb] *n* -**1.** *Br* [dessert] (crème *f*) sabayon *m*. -**2.** [drink] *boisson à base de lait, alcoolisée, relevée et souvent chaude*.

syllabus ['sɪləbəs] (*pl* syllabuses OR syllabi [-baɪ]) *n* programme *m* (d'enseignement) SCOL & UNIV; do you know what's on the ~? savez-vous ce qu'il y a au programme?; the teacher handed out copies of the ~ le professeur distribua des exemplaires du programme.

syllepsis [sɪ'lepsɪs] (*pl* syllepses [-siːz]) *n* syllepse *f*.

syllogism ['sɪlədʒɪzm] *n* syllogisme *m*.

syllogistic [,sɪlə'dʒɪstɪk] *adj* syllogistique.

syllogize, -ise ['sɪlədʒaɪz] *vi* raisonner par syllogismes.

sylph [sɪlf] *n* -**1.** [mythical being] sylphe *m*. -**2.** *lit* [girl, woman] sylphide *f*.

sylphlike ['sɪlflaɪk] *adj lit* [figure] gracile, de sylphe; [woman] gracieuse; you're looking positively ~, my dear *hum* tu es une vraie sylphide, ma chère.

sylvan ['sɪlvən] *adj lit* sylvestre.

sylvanite ['sɪlvənaɪt] *n* sylvanite *f* graphique.

Sylvester [sɪl'vestəʳ] *pr n*: Saint ~ saint Sylvestre.

symbiosis [,sɪmbaɪ'əʊsɪs] *n literal* & *fig* symbiose *f*; in ~ en symbiose.

symbiotic [,sɪmbaɪ'ɒtɪk] *adj literal* & *fig* symbiotique; a ~ relationship une association symbiotique.

symbol ['sɪmbl] *n* symbole *m*.

symbolic(al) [sɪm'bɒlɪk(l)] *adj* symbolique.

symbolically [sɪm'bɒlɪklɪ] *adv* symboliquement.

symbolism ['sɪmbəlɪzm] *n* symbolisme *m*.

symbolist ['sɪmbəlɪst] ◇ *adj* symboliste.
◇ *n* symboliste *mf*.

symbolization [,sɪmbəlaɪ'zeɪʃn] *n* symbolisation *f*.

symbolize, -ise ['sɪmbəlaɪz] *vt* symboliser.

symmetric [sɪ'metrɪk] *adj* LOGIC & MATH symétrique.

symmetrical [sɪ'metrɪkl] *adj* symétrique.

symmetrically [sɪ'metrɪklɪ] *adv* symétriquement.

symmetry ['sɪmətrɪ] *n* symétrie *f*.

sympathetic [,sɪmpə'θetɪk] *adj* -**1.** [compassionate] compatissant; ~ words des paroles compatissantes OR de sympathie; they weren't very ~ ils ne se sont pas montrés très compatissants. -**2.** [well-disposed] bien disposé; [understanding] compréhensif; the public is generally ~ to OR towards the strikers l'opinion publique est dans l'ensemble bien disposée envers les grévistes; she spoke to a ~ audience elle s'adressa à un auditoire bienveillant; the town council was ~ to our grievances la municipalité a accueilli nos revendications avec compréhension. -**3.** [congenial, likeable] sympathique, agréable; he's not a very ~ character ce n'est pas un personnage très sympathique. -**4.** ANAT sympathique; the ~ nervous system le système nerveux sympathique, le sympathique.

-**5.** MUS: ~ string corde *f* qui vibre par résonance.

sympathetically [ˌsɪmpəˈθetɪklɪ] *adv* -**1.** [compassionately] avec compassion; **"I understand how you feel", she said ~** «je vous comprends», dit-elle avec compassion; **he patted me ~ on the hand** il me donna une petite tape sur la main en signe de compassion OR de sympathie. -**2.** [with approval] avec bienveillance; **she received his request ~** elle reçut sa requête avec bienveillance. -**3.** ANAT par sympathie.

sympathize, -ise [ˈsɪmpəθaɪz] *vi* -**1.** [feel compassion] sympathiser, compatir; **we all ~d with him when his wife left** nous avons tous compati à son malheur quand sa femme est partie; **poor Emma, I really ~ with her!** cette pauvre Emma, je la plains vraiment! -**2.** [feel understanding]: **he could not ~ with their feelings** il ne pouvait pas comprendre leurs sentiments; **we understand and ~ with their point of view** nous comprenons et partageons leur point de vue. -**3.** [favour, support] sympathiser; **certain heads of state openly ~d with the terrorists** certains chefs d'État sympathisaient ouvertement avec les terroristes.

sympathizer [ˈsɪmpəθaɪzəʳ] *n* -**1.** [comforter]: **she received many cards from ~s after her husband's death** elle a reçu de nombreuses cartes de condoléances après la mort de son mari. -**2.** [supporter] sympathisant *m*, -e *f*; **she was suspected of being a communist ~** elle était soupçonnée d'être sympathisante communiste.

sympathy [ˈsɪmpəθɪ] (*pl* **sympathies**) *n* -**1.** [compassion] compassion *f*; **to have** OR **to feel ~ for sb** éprouver de la compassion envers qqn; **he showed no ~ for the children** il n'a fait preuve d'aucune compassion envers les enfants; **her tears were only a means of gaining ~** elle ne pleurait que pour qu'on s'attendrisse sur elle; **a ~ card** une carte de condoléances; **you have my deepest sympathies** toutes mes condoléances. -**2.** [approval, support] soutien *m*; **the audience was clearly not in ~ with the speaker** il était évident que le public ne partageait pas les sentiments de l'orateur; **she has strong left-wing sympathies** elle est très à gauche; **I have no ~ for** OR **with terrorism** je désapprouve tout à fait le terrorisme; **his sympathies did not lie with his own class** il ne partageait pas les valeurs de sa propre classe; **to come out in ~ (with sb)** faire grève par solidarité (avec qqn). -**3.** [affinity] sympathie *f*; **there was a strong bond of ~ between them** ils étaient liés par une forte sympathie.

sympathy strike *n* grève *f* de solidarité.

symphonic [sɪmˈfɒnɪk] *adj* symphonique; **a ~ poem** un poème symphonique.

symphony [ˈsɪmfənɪ] (*pl* **symphonies**) ◇ *n* symphonie *f*; **the landscape was a ~ of browns and greens** *fig* & *lit* le paysage était une symphonie de bruns et de verts.
◇ *comp* [concert, orchestra] symphonique.

symposium [sɪmˈpəʊzjəm] (*pl* **symposiums** OR **symposia** [-zjə]) symposium *m*, colloque *m*; **'The Symposium'** *Plato* 'le Banquet'.

symptom [ˈsɪmptəm] *n* MED & *fig* symptôme *m*; **to show ~s of fatigue** donner des signes de fatigue.

symptomatic [ˌsɪmptəˈmætɪk] *adj* MED & *fig* symptomatique.

symptomatology [ˌsɪmptəməˈtɒlədʒɪ] *n* symptomatologie *f*.

synaeresis [sɪˈnɪərəsɪs] (*pl* **synaereses** [-siːz]) = **syneresis**.

synaesthesia *Br*, **synesthesia** *Am* [ˌsɪnɪsˈθiːzjə] *n* synesthésie *f*.

synagogue [ˈsɪnəgɒg] *n* synagogue *f*.

synal(o)epha [ˌsɪnəˈliːfə] *n* synalèphe *f*.

synapse [ˈsaɪnæps] *n* synapse *f*.

synapsis [sɪˈnæpsɪs] *n* synapsis *f*.

sync(h) *inf* [sɪŋk] ◇ *n* (*abbr of* synchronization) synchronisation *f*; **to be in/out of ~** être/ne pas être synchro.
◇ *vt abbr of* **synchronize**.

synchro *inf* [ˈsɪŋkrəʊ] *n* = **synchromesh**.

synchroflash [ˈsɪŋkrəʊflæʃ] *n* flash *m* synchronisé.

synchromesh [ˈsɪŋkrəʊmeʃ] ◇ *adj*: **~ gears** boîte *f* de vitesses avec synchroniseur.
◇ *n* synchroniseur *m*.

synchronic [sɪŋˈkrɒnɪk] *adj* synchronique.

synchronism [ˈsɪŋkrənɪzm] *n* synchronisme *m*.

synchronization [ˌsɪŋkrənaɪˈzeɪʃn] *n* synchronisation *f*.

synchronize, -ise [ˈsɪŋkrənaɪz] ◇ *vt* synchroniser; **~d swimming** natation *f* synchronisée.
◇ *vi* être synchronisé; **the chimes of the clocks ~d perfectly** les carillons des horloges étaient parfaitement synchronisés.

synchronous [ˈsɪŋkrənəs] *adj* synchrone.

syncline [ˈsɪŋklaɪn] *n* synclinal *m*.

syncopate [ˈsɪŋkəpeɪt] *vt* syncoper; **~d rhythm** rythme *m* syncopé.

syncopation [ˌsɪŋkəˈpeɪʃn] *n* syncope *f* MUS.

syncope [ˈsɪŋkəpɪ] *n* syncope *f* LING & MED.

syncretism [ˈsɪŋkrɪtɪzm] *n* syncrétisme *m*.

syncretize, -ise [ˈsɪŋkrətaɪz] ◇ *vt* rendre syncrétique.
◇ *vi* devenir syncrétique.

syndetic [sɪnˈdetɪk] *adj*: **~ clause** clause *f* reliée par syndèse.

syndic [ˈsɪndɪk] *n* syndic *m*.

syndicalism [ˈsɪndɪkəlɪzm] *n* [doctrine] syndicalisme *m* révolutionnaire.

syndicalist [ˈsɪndɪkəlɪst] ◇ *n* syndicaliste *mf* révolutionnaire.
◇ *adj* de syndicalisme révolutionnaire.

syndicate [*n* ˈsɪndɪkət, *vb* ˈsɪndɪkeɪt] ◇ *n* -**1.** COMM & FIN groupement *m*, syndicat *m*; **the loan was underwritten by a ~ of banks** le prêt était garanti par un consortium bancaire; **a ~ of British and French companies** un groupement de sociétés françaises et britanniques. -**2.** [of organized crime] association *f*; **crime ~s** associations de grand banditisme; **the Syndicate** la Mafia. -**3.** PRESS agence *f* de presse *(qui vend des articles, des photos etc à plusieurs journaux pour publication simultanée)*.
◇ *vt* -**1.** COMM & FIN [loan] syndiquer. -**2.** PRESS publier simultanément dans plusieurs journaux; *Am* RADIO vendre à plusieurs stations; *Am* TV vendre à plusieurs chaînes; **she writes a ~d column** elle écrit une chronique qui est publiée dans plusieurs journaux; **the photograph was ~d in all the local newspapers** la photographie a été publiée dans toute la presse régionale; **a ~d TV news programme** des informations télévisées reprises par plusieurs chaînes.
◇ *vi* [form a syndicate] former un groupement OR syndicat.

syndrome [ˈsɪndrəʊm] *n* syndrome *m*.

synecdoche [sɪnˈekdəkɪ] *n* synecdoque *f*.

syneresis [sɪˈnɪərəsɪs] (*pl* **synereses** [-siːz]) *n* synérèse *f*.

synergism [ˈsɪnədʒɪzm] = **synergy**.

synergy [ˈsɪnədʒɪ] (*pl* **synergies**) *n* synergie *f*.

synesthesia *Am* = **synaesthesia**.

synod [ˈsɪnəd] *n* synode *m*; **the (General) Synod** *le Synode général de l'Église d'Angleterre*.

synonym [ˈsɪnənɪm] *n* synonyme *m*.

synonymous [sɪˈnɒnɪməs] *adj literal* & *fig* synonyme; **success is not always ~ with merit** succès n'est pas toujours synonyme de mérite; **the two words are not really ~** les deux mots ne sont pas vraiment synonymes.

synonymy [sɪˈnɒnɪmɪ] *n* synonymie *f*.

synopsis [sɪˈnɒpsɪs] (*pl* **synopses** [-siːz]) *n* [gen] résumé *m*; [of a film] synopsis *m*.

synopsize, -ise [sɪˈnɒpsaɪz] *vt Am* [summarize] résumer, faire un résumé de.

synoptic [sɪˈnɒptɪk] *adj* synoptique; **the ~ gospels** les Évangiles synoptiques.

syntactic [sɪnˈtæktɪk] *adj* syntaxique; **~ analysis** analyse *f* syntaxique.

syntactically [sɪnˈtæktɪklɪ] *adv* du point de vue syntaxique.

syntactics [sɪnˈtæktɪks] *n* *(U)* syntactique *f*.

syntagm [ˈsɪntæm] *n* syntagme *m*.

syntagmatic [ˌsɪntægˈmætɪk] *adj* syntagmatique.

syntax [ˈsɪntæks] *n* syntaxe *f*.

syntax error *n* COMPUT erreur *f* de syntaxe.

synthesis [ˈsɪnθəsɪs] (*pl* **syntheses** [-siːz]) *n* synthèse *f*; **the ~ of vitamin D** la synthèse de la vitamine D; **his work is a ~ of Eastern and Western philosophies** son œuvre est une synthèse des philosophies orientales et occidentales.

synthesize, -ise [ˈsɪnθəsaɪz] *vt* -**1.** BIOL & CHEM [produce by synthesis] synthétiser; **the hormone ~d by this gland** l'hormone synthétisée par cette glande. -**2.** [amalgamate, fuse] synthétiser. -**3.** MUS synthétiser.

synthesizer [ˈsɪnθəsaɪzəʳ] *n* synthétiseur *m*; **voice ~** synthétiseur *m* de voix.

synthetic [sɪnˈθetɪk] ◇ *adj* -**1.** [artificial, electronically produced] synthétique; **~ fibre/rubber** fibre *f*/caoutchouc *m* synthétique; **research on ~ speech** les recherches sur la parole synthétique; **~ image** image *f* de synthèse. -**2.** *fig* & *pej* [food] qui a un goût chimique. -**3.** LING synthétique. -**4.** PHILOS [reasoning, proposition] synthétique.
◇ *n* produit *m* synthétique.
◆ **synthetics** *npl* fibres *fpl* synthétiques.

synthetically [sɪnˈθetɪklɪ] *adv* synthétiquement.

syphilis [ˈsɪfɪlɪs] *n* *(U)* syphilis *f*.

syphilitic [ˌsɪfɪˈlɪtɪk] ◇ *adj* syphilitique.
◇ *n* syphilitique *mf*.

syphon [ˈsaɪfn] = **siphon**.

Syracuse [ˈsaɪərəkjuːz] *pr n* Syracuse.

Syria [ˈsɪrɪə] *pr n* Syrie *f*; **in ~** en Syrie.

Syrian [ˈsɪrɪən] ◇ *n* Syrien *m*, -enne *f*.
◇ *adj* syrien; **the ~ Desert** le désert de Syrie.

syringe [sɪˈrɪndʒ] ◇ *n* seringue *f*.
◇ *vt* seringuer.

syrup [ˈsɪrəp] *n* -**1.** [sweetened liquid] sirop *m*; **peaches in ~** pêches *fpl* au sirop; **~ of figs** sirop de figues. -**2.** [treacle] mélasse *f*. -**3.** MED sirop *m*; **cough ~** sirop *m* contre la toux.

syrupy [ˈsɪrəpɪ] *adj* -**1.** [viscous] sirupeux. -**2.** *pej* [sentimental] sirupeux, à l'eau de rose.

systaltic [sɪˈstæltɪk] *adj* systolique.

system [ˈsɪstəm] *n* -**1.** [organization, structure] système *m*; **the British legal/educational ~** le système juridique/éducatif britannique; **the Social Security ~** le système des prestations sociales; **they live in a democratic/totalitarian ~** ils vivent dans un système démocratique/totalitaire; **the binary/metric ~** le système binaire/métrique ❑ **the solar ~** le système solaire. -**2.** [method] système *m*; **a new ~ of sorting mail** un nouveau système pour trier le courrier. -**3.** ANAT système *m*; **the nervous/muscular/immune ~** le système nerveux/musculaire/immunitaire; **the digestive ~** l'appareil *m* digestif. -**4.** [orderliness] méthode *f*; **you need some ~ in the way you work** vous devriez être plus systématique OR méthodique dans votre travail. -**5.** [human body] organisme *m*; **bad for the ~** nuisible à l'organisme ‖ *fig*: **to get sthg out of one's ~** se débarrasser de qqch; **go on, get it out of your ~!** vas-y, défoule-toi!; **she can't get him out of her ~** elle n'arrive pas à l'oublier. -**6.** [equipment, device, devices]: **the electrical ~ needs to be replaced** l'installation électrique a besoin d'être remplacée; **a fault in the cooling ~** un défaut dans le circuit de refroidissement; **he's on a life-support ~** il est sous assistance respiratoire; **sprinkler ~** installation *f* d'extinction automatique d'incendie; stereo ~ chaîne *f* stéréo. -**7.** [network] réseau *m*; the rail/river/road ~ le réseau ferroviaire/fluvial/routier. -**8.** COMPUT système *m*; operating ~ système *m* d'exploitation. -**9.** [established order] : the ~ le système; they're hoping to overthrow the ~ ils espèrent renverser le système (en place); you can't beat OR buck the ~ *inf* on ne peut rien contre le système. -**10.** GEOL système *m*; the Precambrian ~ le système précambrien.

systematic [ˌsɪstəˈmætɪk] *adj* systématique.

systematically [ˌsɪstəˈmætɪklɪ] *adv* systématiquement.

systematics [ˌsɪstəˈmætɪks] *n (U)* systématique *f*.

systematization [ˌsɪstɪmətaɪˈzeɪʃn] *n* systématisation *f*.

systematize, -ise [ˈsɪstəmətaɪz] *vt* systématiser.

system disk *n* COMPUT disque *m* système.

system error *n* COMPUT erreur *f* système.

systemic [sɪsˈtemɪk] *adj* systémique.

systems analysis *n* analyse *f* fonctionnelle.

systems analyst *n* spécialiste *mf* méthodes.

systems engineer *n* ingénieur *m* système.

systems engineering *n* systémie *f*.

system software *n* COMPUT logiciel *m* d'exploitation.

systole [ˈsɪstəlɪ] *n* systole *f*.

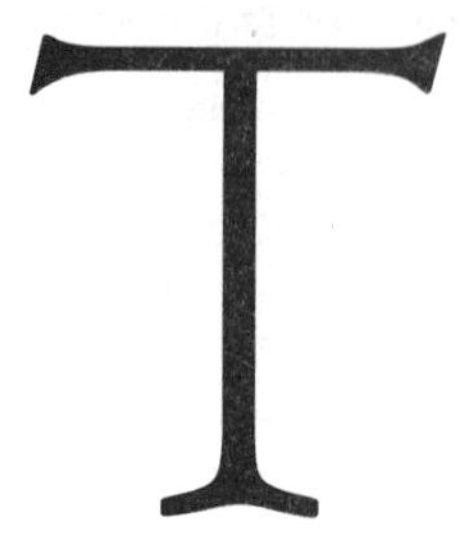

t (*pl* t's OR ts), **T** (*pl* T's OR Ts) [tiː] *n* [letter] t *m*, T *m*; T for Tommy ≃ T comme Thérèse; to a T parfaitement, à merveille; you've described him to a T vous l'avez parfaitement décrit; that's her to a T c'est tout à fait elle; the jacket fits OR suits her to a T la veste lui va à merveille.

ta *inf* [tɑː] *interj Br* merci.

TA *n abbr of* Territorial Army.

tab [tæb] *n* -**1.** [on garment - flap] patte *f*; [- loop] attache *f*; [over ear] oreillette *f*; [on shoelaces] ferret *m*. -**2.** [tag - on clothing, luggage] étiquette *f*; [- on file, dictionary] onglet *m*; *fig*: to keep ~s on sb avoir qqn à l'œil, avoir l'œil sur qqn; I'll keep ~s on how the case progresses je vais surveiller l'évolution de cette affaire. -**3.** [bill] addition *f*, note *f*; to pick up the ~ *literal* payer (la note); *fig* payer l'addition. -**4.** AERON compensateur *m* automatique à ressort. -**5.** *abbr of* tabulator.

tabard ['tæbəd] *n* tabard *m*.

Tabasco® [tə'bæskəʊ] *n* Tabasco® *m*.

tabby ['tæbɪ] (*pl* tabbies) ◇ *n*: ~ (cat) chat *m* tigré, chatte *f* tigrée.
◇ *adj* tigré.

tabernacle ['tæbənækl] *n* -**1.** BIBLE & RELIG tabernacle *m*. -**2.** [place of worship] temple *m*.

table ['teɪbl] ◇ *n* -**1.** [furniture] table *f*; to get round the negotiating ~ s'asseoir à la table des négociations ‖ [for meals] table *f*; to be at ~ être à table; we sat down to ~ nous nous sommes mis à table; may I leave the ~? puis-je sortir de table OR quitter la table? ☐ (coffee) ~ table *f* (basse). -**2.** [people seated] table *f*, tablée *f*; my uncle kept the whole ~ amused mon oncle a diverti toute la tablée; we were seated with a ~ of card players nous étions assis à une table de joueurs de cartes. -**3.** *fml* [food]: she keeps an excellent ~ elle a une excellente table. -**4.** TECH [of machine] table *f*; MUS [of violin] table *f* d'harmonie. -**5.** [list] liste *f*; [chart] table *f*, tableau *m*; [of fares, prices] tableau *m*, barème *m*; the results are set out in the following ~ les résultats sont donnés dans le tableau suivant ‖ SPORT: (league) ~ classement *m*; our team came bottom in the ~ notre équipe s'est classée dernière OR était dernière au classement ‖ SCH: (multiplication) ~ table *f* (de multiplication); we have to learn our 4 times ~ il faut qu'on apprenne la table de 4 ☐ ~ of contents table *f* des matières. -**6.** [slab - of stone, marble] plaque *f*; the Tables of the Law BIBLE les Tables de la Loi. -**7.** GEOG plateau *m*. -**8.** ANAT [of cranium] table *f*. -**9.** *phr*: to put OR to lay sthg on the ~ mettre qqch sur la table; we will not negotiate until they put a better offer on the ~ nous ne négocierons pas tant qu'ils ne mettront pas une meilleure offre sur la table; under the ~: to be under the ~ [drunk] rouler sous la table, être ivre mort; he can drink me under the ~ il peut boire beaucoup plus que moi; the man offered me £100 under the ~ l'homme m'a offert 100 livres en dessous-de-table.
◇ *comp* [lamp, leg, linen] de table.
◇ *vt* -**1.** [submit - bill, motion] présenter. -**2.** *Am* [postpone] ajourner, reporter; the bill has been ~d la discussion du projet de loi a été reportée. -**3.** [tabulate] présenter sous forme de tableau; [classify] classifier. -**4.** [schedule] prévoir, fixer; the discussion is ~d for 4 o'clock la discussion est prévue OR a été fixée à 16 h.

tableau ['tæbləʊ] (*pl* tableaus OR tableaux [-bləʊz]) *n* tableau *m*.

tablecloth ['teɪblklɒθ] *n* nappe *f*.

table lamp *n* lampe *f* (de table).

tableland ['teɪbllænd] *n* plateau *m* GEOG.

table licence *n Br licence autorisant un restaurant à vendre des boissons alcoolisées uniquement avec les repas*.

table manners *npl* manière *f* de se tenir à table; he has terrible/excellent ~ il se tient très mal/très bien à table.

tablemat ['teɪblmæt] *n* dessous-de-plat *m inv*; [of fabric] napperon *m*.

Table Mountain *pr n* la Montagne de la Table.

table salt *n* sel *m* de table, sel *m* fin.

tablespoon ['teɪblspuːn] *n* [for serving] grande cuillère *f*, cuillère *f* à soupe; [as measure] grande cuillerée *f*, cuillerée *f* à soupe.

tablespoonful ['teɪbl,spuːnfʊl] *n* grande cuillerée *f*, cuillerée *f* à soupe.

tablet ['tæblɪt] *n* -**1.** [for writing - stone, wax etc] tablette *f*; [- pad] bloc-notes *m*. -**2.** [pill] comprimé *m*, cachet *m*. -**3.** [of chocolate] tablette *f*; [of soap] savonnette *f*. -**4.** [plaque] plaque *f* (commémorative). -**5.** COMPUT tablette *f*.

table tennis *n* tennis *m* de table, ping-pong *m*.

table top *n* dessus *m* de table, plateau *m* (de table).

table-turning *n pej* [spirituality] spiritisme *m*.

tableware ['teɪblweəʳ] *n* vaisselle *f*.

table wine *n* vin *m* de table.

tabloid ['tæblɔɪd] ◇ *n*: ~ (newspaper) tabloïde *m*; it's front-page news in all the ~s c'est à la une de tous les journaux à sensation.
◇ *adj*: in ~ form condensé, en résumé; the ~ press la presse à sensation.

TABLOID:
Dans les pays anglo-saxons, le format tabloïde est caractéristique des journaux populaires. Les principaux journaux populaires britanniques sont: le Daily Express, le Daily Mail, le Daily Mirror, The Star, The Sun et Today.

taboo [tə'buː] ◇ *adj* [subject, word] tabou.
◇ *n* tabou *m*.
◇ *vt* proscrire, interdire.

tabor ['teɪbəʳ] *n* tambourin *m*.

Tabriz [tæ'briːz] *pr n* Tabriz.

tabu [tə'buː] = **taboo**.

tabular ['tæbjʊləʳ] *adj* -**1.** [statistics, figures] tabulaire; in ~ form sous forme de tableaux. -**2.** [crystal] tabulaire.

tabula rasa ['tæbjʊlə'rɑːzə] (*pl* tabulae rasae ['tæbjʊliː'rɑːziː]) *n* table *f* rase.

tabulate ['tæbjʊleɪt] *vt* -**1.** [in table form] mettre sous forme de table OR tableau; [in columns] mettre en colonnes. -**2.** [classify] classifier.

tabulation [,tæbjʊ'leɪʃn] *n* -**1.** [in tables] présentation *f* OR disposition *f* en tables; [in columns] disposition *f* en colonnes. -**2.** [classification] classification *f*.

tabulator ['tæbjʊleɪtəʳ] *n* tabulateur *m*.

tache *inf* [tæʃ] (*abbr of* moustache) *n* bacchante *f*.

tacheometer [,tækɪ'ɒmɪtəʳ] = **tachymeter**.

tachograph ['tækəgrɑːf] *n* tachygraphe *m*.

tachometer [tæ'kɒmɪtəʳ] *n* tachymètre *m*.

tachycardia [,tækɪ'kɑːdɪə] *n* tachycardie *f*.

tachymeter [tæ'kɪmɪtəʳ] *n* tachéomètre *m*.

tacit ['tæsɪt] *adj* tacite, implicite; ~ approval accord *m* tacite; ~ knowledge connaissances *fpl* implicites.

tacitly ['tæsɪtlɪ] *adv* tacitement.

taciturn ['tæsɪtɜːn] *adj* taciturne, qui parle peu; he was a tall, ~ gentleman c'était un homme grand et taciturne.

Tacitus ['tæsɪtəs] *pr n* Tacite.

tack [tæk] ◇ *n* -**1.** [nail] pointe *f*; [for carpeting, upholstery] semence *f*; ~, thumb-~ punaise *f*. -**2.** *Br* SEW point *m* de bâti. -**3.** NAUT [course] bordée *f*, bord *m*; to make OR to set a ~ courir OR tirer une bordée; in the starboard/port ~ tribord/bâbord amures ‖ *fig*: to be on the right ~ être sur la bonne voie; to be on the wrong ~ faire fausse route; he went off on a quite different ~ il est parti sur une toute autre piste *fig*; she changed ~ in mid-conversation elle changea de sujet en pleine conversation. -**4.** *inf* [food] bouffe *f*. -**5.** [harness] sellerie *f*.
◇ *vt* -**1.** [carpet] clouer. -**2.** SEW faufiler, bâtir.
◇ *vi* NAUT faire OR courir OR tirer une bordée, louvoyer.
◆ **tack down** *vt sep* -**1.** [carpet, board] clouer. -**2.** SEW maintenir en place au point de bâti.
◆ **tack on** *vt sep* -**1.** [with nails] fixer avec des clous. -**2.** SEW bâtir. -**3.** ajouter, rajouter; the conclusion seems ~ed on la conclusion semble avoir été ajoutée après coup; he ~ed a joke on to the end of his story il a rajouté une plaisanterie à la fin de son anecdote.

tackily ['tækɪlɪ] *adv* [shoddily] minablement; [in bad taste] avec mauvais goût.

tacking ['tækɪŋ] *n* SEW bâtissage *m*, faufilage *m*; you'll have to take the ~ out of the skirt il va falloir enlever le faufilage de la jupe.

tacking stitch *n* point *m* de bâti.

tackle ['tækl] ◇ *vt* -**1.** SPORT tacler; *fig* [assailant, bank robber] saisir, empoigner. -**2.** [task, problem] s'attaquer à; [question, subject] s'attaquer à, aborder; to ~ a job se mettre au travail, s'atteler à la tâche; **during the holidays, I hope to ~ Churchill's memoirs** pendant les vacances, j'espère pouvoir m'attaquer aux mémoires de Churchill; **he ~d an enormous plate of chips** il attaqua une énorme assiettée de frites || [confront] interroger; **I ~d him on** OR **about his stand on abortion** je l'ai interrogé sur sa prise de position sur l'avortement; **I'll ~ her about the extra cost** je lui toucherai un mot OR je lui parlerai du coût supplémentaire.
◇ *vi* SPORT tacler.
◇ *n* -**1.** [equipment] attirail *m*, matériel *m*; **fishing ~** matériel *m* OR articles *mpl* de pêche. -**2.** [ropes and pulleys] appareil *m* OR appareils *mpl* de levage; [hoist] palan *m*. -**3.** SPORT [gen] tacle *m*; **good ~!** bien taclé! -**4.** [in American football - player] plaqueur *m*. -**5.** NAUT [rigging] gréement *m*.

tackling ['tæklɪŋ] *n* -**1.** SPORT tacle *m*. -**2.** [of problem, job] manière *f* d'aborder.

tack-room *n* sellerie *f*.

tacky ['tækɪ] (*compar* tackier, *superl* tackiest) *adj* -**1.** [sticky] collant, poisseux; [of paint] pas encore sec; **wait until the glue is ~** attendez que la colle ait commencé à prendre. -**2.** *inf* [shoddy] minable, moche. -**3.** *inf* [vulgar] de mauvais goût, vulgaire; *Am* [person] vulgaire.

taco ['tækəʊ] (*pl* tacos) *n* taco *m* *(crêpe mexicaine farcie)*.

tact [tækt] *n* tact *m*, diplomatie *f*, doigté *m*.

tactful ['tæktfʊl] *adj* [person] plein de tact, qui fait preuve de tact; [remark, suggestion] plein de tact; [inquiry] discret; [behaviour] qui fait preuve de tact OR de délicatesse; **that wasn't a very ~ thing to say** ce n'était pas très diplomatique de dire ça; **try to be more ~** essaie de faire preuve de plus de tact; **we must be ~ with her** nous devons faire preuve de tact avec elle; **they gave us a ~ hint** ils nous ont fait discrètement comprendre.

tactfully ['tæktfʊlɪ] *adv* avec tact OR délicatesse.

tactic ['tæktɪk] *n* tactique *f*; MIL tactique *f*.

tactical ['tæktɪkl] *adj* -**1.** MIL tactique; **~ mistake** erreur *f* tactique; **~ advantage** avantage *m* tactique; **~ nuclear weapons** armes *fpl* nucléaires tactiques. -**2.** [shrewd] adroit; **a purely ~ manoeuvre** une manœuvre purement diplomatique; **~ voting** *(U)*: **there has been a lot of ~ voting** beaucoup de gens ont voté utile.

tactically ['tæktɪklɪ] *adv* du point de vue tactique; **to vote ~** voter utile.

tactician [tæk'tɪʃn] *n* tacticien *m*, -enne *f*.

tactics ['tæktɪks] *n (U)* MIL & SPORT tactique *f*.

tactile ['tæktaɪl] *adj* tactile.

tactless ['tæktlɪs] *adj* [person] dépourvu de tact, qui manque de doigté; [answer] indiscret, peu diplomatique; **what a ~ thing to say/to do!** il faut vraiment manquer de tact pour dire/faire une chose pareille!; **how ~ of him!** quel manque de tact de sa part!

tactlessly ['tæktlɪslɪ] *adv* sans tact.

tactlessness ['tæktlɪsnɪs] *n* manque *m* de tact, indélicatesse *f*.

tad *inf* [tæd] *n Am* -**1.** [boy] mioche *m*, gamin *m*. -**2.** [small bit]: **we only had a ~** on n'en a eu qu'un chouia; **the coat is a ~ expensive** le manteau est un chouia trop cher.

tadpole ['tædpəʊl] *n* têtard *m* ZOOL.

Tadzhik [tɑː'dʒiːk] *n* Tadjik *mf*.

Tadzhiki [tɑː'dʒiːkɪ] ◇ *n* tadjik *m*.
◇ *adj* tadjik.

Tadzhikistan [tɑːˌdʒɪkɪ'stɑːn] *pr n* Tadjikistan *m*; **in ~** au Tadjikistan.

Taff *inf* [tæf] = **Taffy**.

taffeta ['tæfɪtə] ◇ *n* taffetas *m*.
◇ *adj* [dress] en taffetas.

taffrail ['tæfreɪl] *n* NAUT lisse *f* de couronnement, rambarde *f* arrière.

taffy ['tæfɪ] (*pl* taffies) *n Am* bonbon *m* au caramel.

Taffy *inf* ['tæfɪ] (*pl* Taffies) *pr n* *nom péjoratif ou humoristique désignant un Gallois*.

tag [tæg] (*pt* & *pp* tagged, *cont* tagging) ◇ *n* -**1.** [label - on clothes, suitcase] étiquette *f*; [- on file] onglet *m*; **(price) ~** étiquette *f* de prix; **(name) ~** [gen] étiquette *f* (où est marqué le nom); [for dog, soldier] plaque *f* d'identité. -**2.** [on shoelace] ferret *m*. -**3.** [on jacket, coat - for hanging] patte *f*. -**4.** [quotation] citation *f*; [cliché] cliché *m*, lieu *m* commun; [catchword] slogan *m*; **a Latin ~** une citation latine. -**5.** GRAMM: **~ (question)** question-tag *f*. -**6.** GAMES chat *m*; **to play ~** jouer à chat.
◇ *vt* -**1.** [label - package, article, garment] étiqueter; [- animal] marquer; [- file] mettre un onglet à; [- criminal] pincer, épingler; *fig* [- person] étiqueter; **he was tagged as a trouble-maker** il a été classé parmi les agitateurs. -**2.** *Am* [follow] suivre; [subj: detective] filer.
◆ **tag along** *vi insep* suivre; **to ~ along with sb** [follow] suivre qqn; [accompany] aller OR venir avec qqn; **do you mind if I ~ along?** ça vous gêne si je viens?; **the girl tagged along behind the others** [followed] la fille suivit les autres; [lagged behind] la fille était à la traîne derrière les autres.
◆ **tag on** ◇ *vt sep* ajouter.
◇ *vi insep* *inf*: **to ~ on to sb** suivre qqn partout; **to ~ on behind sb** traîner derrière qqn.

Tagalog [tə'gɑːlɒg] *n* -**1.** [person] Tagal *mf*. -**2.** LING tagalog *m*, tagal *m*.

tagboard ['tægbɔːd] *n* carton *m* pour étiquettes.

tag day *n Am journée de vente d'insignes pour une œuvre de bienfaisance*.

tag end *n Am* -**1.** [oddment - of cloth, thread] bout *m*; [of goods] restes *mpl*. -**2.** [end - of performance, day] fin *f*.

tagmeme ['tægmiːm] *n* tagmème *m*.

tagmemic [tæg'miːmɪk] *adj* tagmémique.

tagmemics [tæg'miːmɪks] *n (U)* tagmémique *f*.

Tagus ['teɪgəs] *pr n*: **the ~** le Tage.

tahini [tə'hiːnɪ] *n* CULIN tahini *m*.

Tahiti [tɑː'hiːtɪ] *pr n* Tahiti; **in ~** à Tahiti.

Tahitian [tɑː'hiːʃn] ◇ *n* Tahitien *m*, -enne *f*.
◇ *adj* tahitien.

tail [teɪl] ◇ *n* -**1.** [of animal] queue *f*; **with one's ~ between one's legs** *fig* la queue basse; **it's a case of the ~ wagging the dog** c'est le monde à l'envers; **the detective was still on his ~** *fig* le détective le filait toujours || [of vehicle] *inf*: **the car was right on my ~** *fig* la voiture me collait au derrière OR aux fesses; **to turn ~ and run** prendre ses jambes à son cou. -**2.** [of kite, comet, aircraft] queue *f*; [of musical note] queue *f*. -**3.** [of coat] basque *f*; [of dress] traîne *f*; [of shirt] pan *m*. -**4.** [end - of storm] queue *f*; [- of procession] fin *f*, queue *f*; [- of queue] bout *m*. -**5.** *inf* [follower - police officer, detective] *personne qui file*; **to put a ~ on sb** faire filer qqn. -**6.** *Am inf* [bottom] fesses *fpl*; **he worked his ~ off** il s'est vraiment décarcassé. -**7.** ▽ *(U)* [woman]: **a bit of ~** une gonzesse.
◇ *vt* -**1.** *inf* [follow] suivre, filer. -**2.** [animal] couper la queue à.
◆ **tails** ◇ *npl* *inf* [tailcoat] queue *f* de pie.
◇ *adv* [of coin]: **it's ~s!** (c'est) pile!
◆ **tail along** *vi insep* suivre; **she ~ed along behind** OR **after us** elle traînait derrière nous.
◆ **tail away** *vi insep* [sound] s'affaiblir, décroître; [interest] diminuer petit à petit; [book] se terminer en queue de poisson; [competitors in race] s'espacer; **his voice ~ed slowly away** peu à peu sa voix s'affaiblit.
◆ **tail back** *vi insep* [traffic] être arrêté, former un bouchon; [demonstration, runners] s'égrener, s'espacer; **the line of cars ~ed back for 10 miles/to the slip road** la file de voitures s'étendait sur 16 km/jusqu'à la bretelle d'accès.
◆ **tail off** *vi insep* [quality] baisser; [numbers] diminuer, baisser; [voice] devenir inaudible; [story] se terminer en queue de poisson.

tail assembly *n* AERON dérive *f*.

tailback ['teɪlbæk] *n* bouchon *m* (de circulation); **a 3 mile ~** un bouchon de 5 km.

tailboard ['teɪlbɔːd] *n* hayon *m* *(de camion)*.

tailcoat [ˌteɪl'kəʊt] *n* queue *f* de pie.

tail end *n* [of storm] fin *f*; [of cloth] bout *m*; [of procession] queue *f*, fin *f*; [of story] chute *f*.

tail feather *n* penne *f*.

tailgate ['teɪlgeɪt] ◇ *n* AUT hayon *m*.
◇ *vt* coller au pare-chocs de.

tail lamp, taillight ['teɪllaɪt] *n* feu *m* arrière.

tailor ['teɪlə'] ◇ *n* tailleur *m*.
◇ *vt* [garment] faire sur mesure; [equipment] adapter à un besoin particulier, concevoir en fonction d'un usage particulier; **the kitchen was ~ed to our needs** la cuisine a été faite spécialement pour nous OR conçue en fonction de nos besoins.

tailored ['teɪləd] *adj* [clothes, equipment] (fait) sur mesure; [skirt] ajusté.

tailor-made *adj* [specially made - clothes, equipment] (fait) sur mesure; [very suitable] (comme) fait exprès; **top players have their rackets ~ for them** les joueurs de haut niveau ont des raquettes faites sur mesure; **the job could have been ~ for her** on dirait que le poste est taillé pour elle.

tailor's tack *n* point *m* tailleur.

tailpiece ['teɪlpiːs] *n* -**1.** [addition - to speech] ajout *m*; [- to document] appendice *m*; [- to letter] post-scriptum *m inv*. -**2.** MUS cordier *m* *(d'un violon)*. -**3.** TYPO cul-de-lampe *m*.

tail pipe *n Am* tuyau *m* d'échappement.

tailplane ['teɪlpleɪn] *n* stabilisateur *m* AÉRON.

tail section *n* AERON arrière *m*; **a seat in the ~** une place à l'arrière.

tailskid ['teɪlskɪd] *n* béquille *f* de queue AÉRON.

tailspin ['teɪlspɪn] *n* vrille *f*; **to be in a ~** AERON vriller.

tailwind ['teɪlwɪnd] *n* vent *m* arrière.

taint [teɪnt] ◇ *vt* -**1.** [minds, morals] corrompre, souiller; [person] salir la réputation de; [reputation] salir; **his personal life is ~ed with scandal** sa vie privée fait beaucoup de scandale. -**2.** [food] gâter; [air] polluer, vicier; [water] polluer, infecter.
◇ *n* -**1.** [infection] infection *f*; [contamination] contamination *f*; [decay] décomposition *f*. -**2.** *fig* [of sin, corruption] tache *f*, souillure *f*.

tainted ['teɪntɪd] *adj* -**1.** [morals] corrompu, dépravé; [reputation] terni, sali; [politician] dont la réputation est ternie OR salie; [money] sale; **~ motives** des raisons malhonnêtes. -**2.** [food] gâté; [meat] avarié; [air] vicié, pollué; [water] infecté, pollué; [blood] impur.

Taipei [taɪ'peɪ] *pr n* Taibei.

Taiwan [ˌtaɪ'wɑːn] *pr n* Taiwan; **in ~** à Taiwan.

Taiwanese [ˌtaɪwə'niːz] ◇ *n* Taiwanais *m*, -e *f*.
◇ *adj* taiwanais.

Taj Mahal [ˌtɑːdʒmə'hɑːl] *pr n*: **the ~** le Tadj Mahall, le Taj Mahal.

take [teɪk] (*pt* took [tʊk], *pp* taken ['teɪkən]) ◇ *vt* **A.** -**1.** [get hold of, grip] prendre; [seize] prendre, saisir; **let me ~ your coat** donnez-moi votre manteau; **she took the book from him** elle lui a pris le livre; **to ~ sb's hand** prendre qqn par la main; **she took his arm** elle lui a pris le bras; **Peter took her in his arms** Peter l'a prise dans ses bras; **the wolf took its prey by the throat** le loup a saisi sa proie à la gorge. -**2.** [get control of, capture - person] prendre, capturer; [- fish, game] prendre, attraper; MIL prendre, s'emparer de; **they took the town that night** ils prirent OR s'emparèrent de la ville cette nuit-là; **to ~ sb prisoner** faire qqn prisonnier; **to ~ sb alive** prendre OR capturer qqn vivant; **I took his queen with my rook** j'ai pris sa reine avec ma tour; **to ~ control of a situation** prendre une situation en main; **we took our courage in both hands** nous avons pris notre courage à deux mains; **to ~ the lead in sthg** [in competition] prendre la tête de qqch; [set example] être le premier à faire qqch.
B. -**1.** [carry from one place to another] porter, apporter; [carry along, have in one's possession] prendre, emporter; **she took her mother a cup**

of tea elle a apporté une tasse de thé à sa mère; she took some towels upstairs elle a monté des serviettes; don't forget to ~ your camera n'oubliez pas (de prendre) votre appareil photo; the committee wanted to ~ the matter further *fig* le comité voulait mener l'affaire plus loin ❑ the devil ~ it! que le diable l'emporte! -**2.** [person - lead] mener, emmener; [- accompany] accompagner; her father ~s her to school son père l'emmène à l'école; could you ~ me home? pourriez-vous me ramener OR me raccompagner?; may I ~ you to dinner? puis-je vous inviter à dîner OR vous emmener dîner?; he offered to ~ them to work in the car il leur a proposé de les emmener au bureau en voiture OR de les conduire au bureau; the estate agent took them over the house l'agent immobilier leur a fait visiter la maison; she used to ~ me along to meetings (avant,) elle m'emmenait aux réunions; this road will ~ you to the station cette route vous mènera OR vous conduira à la gare; I don't want to ~ you out of your way je ne veux pas vous faire faire un détour; her job took her all over Africa son travail l'a fait voyager dans toute l'Afrique; that's what first took me to Portugal c'est ce qui m'a amené au Portugal; the record took her to number one in the charts le disque lui a permis d'être première au hit-parade. -**3.** [obtain from specified place] prendre, tirer; [remove from specified place] prendre, enlever; she took a handkerchief from her pocket elle a sorti un mouchoir de sa poche; I took a chocolate from the box j'ai pris un chocolat dans la boîte; ~ a book from the shelf prenez un livre sur l'étagère; ~ your feet off the table enlève tes pieds de la table. -**4.** [appropriate, steal] prendre, voler; to ~ sthg from sb prendre qqch à qqn; someone's taken my wallet quelqu'un a pris mon portefeuille; his article is taken directly from my book le texte de son article est tiré directement de mon livre. -**5.** [draw, derive] prendre, tirer; a passage taken from a book un passage extrait d'un livre; a phrase taken from Latin une expression empruntée au latin.

C. -**1.** [subj: bus, car, train etc] conduire, transporter; the ambulance took him to hospital l'ambulance l'a transporté à l'hôpital; this bus will ~ you to the theatre ce bus vous conduira au théâtre. -**2.** [obj: bus, car, plane, train] prendre; [obj: road] prendre, suivre; ~ a left/a right *Am* prenez à gauche/à droite.

D. -**1.** [have - attitude, bath, holiday] prendre; [make - nap, trip, walk] faire; [- decision] prendre; she took a quick look at him elle a jeté un rapide coup d'œil sur lui; let's ~ five *inf Am* soufflons cinq minutes; he took a flying leap il a bondi; to ~ a wife *arch* OR *lit* prendre femme. -**2.** PHOT: to ~ a picture prendre une photo; she took his picture OR a picture of him elle l'a pris en photo; we had our picture taken nous nous sommes fait photographier OR prendre en photo; he ~s a good photo *inf* [is photogenic] il est photogénique. -**3.** [receive, get] recevoir; he took the blow on his arm il a pris le coup sur le bras; you can ~ the call in my office if you like vous pouvez prendre l'appel dans mon bureau si vous voulez || [earn, win - prize] remporter, obtenir; [- degree, diploma] obtenir, avoir; the bookstore ~s about $3,000 a day la librairie fait à peu près 3 000 dollars (de recette) par jour; how much does he ~ home a month? quel est son salaire mensuel net?; we took all the tricks CARDS nous avons fait toutes les levées; their team took the match leur équipe a gagné OR remporté le match.

E. -**1.** [assume, undertake] prendre; to ~ the blame for sthg prendre la responsabilité de qqch; you'll have to ~ the consequences il va falloir que vous en subissiez les conséquences; she ~s all the credit for our success elle s'attribue tout le mérite de notre réussite; I ~ responsibility for their safety je me charge de leur sécurité. -**2.** [commit oneself to]: he took my side in the argument il a pris parti pour moi dans la dispute; the boy took an oath OR a vow to avenge his family le garçon a fait serment OR a juré de venger sa famille; to ~ the Fifth (Amendment) *Am* invoquer le Cinquième Amendement *(pour refuser de répondre)*. -**3.** [allow oneself]: may I ~ the liberty of inviting you to dinner? puis-je me permettre de vous inviter à dîner?; he took the opportunity to thank them OR of thanking them il a profité de l'occasion pour les remercier.

F. -**1.** [accept - job, gift, payment] prendre, accepter; [- bet] accepter; the doctor only ~s private patients le docteur ne prend pas les patients du service public; the owner won't ~ less than $100 for it le propriétaire en veut au moins 100 dollars; to ~ a bribe se laisser acheter OR corrompre; you'll have to ~ me as I am il faut me prendre comme je suis; ~ things as they come prenez les choses comme elles viennent; I won't ~ "no" for an answer je n'accepterai pas un refus; it's my last offer, (you can) ~ it or leave it c'est ma dernière offre, c'est à prendre ou à laisser; I'll ~ it from here je vais prendre la relève. -**2.** [accept as valid] croire; to ~ sb's advice suivre les conseils de qqn; ~ it from me, he's a crook croyez-moi, c'est un escroc. -**3.** [deal with]: let's ~ things one at a time prenons les choses une par une; the mayor took their questions calmly le maire a entendu leurs questions avec calme; how did she ~ the questioning? comment a-t-elle réagi à OR pris l'interrogatoire?; they took the news well OR in their stride ils ont plutôt bien pris la nouvelle; to ~ sthg badly prendre mal qqch ❑ to ~ things easy *inf* OR it easy *inf* se la couler douce; ~ it easy! [don't get angry] du calme! -**4.** [bear, endure - pain] supporter; [- damage, loss] subir; don't ~ any nonsense! ne te laisse pas faire!; your father won't ~ any nonsense ton père ne plaisante pas avec ce genre de choses; she can ~ it elle tiendra le coup; we couldn't ~ any more on n'en pouvait plus; I find his constant sarcasm rather hard to ~ je trouve ses sarcasmes perpétuels difficiles à supporter; don't expect me to ~ this lying down ne comptez pas sur moi pour accepter ça sans rien dire; those shoes have taken a lot of punishment ces chaussures en ont vu de toutes les couleurs. -**5.** [experience, feel]: to ~ fright prendre peur; to ~ an interest in sthg/sb s'intéresser à qqch/qqn; don't ~ offence ne vous vexez pas, ne vous offensez pas; no offence taken il n'y a pas de mal; we ~ pleasure in travelling nous prenons plaisir à voyager; she ~s pride in her work elle est fière de ce qu'elle fait; to ~ pride in one's appearance prendre soin de sa personne.

G. -**1.** [consider, look at] prendre, considérer; ~ Einstein (for example) prenons (l'exemple d') Einstein; ~ the case of Colombia prenons le cas de la Colombie; taking everything into consideration tout bien considéré; to ~ sthg/sb seriously prendre qqch/qqn au sérieux || [consider as]: do you ~ me for an idiot? vous me prenez pour un idiot?; what do you ~ me for? pour qui me prenez-vous?; he took me for somebody else il m'a pris pour quelqu'un d'autre. -**2.** [suppose, presume] supposer, présumer; he's never been to Madrid, I ~ it si je comprends bien, il n'a jamais été à Madrid; I ~ it you're his mother je suppose que vous êtes sa mère. -**3.** [interpret, understand] prendre, comprendre; we never know how to ~ his jokes on ne sait jamais comment prendre ses plaisanteries; don't ~ that literally ne le prenez pas au pied de la lettre; he was slow to ~ my meaning il lui a fallu un moment avant de comprendre ce que je voulais dire.

H. [require] prendre, demander; how long will it ~ to get there? combien de temps faudra-t-il pour y aller?; the flight ~s three hours le vol dure trois heures; it will ~ you ten minutes vous en avez pour dix minutes; it took him a minute to understand il a mis une minute avant de comprendre; it ~s time to learn a language il faut du temps pour apprendre une langue; what kind of batteries does it ~? quelle sorte de piles faut-il?; he took a bit of coaxing before he accepted il a fallu le pousser un peu pour qu'il accepte; it took four people to stop the brawl il a fallu quatre personnes pour arrêter la bagarre; it ~s courage to admit one's mistakes il faut du courage pour admettre ses erreurs; it ~s patience to work with children il faut de la patience OR il faut être patient pour travailler avec les enfants; one glance was all it took un regard a suffi; the job took some doing *inf* la tâche n'a pas été facile; her story ~s some believing *inf* son histoire n'est pas facile à croire || GRAMM: "falloir" ~s the subjunctive «falloir» est suivi du subjonctif ❑ to have what it ~s to do/to be sthg avoir les qualités nécessaires pour faire/être qqch; we need someone with leadership qualitites — she has what it ~s il nous faut quelqu'un qui ait des qualités de dirigeant — ce n'est pas ce qui lui manque; he's so lazy — it ~s one to know one! *inf* il est vraiment paresseux — tu peux parler!; it ~s two to tango *inf hum* il faut être deux pour faire ça.

I. -**1.** [food, drink etc] prendre; do you ~ milk in your coffee? prenez-vous du lait dans votre café?; I invited him to ~ tea je l'ai invité à prendre le thé; she refused to ~ any food elle a refusé de manger (quoi que ce soit); to ~ drugs se droguer; how many pills has he taken? combien de comprimés a-t-il pris OR absorbé?; 'not to be taken internally' [on bottle] '(à) usage externe'; to ~ the air prendre l'air. -**2.** [wear] faire, porter; she ~s a size 10 dress elle prend du 38 en robe; what size shoe do you ~? quelle pointure faites-vous? -**3.** [pick out, choose] prendre, choisir; [buy] prendre, acheter; [rent] prendre, louer; I'll ~ it je le prends; what newspaper do you ~? quel journal achetez-vous? -**4.** [occupy - chair, seat] prendre, s'asseoir sur; ~ a seat asseyez-vous; is this seat taken? cette place est-elle prise OR occupée? -**5.** [ascertain, find out] prendre; to ~ sb's pulse/temperature prendre le pouls/la température de qqn; to ~ a reading from a meter lire OR relever un compteur. -**6.** [write down - letter, notes] prendre; he took a note of her address il a noté son adresse. -**7.** [subtract] soustraire, déduire; they took 10% off the price ils ont baissé le prix de 10 %; ~ 4 from 9 and you have 5 ôtez 4 de 9, il reste 5. -**8.** SCH & UNIV [exam] passer, se présenter à; [course] prendre, suivre; I took Latin and Greek at A level ≃ j'ai pris latin et grec au bac; she ~s us for maths on l'a en maths. -**9.** [contract, develop]: to ~ a chill, to ~ cold prendre froid; to ~ sick tomber malade; I was taken with a fit of the giggles j'ai été pris d'un fou rire; she took an instant dislike to him elle l'a tout de suite pris en aversion. -**10.** [direct, aim]: she took a swipe at him elle a voulu le gifler. -**11.** [refer]: she ~s all her problems to her sister elle raconte tous ses problèmes à sa sœur; he took the matter to his boss il a soumis la question à son patron; they intend to ~ the case to the High Court JUR ils ont l'intention d'en appeler à la Cour suprême. -**12.** [have recourse to]: he took an axe to the door il a donné des coups de hache dans la porte; they took legal proceedings against him JUR ils lui ont intenté un procès. -**13.** [catch unawares] prendre, surprendre; to ~ sb by surprise OR off guard surprendre qqn, prendre qqn au dépourvu; his death took us by surprise sa mort nous a surpris. -**14.** [negotiate - obstacle] franchir, sauter; [- bend in road] prendre, négocier. -**15.** *inf* [deceive, cheat] avoir, rouler; they took him for every penny (he was worth) ils lui ont pris jusqu'à son dernier sou. -**16.** *arch* OR *lit* [have sex with] prendre.

◇ *vi* -**1.** [work, have desired effect] prendre; did the dye ~? est-ce que la teinture a pris?; it was too cold for the seeds to ~ il faisait trop froid pour que les graines germent. -**2.** [become popular] prendre, avoir du succès. -**3.** [fish] prendre, mordre.

◇ *n* -**1.** [act, capture, catch] prise *f*. -**2.** CIN, PHOT & TV prise *f* de vue; RADIO enregistrement *m*, prise *f* de son. -**3.** *inf Am* [takings] recette *f*; [share] part *f*; **to be on the ~** *inf* toucher des pots-de-vin.

◆ **take aback** *vt sep* [astonish] étonner, ébahir; [disconcert] déconcerter; **her question took him aback** sa question l'a déconcerté; **I was taken aback by the news** la nouvelle m'a beaucoup surpris.

◆ **take after** *vt insep* ressembler à, tenir de; **she ~s after her mother in looks** physiquement, elle tient de sa mère.

◆ **take apart** *vt sep* -**1.** [dismantle] démonter; **they took the room apart looking for evidence** *fig* ils ont mis la pièce sens dessus dessous pour trouver des preuves. -**2.** [criticize] critiquer.

◆ **take aside** *vt sep* prendre à part, emmener à l'écart; **the boss took her aside for a chat** le patron l'a prise à part pour discuter.

◆ **take away** *vt sep* -**1.** [remove] enlever, retirer; **~ that knife away from him** enlevez-lui ce couteau; **they took away his pension** ils lui ont retiré sa pension; **they took their daughter away from the club** ils ont retiré leur fille du club; **the police took his father away** *euph* son père a été arrêté par la police. -**2.** [carry away - object] emporter; [- person] emmener; **'sandwiches to ~ away'** *Br* 'sandwiches à emporter'; **'not to be taken away'** [in library] 'à consulter sur place'. -**3.** MATH soustraire, retrancher; **nine ~ away six is three** neuf moins six font trois.

◆ **take away from** *vt insep* [detract from]: **that doesn't ~ away from his achievements as an athlete** ça n'enlève rien à ses exploits d'athlète.

◆ **take back** *vt sep* -**1.** [after absence, departure] reprendre; **she took her husband back** elle a accepté que son mari revienne vivre avec elle; **the factory took back the workers** l'usine a repris les ouvriers. -**2.** [return] rapporter; [accompany] raccompagner; **~ it back to the shop** rapporte-le au magasin; **he took her back home** il l'a raccompagnée OR ramenée chez elle. -**3.** [retract, withdraw] retirer, reprendre; **I ~ back everything I said** je retire tout ce que j'ai dit; **all right, I ~ it back!** d'accord, je n'ai rien dit! -**4.** [remind of the past] rappeler; **that ~s me back to my childhood** ça me rappelle mon enfance; **that song ~s me back forty years** cette chanson me ramène quarante ans en arrière. -**5.** TYPO transférer à la ligne précédente.

◆ **take down** ◇ *vt sep* -**1.** [lower] descendre; **she took the book down from the shelf** elle a pris le livre sur l'étagère; **can you help me ~ the curtains down?** peux-tu m'aider à décrocher les rideaux?; **she took his picture down from the wall** elle a enlevé sa photo du mur; **he took his trousers down** il a baissé son pantalon. -**2.** [note] prendre, noter; **he took down the registration number** il a relevé le numéro d'immatriculation.

◇ *vi insep* se démonter.

◆ **take in** *vt sep* -**1.** [bring into one's home - person] héberger; [- boarder] prendre; [- orphan, stray animal] recueillir; **she ~s in ironing** elle fait du repassage à domicile ‖ [place in custody]: **the police took him in** la police l'a mis OR placé en garde à vue. -**2.** [air, water, food etc]: **she can only ~ in food intravenously** on ne peut la nourrir que par intraveineuse; **whales ~ in air through their blowhole** les baleines respirent par l'évent. -**3.** [understand, perceive] saisir, comprendre; **he was sitting taking it all in** il était là, assis, écoutant tout ce qui se disait; **he didn't ~ in the real implications of her announcement** il n'a pas saisi les véritables implications de sa déclaration; **I can't ~ in the fact that I've won** je n'arrive pas à croire que j'ai gagné; **she took in the situation at a glance** elle a compris la situation en un clin d'œil. -**4.** [make smaller - garment] reprendre; [- in knitting] diminuer; **you'd better ~ in the slack on the rope** tu ferais bien de tendre OR retendre la corde; **to ~ in a sail** NAUT carguer OR serrer une voile. -**5.** [attend, go to] aller à; **to ~ in a show** aller au théâtre; **she took in the castle while in Blois** elle a visité le château pendant qu'elle était à Blois; **they took in the sights in Rome** ils ont fait le tour des sites touristiques à Rome. -**6.** *inf (usu passive)* [cheat, deceive] tromper, rouler; **don't be taken in by him** ne vous laissez pas rouler par lui; **I'm not going to be taken in by your lies** je ne suis pas dupe de tes mensonges; **he was completely taken in** il marchait complètement.

◆ **take off** ◇ *vt sep* -**1.** [remove - clothing, lid, make-up, tag] enlever; **the boy took his clothes off** le garçon a enlevé ses vêtements OR s'est déshabillé; **she took her glasses off** elle a enlevé ses lunettes; **he often ~s the phone off the hook** il laisse souvent le téléphone décroché; **the surgeon had to ~ her leg off** le chirurgien a dû l'amputer de la jambe; **to ~ off the brake** AUT desserrer le frein (à main) ‖ *fig*: **he didn't ~ his eyes off her all night** il ne l'a pas quittée des yeux de la soirée; **I tried to ~ her mind off her troubles** j'ai essayé de lui changer les idées OR de la distraire de ses ennuis; **his retirement has taken ten years off him** *inf* sa retraite l'a rajeuni de dix ans. -**2.** [deduct] déduire, rabattre; **the teacher took one point off her grade** le professeur lui a retiré un point; **the manager took 10% off the price** le directeur a baissé le prix de 10 %. -**3.** [lead away] emmener; **she was taken off to hospital** on l'a transportée à l'hôpital; **the murderer was taken off to jail** on a emmené l'assassin en prison; **her friend took her off to dinner** son ami l'a emmenée dîner; **she took herself off to Italy** elle est partie en Italie. -**4.** [time]: **~ a few days off** prenez quelques jours (de vacances OR de congé); **she ~s Thursdays off** elle ne travaille pas le jeudi. -**5.** *inf* [copy] imiter; [mimic] imiter, singer. -**6.** THEAT annuler; **the show was taken off after two weeks** le spectacle a été annulé après deux semaines.

◇ *vi insep* -**1.** [aeroplane] décoller; **they took off for OR to Heathrow** ils se sont envolés pour Heathrow. -**2.** [person - depart] partir; **he took off without telling us** il est parti sans nous avertir. -**3.** *inf* [become successful] décoller.

◆ **take on** ◇ *vt sep* -**1.** [accept, undertake] prendre, accepter; **to ~ on the responsibility for sthg** se charger de qqch; **don't ~ on more than you can handle** ne vous surchargez pas; **she took it on herself to tell him** elle a pris sur elle de le lui dire; **he took the job on** [position] il a accepté le poste; [task] il s'est mis au travail; **to ~ on a bet** accepter un pari. -**2.** [contend with, fight against] lutter OR se battre contre; [compete against] jouer contre; **the unions took on the government** les syndicats se sont attaqués OR s'en sont pris au gouvernement; **I shouldn't like to ~ him on** je n'aimerais pas avoir affaire à lui; **he took us on at poker** il nous a défiés au poker. -**3.** [acquire, assume] prendre, revêtir; **her face took on a worried look** elle a pris un air inquiet. -**4.** [load] prendre, embarquer. -**5.** [hire] embaucher, engager.

◇ *vi insep inf* [fret, carry on] s'en faire; **don't ~ on so!** ne t'en fais pas!

◆ **take out** *vt sep* -**1.** [remove - object] prendre, sortir; [- stain] ôter, enlever; [extract - tooth] arracher; **~ the cheese out of the refrigerator** sors le fromage du réfrigérateur; **he took the knife out of his pocket** il a sorti le couteau de sa poche; **~ your hands out of your pockets** enlève les mains de tes poches; **they took their children out of school** ils ont retiré leurs enfants de l'école; **to ~ out sb's appendix/tonsils** MED enlever l'appendice/les amygdales à qqn. -**2.** [carry, lead outside - object] sortir; [- person] faire sortir; [escort] emmener; **to ~ sb out to dinner/to the movies** emmener qqn dîner/au cinéma; **I took her out for a bike ride** je l'ai emmenée faire un tour à vélo; **would you ~ the dog out?** tu veux bien sortir le chien OR aller promener le chien? -**3.** [food] emporter; **'sandwiches to ~ out'** 'sandwiches à emporter'. -**4.** [obtain - subscription] prendre; [- insurance policy] souscrire à, prendre; [- licence] se procurer; COMM & INDUST [- patent] prendre; **to ~ out a mortgage** faire un emprunt-logement. -**5.** *inf* [destroy - factory, town] détruire; [- person] supprimer, liquider; **the planes took the factory out by bombing** les avions ont détruit l'usine (en la bombardant). -**6.** CARDS changer la couleur de *(annoncée par son partenaire)*. -**7.** *phr*: **to ~ sb out of himself/herself** changer les idées à qqn; **working as an interpreter ~s a lot out of you** *inf* le travail d'interprète est épuisant; **the operation really took it out of him** *inf* l'opération l'a mis à plat; **to ~ it out on sb** s'en prendre à qqn; **he took his anger out on his wife** *inf* il a passé sa colère sur sa femme; **don't ~ it out on me!** *inf* ne t'en prends pas à moi!

◆ **take over** ◇ *vt sep* -**1.** [assume responsibility of] reprendre; **he wants his daughter to ~ over the business** il veut que sa fille reprenne l'affaire; **she took over my classes** elle a pris la suite de mes cours; **will you be taking over his job?** est-ce que vous allez le remplacer (dans ses fonctions)? -**2.** [gain control of, invade] s'emparer de; **the military took over the country** l'armée a pris le pouvoir; **fast-food restaurants have taken over Paris** les fast-foods ont envahi Paris. -**3.** FIN [buy out] absorber, racheter. -**4.** [carry across] apporter; [escort across] emmener; **I'll ~ you over by car** je vais vous y conduire en voiture; **the boat took us over to Seattle** le bateau nous a emmenés jusqu'à Seattle. -**5.** TYPO transférer à la ligne suivante.

◇ *vi insep* -**1.** [as replacement]: **who will ~ over now that the mayor has stepped down?** qui va prendre la relève maintenant que le maire a donné sa démission?; **I'll ~ over when he leaves** je le remplacerai quand il partira; **will he allow her to ~ over?** va-t-il lui céder la place?; **compact discs have taken over from records** le (disque) compact a remplacé le (disque) vinyle. -**2.** [army, dictator] prendre le pouvoir.

◆ **take to** *vt insep* -**1.** [have a liking for - person] se prendre d'amitié OR de sympathie pour, prendre en amitié; [- activity, game] prendre goût à; **I think he took to you** je crois que vous lui avez plu; **we took to one another at once** nous avons tout de suite sympathisé; **she didn't ~ to him** il ne lui a pas plu; **we've really taken to golf** nous avons vraiment pris goût au golf. -**2.** [acquire as a habit] se mettre à; **to ~ to drink OR to the bottle** se mettre à boire; **to ~ to doing sthg** se mettre à faire qqch; **she took to wearing black** elle s'est mise à s'habiller en noir. -**3.** [make for, head for]: **he's taken to his bed with the flu** il est alité avec la grippe; **the rebels took to the hills** les insurgés se sont réfugiés dans les collines; **they took to the woods** ils se sont enfuis dans les bois.

◆ **take up** ◇ *vt sep* -**1.** [carry, lead upstairs - object] monter; [- person] faire monter. -**2.** [pick up, lift - object] ramasser, prendre; [- passenger] prendre; **she took up the notes from the table** elle a ramassé OR pris les notes sur la table; **they're taking up the street** le rue est en travaux; **we finally took up the carpet** nous avons enfin enlevé la moquette. -**3.** [absorb] absorber. -**4.** [shorten] raccourcir; **you'd better ~ up the slack in that rope** tu ferais mieux de retendre OR tendre cette corde. -**5.** [fill, occupy - space] prendre, tenir; [- time] prendre, demander; **this table ~s up too much room** cette table prend trop de place OR est trop encombrante; **moving took up the whole day** le déménagement a pris toute la journée; **her work ~s up all her attention** son travail l'absorbe complètement. -**6.** [begin, become interested in - activity, hobby] se mettre à; [- job] prendre; [- career] commencer, embrasser; **when did you ~ up Greek?** quand est-ce que tu t'es mis au grec?; **I've taken up gardening** je me suis mis au jardinage. -**7.** [continue, resume] reprendre, continuer; **I took up the tale where Susan had left off** j'ai repris l'histoire là où Susan l'avait laissée; **she took up her knitting again** elle a repris son tricot. -**8.** [adopt - attitude] prendre, adopter; [- method] adopter; [- place, position] prendre; [- idea] adopter; **they took up**

residence in town ils se sont installés en ville. -**9.** [accept - offer] accepter; [- advice, suggestion] suivre; [- challenge] relever. -**10.** [discuss] discuter, parler de; [bring up] aborder; ~ it up with the boss parlez-en au patron. -**11.** [shares, stock] souscrire à.
◇ *vi insep* reprendre, continuer.
◆ **take upon** *vt sep*: he took it upon himself to organize the meeting il s'est chargé d'organiser la réunion.
◆ **take up on** *vt sep* -**1.** [accept offer, advice of]: his daughter took him up on his advice sa fille a suivi ses conseils; he might ~ you up on that someday! il risque de vous prendre au mot un jour!; she took him up on his promise elle a mis sa parole à l'épreuve. -**2.** [ask to explain]: I'd like to ~ you up on that point j'aimerais revenir sur ce point avec vous.
◆ **take up with** *vt insep* -**1.** [befriend]: to ~ up with sb se lier d'amitié avec qqn, prendre qqn en amitié; she took up with a bad crowd elle s'est mise à fréquenter des vauriens. -**2.** [preoccupy]: to be taken up with doing sthg être occupé à faire qqch; she's very taken up with him elle ne pense qu'à lui; she's taken up with her business elle est très prise par ses affaires; meetings were taken up with talk about the economy on passait les réunions à parler de l'économie.
takeaway ['teɪkə,weɪ] ◇ *n Br & NZ* [shop] *boutique de plats à emporter*; [food] plat *m* à emporter; Chinese ~ [shop] traiteur *m* chinois; [meal] repas *m* chinois à emporter.
◇ *adj*: ~ food plats *mpl* à emporter; ~ restaurant *restaurant qui fait des plats à emporter*.
take-home pay *n* salaire *m* net *(après impôts et déductions sociales)*.
taken ['teɪkn] ◇ *pp* → **take**.
◇ *adj* -**1.** [seat] pris, occupé. -**2.** to be ~ with sthg/sb [impressed] être impressionné par qqch/qqn; [interested] s'intéresser à qqch/qqn; they were quite ~ with the performance l'interprétation leur a beaucoup plu; I'm rather ~ with Aztec art l'art aztèque me plaît beaucoup.
takeoff ['teɪkɒf] *n* -**1.** AERON décollage *m*. -**2.** [imitation] imitation *f*, caricature *f*; the comedian did a ~ of the prime minister le comique a fait une imitation du Premier ministre. -**3.** ECON décollage *m* économique.
takeout ['teɪkaʊt] *Am* = **takeaway**.
takeover ['teɪk,əʊvəʳ] *n* [of power, of government] prise *f* de pouvoir; [of company] prise *f* de contrôle.
takeover bid *n* offre *f* publique d'achat, OPA *f*.
taker ['teɪkəʳ] *n* -**1.** [buyer] acheteur *m*, -euse *f*, preneur *m*, -euse *f*; [of suggestion, offer] preneur *m*, -euse *f*; there were no ~s personne n'en voulait; any ~s? y a-t-il des preneurs? -**2.** [user]: ~s of drugs are at highest risk ce sont les toxicomanes qui courent les plus grands risques.
takeup ['teɪkʌp] *n*: there has been a 75% ~ rate for the new benefit 75 % des gens concernés par la nouvelle allocation l'ont effectivement demandée; ~ has been poor la demande a été faible.
taking ['teɪkɪŋ] ◇ *adj* engageant, séduisant.
◇ *n* [of city, power] prise *f*; [of criminal] arrestation *f*; [of blood, sample] prélèvement *m*; the apples are there for the ~ prenez (donc) une pomme, elles sont là pour ça.
◆ **takings** *npl* COMM recette *f*.
talc [tælk] ◇ *n* talc *m*.
◇ *vt* talquer; to ~ o.s. se mettre du talc, se talquer.
talcum powder ['tælkəm-] *n* talc *m*.
tale [teɪl] *n* -**1.** [story] conte *m*, histoire *f*; [legend] histoire *f*, légende *f*; [account] récit *m*; to tell a ~ raconter une histoire; he told them the ~ of his escape il leur a raconté son évasion OR fait le récit de son évasion; the astronaut lived/didn't live to tell the ~ l'astronaute a survécu/n'a pas survécu pour raconter ce qui s'est passé; this painting tells its own ~ ce tableau est très parlant OR se passe de commentaires; ~s of romance des histoires romantiques ❑ and thereby hangs a ~ *hum* et là-dessus il y en aurait à raconter; 'The Canterbury Tales' *Chaucer* 'les Contes de Cantorbéry'; 'A Tale of Two Cities' *Dickens* 'le Conte des deux villes'; 'Tales from the Vienna Woods' *Strauss* 'Contes des bois de Vienne'; 'The Tales of Hoffman' *Offenbach* 'les Contes d'Hoffmann'. -**2.** [gossip] histoires *fpl*; there's a ~ going around that they're moving on raconte qu'ils vont déménager; to tell ~s on sb raconter des histoires sur le compte de qqn; you shouldn't tell ~s [denounce] il ne faut pas rapporter; [lie] il ne faut pas raconter des histoires.
talebearer ['teɪl,beərəʳ] *n lit* rapporteur *m*, -euse *f*.
talebearing ['teɪl,beərɪŋ] *n lit* rapportage *m*.
talent ['tælənt] *n* -**1.** [gift] talent *m*, don *m*; she has great musical ~ elle est très douée pour la musique, elle a un grand don pour la musique; I have quite a ~ for sewing je suis assez doué pour la OR en couture; it's just one of my many hidden ~s c'est un de mes nombreux talents cachés; you have a ~ for saying the wrong thing vous avez le don pour dire ce qu'il ne faut pas. -**2.** [talented person] talent *m*; she is one of our most promising young ~s c'est un de nos jeunes talents les plus prometteurs. -**3.** *inf* [opposite sex - girls] jolies filles *fpl*, minettes *fpl*; [- boys] beaux mecs *mpl*. -**4.** [coin] talent *m*.
talented ['tæləntɪd] *adj* talentueux, doué; she's a ~ musician c'est une musicienne de talent; she's really ~ elle a beaucoup de talent.
talent scout, talent-spotter *n* [for films] dénicheur *m*, -euse *f* de vedettes; [for sport] dénicheur *m*, -euse *f* de futurs grands joueurs.
tale-telling *n* rapportage *m*.
talisman ['tælɪzmən] (*pl* **talismans**) *n* talisman *m*.
talk [tɔːk] ◇ *vi* -**1.** [speak] parler; [discuss] discuter; [confer] s'entretenir; to ~ to sb parler à qqn; to ~ with sb parler OR s'entretenir avec qqn; to ~ of OR about sthg parler de qqch; we sat ~ing together nous sommes restés à discuter OR à bavarder; to ~ in signs/riddles parler par signes/par énigmes; they were ~ing in Chinese ils parlaient en chinois; I've been teaching my parakeet to ~ j'ai appris à parler à mon perroquet; to ~ for the sake of ~ing parler pour ne rien dire; that's no way to ~! en voilà des façons de parler!; they no longer ~ to each other ils ne se parlent plus, ils ne s'adressent plus la parole; who do you think you're ~ing to? non, mais à qui croyez-vous parler?; don't you ~ to me like that! je t'interdis de me parler sur ce ton!; to ~ to o.s. parler tout seul; I'll ~ to you about it tomorrow morning [converse] je vous en parlerai demain matin; [as threat] j'aurai deux mots à vous dire à ce sujet demain matin; it's no use ~ing to him, he never listens! on perd son temps avec lui, il n'écoute jamais!; to ~ of this and that parler de la pluie et du beau temps OR de choses et d'autres; ~ing of Switzerland, have you ever been skiing? à propos de la Suisse, vous avez déjà fait du ski?; they ~ed of little else ils n'ont parlé que de cela; he's always ~ing big c'est un beau parleur; now you're ~ing! voilà qui s'appelle parler!; you can ~!, look who's ~ing!, you're a fine one to ~! tu peux parler, toi!; it's easy for you to ~, you've never had a gun in your back! c'est facile à dire OR tu as beau jeu de dire ça, on ne t'a jamais braqué un pistolet dans le dos!; ~ about luck! [admirative] qu'est-ce qu'il a comme chance!, quel veinard!; [complaining] tu parles d'une veine! ❑ to ~ through one's hat OR the back of one's neck dire des bêtises OR n'importe quoi. -**2.** [chat] causer, bavarder; [gossip] jaser; you know how people ~ les gens sont tellement bavards. -**3.** [reveal secrets, esp unwillingly] parler; to make sb ~ faire parler qqn; we have ways of making people ~ on a les moyens de faire parler les gens; someone must have ~ed quelqu'un a dû parler.
◇ *vt* -**1.** [language] parler; to ~ slang parler argot; ~ sense! ne dis pas de sottises!, ne dis pas n'importe quoi!; now you're ~ing sense vous dites enfin des choses sensées; stop ~ing nonsense OR rubbish! *inf* arrête de dire des bêtises! ❑ to ~ turkey *inf Am* parler franc. -**2.** [discuss] parler; to ~ business/politics parler affaires/politique; to ~ shop parler métier OR boutique.
◇ *n* -**1.** [conversation] conversation *f*; [discussion] discussion *f*; [chat] causette *f*, causerie *f*; [formal] entretien *m*; to have a ~ with sb about sthg parler de qqch avec qqn, s'entretenir avec qqn de qqch; I'll have a ~ with him about it je lui en parlerai; we had a long ~ nous avons eu une longue discussion; can we have a little ~? je peux vous parler deux minutes?; that's fighting ~! c'est un défi! -**2.** [speech, lecture] exposé *m*; to give a ~ on OR about sthg faire un exposé sur qqch; there was a series of radio ~s on modern Japan il y a eu à la radio une série d'émissions où des gens venaient parler du Japon moderne. -**3.** *(U)* [noise of talking] paroles *fpl*, propos *mpl*; there is a lot of ~ in the background il y a beaucoup de bruit OR de gens qui parlent. -**4.** [speculative] discussion *f*, rumeur *f*; most of the ~ was about the new road il a surtout été question de OR on a surtout parlé de la nouvelle route; there's some ~ of building a concert hall [discussion] il est question OR on parle de construire une salle de concert; [rumour] le bruit court qu'on va construire une salle de concert; enough of this idle ~! assez parlé!; he's all ~ tout ce qu'il dit, c'est du vent. -**5.** *(U)* [gossip] racontars *mpl*, bavardage *m*, bavardages *mpl*, potins *mpl*; it's only ~ ce sont des racontars, tout ça; it's the ~ of the town on ne parle que de ça; the wedding was the ~ of the town on ne parlait que du mariage.
◆ **talks** *npl* [negotiations] négociations *fpl*, pourparlers *mpl*; [conference] conférence *f*; official peace ~s des pourparlers officiels sur la paix; so far there have only been ~s about ~s jusqu'ici il n'y a eu que des négociations préliminaires.
◆ **talk about** *vt insep* -**1.** [discuss] parler de; to ~ to sb about sthg parler de qqch à qqn; what are you ~ing about? [I don't understand] de quoi parles-tu?; [annoyed] qu'est-ce que tu racontes?; there's an important matter I must ~ to you about j'ai à vous parler OR entretenir d'une affaire importante; the new model has been much ~ed about on a beaucoup parlé du nouveau modèle; it gives them something to ~ about ça leur fait un sujet de conversation; they were ~ing about going away for the weekend ils parlaient OR envisageaient de partir pour le week-end. -**2.** [mean]: we're not ~ing about that! il ne s'agit pas de cela!; when it comes to hardship, he knows what he's ~ing about pour ce qui est de souffrir, il sait de quoi il parle; when it comes to cars, he knows what he's ~ing about pour ce qui est des voitures, il connaît son affaire; you don't know what you're ~ing about! tu ne sais pas ce que tu dis!; it's not as if we're ~ing about spending millions qui parle de dépenser des millions?; but I'm ~ing about a matter of principle! pour moi, c'est une question de principe!
◆ **talk at** *vt insep*: to ~ at sb: I hate people who ~ at me not to me je ne supporte pas les gens qui parlent sans se soucier de ce que j'ai à dire.
◆ **talk away** *vi insep* passer le temps à parler, parler sans arrêt; they were still ~ing away at 3 a.m. ils étaient encore en grande conversation à 3 h du matin.
◆ **talk back** *vi insep* [insolently] répondre; to ~ back to sb répondre (insolemment) à qqn; don't you ~ back to me! ne me réponds pas (comme ça)!
◆ **talk down** ◇ *vt sep* -**1.** [silence]: to ~ sb down réduire qqn au silence (en parlant plus fort que lui). -**2.** [aircraft] faire atterrir par radio-contrôle. -**3.** [would-be suicide]: the police managed to ~ him down from the roof la

police a réussi à le convaincre de redescendre du toit.
◇ *vi insep*: to ~ down to sb parler à qqn comme à un enfant.
◆ **talk into** *vt sep*: to ~ sb into doing sthg persuader qqn de faire qqch; **she allowed herself to be ~ed into going** elle s'est laissé convaincre d'y aller.
◆ **talk out** *vt sep* **-1.** [problem, disagreement] débattre de, discuter de; **in the end, they managed to ~ out the problem** finalement, à force de discussions, ils sont arrivés à trouver une solution au problème. **-2.** POL: to ~ **out a bill** *prolonger la discussion d'un projet de loi jusqu'à ce qu'il soit trop tard pour le voter avant la clôture de la séance.*
◆ **talk out of** *vt sep* dissuader; to ~ sb out of doing sthg dissuader qqn de faire qqch; **try to ~ him out of it** essayez de l'en dissuader.
◆ **talk over** *vt sep* discuter OR débattre de; **let's ~ it over** discutons-en, parlons-en; **we'll have to ~ the problem over** il va falloir que l'on parle de ce problème.
◆ **talk round** ◇ *vt sep* [convince] persuader, convaincre; to ~ sb **round to one's way of thinking** amener qqn à sa façon de penser OR à son point de vue; **I'm sure she can be ~ed round** je suis sûr qu'on peut la convaincre.
◇ *vt insep* [problem] tourner autour de; **I'm tired of just ~ing round the subject** j'en ai assez de tourner autour de la question.
◆ **talk up** *vt sep* vanter les mérites de, faire de la publicité pour.

talkative ['tɔːkətɪv] *adj* bavard, loquace.

talkativeness ['tɔːkətɪvnɪs] *n* volubilité *f*, loquacité *f*.

talk-back *n* TV & RADIO émetteur-récepteur *m*.

talker ['tɔːkəʳ] *n* **-1.** [speaker] causeur *m*, -euse *f*, bavard *m*, -e *f*; **she's a real ~** c'est une grande bavarde, c'est un vrai moulin à paroles; **he's a brilliant ~** c'est un beau parleur; **he's a fast ~** [gen] il parle vite; COMM il a du bagout. **-2.** [talking bird] oiseau *m* qui parle.

talkie *inf* ['tɔːkɪ] *n* film *m* parlant.

talk-in *inf n* causerie *f* suivie d'une discussion.

talking ['tɔːkɪŋ] ◇ *n (U)* conversation *f*, propos *mpl*; **he did all the ~** il était le seul à parler.
◇ *adj* [film] parlant; [bird] qui parle.

talking book *n* lecture *f* enregistrée d'un livre *(généralement à l'usage des aveugles)*.

talking head *n* TV présentateur *m*, -trice *f (dont on ne voit que la tête et les épaules)*.

talking point *n* sujet *m* de conversation OR de discussion.

talking-to *inf n* attrapade *f*, réprimande *f*; **he needs a good ~** il a besoin qu'on lui passe un bon savon.

talk show *n* causerie *f* (radiodiffusée OR télévisée), talk-show *m*.

talky ['tɔːkɪ] (*compar* talkier, *superl* talkiest) *adj Am* [film, novel] où il y a beaucoup de dialogues, qui manque d'action.

tall [tɔːl] *adj* **-1.** [person] grand, de grande taille; **how ~ are you?** combien mesurez-vous?; **I'm 6 feet ~** je mesure OR fais 1 m 80; **my sister is ~er than me** ma sœur est plus grande que moi; **she's grown a lot ~er in the past year** elle a beaucoup grandi depuis un an; **he's very ~ and slim** il est très grand et mince ‖ [building] haut, élevé; [tree, glass] grand, haut; **how ~ is that tree?** quelle est la hauteur de cet arbre?; **it's at least 80 feet ~** il fait au moins 25 mètres de haut; **it's a very ~ tree** c'est un très grand arbre. **-2.** *phr*: **a ~ story** une histoire invraisemblable OR abracadabrante, une histoire à dormir debout; **that's a ~ order** c'est beaucoup demander.

tallboy ['tɔːlbɔɪ] *n* (grande) commode *f*.

tallness ['tɔːlnɪs] *n* [of person] (grande) taille *f*; [of tree, building] hauteur *f*.

tallow ['tæləʊ] *n* suif *m*; ~ **candle** chandelle *f*.

tallow wood *n Austr* grand eucalyptus *m*.

tall ship *n* voilier *m* gréé en carré.

tally ['tælɪ] (*pl* tallies, *pt* & *pp* tallied) ◇ *n* **-1.** [record] compte *m*, enregistrement *m*; COMM pointage *m*; *Am* SPORT [score] score *m*; **to keep a ~ of goods/names** pointer des marchandises/des noms sur une liste; **to keep a ~ of the score** compter les points; **automatic counters kept a ~ of passing cars** des appareils automatiques comptaient les voitures qui passaient. **-2.** HIST [stick] taille *f*, baguette *f* à encoches; [mark] encoche *f*. **-3.** [label] étiquette *f*. **-4.** [counterfoil - of cheque, ticket] talon *m*; [duplicate] contrepartie *f*, double *m*.
◇ *vt* **-1.** [record] pointer. **-2.** [count up] compter.
◇ *vi* correspondre; **I couldn't make the figures ~** je ne pouvais faire concorder les chiffres; **your story must ~ with mine** il faut que ta version des faits concorde avec la mienne.

tallyho [,tælɪ'həʊ] (*pl* tallyhos) ◇ *interj* taïaut, tayaut.
◇ *n* cri *m* de taïaut.

tallyman ['tælɪmən] (*pl* tallymen [-mən]) *n* **-1.** [recorder] pointeur *m*, contrôleur *m*. **-2.** *Br* [collector] encaisseur *m* (de traites).

tally sheet *n* COMM bordereau *m*; SPORT feuille *f* de pointage.

Talmud ['tælmʊd] *n* Talmud *m*.

talon ['tælən] *n* **-1.** [of hawk, eagle] serre *f*; [of tiger, lion] griffe *f*. **-2.** CARDS talon *m*.

talus ['teɪləs] *n* GEOL talus *m* d'éboulis.

tamable ['teɪməbl] = **tameable**.

tamales [tə'mɑːlɪz] *npl pâte de farine de maïs contenant de la viande et des épices (spécialité mexicaine)*.

tamarin ['tæmərɪn] *n* tamarin *m (singe)*.

tamarind ['tæmərɪnd] *n* [fruit] tamarin *m*; [tree] tamarinier *m*.

tamarisk ['tæmərɪsk] *n* tamaris *m*, tamarix *m*.

tambour ['tæm,bʊəʳ] *n* **-1.** SEW tambour *m*, métier *m* à broder. **-2.** [on desk, cabinet] rideau *m*. **-3.** ARCHIT & MUS tambour *m*.

tambourine [,tæmbə'riːn] *n* tambour *m* de basque, tambourin *m*.

Tamburlaine ['tæmbəleɪn] *pr n*: ~ **the Great** Tamerlan le Grand.

tame [teɪm] ◇ *adj* **-1.** [as pet - hamster, rabbit] apprivoisé, domestiqué; [normally wild - bear, hawk] apprivoisé; [esp in circus - lion, tiger] dompté; **the deer had become very ~** les cerfs n'étaient plus du tout farouches; **I'll ask our ~ Frenchman if he knows what it means** *hum* je vais demander à notre Français de service s'il sait ce que cela veut dire. **-2.** [insipid, weak] fade, insipide; **the book has a very ~ ending** le livre finit de manière très banale; **it was a very ~ party** cette soirée n'était vraiment pas très folichonne; **the government's measures were considered rather ~** les mesures gouvernementales ont été jugées plutôt modérées.
◇ *vt* **-1.** [as pet - hamster, rabbit] apprivoiser, domestiquer; [normally wild - bear, hawk] apprivoiser; [esp in circus - lion, tiger] dompter. **-2.** [person] mater, soumettre; [natural forces] apprivoiser; [passions] dominer.

tameable ['teɪməbl] *adj* [hawk, bear, rabbit] apprivoisable; [lion, tiger] domptable.

tamely ['teɪmlɪ] *adv* [submit] docilement, sans résistance; [end] platement, de manière insipide; [write] de manière fade, platement.

tameness ['teɪmnɪs] *n* **-1.** [of bird, hamster] nature *f* apprivoisée; [of lion, tiger] nature *f* domptée. **-2.** [of person] docilité *f*. **-3.** [of ending, style] fadeur *f*, insipidité *f*; [of party, film] manque *m* d'intérêt, banalité *f*.

tamer ['teɪməʳ] *n* dresseur *m*, -euse *f*; **lion ~** dresseur *m*, -euse *f* OR dompteur *m*, -euse *f* de lions.

Tamil ['tæmɪl] ◇ *n* **-1.** [person] Tamoul *m*, -e *f*. **-2.** LING tamoul *m*.
◇ *adj* tamoul.

taming ['teɪmɪŋ] *n* [of animal] apprivoisement *m*; [of lions, tigers] domptage *m*, dressage *m*; **'The Taming of the Shrew'** *Shakespeare* 'la Mégère apprivoisée'.

Tammany ['tæmənɪ] *n Am* POL *organisation centrale du parti démocrate de New York (souvent impliquée dans des affaires de corruption)*; ~ **Hall** *siège du parti démocrate new-yorkais aux 18e et 19e siècles*.

Tammanyism ['tæmənɪɪzm] *n Am* POL *corruption dans l'administration politique*.

tammy ['tæmɪ] (*pl* tammies) = **tam-o'-shanter**.

tam-o'-shanter [,tæmə'ʃæntəʳ] *n* béret *m* écossais.

tamp [tæmp] *vt* tasser, damer; [for blasting - drill hole] bourrer (à l'argile OR au sable).
◆ **tamp down** *vt sep* [earth] tasser, damer; [gunpowder, tobacco] tasser.

tamper ['tæmpəʳ]
◆ **tamper with** *vt insep* **-1.** [meddle with - brakes, machinery] trafiquer; [lock] essayer de forcer OR crocheter, fausser; [possessions] toucher à; [falsify - records, accounts, evidence] falsifier, altérer; **someone has been ~ing with my papers** on a touché à mes papiers; **stop ~ing with the radio** arrête de jouer avec la radio; **the TV has been ~ed with** quelqu'un a déréglé la télévision. **-2.** *Am* JUR [witness] suborner; [jury] soudoyer.

tampon ['tæmpɒn] *n* MED tampon *m*; [for feminine use] tampon *m* périodique OR hygiénique.

tam-tam ['tæmtæm] *n* tam-tam *m*.

tan [tæn] (*pt* & *pp* tanned, *cont* tanning) ◇ *n* **-1.** [from sun] bronzage *m*; **I got a good ~ in the mountains** j'ai bien bronzé à la montagne. **-2.** MATH tangente *f*.
◇ *vt* **-1.** [leather, skins] tanner; **to ~ sb's hide** *inf fig* rosser qqn. **-2.** [from sun] bronzer, brunir.
◇ *vi* bronzer; **her skin ~s easily** elle a une peau qui bronze facilement.
◇ *adj* [colour] brun roux, brun clair; [leather] jaune; *Am* [tanned] bronzé.

tandem ['tændəm] ◇ *n* **-1.** [carriage] tandem *m*; **to harness two horses in ~** atteler deux chevaux en tandem OR en flèche; **to work in ~** *fig* travailler en tandem OR en collaboration. **-2.** [bike] tandem *m*.
◇ *adv*: **to ride ~** rouler en tandem.
◇ *adj* double; ~ **exchange** TELEC central *m* tandem.

tandoori [tæn'dʊərɪ] ◇ *n* cuisine *f* tandoori.
◇ *adj* tandoori *(inv)*.

tang [tæŋ] *n* **-1.** [taste] goût *m* (fort); **the ~ of orange juice** le goût acide du jus d'orange; **the ~ of mustard** le goût fort de la moutarde. **-2.** [smell] odeur *f* forte; **the ~ of the sea** l'odeur forte de la mer. **-3.** [hint - of irony] pointe *f*. **-4.** [of knife, sword] soie *f*.

tanga ['tæŋgə] *n* mini-slip *m*.

tangelo ['tændʒələʊ] (*pl* tangelos) *n* tangelo *m*.

tangent ['tændʒənt] *n* MATH tangente *f*; **to be at a ~** former une tangente; **to go off at** OR **on a ~** *fig* partir dans une digression.

tangential [tæn'dʒenʃl] *adj* tangentiel; ~ **line** ligne *f* tangentielle, tangente *f*.

tangentiality [tæn,dʒenʃɪ'ælətɪ] *n* digression *f*.

tangerine [,tændʒə'riːn] ◇ *n* **-1.** [fruit]: ~ **(orange)** mandarine *f*; ~ **(tree)** mandarinier *m*. **-2.** [colour] mandarine *f*.
◇ *adj* [in colour] mandarine *(inv)*.

tangibility [,tændʒə'bɪlətɪ] *n* tangibilité *f*.

tangible ['tændʒəbl] *adj* **-1.** [palpable] tangible; [real, substantial] tangible, réel; **the ~ world** le monde sensible; ~ **proof** des preuves tangibles; **it made no ~ difference** ça n'a pas changé grand-chose. **-2.** JUR [assets] réel, matériel; [property] corporel.

tangibly ['tændʒəblɪ] *adv* tangiblement, manifestement, de manière tangible.

Tangier [tæn'dʒɪəʳ] *pr n* Tanger.

tangle ['tæŋgl] ◇ *n* **-1.** [of wire, string, hair] enchevêtrement *m*; [of branches, weeds] fouillis *m*, enchevêtrement *m*; **this string is in an awful ~** cette ficelle est tout embrouillée; **to get into a ~** [wires, string] s'embrouiller, s'emmêler; [hair] s'emmêler; [traffic] se bloquer; **a ~ of creepers** un enchevêtrement de lianes. **-2.** [muddle] fouillis *m*, confusion *f*; **a legal/**

administrative ~ une affaire compliquée OR embrouillée du point de vue juridique/administratif; to get into a ~ [person] s'empêtrer, s'embrouiller; [records, figures] s'embrouiller; I often get into a ~ with figures/tax returns je m'embrouille souvent dans les chiffres/déclarations d'impôts; she was all in a ~ elle était toute embrouillée, elle ne savait plus où elle en était; the accounts are in a bit of a ~ les comptes sont un peu embrouillés. -**3.** [disagreement] accrochage *m*, différend *m*; they got into a ~ over the new salary scales ils ont eu un différend au sujet de la nouvelle échelle des salaires; I had a ~ with the social security officials j'ai eu des mots OR maille à partir avec les employés de la sécurité sociale.

◇ *vt* [wire, wool] emmêler, enchevêtrer; [figures] embrouiller; to get ~d [string] s'emmêler; [situation, records] s'embrouiller.

◇ *vi* -**1.** [wires, hair] s'emmêler. -**2.** [disagree] avoir un différend OR un accrochage; you'd better not ~ with her il vaut mieux éviter de se frotter à elle; they ~d over who should pay for supper ils se sont disputés pour savoir qui allait payer le repas.

◆ **tangle up** *vt sep* [string, wire] emmêler, enchevêtrer; to get ~d up s'emmêler; she got ~d up with some gangster *fig* elle s'est retrouvée avec un gangster.

tangled ['tæŋgld] *adj* -**1.** [string, creepers] emmêlé, enchevêtré; [undergrowth] touffu; [hair] emmêlé. -**2.** [complex - story, excuse] embrouillé; [- love life] complexe.

tango ['tæŋgəʊ] (*pl* tangos) ◇ *n* tango *m*.

◇ *vi* danser le tango.

tangy ['tæŋɪ] (*compar* tangier, *superl* tangiest) *adj* [in taste] qui a un goût fort; [in smell] qui a une odeur forte.

tank [tæŋk] ◇ *n* -**1.** [container - for liquid, gas] réservoir *m*, cuve *f*, citerne *f*; [- for rainwater] citerne *f*, bac *m*; [- for processing] cuve *f*; [- for transport] réservoir *m*, citerne *f*; [barrel] tonneau *m*, cuve *f*; (petrol *Br* OR fuel) ~ AUT réservoir *m* (d'essence); (domestic) hot water ~ ballon *m* d'eau chaude; (fish) ~ aquarium *m*. -**2.** MIL tank *m*, char *m* d'assaut; armoured ~ blindé *m*.

◇ *comp* de char OR chars d'assaut; ~ regiment régiment *m* de chars (d'assaut).

◇ *vt* mettre en cuve OR en réservoir.

◆ **tank up** *Br* ◇ *vi insep* AUT faire le plein (d'essence).

◇ *vt sep inf*: to get ~ed up se soûler.

tankard ['tæŋkəd] *n* chope *f*.

tank car *n* wagon-citerne *m*.

tank engine *n* locomotive *f* tender, machine *f* tender.

tanker ['tæŋkəʳ] *n* [lorry] camion-citerne *m*; [ship] bateau-citerne *m*, navire-citerne *m*; [plane] avion-ravitailleur *m*; (oil) ~ NAUT pétrolier *m*.

tankful ['tæŋkfʊl] *n* [of petrol] réservoir *m* (plein); [of water] citerne *f* (pleine).

tank top *n* débardeur *m*.

tank trap *n* piège *m* à chars.

tank truck *n* camion-citerne *m*.

tanned [tænd] *adj* -**1.** [person] hâlé, bronzé. -**2.** [leather] tanné.

tanner ['tænəʳ] *n* -**1.** [of leather] tanneur *m*, -euse *f*. -**2.** *inf Br ancienne pièce de six pence*.

tannery ['tænərɪ] (*pl* tanneries) *n* tannerie *f (C)*.

tannic ['tænɪk] *adj* tannique.

tannin ['tænɪn] *n* tanin *m*, tannin *m*.

tanning ['tænɪŋ] *n* -**1.** [of skin] bronzage *m*. -**2.** [of hides] tannage *m*; *fig* raclée *f*; to give sb a ~ *inf* rosser qqn.

Tannoy® ['tænɔɪ] ◇ *n Br* système *m* de haut-parleurs; the delay was announced over the ~ le retard fut annoncé par haut-parleur.

◇ *vt* transmettre par haut-parleur.

tansy ['tænzɪ] (*pl* tansies) *n* tanaisie *f*, barbotine *f*, herbe *f* aux coqs.

tantalic [tæn'tælɪk] *adj* tantalique; ~ acid acide *m* tantalique.

tantalite ['tæntəlaɪt] *n* tantalite *f*.

tantalize, -ise ['tæntəlaɪz] *vt* tourmenter, taquiner.

tantalizing ['tæntəlaɪzɪŋ] *adj* [woman] provocant, aguichant; [smell] alléchant, appétissant; [hint, possibility] tentant.

tantalizingly ['tæntəlaɪzɪŋlɪ] *adv* cruellement; victory was ~ close nous étions si près de la victoire que c'en était frustrant; ~ slow d'une lenteur désespérante.

tantalum ['tæntələm] *n* tantale *m*.

Tantalus ['tæntələs] *pr n* Tantale.

tantamount ['tæntəmaʊnt]

◆ **tantamount to** *prep phr* équivalent à; his statement was ~ to an admission of guilt sa déclaration équivalait à un aveu.

Tantrism ['tæntrɪzm] *n* tantrisme *m*.

tantrum ['tæntrəm] *n* crise *f* de colère OR de rage; to have OR to throw a (temper) ~ piquer une crise (de rage).

Tanzania [,tænzə'nɪə] *pr n* Tanzanie *f*; in ~ en Tanzanie.

Tanzanian [,tænzə'nɪən] ◇ *n* Tanzanien *m*, -enne *f*.

◇ *adj* tanzanien.

tanzanite ['tænzənaɪt] *n* tanzanite *f*.

Taoiseach ['tiːʃək] *n titre du Premier ministre de la République d'Irlande*.

Taoism ['tɑːəʊɪzm] *n* taoïsme *m*.

Taoist ['tɑːəʊɪst] ◇ *adj* taoïste.

◇ *n* taoïste *mf*.

tap [tæp] (*pt* & *pp* tapped, *cont* tapping) ◇ *vt* -**1.** [strike] taper légèrement, tapoter; someone tapped me on the arm/shoulder quelqu'un m'a tapé sur le bras/l'épaule; she was tapping her fingers on the table elle pianotait OR tapotait sur la table; he tapped his feet to the rhythm il marquait le rythme en tapant du pied. -**2.** [barrel, cask] mettre en perce, percer; [gas, water main] faire un branchement sur; [current] capter; [tree] inciser; [pine] gemmer; the trees were tapped for their gum on a incisé les arbres pour en recueillir la résine. -**3.** [exploit, use - resources, market] exploiter; [- talent, service] faire appel à, tirer profit de; [- capital] drainer; to ~ sb for information soutirer des informations à qqn; to ~ sb for a loan *inf* taper qqn; he tapped me for £15 *inf* il m'a tapé de 15 livres. -**4.** TELEC [conversation] capter; to ~ sb's line OR phone mettre qqn sur (table d') écoute. -**5.** TECH [screw] tarauder, fileter. -**6.** ELEC faire une dérivation sur. -**7.** MED poser un drain sur.

◇ *vi* -**1.** [knock] tapoter, taper légèrement; to ~ at the door frapper doucement à la porte; to ~ on the table tapoter sur la table; the boy was tapping on a drum le garçon frappait doucement sur un tambour; the woodpeckers are tapping on the bark les piverts donnent des coups de bec sur l'écorce. -**2.** [dance] faire des claquettes.

◇ *n* -**1.** [for water, gas] robinet *m*; [on barrel] robinet *m*, chantepleure *f*; [plug] bonde *f*; to turn a ~ on/off ouvrir/fermer un robinet; to leave the ~ running laisser le robinet ouvert; on ~ [beer] en fût; *fig inf* [money, person, supply] disponible; they seem to have funds on ~ ils semblent avoir des fonds toujours disponibles. -**2.** [blow] petit coup *m*, petite tape *f*; to give sb a ~ on the shoulder donner une petite tape sur l'épaule à qqn. -**3.** [on shoe] fer *m*. -**4.** [dancing] claquettes *fpl*; to dance ~ faire des claquettes; ~ shoes claquettes *fpl (chaussures)*. -**5.** TECH: (screw) ~ taraud *m*. -**6.** ELEC dérivation *f*, branchement *f*. -**7.** TELEC: to put a ~ on sb's phone mettre (le téléphone de) qqn sur table d'écoute. -**8.** MED drain *m*.

◆ **taps** *n Am* MIL [in evening] *sonnerie pour l'extinction des feux*; [at funeral] sonnerie *f* aux morts.

◆ **tap in** *vt sep* -**1.** [plug] enfoncer à petits coups. -**2.** COMPUT taper.

◆ **tap out** *vt sep* -**1.** [plug] sortir à petits coups; [pipe] vider, débourrer. -**2.** [code, rhythm] taper.

tap dance *n* claquettes *fpl (danse)*.

◆ **tap-dance** *vi* faire des claquettes.

tap dancer *n* danseur *m*, -euse *f* de claquettes.

tap dancing *n (U)* claquettes *fpl (danse)*.

tape [teɪp] ◇ *n* -**1.** [strip] bande *f*, ruban *m*; SEW ruban *m*, ganse *f*; MED sparadrap *m*; to cut the ~ [at ceremony] couper le ruban; sticky ~ ruban *m* adhésif, Scotch® *m*; name ~ ruban *m* de noms tissés. -**2.** [for recording] bande *f* (magnétique); COMPUT bande *f*; [for video, audio] cassette *f*; [recording] enregistrement *m*; on ~ sur bande, enregistré. -**3.** SPORT fil *m* d'arrivée; to breast the ~ franchir la ligne d'arrivée (le premier). -**4.** [for measuring]: ~ (measure) mètre *m* (à ruban).

◇ *vt* -**1.** [record] enregistrer. -**2.** [fasten - package] attacher avec du ruban adhésif; [stick] coller; the address was ~d to the suitcase l'adresse était scotchée sur la valise. -**3.** *Am* [bandage] bander. -**4.** *phr*: she's got him ~d *inf Br* elle sait ce qu'il vaut; we have the situation ~d on a la situation bien en main.

◆ **tape together** *vt sep* [fasten] attacher ensemble avec du ruban adhésif; [stick] coller (avec du ruban adhésif).

◆ **tape up** *vt sep* [fasten - parcel] attacher avec du ruban adhésif; [close - letterbox, hole] fermer avec du ruban adhésif; *Am* [bandage up] bander.

tape cleaner *n* nettoyeur *m* de tête, produit *m* de nettoyage de tête.

tape deck *n* platine *f* de magnétophone.

tape drive *n* dérouleur *m* de bandes (magnétiques), lecteur *m* de bandes (magnétiques).

tape head *n* tête *f* de lecture.

tapeline ['teɪplaɪn] = **tape measure**.

tape machine *n* téléscripteur *m*, téléimprimeur *m*.

tape measure *n* mètre *m* (ruban), centimètre *m*.

taper ['teɪpəʳ] ◇ *vt* [column, trouser leg, plane wing] fuseler; [stick, table leg] effiler, tailler en pointe.

◇ *vi* [column, trouser leg, plane wing] être fuselé; [stick, shape, table leg] se terminer en pointe, s'effiler; [finger] être effilé.

◇ *n longue bougie fine*; RELIG cierge *m*.

◆ **taper off** *vi insep* -**1.** [shape] se terminer en fuseau OR en pointe. -**2.** [noise] diminuer progressivement, décroître, s'affaiblir; [conversation] tomber; [level of interest, activity] décroître progressivement; street crime shows signs of ~ing off tout laisse à penser que les agressions sont en baisse.

tape reader *n* COMPUT lecteur *m* de bande.

tape-record [-rɪ'kɔːd] *vt* enregistrer (sur bande magnétique).

tape recorder *n* magnétophone *m*, lecteur *m* de cassettes.

tape recording *n* enregistrement *m* (sur bande magnétique).

tapered ['teɪpəd], **tapering** ['teɪpərɪŋ] *adj* [trousers] en fuseau; [stick, candle] en pointe, pointu; [table leg] fuselé; ~ fingers des doigts effilés OR fuselés.

tape streamer *n* COMPUT streamer *m*.

tapestry ['tæpɪstrɪ] (*pl* tapestries) *n* tapisserie *f*.

tape transport *n* mécanisme *m* d'entraînement *(d'une bande magnétique)*.

tapeworm ['teɪpwɜːm] *n* ténia *m*, ver *m* solitaire.

tapioca [,tæpɪ'əʊkə] *n* tapioca *m*.

tapir ['teɪpəʳ] (*pl inv* OR tapirs) *n* tapir *m*.

tappet ['tæpɪt] *n* TECH: (valve) ~ poussoir *m* (de soupape), taquet *m*.

taproom ['tæprʊm] *n Br* salle *f (d'un café)*, bar *m*.

taproot ['tæpruːt] *n* racine *f* pivotante.

tap water *n* eau *f* du robinet.

tar [tɑːʳ] (*pt* & *pp* tarred, *cont* tarring) ◇ *n* -**1.** goudron *m*; [on road] goudron *m*, bitume *m*; low-~ cigarettes cigarettes *fpl* à faible teneur en goudron. -**2.** *inf* [sailor] matelot *m*, loup *m* de mer.

◇ *vt* goudronner; [road] goudronner, bitumer; NAUT goudronner; to ~ and feather sb couvrir qqn de goudron et de plumes ❑ **to be tarred with the same brush** être à mettre dans le même panier OR sac.

tara(h) *inf* [tə'rɑː] = **ta-ta**.

taramasalata [ˌtærəməsə'lɑːtə] *n* tarama *m*.

tarantella [ˌtærən'telə] *n* tarentelle *f*.

Taranto [tə'ræntəʊ] *pr n* Tarente.

tarantula [tə'ræntjʊlə] (*pl* tarantulas OR tarantulae [-liː]) *n* tarentule *f*.

taraxacum [tə'ræksəkəm] *n* pissenlit *m*.

tardily ['tɑːdɪlɪ] *adv fml* OR *lit* -**1.** [late] tardivement. -**2.** [slowly] lentement.

tardiness ['tɑːdɪnɪs] *n fml* OR *lit* -**1.** [lateness] retard *m*. -**2.** [slowness] lenteur *f*.

tardy ['tɑːdɪ] (*compar* tardier, *superl* tardiest) *adj* -**1.** *Am* SCH en retard. -**2.** *fml* OR *lit* [late] tardif. -**3.** *fml* OR *lit* [slow] lent, nonchalant.

tare [teə^r] *n* -**1.** [weight] tare *f*, poids *m* à vide. -**2.** BOT vesce *f*.

target ['tɑːgɪt] (*pt* & *pp* targeted, *cont* targeting) ◇ *n* -**1.** [for archery, shooting] cible *f*; MIL cible *f*, but *m*; [objective] cible *f*, objectif *m*; **the ~ of criticism/jokes** la cible de critiques/plaisanteries; **she was an easy ~ for political cartoonists** elle était une cible facile pour les caricaturistes politiques; **to be on ~** [missile] suivre la trajectoire prévue; [plans] se dérouler comme prévu; [productivity] atteindre les objectifs prévus; **to meet production ~s** atteindre les objectifs de production ❑ **moving ~** MIL & *fig* cible *f* mobile. -**2.** ELECTRON & PHYS cible *f*. -**3.** [in surveying] mire *f*. -**4.** CULIN [joint] épaule *f* de mouton.
◇ *comp* -**1.** [date, amount] prévu; **~ figures** chiffres *mpl* prévus; **my ~ weight is 10 stone** je me suis fixé le poids idéal de 63 kg, mon poids idéal est (de) 63 kg. -**2.** MIL: **~ area** zone *f* cible.
◇ *vt* -**1.** [make objective of - enemy troops, city etc] prendre pour cible, viser. -**2.** [aim - missile] diriger; [benefits, advertisement] cibler, s'adresser à; **the benefits are ~ed at one-parent families** les allocations visent les OR sont destinées aux familles monoparentales; **the programme is ~ed at 18-25-year-olds** l'émission s'adresse aux 18-25 ans OR vise les jeunes de 18 à 25 ans.

target language *n* langue *f* cible.

target practice *n* *(U)* [MIL & gen] exercices *mpl* de tir.

tariff ['tærɪf] ◇ *n* -**1.** [customs] tarif *m* douanier; [list of prices] tarif *m*, tableau *m* des prix; **~ reform** réforme *f* des tarifs douaniers. -**2.** *Br* [menu] menu *m*. -**3.** *Br* [rate - of gas, electricity] tarif *m*.
◇ *adj* tarifaire.

Tarmac® ['tɑːmæk] (*pt* & *pp* tarmacked, *cont* tarmacking) *n Br* -**1.** [on road] tarmacadam *m*, macadam *m*. -**2.** [at airport - runway] piste *f*; [- apron] aire *f* de stationnement, piste *f* d'envol.
◆ **tarmac** *vt* macadamiser, goudronner.

Tarmacadam® [ˌtɑːmə'kædəm] = **Tarmac** *n*.

tarn [tɑːn] *n* petit lac *m* de montagne.

tarnation *inf* [tɑː'neɪʃn] *interj Am dated* zut, mince.

tarnish ['tɑːnɪʃ] ◇ *vt* -**1.** [metal] ternir; [mirror] ternir, désargenter. -**2.** [reputation] ternir, salir.
◇ *vi* se ternir.
◇ *n* ternissure *f*.

tarot ['tærəʊ] *n (U)* tarot *m*, tarots *mpl*; **~ card** carte *f* de tarot.

tarp *inf* [tɑːp] *n Am* toile *f* goudronnée.

tarpaulin [tɑː'pɔːlɪn] *n* bâche *f*; NAUT prélart *m*.

tarpon ['tɑːpɒn] (*pl inv* OR tarpons) *n* tarpon *m*.

tarradiddle ['tærədɪdl] *n Br* -**1.** [lie] petit mensonge *m*. -**2.** *(U)* [nonsense] bêtises *fpl*, idioties *fpl*.

tarragon ['tærəgən] *n* estragon *m*; **~ vinegar/sauce** vinaigre *m*/sauce *f* à l'estragon.

Tarragona [ˌtærə'gəʊnə] *pr n* Tarragone.

tarry[1] ['tærɪ] (*pt* & *pp* tarried) *vi lit* [delay] s'attarder, tarder; [remain] rester, demeurer.

tarry[2] ['tɑːrɪ] *adj* goudronneux; [fingers, shoes] plein OR couvert de goudron.

tarsal ['tɑːsl] ◇ *adj* tarsien.
◇ *n* os *m* tarsien.

tarsus ['tɑːsəs] (*pl* tarsi [-saɪ]) *n* tarse *m*.

tart [tɑːt] ◇ *n* -**1.** CULIN tarte *f*; [small] tartelette *f*. -**2.** ▽ *Br* [girl] gonzesse *f*; [prostitute] grue *f*.
◇ *adj* -**1.** [sour - fruit] acide; [- taste] aigre, acide. -**2.** [remark] acerbe, caustique.
◆ **tart up** *inf vt sep Br* [house, restaurant etc] retaper, rénover; **to ~ o.s. up, to get ~ed up** se pomponner.

tartan ['tɑːtn] ◇ *n* [design] tartan *m*; [fabric] tartan *m*, tissu *m* écossais.
◇ *comp* [skirt, trousers] en tissu écossais; [pattern] tartan.

tartar ['tɑːtə^r] *n* -**1.** [on teeth] tartre *m*. -**2.** *Br* [fearsome person] tyran *m*; **she's a real ~** c'est un vrai tyran.
◆ **Tartar** *n* = **Tatar**.

tartar(e) sauce ['tɑːtə^r-] *n* sauce *f* tartare.

tartaric [tɑː'tærɪk] *adj* tartrique; **~ acid** acide *m* tartrique.

Tartary ['tɑːtərɪ] = **Tatary**.

tartlet ['tɑːtlɪt] *n Br* tartelette *f*.

tartly ['tɑːtlɪ] *adv* avec aigreur, de manière acerbe; **"certainly not", he said ~** «certainement pas», dit-il d'un ton acerbe.

tartness ['tɑːtnɪs] *n* [of fruit] aigreur *f*, acidité *f*; [of tone, reply] aigreur *f*, acidité *f*.

tartrazine ['tɑːtrəziːn] *n* tartrazine *f*.

tarty▽ ['tɑːtɪ] (*compar* tartier, *superl* tartiest) *adj Br* vulgaire.

Tarzan ['tɑːzn] ◇ *pr n* Tarzan.
◇ *n*: **he thinks he's a real ~** il aime jouer les Tarzans.

task [tɑːsk] ◇ *n* [chore] tâche *f*, besogne *f*; [job] tâche *f*, travail *m*; SCH devoir *m*; **to set sb a ~** imposer une tâche à qqn; **convincing them will be no easy ~** les convaincre ne sera pas chose facile ❑ **to take sb to ~** réprimander qqn, prendre qqn à partie.
◇ *vt* = **tax** *vt* **3**.

task force *n* MIL corps *m* expéditionnaire; [gen] groupe *m* de travail, mission *f*.

taskmaster ['tɑːskˌmɑːstə^r] *n* tyran *m*; **he's a hard ~** il mène la vie dure à ses subordonnés, c'est un véritable négrier.

task work *n* travail *m* à la tâche OR aux pièces.

Tasmania [tæz'meɪnjə] *pr n* Tasmanie *f*; **in ~** en Tasmanie.

Tasmanian [tæz'meɪnjən] ◇ *n* Tasmanien *m*, -enne *f*.
◇ *adj* tasmanien.

Tasman Sea ['tæzmən-] *pr n*: **the ~** la mer de Tasman.

tassel ['tæsl] (*Br pt* & *pp* tasselled, *cont* tasselling, *Am pt* & *pp* tasseled, *cont* tasseling) ◇ *n* -**1.** [on clothing, furnishing] gland *m*. -**2.** BOT épillets *mpl*, panicule *f*, inflorescence *f* mâle.
◇ *vt* garnir de glands.

taste [teɪst] ◇ *n* -**1.** [sense] goût *m*; **to lose one's sense of ~** perdre le goût, être atteint d'agueusie; **to be sweet/salty to the ~** avoir un goût sucré/salé. -**2.** [flavour] goût *m*, saveur *f*; **these apples have a lovely/strange ~** ces pommes sont délicieuses/ont un drôle de goût; **this cheese doesn't have much ~** ce fromage n'a pas beaucoup de goût OR est assez fade; **the cake has a ~ of almonds** le gâteau a un goût d'amandes; **add sugar to ~** CULIN ajouter du sucre à volonté ❑ **to leave a bad ~ in the mouth** [food] laisser un mauvais goût dans la bouche; *fig* laisser un mauvais souvenir OR un goût amer. -**3.** [small amount - of food] bouchée *f*; [- of drink] goutte *f*; **can I have a ~ of the chocolate cake?** est-ce que je peux goûter au gâteau au chocolat?; **would you like (to have) a ~?** voulez-vous goûter? ❑ **to give sb a ~ of his/her own medicine** rendre la pareille OR la monnaie de sa pièce à qqn; **'A Taste of Honey'** *Delaney* 'Un goût de miel'. -**4.** [liking, preference] goût *m*, penchant *m*; **to have expensive/simple ~s** avoir des goûts de luxe/simples; **to develop a ~ for sthg** prendre goût à qqch; **to have a ~ for sthg** avoir un penchant OR un faible pour qqch; **it's a matter of ~** c'est (une) affaire de goût; **musical/artistic ~s** goûts musicaux/artistiques; **I don't share his ~ in music** je ne partage pas ses goûts en (matière de) musique, nous n'avons pas les mêmes goûts en (matière de) musique; **is it to your ~?** est-ce à votre goût?, est-ce que cela vous convient?, cela vous plaît?; **did you find it to your ~?** l'avez-vous trouvé à votre goût? -**5.** [discernment] goût *m*; **to have good ~** avoir du goût, avoir bon goût; **they have no ~** ils n'ont aucun goût; **she has good ~ in clothes** elle s'habille avec goût; **they don't have much ~ when it comes to art** en matière d'art, ils n'ont pas beaucoup de goût; **the joke was in extremely bad ~** la plaisanterie était de très mauvais goût; **it's bad ~ to ask personal questions** il est de mauvais goût de poser des questions indiscrètes. -**6.** [experience] aperçu *m*; [sample] échantillon *m*; **to have a ~ of freedom/happiness** avoir un aperçu de la liberté/du bonheur; **the sweet ~ of success** les joies OR les délices de la réussite; **he's already had a ~ of prison life** il a déjà tâté OR goûté de la prison; **the experience gave me a ~ of life in the army** l'expérience m'a donné un aperçu de la vie militaire; **a ~ of things to come** un avant-goût de l'avenir.
◇ *vt* -**1.** [flavour, ingredient] sentir (le goût de); **can you ~ the brandy in it?** est-ce que vous sentez le (goût du) cognac?; **you can hardly ~ the mint** on sent à peine (le goût de) la menthe. -**2.** [sample, try] goûter à; [for quality] goûter; **have you ~d the sauce?** avez-vous goûté (à) la sauce?; **to ~ (the) wine** [in restaurant] goûter le vin; [in vineyard] déguster le vin ‖ [eat] manger; [drink] boire; **I've never ~d oysters before** je n'ai jamais mangé d'huîtres; **you don't often get a chance to ~ such good wine** on n'a pas souvent l'occasion de boire un aussi bon vin. -**3.** [experience - happiness, success] goûter, connaître.
◇ *vi* [food]: **to ~ good/bad** avoir bon/mauvais goût; **to ~ salty/burnt** avoir un goût salé/un goût de brûlé; **to ~ funny** avoir un drôle de goût; **it ~s like chicken** cela a un goût de poulet; **to ~ of sthg** avoir le OR un goût de qqch; **it doesn't ~ of anything** cela n'a aucun goût.

taste bud *n* papille *f* gustative.

tasteful ['teɪstfʊl] *adj* [decoration] raffiné, de bon goût; [work of art] de bon goût; [clothing] de bon goût, élégant.

tastefully ['teɪstfʊlɪ] *adv* avec goût.

tastefulness ['teɪstfʊlnɪs] *n* [of decoration] bon goût *m*; [of clothing] chic *m*, élégance *f*.

tasteless ['teɪstlɪs] *adj* -**1.** [food] fade, insipide, sans goût. -**2.** [remark] de mauvais goût; [decoration, outfit, person] qui manque de goût, de mauvais goût.

tastelessly ['teɪstlɪslɪ] *adv* [decorated, dressed] sans goût.

tastelessness ['teɪstlɪsnɪs] *n* -**1.** [of food] fadeur *f*, manque *m* de goût. -**2.** [of remark] mauvais goût *m*; [in decoration, clothes] manque *m* de goût, mauvais goût *m*.

taster ['teɪstə^r] *n* dégustateur *m*, -trice *f*.

tastiness ['teɪstɪnɪs] *n* saveur *f* agréable, bon goût *m*.

tasty ['teɪstɪ] (*compar* tastier, *superl* tastiest) *adj* -**1.** [flavour] savoureux, délicieux; [spicy] relevé, bien assaisonné; [dish] qui a bon goût. -**2.** *inf* [attractive] séduisant.

tat [tæt] (*pt* & *pp* tatted, *cont* tatting) ◇ *vi* [make lace] faire de la frivolité.
◇ *n inf (U) Br pej* [clothes] fripes *fpl*; [goods] camelote *f*.

ta-ta *inf* [tæ'tɑː] *interj Br* au revoir, salut.

Tatar ['tɑːtə^r] ◇ *n* -**1.** [person] Tatar *m*, -e *f*. -**2.** LING tatar *m*.
◇ *adj* tatar.

Tatary ['tɑːtərɪ] *pr n* Tatarie *f*; **in ~** en Tatarie.

tater *inf* ['teɪtə^r] *n* patate *f*.

tattered ['tætəd] *adj* [clothes] en lambeaux, en loques; [page, book] en lambeaux, en morceaux, tout déchiré; [person] en haillons, loqueteux; [reputation] en miettes, ruiné; to be (all) ~ and torn [clothes] être tout en lambeaux; [page, book] être tout déchiré OR en morceaux; [person] être en loques et en guenilles.

tatters ['tætəz] *npl*: to be in ~ *literal* être en lambeaux OR en loques; the original plan is in ~ *fig* le projet initial est complètement à l'eau; her reputation is in ~ *fig* sa réputation est ruinée.

tatting ['tætɪŋ] *n (U)* frivolités *fpl* COUT.

tattle *inf* ['tætl] ◇ *vi* [chatter] jaser, cancaner; [tell secrets] rapporter.
◇ *n (U)* [gossiping] commérages *mpl*, cancans *mpl*.

tattler *inf* ['tætlə^r] *n* commère *f*, bavard *m*, -e *f*.

tattoo [tə'tuː] (*pl* tattoos) ◇ *n* -**1.** [on skin] tatouage *m*; he had ~s across his chest il avait la poitrine tatouée. -**2.** MIL [signal] retraite *f*; to sound the ~ sonner la retraite ‖ [ceremony, parade] parade *f* militaire. -**3.** [on drums] battements *mpl*; to beat a ~ on the drums battre le tambour ‖ *fig* [on door, table]: he beat a furious ~ on the door with his fists il tambourinait violemment sur OR contre la porte avec ses poings.
◇ *vi* & *vt* tatouer.

tatty *inf* ['tætɪ] (*compar* tattier, *superl* tattiest) *adj Br* [clothes] fatigué, défraîchi; [person] défraîchi, miteux; [house] délabré, en mauvais état; [book] écorné, en mauvais état.

taught [tɔːt] *pt* & *pp* → **teach**.

taunt [tɔːnt] ◇ *vt* railler, tourner en ridicule, persifler.
◇ *n* raillerie *f*, sarcasme *m*.

taunting ['tɔːntɪŋ] ◇ *n (U)* railleries *fpl*, sarcasmes *mpl*.
◇ *adj* railleur, sarcastique.

tauntingly ['tɔːntɪŋlɪ] *adv* d'un ton railleur OR persifleur.

taupe [təʊp] *adj* taupe *(inv)*.

tauromachy [ˌtɔː'rɒməkɪ] *n* tauromachie *f*.

Taurus ['tɔːrəs] *pr n* ASTROL & ASTRON Taureau *m*; he's a ~ il est (du signe du) Taureau.

taut [tɔːt] *adj* [rope, cable] tendu, raide; [situation] tendu.

tauten ['tɔːtn] ◇ *vt* [rope, cable etc] tendre, raidir.
◇ *vi* se tendre.

tautness ['tɔːtnɪs] *n* tension *f*, raideur *f*.

tautological [ˌtɔːtə'lɒdʒɪkl] *adj* tautologique, pléonastique.

tautologize, -ise [tɔː'tɒlədʒaɪz] *vi* faire des pléonasmes.

tautology [tɔː'tɒlədʒɪ] (*pl* tautologies) *n* tautologie *f*, pléonasme *m*.

tavern ['tævn] *n* auberge *f*, taverne *f*.

tawdriness ['tɔːdrɪnɪs] *n* [of clothes] mauvais goût *m*, aspect *m* tapageur; [of jewellery] clinquant *m*, faux éclat *m*; [of goods] mauvaise qualité *f*; [of motives, situation] bassesse *f*, indignité *f*.

tawdry ['tɔːdrɪ] (*compar* tawdrier, *superl* tawdriest) *adj* [clothes] voyant, tapageur, de mauvaise qualité; [jewellery] clinquant; [goods] de mauvaise qualité; [motives, situation] bas, indigne.

tawny ['tɔːnɪ] (*compar* tawnier, *superl* tawniest) *adj* [colour] fauve.

tawny owl *n* chouette *f* hulotte.

tax [tæks] ◇ *n* -**1.** [on income] impôt *m*, contributions *fpl* ADMIN; to levy OR to collect ~es lever OR percevoir des impôts; most of my income goes in ~ la plus grande partie de mes revenus va aux impôts; I don't pay much ~ je ne paie pas beaucoup d'impôts; I paid over $5,000 in ~ j'ai payé plus de 5 000 dollars d'impôts. -**2.** [on goods, services, imports] taxe *f*; to levy OR to put a 10% ~ on sthg frapper qqch d'une taxe de 10 %, imposer OR taxer qqch à 10 %; there is a high ~ on whisky le whisky est fortement taxé; baby food is free of ~ les aliments pour bébés sont exempts OR exonérés de taxe; a ~ on books/knowledge une taxe sur les livres/le savoir. -**3.** *fig* [strain - on patience, nerves] épreuve *f*; [- on strength, resources] mise *f* à l'épreuve.
◇ *comp* [burden] fiscal; [assessment] de l'impôt; [liability] à l'impôt.
◇ *vt* -**1.** [person, company] imposer, frapper d'un impôt; [goods] taxer, frapper d'une taxe; the rich will be more heavily ~ed les riches seront plus lourdement imposés OR payeront plus d'impôts; luxury goods are ~ed at 28% les articles de luxe sont taxés à 28 % OR font l'objet d'une taxe de 28 %. -**2.** *Br*: to ~ one's car acheter la vignette (automobile). -**3.** *fig* [strain - patience, resources] mettre à l'épreuve; [- strength, nerves] éprouver. -**4.** [accuse]: to ~ sb with sthg accuser OR taxer qqn de qqch.

taxable ['tæksəbl] *adj* [income, goods, land] imposable.

tax adjustment *n* redressement *m* fiscal OR d'impôt.

tax allowance *n* abattement *m* fiscal.

taxation [tæk'seɪʃn] ◇ *n (U)* -**1.** [of goods] taxation *f*; [of companies, people] imposition *f*. -**2.** [taxes] impôts *mpl*, contributions *fpl*.
◇ *comp* [system] fiscal; ~ authorities administration *f* fiscale, fisc *m*; ~ year année *f* fiscale d'imposition, exercice *m* fiscal.

tax avoidance *n* moyen *m* (légal) pour payer moins d'impôts.

tax bracket *n* tranche *f* d'imposition.

tax code *n* catégorie *f* d'impôt.

tax collector *n* percepteur *m*.

tax-deductible *adj* déductible des impôts, sujet à un dégrèvement d'impôts.

tax disc *n Br* vignette *f* automobile.

taxeme ['tæksiːm] *n* taxème *m*.

tax evasion *n* fraude *f* fiscale.

tax-exempt *Am* = **tax-free**.

tax exile *n personne qui s'expatrie pour des raisons fiscales*.

tax form *n* feuille *f* OR déclaration *f* d'impôts.

tax-free *adj* [goods] exonéré de taxes, non taxé; [interest] exonéré d'impôts, exempt d'impôts.

tax haven *n* paradis *m* fiscal.

taxi ['tæksɪ] (*pl* taxis OR taxies, *pt* & *pp* taxied, *cont* taxying) ◇ *n* taxi *m*; to get OR to take a ~ prendre un taxi; to hail a ~ héler un taxi.
◇ *vi* [aircraft] se déplacer au sol; the plane taxied across the tarmac l'avion traversa lentement l'aire de stationnement.
◇ *vt* [carry passengers] transporter en taxi.

taxicab ['tæksɪkæb] *n* taxi *m*.

taxi dancer *inf n* taxi-girl *f*.

taxidermist ['tæksɪdɜːmɪst] *n* empailleur *m*, -euse *f*, taxidermiste *mf*, naturaliste *mf*.

taxidermy ['tæksɪdɜːmɪ] *n* empaillage *m*, taxidermie *f*, naturalisation *f* des animaux.

taxi driver *n* chauffeur *m* de taxi.

taxi fare *n* [gen] tarif *m* de taxi; [cost of journey] coût *m* du taxi, prix *m* de la course (en taxi); can you pay the ~? pouvez-vous régler OR payer le taxi?

taximan ['tæksɪmæn] (*pl* taximen [-men]) *Br* = **taxi driver**.

taximeter ['tæksɪˌmiːtə^r] *n* taximètre *m*, compteur *m* (de taxi).

tax incentive *n* incitation *f* fiscale.

taxing ['tæksɪŋ] *adj* [problem, time] difficile; [climb] ardu.

tax inspector *n* inspecteur *m* des impôts.

taxiplane ['tæksɪpleɪn] *n* avion-taxi *m*.

taxi rank *Br*, **taxi stand** *Am n* station *f* de taxis.

taxiway ['tæksɪweɪ] *n* AERON taxiway *m*, chemin *m* de roulement.

tax loss *n* déduction *f* fiscale.

taxman ['tæksmæn] (*pl* taxmen [-men]) *n* -**1.** [person] percepteur *m* (du fisc). -**2.** *inf Br* [Inland Revenue]: the ~ le fisc.

taxonomic [ˌtæksə'nɒmɪk] *adj* taxinomique.

taxonomy [tæk'sɒnəmɪ] (*pl* taxonomies) *n* taxinomie *f*, taxonomie *f*.

taxpayer ['tæksˌpeɪə^r] *n* contribuable *mf*.

tax rebate *n* dégrèvement *m* d'impôts.

tax relief *n (U)* dégrèvement *m* fiscal; to get ~ on sthg obtenir un dégrèvement OR allégement fiscal sur qqch.

tax return *n* déclaration *f* de revenus OR d'impôts.

tax shelter *n* avantage *m* fiscal.

tax threshold *n* seuil *m* d'imposition.

tax year *n* année *f* fiscale *(qui commence en avril en Grande-Bretagne)*.

TB *n abbr of* tuberculosis.

T-bar *n* -**1.** [for skiers] téléski *m*, remonte-pente *m*. -**2.** [wrench] clé *f* à pipe en forme de T; [bar] profilé *m* OR fer *m* en T.

T-bone (steak) *n* steak *m* dans l'aloyau *(sur l'os)*.

tbs., tbsp. (*written abbr of* tablespoon(ful)) cs.

Tchaikovsky [tʃaɪ'kɒfskɪ] *pr n* Tchaïkovski.

TCP® (*abbr of* trichlorophonoxyacetic acid) *n Br désinfectant utilisé pour nettoyer des petites plaies ou pour se gargariser*.

TD -**1.** *abbr of* Treasury Department. -**2.** *abbr of* touchdown.

te [tiː] *n* MUS si *m*.

tea [tiː] *n* -**1.** [drink, plant] thé *m*; a cup of ~ une tasse de thé; more ~? encore un peu de thé?; two ~s and a coffee, please deux thés et un café, s'il vous plaît ❑ China ~ thé de Chine; I wouldn't do it for all the ~ in China je ne le ferais à aucun prix OR pour rien au monde. -**2.** [afternoon snack] thé *m*; [evening meal] repas *m* du soir; to ask sb to ~ inviter qqn à prendre le thé ❑ afternoon ~ thé, goûter *m*; high ~ *Br repas léger pris en début de soirée et accompagné de thé (surtout dans le nord de l'Angleterre et en Écosse)*. -**3.** [infusion] infusion *f*, tisane *f*; herbal ~ tisane; rosehip ~ tisane d'églantine.

TEA:
En Grande-Bretagne et en Irlande, le thé est une boisson populaire; il se boit fort, avec du lait et du sucre. Que ce soit au bureau, à l'usine ou sur les chantiers de construction, la journée de travail est traditionnellement ponctuée de «tea breaks» (pauses-thé).

---

tea bag *n* sachet *m* de thé.

tea ball *n Am* boule *f* à thé.

tea biscuit *n Br* gâteau *m* sec.

tea boy *n Br jeune employé chargé de préparer le thé pour ses collègues*.

tea bread *n (U)* ≃ cake *m*.

tea break *n* pause *f* pour prendre le thé, ≃ pause-café *f*; to have OR to take a ~ s'arrêter pour prendre le thé.

tea caddy *n* boîte *f* à thé.

teacake ['tiːkeɪk] *n petite brioche*.

teacart ['tiːkɑːt] *Am* = **tea trolley**.

teach [tiːtʃ] (*pt* & *pp* taught [tɔːt]) ◇ *vt* -**1.** [gen] apprendre; to ~ sb sthg OR sthg to sb apprendre qqch à qqn; she taught herself knitting/French elle a appris à tricoter/elle a appris le français toute seule; you can't ~ them anything! ils savent tout!, ils n'ont plus rien à apprendre!; to ~ sb (how) to do sthg apprendre à qqn à faire qqch; she taught them to play the piano elle leur a appris à jouer du piano; they taught us what to do in emergencies ils nous ont appris OR montré ce qu'il fallait faire en cas d'urgence; didn't anyone ever ~ you not to interrupt people? on ne t'a jamais dit OR appris qu'il ne faut pas couper la parole aux gens? ‖ [as threat]: I'll ~ you to be rude to your elders! je vais t'apprendre à être insolent envers les aînés!; that'll ~ you (not) to go off on your own ça t'apprendra à t'en aller toute seule; that'll ~ you (a lesson)! ça t'apprendra!, c'est bien fait pour toi!; that taught them a lesson they won't forget cela leur a donné une leçon dont ils se souviendront ❑ you can't ~ an old dog new tricks *prov* on ne peut pas apprendre de nouveaux tours à un vieux chien; you can't ~ your grandmother to suck eggs *inf* on n'apprend pas à un vieux singe à faire la grimace *prov*. -**2.** SCH [physics, history etc] enseigner, être professeur de; [pupils, class] faire cours à; she

taught us (to speak) French elle nous a appris OR enseigné le français; she ~es geography elle enseigne la géographie, elle est professeur de géographie; I've been ~ing 3B since Christmas j'ai la 3B depuis Noël, je fais cours à la 3B depuis Noël; to ~ school *Am* être enseignant; she ~es elementary school/high school *Am* elle est institutrice/professeur.
◇ *vi* [as profession] être enseignant, enseigner; [give lessons] faire cours; I started ~ing in 1980 j'ai commencé à enseigner OR je suis entré dans l'enseignement en 1980; she spent the morning ~ing elle a fait cours toute la matinée.

teachable ['tiːtʃəbl] *adj* -1. [subject] que l'on peut enseigner, susceptible d'être enseigné; [children] à qui on peut apprendre quelque chose. -2. *Am* ADMIN scolarisable.

teacher ['tiːtʃəʳ] *n* [in primary school] instituteur *m*, -trice *f*, maître *m*, maîtresse *f*; [in secondary school] professeur *m*, enseignant *m*, -e *f*; [in special school] éducateur *m*, -trice *f*; French/history ~ professeur de français/d'histoire; ~s are threatening to strike les enseignants menacent de se mettre en grève ❑ ~ pupil ratio taux *m* d'encadrement.

teacher certification *n Am* diplôme *m* d'enseignement.

teacher education *n Am* formation *f* pédagogique des enseignants.

teacher evaluation *n Am* UNIV évaluation *f* (des compétences) des enseignants.

teacher's aide *n Am* assistant *m*, -e *f* pédagogique.

teacher's pet *n* chouchou *m*, -oute *f* du professeur.

teacher training *n Br* formation *f* pédagogique des enseignants; ~ certificate diplôme *m* d'enseignement.

teacher training college *n* centre *m* de formation pédagogique, ≃ école *f* normale.

tea chest *n* caisse *f* (à thé).

teach-in *n* séminaire *m*.

teaching ['tiːtʃɪŋ] ◇ *n* -1. [career] enseignement *m*; to go into ~ entrer dans l'enseignement, devenir enseignant. -2. [of subject] enseignement *m*; chemistry/history ~ l'enseignement de la chimie/de l'histoire; EFL ~ l'enseignement de l'anglais (comme) langue étrangère. -3. *(U)* [hours taught] heures *fpl* d'enseignement, (heures *fpl* de) cours *mpl*; she only does a few hours' ~ a week elle ne donne OR n'a que quelques heures de cours par semaine.
◇ *comp* [profession, staff] enseignant.
◆ **teachings** *npl* [of leader, church] enseignements *mpl*.

teaching aid *n* matériel *m* pédagogique.

teaching diploma *n* diplôme *m* d'enseignement.

teaching fellow *n Br* UNIV *étudiant de troisième cycle qui assure quelques heures de cours.*

teaching hospital *n* centre *m* hospitalo-universitaire, CHU *m*.

teaching machine *n tout type d'appareil utilisant des programmes conçus à des fins pédagogiques.*

teaching practice *n (U)* stage *m* pédagogique *(pour futurs enseignants)*; to go on ~ faire un stage pédagogique.

tea cloth *Br* = **tea towel**.

tea cosy *n* cosy *m*.

teacup ['tiːkʌp] *n* -1. [cup] tasse *f* à thé. -2. = **teacupful**.

teacupful ['tiːkʌp,fʊl] *n* tasse *f* à thé *(mesure)*; three ~s of milk trois tasses de lait.

tea dance *n* thé *m* dansant.

tea-drinker *n* buveur *m*, -euse *f* de thé.

tea egg = **tea ball**.

tea garden *n* -1. [garden] *jardin de restaurant qui fait salon de thé.* -2. [plantation] plantation *f* de thé.

teahouse ['tiːhaʊs, *pl* -haʊzɪz] *n* maison *f* de thé *(orientale)*.

teak [tiːk] ◇ *n*: ~ (wood) teck *m*, tek *m*.
◇ *comp* en teck.

teakettle ['tiː,ketl] *n* bouilloire *f*.

teal [tiːl] *(pl inv* OR teals) *n* sarcelle *f*.

tea lady *n Br dame qui prépare ou sert le thé pour les employés d'une entreprise.*

tealeaf ['tiːliːf] *(pl* tealeaves [-liːvz]) *n* -1. feuille *f* de thé; to read the tealeaves ≃ lire dans le marc de café. -2. ▽ *Br hum* [thief] voleur *m*, -euse *f*.

team [tiːm] ◇ *n* -1. [SPORT & gen] équipe *f*; medical/basketball ~ équipe médicale/de basket-ball. -2. [of horses, oxen etc] attelage *m*.
◇ *vt* -1. [workers, players] mettre en équipe; [horses, oxen etc] atteler; I was ~ed with my brother j'ai fait équipe avec mon frère. -2. [colours, garments] assortir, harmoniser.
◆ **team up** ◇ *vt sep* -1. [workers, players] mettre en équipe; [horses, oxen etc] atteler; we're often ~ed up (together) on fait souvent équipe (ensemble); I got ~ed up with Peter on m'a mis en équipe avec Peter. -2. [colours, clothes] assortir, harmoniser.
◇ *vi insep* -1. [workers] faire équipe, travailler en collaboration; to ~ up with sb faire équipe avec qqn; the two villages ~ed up to put on the show les deux villages ont collaboré pour monter le spectacle. -2. [colours, clothes] être assorti, s'harmoniser.

team game *n* jeu *m* d'équipe.

team mate *n* coéquipier *m*, -ère *f*.

team member *n* équipier *m*, -ère *f*.

team spirit *n* esprit *m* d'équipe.

teamster ['tiːmstəʳ] *n Am* routier *m*, camionneur *m*.
◆ **Teamster** *n Am membre du syndicat américain des camionneurs.*

Teamsters' Union *pr n syndicat américain des camionneurs.*

team teaching *n* enseignement *m* en équipe.

teamwork ['tiːmwɜːk] *n* travail *m* d'équipe.

tea party *n* [for adults] thé *m*; [for children] goûter *m*; I'm having a little ~ on Sunday j'ai invité quelques amis à prendre le thé dimanche.

tea plant *n* arbre *m* à thé, théier *m*.

tea plate *n Br* petite assiette *f*, assiette *f* à dessert.

teapot ['tiːpɒt] *n* théière *f*.

tear[1] [teəʳ] *(pt* tore [tɔːʳ], *pp* torn [tɔːn])
◇ *vt* -1. [rip - page, material] déchirer; [- clothes] déchirer, faire un accroc à; [- flesh] déchirer, arracher; I tore my jacket on a nail j'ai fait un accroc à ma veste avec un clou; he tore a hole in the paper il a fait un trou dans le papier; '~ along the dotted line' 'détacher suivant le pointillé'; he tore a hole in his trousers il a fait un trou à son pantalon; the dog was ~ing the meat from a bone le chien déchiquetait la viande d'un os; her heart was torn by grief/remorse elle était déchirée par la douleur/le remords; she tore open the letter elle ouvrit l'enveloppe en la déchirant, elle déchira l'enveloppe; she tore open the wrapper elle déchira l'emballage pour l'ouvrir; to ~ sthg in two OR in half déchirer qqch en deux; you can ~ a piece off this cloth vous pouvez déchirer un morceau de ce tissu; to be torn to shreds être en lambeaux; to ~ sthg to shreds mettre qqch en lambeaux; the critics tore the film to shreds *fig* les critiques ont éreinté le film. -2. [muscle, ligament] froisser, déchirer. -3. [grab, snatch] arracher; he tore the cheque from OR out of my hand il m'a arraché le chèque des mains; the door had been torn from its hinges by the wind le vent avait fait sortir la porte de ses gonds. -4. *fig* [divide] tirailler, déchirer; I'm torn between going and staying je suis tiraillé entre le désir de partir et celui de rester, j'hésite entre partir et rester; the country had been torn by civil war for 30 years ça faisait 30 ans que le pays était déchiré par la guerre civile. -5. *fig* [separate] arracher; sorry to ~ you from your reading, but I need your help je regrette de vous arracher à votre lecture, mais j'ai besoin de votre aide; that's torn it *inf Br*, that ~s it *inf Am* c'est le bouquet, il ne manquait plus que cela.
◇ *vi* -1. [paper, cloth] se déchirer; this cloth ~s easily ce tissu se déchire facilement. -2. [as verb of movement]: to ~ after sb se précipiter OR se lancer à la poursuite de qqn; to ~ along [runner] courir à toute allure; [car] filer à toute allure; to ~ up/down the stairs monter/descendre l'escalier quatre à quatre; the cyclists came ~ing past les cyclistes sont passés à toute allure OR vitesse; the children were ~ing around the playground les enfants couraient de tous les côtés dans la cour de récréation. -3. [hurry]: to ~ through a job faire un travail à toute vitesse; he tore through the book/the report il a lu le livre/le rapport très rapidement.
◇ *n* [in paper, cloth] déchirure *f*; [in clothes] déchirure *f*, accroc *m*; this page has a ~ in it cette page est déchirée; who's responsible for the ~s in the curtains? qui a déchiré les rideaux?
◆ **tear apart** *vt sep* -1. [take to pieces - engine] désassembler, démonter. -2. [divide]: no-one can ~ them apart [friends] on ne peut pas les séparer, ils sont inséparables; [fighters] on n'arrive pas à les séparer; the party was being torn apart by internal strife le parti était déchiré OR divisé par des luttes intestines.
◆ **tear at** *vt insep*: to ~ at sthg déchirer OR arracher qqch; the dogs tore at the meat les chiens arrachèrent OR déchiquetèrent la viande; the children tore impatiently at the wrapping paper dans leur impatience les enfants déchirèrent le papier d'emballage.
◆ **tear away** *vt sep* -1. [remove - wallpaper] arracher, enlever; *fig* [- gloss, façade] enlever. -2. [from activity] arracher; to ~ sb away from sthg arracher qqn à qqch; I just couldn't ~ myself away je ne pouvais tout simplement pas me décider à partir; surely you can ~ yourself away from your work for ten minutes? tu ne vas pas me dire que tu ne peux pas t'éloigner de ton travail pendant dix minutes?, tu peux quand même laisser ton travail dix minutes!
◆ **tear down** *vt sep* -1. [remove - poster] arracher. -2. [demolish - building] démolir; *fig* [- argument] démolir, mettre par terre.
◆ **tear into** *vt insep* -1. [attack, rush at] se précipiter sur; the boxers tore into each other les boxeurs se sont jetés l'un sur l'autre. -2. *inf* [reprimand] enguirlander, passer un savon à; [criticize] taper sur, descendre (en flèche); he really tore into me over my exam results il m'a bien engueulé OR il m'a passé un bon savon au sujet de mes résultats d'examen; the critics have really torn into his latest film les critiques ont complètement descendu son dernier film. -3. [bite into - subj: teeth, knife] s'enfoncer dans; the saw tore into the soft wood la scie s'est enfoncée dans le bois tendre comme dans du beurre. -4. [run]: she came ~ing into the garden elle a déboulé dans le jardin à toute allure, elle s'est précipitée dans le jardin.
◆ **tear off** *vt sep* -1. [tape, wrapper] arracher, enlever en arrachant; [along perforations] détacher; he tore off his trousers and jumped into the water il retira OR enleva son pantalon en toute hâte et sauta dans l'eau ❑ to ~ sb off a strip *inf*, to ~ a strip off sb *inf Br* passer un savon à qqn, enguirlander qqn. -2. *inf* [report, essay etc - do hurriedly] écrire à toute vitesse; [- do badly] bâcler, torcher.
◆ **tear out** *vt sep* [page] arracher; [coupon, cheque] détacher; to ~ one's hair (out) *literal & fig* s'arracher les cheveux.
◆ **tear up** *vt sep* -1. [paper, letter] déchirer (en morceaux); *fig* [agreement, contract] déchirer. -2. [pull up - fence, weeds, surface] arracher; [- tree] déraciner.

tear[2] [tɪəʳ] *n* larme *f*; to be in ~s être en larmes; to burst into ~s fondre en larmes; to shed ~s verser des larmes; I shed no ~s over her resignation sa démission ne m'a pas ému outre mesure OR ne m'a pas arraché de larmes; to shed ~s of joy pleurer de joie, verser des larmes de joie; he had ~s OR there were ~s in his eyes il avait les larmes aux yeux; to be on the verge of ~s, to be near to ~s être au bord des larmes; to be moved to ~s être ému aux larmes; the performance moved me to ~s OR brought ~s to my eyes le spectacle m'a ému aux larmes; to be bored to ~s *fig* s'ennuyer à mourir.

tearaway ['teərə,weɪ] *n Br* casse-cou *mf inv*.

teardrop ['tɪədrɒp] *n* larme *f*.

tear duct [tɪəʳ-] *n* canal *m* lacrymal.

tearful ['tɪəfʊl] *adj* **-1.** [emotional - departure, occasion] larmoyant; [- story, account] larmoyant, à faire pleurer; they said a ~ goodbye ils se sont dit au revoir en pleurant. **-2.** [person] en larmes, qui pleure; [face] en larmes; [voice] larmoyant; I'm feeling a bit ~ j'ai envie de pleurer; she gave me a ~ look elle m'a lancé un regard larmoyant.

tearfully ['tɪəfʊlɪ] *adv* en pleurant, les larmes aux yeux; "I'll be all right", she said ~ «ça va aller», dit-elle avec des sanglots dans la voix OR en pleurant.

tear gas [tɪəʳ-] *n* gaz *m* lacrymogène.
◆ **tear-gas** *vt* envoyer du gaz lacrymogène sur.

tearing ['teərɪŋ] ◇ *n* déchirement *m*.
◇ *adj* **-1.** *literal*: a ~ sound [from paper] un bruit de déchirement; [from stitching] un (bruit de) craquement. **-2.** *Br* [as intensifier]: to be in a ~ hurry être terriblement pressé.

tearjerker *inf* ['tɪə,dʒɜːkəʳ] *n*: the film/the book is a real ~ c'est un film/un livre à faire pleurer.

tearjerking *inf* ['tɪə,dʒɜːkɪŋ] *adj* à faire pleurer.

tearless ['tɪəlɪs] *adj* sans larmes.

tearoom ['tiːrʊm] *n* salon *m* de thé.

tea rose *n* rose thé *f*.

tearstained ['tɪəsteɪnd] *adj* barbouillé de larmes.

tease [tiːz] ◇ *vt* **-1.** [person] taquiner; [animal] tourmenter; she's always teasing her brother elle est toujours à taquiner son frère. **-2.** [fabric] peigner; [wool] peigner, carder. **-3.** *Am* [hair] crêper.
◇ *vi* faire des taquineries; I'm only teasing c'est pour rire.
◇ *n inf* **-1.** [person] taquin *m*, -e *f*; [sexually] allumeuse *f*; don't be such a ~! ne sois pas si taquin! **-2.** [behaviour] taquinerie *f*; it was all a ~ c'était pour rire.
◆ **tease out** *vt sep* **-1.** [wool, hair] démêler. **-2.** [information, facts] faire ressortir; to ~ out a problem débrouiller OR démêler un problème, tirer un problème au clair.

teasel ['tiːzl] (*Br pt* & *pp* teaselled, *cont* teaselling, *Am pt* & *pp* teaseled, *cont* teaseling) ◇ *n* **-1.** BOT cardère *f*. **-2.** TEX carde *f*.
◇ *vt* [cloth] peigner, démêler.

teaser *inf* ['tiːzəʳ] *n* **-1.** [person] taquin *m*, -e *f*. **-2.** [problem] problème *m* difficile, colle *f*.

tea service, tea set *n* service *m* à thé.

tea shop *n Br* salon *m* de thé.

teasing ['tiːzɪŋ] ◇ *n* (*U*) **-1.** [tormenting] taquineries *fpl*. **-2.** TEX peignage *m*.
◇ *adj* taquin.

teasingly ['tiːzɪŋlɪ] *adv* pour me/le *etc* taquiner.

teaspoon ['tiːspuːn] *n* **-1.** [spoon] cuiller *f* OR cuillère *f* à café. **-2.** = **teaspoonful**.

teaspoonful ['tiːspuːn,fʊl] *adj* cuiller *f* OR cuillère *f* à café *(mesure)*.

tea strainer *n* passoire *f* à thé, passe-thé *m inv*.

teat [tiːt] *n* **-1.** [on breast] mamelon *m*, bout *m* de sein; [of animal] tétine *f*, tette *f*; [for milking] trayon *m*. **-2.** *Br* [on bottle] tétine *f*; [dummy] tétine *f*, sucette *f*. **-3.** TECH téton *m*.

tea table *n* table *f* (mise) pour le thé OR à thé.

teatime ['tiːtaɪm] *n* l'heure *f* du thé.

tea towel *n Br* torchon *m* (à vaisselle).

tea tray *n* plateau *m* à thé.

tea trolley *n Br* table *f* roulante *(pour servir le thé)*.

tea urn *n* fontaine *f* à thé.

tea wagon *Am* = **tea trolley**.

teazel ['tiːzl] (*Br pt* & *pp* teazelled, *cont* teazelling, *Am pt* & *pp* teazeled, *cont* teazeling) = **teasel**.

teazle ['tiːzl] = **teasel**.

TEC [tek] (*abbr of* Training and Enterprise Council) *n centre d'emploi et de formation*.

tech *inf* [tek] *n abbr of* technical college.

technetium [tek'niːsɪəm] *n* technétium *m*.

technical ['teknɪkl] *adj* **-1.** [gen & TECH] technique; ~ education enseignement *m* technique; ~ hitch incident *m* technique; ~ term terme *m* technique. **-2.** [according to rules] technique; for ~ reasons pour des raisons d'ordre technique; the judgment was quashed on a ~ point JUR le jugement a été cassé pour vice de forme OR de procédure; it's a purely ~ point *fig* ce n'est qu'un point de détail ❑ ~ foul/knockout SPORT faute *f*/knock-out *m inv* technique; ~ irregularity JUR vice *m* de forme OR de procédure.

technical college *n* ≃ institut *m* de technologie.

technical drawing *n* dessin *m* industriel.

technicality [,teknɪ'kælətɪ] (*pl* technicalities) *n* **-1.** [technical nature] technicité *f*. **-2.** [formal detail] détail *m* OR considération *f* (d'ordre) technique; [technical term] terme *m* technique; it's only a ~ ce n'est qu'un détail technique; to lose one's case on a ~ JUR perdre un procès pour vice de forme.

technically ['teknɪklɪ] *adv* **-1.** [on a technical level] sur un plan technique; [in technical terms] en termes techniques; ~ advanced de pointe, sophistiqué, avancé sur le plan technique; to be ~ minded avoir l'esprit technique. **-2.** [in theory] en théorie, en principe; ~, I'm in charge théoriquement, c'est moi le responsable.

technical school *n* ≃ collège *m* technique, ≃ lycée *m* d'enseignement professionnel.

technician [tek'nɪʃn] *n* technicien *m*, -enne *f*.

Technicolor® ['teknɪ,kʌləʳ] ◇ *n* Technicolor® *m*; in (glorious) ~ en Technicolor.
◇ *adj* en technicolor.

technique [tek'niːk] *n* technique *f*.

technocracy [tek'nɒkrəsɪ] (*pl* technocracies) *n* technocratie *f*.

technocrat ['teknəkræt] *n* technocrate *mf*.

technological [,teknə'lɒdʒɪkl] *adj* technologique.

technologically [,teknə'lɒdʒɪklɪ] *adv* du point de vue OR sur le plan technologique.

technologist [tek'nɒlədʒɪst] *n* technologue *mf*, technologiste *mf*.

technology [tek'nɒlədʒɪ] (*pl* technologies) *n* technologie *f*; new technologies les nouvelles technologies.

tectonic [tek'tɒnɪk] *adj* tectonique; ~ plates plaques *fpl* tectoniques.

tectonics [tek'tɒnɪks] *n* (*U*) tectonique *f*.

ted [ted] (*pt* & *pp* tedded, *cont* tedding) ◇ *vt* [hay] faner.
◇ *n inf abbr of* teddy boy.

tedder ['tedəʳ] *n* [machine] faneuse *f*; [person] faneur *m*, -euse *f*.

teddy ['tedɪ] (*pl* teddies) *n* **-1.** ~ (bear) ours *m* en peluche. **-2.** [garment] teddy *m*.

teddy boy *n Br* ≃ blouson *m* noir *(personne)*.

tedious ['tiːdjəs] *adj* [activity, work] ennuyeux, fastidieux; [time] ennuyeux; [journey] fatigant, pénible; we spent a ~ morning typing address labels on a passé une matinée pénible à taper des étiquettes portant noms et adresses; it's a very ~ job c'est un travail très fastidieux OR pénible; it's a ~ business collecting signatures recueillir des signatures est un travail fastidieux; he can be very ~ sometimes il est vraiment pénible quelquefois.

tediously ['tiːdjəslɪ] *adv* péniblement; [monotonously] de façon monotone, fastidieusement; the journey seemed ~ long le voyage était long et pénible.

tediousness ['tiːdjəsnɪs] *n* ennui *m*, monotonie *f*; the sheer ~ of the job got her down la monotonie de son travail lui mit le moral à zéro; an air of ~ hung over the house un certain ennui pesait sur la maison.

tedium ['tiːdjəm] *n* ennui *m*.

tee [tiː] ◇ *n* [in golf - peg] tee *m*; [- area] tertre *m* OR point *m* de départ; the 17th ~ le départ du 17ᵉ trou.
◇ *vt* placer sur le tee.
◇ *vi* placer la balle sur le tee.
◆ **tee off** ◇ *vi insep* **-1.** [in golf] jouer sa balle OR partir du tee *(du tertre de départ)*; *fig* commencer, démarrer. **-2.** *inf Am* [get angry] se fâcher, s'emporter; to ~ off about sthg se fâcher au sujet de qqch.
◇ *vt sep inf Am* [annoy] agacer, casser les pieds à; he really ~s me off with his arrogance son arrogance m'énerve vraiment; I'm ~d off j'en ai ras le bol OR marre.
◆ **tee up** *vi insep* placer la balle sur le tee.

tee-hee [-'hiː] ◇ *interj* hi! hi!
◇ *n* ricanement *m*.
◇ *vi* ricaner.

teem [tiːm] *vi* **-1.** [be crowded] grouiller, fourmiller; the streets were ~ing (with people) les rues grouillaient (de monde); the river is ~ing with fish la rivière grouille de poissons; the children came ~ing through the gates une horde d'enfants a franchi les grilles. **-2.** [rain]: it's absolutely ~ing (down OR with rain) il pleut à verse OR à torrents.

teeming ['tiːmɪŋ] *adj* **-1.** [streets] grouillant de monde; [crowds, shoppers] grouillant, fourmillant; [ants, insects etc] grouillant. **-2.** [rain] battant, torrentiel.

teen [tiːn] *adj* [teenage - fashion, magazine] pour adolescents OR jeunes; ~ idol idole *f* des jeunes.

teenage ['tiːneɪdʒ] *adj* jeune, adolescent; [habits, activities] d'adolescents; [fashion, magazine] pour les jeunes; the ~ years l'adolescence; ~ boys and girls les adolescents *mpl*.

teenager ['tiːn,eɪdʒəʳ] *n* jeune *mf (entre 13 et 19 ans)*, adolescent *m*, -e *f*.

teens [tiːnz] *npl* **-1.** [age] adolescence *f (entre 13 et 19 ans)*; she's in her ~ c'est une adolescente. **-2.** [numbers] *les chiffres entre 13 et 19*; the upper ~ *les chiffres de 17 à 19*.

teensy(-weensy) *inf* [,tiːnzɪ('wiːnzɪ)] = **teeny-weeny**.

teeny *inf* ['tiːnɪ] *adj* tout petit, minuscule.

teenybopper *inf* ['tiːnɪ,bɒpəʳ] *n jeune qui aime la musique pop*.

teeny-weeny *inf* [-'wiːnɪ] *adj* tout petit, minuscule.

teepee ['tiːpiː] = **tepee**.

tee shirt = **T-shirt**.

teeter ['tiːtəʳ] ◇ *vi* **-1.** [person] chanceler; [pile, object] vaciller, être sur le point de tomber; to ~ on the brink of sthg *fig* être au bord de qqch, friser qqch. **-2.** *Am* [see-saw] se balancer, basculer.
◇ *n Am* jeu *m* de bascule.

teeter-totter *n Am* jeu *m* de bascule.

teeth [tiːθ] *pl* → **tooth**.

teethe [tiːð] *vi* faire OR percer ses premières dents; to be teething commencer à faire ses dents.

teething ['tiːðɪŋ] *n* poussée *f* dentaire, dentition *f*.

teething ring *n* anneau *m* de dentition.

teething troubles *npl literal* douleurs *fpl* provoquées par la poussée des dents; *fig* difficultés *fpl* initiales OR de départ; we're having ~ with the new computer nous avons des problèmes de mise en route avec le nouvel ordinateur.

teetotal [tiː'təʊtl] *adj* [person] *qui ne boit jamais d'alcool*; [organization] antialcoolique.

teetotaller *Br*, **teetotaler** *Am* [tiː'təʊtləʳ] *n personne qui ne boit jamais d'alcool*.

TEFL ['tefl] (*abbr of* Teaching (of) English as a Foreign Language) *n enseignement de l'anglais langue étrangère*.

Teflon® ['teflɒn] *n* Téflon® *m*; a ~-coated pan une casserole téflonisée.

tegument ['tegjʊmənt] *n* tégument *m*.

te-hee ['tiː'hiː] = **tee-hee**.

Tehran, Teheran [ˌteə'rɑːn] *pr n* Téhéran.

tel. (*written abbr of* telephone) tél.

Tel-Aviv [ˌtelə'viːv] *pr n*: ~ (-Jaffa) Tel-Aviv (-Jaffa).

telecamera ['telɪˌkæmərə] *n* caméra *f* de télévision.

telecast ['telɪkɑːst] ◇ *n* émission *f* de télévision, programme *m* télédiffusé.
◇ *vt* diffuser, téléviser.

telecine [ˌtelɪ'sɪnɪ] *n* télécinéma *m*.

telecom(s) ['telɪkɒm(z)] *n abbr of* telecommunications.

telecommunications ['telɪkəˌmjuːnɪ'keɪʃnz] ◇ *n* (*U*) télécommunications *fpl*.
◇ *comp* [engineer] des télécommunications; [satellite] de télécommunication.

telecommuting [ˌtelɪkə'mjuːtɪŋ] *n* télétravail *m*.

Telefax® ['telɪfæks] *n* Téléfax® *m*.

telefilm ['telɪfɪlm] *n* téléfilm *m*.

telegenic [ˌtelɪ'dʒenɪk] *adj* télégénique.

telegram ['telɪgræm] *n* télégramme *m*; [in press, diplomacy] dépêche *f*; by ~ par télégramme.

telegraph ['telɪgrɑːf] ◇ *n* -**1.** [system] télégraphe *m*; the Telegraph PRESS *nom abrégé du Daily Telegraph*; Telegraph reader *lecteur du Daily Telegraph (typiquement conservateur)*. -**2.** [telegram] télégramme *m*.
◇ *comp* [service, wire] télégraphique; ~ pole OR post poteau *m* télégraphique.
◇ *vt* -**1.** [news] télégraphier; [money] télégraphier, envoyer par télégramme; she ~ed us to say she couldn't come elle nous a télégraphié OR envoyé un télégramme pour dire qu'elle ne pouvait pas venir. -**2.** *Can* POL: to ~ votes voter frauduleusement.
◇ *vi* télégraphier; he ~ed to say he'd be late il a télégraphié OR envoyé un télégramme pour dire qu'il serait en retard.

telegrapher [tɪ'legrəfə^r] *n* télégraphiste *mf*.

telegraphese [ˌtelɪgrɑː'fiːz] *n* langage *m* OR style *m* télégraphique.

telegraphic [ˌtelɪ'græfɪk] *adj* télégraphique.

telegraphically [ˌtelɪ'græfɪklɪ] *adv* [by telegram] télégraphiquement, par télégramme; [speak, write] en style télégraphique.

telegraphist [tɪ'legrəfɪst] *n* télégraphiste *mf*.

telegraphy [tɪ'legrəfɪ] *n* télégraphie *f*.

telekinesis [ˌtelɪkaɪ'niːsɪs] *n* télékinésie *f*.

telemarketing ['telɪˌmɑːkɪtɪŋ] *n* vente *f* par téléphone.

Telemessage® ['telɪˌmesɪdʒ] *n Br* télémessagerie *f*, courrier *m* électronique.

telemeter [tə'lemɪtə^r] *n* télémètre *m*.

teleological [ˌtelɪə'lɒdʒɪkl] *adj* téléologique.

teleology [ˌtelɪ'ɒlədʒɪ] *n* téléologie *f*.

telepathic [ˌtelɪ'pæθɪk] *adj* [person] télépathe; [message, means] télépathique.

telepathist [tɪ'lepəθɪst] *n* télépathe *mf*.

telepathy [tɪ'lepəθɪ] *n* télépathie *f*, transmission *f* de pensée; by ~ par télépathie OR transmission de pensée.

telephone ['telɪfəʊn] ◇ *n* téléphone *m*; to be on the ~ [talking] être au téléphone, téléphoner; [subscriber] avoir le téléphone, être abonné au téléphone; she's been on the ~ for nearly an hour ça fait presque une heure qu'elle est au téléphone OR qu'elle téléphone; the boss is on the ~ for you le patron te demande au téléphone; you're wanted on the ~ on vous demande au téléphone; to answer the ~ répondre au téléphone; I use the ~ a lot je téléphone beaucoup.
◇ *comp* [line, receiver] de téléphone; [network, message] téléphonique; [bill, charges] téléphonique, de téléphone; [service] des télécommunications; ~ call appel *m* téléphonique.
◇ *vt* [person] téléphoner à, appeler (au téléphone); [place] téléphoner à, appeler; [news, message, invitation] téléphoner, envoyer par téléphone; I'll ~ him later je lui téléphonerai OR je l'appellerai plus tard; to ~ the United States/home téléphoner aux États-Unis/chez soi; they ~d me (with) the good news ils m'ont téléphoné (pour m'annoncer) la bonne nouvelle.
◇ *vi* [call] téléphoner, appeler; [be on phone] être au téléphone; he ~d to say he'd be late il a téléphoné OR appelé pour dire qu'il serait en retard; where are you telephoning from? d'où appelles-tu OR téléphones-tu?

telephone answering machine *n* répondeur *m* (téléphonique).

telephone book *n* annuaire *m* (téléphonique).

telephone booth, telephone box *n* cabine *f* téléphonique.

telephone directory = **telephone book**.

telephone exchange *n* central *m* téléphonique.

telephone kiosk *Br* = **telephone booth**.

telephone number *n* numéro *m* de téléphone.

telephone subscriber *n* abonné *m*, -e *f* du téléphone.

telephone-tapping [-'tæpɪŋ] *n* mise *f* sur écoute téléphonique.

telephonic [ˌtelɪ'fɒnɪk] *adj* téléphonique.

telephonist [tɪ'lefənɪst] *n Br* standardiste *mf*, téléphoniste *mf*.

telephony [tɪ'lefənɪ] *n* téléphonie *f*.

telephotograph [ˌtelɪ'fəʊtəgrɑːf] *n* photographie *f* prise au téléobjectif, téléphotographie *f*.

telephotography [ˌtelɪfə'tɒgrəfɪ] *n* téléphotographie *f*.

telephoto lens [ˌtelɪ'fəʊtəʊ-] *n* téléobjectif *m*.

teleport ['telɪpɔːt] *vt* faire déplacer par télékinésie.

teleportation [ˌtelɪpɔː'teɪʃn] *n* télékinésie *f*.

teleprint ['telɪprɪnt] *vt* transmettre par téléscripteur OR téléimprimeur.

teleprinter ['telɪˌprɪntə^r] *n Br* téléscripteur *m*, téléimprimeur *m*.

teleprocessing [ˌtelɪ'prəʊsesɪŋ] *n* télétraitement *m*, téléinformatique *f*.

Teleprompter® [ˌtelɪ'prɒmptə^r] *n* prompteur *m*, téléprompteur *m*, télésouffleur *m offic*.

telesales ['telɪseɪlz] *npl* vente *f* par téléphone.

telescope ['telɪskəʊp] ◇ *n* télescope *m*, longue-vue *f*; ASTRON télescope *m*, lunette *f* astronomique.
◇ *vt* [shorten, condense - parts, report] condenser, abréger.
◇ *vi* -**1.** [collapse - parts] s'emboîter. -**2.** [railway carriages] se télescoper; the carriages ~d into each other les wagons se sont télescopés.

telescopic [ˌtelɪ'skɒpɪk] *adj* [aerial] télescopique; [umbrella] pliant; ~ lens téléobjectif *m*; ~ sight lunette *f*.

teleselling [ˌtelɪ'selɪŋ] = **telemarketing**.

telesoftware [ˌtelɪ'sɒftweə^r] *n* télélogiciel *m*, logiciel *m* de télétexte.

telestich [tɪ'lestɪk] *n* acrostiche *m* à l'envers *(ce sont les dernières lettres de chaque vers et non les premières qui composent le mot-clé)*.

teletex ['telɪteks] *n* Télétex® *m*.

teletext ['telɪtekst] *n* télétexte *m*, vidéographie *f* diffusée.

telethon ['telɪθɒn] *n* téléthon *m*.

Teletype® ['telɪtaɪp] ◇ *n* Télétype® *m*.
◇ *vt* transmettre par Télétype.

teletypewriter [ˌtelɪ'taɪpˌraɪtə^r] *n Am* téléscripteur *m*, téléimprimeur *m*.

televangelist [ˌtelɪ'vændʒəlɪst] *n évangéliste qui prêche à la télévision*.

teleview ['telɪvjuː] *vi* regarder la télévision.

televiewer ['telɪvjuːə^r] *n* téléspectateur *m*, -trice *f*.

televiewing ['telɪˌvjuːɪŋ] *n* [watching TV] *action de regarder la télévision*; [programme] programme *m* de télévision.

televise ['telɪvaɪz] *vt* téléviser.

television ['telɪˌvɪʒn] ◇ *n* -**1.** [system, broadcasts] télévision *f*; to watch ~ regarder la télévision; we don't watch much ~ on ne regarde pas souvent la télévision; to go on ~ passer à la télévision; to work in ~ travailler à la télévision. -**2.** [set] téléviseur *m*, (poste *m* de) télévision *f*; I saw her on (the) ~ je l'ai vue à la télévision; to turn the ~ up/down/off/on monter le son de/baisser le son de/éteindre/allumer la télévision; is there anything good on ~ tonight? qu'est-ce qu'il y a de bien à la télévision ce soir?; colour/black-and-white ~ télévision *f* (en) couleur/(en) noir et blanc.
◇ *comp* [camera, engineer, programme, station, screen] de télévision; [picture, news] télévisé; [satellite] de télédiffusion; to make a ~ appearance passer à la télévision; ~ film téléfilm *m*, film *m* pour la télévision; ~ lounge salle *f* de télévision.

television licence *n Br* redevance *f* (de télévision).

television set *n* téléviseur *m*, (poste *m* de) télévision *f*.

television tube *n* tube *m* cathodique.

televisual [ˌtelɪ'vɪʒʊəl] *adj* télévisuel.

teleworking [ˌtelɪ'wɜːkɪŋ] *n* télétravail *m*.

telewriter ['telɪˌraɪtə^r] *n* appareil *m* de téléécriture.

telex ['teleks] ◇ *n* télex *m*.
◇ *vt* envoyer par télex, télexer.

telic ['telɪk] *adj* qui tend vers un but précis; GRAMM de but.

tell [tel] (*pt & pp* told [təʊld]) ◇ *vt* -**1.** [inform of] dire à; to ~ sb sthg dire qqch à qqn; I told him the answer/what I thought je lui ai dit la réponse/ce que je pensais; to ~ sb about OR of *lit* sthg dire qqch à qqn, parler à qqn de qqch; I told her about the new restaurant je lui ai parlé du nouveau restaurant; have you told them about the fire? leur avez-vous parlé de l'incendie?; she told me of her woes *lit* elle m'a parlé de ses malheurs; they told me (that) they would be late ils m'ont dit qu'ils seraient en retard; I'm pleased to ~ you you've won j'ai le plaisir de vous informer OR annoncer que vous avez gagné; let me ~ you how pleased I am laissez-moi vous dire OR permettez-moi de vous dire à quel point je suis heureux; we are told that there is little hope on nous dit qu'il y a peu d'espoir; I'm told he's coming tomorrow j'ai entendu dire OR on m'a dit qu'il venait demain; so I've been told c'est ce qu'on m'a dit; it doesn't ~ us much cela ne nous en dit pas très long, cela ne nous apprend pas grand-chose; can you ~ me the time? pouvez-vous me dire l'heure (qu'il est)?; can you ~ me your name/age? pouvez-vous me dire votre nom/âge? ❑ a little bird told me! c'est mon petit doigt qui me l'a dit! -**2.** [explain to] expliquer à, dire à; this brochure ~s me all I need to know cette brochure m'explique tout ce que j'ai besoin de savoir; I told him what to do in case of an emergency je lui ai dit OR expliqué ce qu'il fallait faire en cas d'urgence; did you ~ them how to get here? leur as-tu expliqué comment se rendre ici?; can you ~ me the way to the station/to Oxford? pouvez-vous m'indiquer le chemin de la gare/la route d'Oxford?; do you want me to ~ you again? voulez-vous que je vous le redise OR répète?; who can ~ me the best way to make omelettes? qui peut me dire OR m'expliquer la meilleure façon de faire des omelettes? ❑ if I've told you once, I've told you a thousand times! je te l'ai dit cent fois!; (I'll) ~ you what, let's play cards j'ai une idée, on n'a qu'à jouer aux cartes. -**3.** [instruct, order]: to ~ sb to do sthg dire à qqn de faire qqch; ~ her to wait outside dites-lui d'attendre dehors; I told them not to interrupt je leur ai dit de ne pas interrompre; I thought I told you not to run? je croyais t'avoir interdit OR défendu de courir?; don't make me ~ you twice ne m'oblige pas à te le dire deux fois; he didn't need to be told twice! il ne s'est pas fait prier!, je n'ai pas eu besoin de lui dire deux fois! -**4.** [recount - story, joke] raconter; [- news] annoncer; [- secret] dire, raconter; to ~ sb about sthg parler à qqn de qqch, raconter qqch à qqn; ~ them about OR of your life as an explorer racontez-leur votre vie d'explorateur; ~ me what you know about it dites-moi ce que vous en savez; could you ~ me a little about yourself? pourriez-vous me parler un peu de vous-même?; I told myself it didn't matter je me suis dit que cela n'avait pas d'importance; I could ~ you a thing or two about his role in it je pourrais vous en dire long sur son rôle dans tout cela; don't ~ me you got lost! ne me dites pas que vous vous êtes perdu!; don't ~ me, let me guess! ne me dites rien, laissez-moi deviner!; ~ it like it is! *inf* n'ayez pas peur de dire la vérité! ❑ ~ that to the marines! *inf*, ~ me another! *inf* à d'autres!, mon œil! -**5.** [recite]: to ~ one's beads dire OR égrener son chapelet. -**6.** [utter - truth, lie] dire, raconter; to ~ sb the truth dire la vérité à qqn; to ~ (you) the truth, truth to ~ à vrai dire, à dire vrai; to ~ lies mentir, dire des mensonges; I ~ a lie! *fig* je me trompe!; to ~ sb's fortune dire la bonne aventure à qqn. -**7.** [assure] dire, assurer; didn't I ~ you?, I told you so! je vous l'avais bien dit!; let me ~ you! [believe me] je vous assure!, croyez-moi!; [as threat] tenez-vous-le pour dit!; I can ~ you! c'est moi qui vous le dis! ❑ you're ~ing me! *inf*, ~ me about it! *inf* à qui le dites-vous! -**8.** [distinguish] distinguer; to ~ right from wrong distinguer le bien du mal; you can hardly ~ the difference between them on voit OR distingue à peine la différence entre eux; how can you ~ one from another? comment les distinguez-vous l'un de l'autre? ‖ [see] voir; [know] savoir; [understand] comprendre; you could ~ he was disappointed on voyait bien qu'il était déçu; how can you ~ when it's ready? à quoi voit-on OR comment peut-on savoir que c'est prêt?; no one could ~ whether the good weather would last personne ne pouvait dire si le beau temps allait durer; there's no ~ing what he might do next/how he'll react (il est) impossible de dire ce qu'il est susceptible de faire ensuite/comment il réagira.

◇ *vi* -**1.** [reveal]: that would be ~ing! ce serait trahir un secret!; I won't ~ je ne dirai rien à personne; time will ~ qui vivra verra, le temps nous le dira; more than words can ~ plus que les mots ne peuvent dire. -**2.** [know] savoir; how can I ~? comment le saurais-je?; who can ~? qui peut savoir?, qui sait?; you never can ~ on ne sait jamais. -**3.** [have effect] se faire sentir, avoir de l'influence; breeding ~s *Br* bon sang ne saurait mentir *prov*; her age is beginning to ~ elle commence à accuser son âge; the strain is beginning to ~ la tension commence à se faire sentir; her aristocratic roots told against/in favour of her ses origines aristocratiques lui nuisaient/jouaient en sa faveur. -**4.** *lit* [story, book]: to ~ of sthg raconter qqch; the first volume ~s of the postwar period le premier volume raconte la période d'après-guerre; I've heard ~ of phantom ships j'ai entendu parler de navires fantômes. -**5.** *lit* [bear witness]: to ~ of témoigner de; the scars told of his reckless life ses cicatrices témoignaient de sa vie mouvementée; the stones told of battles of times past les pierres portaient les traces de batailles des temps passés.

◆ **tell apart** *vt sep* distinguer (entre); I couldn't ~ the twins apart je ne pouvais pas distinguer les jumeaux l'un de l'autre.

◆ **tell off** *vt sep* -**1.** [scold] réprimander, gronder; to ~ sb off for doing sthg gronder OR réprimander qqn pour avoir fait qqch. -**2.** [select] affecter, désigner.

◆ **tell on** *vt insep* -**1.** [denounce] dénoncer; don't ~ on me ne me dénonce pas. -**2.** [have effect on] se faire sentir sur, produire un effet sur; her age is ~ing on her elle accuse son âge; the strain soon began to ~ on her health la tension ne tarda pas à avoir un effet néfaste sur sa santé.

teller ['telə^r] *n* -**1.** [in bank]: (bank) ~ caissier *m*, -ère *f*, guichetier *m*-ère *f*. -**2.** POL [of votes] scrutateur *m*, -trice *f*. -**3.** [of story]: (story) ~ conteur *m*, -euse *f*, narrateur *m*, -trice *f*.

telling ['telɪŋ] ◇ *adj* -**1.** [revealing - smile, figures, evidence] révélateur, éloquent; a ~ look un regard qui en dit long. -**2.** [effective - style] efficace; [- account] saisissant; [- remark, argument] qui porte; it was a ~ blow le coup fut bien asséné OR porta.

◇ *n* récit *m*, narration *f*; the story is long in the ~ l'histoire est longue à raconter.

telling-off (*pl* tellings-off) *n* réprimande *f*; to get a good ~ se faire gronder; to give sb a ~ réprimander qqn.

telltale ['telteɪl] ◇ *n* -**1.** [person] rapporteur *m*, -euse *f*. -**2.** MECH indicateur *m*; ~ lamp lampe *f* témoin.

◇ *adj* [marks] révélateur; [look, blush, nod] éloquent; I was looking for any ~ signs of human settlement je cherchais des traces d'habitation humaine.

tellurium [te'ljʊərɪəm] *n* tellure *m*.

telly *inf* ['telɪ] (*pl* tellies) *n Br* télé *f*; on the ~ à la télé; ~ addict drogué *m*, -e *f* de la télé.

temerity [tɪ'merətɪ] *n* témérité *f*, audace *f*; he had the ~ to suggest I had lied il a eu l'audace OR le front d'insinuer que j'avais menti, il a osé insinuer que j'avais menti.

temp [temp] ◇ *n* (*abbr of* temporary employee) intérimaire *mf*.

◇ *vi*: she's ~ing elle fait de l'intérim.

temp. (*written abbr of* temperature) temp.

temper ['tempə^r] ◇ *n* -**1.** [character] caractère *m*, tempérament *m*; to have an even ~ être d'un tempérament calme OR d'humeur égale; to have a quick OR hot ~ se mettre facilement en colère; he's got a foul OR an awful ~ il a mauvais caractère ‖ [patience] patience *f*; [calm] calme *m*, sang-froid *m inv*; do try and keep your ~ essayez donc de garder votre calme OR sang-froid, essayez donc de vous maîtriser; to lose one's ~ perdre patience, se mettre en colère; to lose one's ~ with sb s'emporter contre qqn; don't try my ~ ne m'énerve pas. -**2.** [mood] humeur *f*; to be in a bad ~ être de mauvaise humeur; he's in a dreadful ~ il est d'une humeur massacrante ‖ [bad mood] (crise *f* de) colère *f*, mauvaise humeur *f*; to be in a ~ être de mauvaise humeur; to fly into a ~ se mettre en colère, s'emporter. -**3.** METALL trempe *f*.

◇ *vt* -**1.** [moderate - passions] modérer, tempérer; [- pain, suffering] adoucir; justice ~ed with mercy la justice tempérée de pitié. -**2.** METALL tremper.

◇ *interj*: ~! on se calme!, du calme!

tempera ['tempərə] *n* [paint] tempera *f*, détrempe *f*; ~ painting détrempe *f*.

temperament ['temprəmənt] *n* [character] tempérament *m*, nature *f*; [moodiness] humeur *f* changeante OR lunatique.

temperamental [,temprə'mentl] *adj* -**1.** [moody - person] capricieux, lunatique; [unpredictable - animal, machine] capricieux. -**2.** [relating to character] du tempérament, de la personnalité.

temperamentally [,temprə'mentəlɪ] *adv* de par son caractère.

temperance ['temprəns] ◇ *n* -**1.** [moderation] modération *f*, sobriété *f*. -**2.** [abstinence from alcohol] tempérance *f*.

◇ *comp* [movement] antialcoolique; ~ hotel *hôtel où l'on ne sert pas de boissons alcoolisées*; ~ society société *f* de tempérance, ligue *f* antialcoolique.

temperate ['temprət] *adj* -**1.** [climate] tempéré. -**2.** [moderate - person] modéré, mesuré; [- character, appetite] modéré; [- reaction, criticism] modéré, sobre.

Temperate Zone *pr n* zone *f* tempérée.

temperature ['temprətʃə^r] ◇ *n* -**1.** MED température *f*; to have OR to run a ~ avoir de la température OR de la fièvre; she has a ~ of 39° elle a 39° de fièvre; to take sb's ~ prendre la température de qqn; to take the ~ of a situation *fig* prendre le pouls d'une situation; her contribution certainly raised the ~ of the debate son intervention a sans aucun doute fait monter le ton du débat. -**2.** METEOR & PHYS température *f*; the cheese should be kept at a ~ of 5° C le fromage doit être conservé à une température de 5° C; a drop in ~ une baisse de température; the ~ fell overnight la température a baissé du jour au lendemain ❑ at room ~ à température ambiante.

◇ *comp* [change] de température; [control] de la température; [gradient] thermique; ~ chart feuille *f* de température.

tempered ['tempəd] *adj* -**1.** [steel] trempé. -**2.** MUS [scale] tempéré.

-tempered *in cpds*: good/bad~ de bonne/mauvaise humeur; an even~ person une personne d'humeur égale.

temper tantrum *n* crise *f* de colère; to have OR to throw a ~ piquer une colère.

tempest ['tempɪst] *n lit* tempête *f*, orage *m*; 'The Tempest' *Shakespeare* 'la Tempête'.

tempestuous [tem'pestjʊəs] *adj* -**1.** [weather] de tempête. -**2.** [person] impétueux, fougueux; [meeting] agité; a ~ love affair une liaison orageuse OR tumultueuse.

tempi ['tempiː] *pl* → **tempo**.

Templar ['templə^r] *n* -**1.** [in crusades]: Knight ~ chevalier *m* du Temple, templier *m*. -**2.** *Br* JUR avocat *m* du Temple.

template ['templɪt] *n* -**1.** TECH gabarit *m*, calibre *m*, patron *m*. -**2.** [beam] traverse *f*.

temple ['templ] *n* -**1.** RELIG temple *m*; the Temple *édifice historique de la City à Londres abritant deux «Inns of Court»*. -**2.** ANAT tempe *f*.

Temple Bar *pr n porte ouest de la City de Londres où le maire vient accueillir le souverain*.

templet ['templɪt] = **template**.

tempo ['tempəʊ] (*pl* tempos OR tempi [-piː]) *n* tempo *m*.

temporal ['tempərəl] *adj* -**1.** [gen & GRAMM] temporel. -**2.** [secular] temporel, séculier.

temporal lobe *n* lobe *m* temporal.

temporarily [*Br* 'tempərərəlɪ, *Am* ,tempə'rerəlɪ] *adv* provisoirement, temporairement.

temporary ['tempərərɪ] (*pl* **temporaries**) ◇ *adj* [accommodation, solution, powers] temporaire, provisoire; [employment] temporaire, intérimaire; [improvement] passager, momentané; on a ~ basis à titre temporaire; a ~ appointment une nomination temporaire OR provisoire; a ~ job un emploi temporaire; ~ teacher SCH professeur *m* suppléant; aspirin can give ~ relief from arthritis l'aspirine peut apporter un soulagement passager à l'arthrite.

◇ *n* intérimaire *mf*.

temporize, -ise ['tempəraɪz] *vi fml* [try to gain time] temporiser, chercher à gagner du temps.

tempt [tempt] *vt* [entice] tenter, donner envie à; [seduce] tenter, séduire; [attract] attirer, tenter; to ~ sb to do sthg OR into doing sthg donner à qqn l'envie de faire qqch; did you hit him? – no, but I was sorely ~ed tu l'as frappé? – non, mais ce n'est pas l'envie qui m'en manquait; I'm ~ed to accept their offer je suis tenté d'accepter leur proposition; and Satan ~ed Christ et Satan tenta le Christ; a rival company tried to ~ him away une entreprise rivale a essayé de le débaucher en lui faisant une offre alléchante; I let myself be ~ed into buying the car je n'ai pas pu résister à la tentation d'acheter la voiture; the mild weather ~ed us into the garden le temps doux nous a incités à aller au jardin; don't ~ me! *hum* n'essayez pas de me tenter!, ne me tentez pas!; can I ~ you to another sandwich? je peux vous proposer encore un sandwich?, vous voulez encore un sandwich? ❑ to ~ fate/providence tenter le diable/le sort.

temptation [temp'teɪʃn] *n* tentation *f*; to put ~ in sb's way exposer qqn à la tentation; it's a great ~ c'est très tentant; to give in to ~ céder OR succomber à la tentation; to resist ~ résister à la tentation.

tempter ['temptə^r] *n* tentateur *m*.

tempting ['temptɪŋ] *adj* [offer] tentant, attrayant; [smell, meal] appétissant.

temptingly ['temptɪŋlɪ] *adv* d'une manière tentante; **it looks ~ easy** c'est tentant parce que cela a l'air facile.

temptress ['temptrɪs] *n lit* OR *hum* tentatrice *f*.

ten [ten] ◇ *num adj* dix; **they're ~ a penny** *Br* il y en a tant qu'on veut OR à revendre.
◇ *n* [figure] dix *m*; **~s of thousands of refugees** des dizaines de milliers de réfugiés; **~ to one** [in ratio, bets] dix contre un; **~ to one we won't sell anything** je te parie que nous ne vendrons rien.
◆ **tens** *npl* MATH dizaines *fpl*; **~ column** colonne *f* des dizaines.

tenable ['tenəbl] *adj* -**1.** [argument, position] défendable, soutenable. -**2.** [post] que l'on occupe, auquel on est nommé; **the appointment is ~ for a five-year period** on est nommé à ce poste pour cinq ans.

tenacious [tɪ'neɪʃəs] *adj* -**1.** [stubborn, persistent - person] entêté, opiniâtre; [- prejudice, opposition] tenace, obstiné; [- tradition] tenace. -**2.** [firm - grip] ferme, solide. -**3.** [tough - stain] tenace. -**4.** [long-lasting - memory] sûr, tenace.

tenaciously [tɪ'neɪʃəslɪ] *adv* avec ténacité, obstinément.

tenacity [tɪ'næsətɪ] *n* ténacité *f*, opiniâtreté *f*.

tenancy ['tenənsɪ] (*pl* **tenancies**) ◇ *n* -**1.** [of house, land] location *f*; **to take up the ~ on a house** prendre une maison en location. -**2.** [period]: **(period of) ~** (période *f* de) location *f*; **during my ~ of the house** quand j'étais locataire de la maison; **during his ~ of Government House** *fig* pendant qu'il était gouverneur. -**3.** [property]: **a council ~** un logement appartenant à la municipalité, ≃ une HLM.
◇ *comp* de location; **~ agreement** contrat *m* de location.

tenant ['tenənt] ◇ *n* locataire *mf*.
◇ *vt* habiter comme locataire, louer.
◇ *comp* [rights] du locataire.

tenant farmer *n* métayer *m*, -ère *f*.

tenantry ['tenəntrɪ] *n* AGR ensemble *m* des tenanciers OR locataires.

ten-cent-store *n Am* bazar *m*.

tench [tenʃ] (*pl inv*) *n* tanche *f*.

tend [tend] ◇ *vi* -**1.** [be inclined]: **to ~ to** avoir tendance à, tendre à; **he does ~ to take himself seriously** il a vraiment tendance à se prendre au sérieux; **I ~ to think (that) politics is a waste of time** j'ai tendance à penser que la politique est une perte de temps; **that does ~ to be the case** c'est souvent le cas. -**2.** [colour]: **red ~ing to orange** rouge tirant sur l'orange. -**3.** [go, move] tendre; **his writings ~ to** OR **towards exoticism** ses écrits tendent vers l'exotisme; **in later life, she ~ed more towards a Marxist view of things** vers la fin de sa vie, elle inclina OR évolua vers des idées marxistes. -**4.** [look after]: **she ~ed to his every wish** elle lui a passé tous ses caprices, elle a fait ses quatre volontés; **to ~ to one's business/one's guests** s'occuper de ses affaires/ses invités; **to ~ to sb's wounds** panser OR soigner les blessures de qqn.
◇ *vt* -**1.** [take care of - sheep] garder; [- sick, wounded] soigner; [- garden] entretenir, s'occuper de; **to ~ sb's wounds** panser OR soigner les blessures de qqn. -**2.** *Am* [customer] servir.

tendency ['tendənsɪ] (*pl* **tendencies**) *n* -**1.** [inclination] tendance *f*; **he has a ~ to forget things** il a tendance à tout oublier; **she has a natural ~ to** OR **towards laziness** elle est d'un naturel paresseux; **to have suicidal tendencies** avoir des tendances suicidaires. -**2.** [trend] tendance *f*; **a growing ~ towards conservatism** une tendance de plus en plus marquée vers le conservatisme; **upward/downward ~** [in prices] tendance à la hausse/à la baisse. -**3.** POL tendance *f*, groupe *m*.

tendentious [ten'denʃəs] *adj* tendancieux.

tendentiously [ten'denʃəslɪ] *adv* tendancieusement.

tendentiousness [ten'denʃəsnɪs] *n* caractère *m* tendancieux.

tender ['tendəʳ] ◇ *adj* -**1.** [affectionate - person] tendre, affectueux, doux; [- heart, smile, words] tendre; [- memories] doux; **they bade each other a ~ farewell** ils se sont fait de tendres adieux ❑ **'Tender is the Night'** *Fitzgerald* 'Tendre est la nuit'. -**2.** [sensitive - skin] délicat, fragile; [sore] sensible, douloureux; **my knee is still ~** mon genou me fait encore mal; **that's rather a ~ subject** c'est un sujet assez délicat; **to touch sb on a ~ spot** *fig* toucher le point sensible de qqn. -**3.** [meat, vegetables] tendre. -**4.** *lit* [innocent - age, youth] tendre; **she gave her first concert at the ~ age of six** elle a donné son premier concert alors qu'elle n'avait que six ans; **to be of ~ years** être d'âge tendre.
◇ *vt* -**1.** [resignation] donner; [apologies] présenter; [thanks] offrir; [bid, offer] faire. -**2.** [money, fare] tendre; **to ~ sthg to sb** tendre qqch à qqn.
◇ *vi* faire une soumission; **to ~ for a contract** faire une soumission pour une adjudication, soumissionner une adjudication.
◇ *n* -**1.** *Br* [statement of charges] soumission *f*; [bid] offre *f*; **to put in** OR **to submit a ~ for a job** soumissionner un travail, faire une soumission pour un travail; **to put a job out to ~, to invite ~s for a job** faire un appel d'offres pour un travail. -**2.** [money]: **legal ~** cours *m* légal. -**3.** RAIL tender *m*. -**4.** NAUT [shuttle] navette *f*; [supply boat] ravitailleur *m*. -**5.** [supply vehicle] véhicule *m* ravitailleur; **(fire) ~** *Br* voiture *f* de pompier.

tenderfoot ['tendəfʊt] (*pl* **tenderfoots** OR **tenderfeet** [-fiːt]) *n* -**1.** [beginner] novice *mf*, nouveau *m*, nouvelle *f*. -**2.** *inf Am* [newcomer] nouveau venu *m*, nouvelle venue *f*.

tenderhearted [ˌtendə'hɑːtɪd] *adj* au cœur tendre, compatissant; **she's too ~** elle est trop bonne.

tenderheartedness [ˌtendə'hɑːtɪdnɪs] *n* compassion *f*, sensibilité *f*.

tenderize, -ise ['tendəraɪz] *vt* attendrir.

tenderizer ['tendəraɪzəʳ] *n* attendrisseur *m*.

tenderloin ['tendəlɔɪn] *n* -**1.** [meat] filet *m*. -**2.** *Am* [district] quartier *m* chaud *(connu pour sa corruption)*.

tenderly ['tendəlɪ] *adv* tendrement, avec tendresse.

tenderness ['tendənɪs] *n* -**1.** [of person, feelings] tendresse *f*, affection *f*; **she feels a certain ~ for the old man** elle éprouve une certaine tendresse pour ce vieux monsieur. -**2.** [of skin] sensibilité *f*; [of plant] fragilité *f*; [soreness] sensibilité *f*. -**3.** [of meat, vegetables] tendreté *f*.

tendon ['tendən] *n* tendon *m*.

tendril ['tendrəl] *n* -**1.** BOT vrille *f*, cirre *m*. -**2.** [of hair] boucle *f*.

tenement ['tenəmənt] *n* -**1.** [block of flats] immeuble *m* (ancien). -**2.** [slum] taudis *m*. -**3.** [dwelling] logement *m*.

tenement building *n* immeuble *m* (ancien).

tenement house *n* maison *f* divisée en appartements.

Tenerife [ˌtenə'riːf] *pr n* Tenerife, Ténériffe; **in ~** à Tenerife.

tenet ['tenɪt] *n* [principle] principe *m*, dogme *m*; [belief] croyance *f*.

tenfold ['tenfəʊld] ◇ *adv* dix fois autant OR plus, au décuple; **to increase ~** décupler.
◇ *adj*: **a ~ increase in applications** dix fois plus de demandes.

ten-gallon hat *n* chapeau *m* de cowboy.

tenner *inf* ['tenəʳ] *n Br* billet *m* de 10 livres.

Tennessee [ˌtenə'siː] *pr n* Tennessee *m*; **in ~** dans le Tennessee.

tennis ['tenɪs] ◇ *n* tennis *m*; **to have** OR **to play a game of ~** faire une partie de tennis; **anyone for ~?** qui veut jouer au tennis?
◇ *comp* [ball, court, player] de tennis.

tennis elbow *n (U)* tennis-elbow *m*, synovite *f* du coude.

tennis shoe *n* (chaussure *f* de) tennis *m ou f*.

tennis whites *npl* tenue *f* de tennis.

tenon ['tenən] ◇ *n* tenon *m*.
◇ *vt* tenonner.

tenor ['tenəʳ] ◇ *n* -**1.** [general sense - of conversation] sens *m* général, teneur *f*; [- of letter] contenu *m*, teneur *f*. -**2.** [general flow - of events] cours *m*, marche *f*; **the accident interrupted the even ~ of their life** l'accident est venu interrompre le cours paisible de leur vie. -**3.** MUS ténor *m*.
◇ *adv*: **to sing ~** avoir une voix de OR être ténor.
◇ *comp* [part, voice] de ténor; [aria] pour (voix de) ténor; **~ recorder** flûte *f* à bec; **~ saxophone** saxophone *m* ténor.

tenpin bowling ['tenpɪn-] *n Br* bowling *m*; **to go ~** aller faire du bowling, aller au bowling.

tenpins ['tenpɪnz] *n Am* bowling *m*.

tense [tens] ◇ *adj* -**1.** [person, relationship, situation] tendu; [smile] crispé; **the audience was ~ with excitement** le public contenait avec peine son enthousiasme; **her voice was ~ with emotion** elle avait la voix étranglée par l'émotion; **we spent several ~ hours waiting for news** nous avons passé plusieurs heures à attendre des nouvelles dans un état de grande tension nerveuse; **the atmosphere was very ~** l'atmosphère était très tendue; **things are getting ~ in the war zone** la situation devient tendue dans la zone de combat. -**2.** [muscles, rope, spring] tendu; **to become ~** se tendre. -**3.** LING [vowel] tendu.
◇ *vt* [muscle] tendre, bander; **to ~ oneself** se raidir.
◇ *n* GRAMM temps *m*; **future ~** futur *m*; **past ~** passé *m*.
◆ **tense up** ◇ *vi insep* [muscle] se tendre, se raidir; [person] se crisper, devenir tendu; **don't ~ up** détends-toi, décontracte-toi.
◇ *vt sep* [person] rendre nerveux; **she's all ~d up** elle est vraiment tendue.

tensely ['tenslɪ] *adv* [move, react] de façon tendue; [speak] d'une voix tendue; **they waited ~ for the doctor to arrive** ils ont attendu le médecin dans un état de grande tension nerveuse.

tenseness ['tensnɪs] *n* tension *f*.

tensile ['tensaɪl] *adj* MECH extensible, élastique.

tensile strength *n* résistance *f* à la tension, limite *f* élastique à la tension.

tension ['tenʃn] *n* -**1.** [of person, situation, voice] tension *f*; **~ between the two countries is mounting** la tension monte entre les deux pays. -**2.** [of muscle, rope, spring] tension *f*. -**3.** ELEC tension *f*, voltage *m*. -**4.** MECH & TECH tension *f*, (force *f* de) traction *f*.

tension headache *n* mal *m* de tête dû à la tension nerveuse.

tensor ['tensəʳ] *n* ANAT & MATH tenseur *m*.

tent [tent] ◇ *n* -**1.** [for camping] tente *f*; **to put up** OR **to pitch a ~** monter une tente. -**2.** MED: **oxygen ~** tente *f* à oxygène.
◇ *comp* [peg, pole] de tente.
◇ *vi* camper.

tentacle ['tentəkl] *n* tentacule *m*.

tentative ['tentətɪv] *adj* -**1.** [provisional] provisoire; [preliminary] préliminaire; [experimental] expérimental; **a ~ offer** une offre provisoire; **our plans are only ~** nos projets ne sont pas définitifs. -**2.** [uncertain - smile] timide; [- person] indécis, hésitant; [- steps] hésitant.

tentatively ['tentətɪvlɪ] *adv* -**1.** [suggest] provisoirement; [act] à titre d'essai. -**2.** [smile] timidement; [walk] d'un pas hésitant.

tent dress *n* robe *f* très ample, robe *f* sac.

tenterhooks ['tentəhʊks] *npl* TEX clous *mpl* à crochet; **to be on ~** être sur des charbons ardents; **to keep sb on ~** tenir qqn en haleine.

tenth [tenθ] ◇ *adj* dixième.
◇ *n* -**1.** [gen & MATH] dixième *m*. -**2.** MUS dixième *f*.

tenuity [te'njuːətɪ] *n* ténuité *f*.

tenuous ['tenjʊəs] *adj* -**1.** [fine - distinction] subtil, ténu; [- thread] ténu; **a ~ voice** une voix grêle OR fluette. -**2.** [flimsy - link, relationship] précaire, fragile; [- evidence] mince, faible; [- argument] faible. -**3.** [precarious - existence] précaire. -**4.** PHYS [gas] raréfié.

tenuously ['tenjʊəslɪ] *adv* de manière ténue OR précaire.

tenuousness ['tenjʊəsnɪs] *n* -**1.** [of distinction] subtilité *f*; [of thread] ténuité *f*; [of voice] faiblesse *f*. -**2.** [of link, relationship] fragilité *f*, précarité *f*; [of evidence] minceur *f*, faiblesse *f*; [of argument] faiblesse *f*. -**3.** [of existence] précarité *f*. -**4.** PHYS raréfaction *f*.

tenure ['tenjəʳ] *n* -**1.** [of land, property] bail *m*. -**2.** [of post] occupation *f*; **during his ~ as chairman** pendant qu'il occupait le poste de président OR était président; **to have ~** *Am* UNIV être titulaire.

tenured ['tenjəd] *adj* [post] titulaire.

tenure-tracked *adj Am*: **he's got a ~ job** son poste est en voie de titularisation.

tepee ['tiːpiː] *n* tipi *m*.

tephra ['tefrə] *n Am* téphra *m*.

tepid ['tepɪd] *adj* -**1.** [water] tiède. -**2.** [welcome, thanks] tiède, réservé.

tepidity [te'pɪdɪtɪ], **tepidness** ['tepɪdnɪs] *n* [of water, welcome] tiédeur *f*.

tequila [tɪ'kiːlə] *n* tequila *f*.

Ter. *written abbr of* terrace.

teratology [terə'tɒlədʒɪ] *n* tératologie *f*.

terbium ['tɜːbɪəm] *n* terbium *m*.

tercentenary [,tɜːsen'tiːnərɪ] (*pl* tercentenaries), **tercentennial** [,tɜːsen'tenjəl] ◇ *n* tricentenaire *m*.
◇ *adj* du tricentenaire.

tercet ['tɜːsɪt] *n* tercet *m*.

Teresa [tə'riːzə] *pr n*: **~ of Avila** sainte Thérèse d'Avila; **Mother ~** Mère Teresa.

term [tɜːm] ◇ *n* -**1.** [period, end of period] terme *m*; [of pregnancy] terme *m*; **in the long/short ~** à long/court terme; **to reach (full) ~** arriver OR être à terme. -**2.** SCH & UNIV trimestre *m*; **in** OR **during ~ (time)** pendant le trimestre; **autumn ~** trimestre d'automne, premier trimestre. -**3.** JUR & POL [of court, parliament] session *f*; [of elected official] mandat *m*; **the president is elected for a 4-year ~** le président est élu pour (une période OR une durée de) 4 ans ❑ **during my ~ of office** [gen] pendant que j'étais en fonction; POL pendant mon mandat. -**4.** [in prison] peine *f*; **~ of imprisonment** peine de prison; **to serve one's ~** purger sa peine. -**5.** [word, expression] terme *m*; **medical/legal ~** terme médical/juridique; **she spoke of you in very flattering ~s** elle a parlé de vous en (des) termes très flatteurs; **she told him what she thought in no uncertain ~s** elle lui a dit carrément ce qu'elle pensait. -**6.** LOGIC & MATH terme *m*.
◇ *vt* appeler, nommer; **I wouldn't ~ it a scientific book exactly** je ne dirais pas vraiment que c'est un livre scientifique; **critics ~ed the play a total disaster** les critiques ont qualifié la pièce d'échec complet.
◆ **terms** *npl* -**1.** [conditions - of employment] conditions *fpl*; [- of agreement, contract] termes *mpl*; **under the ~s of the agreement** selon les termes de l'accord; **~s of payment** modalités *fpl* de paiement; **~s and conditions of sale/of employment** JUR conditions de vente/d'emploi; **what are the inquiry's ~s of reference?** quelles sont les attributions OR quel est le mandat de la commission d'enquête?; **what are your ~s?** quelles sont vos conditions?; **to dictate ~s to sb** imposer des conditions à qqn; **she would only accept on her own ~s** elle n'était disposée à accepter qu'après avoir posé ses conditions; **not on any ~s** à aucun prix, à aucune condition. -**2.** [perspective]: **we must think in less ambitious ~s** il faut voir moins grand; **he refuses to consider the question in international ~s** il refuse d'envisager la question d'un point de vue international; **in personal ~s, it was a disaster** sur le plan personnel, c'était une catastrophe. -**3.** [rates, tariffs] conditions *fpl*, tarifs *mpl*; **we offer easy ~s** nous proposons des facilités de paiement ‖ [in hotel]: **weekly ~s** tarifs à la semaine; **special ~s for travellers** tarifs spéciaux pour VRP. -**4.** [relations]: **to be on good ~s with sb** être en bons termes avec qqn; **we're on the best of ~s** nous sommes en excellents termes; **on equal ~s** d'égal à égal; **they're no longer on speaking ~s** ils ne se parlent plus. -**5.** [agreement] accord *m*; **to make ~s** OR **to come to ~s with sb** arriver à OR conclure un accord avec qqn ‖ [acceptance]: **to come to ~s with sthg** se résigner à qqch, arriver à accepter qqch; **she'll have to come to ~s with her problems eventually** tôt ou tard elle devra faire face à ses problèmes.
◆ **in terms of** *prep phr* en ce qui concerne, pour ce qui est de; **in ~s of profits, we're doing well** pour ce qui est des bénéfices, tout va bien; **I was thinking more in ~s of a Jaguar** je pensais plutôt à une Jaguar; **we really should be thinking more in ~s of foreign competition** il nous faudrait davantage tenir compte de OR penser davantage à la concurrence étrangère.

termagant ['tɜːməgənt] *n* mégère *f*, harpie *f*.

-termer ['tɜːməʳ] *in cpds*: **short/long~** condamné *m*, -e *f* à une courte/longue peine.

terminal ['tɜːmɪnl] ◇ *adj* -**1.** [final] terminal; **~ station** RAIL terminus *m*; **~ velocity** vitesse *f* limite. -**2.** MED [ward] pour malades condamnés OR incurables; [patient] en phase terminale; [disease] qui est dans sa phase terminale; **he has ~ cancer** il a un cancer en phase terminale; **I think I'm suffering from ~ boredom** *hum* je crois que je vais mourir d'ennui. -**3.** [termly] trimestriel.
◇ *n* -**1.** [for bus, underground] terminus *m*; [at airport] terminal *m*, aérogare *f*; **~ B** aérogare OR terminal B; **~ (platform)** PETR terminal. -**2.** COMPUT terminal *m*. -**3.** ELEC [of battery] borne *f*. -**4.** LING terminaison *f*.

terminally ['tɜːmɪnəlɪ] *adv*: **to be ~ ill** être dans la phase terminale d'une maladie; **the ~ ill** les malades condamnés OR qui sont en phase terminale.

terminate ['tɜːmɪneɪt] ◇ *vt* -**1.** [end - project, work] terminer; [- employment] mettre fin OR un terme à; [- contract] résilier, mettre fin OR un terme à; [- pregnancy] interrompre. -**2.** *inf Am* [employee] virer. -**3.** *inf* [kill] descendre.
◇ *vi* -**1.** [end] se terminer; **the row ~d in** OR **with her resignation** la dispute s'est terminée par sa démission. -**2.** LING se terminer. -**3.** RAIL: **this train ~s at Cambridge** ce train ne va pas plus loin que Cambridge.

termination [,tɜːmɪ'neɪʃn] *n* -**1.** [end - gen] fin *f*; [- of contract] résiliation *f*; **~ of employment** licenciement *m*. -**2.** [abortion] interruption *f* de grossesse, avortement *m*. -**3.** LING terminaison *f*, désinence *f*.

termini ['tɜːmɪnaɪ] *pl* → **terminus**.

terminological [,tɜːmɪnə'lɒdʒɪkl] *adj* terminologique; **~ inexactitude** *euph* mensonge *m*.

terminologist [,tɜːmɪ'nɒlədʒɪst] *n* terminologue *mf*.

terminology [,tɜːmɪ'nɒlədʒɪ] (*pl* terminologies) *n* terminologie *f*.

term insurance *n* assurance *f* à terme.

terminus ['tɜːmɪnəs] (*pl* terminuses OR termini [-naɪ]) *n* terminus *m*.

termite ['tɜːmaɪt] *n* termite *m*, fourmi *f* blanche.

termless ['tɜːmlɪs] *adj* -**1.** [endless] illimité, sans limite OR fin. -**2.** [unconditional] sans condition OR conditions, inconditionnel.

termly ['tɜːmlɪ] ◇ *adj* trimestriel.
◇ *adv* trimestriellement, par trimestre.

tern [tɜːn] *n* hirondelle *f* de mer, sterne *f*.

ternary ['tɜːnərɪ] *adj* ternaire.

Terr *written abbr of* terrace.

terrace ['terəs] ◇ *n* -**1.** AGR & GEOL terrasse *f*. -**2.** [patio] terrasse *f*. -**3.** [embankment] terre-plein *m*. -**4.** *Br* [of houses] rangée *f*; **Victorian ~s in Manchester** des rangées de maisons victoriennes à Manchester. -**5.** = **terraced house**.
◇ *vt* AGR cultiver en terrasses.
◆ **terraces** *npl* SPORT gradins *mpl*; **on the ~s** dans les gradins.

> **TERRACE:**
> Ce mot désigne une rangée de maisons à un ou deux étages. A l'origine les «terraced houses» étaient surtout des logements ouvriers (équivalents des corons) construits à proximité d'usines ou de mines de charbon.

terrace cultivation *n* culture *f* en terrasses.

terraced ['terəst] *adj* [garden] suspendu, étagé, «en terrasses»; [hillside] cultivé en terrasses.

terraced house *n Br maison faisant partie d'une «terrace»*; **~s** maisons *fpl* alignées.

terracotta [,terə'kɒtə] ◇ *n* [earthenware] terre *f* cuite.
◇ *comp* [pottery] en terre cuite; [colour] rouille *(inv)*.

terra firma [,terə'fɜːmə] *n lit* OR *hum* terre *f* ferme; **on ~** sur la terre ferme.

terrain [te'reɪn] *n* terrain *m*.

terrapin ['terəpɪn] *n* tortue *f* d'eau douce.

terrarium [tə'reərɪəm] *n* [for plants] mini-serre *f*; [for reptiles] terrarium *m*.

terrazzo [tə'rætsəʊ] (*pl* terrazos) *n* granito *m*.

terrestrial [tə'restrɪəl] ◇ *adj* terrestre.
◇ *n* terrien *m*, -enne *f*.

terrible ['terəbl] *adj* -**1.** [severe, serious - cough, pain] affreux, atroce; [- accident] effroyable, affreux; [- storm] effroyable; **it caused ~ damage** cela a provoqué d'importants dégâts; **it was a ~ blow** ce fut un coup terrible; **the heat was ~** il faisait une chaleur terrible OR épouvantable. -**2.** [very bad - experience, dream] atroce; [- food, smell] épouvantable; [- conditions, poverty] épouvantable, effroyable; **to feel ~** [ill] se sentir très mal; [morally] s'en vouloir beaucoup, avoir des remords; **I feel ~ about the whole situation** je m'en veux beaucoup pour tout ce qui s'est passé; **I feel ~ about leaving them on their own** cela m'ennuie terriblement de les laisser seuls; **she has had a ~ time of it** elle a beaucoup souffert; **I was always ~ at French** j'ai toujours été nul en français; **the food was a ~ disappointment** on a été terriblement déçus par la nourriture.

terribly ['terəblɪ] *adv* -**1.** *inf* [as intensifier] terriblement, extrêmement; **I'm ~ sorry** je suis vraiment désolé; **she'll be ~ disappointed** elle sera terriblement déçue; **the food here isn't ~ good** la nourriture ici n'est pas fameuse; **she's ~ clever** elle est drôlement OR rudement intelligente; **it must have hurt ~** [physically] cela a dû vous faire terriblement mal; [mentally] cela a dû vous faire énormément de peine. -**2.** [very badly] affreusement mal, terriblement mal; **she dresses/plays ~ (badly)** elle s'habille/joue affreusement mal.

terrier ['terɪəʳ] *n* terrier *m (chien)*.
◆ **Terriers** *inf pl pr n Br*: **the Terriers** la territoriale, l'armée *f* territoriale.

terrific [tə'rɪfɪk] *adj* -**1.** [extreme, intense - noise, crash] épouvantable, effroyable; [- speed] fou; [- heat] terrible, épouvantable; [- appetite] énorme, robuste; **these trees grow to a ~ height** ces arbres atteignent une taille énorme; **it must have come as a ~ shock** cela a dû vous faire un choc terrible. -**2.** *inf* [superb, great] terrible, super; **you look ~ in that dress** cette robe te va super bien; **well, I think he's ~** eh bien moi, je le trouve super OR génial.

terrifically *inf* [tə'rɪfɪklɪ] *adv* -**1.** [extremely, enormously] extrêmement, très; **~ happy** super heureux; **~ disappointed** terriblement déçu; **he's grown ~** il a énormément grandi. -**2.** [very well] merveilleusement (bien); **she sings ~** elle chante merveilleusement OR formidablement bien.

terrified ['terɪfaɪd] *adj* terrifié; **to be ~ of sthg** avoir une peur bleue OR avoir très peur de qqch; **I was absolutely ~** j'étais absolument mort de peur OR complètement terrifié OR complètement terrorisé.

terrify ['terɪfaɪ] (*pt* & *pp* terrified) *vt* terrifier, effrayer.

terrifying ['terɪfaɪɪŋ] *adj* [dream] terrifiant; [person] terrible, épouvantable; [weaker use]

terrifiant, effroyable; what a ~ thought! rien que d'y penser, je frémis!
terrifyingly ['terɪfaɪɪŋlɪ] *adv* de façon terrifiante OR effroyable.
terrine [te'riːn] *n* terrine *f*.
territorial [ˌterɪ'tɔːrɪəl] ◇ *adj* territorial; cats are very ~ (animals) les chats sont des animaux farouchement attachés à leur territoire.
◇ *n* territorial *m*; the Territorials l'armée *f* territoriale OR la territoriale britannique.
Territorial Army *pr n* (armée *f*) territoriale *f* britannique.
territorialism [ˌterə'tɔːrɪəlɪzm] *n* territorialisme *m*.
territorial waters *npl* eaux *fpl* territoriales.
territory ['terətrɪ] (*pl* territories) *n* [area] territoire *m*; COMM [of salesperson] territoire *m*, région *f*; [of knowledge] domaine *m*.
terror ['terəʳ] *n* -**1.** [fear] terreur *f*, épouvante *f*; to be OR to go in ~ of one's life craindre pour sa vie; to be in a state of ~ être terrorisé OR terrifié; to have a ~ of (doing) sthg avoir extrêmement peur OR la terreur de (faire) qqch. -**2.** [frightening event or aspect] terreur *f*; the ~s of the night les terreurs de la nuit. -**3.** [terrorism] terreur *f*; campaign of ~ campagne *f* terroriste OR de terreur. -**4.** *inf* [person] terreur *f*; he's a ~ on his bike c'est une terreur en vélo; you little ~! petite terreur!
◆ **Terror** *n*: the Terror HIST la Terreur.
terrorism ['terərɪzm] *n* terrorisme *m*; ecological ~ terrorisme écologique.
terrorist ['terərɪst] ◇ *n* terroriste *mf*.
◇ *adj* [bomb] de terroriste; [campaign, attack, group] terroriste.
terrorize, -ise ['terəraɪz] *vt* terroriser.
terror-stricken, terror-struck *adj* épouvanté, saisi de terreur.
terry (towelling) ['terɪ-] *n*: ~ (cloth) tissu-éponge *m*.
terse [tɜːs] *adj* [concise] concis, succinct; [laconic] laconique; [abrupt] brusque, sec.
tersely ['tɜːslɪ] *adv* [concisely] avec concision; [laconically] laconiquement; [abruptly] brusquement, sèchement.
terseness ['tɜːsnɪs] *n* [concision] concision *f*; [laconicism] laconisme *m*; [abruptness] brusquerie *f*.
tertiary ['tɜːʃərɪ] *adj* [gen & INDUST] tertiaire; [education] postscolaire.
◆ **Tertiary** ◇ *adj* GEOL tertiaire.
◇ *n*: the Tertiary GEOL le tertiaire.
Terylene® ['terəliːn] ◇ *n* Térylène® *m*, ≃ Tergal® *m*.
◇ *adj* en Tergal.
TESL [tesl] (*abbr of* Teaching (of) English as a Second Language) *n* enseignement *m* de l'anglais langue seconde.
TESOL ['tiːsɒl] (*abbr of* Teaching English to Speakers of Other Languages) *n* enseignement *m* de l'anglais aux étrangers OR comme langue étrangère.
TESSA ['tesə] (*abbr of* tax-exempt special savings account) *n en Grande-Bretagne, plan d'épargne exonéré d'impôt*.
tessellated ['tesəleɪtɪd] *adj* en mosaïque.
tessitura [ˌtesɪ'tʊərə] *n* tessiture *f*.
test [test] ◇ *n* -**1.** [examination - gen] test *m*; SCH contrôle *m*, interrogation *f*; to pass a ~ réussir à un examen; biology ~ interrogation de biologie; to sit OR to take a ~ passer un examen ❑ intelligence/general knowledge ~ test d'intelligence/de culture générale; personality ~ test de personnalité; I'm taking my (driving) ~ tomorrow je passe mon permis (de conduire) demain; did you pass your (driving) ~? avez-vous été reçu au permis (de conduire)? -**2.** MED [of blood, urine] test *m*, analyse *f*; [of eyes, hearing] examen *m*; to undergo ~s subir des tests OR examens; to have a blood ~ faire faire une analyse de sang; to have an eye ~ se faire examiner la vue; the lab did a ~ for cholesterol/salmonella le laboratoire a fait une analyse pour déterminer le taux de cholestérol/pour détecter la présence de salmonelles. -**3.** [trial - of equipment, machine] test *m*, essai *m*, épreuve *f*; [- of quality] contrôle *m*; to carry out ~s on sthg effectuer des tests sur qqch; all new drugs undergo clinical ~s tous les nouveaux médicaments subissent des tests cliniques; a ~ for noise levels un contrôle des niveaux sonores; to be on ~ être testé OR à l'essai; to put sthg to the ~ tester qqch, faire l'essai de qqch. -**4.** [of character, endurance, resolve] test *m*; a good ~ of character un bon test de personnalité, un bon moyen de tester la personnalité; to put sb to the ~ éprouver qqn, mettre qqn à l'épreuve; his courage was really put to the ~ son courage fut sérieusement mis à l'épreuve OR éprouvé; it's the first major ~ for the Prime Minister c'est la première fois que le Premier ministre est réellement mis à l'épreuve; to stand the ~ se montrer à la hauteur ❑ ~ of strength *literal* & *fig* épreuve *f* de force; to stand the ~ of time durer, résister à l'épreuve du temps; her books have certainly stood the ~ of time ses livres n'ont pas pris une ride. -**5.** [measure] test *m*; it's a ~ of union solidarity c'est un test de la solidarité syndicale; it will be a ~ of popularity for the new leader ce sera un test de popularité pour le nouveau dirigeant; the by-election will be a good ~ of public opinion l'élection partielle représentera un bon test de l'opinion publique. -**6.** *Br* SPORT test-match *m*.
◇ *comp* [flight, strip etc] d'essai; ~ shot lancement *m* d'essai.
◇ *vt* -**1.** [examine - ability, knowledge, intelligence] tester, mesurer; SCH [pupils] tester, contrôler les connaissances de; we were ~ed in geography and physics nous avons eu un contrôle de géographie et de physique; she was ~ed on her knowledge of plants on a testé OR vérifié ses connaissances botaniques. -**2.** MED [blood, urine] analyser, faire une analyse de; [sight, hearing] examiner; to have one's eyes ~ed se faire examiner la vue; you need your eyes ~ing *Br* OR ~ed *Am*! *fig* il faut mettre des lunettes! -**3.** [try out - prototype, car] essayer, faire l'essai de; [- weapon] tester; [- drug] tester, expérimenter; none of our products are ~ed on animals nos produits ne sont pas testés sur les animaux. -**4.** [check - batteries, pressure, suspension] vérifier, contrôler. -**5.** [measure - reaction, popularity] mesurer, évaluer; the day of action will ~ union solidarity la journée d'action permettra de mesurer OR d'évaluer la solidarité syndicale. -**6.** [analyse - soil] analyser, faire des prélèvements dans; [- water] analyser; the water was ~ed for phosphates on a analysé l'eau pour en déterminer le taux de phosphates; to ~ food for starch rechercher la présence d'amidon dans les aliments ❑ to ~ the water tâter le terrain. -**7.** [tax - machinery, driver, patience] éprouver, mettre à l'épreuve; to ~ sb to the limit pousser qqn à bout OR à la dernière extrémité; to ~ sb's patience to the limit mettre la patience de qqn à rude épreuve.
◇ *vi* -**1.** [make examination]: to ~ for albumin/for salmonella faire une recherche d'albumine/de salmonelles; to ~ for the presence of gas rechercher la présence de gaz. -**2.** RADIO & TELEC: ~ing, ~ing! un, deux, trois!
◆ **test out** *vt sep* -**1.** [idea, theory] tester. -**2.** [prototype, product] essayer, mettre à l'essai; these products used to be ~ed out on animals avant, on testait ces produits sur des animaux.
testament ['testəmənt] *n* -**1.** JUR testament *m*. -**2.** BIBLE testament *m*; the New Testament le Nouveau Testament; the Old Testament l'Ancien Testament.
testamentary [ˌtestə'mentərɪ] *adj* testamentaire.
testate ['testeɪt] *adj*: to die ~ mourir en ayant laissé un testament OR testé.
testator [te'steɪtəʳ] *n* testateur *m*.
testatrix [te'steɪtrɪks] *n* testatrice *f*.
test ban *n* interdiction *f* des essais nucléaires.
test-bed *n* banc *m* d'essai OR d'épreuve.
test card *n Br* TV mire *f*.
test case *n* JUR précédent *m*, affaire *f* qui fait jurisprudence.
test drive (*pt* test-drove, *pp* test-driven) *n* essai *m* sur route; to go for a ~ essayer une voiture.
◆ **test-drive** *vt* [car] essayer.
tester ['testəʳ] *n* -**1.** [person] contrôleur *m*, -euse *f*, vérificateur *m*, -trice *f*. -**2.** [machine] appareil *m* de contrôle OR de vérification. -**3.** [sample - of make-up, perfume] échantillon *m*. -**4.** [over bed] baldaquin *m*, ciel *m*.
testes ['testiːz] *pl* → **testis**.
testicle ['testɪkl] *n* testicule *m*.
testify ['testɪfaɪ] (*pt* & *pp* testified) ◇ *vt* déclarer, affirmer; I can ~ that she remained at home je peux attester qu'elle est restée à la maison.
◇ *vi* [be witness] porter témoignage, servir de témoin; [make statement] déposer, faire une déposition; to ~ for/against sb déposer en faveur de/contre qqn; I can ~ to her honesty je peux attester OR témoigner de son honnêteté; his behaviour testified to his guilt son comportement témoignait de sa culpabilité.
testimonial [ˌtestɪ'məʊnjəl] ◇ *n* -**1.** [certificate] attestation *f*; [reference] recommandation *f*, attestation *f*. -**2.** [tribute] témoignage *m*. -**3.** *Br* SPORT *match en hommage à un grand sportif*.
◇ *comp* qui porte témoignage; they organized a ~ dinner for him ils ont organisé un dîner en son honneur; ~ match *Br match en hommage à un grand sportif*.
testimony [*Br* 'testɪmənɪ, *Am* 'testəməʊnɪ] (*pl* testimonies) *n* -**1.** [statement] déclaration *f*; JUR témoignage *m*, déposition *f*; to call sb in ~ appeler qqn en témoignage. -**2.** [sign, proof] témoignage *m*; to bear ~ to the truth porter OR rendre témoignage de la vérité; the monument is a lasting ~ to OR of his genius ce monument est le témoignage vivant de son génie.
testing ['testɪŋ] ◇ *adj* [difficult] difficile, éprouvant; it's been a ~ time for everyone cela a été une période éprouvante pour tout le monde.
◇ *n* -**1.** [of product, machine, vehicle] (mise *f* à l') essai *m*; nuclear ~ essais *mpl* nucléaires. -**2.** MED [of sight, hearing] examen *m*; [of blood, urine] analyse *f*; [of reaction] mesure *f*. -**3.** [of intelligence, knowledge, skills] évaluation *f*; [of candidate] évaluation *f*, examen *m*.
testing bench *n* banc *m* d'essai.
testing ground *n* terrain *m* d'essai; Scotland is often used as a ~ for new government policies le gouvernement utilise souvent l'Écosse pour tester ses nouvelles mesures politiques.
testis ['testɪs] (*pl* testes [-tiːz]) *n* testicule *m*.
test match *n Br* match *m* international, test-match *m*.
testosterone [te'stɒstərəʊn] *n* testostérone *f*.
test paper *n* -**1.** CHEM papier *m* réactif. -**2.** *Br* SCH interrogation *f* écrite.
test piece *n* MUS morceau *m* imposé OR de concours.
test pilot *n* pilote *m* d'essai.
test run *n* essai *m*; to go for a ~ faire un essai.
test signal *n* signal *m* de mesure.
test tube *n* éprouvette *f*.
◆ **test-tube** *adj* de laboratoire.
test-tube baby *n* bébé-éprouvette *m*.
testy ['testɪ] (*compar* testier, *superl* testiest) *adj* irritable, grincheux.
tetanus ['tetənəs] ◇ *n* tétanos *m*.
◇ *comp* [vaccination, injection] antitétanique.
tetchily ['tetʃɪlɪ] *adv* d'un ton irrité.
tetchiness ['tetʃɪnɪs] *n* irritabilité *f*.
tetchy ['tetʃɪ] (*compar* tetchier, *superl* tetchiest) *adj Br* grincheux, irascible.
tête-à-tête [ˌteɪtɑː'teɪt] ◇ *n* (conversation *f* en) tête-à-tête *m inv*.
◇ *adj* en tête-à-tête.
tether ['teðəʳ] ◇ *n* [for horse] longe *f*, attache *f*; to be at the end of one's ~ [depressed] être au

bout du rouleau; [exasperated] être à bout de patience.
◇ *vt* [horse] attacher.

tetrachloride [ˌtetrəˈklɔːraɪd] *n* tétrachlorure *m*.

tetracycline [ˌtetrəˈsaɪkliːn] *n* tétracycline *f*.

tetrad [ˈtetræd] *n* tétrade *f*.

tetragon [ˈtetrəgən] *n* quadrilatère *m*.

tetrahedron [ˌtetrəˈhiːdrən] (*pl* tetrahedrons OR tetrahedra [-drə]) *n* tétraèdre *m*.

tetrameter [teˈtræmɪtəʳ] *n* tétramètre *m*.

tetraplegic [ˌtetrəˈpliːdʒɪk] ◇ *n* tétraplégique *mf*.
◇ *adj* tétraplégique.

tetrapod [ˈtetrəpɒd] *n* tétrapode *m*.

tetrasyllable [ˈtetrəˌsɪləbl] *n* tétrasyllabe *m*.

tetravalent [ˌtetrəˈveɪlənt] *adj* tétravalent, quadrivalent.

tetrode [ˈtetrəʊd] *n* tétrode *f*, tube *m* à quatre électrodes.

tetter [ˈtetəʳ] *n* éruption *f* cutanée.

Teuton [ˈtjuːtən] *n* Teuton *m*, -onne *f*.

Teutonic [tjuːˈtɒnɪk] *adj* teuton.

Teutonism [ˈtjuːtənɪzm] *n* germanisme *m*.

Tex *n* -**1.** *written abbr of* Texan. -**2.** *written abbr of* Texas.

Texan [ˈteksn] ◇ *n* Texan *m*, -e *f*.
◇ *adj* texan.

Texas [ˈteksəs] *pr n* Texas *m*; in ~ au Texas.

Tex-Mex [ˌteksˈmeks] *n* -**1.** CULIN *cuisine mexicaine adaptée aux goûts américains*. -**2.** [music] musique *f* mexico-américaine.

text [tekst] ◇ *n* [gen & COMPUT] texte *m*.
◇ *comp* COMPUT: ~ mode mode *m* texte; ~ processing traitement *m* automatique de texte sur ordinateur.

textbook [ˈtekstbʊk] ◇ *n* [SCH & gen] manuel *m*.
◇ *comp* [typical] typique; [ideal] parfait, idéal; it's a ~ case c'est un exemple classique OR typique.

textile [ˈtekstaɪl] ◇ *n* textile *m*.
◇ *comp* [industry] textile.

textual [ˈtekstjʊəl] *adj* textuel, de texte; ~ analysis analyse *f* de texte; ~ criticism critique *f* littéraire d'un texte; ~ error erreur *f* de texte.

textually [ˈtekstjʊəlɪ] *adv* textuellement, mot à mot.

texture [ˈtekstʃəʳ] *n* -**1.** [of fabric] texture *f*; [of leather, wood, paper, skin, stone] grain *m*; the paper is grainy in ~ le papier est de texture granuleuse. -**2.** [of food, soil] texture *f*, consistance *f*; [of writing] structure *f*, texture *f*; music is part of the ~ of their lives la musique fait partie intégrante de leur vie.

textured vegetable protein [ˈtekstʃəd-] *n protéine végétale ayant l'aspect et le goût de la viande*.

TGIF *inf* (*abbr of* thank God it's Friday!) encore une semaine de tirée!

TGWU (*abbr of* Transport and General Workers' Union) *pr n le plus grand syndicat interprofessionnel britannique*.

Thai [taɪ] (*pl inv* OR Thais) ◇ *n* -**1.** [person] Thaï *mf*, Thaïlandais *m*, -e *f*. -**2.** LING thaï *m*, thaïlandais *m*.
◇ *adj* thaï, thaïlandais; ~ boxing boxe *f* thaïlandaise.

Thailand [ˈtaɪlænd] *pr n* Thaïlande *f*; in ~ en Thaïlande.

thalamus [ˈθæləməs] (*pl* thalami [-maɪ]) *n* thalamus *m*.

thalassaemia *Br*, **thalassemia** *Am* [ˌθæləˈsiːmɪə] *n* thalassémie *f*.

thalidomide [θəˈlɪdəmaɪd] *n* thalidomide *f*.

thalidomide baby *n bébé victime de la thalidomide*.

thallium [ˈθælɪəm] *n* thallium *m*.

Thames [temz] *pr n*: the (River) ~ la Tamise; he'll never set the ~ on fire *inf Br* il n'a pas inventé la poudre OR le fil à couper le beurre.

than [*weak form* ðən, *strong form* ðæn] ◇ *conj* -**1.** [after comparative adj, adv] que; he plays tennis better ~ I do il joue au tennis mieux que moi; she can walk faster ~ I can run elle va plus vite en marchant que moi en courant; it's quicker by train ~ by bus ça va plus vite en train qu'en bus; I was less/more disappointed ~ angry j'étais moins/plus déçu que fâché. -**2.** [following negative clause]: no sooner had he finished speaking ~ everyone made for the door à peine avait-il fini de parler que tout le monde s'est précipité vers la porte; nothing is worse ~ to spend OR spending the holidays on your own rien n'est pire que de passer les vacances tout seul. -**3.** [with 'rather', 'sooner']: I'd do anything rather ~ have to see him je ferais n'importe quoi plutôt que d'être obligé de le voir; I'd prefer to stay here rather ~ go out, I'd rather OR sooner stay here ~ go out je préférerais rester ici que de sortir. -**4.** [after 'different']: he is different ~ he used to be il n'est plus le même.
◇ *prep* -**1.** [after comparative adj, adv] que; he plays tennis better ~ me OR I il joue au tennis mieux que moi; the cedars are older ~ the oaks les cèdres sont plus vieux que les chênes. -**2.** [indicating quantity, number]: more ~ 15 people plus de 15 personnes; less OR fewer ~ 15 people moins de 15 personnes; I've been invited more ~ once j'ai été invité plus d'une fois; there are more policemen ~ demonstrators il y a plus de policiers que de manifestants. -**3.** [after 'other' in negative clauses]: we have no sizes other ~ 40 or 42 nous n'avons pas d'autres tailles que 40 ou 42; it was none other ~ the Prime Minister who launched the appeal c'est le Premier ministre en personne qui a lancé l'appel. -**4.** [after 'different']: she seems different ~ before elle semble avoir changé; she has different tastes ~ yours elle a des goûts différents des vôtres.

thane [θeɪn] *n* HIST thane *m*, ≃ baron *m*.

thank [θæŋk] *vt* -**1.** remercier; to ~ sb for sthg remercier qqn de OR pour qqch; to ~ sb for doing sthg remercier qqn d'avoir fait qqch; she ~ed us for coming elle nous remercia d'être venus; you have him to ~ for that tu peux lui dire merci; you won't ~ me for it vous allez m'en vouloir; you only have yourself to ~ for that! c'est à toi seul qu'il faut t'en prendre!; ~ God OR goodness! Dieu merci!; ~ heaven OR heavens you're safe! Dieu merci vous êtes sain et sauf! -**2.** [as request]: I'll ~ you to return the book/to keep quiet about it je vous prierai de rapporter le livre/de ne pas en parler.

◆ **thanks** ◇ *npl* -**1.** remerciements *mpl*; give her my ~s for the flowers remerciez-la de ma part pour les fleurs; many ~s for all your help mille mercis OR merci beaucoup pour toute votre aide; received with ~s ADMIN pour acquit. -**2.** RELIG louange *f*, grâce *f*; ~s be to God rendons grâce à Dieu.
◇ *interj* merci; ~s a lot, ~s very much merci beaucoup, merci bien; ~s a million merci mille fois; ~s for coming merci d'être venu; no ~s! (non) merci!; ~s for nothing! je te remercie! *iron*.

◆ **thanks to** *prep phr* grâce à; ~s to you, we saved a lot of money grâce à vous, nous avons économisé beaucoup d'argent; ~s to you, we lost the contract à cause de vous, nous avons perdu le contrat; no ~s to you! ce n'est sûrement pas grâce à vous!

thankful [ˈθæŋkfʊl] *adj* reconnaissant, content; I'm ~ for all their help je leur suis reconnaissant de toute leur aide; I was ~ to get away j'étais content de pouvoir partir; I'm ~ not to have to go back je suis content de ne pas avoir à y retourner; she was just ~ (that) no one recognized her elle s'estimait surtout heureuse que personne ne l'ait reconnue; I'm only ~ everything went off all right je me félicite que tout se soit bien passé; to be ~ for small mercies s'estimer heureux du peu qu'on a.

thankfully [ˈθæŋkfʊlɪ] *adv* -**1.** [with gratitude] avec reconnaissance OR gratitude. -**2.** [with relief] avec soulagement. -**3.** [fortunately] heureusement.

thankfulness [ˈθæŋkfʊlnɪs] *n* gratitude *f*, reconnaissance *f*.

thankless [ˈθæŋklɪs] *adj* [task, person] ingrat.

thanksgiving [ˈθæŋksˌgɪvɪŋ] *n* action *f* de grâce.

Thanksgiving (Day) *n fête nationale américaine*.

THANKSGIVING:
Thanksgiving commémore, le 4e jeudi de novembre, l'installation des premiers colons en Amérique; le dîner en famille qui a généralement lieu à cette occasion est traditionnellement composé d'une dinde aux airelles accompagnée de patates douces, et se termine par une tarte au potiron.

---

thanks offering *n fml* action *f* de grâce; as a ~ [gen] en signe de reconnaissance; RELIG comme action de grâce.

thank you *interj* merci; to say ~ dire merci; ~ very much merci beaucoup OR bien; ~ for the flowers merci pour les fleurs; ~ for coming merci d'être venu.
◆ **thankyou** *n* merci *m*, remerciement *m*; without so much as a thankyou sans même dire merci.

thankyou letter [ˈθæŋkjuː-] *n* lettre *f* de remerciement.

that [ðæt, *weak form of rel pron and conj* ðət] (*pl* those [ðəʊz]) ◇ *dem pron* -**1.** [thing indicated] cela, ce, ça; after/before ~ après/avant cela; what's ~? qu'est-ce que c'est que ça?; who's ~? [gen] qui est-ce?; [on phone] qui est à l'appareil?; is ~ you Susan? c'est toi Susan?; is ~ all you've got to eat? c'est tout ce que vous avez à manger?; what did she mean by ~? qu'est-ce qu'elle voulait dire par là?; those are my parents voilà mes parents; ~ is what he told me c'est OR voilà ce qu'il m'a dit; ~ is where I live c'est là que j'habite; ~ was three months ago il y a trois mois de cela; ~'s strange c'est bizarre; I've only got one coat and ~'s old je n'ai qu'un manteau et encore, il est vieux ☐ it's not as hot as (all) ~! *inf* il ne fait pas si chaud que ça!; so it's come to ~ voilà donc où nous en sommes (arrivés); if it comes to ~, you can always leave si ça en arrive là, vous pouvez toujours partir; ~'s a good boy! en voilà un gentil petit garçon!; ~'s all we need! il ne manquait plus que ça!; ~'s enough (of ~)! ça suffit!; ~'s it! [finished] c'est fini!; [correct] c'est ça!; ~'s it for today! ce sera tout pour aujourd'hui!; ~'s it! you've got it! c'est ça! tu as trouvé!; ~'s life! c'est la vie!; ~'s more like it! voilà qui est déjà mieux!; well, ~'s ~! eh bien voilà!; I said "no" and ~'s ~! j'ai dit «non», un point c'est tout!; ~'s the government all over OR for you! c'est bien l'administration ça!; is she intelligent? — ~ she is! elle est intelligente? — ça oui OR pour sûr! -**2.** [in contrast to 'this'] celui-là *m*, celle-là *f*; those ceux-là *mpl*, celles-là *fpl*; this is an ash, ~ is an oak ceci est un frêne et ça, c'est un chêne; which book do you prefer, this or ~? quel livre préférez-vous, celui-ci ou celui-là?; I'd like some flowers, but not those! j'aimerais des fleurs, mais pas celles-là! -**3.** [used when giving further information] celui *m*, celle *f*; those ceux *mpl*, celles *fpl*; there are those who believe that... il y a des gens qui croient que...; a sound like ~ of a baby crying un bruit comme celui que fait un bébé qui pleure; the symptoms sound like those of malaria les symptômes ressemblent à ceux du paludisme; he spoke with those concerned il a parlé à ceux qui sont concernés; all those interested should contact the club secretary tous ceux qui sont intéressés doivent contacter le secrétaire du club.
◇ *det* -**1.** [the one indicated] ce *m*, cet *m* (*before vowel or mute h*), cette *f*; those ces *mfpl*; ~ man cet homme; those questions ces questions; at ~ moment à ce moment-là; it was raining ~ day il pleuvait ce jour-là; we all agree on ~ point nous sommes tous d'accord là-dessus; did you hear about ~ terrible accident on the motorway? as-tu entendu parler de ce terrible

accident sur l'autoroute?; do you remember ~ play we saw last year? tu te rappelles cette pièce que nous avons vue l'année dernière?; how about ~ drink you offered me? et ce verre que vous m'avez proposé?; I like ~ idea of his j'aime son idée; how's ~ son of yours? comment va ton fils?; if I get hold of ~ son of yours *pej* si je mets la main sur ton sacré fils!; they rode off into the sunset, it was ~ kind of film ils se sont éloignés vers le soleil couchant, c'était ce genre de film, tu vois? -**2.** [in contrast to 'this'] ce...-là *m*, cet...-là *m* (*before vowel or mute h*), cette...-là *f*; those ces...-là *mfpl*; ~ house over there is for sale cette OR la maison là-bas est à vendre; ~ one celui-là *m*, celle-là *f*; choose between this restaurant and ~ one choisissez entre ce restaurant et l'autre.

◇ *adv* -**1.** [so] si, aussi; can you run ~ fast? pouvez-vous courir aussi vite que ça?; he's not (all) ~ good-looking il n'est pas si beau que ça; there's a pile of papers on my desk ~ high! il y a une pile de papiers haute comme ça sur mon bureau! -**2.** *inf* [with result clause] si, tellement; he was ~ weak he couldn't stand il était tellement affaibli qu'il ne tenait plus debout; I could have cried, I was ~ angry j'en aurais pleuré tellement j'étais en colère.

◇ *rel pron* -**1.** [subject of verb] qui; the conclusions ~ emerge from this les conclusions qui en ressortent; nothing ~ matters rien d'important. -**2.** [object or complement of verb] que; the house ~ Jack built la maison que Jack a construite; is this the best ~ you can do? est-ce que c'est ce que vous pouvez faire de mieux?; fool ~ I am, I agreed imbécile que je suis, j'ai accepté; pessimist/optimist ~ he is pessimiste/optimiste comme il est. -**3.** [object of preposition] lequel *m*, laquelle *f*, lesquels *mpl*, lesquelles *fpl*; the box ~ I put it in/on le carton dans lequel/sur lequel je l'ai mis; the songs ~ I was thinking of OR about les chansons auxquelles je pensais; the woman/the film ~ we're talking about la femme/le film dont nous parlons; not ~ I know of pas que je sache. -**4.** [when] où; the week ~ he was sick la semaine où il était malade; during the months ~ we were in Chicago pendant les mois que nous avons passés OR où nous étions à Chicago.

◇ *conj* -**1.** [gen] que; I said ~ I had read it j'ai dit que je l'avais lu; it's natural ~ you should be nervous c'est normal que vous soyez nerveux; it's not ~ she isn't friendly ce n'est pas qu'elle ne soit pas amicale; it was so dark ~ I could barely see il faisait si noir que je voyais à peine; ~ he is capable has already been proven *fml* il a déjà prouvé qu'il était capable; ~ I should live to see the day when... *fml* [expressing incredulity] je n'aurais jamais cru qu'un jour...; oh, ~ it were possible! si seulement c'était possible! -**2.** *arch* OR *lit* [in order that] afin que, pour que; he died ~ we might live il est mort pour que nous puissions vivre.

◆ **and (all) that** *inf adv phr* [and so on] et tout le bastringue; it was a very posh do, waiters in white gloves and (all) ~ c'était très classe, avec des serveurs en gants blancs et tout le bastringue; she went on about friendship and (all) ~ *inf* elle parlait d'amitié et tout ce qui s'ensuit.

◆ **at that** *adv phr* -**1.** [what's more] en plus; it's a forgery and a pretty poor one at ~ c'est une copie et qui plus est elle est mauvaise OR et une mauvaise en plus. -**2.** *inf* [indicating agreement] en fait; perhaps we're not so badly off at ~ *inf* en fait, on n'est peut-être pas tellement à plaindre; it might be worth trying at ~ ça vaudrait peut-être le coup. -**3.** [then] à ce moment-là; at ~, he paused à ce moment-là, il a marqué un temps d'arrêt.

◆ **like that** *inf* ◇ *adj phr* -**1.** [indicating character or attitude] comme ça; she's like ~, she never says thank you elle est comme ça, elle ne dit jamais merci; don't be like ~ ne soyez pas comme ça. -**2.** [close, intimate] comme les deux doigts de la main; the two of them are like ~ *inf* ils sont comme les deux doigts de la main; he's like ~ with the boss *inf* il est au mieux avec le patron.

◇ *adv phr* [in that way] comme ça; stop looking at me like ~! arrête de me regarder comme ça!

◆ **not that** *conj phr*: if he refuses, not ~ he will, is there an alternative? s'il refuse, même si cela est peu probable, est-ce qu'il y a une autre solution?; they've already left, not ~ it matters ils sont déjà partis, encore que ce soit sans importance.

◆ **that is (to say)** *adv phr* enfin; I'll do anything, ~'s to say anything legal je ferais n'importe quoi, enfin du moment que c'est légal; I work at the hospital, as a receptionist ~ is, not as a nurse je travaille à l'hôpital, enfin à la réception, pas comme infirmière; I'd like to ask you something, ~ is, if you've got a minute j'aimerais vous poser une question, enfin, si vous avez un instant.

◆ **that way** *adv phr* -**1.** [in that manner] de cette façon; what makes him act ~ way? qu'est-ce qui le pousse à agir comme ça?; ~ way you'll only make things worse de cette façon, tu ne feras qu'empirer les choses. -**2.** *inf* [in that respect]: she's funny ~ way c'est son côté bizarre; I didn't know he was ~ way inclined je ne connaissais pas ce côté-là de lui.

◆ **with that** *adv phr* là-dessus; with ~, she left sur ce OR là-dessus, elle est partie.

thatch [θætʃ] ◇ *n* -**1.** CONSTR chaume *m*. -**2.** *inf Br fig* [hair] tignasse *f*; a ~ of blonde hair une crinière blonde.

◇ *vt* [roof] couvrir de chaume.

◇ *comp* [roof] de OR en chaume.

thatched [θætʃt] *adj* [roof] en chaume; [house] qui a un toit en chaume; ~ cottage chaumière *f*.

thatcher [ˈθætʃəʳ] *n* couvreur *m* en chaume.

Thatcherism [ˈθætʃərɪzm] *n* POL thatchérisme *m* (*politique de Margaret Thatcher*).

Thatcherite [ˈθætʃəraɪt] ◇ *n* partisan *m* du thatchérisme.

◇ *adj* [policy, view] thatchérien.

thatching [ˈθætʃɪŋ] *n (U)* couverture *f* de chaume.

thaw [θɔː] ◇ *vi* -**1.** [ice, snow] fondre; it's beginning to ~ il commence à dégeler. -**2.** [frozen food] dégeler, se décongeler. -**3.** [hands, feet] se réchauffer. -**4.** *fig* [person, relations] se dégeler, être plus détendu; she seems at last to be ~ing towards me elle semble enfin perdre sa réserve OR sa froideur à mon égard.

◇ *vt* -**1.** [ice, snow] faire dégeler OR fondre. -**2.** [frozen food] dégeler, décongeler.

◇ *n* -**1.** METEOR dégel *m*. -**2.** POL détente *f*, dégel *m*.

◆ **thaw out** ◇ *vt sep* -**1.** [frozen food] décongeler, dégeler. -**2.** [feet, hands] réchauffer; come and ~ yourself out in the sitting room venez vous réchauffer au salon. -**3.** *fig* [make relaxed - person] dégeler, mettre à l'aise.

◇ *vi insep* -**1.** [frozen food] décongeler, dégeler. -**2.** [hands, feet] se réchauffer; I'm beginning to ~ out now je commence à me réchauffer maintenant. -**3.** *fig* [become relaxed] se dégeler, perdre sa froideur OR réserve.

the [*weak form* ðə, *before vowel* ðɪ, *strong form* ðiː] *det* -**1.** [with noun, adj] le *m*, la *f*, l' *mf* (*before vowel or mute h*), les *mfpl*; ~ blue dress is ~ prettiest la robe bleue est la plus jolie; ~ dead/poor/French les morts/pauvres/Français; I can't do ~ impossible je ne peux pas faire l'impossible; translated from ~ Latin traduit du latin. -**2.** [with names, titles]: ~ Smiths/Martins les Smith/Martin; Alexander ~ Great Alexandre le Grand. -**3.** [with numbers, dates]: Monday June ~ tenth OR ~ tenth of June le lundi 10 juin; ~ 80s les années 80; ~ 1820s les années 1820 à 1830; ~ second from the left le second en partant de la gauche. -**4.** [in prices, quantities]: tomatoes are 40p ~ pound les tomates sont à 40 pence la livre; the car does 40 miles to ~ gallon la voiture consomme 7 litres aux 100. -**5.** [with comparatives]: ~ more ~ better plus il y en a, mieux c'est; ~ less said ~ better moins on en parlera, mieux cela vaudra. -**6.** [stressed form]: for him Bach is THE composer pour lui, Bach est le compositeur par excellence; the Olympics are THE event this winter les jeux Olympiques sont l'événement à ne pas manquer cet hiver; do you mean THE John Irving? vous voulez dire le célèbre John Irving? -**7.** [enough] le *m*, la *f*, l' (*before vowel or mute h*), les *mfpl*; I haven't ~ time/money to do it je n'ai pas le temps de/l'argent pour le faire. -**8.** [instead of 'your', 'my' etc]: she took him by ~ hand elle l'a pris par la main; how's ~ wife? *inf* comment va la femme?; I've brought ~ family along j'ai emmené la famille.

theatre *Br*, **theater** *Am* [ˈθɪətəʳ] ◇ *n* -**1.** [building] théâtre *m*; to go to the ~ aller au théâtre; a night at the ~ une soirée au théâtre; movie ~ *Am* cinéma *m*. -**2.** [form] théâtre *m*, art *m* dramatique; [plays in general] théâtre *m*; [profession] théâtre *m*; Greek/modern ~ le théâtre antique/moderne; Shakespeare's ~ le théâtre de Shakespeare; I've been in the ~ for over 30 years je fais du théâtre depuis plus de 30 ans. -**3.** [hall] salle *f* de spectacle; [for lectures] salle *f* de conférences; UNIV amphithéâtre *m*. -**4.** MED: (operating) ~ salle *f* d'opération; she's in (the) ~ [doctor] elle est en salle d'opération; [patient] elle est sur la table d'opération. -**5.** *fig* [for important event] théâtre *m*; ~ of war MIL théâtre des hostilités; the southern/eastern ~s MIL les fronts du sud/de l'est.

◇ *comp* -**1.** [programme, tickets] de théâtre; [manager] du théâtre; ~ company troupe de théâtre, compagnie théâtrale; ~ workshop atelier *m* de théâtre. -**2.** MED [staff, nurse] de salle d'opération; [routine, job] dans la salle d'opération.

theatregoer [ˈθɪətəˌgəʊəʳ] *n* amateur *m* de théâtre; they're regular ~s ils vont régulièrement au théâtre.

theatre in the round *n* théâtre *m* en rond.

theatreland [ˈθɪətəlænd] *n Br* quartier *m* des théâtres; in ~ dans le quartier des théâtres.

theatrical [θɪˈætrɪkl] *adj* -**1.** THEAT [performance, season] théâtral. -**2.** *fig* [exaggerated - gesture, behaviour] théâtral, affecté; there's no need to resort to such ~ behaviour c'est inutile de faire toute cette comédie.

◆ **theatricals** *npl* -**1.** THEAT théâtre *m* d'amateur. -**2.** *fig* comédie *f*; I'm fed up with all her ~s j'en ai assez de toutes ses manières.

theatrically [θɪˈætrɪklɪ] *adv* théâtralement.

Theban [ˈθiːbən] ◇ *n* Thébain *m*, -e *f*.

◇ *adj* thébain.

Thebes [θiːbz] *pr n* Thèbes.

thee [ðiː] *pron* BIBLE & *arch* te; [before vowel] t'; [after prep] toi; we beseech ~ nous te supplions.

theft [θeft] *n* vol *m*; to commit ~ commettre un vol; to be charged with ~ être inculpé de vol.

their [*weak form* ðəʳ, *strong form* ðeəʳ] *det* leur *(sg)*, leurs *(pl)*; ~ car leur voiture; ~ clothes leurs vêtements; somebody's left their umbrella behind quelqu'un a oublié son parapluie; a house of ~ own leur propre maison, une maison à eux; everyone must bring ~ own book chacun doit apporter son livre; nobody in ~ right mind would do such a thing! personne de sensé ne ferait une chose pareille!; ~ highnesses the King and the Queen Leurs Majestés le roi et la reine.

theirs [ðeəz] *pron* le leur *m*, la leur *f*, les leurs *mfpl*; our car is sturdier than ~ notre voiture est plus solide que la leur; I like that painting of ~ j'aime leur tableau; I really can't stand that dog of ~ je ne supporte pas leur sacré chien; a friend of ~ un de leurs amis; is this yours or ~? est-ce que ceci est à vous ou à eux?; it is not ~ to choose ce n'est pas à eux de choisir, le choix ne leur appartient pas.

theism [ˈθiːɪzm] *n* théisme *m* RELIG.

theist [ˈθiːɪst] ◇ *adj* théiste.

◇ *n* théiste *mf*.

theistic(al) [ˈθiːɪstɪkl] *adj* théiste.

them [*weak form* ðəm, *strong form* ðem] *pron* -**1.** [direct obj] les; **I met ~ last week** je les ai rencontrés la semaine dernière. -**2.** [indirect obj] leur; **we bought/gave ~ some flowers** nous leur avons acheté/donné des fleurs. -**3.** [after preposition]: **it's for ~** c'est pour eux; **the yacht belongs to ~** le yacht leur appartient; **both of ~ are wool** ils sont tous les deux en laine; **she's brighter than ~** elle est plus intelligente qu'eux; **neither of ~ is happy** ils ne sont heureux ni l'un ni l'autre; **I don't want any of ~** je n'en veux aucun; **a few of ~ seemed genuinely interested** quelques-uns d'entre eux semblaient vraiment intéressés; **all of ~ came** ils sont tous venus; **most of ~ are busy** la plupart d'entre eux sont occupés; **it was good of ~ to come** c'était gentil de leur part OR à eux de venir.

thematic [θɪ'mætɪk] *adj* thématique.

theme [θiːm] *n* -**1.** [subject, topic] thème *m*, sujet *m*. -**2.** MUS thème *m*; **~ and variations** thème et variations. -**3.** GRAMM & LING thème *m*.

theme park *n* parc *m* à thème.

theme pub *n* bar *m* à thème.

theme song *n* -**1.** [from film] chanson *f* (de film); **the ~ from "The Graduate"** la chanson du film «Le Lauréat». -**2.** *Am* [signature tune] indicatif *m*.

theme tune *n* -**1.** [from film] musique *f* (de film). -**2.** *Br* [signature tune] indicatif *m*; **the ~ from "Dallas"** l'indicatif de «Dallas».

themselves [ðəm'selvz] *pron* -**1.** [reflexive use]: **they hurt ~** ils se sont fait mal; **the girls enjoyed ~** les filles se sont bien amusées; **the children could see ~ in the mirror** les enfants se voyaient dans la glace. -**2.** [emphatic use] eux-mêmes *mpl*, elles-mêmes *fpl*; **they had to come ~** ils ont dû venir eux-mêmes OR en personne; **they painted the house ~** ils ont peint la maison eux-mêmes; **they came by ~** ils sont venus tout seuls. -**3.** [referring to things] eux-mêmes *mpl*, elles-mêmes *fpl*; **the boxes ~ aren't very heavy** les boîtes (en) elles-mêmes ne sont pas très lourdes; **the details in ~ are not important** ce ne sont pas les détails en eux-mêmes qui sont importants.

then [ðen] ◇ *adv* -**1.** [at a particular time] alors, à ce moment-là; [in distant past] à l'époque, à cette époque, à cette époque-là; **we were very young ~** nous étions très jeunes à l'époque; **we can talk about it ~** nous pourrons en parler à ce moment-là; **Marilyn, or Norma Jean as she ~ was known** Marilyn, ou Norma Jean comme elle s'appelait alors; **by ~** [in future] d'ici là; [in past] entre-temps; **from ~ on** à partir de ce moment-là; **since ~** depuis (lors); **until ~** [in future] jusque-là; [in past] jusqu'alors, jusqu'à ce moment-là. -**2.** [afterwards, next] puis, ensuite; **we went shopping, ~ we had lunch** nous avons fait des courses, puis nous avons déjeuné; **do your homework first, ~ you can watch TV** fais d'abord tes devoirs, et ensuite tu pourras regarder la télé; **you ~ take the chopped onions...** prenez ensuite les oignons coupés en lamelles... -**3.** [so, in that case] donc, alors; **what do you suggest ~?** qu'est-ce que vous suggérez alors?; **you were right ~!** mais alors, vous aviez raison!; **I'll see you at 6 ~** bon, je te retrouve à 6 h alors; **right ~, anyone for more tea?** bon alors, qui d'autre veut du thé?; **if... ~...** si... alors...; **if x equals 10 ~ y...** si x égale 10 alors y...; **if it's not in my bag, ~ look in the cupboard** si ce n'est pas dans mon sac, regarde dans le placard. -**4.** [also] et puis; **~ there's Peter to invite** et puis il faut inviter Peter. -**5.** [therefore] donc; **these ~ are the main problems** voici donc les principaux problèmes; **its significance, ~, is twofold** sa signification, donc, est double.
◇ *adj* d'alors, de l'époque; **the ~ head of department** le chef du département d'alors OR de l'époque.
◆ **then again** *adv phr*: **and ~ again, you may prefer to forget it** mais enfin peut-être que vous préférez ne plus y penser; **but ~ again, no one can be sure** mais après tout, on ne sait jamais.

thence [ðens] *adv lit & fml* -**1.** [from that place] de là, de ce lieu, de ce lieu-là. -**2.** [from that time] depuis lors. -**3.** [therefore] par conséquent.

thenceforth [,ðens'fɔːθ], **thenceforward** [ðens'fɔːwəd] *adv lit & fml* dès lors, désormais.

theocentric [θɪə'sentrɪk] *adj* théocentrique.

theocracy [θɪ'ɒkrəsɪ] (*pl* **theocracies**) *n* théocratie *f*.

theocratic [θɪə'krætɪk] *adj* théocratique.

theodolite [θɪ'ɒdəlaɪt] *n* théodolite *m*.

Theodore ['θɪədɔːʳ] *pr n*: **Saint ~** saint Théodore.

Theodosius [,θɪə'dəʊsjəs] *pr n* Théodose.

theologian [θɪə'ləʊdʒən] *n* théologien *m*, -enne *f*.

theological [θɪə'lɒdʒɪkl] *adj* théologique; **~ college** séminaire *m*.

theology [θɪ'ɒlədʒɪ] *n* théologie *f*.

theorem ['θɪərəm] *n* théorème *m*.

theoretical [θɪə'retɪkl] *adj* théorique.

theoretically [θɪə'retɪklɪ] *adv* théoriquement, en principe.

theoretician [,θɪərə'tɪʃn] *n* théoricien *m*, -enne *f*.

theorist ['θɪərɪst] *n* théoricien *m*, -enne *f*.

theorize, -ise ['θɪəraɪz] ◇ *vi* -**1.** [speculate] théoriser, faire des théories; **analysts have ~d about the reasons for this** les analystes ont émis toutes sortes de théories pour expliquer cela; **it's no use theorizing, we have to make a decision** ça ne sert à rien de faire de grandes théories, il faut qu'on prenne une décision. -**2.** [scientist] élaborer des théories.
◇ *vt*: **scientists ~d that the space probe would disintegrate** les scientifiques émirent l'hypothèse que la sonde spatiale se désintègrerait.

theory ['θɪərɪ] (*pl* **theories**) *n* -**1.** [hypothesis] théorie *f*; **I have a ~ about his disappearance** j'ai mon idée sur sa disparition. -**2.** [principles, rules] théorie *f*; **musical ~** théorie musicale.
◆ **in theory** *adv phr* en théorie, théoriquement, en principe.

theosophical [θɪə'sɒfɪkl] *adj* théosophique.

theosophist [θɪ'ɒsəfɪst] *n* théosophe *mf*.

theosophy [θɪ'ɒsəfɪ] *n* théosophie *f*.

therapeutic [,θerə'pjuːtɪk] *adj* thérapeutique.

therapeutically [,θerə'pjuːtɪklɪ] *adv*: **used ~** utilisé comme thérapeutique.

therapist ['θerəpɪst] *n* thérapeute *mf*.

therapy ['θerəpɪ] (*pl* **therapies**) *n* thérapie *f*; **to go for** OR **to be in ~** suivre une thérapie.

there [*weak form* ðəʳ, *strong form* ðeəʳ] ◇ *adv* -**1.** [in or to a particular place] là, y; **they aren't ~** ils ne sont pas là, ils n'y sont pas; **we never go ~** nous n'y allons jamais; **who's ~?** qui est là?; **is Maureen ~?** est-ce que Maureen est là?; **see that woman ~? that's Margot** tu vois cette femme là-bas? c'est Margot; **so ~ we were/I was** donc, on était/j'étais là; **she got ~ in the end** [reached a place] elle a fini par arriver; [completed a task] elle a fini par y arriver; **it's ~ on the desk** c'est là sur le bureau; **she just sat/stood ~** elle était assise/debout là; **here and ~** çà et là; **~ it is** le voilà; **it's around ~ somewhere** c'est quelque part par là; **back ~** là-bas; **in ~** là-dedans; **on ~** là-dessus; **over ~** là-bas; **under ~** là-dessous; **that car ~** cette voiture-là; **those cars ~** ces voitures-là. -**2.** [available] là; **it's ~ if you need it** c'est là si tu en as besoin; **she's always been ~ for me** elle a toujours été là quand j'avais besoin d'elle. -**3.** [in existence] là; **I couldn't believe he was really ~** je n'arrivais pas à croire qu'il était vraiment là; **the central problem is still ~** le principal problème est toujours là. -**4.** [on or at a particular point] là; **we disagree ~, we disagree** nous ne sommes pas d'accord là-dessus; **~ you're wrong** là vous vous trompez; **you're right ~** là vous avez raison; **let's leave it ~** restons-en là; **could I just stop you ~?** puis-je vous interrompre ici?; **as for the food, I've no complaints ~** pour ce qui est de la nourriture, là je n'ai pas à me plaindre; **you've got me ~!** *inf* là, je ne sais pas quoi vous répondre OR dire! -**5.** [drawing attention to someone or something]: **hello** OR **hi ~!** salut!; **hey ~!** hep, vous là-bas!; **~ they are!** les voilà!; **~ they come** les voilà (qui arrivent); **~ you go again!** ça y est, vous recommençez!; **~ she goes, complaining again!** voilà qu'elle recommence à se plaindre!; **~'s the bell, I must be going** tiens ça sonne, je dois partir; **~'s gratitude for you** *iron* c'est beau la reconnaissance! *iron*; **now finish your homework, ~'s a good boy** maintenant sois un grand garçon et finis tes devoirs. -**6.** *phr*: **he's not all** OR **not quite ~** [stupid] il n'a pas toute sa tête; [senile] il n'a plus toute sa tête.
◇ *pron*: **~ is** *(before singular noun)* il y a; **~ are** *(before plural noun)* il y a; **~ is** OR **~'s a book on the table** il y a un livre sur la table; **~ are some books on the table** il y a des livres sur la table; **~'s a bus coming** il y a un bus qui arrive; **~'s that girl I was telling you about before** il y a bien cette fille dont je t'ai déjà parlé; **what happens if ~'s a change of plan?** qu'est-ce qui se passe si on change d'idée?; **~ must have been a mistake** il a dû y avoir une erreur; **~ were some pieces missing** il manquait des pièces; **~ weren't any more, were ~?** il n'en restait pas, si?; **~'s no stopping her** rien ne peut l'arrêter; **~'s no knowing what he'll do next** il est impossible de prévoir ce qu'il fera ensuite; **~ was no denying it** c'était indéniable; **~ follows a party political broadcast** *formule annonçant la diffusion télévisée des messages électoraux des différents partis*; **~ comes a time when you have to slow down** il arrive un moment où il faut ralentir le rythme; **~ still remain several points to be resolved** il reste encore plusieurs problèmes à résoudre; **~ arose a murmur of disapproval** un murmure de désapprobation s'éleva.
◇ *interj* -**1.** [soothing]: **~ now, don't cry!** allons! OR là! ne pleure pas!; **~, that wasn't so bad, was it?** voilà, ça n'était pas si terrible que ça, si?; **~, ~!** allez! -**2.** [aggressive]: **~ now, what did I say?** voilà, qu'est-ce que je t'avais dit?; **~, now you've made me lose count!** et voilà, tu m'as fait perdre le compte! -**3.** [after all]: **but, ~, it's not surprising** mais enfin, ce n'est pas surprenant.
◆ **so there** *adv phr* voilà.
◆ **there again** *adv phr* après tout; **but ~ again, no one really knows** mais après tout, personne ne sait vraiment.
◆ **there and back** *adv phr*: **we did the trip ~ and back in three hours** nous avons fait l'aller retour en trois heures; **it will take you about an hour/cost you about £50 ~ and back** l'aller retour vous prendra à peu près une heure/vous coûtera environ 50 livres.
◆ **there and then, then and there** *adv phr* sur-le-champ; **I decided ~ and then to have no more to do with him** j'ai tout de suite décidé de ne plus avoir affaire à lui.
◆ **there you are, there you go** *adv phr* -**1.** [never mind]: **it wasn't the ideal solution, but ~ you are** OR **go** ce n'était pas l'idéal, mais enfin OR mais qu'est-ce que vous voulez. -**2.** [I told you so] voilà, ça y est. -**3.** [here you are] tenez, voilà.

thereabout ['ðeərəbaʊt] *Am* = **thereabouts**.

thereabouts ['ðeərəbaʊts] *adv* -**1.** [indicating place] par là, dans les environs, pas loin; **somewhere ~** quelque part par là. -**2.** [indicating quantity, weight] à peu près, environ. -**3.** [indicating price] environ; **£10 or ~** 10 livres environ. -**4.** [indicating time] aux alentours de; **at 10 p.m. or ~** aux alentours de 22 h, vers 10 h du soir.

thereafter [,ðeər'ɑːftəʳ] *adv fml* -**1.** [subsequently] par la suite. -**2.** [below] ci-dessous.

thereat [,ðeər'æt] *adv arch* OR *fml* -**1.** [of place] là. -**2.** [of time] alors.

thereby [,ðeər'baɪ] *adv* -**1.** *fml* de ce fait, ainsi. -**2.** *phr*: **~ hangs a tale!** c'est une longue histoire!

therefore ['ðeəfɔːʳ] *adv* donc, par conséquent.

therefrom [,ðeə'frɒm] *adv arch* OR *fml* de là.

therein [,ðeər'ɪn] *adv* JUR OR *fml* -**1.** [within] à l'intérieur; the box and all that is contained ~ la boîte et son contenu. -**2.** [in that respect] là; ~ lies the difficulty là est la difficulté.

thereof [,ðeər'ɒv] *adv arch* OR *fml* de cela, en; all citizens of the republic are subject to the laws ~ tous les citoyens de la république doivent se soumettre aux lois de celle-ci; he ate ~ il en mangea.

thereon [,ðeər'ɒn] *adv arch* OR *fml* -**1.** [on that subject] là-dessus. -**2.** = **thereupon 1**.

thereto [,ðeə'tu:] *adv* JUR OR *fml* y; a copy of the Bill and the amendments ~ une copie du projet de loi et de ses amendements.

theretofore [,ðeətu:'fɔ:ʳ] *adv* JUR OR *fml* jusqu'alors, avant cela.

thereunder [ðeər'ʌndəʳ] *adv* JUR OR *fml* là-dessous, en dessous.

thereupon [,ðeərə'pɒn] *adv fml* -**1.** [then] sur ce. -**2.** JUR [on that subject] à ce sujet, là-dessus.

therewith [,ðeə'wɪð] *adv* -**1.** JUR [with] avec cela; [in addition] en outre. -**2.** *arch* = **thereupon 1**.

therm [θɜ:m] *n Br* ≃ 1,055 X 10^8 joules *(unité de chaleur)*.

thermal ['θɜ:ml] ◇ *adj* -**1.** PHYS [energy, insulation] thermique; [conductor, unit] thermique, de chaleur; ~ shield bouclier *m* thermique. -**2.** [spring, stream] thermal; ~ baths thermes *mpl*. -**3.** [underwear] en chlorofibres, en Rhovyl® OR Thermolactyl®.
◇ *n* AERON & METEOR thermique *m*, ascendance *f* thermique.

thermal paper *n* papier *m* thermique.

thermal printer *n* imprimante *f* thermique.

thermal reactor *n* réacteur *m* thermique.

thermic ['θɜ:mɪk] *adj* PHYS thermique.

thermionic [,θɜ:mɪ'ɒnɪk] *adj* thermoïonique; ~ valve *Br*, ~ tube *Am* tube *m* thermoïonique OR thermoélectronique.

thermocouple ['θɜ:məʊkʌpl] *n* thermocouple *m*.

thermodynamic [,θɜ:məʊdaɪ'næmɪk] *adj* thermodynamique.

thermodynamics [,θɜ:məʊdaɪ'næmɪks] *n (U)* thermodynamique *f*.

thermoelectric(al) [,θɜ:məʊɪ'lektrɪk(l)] *adj* thermoélectrique.

thermoelectricity [,θɜ:məʊɪlek'trɪsətɪ] *n* thermoélectricité *f*.

thermograph [,θɜ:məʊ'grɑ:f] *n* thermographe *m*.

thermography [θɜ:'mɒgrəfɪ] *n* thermographie *f*.

thermometer [θə'mɒmɪtəʳ] *n* thermomètre *m*.

thermonuclear [,θɜ:məʊ'nju:klɪəʳ] *adj* thermonucléaire.

thermopile ['θɜ:məʊpaɪl] *n* thermopile *f*.

thermoplastic [,θɜ:məʊ'plæstɪk] ◇ *adj* thermoplastique.
◇ *n* thermoplastique *m*.

Thermos® ['θɜ:mɒs] *n*: ~ (flask) Thermos® *f*.

thermosetting ['θɜ:məʊ,setɪŋ] *adj* thermodurcissable.

thermostat ['θɜ:məstæt] *n* thermostat *m*.

thermostatic [,θɜ:mə'stætɪk] *adj* thermostatique.

thermostatically [,θɜ:mə'stætɪklɪ] *adv*: ~ controlled contrôlé par thermostat.

thesaurus [θɪ'sɔ:rəs] (*pl* thesauri [-raɪ] OR thesauruses [-sɪz]) *n* -**1.** [book of synonyms] ≃ dictionnaire *m* analogique. -**2.** COMPUT thésaurus *m*.

these [ði:z] *pl* → **this**.

Theseus ['θi:sju:s] *pr n* Thésée.

thesis ['θi:sɪs] (*pl* theses [-si:z]) *n* [gen & UNIV] thèse *f*.

thespian ['θespɪən] *fml* OR *hum* ◇ *adj* dramatique, de théâtre.
◇ *n* acteur *m*, -trice *f*.

Thessalonian [,θesə'ləʊnjən] *n*: the Epistle of Paul to the ~s l'Épître de saint Paul aux Thessaloniciens.

Thessaly ['θesəlɪ] *pr n* Thessalie *f*; in ~ en Thessalie.

they [ðeɪ] *pron* ils *mpl*, elles *fpl*; [stressed form] eux *mpl*, elles *fpl*; ~'ve left ils sont partis; THEY bought the flowers ce sont eux qui ont acheté les fleurs; oh, there ~ are! ah, les voilà!; ~ say that... on prétend que...

thiamin(e) ['θaɪəmi:n] *n* thiamine *f*.

thiazol(e) ['θaɪəzəʊl] *n* thiazole *m*.

thick [θɪk] ◇ *adj* -**1.** [wall, slice, writing] épais, gros; [print] gras; [lips] épais, charnu; [shoes, boots] gros; the boots have a ~ fur lining les bottes sont doublées de fourrure épaisse; the snow was ~ on the ground il y avait une épaisse couche de neige sur le sol; the boards are 20 cm ~ les planches ont une épaisseur de 20 cm, les planches font 20 cm d'épaisseur ❑ to give sb a ~ ear *Br* donner une gifle à qqn; he got a ~ ear il a reçu une bonne gifle. -**2.** [beard, eyebrows, hair] épais, touffu; [grass, forest, crowd] épais, dense; pubs are not very ~ on the ground round here les pubs sont plutôt rares par ici. -**3.** [soup, cream, sauce] épais; to become OR to get ~ épaissir, durcir. -**4.** [fog, smoke] épais, dense; [clouds] épais; [darkness, night] profond; the air is rather ~ in here on respire mal ici ❑ my head feels a bit ~ this morning *inf* j'ai un peu mal au crâne OR aux cheveux ce matin. -**5.** ~ with: the shelves were ~ with dust les étagères étaient recouvertes d'une épaisse couche de poussière; the air was ~ with smoke [from smokers] la pièce était enfumée; [from fire, guns] l'air était empli d'une épaisse fumée; the streets were ~ with police les rues étaient pleines de policiers. -**6.** [voice - with emotion] voilé; [- after late night, drinking] pâteux. -**7.** [accent] fort, prononcé. -**8.** *inf* [intimate] intime, très lié; Sharon seems to be very ~ with Henry Sharon semble être très liée OR intime avec Henry ❑ those two are as ~ as thieves ces deux-là s'entendent comme larrons en foire. -**9.** *inf* [stupid] obtus, bouché; he's as ~ as two short planks OR as a brick il est bête comme ses pieds. -**10.** *inf Br* [unreasonable]: that's OR it's a bit ~ ça, c'est un peu fort OR raide OR dur à avaler; it's a bit ~ expecting us to pay nous demander de payer, ils abusent.
◇ *adv* [spread] en couche épaisse; [cut] en tranches épaisses, en grosses tranches; the snow lay ~ on the ground il y avait une épaisse couche de neige sur le sol; the grass grows ~ at the bottom of the hill l'herbe pousse dru en bas de la colline ❑ he really laid it on ~ *inf* il n'y est pas allé avec le dos de la cuiller, il a insisté lourdement; ~ and fast: arrows started falling ~ and fast around them les flèches pleuvaient autour d'eux; invitations/phone calls began to come in ~ and fast il y eut une avalanche d'invitations/de coups de téléphone.
◇ *n phr*: to stick OR to stay with sb through ~ and thin rester fidèle à qqn contre vents et marées OR quoi qu'il arrive.
◆ **in the thick of** *prep phr* au milieu OR cœur de, en plein, en plein milieu de; in the ~ of the battle en plein milieu OR au plus fort de la bataille; in the ~ of the discussion en pleine discussion; he's really in the ~ of it [dispute, activity] il est vraiment dans le feu de l'action.

thicken ['θɪkn] ◇ *vi* -**1.** [fog, clouds, smoke] s'épaissir, devenir plus épais; [bushes, forest] s'épaissir. -**2.** [sauce] épaissir; [jam, custard] durcir. -**3.** [crowd] grossir. -**4.** [mystery] s'épaissir; the plot ~s les choses se compliquent OR se corsent, l'histoire se corse.
◇ *vt* [sauce, soup] épaissir.

thickener ['θɪknəʳ] *n* [for sauce, soup] liant *m*; [for oil, paint] épaississant *m*.

thickening ['θɪknɪŋ] ◇ *n* -**1.** [process, act - of fog, smoke] épaississement *m*; [- of sauce] liaison *f*. -**2.** CULIN [thickener] liant *m*.
◇ *adj* [agent] épaississant; [process] d'épaississement.

thicket ['θɪkɪt] *n* fourré *m*.

thickhead *inf* ['θɪkhed] *n* bêta *m*, -asse *f*, imbécile *mf*, andouille *f*.

thickheaded *inf* [,θɪk'hedɪd] *adj* obtus, bouché.

thickie *inf* ['θɪkɪ] (*pl* thickies) *n Br* bêta *m*, -asse *f*, imbécile *mf*, andouille *f*.

thickly ['θɪklɪ] *adv* -**1.** [spread] en couche épaisse; [cut] en tranches épaisses; the windows were ~ covered in OR with ice les vitres étaient recouvertes d'une épaisse couche de givre; ~ buttered toast pain grillé avec une épaisse couche de beurre. -**2.** [densely] dru; to grow ~ [vegetation, beard] pousser dru; ~ populated très peuplé, à forte densité de population; the snow fell ~ la neige tombait dru. -**3.** [speak] d'une voix rauque OR pâteuse.

thickness ['θɪknɪs] *n* -**1.** [of wall, snow, layer] épaisseur *f*; [of string, bolt] épaisseur *f*, grosseur *f*. -**2.** [of beard, hair] épaisseur *f*, abondance *f*. -**3.** [of fog, smoke, forest] épaisseur *f*, densité *f*.

thicko▽ ['θɪkəʊ] *n* débile *mf*.

thickset [,θɪk'set] *adj* trapu, costaud.

thick-skinned *adj* peu sensible; she's very ~ elle est capable de supporter beaucoup de choses.

thicky *inf* ['θɪkɪ] (*pl* thickies) *Br* = **thickie**.

thief [θi:f] (*pl* thieves [θi:vz]) *n* voleur *m*, -euse *f*; stop ~! au voleur! ❑ thieves' kitchen repaire *m* de brigands; 'The Thief of Baghdad' *Powell* 'le Voleur de Bagdad'.

thieve *inf* [θi:v] *vi* & *vt* voler.

thieves [θi:vz] *pl* → **thief**.

thieving *inf* ['θi:vɪŋ] ◇ *adj* voleur; keep your ~ hands off! arrête de rôder autour de ce truc comme un voleur! ❑ 'The Thieving Magpie' *Rossini* 'la Pie voleuse'.
◇ *n (U)* vol *m*, vols *mpl*.

thigh [θaɪ] *n* cuisse *f*.

thighbone ['θaɪbəʊn] *n* fémur *m*.

thigh boots, **thigh-high boots** *npl* cuissardes *fpl*.

thimble ['θɪmbl] *n* dé *m* à coudre.

thimbleful ['θɪmblfʊl] *n fig* [of liquid] doigt *m*, goutte *f*.

thin [θɪn] (*compar* thinner, *superl* thinnest, *pt* & *pp* thinned, *cont* thinning) ◇ *adj* -**1.** [layer, wall, wire etc] mince, fin; [person, leg, neck] mince, maigre; [clothing, blanket] léger, fin; [carpet] ras; [crowd] peu nombreux, épars; to become OR to get OR to grow ~ [person] maigrir ❑ he's as ~ as a rake *Br* OR as a rail *Am* il est maigre comme un clou; it's the ~ end of the wedge cela ne présage rien de bon; cheap hotels are ~ on the ground les hôtels bon marché sont rares. -**2.** [beard, hair] clairsemé; he's getting a bit ~ on top il commence à perdre ses cheveux, il se dégarnit. -**3.** [soup, sauce] clair; [cream] liquide; [paint, ink] délayé, dilué; [blood] appauvri, anémié. -**4.** [smoke, clouds, mist] léger; [air] raréfié; she seemed to vanish into ~ air elle semblait s'être volatilisée. -**5.** [excuse, argument] mince, peu convaincant; the report is rather ~ on facts le rapport ne présente pas beaucoup de faits concrets. -**6.** [profits] maigre; to have a ~ time of it passer une période OR un moment difficile. -**7.** [voice] grêle.
◇ *adv* [spread] en fine couche, en couche mince; [cut] en tranches minces OR fines.
◇ *vt* [sauce, soup] allonger, délayer, éclaircir.
◇ *vi* [crowd] s'éclaircir, se disperser; [fog] se lever, devenir moins dense OR épais; [smoke] devenir moins dense OR épais; [population] se réduire; his hair is thinning il perd ses cheveux.
◆ **thin down** ◇ *vt sep* [sauce, soup] allonger, éclaircir, délayer; [paint] délayer, diluer.
◇ *vi insep* [person] maigrir.
◆ **thin out** ◇ *vt sep* [plants] éclaircir.
◇ *vi insep* [crowd] se disperser; [population] se réduire, diminuer; [fog] se lever.

thine [ðaɪn] BIBLE OR *arch* ◇ *poss adj* ton, ta, tes.
◇ *pron* le tien, la tienne, les tiens, les tiennes; for thee and ~ pour toi et les tiens.

thing [θɪŋ] *n* **A.** -**1.** [object, item] chose *f*, objet *m*; what's that yellow ~ on the floor? qu'est-ce que c'est que ce truc jaune par terre?;

what's that ~ for? à quoi ça sert, ça?; what's this knob ~ for? à quoi sert cette espèce de bouton?; where's my hat? I can't find the ~ anywhere où est mon chapeau? je ne le trouve nulle part; the only ~ I could hear was a dripping tap la seule chose que j'entendais c'était un robinet qui fuyait; any idea how to work this ~? tu sais comment ça marche?; I had to rewrite the whole ~ j'ai dû tout réécrire; the ~ he loves most is his pipe ce qu'il aime le plus, c'est sa pipe; I need a few ~s from the shop j'ai besoin de faire quelques courses; she loves books and posters and ~s, she loves ~s like books and posters elle aime les livres, les posters, ce genre de choses; he likes making ~s with his hands il est très manuel; she enjoys the good ~s in life elle apprécie les bonnes choses de la vie; I must be seeing ~s je dois avoir des visions; I must be hearing ~s je dois rêver, j'entends des voix; ~s that go bump in the night *hum* les choses qui font du bruit la nuit; they were treated as ~s not people on les traitait comme des choses, pas comme des êtres humains. -**2.** [activity, event] chose *f*; he likes ~s like gardening il aime le jardinage et les choses dans ce goût-là; she's still into this art ~ in a big way *inf* elle est encore très branchée art; the ~ to do is to pretend you're asleep vous n'avez qu'à faire semblant de dormir; the first ~ to do is (to) ring the police la première chose à faire, c'est d'appeler la police; the next ~ on the agenda le point suivant à l'ordre du jour; it's the best ~ to do c'est ce qu'il y a de mieux à faire; that was a silly ~ to do! ce n'était pas la chose à faire!; how could you do such a ~? comment avez-vous pu faire une chose pareille?; I have lots of ~s to do j'ai des tas de choses à faire; she certainly gets ~s done avec elle, ça ne traîne pas. -**3.** [in negative clauses]: I don't know a ~ about what happened j'ignore tout de ce qui s'est passé; not a ~ was overlooked pas un détail n'a été négligé; I didn't understand a ~ she said je n'ai rien compris à ce qu'elle disait, je n'ai pas compris un mot de ce qu'elle disait; we couldn't do a ~ about it nous n'y pouvions absolument rien; I couldn't do a ~ to help je n'ai rien pu faire pour me rendre utile; she hadn't got a ~ on elle était entièrement nue; I haven't got a ~ to wear je n'ai rien à me mettre sur le dos. -**4.** [creature, being] créature *f*, être *m*; the ~ he loves most is his dog ce qu'il aime le plus, c'est son chien; there wasn't a living ~ around il n'y avait pas âme qui vive; what a sweet little ~! quel amour!; she's a dear old ~ c'est une charmante petite vieille; you silly ~ espèce d'idiot; poor ~! [said about somebody] le/la pauvre!; [said to somebody] mon/ma pauvre!; [animal] (la) pauvre bête! -**5.** [monster]: the ~ from outer space le monstre de l'espace.

B. -**1.** [idea, notion] idée *f*, chose *f*; the best ~ would be to ask them le mieux serait de leur demander; it would be a good ~ if we all went together ce serait une bonne chose que nous y allions tous ensemble; it's a good ~ (for you) no one knew heureusement (pour vous) que personne ne savait; to be on to a good ~ être sur une bonne affaire ❑ to know a ~ or two about sthg s'y connaître en qqch; I could show him a ~ or two about hang gliding je pourrais lui apprendre une ou deux petites choses en deltaplane. -**2.** [matter, question] chose *f*, question *f*; the ~ is, we can't really afford it le problème, c'est qu'on n'a pas vraiment les moyens; the ~ is, will she want to come? le problème c'est qu'on ne sait pas si elle voudra venir; the main ~ is to succeed ce qui importe, c'est de réussir; the important ~ is not to stop ce qui compte, c'est de ne pas arrêter ❑ it's one ~ to talk but quite another to act parler est une chose, agir en est une autre; we talked of one ~ and another nous avons parlé de choses et d'autres; what with one ~ and another, I haven't had time avec tout ce qu'il y avait à faire, je n'ai pas eu le temps; if it's not one ~, it's another ça ne s'arrête jamais; taking one ~ with another à tout prendre, somme toute. -**3.** [remark]: that's not a very nice ~ to say ce n'est pas très gentil de dire ça; she said some nasty ~s about him elle a dit des méchancetés sur lui; how can you say such a ~? comment pouvez-vous dire une chose pareille?; I said no such ~! je n'ai rien dit de tel!; I said the first ~ that came into my head j'ai dit la première chose qui m'est venue à l'esprit. -**4.** [quality, characteristic] chose *f*; one of the ~s I like about her is her sense of humour une des choses que j'aime chez elle, c'est son sens de l'humour; the town has a lot of ~s going for it la ville a beaucoup de bons côtés.

C. -**1.** *inf* [strong feeling]: to have a ~ about sthg [like] aimer qqch; [dislike] ne pas aimer qqch; I have a ~ about jazz [like] j'aime vraiment le jazz; [dislike] je n'aime vraiment pas le jazz; he has a ~ about red hair [likes] il adore les cheveux roux; [dislikes] il a quelque chose contre les cheveux roux; it's a bit of a ~ with me j'aime assez ça. -**2.** [interest]: it's not really my ~ ce n'est pas vraiment mon truc; to do one's own ~: he went off to the States to do his own ~ il est parti aux États-Unis faire ce qui lui plaît. -**3.** [what is needed, required] idéal *m*; hot cocoa is just the ~ on a winter's night un chocolat chaud c'est l'idéal les soirs d'hiver; that's the very ~ for my bad back! c'est juste ce dont j'avais besoin pour mon mal de dos! -**4.** [fashion] mode *f*; it's the latest ~ in swimwear c'est la dernière mode en matière de maillots de bain; it's really quite the ~ ça se fait vraiment beaucoup; natural food is the ~ just now les aliments biologiques sont la grande mode en ce moment; a ~ of the past une chose du passé. -**5.** [fuss]: to make a big ~ about sthg faire (tout) un plat de qqch; he made a big ~ out of my not going il a fait tout un plat parce que je n'y allais pas; there's no need to make a big ~ out of it! ce n'est pas la peine d'en faire tout un plat OR toute une montagne!

◆ **things** *npl* -**1.** [belongings] effets *mpl*, affaires *fpl*; [clothes] affaires *fpl*; [equipment] affaires *fpl*, attirail *m*; [tools] outils *mpl*, ustensiles *mpl*; put your ~s away ramassez vos affaires; take your wet ~s off enlevez vos affaires humides; you can take your ~s off in the bedroom vous pouvez vous déshabiller dans la chambre; have you brought your fishing/swimming ~s? avez-vous apporté votre attirail de pêche/vos affaires de piscine?; have you washed the breakfast ~s? as-tu fait la vaisselle du petit déjeuner?; to take the tea ~s away desservir la table (après le thé). -**2.** [situation, circumstances] choses *fpl*; how's *inf* OR how are ~s? comment ça va?; ~s are getting better les choses vont mieux; ~s began to get rather dangerous les choses ont commencé à devenir assez dangereuses; I feel rather out of ~s je n'ai pas l'impression d'être vraiment dans le bain; you take ~s too seriously vous prenez les choses trop au sérieux; I need time to think ~s over j'ai besoin de temps pour réfléchir; as ~s are OR stand dans l'état actuel des choses, les choses étant ce qu'elles sont ❑ it's just one of those ~s ce sont des choses qui arrivent. -**3.** [specific aspect of life] choses *fpl*; ~s of the mind les choses de l'esprit; she's interested in all ~s French elle s'intéresse à tout ce qui est français; moderation in all ~s de la modération en tout; she wants to be an airline pilot of all ~s! elle veut être pilote de l'air, non mais vraiment! -**4.** [facts, actions etc] choses *fpl*; they did terrible ~s to their prisoners ils ont fait des choses atroces à leurs prisonniers; I've heard good ~s about his work on dit du bien de son travail. -**5.** JUR [property] biens *mpl*.

◆ **for one thing** *adv phr* (tout) d'abord; for one ~... for another (tout) d'abord... et puis; well for one ~, we can't afford it pour commencer, nous n'en avons pas les moyens.

thingahoochie *inf* [ˈθɪŋəˌhuːtʃɪ] *n Am* truc *m*.

thingamabob [ˈθɪŋəmɪˌbɒb], **thingamajig, thingumajig** [ˈθɪŋəmədʒɪg], **thingummy** *inf* [ˈθɪŋəmɪ] *n* machin *m*, truc *m*, bidule *m*; do you remember Mr ~? tu te souviens de M. Machin?

thingy *inf* [ˈθɪŋɪ] *n* [object] truc *m*, bidule *m*, machin *m*, bitoniau *m*; have you seen the ~ for the food processor? tu as vu le bitoniau du robot de cuisine? || [person] Machin-Chose, Trucmuche; I saw ~ who you used to work with last week la semaine dernière, j'ai vu Machin-Chose avec qui tu travaillais dans le temps.

think [θɪŋk] (*pt* & *pp* **thought** [θɔːt])

◇ *vi* -**1.** [reason] penser, raisonner; to ~ for oneself se faire ses propres opinions; sorry, I wasn't ~ing clearly désolé, je n'avais pas les idées claires; to ~ aloud penser tout haut; to ~ big *inf* voir les choses en grand; she always ~s big elle voit toujours les choses en grand; ~ big! sois ambitieux!; ~ thin! pensez minceur! ❑ to ~ on one's feet réfléchir vite; you couldn't hear yourself ~ il n'était pas possible de se concentrer; I can't ~ straight with this headache ce mal de tête m'embrouille les idées. -**2.** [ponder, reflect] penser, réfléchir; he thought for a moment il a réfléchi un instant; she doesn't say much but she ~s a lot elle ne dit pas grand-chose, mais elle n'en pense pas moins; ~ before you speak réfléchissez avant de parler; ~ again! [reconsider] repensez-y!; [guess] vous n'y êtes pas, réfléchissez donc!; let me ~ laisse-moi réfléchir; ~ carefully before deciding réfléchissez bien avant de vous décider; I thought hard j'ai beaucoup réfléchi; I thought twice before accepting j'ai réfléchi à deux fois avant d'accepter; to act without ~ing agir sans réfléchir; that's what set me ~ing c'est ce qui m'a fait réfléchir. -**3.** [imagine] (s')imaginer; if you ~ I'd lend you my car again... si tu t'imagines que je te prêterai encore ma voiture...; just ~! imaginez (-vous) un peu!; just ~, you might have married him! imagine (-toi) que tu aurais pu l'épouser! -**4.** [believe, have as opinion] penser, croire; she ~s as I do elle pense comme moi; to her way of ~ing à son avis; it's a lot harder than I thought c'est beaucoup plus difficile que je ne croyais ❑ oh, he's so honest, I don't ~! honnête, mon œil, oui!

◇ *vt* -**1.** [ponder, reflect on] penser à, réfléchir à; he was ~ing what they could do next il se demandait ce qu'ils allaient pouvoir faire ensuite; I'm ~ing how to go about it je me demande comment il faudrait s'y prendre; I was just ~ing how ironic it all is je pensais simplement à l'ironie de la chose; guess what we're ~ing essaye de deviner à quoi nous pensons; I kept ~ing: why me? je n'arrêtais pas de me dire: pourquoi moi?; I'm happy to ~ she's not all alone je suis content de savoir qu'elle n'est pas toute seule; to ~ deep/evil thoughts avoir des pensées profondes/de mauvaises pensées. -**2.** [believe] penser, croire; I ~ so je crois; I ~ not je ne crois pas; he's a crook – I thought so OR I thought as much c'est un escroc – je m'en doutais; I ~ you mean Johnson not Boswell je crois que tu veux dire Johnson, pas Boswell; more tea? – I don't ~ I will, thank you encore un peu de thé? – non merci, je ne pense pas; she didn't ~ he would actually leave elle ne pensait pas qu'il partirait vraiment; she ~s you should leave town elle croit que tu devrais quitter la ville; they asked me what I thought ils m'ont demandé mon avis; what does he ~ I should do? que pense-t-il OR croit-il que je doive faire?; he wants cream walls – what do you ~? il veut des murs crème – qu'est-ce que tu en penses?; I thought I heard a noise j'ai cru OR il m'a semblé entendre un bruit; it's expensive, don't you ~? c'est cher, tu ne trouves pas?; I don't know what to ~ je ne sais pas quoi penser; he ~s he knows everything il croit tout savoir; she ~s she's talented elle se croit OR se trouve douée; that's what you ~! tu te fais des

illusions!; what will people ~? qu'en dira-t-on?, qu'est-ce que les gens vont penser?; anyone would ~ he owned the place on croirait que c'est lui le propriétaire; anybody would ~ it was Sunday on dirait un dimanche; (just) who does he ~ he is? (mais) pour qui se prend-il?; you always ~ the best/the worst of everyone vous avez toujours une très bonne/mauvaise opinion de tout le monde. -**3.** [judge, consider] juger, considérer; we ~ the rule unfair nous trouvons le règlement injuste; you must ~ me very nosy vous devez me trouver très curieux; she is thought to be one of the best on dit qu'elle fait partie des meilleurs; if you ~ it necessary si vous le jugez nécessaire. -**4.** [imagine] (s') imaginer; I can't ~ why he refused je ne vois vraiment pas pourquoi il a refusé; you'd ~ she'd be pleased elle devrait être contente; who'd have thought she'd become president! qui aurait dit qu'elle serait un jour président!; who'd have thought it! qui l'eût cru!; just ~ what we can do with all that money! imaginez ce qu'on peut faire avec tout cet argent!; and to ~ she did it all by herself et dire OR quand on pense qu'elle a fait cela toute seule. -**5.** [remember] penser à, se rappeler; I can't ~ what his name is je n'arrive pas à me rappeler son nom, son nom m'échappe; he couldn't ~ which countries belonged to the EC il n'arrivait pas à se rappeler quels pays étaient membres de la CEE; to ~ to do sthg penser à faire qqch; they didn't ~ to invite her ils n'ont pas pensé à l'inviter; did you ~ to buy some bread? as-tu pensé à acheter du pain? -**6.** [expect] penser, s'attendre à; I don't ~ she'll come je ne pense pas qu'elle viendra OR vienne; I didn't ~ to find you here je ne m'attendais pas à vous trouver ici. -**7.** [have as intention]: I ~ I'll go for a walk je crois que je vais aller me promener. -**8.** [in requests]: do you ~ you could help me? pourriez-vous m'aider?
◇ *n*: we've had a ~ about it nous y avons réfléchi; she had a good ~ about their offer elle a bien réfléchi à leur proposition; I'll have another ~ about it je vais encore y réfléchir ❑ you've got another ~ coming! *inf* tu te fais des illusions!

◆ **think about** *vt insep* -**1.** [ponder, reflect on]: to ~ about sthg/doing sthg penser à qqch/à faire qqch; what are you ~ing about? à quoi pensez-vous?; we were just ~ing about the holidays nous pensions justement aux vacances; I've thought about your proposal j'ai réfléchi à votre proposition; it's not a bad idea, if you ~ about it ce n'est pas une mauvaise idée, si tu réfléchis bien; she's ~ing about starting a business elle pense à OR envisage de monter une affaire; we'll ~ about it nous allons y penser OR réfléchir; she has a lot to ~ about just now elle est très préoccupée en ce moment; there's so much to ~ about when you buy a house il y a tant de choses à prendre en considération quand on achète une maison; the conference gave us much to ~ about la conférence nous a donné matière à réflexion; I'll give you something to ~ about! je vais te donner de quoi réfléchir! -**2.** [consider seriously] penser; all he ~s about is money il n'y a que l'argent qui l'intéresse; he's always ~ing about food – what else is there to ~ about? il ne pense qu'à manger – c'est ce qu'il y a de plus intéressant, non?

◆ **think ahead** *vi insep* prévoir; you have to learn to ~ ahead il faut apprendre à prévoir.

◆ **think back** *vi insep*: to ~ back to sthg se rappeler qqch; ~ back to that night essayez de vous souvenir de OR vous rappeler cette nuit-là; I thought back over the years j'ai repensé aux années passées.

◆ **think of** *vt insep* -**1.** [have as tentative plan] penser à, envisager de; she's ~ing of starting a business elle pense à OR envisage de monter une affaire. -**2.** [have in mind]: whatever were you ~ing of? où avais-tu la tête? ❑ come to ~ of it, that's not a bad idea à la réflexion, ce n'est pas une mauvaise idée. -**3.** [remember] penser à, se rappeler; I can't ~ of the address je n'arrive pas à me rappeler l'adresse; he couldn't ~ of the name il ne se rappelait pas le nom, le nom ne lui venait pas; that makes me ~ of my childhood ça me rappelle mon enfance. -**4.** [come up with - idea, solution]: she's the one who thought of double-checking it c'est elle qui a eu l'idée de le vérifier; it's the only way they could ~ of doing it ils ne voyaient pas d'autre façon de s'y prendre; I thought of the answer j'ai trouvé la réponse; I've just thought of something, she'll be out j'avais oublié OR je viens de me rappeler, elle ne sera pas là; I've just throught of something else attendez, il y a autre chose; I'd never have thought of that je n'y aurais jamais pensé; whatever will they ~ of next? qu'est-ce qu'ils vont bien pouvoir trouver ensuite?; ~ of a number between 1 and 10 pensez à un chiffre entre 1 et 10; I thought better of it je me suis ravisé; he thought nothing of leaving the baby alone for hours at a time il trouvait (ça) normal de laisser le bébé seul pendant des heures; thank you – ~ nothing of it! merci – mais je vous en prie OR mais c'est tout naturel! -**5.** [judge, have as opinion] estimer; what do you ~ of the new teacher? comment trouvez-vous le OR que pensez-vous du nouveau professeur?; she ~s very highly of OR very well of him elle a une très haute opinion de lui; he ~s of himself as an artist il se prend pour un artiste; as a doctor she is very well thought of elle est très respectée en tant que médecin; I hope you won't ~ badly of me if I refuse j'espère que vous ne m'en voudrez pas si je refuse; I don't ~ much of that idea cette idée ne me dit pas grand-chose; he doesn't ~ much of his brother il n'a pas une haute opinion de son frère. -**6.** [imagine] penser à, imaginer; I always thought of her as being blonde je la croyais blonde; just ~ of it, me as president! imaginez un peu: moi président!, vous m'imaginez président?; when I ~ of how things might have turned out quand je pense à la manière dont les choses auraient pu finir; you might have married him, ~ of that! tu aurais pu l'épouser, imagine un peu! -**7.** [take into consideration] penser à, considérer; I have my family to ~ of il faut que je pense à ma famille; she never ~s of anyone but herself elle ne pense qu'à elle-même; ~ of your mother's feelings pense un peu à ta mère; he never ~s of her il n'a aucun égard OR aucune considération pour elle; you never ~ of the expense tu ne regardes jamais à la dépense; ~ of how much it will cost! pense un peu à ce que ça va coûter!; you can't ~ of everything on ne peut pas penser à tout.

◆ **think out** *vt sep* [plan] élaborer, préparer; [problem] bien étudier OR examiner; [solution] bien étudier; it needs ~ing out cela demande mûre réflexion; a carefully thought-out answer une réponse bien pesée; a well-thought-out plan un projet bien conçu OR ficelé.

◆ **think over** *vt sep* bien examiner, bien réfléchir à; we'll have to ~ it over il va falloir que nous y réfléchissions; this needs ~ing over cela mérite réflexion; ~ the offer over carefully réfléchissez bien à cette proposition; on ~ing things over we've decided not to sell the house réflexion faite, on a décidé de ne pas vendre la maison; I need some time to ~ things over j'ai besoin de temps pour réfléchir.

thinkable [ˈθɪŋkəbl] *adj* pensable, concevable, imaginable.

thinker [ˈθɪŋkəʳ] *n* penseur *m*, -euse *f*; 'The Thinker' *Rodin* 'le Penseur'.

thinking [ˈθɪŋkɪŋ] ◇ *adj* [person] pensant, rationnel, qui réfléchit; it's the ~ man's answer to pulp fiction c'est un roman de hall de gare en plus intelligent.
◇ *n* -**1.** [act] pensée *f*, pensées *fpl*, réflexion *f*; I've done some serious ~ about the situation j'ai bien OR sérieusement OR mûrement réfléchi à la situation. -**2.** [opinion, judgment] point *m* de vue, opinion *f*, opinions *fpl*; my ~ on disarmament has changed mes opinions sur le désarmement ont changé; she finally came round to my way of ~ elle s'est finalement ralliée à mon point de vue; to his way of ~ it was wrong pour lui, ce n'était pas bien.

thinking cap *n*: to put on one's ~ *inf fig* se mettre à réfléchir, cogiter.

think tank *n* groupe *m* d'experts.

thin-lipped *adj* aux lèvres minces OR fines.

thinly [ˈθɪnlɪ] *adv* [spread] en couche mince; [cut] en fines tranches; a ~ disguised insult une insulte à peine voilée; a ~ clad child un enfant insuffisamment OR trop légèrement vêtu; the area is ~ populated la région n'est pas très peuplée.

thinner [ˈθɪnəʳ] ◇ *compar* → **thin**.
◇ *n* [solvent] diluant *m*.

thinness [ˈθɪnnɪs] *n* -**1.** [of layer, wall] minceur *f*, finesse *f*; [of person] minceur *f*, maigreur *f*; [of wire] finesse *f*; [of clothing, blanket, carpet] légèreté *f*, finesse *f*. -**2.** [of beard, hair] finesse *f*, rareté *f*. -**3.** [of excuse] faiblesse *f*, insuffisance *f*.

thin-skinned *adj fig* susceptible.

third [θɜːd] ◇ *adj* troisième; ~ finger annulaire *m*; ~ person GRAMM troisième personne *f*; in the ~ person à la troisième personne; ~ time lucky la troisième fois sera la bonne; 'The Third Man' *Greene, Reed* 'le Troisième Homme'.
◇ *n* -**1.** [gen] troisième *mf*. -**2.** [fraction] tiers *m*. -**3.** MUS tierce *f*. -**4.** AUT: ~ (gear) troisième *f*; in ~ (gear) en troisième. -**5.** *Br* UNIV ≃ licence *f* sans mention.
◇ *adv* en troisième place *f* OR position *f*.

third class ◇ *n* -**1.** [for travel] troisième classe *f*; [for accommodation] troisième catégorie *f*. -**2.** *Am* [for mail] ≃ tarif *m* «imprimés», ≃ tarif *m* lent.
◇ *adv* -**1.** [travel] en troisième classe. -**2.** *Am*: to mail a package ~ ≃ envoyer un colis au tarif lent.

◆ **third-class** *adj* -**1.** [ticket, compartment] de troisième classe; [hotel, accommodation] de troisième catégorie. -**2.** [inferior - merchandise] de qualité inférieure, de pacotille; [- restaurant, food] de qualité inférieure. -**3.** *Br* UNIV: third-class degree ≃ licence *f* sans mention. -**4.** *Am* [mail] au tarif «imprimés», au tarif lent.

third degree *inf n*: to get the ~ passer à l'interrogatoire; to give sb the ~ [torture] passer qqn à tabac; [interrogate] cuisiner qqn.

third-degree burn *n* brûlure *f* au troisième degré.

Third Estate *n* HIST: the ~ le Tiers état.

thirdhand [ˌθɜːdˈhænd] ◇ *adj* [car, information] de troisième main.
◇ *adv* [buy] en troisième main.

thirdly [ˈθɜːdlɪ] *adv* troisièmement, en troisième lieu, tertio.

third party *n* tierce personne *f*, tiers *m*.

◆ **third-party** *adj*: third-party insurance assurance *f* au tiers.

third-rate *adj* de qualité inférieure.

third reading *n* [of a bill] *dernière lecture*.

Third World *n*: the ~ le tiers-monde.

◆ **Third-World** *comp* du tiers-monde.

thirst [θɜːst] ◇ *n literal & fig* soif *f*; all that hard work has given me a ~ ça m'a donné soif de travailler dur comme ça; he has a ~ for adventure *fig* il a soif d'aventure.
◇ *vi*: to ~ for sthg avoir soif de qqch; he was ~ing for a beer il avait soif d'une bière; a jealous husband ~ing for revenge *fig* un mari jaloux assoiffé de vengeance; to ~ for knowledge *fig* être avide de connaissances.

thirsty [ˈθɜːstɪ] (*compar* thirstier, *superl* thirstiest) *adj* -**1.** to be ~ avoir soif; I feel very ~ j'ai très soif; salted peanuts make you ~ les cacahuètes salées donnent soif; it's ~ work ça donne soif. -**2.** *fig* [for knowledge, adventure] assoiffé; she was ~ for revenge elle était assoiffée de vengeance. -**3.** [plant] qui a besoin de beaucoup d'eau; [soil] desséché.

thirteen [ˌθɜːˈtiːn] ◇ *adj* treize.
◇ *n* treize *m inv*.

thirteenth [ˌθɜːˈtiːnθ] ◇ *adj* treizième.
◇ *n* treizième *mf*.

thirtieth [ˈθɜːtɪəθ] ◇ *adj* trentième.
◇ *n* trentième *mf*.

thirty [ˈθɜːtɪ] (*pl* thirties) ◇ *n* trente *m inv*.
◇ *adj* trente; the Thirty Years' War HIST la guerre de Trente Ans; 'The Thirty-Nine Steps' *Buchan, Hitchcock* 'les Trente-Neuf Marches'.

thirty-second note *n Am* triple croche *f*.

thirty-second rest *n* huitième *m* de soupir.

thirty-something *adj caractéristique de certaines personnes ayant la trentaine et issues de milieu aisé*.

thirty-three *n* [record] trente-trois tours *m inv*.

this [ðɪs] (*pl* these [ðiːz]) ◇ *dem pron* -**1.** [person, situation, statement, thing indicated] ceci, ce; what's ~? qu'est-ce que c'est (que ça)?; who's ~? [gen] qui est-ce?; [on phone] qui est à l'appareil?; ~ is for you tiens, c'est pour toi; ~ is Mr Smith speaking [on phone] M. Smith à l'appareil, c'est M. Smith; ~ is my mother [in introduction] je vous présente ma mère; [in picture] c'est ma mère; ~ is the place I was talking about c'est OR voici l'endroit dont je parlais; ~ is terrible c'est affreux; ~ is what he told me voici ce qu'il m'a dit; ~ is where I live c'est ici que j'habite; what's ~ I hear about your leaving? on me dit que vous partez?; it was like ~ voici comment les choses se sont passées; do it like ~ voici comment il faut faire; I didn't want it to end like ~ je ne voulais pas que ça finisse OR se termine comme ça; that it should come to ~ qu'on en arrive là; and there's no way she could live with you? – well, ~ is it et elle ne pourrait pas vivre avec toi? – non, justement; ~ is it, wish me luck voilà, souhaite-moi bonne chance; I'll tell you ~... je vais te dire une chose...; after/before ~ après/avant ça; at OR with ~, he left the room là-dessus OR sur ce, il a quitté la pièce ❑ what did you talk about? – oh, ~ and that de quoi avez-vous parlé? – oh, de choses et d'autres; they sat chatting about ~, that and the other ils étaient là, assis, à bavarder de choses et d'autres; it's always Johnny ~ and Johnny that c'est Johnny par-ci, Johnny par-là. -**2.** [contrasted with 'that'] celui-ci *m*, celle-ci *f*; these ceux-ci *mpl*, celles-ci *fpl*; ~ is a rose, that is a peony ceci est une rose, ça c'est une pivoine; I want these, not those! je veux ceux-ci, pas ceux-là!; is ~ more expensive than that? celui-ci est-il plus cher que celui-là?
◇ *det* -**1.** [referring to a particular person, idea, time or thing] ce *m*, cet *m* (*before vowel or mute h*), cette *f*; these ces *mfpl*; ~ man cet homme; these ideas ces idées; ~ plan of yours won't work votre projet ne marchera pas; ~ book you wanted le livre que vous vouliez; he's lived in ~ country for years ça fait des années qu'il vit dans ce pays; ~ way please par ici s'il vous plaît; ~ funny little man came up to me un petit bonhomme à l'air bizarre est venu vers moi; there were these two Germans... il y avait ces deux Allemands...; who's ~ friend of yours? c'est qui, cet ami?; ~ here bicycle *dial* ce vélo-ci; by ~ time tomorrow he'll be gone demain à cette heure-ci, il sera parti; ~ time last week la semaine dernière à la même heure; ~ time next year l'année prochaine à la même époque; ~ coming week la semaine prochaine OR qui vient; saving money isn't easy these days faire des économies n'est pas facile aujourd'hui OR de nos jours; he's worked hard these last two months il a beaucoup travaillé ces deux derniers mois; I've been watching you ~ past hour ça fait une heure OR voici une heure que je vous regarde; what are you doing ~ Christmas? qu'est-ce que vous faites pour Noël cette année? -**2.** [contrasted with 'that'] ce... -ci *m*, cet... -ci *m* (*before vowel or mute h*), cette... -ci *f*; these ces... -ci *mfpl*; ~ table over here cette table-ci; which do you prefer, ~ one or that one? lequel tu préfères, celui-ci ou celui-là?; ~ dress is cheaper than that one cette robe-ci est moins chère que celle-là OR que l'autre; people ran ~ way and that les gens couraient dans tous les sens.
◇ *adv* aussi, si; it was ~ high c'était haut comme ça; we've come ~ far, we might as well go on [on journey] nous sommes venus jusqu'ici, alors autant continuer; [in project] maintenant que nous en sommes là, autant continuer.

thistle [ˈθɪsl] *n* chardon *m*.

thistledown [ˈθɪsəldaʊn] *n* duvet *m* de chardon.

thistly [ˈθɪslɪ] *adj* couvert de chardons.

thither [ˈðɪðəʳ] *adv fml* & *lit* là; go ~ allez-y.

thitherto [ˌðɪðəˈtuː] *adv fml* & *lit* jusqu'alors.

tho, tho' *Am* OR *lit* [ðəʊ] = **though**.

thole [θəʊl], **tholepin** [ˈθəʊlpɪn] *n* NAUT tolet *m*, dame *f* de nage.

Thomas [ˈtɒməs] *pr n*: Saint ~ saint Thomas; he's a doubting ~ il est comme saint Thomas.

thong [θɒŋ] *n* -**1.** [strip - of leather, rubber] lanière *f*. -**2.** [G-string] cache-sexe *m*.
◆ **thongs** *npl Am* tongs *fpl*.

Thor [θɔːʳ] *pr n* Thor.

thoraces [ˈθɔːrəsiːz] *pl* → **thorax**.

thoracic [θɔːˈræsɪk] *adj* thoracique.

thorax [ˈθɔːræks] (*pl* thoraxes OR thoraces [-rəsiːz]) *n* thorax *m*.

thorium [ˈθɔːrɪəm] *n* thorium *m*; ~ series famille *f* du thorium.

thorn [θɔːn] *n* -**1.** [prickle] épine *f*; it's a ~ in his side OR flesh c'est une source d'irritation constante pour lui, c'est sa bête noire. -**2.** [tree, shrub] arbuste *m* épineux; [hawthorn] aubépine *f*.

thorn apple *n* stramoine *f*.

thornback [ˈθɔːnbæk] *n* raie *f* bouclée.

thornbill [ˈθɔːnbɪl] *n* colibri *m*.

thornbush [ˈθɔːnbʊʃ] *n* buisson *m* épineux.

thornless [ˈθɔːnlɪs] *adj* sans épines.

thorny [ˈθɔːnɪ] (*compar* thornier, *superl* thorniest) *adj literal* & *fig* épineux.

thorough [ˈθʌrə] *adj* -**1.** [complete - inspection, research] minutieux, approfondi; to give sthg a ~ cleaning/dusting nettoyer/épousseter qqch à fond; she has a ~ knowledge of her subject elle a une connaissance parfaite de son sujet, elle connaît son sujet à fond OR sur le bout des doigts; she was subjected to a ~ cross-examination elle a subi un contre-interrogatoire minutieux; they were given a ~ telling-off ils ont reçu un bon savon. -**2.** [conscientious -work, worker] consciencieux, sérieux. -**3.** [as intensifier] absolu, complet; what a ~ bore this book is! qu'est-ce qu'il est ennuyeux, ce livre!; the man is a ~ scoundrel! ce type est une crapule finie!; it's a ~ nuisance! c'est vraiment très embêtant!

thoroughbred [ˈθʌrəbred] ◇ *adj* [horse] pur-sang *(inv)*; [animal - gen] de race.
◇ *n* -**1.** [horse] pur-sang *m inv*; [animal - gen] bête *f* de race. -**2.** [person]: she's a ~ elle a de la classe, elle est racée.

thoroughfare [ˈθʌrəfeəʳ] *n* voie *f* de communication; the main ~ la rue OR l'artère *f* principale; 'no ~' [no entry] 'passage interdit'; [cul-de-sac] 'voie sans issue' ❑ public ~ voie publique.

thoroughgoing [ˈθʌrəˌgəʊɪŋ] *adj* [search, investigation] minutieux, approfondi, complet; he's a ~ nuisance il est vraiment pénible.

thoroughly [ˈθʌrəlɪ] *adv* -**1.** [minutely, in detail - search] à fond, de fond en comble; [- examine] à fond, minutieusement; the carpet has been ~ cleaned le tapis a été nettoyé à fond; read all the questions ~ lisez très attentivement toutes les questions. -**2.** [as intensifier] tout à fait, absolument; it's ~ disgraceful c'est absolument honteux, c'est un véritable scandale, c'est une honte; I ~ agree je suis tout à fait d'accord.

thoroughness [ˈθʌrənɪs] *n* minutie *f*.

those [ðəʊz] *pl* → **that**.

thou[1] [ðaʊ] *pron* BIBLE OR *dial* tu; [stressed form] toi.

thou[2] [θaʊ] (*pl inv* OR thous) *n* -**1.** *abbr of* thousand. -**2.** *abbr of* thousandth of an inch.

though [ðəʊ] ◇ *conj* bien que, quoique; ~ young, she's very mature bien qu'elle soit jeune OR quoique jeune, elle est très mûre; ~ it's a difficult language, I intend to persevere bien que ce soit une langue difficile, j'ai l'intention de persévérer; he enjoyed the company ~ not the food il appréciait les gens avec qui il était mais pas ce qu'il mangeait; kind ~ she was, we never really got on malgré sa gentillesse, nous ne nous sommes jamais très bien entendus; it's an excellent book, ~ I say so myself c'est un très bon livre, sans fausse modestie; strange ~ it may seem aussi étrange que cela puisse paraître.
◇ *adv* pourtant; he's a difficult man; I like him ~ il n'est pas facile à vivre; pourtant je l'aime bien; it's nice, ~, isn't it? c'est joli quand même, tu ne trouves pas?

thought [θɔːt] ◇ *pt* & *pp* → **think**.
◇ *n* -**1.** *(U)* [reflection] pensée *f*, réflexion *f*; to give a problem much OR a lot of ~ bien réfléchir à un problème; after much ~ après mûre réflexion, après avoir mûrement réfléchi; we gave some ~ to the matter nous avons réfléchi à la question; this problem needs careful ~ nous devons bien réfléchir à ce problème; she was lost OR deep in ~ elle était absorbée par ses pensées OR plongée dans ses pensées. -**2.** *(C)* [consideration] considération *f*, pensée *f*; have you given my proposal a single ~? avez-vous pensé un seul instant à ma proposition?; I haven't given it a ~ je n'y ai pas pensé; don't give it another ~ n'y pensez plus; to collect one's ~s rassembler ses esprits; my ~s were elsewhere j'avais l'esprit ailleurs; my ~s went back to the time I had spent in Tunisia j'ai repensé au temps où j'étais en Tunisie; she accepted the job with no ~ of her family elle a accepté le travail sans tenir compte de sa famille; he had no ~ for his own safety il ne pensait pas à sa propre sécurité. -**3.** *(C)* [idea, notion] idée *f*, pensée *f*; the ~ occurred to me that you might like to come l'idée m'est venue OR je me suis dit que cela vous ferait peut-être plaisir de venir; I had to give up all ~ OR ~s of finishing on time j'ai dû finalement renoncer à l'idée de terminer à temps; the mere ~ of it makes me feel ill rien que d'y penser, ça me rend malade; that's a ~! ça, c'est une idée!; what an awful ~! quelle horreur!; what a kind ~! quelle aimable attention! -**4.** *(C)* [intention] idée *f*, intention *f*; we have ~s of going to Australia nous avons dans l'idée d'aller OR nous songeons à aller en Australie; her one ~ was to reach the top sa seule idée était d'atteindre le sommet; I have no ~ of resigning je n'ai pas l'intention de démissionner; it's the ~ that counts c'est l'intention qui compte. -**5.** *(C)* [opinion] opinion *f*, avis *m*; we'd like your ~s on the matter nous aimerions savoir ce que vous en pensez. -**6.** *(U)* [doctrine, ideology] pensée *f*; contemporary political ~ la pensée politique contemporaine. -**7.** *dated* [small amount]: a ~ too salty un tout petit peu trop salé.

thoughtful [ˈθɔːtfʊl] *adj* -**1.** [considerate, kind] prévenant, gentil, attentionné; it was a ~ gesture c'était un geste plein d'attention; be more ~ next time pensez un peu plus aux autres la prochaine fois; it was very ~ of them to send the flowers c'était très aimable à eux OR gentil de leur part d'envoyer les fleurs. -**2.** [pensive] pensif. -**3.** [reasoned - decision, remark, essay] réfléchi; [- study] sérieux.

thoughtfully [ˈθɔːtfʊlɪ] *adv* -**1.** [considerately, kindly] avec prévenance OR délicatesse, gentiment; she very ~ offered to help elle a très gentiment proposé de m'aider. -**2.** [pensively] pensivement. -**3.** [with careful thought] d'une manière réfléchie; it's a ~ written article c'est un article écrit de façon réfléchie.

thoughtfulness [ˈθɔːtfʊlnɪs] *n* -**1.** [kindness] prévenance *f*, délicatesse *f*, gentillesse *f*. -**2.** [pensiveness] air *m* pensif.

thoughtless [ˈθɔːtlɪs] *adj* -**1.** [inconsiderate - person, act, behaviour] inconsidéré, irréfléchi, qui manque de délicatesse; [- remark] irréfléchi; it was ~ of me ce n'était pas très délicat de ma part; what a ~ thing to do! quel manque de

délicatesse! -**2.** [hasty, rash - decision, action] irréfléchi, hâtif; [- person] irréfléchi, léger.
thoughtlessly ['θɔːtlɪslɪ] *adv* -**1.** [inconsiderately] sans aucun égard, sans aucune considération. -**2.** [hastily] hâtivement, sans réfléchir.
thought-provoking *adj* qui pousse à la réflexion, stimulant.
thought transference *n* transmission *f* de pensée.
thousand ['θaʊznd] ◇ *adj* mille; a ~ years mille ans, un millénaire; five ~ people cinq mille personnes; I've already told you a ~ times je te l'ai déjà dit mille fois ❑ 'The Thousand and One Nights' 'les Mille et une nuits'.
◇ *n* mille *m inv*; in the year two ~ en l'an deux mille; there were ~s of people il y avait des milliers de personnes.
thousandfold ['θaʊzndfəʊld] ◇ *adj* multiplié par mille.
◇ *adv* mille fois autant.
Thousand Island dressing *n sauce à base de mayonnaise, de ketchup et de cornichons hachés.*
thousandth ['θaʊzntθ] ◇ *adj* millième.
◇ *n* millième *m*.
Thrace [θreɪs] *pr n* Thrace *f*.
thraldom *Br*, **thralldom** *Am* ['θrɔːldəm] *n fml* servitude *f*, esclavage *m*.
thrall [θrɔːl] *n fml* -**1.** [state] servitude *f*, esclavage *m*; to be in ~ to sb être l'esclave de qqn. -**2.** [person] esclave *mf*.
thralldom *Am* = **thraldom**.
thrash [θræʃ] ◇ *vt* -**1.** [in punishment - person, animal] battre; he ~ed the hedge with a stick il donna des grands coups de bâton dans la haie; the horse reared and ~ed the air with its hooves le cheval se cabra et fouetta l'air de ses sabots. -**2.** SPORT [defeat] battre à plate couture OR à plates coutures; Liverpool ~ed Arsenal Liverpool a battu Arsenal à plate couture. -**3.** [move vigorously]: to ~ one's arms/legs (about) battre des bras/jambes; the dolphin ~ed its tail and disappeared le dauphin donna de grands coups de queue et disparut. -**4.** [thresh - corn] battre.
◇ *vi* [move violently] se débattre; the waves ~ed against the rocks/boat les vagues battaient violemment contre les rochers/le bateau.
◇ *n* -**1.** [stroke] battement *m*; with a few ~es of its tail, the fish was gone quelques battements de queue et le poisson disparut. -**2.** *inf Br* [party] sauterie *f*.
◆ **thrash about, thrash around** ◇ *vi insep* [person, fish] se débattre; she was ~ing about in bed elle se débattait OR elle remuait dans le lit; he ~ed about to free himself il se débattait pour se libérer; he was ~ing about in the undergrowth with a stick il battait les broussailles de son bâton.
◇ *vt sep* [arms, legs, tail] battre de; [stick] agiter.
◆ **thrash out** *vt sep* [problem] débattre de; [agreement] finir par trouver; we'll ~ it out over lunch on démêlera OR éclaircira cette affaire pendant le repas.
thrashing ['θræʃɪŋ] *n* -**1.** [punishment] raclée *f*, correction *f*; I gave him a good ~ je lui ai donné une bonne correction. -**2.** SPORT: to get a ~ se faire battre à plates coutures; we gave the team a ~ on a battu l'équipe à plates coutures. -**3.** [of corn] battage *m*.
thread [θred] ◇ *n* -**1.** SEW & MED fil *m*; polyester ~ fil polyester; his life hung by a ~ *fig* sa vie ne tenait qu'à un fil. -**2.** *fig* [of water, smoke] filet *m*; [of light] mince rayon *m*; [of story, argument] fil *m*; I've lost the ~ of what I was saying j'ai perdu le fil de ce que je disais; it's difficult to follow the ~ of her argument il est difficile de suivre le fil de ses idées. -**3.** TECH [of screw] pas *m*, filetage *m*.
◇ *vt* -**1.** [needle, beads, cotton] enfiler; she ~ed black cotton through the needle elle a enfilé une aiguillée de coton noir; she ~ed the needle elle a enfilé l'aiguille; she quickly ~ed the film into the projector elle a vite monté le film sur le projecteur; you have to ~ the elastic through the loops il faut enfiler OR faire passer l'élastique dans les boucles; she ~ed her way through the crowd/market *fig* elle s'est faufilée parmi la foule/à travers le marché. -**2.** TECH [screw] tarauder, fileter.
◇ *vi* [needle, cotton] s'enfiler; the tape ~s through the slot la bande passe dans la fente.
◆ **threads** *inf npl Am* [clothes] fringues *fpl*.
◆ **thread together** *vt sep* [beads] enfiler.
threadbare ['θredbeə^r] *adj* -**1.** [carpet, clothing] usé, râpé; he lived a ~ existence il menait une existence miséreuse. -**2.** [joke, excuse, argument] usé, rebattu.
thread mark *n* filigrane *m (des billets de banque)*.
threadworm ['θredwɜːm] *n* oxyure *m*.
threat [θret] *n literal & fig* menace *f*; to make ~s against sb proférer des menaces contre qqn; they got what they wanted by ~s ils ont obtenu ce qu'ils voulaient par la menace; terrorist attacks are a constant ~ to our security les attentats terroristes représentent une menace constante pour notre sécurité; he's a ~ to our security il constitue une menace pour notre sécurité; political unrest poses a ~ to peace in the area l'agitation politique menace la paix dans la région; he is under ~ of death il est menacé de mort; the country lives under (the) ~ of war le pays vit sous la menace de la guerre.
threaten ['θretn] ◇ *vt* -**1.** [make threats against - person] menacer; to ~ to do sthg menacer de faire qqch; he ~ed her with a gun il l'a menacée avec un pistolet; he started ~ing me il s'est fait menaçant, il s'est mis à me menacer; we were ~ed with the sack on nous a menacés de licenciement; to ~ proceedings against sb, to ~ sb with proceedings JUR menacer de poursuivre qqn, menacer qqn de poursuites. -**2.** [subj: danger, unpleasant event] menacer; the species is ~ed with extinction l'espèce est menacée OR en voie de disparition; our jobs are ~ed nos emplois sont menacés; it's ~ing to rain/to snow la pluie/la neige menace. -**3.** [be a danger for - society, tranquillity] menacer, être une menace pour.
◇ *vi* [danger, storm] menacer.
threatened ['θretnd] *adj* menacé.
threatening ['θretnɪŋ] *adj* [danger, sky, storm, person] menaçant; [letter] de menaces; [gesture] menaçant, de menace; she gave me a ~ look elle m'a lancé un regard menaçant; to use ~ language prononcer des paroles menaçantes.
threateningly ['θretnɪŋlɪ] *adv* [behave, move] de manière menaçante, d'un air menaçant; [say] d'un ton OR sur un ton menaçant.
three [θriː] ◇ *adj* trois; the Three Wise Men les Rois mages *mpl*; 'Three Men in a Boat' *Jerome* 'Trois hommes dans un bateau'; 'The Three Musketeers' *Dumas* 'les Trois mousquetaires'; 'The Three Sisters' *Chekhov* 'les Trois sœurs'.
◇ *n* trois *m*.
three-card trick *n* bonneteau *m*.
three-cornered *adj* triangulaire; ~ discussion débat *m* à trois; ~ hat tricorne *m*.
3-D [ˌθriːˈdiː] = **three-D**.
three-day event *n* EQUIT concours *m* hippique sur trois jours.
three-D, three-dimensional [-dɪˈmenʃənl] *adj* -**1.** [object] à trois dimensions, tridimensionnel; [film] en relief; [image] en trois dimensions. -**2.** [character - in book, play etc] qui semble réel.
threefold ['θriːfəʊld] ◇ *adj* triple.
◇ *adv* trois fois autant.
three-four time *n* MUS trois-quatre *m inv*; in ~ en trois-quatre.
three-legged *adj* [stool, table] à trois pieds; [animal] à trois pattes.
three-legged race *n course où les participants courent par deux, la jambe gauche de l'un attachée à la droite de l'autre.*
three-line whip *n* POL *invitation urgente faite à un député par un «whip» à prendre part à un débat ou à un vote.*
Three Mile Island *pr n* Three Mile Island *(théâtre d'un accident dans une centrale nucléaire aux États-Unis en 1979).*
threepence ['θrepəns] *n Br* trois (anciens) pence *mpl*.
threepenny ['θrepənɪ] *Br* ◇ *n*: ~ (bit OR piece) *ancienne pièce de trois pence.*
◇ *adj* à trois pence, coûtant trois pence; 'The Threepenny Opera' *Brecht* 'l'Opéra de quat' sous'.
three-phase *adj* triphasé.
three-piece *adj*: ~ suite *Br*, ~ set *Am salon comprenant un canapé et deux fauteuils assortis*; ~ (suit) (costume *m*) trois-pièces *m inv*.
three-ply *adj* [wool] à trois fils; [rope] à trois brins; ~ wood contre-plaqué *m (à trois épaisseurs)*.
three-point landing *n* AERON atterrissage *m* trois points.
three-point turn *n* AUT demi-tour *m* en trois manœuvres.
three-quarter ◇ *adj* [sleeve] trois-quarts *(inv)*; [portrait] de trois-quarts; ~ (length) jacket veste *f* trois-quarts.
◇ *n* [in rugby]: ~ (back) trois-quart *m inv*.
three quarters ◇ *npl* trois quarts *mpl*.
◇ *adv* aux trois quarts; the tank is ~ full le réservoir est aux trois quarts plein.
three-ring circus *n Am* cirque *m* à trois pistes; it's a real ~ *fig* c'est un véritable cirque.
three R's *npl* SCH: the ~ *la lecture, l'orthographe, l'arithmétique, traditionnellement considérés comme le fondement de toute éducation.*
threescore [ˌθriːˈskɔː^r] *lit* ◇ *adj* soixante.
◇ *n* soixante *m*.
three-sided *adj* [shape] à trois côtés OR faces; [discussion] à trois.
threesome ['θriːsəm] *n* -**1.** [group] groupe *m* de trois personnes; we went as a ~ nous y sommes allés à trois. -**2.** [in cards, golf] partie *f* OR jeu *m* à trois; she came along to make up a ~ elle est venue pour que nous soyons trois (joueurs).
three-way *adj* [discussion, conversation] à trois; [division] en trois; [switch] à trois voies OR directions.
three-wheeler *n* [tricycle] tricycle *m*; [car] voiture *f* à trois roues.
threnody ['θrenədɪ] (*pl* **threnodies**) *n* thrène *m*, chant *m* funèbre.
thresh [θreʃ] *vt* [corn, wheat] battre.
thresher ['θreʃə^r] *n* AGR -**1.** [person] batteur *m*, -euse *f*. -**2.** [machine] batteuse *f*.
threshing ['θreʃɪŋ] *n* battage *m*.
threshing machine *n* batteuse *f*.
threshold ['θreʃhəʊld] ◇ *n* -**1.** [doorway] seuil *m*, pas *m* de la porte; to cross the ~ franchir le seuil. -**2.** *fig* seuil *m*, début *m*; we are on the ~ of new discoveries nous sommes sur le point de faire de nouvelles découvertes; she is on the ~ of a new career elle débute une nouvelle carrière. -**3.** ECON & FIN niveau *m*, limite *f*; the government has raised tax ~s in line with inflation le gouvernement a relevé les tranches de l'impôt pour tenir compte de l'inflation. -**4.** ANAT & PSYCH seuil *m*.
◇ *comp* -**1.** *Br* ECON: ~ wage agreement/policy accord *m*/politique *f* d'indexation des salaires sur les prix. -**2.** ELEC [current, voltage] de seuil. -**3.** LING: ~ level niveau *m* seuil.
threw [θruː] *pt* → **throw**.
thrice [θraɪs] *adv lit & arch* trois fois.
thrift [θrɪft] *n* -**1.** [care with money] économie *f*, esprit *m* d'économie. -**2.** *Am* [savings bank]: ~ (institution) caisse *f* d'épargne.
thriftiness ['θrɪftɪnɪs] *n* sens *m* de l'économie.
thriftless ['θrɪftlɪs] *adj* dépensier, peu économe.
thrift shop *n magasin vendant des articles d'occasion au profit d'œuvres charitables.*
thrifty ['θrɪftɪ] (*compar* **thriftier**, *superl* **thriftiest**) *adj* économe, peu dépensier.

thrill [θrɪl] ◇ *n* [feeling of excitement] frisson *m*; [exciting experience, event] sensation *f*, émotion *f*; with a ~ of anticipation/pleasure en frissonnant d'avance/de plaisir; it was a real ~ to meet the president j'ai ressenti une grande émotion à rencontrer le président; the film gave the audience plenty of ~s le film a procuré aux spectateurs beaucoup de sensations fortes; they got quite a ~ out of the experience ils ont été ravis OR enchantés de l'expérience; what a ~ for you! quelle émotion vous avez dû ressentir!

◇ *vt* transporter, électriser; the magician ~ed the audience with his tricks le prestidigitateur a électrisé les spectateurs avec ses tours; the sight of the pyramids ~ed us le spectacle des pyramides nous a procuré une vive émotion.

◇ *vi* [with joy] tressaillir, frissonner; they ~ed to the sound of the drums le bruit des tambours les fit frissonner; I ~ed at the sight à la vue de ce spectacle, j'ai ressenti une vive émotion.

thrilled [θrɪld] *adj* ravi; she was ~ to be chosen elle était ravie d'avoir été choisie; I was ~ with the new chairs j'étais très content des nouvelles chaises ❑ to be ~ to bits *inf* être aux anges.

thriller [ˈθrɪləʳ] *n* [film, book] thriller *m*.

thrilling [ˈθrɪlɪŋ] *adj* [adventure, film, story] palpitant, saisissant, excitant; [speech] passionnant; what a ~ experience! quelle expérience excitante!

thrips [θrɪps] (*pl inv*) *n* thrips *m*.

thrive [θraɪv] (*pt* thrived OR throve [θrəʊv], *pp* thrived OR thriven [ˈθrɪvn]) *vi* -**1.** [plant] pousser, se développer; [child] grandir, se développer; [adult] se porter bien, respirer la santé; the plants ~ in peaty soil les plantes poussent bien dans un sol tourbeux; she ~d on the mountain air l'air des montagnes lui réussissait très bien; he ~s on hard work il aime bien travailler dur. -**2.** [business, company] prospérer, être florissant; [businessman] prospérer, réussir.

thriving [ˈθraɪvɪŋ] *adj* -**1.** [person] florissant de santé, vigoureux; [animal] vigoureux; [plant] robuste, vigoureux. -**2.** [business, company] prospère, florissant; [businessman] prospère.

thro' [θruː] *lit* = **through**.

throat [θrəʊt] *n* gorge *f*; he was wearing a scarf round his ~ il portait une écharpe autour du cou; get this drink/medicine down your ~! *hum* avalez-moi cette boisson/ce médicament!; he grabbed him by the ~ il l'a pris à la gorge; to clear one's ~ s'éclaircir la voix ❑ the two brothers are always at each other's ~s les deux frères sont toujours en train de se battre; she's always jumping down my ~ *inf* elle est toujours à me crier dessus; he never misses the chance to ram OR to shove his success down my ~ *inf* il ne manque jamais une occasion de me rebattre les oreilles avec sa réussite.

throat-microphone, **throat-mike** *n* laryngophone *m*.

throaty [ˈθrəʊtɪ] (*compar* throatier, *superl* throatiest) *adj* [voice, laugh etc] guttural, rauque; a ~ cough une toux rauque.

throb [θrɒb] (*pt* & *pp* throbbed, *cont* throbbing) ◇ *vi* -**1.** [music] vibrer; [drums] battre (rythmiquement); [engine, machine] vrombir, vibrer; the place was throbbing (with life) *fig* l'endroit grouillait de vie. -**2.** [heart] battre fort, palpiter. -**3.** [pain] lanciner; my head is throbbing j'ai très mal à la tête; my finger still ~s where I hit it j'ai encore des élancements dans le doigt là où je l'ai cogné.

◇ *n* -**1.** [of music, drums] rythme *m*, battement *m* rythmique, battements *mpl* rythmiques; [of engine, machine] vibration *f*, vibrations *fpl*, vrombissement *m*, vrombissements *mpl*. -**2.** [of heart] battement *m*, battements *mpl*, pulsation *f*, pulsations *fpl*. -**3.** [of pain] élancement *m*.

throbbing [ˈθrɒbɪŋ] *adj* -**1.** [rhythm] battant; [drum] qui bat rythmiquement; [engine, machine] vibrant, vrombissant. -**2.** [heart] battant, palpitant. -**3.** [pain] lancinant; I've got a ~ headache j'ai un mal de tête lancinant.

throes [θrəʊz] *npl* [pains] douleurs *fpl*, agonie *f*; death ~ agonie *f*.

◆ **in the throes of** *prep phr*: in the ~ of war/illness en proie à la guerre/la maladie; to be in the ~ of doing sthg être en train de faire qqch; they are in the ~ of moving house ils sont en plein déménagement.

thrombi [ˈθrɒmbaɪ] *pl* → **thrombus**.

thrombosis [θrɒmˈbəʊsɪs] (*pl* thromboses [-siːz]) *n* thrombose *f*, thromboses *fpl*; coronary ~ infarctus *m* (du myocarde).

thrombus [ˈθrɒmbəs] (*pl* thrombi [-baɪ]) *n* thrombus *m*, caillot *m* de sang.

throne [θrəʊn] ◇ *n* trône *m*; to come to the ~ monter sur le trône; she has been on the ~ for nearly 50 years elle est sur le trône depuis presque 50 ans.

◇ *vt* [monarch] mettre sur le trône; [bishop] introniser.

throne room *n* salle *f* du trône.

throng [θrɒŋ] ◇ *n* foule *f*, multitude *f*; ~s of people were doing their Christmas shopping une foule de gens faisaient leurs achats de Noël OR faisait ses achats de Noël.

◇ *vt*: demonstrators ~ed the streets des manifestants se pressaient dans les rues; the shops were ~ed with people les magasins grouillaient de monde OR étaient bondés.

◇ *vi* affluer, se presser; crowds of people ~ed towards the stadium les gens se dirigeaient en masse vers le stade; people ~ed into the square to get a glimpse of the president les gens se sont pressés sur la place pour apercevoir le président.

throttle [ˈθrɒtl] ◇ *n* [of car] accélérateur *m*; [of motorcycle] poignée *f* d'accélération OR des gaz; [of aircraft] commande *f* des gaz; to open/to close the ~ mettre/réduire les gaz; at full ~ (à) pleins gaz.

◇ *vt* [strangle] étrangler; I could ~ you! je pourrais te tuer!

◇ *comp* [controls]: ~ valve papillon *m* des gaz, soupape *f* d'étranglement.

◆ **throttle down**, **throttle back** *vt sep* mettre au ralenti.

through [θruː] ◇ *prep* -**1.** [from one end or side to the other] à travers; to walk ~ the streets se promener dans OR à travers les rues; they drove ~ the countryside ils ont roulé à travers la campagne; we travelled ~ America nous avons parcouru les États-Unis; he swam quickly ~ the water il nageait rapidement; the river flows ~ a deep valley le fleuve traverse une vallée profonde; the police let them ~ the roadblock la police les a laissés passer à travers le barrage routier; the bullet went straight ~ his shoulder la balle lui a traversé l'épaule de part en part; we went ~ a door nous avons passé une porte; water poured ~ the hole l'eau coulait par le trou; he could see her ~ the window il pouvait la voir par la fenêtre; can you see ~ it? est-ce que tu peux voir au travers?; I can't see much ~ the fog je ne vois pas grand-chose à travers le brouillard; what can you see ~ the telescope? qu'est-ce que vous voyez dans OR à travers le télescope?; I could hear them ~ the wall je les entendais à travers le mur; she couldn't feel anything ~ her gloves elle ne sentait rien à travers ses gants; a shiver ran ~ him il fut parcouru d'un frisson; he drove ~ a red light il a brûlé un feu rouge; to slip ~ the net *literal* & *fig* passer à travers les mailles du filet; he goes ~ his money very quickly l'argent lui brûle les doigts; she ate her way ~ a whole box of chocolates elle a mangé toute une boîte de chocolats. -**2.** [in] dans, à travers; he got a bullet ~ the leg une balle lui a traversé la jambe; she was shot ~ the heart on lui a tiré une balle dans le cœur; the bull had a ring ~ its nose le taureau avait un anneau dans le nez; to make a hole ~ sthg percer un trou à travers qqch. -**3.** [from beginning to end of] à travers; ~ the ages à travers les âges; halfway ~ the performance à la moitié OR au milieu de la représentation; she has lived ~ some difficult times elle a connu OR traversé des moments difficiles; we had to sit ~ a boring lecture nous avons dû rester à écouter une conférence ennuyeuse; I slept ~ the storm l'orage ne m'a pas réveillé; will he live ~ the night? passera-t-il la nuit?; the war lasted all ~ 1914-18 la guère a duré de 1914 jusqu'en 1918; she maintained her dignity ~ it all elle a toujours gardé sa dignité. -**4.** *Am* [to, until]: 80 ~ 100 de 80 à 100; April ~ July d'avril jusqu'en juillet, d'avril à juillet. -**5.** [by means of] par, grâce à; I sent it ~ the post je l'ai envoyé par la poste; she can only be contacted ~ her secretary on ne peut la contacter que par l'intermédiaire de sa secrétaire; it was only ~ his intervention that we were allowed out c'est uniquement grâce à son intervention qu'on nous a laissés sortir; I met a lot of people ~ him il m'a fait rencontrer beaucoup de gens; she was interviewed ~ an interpreter on l'a interviewée par l'intermédiaire d'un interprète; change must be achieved ~ peaceful means le changement doit être obtenu par des moyens pacifiques. -**6.** [because of] à cause de; ~ no fault of his own, he lost his job il a perdu son emploi sans que ce soit de sa faute; it all came about ~ a misunderstanding tout est arrivé à cause d'un malentendu.

◇ *adv* -**1.** [from one side to the other]: please go ~ into the lounge passez dans le salon, s'il vous plaît; I couldn't get ~ je ne pouvais pas passer; we shoved our way ~ nous nous sommes frayé un chemin en poussant; the police let us ~ la police nous a laissés passer; the rain was coming ~ la pluie passait au travers; the nail had gone right ~ le clou était passé au travers. -**2.** [from beginning to end]: I slept ~ until 8 j'ai dormi (sans me réveiller) jusqu'à 8 h; I slept the whole night ~ j'ai dormi d'un trait jusqu'au matin; I saw the film all the way ~ j'ai vu le film jusqu'au bout; I read the letter ~ j'ai lu la lettre jusqu'au bout; I left halfway ~ je suis parti au milieu. -**3.** [directly]: the train goes ~ to Paris without stopping le train va directement à Paris OR est sans arrêt jusqu'à Paris; can you get a bus right ~ to the port? est-ce qu'il y a un bus direct pour le port? -**4.** [completely]: to be wet ~ être complètement trempé; she's an aristocrat ~ and ~ c'est une aristocrate jusqu'au bout des ongles. -**5.** TELEC: can you put me ~ to Elaine/to extension 363? pouvez-vous me passer Elaine/le poste 363?; I'm putting you ~ now je vous passe votre correspondant OR communication; I tried ringing him, but I couldn't get ~ j'ai essayé de l'appeler mais je n'ai pas réussi à l'avoir; you're ~ now vous êtes en ligne.

◇ *adj* -**1.** [direct - train, ticket] direct; [traffic] en transit, de passage; all ~ passengers must remain seated tous les passagers en transit doivent garder leur place; a ~ train to London un train direct pour Londres; 'no ~ road' *Br*, 'not a ~ street' *Am* 'voie sans issue'. -**2.** [finished]: are you ~? avez-vous fini?, c'est fini?; he's ~ with his work at last il a enfin terminé tout son travail; I'll be ~ reading the newspaper in a minute j'aurai fini de lire le journal dans un instant; I'm ~ with smoking la cigarette, c'est fini; she's ~ with him elle en a eu assez de lui; you can do your own typing, I'm ~! tu n'as qu'à le taper toi-même, moi c'est fini OR j'en ai assez!

throughout [θruːˈaʊt] ◇ *prep* -**1.** [in space] partout dans; ~ the world dans le monde entier, partout dans le monde; ~ Europe à travers OR dans toute l'Europe, partout en Europe. -**2.** [in time]: ~ the year pendant toute l'année; ~ my life (durant) toute ma vie; ~ this period pendant toute cette période.

◇ *adv* -**1.** [everywhere] partout; the house has been repainted ~ la maison a été entièrement repeinte. -**2.** [all the time] (pendant) tout le temps; she remained silent ~ elle est restée silencieuse du début jusqu'à la fin.

throughput ['θru:put] *n* COMPUT débit *m*.

throughway ['θru:weɪ] = **thruway**.

throve [θrəʊv] *pt* → **thrive**.

throw [θrəʊ] (*pt* threw [θru:], *pp* thrown [θrəʊn]) ⋄ *vt* -**1.** [stone] lancer, jeter; [ball] lancer; [coal onto fire] mettre; ~ me the ball, ~ the ball to me lance-moi le ballon; he threw the ball over the wall il a lancé OR envoyé le ballon par-dessus le mur; a bomb was ~n into the crowded waiting room une bombe a été lancée dans la salle d'attente bondée; could you ~ me my lighter? peux-tu me lancer mon briquet?; she threw the serviette into the bin elle a jeté la serviette à la poubelle; children were ~ing bread to the birds les enfants jetaient OR lançaient du pain aux oiseaux; he threw his jacket over a chair il a jeté sa veste sur une chaise; she threw a few clothes into a suitcase elle a jeté quelques affaires dans une valise; I threw some cold water on my face je me suis aspergé la figure avec de l'eau froide; a group of rioters threw stones at the police un groupe de manifestants a lancé OR jeté des pierres sur les policiers; he threw two sixes [in dice] il a jeté deux six; to ~ sb into prison OR jail jeter qqn en prison; to ~ sb overboard jeter qqn par-dessus bord. -**2.** [opponent, rider] jeter (par terre); his opponent threw him to the ground [in fight] son adversaire l'a jeté à terre; [in wrestling match] son adversaire l'a envoyé au sol OR au tapis; the horse threw him le cheval le désarçonna OR le jeta à terre. -**3.** [with force, violence] projeter; she was ~n clear [in car accident] elle a été éjectée; the force of the explosion threw them against the wall la force de l'explosion les a projetés contre le mur; to ~ open ouvrir en grand OR tout grand; she threw open the door/windows elle a ouvert la porte/les fenêtres en grand; the House of Commons has been ~n open to television cameras *fig* la Chambre des communes a été ouverte aux caméras de télévision; she threw herself into an armchair elle s'est jetée dans un fauteuil; he threw himself at her feet il s'est jeté à ses pieds; she threw herself at him [attacked] elle s'est jetée OR s'est ruée sur lui; [as lover] elle s'est jetée sur lui OR à sa tête; he threw himself on the mercy of the king *fig* il s'en est remis au bon vouloir du roi. -**4.** [plunge] plonger; the news threw them into confusion/a panic les nouvelles les ont plongés dans l'embarras/les ont affolés; the scandal has ~n the country into confusion le scandale a semé la confusion dans le pays; to ~ o.s. into one's work se plonger dans son travail; she threw herself into the job of organizing the wedding elle s'est plongée avec enthousiasme dans l'organisation des noces. -**5.** [direct, aim - look, glance] jeter, lancer; [- accusation, reproach] lancer, envoyer; [- punch] lancer, porter; [cast - light, shadows] projeter; to ~ a question at sb poser une question à brûle-pourpoint à qqn; don't ~ that one at me! ne me faites pas ce reproche!, ne me jetez pas ça à la figure!; to ~ one's voice THEAT projeter sa voix; to ~ a bridge over a river CONSTR jeter un pont sur une rivière; this ~s new light on the matter *fig* ceci éclaire l'affaire d'un jour nouveau. -**6.** [confuse] désarçonner, dérouter, déconcerter; that question really threw me! cette question m'a vraiment désarçonné!, je ne savais vraiment pas quoi répondre à cette question!; I was completely ~n for a few seconds je suis resté tout interdit pendant quelques secondes. -**7.** [activate - switch, lever, clutch] actionner. -**8.** SPORT [race, match] perdre délibérément. -**9.** [silk] tordre; [subj: potter]: to ~ a pot tourner un vase. -**10.** VETER [subj: cat, pig]: to ~ a litter mettre bas. -**11.** *inf phr*: to ~ a fit/tantrum piquer une crise (de nerfs)/une colère; he nearly threw a fit when he heard the news il a failli exploser quand il a appris la nouvelle; to ~ a party organiser une petite fête; they threw a party in his honour ils ont donné une fête en son honneur.

⋄ *n* -**1.** [of ball, javelin] jet *m*, lancer *m*; [of dice] lancer *m*; his whole fortune depended on a single ~ of the dice toute sa fortune dépendait d'un seul coup de dés; a free ~ SPORT un lancer franc; that was a good ~! vous avez bien visé! -**2.** *inf* [go, turn] coup *m*, tour *m*; 10p a ~ 10 pence le coup; at £20 a ~ I can't afford it à 20 livres chaque fois, je ne peux pas me l'offrir; give me another ~ laissez-moi encore une chance; it's your ~ à toi. -**3.** [cover] couverture *f*.

◆ **throw about** *Br*, **throw around** *vt sep* -**1.** [toss] lancer; [scatter] jeter, éparpiller; the boys were ~ing a ball about les garçons jouaient à la balle; don't ~ your books/toys about like that ne lance pas tes livres/jouets comme ça; to be ~n about être ballotté. -**2.** [move violently]: to ~ o.s. about s'agiter, se débattre; she was ~ing her arms about wildly elle agitait frénétiquement les bras.

◆ **throw aside** *vt sep* [unwanted object] rejeter, laisser de côté; [friend, work] laisser tomber, laisser de côté; [idea, suggestion] rejeter, repousser.

◆ **throw away** ⋄ *vt sep* -**1.** [old clothes, rubbish] jeter. -**2.** *fig* [waste - advantage, opportunity, talents] gaspiller, gâcher; [- affection, friendship] perdre; don't ~ your money away on expensive toys ne gaspille pas ton argent à acheter des jouets coûteux; you're ~ing away your only chance of happiness vous êtes en train de gâcher votre seule chance de bonheur; his presents are just ~n away on her elle ne sait pas apprécier les cadeaux qu'il lui fait. -**3.** THEAT [line, remark] laisser tomber.

⋄ *vi insep* [in cards] se défausser.

◆ **throw back** *vt sep* -**1.** [gen] relancer, renvoyer; [fish] rejeter (à l'eau); *fig* [image, light] réfléchir, renvoyer; she threw his words of love back at him *fig* elle lui a jeté tous ses mots d'amour à la tête. -**2.** [hair, head] rejeter en arrière; [shoulders] redresser, jeter en arrière. -**3.** [curtains] ouvrir; [shutters] repousser, ouvrir tout grand; [bedclothes] repousser. -**4.** *phr* [force to rely on]: we were ~n back on our own resources on a dû se rabattre sur nos propres ressources.

◆ **throw down** *vt sep* -**1.** [to lower level] jeter; can you ~ the towel down to me? pouvez-vous me lancer la serviette?; she threw her bag down on the floor elle a jeté son sac par terre; to ~ o.s. down on the ground/on one's knees se jeter par terre/à genoux; he threw his cards down on the table il a jeté ses cartes sur la table; I threw the money down on the counter j'ai jeté l'argent sur le comptoir. -**2.** [weapons] jeter, déposer; they threw down their arms ils ont déposé les armes. -**3.** *fig* [challenge] lancer. -**4.** *Br phr*: it's ~ing it down [raining] il pleut à verse, il tombe des cordes.

◆ **throw in** ⋄ *vt sep* -**1.** [into box, cupboard etc] jeter; [through window] jeter, lancer; to ~ in the towel *fig* & SPORT jeter l'éponge; to ~ in one's hand abandonner la partie, s'avouer vaincu. -**2.** [interject - remark, suggestion] placer; she threw in a few comments about housing problems elle a placé quelques remarques sur les problèmes de logement ‖ [include]: breakfast is ~n in le petit déjeuner est compris; the salesman said he'd ~ in a free door if we bought new windows le vendeur nous a promis une porte gratuite pour l'achat de fenêtres neuves; with a special trip to Stockholm ~n in avec en prime une excursion à Stockholm. -**3.** SPORT [ball] remettre en jeu.

⋄ *vi insep Am*: to ~ in with sb s'associer à OR avec qqn.

◆ **throw off** *vt sep* -**1.** [discard - clothes] enlever OR ôter (à la hâte); [- mask, disguise] jeter; he threw off his shirt and dived into the water il enleva sa chemise et plongea dans l'eau. -**2.** [get rid of - habit, inhibition] se défaire de, se débarrasser de; [- burden] se libérer de, se débarrasser de; [- cold, infection] se débarrasser de. -**3.** [elude - pursuer] perdre, semer; he managed to ~ the dogs off the trail il a réussi à dépister les chiens.

◆ **throw on** *vt sep* [clothes] enfiler OR passer (à la hâte); she threw on some make-up/an old coat elle s'est maquillée/a enfilé un vieux manteau à la hâte.

◆ **throw out** *vt sep* -**1.** [rubbish, unwanted items] jeter, mettre au rebut. -**2.** [eject - from building] mettre à la porte, jeter dehors; [- from night club] jeter dehors, vider; [evict - from accommodation] expulser; [expel - from school, army] renvoyer, expulser; we were ~n out of our jobs on s'est fait mettre à la porte. -**3.** [reject - bill, proposal] rejeter, repousser. -**4.** [extend - arms, leg] tendre, étendre; to ~ out one's chest bomber le torse. -**5.** [make - remark, suggestion] émettre, laisser tomber; to ~ out a challenge lancer un défi. -**6.** [disturb - person] déconcerter, désorienter; [upset - calculation, results] fausser. -**7.** [emit - light] émettre, diffuser; [- smoke, heat] émettre, répandre.

◆ **throw over** *inf vt sep* [girlfriend, boyfriend] quitter, laisser tomber; [plan] abandonner, renoncer à; she threw me over for another guy elle m'a laissé tomber pour un autre.

◆ **throw together** *vt sep* -**1.** *inf* [make quickly - equipment, table] fabriquer à la hâte, bricoler; he managed to ~ a meal together il a réussi à improviser un repas; she threw the report together the night before elle a rédigé le rapport en vitesse la veille au soir. -**2.** [gather] rassembler à la hâte; she threw a few things together and rang for a taxi elle a jeté quelques affaires dans un sac et a appelé un taxi. -**3.** [by accident] réunir par hasard; Fate had ~n them together le destin les avait réunis.

◆ **throw up** ⋄ *vt sep* -**1.** [above one's head] jeter OR lancer en l'air; can you ~ me up my towel? peux-tu me lancer ma serviette?; they threw their hats up into the air ils ont lancé leur chapeau en l'air; she threw up her hands in horror elle a levé les bras en signe d'horreur. -**2.** [produce - problem] produire, créer; [- evidence] mettre à jour; [- dust, dirt] soulever; [- artist] produire. -**3.** [abandon - career, studies] abandonner, laisser tomber; [- chance, opportunity] laisser passer, gaspiller. -**4.** *pej* [construct - building] construire OR bâtir en moins de deux. -**5.** *inf* [vomit] vomir.

⋄ *vi insep inf* vomir, rendre; it makes you want to ~ up c'est à vomir.

throwaway ['θrəʊə,weɪ] ⋄ *adj* [line, remark] fait comme par hasard OR comme si de rien n'était.

⋄ *n* -**1.** [bottle] bouteille *f* sans consigne; [container] emballage *m* perdu OR jetable. -**2.** *Am* [handbill] prospectus *m*.

⋄ *comp* [bottle, carton etc] jetable, à jeter, à usage unique; we live in a ~ society nous vivons dans une société de gaspillage.

throwback ['θrəʊbæk] *n* -**1.** ANTHR & BIOL régression *f* atavique. -**2.** [of fashion, custom]: those new hats are a ~ to the 1930s ces nouveaux chapeaux marquent un retour aux années 30 OR sont inspirés des années 30.

thrower ['θrəʊəʳ] *n* lanceur *m*, -euse *f*.

throw-in *n* FTBL rentrée *f* en touche.

thrown [θrəʊn] *pp* → **throw**.

thru [θru:] *Am* = **through**.

thrum [θrʌm] ⋄ *vi* -**1.** [engine, machine] vibrer, vrombir; [rain] tambouriner. -**2.** [guitarist] gratter les cordes; to ~ on a guitar gratter de la guitare.

⋄ *vt* -**1.** [repeat] réciter OR répéter d'une manière monotone. -**2.** [guitar] gratter de, taquiner; to ~ a tune on the guitar racler un air sur la guitare.

thrush [θrʌʃ] *n* -**1.** [bird] grive *f*. -**2.** MED [oral] muguet *m*; [vaginal] mycose *f*, candidose *f*.

thrust [θrʌst] (*pt* & *pp* thrust) ⋄ *vt* -**1.** [push, shove] enfoncer, fourrer, plonger; he ~ his finger/elbow into my ribs il m'a enfoncé le doigt/le coude dans les côtes; I ~ the stick into the jar j'ai plongé le bâton dans le pot; he ~ his sword into its scabbard il a glissé son épée dans son fourreau; to ~ one's hands into one's pockets enfoncer OR fourrer les mains dans ses

poches; he ~ her into the cell il l'a poussée violemment dans la cellule; she ~ the money towards him elle a brusquement poussé l'argent vers lui; she ~ the money into his hands/into his bag elle lui a fourré l'argent dans les mains/dans le sac; I had a gun ~ at me on a brandi un pistolet dans ma direction; she ~ me to the front elle m'a poussé devant; to ~ one's way through the crowd/to the front se frayer un chemin à travers la foule/pour être devant. -**2.** [force - responsibility, fame] imposer; the job was ~ upon me on m'a imposé ce travail; fame was ~ upon her overnight la gloire lui est tombée dessus du jour au lendemain; he was ~ into the limelight il a été mis en vedette; to ~ o.s. on OR upon sb imposer sa présence à qqn, s'imposer à qqn.
◇ *vi* -**1.** [push]: he ~ past her [rudely] il l'a bousculée en passant devant elle; [quickly] il est passé devant elle comme une flèche; towers ~ing upwards into the sky *fig* des tours qui s'élancent vers le ciel. -**2.** FENCING allonger OR porter une botte; he ~ at him with a knife il a essayé de lui donner un coup de couteau.
◇ *n* -**1.** [lunge] poussée *f*; [stab] coup *m*; with a single ~ of his sword d'un seul coup d'épée. -**2.** *fig* [remark] pointe *f*; a few well-aimed ~s at the opposition parties quelques pointes bien senties contre les partis de l'opposition. -**3.** *(U)* [force - of engine] poussée *f*; *fig* [drive] dynamisme *m*, élan *m*. -**4.** [of argument, story] sens *m*, idée *f*; [of policy] idée *f* directrice; [of research] aspect *m* principal; the main ~ of her argument l'idée maîtresse de son argument. -**5.** *(U)* ARCHIT & GEOL poussée *f*.
◆ **thrust aside** *vt sep* [person, thing] écarter brusquement; [suggestion] écarter OR rejeter brusquement.
◆ **thrust away** *vt sep* repousser.
◆ **thrust forward** *vt sep* pousser en avant brusquement; to ~ o.s. forward *literal* se frayer un chemin; *fig* se mettre en avant.
◆ **thrust in** ◇ *vi insep* [physically] s'introduire de force.
◇ *vt sep* [finger, pointed object] enfoncer; she ~ her hand in elle a brusquement mis la main dedans; to ~ one's way in se frayer un passage pour entrer.
◆ **thrust out** *vt sep* -**1.** [arm, leg] allonger brusquement; [hand] tendre brusquement; [chin] projeter en avant; she ~ her head out of the window elle a brusquement passé la tête par la fenêtre; to ~ out one's chest bomber la poitrine; to ~ one's way out se frayer un chemin pour sortir. -**2.** [eject] pousser dehors.
◆ **thrust up** *vi insep* s'élancer, jaillir.

thruster ['θrʌstəʳ] *n* ASTRONAUT [rocket] micropropulseur *m*.

thrusting ['θrʌstɪŋ] *adj* [dynamic] dynamique, entreprenant, plein d'entrain; *pej* qui se fait valoir, qui se met en avant; one of these ~ young salesmen un de ces jeunes vendeurs qui cherchent à se mettre en avant.

thruway ['θruːweɪ] *n Am* ≃ autoroute *f* (à cinq ou six voies).

thud [θʌd] (*pt* & *pp* thudded, *cont* thudding) ◇ *vi* -**1.** faire un bruit sourd; [falling object] tomber en faisant un bruit sourd; we could hear the cannon thudding in the distance on entendait gronder les canons au loin. -**2.** [walk or run heavily]: to ~ across/in/past traverser/entrer/passer à pas pesants; we could hear people thudding about in the flat above on entendait les gens du dessus marcher à pas lourds; footsteps thudded up the stairs quelqu'un montait l'escalier d'un pas lourd. -**3.** [heart] battre fort.
◇ *n* bruit *m* sourd; the book fell to the floor with a ~ le livre est tombé par terre avec un bruit sourd.

thug [θʌg] *n* voyou *m*; a gang of ~s une bande de voyous.

thuggery ['θʌgərɪ] *n* brutalité *f*, violence *f*.

thulium ['θuːlɪəm] *n* thulium *m*.

thumb [θʌm] ◇ *n* pouce *m*; to be under sb's ~ être sous la coupe de qqn; his mother's really got him under her ~ sa mère a vraiment de l'emprise sur lui OR en fait vraiment ce qu'elle veut; to be all (fingers and) ~s être maladroit ❑ to stick out like a sore ~ [be obvious] crever les yeux; [be obtrusive]: that factory sticks out like a sore ~ cette usine gâche le paysage.
◇ *vt* -**1.** [book, magazine] feuilleter, tourner les pages de; [pages] tourner; the catalogue has been well ~ed les pages du catalogue sont bien écornées. -**2.** [hitch]: to ~ a lift *Br* OR ride *Am* faire du stop OR de l'auto-stop; they ~ed a lift to Exeter ils sont allés à Exeter en stop; I had to ~ a lift home j'ai dû rentrer (chez moi) en stop; she ~ed a lift from a passing motorist elle a réussi à se faire prendre en stop par une voiture qui passait. -**3.** *phr*: to ~ one's nose at sb faire un pied de nez à qqn.
◇ *vi inf Am* faire du stop OR de l'auto-stop.
◆ **thumb through** *vt insep* [book, magazine] feuilleter; [files] consulter rapidement; [pages] tourner.

thumb index *n* répertoire *m* à onglets.

thumbnail ['θʌmneɪl] *n* ongle *m* du pouce; ~ sketch [of plan] aperçu *m*, croquis *m* rapide; [of personality] bref portrait *m*.

thumbprint ['θʌmprɪnt] *n* empreinte *f* du pouce.

thumbscrew ['θʌmskruː] *n* -**1.** TECH vis *f* à papillon OR à ailettes. -**2.** [instrument of torture] poucettes *fpl*.

thumbs-down *n*: he gave her the ~ as he came out en sortant, il lui a fait signe que cela avait mal marché; my proposal was given the ~ ma proposition a été rejetée.

thumbstall ['θʌmstɔːl] *n* poucier *m*.

thumbs-up *n*: to give sb the ~ [all OK] faire signe à qqn que tout va bien; [in encouragement] faire signe à qqn pour l'encourager; he gave her the ~ as he came out en sortant, il lui a fait signe que cela avait bien marché; they've given me the ~ for my thesis ils m'ont donné le feu vert pour ma thèse.

thumbtack ['θʌmtæk] *n Am* punaise *f*.

thump [θʌmp] ◇ *vt* donner un coup de poing à, frapper d'un coup de poing; he ~ed me in the stomach/on the head il m'a donné un coup de poing à l'estomac/à la tête; to ~ sb on the back donner une grande tape dans le dos à qqn; he ~ed his fist on the table il a frappé du poing sur la table.
◇ *vi* -**1.** [bang] cogner; he ~ed on the door/wall il a cogné à la porte/contre le mur; she was ~ing away on the piano elle tapait sur le piano comme une sourde; my heart was ~ing with fear/excitement la peur/l'émotion me faisait battre le cœur. -**2.** [run or walk heavily]: to ~ in/out/past entrer/sortir/passer à pas lourds; heavy boots ~ed up the stairs on entendait de lourds bruits de bottes dans l'escalier.
◇ *n* -**1.** [blow - gen] coup *m*; [- with fist] coup *m* de poing; [- with stick] coup *m* de bâton; to give sb a ~ assener un coup de poing à qqn; he got a ~ in the stomach il a reçu un coup de poing à l'estomac; he gave me a friendly ~ on the back il m'a donné une tape amicale dans le dos. -**2.** [sound] bruit *m* sourd; the log fell to the ground with a ~ la bûche est tombée par terre lourdement OR avec un bruit sourd.
◇ *adv*: to go ~ *inf* faire boum.
◆ **thump out** *vt sep*: to ~ out a tune on the piano marteler un air au piano.

thumping *inf* ['θʌmpɪŋ] *Br* ◇ *adj* [success] énorme, immense, phénoménal; [difference] énorme.
◇ *adv dated* [as intensifier]: a ~ great meal un repas énorme; that was a ~ good show! ce spectacle était formidable!

thunder ['θʌndəʳ] ◇ *n* -**1.** METEOR tonnerre *m*; there was a lot of ~ last night il a beaucoup tonné la nuit dernière; there's ~ in the air le temps est à l'orage ❑ to be as black as ~ [angry] être dans une colère noire. -**2.** [of applause, guns] tonnerre *m*; [of engine, traffic] bruit *m* de tonnerre; [of hooves] fracas *m*; we could hear the ~ of the waves crashing on the rocks below on entendait le fracas des vagues qui s'écrasaient sur les rochers en contre-bas; his voice was like ~ il avait une voix de tonnerre. -**3.** *Br dated*: by ~! tonnerre!
◇ *vi* -**1.** METEOR tonner; it's ~ing il tonne, ça tonne. -**2.** [guns, waves] tonner, gronder; [hooves] retentir; a train ~ed past le train est passé dans un grondement de tonnerre. -**3.** [shout]: to ~ at sb/against sthg tonner contre qqn/contre qqch.
◇ *vt* [order, threat, applause] lancer d'une voix tonitruante OR tonnante; "damn them!", he ~ed «qu'ils aillent au diable!», tonna-t-il; the audience ~ed their delight le public manifesta son plaisir par un tonnerre d'applaudissements.
◆ **thunder out** *vt sep* [order] lancer d'une voix tonitruante.

thunderbolt ['θʌndəbəʊlt] *n* METEOR éclair *m*; *fig* coup *m* de tonnerre.

thunderbox *inf* ['θʌndəbɒks] *n hum* petit coin *m*, cabinets *mpl*.

thunderclap ['θʌndəklæp] *n* coup *m* de tonnerre.

thundercloud ['θʌndəklaʊd] *n* METEOR nuage *m* orageux; *fig* nuage *m* noir.

Thunderer ['θʌndərəʳ] *n* MYTH: the ~ Jupiter.

thunderhead ['θʌndəhed] *n esp Am* cumulonimbus *m*.

thundering *inf* ['θʌndərɪŋ] *Br dated* ◇ *adj* -**1.** [terrible]: to be in a ~ temper OR rage être dans une colère noire OR hors de soi; it's a ~ nuisance! quelle barbe! -**2.** [superb - success] foudroyant, phénoménal.
◇ *adv*: it's a ~ good read c'est un livre formidable.

thunderous ['θʌndərəs] *adj* [shouts, noise] retentissant; there was ~ applause il y eut un tonnerre d'applaudissements.

thunder sheet *n* THEAT *plaque de métal servant à imiter le bruit du tonnerre.*

thunderstorm ['θʌndəstɔːm] *n* orage *m*.

thunderstruck ['θʌndəstrʌk] *adj* foudroyé, abasourdi; she was ~ by the news la nouvelle la foudroya.

thundery ['θʌndərɪ] *adj* METEOR orageux; ~ weather is forecast la météo prévoit de l'orage.

Thur, Thurs (*written abbr of* Thursday) jeu.

thurible ['θjʊərɪbl] *n* encensoir *m*.

thurifer ['θjʊərɪfəʳ] *n* thuriféraire *m*.

Thuringia [θjʊ'rɪndʒɪə] *pr n* Thuringe *f*; in ~ en Thuringe.

Thursday ['θɜːzdɪ] *n* jeudi *m*; Black Thursday jeudi noir *(jour du krach de Wall Street qui déclencha la crise de 1929)*.

thus [ðʌs] *adv* [so] ainsi, donc; [as a result] ainsi, par conséquent; [in this way] ainsi; ~ far [in present] jusqu'ici; [in past] jusque-là ❑ 'Thus Spake Zarathustra' *Nietzsche* 'Ainsi parlait Zarathoustra'.

thwack [θwæk] ◇ *n* -**1.** [blow] grand coup *m*; [slap] claque *f*; he gave the hedge a ~ with his stick il donna un grand coup de canne dans la haie. -**2.** [sound] claquement *m*, coup *m* sec.
◇ *vt* donner un coup sec à; [slap - person] gifler; the player ~ed the ball into the crowd le joueur envoya la balle dans le public d'un vigoureux coup de pied.

thwart [θwɔːt] *vt* [plan] contrecarrer, contrarier; [person - in efforts] contrarier les efforts de; [- in plans] contrarier les projets de; [- in attempts] contrecarrer les tentatives de; I was ~ed in my attempts to leave the country mes tentatives de quitter le pays ont été contrecarrées.

thy [ðaɪ] *poss adj* BIBLE, *dial* OR *lit* ton, ta, tes.

thyme [taɪm] *n (U)* thym *m*.

thymine ['θaɪmiːn] *n* thymine *f*.

thymol ['θaɪmɒl] *n* thymol *m*.

thymus ['θaɪməs] *n* thymus *m*.

thyristor [θaɪ'rɪstəʳ] *n* thyristor *m*.

thyroid ['θaɪrɔɪd] ◇ *n* thyroïde *f*.
◇ *adj* thyroïde.

thyroxin(e) [θaɪ'rɒksɪn] *n* thyroxine *f*.

thyself [ðaɪ'self] *pers pron* BIBLE, *dial* OR *lit (reflexive)* te; *(intensifier)* toi-même.

ti [tiː] = **te**.

Tiananmen Square ['tjænənmen-] *pr n* la place Tian'anmen.

tiara [tɪ'ɑːrə] *n* [gen] diadème *m*; RELIG tiare *f*.

Tiber ['taɪbəʳ] *pr n*: the (River) ~ le Tibre.

Tiberias [taɪ'bɪərɪæs] *pr n*: Lake ~ le lac de Tibériade.

Tiberius [taɪ'bɪərɪəs] *pr n* Tibère.

Tibesti [tɪ'bestɪ] *pr n*: the ~ (Massif) le Tibesti.

Tibet [tɪ'bet] *pr n* Tibet *m*; in ~ au Tibet.

Tibetan [tɪ'betn] ◇ *n* -**1.** [person] Tibétain *m*, -e *f*. -**2.** LING tibétain *m*.
◇ *adj* tibétain.

tibia ['tɪbɪə] (*pl* **tibias** OR **tibiae** [-bɪiː]) *n* tibia *m*.

tic [tɪk] *n*: (nervous) ~ tic *m* (nerveux).

tich *inf* [tɪtʃ] *n Br* microbe *m*; he's a real ~ [person] il est haut comme trois pommes.

tichy *inf* ['tɪtʃɪ] *adj Br* minuscule, tout petit.

Ticino [tɪ'tʃiːnəʊ] *pr n* Tessin *m*.

tick [tɪk] ◇ *vi* [clock, time-bomb] faire tic-tac; [motivation]: I wonder what makes him ~ je me demande ce qui le motive.
◇ *vt Br* [mark - name, item] cocher, pointer; [- box, answer] cocher; SCH [- as correct] marquer juste.
◇ *n* -**1.** [of clock] tic-tac *m*. -**2.** *inf Br* [moment] instant *m*; just a ~! un instant!; I'll be ready in a ~/in a couple of ~s je serai prêt dans une seconde/en moins de deux; I'll only be a ~ j'en ai pour une seconde. -**3.** *Br* [mark] coche *f*; to put a ~ against sthg cocher qqch. -**4.** ZOOL tique *f*. -**5.** *inf Br* [credit] crédit *m*; to buy sthg on ~ acheter qqch à crédit. -**6.** TEX [ticking] toile *f* à matelas; [covering - for mattress] housse *f* (de matelas); [- for pillow] housse *f* (d'oreiller), taie *f*.
◆ **tick away** *vi insep* -**1.** [clock] faire tic-tac; [taximeter] tourner. -**2.** [time] passer; the minutes ~ed away les minutes passaient.
◆ **tick off** *vt sep* -**1.** [name, item] cocher, pointer. -**2.** *fig* [count - reasons, chapters] compter, énumérer; he ~ed off the EC countries on his fingers il compta les pays de la CEE sur ses doigts. -**3.** *inf Br* [scold] attraper, passer un savon à; she got ~ed off for being late elle s'est fait attraper pour être arrivée en retard. -**4.** *inf Am* [annoy] agacer, taper sur le système à.
◆ **tick over** *vi insep* -**1.** *Br* [car engine] tourner au ralenti; [taximeter] tourner. -**2.** *fig* [business, production] tourner normalement; everything's ~ing over nicely tout tourne bien.

ticked *inf* [tɪkt] *adj Am* en rogne.

ticker ['tɪkəʳ] *n* -**1.** *Am* [printer] téléscripteur *m*, téléimprimeur *m*. -**2.** *inf* [heart] palpitant *m*, cœur *m*. -**3.** *inf* [watch] tocante *f*, toquante *f*.

tickertape ['tɪkəteɪp] *n* -**1.** [tape] bande *f* de téléscripteur OR de téléimprimeur. -**2.** *Am fig*: to get a ~ reception OR welcome recevoir un accueil triomphal.

tickertape parade *n aux États-Unis, défilé où l'on accueille un héros national sous une pluie de serpentins.*

ticket ['tɪkɪt] ◇ *n* -**1.** [for travel - on coach, plane, train] billet *m*; [- on bus, underground] billet *m*, ticket *m*; [for entry - to cinema, theatre, match] billet *m*; [- to car park] ticket *m* (de parking); [for membership - of library] carte *f*; to buy a ~ prendre OR acheter un billet ❑ this play's the hottest ~ in town c'est le spectacle dont tout le monde parle en ce moment. -**2.** [receipt - in shop] ticket *m* (de caisse), reçu *m*; [- for left-luggage, cloakroom] ticket *m* (de consigne); [- from pawnshop] reconnaissance *f*. -**3.** [label] étiquette *f*. -**4.** AUT [fine] P-V *m*, contravention *f*, amende *f*; to give sb a ~ mettre un P-V OR une contravention à qqn; to get a ~ avoir un P-V. -**5.** *Am* POL [set of principles]: he fought the election on a Democratic ~ il a basé son programme électoral sur les principes du Parti démocrate ‖ [list of candidates]: to vote a straight ~ voter pour une liste sans panachage. -**6.** *inf* AERON & NAUT [certificate] brevet *m*. -**7.** *Br mil sl*: to get one's ~ être libéré des obligations militaires. -**8.** *phr*: that's (just) the ~! *inf* voilà exactement ce qu'il faut!
◇ *vt* -**1.** [label] étiqueter. -**2.** [earmark] désigner, destiner. -**3.** *Am* [issue with a ticket] donner un billet à; I'm ~ed on the 7.30 flight j'ai un billet pour le vol de 7 h 30. -**4.** *Am* [issue with a parking ticket] mettre un P-V à.

ticket agency *n* -**1.** THEAT agence *f* de spectacles. -**2.** RAIL agence *f* de voyages.

ticket collector *n* RAIL contrôleur *m*, -euse *f*.

ticket day *n Br* ST. EX jour *m* de déclaration des noms.

ticket holder *n* personne *f* munie d'un billet.

ticket inspector = **ticket collector**.

ticket machine *n* distributeur *m* de tickets, billetterie *f* automatique.

ticket office *n* bureau *m* de vente des billets, guichet *m*.

ticket tout *n Br* revendeur *m*, -euse *f* de billets *(sur le marché noir)*.

ticking ['tɪkɪŋ] *n* -**1.** [of clock] tic-tac *m*. -**2.** TEX toile *f* (à matelas).

ticking off *inf* (*pl* **tickings off**) *n Br*: to give sb a ~ enguirlander qqn, tirer les oreilles à qqn; she got a ~ for being late elle s'est fait enguirlander parce qu'elle était en retard; he needs a good ~ il a besoin de se faire enguirlander OR tirer les oreilles.

tickle ['tɪkl] ◇ *vt* -**1.** *literal* [by touching] chatouiller; don't ~ my feet! ne me chatouille pas les pieds!; to ~ sb in the ribs/under the chin chatouiller les côtes/le menton à qqn; the blanket ~d her nose la couverture lui chatouillait le nez. -**2.** *fig* [curiosity, vanity] chatouiller; something about the idea really ~d my fancy cette idée avait quelque chose qui me séduisait vraiment. -**3.** *fig* [amuse] amuser, faire rire; [please] faire plaisir à; she was really ~d by the news [amused] la nouvelle l'a vraiment amusée; [pleased] la nouvelle lui a vraiment fait plaisir ❑ to be ~d pink OR to death être ravi OR aux anges; he was ~d pink at becoming a grandfather il était ravi de devenir grand-père; she was ~d to death to think he actually liked her elle était enchantée de penser qu'en fait il l'aimait bien. -**4.** *phr*: to ~ the ivories *inf hum* jouer du piano, pianoter.
◇ *vi* [person, blanket] chatouiller; [beard] piquer; don't ~! ne me chatouille pas!
◇ *n* [on body] chatouillement *m*; to give sb a ~ chatouiller qqn, faire des chatouilles à qqn ‖ [in throat] picotement *m*; I've got an awful ~ in my throat j'ai la gorge qui picote atrocement.

tickler ['tɪkləʳ] *n* -**1.** *inf* [question] colle *f*; [problem] casse-tête *m inv*; [situation] situation *f* délicate OR épineuse. -**2.** *Am* [memorandum book] pense-bête *m*.

tickling ['tɪklɪŋ] ◇ *n (U)* [of person] chatouilles *fpl*; [of blanket] picotement *m*.
◇ *adj* [throat] qui gratouille OR picote; [cough] d'irritation, qui gratte la gorge; you get a ~ sensation in your feet on a une sensation de picotement dans les pieds.

ticklish ['tɪklɪʃ] *adj* -**1.** [person, feet] chatouilleux; [sensation] de chatouillement. -**2.** *inf* [touchy] chatouilleux; she's very ~ about certain subjects il y a des sujets qu'il ne faut pas aborder avec elle. -**3.** *inf* [delicate - situation, topic] délicat, épineux; [- moment] crucial; [- negotiations] délicat.

tickly *inf* ['tɪklɪ] *adj* [sensation] de chatouillis; [blanket] qui chatouille; [beard] qui pique.

ticktack ['tɪk,tæk] = **tic tac**.

tick-tack man = **tic tac man**.

tick-tack-toe *Am* = **tic-tac-toe**.

ticktock ['tɪktɒk] *n* [of clock] tic-tac *m*.

ticky-tacky *inf* ['tɪkɪ,tækɪ] ◇ *adj* de pacotille.
◇ *n* pacotille *f*.

tic tac ['tɪk,tæk] *n* -**1.** *Br* gestuelle *f* des bookmakers *(pour indiquer la cote)*. -**2.** *Am* tic-tac *m*.

tic tac man *n sur un terrain de courses, bookmaker qui donne des renseignements à des collègues en faisant des signaux avec les mains et les bras.*

tic-tac-toe *n Am* morpion *m (jeu)*.

tidal ['taɪdl] *adj* [estuary, river] qui a des marées; [current, cycle, force] de la marée; [ferry] dont les horaires sont fonction de la marée; [energy] marémoteur.

tidal wave *n* raz-de-marée *m inv*; *fig* [of sympathy] élan *m*.

tidbit ['tɪdbɪt] *Am* = **titbit**.

tiddledywinks ['tɪdldɪwɪŋks] *n Am* = **tiddlywinks**.

tiddler *inf* ['tɪdləʳ] *n* -**1.** [fish] petit poisson *m*; [minnow] fretin *m*; [stickleback] épinoche *f*. -**2.** *Br* [child] mioche *m*.

tiddly *inf* ['tɪdlɪ] (*compar* **tiddlier**, *superl* **tiddliest**) *adj Br* -**1.** [tiny] tout petit, minuscule. -**2.** [tipsy] éméché, paf.

tiddlywink ['tɪdlɪwɪŋk] *n* pion *m* (du jeu de puce).
◆ **tiddlywinks** *n (U)* jeu *m* de puce.

tide [taɪd] *n* -**1.** [of sea] marée *f*; at high/low ~ à marée haute/basse; high ~ is at 17.29 la mer est haute à 17 h 29, la marée haute est à 17 h 29; the ~ is on the turn la mer est étale; the raft was swept out to sea on the ~ la marée a emporté le radeau au large; they left on the first ~ ils sont partis avec la première marée. -**2.** [of opinion] courant *m*; [of discontent, indignation] vague *f*; [of events] cours *m*, marche *f*; the ~ has turned la chance a tourné; there is a rising ~ of unrest amongst the workforce il y a une agitation grandissante parmi le personnel.
◆ **tide over** *vt sep* dépanner; to ~ sb over a difficult patch dépanner qqn qui se trouve en difficulté; here's £20 to ~ you over until Monday voici 20 livres pour vous dépanner jusqu'à lundi.

tide gauge *n* marégraphe *m*.

tideland ['taɪdlænd] *n Am* laisse *f* (de la marée).

tideline ['taɪdlaɪn] = **tidemark 1**.

tidemark ['taɪdmɑːk] *n* -**1.** [on shore] laisse *f* de haute mer. -**2.** *fig* & *hum* [round bath, neck] marque *f* de crasse.

tide race *n* courant *m* de marée rapide.

tide table *n* échelle *f* OR table *f* des marées, almanach *m* (des marées).

tidewater ['taɪd,wɔːtəʳ] *n (U)* -**1.** *Br* [water] (eaux *fpl* de) marée *f*. -**2.** *Am* [land] côte *f* (baignée par des eaux de marée).

tideway ['taɪdweɪ] *n* [channel] lit *m* de la marée; [part of river] estuaire *m*, aber *m*.

tidily ['taɪdɪlɪ] *adv* [pack, fold] soigneusement, avec soin; ~ dressed [adult] bien habillé OR mis; [child] habillé proprement; her hair was tied back ~ ses cheveux étaient soigneusement attachés; put your books/clothes away ~ range bien tes livres/habits.

tidiness ['taɪdɪnɪs] *n* -**1.** [of drawer, desk, room] ordre *m*; lack of ~ désordre *m*. -**2.** [of appearance] netteté *f*. -**3.** [of work, exercise book] propreté *f*, netteté *f*; [of writing] netteté *f*.

tidings ['taɪdɪŋz] *npl arch* OR *lit* nouvelles *fpl*; we bring you ~ of great joy nous vous apportons de joyeuses nouvelles.

tidy ['taɪdɪ] (*compar* **tidier**, *superl* **tidiest**, *pl* **tidies**, *pt* & *pp* **tidied**) ◇ *adj* -**1.** [room, house, desk] rangé, ordonné, en ordre; [garden, town] propre; neat and ~ propre et net; he keeps his flat very ~ il tient son appartement bien rangé; can't you make the room a bit tidier? tu ne peux pas mettre un peu (plus) d'ordre dans cette pièce? -**2.** [in appearance - person] soigné; [- clothes, hair] soigné, net. -**3.** [work, writing] soigné, net. -**4.** [in character - person] ordonné, méthodique; she has a very ~ mind elle a l'esprit très méthodique. -**5.** *inf* [sum, profit] joli, coquet; a ~ bit of my income goes in tax une bonne partie de mes revenus part en impôts.
◇ *n* -**1.** [receptacle] vide-poches *m inv*. -**2.** *Am* [on chair] têtière *f*.
◇ *vt* [room] ranger, mettre de l'ordre dans;

[desk, clothes, objects] ranger; to ~ one's hair se recoiffer; ~ those books into a cupboard range ces livres dans un placard.

◆ **tidy away** *vt sep* ranger, ramasser.

◆ **tidy out** *vt sep* [drawer, wardrobe, garden shed] ranger de fond en comble, mettre de l'ordre dans; [newspapers] ranger, trier; go and ~ out your room va mettre de l'ordre dans OR ranger ta chambre.

◆ **tidy up** ◇ *vi insep* -**1.** [in room] tout ranger; after the last guests had gone she was left to ~ up elle a dû tout remettre en ordre OR tout ranger après le départ des derniers invités. -**2.** [in appearance] s'arranger; you'd better ~ up before they arrive tu ferais mieux de t'arranger un peu avant qu'ils arrivent.

◇ *vt sep* [room, clothes] ranger, mettre de l'ordre dans; [desk] ranger; to ~ o.s. up s'arranger; ~ your things up [make tidy] range tes affaires; [put away] range OR ramasse tes affaires.

tidy-out *inf n*: to have a ~ [make tidy] faire du (grand) rangement; [clear out] faire du rangement par le vide; we gave the room a good ~ on a rangé la pièce de fond en comble.

tidy-up *inf n*: to have a ~ faire du rangement; we'll have to give the place a ~ before the guests arrive il va falloir mettre de l'ordre OR faire du rangement dans la maison avant l'arrivée des invités.

tie [taɪ] ◇ *n* -**1.** [necktie] cravate *f*. -**2.** [fastener - gen] attache *f*; [- on apron] cordon *m*; [- for curtain] embrasse *f*; [- on shoes] lacet *m*. -**3.** [bond, link] lien *m*, attache *f*; emotional ~s liens affectifs; family ~s liens de parenté OR familiaux; there are strong ~s between the two countries les deux pays entretiennent d'étroites relations. -**4.** [restriction] entrave *f*; pets/young children can be a ~ les animaux/les jeunes enfants peuvent être une entrave. -**5.** SPORT [draw] égalité *f*; [drawn match] match *m* nul; the match ended in a ~ les deux équipes ont fait match nul ‖ [in competition] *compétition dont les gagnants sont ex aequo*; it was a ~ for first/second place il y avait deux premiers/seconds ex aequo ‖ POL égalité *f* de voix; the election resulted in a ~ les candidats ont obtenu le même nombre de voix OR étaient à égalité des voix. -**6.** FTBL [match] match *m*; a championship ~ un match de championnat; a European cup ~ un match de la coupe européenne. -**7.** MUS liaison *f*. -**8.** *Am* RAIL traverse *f*. -**9.** CONSTR tirant *m*.

◇ *vt* -**1.** [with string, rope - parcel] attacher, ficeler; is it ~d properly? est-ce que c'est bien attaché?; they ~d him to a tree il l'ont attaché OR ligoté à un arbre; his hands and feet were ~d ses mains et ses pieds étaient ligotés; they ~d my hands behind my back ils m'ont lié OR attaché les mains dans le dos; my hands are ~d *fig* j'ai les mains liées. -**2.** [necktie, scarf, shoelaces] attacher, nouer; to ~ one's shoelaces attacher OR nouer ses lacets (de chaussures); to ~ a scarf round one's neck nouer une écharpe autour de son cou; why not ~ some string to the handle? pourquoi ne pas attacher une ficelle à la poignée?; she ~d the ribbon in a bow elle a fait un nœud au ruban; she ~d a bow/a ribbon in her hair elle s'est mis un nœud/un ruban dans les cheveux; to ~ a knot in sthg, to ~ sthg in a knot faire un nœud à qqch ❑ he's still ~d to his mother's apron strings il n'a pas encore quitté les jupes de sa mère; to get ~d (up) in knots *inf*, to ~ o.s. (up) in knots *inf* s'emmêler les pinceaux; ~ a knot in it! *inf Br* ferme-la! -**3.** [confine - subj: responsibility, job etc]: she's ~d to the house [unable to get out] elle est clouée à la maison; [kept busy] la maison l'accapare beaucoup; the job keeps me very much ~d to my desk mon travail m'oblige à passer beaucoup de temps devant mon bureau; they're ~d to OR by the conditions of the contract ils sont liés par les conditions du contrat. -**4.** MUS lier.

◇ *vi* -**1.** [apron, shoelace etc] s'attacher, se nouer; the dress ~s at the back la robe s'attache par derrière. -**2.** [draw - players] être à égalité; [- in match] faire match nul; [- in exam, competition] être ex aequo; [- in election] obtenir le même score OR nombre de voix; they ~d for third place in the competition ils étaient troisième ex aequo au concours.

◆ **tie back** *vt sep* [hair] attacher (en arrière); [curtains, plant] attacher; her hair was ~d back in a bun ses cheveux étaient ramassés en chignon.

◆ **tie down** *vt sep* -**1.** [with string, rope - person, object] attacher; they had to ~ him down ils ont dû l'attacher. -**2.** *fig* [restrict] accaparer; she doesn't want to feel ~d down elle ne veut pas perdre sa liberté; children can really ~ you down il arrive que les enfants vous accaparent totalement; I'd rather not be ~d down to a specific time je préférerais qu'on ne fixe pas une heure précise; we must ~ them down to the terms of the contract il faut les obliger à respecter les termes du contrat.

◆ **tie in** ◇ *vi insep* -**1.** [be connected] être lié OR en rapport; everything seems to ~ in tout semble se tenir; this ~s in with what I said before cela rejoint ce que j'ai dit avant. -**2.** [correspond] correspondre, concorder; the evidence doesn't ~ in with the facts les indices dont nous disposons ne correspondent pas aux faits OR ne cadrent pas avec les faits.

◇ *vt sep*: how is this ~d in with your previous experiments? quel est le lien OR le rapport avec vos expériences antérieures?; she's trying to ~ her work experience in with her research elle essaie de faire coïncider son expérience professionnelle et ses recherches.

◆ **tie on** *vt sep* attacher, nouer; she had a basket ~d on to the handlebars elle avait un panier attaché à son guidon.

◆ **tie together** ◇ *vi insep*: it all ~s together tout se tient; his story doesn't ~ together very well son histoire ne tient pas vraiment debout.

◇ *vt sep* [papers, sticks] attacher (ensemble); to ~ sb's hands/feet together attacher les mains/les pieds de qqn; the letters had been ~d together in bundles les lettres avaient été mises en liasses.

◆ **tie up** ◇ *vt sep* -**1.** [parcel, papers] ficeler; [plant, animal] attacher; [prisoner] attacher, ligoter; [boat] attacher, arrimer; [shoelace] nouer, attacher; the letters were ~d up in bundles les lettres étaient ficelées en liasses; the dog was ~d up to a post le chien était attaché à un poteau. -**2.** *(usu pass)* [money, supplies] immobiliser; their money is all ~d up in shares leur argent est entièrement investi dans des actions; her inheritance is ~d up until her 21st birthday elle ne peut toucher à son héritage avant son 21e anniversaire. -**3.** [connect - company, organization] lier par des accords. -**4.** [complete, finalize - deal] conclure; [- terms of contract] fixer; I'd like to get everything ~d up before the holidays je voudrais arriver à tout régler avant les vacances; there are still a few loose ends to ~ up il y a encore quelques points de détail à régler. -**5.** [impede - traffic] bloquer; [- progress, production] freiner, entraver.

◇ *vi insep* -**1.** [be connected] être lié; how does this ~ up with the Chicago gang killings? quel est le rapport avec les assassinats du gang de Chicago?; it's all beginning to ~ up tout commence à s'expliquer. -**2.** NAUT accoster.

tieback ['taɪbæk] *n* [cord] embrasse *f* (de rideaux); [curtain] rideau *m (retenu par une embrasse)*.

tie beam *n* CONSTR longrine *f*.

tiebreak ['taɪbreɪk] = **tiebreaker**.

tiebreaker ['taɪbreɪkə^r] *n* TENNIS tie-break *m*; [in game, contest] épreuve *f* subsidiaire; [in quiz] question *f* subsidiaire.

tie clasp, tie clip *n* fixe-cravate *m*.

tied [taɪd] *adj* -**1.** SPORT: to be ~ [players] être à égalité; [game] être nul. -**2.** [person - by obligation, duties] pris, occupé; he doesn't want to feel ~ il ne veut pas s'engager; she feels very ~ by the new baby elle est très prise par le nouveau bébé; she isn't ~ by any family obligations elle n'a OR elle n'est tenue par aucune obligation familiale. -**3.** MUS [note] lié.

tied cottage *n Br logement attaché à une ferme et occupé par un employé agricole*.

tied house *n* [pub] *pub lié par contrat à une brasserie qui l'approvisionne*; [house] logement *m* de fonction.

tied up *adj* [busy]: to be ~ être occupé OR pris; she's ~ with the children every Wednesday elle est prise par les enfants tous les mercredis; he's ~ in a meeting until 5 il est en réunion jusqu'à 17 h; I'll be ~ all weekend writing these wretched reports je vais devoir passer tout le week-end à rédiger ces maudits rapports.

tie-dye *vt* teindre en nouant *(pour obtenir une teinture non uniforme)*.

tie-dyeing *n procédé de teinture qui consiste à nouer le tissu pour qu'il prenne la couleur de manière irrégulière*.

tie-in *n* -**1.** [connection] lien *m*, rapport *m*. -**2.** *Am* COMM [sale] vente *f* par lots; [items] lot *m*. -**3.** [in publishing] *livre, cassette etc lié à un film ou une émission*; there may be a film ~ on pourrait en tirer un film.

tie line *n* TELEC ligne *f* interautomatique.

tie-on *adj* [label] à œillet.

tiepin ['taɪpɪn] *n* épingle *f* de cravate.

tier [tɪə^r] ◇ *n* -**1.** [row of seats - in theatre, stadium] gradin *m*, rangée *f*; [level] étage *m*; to arrange seats in ~s disposer des sièges en gradins. -**2.** ADMIN échelon *m*, niveau *m*; a five-~ system un système à cinq niveaux. -**3.** [of cake] étage *m*; a three-~ wedding cake un gâteau de mariage à trois étages.

◇ *vt* [seating] disposer en gradins.

tie-rod *n* AUT tirant *m*.

Tierra del Fuego [tɪˌerədel'fweɪgəʊ] *pr n* Terre de Feu *f*; in ~ en Terre de Feu.

tie-tack *n Am* fixe-cravate *m*.

tie-up *n* -**1.** [connection] lien *m*, rapport *m*. -**2.** FIN [merger] fusion *f*. -**3.** *Am* [stoppage] arrêt *m*, interruption *f*. -**4.** *Am* [traffic jam] embouteillage *m*, bouchon *m*.

tiff *inf* [tɪf] *n Br* prise *f* de bec; they've had a bit of a ~ ils se sont un peu disputés; a lover's ~ une dispute d'amoureux.

tiffin ['tɪfɪn] *n Br dated* repas *m* de midi.

tig [tɪg] *n* (jeu *m* du) chat *m*; to play ~ jouer à chat.

tiger ['taɪgə^r] *n* tigre *m*; to fight like a ~ se battre comme un tigre to hunt ~ aller à la chasse au tigre ❑ to get off the ~ OR the ~'s back se tirer d'embarras; to have a ~ by the tail se trouver pris dans une situation dont on n'est plus maître; to ride the ~ vivre dangereusement.

Tiger balm® *n* baume *m* du tigre *(pommade mentholée utilisée comme panacée)*.

tiger lily *n* lis *m* tigré.

tiger moth *n* écaille *f* ENTOM.

tiger's-eye *n* [stone] œil-de-tigre *m*.

tiger shark *n* requin-tigre *m*.

tight [taɪt] ◇ *adj* -**1.** [garment, footwear] serré, étroit; these shoes are a bit ~ ces chaussures sont un peu trop serrées; it's a ~ fit c'est trop serré OR juste; ~ jeans [too small] un jean trop serré; [close-fitting] un jean moulant; a ~ skirt [too small] une jupe trop serrée; [close-fitting] une jupe moulante; my tie is too ~ ma cravate est trop serrée. -**2.** [stiff - drawer, door] dur à ouvrir; [- tap] dur à tourner; [- lid] dur à enlever; [- screw] serré; [constricted] pesant; I've got a ~ feeling across my chest j'ai comme un poids sur la poitrine; it was a ~ squeeze but we got everyone in on a eu du mal mais on a réussi à faire entrer tout le monde ❑ to be in a ~ corner OR spot être dans une situation difficile. -**3.** [taut - rope] raide, tendu; [- bow] tendu; [- net, knitting, knot] serré; [- skin] tiré; [- group] serré; her face looked ~ and drawn elle avait les traits tirés; they marched in ~ formation ils marchaient en ordre serré ‖ [firm]: to keep (a) ~ hold OR grasp on sthg bien tenir qqch; she kept a ~ hold on the rail elle s'agrippait à la balustrade; she kept a ~ hold

on the expenses *fig* elle surveillait les dépenses de près; you should keep a ~er rein on the children/your emotions *fig* il faudrait surveiller les enfants de plus près/mieux maîtriser vos émotions. -**4.** [sharp - bend, turn] brusque; we had to make a ~ turn to avoid the car nous avons dû effectuer un virage serré pour éviter la voiture. -**5.** [strict - control, restrictions] strict, sévère; [- security] strict; to run a ~ ship mener son monde à la baguette. -**6.** [limited - budget, credit] serré, resserré; to work on a ~ budget travailler avec un budget serré; money is a bit ~ OR things are a bit ~ at the moment l'argent manque un peu en ce moment. -**7.** [close - competition] serré. -**8.** [busy - schedule] serré, chargé; it was ~ but I made it in time c'était juste, mais je suis arrivé à temps. -**9.** *inf* [mean] radin, pingre; he's very ~ with his money il est très près de ses sous. -**10.** *inf* [drunk] soûl, rond; he gets ~ on one glass of wine un verre de vin suffit à le soûler.
◇ *adv* [close, fasten] bien; packed ~ [bag] bien rempli OR plein; [pub, room] bondé; hold ~! tenez-vous bien!, accrochez-vous bien!; she held the rabbit ~ in her arms elle serrait le lapin dans ses bras; pull the thread ~ tirez OR tendez bien le fil; is that window shut ~? cette fenêtre est-elle bien fermée?; it needs to be turned/screwed ~ il faut le serrer/le visser à fond.
◆ **tights** *npl*: (pair of) ~s collant *m*, collants *mpl*.

tight-arsed▼ *Br* [-ɑːst], **tight-assed**▼ *Am* [-æst] *adj* coincé, constipé.

tighten ['taɪtn] ◇ *vt* -**1.** [belt, strap] resserrer; he ~ed his grasp on the rail il agrippa plus fermement la balustrade ❑ to ~ one's belt *literal* resserrer sa ceinture; *fig* se serrer la ceinture. -**2.** [nut, screw] serrer, bien visser; [knot] serrer; [cable, rope] serrer, tendre. -**3.** [control, security, regulations] renforcer; [credit] resserrer.
◇ *vi* -**1.** [grip]: his finger ~ed on the trigger son doigt se serra sur la gâchette; her grasp ~ed on my arm elle serra mon bras plus fort. -**2.** [nut, screw, knot] se resserrer; [cable, rope] se raidir, se tendre. -**3.** [control, security, regulation] être renforcé; [credit] se resserrer. -**4.** [throat, stomach] se nouer.
◆ **tighten up** *vt sep* -**1.** [nut, screw] serrer. -**2.** [control, security, regulation] renforcer; the law on drug peddling has been ~ed up la loi sur le trafic de drogue a été renforcée.
◆ **tighten up on** *vt insep*: to ~ up on discipline/security renforcer la discipline/la sécurité; the government are ~ing up on drug pushers/tax evasion le gouvernement renforce la lutte contre les revendeurs de drogue/la fraude fiscale.

tightening ['taɪtnɪŋ] *n* [of screw, credit] resserrement *m*; [of control, regulation] renforcement *m*; he felt a ~ in his throat il sentit sa gorge se nouer.

tightfisted [,taɪt'fɪstɪd] *adj pej* avare, pingre.

tight-fitting *adj* [skirt, trousers] moulant; [lid] qui ferme bien.

tight-knit *adj* [community, family] (très) uni.

tight-lipped *adj*: he sat ~ and pale il était assis, pâle et muet; she sat in ~ silence elle se tenait assise, sans desserrer les dents.

tightly ['taɪtlɪ] *adv* -**1.** [firmly - hold, fit, screw] (bien) serré; he held his daughter ~ to him il serrait sa fille tout contre lui; hold on ~ tenez-vous OR accrochez-vous bien; we held on ~ to the rail nous nous sommes agrippés fermement à la balustrade; make sure the lid fits ~ vérifiez que le couvercle est bien fermé; the cases were ~ sealed les caisses étaient bien scellées; her eyes were ~ shut elle avait les yeux bien fermés; news is ~ controlled les informations sont soumises à un contrôle rigoureux; ~ curled hair des cheveux frisés. -**2.** [densely]: the lecture hall was ~ packed l'amphithéâtre était bondé OR plein à craquer.

tightness ['taɪtnɪs] *n* -**1.** [of garment, shoes] étroitesse *f*. -**2.** [stiffness - of drawer, screw, tap] dureté *f*. -**3.** [tautness - of bow, rope] raideur *f*; he felt a sudden ~ in his throat il sentit soudain sa gorge se nouer; he felt a sudden ~ in his chest [physical] il ressentit soudain une douleur dans la poitrine; [emotional] il sentit soudain son cœur se serrer. -**4.** [strictness - of control, regulation] rigueur *f*, sévérité *f*; [- of security] rigueur *f*.

tightrope ['taɪtrəʊp] *n* corde *f* raide; to walk the ~ marcher sur la corde raide; she's walking a political ~ *fig* elle s'est aventurée sur un terrain politique glissant OR dangereux.

tightrope walker *n* funambule *mf*.

tightwad *inf* ['taɪtwɒd] *n Am pej* radin *m*, -e *f*; he's a real ~ il est vraiment grippe-sou.

Tigré ['tiːgreɪ] *pr n* Tigré *m*; in ~ dans le Tigré.

tigress ['taɪgrɪs] *n* ZOOL & *fig* tigresse *f*.

Tigris ['taɪgrɪs] *pr n*: the (River) ~ le Tigre.

tike [taɪk] = **tyke**.

tilde ['tɪldə] *n* tilde *m*.

tile [taɪl] ◇ *n* [for roof] tuile *f*; [for wall, floor] carreau *m*; to have a night (out) on the ~s *inf* faire la noce.
◇ *vt* [roof] couvrir de tuiles; [floor, wall] carreler; ~d bathroom salle de bains *f* carrelée; ~d floor sol *m* carrelé; ~d roof toit *m* de tuiles.

tiler ['taɪlər] *n* [of roof] couvreur *m* *(de toits en tuiles)*; [of floor, wall] carreleur *m*.

tiling ['taɪlɪŋ] *n* *(U)* -**1.** [putting on tiles - on roof] pose *f* des tuiles; [- on floor, in bathroom] carrelage *m*. -**2.** [tiles - on roof] tuiles *fpl*; [- on floor, wall] carrelage *m*, carreaux *mpl*.

till [tɪl] ◇ *conj* = **until**.
◇ *prep* = **until**.
◇ *n* -**1.** [cash register] caisse *f* (enregistreuse); [drawer] tiroir-caisse *m*; to be caught with one's fingers OR hands in the ~ être pris en flagrant délit OR la main dans le sac; pay at the ~ payez à la caisse. -**2.** [money] caisse *f*.
◇ *vt* AGR labourer; to ~ the soil labourer la terre.

tillage ['tɪlɪdʒ] *n* -**1.** [act] labour *m*, labourage *m*. -**2.** [land] labour *m*, pièce *f* labourée.

tiller ['tɪlər] *n* -**1.** NAUT barre *f*, gouvernail *m*. -**2.** BOT pousse *f*, talle *f*.

tilt [tɪlt] ◇ *vt* -**1.** [lean] pencher, incliner; to ~ one's chair (back) se balancer sur sa chaise; he ~ed his head to one side il pencha OR inclina la tête sur le côté; to ~ one's head back renverser la tête en arrière; her hat was ~ed over one eye son chapeau était penché sur le côté; this may ~ the odds in our favour *fig* cela peut faire pencher la balance de notre côté. -**2.** [cover - gen] bâcher; NAUT tauder.
◇ *vi* -**1.** [lean] se pencher, s'incliner; to ~ backwards/forwards se pencher en arrière/en avant; don't ~ back on your chair ne te balance pas sur ta chaise. -**2.** HIST [joust] jouter; to ~ at sb HIST diriger un coup de lance contre qqn; *fig* lancer des piques à qqn ❑ to ~ at windmills se battre contre des moulins à vent.
◇ *n* -**1.** [angle] inclinaison *f*; [slope] pente *f*; the room has a definite ~ to it la pièce penche nettement; she wore her hat at a ~ elle portait son chapeau incliné; I'm sure that picture's on a ~ je suis sûr que le tableau penche. -**2.** HIST [joust] joute *f*; [thrust] coup *m* de lance; *fig*: to have a ~ at sb s'en prendre à qqn, décocher des pointes à qqn; that was obviously a ~ at you c'était une pointe qui vous était destinée. -**3.** [awning] store *m* (de toile), bâche *f*; NAUT taud *m*.
◆ **full tilt** *adv phr*: he ran full ~ into her il lui est rentré en plein dedans; he ran full ~ into the door il est rentré en plein dans la porte.
◆ **tilt over** *vi insep* -**1.** [slant] pencher. -**2.** [overturn] se renverser, basculer.

tilth [tɪlθ] *n* [act of tilling] labourage *m*; [soil] terre *f* arable.

timber ['tɪmbər] ◇ *n* -**1.** [wood] bois *m* de charpente OR de construction OR d'œuvre. -**2.** *(U)* [trees] arbres *mpl*, bois *m*; land under ~ terre *f* boisée; to put land under ~ boiser un terrain; standing ~ bois sur pied. -**3.** [beam] madrier *m*, poutre *f*; [on ship] membrure *f*. -**4.** shiver me ~s! *expression stéréotypée de marin*, ≃ mille sabords!
◇ *comp* [roof, fence] en bois.
◇ *vt* [tunnel] boiser.
◇ *interj*: ~! attention!

timbered ['tɪmbəd] *adj* [region, land] boisé; [house] en bois.

timberhead ['tɪmbəhed] *n* NAUT bitte *f* (d'amarrage), bollard *m*.

timbering ['tɪmbərɪŋ] *n* boisage *m*.

timberland ['tɪmbəlænd] *n Am* terre *f* OR région *f* boisée *(pour l'abattage)*.

timberline ['tɪmbəlaɪn] *n* limite *f* des arbres.

timber merchant *n* marchand *m* de bois.

timber wolf *n* loup *m* gris.

timberwork ['tɪmbəwɜːk] *n* structure *f* en bois.

timberyard ['tɪmbəjɑːd] *n* chantier *m* de bois.

timbre ['tæmbrə, 'tɪmbər] *n* LING & MUS timbre *m*.

Timbuktu [,tɪmbʌk'tuː] *pr n* Tombouctou.

time [taɪm] ◇ *n* -**1.** [continuous stretch of time] temps *m*; as ~ goes by avec le temps; the price has gone up over ~ le prix a augmenté avec le temps; it's only a matter OR a question of ~ ce n'est qu'une question de temps; these things take ~ cela ne se fait pas du jour au lendemain; to have ~ on one's hands OR ~ to spare avoir du temps; ~ hangs heavy on his hands le temps lui pèse, il trouve le temps long; since the dawn of ~ depuis la nuit des temps; ~ flies le temps passe vite; doesn't ~ fly! comme le temps passe vite!; ~ heals all wounds le temps guérit tout; only ~ will tell seul l'avenir nous le dira; ~ will prove me right l'avenir me donnera raison; it's a race against ~ c'est une course contre la montre; they're working against ~ to save her ils ne disposent que de très peu de temps pour la sauver; ~ is on our side le temps joue en notre faveur; ~ out of mind de temps immémorial, de toute éternité ❑ to take Time by the forelock *lit* saisir l'occasion (par les cheveux); ~ is money *prov* le temps, c'est de l'argent *prov*; ~ and tide wait for no man *prov* les événements n'attendent personne. -**2.** [period of time spent on particular activity] temps *m*; there's no ~ to lose il n'y a pas de temps à perdre; he lost no ~ in telling me il s'est empressé de me le dire; to make up for lost ~ rattraper le temps perdu; to make good/poor ~ doing sthg mettre peu de temps/longtemps à faire qqch; I passed the ~ reading j'ai passé mon temps à lire; take your ~ prenez votre temps; take your ~ over it prenez le temps qu'il faudra; it took me all my ~ just to get here! *fig* avec le temps que j'ai mis pour arriver ici! you took your ~ about it! tu en as mis du temps!; I took ~ out to travel [from work] je me suis mis en congé pour voyager; [from studies] j'ai interrompu mes études pour voyager; she took ~ out OR made the ~ to read the report elle a pris le temps de lire le rapport; I spend half/all my ~ cleaning up je passe la moitié de/tout mon temps à faire le ménage; half the ~ he doesn't know what he's doing la moitié du temps il ne sait pas ce qu'il fait; most of the ~ la plupart du temps; he was ill part OR some of the ~ il a été malade une partie du temps; it rained part OR some of the ~ il a plu par moments; we spend the better part of our ~ working nous passons le plus clair de notre temps à travailler; I start in three weeks' ~ je commence dans trois semaines; they'll have finished the project in three weeks' ~ ils auront terminé le projet dans trois semaines ❑ all in good ~! chaque chose en son temps!; I'll finish it in my own good ~ je le finirai quand bon me semblera. -**3.** [available period of time] temps *m*; I haven't (the) ~ to do the shopping je n'ai pas le temps de faire les courses; I've no ~ for gossip *literal* je n'ai pas le temps de papoter; *fig* jen'ai pas de temps à perdre en bavardages; my ~ is my own mon temps m'appartient; my ~ is not my own je ne suis pas libre de mon temps; he has no ~ for sycophants il n'a pas de temps à perdre avec les flatteurs; we've just got ~ to catch the train on a juste le temps d'attraper le train; that doesn't leave them much ~ to get ready cela ne leur laisse guère de temps pour se préparer; you'll have to find the ~ to see her il faut que tu trouves le temps de la voir; you have plenty of ~ to finish it vous avez largement le temps de le finir; we've got plenty of ~ OR all the ~ in the world nous avons tout le temps. -4. [while] temps *m*; after a ~ après un (certain) temps; a long ~ longtemps; a long ~ ago il y a longtemps; it's a long ~ since we've been out for a meal together ça fait longtemps que nous ne sommes pas sortis dîner ensemble; she's been dreaming of this for a long ~ now voilà longtemps qu'elle en rêve; he waited for a long ~ il a attendu longtemps; I worked for a long ~ as a translator j'ai travaillé (pendant) longtemps comme traducteur; for a long ~ he refused to eat meat il a (pendant) longtemps refusé de manger de la viande; it'll be a long ~ before I do that again je ne suis pas près de recommencer, je ne recommencerai pas de si tôt OR de sitôt; the car takes a long ~ to warm up la voiture met longtemps à chauffer; you took a long ~! tu en as mis du temps!, il t'en a fallu du temps!; long ~ no see! *inf* ça faisait longtemps!; a short ~ peu de temps; after a short ~ peu (de temps) après; a short ~ before their wedding peu avant leur mariage; she's going to stay with us for a short ~ elle va rester avec nous pendant quelque temps; in the shortest possible ~ dans les plus brefs délais, le plus vite OR tôt possible; after some ~ au bout de quelque temps, après un certain temps; some ~ after their trip quelque temps après leur voyage; some ~ ago il y a quelque temps; it's the best film I've seen for some ~ c'est le meilleur film que j'aie vu depuis un moment; it will take (quite) some ~ to repair il va falloir pas mal de temps pour le réparer. -5. [time taken or required to do something] temps *m*, durée *f*; the flying ~ to Madrid is two hours la durée du vol pour Madrid est de deux heures; the cooking ~ is two hours le temps de cuisson est de deux heures; the winner's ~ was under four minutes le gagnant a fait un temps de moins de quatre minutes; how much ~ will it take? combien de temps cela prendra-t-il?; she finished in half the ~ it took me to finish elle a mis deux fois moins de temps que moi pour finir. -6. [by clock] heure *f*; what ~ is it?, what's the ~? quelle heure est-il?; what ~ do you make it? quelle heure avez-vous?; have you got the right ~ on you? avez-vous l'heure juste?; the ~ is twenty past three il est trois heures vingt; what ~ are we leaving? à quelle heure partons-nous?; do you know how to tell the ~? est-ce que tu sais lire l'heure?; could you tell me the ~? pourriez-vous me dire l'heure (qu'il est)?; have you seen the ~? avez-vous vu l'heure?; I looked at the ~ j'ai regardé l'heure; this old watch still keeps good ~ cette vieille montre est toujours à l'heure OR exacte; at this ~ of day à cette heure de la journée; we'll have to keep an eye on the ~ il faudra surveiller l'heure; it is almost ~ to leave/for my bus il est presque l'heure de partir/de mon bus; it's ~ I was going il est temps que je parte; it's dinner ~, it's ~ for dinner c'est l'heure de dîner; there you are, it's about ~! te voilà, ce n'est pas trop tôt! ❑ I wouldn't give him the ~ of day je ne lui dirais même pas bonjour; to pass the ~ of day with sb échanger quelques mots avec qqn. -7. [system]: local ~ heure *f* locale; it's 5 o'clock Tokyo ~ il est 5 h, heure de Tokyo. -8. [schedule]: is the bus running to ~? est-ce que le bus est à l'heure?; within the required ~ dans les délais requis. -9. [particular point in time] moment *m*; at that ~ I was in Madrid à ce moment-là j'étais OR j'étais alors à Madrid; I worked for her at one ~ à un moment donné j'ai travaillé pour elle; at the present ~ en ce moment, à présent; he is president at the present ~ il est actuellement président; at a later ~ plus tard; at a given ~ à un moment donné; at any one ~ à la fois; there's room for 15 people at any one ~ il y a de la place pour 15 personnes à la fois; an inconvenient ~ un moment inopportun; you called at a most inconvenient ~ vous avez appelé à un très mauvais moment; there are ~s when I could scream il y a des moments où j'ai envie de hurler; at the best of ~s même quand tout va bien; even at the best of ~s he is not that patient même dans ses bons moments il n'est pas particulièrement patient; at no ~ did I agree to that je n'ai jamais donné mon accord pour cela; by the ~ you get this... le temps que tu reçoives ceci..., quand tu auras reçu ceci...; by that ~ it will be too late à ce moment-là il sera trop tard; by that ~ we'll all be dead d'ici là nous serons tous morts; by this ~ next week d'ici une semaine, dans une semaine; this ~ next week la semaine prochaine à cette heure-ci; this ~ last week il y a exactement une semaine; from that ~ on we had nothing to do with them à partir de ce moment-là, nous avons refusé d'avoir affaire à eux; in between ~s entre-temps; until such ~ as I hear from them jusqu'à ce que OR en attendant que j'aie de leurs nouvelles. -10. [suitable moment] moment *m*; she chose her ~ badly elle a mal choisi son moment; this is no ~ for you to leave ce n'est pas le moment de partir; now's our ~ to tell her c'est maintenant que nous devrions OR voici venu le moment de le lui dire; now is the ~ to invest c'est maintenant qu'il faut investir; when the ~ comes (quand) le moment (sera) venu; we'll talk about that when the ~ comes nous en parlerons en temps utile; the ~ has come to make a stand c'est le moment d'avoir le courage de ses opinions; it's about ~ we taught her a lesson il est grand temps que nous lui donnions une bonne leçon; there's no ~ like the present [let's do it now] faisons-le maintenant; there's a ~ and a place for everything il y a un temps et un lieu pour OR à tout. -11. [occasion, instance] fois *f*; I'll forgive you this ~ je vous pardonne cette fois-ci OR pour cette fois; each OR every ~ chaque fois; she succeeds every ~ elle réussit à chaque fois; the last ~ he came la dernière fois qu'il est venu; the ~ before la fois précédente OR d'avant; another OR some other ~ une autre fois; I called her three ~s je l'ai appelée trois fois; many ~s bien des fois, très souvent; many a ~ I've wondered... je me suis demandé plus d'une OR bien des fois...; several ~s plusieurs fois; several ~s in the past plusieurs fois déjà; he asked me several ~s if... il m'a demandé plusieurs fois si...; it costs 15 cents a ~ ça coûte 15 cents à chaque fois; the one ~ I win, he wants to stop playing pour une fois que je gagne, il veut arrêter de jouer; nine ~s out of ten the machine doesn't work neuf fois sur dix la machine ne marche pas; we'll have to decide some ~ or other tôt ou tard OR un jour ou l'autre il va falloir nous décider; do you remember that ~ we went to Germany? tu te rappelles la fois où nous sommes allés en Allemagne?; there's always a first ~ il y a un début à tout; I've told you a hundred ~s! je te l'ai dit vingt OR cent fois!; give me a good detective story every ~! rien ne vaut un bon roman policier! -12. [experience]: to have a good ~ bien s'amuser; I had the ~ of my life jamais je ne me suis si bien OR autant amusé; we had an awful ~ at the picnic nous nous sommes ennuyés à mourir au pique-nique; it was a difficult ~ for all of us c'était une période difficile pour nous tous; she had a hard ~ bringing up five children alone ça a été difficile pour elle d'élever cinq enfants seule; what a ~ I had with him! [fun] qu'est-ce que j'ai pu m'amuser avec lui!; [trouble] qu'est-ce qu'il m'en a fait voir! -13. [hours of work]: to put in ~ faire des heures (de travail); to work part/full ~ travailler à temps partiel/à plein temps; in company ~ *Br*, on company ~ *Am* pendant les heures de travail; in your own ~ *Br*, on your own ~ *Am* pendant votre temps libre, en dehors des heures de travail; ~ off temps *m* libre; what do you do in your ~ off? qu'est-ce que vous faites de votre temps libre? -14. [hourly wages]: we pay ~ and a half on weekends nous payons les heures du week-end une fois et demie le tarif normal; overtime is paid at double ~ les heures supplémentaires sont payées OR comptées double. -15. *(usu plural)* [era] époque *f*, temps *m*; in Victorian ~s à l'époque victorienne; in the ~ of Henry IV à l'époque d'Henri IV, du temps d'Henri IV; ancient ~s l'Antiquité *f*; in ~s past, in former ~s autrefois, jadis; in ~s to come à l'avenir; at one ~, things were different autrefois OR dans le temps les choses étaient différentes; the house has seen better ~s la maison a connu des jours meilleurs; in ~(s) of need/war en temps de pénurie/de guerre; ~ was when doctors made house calls il fut un temps où les médecins faisaient des visites à domicile; those were happy ~s! c'était le bon (vieux) temps!; ~s are hard les temps sont durs; in our ~ de nos jours; the ~s we live in l'époque où nous vivons; in my ~ children didn't talk back de mon temps les enfants ne répondaient pas ❑ to be ahead of OR before one's ~ être en avance sur son époque OR sur son temps; to be behind the ~s être en retard sur son époque OR sur son temps; to keep up with the ~s vivre avec son temps; to move with the ~s évoluer avec son temps; ~s have changed autres temps, autres mœurs *prov*. -16. [lifetime]: I've heard some odd things in my ~! j'en ai entendu, des choses, dans ma vie!; it won't happen in our ~ nous ne serons pas là pour voir ça; at my ~ of life à mon âge; that was before your ~ [birth] vous n'étiez pas encore né; [arrival] vous n'étiez pas encore là; her ~ has come [childbirth] elle arrive à son terme; [death] son heure est venue OR a sonné; [success] son heure est venue; he died before his ~ il est mort avant l'âge. -17. [season]: it's hot for the ~ of year il fait chaud pour la saison. -18. [end of period] fin *f*; ~'s up [on exam, visit] c'est l'heure; [on meter, telephone] le temps est écoulé; ~, (gentlemen) please! [in pub] *Br* on ferme!; the referee called ~ SPORT l'arbitre a sifflé la fin du match. -19. *Am* COMM: to buy sthg on ~ acheter qqch à tempérament OR à terme OR à crédit. -20. ▽ [in prison]: to do ~ faire de la taule; he's serving ~ for murder il est en taule pour meurtre. -21. MUS mesure *f*; he beat ~ with his foot il battait OR marquait la mesure du pied; in triple OR three-part ~ à trois temps; ~ (value) valeur *f (d'une note)*. -22. RADIO & TV espace *m*; to buy/to sell ~ on television acheter/vendre de l'espace publicitaire à la télévision. -23. *inf Am phr*: to make ~ with sb [pursue] draguer qqn; [be with] être avec qqn *(en couple)*.

◇ *vt* -1. [on clock - runner, worker] chronométrer; they ~d her at four minutes a mile ils l'ont chronométrée OR ils ont chronométré son temps à quatre minutes au mille; ~ how long she takes to finish regardez combien de temps elle met pour finir; he ~d his speech to last 20 minutes il a fait en sorte que son discours dure 20 minutes; to ~ an egg minuter le temps de cuisson d'un œuf. -2. [schedule] fixer OR prévoir (l'heure de); they ~d the attack for 6 o'clock l'attaque était prévue pour 6 h. -3. [choose right moment for] choisir OR calculer le moment de; she ~d her entrance well elle a bien choisi le moment pour faire son entrée; he ~d the blow perfectly il a frappé au bon moment; your remark was perfectly/badly ~d votre observation est venue au bon/au mauvais moment. -4. [synchronize] régler, ajuster; she tried to ~ her steps to the music elle essayait de régler ses pas sur la musique.

◆ **times** ◇ *npl* [indicating degree] fois *f*; she's ten ~s cleverer than you are elle est dix fois plus intelligente que toi; he ate four ~s as much cake as I did il a mangé quatre fois plus de gâteau que moi.

◇ *prep* MATH: 3 ~s 5 is 15 3 fois 5 font OR égalent 15; 1 ~s 6 is 6 une fois six fait OR égale six.

◆ **ahead of time** *adv phr* en avance; I'm ten minutes ahead of ~ j'ai dix minutes d'avance.

◆ **all the time** *adv phr*: he talked all the ~ we were at lunch il a parlé pendant tout le déjeuner; he's been watching us all the ~ il n'a pas cessé de nous regarder; I knew it all the ~ je le savais depuis le début.

◆ **any time** *adv phr* n'importe quand; come over any ~ venez quand vous voulez; you're welcome any ~ vous serez toujours le bienvenu; thanks for all your help – any ~ merci de votre aide – de rien.

◆ **at a time** *adv phr*: for days at a ~ pendant des journées entières, des journées durant; take one book at a ~ prenez les livres un par un OR un (seul) livre à la fois; she ran up the stairs two at a ~ elle a monté les marches quatre à quatre.

◆ **at all times** *adv phr* à tous moments.

◆ **at any time** *adv phr* à toute heure; hot meals at any ~ repas chauds à toute heure; at any ~ of day or night à n'importe quelle heure du jour ou de la nuit; at any ~ during office hours n'importe quand pendant les heures de bureau; he could die at any ~ il peut mourir d'un moment à l'autre.

◆ **at the same time** *adv phr* -**1.** [simultaneously] en même temps; they all spoke at the same ~ ils se sont mis à parler tous en même temps; they arrived at the same ~ (as) he did ils sont arrivés en même temps que lui. -**2.** [yet] en même temps; she was pleased but at the same ~ a bit concerned elle était contente mais en même temps un peu inquiète. -**3.** [nevertheless] pourtant, cependant; at the same ~, we must not forget... pourtant OR cependant, il ne faut pas oublier...

◆ **at the time** *adv phr*: at the ~ of their wedding au moment de leur mariage; I didn't pay much attention at the ~ sur le moment je n'ai pas fait vraiment attention.

◆ **at times** *adv phr* parfois, par moments.

◆ **behind time** *adv phr* en retard; we're a bit behind ~ nous sommes légèrement en retard; the project was running behind ~ le projet avait du retard.

◆ **for a time** *adv phr* pendant un (certain) temps; for a ~, he was unable to walk pendant un certain temps, il n'a pas pu marcher.

◆ **for all time** *adv phr* pour toujours.

◆ **for the time being** *adv phr* pour le moment.

◆ **from time to time** *adv phr* de temps en temps, de temps à autre.

◆ **in time** *adv phr* -**1.** [eventually]: she'll come to her senses in ~ elle finira par revenir à la raison; he'll forget about it in (the course of) ~ il finira par l'oublier (avec le temps). -**2.** [not too late]: let me know in (good) ~ prévenez-moi (bien) à l'avance; she arrived in ~ for the play elle est arrivée à l'heure pour la pièce; you're just in ~ to greet our guests tu arrives juste à temps pour accueillir nos invités; I'll be back in ~ for the film je serai de retour à temps pour le film. -**3.** MUS mesure *f*; to be OR keep in ~ (with the music) être en mesure (avec la musique).

◆ **in (next to) no time** *adv phr* en un rien de temps.

◆ **of all time** *adv phr* de tous les temps.

◆ **of all times** *adv phr*: why now of all ~s? pourquoi faut-il que ce soit juste maintenant?

◆ **on time** *adv phr* à l'heure; she arrived right on ~ elle est arrivée juste à l'heure; is the bus on ~? est-ce que le bus est à l'heure?

◆ **out of time** *adv phr*: he got out of ~ il a perdu la mesure.

◆ **time after time, time and (time) again** *adv phr* maintes et maintes fois.

time-and-motion *n*: ~ study étude *f* de productivité *(qui se concentre sur l'efficacité des employés)*; ~ expert expert *m* en productivité.

time bomb *n literal* & *fig* bombe *f* à retardement.

time capsule *n* capsule *f* témoin *(qui doit servir de témoignage historique aux générations futures)*.

time card *n* INDUST carte *f* OR fiche *f* de pointage.

time chart *n* -**1.** [showing time zones] carte *f* des fuseaux horaires. -**2.** [showing events] table *f* d'événements historiques. -**3.** [showing planning] calendrier *m*, planning *m*.

time check *n* [on radio] rappel *m* de l'heure.

time clock *n* INDUST pointeuse *f*.

time code *n* code *m* temporel.

time-consuming *adj* [work] qui prend beaucoup de temps, prenant; [tactics] dilatoire.

time deposit *n Am* FIN dépôt *m* à terme.

time exposure *n* -**1.** [of film] pose *f*. -**2.** [photograph] photo *f* prise en pose.

time-filler *n*: I'm just doing this job as a ~ je fais ce travail uniquement pour tuer le temps.

time frame *n* délai *m*; what's our ~? de combien de temps disposons-nous?

time fuse *n* détonateur *m* OR fusée *f* à retardement.

time-honoured *adj* consacré (par l'usage).

timekeeper ['taɪm,kiːpəʳ] *n* -**1.** [watch] montre *f*; [clock] horloge *f*; [stopwatch] chronomètre *m*; this watch is a good ~ cette montre est toujours à l'heure. -**2.** [supervisor] pointeau *m*. -**3.** [employee, friend]: he's a good ~ il est toujours à l'heure, il est toujours très ponctuel; he's a bad ~ il n'est jamais à l'heure. -**4.** SPORT chronométreur *m* (officiel), chronométreuse *f* (officielle).

time lag *n* -**1.** [delay] décalage *m* dans le temps. -**2.** [in time zones] décalage *m* horaire.

time lapse *n* décalage *m* horaire.

time-lapse photography *n* photographie *f* accélérée.

timeless ['taɪmlɪs] *adj* éternel, hors du temps, intemporel.

time limit *n* [gen] délai *m*, date *f* limite; JUR délai *m* de forclusion; there is a strict ~ for applications il y a un délai impératif OR de rigueur pour la remise des dossiers de candidature; we'll have to set ourselves a ~ for the work il va falloir nous imposer un délai pour finir ce travail; the work must be completed within the ~ le travail doit être terminé avant la date limite.

timeliness ['taɪmlɪnɪs] *n* [of remark] à-propos *m*, opportunité *f*; [of visit] opportunité *f*.

time loan *n* emprunt *m* à terme.

timely ['taɪmlɪ] *adj* [remark, intervention, warning] qui tombe à point nommé, opportun; [visit] opportun; he made a ~ escape il s'est échappé juste à temps.

time machine *n* machine *f* à voyager dans le temps; 'The Time Machine' *Wells* 'la Machine à explorer le temps'.

time-out *n* SPORT temps *m* mort; [in chess match] temps *m* de repos; [in work] pause *f*.

timepiece ['taɪmpiːs] *n fml* OR *dated* [watch] montre *f*; [clock] horloge *f*, pendule *f*.

timer ['taɪməʳ] *n* -**1.** CULIN minuteur *m*; (egg) ~ sablier *m*, compte-minutes *m inv*. -**2.** [counter] compteur *m*. -**3.** [for lighting] minuterie *f*. -**4.** [stopwatch] chronomètre *m*. -**5.** [timekeeper] chronométreur *m*, -euse *f*. -**6.** AUT distributeur *m* (d'allumage).

time-saver *n*: a dishwasher is a great ~ on gagne beaucoup de temps avec un lave-vaisselle, un lave-vaisselle permet de gagner beaucoup de temps.

time-saving ◇ *adj* qui économise OR fait gagner du temps; it's a ~ device cet appareil fait gagner du temps.

◇ *n* gain *m* de temps.

time scale *n* échelle *f* dans le temps.

timeserver ['taɪm,sɜːvəʳ] *n* -**1.** [opportunist] opportuniste *mf*. -**2.** [employee] tire-au-flanc *m inv*.

time-serving ◇ *adj* opportuniste.

◇ *n* opportunisme *m*.

time-share ◇ *n*: to buy a ~ in a flat acheter un appartement en multipropriété.

◇ *adj* [flat] en multipropriété; [computer] en temps partagé.

time-sharing *n* -**1.** [of flat, villa] multipropriété *f*. -**2.** COMPUT temps *m* partagé.

time sheet *n* fiche *f* horaire.

time signal *n* RADIO signal *m* OR top *m* horaire.

time signature *n* MUS indication *f* de la mesure.

time slice *n* COMPUT tranche *f* de temps.

time switch *n* [for oven, heating] minuteur *m*; [for lighting] minuterie *f*.

timetable ['taɪm,teɪbl] ◇ *n* -**1.** [for transport] horaire *m*; bus ~ indicateur *m* OR horaire des autobus. -**2.** [schedule] emploi *m* du temps; I have a very full ~ j'ai un emploi du temps très chargé. -**3.** [calendar] calendrier *m*; exam ~ dates *fpl* OR calendrier des examens.

◇ *vt* [meeting - during day] fixer une heure pour; [- during week, month] fixer une date pour; SCH [classes, course] établir un emploi du temps pour; the train is ~d to arrive at six o'clock l'arrivée du train est prévue à 6 h; her visit is ~d to coincide with the celebrations sa visite devrait coïncider avec les festivités.

time travel *n* voyage *m* dans le temps.

time trial *n* SPORT course *f* contre la montre.

time value *n* MUS valeur *f*.

time warp *n*: it's like living in a ~ c'est comme si on vivait hors du temps; the country seems to have entered a ~ le temps semble s'être arrêté dans le pays.

timework ['taɪmwɜːk] *n* [hourly] travail *m* payé à l'heure; [daily] travail *m* payé à la journée; to be on ~ [hourly] être payé OR travailler à l'heure; [daily] être payé OR travailler à la journée.

timeworker ['taɪmwɜːkəʳ] *n* [paid - hourly] horaire *mf*; [- daily] journalier *m*, -ère *f*.

timeworn ['taɪmwɔːn] *adj* [object] usé par le temps, vétuste; *fig* [idea, phrase] rebattu, éculé.

time zone *n* fuseau *m* horaire.

timid ['tɪmɪd] *adj* timide.

timidity [tɪ'mɪdətɪ] *n* timidité *f*.

timidly ['tɪmɪdlɪ] *adv* timidement.

timidness ['tɪmɪdnɪs] *n* timidité *f*.

timing ['taɪmɪŋ] *n* -**1.** [of actor] minutage *m* (du débit); [of musician] sens *m* du rythme; [of tennis player] timing *m*; [of stunt driver] synchronisation *f*; you need a good sense of ~ il faut savoir choisir le bon moment; cooking such a big meal requires careful ~ pour préparer un si grand repas, il faut organiser son temps avec soin; that was good ~! voilà qui était bien calculé! -**2.** [chosen moment - of operation, visit] moment *m* choisi; the ~ of the statement was unfortunate cette déclaration est vraiment tombée à un très mauvais moment. -**3.** SPORT chronométrage *m*. -**4.** AUT réglage *m* de l'allumage.

timing device *n* [for bomb] mécanisme *m* d'horlogerie; [for lights] minuterie *f*.

timing mechanism *n* [for bomb, in clock] mécanisme *m* d'horlogerie.

timorous ['tɪmərəs] *adj* timoré, craintif.

timorously ['tɪmərəslɪ] *adv* craintivement.

Timothy ['tɪməθɪ] *pr n* Timothée.

timpani ['tɪmpənɪ] *npl* timbales *fpl* MUS.

timpanist ['tɪmpənɪst] *n* timbalier *m*.

tin [tɪn] (*pt* & *pp* **tinned**, *cont* **tinning**) ◇ *n* -**1.** [metal] étain *m*; ~ (plate) fer-blanc *m*. -**2.** *Br* [can] boîte *f* (en fer-blanc); ~s of beans/of food des boîtes de haricots/de conserve; a ~ of paint un pot de peinture; to live out of ~s se nourrir de conserves. -**3.** [for storing] boîte *f* en fer; biscuit ~ [empty] boîte *f* à biscuits; [full] boîte *f* de biscuits. -**4.** [for cooking]: roasting ~ plat *m* à rôtir; baking OR cake ~ moule *m* à gâteau.

◇ *comp* [made of tin] en étain; [made of tinplate] en fer-blanc; [box] en fer; [roof] en tôle; 'The Tin Drum' *Grass* 'le Tambour'.

◇ *vt* -**1.** *Br* [food] mettre en conserve OR en boîte. -**2.** [plate] étamer.

tin can *n* boîte *f* (en fer-blanc).

tincture ['tɪŋktʃəʳ] ◇ *n* -**1.** CHEM & PHARM teinture *f*; ~ of iodine teinture d'iode. -**2.** [colour, tint] teinte *f*, nuance *f*. -**3.** *lit* [trace, hint] teinte *f*, touche *f*.
◇ *vt literal* & *fig* teinter.

tinder ['tɪndəʳ] *n* *(U)* [in tinderbox] amadou *m*; [dry wood] petit bois *m*; [dry grass] herbes *fpl* sèches; **his words were ~ to the mob's fury** *fig* ses paroles ont eu un effet incendiaire sur la foule en colère.

tinderbox ['tɪndəbɒks] *n* -**1.** [lighter] briquet *m* à amadou. -**2.** [dry place] endroit *m* sec. -**3.** *fig* [explosive situation] poudrière *f*, situation *f* explosive.

tinder-dry *adj* très sec.

tindery ['tɪndərɪ] *adj* hautement inflammable, sec (comme de l'amadou).

tine [taɪn] *n* [of fork] dent *f*; [of antler] andouiller *m*.

tinfoil ['tɪnfɔɪl] *n* papier *m* d'aluminium.

ting [tɪŋ] ◇ *onomat* ding.
◇ *vi* tinter.
◇ *vt* faire tinter.

ting-a-ling ◇ *onomat* [of phone, doorbell, bike] dring-dring.
◇ *n* dring-dring *m*.

tinge [tɪndʒ] ◇ *n* teinte *f*, nuance *f*.
◇ *vt* teinter; **her smile was ~d with sadness** *fig* son sourire était empreint de tristesse.

tingle ['tɪŋgl] ◇ *vi* -**1.** [with heat, cold - ears, cheeks, hands] fourmiller, picoter; **the cold wind made my face ~** le vent froid me piquait le visage; **his cheeks were tingling** les joues lui picotaient; **my whole body was tingling** j'avais des picotements OR des fourmis dans tout le corps; **my face still ~d from the blow** le visage me cuisait encore à cause du coup (que j'avais) reçu; **it makes my tongue ~** ça me pique la langue. -**2.** [with excitement, pleasure] frissonner, frémir; **she was tingling with excitement** elle tremblait d'excitation; **the insult left me tingling with indignation** l'insulte me fit frémir d'indignation.
◇ *n* -**1.** [stinging] picotements *mpl*, fourmillements *mpl*. -**2.** [thrill] frisson *m*, frémissement *m*.

tingling ['tɪŋglɪŋ] ◇ *n* [stinging] picotement *m*, fourmillement *m*; [from excitement] frisson *m*, frémissement *m*.
◇ *adj* [sensation] de picotement, de fourmillement.

tingly ['tɪŋglɪ] *adj* [sensation] de picotement, de fourmillement; **my fingers have gone all ~** j'ai des fourmis dans les doigts.

tin god *n* demi-dieu *m*; **he's nothing but a little ~** il se croit sorti de la cuisse de Jupiter.

tin hat *n* casque *m* (militaire).

tinhorn *inf* ['tɪnhɔːn] ◇ *n* *Am* petit prétentieux *m*, petite prétentieuse *f*.
◇ *adj* de pacotille, clinquant.

tinker ['tɪŋkəʳ] ◇ *n* -**1.** [pot mender] rétameur *m*; [gipsy] romanichel *m*, -elle *f* ❑ **I don't give a ~'s cuss** OR **damn!** *inf* je m'en fiche comme de ma première chemise!; **it's not worth a ~'s cuss** *inf* ça vaut des clopinettes; **~, tailor, soldier, sailor** [child's rhyme] ≃ il m'aime un peu, beaucoup, passionnément, à la folie, pas du tout. -**2.** *inf Br* [child] voyou *m*, garnement *m*; **you little ~!** petit garnement! -**3.** [act of tinkering] bricolage *m*.
◇ *vi*: **to ~ about** bricoler; **he spends hours ~ing with that car** il passe des heures à bricoler cette voiture; **someone has been ~ing with my papers** quelqu'un a touché à mes papiers; **so far you've only been ~ing with the problem** pour l'instant, tu n'as résolu le problème qu'à moitié.

tinkle ['tɪŋkl] ◇ *vi* [bell] tinter.
◇ *vt* faire tinter.
◇ *n* -**1.** [ring] tintement *m*; **I heard the ~ of a bell** j'ai entendu tinter une sonnette. -**2.** *Br* [phone call]: **to give sb a ~** *inf* donner OR passer un coup de fil à qqn. -**3.** *inf* [act of urinating]: **to go for a ~** aller faire pipi.

tinkling ['tɪŋklɪŋ] ◇ *n* tintement *m*.
◇ *adj* [bell] qui tinte; [water] qui murmure.

tinkly ['tɪŋklɪ] = **tinkling** *adj*.

tin lizzie *inf* [-'lɪzɪ] *n* vieille guimbarde *f*.

tin mine *n* mine *f* d'étain.

tinned [tɪnd] *adj Br* [sardines, fruit etc] en boîte, en conserve; **~ food** conserves *fpl*.

tinnitus [tɪ'naɪtəs] *n* *(U)* MED acouphène *m*.

tinny ['tɪnɪ] (*compar* **tinnier**, *superl* **tinniest**) *adj* -**1.** [sound] métallique, de casserole; [taste] métallique. -**2.** *inf* [poor quality] de quatre sous; **~ piano** casserole *f*.

tin opener *n* *Br* ouvre-boîte *m*, ouvre-boîtes *m inv*.

Tin Pan Alley *n*: **he works in ~** il travaille dans la musique pop.

tinplate ['tɪnpleɪt] *n* fer-blanc *m*.

tin-pot *adj Br* -**1.** [worthless - car, machine] qui ne vaut rien. -**2.** [insignificant, hopeless] médiocre; **a ~ regime/dictator** un régime/un dictateur fantoche; **a ~ frontier town** une petite ville frontalière sans importance.

tinsel ['tɪnsl] (*Br pt* & *pp* **tinselled**, *cont* **tinselling**, *Am pt* & *pp* **tinseled**, *cont* **tinseling**) ◇ *n* *(U)* -**1.** [for Christmas tree] guirlandes *fpl* de Noël; [in fine strands] cheveux *mpl* d'ange. -**2.** *fig* clinquant *m*; **Tinsel Town** *inf Hollywood*.
◇ *vt* [tree] orner OR décorer de guirlandes.

tinsmith ['tɪnsmɪθ] *n* étameur *m*, ferblantier *m*.

tin soldier *n* soldat *m* de plomb.

tint [tɪnt] ◇ *n* -**1.** [colour, shade] teinte *f*, nuance *f*. -**2.** [hair dye] shampooing *m* colorant. -**3.** [in engraving, printing] hachure *f*, hachures *fpl*.
◇ *vt* teinter; **blue-~ed walls** des murs bleutés; **~ed lenses** verres *mpl* teintés; **to ~ one's hair** se faire un shampooing colorant; **she ~s her hair** elle se teint les cheveux.

tintack ['tɪntæk] *n* clou *m* de tapissier, semence *f*.

tintinnabulation ['tɪntɪ,næbjʊ'leɪʃn] *n lit* tintamarre *m*.

Tintoretto [,tɪntə'retəʊ] *pr n* le Tintoret; **a painting by ~** un tableau du Tintoret.

tinware ['tɪnweəʳ] *n* *(U)* articles *mpl* en fer-blanc.

tin whistle *n* flûtiau *m*, pipeau *m*.

tinworks ['tɪnwɜːks] (*pl inv*) *n* ferblanterie *f*.

tiny ['taɪnɪ] (*compar* **tinier**, *superl* **tiniest**) *adj* tout petit, minuscule; **a ~ baby** un tout petit bébé; **a ~ bit** un tout petit peu; **the meat is a ~ bit overdone** la viande est un tantinet trop cuite.

tip [tɪp] (*pt* & *pp* **tipped**, *cont* **tipping**) ◇ *n* -**1.** [extremity - of ear, finger, nose] bout *m*; [- of tongue] bout *m*, pointe *f*; [- of cigarette, stem, wing] bout *m*; [- of blade, knife, fork] pointe *f*; **stand on the ~s of your toes** mettez-vous sur la pointe des pieds; **six metres from ~ to ~** six mètres d'envergure OR de long ❑ **his name is on the ~ of my tongue** j'ai son nom sur le bout de la langue; **asparagus ~s** CULIN pointes d'asperge. -**2.** [of iceberg] pointe *f*; [of island, peninsula] extrémité *f*, pointe *f*; **it's just the ~ of the iceberg** ce n'est que la partie émergée de l'iceberg. -**3.** [cap - on walking stick, umbrella] embout *m*; [- on snooker cue] procédé *m*. -**4.** *Br* [dump - for rubbish] dépotoir *m*, dépôt *m* d'ordures; [- for coal] terril *m*; *fig*: **your room is a real ~!** *inf* quel bazar, ta chambre!; **the house is a bit of a ~** *inf* la maison est un peu en désordre. -**5.** [hint - for stock market, race] tuyau *m*; [advice] conseil *m*; **to give sb a ~** [for race] donner un tuyau à qqn; [for repairs, procedure] donner un tuyau OR un conseil à qqn; **if you take my ~, you'll wait a bit longer before selling** si vous voulez un bon conseil, attendez encore un peu avant de vendre; **any ~s for the 4.30?** avez-vous un tuyau pour la course de 16 h 30?; **Orlando's my ~** je pense qu'Orlando va gagner; **"Handy Tips for Successful Gardening"** [book title] «Comment réussir votre jardin». -**6.** [money] pourboire *m*; **to give sb a ~** donner un pourboire à qqn; **how much ~ shall I leave?** combien de pourboire dois-je laisser?
◇ *vt* -**1.** [cane] mettre un embout à; [snooker cue] mettre un procédé à; **an ivory-tipped cane** une canne à pommeau d'ivoire; **arrows tipped with poison** des flèches empoisonnées. -**2.** [tilt, lean] incliner, pencher; **she tipped her head to one side** elle a penché la tête sur le côté; **to ~ one's hat to sb** saluer qqn d'un coup de chapeau; **the boxer tipped the scales at 80 kg** le boxeur pesait 80 kg; **to ~ the scales in sb's favour** *fig* faire pencher la balance en faveur de qqn; **the election tipped the balance of power** avec les élections, l'équilibre des forces politiques a été inversé. -**3.** [upset, overturn] renverser, faire chavirer; **I was tipped off my stool/into the water** on m'a fait tomber de mon tabouret/dans l'eau. -**4.** *Br* [empty, pour] verser; [unload] déverser, décharger; **she tipped the sugar into the bowl** elle a versé OR vidé le sucre dans le bol; **the lorry tipped the rubbish into the field** le camion a déchargé OR déversé les déchets dans le champ. -**5.** [winning horse] pronostiquer; **Orlando is tipped for the 2.30** OR **to win the 2.30** Orlando est donné gagnant dans la course de 14 h 30; **he tipped the winner** il a pronostiqué OR donné le cheval gagnant; **you've tipped a winner there** *fig* vous avez trouvé un bon filon; **he's tipped to be the next president** OR **as the next president** on pronostique qu'il sera le prochain président ❑ **to ~ sb the wink** *inf* avertir OR prévenir qqn. -**6.** [porter, waiter] donner un pourboire à; **she tipped him £1** elle lui a donné une livre de pourboire.
◇ *vi* -**1.** *Br* [tilt] incliner, pencher; **to ~ to the left** pencher à gauche. -**2.** *Br* [overturn] basculer, se renverser. -**3.** *Br* [rubbish]: **'no tipping'** 'défense de déposer des ordures'. -**4.** [give money]: **how much do you usually ~?** combien de pourboire laissez-vous habituellement?

◆ **tip back** ◇ *vi insep* se rabattre en arrière, s'incliner en arrière; **don't ~ back on your chair** ne te balance pas sur ta chaise.
◇ *vt sep* faire basculer (en arrière); **don't ~ your chair back too far** ne te penche pas trop en arrière sur ta chaise.

◆ **tip down** *inf Br* ◇ *vi insep*: **the rain is tipping down, it's tipping down (with rain)** il pleut des cordes.
◇ *vt sep phr*: **it's tipping it down** il pleut des cordes.

◆ **tip off** *vt sep* avertir, prévenir; **the police had been tipped off about the robbery** la police avait été avertie que le hold-up aurait lieu; **someone must have tipped them off** quelqu'un a dû les prévenir.

◆ **tip out** *vt sep Br* -**1.** [empty - liquid, small objects] vider, verser; [- rubbish, larger objects] déverser, décharger; **~ the tea out into the sink** vide OR verse le thé dans l'évier; **she tipped the coins out into my hand** elle a fait tomber les pièces dans ma main. -**2.** [overturn, toss] faire basculer; **we were tipped out of the cart into the water** on nous a fait basculer de la charrette pour nous faire tomber dans l'eau.

◆ **tip over** ◇ *vi insep* -**1.** [tilt] pencher. -**2.** [overturn - boat] chavirer, se renverser.
◇ *vt sep* faire basculer, renverser.

◆ **tip up** ◇ *vi insep* -**1.** [cinema seat] se rabattre; [bunk, plank, cart] basculer; **the table tipped up when I sat on it** la table a basculé quand je me suis assis dessus. -**2.** [bucket, cup, vase] se renverser.
◇ *vt sep* -**1.** [seat, table] faire basculer, rabattre. -**2.** [upside down - bottle, barrel] renverser.

tip cart *n* tombereau *m*.

tip-off *inf n*: **to give sb a ~** [hint] filer un tuyau à qqn; [warning] avertir OR prévenir qqn; **a ~ to the police led to his arrest** quelqu'un l'a donné à la police.

tipped [tɪpt] *adj*: **~ with felt/steel** à bout feutré/ferré ‖ [cigarettes] (à) bout filtre *(inv)*.

-tipped *in cpds* à bout...; steel/felt~ à bout ferré/feutré; a felt~ pen un crayon-feutre, un feutre.

tipper ['tɪpəʳ] *n* -**1.** = **tipper truck**. -**2.** [tipping device] benne *f* (basculante). -**3.** [customer]: he's a generous ~ il laisse toujours de bons pourboires.

tipper truck *n* camion *m* à benne (basculante).

tippet ['tɪpɪt] *n* étole *f*.

Tipp-Ex® ['tɪpeks] *n* correcteur *m* liquide, Tipp-Ex® *m*.

◆ **tippex out** *vt sep*: to ~ sthg out effacer qqch (avec du Tipp-Ex®).

tipple ['tɪpl] ◇ *vi inf* picoler.

◇ *n* -**1.** *inf* [drink]: he likes a ~ now and then il aime boire un coup de temps à autre; what's your ~ then? qu'est-ce que vous prendrez? -**2.** MIN [device] culbuteur *m*; [place - for loading] aire *f* de chargement; [- for unloading] aire *f* de déchargement.

tippler *inf* ['tɪpləʳ] *n* picoleur *m*, -euse *f*.

tipsily *inf* ['tɪpsɪlɪ] *adv*: he got ~ to his feet il s'est levé en titubant.

tipstaff ['tɪpstɑːf] *n* -**1.** *Br* JUR huissier *m*. -**2.** [staff] bâton *m* ferré (cérémonial).

tipster ['tɪpstəʳ] *n* pronostiqueur *m*, -euse *f*.

tipsy *inf* ['tɪpsɪ] (*compar* **tipsier**, *superl* **tipsiest**) *adj* pompette, rond; to get ~ se griser; white wine makes me ~ le vin blanc me monte à la tête.

tipsy cake *n Br* gâteau *m* imbibé d'alcool, ≃ baba *m* au rhum.

tiptoe ['tɪptəʊ] ◇ *n*: on ~ sur la pointe des pieds.

◇ *vi* marcher sur la pointe des pieds; to ~ in/out entrer/sortir sur la pointe des pieds; he ~d downstairs il est descendu sur la pointe des pieds OR sans faire de bruit.

tip-top *inf adj* de premier ordre, de toute première qualité; in ~ condition en excellent état.

tip-up *adj*: ~ seat [in cinema, theatre] siège *m* rabattable, strapontin *m*; [in metro] strapontin *m*; ~ truck *Br* camion *m* à benne (basculante).

tirade [taɪ'reɪd] *n* diatribe *f*; a ~ of abuse une bordée d'injures; he launched into a long ~ against bureaucrats il s'est lancé dans une longue diatribe contre les bureaucrates.

Tirana, Tiranë [tɪ'rɑːnə] *pr n* Tirana.

tire ['taɪəʳ] ◇ *vi* -**1.** [become exhausted] se fatiguer; she ~s easily elle est vite fatiguée. -**2.** [become bored] se fatiguer, se lasser; he soon ~d of her/of her company il se lassa vite d'elle/de sa compagnie; he never ~s of talking about the war il ne se lasse jamais de parler de la guerre.

◇ *vt* -**1.** [exhaust] fatiguer. -**2.** [bore] fatiguer, lasser.

◇ *n Am* = **tyre**.

◆ **tire out** *vt sep* épuiser, éreinter; the long walk had ~d us all out cette longue marche nous avait tous épuisés; I'm ~d out! je n'en peux plus!; you'll ~ yourself out moving all those boxes vous allez vous épuiser à déplacer toutes ces caisses.

tired ['taɪəd] *adj* -**1.** [exhausted] fatigué; to feel ~ se sentir fatigué; to get ~ se fatiguer; the walk made me ~ la marche m'a fatigué; I'm so ~ I could drop je tombe de sommeil; my eyes are ~ j'ai les yeux fatigués; in a ~ voice d'une voix lasse. -**2.** [fed up] fatigué, las; to be ~ of sthg/sb en avoir assez de qqch/qqn; I'm ~ of their excuses j'en ai assez de leurs excuses; I'm ~ of telling them j'en ai assez de le leur répéter; she soon got ~ of him elle se fatigua OR se lassa vite de lui; I got rather ~ of playing cards j'en ai eu assez de jouer aux cartes; the children make me ~ with their constant whining les enfants me fatiguent avec leur pleurnicheries continuelles. -**3.** [hackneyed] rebattu. -**4.** *fig* [old - skin] desséché; [- vegetable] défraîchi, flétri; [- upholstery, springs, car] fatigué.

tiredly ['taɪədlɪ] *adv* [say] d'une voix lasse; [move, walk] avec lassitude.

tiredness ['taɪədnɪs] *n* -**1.** [exhaustion] fatigue *f*; ~ began to set in la fatigue commença à se faire sentir. -**2.** [tedium] fatigue *f*, lassitude *f*.

tireless ['taɪəlɪs] *adj* [effort] infatigable, inlassable; [energy] inépuisable.

tirelessly ['taɪəlɪslɪ] *adv* infatigablement, inlassablement, sans ménager ses efforts.

tiresome ['taɪəsəm] *adj* [irritating] agaçant, ennuyeux; [boring] assommant, ennuyeux; how ~! que c'est ennuyeux!; you're being very ~! tu m'ennuies!, tu es vraiment agaçant!

tiring ['taɪərɪŋ] *adj* fatigant.

tiro ['taɪrəʊ] = **tyro**.

Tirol [tɪ'rəʊl] = **Tyrol**.

'tis [tɪz] *dial* OR *lit* = **it is**.

tisane [tiː'zæn] *n* tisane *f*.

tissue ['tɪʃuː] *n* -**1.** ANAT & BOT tissu *m*. -**2.** TEX tissu *m*, étoffe *f*; a ~ of lies *fig* un tissu de mensonges. -**3.** [paper handkerchief] mouchoir *m* en papier; [toilet paper] papier *m* hygiénique.

tissue paper *n* papier *m* de soie.

tissue type *n* groupe *m* tissulaire.

tit [tɪt] *n* -**1.** ORNITH mésange *f*. -**2.** ▽ [breast] nichon *m*. -**3.** ▽ *pej* imbécile *mf*. -**4.** *phr*: it's ~ for tat! c'est un prêté pour un rendu!

Titan ['taɪtn] *n* ASTRON Titan; MYTH Titan *m*; the ~s les Titans.

titanic [taɪ'tænɪk] *adj* -**1.** [huge] titanesque, colossal. -**2.** CHEM au titane; ~ acid acide *m* de titane.

titanium [taɪ'teɪnɪəm] *n* titane *m*.

titbit ['tɪtbɪt] *n* -**1.** CULIN bon morceau *m*, morceau *m* de choix. -**2.** [of information, of scandal] détail *m* croustillant; ~ of gossip potin *m*, racontar *m*.

titch [tɪtʃ] = **tich**.

titchy ['tɪtʃɪ] = **tichy**.

titfer *inf* ['tɪtfəʳ] *n Br dated* galurin *m*.

tithe [taɪð] ◇ *n* HIST dîme *f*; to pay ~s payer la dîme.

◇ *vt* lever la dîme sur.

tithe barn *n grange où l'on mettait les recettes de la dîme*.

titian ['tɪʃn] *adj* blond vénitien *(inv)*.

Titian ['tɪʃn] *pr n* (le) Titien.

titillate ['tɪtɪleɪt] *vt* titiller.

titillation [,tɪtɪ'leɪʃn] *n* titillation *f*.

titivate *inf* ['tɪtɪveɪt] *hum* ◇ *vi* se bichonner, se pomponner.

◇ *vt* bichonner.

titivation *inf* [,tɪtɪ'veɪʃn] *n* bichonnage *m*.

title ['taɪtl] ◇ *n* -**1.** [indicating rank, status] titre *m*; he has the ~ of Chief Executive Officer son titre officiel est directeur général; he was given a ~ for services to industry [sir] on lui a conféré un titre pour services rendus à l'industrie; [lord] on l'a anobli pour services rendus à l'industrie; the monarch bears the ~ of Defender of the Faith le monarque porte le titre de défenseur de la foi ‖ [nickname] surnom *m*; she earned the ~ "Iron Lady" on l'a surnommée «la Dame de Fer». -**2.** [of book, film, play, song] titre *m*; [of newspaper article] titre *m*, intitulé *m*. -**3.** PRINT titre *m*; they published 200 ~s last year ils ont publié 200 titres l'an dernier. -**4.** SPORT titre *m*; to win the ~ remporter le titre; he holds the world heavyweight boxing ~ il détient le titre de champion du monde de boxe des poids lourds. -**5.** JUR droit *m*, titre *m*.

◇ *comp* [music] du générique.

◇ *vt* [book, chapter, film] intituler.

◆ **titles** *npl* CIN & TV [credits] générique *m*.

titled ['taɪtld] *adj* [person, family] titré; the ~ classes les classes *fpl* titrées.

title deed *n* titre *m* de propriété.

titleholder ['taɪtl,həʊldəʳ] *n* détenteur *m*, -trice *f* du titre, tenant *m*, -e *f* du titre.

title page *n* page *f* de titre.

title role *n* rôle-titre *m*; with Vanessa Redgrave in the ~ avec Vanessa Redgrave dans le rôle-titre.

title track *n* morceau *m* qui donne son titre à l'album.

titmouse ['tɪtmaʊs] (*pl* titmice [-maɪs]) *n* ORNITH mésange *f*.

Titoism ['tiːtəʊɪzm] *n* titisme *m*.

Titoist ['tiːtəʊɪst] ◇ *adj* titiste.

◇ *n* titiste *mf*.

titrate [*Br* 'taɪtreɪt, *Am* taɪ'treɪt] *vt* CHEM titrer.

titration [taɪ'treɪʃn] *n* CHEM titrage *m*.

titter ['tɪtəʳ] ◇ *vi* rire bêtement OR sottement, glousser.

◇ *n* petit rire *m* bête OR sot, gloussement *m*.

tittivate *inf etc* ['tɪtɪveɪt] = **titivate**.

tittle ['tɪtl] *n* TYPO signe *m* diacritique, iota *m*.

tittle-tattle [-,tætl] ◇ *n (U)* potins *mpl*, cancans *mpl*.

◇ *vi* jaser, cancaner.

titty▽ ['tɪtɪ] *n* néné *m*; tough ~!▽ tant pis!

titular ['tɪtjʊləʳ], **titulary** ['tɪtjʊlərɪ] *adj* nominal.

Titus ['taɪtəs] *pr n* Tite; 'Titus Andronicus' *Shakespeare* 'Titus Andronicus'.

tiz-woz *inf* ['tɪzwɒz] *Br* = **tizzy**.

tizz *inf* [tɪz] = **tizzy**.

tizzy *inf* ['tɪzɪ] *n* panique *f*; to be in a ~ paniquer; don't get into a ~ about it ne t'affole pas pour ça.

T-joint *n* assemblage *m* en T.

T-junction *n* intersection *f* en T.

TLS *pr n abbr of* Times Literary Supplement.

TM ◇ *n* (*abbr of* transcendental meditation) MT *f*.

◇ *written abbr of* trademark.

tmesis ['tmiːsɪs] *n* tmèse *f*.

TN *written abbr of* Tennessee.

TNT (*abbr of* trinitrotoluene) *n* TNT *m*.

to [*strong form* tuː, *weak form before vowel* tʊ, *weak form before consonant* tə] ◇ *prep* **A.** -**1.** [indicating direction]: to go to school/the cinema aller à l'école/au cinéma; let's go to town allons en ville; he climbed to the top il est monté jusqu'au sommet OR jusqu'en haut; she ran to where her mother was sitting elle a couru (jusqu') à l'endroit où sa mère était assise; we've been to it before nous y sommes déjà allés; the vase fell to the ground le vase est tombé par OR à terre; I invited them to dinner je les ai invités à dîner; he returned to his work il est retourné à son OR il a repris son travail; let's go to Susan's allons chez Susan; to go to the doctor OR doctor's aller chez le médecin; he pointed to the door il a pointé son doigt vers la porte; the road to the south la route du sud; our house is a mile to the south notre maison est à un mille au sud; it's 12 miles to the nearest town [from here] nous sommes à 12 miles de la ville la plus proche; [from there] c'est à 12 miles de la ville la plus proche; what's the best way to the station? quel est le meilleur chemin pour aller à la gare?; she turned his photograph to the wall elle a retourné sa photo contre le mur; I sat with my back to her j'étais assis lui tournant le dos; tell her to her face dites-le-lui en face. -**2.** [indicating location, position] à; the street parallel to this one la rue parallèle à celle-ci; she lives next door to us elle habite à côté de chez nous; to one side d'un côté; to the left/right à gauche/droite. -**3.** [with geographical names]: to Madrid à Madrid; to Le Havre au Havre; to France en France; to Argentina en Argentine; to Japan au Japon; to the United States aux États-Unis; I'm off to Paris je pars à OR pour Paris; the road to Chicago la route de Chicago; on the way to Milan en allant à Milan, sur la route de Milan; planes to and from Europe les vols à destination et en provenance de l'Europe. -**4.** [indicating age, amount or level reached] jusqu'à; the snow came (up) to her knees la neige lui arrivait aux genoux; unemployment is up to nearly 9% le (taux de) chômage atteint presque les 9 %; they cut expenses down to a minimum ils ont réduit les frais au minimum; she can count (up) to one hundred elle sait compter jusqu'à cent; it's accurate to the millimetre c'est exact au millimètre près; it weighs 8 to 9 pounds ça pèse entre 8 et 9 livres; moderate to cool temperatures des températures douces ou fraîches; to live to a great age vivre jusqu'à un âge avancé. -**5.** [so as to make contact with] à, contre; she pinned the brooch to her dress elle a épinglé la broche sur sa robe; they sat in bumper-to-bumper traffic ils étaient coincés pare-chocs contre pare-chocs; they danced cheek to cheek ils dansaient joue contre joue; he clutched the baby to his chest il a serré l'enfant contre lui.

B. -**1.** [before the specified hour or date]: it's ten minutes to three il est trois heures moins dix; we left at a quarter to six nous sommes partis à six heures moins le quart; it's twenty to il est moins vingt; how long is it to dinner? on dîne dans combien de temps?; there's only two weeks to Christmas il ne reste que deux semaines avant Noël. -**2.** [up to and including] (jusqu') à ; from Tuesday night to Thursday morning du mardi soir (jusqu') au jeudi matin; from March to June de mars (jusqu') à juin; a nine-to-five job des horaires de fonctionnaire; it was three years ago to the day since I saw her last il y a trois ans jour pour jour que je l'ai vue pour la dernière fois; to this day jusqu'à ce jour, jusqu'à aujourd'hui; he was brave (up) to the last il a été courageux jusqu'au bout OR jusqu'à la fin; from day to day de jour en jour; I read it from beginning to end je l'ai lu du début (jusqu') à la fin; from bad to worse de mal en pis; I do everything from scrubbing the floor to keeping the books je fais absolument tout, depuis le ménage jusqu'à la comptabilité.

C. -**1.** [before infinitive]: to talk parler; to open ouvrir; to answer répondre. -**2.** [after verb]: she lived to be 100 elle a vécu jusqu'à 100 ans; we are to complete the work by Monday nous devons finir le travail pour lundi; she went on to become a brilliant guitarist elle est ensuite devenue une excellente guitariste; I finally accepted (only) to find that they had changed their mind lorsque je me suis décidé à accepter, ils avaient changé d'avis; she turned round to find him standing right in front of her lorsqu'elle s'est retournée, elle s'est retrouvée nez à nez avec lui; he dared to speak out against injustice il a osé s'élever contre l'injustice; you can leave if you want to vous pouvez partir si vous voulez; why? — because I told you to pourquoi? — parce que je t'ai dit de le faire; would you like to come? — we'd love to voulez-vous venir? — avec plaisir OR oh, oui! -**3.** [after noun]: I have a lot to do j'ai beaucoup à faire; that's no reason to leave ce n'est pas une raison pour partir; I haven't got money to burn *inf* je n'ai pas d'argent à jeter par les fenêtres; the first to complain le premier à se plaindre; the house to be sold la maison à vendre; that's the way to do it voilà comment il faut faire. -**4.** [after adjective]: I'm happy/sad to see her go je suis content/triste de la voir partir; pleased to meet you enchanté (de faire votre connaissance); difficult/easy to do difficile/facile à faire; it was strange to see her again c'était bizarre de la revoir; she's too proud to apologize elle est trop fière pour s'excuser; he's old enough to understand il est assez grand pour comprendre. -**5.** [after 'how', 'which', 'where' etc]: do you know where to go? savez-vous où aller?; he told me how to get there il m'a dit comment y aller; can you tell me when to get off? pourriez-vous me dire quand je dois descendre?; she can't decide whether to go or not elle n'arrive pas à décider si elle va y aller ou non. -**6.** [indicating purpose] pour; I did it to annoy her je l'ai fait exprès pour l'énerver; to answer that question, we must... pour répondre à cette question, il nous faut... -**7.** [introducing statement] pour; to be honest/frank pour être honnête/franc; to put it another way en d'autres termes. -**8.** [in exclamations]: oh, to be in England! ah, si je pouvais être en Angleterre!; and to think I nearly married him! quand je pense que j'ai failli l'épouser! -**9.** [in headlines]: unions to strike les syndicats s'apprêtent à déclencher la grève; Russia to negotiate with Baltic States l'URSS va négocier avec les pays Baltes.

D. -**1.** [indicating intended recipient, owner] à; I showed the picture to her je lui ai montré la photo; I showed it to her je le lui ai montré; show it to her montrez-le-lui; the person I spoke to la personne à qui j'ai parlé; that book belongs to her ce livre lui appartient; be kind to him/to animals soyez gentil avec lui/bon envers les animaux; what's it to him? qu'est-ce que cela peut lui faire?; it doesn't matter to her ça lui est égal; did you have a room to yourself? avais-tu une chambre à toi OR pour toi tout seul?; to keep sthg to o.s. garder qqch pour soi; I said to myself je me suis dit; he is known to the police il est connu de la police. -**2.** [in the opinion of] pour; $2 is a lot of money to some people il y a des gens pour qui 2 dollars représentent beaucoup d'argent; it sounds suspicious to me cela me semble bizarre; it didn't make sense to him ça n'avait aucun sens pour lui. -**3.** [indicating intention]: with a view to clarifying matters dans l'intention d'éclaircir la situation; it's all to no purpose tout cela ne sert à rien OR est en vain. -**4.** [indicating resulting state]: the light changed to red le feu est passé au rouge; the noise drove him to distraction le bruit le rendait fou; the rain turned to snow la pluie avait fait place à la neige; her admiration turned to disgust son admiration s'est transformée en dégoût; (much) to my relief/surprise/delight à mon grand soulagement/mon grand étonnement/ma grande joie; (much) to my horror, I found the money was missing c'est avec horreur que je me suis rendu compte que l'argent avait disparu; the meat was done to perfection la viande était cuite à la perfection; smashed to pieces brisé en mille morceaux; he was beaten to death il a été battu à mort; they starved to death ils sont morts de faim; she rose rapidly to power elle est arrivée au pouvoir très rapidement; she sang the baby to sleep elle a chanté jusqu'à ce que le bébé s'endorme; the court sentenced him to death le juge l'a condamné à mort. -**5.** [as regards]: the answer to your question la réponse à votre question; a hazard to your health un danger pour votre santé; what's your reaction to all this? comment réagissez-vous à tout ça?; no one was sympathetic to his ideas ses idées ne plaisaient à personne; what would you say to a game of bridge? que diriez-vous d'un bridge?, si on faisait un bridge?; that's all there is to it [it's simple] ce n'est pas plus difficile que ça; [it's above board] c'est aussi simple que ça; there's nothing to it il n'y a rien de plus simple; 'to translating annual report: $300' COMM [on bill] 'traduction du rapport annuel: 300 dollars'; 'to services rendered' 'pour services rendus'. -**6.** [indicating composition or proportion]: there are 16 ounces to a pound il y a 16 onces dans une livre; there are 6 francs to the dollar un dollar vaut 6 francs; there are 25 chocolates to a box il y a 25 chocolats dans chaque OR par boîte; one cup of sugar to every three cups of fruit une tasse de sucre pour trois tasses de fruits; Milan beat Madrid by 4 (points) to 3 Milan a battu Madrid 4 (points) à 3; I'll bet 100 to 1 je parierais 100 contre 1; the odds are 1000 to 1 against it happening again il y a 1 chance sur 1000 que cela se produise à nouveau; the vote was 6 to 3 il y avait 6 voix contre 3. -**7.** [per]: how many miles do you get to the gallon? vous faites combien de litres au cent? -**8.** [indicating comparison]: inferior to inférieur à; they compare her to Callas on la compare à (la) Callas; that's nothing compared to what I've seen ce n'est rien à côté de ce que j'ai vu; inflation is nothing (compared) to last year l'inflation n'est rien à côté de OR en comparaison de l'année dernière; as a cook she's second to none comme cuisinière on ne fait pas mieux; to prefer sthg to sthg préférer qqch à qqch. -**9.** [of] de; the key to this door la clé de cette porte; he's secretary to the director/to the committee c'est le secrétaire du directeur/du comité; she's assistant to the president c'est l'adjointe du président; the French ambassador to Algeria l'ambassadeur français en Algérie; ambassador to the King of Thailand ambassadeur auprès du roi de Thaïlande; she's interpreter to the president c'est l'interprète du président; Susan, sister to Mary Suzanne, sœur de Marie; he's been like a father to me il est comme un père pour moi. -**10.** [in accordance with]: to his way of thinking, to his mind à son avis; to hear him talk, you'd think he was an expert à l'entendre parler, on croirait que c'est un expert; to my knowledge, she never met him elle ne l'a jamais rencontré (pour) autant que je sache; it's to your advantage to do it c'est (dans) ton intérêt de le faire; the climate is not to my liking le climat ne me plaît pas; add salt to taste salez selon votre goût OR à volonté; she made out a cheque to the amount of £15 elle a fait un chèque de 15 livres. -**11.** [indicating accompaniment, simultaneity]: we danced to live music nous avons dansé sur la musique d'un orchestre; in time to the music en mesure avec la musique. -**12.** [in honour of] à; let's drink to his health buvons à sa santé; (here's) to your health! à la vôtre!; (here's) to the bride! à la mariée!; to my family [in dedication] à ma famille; his book is dedicated to his mother son livre est dédié à sa mère; a monument to the war dead un monument aux morts.

E. -**1.** [indicating addition]: add flour to the list ajoutez de la farine sur la liste; add 3 to 6 additionnez 3 et 6, ajoutez 3 à 6; in addition to Charles, there were three women en plus de Charles, il y avait trois femmes. -**2.** MATH: to the power... à la puissance...; 2 to the 3rd power, 2 to the 3rd 2 (à la) puissance 3.

◇ *adv* -**1.** [closed] fermé; the wind blew the door to un coup de vent a fermé la porte. -**2.** [back to consciousness]: to come to revenir à soi, reprendre connaissance. -**3.** NAUT: to bring a ship to mettre un bateau en panne.

toad [təʊd] *n* -**1.** ZOOL crapaud *m*. -**2.** *inf fig* [person] rat *m*.

toad-in-the-hole *n Br* CULIN *plat composé de saucisses cuites au four dans une sorte de pâte à crêpes.*

toadstool ['təʊdstuːl] *n* champignon *m* (vénéneux).

toady ['təʊdɪ] (*pl* toadies, *pt* & *pp* toadied) *pej*
◇ *n* flatteur *m*, -euse *f*.
◇ *vi* être flatteur; to ~ to sb passer de la pommade à qqn.

toadying ['təʊdɪɪŋ] *n pej* flagornerie *f*.

to and fro *adv phr*: to go ~ aller et venir, se promener de long en large; to swing ~ se balancer d'avant en arrière.
◆ **to-and-fro** *adj* : a to-and-fro movement un mouvement de va-et-vient.

toast [təʊst] ◇ *n* -**1.** [bread] pain *m* grillé; a piece OR slice of ~ une tartine grillée, un toast; three slices OR rounds of ~ trois tartines grillées; don't burn the ~ ne brûle pas le pain; cheese/sardines on ~ fromage fondu/sardines sur du pain grillé. -**2.** [drink] toast *m*; to drink a ~ to sb porter un toast à qqn, boire à la santé de qqn; we drank a ~ to their success/future happiness on a bu à leur succès/bonheur futur; to propose a ~ to sb porter un toast à qqn; she was the ~ of the town elle était la coqueluche de la ville.
◇ *vt* -**1.** [grill] griller; ~ed cheese fromage *m* fondu; ~ed cheese sandwich ≃ croque-monsieur *m inv*; he was ~ing himself/his toes by the fire *fig* il se chauffait/il se rôtissait les orteils devant la cheminée. -**2.** [drink to - person] porter un toast à, boire à la santé de; [- success, win] arroser; to ~ sb's success arroser la réussite de qqn; to ~ sb's health boire à la santé de qqn; they ~ed her victory in champagne ils ont arrosé sa victoire au champagne.

toaster ['təʊstəʳ] *n* grille-pain *m inv* (électrique), toaster *m*.

toastie *inf* ['təʊstɪ] *n* sandwich *m* grillé.

toasting fork ['təʊstɪŋ] *n* fourchette *f* à griller le pain.

toastmaster ['təʊst,mɑːstə^r] *n* animateur *m* *(qui annonce les toasts ou les discours lors d'une réception)*.

toast rack *n* porte-toasts *m inv*.

toasty *inf* ['təʊstɪ] ◇ *Am adj* [warm]: it's ~ in here il fait bon ici.
◇ *n* [sandwich] = **toastie**.

tobacco [tə'bækəʊ] (*pl* tobaccos) ◇ *n* -1. tabac *m*; chewing ~ tabac *m* à chiquer. -2. BOT: ~ (plant) (pied *m* de) tabac *m*.
◇ *comp* [leaf, plantation, smoke] de tabac; [industry] du tabac.

tobacco brown ◇ *adj* tabac *(inv)*.
◇ *n* couleur *f* tabac.

tobacconist [tə'bækənɪst] *n* marchand *m*, -e *f* de tabac, buraliste *mf*; ~'s (shop) (bureau *m* de) tabac *m*.

tobacco pouch *n* blague *f* à tabac.

-to-be *in cpds*: mother~ future mère *f*; father~ futur père *m*.

toboggan [tə'bɒgən] ◇ *n* luge *f*.
◇ *comp* [race] de luge.
◇ *vi* -1. to ~ OR go ~ing faire de la luge; they ~ed down the slope ils ont descendu la pente en luge. -2. *Am* [prices, sales] dégringoler.

toboggan run *n* piste *f* de luge.

Tobruk [tə'brʊk] *pr n* Tobrouk.

toby jug ['təʊbɪ] *n tasse ou cruche en forme d'homme assis portant un tricorne et fumant la pipe*.

toccata [tə'kɑːtə] *n* toccata *f*.

tocsin ['tɒksɪn] *n* tocsin *m*.

tod *inf* [tɒd] *n Br phr*: to be on one's ~ être tout seul.

today [tə'deɪ] ◇ *adv* aujourd'hui; a week ~ [past] il y a huit jours aujourd'hui; [future] dans huit jours aujourd'hui; they arrived a week ago ~ ils sont arrivés il y a huit jours; they've been here a week ~ ils sont là depuis exactement une semaine; he died 5 years ago ~ cela fait 5 ans aujourd'hui qu'il est mort; she's more popular ~ than she was 10 years ago elle est plus populaire aujourd'hui qu'il y a 10 ans ❑ here ~ and gone tomorrow ça va ça vient.
◇ *n* aujourd'hui *m*; what's ~'s date? quelle est la date d'aujourd'hui?; what day is it ~? quel jour est-on (aujourd'hui)?; ~ is March 17th aujourd'hui, on est le 17 mars; it's Monday ~ on est lundi aujourd'hui; a week from ~ dans une semaine aujourd'hui; three weeks from ~ dans trois semaines; as from ~ à partir d'aujourd'hui; have you seen ~'s paper? as-tu vu le journal d'aujourd'hui?; the youth of ~, ~'s youth la jeunesse d'aujourd'hui ❑ ~'s the day! c'est le grand jour!; 'Today' PRESS *quotidien britannique populaire de tendance conservatrice*.

toddle ['tɒdl] ◇ *vi* -1. [start to walk - child] faire ses premiers pas; [walk unsteadily] marcher d'un pas chancelant; he's just started to ~ il vient de commencer à marcher; he managed to ~ across the room il a réussi à faire quelques pas dans la pièce. -2. *inf* [go] aller; [stroll] se balader; [go away] s'en aller, partir; she ~d along after him elle trottinait derrière lui; could you just ~ down to the shops for me? pourrais-tu faire une ou deux courses pour moi?
◇ *n inf*: I'm just going for a little ~ je vais faire un petit tour OR une petite balade.
◆ **toddle off** *inf vi insep* [go] aller; [go away] s'en aller, partir bien gentiment; she ~d off somewhere on her own elle est partie faire un tour toute seule; he ~d off to the pub il est allé au bistrot.

toddler ['tɒdlə^r] *n* tout petit *m*, toute petite *f* *(qui fait ses premiers pas)*; he's just a ~ il sait à peine marcher; their children are still ~s leurs enfants sont tout juste en âge de marcher.

toddy ['tɒdɪ] (*pl* toddies) *n* -1. [drink] ≃ grog *m*. -2. [sap] sève *f* de palmier *(utilisée comme boisson)*.

to-do *inf n* -1. [fuss] remue-ménage *m inv*, tohu-bohu *m inv*; she made a great ~ about it elle en a fait tout un plat; there was a great ~ over her wedding son mariage a fait grand bruit; what a ~! quelle affaire!, quelle histoire! -2. *Am* [party] bringue *f*.

toe [təʊ] ◇ *n* -1. ANAT orteil *m*, doigt *m* de pied; big/little ~ gros/petit orteil; to stand on one's ~s se dresser sur la pointe des pieds ❑ to step OR to tread on sb's ~s *literal* & *fig* marcher sur les pieds de qqn; to keep sb on their ~s: she kept us on our ~s elle ne nous laissait aucun répit. -2. [of sock, shoe] bout *m*; there's a hole in the ~ le bout est troué; the ~ of Italy *fig* le bout de l'Italie.
◇ *vt* -1. [ball] toucher du bout du pied. -2. *phr*: to ~ the line OR *Am* mark se mettre au pas, obtempérer; to ~ the party line POL s'aligner sur le OR suivre la ligne du parti.

toe cap *n* bout *m* renforcé *(de soulier)*; steel ~ bout *m* ferré.

toe clip *n* cale-pied *m*.

-toed [təʊd] *in cpds*: six~ à six orteils.

toehold ['təʊhəʊld] *n* prise *f* de pied; to get OR to gain a ~ [climber] trouver une prise (pour le pied); *fig* prendre pied, s'implanter; the company now has a ~ in the foreign market *fig* l'entreprise a désormais un pied sur le marché étranger.

toeless ['təʊlɪs] *adj* -1. ANAT sans orteil OR orteils. -2. [sock, shoe] (à bout) ouvert.

toenail ['təʊneɪl] *n* ongle *m* de pied.

toe-piece *n* [of ski] butée *f*.

toerag^▽ ['təʊræg] *n Br pej* ordure *f*.

toe-strap *n* lanière *f* de gros orteil.

toff *inf* [tɒf] *n Br* aristo *m*.

toffee ['tɒfɪ] *n Br* caramel *m* (au beurre); he can't dance for ~ *inf* il danse comme un pied; I can't speak Italian for ~ *inf* je suis incapable de parler italien.

toffee apple *n* pomme *f* d'amour.

toffee-nosed *inf adj Br* bêcheur, snob.

tofu ['təʊfuː] *n* tofu *m inv*.

tog [tɒg] (*pt* & *pp* togged, *cont* togging) *n* [measurement of warmth] pouvoir *m* adiathermique, PA *m*; ~ number indice *m* de PA.
◆ **togs** *inf npl* [clothes] fringues *fpl*; SPORT affaires *fpl*.
◆ **tog out** *inf*, **tog up** *inf vt sep* nipper, fringuer; she was all togged up in her best clothes elle était super sapée; he hates getting togged up for special occasions il a horreur de se saper pour les grandes occasions; they were all togged out for the match ils s'étaient tous mis en tenue pour le match.

toga ['təʊgə] *n* toge *f*.

together [tə'geðə^r] ◇ *adv* -1. [with each other] ensemble; we went shopping ~ nous sommes allés faire des courses ensemble; are you ~? êtes-vous ensemble?; they get on well ~ ils s'entendent bien; we're all in this ~! on est tous logés à la même enseigne!; those colours go well ~ ces couleurs vont bien ensemble; they were ~ for six years before getting married ils ont été ensemble six ans avant de se marier. -2. [jointly]: she's cleverer than both of them put ~ elle est plus intelligente qu'eux deux réunis; even taken ~, their efforts don't amount to much même si on les considère dans leur ensemble, leurs efforts ne représentent pas grand-chose; ~ we can change things ensemble, nous pouvons changer les choses. -3. [indicating proximity]: tie the two ribbons ~ attachez les deux rubans l'un à l'autre; she tried to bring the two sides ~ elle a essayé de rapprocher les deux camps; we were crowded ~ into the room on nous a tous entassés dans la pièce; they were bound ~ by their beliefs leurs convictions les unissaient. -4. [at the same time] à la fois, en même temps, ensemble; all ~ now! [pull] tous ensemble!, ho hisse!; [sing, recite] tous ensemble OR en chœur! -5. [consecutively]: for 12 hours ~ pendant 12 heures d'affilée OR de suite.
◇ *adj inf* [person] équilibré, bien dans sa peau.
◆ **together with** *conj phr* ainsi que, en même temps que; pick up a leaflet ~ with an entry form prenez un imprimé et une feuille d'inscription.

togetherness [tə'geðənɪs] *n* [unity] unité *f*; [solidarity] solidarité *f*; [comradeship] camaraderie *f*.

toggle ['tɒgl] ◇ *n* -1. [peg] cheville *f*. -2. SEW bouton *m* de duffle-coat. -3. NAUT cabillot *m*.
◇ *vt* attacher avec un cabillot.
◇ *vi* COMPUT basculer; to ~ between alterner entre.

toggle joint *n* TECH genouillère *f*.

toggle switch *n* ELEC & COMPUT bouton *m* (à levier), basculeur *m*.

Togo ['təʊgəʊ] *pr n* Togo *m*; in ~ au Togo.

Togolese [,təʊgə'liːz] ◇ *n* Togolais *m*, -e *f*.
◇ *adj* togolais.

toil [tɔɪl] ◇ *vi* -1. [labour] travailler dur, peiner; he ~ed over his essay for weeks il a peiné OR il a sué sur sa dissertation pendant des semaines. -2. [as verb of movement] avancer péniblement; they ~ed up the hill on their bikes/on foot ils montèrent péniblement la colline à vélo/à pied; they ~ed on over the rough ground ils poursuivirent péniblement leur chemin sur le terrain accidenté.
◇ *n* labeur *m lit*, travail *m* (pénible).
◆ **toil away** *vi insep* travailler dur, peiner.

toile [twɑːl] *n* TEX toile *f*.

toilet ['tɔɪlɪt] *n* -1. [lavatory] toilettes *fpl*; to go to the ~ aller aux toilettes OR aux cabinets; the ~ won't flush la chasse d'eau ne marche pas; he threw it down the ~ il l'a jeté dans les toilettes; 'Public Toilets' 'Toilettes', 'W-C Publics'. -2. *dated* & *fml* [dressing, washing] toilette *f*.

toilet bag *n* trousse *f* de toilette.

toilet paper *n* papier *m* hygiénique.

toiletries ['tɔɪlɪtrɪz] *npl* articles *mpl* de toilette.

toilet roll *n* rouleau *m* de papier hygiénique.

toilet seat *n* siège *m* des cabinets OR W-C OR toilettes.

toilet soap *n* savon *m* de toilette.

toilette [twɑː'let] *n* toilette *f (action de se laver)*.

toilet tissue = **toilet paper**.

toilet-train *vt*: to ~ a child apprendre à un enfant à être propre; is he ~ed? est-ce qu'il est propre?

toilet training *n* apprentissage *m* de la propreté *(pour un enfant)*.

toilet water *n* eau *f* de toilette.

toils [tɔɪlz] *npl lit* rets *mpl lit*, filets *mpl*.

toilsome ['tɔɪlsəm] *adj* pénible, laborieux.

to-ing and fro-ing *inf* [,tuːɪŋən'frəʊɪŋ] *n (U)* allées et venues *fpl*.

toke *inf* [təʊk] ◇ *n Am* [of cigarette] taffe *f*.
◇ *vi* prendre une taffe.

token ['təʊkn] ◇ *n* -1. [of affection, appreciation, esteem etc] marque *f*, témoignage *m*; as a ~ of OR in ~ of my gratitude en témoignage OR en gage de ma reconnaissance; a love ~ un gage d'amour; as a ~ of our love en gage de notre amour. -2. [indication] signe *m*. -3. [souvenir, gift] souvenir *m*; we'd like you to accept this little ~ to remind you of your visit nous aimerions que vous acceptiez ce petit cadeau en souvenir de votre visite. -4. [for machine] jeton *m*. -5. [voucher] bon *m*; book ~ bon *m* d'achat de livres; gift ~ bon d'achat; record ~ chèque-disque *m*. -6. LING occurrence *f*.
◇ *adj* [gesture, effort] symbolique, pour la forme; [increase, protest] symbolique, de pure forme; they only pay a ~ rent ils ne paient qu'un loyer symbolique; to put up a ~ resistance opposer une résistance symbolique.
◆ **by the same token** *adv phr* de même, pareillement.

tokenism ['təʊkənɪzm] *n* politique *f* minimaliste OR de pure forme.

token money *n* monnaie *f* fiduciaire.

token payment *n* paiement *m* symbolique (d'intérêts).

token strike *n* grève *f* symbolique OR d'avertissement.

token vote *n* vote *m* symbolique.

Tokyo ['təʊkjəʊ] *pr n* Tokyo.

told [təʊld] *pt* & *pp* → **tell**.

Toledo [tɒ'leɪdəʊ] *pr n* Tolède.

tolerable ['tɒlərəbl] *adj* -**1.** [pain, situation, behaviour] tolérable; [standard] admissible. -**2.** [not too bad] pas trop mal, passable.

tolerably ['tɒlərəblɪ] *adv* passablement; she performed ~ (well) elle n'a pas trop mal joué; I'm ~ well je me porte assez bien; they were ~ pleased with the results ils étaient assez contents des résultats.

tolerance ['tɒlərəns] *n* tolérance *f*; they showed great ~ ils ont fait preuve de beaucoup de tolérance, ils ont été très tolérants; religious/racial ~ tolérance religieuse/raciale; to develop (a) ~ to a drug développer une accoutumance à un médicament; they have little ~ to cold ils ont peu de résistance au froid; a ~ of a thousandth of a millimetre TECH une tolérance d'un millième de millimètre.

tolerant ['tɒlərənt] *adj* tolérant; he's not very ~ of others il n'est pas très tolérant envers les autres; she's not very ~ of criticism elle ne supporte pas bien les critiques; ~ to heat/cold PHYS résistant à la chaleur/au froid.

tolerantly ['tɒlərəntlɪ] *adv* avec tolérance.

tolerate ['tɒləreɪt] *vt* tolérer.

toleration [,tɒlə'reɪʃn] *n* tolérance *f*.

toll [təʊl] ◇ *n* -**1.** [on bridge, road] péage *m*. -**2.** [of victims] nombre *m* de victimes; [of casualties] nombre *m* de blessés; [of deaths] nombre *m* de morts; the death ~ has risen on déplore de nouvelles victimes; the epidemic took a heavy ~ of OR among the population l'épidémie a fait beaucoup de morts OR de victimes parmi la population; the years have taken their ~ les années ont laissé leurs traces; her illness took its ~ on her family sa maladie a ébranlé sa famille. -**3.** [of bell] sonnerie *f*.
◇ *vt* [bell] sonner; to ~ sb's death sonner le glas pour qqn.
◇ *vi* [bell] sonner.

tollbooth ['təʊlbu:θ] *n* (poste *m* de) péage *m*.

toll bridge *n* pont *m* à péage.

toll call *n Am* & *NZ* TELEC appel *m* interurbain.

toll charge *n* -**1.** [for bridge] (coût *m* du) péage *m*. -**2.** *NZ* TELEC tarif *m* interurbain.

toll-free *Am* ◇ *adj*: ~ number numéro *m* vert.
◇ *adv*: to call ~ appeler un numéro vert.

tollgate ['təʊlgeɪt] *n* (barrière *f* de) péage *m*.

tollhouse ['təʊlhaʊs, *pl* -haʊzɪz] *n* (bureau *m* de) péage *m*.

tollroad ['təʊlrəʊd] *n* route *f* à péage.

Tolstoy ['tɒlstɔɪ] *pr n*: Leon ~ Léon Tolstoï.

tom [tɒm] *n* [cat] matou *m*.

Tom [tɒm] *pr n* [dimin of Thomas]: any OR every ~, Dick or Harry n'importe qui, le premier venu; 'The Adventures of ~ Sawyer' *Twain* 'les Aventures de Tom Sawyer'; '~ Thumb' 'Tom Pouce'.

tomahawk ['tɒməhɔ:k] *n* tomahawk *m*.

tomato [*Br* tə'mɑ:təʊ, *Am* tə'meɪtəʊ] (*pl* tomatoes) ◇ *n* tomate *f*.
◇ *comp* [juice, salad, soup] de tomates; ~ ketchup ketchup *m*; ~ plant (pied *m* de) tomate *f*; ~ sauce sauce *f* tomate.

tomb [tu:m] *n* tombeau *m*, tombe *f*.

tombola [tɒm'bəʊlə] *n Br* tombola *f*.

tomboy ['tɒmbɔɪ] *n* garçon *m* manqué; she looks a bit of a ~ elle fait un peu garçon manqué.

tomboyish ['tɒmbɔɪɪʃ] *adj* de garçon manqué, garçonnier.

tombstone ['tu:mstəʊn] *n* pierre *f* tombale.

tomcat ['tɒmkæt] *n* chat *m*, matou *m*.

Tom Collins [-'kɒlɪns] *n boisson glacée au gin et au jus de citron*.

tome [təʊm] *n* gros volume *m*.

tomfool *inf* [,tɒm'fu:l] ◇ *n* idiot *m*, -e *f*, imbécile *mf*.
◇ *adj* idiot, imbécile.

tomfoolery *inf* [tɒm'fu:lərɪ] *n (U)* [foolish words] absurdités *fpl*, idioties *fpl*, bêtises *fpl*; [foolish behaviour] bêtises *fpl*.

Tommy ['tɒmɪ] (*pl* Tommies) *pr n dated surnom donné autrefois aux soldats britanniques*.

tommy gun *inf n* mitraillette *f*.

tommyrot *inf* ['tɒmɪrɒt] *n (U) Br dated* balivernes *fpl*, bêtises *fpl*; ~! mon œil!

tomorrow [tə'mɒrəʊ] ◇ *adv* demain; ~ morning/evening demain matin/soir; see you ~! à demain!; a week ~ [past] cela fera huit jours demain; [future] dans une semaine demain; they arrived/they will have been here a week ~ ça fera huit jours demain qu'ils sont arrivés/qu'ils sont là.
◇ *n* -**1.** *literal* demain *m*; what's ~'s date? le combien serons-nous demain?; what day is it OR will it be ~? quel jour serons-nous demain?; ~ is OR will be March 17th demain, on sera le 17 mars; ~ is Monday demain, c'est lundi; a week from ~ dans une semaine demain; three weeks from ~ dans trois semaines demain; the day after ~ après-demain, dans deux jours; ~ may never come qui sait où nous serons demain; ~ never comes demain n'arrive jamais; ~ is another day demain il fera jour ❑ never put off till ~ what you can do today *prov* il ne faut jamais remettre au lendemain ce que l'on peut faire le jour même *prov*. -**2.** *fig* [future] demain *m*, lendemain *m*; we look forward to a bright ~ nous espérons des lendemains qui chantent; ~'s world le monde de demain ❑ he spends money like there was no ~ *inf* il dépense (son argent) comme si demain n'existait pas.

tomtit ['tɒmtɪt] *n* mésange *f*.

tom-tom *n* tam-tam *m*.

ton [tʌn] *n* -**1.** [weight] tonne *f*; a 35-~ lorry un 35 tonnes ‖ *fig*: it's a ~ weight! ça pèse une tonne!; this suitcase weighs a ~! cette valise pèse une tonne! ❑ (register) ~ NAUT tonneau *m*; she came down on me like a ~ of bricks! elle m'est tombée dessus! -**2.** *inf* [speed]: to do a ~ rouler à plus de 150.
◆ **tons** *inf npl* [lots]: ~s of money des tas OR des tonnes d'argent; ~s of people des tas de gens; ~s better beaucoup mieux.

tonal ['təʊnl] *adj* tonal.

tonality [tə'nælətɪ] (*pl* tonalities) *n* tonalité *f* MUS.

tone [təʊn] ◇ *n* -**1.** [of voice] ton *m* (de la voix); don't (you) speak to me in that ~ (of voice)! ne me parle pas sur ce ton!; I don't like your ~! je n'aime pas votre ton!; I didn't much like the ~ of her remarks je n'ai pas beaucoup aimé le ton de ses remarques; to raise/to lower the ~ of one's voice hausser/baisser le ton; he spoke to me in soft ~s OR in a soft ~ il m'a parlé d'une voix douce. -**2.** [sound - of voice, musical instrument] sonorité *f*; [of singer] timbre *m* (de la voix); the rich bass ~s of his voice la richesse de sa voix dans les tons graves; the stereo has an excellent ~ la stéréo a une excellente sonorité; I thought I recognized those dulcet ~s *hum* j'ai cru reconnaître cette douce voix. -**3.** MUS ton *m*. -**4.** LING ton *m*; rising/falling ~ ton ascendant/descendant. -**5.** TELEC tonalité *f*; please speak after the ~ veuillez parler après le signal sonore. -**6.** [control - of amplifier, radio] tonalité *f*. -**7.** [shade] ton *m*; in matching ~s of red and gold dans des tons rouge et or assortis; soft blue ~s des tons bleu pastel; a two-~ colour scheme une palette de couleurs à deux tons. -**8.** [style, atmosphere - of poem, article] ton *m*; to set the ~ donner le ton. -**9.** [classiness] chic *m*, classe *f*; to give/to lend ~ to sthg donner de la classe/apporter un plus à qqch; it lowers/raises the ~ of the neighbourhood cela rabaisse/rehausse le standing du quartier. -**10.** FIN [of market] tenue *f*. -**11.** PHYSIOL [of muscle, nerves] tonus *m*. -**12.** *Am* [single musical sound] note *f*.
◇ *vi* [colour] s'harmoniser; the wallpaper doesn't ~ well with the carpet le papier peint n'est pas bien assorti à la moquette.
◇ *vt* = **tone up**.
◆ **tone down** *vt sep* -**1.** [colour, contrast] adoucir. -**2.** [sound, voice] atténuer, baisser. -**3.** [moderate - language, statement, views] tempérer, modérer; [- effect] adoucir, atténuer; his article had to be ~d down for publication son article a dû être édulcoré avant d'être publié.
◆ **tone in** *vi insep* s'harmoniser, s'assortir; the curtains ~ in well with the carpet les rideaux sont bien dans le ton du tapis.
◆ **tone up** *vt sep* [body, muscles] tonifier.

tone arm *n* bras *m* de lecture.

tone colour *n* timbre *m*.

tone control *n* bouton *m* de tonalité.

tone-deaf *adj*: to be ~ ne pas avoir d'oreille.

tone deafness *n* manque *m* d'oreille.

tone language *n* LING langue *f* à tons.

toneless ['təʊnlɪs] *adj* [voice] blanc, sans timbre; [colour] terne.

tonelessly ['təʊnlɪslɪ] *adv* [say, speak] d'une voix blanche.

toneme ['təʊni:m] *n* tonème *m*.

tone poem *n* poème *m* symphonique.

toner ['təʊnə[r]] *n* [for hair] colorant *m*; [for skin] lotion *f* tonique; PHOT toner *m*, encre *f*.

tonetic [təʊ'netɪk] *adj* tonétique.

Tonga ['tɒŋgə] *pr n* Tonga; in ~ à Tonga.

Tongan ['tɒŋgən] ◇ *n* -**1.** [person] Tongan *m*, -e *f*. -**2.** LING tongan *m*.
◇ *adj* tongan.

tongs [tɒŋz] *npl*: (pair of) ~ pinces *fpl*; fire ~ pincettes *fpl*; (sugar) ~ pince *f* (à sucre).

tongue [tʌŋ] ◇ *n* -**1.** ANAT langue *f*; to put OR to stick one's ~ out (at sb) tirer la langue (à qqn); his ~ was practically hanging out *fig* [very eager] il en salivait littéralement; [very thirsty] il était pratiquement mort de soif. -**2.** *fig* [for speech] langue *f*; to lose/to find one's ~ perdre/retrouver sa langue; hold your ~! tenez votre langue!, taisez-vous!; try to keep a civil ~ in your head! essayez de rester courtois OR correct!; I can't get my ~ round his name *Br* je n'arrive pas à prononcer correctement son nom; to have a sharp ~ avoir la langue acérée; she has a quick ~ elle n'a pas sa langue dans sa poche; ~s will wag les langues iront bon train, ça va jaser; the news set ~s wagging la nouvelle a fait jaser (les gens) ❑ ~ in cheek ironiquement; she said it (with) ~ in cheek elle l'a dit avec une ironie voilée, il ne faut pas prendre au sérieux ce qu'elle a dit; a ~-in-cheek remark une réflexion ironique. -**3.** [language] *fml* OR *lit* langue *f*; to speak in ~s RELIG avoir le don des langues. -**4.** *(U)* CULIN langue *f* (de bœuf). -**5.** [of shoe] languette *f*; [of bell] battant *m*; [of buckle] ardillon *m*; TECH langue *f*, languette *f*. -**6.** [of flame, land, sea] langue *f*.
◇ *vt* -**1.** MUS [note] détacher; [phrase] détacher les notes de. -**2.** [in woodworking] langueter.

tongue-and-groove *adj* [joint] à tenon et mortaise; [boarding] avec jointures à tenons et mortaises.

tongue-in-cheek → **tongue** *n* **2**.

tongue-lashing *inf n*: to give sb a ~ sonner les cloches à qqn.

tongue-tied *adj* muet *fig*, trop timide (pour parler); she was completely ~ elle semblait avoir perdu sa langue.

tongue-twister *n mot ou phrase très difficile à prononcer*; his name's a real ~ son nom est impossible à prononcer.

tonguing ['tʌŋɪŋ] *n* MUS coup *m* de langue.

tonic ['tɒnɪk] ◇ *n* -**1.** MED tonique *m*, fortifiant *m*; *fig*: the news was a ~ to us all la nouvelle nous a remonté le moral à tous; it's a ~ to see you looking so happy ça me fait du bien OR me remonte le moral de te voir si heureux. -**2.** [cosmetic] lotion *f* tonique; hair ~ lotion *f* capillaire. -**3.** [drink] tonic *m*; gin and ~ gin-tonic *m*. -**4.** MUS tonique *f*. -**5.** LING syllabe *f* tonique OR accentuée.

◇ *adj* tonique; the ~ effect of sea air l'effet tonique OR vivifiant de l'air marin; ~ **syllable/stress** LING syllabe *f*/accent *m* tonique.

tonicity [tə'nɪsətɪ] *n* [gen] tonicité *f*; PHYSIOL tonus *m*.

tonic sol-fa *n* solfège *m*.

tonic water *n* tonic *m*, ≃ Schweppes®.

tonic wine *n* vin *m* tonique.

tonight [tə'naɪt] ◇ *n* [this evening] ce soir; [this night] cette nuit; **in ~'s newspaper** dans le journal de ce soir; **~'s the night** c'est le grand soir.

◇ *adv* [this evening] ce soir; **shall we go dancing ~?** si on allait danser ce soir? || [this night] cette nuit *f*; **I hope I sleep well ~** j'espère que je dormirai bien cette nuit.

tonnage ['tʌnɪdʒ] *n* **-1.** [total weight] poids *m* total d'une chose. **-2.** [capacity - of a ship] tonnage *m*, jauge *f*; [of a port] tonnage *m*; **registered ~** jauge *f (telle que définie officiellement)*.

tonne [tʌn] *n* tonne *f* (métrique).

tonneau ['tɒnəʊ] (*pl* **tonneaus** OR **tonneaux** ['tɒnəʊz]) *n* **-1.** AUT capote *f*. **-2.** [of wine] tonneau *m*.

-tonner ['tʌnə^r] *in cpds*: **a thousand~** un navire de mille tonneaux.

tonometer [təʊ'nɒmɪtə^r] *n* MED & MUS tonomètre *m*.

tonsil ['tɒnsl] *n* (*usu pl*) amygdale *f*; **enlarged ~s** des amygdales hypertrophiées; **your ~s are inflamed** vous avez une inflammation des amygdales; **to have one's ~s out** être opéré des amygdales.

tonsillectomy [,tɒnsɪ'lektəmɪ] (*pl* **tonsillectomies**) *n* amygdalectomie *f*, tonsillectomie *f*.

tonsillitis [,tɒnsɪ'laɪtɪs] *n (U)* angine *f*, amygdalite *f spec*; **to have ~** avoir une angine.

tonsure ['tɒnʃə^r] ◇ *n* tonsure *f*.

◇ *vt* tonsurer.

tontine [tɒn'tiːn] *n* FIN tontine *f*.

ton-up boy *inf n Br* fou *m* de moto.

tonus ['təʊnəs] *n* PHYSIOL tonus *m*.

tony *inf* ['təʊnɪ] (*compar* **tonier**, *superl* **toniest**) *adj Am* chic, de grande classe; **a ~ neighbourhood** un quartier élégant.

too [tuː] *adv* **-1.** [as well] aussi, également; **I like jazz — I do ~** OR **me ~** j'aime le jazz — moi aussi; **he's a professor ~** [as well as sthg else] il est également professeur; [as well as sb else] lui aussi est professeur; **would I ~ fail?** *lit* allais-je échouer moi aussi?; **stylistically, ~, they are similar** du point de vue du style également, ils se ressemblent. **-2.** [excessively] trop; **she works ~ hard** elle travaille trop; **I have one apple ~ many** j'ai une pomme de trop; **that's ~ bad** c'est vraiment dommage; *iron* tant pis!; **~ little money** trop peu d'argent; **~ few people** trop peu de gens; **she's ~ tired to go out** elle est trop fatiguée pour sortir; **all ~ soon we had to go home** très vite, nous avons dû rentrer; **you're going ~ far** *fig* tu exagères, tu vas trop loin; **you're ~ kind** vous êtes trop aimable. **-3.** [with negatives] trop; **the first ski slope wasn't ~ bad** la première descente n'était pas trop difficile; **I wasn't ~ happy about it** ça ne me réjouissait pas trop; **she hasn't been ~ well** elle ne va pas trop bien depuis quelque temps. **-4.** [moreover] en outre, en plus; **he's so silly! — and a grown man ~!** qu'est-ce qu'il peut être bête! — et il en a passé l'âge en plus! **-5.** [for emphasis]: **and quite right ~!** tu as/il a *etc* bien fait!; **about time ~!** ce n'est pas trop tôt!; **I should think so ~!** j'espère bien!; **~ true!** ça, c'est vrai! **-6.** *Am* [indeed]: **you didn't do your homework — I did ~!** tu n'as pas fait tes devoirs — si!; **you will ~ behave!** si, tu vas être sage!

toodle-oo *inf* [,tuːdl'uː], **toodle-pip** *inf interj Br dated* salut.

took [tʊk] *pt* → **take**.

tool [tuːl] ◇ *n* **-1.** [instrument] outil *m*; **set of ~s** outillage *m*; **garden ~s** outils de jardinage; **the ~s of the trade** les instruments de travail; **the computer has become an essential ~ for most business** l'ordinateur est devenu un outil essentiel pour la plupart des entreprises ❑ **to down ~s** cesser le travail, se mettre en grève, débrayer. **-2.** TYPO fer *m* de reliure. **-3.** [dupe]: **he was nothing but a ~ of the government** il n'était que le jouet OR l'instrument du gouvernement. **-4.** ▼ [penis] engin *m*. **-5.** *Br crime sl* [gun] arme *f*.

◇ *vt* [decorate - wood] travailler, façonner; [- stone] sculpter; [- book cover] ciseler; **~ed leather** cuir *m* repoussé.

◇ *vi inf* rouler (en voiture); **I was ~ing along at 30 mph** je roulais peinardement à 50 km/h.

◆ **tool around** *inf vi insep Am* traîner; **all I ever did in high school was ~ around with the guys** je n'ai jamais rien fait au lycée à part traîner avec les copains.

◆ **tool up** ◇ *vi insep* s'équiper.

◇ *vt sep* outiller, équiper; **they are preparing to ~ up the new factory** ils s'apprêtent à outiller OR équiper la nouvelle usine.

toolbag ['tuːlbæg] *n* trousse *f* à outils.

toolbox ['tuːlbɒks] (*pl* **toolboxes**) *n* boîte *f* à outils.

toolcase ['tuːlkeɪs] *n* caisse *f* à outils.

toolchest ['tuːltʃest] *n* coffre *m* à outils.

toolholder ['tuːl,həʊldə^r] *n* porte-outil *m*.

tooling ['tuːlɪŋ] *n* **-1.** [decoration] façonnage *m*; [on leather] repoussé *m*; [in stone] ciselure *f*. **-2.** [equipment] outillage *m*.

toolkit ['tuːlkɪt] *n* jeu *m* d'outils.

toolmaker ['tuːl,meɪkə^r] *n* outilleur *m*.

toolmaking ['tuːl,meɪkɪŋ] *n* fabrication *f* d'outils.

toolroom ['tuːlrʊm] *n* atelier *m* d'outillage.

toolshed ['tuːlʃed] *n* remise *f*, resserre *f*.

toot [tuːt] ◇ *vi* [car] klaxonner; [train] siffler.

◇ *vt*: **he ~ed his horn** AUT il a klaxonné OR donné un coup de klaxon.

◇ *n* **-1.** [sound] appel *m*; **the tugboat gave a ~** le remorqueur a donné un coup de sirène; **a ~ of the horn** AUT un coup de klaxon. **-2.** *drugs sl* drogue *f* à sniffer. **-3.** ▽ *Am* [drinking spree]: **to go on the ~** prendre une cuite.

tooth [tuːθ] (*pl* **teeth**) ◇ *n* **-1.** ANAT dent *f*; **permanent teeth** dents permanentes; **a set of teeth** une denture, une dentition; **a false ~** une fausse dent; **a set of false teeth** un dentier; **to have a ~ out** se faire arracher une dent; **to have good/bad teeth** avoir de bonnes/mauvaises dents; **to bare** OR **to show one's teeth** montrer les dents ❑ **baby teeth** dents *fpl* de lait; **to have no teeth** *literal* être édenté; *fig* manquer de force; **the amendment will give the law some teeth** l'amendement renforcera quelque peu le pouvoir de la loi. **-2.** [of comb, file, cog, saw, wheel] dent *f*. **-3.** *phr*: **to be fed up** OR **sick to the back teeth** *inf* en avoir plein le dos OR ras le bol; **to fight ~ and nail** se battre bec et ongles; **to get one's teeth into sthg** se mettre à fond à qqch; **she needs something to get her teeth into** elle a besoin de quelque chose qui la mobilise; **the play gives you nothing to get your teeth into** la pièce manque de substance; **it was a real kick in the teeth** *inf* ça m'a fichu un sacré coup; **it's better than a kick in the teeth** c'est mieux que rien; **to set sb's teeth on edge** faire grincer qqn des dents; **she's a bit long in the ~** elle n'est plus toute jeune.

◇ *vi* [cogwheels] s'engrener.

◆ **in the teeth of** *prep phr* malgré; **he acted in the teeth of fierce opposition** il a agi malgré une opposition farouche.

toothache ['tuːθeɪk] *n* mal *m* de dents; **to have ~** OR *Am* **a ~** avoir mal aux dents.

toothbrush ['tuːθbrʌʃ] (*pl* **toothbrushes**) *n* brosse *f* à dents.

toothcomb ['tuːθkəʊm] → **fine-tooth comb**.

toothed [tuːθt] *adj* [wheel] denté.

-toothed *in cpds*: **gap~** aux dents écartées.

tooth glass *n* verre *m* à dents.

toothless ['tuːθlɪs] *adj* **-1.** *literal* édenté, sans dents. **-2.** *fig* sans pouvoir OR influence.

tooth mug *n* verre *m* à dents.

toothpaste ['tuːθpeɪst] *n* dentifrice *m*, pâte *f* dentifrice; **a tube of ~** un tube de dentifrice.

toothpick ['tuːθpɪk] *n* cure-dents *m inv*.

tooth powder *n* poudre *f* dentifrice.

toothsome ['tuːθsəm] *adj lit* OR *hum* **-1.** [food] appétissant. **-2.** [person] séduisant.

toothy *inf* ['tuːθɪ] (*compar* **toothier**, *superl* **toothiest**) *adj*: **a ~ grin** un sourire tout en dents.

tootle *inf* ['tuːtl] ◇ *vi* **-1.** [on musical instrument] jouer un petit air; **he was tootling on a recorder** il jouait un petit air sur sa flûte. **-2.** *Br* [drive]: **we were tootling along quite nicely until the tyre burst** nous suivions notre petit bonhomme de chemin lorsque le pneu a éclaté; **I'm going to ~ into town this afternoon** je vais aller faire un petit tour en ville cet après-midi.

◇ *n* **-1.** [on musical instrument] petit air *m*. **-2.** [drive] petit tour *m* en voiture.

toots *inf* [tʊts] (*pl* **tootses**) = **tootsie 2**.

tootsie *inf*, **tootsy** *inf* ['tʊtsɪ] (*pl* **tootsies**) *n* **-1.** *baby talk* [foot] pied *m*, peton *m*; [toe] doigt *m* de pied, orteil *m*. **-2.** [term of address] chéri *m*, -e *f*, mon petit chou *m*.

tootsie-wootsie *inf* [-'wʊtsɪ] *n baby talk* petit peton *m*.

top [tɒp] (*pt* & *pp* **topped**, *cont* **topping**) ◇ *n* **-1.** [highest point] haut *m*, sommet *m*; [of tree] sommet *m*, cime *f*; **carrot ~s** fanes *fpl* de carottes; **at the ~ of the stairs** en haut de l'escalier; **he searched the house from ~ to bottom** il a fouillé la maison de fond en comble; **she filled the jar right to the ~** elle a rempli le bocal à ras bord; **the page number is at the ~ of the page** la numérotation se trouve en haut de la page; **the wreckage floated on ~ of the water** l'épave flottait sur l'eau || [surface] dessus *m*, surface *f*; [end]: **at the ~ of the street** au bout de la rue; **at the ~ of the garden** au fond du jardin ❑ **to blow one's ~** *inf* piquer une crise, exploser; **from ~ to toe** *Br* de la tête aux pieds; **he's talking off the ~ of his head** il raconte n'importe quoi; **he's getting thin on ~** il commence à se dégarnir; **to come out on ~** avoir le dessus; **he doesn't have much up ~** *inf Br* il n'est pas très futé; **over the ~: the soldiers went over the ~** *literal* les soldats sont montés à l'assaut; **I think he went a bit over the ~** *inf Br fig* à mon avis, il est allé trop loin; **he's a bit over the ~** il en fait un peu trop. **-2.** [cap, lid] couvercle *m*; **where's the ~ to my pen?** où est le capuchon de mon stylo?; **bottle ~** [screw-on] bouchon *m* (de bouteille); [on beer bottle] capsule *f* (de bouteille). **-3.** [highest degree]: **he is at the ~ of his form** il est au meilleur de sa forme; **at the ~ of one's voice** à tue-tête. **-4.** [most important position]: **at the ~ of the table** *Br* à la place d'honneur; **she's ~ of her class** elle est première de sa classe; **someone who has reached the ~ in their profession** quelqu'un qui est arrivé en haut de l'échelle dans sa profession; **to be (at the) ~ of the bill** THEAT être en tête d'affiche; **to reach the ~ of the tree** arriver en haut de l'échelle; **it's tough at the ~!** c'est la rançon de la gloire! *hum*, c'est dur, la vie!; **this car is the ~ of the range** c'est une voiture haut de gamme ❑ **~ of the morning!** *Ir* bien le bonjour! **-5.** *Br* AUT: **she changed into ~** elle a enclenché la quatrième OR la cinquième. **-6.** [garment] haut *m*; **does this ~ go with my skirt?** est-ce que ce haut va avec ma jupe? **-7.** [beginning]: **play it again from the ~** reprends au début; **let's take it from the ~** commençons par le commencement. **-8.** [toy] toupie *f*; **to spin a ~** lancer OR fouetter une toupie ❑ **to sleep like a ~** *Br* dormir comme un loir.

◇ *vt* **-1.** [form top of] couvrir; **a cake topped with chocolate** un gâteau recouvert de chocolat; **snow topped the mountains** les sommets (des montagnes) étaient recouverts de neige. **-2.** *Br* [trim] écimer, étêter; **she was topping the carrots** elle coupait les fanes des carottes; **to ~ and tail gooseberries** équeuter des groseilles. **-3.** [exceed] dépasser; **production topped five tons last month** le mois dernier, la production

a dépassé les cinq tonnes; **he topped her offer** il a renchéri sur son offre; **his score ~s the world record** avec ce score, il bat le record du monde; **his story topped them all** son histoire était la meilleure de toutes; **that ~s the lot!** *Br* ça, c'est le bouquet! -**4.** [be at the top of]: **the book topped the best-seller list** ce livre est arrivé en tête des best-sellers; **she topped the polls in the last election** aux dernières élections, elle est arrivée en tête de scrutin. -**5.** *inf Br* [kill] faire la peau à; **to ~ o.s.** faire hara-kiri.
◇ *adj*: **the ~ floor** OR **storey** le dernier étage; **the ~ shelf** l'étagère du haut; **the ~ button of her dress** le premier bouton de sa robe; **in the ~ right-hand corner** dans le coin en haut à droite; **this job should be given ~ priority** ce travail doit absolument être fait en priorité; **~ management** la direction générale; **the ~ banks in the country** les grandes banques du pays; **to have ~ billing** être en tête d'affiche; **the ~ speed of this car is 150 mph** la vitesse maximum de cette voiture est de 240 km/h; **at ~ speed** à toute vitesse; **to be on ~ form** être en pleine forme ❑ **the ~ brass** *inf Br* MIL les officiers *mpl* supérieurs, les gros bonnets *mpl*; **the ~ ten** *hit parade des dix meilleures ventes de disques pop et rock*; **to pay ~ whack for sthg** *inf Br* payer qqch au prix fort; **I can offer you £20 ~ whack** *inf* je vous en donne 20 livres, c'est mon dernier prix.
◆ **on top of** *prep phr*: **suddenly the lorry was on ~ of him** d'un seul coup, il s'est retrouvé sous le camion; **we're living on ~ of each other** nous vivons les uns sur les autres; **on ~ of everything else** pour couronner le tout; **it's just one thing on ~ of another** ça n'arrête pas ❑ **don't worry, I'm on ~ of things** ne t'inquiète pas, je m'en sors très bien; **it's all getting on ~ of him** il est dépassé par les événements; **to feel on ~ of the world** avoir la forme.
◆ **top off** *vt sep* -**1.** *Br* [conclude] terminer, couronner; **and to ~ off a miserable day, it started to rain** et pour conclure cette triste journée, il s'est mis à pleuvoir. -**2.** *Am* [fill to top] remplir.
◆ **top out** *vt insep* [building] fêter l'achèvement de.
◆ **top up** *vt sep Br* [fill up] remplir; **can I ~ up your drink** OR **~ you up?** encore une goutte?; **to ~ up the battery** AUT ajouter de l'eau dans la batterie.

topaz ['təʊpæz] *n* topaze *f*; **a ~ bracelet** un bracelet de topazes.
top boots *npl Br* bottes *f* hautes.
top-class *adj* excellent.
topcoat ['tɒpkəʊt] *n* -**1.** [clothing] pardessus *m*, manteau *m*. -**2.** [paint] couche *f* de finition.
top dog *inf n* chef *m*; **he's ~ around here** c'est lui qui commande ici.
top-down *adj* hiérarchisé.
top drawer *inf n Br*: **a family right out of the ~** une famille de la haute.
◆ **top-drawer** *inf adj Br* de tout premier rang; **he's a top-drawer musician** c'est un musicien de haute volée.
top-dress *vt* AGR fumer en surface.
top-dressing *n* AGR fumure *f* en surface.
tope [təʊp] *vi lit* boire.
topee ['təʊpiː] *n Br* casque *m* colonial *(des Indes)*.
toper ['təʊpəʳ] *n lit* alcoolique *mf*, buveur *m*, -euse *f*.
top-flight *adj* de premier ordre.
top gear *n* vitesse *f* supérieure.
top hat *n* (chapeau *m*) haut-de-forme *m*.
top-hatted [-'hætɪd] *adj* qui porte un haut-de-forme.
top-heavy *adj* -**1.** [unbalanced] trop lourd du haut, déséquilibré; **a ~ bureaucracy** *fig* une bureaucratie à structure dirigeante trop lourde. -**2.** FIN surcapitalisé.
top-hole *inf adj Br dated* épatant, formidable.
topi ['təʊpɪ] = **topee**.
topiary ['təʊpjərɪ] *adj* topiaire.
topic ['tɒpɪk] *n* [theme] sujet *m*, thème *m*; **tonight's ~ for debate is unemployment** le débat de ce soir porte sur le chômage.
topical ['tɒpɪkl] *adj* -**1.** [current] actuel; **a ~ question** une question d'actualité; **a timely and ~ report** un rapport qui vient à point nommé. -**2.** MED topique, à usage local.
topicality [,tɒpɪ'kælətɪ] (*pl* **topicalities**) *n* actualité *f*.
topknot ['tɒpnɒt] *n* -**1.** [of hair] chignon *m*; [of ribbons] ornement *m* fait de rubans; [of feathers] aigrette *f*. -**2.** ZOOL pleuronectidé *m*.
topless ['tɒplɪs] *adj* [sunbather] aux seins nus; **to go ~** ne pas porter de haut; **~ bar** bar *m* topless.
top-level *adj* de très haut niveau.
topmast ['tɒpmɑːst] *n* mât *m* de hune.
topmost ['tɒpməʊst] *adj* le plus haut, le plus élevé.
topnotch *inf* ['tɒp'nɒtʃ] *adj* excellent.
topographer [tə'pɒgrəfəʳ] *n* topographe *mf*.
topographic(al) [,tɒpə'græfɪk(l)] *adj* topographique.
topography [tə'pɒgrəfɪ] *n* topographie *f*.
topological [,tɒpə'lɒdʒɪkl] *adj* topologique.
topology [tə'pɒlədʒɪ] *n* topologie *f*.
toponym ['tɒpənɪm] *n* toponyme *m*.
toponymy [tə'pɒnəmɪ] *n* toponymie *f*.
topper *inf* ['tɒpəʳ] *n Br* [top hat] (chapeau *m*) haut-de-forme *m*.
topping ['tɒpɪŋ] ◇ *n* dessus *m*; CULIN garniture *f*; **a cake with a chocolate ~** un gâteau recouvert de chocolat.
◇ *adj inf Br dated* épatant, formidable.
topple ['tɒpl] ◇ *vi* [fall] basculer; [totter] vaciller; **the whole pile ~d over** toute la pile s'est effondrée; **he ~d over backwards** il a perdu l'équilibre et est tombé en arrière.
◇ *vt* -**1.** [cause to fall] faire tomber, faire basculer. -**2.** *fig* renverser; **the scandal almost ~d the government** ce scandale a failli faire tomber le gouvernement.
top-ranking *adj* de premier rang, haut placé; **a ~ official** un haut fonctionnaire.
tops *inf* [tɒps] *n dated*: **it's the ~!** c'est bath!
TOPS [tɒps] (*abbr of* **Training Opportunities Scheme**) *pr n progamme du recyclage professionnel en Grande-Bretagne*.
topsail ['tɒpsl, 'tɒpseɪl] *n* hunier *m*.
top-secret *adj* top secret *(inv)*.
top-security *adj* de haute sécurité; **~ prison** ≃ quartier *m* de haute sécurité.
topside ['tɒpsaɪd] *n Br* [of beef] tende-de-tranche *m*.
◆ **topsides** *npl* NAUT accastillage *m*.
topsoil ['tɒpsɔɪl] *n* terre *f* superficielle, couche *f* arable.
topspin ['tɒpspɪn] *n*: **to put ~ on a ball** donner de l'effet à une balle.
topsy-turvy [,tɒpsɪ'tɜːvɪ] *adj & adv* sens dessus dessous; **a ~ world** le monde à l'envers; **everything is ~** tout est sens dessus dessous; **the war turned their lives ~** la guerre a bouleversé leur vie.
top ten *n* hit-parade *m*; **in the ~** au hit-parade.
top-up *n Br*: **can I give you a ~?** je vous ressers?, encore une goutte?
toque [təʊk] *n* toque *f*; *Can* bonnet *m*.
tor [tɔːʳ] *n* colline *f* rocailleuse *(notamment dans le sud-ouest de l'Angleterre)*.
Torah ['tɔːrə] *pr n* Torah *f*.
torch [tɔːtʃ] (*pl* **torches**) ◇ *n* -**1.** *Br* [electric] lampe *f* de poche. -**2.** [flaming stick] torche *f*, flambeau *m*; **to put a ~ to sthg** mettre le feu à qqch ❑ **to carry a ~ for sb** en pincer pour qqn. -**3.** TECH [for welding, soldering etc] chalumeau *m*.
◇ *vt* mettre le feu à; **they ~ed the old barn** ils ont mis le feu à la vieille grange.
torchbearer ['tɔːtʃ,beərəʳ] *n* porteur *m* de flambeau.
torchlight ['tɔːtʃlaɪt] ◇ *n* lumière *f* de flambeau OR de torche; **by ~** à la lueur des flambeaux.
◇ *comp*: **a ~ procession** une retraite aux flambeaux.
torch song *n* chanson *f* d'amour populaire.
tore [tɔːʳ] *pt* → **tear**.
toreador ['tɒrɪədɔːʳ] *n* torero *m*, toréador *m*.
toreador pants *npl* pantalon *m* corsaire.
torero [tɒ'reərəʊ] *n* torero *m*.
torment [*n* 'tɔːment, *vb* tɔː'ment] ◇ *n* -**1.** [suffering] supplice *m*; *lit* tourment *m*; **to be in ~** être au supplice; **her face showed her inner ~** son tourment intérieur se lisait sur son visage; **to suffer ~** souffrir le martyre. -**2.** [ordeal] rude épreuve *f*. -**3.** [pest] démon *m*; **that child is a real ~** cet enfant est vraiment insupportable.
◇ *vt* -**1.** [cause pain to] torturer; **~ed by doubt** harcelé de doutes. -**2.** [harass] tourmenter, harceler; **stop ~ing your sister!** laisse ta sœur tranquille!
tormenter, **tormentor** [tɔː'mentəʳ] *n* persécuteur *m*, -trice *f*, bourreau *m*.
torn [tɔːn] *pp* → **tear**.
tornado [tɔː'neɪdəʊ] (*pl* **tornados** OR **tornadoes**) *n* [storm] tornade *f*; *fig* [person, thing] ouragan *m*.
Toronto [tə'rɒntəʊ] *pr n* Toronto.
torpedo [tɔː'piːdəʊ] (*pl* **torpedoes**, *pt & pp* **torpedoed**) ◇ *n* -**1.** MIL torpille *f*. -**2.** *Am* [firework] pétard *m*.
◇ *vt* -**1.** MIL torpiller. -**2.** *fig* [destroy - plan] faire échouer, torpiller.
torpedo boat *n* torpilleur *m*, vedette *f* lance-torpilles.
torpedo tube *n* tube *m* lance-torpilles.
torpid ['tɔːpɪd] *adj fml* léthargique; **a ~ mind** un esprit engourdi.
torpor ['tɔːpəʳ] *n fml* torpeur *f*, léthargie *f*, engourdissement *m*.
torque [tɔːk] *n* -**1.** [rotational force] moment *m* de torsion; AUT couple *m* moteur. -**2.** HIST [collar] torque *m*.
torque converter *n* convertisseur *m* de couple.
torque wrench *n* clef *f* dynamométrique.
torrent ['tɒrənt] *n* -**1.** [of liquid] torrent *m*; **the rain came down in ~s** il pleuvait à torrents OR à verse. -**2.** [of emotion, abuse etc] torrent *m*; **a ~ of insults** un torrent OR flot d'injures.
torrential [tə'renʃl] *adj* torrentiel.
torrid ['tɒrɪd] *adj* -**1.** [hot] torride; **the ~ zone** la zone intertropicale. -**2.** [passionate] passionné, ardent.
torsion ['tɔːʃn] *n* torsion *f*.
torsion balance *n* balance *f* de torsion.
torsion bar *n* barre *f* de torsion.
torso ['tɔːsəʊ] (*pl* **torsos**) *n* [human] torse *m*; [sculpture] buste *m*.
tort [tɔːt] *n* JUR acte *m* délictuel, préjudice *m*; **~s lawyer** *Am* avocat *m* spécialisé en droit civil.
tortilla [tɔː'tiːlə] *n* tortilla *f (crêpe mexicaine faite avec de la farine de maïs)*.
tortoise ['tɔːtəs] *n* tortue *f*.
tortoiseshell ['tɔːtəʃel] ◇ *n* -**1.** [substance] écaille *f* (de tortue). -**2.** [cat] chat *m* roux tigré. -**3.** [butterfly] vanesse *f*.
◇ *adj* -**1.** [comb, ornament] en écaille. -**2.** [cat] roux tigré.
tortuous ['tɔːtjʊəs] *adj* -**1.** [path] tortueux, sinueux. -**2.** [argument, piece of writing] contourné, tarabiscoté; [mind] retors.
tortuously ['tɔːtjʊəslɪ] *adv* tortueusement, de manière tortueuse.
torture ['tɔːtʃəʳ] ◇ *n* -**1.** [cruelty] torture *f*, supplice *m*; **to be subjected to ~** être torturé, subir des tortures; **instruments of ~** instruments *mpl* de torture. -**2.** *fig* torture *f*, tourment *m*; **the waiting was sheer ~!** cette attente fut un vrai supplice!
◇ *vt* -**1.** [inflict pain on] torturer; **they ~d her until she confessed** ils l'ont torturée jusqu'à ce qu'elle avoue. -**2.** [torment] torturer; **~d by remorse** tenaillé par le remords. -**3.** [distort]:

she ~s the Spanish language elle écorche la langue espagnole; to ~ a song massacrer une chanson.

torture chamber *n* chambre *f* de torture.

torturer ['tɔːtʃərə^r] *n* tortionnaire *mf*, bourreau *m*.

Tory ['tɔːrɪ] (*pl* Tories) ◇ *n* POL tory *m*, membre *m* du parti conservateur.
◇ *adj* [party, MP] tory, conservateur.

Toryism ['tɔːrɪɪzm] *n* POL torysme *m*.

tosh *inf* [tɒʃ] *n (U) Br* sornettes *fpl*; absolute ~! n'importe quoi!

toss [tɒs] ◇ *vt* -**1.** [throw] lancer, jeter; she ~ed him the ball elle lui a lancé la balle; I ~ed some herbs into the soup j'ai ajouté une poignée de fines herbes à la soupe; the horse nearly ~ed its rider into the ditch le cheval a failli faire tomber son cavalier dans le fossé; he was ~ed by the bull le taureau l'a projeté en l'air; to ~ pancakes *Br* faire sauter des crêpes; to ~ a coin jouer à pile ou face; she ~ed back her head with a laugh elle rejeta la tête en arrière en riant; ~ing the caber *jeu écossais consistant à lancer un tronc d'arbre et à le faire basculer*. -**2.** CULIN mélanger; to ~ the salad remuer OR retourner la salade; ~ the carrots in butter ajoutez du beurre et mélangez aux carottes.
◇ *vi* s'agiter; to ~ and turn in bed avoir le sommeil agité; the trees were ~ing in the wind le vent secouait les arbres; to pitch and ~ [boat] tanguer; shall we ~ for it? on joue à pile ou face?
◇ *n* -**1.** [throw - gen] lancer *m*, lancement *m*; [- of a coin] coup *m* de pile ou face; SPORT tirage *m* au sort; to win/to lose the ~ gagner/perdre à pile ou face; our team won the ~ notre équipe a gagné au tirage au sort ❑ to argue the ~ *Br* discuter pour rien; I don't give a ~ *inf Br* je m'en fiche. -**2.** [of head] mouvement *m* brusque. -**3.** [fall from horse] chute *f*; to take a ~ [from horse] être désarçonné, faire une chute.
◆ **toss about** *Br*, **toss around** ◇ *vt sep* -**1.** [rock, buffet] ballotter, secouer; we were ~ed about by the bumpy road nous avons été ballottés sur cette route cahoteuse; the boat was ~ed about by the waves les vagues faisaient tanguer le bateau. -**2.** *fig*: they were ~ing ideas about ils lançaient toutes sortes d'idées; figures of £5,000 were being ~ed around on avançait allègrement des chiffres de l'ordre de 5000 livres.
◇ *vi insep* = **toss** *vi*.
◆ **toss off** ◇ *vt sep* -**1.** [do hastily] expédier; to ~ off a letter écrire une lettre au pied levé. -**2.** [drink quickly] boire d'un coup, lamper. -**3.** ▼ *Br* [masturbate] branler.
◇ *vi insep* ▼ *Br* [masturbate] se branler.
◆ **toss up** ◇ *vt sep* lancer, jeter; she ~ed the ball up into the air elle a lancé le ballon en l'air.
◇ *vi insep*: the two captains ~ed up les deux capitaines ont joué à pile ou face.

tosspot ['tɒspɒt] *n arch* OR *lit* ivrogne *m*.

toss-up *n* coup *m* de pile ou face; it's a ~ as to which is best *fig* c'est blanc bonnet et bonnet blanc.

tot [tɒt] (*pt* & *pp* totted, *cont* totting) *n* -**1.** *inf* [child] petit enfant *m*; tiny ~s les tout petits *mpl*. -**2.** *Br* [of alcohol] goutte *f*; a ~ of rum un petit verre de rhum.
◆ **tot up** *Br* ◇ *vt sep* additionner; I'll ~ up your bill je vais vous faire l'addition.
◇ *vi insep*: that ~s up to £3 ça fait 3 livres en tout.

total ['təʊtl] (*Br pt* & *pp* totalled, *cont* totalling, *Am pt* & *pp* totaled, *cont* totaling) ◇ *adj* -**1.** [amount, number] total; the ~ cost le coût total; the ~ gains/losses le total des profits/pertes. -**2.** [as intensifier] complet; ~ silence un silence absolu; we are in ~ disagreement nous ne sommes pas d'accord du tout; that's ~ nonsense! c'est complètement absurde!; he was a ~ stranger to me je ne le connaissais ni d'Ève ni d'Adam.
◇ *n* total *m*; she wrote a ~ of ten books elle a écrit dix livres en tout; that comes to a ~ of £2 ça fait 2 livres en tout.
◇ *vt* -**1.** [add up] additionner, faire le total de. -**2.** [amount to] s'élever à; the groceries ~ £10 la note d'épicerie s'élève à 10 livres; the collection totalled 500 paintings cette collection comptait 500 tableaux en tout. -**3.** *inf Am* [wreck] démolir; he ~ed his car sa voiture est bonne pour la casse.
◆ **in total** *adv phr* au total; there are three hundred students in ~ au total, il y a trois cents étudiants.

totalitarian [ˌtəʊtælɪ'teərɪən] *adj* totalitaire.

totalitarianism [ˌtəʊtælɪ'teərɪənɪzm] *n* totalitarisme *m*.

totality [təʊ'tælətɪ] (*pl* totalities) *n* -**1.** totalité *f*; in its ~ dans sa totalité, intégralement. -**2.** ASTRON occultation *f* totale.

totalizator ['təʊtəlaɪzeɪtə^r] *n* -**1.** [adding machine] totalisateur *m*, machine *f* totalisatrice. -**2.** *Br* [in betting] pari *m* mutuel.

totalize, -ise ['təʊtəlaɪz] *vt* totaliser, additionner.

totalizer ['təʊtəlaɪzə^r] = **totalizator**.

totally ['təʊtəlɪ] *adv* totalement, entièrement, complètement; do you agree? – yes, ~ êtes-vous d'accord? – oui, tout à fait.

tote [təʊt] ◇ *n* (*abbr of* totalizator) pari *m* mutuel; ~ board tableau *m* électronique.
◇ *vt inf* porter; I've been toting that thing around all day j'ai trimballé ce truc toute la journée; he was toting a gun il avait un fusil sur lui.

tote bag *n* grand sac *m*, fourre-tout *m inv*.

totem ['təʊtəm] *n* totem *m*.

totemic [təʊ'temɪk] *adj* totémique.

totemism ['təʊtəmɪzm] *n* totémisme *m*.

totem pole *n* mât *m* totémique.

totter ['tɒtə^r] ◇ *vi* -**1.** *literal* [person] chanceler, tituber; [pile, vase] chanceler; he ~ed down the stairs il descendit les escaliers en chancelant; the child ~ed into/out of the room l'enfant est entré dans/sorti de la pièce d'un pas mal assuré. -**2.** *fig* [government, company etc] chanceler, être dans une mauvaise passe.
◇ *n* vacillement *m*; [gait] démarche *f* titubante OR chancelante; with a ~ d'un pas chancelant, en chancelant.

tottering ['tɒtərɪŋ], **tottery** ['tɒtərɪ] *adj* chancelant; [building] branlant; [government] chancelant, déstabilisé; with ~ steps en titubant.

totting *inf* ['tɒtɪŋ] *n Br recherche d'objets récupérables dans les décharges*.

toucan ['tuːkən] *n* toucan *m*.

touch [tʌtʃ] (*pl* touches) ◇ *n* -**1.** [sense] toucher *m*; sense of ~ sens *m* du toucher; soft to the ~ doux au toucher. -**2.** [physical contact] toucher *m*, contact *m*; [light brushing] effleurement *m*, frôlement *m*; she felt the ~ of his hand elle a senti le frôlement de sa main; she felt a ~ on her shoulder elle sentit qu'on lui touchait l'épaule; the machine works at the ~ of a button il suffit de toucher un bouton pour mettre en marche cet appareil. -**3.** [style] touche *f*; this painting has the Hopper ~ on reconnaît dans ce tableau la patte de Hopper; the pianist has a light ~ ce pianiste a le toucher léger || *fig*: to give sthg a personal ~ ajouter une note personnelle à qqch; to have the right ~ with sthg/sb savoir s'y prendre avec qqch/qqn; the house needed a woman's ~ il manquait dans cette maison une présence féminine; the cook has lost his ~ le cuisinier a perdu la main. -**4.** [detail]: to put the final OR finishing ~es to sthg mettre la dernière main à qqch; that logo in the bottom corner is a nice ~ c'est une bonne idée d'avoir mis ce logo dans le coin en bas || [slight mark] coup *m*; with a ~ of the pen d'un coup de stylo; to add a few ~es to a picture faire quelques retouches à un tableau. -**5.** [small amount, hint] note *f*, pointe *f*; a ~ of madness un grain de folie; there's a ~ of spring in the air ça sent le printemps; he answered with a ~ of bitterness il a répondu avec une pointe d'amertume; I got a ~ of sunstroke j'ai eu une petite insolation; I've got a ~ of flu je suis un peu grippé, j'ai une petite grippe; to add a ~ of class to sthg rendre qqch plus distingué. -**6.** [communication]: to be/to keep in ~ with sb être/rester en contact avec qqn; I'll be in ~! je te contacterai!; keep OR stay in ~! donne-nous de tes nouvelles!; to get in ~ with sb contacter qqn; you can get in ~ with me at this address vous pouvez me joindre à cette adresse; he put me in ~ with the director il m'a mis en relation avec le directeur; she is OR keeps in ~ with current events elle se tient au courant de l'actualité; I'll keep in ~ with developments je me tiendrai au courant de la situation; I am out of ~ with her now je ne suis plus en contact avec elle; she is out of ~ with politics elle ne suit plus l'actualité politique; they lost ~ long ago ils se sont perdus de vue il y a longtemps; he has lost ~ with reality il a perdu le sens des réalités. -**7.** [of an instrument] toucher *m*; [typewriter] frappe *f*; a keyboard with a light ~ un clavier à frappe légère. -**8.** SPORT touche *f*; to kick the ball into ~ mettre le ballon en touche; the ball landed in ~ le ballon est sorti en touche; to kick sthg into ~ *fig* mettre qqch au rencart. -**9.** *inf phr*: to be an easy OR soft ~ se laisser taper trop facilement.
◇ *vt* -**1.** [make contact with] toucher; to ~ lightly frôler, effleurer; his arm ~ed hers son bras a touché le sien; she ~ed it with her foot elle l'a touché du pied; he loved to ~ her hair il adorait lui caresser les cheveux; a smile ~ed her lips un sourire effleura ses lèvres; he ~ed his hat to her il a porté la main à son chapeau pour la saluer; since they met, her feet haven't ~ed the ground depuis leur rencontre, elle est sur un nuage; can you ~ the bottom? as-tu pied?; the boat ~ed land le bateau a accosté; the law can't ~ him la loi ne peut rien contre lui ❑ ~ wood! touchons du bois! -**2.** [handle] toucher à; don't ~ her things ne dérangez pas ses affaires; I didn't ~ it! je n'y ai pas touché!; don't ~ anything until I get home ne touchez à rien avant mon retour; he swears he never ~ed her il jure qu'il ne l'a jamais touchée; I didn't ~ him! je n'ai pas touché à un cheveu de sa tête! ❑ I wouldn't ~ that with a ten-foot pole OR *Br* bargepole je n'en voudrais à aucun prix. -**3.** [adjoin] jouxter; Alaska ~es Canada l'Alaska et le Canada sont limitrophes. -**4.** [eat, drink] (*usu neg*) toucher à; I never ~ meat je ne mange jamais de viande; she didn't ~ her vegetables elle n'a pas touché aux légumes. -**5.** [move emotionally] émouvoir, toucher; he ~ed the right note il a touché la corde sensible; he was very ~ed by her generosity il a été très touché par sa générosité; his remark ~ed a (raw) nerve sa réflexion a touché un point sensible; to ~ sb to the quick *Br* toucher qqn au vif. -**6.** [damage]: fruit ~ed by frost fruits abîmés par le gel; the fire didn't ~ the pictures l'incendie a épargné les tableaux; the war didn't ~ this area cette région a été épargnée par la guerre. -**7.** [concern] concerner, toucher; the problem ~es us all ce problème nous concerne tous. -**8.** *inf* [rival] valoir, égaler; nothing can ~ butter for cooking rien ne vaut la cuisine au beurre; no professor can ~ him c'est un professeur sans égal. -**9.** *Am* [dial]: ~ 645 faites le 645. -**10.** *inf phr*: to ~ sb for a loan taper qqn.
◇ *vi* -**1.** [be in contact] se toucher. -**2.** [adjoin - properties, areas] se toucher, être contigus. -**3.** [handle]: 'do not ~!' 'défense de toucher'. -**4.** NAUT: the ship ~es at Hong Kong le navire fait escale à Hong Kong.
◆ **a touch** *adv phr*: there was a ~ too much pepper in the soup le potage était un petit peu trop poivré.
◆ **touch down** ◇ *vi insep* -**1.** [aeroplane, spacecraft - on land] atterrir; [- on sea] amerrir. -**2.** RUGBY marquer un essai.

◇ *vt sep* RUGBY: to ~ the ball down marquer un essai.

◆ **touch off** *vt sep* [explosive] faire exploser, faire détoner; *fig* déclencher, provoquer; the ruling ~ed off widespread rioting cette décision a provoqué une vague d'émeutes.

◆ **touch on** *vt insep* aborder; his speech barely ~ed on the problem of unemployment son discours a à peine effleuré le problème du chômage.

◆ **touch up** *vt sep* -**1.** [painting, photograph] faire des retouches à, retoucher; [paintwork] refaire. -**2.** ▽ *Br* [sexually] peloter.

touch-and-go *adj*: a ~ situation une situation dont l'issue est incertaine; it was ~ with him il revient de loin; it was ~ whether we'd make it in time nous avons bien failli ne pas arriver à temps.

touchdown ['tʌtʃdaʊn] *n* -**1.** [on land] atterrissage *m*; [on sea] amerrissage *m*. -**2.** [in American football] but *m*.

touché ['tu:ʃeɪ] *interj* -**1.** [fencing] touché. -**2.** *fig* très juste.

touched [tʌtʃt] *adj* -**1.** [with gratitude] touché; she was ~ by his thoughtfulness elle était touchée par sa délicatesse. -**2.** *inf Br* [mad] toqué, timbré.

touch football *n Am sorte de football sans «tackling»*.

touchiness ['tʌtʃɪnɪs] *n* susceptibilité *f*.

touching ['tʌtʃɪŋ] ◇ *adj* touchant, émouvant.
◇ *prep lit* touchant.

touchingly ['tʌtʃɪŋlɪ] *adv* d'une manière touchante.

touch-in-goal *n* RUGBY en-but *m*.

touch judge *n* RUGBY juge *m* de touche.

touch kick *n* RUGBY mise *f* en touche.

touchline ['tʌtʃlaɪn] *n* SPORT ligne *f* de touche.

touch-me-not *n* impatiens *f*, balsamine *f*.

touchpaper ['tʌtʃ,peɪpəʳ] *n* papier *m* nitraté.

touch rugby *n sorte de rugby sans «tackling»*.

touchstone ['tʌtʃstəʊn] *n* MINER & *fig* pierre *f* de touche.

touch-tone *adj*: ~ telephone téléphone *m* à touches.

touch-type *vi* taper sans regarder le clavier.

touch-typing [-,taɪpɪŋ] *n* dactylographie *f* (sans regarder le clavier).

touch-up *n* ART & PHOT retouche *f*; [of object] restauration *f*.

touchy ['tʌtʃɪ] (*compar* touchier, *superl* touchiest) *adj* -**1.** [oversensitive] susceptible, ombrageux; she's ~ about her weight elle est susceptible OR chatouilleuse sur la question de son poids; he's very ~ il se froisse OR vexe pour un rien. -**2.** [matter, situation] délicat, épineux.

tough [tʌf] ◇ *adj* -**1.** [resilient - person] solide, résistant, robuste; [- meat] dur, coriace; [- animal, plant] résistant, robuste; [- substance, fabric] solide, résistant; you have to be ~ to make it here il faut être solide pour s'en tirer ici; she's ~ enough to win elle a assez d'endurance pour gagner ❑ he's as ~ as old boots *Br* il est coriace; this steak is as ~ as old boots ce n'est pas du bifteck, c'est de la semelle. -**2.** [difficult] dur, pénible; a ~ problem un problème épineux; it's ~ on him c'est un coup dur pour lui; she made it ~ for him elle lui a mené la vie dure; that's a ~ act to follow c'est difficile de faire mieux; I gave them a ~ time je leur en ai fait voir de toutes les couleurs; it's ~ work c'est un travail pénible; she had a ~ life elle n'a pas eu une vie facile; he had a ~ time passing the exam il a eu du mal à réussir son examen; Wall Street is a ~ environment Wall Street est un milieu très dur. -**3.** [severe] sévère; a ~ economic policy une politique économique draconienne; a ~ boss un patron sévère; to get ~ with sb se montrer dur avec qqn; the boss takes a ~ line with people who are late le patron ne plaisante pas avec les retardataires ‖ [resolute] dur, inflexible; she's a ~ person to deal with elle ne fait pas de concessions ❑ he's a ~ cookie *inf Am* il n'est pas commode; they're ~ customers ce sont des durs à cuire. -**4.** [rough, hardened] dur; a ~ criminal un criminel endurci; a real ~ guy *inf* un vrai dur; stay out of the ~ neighbourhoods évitez les quartiers dangereux. -**5.** *inf* [unfortunate] malheureux; that's really ~ ça, c'est vraiment vache; ~ luck! pas de pot!; that's your ~ luck! tant pis pour vous!
◇ *adv inf*: to talk ~, to act ~ jouer au dur.
◇ *vt phr*: to ~ it out *inf Br* tenir bon.
◇ *n inf* dur *m*, -e *f*.

toughen ['tʌfn] ◇ *vt* [metal, leather] rendre plus solide, renforcer; [person] endurcir; [conditions] rendre plus sévère; ~ed glass verre *m* trempé.
◇ *vi* [metal, glass, leather] durcir; [person] s'endurcir.

◆ **toughen up** *vt sep* & *vi insep* = **toughen**.

toughie *inf* ['tʌfɪ] *n* [person] dur *m*, -e *f*; [problem] casse-tête *m*, cactus *m*.

toughly ['tʌflɪ] *adv* [fight] avec acharnement, âprement; [speak] durement, sans ménagement.

tough-minded *adj*: he's a ~ man il a la tête froide.

toughness ['tʌfnɪs] *n* -**1.** [of fabric, glass, leather] solidité *f*; [of meat] dureté *f*; [of metal] ténacité *f*, résistance *f*. -**2.** [of job] difficulté *f*; [of struggle] acharnement *m*, âpreté *f*. -**3.** [of character - strength] force *f*, résistance *f*; [- hardness] dureté *f*; [- severity] inflexibilité *f*, sévérité *f*.

toupee ['tu:peɪ] *n* postiche *m*.

tour [tʊəʳ] ◇ *n* -**1.** [trip] voyage *m*; we're going on a ~ of Eastern Europe nous allons visiter les pays de l'Est; a day ~ une excursion (d'un jour) ❑ guided ~ visite *f* guidée; package ~ voyage *m* organisé; she's on a walking ~ in Wales elle fait une randonnée à pied dans le pays de Galles; they're off on a world ~ ils sont partis faire le tour du monde; the Grand Tour HIST le tour d'Europe. -**2.** [of a building] visite *f*; we went on a ~ of the factory nous avons visité l'usine; a guided ~ of the museum une visite guidée du musée. -**3.** [official journey] tournée *f*; the dance company is on ~ la troupe de danseurs est en tournée; to go on ~ faire une tournée; is he taking the team on ~? est-ce qu'il emmène l'équipe en tournée?; she's taking the play on ~ elle donne la pièce en tournée; the Tour of Spain SPORT le Tour d'Espagne ❑ ~ of duty MIL service *m*; ~ of inspection tournée *f* d'inspection.
◇ *vt* -**1.** [visit] visiter; they're ~ing Italy ils visitent l'Italie, ils font du tourisme en Italie. -**2.** SPORT & THEAT: the orchestra is ~ing the provinces l'orchestre est en tournée en province.
◇ *vi* voyager, faire du tourisme.

tourer ['tʊərəʳ] *n* voiture *f* de tourisme.

tour guide *n* [person] guide *m*; [book] guide *m* touristique.

touring ['tʊərɪŋ] ◇ *adj*: ~ bicycle vélo *m* de randonnée; ~ company THEAT [permanently] troupe *f* ambulante; [temporarily] troupe *f* en tournée; ~ party SPORT équipe *f* en tournée.
◇ *n (U)* tourisme *m*, voyages *mpl* touristiques.

tourism ['tʊərɪsm] *n* tourisme *m*.

tourist ['tʊərɪst] ◇ *n* touriste *mf*.
◇ *comp* [agency, centre] de tourisme; [attraction, information, ticket] touristique; ~ office office *m* de tourisme, syndicat *m* d'initiative.

tourist class *n Br* classe *f* touriste.

tourist trade *n* tourisme *m*; the country relies on its ~ le pays vit du tourisme.

tourist traffic *n* flot *m* des touristes.

tourist trap *n* attrape-touristes *m inv*.

touristy *inf* ['tʊərɪstɪ] *adj pej* trop touristique.

tournament ['tɔ:nəmənt] *n* tournoi *m*.

tourney ['tʊənɪ] *n* tournoi *m*.

tourniquet ['tʊənɪkeɪ] *n* garrot *m*.

tour operator *n* [travel agency] tour-opérateur *m*, voyagiste *m*; [bus company] compagnie *f* de cars *(qui organise des voyages)*.

tousle ['taʊzl] *vt* [hair] ébouriffer; [clothes] friper, froisser.

tousled ['taʊzld] *adj* [hair] ébouriffé; [clothes] fripé, froissé; his ~ appearance son aspect débraillé.

tout [taʊt] *Br* ◇ *n* -**1.** (ticket) ~ revendeur *m*, -euse *f* de billets *(au marché noir)*. -**2.** [in racing] pronostiqueur *m*, -euse *f*.
◇ *vt* -**1.** [peddle - tickets] revendre *(au marché noir)*; [- goods] vendre *(en vantant sa marchandise)*; the cries of the market traders ~ing their wares les cris des marchands essayant de raccrocher les clients; he's been ~ing those records around for days ça fait des jours qu'il essaie de revendre ces disques. -**2.** [promote]: he is being ~ed as a future prime minister on veut faire de lui un futur premier ministre.
◇ *vi* -**1.** salesmen ~ing for custom des vendeurs qui essaient d'attirer les clients; they've been ~ing around for work/business ils essayaient de trouver du travail/de se constituer une clientèle. -**2.** [racing] vendre des pronostics.

tow [təʊ] ◇ *vt* tirer; [boat, car] remorquer; [barge] haler; to ~ a car remorquer une voiture; the police ~ed my car away la police a emmené ma voiture à la fourrière; the ship was ~ed out of harbour le navire a été remorqué hors du port; they were ~ing a trailer leur voiture tirait une remorque.
◇ *n* -**1.** [action] remorquage *m*; [vehicle] véhicule *m* en remorque; to be on ~ être en remorque; can you give me a ~? pourriez-vous remorquer ma voiture?; he took my car in ~ il a pris ma voiture en remorque; they arrived with all the kids in ~ *fig* ils sont arrivés avec tous leurs enfants. -**2.** [line] câble *m* de remorquage. -**3.** TEX filasse *f*, étoupe *f*.
◇ *comp* AUT: ~-start: to give sb a ~-start faire démarrer qqn en remorque.

towage ['təʊɪdʒ] *n (U)* [act] remorquage *m*; [fee] frais *mpl* de remorquage.

towards [tə'wɔ:dz] *Br*, **toward** [tə'wɔ:d] *Am prep* -**1.** [in the direction of] dans la direction de, vers; he turned ~ her il s'est tourné vers elle; we headed ~ Chicago nous avons pris la direction de Chicago; she was standing with her back ~ him elle lui tournait le dos; the negotiations are a first step ~ peace *fig* les négociations sont un premier pas sur le chemin de la paix; they are working ~ a solution *fig* ils cherchent une solution; 'Towards a New Humanism' 'Vers un nouvel humanisme'. -**2.** [indicating attitude] envers; she's very hostile ~ me elle est très hostile à mon égard; the public's attitude ~ crime l'attitude de l'opinion publique face à la criminalité; his feelings ~ her ses sentiments pour elle, les sentiments qu'il éprouve pour elle. -**3.** [as contribution to] pour; the money is going ~ a new car l'argent contribuera à l'achat d'une nouvelle voiture; I'll give you something ~ your expenses je vous donnerai quelque chose pour vous payer une partie de vos frais. -**4.** [near - in time] vers; [- in space] près de; ~ the end of his life vers OR sur la fin de sa vie; ~ the end of the century vers la fin du siècle; ~ the middle vers le milieu.

tow-away zone *n Am zone de ramassage des véhicules en infraction*.

towbar ['təʊbɑ:ʳ] *n* barre *f* de remorquage.

towboat ['təʊbəʊt] *n* remorqueur *m*.

towel ['taʊəl] (*Br pt* & *pp* towelled, *cont* towelling, *Am pt* & *pp* toweled OR towelled, *cont* toweling OR towelling) ◇ *n* serviette *f* (de toilette); [for hands] essuie-mains *m inv*; [for glasses] essuie-verres *m inv*; (dish) ~ torchon *m* à vaisselle; paper ~ serviette *f* en papier; ~ rack OR rail OR ring porte-serviettes *m inv*.
◇ *vt* frotter avec une serviette; to ~ o.s. dry OR down s'essuyer OR se sécher avec une serviette.

towelling *Br*, **toweling** *Am* ['taʊəlɪŋ] ◇ *n* -**1.** [material] tissu *m* éponge. -**2.** [drying]: to give sb a ~ (down) frictionner qqn avec une serviette.
◇ *comp* [robe, shirt] en tissu éponge.

tower ['taʊəʳ] ◇ *n* tour *f*; church ~ clocher *m*; clock ~ tour (de l'horloge); water ~ château *m* d'eau; he's a ~ of strength c'est un roc; you've been a ~ of strength to me ton soutien m'a été précieux; 'Barchester Towers' *Trollope* 'les Tours de Barchester'.
◇ *vi*: the skyscraper ~s above OR over the city le gratte-ciel domine la ville; he ~ed above OR over me j'étais tout petit à côté de lui; she ~s above OR over her contemporaries *fig* elle domine de loin ses contemporains.

tower block *n Br* tour *f* (d'habitation), gratte-ciel *m*.

tower crane *n* grue *f* à pylône.

towering ['taʊərɪŋ] *adj* -**1.** [very high - skyscraper, tree, statue] très haut, imposant. -**2.** [excessive] démesuré; in a ~ rage dans une colère noire.

tow-headed *adj Br* aux cheveux (blonds) filasse.

towline ['təʊlaɪn] = **towrope**.

town [taʊn] *n* ville *f*; a country ~ une ville de province; I work in ~ je travaille en ville; to live in a small ~ habiter une OR dans une petite ville; she's going into ~ elle va en ville; he's out of ~ this week il n'est pas là OR il est en déplacement cette semaine; we're from out of ~ *Am* nous ne sommes pas d'ici ❑ ~ gas gaz *m* de ville; a small market ~ *Br* une bourgade; it's the talk of the ~ toute la ville en parle; ~ and gown *expression désignant collectivement les habitants et les étudiants de certaines villes universitaires et soulignant les différences de culture entre les deux milieux*; they went out on the ~ last night *inf* hier soir, ils ont fait une virée en ville; to have a night (out) on the ~ *inf* faire la noce OR la java en ville; they really went to ~ on the new school *inf* pour la nouvelle école, ils n'ont pas fait les choses à moitié OR ils ont vraiment mis le paquet.

town centre *n* centre-ville *m*.

town clerk *n* secrétaire *m* de mairie.

town council *n* conseil *m* municipal.

town councillor *n* conseiller *m* municipal, conseillère *f* municipale.

town crier *n* garde-champêtre *m*.

town dweller *n* citadin *m*, -e *f*.

townee *inf Br*, **townie** *inf Am* [taʊ'niː] *n* citadin *m*, -e *f*, rat *m* des villes.

town hall *n* hôtel de ville *m*, mairie *f*.

town house *n* -**1.** [gen] maison *f* en ville; [more imposing] ≃ hôtel *m* particulier. -**2.** *Am* maison *f* mitoyenne (en ville).

town meeting *n Am assemblée générale des habitants d'une ville*.

town planner *n* urbaniste *mf*.

town planning *n* urbanisme *m*.

townscape ['taʊnskeɪp] *n* paysage *m* urbain.

townsfolk ['taʊnzfəʊk] *npl* citadins *mpl*.

township ['taʊnʃɪp] *n* -**1.** [gen] commune *f*; *Am* canton *m*. -**2.** *SAfr* township *f*.

townsman ['taʊnzmən] (*pl* townsmen [-mən]) *n* citadin *m*; my fellow townsmen mes concitoyens.

townspeople ['taʊnz,piːpl] *npl* citadins *mpl*.

towny *inf* ['taʊniː] (*pl* townies) = **townee**.

towpath ['təʊpɑːθ, *pl* -pɑːðz] *n* chemin *m* de halage.

towrope ['təʊrəʊp] *n* câble *m* de remorque; [to towpath] câble *m* de halage.

towtruck ['təʊtrʌk] *Am* = **breakdown lorry**.

toxaemia *Br*, **toxemia** *Am* [tɒk'siːmɪə] *n* toxémie *f*.

toxic ['tɒksɪk] *adj* toxique.

toxicant ['tɒksɪkənt] ◇ *adj* toxique.
◇ *n* toxique *m*.

toxicity [tɒk'sɪsətɪ] *n* toxicité *f*.

toxicological [,tɒksɪkə'lɒdʒɪkl] *adj* toxicologique.

toxicologist [,tɒksɪ'kɒlədʒɪst] *n* toxicologue *mf*.

toxicology [,tɒksɪ'kɒlədʒɪ] *n* toxicologie *f*.

toxicosis [,tɒksɪ'kəʊsɪs] (*pl* toxicoses [-siːz]) *n* toxicose *f*.

toxin ['tɒksɪn] *n* toxine *f*.

toy [tɔɪ] (*pl* toys) ◇ *n* jouet *m*; cuddly ~ peluche *f*.
◇ *comp* -**1.** [car, train] miniature; ~ soldier soldat *m* de plomb; ~ theatre théâtre *m* de marionnettes; ~ trumpet trompette *f* d'enfant. -**2.** [box, chest, drawer] à jouets. -**3.** [dog] nain.
◆ **toy with** *vt insep* jouer avec; [idea] caresser; to ~ with one's food manger du bout des dents; she ~ed with the idea of going home elle songeait à rentrer chez elle; he was ~ing with her affections il jouait avec ses sentiments.

toy boy *inf n pej* OR *hum jeune homme sortant avec une femme mûre*.

toy dog *n* chien *m* nain.

toymaker ['tɔɪ,meɪkəʳ] *n* fabricant *m* de jouets.

toyshop ['tɔɪʃɒp] *n* magasin *m* de jouets.

trace [treɪs] ◇ *n* -**1.** [sign] trace *f*; to disappear OR to sink without ~ disparaître sans laisser de traces; there is no ~ of it now il n'en reste plus aucune trace; we've lost all ~ of her nous ignorons ce qu'elle est devenue; ~s of cocaine were found in his blood l'analyse de son sang a révélé des traces de cocaïne; a ~ of a smile un sourire à peine esquissé; without a ~ of fear sans la moindre peur. -**2.** [trail] trace *f* de pas, piste *f*; *Am* [path] piste *f*, sentier *m*. -**3.** [drawing] tracé *m*. -**4.** TECH: a radar ~ la trace d'un spot. -**5.** [harness] trait *m*.
◇ *vt* -**1.** [follow trail of] suivre la trace de; [track down - object] retrouver; she ~d him as far as New York elle a suivi sa piste jusqu'à New York; I can't ~ any reference to that letter je ne trouve aucune mention de cette lettre; they ~d the murder to him ils ont finalement établi qu'il était le meurtrier; they ~d the lost shipment ils ont retrouvé la cargaison égarée; we eventually ~d the problem to a computer error nous avons finalement découvert que le problème était dû à une erreur de l'ordinateur. -**2.** [follow development of] suivre; the film ~s the rise to power of a gangland boss ce film relate l'ascension d'un chef de gang. -**3.** [mark outline of] tracer, dessiner; [with tracing paper] décalquer; he ~d (out) a map in the sand with his finger avec son doigt, il a dessiné un plan sur le sable.
◆ **trace back** ◇ *vt sep* : to ~ sthg back to its source retrouver l'origine de qqch; she can ~ her ancestry back to the 15th century sa famille remonte au XVᵉ siècle; he ~d the rumour back to her il a découvert qu'elle était à l'origine de cette rumeur; the cause of the epidemic was ~d back to an infected water supply on a découvert que l'épidémie était due à la contamination de l'alimentation en eau.
◇ *vi insep Am* -**1.** [go back]: to ~ back to remonter à; his family ~s back to the Norman Conquest sa famille remonte à la conquête de l'Angleterre par les Normands. -**2.** [be due to] être dû à.

traceable ['treɪsəbl] *adj* [object] retrouvable, qui peut être retrouvé.

trace element *n* oligo-élément *m*.

tracer ['treɪsəʳ] *n* -**1.** [person] traceur *m*, -euse *f*; [device] traçoir *m*. -**2.** CHEM traceur *m*.

tracer bullet *n* balle *f* traçante.

traceried ['treɪsərɪd] *adj* à nervures.

tracery ['treɪsərɪ] (*pl* traceries) *n* filigrane *m*, dentelles *fpl*; [on leaf, insect wing] nervures *fpl*; ARCHIT réseau *m*.

trachea [trə'kiːə] (*pl* tracheae [-'kiːiː] OR tracheas) *n* trachée *f*.

tracheotomy [,trækɪ'ɒtəmɪ] (*pl* tracheotomies) *n* trachéotomie *f*.

trachoma [trə'kəʊmə] *n* trachome *m*.

tracing ['treɪsɪŋ] *n* [process] calquage *m*; [result] calque *m*.

tracing paper *n* papier-calque *m inv*, papier *m* à décalquer.

track [træk] ◇ *n* -**1.** [path, route] chemin *m*, sentier *m*; [of planet, star, aeroplane] trajectoire *f*; a mountain ~ un sentier de montagne; a farm ~ un chemin de campagne ‖ *fig*: to be on the right ~ être sur la bonne voie; he's on the wrong ~ il fait fausse route; you're way off ~! *inf* tu es complètement à côté de la plaque! -**2.** SPORT: cinder ~ cendrée *f*; greyhound ~ *Br* cynodrome *m*; motor-racing ~ *Br* autodrome *m*; race ~ piste *f*; test ~ piste *f* d'essai; ~ and field athlétisme *m*; ~ and field events épreuves *fpl* d'athlétisme. -**3.** RAIL voie *f*, rails *mpl*; the train jumped the ~s le train a déraillé OR a quitté les rails ❑ to come from the wrong side of the ~s *inf* venir d'un milieu pauvre. -**4.** [mark, trail] trace *f*, piste *f*; [of animal, person] piste *f*; [of boat] sillage *m*; to be on sb's ~ OR ~s être sur la piste de qqn; the terrorists had covered their ~s well les terroristes n'avaient pas laissé de traces; that should throw them off my ~ avec ça, je devrais arriver à les semer; to keep ~ of suivre; it's hard to keep ~ of her, she moves around so much il est difficile de rester en contact avec elle, elle bouge tout le temps; we like to keep ~ of current events nous aimons nous tenir au courant de l'actualité; why can't you keep ~ of your things? tu ne peux pas faire attention où tu mets tes affaires?; we'll have to keep ~ of the time! il ne faudra pas oublier l'heure!; to lose ~ of perdre; don't lose ~ of those files n'égarez pas ces dossiers; they've lost ~ of the situation ils ne suivent plus OR ne sont plus au courant de ce qui se passe; I lost ~ of them years ago j'ai perdu le contact avec eux OR je les ai perdus de vue il y a des années; she lost all ~ of time elle a perdu toute notion du temps; he lost ~ of what he was saying il a perdu le fil de ce qu'il disait ❑ to make ~s *inf* mettre les voiles; she made ~s for home elle a filé chez elle. -**5.** [on LP, tape] plage *f*; COMPUT piste *f*. -**6.** AUT [tyre tread] chape *f*; [space between wheels] écartement *m*; caterpillar ~ chenille *f*; ~ vehicle véhicule *m* chenillé. -**7.** *Am* SCH classe *f* de niveau; ~ system *répartition des élèves en sections selon leurs aptitudes*. -**8.** *drugs sl* trace *f* de piqûre.
◇ *vt* -**1.** [follow - animal] suivre à la trace, filer; [- rocket] suivre la trajectoire de; [criminal] traquer. -**2.** *Am*: don't ~ mud into the house! ne traîne pas de boue dans la maison!
◇ *vi* -**1.** [stylus] suivre le sillon. -**2.** [with camera] faire un traveling OR travelling.
◆ **track down** *vt sep* retrouver, localiser; [animal, criminal] traquer et capturer.

tracked [trækt] *adj* chenillé, à chenilles.

tracker ['trækəʳ] *n* -**1.** [person - gen] poursuivant *m*, -e *f*; [- in hunting] traqueur *m*, -euse *f*. -**2.** [device] appareil *m* de poursuite.

tracker dog *n* chien *m* policier.

track event *n* épreuve *f* sur piste.

tracking ['trækɪŋ] ◇ *n* -**1.** poursuite *f*; [of missile] repérage *m*. -**2.** *Am* SCH *répartition des élèves en sections selon leurs aptitudes*.
◇ *comp* [radar, satellite] de poursuite.

tracking shot *n* CIN traveling *m*, travelling *m*.

tracking station *n* station *f* d'observation.

tracklayer ['træk,leɪəʳ] *n Am* poseur *m* de rails.

trackless ['træklɪs] *adj* -**1.** [forest] sans chemins, sans sentiers. -**2.** [vehicle] sans chenilles.

trackman ['trækmən] (*pl* trackmen [-mən]) *n Am responsable de l'entretien de la voie*.

track meet *n Am* rencontre *f* d'athlétisme.

track racing *n* (U) courses *fpl* sur piste.

track record *n* SPORT & *fig* dossier *m*, carrière *f*; she has a good ~ elle a fait ses preuves; given his ~ vu ce qu'il a déjà accompli.

track rod *n Br* biellette *f* de connexion.

track shoe *n* chaussure *f* d'athlétisme.

tracksuit ['træk,suːt] *n* survêtement *m*.

tract [trækt] *n* -**1.** [pamphlet] tract *m*. -**2.** [large area] étendue *f*; *Am* [housing estate] lotissement *m*; [mining] gisement *m*; a ~ house un pavillon. -**3.** ANAT: digestive/respiratory ~ appareil *m* OR système *m* digestif/respiratoire.

tractable ['træktəbl] *adj* [person, animal] accommodant; [material] malléable; [problem] soluble, facile à résoudre.

Tractarianism [træk'teərɪənɪzm] *n* tractarianisme *m.*

traction ['trækʃn] *n* **-1.** MECH traction *f*; electric/steam ~ traction électrique/à vapeur. **-2.** MED: to be in ~ être en extension; ~ splint attelle *f* d'extension; ~ of the tongue [artificial respiration] tractions *fpl* rythmées de la langue.

traction engine *n* locomotive *f.*

tractive force ['træktɪv-] *n* effort *m* de traction.

tractor ['træktəʳ] *n* [on farm] tracteur *m*; TECH locomobile *f.*

tractorfeed ['træktəfiːd] *n* COMPUT dispositif *m* d'entraînement à picots.

tractor-trailer *n Am* semi-remorque *m.*

trad *inf* [træd] ◇ *adj* MUS traditionnel.
◇ *n*: ~ (jazz) jazz traditionnel des années 30.

trade [treɪd] ◇ *n* **-1.** *(U)* COMM commerce *m*, affaires *fpl*; the clothing ~ la confection, l'industrie *f* de la confection; she is in the tea ~ elle est dans le commerce du thé, elle est négociante en thé; the tourist ~ le tourisme; ~ is brisk les affaires vont bien; to do a good OR roaring ~ faire des affaires en or; domestic/foreign ~ commerce intérieur/extérieur; retail/wholesale ~ commerce de détail/de gros; Board of Trade *Br*, Department of Trade *Am* ministère *m* du Commerce; Minister of Trade *Br*, Secretary of Trade *Am* ministre *m* du Commerce; Department of Trade and Industry *Br* ≃ ministère *m* de l'Industrie et du Commerce. **-2.** [illicit dealings] trafic *m*; the drug ~ le trafic de drogue; the slave ~ la traite des esclaves. **-3.** [vocation, occupation] métier *m*; she is an electrician by ~ elle est électricienne de son métier OR de son état; to be in the ~ être du métier; as we say in the ~ comme on dit dans le métier; open to members of the ~ only pour les membres de la profession seulement. **-4.** [exchange] échange *m*; fair ~ échange équitable. **-5.** [regular customers] clientèle *f.* **-6.** *Am* [transaction] transaction *f* commerciale.
◇ *comp* **-1.** COMM [agreement, balance] commercial; ~ deficit balance *f* commerciale déficitaire, déficit *m* extérieur; ~ figures résultats *mpl* financiers. **-2.** [publication] spécialisé.
◇ *vt* [exchange] échanger, troquer; he ~d a marble for a toffee il a échangé OR troqué une bille contre un caramel; they ~d insults over the dinner table ils ont échangé des insultes pendant le dîner.
◇ *vi* **-1.** [businessman, country] faire du commerce; he ~s in clothing il est négociant en confection, il est dans la confection; what name do you ~ under? quel est votre raison sociale?; to ~ at a loss vendre à perte; to ~ with sb avoir OR entretenir des relations commerciales avec qqn; they stopped trading with Iran ils ont arrêté toute relation commerciale avec l'Iran. **-2.** *Am* [private individual] faire ses achats; to ~ at OR with faire ses courses à OR chez. **-3.** ST. EX [currency, commodity]: corn is trading at £25 le maïs se négocie à 25 livres.
◆ **trades** *npl* [winds] alizés *mpl.*
◆ **trade in** *vt sep* faire reprendre; I ~d my television in for a new one ils ont repris mon vieux téléviseur quand j'ai acheté le nouveau.
◆ **trade off** ◇ *vt sep* échanger, troquer; [as a compromise] accepter en compensation; to ~ sthg off against sthg laisser OR abandonner qqch pour qqch.
◇ *vi insep Am*: they ~ off every year for first place ils sont premiers chacun leur tour tous les ans.
◆ **trade on** *vt insep* exploiter, profiter de; he ~s on her gullibility il profite de sa crédulité; I'd hate to ~ on OR upon your kindness je ne voudrais pas abuser de votre gentillesse.

trade association *n* association *f* professionnelle.

trade barriers *npl* barrières *fpl* douanières.

trade cycle *n* cycle *m* économique.

Trade Descriptions Act *pr n loi britannique contre la publicité mensongère.*

trade discount *n* remise *f* professionnelle OR au détaillant.

trade fair *n* foire *f* OR exposition *f* commerciale.

trade gap *n* déficit *m* commercial.

trade-in *n* reprise *f*; will he accept a ~? acceptera-t-il la reprise?; they took my old refrigerator as a ~ ils ont repris mon vieux réfrigérateur; the ~ price/value of your old car le prix/la valeur à la reprise de votre ancienne voiture.

trademark ['treɪdmɑːk] ◇ *n* marque *f* (de fabrique); *fig* signe *m* caractéristique.
◇ *vt* [label a product] apposer une marque sur; [register a product] déposer.

trade name *n* [of product] nom *m* de marque; [of firm] raison *f* commerciale.

trade-off *n* échange *m*; [compromise] compromis *m*; there's always a ~ between speed and accuracy il faut toujours faire un compromis entre la vitesse et la précision.

trade paper *n* revue *f* spécialisée.

trade plate *n* plaque *f* d'immatriculation provisoire.

trade price *n* prix *m* de gros.

trader ['treɪdəʳ] *n* **-1.** [gen] commerçant *m*, -e *f*, marchand *m*, -e *f*; [on large scale] négociant *m*, -e *f.* **-2.** [ship] navire *m* marchand OR de commerce. **-3.** *Am* ST. EX contrepartiste *m.*

trade route *n* route *f* commerciale.

trade secret *n* secret *m* de fabrication; she won't tell me her recipe, she says it's a ~! *hum* elle ne veut pas me donner sa recette, elle dit que c'est un secret!

tradesman ['treɪdzmən] (*pl* tradesmen [-mən]) *n* **-1.** [trader] commerçant *m*, marchand *m*; ~'s entrance entrée *f* de service OR des fournisseurs. **-2.** [skilled workman] ouvrier *m* qualifié.

tradespeople ['treɪdz,piːpl] *npl esp Br* commerçants *mpl.*

trade(s) union *n* syndicat *m*; to join a ~ se syndiquer; the workers formed a ~ les ouvriers ont formé un syndicat; I am in the ~ je suis syndiqué, j'appartiens au syndicat.

Trades Union Congress *n confédération des syndicats britanniques.*

trade(s) unionism *n* syndicalisme *m.*

trade(s) unionist *n* syndicaliste *mf.*

trade wind *n* alizé *m.*

trading ['treɪdɪŋ] ◇ *n* commerce *m*, négoce *m*; [illicit dealing] trafic *m*; ~ on the Stock Exchange was heavy le volume de transactions à la Bourse était important; ~ losses for the past year were heavy les pertes subies pour l'exercice de l'année écoulée ont été lourdes.
◇ *comp* [company, partner] commercial; ~ nation nation *f* commerçante; ~ standards normes *fpl* de conformité; ~ standards office ≃ Direction *f* de la consommation et de la répression des fraudes; ~ year COMM année *f* d'exploitation, exercice *m.*

trading estate *n Br* zone *f* artisanale et commerciale.

trading post *n Am* comptoir *m* commercial.

trading stamp *n* timbre-prime *m.*

tradition [trə'dɪʃn] *n* tradition *f*, coutume *f*; it's in the best ~ of New Year's Eve parties c'est dans la plus pure tradition des réveillons du Nouvel An; ~ has it that... la tradition veut que...; the ~ that... la tradition selon laquelle... OR qui veut que...; a comedian in the ~ of Chaplin un comédien dans la lignée de Chaplin; to break with ~ rompre avec la tradition.

traditional [trə'dɪʃənl] *adj* traditionnel; it is ~ to sing Auld Lang Syne at New Year il est de tradition de chanter Auld Lang Syne au Nouvel An; ~ dress costume *m* traditionnel; this school is a very ~ one cette école est très traditionnelle.

traditionalism [trə'dɪʃnəlɪzm] *n* traditionalisme *m.*

traditionalist [trə'dɪʃnəlɪst] ◇ *n* traditionaliste *mf.*
◇ *adj* traditionaliste.

traditionally [trə'dɪʃnəlɪ] *adv* traditionnellement.

traduce [trə'djuːs] *vt fml* [malign] calomnier, diffamer.

traffic ['træfɪk] (*pt* & *pp* trafficked, *cont* trafficking) ◇ *n* **-1.** [on roads] circulation *f*; [rail, air, maritime] trafic *m*; holiday ~ [outward] la circulation des grands départs; [homeward] la circulation des grands retours; the ~ is heavy/light la circulation est dense/fluide; ~ is building up la circulation augmente; there is a great deal of ~ on the roads les routes sont encombrées; ~ in and out of the city circulation à destination et en provenance de la ville; watch out for ~ when crossing! (fais) attention aux voitures en traversant!; road closed to heavy ~ route interdite aux poids lourds; eastbound ~ circulation ouest-est; the cyclist weaved through the ~ le cycliste se faufila entre les voitures; the resort experiences heavy ski ~ in winter *fig* il y a beaucoup de skieurs en hiver dans cette station ❑ road ~ circulation *f* routière; sea ~ navigation *f* OR trafic *m* maritime; rail OR railway ~ trafic *m* ferroviaire; through ~ circulation *f* de transit; ~ calming *mesures visant à ralentir la circulation.* **-2.** COMM commerce *m*; [illicit] trafic *m*; *Am* [customers] clientèle *f*; the ~ in arms/drugs le trafic des armes/de drogue. **-3.** *Br* [dealings] échange *m*; you should have no ~ with these people évitez d'avoir affaire à ces gens.
◇ *vi*: to ~ in faire le commerce de; organizations trafficking in arms/drugs des organisations spécialisées dans le trafic d'armes/de drogue.

trafficator ['træfɪkeɪtəʳ] *n Br dated* flèche *f* de direction.

traffic circle *n Am* rond-point *m*, sens *m* giratoire.

traffic control *n* régulation *f* de la circulation; AERON, NAUT & RAIL contrôle *m* du trafic; ~ tower tour *f* de contrôle.

traffic controller *n* contrôleur *m*, -euse *f* de la navigation aérienne, aiguilleur *m* du ciel.

traffic cop *inf n Am* agent *m* de la circulation.

traffic island *n* refuge *m.*

traffic jam *n Br* embouteillage *m*, bouchon *m.*

trafficker ['træfɪkəʳ] *n* trafiquant *m*, -e *f*; drug ~ trafiquant *m* de drogue.

traffic light *n* feu *m* de signalisation; the ~s are (on) green le feu est (au) vert; carry on to the next set of ~s continuez jusqu'aux prochains feux.

traffic offence *n* infraction *f* au code de la route.

traffic pattern *n* AERON couloir *m* OR position *f* d'approche.

traffic police *n* [speeding, safety] police *f* de la route; [point duty] police *f* de la circulation.

traffic policeman *n* agent *m* de police; [on point duty] agent *m* de la circulation.

traffic sign *n* panneau *m* de signalisation, poteau *m* indicateur.

traffic signal *n* feu *m* de signalisation.

traffic warden *n Br* contractuel *m*, -elle *f.*

TRAFFIC WARDEN:
En Grande-Bretagne, les contractuels sont habilités à dresser les procès-verbaux mais aussi à régler la circulation.

---

tragedian [trə'dʒiːdɪən] *n* [author] auteur *m* tragique; [actor] tragédien *m.*

tragedienne [trə,dʒiːdɪ'en] *n* tragédienne *f.*

tragedy ['trædʒədɪ] (*pl* tragedies) *n* [gen & THEAT] tragédie *f*; it's a ~ that this should happen to her c'est tragique que ça lui arrive à elle; what a ~! quel malheur!, quelle tragédie!

tragic(al) ['trædʒɪk(l)] *adj* tragique.

tragically ['trædʒɪklɪ] *adv* tragiquement; the trip went ~ wrong le voyage a tourné au drame.

tragic irony *n* ironie *f* tragique.

tragicomedy [,trædʒɪ'kɒmədɪ] (*pl* tragicomedies) *n* tragi-comédie *f.*

tragicomic(al) [,trædʒɪ'kɒmɪk(l)] *adj* tragicomique.

trail [treɪl] ◇ *n* -**1.** [path] sentier *m*, chemin *m*; [through jungle] piste *f*; ski ~ piste de ski; to break a ~ faire la trace, tracer; **he hit the campaign** ~ *fig* il est parti en campagne (électorale); **the end of the** ~ *Am* le bout de la piste *(nom donné à la Californie par les pionniers américains)*; the ~ of tears *Am* HIST le chemin des larmes. -**2.** [traces of passage] piste *f*, trace *f*; to be on the ~ of sb/sthg être sur la piste de qqn/qqch; **the police were on his** ~ la police était sur sa trace; **a false** ~ une fausse piste; **the storm left a** ~ **of destruction** l'orage a tout détruit sur son passage; **she leaves a** ~ **of broken hearts behind her** *fig* elle laisse beaucoup de cœurs brisés derrière elle. -**3.** [of blood, smoke] traînée *f*; [of comet] queue *f*. -**4.** [of gun] crosse *f* OR flèche *f* d'affût.
◇ *vt* -**1.** [follow] suivre, filer; [track] suivre la piste de; [animal, criminal] traquer. -**2.** [drag behind, tow] traîner; [boat, trailer] tirer, remorquer; **she** ~**ed her hand in the water** elle laissait traîner sa main dans l'eau; **he was** ~**ing a sack of coal behind him** il traînait OR tirait un sac de charbon derrière lui ❑ **to** ~ **one's coat** chercher la bagarre. -**3.** [lag behind] être en arrière par rapport à; **he** ~**s all his classmates** il est en retard par rapport aux autres élèves. -**4.** [gun] porter à la main. -**5.** [advertise] diffuser (une bande-annonce).
◇ *vi* -**1.** [long garment] traîner; [plant] ramper; **smoke** ~**ed from the chimney** de la fumée sortait de la cheminée. -**2.** [move slowly] traîner; **he** ~**ed along at a snail's pace** il avançait comme un escargot; **the prisoners** ~**ed slowly past** les prisonniers passaient lentement à la queue leu leu; **he** ~**ed in last** SPORT il est arrivé bon dernier. -**3.** [lag behind in contest] être à la traîne; **he's** ~**ing in the polls** il est à la traîne dans les sondages. -**4.** [follow] suivre, filer; **with five children** ~**ing behind her** avec cinq enfants dans son sillage.
◆ **trail away** *vi insep* s'estomper; **his voice** ~**ed away to a whisper** sa voix ne fut plus qu'un murmure.
◆ **trail off** *vi insep* s'estomper; **he** ~**ed off in mid sentence** il n'a pas terminé sa phrase.

THE TRAIL OF TEARS:
Nom donné au chemin parcouru, en 1838, par les Indiens d'Amérique transférés de force dans des réserves à l'ouest du Mississippi et sur lequel nombre d'entre eux succombèrent à la maladie et aux mauvais traitements.

---

trail bike *n* moto *f* de cross.
trailblazer ['treɪl,bleɪzəʳ] *n fig* pionnier *m*, -ère *f*.
trailblazing ['treɪl,bleɪzɪŋ] *adj* de pionnier.
trailer ['treɪləʳ] *n* -**1.** AUT remorque *f*; *Am* camping-car *m*; ~ **court**, ~ **park** *Am terrain aménagé pour les camping-cars*; ~ **tent** tente *f* remorque. -**2.** CIN & TV bande-annonce *f*. -**3.** [end of film roll] amorce *f*.
trailing ['treɪlɪŋ] *adj* traînant; [plant] rampant; ~ **edge** AERON bord *m* de fuite.
train [treɪn] ◇ *n* -**1.** [railway] train *m*; [underground] métro *m*, rame *f*; **to go by** ~ prendre le train, aller en train; **I met a friend on the** ~ j'ai rencontré un ami dans le train; **to transport goods by** ~ transporter des marchandises par voie ferrée OR rail; 'to the ~s' 'accès aux quais'. -**2.** [procession - of vehicles] file *f*, cortège *m*; [- of mules] file *f*; [- of camels] caravane *f*; MIL convoi *m*; [retinue] suite *f*, équipage *m*; MIL équipage *m*; **the famine brought disease in its** ~ la maladie succéda à la famine. -**3.** [of dress] traîne *f*. -**4.** [connected sequence] suite *f*, série *f*; **in an unbroken** ~ en succession ininterrompue; **a** ~ **of thought** un enchaînement d'idées; **a** ~ **of events** une suite d'événements; **my remark interrupted her** ~ **of thought** ma remarque a interrompu le fil de sa pensée OR ses pensées; **to follow sb's** ~ **of thought** suivre le raisonnement de qqn. -**5.** MECH train *m*; ~ **of gears** train d'engrenage. -**6.** *fml* [progress]: **in** ~ en marche; **to set sthg in** ~ mettre qqch en marche. -**7.** [fuse] amorce *f*; [of gunpowder] traînée *f* (de poudre).
◇ *comp* [dispute, strike] des cheminots, des chemins de fer; [reservation, ticket] de train; **there is a good** ~ **service to the city** la ville est bien desservie par le train; **there is an hourly** ~ **service** il y a des trains toutes les heures.
◇ *vt* -**1.** [employee, soldier] former; [voice] travailler; [animal] dresser; [mind] former; SPORT entraîner; [plant - by pruning] tailler; [- by tying] palisser; [climbing plant] diriger, faire grimper; **he is** ~**ing sb to take over from him** il forme son successeur; **to** ~ **sb in a trade** apprendre un métier à qqn, préparer qqn à un métier; **she was** ~**ed in economics** elle a reçu une formation d'économiste; **he was** ~**ed at Sandhurst** il a fait ses classes à Sandhurst; **to** ~ **sb to use sthg** apprendre à qqn à utiliser qqch; **to** ~ **sb up** former OR préparer qqn; **he has been** ~**ed in the use of explosives** il a été formé au maniement des explosifs; **the dogs have been** ~**ed to detect explosives** les chiens ont été dressés pour détecter les explosifs. -**2.** [direct, aim] viser; **he** ~**ed his gun on us** il a braqué son arme sur nous. -**3.** *inf* RAIL: **we** ~**ed it down to the South of France** nous sommes allés en train jusque dans le Midi de la France.
◇ *vi* -**1.** recevoir une formation; **I** ~**ed as a translator** j'ai reçu une formation de traducteur; **she's** ~**ing as a teacher** elle suit une formation pédagogique; **where did you** ~? où avez-vous reçu votre formation? -**2.** SPORT s'entraîner, se préparer.
trainbearer ['treɪn,beərəʳ] *n personne qui porte la traîne d'un dignitaire*; [at wedding] demoiselle *f* OR dame *f* d'honneur; [boy] page *m*.
trained [treɪnd] *adj* compétent, qualifié; [engineer] breveté, diplômé; [nurse, translator] diplômé, qualifié; **he's not** ~ **for this job** il n'est pas qualifié OR n'a pas la formation requise pour ce poste; **we need a well** ~ **employee** il nous faut quelqu'un qui ait une bonne formation; **she has her boss well** ~! *hum* elle a bien dressé son patron!; **a** ~ **eye** un œil exercé; **a** ~ **ear** une oreille exercée; **he has a** ~ **voice** il a travaillé sa voix || [animal] dressé; **a** ~ **parrot** un perroquet savant; **a well** ~ **horse** un cheval bien dressé.
trainee [treɪ'ni:] ◇ *n* stagiaire *mf*; **sales** ~ stagiaire de vente.
◇ *comp* stagiaire, en stage; [in trades] en apprentissage; ~ **journalist** journaliste *mf* stagiaire; ~ **computer programmer** élève *mf* programmeur.
trainer ['treɪnəʳ] *n* -**1.** SPORT entraîneur *m*. -**2.** [of animal] dresseur *m*, -euse *f*; [of racehorses] entraîneur *m*; [of lion] dompteur *m*, -euse *f*. -**3.** AERON [simulator] simulateur *m*; ~ **(aircraft)** avion-école *m*. -**4.** [shoe] chaussure *f* de sport.
training ['treɪnɪŋ] ◇ *n* -**1.** formation *f*; [of soldier] instruction *f*; [of animal] dressage *m*; **further** ~ perfectionnement *m*; **he is a carpenter by** ~ il est menuisier de formation; **I have had some business** ~ j'ai suivi une petite formation commerciale ❑ **in-service** ~ formation continue; **staff** ~ formation du personnel; **vocational** ~ formation professionnelle; **to do one's basic** ~ MIL faire ses classes. -**2.** SPORT entraînement *m*, préparation *f*; **to be in** ~ être en cours d'entraînement OR de préparation; **I'm out of** ~ j'ai perdu la forme; **she's in** ~ **for the tennis tournament** elle s'entraîne pour le tournoi OR se prépare au tournoi de tennis.
◇ *comp* [centre, programme, scheme] de formation; ~ **manual** manuel *m* d'instruction.
Training Agency *pr n*: **the** ~ *organisme britannique créé en 1989, qui propose des stages de formation et de recyclage*.
training camp *n* camp *m* d'entraînement; MIL base *f* école.
training college *n* école *f* spécialisée OR professionnelle.
training course *n* stage *m* de formation.
training ship *n* navire-école *m*.
training shoes *npl* chaussures *fpl* de sport.
train set *n* train *m* électrique.
trainsick ['treɪnsɪk] *adj*: **to be** OR **to get** ~ être malade en train.
train spotter *n Br amateur de trains dont la passion consiste à relever les numéros d'immatriculation des locomotives*.
train spotting [-'spɒtɪŋ] *n*: **to go** ~ observer les trains.
traipse *inf* [treɪps] ◇ *vi*: **we all** ~**d off to the shops** nous sommes tous partis traîner dans les magasins; **she came traipsing in** elle est entrée en traînassant; **to** ~ **about** OR **around** se balader, vadrouiller; **they** ~**d from one museum to another** ils ont fait tous les musées.
◇ *n* longue promenade; **it's quite a** ~ ça fait une trotte.
trait [treɪ, treɪt] *n* trait *m*.
traitor ['treɪtəʳ] *n* traître *m*; **a** ~ **to his country** un traître envers son pays; **you're a** ~ **to your country/to the cause** vous trahissez votre pays/la cause; **he turned** ~ il est passé à l'ennemi.
traitorous ['treɪtərəs] *adj fml* traître, perfide.
traitress ['treɪtrɪs] *n* traîtresse *f*.
trajectory [trə'dʒektərɪ] (*pl* **trajectories**) *n* trajectoire *f*.
tra-la(-la) [trɑ:'lɑ:, ,trɑ:lɑ:'lɑ:] *onomat refrain de chanson sans sens particulier*.
tram [træm] *n Br* tram *m*, tramway *m*; MIN berline *f*, benne *f* roulante; **to go by** ~ prendre le tram; **the** ~**s** le réseau des tramways; **to work on the** ~**s** travailler dans les tramways.
tramcar ['træmkɑ:ʳ] *n Br* tram *m*, tramway *m*.
tramline ['træmlaɪn] *n Br* [rails] voie *f* de tramway; [route] ligne *f* de tramway.
◆ **tramlines** *npl* [in tennis, badminton] lignes *fpl* de côté.
trammel ['træml] (*Br pt* & *pp* **trammelled**, *cont* **trammelling**, *Am pt* & *pp* **trammeled**, *cont* **trammeling**) ◇ *vt literal* & *fig* entraver.
◇ *n* -**1.** **the** ~**s of society** les entraves de la société. -**2.** FISHING tramail *m*, trémail *m*.
tramp [træmp] ◇ *n* -**1.** [vagabond] clochard *m*, -e *f*, chemineau *m dated*; 'The Tramp' *Chaplin* 'le Vagabond'. -**2.** [sound] bruit *m* de pas; **I could hear the** ~ **of soldiers' feet** j'entendais le pas lourd des soldats. -**3.** [long walk] randonnée *f* (à pied), promenade *f*; **it's a long** ~ **into town** il y a un bon bout de chemin à faire jusqu'à la ville. -**4.** [ship]: ~ **(steamer)** tramp *m*. -**5.** *inf Am pej* traînée.
◇ *vi* [hike] marcher, se promener; [walk heavily] marcher d'un pas lourd; **we** ~**ed along in silence for a while** nous avons poursuivi notre chemin en silence pendant un moment; **to** ~ **up and down** faire les cent pas.
◇ *vt* parcourir; **he** ~**ed the streets in search of work** il a battu le pavé pour trouver du travail.
◆ **tramp down, tramp in** *vt sep* tasser du pied.
trample ['træmpl] ◇ *vt* piétiner, fouler aux pieds; **the crowd** ~**d the man to death** l'homme est mort piétiné par la foule || [sb's feelings] bafouer; **he** ~**d my arguments underfoot** il a piétiné OR pulvérisé mes arguments.
◇ *vi* marcher d'un pas lourd.
◇ *n* [action] piétinement *m*; [sound] bruit *m* de pas.
◆ **trample on, trample over** *vt insep* piétiner; *fig* [sb's feelings] bafouer; [objections] passer outre à.
trampoline ['træmpəli:n] ◇ *n* trampoline *m*.
◇ *vi*: **to** ~, **to go trampolining** faire du trampoline.
tramway ['træmweɪ] (*pl* **tramways**) *n Br* [rails] voie *f* de tramway; [route] ligne *f* de tramway.
trance [trɑ:ns] *n* transe *f*; MED catalepsie *f*; **to go** OR **to fall into a** ~ entrer en transe; MED tomber en catalepsie; **he put me into a** ~ il m'a hypnotisé, il m'a fait entrer en transe.
trannie *inf*, **tranny** *inf* ['trænɪ] (*pl* **trannies**) *n Br* [transistor radio] transistor *m*.
tranquil ['træŋkwɪl] *adj* tranquille, paisible.

tranquillity *Br*, **tranquility** *Am* [træŋ'kwɪlətɪ] *n* tranquillité *f*, calme *m*.

tranquillize, -ise *Br*, **tranquilize** *Am* ['træŋkwɪlaɪz] *vt* calmer, apaiser; MED mettre sous tranquillisants.

tranquillizer *Br*, **tranquilizer** *Am* ['træŋkwɪlaɪzə^r] *n* tranquillisant *m*, calmant *m*.

transact [træn'zækt] *vt* traiter, régler; **the deal was successfully ~ed** l'affaire a été conclue avec brio.

transaction [træn'zækʃn] *n* -**1.** [gen & BANK] opération *f*, affaire *f*; **cash ~** opération *f* au comptant ‖ ECON, FIN & ST. EX transaction *f*; **cash ~s have increased** les mouvements d'espèces ont augmenté; **Stock Exchange ~s** opérations *fpl* de Bourse. -**2.** [act of transacting] conduite *f*, gestion *f*; **~ of business will continue as normal** la conduite des affaires se poursuivra comme à l'accoutumée. -**3.** COMPUT mouvement *m*.
◆ **transactions** *npl* [proceedings of an organization] travaux *mpl*; [minutes] actes *mpl*.

transactional [træn'zækʃənl] *adj* transactionnel; **~ analysis** PSYCH analyse *f* transactionnelle.

transalpine [,trænz'ælpaɪn] *adj* transalpin.

transatlantic [,trænzət'læntɪk] *adj* transatlantique.

Transcaucasia [,trænskɔː'keɪzjə] *pr n* Transcaucasie *f*.

transceiver [træn'siːvə^r] *n* émetteur-récepteur *m*.

transcend [træn'send] *vt* -**1.** [go beyond] transcender, dépasser; PHILOS & RELIG transcender; **the issue ~s party loyalties** le problème dépasse les clivages partisans. -**2.** [surpass] surpasser.

transcendence [træn'sendəns], **transcendency** [træn'sendənsɪ] *n* transcendance *f*.

transcendent [træn'sendənt] *adj* transcendant.

transcendental [,trænsen'dentl] *adj* transcendantal.

transcendentalism [,trænsen'dentəlɪzm] *n* transcendantalisme *m*.

transcendental meditation *n* méditation *f* transcendantale.

transcontinental ['trænz,kɒntɪ'nentl] *adj* transcontinental; **the Transcontinental Railroad** la Transcontinentale.

THE TRANSCONTINENTAL RAILROAD:
Voie de chemin de fer traversant les États-Unis d'est en ouest. Achevée en 1869, elle fut construite par deux compagnies: la «Union Pacific» et la «Central Pacific», qui, parties respectivement de la côte est et de la côte ouest, se rejoignirent dans l'Utah.

transcribe [træn'skraɪb] *vt* transcrire.

transcript ['trænskrɪpt] *n* transcription *f*; SCH & UNIV *dossier complet de la scolarité*.

transcription [træn'skrɪpʃn] *n* transcription *f*; **broad/narrow ~** LING transcription large/étroite.

transduce [trænz'djuːs] *vt* transformer, convertir.

transducer [trænz'djuːsə^r] *n* transducteur *m*.

transduction [trænz'dʌkʃn] *n* transduction *f*.

transect [træn'sekt] *vt* sectionner transversalement.

transection [træn'sekʃn] *n* coupe *f* OR section *f* transversale.

transept ['trænsept] *n* transept *m*.

transfer [*vb* træns'fɜː^r, *n* 'trænsfɜː^r] ◇ *vt* -**1.** [move] transférer; [employee, civil servant] transférer, muter; [soldier] muter; [player] transférer; [passenger] transférer, transborder; [object, goods] transférer, transporter; [money] virer; **can this ticket be transferred to another airline?** peut-on utiliser ce billet d'avion sur une autre compagnie?; **I transferred the funds to my bank account** j'ai fait virer l'argent sur mon compte bancaire. -**2.** [convey - property, ownership] transmettre, transférer; [- power, responsibility] passer; JUR faire cession de, céder; **she will ~ the rights over to him** elle va lui céder OR passer les droits. -**3.** TELEC: **I'd like to ~ the charges** *Br* je voudrais téléphoner en PCV; **I'm transferring you now** [operator] je vous mets en communication ❑ **transferred charge call** *Br* communication *f* en PCV. -**4.** [displace - design, picture] reporter, décalquer; **to ~ a design from one surface to another** décalquer un dessin d'un support sur un autre; **she transferred her affection/allegiance to him** *fig* elle a reporté son affection/sa fidélité sur lui.
◇ *vi* -**1.** [move] être transféré; [employee, civil servant] être muté OR transféré; [soldier] être muté; SPORT [player] être transféré; **she transferred to another school** *Am* elle a changé d'école; **I'm transferring to history** je me réoriente en histoire. -**2.** [change mode of transport] être transféré OR transbordé; **they had to ~ to a train** ils ont dû changer et prendre le train.
◇ *n* -**1.** [gen] transfert *m*; [of employee, civil servant] mutation *f*; [of passenger] transfert *m*, transbordement *m*; [of player] transfert *m*; [of goods, objects] transfert *m*, transport *m*; [of money] virement *m*; **he has asked for a ~** il a demandé son transfert OR à être muté; **~ of a debt** cession *f* OR revirement *m* d'une créance; **bank ~** virement *m* bancaire. -**2.** JUR transmission *f*, cession *f*; **~ of ownership from sb to sb** transfert *m* OR translation *f* de propriété de qqn à qqn; **application for ~ of proceedings** demande *f* de renvoi devant une autre juridiction. -**3.** POL: **~ of power** passation *f* de pouvoir. -**4.** [design, picture] décalcomanie *f*; [rub-on] autocollant *m*; [sew-on] décalque *m*. -**5.** [change of mode of travel] transfert *m*; [at airport, train station] correspondance *f*; **~ (ticket)** billet *m* de correspondance.

transferable [træns'fɜːrəbl] *adj* transmissible; JUR cessible; **this ticket is not ~** ce billet est strictement personnel; **~ securities** FIN valeurs *fpl* négociables.

transferable vote *n voix pouvant se reporter sur un autre candidat*.

transferee [,trænsfɜː'riː] *n* JUR & FIN cessionnaire *mf*, bénéficiaire *mf*.

transference ['trænsfərəns] *n* [gen & PSYCH] transfert *m*; [of employee, civil servant] mutation *f*; [of money] virement *m*; [of power] passation *f*; [of ownership] transfert *m* OR translation *f* de propriété.

transfer fee *n* FTBL prix *m* du transfert.

transfer list *n Br* liste *f* des joueurs transférables.

transfer-listed *adj Br*: **to be ~** être sur la liste des joueurs transférables.

transferor, transferrer [træns'fɜːrə^r] *n* JUR cédant *m*, -e *f*.

transfer passenger *n* [between flights] voyageur *m*, -euse *f* en transit.

transfiguration [,trænsfɪgə'reɪʃn] *n* transfiguration *f*; **the Transfiguration** RELIG la Transfiguration.

transfigure [træns'fɪgə^r] *vt* transfigurer.

transfinite [træns'faɪnaɪt] *adj* transfini.

transfix [træns'fɪks] *vt literal* transpercer; *fig* pétrifier; **to be ~ed with fear** être paralysé par la peur; **she stood ~ed** elle est restée clouée sur place.

transform [træns'fɔːm] ◇ *vt* -**1.** [change - gen] transformer, métamorphoser; **to ~ sthg into sthg** transformer qqch en qqch; **her year abroad has completely ~ed her** son année à l'étranger l'a complètement métamorphosée. -**2.** ELEC transformer; CHEM, MATH & PHYS transformer, convertir. -**3.** GRAMM transformer.
◇ *n* -**1.** LING transformation *f*. -**2.** MATH transformée *f*.

transformation [,trænsfə'meɪʃn] *n* transformation *f*, métamorphose *f*; ELEC & MATH transformation *f*; CHEM & PHYS conversion *f*; LING transformation *f*.

transformational grammar [,trænsfə'meɪʃənl-] *n* grammaire *f* transformationnelle.

transformer [træns'fɔːmə^r] ◇ *n* transformateur *m*.
◇ *comp*: **~ station** station *f* de transformation.

transfuse [træns'fjuːz] *vt* [gen & MED] transfuser.

transfusion [træns'fjuːʒn] *n* [gen & MED] transfusion *f*; **they gave him a ~** ils lui ont fait une transfusion; **blood ~** transfusion sanguine OR de sang.

transgress [træns'gres] *fml* ◇ *vt* transgresser, enfreindre.
◇ *vi* pécher.

transgression [træns'greʃn] *n fml* -**1.** [overstepping] transgression *f*. -**2.** [crime] faute *f*, violation *f* (d'une loi); RELIG péché *m*.

transgressor [træns'gresə^r] *n* [gen & JUR] transgresseur *m*; RELIG pécheur *m*, -eresse *f*.

tranship [træns'ʃɪp] = **transship**.

transience ['trænzɪəns] *n* caractère *m* éphémère OR transitoire.

transient ['trænzɪənt] ◇ *adj* [temporary] transitoire, passager; [fleeting] éphémère.
◇ *n* -**1.** [person] voyageur *m*, -euse *f* en transit. -**2.** [goods] marchandise *f* en transit.

transistor [træn'zɪstə^r] *n* transistor *m*.

transistorize, -ise [træn'zɪstəraɪz] *vt* transistoriser; **~d circuit** circuit *m* à transistors.

transistor radio *n* transistor *m*.

transit ['trænsɪt] ◇ *n* [of goods, passengers] transit *m*; ASTRON passage *m*; **in ~** en transit; **goods lost in ~** marchandises égarées pendant le transport.
◇ *comp* [goods, passengers] en transit; [documents, lounge, port] de transit; **~ authority** *Am* régie *f* des transports (en commun).
◇ *vt* [goods, passengers] transiter; ASTRON passer sur.

transit camp *n* camp *m* de transit.

transition [træn'zɪʃn] ◇ *n* transition *f*, passage *m*; **the ~ from childhood to maturity** le passage de l'enfance à l'âge adulte.
◇ *comp* [period] de transition.

transitional [træn'zɪʃənl] *adj* de transition, transitoire; **~ relief** *Br* ADMIN *aide financière de l'État pour faciliter la mise en place d'une réforme administrative*.

transitive ['trænsətɪv] *adj* transitif.

transitively ['trænsətɪvlɪ] *adv* transitivement.

transitory ['trænsɪtrɪ] *adj* transitoire, passager.

translatable [træns'leɪtəbl] *adj* traduisible.

translate [træns'leɪt] ◇ *vt* -**1.** traduire; **to ~ sthg from Spanish into English** traduire qqch de l'espagnol en anglais; **how do you ~ "hunger"?** comment traduit-on «hunger»?; **it can be ~d as...** on peut le traduire par...; **~d into Fahrenheit** exprimé OR converti en Fahrenheit; **he ~d her silence as a refusal** *fig* il a interprété son silence comme un refus; **to ~ ideas into action** traduire des idées en actes. -**2.** RELIG [transfer - cleric, relics] transférer; [convey to heaven] ravir.
◇ *vi* -**1.** [words] se traduire; **it doesn't ~** c'est intraduisible. -**2.** [person] traduire.

translation [træns'leɪʃn] *n* -**1.** traduction *f*; SCH version *f*; **the book is a ~ from (the) Chinese** le livre est traduit du chinois; **the text loses something in the ~** le texte perd quelque chose à la traduction. -**2.** RELIG [of cleric, relics] translation *f*; [conveying to heaven] ravissement *m*.

translator [træns'leɪtə^r] *n* traducteur *m*, -trice *f*.

transliterate [trænz'lɪtəreɪt] *vt* translitérer, translittérer.

transliteration [,trænzlɪtə'reɪʃn] *n* translitération *f*, translittération *f*, transcription *f*.

translocate [,trænzləʊ'keɪt] *vt* déplacer.

translucence [trænz'luːsns] *n* translucidité *f*.

translucent [trænz'luːsnt] *adj* translucide, diaphane.

transmigrate [ˌtrænzmaɪ'greɪt] *vi* [soul] transmigrer; [people] émigrer.

transmigration [ˌtrænzmaɪ'greɪʃn] *n* [of souls] transmigration *f*; [of people] émigration *f*.

transmissible [trænz'mɪsəbl] *adj* transmissible.

transmission [trænz'mɪʃn] *n* **-1.** transmission *f*; [broadcast] retransmission *f*. **-2.** AUT transmission *f*; *Am* boîte *f* de vitesses; ~ shaft arbre *m* de transmission.

transmit [trænz'mɪt] (*pt* & *pp* **transmitted**, *cont* **transmitting**) ◇ *vt* transmettre; TELEC émettre, diffuser.
◇ *vi* RADIO, TELEC & TV émettre, diffuser.

transmitter [trænz'mɪtə^r] *n* transmetteur *m*; RADIO & TV émetteur *m*; [in telephone] microphone *m* (téléphonique).

transmitting [trænz'mɪtɪŋ] ◇ *adj* TELEC émetteur *m*.
◇ *n* transmission *f*.

transmogrify [trænz'mɒgrɪfaɪ] (*pt* & *pp* **transmogrified**) *vt hum* métamorphoser, changer.

transmutable [trænz'mjuːtəbl] *adj* transmuable, transmutable.

transmutation [ˌtrænzmjuː'teɪʃn] *n* transmutation *f*.

transmute [trænz'mjuːt] *vt* transmuer, transmuter; the process ~s the metal into gold le processus transforme OR transmute le métal en or.

transnational [ˌtrænz'næʃənl] *adj* transnational.

transom ['trænsəm] *n* **-1.** [in window] petit bois *m* horizontal; [above door] traverse *f* d'imposte. **-2.** *Am* [fanlight]: ~ (window) imposte *f* (semi-circulaire).

transonic [træn'sɒnɪk] *adj* transsonique.

transparency [træns'pærənsɪ] (*pl* **transparencies**) *n* **-1.** [gen & PHYS] transparence *f*. **-2.** [for overhead projector] transparent *m*; *esp Br* [slide] diapositive *f*.

transparent [træns'pærənt] *adj* [gen & PHYS] transparent.

transpiration [ˌtrænspɪ'reɪʃn] *n* BOT & PHYSIOL transpiration *f*.

transpire [træn'spaɪə^r] ◇ *vi* **-1.** [be discovered, turn out] apparaître; it ~d that he had been embezzling funds on a appris OR on s'est aperçu qu'il avait détourné des fonds. **-2.** [happen] se passer, arriver; the events that ~d later that day les événements intervenus plus tard dans la journée. **-3.** BOT & PHYSIOL transpirer.
◇ *vt* **-1.** BOT & PHYSIOL transpirer.

transplant [*vb* træns'plɑːnt, *n* 'trænsˌplɑːnt] ◇ *vt* **-1.** BOT [plant] transplanter; [seedling] repiquer. **-2.** MED [organ] greffer, transplanter; [tissue] greffer. **-3.** [population] transplanter.
◇ *n* MED [organ] transplant *m*; [tissue] greffe *f*; [operation] greffe *f*; she's had a kidney ~ on lui a fait une greffe du rein; she's had a heart ~ on lui a greffé un cœur.

transplantation [ˌtrænsplɑːn'teɪʃn] *n* **-1.** BOT [of seedling] repiquage *m*; [of plant] transplantation *f*. **-2.** *fig* [of people] transplantation *f*.

transponder [træn'spɒndə^r] *n* transpondeur *m*.

transport [*n* 'trænspɔːt, *vb* træn'spɔːt] ◇ *n* **-1.** (*U*) *Br* [system] transport *m*, transports *mpl*; public ~ transports *mpl* publics OR en commun; he went by public ~ [bus] il est allé en bus; [train] il est allé en train. **-2.** [means] moyen *m* de transport OR de locomotion; have you got ~ for tonight? *inf Br* tu as un moyen de locomotion pour ce soir? ❑ ~ plane avion *m* de transport; ~ ship navire *m* de transport; troop ~ MIL transport *m* de troupes. **-3.** [of goods] transport *m*. **-4.** *lit* [of joy] transport *m*; [of anger] accès *m*; he went into ~s of delight il fut transporté de joie.
◇ *vt* transporter.

transportable [træn'spɔːtəbl] *adj* transportable.

transportation [ˌtrænspɔː'teɪʃn] *n* **-1.** *Am* [transport] transport *m*; public ~ transports publics; ~ system système *m* des transports; Secretary of Transportation POL ministre *m* des Transports. **-2.** [of criminals] transportation *f*.

transport café *n Br* ≃ routier *m (restaurant)*.

transporter [træn'spɔːtə^r] *n* **-1.** MIL [for troops - lorry] camion *m* de transport; [- ship] navire *m* de transport; [for tanks] camion *m* porte-char. **-2.** [for cars - lorry] camion *m* pour transport d'automobiles; [- train] wagon *m* pour transport d'automobiles.

transporter bridge *n* pont *m* transbordeur.

Transport House *pr n bâtiment à Londres abritant le siège de la TGWU et, jusqu'en 1980, le parti travailliste.*

transpose [træns'pəʊz] *vt* transposer.

transposition [ˌtrænspə'zɪʃn] *n* transposition *f*.

transputer [træns'pjuːtə^r] *n* COMPUT transputer *m*.

transsexual [træns'sekʃʊəl] *n* transsexuel *m*, -elle *f*.

transship [træns'ʃɪp] (*pt* & *pp* **transshipped**, *cont* **transshipping**) *vt* transborder.

Trans-Siberian ['trænz-] *adj*: the ~ (Railway) le Transsibérien.

transsonic [træn'sɒnɪk] = **transonic**.

transubstantiate [ˌtrænsəb'stænʃɪeɪt] ◇ *vt* transmuer, transmuter.
◇ *vi* RELIG subir la transsubstantiation.

transubstantiation ['trænsəbˌstænʃɪ'eɪʃn] *n* transsubstantiation *f*.

transuranic [ˌtrænsjʊ'rænɪk] *adj* transuranien.

Transvaal ['trænzvɑːl] *pr n* Transvaal *m*; in the ~ au Transvaal.

transversal [trænz'vɜːsl] ◇ *adj* transversal.
◇ *n* GEOM transversale *f*.

transversally [trænz'vɜːsəlɪ] *adv* transversalement.

transverse ['trænzvɜːs] ◇ *adj* [beam, line] transversal; ANAT transverse; ~ engine AUT moteur *m* transversal.
◇ *n* [gen] partie *f* transversale; GEOM axe *m* transversal *(d'une hyperbole)*.

transversely [ˌtrænz'vɜːslɪ] *adv* transversalement.

transverter [trænz'vɜːtə^r] *n* RADIO émetteur-récepteur *m* additionnel.

transvestism [trænz'vestɪzm] *n* travestisme *m*, transvestisme *m*.

transvestite [trænz'vestaɪt] *n* travesti *m*.

Transylvania [ˌtrænsɪl'veɪnjə] *pr n* Transylvanie *f*; in ~ en Transylvanie.

Transylvanian [ˌtrænsɪl'veɪnjən] ◇ *n* Transylvanien *m*, -enne *f*.
◇ *adj* transylvanien.

trap [træp] (*pt* & *pp* **trapped**, *cont* **trapping**) ◇ *n* **-1.** [snare] piège *m*; [dug in ground] trappe *f*; [gintrap] collet *m*; to set OR to lay a ~ for hares dresser OR tendre un piège pour les lièvres; the badger was caught in a ~ le blaireau était pris dans un piège. **-2.** *fig* piège *m*, traquenard *m*; to set OR to lay a ~ for sb tendre un piège à qqn; they fell into the ~ ils sont tombés dans le piège; the poverty ~ le piège de la pauvreté. **-3.** [in drain] siphon *m*. **-4.** SPORT [in dog racing] box *m* de départ; [for shooting] ball-trap *m*. **-5.** [carriage] cabriolet *m*, charrette *f* anglaise. **-6.** [trapdoor] trappe *f*. **-7.** ▽ [mouth] gueule *f*; shut your ~! ta gueule!, ferme-la!
◇ *vt* **-1.** [animal] prendre au piège, piéger. **-2.** *fig* [opponent] piéger; now you're trapped! maintenant vous êtes piégé OR pris!; he trapped me into thinking I was safe il m'a piégé en me faisant croire que j'étais hors de danger; we got trapped into going on s'est fait piéger et on a dû y aller; she trapped him into marrying her elle l'a piégé en le forçant à l'épouser. **-3.** [immobilize, catch] bloquer, immobiliser; they were trapped OR they got trapped in the lift ils ont été bloqués dans l'ascenseur; we were trapped by the incoming tide on a été surpris par la marée montante; I trapped my leg OR my leg got trapped under the table je me suis coincé la jambe OR j'avais la jambe coincée sous la table; she trapped her fingers in the door elle s'est pris les doigts dans la porte; the window blew shut and trapped my hand un coup de vent a fermé la fenêtre et ma main est restée coincée; they were trapped in the rubble ils étaient coincés OR immobilisés sous les décombres; he trapped the ball skilfully FTBL il a habilement bloqué le ballon. **-4.** [hold back - water, gas] retenir; there's a grid to ~ dead leaves il y a une grille pour retenir les feuilles mortes.

trapdoor [ˌtræp'dɔː^r] *n* trappe *f*.

trapdoor spider *n* mygale *f*.

trapes *inf* [treɪps] = **traipse**.

trapeze [trə'piːz] *n* trapèze *m* (de cirque); ~ artist trapéziste *mf*.

trapezium [trə'piːzjəm] (*pl* **trapeziums** OR **trapezia** [-zjə]) *n* **-1.** GEOM *Br* trapèze *m*; *Am* quadrilatère *m* trapézoïdal. **-2.** ANAT trapèze *m*.

trapezoid ['træpɪzɔɪd] ◇ *n* **-1.** GEOM *Br* quadrilatère *m* trapézoïdal; *Am* trapèze *m*. **-2.** ANAT trapézoïde *m*.
◇ *adj* trapézoïde.

trapper ['træpə^r] *n* trappeur *m*.

trappings ['træpɪŋz] *npl* **-1.** [accessories] ornements *mpl*; the ~ of power les signes extérieurs du pouvoir. **-2.** [harness] harnachement *m*, caparaçon *m*.

Trappist ['træpɪst] ◇ *n* trappiste *m*.
◇ *comp* [monk, monastery] de la Trappe.

traps [træps] *npl* [luggage] bagages *mpl*, affaires *fpl*.

trapshooting ['træpˌʃuːtɪŋ] *n* ball-trap *m*; to go ~ faire du ball-trap.

trash [træʃ] ◇ *n* (*U*) **-1.** [nonsense] bêtises *fpl*, âneries *fpl*; he talks/writes a lot of ~ il dit/écrit beaucoup d'âneries; what utter ~! c'est vraiment n'importe quoi!; how can you watch that ~? comment peux-tu regarder de telles nullités OR idioties? **-2.** [goods] camelote *f*; they sell a lot of ~ ils vendent beaucoup de camelote. **-3.** *Am* [waste] ordures *fpl*; ~ heap tas *m* d'ordures. **-4.** *inf* [people] racaille *f*; he's just ~, they're just ~ c'est de la racaille.
◇ *vt inf* **-1.** [reject] jeter, bazarder; they ~ed all my ideas ils ont rejeté toutes mes idées. **-2.** [criticize] débiner, éreinter. **-3.** [vandalize] vandaliser, saccager. **-4.** *Am* SPORT [opponent] démolir.

trashcan ['træʃkæn] *n Am* poubelle *f*.

trasher ['træʃə^r] *n Am* vandale *m*, voyou *m*.

trashman ['træʃmæn] (*pl* **trashmen** [-men]) *n Am* éboueur *m*.

trashy ['træʃɪ] (*compar* **trashier**, *superl* **trashiest**) *adj* [goods] de pacotille; [magazine, book] de quatre sous; [idea, article] qui ne vaut rien; [programme] lamentable, au-dessous de tout.

trauma [*Br* 'trɔːmə, *Am* 'traʊmə] (*pl* **traumas** OR **traumata** [-mətə]) *n* [gen & PSYCH] trauma *m spec*, traumatisme *m*; MED traumatisme *m*.

traumatic [trɔː'mætɪk] *adj* [gen & PSYCH] traumatisant; MED traumatique.

traumatism [*Br* 'trɔːmətɪzm, *Am* 'traʊmətɪzm] *n* traumatisme *m*.

traumatize, -ise [*Br* 'trɔːmətaɪz, *Am* 'traʊmətaɪz] *vt* traumatiser.

travail ['træveɪl] ◇ *n arch* OR *lit* **-1.** [work] labeur *m*. **-2.** [in childbirth] douleurs *fpl* de l'enfantement, travail *m*.
◇ *vi arch* OR *lit* **-1.** [work] peiner. **-2.** [in childbirth] être en travail OR en couches.

travel ['trævl] (*Br pt* & *pp* **travelled**, *cont* **travelling**, *Am pt* & *pp* **traveled**, *cont* **traveling**) ◇ *vi* **-1.** [journey - traveller] voyager; to ~ by air/car voyager en avion/en voiture; they travelled to Greece by boat ils sont allés en Grèce en bateau; they've travelled a lot together ils ont beaucoup voyagé ensemble; to ~ round the world faire le tour du monde; she's travelling (about OR around) somewhere in Asia elle est en voyage quelque part en Asie; we travelled across France by train nous avons traversé la France en train; they've travelled far

and wide ils ont voyagé partout dans le monde; to ~ light voyager avec peu de bagages; to ~ back revenir, rentrer; let's ~ back in time to 1940 retournons en 1940. -**2.** COMM être voyageur OR représentant de commerce; he ~s in confectionery *Br* il est représentant en confiserie. -**3.** [go, move - person] aller; [- vehicle, train] aller, rouler; [- piston, shuttle] se déplacer; [- light, sound] se propager; the train travelled at high speed through the countryside le train roulait à toute vitesse à travers la campagne; we were travelling at an average speed of 60 m.p.h. on faisait du 90 km/h de moyenne; the signals ~ along different routes les signaux suivent des trajets différents; the components ~ along a conveyor belt les pièces détachées sont transportées sur un tapis roulant. -**4.** *inf* [go very fast] rouler (très) vite; we were really travelling on roulait vraiment très vite; this car certainly ~s! elle bombe, cette voiture! -**5.** *fig* [thoughts, mind]: my mind travelled back to last June mes pensées m'ont ramené au mois de juin dernier. -**6.** [news, rumour] se répandre, se propager, circuler; news ~s fast les nouvelles vont vite. -**7.** [food] supporter le voyage.
◇ *vt* -**1.** [distance] faire, parcourir; I travelled 50 miles to get here j'ai fait 80 km pour venir ici. -**2.** [area, road] parcourir; I've travelled these roads for years j'ai parcouru ces routes pendant des années; we travelled the country from west to east on a parcouru OR traversé le pays d'ouest en est.
◇ *n (U)* [journeys] voyage *m*, voyages *mpl*; ~ broadens the mind les voyages ouvrent l'esprit; I've done a lot of foreign ~ j'ai beaucoup voyagé à l'étranger.
◇ *comp* [book] de voyages; [guide, brochure] touristique; [writer] qui écrit des récits de voyage.
◆ **travels** *npl* [journeys] voyages *mpl*; [comings and goings] allées et venues *fpl*; I met them on my ~s in China je les ai rencontrés au cours de mes voyages en Chine; did you see my glasses on your ~s? *hum* tu n'as pas vu mes lunettes quelque part? ❑ 'Gulliver's Travels' *Swift* 'les Voyages de Gulliver'.

travel agency *n* agence *f* de voyages.

travel agent *n* agent *m* de voyages; ~'s agence *f* de voyages.

travelator ['trævəleɪtəʳ] = **travolator**.

travel book *n* récit *m* de voyages.

travel brochure *n* dépliant *m* touristique.

travel bureau *n* agence *f* de voyages.

Travelcard ['trævlkɑːd] *n* carte *f* d'abonnement *(pour les transports en commun à Londres)*.

travel insurance *n (U)*: to take out ~ prendre une assurance-voyage.

travelled *Br*, **traveled** *Am* ['trævld] *adj* -**1.** [person] qui a beaucoup voyagé; he's a well-~ man il a beaucoup voyagé. -**2.** [road, path] fréquenté; this is a much ~ road c'est une route très fréquentée.

traveller *Br*, **traveler** *Am* ['trævləʳ] *n* -**1.** [gen] voyageur *m*, -euse *f*; I'm not a good ~ je supporte mal les voyages. -**2.** [salesman] voyageur *m*, -euse *f* de commerce. -**3.** [gipsy] bohémien *m*, -enne *f*.

traveller's cheque *n* chèque *m* de voyage, traveller's cheque *m*.

travelling *Br*, **traveling** *Am* ['trævlɪŋ] ◇ *n (U)* voyage *m*, voyages *mpl*.
◇ *adj* [companion, bag] de voyage; [preacher, musician] itinérant; [crane] mobile.

travelling clock *n* réveil *m* de voyage.

travelling expenses *npl* frais *mpl* de déplacement.

travelling library *n* ≃ bibliobus *m*.

travelling people *npl* gens *mpl* du voyage.

travelling salesman *n* représentant *m* OR voyageur *m* de commerce.

travelogue *Br*, **travelog** *Am* ['trævəlɒg] *n* [lecture, book] récit *m* de voyage; [film] film *m* de voyage.

travel-sick *adj Br*: to be ~ [in car] avoir mal au cœur en voiture, avoir le mal de la route; [in boat] avoir le mal de mer; [in plane] avoir le mal de l'air; I get ~ in buses je suis malade OR j'ai mal au cœur en bus.

travel sickness *n* mal *m* de la route.

travel-stained *adj* sali par le voyage OR les voyages.

traverse ['trævəs, ˌtrə'vɜːs] ◇ *vt fml* traverser.
◇ *vi* [in climbing, skiing] faire une traversée, traverser.
◇ *n* -**1.** [beam] traverse *f*. -**2.** [gallery] galerie *f* transversale.

travesty ['trævəstɪ] (*pl* travesties, *pt* & *pp* travestied) ◇ *n* [parody] parodie *f*, pastiche *m*; *pej* [mockery, pretence] simulacre *m*, travestissement *m*; the trial was a ~ of justice le procès n'était qu'un simulacre de justice.
◇ *vt* [justice] bafouer.

travolator ['trævəleɪtəʳ] *n* tapis *m* OR trottoir *m* roulant.

trawl [trɔːl] ◇ *n* -**1.** FISHING: ~ (net) chalut *m*; ~ line palangre *f*. -**2.** [search] recherche *f*.
◇ *vi* -**1.** FISHING pêcher au chalut; to ~ for mackerel pêcher le maquereau au chalut. -**2.** [search] chercher; to ~ for information chercher des renseignements, aller à la pêche (aux renseignements).
◇ *vt* [net] traîner, tirer; [sea] pêcher dans.

trawler ['trɔːləʳ] *n* [boat, fisherman] chalutier *m*.

tray [treɪ] *n* -**1.** [for carrying] plateau *m*. -**2.** [for papers] casier *m* (de rangement); [for mail] corbeille *f*; in/out ~ corbeille entrée/sortie.

traycloth ['treɪklɒθ] *n* napperon *m* (de plateau).

treacherous ['tretʃərəs] *adj* -**1.** [disloyal - ally] traître, perfide; *fig* [memory] infidèle. -**2.** [dangerous - water, current, ice] traître; the roads are ~ les routes sont très glissantes.

treacherously ['tretʃərəslɪ] *adv* [act] traîtreusement; the currents are ~ strong les courants sont traîtres tellement ils sont forts.

treachery ['tretʃərɪ] (*pl* treacheries) *n* perfidie *f*, traîtrise *f*.

treacle ['triːkl] *n Br* [molasses] mélasse *f*; [golden syrup] mélasse *f* raffinée.

treacle pudding *n Br* pudding *m* à la mélasse.

treacle tart *n Br* tarte *f* à la mélasse.

treacly ['triːklɪ] *adj* [sweet] sirupeux; *fig* [sentimental] mièvre, sirupeux.

tread [tred] (*pt* trod [trɒd], *pp* trod OR trodden ['trɒdn]) ◇ *vt* -**1.** [walk]: a path had been trodden through the grass les pas des marcheurs avaient tracé un chemin dans l'herbe; she trod the streets looking for him elle a battu le pavé OR parcouru la ville à sa recherche; the path had been trodden by generations of hikers des générations de randonneurs avaient foulé ce chemin ❑ to ~ the boards monter sur les planches. -**2.** [trample] fouler; to ~ grapes fouler du raisin; to ~ sthg underfoot fouler qqch aux pieds, piétiner qqch ❑ to ~ water nager sur place. -**3.** [stamp] enfoncer, écraser; she trod the cigarette into the sand elle a écrasé du pied le mégot dans le sable; don't ~ the crumbs into the carpet ne piétinez pas les miettes sur la moquette.
◇ *vi* -**1.** [walk] marcher; to ~ lightly marcher d'un pas léger; to ~ carefully OR warily *fig* y aller doucement OR avec précaution. -**2.** [step]: to ~ on sthg [accidentally] marcher sur qqch; [deliberately] marcher (exprès) sur qqch; I must have trodden in something j'ai dû marcher sur OR dans quelque chose; he trod on my foot il m'a marché sur le pied ❑ to ~ on sb's heels talonner qqn, suivre qqn de près; to ~ on sb's toes marcher sur les pieds de qqn.
◇ *n* -**1.** [footstep] pas *m*; to walk with a heavy ~ marcher d'un pas lourd || [sound of steps] bruit *m* de pas. -**2.** [of stairs] marche *f*, giron *m spec*. -**3.** [of shoe] semelle *f*; [of tyre - depth] bande *f* de roulement; [- pattern] sculptures *fpl*; there's no ~ left [on shoe] la semelle est usée; [on tyre] le pneu est lisse.
◆ **tread down** *vt sep* tasser (du pied).
◆ **tread in** *vt sep* [plant] tasser la terre autour de.

treadle ['tredl] ◇ *n* pédale *f (sur un tour ou sur une machine à coudre)*.
◇ *vi* actionner la pédale.

treadmill ['tredmɪl] *n* [machine] manège *m*; HIST *roue ou manège mûs par un homme ou un animal et actionnant une machine*; I feel like I'm on a ~ je ne supporte pas cette routine.

treas. (*written abbr of* treasurer) trés.

treason ['triːzn] *n* trahison *f*; high ~ haute trahison.

treasonable ['triːznəbl] *adj* [action, statement] qui constitue une trahison.

treasure ['treʒəʳ] ◇ *n* -**1.** [valuables] trésor *m*; 'Treasure Island' *Stevenson* 'l'Île au trésor'. -**2.** [art] joyau *m*, trésor *m*; the museum has many ~s of Renaissance art le musée contient de nombreux joyaux de la Renaissance. -**3.** *inf* [person] trésor *m*, ange *m*; she's a real ~ c'est un vrai trésor; come here, my little ~ viens là, mon (petit) trésor.
◇ *vt* -**1.** [friendship, possession] tenir beaucoup à. -**2.** [gift] garder précieusement, être très attaché à; [memory] conserver précieusement, chérir *fml*; [moment] chérir *fml*.

treasure house *n* -**1.** [museum] trésor *m (lieu)*. -**2.** [room, library] mine *f*, trésor *m*. -**3.** *fig* [person]: she's a ~ of information c'est un puits de science OR une mine de renseignements.

treasure hunt *n* chasse *f* au trésor.

treasurer ['treʒərəʳ] *n* -**1.** [of club] trésorier *m*, -ère *f*. -**2.** *Am* [of company] directeur *m* financier.

treasure trove *n* trésor *m*.

treasury ['treʒərɪ] (*pl* treasuries) *n* -**1.** [building] trésorerie *f*. -**2.** *fig* [of information] mine *f*; [of poems] recueil *m*. -**3.** ADMIN: the Treasury la Trésorerie, ≃ le ministère des Finances; Secretary/Department of the Treasury *Am* ≃ ministre *m*/ministère *m* des Finances.

Treasury bench *n* banc *m* des ministres *(au Parlement britannique)*.

treasury bill *n* ≃ bon *m* du Trésor.

treat [triːt] ◇ *vt* -**1.** [deal with] traiter; he ~s them with contempt il est méprisant envers eux; teachers expect to be ~ed with respect by their pupils les professeurs exigent que leurs élèves se conduisent respectueusement envers eux; you shouldn't ~ them like children vous ne devriez pas les traiter comme des enfants; the firm ~s its customers extremely well/badly la compagnie traite extrêmement bien/mal ses clients; the hostages said that they had been well ~ed les otages ont déclaré qu'ils avaient été bien traités. -**2.** [handle - substance, object] utiliser, se servir de; the weedkiller needs to be ~ed with great care il faut se servir du désherbant avec beaucoup de précaution || [claim, request] traiter. -**3.** [consider - problem, question] traiter, considérer; the whole episode was ~ed as a joke on a pris OR on a considéré tout cet épisode comme une plaisanterie; she ~ed the subject rather superficially elle a traité le sujet assez superficiellement. -**4.** MED [patient] soigner; [illness] traiter; she's being ~ed for cancer on la soigne pour un cancer. -**5.** [fruit, timber, crops] traiter; the land has been ~ed with fertilizer la terre a été traitée aux engrais. -**6.** [buy]: to ~ sb to sthg offrir OR payer qqch à qqn; she ~ed them all to ice cream elle a payé OR offert une glace à tout le monde; I ~ed myself to a new coat je me suis offert OR payé un manteau neuf; go on, ~ yourself! vas-y, gâte-toi OR fais-toi plaisir!
◇ *vi fml* -**1.** to ~ of [deal with] traiter de; the book ~s of love le livre traite de l'amour. -**2.** [negotiate]: to ~ with sb traiter avec qqn; the government refuses to ~ with terrorists le gouvernement refuse de traiter avec les terroristes.
◇ *n* -**1.** [on special occasion - enjoyment] gâterie *f*, (petit) plaisir *m*; [- surprise] surprise *f*; [- present] cadeau *m*; [- outing] sortie *f*; as a special ~ we went to the planetarium on nous a offert tout spécialement une visite au plané-

tarium; I've got a ~ for you j'ai une bonne surprise pour toi; let's give her a ~ faisons-lui un petit plaisir; this is my ~ c'est moi qui offre; you've got a ~ in store on te réserve une surprise, attends-toi à une surprise; it used to be a real ~ to travel by train autrefois, on se faisait une vraie fête de voyager en train. -2. [pleasure] plaisir *m*; it's a ~ for us to see you looking so happy cela nous fait vraiment plaisir OR pour nous c'est une grande joie de vous voir si heureuse.

◆ **a treat** *inf adv phr Br* à merveille; he's coming on a ~ il fait de sacrés progrès; the idea worked a ~ l'idée a marché à merveille.

treatise ['triːtɪz] *n* traité *m*; a ~ on racism un traité sur le racisme.

treatment ['triːtmənt] *n* -1. [of person] traitement *m*; we complained of ill ~ nous nous sommes plaints d'avoir été mal traités; they gave him preferential ~ ils lui ont accordé un traitement préférentiel OR de faveur; I got very good ~ on m'a très bien traité; to give sb the (full) ~ traiter qqn avec tous les égards. -2. *(U)* MED soins *mpl*, traitement *m*; a course of ~ un traitement; she was sent to Madrid for ~ on l'a envoyée se faire soigner à Madrid; to receive/to undergo ~ recevoir/suivre un traitement; is he responding to ~? est-ce qu'il réagit au traitement?; no doctor has the right to refuse ~ aucun médecin n'a le droit de refuser ses soins à un malade; cancer ~ traitement du cancer; X-ray ~ traitement par rayons X. -3. [of subject] traitement *m*, façon *f* de traiter. -4. [of crops, timber] traitement *m*. -5. [chemical] produit *m* chimique. -6. CIN traitement *m*.

treaty ['triːtɪ] *(pl* treaties) *n* -1. POL traité *m*; to sign a ~ (with sb) signer OR conclure un traité (avec qqn); there is a ~ between the two countries les deux pays sont liés par traité. -2. JUR: they sold the property by private ~ ils ont vendu la propriété par accord privé.

treble ['trebl] ◇ *adj* -1. [triple] triple; my phone number is 70~4 *Br* mon numéro de téléphone est le soixante dix, quatre cent quarante-quatre. -2. MUS [voice] de soprano; [part] pour voix de soprano.

◇ *n* -1. MUS [part, singer] soprano *m*. -2. *(U)* [in hi-fi] aigus *mpl*.

◇ *vt & vi* tripler.

◇ *adv*: to sing ~ chanter dans un registre de soprano.

treble chance *n Br méthode de pari en football.*

treble clef *n* clef *f* de sol.

trebly ['treblɪ] *adv* triplement, trois fois plus; ~ difficult trois fois plus difficile.

tree [triː] ◇ *n* -1. BOT arbre *m*; apple ~ pommier *m*; plum ~ prunier *m*; rose ~ rosier *m*; the Tree of Knowledge/Life BIBLE l'arbre de la science du bien et du mal/de vie ❑ to be up a ~ *Am* être dans une impasse. -2. [diagram]: ~ (diagram) représentation *f* en arbre OR arborescente, arborescence *f*. -3. [for shoes] embauchoir *m*, forme *f*. -4. [of saddle] arçon *m*.

◇ *vt* -1. [hunter, animal] forcer OR obliger à se réfugier dans un arbre. -2. *inf Am fig* [trap] piéger.

tree creeper *n* ORNITH grimpereau *m*.

tree fern *n* fougère *f* arborescente.

tree frog *n* rainette *f*.

treehouse ['triːhaus, *pl* -hauzɪz] *n cabane construite dans un arbre.*

treeless ['triːlɪs] *adj* sans arbres, dénudé.

tree-lined *adj* bordé d'arbres.

tree ring *n* cercle *m* d'arbres.

tree surgeon *n* arboriculteur *m*, -trice *f (qui s'occupe de soigner et d'élaguer les arbres).*

tree surgery *n* arboriculture *f (traitement des arbres malades).*

treetop ['triːtɒp] *n* cime *f* OR haut *m* OR faîte *m* d'un arbre; the birds in the ~s les oiseaux au faîte OR en haut des arbres.

tree trunk *n* tronc *m* d'arbre.

trefoil ['trefɔɪl] *n* ARCHIT & BOT trèfle *m*.

trek [trek] *(pt & pp* trekked, *cont* trekking) ◇ *n* -1. [walk] marche *f*; [hike] randonnée *f*; to go on a ~ faire une marche OR une randonnée ‖ [arduous trip] marche *f* pénible; it was a real ~ to get here ça a été une véritable expédition pour arriver ici; it's a bit of a ~ to the shops il y a un bout de chemin jusqu'aux magasins. -2. *SAfr* HIST voyage *m* en char à bœufs.

◇ *vi* -1. [walk] avancer avec peine; [hike] faire de la randonnée; we had to ~ across fields to get here il a fallu passer à travers champs pour arriver ici ‖ [drag o.s.] se traîner; they trekked all the way out here to see us ils ont fait tout ce chemin pour venir nous voir; I can't be bothered to ~ over to the supermarket again je n'ai pas le courage de refaire tout ce chemin jusqu'au supermarché. -2. *SAfr* HIST voyager en char à bœufs.

◇ *vt SAfr* [load] tirer, traîner.

trellis ['trelɪs] ◇ *n* treillage *m*, treillis *m*.

◇ *vt* [wood strips] faire un treillage de; [plant] treillager.

trelliswork ['trelɪs,wɜːk] *n* treillage *m*.

tremble ['trembl] ◇ *vi* -1. [person - with cold] trembler, frissonner; [- from fear, excitement, rage] trembler, frémir; [hands] trembler; to ~ with fear trembler de peur. -2. [voice - from emotion] trembler, vibrer; [- from fear] trembler; [- from old age] trembler, chevroter; her voice ~d with emotion sa voix tremblait d'émotion. -3. [bridge, house, ground] trembler; [engine] vibrer. -4. *fig* [be anxious] frémir; he ~d for their safety il tremblait pour eux; she ~d at the thought elle frémissait à cette seule pensée.

◇ *n* -1. [from fear] tremblement *m*; [from excitement, rage] frémissement *m*; [from cold] frissonnement *m*; to be all of a ~ *inf* trembler comme une feuille. -2. [in voice] frémissement *m*, frisson *m*.

trembling ['tremblɪŋ] ◇ *adj* -1. [body - with cold] frissonnant, grelottant; [- in fear, excitement] frémissant, tremblant; [hands] tremblant. -2. [voice - with emotion] vibrant; [- with fear] tremblant; [- because of old age] chevrotant; with a ~ voice [speaker] d'une OR la voix tremblante; [singer] d'une OR la voix chevrotante.

◇ *n* [from cold] tremblement *m*, frissonnement *m*; [from fear] tremblement *m*, frémissement *m*.

tremendous [trɪ'mendəs] *adj* -1. [number, amount] énorme, très grand; [cost, speed] très élevé, vertigineux; [building, arch] énorme; [height] vertigineux, très grand; [undertaking] énorme, monumental; [admiration, disappointment, pride] très grand, extrême; [crash, noise] terrible, épouvantable; the fair was a ~ success la foire a été une très grande réussite; there's been a ~ improvement in her work son travail s'est énormément amélioré; there was a ~ crowd il y avait un monde fou OR une foule énorme; you've been a ~ help vous m'avez été d'une aide précieuse. -2. [wonderful] sensationnel, formidable; I had a ~ time je me suis amusé comme un fou; she looks ~ in black elle a beaucoup d'allure en noir; he scored a ~ goal il a mis un but de toute beauté.

tremendously [trɪ'mendəslɪ] *adv* [as intensifier] extrêmement; we heard a ~ loud explosion on a entendu une formidable explosion; we enjoyed it ~ cela nous a énormément plu; he did ~ well il a extrêmement bien réussi; I'm not ~ keen on his plays je n'aime pas vraiment ses pièces.

tremolo ['treməlәʊ] *(pl* tremolos) *n* MUS trémolo *m*; ~ arm *levier sur une guitare électrique qui sert à varier le ton d'une note.*

tremor ['tremәʳ] *n* -1. GEOL secousse *f* (sismique). -2. [in voice] frémissement *m*, frisson *m*, tremblement *m*. -3. [of fear, thrill] frisson *m*; a ~ of anticipation ran through the audience à l'idée de ce qui allait suivre, la salle fut parcourue d'un frisson.

tremulous ['tremjʊləs] *adj lit* -1. [with fear] tremblant; [with excitement, nervousness] frémissant; [handwriting] tremblé; he was ~ with emotion/fear il tremblait d'émotion/de peur; her voice was ~ with joy sa voix vibrait de joie. -2. [timid - person, manner] timide, craintif; [- animal] craintif, effarouché; [- smile] timide.

tremulously ['tremjʊləslɪ] *adv lit* -1. [with fear, emotion] en tremblant; to sing/to answer ~ chanter/répondre d'une voix tremblante. -2. [timidly] timidement, craintivement.

trench [trentʃ] ◇ *n* [gen, CONSTR & MIL] tranchée *f*; [ditch] fossé *m*; life in the ~es la vie dans les tranchées; my grandfather fought in the ~es mon grand-père a fait la guerre des tranchées.

◇ *vt* [field] creuser une tranchée OR des tranchées dans; MIL retrancher.

◇ *vi* creuser une tranchée OR des tranchées.

trenchant ['trentʃənt] *adj* incisif, tranchant.

trenchantly ['trentʃəntlɪ] *adv* [speak] d'un ton tranchant OR incisif; [write] d'une manière incisive.

trench coat *n* trench-coat *m*.

trencher ['trentʃəʳ] *n* tranchoir *m*.

trencherman ['trentʃəmən] *(pl* trenchermen [-mən]) *n lit* OR *hum* gros mangeur *m*; he's a good/great ~ il a un bon coup de fourchette.

trench fever *n (U)* fièvre *f* des tranchées, rickettsiose *f*.

trench foot *n (U) sorte de gelure au pied due au froid ou à l'humidité.*

trench mouth *n (U)* angine *f* ulcéreuse OR de Vincent.

trench warfare *n* guerre *f* de tranchées.

trend [trend] ◇ *n* [tendency] tendance *f*; [fashion] mode *f*; the ~ is towards shorter skirts la tendance est aux jupes plus courtes; there is a ~ away from going abroad for holidays on a tendance à délaisser les vacances à l'étranger; political/electoral ~s tendances politiques/électorales; house prices are on an upward ~ again le prix des maisons est de nouveau à la hausse; the ~ of events le cours OR la tournure des événements; the latest ~s la dernière mode; to set a/the ~ [style] donner un/le ton; [fashion] lancer une/la mode.

◇ *vi* [extend - mountain range] s'étendre; [veer - coastline] s'incliner; [turn - prices, opinion] s'orienter.

trendily *inf* ['trendɪlɪ] *adv* [dress] branché *adv*.

trendsetter ['trend,setəʳ] *n* [person - in style] personne *f* qui donne le ton; [- in fashion] personne *f* qui lance une mode.

trendsetting ['trend,setɪŋ] ◇ *adj* [person] qui lance une mode; [idea, garment] d'avant-garde.

◇ *n* lancement *m* d'une mode.

trendy *inf* ['trendɪ] *(compar* trendier, *superl* trendiest, *pl* trendies) ◇ *adj* [music, appearance] branché; [ideas] à la mode, branché; [clothes] branché; [place, resort] à la mode, branché; he's a very ~ dresser il est toujours habillé à la dernière mode; ~ lefty *inf* intello *mf* de gauche.

◇ *n pej* branché *m*, -e *f*.

Trento ['trentəʊ] *pr n* Trente.

trepan [trɪ'pæn] *(pt & pp* trepanned, *cont* trepanning) ◇ *vt* -1. MIN forer. -2. MED trépaner.

◇ *n* -1. MIN foreuse *f*; [for metal, plastic] foret *m*. -2. MED trépan *m*.

trepidation [,trepɪ'deɪʃn] *n* -1. [alarm] inquiétude *f*; with great ~ avec une vive inquiétude. -2. [excitement] agitation *f*.

trespass ['trespəs] ◇ *vi* -1. JUR s'introduire dans une propriété privée; you're ~ing vous êtes sur une propriété privée; to ~ on sb's land s'introduire OR entrer sans autorisation dans une propriété privée; 'no ~ing' 'défense d'entrer', 'propriété privée'. -2. *fig* [encroach]: I don't want to ~ on your time/hospitality je ne veux pas abuser de votre temps/hospitalité; he's ~ing on my area of responsibility il empiète sur mon terrain. -3. BIBLE: to ~ against sb offenser qqn; to ~ against the law enfreindre la loi (divine).

◇ *n* -1. *(U)* JUR entrée *f* non autorisée; to commit ~ s'introduire dans une propriété privée. -2. BIBLE péché *m*; forgive us our ~es pardonne-nous nos offenses.

trespasser ['trespəsəʳ] *n* -**1.** JUR intrus *m*, -e *f* *(dans une propriété privée)*; '~s will be prosecuted' 'défense d'entrer sous peine de poursuites'. -**2.** BIBLE pécheur *m*, -eresse *f*.

tress [tres] *n lit*: a ~ (of hair) une mèche OR une boucle de cheveux; her golden ~es sa blonde chevelure.

trestle ['tresl] *n* -**1.** [for table] tréteau *m*. -**2.** CONSTR chevalet *m*.

trestle bridge *n* pont *m* sur chevalets.

trestle table *n* table *f* à tréteaux.

trews [tru:z] *npl Scot* pantalon *m* (écossais).

triable ['traɪəbl] *adj* JUR [case] susceptible d'être porté en justice.

triad ['traɪæd] *n* [gen] triade *f*; MUS accord *m* parfait.

triage ['tri:ɑ:ʒ] *n* MED triage *m (des malades, des blessés)*.

trial ['traɪəl] ◇ *n* -**1.** JUR procès *m*; he pleaded guilty at the ~ il a plaidé coupable à son procès OR devant le tribunal; many witnesses were brought forward at the ~ de nombreux témoins sont venus à la barre au cours du procès; to be OR to go on ~ for sthg, to stand ~ for sthg passer en jugement OR en justice pour qqch; he was put on OR sent for ~ for murder il a été jugé pour meurtre; to bring sb to ~ faire passer OR traduire qqn en justice; his case comes up for ~ in September son affaire passe en jugement en septembre; ~ by jury jugement *m* par jury ❑ 'The Trial' *Kafka* 'le Procès'. -**2.** [test] essai *m*; to give sthg a ~ mettre qqch à l'essai, essayer qqch; to be on ~ être à l'essai; give her a month's ~ before you take her on prenez-la un mois à l'essai avant de l'embaucher; it was a ~ of strength c'était une épreuve de force ❑ clinical ~s tests *mpl* cliniques; by ~ and error par tâtonnements, par essais et erreurs; it was just ~ and error ce n'était qu'une suite d'approximations. -**3.** [hardship, adversity] épreuve *f*; the ~s of married life les vicissitudes de la vie conjugale; ~s and tribulations tribulations *fpl*; her arthritis was a great ~ to her son arthrite l'a beaucoup fait souffrir ‖ [person]: he's always been a ~ to his parents il a toujours donné du souci à ses parents.
◇ *adj* -**1.** [test - flight] d'essai; [- marriage, separation] à l'essai; on a ~ basis à titre d'essai; for a ~ period pendant une période d'essai ❑ ~ balloon *literal* & *fig* ballon *m* d'essai; ~ run essai *m*; can we give the car a ~ run? est-ce qu'on peut essayer la voiture OR faire un essai avec la voiture?; we'll have a ~ run before we record on fera un essai avant d'enregistrer. -**2.** *Am* JUR: ~ attorney OR lawyer avocat *m*; ~ court tribunal *m* de première instance; ~ judge ≃ juge *m* d'instance; ~ jury jury *m*.
◆ **trials** *npl* [competition] concours *m*; [for selection - match] match *m* de sélection; [- race] épreuve *f* de sélection; sheepdog/horse ~s concours de chiens de berger/hippique.

trial balance *n* FIN balance *f* d'inventaire.

triangle ['traɪæŋgl] *n* -**1.** GEOM triangle *m*; *Am* [set square] équerre *f*. -**2.** MUS triangle *m*.

triangular [traɪ'æŋgjʊləʳ] *adj* triangulaire.

triangulate [traɪ'æŋgjʊleɪt] *vt* -**1.** GEOM diviser en triangles. -**2.** GEOG [region] trianguler.

triangulation [traɪˌæŋgjʊ'leɪʃn] *n* triangulation *f*.

triangulation station *n* station *f* géodésique.

Triassic [traɪ'æsɪk] ◇ *n* trias *m*.
◇ *adj* triasique.

triathlon [traɪ'æθlɒn] *n* triathlon *m*.

tribadism ['trɪbədɪzm] *n* tribadisme *m*.

tribal ['traɪbl] *adj* [games, rites, warfare] tribal; [loyalty] à la tribu.

tribalism ['traɪbəlɪzm] *n* tribalisme *m*.

tribalistic [ˌtraɪbə'lɪstɪk] *adj* tribal.

tribe [traɪb] *n* -**1.** HIST, SOCIOL & ZOOL tribu *f*. -**2.** *inf fig* tribu *f*, smala *f*.

tribesman ['traɪbzmən] (*pl* **tribesmen** [-mən]) *n* membre *m* d'une tribu; [of particular tribe] membre *m* de la tribu.

triboelectricity ['traɪbəʊɪlek'trɪsətɪ] *n* triboélectricité *f*.

tribrach ['trɪbræk] *n* LITERAT tribraque *m*.

tribulation [ˌtrɪbjʊ'leɪʃn] *n lit* affliction *f lit*, malheur *m*; in times of ~ en temps de malheurs.

tribunal [traɪ'bju:nl] *n* [gen & JUR] tribunal *m*; the ~ of public opinion *fig* le jugement de l'opinion publique ❑ ~ of inquiry commission *f* d'enquête; military ~ tribunal militaire.

tribune ['trɪbju:n] *n* -**1.** ANTIQ tribun *m*. -**2.** [platform] tribune *f*; the newspaper provides a ~ for the views of young people *fig* le journal offre une tribune à des jeunes pour faire connaître leurs points de vue ❑ Tribune PRESS *magazine politique et littéraire exprimant le point de vue de l'aile gauche du parti travailliste*. -**3.** [defender] tribun *m*.

Tribune Group *pr n* POL: the ~ *le groupe des députés de gauche du parti travailliste britannique*.

tributary ['trɪbjʊtrɪ] (*pl* **tributaries**) ◇ *n* -**1.** [ruler, state] tributaire *m*. -**2.** GEOG [stream] affluent *m*.
◇ *adj* tributaire.

tribute ['trɪbju:t] *n* -**1.** [mark of respect] hommage *m*; to pay ~ to sb rendre hommage à qqn; we stood in silent ~ nous lui avons rendu un hommage silencieux; floral ~ couronne *f* (de fleurs). -**2.** [indication of efficiency] témoignage *m*; it was a ~ to their organizational skills that everything went so smoothly si tout a si bien marché, c'est grâce à leurs qualités d'organisateurs. -**3.** HIST & POL tribut *m*.

trice [traɪs] ◇ *n* [moment]: in a ~ en un clin d'œil, en un rien de temps.
◇ *vt* NAUT [sail] hisser.

tricentennial [ˌtraɪsen'tenjəl] ◇ *n* tricentenaire *m*.
◇ *adj* tricentenaire; [celebrations] du tricentenaire.

triceps ['traɪseps] (*pl* **tricepses** [-sɪz]) *n* triceps *m*.

triceratops [traɪ'serətɒps] *n* tricératops *m*.

trichloride [traɪ'klɔ:raɪd] *n* trichlorure *m*.

trichology [trɪ'kɒlədʒɪ] *n* trichologie *f*.

trichromatic [ˌtraɪkrəʊ'mætɪk] *adj* trichrome.

trichromatism [traɪ'krəʊmətɪzm] *n* trichromie *f*.

trick [trɪk] ◇ *n* -**1.** [deception, ruse] ruse *f*, astuce *f*; [stratagem] stratagème *m*; it's just a ~ to get you to open the door c'est une ruse OR une astuce pour vous amener à ouvrir la porte; a ~ of the light un effet d'optique. -**2.** [joke, prank] tour *m*, farce *f*, blague *f*; to play a ~ on sb faire une farce OR jouer un tour à qqn; what a dirty OR mean OR nasty ~ to play! quel sale tour! ❑ "~ or treat" «une gâterie ou une farce» *(phrase rituelle des enfants déguisés qui font la quête la veille de la fête de Halloween)*. -**3.** (*usu pl*) [silly behaviour] bêtise *f*; none of your ~s! et pas de bêtises, hein!; he's up to his old ~s again il fait encore des siennes. -**4.** [knack] truc *m*, astuce *f*; [in conjuring, performance] tour *m*; there, that should do the ~ voilà, ça fera l'affaire; he knows a ~ or two il a plus d'un tour dans son sac, c'est un malin ❑ card ~ tour de cartes; she still has a few ~s up her sleeve il lui reste plus d'un tour dans son sac; it's one of the ~s of the trade c'est une vieille ficelle OR un truc du métier. -**5.** [habit] habitude *f*, manie *f*; [particularity] particularité *f*; [gift] don *m*; [mannerism] manie *f*, tic *m*; he has a ~ of turning up at mealtimes il a le don d'arriver à l'heure des repas. -**6.** [in card games] pli *m*, levée *f*; to make OR to take a ~ faire un pli OR une levée. -**7.** ▽ *Am* [prostitute's client] micheton *m*. -**8.** NAUT tour *m* de barre. -**9.** *phr*: how's ~s? *inf* comment va?, quoi de neuf?
◇ *adj* -**1.** [for jokes] d'attrape, faux, de farces et attrapes; ~ soap savon *m* d'attrape, faux savon; ~ spoon cuiller *f* d'attrape, fausse cuiller. -**2.** [deceptive - lighting] truqué; ~ photograph photo *f* truquée; ~ photography truquage *m* photographique; ~ question question-piège *f*. -**3.** *Am* [weak - knee] faible; [- leg] boîteux.
◇ *vt* [deceive] tromper, rouler; [swindle] escroquer; [catch out] attraper; you've been ~ed! vous vous êtes fait rouler!; I was ~ed into leaving on a manœuvré pour me faire partir; she was ~ed out of her inheritance on lui a escroqué son héritage.
◆ **trick out, trick up** *vt sep lit* parer; they were ~ed out to look like circus performers ils étaient déguisés en artistes de cirque; she was ~ed out in all her finery elle était sur son trente et un.

trick cyclist *n* -**1.** [in circus] cycliste *m* acrobate. -**2.** ▽ *Br pej* [psychiatrist] psy *mf*.

trickery ['trɪkərɪ] *n* ruse *f*, supercherie *f*; he got what he wanted through OR by ~ il a eu ce qu'il voulait par la ruse.

trickle ['trɪkl] ◇ *vi* -**1.** [liquid] dégoutter, tomber en un (mince) filet; rainwater ~d from the gutters l'eau de pluie coulait peu à peu des gouttières; I felt the blood ~ slowly down my leg je sentis le sang couler doucement le long de ma jambe; water ~d down the window pane un filet d'eau coulait OR dégoulinait le long de la vitre; tears ~d down his face les larmes coulaient OR dégoulinaient sur son visage. -**2.** *fig*: information began to ~ out from behind enemy lines l'information commença à filtrer depuis l'arrière des lignes ennemies; cars began to ~ over the border la circulation a repris progressivement à la frontière; the ball ~d into the goal le ballon roula tranquillement dans les buts.
◇ *vt* -**1.** [liquid] faire couler goutte à goutte; he ~d a few drops of milk into the flour il a versé quelques gouttes de lait dans la farine; she ~d some oil out of the can elle a versé un peu d'huile de la boîte. -**2.** [sand, salt] faire glisser OR couler; to ~ sand through one's fingers faire glisser OR couler du sable entre ses doigts.
◇ *n* -**1.** [liquid] filet *m*; the flow from the spring dwindled to a ~ la source ne laissait plus échapper qu'un mince filet d'eau; the ~ of lava soon became a torrent le filet de lave se transforma bientôt en torrent; there was only a ~ of water from the tap un maigre filet d'eau coulait du robinet. -**2.** *fig*: a ~ of applications began to come in les candidatures commencèrent à arriver au compte-gouttes; there was only a ~ of visitors il n'y avait que quelques rares visiteurs, les visiteurs étaient rares.
◆ **trickle away** *vi insep* -**1.** [liquid] s'écouler lentement; the water ~d away down the plughole l'eau s'écoulait lentement dans le trou de l'évier. -**2.** *fig* [money, savings] disparaître petit à petit; [crowd] se disperser petit à petit; [people] s'en aller progressivement.
◆ **trickle in** *vi insep* -**1.** [rain] entrer goutte à goutte. -**2.** [spectators] entrer par petits groupes. -**3.** *fig*: offers of help began to ~ in quelques offres d'aide commençaient à arriver; information on the disaster only ~d in at first au début les informations sur le désastre arrivaient au compte-gouttes.

trickle charger *n* chargeur *m* à régime lent.

trickster ['trɪkstəʳ] *n* [swindler] filou *m*, escroc *m*.

tricksy ['trɪksɪ] (*compar* **tricksier**, *superl* **tricksiest**) *adj* -**1.** [mischievous] espiègle. -**2.** [sly] malin, rusé.

tricky ['trɪkɪ] (*compar* **trickier**, *superl* **trickiest**) *adj* -**1.** [complex, delicate - job, situation, negotiations] difficile, délicat; [- problem] épineux, difficile; the path is ~ in places le chemin est difficile OR peu praticable par endroits. -**2.** [sly - person] rusé, fourbe.

tricolour *Br*, **tricolor** *Am* ['trɪkələʳ] *n* drapeau *m* tricolore.

tricorn ['traɪkɔ:n] ◇ *adj* à trois cornes.
◇ *n* tricorne *m*.

trictrac, tricktrack ['trɪkˌtræk] *n* trictrac *m*.

tricuspid [traɪ'kʌspɪd] *adj* tricuspide.

tricycle ['traɪsɪkl] ◇ *n* tricycle *m*.
◇ *vi* faire du tricycle.

trident ['traɪdnt] *n* trident *m*.

Tridentine Mass [trɪ'dentaɪn-] *n* messe *f* traditionnelle en latin.

tried [traɪd] *pt* & *pp* → **try**.

triennial [traɪ'enjəl] ◇ *adj* triennal; BOT trisannuel.
◇ *n* -**1.** [anniversary] troisième anniversaire *m*. -**2.** [period] période *f* de trois ans. -**3.** BOT plante *f* trisannuelle.

triennially [traɪ'enjəlɪ] *adv* tous les trois ans.

trier ['traɪəʳ] *n*: to be a ~ être persévérant; **he's a real** ~ il ne se laisse jamais décourager.

Trier ['trɪəʳ] *pr n* Trèves.

Trieste [triː'est] *pr n* Trieste.

trifle ['traɪfl] *n* -**1.** [unimportant thing, small amount] bagatelle *f*, broutille *f*, rien *m*; **don't waste your time on ~s** ne perdez pas votre temps à des bagatelles; **she doesn't worry over ~s like money** l'argent est le cadet de ses soucis; **they quarrel over ~s** il se disputent pour un oui pour un non OR pour un rien; **I bought it for a** ~ je l'ai acheté pour une bouchée de pain OR pour trois fois rien; **£100 is a mere ~ to them** 100 livres, c'est peu de chose pour eux. -**2.** CULIN ≃ charlotte *f*.
◆ **a trifle** *adv phr* un peu, un tantinet; **it's a ~ easier than it was** c'est un peu OR un rien plus facile qu'avant.
◆ **trifle with** *vt insep*: to ~ **with sb's affections** jouer avec les sentiments de qqn; **he's not a man to be ~d with** avec lui, on ne plaisante pas.

trifling ['traɪflɪŋ] *adj* insignifiant.

trifocal [traɪ'fəʊkl] ◇ *adj* [lens] à triple foyer.
◇ *n* [lens] lentille *f* à triple foyer.
◆ **trifocals** *npl* [spectacles] lunettes *fpl* à triple foyer.

trifoliate [traɪ'fəʊlɪɪt] *adj* à trois feuilles; BOT trifolié.

triforium [traɪ'fɔːrɪəm] (*pl* **triforia** [-rɪə]) *n* triforium *m*.

triform ['traɪfɔːm] *adj* en OR à trois parties.

trig *inf* [trɪg] *n abbr of* **trigonometry**.

trigger ['trɪgəʳ] ◇ *n* -**1.** [in gun] gâchette *f*, détente *f*; **to pull** OR **to squeeze the** ~ appuyer sur la gâchette; **he's fast** OR **quick on the** ~ *literal* il tire vite; *fig* il réagit vite. -**2.** *fig* [initiator] déclenchement *m*; **the strike was the ~ for nationwide protests** la grève a donné le signal d'un mouvement de contestation dans tout le pays.
◇ *vt* [mechanism, explosion, reaction] déclencher; [revolution, protest] déclencher, provoquer, soulever.
◆ **trigger off** *vt sep* = **trigger** *vt*.

trigger finger *n* index *m* (*avec lequel on appuie sur la gâchette*).

trigger-happy *inf adj* [individual] qui a la gâchette facile; [country] prêt à déclencher la guerre pour un rien, belliqueux.

trigonometric(al) [,trɪgənə'metrɪk(l)] *adj* trigonométrique.

trigonometry [,trɪgə'nɒmətrɪ] *n* trigonométrie *f*.

trig point *n* station *f* géodésique.

trigram ['traɪgræm] *n* trigramme *m*.

trigraph ['traɪgrɑːf] *n* trigramme *m*.

trike *inf* [traɪk] *n* tricycle *m*.

trilateral [,traɪ'lætərəl] *adj* trilatéral, à trois côtés.

trilby ['trɪlbɪ] *n Br*: ~ **(hat)** (chapeau *m* en) feutre *m*.

trilingual [traɪ'lɪŋgwəl] *adj* trilingue.

trill [trɪl] ◇ *n* MUS & ORNITH trille *m*; LING consonne *f* roulée.
◇ *vi* triller, faire des trilles.
◇ *vt* -**1.** [note, word] triller. -**2.** [consonant] rouler.

trillion ['trɪljən] *n Br* trillion *m*; *Am* billion *m*; **~s of stars** des milliards d'étoiles.

trilogy ['trɪlədʒɪ] (*pl* **trilogies**) *n* trilogie *f*.

trim [trɪm] (*compar* **trimmer**, *superl* **trimmest**, *pt* & *pp* **trimmed**, *cont* **trimming**) ◇ *adj* -**1.** [neat - appearance] net, soigné; [- person] d'apparence soignée; [- garden, flowerbed] bien tenu, bien entretenu; [- ship] en bon ordre; **the garden is looking very** ~ le jardin a l'air très bien entretenu. -**2.** [svelte - figure] svelte, mince. -**3.** [fit] en bonne santé, en forme.
◇ *vt* -**1.** [cut - roses] tailler, couper; [- hair, nails] couper; [- beard] tailler; [- candle wick] tailler, moucher; [- paper, photo] rogner; **to ~ one's nails** se couper les ongles; **I had my hair trimmed** je me suis fait égaliser les cheveux; ~ **the frayed edges off** égalisez les bords du tissu. -**2.** [edge] orner, garnir; **a hat trimmed with fur** un chapeau bordé OR orné de fourrure; **the collar was trimmed with lace** le col était bordé OR garni de dentelle ‖ [decorate]: **we trimmed the Christmas tree with tinsel** on a décoré le sapin de Noël avec des guirlandes. -**3.** AERON & NAUT [plane, ship] équilibrer; [sails] régler; **to ~ one's sails** *fig* réviser son jugement. -**4.** [cut back - budget, costs] réduire, limiter; **they were able to ~ several thousand pounds from the budget** ils ont pu réduire le budget de plusieurs milliers de livres.
◇ *n* -**1.** [neat state] ordre *m*, bon état *m*; **to be in good ~** être en bon état OR ordre; **the garden doesn't look in very good ~** le jardin a l'air un peu à l'abandon. -**2.** [fitness] forme *f*; **to get in** OR **into ~** se remettre en forme; **are you in (good) ~ for the match?** êtes-vous en forme pour le match? -**3.** [cut] coupe *f*, taille *f*; **she gave the hedge a ~** elle a taillé la haie; **she gave her nails a ~** elle s'est coupé les ongles; **to have a ~** [at hairdresser's] se faire égaliser les cheveux; **just a ~, please** simplement rafraîchi, s'il vous plaît. -**4.** (*U*) [moulding, decoration] moulures *fpl*; [on car] aménagement *m* intérieur, garnitures *fpl*; [on dress] garniture *f*; *Am* [in shop window] composition *f* d'étalage. -**5.** NAUT [of sails] orientation *f*, réglage *m*. -**6.** CIN coupe *f*.
◆ **trim down** *vt sep* -**1.** [wick] tailler, moucher. -**2.** [budget, costs] réduire.
◆ **trim off** *vt sep* [edge] enlever, couper; [hair] couper; [branch] tailler; [jagged edges] ébarber.

trimaran ['traɪməræn] *n* trimaran *m*.

trimester [traɪ'mestəʳ] *n* -**1.** *Am* trimestre *m*. -**2.** [gen] trois mois *mpl*.

trimmer ['trɪməʳ] *n* -**1.** CONSTR linçoir *m*, linsoir *m*. -**2.** [for timber] trancheuse *f* (*pour le bois*); **(hedge)** ~ taille-haie *m*. -**3.** ELECTRON trimmer *m*, condensateur *m* ajustable. -**4.** *pej* [person] opportuniste *mf*.

trimming ['trɪmɪŋ] *n* -**1.** SEW parement *m*; [lace, ribbon] passement *m*. -**2.** CULIN garniture *f*, accompagnement *m*; **turkey with all the ~s** la dinde avec sa garniture habituelle. -**3.** [accessory] accessoire *m*; **it's the ~s you pay for** ce sont les accessoires que vous payez. -**4.** *inf Am* [defeat] raclée *f*; **to get a ~** prendre une raclée, se faire battre à plate couture.
◆ **trimmings** *npl* [scraps] chutes *fpl*, rognures *fpl*.

trimonthly [traɪ'mʌnθlɪ] *adj* trimestriel.

trinary ['traɪnərɪ] *adj* ternaire.

Trinidad ['trɪnɪdæd] *pr n* (l'île *f* de) la Trinité *f*; **in ~** à la Trinité.

Trinidad and Tobago [-tə'beɪgəʊ] *pr n* Trinité-et-Tobago; **in ~** à Trinité-et-Tobago.

Trinidadian [,trɪnɪ'dædɪən] ◇ *n* Trinidadien *m*, -enne *f*, habitant *m*, -e *f* de la Trinité.
◇ *adj* trinidadien, de la Trinité.

trinitroglycerin [traɪ,naɪtrəʊ'glɪsəriːn] *n* nitroglycérine *f*.

trinitrotoluene [traɪ,naɪtrəʊ'tɒljʊiːn] *n* trinitrotoluène *m*.

trinity ['trɪnətɪ] (*pl* **trinities**) *n fml* OR *lit* trio *m*, groupe *m* de trois.
◆ **Trinity** *n* RELIG -**1.** [union]: **the Trinity** la Trinité. -**2.** [feast]: **Trinity (Sunday)** (la fête de) la Trinité; **the first Sunday after Trinity** le premier dimanche après la Trinité.

Trinity term *n* UNIV troisième trimestre *m*.

trinket ['trɪŋkɪt] *n* [bauble] bibelot *m*, babiole *f*; [jewel] colifichet *m*; [on bracelet] breloque *f*.

trinomial [traɪ'nəʊmjəl] ◇ *n* trinôme *m*.
◇ *adj* à trois termes.

trio ['triːəʊ] (*pl* **trios**) *n* -**1.** MUS trio *m* (*morceau*). -**2.** [group] trio *m*, groupe *m* de trois; MUS trio (*joueurs*).

triode ['traɪəʊd] *n* triode *f*.

triolet ['triːəʊlet] *n* triolet *m*.

trio sonata *n* sonate *f* en trio.

trip [trɪp] (*pt* & *pp* **tripped**, *cont* **tripping**)
◇ *n* -**1.** [journey] voyage *m*; **to go on a ~** partir OR aller en voyage; **we went on a long bus ~** on a fait un long voyage en bus; **I had to make three ~s into town** j'ai dû aller trois fois en ville OR faire trois voyages en ville; **to make a ~ to the dentist's** aller chez le dentiste ❑ **business ~** voyage *m* d'affaires; **it's a 2-hour round ~** le voyage aller-retour OR l'aller-retour dure 2 heures. -**2.** [excursion] promenade *f*, excursion *f*; **we had a lovely ~ to Devon** nous avons fait une très belle promenade dans le Devon; **she took the children on a ~ to the seaside** elle a emmené les enfants en promenade au bord de la mer ‖ [outing] promenade *f*, sortie *f*; **the annual school ~** la sortie scolaire annuelle. -**3.** *drugs sl* trip *m*; **an LSD ~** un trip au LSD; **to have a bad ~** faire un mauvais trip OR voyage ‖ *fig* [experience]: **he seems to be on some kind of nostalgia/ego ~** il semble être en pleine crise de nostalgie/d'égocentrisme.
◇ *vt* -**1.** [person - make stumble] faire trébucher; [- make fall] faire tomber; [intentionally] faire un croche-pied OR un croc-en-jambe à; **he tripped me** il m'a fait un croche-pied. -**2.** [switch, alarm] déclencher. -**3.** *phr*: **to ~ the light fantastic** *hum* danser.
◇ *vi* -**1.** [stumble] trébucher; **I tripped and fell** j'ai trébuché et je suis tombé; **she tripped on** OR **over the wire** elle s'est pris le pied dans le fil; **I tripped on a pile of books** j'ai buté contre OR trébuché sur une pile de livres. -**2.** [step lightly]: **to ~ in/out** entrer/sortir en sautillant; **she tripped down the lane** elle descendit le chemin d'un pas léger; **her name doesn't exactly ~ off the tongue** *fig* son nom n'est pas très facile à prononcer. -**3.** *drugs sl* faire un trip; **to ~ on acid** faire un trip à l'acide.
◆ **trip out** *vi insep drugs sl* faire un trip.
◆ **trip over** ◇ *vi insep* trébucher, faire un faux pas.
◇ *vt insep* buter sur OR contre, trébucher sur OR contre.
◆ **trip up** ◇ *vt sep* -**1.** [cause to fall] faire trébucher; [deliberately] faire un croche-pied à. -**2.** [trap] désarçonner; **her questions are often designed to ~ people up** ses questions sont souvent conçues pour désarçonner les gens.
◇ *vi insep* -**1.** [fall] trébucher; **I tripped up on a stone** j'ai trébuché OR buté contre une pierre. -**2.** [make a mistake] gaffer, faire une gaffe; **I tripped up badly there** là-dessus, j'ai fait une grosse gaffe.

tripartite [,traɪ'pɑːtaɪt] *adj* [division, agreement] tripartite, triparti.

tripe [traɪp] *n* (*U*) -**1.** CULIN tripes *fpl*. -**2.** *inf Br* [nonsense] foutaises *fpl*, bêtises *fpl*; **what a load of ~!** quelles foutaises!; **the film is utter ~** le film est vraiment nul.

triphammer ['trɪp,hæməʳ] *n* marteau *m* à bascule.

triphase ['traɪfeɪz] *adj* ELEC triphasé.

triphthong ['trɪfθɒŋ] *n* triphtongue *f*.

triplane ['traɪpleɪn] *n* triplan *m*.

triple ['trɪpl] ◇ *adj* -**1.** [in three parts] triple; **she has a ~ role of actress, director and producer** elle a le triple rôle d'actrice, de metteur en scène et de productrice; **the organization serves a ~ purpose** le but de l'organisation est triple. -**2.** [treble] triple; **a ~ brandy** un triple cognac; **a ~ murder** un triple meurtre; ~ **the usual amount** trois fois la dose habituelle.
◇ *n* triple *m*.
◇ *vi* & *vt* tripler.

Triple Alliance *pr n* HIST: **the ~** la Triple Alliance *f*.

triple jump *n* triple saut *m*.

triplet ['trɪplɪt] *n* -**1.** [child] triplé *m*, -e *f*; ~s des triplés *mpl*, des triplées *fpl*. -**2.** MUS triolet *m*; LITERAT tercet *m*.

triple time *n*: in ~ à trois temps.

triplex ['trɪpleks] ◇ *adj* [triple] triple.
◇ *n Am* [apartment] triplex *m*.

Triplex® ['trɪpleks] *n Br*: ~ (glass) Triplex® *m*, (verre *m*) Sécurit® *m*; ~ windscreen pare-brise *m inv* en (verre) Sécurit®.

triplicate [*adj* & *n* 'trɪplɪkət, *vb* 'trɪplɪkeɪt]
◇ *adj* en trois exemplaires, en triple exemplaire.
◇ *n* -**1.** [document]: in ~ en trois exemplaires, en triple exemplaire. -**2.** [third copy] triplicata *m*.
◇ *vt* multiplier par trois, tripler.

triply ['trɪplɪ] *adv* triplement.

tripod ['traɪpɒd] *n* trépied *m*.

Tripoli ['trɪpəlɪ] *pr n* Tripoli.

tripos ['traɪpɒs] *n examen de licence (BA) à l'université de Cambridge*.

tripper ['trɪpəʳ] *n Br* [on day trip] excursionniste *mf*; [on holiday] vacancier *m*, -ère *f*.

trip recorder *n* AUT compteur *m* journalier, totalisateur *m* partiel.

trip switch *n* interrupteur *m*.

triptych ['trɪptɪk] *n* triptyque *m*.

trip wire *n* fil *m* de détente.

trireme ['traɪriːm] *n* trirème *f*, trière *f*.

trisect [traɪ'sekt] *vt* diviser en trois parties égales.

Tristan ['trɪstən] *pr n*: '~ and Isolde' *Wagner* 'Tristan et Isolde'.

trisyllabic [ˌtraɪsɪ'læbɪk] *adj* trisyllabique, trisyllabe.

trisyllable [ˌtraɪ'sɪləbl] *n* trisyllabe *m*.

trite [traɪt] *adj* [theme, picture] banal; he made a ~ remark il a dit une banalité; I know it sounds a bit ~, but I do care je sais que ça peut paraître banal de dire ça, mais vraiment je me sens concernée.

tritely ['traɪtlɪ] *adv* banalement.

tritium ['trɪtɪəm] *n* tritium *m*.

triton [*sense 1* 'traɪtn, *sense 2* 'traɪtɒn] *n* -**1.** ZOOL triton *m*. -**2.** PHYS triton *m*.
◆ **Triton** *pr n* MYTH Triton.

tritone ['traɪtəʊn] *n* triton *m* MUS.

triturate ['trɪtjʊreɪt] *vt* triturer.

trituration [ˌtrɪtjʊ'reɪʃn] *n* trituration *f*.

triumph ['traɪəmf] ◇ *n* -**1.** [jubilation] (sentiment *m* de) triomphe *m*; to return in ~ rentrer triomphalement; she had a look of ~ on her face elle avait une expression triomphante. -**2.** [victory] victoire *f*, triomphe *m*; [success] triomphe *m*, (grande) réussite *f*; the musical was an absolute ~ la comédie musicale a été OR a fait un véritable triomphe; the ~ of reason over passion le triomphe de la raison sur la passion; the agreement will be seen as a personal ~ for the President cet accord sera considéré comme un triomphe personnel pour le président. -**3.** [in ancient Rome] triomphe *m*.
◇ *vi* triompher; to ~ over difficulties/a disability triompher des difficultés/d'une infirmité, vaincre les difficultés/une infirmité.

triumphal [traɪ'ʌmfl] *adj* triomphal.

triumphalist [traɪ'ʌmfəlɪst] *adj* triomphaliste.

triumphant [traɪ'ʌmfənt] *adj* [team] victorieux, triomphant; [return] triomphal; [cheer, smile] de triomphe, triomphant; [success] triomphal.

triumphantly [traɪ'ʌmfəntlɪ] *adv* [march] en triomphe, triomphalement; [cheer, smile] triomphalement; [announce] d'un ton triomphant, triomphalement; [look] d'un air triomphant, triomphalement.

triumvirate [traɪ'ʌmvɪrət] *n* triumvirat *m*.

triune ['traɪjuːn] *adj* RELIG trin.

trivalent [traɪ'veɪlənt] *adj* trivalent.

trivet ['trɪvɪt] *n* [when cooking] trépied *m*, chevrette *f*; [for table] dessous-de-plat *m inv*.

trivia ['trɪvɪə] *npl* [trifles] bagatelles *fpl*, futilités *fpl*; [details] détails *mpl*; the ~ of everyday life les petites choses de la vie quotidienne.

trivial ['trɪvɪəl] *adj* -**1.** [insignificant - sum, reason] insignifiant, dérisoire; it's only a ~ offence ce n'est qu'une peccadille, c'est sans gravité. -**2.** [pointless - discussion, question] sans intérêt, insignifiant. -**3.** [banal - story] banal.

triviality [ˌtrɪvɪ'ælətɪ] (*pl* trivialities) *n* -**1.** [of sum] insignifiance *f*, caractère *m* insignifiant; [of discussion] insignifiance *f*, caractère *m* oiseux; [of film] banalité *f*. -**2.** [trifle] futilité *f*, bagatelle *f*; don't waste your time on trivialities ne perdez pas votre temps à des bagatelles.

trivialize, -ise ['trɪvɪəlaɪz] *vt* [make insignificant] banaliser, dévaloriser; her work's very important to her, don't ~ it son travail est très important pour elle, ne le dévalorisez pas; the tabloids ~ even the most important events la presse populaire banalise même les événements les plus importants.

triweekly [traɪ'wiːklɪ] (*pl* triweeklies) ◇ *adv* -**1.** [every three weeks] toutes les trois semaines. -**2.** [three times a week] trois fois par semaine.
◇ *adj* [newspaper] qui paraît toutes les trois semaines; [visit, class] qui se produit trois fois par semaine.
◇ *n* journal *m* qui paraît toutes les trois semaines.

t-RNA (*abbr of* transfer RNA) *n* ARN *m* de transfert.

trochaic [trəʊ'keɪɪk] *adj* trochaïque.

trochee ['trəʊkiː] *n* trochée *m*.

trod [trɒd] *pt* & *pp* → **tread**.

trodden ['trɒdn] *pp* → **tread**.

trog *inf* [trɒg] (*pt* & *pp* trogged, *cont* trogging) *vi Br* se traîner.

troglodyte ['trɒglədaɪt] ◇ *n* troglodyte *m*.
◇ *adj* troglodytique.

troilism ['trɔɪlɪzm] *n* triolisme *m*.

Troilus ['trɔɪləs] *pr n*: '~ and Cressida' *Shakespeare* 'Troïlus et Cressida'.

Trojan ['trəʊdʒən] ◇ *adj* troyen; ~ work travail *m* de titan; 'The ~ Women' *Euripides* 'les Troyennes'.
◇ *n* Troyen *m*, -enne *f*; to work like a ~ travailler comme un forçat.

Trojan Horse *n* HIST & *fig* cheval *m* de Troie.

Trojan War *pr n* guerre *f* de Troie.

troll [trəʊl] ◇ *n* [goblin] troll *m*.
◇ *vi* -**1.** FISHING pêcher à la traîne. -**2.** *inf Br* [stroll] se balader. -**3.** *arch* [sing] chanter vigoureusement.

trolley ['trɒlɪ] (*pl* trolleys) *n* -**1.** [handcart] chariot *m*; [two-wheeled] diable *m*; [for child] poussette *f*; [in supermarket, station] chariot *m*, caddie *m*; [in restaurant] chariot *m*; tea ~ table *f* roulante; drinks ~ chariot *m* à boissons; to be off one's ~ *inf Br* être cinglé. -**2.** [on rails - in mine] wagonnet *m*, benne *f*. -**3.** [for tram] trolley *m* ÉLECTR. -**4.** *Am* [tram] tramway *m*, tram *m*.

trolleybus ['trɒlɪbʌs] *n* trolleybus *m*, trolley *m*.

trolley car *n Am* tramway *m*, tram *m*.

trollop ['trɒləp] *n dated* & *pej* [prostitute] putain *f*; [slut] souillon *f*.

trombone [trɒm'bəʊn] *n* trombone *m (instrument)*.

trombonist [trɒm'bəʊnɪst] *n* tromboniste *mf*, trombone *m (musicien)*.

troop [truːp] ◇ *n* [band - of schoolchildren] bande *f*, groupe *m*; [- of scouts] troupe *f*; [- of animals] troupe *f*; MIL [of cavalry, artillery] escadron *m*.
◇ *vi*: to ~ by OR past passer en troupe; to ~ in/out entrer/sortir en troupe; the children ~ed back to school les enfants sont repartis à l'école en bande.
◇ *vt Br* MIL: to ~ the colour faire le salut au drapeau.
◆ **troops** *npl* [gen & MIL] troupes *fpl*.

troop carrier *n* [ship] transport *m* de troupes; [plane] avion *m* de transport militaire.

trooper ['truːpəʳ] *n* -**1.** [soldier] soldat *m* de cavalerie. -**2.** *Am* & *Austr* [mounted policeman] membre *m* de la police montée; (state) ~ ≃ gendarme *m*. -**3.** *Br* MIL [ship] transport *m* de troupes.

trooping ['truːpɪŋ] *n Br*: ~ (of) the colour salut *m* au drapeau; Trooping the Colour *défilé de régiments ayant lieu chaque année le jour officiel de l'anniversaire de la reine d'Angleterre*.

troopship ['truːpʃɪp] *n* navire *m* de transport.

trope [trəʊp] *n* trope *m*.

trophic ['trɒfɪk] *adj* trophique.

trophy ['trəʊfɪ] (*pl* trophies) *n* trophée *m*.

tropic ['trɒpɪk] ◇ *n* tropique *m*; in the ~s sous les tropiques; the Tropic of Capricorn/Cancer le tropique du Capricorne/du Cancer.
◇ *adj lit* = **tropical**.

tropical ['trɒpɪkl] *adj* [region] des tropiques, tropical; [weather, forest, medicine] tropical.

tropism ['trəʊpɪzm] *n* tropisme *m*.

troposphere ['trɒpəsfɪəʳ] *n* troposphère *f*.

trot [trɒt] (*pt* & *pp* trotted, *cont* trotting)
◇ *n* -**1.** [of horse] trot *m*; to go at a ~ aller au trot, trotter ‖ [of person]: he went off at a ~ il est parti au pas de course. -**2.** [ride] promenade *f* à cheval; [run] *inf* petite course *f*; to go for a ~ [on horseback] aller faire une promenade à cheval; [on foot] *inf* aller faire une promenade ❑ on the ~ *inf Br* [busy] affairé; [in succession] d'affilée, de suite; they kept me on the ~ all afternoon ils m'ont fait courir tout l'après-midi, ils ne m'ont pas accordé un moment de répit de tout l'après-midi; he conducted ten interviews on the ~ (that morning) (ce matin-là,) il a fait dix interviews d'affilée OR de suite. -**3.** *inf Am* [crib] anti-sèche *f*.
◇ *vi* -**1.** [horse, rider] trotter; he trotted up to us il est venu vers nous au trot. -**2.** [on foot]: to ~ in/out/past entrer/sortir/passer en courant; can you ~ down to the shops for me? peux-tu faire un saut pour moi jusqu'aux magasins?
◇ *vt* [horse] faire trotter.
◆ **trot along** *vi insep* -**1.** [horse] trotter, aller au trot. -**2.** *inf* [person] partir; ~ along now sauve-toi maintenant.
◆ **trot away** *vi insep* -**1.** [horse] partir au trot. -**2.** *inf* [person] partir au pas de course.
◆ **trot out** *inf vt sep Br* [excuse, information] débiter *pej*; [story, list] débiter *pej*, réciter *pej*; she trotted out the usual excuses elle débita OR sortit les excuses habituelles.
◆ **trot over** *vi insep* -**1.** [rider] venir à cheval. -**2.** *inf* [person] venir, faire un saut; why don't you ~ over to see me some time? viens donc faire un saut un de ces jours; she trotted over to the shops elle a fait un saut jusqu'aux magasins.
◆ **trots** *inf npl Br* diarrhée *f*; to have the ~s avoir la courante.

Trot *inf* [trɒt] *n pej abbr of* Trotskyist

troth [trəʊθ] *n arch*: by my ~! ma foi!, pardieu! *arch*; in ~ en vérité.

trotline ['trɒtlaɪn] *n* FISHING *ligne qui traverse une rivière et à laquelle on suspend des hameçons*.

Trotsky ['trɒtskɪ] *pr n* Trotski.

Trotskyism ['trɒtskɪɪzm] *n* trotskisme *m*.

Trotskyist ['trɒtskɪɪst] ◇ *adj* trotskiste.
◇ *n* trotskiste *mf*.

Trotskyite ['trɒtskɪaɪt] ◇ *adj* trotskiste.
◇ *n* trotskiste *mf*.

trotter ['trɒtəʳ] *n* -**1.** [horse] trotteur *m*, -euse *f*. -**2.** CULIN: pig's/sheep's ~s pieds *mpl* de porc/de mouton.

troubadour ['truːbədɔːʳ] *n* troubadour *m*.

trouble ['trʌbl] ◇ *n* -**1.** *(U)* [conflict - esp with authority] ennuis *mpl*, problèmes *mpl*; [discord] discorde *f*; to be in ~ avoir des ennuis; you're really in ~ now! tu es dans de beaux draps OR te voilà bien maintenant!; I've never been in ~ with the police je n'ai jamais eu d'ennuis OR d'histoires avec la police; to get into ~ s'attirer des ennuis, se faire attraper; her sharp tongue often gets her into ~ sa causticité lui attire souvent des ennuis; he got into ~ for stealing apples il s'est fait attraper pour avoir volé des

trustingly ['trʌstɪŋlɪ] *adv* en toute confiance; he looked at me ~ il m'a lancé un regard confiant.

trust territory *n* territoire *m* sous tutelle.

trustworthiness ['trʌst,wɜːðɪnɪs] *n* -**1.** [reliability - of person] loyauté *f*, sérieux *m*; [- of information, source] fiabilité *f*. -**2.** [accuracy - of report, figures] fiabilité *f*, justesse *f*. -**3.** [honesty] honnêteté *f*.

trustworthy ['trʌst,wɜːðɪ] *adj* -**1.** [reliable - person] sur qui on peut compter, à qui on peut faire confiance; [- information, source] sûr, fiable. -**2.** [accurate - report, figures] fidèle, précis. -**3.** [honest] honnête.

trusty ['trʌstɪ] (*compar* trustier, *superl* trustiest, *pl* trusties) ◇ *adj arch* OR *hum* [steed, sword] loyal, fidèle.

◇ *n* [prisoner] *détenu bénéficiant d'un régime de faveur.*

truth [truːθ] (*pl* truths [truːðz]) *n* -**1.** [true facts] vérité *f*; I then discovered the ~ about Neil j'ai alors découvert la vérité sur Neil; there isn't a grain OR an ounce of ~ in what he says il n'y a pas une once de vérité dans ce qu'il dit; there's some ~ in what he says il y a du vrai dans ce qu'il dit; there is no ~ in the rumour il n'y a rien de vrai dans cette rumeur; the ~ of the matter is I really don't care any more la vérité c'est que maintenant je m'en fiche vraiment; to tell the ~ dire la vérité ☐ to tell (you) the ~ à vrai dire, à dire vrai; ~ to tell *lit* à dire vrai; (the) ~ will out *prov* la vérité finit toujours par se savoir. -**2.** [fact, piece of information] vérité *f*; he learned some important ~s about himself on lui a dit ses quatre vérités; universal ~s vérités universelles.

◆ **in truth** *adv phr* en vérité.

truth-condition *n* LOGIC & PHILOS condition *f* nécessaire et préalable.

truth drug *n* sérum *m* de vérité.

truthful ['truːθfʊl] *adj* [person] qui dit la vérité; [character] honnête; [article, statement] fidèle à la réalité, vrai; [story] véridique, vrai; [portrait] fidèle.

truthfully ['truːθfʊlɪ] *adv* [answer, speak] honnêtement, sans mentir; [sincerely] sincèrement, vraiment.

truthfulness ['truːθfʊlnɪs] *n* [of person] honnêteté *f*; [of portrait] fidélité *f*; [of story, statement] véracité *f*.

truth-function *n* LOGIC fonction *f* vériconditionnelle.

truth set *n* LOGIC & MATH *ensemble qui n'a pas de solution unique.*

truth-value *n* LOGIC & PHILOS valeur *f* de vérité.

try [traɪ] (*pt* & *pp* tried, *pl* tries) ◇ *vt* -**1.** [attempt] essayer; to ~ to do OR doing sthg essayer OR tâcher de faire qqch, chercher à faire qqch; I've tried to give up smoking before j'ai déjà essayé d'arrêter de fumer; ~ phoning later essaie de rappeler plus tard; she tried not to think about it elle essaya de ne pas y penser OR d'éviter d'y penser; I tried hard to understand j'ai tout fait pour essayer de comprendre, j'ai vraiment cherché à comprendre; to ~ one's best OR hardest faire de son mieux; he tried his best to explain il a essayé d'expliquer de son mieux; I'm willing to ~ anything once! je suis prêt à tout essayer au moins une fois!; it's ~ing to rain on dirait qu'il va pleuvoir; and don't ~ any funny business! *inf* et pas d'entourloupe!; just you ~ it! [as threat] essaie un peu pour voir! ☐ to ~ one's hand at (doing) sthg s'essayer à (faire) qqch. -**2.** [test - method, approach, car] essayer; have you tried acupuncture? avez-vous essayé l'acupuncture?; the method has been tried and tested la méthode a fait ses preuves; he has been tried and found wanting il ne s'est pas montré à la hauteur; (just) ~ me! *inf* essaie toujours!; to ~ one's strength against sb se mesurer à qqn; to ~ one's luck (at sthg) tenter sa chance (à qqch). -**3.** [sample - recipe, wine] essayer, goûter à; [- clothes] essayer; ~ it, you'll like it essayez OR goûtez-y donc, vous aimerez; just ~ the dress and see if it suits you essaie donc la robe, pour voir si elle te va; ~ this for size *literal* [garment] essayez ceci pour voir la taille; [shoe] essayez ceci pour voir la pointure; *fig* essayez ceci pour voir si ça va. -**4.** [attempt to open - door, window] essayer; we tried the door, but it was locked on a essayé la porte, mais elle était fermée à clé. -**5.** TELEC essayer; ~ the number again refaites le numéro; ~ him later *inf* essayez de le rappeler plus tard. -**6.** [visit] essayer; I've tried six shops already j'ai déjà essayé six magasins; he tried the embassy first il a d'abord essayé l'ambassade. -**7.** JUR [person, case] juger; he was tried for murder il a été jugé pour meurtre. -**8.** [tax, strain - patience] éprouver, mettre à l'épreuve; these things are sent to ~ us! c'est le ciel qui nous envoie ces épreuves!; it's enough to ~ the patience of a saint même un ange n'aurait pas la patience; to be sorely tried *lit* OR *hum* être durement éprouvé.

◇ *vi* essayer; to ~ and do sthg essayer de faire qqch; ~ again refaites un essai, recommencez; ~ later essayez plus tard; we can but ~ on peut toujours essayer; you can do it if you ~ quand on veut, on peut; just (you) ~! essaie donc un peu!; to ~ for sthg essayer d'obtenir qqch; she's ~ing for a place at Oxford elle essaie d'être admise à l'université d'Oxford; why don't you at least ~ for the job? pourquoi ne pas au moins vous présenter pour le poste?; she's ~ing for a gold medal elle essaie de décrocher une médaille d'or.

◇ *n* -**1.** [attempt] essai *m*, tentative *f*; to have a ~ at sthg/at doing sthg essayer qqch/de faire qqch; good ~! bien essayé!; it's worth a ~ cela vaut la peine d'essayer; I managed it at the first ~ j'ai réussi du premier coup; he had several tries at opening the box il a essayé plusieurs fois d'ouvrir la boîte. -**2.** [test, turn] essai *m*; to give sthg a ~ essayer qqch; do you want a ~ on my bike? veux-tu essayer mon vélo? -**3.** SPORT [in rugby] essai *m*; to score a ~ marquer un essai.

◆ **try on** *vt sep* -**1.** [garment] essayer; ~ it on for size essayez-le pour voir la taille. -**2.** *phr*: to ~ it on with sb *inf Br* essayer de voir jusqu'où on peut pousser qqn; he's just ~ing it on to see how far he can go il essaie juste de voir jusqu'où il peut aller; don't you ~ anything on with me! [gen] ne fais pas le malin avec moi!; [flirt] n'essaie pas de flirter avec moi!

◆ **try out** ◇ *vt sep* [new car, bicycle] essayer, faire un essai avec, faire l'essai de; [method, chemical, recipe] essayer; [employee] mettre à l'essai.

◇ *vi insep Am*: to ~ out for a team faire un essai pour se faire engager dans une équipe.

◆ **try over** *vt sep* [music] jouer à titre d'essai.

trying ['traɪɪŋ] *adj* [experience] pénible, douloureux, éprouvant; [journey, job] ennuyeux, pénible; [character, person] fatigant, pénible; he had a very ~ time [moment] il a passé un moment très difficile; [period] il a vécu une période difficile; [experience] il a vécu une expérience très difficile OR éprouvante.

try-on *inf n Br*: it's a ~ c'est du bluff.

try-out *n* essai *m*.

trysail ['traɪsəl] *n* voile *f* goélette.

tryst [trɪst] *n lit* rendez-vous *m* (d'amour).

tsar [zɑː^{r}] *n* tsar *m*, tzar *m*, czar *m*.

tsarevitch ['zɑːrəvɪtʃ] *n* tsarévitch *m*, tzarévitch *m*.

tsarina [zɑː'riːnə] *n* tsarine *f*, tzarine *f*.

tsarism ['zɑːrɪzm] *n* tsarisme *m*.

tsarist ['zɑːrɪst] ◇ *adj* tsariste.

◇ *n* tsariste *mf*.

T-section *n* profil *m* en T.

tsetse fly ['tsetsɪ-] *n* mouche *f* tsé-tsé.

T-shaped *adj* en forme de T.

T-shirt *n* tee-shirt *m*, t-shirt *m*.

tsp. (*written abbr of* teaspoon) cc.

T-square *n* équerre *f* en T, té *m*, T *m* *(règle)*.

T-stop *n* PHOT diaphragme *m*.

T-strap *n* [on shoe] fermeture *f* en té.

TT ◇ *adj abbr of* teetotal.

◇ *pr n* (*abbr of* Tourist Trophy): ~ races *courses de moto sur l'île de Man.*

TTL (*abbr of* through the lens) *adj*: ~ measurement mesure *f* à travers l'objectif OR TTL.

TU *n abbr of* trade union.

Tuareg ['twɑːreg] (*pl inv* OR Tuaregs) ◇ *n* -**1.** [person] Touareg *m*, -ègue *f*. -**2.** LING touareg *m*.

◇ *adj* touareg.

tub [tʌb] *n* -**1.** [container - for liquid] cuve *f*, bac *m*; [- for flowers] bac *m*; [- for washing clothes] baquet *m*; [- in washing machine] cuve *f*. -**2.** [contents - of washing powder] baril *m*; [- of wine, beer] tonneau *m*; [- of ice cream, yoghurt] pot *m*. -**3.** *inf* [bath]: he's in the ~ il prend un bain. -**4.** *inf* [boat] rafiot *m*.

tuba ['tjuːbə] *n* tuba *m*.

tubby *inf* ['tʌbɪ] (*compar* tubbier, *superl* tubbiest) *adj* dodu, rondelet.

tube [tjuːb] ◇ *n* -**1.** [pipe] tube *m*; he was fed through a ~ on l'a nourri à la sonde. -**2.** ANAT tube *m*, canal *m*; bronchial ~s bronches *fpl*. -**3.** [of glue, toothpaste] tube *m*. -**4.** [in tyre]: (inner) ~ chambre *f* à air. -**5.** TV: what's on the ~ tonight? *inf* qu'est-ce qu'il y a à la télé ce soir?; (cathode-ray) ~ tube *m* (cathodique). -**6.** *Br* [underground]: the ~ *le métro londonien*; to go by ~, to take the ~ aller en métro, prendre le métro. -**7.** *phr*: to go down the ~s *inf* tomber à l'eau.

◇ *comp* [map, station] de métro.

tube dress *n Br* robe *f* tube.

tube-feed *vt* nourrir à la sonde.

tubeless ['tjuːblɪs] *adj Br*: ~ tyre pneu *m* sans chambre (à air).

tuber ['tjuːbə^{r}] *n* ANAT & BOT tubercule *m*.

tubercle ['tjuːbəkl] *n* tubercule *m*.

tubercular [tjuː'bɜːkjʊlə^{r}] *adj* tuberculeux.

tuberculin [tjuː'bɜːkjʊlɪn] *n* tuberculine *f*.

tuberculin-tested [-'testɪd] *adj* [cow] tuberculinisé, tuberculiné; ~ milk ≃ lait *m* certifié.

tuberculosis [tjuː,bɜːkjʊ'ləʊsɪs] *n* (*U*) tuberculose *f*; he has ~ il a la tuberculose, il est tuberculeux.

tuberculous [tjuː'bɜːkjʊləs] *adj* tuberculeux.

tube skirt *n Br* jupe *f* tube.

tubing ['tjuːbɪŋ] *n* (*U*) tubes *mpl*, tuyaux *mpl*; a piece of plastic ~ un tube en plastique.

tub-thumper *inf* [-'θʌmpə^{r}] *n Br* orateur *m* démagogue.

tub-thumping *inf* ◇ *n Br* démagogie *f*.

◇ *adj* démagogique.

Tubuai Islands [,tuːbuː'aɪ-] *pl pr n*: the ~ les îles *fpl* Australes.

tubular ['tjuːbjʊlə^{r}] *adj* [furniture, shape] tubulaire; ~ bells MUS carillon *m* d'orchestre.

TUC (*abbr of* Trades Union Congress) *pr n la Confédération des syndicats britanniques*; the ~ annual conference le congrès annuel des syndicats.

tuck [tʌk] ◇ *vt* -**1.** [shirt] rentrer; [sheet] rentrer, border; he ~ed his shirt into his trousers il rentra sa chemise dans son pantalon; she ~ed the sheets under the mattress elle borda le lit. -**2.** [put] mettre; [slip] glisser; she ~ed the book under the bedclothes elle glissa le livre sous les draps; he had a newspaper ~ed under his arm il avait un journal sous le bras; she ~ed her hair behind her ears elle ramena ses cheveux derrière ses oreilles; his mother came to ~ him into bed sa mère est venue le border dans son lit.

◇ *n* -**1.** SEW rempli *m*; to put OR to make a ~ in sthg faire un rempli dans qqch. -**2.** [in diving] plongeon *m* groupé. -**3.** *inf Br* SCH boustifaille *f*.

◆ **tuck away** *vt sep* -**1.** [hide] cacher; [put] mettre, ranger; the house was ~ed away in the hills la maison était cachée OR perdue dans les collines. -**2.** *inf* [food] s'enfiler, avaler; he ~ed away three helpings il s'est enfilé trois portions.

◆ **tuck in** ◇ *vt sep* -**1.** [shirt, stomach] rentrer. -**2.** [child] border; he ~ed her in for the night il la borda pour la nuit.

◇ *vi insep inf* [eat]: we ~ed in to a lovely meal nous avons attaqué un excellent repas; don't wait for me, ~ in! ne m'attendez pas, attaquez!
◆ **tuck up** *vt sep* -**1.** [person] border (dans son lit); all the children were safely ~ed up in bed les enfants étaient tous bien bordés dans leurs lits. -**2.** [skirt, sleeves] remonter; [hair] rentrer. -**3.** [legs] replier, rentrer.
tuckbox ['tʌkbɒks] *n Br* SCH gamelle *f (d'écolier)*.
tucker ['tʌkəʳ] ◇ *n* -**1.** [on dress] fichu *m*. -**2.** *inf Austr & NZ* [food] bouffe *f*.
◇ *vt inf Am* [exhaust] crever; you look ~ed out! tu as l'air complètement crevé!
tuck-in *inf n Br*: we had a great ~ on a bien bouffé.
tuckshop ['tʌkʃɒp] *n Br* SCH *petite boutique où les écoliers achètent bonbons, gâteaux etc.*
Tudor ['tju:dəʳ] ◇ *adj* [family, period] des Tudor; [king, architecture] Tudor *(inv)*.
◇ *n* Tudor *m inv*, membre *m* de la famille des Tudor.
Tue., Tues. (*written abbr of* Tuesday) mar.
Tuesday ['tju:zdɪ] *n* mardi *m*.
tufa ['tju:fə] *n* tuf *m* calcaire.
tuffet ['tʌfɪt] *n arch* -**1.** [of grass] touffe *f* d'herbe. -**2.** [stool] petit tabouret *m*.
tuft [tʌft] *n* -**1.** [of hair, grass] touffe *f*. -**2.** ORNITH: ~ (of feathers) huppe *f*, aigrette *f*.
tufted ['tʌftɪd] *adj* -**1.** [bird] huppé. -**2.** [grass] en touffe OR touffes. -**3.** [carpet] en velours coupé, tufté.
tufted duck *n* morillon *m*.
tug [tʌg] (*pt & pp* tugged, *cont* tugging)
◇ *n* -**1.** [pull] petit coup *m*; give the rope a ~, will you? tire un peu sur la corde, tu veux?; he felt a ~ at his sleeve il sentit qu'on le tirait par la manche. -**2.** NAUT remorqueur *m*.
◇ *vt* -**1.** [handle, sleeve] tirer sur; [load] tirer, traîner; he tugged the heavy crate along the path il traîna la lourde caisse le long de l'allée. -**2.** NAUT remorquer.
◇ *vi*: to ~ at OR on sthg tirer sur qqch; the music tugged at her heartstrings *fig* cette musique l'émouvait.
tugboat ['tʌgbəʊt] *n* remorqueur *m*.
tug-of-love *inf n Br conflit entre des parents en instance de divorce pour avoir la garde d'un enfant*; ~ children *les enfants dont les parents se disputent la garde*.
tug-of-war *n* SPORT lutte *f* à la corde; *fig* lutte *f* acharnée.
tuition [tju:'ɪʃn] *n (U)* -**1.** *Br* [instruction] cours *mpl*; I give ~ in Spanish je donne des cours d'espagnol. -**2.** UNIV: ~ (fees) frais *mpl* de scolarité.
tulip ['tju:lɪp] *n* tulipe *f*.
tulip tree *n* tulipier *m*.
tulle [tju:l] *n* tulle *m*.
tum *inf* [tʌm] *n Br* ventre *m*.
tumble ['tʌmbl] ◇ *vi* -**1.** [fall - person] faire une chute, dégringoler; [- ball, objects] dégringoler; he ~d down the stairs il a fait une culbute dans OR il a dégringolé (dans) l'escalier; to ~ head over heels faire une culbute OR un roulé-boulé; the bottles came tumbling off the shelf les bouteilles ont dégringolé de l'étagère. -**2.** [collapse - prices] dégringoler, s'effondrer; the Chancellor's resignation sent share prices tumbling la démission du ministre des Finances a fait dégringoler le prix des actions. -**3.** [rush] se précipiter; the children ~d into the kitchen les enfants se ruèrent OR se précipitèrent dans la cuisine; they came tumbling after me ils se sont lancés à ma poursuite. -**4.** [perform somersaults] faire des sauts périlleux.
◇ *vt* [knock, push - person] renverser, faire tomber OR dégringoler; she ~d me into the pool elle m'a fait tomber dans la piscine.
◇ *n* [fall] chute *f*, culbute *f*, roulé-boulé *m*; [somersault] culbute *f*, cabrioles *fpl*; he had a bad ~ on the ice il a fait une mauvaise chute sur la glace; to take a ~ faire une chute OR une culbute; his pride took a ~ *fig* son orgueil a souffert; share prices took a ~ today le prix des actions s'est effondré aujourd'hui.
◆ **tumble about** ◇ *vi insep* [children] gambader, batifoler; [acrobat] faire des cabrioles; [swimmer] s'ébattre; [water] clapoter.
◇ *vt sep* mettre en désordre; the waves ~d us about nous étions ballotés par les vagues.
◆ **tumble down** *vi insep* [person] faire une culbute, dégringoler; [pile] dégringoler; [wall, building] s'effondrer; the whole building came tumbling down tout l'édifice s'est effondré OR écroulé.
◆ **tumble out** ◇ *vi insep* -**1.** [person - from tree, loft] faire une culbute, dégringoler; [- from bus, car] se jeter, sauter; [possessions, contents] tomber (en vrac); the apples ~d out of her basket les pommes ont roulé de son panier; the tablets ~d out onto the table les comprimés ont roulé sur la table; he ~d out of bed at midday il est tombé du lit à midi *hum*. -**2.** [news, confession] s'échapper; all their secrets came tumbling out ils nous ont déballé tous leurs secrets.
◇ *vt sep* faire tomber en vrac OR en tas.
◆ **tumble over** ◇ *vi insep* [person] culbuter, faire une culbute; [pile, vase] se renverser.
◇ *vt sep* renverser, faire tomber.
◆ **tumble to** *inf vt insep Br* [fact, secret, joke] piger, saisir, comprendre; I finally ~d to their little game j'ai enfin compris leur petit manège.
tumbledown ['tʌmbldaʊn] *adj* en ruines, délabré.
tumble-dry *vt* faire sécher dans le sèche-linge.
tumble dryer *n* sèche-linge *m inv*.
tumbler ['tʌmbləʳ] *n* -**1.** [glass] verre *m* (droit); [beaker] gobelet *m*, timbale *f*; a ~ of orange (juice) un verre de jus d'orange. -**2.** [acrobat] acrobate *mf*. -**3.** [in lock] gorge *f* (de serrure). -**4.** = **tumble dryer**. -**5.** [pigeon] pigeon *m* culbutant.
tumbler switch *n* interrupteur *m* à bascule.
tumbleweed ['tʌmblwi:d] *n* amarante *f*.
tumbrel ['tʌmbrəl], **tumbril** ['tʌmbrɪl] *n* tombereau *m*.
tumefaction [,tju:mɪ'fækʃn] *n* tuméfaction *f*.
tumescent [,tju:'mesnt] *adj* tumescent.
tumid ['tju:mɪd] *adj* -**1.** MED tuméfié. -**2.** *lit* [style] ampoulé, boursouflé.
tummy *inf* ['tʌmɪ] ◇ *n* ventre *m*.
◇ *comp*: to have (a) ~ ache avoir mal au ventre; ~ button nombril *m*.
tumour *Br*, **tumor** *Am* ['tju:məʳ] *n* tumeur *f*.
tumuli ['tju:mjʊlaɪ] *pl* → **tumulus**.
tumult ['tju:mʌlt] *n* -**1.** [noise] tumulte *m*; [agitation] tumulte *m*, agitation *f*; in (a) ~ dans le tumulte. -**2.** *fml* OR *lit* [of feelings] émoi *m*.
tumultuous ['tju:mʌltjʊəs] *adj* [crowd, noise] tumultueux; [applause] frénétique; [period] tumultueux, agité; he got a ~ welcome il a reçu un accueil enthousiaste.
tumulus ['tju:mjʊləs] (*pl* tumuli [-laɪ]) *n* tumulus *m*.
tun [tʌn] *n* fût *m*, tonneau *m*.
tuna ['tju:nə, 'tu:nə] *n*: ~ (fish) thon *m*.
tundra ['tʌndrə] *n* toundra *f*.
tune [tju:n] ◇ *n* [melody] air *m*, mélodie *f*; give us a ~ on the mouth organ joue-nous un petit air d'harmonica; the band played some old Irish ~s l'orchestre joua de vieilles mélodies irlandaises; the soldiers marched to the ~ of Rule Britannia les soldats marchèrent sur l'air de OR aux accents de Rule Britannia; it's got no ~ to it cela manque de mélodie, ce n'est pas mélodieux.
◇ *vt* -**1.** [musical instrument] accorder; the strings are ~d to the key of G les cordes sont en sol. -**2.** [regulate - engine, machine] mettre au point, régler. -**3.** [radio, television] régler; the radio is ~d to Voice of America la radio est réglée sur la Voix de l'Amérique; we can't ~ our TV to Channel 5 nous ne pouvons pas capter la chaîne 5 sur notre télé; stay ~d! restez à l'écoute! -**4.** [adapt]: politicians always ~ their remarks to suit their audience les hommes politiques se mettent toujours au diapason de leur auditoire, les hommes politiques adaptent toujours leurs commentaires à leur auditoire.
◆ **in tune** ◇ *adj phr* [instrument] accordé, juste; [singer] qui chante juste; the violins are not in ~ with the piano les violons ne sont pas accordés avec le piano; he is completely in ~ with current political thinking *fig* il est complètement en accord avec la pensée politique actuelle.
◇ *adv phr* juste; to play/to sing in ~ jouer/chanter juste.
◆ **out of tune** ◇ *adj phr* [instrument] faux, désaccordé; [singer] qui chante faux; the MP was out of ~ with the rest of his party *fig* le député n'était pas sur la même longueur d'onde que les autres membres de son parti OR était en désaccord avec les autres membres de son parti.
◇ *adv phr* faux; to play/to sing out of ~ jouer/chanter faux.
◆ **to the tune of** *prep phr*: they were given grants to the ~ of £100,000 on leur a accordé des subventions qui s'élevaient à 100 000 livres.
◆ **tune in** ◇ *vi insep* RADIO & TV se mettre à l'écoute; ~ in to this channel next week soyez à l'écoute de cette chaîne la semaine prochaine; I ~d in to Radio Ultra je me suis mis à l'écoute de Radio Ultra.
◇ *vt sep* -**1.** [radio, television] régler sur. -**2.** *inf fig*: to be ~d in to sthg être branché sur qqch.
◆ **tune out** *Am* ◇ *vi insep* [refuse to listen] faire la sourde oreille; [stop listening] décrocher.
◇ *vt sep* -**1.** [remark] ignorer. -**2.** [radio] éteindre; he is completely ~d out *inf fig* il n'est pas du tout branché.
◆ **tune up** ◇ *vi insep* MUS [player] accorder son instrument; [orchestra] accorder ses instruments.
◇ *vt sep* -**1.** MUS accorder. -**2.** AUT mettre au point, régler.
tuned-in *inf* [tju:nd-] *adj* branché.
tuneful ['tju:nfʊl] *adj* [song, voice] mélodieux; [singer] à la voix mélodieuse.
tunefully ['tju:nfʊlɪ] *adv* mélodieusement.
tuneless ['tju:nlɪs] *adj* peu mélodieux, discordant.
tunelessly ['tju:nlɪslɪ] *adv* [with no tune] de manière peu mélodieuse; [out of tune] faux *(adv)*.
tuner ['tju:nəʳ] *n* -**1.** [of piano] accordeur *m*. -**2.** RADIO & TV tuner *m*, syntonisateur *m spec*.
tuner amplifier *n* ampli-tuner *m*.
tune-up *n* AUT réglage *m*, mise *f* au point; to have a ~ faire faire une mise au point OR un réglage.
tungsten ['tʌŋstən] *n* tungstène *m*.
tungsten carbide *n* carbure *m* de tungstène.
tungsten lamp *n* lampe *f* au tungstène.
tungsten steel *n* acier *m* au tungstène.
tunic ['tju:nɪk] *n* [gen & BOT] tunique *f*.
tuning ['tju:nɪŋ] *n* -**1.** MUS accord *m*. -**2.** RADIO & TV réglage *m*. -**3.** AUT réglage *m*, mise *f* au point.
tuning fork *n* diapason *m*.
tuning key *n* accordoir *m*.
tuning knob *n* bouton *m* de réglage.
Tunis ['tju:nɪs] *pr n* Tunis.
Tunisia [tju:'nɪzɪə] *pr n* Tunisie *f*; in ~ en Tunisie.
Tunisian [tju:'nɪzɪən] ◇ *n* Tunisien *m*, -enne *f*.
◇ *adj* tunisien.
tunnage ['tʌnɪdʒ] = **tonnage**.
tunnel ['tʌnl] (*Br pt & pp* tunnelled, *cont* tunnelling, *Am pt & pp* tunneled, *cont* tunneling)
◇ *n* [gen & RAIL] tunnel *m*; MIN galerie *f*; [of mole, badger] galerie *f*; to make OR to dig a ~ [gen] percer OR creuser un tunnel; MIN percer OR creuser une galerie.
◇ *vt* [hole, passage] creuser, percer; to ~ one's way through the earth CONSTR creuser un tunnel dans la terre; [mole] creuser une galerie dans la terre; the prisoners tunnelled their way to freedom les prisonniers se sont évadés en creusant un tunnel.

◇ *vi* [person] creuser OR percer un tunnel OR des tunnels; [badger, mole] creuser une galerie OR des galeries; **they tunnelled into the mountain** CONSTR ils ont percé un tunnel dans la montagne; MIN ils ont percé une galerie dans la montagne; **the machines had to ~ through granite** les machines ont dû creuser dans le granit.

tunnel effect *n* effet *m* tunnel.

tunnelling machine [ˈtʌnlɪŋ-] *n* foreuse *f*.

tunnel vision *n* -**1.** OPT rétrécissement *m* du champ visuel. -**2.** *fig* esprit *m* borné; **to have ~** avoir des vues étroites, voir les choses par le petit bout de la lorgnette.

tunny [ˈtʌnɪ] = **tuna**.

tup [tʌp] (*pt* & *pp* **tupped**, *cont* **tupping**) ◇ *n* -**1.** *Br* [ram] bélier *m*. -**2.** [on pile-driver] mouton *m*.

◇ *vt* [subj: ram] s'accoupler à; [ram] accoupler.

tuppence [ˈtʌpəns] *n Br* deux pence *mpl*; **the picture isn't worth ~** *inf* [in price] le tableau ne vaut pas un rond OR ne vaut rien; [in quality] le tableau ne vaut pas un clou; **I don't care ~ for your opinion** *inf* je me fiche pas mal de votre opinion OR de ce que vous pensez.

tuppenny *inf* [ˈtʌpnɪ] *adj Br* de OR à deux pence; **I don't give a ~ damn** je m'en fiche (et je m'en contrefiche).

tuppenny-ha'penny *inf* [ˈtʌpnɪˌheɪpnɪ] *adj Br* de rien du tout, de quatre sous.

Tupperware® [ˈtʌpəweəʳ] ◇ *n* Tupperware® *m*; **~ party** réunion *f* Tupperware.

◇ *comp* en Tupperware®.

turban [ˈtɜːbən] *n* turban *m*.

turban(n)ed [ˈtɜːbənd] *adj* [person] en turban; [head] coiffé d'un turban, enturbanné.

turbid [ˈtɜːbɪd] *adj* trouble.

turbine [ˈtɜːbaɪn] *n* turbine *f*; **gas/steam ~** turbine *f* à gaz/à vapeur.

turbo [ˈtɜːbəʊ] (*pl* **turbos**) *n* -**1.** AUT turbo *m*. -**2.** [turbine] turbine *f*.

turbocharged [ˈtɜːbəʊtʃɑːdʒd] *adj* turbo.

turbocharger [ˈtɜːbəʊtʃɑːdʒəʳ] *n* turbocompresseur *m*.

turboelectric [ˌtɜːbəʊɪˈlektrɪk] *adj* turboélectrique.

turbofan [ˈtɜːbəʊfæn] *n*: **~ engine** turboventilateur *m*, turbofan *m*.

turbogenerator [ˌtɜːbəʊˈdʒenəreɪtəʳ] *n* turbogénérateur *m*.

turbojet [ˌtɜːbəʊˈdʒet] *n* [engine] turboréacteur *m*; [plane] avion *m* à turboréacteur.

turboprop [ˌtɜːbəʊˈprɒp] *n* [engine] turbopropulseur *m*; [plane] avion *m* à turbopropulseur.

turbosupercharger [ˌtɜːbəʊˈsuːpəˌtʃɑːdʒəʳ] *n* turbocompresseur *m* de suralimentation.

turbot [ˈtɜːbət] (*pl inv* OR **turbots**) *n* turbot *m*.

turbulence [ˈtɜːbjʊləns] *n* -**1.** [unrest] turbulence *f*, agitation *f*. -**2.** [in air] turbulence *f*; [in sea] agitation *f*. -**3.** PHYS turbulence *f*.

turbulent [ˈtɜːbjʊlənt] *adj* [crowd, period, emotions] tumultueux; [sea] agité.

Turco- [ˈtɜːkəʊ] *in cpds* turco-; **~Persian** turco-persan.

turd▽ [tɜːd] *n* -**1.** [excrement] merde *f*. -**2.** *pej* [person] con *m*, salaud *m*.

tureen [təˈriːn] *n* soupière *f*.

turf [tɜːf] (*pl* **turfs** OR **turves** [tɜːvz]) ◇ *n* -**1.** [grass] gazon *m*. -**2.** [sod] motte *f* de gazon. -**3.** SPORT turf *m*; **to follow the ~** être turfiste. -**4.** [peat] tourbe *f*. -**5.** ▽*Am* [of gang] territoire *m* réservé, chasse *f* gardée.

◇ *vt* -**1.** [with grass]: **~ (over)** gazonner. -**2.** *inf Br* [throw] balancer, flanquer, jeter; **she ~ed the old magazines into the box** elle a balancé les vieux magazines dans la boîte.

◆ **turf out** *inf vt sep Br* [eject, evict - person] vider, flanquer à la porte; [remove - furniture, possessions] sortir, enlever; [throw away - rubbish] bazarder; **he ~ed everything out of the cupboard** il a tout sorti du placard, il a bazardé tout ce qu'il y avait dans le placard; **he was ~ed out of the club** il s'est fait virer OR vider du club.

turf accountant *n fml Br* bookmaker *m*.

turfman [ˈtɜːfmən] (*pl* **turfmen** [-mən]) *n Am* turfiste *m*.

Turgenev [tɜːˈgeɪnjev] *pr n* Tourgueniev.

turgid [ˈtɜːdʒɪd] *adj* -**1.** [style, prose] ampoulé, boursouflé. -**2.** MED enflé, gonflé.

Turin [tjʊˈrɪn] *pr n* Turin.

Turk [tɜːk] *n* Turc *m*, Turque *f*.

Turkestan, Turkistan [ˌtɜːkɪˈstɑːn] *pr n* Turkistan *m*; **in ~** au Turkistan.

turkey [ˈtɜːkɪ] (*pl inv* OR **turkeys**) *n* -**1.** [bird - cock] dindon *m*; [- hen] dinde *f*. -**2.** CULIN dinde *f*. -**3.** *inf Am* [fool] idiot *m*, -e *f*, imbécile *mf*. -**4.** *inf Am* [flop] bide *m*; THEAT four *m*.

Turkey [ˈtɜːkɪ] *pr n* Turquie *f*; **in ~** en Turquie.

turkey buzzard *n* vautour *m* aura.

turkey cock *n* dindon *m*; *fig inf* crâneur *m*, -euse *f*.

Turkish [ˈtɜːkɪʃ] ◇ *n* LING turc *m*.

◇ *adj* turc.

Turkish bath *n* bain *m* turc.

Turkish coffee *n* café *m* turc.

Turkish delight *n* loukoum *m*.

Turkman [ˈtɜːkmən] (*pl* **Turkmans** OR **Turkmen** [-mən]) ◇ *n* Turkmène *mf*.

◇ *adj* turkmène.

Turkmen [ˈtɜːkmen] *n* LING turkmène *m*.

Turkmenistan [ˌtɜːkmenɪˈstɑːn] *pr n* Turkménistan *m*; **in ~** au Turkménistan.

Turks and Caicos Islands [-ˈkeɪkəs-] *pl pr n*: **the ~** les îles *fpl* Turks et Caïcos; **in the ~** aux îles Turks et Caïcos.

turmeric [ˈtɜːmərɪk] *n* curcuma *m*, safran *m* des Indes.

turmoil [ˈtɜːmɔɪl] *n* -**1.** [confusion] agitation *f*, trouble *m*, chaos *m*; **the country was in ~** le pays était en ébullition OR en effervescence. -**2.** [emotional] trouble *m*, émoi *m*; **her mind was in (a) ~** elle avait l'esprit troublé, elle était en émoi.

turn [tɜːn] ◇ *vt* **A.** -**1.** [cause to rotate, move round] tourner; [shaft, axle] faire tourner, faire pivoter; [direct] diriger; **she ~ed the key in the lock** [to lock] elle a donné un tour de clé (à la porte), elle a fermé la porte à clé; [to unlock] elle a ouvert la porte avec la clé; **~ the wheel all the way round** faites faire un tour complet à la roue; **to ~ the (steering) wheel** AUT tourner le volant; **~ the knob to the right** tournez le bouton vers la droite; **~ the knob to "record"** mettez le bouton en position «enregistrer»; **she ~ed the oven to its highest setting** elle a allumé OR mis le four à la température maximum; **she ~ed her chair towards the window** elle a tourné sa chaise face à la fenêtre; **he ~ed the car into the drive** il a engagé la voiture dans l'allée; **we ~ed our steps homeward** nous avons dirigé nos pas vers la maison; **~ your head this way** tournez la tête de ce côté. -**2.** *fig* [change orientation of]: **she ~ed the conversation to sport** elle a orienté la conversation vers le sport; **their votes could ~ the election in his favour** leurs voix pourraient faire basculer les élections en sa faveur; **he would not be ~ed from his decision to resign** il n'y a pas eu moyen de le faire revenir sur sa décision de démissionner; **nothing would ~ the rebels from their cause** rien ne pourrait détourner les rebelles de leur cause; **you've ~ed my whole family against me** vous avez monté toute ma famille contre moi; **we ~ed his joke against him** nous avons retourné la plaisanterie contre lui; **let's ~ our attention to the matter in hand** occupons-nous de l'affaire en question; **she ~ed her attention to the problem** elle s'est concentrée sur le problème; **research workers have ~ed the theory to practical use** les chercheurs ont mis la théorie en pratique; **how can we ~ this policy to our advantage** OR **account?** comment tirer parti de cette politique?, comment tourner cette politique à notre avantage?; **she can ~ her hand to anything** elle sait tout faire ❑ **to ~ one's back on sb** *literal* tourner le dos à qqn; **she looked at the letter the minute his back was ~ed** dès qu'il a eu le dos tourné, elle a jeté un coup d'œil à la lettre; **how can you ~ your back on your own family?** comment peux-tu abandonner ta famille?; **she ~ed her back on her friends** elle a tourné le dos à ses amis; **to ~ one's back on the past** tourner la page, tourner le dos au passé; **he took the news without ~ing a hair** *Br* il a appris la nouvelle sans broncher OR sourciller; **she was so pretty that she ~ed heads wherever she went** elle était si jolie que tout le monde se retournait sur son passage; **success had not ~ed his head** la réussite ne lui avait pas tourné la tête, il ne s'était pas laissé griser par la réussite; **all their compliments had ~ed her head** tous leurs compliments lui étaient montés à la tête OR lui avaient tourné la tête; **to ~ the tables on sb** reprendre l'avantage sur qqn; **now the tables are ~ed** maintenant les rôles sont renversés, tel est pris qui croyait prendre *prov*.

B. -**1.** [flip over - page] tourner; [- collar, mattress, sausages, soil] retourner; **the very thought of food ~s my stomach** l'idée même de manger me soulève le cœur; **to ~ sthg on its head** bouleverser qqch, mettre qqch sens dessus dessous. -**2.** [send away]: **he ~ed the beggar from his door** il a chassé le mendiant; **they ~ed the poachers off their land** ils ont chassé les braconniers de leurs terres. -**3.** [release, let loose]: **he ~ed the cattle into the field** il a fait rentrer le bétail dans le champ. -**4.** [go round - corner] tourner; **the car ~ed the corner** la voiture a tourné le OR au coin de la rue; **the economy has ~ed the corner** *fig* l'économie a passé le cap OR le moment critique. -**5.** [reach - in age, time] passer, franchir; **I had just ~ed twenty** je venais d'avoir vingt ans; **she's ~ed thirty** elle a trente ans passés, elle a dépassé le cap de la trentaine; **it has only just ~ed four o'clock** il est quatre heures passées de quelques secondes. -**6.** [do, perform] faire; **the skater ~ed a circle on the ice** la patineuse a décrit un cercle sur la glace; **to ~ a cartwheel** faire la roue. -**7.** [ankle] tordre; **I've ~ed my ankle** je me suis tordu la cheville.

C. -**1.** [transform, change] changer, transformer; [make] faire devenir, rendre; **to ~ sthg into sthg** transformer OR changer qqch en qqch; **bitterness ~ed their love into hate** l'amertume a transformé leur amour en haine; **she ~ed the remark into a joke** elle a tourné la remarque en plaisanterie; **they're ~ing the book into a film** ils adaptent le livre pour l'écran; **the sight ~ed his heart to ice** le spectacle lui a glacé le cœur OR l'a glacé; **you should ~ your shares into cash** ST. EX vous devriez réaliser vos actions || [in colour]: **time had ~ed the pages yellow** le temps avait jauni les pages. -**2.** [make bad, affect]: **the lemon juice ~ed the milk (sour)** le jus de citron a fait tourner le lait. -**3.** *Am* COMM [goods] promouvoir la vente de; [money] gagner; **to ~ a good profit** faire de gros bénéfices; **he ~s an honest penny** il gagne sa vie honnêtement; **he was out to ~ a fast buck** *inf* il cherchait à gagner OR faire du fric facilement. -**4.** TECH [shape] tourner, façonner au tour; **a well ~ed leg** une jambe bien faite; **to ~ a phrase** *fig* faire des phrases.

◇ *vi* -**1.** [rotate, move round - handle, key, screw, wheel] tourner; [- shaft] tourner, pivoter; [- person] se tourner; **to ~ on an axis** tourner autour d'un axe; **the crane ~ed (through) 180°** la grue a pivoté de 180°; **the key won't ~** la clé ne tourne pas; **he ~ed right round** il a fait volte-face; **they ~ed towards me** ils se sont tournés vers moi OR de mon côté; **they ~ed from the gruesome sight** ils se sont détournés de cet horrible spectacle; **~ (round) and face the front** tourne-toi et regarde devant toi. -**2.** [flip over - page] tourner; [- car, person, ship] se retourner; *fig*: **the smell made my stomach ~** l'odeur m'a soulevé le cœur; **your father would ~ in his grave if he could hear you now** ton père se retournerait dans sa tombe s'il t'entendait. -**3.** [change direction - person] tourner; [- vehicle] tourner, virer; [- luck, wind] tourner, changer; [- river, road] faire un coude; [- tide] changer de direction; ~ (to the) right [walking] tournez à droite; [driving] tournez OR prenez à droite; we ~ed towards town nous nous sommes dirigés vers la ville; he ~ed (round) and went back il a fait demi-tour et est revenu sur ses pas; the road ~s south la route tourne vers le sud; the car ~ed into our street la voiture a tourné dans notre rue; we ~ed onto the main road nous nous sommes engagés dans OR nous avons pris la grand-route; the market ~ed downwards/upwards ST. EX le marché était à la baisse/à la hausse; I don't know where OR which way to ~ *fig* je ne sais plus quoi faire. -**4.** *(with adj or noun complement)* [become] devenir; the weather's ~ed bad le temps s'est gâté; the argument ~ed nasty la dispute s'est envenimée; she ~ed angry when he refused elle s'est mise en colère quand il a refusé; a lawyer ~ed politician un avocat devenu homme politique; he ~ed traitor [gen] il s'est mis à trahir; [diplomat, soldier, spy] il est passé OR s'est vendu à l'ennemi; to ~ professional passer OR devenir professionnel; the whole family ~ed Muslim toute la famille s'est convertie à l'islam. -**5.** [change in the specified way] se changer, se transformer; the pumpkin ~ed into a carriage la citrouille s'est transformée en carrosse; the rain ~ed to snow la pluie s'est transformée en neige; the little girl had ~ed into a young woman la petite fille était devenue une jeune femme; their love ~ed to hate leur amour se changea en haine OR fit place à la haine. -**6.** [leaf] tourner, jaunir; [milk] tourner; the weather has ~ed le temps a changé.

◇ *n* -**1.** [revolution, rotation] tour *m*; he gave the handle a ~ il a tourné la poignée; give the screw another ~ donnez un autre tour de vis ❑ 'The Turn of the Screw' *James* 'le Tour d'écrou'. -**2.** [change of course, direction] tournant *m*; [in skiing] virage *m*; to make a right ~ [walking] tourner à droite; [driving] tourner OR prendre à droite; take the second ~ on the right prenez la deuxième à droite; 'no right ~' 'défense de tourner à droite' || *fig*: at every ~ à tout instant, à tout bout de champ; the twists and ~s of the story les tours et détours de l'histoire. -**3.** [bend, curve in road] virage *m*, tournant *m*; there is a sharp ~ to the left la route fait un brusque virage OR tourne brusquement à gauche. -**4.** [change in state, nature] tour *m*, tournure *f*; the conversation took a new ~ la conversation a pris une nouvelle tournure; it was an unexpected ~ of events les événements ont pris une tournure imprévue; things took a ~ for the worse/better les choses se sont aggravées/améliorées; the patient took a ~ for the worse/better l'état du malade s'est aggravé/amélioré; the situation took a tragic ~ la situation a tourné au tragique; to be on the ~ *Br* être sur le point de changer; the milk is on the ~ le lait a commencé à tourner; the tide is on the ~ *literal* c'est le changement de marée; *fig* le vent tourne. -**5.** [time of change]: at the ~ of the year vers la fin de l'année; at the ~ of the century au tournant du siècle. -**6.** [in game, order, queue] tour *m*; it's my ~ c'est à moi, c'est mon tour; whose ~ is it? [in queue] (c'est) à qui le tour?; [in game] c'est à qui de jouer?; it's his ~ to do the dishes c'est à lui OR c'est son tour de faire la vaisselle; you'll have to wait your ~ il faudra attendre ton tour; they laughed and cried by ~s ils passaient tour à tour du rire aux larmes; to take it in ~s to do sthg faire qqch à tour de rôle; let's take it in ~s to drive relayons-nous au volant; we took ~s sleeping on the floor nous avons dormi par terre à tour de rôle; ~ and ~ about à tour de rôle || [shift]: ~ of duty [gen] tour *m* de service; MIL tour *m* de garde. -**7.** [action, deed]: to do sb a good/bad ~ rendre service/jouer un mauvais tour à qqn; he did them a bad ~ il leur a joué un mauvais tour; I've done my good ~ for the day j'ai fait ma bonne action de la journée ❑ one good ~ deserves another *prov* un service en vaut un autre, un service rendu en appelle un autre. -**8.** *inf* [attack of illness] crise *f*, attaque *f*; she had one of her (funny) ~s this morning elle a eu une de ses crises ce matin. -**9.** *inf* [shock]: you gave me quite a ~! tu m'as fait une sacrée peur!, tu m'as fait une de ces peurs! -**10.** *dated* [short trip, ride, walk] tour *m*; let's go for OR take a ~ in the garden allons faire un tour dans le jardin. -**11.** [tendency, style]: to have an optimistic ~ of mind être optimiste de nature OR d'un naturel optimiste; he has a strange ~ of mind il a une drôle de mentalité; to have a good ~ of speed rouler vite; ~ of phrase tournure *f* OR tour *m* de phrase; she has a witty ~ of phrase elle est très spirituelle OR pleine d'esprit. -**12.** [purpose, requirement] exigence *f*, besoin *m*; this book has served its ~ ce livre a fait son temps. -**13.** MUS doublé *m*. -**14.** ST. EX [transaction] transaction *f (qui comprend l'achat et la vente)*; *Br* [difference in price] écart *m* entre le prix d'achat et le prix de vente. -**15.** *Br* THEAT numéro *m*; a comedy ~ un numéro de comédie. -**16.** *Br phr*: done to a ~ *inf*: the chicken was done to a ~ CULIN le poulet était cuit à point.

◆ **in turn** *adv phr*: she interviewed each of us in ~ elle a eu un entretien avec chacun de nous l'un après l'autre; I told Sarah and she in ~ told Paul je l'ai dit à Sarah qui, à son tour, l'a dit à Paul; I worked in ~ as a waiter, an actor and a teacher j'ai travaillé successivement OR tour à tour comme serveur, acteur et enseignant.

◆ **out of turn** *adv phr*: don't play out of ~ attends ton tour pour jouer; to speak out of ~ *fig* faire des remarques déplacées, parler mal à propos.

◆ **turn against** *vt insep* se retourner contre, s'en prendre à.

◆ **turn around** = **turn round**.

◆ **turn aside** ◇ *vi insep* [move to one side] s'écarter; *literal* & *fig* [move away] se détourner; she ~ed aside to blow her nose elle se détourna pour se moucher.

◇ *vt sep literal* & *fig* écarter, détourner.

◆ **turn away** ◇ *vt sep* -**1.** [avert] détourner; she ~ed her head away from him elle s'est détournée de lui. -**2.** [reject - person] renvoyer; [stronger] chasser; the college ~ed away hundreds of applicants l'université a refusé des centaines de candidats; she ~ed the salesman away elle chassa le représentant.

◇ *vi insep* se détourner; he ~ed away from them in anger en OR de colère, il leur a tourné le dos.

◆ **turn back** ◇ *vi insep* -**1.** [return - person] revenir, rebrousser chemin; [- vehicle] faire demi-tour; it was getting dark so we decided to ~ back comme il commençait à faire nuit, nous avons décidé de faire demi-tour; my mind is made up, there is no ~ing back ma décision est prise, je n'y reviendrai pas. -**2.** [go back in book]: ~ back to chapter one revenez OR retournez au premier chapitre.

◇ *vt sep* -**1.** [force to return] faire faire demi-tour à; [refugee] refouler. -**2.** [fold - collar, sheet] rabattre; [- sleeves] remonter, retrousser; [- corner of page] corner. -**3.** *phr*: to ~ the clock back remonter dans le temps, revenir en arrière.

◆ **turn down** ◇ *vt sep* -**1.** [heating, lighting, sound] baisser. -**2.** [fold - sheet] rabattre, retourner; [- collar] rabattre; to ~ down the corner of a page corner une page. -**3.** [reject - offer, request, suitor] rejeter, repousser; [- candidate, job] refuser; she ~ed me down flat *inf* elle m'a envoyé balader.

◇ *vi insep* [move downwards] tourner vers le bas; the corners of his mouth ~ed down il a fait la moue OR une grimace désapprobatrice.

◆ **turn in** ◇ *vt sep* -**1.** [return, give in - borrowed article, equipment, piece of work] rendre, rapporter; [- criminal] livrer à la police; they ~ed the thief in [took him to the police] ils ont livré le voleur à la police; [informed on him] ils ont dénoncé le voleur à la police. -**2.** [fold in]: ~ in the edges rentrez les bords. -**3.** [produce]: the actor ~ed in a good performance l'acteur a très bien joué; the company ~ed in record profits l'entreprise a fait des bénéfices record.

◇ *vi insep* -**1.** [feet, toes]: my toes ~ in j'ai les pieds en dedans. -**2.** *inf* [go to bed] se coucher. -**3.** *phr*: to ~ in on o.s. se replier sur soi-même.

◆ **turn off** ◇ *vt sep* -**1.** [switch off - light] éteindre; [- heater, radio, television] éteindre, fermer; [cut off at mains] couper; [tap] fermer; she ~ed the ignition/engine off elle a coupé le contact/arrêté le moteur. -**2.** *inf* [fail to interest] rebuter; her superior attitude really ~s me off *inf* son air suffisant me rebute || [sexually] couper l'envie à.

◇ *vi insep* -**1.** [leave road] tourner; we ~ed off at junction 5 nous avons pris la sortie d'autoroute 5. -**2.** [switch off] s'éteindre; the heater ~s off automatically l'appareil de chauffage s'éteint OR s'arrête automatiquement.

◆ **turn on** ◇ *vt sep* -**1.** [switch on - electricity, heating, light, radio, television] allumer; [- engine] mettre en marche; [- water] faire couler; [- tap] ouvrir; [open at mains] ouvrir; she can ~ on the charm/the tears whenever necessary *inf fig* elle sait faire du charme/pleurer quand il le faut. -**2.** *inf* [person - interest] intéresser; [- sexually] exciter; [- introduce to drugs] initier à la drogue; the movie didn't ~ me on at all le film ne m'a vraiment pas emballé; he ~ed us on to this new pianist il nous a fait découvrir ce nouveau pianiste.

◇ *vt insep* [attack] attaquer; the dogs ~ed on him les chiens l'ont attaqué OR se sont jetés sur lui; his colleagues ~ed on him and accused him of stealing ses collègues s'en sont pris à lui et l'ont accusé de vol.

◇ *vi insep* -**1.** [switch on] s'allumer; the oven ~s on automatically le four s'allume automatiquement. -**2.** [depend, hinge on] dépendre de, reposer sur; the whole case ~ed on OR upon this detail toute l'affaire reposait sur ce détail; everything ~s on whether he continues as president tout dépend s'il reste président ou non.

◆ **turn out** ◇ *vt sep* -**1.** [switch off - light] éteindre; [- gas] éteindre, couper. -**2.** [point outwards]: she ~s her toes out when she walks elle marche en canard. -**3.** [dismiss, expel] mettre à la porte; [tenant] expulser, déloger; he ~ed his daughter out of the house il a mis sa fille à la porte OR a chassé sa fille de la maison; he was ~ed out of his job il a été renvoyé. -**4.** [empty - container, pockets] retourner, vider; [- contents] vider; [- jelly] verser; ~ the cake out onto a plate démoulez le gâteau sur une assiette. -**5.** *Br* [clean] nettoyer à fond; to ~ out a room faire une pièce à fond. -**6.** [produce] produire, fabriquer; he ~s out a book a year il écrit un livre par an; few schools ~ out the kind of people we need peu d'écoles forment le type de gens qu'il nous faut. -**7.** [police, troops] envoyer; ~ out the guard! faites sortir la garde! -**8.** *(usu passive)* [dress] habiller; nicely OR smartly ~ed out élégant; he was ~ed out in a suit and a tie il portait un costume-cravate; she always ~s her children out beautifully elle habille toujours bien ses enfants.

◇ *vi insep* -**1.** [show up] venir, arriver; MIL [guard] (aller) prendre la faction; [troops] aller au rassemblement; thousands ~ed out for the concert des milliers de gens sont venus OR ont assisté au concert. -**2.** [car, person] sortir, partir; the car ~ed out of the car park la voiture est sortie du parking. -**3.** [point outwards]: my feet ~ out j'ai les pieds en canard OR en dehors. -**4.** [prove] se révéler, s'avérer; his statement ~ed out to be false sa déclaration s'est révélée fausse; her story ~ed out to be true ce qu'elle a raconté était vrai; he ~ed out to be a scoundrel il s'est révélé être un vaurien, on s'est rendu compte que c'était un vaurien || [end up]: I don't know how it ~ed out je ne sais pas comment cela a fini; the story ~ed out happily l'histoire s'est bien terminée OR a bien fini;

the evening ~ed out badly la soirée a mal tourné; everything will ~ out fine tout va s'arranger OR ira bien; as it ~s out, he needn't have worried en l'occurrence OR en fin de compte, ce n'était pas la peine de se faire du souci. -**5.** *inf Br* [get out of bed] se lever, sortir du lit.

◆ **turn over** ◇ *vt sep* -**1.** [playing card, mattress, person, stone] retourner; [page] tourner; [vehicle] retourner; [boat] faire chavirer; I was ~ing over the pages of the magazine je feuilletais la revue ☐ to ~ over a new leaf s'acheter une conduite. -**2.** [consider] réfléchir à OR sur; I was ~ing the idea over in my mind je tournais et retournais OR ruminais l'idée dans ma tête. -**3.** [hand over, transfer] rendre, remettre; he ~ed the responsibility over to his deputy il s'est déchargé de la responsabilité sur son adjoint; to ~ sb over to the authorities livrer qqn aux autorités. -**4.** [change] transformer, changer; he's ~ing the land over to cattle farming il reconvertit sa terre dans l'élevage du bétail. -**5.** COMM: the store ~s over £1,000 a week la boutique fait un chiffre d'affaires de 1 000 livres par semaine. -**6.** [search through] fouiller. -**7.** *inf Br* [rob - person] voler, dévaliser; [- store] dévaliser; [- house] cambrioler.

◇ *vi insep* -**1.** [roll over - person] se retourner; [- vehicle] se retourner, faire un tonneau; [- boat] se retourner, chavirer. -**2.** [engine] commencer à tourner. -**3.** [when reading] tourner; please ~ over [in letter] → **PTO**. -**4.** COMM [merchandise] s'écouler, se vendre.

◆ **turn round** ◇ *vi insep Br* -**1.** [rotate - person] se retourner; [- object] tourner; she ~ed round and waved goodbye elle se retourna et dit au revoir de la main; the dancers ~ed round and round les danseurs tournaient OR tournoyaient (sur eux-mêmes). -**2.** [face opposite direction - person] faire volte-face, faire demi-tour; [- vehicle] faire demi-tour; she ~ed round and accused us of stealing *fig* elle s'est retournée contre nous et nous a accusés de vol.

◇ *vt sep* -**1.** [rotate - head] tourner; [- object, person] tourner, retourner; [- vehicle] faire faire demi-tour à; could you ~ the car round please? tu peux faire demi-tour, s'il te plaît? -**2.** [quantity of work] traiter. -**3.** [change nature of]: to ~ a situation round renverser une situation; to ~ a company round COMM faire prospérer une entreprise qui périclitait, sauver une entreprise de la faillite. -**4.** [sentence, idea] retourner.

◆ **turn to** *vt insep* -**1.** *literal* [person] se tourner vers; [- page] aller à; ~ to chapter one allez au premier chapitre. -**2.** [seek help from] s'adresser à, se tourner vers; to ~ to sb for advice consulter qqn, demander conseil à qqn; I don't know who to ~ to je ne sais pas à qui m'adresser OR qui aller trouver; he ~ed to his mother for sympathy il s'est tourné vers sa mère pour qu'elle le console; she won't ~ to me for help elle ne veut pas me demander de l'aide; he ~ed to the bottle il s'est mis à boire. -**3.** *fig* [shift, move on to]: her thoughts ~ed to her sister elle se mit à penser à sa sœur; the discussion ~ed to the war on se mit à discuter de la guerre|| [address - subject, issue etc] aborder, traiter; we shall now ~ to the problem of housing nous allons maintenant aborder le problème du logement; let us ~ to another topic passons à un autre sujet.

◆ **turn up** ◇ *vt sep* -**1.** [heat, lighting, radio, TV] mettre plus fort; to ~ the sound up augmenter OR monter le volume; she ~ed the oven up elle a mis OR réglé le four plus fort, elle a augmenté la température du four ☐ ~ it up! *inf Br* la ferme! -**2.** [find, unearth] découvrir, dénicher; [buried object] déterrer; her research ~ed up some interesting new facts sa recherche a révélé de nouveaux détails intéressants. -**3.** [point upwards] remonter, relever; she has a ~ed-up nose elle a le nez retroussé. -**4.** [collar] relever; [trousers] remonter; [sleeve] retrousser, remonter.

◇ *vi insep* -**1.** [appear] apparaître; [arrive] arriver; she ~ed up at my office this morning elle s'est présentée à mon bureau ce matin; he'll ~ up again one of these days il reviendra bien un de ces jours; I'll take the first job that ~s up je prendrai le premier poste qui se présentera ☐ he ~s up like a bad penny il arrive (toujours) au mauvais moment OR mal. -**2.** [be found] être trouvé OR retrouvé; her bag ~ed up eventually elle a fini par retrouver son sac. -**3.** [happen] se passer, arriver; don't worry, something will ~ up ne t'en fais pas, tu finiras par trouver quelque chose; until something better ~s up en attendant mieux.

turnabout ['tɜːnəbaʊt] *n* volte-face *f inv*.

turnaround ['tɜːnəraʊnd] *Am* = **turnround**.

turncoat ['tɜːnkəʊt] *n* renégat *m*, -e *f*, transfuge *mf*.

turndown ['tɜːndaʊn] ◇ *n* -**1.** [rejection] refus *m*. -**2.** [in prices] tendance *f* à la baisse; [in the economy] (tendance à la) baisse *f*.

◇ *adj* [collar] rabattu; [edge] à rabattre.

turned [tɜːnd] *adj* -**1.** [milk] tourné. -**2.** TYPO: ~ comma ≃ guillemet *m*; ~ period point *m* décimal, ≃ virgule *f*.

turned-on *inf adj* -**1.** [up-to-date] branché, câblé. -**2.** [aroused] excité; to get ~ s'exciter.

turner ['tɜːnəʳ] *n* -**1.** [lathe operator] tourneur *m*. -**2.** *Am* [gymnast] gymnaste *mf*.

turnery ['tɜːnərɪ] (*pl* turneries) *n* atelier *m* de tournage.

turning ['tɜːnɪŋ] *n* -**1.** *Br* [side road] route *f* transversale; [side street] rue *f* transversale, petite rue; take the third ~ on the right prenez la troisième à droite. -**2.** *Br* [bend - in river] coude *m*; [- in road] virage *m*; [fork] embranchement *m*, carrefour *m*. -**3.** INDUST tournage *m*.

turning circle *n Br* AUT rayon *m* de braquage.

turning point *n* [decisive moment] moment *m* décisif; [change] tournant *m*; 1989 marked a ~ in my career l'année 1989 marqua un tournant dans ma carrière; it was a ~ in her life ce fut un tournant dans sa vie.

turning radius *Am* = **turning circle**.

turnip ['tɜːnɪp] *n* navet *m*.

turnkey ['tɜːnkiː] ◇ *n* [jailer] geôlier *m*, -ère *f*.

◇ *adj* CONSTR [project] clés en main.

turnkey system *n* COMPUT système *m* clés en main.

turn-off *n* -**1.** [road] sortie *f* (de route), route *f* transversale, embranchement *m*. -**2.** *inf* [loss of interest]: it's a real ~ [gen] c'est vraiment à vous dégoûter; [sexual] ça vous coupe vraiment l'envie.

turn-on *inf n*: what a ~! c'est excitant!; he finds leather a ~ il trouve le cuir excitant, le cuir l'excite.

turnout ['tɜːnaʊt] *n* -**1.** [attendance - at meeting, concert] assistance *f*; POL [at election] (taux *m* de) participation *f*; there was a good ~ [gen] il y avait beaucoup de monde, beaucoup de gens sont venus; POL il y avait un fort taux de participation. -**2.** [dress] mise *f*, tenue *f*. -**3.** *Br* [clearout]: we had a good ~ of the attic on a nettoyé OR fait le grenier à fond; I had a ~ of my old clothes for the jumble sale j'ai trié mes vieux vêtements pour la vente de charité. -**4.** *Am* AUT refuge *m (pour se laisser doubler)*.

turnover ['tɜːnˌəʊvəʳ] *n* -**1.** *Br* FIN chiffre *m* d'affaires. -**2.** [of staff, tenants] renouvellement *m*; there is a high ~ of tenants les locataires changent souvent. -**3.** *Am* [of stock] vitesse *f* de rotation; [of shares] mouvement *m*; computer magazines have a high ~ les revues d'informatique se vendent bien. -**4.** CULIN: apple ~ chausson *m* aux pommes.

turnpike ['tɜːnpaɪk] *n* -**1.** [barrier] barrière *f* de péage. -**2.** *Am* [road] autoroute *f* à péage.

turnround ['tɜːnraʊnd] *n* -**1.** ~ (time) [of passenger ship, plane] temps *m* nécessaire entre deux voyages; [for freight] temps nécessaire pour le déchargement; NAUT estarie *f*, starie *f*; COMPUT temps de retournement, délai *m* d'exécution. -**2.** [reversal - of fortunes] retournement *m*, renversement *m*; [- of opinions] revirement *m*, volte-face *f inv*.

turn signal lever *n Am* (manette *f* de) clignotant *m*.

turnstile ['tɜːnstaɪl] *n* tourniquet *m (barrière)*.

turntable ['tɜːnˌteɪbl] *n* -**1.** [on record player] platine *f*. -**2.** RAIL plaque *f* tournante. -**3.** [on microscope] platine *f*. -**4.** *Austr* [turning space] endroit *m* pour manœuvrer.

turntable ladder *n* échelle *f* pivotante (des pompiers).

turn-up *n* -**1.** [on trousers] revers *m*. -**2.** *inf Br* [surprise] surprise *f*; that's a ~ for the book OR books c'est une sacrée surprise.

turpentine ['tɜːpəntaɪn] *n Br* (essence *f* de) térébenthine *f*.

turpitude ['tɜːpɪtjuːd] *n* turpitude *f*.

turps [tɜːps] *(U) Br* = **turpentine**.

turquoise ['tɜːkwɔɪz] ◇ *n* -**1.** [gem] turquoise *f*. -**2.** [colour] turquoise *m inv*.

◇ *adj* -**1.** [bracelet, ring] de OR en turquoise. -**2.** [in colour] turquoise *(inv)*.

turret ['tʌrɪt] *n* tourelle *f*.

turret gun *n* canon *m* de tourelle.

turtle ['tɜːtl] *n* -**1.** [in sea] tortue *f* marine; *Am* [on land] tortue *f*. -**2.** *phr*: to turn ~ se renverser.

turtleback ['tɜːtlbæk] *n* NAUT pont *m* en carapace de tortue.

turtledove ['tɜːtldʌv] *n* tourterelle *f*.

turtleneck ['tɜːtlnek] ◇ *adj* [sweater, dress] à col montant, à encolure montante; *Am* à col roulé.

◇ *n* col *m* montant, encolure *f* montante; *Am* (pull *m* à) col *m* roulé.

Tuscan ['tʌskən] ◇ *n* -**1.** [person] Toscan *m*, -e *f*. -**2.** LING toscan *m*.

◇ *adj* toscan.

Tuscany ['tʌskənɪ] *pr n* Toscane *f*; in ~ en Toscane.

tush *inf* [tʌʃ] *n Am* [buttocks] fesses *fpl*.

tusk [tʌsk] *n* [of elephant, boar] défense *f*.

tusker ['tʌskəʳ] *n* [elephant] éléphant *m (adulte)*; [boar] sanglier *m (adulte)*.

tussle *inf* ['tʌsl] ◇ *n* -**1.** [scuffle] mêlée *f*, bagarre *f*; to have a ~ with sb se battre contre qqn, en venir aux mains avec qqn. -**2.** [struggle] lutte *f*; it was quite a ~ to get him to agree il a fallu pas mal lutter OR faire des pieds et des mains pour qu'il accepte. -**3.** [quarrel] dispute *f*; to have a ~ with sb se disputer avec qqn.

◇ *vi* [scuffle, fight] se battre; I ~d with her for the ball je me suis battu avec elle pour avoir la balle, on s'est disputé la balle; the kids were tussling over the toy les gosses se disputaient le jouet.

tussock ['tʌsək] *n* touffe *f* d'herbe.

tut [tʌt] (*pt* & *pp* tutted, *cont* tutting) ◇ *interj*: ~!, ~-~! [in disapproval] allons donc!; [in annoyance] zut!

◇ *vi* [in disapproval] pousser une exclamation désapprobatrice; [in annoyance] exprimer son mécontentement; she tutted with disapproval elle eut une exclamation désapprobatrice.

Tutankhamen [ˌtuːtəŋ'kɑːmən], **Tutankhamun** [ˌtuːtəŋkɑː'muːn] *pr n* Toutankhamon.

tutelage ['tjuːtɪlɪdʒ] *n fml* tutelle *f*; under his ~ sous sa tutelle.

tutelary ['tjuːtɪlərɪ] *adj fml* tutélaire.

tutor ['tjuːtəʳ] ◇ *n* -**1.** [teacher] professeur *m* particulier; [full-time] précepteur *m*, -trice *f*; piano ~ professeur de piano; she has a private German ~ elle prend des cours particuliers avec un professeur d'allemand. -**2.** *Br* UNIV [teacher] professeur *m (qui dirige et supervise les travaux d'un groupe d'étudiants)*; *Br* SCH professeur *m* principal *(surtout dans les écoles privées)*. -**3.** *Scot* JUR [guardian] tuteur *m*, -trice *f*.

◇ *vt* -**1.** [instruct] donner des cours (particuliers) à; I'm ~ing her in maths je lui donne des cours particuliers de maths. -**2.** *Br* UNIV diriger les études de. -**3.** *Scot* JUR être le tuteur de.

◇ *vi* -**1.** [pupil] suivre des cours particuliers. -**2.** [teacher] donner des cours particuliers.

tutorial [tjuː'tɔːrɪəl] UNIV ◇ *n* (séance *f* de) travaux *mpl* dirigés, TD *mpl*; a maths ~ des TD de maths.

◇ *adj* [work] de travaux dirigés; [duties] de directeur d'études.

tutti frutti [ˌtuːtɪ'fruːtɪ] (*pl* tutti fruttis) ◇ *n* plombières *f*, tutti-frutti *m*.
◇ *adj* [ice cream, flavour] tutti-frutti.

tut-tut = **tut**.

tutu ['tuːtuː] *n* tutu *m*.

tu-whit tu-whoo [tə'wɪttə'wuː] *onomat* hou-hou.

tux *inf* [tʌks] *n* *abbr of* tuxedo

tuxedo [tʌk'siːdəʊ] (*pl* tuxedos) *n Am* smoking *m*.

TV ◇ *n* (*abbr of* television) TV *f*.
◇ *comp* [programme, set, star] de télé; ~ dinner plateau-repas *m*, repas *m* tout prêt OR prêt à consommer *(que l'on mange devant la télé)*.

twaddle *inf* ['twɒdl] *n Br (U)* bêtises *fpl*, âneries *fpl*, imbécillités *fpl*; what a load of ~! quelles âneries!

twain [tweɪn] *n lit*: never the ~ shall meet les deux sont inconciliables, les deux ne pourront jamais se mettre d'accord.

twang [twæŋ] ◇ *n* -**1.** [of wire, guitar] son *m* de corde pincée. -**2.** [in voice] ton *m* nasillard; she speaks with a ~ elle parle du nez, elle nasille. -**3.** [accent] accent *m*; he has a slight Australian ~ il a un léger accent australien.
◇ *vt* [string instrument] pincer les cordes de.
◇ *vi* [arrow, bow, wire] vibrer; the arrow ~ed through the air la flèche a traversé l'air en vibrant.

'twas [twɒz] *lit* OR *dial* = **it was**.

twat▼ [twɒt, twæt] *n* -**1.** [female genitals] chatte *f*. -**2.** [fool] con *m*.

tweak [twiːk] ◇ *vt* -**1.** [twist - ear, nose] tordre (doucement), pincer; [pull] tirer (sur). -**2.** AUT mettre au point; COMPUT peaufiner, mettre au point.
◇ *n* (petit) coup *m* sec; he gave my ear a ~ il m'a tiré l'oreille.

twee *inf* [twiː] *adj Br* [person] chichiteux; [idea, sentiment] mièvre; [decor] cucul *(inv)*.

tweed [twiːd] ◇ *n* [cloth] tweed *m*.
◇ *comp* [jacket, skirt] de tweed, en tweed.
◆ **tweeds** *npl* [clothes] vêtements *mpl* de tweed; [suit] costume *m* de tweed; a smart lady in ~s une femme élégante en tailleur de tweed.

tweedy ['twiːdɪ] (*compar* tweedier, *superl* tweediest) *adj* -**1.** [fabric] qui ressemble au tweed. -**2.** *pej* [man] qui a le genre gentleman-farmer; [woman] qui fait bourgeoise de campagne.

'tween [twiːn] *lit* = **between**.

tweeny *inf* ['twiːnɪ] (*pl* tweenies) *n Br* [maid] bonne *f*.

tweet [twiːt] ◇ *n* pépiement *m*.
◇ *onomat* cui-cui.
◇ *vi* pépier.

tweeter ['twiːtəʳ] *n* tweeter *m*, haut-parleur *m* d'aigus.

tweeze [twiːz] *vt Am* [eyebrows] épiler.

tweezers ['twiːzəz] *npl*: (pair of) ~ pince *f* à épiler.

twelfth [twelfθ] ◇ *adj* douzième.
◇ *n* -**1.** [ordinal] douzième *mf*. -**2.** [fraction] douzième *m*.

Twelfth Night *n* la fête des Rois.

twelve [twelv] ◇ *adj* douze *(inv)*; the Twelve Apostles les douze apôtres.
◇ *n* douze *m inv*.

twelvemonth ['twelvmʌnθ] *n Br arch* OR *lit* année *f*, an *m*.

twelve-tone *adj* MUS dodécaphonique; ~ system dodécaphonisme *m*.

twentieth ['twentɪəθ] ◇ *adj* vingtième.
◇ *n* -**1.** [ordinal] vingtième *mf*. -**2.** [fraction] vingtième *m*.

twenty ['twentɪ] ◇ *adj* vingt *(inv)*; 'Twenty Thousand Leagues under the Sea' *Verne* 'Vingt Mille Lieues sous les mers'.
◇ *n* vingt *m*.

twenty-first *n* [birthday] vingt-et-unième anniversaire *m*.

twenty-four *adj*: a ~-hour petrol station une station-service ouverte jour et nuit OR vingt-quatre heures sur vingt-quatre; ~-hour service service *m* vingt-quatre heures sur vingt-quatre OR jour et nuit; open ~ hours a day ouvert vingt-quatre heures sur vingt-quatre.

twenty-one *n* [pontoon] vingt-et-un *m inv (jeu)*.

twenty-twenty vision *n*: to have ~ avoir dix dixièmes à chaque œil.

'twere [twɜːʳ] *lit* OR *dial* = **it were**.

twerp *inf* [twɜːp] *n* andouille *f*, crétin *m*, -e *f*.

twice [twaɪs] *adv* -**1.** *(+ noun)* deux fois; ~ a day deux fois par jour; ~ the price deux fois plus cher; he's almost ~ your height il est presque deux fois plus grand que vous; ~ 3 is 6 deux fois 3 font 6; since the operation he is ~ the man he was depuis son opération il est transformé OR en pleine forme; he's ~ the man you are! il vaut deux fois mieux que toi! -**2.** *(+ verb)* deux fois; I've already told you ~ je te l'ai déjà dit deux fois, je te l'ai déjà répété; they didn't need to be asked OR told ~ ils ne se sont pas fait prier, ils ne se le sont pas fait dire deux fois. -**3.** *(+ adj or adv)*: ~ weekly/daily deux fois par semaine/jour; she can run ~ as fast as me elle court deux fois plus vite que moi; it's ~ as good c'est deux fois mieux; ~ as much time/as many apples deux fois plus de temps/de pommes.

twiddle ['twɪdl] ◇ *vt* [knob, dial] tourner, manier; [moustache] tripoter, jouer avec; to ~ one's thumbs *literal* & *fig* se tourner les pouces.
◇ *vi*: to ~ with the knob tourner le bouton; to ~ with the radio jouer avec la radio; she sat there twiddling with a ruler elle était assise là à jouer avec une règle.
◇ *n*: give the knob a ~ tournez le bouton.

twig [twɪg] (*pt* & *pp* twigged, *cont* twigging) ◇ *vi inf Br* [understand] piger.
◇ *n* [for fire] brindille *f*; [on tree] petite branche *f*.

twilight ['twaɪlaɪt] ◇ *n* -**1.** [in evening] crépuscule *m*; [in morning] aube *f*; at ~ [evening] au crépuscule; [morning] à l'aube. -**2.** [half-light] pénombre *f*, obscurité *f*, demi-jour *m*; I could hardly see you in the ~ je vous voyais à peine dans la pénombre. -**3.** *fig* [last stages, end] crépuscule *m*; in the ~ of his life au crépuscule de sa vie.
◇ *comp*: a ~ world un monde nébuleux; his ~ years les dernières années de sa vie; ~ sleep MED demi-sommeil *m* provoqué.

twilight zone *n* -**1.** [in city] quartier *m* délabré *(qui entoure un quartier commercial)*. -**2.** [in ocean] zone *f* crépusculaire. -**3.** *fig* zone *f* d'ombre, zone floue.

twill [twɪl] *n* sergé *m*.

'twill [twɪl] *lit* OR *dial* = **it will**.

twin [twɪn] (*pt* & *pp* twinned, *cont* twinning) ◇ *n* jumeau *m*, -elle *f*; she gave birth to ~s elle a donné naissance à des jumeaux.
◇ *adj* -**1.** [child, sibling]: they have ~ boys/girls ils ont des jumeaux/des jumelles; my ~ sister ma sœur jumelle. -**2.** [dual - spires, hills] double, jumeau; [- aims] double; the ~ towers overlooking the bay les deux tours qui surplombent la baie; the Twin Cities *surnom des villes jumelles de Saint-Paul et Minneapolis*.
◇ *vt* [town] jumeler; our town is twinned with Hamburg notre ville est jumelée avec Hambourg.

twin-bedded *adj* [room] à deux lits.

twin beds *npl* lits *m* jumeaux.

twin bill *inf n Am* CIN programme *m* de deux longs métrages.

twin cylinder ◇ *n* moteur *m* à deux cylindres.
◇ *adj* à deux cylindres.

twine [twaɪn] ◇ *vt* -**1.** [wind - hair, string] entortiller, enrouler; she ~d the rope round a post elle enroula la corde autour d'un poteau; the honeysuckle had ~d itself around the tree le chèvrefeuille s'était enroulé autour de l'arbre. -**2.** [weave] tresser.
◇ *vi* -**1.** [stem, ivy] s'enrouler; the honeysuckle had ~d around the tree le chèvrefeuille s'était enroulé autour de l'arbre. -**2.** [path, river] serpenter.
◇ *n (U)* (grosse) ficelle *f*.

twin-engined *adj* bimoteur.

twinge [twɪndʒ] *n* -**1.** [of guilt, shame] sentiment *m*; to have OR to feel a ~ of remorse ressentir un certain remords; he watched her leave with a ~ of sadness il la regarda partir avec (une certaine) tristesse. -**2.** [of pain] élancement *m*, tiraillement *m*; she felt a ~ in her back elle sentit une petite douleur dans le dos.

twining ['twaɪnɪŋ] *adj* [plant] volubile.

Twinkie® ['twɪŋkɪ] *n Am* -**1.** [cake] *petit gâteau fourré à la crème*. -**2.** *inf* [effeminate youth] *jeune homme efféminé*.

twinkle ['twɪŋkl] ◇ *vi* -**1.** [star, diamond] briller, scintiller. -**2.** [eyes] briller, pétiller; her eyes ~d with excitement ses yeux brillaient de plaisir.
◇ *n* -**1.** [of star, diamond, light] scintillement *m*. -**2.** [in eye] pétillement *m*; he had a ~ in his eye il avait les yeux pétillants; when you were just a ~ in your father's eye *hum* bien avant que tu ne fasses ton entrée dans le monde.

twinkling ['twɪŋklɪŋ] ◇ *adj* -**1.** [star, gem, sea] scintillant, brillant. -**2.** [eyes] pétillant, brillant. -**3.** *fig* [feet] agile.
◇ *n (U)* -**1.** [of star, light, gem] scintillement *m*. -**2.** [in eyes] pétillement *m*; in the ~ of an eye en un clin d'œil.

twin-lens reflex *n* PHOT: ~ (camera) appareil *m* reflex à deux objectifs.

twinning ['twɪnɪŋ] *n* jumelage *m* (de villes).

twin-screw *adj* [boat] à deux hélices.

twinset ['twɪnˌset] *n* twin set *m*; she's a bit ~ and pearls *inf Br pej* ≃ elle fait un peu foulard Hermès et collier de perles, ≃ elle fait plutôt BCBG.

twin town *n* ville *f* jumelée OR jumelle.

twin-tub *n* machine *f* à laver à deux tambours.

twirl [twɜːl] ◇ *vt* -**1.** [spin - stick, parasol, handle] faire tournoyer; [- lasso] faire tourner; she ~ed the stick (round) in the air elle jeta le bâton en l'air en le faisant tournoyer. -**2.** [twist - moustache, hair] tortiller, friser.
◇ *vi* [dancer, lasso, handle] tournoyer; she ~ed round to face us elle se tourna pour nous faire face, elle fit volte-face vers nous.
◇ *n* -**1.** [whirl - of body, stick] tournoiement *m*; [pirouette] pirouette *f*; I gave the top/wheel a ~ j'ai fait tourner la toupie/la roue; to do a ~ tourner sur soi-même, faire une pirouette. -**2.** [written flourish] fioriture *f*.

twirp *inf* [twɜːp] = **twerp**.

twist [twɪst] ◇ *vt* -**1.** [turn - round and round] tourner; [- round axis] tourner, visser; [- tightly] tordre; try ~ing the dial to the left essaie de tourner le cadran vers la gauche; you have to ~ the lid clockwise il faut visser le couvercle dans le sens des aiguilles d'une montre; she ~ed her hankie nervously elle tordait nerveusement son mouchoir; to ~ sthg into a ball faire une boule de qqch; he ~ed the wire into the shape of a dog il a tordu le fil pour lui donner la forme d'un chien; the railings were ~ed out of shape les grilles étaient toutes tordues; he ~ed the keys from my hand il m'a arraché les clés des mains. -**2.** [twine] tresser, entortiller; [wind] enrouler, tourner; she ~ed her hair into a bun elle s'est coiffée en chignon, elle a torsadé ses cheveux pour faire un chignon; the seat-belt got ~ed la ceinture (de sécurité) s'est entortillée; the wires got ~ed les fils se sont entortillés; he ~ed the threads into a rope il a tressé OR torsadé les fils pour en faire une corde. -**3.** [body, part of body] tourner; I ~ed my head (round) to the left j'ai tourné la tête vers la gauche; he ~ed himself free il s'est dégagé en se tortillant; her face was ~ed with pain *fig* ses traits étaient tordus par la douleur, la douleur lui tordait le visage ❑ to ~ sb's arm *literal* tordre le bras à qqn; *fig* forcer la main à qqn; if you ~ his arm, he'll agree to go si tu insistes un peu, il voudra bien y aller; she can ~ him round her little finger *inf Br* elle le mène par le bout du nez, elle en fait ce qu'elle veut.

-**4.** [sprain - ankle, wrist] tordre, fouler; **I've ~ed my ankle** je me suis tordu OR foulé la cheville; **I seem to have ~ed my neck** je crois que j'ai attrapé un torticolis. -**5.** [distort - words] déformer; [- argument] déformer, fausser; **don't ~ the facts to suit your argument** ne déformez pas les faits pour étayer votre argument; **she ~s everything I say** elle déforme tout ce que je dis. -**6.** *inf Br* [cheat, swindle] arnaquer; **I've been ~ed** je me suis fait avoir.
◇ *vi* -**1.** [road, stream] serpenter; **the path ~ed and turned through the forest** le chemin zigzaguait à travers la forêt. -**2.** [become twined] s'enrouler; **the ivy ~ed round the tree** le lierre s'enroulait autour de l'arbre. -**3.** [body, part of body] se tortiller; **he ~ed and turned to get himself free** il s'est tortillé tant qu'il a pu pour se dégager; **the dog ~ed out of my arms** le chien s'est dégagé de mes bras en se tortillant; **his mouth ~ed into a smile** il eut un rictus. -**4.** [be sprained - ankle] se tordre, se fouler; [- knee] se tordre. -**5.** [dance] twister. -**6.** [in pontoon]: **~!** encore une carte!
◇ *n* -**1.** [turn, twirl] tour *m*, torsion *f*; **to give sthg a ~** [dial, handle, lid] (faire) tourner qqch; [wire] tordre qqch; **there's a ~ in the tape** la bande est entortillée; **to get (o.s.) into a ~ about sthg** [get angry] se fâcher OR s'énerver au sujet de qqch; [get upset] prendre qqch au tragique, se mettre dans tous ses états; **the string is in an awful ~** la ficelle est tout emmêlée. -**2.** [in road] tournant *m*, virage *m*; [in river] coude *m*; [in staircase] tournant *m*; *fig* [in thinking] détour *m*; **the road has many ~s and turns** la route a beaucoup de tournants et de virages OR fait de nombreux tours et détours; **it's difficult to follow the ~s and turns of his argument/of government policy** il est difficile de suivre les méandres de son argumentation/de la politique gouvernementale. -**3.** [coil - of tobacco] rouleau *m*; [- of paper] tortillon *m*. -**4.** CULIN: **a ~ of lemon** un zeste de citron. -**5.** [in story, plot] tour *m*; **the film has an exciting ~ at the end** le film se termine par un coup de théâtre passionnant; **there is an ironic ~ to the story** l'histoire comporte un tour ironique; **the book gives a new ~ to the old story** le livre donne une nouvelle tournure OR un tour nouveau à cette vieille histoire; **by a strange ~ of fate, we met again years later in Zimbabwe** par un hasard extraordinaire OR un caprice du destin, nous nous sommes retrouvés au Zimbabwe des années après. -**6.** [dance] twist *m*; **to do** OR **to dance the ~** twister. -**7.** *inf Br* [cheat] arnaque *f*; **it's a real ~!** c'est vraiment de l'arnaque OR du vol!; **what a ~!** on s'est bien fait avoir! -**8.** *inf Br phr*: **to be completely round the ~** être complètement dingue OR cinglé; **they're driving me round the ~!** ils me rendent dingue!

◆ **twist about** *Br*, **twist around** *vi insep* -**1.** [wire, rope] s'entortiller, s'emmêler. -**2.** [road] serpenter, zigzaguer.

◆ **twist off** ◇ *vt sep* [lid] dévisser; [cork] enlever en tournant; [branch] enlever OR arracher en tordant.
◇ *vi insep* [cap, lid] se dévisser.

◆ **twist out** *vt sep* [nail, cork] enlever en vissant OR en tournant.

◆ **twist round** *Br* ◇ *vt sep* [rope, tape] enrouler; [lid] tourner, visser; [handle] (faire) tourner; [swivel chair] faire tourner OR pivoter; [hat] tourner; [head] tourner; **I ~ed myself round on my chair** je me suis retourné sur ma chaise.
◇ *vi insep* -**1.** [person] se retourner. -**2.** [strap, rope] se tortiller; [swivel chair] se tourner, pivoter. -**3.** [path] serpenter, zigzaguer.

◆ **twist together** *vt sep* [threads] tresser, enrouler; [wires] enrouler.

◆ **twist up** ◇ *vt sep* [threads, wires] enrouler, emmêler.
◇ *vi insep* -**1.** [threads, wires] s'emmêler, s'enchevêtrer. -**2.** [smoke] monter en volutes.

twisted ['twɪstɪd] *adj* -**1.** [personality, smile] tordu; [mind] tordu, mal tourné. -**2.** [logic, argument] faux, tordu; **by a kind of ~ logic** selon une sorte de logique tordue OR fausse. -**3.** [dishonest] malhonnête; [politician, lawyer, businessman] malhonnête, véreux. -**4.** *inf* [crazy] tordu.

twister *inf* ['twɪstəʳ] *n* -**1.** *Br* [crook] escroc *m*. -**2.** *Am* [tornado] tornade *f*.

twist grip *n* [accelerator] poignée *f* d'accélération; [gear change] poignée *f* de changement de vitesses.

twisty ['twɪstɪ] *adj* [road, river] sinueux, qui serpente.

twit [twɪt] (*pt* & *pp* **twitted**, *cont* **twitting**)
◇ *vt dated* [tease] taquiner; **they twitted him about his hat** ils l'ont taquiné sur OR à propos de son chapeau.
◇ *n inf Br* [idiot] crétin *m*, -e *f*, imbécile *mf*; **you silly ~!** espèce d'idiot OR de crétin!

twitch [twɪtʃ] ◇ *vi* -**1.** [jerk - once] avoir un mouvement convulsif; [- habitually] avoir un tic; [muscle] se contracter convulsivement; **his hands ~ed nervously** ses mains se contractaient nerveusement; **his right eye ~es** il a un tic à l'œil droit; **the rabbit's nose ~ed** le lapin a remué le nez. -**2.** [wriggle] s'agiter, se remuer; **stop ~ing about on your chair!** arrête de t'agiter OR de te tortiller sur ta chaise!
◇ *vt* [ears, nose] remuer, bouger; [curtain, rope] tirer d'un coup sec, donner un coup sec à; **she ~ed my sleeve** elle tira ma manche d'un petit coup sec; **she ~ed the scarf out of my hands** elle m'arracha l'écharpe des mains.
◇ *n* -**1.** [nervous tic] tic *m*; [muscular spasm] spasme *m*; **to have a (nervous) ~** avoir un tic (nerveux); **the rabbit's ears gave a ~** le lapin a remué les oreilles. -**2.** [tweak, pull - on hair, rope] coup *m* sec, saccade *f*; **a ~ of the whip** un petit coup de fouet.

twitchy ['twɪtʃɪ] *adj* [person] agité, nerveux.

twitter ['twɪtəʳ] ◇ *vi* -**1.** [bird] gazouiller, pépier. -**2.** [person - chatter] jacasser; **she's always ~ing (on) about her daughter** elle ne parle que de sa fille.
◇ *n* -**1.** [of bird] gazouillement *m*, pépiement *m*. -**2.** [of person] bavardage *m*. -**3.** *inf* [agitation] état *m* d'agitation; **to be all of a** OR **in a ~ about sthg** être dans tous ses états OR sens dessus dessous à cause de qqch.

'twixt [twɪkst] *lit* = **betwixt**.

two [tuː] (*pl* twos) ◇ *adj* deux *(inv)*; 'The Two Gentlemen of Verona' *Shakespeare* 'les Deux Gentilshommes de Vérone'.
◇ *n* -**1.** deux *m inv*; **to cut sthg in ~** couper qqch en deux; **in ~s, ~ by ~** deux par deux; **in ~s and threes** par (groupes de) deux ou trois; **~ at a time** deux à la fois. -**2.** *phr*: **to put ~ and ~ together** faire le rapport (entre deux choses) et tirer ses conclusions; **she put ~ and ~ together, and made five** elle en a tiré des conclusions erronées; **they're ~ of a kind** ils sont du même genre, ils se ressemblent tous les deux; **that makes ~ of us** vous n'êtes pas le seul, moi c'est pareil; **~'s company, three's a crowd** deux ça va, trois c'est trop; **~ can play at that game** à bon chat, bon rat *prov*.
◇ *pron* deux *mfpl*; **there are ~ (of them)** il y en a deux.

two-bit *inf adj Am pej* de pacotille.

two-by-four ◇ *n bois d'œuvre de 2 pouces sur 4 de section*.
◇ *adj inf Am* [small] exigu; [worthless] minable.

two-chamber system *n* POL système *m* bicaméral.

two-cycle *adj Am* [engine] à deux temps.

two-cylinder *adj* à deux cylindres.

two-dimensional *adj* -**1.** [figure, drawing] à deux dimensions. -**2.** [simplistic - character] sans profondeur, simpliste.

two-door *adj* [car] à deux portes.

two-edged *adj* [sword, policy, argument] à double tranchant.

two-faced *adj* hypocrite.

twofold ['tuːfəʊld] ◇ *adj* double; **their aims are ~** ils ont deux objectifs OR un objectif double; **there has been a ~ increase in attendance** l'assistance a doublé.
◇ *adv* [increase] au double; **prices have risen ~** les prix ont doublé.

two-four time *n* MUS mesure *f* à deux temps, deux-quatre *m inv*.

two-handed *adj* [tool] à deux poignées; [saw] à deux mains, forestière; [sword] à deux mains; [game] qui se joue à deux, pour deux joueurs; **a ~ backhand** [in tennis] un revers à deux mains.

two-legged *adj* bipède.

two-level *adj* à deux niveaux.

two-party *adj* [coalition, system] biparti, bipartite.

twopence ['tʌpəns] *n Br* deux pence *mpl*; **I don't give ~ for what he thinks** *inf* je me moque bien OR je me fiche pas mal de ce qu'il pense.

twopenny *inf* ['tʌpnɪ] *adj Br* à OR de deux pence.

twopenny-halfpenny *inf adj* qui ne vaut rien, de quatre sous.

two-phase *adj* ELEC diphasé, biphasé.

two-piece ◇ *adj* en deux parties; **~ swimming costume** (maillot *m* de bain) deux-pièces *m*; **~ suit** [man's] costume *m* deux-pièces; [woman's] tailleur *m*.
◇ *n* [bikini] deux-pièces *m*; [man's suit] costume *m* deux-pièces; [woman's suit] tailleur *m*.

two-ply *adj* [wool] à deux fils; [rope] à deux brins; [tissue] double, à double épaisseur; [wood] à deux épaisseurs.

two-seater ◇ *adj* à deux places.
◇ *n* [plane] avion *m* à deux places; [car] voiture *f* à deux places.

two-sided *adj* [problem] qui a deux aspects; [argument] discutable, qui comporte deux points de vue.

twosome ['tuːsəm] *n* -**1.** [couple] couple *m*. -**2.** [match] partie *f* à deux.

two-star ◇ *adj* -**1.** [restaurant, hotel] deux étoiles. -**2.** *Br* [petrol] ordinaire.
◇ *n Br* [petrol] (essence *f*) ordinaire *m*.

two-step *n* [dance, music] pas *m* de deux.

two-storey *adj* à deux étages.

two-stroke *adj* [engine] à deux temps.

two-tier *adj* [cake, management, financing] à deux étages.

two-time *inf vt* [lover] tromper, être infidèle à.

two-timer *inf n* [lover] amant *m*, maîtresse *f* infidèle.

two-tone *adj* [in colour] à deux tons; [in sound] de deux tons.

'twould [twʊd] *lit* OR *dial* = **it would**.

two-way *adj* [traffic] dans les deux sens; [street] à double sens; [agreement, process] bilatéral; **~ mirror** glace *f* sans tain; **~ radio** TELEC émetteur-récepteur *m*; **~ switch** ELEC va-et-vient *m inv*.

two-wheeler *n* [motorbike] deux-roues *m*; [bicycle] bicyclette *f*, deux-roues *m*.

TX *written abbr of* Texas.

tycoon [taɪˈkuːn] *n* homme *m* d'affaires important, magnat *m*; **oil/newspaper ~** magnat du pétrole/de la presse.

tyke [taɪk] *n* -**1.** [dog] chien *m* bâtard. -**2.** *inf* [child] sale gosse *mf*.

tympani ['tɪmpənɪ] = **timpani**.

tympanist ['tɪmpənɪst] = **timpanist**.

tympanum ['tɪmpənəm] (*pl* tympana [-nə] OR tympanums) *n* -**1.** ANAT, ARCHIT & ZOOL tympan *m*. -**2.** MUS tymbale *f*.

type [taɪp] ◇ *n* -**1.** [gen & BIOL]: **blood/hair ~** type *m* sanguin/de cheveux. -**2.** [sort, kind] sorte *f*, genre *m*, espèce *f*; [make - of coffee, shampoo etc] marque *f*; [model - of car, plane, equipment etc] modèle *m*; **what ~ of washing powder do you use?** quelle (marque de) lessive utilisez-vous?; **what ~ of car do you drive?** qu'est-ce que vous avez comme voiture?, quel modèle de voiture avez-vous?; **a new ~ of warship/of phone** un nouveau modèle de navire de guerre/de téléphone. -**3.** [referring to person] genre *m*, type *m*; **she's not that ~ (of person)** ce n'est pas son genre; **he's not my ~** ce n'est pas mon type (d'homme); **men of his ~** les hommes de son genre OR son espèce; **I know his/their ~** je connais les gens de son espèce/de cette espèce; **the blond fair-skinned ~** le type cheveux blonds et peau blanche; **she's one of those sporty ~s** elle est du genre sportif. -**4.** [typical example] type *m*, exemple *m*. -**5.** *(U)* TYPO [single character] caractère *m*; [block of print] caractères *mpl* (d'imprimerie); **to set ~** composer.

◇ *vt* -**1.** [subj: typist] taper (à la machine); **to ~ sthg into a computer** saisir qqch à l'ordinateur; **to ~ a letter** taper une lettre. -**2.** MED [blood sample] classifier, déterminer le type de.

◇ *vi* [typist] taper (à la machine); **I can only ~ with two fingers** je ne tape qu'avec deux doigts.

◆ **type out** *vt sep* -**1.** [letter] taper (à la machine). -**2.** [error] effacer (à la machine).

◆ **type over** *vt insep* COMPUT écraser.

◆ **type up** *vt sep* [report, notes] taper (à la machine).

-type *in cpds* du type, genre; **western~ governments** des gouvernements du type occidental; **collie~ dogs** des chiens genre colley.

typebar ['taɪpbɑːʳ] *n* barre *f* porte-caractères, barre *f* d'impression.

typecase ['taɪpkeɪs] *n* TYPO casse *f*.

typecast ['taɪpkɑːst] (*pt* & *pp* **typecast**) *vt* [actor] enfermer dans le rôle de; **he is always ~ as a villain** on lui fait toujours jouer des rôles de bandit.

typeface ['taɪpfeɪs] *n* œil *m* du caractère; **try another ~** essaie avec un autre caractère.

typeover ['taɪp,əʊvəʳ] *n*: **'typeover'** '(mode) écraser'.

typescript ['taɪpskrɪpt] *n* texte *m* dactylographié, tapuscrit *m*.

typeset ['taɪpset] (*pt* & *pp* **typeset**, *cont* **typesetting**) *vt* composer IMPR.

typesetter ['taɪp,setəʳ] *n* [worker] compositeur *m*, -trice *f*; [machine] linotype *f*.

typesetting ['taɪp,setɪŋ] *n* composition *f* IMPR.

typewrite ['taɪpraɪt] *vi* & *vt* taper à la machine.

typewriter ['taɪp,raɪtəʳ] *n* machine *f* à écrire.

typewritten ['taɪp,rɪtn] *adj* dactylographié, tapé à la machine.

typhlology [tɪf'lɒlədʒɪ] *n* soin *m* des aveugles.

typhoid ['taɪfɔɪd] ◇ *n (U)* typhoïde *f*.

◇ *comp* [injection] antityphoïdique; [symptoms] de la typhoïde; **~ fever** (fièvre *f*) typhoïde *f*.

typhoon [taɪ'fuːn] *n* typhon *m*.

typhus ['taɪfəs] *n* typhus *m*.

typical ['tɪpɪkl] *adj* typique, caractéristique; **such behaviour is ~ of young people nowadays** un tel comportement est typique OR caractéristique des jeunes d'aujourd'hui; **it was ~ of him to offer to pay** c'était bien son genre de proposer de payer; **it's a ~ example of Aztec pottery** c'est un exemple type de poterie aztèque; **the ~ American** l'Américain typique OR type; **that's ~ of her!** *pej* c'est bien d'elle!; **he said with ~ self-deprecation** il dit avec son humilité habituelle; **~ man!** c'est bien un homme!

typically ['tɪpɪklɪ] *adv* -**1.** [normally] d'habitude; **we ~ deal with 20 phone calls a day** d'habitude nous répondons à 20 appels téléphoniques par jour; **it was a ~ sunny day** c'était une journée ensoleillée comme d'habitude. -**2.** [characteristically] typiquement; **she's ~ English** elle est typiquement anglaise, c'est l'Anglaise type OR typique; **it's a ~ French scene** c'est une scène bien française OR typiquement française; **a group of ~ noisy schoolboys** un groupe de lycéens bruyants comme le sont tous les lycéens; **~, she changed her mind at the last minute** comme à son habitude, elle a changé d'avis au dernier moment.

typify ['tɪpɪfaɪ] (*pt* & *pp* **typified**) *vt* -**1.** [be typical of] être typique OR caractéristique de; **the building typifies the Baroque style** l'édifice est caractéristique du style baroque. -**2.** [embody, symbolize] symboliser, être le type même de; **she typifies the modern career woman** c'est le type même de la femme moderne qui poursuit une carrière.

typing ['taɪpɪŋ] *n* -**1.** [typing work]: **he had 10 pages of ~ to do** il avait 10 pages à taper OR dactylographier. -**2.** [typescript] tapuscrit *m*, texte *m* dactylographié. -**3.** [skill] dactylo *f*, dactylographie *f*.

typing paper *n* papier *m* machine.

typing pool *n* bureau *m* OR pool *m* des dactylos.

typing speed *n* vitesse *f* de frappe; **I only have a ~ of 30 words a minute** je ne tape que 30 mots par minute.

typist ['taɪpɪst] *n* dactylo *mf*, dactylographe *mf*.

typo *inf* ['taɪpəʊ] (*pl* **typos**) *n* [in typescript] faute *f* de frappe; [in printed text] coquille *f*.

typographer [taɪ'pɒgrəfəʳ] *n* typographe *mf*.

typographic(al) [,taɪpə'græfɪk(l)] *adj* typographique.

typography [taɪ'pɒgrəfɪ] *n* typographie *f*.

typological [,taɪpə'lɒdʒɪkl] *adj* typologique.

typology [taɪ'pɒlədʒɪ] *n* typologie *f*.

tyramine ['taɪrəmiːn] *n* tyramine *f*.

tyrannic(al) [tɪ'rænɪk(l)] *adj* tyrannique.

tyrannically [tɪ'rænɪklɪ] *adv* tyranniquement, avec tyrannie.

tyrannicide [tɪ'rænɪsaɪd] *n* -**1.** [person] tyrannicide *mf*. -**2.** [act] tyrannicide *m*.

tyrannize, -ise ['tɪrənaɪz] ◇ *vt* tyranniser.

◇ *vi*: **to ~ over sb** tyranniser qqn.

tyrannosaur [tɪ'rænəsɔːʳ], **tyrannosaurus** [tɪ,rænə'sɔːrəs] *n* tyrannosaure *m*.

tyranny ['tɪrənɪ] (*pl* **tyrannies**) *n* tyrannie *f*.

tyrant ['taɪrənt] *n* tyran *m*.

tyre *Br*, **tire** *Am* ['taɪəʳ] *n* pneu *m*; **~ pressure** pression *f* des pneus.

Tyre ['taɪəʳ] *pr n* Tyr.

tyre fitter *n* monteur *m* de pneus.

tyre gauge *n* manomètre *m (pour pneus)*.

tyre lever *n* démonte-pneu *m*.

tyro ['taɪrəʊ] (*pl* **tyros**) *n fml* débutant *m*, -e *f*, novice *mf*.

Tyrol [tɪ'rəʊl] *pr n* Tyrol *m*; **in the ~** dans le Tyrol.

Tyrolean [tɪ'rəʊlɪən], **Tyrolese** [,tɪrə'liːz] ◇ *n* Tyrolien *m*, -enne *f*.

◇ *adj* tyrolien.

Tyrrhenian Sea [tɪ'riːnɪən-] *pr n*: **the ~** la mer Tyrrhénienne.

tzar *etc* [zɑːʳ] = **tsar**.

tzetze fly ['tsetsɪ-] = **tsetse fly**.

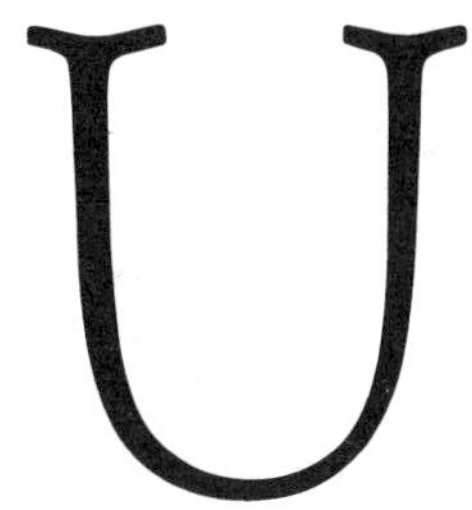

u (*pl* u's OR us), **U** (*pl* U's OR Us) [juː] *n* [letter] u *m*, U *m*.

U ◇ *n* (*abbr of* universal) *désigne un film tous publics en Grande-Bretagne*.
◇ -**1.** *written abbr of* united. -**2.** *written abbr of* unionist.
◇ *adj inf Br* [upper-class - expression, activity] ≃ distingué; U/non-U language langage *m* distingué/vulgaire.

UAE (*abbr of* United Arab Emirates) *pr n* EAU *mpl*.

UAR (*abbr of* United Arab Republic) *pr n* RAU *f*.

UAW (*abbr of* United Automobile Workers) *pr n syndicat américain de l'industrie automobile*.

UB40 (*abbr of* unemployment benefit form 40) *n* -**1.** [card] *en Grande-Bretagne, carte de pointage pour bénéficier de l'allocation de chômage*. -**2.** *inf* [person] chômeur *m*, -euse *f*.

U-bend *n* -**1.** [in pipe] coude *m*; [under sink] siphon *m*. -**2.** *Br* [in road] virage *m* en épingle à cheveux.

ubiquitous [juːˈbɪkwɪtəs] *adj* [gen] omniprésent, que l'on trouve partout; [person] doué d'ubiquité, omniprésent.

ubiquity [juːˈbɪkwətɪ] *n* ubiquité *f*, omniprésence *f*.

U-boat *n* sous-marin *m* allemand.

U-bolt *n* agrafe *f* filetée, étrier *m*.

UCCA [ˈʌkə] (*abbr of* Universities Central Council on Admissions) *pr n organisme centralisant les demandes d'inscription dans les universités britanniques*.

UCL (*abbr of* University College, London) *pr n l'une des facultés de l'Université de Londres*.

UDA (*abbr of* Ulster Defence Association) *pr n organisation paramilitaire protestante en Irlande du Nord déclarée hors la loi en 1992*.

UDC (*abbr of* Urban District Council) *n Br conseil d'une communauté urbaine*.

udder [ˈʌdəʳ] *n* mamelle *f*, pis *m*.

UDI (*abbr of* Unilateral Declaration of Independence) *n déclaration unilatérale d'indépendance*.

UDM (*abbr of* Union of Democratic Mineworkers) *pr n syndicat britannique de mineurs*.

UDR (*abbr of* Ulster Defence Regiment) *pr n ancien régiment de réservistes en Irlande du Nord qui fait aujourd'hui partie du Royal Irish Regiment*.

UEFA [juːˈeɪfə] (*abbr of* Union of European Football Associations) *pr n* UEFA *f*.

UFO [ˌjuːefˈəʊ, ˈjuːfəʊ] (*abbr of* unidentified flying object) *n* OVNI *m*, ovni *m*.

ufology [ˌjuːˈfɒlədʒɪ] *n* ufologie *f*.

Uganda [juːˈgændə] *pr n* Ouganda *m*; in ~ en Ouganda.

Ugandan [juːˈgændən] ◇ *n* Ougandais *m*, -e *f*.
◇ *adj* ougandais.

UGC (*abbr of* University Grants Committee) *pr n organisme répartissant les crédits entre les universités en Grande-Bretagne*.

ugh [ʌg] *interj*: ~! beurk!, berk!, pouah!

Ugli ® [ˈʌglɪ] (*pl* Uglis OR Uglies) *n* tangelo *m*.

uglify *inf* [ˈʌglɪfaɪ] (*pt* & *pp* uglified) *vt* [city, building] enlaidir.

ugliness [ˈʌglɪnɪs] *n* laideur *f*.

ugly [ˈʌglɪ] (*compar* uglier, *superl* ugliest) *adj* -**1.** [in appearance - person, face, building] laid, vilain; it was an ~ sight ce n'était pas beau à voir; as ~ as sin laid à faire peur ❑ 'The Ugly Duckling' *Andersen* 'le Vilain Petit Canard'. -**2.** [unpleasant, nasty - habit] sale, désagréable; [- behaviour] répugnant; [- quarrel] mauvais; [- clouds, weather] vilain, sale; [- rumour, word] vilain; [- situation] fâcheux, mauvais; there were some ~ scenes il y a eu du vilain; he has an ~ bruise on his face il a un vilain bleu au visage; the ~ truth is... la vérité, dans toute son horreur, c'est que...; he was in an ~ mood il était d'une humeur massacrante, il était de fort méchante humeur; she gave me an ~ look elle m'a regardé d'un sale œil; he's an ~ customer c'est un sale individu, il n'est pas commode; to turn OR to get ~ [person] devenir OR se faire menaçant; [situation] prendre mauvaise tournure OR une sale tournure; things took an ~ turn les choses ont pris une mauvaise OR vilaine tournure.

ugly ducking *n* vilain petit canard *m*.

UHF (*abbr of* ultra-high frequency) *n* UHF *f*.

uh-huh *inf* [ʌˈhʌ] *interj*: ~! [as conversation filler] ah ah!; [in assent] oui oui!, OK!; ~? [in question] ah ha?; [in surprise] ah bon?, ah ouais?

UHT (*abbr of* ultra heat treated) *adj* UHT.

uh-uh *inf* [ʌʌ] *interj* [no] non non!; [in warning] hé!, hein!

UK ◇ *pr n* (*abbr of* United Kingdom) Royaume-Uni *m*; in the ~ au Royaume-Uni.
◇ *comp* du Royaume-Uni.

uke *inf* [juːk] *n abbr of* ukulele.

ukelele [ˌjuːkəˈleɪlɪ] = **ukulele**.

Ukraine [juːˈkreɪn] *pr n*: the ~ l'Ukraine *f*; in the ~ en Ukraine.

Ukrainian [juːˈkreɪnjən] ◇ *n* -**1.** [person] Ukrainien *m*, -enne *f*. -**2.** LING ukrainien *m*.
◇ *adj* ukrainien; the ~ Soviet Socialist Republic la République soviétique d'Ukraine.

ukulele [ˌjuːkəˈleɪlɪ] *n* guitare *f* hawaïenne, ukulélé *m*.

Ulan Bator [ʊˈlɑːnˈbɑːtɔːʳ] *pr n* Oulan-Bator.

ulcer [ˈʌlsəʳ] *n* -**1.** MED [in stomach] ulcère *m*; [in mouth] aphte *m*. -**2.** *fig* plaie *f*.

ulcerate [ˈʌlsəreɪt] ◇ *vt* ulcérer.
◇ *vi* s'ulcérer.

ulcerated [ˈʌlsəreɪtɪd] *adj* ulcéreux.

ulceration [ˌʌlsəˈreɪʃn] *n* ulcération *f*.

ulcerous [ˈʌlsərəs] *adj* -**1.** [ulcerated] ulcéreux. -**2.** [causing ulcers] ulcératif.

ullage [ˈʌlɪdʒ] *n* -**1.** [in transport] *quantité de liquide perdue par l'évaporation ou par des fuites au cours du transport*. -**2.** [in wine bottle] ouillage *m*.

'ullo *inf* [ʌˈləʊ] *interj* [greeting] salut; [doubtful] tiens, tiens.

ulna [ˈʌlnə] (*pl* ulnae [-niː] OR ulnas) *n* cubitus *m*.

ulster [ˈʌlstəʳ] *n* [coat] *gros pardessus*.

Ulster [ˈʌlstəʳ] *pr n* -**1.** [province] Ulster *m*; in ~ dans l'Ulster. -**2.** [N.Ireland] Irlande *f* du Nord, Ulster *m*.

Ulster Democratic Unionist Party *pr n parti politique essentiellement protestant exigeant le maintien de l'Ulster au sein du Royaume-Uni*.

Ulsterman [ˈʌlstəmən] (*pl* Ulstermen [-mən]) *n* Ulstérien *m*, habitant *m* de l'Irlande du Nord.

Ulsterwoman [ˈʌlstəˌwʊmən] (*pl* Ulsterwomen [-ˌwɪmɪn]) *n* Ulstérienne *f*, habitante *f* de l'Irlande du Nord.

ult [ʌlt] *fml written abbr of* ultimo.

ulterior [ʌlˈtɪərɪəʳ] *adj* [hidden, secret] secret, dissimulé; ~ motive arrière-pensée *f*.

ultima [ˈʌltɪmə] *n* dernière syllabe *f* d'un mot.

ultimata [ˌʌltɪˈmeɪtə] *pl* → **ultimatum**.

ultimate [ˈʌltɪmət] ◇ *adj* -**1.** [eventual, final - ambition, power, responsibility] ultime; [- cost, destination, objective] ultime, final; [- solution, decision, answer] final, définitif; her tragic illness and ~ death deprived the world of a great artist sa mort survenue à l'issue d'une tragique maladie a privé le monde d'une grande artiste; I believe in the party's ~ victory je crois à la victoire finale du parti; they regard nuclear weapons as the ~ deterrent ils considèrent les armes nucléaires comme l'ultime moyen de dissuasion. -**2.** [basic, fundamental - cause] fondamental, premier; [- truth] fondamental, élémentaire; the ~ meaning of life le sens fondamental de la vie. -**3.** [extreme, supreme - authority, insult] suprême; [- cruelty, stupidity] suprême, extrême; it's their idea of the ~ holiday c'est ce qu'ils appellent de vraies vacances, c'est leur conception des vacances idéales; the ~ sacrifice le sacrifice suprême. -**4.** [furthest] le plus éloigné; the ~ origins of mankind les origines premières de l'homme.
◇ *n* comble *m*, summum *m*; the ~ in comfort le summum du confort; the ~ in hi-fi le nec plus ultra de la hi-fi.

ultimately [ˈʌltɪmətlɪ] *adv* -**1.** [eventually, finally] finalement, en fin de compte, à la fin; [later] par la suite; a solution will ~ be found on finira bien par trouver une solution; ~ there will be peace tôt ou tard, il y aura la paix. -**2.** [basically] en dernière analyse, en fin de compte; ~, the problem is a shortage of money en dernière analyse, le problème est lié à un manque d'argent; **responsibility ~ lies with you** en fin de compte c'est vous qui êtes responsable.

ultimatum [ˌʌltɪˈmeɪtəm] (*pl* **ultimatums** OR **ultimata** [-tə]) *n* ultimatum *m*; **to give** OR **to issue** OR **to deliver an ~ to sb** adresser un ultimatum à qqn.

ultimo [ˈʌltɪməʊ] *adv fml* du mois dernier; **the 16th ~** le 16 du mois dernier.

ultra [ˈʌltrə] (*pl* **ultras**) ◇ *adj* ultra, extrémiste.
◇ *n* ultra *mf*.

ultra- *in cpds* ultra-, hyper-; **~trendy** *inf* hyper-branché; **~right-wing** d'extrême droite; **~bright** ultralumineux.

ultraclean [ˌʌltrəˈkliːn] *adj* hyper-propre.

ultraconservative [ˌʌltrəkənˈsɜːvətɪv] ◇ *adj* ultraconservateur.
◇ *n* ultraconservateur *m*, -trice *f*.

ultra-fashionable *adj* ultra-chic.

ultrafiche [ˈʌltrəfiːʃ] *n* microfiche *f*.

ultrahigh frequency [ˌʌltrəˈhaɪ-] *n* très haute fréquence *f*.

ultralight [*adj* ˌʌltrəˈlaɪt, *n* ˈʌltrəlaɪt] ◇ *adj* ultra-léger.
◇ *n* ULM *m*, ultra-léger motorisé *m*.

ultramarine [ˌʌltrəməˈriːn] *adj* bleu outremer *(inv)*.

ultramicroscope [ˌʌltrəˈmaɪkrəskəʊp] *n* ultra-microscope *m*.

ultramicroscopic [ˈʌltrəˌmaɪkrəˈskɒpɪk] *adj* ultramicroscopique.

ultramodern [ˌʌltrəˈmɒdən] *adj* ultramoderne.

ultramontane [ˌʌltrəˈmɒnteɪn] ◇ *adj* ultramontain.
◇ *n* ultramontain *m*, -e *f*.

ultranationalist [ˌʌltrəˈnæʃnəlɪst] ◇ *n* extrémiste *mf* nationaliste, ultranationaliste *mf*.
◇ *adj* d'un nationalisme extrémiste, ultranationaliste.

ultrashort [ˌʌltrəˈʃɔːt] *adj* ultracourt.

ultrasonic [ˌʌltrəˈsɒnɪk] *adj* ultrasonique.
◆ **ultrasonics** *n (U)* science *f* des ultrasons.

ultrasound [ˌʌltrəˈsaʊnd] *n* ultrason *m*.

ultrasound scan *n* échographie *f*.

ultraviolet [ˌʌltrəˈvaɪələt] ◇ *adj* ultraviolet.
◇ *n* ultraviolet *m*.

ultra vires [-ˈvaɪəriːz] *adj* & *adv* au-delà des pouvoirs.

ultravirus [ˌʌltrəˈvaɪərəs] *n* ultravirus *m*.

ululate [ˈjuːljʊleɪt] *vi fml* [owl] ululer, hululer; [wolf, dog] hurler.

ululation [ˌjuːljʊˈleɪʃn] *n fml* [of owl] ululement *m*, hululement *m*; [of wolf, dog] hurlement *m*.

Ulysses [juːˈlɪsiːz] *pr n* Ulysse; **'Ulysses'** *Joyce* 'Ulysse'.

um *inf* [ʌm] (*pt* & *pp* **ummed**, *cont* **umming**) ◇ *interj* euh.
◇ *vi* dire euh; **to ~ and ah** tergiverser, hésiter; **he's always umming and ahing** il n'arrive jamais à se décider.

umbelliferous [ˌʌmbeˈlɪfərəs] *adj* ombellifère.

umber [ˈʌmbəʳ] ◇ *adj* [colour, paint] terre d'ombre *(inv)*.
◇ *n* [clay] terre *f* d'ombre OR de Sienne.

umbilical [ʌmˈbɪlɪkl] *adj* ombilical.

umbilical cord *n* cordon *m* ombilical.

umbilicus [ʌmˈbɪlɪkəs] (*pl* **umbilici** [-saɪ]) *n* MED ombilic *m*, nombril *m*.

umbra [ˈʌmbrə] (*pl* **umbras** OR **umbrae** [-briː]) *n* ASTRON ombre *f*.

umbrage [ˈʌmbrɪdʒ] *n* [offence]: **to take ~ (at sthg)** prendre ombrage de qqch, s'offenser de qqch.

umbrella [ʌmˈbrelə] ◇ *n* -**1.** parapluie *m*; **to put up/down an ~** ouvrir/fermer un parapluie; **beach ~** parasol *m*; **~ stand** porte-parapluies *m inv*. -**2.** *fig* [protection, cover] protection *f*; MIL écran *m* OR rideau *m* de protection; **under the ~ of the WHO** sous l'égide OR les auspices de l'OMS. -**3.** [of jellyfish] ombrelle *f*.
◇ *comp* [term] général; [organization] qui en recouvre OR chapeaute plusieurs autres.

umbrella pine *n* pin *m* parasol.

umbrella plant *n* laîche *f*, carex *m*.

umbrella tree *n* magnolia *m* parasol.

Umbria [ˈʌmbrɪə] *pr n* Ombrie *f*.

Umbrian [ˈʌmbrɪən] ◇ *n* Ombrien *m*, -enne *f*.
◇ *adj* ombrien.

UMIST [ˈjuːmɪst] (*abbr of* University of Manchester Institute of Science and Technology) *pr n institut de science et de technologie de l'université de Manchester, en Grande-Bretagne*.

umlaut [ˈʊmlaʊt] *n* [in German] umlaut *m*, inflexion *f* vocalique; [diaeresis] tréma *m*.

umpire [ˈʌmpaɪəʳ] ◇ *n* arbitre *m*.
◇ *vt* [match, contest] arbitrer.
◇ *vi* servir d'arbitre, être arbitre.

umpteen *inf* [ˌʌmpˈtiːn] ◇ *adj* je ne sais combien de, des tas de; **she's got ~ dresses** elle a je ne sais combien de robes OR des quantités de robes; **I've told you ~ times** je te l'ai dit trente-six fois OR cent fois; **~ people** des dizaines de gens, des tas de gens.
◇ *pron*: **there were ~ of them** il y en avait des quantités OR je ne sais combien.

umpteenth *inf* [ˌʌmpˈtiːnθ] *adj ord* énième, nième; **for the ~ time** pour la nième fois.

UMW (*abbr of* United Mineworkers of America) *pr n syndicat américain de mineurs*.

'un *inf* [ʌn] *pron*: **he's only a young ~** ce n'est qu'un petit gars; **the little ~s** les petiots *mpl*; **the young ~s** les jeunots *mpl*.

UN (*abbr of* United Nations) ◇ *pr n*: **the ~** l'ONU *f*, l'Onu *f*.
◇ *comp* de l'ONU.

unabashed [ˌʌnəˈbæʃt] *adj* -**1.** [undeterred] nullement décontenancé OR déconcerté, imperturbable; **she was quite ~ by the criticism** elle ne se laissa pas intimider OR elle ne fut nullement décontenancée par les critiques; **to carry on ~** continuer sans se démonter OR décontenancer. -**2.** [unashamed] sans honte, qui n'a pas honte.

unabated [ˌʌnəˈbeɪtɪd] ◇ *adv* [undiminished] sans diminuer; **the storm/the noise continued ~ for most of the night** la tempête/le bruit a continué sans perdre de son intensité OR sans répit pendant une grande partie de la nuit.
◇ *adj* non diminué; **their enthusiasm was ~** leur enthousiasme ne diminuait pas, ils montraient toujours autant d'enthousiasme.

unabbreviated [ˌʌnəˈbriːvɪeɪtɪd] *adj* [word] sans abréviation; **in its ~ form** sous sa forme non abrégée, en toutes lettres.

unable [ʌnˈeɪbl] *adj*: **to be ~ to do sthg** [gen] ne pas pouvoir faire qqch; [not know how to] ne pas savoir faire qqch; [be incapable of] être incapable de faire qqch; [not be in a position to] ne pas être en mesure de faire qqch; [be prevented from] être dans l'impossibilité de faire qqch; **children who are ~ to read/swim** les enfants qui ne savent pas lire/nager; **he seems totally ~ to understand** il semble tout à fait incapable de comprendre; **he was ~ to pay** il n'était pas en mesure de payer; **unfortunately I'm ~ to come** malheureusement, je ne peux pas venir OR il m'est impossible de venir.

unabridged [ˌʌnəˈbrɪdʒd] *adj* [text, version, edition] intégral; **the film is ~** le film est dans sa version intégrale.

unacceptable [ˌʌnəkˈseptəbl] *adj* -**1.** [intolerable - violence, behaviour] inadmissible, intolérable; [- language] inacceptable; **it is ~ that anyone should have to** OR **for anyone to have to sleep rough** il est inadmissible que des gens soient obligés de coucher dehors; **the ~ face of capitalism** *allusion Edward Heath* la face honteuse du capitalisme. -**2.** [gift, proposal] inacceptable.

unacceptably [ˌʌnəkˈseptəblɪ] *adv* [noisy, rude] à un point inacceptable OR inadmissible; **the film was ~ violent** le film était d'une violence inacceptable.

unaccompanied [ˌʌnəˈkʌmpənɪd] *adj* -**1.** [child, traveller] non accompagné, seul; **~ by an adult** non accompagné par un adulte. -**2.** MUS [singing] sans accompagnement, a capella; [singer] non accompagné, a capella; [song] sans accompagnement; [choir] a capella; **for ~ violin** pour violon seul.

unaccomplished [ˌʌnəˈkʌmplɪʃt] *adj* -**1.** [incomplete - task] inachevé, inaccompli. -**2.** [unfulfilled - wish, plan] non réalisé, non accompli. -**3.** [untalented - actor, player] sans grand talent, médiocre; [- performance] médiocre.

unaccountable [ˌʌnəˈkaʊntəbl] *adj* -**1.** [inexplicable - disappearance, reason] inexplicable. -**2.** [to electors, public etc]: **representatives who are ~ to the general public** les représentants qui ne sont pas responsables envers le grand public.

unaccountably [ˌʌnəˈkaʊntəblɪ] *adv* inexplicablement, de manière inexplicable; **she was ~ delayed** pour des raisons que l'on ne s'explique pas, elle a été retardée, elle a été retardée sans que l'on sache trop pourquoi.

unaccounted [ˌʌnəˈkaʊntɪd]
◆ **unaccounted for** *adj phr* -**1.** [money] qui manque; **there is still a lot of money ~ for** il manque encore beaucoup d'argent. -**2.** [person] qui manque, qui a disparu; [plane] qui n'est pas rentré; **by nightfall, 2 children were still ~ for** à la tombée de la nuit, il manquait encore 2 enfants.

unaccustomed [ˌʌnəˈkʌstəmd] *adj* -**1.** [not used to - person] peu familier OR habitué; **he is ~ to wearing a tie** il n'a pas l'habitude de mettre des cravates; **~ as I am to public speaking** bien que je n'aie guère l'habitude de prendre la parole en public. -**2.** [unusual, uncharacteristic - rudeness, light-heartedness] inhabituel, inaccoutumé.

unacknowledged [ˌʌnəkˈnɒlɪdʒd] *adj* -**1.** [unrecognized - truth, fact] non reconnu; [- qualities, discovery] non reconnu, méconnu; **he's an ~ genius** c'est un génie méconnu. -**2.** [ignored - letter] resté sans réponse.

unacquainted [ˌʌnəˈkweɪntɪd] *adj* -**1.** [ignorant]: **to be ~ with sthg** ne pas être au courant de qqch. -**2.** [two people]: **I am ~ with her** je ne la connais pas, je n'ai pas fait sa connaissance.

unadopted [ˌʌnəˈdɒptɪd] *adj* -**1.** *Br* [road] non pris en charge OR entretenu par la commune. -**2.** [resolution, bill] non adopté, rejeté. -**3.** [child] qui n'est pas adopté.

unadorned [ˌʌnəˈdɔːnd] *adj* [undecorated] sans ornement, naturel, simple.

unadulterated [ˌʌnəˈdʌltəreɪtɪd] *adj* -**1.** [milk, flour] pur, naturel; [wine] non frelaté. -**2.** [pleasure, joy] pur (et simple), parfait; **it's ~ rubbish!** c'est de la pure bêtise!

unadventurous [ˌʌnədˈventʃərəs] *adj* [person] qui ne prend pas de risques, qui manque d'audace; [lifestyle] conventionnel, banal; [performance] terne; [holiday] banal; **she is an ~ cook** c'est une cuisinière qui manque d'imagination.

unadvertised [ˌʌnˈædvətaɪzd] *adj* [job] non affiché, pour lequel il n'y a pas eu d'annonce; [meeting, visit] discret, sans publicité.

unadvisable [ˌʌnədˈvaɪzəbl] *adj* imprudent, à déconseiller; **it is ~ for her to travel** les voyages lui sont déconseillés, il vaut mieux qu'elle évite de voyager.

unaffected [ˌʌnəˈfektɪd] *adj* -**1.** [resistant] non affecté, qui résiste; **~ by cold** qui n'est pas affecté par le OR qui résiste au froid; **~ by heat** qui résiste à la chaleur. -**2.** [unchanged, unaltered] qui n'est pas touché OR affecté; **we were ~ by the war** nous n'avons pas été affectés OR touchés par la guerre; **children cannot remain ~ by TV violence** il est impossible que les enfants ne soient pas affectés OR marqués par la violence qu'ils voient à la télé. -**3.** [indifferent] indifférent, insensible; **he seems quite ~ by his loss** sa perte ne semble pas l'émouvoir, sa perte n'a pas du tout l'air de le toucher. -**4.** [natural - person, manners, character] simple, naturel, sans affectation; [- style] simple, sans recherche.

unaffectedly [ˌʌnəˈfektɪdlɪ] *adv* [speak, behave] sans affectation; [write, dress] simplement, sans recherche.

unaffectionate [ˌʌnəˈfekʃənət] *adj* [person] froid, qui n'est pas affectueux; [kiss] sans affection OR tendresse.

unaffiliated [ˌʌnəˈfɪlɪeɪtɪd] *adj* [unions] non affilié.

unafraid [ˌʌnəˈfreɪd] *adj* sans peur, qui n'a pas peur; **he was quite ~** il n'avait pas du tout peur.

unaided [ˌʌnˈeɪdɪd] ◇ *adj* sans aide (extérieure); **it is his own ~ work** c'est un travail qu'il a fait tout seul OR sans l'aide de personne; **an impossible task for an ~ person** une tâche qu'il est impossible d'accomplir seul OR sans se faire aider.
◇ *adv* [work] tout seul, sans être aidé.

unaligned [ˌʌnəˈlaɪnd] *adj* -**1.** [wheels, posts] non aligné, qui n'est pas aligné. -**2.** POL non-aligné.

unalike [ˌʌnəˈlaɪk] *adj* différent, peu ressemblant; **the two sisters are quite ~** les deux sœurs ne se ressemblent pas du tout, les deux sœurs sont très différentes; **they look** OR **seem quite ~** ils ne se ressemblent absolument pas.

unalloyed [ˌʌnəˈlɔɪd] *adj* -**1.** [joy, enthusiasm] sans mélange, parfait. -**2.** [metal] pur, sans alliage.

unalterable [ʌnˈɔːltərəbl] *adj* [fact] immuable; [decision] irrévocable; [truth] certain, immuable.

unaltered [ʌnˈɔːltəd] *adj* inchangé, non modifié; **the original building remains ~** le bâtiment d'origine reste tel quel OR n'a pas subi de modifications.

unambiguous [ˌʌnæmˈbɪgjʊəs] *adj* [wording, rule] non ambigu, non équivoque; [thinking] clair.

unambiguously [ˌʌnæmˈbɪgjʊəslɪ] *adv* sans ambiguïté, sans équivoque.

unambitious [ˌʌnæmˈbɪʃəs] *adj* sans ambition, peu ambitieux.

un-American *adj* -**1.** [uncharacteristic] peu américain; **it's very ~** ce n'est pas du tout américain. -**2.** [anti-American] antiaméricain.

unamused [ˌʌnəˈmjuːzd] *adj* qui n'est pas amusé.

unanimity [ˌjuːnəˈnɪmətɪ] *n* unanimité *f*; **there must be ~ on the issue** il faut qu'il y ait unanimité à ce sujet.

unanimous [juːˈnænɪməs] *adj* unanime; **passed by a ~ vote** voté à l'unanimité; **we must give him our ~ support** il faut qu'on soit unanimes à le soutenir; **the audience was ~ in its approval** le public a approuvé à l'unanimité.

unanimously [juːˈnænɪməslɪ] *adv* [decide, agree] à l'unanimité, unanimement; [vote] à l'unanimité.

unannounced [ˌʌnəˈnaʊnst] ◇ *adj* [arrival, event] inattendu; **their ~ arrival caused some confusion** leur arrivée inattendue a provoqué une certaine confusion.
◇ *adv* [unexpectedly] de manière inattendue, sans se faire annoncer; [suddenly] subitement; **he turned up ~** il est arrivé à l'improviste.

unanswerable [ˌʌnˈɑːnsərəbl] *adj* -**1.** [impossible - question, problem] auquel il est impossible de répondre. -**2.** [irrefutable - argument, logic] irréfutable, incontestable.

unanswered [ˌʌnˈɑːnsəd] *adj* -**1.** [question] qui reste sans réponse; [prayer] inexaucé; **my main argument was left ~** on n'a toujours pas réfuté mon argument principal; **an ~ charge** JUR une accusation non réfutée OR irréfutée. -**2.** [unsolved - mystery, puzzle] non résolu. -**3.** [letter] (resté) sans réponse; **I have 6 ~ letters to deal with** il y a 6 lettres auxquelles je n'ai pas encore répondu.

unanticipated [ˌʌnænˈtɪsɪpeɪtɪd] *adj* [success, arrival] inattendu; [situation, event, result, outcome] imprévu, inattendu; [announcement] inattendu, surprenant.

unappealing [ˌʌnəˈpiːlɪŋ] *adj* peu attrayant, peu attirant.

unappetizing, -ising [ˌʌnˈæpɪtaɪzɪŋ] *adj* peu appétissant.

unappreciated [ˌʌnəˈpriːʃɪeɪtɪd] *adj* [person, talents] méconnu, incompris; [efforts, kindness] non apprécié, qui n'est pas apprécié.

unapproachable [ˌʌnəˈprəʊtʃəbl] *adj* -**1.** [person] inabordable, d'un abord difficile. -**2.** [place] inaccessible, inabordable; **~ by road** inaccessible par la route.

unarguable [ʌnˈɑːgjʊəbl] *adj* incontestable.

unarguably [ʌnˈɑːgjʊəblɪ] *adv* incontestablement.

unarmed [ˌʌnˈɑːmd] *adj* -**1.** [person, vehicle] sans armes, non armé. -**2.** BOT sans épines.

unarmed combat *n* combat *m* sans armes.

unary [ˈjuːnərɪ] *adj* unaire, monadique.

unashamed [ˌʌnəˈʃeɪmd] *adj* [curiosity, gaze] sans gêne; [greed, lie, hypocrisy] effronté, sans scrupule; [person] sans honte; **he was quite ~ about** OR **of his huge wealth** il ne se cachait pas de son immense richesse, il étalait son immense richesse sans vergogne OR sans pudeur.

unashamedly [ˌʌnəˈʃeɪmɪdlɪ] *adv* [brazenly] sans honte, sans scrupule; [openly] sans honte, sans se cacher; **she lied quite ~** elle mentait absolument sans vergogne, c'était une menteuse tout à fait éhontée; **he is ~ greedy** il est d'une gourmandise éhontée.

unasked [ˌʌnˈɑːskt] ◇ *adj* [question] que l'on n'a pas posé; **the central question is still ~** la question essentielle reste à poser.
◇ *adv*: **he came ~** il est venu de son propre chef OR sans avoir été invité; **they did the job ~** ils ont fait le travail sans qu'on le leur ait demandé OR spontanément.

unassailable [ˌʌnəˈseɪləbl] *adj* [fort, city] imprenable, inébranlable; [certainty, belief] inébranlable; [reputation] inattaquable; [argument, reason] inattaquable, irréfutable; **to be in an ~ position** être dans une position inattaquable.

unassigned [ˌʌnəˈsaɪnd] *adj* [office, room - for person] non attribué; [- for purpose] non affecté; [task] non assigné.

unassisted [ˌʌnəˈsɪstɪd] ◇ *adv* sans aide, tout seul.
◇ *adj* sans aide.

unassuming [ˌʌnəˈsjuːmɪŋ] *adj* modeste, sans prétentions.

unassumingly [ˌʌnəˈsjuːmɪŋlɪ] *adv* modestement, sans prétention.

unattached [ˌʌnəˈtætʃt] *adj* -**1.** [unconnected - building, part, group] indépendant. -**2.** [not married] libre, sans attaches.

unattainable [ˌʌnəˈteɪnəbl] *adj* [goal, place] inaccessible.

unattended [ˌʌnəˈtendɪd] *adj* -**1.** [vehicle, luggage] laissé sans surveillance; **do not leave small children ~** ne laissez pas de jeunes enfants sans surveillance OR tout seuls; **do not leave luggage ~** ne laissez pas vos bagages sans surveillance. -**2.** [person] sans escorte, seul; **I can't even go to the toilet ~** je ne peux même pas aller aux toilettes seul.

unattractive [ˌʌnəˈtræktɪv] *adj* [face, room, wallpaper] peu attrayant, assez laid; [habit] peu attrayant, désagréable; [personality] déplaisant, peu sympathique; [prospect] désagréable, peu attrayant, peu agréable.

unauthenticated [ˌʌnɔːˈθentɪkeɪtɪd] *adj* [story] non vérifié; [painting, handwriting] non authentifié; [evidence] non établi.

unauthorized, -ised [ˌʌnˈɔːθəraɪzd] *adj* [absence, entry] non autorisé, fait sans autorisation.

unavailable [ˌʌnəˈveɪləbl] *adj* [person] indisponible, qui n'est pas libre; [resources] indisponible, qu'on ne peut se procurer; **the book is ~** [in library, bookshop] le livre n'est pas disponible; [from publisher] le livre est épuisé; **Mr Fox is ~** M. Fox n'est pas disponible OR libre; **the Minister was ~ for comment** le ministre s'est refusé à tout commentaire.

unavailing [ˌʌnəˈveɪlɪŋ] *adj* [effort, attempt] vain, inutile; [method] inefficace.

unavailingly [ˌʌnəˈveɪlɪŋlɪ] *adv* en vain, sans succès.

unavoidable [ˌʌnəˈvɔɪdəbl] *adj* [accident, delay] inévitable; **it is ~ that some people will suffer from the new regulations** il est inévitable que certaines personnes pâtissent des nouvelles lois, les nouvelles lois affecteront forcément OR fatalement certaines personnes.

unavoidably [ˌʌnəˈvɔɪdəblɪ] *adv* [happen] inévitablement; [detain] malencontreusement; **I was ~ delayed** j'ai été retardé malgré moi OR pour des raisons indépendantes de ma volonté.

unaware [ˌʌnəˈweəʳ] *adj* [ignorant] inconscient, qui ignore; **to be ~ of** [facts] ignorer, ne pas être au courant de; [danger] être inconscient de, ne pas avoir conscience de; **I was ~ that they had arrived** j'ignorais OR je ne savais pas qu'ils étaient arrivés; **he continued ~ of what was happening** il a continué, ignorant de ce qui se passait OR sans savoir ce qui se passait; **she is politically ~** elle n'a aucune conscience politique, elle ignore tout de la politique; **he seemed quite ~ that he was being watched** il semblait tout à fait ignorer qu'on l'observait, il ne semblait pas du tout remarquer qu'on l'observait.

unawares [ˌʌnəˈweəz] *adv* -**1.** [by surprise] au dépourvu, à l'improviste; **to catch** OR **to take sb ~** prendre qqn à l'improviste OR au dépourvu; **the photographer caught us ~** le photographe nous a pris sans qu'on s'en rende compte OR à notre insu. -**2.** [unknowingly] inconsciemment. -**3.** [by accident] par mégarde, par inadvertance.

unbalance [ˌʌnˈbæləns] ◇ *vt* déséquilibrer.
◇ *n* déséquilibre *m*.

unbalanced [ˌʌnˈbælənst] *adj* -**1.** [load] mal équilibré. -**2.** [person, mind] déséquilibré, désaxé. -**3.** [reporting] tendancieux, partial. -**4.** FIN [economy] déséquilibré; [account] non soldé. -**5.** ELEC [circuit, load] déséquilibré.

unbaptized, -ised [ˌʌnbæpˈtaɪzd] *adj* non baptisé.

unbar [ˌʌnˈbɑːʳ] (*pt* & *pp* **unbarred**, *cont* **unbarring**) *vt* -**1.** [door, gate] enlever la barre de. -**2.** *fig* [path, road] ouvrir; **the decision could ~ the way to a lasting solution** cette décision pourrait bien ouvrir la voie à une solution durable.

unbearable [ʌnˈbeərəbl] *adj* insupportable; **'The Unbearable Lightness of Being'** *Kundera* 'l'Insoutenable Légèreté de l'être'.

unbearably [ʌnˈbeərəblɪ] *adv* insupportablement; **he is ~ conceited** il est d'une vanité insupportable; **it's ~ hot** il fait une chaleur insupportable.

unbeatable [ˌʌnˈbiːtəbl] *adj* [champion, prices] imbattable; **it's ~ value for money** le rapport qualité-prix est imbattable.

unbeaten [ˌʌnˈbiːtn] *adj* [fighter, team] invaincu; [record, price] non battu; **the record has remained ~ for 20 years** le record n'a pas été battu depuis 20 ans.

unbecoming [ˌʌnbɪˈkʌmɪŋ] *adj* -**1.** [dress, colour, hat] peu seyant, qui ne va pas; **that coat is rather ~** ce manteau ne lui va pas. -**2.** [behaviour] malséant.

unbeknown(st) [ˌʌnbɪˈnəʊn(st)] *adv*: **~ to** à l'insu de; **~ to him** à son insu, sans qu'il le sache.

unbelief [ˌʌnbɪˈliːf] *n* -**1.** [incredulity] incrédulité *f*. -**2.** RELIG incroyance *f*.

unbelievable [ˌʌnbɪˈliːvəbl] *adj* -**1.** [extraordinary] incroyable; **it's ~ that they should want to marry so young** il est incroyable OR je n'arrive pas à croire qu'ils veuillent se marier si jeunes; **~ stupidity** stupidité incroyable; **~ good fortune** chance insolente OR incroyable. -**2.** [implausible] incroyable, invraisemblable; **his story was totally ~** son histoire était totalement incroyable OR à dormir debout.

unbelievably [ˌʌnbɪˈliːvəblɪ] *adv* -**1.** [extraordinarily] incroyablement, extraordinairement; **~ beautiful/cruel** d'une beauté/cruauté incroyable OR extraordinaire; ~, he agreed aussi incroyable que cela puisse paraître, il a accepté. -**2.** [implausibly] invraisemblablement, incroyablement.

unbeliever [,ʌnbɪ'li:vəʳ] *n* incroyant *m*, -e *f*.

unbelieving [,ʌnbɪ'li:vɪŋ] *adj* [gen] incrédule, sceptique; RELIG incroyant.

unbelievingly [,ʌnbɪ'li:vɪŋlɪ] *adv* [look, speak] d'un air incrédule.

unbend [,ʌn'bend] (*pt* & *pp* unbent [-'bent]) ◇ *vt* [fork, wire] redresser, détordre. ◇ *vi* [relax] se détendre.

unbending [,ʌn'bendɪŋ] *adj* -**1.** [will, attitude] intransigeant, inflexible; **she remained ~ on the issue** elle est restée intransigeante sur la question; **his ~ puritanism** son puritanisme rigide. -**2.** [pipe, metal] rigide, non flexible.

unbias(s)ed [,ʌn'baɪəst] *adj* impartial.

unbidden [,ʌn'bɪdn] *adv lit* spontanément, sans que l'on demande; **she did it ~** elle l'a fait de son propre chef OR sans qu'on le lui ait demandé; **she entered ~** elle est entrée sans y avoir été invitée; **the thought came ~ to my mind** l'idée m'est venue spontanément.

unbind [,ʌn'baɪnd] (*pt* & *pp* unbound [-'baʊnd]) *vt* [prisoner] délier; [bandage] défaire, dérouler.

unblemished [,ʌn'blemɪʃt] *adj* [purity, skin, colour, reputation] sans tache, sans défaut; **an ~ record** un parcours sans faute.

unblinking [,ʌn'blɪŋkɪŋ] *adj* [impassive] impassible; [fearless] impassible, imperturbable; **she stared at me with ~ eyes** elle me regarda fixement sans ciller.

unblock [,ʌn'blɒk] *vt* [sink] déboucher; [traffic jam] dégager.

unblushing [,ʌn'blʌʃɪŋ] *adj* éhonté.

unbolt [,ʌn'bəʊlt] *vt* [door] déverrouiller, tirer le verrou de; [scaffolding] déboulonner.

unborn [,ʌn'bɔ:n] *adj* [child] qui n'est pas encore né.

unbosom [,ʌn'bʊzəm] *vt lit* [secret, emotions] confesser; **to ~ o.s. to sb** ouvrir son cœur à qqn, se confier à qqn.

unbound [,ʌn'baʊnd] ◇ *pt* & *pp* → **unbind**. ◇ *adj* -**1.** [prisoner, hands] non lié; **'Prometheus Unbound'** *Shelley* 'Prométhée délivré'. -**2.** [book,periodical] non relié. -**3.** LING [morpheme] libre.

unbounded [,ʌn'baʊndɪd] *adj* [gratitude, admiration] illimité, sans borne; [pride, greed] démesuré.

unbowed [,ʌn'baʊd] *adj* insoumis, invaincu; **they stood with their heads ~** ils étaient debout, la tête haute.

unbreakable [,ʌn'breɪkəbl] *adj* -**1.** [crockery] incassable. -**2.** [habit] dont on ne peut pas se débarrasser. -**3.** [promise] sacré; [will, spirit] inébranlable, que l'on ne peut briser OR abattre.

unbridled [,ʌn'braɪdld] *adj* [horse] débridé, sans bride; [anger, greed] sans retenue, effréné.

unbroken [,ʌn'brəʊkn] *adj* -**1.** [continuous in space - line] continu; [- surface, expanse] continu, ininterrompu; [continuous in time - sleep, tradition, peace] ininterrompu. -**2.** [intact - crockery, eggs] intact, non cassé; [- fastening, seal] intact, non brisé; [- record] non battu. -**3.** *fig* [promise] tenu, non rompu; **despite all her troubles, her spirit remains ~** malgré tous ses ennuis, elle garde le moral OR elle ne se laisse pas abattre. -**4.** [voice] qui n'a pas (encore) mué. -**5.** [horse] indompté.

unbuckle [,ʌn'bʌkl] *vt* [belt] déboucler, dégrafer; [shoe] défaire la boucle de.

unburden [,ʌn'bɜ:dn] *vt* -**1.** *literal* & *fml* décharger (d'un fardeau); **can I ~ you of your bags?** puis-je vous décharger de vos sacs? -**2.** *fig* [heart] livrer, épancher, soulager; [grief, guilt] se décharger de; [conscience, soul] soulager; **to ~ o.s. to sb** se confier à qqn, s'épancher auprès de qqn; **she ~ed her heart to me** elle s'est confiée à moi, elle m'a ouvert son cœur.

unburied [,ʌn'berɪd] *adj* non enterré, non enseveli.

unbutton [,ʌn'bʌtn] ◇ *vt* [shirt, jacket] déboutonner. ◇ *vi inf fig* se déboutonner.

uncalled-for [,ʌn'kɔ:ld-] *adj* [rudeness, outburst] qui n'est pas nécessaire, injustifié; [remark] mal à propos, déplacé.

uncannily [ʌn'kænɪlɪ] *adv* [accurate, familiar] étrangement; [quiet] mystérieusement, étrangement.

uncanny [ʌn'kænɪ] (*compar* uncannier, *superl* uncanniest) *adj* -**1.** [eerie - place] sinistre, qui donne le frisson; [- noise] mystérieux, sinistre; [- atmosphere] étrange, sinistre. -**2.** [strange - accuracy, likeness, ability] troublant, étrange; **it's ~ how you always know what I'm thinking** c'est curieux OR bizarre ce don que tu as de toujours savoir ce que je pense.

uncap [,ʌn'kæp] (*pt* & *pp* uncapped, *cont* uncapping) *vt* [bottle, jar] décapsuler, déboucher; [pen] enlever le capuchon de.

uncared-for [,ʌn'keəd-] *adj* [appearance] négligé, peu soigné; [house, bicycle] négligé, (laissé) à l'abandon; [child] laissé à l'abandon, délaissé.

uncaring [,ʌn'keərɪŋ] *adj* [unfeeling] insensible, dur.

uncaught [,ʌn'kɔ:t] *adj* [escapee] qui n'a pas été appréhendé.

unceasing [,ʌn'si:sɪŋ] *adj* incessant, continuel.

unceasingly [,ʌn'si:sɪŋlɪ] *adv* sans cesse, continuellement.

uncelebrated [,ʌn'selɪbreɪtɪd] *adj* [birthday, success] non célébré OR fêté.

uncensored [,ʌn'sensəd] *adj* non censuré.

unceremonious ['ʌn,serɪ'məʊnjəs] *adj* -**1.** [abrupt] brusque. -**2.** [without ceremony] sans façon; **his ~ dismissal** son brusque renvoi.

unceremoniously ['ʌn,serɪ'məʊnjəslɪ] *adv* -**1.** [abruptly] avec brusquerie, brusquement. -**2.** [without ceremony] sans cérémonie; **they were pushed ~ into the back of the police van** on les a poussés brutalement à l'arrière de la voiture cellulaire.

uncertain [ʌn'sɜ:tn] *adj* -**1.** [unsure] incertain; **we were ~ whether to continue** OR **we should continue** nous ne savions pas trop si nous devions continuer; **they were ~ how to begin** ils ne savaient pas trop comment commencer; **to be ~ about the future** être inquiet au sujet de OR incertain de l'avenir. -**2.** [unpredictable - result, outcome] incertain, aléatoire; [- weather] incertain; **it's ~ whether we'll succeed or not** il n'est pas sûr OR certain que nous réussissions; **in no ~ terms** en termes on ne peut plus clairs, sans mâcher ses mots. -**3.** [unknown] inconnu, incertain; **the cause of her death is still ~** la cause de sa mort reste inconnue, on ignore encore la cause de sa mort. -**4.** [unsteady - voice, steps, smile] hésitant, mal assuré. -**5.** [undecided - plans] incertain, pas sûr.

uncertainly [ʌn'sɜ:tnlɪ] *adv* avec hésitation, d'une manière hésitante.

uncertainty [ʌn'sɜ:tntɪ] (*pl* uncertainties) *n* incertitude *f*, doute *m*; **I am in some ~ as to whether I should tell him** je ne sais pas trop OR je ne suis pas trop sûre si je dois le lui dire ou non; **is there any ~ about what to do?** est-ce que quelqu'un a des doutes sur ce qu'il faut faire?; **financial uncertainties** incertitudes financières.

uncertainty principle *n* principe *m* d'incertitude OR d'indétermination de Heisenberg.

uncertified [,ʌn'sɜ:tɪfaɪd] *adj* [copy] non certifié; [doctor, teacher] non diplômé; **~ teacher** *Am* ≃ maître *m* auxiliaire.

unchain [,ʌn'tʃeɪn] *vt* [door, dog] enlever OR défaire les chaînes de, désenchaîner; [emotions] déchaîner.

unchallenged [,ʌn'tʃæləndʒd] ◇ *adj* -**1.** [authority, leader] incontesté, indiscuté; [version] non contesté; **his position/his authority remains ~** sa position/son autorité reste incontestée. -**2.** JUR [witness] non récusé; [evidence] non contesté. ◇ *adv* -**1.** [unquestioned] sans discussion, sans protestation; **her decisions always go ~** ses décisions ne sont jamais contestées OR discutées; **that remark cannot go ~** on ne peut pas laisser passer cette remarque sans protester. -**2.** [unchecked] sans rencontrer d'opposition; **he walked into the army base ~** il est entré dans la base militaire sans être interpellé OR sans rencontrer d'opposition.

unchangeable [,ʌn'tʃeɪndʒəbl] *adj* immuable, invariable.

unchanged [,ʌn'tʃeɪndʒd] *adj* inchangé.

unchanging [,ʌn'tʃeɪndʒɪŋ] *adj* invariable, immuable.

uncharacteristic ['ʌn,kærəktə'rɪstɪk] *adj* peu caractéristique, peu typique; **it's ~ of him** cela ne lui ressemble pas.

uncharacteristically ['ʌn,kærəktə'rɪstɪklɪ] *adv* d'une façon peu caractéristique.

uncharitable [,ʌn'tʃærɪtəbl] *adj* [unkind] peu charitable, peu indulgent.

uncharted [,ʌn'tʃɑ:tɪd] *adj* -**1.** [unmapped - region, forest, ocean] dont on n'a pas dressé la carte; [not on map] qui n'est pas sur la carte. -**2.** *fig*: **we're moving into ~ waters** nous faisons un saut dans l'inconnu; **we're sailing in ~ waters** nous ne savons pas où nous allons; **the ~ regions of the mind** les coins inexplorés de l'esprit.

unchaste [,ʌn'tʃeɪst] *adj lit* impudique, non chaste.

unchecked [,ʌn'tʃekt] ◇ *adj* -**1.** [unrestricted - growth, expansion, tendency] non maîtrisé; [anger, instinct] non réprimé, auquel on laisse libre cours. -**2.** [unverified - source, figures] non vérifié; [proofs] non relu. ◇ *adv* -**1.** [grow, expand] continuellement, sans arrêt; [continue] impunément, sans opposition; **such rudeness can't go ~** on ne peut pas laisser passer une telle impolitesse OR grossièreté; **the growth of industry continued ~** la croissance industrielle s'est poursuivie de façon constante. -**2.** [advance] sans rencontrer d'opposition.

unchivalrous [,ʌn'ʃɪvəlrəs] *adj* peu galant, discourtois.

unchristian [,ʌn'krɪstʃən] *adj* -**1.** RELIG peu chrétien. -**2.** *fig* barbare; **this is an ~ hour to phone someone!** on ne téléphone pas aux gens à des heures indues!

uncial ['ʌnsɪəl] ◇ *adj* oncial. ◇ *n* onciale *f*.

uncircumcised [,ʌn'sɜ:kəmsaɪzd] *adj* incirconcis.

uncivil [,ʌn'sɪvl] *adj* impoli, grossier; **to be ~ to sb** être impoli envers OR à l'égard de qqn.

uncivilized, -ised [,ʌn'sɪvɪlaɪzd] *adj* -**1.** [people, tribe] non civilisé. -**2.** [primitive, barbaric - behaviour, conditions] barbare; [- people] barbare, inculte. -**3.** *fig* [ridiculous] impossible, extraordinaire; **the plane arrives at the ~ hour of 4 a.m.** l'avion arrive à une heure indue, 4 h du matin.

unclad [,ʌn'klæd] *adj lit* sans vêtements, nu.

unclaimed [,ʌn'kleɪmd] *adj* [property, reward] non réclamé; [rights] non revendiqué.

unclasp [,ʌn'klɑ:sp] *vt* [hands] ouvrir; [bracelet] dégrafer, défaire; **he was continually clasping and ~ing his hands** il n'arrêtait pas de se tordre les mains nerveusement.

unclassified [,ʌn'klæsɪfaɪd] *adj* -**1.** [not sorted - books, papers] non classé. -**2.** *Br* [road] non classé. -**3.** [information] non secret.

uncle ['ʌŋkl] *n* -**1.** [relative] oncle *m*; **"hello Uncle"** «bonjour mon oncle», «bonjour tonton»; **Uncle Peter** l'oncle Peter, tonton Peter ❑ **to cry** OR **to say ~** *inf Am* s'avouer vaincu, se rendre; **'Uncle Tom's Cabin'** *Stowe* 'la Case de l'oncle Tom'; **'Uncle Vanya'** *Chekhov* 'Oncle Vania'. -**2.** *inf Br dated* [pawnbroker] prêteur *m* sur gages.

unclean [,ʌn'kli:n] *adj* -**1.** [dirty - water] sale; [- habits] sale. -**2.** RELIG impur.

unclear [,ʌn'klɪəʳ] *adj* -**1.** [confused, ambiguous - thinking, purpose, reason] pas clair, pas évident; **the instructions were ~** les instructions n'étaient pas claires; I'm still ~ about what exactly I have to do je ne sais pas encore très bien ce que je dois faire exactement. -**2.** [uncertain - future, outcome] incertain; it is now ~ whether the talks will take place or not nous ne savons pas bien pour le moment si la conférence va avoir lieu. -**3.** [indistinct - sound, speech] indistinct, inaudible; [- outline] flou.

unclench [ˌʌnˈklentʃ] *vt* [fist, teeth] desserrer.

Uncle Sam [-sæm] *pr n* Oncle Sam *(personnage représentant les États-Unis dans la propagande pour l'armée)*.

Uncle Tom▽ *n Am pej Noir qui se comporte de façon obséquieuse avec les Blancs.*

uncloak [ˌʌnˈkləʊk] *vt* [mystery] dévoiler.

unclog [ˌʌnˈklɒg] (*pt* & *pp* unclogged, *cont* unclogging) *vt* [drain] déboucher; [wheel] débloquer.

unclothed [ˌʌnˈkləʊðd] *adj* dévêtu, nu.

unclouded [ˌʌnˈklaʊdɪd] *adj* -**1.** [sky] dégagé, sans nuages; *fig* [thinking] limpide; [mind] clair; a future ~ by financial worries un avenir sans soucis financiers. -**2.** [liquid] clair, limpide.

uncluttered [ˌʌnˈklʌtəd] *adj* [room] dépouillé, simple; [style of writing] sobre; [design] dépouillé; [mind, thinking] clair, net; the room is spacious and ~ la pièce est spacieuse et simple; the diagram should be neat and ~ le diagramme devrait être net et concis.

uncoil [ˌʌnˈkɔɪl] ◇ *vt* dérouler.
◇ *vi* se dérouler.

uncombed [ʌnˈkəʊmd] *adj* [hair] mal peigné, ébouriffé; [wool] non peigné.

uncomfortable [ʌnˈkʌmftəbl] *adj* -**1.** [physically - chair, bed, clothes] inconfortable, peu confortable; [- position] inconfortable, peu commode; this chair is very ~ cette chaise n'est pas du tout confortable, on est très mal sur cette chaise; I feel most ~ perched on this stool je ne me sens pas du tout à l'aise perché sur ce tabouret. -**2.** *fig* [awkward, uneasy - person] mal à l'aise, gêné; [difficult, embarrassing - situation, truth] difficile, gênant; [unpleasant] désagréable; I feel ~ about the whole thing je me sens mal à l'aise avec tout ça; to make sb (feel) ~ mettre qqn mal à l'aise; I've an ~ feeling this isn't going to work je ne peux pas m'empêcher de penser que ça ne va pas marcher; to make life OR things (very) ~ for sb créer des ennuis à qqn.

uncomfortably [ʌnˈkʌmftəblɪ] *adv* -**1.** [lie, sit, stand] inconfortablement, peu confortablement; [dressed] mal, inconfortablement. -**2.** [unpleasantly - heavy, hot] désagréablement; the train was ~ crowded le train était désagréablement bondé; he came ~ close to discovering the truth il a été dangereusement près de découvrir la vérité. -**3.** [uneasily] avec gêne; he shifted ~ in his seat il bougeait avec embarras sur son siège.

uncommercial [ˌʌnkəˈmɜːʃl] *adj* peu commercial.

uncommitted [ˌʌnkəˈmɪtɪd] *adj* [person, literature] non engagé; he remains politically ~ il reste neutre politiquement; an ~ relationship une relation libre.

uncommon [ʌnˈkɒmən] *adj* -**1.** [rare, unusual - disease, species] rare, peu commun; it's not ~ for the heating to break down il n'est pas rare que le chauffage soit en panne. -**2.** *fml* [exceptional] singulier, extraordinaire; a child of ~ abilities un enfant aux dons singuliers.

uncommonly [ʌnˈkɒmənlɪ] *adv* -**1.** [rarely] rarement, inhabituellement. -**2.** *fig* [exceptionally - clever, cold, polite] singulièrement, exceptionnellement.

uncommunicative [ˌʌnkəˈmjuːnɪkətɪv] *adj* peu communicatif, taciturne; to be ~ about sthg se montrer réservé sur qqch.

uncomplaining [ˌʌnkəmˈpleɪnɪŋ] *adj* qui ne se plaint pas; he has a calm and ~ wife il a une femme calme et résignée.

uncomplainingly [ˌʌnkəmˈpleɪnɪŋlɪ] *adv* sans se plaindre.

uncompleted [ˌʌnkəmˈpliːtɪd] *adj* inachevé.

uncomplicated [ˌʌnˈkɒmplɪkeɪtɪd] *adj* peu compliqué, simple.

uncomplimentary [ˈʌnˌkɒmplɪˈmentərɪ] *adj* peu flatteur; he was very ~ about you ce qu'il a dit de vous était loin d'être flatteur.

uncomprehending [ˈʌnˌkɒmprɪˈhendɪŋ] *adj* qui ne comprend pas.

uncomprehendingly [ˈʌnˌkɒmprɪˈhendɪŋlɪ] *adv* sans comprendre.

uncompromising [ʌnˈkɒmprəmaɪzɪŋ] *adj* [rigid - attitude, behaviour] rigide, intransigeant, inflexible; [committed - person] convaincu, ardent.

uncompromisingly [ʌnˈkɒmprəmaɪzɪŋlɪ] *adv* sans concession, de manière intransigeante; ~ honest d'une honnêteté absolue.

unconcealed [ˌʌnkənˈsiːld] *adj* [joy, anger] évident, non dissimulé.

unconcern [ˌʌnkənˈsɜːn] *n* -**1.** [indifference] indifférence *f*; ~ for others/for danger indifférence envers les autres/au danger. -**2.** [calm] sang-froid *m inv*; she continued with apparent ~ elle poursuivit avec un sang-froid apparent.

unconcerned [ˌʌnkənˈsɜːnd] *adj* -**1.** [unworried, calm] qui ne s'inquiète pas, insouciant; he seemed quite ~ about the exam/her health il ne semblait pas du tout s'inquiéter de l'examen/de sa santé. -**2.** [uninterested] indifférent; she's ~ with political matters elle est indifférente aux questions politiques.

unconcernedly [ˌʌnkənˈsɜːnɪdlɪ] *adv* -**1.** [calmly] sans s'inquiéter, sans se laisser troubler. -**2.** [uninterestedly] avec indifférence OR insouciance.

unconditional [ˌʌnkənˈdɪʃənl] *adj* -**1.** [support, submission] inconditionnel, sans condition; ~ discharge JUR libération *f* inconditionnelle; ~ surrender reddition *f* inconditionnelle. -**2.** MATH [equality] sans conditions.

unconditionally [ˌʌnkənˈdɪʃnəlɪ] *adv* [accept, surrender] inconditionnellement, sans condition.

unconditioned [ˌʌnkənˈdɪʃənd] *adj* -**1.** PSYCH [reflex] inconditionnel; ~ response réponse *f* inconditionnelle; ~ stimulus stimulus *m* inconditionnel. -**2.** PHILOS absolu, inconditionné.

unconfined [ˌʌnkənˈfaɪnd] *adj lit* illimité, sans bornes; let joy be ~ que la joie éclate.

unconfirmed [ˌʌnkənˈfɜːmd] *adj* [report, booking] non confirmé.

uncongenial [ˌʌnkənˈdʒiːnjəl] *adj* [surroundings] peu agréable; [personality] antipathique.

unconnected [ˌʌnkəˈnektɪd] *adj* [unrelated - facts, incidents] sans rapport; [- ideas, thoughts] sans suite, décousu; the riot was ~ with food prices l'émeute n'avait pas de rapport OR était sans rapport avec les prix alimentaires; the two incidents are not ~ les deux incidents ne sont pas sans lien.

unconquerable [ʌnˈkɒŋkərəbl] *adj* [opponent, peak] invincible; [obstacle, problem] insurmontable; [instinct, will] irrépressible.

unconquered [ʌnˈkɒŋkəd] *adj* [nation, territory] qui n'a pas été conquis; [mountain] invaincu.

unconscionable [ʌnˈkɒnʃənəbl] *adj fml* -**1.** [liar] sans scrupules. -**2.** [demand] déraisonnable; [time] extraordinaire.

unconscionably [ʌnˈkɒnʃənəblɪ] *adv fml* -**1.** [shamelessly] sans vergogne OR scrupules. -**2.** [excessively] excessivement, démesurément.

unconscious [ʌnˈkɒnʃəs] ◇ *adj* -**1.** [in coma] sans connaissance; to knock sb ~ assommer qqn; he lay ~ for 5 days il est resté sans connaissance pendant 5 jours ‖ [in faint] évanoui; she remained ~ for some minutes elle est restée évanouie pendant quelques minutes. -**2.** [unaware] inconscient; she seemed ~ of all the noise around her elle semblait ne pas avoir conscience de tout le bruit autour d'elle; they are ~ of the fact ils ne sont pas conscients du fait. -**3.** [unintentional] inconscient, involontaire; it was an ~ pun c'était un jeu de mots involontaire; there was an ~ bias in his selection of candidates il y avait un parti pris involontaire dans sa sélection des candidats. -**4.** PSYCH [motives] inconscient; the ~ mind l'inconscient *m*.
◇ *n* [gen & PSYCH] inconscient *m*; the ~ l'inconscient.

unconsciously [ʌnˈkɒnʃəslɪ] *adv* inconsciemment, sans s'en rendre compte; I think, ~, she resents me je crois qu'inconsciemment, elle ne m'apprécie pas.

unconsciousness [ʌnˈkɒnʃəsnɪs] *n (U)* -**1.** MED [coma] perte *f* de connaissance; [fainting] évanouissement *m*; in a state of ~ sans connaissance. -**2.** [lack of awareness] inconscience *f*.

unconsecrated [ˌʌnˈkɒnsɪkreɪtɪd] *adj* non consacré.

unconsidered [ˌʌnkənˈsɪdəd] *adj* -**1.** [thought, action] irréfléchi. -**2.** *fml* [object] sans importance.

unconstitutional [ˈʌnˌkɒnstɪˈtjuːʃənl] *adj* inconstitutionnel.

unconstrained [ˌʌnkənˈstreɪnd] *adj* [feelings] sans contrainte, non contraint; [action] spontané; [manner] aisé; he is ~ by inhibitions les inhibitions ne l'arrêtent pas.

unconsummated [ˌʌnˈkɒnsəmeɪtɪd] *adj* [marriage] non consommé.

uncontested [ˌʌnkənˈtestɪd] *adj* [position, authority] non disputé, incontesté; the seat was ~ POL il n'y avait qu'un candidat pour le siège.

uncontrollable [ˌʌnkənˈtrəʊləbl] *adj* -**1.** [irrepressible - fear, desire, urge] irrésistible, irrépressible; [- stammer] que l'on ne peut maîtriser OR contrôler; to be seized by ~ laughter/anger être pris d'un fou rire/d'un accès de colère. -**2.** [animal] indomptable; [child] impossible à discipliner. -**3.** [growth, inflation] qui ne peut être freiné, galopant.

uncontrollably [ˌʌnkənˈtrəʊləblɪ] *adv* -**1.** [helplessly] irrésistiblement; he was laughing ~ il avait le fou rire; I shook ~ je tremblais sans pouvoir m'arrêter. -**2.** [out of control]: the boat rocked ~ on n'arrivait pas à maîtriser le tangage du bateau. -**3.** [fall, increase] irrésistiblement; prices are rising ~ les prix augmentent irrésistiblement.

uncontrolled [ˌʌnkənˈtrəʊld] *adj* -**1.** [unrestricted - fall, rise] effréné, incontrôlé; [- population growth] non contrôlé; inflation cannot remain ~ l'inflation ne peut demeurer incontrôlée; scenes of ~ violence des scènes de violence incontrôlée OR d'une extrême violence. -**2.** [unverified - experiment] non contrôlé.

uncontroversial [ˈʌnˌkɒntrəˈvɜːʃl] *adj* qui ne prête pas à controverse, incontestable.

unconventional [ˌʌnkənˈvenʃənl] *adj* non conformiste.

unconventionally [ˌʌnkənˈvenʃnəlɪ] *adv* [live, think] d'une manière originale OR peu conventionnelle; [dress] d'une manière originale.

unconvinced [ˌʌnkənˈvɪnst] *adj* incrédule, sceptique; I'm ~ je ne suis pas convaincu, je reste sceptique; to be/to remain ~ by sthg être/rester sceptique à l'égard de qqch.

unconvincing [ˌʌnkənˈvɪnsɪŋ] *adj* peu convaincant.

unconvincingly [ˌʌnkənˈvɪnsɪŋlɪ] *adv* [argue, lie] d'un ton OR d'une manière peu convaincante, peu vraisemblablement.

uncooked [ʌnˈkʊkt] *adj* non cuit, cru.

uncool *inf* [ʌnˈkuːl] *adj* -**1.** [unrelaxed] pas cool. -**2.** *dated* pas branché.

uncooperative [ˌʌnkəʊˈɒpərətɪv] *adj* peu coopératif.

uncoordinated [ˌʌnkəʊˈɔːdɪneɪtɪd] *adj* -**1.** [movements] mal coordonné; her hand and eye movements are ~ les mouvements de ses yeux et de ses mains ne sont pas coordonnés. -**2.** [clumsy] maladroit. -**3.** [unorganized - efforts] qui manque de coordination, mal organisé.

uncork [ˌʌnˈkɔːk] *vt* [bottle] déboucher; *fig* [emotions] déchaîner.

uncorroborated [ˌʌnkəˈrɒbəreɪtɪd] *adj* non corroboré.

uncountable [ˌʌnˈkaʊntəbl] *adj* -**1.** [numberless] incalculable, innombrable. -**2.** GRAMM non dénombrable; ~ **noun** nom *m* non dénombrable.

uncouple [ˌʌnˈkʌpl] *vt* [engine] découpler; [carriage] dételer; [cart, trailer] détacher.

uncouth [ʌnˈkuːθ] *adj* [language, manners, person] grossier, fruste.

uncover [ʌnˈkʌvəʳ] *vt* découvrir.

uncovered [ʌnˈkʌvəd] *adj* -**1.** *literal* découvert; **food should not be left** ~ la nourriture ne doit pas rester à l'air. -**2.** FIN sans couverture.

uncritical [ˌʌnˈkrɪtɪkl] *adj* [naïve] dépourvu d'esprit critique, non critique; [unquestioning] inconditionnel.

uncross [ˌʌnˈkrɒs] *vt* décroiser.

uncrossed [ˌʌnˈkrɒst] *adj* -**1.** [cheque] non barré. -**2.** [legs] décroisé.

uncrowded [ˌʌnˈkraʊdɪd] *adj* où il n'y a pas beaucoup de monde; **long,** ~ **beaches** de longues plages presque désertes.

uncrowned [ˌʌnˈkraʊnd] *adj* sans couronne, non couronné; **the** ~ **king of rock and roll** le roi sans couronne du rock'n'roll.

unction [ˈʌŋkʃn] *n* onction *f.*

unctuous [ˈʌŋktjʊəs] *adj fml* mielleux, onctueux.

unctuously [ˈʌŋktjʊəslɪ] *adv fml* mielleusement, onctueusement.

unctuousness [ˈʌŋktjʊəsnɪs] *n (U) fml* manières *fpl* onctueuses.

uncultivated [ˌʌnˈkʌltɪveɪtɪd] *adj* -**1.** [land] inculte, en friche. -**2.** = **uncultured**.

uncultured [ˌʌnˈkʌltʃəd] *adj* [manners, person] inculte; [accent, speech] qui manque de raffinement.

uncurl [ˌʌnˈkɜːl] ◇ *vt* [rope] dérouler; [body, toes] étirer.
◇ *vi* [leaf] s'ouvrir.

uncut [ˌʌnˈkʌt] *adj* -**1.** [hair, nails] non coupé; [hedge, stone] non taillé; [diamond] non taillé, brut; [corn, wheat] non récolté, sur pied; [pages] non rogné. -**2.** [uncensored - film, text] intégral, sans coupures.

undamaged [ˌʌnˈdæmɪdʒd] *adj* -**1.** [car, contents, merchandise, building, roof] indemne, intact, non endommagé. -**2.** *fig* [reputation] intact.

undamped [ˌʌnˈdæmpt] *adj* -**1.** [enthusiasm, feelings] intact, non affaibli. -**2.** [piano string] non étouffé. -**3.** RADIO [oscillation] non amorti, entretenu.

undated [ˌʌnˈdeɪtɪd] *adj* non daté, sans date.

undaunted [ˌʌnˈdɔːntɪd] *adj* -**1.** [not discouraged] qui ne se laisse pas décourager OR démonter; **she was** ~ **by their criticism** leurs critiques ne la décourageaient pas; **he carried on** ~ il a continué sans se laisser décourager. -**2.** [fearless] sans peur.

undecagon [ˌʌnˈdekəgən] *n* hendécagone *m.*

undeceive [ˌʌndɪˈsiːv] *vt lit* détromper.

undecided [ˌʌndɪˈsaɪdɪd] *adj* [person, issue] indécis; [outcome] incertain; **he is** ~ **whether to stay or go** il n'a pas décidé s'il restera ou s'il partira; **the matter is still** ~ la question n'a pas encore été résolue.

undecipherable [ˌʌndɪˈsaɪfərəbl] *adj* [writing] indéchiffrable, illisible; [code] indéchiffrable.

undeclared [ˌʌndɪˈkleəd] *adj* [goods] non déclaré; [love] non avoué.

undefeated [ˌʌndɪˈfiːtɪd] *adj* invaincu.

undefended [ˌʌndɪˈfendɪd] *adj* -**1.** MIL [fort, town] sans défense. -**2.** JUR [lawsuit] où on ne présente pas de défense.

undefinable [ˌʌndɪˈfaɪnəbl] *adj* indéfinissable, impossible à définir.

undelivered [ˌʌndɪˈlɪvəd] *adj* [letter] non remis, non distribué; **if** ~ **please return to sender** en cas de non-distribution, prière de retourner à l'expéditeur.

undemanding [ˌʌndɪˈmɑːndɪŋ] *adj* [person] facile à vivre, qui n'est pas exigeant; [work] simple, qui n'est pas astreignant.

undemocratic [ˈʌnˌdeməʊˈkrætɪk] *adj* antidémocratique, peu démocratique.

undemonstrative [ˌʌndɪˈmɒnstrətɪv] *adj* réservé, peu démonstratif.

undeniable [ˌʌndɪˈnaɪəbl] *adj* indéniable, incontestable.

undeniably [ˌʌndɪˈnaɪəblɪ] *adv* [true] incontestablement, indiscutablement; **he's** ~ **a very clever man** c'est incontestablement un homme très intelligent.

undenominational [ˈʌndɪˌnɒmɪˈneɪʃənl] *adj* non confessionnel.

under [ˈʌndəʳ] ◇ *prep* -**1.** [beneath, below] sous; **the newspaper was** ~ **the chair/cushion** le journal était sous la chaise/le coussin; **the pantry is** ~ **the stairs** le garde-manger est sous l'escalier; **I can't see anything** ~ **it** je ne vois rien (en-) dessous; **there is a coat of paint** ~ **the wallpaper** il y a une couche de peinture sous le papier peint; **the body was lying** ~ **a sheet** le cadavre était étendu sous un drap; **he wore a white shirt** ~ **his jacket** il portait une chemise blanche sous sa veste; **he pulled a wallet from** ~ **his jersey** il a sorti un portefeuille de sous son pull; **he was carrying a paper** ~ **his arm** il portait un journal sous le bras; **hold your hand** ~ **the tap** mettez votre main sous le robinet; **stand** ~ **my umbrella** mettez-vous sous mon parapluie; **we took shelter** ~ **a tree** nous nous sommes abrités sous un arbre; **to be born** ~ **Aries/Leo** être né sous le signe du Bélier/du Lion; **it can only be seen** ~ **a microscope** on ne peut le voir qu'au microscope ‖ [with verbs of movement] : **we had to crawl** ~ **the barbed wire** on a dû passer sous les barbelés en rampant; **the tunnel ran** ~ **the sea** le tunnel passait sous la mer; **she was swimming** ~ **water/**~ **the bridge** elle nageait sous l'eau/sous le pont; **it's unlucky to walk** ~ **a ladder** ça porte malheur de passer sous une échelle. -**2.** [less than] moins de, au-dessous de; ~ **£7,000** moins de 7 000 livres; **everything is** ~ **£5** tout est à moins de 5 livres; **is she** ~ **16?** est-ce qu'elle a moins de 16 ans? -**3.** [weighed down by] sous le poids de; **he staggered** ~ **his heavy load** il chancelait sous le poids de son lourd chargement; **to sink** ~ **the weight of one's debts** *fig* sombrer sous le poids de ses dettes. -**4.** [indicating conditions or circumstances] sous, dans; **we had to work** ~ **appalling conditions** on a dû travailler dans des conditions épouvantables; **she was murdered** ~ **strange circumstances** elle a été tuée dans d'étranges circonstances ‖ [subject to] sous; ~ **duress/threat** sous la contrainte/la menace ‖ MED sous; ~ **sedation/treatment** sous calmants/traitement. -**5.** [directed, governed by] sous (la direction de); **he studied** ~ **Fox** il a été l'élève de Fox; **she has two assistants** ~ **her** elle a deux assistants sous ses ordres; **the Bristol Chamber Orchestra** ~ **Martin Davenport** MUS l'orchestre de (musique de) chambre de Bristol sous la direction de Martin Davenport; **I served** ~ **General White** j'ai servi sous le général White; **the book describes Uganda** ~ **Amin** le livre décrit l'Ouganda sous (le régime d') Amin Dada; ~ **her management, the firm prospered** sous sa direction, l'entreprise prospérait; ~ **fascism, many groups were outlawed** sous le régime fasciste, de nombreux groupes furent interdits. -**6.** [according to] conformément à, en vertu de, selon; ~ **the new law, all this will change** avec la nouvelle loi, tout ceci va changer; ~ **the new law, elections will be held every four years** en vertu de OR selon la nouvelle loi, les élections auront lieu tous les quatre ans; ~ **the Emergency Powers Act** conformément à la loi instituant l'état d'urgence; ~ **this system, the President has little real power** dans ce système, le Président a peu de pouvoir véritable; ~ **(the terms of) his will/the agreement** selon (les termes de) son testament/l'accord. -**7.** [in the process of] en cours de; ~ **construction** en cours de construction; **the matter is** ~ **consideration/discussion** on est en train d'étudier/de discuter la question. -**8.** AGR: **fields** ~ **cultivation** des terres cultivées; ~ **wheat/barley** en blé/orge. -**9.** [in classification]: **you'll find the book** ~ **philosophy** vous trouverez le livre sous la rubrique philosophie; **you'll find my number** ~ **Magee** vous trouverez mon numéro sous Magee; **she writes** ~ **the name of Heidi Croft** elle écrit sous le nom de Heidi Croft; **few singers perform** ~ **their own name** peu de chanteurs gardent leur vrai nom.
◇ *adv* -**1.** *(with verbs)* [below ground, water, door etc] : **to slide** OR **to slip** ~ se glisser dessous; **to pass** ~ passer dessous; **to stay** ~ [under water] rester sous l'eau ❑ **to be six feet** ~ *inf* être à six pieds sous terre. -**2.** MED [anaesthetized] sous l'effet de l'anesthésie. -**3.** [less - in age, price]: **you have to be 16 or** ~ **to enter** il faut avoir 16 ans ou moins pour se présenter; **items at £20 and** ~ des articles à 20 livres et au-dessous.

under- *in cpds* -**1.** [below] sous-; **holidays for the** ~**30s** vacances pour les moins de 30 ans. -**2.** [junior] sous-; ~**gardener** sous-jardinier *m.*

under-18 *n (usu pl)* personne *f* de moins de 18 ans, mineur *m,* -e *f.*

underachieve [ˌʌndərəˈtʃiːv] *vi* ne pas obtenir les résultats attendus; **he constantly** ~**s** il n'obtient jamais les résultats dont il est capable.

underachiever [ˌʌndərəˈtʃiːvəʳ] *n* [gen] personne *f* qui n'obtient pas les résultats escomptés; *Am* SCH élève *mf* médiocre; **he's always been an** ~ il a toujours été en deçà de ses possibilités.

underage [ˌʌndərˈeɪdʒ] *adj* [person] mineur; ~ **drinking** consommation *f* d'alcool par les mineurs; ~ **sex** rapports *mpl* sexuels entre mineurs.

underarm [ˈʌndərɑːm] ◇ *adv* SPORT [bowl, hit] (par) en dessous.
◇ *adj* [deodorant] pour les aisselles; [hair] sous les bras OR les aisselles; SPORT [bowling, throw] par en dessous.

underbelly [ˈʌndəˌbelɪ] (*pl* **underbellies**) *n* -**1.** *literal* bas-ventre *m.* -**2.** *fig* point *m* faible; **the soft** ~ **of society** le point faible de la société.

underbid [ˌʌndəˈbɪd] (*pt* & *pp* **underbid,** *cont* **underbidding**) *vi* [in bridge] annoncer au-dessous de sa force; [in auction] ne pas offrir assez, faire une enchère insuffisamment élevée.

underblanket [ˈʌndəˌblæŋkɪt] *n* alaise *f.*

underbody [ˈʌndəˌbɒdɪ] *n* AUT dessous *m* de caisse.

underbrush [ˈʌndəbrʌʃ] *n (U) Am* sous-bois *m,* broussailles *fpl.*

undercapitalized, -ised [ˌʌndəˈkæpɪtəlaɪzd] *adj* [entrepreneur, company] qui n'a pas OR ne dispose pas de fonds suffisants.

undercarriage [ˈʌndəˌkærɪdʒ] *n* [of aeroplane] train *m* d'atterrissage; [of vehicle] châssis *m;* **to get the** ~ **down** sortir le train d'atterrissage.

undercharge [ˌʌndəˈtʃɑːdʒ] *vt* -**1.** [customer] faire payer insuffisamment OR moins cher à; **I was** ~**d** on m'a fait payer moins cher, on ne m'a pas fait payer le prix indiqué; **she** ~**d him by £6** elle lui a fait payer 6 livres de moins que le prix. -**2.** [gun] charger insuffisamment.

underclothes [ˈʌndəkləʊðz] *npl* sous-vêtements *mpl;* [for women] lingerie *f,* dessous *mpl.*

underclothing [ˈʌndəˌkləʊðɪŋ] *n (U)* = **underclothes**.

undercoat [ˈʌndəkəʊt] *n* [of paint] sous-couche *f;* [of anti-rust] couche *f* d'antirouille.

undercook [ˌʌndəˈkʊk] *vt* ne pas assez cuire; **the potatoes were** ~**ed** les pommes de terre n'étaient pas assez cuites OR n'avaient pas cuit assez longtemps.

undercover [ˈʌndəˌkʌvəʳ] *adj* [methods, work] secret, clandestin; ~ **agent** agent *m* secret.

undercurrent [ˈʌndəˌkʌrənt] *n* -**1.** [in sea] courant *m* sous-marin; [in river] courant *m.* -**2.** *fig* [feeling] sentiment *m* sous-jacent; **there was an** ~ **of hostility throughout the discussion** il y eut une hostilité sous-jacente tout au long de la discussion.

undercut [ˌʌndəˈkʌt] (*pt* & *pp* undercut, *cont* undercutting) ◇ *vt* -**1.** COMM [competitor] vendre moins cher que; [prices] casser. -**2.** [undermine - efforts, principle] amoindrir. -**3.** SPORT [ball] lifter.
◇ *n* -**1.** SPORT lift *m*. -**2.** CULIN [meat] (morceau *m* de) filet *m*.

underdeveloped [ˌʌndədɪˈveləpt] *adj* -**1.** [country, society] en voie de développement. -**2.** [stunted - foetus, plant] qui n'est pas complètement développé OR formé. -**3.** *fig* [argument, idea] insuffisamment développé OR exposé. -**4.** PHOT [film, print] insuffisamment développé.

underdo [ˌʌndəˈduː] (*pt* & *pp* underdone [-ˈdʌn]) *vt* [food] faire cuire insuffisamment.

underdog [ˈʌndədɒg] *n*: the ~ [in fight, contest] celui *m*, celle *f* qui risque de perdre OR qui part perdant; [in society] laissé-pour-compte *m*, laissée-pour-compte *f*, opprimé *m*, -e *f*.

underdone [ˌʌndəˈdʌn] *adj* [accidentally] pas assez cuit; [deliberately - meat] saignant; [- vegetable, cake] pas trop cuit.

underdressed [ˌʌndəˈdrest] *adj* [lightly clad] trop légèrement vêtu; [informally dressed] habillé trop sport; **I feel positively ~ in these jeans** avec ce jean, je me trouve très mal habillé pour la circonstance.

underemployed [ˌʌndərɪmˈplɔɪd] *adj* [worker, equipment] sous-employé; [resources] sous-exploité; **he feels ~** il trouve qu'il n'a pas assez de travail.

underemployment [ˌʌndərɪmˈplɔɪmənt] *n* [of workers] sous-emploi *m*; [of resources] sous-exploitation *f*.

underestimate [*vb* ˌʌndərˈestɪmeɪt, *n* ˌʌndərˈestɪmət] ◇ *vt* [size, strength] sous-estimer; [person, value] sous-estimer, mésestimer.
◇ *n* sous-estimation *f*.

underestimation [ˈʌndərˌestɪˈmeɪʃn] *n* sous-estimation *f*.

underexpose [ˌʌndərɪkˈspəʊz] *vt* -**1.** PHOT [print, film] sous-exposer. -**2.** [person] faire insuffisamment la publicité de.

underexposure [ˌʌndərɪkˈspəʊʒəʳ] *n* -**1.** PHOT [lack of exposure] sous-exposition *f*; [photo, print] photo *f* sous-exposée. -**2.** [to publicity] manque *m* de publicité; **the campaign suffered from ~ in the media** la campagne a souffert d'un manque de publicité dans les médias ‖ [social]: **~ to other children may inhibit development** le manque de contact avec d'autres enfants freine le développement.

underfed [ˌʌndəˈfed] ◇ *pt* & *pp* → **underfeed**.
◇ *adj* [person] sous-alimenté.

underfeed [ˌʌndəˈfiːd] (*pt* & *pp* underfed [-ˈfed]) *vt* sous-alimenter.

underfelt [ˈʌndəfelt] *n* thibaude *f*.

underfinanced [ˌʌndəˈfaɪnænst] *adj* [business, scheme, school] qui manque de fonds.

underfloor [ˈʌndəflɔːʳ] *adj* [pipes, wiring] qui se trouve sous le plancher; **~ heating** chauffage *m* par le sol.

underflow [ˈʌndəfləʊ] *n* -**1.** [current - in sea] courant *m* sous-marin. -**2.** COMPUT dépassement *m* par valeurs inférieures.

underfoot [ˌʌndəˈfʊt] *adv* sous les pieds; **the grass is wet ~** l'herbe est humide; **I felt the gravel crunch ~** j'ai senti les graviers crisser sous mes pieds; **to trample sb/sthg ~** *literal* & *fig* [person] fouler qqn/qqch aux pieds; [animal] piétiner qqn/qqch.

undergarment [ˈʌndəˌgɑːmənt] *n* sous-vêtement *m*.

underglaze [ˈʌndəgleɪz] *n* sous-couche *f*.

undergo [ˌʌndəˈgəʊ] (*pt* underwent [-ˈwent], *pp* undergone [-ˈgɒn]) *vt* -**1.** [experience - change] subir; [- hardship] subir, éprouver. -**2.** [test, trials] subir, passer; [training] suivre. -**3.** [be subject to] subir; **the building/the system is ~ing modernization** l'immeuble/le système est en cours de modernisation. -**4.** MED: **to ~ an operation** subir une intervention chirurgicale; **to ~ treatment** suivre un traitement.

undergrad *inf* [ˈʌndəgræd] *n* étudiant *m*, -e *f* *(qui prépare une licence)*.

undergraduate [ˌʌndəˈgrædʒʊət] ◇ *n* étudiant *m*, -e *f (qui prépare une licence)*; **she was an ~ at Manchester** elle était en licence à Manchester; **~ student** étudiant *m*, -e *f* en licence.
◇ *adj* [circles, life] estudiantin, étudiant; [course] pour les étudiants de licence; [accommodation, grant] pour étudiants; [humour] d'étudiant.

underground [*adj* & *n* ˈʌndəgraʊnd, *adv* ˌʌndəˈgraʊnd] ◇ *adj* -**1.** [subterranean - explosion] souterrain; [- car park] en sous-sol, souterrain; **~ railway** métro *m*. -**2.** [secret] secret, clandestin; **they joined an ~ movement** [clandestine] ils sont entrés dans un mouvement clandestin; [resistance] ils sont entrés dans un mouvement de résistance; **the ~ press** la presse clandestine; **the Underground Railroad** HIST *réseau clandestin qui permettait aux fugitifs noirs des États esclavagistes de rejoindre le nord des États-Unis ou le Canada*. -**3.** [unofficial - literature, theatre] d'avant-garde, underground *(inv)*; [- institutions] parallèle. -**4.** [illegal - methods] illégal.
◇ *n* -**1.** MIL & POL [resistance] résistance *f*; [secret army] armée *f* secrète. -**2.** ART, MUS & THEAT avant-garde *f*, underground *m inv*. -**3.** *Br* [railway] métro *m*; **to go by ~** aller en métro.
◇ *adv* -**1.** [below surface] sous (la) terre. -**2.** [in hiding]: **to go ~** passer dans la clandestinité, prendre le maquis.

undergrowth [ˈʌndəgrəʊθ] *n (U)* sous-bois *m*; [scrub] broussailles *fpl*.

underhand [ˌʌndəˈhænd] ◇ *adj* -**1.** [action] en dessous, en sous-main; [person] sournois; **in an ~ way** sournoisement. -**2.** SPORT par en dessous.
◇ *adv* sournoisement.

underhanded [ˌʌndəˈhændɪd] *adj* -**1.** = **underhand**. -**2.** [shorthanded] qui manque de personnel.

underhandedly [ˌʌndəˈhændɪdlɪ] *adv* en dessous, sournoisement.

underhung [ˌʌndəˈhʌŋ] *adj* -**1.** [jaw] prognathe, saillant. -**2.** [door] à coulisse.

underinsure [ˌʌndərɪnˈʃɔːʳ] *vt* sous-assurer.

underinvestment [ˌʌndərɪnˈvestmənt] *n* insuffisance *f* d'investissement.

underlain [ˌʌndəˈleɪn] *pp* → **underlie**.

underlay [*vb* ˌʌndəˈleɪ, *n* ˈʌndəleɪ] (*pt* & *pp* underlaid [-ˈleɪd]) ◇ *pt* → **underlie**.
◇ *vt* [carpet] doubler.
◇ *n* [felt] thibaude *f*; [foam] doublure *f*.

underlie [ˌʌndəˈlaɪ] (*pt* underlay [-ˈleɪ], *pp* underlain [-ˈleɪn]) *vt* sous-tendre, être à la base de.

underline [ˌʌndəˈlaɪn] *vt literal* & *fig* souligner.

underling [ˈʌndəlɪŋ] *n pej* subalterne *mf*, sous-fifre *m*.

underlining [ˌʌndəˈlaɪnɪŋ] *n* soulignage *m*, soulignement *m*.

underlying [ˌʌndəˈlaɪɪŋ] *adj* sous-jacent.

undermanned [ˌʌndəˈmænd] *adj* à court de personnel; NAUT à équipage incomplet.

undermentioned [ˌʌndəˈmenʃnd] *adj fml* & ADMIN ci-dessous (mentionné).

undermine [ˌʌndəˈmaɪn] *vt* [cliff] miner, saper; [authority, person] saper; [health] user; [confidence] ébranler.

undermost [ˈʌndəməʊst] ◇ *adj* [in heap] le dernier, le plus bas; [in depth] le plus profond OR bas.
◇ *adv* tout en bas.

undernamed [ˌʌndəˈneɪmd] (*pl inv*) ◇ *n* personne *f* nommée ci-dessous OR dont le nom suit.
◇ *adj* nommé ci-dessous.

underneath [ˌʌndəˈniːθ] ◇ *prep* sous, au-dessous de, en dessous de; **the cat slipped ~ the fence** le chat s'est glissé OR est passé sous OR par-dessous le grillage; **she was wearing two pullovers ~ her coat** elle portait deux pullovers sous son manteau; **the noise was coming from ~ the floorboards** le bruit venait de sous le plancher.
◇ *adv* -**1.** [in space] (en) dessous, au-dessous; **I've got a pullover on ~** j'ai un pull dessous. -**2.** [within oneself]: **he smiled, but ~ he felt afraid/helpless** il a souri, mais dans le fond il avait peur/il se sentait impuissant.
◇ *n* dessous *m*; **what's written on the ~?** qu'est-ce qui est écrit sur le dessous?
◇ *adj* de dessous, d'en dessous.

undernourished [ˌʌndəˈnʌrɪʃt] *adj* sous-alimenté.

undernourishment [ˌʌndəˈnʌrɪʃmənt] *n* sous-alimentation *f*.

underpaid [*adj* ˈʌndəpeɪd, *pt* & *pp* ˌʌndəˈpeɪd] ◇ *adj* sous-payé.
◇ *pt* & *pp* → **underpay**.

underpants [ˈʌndəpænts] *npl* -**1.** [for men] slip *m (d'homme)*; **a pair of ~** un caleçon. -**2.** *Am* [for women] culotte *f*.

underpart [ˈʌndəpɑːt] *n* ZOOL [underside] dessous *m*, partie *f* inférieure.
◆ **underparts** *npl* [abdomen] ventre *m*.

underpass [ˈʌndəpɑːs] *n* -**1.** [subway] passage *m* souterrain. -**2.** [road] route *f* inférieure.

underpay [ˌʌndəˈpeɪ] (*pt* & *pp* underpaid [-ˈpeɪd]) *vt* sous-payer.

underperform [ˌʌndəpəˈfɔːm] *vi* rester en deçà de ses possibilités.

underpin [ˌʌndəˈpɪn] (*pt* & *pp* underpinned, *cont* underpinning) *vt literal* & *fig* soutenir, étayer.

underpinning [ˌʌndəˈpɪnɪŋ] *n* soutien *m*, étayage *m*.

underplay [ˌʌndəˈpleɪ] ◇ *vt* -**1.** [minimize - importance] minimiser; [- event] réduire OR minimiser l'importance de; **to ~ one's hand** [in cards] jouer volontairement une petite carte; *fig* cacher son jeu. -**2.** THEAT [role] jouer avec retenue.
◇ *vi* [in cards] jouer volontairement une petite carte.

underpopulated [ˌʌndəˈpɒpjʊleɪtɪd] *adj* sous-peuplé.

underpowered [ˌʌndəˈpaʊəd] *adj* qui manque de puissance; **an ~ performance** *fig* un jeu qui manque de puissance.

underprice [ˌʌndəˈpraɪs] *vt* -**1.** [for sale] vendre au-dessous de sa valeur. -**2.** [for estimate] sous-évaluer.

underprivileged [ˌʌndəˈprɪvɪlɪdʒd] ◇ *adj* [person, social class] défavorisé, déshérité.
◇ *npl*: **the ~** les économiquement faibles *mpl*.

underproduce [ˌʌndəprəˈdjuːs] ◇ *vt* produire insuffisamment de.
◇ *vi* produire insuffisamment.

underproduction [ˌʌndəprəˈdʌkʃn] *n* sous-production *f*.

underquote [ˌʌndəˈkwəʊt] *vt* -**1.** [goods, securities, services] *proposer à un prix inférieur à celui du marché*. -**2.** [competitor] vendre moins cher que.

underrate [ˌʌndəˈreɪt] *vt* sous-estimer.

underrehearsed [ˌʌndərɪˈhɜːst] *adj* MUS & THEAT insuffisamment répété.

underripe [ˌʌndəˈraɪp] *adj* pas mûr.

underscore [ˌʌndəˈskɔːʳ] ◇ *vt* souligner.
◇ *n* soulignage *m*, soulignement *m*.

undersea [ˈʌndəsiː] ◇ *adj* sous-marin.
◇ *adv* sous la mer.

underseal [ˈʌndəsiːl] *Br* AUT ◇ *n* -**1.** [product] produit *m* antirouille. -**2.** [act, result] couche *f* antirouille.
◇ *vt* faire un traitement antirouille.

underseas [ˌʌndəˈsiːz] = **undersea** *adv*.

undersecretary [ˌʌndəˈsekrətərɪ] (*pl* undersecretaries) *n* POL -**1.** *Br* [in department] chef *m* de cabinet. -**2.** [politician] sous-secrétaire *m*; **~ of state** sous-secrétaire d'État.

undersell [ˌʌndəˈsel] (*pt* & *pp* undersold [-ˈsəʊld]) ◇ *vt* [competitor] vendre moins cher que; [goods] vendre au rabais; **to ~ o.s.** *fig* se sous-estimer.
◇ *vi* [goods] se vendre mal.

undersexed [ˌʌndəˈsekst] *adj* qui manque de libido.
undershirt [ˈʌndəʃɜːt] *n Am* maillot *m* OR tricot *m* de corps.
undershoot [ˌʌndəˈʃuːt] (*pt* & *pp* undershot [ˈʃɒt]) *vt*: the plane undershot the runway l'avion s'est posé avant d'atteindre la piste d'atterrissage; he undershot the target son coup n'a pas atteint la cible.
undershorts [ˈʌndəʃɔːts] *npl Am* caleçon *m*, slip *m*.
undershot [ˌʌndəˈʃɒt] ◇ *pt* & *pp* → **undershoot**.
◇ *adj* -**1.** [jaw] proéminent, saillant. -**2.** [waterwheel] à aubes.
underside [ˈʌndəsaɪd] *n*: the ~ le dessous, la face inférieure.
undersigned [ˈʌndəsaɪnd] (*pl inv*) *fml* ◇ *n*: the ~ le soussigné, la soussignée; I, the ~ je soussigné.
◇ *adj* soussigné.
undersize(d) [ˌʌndəˈsaɪz(d)] *adj* trop petit.
underskirt [ˈʌndəskɜːt] *n* jupon *m*.
underslung [ˌʌndəˈslʌŋ] *adj* très bas; AUT surbaissé.
undersoil [ˈʌndəsɔɪl] *n* sous-sol *m* AGR.
understaffed [ˌʌndəˈstɑːft] *adj* qui manque de personnel.
understand [ˌʌndəˈstænd] (*pt* & *pp* understood [-ˈstʊd]) ◇ *vt* -**1.** [meaning] comprendre; I ~ what you mean je comprends ce que vous voulez dire; is that understood? est-ce compris?; to make o.s. understood se faire comprendre; do I make myself understood? [as threat] est-ce que je me suis bien fait comprendre?; she didn't ~ a single word elle n'a pas compris un traître mot; I can't ~ it! je ne comprends pas!, cela me dépasse! -**2.** [subject, theory] comprendre, entendre; I don't ~ a thing about economics je ne comprends rien à l'économie. -**3.** [character, person] comprendre; he claims his wife doesn't ~ him il affirme que sa femme ne le comprend pas; I ~ your need to be independent je comprends bien que vous ayez besoin d'être indépendant; we ~ each other perfectly nous nous comprenons parfaitement; she didn't ~ why no one was interested elle ne comprenait pas pourquoi personne n'était intéressé. -**4.** [believe] comprendre, croire; I ~ you need a loan j'ai cru comprendre que OR si j'ai bien compris, vous avez besoin d'un prêt; am I to ~ that they refused? dois-je comprendre qu'ils ont refusé?; they are understood to have fled the country il paraît qu'ils ont fui le pays; we were given to ~ that he was very ill on nous a fait comprendre OR donné à entendre qu'il était très malade; so I ~ c'est ce que j'ai compris. -**5.** [interpret] entendre; what do you ~ by "soon"? qu'est-ce que vous entendez par «bientôt»?; as I ~ it, there's nothing to pay d'après ce que j'ai compris, il n'y a rien à payer. -**6.** [leave implicit] entendre, sous-entendre; she let it be understood that she preferred to be alone elle a laissé entendre OR donné à entendre qu'elle préférait être seule; the object of the sentence is understood GRAMM l'objet de la phrase est sous-entendu.
◇ *vi* comprendre; of course, I ~ bien sûr, je comprends (bien); if you do that once more you're out, ~? faites ça encore une fois et vous êtes viré, compris?; they ~ about international finance ils comprennent la OR ils s'y connaissent en finance internationale.
understandable [ˌʌndəˈstændəbl] *adj* compréhensible; that's perfectly ~ cela se comprend parfaitement.
understandably [ˌʌndəˈstændəblɪ] *adv* -**1.** [naturally] naturellement; they were, ~ (enough), deeply embarrassed ils étaient profondément gênés, ce qui se comprend parfaitement. -**2.** [speak, write] de manière compréhensible.
understanding [ˌʌndəˈstændɪŋ] ◇ *n* -**1.** *(U)* [comprehension] compréhension *f*; [intelligence] intelligence *f*; [knowledge] connaissance *f*, connaissances *fpl*; it is our ~ that they have now left the country d'après ce que nous avons compris, ils ont quitté le pays à présent; they have little ~ of what the decision involves ils ne comprennent pas très bien ce que la décision entraînera; it's beyond all ~! cela dépasse l'entendement!, c'est à n'y rien comprendre! -**2.** [agreement] accord *m*, arrangement *m*; to come to an ~ about sthg (with sb) s'entendre (avec qqn) sur qqch; there's some kind of ~ between them il y a quelque arrangement entre eux. -**3.** [interpretation] compréhension *f*, interprétation *f*; [conception] conception *f*; my ~ of the matter is that he's resigned ma conception des choses, c'est qu'il a démissionné. -**4.** [relationship - between people] bonne intelligence *f*, entente *f*; [- between nations] entente *f*. -**5.** [sympathy]: he showed great ~ il a fait preuve de beaucoup de compréhension. -**6.** [condition] condition *f*.
◇ *adj* compréhensif, bienveillant.
◆ **on the understanding that** *conj phr* à condition que; on the ~ that the money is given to charity à condition que l'argent soit donné à des bonnes œuvres.
understandingly [ˌʌndəˈstændɪŋlɪ] *adv* avec compréhension, avec bienveillance.
understate [ˌʌndəˈsteɪt] *vt* -**1.** [minimize] minimiser (l'importance de). -**2.** [state with restraint] dire avec retenue, modérer l'expression de.
understated [ˌʌndəˈsteɪtɪd] *adj* discret.
understatement [ˌʌndəˈsteɪtmənt] *n* -**1.** affirmation *f* en dessous de la vérité; that's a bit of an ~! c'est peu dire!; I'd say that calling him lazy was something of an ~ à mon avis, le traiter de paresseux, c'est peu dire; that's the ~ of the year! *hum* c'est le moins qu'on puisse dire! -**2.** LING & LITERAT litote *f*; typical British ~ euphémisme *m* typique des Britanniques.
understeer [ˌʌndəˈstɪəʳ] *vi* AUT sous-virer.
understock [ˌʌndəˈstɒk] *vt* [shop] mal approvisionner; the farm is ~ed la ferme manque de bétail.
understood [ˌʌndəˈstʊd] *pt* & *pp* → **understand**.
understudy [ˈʌndəˌstʌdɪ] (*pl* understudies, *pt* & *pp* understudied) ◇ *n* THEAT doublure *f*.
◇ *vt* [role] apprendre un rôle en tant que doublure; [actor] doubler.
undertake [ˌʌndəˈteɪk] (*pt* undertook [-ˈtʊk], *pp* undertaken [-ˈteɪkn]) *vt fml* -**1.** [take up - job, project] entreprendre; [- experiment] entreprendre, se lancer dans; [- responsibility] assumer, se charger de; [- change] entreprendre, mettre en œuvre. -**2.** [agree, promise] s'engager à; he undertook to pay half the costs il s'est engagé à payer la moitié des frais.
undertaker [ˈʌndəˌteɪkəʳ] *n* ordonnateur *m* des pompes funèbres.
undertaking [ˌʌndəˈteɪkɪŋ] *n* -**1.** [promise] engagement *m*; to give a (written) ~ to do sthg s'engager (par écrit) à faire qqch; she gave an ~ that she wouldn't intervene elle a promis de ne pas intervenir. -**2.** [enterprise] entreprise *f*.
under-the-counter *inf* ◇ *adj* [agreement, offer, sale] en douce, clandestin; an ~ payment un dessous-de-table.
◇ *adv* clandestinement, sous le manteau; to sell sthg ~ vendre qqch sous le manteau.
underthings *inf* [ˈʌndəθɪŋz] *npl* dessous *mpl*, sous-vêtements *mpl*.
undertip [ˌʌndəˈtɪp] (*pt* & *pp* undertipped, *cont* undertipping) *vi* donner un pourboire trop petit.
undertone [ˈʌndətəʊn] *n* -**1.** [in speech] voix *f* basse; to speak in an ~ parler à voix basse OR à mi-voix. -**2.** [of feeling] nuance *f*; the situation had distinctly comic ~s la situation avait un net comique sous-jacent; all her poetry has a tragic ~ toute sa poésie a un fond de tragique.
undertook [ˌʌndəˈtʊk] *pt* → **undertake**.
undertow [ˈʌndətəʊ] *n* courant *m* de retour; I sensed an ~ of resentment in her words *fig* je sentais un vague ressentiment dans ses paroles.
undertrick [ˈʌndətrɪk] *n* [in bridge] *trick qui ne remplit pas le contrat*.
undertrump [ˌʌndəˈtrʌmp] *vt* CARDS *jouer un atout inférieur à un autre déjà joué*.
underuse [ˌʌndəˈjuːz] *vt* sous-utiliser.
underused [ˌʌndəˈjuːzd], **underutilized** [ˌʌndəˈjuːtəlaɪzd] *adj* [facilities, land, resources] sous-exploité.
undervalue [ˌʌndəˈvæljuː] *vt* [object] sous-évaluer, sous-estimer; [person, help] sous-estimer.
undervest [ˈʌndəvest] *n Br* tricot *m* OR maillot *m* de corps.
underwater [ˌʌndəˈwɔːtəʳ] ◇ *adj* sous-marin.
◇ *adv* sous l'eau.
underwear [ˈʌndəweəʳ] *n (U)* sous-vêtements *mpl*.
underweight [ˌʌndəˈweɪt] *adj* -**1.** [person] qui ne pèse pas assez, trop maigre; to be ~ être en dessous de son poids normal. -**2.** [goods] d'un poids insuffisant; all the packets are 20 grams ~ il manque 20 grammes à chaque paquet.
underwent [ˌʌndəˈwent] *pt* → **undergo**.
underwhelm [ˌʌndəˈwelm] *vt hum* décevoir, désappointer; I found the whole affair distinctly ~ing j'ai trouvé toute l'affaire vraiment décevante; she felt rather ~ed by it all elle a été plutôt déçue par tout ça.
underworld [ˈʌndəˌwɜːld] ◇ *n* -**1.** [of criminals] pègre *f*, milieu *m*. -**2.** MYTH: the ~ les Enfers *mpl*.
◇ *comp* [activity] du milieu; [contact] dans OR avec le milieu.
underwrite [ˈʌndəraɪt] (*pt* underwrote [-rəʊt], *pp* underwritten [-ˌrɪtn]) *vt* -**1.** [for insurance - policy] garantir; [- risk] garantir, assurer contre. -**2.** ST. EX [shares] garantir. -**3.** [support - financially] soutenir OR appuyer financièrement; [- by agreement] soutenir, souscrire à.
underwriter [ˈʌndəˌraɪtəʳ] *n* -**1.** [of insurance] assureur *m*. -**2.** ST. EX syndicataire *mf*.
undescended [ˌʌndɪˈsendɪd] *adj* ANAT [testis] qui n'est pas descendu.
undeserved [ˌʌndɪˈzɜːvd] *adj* immérité, injuste.
undeservedly [ˌʌndɪˈzɜːvɪdlɪ] *adv* injustement, indûment.
undeserving [ˌʌndɪˈzɜːvɪŋ] *adj* [person] peu méritant; [cause] peu méritoire; he is quite ~ of such praise il est parfaitement indigne de OR il ne mérite pas du tout de telles louanges.
undesirable [ˌʌndɪˈzaɪərəbl] ◇ *adj* indésirable; ~ alien étranger *m* indésirable; highly ~ tout à fait inopportun.
◇ *n* indésirable *mf*.
undetected [ˌʌndɪˈtektɪd] *adj* [error] non détecté, non décelé; [disease] non détecté, non dépisté; to go ~ passer inaperçu.
undetermined [ˌʌndɪˈtɜːmɪnd] *adj* -**1.** [unknown] inconnu, indéterminé; an artefact of ~ origin un objet fabriqué d'origine inconnue; for an ~ sum of money pour une somme d'argent non fixée. -**2.** [hesitant] irrésolu, indécis.
undeterred [ˌʌndɪˈtɜːd] *adj* sans se laisser décourager; she was ~ by this setback elle ne s'est pas laissé décourager par ce revers.
undeveloped [ˌʌndɪˈveləpt] *adj* -**1.** non développé; [country] en développement; [muscles, organs] non formé; [land, resources] non exploité. -**2.** [immature] immature.
undid [ˌʌnˈdɪd] *pt* → **undo**.
undies *inf* [ˈʌndɪz] *npl* dessous *mpl*.
undigested [ˌʌndɪˈdʒestɪd] *adj* mal digéré, non digéré.
undignified [ʌnˈdɪgnɪfaɪd] *adj* [behaviour, person] qui manque de dignité.
undiluted [ˌʌndaɪˈljuːtɪd] *adj* -**1.** [juice] non dilué. -**2.** *fig* [emotion] sans mélange, parfait; it's pure, ~ maliciousness c'est de la méchanceté à l'état pur.
undiminished [ˌʌndɪˈmɪnɪʃt] *adj* intact, non diminué.

undimmed [ˌʌnˈdɪmd] *adj lit* -**1.** [light, faculty] non diminué. -**2.** *fig* [fame, lustre] non terni; [memory] intact.
undiplomatic [ˌʌndɪpləˈmætɪk] *adj* [action] peu diplomatique; [person] peu diplomate, qui manque de diplomatie.
undipped [ˌʌnˈdɪpt] *adj Br* AUT: to drive on ~ headlights rouler en pleins phares.
undirected [ˌʌndɪˈrektɪd] *adj* -**1.** [effort] sans but. -**2.** [mail] sans adresse.
undischarged [ˌʌndɪsˈtʃɑːdʒd] *adj* JUR [bankrupt] non réhabilité; [debt] non liquidé.
undisciplined [ʌnˈdɪsɪplɪnd] *adj* indiscipliné.
undisclosed [ˌʌndɪsˈkləʊzd] *adj* non divulgué; for an ~ sum pour une somme dont le montant n'a pas été révélé.
undiscovered [ˌʌndɪˈskʌvəd] *adj* non découvert; the manuscript lay ~ for centuries le manuscrit est resté inconnu des siècles durant; an ~ land une terre inconnue.
undiscriminating [ˌʌndɪsˈkrɪmɪneɪtɪŋ] *adj* qui manque de discernement.
undisguised [ˌʌndɪsˈgaɪzd] *adj* non déguisé, non dissimulé.
undismayed [ˌʌndɪsˈmeɪd] *adj* qui ne se laisse pas décourager; he seemed quite ~ by his defeat sa défaite ne semblait pas du tout l'avoir découragé.
undisputed [ˌʌndɪˈspjuːtɪd] *adj* incontesté.
undistinguished [ˌʌndɪˈstɪŋgwɪʃt] *adj* -**1.** [person] peu distingué, sans distinction. -**2.** [style, taste] banal, quelconque.
undisturbed [ˌʌndɪˈstɜːbd] *adj* -**1.** [in peace] tranquille; I want to be left ~ for a while je veux qu'on me laisse tranquille un moment. -**2.** [unchanged, untroubled] inchangé, tranquille; village life has gone on here ~ for centuries la vie du village s'est poursuivie tranquillement depuis des siècles; the population remained largely ~ by the war en général, la population n'a pas été affectée par la guerre. -**3.** [untouched - body, ground, papers] non dérangé, non déplacé.
undivided [ˌʌndɪˈvaɪdɪd] *adj* -**1.** [whole] entier; this job requires your ~ attention ce travail nécessite toute votre attention OR votre entière attention; you have my ~ love vous avez tout mon amour. -**2.** [unanimous] unanime.
undo [ʌnˈduː] (*pt* undid [-ˈdɪd], *pp* undone [-ˈdʌn]) *vt* -**1.** [bow, knot] défaire; to come undone se défaire. -**2.** [ruin - work] détruire; [- effect] annuler; [- plan] mettre en échec. -**3.** [repair -wrong] réparer.
undock [ˌʌnˈdɒk] ◇ *vt* ASTRONAUT larguer.
◇ *vi* -**1.** ASTRONAUT se séparer; ~ing manoeuvre manœuvre *f* de désaccouplement. -**2.** NAUT quitter le quai.
undocumented [ˌʌnˈdɒkjʊmentɪd] *adj* non documenté.
undoing [ˌʌnˈduːɪŋ] *n* (cause *f* de) perte *f*; his indecision proved to be his ~ son indécision aura causé sa perte.
undone [ʌnˈdʌn] ◇ *pp* → **undo**.
◇ *adj* -**1.** [button, clothes, hair] défait. -**2.** [task] non accompli. -**3.** *arch* [hope, plan] ruiné, anéanti; we are ~! *arch* OR *hum* nous sommes perdus!
undoubted [ʌnˈdaʊtɪd] *adj* indubitable.
undoubtedly [ʌnˈdaʊtɪdlɪ] *adv* indubitablement.
undrawn [ˌʌnˈdrɔːn] *adj* [cheque] qu'on n'a pas tiré.
undreamed-of [ʌnˈdriːmdɒv], **undreamt-of** [ʌnˈdremtɒv] *adj* inconcevable, impensable, auquel on ne songe pas.
undress [ʌnˈdres] ◇ *vt* déshabiller.
◇ *vi* se déshabiller.
◇ *n*: in a state of ~ *hum* en petite tenue.
undressed [ˌʌnˈdrest] *adj* -**1.** [person] déshabillé; to get ~ se déshabiller. -**2.** [wound] non pansé. -**3.** [salad] non assaisonné.
undrinkable [ˌʌnˈdrɪŋkəbl] *adj* -**1.** [bad-tasting] imbuvable. -**2.** [unfit for drinking] non potable.
undue [ˌʌnˈdjuː] *adj* excessif; with ~ haste avec une hâte excessive.
undulate [ˈʌndjʊleɪt] *vi* onduler.
undulating [ˈʌndjʊleɪtɪŋ] *adj* [curves, hills] onduleux.
undulation [ˌʌndjʊˈleɪʃn] *n* ondulation *f*.
undulatory [ˈʌndjʊlətrɪ] *adj* [gen] ondulant; PHYS ondulatoire.
unduly [ˌʌnˈdjuːlɪ] *adv* excessivement, trop.
undying [ʌnˈdaɪɪŋ] *adj* [faith] éternel; to swear one's ~ love (for sb) jurer un amour éternel (à qqn).
unearned [ˌʌnˈɜːnd] *adj* -**1.** [undeserved - fame, privilege] non mérité, immérité. -**2.** ECON non gagné en travaillant OR par le travail; ~ increment plus-value *f*.
unearned income *n* (*U*) revenus *mpl* non professionnels, rentes *fpl*.
unearth [ˌʌnˈɜːθ] *vt* -**1.** [dig up] déterrer. -**2.** *fig* [find - equipment, fact] dénicher, trouver; [- old ideas] ressortir, ressusciter.
unearthly [ʌnˈɜːθlɪ] *adj* -**1.** [weird] étrange; [unnatural] surnaturel; [mysterious] mystérieux; [sinister] sinistre. -**2.** *fig*: at an ~ hour à une heure indue.
unease [ʌnˈiːz] *n lit* -**1.** [of mind] inquiétude *f*, malaise *m*; [embarrassment] malaise *m*, gêne *f*; I tried to ignore my growing ~ j'essayais d'ignorer mon malaise grandissant. -**2.** POL [unrest] troubles *mpl*; [tension] tension *f*.
uneasily [ʌnˈiːzɪlɪ] *adv* -**1.** [anxiously - wait, watch] anxieusement, avec inquiétude; [- sleep] d'un sommeil agité. -**2.** [with embarrassment] avec gêne, mal à l'aise.
uneasiness [ʌnˈiːzɪnɪs] *n* -**1.** [of mind] inquiétude *f*, malaise *m*; [of conscience] trouble *m*; [of sleep] agitation *f*; she felt a growing ~ elle sentait une inquiétude croissante. -**2.** [embarrassment] malaise *m*, gêne *f*.
uneasy [ʌnˈiːzɪ] (*compar* uneasier, *superl* uneasiest) *adj* -**1.** [troubled - person] inquiet; [- sleep] agité; I had the ~ feeling we were being followed j'avais la désagréable impression que l'on nous suivait; she was ~ in her mind elle se sentait inquiète; to feel ~ about (doing) sthg se sentir inquiet à l'idée de (faire) qqch; I had an ~ conscience about it je n'avais pas la conscience tranquille à ce sujet. -**2.** [embarrassed - person] mal à l'aise, gêné; [- silence] gêné; I feel ~ in her presence je me sens mal à l'aise en sa présence. -**3.** [uncertain - peace, situation] précaire.
uneatable [ˌʌnˈiːtəbl] *adj* immangeable.
uneaten [ˌʌnˈiːtn] *adj* qui n'a pas été mangé; he left his meal ~ il n'a pas touché à son repas.
uneconomic [ˈʌnˌiːkəˈnɒmɪk] *adj* -**1.** [expensive] peu économique; [unproductive] non rentable. -**2.** = **uneconomical**.
uneconomical [ˈʌnˌiːkəˈnɒmɪkl] *adj* [wasteful] peu rentable.
unedifying [ˌʌnˈedɪfaɪɪŋ] *adj* peu édifiant.
unedited [ˌʌnˈedɪtɪd] *adj* CIN & TV non monté; [speech, text] non édité, non révisé.
uneducated [ˌʌnˈedjʊkeɪtɪd] *adj* -**1.** [person] sans instruction. -**2.** [unrefined - behaviour, manners] sans éducation, inculte; [- writing] informe; [- speech] populaire.
unelectable [ˌʌnɪˈlektəbl] *adj* [person] inéligible; [party] incapable de remporter des élections.
unemotional [ˌʌnɪˈməʊʃənl] *adj* [person] impassible; [behaviour, reaction] qui ne trahit aucune émotion; [voice] neutre; [account, style] sans passion, neutre.
unemployable [ˌʌnɪmˈplɔɪəbl] *adj* [person] inapte au travail, que l'on ne peut pas embaucher.
unemployed [ˌʌnɪmˈplɔɪd] ◇ *npl*: the ~ les chômeurs *mpl*, les demandeurs *mpl* d'emploi.
◇ *adj* en OR au chômage.
unemployment [ˌʌnɪmˈplɔɪmənt] ◇ *n* chômage *m*.
◇ *comp* [benefit, compensation, rate] de chômage; ~ figures les chiffres *mpl* du chômage; ~ insurance assurance *f* chômage.
unemployment benefit *n Br* allocation *f* de chômage.
unencumbered [ˌʌnɪnˈkʌmbəd] *adj* [passage] dégagé, non encombré; [person] non encombré; ~ by children or mortgage sans enfants ni hypothèque.
unending [ʌnˈendɪŋ] *adj* sans fin, interminable.
unendurable [ˌʌnɪnˈdjʊərəbl] *adj* intolérable.
unenforceable [ˌʌnɪnˈfɔːsəbl] *adj* inapplicable.
unenlightened [ˌʌnɪnˈlaɪtnd] *adj* [person] ignorant, peu éclairé; [practice] arriéré.
unenterprising [ˌʌnˈentəpraɪzɪŋ] *adj* [person] peu entreprenant; [measure] timoré.
unenthusiastic [ˌʌnɪnˌθjuːzɪˈæstɪk] *adj* peu enthousiaste; she seemed rather ~ about it ça n'avait pas l'air de l'enthousiasmer.
unenviable [ˌʌnˈenvɪəbl] *adj* [conditions, situation, task] peu enviable.
unequal [ˌʌnˈiːkwəl] *adj* -**1.** [amount, number, result] inégal. -**2.** [contest, struggle] inégal, non équilibré. -**3.** *fml* [incapable]: to be ~ to a job/to a task ne pas être à la hauteur d'un travail/d'une tâche.
unequalled *Br*, **unequaled** *Am* [ˌʌnˈiːkwəld] *adj* inégalé, sans pareil.
unequally [ˌʌnˈiːkwəlɪ] *adv* inégalement.
unequivocal [ˌʌnɪˈkwɪvəkl] *adj* sans équivoque.
unequivocally [ˌʌnɪˈkwɪvəklɪ] *adv* sans équivoque, clairement.
unerring [ˌʌnˈɜːrɪŋ] *adj* infaillible, sûr; [accuracy, judgement] infaillible, sûr; [aim] sûr.
unerringly [ˌʌnˈɜːrɪŋlɪ] *adv* infailliblement.
UNESCO [juːˈneskəʊ] (*abbr of* United Nations Educational, Scientific and Cultural Organization) *pr n* Unesco *f*.
unescorted [ˌʌnɪˈskɔːtɪd] *adj* non accompagné; an ~ woman une femme non accompagnée.
unessential [ˌʌnɪˈsenʃl] = **inessential**.
unethical [ʌnˈeθɪkl] *adj* contraire à l'éthique.
uneven [ˌʌnˈiːvn] *adj* -**1.** [line] irrégulier, qui n'est pas droit; [surface] irrégulier, rugueux; [ground] raboteux, accidenté; [edge] inégal; she has ~ teeth ses dents sont irrégulières. -**2.** [unequal - contest, quality, distribution] inégal; his performance was very ~ *fig* il a joué de façon très inégale. -**3.** [number] impair.
unevenly [ˌʌnˈiːvnlɪ] *adv* -**1.** [divide, spread] inégalement; the contestants are ~ matched les adversaires ne sont pas de force égale. -**2.** [cut, draw] irrégulièrement.
unevenness [ˌʌnˈiːvnnɪs] *n* -**1.** [of edge, ground, line, surface] irrégularité *f*. -**2.** [of contest, distribution, quality] inégalité *f*.
uneventful [ˌʌnɪˈventfʊl] *adj* [day] sans événement marquant, sans histoires; to lead an ~ life mener une vie sans histoires OR paisible; an ~ journey un voyage sans histoires OR sans encombre; an ~ career une carrière sans histoires.
uneventfully [ˌʌnɪˈventfʊlɪ] *adv* sans incidents.
unexceptionable [ˌʌnɪkˈsepʃnəbl] *adj fml* irréprochable.
unexceptional [ˌʌnɪkˈsepʃənl] *adj* qui n'a rien d'exceptionnel, banal.
unexciting [ˌʌnɪkˈsaɪtɪŋ] *adj* [life] peu passionnant; [film] sans grand intérêt; [food] quelconque.
unexpected [ˌʌnɪkˈspektɪd] *adj* inattendu, imprévu; their marriage was totally ~ leur mariage était totalement inattendu.
unexpectedly [ˌʌnɪkˈspektɪdlɪ] *adv* -**1.** [arrive] à l'improviste, de manière imprévue; [fail, succeed] contre toute attente, de manière inattendue. -**2.** [surprisingly] étonnamment.
unexplained [ˌʌnɪkˈspleɪnd] *adj* [mystery, reason] inexpliqué.
unexploded [ˌʌnɪkˈspləʊdɪd] *adj* non explosé.
unexplored [ˌʌnɪkˈsplɔːd] *adj* inexploré, inconnu; [solution, possibility] inexploré.
unexposed [ˌʌnɪkˈspəʊzd] *adj* PHOT [film] vierge.
unexpressed [ˌʌnɪkˈsprest] *adj* inexprimé.

unexpurgated [ˌʌnˈekspəgeɪtɪd] *adj* non expurgé, intégral.
unfading [ʌnˈfeɪdɪŋ] *adj* [colour, feeling, pleasure] toujours vif *(malgré le temps)*; [memory] toujours vif, ineffaçable.
unfailing [ʌnˈfeɪlɪŋ] *adj* [loyalty, support] sûr, à toute épreuve; [courage] inébranlable, à toute épreuve; [energy, supply] intarissable, inépuisable; [good mood, interest] constant, inaltérable.
unfailingly [ʌnˈfeɪlɪŋlɪ] *adv* inlassablement, toujours.
unfair [ˌʌnˈfeəʳ] *adj* [advantage, decision, treatment] injuste; [system] injuste, inique; [judgement] inique; [competition, play] déloyal; to be ~ to sb se montrer injuste envers qqn ❑ ~ dismissal INDUST licenciement *m* abusif.
unfairly [ˌʌnˈfeəlɪ] *adv* [treat] inéquitablement, injustement; [compete] déloyalement; to be ~ dismissed INDUST être victime d'un licenciement abusif.
unfairness [ˌʌnˈfeənɪs] *n (U)* injustice *f*.
unfaithful [ˌʌnˈfeɪθfʊl] *adj* infidèle; to be ~ to sb être infidèle à qqn.
unfaithfully [ˌʌnˈfeɪθfʊlɪ] *adv* infidèlement.
unfaithfulness [ˌʌnˈfeɪθfʊlnɪs] *n* infidélité *f*.
unfaltering [ʌnˈfɔːltərɪŋ] *adj* [speech, steps] ferme, assuré; she was ~ in her support elle était décidée dans son soutien.
unfalteringly [ʌnˈfɔːltərɪŋlɪ] *adv* fermement, sans hésitation.
unfamiliar [ˌʌnfəˈmɪljəʳ] *adj* [face, person, surroundings] inconnu; [ideas] peu familier, que l'on connaît mal; I'm ~ with his writings je connais mal ses écrits.
unfamiliarity [ˈʌnfəˌmɪlɪˈærətɪ] *n* [strangeness - of faces, ideas, surroundings] aspect *m* peu familier, étrangeté *f*; [newness] nouveauté *f*; my ~ with the city put me at a disadvantage mon inexpérience de la ville a été un inconvénient.
unfashionable [ˌʌnˈfæʃnəbl] *adj* -**1.** [clothes, ideas] démodé. -**2.** [area] peu chic.
unfasten [ˌʌnˈfɑːsn] *vt* [button, lace] défaire; [gate] ouvrir; [belt, bonds, rope] détacher.
unfathomable [ʌnˈfæðəməbl] *adj* insondable.
unfathomed [ʌnˈfæðəmd] *adj* inexploré, insondé.
unfavourable *Br*, **unfavorable** *Am* [ˌʌnˈfeɪvrəbl] *adj* défavorable.
unfavourably *Br*, **unfavorably** *Am* [ˌʌnˈfeɪvrəblɪ] *adv* défavorablement.
unfeeling [ʌnˈfiːlɪŋ] *adj* insensible, dur.
unfeelingly [ʌnˈfiːlɪŋlɪ] *adv* avec dureté, sans pitié.
unfeigned [ʌnˈfeɪnd] *adj* non feint, réel.
unfeminine [ʌnˈfemɪnɪn] *adj* qui manque de féminité, peu féminin.
unfettered [ˌʌnˈfetəd] *adj fml* [action] sans contrainte, sans entrave; [imagination, violence] débridé; ~ by moral constraints libre de toute contrainte morale.
unfinished [ˌʌnˈfɪnɪʃt] *adj* -**1.** [incomplete] incomplet, inachevé; an ~ piece of work un travail inachevé ❑ ~ business *literal* affaires *fpl* à régler; *fig* questions *fpl* à régler; 'The Unfinished Symphony' *Schubert* 'la Symphonie inachevée'. -**2.** [rough - furniture] brut, non fini; TEX sans apprêt.
unfit [ˌʌnˈfɪt] (*pt* & *pp* unfitted, *cont* unfitting)
◇ *adj* -**1.** [unsuited - permanently] inapte; [- temporarily] qui n'est pas en état; he is ~ for life in the army il est inapte à la vie militaire; ~ for human consumption impropre à la consommation; she is ~ for social work OR to be a social worker elle n'est pas faite pour être assistante sociale; he's still ~ for work il n'est toujours pas en état de reprendre le travail. -**2.** [unhealthy - person] qui n'est pas en forme, qui est en mauvaise forme; [- condition] mauvais; three of our star players have been declared ~ trois de nos joueurs vedettes ont été déclarés hors d'état de jouer.
◇ *vt fml* rendre inapte; his past record unfitted him for public office sa conduite passée lui interdisait toute fonction officielle.
unfitness [ˌʌnˈfɪtnɪs] *n* -**1.** [unsuitability] inaptitude *f*, incapacité *f*; ~ for public office inaptitude à toute fonction officielle. -**2.** [lack of health, physical fitness] mauvaise forme *f*.
unfitted [ˌʌnˈfɪtɪd] *adj fml* [unprepared] mal préparé; [unsuitable] inapte; to be ~ to do sthg être inapte à faire qqch; he is quite ~ for a job in management il est totalement inapte à un poste de direction.
unfitting [ˌʌnˈfɪtɪŋ] *adj* [remarks] déplacé, inconvenant; [behaviour] inconvenant.
unfix [ˌʌnˈfɪks] *vt* [bayonet] remettre.
unflagging [ˌʌnˈflægɪŋ] *adj* [courage] infatigable, inlassable; [enthusiasm] inépuisable; with ~ interest avec un intérêt toujours soutenu.
unflaggingly [ˌʌnˈflægɪŋlɪ] *adv* infatigablement, inlassablement.
unflappable *inf* [ˌʌnˈflæpəbl] *adj Br* imperturbable, qui ne se laisse pas démonter.
unflattering [ˌʌnˈflætərɪŋ] *adj* peu flatteur.
unfledged [ˌʌnˈfledʒd] *adj* -**1.** ZOOL sans plumes. -**2.** *fig* inexpérimenté, novice.
unflinching [ʌnˈflɪntʃɪŋ] *adj* intrépide, qui ne bronche pas.
unflinchingly [ʌnˈflɪntʃɪŋlɪ] *adv* stoïquement, sans broncher.
unfocus(s)ed [ˌʌnˈfəʊkəst] *adj* [gaze, photo] flou; ~ energy *fig* énergie sans but.
unfold [ʌnˈfəʊld] ◇ *vt* -**1.** [spread out - cloth, map] déplier. -**2.** [reveal - intentions, plans] exposer, révéler; [- story] raconter, dévoiler; [- secret] dévoiler; [- reasons] faire connaître.
◇ *vi* -**1.** [cloth, map] se déplier; [wings] se déployer. -**2.** [plan, story] se dévoiler, se développer; [view] se dérouler, s'étendre; the drama ~ed before our eyes le drame se déroulait devant nos yeux; a spectacular view ~ed before us un spectaculaire panorama s'étendait devant nous.
unforeseeable [ˌʌnfɔːˈsiːəbl] *adj* imprévisible.
unforeseen [ˌʌnfɔːˈsiːn] *adj* imprévu, inattendu.
unforgettable [ˌʌnfəˈgetəbl] *adj* inoubliable.
unforgettably [ˌʌnfəˈgetəblɪ] *adv* inoubliablement.
unforgivable [ˌʌnfəˈgɪvəbl] *adj* impardonnable.
unforgivably [ˌʌnfəˈgɪvəblɪ] *adv* impardonnablement.
unforgiving [ˌʌnfəˈgɪvɪŋ] *adj* implacable, impitoyable, sans merci.
unforgotten [ˌʌnfəˈgɒtn] *adj* inoublié.
unformatted [ˌʌnˈfɔːmætɪd] *adj* COMPUT non formaté.
unformed [ˌʌnˈfɔːmd] *adj* -**1.** [undeveloped] non formé. -**2.** [shapeless] informe, sans forme.
unforthcoming [ˌʌnˌfɔːθˈkʌmɪŋ] *adj*: he was very ~ about the date of the elections il s'est montré très discret sur la date des élections.
unfortunate [ʌnˈfɔːtʃnət] ◇ *adj* -**1.** [unlucky] malheureux, malchanceux; hundreds of ~ people are now homeless des centaines de malheureux sont maintenant sans abri. -**2.** [regrettable - incident, situation] fâcheux, regrettable; [- joke, remark] malencontreux; it's just ~ things turned out this way il est malheureux OR regrettable que les choses se soient passées ainsi.
◇ *n euph* & *fml* malheureux *m*, -euse *f*.
unfortunately [ʌnˈfɔːtʃnətlɪ] *adv* malheureusement; ~ not malheureusement pas.
unfounded [ˌʌnˈfaʊndɪd] *adj* infondé, dénué de fondement.
unframed [ˌʌnˈfreɪmd] *adj* sans cadre.
unfreeze [ʌnˈfriːz] (*pt* unfroze [-ˈfrəʊz], *pp* unfrozen [-ˈfrəʊzn]) ◇ *vt* -**1.** [de-ice] dégeler. -**2.** FIN [credit, rent] débloquer, dégeler.
◇ *vi* (se) dégeler.
unfrequented [ˌʌnfrɪˈkwentɪd] *adj* peu fréquenté.
unfriendliness [ˌʌnˈfrendlɪnɪs] *n* hostilité *f*, froideur *f*.
unfriendly [ˌʌnˈfrendlɪ] (*compar* unfriendlier, *superl* unfriendliest) *adj* inamical, froid.
unfrock [ˌʌnˈfrɒk] *vt* défroquer.
unfroze [ˌʌnˈfrəʊz] *pt* → **unfreeze**.
unfrozen [ˌʌnˈfrəʊzn] *pp* → **unfreeze**.
unfruitful [ˌʌnˈfruːtfʊl] *adj* -**1.** [barren] stérile, improductif. -**2.** *fig* [efforts, search] infructueux, vain.
unfulfilled [ˌʌnfʊlˈfɪld] *adj* [person] insatisfait, frustré; [dream] non réalisé; [ambition, hopes] inaccompli; [promise] non tenu; to feel ~ éprouver un sentiment d'insatisfaction.
unfunded [ˌʌnˈfʌndɪd] *adj* sans subvention; ~ debt FIN dette *f* flottante.
unfunny [ˌʌnˈfʌnɪ] *adj* [experience, joke, situation] qui n'a rien d'amusant; I find that most ~ je ne trouve pas ça amusant du tout.
unfurl [ˌʌnˈfɜːl] ◇ *vt* [flag, sail] déferler, déployer.
◇ *vi* se déployer.
unfurnished [ˌʌnˈfɜːnɪʃt] *adj* [flat, room] non meublé.
unfussy [ˌʌnˈfʌsɪ] *adj* [clothes, manners, person] simple, pas compliqué; [design, furniture] simple.
ungainliness [ʌnˈgeɪnlɪnɪs] *n* maladresse *f*, gaucherie *f*.
ungainly [ʌnˈgeɪnlɪ] (*compar* ungainlier, *superl* ungainliest) *adj* [in movement] maladroit, gauche; [in appearance] dégingandé, disgracieux.
ungallant [ʌnˈgælənt] = **ungentlemanly**.
ungenerous [ˌʌnˈdʒenərəs] *adj* -**1.** [allowance, person] peu généreux; the offer was not ~ l'offre n'était pas peu généreuse. -**2.** [criticism, remark] mesquin.
ungentlemanly [ʌnˈdʒentlmənlɪ] *adj* [attitude, conduct, remark] peu courtois, peu galant.
ungetatable *inf* [ˌʌngetˈætəbl] *adj* inaccessible, hors de portée.
ungodliness [ˌʌnˈgɒdlɪnɪs] *n* impiété *f*.
ungodly [ˌʌnˈgɒdlɪ] *adj* -**1.** *lit* irréligieux, impie. -**2.** *inf fig* [noise] infernal; why are you phoning me at this ~ hour? pourquoi me téléphonez-vous à cette heure impossible?
ungovernable [ˌʌnˈgʌvənəbl] *adj* -**1.** [feelings, temper] irrépressible. -**2.** [country] ingouvernable.
ungracious [ˌʌnˈgreɪʃəs] *adj* désagréable.
ungraciously [ˌʌnˈgreɪʃəslɪ] *adv* de mauvaise grâce.
ungrammatical [ˌʌngrəˈmætɪkl] *adj* agrammatical, non grammatical.
ungrammatically [ˌʌngrəˈmætɪklɪ] *adv* incorrectement LING.
ungrateful [ʌnˈgreɪtfʊl] *adj* -**1.** [person] ingrat; to be ~ to sb manquer de reconnaissance envers qqn. -**2.** *fml* OR *lit* [task] ingrat.
ungratefully [ʌnˈgreɪtfʊlɪ] *adv* de manière ingrate, avec ingratitude.
ungratefulness [ʌnˈgreɪtfʊlnɪs] *n* ingratitude *f*.
ungrudging [ˌʌnˈgrʌdʒɪŋ] *adj* [expense, help] généreux, sans compter.
ungrudgingly [ˌʌnˈgrʌdʒɪŋlɪ] *adv* généreusement, de bon cœur.
unguarded [ˌʌnˈgɑːdɪd] *adj* -**1.** [house] non surveillé, non gardé; [suitcase] sans surveillance, non surveillé. -**2.** [fire] sans pare-feu. -**3.** [remark] irréfléchi; in an ~ moment dans un moment d'inattention. -**4.** [feelings] franc; she gave ~ support for the scheme elle n'a pas hésité à soutenir ce projet.
unguent [ˈʌŋgwənt] *n lit* onguent *m*, pommade *f*.
ungulate [ˈʌŋgjʊleɪt] ◇ *adj* ongulé.
◇ *n* ongulé *m*.
unhallowed [ˌʌnˈhæləʊd] *adj* -**1.** RELIG [ground] non consacré. -**2.** [ungodly - act, behaviour] impie.
unhampered [ˌʌnˈhæmpəd] *adj* non entravé, libre.
unhand [ˌʌnˈhænd] *vt arch* OR *hum* lâcher; ~ me, sir! monsieur, lâchez-moi!

unhappily [ʌn'hæpɪlɪ] *adv* **-1.** [sadly] tristement; she looked at me ~ elle me regarda d'un air triste OR malheureux. **-2.** *fml* [unfortunately] malheureusement; ~, all her friends had left malheureusement OR par malheur tous ses amis étaient partis.

unhappiness [ʌn'hæpɪnɪs] *n* chagrin *m*, peine *f*; her departure caused me great ~ son départ m'a fait beaucoup de peine.

unhappy [ʌn'hæpɪ] (*compar* unhappier, *superl* unhappiest) *adj* **-1.** [sad] triste, malheureux; to make sb ~ rendre qqn malheureux; he had an ~ time abroad il a fait un mauvais séjour à l'étranger. **-2.** *fml* [unfortunate - coincidence] malheureux, regrettable; [- remark] malheureux, malencontreux; an ~ turn of phrase une tournure malheureuse; it's a most ~ state of affairs c'est une situation tout à fait regrettable OR fâcheuse; the ~ fellow drowned *Br* le pauvre malheureux s'est noyé. **-3.** [displeased] mécontent; [worried] inquiet; to be ~ about OR with sthg être mécontent de qqch; she was ~ about me spending so much time away from home [displeased] elle n'aimait pas que je passe tant de temps loin de la maison; [worried] cela l'inquiétait que je passe tant de temps loin de la maison.

unharmed [ʌn'hɑːmd] *adj* **-1.** [person] sain et sauf, indemne; to escape ~ s'en sortir indemne; they released two boys ~ ils ont relâché deux garçons sains et saufs. **-2.** [vase] intact; [house, paintwork] non endommagé.

unharness [ʌn'hɑːnɪs] *vt* [remove harness from] déharnacher; [unhitch] dételer.

unhealthily [ʌn'helθɪlɪ] *adv* d'une manière malsaine; to be ~ thin être d'une maigreur malsaine.

unhealthy [ʌn'helθɪ] (*compar* unhealthier, *superl* unhealthiest) *adj* **-1.** [person] malade; [complexion] maladif; he had an ~ look about him il avait un air maladif. **-2.** [air, place] malsain, insalubre. **-3.** *fig* [curiosity, interest] malsain, morbide.

unheard [ʌn'hɜːd] *adj* non entendu; his cries for help went ~ personne n'a entendu ses appels à l'aide || JUR [case] non jugé; to be judged ~ être jugé sans être entendu.

unheard-of *adj* **-1.** [extraordinary] inouï, sans précédent; ~ cruelty une cruauté inouïe. **-2.** [unprecedented] inconnu, sans précédent; such an occurrence is quite unheard of pareil événement n'est pratiquement jamais arrivé. **-3.** [unknown] inconnu, ignoré; several previously ~ painters were included in the exhibition plusieurs peintres inconnus jusqu'alors ont participé à l'exposition.

unheated [ʌn'hiːtɪd] *adj* sans chauffage.

unheeded [ʌn'hiːdɪd] *adj* [ignored - message, warning] ignoré, dont on ne tient pas compte; his instructions went OR were ~ ses instructions n'ont pas été suivies || [unnoticed] inaperçu; the announcement went ~ on n'a pas tenu compte de l'annonce.

unheeding [ʌn'hiːdɪŋ] *adj* **-1.** [unconcerned] insouciant, indifférent. **-2.** [inattentive] inattentif.

unhelpful [ʌn'helpfʊl] *adj* [person] peu secourable OR serviable; [instructions, map] qui n'est d'aucun secours; [advice] inutile; you're being deliberately ~ vous faites exprès de ne pas nous aider.

unhelpfully [ʌn'helpfʊlɪ] *adv* **-1.** [act] sans aider, sans coopérer. **-2.** [advise, say, suggest] inutilement.

unhelpfulness [ʌn'helpfʊlnɪs] *n* inutilité *f*; [of person] manque *m* d'obligeance.

unheralded [ʌn'herəldɪd] *adj* [unannounced] non annoncé; [unexpected] inattendu.

unhesitating [ʌn'hezɪteɪtɪŋ] *adj* [reply] immédiat, spontané; [belief] résolu, ferme; [person] résolu, qui n'hésite pas.

unhesitatingly [ʌn'hezɪteɪtɪŋlɪ] *adv* sans hésitation.

unhindered [ʌn'hɪndəd] *adj* sans entrave OR obstacle; we crossed the border ~ nous avons passé la frontière sans encombre.

unhinge [ʌn'hɪndʒ] *vt* **-1.** [door, window] démonter, enlever de ses gonds. **-2.** *fig* [mind, person] déséquilibrer, déranger.

unhinged [ʌn'hɪndʒd] *adj* déséquilibré.

unhitch [ʌn'hɪtʃ] *vt* **-1.** [rope] détacher, décrocher. **-2.** [horse, ox] dételer.

unholy [ʌn'həʊlɪ] (*compar* unholier, *superl* unholiest) *adj* **-1.** RELIG profane, impie; an ~ alliance *fig* une alliance *f* contre nature. **-2.** *inf* [awful - noise, mess] impossible, invraisemblable; at an ~ hour à une heure impossible OR indue.

unhook [ʌn'hʊk] ◇ *vt* **-1.** [remove, take down] décrocher. **-2.** [bra, dress] dégrafer, défaire.
◇ *vi* [bra, dress] se dégrafer.

unhoped-for [ʌn'həʊpt-] *adj* inespéré.

unhopeful [ʌn'həʊpfʊl] *adj* **-1.** [person] pessimiste, sans illusion. **-2.** [situation] décourageant.

unhorse [ʌn'hɔːs] *vt* **-1.** EQUIT démonter, désarçonner. **-2.** *fig* [from power] faire tomber, renverser.

unhurried [ʌn'hʌrɪd] *adj* [person] qui ne se presse pas; [manner] tranquille, serein; we enjoyed an ~ lunch nous avons pris plaisir à déjeuner sans nous presser.

unhurriedly [ʌn'hʌrɪdlɪ] *adv* calmement, sans se presser.

unhurt [ʌn'hɜːt] *adj* indemne, sans blessure; to escape ~ sortir sain et sauf OR indemne.

unhygienic [ˌʌnhaɪ'dʒiːnɪk] *adj* antihygiénique, non hygiénique.

uni *inf* ['juːnɪ] (*abbr of* university) *n* fac *f*.

unicameral [ˌjuːnɪ'kæmərəl] *adj* monocaméral.

UNICEF ['juːnɪˌsef] (*abbr of* United Nations International Children's Emergency Fund) *pr n* Unicef *m*.

unicellular [ˌjuːnɪ'seljʊlə^r] *adj* unicellulaire.

unicorn ['juːnɪkɔːn] *n* MYTH licorne *f*.

unicycle ['juːnɪsaɪkl] *n* monocycle *m*.

unidentifiable [ˌʌnaɪ'dentɪfaɪəbl] *adj* non identifiable.

unidentified [ˌʌnaɪ'dentɪfaɪd] *adj* non identifié.

unidentified flying object *n* objet *m* volant non identifié.

unidirectional [ˌjuːnɪdɪ'rekʃənl] *adj* unidirectionnel.

unification [ˌjuːnɪfɪ'keɪʃn] *n* unification *f*.

uniform ['junɪfɔːm] ◇ *n* uniforme *m*; in ~ [gen] en uniforme; MIL sous les drapeaux; in school ~ en uniforme d'école; to wear ~ porter l'uniforme.
◇ *adj* [identical] identique, pareil; [constant] constant; [unified] uniforme.

uniformed ['juːnɪfɔːmd] *adj* [gen] en uniforme; [policeman, soldier] en tenue.

uniformity [ˌjuːnɪ'fɔːmətɪ] (*pl* uniformities) *n* uniformité *f*.

uniformly ['juːnɪfɔːmlɪ] *adv* uniformément.

unify ['juːnɪfaɪ] (*pt* & *pp* unified) *vt* **-1.** [unite - country] unifier. **-2.** [make uniform - legislation, prices, system] uniformiser.

unifying ['juːnɪfaɪɪŋ] *adj* unificateur.

unilateral [ˌjuːnɪ'lætərəl] *adj* **-1.** [action, decision] unilatéral; ~ declaration of independence déclaration *f* unilatérale d'indépendance. **-2.** MED [paralysis] hémiplégique.

unilateral disarmament *n* désarmement *m* unilatéral.

unilateralism [ˌjuːnɪ'lætərəlɪzm] *n* doctrine *f* du désarmement unilatéral.

unilateralist [ˌjuːnɪ'lætərəlɪst] *n* partisan *m* du désarmement unilatéral.

unilaterally [ˌjuːnɪ'lætərəlɪ] *adv* **-1.** [act, decide] unilatéralement. **-2.** MED: to be paralysed ~ être paralysé d'un seul côté, être hémiplégique.

unilingual [ˌjuːnɪ'lɪŋgwəl] *adj* monolingue, unilingue.

unimaginable [ˌʌnɪ'mædʒɪnəbl] *adj* inimaginable, inconcevable.

unimaginably [ˌʌnɪ'mædʒɪnəblɪ] *adv* incroyablement, invraisemblablement.

unimaginative [ˌʌnɪ'mædʒɪnətɪv] *adj* manquant d'imagination, peu imaginatif.

unimaginatively [ˌʌnɪ'mædʒɪnətɪvlɪ] *adv* sans imagination.

unimpaired [ˌʌnɪm'peəd] *adj* [faculty, health, strength] non diminué; her political prestige remains ~ son prestige politique demeure intact.

unimpeachable [ˌʌnɪm'piːtʃəbl] *adj fml* [source, evidence] incontestable; [reputation, honesty] irréprochable.

unimpeded [ˌʌnɪm'piːdɪd] *adj* sans obstacle, libre.

unimportant [ˌʌnɪm'pɔːtənt] *adj* **-1.** [detail, matter, question] sans importance, insignifiant. **-2.** [person] sans influence, sans importance.

unimposing [ˌʌnɪm'pəʊzɪŋ] *adj* **-1.** [unimpressive] peu imposant OR impressionnant. **-2.** [insignificant] insignifiant.

unimpressed [ˌʌnɪm'prest] *adj* non impressionné; I was ~ by her elle ne m'a pas fait une grosse impression; they were obviously ~ by your threats ils n'étaient manifestement pas impressionnés par vos menaces.

unimpressive [ˌʌnɪm'presɪv] *adj* guère impressionnant; their record is ~ leur dossier n'est pas très impressionnant OR est très quelconque.

unimproved [ˌʌnɪm'pruːvd] *adj* **-1.** [no better] non amélioré; his condition is ~ son état ne s'est pas amélioré. **-2.** [land] non amendé; [resources] inexploité, inutilisé; ~ value valeur *f* non bâtie *(d'un terrain)*.

unincorporated [ˌʌnɪn'kɔːpəreɪtɪd] *adj* **-1.** [not included] non incorporé OR intégré. **-2.** COMM & JUR non enregistré.

uninformative [ˌʌnɪn'fɔːmətɪv] *adj* [book, leaflet, person] qui n'apprend rien; [conversation] qui n'est pas très instructif.

uninformed [ˌʌnɪn'fɔːmd] *adj* [person] non informé; [opinion] mal informé; [reader] non averti; ~ critics critiques non avertis; to make an ~ guess deviner au hasard.

uninhabitable [ˌʌnɪn'hæbɪtəbl] *adj* inhabitable.

uninhabited [ˌʌnɪn'hæbɪtɪd] *adj* inhabité.

uninhibited [ˌʌnɪn'hɪbɪtɪd] *adj* [person] sans inhibition OR inhibitions; [behaviour, reaction] non réfréné, non réprimé; [laughter] franc et massif, sans retenue.

uninitiated [ˌʌnɪ'nɪʃɪeɪtɪd] ◇ *npl*: the ~ les profanes *mpl*, les non-initiés *mpl*, les non-initiées *fpl*; to OR for the ~ pour le profane.
◇ *adj* non initié.

uninjured [ʌn'ɪndʒəd] *adj* [person] indemne, sain et sauf; miraculously she was ~ par miracle, elle était indemne.

uninspired [ˌʌnɪn'spaɪəd] *adj* qui manque d'inspiration.

uninspiring [ˌʌnɪn'spaɪrɪŋ] *adj* [dull] qui n'inspire pas; [mediocre] médiocre; [unexciting] qui n'est pas passionnant; [uninteresting] sans intérêt.

unintelligent [ˌʌnɪn'telɪdʒənt] *adj* inintelligent, qui manque d'intelligence; he's not an ~ lad ce garçon n'est pas bête.

unintelligible [ˌʌnɪn'telɪdʒəbl] *adj* inintelligible; [writing] illisible.

unintended [ˌʌnɪn'tendɪd] *adj* non intentionnel, accidentel, fortuit.

unintentional [ˌʌnɪn'tenʃənl] *adj* involontaire, non intentionnel.

unintentionally [ˌʌnɪn'tenʃnəlɪ] *adv* sans le vouloir, involontairement.

uninterested [ʌn'ɪntrəstɪd] *adj* [indifferent] indifférent; to be ~ in sb/sthg être indifférent à qqn/qqch.

uninteresting [ʌn'ɪntrəstɪŋ] *adj* [subject] inintéressant, sans intérêt; [book] inintéressant, ennuyeux; [person] ennuyeux.

uninterrupted ['ʌnˌɪntə'rʌptɪd] *adj* continu, ininterrompu.

uninterruptedly ['ʌnˌɪntə'rʌptɪdlɪ] *adv* de façon ininterrompue, sans interruption.

uninvited [ˌʌnɪnˈvaɪtɪd] *adj* -**1.** [person] qu'on n'a pas invité; an ~ guest un invité inattendu; he turned up ~ at the party il a débarqué à la soirée sans y avoir été invité. -**2.** [comment] non sollicité.

uninviting [ˌʌnɪnˈvaɪtɪŋ] *adj* [place] peu accueillant; [prospect] peu attrayant; [smell] peu attirant.

union [ˈjuːnjən] ◇ *n* -**1.** [act of linking, uniting] union *f*; COMM regroupement *m*, fusion *f*. -**2.** INDUST syndicat *m*. -**3.** [association] association *f*, union *f*; students' ~ union des étudiants. -**4.** [marriage] union *f*, mariage *m*. -**5.** MATH union *f*.
◇ *comp* [dues, leader, meeting] syndical; [member] d'un OR du syndicat; ~ shop *Am* atelier *m* d'ouvriers syndiqués, union shop *m*.
◆ **Union** *n* -**1.** POL [country]: the Union of South Africa la République d'Afrique du Sud; the Soviet Union l'Union *f* soviétique. -**2.** HIST: the Union *Br* [with Scotland] l'Union *f* de l'Angleterre et de l'Écosse; [with Northern Ireland] l'Union de l'Angleterre et de l'Irlande du Nord; *Am* les États *mpl* de l'Union.

union-bashing *n Br* antisyndicalisme *m*.

Union Flag = **Union Jack**.

unionism [ˈjuːnjənɪzm] *n* -**1.** INDUST syndicalisme *m*. -**2.** POL unionisme *m*.

unionist [ˈjuːnjənɪst] ◇ *adj* INDUST syndicaliste.
◇ *n* -**1.** INDUST syndicaliste *mf*. -**2.** POL unioniste *mf*; [in American Civil War] nordiste *mf*.

unionize, -ise [ˈjuːnjənaɪz] ◇ *vi* se syndicaliser, se syndiquer.
◇ *vt* syndicaliser, syndiquer.

Union Jack *n* Union Jack *m (drapeau officiel du Royaume-Uni)*.

uniparous [juːˈnɪpərəs] *adj* unipare.

uniprocessor [ˌjuːnɪˈprəʊsesəʳ] *n* COMPUT monoprocesseur *m*.

uniprogramming [ˌjuːnɪˈprəʊgræmɪŋ] *n* COMPUT monoprogrammation *f*.

unique [juːˈniːk] *adj* -**1.** [sole, single] unique; [particular] particulier, propre; a problem ~ to this region un problème propre à cette région. -**2.** [exceptional] exceptionnel, remarquable; his work is quite ~ son travail est tout à fait exceptionnel.

uniquely [juːˈniːklɪ] *adv* [particularly] particulièrement; [remarkably] exceptionnellement, remarquablement.

uniqueness [juːˈniːknɪs] *n* originalité *f*.

unironed [ʌnˈaɪənd] *adj* non repassé.

unisex [ˈjuːnɪseks] *adj* unisexe.

unison [ˈjuːnɪzn] *n* unisson *m*; in ~ à l'unisson.

UNISON [ˈjuːnɪzn] *pr n «super-syndicat» de la fonction publique en Grande-Bretagne*.

unit [ˈjuːnɪt] ◇ *n* -**1.** [constituent, component] unité *f*; administrative ~ unité administrative; the parish is the basic church ~ la paroisse est l'unité de base de l'Église. -**2.** [group] unité *f*; [team] équipe *f*, unité *f*; army ~ unité de l'armée; family ~ cellule *f* familiale; production ~ unité de production. -**3.** [department] service *m*; [centre] centre *m*; [building] locaux *mpl*; [offices] bureaux *mpl*; child care ~ service de pédiatrie; operating ~ bloc *m* opératoire. -**4.** [in amounts, measurement] unité *f*; ~ of length/time unité de longueur/de temps; two ~s of morphine MED deux unités de morphine; ~ of currency unité monétaire. -**5.** [part, element - of furniture] élément *m*; [- of mechanism, system] bloc *m*, élément *m*; kitchen ~s éléments de cuisine; sink ~ bloc-évier *m*; transformer ~ bloc transformateur. -**6.** SCH [lesson] unité *f*; ~ 5 unité 5.
◇ *comp* [furniture] par éléments, modulaire.
◆ **units** *npl* MATH: the ~s les unités *fpl*.

Unitarian [ˌjuːnɪˈteərɪən] ◇ *n* RELIG unitaire *mf*, unitarien *m*, -enne *f*.
◇ *adj* unitaire, unitarien.

Unitarianism [ˌjuːnɪˈteərɪənɪzm] *n* RELIG unitarisme *m*.

unitary [ˈjuːnɪtrɪ] *adj* -**1.** [united, single] unitaire. -**2.** [government] centralisé.

unit charge *n* TELEC taxe *f* unitaire.

unit cost *n* COMM coût *m* unitaire.

unite [juːˈnaɪt] ◇ *vt* -**1.** [join, link - forces] unir, rassembler. -**2.** [unify - country, party] unifier, unir. -**3.** [bring together - people, relatives] réunir.
◇ *vi* s'unir; they ~d in their efforts to defeat the enemy ils ont conjugué leurs efforts pour vaincre l'ennemi; the two countries ~d in opposing OR to oppose oppression les deux pays se sont unis pour s'opposer à l'oppression; they seem to have ~d against me ils semblent s'être unis contre moi.

united [juːˈnaɪtɪd] *adj* [family] uni; [efforts] conjugué; [country, party] uni, unifié; to present a ~ front montrer un front uni; they are ~ against her/against fascism ils sont unis contre elle/contre le fascisme; we are ~ in our aims nous sommes d'accord dans nos objectifs, nous partageons les mêmes objectifs ❑ Melchester United SPORT Melchester United; ~ we stand, divided we fall *prov* l'union fait la force *prov*.

United Arab Emirates *pl pr n*: the ~ les Émirats *mpl* arabes unis; in the ~ dans les Émirats arabes unis.

United Arab Republic *pr n* République *f* arabe unie; in the ~ dans la République arabe unie.

United Kingdom *pr n* Royaume-Uni *m*; in the ~ au Royaume-Uni.

United Nations *pr n* Nations *fpl* unies.

United Provinces *pl pr n*: the ~ les Provinces-Unies *fpl*; in the ~ dans les Provinces-Unies.

United States *pr n* États-Unis *mpl*; in the ~ aux États-Unis; the ~ of America les États-Unis d'Amérique.

unit price *n* prix *m* unitaire OR à l'unité.

unit trust *n Br* FIN fonds *m* commun de placement, SICAV *f*.

unity [ˈjuːnətɪ] (*pl* **unities**) *n* -**1.** [union] unité *f*, union *f*; national/political ~ unité nationale/politique; strength lies in ~ l'union fait la force. -**2.** [identity - of purpose] identité *f*; [- of views] unité *f*. -**3.** [harmony] harmonie *f*; to live in ~ vivre en harmonie. -**4.** THEAT unité *f*; the dramatic unities les unités dramatiques. -**5.** MATH unité *f*.

Univ. *written abbr of* university.

univalent [ˌjuːnɪˈveɪlənt] ◇ *adj* BIOL & CHEM univalent, monovalent.
◇ *n* chromosome *m* univalent.

univalve [ˈjuːnɪvælv] ◇ *adj* ZOOL univalve.
◇ *n* mollusque *m* univalve.

universal [ˌjuːnɪˈvɜːsl] ◇ *adj* [belief, education, language] universel; topics of ~ interest sujets qui intéressent tout le monde ❑ ~ product code *Am* code *m* barres.
◇ *n* -**1.** [truth] vérité *f* universelle; [proposition] proposition *f* universelle. -**2.** LING & PHILOS: ~s universaux *mpl*.

universal grammar *n* grammaire *f* universelle.

universality [ˌjuːnɪvɜːˈsælətɪ] *n* universalité *f*.

universalize, -ise [ˌjuːnɪˈvɜːsəlaɪz] *vt* universaliser, généraliser.

universal joint *n* (joint *m* de) cardan *m*.

universally [ˌjuːnɪˈvɜːsəlɪ] *adv* universellement; a ~ held opinion une opinion qui prévaut partout; he is ~ liked/admired tout le monde l'aime bien/l'admire.

universe [ˈjuːnɪvɜːs] *n* univers *m*; in the ~ dans l'univers.

university [ˌjuːnɪˈvɜːsətɪ] (*pl* **universities**) ◇ *n* université *f*; to go to ~ aller à l'université, faire des études universitaires; to be at ~ être à l'université OR en faculté; she studied at Cambridge ~ elle était à l'université de Cambridge.
◇ *comp* [building, campus, team] universitaire; [professor, staff] d'université; [education, studies] supérieur, universitaire; ~ fees frais *mpl* d'inscription à l'université.

univocal [ˌjuːnɪˈvəʊkl] ◇ *adj* [message, term, text] univoque.
◇ *n* LING mot *m* univoque.

unjust [ʌnˈdʒʌst] *adj* injuste.

unjustifiable [ʌnˈdʒʌstɪfaɪəbl] *adj* [behaviour] injustifiable, inexcusable; [claim] que l'on ne peut justifier; [error] injustifié.

unjustifiably [ʌnˈdʒʌstɪfaɪəblɪ] *adv* sans justification.

unjustified [ʌnˈdʒʌstɪfaɪd] *adj* [unwarranted] injustifié; ~ absences absences sans motif valable; such accusations are ~ de telles plaintes sont sans fondement OR sont injustifiées.

unjustly [ʌnˈdʒʌstlɪ] *adv* injustement, à tort.

unkempt [ʌnˈkempt] *adj* [hair] mal peigné, en bataille; [beard] hirsute; [appearance, person] négligé, débraillé; [garden] mal entretenu, en friche.

unkind [ʌnˈkaɪnd] *adj* -**1.** [person] peu aimable, qui n'est pas gentil; [manner] peu aimable; [thought] vilain, méchant; [remark] désobligeant, méchant; he was rather ~ to me il n'a pas été très gentil à mon égard OR avec moi. -**2.** [climate] rigoureux, rude.

unkindly [ʌnˈkaɪndlɪ] ◇ *adv* [cruelly] méchamment, cruellement; [roughly] sans ménagement; I hope you won't take it ~ but I'll have to decline your invitation j'espère que vous ne le prendrez pas mal OR vous ne serez pas offensé mais je dois décliner votre invitation; she didn't mean it ~ elle n'a voulu blesser OR offenser personne.
◇ *adj lit* [person] peu aimable OR gentil; [action] vilain; [remark] désobligeant.

unkindness [ʌnˈkaɪndnɪs] *n* -**1.** [of person] manque *m* de gentillesse, méchanceté *f*; [of behaviour, manner] méchanceté *f*. -**2.** [of climate] rigueur *f*.

unknit [ʌnˈnɪt] (*pt* & *pp* unknitted, *cont* unknitting) *vt* -**1.** [pullover] défaire, détricoter. -**2.** *fig* & *lit* [alliance, friendship] rompre.

unknowable [ˌʌnˈnəʊəbl] ◇ *adj* inconnaissable.
◇ *n* inconnaissable *m*.

unknowing [ʌnˈnəʊɪŋ] *adj* inconscient; they went, all ~, to their deaths ils allaient, sans le savoir, au-devant de leur mort.

unknowingly [ʌnˈnəʊɪŋlɪ] *adv* à mon/son *etc* insu, sans m'en/s'en *etc* apercevoir.

unknown [ʌnˈnəʊn] ◇ *adj* -**1.** [not known] inconnu; for reasons ~ to us pour des raisons que nous ignorons OR qui nous sont inconnues; ~ to his son, he sold the house à l'insu de son fils OR sans que son fils le sache, il a vendu la maison; these drugs are ~ to most family doctors ces médicaments sont inconnus OR ignorés de la plupart des généralistes ❑ ~ quantity MATH & *fig* inconnue *f*. -**2.** [obscure - cause] inconnu, mystérieux; [- place] inconnu. -**3.** [obscure - actor, writer] inconnu, méconnu.
◇ *n* -**1.** [person] inconnu *m*, -e *f*. -**2.** [place, situation] inconnu *m*; the great ~ le grand inconnu; the explorers set off into the ~ les explorateurs se lancèrent vers l'inconnu. -**3.** MATH & LOGIC inconnue *f*.

Unknown Soldier, Unknown Warrior *n*: the ~ le Soldat *m* inconnu.

unlabelled [ʌnˈleɪbld] *adj* non étiqueté, sans étiquette.

unlace [ʌnˈleɪs] *vt* [bodice, shoe] délacer, défaire le lacet OR les lacets de.

unladen [ʌnˈleɪdn] *adj* -**1.** [goods] déchargé. -**2.** [lorry, ship] à vide; ~ weight poids *m* à vide.

unladylike [ʌnˈleɪdɪlaɪk] *adj* [girl] mal élevé; [behaviour, posture] peu distingué, qui ne sied pas à une jeune fille; it's ~ to whistle une jeune fille bien élevée ne siffle pas.

unlamented [ˌʌnləˈmentɪd] *adj* regretté de personne; his death was ~, he died ~ personne n'a pleuré sa mort.

unlatch [ʌnˈlætʃ] ◇ *vt* [door] soulever le loquet de, ouvrir; the door was left ~ed la porte est

restée entrouverte, on n'avait pas fermé le loquet de la porte.
◇ *vi* [door] s'ouvrir.

unlawful [,ʌn'lɔːfʊl] *adj* illicite, illégal; it is ~ to use a television set without a licence il est interdit d'utiliser une télévision sans payer de redevance; their marriage was deemed ~ leur mariage fut jugé illégitime; the demonstration is ~ la manifestation est interdite ❑ ~ assembly JUR réunion *f* illégale, attroupement *m* illégal; ~ killing meurtre *m*.

unlawfully [,ʌn'lɔːfʊlɪ] *adv* illicitement, illégalement.

unleaded [,ʌn'ledɪd] *adj* [petrol] sans plomb.

unlearn [,ʌn'lɜːn] (*pt* & *pp* unlearned OR unlearnt [-'lɜːnt]) *vt* désapprendre.

unlearned [*sense 1* ,ʌn'lɜːnɪd, *sense 2* ,ʌn'lɜːnd] *adj* -**1.** [person] non instruit, ignorant. -**2.** = **unlearnt**.

unlearnt [,ʌn'lɜːnt] *adj* [lesson] non appris; [reflex] inné, non acquis.

unleash [,ʌn'liːʃ] *vt* -**1.** [dog] lâcher. -**2.** *fig* [anger, violence] déchaîner; she ~ed a stream of invective elle lâcha une bordée d'injures.

unleavened [,ʌn'levnd] *adj* [bread] CULIN sans levain; RELIG azyme; the speech was ~ by even a trace of humour *lit* le discours n'était même pas égayé par une pointe d'humour.

unless [ən'les] *conj* à moins que (+ *subjunctive*), à moins de (+ *infinitive*); I'll go ~ he phones first j'irai, à moins qu'il téléphone d'abord; ~ I'm very much mistaken à moins que je ne me trompe; you won't win ~ you practise vous ne gagnerez pas si vous ne vous entraînez pas; they won't agree ~ I go myself ils n'accepteront pas si je n'y vais pas moi-même; don't speak ~ spoken to ne parle que lorsqu'on t'adresse la parole; ~ I hear otherwise OR to the contrary sauf avis contraire, sauf contrordre.

unlettered [,ʌn'letəd] *adj lit* [uneducated] sans instruction; [illiterate] illettré, analphabète.

unliberated [,ʌn'lɪbəreɪtɪd] *adj* non libéré; ~ slaves les esclaves non émancipés; the ~ woman la femme non libérée.

unlicensed [,ʌn'laɪsənst] *adj* [parking, sale] illicite, non autorisé; [fishing, hunting] sans permis, illicite; [car] sans vignette; [premises, restaurant] qui n'a pas de licence de débit de boissons.

unlikable [,ʌn'laɪkəbl] *adj* [person] peu sympathique; [place, thing] peu agréable.

unlike [,ʌn'laɪk] ◇ *adj* [dissimilar] dissemblable; [different] différent; [showing no likeness] peu ressemblant; [unequal] inégal; the two sisters are quite ~ each other les deux sœurs ne se ressemblent pas du tout.
◇ *prep* -**1.** [different from] différent de, qui ne ressemble pas à; he's quite ~ his brother il ne ressemble pas à son frère; she is not ~ Meryl Streep in looks elle n'est pas sans ressembler à Meryl Streep; your situation is quite ~ mine votre situation est très différente de la mienne. -**2.** [uncharacteristic of]: that's (very) ~ him! cela ne lui ressemble pas (du tout)! -**3.** [in contrast to] à la différence de, contrairement à; ~ you, I prefer a quiet life contrairement à vous, je préfère une vie tranquille.

unlikeable [,ʌn'laɪkəbl] = **unlikable**.

unlikelihood [ʌn'laɪklɪhʊd] *n* improbabilité *f*.

unlikely [ʌn'laɪklɪ] *adj* -**1.** [improbable - event, outcome] improbable, peu probable; it is very OR most ~ that it will rain il est très peu probable qu'il pleuve, il y a peu de chances pour qu'il pleuve; in the ~ event of my winning au cas improbable où je gagnerais. -**2.** [person] peu susceptible, qui a peu de chances; he is ~ to come/to fail il est peu probable qu'il vienne/échoue, il est peu susceptible de venir/d'échouer; she is ~ to choose him elle a peu de chances de le choisir, il y a peu de chances pour qu'elle le choisisse. -**3.** [implausible - excuse, story] invraisemblable. -**4.** [unexpected - situation, undertaking, costume etc] extravagant, invraisemblable; he turns up at the most ~ times il débarque à des heures invraisemblables; the manager chose the most ~ person to run the department le directeur a choisi la personne la moins indiquée au monde pour diriger le service; he seems an ~ choice il semble un choix peu judicieux.

unlimited [ʌn'lɪmɪtɪd] *adj* -**1.** [possibilities, space] illimité, sans limites; [power] illimité, sans bornes; we don't have ~ time at our disposal nous ne disposons pas d'un temps infini OR illimité. -**2.** *Br* FIN: ~ liability responsabilité *f* illimitée.

unlined [,ʌn'laɪnd] *adj* -**1.** [paper] non réglé, uni. -**2.** [clothes, curtain] sans doublure. -**3.** [face] sans rides.

unlisted [,ʌn'lɪstɪd] *adj* -**1.** [not on list - name] qui ne paraît pas sur la liste. -**2.** *Am* TELEC: the number is ~ le numéro est sur la liste rouge. -**3.** ST. EX non coté (en Bourse).

unlit [,ʌn'lɪt] *adj* -**1.** [candle, fire] non allumé. -**2.** [room, street] non éclairé.

unload [,ʌn'ləʊd] ◇ *vt* -**1.** [remove load from - gun, ship, truck] décharger; have you ~ed the washing machine? avez-vous enlevé le linge de la machine? -**2.** [remove - cargo, furniture] décharger; to ~ bricks from a cart décharger les briques d'une charrette; to ~ a film (from a camera) enlever la pellicule (d'un appareil photo). -**3.** *inf* [get rid of] se débarrasser de, se défaire de; to ~ sthg onto sb se décharger de qqch sur qqn. -**4.** *fig* [responsibility, worries] décharger.
◇ *vi* [ship, truck] décharger.

unloading [,ʌn'ləʊdɪŋ] *n* déchargement *m*.

unlock [,ʌn'lɒk] ◇ *vt* -**1.** [door] ouvrir. -**2.** *fig* [mystery, puzzle] résoudre, donner la clé de; [secret] dévoiler.
◇ *vi* s'ouvrir.

unlooked-for [,ʌn'lʊkt-] *adj* inattendu, imprévu.

unloose [,ʌn'luːs] = **unleash**.

unloose(n) [,ʌn'luːs(n)] *vt* [belt, bonds, grip] relâcher, desserrer.

unlovable [,ʌn'lʌvəbl] *adj* peu attachant.

unloved [,ʌn'lʌvd] *adj* privé d'affection, aimé de personne; to feel ~ se sentir mal aimé.

unlovely [,ʌn'lʌvlɪ] *adj* laid, déplaisant.

unloving [,ʌn'lʌvɪŋ] *adj* peu affectueux.

unluckily [ʌn'lʌkɪlɪ] *adv* malheureusement; ~ for us, it rained malheureusement pour nous, il a plu.

unlucky [ʌn'lʌkɪ] (*compar* unluckier, *superl* unluckiest) *adj* -**1.** [person] malchanceux; [day] de malchance; she was rather ~ elle a été plutôt malchanceuse; we were ~ enough to get caught in a jam nous avons eu la malchance d'être pris dans un embouteillage; to be ~ in love être malheureux en amour. -**2.** [colour, number] qui porte malheur; [omen] funeste, mauvais; it's supposed to be ~ to break a mirror c'est censé porter malheur de casser un miroir.

unmade [,ʌn'meɪd] ◇ *pt* & *pp* → **unmake**.
◇ *adj* -**1.** [bed] défait. -**2.** *Br* [road] non goudronné.

unmade-up *adj* [face] non maquillé, sans maquillage.

unmake [,ʌn'meɪk] (*pt* & *pp* unmade [-'meɪd]) *vt* -**1.** [bed] défaire. -**2.** *fml* OR *lit* [reputation] démolir, ruiner; [man] briser, ruiner; [ruler] déposer.

unman [,ʌn'mæn] (*pt* & *pp* unmanned, *cont* unmanning) *vt* -**1.** NAUT renvoyer l'équipage de. -**2.** *lit* [person] faire perdre courage à.

unmanageable [ʌn'mænɪdʒəbl] *adj* -**1.** [unwieldy - vehicle] peu maniable; [- object] peu maniable, difficile à manier; the trailer was of an ~ length à cause de sa longueur, la caravane était difficile à manœuvrer. -**2.** [animal] difficile, indocile; [children] difficile, impossible. -**3.** [situation] difficile à gérer; the problem has become ~ le problème est devenu impossible à gérer OR à régler. -**4.** [hair] difficile à coiffer, rebelle.

unmanly [,ʌn'mænlɪ] *adj* -**1.** [effeminate] efféminé, peu viril. -**2.** [cowardly] lâche.

unmanned [,ʌn'mænd] *adj* [without crew - plane, ship] sans équipage; [- spacecraft, flight] inhabité; RAIL [- station] sans personnel; [- level crossing] non gardé, automatique; ~ space travel vols *mpl* spatiaux non habités; the border post/switchboard was ~ il n'y avait personne au poste frontière/au standard; the control centre was left ~ for half an hour le centre de contrôle est resté sans surveillance pendant une demi-heure.

unmannerly [ʌn'mænəlɪ] *adj fml* [person] discourtois, mal élevé; [behaviour] mal élevé.

unmapped [,ʌn'mæpt] *adj* [area] pour lequel il n'existe pas de carte, dont on n'a pas dressé la carte.

unmarked [,ʌn'mɑːkt] *adj* -**1.** [face, furniture, page] sans marque, sans tache. -**2.** [without identifying features]: the radioactive waste was carried in ~ drums les déchets radioactifs étaient transportés dans des barils non identifiés; an ~ police car une voiture de police banalisée. -**3.** [without name tag, label] sans nom, non marqué. -**4.** [essay] non corrigé. -**5.** LING non marqué. -**6.** SPORT [player] démarqué.

unmarketable [,ʌn'mɑːkɪtəbl] *adj* invendable.

unmarred [,ʌn'mɑːd] *adj lit* non abîmé; [reputation] sans tache, entier.

unmarriageable [,ʌn'mærɪdʒəbl] *adj* immariable.

unmarried [,ʌn'mærɪd] *adj* non marié, célibataire; ~ mother mère *f* célibataire.

unmask [,ʌn'mɑːsk] *vt* démasquer.

unmatched [,ʌn'mætʃt] *adj* inégalé, sans égal OR pareil.

unmeasurable [,ʌn'meʒərəbl] *adj* incommensurable.

unmeasured [,ʌn'meʒəd] *adj* -**1.** [gen] sans mesure, démesuré. -**2.** MUS sans mesure, non mesuré.

unmentionable [ʌn'menʃnəbl] ◇ *adj* [subject] dont il ne faut pas parler, interdit; [word] qu'il ne faut pas prononcer, interdit.
◇ *n*: the ~ [forbidden subject] le sujet interdit OR dont il ne faut pas parler; [taboo] le sujet tabou.
◆ **unmentionables** *npl euph* & *hum* [underwear] dessous *mpl*, sous-vêtements *mpl*.

unmerciful [ʌn'mɜːsɪfʊl] *adj* impitoyable, sans pitié; to be ~ to OR towards sb être sans pitié pour qqn.

unmercifully [ʌn'mɜːsɪfʊlɪ] *adv* [treat] impitoyablement, sans pitié; [tease] sans répit.

unmerited [,ʌn'merɪtɪd] *adj* [undeserved] immérité; [unjust] injuste.

unmindful [ʌn'maɪndfʊl] *adj fml* [uncaring] peu soucieux; [forgetful] oublieux; [inattentive] inattentif; he is ~ of other people's feelings il est peu soucieux des sentiments des autres, il ne tient pas compte des sentiments des autres.

unmistakable [,ʌnmɪ'steɪkəbl] *adj* [not mistakeable] facilement reconnaissable; the ~ sound of bagpipes le son aisément reconnaissable de la cornemuse ‖ [clear, obvious] indubitable, manifeste, évident; she began to show ~ signs of fatigue elle commença à montrer des signes évidents de fatigue.

unmistakably [,ʌnmɪ'steɪkəblɪ] *adv* -**1.** [undeniably] indéniablement, sans erreur possible. -**2.** [visibly] visiblement, manifestement.

unmistakeable [,ʌnmɪ'steɪkəbl] = **unmistakable**.

unmitigated [ʌn'mɪtɪgeɪtɪd] *adj* -**1.** [total - disaster, chaos] total; [- stupidity] pur, total; the whole project was an ~ disaster tout le projet a été un véritable désastre. -**2.** [undiminished] non mitigé.

unmixed [,ʌn'mɪkst] *adj* non mélangé, pur.

unmounted [,ʌn'maʊntɪd] *adj* -**1.** [rider] non monté, sans monture. -**2.** [photograph] non monté. -**3.** [jewel] non monté OR serti.

unmourned [,ʌn'mɔːnd] *adj*: he died ~ personne ne l'a pleuré.

unmoved [ˌʌn'muːvd] *adj* indifférent, insensible; to be ~ by sthg rester insensible à qqch; the music left me ~ la musique ne m'a pas ému; he remained ~ il a continué, imperturbable OR impassible.
unmusical [ˌʌn'mjuːzɪkl] *adj* -**1.** [sound] peu musical. -**2.** [person] peu musicien.
unnameable [ˌʌn'neɪməbl] *adj* innommable, sans nom.
unnamed [ˌʌn'neɪmd] *adj* -**1.** [anonymous] anonyme; [unspecified] non précisé. -**2.** [having no name - child] sans nom, qui n'a pas reçu de nom; [- desire, fear] inavoué.
unnatural [ʌn'nætʃrəl] *adj* -**1.** [affected - behaviour, manner, tone] affecté, peu naturel; [- laughter] peu naturel, forcé. -**2.** [odd, abnormal - circumstances, state] anormal; [- phenomenon] surnaturel. -**3.** [perverse - love, passion] contre nature.
unnaturally [ʌn'nætʃrəlɪ] *adv* [behave, laugh, walk] bizarrement, de façon peu naturelle; he not ~ decided to resign naturellement, il a décidé de démissionner.
unnecessarily [*Br* ʌn'nesəsərɪlɪ, *Am* ˌʌnnesə'serəlɪ] *adv* sans nécessité OR raison.
unnecessary [ʌn'nesəsərɪ] *adj* superflu, inutile; it's quite ~ for you all to attend il n'est vraiment pas nécessaire OR utile que vous y alliez tous; it's a lot of ~ fuss c'est beaucoup d'agitation pour rien.
unneighbourly *Br*, **unneighborly** *Am* [ˌʌn'neɪbəlɪ] *adj* [unfriendly] peu obligeant, qui n'agit pas en bon voisin; [unhelpful] peu serviable.
unnerve [ˌʌn'nɜːv] *vt* démonter, déconcerter.
unnerving [ˌʌn'nɜːvɪŋ] *adj* [event, experience] déconcertant, perturbant.
unnoticed [ˌʌn'nəʊtɪst] *adj* inaperçu; to pass ~ passer inaperçu.
unnumbered [ˌʌn'nʌmbəd] *adj* -**1.** [seats, tickets, copies] non numéroté. -**2.** *fig* & *fml* [descendants, followers, stars] innombrable, sans nombre.
UNO (*abbr of* United Nations Organization) *pr n* ONU *f*.
unobjectionable [ˌʌnəb'dʒekʃnəbl] *adj* [idea, activity] acceptable; [behaviour, person] qui ne peut être critiqué.
unobservant [ˌʌnəb'zɜːvənt] *adj* peu observateur.
unobserved [ˌʌnəb'zɜːvd] *adj* inaperçu; she crept past ~ elle s'est faufilée sans se faire remarquer.
unobstructed [ˌʌnəb'strʌktɪd] *adj* -**1.** [entry, passage, view] non obstrué, libre. -**2.** [activity, progress] sans obstacle.
unobtainable [ˌʌnəb'teɪnəbl] *adj* impossible à obtenir; the ~ tone *Br* TELEC *tonalité continue indiquant qu'un numéro n'est pas en service*.
unobtrusive [ˌʌnəb'truːsɪv] *adj* [person] discret, effacé; [object] discret, pas trop visible; [smell] discret.
unobtrusively [ˌʌnəb'truːsɪvlɪ] *adv* discrètement; she stood ~ in a corner elle se tenait dans un coin sans se faire remarquer.
unoccupied [ʌn'ɒkjʊpaɪd] *adj* -**1.** [person] qui ne fait rien, oisif. -**2.** [house] inoccupé, vide; [seat] libre. -**3.** MIL [zone, territory] non occupé, libre.
unofficial [ˌʌnə'fɪʃl] *adj* -**1.** [unconfirmed - report] officieux, non officiel. -**2.** [informal - appointment] non officiel, privé. -**3.** INDUST: ~ strike grève *f* sauvage.
unofficially [ˌʌnə'fɪʃəlɪ] *adv* [informally] officieusement; [in private] en privé.
unopened [ˌʌn'əʊpənd] *adj* -**1.** [letter, bottle] fermé. -**2.** BOT non éclos.
unopposed [ˌʌnə'pəʊzd] *adj*: she was elected ~ elle était la seule candidate (et elle a été élue).
unorganized, -ised [ˌʌn'ɔːgənaɪzd] *adj* inorganisé, non organisé.
unoriginal [ˌʌnə'rɪdʒənl] *adj* sans originalité.
unorthodox [ˌʌn'ɔːθədɒks] *adj* non orthodoxe, pas très orthodoxe; RELIG hétérodoxe.

unpack [ˌʌn'pæk] ◇ *vt* -**1.** [bag, suitcase] défaire; [books, clothes, shopping] déballer; to get ~ed défaire ses bagages; can you ~ the cases from the boot? pouvez-vous sortir les valises du coffre? -**2.** COMPUT décompresser.
◇ *vi* défaire ses bagages.
unpacking [ˌʌn'pækɪŋ] *n* déballage *m*; to do the ~ déballer ses affaires.
unpaid [ˌʌn'peɪd] *adj* -**1.** [helper, job] bénévole, non rémunéré. -**2.** [bill, salary] impayé; [employee] non payé; ~ holiday congé *m* sans solde.
unpalatable [ʌn'pælətəbl] *adj* [food] immangeable; *fig* [idea] dérangeant; [truth] désagréable à entendre.
unparalleled [ʌn'pærəleld] *adj* [unequalled] sans pareil; [unprecedented] sans précédent.
unpardonable [ʌn'pɑːdnəbl] *adj* impardonnable, inexcusable.
unpardonably [ʌn'pɑːdnəblɪ] *adv* de manière inexcusable; he was ~ rude il a été d'une impolitesse inexcusable OR impardonnable.
unparliamentary ['ʌnˌpɑːlə'mentərɪ] *adj* [behaviour] peu courtois OR parlementaire *dated*; ~ language *Br* POL langage *m* grossier.
unpatriotic ['ʌnˌpætrɪ'ɒtɪk] *adj* [person] peu patriote; [sentiment, song] peu patriotique.
unpaved [ˌʌn'peɪvd] *adj* [street] non pavé.
unperturbed [ˌʌnpə'tɜːbd] *adj* imperturbable, impassible; to be ~ by sthg rester imperturbable face à qqch; he remained ~ il est resté impassible.
unpick [ˌʌn'pɪk] *vt* découdre.
unpin [ˌʌn'pɪn] (*pt* & *pp* unpinned, *cont* unpinning) *vt* [seam] enlever les épingles de.
unplaced [ˌʌn'pleɪst] *adj* [horse, competitor] non placé.
unplanned [ˌʌn'plænd] *adj* [visit, activity] imprévu.
unplayable [ˌʌn'pleɪəbl] *adj* [pitch] impraticable; [ball, shot - in tennis, squash etc] qu'on ne peut rattraper; [- in golf] impossible à jouer.
unpleasant [ʌn'pleznt] *adj* [person] désagréable; [smell, weather] désagréable, mauvais; [remark] désagréable, désobligeant; [memory] pénible; it was a most ~ experience ce fut une expérience fort *fml* OR extrêmement désagréable; the boss was most ~ to her le patron était très désagréable avec elle.
unpleasantly [ʌn'plezntlɪ] *adv* désagréablement, de façon déplaisante; her remarks were ~ close to the truth ses remarques tombaient si juste que c'en était désagréable.
unpleasantness [ʌn'plezntnɪs] *n* -**1.** [of person] côté *m* désagréable; [of experience, weather] désagrément *m*. -**2.** [discord] friction *f*, dissension *f*; the disputes caused a lot of ~ le conflit a provoqué beaucoup de frictions.
unpleasing [ˌʌn'pliːzɪŋ] *adj* déplaisant, désagréable.
unplug [ʌn'plʌg] (*pt* & *pp* unplugged, *cont* unplugging) *vt* ELEC débrancher.
unplumbed [ˌʌn'plʌmd] *adj* [depths, area of knowledge] insondé.
unpolished [ˌʌn'pɒlɪʃt] *adj* -**1.** [furniture, brass] non poli; [floor, shoes] non ciré. -**2.** *fig* [person] qui manque de savoir-vivre; [manners, style] peu raffiné, peu élégant.
unpolluted [ˌʌnpə'luːtɪd] *adj* non pollué.
unpopular [ˌʌn'pɒpjʊlə^r] *adj* impopulaire, peu populaire; this style is ~ with the younger generation ce style est peu populaire chez les jeunes, les jeunes n'aiment pas beaucoup ce style; I'm rather ~ with the bosses just now je ne suis pas très bien vu des patrons en ce moment; to make o.s. ~ se rendre impopulaire.
unpopularity ['ʌnˌpɒpjʊ'lærətɪ] *n* impopularité *f*.
unpractised *Br*, **unpracticed** *Am* [ʌn'præktɪst] *adj* inexpérimenté.
unprecedented [ʌn'presɪdəntɪd] *adj* sans précédent.

unpredictable [ˌʌnprɪ'dɪktəbl] *adj* imprévisible.
unpredictably [ˌʌnprɪ'dɪktəblɪ] *adv* de façon imprévisible.
unprejudiced [ˌʌn'predʒʊdɪst] *adj* impartial, sans parti pris.
unpremeditated [ˌʌnprɪ'medɪteɪtɪd] *adj* sans préméditation.
unprepared [ˌʌnprɪ'peəd] *adj* mal préparé; we were ~ for what happened nous n'étions pas préparés à ce qui s'est passé.
unpreparedness [ˌʌnprɪ'peərɪdnɪs] *n* manque *m* de préparation.
unprepossessing ['ʌnˌpriːpə'zesɪŋ] *adj* [place, smile] peu attrayant, qui n'a rien d'attrayant; [person] peu avenant.
unpretentious [ˌʌnprɪ'tenʃəs] *adj* sans prétention.
unpriced [ˌʌn'praɪst] *adj* non étiqueté, qui n'a pas d'étiquette de prix.
unprincipled [ʌn'prɪnsəpld] *adj* [person, behaviour] sans scrupules.
unprintable [ˌʌn'prɪntəbl] *adj* [language] grossier; her reply was ~ la décence m'empêche de rapporter sa réponse.
unprocessed [ʌn'prəʊsest] *adj* -**1.** [food, wool] non traité, naturel. -**2.** PHOT [film] non développé. -**3.** [data] brut.
unproductive [ˌʌnprə'dʌktɪv] *adj* [land] improductif, stérile; [discussion, weekend] improductif.
unprofessional [ˌʌnprə'feʃənl] *adj* [attitude, conduct] peu professionnel.
unprofitable [ˌʌn'prɒfɪtəbl] *adj* -**1.** [business] peu rentable. -**2.** [discussions] peu profitable; [action] inutile.
unpromising [ˌʌn'prɒmɪsɪŋ] *adj* peu prometteur.
unprompted [ˌʌn'prɒmptɪd] *adj* [action, words] spontané.
unpronounceable [ˌʌnprə'naʊnsəbl] *adj* imprononçable.
unprotected [ˌʌnprə'tektɪd] *adj* -**1.** [person] sans protection, non défendu; children over 15 are ~ by the legislation les enfants de plus de 15 ans ne sont pas protégés par la législation; ~ sex rapports *mpl* non protégés. -**2.** [machinery] sans protection, non protégé. -**3.** [wood] non traité. -**4.** [exposed] exposé (aux intempéries); the house is ~ from the east wind la maison est exposée aux vents d'est.
unprovoked [ˌʌnprə'vəʊkt] *adj* [attack, insult] injustifié.
unpublishable [ˌʌn'pʌblɪʃəbl] *adj* impubliable; an ~ manuscript un très mauvais manuscrit.
unpublished [ˌʌn'pʌblɪʃt] *adj* [manuscript, book] inédit, non publié.
unpunctual [ˌʌn'pʌŋktʃʊəl] *adj* peu ponctuel, souvent en retard.
unpunished [ˌʌn'pʌnɪʃt] *adj* impuni; he can't be allowed to go ~ il ne peut pas rester impuni.
unputdownable *inf* [ˌʌnpʊt'daʊnəbl] *adj Br* [book, novel] passionnant, dont on a du mal à s'arracher.
unqualified [ˌʌn'kwɒlɪfaɪd] *adj* -**1.** [unskilled] non qualifié; [without diploma] qui n'a pas les diplômes requis; [unsuitable] qui n'a pas les qualités requises; he is ~ for the job of chairman il n'est pas qualifié pour le poste de président. -**2.** [not competent] non qualifié OR compétent; she is ~ to decide elle n'est pas qualifiée pour décider. -**3.** [unrestricted - admiration, approval] inconditionnel, sans réserve; [- success] complet.
unquenchable [ˌʌn'kwentʃəbl] *adj lit* [curiosity, desire, thirst] insatiable.
unquestionable [ʌn'kwestʃənəbl] *adj* -**1.** [undeniable] incontestable, indubitable. -**2.** [above suspicion] qui ne peut être mis en question.
unquestionably [ʌn'kwestʃənəblɪ] *adv* indéniablement, incontestablement.
unquestioned [ʌn'kwestʃənd] *adj* [decision, leader, principle] indiscuté, incontesté.

unquestioning [ʌn'kwestʃənɪŋ] *adj* [faith, love, obedience, belief] absolu, aveugle.

unquestioningly [ʌn'kwestʃənɪŋlɪ] *adv* aveuglément.

unquiet [ˌʌn'kwaɪət] *adj lit* [person] troublé, inquiet, tourmenté; [mind] perturbé, tourmenté; [period] troublé, agité.

unquote [ˌʌn'kwəʊt] *adv* fin de citation; [in dictation] fermez les guillemets.

unquoted [ˌʌn'kwəʊtɪd] *adj*: ~ company *Br* société *f* non cotée (en Bourse); ~ shares actions *fpl* non cotées (en Bourse).

unravel [ʌn'rævl] (*Br pt & pp* unravelled, *cont* unravelling, *Am pt & pp* unraveled, *cont* unraveling) ◇ *vt* -1. [knitting] défaire; [textile] effiler, effilocher. -2. [untangle - knots, string] démêler; *fig* [mystery] débrouiller, éclaircir.
◇ *vi* [knitting] se défaire; [textile] s'effilocher.

unread [ˌʌn'red] *adj* -1. [person] qui a peu lu. -2. [book, report] qui n'a pas été lu.

unreadable [ˌʌn'riːdəbl] *adj* -1. [handwriting, signature] illisible. -2. [book, report] illisible, ennuyeux.

unreadiness [ˌʌn'redɪnɪs] *n* -1. [unpreparedness] manque *m* de préparation. -2. [unwillingness] manque *m* d'empressement.

unready [ˌʌn'redɪ] *adj* -1. [unprepared] non préparé, qui n'est pas prêt. -2. [unwilling] peu disposé.

unreal [ˌʌn'rɪəl] *adj* -1. [appearance, feeling]: it all seems so ~ tout paraît si irréel; an ~ situation une situation artificielle. -2. ▽ [very good] incroyable.

unrealistic [ˌʌnrɪə'lɪstɪk] *adj* irréaliste, peu réaliste.

unrealistically [ˌʌnrɪə'lɪstɪklɪ] *adv*: his hopes were ~ high ses espoirs étaient trop grands pour être réalistes.

unreality [ˌʌnrɪ'ælətɪ] *n* irréalité *f*.

unrealizable, -isable [ˌʌn'rɪəlaɪzəbl] *adj* [aim, dream] irréalisable; [fact, situation, state] inconcevable.

unreason [ˌʌn'riːzn] *n fml* déraison *f*, folie *f*.

unreasonable [ʌn'riːznəbl] *adj* -1. [absurd, preposterous] déraisonnable; you're being ~ vous n'êtes pas raisonnable; it's ~ to stay up so late ce n'est pas raisonnable de veiller si tard. -2. [excessive] excessif, déraisonnable.

unreasonably [ʌn'riːznəblɪ] *adv* déraisonnablement.

unreasoning [ʌn'riːznɪŋ] *adj* irrationnel.

unreclaimed [ˌʌnrɪ'kleɪmd] *adj* -1. [belongings, parcel] non réclamé. -2. [land] non défriché, laissé en friche; [marshes] non asséché.

unrecognizable, -isable [ˌʌn'rekəgnaɪzəbl] *adj* méconnaissable.

unrecognized, -ised [ˌʌn'rekəgnaɪzd] *adj* -1. [without being recognized]: he slipped out ~ il s'est glissé vers la sortie sans être reconnu. -2. [not acknowledged - talent, achievement] méconnu; he is ~ by the scientific community il n'est pas reconnu par la communauté scientifique; her discoveries went largely ~ ses découvertes sont restées méconnues pour la plupart.

unreconstructed [ˌʌnriːkən'strʌktɪd] *adj* [person, ideas] rétrograde.

unrecorded [ˌʌnrɪ'kɔːdɪd] *adj* -1. [remark, fact] qui n'a pas été enregistré. -2. [music] qui n'a pas encore été enregistré.

unredeemed [ˌʌnrɪ'diːmd] *adj* -1. [from pawn] non dégagé OR racheté. -2. [promise] non tenu; [obligation] non rempli. -3. [sinner] impénitent; [sin] inexpié, non racheté.

unreel [ˌʌn'riːl] ◇ *vt* dérouler.
◇ *vi* se dérouler.

unrefined [ˌʌnrɪ'faɪnd] *adj* -1. [petrol] brut, non raffiné; [sugar] non raffiné; [flour] non bluté. -2. [person, manners] peu raffiné, fruste.

unreflecting [ˌʌnrɪ'flektɪŋ] *adj* -1. [person, action, behaviour] irréfléchi. -2. [surface] non réfléchissant.

unregistered [ˌʌn'redʒɪstəd] *adj* -1. [luggage, complaint] non enregistré. -2. [mail] non recommandé. -3. [car] non immatriculé. -4. [voter, student] non inscrit; [birth] non déclaré; ~ childminder *Br* nourrice *f* non agréée.

unrehearsed [ˌʌnrɪ'hɜːst] *adj* -1. [improvised] improvisé, spontané. -2. MUS & THEAT sans répétition, qui n'a pas été répété.

unrelated [ˌʌnrɪ'leɪtɪd] *adj* -1. [unconnected] sans rapport; the two incidents are ~ les deux incidents sont sans rapport l'un avec l'autre; his answer was completely ~ to the question sa réponse n'avait absolument aucun rapport OR absolument rien à voir avec la question. -2. [people] sans lien de parenté.

unrelenting [ˌʌnrɪ'lentɪŋ] *adj* -1. [activity, effort] soutenu, continuel. -2. [person] tenace, obstiné.

unrelentingly [ˌʌnrɪ'lentɪŋlɪ] *adv* sans répit.

unreliability ['ʌnrɪˌlaɪə'bɪlətɪ] *n* -1. [of person] manque *m* de sérieux. -2. [of method, machine] manque *m* de fiabilité.

unreliable [ˌʌnrɪ'laɪəbl] *adj* -1. [person] peu fiable, sur qui on ne peut pas compter; he's too ~ on ne peut vraiment pas compter sur lui OR lui faire confiance. -2. [car, machinery] peu fiable. -3. [delivery, service] peu fiable, peu sûr; [business, company] qui n'inspire pas confiance. -4. [documents, information, memory] peu fiable.

unreliably [ˌʌnrɪ'laɪəblɪ] *adv* de manière peu fiable.

unrelieved [ˌʌnrɪ'liːvd] *adj* [pain] constant, non soulagé; [gloom, misery] constant, permanent; [boredom] mortel; [black] uniforme; [landscape, routine] monotone.

unremarkable [ˌʌnrɪ'mɑːkəbl] *adj* peu remarquable, quelconque.

unremarked [ˌʌnrɪ'mɑːkt] *adj* inaperçu.

unremitting [ˌʌnrɪ'mɪtɪŋ] *adj* [activity, rain] incessant, ininterrompu; [demands, efforts] inlassable, infatigable; [opposition] implacable, opiniâtre; they were ~ in their efforts to find a solution ils se sont efforcés avec assiduité de trouver une solution.

unremittingly [ˌʌnrɪ'mɪtɪŋlɪ] *adv* [work] sans cesse, inlassablement; [rain] sans cesse, sans interruption; [hostile, opposed] implacablement, opiniâtrement.

unrepeatable [ˌʌnrɪ'piːtəbl] *adj* [remark] qu'on n'ose pas répéter, trop grossier pour être répété; [offer, performance] exceptionnel, unique.

unrepentant [ˌʌnrɪ'pentənt] *adj* impénitent.

unreported [ˌʌnrɪ'pɔːtɪd] *adj* non signalé OR mentionné; the accident went ~ l'accident n'a pas été signalé.

unrepresentative [ˌʌnreprɪ'zentətɪv] *adj* non représentatif; his opinions are ~ of the group ses opinions ne représentent pas celles du groupe.

unrepresented [ˌʌnreprɪ'zentɪd] *adj* POL qui n'est pas représenté.

unrequited [ˌʌnrɪ'kwaɪtɪd] *adj lit* non réciproque, non partagé; ~ love amour non partagé.

unreserved [ˌʌnrɪ'zɜːvd] *adj* -1. [place] non réservé. -2. [unqualified] sans réserve, entier.

unreservedly [ˌʌnrɪ'zɜːvɪdlɪ] *adv* -1. [without qualification] sans réserve, entièrement. -2. [frankly] sans réserve, franchement.

unresolved [ˌʌnrɪ'zɒlvd] *adj* [issue, problem] non résolu.

unresponsive [ˌʌnrɪ'spɒnsɪv] *adj* [without reaction] qui ne réagit pas; [unaffected] insensible; an ~ audience un auditoire passif; management was ~ to workers' demands l'administration n'a pas répondu aux exigences des ouvriers.

unrest [ˌʌn'rest] *n (U)* agitation *f*, troubles *mpl*.

unrestrained [ˌʌnrɪ'streɪnd] *adj* [anger, growth, joy] non contenu; the ~ use of force l'usage sans limites de la force.

unrestricted [ˌʌnrɪ'strɪktɪd] *adj* [access, parking] libre; [number, time] illimité; [power] absolu.

unrewarded [ˌʌnrɪ'wɔːdɪd] *adj* [person] non récompensé; [effort, search] vain, infructueux; our efforts went ~ nos efforts sont restés sans récompense.

unrewarding [ˌʌnrɪ'wɔːdɪŋ] *adj* -1. [financially] pas très intéressant financièrement. -2. *fig* [work, experience] ingrat.

unrighteous [ʌn'raɪtʃəs] *npl lit*: the ~ [not pious] les impies *mpl*; [sinful] les pécheurs *mpl*.

unripe [ˌʌn'raɪp] *adj* vert.

unrivalled *Br*, **unrivaled** *Am* [ʌn'raɪvld] *adj* sans égal OR pareil, incomparable.

unroadworthy [ˌʌn'rəʊdˌwɜːðɪ] *adj* [vehicle] qui n'est pas en état de rouler.

unroll [ˌʌn'rəʊl] *vt* dérouler.

unromantic [ˌʌnrə'mæntɪk] *adj* [person - unsentimental] peu romantique; [- down-to-earth] prosaïque, terre à terre *(inv)*; [ideas, place] peu romantique.

unruffled [ˌʌn'rʌfld] *adj* -1. [person] imperturbable, qui ne perd pas son calme; she remained completely ~ elle n'a pas sourcillé OR bronché. -2. [hair] lisse; [water] calme, lisse.

unruled [ˌʌn'ruːld] *adj* blanc, non réglé.

unruly [ʌn'ruːlɪ] *adj* -1. [children] indiscipliné, turbulent; [mob] incontrôlé. -2. [hair] indiscipliné.

unsaddle [ˌʌn'sædl] *vt* [horse] desseller; [rider] désarçonner.

unsafe [ˌʌn'seɪf] *adj* -1. [dangerous - machine, neighbourhood] peu sûr, dangereux; [- building, bridge] peu solide, dangereux; the water is ~ to drink l'eau n'est pas potable. -2. [endangered] en danger; I feel very ~ here je ne me sens pas du tout en sécurité ici.

unsaid [ˌʌn'sed] *adj* non dit, inexprimé; a lot was left ~ beaucoup de choses ont été passées sous silence.

unsal(e)able [ˌʌn'seɪləbl] *adj* invendable.

unsalted [ˌʌn'sɔːltɪd] *adj* non salé.

unsatisfactory ['ʌnˌsætɪs'fæktərɪ] *adj* peu satisfaisant, qui laisse à désirer.

unsatisfied [ˌʌn'sætɪsfaɪd] *adj* -1. [person - unhappy] insatisfait, mécontent; [- unconvinced] non convaincu; they remain ~ with her work ils sont toujours mécontents de son travail. -2. [desire] insatisfait, inassouvi.

unsatisfying [ˌʌn'sætɪsfaɪɪŋ] *adj* -1. [activity, task] peu gratifiant, ingrat. -2. [unconvincing] peu convaincant. -3. [meal - insufficient] insuffisant, peu nourrissant; [- disappointing] décevant.

unsaturated [ˌʌn'sætʃəreɪtɪd] *adj* non saturé.

unsavoury *Br*, **unsavory** *Am* [ˌʌn'seɪvərɪ] *adj* -1. [behaviour, habits] répugnant, très déplaisant; [person] peu recommandable; [place] louche; [reputation] douteux. -2. [smell] fétide, nauséabond.

unsay [ˌʌn'seɪ] (*pt & pp* unsaid [-'sed]) *vt* retirer, revenir sur.

unscathed [ˌʌn'skeɪðd] *adj* [physically] indemne, sain et sauf; [psychologically] non affecté.

unscheduled [*Br* ˌʌn'ʃedjuːld, *Am* ˌʌn'skedʒuːld] *adj* imprévu.

unschooled [ˌʌn'skuːld] *adj fml* -1. [person] qui n'a pas d'instruction. -2. [talent] inné, naturel.

unscientific ['ʌnˌsaɪən'tɪfɪk] *adj* non OR peu scientifique.

unscramble [ˌʌn'skræmbl] *vt* [code, message] déchiffrer; *fig* [problem] résoudre.

unscrambler [ˌʌn'skræmblər] *n* déchiffreur *m*.

unscrew [ˌʌn'skruː] ◇ *vt* dévisser.
◇ *vi* se dévisser.

unscripted [ˌʌn'skrɪptɪd] *adj* [play, speech] improvisé; [item, subject] non programmé.

unscrupulous [ʌn'skruːpjʊləs] *adj* [person] sans scrupules, peu scrupuleux; [behaviour, methods] malhonnête, peu scrupuleux.

unscrupulously [ʌn'skruːpjʊləslɪ] *adv* sans scrupules, peu scrupuleusement.

unscrupulousness [ʌn'skruːpjʊləsnɪs] *n* [of person] manque *m* de scrupules, malhonnêteté *f*; [of behaviour, methods] malhonnêteté *f*.

unseal [ˌʌn'siːl] *vt* [open - letter] ouvrir, décacheter; [- deed, testament] desceller; to ~ one's lips *fig* rompre le silence, parler.

unsealed [ˌʌn'siːld] *adj* [letter] ouvert, décacheté; [deed, testament] descellé.

unseasonable [ʌn'siːznəbl] *adj* [clothing, weather] qui n'est pas de saison.

unseasonably [ʌn'siːznəblɪ] *adv*: **an ~ cold night** une nuit fraîche pour la saison.

unseasoned [ˌʌn'siːznd] *adj* -**1.** [food] non assaisonné. -**2.** [wood] vert.

unseat [ˌʌn'siːt] *vt* [rider] désarçonner; [government, king] faire tomber.

unsecured [ˌʌnsɪ'kjʊəd] *adj* -**1.** [door, window - unlocked] qui n'est pas fermé à clé; [- open] mal fermé. -**2.** FIN [creditor, loan] sans garantie.

unseeded [ˌʌn'siːdɪd] *adj* SPORT non classé.

unseeing [ˌʌn'siːɪŋ] *adj lit* aveugle; **he looked at her with ~ eyes** il l'a regardée sans (vraiment) la voir.

unseemly [ʌn'siːmlɪ] *adj lit* [improper - behaviour] inconvenant, déplacé; [- dress] inconvenant, peu convenable; [rude] indécent, grossier.

unseen [ˌʌn'siːn] ◇ *adj* -**1.** [invisible] invisible; [unnoticed] inaperçu; **she passed ~ through the crowd** elle est passée inaperçue dans la foule. -**2.** [not seen previously]: **to buy sthg sight ~** acheter qqch sans l'avoir vu; **an ~ translation** *Br* SCH & UNIV une traduction sans préparation OR à vue.
◇ *n Br* SCH & UNIV traduction *f* sans préparation OR à vue.

unsegregated [ˌʌn'segrɪgeɪtɪd] *adj* où la ségrégation n'est pas appliquée.

unselfconscious [ˌʌnself'kɒnʃəs] *adj* naturel; **she's quite ~ about speaking up** elle n'a vraiment pas peur de dire ce qu'elle pense, elle dit ce qu'elle pense sans la moindre gêne.

unselfish [ˌʌn'selfɪʃ] *adj* [person, act] généreux, désintéressé.

unselfishly [ˌʌn'selfɪʃlɪ] *adv* généreusement, sans penser à soi.

unselfishness [ˌʌn'selfɪʃnɪs] *n* [of person, act] générosité *f*, désintéressement *m*.

unset [ʌn'set] *adj* [diamond, emerald] non serti, non enchâssé.

unsettle [ˌʌn'setl] *vt* -**1.** [person] inquiéter, troubler. -**2.** [stomach] déranger.

unsettled [ˌʌn'setld] *adj* -**1.** [unstable - conditions, situation] instable, incertain; [- person] troublé, perturbé, inquiet; [- stomach] dérangé; [- weather] incertain, changeant; **I feel ~ in my job** je ne suis pas bien dans mon boulot. -**2.** [unfinished - issue, argument, dispute] qui n'a pas été réglé. -**3.** [account, bill] non réglé, impayé. -**4.** [area, region] inhabité, sans habitants.

unsettling [ˌʌn'setlɪŋ] *adj* [disturbing] troublant, perturbateur.

unsex [ˌʌn'seks] *vt lit* [woman] faire perdre sa féminité à; [man] faire perdre sa virilité à.

unshackle [ˌʌn'ʃækl] *vt literal* désenchaîner, ôter ses fers à; *fig* libérer, émanciper.

unshakeable [ʌn'ʃeɪkəbl] *adj* [conviction, faith] inébranlable; [decision] ferme.

unshakeably [ʌn'ʃeɪkəblɪ] *adv* irréductiblement.

unshaken [ˌʌn'ʃeɪkən] *adj* inébranlable.

unshaven [ˌʌn'ʃeɪvn] *adj* non rasé.

unsheathe [ˌʌn'ʃiːð] *vt* dégainer.

unshockable [ˌʌn'ʃɒkəbl] *adj* imperturbable, impassible.

unshod [ˌʌn'ʃɒd] *adj* [horse] qui n'est pas ferré.

unsighted [ˌʌn'saɪtɪd] *adj* SPORT: **the goalkeeper was ~** quelqu'un empêchait le gardien de but de voir le ballon.

unsightliness [ʌn'saɪtlɪnɪs] *n* laideur *f*, aspect *m* disgracieux.

unsightly [ʌn'saɪtlɪ] *adj* disgracieux, laid.

unsigned [ˌʌn'saɪnd] *adj* non signé, sans signature.

unsinkable [ˌʌn'sɪŋkəbl] *adj* [boat] insubmersible; *fig* [person] qui ne se démonte pas facilement.

unskilful *Br*, **unskillful** *Am* [ˌʌn'skɪlfʊl] *adj* [lacking skill] inexpert, malhabile; [clumsy] maladroit.

unskilled [ˌʌn'skɪld] *adj* -**1.** [worker] sans formation professionnelle, non spécialisé, non qualifié; **~ labourer** *Br* ouvrier *m* non spécialisé, ouvrière *f* non spécialisée. -**2.** [job, work] qui ne nécessite pas de connaissances professionnelles.

unskillful *Am* = **unskilful**.

unsmiling [ˌʌn'smaɪlɪŋ] *adj* [person, face] austère, sérieux.

unsociable [ʌn'səʊʃəbl] *adj* [person] sauvage, peu sociable; [place] peu accueillant; **to feel ~** ne pas avoir envie de voir du monde; **don't be so ~!** ne sois pas si sauvage!

unsocial [ˌʌn'səʊʃl] *adj*: **she works ~ hours** elle travaille en dehors des heures normales.

unsold [ˌʌn'səʊld] *adj* invendu.

unsolicited [ˌʌnsə'lɪsɪtɪd] *adj* non sollicité.

unsolved [ˌʌn'sɒlvd] *adj* [mystery] non résolu, inexpliqué; [problem] non résolu.

unsophisticated [ˌʌnsə'fɪstɪkeɪtɪd] *adj* -**1.** [person - in dress, tastes] simple; [- in attitude] simple, naturel. -**2.** [dress, style] simple, qui n'est pas sophistiqué. -**3.** [device, machine] (de conception) simple; [approach, method] rudimentaire, simpliste *pej*.

unsorted [ˌʌn'sɔːtɪd] *adj* [clothing, mail] non trié; [documents] non classé.

unsought [ˌʌn'sɔːt] *adj* [advice, compliment] non sollicité, non recherché.

unsound [ˌʌn'saʊnd] *adj* -**1.** [argument, conclusion, reasoning] mal fondé, peu pertinent; [advice, decision] peu judicieux, peu sensé; [enterprise, investment] peu sûr, risqué; [business] peu sûr, précaire; **the project is economically ~** le projet n'est pas sain OR viable sur le plan économique. -**2.** [building, bridge] peu solide, dangereux. -**3.** *phr*: **to be of ~ mind** ne pas jouir de toutes ses facultés mentales.

unsparing [ʌn'speərɪŋ] *adj* -**1.** [generous] généreux, prodigue; **they were ~ in their efforts to help us** ils n'ont pas ménagé leurs efforts pour nous aider. -**2.** [harsh] sévère.

unsparingly [ʌn'speərɪŋlɪ] *adv* -**1.** [lavishly] généreusement, libéralement. -**2.** [criticize, mock] sévèrement, sans mâcher ses mots.

unspeakable [ʌn'spiːkəbl] *adj* -**1.** [crime, pain] épouvantable, atroce. -**2.** [beauty, joy] indicible, ineffable.

unspeakably [ʌn'spiːkəblɪ] *adv* [cruel, rude] épouvantablement, atrocement; [beautiful] indiciblement, ineffablement.

unspecified [ˌʌn'spesɪfaɪd] *adj* non spécifié.

unspent [ˌʌn'spent] *adj* non dépensé, restant.

unspoiled [*Br* ˌʌn'spɔɪlt, *Am* ˌʌn'spɔɪld] *adj* -**1.** [person] (qui est resté) naturel; **they were ~ by fame** ils sont restés simples OR naturels malgré leur succès. -**2.** [beauty, town] qui n'est pas gâté OR défiguré. -**3.** [flavour] naturel.

unspoken [ˌʌn'spəʊkən] *adj* -**1.** [agreement] tacite. -**2.** [thought, wish] inexprimé; [word] non prononcé.

unsporting [ˌʌn'spɔːtɪŋ] *adj* déloyal; **it was ~ of him just to quit like that** ce n'était pas fair-play de sa part d'abandonner comme ça.

unsprung [ˌʌn'sprʌŋ] *adj* -**1.** [mattress] sans ressorts. -**2.** [trap] qui ne s'est pas déclenché.

unstable [ˌʌn'steɪbl] *adj* -**1.** [chair, government, price, situation] instable. -**2.** [marriage] peu solide. -**3.** [person] déséquilibré, instable.

unstained [ˌʌn'steɪnd] *adj* -**1.** [reputation] sans tache. -**2.** [wood] non teinté.

unstamped [ˌʌn'stæmpt] *adj* [letter] non affranchi, non timbré; [document] non tamponné.

unstated [ˌʌn'steɪtɪd] *adj* -**1.** [agreement] tacite. -**2.** [desire] inexprimé.

unstatesmanlike [ˌʌn'steɪtsmənlaɪk] *adj* peu digne.

unsteadily [ˌʌn'stedɪlɪ] *adv* [walk] d'un pas chancelant OR incertain, en titubant; [speak] d'une voix mal assurée; [hold, write] d'une main tremblante.

unsteadiness [ˌʌn'stedɪnɪs] *n* [of step, voice, writing] manque *m* d'assurance; [of table] manque de stabilité *f*.

unsteady [ˌʌn'stedɪ] (*compar* **unsteadier**, *superl* **unsteadiest**) *adj* -**1.** [chair, ladder] instable, branlant. -**2.** [step, voice] mal assuré, chancelant; [hand] tremblant; **to be ~ on one's feet** [from illness, tiredness] marcher d'un pas chancelant OR incertain, ne pas être très solide sur ses jambes; [from drink] tituber. -**3.** [rhythm, speed, temperature] irrégulier; [flame] vacillant.

unstick [ˌʌn'stɪk] (*pt* & *pp* **unstuck** [-'stʌk])
◇ *vt* décoller.
◇ *vi* se décoller.

unstinting [ˌʌn'stɪntɪŋ] *adj* [care] infini; [help] généreux; [efforts] incessant, illimité; [person] généreux, prodigue; **the firm has been ~ in its efforts to help us** l'entreprise ne ménage pas ses efforts pour nous aider.

unstitch [ˌʌn'stɪtʃ] *vt* découdre; **the hem came ~ed** l'ourlet s'est décousu.

unstop [ˌʌn'stɒp] (*pt* & *pp* **unstopped**, *cont* **unstopping**) *vt* [drain, sink] déboucher.

unstoppable [ˌʌn'stɒpəbl] *adj* qu'on ne peut pas arrêter.

unstressed [ˌʌn'strest] *adj* LING inaccentué, atone.

unstructured [ˌʌn'strʌktʃəd] *adj* [activity] non structuré; [group] non organisé.

unstuck [ˌʌn'stʌk] ◇ *pt* & *pp* → **unstick**.
◇ *adj* [envelope, label] décollé; **to come ~** *literal* se décoller; *fig* [plan, system] tomber à l'eau; [person] échouer.

unstudied [ˌʌn'stʌdɪd] *adj* [natural] naturel; [spontaneous] spontané.

unsubstantiated [ˌʌnsəb'stænʃɪeɪtɪd] *adj* [report, story] non confirmé; [accusation] non fondé.

unsubtle [ˌʌn'sʌtl] *adj* [person, remark] peu subtil, sans finesse; [joke] gros.

unsuccessful [ˌʌnsək'sesfʊl] *adj* [plan, project] qui est un échec, qui n'a pas réussi; [attempt] vain, infructueux; [person] qui n'a pas de succès; [application, demand] refusé, rejeté; [marriage] malheureux; **after several ~ attempts** après plusieurs essais infructueux; **to be ~** échouer; **I was ~ in my attempts to find her** je n'ai pas réussi OR je ne suis pas arrivé à la trouver, je l'ai cherchée en vain OR sans succès; **to be ~ in an exam** échouer OR ne pas être reçu à un examen.

unsuccessfully [ˌʌnsək'sesfʊlɪ] *adv* en vain, sans succès.

unsuitable [ˌʌn'suːtəbl] *adj* [arrangement, candidate, qualities] qui ne convient pas; [behaviour, language] inconvenant; [moment, time] inopportun; [clothing] peu approprié, inadéquat; **he chose an ~ time to call** il a mal choisi le moment pour appeler; '**~ for children**' 'ne convient pas aux enfants'; **the land is ~ for farming** le sol n'est pas propice aux cultures OR n'est pas cultivable.

unsuitably [ˌʌn'suːtəblɪ] *adv* [behave] de façon inconvenante; [dress] d'une manière inadéquate.

unsuited [ˌʌn'suːtɪd] *adj* [person] inapte; [machine, tool] mal adapté, impropre; **he is ~ to politics** il n'est pas fait pour le monde politique, le monde politique ne lui convient pas; **as a couple they seem totally ~** ils forment un couple mal assorti, ils ne vont pas du tout ensemble.

unsullied [ˌʌn'sʌlɪd] *adj lit* sans souillure *lit*, sans tache.

unsung [ˌʌn'sʌŋ] *adj lit* [deed, hero] méconnu.

unsupported [ˌʌnsə'pɔːtɪd] *adj* -**1.** [argument, theory] non vérifié; [accusation, statement] non fondé. -**2.** [wall, aperture] sans support. -**3.** *fig* [person - financially, emotionally]: **to be ~** n'avoir aucun soutien.

unsure [ˌʌn'ʃɔːʳ] *adj* [lacking self-confidence] qui manque d'assurance, qui n'est pas sûr de soi; [hesitant] incertain; **to be ~ of o.s.** manquer d'assurance; **I'm ~ about going** je ne suis pas certain d'y aller; they were ~ of his reaction ils ignoraient quelle serait sa réaction.

unsurpassed [ˌʌnsəˈpɑːst] *adj* sans égal OR pareil.

unsurprisingly [ˌʌnsəˈpraɪzɪŋlɪ] *adv* bien entendu, évidemment.

unsuspected [ˌʌnsəˈspektɪd] *adj* insoupçonné.

unsuspecting [ˌʌnsəˈspektɪŋ] *adj* qui ne soupçonne rien, qui ne se doute de rien.

unsuspectingly [ˌʌnsəˈspektɪŋlɪ] *adv* sans se douter de rien, sans se méfier.

unsweetened [ˌʌnˈswiːtnd] *adj* sans sucre, non sucré.

unswerving [ʌnˈswɜːvɪŋ] *adj* [devotion, loyalty] indéfectible, à toute épreuve; [determination] inébranlable.

unswervingly [ʌnˈswɜːvɪŋlɪ] *adv*: ~ loyal d'une loyauté à toute épreuve.

unsympathetic [ˈʌnˌsɪmpəˈθetɪk] *adj* **-1.** [unfeeling] insensible, incompréhensif; to be ~ to a cause être opposé OR hostile à une cause. **-2.** [unlikeable] antipathique.

unsympathetically [ˈʌnˌsɪmpəˈθetɪklɪ] *adv* [speak, behave] sans montrer la moindre sympathie.

unsystematic [ˌʌnsɪstəˈmætɪk] *adj* non systématique, non méthodique.

untainted [ˌʌnˈteɪntɪd] *adj* [water] pur; *fig* [reputation] sans tache; **his work is ~ by commercialism** son œuvre n'est pas commerciale.

untamed [ˌʌnˈteɪmd] *adj* **-1.** [animal - undomesticated] sauvage, inapprivoisé; [- untrained] non dressé; [lion, tiger] indompté. **-2.** [land] sauvage. **-3.** [person] insoumis, indompté; [spirit] indompté, rebelle.

untangle [ˌʌnˈtæŋgl] *vt* [hair, necklace, rope] démêler; *fig* [mystery] débrouiller, éclaircir.

untapped [ˌʌnˈtæpt] *adj* inexploité.

untarnished [ˌʌnˈtɑːnɪʃt] *adj* [silver] non terni; *fig* [reputation] non terni, sans tache.

untasted [ˌʌnˈteɪstɪd] *adj* auquel on n'a pas goûté; **he sent the wine back ~** il a renvoyé le vin sans y avoir goûté OR touché.

untaxed [ˌʌnˈtækst] *adj* [items] non imposé, exempt de taxes; [income] non imposable, exonéré d'impôts.

unteachable [ˌʌnˈtiːtʃəbl] *adj* [person] à qui on ne peut rien apprendre; [skill] impossible à enseigner OR à inculquer.

untenable [ˌʌnˈtenəbl] *adj* [argument, theory] indéfendable; [position] intenable.

untenanted [ˌʌnˈtenəntɪd] *adj* inoccupé, sans locataire.

untested [ˌʌnˈtestɪd] *adj* [employee, method, theory] qui n'a pas été mis à l'épreuve; [invention, machine, product] qui n'a pas été essayé; [drug] non encore expérimenté.

unthinkable [ʌnˈθɪŋkəbl] *adj* impensable, inconcevable.

unthinking [ʌnˈθɪŋkɪŋ] *adj* [action, remark] irréfléchi, inconsidéré; [person] irréfléchi, étourdi.

unthinkingly [ʌnˈθɪŋkɪŋlɪ] *adv* sans réfléchir, inconsidérément.

untidily [ʌnˈtaɪdɪlɪ] *adv* sans soin, d'une manière négligée; **the children's clothes were strewn ~ across the floor** les vêtements des enfants jonchaient le plancher; **she stuffed everything ~ into a drawer** elle a tout fourré pêle-mêle dans un tiroir.

untidiness [ʌnˈtaɪdɪnɪs] *n* [of dress] manque *m* de soin, débraillé *m*; [of a person] manque *m* d'ordre; [of room] désordre *m*.

untidy [ʌnˈtaɪdɪ] (*compar* untidier, *superl* untidiest) *adj* [cupboard, desk, room] mal rangé, en désordre; [appearance] négligé, débraillé; [person] désordonné.

untie [ˌʌnˈtaɪ] *vt* [string] dénouer; [knot] défaire; [bonds] défaire, détacher; [package] défaire, ouvrir; [prisoner] détacher, délier.

until [ənˈtɪl] ◇ *prep* **-1.** [up to] jusqu'à; ~ **midnight/Monday** jusqu'à minuit/lundi; **stay on the motorway ~ junction 13** restez sur l'autoroute jusqu'à la sortie 13; ~ **such time as you are ready** jusqu'à ce que OR en attendant que vous soyez prêt; **she was here (up) ~ February** elle était ici jusqu'en février; **(up) ~ now** jusqu'ici, jusqu'à présent; **(up) ~ then** jusque-là. **-2.** *(with negative)* [before]: **they didn't arrive ~ 8 o'clock** ils ne sont arrivés qu'à 8 h; **your car won't be ready ~ next week** votre voiture ne sera pas prête avant la semaine prochaine.
◇ *conj* [up to the specified moment - in present] jusqu'à ce que; [- in past] avant que, jusqu'à ce que; **I'll wait here ~ you come back** j'attendrai ici jusqu'à ce que tu reviennes; **wait ~ she says hello** attendez qu'elle dise bonjour; **they stayed ~ everybody had gone** ils sont restés jusqu'à ce que tout le monde soit parti; **I laughed ~ I cried** j'ai ri aux larmes ‖ *(with negative main clause)*: ~ **she spoke I didn't realize she was Spanish** jusqu'à ce qu'elle commence à parler, je ne m'étais pas rendu compte qu'elle était espagnole; **she won't go to sleep ~ her mother comes home** elle ne s'endormira pas avant que sa mère (ne) soit rentrée OR tant que sa mère n'est pas rentrée; **he can't leave hospital ~ the wound has completely healed** il ne peut pas quitter l'hôpital tant que sa blessure n'est pas complètement guérie, il ne quittera pas l'hôpital avant que sa blessure (ne) soit complètement guérie; **don't sign anything ~ the boss gets there** ne signez rien avant que le patron n'arrive, attendez le patron pour signer quoi que ce soit; **the play didn't start ~ everyone was seated** la pièce n'a commencé qu'une fois que tout le monde a été assis.

untilled [ˌʌnˈtɪld] *adj* [uncultivated] non cultivé; [not ploughed] non labouré.

untimely [ʌnˈtaɪmlɪ] *adj* **-1.** [premature] prématuré, précoce; **an ~ death** une mort prématurée. **-2.** [inopportune - remark] inopportun, déplacé; [- moment] inopportun, mal choisi; [- visit] intempestif.

untiring [ʌnˈtaɪərɪŋ] *adj* [efforts] inlassable, infatigable; **they were ~ in their efforts** ils n'ont pas ménagé leurs efforts.

untiringly [ʌnˈtaɪərɪŋlɪ] *adv* inlassablement, infatigablement.

untitled [ˌʌnˈtaɪtld] *adj* [painting] sans titre; [person] non titré.

unto [ˈʌntuː] *prep arch* OR *lit* **-1.** *(indicating dative)* [to] à; **do ~ others as you would have them do ~ you** ne faites pas à autrui ce que vous ne voudriez pas qu'il vous fît. **-2.** [until] jusqu'à; ~ **death** jusqu'à la mort.

untogether *inf* [ˌʌntəˈgeðəʳ] *adj*: **he's very ~** [in work] il est très mal organisé; [emotionally] il est vraiment mal dans sa peau.

untold [ˌʌnˈtəʊld] *adj* **-1.** [tale] jamais raconté; [secret] jamais dévoilé; **the story remains ~** cette histoire reste secrète OR n'a jamais été racontée. **-2.** [great - joy, suffering] indicible, indescriptible; [- amount, number] incalculable.

untouchable [ˌʌnˈtʌtʃəbl] ◇ *adj* intouchable.
◇ *n* [in India] intouchable *mf*; *fig* paria *m*.

untouched [ˌʌnˈtʌtʃt] *adj* **-1.** [not changed] auquel on n'a pas touché, intact; **her coffee was ~** elle n'a pas touché à son café. **-2.** [unharmed - person] indemne, sain et sauf; [- thing] indemne, intact.

untoward [ˌʌntəˈwɔːd] *adj fml* [unfortunate - circumstances, event] fâcheux, malencontreux; [- effect] fâcheux, défavorable; **I hope nothing ~ has happened** j'espère qu'il n'est rien arrivé de fâcheux.

untrained [ˌʌnˈtreɪnd] *adj* [person] sans formation; [ear] inexercé; [mind] non formé; [voice] non travaillé; [dog, horse] non dressé; **to the ~ eye** pour un œil inexercé.

untrammelled *Br*, **untrammeled** *Am* [ʌnˈtræmәld] *adj lit* sans contrainte, sans entraves; ~ **by convention** libre de toute convention.

untranslatable [ˌʌntrænsˈleɪtəbl] *adj* intraduisible.

untravelled *Br*, **untraveled** *Am* [ˌʌnˈtrævld] *adj* [road] peu utilisé OR fréquenté; [person] qui n'a pas voyagé.

untreated [ˌʌnˈtriːtɪd] *adj* **-1.** [unprocessed - food] non traité; [- wood] non traité; [- sewage] brut. **-2.** [infection, tumour] non traité, non soigné; **her condition will worsen if left ~** son état empirera si elle ne reçoit pas de traitement.

untried [ˌʌnˈtraɪd] *adj* [method, recruit, theory] qui n'a pas été mis à l'épreuve; [invention, product] qui n'a pas été essayé.

untrodden [ˌʌnˈtrɒdn] *adj* [ground, wilderness] inexploré, vierge; [path] non utilisé OR fréquenté.

untroubled [ˌʌnˈtrʌbld] *adj* tranquille, paisible; **they seemed ~ by the situation** ils ne semblaient pas (être) affectés par la situation.

untrue [ˌʌnˈtruː] *adj* **-1.** [incorrect - belief, statement] faux, erroné; [- measurement, reading] erroné, inexact. **-2.** [disloyal]: **to be ~ to sb** être déloyal envers OR infidèle à qqn.

untrustworthy [ˌʌnˈtrʌstˌwɜːðɪ] *adj* [person] qui n'est pas digne de confiance.

untruth [ˌʌnˈtruːθ] *n euph* & *fml* [lie] mensonge *m*, invention *f*; **to tell an ~** mentir, dire un mensonge.

untruthful [ˌʌnˈtruːθfʊl] *adj* [statement] mensonger; [person] menteur; **to say ~ things** mentir, dire des mensonges.

untuneful [ˌʌnˈtjuːnfʊl] *adj* [song, voice] peu mélodieux.

untutored [ˌʌnˈtjuːtəd] *adj* **-1.** [person] sans instruction; [eye, ear] inexercé; [voice] non travaillé; [mind] non formé. **-2.** [skill, talent] inné, naturel.

unusable [ˌʌnˈjuːzəbl] *adj* inutilisable.

unused [*sense 1* ˌʌnˈjuːzd, *sense 2* ʌnˈjuːst] *adj* **-1.** [not in use] inutilisé; [new - machine, material] neuf, qui n'a pas servi; [- clothing, shoes] neuf, qui n'a pas été porté. **-2.** [unaccustomed] peu habitué, peu accoutumé; **I'm ~ to spicy food** je n'ai pas l'habitude de manger OR je suis peu habitué à manger épicé.

unusual [ʌnˈjuːʒl] *adj* [uncommon] peu commun, inhabituel; [odd] étrange, bizarre; **it's ~ for her to be so brusque** il est rare qu'elle soit si brusque, ça ne lui ressemble pas OR ce n'est pas son genre d'être aussi brusque; **it's not ~ to see flooding in these parts** il n'est pas rare OR il arrive assez fréquemment qu'il y ait des inondations par ici.

unusually [ʌnˈjuːʒəlɪ] *adv* [exceptionally] exceptionnellement, extraordinairement; **she is ~ intelligent** elle est d'une intelligence exceptionnelle ‖ [abnormally] exceptionnellement, anormalement; **he was ~ silent that day** il était étrangement OR anormalement silencieux ce jour-là; **~, it wasn't raining** chose rare, il ne pleuvait pas.

unutterable [ʌnˈʌtərəbl] *adj fml* [misery, pain] indicible, indescriptible; [boredom] mortel; [joy] inexprimable; **he's an ~ fool!** c'est vraiment un imbécile fini!

unutterably [ʌnˈʌtərəblɪ] *adv fml* [miserable, tired] terriblement, horriblement; [happy] extrêmement, extraordinairement; **he's ~ stupid** il est d'une stupidité invraisemblable OR inouïe.

unuttered [ˌʌnˈʌtəd] *adj* inexprimé.

unvaried [ʌnˈveərɪd] *adj* qui manque de variété, monotone; **an ~ diet** une alimentation peu variée.

unvarnished [ˌʌnˈvɑːnɪʃt] *adj* **-1.** [furniture] non verni. **-2.** *fig* [plain, simple] simple, sans fard; **the ~ truth** la vérité pure et simple OR toute nue.

unvarying [ʌnˈveərɪɪŋ] *adj* invariable, uniforme.

unvaryingly [ʌnˈveərɪŋlɪ] *adv* invariablement.

unveil [ˌʌnˈveɪl] *vt* [painting, sculpture] dévoiler, inaugurer; *fig* [secret] dévoiler, révéler.

unveiling [ˌʌnˈveɪlɪŋ] *n* [of painting, sculpture] dévoilement *m*, inauguration *f*; [of secret] dévoilement *m*, révélation *f*.

unverified [ˌʌnˈverɪfaɪd] *adj* non vérifié.

unversed [ˌʌnˈvɜːst] *adj fml* peu versé *fml*, peu expérimenté; to be ~ in sthg être peu versé dans qqch.

unvoiced [ˌʌnˈvɔɪst] *adj* -**1.** [desire, objection] inexprimé. -**2.** PHON non voisé, sourd.

unwaged [ˌʌnˈweɪdʒd] ◇ *adj* [unsalaried] non salarié; [unemployed] sans emploi, au chômage. ◇ *npl*: the ~ les sans-emploi *mpl*.

unwanted [ˌʌnˈwɒntɪd] *adj* [child, pregnancy] non désiré, non souhaité; [books, clothing] dont on n'a plus besoin, dont on veut se séparer; I felt ~ as a child j'ai été privé d'affection dans mon enfance.

unwarranted [ʌnˈwɒrəntɪd] *adj* [concern, criticism] injustifié; [remark, interference] déplacé.

unwary [ʌnˈweərɪ] *adj* [person, animal] qui n'est pas méfiant OR sur ses gardes.

unwashed [ˌʌnˈwɒʃt] ◇ *adj* [dishes, feet, floor] non lavé; [person] qui ne s'est pas lavé. ◇ *npl*: the great ~ *Br hum* & *pej* la populace.

unwavering [ʌnˈweɪvərɪŋ] *adj* [devotion, support] indéfectible, à toute épreuve; [look] fixe; [person] inébranlable, ferme; they were ~ in their belief ils étaient inébranlables dans leur conviction.

unwaveringly [ʌnˈweɪvərɪŋlɪ] *adv* [believe, support] sans réserve, fermement; [look] fixement.

unwed [ˌʌnˈwed] *adj* célibataire.

unwelcome [ʌnˈwelkəm] *adj* [advances, attention] importun; [advice] non sollicité; [visit] inopportun; [visitor] importun, gênant; [news, situation] fâcheux; he made his mother feel ~ il a donné l'impression à sa mère qu'elle gênait.

unwelcoming [ʌnˈwelkəmɪŋ] *adj* [person, look] hostile, froid; [place] peu accueillant.

unwell [ˌʌnˈwel] *adj* [indisposed] souffrant, indisposé *fml*; [ill] malade.

unwholesome [ˌʌnˈhəʊlsəm] *adj* [climate] malsain, insalubre; [activity, habits, thoughts] malsain, pernicieux; [fascination, interest] malsain, morbide; [drink, food] peu sain, nocif.

unwieldy [ʌnˈwiːldɪ] *adj* -**1.** [chair, package] peu maniable, encombrant. -**2.** [argument, method] maladroit; [bureaucracy, system] lourd.

unwilling [ˌʌnˈwɪlɪŋ] *adj* [helper, student] réticent, peu enthousiaste; he was ~ to cooperate il n'était pas vraiment disposé à coopérer; I was their ~ accomplice j'étais leur complice malgré moi OR à mon corps défendant.

unwillingly [ʌnˈwɪlɪŋlɪ] *adv* à contrecœur, contre son gré.

unwillingness [ʌnˈwɪlɪŋnɪs] *n* manque *m* d'enthousiasme, réticence *f*; she showed her usual ~ to compromise comme d'habitude, elle s'est montrée réticente à accepter le compromis.

unwind [ˌʌnˈwaɪnd] (*pt* & *pp* unwound [-ˈwaʊnd]) ◇ *vt* dérouler. ◇ *vi* -**1.** [bail of yarn, cord] se dérouler. -**2.** *fig* [relax] se détendre, se relaxer.

unwise [ʌnˈwaɪz] *adj* [action, decision] peu judicieux, imprudent; it would be ~ of you to go vous auriez tort OR il serait imprudent de votre part d'y aller.

unwisely [ˌʌnˈwaɪzlɪ] *adv* imprudemment.

unwitting [ʌnˈwɪtɪŋ] *adj fml* [accomplice] involontaire, malgré soi; [insult] non intentionnel, involontaire.

unwittingly [ʌnˈwɪtɪŋlɪ] *adv* involontairement, sans (le) faire exprès.

unwomanly [ʌnˈwʊmənlɪ] *adj* peu féminin.

unwonted [ʌnˈwəʊntɪd] *adj fml* [event] exceptionnel; [generosity, kindness] inaccoutumé, inhabituel.

unworkable [ʌnˈwɜːkəbl] *adj* [idea, plan] impraticable, impossible à réaliser; your project is ~ votre projet ne marchera pas OR est infaisable.

unworldly [ˌʌnˈwɜːldlɪ] *adj* -**1.** [spiritual] spirituel, détaché de ce monde; [ascetic] d'ascète, ascétique. -**2.** [naive] naïf, ingénu.

unworn [ˌʌnˈwɔːn] *adj* [clothing] qui n'a pas été porté, (comme) neuf; [carpet] qui n'est pas usé.

unworthiness [ʌnˈwɜːðɪnɪs] *n* [of person] indignité *f*, manque *m* de mérite; [of action] indignité *f*.

unworthy [ʌnˈwɜːðɪ] *adj* [unbefitting] indigne; [undeserving] indigne, peu méritant; he felt ~ of such praise il se croyait indigne de OR il ne croyait pas mériter de telles louanges; such behaviour is ~ of you! une telle conduite est indigne de vous!; such details are ~ of her attention de tels détails ne méritent pas son attention OR qu'elle s'y arrête.

unwound [ˌʌnˈwaʊnd] ◇ *pt* & *pp* → **unwind**. ◇ *adj*: to come ~ se dérouler.

unwounded [ˌʌnˈwuːndɪd] *adj* non blessé, indemne.

unwrap [ˌʌnˈræp] (*pt* & *pp* unwrapped, *cont* unwrapping) *vt* déballer, ouvrir.

unwritten [ˌʌnˈrɪtn] *adj* [legend, story] non écrit; [agreement] verbal, tacite; an ~ rule une règle tacitement admise; ~ law droit *m* coutumier.

unyielding [ʌnˈjiːldɪŋ] *adj* [ground, material] très dur; [person] inflexible, intransigeant; [determination, principles] inébranlable.

unyoke [ˌʌnˈjəʊk] *vt* dételer.

unzip [ˌʌnˈzɪp] (*pt* & *pp* unzipped, *cont* unzipping) ◇ *vt* ouvrir OR défaire (la fermeture Éclair® de). ◇ *vi* se dégrafer.

up [ʌp] (*pt* & *pp* upped, *cont* upping) ◇ *adv* **A.** -**1.** [towards a higher position or level] en haut; he's on his way up il monte; they had coffee sent up ils ont fait monter du café; hang it higher up accrochez-le plus haut; wait till the moon comes up attends que la lune se lève. -**2.** [in a higher position, at a higher level]: she wears her hair up elle porte ses cheveux relevés; hold your head up high! redressez la tête!; heads up! attention! || [in a high place or position]: up above au-dessus; the glasses are up above the plates les verres sont au-dessus des assiettes; up in the air en l'air; look at the kite up in the sky regardez le cerf-volant (là-haut) dans le ciel; I live eight floors up j'habite au huitième (étage); she lives three floors up from us elle habite trois étages au-dessus de chez nous; she's up in her room elle est en haut dans sa chambre; we spend our holidays up in the mountains nous passons nos vacances à la montagne; from up on the mountain du haut de la montagne; do you see her up on that hill? la voyez-vous en haut de OR sur cette colline?; what are you doing up there? qu'est-ce que vous faites là-haut?; the captain is up on deck le capitaine est en haut sur le pont; have you ever been up in a plane? avez-vous déjà pris l'avion?; up the top tout en haut; it's up on top of the wardrobe c'est sur le dessus de l'armoire; she's up there with the best (of them) *fig* elle est parmi OR dans les meilleurs. -**3.** [in a raised position] levé; Charles has his hand up Charles a la main levée; wind the window up [in car] remontez la vitre; put your hood up relève OR mets ta capuche; she turned her collar up elle a relevé son col. -**4.** [into an upright position] debout; up you get! debout!; he helped me up il m'a aidé à me lever OR à me mettre debout; sit up straight! tiens-toi droit!; the trunk was standing up on end la malle était debout ❑ up and at them! *inf* grouillez-vous! -**5.** [out of bed]: get up! debout!; she got up late this morning elle s'est levée tard ce matin; she's always up and doing elle n'arrête jamais. -**6.** [facing upwards]: the body was lying face up le corps était couché sur le dos; I turned the poster right side up j'ai mis l'affiche dans le bon sens OR à l'endroit; he turned his hand palm up il a tourné la main paume vers le haut; 'fragile – this way up' 'fragile – haut'; I don't know which end is up anymore *fig* je suis complètement déboussolé. -**7.** [erected, installed]: they're putting up a new hotel there ils construisent un nouvel hôtel là-bas; help me get the curtains/the pictures up aide-moi à accrocher les rideaux/les tableaux. -**8.** [on wall]: up on the blackboard au tableau; I saw an announcement up about it je l'ai vu sur une affiche.

B. -**1.** [towards north]: they came up for the weekend ils sont venus pour le week-end; it's cold up here il fait froid ici; up there là-bas; up north dans le nord. -**2.** [in, to or from a larger place]: up in Madrid à Madrid; she's up in Maine for the week elle passe une semaine dans le Maine; we're up from Munich nous venons OR arrivons de Munich; he was on his way up to town il allait en ville. -**3.** *Br* [at university]: he's up at Oxford/Cambridge il est à Oxford/Cambridge. -**4.** [further]: there's a café up ahead il y a un café plus loin; the sign up ahead says 10 miles la pancarte là-bas indique 10 milles. -**5.** [in phrasal verbs]: the clerk came up to him le vendeur s'est approché de lui OR est venu vers lui; a car drew up at the petrol pump une voiture s'est arrêtée à la pompe à essence; up came a small, blonde child (alors,) un petit enfant blond s'est approché. -**6.** [close to]: up close de près; I like to sit up front j'aime bien m'asseoir devant; when you get right up to her quand vous la voyez de près; they stood up close to one another ils se tenaient l'un contre l'autre OR tout près l'un de l'autre.

C. -**1.** [towards a higher level]: prices have gone up by 10 per cent les prix ont augmenté OR monté de 10 pour cent; bread has gone up again le pain a encore augmenté; the temperature soared up into the thirties la température est montée au-dessus de trente degrés; they can cost anything from £750 up ils coûtent au moins 750 livres, on en trouve à partir de 750 livres. -**2.** [more loudly, intensely] plus fort; speak up parlez plus fort; he turned the radio up il a mis la radio plus fort.

D. -**1.** [indicating completion]: drink up! finissez vos verres!; eat up your greens mange tes légumes; the river had dried up la rivière s'était asséchée. -**2.** [into small pieces]: he ripped the shirt up il a mis la chemise en lambeaux; I tore up the letter j'ai déchiré la lettre (en petits morceaux). -**3.** [together]: add these figures up additionnez ces chiffres; the teacher gathered up his notes le professeur a ramassé ses notes.

E. -**1.** [before an authority]: he came up before the judge for rape il a comparu devant le juge pour viol; the murder case came up before the court today le meutre a été jugé aujourd'hui; she comes up before the board tomorrow elle paraît devant le conseil demain. -**2.** *inf* [indicating support]: up (with) the Revolution! vive la Révolution!; up the Lakers! SPORT allez les Lakers!

◇ *adj* **A.** -**1.** [at or moving towards higher level] haut; the river is up le fleuve est en crue; the tide is up la marée est haute; prices are up on last year les prix ont augmenté par rapport à l'année dernière; the temperature is up in the twenties la température a dépassé les vingt degrés. -**2.** [in a raised position] levé; the blinds are up les stores sont levés; keep the windows up [in car] n'ouvrez pas les fenêtres; her hair was up (in a bun) elle avait un chignon; her hood was up so I couldn't see her face sa capuche était relevée, si bien que je ne voyais pas sa figure; his defences were up *fig* il était sur ses gardes. -**3.** [in an upwards direction]: the up escalator l'escalier roulant ascendant. -**4.** *Br* RAIL [heading for a larger city]: the up train le train qui va en ville; the up platform le quai où l'on prend le train qui va en ville. -**5.** [out of bed]: is she up yet? est-elle déjà levée OR debout?; we're normally up at 6 d'habitude nous nous levons à 6 h; she was up late last night elle s'est couchée OR elle a veillé tard hier soir; they were up all night ils ne se sont pas couchés de la nuit, ils ont passé une nuit blanche. -**6.** [in tennis]: was the ball up? la balle était-elle bonne?

B. -**1.** [road] en travaux; 'road up' 'travaux'. -**2.** [erected, installed]: these buildings haven't been up long ça ne fait pas longtemps que ces immeubles ont été construits; are the new curtains up yet? les nouveaux rideaux ont-ils été posés?

C. -**1.** [finished, at an end] terminé; **time is up!** [on exam, visit] c'est l'heure!; [in game, on meter] le temps est écoulé!; **when the month was up he left** à la fin du mois, il est parti. -**2.** [ahead] : **I'm $50 up on you** *inf* j'ai 50 dollars de plus que vous; **Madrid was two goals up** SPORT Madrid menait de deux buts; **Georgetown was 13 points up on Baltimore** SPORT Georgetown avait 13 points d'avance sur Baltimore ❑ **to be one up on sb** *inf* avoir un avantage sur qqn. -**3.** [ready] prêt; **dinner's up** le dîner est prêt. -**4.** [in operation] : **the computer's up again** l'ordinateur fonctionne à nouveau.

D. *inf* -**1.** [cheerful] gai; **he seemed very up when I saw him** il avait l'air en pleine forme quand je l'ai vu. -**2.** [well-informed] : **he's really up on history** il est fort OR calé en histoire; **she's always up with the latest trends** elle est toujours au courant de la dernière mode.

E. -**1.** [before an authority] comparaître; **to be up before a court/a judge** comparaître devant un tribunal/un juge; **she's up before the board tomorrow** elle comparaît devant le conseil demain. -**2.** *inf phr*: **something's up** [happening] il se passe quelque chose; [wrong] quelque chose ne va pas; **what's up?** [happening] qu'est-ce qui se passe?; [wrong] qu'est-ce qu'il y a?; *Am* [as greeting] quoi de neuf?; **what's up with you?** [happening] quoi de neuf?; [wrong] qu'est-ce que tu as?; **do you know what's up?** est-ce que tu sais ce qui se passe?; **something's up with Mum** il y a quelque chose qui ne va pas chez maman, maman a quelque chose.

◇ *prep* -**1.** [indicating motion to a higher place or level] : **we carried our suitcases up the stairs** nous avons monté nos valises; **he ran up the stairs** il a monté l'escalier en courant; **she was up and down stairs all day** elle montait et descendait les escaliers toute la journée; **I climbed up the ladder** je suis monté à l'échelle; **the cat climbed up the tree** le chat a grimpé dans l'arbre; **further up the wall** plus haut sur le mur ❑ **up hill and down dale** *lit* par monts et par vaux. -**2.** [at or to the far end of] : **her flat is up those stairs** son appartement est en haut de cet escalier; **we walked up the street** nous avons monté la rue; **she pointed up the street** elle a montré le haut de la rue; **she lives up this street** elle habite dans cette rue; **the café is just up the road** le café se trouve plus loin OR plus haut dans la rue. -**3.** [towards the source of] : **up the river** en amont; **a voyage up the Amazon** une remontée de l'Amazone. -**4.** ▽ *Br* [out at] à; **he's up the pub** il est au pub. -**5.** *phr*: **up yours!** ▽ va te faire voir!

◇ *vt* -**1.** [increase] augmenter; **they have upped their prices by 25 per cent** ils ont augmenté leurs prix de 25 pour cent. -**2.** [promote] lever, relever; **the boss upped him to district manager** le patron l'a bombardé directeur régional.

◇ *vi* *inf*: **she upped and left** elle a fichu le camp; **he upped and married her** en moins de deux, il l'a épousée.

◇ *n* -**1.** [high point] haut *m*; **ups and downs** [in land, road] accidents *mpl*; [of market] fluctuations *fpl* ‖ [in life] : **I've had a lot of ups and downs in my life** j'ai connu des hauts et des bas; **we all have our ups and downs** nous avons tous des hauts et des bas. -**2.** [increase] : **the market is on the up** le marché est à la hausse; **prices are on the up** les prix sont en train d'augmenter.

◆ **up against** *prep phr* -**1.** [touching] contre; **lean the ladder up against the window** appuyez l'échelle contre la fenêtre. -**2.** [in competition or conflict with] : **you're up against some good candidates** vous êtes en compétition avec de bons candidats; **they don't know what they're up against!** ils ne se rendent pas compte de ce qui les attend!; **to be up against the law** être dans l'illégalité ❑ **to be up against it** *inf* être dans le pétrin.

◆ **up and about, up and around** *adj phr* [gen] : **I've been up and about since 7 o'clock** je suis levé depuis 7 h ‖ [after illness] : **so you're up and about again?** alors tu n'es plus alité?

◆ **up and down** ◇ *adv phr* -**1.** [upwards and downwards] : **the boy was jumping up and down** le garçon sautait sur place; **she looked us up and down** elle nous a regardé de haut en bas; **the bottle bobbed up and down on the waves** la bouteille montait et descendait sur les vagues; **I was up and down all night** [in and out of bed] je n'ai pas arrêté de me lever la nuit dernière. -**2.** [to and fro] de long en large; **I could hear him walking up and down** je l'entendais faire les cent pas OR marcher de long en large; **she walked up and down the platform** elle faisait les cent pas sur le quai. -**3.** [in all parts of] : **up and down the country** dans tout le pays.

◇ *adj phr*: **she's been very up and down lately** elle a eu beaucoup de hauts et de bas ces derniers temps.

◆ **up for** *prep phr* -**1.** [under consideration, about to undergo] à; **the house is up for sale** la maison est à vendre; **the project is up for discussion** on va discuter du projet; **she's up for election** elle est candidate OR elle se présente aux élections. -**2.** [due to be tried for] être jugé; **he's up for murder/speeding** il va être jugé pour meurtre/excès de vitesse. -**3.** *inf* [interested in, ready for] : **are you still up for supper tonight?** tu veux toujours qu'on dîne ensemble ce soir?; **he's up for anything** il est toujours partant.

◆ **up to** *prep phr* -**1.** [as far as] jusqu'à; **he can count up to 100** il sait compter jusqu'à 100; **the river is up to 25 feet wide** le fleuve a jusqu'à 25 pieds de largeur; **the bus can take up to 50 passengers** le bus peut accueillir jusqu'à 50 passagers; **I'm up to page 120** j'en suis à la page 120; **up to and including Saturday** jusqu'à samedi inclus; **up to here** jusqu'ici; **up to** OR **up until now** jusqu'à maintenant, jusqu'ici; **up to** OR **up until then** jusqu'alors, jusque-là; **we were up to our knees in mud** nous avions de la boue jusqu'aux genoux. -**2.** [the responsibility of] : **should he attend the meeting? — that's up to him** devrait-il assister à la réunion? — il fait ce qu'il veut OR c'est à lui de voir; **which film do you fancy seeing? — it's up to you** quel film est-ce que tu veux voir? — c'est comme tu veux; **if it were up to me...** si c'était moi qui décidais OR à moi de décider...; **it's up to them to pay damages** c'est à eux OR il leur appartient de payer les dégâts. -**3.** [capable of] : **to be up to doing sthg** être capable de faire qqch; **he's not up to heading the team** il n'est pas capable de diriger l'équipe; **my German is not up to translating novels** mon niveau d'allemand ne me permet pas de traduire des romans; **are you going out tonight? — no, I don't feel up to it** tu sors ce soir? — non, je n'en ai pas tellement envie; **are you up to working** OR **to work?** êtes-vous capable de OR en état de travailler?; **I'm not up to going back to work** je ne suis pas encore en état de reprendre le travail ❑ **the football team isn't up to much** *inf* l'équipe de foot ne vaut pas grand-chose. -**4.** [as good as] : **his work is not up to his normal standard** son travail n'est pas aussi bon que d'habitude; **the levels are up to standard** les niveaux sont conformes aux normes; **I don't feel up to par** je ne me sens pas en forme. -**5.** [engaged in, busy with] : **let's see what she's up to** allons voir ce qu'elle fait OR fabrique; **what have you been up to lately?** qu'est-ce que tu deviens?; **what's he been up to now?** qu'est-ce qu'il a encore inventé?; **they're up to something** ils manigancent quelque chose; **she's up to no good** elle prépare un mauvais coup; **the things we got up to in our youth!** qu'est-ce qu'on OR ce qu'on ne faisait pas quand on était jeunes!

up-and-coming *adj* plein d'avenir, qui promet, qui monte.

up-and-down *adj* -**1.** [movement] qui monte et qui descend, ascendant et descendant. -**2.** [unstable] : **his career has been very up and down** sa carrière a connu des hauts et des bas; **I've been very up and down lately** *Br* j'ai eu des hauts et des bas ces derniers temps.

up-and-over *adj*: ~ **door** porte *f* basculante *(d'un garage etc)*.

up-and-under *n* [in rugby] chandelle *f*.

upbeat ['ʌpbi:t] ◇ *adj* [mood, person] optimiste; [music] entraînant.

◇ *n* MUS levé *m*.

upbraid [ʌp'breɪd] *vt fml* réprimander.

upbringing ['ʌp,brɪŋɪŋ] *n* éducation *f*; **to rebel against one's ~** se révolter contre son éducation.

upchuck▽ ['ʌptʃʌk] *vi Am* dégueuler, vomir.

upcoming ['ʌp,kʌmɪŋ] *adj* [event] à venir, prochain; [book] à paraître, qui va paraître; [film] qui va sortir; **Ford's ~ film** le prochain film de Ford; **the ~ elections** les élections qui vont bientôt avoir lieu; **'~ attractions'** 'prochains spectacles', 'prochainement'.

up-country ◇ *adj* [inland] de l'intérieur; *pej* [unsophisticated] provincial.

◇ *n* intérieur *m*.

◇ *adv* [go, move] vers l'intérieur; [live] à l'intérieur.

update [*vb* ,ʌp'deɪt, *n* 'ʌpdeɪt] ◇ *vt* [information, record] mettre à jour, actualiser; [army, system] moderniser.

◇ *n* [of information, record] mise *f* à jour, actualisation *f*; [of army, system] modernisation *f*; **an ~ on the situation** une mise au point sur la situation.

updated [,ʌp'deɪtɪd] *adj* [records] mis à jour; [army, system] modernisé.

upend [ʌp'end] *vt* -**1.** *literal* [object] mettre debout; [person] mettre la tête en bas. -**2.** *fig* [upset] bouleverser.

upfront *inf* [,ʌp'frʌnt] *adj* -**1.** [frank - person] franc, ouvert; [- remark] franc, direct. -**2.** [payment] d'avance.

◆ **up front** *adv* [pay] d'avance.

upgradable [ʌp'greɪdəbl] *adj* COMPUT extensible.

upgrade [*vb* ,ʌp'greɪd, *n* 'ʌpgreɪd] ◇ *vt* -**1.** [improve] améliorer; [increase] augmenter; [modernize - computer system] moderniser, actualiser; **I was ~d to business class** [on plane] on m'a mis en classe affaires. -**2.** [job] revaloriser; [employee] promouvoir; **I was ~d** je suis monté en grade; **she was ~d to sales manager** elle a été promue directrice des ventes.

◇ *vi*: **we've ~d to a more powerful system** on est passés à un système plus puissant.

◇ *n* -**1.** *phr*: **to be on the ~** [price, salary] augmenter, être en hausse; [business, venture] progresser, être en bonne voie; [sick person] être en voie de guérison; **his career is on the ~** sa carrière est en bonne voie. -**2.** *Am* [slope] montée *f*. -**3.** COMPUT [of software] actualisation *f*; [of system] extension *f*.

upheaval [ʌp'hi:vl] *n* [emotional, political etc] bouleversement *m*; [social unrest] agitation *f*, perturbations *fpl*; **the war brought a lot of ~** la guerre a entraîné de nombreux bouleversements.

upheld [ʌp'held] *pt* & *pp* → **uphold**.

uphill [,ʌp'hɪl] ◇ *adj* -**1.** [road, slope] qui monte. -**2.** *fig* [task] ardu, pénible; [battle] rude, acharné; **it was an ~ struggle convincing him** j'ai eu beaucoup de mal à le convaincre.

◇ *adv*: **to go ~** [car, person] monter (la côte); [road] monter.

uphold [ʌp'həʊld] (*pt* & *pp* **upheld** [-'held]) *vt* -**1.** [right] défendre, faire respecter; [law, rule] faire respecter OR observer. -**2.** JUR [conviction, decision] maintenir, confirmer.

upholder [ʌp'həʊldə^r] *n* défendeur *m*.

upholster [ʌp'həʊlstə^r] *vt* recouvrir, tapisser; **~ed in leather** recouvert OR tapissé de cuir; **to be well ~ed** *hum* être enrobé OR bien en chair.

upholsterer [ʌp'həʊlstərə^r] *n* tapissier *m*, -ère *f*.

upholstery [ʌp'həʊlstərɪ] *n* *(U)* -**1.** [covering - fabric] tissu *m* d'ameublement; [- leather] cuir *m*; [- in car] garniture *f*. -**2.** [trade] tapisserie *f*.

upkeep ['ʌpkiːp] *n (U)* [maintenance] entretien *m*; [cost] frais *mpl* d'entretien.

upland ['ʌplənd] ◇ *n*: the ~ OR ~s les plateaux *mpl*, les hautes terres *fpl*.
◇ *adj* des plateaux.

uplift [*vb* ʌp'lɪft, *comp* 'ʌplɪft] ◇ *vt* [person - spiritually] élever (l'esprit de); [- morally] encourager; he felt ~ed by the news la nouvelle lui a redonné courage.
◇ *comp*: ~ bra soutien-gorge *m* de maintien.

uplifting [ʌp'lɪftɪŋ] *adj* édifiant.

upload ['ʌpləʊd] *vt* COMPUT télécharger *(vers un gros ordinateur)*.

up-market ◇ *adj* [goods, service, area] haut de gamme, de première qualité; [newspaper, television programme] qui vise un public cultivé; [audience] cultivé.
◇ *adv*: she's moved ~ elle fait dans le haut de gamme maintenant.

upmost ['ʌpməʊst] = **uppermost**.

upon [ə'pɒn] *prep* -**1.** *fml* [indicating position or place] sur, à; ~ the grass/the table sur la pelouse/la table; she had a sad look ~ her face elle avait l'air triste; the ring ~ her finger la bague à son doigt. -**2.** *fml* [indicating person or thing affected]: attacks ~ old people are on the increase les attaques contre les personnes âgées sont de plus en plus fréquentes. -**3.** *fml* [immediately after] à; ~ our arrival in Rome à notre arrivée à Rome; ~ hearing the news, he rang home lorsqu'il a appris la nouvelle, il a appelé chez lui; ~ request sur simple demande. -**4.** [indicating large amount] et; mile ~ mile of desert des kilomètres et des kilomètres de désert; we receive thousands ~ thousands of offers each year nous recevons plusieurs milliers de propositions chaque année. -**5.** [indicating imminence]: the holidays are nearly ~ us les vacances approchent. -**6.** *phr*: ~ my word! *dated* ma parole!

upper ['ʌpəʳ] ◇ *adj* -**1.** [physically higher] supérieur, plus haut OR élevé; [top] du dessus, du haut; ~ lip lèvre supérieure; temperatures are in the ~ 30s la température dépasse 30 degrés ❑ to have the ~ hand avoir le dessus; to get OR to gain the ~ hand prendre le dessus OR l'avantage. -**2.** [higher in order, rank] supérieur; the Upper House [gen] la Chambre haute; [in England] la Chambre des lords. -**3.** GEOG [inland] haut; the ~ valley of the Nile la haute vallée du Nil.
◇ *n* -**1.** [of shoe] empeigne *f*; to be on one's ~s *inf Br* manger de la vache enragée, être fauché. -**2.** *drugs sl* excitant *m*, stimulant *m*.

upper case *n* TYPO haut *m* de casse.
◆ **upper-case** *adj*: an upper-case letter une majuscule.

upper class *n*: the ~, the ~es *l'aristocratie et la haute bourgeoisie*.
◆ **upper-class** *adj* -**1.** [accent, family] aristocratique; ~ twit *inf expression péjorative caricaturant l'aristocratie peu intelligente*. -**2.** *Am* UNIV [student] *de troisième ou quatrième année*.

upper-crust *inf adj* aristocratique.

uppercut ['ʌpəkʌt] (*pt* & *pp* uppercut, *cont* uppercutting) ◇ *n* uppercut *m*.
◇ *vt* frapper d'un uppercut.

upper middle class *n*: the ~ *classe sociale réunissant les professions libérales et universitaires, les cadres de l'industrie et les hauts fonctionnaires*.

uppermost ['ʌpəməʊst] ◇ *adj* -**1.** [part, side] le plus haut OR élevé; [drawer, storey] du haut, du dessus. -**2.** [most prominent] le plus important; it's not ~ in my mind ce n'est pas ma préoccupation essentielle en ce moment; human rights are ~ on his list of priorities les droits de l'homme sont en tête de ses priorités.
◇ *adv* [most prominently]: the question that comes ~ in my mind la question que je me pose en premier OR avant toute autre.

upper school *n Br*: the ~ les grandes classes *fpl*.

upper sixth *n Br* SCH (classe *f*) terminale *f*.

Upper Volta [-'vɒltə] *pr n* Haute-Volta *f*; in ~ en Haute-Volta.

uppish *inf* ['ʌpɪʃ] *Br*, **uppity** *inf* ['ʌpətɪ] *adj* [arrogant] arrogant, suffisant; [snobbish] snob *(inv)*; you don't have to get so ~ about it! inutile de le prendre de si haut!

Uppsala ['ʌpsɑːlə] *pr n* Uppsala.

upraised [ʌp'reɪzd] *adj* levé.

upright [*adj sense 1* & *adv* ,ʌp'raɪt, *adj sense 2* & *n* 'ʌpraɪt] ◇ *adj* -**1.** [erect] droit; ~ piano piano *m* droit. -**2.** [honest] droit.
◇ *adv* -**1.** [sit, stand] droit; he sat bolt ~ il se redressa (sur son siège). -**2.** [put] droit, debout.
◇ *n* -**1.** [of door, bookshelf] montant *m*, portant *m*; [of goal post] montant *m* du but; ARCHIT pied-droit *m*. -**2.** [piano] piano *m* droit.

uprising ['ʌp,raɪzɪŋ] *n* soulèvement *m*, révolte *f*.

upriver [,ʌp'rɪvəʳ] ◇ *adj* (situé) en amont, d'amont.
◇ *adv* [be] en amont; [move] vers l'amont; [row, swim] contre le courant.

uproar ['ʌprɔːʳ] *n* [noise] tumulte *m*, vacarme *m*; [protest] protestations *fpl*, tollé *m*; his speech caused quite an ~ [protests] son discours a mis le feu aux poudres; [shouting] son discours a déclenché le tumulte; the town was in (an) ~ over the new taxes la ville entière s'est élevée contre le nouvel impôt.

uproarious [ʌp'rɔːrɪəs] *adj* [crowd, group] hilare; [film, joke] hilarant, désopilant; [laughter] tonitruant.

uproariously [ʌp'rɔːrɪəslɪ] *adv* [laugh] aux éclats; ~ funny désopilant, tordant.

uproot [ʌp'ruːt] *vt literal* & *fig* déraciner.

upsadaisy *inf* [,ʌpsə'deɪzɪ] *Br* = **upsydaisy**.

upscale ['ʌpskeɪl] *adj Am* haut de gamme.

upset [*vb* & *adj* ʌp'set, *n* 'ʌpset] (*pt* & *pp* upset, *cont* upsetting) ◇ *vt* -**1.** [overturn - chair, pan] renverser; [- milk, paint] renverser, répandre; [- boat] faire chavirer; don't ~ the applecart! ne gâche pas tout! -**2.** [disturb - plans, routine] bouleverser, déranger; [- procedure] bouleverser; [- calculations, results] fausser; [- balance] rompre, fausser. -**3.** [person - annoy] contrarier, ennuyer; [- offend] fâcher, vexer; [- worry] inquiéter, tracasser; the least little thing ~s her elle se fait du mauvais sang pour rien; it's not worth upsetting yourself over ce n'est pas la peine de vous en faire. -**4.** [make ill - stomach] déranger; [- person] rendre malade; sea food always ~s me OR my stomach les fruits de mer me rendent toujours malade.
◇ *adj* -**1.** [annoyed] ennuyé, contrarié; [offended] fâché, vexé; [worried] inquiet; there's no reason to get so ~ il n'y a pas de quoi en faire un drame OR te fâcher; he's ~ about losing the deal cela l'ennuie d'avoir perdu l'affaire; I was most ~ that she left j'étais très ennuyé qu'elle soit partie; why is she so ~? qu'est-ce qu'elle a? -**2.** [stomach] dérangé; to have an ~ stomach avoir une indigestion.
◇ *n* -**1.** [in plans] bouleversement *m*; [of government] renversement *m*; [of team] défaite *f*; the result caused a major political ~ le résultat a entraîné de grands bouleversements politiques. -**2.** [emotional] bouleversement *m*. -**3.** [of stomach] indigestion *f*; he often gets stomach ~s il a souvent des indigestions.

upset price ['ʌpset-] *n Am* & *Scot* mise *f* à prix.

upsetting [ʌp'setɪŋ] *adj* [annoying] ennuyeux, contrariant; [offensive] vexant; [saddening] attristant, triste; [worrying] inquiétant.

upshot ['ʌpʃɒt] *n* résultat *m*, conséquence *f*.

upside ['ʌpsaɪd] *n* -**1.** [surface] dessus *m*. -**2.** [of situation] avantage *m*, bon côté *m*.

upside down ◇ *adj* -**1.** [cup, glass] à l'envers, retourné; upside-down logic *fig* raisonnement *m* tordu; upside-down cake gâteau *m* renversé. -**2.** [room, house] sens dessus dessous.
◇ *adv* -**1.** [in inverted fashion] à l'envers; she hung ~ from the bar elle s'est suspendue à la barre la tête en bas; to read sthg ~ lire qqch à l'envers. -**2.** [in disorderly fashion] sens dessus dessous; we turned the house ~ looking for the keys nous avons mis la maison sens dessus dessous en cherchant les clés; the news turned our world ~ la nouvelle a bouleversé notre univers.

upstage [,ʌp'steɪdʒ] ◇ *adv* [move] vers le fond de la scène; [enter, exit] par le fond de la scène; [stand] au fond de la scène.
◇ *vt fig* éclipser, voler la vedette à.

upstairs [,ʌp'steəz] ◇ *adv* en haut, à l'étage; there are three bedrooms ~ il y a trois chambres en haut OR à l'étage; to go ~ monter (à l'étage); she ran back ~ elle est remontée en courant; I'll take your bags ~ je monterai vos bagages; let me show you ~ permettez que je vous fasse monter ❑ he hasn't got much ~ il n'est pas très futé OR dégourdi.
◇ *adj* [room, window] du haut, (situé) à l'étage; [flat, neighbour] du dessus.
◇ *n* étage *m*; we rent out the ~ nous louons (les pièces de) l'étage.

upstanding [,ʌp'stændɪŋ] *adj* -**1.** [in character] intègre, droit; [in build] bien bâti. -**2.** *fml*: be ~ levez-vous.

upstart ['ʌpstɑːt] *n pej* parvenu *m*, -e *f*; that young ~! ce petit morveux!

upstate [,ʌp'steɪt] *Am* ◇ *adv* [live] dans le nord (de l'État); [move] vers le nord (de l'État); he moved ~ il est allé s'installer dans le nord (de l'État).
◇ *adj* au nord (de l'État); ~ New York *la partie nord de l'État de New York*.

upstream [,ʌp'striːm] ◇ *adv* [live] en amont; [move] vers l'amont; [row, swim] contre le courant.
◇ *adj* d'amont, (situé) en amont.

upstroke ['ʌpstrəʊk] *n* [of pen] délié *m*; [of piston] mouvement *m* ascendant.

upsurge ['ʌpsɜːdʒ] *n* [gen] mouvement *m* vif; [of anger, enthusiasm] vague *f*, montée *f*; [of interest] renaissance *f*, regain *m*; [in production, sales] montée *f*, augmentation *f*.

upswing ['ʌpswɪŋ] *n* -**1.** [movement] mouvement *m* ascendant, montée *f*. -**2.** [improvement] amélioration *f*; the stock market is on the ~ la Bourse est en hausse; there's been an ~ in sales il y a eu une progression des ventes.

upsydaisy *inf* [,ʌpsə'deɪzɪ] *interj*: ~! allez, hop!

uptake ['ʌpteɪk] *n* -**1.** [of air] admission *f*; [of water] prise *f*, adduction *f*. -**2.** *phr*: to be quick on the ~ avoir l'esprit vif OR rapide, comprendre vite; to be slow on the ~ être lent à comprendre OR à saisir. -**3.** [of offer, allowance]: a government campaign to improve the ~ of child benefit une campagne gouvernementale pour inciter les gens à réclamer leurs allocations familiales.

upthrust ['ʌpθrʌst] *n* [of piston] poussée *f* ascendante; GEOL soulèvement *m*.

uptight *inf* [ʌp'taɪt] *adj* -**1.** [tense] tendu, crispé; [irritable] irritable, énervé; [nervous] nerveux, inquiet; he gets so ~ whenever I mention it [tense] il se crispe chaque fois que j'en parle; [annoyed] il s'énerve chaque fois que j'en parle. -**2.** [prudish] coincé, collet monté *(inv)*; he's very ~ about sex il est très coincé quand il s'agit de sexe.

uptime ['ʌptaɪm] *n* COMPUT temps *m* de bon fonctionnement.

up-to-date *adj* -**1.** [information, report - updated] à jour; [- most current] le plus récent; I try to keep ~ on the news j'essaie de me tenir au courant de l'actualité; to bring sb ~ on sthg mettre qqn au courant de qqch; they brought the reports ~ ils ont mis les rapports à jour. -**2.** [modern - machinery, methods] moderne.

up-to-the-minute *adj* le plus récent; ~ news reporting bulletins *mpl* (d'information) de dernière minute.

uptown [,ʌp'taʊn] *Am* ◇ *adj* des quartiers résidentiels.
◇ *adv* [be, live] dans les quartiers résidentiels; [move] vers les quartiers résidentiels.
◇ *n* les quartiers *mpl* résidentiels.

upturn [*n* 'ʌptɜːn, *vb* ʌp'tɜːn] ◇ *n* [in economy, situation] amélioration *f*; [in production, sales]

progression *f*, reprise *f*; there's been an ~ in the market il y a eu une progression du marché.
◇ *vt* [turn over] retourner; [turn upside down] mettre à l'envers; [overturn] renverser.

upturned [ʌp'tɜːnd] *adj* -**1.** [nose] retroussé; ~ faces visages tournés vers le haut. -**2.** [upside down] retourné, renversé.

upward ['ʌpwəd] ◇ *adj* [movement] ascendant; [trend] à la hausse.
◇ *adv Am* = **upwards**.

upwardly mobile ['ʌpwədlɪ-] *adj* susceptible de promotion sociale.

upward mobility *n* ascension *f* sociale.

upwards ['ʌpwədz] *adv* -**1.** [move, climb] vers le haut; to slope ~ monter; we looked ~ nous avons levé les yeux OR regardé vers le haut; if you look ~ you can see... si vous levez la tête OR les yeux, vous voyez...; prices are moving ~ les prix sont à la hausse. -**2.** [facing up]: she placed the photos (face) ~ on the table elle a posé les photos sur la table face vers le haut; he lay on the floor face ~ il était allongé par terre sur le dos. -**3.** [onwards]: from 15 years ~ à partir de 15 ans; from her youth ~ depuis sa jeunesse.
◆ **upwards of** *prep phr*: ~ of 100 candidates applied plus de 100 candidats se sont présentés; they can cost ~ of £150 ils peuvent coûter 150 livres et plus.

upwind [ʌp'wɪnd] ◇ *adv* du côté du vent, contre le vent.
◇ *adj* dans le vent, au vent; to be ~ of sthg être dans le vent OR au vent par rapport à qqch.

Ur [ɜː] *pr n* Our, Ur.

uraemia [jʊə'riːmjə] *Br* = **uremia**.

Ural ['jʊərəl] *adj*: the ~ Mountains les monts *mpl* Oural, l'Oural *m*; the ~ River l'Oural *m*.

Urals ['jʊərəlz] *pl pr n*: the ~ l'Oural *m*; in the ~ dans l'Oural.

uranite ['jʊərənaɪt] *n* uranite *f*.

uranium [jʊ'reɪnjəm] *n* uranium *m*; ~ series série *f* uranique.

Uranus ['jʊərənəs] *pr n* ASTRON & MYTH Uranus.

urban ['ɜːbən] *adj* urbain; ~ area zone *f* urbaine, agglomération *f*; ~ district *Br* ADMIN district *m* urbain; ~ guerrilla personne *f* qui pratique la guérilla urbaine; ~ renewal rénovations *fpl* urbaines; ~ unemployment chômage *m* dans les zones urbaines.

urbane [ɜː'beɪn] *adj* [person] poli, qui a du savoir-vivre; [manner] poli, raffiné.

urbanely [ɜː'beɪnlɪ] *adv* avec mondanité.

urbanism ['ɜːbənɪzm] *n* urbanisme *m*.

urbanite ['ɜːbənaɪt] *n* citadin *m*, -e *f*.

urbanity [ɜː'bænətɪ] *n* urbanité *f fml*, savoir-vivre *m*.

urbanization [ˌɜːbənaɪ'zeɪʃn] *n* urbanisation *f*.

urbanize, -ise ['ɜːbənaɪz] *vt* urbaniser.

urchin ['ɜːtʃɪn] *n* galopin *m*, polisson *m*, -onne *f*.

urchin cut *n* coupe *f* OR coiffure *f* à la garçonne.

Urdu ['ʊəduː] *n* ourdou *m*, urdu *m*.

urea ['jʊərɪə] *n* urée *f*.

uremia [ˌjʊə'riːmjə] *n esp Am* urémie *f*.

ureter [ˌjʊə'riːtə] *n* uretère *m*.

urethra [ˌjʊə'riːθrə] *n* urètre *m*.

urethritis [ˌjʊərɪ'θraɪtɪs] *n (U)* urétrite *f*.

urge [ɜːdʒ] ◇ *n* forte envie *f*, désir *m*; I felt OR I had a sudden ~ to tell her j'avais tout à coup très envie de lui dire; the sexual ~ les pulsions *fpl* sexuelles.
◇ *vt* -**1.** [person - incite] exhorter, presser; I ~ you to reconsider je vous conseille vivement de reconsidérer votre position; she ~d us not to sell the house elle nous a vivement déconseillé de vendre la maison; he ~d them to revolt il les a incités à la révolte OR à se révolter. -**2.** [course of action] conseiller vivement, préconiser; [need, point] insister sur; they ~d the need for new schools ils ont insisté sur la nécessité de construire de nouvelles écoles; we ~d caution nous avons préconisé la prudence.
◆ **urge on** *vt sep* talonner, presser; [person, troops] faire avancer; to ~ sb on to do sthg inciter qqn à faire qqch.

urgency ['ɜːdʒənsɪ] *n* urgence *f*; it's a matter of great ~ c'est une affaire très urgente; there's no great ~ cela n'est pas urgent OR ne presse pas; there was a note of ~ in her voice il y avait de l'insistance dans sa voix.

urgent ['ɜːdʒənt] *adj* -**1.** [matter, need] urgent, pressant; [message] urgent; it's not ~ ce n'est pas urgent, ça ne presse pas; is it ~? est-ce urgent?; the roof is in ~ need of repair le toit a un besoin urgent d'être réparé. -**2.** [manner, voice] insistant; he was ~ in his demands for help il a insisté pour qu'on lui vienne en aide.

urgently ['ɜːdʒəntlɪ] *adv* d'urgence, de toute urgence; they appealed ~ for help ils ont demandé du secours avec insistance; the matter is ~ in need of attention l'affaire demande à être traitée immédiatement OR sans délais; supplies are ~ needed un ravitaillement est absolument nécessaire.

uric ['jʊərɪk] *adj* urique; ~ acid acide *m* urique.

urinal ['jʊərɪnl] *n* [apparatus] urinal *m*; [building] urinoir *m*.

urinary ['jʊərɪnərɪ] *adj* urinaire; ~ tract appareil *m* urinaire.

urinate ['jʊərɪneɪt] *vi* uriner.

urine ['jʊərɪn] *n* urine *f*.

urinogenital [ˌjʊərɪnəʊ'dʒenɪtl] = **urogenital**.

urn [ɜːn] *n* -**1.** [container - gen] urne *f*. -**2.** [for ashes] urne *f* (funéraire). -**3.** [for coffee, tea] fontaine *f*; tea ~ fontaine à thé.

urogenital [ˌjʊərəʊ'dʒenɪtl] *adj* urogénital.

urologist [jʊə'rɒlədʒɪst] *n* urologue *mf*.

urology [jʊə'rɒlədʒɪ] *n* urologie *f*.

Ursa ['ɜːsə] *pr n*: ~ Major/Minor la Grande/Petite Ourse.

urticaria [ˌɜːtɪ'keərɪə] *n* urticaire *f*.

Uruguay ['jʊərəgwaɪ] *pr n* Uruguay *m*; in ~ en Uruguay.

Uruguayan [ˌjʊərʊ'gwaɪən] ◇ *n* Uruguayen *m*, -enne *f*.
◇ *adj* uruguayen.

us [ʌs] *pron* -**1.** [object form of 'we'] nous; tell us the truth dites-nous la vérité; it's us! c'est nous!; it's us she's looking for c'est nous qu'elle cherche; most of us are students nous sommes presque tous des étudiants; all four of us went nous y sommes allés tous les quatre; there are three of us nous sommes trois; they're with us ils sont avec nous. -**2.** *inf* [me - direct object] me; [- indirect object] me, moi; give us a kiss! embrasse-moi!; give us a chance, I've only just got here! je t'en prie, je viens d'arriver!

US ◇ *pr n* (*abbr of* United States): the ~ les USA *mpl*; in the ~ aux USA, aux États-Unis.
◇ *comp* des États-Unis, américain.

USA *pr n* -**1.** (*abbr of* United States of America): the ~ les USA *mpl*; in the ~ aux USA, aux États-Unis. -**2.** (*abbr of* United States Army) *armée des États-Unis*.

usable ['juːzəbl] *adj* utilisable.

USAF (*abbr of* United States Air Force) *pr n armée de l'air des États-Unis*.

usage ['juːzɪdʒ] *n* -**1.** [custom, practice] coutume *f*, usage *m*. -**2.** [of term, word] usage *m*; the term is in common ~ le terme est employé couramment; that phrase has long since dropped out of ~ cette expression n'est plus usitée depuis longtemps. -**3.** [employment] usage *m*, emploi *m*; [treatment - of material, tool] manipulation *f*; [- of person] traitement *m*; designed for rough ~ conçu pour résister aux chocs; these books are not meant for rough ~ ces livres ne sont pas faits pour être malmenés.

USCG (*abbr of* United States Coast Guard) *pr n service de surveillance côtière américain*.

USDA (*abbr of* United States Department of Agriculture) *pr n ministère américain de l'Agriculture*.

USDAW ['ʌzdɔː] (*abbr of* Union of Shop, Distributive and Allied Workers) *pr n syndicat britannique des personnels de la distribution*.

USDI (*abbr of* United States Department of the Interior) *pr n ministère américain de l'Intérieur*.

use[1] [juːs] *n* -**1.** [utilization - of materials] utilisation *f*, emploi *m*; [consumption - of water, resources etc] consommation *f*; [being used, worn etc] usage *m*; the ~ of brick in building l'emploi OR l'utilisation de la brique dans la construction; to stretch out with ~ se détendre à l'usage; to wear out with ~ s'user; the dishes are for everyday ~ c'est la vaisselle de tous les jours; ready for ~ prêt à l'emploi; 'directions for ~' 'mode d'emploi'; 'for your personal ~' pour votre usage personnel; 'for customer ~ only' 'réservé à notre clientèle'; 'for external/internal ~ only' MED 'à usage externe/interne'; 'for ~ in case of emergency' 'à utiliser en cas d'urgence'; the film is for ~ in teaching le film est destiné à l'enseignement ❑ in ~ [machine, system] en usage, utilisé; [lift, cash point] en service; [phrase, word] usité; in general ~ d'emploi courant, d'utilisation courante; 'not in ~', 'out of ~' 'hors d'usage'; [lift, cash point] 'hors service'; the phrase is no longer in ~ l'expression est inusitée OR ne s'utilise plus; to come into ~ entrer en service; to go out of ~ [machine] être mis au rebut; steam engines went out of ~ in 1950 on a cessé d'utiliser OR d'employer les machines à vapeur en 1950; to make ~ of sthg utiliser qqch; schools are making increasing ~ of audio-visual aids les écoles se servent de plus en plus de supports audiovisuels; to make good ~ of, to put to good ~ [machine, money] faire bon usage de; [opportunity, experience] tirer profit de. -**2.** [ability or right to use] usage *m*, utilisation *f*; we gave them the ~ of our car nous leur avons laissé l'usage de notre voiture; he only has the ~ of one arm il n'a l'usage que d'un bras; she lost the ~ of her legs elle a perdu l'usage de ses jambes; the old man still has the full ~ of his faculties le vieil homme jouit encore de toutes ses facultés. -**3.** [practical application] usage *m*, emploi *m*; this tool has many ~s cet outil a de nombreux usages OR emplois; we found a ~ for the old fridge nous avons trouvé un emploi pour le vieux frigo ❑ I have my ~s *hum* il m'arrive de servir à quelque chose. -**4.** [need] besoin *m*, usage *m*; do you have any ~ for this book? avez-vous besoin de ce livre?; to have no ~ for sthg *literal* ne pas avoir besoin de qqch; *fig* n'avoir que faire de qqch; I have no ~ for idle gossip je n'ai que faire des cancans; this department has no ~ for slackers il n'y a pas de place pour les fainéants dans ce service. -**5.** [usefulness]: to be of ~ (to sb) être utile (à qqn), servir (à qqn); this dictionary might be of ~ to you ce dictionnaire pourrait vous être utile OR vous servir; were the instructions (of) any ~? est-ce que le mode d'emploi a servi à quelque chose?; I found his advice to be of little ~, his advice was of little ~ to me je n'ai pas trouvé ses conseils très utiles; the book would be of more ~ if it had illustrations le livre serait plus utile s'il contenait des illustrations; he's not much ~ as a secretary il n'est pas brillant comme secrétaire; to be (of) no ~ [thing] ne servir à rien; [person] n'être bon à rien; they were no ~ at all during the move ils n'ont rien fait pendant le déménagement; you're no ~! tu n'es bon à rien!; it's OR there's no ~ complaining inutile de OR ça ne sert à rien de se plaindre; there's no ~ shouting ça ne sert à rien de OR inutile de crier; it's no ~, we might as well give up c'est inutile OR ça ne sert à rien, autant abandonner; I tried to convince her but it was no ~ j'ai essayé de la convaincre mais il n'y avait rien à faire; is it any ~ calling her? est-ce que ça servira à quelque chose de l'appeler?; what's the ~ of waiting? à quoi bon attendre?, à quoi ça sert d'attendre?; oh, what's the ~? à quoi bon?; that's a fat lot of ~! *inf iron* ça nous fait une belle jambe! -**6.** LING usage *m*; that's an old-fashioned ~ c'est un usage vieilli. -**7.** RELIG usage *m*.

use2 [juːz] ◇ *vt* -**1.** [put into action - service, tool] se servir de, utiliser; [- product] utiliser; [- method, phrase, word] employer; [- name] utiliser, faire usage de; [- vehicle, form of transport] prendre; **these are the notebooks he ~d** ce sont les cahiers dont il s'est servi OR qu'il a utilisés; **is anyone using this book?** est-ce que quelqu'un se sert de OR a besoin de ce livre?; **it's very easy to ~** c'est très facile à utiliser; **it's no longer ~d** [machine, tool] ça ne sert plus; **am I using the term correctly?** est-ce comme ça qu'on utilise le terme?; **I'd like to ~ my language skills more** j'aimerais utiliser davantage mes connaissances en langues; **I always ~ public transport** je prends toujours les transports en commun; **we ~ this room as an office** nous nous servons de cette pièce comme bureau, cette pièce nous sert de bureau; **what is this ~d for** OR **as?** à quoi cela sert-il?; **it's ~d for identifying the blood type** cela sert à identifier le groupe sanguin; **I ~ it for opening** OR **to open letters** je m'en sers OR je l'utilise pour ouvrir les lettres; **what battery does this radio ~?** quelle pile faut-il pour cette radio?; **my car ~s unleaded petrol** ma voiture marche à l'essence sans plomb; **may I ~ the phone?** puis-je téléphoner?; **he asked to ~ the toilet** OR **bathroom** il a demandé à aller aux toilettes; **to ~ force/violence** avoir recours à la force/violence; **the police often ~ tear gas** la police a souvent recours au gaz lacrymogène; **~ your imagination!** utilise ton imagination!; **~ your initiative!** fais preuve d'initiative!; **~ your head** OR **your brains!** réfléchis un peu!; **~ your eyes!** ouvrez l'œil! ❑ **he could certainly ~ some help** *inf* un peu d'aide ne lui ferait pas de mal; **we could all ~ a holiday!** *inf* nous aurions tous bien besoin de vacances! -**2.** [exploit, take advantage of - opportunity] profiter de; [- person] se servir de; **~ it to your advantage!** profitez-en!; **he's only using you to get ahead** il ne fait que se servir de toi pour avancer; **I feel ~d** j'ai l'impression qu'on s'est servi de moi. -**3.** [consume] consommer, utiliser; [finish, use up] finir, épuiser; **the car's using a lot of oil** la voiture consomme beaucoup d'huile; **have you ~d all the shampoo?** as-tu utilisé tout le shampooing? -**4.** *fml* [treat physically] traiter; [behave towards] agir envers; **they ~d the workers well** ils ont bien traité les ouvriers, ils ont bien agi envers les ouvriers; **I consider I was ill ~d** je considère qu'on ne m'a pas traité comme il faut. -**5.** ▽ [drug] prendre.

◇ *modal vb* (*only in past tense*): **they ~d to live here** (avant) ils habitaient ici; **he ~d to drink a lot** il buvait beaucoup avant; **it ~d to be true** c'était vrai autrefois; **she can't get about the way she ~d to** elle ne peut plus se déplacer comme avant; **she never ~d to smoke** elle ne fumait pas avant; **we ~d not** OR **we didn't ~ to eat meat** avant, nous ne mangions pas de viande; **did he ~ to visit her?** venait-il la voir avant?

◆ **use up** *vt sep* [consume] consommer, prendre; [exhaust - paper, soap] finir; [- patience, energy, supplies] épuiser; **she ~d up the leftovers to make the soup** elle a utilisé les restes pour faire un potage; **did you ~ up all your money?** as-tu dépensé tout ton argent?; **the paper was all ~d up** il ne restait plus de papier.

used1 [juːzd] *adj* [book, car] d'occasion; [clothing] d'occasion, usagé; [glass, linen] sale, qui a déjà servi.

used2 [juːst] *adj* [accustomed]: **to be ~ to sthg** avoir l'habitude de OR être habitué à qqch; **I'm ~ to working alone** j'ai l'habitude de OR je suis habitué à travailler tout seul; **they're not ~ to it** ils n'y sont pas habitués, ils n'en ont pas l'habitude; **to be ~ to sb** être habitué à qqn; **to get ~ to sthg** s'habituer à qqch; **he can't get ~ to it** il n'arrive pas à s'y habituer; **you'll soon get ~ to the idea** tu te feras à l'idée.

useful ['juːsfʊl] *adj* -**1.** [handy - book, information, machine] utile, pratique; [- discussion, experience] utile, profitable; [- method] utile, efficace; **does it serve any ~ purpose?** est-ce utile?, est-ce que cela sert à quelque chose?; **I felt as if I was doing something ~** j'avais l'impression de faire quelque chose d'utile OR de me rendre utile; **you could be ~ to the director** vous pourriez rendre service au directeur; **the information was ~ to us in making a decision** les renseignements nous ont aidés à prendre une décision; **make yourself ~ and help me tidy up** rends-toi utile et aide-moi à ranger; **she's a ~ person to know** c'est une femme qu'il est bon de connaître; **he's very ~ around the house** il est très utile OR il rend beaucoup de services dans la maison; **they're ~ when it comes to financial affairs** ils sont très compétents dans le domaine financier; **this map could be very ~** cette carte pourrait être très utile OR d'une grande utilité. -**2.** *inf* [satisfactory - performance, score] honorable; **he's a very ~ player** c'est un joueur très compétent.

usefully ['juːsfʊlɪ] *adv* utilement; **his free time was ~ employed in improving his languages** il a employé utilement son temps libre à améliorer ses langues; **you could ~ devote a further year's study to the subject** tu pourrais consacrer avec profit une année d'étude supplémentaire au sujet.

usefulness ['juːsfʊlnɪs] *n* utilité *f*; **it's outlived its ~** ça a fait son temps, ça ne sert plus à rien.

useless ['juːslɪs] *adj* -**1.** [bringing no help - book, information, machine] inutile; [- discussion, experience] vain, qui n'apporte rien; [- advice, suggestion] qui n'apporte rien, qui ne vaut rien; [- attempt, effort] inutile, vain; **the contract is ~ to them** le contrat leur est inutile; **it's ~ trying to reason with him, it's ~ to try and reason with him** ça ne sert à rien OR c'est inutile d'essayer de lui faire entendre raison; **the computer is ~ without the instructions** l'ordinateur est inutilisable OR on ne peut pas se servir de l'ordinateur sans mode d'emploi. -**2.** *inf* [incompetent] nul; **she makes me feel ~** elle me donne l'impression d'être bon à rien; **I'm ~ at history/maths** je suis nul en histoire/math; **she's ~ as a navigator** elle est nulle OR elle ne vaut rien en tant que navigateur; **her brother is absolutely ~** son frère est nul OR bon à rien.

uselessly ['juːslɪslɪ] *adv* inutilement.

user ['juːzəʳ] ◇ *n* [of computer, machine] utilisateur *m*, -trice *f*; [of airline, public service, road] usager *m*; [of electricity, gas, oil] usager *m*, utilisateur *m*, -trice *f*; [of drugs] consommateur *m*, -trice *f*, usager *m*; **road ~s** usagers de la route; **~s of public transport** usagers des transports en commun.

◇ *in cpds* par l'utilisateur; **~-definable** définissable par l'utilisateur; **~-programmable** programmable par l'utilisateur.

user-defined [-dɪ'faɪnd] *adj* COMPUT programmé par l'utilisateur.

user-friendliness *n* COMPUT convivialité *f*.

user-friendly *adj* COMPUT convivial, facile à utiliser.

user-interface *n* COMPUT & *fig* interface *f* utilisateur.

USES (*abbr of* United States Employment Service) *pr n services américains de l'emploi*.

U-shaped *adj* en (forme de) U.

usher ['ʌʃəʳ] ◇ *vt* conduire, accompagner; **I ~ed them to their seats** je les ai conduits à leur place; **he ~ed us into/out of the living room** il nous a fait entrer au/sortir du salon.

◇ *n* -**1.** [at concert, theatre] placeur *m*, -euse *f*. -**2.** [doorkeeper] portier *m*; JUR huissier *m*.

◆ **usher in** *vt sep fig* inaugurer, marquer le début de; **the printing press ~ed in a new era** l'imprimerie a inauguré OR annoncé une nouvelle ère.

usherette [,ʌʃə'ret] *n* ouvreuse *f*.

USIA (*abbr of* United States Information Agency) *pr n agence américaine de renseignements*.

USM *pr n* -**1.** (*abbr of* United States Mail) ≃ la Poste *(aux États-Unis)*. -**2.** (*abbr of* United States Mint) ≃ la Monnaie *(aux États-unis)*.

USN (*abbr of* United States Navy) *pr n marine de guerre des États-Unis*.

USPHS (*abbr of* United States Public Health Service) *pr n direction américaine des Affaires sanitaires et sociales*.

USS (*abbr of* United States Ship) *initiales précédant le nom des navires américains*; **the ~ Washington** le Washington.

USSR (*abbr of* Union of Soviet Socialist Republics) *pr n*: **the ~** l'URSS *f*; **in the ~** en URSS.

usu. *written abbr of* usually.

usual ['juːʒl] ◇ *adj* [customary - activity, place, road] habituel; [- practice, price] habituel, courant; [- expression, word] courant, usité; **we sat at our ~ table** nous nous sommes assis à notre table habituelle; **our ~ doctor** notre médecin habituel OR traitant OR de famille; **they asked the ~ questions** ils ont posé les questions habituelles; **my ~ diet consists of fish and vegetables** généralement OR d'habitude je mange du poisson et des légumes; **let's meet at the ~ time** retrouvons-nous à l'heure habituelle OR à la même heure que d'habitude; **6 o'clock is the ~ time he gets home** d'habitude OR en général il rentre à 18 h; **earlier/later than ~** plus tôt/plus tard que d'habitude; **he drank more than ~** il a bu plus que d'habitude; **she was her ~ cheery self** elle était gaie comme d'habitude; **she's her ~ self again** elle est redevenue elle-même; **with her ~ optimism** avec son optimisme habituel, avec l'optimisme qui est le sien OR qui la caractérise; **it's not ~ for him to be so bitter** il est rarement si amer, c'est rare qu'il soit si amer; **it's the ~ story** c'est toujours la même histoire; **it's quite ~ to see flooding in the spring** il y a souvent des inondations au printemps; **I believe it's the ~ practice** je crois que c'est ce qui se fait d'habitude; **as is ~ with young mothers** comme toujours OR comme d'habitude avec les jeunes mamans.

◇ *n inf* [drink, meal]: **what will you have? — the ~, please** que prends-tu? — comme d'habitude, s'il te plaît.

◆ **as usual, as per usual** *adv phr* comme d'habitude; **as ~, the opposition objected** comme d'habitude OR comme toujours, l'opposition a élevé une objection; **life goes on as ~** la vie continue; **'business as ~'** [during building work] 'le magasin reste ouvert pendant la durée des travaux'; **it's business as ~** il n'y a rien à signaler.

usually ['juːʒəlɪ] *adv* généralement, d'habitude, d'ordinaire; **I ~ get to work early** généralement OR d'habitude j'arrive tôt au bureau; **she's not ~ late** il est rare qu'elle soit en retard, elle est rarement en retard; **we don't ~ eat dessert** d'habitude nous ne mangeons pas de dessert; **what route do you ~ take?** quelle route prenez-vous d'habitude OR d'ordinaire?; **the roads were more than ~ busy** il y avait encore plus de trafic que d'habitude OR d'ordinaire OR de coutume sur les routes.

usufruct ['juːsjuːfrʌkt] *n* usufruit *m*.

usurer ['juːʒərəʳ] *n* usurier *m*, -ère *f*.

usurp [juː'zɜːp] *vt* usurper.

usurpation [,juːzɜː'peɪʃn] *n* usurpation *f*.

usurper [juː'zɜːpəʳ] *n* usurpateur *m*, -trice *f*.

usury ['juːʒʊrɪ] *n* usure *f (intérêt)*.

UT *written abbr of* Utah.

Utah ['juːtɑː] *pr n* Utah *m*; **in ~** dans l'Utah.

utensil [juː'tensl] *n* ustensile *m*, outil *m*; **cooking ~s** ustensiles de cuisine.

uterine ['juːtəraɪn] *adj* utérin.

uterus ['juːtərəs] (*pl* uteri [-raɪ] OR uteruses) *n* utérus *m*.

utilitarian [,juːtɪlɪ'teərɪən] ◇ *adj* -**1.** [functional] utilitaire, fonctionnel. -**2.** PHILOS utilitariste.

◇ *n* utilitariste *mf*.

utilitarianism [,juːtɪlɪ'teərɪənɪzm] *n* utilitarisme *m*.

utility [juːˈtɪlətɪ] (*pl* **utilities**) ◇ *n* -**1.** [usefulness] utilité *f*. -**2.** [service] service *m*; **they plan to improve (public) utilities** ils ont l'intention d'améliorer les services publics. -**3.** COMPUT utilitaire *m*, programme *m* utilitaire. -**4.** *Am* [room] = **utility room**.
◇ *adj* [fabric, furniture] utilitaire, fonctionnel; [vehicle] utilitaire.

utility man *n Am* [worker] *ouvrier capable d'occuper différents postes*; [for gas, electricity] *employé des services publics*; [actor] *acteur qui joue les utilités*.

utility player *n* SPORT *joueur capable d'occuper différents postes*.

utility program *n* COMPUT (logiciel *m*) utilitaire *m*.

utility room *n pièce servant à ranger les appareils ménagers, provisions etc*.

utilizable [ˈjuːtɪlaɪzəbl] *adj* utilisable.

utilization [ˌjuːtɪlaɪˈzeɪʃn] *n* utilisation *f*.

utilize, -ise [ˈjuːtɪlaɪz] *vt* [use] utiliser, se servir de; [make best use of] exploiter; **you could have ~d your time better** vous auriez pu tirer meilleur parti de votre temps OR mieux profiter de votre temps.

utmost [ˈʌtməʊst] ◇ *adj* -**1.** [greatest] le plus grand; **it's a matter of the ~ seriousness** c'est une affaire extrêmement sérieuse; **in the ~ secrecy** dans le plus grand secret; **it's of the ~ importance that I see him** il est extrêmement important OR il est d'une importance capitale que je le voie; **with the ~ respect, I cannot agree with your conclusions** avec tout le respect que je vous dois, je ne peux pas partager vos conclusions. -**2.** [farthest] : **to the ~ ends of the earth** au bout du monde.
◇ *n* -**1.** [maximum] maximum *m*, plus haut degré *m*; **the ~ in comfort** ce qui se fait de mieux en matière de confort. -**2.** [best effort] : **we did our ~ to fight the new taxes** nous avons fait tout notre possible OR tout ce que nous pouvions pour lutter contre les nouveaux impôts; **she tried her ~** elle a fait de son mieux.

utopia, Utopia [juːˈtəʊpjə] *n* utopie *f*; **'Utopia'** *More* 'l'Utopie'.

utopian, Utopian [juːˈtəʊpjən] ◇ *adj* utopique.
◇ *n* utopiste *mf*.

utopianism, Utopianism [juːˈtəʊpjənɪzm] *n* utopisme *m*.

Utrecht [ˈjuːtrekt] *pr n* Utrecht.

utter [ˈʌtəʳ] ◇ *vt* -**1.** [pronounce - word] prononcer, proférer; [- cry, groan] pousser; **he didn't ~ a sound** il n'a pas ouvert la bouche, il n'a pas soufflé mot. -**2.** JUR [libel] publier; [counterfeit money] émettre, mettre en circulation.
◇ *adj* [amazement, bliss] absolu, total; [fool] parfait, fini; **he shows an ~ disregard for his family's welfare** il affiche une indifférence absolue pour le bien-être de sa famille; **he's talking ~ rubbish** ce qu'il dit n'a aucun sens OR est absolument idiot; **it's an ~ scandal** c'est un véritable scandale; **an ~ fool** un parfait crétin, un crétin fini.

utterance [ˈʌtərəns] *n* -**1.** [statement] déclaration *f*; LING énoncé *m*. -**2.** [expression] expression *f*, énonciation *f*; **to give ~ to sthg** exprimer qqch.

utterly [ˈʌtəlɪ] *adv* complètement, tout à fait.

uttermost [ˈʌtəməʊst] = **utmost**.

U-turn *n* -**1.** AUT demi-tour *m*; **to make a ~** faire (un) demi-tour; **'no ~s'** 'défense de faire demi-tour'. -**2.** *fig* volte-face *f inv*, revirement *m*; **the government were accused of making a ~ on health policy** le gouvernement a été accusé de faire volte-face en matière de politique de santé.

UV (*abbr of* **ultra-violet**) *n* UV *m*.

UV-A, UVA (*abbr of* **ultra-violet-A**) *n* UVA *m*.

UV-B, UVB (*abbr of* **ultra-violet-B**) *n* UVB *m*.

uvula [ˈjuːvjʊlə] (*pl* **uvulas** OR **uvulae** [-liː]) *n* luette *f*, uvule *f spec*, uvula *f spec*.

uvular [ˈjuːvjʊləʳ] *adj* uvulaire.

uxorious [ʌkˈsɔːrɪəs] *adj fml* OR *lit* excessivement soumis à sa femme.

Uzbek [ˈʊzbek] *n* -**1.** [person] Ouzbek *mf*. -**2.** LING ouzbek *m*.

Uzbekistan [ʊzˌbekɪˈstɑːn] *pr n* Ouzbékistan *m*; **in ~** en Ouzbékistan.

v (*pl* v's OR vs), **V** (*pl* V's OR Vs) [viː] *n* [letter] v *m*, V *m*; V for Victor V comme Victor; V-shaped en (forme de) V; V-1 (bomb) V1 *m*; V-2 (rocket) V2 *m*; V-8 (engine) moteur *m* à huit cylindres en V.

v -**1.** *written abbr of* velocity. -**2.** (*written abbr of* verb) v. -**3.** (*written abbr of* verse) v. -**4.** *written abbr of* versus. -**5.** (*written abbr of* vide) v.

V ◇ *n* [Roman numeral] V *m*.
◇ (*written abbr of* volt) V.

VA *written abbr of* Virginia.

vac *inf* [væk] (*abbr of* vacation) *n Br* UNIV [recess] vacances *fpl*; the Easter ~ les vacances de Pâques.

vacancy ['veɪkənsɪ] (*pl* vacancies) *n* -**1.** [emptiness] vide *m*. -**2.** [lack of intelligence] ineptie *f*, esprit *m* vide; he had a look of utter ~ on his face il avait l'air complètement idiot. -**3.** [in hotel] chambre *f* libre; 'no vacancies' 'complet'. -**4.** [job] poste *m* vacant OR libre, vacance *f*; do you have any vacancies? avez-vous des postes à pourvoir?, est-ce qu'il y a de l'embauche?; we have a ~ for a sales clerk nous avons un poste de vendeur à pourvoir, nous cherchons un vendeur; the ~ has been filled le poste a été pourvu; 'no vacancies' pas d'embauche; 'vacancies for waitresses' 'cherchons serveuses'.

vacant ['veɪkənt] *adj* -**1.** [house, room - to rent] libre, à louer; [- empty] inoccupé; [seat] libre, inoccupé; is this seat ~? y a-t-il quelqu'un à cette place?, est-ce que cette place est libre?; the room becomes ~ tomorrow la chambre sera libérée OR disponible demain; apartments sold with ~ possession appartements libres à la vente. -**2.** [job, position] vacant, libre; there are several ~ places to be filled il y a plusieurs postes à pourvoir; I found the job through the "situations ~" column j'ai trouvé le poste grâce à la rubrique des offres d'emploi; a secretarial job became OR fell ~ un poste de secrétaire est devenu disponible OR vacant. -**3.** [empty - mind, look, stare] vide; [stupid - person, look, stare] niais, idiot; I asked a question and she just looked ~ j'ai posé une question et elle a eu l'air de ne pas comprendre. -**4.** [time] de loisir, perdu; [hour] creux, de loisir.

vacantly ['veɪkəntlɪ] *adv* [expressionlessly] d'un air absent OR vague; [stupidly] d'un air niais OR idiot; he looked at us ~ [expressionlessly] il nous a regardés avec des yeux vides OR sans expression; [stupidly] il nous a regardés niaisement; she stared ~ into space elle avait le regard perdu dans le vague.

vacate [və'keɪt] *vt* [hotel room] libérer, quitter; [flat, house] quitter, déménager de; [job] démissionner de; they ~d the premises yesterday ils ont vidé les lieux hier.

vacation [və'keɪʃn] ◇ *n* -**1.** *Br* UNIV [recess] vacances *fpl*; JUR vacations *fpl*, vacances *fpl* judiciaires; over the ~ pendant les vacances; ~ course UNIV cours *mpl* d'été. -**2.** *Am* [holiday] vacances *fpl*; they went to Italy on ~ ils ont passé leurs vacances en Italie; when are you going on OR taking ~? quand est-ce que vous prenez vos vacances?
◇ *vi Am* prendre OR passer des vacances; they're ~ing in the mountains ils sont en vacances à la montagne.

vacationer [və'keɪʃənər], **vacationist** [və'keɪʃənɪst] *n Am* vacancier *m*, -ère *f*.

vaccinate ['væksɪneɪt] *vt* vacciner; have you been ~d against polio? est-ce que vous êtes vacciné OR est-ce que vous vous êtes fait vacciner contre la polio?

vaccination [,væksɪ'neɪʃn] *n* vaccination *f*; polio ~, ~ against polio vaccination contre la polio; the children all had ~s against polio les enfants étaient tous vaccinés contre la polio.

vaccine [*Br* 'væksiːn, *Am* væk'siːn] *n* vaccin *m*; smallpox ~ vaccination contre la variole.

vacillate ['væsəleɪt] *vi* hésiter.

vacillating ['væsəleɪtɪŋ] ◇ *adj* [behaviour] indécis, irrésolu.
◇ *n* indécision *f*.

vacillation [,væsə'leɪʃn] *n* hésitation *f*, indécision *f*.

vacuity [væ'kjuːətɪ] (*pl* vacuities) *n fml* -**1.** [of person, reasoning] vacuité *f*. -**2.** [statement] ânerie *f*, niaiserie *f*.

vacuous ['vækjʊəs] *adj fml* [eyes, look] vide, sans expression; [remark] sot, niais; [film, novel] idiot, dénué de tout intérêt; [life] vide de sens.

vacuum ['vækjʊəm] (*pl* vacuums OR vacua [-jʊə]) ◇ *n* -**1.** [void] vide *m*; his death left a ~ in her life sa mort a laissé un vide dans sa vie. -**2.** PHYS vacuum *m*. -**3.** [machine]: ~ (cleaner) aspirateur *m*; I gave the room a quick ~ j'ai passé l'aspirateur en vitesse dans la pièce.
◇ *vt* [carpet] passer l'aspirateur sur; [flat, room] passer l'aspirateur dans.

vacuum bottle *Am* = **vacuum flask**.

vacuum brake *n* frein *m* à vide.

vacuum-clean = **vacuum** *vt*.

vacuum cleaner *n* aspirateur *m*.

vacuum flask *n Br* (bouteille *f*) Thermos® *f*.

vacuum-packed *adj* emballé sous vide.

vacuum pump *n* pompe *f* à vide.

vacuum tube *n Am* tube *m* électronique OR à vide.

vade mecum [,vɑːdɪ'meɪkʊm] (*pl* vade mecums) *n* vade-mecum *m inv*.

vagabond ['vægəbɒnd] ◇ *n* [wanderer] vagabond *m*, -e *f*; [tramp] clochard *m*, -e *f*.
◇ *adj* vagabond, errant.

vagary ['veɪgərɪ] (*pl* vagaries) *n* caprice *m*.

vagina [və'dʒaɪnə] (*pl* vaginas OR vaginae [-niː]) *n* vagin *m*.

vaginal [və'dʒaɪnl] *adj* vaginal; ~ discharge pertes *fpl* blanches; ~ smear frottis *m* vaginal.

vaginismus [,vædʒɪ'nɪzməs] *n* vaginisme *m*.

vaginitis [,vædʒɪ'naɪtɪs] *n* vaginite *f*.

vagrancy ['veɪgrənsɪ] *n* [gen & JUR] vagabondage *m*.

vagrant ['veɪgrənt] ◇ *n* [wanderer] vagabond *m*, -e *f*; [tramp] clochard *m*, -e *f*; [beggar] mendiant *m*, -e *f*.
◇ *adj* vagabond.

vague [veɪg] *adj* -**1.** [imprecise - promise, statement] vague, imprécis; [- person] vague; she had only a ~ idea of what he meant elle ne comprenait que vaguement ce qu'il voulait dire; he made a ~ gesture toward the office d'un geste vague il désigna le bureau; don't be so ~ précisez ce que vous voulez dire, soyez plus précis; his instructions were ~ ses instructions manquaient de précision; they were ~ about their activities [imprecise] ils n'ont pas précisé la nature de leurs activités; [evasive] ils sont restés vagues sur la nature OR ils ont évité de préciser la nature de leurs activités || [unsure]: I'm still ~ about how to get there je ne comprends toujours pas comment y aller; I haven't the vaguest idea je n'en ai pas la moindre idée. -**2.** [dim - memory, feeling] vague, confus; I have a ~ recollection of summers spent in Greece je me rappelle vaguement les étés passés en Grèce. -**3.** [indistinct - shape] flou, indistinct. -**4.** [absent-minded] distrait; she looked ~ elle avait un air distrait.

vaguely ['veɪglɪ] *adv* -**1.** [not clearly - promise, say] vaguement; [- remember, understand] vaguement, confusément; I ~ remember dining here before j'ai le vague souvenir OR je me souviens vaguement d'avoir déjà mangé ici. -**2.** [a little] vaguement, peu; it tastes ~ like coffee cela a vaguement un goût de café; she resembles her sister only ~ elle ne ressemble pas beaucoup à sa sœur. -**3.** [absent-mindedly] distraitement; he looked ~ around him il regardait autour de lui d'un air vague OR distrait.

vagueness ['veɪgnɪs] *n* -**1.** [imprecision - of instructions, statement] imprécision *f*, manque *m* de clarté. -**2.** [dimness - of memory] imprécision *f*, manque *m* de précision; [- of feeling] vague *m*, caractère *m* vague OR indistinct. -**3.** [of shape] flou *m*, caractère *m* indistinct. -**4.** [absent-mindedness] distraction *f*.

vagus ['veɪgəs] (*pl* vagi [-dʒaɪ]) *n* nerf *m* vague OR pneumogastrique, pneumogastrique *m*.

vain [veɪn] *adj* -**1.** [conceited] vaniteux; he's very ~ about his looks il s'occupe beaucoup de sa petite personne. -**2.** [unsuccessful - attempt, effort] vain, inutile; [- hope, plea, search] vain, futile. -**3.** [idle - promise] vide, en l'air; [- word] creux, en l'air.

◆ **in vain** *adv phr* [unsuccessfully] en vain, inutilement; they tried in ~ to free the driver ils ont essayé sans succès OR en vain de libérer le conducteur; all their efforts were in ~ leurs efforts n'ont servi à rien OR étaient vains; it was all in ~ c'était peine perdue; to take sb's name in ~ [show disrespect] manquer de respect envers le nom de qqn; [mention name] parler de qqn en son absence; are you taking my name in ~ again? *hum* vous parlez encore de moi derrière mon dos?

vainglorious [ˌveɪnˈglɔːrɪəs] *adj lit* [proud] vaniteux, orgueilleux; [boastful] vantard.

vainly [ˈveɪnlɪ] *adv* -**1.** [conceitedly] avec vanité, vaniteusement. -**2.** [unsuccessfully - try] en vain, inutilement; [- hope] en vain.

valance [ˈvæləns] *n* [round bed frame] frange *f* de lit; [round shelf, window] lambrequin *m*, frange *f*.

vale [veɪl] *n lit* vallée *f*, val *m lit*.

valediction [ˌvælɪˈdɪkʃn] *n* [act] adieux *mpl*; [speech] discours *m* d'adieu; to give the ~ prononcer le discours d'adieu.

valedictorian [ˌvælɪdɪkˈtɔːrɪən] ◇ *adj* d'adieu.
◇ *n Am* SCH & UNIV *major de la promotion (qui prononce le discours d'adieu)*.

valedictory [ˌvælɪˈdɪktərɪ] (*pl* valedictories) *fml*
◇ *adj* d'adieu.
◇ *n* discours *m* d'adieu.

valence [ˈveɪləns] *n* -**1.** *Am* = **valency**. -**2.** [bonding capacity] atomicité *f*.

Valencia [vəˈlenʃɪə] *pr n* Valence.

valency [ˈveɪlənsɪ] (*pl* valencies) *n* CHEM & LING valence *f*.

valentine [ˈvæləntaɪn] *n* -**1.** [card]: ~ (card) carte *f* de la Saint-Valentin. -**2.** [person] bien-aimé *m*, -e *f*; be my ~ c'est toi que j'aime.

Valentine [ˈvæləntaɪn] *pr n*: Saint ~ Saint Valentin; Saint ~'s Day la saint-Valentin; the Saint ~'s Day Massacre *Am* HIST le massacre de la Saint-Valentin.

THE SAINT VALENTINE'S DAY MASSACRE:
Massacre particulièrement sanglant de cinq membres d'un gang de Chicago par une bande rivale, le 14 février 1929. Bien que sa culpabilité n'ait jamais pu être prouvée, Al Capone fut soupçonné d'en avoir été l'instigateur.

---

valerian [vəˈlɪərɪən] *n* valériane *f*.

Valerian [vəˈlɪərɪən] *pr n* Valérien.

valet [ˈvælɪt] *n* -**1.** [manservant] valet *m* de chambre; ~ service le pressing de l'hôtel. -**2.** [clothing rack] valet *m*. -**3.** *Am*: '~ parking' voiturier *m*.

Valetta [vəˈletə] = **Valletta**.

valetudinarian [ˌvælɪtjuːdɪˈneərɪən] *arch* OR *lit*
◇ *adj* valétudinaire.
◇ *n* valétudinaire *mf*.

Valhalla [vælˈhælə] *n* Walhalla *m*.

valiance [ˈvæljəns] *n lit* vaillance *f lit*, bravoure *f*, courage *m*.

valiant [ˈvæljənt] *adj* [person] vaillant, courageux; [behaviour, deed] courageux, brave; she made a ~ attempt to put out the fire elle a tenté avec courage OR courageusement d'éteindre l'incendie; he made a ~ effort not to cry out il a fait un gros effort pour ne pas crier.

valiantly [ˈvæljəntlɪ] *adv* vaillamment, courageusement.

valid [ˈvælɪd] *adj* -**1.** [argument, reasoning] valable, bien fondé; [excuse] valable. -**2.** [contract, passport] valide, valable; a ~ driving licence un permis de conduire valable OR valide OR en règle; my driver's licence is no longer ~ mon permis de conduire est périmé; ~ for two months [on train ticket] valable deux mois.

validate [ˈvælɪdeɪt] *vt* -**1.** [argument, claim] confirmer, prouver la justesse de. -**2.** [document] valider.

validation [ˌvælɪˈdeɪʃn] *n* -**1.** [of argument, claim] confirmation *f*, preuve *f*. -**2.** [of document] validation *f*.

validity [vəˈlɪdətɪ] *n* -**1.** [of argument, reasoning] justesse *f*, solidité *f*. -**2.** [of document] validité *f*.

valine [ˈveɪliːn] *n* valine *f*.

valise [*Br* vəˈliːz, *Am* vəˈliːs] *n* mallette *f*.

Valium® [ˈvælɪəm] (*pl inv*) *n* valium® *m*.

Valkyrie [vælˈkɪərɪ] *n* Walkyrie *f*, Valkyrie *f*; 'The ~' *Wagner* 'la Walkyrie'.

Valletta [vəˈletə] *pr n* La Valette.

valley [ˈvælɪ] *n* vallée *f*; [small] vallon *m*; the Valleys *le sud du pays de Galles*; the Loire/Rhone ~ la vallée de la Loire/du Rhône; 'How Green Was My Valley' *Llewellyn* 'Qu'elle était verte, ma vallée'; 'Valley of the Dolls' *Robson* 'la Vallée des poupées'.

Valley Forge *pr n* Valley Forge.

VALLEY FORGE:
Vallée de l'État de Pennsylvanie où l'armée de George Washington prit ses quartiers d'hiver en 1777-78, pendant la guerre d'Indépendance américaine. Le courage des troupes face aux difficiles conditions de vie dans les campements a fait de cette vallée un lieu hautement symbolique.

---

valor *Am* = **valour**.

valorize, -ise [ˈvæləraɪz] *vt* valoriser.

valour *Br*, **valor** *Am* [ˈvæləʳ] *n lit* courage *m*, bravoure *f*, vaillance *f lit*.

Valparaiso [ˌvælpəˈraɪzəʊ] *pr n* Valparaiso.

valuable [ˈvæljʊəbl] ◇ *adj* -**1.** [of monetary worth] de (grande) valeur. -**2.** [advice, friendship] précieux; we're wasting ~ time nous perdons un temps précieux.
◇ *n* (*usu pl*): ~s objets *mpl* de valeur; take your ~s with you emportez tous vos objets de valeur.

valuate [ˈvæljʊeɪt] *vt Am* estimer, expertiser; the house was ~d at $100,000 la maison a été expertisée OR estimée OR évaluée à 100 000 dollars.

valuation [ˌvæljʊˈeɪʃn] *n* expertise *f*, estimation *f*; we asked for a ~ of the house nous avons fait expertiser OR estimer la maison; the ~ of OR the ~ (put) on the business is £50,000 l'affaire a été expertisée OR estimée OR évaluée à 50 000 livres.

valuator [ˈvæljʊeɪtəʳ] *n* expert *m (en expertise de biens)*.

value [ˈvæljuː] ◇ *n* -**1.** [monetary worth] valeur *f*; they own nothing of ~ ils ne possèdent rien de valeur OR rien qui ait de la valeur; this necklace is of great ~ ce collier vaut cher; this necklace is of little ~ ce collier ne vaut pas grand-chose OR a peu de valeur; it's of no ~ c'est sans valeur; it's excellent ~ for money le rapport qualité-prix est excellent; it's good ~ at £10 ce n'est pas cher à 10 livres; we got good ~ for our money nous en avons eu pour notre argent; which of the brands gives the best ~? laquelle des marques est la plus avantageuse?; the airline paid her the ~ of the lost luggage la compagnie aérienne l'a dédommagée de la perte de ses bagages; property is going up/down in ~ l'immobilier prend/perd de la valeur; to depreciate in ~ se déprécier; the increase in ~ la hausse de valeur, l'appréciation; the loss in ~ la perte de valeur, la dépréciation; to put a ~ on sthg évaluer OR estimer qqch; they put a ~ of £50,000 on the house ils ont estimé OR expertisé la maison à 50 000 livres. -**2.** [merit, importance - of method, work] valeur *f*; [- of person] valeur *f*, mérite *m*; he had nothing of ~ to add il n'avait rien d'important OR de valable à ajouter; these books may be of ~ to them ces livres peuvent leur servir, ils peuvent avoir besoin de ces livres; they place little/a high ~ on punctuality ils font peu de cas/grand cas de l'exactitude, ils attachent peu d'importance/beaucoup d'importance à l'exactitude. -**3.** (*usu pl*) [principles]: ~s valeurs *fpl*; he has old-fashioned ~s il est très vieux jeu. -**4.** [feature] particularité *f*; it has novelty ~ cela a la particularité d'être nouveau OR de la nouveauté. -**5.** [of colour] valeur *f*. -**6.** LING, LOGIC, MATH & MUS valeur *f*.
◇ *vt* -**1.** [assess worth of] expertiser, estimer, évaluer; they ~d the house at £50,000 ils ont estimé OR évalué la maison à 50 000 livres; we had our paintings ~d nous avons fait expertiser OR estimer OR évaluer nos tableaux. -**2.** [have high regard for - friendship] apprécier, estimer; [- honesty, punctuality] faire grand cas de; if you ~ your freedom/your life you'd better leave si vous tenez à votre liberté/à la vie, vous feriez mieux de partir; we greatly ~ your help nous apprécions beaucoup OR nous vous sommes très reconnaissants de votre aide; does he ~ your opinion? votre opinion lui importe-t-elle?

value-added tax *n Br* taxe *f* sur la valeur ajoutée.

valued [ˈvæljuːd] *adj* [opinion] estimé; [advice, friend] précieux.

value judgment *n* jugement *m* de valeur.

valueless [ˈvæljʊlɪs] *adj* sans valeur.

valuer [ˈvæljʊəʳ] *n* expert *m (en expertise de biens)*.

valve [vælv] *n* -**1.** [in pipe, tube, air chamber] valve *f*; [in machine] soupape *f*, valve *f*. -**2.** ANAT valve *f*; [small] valvule *f*. -**3.** BOT & ZOOL valve *f*. -**4.** MUS piston *m*.

valvular [ˈvælvjʊləʳ] *adj* -**1.** [machine] à soupapes OR valves. -**2.** ANAT, BOT & ZOOL valvulaire. -**3.** [musical instrument] à pistons.

vamoose *inf* [vəˈmuːs] *vi Am* filer; ~! fiche le camp!

vamp [væmp] ◇ *n* -**1.** *inf* [woman] vamp *f*. -**2.** [piecing together] rafistolage *m*. -**3.** [of story] enjolivement *m*; MUS improvisation *f*. -**4.** [of shoe] devant *m*.
◇ *vt* -**1.** *inf* [seduce] vamper. -**2.** [repair] rafistoler; [renovate] rénover. -**3.** [story] enjoliver. -**4.** MUS [piece, song] improviser des accompagnements à; [accompaniment] improviser.
◇ *vi* [woman] jouer la vamp.
◆ **vamp up** *vt sep* = **vamp** *vt* **2,3,4**.

vampire [ˈvæmpaɪəʳ] *n* [bat, monster] vampire *m*; [person] vampire *m*, sangsue *f*.

vampire bat *n* vampire *m (chauve-souris)*.

vampirism [ˈvæmpaɪərɪzm] *n* vampirisme *m*.

van [væn] *n* -**1.** [small vehicle] camionnette *f*, fourgonnette *f*; [large vehicle] camion *m*, fourgon *m*. -**2.** *Br* RAIL fourgon *m*, wagon *m*. -**3.** [caravan] caravane *f*. -**4.** *inf Br* [advantage - in tennis] avantage *m*; ~ in/out avantage dedans/dehors. -**5.** MIL [vanguard] avant-garde *f*; in the ~ en tête; in the ~ of abstract art *fig* à l'avant-garde de l'art abstrait.

vanadium [vəˈneɪdɪəm] *n* vanadium *m*.

Vancouver [vænˈkuːvəʳ] *pr n* Vancouver.

V and A (*abbr of* Victoria and Albert Museum) *pr n grand musée londonien des arts décoratifs*.

vandal [ˈvændl] *n* [hooligan] vandale *mf*.
◆ **Vandal** *n* HIST Vandale *mf*.

vandalism [ˈvændəlɪzm] *n* vandalisme *m*.

vandalize, -ise [ˈvændəlaɪz] *vt* saccager.

Vandyke [ˌvænˈdaɪk] *n*: ~ (beard) barbiche *f*, bouc *m*.

vane [veɪn] *n* -**1.** [blade - of propeller] pale *f*; [- of windmill] aile *f*; [- of turbine] aube *f*. -**2.** (weather) ~ girouette *f*. -**3.** ORNITH [of feather] barbe *f*.

vanguard [ˈvængɑːd] *n* MIL avant-garde *f*; in the ~ of the division en tête de la division; in the ~ of progress *fig* à l'avant-garde OR à la pointe du progrès.

vanilla [vəˈnɪlə] *n* [plant] vanillier *m*; [flavour] vanille *f*; ~ ice cream/flavour glace *f*/parfum *m* à la vanille; ~ essence extrait *m* de vanille.

vanilla bean *n* gousse *f* de vanille.

vanilla pod *n* gousse *f* de vanille.

vanilla sugar *n* sucre *m* vanillé.

vanillin [ˈvænɪlɪn] *n* vanilline *f*.

vanish [ˈvænɪʃ] *vi* [object, person, race] disparaître; [hopes, worries] disparaître, se dissiper; the aeroplane ~ed from sight l'avion a disparu; the sun ~ed behind the mountains le soleil a disparu derrière les montagnes; she ~ed into the crowd elle s'est perdue dans la foule; they ~ed into thin air ils se sont volatilisés; entire species have ~ed from the face of the earth des espèces entières ont disparu de la surface du globe; just when you need him he ~es! dès que vous avez besoin de lui, il s'éclipse!; she did a ~ing act *fig* elle s'est éclipsée.

vanishing cream ['vænɪʃɪŋ] *n* crème *f* de beauté.

vanishing point *n* point *m* de fuite.

vanishing trick *n* tour *m* de passe-passe.

vanity ['vænətɪ] (*pl* vanities) *n* -**1.** [conceit] vanité *f*, orgueil *m*; she refused to use a walking stick out of (sheer) ~ par (pure) vanité elle a refusé d'utiliser une canne; I think I can without ~ claim to be the most competent sans vanité OR sans vouloir me vanter, je peux prétendre être le plus compétent ❑ 'Vanity Fair' *Thackeray* 'la Foire aux vanités'. -**2.** *fml* OR *lit* [futility] futilité *f*, insignifiance *f*, vanité *f lit*; all is ~ tout n'est que vanité. -**3.** *Am* [dressing table] coiffeuse *f*, table *f* de toilette.

vanity bag *n* trousse *f* de toilette *(pour femme)*.

vanity case *n* petite valise *f* de toilette, vanity-case *m*.

vanity mirror *n* miroir *m* de courtoisie.

vanity press *n* maison *f* d'édition à compte d'auteur.

vanity table *n* coiffeuse *f*, table *f* de toilette.

vanity unit *n meuble de salle de bains avec lavabo encastré.*

vanquish ['væŋkwɪʃ] *vt* vaincre.

vanquisher ['væŋkwɪʃəʳ] *n* vainqueur *m*.

vantage ['vɑːntɪdʒ] *n* -**1.** [advantageous situation] avantage *m*, supériorité *f*; point of ~ point de vue *m* (privilégié). -**2.** [in tennis] avantage *m*.

vantage ground *n* [gen] point de vue *m* (privilégié); MIL position *f* stratégique.

vantage point *n* point de vue *m* (privilégié).

Vanuatu [vænuːˈætuː] *pr n* Vanuatu.

vapid ['væpɪd] *adj* [conversation, remark] fade, insipide; [style] fade, plat; [person] écervelé.

vapidity [væ'pɪdətɪ] *n* [of conversation] insipidité *f*; [of style] platitude *f*, caractère *m* plat; [of person] frivolité *f*, fadeur *f*.

vapor *Am* = **vapour**.

vaporization [ˌveɪpəraɪ'zeɪʃn] *n* vaporisation *f*.

vaporize, -ise ['veɪpəraɪz] ◇ *vt* vaporiser.
◇ *vi* se vaporiser.

vaporizer ['veɪpəraɪzəʳ] *n* -**1.** [gen] vaporisateur *m*; [for perfume, spray] atomiseur *m*, pulvérisateur *m*. -**2.** MED [inhaler] inhalateur *m*; [for throat] pulvérisateur *m*.

vaporous ['veɪpərəs] *adj* vaporeux.

vapour *Br*, **vapor** *Am* ['veɪpəʳ] ◇ *n* vapeur *f*; [on window] buée *f*.
◇ *vi* -**1.** PHYS s'évaporer. -**2.** *inf Am* [brag] se vanter, fanfaronner.
◆ **vapours** *npl arch*: to have (an attack of) the ~s avoir des vapeurs.

vapour bath *n* bain *m* de vapeur.

vapour density *n* densité *f* de vapeur.

vapour lock *n* bouchon *m* de vapeur.

vapour pressure *n* pression *f* de vapeur.

vapour trail *n* AERON traînée *f* de condensation.

variability [ˌveərɪə'bɪlətɪ] *n* variabilité *f*.

variable ['veərɪəbl] ◇ *adj* -**1.** [weather] variable, changeant; [quality] variable, inégal; [performance, work] de qualité inégale, inégal. -**2.** COMPUT & MATH variable.
◇ *n* variable *f*.

variable star *n* étoile *f* variable.

variance ['veərɪəns] *n* -**1.** [in statistics] désaccord *m*, divergence *f*; [in law] divergence *f*, différence *f*. -**2.** CHEM & MATH variance *f*. -**3.** *phr*: to be at ~ with sb être en désaccord avec qqn; to be at ~ with sthg ne pas cadrer avec OR ne pas concorder avec qqch; she is at ~ with her colleagues on OR over this issue elle est en désaccord avec ses collègues à ce sujet; this announcement is at ~ with his previous statements cette annonce est en contradiction avec OR ne s'accorde pas avec ses déclarations antérieures.

variant ['veərɪənt] ◇ *n* [gen & LING] variante *f*.
◇ *adj* -**1.** [different] autre, différent; ~ interpretation OR reading une interprétation OR lecture différente; a ~ spelling une variante orthographique. -**2.** [various] varié, divers. -**3.** LING variant.

variation [ˌveərɪ'eɪʃn] *n* -**1.** [change, modification] variation *f*, modification *f*; ~s in temperature variations OR changements de température; the level of demand is subject to considerable ~ le niveau de la demande peut varier considérablement; the different legends are ~s of the same basic story ces différentes légendes sont inspirées d'une même histoire. -**2.** MUS variation *f*; theme and ~s thème et variations; ~s on a theme variations sur un thème. -**3.** BIOL variation *f*.

varicoloured *Br*, **varicolored** *Am* ['veərɪˌkʌləd] *adj* multicolore, aux couleurs variées, bigarré; *fig* divers.

varicose ['værɪkəʊs] *adj* [ulcer] variqueux; to have OR to suffer from ~ veins avoir des varices.

varied ['veərɪd] *adj* varié, divers.

variegated ['veərɪgeɪtɪd] *adj* -**1.** [gen] bigarré. -**2.** BOT panaché.

variegation [ˌveərɪ'geɪʃn] *n* bigarrure *f*.

varietal [və'raɪətl] *adj* variétal.

variety [və'raɪətɪ] (*pl* varieties) ◇ *n* -**1.** [diversity] variété *f*, diversité *f*; there isn't much ~ in the menu le menu n'est pas très varié OR n'offre pas un grand choix; he needs more ~ in his diet il a besoin d'un régime plus varié; the work lacks ~ le travail manque de variété OR n'est pas assez varié ❑ ~ is the spice of life *prov* la diversité est le sel de la vie. -**2.** [number, assortment] nombre *m*, quantité *f*; for a ~ of reasons [various] pour diverses raisons; [many] pour de nombreuses raisons; in a ~ of ways de diverses manières; the dresses come in a ~ of sizes les robes sont disponibles dans un grand nombre de tailles; there is a wide ~ of colours/styles to choose from il y a un grand choix de couleurs/styles. -**3.** [type] espèce *f*, genre *m*; different varieties of cheese différents types OR différentes variétés de fromage. -**4.** BOT & ZOOL [strain] variété *f*. -**5.** *(U)* THEAT & TV variétés *fpl*.
◇ *comp* [artiste, show, theatre] de variétés, de music-hall.

variety meat *n Am* abats *mpl*.

variety store *n Am* grand magasin *m*.

variola [və'raɪələ] *n* variole *f*, petite vérole *f*.

variorum [ˌveərɪ'ɔːrəm] ◇ *n* (édition *f*) variorum *m inv*.
◇ *adj* variorum *(inv)*.

various ['veərɪəs] *adj* -**1.** [diverse] divers, différent; [several] plusieurs; she writes under ~ names elle écrit sous des noms divers; at ~ times in his life à différents moments OR à plusieurs reprises dans sa vie; at ~ intervals de temps à autre. -**2.** [varied, different] varié; his reasons were many and ~ ses raisons étaient nombreuses et variées.

variously ['veərɪəslɪ] *adv* [in different ways] diversement, de différentes OR diverses façons; he was ~ known as soldier, king and emperor on le connaissait à la fois comme soldat, roi et empereur.

varlet ['vɑːlɪt] *n* -**1.** *arch* [servant] valet *m*. -**2.** *pej* & *lit* fripon *m*, gredin *m*.

varmint *inf* ['vɑːmɪnt] *n dated* coquin *m*, -e *f*, vaurien *m*, -enne *f*.

varnish ['vɑːnɪʃ] ◇ *n literal* & *fig* vernis *m*.
◇ *vt* [nails, painting, wood] vernir; [pottery] vernir, vernisser; to ~ (over) the truth *fig* maquiller la vérité.

varnishing ['vɑːnɪʃɪŋ] *n* vernissage *m*.

varnishing day *n* ART (jour *m* du) vernissage *m*.

varoom [və'ruːm] = **vroom**.

varsity *inf* ['vɑːsətɪ] (*pl* varsities) ◇ *n Br dated* université *f*, fac *f*; ~ match match *m* interuniversitaire *(entre Oxford et Cambridge)*.
◇ *adj Am* SPORT *qui représente l'université au plus haut niveau*.

vary ['veərɪ] ◇ *vi* -**1.** [be different] varier; opinions on this question ~ les opinions varient sur ce sujet; the students ~ considerably in ability les étudiants ont des niveaux très différents; they ~ in size from small to extra large ils vont de la plus petite taille à la plus grande. -**2.** [change, alter] changer, se modifier; his mood varies with the weather il est très lunatique; the colour of the wood varies with age ce bois change de couleur en vieillissant.
◇ *vt* [diet, menu] varier; [temperature] faire varier.

varying ['veərɪɪŋ] *adj* variable, qui varie; with ~ degrees of enthusiasm/of success avec plus ou moins d'enthousiasme/de succès.

vascular ['væskjʊləʳ] *adj* vasculaire.

vas deferens ['væs'defərenz] (*pl* vasa deferentia [ˌveɪsədefə'renʃɪə]) *n* canal *m* déférent.

vase [*Br* vɑːz, *Am* veɪz] *n* vase *m*.

vasectomy [væ'sektəmɪ] (*pl* vasectomies) *n* vasectomie *f*; to have a ~ subir une vasectomie.

Vaseline® ['væsɪliːn] ◇ *n*: ~ (jelly) vaseline *f*.
◇ *vt* enduire de vaseline.

vasoconstrictor [ˌveɪzəʊkən'strɪktəʳ] *n* vasoconstricteur *m*.

vasodilator [ˌveɪzəʊdaɪ'leɪtəʳ] *n* vasodilatateur *m*.

vasomotor [ˌveɪzəʊ'məʊtəʳ] *adj* vasomoteur.

vassal ['væsl] ◇ *adj* vassal.
◇ *n* vassal *m*.

vassalage ['væsəlɪdʒ] *n* vassalité *f*, vasselage *m*.

vast [vɑːst] *adj* vaste, immense, énorme; ~ sums of money des sommes énormes, énormément d'argent; it's a ~ improvement on his last performance c'est infiniment mieux que sa dernière interprétation; she has ~ experience in this area elle a beaucoup d'expérience dans ce domaine.

vastly ['vɑːstlɪ] *adv* [wealthy] extrêmement, immensément; [grateful] infiniment; the show was ~ successful le spectacle a eu un immense succès; he is ~ improved [in health] il va infiniment mieux; [in work, performance] ce qu'il a fait est infiniment mieux.

vastness ['vɑːstnɪs] *n* immensité *f*.

vat [væt] *n* cuve *f*, bac *m*.

VAT [væt, ˌviːeɪ'tiː] (*abbr of* value added tax) *n* TVA *f*.

Vatican ['vætɪkən] ◇ *pr n*: the ~ le Vatican; in the ~ au Vatican.
◇ *comp* [edict, bank, policy] du Vatican.

Vatican City *pr n* l'État *m* de la cité du Vatican, le Vatican; in ~ au Vatican.

Vatican council *n*: the first/second ~ le premier/deuxième concile du Vatican.

vatman *inf* ['vætmæn] (*pl* vatmen [-men]) *n Br*: the ~ le service de la TVA.

vaudeville ['vɔːdəvɪl] ◇ *n Am* vaudeville *m*.
◇ *comp* [artiste, theatre] de vaudeville, de music-hall.

vault [vɔːlt] ◇ *n* -**1.** ARCHIT voûte *f*; the ~ of heaven *fig* la voûte céleste. -**2.** ANAT voûte *f*. -**3.** [cellar] cave *f*, cellier *m*; [burial chamber] caveau *m*; a family ~ un caveau de famille. -**4.** [in bank] chambre *f* forte; a bank ~ les coffres d'une banque, la salle des coffres. -**5.** [jump] (grand) saut *m*; SPORT saut *m* (à la perche).
◇ *vi* [jump] sauter; SPORT sauter (à la perche); he ~ed over the fence il a sauté par-dessus la clôture.
◇ *vt* -**1.** ARCHIT voûter, cintrer. -**2.** [jump] sauter par-dessus.

vaulted ['vɔːltɪd] *adj* ARCHIT voûté, en voûte.

vaulting ['vɔːltɪŋ] ◇ *n* -**1.** ARCHIT voûte *f*, voûtes *fpl*. -**2.** SPORT saut *m* à la perche.
◇ *adj* -**1.** SPORT [pole] de saut. -**2.** *fig* & *lit* [arrogance] outrecuidant; [ambition] démesuré.

vaulting horse *n* cheval-d'arçons *m inv*.

vaunt [vɔːnt] ◇ *vt lit* vanter, se vanter de; her much ~ed charms ses charmes tant vantés.
◇ *vi lit* se vanter, fanfaronner.

VC ◇ *n* -**1.** *abbr of* Victoria Cross. -**2.** *abbr of* vice-chancellor. -**3.** *abbr of* vice-chairman.
◇ *pr n* *abbr of* Vietcong.
VCR (*abbr of* video cassette recorder) *n* magnétoscope *m*.
VD (*abbr of* venereal disease) *n* *(U)* MST *f*.
VDT (*abbr of* visual display terminal) *n* moniteur *m*.
VDU (*abbr of* visual display unit) *n* moniteur *m*.
veal [viːl] ◇ *n* veau *m* CULIN.
◇ *comp* [cutlet] de veau.
vector [ˈvektəʳ] ◇ *n* -**1.** MATH & MED vecteur *m*. -**2.** AERON direction *f*.
◇ *vt* AERON radioguider.
◇ *comp* MATH vectoriel.
vectorial [vekˈtɔːrɪəl] *adj* vectoriel.
Veda [ˈveɪdə] *n* Veda *mpl*.
VE day (*abbr of* Victory in Europe Day) *n jour l'armistice du 8 mai 1945*.
vedette [vɪˈdet] *n* MUS & NAUT vedette *f*.
vee [viː] *n objet en forme de V*.
veep *inf* [viːp] *n Am* vice-président *m*, -e *f*.
veer [vɪəʳ] ◇ *vi* -**1.** [vehicle, road] virer, tourner; [ship] virer de bord; [wind] tourner, changer de direction; **the car ~ed (over) to the left** la voiture a viré vers la OR à gauche; **the wind has ~ed (round) to the east** le vent a tourné à l'est; **the deer ~ed away from us** le cerf s'est éloigné de nous; **the car ~ed off into the ditch** la voiture a quitté la route et a basculé dans le fossé; **to ~ off course** [car] quitter sa route; [boat, plane, wind-surfer] quitter sa trajectoire. -**2.** *fig*: **the conversation ~ed round to the elections** la conversation a dévié sur les élections; **the speaker kept ~ing off the subject** l'orateur s'éloignait sans cesse du sujet; **her mood ~s between euphoria and black depression** son humeur oscille entre l'euphorie et un profond abattement OR va de l'euphorie à un profond abattement.
◇ *vt* -**1.** [ship, car] faire virer. -**2.** [cable] filer.
veg *inf* [vedʒ] (*abbr of* **vegetable/vegetables**) *n* légumes *mpl*; **meat and two ~** viande avec deux légumes différents.
vegan [ˈviːgən] ◇ *n* végétalien *m*, -enne *f*.
◇ *adj* végétalien.
veganism [ˈviːgənɪzm] *n* végétalisme *m*.
vegetable [ˈvedʒtəbl] ◇ *n* -**1.** CULIN & HORT légume *m*; BOT [plant] végétal *m*; **early ~s** primeurs *mpl*; **green ~s** légumes *mpl* verts; **root ~s** racines *fpl (comestibles)*. -**2.** *inf fig*: **he's little more than a ~ now** [brain damaged] ce n'est plus qu'un légume.
◇ *comp* [matter] végétal; [soup] de légumes; **he's reduced to a ~ existence** il est réduit à un état végétatif.
vegetable butter *n* beurre *m* végétal.
vegetable dish *n* plat *m* à légumes, légumier *m*.
vegetable garden *n* (jardin *m*) potager *m*.
vegetable kingdom *n* règne *m* végétal.
vegetable knife *n* couteau *m* à légumes, éplucheur *m*.
vegetable marrow *n* courge *f*.
vegetable oil *n* huile *f* végétale.
vegetable peeler = **vegetable knife**.
vegetable slicer *n* coupe-légumes *m inv*.
vegetal [ˈvedʒɪtl] *adj* végétal.
vegetarian [ˌvedʒɪˈteərɪən] ◇ *n* végétarien *m*, -enne *f*.
◇ *adj* végétarien.
vegetarianism [ˌvedʒɪˈteərɪənɪzm] *n* végétarisme *m*.
vegetate [ˈvedʒɪteɪt] *vi literal* & *fig* végéter.
vegetation [ˌvedʒɪˈteɪʃn] *n* végétation *f*.
vegetative [ˈvedʒɪtətɪv] *adj literal* & *fig* végétatif.
veggie *inf* [ˈvedʒɪ] *n* & *adj abbr of* **vegetarian**.
vehemence [ˈviːɪməns] *n* [of emotions] ardeur *f*, véhémence *f*; [of actions, gestures] violence *f*, véhémence *f*; [of language] véhémence *f*, passion *f*.
vehement [ˈviːɪmənt] *adj* [emotions] ardent, passionné, véhément; [actions, gestures] violent, véhément; [language] véhément, passionné; **she launched a ~ attack on the government** elle s'est lancée dans une attaque véhémente contre OR elle a violemment attaqué le gouvernement.
vehemently [ˈviːɪməntlɪ] *adv* [speak] avec passion, avec véhémence; [attack] avec violence; [gesticulate] frénétiquement.
vehicle [ˈviːɪkl] *n* -**1.** [AUT & gen] véhicule *m*; **'heavy ~s turning'** 'passage d'engins'. -**2.** PHARM véhicule *m*. -**3.** *fig* véhicule *m*; **the newspaper is merely a ~ for state propaganda** le journal n'est qu'un véhicule de la propagande gouvernementale.
vehicular [vɪˈhɪkjʊləʳ] *adj* [AUT & gen] de véhicules, de voitures; **~ traffic** circulation automobile; **~ access** accès aux véhicules.
veil [veɪl] ◇ *n* -**1.** [over face] voile *m*; [on hat] voilette *f*, voile *m*; **she was wearing a ~** elle était voilée. -**2.** *fig* voile *m*; **to draw a ~ over sthg** mettre un voile sur qqch; **under the ~ of secrecy** sous le voile du secret; **a ~ of mist/of silence** un voile de brume/de silence. -**3.** RELIG: **to take the ~** prendre le voile.
◇ *vt* -**1.** [face] voiler, couvrir d'un voile; **to ~ o.s.** se voiler. -**2.** *fig* [truth, feelings, intentions] voiler, dissimuler, masquer.
veiled [veɪld] *adj* -**1.** [wearing a veil] voilé. -**2.** [hidden, disguised - expression, meaning] voilé, caché; [- allusion, insult] voilé; [- hostility] sourd.
veiling [ˈveɪlɪŋ] *n* -**1.** TEX voilage *m*. -**2.** *fig* [of truth] dissimulation *f*.
vein [veɪn] *n* -**1.** ANAT veine *f*; **she has Polish blood in her ~s** elle a du sang polonais dans les veines. -**2.** [on insect wing] veine *f*; [on leaf] nervure *f*. -**3.** [in cheese, wood, marble] veine *f*; [of ore, mineral] filon *m*, veine *f*; **a rich ~ of irony runs through the book** le livre est parcouru d'une ironie sous-jacente. -**4.** [mood] esprit *m*; [style] veine *f*, style *m*; **in a more frivolous ~** dans un esprit plus frivole; **in the same ~** dans le même style OR la même veine; **written in an imaginative ~** écrit dans un style plein d'imagination.
veined [veɪnd] *adj* -**1.** [hand, skin] veiné. -**2.** [leaf] nervuré. -**3.** [cheese, stone] marbré, veiné; **green-~ marble** marbre veiné de vert.
veining [ˈveɪnɪŋ] *n (U)* -**1.** ANAT veines *fpl*. -**2.** BOT [on leaf] nervures *fpl*. -**3.** [in wood, marble, cheese] veines *fpl*.
velar [ˈviːləʳ] *adj* ANAT & LING vélaire.
velarize, -ise [ˈviːləraɪz] *vt* vélariser.
Velcro® [ˈvelkrəʊ] *n* (bande *f*) Velcro® *m*.
veld(t) [velt] *n* veld *m*, veldt *m*.
vellum [ˈveləm] ◇ *n* vélin *m*.
◇ *adj* de vélin; **~ paper** papier *m* vélin.
velocipede [vɪˈlɒsɪpiːd] *n* vélocipède *m*.
velocity [vɪˈlɒsətɪ] (*pl* **velocities**) *n* vélocité *f*.
velodrome [ˈvelədrəʊm] *n* vélodrome *m*.
velour(s) [vəˈlʊəʳ] (*pl* **velours** [-ˈlʊəz]) ◇ *n* velours *m*.
◇ *comp* de OR en velours.
velum [ˈviːləm] *n* ANAT voile *m* du palais.
velvet [ˈvelvɪt] ◇ *n* velours *m*; **to be on ~** *inf fig* jouer sur le velours.
◇ *comp* [curtains, dress] de OR en velours; *fig* [skin, voice] velouté, de velours; **to walk with a ~ tread** marcher à pas de velours OR à pas feutrés; **an iron hand in a ~ glove** *fig* une main de fer dans un gant de velours.
velveteen [ˌvelvɪˈtiːn] ◇ *n* velvet *m*, velventine *f*, velvantine *f*.
◇ *adj* en OR de velventine.
Velvet Revolution *pr n*: **the ~** la Révolution de Velours.
velvety [ˈvelvɪtɪ] *adj* [cloth, complexion, texture] velouteux, velouté; *fig* [cream, voice] velouté.
venal [ˈviːnl] *adj* vénal.
venality [viːˈnælətɪ] *n* vénalité *f*.
vend [vend] *vt* JUR OR *fml* vendre.
vendetta [venˈdetə] *n* vendetta *f*.
vending [ˈvendɪŋ] *n* JUR OR *fml* vente *f*.
vending machine *n* distributeur *m* automatique.
vendor [ˈvendɔːʳ] *n* -**1.** COMM marchand *m*, -e *f*; **ice-cream/news ~** marchand de glaces/de journaux. -**2.** [machine] distributeur *m* automatique. -**3.** JUR vendeur *m*, -euse *f*.
veneer [vəˈnɪəʳ] ◇ *n* -**1.** [of wood] placage *m* (de bois); **walnut ~** placage noyer. -**2.** *fig* vernis *m*, masque *m*, apparence *f*; **a ~ of respectability** un vernis de respectabilité.
◇ *vt* plaquer; **~ed in** OR **with walnut** plaqué noyer.
venepuncture [ˈvenɪˌpʌŋktʃəʳ] *n* MED ponction *f* d'une veine.
venerable [ˈvenərəbl] *adj* [gen & RELIG] vénérable; **the Venerable Bede** Bède le Vénérable.
venerate [ˈvenəreɪt] *vt* vénérer.
veneration [ˌvenəˈreɪʃn] *n* vénération *f*.
venereal [vɪˈnɪərɪəl] *adj* vénérien.
venereal disease *n* maladie *f* vénérienne.
venereology [vɪˌnɪərɪˈɒlədʒɪ] *n* vénéréologie *f*, vénérologie *f*.
Venetian [vɪˈniːʃn] ◇ *n* Vénitien *m*, -enne *f*.
◇ *adj* vénitien, de Venise; **~ glass** verre *m* OR cristal *m* de Venise; **~ blind** store *m* vénitien.
Veneto [ˈvenətəʊ] *pr n* Vénétie *f*.
Venezuela [ˌvenɪˈzweɪlə] *pr n* Venezuela *m*; **in ~** au Venezuela.
Venezuelan [ˌvenɪˈzweɪlən] ◇ *n* Vénézuélien *m*, -enne *f*.
◇ *adj* vénézuélien.
vengeance [ˈvendʒəns] *n* -**1.** [revenge] vengeance *f*; **to take** OR **to wreak ~ on** OR **upon sb (for sthg)** se venger sur qqn (de qqch); **to seek ~ for sthg** vouloir tirer vengeance de qqch, chercher à se venger de qqch. -**2.** *phr*: **with a ~** très fort; **by then it was raining with a ~** à ce moment-là, la pluie tombait à torrents; **to work with a ~** travailler d'arrache-pied OR à un rythme d'enfer; **she's back with a ~** elle fait un retour en force.
vengeful [ˈvendʒfʊl] *adj* vindicatif.
venial [ˈviːnjəl] *adj* [RELIG & gen] véniel.
veniality [ˌviːnɪˈælətɪ] *n* caractère *m* véniel.
Venice [ˈvenɪs] *pr n* Venise.
venipuncture [ˈvenɪˌpʌŋktʃəʳ] = **venepuncture**.
venisection [ˈvenɪsekʃn] *n* phlébotomie *f*.
venison [ˈvenɪzn] *n* venaison *f*.
Venn diagram [ven-] *n* diagramme *m* de Venn.
venom [ˈvenəm] *n literal* & *fig* venin *m*; **with ~** *fig* d'une manière venimeuse.
venomous [ˈvenəməs] *adj literal* venimeux; *fig* [remark, insult] venimeux, malveillant; [look] haineux, venimeux; **he has a ~ tongue** il a une langue de vipère.
venomously [ˈvenəməslɪ] *adv* d'une manière venimeuse.
venous [ˈviːnəs] *adj* veineux.
vent [vent] ◇ *n* -**1.** [outlet - for air, gas, liquid] orifice *m*, conduit *m*; [- in chimney] conduit *m*, tuyau *m*; [- in volcano] cheminée *f*; [- in barrel] trou *m*; [- for ventilation] conduit *m* d'aération. -**2.** *phr*: **to give ~ to sthg** donner OR laisser libre cours à qqch; **he gave full ~ to his feelings** il a donné OR laissé libre cours à ses émotions; **she gave ~ to her anger** elle a laissé échapper sa colère. -**3.** [in jacket, skirt] fente *f*.
◇ *vt* -**1.** [barrel] pratiquer un trou dans, trouer; [pipe, radiator] purger. -**2.** [release - smoke] laisser échapper; [- gas] évacuer. -**3.** *fig* [express - anger] décharger; **to ~ one's anger/one's spleen on sb** décharger sa colère/sa bile sur qqn.
ventilate [ˈventɪleɪt] *vt* -**1.** [room] ventiler, aérer; **a well/badly ~d room** une pièce bien/mal aérée. -**2.** *fig* [controversy, question] agiter (au grand jour); [grievance] étaler (au grand jour). -**3.** MED [blood] oxygéner.
ventilation [ˌventɪˈleɪʃn] *n* aération *f*, ventilation *f*; **a ~ shaft** un conduit d'aération OR de ventilation.
ventilator [ˈventɪleɪtəʳ] *n* -**1.** [in room, building] ventilateur *m*; AUT déflecteur *m*. -**2.** MED respirateur *m* (artificiel).

Ventimiglia [ventɪ'mɪljə] *pr n* Vintimille.
ventral ['ventrəl] *adj* ventral.
ventricle ['ventrɪkl] *n* ventricule *m*.
ventriloquism [ven'trɪləkwɪzm] *n* ventriloquie *f*.
ventriloquist [ven'trɪləkwɪst] *n* ventriloque *mf*.
ventriloquy [ven'trɪləkwɪ] = **ventriloquism**.
venture ['ventʃəʳ] ◇ *n* -**1.** [undertaking] entreprise *f* périlleuse OR risquée; [adventure] aventure *f*; [project] projet *m*, entreprise *f*; **his latest film ~** sa dernière entreprise cinématographique; **it's his first ~ into politics** c'est la première fois qu'il s'aventure dans le domaine politique. -**2.** COMM & FIN [firm] entreprise *f*; **a business ~** une entreprise commerciale, un coup d'essai commercial; **joint ~** coentreprise *f*, joint-venture *m*. -**3.** *phr*: **at a ~** au hasard.
◇ *vt* -**1.** [risk - fortune, life] hasarder, risquer; **he ~d a glance at her** il risqua un coup d'œil dans sa direction; **nothing ~d nothing gained** *prov* qui ne risque rien n'a rien *prov*. -**2.** [proffer - opinion, suggestion] hasarder, avancer, risquer; **she didn't dare ~ an opinion on the subject** elle n'a pas osé exprimer sa pensée à ce sujet; **if I may ~ a guess/an opinion** si je peux me permettre d'avancer une hypothèse/une opinion. -**3.** [dare] oser; **to ~ to do sthg** s'aventurer OR se hasarder à faire qqch; **he ~d to contradict her** il a osé la contredire.
◇ *vi* -**1.** [embark] se lancer; **the government has ~d on a new defence policy** le gouvernement s'est lancé dans OR a entrepris une nouvelle politique de défense; **to ~ into politics** se lancer dans la politique. -**2.** *(verb of movement)*: **to ~ in/out** prendre le risque d'entrer/de sortir, se risquer à entrer/à sortir; **I wouldn't ~ out of doors in this weather** je ne me risquerais pas à sortir par ce temps; **don't ~ too far across the ice** ne va pas trop loin sur la glace; **don't ~ too far from the beach** ne t'éloigne pas trop de la plage; **he ~d into the woods** il s'est hasardé dans les bois; **the explorers ~d forth into the jungle** *lit* les explorateurs se sont lancés dans la jungle.
venture capital *n* capital-risque *m*.
Venture Scout *n Br* éclaireur *m (de grade supérieur)*.
venturesome ['ventʃəsəm] *adj lit* -**1.** [daring - nature, person] aventureux, entreprenant. -**2.** [hazardous - action, journey] hasardeux, risqué.
venue ['venju:] *n* -**1.** [setting] lieu *m* (de rendez-vous OR de réunion); **they haven't yet decided on a ~ for the concert** ils n'ont pas encore décidé où le concert aura lieu; **they've changed the ~ for tonight's meeting** ils ont changé le lieu de réunion de ce soir. -**2.** JUR lieu *m* du procès.
Venus ['vi:nəs] *pr n* ASTRON & MYTH Vénus *f*; **'The ~ de Milo'** 'la Vénus de Milo'.
Venus flytrap *n* dionée *f*.
veracious [və'reɪʃəs] *adj* véridique.
veracity [və'ræsətɪ] *n* véracité *f*.
veranda(h) [və'rændə] *n* véranda *f*.
verb [vɜ:b] *n* verbe *m*; **~ phrase** syntagme *m* OR groupe *m* verbal.
verbal ['vɜ:bl] *adj* -**1.** [spoken - account, agreement, promise] verbal, oral; [- confession] oral; **~ memory** mémoire *f* auditive. -**2.** [related to words]: **~ skills** aptitudes *fpl* à l'oral. -**3.** [literal - copy, translation] mot à mot, littéral, textuel. -**4.** GRAMM verbal.
◆ **verbals** *npl* JUR aveux *mpl* faits oralement OR de vive voix.
verbalize, -ise ['vɜ:bəlaɪz] *vt* [feelings, ideas] verbaliser, exprimer par des mots.
verbally ['vɜ:bəlɪ] *adv* verbalement, oralement; **~ deficient** illettré, analphabète.
verbal noun *n* GRAMM nom *m* verbal.
verbatim [vɜ:'beɪtɪm] ◇ *adj* mot pour mot; **~ report** procès-verbal *m (d'une réunion)*.
◇ *adv* textuellement.
verbena [vɜ:'bi:nə] *n* [herb, plant] verveine *f*; [genus] verbénacées *fpl*.
verbiage ['vɜ:bɪɪdʒ] *n* verbiage *m*.
verbose [vɜ:'bəʊs] *adj* verbeux, prolixe.
verbosity [vɜ:'bɒsətɪ] *n* verbosité *f*.
verdant ['vɜ:dənt] *adj lit* verdoyant.
verdict ['vɜ:dɪkt] *n* -**1.** JUR verdict *m*; **to reach a ~** arriver à un verdict; **the jury brought in** OR **returned a ~ of not guilty** le jury a rendu OR prononcé un verdict de non-culpabilité. -**2.** *fig* [conclusion] verdict *m*, jugement *m*; **to give one's ~ on sthg** donner son verdict OR se prononcer sur qqch; **what is your/the ~?** quel est votre/le verdict?
verdigris ['vɜ:dɪgrɪs] ◇ *n* vert-de-gris *m inv*.
◇ *adj* vert-de-grisé.
verdure ['vɜ:dʒəʳ] *n lit* verdure *f*.
verge [vɜ:dʒ] ◇ *n* -**1.** [edge - of lawn] bord *m*; [- by roadside] accotement *m*, bas-côté *m*; [- of forest] orée *f*; **grass ~** [round flowerbed] bordure *f* en gazon; [by roadside] herbe *f* au bord de la route; [in park, garden] bande *f* d'herbe; **the car skidded onto the ~** la voiture a dérapé et est montée sur l'accotement OR sur le bas-côté. -**2.** *fig* [brink] bord *m*; [threshold] seuil *m*; **to be on the ~ of tears** être au bord des larmes; **to be on the ~ of bankruptcy/of a nervous breakdown** être au bord de la faillite/de la dépression nerveuse; **to be on the ~ of adolescence/old age** être au seuil de l'adolescence/de la vieillesse; **to be on the ~ of doing sthg** être sur le point de faire qqch; **I was on the ~ of telling him** j'étais sur le point de lui dire, j'étais à deux doigts de lui dire; **he's on the ~ of sixty** il frôle OR frise la soixantaine; **the country has been brought to the ~ of civil war** le pays a été amené au seuil de la guerre civile.
◇ *vt* [road, lawn] border.
◆ **verge on, verge upon** *vt insep* [be close to] côtoyer, s'approcher de; **they are verging on bankruptcy** ils sont au bord de la faillite, la faillite les menace; **his feeling was one of panic verging on hysteria** il ressentait une sorte de panique proche de l'hystérie OR qui frôlait l'hystérie; **she's verging on thirty** elle frise la trentaine; **green verging on blue** du vert qui tire sur le bleu.
verger ['vɜ:dʒəʳ] *n* RELIG bedeau *m*, suisse *m*; [at ceremony] huissier *m* à verge, massier *m*.
Vergil ['vɜ:dʒɪl] = **Virgil**.
verifiable ['verɪfaɪəbl] *adj* vérifiable.
verification [,verɪfɪ'keɪʃn] *n* vérification *f*.
verify ['verɪfaɪ] (*pt* & *pp* verified) *vt* [prove - information, rumour] vérifier; [confirm - truth] vérifier, confirmer; **this verifies my worst suspicions** ceci vérifie OR confirme mes pires soupçons; **I have witnesses who can ~ what I have said** j'ai des témoins qui peuvent confirmer mes dires.
verily ['verəlɪ] *adv arch* vraiment, véritablement.
verisimilitude [,verɪsɪ'mɪlɪtju:d] *n fml* vraisemblance *f*.
verism ['vɪərɪzm] *n* vérisme *m*.
veritable ['verɪtəbl] *adj* véritable; **he is a ~ genius** c'est un véritable OR un vrai génie.
veritably ['verɪtəblɪ] *adv* véritablement.
verity ['verətɪ] (*pl* verities) *n fml* vérité *f*.
vermicelli [,vɜ:mɪ'selɪ] *n (U)* vermicelle *m*, vermicelles *mpl*.
vermicide ['vɜ:mɪsaɪd] *n* vermicide *m*.
vermifugal [,vɜ:mɪ'fju:gəl] *adj* vermifuge.
vermil(l)ion [və'mɪljən] ◇ *n* vermillon *m*.
◇ *adj* vermillon *(inv)*.
vermin ['vɜ:mɪn] *npl* -**1.** ZOOL [rodents] animaux *mpl* nuisibles; [insects] vermine *f*. -**2.** *pej* [people] vermine *f*, racaille *f*.
verminous ['vɜ:mɪnəs] *adj* -**1.** [place] infesté de vermine OR d'animaux nuisibles, pouilleux; [clothes] pouilleux, couvert de vermine; MED [disease] vermineux. -**2.** *pej* [person] infect, ignoble.
Vermont [vɜ:'mɒnt] *pr n* Vermont *m*; **in ~** dans le Vermont.
vermouth ['vɜ:məθ] *n* vermouth *m*.
vernacular [və'nækjʊləʳ] ◇ *n* -**1.** LING (langue *f*) vernaculaire *m*; **in the ~** LING en langue vernaculaire; [everyday language] en langage courant. -**2.** BOT & ZOOL nom *m* vernaculaire. -**3.** ARCHIT style *m* typique (du pays).
◇ *adj* -**1.** BOT, LING & ZOOL vernaculaire. -**2.** [architecture, style] indigène.
vernal ['vɜ:nl] *adj lit* [flowers, woods, breeze] printanier.
vernal equinox *n* point *m* vernal.
vernier ['vɜ:njəʳ] *n* vernier *m*.
Verona [və'rəʊnə] *pr n* Vérone.
Veronese [,verə'neɪzɪ] *pr n* Véronèse.
veronica [və'rɒnɪkə] *n* BOT véronique *f*.
verruca [və'ru:kə] *n* verrue *f* (plantaire).
versatile ['vɜ:sətaɪl] *adj* -**1.** [person] aux talents variés, doué dans tous les domaines; [mind] souple; [tool] polyvalent, à usages multiples; **a politician has to be very ~** un politicien doit avoir des talents variés. -**2.** BOT versatile. -**3.** ZOOL mobile, pivotant.
versatility [,vɜ:sə'tɪlətɪ] *n* -**1.** [of person] faculté *f* d'adaptation, variété *f* de talents; [of mind] souplesse *f*; [of tool] polyvalence *f*. -**2.** BOT & ZOOL versatilité *f*.
verse [vɜ:s] ◇ *n* -**1.** [stanza - of poem] strophe *f*; [- of song] couplet *m*; [- in bible] verset *m*. -**2.** *(U)* [poetry] vers *mpl*, poésie *f*; **in ~** en vers.
◇ *comp* [line, epic] en vers.
versed [vɜ:st] *adj*: **~ in** [knowledgeable] versé dans; [experienced] rompu à; **he is well/not very well ~ in current affairs** il est très/peu versé dans les questions d'actualité.
versification [,vɜ:sɪfɪ'keɪʃn] *n* versification *f*.
versifier ['vɜ:sɪfaɪəʳ] *n pej* versificateur *m*, -trice *f*.
versify ['vɜ:sɪfaɪ] (*pt* & *pp* versified) ◇ *vt* versifier, mettre en vers.
◇ *vi* rimer, faire des vers.
version ['vɜ:ʃn] *n* -**1.** [account of events] version *f*. -**2.** [form - of book, film, song] version *f*; **did you see the film in the original ~?** est-ce que vous avez vu le film dans sa version originale?; **the screen** OR **film ~ of the book** l'adaptation cinématographique du livre; **he looks like a younger ~ of his father** *fig* c'est l'image de son père en plus jeune. -**3.** [model - of car, plane] modèle *m*, version *f*. -**4.** [translation] version *f*.
verso ['vɜ:səʊ] (*pl* versos) *n* [of page] verso *m*; [of coin, medal] revers *m*.
versus ['vɜ:səs] *prep* -**1.** [against] contre; **it's the government ~ the trade unions** c'est le gouvernement contre les syndicats, c'est une lutte entre le gouvernement et les syndicats; **Italy ~ France** SPORT Italie-France; **Dickens ~ Dickens** JUR Dickens contre Dickens. -**2.** [compared with] par rapport à, par opposition à; **country ~ city life** la vie à la campagne par opposition à OR par rapport à la vie citadine; **the advantages of living in a house ~ (living in) a flat** les avantages d'une maison OR d'habiter une maison par rapport à un appartement.
vertebra ['vɜ:tɪbrə] (*pl* vertebras OR vertebrae [-bri:]) *n* vertèbre *f*.
vertebral ['vɜ:tɪbrəl] *adj* vertébral; **~ column** colonne *f* vertébrale.
vertebrate ['vɜ:tɪbreɪt] ◇ *adj* vertébré.
◇ *n* vertébré *m*.
vertex ['vɜ:teks] (*pl* vertexes OR vertices [-tɪsi:z]) *n* MATH sommet *m*; ASTRON apex *m*; ANAT vertex *m*.
vertical ['vɜ:tɪkl] ◇ *adj* -**1.** [gen & GEOM] vertical; **a ~ cliff** une falaise à pic OR qui s'élève à la verticale; **a ~ line** une ligne verticale; **a ~ drop** une descente OR une pente verticale. -**2.** *fig* [structure, organization] vertical; **~ integration** intégration *f* verticale.
◇ *n* verticale *f*; **out of the ~** écarté de la verticale, hors d'aplomb.
vertical angles *npl* GEOM angles *mpl* de pointe.
vertical circle *n* vertical *m* ASTRON.
vertically ['vɜ:tɪklɪ] *adv* verticalement; **to take off ~** AERON décoller à la verticale.

vertical takeoff ◇ *n* décollage *m* vertical.
◇ *comp*: ~ aircraft avion *m* à décollage vertical.

vertical union *n Am* confédération *f* syndicale.

vertiginous [vɜːˈtɪdʒɪnəs] *adj fml* vertigineux.

vertigo [ˈvɜːtɪgəʊ] *n* vertige *m*; **to suffer from** OR **to have** ~ avoir le vertige; **heights give me** ~ les hauteurs me donnent le vertige ❑ **'Vertigo'** *Hitchcock* 'Sueurs froides'.

verve [vɜːv] *n* verve *f*, brio *m*.

very [ˈverɪ] (*compar* verier, *superl* veriest) ◇ *adv* **-1.** [with adj or adv] très, bien; **it was** ~ **pleasant** c'était très OR bien agréable; **was the pizza good?** – ~/**not** ~ la pizza était-elle bonne? – très/pas très; **I'm not** ~ **impressed with the results** je ne suis pas très OR tellement impressionné par les résultats; **be** ~ **careful** faites très OR bien attention; **he was** ~ **hungry/thirsty** il avait très faim/soif; **I** ~ **nearly fell** j'ai bien failli tomber; ~ **few/little** très peu; **there were** ~ **few of them** [people] ils étaient très peu nombreux; [objets] il y en avait très peu; **he takes** ~ **little interest in what goes on** il s'intéresse très peu à ce qui se passe; **there weren't** ~ **many people** il n'y avait pas beaucoup de gens, il n'y avait pas grand monde ❑ ~ **good!**, ~ **well!** [expressing agreement, consent] très bien!; **you can't** ~ **well ask outright** tu ne peux pas vraiment demander directement; **that's all** ~ **well but...** tout ça, c'est très bien mais... **-2.** *(with superlative)* [emphatic use]: **our** ~ **best wine** notre meilleur vin; **the** ~ **best of friends** les meilleurs amis du monde; **it's the** ~ **worst thing that could have happened** c'est bien la pire chose qui pouvait arriver; **the** ~ **latest designs** les créations les plus récentes; **at the** ~ **latest** au plus tard; **at the** ~ **least/most** tout au moins/plus; **the** ~ **first/last person** la (toute) première/dernière personne; **the** ~ **next day** le lendemain même, dès le lendemain; **the** ~ **next person I met was his brother** la première personne que j'ai rencontrée était son frère; **we'll stop at the** ~ **next town** nous nous arrêterons à la prochaine ville; **it's nice to have your** ~ **own car** OR **a car of your** ~ **own** c'est agréable d'avoir sa voiture à soi; **it's my** ~ **own** c'est à moi; **the** ~ **same day** le jour même; **on the** ~ **same date** exactement à la même date.
◇ *adj* **-1.** [extreme, far]: **at the** ~ **end** [of street, row etc] tout au bout; [of story, month etc] tout à la fin; **to the** ~ **end** [in space] jusqu'au bout; [in time] jusqu'à la fin; **at the** ~ **back** tout au fond; **at the** ~ **top/bottom of the page** tout en haut/en bas de la page; **at the** ~ **bottom of the sea** au plus profond de la mer. **-2.** [exact]: **at that** ~ **moment** juste à ce moment-là; **the** ~ **man I need** juste l'homme qu'il me faut; **those were his** ~ **words** ce sont ses propos mêmes, c'est exactement ce qu'il a dit; **this is the** ~ **room where they were murdered** c'est dans cette pièce même qu'ils ont été tués. **-3.** [emphatic use]: **the** ~ **idea!** quelle idée!; **the** ~ **thought of eating raw fish makes me shiver** la simple idée de manger du poisson cru me donne des frissons; **it happened before my** ~ **eyes** cela s'est passé sous mes yeux.
◆ **very much** ◇ *adv phr* **-1.** [greatly] beaucoup, bien; **I like jazz** ~ **much** j'aime beaucoup le jazz; **I** ~ **much hope to be able to come** j'espère bien que je pourrai venir; ~ **much better/bigger** beaucoup mieux/plus grand; **unless I'm** ~ **much mistaken** à moins que je ne me trompe; **were you impressed?** – ~ **much** so ça vous a impressionné? – beaucoup. **-2.** [to a large extent]: **the situation remains** ~ **much the same** la situation n'a guère évolué; **it's** ~ **much a question of who to believe** la question est surtout de savoir qui on doit croire.
◇ *det phr* beaucoup de; **there wasn't** ~ **much wine** il n'y avait pas beaucoup de vin.
◇ *pron phr* beaucoup; **she doesn't say** ~ **much** elle parle peu, elle ne dit pas grand-chose.

very high frequency [ˈverɪ-] *n (U)* très haute fréquence *f*, (gamme *f* des) ondes *fpl* métriques.

Very light [ˈvɪərɪ-] *n* fusée *f* éclairante.

very low frequency [ˈverɪ-] *n* très basse fréquence *f*.

Very pistol [ˈvɪərɪ-] *n* pistolet *m* lance-fusées.

Very Reverend [ˈverɪ-] *adj* RELIG: **the** ~ **Alan Scott** le très révérend Alan Scott.

vesicle [ˈvesɪkl] *n* vésicule *f*.

vespers [ˈvespəz] *npl* vêpres *fpl*.

vessel [ˈvesl] *n* **-1.** *lit* [container] récipient *m*; **a drinking** ~ une timbale, un gobelet. **-2.** NAUT vaisseau *m*. **-3.** ANAT & BOT vaisseau *m*.

vest [vest] ◇ *n* **-1.** *Br* [singlet – for boy, man] maillot *m* de corps, tricot *m* de peau; [– for woman] chemise *f*. **-2.** *Am* [waistcoat] gilet *m* (de costume).
◇ *vt fml* investir; **to** ~ **sb with power/authority** investir qqn de pouvoir/d'autorité; **to** ~ **sthg in sb** assigner OR attribuer qqch à qqn; **the power** ~**ed in the government** le pouvoir dont le gouvernement est investi; **the president is** ~**ed with the power to veto the government** le président est doté du pouvoir d'opposer son veto aux projets du gouvernement; **legislative authority is** ~**ed in Parliament** le Parlement est investi du pouvoir législatif.

vestal virgin [ˈvestl-] *n* vestale *f*.

vested interest [ˈvestɪd-] *n*: ~**s** [rights] droits *mpl* acquis; [investments] capitaux *mpl* investis; [advantages] intérêts *mpl*; **there are** ~**s in industry opposed to trade union reform** ceux qui ont des intérêts dans l'industrie s'opposent à la réforme des syndicats; **there are too many** ~**s** cela dérange trop de gens influents; **to have a** ~ **in doing sthg** avoir directement intérêt à faire qqch; **she has a** ~ **in keeping it secret** elle a tout intérêt à garder le secret.

vestibule [ˈvestɪbjuːl] *n* **-1.** [in house, church] vestibule *m*; [in hotel] vestibule *m*, hall *m* d'entrée. **-2.** ANAT vestibule *m*. **-3.** *Am* RAIL sas *m*.

vestige [ˈvestɪdʒ] *n* **-1.** [remnant] vestige *m*; **he clung on to the last** ~**s of power** il s'est accroché aux derniers vestiges de son autorité; **not a** ~ **of the original building remains** il ne reste plus un seul vestige de l'édifice d'origine; **there's not a** ~ **of truth in the story** il n'y a pas un grain OR une once de vérité dans cette histoire. **-2.** ANAT & ZOOL organe *m* rudimentaire; **the** ~ **of a tail** une queue rudimentaire.

vestigial [veˈstɪdʒɪəl] *adj* **-1.** [remaining] résiduel. **-2.** ANAT & ZOOL [organ, tail] rudimentaire, atrophié.

vestment [ˈvestmənt] *n* habit *m* de cérémonie; RELIG vêtement *m* sacerdotal.

vest-pocket *Am* ◇ *n* poche *f* de gilet.
◇ *adj* [book, object] de poche; *fig* minuscule, tout petit.

vestry [ˈvestrɪ] (*pl* vestries) *n* **-1.** [room] sacristie *f*. **-2.** [committee] conseil *m* paroissial.

Vesuvius [vɪˈsuːvjəs] *pr n*: (Mount) ~ le Vésuve.

vet [vet] (*pt* & *pp* vetted, *cont* vetting) ◇ *n* **-1.** (*abbr of* **veterinary surgeon/veterinary**) vétérinaire *mf*. **-2.** *inf Am* (*abbr of* **veteran**) ancien combattant *m*, vétéran *m*.
◇ *adj inf Am* (*abbr of* **veteran**) [association, rally] d'anciens combattants.
◇ *vt* **-1.** [check – application] examiner minutieusement, passer au crible; [– claims, facts, figures] vérifier soigneusement, passer au crible; [– documents] contrôler; [– person] enquêter sur; **she was thoroughly vetted for the job** ils ont soigneusement examiné sa candidature avant de l'embaucher; **all sources must be carefully vetted before publication** toutes les sources doivent être soigneusement vérifiées avant publication; **the committee has to** ~ **any expenditure exceeding £100** le comité doit approuver toute dépense au-delà de 100 livres. **-2.** VETER [examine] examiner; [treat] soigner.

vetch [vetʃ] *n* vesce *f*.

veteran [ˈvetrən] ◇ *n* **-1.** MIL ancien combattant *m*, vétéran *m*; **Veteran's Day** *Am* fête *f* de l'armistice *(le 11 novembre)*. **-2.** [experienced person] personne *f* chevronnée OR expérimentée, vieux *m* de la vieille. **-3.** [car] voiture *f* ancienne OR d'époque; [machinery] vieille machine *f*.
◇ *adj* [experienced] expérimenté, chevronné; **she's a** ~ **politician/campaigner for civil rights** c'est un vétéran de la politique/de la campagne pour les droits civiques.

veteran car *n Br* voiture *f* de collection *(normalement antérieure à 1905)*.

veterinarian [ˌvetərɪˈneərɪən] *n Am* vétérinaire *mf*.

veterinary [ˈvetərɪnrɪ] *adj* [medicine, practice] vétérinaire.

veterinary surgeon *n Br* vétérinaire *mf*.

veto [ˈviːtəʊ] (*pl* vetoes) ◇ *n* **-1.** *(U)* [power] droit *m* de veto; **to use one's** ~ exercer son droit de veto. **-2.** [refusal] veto *m*; **to put a** ~ **on sthg** mettre OR opposer son veto à qqch.
◇ *vt* POL & *fig* mettre OR opposer son veto à.

vetting [ˈvetɪŋ] *n (U)* enquêtes *fpl*; **security** ~ enquêtes de sécurité.

vex [veks] *vt* contrarier, ennuyer.

vexation [vekˈseɪʃn] *n fml* **-1.** [anger] ennui *m*, agacement *m*; **she threw it down in** ~ elle le jeta avec agacement. **-2.** [difficulty, annoyance] ennui *m*, tracasserie *f*; **one of life's** ~**s** une de ces contrariétés que nous réserve la vie.

vexatious [vekˈseɪʃəs] *adj fml* contrariant, ennuyeux.

vexed [vekst] *adj fml* **-1.** [annoyed] fâché, ennuyé, contrarié; **to become** ~ se fâcher; **to be** ~ **with sb** être fâché contre qqn, en vouloir à qqn; **she was** ~ **at his behaviour** elle était contrariée par son comportement, son comportement l'avait contrariée; **she was** ~ **to discover that she had left her purse behind** elle a été contrariée quand elle a réalisé qu'elle avait oublié son porte-monnaie. **-2.** [controversial] controversé; **we have to deal with the** ~ **question of what to do about a salary increase** nous devons aborder la question épineuse d'une éventuelle hausse des salaires; **it's a very** ~ **period in our history** c'est une période délicate de notre histoire.

vexing [ˈveksɪŋ] *adj* **-1.** [annoying] contrariant, ennuyeux, fâcheux. **-2.** [frustrating – issue, riddle] frustrant.

VG (*written abbr of* **very good**) TB.

vgc (*written abbr of* **very good condition**) tbe.

VHF (*abbr of* **very high frequency**) *n* VHF *f*.

VHS (*abbr of* **video home system**) *n* VHS *m*.

VI *written abbr of* **Virgin Islands**.

via [ˈvaɪə] *prep* **-1.** [by way of] via, par; **they travelled from Paris to Rome** ~ **Florence** ils ont voyagé de Paris à Rome via OR en passant par Florence; **the trip is shorter if you travel** ~ **Calais** le trajet est plus court par Calais. **-2.** [by means of] par, au moyen de; **contact me** ~ **this number/**~ **my secretary** contactez-moi à ce numéro/par l'intermédiaire de ma secrétaire; **she sent him the letter** ~ **her sister** elle lui a envoyé la lettre par l'intermédiaire de sa sœur; **these pictures come** ~ **satellite** ces images arrivent par satellite; **the best way to get into films is** ~ **drama school** le meilleur moyen d'entrer dans le monde du cinéma est de passer par une école d'art dramatique; **the patient was fed** ~ **a tube** le malade était alimenté au moyen d'un tube.

viability [ˌvaɪəˈbɪlətɪ] *n (U)* **-1.** ECON [of company, state] viabilité *f*. **-2.** [of plan, programme, scheme] chances *fpl* de réussite, viabilité *f*. **-3.** ANAT & BOT viabilité *f*.

viable [ˈvaɪəbl] *adj* **-1.** ECON [company, economy, state] viable. **-2.** [practicable – plan, programme] viable, qui a des chances de réussir; **there is no** ~ **alternative** il n'y a pas d'autre solution viable; **it's not a** ~ **proposition** cette proposition n'est pas viable. **-3.** ANAT & BOT viable.

viaduct [ˈvaɪədʌkt] *n* viaduc *m*.

vial [ˈvaɪəl] *n lit* fiole *f*; PHARM ampoule *f*.

viand [ˈvaɪənd] *n arch* OR *lit* friandise *f*.
◆ **viands** *npl arch* aliments *mpl*.

viaticum [vaɪˈætɪkəm] (*pl* viaticums OR viatica [-kə]) *n* viatique *m*.

vibes *inf* [vaɪbz] *npl* -**1.** *abbr of* vibraphone. -**2.** (*abbr of* vibrations) atmosphère *f*, ambiance *f*; they give off really good/bad ~ avec eux le courant passe vraiment bien/ne passe vraiment pas; I don't like the ~ in this place je n'aime pas l'ambiance ici.
vibraharp ['vaɪbrəhɑːp] *Am* = **vibraphone**.
vibrancy ['vaɪbrənsɪ] *n* enthousiasme *m*.
vibrant ['vaɪbrənt] ◇ *adj* -**1.** [vigorous, lively - person] vif; [- speech, programme, atmosphere] vibrant, touchant, émouvant; to be ~ with life être plein de vie. -**2.** [resonant - sound, voice] vibrant, résonant. -**3.** [bright - colour, light] brillant.
◇ *n* LING vibrante *f*.
vibraphone ['vaɪbrəfəʊn] *n* vibraphone *m*.
vibrate [vaɪ'breɪt] *vi* -**1.** [shake, quiver] vibrer. -**2.** [sound] vibrer, retentir. -**3.** PHYS [oscillate] osciller, vibrer.
vibration [vaɪ'breɪʃn] *n* vibration *f*.
◆ **vibrations** *inf npl* [feeling] ambiance *f*; good ~s bonne ambiance.
vibrato [vɪ'brɑːtəʊ] (*pl* **vibratos**) ◇ *n* MUS vibrato *m*.
◇ *adv* avec vibrato.
vibrator [vaɪ'breɪtə^r] *n* -**1.** ELEC vibrateur *m*. -**2.** [medical or sexual] vibromasseur *m*.
vibratory ['vaɪbrətrɪ] *adj* vibratoire.
viburnum [vaɪ'bɜːnəm] *n* viorne *f*.
vicar ['vɪkə^r] *n* pasteur *m*; the Vicar of Christ le vicaire de Jésus-Christ.
vicarage ['vɪkərɪdʒ] *n* presbytère *m*.
vicar apostolic *n* vicaire *m* apostolique.
vicar general *n* vicaire *m* général.
vicarious [vɪ'keərɪəs] *adj* -**1.** [indirect, second-hand - feeling, pride, enjoyment] indirect, par procuration OR contrecoup; they got ~ satisfaction from their son's success le succès de leur fils les a satisfaits par procuration. -**2.** [punishment] (fait) pour autrui; [suffering, pain] subi pour autrui. -**3.** [power, authority] délégué. -**4.** MED vicariant.
vicariously [vɪ'keərɪəslɪ] *adv* -**1.** [experience] indirectement; she lived ~ through her reading elle vivait par procuration à travers ses lectures. -**2.** [authorize] par délégation, par procuration.
vice [*n* vaɪs, *prep* 'vaɪsɪ] ◇ *n* -**1.** [depravity] vice *m*. -**2.** [moral fault] vice *m*; [less serious] défaut *m*; I'm afraid chocolate is one of my little ~s j'ai bien peur que le chocolat ne soit l'un de mes petits vices. -**3.** TECH étau *m*; he held her in a ~-like grip il la serrait comme dans un étau. -**4.** *Am* = **vice squad**.
◇ *prep fml* à la place de, en remplacement de.
vice-admiral [,vaɪs-] *n* vice-amiral *m* d'escadre.
vice-chairman [,vaɪs-] *n* vice-président *m*, -e *f*.
vice-chancellor [,vaɪs-] *n* -**1.** *Br* UNIV président *m*, -e *f* d'université. -**2.** *Am* JUR vice-chancelier *m*.
vice-consul [,vaɪs-] *n* vice-consul *m*.
Vicenza [viː'tʃentsə] *pr n* Vicence.
vice-premier [,vaɪs-] *n* vice-premier ministre *m*.
vice-presidency [,vaɪs-] *n* vice-présidence *f*.
vice-president [,vaɪs-] *n* vice-président *m*, -e *f*.
vice-presidential [,vaɪs-] *adj* vice-présidentiel; ~ candidate candidat *m* à la vice-présidence.
vice-principal [,vaɪs-] *n* SCH directeur *m* adjoint, directrice *f* adjointe.
viceregal [,vaɪs'riːgl] *adj* de OR du vice-roi.
vicereine [,vaɪs'reɪn] *n* vice-reine *f*.
viceroy ['vaɪsrɔɪ] *n* vice-roi *m*.
viceroyalty ['vaɪsrɔɪəltɪ] *n* vice-royauté *f*.
vice squad [,vaɪs-] *n* brigade *f* des mœurs.
vice versa [,vaɪsɪ'vɜːsə] *adv* vice versa, inversement.
Vichy ['viːʃiː] *pr n* Vichy.
Vichy water *n* eau *f* de Vichy.
vicinity [vɪ'sɪnətɪ] (*pl* **vicinities**) *n* -**1.** [surrounding area] environs *mpl*, alentours *mpl*; [neighbourhood] voisinage *m*, environs *mpl*; [proximity] proximité *f*; is there a good school in the ~? est-ce qu'il y a une bonne école dans les alentours OR dans le quartier?; he's somewhere in the ~ il est quelque part dans les environs OR dans le coin; in the ~ of the town centre [in the area] dans les environs du centre-ville; [close] à proximité du centre-ville; in the immediate ~ dans les environs immédiats; one good thing about the house is its ~ to the station *fml* un des bons côtés de la maison, c'est qu'elle est située tout près de la gare. -**2.** [approximate figures, amounts]: his salary is in the ~ of £18,000 son salaire est aux alentours de OR de l'ordre de 18 000 livres; its weight is in the ~ of £500 lb cela pèse dans les 500 livres.
vicious ['vɪʃəs] *adj* -**1.** [cruel, savage - attack, blow] brutal, violent; a ~ wind un vent violent. -**2.** [malevolent - criticism, gossip, remarks] méchant, malveillant; he has a ~ tongue il a une langue de vipère. -**3.** [dog] méchant; [horse] vicieux, rétif. -**4.** [perverse - behaviour, habits] vicieux, pervers.
vicious circle *n* cercle *m* vicieux.
viciously ['vɪʃəslɪ] *adv* [attack, beat] brutalement, violemment; [criticize] avec malveillance, méchamment.
viciousness ['vɪʃəsnɪs] *n* [of attack, beating] brutalité *f*, violence *f*; [of criticism, gossip] méchanceté *f*, malveillance *f*.
vicissitude [vɪ'sɪsɪtjuːd] *n fml* vicissitude *f*.
victim ['vɪktɪm] *n* -**1.** [physical sufferer] victime *f*; to fall ~ to sthg devenir la victime de qqch; the fire claimed many ~s l'incendie a fait de nombreuses victimes; road accident ~s les victimes OR les accidentés de la route; a fund for ~s of cancer des fonds pour les cancéreux OR les malades du cancer. -**2.** *fig* victime *f*; to fall ~ to sb's charms succomber aux charmes de qqn; many people fall ~ to these fraudulent schemes beaucoup de gens se font avoir par ces combines frauduleuses; he was a ~ of his own ambition il a été victime de sa propre ambition; education is always the first ~ of government spending cuts l'éducation est toujours la première à souffrir des réductions des dépenses publiques.
victimization [,vɪktɪmaɪ'zeɪʃn] *n* [for beliefs, race, differences] fait *m* de prendre pour victime; [reprisals] représailles *fpl*; there must be no further ~ of workers il ne doit pas y avoir d'autres représailles contre les ouvriers.
victimize, -ise ['vɪktɪmaɪz] *vt* [make victim of] faire une victime de, prendre pour victime; [take reprisals against] exercer des OR user de représailles sur; she was ~d at school because of her accent/of her colour elle a été prise pour victime à l'école à cause de son accent/de la couleur de sa peau; immigrant workers are being ~d by some of the foremen les travailleurs immigrés sont pris pour victimes OR pour cibles par certains contremaîtres; the strikers feel they are being ~d les grévistes estiment qu'ils sont victimes de représailles.
victor ['vɪktə^r] *n* vainqueur *m*; Labour were the ~s in the election le Parti travailliste a remporté la victoire aux élections.
Victoria [vɪk'tɔːrɪə] *pr n* -**1.** [person]: Queen ~ la reine Victoria. -**2.** [state] Victoria *m*; in ~ dans le Victoria.
Victoria Cross *n* MIL croix *f* de Victoria *(en Grande-Bretagne, décoration militaire très prestigieuse)*.
Victoria Falls *pl pr n* les chutes *fpl* Victoria.
Victorian [vɪk'tɔːrɪən] ◇ *adj* victorien; a return to ~ values un retour aux valeurs victoriennes OR de l'époque victorienne.
◇ *n* Victorien *m*, -enne *f*.
Victoriana [,vɪktɔːrɪ'ɑːnə] *n (U)* antiquités *fpl* victoriennes, objets *mpl* de l'époque victorienne.
victorious [vɪk'tɔːrɪəs] *adj* [army, campaign, party] victorieux; [army] vainqueur; [cry] de victoire; to be ~ over sb être victorieux de qqn, remporter la victoire sur qqn.
victoriously [vɪk'tɔːrɪəslɪ] *adv* victorieusement.
victory ['vɪktərɪ] (*pl* **victories**) *n* victoire *f*; to gain OR to win a ~ over sb remporter la victoire sur qqn.
victory roll *n* AERON *looping pour marquer une victoire*.
victory sign *n* V *m* de la victoire.
victual ['vɪtl] (*pt & pp* **victualled**, *cont* **victualling**) *arch* ◇ *vt* ravitailler, approvisionner.
◇ *vi* se ravitailler, s'approvisionner.
◆ **victuals** *npl arch* victuailles *fpl*.
victualler ['vɪtlə^r] *n* fournisseur *m* (de provisions).
vide ['vaɪdiː] *impers vb* [in text] voir, cf.
videlicet [vɪ'diːlɪset] *adv fml* à savoir.
video ['vɪdɪəʊ] (*pl* **videos**) ◇ *n* -**1.** [medium] vidéo *f*; I use ~ a lot in my teaching j'utilise beaucoup la vidéo pendant mes cours. -**2.** [VCR] magnétoscope *m*; they recorded the series on ~ ils ont enregistré le feuilleton au magnétoscope. -**3.** [cassette] vidéocassette *f*; [recording] vidéo *f*; [for pop-song] clip *m*, vidéoclip *m*; they rented a ~ for the night ils ont loué une vidéo OR vidéocassette pour la soirée; we've got a ~ of the film on a le film en vidéocassette. -**4.** *inf Am* [television] télé *f*.
◇ *vt* enregistrer sur magnétoscope, magnétoscoper.
◇ *comp* -**1.** [film, version] (en) vidéo; [services, equipment, signals] vidéo *(inv)*; a ~ shop un magasin vidéo. -**2.** *Am* [on TV] télévisé.
video art *n* art *m* vidéo.
video camera *n* caméra *f* vidéo.
video cartridge *n* cartouche *f* vidéo.
video cassette *n* vidéocassette *f*.
video cassette recorder *n* magnétoscope *m*.
video clip *n* clip *m*, vidéoclip *m*, clip *m* vidéo.
video club *n* club *m* vidéo.
video conference *n* vidéoconférence *f*, visioconférence *f*.
videodisc ['vɪdɪəʊdɪsk] *n* vidéodisque *m*.
video frequency *n* vidéofréquence *f*.
video game *n* jeu *m* vidéo.
video library *n* vidéothèque *f*.
video nasty *inf n Br film vidéo à caractère violent et souvent pornographique*.
videophone ['vɪdɪəʊfəʊn] *n* vidéophone *m*, visiophone *m*.
video-record *vt* enregistrer sur magnétoscope, magnétoscoper.
videorecorder ['vɪdɪəʊrɪ,kɔːdə^r] *n* magnétoscope *m*.
video recording *n* enregistrement *m* sur magnétoscope.
video shop *n* vidéo-club *m*.
videotape ['vɪdɪəʊteɪp] ◇ *n* bande *f* vidéo.
◇ *vt* enregistrer sur magnétoscope, magnétoscoper.
videotext ['vɪdɪəʊtekst] *n* vidéotex *m*, vidéographie *f* interactive.
vidicon ['vɪdɪkɒn] *n* vidicon *m*.
vie [vaɪ] (*pt & pp* **vied**, *cont* **vying**) *vi* rivaliser, lutter; to ~ with sb for sthg disputer qqch à qqn; the two children ~d with each other for attention les deux enfants rivalisaient l'un avec l'autre pour attirer l'attention; several companies were vying with each other to sponsor the event plusieurs firmes se battaient pour parrainer l'évènement.
Vienna [vɪ'enə] ◇ *pr n* Vienne; the Congress of ~ le congrès de Vienne.
◇ *comp* viennois, de Vienne.
Viennese [,vɪə'niːz] (*pl inv*) ◇ *n* Viennois *m*, -e *f*.
◇ *adj* viennois.
Vietcong [,vjet'kɒŋ] (*pl inv*) *n* Viêt-cong *mf*.
Vietnam [*Br* ,vjet'næm, *Am* ,vjet'nɑːm] *pr n* Viêt-nam *m*; in ~ au Viêt-nam; the ~ War la guerre du Viêt-nam.

THE VIETNAM WAR:
Conflit opposant, de 1954 à 1975, le Viêt-nam du Nord communiste au Viêt-nam du Sud, soutenu militairement par les États-Unis. Aussitôt critiqué par l'opinion publique nationale, l'effort de guerre américain s'intensifia considérablement au milieu des années 60, sans parvenir pour autant à faire basculer l'issue du conflit. À partir de 1970, sous la présidence de R. Nixon, un processus de cessez-le-feu fut engagé, aboutissant au retrait des troupes américaines en 1973. Un an plus tard, le sud du pays passa aux mains des communistes.
Véritable traumatisme national, la guerre du Viêt-nam est peut-être l'épisode le plus pénible de l'histoire des États-Unis. La longueur du conflit, les atrocités commises de part et d'autre, le nombre très élevé de victimes, mais surtout les interrogations sur la finalité de cette guerre remirent dramatiquement en question la légitimité de l'ingérence américaine et provoquèrent chez les jeunes Américains de l'époque un mouvement antimilitariste d'une ampleur sans précédent.

Vietnamese [ˌvjetnəˈmiːz] (*pl inv*) ◇ *n* -**1.** [person] Vietnamien *m*, -enne *f*. -**2.** LING vietnamien *m*.
◇ *adj* vietnamien.

view [vjuː] ◇ *n* -**1.** [sight] vue *f*; **to come into ~** apparaître; **we came into ~ of the shore** nous sommes arrivés en vue du rivage, nous avons aperçu le rivage; **he turned the corner and disappeared from ~** il a tourné au coin et on l'a perdu de vue OR il a disparu; **it happened in full ~ of the television cameras/police** cela s'est passé juste devant les caméras de télévision/sous les yeux de la police; **to be on ~** [house] être ouvert aux visites; [picture] être exposé; **the woods are within ~ of the house** de la maison on voit les bois; **to hide sthg from ~** [accidentally] cacher qqch de la vue; [deliberately] cacher qqch aux regards. -**2.** [prospect] vue *f*; **the house has a good ~ of the sea** la maison a une belle vue sur la mer; **a room with a ~** une chambre avec vue; **there's a nice ~ from the window** de la fenêtre il y a une très belle vue; **there are nice ~s of the coast from that hill** de cette colline on a de belles vues sur la côte; **from here we have a side ~ of the cathedral** d'ici nous avons une vue de profil de la cathédrale; **you get a better ~ from here** on voit mieux d'ici; **the man in front of me blocked my ~ of the stage** l'homme devant moi m'empêchait de voir la scène; **a comprehensive ~ of English literature** *fig* une vue d'ensemble de la littérature anglaise. -**3.** [future perspective]: **in ~** en vue; **there appears to be no solution in ~** il semble n'y avoir aucune solution en vue; **what do you have in ~ as regards work?** quelles sont vos intentions en ce qui concerne le travail?; **with this end in ~** avec OR dans cette intention; **she has in ~ the publication of a new book** elle envisage de publier un nouveau livre; **to take the long ~ of sthg** voir qqch à long terme. -**4.** [aim, purpose] but *m*, intention *f*; **with a ~ to doing sthg** en vue de faire qqch, dans l'intention de faire qqch; **they bought the house with a ~ to their retirement** ils ont acheté la maison en pensant à leur retraite. -**5.** [interpretation] vue *f*; **an overall ~** une vue d'ensemble; **he has OR takes a gloomy ~ of life** il a une vue pessimiste de la vie, il envisage la vie d'une manière pessimiste. -**6.** [picture, photograph] vue *f*; **~s of Venice** vues de Venise; **an aerial ~ of New York** une vue aérienne de New York. -**7.** [opinion] avis *m*, opinion *f*; **in my ~** à mon avis; **I respect her political ~s** je respecte ses opinions politiques; **that seems to be the generally accepted ~** ceci semble être l'opinion générale OR courante; **that's the official ~** c'est le point de vue officiel; **everybody has their own ~ of the situation** chacun comprend la situation à sa façon, chacun a sa propre façon de voir la situation; **he takes the ~ that they are innocent** il pense OR estime OR soutient qu'ils sont innocents; **I don't take that ~** je ne partage pas cet avis; **she took a poor OR dim ~ of his behaviour** elle n'appréciait guère son comportement; **she holds OR has strong ~s on the subject** elle a des opinions OR des idées bien nettes sur le sujet; **he's changed his ~s on disarmament** il a changé d'avis sur le désarmement.
◇ *vt* -**1.** [look at] voir, regarder; [film] regarder; **~ed from above/from afar** vu d'en haut/de loin. -**2.** [examine - slides] visionner; [- through microscope] regarder; [- flat, showhouse] visiter, inspecter; **the house may be ~ed at weekends only** on peut visiter la maison pendant les week-ends uniquement. -**3.** *fig* [consider, judge] considérer, envisager; **the committee ~ed his application favourably** la commission a porté un regard favorable sur sa candidature; **he was ~ed as a dangerous maniac** on le considérait comme un fou dangereux; **how do you ~ this matter?** quel est votre avis sur cette affaire?; **the government ~s the latest international developments with alarm** le gouvernement porte un regard inquiet sur les derniers développements internationaux; **I would ~ his departure with equanimity** j'envisagerais son départ avec sérénité. -**4.** HUNT [fox] apercevoir.
◇ *vi* TV regarder la télévision.
◆ **in view of** *prep phr* étant donné, vu; **in ~ of his age** étant donné son âge, vu son âge; **in ~ of what has happened** en raison de OR étant donné ce qui s'est passé; **in ~ of this** ceci étant.

Viewdata® [ˈvjuːˌdeɪtə] *pr n* vidéotex *m*, vidéographie *f* interactive.

viewer [ˈvjuːəʳ] *n* -**1.** TV téléspectateur *m*, -trice *f*; **the programme has OR attracts a lot of women ~s/young ~s** l'émission est beaucoup regardée par les femmes/les jeunes. -**2.** PHOT [for slides] visionneuse *f*; [viewfinder] viseur *m*.

viewfinder [ˈvjuːˌfaɪndəʳ] *n* viseur *m* PHOT.

viewing [ˈvjuːɪŋ] ◇ *n* (*U*) -**1.** TV programme *m*, programmes *mpl*, émissions *fpl*; **late-night ~ on BBC 2** émissions de fin de soirée sur BBC 2; **his latest film makes exciting ~** son dernier film est un spectacle passionnant; **a good evening's ~** une soirée passée devant de bons programmes de télévision. -**2.** [of showhouse, exhibition] visite *f*; **~ at weekends only** visites uniquement le week-end. -**3.** ASTRON observation *f*.
◇ *comp* -**1.** TV [time, patterns] d'écoute; **a young ~ audience** de jeunes téléspectateurs; **~ figures** taux *m* OR indice *m* d'écoute; **~ hours** heures *fpl* d'écoute; **at peak ~ hours** aux heures de grande écoute. -**2.** ASTRON & METEOR [conditions] d'observation.

viewless [ˈvjuːlɪs] *adj* -**1.** [site, windows] qui n'offre pas de vue. -**2.** [person] sans opinion OR opinions.

viewphone [ˈvjuːfəʊn] *n* vidéophone *m*, visiophone *m*.

viewpoint [ˈvjuːpɔɪnt] *n* -**1.** [opinion] point de vue *m*. -**2.** [viewing place] point de vue *m*, panorama *m*.

vig▽ [vɪg] *n Am* intérêts *mpl*.

vigil [ˈvɪdʒɪl] *n* -**1.** [watch] veille *f*; [in sickroom] veillée *f*; [for dead person] veillée *f* funèbre; **to keep (an all-night) ~ by sb's bedside** veiller (toute la nuit) au chevet de qqn. -**2.** [demonstration] manifestation *f* silencieuse (nocturne). -**3.** RELIG vigile *f*.

vigilance [ˈvɪdʒɪləns] *n* vigilance *f*.

vigilance committee *n Am* groupe *m* d'autodéfense.

vigilant [ˈvɪdʒɪlənt] *adj* vigilant, éveillé.

vigilante [ˌvɪdʒɪˈlæntɪ] *n* membre *m* d'un groupe d'autodéfense; **~ group** groupe *m* d'autodéfense.

vigilantism [ˌvɪdʒɪˈlæntɪzm] *n attitude agressive typique des groupes d'autodéfense*.

vigilantly [ˈvɪdʒɪləntlɪ] *adv* avec vigilance, attentivement.

vignette [vɪˈnjet] ◇ *n* [illustration] vignette *f*; ART & PHOT portrait *m* en buste dégradé; LITERAT esquisse *f* de caractère, portrait *m*.
◇ *vt* [picture, photograph] dégrader, estomper; [character] esquisser; [book, page] orner de vignettes.

vigor *Am* = **vigour**.

vigorous [ˈvɪgərəs] *adj* -**1.** [robust - person, plant] vigoureux; [enthusiastic - person] enthousiaste. -**2.** [forceful - opposition, campaign, support] vigoureux, énergique. -**3.** [energetic - exercise] énergique.

vigorously [ˈvɪgərəslɪ] *adv* vigoureusement, énergiquement; **he nodded his head ~** il acquiesça vivement de la tête.

vigour *Br*, **vigor** *Am* [ˈvɪgəʳ] *n* -**1.** [physical vitality] vigueur *f*, énergie *f*, vitalité *f*; [mental vitality] vigueur *f*, vivacité *f*; **he is no longer in the full ~ of youth** il n'a plus toute la vigueur de la jeunesse. -**2.** [of attack, style] vigueur *f*; [of storm] violence *f*. -**3.** *Am* JUR: **in ~** en vigueur.

Viking [ˈvaɪkɪŋ] ◇ *adj* viking.
◇ *n* Viking *mf*.

Viking ship *n* drakkar *m*.

vile [vaɪl] *adj* -**1.** [morally wrong - deed, intention, murder] vil, ignoble, infâme; **he made some ~ accusations** il a porté des accusations ignobles OR infâmes. -**2.** [disgusting - person, habit, food, taste] abominable, exécrable; [- smell] infect, nauséabond; **it smells ~!** ça pue!; **spitting is a ~ habit** cracher est une sale habitude; **he used some ~ language** il a employé des termes ignobles. -**3.** [very bad - temper] exécrable, massacrant; [- weather] exécrable; **to be in a ~ temper** être d'une humeur massacrante; **what ~ weather!** quel sale temps!

vilely [ˈvaɪllɪ] *adv* vilement, bassement.

vileness [ˈvaɪlnɪs] *n* -**1.** [of deed, intention] vilenie *f*, bassesse *f*. -**2.** [of smell, taste, weather] caractère *m* exécrable OR abominable.

vilification [ˌvɪlɪfɪˈkeɪʃn] *n fml* diffamation *f*, calomnie *f*.

vilify [ˈvɪlɪfaɪ] *vt fml* diffamer, calomnier.

villa [ˈvɪlə] *n* [in country] maison *f* de campagne; [by sea] villa *f*; *Br* [in town] villa *f* OR pavillon *m* (de banlieue); HIST villa *f*.

village [ˈvɪlɪdʒ] ◇ *n* village *m*.
◇ *comp* du village.

village green *n pelouse au centre du village.*

VILLAGE GREEN:
Souvent situé au centre du village, le «village green» accueille les kermesses et des manifestations sportives.

village hall *n* salle *f* des fêtes.

village idiot *n* idiot *m* du village.

villager [ˈvɪlɪdʒəʳ] *n* villageois *m*, -e *f*.

villain [ˈvɪlən] *n* -**1.** [ruffian, scoundrel] scélérat *m*, -e *f*, vaurien *m*, -enne *f*; [in film, story] méchant *m*, -e *f*, traître *m*, -esse *f*; **the ~ of the piece** THEAT & *fig* le méchant, le coupable. -**2.** *inf* [rascal] coquin *m*, -e *f*, vilain *m*, -e *f*; **you little ~!** petit coquin!, vilain! -**3.** *crime sl* [criminal] bandit *m*, malfaiteur *m*.

villainous [ˈvɪlənəs] *adj* -**1.** [evil - act, intention, person] vil, ignoble, infâme; **a ~ deed** une infamie OR bassesse. -**2.** [foul - food, weather] abominable, exécrable.

villainy [ˈvɪlənɪ] (*pl* **villainies**) *n* infamie *f*, bassesse *f*.

villein [ˈvɪlɪn] *n* HIST [free] vilain *m*, -e *f*; [unfree] serf *m*, serve *f*.

villus [ˈvɪləs] (*pl* **villi** [-laɪ]) *n* BOT poil *m*; ANAT & ZOOL villosité *f*.

Vilnius [ˈvɪlnɪəs] *pr n* Vilnious.

vim *inf* [vɪm] *n* énergie *f*, entrain *m*; **full of ~ (and vigour)** plein d'entrain.

vinaigrette [ˌvɪnɪˈgret] *n* vinaigrette *f*.

vindaloo [vɪndəˈluː] *n plat indien au curry très épicé*.

vindicate [ˈvɪndɪkeɪt] *vt* -**1.** [justify] justifier; **this ~s my faith in him** ceci prouve que j'avais raison d'avoir confiance en lui, ceci prouve que la confiance que j'avais en lui était justifiée; **his opinions were ~d** ses opinions ont été justifiées. -**2.** [uphold - claim, right] faire valoir, revendiquer.

vindication [ˌvɪndɪˈkeɪʃn] *n* justification *f*; he spoke in ~ of his behaviour il s'expliqua pour justifier son comportement.
vindictive [vɪnˈdɪktɪv] *adj* vindicatif.
vindictively [vɪnˈdɪktɪvlɪ] *adv* vindicativement.
vindictiveness [vɪnˈdɪktɪvnɪs] *n* caractère *m* vindicatif; she did it out of sheer ~ elle l'a fait par simple envie de vengeance.
vine [vaɪn] ◇ *n* -**1.** [grapevine] vigne *f*. -**2.** [plant - climbing] plante *f* grimpante; [- creeping] plante *f* rampante.
◇ *comp* [leaf] de vigne; [disease] de la vigne; ~ grower viticulteur *m*, vigneron *m*; ~ growing viticulture *f*; ~ harvest vendange *f*, vendanges *fpl*.
vinegar [ˈvɪnɪgəʳ] *n* vinaigre *m*.
vinegar fly *n* mouche *f* du vinaigre.
vinegary [ˈvɪnɪgərɪ] *adj* -**1.** [smell, taste] de vinaigre; [wine] qui a un goût de vinaigre. -**2.** *fig* [tone, reply] acide, acerbe; [temper] acide, acariâtre.
vineyard [ˈvɪnjəd] *n* vignoble *m*.
viniculture [ˈvɪnɪkʌltʃəʳ] *n* viniculture *f*.
vinification [ˌvɪnɪfɪˈkeɪʃn] *n* vinification *f*.
vino *inf* [ˈviːnəʊ] *n* pinard *m*.
vinous [ˈvaɪnəs] *adj* vineux.
vintage [ˈvɪntɪdʒ] ◇ *n* -**1.** VINIC [wine] vin *m* de cru; [year] cru *m*, millésime *m*; this claret is an excellent ~ ce bordeaux est un très grand cru; 1982 was a good ~ 1982 a été une bonne année pour le vin; a 1983 ~ un vin de 1983; what ~ is this wine? quel est le millésime OR quelle est l'année de ce vin? -**2.** [crop] récolte *f*; [harvesting] vendange *f*, vendanges *fpl*. -**3.** [period] époque *f*; an old radio of pre-war ~ une vieille radio d'avant-guerre.
◇ *adj* -**1.** [old] antique, ancien. -**2.** [classic, superior] classique; a season of ~ films une saison de films classiques; it was ~ Agatha Christie c'était de l'Agatha Christie du meilleur style OR cru. -**3.** [port, champagne] de cru.
◇ *vt* vendanger.
vintage car *n Br* voiture *f* de collection *(normalement construite entre 1919 et 1930)*.
vintage model *n* modèle *m* OR pièce *f* d'époque.
vintage wine *n* vin *m* de grand cru, grand vin *m*.
vintage year *n* [for wine] grand cru *m*, grande année *f*; [for books, films] très bonne année *f*; it was a ~ for the British film industry ce fut une excellente année pour l'industrie cinématographique britannique.
vintner [ˈvɪntnəʳ] *n* négociant *m* en vins.
vinyl [ˈvaɪnɪl] ◇ *n* vinyle *m*.
◇ *adj* [wallpaper, tiles, coat] de OR en vinyle; [paint] vinylique.
viol [ˈvaɪəl] ◇ *n* viole *f*.
◇ *comp*: ~ player violiste *mf*.
viola [vɪˈəʊlə] ◇ *n* -**1.** MUS alto *m*. -**2.** BOT [genus] violacée *f*; [flower] pensée *f*, violette *f*.
◇ *comp*: ~ player altiste *mf*.
viola da gamba [vɪˌəʊlədəˈgæmbə] (*pl* **viole da gamba** [vɪˌəʊle-]) *n* viole *f* de gambe.
viola d'amore [vɪˌəʊlədæˈmɔːrɪ] (*pl* **viole d'amore** [vɪˌəʊle-]) *n* viole *f* d'amour.
violate [ˈvaɪəleɪt] *vt* -**1.** [promise, secret, treaty] violer; [law] violer, enfreindre; [rights] violer, bafouer. -**2.** [frontier, property] violer. -**3.** [peace, silence] troubler, rompre; to ~ sb's privacy déranger qqn dans son intimité OR dans sa vie privée. -**4.** [sanctuary, tomb] violer, profaner. -**5.** *fml* [rape] violer, violenter.
violation [ˌvaɪəˈleɪʃn] *n* -**1.** [of promise, rights, secret] violation *f*; [of law] violation *f*, infraction *f*; SPORT faute *f*; they acted in ~ of the treaty/of the regulations ils ont contrevenu au traité/au règlement. -**2.** [of frontier, property] violation *f*; it's a ~ of my privacy c'est une atteinte à ma vie privée. -**3.** ADMIN: ~ of the peace trouble *m* de l'ordre public. -**4.** [of sanctuary, tomb] violation *f*, profanation *f*. -**5.** *Am* JUR infraction *f*; a traffic ~ une infraction au Code de la route. -**6.** *fml* [rape] viol *m*.
violator [ˈvaɪəleɪtəʳ] *n* -**1.** [gen] violateur *m*. -**2.** *Am* JUR contrevenant *m*.
violence [ˈvaɪələns] *n (U)* -**1.** [physical] violence *f*; acts/scenes of ~ actes *mpl*/scènes *fpl* de violence; football/TV ~ violence sur les terrains de football/à la télévision; the men of ~ [terrorists] les terroristes *mpl*; ~ broke out in the streets of the capital il y a eu de violents incidents OR des bagarres ont éclaté dans les rues de la capitale. -**2.** JUR violences *fpl*; crimes of ~ crimes *mpl* de violence; robbery with ~ vol avec coups et blessures. -**3.** [of language, passion, storm] violence *f*. -**4.** *phr*: to do ~ to sb/sthg faire violence à qqn/qqch.
violent [ˈvaɪələnt] *adj* -**1.** [attack, crime, person] violent; by ~ means par la violence; to be ~ with sb se montrer OR être violent avec qqn; he began to get ~ il a commencé à se montrer violent; he gave the door a ~ kick il a donné un violent coup de pied dans la porte; to die a ~ death mourir de mort violente. -**2.** [intense - pain] violent, aigu; [furious - temper] violent; [strong, great - contrast, change] violent, brutal; [- explosion] violent; she took a ~ dislike to him elle s'est prise d'une vive aversion à son égard; I've got a ~ toothache/headache j'ai une rage de dents/un mal de tête atroce. -**3.** [forceful, impassioned - argument, language, emotions] violent. -**4.** [wind, weather] violent. -**5.** [colour] criard, voyant; the walls had been painted a ~ red on avait peint les murs d'un rouge criard.
violently [ˈvaɪələntlɪ] *adv* [attack, shake, struggle] violemment; [act, react] violemment, avec violence; to behave ~ avoir un comportement violent; he was ~ sick il fut pris de vomissements violents; he was shaking/shivering ~ il était secoué de tremblements/de frissons violents.
violet [ˈvaɪələt] ◇ *n* -**1.** BOT violette *f*. -**2.** [colour] violet *m*.
◇ *adj* violet.
violin [ˌvaɪəˈlɪn] ◇ *n* violon *m*.
◇ *comp* [concerto] pour violon; [lesson] de violon; ~ case étui *m* à violon; ~ maker luthier *m*.
violinist [ˌvaɪəˈlɪnɪst] *n* violoniste *mf*.
violoncellist [ˌvaɪələnˈtʃelɪst] *n* violoncelliste *mf*.
violoncello [ˌvaɪələnˈtʃeləʊ] *n* violoncelle *m*.
VIP (*abbr of* **very important person**) ◇ *n* VIP *mf*, personnalité *f*, personnage *m* de marque.
◇ *comp* [guests, visitors] de marque, éminent, très important; to give sb the ~ treatment traiter qqn comme un personnage de marque; we got ~ treatment on nous a réservé un accueil princier, on nous a traités comme des rois ❑ ~ **lounge** *salon d'accueil (dans un aéroport) réservé aux personnages de marque*.
viper [ˈvaɪpəʳ] *n* ZOOL & *fig* vipère *f*; a ~s' nest *fig* un nœud de vipères.
viperish [ˈvaɪpərɪʃ] *adj* [tongue] de vipère; [person] qui a une langue de vipère.
virago [vɪˈrɑːgəʊ] (*pl* **viragoes** OR **viragos**) *n* mégère *f*, virago *f*.
viral [ˈvaɪrəl] *adj* viral; a ~ infection une infection virale.
Virgil [ˈvɜːdʒɪl] *pr n* Virgile.
Virgilian [vɜːˈdʒɪlɪən] *adj* virgilien.
virgin [ˈvɜːdʒɪn] ◇ *n* [girl] vierge *f*, pucelle *f*; [boy] puceau *m*.
◇ *adj* -**1.** [sexually] vierge. -**2.** [forest, soil] vierge; [fresh] virginal; ~ snow neige *f* fraîche; ~ white sheets draps d'un blanc immaculé.
◆ **Virgin** *pr n* RELIG: the (Blessed) Virgin la (Sainte) Vierge.
virginal [ˈvɜːdʒɪnl] ◇ *n* MUS: ~s virginal *m*.
◇ *adj* virginal.
Virgin birth *n*: the ~ l'Immaculée Conception *f*.
Virginia [vəˈdʒɪnjə] *pr n* Virginie *f*; in ~ en Virginie.
Virginia creeper *n* vigne *f* vierge.
Virginian [vəˈdʒɪnjən] ◇ *n* Virginien *m*, -enne *f*.
◇ *adj* virginien.
Virginia stock *n* malcolmia *m*.
Virginia tobacco *n* virginie *m*, tabac *m* de Virginie.
Virgin Islands *pl pr n*: the ~ les îles *fpl* Vierges; in the ~ dans les îles Vierges.
virginity [vəˈdʒɪnətɪ] *n* virginité *f*; to lose one's ~ perdre sa virginité.
Virgin Mary *pr n*: the ~ la Vierge Marie.
Virgo [ˈvɜːgəʊ] *pr n* ASTROL & ASTRON Vierge *f*; he's a ~ il est (du signe de la) Vierge.
virile [ˈvɪraɪl] *adj* viril.
virility [vɪˈrɪlətɪ] *n* virilité *f*.
virologist [ˌvaɪˈrɒlədʒɪst] *n* virologue *mf*, virologiste *mf*.
virology [ˌvaɪˈrɒlədʒɪ] *n* virologie *f*.
virtual [ˈvɜːtʃʊəl] *adj* -**1.** [near, as good as]: the country is in a state of ~ anarchy c'est pratiquement l'anarchie dans le pays; the strike led to a ~ halt in production la grève a provoqué une interruption quasi totale de la production; it's a ~ impossibility/dictatorship c'est une quasi-impossibilité/une quasi-dictature. -**2.** [actual, effective]: they are the ~ rulers of the country en fait ce sont eux qui dirigent le pays, ce sont eux les dirigeants de fait du pays. -**3.** COMPUT & PHYS virtuel.
virtual image *n* image *f* virtuelle.
virtually [ˈvɜːtʃʊəlɪ] *adv* -**1.** [almost] pratiquement, quasiment, virtuellement; it's ~ impossible c'est pratiquement OR quasiment impossible; it's ~ finished c'est presque OR quasiment fini; I'm ~ certain je suis pratiquement certain; she ~ insulted me elle m'a pratiquement insulté. -**2.** [actually, in effect] en fait; he is ~ the manager en fait OR en pratique, c'est lui le directeur.
virtual memory *n* COMPUT mémoire *f* virtuelle.
virtual reality *n* réalité *f* virtuelle.
virtual storage = **virtual memory**.
virtue [ˈvɜːtjuː] *n* -**1.** [goodness] vertu *f*; to make a ~ of necessity faire de nécessité vertu; a woman of easy ~ une femme de petite vertu ❑ ~ is its own reward *prov* la vertu est sa propre récompense. -**2.** [merit] mérite *m*, avantage *m*; she at least has the ~ of being discreet elle a au moins le mérite d'être discrète; the flat has the ~ of being centrally heated l'appartement a l'avantage d'avoir le chauffage central. -**3.** *arch* [efficacy] vertu *f*, efficacité *f*.
◆ **by virtue of** *prep phr* en vertu OR en raison de; by ~ of her age en vertu OR en raison de son âge; by ~ of being the eldest en vertu OR en raison du fait qu'il est l'aîné.
virtuosity [ˌvɜːtjʊˈɒsɪtɪ] *n* virtuosité *f*.
virtuoso [ˌvɜːtjʊˈəʊzəʊ] (*pl* **virtuosos** OR **virtuosi** [-siː]) ◇ *n* [gen & MUS] virtuose *mf*.
◇ *adj* de virtuose; it was a ~ performance MUS c'était une interprétation de virtuose; *fig* c'était un tour de force.
virtuous [ˈvɜːtʃʊəs] *adj* vertueux.
virtuously [ˈvɜːtʃʊəslɪ] *adv* vertueusement.
virulence [ˈvɪrʊləns] *n* virulence *f*.
virulent [ˈvɪrʊlənt] *adj* virulent.
virulently [ˈvɪrʊləntlɪ] *adv* avec virulence.
virus [ˈvaɪrəs] ◇ *n* virus *m*; the flu/rabies ~ le virus de la grippe/de la rage.
◇ *comp*: a ~ infection une infection virale.
visa [ˈviːzə] ◇ *n* visa *m*; he has applied for an American ~ il a demandé un visa pour l'Amérique.
◇ *vt* ADMIN viser.
visage [ˈvɪzɪdʒ] *n lit* visage *m*, figure *f*.
vis-à-vis [ˌviːzɑːˈviː] (*pl inv*) ◇ *prep* -**1.** [in relation to] par rapport à. -**2.** [opposite] vis-à-vis de.
◇ *adv* vis-à-vis.
◇ *n* -**1.** [person or thing opposite] vis-à-vis *m inv*. -**2.** [counterpart] homologue *mf*.
viscera [ˈvɪsərə] *npl* viscères *mpl*.
visceral [ˈvɪsərəl] *adj* viscéral.
viscid [ˈvɪsɪd] *adj* visqueux.
viscose [ˈvɪskəʊs] ◇ *n* viscose *f*.
◇ *adj* visqueux.
viscosity [vɪˈskɒsətɪ] (*pl* **viscosities**) *n* viscosité *f*.

viscount ['vaɪkaʊnt] *n* vicomte *m*.
viscountcy ['vaɪkaʊntsɪ] *n* vicomté *f*.
viscountess ['vaɪkaʊntɪs] *n* vicomtesse *f*.
viscounty ['vaɪkaʊntɪ] = **viscountcy**.
viscous ['vɪskəs] *adj* visqueux, gluant.
vise [vaɪs] *Am* = **vice 4**.
visibility [,vɪzɪ'bɪlətɪ] *n* visibilité *f*; ~ is down to a few yards la visibilité est réduite à OR ne dépasse pas quelques mètres.
visible ['vɪzəbl] *adj* -**1.** [gen & OPTICS] visible; to become ~ devenir visible; clearly ~ to the naked eye clairement visible à l'œil nu; only ~ under a microscope seulement visible au microscope. -**2.** [evident] visible, apparent, manifeste; his nervousness was clearly ~ sa nervosité était manifeste OR évidente; it serves no ~ purpose on n'en voit pas vraiment l'utilité, on ne voit pas vraiment à quoi cela sert; with no ~ means of support ADMIN sans ressources apparentes. -**3.** *inf* ECON visible.
visibly ['vɪzəblɪ] *adv* visiblement; he was ~ surprised/annoyed il était visiblement surpris/ennuyé, sa surprise/son ennui était manifeste.
Visigoth ['vɪzɪgɒθ] *pr n* Visigoth *m*, -e *f*, Wisigoth *m*, -e *f*.
Visigothic [,vɪzɪ'gɒθɪk] *adj* visigoth, wisigoth.
vision ['vɪʒn] *n* -**1.** *(U)* OPTICS [sight] vision *f*, vue *f*; to suffer from defective ~ avoir une vision défectueuse; outside/within one's field of ~ hors de/en vue. -**2.** [insight] vision *f*, clairvoyance *f*; a man of ~ un homme clairvoyant; we need people with ~ and imagination nous avons besoin de gens inspirés et imaginatifs. -**3.** [dream, fantasy] vision *f*; to have a ~ RELIG avoir une vision; to have ~s MED & PSYCH avoir des visions; he has ~s of being rich and famous il se voit riche et célèbre; I had ~s of you lying in a hospital bed je vous voyais couché dans un lit d'hôpital. -**4.** [conception] vision *f*, conception *f*; what is your ~ of the new town centre? comment voyez-vous OR comment concevez-vous le nouveau centre-ville? -**5.** [apparition] vision *f*, apparition *f*; [lovely sight] magnifique spectacle *m*; she was a ~ in white lace elle était ravissante en dentelle blanche; a ~ of loveliness une apparition de charme. -**6.** TV image *f*.
visionary ['vɪʒənrɪ] (*pl* visionaries) ◇ *adj* visionnaire.
◇ *n* visionnaire *mf*.
vision mixer *n* TV -**1.** [equipment] mixeur *m*, mélangeur *m* de signaux. -**2.** [person] opérateur *m* de mixage.
vision mixing *n* TV mixage *m* d'images.
visit ['vɪzɪt] ◇ *n* -**1.** [call] visite *f*; to pay sb a ~ rendre visite à qqn; I haven't paid a ~ to the cathedral yet je n'ai pas encore visité OR je ne suis pas encore allé voir la cathédrale; you must pay them a return ~ il faut leur rendre leur visite; she met him on a return ~ to her home town elle l'a rencontré quand elle est retournée en visite dans sa ville natale ☐ to pay a ~ *inf Br euph* aller au petit coin. -**2.** [stay] visite *f*, séjour *m*; [trip] voyage *m*, séjour *m*; she's on a ~ to her aunt's elle est en visite chez sa tante; she's on a ~ to Amsterdam elle fait un séjour à Amsterdam; did you enjoy your ~ to California? avez-vous fait un bon séjour en Californie?; the President is on an official ~ to Australia le président est en visite officielle en Australie. -**3.** *Am* [chat] causette *f*, bavardage *m*.
◇ *vt* -**1.** [person - go to see] rendre visite à, aller voir; [- stay with] rendre visite à, séjourner chez; she went to ~ her aunt in hospital elle est allée rendre visite à sa tante OR allée voir sa tante à l'hôpital; not many people come to ~ her il n'y a pas beaucoup de gens qui viennent lui rendre visite; to ~ the sick visiter les malades; he's away ~ing friends at the moment il séjourne chez des amis en ce moment. -**2.** [museum, town] visiter, aller voir; in the afternoon they went to ~ Pisa l'après-midi ils sont allés voir OR visiter Pise. -**3.** [inspect - place, premises] visiter, inspecter, faire une visite d'inspection à; to ~ the scene of the crime JUR se rendre sur les lieux du crime. -**4.** *lit* [inflict]: to ~ a punishment on sb punir qqn; the sins of the fathers are ~ed upon their sons les fils sont punis pour les péchés de leurs pères; the city was ~ed by the plague in the 17th century la ville a été atteinte par la peste au 17ᵉ siècle.
◇ *vi* visiter; we're just ~ing nous sommes simplement en visite OR de passage.
◆ **visit with** *vt insep Am* [call on] passer voir; [talk with] bavarder avec.
visitant ['vɪzɪtənt] *n* -**1.** *lit* [ghost] revenant *m*, fantôme *m*. -**2.** [bird] oiseau *m* migrateur OR de passage.
visitation [,vɪzɪ'teɪʃn] *n* -**1.** [official visit, inspection] visite *f* OR tour *m* d'inspection; RELIG visite *f* épiscopale OR pastorale. -**2.** [social visit] visite *f*; *hum* [prolonged] visite *f* trop prolongée. -**3.** *fml* [affliction] punition *f* du ciel; [reward] récompense *f* divine.
◆ **Visitation** *n* RELIG: the Visitation la Visitation.
visiting ['vɪzɪtɪŋ] *adj* [circus, performers] de passage; [lecturer] invité; [birds] de passage, migrateur; the ~ team SPORT les visiteurs.
visiting card *n Br* carte *f* de visite; the dog left its ~ *hum & euph* le chien a laissé sa carte de visite.
visiting fireman *inf n Am* visiteur *m* de marque.
visiting hours *npl* heures *fpl* de visite.
visiting nurse *n Am* infirmier *m*, -ère *f* à domicile.
visiting professor *n* UNIV professeur *m* associé OR invité.
visiting time = **visiting hours**.
visitor ['vɪzɪtəʳ] *n* -**1.** [caller - at hospital, house, prison] visiteur *m*, -euse *f*; you have a ~ vous avez de la visite; they are not allowed any ~s after 10 p.m. ils n'ont pas le droit de recevoir des visiteurs OR des visites après 22 h. -**2.** [guest - at private house] visiteur *m*, -euse *f*, invité *m*, -e *f*; [- at hotel] client *m*, -e *f*; we have ~s on a du monde OR des invités. -**3.** [tourist] visiteur *m*, -euse *f*, touriste *mf*; ~s to the exhibition are requested not to smoke il est demandé aux personnes visitant l'exposition de ne pas fumer; we had 40,000 ~s last year on a eu 40 000 visiteurs l'an dernier; we get lots of American ~s in the town nous avons énormément de visiteurs américains dans la ville. -**4.** ORNITH oiseau *m* passager; this bird is a ~ to these shores cet oiseau est seulement de passage sur ces côtes.
visitors' book *n* [in house, museum] livre *m* d'or; [in hotel] registre *m*.
visitors' gallery *n* tribune *f* du public.
visitor's passport *n* passeport *m* temporaire.
visor, vizor ['vaɪzəʳ] *n* visière *f*.
vista ['vɪstə] *n* -**1.** [view] vue *f*, perspective *f*; a mountain ~ une vue sur les montagnes, une perspective de montagnes. -**2.** *fig* [perspective, horizon] perspective *f*, horizon *m*; [image - of past] vue *f*, vision *f*; [- of future] perspective *f*, vision *f*; to open up new ~s ouvrir de nouvelles perspectives OR de nouveaux horizons.
VISTA ['vɪstə] (*abbr of* Volunteers in Service to America) *pr n programme américain d'aide aux personnes les plus défavorisées*.
visual ['vɪʒʊəl] *adj* -**1.** [gen & OPTICS - image, impression, faculty] visuel; ~ memory mémoire *f* visuelle. -**2.** AERON [landing, navigation] à vue.
◆ **visuals** *npl* supports *mpl* visuels.
visual aid *n* support *m* visuel.
visual arts *npl* arts *mpl* plastiques.
visual display terminal, visual display unit *n* visuel *m*, écran *m* de visualisation.
visual field *n* champ *m* visuel.
visual handicap *n* handicap *m* visuel.
visualization [,vɪʒʊəlaɪ'zeɪʃn] *n* -**1.** [visual presentation] visualisation *f*. -**2.** [imagination] visualisation *f*, évocation *f*.
visualize, -ise ['vɪʒʊəlaɪz] *vt* -**1.** [call to mind - scene] se représenter, évoquer; [imagine] s'imaginer, visualiser, se représenter; I remember the name but I can't ~ his face je me souviens de son nom mais je ne revois plus son visage; he tried to ~ what it would be like il essaya de s'imaginer comment ce serait; she tried to ~ herself travelling through the Amazon elle essayait de se représenter OR s'imaginer en train de traverser l'Amazone. -**2.** [foresee] envisager, prévoir; I can't ~ things getting any better je n'envisage aucune amélioration. -**3.** TECH [make visible] visualiser; MED rendre visible par radiographie.
visually ['vɪʒʊəlɪ] *adv* visuellement.
visually handicapped, visually impaired
◇ *adj* malvoyant, amblyope *spec*.
◇ *npl*: the ~ les malvoyants *mpl*.
vital ['vaɪtl] *adj* -**1.** [essential - information, services, supplies] vital, essentiel, indispensable; the question is of ~ importance la question est d'une importance capitale; this drug is ~ to the success of the operation ce médicament est indispensable au succès de l'opération; it's ~ that I know the truth il est indispensable que je sache la vérité. -**2.** [very important - decision, matter] vital, fondamental; tonight's match is ~ le match de ce soir est décisif. -**3.** BIOL [function, organ] vital; a ~ force une force vitale. -**4.** [energetic] plein d'entrain, dynamique.
◆ **vitals** *npl* -**1.** *hum* OU ANAT organes *mpl* vitaux. -**2.** [essential elements] parties *fpl* essentielles.
vital capacity *n* MED capacité *f* thoracique.
vitality [vaɪ'tælətɪ] *n* vitalité *f*.
vitalize, -ise ['vaɪtəlaɪz] *vt* vivifier, dynamiser.
vitally ['vaɪtəlɪ] *adv* absolument; it's ~ important that you attend this meeting il est extrêmement important OR il est essentiel que vous assistiez à cette réunion; this question is ~ important cette question est d'une importance capitale.
vital statistics *npl* -**1.** [demographic] statistiques *fpl* démographiques. -**2.** *hum* [of woman] mensurations *fpl*.
vitamin [*Br* 'vɪtəmɪn, *Am* 'vaɪtəmɪn] *n* vitamine *f*; ~ C/E vitamine C/E.
vitamin deficiency *n* carence *f* vitaminique.
vitamin pill *n* comprimé *m* de vitamines.
vitiate ['vɪʃɪeɪt] *vt fml* vicier.
viticulture ['vɪtɪkʌltʃəʳ] *n* viticulture *f*.
vitreous ['vɪtrɪəs] *adj* -**1.** [china, rock] vitreux; [enamel] vitrifié. -**2.** ANAT vitré; ~ humour humeur *f* vitrée.
vitrifaction [,vɪtrɪ'fækʃn], **vitrification** [,vɪtrɪfɪ'keɪʃn] *n* vitrification *f*.
vitrify ['vɪtrɪfaɪ] (*pt & pp* vitrified) ◇ *vt* vitrifier.
◇ *vi* se vitrifier.
vitriol ['vɪtrɪəl] *n* CHEM & *fig* vitriol *m*.
vitriolic [,vɪtrɪ'ɒlɪk] *adj* -**1.** CHEM de vitriol. -**2.** [attack, description, portrait] au vitriol; [tone] venimeux.
vitriolize, -ise ['vɪtrɪəlaɪz] *vt* vitrioler.
vittle ['vɪtl] *dial* = **victual**.
vituperate [vɪ'tju:pəreɪt] *lit* ◇ *vt* vitupérer (contre), vilipender.
◇ *vi* vitupérer; to ~ against sthg/sb vitupérer (contre) qqch/qqn.
vituperation [vɪ,tju:pə'reɪʃn] *n (U)* vitupérations *fpl*.
vituperative [vɪ'tju:pərətɪv] *adj* injurieux.
viva[1] ['vi:və] ◇ *interj*: ~! vive!
◇ *n* vivat *m*.
viva[2] ['vaɪvə] = **viva voce** *n*.
vivacious [vɪ'veɪʃəs] *adj* -**1.** [manner, person] enjoué, exubérant. -**2.** BOT vivace.
vivaciously [vɪ'veɪʃəslɪ] *adv* avec vivacité.
vivacity [vɪ'væsətɪ] *n* [in action] vivacité *f*; [in speech] verve *f*.
vivarium [vaɪ'veərɪəm] (*pl* vivariums OR vivaria [-rɪə]) *n* vivarium *m*.
viva voce [,vaɪvə'vəʊsɪ] ◇ *n Br* UNIV [gen] épreuve *f* orale, oral *m*; [for thesis] soutenance *f* de thèse.
◇ *adj* oral.
◇ *adv* de vive voix, oralement.

vivid ['vɪvɪd] *adj* -**1.** [bright - colour, light] vif, éclatant; [- clothes] voyant; ~ green paint peinture d'un vert éclatant. -**2.** [intense - feeling] vif; the book has a ~ sense of place le livre a un sens très vif des lieux. -**3.** [lively - personality] vif, vivant; [- imagination] vif; [- language] coloré; it was a very ~ performance c'était une interprétation pleine de verve. -**4.** [graphic - account, description] vivant; [- memory] vif, net; [- example] frappant; he paints a ~ picture of 18th century life il dresse un tableau très vivant de la vie au XVIIIe siècle.

vividly ['vɪvɪdlɪ] *adv* -**1.** [coloured] de façon éclatante; [painted, decorated] avec éclat, de façon éclatante. -**2.** [describe] de façon frappante OR vivante; I can ~ remember the day we first met j'ai un vif souvenir du jour où nous nous sommes rencontrés.

vividness ['vɪvɪdnɪs] *n* -**1.** [of colour, light] éclat *m*, vivacité *f*. -**2.** [of description, language, style] vivacité *f*; [of memory] clarté *f*; she could remember him with great ~ elle se souvenait très nettement de lui.

vivify ['vɪvɪfaɪ] (*pt* & *pp* vivified) *vt* vivifier.

viviparous [vɪ'vɪpərəs] *adj* vivipare.

vivisect [,vɪvɪ'sekt] *vt* pratiquer la vivisection sur.

vivisection [,vɪvɪ'sekʃn] *n* vivisection *f*.

vivisectionist [,vɪvɪ'sekʃənɪst] *n* -**1.** [practitioner] vivisecteur *m*. -**2.** [advocate] partisan *m*, -e *f* de la vivisection.

vixen ['vɪksn] *n* -**1.** ZOOL renarde *f*. -**2.** *pej* [woman] mégère *f*.

Viyella® [vaɪ'elə] *n* *tissu mélangé (laine et coton)*.

viz [vɪz] (*abbr of* videlicet) c-à-d.

vizier [vɪ'zɪə^r] *n* vizir *m*.

vizor ['vaɪzə^r] = **visor**.

VLF *n* *abbr of* very low frequency.

VLSI *n* COMPUT *abbr of* very large-scale integration.

V-neck ◇ *n* encolure *f* en V.
◇ *adj* = **V-necked**.

V-necked *adj* [pullover] à encolure OR col en V.

VOA (*abbr of* Voice of America) *pr n* *station de radio américaine émettant dans le monde entier*.

vocab *inf* ['vəʊkæb] *n* *abbr of* vocabulary.

vocable ['vəʊkəbl] *n* vocable *m*.

vocabulary [və'kæbjʊlərɪ] (*pl* vocabularies) *n* vocabulaire *m*; LING vocabulaire *m*, lexique *m*.

vocal ['vəʊkl] ◇ *adj* -**1.** ANAT vocal; the ~ organs les organes *mpl* vocaux. -**2.** [oral - communication] oral, verbal. -**3.** [outspoken - person, minority] qui se fait bien entendre; the most ~ member of the delegation le membre de la délégation qui s'est fait le plus entendre OR qui s'est exprimé le plus énergiquement. -**4.** [noisy - assembly, meeting] bruyant. -**5.** MUS vocal. -**6.** LING [sound] vocalique; [consonant] voisé.
◇ *n* LING son *m* vocalique.
◆ **vocals** *npl* MUS chant *m*, musique *f* vocale; Chrissie Webb on ~s chanteuse: Chrissie Webb.

vocal cords *npl* cordes *fpl* vocales; false ~ fausses cordes vocales, bandes *fpl* ventriculaires; true ~ (vraies) cordes vocales.

vocalic [və'kælɪk] *adj* vocalique.

vocalist ['vəʊkəlɪst] *n* chanteur *m*, -euse *f (dans un groupe pop)*.

vocalization [,vəʊkəlaɪ'zeɪʃn] *n* vocalisation *f*.

vocalize, -ise ['vəʊkəlaɪz] ◇ *vt* -**1.** [gen - articulate] exprimer. -**2.** LING [sound] vocaliser. -**3.** [text] vocaliser, marquer des points-voyelles sur.
◇ *vi* MUS vocaliser, faire des vocalises.

vocally ['vəʊkəlɪ] *adv* vocalement.

vocal score *n* partition *f* chorale.

vocation [vəʊ'keɪʃn] *n* [gen & RELIG] vocation *f*; he has no ~ for teaching/acting il n'a pas la vocation de l'enseignement/du théâtre.

vocational [vəʊ'keɪʃənl] *adj* professionnel; ~ course [short] stage *m* de formation professionnelle; [longer] enseignement *m* professionnel; ~ guidance orientation *f* professionnelle; ~ training formation *f* professionnelle.

vocationally [vəʊ'keɪʃnəlɪ] *adv*: ~ oriented à vocation professionnelle; ~ relevant subjects des matières à vocation professionnelle.

vocative ['vɒkətɪv] ◇ *n* GRAMM vocatif *m*; in the ~ au vocatif.
◇ *adj* vocatif; the ~ case le vocatif.

vociferate [vəʊ'sɪfəreɪt] *vi* vociférer, hurler.

vociferous [vəʊ'sɪfərəs] *adj* bruyant, vociférateur.

vociferously [vəʊ'sɪfərəslɪ] *adv* bruyamment, en vociférant.

vocoder [,vəʊ'kəʊdə^r] *n* vocodeur *m*.

vodka ['vɒdkə] *n* vodka *f*.

vogue [vəʊg] ◇ *n* [fashion] vogue *f*, mode *f*; to come into ~ devenir à la mode; that hairstyle was much in ~ in the 1930s cette coiffure était très en vogue OR très à la mode dans les années trente; the ~ for long hair is on the way out les cheveux longs passent de mode; mini skirts are back in ~ les minijupes sont de nouveau à la mode.
◇ *adj* [style, word] en vogue, à la mode.

voice [vɔɪs] ◇ *n* -**1.** [speech] voix *f*; in a low ~ à voix basse; in a loud ~ d'une voix forte; to have a good speaking ~ avoir une bonne voix; we heard the sound of ~s on entendait des gens parler; he likes the sound of his own ~ [talkative] il parle beaucoup; [conceited] il s'écoute parler; to shout at the top of one's ~ crier à tue-tête; to give ~ to sthg exprimer qqch; to hear ~s [gen & RELIG] entendre des voix; keep your ~s down ne parlez pas si fort; to raise one's ~ [speak louder] parler plus fort; [get angry] hausser le ton; don't you raise your ~ at OR to me! ne prenez pas ce ton-là avec moi!; several ~s were raised in protest plusieurs voix se sont élevées pour protester; the ~ of conscience/reason *fig* la voix de la conscience/de la raison; with one ~ d'une seule voix; the government must be seen to speak with one ~ le gouvernement doit donner l'impression qu'il parle d'une seule voix. -**2.** [of singer] voix *f*; to have a good (singing) ~ avoir une belle voix; to be in good ~ être bien en voix. -**3.** [say] voix *f*; did you have a ~ in deciding who should be invited? avez-vous participé à l'élaboration de la liste des invités? -**4.** GRAMM voix *f*; in the active/passive ~ à la voix active/passive.
◇ *vt* -**1.** [express - feelings] exprimer, formuler; [- opposition, support] exprimer. -**2.** LING [consonant] voiser. -**3.** MUS [organ] harmoniser.

voice-activated *adj* à commande vocale.

voice box *n* larynx *m*.

voiced [vɔɪst] *adj* LING [consonant] voisé.

-voiced *in cpds*: low/soft~ à voix basse/douce.

voice input *n* COMPUT commande *f* verbale.

voiceless ['vɔɪslɪs] *adj* -**1.** MED aphone. -**2.** [with no say] sans voix; the ~ masses les masses sans voix OR qui ne peuvent pas s'exprimer. -**3.** LING [consonant] non-voisé, sourd.

voice-over *n* CIN & TV voix *f* off.

voiceprint ['vɔɪsprɪnt] *n* empreinte *f* vocale.

voice recognition *n* COMPUT reconnaissance *f* de la parole.

voice response *n* COMPUT sortie *f* verbale.

voice training *n (U)* MUS cours *mpl* de chant; THEAT cours *mpl* de diction OR d'élocution.

voice vote *n* *Am* POL vote *m* par acclamation.

void [vɔɪd] ◇ *n* -**1.** PHYS & ASTRON vide *m*. -**2.** [chasm] vide *m*. -**3.** [emptiness] vide *m*; to fill a ~ combler un vide; her husband's death left an aching ~ in her life la mort de son mari a laissé un grand vide OR un vide douloureux dans sa vie.
◇ *adj* -**1.** [empty] vide; ~ of interest dépourvu d'intérêt, sans aucun intérêt. -**2.** JUR nul; to make sthg ~ annuler OR rendre nul qqch. -**3.** [vacant - position] vacant.
◇ *vt* -**1.** *fml* [empty] vider; [discharge - bowels] évacuer. -**2.** JUR annuler, rendre nul.

voidance ['vɔɪdəns] *n* JUR annulation *f*.

voile [vɔɪl] *n* voile *m* TEX.

Vojvodina ['vɔɪvɒdiːnə] *pr n* Vojvodine *f*.

vol. (*written abbr of* volume) vol.

volatile [*Br* 'vɒlətaɪl, *Am* 'vɒlətl] ◇ *adj* -**1.** CHEM volatil. -**2.** [person - changeable] versatile, inconstant; [- temperamental] lunatique. -**3.** [unstable - situation] explosif, instable; [- market] instable. -**4.** *lit* [transitory] fugace. -**5.** COMPUT [memory] volatil.
◇ *n* CHEM substance *f* volatile.

volatility [,vɒlə'tɪlətɪ] *n* -**1.** CHEM volatilité *f*. -**2.** [of person - changeability] versatilité *f*, inconstance *f*. -**3.** [of situation, market] instabilité *f*.

volatilize, -ise [vɒ'lætɪlaɪz] ◇ *vt* volatiliser.
◇ *vi* se volatiliser, s'évaporer.

vol-au-vent ['vɒləʊvɑ̃] *n* vol-au-vent *m inv*.

volcanic [vɒl'kænɪk] *adj* volcanique.

volcano [vɒl'keɪnəʊ] (*pl* volcanoes OR volcanos) *n* volcan *m*.

vole [vəʊl] *n* ZOOL campagnol *m*.

Volga ['vɒlgə] *pr n*: the (River) ~ la Volga.

volition [və'lɪʃn] *n* [gen & PHILOS] volition *f*, volonté *f*; of one's own ~ de son propre gré.

volitive ['vɒlɪtɪv] *adj fml* volitif.

volley ['vɒlɪ] ◇ *n* -**1.** [of gunshots] volée *f*, salve *f*; [of arrows, missiles, stones] volée *f*, grêle *f*; [of blows] volée *f*. -**2.** [of insults] grêle *f*, bordée *f*, torrent *m*; [of curses] bordée *f*, torrent *m*; [of questions] feu *m* roulant; [of applause] salve *f*. -**3.** SPORT volée *f*.
◇ *vt* -**1.** [missile, shot] tirer une volée OR une salve de. -**2.** [curses, insults] lâcher une bordée OR un torrent de. -**3.** SPORT reprendre de volée.
◇ *vi* -**1.** MIL tirer par salves. -**2.** SPORT [in tennis] volleyer; [in football] reprendre le ballon de volée.

volleyball ['vɒlɪbɔːl] *n* volley-ball *m*, volley *m*; ~ player volleyeur *m*, -euse *f*.

volt [vəʊlt] *n* volt *m*.

Volta ['vɒltə] *pr n* Volta *f*; the Black ~ la Volta Noire; the White ~ la Volta Blanche.

voltage ['vəʊltɪdʒ] *n* voltage *m*, tension *f spec*; high/low ~ haute/basse tension.

voltaic [vɒl'teɪk] *adj* voltaïque.

voltaic pile *n* pile *f* voltaïque.

voltameter [vɒl'tæmɪtə^r] *n* voltamètre *m*.

volt-ampere *n* voltampère *m*.

volte-face [,vɒlt'fɑːs] *n* volte-face *f inv*; the speech represents a complete ~ ce discours marque un revirement complet.

voltmeter ['vəʊlt,miːtə^r] *n* voltmètre *m*.

volubility [,vɒljʊ'bɪlətɪ] *n* volubilité *f*.

voluble ['vɒljʊbl] *adj* volubile, loquace.

volubly ['vɒljʊblɪ] *adv* avec volubilité.

volume ['vɒljuːm] *n* -**1.** [as measure - gen & PHYS] volume *m*; [capacity] volume *m*, capacité *f*; [amount] volume *m*, quantité *f*; to increase in ~ augmenter de volume; the ~ of traffic has greatly increased le volume de la circulation a beaucoup augmenté; the ~ of business/imports le volume des affaires/des importations. -**2.** ACOUST volume *m*; to turn the ~ up/down augmenter/baisser le volume. -**3.** [book] volume *m*, tome *m*; an encyclopedia in 20 ~s une encyclopédie en 20 volumes; the third ~ of his memoirs le troisième tome OR volume de ses mémoires; a rare ~ un exemplaire OR un livre rare. -**4.** [in hairstyle] volume *m*.

volume control *n* RADIO & TV bouton *m* de réglage du volume.

volumetric [,vɒljʊ'metrɪk] *adj* volumétrique.

voluminous [və'luːmɪnəs] *adj* volumineux.

voluntarily [*Br* 'vɒləntrɪlɪ, *Am* ,vɒlən'terəlɪ] *adv* -**1.** [willingly] volontairement, de son plein gré. -**2.** [without payment] bénévolement.

voluntary ['vɒləntrɪ] (*pl* voluntaries) ◇ *adj* -**1.** [freely given - statement, donation, gift] volontaire, spontané. -**2.** [optional] facultatif; attendance on the course is purely ~ la participation au cours est facultative. -**3.** [unpaid - help, service] bénévole; the shop is run on a ~ basis le personnel du magasin se compose de bénévoles, le magasin est tenu par des bénévoles ☐ ~ shop magasin *m* tenu par des bénévoles. -4. PHYSIOL volontaire.

◇ *n* -1. RELIG & MUS morceau *m* d'orgue. -2. [unpaid work] travail *m* bénévole, bénévolat *m*.

voluntary agency, voluntary body *n* organisme *m* bénévole.

voluntary liquidation *n Br* dépôt *m* de bilan; to go into ~ déposer son bilan.

voluntary manslaughter *n* homicide *m* volontaire.

voluntary redundancy *n Br* licenciement *m* consenti; he decided to take ~ il a accepté d'être licencié en échange d'indemnités.

voluntary school *n* école *f* libre.

Voluntary Service Overseas *n coopération technique à l'étranger (non rémunérée).*

voluntary work *n* travail *m* bénévole, bénévolat *m*.

voluntary worker *n* bénévole *mf*.

volunteer [ˌvɒlənˈtɪəʳ] ◇ *n* -1. [gen & MIL] volontaire *mf*. -2. [unpaid worker] bénévole *mf*.

◇ *comp* -1. [army, group] de volontaires. -2. [work, worker] bénévole.

◇ *vt* -1. [advice, information, statement] donner OR fournir spontanément; [help, services] donner OR proposer volontairement; he ~ed his services as a guide il s'est offert OR s'est proposé comme guide; to ~ to do sthg se proposer pour OR offrir de faire qqch. -2. [say] dire spontanément; "I saw them yesterday" she ~ed «je les ai vus hier» dit-elle spontanément.

◇ *vi* [gen] se porter volontaire; MIL s'engager comme volontaire; to ~ for extra work/guard duty se porter volontaire pour (faire) du travail supplémentaire/pour être de garde; why not ~ for the Marines? pourquoi ne pas vous engager comme volontaire dans la marine?

voluptuary [vəˈlʌptʃʊərɪ] (*pl* **voluptuaries**) *lit*

◇ *n* voluptueux *m*, -euse *f*, sybarite *mf*.

◇ *adj* = **voluptuous**.

voluptuous [vəˈlʌptʃʊəs] *adj* voluptueux, sensuel.

voluptuously [vəˈlʌptʃʊəslɪ] *adv* voluptueusement.

voluptuousness [vəˈlʌptʃʊəsnɪs] *n* volupté *f*, sensualité *f*.

volute [vəˈluːt] *n* volute *f*.

voluted [vəˈluːtɪd] *adj* en volute.

volution [vəˈluːʃn] *n* enroulement *m*.

volva [ˈvɒlvə] (*pl* volvas OR volvae [-viː]) *n* volve *f*.

vomit [ˈvɒmɪt] ◇ *n* vomissement *m*, vomi *m*.

◇ *vt literal* & *fig* vomir; to ~ blood vomir du sang.

◆ **vomit out, vomit up** *vt sep* vomir.

vomiting [ˈvɒmɪtɪŋ] *n (U)* vomissements *mpl*.

voodoo [ˈvuːduː] (*pl* voodoos) ◇ *n* vaudou *m*.

◇ *adj* vaudou *(inv)*.

◇ *vt* envoûter, ensorceler.

voodooism [ˈvuːduːɪzm] *n* vaudou *m*.

voracious [vəˈreɪʃəs] *adj* [appetite, energy, person] vorace; [reader] avide.

voraciously [vəˈreɪʃəslɪ] *adv* [consume, eat] voracement, avec voracité; [read] avec voracité, avidement.

voracity [vɒˈræsətɪ] *n* voracité *f*.

vortex [ˈvɔːteks] (*pl* vortexes OR vortices [-tɪsiːz]) *n* [of water, gas] vortex *m*, tourbillon *m*; *fig* tourbillon *m*, maelström *m*.

Vorticism [ˈvɔːtɪsɪzm] *n* vorticisme *m (mouvement artistique et littéraire, lié au cubisme et au futurisme, fondé en Angleterre vers 1914).*

votary [ˈvəʊtərɪ] (*pl* votaries) *n* RELIG OR *fig* fervent *m*, -e *f*.

vote [vəʊt] ◇ *n* -1. [ballot] vote *m*; to have a ~ on sthg voter sur qqch, mettre qqch au vote; to put a question to the ~ mettre une question au vote OR aux voix; to take a ~ on sthg [gen] voter sur qqch; ADMIN & POL procéder au vote de qqch; if it comes to a OR the ~, I know where I stand s'il est procédé à un vote, je sais quelle est ma position ☐ ~ of thanks discours *m* de remerciement; I propose a ~ of thanks to our charming hostesses je propose que l'on remercie chaleureusement nos charmantes hôtesses. -2. [in parliament] vote *m*, scrutin *m*; 70 MPs were present for the ~ 70 députés étaient présents pour le vote; the ~ went in the government's favour/against the government les députés se sont prononcés en faveur du/contre le gouvernement ☐ free ~ vote libre; ~ of confidence vote de confiance; ~ of no confidence motion *f* de censure. -3. [individual choice] vote *m*, voix *f*; to give one's ~ to sb voter pour qqn; to cast one's ~ voter; to count the ~s [gen] compter les votes OR les voix; POL dépouiller le scrutin; the candidate got 15,000 ~s le candidat a recueilli 15 000 voix; one man, one ~ ≃ suffrage *m* universel. -4. [ballot paper] bulletin *m* de vote. -5. [suffrage] droit *m* de vote; to have the ~ avoir le droit de vote; to give the ~ to sb accorder le droit de vote à qqn; the suffragettes campaigned for ~s for women les suffragettes ont fait campagne pour qu'on accorde le droit de vote aux femmes. -6. *(U)* [collectively - voters] vote *m*, voix *fpl*; [- votes cast] voix *fpl* exprimées; they hope to win the working-class ~ ils espèrent gagner les voix des ouvriers; the Scottish ~ went against the government le vote écossais a été défavorable au gouvernement; they won 40 % of the ~ ils ont remporté 40 % des voix OR des suffrages. -7. *Br* POL [grant] vote *m* de crédits; a ~ of £100,000 un vote de crédits de 100 000 livres.

◇ *vt* -1. [in election] voter; ~ Malone! votez Malone!; to ~ Labour/Republican voter travailliste/républicain; our family have always ~d Conservative notre famille a toujours voté conservateur OR pour le parti conservateur. -2. [in parliament, assembly - motion, law, money] voter; they ~d that the sitting (should) be suspended ils ont voté la suspension de la séance. -3. [elect] élire; [appoint] nommer; she was ~d president elle a été élue présidente. -4. [declare] proclamer; the party was ~d a great success de l'avis de tous, la soirée a été un grand succès. -5. [suggest] proposer; I ~ we all go to bed je propose qu'on aille tous se coucher.

◇ *vi* voter; France is voting this weekend la France va aux urnes ce week-end; how did the country ~? comment est-ce que le pays a voté?; I'm going to ~ for Barron je vais voter (pour) Barron OR donner ma voix à Barron; most of the delegates ~d against the chairman la plupart des délégués ont voté contre le président; I've always ~d in favour of/against military intervention j'ai toujours voté pour/contre l'intervention militaire; the party conference ~d on the question of nuclear disarmament le congrès du parti a voté sur la question du désarmement nucléaire; let's ~ on it! mettons cela aux voix!; to ~ by a show of hands voter à main levée ☐ to ~ with one's feet *Br* partir en signe de désaccord OR pour montrer son désaccord.

◆ **vote down** *vt sep* [bill, proposal] rejeter *(par le vote)*.

◆ **vote in** *vt sep* [person, government] élire; [new law] voter, adopter.

◆ **vote out** *vt sep* [suggestion] rejeter; [minister] relever de ses fonctions; the bill was ~d out le projet de loi n'a pas été adopté OR a été rejeté; the chairman was ~d out (of office) le président n'a pas été réélu.

◆ **vote through** *vt sep* [bill, reform] voter, ratifier.

vote-catcher *n* politique *f* électoraliste.

vote-loser *n* politique *f* qui risque de faire perdre des voix, politique *f* peu populaire.

voter [ˈvəʊtəʳ] *n* électeur *m*, -trice *f*.

voter registration *n* inscription *f* sur les listes électorales.

voting [ˈvəʊtɪŋ] *n* vote *m*, scrutin *m*; ~ takes place on Sunday le scrutin a lieu dimanche, les électeurs vont aux urnes dimanche; nobody knows how the ~ will go personne ne sait comment les gens vont voter.

voting booth *n* isoloir *m*.

voting machine *n Am* machine *f* pour enregistrer les votes.

voting paper *n* bulletin *m* de vote.

votive [ˈvəʊtɪv] *adj* votif.

vouch [vaʊtʃ] *vi*: to ~ for sb/sthg se porter garant de qqn/qqch, répondre de qqn/qqch; he needs somebody to ~ for his honesty il lui faut quelqu'un qui se porte garant de son honnêteté; I can ~ for the truth of her statement je peux attester OR témoigner de la véracité de sa déclaration.

voucher [ˈvaʊtʃəʳ] *n* -1. *Br* [for restaurant, purchase, petrol] bon *m*; when you've collected five ~s, you get a free car wash quand vous avez réuni cinq bons, vous avez droit à un lavage auto gratuit ☐ cash ~ bon *m* de caisse; credit ~ bon *m*; gift ~ bon *m* d'achat. -2. [receipt] reçu *m*, récépissé *m*. -3. JUR pièce *f* justificative.

vouchsafe [vaʊtʃˈseɪf] *vt fml* -1. [grant - help, support] accorder, octroyer; [- answer] accorder; he ~d us no reply il n'a pas daigné nous répondre. -2. [undertake]: to ~ to do sthg [willingly] accepter gracieusement de faire qqch; [reluctantly] condescendre à OR daigner faire qqch.

vow [vaʊ] ◇ *n* -1. [promise] serment *m*, promesse *f*; to make a ~ to do sthg promettre OR jurer de faire qqch; I'm under a ~ of silence j'ai promis de ne rien dire; she took a solemn ~ to return once a year elle a juré solennellement de revenir une fois par an. -2. RELIG vœu *m*; to take one's ~s prononcer ses vœux; to take a ~ of poverty/chastity faire vœu de pauvreté/de chasteté.

◇ *vt* [swear] jurer; to ~ to do sthg jurer de faire qqch; to ~ obedience/secrecy faire vœu d'obéissance/de discrétion; she ~ed never to return OR that she would never return elle s'est juré de ne jamais revenir.

vowel [ˈvaʊəl] ◇ *n* voyelle *f*.

◇ *comp* [harmony, pattern, sound] vocalique.

vowel point *n* point-voyelle *m*.

vowel shift *n* mutation *f* vocalique.

vox pop *inf* [ˌvɒksˈpɒp] *n Br émission de radio ou de TV avec intervention du public.*

vox populi [vɒksˈpɒpjʊlaɪ] *n* vox populi *f inv*.

voyage [ˈvɔɪɪdʒ] ◇ *n* voyage *m*; a transatlantic ~ un voyage OR une traversée transatlantique; to go on a ~ partir en voyage; a round-the-world ~ un voyage autour du monde; a ~ into the unknown un voyage dans l'inconnu; a ~ to Jupiter un voyage vers Jupiter; great ~s of discovery grands voyages d'exploration ☐ 'Voyage to the Centre of the Earth' *Verne* 'Voyage au centre de la terre'.

◇ *vt* NAUT traverser, parcourir.

◇ *vi* -1. NAUT voyager par mer; they ~d across the Atlantic ils ont traversé l'Atlantique; to ~ round the world voyager autour du monde; to ~ across the desert traverser le désert. -2. *Am* AERON voyager par avion.

voyager [ˈvɔɪədʒəʳ] *n* -1. [traveller] voyageur *m*, -euse *f*. -2. [explorer] navigateur *m*, -trice *f*.

voyeur [vwɑːˈjɜːʳ] *n* voyeur *m*, -euse *f*.

voyeurism [vwɑːˈjɜːrɪzm] *n* voyeurisme *m*.

voyeuristic [ˌvɔɪəˈrɪstɪk] *adj* de voyeur.

VP *n abbr of* vice-president.

vroom [vruːm] *interj*: ~! vroom!, vroum!

vs *written abbr of* versus.

V-shaped *adj* en (forme de) V.

V-sign *n*: to give the ~ [for victory, approval] faire le V de la victoire; to give sb a ~ *Br* ≃ faire un bras d'honneur à qqn.

VSO (*abbr of* Voluntary Service Overseas) *n coopération technique à l'étranger (non rémunérée).*

VSOP (*abbr of* very special old pale) VSOP.

VT *written abbr of* Vermont.

VTOL [ˈviːtɒl] (*abbr of* vertical take off and landing) *n* [system] décollage *m* et atterrissage *m* vertical; [plane] ADAV *m*, avion *m* à décollage et atterrissage vertical.

VTR *n abbr of* video tape recorder.

Vulcan ['vʌlkən] *pr n* MYTH Vulcain.

vulcanite ['vʌlkənaɪt] *n* ébonite *f*.

vulcanization [ˌvʌlkənaɪ'zeɪʃn] *n* vulcanisation *f*.

vulcanize, -ise ['vʌlkənaɪz] *vt* vulcaniser.

vulgar ['vʌlgəʳ] *adj* -**1.** [rude] vulgaire, grossier. -**2.** [common - person] vulgaire, commun; [- taste, decor] vulgaire; the ~ tongue la langue commune.

vulgar fraction *n* fraction *f* vulgaire.

vulgarian [vʌl'geərɪən] *n* personne *f* vulgaire.

vulgarism ['vʌlgərɪzm] *n* -**1.** [uneducated language] vulgarisme *m*; [rude word] grossièreté *f*. -**2.** = **vulgarity**.

vulgarity [vʌl'gærətɪ] *n* vulgarité *f*.

vulgarization [ˌvʌlgəraɪ'zeɪʃn] *n* vulgarisation *f*.

vulgarize, -ise ['vʌlgəraɪz] *vt* -**1.** [appearance, language] rendre vulgaire. -**2.** [popularize] vulgariser, populariser.

Vulgar Latin *n* latin *m* vulgaire.

vulgarly ['vʌlgəlɪ] *adv* -**1.** [coarsely] vulgairement, grossièrement. -**2.** [commonly] vulgairement, communément.

Vulgate ['vʌlgeɪt] *n* Vulgate *f*.

vulnerability [ˌvʌlnərə'bɪlətɪ] *n* vulnérabilité *f*.

vulnerable ['vʌlnərəbl] *adj* vulnérable; we are very ~ to attack/criticism nous sommes très vulnérables à l'attaque/à la critique.

vulpine ['vʌlpaɪn] *adj literal* vulpin; *fig* & *lit* sournois.

vulture ['vʌltʃəʳ] *n* ORNITH OR *fig* vautour *m*.

vulva ['vʌlvə] (*pl* **vulvas** OR **vulvae** [-viː]) *n* vulve *f*.

vying ['vaɪɪŋ] *n* rivalité *f*.

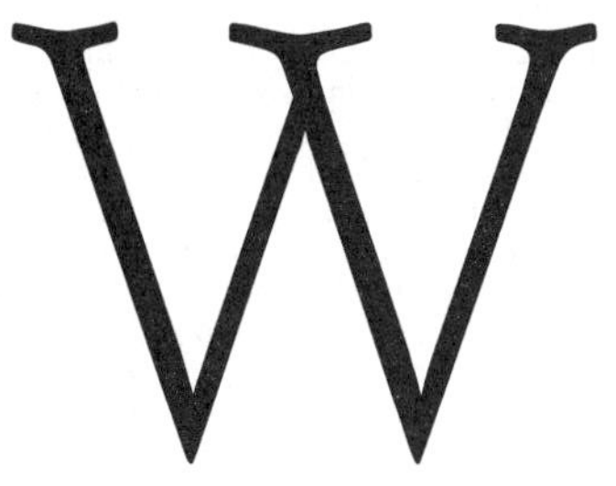

w (*pl* w's OR ws), **W** (*pl* W's OR Ws) ['dʌblju:] *n* [letter] w *m*, W *m*.

W -**1.** (*written abbr of* west) O. -**2.** (*written abbr of* watt) w.

WA -**1.** *written abbr of* Washington (State). -**2.** *written abbr of* Western Australia.

WAAC [wæk] (*abbr of* Women's Army Auxiliary Corps) *pr n* HIST *pendant la deuxième guerre mondiale, section féminine auxiliaire de l'armée de terre britannique*.

WAAF [wæf] (*abbr of* Women's Auxiliary Air Force) *pr n pendant la deuxième guerre mondiale, section féminine auxiliaire de l'armée de l'air britannique*.

wack *inf* ['wæk] *n Br dial*: hiya ~! salut, mon pote!

wacky *inf* ['wækɪ] (*compar* wackier, *superl* wackiest) *adj* cinglé, dingue, farfelu.

wad [wɒd] (*pt* & *pp* wadded, *cont* wadding)
◇ *n* -**1.** [of cotton wool, paper] tampon *m*, bouchon *m*; [of tobacco] chique *f*; [of straw] bouchon *m*; [of gum] boulette *f*; [for cannon, gun] bourre *f*. -**2.** [of letters, documents] liasse *f*, paquet *m*; he pulled out a thick ~ of banknotes il a sorti une grosse liasse de billets.
◇ *vt* -**1.** [cloth, paper] faire un tampon de; [tobacco, chewing gum] faire une boulette de. -**2.** [hole, aperture] boucher (avec un tampon); MIL [barrel, cannon] bourrer. -**3.** [quilt, garment] rembourrer; a wadded jacket une veste ouatée OR doublée d'ouate.

Waddenzee [wædənzeɪ] *pr n*: the ~ la mer des Wadden.

wadding ['wɒdɪŋ] *n* -**1.** MIL [in gun, cartridge] bourre *f*. -**2.** [stuffing - for furniture, packing] rembourrage *m*, capitonnage *m*; [- for clothes] ouate *f*, ouatine *f*.

waddle ['wɒdl] ◇ *vi* [duck, person] se dandiner; to ~ along/in/out avancer/entrer/sortir en se dandinant.
◇ *n* dandinement *m*.

wade [weɪd] ◇ *vi* patauger, avancer en pataugeant; they ~d across the stream ils ont traversé le ruisseau en pataugeant; we ~d into the water nous sommes entrés dans l'eau en pataugeant; she ~d out to the boat elle s'avança dans l'eau vers le bateau.
◇ *vt* [river] passer OR traverser à gué.
◆ **wade in** *vi insep Br* [in fight, quarrel] s'y mettre.
◆ **wade into** *vt insep Br* [work, task] attaquer, s'atteler à, se mettre à; [meal] attaquer, entamer.
◆ **wade through** *vt insep* avancer OR marcher péniblement dans; *fig*: I'm still wading through "War and Peace" je suis toujours aux prises avec «Guerre et paix»; it took me two weeks to ~ through that book il m'a fallu deux semaines pour venir à bout de ce livre; she's got a 100-page report to ~ through elle a un rapport de 100 pages à lire, elle doit se taper un rapport de 100 pages.

wader ['weɪdə^r] *n* échassier *m*.

waders ['weɪdəz] *npl* cuissardes *fpl (de pêcheur)*.

wadge *inf* [wɒdʒ] *n Br* paquet *m*; ~s of notes des liasses de billets.

wadi ['wɒdɪ] *n* oued *m*.

wading ['weɪdɪŋ] *n* pataugeage *m*, barbotage *m*.

wading pool *n Am* petit bassin *m*.

wafer ['weɪfə^r] ◇ *n* -**1.** CULIN gaufrette *f*. -**2.** RELIG hostie *f*. -**3.** [seal] cachet *m* (de papier rouge). -**4.** COMPUT & TECH tranche *f*.
◇ *vt* -**1.** [seal] cacheter (avec du papier rouge). -**2.** COMPUT & TECH diviser en tranches.

wafer-thin, **wafery** ['weɪfərɪ] *adj* mince comme une feuille de papier à cigarette OR comme une pelure d'oignon.

waffle ['wɒfl] ◇ *n* -**1.** CULIN gaufre *f*. -**2.** *inf Br* [spoken] baratin *m*, bla-bla *m inv*; [written] remplissage *m*, baratin *m*; it's just a load of ~ ce n'est que du baratin; cut the ~ and get to the point arrêtez de parler pour ne rien dire et venez-en au fait.
◇ *vi inf* [in speaking] baratiner, parler pour ne rien dire; [in writing] faire du remplissage; he's been waffling away for over an hour cela fait plus d'une heure qu'il raconte son baratin; to ~ on *Br* bavarder, faire des laïus; she's always waffling on about poetry/her children elle n'arrête pas de parler poésie/de ses enfants.

waffle iron *n* gaufrier *m*.

waffler *inf* ['wɒflə^r] *n Br* baratineur *m*, -euse *f*.

waffling *inf* ['wɒflɪŋ] *n Br* [spoken] baratin *m*, bla-bla *m inv*; [written] baratin *m*, remplissage *m*.

waffly *inf* ['wɒflɪ] *adj* [speech, essay] plein de baratin.

waft [wɑ:ft, wɒft] ◇ *vt* [scent, sound] porter, transporter; the breeze ~ed the curtains gently to and fro le vent léger faisait ondoyer les rideaux.
◇ *vi* [scent, sound] flotter; a delicious smell ~ed into the room une délicieuse odeur envahit la pièce; the papers ~ed off the table un souffle d'air emporta les papiers qui étaient sur la table; Vanessa ~ed into/out of the room *fig* Vanessa entra dans/sortit de la pièce d'un pas léger.
◇ *n* [of smoke, air] bouffée *f*.

wag [wæg] (*pt* & *pp* wagged, *cont* wagging)
◇ *vt* [tail] agiter, remuer; the dog wagged its tail enthusiastically le chien agita la queue de contentement; she wagged her finger at him elle le menaça du doigt.
◇ *vi* [tail] remuer, frétiller.
◇ *n* -**1.** [of tail] remuement *m*, frétillement *m*; with a ~ of its tail en agitant OR en remuant la queue. -**2.** *Br* [person] plaisantin *m*, farceur *m*, -euse *f*.

wage [weɪdʒ] ◇ *n* -**1.** [pay - of worker] salaire *m*, paye *f*, paie *f*; [- of servant] gages *mpl*; her wage is OR her ~s are only £100 a week elle ne gagne que 100 livres par semaine; his employers took it out of his ~s ses employeurs l'ont prélevé sur sa paie; a ~s and prices OR a ~-price spiral *Br* une spirale des prix et des salaires. -**2.** [reward] salaire *m*, récompense *f*; the ~s of sin is death BIBLE la mort est le salaire du péché.
◇ *comp* [claim, demand, settlement] salarial; [increase, incentive] de salaire.
◇ *vt*: to ~ war on OR against faire la guerre contre; the government have decided to ~ war on drug trafficking le gouvernement a résolu de partir en guerre contre les trafiquants de drogue; to ~ a campaign for/against sthg faire campagne pour/contre qqch.

wage bargaining *n (U)* négociations *fpl* salariales.

wage earner *n* salarié *m*, -e *f*; they are both ~s ils sont salariés tous les deux, ils ont tous les deux un salaire.

wage freeze *n* blocage *m* des salaires.

wage packet *n Br* paie *f*, paye *f (surtout en espèces)*.

wager ['weɪdʒə^r] *fml* ◇ *vt* parier; I'll ~ £10 that he'll come je parie 10 livres qu'il viendra.
◇ *vi* parier, faire un pari.
◇ *n* pari *m*; to make OR to lay a ~ faire un pari.

wage scale *n* échelle *f* des salaires.

wage slave *n hum*: I'm fed up with being a ~ j'en ai assez d'être obligé de gagner ma vie.

wage slip *n* fiche *f* de paie, bulletin *m* de salaire.

wageworker ['weɪdʒ,wɜ:kə^r] *n Am* salarié *m*, -e *f*.

waggish ['wægɪʃ] *adj* badin, facétieux.

waggishly ['wægɪʃlɪ] *adv* d'un ton badin OR facétieux, facétieusement.

waggle ['wægl] ◇ *vt* [tail] agiter, remuer; [pencil] agiter; [loose tooth, screw] faire jouer; can you ~ your ears/nose? tu sais remuer les oreilles/le nez?
◇ *vi* [tail] bouger, frétiller; [loose tooth, screw] bouger, branler; the knob ~s if you touch it le bouton bouge si on y touche.
◇ *n*: to give sthg a ~ agiter OR remuer qqch.

waggon *etc* ['wægən] *Br* = **wagon**.

Wagner ['vɑ:gnə] *pr n* Wagner.

Wagnerian [vɑ:g'nɪərɪən] ◇ *adj* wagnérien.
◇ *n* wagnérien *m*, -enne *f*.

wagon ['wægən] *n* -**1.** [horse-drawn] chariot *m*. -**2.** [truck, van] camionnette *f*, fourgon *m*; (patrol) ~ *Am* fourgon cellulaire; (station) ~ *Am* break *m*. -**3.** *Br* RAIL wagon *m* (de marchandises). -**4.** *Am* [drinks trolley] chariot *m*. -**5.** *phr*: to be on the ~ *inf* être OR se mettre au régime sec, arrêter de boire.

wagoner ['wægənər] *n* charretier *m*.

wagonette [,wægə'net] *n* break *m* (attelé).

wagonload ['wægənləʊd] *n* AGR charretée *f*; RAIL wagon *m*.

wagon train *n* convoi *m* de chariots *(en particulier de colons américains)*.

wagtail ['wægteɪl] *n* hochequeue *m*, bergeronnette *f*.

Wahhabi [wə'hɑːbɪ] ◇ *adj* wahhabite.
◇ *n* Wahhabite *mf*.

wah-wah ['wɑː,wɑː] *n* & *onomat* effet *m* wah-wah OR wa-wa.

wah-wah pedal *n* pédale *f* wah-wah.

waif [weɪf] *n* [child - neglected] enfant *m* malheureux, enfant *f* malheureuse; [- homeless] enfant *m* abandonné, enfant *f* abandonnée; **~s and strays** [animals] animaux errants.

waiflike ['weɪflaɪk] *adj* frêle.

wail [weɪl] ◇ *vi* -**1.** [person - whine, moan] gémir, pousser des gémissements; [baby - cry] hurler; [- weep] pleurer bruyamment; **that's enough weeping and ~ing!** assez pleuré et gémi comme ça! -**2.** [wind] gémir; [siren] hurler.
◇ *vt* dire en gémissant, gémir; **"you've broken it!" she ~ed** «tu l'as cassé!» gémit-elle.
◇ *n* -**1.** [of person] gémissement *m*; **he gave a loud ~** il poussa un profond gémissement; **"he's gone!" she said with a ~** «il est parti!» dit-elle en gémissant. -**2.** [of wind] gémissement *m*; [of siren] hurlement *m*.

wailing ['weɪlɪŋ] ◇ *n (U)* [of person] gémissements *mpl*, plaintes *fpl*; [of wind] gémissements *mpl*, plainte *f*; [of siren] hurlement *m*, hurlements *mpl*.
◇ *adj* [person] gémissant; [sound] plaintif.

Wailing Wall *pr n*: **the ~** le mur des Lamentations.

wain [weɪn] *n lit* chariot *m (de ferme)*.
◆ **Wain** *pr n* ASTRON: **the Wain** le Grand Chariot, la Grande Ourse.

wainscot ['weɪnskət] *n Br* lambris *m (en bois)*.

wainscotting ['weɪnskətɪŋ] *n Br* lambrissage *m (en bois)*.

wainwright ['weɪnraɪt] *n Br* charron *m*.

waist [weɪst] *n* -**1.** [of person, garment] taille *f*; **he measures 80 cm around the ~, his ~ measures 80 cm** il fait 80 cm de tour de taille, son tour de taille est de 80 cm; **he put his arm around her ~** il l'a prise par la taille; **he was up to the** OR **his ~ in water** l'eau lui arrivait à la ceinture OR à la taille ❑ **~ measurement, ~ size** tour *m* de taille. -**2.** [of ship, plane] partie *f* centrale; [of violin] partie *f* resserrée de la table.

waistband ['weɪstbænd] *n* ceinture *f (d'un pantalon ou d'une jupe)*.

waistcoat ['weɪskəʊt] *n Br* gilet *m (de costume)*.

waist-deep *adj*: **he was ~ in water** l'eau lui arrivait à la ceinture OR à la taille; **the water was ~** l'eau arrivait à la ceinture.

-waisted ['weɪstɪd] *in cpds*: **a low/high~ dress** une robe à taille basse/haute; **to be slim/thick~** avoir la taille fine/épaisse.

waist-high = **waist-deep**.

waistline ['weɪstlaɪn] *n* taille *f*; **to watch one's ~** surveiller sa ligne.

wait [weɪt] ◇ *vi* -**1.** [person, bus, work] attendre; **I've been ~ing for half an hour/since Easter** j'attends depuis une demi-heure/depuis Pâques; **just you ~!** [as threat] tu vas voir ce que tu vas voir!, tu ne perds rien pour attendre!; **we'll just have to ~ and see** on verra bien; **he didn't ~ to be told twice** il ne se l'est pas fait dire deux fois; **letters ~ing to be delivered** lettres en souffrance ADMIN OR qui attendent d'être distribuées; **to keep sb ~ing** faire attendre qqn; **you shouldn't keep people ~ing** vous ne devriez pas vous faire attendre OR faire attendre les gens; **they do it while you ~** ils le font devant vous; **'repairs while you ~'** 'réparations minute'; **'keys cut while you ~'** 'clés minute' ❑ **everything comes to him who ~s** *prov* tout vient à point à qui sait attendre *prov*. -**2.** [with 'can']: **it can ~** cela peut attendre; **he can ~** laisse-le attendre; **I can't ~!** *iron* je brûle d'impatience!; **it can't ~** cela ne peut pas attendre, c'est très urgent; **I can hardly ~ to see them again** j'ai hâte de les revoir; **I can't ~ for the weekend to arrive** j'attends le week-end avec impatience!, vivement le week-end! -**3.** [with 'until' or 'till']: **~ until I've finished** attendez que j'aie fini; **~ until the film is over** attendez la fin du film; **you'll have to ~ until you're old enough** il va falloir attendre que tu sois plus grand; **can't that ~ until tomorrow?** cela ne peut pas attendre jusqu'à demain?; **just ~ till your parents hear about it** attends un peu que tes parents apprennent cela. -**4.** [serve] servir, faire le service; **to ~ at table** *Br* OR **on table** *Am* servir à table, faire le service.
◇ *vt* -**1.** [period of time] attendre; **I ~ed half an hour** j'ai attendu (pendant) une demi-heure; **I ~ed all day for the repairman to come** j'ai passé toute la journée à attendre le réparateur; **~ a minute!** (attendez) une minute OR un instant!; **~ your turn!** attendez votre tour! -**2.** *Am* [delay]: **don't ~ dinner for me** ne m'attendez pas pour vous mettre à table. -**3.** *Am* [serve at]: **to ~ tables** servir à table, faire le service.
◇ *n* attente *f*; **we had a long ~** nous avons dû attendre (pendant) longtemps; **she had a half hour** OR **half hour's ~ at Gatwick** il a fallu qu'elle attende une demi-heure OR elle a eu une demi-heure d'attente à Gatwick; **there was an hour's ~ between trains** il y avait une heure de battement OR d'attente entre les trains; **to lie in ~ for** être à l'affût de, guetter; **the foxes lay in ~ for the hares** les renards étaient à l'affût des lièvres; **the gunmen were lying in ~ for the convoy** les bandits guettaient l'arrivée du convoi; **the detective was lying in ~ for her outside her house** [arrival] le détective guettait son arrivée à la maison; [departure] le détective guettait son départ de la maison.
◆ **waits** *npl Br* MUS chanteurs *mpl* de Noël.
◆ **wait about** *vi insep Br* traîner, faire le pied de grue; **to ~ about for sb** attendre qqn, faire le pied de grue en attendant qqn; **I can't stand all this ~ing about** cela m'énerve d'être obligé d'attendre OR de traîner comme ça; **I can't ~ about all evening until he comes home** je ne peux pas traîner toute la soirée à attendre qu'il rentre.
◆ **wait around** = **wait about**.
◆ **wait behind** *vi insep* rester; **to ~ behind for sb** rester pour attendre qqn; **they ~ed behind after the meeting** ils sont restés après la réunion.
◆ **wait for** *vt insep*: **to ~ for sb/sthg** attendre qqn/qqch; **I'm ~ing for the children/the next train** j'attends les enfants/le prochain train; **I'm ~ing for the bank to open/the workmen to arrive** j'attends que la banque soit ouverte/que les ouvriers arrivent, j'attends l'ouverture de la banque/l'arrivée des ouvriers; **~ for the signal** attendez le signal; **that was worth ~ing for** cela valait la peine d'attendre; **what are you ~ing for?** qu'est-ce que vous attendez?; **~ for it!** *Br hum* tiens-toi bien! ❑ **'Waiting for Godot'** *Beckett* 'En attendant Godot'.
◆ **wait in** *vi insep* rester à la maison; **I ~ed in all evening for her** je suis resté chez moi toute la soirée à l'attendre.
◆ **wait on** *vt insep* -**1.** [serve]: **I'm not here to ~ on you!** [male] je ne suis pas ton serviteur!; [female] je ne suis pas ta servante OR ta bonne! ❑ **to ~ on sb hand and foot** être aux petits soins pour qqn; **he expects to be ~ed on hand and foot** il veut que tout le monde soit à son service OR à ses petits soins. -**2.** *Am* [in restaurant]: **to ~ on tables** faire le service, servir à table.
◆ **wait out** *vt sep* [concert, film] rester jusqu'à la fin OR jusqu'au bout de, attendre la fin de.
◆ **wait up** *vi insep* -**1.** [at night] rester debout, veiller; **I'll be late so don't ~ up (for me)** je rentrerai tard, ne veillez pas pour moi OR couchez-vous sans m'attendre; **her parents always ~ up for her** ses parents ne se couchent jamais avant qu'elle soit rentrée OR attendent toujours qu'elle rentre pour se coucher; **the children were allowed to ~ up until midnight** on a permis aux enfants de veiller jusqu'à minuit. -**2.** *inf Am* [wait]: **hey, ~ up!** attendez-moi!
◆ **wait upon** = **wait on 1**.

waiter ['weɪtər] *n* serveur *m*, garçon *m*; **~!** s'il vous plaît!, monsieur!

waiting ['weɪtɪŋ] ◇ *n* attente *f*; **after two hours of ~** après deux heures d'attente, après avoir attendu deux heures; **this ~ is nerve-wracking** c'est angoissant d'avoir à attendre, cette attente est angoissante; **'no ~'** 'stationnement interdit'; **to be in ~ on sb** être au service de qqn.
◇ *adj* -**1.** [person, taxi] qui attend. -**2.** [period] d'attente.

waiting game *n*: **to play a ~** *fig* jouer la montre, attendre son heure; MIL & POL mener une politique d'attentisme.

waiting list *n* liste *f* d'attente.

waiting room *n* [for clients, patients] salle *f* d'attente; [in airport, station] salle *f* des pas perdus, salle *f* d'attente.

waitress ['weɪtrɪs] *n* serveuse *f*; **~!** s'il vous plaît!, mademoiselle!

wait state *n* COMPUT état *m* d'attente.

waive [weɪv] *vt* [condition, requirement] ne pas insister sur, abandonner; [law, rule] déroger à; [claim, right] renoncer à, abandonner.

waiver ['weɪvər] *n* [of condition, requirement] abandon *m*; [of law, rule] dérogation *f*; [of claim, right] renonciation *f*, abandon *m*; **full-collision ~** *Am* assurance *f* tous risques.

wake [weɪk] (*pt* **woke** [wəʊk] OR **waked**, *pp* **woken** ['wəʊkn] OR **waked**) ◇ *vi* -**1.** [stop sleeping] se réveiller, s'éveiller; **the baby woke at six** le bébé s'est réveillé à 6 h; **I woke with a start** je me suis réveillé en sursaut; **he woke to the news that war had broken out** à son réveil OR en se réveillant, il a appris que la guerre avait éclaté; **they woke to find themselves famous** du jour au lendemain, ils se sont retrouvés célèbres. -**2.** = **wake up** *vi insep* **2**.
◇ *vt* -**1.** [rouse from sleep] réveiller, tirer OR sortir du sommeil; **~ me at seven** réveillez-moi à 7 h; **the noise was enough to ~ the dead** il y avait un bruit à réveiller les morts. -**2.** [arouse - curiosity, jealousy] réveiller, éveiller, exciter; [- memories] réveiller, éveiller, ranimer. -**3.** [alert] éveiller l'attention de.
◇ *n* -**1.** [vigil] veillée *f* (mortuaire); **'Finnegan's Wake'** *Joyce* 'Finnegan's Wake'. -**2.** [of ship] sillage *m*, eaux *fpl*; *fig* sillage *m*; **famine followed in the ~ of the drought** la famine a suivi la sécheresse; **he always brings trouble in his ~** il amène toujours des ennuis (dans son sillage); **in the ~ of the storm** après l'orage. -**3.** = **wakes**.
◆ **wakes** *n* OR *npl* [in Northern England]: **~s week** *la semaine de congé annuel (dans le Nord de l'Angleterre)*.
◆ **wake up** ◇ *vi insep* -**1.** [stop sleeping] se réveiller, s'éveiller; **~ up!** réveille-toi!; **they woke up to find themselves famous** du jour au lendemain, ils se sont retrouvés célèbres. -**2.** [become alert] se réveiller, prendre conscience; **~ up and get down to work!** mais enfin réveille-toi OR remue-toi OR secoue-toi et mets-toi au travail!; **it's time you woke up to the truth** il est temps que tu regardes la vérité en face.
◇ *vt sep* -**1.** [rouse from sleep] réveiller, tirer OR sortir du sommeil; **~ me up at seven** réveillez-moi à 7 h. -**2.** [alert] réveiller, secouer; **a little exercise will ~ you up!** un peu d'exercice va vous réveiller!; **the accident woke us up to the dangers of nuclear power** l'accident a attiré OR éveillé notre attention sur les dangers de l'énergie nucléaire.

wakeful ['weɪkfʊl] *adj* -**1.** [person - unable to sleep] qui ne dort pas, éveillé; [- alert] vigilant. -**2.** [night, week] sans sommeil; **I had** OR **I spent a ~ night** j'ai passé une nuit blanche.

wakefulness ['weɪkfʊlnɪs] *n* [sleeplessness] insomnie *f*; [alertness] vigilance *f*.

waken ['weɪkən] *lit* ◇ *vi* se réveiller, s'éveiller; to ~ from sleep se réveiller, s'éveiller, sortir du sommeil.
◇ *vt* réveiller, tirer OR sortir du sommeil.

wake-up call *n* réveil *m* téléphonique.

wakey wakey *inf* [,weɪkɪ'weɪkɪ] *interj Br*: ~! réveille-toi!, debout!

waking ['weɪkɪŋ] ◇ *adj* [hours] de veille; she spends her ~ hours reading elle passe tout son temps à lire; a ~ dream une rêverie, une rêvasserie.
◇ *n* [state] (état *m* de) veille *f*.

waky waky *inf* [,weɪkɪ'weɪkɪ] = **wakey wakey**.

Waldorf salad ['wɔːldɔːf-] *n salade composée de pommes, de céleri et de noix, assaisonnée avec de la mayonnaise*.

wale [weɪl] *n* zébrure *f*, marque *f* de coup.

Wales [weɪlz] *pr n* pays *m* de Galles; in ~ au pays de Galles.

walk [wɔːk] ◇ *vi* -**1.** marcher; [go for a walk] se promener; ~, don't run! ne cours pas!; he ~ed along the beach il marchait OR se promenait le long de la plage; we ~ed down/up the street nous avons descendu/monté la rue à pied; they ~ed through the park ils ont traversé le parc à pied; he ~ed slowly towards the door il s'est dirigé lentement vers la porte; she ~ed back and forth elle marchait de long en large, elle faisait les cent pas; let's ~ a little si nous marchions un peu?; ~ with me to the shop accompagnez-moi au magasin; he ~s in his sleep il est somnambule; he ~ed downstairs in his sleep il a descendu l'escalier en dormant; to ~ on one's hands marcher sur les mains, faire l'arbre fourchu; you have to ~ before you can run *fig* il faut apprendre petit à petit ❑ I'm ~ing on air! je suis aux anges!; he's ~ing tall *Am* il marche la tête haute. -**2.** [as opposed to drive, ride] aller à pied; I ~ to work je vais au travail à pied; did you ~ all the way? avez-vous fait tout le chemin à pied?; is it too far to ~? est-ce trop loin pour y aller à pied?
◇ *vt* -**1.** [cover on foot] faire à pied; we ~ 3 km a day nous faisons 3 km (de marche) à pied par jour; you can ~ it in 10 minutes il faut 10 minutes (pour y aller) à pied; she ~s this road every day elle passe à pied par cette rue tous les jours; to ~ the streets [wander] se promener dans les rues; [looking for something] arpenter les rues, battre le pavé; [as prostitute] faire le trottoir; to ~ a beat [policeman] faire sa ronde; to ~ a tightrope *literal* marcher sur la corde raide; *fig* être sur la corde raide. -**2.** [escort] accompagner, marcher avec; I'll ~ you to the station je vais vous accompagner (à pied) à la gare; may I ~ you home? puis-je vous raccompagner? -**3.** [take for walk - person] faire marcher; [- dog] promener; [- horse] conduire à pied; his friend ~ed him up and down the room son ami l'a fait marcher en long et en large dans la pièce; she ~ed her mother round the garden elle a fait faire un tour de jardin à sa mère; they ~ed him forcibly to the door ils l'ont dirigé de force vers la porte; she ~ed the bike up the hill elle a poussé le vélo pour monter la colline ❑ she ~ed me off my feet *inf Br* elle m'a fait tellement marcher que je ne tiens plus debout.
◇ *n* -**1.** [movement]: she slowed to a ~ elle a ralenti et s'est mise à marcher; they moved along at a brisk ~ ils marchaient d'un pas rapide. -**2.** [stroll] promenade *f*; [long] randonnée *f*; to go for OR to take a ~ aller se promener, faire une promenade OR un tour; we had a long ~ through the woods nous avons fait une grande promenade OR balade en forêt; it'll be a nice ~ for you cela vous fera une belle promenade; I take a 5 km ~ each day je fais chaque jour une promenade de 5 km; it's a long ~ to the office ça fait loin pour aller à pied au bureau; the station is a five-minute ~ from here la gare est à cinq minutes de marche OR à cinq minutes à pied d'ici; I took my mother for a ~ j'ai emmené ma mère en promenade OR faire un tour; did you take the dog for a ~? as-tu promené OR sorti le chien? ❑ take a ~! *inf Am* dégage! -**3.** [gait] démarche *f*, façon *f* de marcher; you'll recognize her from her ~ tu la reconnaîtras à sa démarche OR à sa façon de marcher OR à la façon dont elle marche; his ~ reminds me of Groucho Marx quand il marche, il me fait penser à Groucho Marx. -**4.** [path] promenade *f*; [in garden] allée *f*; [in forest] sentier *m*, chemin *m*; a coastal ~ un chemin côtier; the front ~ *Am* l'allée *f (de devant la maison)*. -**5.** [occupation]: we meet people from all ~s OR from every ~ of life nous rencontrons des gens de tous milieux. -**6.** *Am* [sidewalk] trottoir *m*.

◆ **walk about** *vi insep Br* se promener, se balader.

◆ **walk across** ◇ *vi insep* traverser (à pied).
◇ *vt sep* faire traverser (à pied).

◆ **walk around** = **walk about**.

◆ **walk away** *vi insep* partir, s'en aller; she ~ed away from the group elle s'est éloignée du groupe, elle a quitté le groupe; he ~ed away from the accident il est sorti de l'accident indemne; you can't just ~ away from the situation tu ne peux pas te désintéresser comme ça de la situation.

◆ **walk away with** *vt insep*: to ~ away with sthg *literal* emporter qqch; *fig* remporter OR gagner qqch haut la main; she ~ed away with all the credit c'est elle qui a reçu tous les honneurs.

◆ **walk back** ◇ *vi insep* [return] revenir OR retourner (à pied).
◇ *vt sep* raccompagner (à pied).

◆ **walk in** ◇ *vi insep* entrer; she ~ed in and started complaining elle est entrée et a commencé à se plaindre; we ~ed in on her as she was getting dressed nous sommes entrés sans prévenir pendant qu'elle s'habillait.
◇ *vt sep* faire entrer.

◆ **walk into** *vt insep* -**1.** [enter - house, room] entrer dans; [- job] obtenir (sans problème); [- situation] se retrouver dans; [- trap] tomber dans; you ~ed right into that one! *inf* tu es vraiment tombé dans le panneau! -**2.** [bump into - chair, wall] se cogner à, rentrer dans; [- person] rentrer dans.

◆ **walk off** ◇ *vi insep* partir, s'en aller.
◇ *vt sep* [get rid of - headache] faire passer en marchant; [- weight] perdre en faisant de la marche.

◆ **walk off with** *vt insep*: to ~ off with sthg [take] emporter qqch; [steal] voler qqch; he ~ed off with all the prizes il a remporté OR gagné tous les prix (haut la main).

◆ **walk out** *vi insep* -**1.** [go out] sortir; [leave] partir, s'en aller; we ~ed out of the meeting nous avons quitté la réunion OR nous sommes partis de la réunion (en signe de protestation). -**2.** [worker] se mettre en grève. -**3.** *Br dated* [court]: to ~ out with sb faire la cour à qqn, courtiser qqn.

◆ **walk out on** *vt insep* [family, lover] quitter.

◆ **walk over** ◇ *vt insep* [bridge] traverser; don't let them ~ all over you *fig* ne vous laissez pas avoir, ne vous laissez pas marcher sur les pieds.
◇ *vi insep* aller, faire un saut; I'll ~ over to her place tomorrow je ferai un saut OR je passerai chez elle demain; the boss ~ed over to congratulate him le patron s'est approché de lui pour le féliciter.

◆ **walk up** *vi insep* -**1.** [go upstairs] monter. -**2.** [come close] s'approcher; a complete stranger ~ed up to her un inconnu s'est approché d'elle.

walkable ['wɔːkəbl] *adj*: it's ~ on peut y aller à pied.

walkabout ['wɔːkə,baʊt] *n* -**1.** *Br*: to go on a ~ [actor, politician] prendre un bain de foule. -**2.** [of an Aborigine] *excursion périodique dans la brousse*.

walkaway *inf* ['wɔːkə,weɪ] *n Am*: the race was a ~ for him il a gagné la course haut la main OR dans un fauteuil.

walker ['wɔːkəʳ] *n* -**1.** [person - stroller] promeneur *m*, -euse *f*, marcheur *m*, -euse *f*; [- in mountains] randonneur *m*, -euse *f*; SPORT marcheur *m*, -euse *f*; are you a keen ~? êtes-vous bon marcheur?, aimez-vous la marche?; she's a fast/slow ~ elle marche vite/lentement. -**2.** [apparatus - for babies] trotte-bébé *m*; [- for invalids] déambulateur *m*.

walkies *inf* ['wɔːkɪz] *n Br*: (let's go) ~! allez, on va se promener!

walkie-talkie [,wɔːkɪ'tɔːkɪ] *n* (poste *m*) émetteur-récepteur *m* portatif, talkie-walkie *m*.

walk-in *adj* -**1.** [safe, wardrobe] de plain-pied; ~ cupboard [gen] débarras *m*; [for clothes] dressing *m*. -**2.** *inf Am* [victory] facile.

walking ['wɔːkɪŋ] ◇ *n* -**1.** [activity - gen] marche *f* (à pied), promenade *f*, promenades *fpl*; [- hiking] randonnée *f*; SPORT marche *f* (athlétique). -**2.** [in basketball] marcher *m*.
◇ *adj* [clothing, shoes] de marche; is it within ~ distance? est-ce qu'on peut y aller à pied?; a ~ holiday in the Vosges un séjour de randonnée dans les Vosges; we went on a ~ tour of the Alps nous avons fait de la randonnée dans les Alpes; the ~ wounded les blessés qui peuvent encore marcher; he's a ~ dictionary *hum* c'est un vrai dictionnaire ambulant.

walking frame *n* déambulateur *m*.

walking papers *inf npl Am*: to hand OR to give sb their ~ [employee] renvoyer qqn, mettre OR flanquer qqn à la porte; [lover] plaquer qqn; to get one's ~ se faire mettre à la porte.

walking race *n* épreuve *f* de marche.

walking shoes *n* chaussures *fpl* de marche.

walking stick *n* canne *f*.

Walkman® ['wɔːkmən] (*pl* Walkmans) *n* baladeur *m offic*, Walkman® *m*.

walk-on ◇ *n* rôle *m* de figurant.
◇ *comp*: ~ part rôle *m* de figurant.

walkout ['wɔːkaʊt] *n* [of members, spectators] départ *m* (en signe de protestation); [of workers] grève *f*; to stage a ~ [negotiators, students] partir (en signe de protestation); [workers] se mettre en grève.

walkover ['wɔːk,əʊvəʳ] *n* -**1.** *inf Br* [victory] victoire *f* dans un fauteuil; the race was a ~ for the German team l'équipe allemande a gagné la course haut la main OR dans un fauteuil. -**2.** [in horse racing] walk-over *m inv*.

walk-through *n* THEAT répétition *f*.

walk-up *Am* ◇ *adj* [apartment] situé dans un immeuble sans ascenseur; [building] sans ascenseur.
◇ *n appartement ou bureau situé dans un immeuble sans ascenseur*; [building] *immeuble sans ascenseur*; they live in a fifth-floor ~ ils habitent au quatrième étage sans ascenseur.

walkway ['wɔːkweɪ] *n* [path] sentier *m*, chemin *m*; [passage] passage *m* OR passerelle *f (pour piétons, entre deux bâtiments)*.

walky-talky [,wɔːkɪ'tɔːkɪ] (*pl* walky-talkies) = **walkie-talkie**.

wall [wɔːl] ◇ *n* -**1.** [of building, room] mur *m*; [round field, garden] mur *m* de clôture; [round castle, city] murs *mpl*, murailles *fpl*, remparts *mpl*; the city ~s of Langres les remparts OR murs de Langres; within the city ~s dans les murs, dans la ville, intra-muros; the Great Wall of China la Grande Muraille de Chine; a ~ of fire une muraille de feu; the prisoners went over the ~ les prisonniers se sont évadés; a ~ of silence *fig* un mur de silence ❑ our backs are to the ~ *inf* nous sommes le dos au mur OR acculés; to drive OR to send sb up the ~ *inf* rendre qqn fou OR dingue; to go to the ~ *Br* [business] faire faillite; [employee] perdre la partie; I'll go up the ~ if I have to work with her *inf* je vais devenir fou si je dois travailler avec elle; ~s have ears les murs ont des oreilles. -**2.** [side - of box, cell, vein] paroi *f*; [- of tyre] flanc *m*. -**3.** [of mountain] paroi *f*, face *f*.
◇ *vt* [garden, land] clôturer, entourer d'un mur; [city] fortifier; ~ed garden jardin *m* clos.

◆ **wall in** *vt sep* [garden] clôturer, entourer d'un mur; she felt ~ed in by social convention *fig* elle se sentait prisonnière des convenances.

◆ **wall off** *vt sep* séparer par un mur OR par une cloison.

◆ **wall up** *vt sep* [door, window] murer, condamner; [body, treasure] emmurer.

wallaby ['wɒləbɪ] (*pl* wallabies) *n* wallaby *m*.

wallah *inf* ['wɒlə] *n dated* OR *hum* préposé *m*.

wall bars *npl* espalier *m (pour exercices)*.

wallboard ['wɔːlbɔːd] *n* plaque *f* de plâtre.

wall bracket *n* support *m* mural.

wallchart ['wɔːltʃɑːt] *n* panneau *m* mural.

wall cupboard *n* placard *m* mural.

wallet ['wɒlɪt] *n* portefeuille *m*.

walleye ['wɔːlˌaɪ] *n* -**1.** [squint] strabisme *m*; to have a ~ loucher, avoir un strabisme. -**2.** [eye] œil *m* vairon.

walleyed ['wɔːlˌaɪd] *adj* -**1.** [person] qui louche. -**2.** [eyes] aux yeux vairons.

wallflower ['wɔːlˌflaʊəʳ] *n* -**1.** BOT giroflée *f*. -**2.** *inf* [person]: I'm tired of being a ~ j'en ai assez de faire tapisserie.

wall game *n sorte de football pratiqué à Eton*.

wall hanging *n* tenture *f* murale.

Wallis and Futuna Islands ['wɒlɪsnfuːˌtjuːnə-] *pl pr n*: the ~ Wallis-et-Futuna; in the ~ à Wallis-et-Futuna.

wall lamp, wall light *n* applique *f (lampe)*.

wall lighting *n* éclairage *m* par appliques.

Walloon [wɒ'luːn] ◇ *n* -**1.** [person] Wallon *m*, -onne *f*. -**2.** LING wallon *m*.
◇ *adj* wallon.

wallop *inf* ['wɒləp] ◇ *vt* -**1.** [hit - person] flanquer un coup à, cogner sur; [- ball] taper sur, donner un grand coup dans; she ~ed him on the jaw elle lui a flanqué son poing sur la figure; ~ him one! fiche-lui une beigne! -**2.** [defeat] écraser, battre à plate couture.
◇ *n* -**1.** [blow] beigne *f*, coup *m*; he packs a real ~ il a du punch. -**2.** [impact]: she fell down with a ~ et vlan! elle est tombée par terre. -**3.** ▽ *Br* [beer] bière *f*.
◇ *adv Br*: to run ~ into sthg rentrer en plein dans qqch.

walloping *inf* ['wɒləpɪŋ] ◇ *adj* énorme, phénoménal.
◇ *adv* vachement.
◇ *n* -**1.** [beating] raclée *f*, rossée *f*; his mother gave him a good ~ sa mère lui a flanqué une rossée. -**2.** [defeat]: they gave our team a ~ ils ont écrasé notre équipe, ils ont battu notre équipe à plate couture.

wallow ['wɒləʊ] ◇ *vi* -**1.** [roll about] se vautrer, se rouler. -**2.** [indulge] se vautrer, se complaire; to ~ in misery se complaire dans la tristesse; to ~ in self-pity s'apitoyer sur soi-même. -**3.** NAUT être ballotté.
◇ *n* -**1.** [mud] boue *f*, bourbe *f*; [place] mare *f* bourbeuse. -**2.** *inf* [act of wallowing]: to have a good ~ [in a bath] prendre un bon bain; [in self-pity] s'apitoyer sur soi-même.

wall painting *n* peinture *f* murale.

wallpaper ['wɔːlˌpeɪpəʳ] ◇ *n* papier *m* peint.
◇ *vt* tapisser (de papier peint).

wallposter ['wɔːlˌpəʊstəʳ] *n* affiche *f* murale.

wall socket *n* prise *f* murale.

Wall Street *pr n* Wall Street; the ~ Crash le krach de Wall Street.

THE WALL STREET CRASH:
Krach financier à la Bourse de New York le 24 octobre 1929 («jeudi noir»). Il entraîna la ruine de plusieurs milliers de personnes, acculant même certains au suicide. Cet événement est considéré comme le point de départ de la crise économique qu'allaient vivre les États-Unis pendant dix ans (la grande dépression).

---

wall-to-wall *adj*: ~ carpet OR carpeting moquette *f*; ~ sound son enveloppant.

wall unit *n* élément *m* mural.

wally *inf* ['wɒlɪ] (*pl* wallies) *n Br* imbécile *mf*, andouille *mf*.

walnut ['wɔːlnʌt] ◇ *n* [tree, wood] noyer *m*; [fruit] noix *f*.
◇ *comp* [furniture] de OR en noyer; [oil] de noix; [cake] aux noix.

walrus ['wɔːlrəs] (*pl inv* OR walruses) *n* morse *m*; ~ moustache moustache *f* à la gauloise.

waltz [wɔːls] ◇ *n* valse *f*.
◇ *vi* -**1.** [dancer] valser, danser une valse. -**2.** [move] danser; she ~ed in/out of his office [jauntily] elle est entrée dans/sortie de son bureau d'un pas joyeux; [brazenly] elle est entrée dans/sortie de son bureau avec effronterie; he ~ed right up to the boss il s'est approché du patron sans hésitation; to ~ off partir, s'en aller; he ~ed off with her purse il lui a volé son sac à main; they ~ed off with first prize ils ont remporté le premier prix haut la main.
◇ *vt* -**1.** [dance] valser avec, faire valser; he ~ed her round the room il s'est mis à valser OR danser avec elle à travers la chambre. -**2.** [propel] pousser, propulser.

Walworth Road ['wɒlwəθ-] *pr n rue de Londres où se trouve le siège du parti travailliste*.

wampum ['wɒmpəm] *n* *(U)* -**1.** [beads] *colliers faits de coquilles (servant d'argent ou de décoration)*. -**2.** *inf Am* [money] pognon *m*.

wan [wɒn] (*compar* wanner, *superl* wannest) *adj* [person - pale] pâle, blême, blafard; [- sad] triste; [smile] pâle, faible; [light, star] pâle.

WAN [wæn] *n abbr of* wide area network.

wand [wɒnd] *n* [of fairy, magician] baguette *f* (magique).

wander ['wɒndəʳ] ◇ *vi* -**1.** [meander - person] errer, flâner; [- stream] serpenter, faire des méandres; she ~ed into a café elle est entrée dans un café d'un pas nonchalant; we ~ed round the town nous avons flâné en ville, nous nous sommes promenés au hasard dans la ville; her eyes ~ed over the crowd elle a promené son regard sur la foule. -**2.** [stray - person] s'égarer; he's ~ed off somewhere il est parti mais il n'est pas loin; the tourists ~ed into the red light district les touristes se sont retrouvés par hasard dans le quartier chaud; don't ~ off the path ne vous écartez pas du chemin. -**3.** [mind, thoughts] vagabonder, errer; the speaker ~ed off the topic le conférencier s'est écarté du sujet; her attention began to ~ elle commença à être de moins en moins attentive; I can't concentrate, my mind keeps ~ing je ne peux pas me concentrer, je suis trop distrait; my mind ~ed back to when we first met mes pensées se sont reportées à l'époque où nous nous sommes connus; her thoughts ~ed to her holiday plans sa pensée erra sur ses projets de vacances. -**4.** [become confused] divaguer, déraisonner; her mother's mind OR her mother has begun to ~ sa mère commence à divaguer.
◇ *vt* errer dans, parcourir (au hasard); their children ~ the streets at night leurs enfants errent dans les rues OR courent les rues le soir; the nomads ~ the desert les nomades parcourent le désert; he spent his life ~ing the world il a passé sa vie à parcourir le monde.
◇ *n* promenade *f*, tour *m*; we went for a ~ round the town nous sommes allés faire un tour OR nous nous sommes promenés dans la ville.

◆ **wander about** *Br*, **wander around** *vi insep* [without destination] errer, aller sans but; [without hurrying] flâner, aller sans se presser.

wanderer ['wɒndərəʳ] *n* vagabond *m*, -e *f*; she's a bit of a ~ *fig* elle n'aime pas trop se fixer.

wandering ['wɒndərɪŋ] ◇ *adj* -**1.** [roaming - person] errant, vagabond; [- tribe] nomade; [- stream] qui serpente, qui fait des méandres; ~ minstrels ménestrels *mpl*; the Wandering Jew le Juif errant. -**2.** [distracted - mind, thoughts, attention] distrait, vagabond. -**3.** [confused - mind, person] qui divague, qui délire; [- thoughts] incohérent.
◇ *n* -**1.** [trip] = **wanderings**. -**2.** [of mind] délire *m*.

◆ **wanderings** *npl* [trip] vagabondage *m*, voyages *mpl*; during his ~s pendant ses voyages.

wanderlust ['wɒndəlʌst] *n* envie *f* de voyager.

Wandsworth Prison ['wɒnzwəθ-] *pr n la plus grande prison de Grande-Bretagne*.

wane [weɪn] ◇ *vi* [moon] décroître, décliner; [interest, power] diminuer; [civilization, empire] décliner, être en déclin.
◇ *n*: to be on the ~ [moon] décroître, décliner; [interest, power] diminuer; [civilization, empire] décliner, être en déclin.

wangle *inf* ['wæŋgl] *vt* [obtain - through cleverness] se débrouiller pour avoir; [- through devious means] obtenir par subterfuge, carotter; can you ~ me an invitation? est-ce que tu peux m'avoir OR me dégotter une invitation?; can you ~ it? peux-tu arranger ça?; he ~d his way into the job c'est par combine qu'il a décroché le poste; they ~d their way out of paying the fine ils se sont débrouillés pour ne pas payer l'amende.

waning ['weɪnɪŋ] ◇ *n* [of moon] décroissement *m*; [of interest, power] diminution *f*; [of empire] déclin *m*.
◇ *adj* [moon] décroissant, à son déclin; [interest, power] qui diminue; [empire] sur son déclin, en déclin.

wank▼ [wæŋk] *Br* ◇ *vi* se branler.
◇ *n* branlette *f*; to have a ~ se faire une branlette.

wanker▼ ['wæŋkəʳ] *n Br* branleur *m*.

wanly ['wɒnlɪ] *adv* -**1.** [answer, smile] faiblement, tristement. -**2.** [shine] faiblement, avec une pâle OR faible clarté.

wanna▽ ['wɒnə] -**1.** = **want to**. -**2.** = **want a**.

wannabe *inf* ['wɒnəˌbiː] *n se dit de quelqu'un qui veut être ce qu'il ne peut pas être*; a Michael Jackson ~ un clone de Michael Jackson.

wanness ['wɒnnɪs] *n* [of person - paleness] pâleur *f*; [- sadness] tristesse *f*; [of light] pâleur *f*, manque *m* de clarté.

want [wɒnt] ◇ *vt* -**1.** [expressing a wish or desire] vouloir, désirer; to ~ sthg badly avoir très envie de qqch; what do you ~? qu'est-ce que vous voulez?; what do you ~ now? qu'est-ce que tu veux encore?; I ~ a cup of coffee je veux OR voudrais une tasse de café; I ~ my Mummy! je veux ma maman!; all he ~s is to go to bed tout ce qu'il veut, c'est aller se coucher; to ~ to do sthg avoir envie de OR vouloir faire qqch; they ~ to go to Spain on holiday ils ont envie d'aller OR ils veulent aller en vacances en Espagne; she doesn't ~ to go elle n'a pas envie d'y aller, elle ne veut pas y aller; she doesn't ~ to elle n'en a pas envie; he doesn't ~ to know il ne veut rien savoir; I ~ you to wait here je veux que tu attendes ici; they never ~ed (to have) children ils n'ont jamais eu envie d'avoir des enfants, ils n'ont jamais voulu (avoir) d'enfants; I don't ~ (to have) any trouble je ne veux pas d'ennuis; how much OR what do you ~ for this table? combien voulez-vous pour cette table?; what do you ~ with her? qu'est-ce que tu lui veux?; she doesn't ~ much! *iron* elle n'est pas difficile, elle au moins; now I've got you where I ~ you! *fig* je te tiens! -**2.** [desire sexually] désirer, avoir envie de. -**3.** [require to be present] demander, vouloir voir; the boss ~s you le patron vous demande OR veut vous voir OR demande à vous voir; someone ~s you OR you're ~ed on the phone quelqu'un vous demande au téléphone; where do you ~ this wardrobe? où voulez-vous qu'on mette cette armoire?; you won't be ~ed this afternoon on n'aura pas besoin de vous cet après-midi; go away, you're not ~ed here va-t-en, tu n'es pas le bienvenu ici; I know when I'm not ~ed je sais quand je suis de trop. -**4.** [hunt, look for] chercher, rechercher; to be ~ed by the police être recherché par la police; he's ~ed for armed robbery il est recherché pour attaque à main armée. -**5.** [need - subj: person] avoir besoin de; [- subj: task, thing] avoir besoin de, nécessiter; **do you have everything you ~?** avez-vous tout ce qu'il vous faut?; **I have more than I ~** j'en ai plus qu'il n'en faut; **this room ~s a fresh coat of paint** cette pièce a besoin d'une nouvelle couche de peinture; **that child ~s a good hiding** cet enfant a besoin d'une bonne correction; **this coat ~s cleaning very badly** ce manteau a besoin d'un bon nettoyage; **there are still a couple of things that ~ doing** il y a encore quelques petites choses à faire OR qu'il faut faire; **what do you ~ with a car that size?** qu'allez-vous faire d'une voiture de cette taille? -**6.** *inf* [ought]: **you ~ to see a doctor about that leg** vous devez montrer OR il faut que vous montriez cette jambe à un médecin; **she ~s to watch out, the boss is gunning for her** elle devrait faire attention, le patron la cherche. -**7.** *lit* [lack - food, shelter] manquer de.

◇ *vi inf*: **the cat ~s in/out** le chat veut entrer/sortir ‖ *fig*: **he ~s in (on the deal)** il veut une part du gâteau; **I ~ out!** je ne suis plus de la partie!

◇ *n* -**1.** [desire, wish] désir *m*, envie *f*; **to satisfy sb's ~s** satisfaire les envies OR les désirs de qqn. -**2.** [requirement] besoin *m*; **to have few ~s** avoir peu de besoins, avoir besoin de peu; **she attends to all his ~s** elle pourvoit à tous ses besoins. -**3.** [lack] manque *m*; **a ~ of generosity** un manque de générosité; **there's certainly no ~ of goodwill** ce ne sont certainement pas les bonnes volontés qui manquent; **to be in ~ of sthg** avoir besoin de qqch. -**4.** [poverty] misère *f*, besoin *m*; **to be in ~** être dans le besoin OR dans la misère.

◆ **want for** *vt insep* manquer de; **they never ~ed for friends** ils n'ont jamais manqué d'amis; **he ~s for nothing** il ne manque de rien.

◆ **for want of** *prep phr* faute de; **I'll take this novel for ~ of anything better** faute de mieux je vais prendre ce roman; **for ~ of anything better to do, she went for a walk** n'ayant rien de mieux à faire, elle est allée se promener; **the project fell through for ~ of funding** faute de financement, le projet est tombé à l'eau; **if we failed, it wasn't for ~ of trying** nous avons échoué mais ce n'est pas faute d'avoir essayé.

want ad *n* petite annonce *f*.

wanted [ˈwɒntɪd] *adj* -**1.** [in advertisements]: **'carpenter/cook ~'** 'on recherche (un) charpentier/(un) cuisinier'; **'accommodation ~'** 'cherche appartement'. -**2.** [murderer, thief] recherché; **'~ for armed robbery'** recherché pour vol à main armée; **~ notice** avis *m* de recherche.

wanting [ˈwɒntɪŋ] *adj* -**1.** [inadequate]: **to be found ~** [person] ne pas convenir, ne pas faire l'affaire; [machine] ne pas convenir, ne pas être au point. -**2.** [lacking] manquant; **to be ~ in sthg** manquer de qqch. -**3.** *euph* [weak-minded] simple d'esprit.

wanton [ˈwɒntən] ◇ *adj* -**1.** [malicious - action, cruelty] gratuit, injustifié; [- destroyer] vicieux. -**2.** *fml* [immoral - behaviour, thoughts] licencieux; [- person] dévergondé. -**3.** *arch* OR *lit* [uncontrolled - vegetation] abondant, exubérant. -**4.** *arch* OR *lit* [playful - breeze] capricieux.

◇ *n lit* [man] dévergondé *m*; [woman] dévergondée *f*, femme *f* légère.

wantonly [ˈwɒntənlɪ] *adv* -**1.** [maliciously] gratuitement, sans justification. -**2.** *fml* [immorally] licencieusement. -**3.** *arch* OR *lit* [playfully] capricieusement.

Wapping [ˈwɒpɪŋ] *pr n quartier de l'Est de Londres où se trouvent les sièges de plusieurs journaux détenus par Rupert Murdoch.*

war [wɔːʳ] (*pt* & *pp* **warred**, *cont* **warring**) ◇ *n* -**1.** [armed conflict] guerre *f*; **Japan was at ~ with Russia** le Japon était en guerre avec la Russie; **Israel went to ~ with Syria over border disagreements** Israël est entré en guerre avec OR contre la Syrie pour des problèmes territoriaux; **the Allies waged ~ against** OR **on the Axis** les Alliés ont fait la guerre aux puissances de l'Axe; **he fought in the ~** il a fait la guerre; **the troops went off to ~** les troupes sont parties pour OR sont allées à la guerre; **you've been in the ~s!** *inf hum* on dirait que tu reviens de la guerre!, tu t'es bien arrangé!; **to have a good ~** [soldier] être vaillant au combat; **the period between the two (World) Wars** l'entre-deux-guerres *m inv* ❑ **~ of attrition** guerre d'usure; **~ museum** musée *m* de guerre; **the American War of Independence** la guerre d'Indépendance américaine; **the War between the States, the War of Secession** la guerre de Sécession; **the Wars of the Roses** la guerre des Deux-Roses; **'War and Peace'** *Tolstoy* 'Guerre et paix'; **'The War of the Worlds'** *Wells* 'la Guerre des mondes'. -**2.** [conflict, struggle] guerre *f*, lutte *f*; **to declare** OR **to wage ~ on sthg** partir en guerre contre OR déclarer la guerre à qqch; **a ~ of nerves/words** une guerre des nerfs/des mots; **the ~ against crime/drugs** la lutte contre le crime/la drogue; **price ~** guerre *f* des prix.

◇ *comp* [criminal, diary, film, hero, pension, wound, zone] de guerre; **~ victims** victimes *mpl* de guerre; **during the ~ years** pendant la guerre; **the ~ effort** l'effort *m* de guerre; **~ record** passé *m* militaire; **he has a good ~ record** il s'est conduit honorablement pendant la guerre; **what's his ~ record?** qu'est-ce qu'il a fait pendant la guerre?

◇ *vi* faire la guerre; **to ~ with sb** faire la guerre à qqn.

THE WARS OF THE ROSES:
Guerres qui, au XVe siècle, opposèrent les deux familles pouvant prétendre au trône d'Angleterre: la maison d'York, dont l'emblème était une rose blanche, et la maison de Lancastre, représentée par une rose rouge. Ces guerres prirent fin en 1485 par la victoire d'un Lancastre, qui devint Henri VII et réconcilia les deux familles en épousant Élizabeth d'York.

THE WAR OF THE WORLDS:
Pièce radiophonique adaptée du roman de H.G. Wells et mise en scène par Orson Welles, diffusée le 30 octobre 1938 par une radio new-yorkaise à l'occasion de Halloween. La description très réaliste de l'arrivée sur terre de martiens fut prise au sérieux par les auditeurs, ce qui provoqua une panique générale: désertion des villes, embouteillages monstres, mais aussi crises d'hystérie, crises cardiaques et suicides.

War. = **Warks.**

war baby *n* enfant *mf* de la guerre.

warble [ˈwɔːbl] ◇ *vi* & *vt* [subj: bird] gazouiller; [subj: person] chanter (avec des trilles).

◇ *n* gazouillis *m*, gazouillement *m*.

warbler [ˈwɔːbləʳ] *n* fauvette *f*, pouillot *m*.

warbling [ˈwɔːblɪŋ] *n* gazouillis *m*, gazouillement *m*.

war bond *n* titre *m* d'emprunt de guerre *(issu pendant la Deuxième Guerre mondiale)*.

war bride *n* mariée *f* de la guerre.

war cabinet *n* cabinet *m* de guerre.

war chest *n literal* caisse *f* spéciale *(affectée à une guerre)*; *fig* caisse *f* spéciale *(d'un parti politique, d'hommes d'affaires etc)*.

war clouds *npl* nuages *mpl* OR signes *mpl* précurseurs de guerre; **the ~ are gathering** la guerre menace.

war correspondent *n* correspondant *m*, -e *f* de guerre.

war crime *n* crime *m* de guerre.

war cry *n* cri *m* de guerre.

ward [wɔːd] *n* -**1.** [of hospital - room] salle *f*; [- section] pavillon *m*; [of prison] quartier *m*. -**2.** POL [district] circonscription *f* électorale. -**3.** JUR [person] pupille *mf*; [guardianship] tutelle *f*; **to be in ~** être sous tutelle judiciaire; **she was placed in ~** elle a été placée sous tutelle judiciaire ❑ **~ of court** pupille *mf* sous tutelle judiciaire.

◆ **ward off** *vt sep* [danger, disease] éviter; [blow] parer, éviter.

war dance *n* danse *f* de guerre OR guerrière.

warden [ˈwɔːdn] *n* -**1.** [director - of building, institution] directeur *m*, -trice *f*; *Am* [- of prison] directeur *m*, -trice *f* de prison. -**2.** [public official - of fortress, town] gouverneur *m*; [- of park, reserve] gardien *m*, -enne *f*; **Warden of the Cinque Ports** *Br* gouverneur des Cinq Ports. -**3.** *Br* UNIV portier *m*.

warder [ˈwɔːdəʳ] *n Br* [guard] gardien *m* OR surveillant *m* (de prison).

ward heeler [-ˌhiːləʳ] *n Am* POL agent *m* électoral *(qui sollicite des voix)*.

wardress [ˈwɔːdrɪs] *n Br* gardienne *f* OR surveillante *f* (de prison).

wardrobe [ˈwɔːdrəʊb] *n* -**1.** [cupboard] armoire *f*, penderie *f*. -**2.** [clothing] garde-robe *f*; THEAT costumes *mpl*; **Peter Taylor's ~ by...** CIN & THEAT Peter Taylor est habillé par..., les costumes de Peter Taylor sont de chez...; **this is my summer ~** c'est ma garde-robe d'été.

wardrobe mistress *n* costumière *f*.

wardrobe trunk *n* malle *f (penderie)*.

wardroom [ˈwɔːdrʊm] *n* [quarters] quartiers *mpl* des officiers *(excepté le capitaine)*; [officers] officiers *mpl (excepté le capitaine)*.

wardship [ˈwɔːdʃɪp] *n* tutelle *f*.

wares [weəz] *npl* marchandises *fpl*.

warehouse [*n* ˈweəhaʊs, *pl* -haʊzɪz, *vb* ˈweəhaʊz] ◇ *n* entrepôt *m*, magasin *m*.

◇ *vt* entreposer, emmagasiner.

warehouseman [ˈweəhaʊsmən] (*pl* **warehousemen** [-mən]) *n* magasinier *m*.

warfare [ˈwɔːfeəʳ] *n* MIL guerre *f*; *fig* lutte *f*, guerre *f*; **class ~** lutte des classes; **economic ~** guerre économique; **open ~** MIL & *fig* guerre ouverte.

war game *n (usu pl)* -**1.** MIL [simulated battle with maps] kriegspiel *m*, wargame *m*; [manoeuvres] manœuvres *fpl* militaires. -**2.** GAMES wargame *m*.

war grave *n tombeau d'un soldat tombé au champ d'honneur.*

warhead [ˈwɔːhed] *n* ogive *f*; **nuclear ~** ogive OR tête *f* nucléaire.

warhorse [ˈwɔːhɔːs] *n* [horse] cheval *m* de bataille; *fig* [person] *inf* dur *m*, -e *f* à cuire; **he's an old ~ of the party** c'est un vétéran du parti.

warily [ˈweərəlɪ] *adv* [carefully] prudemment, avec prudence OR circonspection; [distrustfully] avec méfiance.

wariness [ˈweərɪnɪs] *n* [caution] prudence *f*, circonspection *f*; [distrust] méfiance *f*.

Warks. *written abbr of* Warwickshire.

warlike [ˈwɔːlaɪk] *adj* guerrier, belliqueux.

war loan *n Br* titre *m* d'emprunt de guerre.

warlock [ˈwɔːlɒk] *n* sorcier *m*.

warlord [ˈwɔːlɔːd] *n* seigneur *m* de la guerre.

warm [wɔːm] ◇ *adj* -**1.** [moderately hot] chaud; **a ~ front** METEOR un front chaud; **a ~ oven** un four moyen; **~ milk** lait chaud; **I can't wait for the ~ weather** j'ai hâte qu'il fasse chaud; **this soup is barely ~** cette soupe est à peine chaude OR est tiède; **will you keep dinner ~ for me?** peux-tu me garder le dîner au chaud?; **does that coat keep you ~?** est-ce que ce manteau te tient chaud?; **it's a difficult house to keep ~** c'est une maison difficile à chauffer; **are you ~ enough?** avez-vous assez chaud?; **I can't seem to get ~** je n'arrive pas à me réchauffer; **the room is too ~** il fait trop chaud OR on étouffe dans cette pièce; **the bedroom was nice and ~** il faisait bon OR agréablement chaud dans la chambre ❑ **am I right?—you're getting ~er!** *fig* est-ce que j'y suis? — tu chauffes! -**2.** [clothing] chaud, qui tient chaud. -**3.** [work] qui donne chaud. -**4.** [affectionate - feelings] chaud, chaleureux; [- personality] chaleureux; **he's a very ~ person, he has a ~ heart** il est très chaleureux; **she has a ~ relationship with her mother** elle a une relation très affectueuse avec sa mère; **give my ~est wishes to your wife** toutes mes

amitiés à votre femme. -**5.** [hearty - greeting, welcome] chaleureux, cordial; [- thanks] vif; [- admirer, support] ardent, enthousiaste; [- applause] chaleureux, enthousiaste. -**6.** [colour, sound] chaud; [voice] chaud, chaleureux. -**7.** [scent, trail] récent.
◇ *vt* -**1.** [heat - person, room] réchauffer; [- food] (faire) chauffer; she **~ed her hands by the fire** elle s'est réchauffé les mains au-dessus du feu; **come and ~ yourself at the fire** viens te chauffer OR réchauffer près du feu ❑ **the sight was enough to ~ the cockles of your heart!** c'était un spectacle à vous chauffer OR réchauffer OR réjouir le cœur! -**2.** [reheat] (faire) réchauffer.
◇ *vi*: to ~ to sb/sthg: **she ~ed to the new neighbours** elle s'est prise de sympathie pour les nouveaux voisins; **you'll soon ~ to the idea** tu verras, cette idée finira par te plaire; **the speaker began to ~ to his subject** le conférencier s'est laissé entraîner par son sujet.
◇ *n inf*: **come into the ~** viens au chaud OR où il fait chaud; **I'll give the coffee a ~** je vais réchauffer le café.
◆ **warm down** *vi insep* [after physical effort] *travailler lentement en étirement après un échauffement intense.*
◆ **warm over** *vt sep Am* [food] (faire) réchauffer; *pej* [idea] ressasser.
◆ **warm through** *vt sep* (faire) réchauffer complètement.
◆ **warm up** ◇ *vt sep* -**1.** [heat - person, room] réchauffer; [- food] (faire) chauffer; [- engine, machine] faire chauffer. -**2.** [reheat] (faire) réchauffer. -**3.** [animate - audience] mettre en train, chauffer.
◇ *vi insep* -**1.** [become hotter - person] se chauffer, se réchauffer; [- room, engine, food] se réchauffer; [- weather] devenir plus chaud, se réchauffer. -**2.** [get ready - athlete, comedian] s'échauffer, se mettre en train; [- audience] commencer à s'animer. -**3.** [debate, discussion] s'animer; **the party began to ~ up** la soirée commençait à s'animer.

war machine *n* machine *f* de guerre.

warm-blooded *adj* ZOOL à sang chaud; *fig* [ardent] ardent, qui a le sang chaud.

war memorial *n* monument *m* aux morts.

warm-hearted *adj* [kindly] chaleureux, bon; [generous] généreux.

warming pan ['wɔːmɪŋ] *n* bassinoire *f*.

warmly ['wɔːmlɪ] *adv* -**1.** [dress] chaudement; **the sun shone ~** le soleil chauffait. -**2.** [greet, smile, welcome] chaleureusement, chaudement; [recommend, thank] vivement, chaudement; [support] avec enthousiasme, ardemment; [applaud] avec enthousiasme, chaleureusement.

warmonger ['wɔːˌmʌŋgəʳ] *n* belliciste *mf*.

warmongering ['wɔːˌmʌŋgərɪŋ] ◇ *n (U)* [activities] activités *fpl* bellicistes; [attitude] bellicisme *m*; [propaganda] propagande *f* belliciste.
◇ *adj* belliciste.

warmth [wɔːmθ] *n* [of temperature] chaleur *f*; [of greeting, welcome] chaleur *f*, cordialité *f*; [of recommendation, thanks] chaleur *f*, vivacité *f*; [of applause, support] enthousiasme *m*; [of colour] chaleur *f*.

warm-up ◇ *n* [gen] préparation *f*, préparations *fpl*; [of athlete, singer] échauffement *m*; [of audience] mise *f* en train.
◇ *comp*: **~ exercises** exercices *mpl* d'échauffement.

warmups ['wɔːmʌps] *npl Am* survêtement *m*.

warn [wɔːn] *vt* -**1.** [inform] avertir, prévenir; **I ~ed them of the danger** je les ai avertis OR prévenus du danger; **~ them that the bridge is unsafe** prévenez-les OR avertissez-les que le pont n'est pas sûr; **she ~ed them that she would be late** elle les a prévenus qu'elle serait en retard; **consider yourself ~ed!** on vous aura averti OR prévenu!, vous êtes prévenu!; **~ the police!** alertez la police! -**2.** [advise] conseiller, recommander; **he ~ed her about** OR **against travelling at night**, **he ~ed her not to travel at night** il lui a déconseillé de voyager la nuit, il l'a mise en garde contre les voyages de nuit.
◆ **warn off** *vt sep* décourager; **the doctor has ~ed him off alcohol** le médecin lui a vivement déconseillé l'alcool; **the barbed wire is there to ~ off intruders** des barbelés ont été installés pour décourager les intrus.

warning ['wɔːnɪŋ] ◇ *n* -**1.** [caution, notice] avertissement *m*; **let that be a ~ to you** que cela vous serve d'avertissement; **thanks for the ~** merci de m'avoir prévenu OR m'avoir averti; **the boss visited the office without (any) ~** le patron est venu visiter le bureau inopinément OR à l'improviste; **he left without any ~** il est parti sans prévenir; **they gave us advance ~ of the meeting** ils nous ont prévenus de la réunion; **there was a note of ~ in her voice** il y avait comme un avertissement dans sa voix; **the police gave him a ~ (about speeding)** la police lui a donné un avertissement (pour excès de vitesse); **to issue a ~ against sthg** mettre qqn en garde contre qqch ❑ **fog/gale ~** METEOR avis *m* de brouillard/de coup de vent. -**2.** [alarm, signal] alerte *f*, alarme *f*. -**3.** [advice] conseil *m*; **he gave them a stern ~ about the dangers of smoking** il les a sévèrement mis en garde contre les dangers du tabac.
◇ *adj* d'avertissement; **they fired a ~ shot** [gen & MIL] ils ont tiré une fois en guise d'avertissement; NAUT ils ont tiré un coup de semonce ❑ **~ device** avertisseur *m*; **~ light** voyant *m* (avertisseur), avertisseur *m* lumineux; **~ notice** avis *m*, avertissement *m*; **~ sign** panneau *m* avertisseur; **~ signal** [gen] signal *m* d'alarme OR d'alerte; AUT signal *m* de détresse.

War Office *n ancien nom du ministère de la Défense britannique.*

warp [wɔːp] ◇ *vt* -**1.** [wood] gauchir, voiler; [metal, plastic] voiler. -**2.** *fig* [character, mind] pervertir; [thinking] fausser, pervertir.
◇ *vi* [wood] gauchir, se voiler; [metal, plastic] se voiler.
◇ *n* -**1.** [fault - in wood] gauchissement *m*, voilure *f*; [- in metal, plastic] voilure *f*. -**2.** TEX [of yarn] chaîne *f*.

war paint *n* [of Indian] peinture *f* de guerre; *fig* & *hum* [make-up] maquillage *m*, peinture *f* de guerre *hum*.

warpath ['wɔːpɑːθ] *n*: **to be on the ~** *literal* être sur le sentier de la guerre; **be careful, the boss is on the ~** *fig* fais attention, le patron est d'une humeur massacrante.

warped [wɔːpt] *adj* -**1.** [wood] gauchi, voilé; [metal, plastic] voilé. -**2.** *fig* [character, person] perverti; [thinking, view] faux, perverti; **you've got a ~ mind!**, **your mind is ~!** tu as l'esprit tordu!; **what a ~ sense of humour!** quel humour morbide!

warplane ['wɔːpleɪn] *n* avion *m* de guerre.

warrant ['wɒrənt] ◇ *n* -**1.** JUR [written order] mandat *m*; **there's a ~ (out) for his arrest** il y a un mandat d'arrêt contre lui; **search ~** mandat *m* de perquisition. -**2.** COMM & FIN [for payment] bon *m*; [guarantee] garantie *f*. -**3.** MIL brevet *m*.
◇ *vt* -**1.** [justify] justifier; **the situation ~s a new approach** la situation demande que l'on s'y prenne autrement; **costs are too high to ~ further investment** les frais sont trop élevés pour permettre OR justifier d'autres investissements. -**2.** [declare with certainty] assurer, certifier; **I'll ~ (you) that's the last we see of her** c'est la dernière fois qu'on la voit, je vous le promets OR je vous le certifie.

warrantee [ˌwɒrən'tiː] *n* JUR titulaire *mf* d'une garantie.

warranter ['wɒrəntə] = **warrantor**.

warrant officer *n* adjudant *m (auxiliaire d'un officier)*.

warrantor ['wɒrəntɔːʳ] *n* JUR garant *m*, -e *f*, débiteur *m*, -trice *f*.

warranty ['wɒrəntɪ] (*pl* warranties) *n* -**1.** [guarantee] garantie *f*; **a one-year ~** une garantie d'un an. -**2.** JUR garantie *f*.

warren ['wɒrən] *n* -**1.** [of rabbit] terriers *mpl*, garenne *f*. -**2.** *fig* [maze of passageways] labyrinthe *m*, dédale *m*.

warring ['wɔːrɪŋ] *adj* [nations, tribes] en guerre; *fig* [beliefs] en conflit; [interests] contradictoire, contraire.

warrior ['wɒrɪəʳ] *n* guerrier *m*, -ère *f*.

Warsaw ['wɔːsɔː] *pr n* Varsovie.

Warsaw Pact *pr n*: **the ~** le pacte de Varsovie; **~ countries** pays *mpl* (membres) du pacte de Varsovie.

warship ['wɔːʃɪp] *n* navire *m* OR bâtiment *m* de guerre.

wart [wɔːt] *n* -**1.** MED verrue *f*; **she described her family ~s and all** *fig* elle a fait un portrait sans complaisance de sa famille. -**2.** BOT excroissance *f*.

wart hog *n* phacochère *m*.

wartime ['wɔːtaɪm] ◇ *n* période *f* de guerre; **in ~** en temps de guerre.
◇ *comp* de guerre; **~ rations** rations *fpl* de guerre.

war-torn *adj* déchiré par la guerre.

warty ['wɔːtɪ] (*compar* wartier, *superl* wartiest) *adj* couvert de verrues, verruqueux *spec*.

war-weary *adj* las de la guerre.

war widow *n* veuve *f* de guerre; **a ~'s pension** une pension de veuve de guerre.

wary ['weərɪ] (*compar* warier, *superl* wariest) *adj* [prudent - person] prudent, sur ses gardes; [- look] prudent; [- smile] hésitant; [distrustful] méfiant; **I'm ~ about promoting these ideas** j'hésite à promouvoir ces idées; **the people were ~ of the new regime** les gens se méfiaient du nouveau régime; **he kept a ~ eye on the dog** il surveillait le chien attentivement.

was [*weak form* wəz, *strong form* wɒz] *pt* → **be**.

wash [wɒʃ] ◇ *vt* -**1.** [clean] laver; **to ~ o.s.** [person] se laver, faire sa toilette; [cat, dog] faire sa toilette; **go and ~ your hands** va te laver les mains; **she ~ed her hair** elle s'est lavé la tête OR les cheveux; **he ~ed the walls clean** il a bien lavé OR nettoyé les murs; **to ~ the dishes** faire OR laver la vaisselle; **to ~ clothes** faire la lessive; **'~ in cold/hot water'** 'laver à l'eau froide/chaude' ❑ **to ~ one's hands of sb/sthg**: **I ~ my hands of the whole affair** je me lave les mains de toute cette histoire; **she ~ed her hands of him** elle s'est désintéressée de lui; **to ~ one's dirty linen in public** *Br* laver son linge sale en public. -**2.** [subj: current, river, waves - move over] baigner; [- carry away] emporter, entraîner; **the waves ~ed the shore** les vagues baignaient la côte; **the body was ~ed ashore** le cadavre s'est échoué OR a été rejeté sur la côte; **the crew was ~ed overboard** l'équipage a été emporté par une vague; **he was ~ed out to sea** il a été emporté par la mer. -**3.** [coat, cover] badigeonner. -**4.** MIN [gold, ore] laver.
◇ *vi* -**1.** [to clean oneself - person] se laver, faire sa toilette; **have you ~ed properly?** est-ce que tu as bien fait ta toilette? -**2.** [be washable] se laver, être lavable; **this dress doesn't ~ very well** cette robe ne supporte pas bien le lavage ❑ **his story just doesn't ~ with me** *Br inf* son histoire ne marche pas avec moi, il ne me fera pas avaler cette histoire.
◇ *n* -**1.** [act of cleaning] nettoyage *m*; **this floor needs a good ~** ce plancher a bien besoin d'être lavé OR nettoyé; **your hair needs a ~** il faut que tu te laves la tête; **I gave the car a ~** j'ai lavé la voiture; **he's having a ~** il se lave, il fait sa toilette; **I could do with a quick ~ and brush-up** j'aimerais faire un brin de toilette OR me débarbouiller. -**2.** [clothes to be washed] lessive *f*, linge *m* sale; **your shirt is in the ~** [laundry basket] ta chemise est au (linge) sale; [machine] ta chemise est à la lessive; **the stain came out in the ~** la tache est partie au lavage ❑ **it'll all come out in the ~** *Br* [become known] ça finira par se savoir; [turn out for the best] tout cela finira par s'arranger. -**3.** [movement of water - caused by current] remous *m*; [- caused by ship] sillage *m*, remous *m*; [sound of water] cla-

potis *m*. -**4.** [of paint] badigeon *m*. -**5.** MED [lotion] solution *f*. -**6.** ART: ~ (drawing) (dessin *m* au) lavis *m*.
◇ *adj Am* lavable.
◆ **wash away** *vt sep* [carry off - boat, bridge, house] emporter; [- river bank, soil] éroder; the rain ~ed away the road la route s'est effondrée sous l'action de la pluie; to ~ one's sins away *fig* laver ses péchés.
◆ **wash down** *vt sep* -**1.** [clean] laver (à grande eau). -**2.** [food] arroser; she ~ed down the aspirin with water elle a pris de l'aspirine OR a fait descendre le comprimé d'aspirine avec de l'eau; roast beef ~ed down with Burgundy wine rosbif arrosé d'un bourgogne.
◆ **wash off** ◇ *vt sep* [remove - with soap] enlever OR faire partir au lavage; [- with water] enlever OR faire partir à l'eau.
◇ *vi insep* [disappear - with soap] s'en aller OR partir au lavage; [- with water] s'en aller OR partir à l'eau; the paint won't ~ off la peinture ne s'en va pas OR ne part pas.
◆ **wash out** ◇ *vt sep* -**1.** [remove - with soap] enlever OR faire partir au lavage; [- with water] enlever OR faire partir à l'eau. -**2.** [clean] laver. -**3.** [carry away - bridge] emporter; [- road] dégrader. -**4.** [cancel, prevent]: the game was ~ed out le match a été annulé à cause de la pluie.
◇ *vi insep* = **wash off**.
◆ **wash up** ◇ *vi insep* -**1.** *Br* [wash dishes] faire OR laver la vaisselle. -**2.** *Am* [wash oneself] se laver, faire sa toilette.
◇ *vt sep* -**1.** *Br* [glass, dish] laver; whose turn is it to ~ up the dishes? à qui le tour de faire OR laver la vaisselle? -**2.** [subj: sea] rejeter; several dolphins were ~ed up on shore plusieurs dauphins se sont échoués sur la côte.

washable [ˈwɒʃəbl] *adj* lavable, lessivable.
wash-and-wear *adj* qui ne nécessite aucun repassage.
washbag [ˈwɒʃˌbæg] *n* trousse *f* de toilette.
washbasin [ˈwɒʃˌbeɪsn] *n* [basin] cuvette *f*, bassine *f*; [sink] lavabo *m*.
washboard [ˈwɒʃˌbɔːd] *n* planche *f* à laver.
washbowl [ˈwɒʃbəʊl] *Am* = **washbasin**.
washcloth [ˈwɒʃˌklɒθ] *n* [for dishes] lavette *f*; *Am* [face flannel] ≃ gant *m* de toilette.
washday [ˈwɒʃˌdeɪ] *n* jour *m* de lessive.
washed-out [wɒʃt-] *adj* -**1.** [faded - colour] délavé; [- curtain, jeans] décoloré, délavé. -**2.** *inf* [exhausted] épuisé, lessivé.
washed-up *inf adj* fichu; he's ~ as a singer sa carrière de chanteur est fichue OR finie; their marriage is ~ leur mariage est fichu OR se casse la figure.
washer [ˈwɒʃəʳ] *n* -**1.** CONSTR joint *m*, rondelle *f*; [in tap] joint *m*. -**2.** [washing machine] machine *f* à laver, lave-linge *m inv*.
washer-dryer *n* machine *f* à laver séchante.
washer-up *inf* (*pl* washers-up) *n Br* [gen] laveur *m*, -euse *f* de vaisselle; [in restaurant] plongeur *m*, -euse *f*.
washerwoman [ˈwɒʃəˌwʊmən] (*pl* washerwomen [-ˌwɪmɪn]) *n* blanchisseuse *f*.
wash-hand basin *Br* = **washbasin**.
washhouse [ˈwɒʃhaʊs, *pl* -haʊzɪz] *n* lavoir *m*.
washing [ˈwɒʃɪŋ] *n* -**1.** [act - of car, floors] lavage *m*; [- of laundry] lessive *f*. -**2.** [laundry] linge *m*, lessive *f*; a pile of dirty ~ une pile de linge sale; to do the ~ faire la lessive, laver le linge; where can I hang the ~? où puis-je étendre le linge?; do you have a lot of ~ to do? avez-vous beaucoup de lessive OR une grande lessive à faire?
washing day = **washday**.
washing line *n* corde *f* à linge.
washing machine *n* machine *f* à laver, lave-linge *m inv*.
washing powder *n* lessive *f* OR détergent *m (en poudre)*.
washing soda *n* cristaux *mpl* de soude.
Washington [ˈwɒʃɪŋtən] *pr n* -**1.** [state]: ~ (State) l'État *m* de Washington; in ~ dans l'État de Washington. -**2.** [town]: ~ (DC) Washington.
washing-up *n Br* vaisselle *f (à laver)*; to do the ~ faire la vaisselle.
washing-up liquid *n Br* produit *m* à vaisselle.
wash-leather *n Br* peau *f* de chamois.
washout *inf* [ˈwɒʃaʊt] *n* [party, plan] fiasco *m*, échec *m*; [person] raté *m*, -e *f*.
washrag [ˈwɒʃræg] *n Am* lavette *f*.
washroom [ˈwɒʃrʊm] *n* -**1.** [for laundry] buanderie *f*. -**2.** *Am euph* [lavatory] toilettes *fpl*.
washstand [ˈwɒʃstænd] *n* table *f* de toilette.
washtub [ˈwɒʃtʌb] *n* [for laundry] bassine *f*, cuvette *f*.
wasn't [wɒznt] = **was not**.
wasp [wɒsp] *n* guêpe *f*; a ~'s nest un guêpier.
Wasp, WASP *inf* [wɒsp] (*abbr of* White Anglo-Saxon Protestant) *n Am Blanc d'origine anglo-saxonne et protestante, appartenant aux classes aisées et influentes*.
waspish [ˈwɒspɪʃ] *adj* [person - by nature] qui a mauvais caractère; [- in bad mood] qui est de mauvaise humeur; [reply, remark] mordant, méchant.
wasp waist *n*: to have a ~ avoir une taille de guêpe.
wasp-waisted *adj* à la taille de guêpe.
wassail [ˈwɒseɪl] *arch* ◇ *n* -**1.** [drink - beer] bière *f* épicée; [- wine] vin *m* chaud. -**2.** [festivity] beuverie *f*. -**3.** [toast] toast *m*.
◇ *vi* chanter (des chants de Noël); to go ~ing aller de maison en maison en chantant (des noëls).
wast [*weak form* wəst, *strong form* wɒst] *arch* = **(you) were**.
wastage [ˈweɪstɪdʒ] *n* *(U)* -**1.** [loss - of materials, money] gaspillage *m*, gâchis *m*; [- of time] perte *f*; [- through leakage] fuites *fpl*, pertes *fpl*. -**2.** [in numbers, workforce] réduction *f*; many students are lost by ~ beaucoup d'étudiants abandonnent en cours de route.
waste [weɪst] ◇ *vt* -**1.** [misuse - materials, money] gaspiller; [- time] perdre; very little is ~d in this family on ne gaspille pas dans cette famille; don't ~ your life hanging around pubs ne gâche pas ta vie à traîner dans les pubs; I ~d an hour at the post office j'ai perdu une heure à la poste; don't ~ your time worrying about her ne t'en fais pas pour elle, tu perds ton temps; she ~d no time in telling us about it elle s'est empressée de nous le raconter; her wit was ~d on them ils n'ont pas compris OR su apprécier son esprit ❑ you're wasting your breath! tu uses ta salive pour rien!; don't ~ your breath trying to convince them ne te fatigue pas OR ne perds pas ton temps à essayer de les convaincre; ~ not, want not *prov* l'économie protège du besoin. -**2.** [wear away - limb, muscle] atrophier; [- body, person] décharner; her body was completely ~d by cancer son corps était complètement miné par le cancer. -**3.** ▽ *Am* [kill] liquider.
◇ *n* -**1.** [misuse - of materials, money] gaspillage *m*, gâchis *m*; [- of time] perte *f*; what a ~! quel gâchis OR gaspillage!; it's a ~ of breath arguing about it ce n'est pas la peine d'en discuter; that book was a complete ~ of money ce livre, c'était de l'argent jeté par les fenêtres; it's a ~ of time talking to her tu perds ton temps à discuter avec elle; what a ~ of time! que de temps perdu!; our trip was a ~ of time and energy notre voyage a été une perte de temps et d'énergie; it's an enormous ~ of talent c'est énormément de talent gâché; to go to ~ [gen] se perdre, être gaspillé; [land] tomber en friche; don't let all this food go to ~! ne laissez pas OR n'allez pas laisser tout ça se perdre!; I'm not going to let the opportunity go to ~ je ne vais pas laisser passer l'occasion. -**2.** *(U)* [refuse - gen] déchets *mpl*; [- household] ordures *fpl* (ménagères); [- water] eaux *fpl* usées; industrial/radioactive ~ déchets industriels/radioactifs. -**3.** [land] terrain *m* vague. -**4.** *phr*: to lay ~ to sthg, to lay sthg ~ ravager OR dévaster qqch.
◇ *adj* -**1.** [paper] de rebut; [energy] perdu; [water] sale, usé; [food] qui reste; ~ material déchets *mpl*. -**2.** [ground] en friche; [region] désert, désolé; 'The Waste Land' *Eliot* 'la Terre Gaste'.
◆ **wastes** *npl* terres *fpl* désolées, désert *m*; the polar ~s le désert polaire.
◆ **waste away** *vi insep* dépérir.
wastebasket [ˈweɪstˌbɑːskɪt] *n esp Am* corbeille *f* (à papier).
waste bin *n Br* [in kitchen] poubelle *f*, boîte *f* à ordures; [for paper] corbeille *f* (à papier).
wasted [ˈweɪstɪd] *adj* -**1.** [material, money] gaspillé; [energy, opportunity, time] perdu; [attempt, effort] inutile, vain; [food] inutilisé; a ~ journey un voyage raté. -**2.** [figure, person] décharné; [limb - emaciated] décharné; [- enfeebled] atrophié.
waste disposal unit *n* broyeur *m* d'ordures.
wasteful [ˈweɪstfʊl] *adj* [habits] de gaspillage; [person] gaspilleur; [procedure] inefficace, peu rentable; a ~ use of natural resources un gaspillage des ressources naturelles.
wastefully [ˈweɪstfʊlɪ] *adv* en gaspillant; we spend our time so ~ on gaspille un temps fou.
wastefulness [ˈweɪstfʊlnɪs] *n* [of person] gaspillage *m*, manque *m* d'économie; [of procedure] inefficacité *f*.
waste ground *n* *(U)*: the children were playing on ~ les enfants jouaient sur un terrain vague.
wasteland [ˈweɪstˌlænd] *n* [land - disused] terrain *m* vague; [- uncultivated] terres *fpl* en friche OR abandonnées; [of desert, snow] désert *m*; a cultural ~ *fig* un désert culturel.
waste paper *n (U)* papier *m* OR papiers *mpl* de rebut.
wastepaper basket [ˌweɪstˈpeɪpəʳ] *n Br* corbeille *f* (à papier).
waste pipe *n* (tuyau *m* de) vidange *f*.
waste product *n* INDUST déchet *m* de production OR de fabrication; PHYSIOL déchet *m (de l'organisme)*.
waster [ˈweɪstəʳ] *n* -**1.** [gen] gaspilleur *m*, -euse *f*; [of money] dépensier *m*, -ère *f*. -**2.** [good-for-nothing] bon *m* à rien, bonne *f* à rien.
wasting [ˈweɪstɪŋ] *adj* qui mine; a ~ disease une maladie qui ronge OR mine.
wastrel [ˈweɪstrəl] = **waster**.
watch [wɒtʃ] ◇ *vt* -**1.** [look at, observe - event, film] regarder; [- animal, person] regarder, observer; they ~ a lot of television ils regardent beaucoup la télévision; the crowds were ~ing the lions being fed la foule regardait les lions qu'on était en train de nourrir; we sat outside ~ing the world go by nous étions assis dehors à regarder les gens passer; ~ how I do it regardez OR observez comment je fais; I bet he ignores us, just you ~! je parie qu'il va nous ignorer, tu vas voir! ❑ a ~ed pot never boils *prov* inutile de s'inquiéter, ça ne fera pas avancer les choses. -**2.** [spy on - person] surveiller, observer; [- activities, suspect] surveiller; you'd better ~ him vous feriez bien de le surveiller OR de l'avoir à l'œil; I think we're being ~ed [gen] j'ai l'impression qu'on nous observe OR surveille; [by police, thieves] j'ai l'impression qu'on nous surveille. -**3.** [guard, tend - children, pet] surveiller, s'occuper de; [- belongings, house] surveiller, garder; MIL monter la garde devant, garder. -**4.** [pay attention to - health, weight] faire attention à; [- development, situation] suivre de près; ~ where you're going! regardez devant vous!; ~ what you're doing! faites attention (à ce que vous faites)!; ~ you don't spill the coffee fais attention à OR prends garde de ne pas renverser le café; can you ~ the milk? peux-tu surveiller le lait?; I'm ~ing the classifieds for any job opportunities je regarde les petites annonces pour les offres d'emploi; ~ you don't break anything faites attention à ne rien casser; we'd better ~ the time il faut que nous surveillions l'heure; stop ~ing the clock and do some work! arrêtez de surveiller

la pendule et travaillez un peu!; '~ this space' *annonce d'une publicité ou d'informations à paraître*; ~ your head! attention OR gare à votre tête!; ~ your language! surveille ton langage! ❑ ~ it! [warning] (fais) attention!; [threat] attention!, gare à vous!; ~ your step *literal* & *fig* faites attention OR regardez où vous mettez les pieds; you should ~ your step OR ~ yourself with the boss vous feriez bien de vous surveiller quand vous êtes avec le patron.

◇ *vi* -**1.** [observe] regarder, observer; I ~ed to see how she would react j'ai attendu pour voir quelle serait sa réaction; he ~ed closely as I removed the bandage il a regardé OR observé attentivement quand j'ai enlevé le bandage; I just came to ~ je suis simplement venu regarder, je suis venu en simple spectateur. -**2.** [keep vigil] veiller; his mother ~ed by his bedside sa mère a veillé à son chevet.

◇ *n* -**1.** [timepiece] montre *f*; it's 6 o'clock by my ~ il est 6 h à ma montre. -**2.** [lookout] surveillance *f*; be on the ~ for pickpockets *Br* faites attention OR prenez garde aux voleurs à la tire; tax inspectors are always on the ~ for fraud *Br* les inspecteurs des impôts sont toujours à l'affût des fraudeurs; a sentry was on ~ OR kept ~ une sentinelle montait la garde; to keep ~ by sb's bed veiller au chevet de qqn; the police kept a close ~ on the suspect la police a surveillé le suspect de près; we'll keep ~ on your house during your absence nous surveillerons votre maison pendant votre absence; we're keeping a ~ on inflation rates nous surveillons de près les taux d'inflation. -**3.** [person on guard - gen & MIL] sentinelle *f*; NAUT homme *m* de quart; [group of guards - gen & MIL] garde *f*; NAUT quart *m*. -**4.** [period of duty - gen & MIL] garde *f*; NAUT quart *m*; who's on ~? [gen & MIL] qui monte la garde?; NAUT qui est de quart? -**5.** *lit* [period of the night]: in the slow ~es of the night pendant les longues nuits sans sommeil.

◆ **watch for** *vt insep* guetter, surveiller; he ~ed for a chance to approach the President il attendait une occasion d'approcher le Président; ~ for any sudden changes in temperature surveillez toute variation soudaine de la température.

◆ **watch out** *vi insep* faire attention, prendre garde; ~ out! [warning] (faites) attention!; to ~ out for sthg [be on lookout for] guetter qqch; [be careful of] faire attention OR prendre garde à qqch; ~ out for the bus guettez le bus; ~ out for the fine print faites bien attention à toutes les clauses.

◆ **watch over** *vt insep* garder, surveiller; the shepherds were ~ing over their flocks les bergers gardaient OR surveillaient leurs troupeaux; she ~ed over the children while we were gone elle a surveillé les enfants OR elle s'est occupée des enfants pendant notre absence; God will ~ over you Dieu vous protègera.

watchband ['wɒtʃ,bænd] *n Am* bracelet *m* de montre.

watch-case *n* étui *m* de montre.

watch chain *n* chaîne *f* de montre.

watchdog ['wɒtʃdɒg] ◇ *n* [dog] chien *m*, -enne *f* de garde; *fig* [person] gardien *m*, -enne *f*; the committee acts as ~ on environmental issues le comité veille aux problèmes d'environnement.

◇ *comp* [body, committee] de surveillance.

watcher ['wɒtʃər] *n* observateur *m*, -trice *f*; [spectator] spectateur *m*, -trice *f*; [idle onlooker] curieux *m*, -euse *f*.

watchful ['wɒtʃʊl] *adj* vigilant, attentif; he was ~ for any unusual behaviour il était attentif à tout comportement inhabituel; under the ~ eye of her mother sous l'œil vigilant de sa mère; to keep a ~ eye on sthg/sb avoir qqch/qqn à l'œil; she kept a ~ eye on the situation elle a suivi la situation de près.

watchglass ['wɒtʃglɑːs] *n* verre *m* de montre.

watchmaker ['wɒtʃ,meɪkər] *n* horloger *m*, -ère *f*.

watchmaking ['wɒtʃ,meɪkɪŋ] *n* horlogerie *f*.

watchman ['wɒtʃmən] (*pl* watchmen [-mən]) *n* gardien *m*.

watch night *n* nuit *f* de la Saint-Sylvestre; ~ service messe *f* (de minuit) de la Saint-Sylvestre.

watch pocket *n* gousset *m*.

watchstrap ['wɒtʃstræp] *n* bracelet *m* de montre.

watchtower ['wɒtʃ,taʊər] *n* tour *f* de guet.

watchword ['wɒtʃwɜːd] *n* [password] mot *m* de passe; [slogan] mot *m* d'ordre.

water ['wɔːtər] ◇ *n* -**1.** [liquid - gen] eau *f*; I took a drink of ~ j'ai bu de l'eau OR un verre d'eau; hot and cold running ~ eau courante chaude et froide; turn on the ~ [at main] ouvre l'eau; [at tap] ouvre le robinet; prisoners were put on bread and ~ on avait mis les prisonniers au pain (sec) et à l'eau; they held his head under ~ ils lui ont tenu la tête sous l'eau; the cellar is under 2 metres of ~ il y a 2 mètres d'eau dans la cave; the ~ OR ~s of the Seine l'eau OR les eaux de la Seine; the ship was making ~ le bateau prenait l'eau OR faisait eau; they're in rough financial ~s *fig* ils sont dans une situation financière difficile ❑ that idea won't hold ~ cette idée ne tient pas debout; you're in hot ~ now *inf* tu vas avoir de gros ennuis, tu es dans de beaux draps; her statement got us into hot ~ sa déclaration nous a mis dans le pétrin OR dans de beaux draps; I'm trying to keep my head above ~ OR to stay above ~ *inf* j'essaye de me maintenir à flot OR de faire face; the wine flowed like ~ le vin coulait à flots; to spend money like ~ jeter l'argent par les fenêtres; he's an artist of the first ~ *Br fml* c'est un artiste de premier ordre; they poured OR threw cold ~ on our suggestion ils n'ont pas été enthousiasmés par notre suggestion; it's like ~ off a duck's back ça glisse comme sur les plumes d'un canard; it's ~ under the bridge c'est du passé; a lot of ~ has passed under the bridge since then il a coulé beaucoup d'eau sous les ponts depuis. -**2.** [body of water] eau *f*; the children played at the ~'s edge les enfants ont joué au bord de l'eau; she fell in the ~ elle est tombée à l'eau; they sent the goods by ~ ils ont envoyé la marchandise par bateau. -**3.** [tide] marée *f*; at high/low ~ à marée haute/basse. -**4.** *euph* [urine] urine *f*; to make OR to pass ~ uriner. -**5.** MED: ~ on the brain hydrocéphalie *f*; the baby has ~ on the brain le bébé est hydrocéphale; to have ~ on the knee avoir un épanchement de synovie. -**6.** TEX [of cloth] moiré *m*.

◇ *vt* -**1.** [land, plants] arroser; the land here is ~ed by the Seine ici, la terre est arrosée OR irriguée par la Seine. -**2.** [animal] donner à boire à, faire boire. -**3.** [dilute - alcohol] couper (d'eau). -**4.** TEX [cloth] moirer.

◇ *vi* -**1.** [eyes] larmoyer. -**2.** [mouth]: the smell made my mouth ~ l'odeur m'a fait venir l'eau à la bouche.

◆ **waters** *npl* -**1.** [territorial] eaux *fpl*; in Japanese ~s dans les eaux (territoriales) japonaises. -**2.** [spa water]: to take the ~s prendre les eaux, faire une cure thermale. -**3.** [of pregnant woman] poche *f* des eaux; her ~s broke elle a perdu les eaux, la poche des eaux s'est rompue.

◆ **water down** *vt sep* [alcohol] couper (d'eau); *fig* [speech] édulcorer; [complaint, criticism] atténuer.

water bag *n* outre *f* à eau.

water bailiff *n Br* garde-pêche *m (personne)*.

water bed *n* matelas *m* à eau.

water beetle *n* gyrin *m*, tourniquet *m*.

water bird *n* oiseau *m* aquatique.

water biscuit *n Br* biscuit *m* salé craquant.

water blister *n* ampoule *f*, phlyctène *f spec*.

water boatman *n* ENTOM notonecte *f*.

water bomb *n* bombe *f* à eau.

waterborne ['wɔːtəbɔːn] *adj* [vehicle] flottant; [commerce, trade] effectué par voie d'eau; [disease] d'origine hydrique.

water bottle *n* [gen] bouteille *f* d'eau; [soldier's, worker's] bidon *m* à eau; [in leather] outre *f*.

water buffalo *n* [India] buffle *m* d'Inde; [Malaysia] karbau *m*, kérabau *m*; [Asia] buffle *m* d'Asie.

water bug *n* nèpe *f*.

water bus *n* navette *f (sur eau)*.

water butt *n* citerne *f* (à eau de pluie).

water cannon *n* canon *m* à eau.

water carrier *n* -**1.** [container] bidon *m* à eau. -**2.** [person] porteur *m*, -euse *f* d'eau.

◆ **Water Carrier** *pr n* ASTROL & ASTRON: the Water Carrier le Verseau.

water cart *n* [to sprinkle water] arroseuse *f*; [to sell water] voiture *f* de marchand d'eau.

water chestnut *n* châtaigne *f* d'eau.

water chute *n* [in swimming pool] cascade *f*.

water closet *n* W-C *mpl*, toilettes *fpl*, cabinets *mpl*.

watercolour *Br*, **watercolor** *Am* ['wɔːtə,kʌlər] ◇ *n* [paint] couleur *f* pour aquarelle; [painting] aquarelle *f*; painted in ~ peint à l'aquarelle.

◇ *adj* [paint] pour aquarelle, à l'eau; [landscape, portrait] à l'aquarelle.

watercolourist *Br*, **watercolorist** *Am* ['wɔːtə,kʌlərɪst] *n* aquarelliste *mf*.

water-cooled [-kuːld] *adj* à refroidissement par eau.

water cooler *n* distributeur *m* d'eau fraîche.

watercourse ['wɔːtəkɔːs] *n* [river, stream] cours *m* d'eau; [bed] lit *m (d'un cours d'eau)*.

watercress ['wɔːtəkres] *n* cresson *m*.

water-diviner *n* sourcier *m*, -ère *f*, radiesthésiste *mf*.

watered-down [,wɔːtəd-] *adj* [alcohol] coupé (d'eau); [speech] édulcoré; [complaint, criticism] atténué.

watered silk *n* soie *f* moirée.

waterfall ['wɔːtəfɔːl] *n* cascade *f*, chute *f* d'eau.

waterfinder ['wɔːtə,faɪndər] *Am* = **water-diviner**.

water flea *n* daphnie *f*, puce *f* d'eau.

water fountain *n* [for decoration] jet *m* d'eau; [for drinking] distributeur *m* d'eau fraîche.

waterfowl ['wɔːtəfaʊl] (*pl inv* OR waterfowls) *n* [bird] oiseau *m* aquatique; [collectively] gibier *m* d'eau.

waterfront ['wɔːtəfrʌnt] *n* [at harbour] quais *mpl*; [seafront] front *m* de mer; on the ~ [at harbour] sur les quais; [on seafront] face à la mer ❑ 'On the Waterfront' *Kazan* 'Sur les quais'.

water gas *n* gaz *m* à l'eau.

Watergate ['wɔːtəgeɪt] *pr n* Watergate *m*.

WATERGATE:

Scandale politique qui entraîna en août 1974 la démission du président américain républicain Richard Nixon, impliqué dans un vol de documents au siège du parti démocrate (situé dans l'immeuble de Watergate à Washington) et dans une affaire d'écoute clandestine. Alors que plusieurs de ses collaborateurs furent jugés et condamnés, R. Nixon démissionna avant sa mise en accusation, ce qui contribua à ébranler la confiance des Américains dans leur gouvernement.

water gauge *n* jauge *f* d'eau.

water glass *n* -**1.** [for drinking] verre *m* à eau. -**2.** [water gauge] jauge *f* d'eau. -**3.** CHEM silicate *m* de potasse.

water gun = **water pistol**.

water heater *n* chauffe-eau *m inv*.

water hen *n* poule *f* d'eau.

waterhole ['wɔːtəhəʊl] *n* point *m* d'eau; [in desert] oasis *f*.

water ice *n Br* sorbet *m*.

watering ['wɔːtərɪŋ] *n* [of garden, plants] arrosage *m*; [of crops, fields] irrigation *f*; azaleas need daily ~ il faut arroser les azalées chaque jour.

watering can *n* arrosoir *m*.

watering hole *n* [for animals] point *m* d'eau; *fig* & *hum inf* [pub] ≃ bistrot *m*, ≃ bar *m*.

watering place *n* **-1.** [waterhole] point *m* d'eau. **-2.** *Br* [spa] station *f* thermale. **-3.** *Br* [seaside resort] station *f* balnéaire.

watering pot *n* arrosoir *m*.

water jacket *n* chemise *f* d'eau.

water jump *n* brook *m*.

water level *n* [of river, sea] niveau *m* de l'eau; [in tank] niveau *m* d'eau.

water lily *n* nénuphar *m*.

waterline ['wɔːtəlaɪn] *n* **-1.** [left by river] ligne *f* des hautes eaux; [left by tide] laisse *f* de haute mer. **-2.** NAUT [on ship] ligne *f* de flottaison.

waterlogged ['wɔːtəlɒgd] *adj* [land, soil] détrempé; [boat] plein d'eau; [clothing, shoes] imbibé d'eau.

Waterloo [,wɔːtə'luː] ◇ *pr n* Waterloo; the Battle of ~ la bataille de Waterloo.
◇ *n*: to meet one's ~ essuyer un revers.

water main *n* conduite *f* OR canalisation *f* d'eau.

waterman ['wɔːtəmən] (*pl* watermen [-mən]) *n* batelier *m*.

watermark ['wɔːtəmɑːk] ◇ *n* **-1.** = **waterline 1.** **-2.** [on paper] filigrane *m*.
◇ *vt* filigraner.

water meadow *n* prairie *f* *(souvent inondée)*.

watermelon ['wɔːtə,melən] *n* pastèque *f*, melon *m* d'eau.

water meter *n* compteur *m* d'eau.

watermill ['wɔːtəmɪl] *n* moulin *m* à eau.

water nymph *n* naïade *f*.

water ox = **water buffalo**.

water pipe *n* **-1.** CONSTR conduite *f* OR canalisation *f* d'eau. **-2.** [hookah] narguilé *m*.

water pistol *n* pistolet *m* à eau.

water polo *n* water-polo *m*.

water power *n* énergie *f* hydraulique, houille *f* blanche.

waterproof ['wɔːtəpruːf] ◇ *adj* [clothing, material] imperméable; [container, wall, watch] étanche.
◇ *n* imperméable *m*.
◇ *vt* [clothing, material] imperméabiliser; [barrel, wall] rendre étanche.

waterproofing ['wɔːtəpruːfɪŋ] *n* [process - for clothing, material] imperméabilisation *f*; [- for barrel, wall] action *f* de rendre étanche; [coating] imperméabilisation *f*.

water rat *n* rat *m* d'eau.

water rate *n* *Br* taxe *f* sur l'eau.

water-repellent *adj* imperméable, hydrofuge.

water-resistant *adj* [material] semi-imperméable; [lotion] qui résiste à l'eau; [ink] indélébile, qui résiste à l'eau.

watershed ['wɔːtəʃed] *n* [area of ground] ligne *f* de partage des eaux; *fig* [event] grand tournant *m*; the concert was a ~ in her career as a singer ce concert fut un moment décisif OR un grand tournant dans sa carrière de chanteuse.

waterside ['wɔːtəsaɪd] ◇ *n* bord *m* de l'eau.
◇ *adj* [house, path] au bord de l'eau; [resident] riverain; [flower] du bord de l'eau.

water ski *n* ski *m* nautique.
◆ **water-ski** *vi* faire du ski nautique.

water skier *n* skieur *m*, -euse *f* nautique.

water skiing *n* ski *m* nautique.

water snake *n* serpent *m* d'eau.

water softener *n* adoucisseur *m* d'eau.

water-soluble *adj* soluble dans l'eau.

water spaniel *n* épagneul *m* *(qui chasse du gibier d'eau)*.

water spider *n* araignée *f* d'eau.

water sport *n* sport *m* nautique.

waterspout ['wɔːtəspaʊt] *n* **-1.** [pipe] (tuyau *m* de) descente *f*. **-2.** METEOR trombe *f*.

water supply *n* [for campers, troops] provision *f* d'eau; [to house] alimentation *f* en eau; [to area, town] distribution *f* des eaux, approvisionnement *m* en eau; the ~ has been cut off l'eau a été coupée.

water table *n* nappe *f* phréatique, niveau *m* hydrostatique.

water tank *n* réservoir *m* d'eau, citerne *f*.

watertight ['wɔːtətaɪt] *adj* [box, door] étanche; *fig* [argument, reasoning] inattaquable, indiscutable.

water torture *n* supplice *m* de l'eau.

water tower *n* château *m* d'eau.

water vapour *n* vapeur *f* d'eau.

water vole *n* rat *m* d'eau.

waterway ['wɔːtəweɪ] *n* cours *m* d'eau, voie *f* navigable.

waterweed ['wɔːtəwiːd] *n* élodée *f*.

waterwheel ['wɔːtəwiːl] *n* roue *f* hydraulique.

waterwings ['wɔːtəwɪŋz] *npl* bouée *f* *(pour apprendre à nager)*.

waterworks ['wɔːtəwɜːks] (*pl inv*) ◇ *n* [establishment] station *f* hydraulique; [system] système *m* hydraulique.
◇ *npl* **-1.** [fountain] jet *m* d'eau. **-2.** *inf Br euph* & *hum* [urinary system] voies *fpl* urinaires; he has problems with his ~ il a des problèmes de vessie. **-3.** *inf hum* [tears]: she turned on the ~ elle s'est mise à pleurer comme une Madeleine.

watery ['wɔːtərɪ] *adj* **-1.** [surroundings, world] aquatique; [ground, soil] détrempé, saturé d'eau; the sailors found a ~ grave les marins ont été ensevelis par les eaux. **-2.** [eyes] larmoyant, humide. **-3.** [coffee, tea] trop léger; [soup] trop liquide, fade; [milk] qui a trop d'eau; [taste] fade, insipide. **-4.** [light, sun, smile] faible; [colour] délavé, pâle.

watt [wɒt] *n* watt *m*.

wattage ['wɒtɪdʒ] *n* puissance *f* OR consommation *f* (en watts).

watt-hour *n* wattheure *m*.

wattle ['wɒtl] *n* **-1.** [of bird, lizard] caroncule *f*. **-2.** [sticks] clayonnage *m*; ~ and daub clayonnage enduit de torchis; ~ walls murs *mpl* en clayonnage.

wattmeter ['wɒt,miːtəʳ] *n* wattmètre *m*.

wave [weɪv] ◇ *n* **-1.** [in sea] vague *f*, lame *f*; [on lake] vague *f*; the ~s les flots *mpl*; don't make ~s *fig* ne faites pas de vagues, ne créez pas de remous. **-2.** [of earthquake, explosion] onde *f*; *fig* [of crime, panic] vague *f*; a ~ of anger une bouffée de colère; a ~ of disgust swept over him une vague de dégoût le submergea; the refugees arrived in ~s les réfugiés sont arrivés par vagues; there were several ~s of attack MIL il y eut plusieurs vagues d'assaut. **-3.** [in hair] cran *m*, ondulation *f*; her hair has a natural ~ to it ses cheveux ondulent naturellement. **-4.** [gesture] geste *m* OR signe *m* de la main; our neighbour gave us a friendly ~ notre voisin nous a fait un signe amical; with a ~ of the hand d'un geste OR signe de la main. **-5.** RADIO onde *f*.
◇ *vi* **-1.** [gesture] faire un signe OR un geste de la main; his sister ~d at OR to him [greeted] sa sœur l'a salué d'un signe de la main; [signalled] sa sœur lui a fait signe de la main; she ~d at OR to them to come in elle leur a fait signe d'entrer; he ~d vaguely towards the door il a montré vaguement la porte d'un geste de la main. **-2.** [move - flag] flotter; [- wheat] onduler, ondoyer; [- branch] être agité.
◇ *vt* **-1.** [brandish - flag] agiter, brandir; [- pistol, sword] brandir. **-2.** [gesture]: his mother ~d him away sa mère l'a écarté d'un geste de la main; the guard ~d us back/on le garde nous a fait signe de reculer/d'avancer; the policeman ~d us through the crossroads le policier nous a fait signe de traverser le carrefour; we ~d goodbye nous avons fait au revoir de la main; you can ~ goodbye to your promotion! *inf fig* tu peux dire adieu à ta promotion! **-3.** [hair] onduler.
◆ **wave about** ◇ *vi insep* = **wave** *vi* **2**.
◇ *vt sep Br* [flag, sign] agiter, brandir; [pistol, sword] brandir; he was waving his hands about il gesticulait.
◆ **wave aside** *vt sep* [person] écarter OR éloigner d'un geste; [protest] écarter; [help, suggestion] refuser, rejeter.
◆ **wave down** *vt sep*: to ~ sb/a car down faire signe à qqn/à une voiture de s'arrêter.

wave band *n* bande *f* de fréquences.

waveform ['weɪvfɔːm] *n* courbe *f* d'onde.

wave function *n* fonction *f* d'onde.

waveguide ['weɪvgaɪd] *n* guide *m* d'ondes.

wavelength ['weɪvleŋkθ] *n* PHYS & RADIO longueur *f* d'onde; we're just not on the same ~ *fig* nous ne sommes pas sur la même longueur d'onde.

wavelet ['weɪvlɪt] *n* vaguelette *f*.

wave mechanics *n* *(U)* mécanique *f* ondulatoire.

wave power *n* énergie *f* des vagues.

waver ['weɪvəʳ] *vi* **-1.** [person] vaciller, hésiter; [confidence, courage] vaciller, faiblir; they didn't ~ in their loyalty to the cause leur attachement à la cause n'a pas faibli. **-2.** [flame, light] vaciller, osciller; [temperature] osciller. **-3.** [voice] trembloter, trembler.

waverer ['weɪvərəʳ] *n* irrésolu *m*, -e *f*, indécis *m*, -e *f*.

wavering ['weɪvərɪŋ] ◇ *adj* **-1.** [person] irrésolu, indécis; [confidence, courage] vacillant, défaillant. **-2.** [flame, light] vacillant, oscillant; [steps] vacillant, chancelant; [temperature] oscillant. **-3.** [voice] tremblotant, tremblant.
◇ *n* **-1.** [of person] irrésolution *f*, indécision *f*; [of confidence, courage] défaillance *f*. **-2.** [of flame, light] vacillement *m*, oscillation *f*; [of temperature] oscillation *f*.

wavy ['weɪvɪ] (*compar* wavier, *superl* waviest) *adj* **-1.** [line] qui ondule, ondulant. **-2.** [hair] ondulé, qui a des crans.

wavy-haired *adj* aux cheveux ondulés.

wax [wæks] ◇ *n* **-1.** [for car, floor, furniture] cire *f*; [in ear] cérumen *m*; [for skis] fart *m*. **-2.** *Br dated*: to be in a ~ *inf* être en rogne OR en colère.
◇ *comp* [candle, figure] de OR en cire; ~ crayons pastels *mpl*.
◇ *vt* **-1.** [floor, table] cirer, encaustiquer; [skis] farter; [car] enduire de cire. **-2.** [legs] épiler (à la cire).
◇ *vi* **-1.** [moon] croître; [influence, power] croître, augmenter; to ~ and wane [moon] croître et décroître; [influence, power] croître et décliner. **-2.** *arch* OR *hum* [become] devenir; he ~ed poetic/sentimental il se fit poète/sentimental; she ~ed eloquent OR lyrical on the subject of country life elle s'est montrée éloquente sur le thème de la vie à la campagne.

waxed paper [wækst-] *n* papier *m* paraffiné OR sulfurisé.

waxen ['wæksən] *adj* [candle, figure] de OR en cire; [complexion, face] cireux.

wax paper = **waxed paper**.

waxwing ['wækswɪŋ] *n* ORNITH jaseur *m*.

waxwork ['wækswɜːk] *n* [object] objet *m* de OR en cire; [statue of person] statue *f* de cire.

waxworks ['wækswɜːks] (*pl inv*) *n* musée *m* de cire.

waxy ['wæksɪ] (*compar* waxier, *superl* waxiest) *adj* [complexion, texture] cireux; [colour] cireux, jaunâtre; [potato] ferme, pas farineux.

way [weɪ] ◇ *n* **A.** **-1.** [thoroughfare, path] chemin *m*, voie *f*; [for cars] rue *f*, route *f*; we took the ~ through the woods nous avons pris le chemin qui traverse le bois; they're building a ~ across the desert ils ouvrent une route à travers le désert; they live across OR over the ~ from the school ils habitent en face de l'école ❑ pedestrian ~ voie OR rue piétonne; private/public ~ voie privée/publique; the Appian Way la voie Appienne; the Way of the Cross RELIG le chemin de Croix. **-2.** [route leading to a specified place] chemin *m*; this is the ~ to the library la bibliothèque est par là; could you tell me the ~ to the library? pouvez-vous me dire comment aller à la bibliothèque?; what's the shortest OR quickest ~ to town? quel est le chemin le plus court pour aller en ville?; we took the long ~ (round) nous avons pris le chemin le plus long; which ~ does this bus go? par où passe ce bus?; I had to ask the OR my ~ il a fallu que je demande mon chemin; she knows the ~ to school elle connaît le chemin de l'école; they went the wrong ~ ils se sont trompés de chemin, ils ont pris le mauvais chemin ❑ to lose one's ~ *literal* s'égarer, perdre son chemin; *fig* s'égarer, se fourvoyer; to know one's ~ around *inf literal* savoir s'orienter; *fig* savoir se débrouiller. - **3.** [route leading in a specified direction] chemin *m*, route *f*; the ~ back le chemin OR la route du retour; I got lost on the ~ back home je me suis perdu sur le chemin du retour; he couldn't find the ~ back home il n'a pas trouvé le chemin pour rentrer (à la maison); on our ~ back we stopped for dinner au retour OR sur le chemin du retour nous nous sommes arrêtés pour dîner; she showed us the easiest ~ down/up elle nous a montré le chemin le plus facile pour descendre/monter; the ~ up is difficult but the ~ down will be easier la montée est difficile mais la descente sera plus facile; do you know the ~ down/up? savez-vous par où on descend/on monte?; the ~ in l'entrée *f*; the ~ out la sortie; we looked for a ~ in/out nous cherchions un moyen d'entrer/de sortir; I took the back ~ out je suis sorti par derrière; '~ in' 'entrée'; '~ out' 'sortie' ‖ *fig*: miniskirts are on the ~ back in la minijupe est de retour; miniskirts are on the ~ out la minijupe n'est plus tellement à la mode; the director is on the ~ out le directeur ne sera plus là très longtemps; they found a ~ out of the deadlock ils ont trouvé une solution pour sortir de l'impasse; is there no ~ out of this nightmare? n'y a-t-il pas moyen de mettre fin à ce cauchemar?; their decision left her no ~ out leur décision l'a mise dans une impasse; he left himself a ~ out il s'est ménagé une porte de sortie. - **4.** [direction] direction *f*, sens *m*; come this ~ venez par ici; he went that ~ il est allé par là; 'this ~ to the chapel' 'vers la chapelle'; this ~ and that de-ci de-là, par-ci par-là; look this ~ regarde par ici; I never looked their ~ je n'ai jamais regardé dans leur direction; to look the other ~ *literal* détourner les yeux; *fig* fermer les yeux; he didn't know which ~ to look [embarrassed] il ne savait plus où se mettre; which ~ is the wind blowing? *literal* d'où vient le vent?; I could tell which ~ the wind was blowing *fig* je voyais très bien ce qui allait se passer; which ~ do I go from here? *literal* où est-ce que je vais maintenant?; *fig* qu'est-ce que je fais maintenant?; get in, I'm going your ~ montez, je vais dans la même direction que vous; we each went our separate ~s [on road] nous sommes partis chacun de notre côté; [in life] chacun de nous a suivi son propre chemin; he went the wrong ~ il a pris la mauvaise direction; [down one-way street] il a pris la rue en sens interdit ❑ to come one's ~ se présenter; any job that comes my ~ n'importe quel travail qui se présente; if ever the opportunity comes your ~ si jamais l'occasion se présente; everything's going my ~ *inf* tout marche comme je veux en ce moment; the vote went our ~ le vote nous a été favorable; the vote couldn't have gone any other ~ les résultats du vote étaient donnés d'avance; to go one's own ~ n'en faire qu'à sa tête, vivre à sa guise; to go the ~ of all flesh OR of all things mourir. - **5.** [side] sens *m*; stand the box the other ~ up posez le carton dans l'autre sens; 'this ~ up' 'haut'; hold the picture the right ~ up tenez le tableau dans le bon sens; it's the wrong ~ up c'est dans le mauvais sens; the curtains are the wrong ~ round les rideaux sont à l'envers OR dans le mauvais sens; your sweater is the right/wrong ~ out votre pull est à l'endroit/à l'envers; cats hate having their fur brushed the wrong ~ les chats détestent qu'on les caresse à rebrousse-poil; SHE insulted him? you've got it the wrong ~ round elle, elle l'a insulté? mais c'est le contraire; he invited her tonight, last time it was the other ~ round ce soir c'est lui qui l'a invitée, la dernière fois c'était l'inverse ❑ to rub sb up the right ~ caresser qqn dans le sens du poil; to rub sb up the wrong ~ prendre qqn à rebrousse-poil. - **6.** [area, vicinity] parages *mpl*; call in when you're up our ~ passez nous voir quand vous êtes dans le coin OR dans les parages; I was out OR over your ~ yesterday j'étais près de OR du côté de chez vous hier; the blast came from Chicago ~ l'explosion venait du côté de Chicago. - **7.** [distance - in space]: we came part of the ~ by foot nous avons fait une partie de la route à pied; they were one-third of the ~ through their trip ils avaient fait un tiers de leur voyage; we've come most of the ~ nous avons fait la plus grande partie du chemin; he can swim quite a ~ il peut nager assez longtemps; a long ~ off OR away loin; a little OR short ~ off pas très loin, à courte distance; Susan sat a little ~ off Susan était assise un peu plus loin; I saw him from a long ~ off je l'ai aperçu de loin; it's a long ~ to Berlin Berlin est loin; it's a long ~ from Paris to Berlin la route est longue de Paris à Berlin; we're a long ~ from home nous sommes loin de chez nous; we've come a long ~ [from far away] nous venons de loin; [made progress] nous avons fait du chemin; we've a long ~ to go [far to travel] il nous reste beaucoup de route à faire; [a lot to do] nous avons encore beaucoup à faire; [a lot to collect, pay] nous sommes encore loin du compte; he has a long ~ to go to be ready for the exam il est loin d'être prêt pour l'examen ‖ [in time]: it's a long ~ to Christmas Noël est encore loin; you have to go back a long ~ il faut remonter loin ‖ *fig*: I'm a long ~ from trusting him je suis loin de lui faire confiance; you're a long ~ off OR out [in guessing] vous n'y êtes pas du tout; that's a long ~ from what we thought ce n'est pas du tout ce qu'on croyait; she'll go a long ~ elle ira loin; the scholarship will go a long ~ towards helping with expenses la bourse va beaucoup aider à faire face aux dépenses; a little goodwill goes a long ~ un peu de bonne volonté facilite bien les choses; she makes her money go a long ~ elle sait ménager son argent ❑ a little bit goes a long ~ il en faut très peu; a little of him goes a long ~ *hum* il est sympa, mais à petites doses *hum*. - **8.** [space in front of person, object]: a tree was in the ~ un arbre bloquait OR barrait le passage; a car was in his ~ une voiture lui barrait le passage OR l'empêchait de passer; I can't see, the cat is in the ~ je ne vois pas, le chat me gêne; is the lamp in your ~? la lampe vous gêne-t-elle?; put the suitcases under the bed out of the ~ rangez les valises sous le lit, pour qu'elles ne gênent pas; to get out of the ~ s'écarter (du chemin); we got out of his ~ nous l'avons laissé passer; out of my ~! pousse-toi!, laisse-moi passer!; the cars got out of the ambulance's ~ les voitures ont laissé passer l'ambulance; keep out of the ~! ne reste pas là!; make ~! écartez-vous!; make ~ for the parade! laissez passer le défilé!; make ~ for the President! faites place au Président! ‖ *fig*: her social life got in the ~ of her studies ses sorties l'empêchaient d'étudier; I don't want to get in the ~ of your happiness je ne veux pas entraver votre bonheur; I kept out of the boss's ~ j'ai évité le patron; he wants his boss out of the ~ *inf* il veut se débarrasser de son patron; once the meeting is out of the ~ *inf* dès que nous serons débarrassés de la réunion; they tore down the slums to make ~ for blocks of flats ils ont démoli les taudis pour pouvoir construire des immeubles ❑ to clear OR prepare the ~ for sthg préparer la voie à qqch; to put difficulties in sb's ~ créer des difficultés à qqn. - **9.** [indicating a progressive action]: the acid ate its ~ through the metal l'acide est passé à travers le métal; I fought OR pushed my ~ through the crowd je me suis frayé un chemin à travers la foule; we made our ~ towards the train nous nous sommes dirigés vers le train; I made my ~ back to my seat je suis retourné à ma place; they made their ~ across the desert ils ont traversé le désert; they made their ~ down/up the hill ils ont descendu/monté la colline; she made her ~ up through the hierarchy elle a gravi les échelons de la hiérarchie un par un; she had to make her own ~ in the world elle a dû faire son chemin toute seule; she talked her ~ out of it elle s'en est sortie avec de belles paroles; he worked OR made his ~ through the pile of newspapers il a lu les journaux un par un; I worked my ~ through college j'ai travaillé pour payer mes études.

B. - **1.** [means, method] moyen *m*, méthode *f*; in what ~ can I help you? comment OR en quoi puis-je vous être utile?; there are several ~s to go OR of going about it il y a plusieurs façons OR moyens de s'y prendre; I do it this ~ voilà comment je fais; they thought they would win that ~ ils pensaient pouvoir gagner comme ça; he's going to handle it his ~ il va faire ça à sa façon; she has her own ~ of cooking fish elle a sa façon à elle de cuisiner le poisson; the right/wrong ~ to do it la bonne/mauvaise façon de le faire; you're doing it the right/wrong ~ c'est comme ça/ce n'est pas comme ça qu'il faut (le) faire; do it the usual ~ faites comme d'habitude; there's no ~ OR I can't see any ~ we'll finish on time nous ne finirons jamais OR nous n'avons aucune chance de finir à temps ❑ ~s and means POL financement *m*; love will find a ~ *hum* l'amour finit toujours par triompher; that's the ~ to do it! c'est comme ça qu'il faut faire!, voilà comment il faut faire!; well done! that's the ~ (to go)! *Am inf* bravo! c'est bien!; what a ~ to go! [manner of dying] quelle belle mort!; [congratulations] bravo! - **2.** [particular manner, fashion] façon *f*, manière *f*; in a friendly ~ gentiment; he spoke in a general ~ about the economy il a parlé de l'économie d'une façon générale; she doesn't like the ~ he is dressed elle n'aime pas la façon dont il est habillé; he doesn't speak the ~ his family does il ne parle pas comme sa famille; they see things in the same ~ ils voient les choses de la même façon; in their own (small) ~ they fight racism à leur façon OR dans la limite de leurs moyens, ils luttent contre le racisme; in the same ~, we note that... de même, on notera que...; that's one ~ to look at it OR ~ of looking at it c'est une façon OR manière de voir les choses; my ~ of looking at it mon point de vue sur la question; try to see it my ~ mettez-vous à ma place; to her ~ of thinking à son avis; the ~ she feels about him les sentiments qu'elle éprouve à son égard; I didn't think you would take it this ~ je ne pensais pas que vous le prendriez comme ça; if that's the ~ you feel about it! si c'est comme ça que vous le prenez! ❑ the American ~ of life la manière de vivre des Américains, le mode de vie américain; being on the move is a ~ of life for the gypsy le voyage est un mode de vie pour les gitans; yearly strikes have become a ~ of life les grèves annuelles sont devenues une habitude. - **3.** [custom] coutume *f*, usage *m*; [habitual manner of acting] manière *f*, habitude *f*; we soon got used to her ~s nous nous sommes vite habitués à ses manières; the ~s of God and men les voies de Dieu et de l'homme; he knows nothing of their ~s il les connaît très mal OR ne les comprend pas du tout; she has a ~ of tossing her head when she laughs elle a une façon OR manière de rejeter la tête en arrière quand elle rit; they're happy in their own ~ ils sont heureux à leur manière; it's not my ~ to criticize ce n'est pas mon genre OR ce n'est pas dans mes habitudes de critiquer; he's not in a bad mood, it's just his ~ il n'est pas de mauvaise humeur, c'est sa façon d'être habituelle ❑ she got into/out of the ~ of rising early elle a pris/perdu l'habitude de se lever tôt. - **4.** [facility, knack]: she has a (certain) ~ with her elle a le chic; he has a ~ with children il sait (comment) s'y prendre OR il a le chic avec les enfants; she has a ~ with words elle a le chic pour s'exprimer; trouble has a ~ of showing up when least expected les ennuis ont le chic pour se manifester quand on ne s'y attend pas. -**5.** [indicating a condition, state of affairs] : **let me tell you the ~ it was** laisse-moi te raconter comment ça s'est passé; **we can't invite him given the ~ things are** on ne peut pas l'inviter étant donné la situation; **we left the flat the ~ it was** nous avons laissé l'appartement tel qu'il était OR comme il était; **is he going to be staying here? – it looks that ~** est-ce qu'il va loger ici? – on dirait (bien); **it's not the ~ it looks!** ce n'est pas ce que vous pensez!; **it's not the ~ it used to be** ce n'est pas comme avant; **that's the ~ things are** c'est comme ça; **that's the ~ of the world** ainsi va le monde; **business is good and we're trying to keep it that ~** les affaires vont bien et nous faisons en sorte que ça dure; **the train is late – that's always the ~** le train est en retard – c'est toujours comme ça OR pareil; **life goes on (in) the same old ~** la vie va son train OR suit son cours; **I don't like the ~ things are going** je n'aime pas la tournure que prennent les choses; **we'll never finish the ~ things are going** au train où vont les choses, on n'aura jamais fini ❑ **to be in a bad ~** être en mauvais état; **he's in a bad ~** il est dans un triste état; **their business is in a bad/good ~** leurs affaires marchent mal/bien; **she's in a fair ~ to succeed/to becoming president** elle est bien partie pour réussir/pour devenir président. -**6.** [respect, detail] égard *m*, rapport *m*; **in what ~?** à quel égard?, sous quel rapport?; **in this ~** à cet égard, sous ce rapport; **it's important in many ~s** c'est important à bien des égards; **in some ~s** à certains égards, par certains côtés; **the job suits her in every ~** le poste lui convient à tous égards OR à tous points de vue; **I'll help you in every possible ~** je ferai tout ce que je peux pour vous aider; **she studied the problem in every ~ possible** elle a examiné le problème sous tous les angles possibles; **useful in more ~s than one** utile à plus d'un égard; **these two books, each interesting in its (own) ~** ces deux livres, qui sont intéressants chacun dans son genre; **he's clever that ~** sur ce plan-là il est malin ❑ **in a ~ you're right** en un sens vous avez raison; **I see what you mean in a ~** d'un certain point de vue OR d'une certaine manière, je vois ce que tu veux dire; **I am in no ~ responsible** je ne suis absolument pas OR aucunement responsable; **this in no ~ changes your situation** ceci ne change en rien votre situation; **without wanting in any ~ to criticize** sans vouloir le moins du monde critiquer. -**7.** [scale] : **to do things in a big ~** faire les choses en grand; **she went into politics in a big ~** elle s'est lancée à fond dans la politique; **they're in the arms business in a big ~** ils font de grosses affaires dans l'armement; **they helped out in a big ~** ils ont beaucoup aidé; **a grocer in a big/small ~** un gros/petit épicier; **we live in a small ~** nous vivons modestement; **it does change the situation in a small ~** ça change quand même un peu la situation. -**8.** *(usu pl)* [part, share] : **we divided the money four ~s** nous avons partagé l'argent en quatre; **the committee was split three ~s** le comité était divisé en trois groupes. -**9.** NAUT: **we're gathering/losing ~** nous prenons/perdons de la vitesse; **the ship has ~ on** le navire a de l'erre. -**10.** *phr*: **she always gets** OR **has her ~** elle arrive toujours à ses fins; **he only wants it his ~** il n'en fait qu'à sa tête; **I'm not going to let you have it all your ~** je refuse de te céder en tout; **if I had my ~, he'd be in prison** si cela ne tenait qu'à moi, il serait en prison; **I refuse to go – have it your ~** je refuse d'y aller – fais ce que OR comme tu veux; **no, it was 1789 – have it your ~** non, c'était en 1789 – soit; **you can't have it both ~s** il faut choisir; **I can stop too, it works both ~s** je peux m'arrêter aussi, ça marche dans les deux sens; **there are no two ~s about it** il n'y a pas le choix; **no two ~s about it, he was rude** il n'y a pas à dire, il a été grossier; **to have one's (wicked) ~ with sb** *hum* coucher avec qqn.

◇ *adv inf* -**1.** [far – in space, time] très loin; **they live ~ over yonder** ils habitent très loin par là-bas; **~ up the mountain** très haut dans la montagne; **~ back in the distance** au loin derrière; **~ back in the 1930s** déjà dans les années 30. -**2.** *fig*: **we've been friends from ~ back** nous sommes amis depuis très longtemps; **you're ~ below the standard** tu es bien en-dessous du niveau voulu; **he's ~ over forty** il a largement dépassé la quarantaine; **she's ~ ahead of her class** elle est très en avance sur sa classe; **he's ~ off in his guess** il est loin d'avoir deviné.

◆ **ways** *npl* NAUT [in shipbuilding] cale *f*.

◆ **all the way** *adv phr*: **the baby cried all the ~** le bébé a pleuré tout le long du chemin; **don't close the curtains all the ~** ne fermez pas complètement les rideaux; **prices go all the ~ from 200 to 1,000 dollars** les prix vont de 200 à 1 000 dollars; **I'm with you all the ~** *fig* je vous suis OR je vous soutiens jusqu'au bout ❑ **to go all the ~ (with sb)** *inf* aller jusqu'au bout (avec qqn).

◆ **along the way** *adv phr* en route; **I stopped several times along the ~** je me suis arrêté plusieurs fois en (cours de) route; **their project had some problems along the ~** *fig* leur projet a connu quelques problèmes en cours de route.

◆ **by a long way** *adv phr*: **I prefer chess by a long ~** je préfère de loin OR de beaucoup les échecs; **this is bigger by a long ~** c'est nettement OR beaucoup plus grand; **he's not as capable as you are by a long ~** il est loin d'être aussi compétent que toi; **is your project ready? – not by a long ~!** ton projet est-il prêt? – loin de là!

◆ **by the way** ◇ *adv phr* [incidentally] à propos; **by the ~, where did he go?** à propos, où est-il allé?; **by the ~, her brother sings much better** soit dit en passant, son frère chante beaucoup mieux; **I bring up this point by the ~** je signale ce point au passage OR en passant. ◇ *adj phr* [incidental] secondaire; **that point is quite by the ~** ce détail est tout à fait secondaire.

◆ **by way of** *prep phr* -**1.** [via] par, via; **to go by ~ of Brussels** passer par Bruxelles. -**2.** [as a means of] : **by ~ of illustration** à titre d'exemple; **she outlined the situation by ~ of introduction** elle a présenté un aperçu de la situation en guise d'introduction; **by ~ of introducing himself, he gave us his card** en guise de présentation, il nous a donné sa carte; **they receive money by ~ of grants** ils reçoivent de l'argent sous forme de bourses.

◆ **either way** *adv phr* -**1.** [in either case] dans les deux cas; **either ~ I lose** dans les deux cas je suis perdant; **shall we take the car or the bus? – it's fine by me either ~** tu préfères prendre la voiture ou le bus? – n'importe, ça m'est égal. -**2.** [more or less] en plus ou en moins; **a few days either ~ could make all the difference** quelques jours en plus ou en moins pourraient tout changer. -**3.** [indicating advantage] : **the match could have gone either ~** le match était ouvert; **there's nothing in it either ~** c'est pareil.

◆ **in such a way as to** *conj phr* de façon à ce que; **she answered in such a ~ as to make me understand** elle a répondu de façon à ce que je comprenne.

◆ **in such a way that** *conj phr* de telle façon OR manière que.

◆ **in the way of** *prep phr* -**1.** [in the form of] : **she receives little in the ~ of salary** son salaire n'est pas bien gros; **what is there in the ~ of food?** qu'est-ce qu'il y a à manger?; **do you need anything in the ~ of paper?** avez-vous besoin de papier?; **he doesn't have much in the ~ of brains** il n'a rien dans la tête. -**2.** [within the context of] : **we met in the ~ of business** nous nous sommes rencontrés dans le cadre du travail ❑ **they put me in the ~ of making some money** ils m'ont indiqué un moyen de gagner de l'argent.

◆ **no way** *inf adv phr* pas question; **will you do it for me? – no ~!** tu feras ça pour moi? – pas question!; **no ~ am I going to tell him!** (il n'est) pas question que je le lui dise!

◆ **on one's way, on the way** *adv & adj phr* -**1.** [along the route] : **it's on my ~** c'est sur mon chemin; **you pass it on your ~ to the office** vous passez devant en allant au bureau; **I'll catch up with you on the ~** je te rattraperai en chemin OR en route || [coming, going] : **on the ~ to work** en allant au bureau; **I'm on my ~!** j'y vais!; **she's on her ~ home** elle rentre chez elle; **on his ~ to town he met his father** en allant en ville, il a rencontré son père ❑ **we must be on our ~** il faut que nous y allions; **to go one's ~** repartir, reprendre son chemin. -**2.** *fig*: **she has a baby on the ~** elle attend un bébé; **her second book is on the ~** [being written] elle a presque fini d'écrire son deuxième livre; [being published] son deuxième livre est sur le point de paraître; **she's on the ~ to success** elle est sur le chemin de la réussite; **the patient is on the ~ to recovery** le malade est en voie de guérison; **she's (well) on the ~ to becoming president** elle est en bonne voie de devenir président; **the new school is well on the ~ to being finished** la nouvelle école est presque terminée.

◆ **one way and another** *adv phr* en fin de compte; **I've done quite well for myself one ~ and another** je me suis plutôt bien débrouillé en fin de compte.

◆ **one way or the other, one way or another** *adv phr* -**1.** [by whatever means] d'une façon ou d'une autre; **one ~ or the other I'm going to get that job!** d'une façon ou d'une autre, j'aurai ce boulot! -**2.** [expressing impartiality or indifference] : **I've nothing to say one ~ or the other** je n'ai rien à dire, ni pour ni contre; **it doesn't matter to them one ~ or another** ça leur est égal. -**3.** [more or less] : **a month one ~ or the other** un mois de plus ou de moins.

◆ **out of one's way** *adv phr*: **I don't want to take you out of your ~** je ne veux pas vous faire faire un détour; **don't go out of your ~ for me!** *fig* ne vous dérangez pas pour moi!; **she went out of her ~ to find me a job** *fig* elle s'est donné du mal pour me trouver du travail.

◆ **under way** *adj & adv phr*: **to be under ~** [person, vehicle] être en route; *fig* [meeting, talks] être en cours; [plans, project] être en train; **to get under ~** [person, train] se mettre en route, partir; [car] se mettre en route, démarrer; *fig* [meeting, plans, talks] démarrer; **the meeting was already under ~** la réunion avait déjà commencé; **they got the plans under ~** ils ont mis le projet en route; **the project is well under ~** le projet est en bonne voie de réalisation || NAUT: **the ship is under ~** le navire est en route; **the captain got (the ship) under ~** le capitaine a appareillé; **the ship got under ~** le navire a appareillé OR a levé l'ancre.

-way *in cpds*: **one~ street** rue *f* à sens unique; **a four~ discussion** une discussion à quatre participants; **there was a three~ split of the profits** les bénéfices ont été divisés en trois.

waybill ['weɪbɪl] *n* feuille *f* de route, lettre *f* de voiture.

wayfarer ['weɪfeərəʳ] *n* voyageur *m*, -euse *f*.

wayfaring ['weɪfeərɪŋ] ◇ *n (U)* voyages *mpl*. ◇ *adj* voyageur.

waylay [,weɪ'leɪ] (*pt & pp* waylaid) *vt* [attack] attaquer, assaillir; [stop] intercepter, arrêter (au passage).

way-out *inf adj* [unusual – film, style] bizarre, curieux; [– person] excentrique, bizarre.

Ways and Means Committee *pr n commission américaine du budget à la Chambre des représentants*.

wayside ['weɪsaɪd] ◇ *n* bord *m* OR côté *m* de la route.
◇ *adj* au bord de la route; **a ~ inn** une auberge au bord de la route; **~ flowers** les fleurs qui bordent la route.

way station *n Am* RAIL petite gare *f*; **a ~ on the road to success** *fig* une étape sur la route du succès.

wayward ['weɪwəd] *adj* -**1.** [person – wilful] entêté, têtu; [– unpredictable] qui n'en fait qu'à sa tête, imprévisible; [behaviour] imprévisible; [horse] rétif. -2. [fate] fâcheux, malencontreux.

WBC (*abbr of* World Boxing Council) *pr n* Conseil *m* mondial de la boxe.

WC (*abbr of* water closet) *n* W-C *mpl*.

WCC *pr n abbr of* World Council of Churches.

we [wiː] *pron* -1. [oneself and others] nous; we went for a walk nous sommes allés nous promener; we all stood up nous nous sommes tous levés; we, the people nous, le peuple; we Democrats believe that... nous, les démocrates, croyons que...; as we say back home comme on dit chez nous; as we will see in chapter two comme nous le verrons OR comme on le verra dans le chapitre deux; we all make mistakes tout le monde peut se tromper. -2. *fml* [royal] nous; the royal we le nous OR pluriel de majesté. -3. *inf* [you]: and how are we today, John/Mrs Smith? alors, comment allons-nous aujourd'hui, John/Madame Smith?

weak [wiːk] ◇ *adj* -1. [physically - animal, person] faible; [- health] fragile, délicat; [- eyes, hearing] faible, mauvais; to become OR to get OR to grow ~ OR ~er s'affaiblir; we were ~ with OR from hunger nous étions affaiblis par la faim; he felt ~ with fear il avait les jambes molles de peur; I went ~ at the knees mes jambes se sont dérobées sous moi, j'avais les jambes en coton; it's always the ~est who go to the wall *Br* ce sont toujours les plus faibles qui trinquent; the ~er sex le sexe faible. -2. [morally, mentally] mou, faible; he's far too ~ to be a leader il est beaucoup trop mou pour être un meneur; in a ~ moment dans un moment de faiblesse; to be ~ in the head être faible d'esprit. -3. [feeble - argument, excuse] faible, peu convaincant; [- army, government, institution] faible, impuissant; [- structure] fragile, peu solide; [- light, signal, currency, economy, stock market] faible; she managed a ~ smile elle a réussi à sourire faiblement; she answered in a ~ voice elle répondit d'une voix faible; to have a ~ hand [in cards] avoir des cartes faibles; he's the ~ link in the chain c'est lui le maillon faible de la chaîne. -4. [deficient, poor - pupil, subject] faible; I'm ~ in geography, geography is my ~ subject je suis faible en géographie; she's rather ~ on discipline elle est plutôt laxiste. -5. [chin] fuyant; [mouth] tombant. -6. [acid, solution] faible; [drink, tea] léger; AUT & MECH [mixture] pauvre. -7. GRAMM & LING [verb] faible, régulier; [syllable] faible, inaccentué.
◇ *npl*: the ~ les faibles *mpl*.

weaken ['wiːkn] ◇ *vt* -1. [person] affaiblir; [heart] fatiguer; [health] miner. -2. [government, institution, team] affaiblir; FIN [dollar, mark] affaiblir, faire baisser. -3. [argument] enlever du poids OR de la force à; [position] affaiblir; [determination] affaiblir, faire fléchir. -4. [structure] affaiblir, rendre moins solide; [foundations, cliff] miner, saper.
◇ *vi* -1. [person - physically] s'affaiblir, faiblir; [- morally] faiblir; [voice, health] faiblir; her resolution began to ~ sa détermination commençait à faiblir; he finally ~ed and gave in il s'est finalement laissé fléchir et a cédé. -2. [influence, power] diminuer, baisser. -3. [structure] faiblir, devenir moins solide. -4. FIN [dollar, mark] s'affaiblir; [prices] fléchir, baisser.

weakening ['wiːkənɪŋ] *n* [of person, resolve] affaiblissement *m*; [of currency or structure] fléchissement *m*, affaiblissement *m*.

weak-kneed [-niːd] *adj* mou, lâche.

weakling ['wiːklɪŋ] *n* -1. [physically] gringalet *m*, petite nature *f*. -2. [morally] faible *mf*, mauviette *f*.

weakly ['wiːklɪ] *adv* [get up, walk] faiblement; [speak] faiblement, mollement.

weak-minded *adj* -1. [not intelligent] faible OR simple d'esprit. -2. [lacking willpower] faible, irrésolu.

weakness ['wiːknɪs] *n* -1. [of person - physical] faiblesse *f*; [- moral] point *m* faible; in a moment of ~ dans un moment de faiblesse; sweets are one of his ~es la confiserie est un de ses points faibles; he has a ~ for sports cars il a un faible pour les voitures de sport. -2. [of government, institution] faiblesse *f*, fragilité *f*. -3. [of structure] fragilité *f*. -4. FIN [of currency] faiblesse *f*.

weak-willed *n* faible, velléitaire.

weal [wiːl] *n* -1. [mark] marque *f* de coup, zébrure *f*; his back was covered in ~s il avait le dos couvert de traces de coups. -2. *arch* OR *lit* [wellbeing] bien *m*, bonheur *m*; the common OR public ~ le bien public.

weald [wiːld] *n Br arch* [open country] pays *m* découvert; [wooded country] pays *m* boisé.

Weald [wiːld] *pr n* [region]: the ~ *région du sud-est de l'Angleterre*.

wealth [welθ] *n (U)* -1. [richness - of family, person] richesse *f*, richesses *fpl*, fortune *f*; [- of nation] richesse *f*, prospérité *f*; a young woman of great ~ une jeune femme très fortunée; they have acquired considerable ~ ils ont acquis une fortune considérable OR des biens considérables ❑ 'The Wealth of Nations' *Smith* 'Recherches sur la nature et les causes de la richesse des nations'. -2. [large amount - of details, ideas] abondance *f*, profusion *f*; he showed a ~ of knowledge about Egyptian art il fit preuve d'une profonde connaissance de l'art égyptien.

wealth tax *n Br* impôt *m* sur la fortune.

wealthy ['welθɪ] (*compar* wealthier, *superl* wealthiest) ◇ *adj* [person] riche, fortuné; [country] riche; a ~ heiress une riche héritière.
◇ *npl*: the ~ les riches *mpl*.

wean [wiːn] *vt* [baby] sevrer; a generation ~ed on television une génération qui a grandi avec la télévision.
◆ **wean off** *vt sep*: to ~ sb off sthg détourner qqn de qqch; I've ~ed him off cigarettes je lui ai fait perdre l'habitude de fumer.

weaning ['wiːnɪŋ] ◇ *n* sevrage *m*.
◇ *adj*: a ~ kitten/calf un chaton/un veau en sevrage.

weapon ['wepən] *n* arme *f*; carrying a ~ is illegal le port d'armes est illégal; patience is your best ~ in this situation *fig* la patience est votre meilleure arme dans cette situation; high interest rates are seen as a ~ against inflation des taux d'intérêt élevés sont considérés comme une arme contre l'inflation ❑ nuclear ~s armes nucléaires.

weaponry ['wepənrɪ] *n (U)* armes *fpl*; MIL matériel *m* de guerre, armements *mpl*.

weapon system *n* dispositif *m* OR système *m* militaire.

wear [weəʳ] (*pt* wore [wɔːʳ], *pp* worn [wɔːn]) ◇ *vt* -1. [beard, spectacles, clothing etc] porter; what shall I ~? qu'est-ce que je vais mettre?; I haven't a thing to ~ je n'ai rien à me mettre; she wore a miniskirt elle portait une minijupe, elle était en minijupe; to ~ a seat belt AUT mettre la ceinture (de sécurité); the miniskirt is being worn again this year la minijupe se porte de nouveau cette année; he always ~s good clothes il est toujours bien habillé, il s'habille toujours bien; he was ~ing slippers/a dressing gown il était en chaussons/en robe de chambre; he ~s a beard il porte la barbe; she wore a ribbon in her hair elle portait OR avait un ruban dans les cheveux; she ~s her hair in a bun elle a un chignon; do you always ~ make-up? tu te maquilles tous les jours?; she wore lipstick elle s'était mis OR elle avait mis du rouge à lèvres; I often ~ perfume/aftershave je mets souvent du parfum/de la lotion après-rasage ❑ to ~ the trousers *Br* OR the pants *Am inf* porter la culotte, commander. -2. [expression] avoir, afficher; [smile] arborer; she wore an anxious look son regard exprimait l'inquiétude, elle avait un air inquiet; he wore a frown il fronçait les sourcils ❑ to ~ one's heart on one's sleeve laisser voir ses sentiments. -3. [make by rubbing] user; to ~ holes in sthg trouer OR percer peu à peu qqch; her shoes were worn thin ses chaussures étaient complètement usées; he wore his coat threadbare il a usé son manteau jusqu'à la corde; a path had been worn across the lawn un sentier avait été creusé à travers la pelouse par le passage des gens; the wheel had worn a groove in the wood la roue avait creusé le bois. -4. *inf Br* [accept - argument, behaviour] supporter, tolérer; I won't ~ it! je ne marcherai pas! -5. *phr*: to ~ o.s. to a frazzle OR a shadow s'éreinter.
◇ *vi* -1. [endure, last] durer; wool ~s better than cotton la laine résiste mieux à l'usure OR fait meilleur usage que le coton; this coat has worn well ce manteau a bien servi; this rug should ~ for years ce tapis devrait durer OR faire des années; it will ~ forever cela durera pour toujours, c'est inusable ‖ *fig*: their friendship has worn well leur amitié est restée intacte malgré le temps; she's worn well *inf Br* elle est bien conservée. -2. [be damaged through use] s'user; this rug has worn badly in the middle ce tapis est très usé au milieu; the carpet had worn thin le tapis était usé OR élimé; the stone had worn smooth la pierre était polie par le temps ‖ *fig*: her patience was ~ing thin elle était presque à bout de patience; his excuses are ~ing a bit thin ses excuses ne prennent plus; his jokes are ~ing a bit thin ses plaisanteries ne sont plus drôles. -3. *lit* [time] passer; as morning wore into afternoon comme la matinée passait OR l'après-midi approchait; as the year wore to its close comme l'année tirait à sa fin.
◇ *n (U)* -1. [of clothes]: for everyday ~ pour porter tous les jours; clothes suitable for evening ~ tenue de soirée; a suit for business ~ un costume pour le bureau ❑ women's ~ vêtements *mpl* pour femmes; winter ~ vêtements *mpl* d'hiver. -2. [use] usage *m*; these shoes will stand hard ~ ces chaussures feront un bon usage OR résisteront bien à l'usure; there's still plenty of ~ in that dress cette robe est encore très portable; to get a lot of ~ from OR out of sthg faire durer qqch; is there any ~ left in them? feront-ils encore de l'usage? -3. [deterioration]: ~ (and tear) usure *f*; fair OR normal ~ and tear usure normale; living in the big city puts a lot of ~ and tear on people les grandes villes sont une source de stress pour leurs habitants; the sheets are beginning to show signs of ~ les draps commencent à être un peu usés OR fatigués.
◆ **wear away** ◇ *vt sep* [soles] user; [cliff, land] ronger, éroder; [paint, design] effacer.
◇ *vi insep* [metal] s'user; [land] être rongé OR érodé; [grass, topsoil] disparaître *(par usure)*; [design] s'effacer.
◆ **wear down** ◇ *vt sep* [steps] user; *fig* [patience, strength] épuiser petit à petit; [courage, resistance] saper, miner; in the end she wore me down [I gave in to her] elle a fini par me faire céder; the busy schedule finally wore her down son emploi du temps chargé a fini par l'épuiser OR l'exténuer.
◇ *vi insep* [pencil, steps, tyres] s'user; [courage] s'épuiser; the heels have worn down les talons sont usés.
◆ **wear off** ◇ *vi insep* -1. [marks, design] s'effacer, disparaître. -2. [excitement] s'apaiser, passer; [anaesthetic, effects] se dissiper, disparaître; [pain] se calmer, passer; the novelty soon wore off l'attrait de la nouveauté a vite passé.
◇ *vt sep* effacer par l'usure, user.
◆ **wear on** *vi insep* [day, season] avancer lentement; [battle, discussion] se poursuivre lentement; as time wore on au fur et à mesure que le temps passait.
◆ **wear out** ◇ *vt sep* -1. [clothing, machinery] user. -2. [patience, strength, reserves] épuiser; to ~ out one's welcome abuser de l'hospitalité de ses hôtes. -3. [tire] épuiser; you're ~ing yourself out working so hard tu t'épuises OR t'exténues à tant travailler; to be worn out être exténué OR éreinté; worn out from arguing, he finally accepted their offer de guerre lasse, il a fini par accepter leur offre; their constant bickering ~s me out leurs chamailleries continuelles me fatiguent OR m'épuisent.

◇ *vi insep* [clothing, shoes] s'user; this material will never ~ out ce tissu est inusable.

◆ **wear through** ◇ *vt sep* trouer, percer.

◇ *vi insep* se trouer; my jeans have worn through at the knees mon jean est troué aux genoux.

wearable [ˈweərəbl] *adj* portable.

wearer [ˈweərəʳ] *n*: good news for ~s of glasses bonnes nouvelles pour les personnes qui portent des lunettes.

wearily [ˈwɪərɪlɪ] *adv* avec lassitude; "all right, if I must", she said ~ «bien, s'il le faut», dit-elle d'un ton las; he smiled ~ il sourit d'un air fatigué; we shuffled ~ along the platform nous traînions les pieds sur le quai avec lassitude.

weariness [ˈwɪərɪnɪs] *n* -**1.** [physical] lassitude *f*, fatigue *f*; [moral] lassitude *f*, abattement *m*. -**2.** [boredom] lassitude *f*, ennui *m*.

wearing [ˈweərɪŋ] *adj* fatigant, épuisant.

wearisome [ˈwɪərɪsəm] *adj* -**1.** [tiring] fatigant, épuisant. -**2.** [annoying] ennuyeux, lassant.

weary [ˈwɪərɪ] (*compar* wearier, *superl* weariest, *pt* & *pp* wearied) ◇ *adj* -**1.** [tired - physically, morally] las *fml*, fatigué; she grew ~ of reading elle s'est lassée de lire; I'm ~ of his silly jokes j'en ai assez de ses plaisanteries stupides; he gave a ~ sigh il a soupiré d'un air las; he spoke in a ~ voice il parlait d'une voix lasse; I'm ~ of life j'en ai assez OR je suis las de la vie. -**2.** [tiring - day, journey] fatigant, lassant.

◇ *vt* [tire] fatiguer, lasser; [annoy] lasser, agacer; they ~ me with all their complaining ils m'ennuient avec leurs plaintes continuelles.

◇ *vi* se lasser; she began to ~ of life in the country elle commença à se lasser de la vie à la campagne.

weasel [ˈwiːzl] ◇ *n* belette *f*; *pej* [person] fouine *f*.

◇ *vi Am* ruser; [in speaking] parler d'une façon ambiguë.

◇ *vt*: he ~ed his way into the conversation il s'est insinué dans la conversation.

◆ **weasel out** *inf vi insep Am*: to ~ out of sthg se tirer de qqch; he ~ed out of the contract il s'est débrouillé pour se dégager du contrat; she always ~s out of doing the dishes elle se débrouille toujours pour échapper à la vaisselle.

weasel words *npl* paroles *fpl* ambiguës OR équivoques, discours *m* ambigu OR équivoque.

weather [ˈweðəʳ] ◇ *n* -**1.** METEOR temps *m*; what's the ~ (like) today? quel temps fait-il aujourd'hui?; it's beautiful/terrible ~ il fait beau/mauvais; the ~ is awful OR foul il fait un temps de chien; ~ permitting si le temps le permet; surely you're not going out in this ~? vous n'allez tout de même pas sortir par un temps pareil?; in hot ~ par temps chaud, en période de chaleur; in all ~s par tous les temps; there was a change in the ~ il y eut un changement de temps, le temps changea. -**2.** RADIO & TV: ~ (forecast) (bulletin *m*) météo *f*; did you listen to the ~? as-tu écouté la météo? -**3.** *phr*: to feel under the ~ *inf* ne pas être dans son assiette.

◇ *comp* [forecast, map] météorologique; [conditions] climatique, atmosphérique; NAUT [side] du vent; keep your ~ eye open! *inf* veillez au grain!; I'll keep a ~ eye on the kids *inf* je vais surveiller les enfants.

◇ *vt* -**1.** [survive - storm] réchapper à; [- crisis] survivre à, réchapper à; the ship ~ed the storm le navire a traversé la tempête; will he ~ the storm? *fig* va-t-il se tirer d'affaire OR tenir le coup? -**2.** [wood] exposer aux intempéries.

◇ *vi* [bronze, wood] se patiner; [rock] s'éroder; this paint ~s well cette peinture vieillit bien OR résiste bien aux intempéries.

weather balloon *n* ballon-sonde *m*.

weather-beaten *adj* [face, person] buriné; [building, stone] dégradé par les intempéries.

weatherboard [ˈweðəbɔːd] *n* -**1.** *(U)* [on outer walls] planche *f* OR planches *fpl* à recouvrement. -**2.** [on door] planche *f* de recouvrement.

weatherboarding [ˈweðəbɔːdɪŋ] *n (U)* planches *fpl* à recouvrement.

weather-bound *adj* [aircraft, ship] immobilisé par le mauvais temps; [event] reporté pour cause de mauvais temps.

weather bureau *n Am* ≃ office *m* national de la météorologie.

weather centre *n Br* ≃ centre *m* météorologique régional; the London ~ la station de météorologie de Londres.

weathercock [ˈweðəkɒk] *n literal* & *fig* girouette *f*.

weather deck *n* [on ship] pont *m* découvert; [on bus] impériale *f* découverte.

weathered [ˈweðəd] *adj* [bronze, wood] patiné par le temps; [building, stone] érodé par le temps, usé par les intempéries; [face] buriné.

weatherglass [ˈweðəglɑːs] *n* baromètre *m*.

weather house *n sorte de baromètre décoratif représentant une petite maison d'où sortent deux figurines, l'une par beau temps, l'autre par mauvais temps.*

weathering [ˈweðərɪŋ] *n* désagrégation *f*, érosion *f*.

weatherly [ˈweðəlɪ] *adj* qui tient bien près du vent; a ~ ship un bateau ardent.

weatherman [ˈweðəmæn] (*pl* weathermen [-men]) *n*: the ~ le météorologue, le météorologiste; RADIO & TV le journaliste météo.

weatherproof [ˈweðəpruːf] ◇ *adj* [clothing] imperméable; [building] étanche.

◇ *vt* [clothing] imperméabiliser; [building] rendre étanche.

weather report *n* bulletin *m* météorologique.

weather satellite *n* satellite *m* météorologique.

weather ship *n* navire *m* météorologique.

weather station *n* station *f* OR observatoire *m* météorologique.

weather strip, weather stripping [ˈstrɪpɪŋ] *n* bourrelet *m* étanche.

weather vane *n* girouette *f*.

weatherwoman [ˈweðə,wʊmən] (*pl* weatherwomen [-,wɪmɪn]) *n*: the ~ la météorologue, la météorologiste; the BBC ~ RADIO & TV celle qui fait OR qui présente la météo à la BBC.

weatherworn [ˈweðəwɔːn] *adj* [face, person] buriné; [building, stone] dégradé par le temps.

weave [wiːv] (*vt senses 1,2,3 & vi senses 1,2 pt* wove [wəʊv], *pp* woven [ˈwəʊvn], *vt sense 4 & vi sense 3 pt & pp* weaved) ◇ *vt* -**1.** [cloth, web] tisser; [basket, garland] tresser; she wove the strands together into a necklace elle a tressé OR entrelacé les fils pour en faire un collier. -**2.** [story] tramer, bâtir; [plot] tisser, tramer; a tightly woven plot une intrigue bien ficelée; to ~ a spell jeter un sort. -**3.** [introduce] introduire, incorporer; he managed to ~ all the facts together to make a fascinating report il a réussi à incorporer tous les faits dans un rapport passionnant. -**4.** [as verb of movement]: he ~d his way across the room/towards the bar il s'est frayé un chemin à travers la salle/vers le bar; I had to ~ my way through the crowd j'ai dû me frayer un chemin OR me faufiler à travers la foule; the cyclist ~d his way through the traffic le cycliste se faufilait OR se glissait à travers la circulation.

◇ *vi* -**1.** TEX tisser. -**2.** [road, river] serpenter. -**3.** [as verb of movement] se faufiler, se glisser; he ~d unsteadily across the street il a traversé la rue en titubant OR en zigzaguant; the boxer ducked and ~d le boxeur a esquivé tous les coups; come on, get weaving! *inf* allons, grouillez-vous!

◇ *n* tissage *m*; the basket has a loose ~ le panier a un tissage lâche.

weaver [ˈwiːvəʳ] *n* -**1.** TEX tisserand *m*, -e *f*. -**2.** ORNITH tisserin *m*.

weaving [ˈwiːvɪŋ] ◇ *n* -**1.** [of cloth] tissage *m*; [of baskets, garlands] tressage *m*. -**2.** [of story] récit *m*; [of plot] trame *f*.

◇ *comp* [industry, mill] de tissage.

web [web] *n* -**1.** [of fabric, metal] tissu *m*; [of spider] toile *f*; a ~ of lies *fig* un tissu de mensonges; he was caught in a ~ of intrigue *fig* il a été pris dans un réseau d'intrigues. -**2.** [on feet - of duck, frog] palmure *f*; [- of humans] palmature *f*.

webbed [webd] *adj* palmé; to have ~ feet OR toes [duck, frog] avoir les pattes palmées; [human] avoir une palmature.

webbing [ˈwebɪŋ] *n (U)* -**1.** TEX [material] toile *f* à sangles; [on chair] sangles *fpl*. -**2.** ANAT [animal] palmure *f*; [human] palmature *f*.

weber [ˈveɪbəʳ] *n* weber *m*.

webfoot [ˈwebfʊt] (*pl* webfeet [-fiːt]) *n* -**1.** [foot - of animal] patte *f* palmée; [- of human] palmature *f*. -**2.** [kind of animal] palmipède *m*.

web-footed *adj* [animal] palmipède, qui a les pattes palmées; [human] qui a une palmature.

wed [wed] (*pt* & *pp* wed OR wedded, *cont* wedding) ◇ *vt lit* -**1.** [marry] épouser, se marier avec; to get ~ se marier. -**2.** *(usu pass)* [unite] allier; intelligence wedded to beauty l'intelligence alliée à la beauté; he's wedded to the cause il est véritablement marié à cette cause. -**3.** [subj: priest] marier.

◇ *vi* [in headline] se marier; PM's son to ~ le fils du Premier ministre se marie.

we'd [wiːd] -**1.** = **we would**. -**2.** = **we had**.

Wed. (*written abbr of* Wednesday) mer.

wedded [ˈwedɪd] *adj* [person] marié; [bliss, life] conjugal; her lawful ~ husband son époux légitime; the newly ~ couple les jeunes mariés *mpl*.

wedding [ˈwedɪŋ] ◇ *n* -**1.** [marriage] mariage *m*, noces *fpl*; to have a church ~ se marier à l'église; to have a civil ~ faire un mariage civil, se marier à la mairie; we had a quiet ~ nous nous sommes mariés OR nous avons célébré le mariage dans l'intimité; silver/golden/diamond ~ noces d'argent/d'or/de diamant. -**2.** [uniting] union *f*.

◇ *comp* [cake, night, trip] de noces; [ceremony, photograph, present] de mariage; ~ invitation faire-part *m inv* de mariage.

wedding anniversary *n* anniversaire *m* de mariage; our 10th ~ notre 10e anniversaire de mariage.

wedding band = **wedding ring**.

wedding breakfast *n lunch servi après la cérémonie du mariage.*

wedding day *n* jour *m* du mariage; on their ~ le jour de leur mariage.

wedding dress *n* robe *f* de mariée.

wedding list *n* liste *f* de mariage.

wedding march *n* marche *f* nuptiale.

wedding ring *n* alliance *f*, anneau *m* de mariage.

wedeln [ˈveɪdəln] *n* godille *f*.

wedge [wedʒ] ◇ *n* -**1.** [under door, wheel] cale *f*; put a ~ under the door calez la porte, mettez une cale sous la porte; their political differences drove a ~ between the two friends *fig* les deux amis se sont brouillés à cause de leurs divergences politiques. -**2.** [for splitting wood] coin *m*. -**3.** [of cheese, cake, pie] morceau *m*, part *f*. -**4.** [golf club] cale *f*. -**5.** [for climber] coin *m*.

◇ *vt* -**1.** [make fixed or steady] caler; the window was ~d open la fenêtre était maintenue ouverte à l'aide d'une cale; I ~d the door open/shut j'ai maintenu la porte ouverte/fermée par une cale; can you ~ the table with something? it's wobbling pouvez-vous caler la table avec quelque chose OR mettre une cale sous la table? elle est branlante. -**2.** [squeeze, push] enfoncer; to ~ sthg apart fendre OR forcer qqch; he ~d his foot in the door il a bloqué la porte avec son pied; she sat ~d between her two aunts elle était assise coincée entre ses deux tantes; I found the ring ~d down behind the cushion j'ai trouvé la bague enfoncée derrière le coussin.

◆ **wedge in** *vt sep* [object] faire rentrer, enfoncer; [person] faire rentrer; she was ~d in between two Italians elle était coincée entre deux Italiens; I ~d myself in at the back of the crowded hall je me suis glissé au fond de la salle

bondée; the photo was ~d in between two books la photo était glissée entre deux livres.
wedge heel *n* semelle *f* compensée.
wedge-heeled shoe [-hiːld], **wedgie** *inf* [ˈwedʒiː] *n* chaussure *f* à semelle compensée.
wedge-shaped *adj* en forme de coin.
wedlock [ˈwedlɒk] *n fml* mariage *m*; to be born out of ~ être un enfant naturel OR illégitime, être né hors du mariage.
Wednesday [ˈwenzdɪ] *n* mercredi *m*.
wee [wiː] ◇ *adj esp Scot* tout petit; a ~ bit un tout petit peu; a ~ drop of whisky une larme de whisky; in the ~ (small) hours of the morning au petit matin, aux premières heures du jour; a ~ boy un petit garçon.
◇ *vi inf* faire pipi.
◇ *n inf* pipi *m*; to have a ~ faire pipi.
weed [wiːd] ◇ *n* -**1.** [plant] mauvaise herbe *f*; that plant grows like a ~ cette plante pousse comme du chiendent. -**2.** *pej* [person] mauviette *f*. -**3.** *inf* [tobacco]: the ~ le tabac. -**4.** *drugs sl* herbe *f*.
◇ *vt* désherber, arracher les mauvaises herbes de; [with hoe] sarcler.
◇ *vi* désherber, arracher les mauvaises herbes.
◆ **weeds** *npl* vêtements *mpl* de deuil; in widow's ~s en deuil.
◆ **weed out** *vt sep* éliminer; [troublemakers] expulser; to ~ out the bad from the good faire le tri.
weeding [ˈwiːdɪŋ] *n* désherbage *m*; [with hoe] sarclage *m*; he does a little ~ every day il désherbe un peu OR enlève quelques mauvaises herbes tous les jours.
weedkiller [ˈwiːdˌkɪləʳ] *n* herbicide *m*, désherbant *m*.
weedy [ˈwiːdɪ] (*compar* weedier, *superl* weediest) *adj* -**1.** [ground] couvert OR envahi de mauvaises herbes. -**2.** *inf pej* [person] malingre.
Weejun® [ˈwiːdʒn] *n Am* mocassin *m*.
week [wiːk] *n* semaine *f*; next/last ~ la semaine prochaine/dernière; see you next ~ à la semaine prochaine; in one ~, in one ~'s time dans huit jours, d'ici une semaine; two ~s ago il y a deux semaines OR quinze jours; within a ~ [gen] dans la semaine, d'ici une semaine; ADMIN & COMM sous huitaine; ~ ending 25th March la semaine du 21 mars; a ~ from today d'ici huit jours; a ~ from tomorrow demain en huit; yesterday ~, a ~ yesterday il y a eu une semaine hier; Monday ~, a ~ on Monday lundi en huit; twice a ~ deux fois par semaine; ~ in ~ out, ~ after ~, ~ by ~ semaine après semaine; the rate changes from ~ to ~ le taux varie de semaine en semaine; it rained for ~s on end il a plu pendant des semaines; I haven't seen you in OR for ~s ça fait des semaines que je ne t'ai pas vu; we're taking a ~'s holiday nous prenons huit jours de congé; the working ~ la semaine de travail; a 40-hour ~ une semaine de 40 heures; she's paid by the ~ elle est payée à la semaine; I lost a ~'s pay j'ai perdu une semaine de salaire.
weekday [ˈwiːkˌdeɪ] ◇ *n* jour *m* de la semaine; ADMIN & COMM jour *m* ouvrable; on ~s en semaine; ~s only la semaine seulement, sauf samedi et dimanche.
◇ *comp* [activities] de la semaine; on ~ mornings le matin en semaine.
weekend [ˌwiːkˈend] ◇ *n* fin *f* de semaine, week-end *m*; at *Br* OR on *Am* the ~ le week-end; I'll do it at the ~ je le ferai pendant le week-end; what do you do at ~s? que faites-vous (pendant) le week-end OR les week-ends?; what are you doing this ~? quels sont tes projets pour le week-end?; he's staying with them for the ~ il passe le week-end chez eux; I'm going away for the ~ je pars pour le week-end; a long ~ un week-end prolongé.
◇ *comp* [schedule, visite] de OR du week-end; ~ bag OR case sac *m* de voyage, mallette *f*; ~ break *séjour d'un week-end*; a ~ cottage une maison secondaire OR de campagne; ~ return RAIL *billet aller et retour valable du vendredi au dimanche soir*.
◇ *vi* passer le week-end.
weekender [ˌwiːkˈendeʳ] *n personne en voyage pour le week-end*; he's one of the ~s who come here to ski il fait partie des gens qui viennent skier ici le week-end; most of the cottages belong to ~s la plupart des maisons sont des résidences secondaires.
weekly [ˈwiːklɪ] ◇ *adj* [visit, meeting] de la semaine, hebdomadaire; [publication, payment, wage] hebdomadaire.
◇ *n* hebdomadaire *m*.
◇ *adv* [once a week] chaque semaine, une fois par semaine; [each week] chaque semaine, tous les huit jours; twice ~ deux fois par semaine; he's paid ~ il est payé à la semaine.
weeknight [ˈwiːkˌnaɪt] *n* soir *m* de la semaine; I can't go out on ~s je ne peux pas sortir le soir en semaine.
weenie *inf* [ˈwiːnɪ] *n Am* -**1.** [frankfurter] saucisse *f* (de Francfort); ~ stand *kiosque où l'on vend des hot-dogs*. -**2.** [penis] zizi *m*. -**3.** [person] imbécile *mf*.
weeny *inf* [ˈwiːnɪ] (*compar* weenier, *superl* weeniest) *adj* tout petit, minuscule; would you like a brandy? — just a ~ one voulez-vous un cognac? — (j'en prendrai) juste un tout petit.
weenybopper *inf* [ˌwiːnɪˌbɒpəʳ] *n jeune qui aime la musique pop*.
weep [wiːp] (*pt* & *pp* wept [wept])
◇ *vi* -**1.** [person] pleurer, verser des larmes; to ~ for joy/with vexation pleurer de joie/de dépit; she wept for her lost youth elle pleurait sa jeunesse perdue; to ~ for sb pleurer qqn; the little girl wept over her broken doll la petite fille pleurait sur sa poupée cassée; he wept to see her so ill il a pleuré de la voir si malade; that's nothing to ~ about OR over il n'y a pas de quoi pleurer; it's enough to make you ~! *hum* c'est à faire pleurer!; I could have wept! j'en aurais pleuré! -**2.** [walls, wound] suinter, suer.
◇ *vt* [tears] verser, pleurer; he wept bitter tears il pleura amèrement.
◇ *n*: to have a ~ pleurer; she had a little ~ elle a versé quelques larmes.
weeping [ˈwiːpɪŋ] ◇ *adj* [person] qui pleure; [walls, wound] suintant.
◇ *n (U)* larmes *fpl*, pleurs *mpl*; a fit of ~ une crise de larmes.
weeping willow *n* saule *m* pleureur.
weepy [ˈwiːpɪ] (*compar* weepier, *superl* weepiest, *pl* weepies) ◇ *adj* -**1.** [tone, voice] larmoyant; [person] qui pleure; she is OR feels ~ elle a envie de pleurer, elle est au bord des larmes. -**2.** [film, story] sentimental, larmoyant.
◇ *n inf Br* [film] mélo *m*, film *m* sentimental; [book] mélo *m*, roman *m* à l'eau de rose.
weever [ˈwiːvəʳ] *n* vive *f*.
weevil [ˈwiːvl] *n* charançon *m*.
wee-wee *inf baby talk* ◇ *n* pipi *m*; to go (for a) ~ faire pipi.
◇ *vi* faire pipi.
weft [weft] *n* trame *f* TEXT.
weigh [weɪ] ◇ *vt* -**1.** [person, thing] peser; to ~ oneself se peser; to ~ sthg in one's hand soupeser qqch *pr*. -**2.** [consider] considérer, peser; let's ~ the evidence considérons les faits; she ~ed her words carefully elle a bien pesé ses mots; you have to ~ the pros and cons il faut peser le pour et le contre; to ~ one thing against another mettre deux choses en balance. -**3.** NAUT: to ~ anchor lever l'ancre.
◇ *vi* -**1.** [person, object] peser; how much do you ~? combien pesez-vous?, quel poids faites-vous?; the fish ~s one kilo le poisson pèse un kilo; he doesn't ~ much il ne pèse pas lourd. -**2.** [influence]: his silence began to ~ (heavy) son silence commençait à devenir pesant; the facts ~ heavily against him les faits plaident lourdement en sa défaveur.
◆ **under weigh** *adj phr* NAUT appareillé, en marche.
◆ **weigh down** *vt sep* -**1.** *literal* faire plier, courber; the branches were ~ed down with snow les branches ployaient sous le poids de la neige; she was ~ed down with suitcases elle pliait sous le poids des valises. -**2.** *fig*: she's ~ed down with financial problems elle est en proie à des OR accablée de problèmes financiers; he was ~ed down with debts/with sorrow il était accablé de dettes/de tristesse.
◆ **weigh in** *vi insep* -**1.** SPORT se faire peser *(avant une épreuve)*; the boxer ~ed in at 85 kilos le boxeur faisait 85 kilos avant le match; the jockey ~ed in at 45 kilos le jockey pesait 45 kilos avant la course. -**2.** [join in] intervenir; he always has to ~ in with his opinions il faut toujours qu'il intervienne pour imposer ses opinions.
◆ **weigh on** *vt insep* peser; his worries ~ed heavily on him ses soucis lui pesaient beaucoup; the exam ~ed on his mind l'examen le préoccupait OR tracassait.
◆ **weigh out** *vt sep* peser.
◆ **weigh up** *vt sep* -**1.** [consider] examiner, calculer; [compare] mettre en balance; to ~ up the situation peser la situation; I'm ~ing up whether to take the job or not je me demande si je devrais prendre le poste; to ~ up the pros and cons peser le pour et le contre. -**2.** [size up] mesurer; I looked round, ~ing up the opposition je me suis retourné pour mesurer l'adversaire.
weighbridge [ˈweɪbrɪdʒ] *n* pont-bascule *m*.
weigh-in *n* SPORT pesage *m*, pesée *f*.
weighing machine [ˈweɪɪŋ] *n* [for people] balance *f*; [for loads] bascule *f*.
weight [weɪt] ◇ *n* -**1.** [of person, package, goods] poids *m*; she tested OR felt the ~ of the package elle a soupesé le paquet; what's your normal ~? combien pesez-vous OR quel poids faites-vous normalement?; my ~ is 50 kg, I'm 50 kilos in ~ je pèse OR je fais 50 kilos; we're the same ~ nous faisons le même poids; he's twice your ~ il pèse deux fois plus lourd que toi; to gain OR to put on ~ grossir, prendre du poids; to lose ~ maigrir, perdre du poids; she's watching her ~ elle fait attention à sa ligne; what a ~! [person] qu'il est lourd!; [stone, parcel] que c'est lourd!; to sell sthg by ~ vendre qqch au poids ☐ she's worth her ~ in gold elle vaut son pesant d'or; take the ~ off your feet *hum* assieds-toi un peu. -**2.** [force] poids *m*; he put his full ~ behind the blow il a frappé de toutes ses forces ☐ to pull one's ~ faire sa part du travail, y mettre du sien; to throw one's ~ about OR around bousculer les gens. -**3.** [burden] poids *m*; the ~ of years le poids des années; he quailed under the ~ of responsibility le poids de la responsabilité l'a effrayé; that's a ~ off my mind je suis vraiment soulagé. -**4.** [importance, influence] poids *m*, influence *f*; the facts lend considerable ~ to her argument les faits donnent un poids considérable à son raisonnement; their opinion carries quite a lot of ~ leur opinion a un poids OR une autorité considérable; she put OR threw all her ~ behind the candidate elle a apporté tout son soutien au candidat; she carries little ~ with the authorities elle n'a pas beaucoup d'influence OR de poids auprès de l'administration. -**5.** [for scales] poids *m*; ~s and measures poids et mesures; a set of ~s une série de poids; a one kilogramme ~ un poids d'un kilogramme. -**6.** SPORT poids *m*; to lift ~s soulever des poids OR des haltères. -**7.** PHYS pesanteur *f*, poids *m*; atomic ~ poids atomique.
◇ *comp*: ~ allowance [in aeroplane] poids *m* de bagages autorisé; to have a ~ problem avoir un problème de poids.
◇ *vt* -**1.** [put weights on] lester. -**2.** [hold down] retenir OR maintenir avec un poids. -**3.** [bias]: the system is ~ed in favour of the wealthy le système est favorable aux riches OR privilégie les riches; the electoral system was ~ed against him le système électoral lui était défavorable OR jouait contre lui.

◆ **weight down** *vt sep* -**1.** [body, net] lester. -**2.** [papers, tarpaulin] maintenir OR retenir avec un poids.

weighted ['weɪtɪd] *adj* -**1.** [body, net] lesté. -**2.** [statistics, average] pondéré.

weighting ['weɪtɪŋ] *n* -**1.** [extra salary] indemnité *f*, allocation *f*; **London ~** indemnité de résidence à Londres. -**2.** [of statistics] pondération *f*; SCH coefficient *m*.

weightless ['weɪtlɪs] *adj* très léger; ASTRONAUT en état d'apesanteur.

weightlessness ['weɪtlɪsnɪs] *n* extrême légèreté *f*; ASTRONAUT apesanteur *f*.

weightlifter ['weɪt,lɪftəʳ] *n* haltérophile *mf*.

weightlifting ['weɪt,lɪftɪŋ] *n* haltérophilie *f*.

weight loss *n* perte *f* de poids.

weight training *n* entraînement *m* aux haltères.

weightwatcher ['weɪt,wɒtʃəʳ] *n* [person - on diet] personne *f* qui suit un régime; [- figure-conscious] personne *f* qui surveille son poids.

weighty ['weɪtɪ] (*compar* **weightier**, *superl* **weightiest**) *adj* -**1.** [suitcase, tome] lourd. -**2.** [responsibility] lourd; [problem] important, grave; [argument, reasoning] probant, de poids; **we're not qualified to consider such ~ matters** nous n'avons pas les compétences requises pour examiner des questions aussi importantes.

weir [wɪəʳ] *n* barrage *m (sur un cours d'eau)*.

weird [wɪəd] *adj* -**1.** [mysterious] mystérieux, surnaturel. -**2.** *inf* [peculiar] bizarre, étrange; **he has some ~ ideas** il a de drôles d'idées.

weirdly ['wɪədlɪ] *adv* -**1.** [mysteriously] mystérieusement. -**2.** [oddly] bizarrement, singulièrement.

weirdness ['wɪədnɪs] *n* étrangeté *f*, singularité *f*.

weirdo *inf* ['wɪədəʊ] (*pl* **weirdos**) ◇ *n* drôle d'oiseau *m* OR de zèbre *m*.
◇ *comp* [hairdo] extravagant.

welch [welʃ] = **welsh**.

welcher ['welʃəʳ] = **welsher**.

welcome ['welkəm] ◇ *vt* -**1.** [greet, receive - people] accueillir; **I ~d her warmly** je lui ai fait bon accueil OR un accueil chaleureux; **they ~d me in** ils m'ont chaleureusement invité à entrer; **we ~d him with open arms** nous l'avons accueilli à bras ouverts; **a dinner to ~ the new members** un dîner pour accueillir les nouveaux membres; **the dog ~s them home every evening** le chien leur fait la fête chaque soir lorsqu'ils rentrent; **would you please ~ Peter Robinson!** [to audience] voulez-vous applaudir Peter Robinson! -**2.** [accept gladly] être heureux d'avoir, recevoir avec plaisir; **I ~d the opportunity to speak to her** j'étais content d'avoir l'occasion de lui parler; **he ~d the news** il s'est réjoui de la nouvelle, il a accueilli la nouvelle avec joie; **she ~d any comments** elle accueillait volontiers les remarques que l'on pouvait lui faire; **we'd ~ a cup of coffee** nous prendrions volontiers une tasse de café.
◇ *n* accueil *m*; **she said a few words of ~** elle a prononcé quelques mots de bienvenue; **we bid them ~** nous leur souhaitons la bienvenue; **they gave him a warm ~** ils lui ont fait bon accueil OR réservé un accueil chaleureux; **we gave her a big ~ home** nous lui avons fait fête à son retour à la maison; **let's give a warm ~ to Louis Armstrong!** [to audience] applaudissons très fort Louis Armstrong!; **to overstay** OR **to outstay one's ~** abuser de l'hospitalité de ses hôtes; **I don't want to outstay my ~** je ne veux pas abuser de sa/votre *etc* hospitalité.
◇ *adj* -**1.** [person] bienvenu; **to be ~** être le bienvenu; **she's always ~ here** elle est toujours la bienvenue ici; **they made us very ~** ils nous ont fait un très bon accueil; **she didn't feel very ~** elle s'est sentie de trop ❑ **to put out the ~ mat (for sb)** faire un accueil chaleureux (à qqn). -**2.** [pleasant, desirable - arrival] bienvenu; [- change, interruption, remark] opportun; **that's ~ news** nous sommes heureux de l'apprendre; **their offer was most ~** leur suggestion m'a fait grand plaisir; **this cheque is most ~** ce chèque arrive opportunément OR tombe bien; **that's a ~ sight!** c'est un spectacle à réjouir le cœur!; **a helping hand is always ~** un coup de main est toujours le bienvenu OR ne fait jamais de mal; **the news came as a ~ relief to him** la nouvelle a été un vrai soulagement pour lui, il a été vraiment soulagé d'apprendre la nouvelle; **the holiday came as a ~ break** les vacances ont été une coupure bienvenue OR appréciable. -**3.** [permitted]: **you're ~ to join us** n'hésitez pas à vous joindre à nous; **he's ~ to borrow my book** qu'il n'hésite pas à emprunter mon livre; **you're ~ to anything you need** servez-vous si vous avez besoin de quelque chose; **you're ~ to try** je vous en prie, essayez ‖ [grudgingly]: **he's ~ to try!** libre à lui d'essayer!, qu'il essaie donc!; **I don't need it, she's ~ to it** je n'en ai pas besoin, elle peut bien le prendre OR je le lui donne volontiers; **she's ~ to him!** je ne le lui envie pas!; **take it and ~!** je te le donne bien volontiers! -**4.** [acknowledgment of thanks]: **you're ~!** je vous en prie!, il n'y a pas de quoi!
◇ *interj*: **~!** soyez le bienvenu!; **~ back** OR **home!** content de vous revoir!; **~ to my home!** bienvenue chez moi OR à la maison!; '**~ to Wales**' 'bienvenue au pays de Galles'.

◆ **welcome back** *vt sep* accueillir (à son retour); **we ~d her back after her illness** nous lui avons fait fête OR l'avons accueillie chaleureusement après sa maladie.

welcoming ['welkəmɪŋ] *adj* [greeting, smile] accueillant; [ceremony, committee] d'accueil; **the ~ party took them to their hotel** la délégation venue les accueillir les a conduits à leur hôtel.

weld [weld] ◇ *vt* -**1.** MECH & TECH souder; **to ~ parts together** souder des pièces ensemble; **he ~ed the bracket onto the shelf** il a soudé le support à l'étagère. -**2.** [unite] amalgamer, réunir; **a set of policies that will ~ the party into a united political force** un ensemble de mesures qui cimentera le parti et en fera une force politique unie.
◇ *vi* souder.
◇ *n* soudure *f*.

welder ['weldəʳ] *n* [person] soudeur *m*, -euse *f*; [machine] soudeuse *f*, machine *f* à souder.

welding ['weldɪŋ] *n* soudage *m*; [of groups] union *f*.

welding torch *n* chalumeau *m*.

welfare ['welfeəʳ] ◇ *n* -**1.** [well-being] bien-être *m*; **the ~ of the nation** le bien public; **child ~** protection *f* de l'enfance; **the physical and spiritual ~ of the people** le bien-être physique et moral du peuple; **I am concerned about** OR **for her ~** je m'inquiète pour elle; **she's looking after his ~** elle s'occupe de lui. -**2.** *Am* [state aid] assistance *f* publique; **his family is on ~** sa famille touche des prestations sociales OR reçoit l'aide sociale; **to live on ~** vivre de l'aide sociale.
◇ *comp* [meals, milk] gratuit; **~ benefits** *Am* avantages *mpl* sociaux; **~ check** *Am* (chèque *m* d') allocations *fpl*; **payments** prestations *fpl* sociales; **~ work** travail *m* social; **~ worker** assistant *m* social, assistante *f* sociale.

welfare centre *n* ≃ centre *m* d'assistance sociale.

welfare officer *n travailleur social ayant la charge d'une personne mise en liberté surveillée.*

welfare service *n* ≃ service *m* d'assistance sociale.

Welfare State *n*: **the ~** l'État *m* providence.

welfarism ['welfeərɪzm] *n* théorie *f* de l'État providence.

well1 [wel] ◇ *n* -**1.** [for water, oil] puits *m*. -**2.** [for lift, staircase] cage *f*; [between buildings] puits *m*, cheminée *f*. -**3.** *Br* JUR barreau *m (au tribunal)*.
◇ *vi* = **well-up**.

◆ **well out** *vi insep* [water] jaillir.

◆ **well up** *vi insep* [blood, spring, tears] monter, jaillir; **tears ~ed up in her eyes** les larmes lui montèrent aux yeux; **joy ~ed up within her** la joie monta en elle.

well2 [wel] (*compar* **better** [betəʳ], *superl* **best** [best]) ◇ *adv* -**1.** [satisfactorily, successfully] bien; **she speaks French very ~** elle parle très bien (le) français; **he plays the piano ~** il joue bien du piano; **she came out of it rather ~** elle s'en est plutôt bien sortie; **it's extremely ~ done** c'est vraiment très bien fait; **everything is going ~** tout se passe bien; **the meeting went ~** la réunion s'est bien passée; **those colours go really ~ together** ces couleurs vont vraiment bien ensemble; **the machine/system works ~** la machine/le système marche bien; **things have worked out ~** les choses se sont bien passées; **does she work as ~ as I do?** fait-elle son travail aussi bien que moi? ❑ **to do ~** s'en sortir; **she's doing very ~** elle s'en sort très bien; **he did very ~ for a beginner** il s'est très bien débrouillé pour un débutant; **you did quite ~ in the exam** vous vous en êtes assez bien sorti à l'examen; **to do ~ for o.s.** bien se débrouiller; **to do ~ out of sb/sthg** bien s'en sortir avec qqn/qqch; **that boy will do ~!** ce garçon ira loin!; **the patient is doing ~** le malade se rétablit bien OR est en bonne voie de guérison; **we would do ~ to keep quiet** nous ferions bien de nous taire; **~ done!** bravo!; **~ said!** bien dit!; **it was money ~ spent** ce n'était pas de l'argent gaspillé. -**2.** [favourably, kindly] bien; **she treats her staff very ~** elle traite très bien son personnel; **everyone speaks ~ of you** tout le monde dit du bien de vous; **his action speaks ~ of his courage** son geste montre bien son courage; **she won't take it ~** elle ne va pas apprécier; **she thinks ~ of you** elle a de l'estime pour vous; **he wished her ~** il lui souhaita bonne chance; **it's a card from someone wishing you ~** c'est une carte de quelqu'un qui vous veut du bien ❑ **to do ~ by sb** traiter qqn comme il se doit. -**3.** [easily, readily] bien; **he could ~ decide to leave** il se pourrait tout à fait qu'il décide de partir; **I couldn't very ~ accept** je ne pouvais guère accepter; **you may ~ be right** il se peut bien que tu aies raison; **I can ~ believe it** je le crois facilement OR sans peine; **she was angry, and ~ she might be** elle était furieuse, et à juste titre. -**4.** [to a considerable extent or degree] bien; **she's ~ over** OR **past forty** elle a bien plus de quarante ans; **he's ~ into his seventies** il a largement dépassé les soixante-dix ans; **there were ~ over 5,000 demonstrators** il y avait bien plus de 5 000 manifestants; **he's ~ on in years** il n'est plus tout jeune; **~ on into the morning** jusque tard dans la matinée; **the fashion lasted ~ into the 1960s** cette mode a duré une bonne partie des années 60; **it's ~ above/within the limit** c'est bien au-dessus de/inférieur à la limite; **it's ~ after midday** il est bien plus de midi; **the play went on until ~ after midnight** la partie s'est prolongée bien au-delà de minuit; **I woke ~ before dawn** je me suis réveillé bien avant l'aube; **let me know ~ in advance** prévenez-moi longtemps à l'avance; **the team finished ~ up the league** l'équipe a fini parmi les premières de sa division. -**5.** [thoroughly] bien; **shake/stir ~** bien secouer/agiter; **be sure to cook it ~** veillez à ce que ce soit bien cuit; **~ cooked** OR **done** bien cuit; **let it dry ~ first** attendez d'abord que ce soit bien sec; **I know her ~** je la connais bien; **you know your subject ~** vous connaissez bien votre sujet; **I know only too ~ how hard it is** je ne sais que trop bien à quel point c'est difficile; **how ~ I understand her feelings!** comme je comprends ce qu'elle ressent!; **I'm ~ aware of the problem** je suis bien conscient OR j'ai bien conscience du problème; **I bet he was ~ pleased!** *iron* il devait être content! *iron*; **I like him ~ enough** il ne me déplaît pas; **we got ~ and truly soaked** nous nous sommes fait tremper jusqu'aux os; **it's ~ and truly over** c'est bel et bien fini; **it's ~ worth the money** ça vaut largement la dépense; **it's ~ worth trying** ça vaut vraiment la peine d'essayer. -**6.** *phr*: **to be ~ away** [making good progress] être sur la bonne voie; [drunk] être complètement parti; to be ~ in with sb être bien avec qqn; **she's ~ in with all the right people** elle est très bien avec tous les gens qui peuvent servir; to be ~ out of it s'en sortir à bon compte; **you're ~ out of it** tu as bien fait de partir; to be ~ rid of sb/sthg: **she's ~ rid of him/it!** quel bon débarras pour elle!; to be ~ up on sthg s'y connaître en qqch; **she's ~ up on European law** elle s'y connait en droit européen; to leave OR let ~ alone [equipment] ne pas toucher; [situation] ne pas s'occuper de; [person] laisser tranquille.

◇ *adj* -**1.** [good] bien, bon; **all is not ~ with them** il y a quelque chose qui ne va pas chez eux; **owning a home is all very ~, but...** c'est bien beau d'être propriétaire, mais...; **it's all very ~ pretending you don't care, but...** c'est bien beau de dire que ça t'est égal, mais... ❑ **all's ~!** MIL rien à signaler!; **all's ~ that ends ~** *prov* tout est bien qui finit bien *prov.* -**2.** [advisable] bien; **it would be ~ to start soon** nous ferions bien de commencer bientôt. -**3.** [in health]: to be ~ aller OR se porter bien; **how are you? — ~, thank you** comment allez-vous? — bien, merci; **he's been ill, but he's better now** il a été malade, mais il va mieux (maintenant); **I don't feel ~** je ne me sens pas bien; **she's not very ~** elle ne va pas très bien; to get ~ se remettre, aller mieux; **'get ~ soon'** [on card] 'bon rétablissement'; **I hope you're ~** j'espère que vous allez bien; **you're looking OR you look ~** vous avez l'air en forme; **he's not a ~ man** il ne se porte pas bien ❑ ~ **woman clinic** centre *m* de santé pour femmes.

◇ *interj* -**1.** [indicating start or continuation of speech] bon, bien; **~, I would just say one thing** bon, je voudrais simplement dire une chose; **~, let me just add that...** alors, laissez-moi simplement ajouter que...; **~, here we are again!** et nous y revoilà! -**2.** [indicating change of topic or end of conversation]: **~, as I was saying...** donc, je disais que..., je disais donc que...; **right, ~, let's move on to the next subject** bon, alors passons à la question suivante; **~ thank you Mr Alderson, I'll be in touch** eh bien merci M. Alderson, je vous contacterai. -**3.** [softening a statement]: **~, obviously I'd like to come but...** disons que, bien sûr, j'aimerais venir mais...; **he was, ~, rather unpleasant really** il a été, disons, assez désagréable, c'est le mot. -**4.** [expanding on or explaining a statement]: **he was rather fat, ~ stout might be a better word** il était plutôt gros, enfin disons corpulent; **I've known her for ages, ~ at least three years** ça fait des années que je la connais, enfin au moins trois ans; **you know John? ~ I saw him yesterday** tu connais John? eh bien je l'ai vu hier. -**5.** [expressing hesitation or doubt] ben, eh bien; **did you ask? — ~... I didn't dare actually** as-tu demandé? — eh bien OR ben, je n'ai pas osé; **are you ready? — ~, I should really stay in and work** tu viens? — eh bien, il vaudrait mieux que je reste à la maison pour travailler. -**6.** [asking a question] eh bien, alors; **~, who was it?** alors OR eh bien, qui était-ce?; **~, what of it?** et alors? -**7.** [expressing surprise or anger]: **~, look who's here!** ça alors, regardez qui est là!; **~, ~, ~** tiens, tiens; **~, really!** ça alors!; **~ I never!** *inf* ça par exemple!; **(~,) ~, what do you know!** eh bien OR ça alors, qui l'aurait cru! -**8.** [in relief] eh bien; **~, at least that's over!** eh bien, en tout cas, c'est terminé! -**9.** [in resignation] bon; **(oh) ~, it can't be helped** bon tant pis, on n'y peut rien; **(oh) ~, that's life** bon enfin, c'est la vie; **(oh) ~, all right** bon allez, d'accord; **can I come too? — oh, very ~, if you must** je peux venir aussi? — bon allez, si tu y tiens.

◇ *npl*: the ~ ceux *mpl* qui sont en bonne santé.

◆ **all well and good** *adv phr* tout ça, c'est très bien; **so you want to go to drama school, all ~ and good, but...** alors comme ça, tu veux faire une école de théâtre? tout ça, c'est très bien mais...

we'll [wiːl] = **we shall, we will.**

well-adjusted *adj* [person - psychologically] équilibré; [- to society, work] bien adapté.

well-advised *adj* sage, prudent; **he would be ~ to leave as soon as possible** il aurait intérêt à partir le plus vite possible.

well-aimed [-eɪmd] *adj* [shot] bien ajusté; [criticism, remark] qui porte.

well-appointed [-əˈpɔɪntɪd] *adj Br fml* [house] bien équipé; [hotel] de catégorie supérieure.

well-argued [-ˈɑːgjuːd] *adj* bien argumenté; **a ~ case** un point de vue bien argumenté.

well-balanced *adj* [person] équilibré, posé; [diet] bien équilibré; [sentence] bien construite.

well-behaved [-bɪˈheɪvd] *adj* [person] bien élevé; [animal] bien dressé.

wellbeing [ˌwelˈbiːɪŋ] *n* bien-être *m inv*; **the general ~ of the population** le bien-être général de la population; **he felt a sense of ~** il éprouvait une impression de bien-être; **for your own ~** pour votre bien.

well-beloved *adj lit* bien-aimé.

well-bred *adj* -**1.** [well-behaved] bien élevé. -**2.** [from good family] de bonne famille. -**3.** [animal] de (bonne) race; [horse] pur-sang *(inv)*.

well-brought-up *adj* bien élevé.

well-built *adj* -**1.** [person] bien bâti. -**2.** [building] bien construit.

well-chosen *adj* [present, words] bien choisi.

well-connected *adj* [of good family] de bonne famille; [having influential friends] qui a des relations.

well-defined [-dɪˈfaɪnd] *adj* -**1.** [distinct - colour, contrasts, shape] bien défini, net. -**2.** [precise - problem] bien défini, précis; **within ~ limits** dans des limites bien définies.

well-deserved [-dɪˈzɜːvd] *adj* bien mérité.

well-developed *adj* -**1.** [person] bien fait; [body, muscles] bien développé. -**2.** [scheme] bien développé; [idea] bien exposé.

welldigger [ˈwelˌdɪgəʳ] *n* puisatier *m*.

well-disposed [-dɪˈspəʊzd] *adj* bien disposé; to be ~ to OR **towards sb** être bien disposé envers qqn; to be ~ to OR **towards sthg** voir qqch d'un bon œil.

well-done *adj* [work] bien fait; [meat] bien cuit.

well-dressed *adj* bien habillé.

well-earned [-ɜːnd] *adj* bien mérité.

well-educated *adj* cultivé, instruit.

well-endowed [-ɪnˈdaʊd] *adj euph*: **a ~ young man/woman** *fig* un jeune homme bien doté/une jeune femme bien dotée par la nature.

well-equipped [-ɪˈkwɪpt] *adj* [garage, kitchen, person] bien équipé; [with tools] bien outillé; **the vans are ~ to deal with any emergency** les camionnettes sont équipées pour faire face à toute urgence.

well-established *adj* bien établi.

well-favoured *adj arch* beau.

well-fed *adj* [animal, person] bien nourri.

well-formed *adj* [gen & LING] bien formé.

well-founded [-ˈfaʊndɪd] *adj* [doubt, suspicion] fondé, légitime.

well-groomed *adj* [person] soigné; [hair] bien coiffé; [horse] bien pansé; [garden, lawn] bien entretenu.

wellhead [ˈwelhed] *n literal & fig* source *f*.

well-heeled *inf* [-hiːld] *adj* à l'aise.

well-hung *adj* -**1.** [game] bien faisandé. -**2.** ▽ [man] bien monté.

wellie [ˈwelɪ] = **welly**.

well-informed *adj* [having information] bien informé OR renseigné; [knowledgeable] instruit; **in ~ circles** dans les milieux bien informés; **he's very ~ about current affairs** il est très au courant de l'actualité.

Wellington [ˈwelɪŋtən] ◇ *pr n* Wellington.

◇ *n Br*: ~ **(boot)** botte *f* (en caoutchouc).

well-intentioned [-ɪnˈtenʃnd] *adj* bien intentionné.

well-judged [-ˈdʒʌdʒd] *adj* [remark] bien vu, judicieux; [shot, throw] bien ajusté; [estimate] juste; [moment] opportun.

well-kept *adj* -**1.** [hands, nails] soigné; [hair] bien coiffé; [house] bien tenu; [garden] bien entretenu. -**2.** [secret] bien gardé.

well-knit *adj* [person, body] bien bâti; [argument] bien enchaîné.

well-known *adj* [person] connu, célèbre; [fact] bien connu; **it is ~ OR it is a ~ fact that she disagrees with the policy** tout le monde sait qu'elle n'est pas d'accord avec cette politique; **what is less ~ is that she's an accomplished actress** ce qu'on sait moins c'est que c'est une très bonne actrice.

well-made *adj* bien fait.

well-mannered *adj* qui a de bonnes manières, bien élevé.

well-meaning *adj* bien intentionné.

well-meant *adj* [action, remark] bien intentionné.

well-nigh *adv* presque; **it's ~ impossible** c'est presque OR quasi impossible.

well-off ◇ *adj* -**1.** [financially] aisé. -**2.** [in a good position]: **they were still ~ for supplies** ils avaient encore largement assez de provisions; **you don't know when you're ~** *fig* vous ne connaissez pas votre bonheur.

◇ *npl*: **the ~** les riches *mpl*; **the less ~** ceux qui ont des moyens modestes.

well-oiled *adj* -**1.** [machinery] bien graissé; **the operation ran like a ~ machine** l'opération s'est parfaitement déroulée. -**2.** *inf* [drunk] pompette.

well-padded *inf adj euph* bien enveloppé.

well-paid *adj* bien payé.

well-preserved [-prɪˈzɜːvd] *adj* [person, building] bien conservé.

well-read [-red] *adj* cultivé, érudit; **she's very ~** elle est très cultivée.

well-rounded *adj* -**1.** [complete - education] complet; [- life] bien rempli. -**2.** [figure] rondelet. -**3.** [style] harmonieux; [sentence] bien tourné.

well-spent *adj* [time] bien utilisé, qui n'est pas perdu; [money] utilement dépensé, que l'on n'a pas gaspillé; **it's money ~** c'est un bon investissement.

well-spoken *adj* [person] qui sait s'exprimer.

well-spoken-of *adj*: **she's very ~ in business circles** on dit beaucoup de bien d'elle dans le milieu des affaires.

wellspring [ˈwelsprɪŋ] *n literal* source *f*; *fig* source *f* intarissable.

well-stacked▽ *adj Br* [woman] plantureux.

well-thought-of *adj* bien considéré.

well-thought-out *adj* bien conçu.

well-thumbed [-θʌmd] *adj* [magazine] qui a été beaucoup feuilleté; [book] lu et relu.

well-timed [-ˈtaɪmd] *adj* [arrival, remark] opportun, qui tombe à point; [blow] bien calculé.

well-to-do *inf* ◇ *adj* aisé, riche.

◇ *npl*: **the ~** les nantis *mpl*.

well-tried *adj* éprouvé, qui a fait ses preuves.

well-turned *adj* [ankle] fin; [leg] bien galbé; *Br* [sentence] bien tourné.

well-versed *adj*: to be ~ in sthg bien connaître qqch.

well-wisher [-ˌwɪʃəʳ] *n* [gen] personne *f* qui offre son soutien; [of cause, group] sympathisant *m*, -e *f*, partisan *m*; **surrounded by ~s** entouré d'admirateurs.

well-woman clinic *n* centre *m* de santé pour femmes.

well-worn *adj* -**1.** [carpet, clothes] usé, usagé. -**2.** [path] battu. -**3.** [expression, joke] rebattu; **a ~ phrase** une banalité, un lieu commun.

welly *inf* [ˈwelɪ] (*pl* **wellies**) *n Br* -**1.** [boot] botte *f* (en caoutchouc). -**2.** *phr*: **give it some ~!** *inf* du nerf!

welsh *inf* [welʃ] *vi Br* partir OR décamper sans payer; to ~ **on a debt** partir sans payer une dette; to ~ **on a promise** ne pas tenir une promesse.

Welsh [welʃ] ◇ *npl*: the ~ les Gallois *mpl*.
◇ *n* LING gallois *m*.
◇ *adj* gallois.

Welsh dresser *n* vaisselier *m*.

Welshman ['welʃmən] (*pl* Welshmen [-mən]) *n* Gallois *m*.

Welsh rabbit, Welsh rarebit *n Br* ≃ toast *m* au fromage.

Welshwoman ['welʃ,wʊmən] (*pl* Welshwomen [-,wɪmɪn]) *n* Galloise *f*.

welt [welt] *n* -**1.** [on skin] zébrure *f*. -**2.** [on garment] bordure *f*; [on shoe] trépointe *f*.

welter ['weltəʳ] ◇ *vi lit* se vautrer, se rouler.
◇ *n* confusion *f*; a ~ of detail une profusion de détails; a ~ of conflicting information une avalanche d'informations contradictoires.

welterweight ['weltəweɪt] ◇ *n* poids *m* welter.
◇ *comp* [champion] des poids welter; [fight, title] de poids welter.

wen [wen] *n* -**1.** MED loupe *f*, kyste *m* sébacé *spec*. -**2.** [city]: the great ~ Londres.

Wenceslas ['wensɪsləs] *pr n* Venceslas.

wench [wentʃ] ◇ *n arch* OR *hum* jeune fille *f*, jeune femme *f*.
◇ *vi arch*: to go ~ing aller courir le jupon.

wend [wend] *vt lit* s'acheminer; to ~ one's way home s'acheminer vers chez soi; he ~ed his way through the forest il s'achemina à travers la forêt.

Wendy house ['wendɪ-] *n Br maison en miniature dans laquelle les jeunes enfants peuvent jouer*.

Wensleydale ['wenzlɪdeɪl] *n fromage anglais originaire de Wensleydale*.

went [went] *pt* → **go**.

wept [wept] *pt* & *pp* → **weep**.

were [wɜːʳ] *pt* → **be**.

we're [wɪəʳ] = **we are**.

weren't [wɜːnt] = **were not**.

werewolf ['wɪəwʊlf] (*pl* werewolves [-wʊlvz]) *n* loup-garou *m*.

wert [wɜːt] *Br dial* & BIBLE = **were**.

Wesleyan ['wezlɪən] ◇ *adj* de Wesley, wesleyen; ~ Methodists méthodistes *mpl* wesleyens.
◇ *n* disciple *m* de Wesley.

west [west] ◇ *n* [direction] ouest *m*; in the ~ of the country dans l'ouest du pays; the house lies three kilometres to the ~ (of the town) la maison se trouve à trois kilomètres à l'ouest (de la ville); two miles to the ~ trois kilomètres à l'ouest; look towards the ~ regardez vers l'ouest; the wind is coming from the ~ le vent vient OR souffle de l'ouest; a storm is brewing in the ~ un orage couve à l'ouest; the wind is in the ~ le vent est à l'ouest.
◇ *adj* ouest *(inv)*; on the ~ side du côté ouest; the ~ coast la côte ouest; a ~ wind un vent d'ouest; in ~ London dans l'ouest de Londres ❑ 'West Side Story' *Bernstein* 'West Side Story'.
◇ *adv* [to the west] vers l'ouest; [from the west] de l'ouest; he travelled ~ for three days pendant trois jours il s'est dirigé en direction de OR vers l'ouest; the school lies further ~ of the town hall l'école se trouve plus à l'ouest de la mairie; drive due ~ roulez droit vers l'ouest; to face ~ [house] être exposé à l'ouest ❑ to go ~ *literal* aller à OR vers l'ouest; *hum inf* [person] passer l'arme à gauche; [thing] tomber à l'eau; there's another job gone ~! *inf* encore un emploi de perdu!
◆ **West** *n* -**1.** POL: the West l'Occident *m*, les pays *mpl* occidentaux. -**2.** [in the U.S.]: the West l'Ouest *m*.

West Africa *pr n* Afrique *f* occidentale.

West African ◇ *n* habitant *m*, -e *f* de l'Afrique occidentale.
◇ *adj* [languages, states] de l'Afrique occidentale, ouest-africain.

West Bank ◇ *pr n*: the ~ la Cisjordanie; on the ~ en Cisjordanie.
◇ *comp* de Cisjordanie.

West Berlin *pr n* Berlin-Ouest.

westbound ['westbaʊnd] *adj* [traffic] en direction de l'ouest; [lane, carriageway] de l'ouest; [road] vers l'ouest.

West Coast *n* côte *f* ouest *(des États-Unis)*.

West Country *pr n*: the ~ *le sud-ouest de l'Angleterre (Cornouailles, Devon et Somerset)*; in the ~ dans le sud-ouest de l'Angleterre.

West End ◇ *pr n*: the ~ le West End *(centre touristique et commercial de la ville de Londres connu pour ses théâtres)*; in the ~ dans le West End.
◇ *comp* qui se situe dans le West End.

wester ['westəʳ] *vi* [subj: sun, moon] passer à l'ouest.

westering ['westərɪŋ] *adj lit* qui passe à l'ouest; the ~ sun le soleil couchant.

westerly ['westəlɪ] (*pl* westerlies) ◇ *adj* [wind] d'ouest; [position] à l'ouest, au couchant; to head in a ~ direction se diriger vers OR en direction de l'ouest; the most ~ point on the island le point le plus à l'ouest de l'île.
◇ *adv* vers l'ouest.
◇ *n* vent *m* d'ouest.
◆ **Westerlies** *npl*: the Westerlies les Westerlies *mpl (vents d'ouest dominants)*.

western ['westən] ◇ *adj* -**1.** [in direction] ouest, de l'ouest; in ~ Spain dans l'ouest de l'Espagne; the ~ coast la côte ouest OR occidentale; on the ~ side of the state dans l'ouest de l'État. -**2.** POL [powers, technology, world] occidental; Western Europe l'Europe *f* de l'Ouest OR occidentale.
◇ *n* [film] western *m*; [book] roman-western *m*.

Western Australia *pr n* Australie-Occidentale *f*; in ~ en Australie-Occidentale.

Western Church *n*: the ~ l'Église *f* d'Occident OR latine.

Westerner ['westənəʳ] *n* habitant *m*, -e *f* de l'ouest; POL Occidental *m*, -e *f*.

Western Isles *pl pr n*: the ~ les Hébrides *fpl*; in the ~ aux Hébrides.

westernization [,westənaɪ'zeɪʃn] *n* occidentalisation *f*.

westernize, -ise ['westənaɪz] *vt* occidentaliser; Japan is becoming increasingly ~d le Japon s'occidentalise de plus en plus.

westernmost ['westənməʊst] *adj* le plus à l'ouest.

Western Sahara *pr n*: the ~ le Sahara occidental; in the ~ au Sahara occidental.

Western Samoa *pr n* Samoa *fpl* occidentales; in ~ dans les Samoa occidentales.

Western Union *pr n compagnie américaine privée des télégraphes*.

west-facing *adj* orienté à l'ouest OR au couchant.

West German ◇ *n* Allemand *m*, -e *f* de l'Ouest.
◇ *adj* ouest-allemand.

West Germany *pr n*: (former) ~ (ex-) Allemagne *f* de l'Ouest; in ~ en Allemagne de l'Ouest.

West Indian ◇ *n* Antillais *m*, -e *f*.
◇ *adj* antillais.

West Indies *pl pr n* Antilles *fpl*; in the ~ aux Antilles; the French ~ les Antilles françaises; the Dutch ~ les Antilles néerlandaises.

westing ['westɪŋ] *n* NAUT route *f* vers l'ouest, chemin *m* ouest.

Westminster ['westmɪnstəʳ] *pr n quartier du centre de Londres*.

WESTMINSTER:
C'est dans ce quartier que se trouvent le Parlement et le palais de Buckingham. Le nom de «Westminster» est également employé pour désigner le Parlement lui-même.

---

west-northwest ◇ *n* ouest-nord-ouest *m*.
◇ *adj* à OR de l'ouest-nord-ouest; a ~ wind un vent d'ouest-nord-ouest.
◇ *adv* vers l'ouest-nord-ouest.

Westphalia [west'feɪljə] *pr n* Westphalie *f*.

West Point *pr n importante école militaire américaine*.

west-southwest ◇ *n* ouest-sud-ouest *m*.
◇ *adj* à OR de l'ouest-sud-ouest; a ~ wind un vent d'ouest-sud-ouest.
◇ *adv* vers l'ouest-sud-ouest.

West Virginia *pr n* Virginie-Occidentale *f*; in ~ en Virginie-Occidentale.

westward ['westwəd] ◇ *adj* [to the west] vers l'ouest.
◇ *adv* en direction de OR vers l'ouest.

westwards ['westwədz] *adv* vers l'ouest.

wet [wet] (*compar* wetter, *superl* wettest, *pt* & *pp* wet OR wetted, *cont* wetting) ◇ *adj* -**1.** [ground, person, umbrella - gen] mouillé; [- damp] humide; [- soaked] trempé; to get ~ se faire mouiller; I got my jacket ~ j'ai mouillé ma veste; I got my feet ~ je me suis mouillé les pieds; try not to get your shoes ~ essaie de ne pas mouiller tes chaussures; to be ~ through [person] être trempé jusqu'aux os OR complètement trempé; [clothes, towel] être complètement trempé; her eyes were ~ with tears elle avait les yeux baignés de larmes; the roads can be slippery when ~ les routes mouillées peuvent être glissantes ❑ to be (still) ~ behind the ears manquer d'expérience. -**2.** [ink, paint, concrete] frais; '~ paint!' 'peinture fraîche!'. -**3.** [climate, weather - damp] humide; [- rainy] pluvieux; [day] pluvieux, de pluie; it's going to be very ~ all weekend il va beaucoup pleuvoir tout ce week-end; in ~ weather par temps de pluie, quand il pleut; the ~ season la saison des pluies. -**4.** *inf Br* [feeble]: don't be so ~! tu es une vraie lavette! -**5.** *inf Br* POL mou, modéré. -**6.** *Am* [wrong]: to be all ~ avoir tort. -**7.** *Am* [state, town] *où l'on peut acheter librement des boissons alcoolisées*.
◇ *vt* [hair, sponge, towel] mouiller; to ~ o.s. OR one's pants mouiller sa culotte; to ~ the bed faire pipi au lit; to ~ one's lips s'humecter les lèvres ❑ to ~ o.s. *inf* [from worry] se faire de la bile; [from laughter] rire aux larmes; to ~ one's whistle boire un coup.
◇ *n* -**1.** *Br* [rain] pluie *f*; [damp] humidité *f*; to go out in the ~ sortir sous la pluie; let's get in out of the ~ entrons, ne restons pas sous la pluie; he left his bike out in the ~ il a laissé son vélo dehors sous la pluie. -**2.** *Austr*: the ~ la saison des pluies. -**3.** *inf Br* POL modéré *m*, -e *f* OR mou *m*, molle *f (du parti conservateur)*. -**4.** *inf Br pej* [feeble person] lavette *f*.

wet and dry *n toile d'émeri très fine*.

wetback▼ ['wetbæk] *n Am terme injurieux désignant un ouvrier mexicain entré illégalement aux États-Unis*.

wet bar *n Am minibar avec un petit évier*.

wet blanket *inf n* rabat-joie *m inv*.

wet dock *n* bassin *m* à flot.

wet dream *n* éjaculation *f* OR pollution *f* nocturne.

wet fish *n* poisson *m* frais.

wether ['weðəʳ] *n* bélier *m* châtré, mouton *m*.

wetland ['wetlənd] *n* marécage *m*, marais *m*.

wet-look ◇ *adj* brillant; a ~ dress une robe qui brille.
◇ *n* aspect *m* brillant.

wetness ['wetnɪs] *n* humidité *f*.

wet nurse *n* nourrice *f*.
◆ **wet-nurse** *vt* servir de nourrice à, élever au sein.

wet rot *n (U)* moisissure *f* humide.

wet suit *n* combinaison *f* OR ensemble *m* de plongée.

wetting agent ['wetɪŋ-] *n* CHEM (agent *m*) mouillant *m*.

WEU (*abbr of* Western European Union) *pr n* UEO *f*.

we've [wiːv] = **we have**.

WFTU (*abbr of* World Federation of Trade Unions) *pr n* FSM *f*.

whack *inf* [wæk] ◇ *n* -**1.** [thump] claque *f*, grand coup *m*; [sound] claquement *m*, coup *m* sec; to give sb/sthg a ~ donner un grand coup à qqn/qqch. -**2.** [try] essai *m*; to have a ~ at sthg essayer qqch. -**3.** *Br* [share] part *f*; he paid more than his ~ il a payé plus que sa part; she didn't do her fair ~ elle n'a pas fait sa part du travail. -**4.** *Am phr*: out of the ~ déglingué.

◇ *vt* -**1.** [thump] donner un coup OR des coups à; [spank] donner une claque sur les fesses à. -**2.** *Br* [defeat] flanquer une dérouillée OR raclée à.

◇ *interj* vlan!

◆ **whack off**▼ *vi insep* se branler.

whacked *inf* [wækt] *adj Br* vanné, crevé.

whacker *inf* ['wækəʳ] *Br* = **whopper 1**.

whacking *inf* ['wækɪŋ] ◇ *adj Br* énorme, colossal.

◇ *adv* extrêmement; a ~ great dog/house un chien/une maison absolument énorme.

◇ *n*: to get a ~ [beating] prendre une raclée; [defeat] prendre une raclée OR une déculottée.

whacko *inf* [ˌwæk'əʊ] *interj dated* épatant, bath.

whacky *inf* ['wækɪ] (*compar* whackier, *superl* whackiest) = **wacky**.

whale [weɪl] ◇ *n* -**1.** *literal* baleine *f*. -**2.** *phr*: we had a ~ of a time *inf* on s'est drôlement bien amusés.

◇ *vi* -**1.** pêcher la baleine. -**2.** *inf Am*: to ~ away at sthg s'en prendre à qqch.

◇ *vt inf Am* -**1.** [thump] mettre une raclée à, rosser; I'll ~ the living daylights out of you! je vais te mettre une de ces raclées! -**2.** SPORT [defeat] mettre une raclée à, battre à plate couture.

whaleboat ['weɪlbəʊt] *n* baleinière *f*.

whalebone ['weɪlbəʊn] *n* fanon *m* de baleine; [in corset, dress] baleine *f*.

whale oil *n* huile *f* de baleine.

whaler ['weɪləʳ] *n* -**1.** [person] pêcheur *m* de baleine. -**2.** [ship] baleinier *m*.

whale shark *n* requin-baleine *m*.

whaling ['weɪlɪŋ] ◇ *n* -**1.** [industry] pêche *f* à la baleine. -**2.** *inf Am* [thrashing] rossée *f*, raclée *f*.

◇ *comp* [industry, port] baleinier; ~ **ship** baleinier *m*; **International Whaling Commission** Commission *f* internationale baleinière.

wham *inf* [wæm] (*pt & pp* whammed, *cont* whamming) ◇ *n*: **we hit the wall with a ~** et vlan! on est rentrés dans le mur.

◇ *interj* vlan.

◇ *vt* -**1.** [hit - person] donner une raclée à; [- ball] donner un grand coup dans; **she whammed the ball over the net** d'un grand coup elle a envoyé la balle par-dessus le filet. -**2.** [crash - heavy object, vehicle] rentrer dans.

wharf [wɔːf] (*pl* wharves [wɔːvz] OR wharfs) *n* quai *m* NAUT.

wharfage ['wɔːfɪdʒ] *n* droits *mpl* de quai.

what [wɒt] ◇ *pron* -**1.** [in direct questions - as subject] qu'est-ce qui, que; [- as object] (qu'est-ce) que, quoi; ~ **do you want?** qu'est-ce que tu veux?, que veux-tu?; ~**'s happening?** qu'est-ce qui se passe?, que se passe-t-il?; ~**'s new?** quoi de neuf?; ~**'s up?** *inf* qu'est-ce qu'il y a?; ~**'s the matter?**, ~ **is it?** qu'est-ce qu'il y a?; ~**'s it to you?** *inf* qu'est-ce que ça peut te faire?; ~**'s that?** qu'est-ce que c'est que ça?; ~**'s that building?** qu'est-ce que c'est que ce bâtiment?; ~**'s your phone number?** quel est votre numéro de téléphone?; ~**'s her name?** comment s'appelle-t-elle?; ~**'s the Spanish for "light"?** comment dit-on «lumière» en espagnol?; ~**'s the boss like?** comment est le patron?; ~ **is life without friends?** que vaut la vie sans amis?; ~**'s up with him?** *inf* qu'est-ce qu'il a?; ~ **did I tell you?** [gen] qu'est-ce que je vous ai dit?; [I told you so] je vous l'avais bien dit!; **she must be**, ~, **50?** elle doit avoir, quoi, 50 ans?; **Mum?** — ~? — **can I go out?** Maman? — quoi? — est-ce que je peux sortir? || [with preposition] quoi; ~ **are you thinking about?** à quoi pensez-vous?; ~ **did he die of?** de quoi est-il mort?; ~ **do you take me for?** pour qui me prenez-vous?; **to ~ do I owe this honour?** *fml* OR *hum* qu'est-ce qui me vaut cet honneur? -**2.** [in indirect questions - as subject] ce qui; [- as object] ce que, quoi; **tell us ~ happened** dites-nous ce qui s'est passé; **I wonder ~ she was thinking about!** je me demande ce qui lui est passé par la tête!; **I asked ~ it was all about** j'ai demandé de quoi il était question; **he didn't understand ~ I said** il n'a pas compris ce que j'ai dit; **I don't know ~ to do** je ne sais pas quoi faire; **I don't know ~ to do to help him** je ne sais pas quoi faire pour l'aider; **I don't know ~ that building is** je ne sais pas ce qu'est ce bâtiment. -**3.** [asking someone to repeat something] comment; ~**'s that?** qu'est-ce que tu dis?; **they bought ~?** quoi, qu'est-ce qu'ils ont acheté? -**4.** [expressing surprise]: ~, **another new dress?** quoi, encore une nouvelle robe?; ~, **no coffee!** comment OR quoi? pas de café?; **he's going into the circus** — ~! il va travailler dans un cirque — quoi?; **I found $350** — **you ~!** j'ai trouvé 350 dollars — quoi?; **I told her to leave** — **you did ~!** je lui ai dit de partir — tu lui as dit quoi? -**5.** [how much]: ~**'s 17 minus 4?** combien OR que fait 17 moins 4?; ~ **does it cost?** combien est-ce que ça coûte?; ~ **do I owe you?** combien vous dois-je?; **do you know ~ he was asking for it?** savez-vous combien il en demandait? -**6.** [that which - as subject] ce qui; [- as object] ce que, quoi; ~ **you need is a hot bath** ce qu'il vous faut, c'est un bon bain chaud; **they spent ~ amounted to a week's salary** ils ont dépensé l'équivalent d'une semaine de salaire; **she has ~ it takes to succeed** elle a ce qu'il faut pour réussir; **that's ~ life is all about!** c'est ça la vie!; **education is not ~ it used to be** l'enseignement n'est plus ce qu'il était; **it was pretty much ~ we expected** c'était plus ou moins ce qu'on avait imaginé; ~**'s done cannot be undone** ce qui est fait est fait; **and ~ is worse,...** et ce qui est pire,... -**7.** [whatever, everything that]: **they rescued ~ they could** ils ont sauvé ce qu'ils ont pu; **say ~ you will** vous pouvez dire OR vous direz tout ce que vous voudrez; **say ~ you will, I don't believe you** racontez tout ce que vous voulez, je ne vous crois pas; **come ~ may** advienne que pourra. -**8.** *inf Br dated* [inviting agreement] n'est-ce pas; **an interesting book,** ~? un livre intéressant, n'est-ce pas OR pas vrai? -**9.** *phr*: **I'll tell you ~...**, **you know ~...?** tu sais quoi...?; **I know ~** j'ai une idée; **you'll never guess ~** tu ne devineras jamais (quoi) ❑ **documents, reports and ~ have you** *inf* OR **and ~ not** *inf* des documents, des rapports et je ne sais quoi encore; **and I don't know ~** *inf* et que sais-je encore; **and God knows ~** *inf* et Dieu sait quoi; **have you got a flat, rooms or ~?** vous avez un appartement, une chambre ou quoi?; **look, do you want to come or ~?** alors, tu veux venir ou quoi?; **a trip to Turkey?** — ~ **next!** un voyage en Turquie? — et puis quoi encore!; ~ **ho!** *dated* eh! ho!; [as greeting] salut!; **we need to find out ~'s ~** *inf* il faut qu'on sache où en sont les choses; **she told me ~ was ~** *inf* elle m'a mis au courant; **they know ~'s ~ in art** *inf* ils s'y connaissent en art; **I'll show him ~'s ~!** *inf* je vais lui montrer de quel bois je me chauffe!

◇ *det* -**1.** [in questions] quel *m*, quelle *f*, quels *mpl*, quelles *fpl*; ~ **books did you buy?** quels livres avez-vous achetés?; ~ **colour/size is it?** de quelle couleur/taille c'est?; **(at) ~ time will you be arriving?** à quelle heure arriverez-vous?; ~ **day is it?** quel jour sommes-nous? -**2.** [as many as, as much as]: **I gave her ~ money I had** je lui ai donné le peu d'argent que j'avais; **he gathered ~ strength he had** il a rassemblé le peu de forces qui lui restaient; ~ **time we had left was spent (in) packing** on a passé le peu de temps qui nous restait à faire les valises; **they stole ~ little money she had** ils lui ont volé le peu d'argent qu'elle avait; **I gave her ~ comfort I could** je l'ai consolée autant que j'ai pu.

◇ *predet* [expressing an opinion or reaction]: ~ **a suggestion!** quelle idée!; ~ **a strange thing!** comme c'est bizarre!; ~ **a pity!** comme c'est OR quel dommage!; ~ **an idiot he is!** comme il est bête!, qu'il est bête!; ~ **lovely children you have!** quels charmants enfants vous avez!; **you can't imagine ~ a time we had getting here** vous ne pouvez pas vous imaginer le mal qu'on a eu à venir jusqu'ici.

◇ *adv* [in rhetorical questions]: ~ **do I care?** qu'est-ce que ça peut me faire?; ~ **does it matter?** qu'est-ce que ça peut faire?

◆ **what about** *adv phr*: ~ **about lunch?** et si on déjeunait?; **when shall we go?** — ~ **about Monday?** quand est-ce qu'on y va? — (et si on disait) lundi?; ~ **about your promise?** — ~ **about my promise?** et ta promesse? — ben quoi, ma promesse?; ~ **about it?** *inf* et alors?; **do you remember Mary?** — ~ **about her?** tu te souviens de Mary? — oui, et alors?; **and ~ about you?** et vous donc?

◆ **what for** *adv phr* -**1.** [why]: ~ **for?** pourquoi?; ~ **did you say that for?** pourquoi as-tu dit cela?; **I'm leaving town** — ~ **for?** je quitte la ville — pourquoi? -**2.** *phr*: **to give sb ~ for** *inf* passer un savon à qqn.

◆ **what if** *conj phr*: ~ **if we went to the beach?** et si on allait à la plage?; **he won't come** — **and ~ if he doesn't?** [supposing] il ne va pas venir — et alors?

◆ **what with** *conj phr*: ~ **with work and the children I don't get much sleep** entre le travail et les enfants je ne dors pas beaucoup; ~ **with paying for dinner and the cab he was left with no cash** après avoir payé le dîner et le taxi il n'avait plus d'argent; ~ **with one thing and another I never got there** pour un tas de raisons je n'y suis jamais allé.

whatchamacallit *inf* ['wɒtʃəməˌkɔːlɪt], **what-d'you-call-it** *inf* ['wɒtdjʊˌkɔːlɪt] *n* machin *m*, truc *m*.

whate'er [wɒt'eəʳ] *lit* = **whatever**.

whatever [wɒt'evəʳ] ◇ *pron* -**1.** [anything, everything] tout ce que; **do ~ he asks (you)** faites tout ce qu'il vous demande; **take ~ you need** prenez tout ce dont vous avez besoin; **I'll do ~ is necessary** je ferai le nécessaire. -**2.** [no matter what] quoi que; ~ **I say, he always disagrees** quoi que je dise, il n'est jamais d'accord; ~ **happens, stay calm** quoi qu'il arrive, restez calme; ~ **it may be** quoi que ce soit; ~ **the reason** quelle que soit la raison; **the doctors must operate ~ the risk** les médecins doivent opérer quel que soit le risque; ~ **it costs, I want that house** je veux cette maison à tout prix; **I won't do it,** ~ **you say** vous aurez beau dire OR vous pouvez dire tout ce que vous voulez, je ne le ferai pas; ~ **you say,** ~ **you think best** comme tu voudras; ~ **you may think, I am telling the truth** vous pouvez penser ce que vous voulez, mais je dis la vérité. -**3.** [indicating surprise]: ~ **can that mean?** qu'est-ce que ça peut bien vouloir dire?; ~ **do you want to do that for?** et pourquoi donc voulez-vous faire ça?; **he wants to join the circus** — ~ **next!** il veut travailler dans un cirque — et puis quoi encore! || [indicating uncertainty]: **it's an urban regeneration area,** ~ **that means** c'est une zone de rénovation urbaine, si tu sais ce qu'ils entendent par là. -**4.** *inf* [some similar thing or things]: **they sell newspapers, magazines and ~** ils vendent des journaux, des revues et ainsi de suite OR et que sais-je encore; **I don't want to study English or philosophy or ~** je ne veux étudier ni l'anglais, ni la philosophie, ou que sais-je encore. -**5.** [indicating lack of interest]: **shall I take the red or the green?** — ~ *inf* je prends le rouge ou le vert? — n'importe.

◇ *det* -**1.** [any, all] tout, n'importe quel; **she read ~ books she could find** elle lisait tous les livres qui lui tombaient sous la main; **he gave up ~ ambitions he still had** il a abandonné ce qui lui restait d'ambition; **I'll take ~ fruit you have** je prendrai ce que vous avez comme fruits. -**2.** [no matter what]: **for ~ reason, he changed his mind** pour une raison quelconque, il a changé d'avis; **she likes all films,** ~ **subject they have** elle aime tous les films quel qu'en soit le sujet.

◇ *adv*: **choose any topic ~** choisissez n'importe quel sujet; **I have no doubt ~** je n'ai pas le moindre doute; **I see no reason ~ to go** je ne vois absolument aucune raison d'y aller; we have no intention ~ of giving up nous n'avons pas la moindre intention d'abandonner; he knew nothing ~ about it il n'en savait absolument rien OR rien du tout; she has no money ~ elle n'a pas un sou.

whatnot ['wɒtnɒt] *n* -**1.** *phr*: and ~ *inf* et ainsi de suite. -**2.** [furniture] étagère *f*.

what's [wɒts] = **what is**.

whatshername *inf* ['wɒtsəneɪm] *n* Machine *f*; (Mrs) ~ Madame Machin.

whatshisname *inf* ['wɒtsɪzneɪm] *n* Machin *m*, Machin Chouette *m*; Mr ~ Monsieur Machin.

whatsit *inf* ['wɒtsɪt] *n* machin *m*, truc *m*.

whatsitsname *inf* ['wɒtsɪtsneɪm] *n* machin *m*, truc *m*.

whatsoever [,wɒtsəʊ'evəʳ] *pron*: none ~ aucun; he gave us no encouragement ~ il ne nous a pas prodigué le moindre encouragement.

wheat [wiːt] ◇ *n* blé *m*; to separate the ~ from the chaff séparer le bon grain de l'ivraie. ◇ *comp* [flour] de blé, de froment; ~ field champ *m* de blé.

wheatear ['wiːt,ɪəʳ] *n* traquet *m*, motteux *m*.

wheaten ['wiːtn] *adj* -**1.** [bread] de blé OR froment. -**2.** [colour] blond comme les blés.

wheat germ *n* germe *m* de blé.

wheatmeal ['wiːtmiːl] *n*: ~ (flour) farine *f* complète.

wheat rust *n* rouille *f* du blé.

Wheatstone bridge ['wiːtstən-] *n* pont *m* de Wheatstone.

whee [wiː] *interj*: ~! ooooh!

wheedle [wiːdl] *vt* enjôler; to ~ sb into doing sthg convaincre qqn de faire qqch à force de cajoleries; to ~ sthg out of sb obtenir qqch de qqn par des cajoleries.

wheedling ['wiːdlɪŋ] ◇ *n (U)* cajolerie *f*, cajoleries *fpl*.
◇ *adj* cajoleur, enjôleur; a ~ voice une voix pateline.

wheel [wiːl] ◇ *n* -**1.** [of bicycle, car, train] roue *f*; [smaller] roulette *f*; [for potter] tour *m*; on ~s sur roues OR roulettes; the ~ has come full circle *fig* la boucle est bouclée ❑ ~ alignment AUT parallélisme *m* des roues; the ~ of fortune la roue de la fortune; she's a big ~ around here *Am* elle est considérée comme une huile par ici. -**2.** AUT: to be at the ~ *literal* être au volant; *fig* être aux commandes; to get behind OR to take the ~ se mettre au OR prendre le volant ❑ (steering) ~ volant *m*; the City on Wheels *surnom de Los Angeles*. -**3.** NAUT barre *f*, gouvernail *m*; at the ~ à la barre. -**4.** [of torture] roue *f*.
◇ *vi* -**1.** [birds] tournoyer; [procession] faire demi-tour; MIL [column] effectuer une conversion; to ~ to the left tourner sur la gauche; left ~! MIL à gauche!; to ~ (round) [person] se retourner, faire une volte-face; [procession] faire demi-tour; [horse] pirouetter; [birds] tournoyer. -**2.** *phr*: to ~ and deal *inf* [do business] brasser des affaires; *pej* magouiller.
◇ *vt* [bicycle, trolley] pousser; [suitcase] tirer; she ~ed the baby around the park elle a promené le bébé dans le parc; she ~ed in a trolley full of cakes elle entra en poussant un chariot plein de gâteaux; they ~ed on OR out the usual celebrities *fig* ils ont ressorti les mêmes célébrités.
◆ **wheels** *npl* -**1.** [workings] rouages *mpl*; the ~s of government les rouages du gouvernement ❑ there are ~s within ~s c'est plus compliqué que ça n'en a l'air. -**2.** *inf* AUT [car] bagnole *f*; he's got a new set of ~s il a une nouvelle bagnole.

wheelbarrow ['wiːl,bærəʊ] *n* brouette *f*.

wheelbase ['wiːlbeɪs] *n* empattement *m* AUT.

wheel brace *n* clef *f* en croix.

wheelchair [,wiːl'tʃeəʳ] *n* fauteuil *m* roulant; ~ access accès *m* aux handicapés; the Wheelchair Olympics les jeux Olympiques handisport OR pour handicapés.

wheelclamp ['wiːlklæmp] ◇ *n* sabot *m* de Denver.
◇ *vt*: my car was ~ed on a mis un sabot à ma voiture.

wheeled [wiːld] *adj* à roues, muni de roues.

-wheeled *in cpds* à roues; four~ à quatre roues.

wheeler ['wiːləʳ] *n* -**1.** [wheelmaker] charron *m*. -**2.** [horse] timonier *m*.

-wheeler *in cpds* à roues; three~ véhicule *m* à trois roues.

wheeler-dealer *inf n pej* affairiste *mf*.

wheelhouse ['wiːlhaʊs, *pl* -haʊzɪz] *n* timonerie *f*.

wheelie *inf* ['wiːlɪ] *n manœuvre sur bicyclette ou moto qui consiste à lever la roue avant*.

wheeling and dealing *inf* ['wiːlɪŋ-] *n (U)* combines *fpl*, manigances *fpl*.

wheelspin ['wiːlspɪn] *n* patinage *m* AUT.

wheelwright ['wiːlraɪt] *n* charron *m*.

wheeze [wiːz] ◇ *vi* [person] respirer bruyamment OR comme un asthmatique; [animal] souffler.
◇ *vt* dire d'une voix rauque; the old accordion can still ~ out a note or two on peut encore tirer quelques notes du vieil accordéon.
◇ *n* -**1.** [sound of breathing] respiration *f* difficile OR sifflante. -**2.** *inf Br dated* [trick] combine *f*. -**3.** *inf Br* [joke] blague *f*. -**4.** *Am* [saying] dicton *m*.

wheezy ['wiːzɪ] (*compar* **wheezier**, *superl* **wheeziest**) *adj* [person] asthmatique; [voice, chest] d'asthmatique; [musical instrument, horse] poussif.

whelk [welk] *n* bulot *m*, buccin *m*.

whelp [welp] ◇ *n* -**1.** [animal] petit *m*, -e *f*. -**2.** *pej* [youth] petit morveux *m*, petite morveuse *f*.
◇ *vi* [of animals] mettre bas.

when [wen] ◇ *adv* quand; ~ are we leaving? quand partons-nous?; ~ is the next bus? à quelle heure est OR quand passe le prochain bus?; ~ did the war end? quand la guerre s'est-elle terminée?; ~ did the accident happen? quand l'accident a-t-il eu lieu?; ~ was the Art Nouveau period? à quand remonte l'époque de l'Art nouveau?; ~ do you start your new job? quand commencez-vous votre nouveau travail?; ~ do you use the subjunctive? quand emploie-t-on le subjonctif?; you're open until ~? vous êtes ouvert jusqu'à quand?; ~ did you last see her? quand l'avez-vous vue pour la dernière fois?; ~ do the Easter holidays begin? quand est-ce que commencent les vacances de Pâques?; ~ is the best time to call? quel est le meilleur moment pour appeler?; the homework is due ~? quand doit-on rendre les devoirs?
◇ *conj* -**1.** [how soon] quand; I don't know ~ we'll see you again je ne sais pas quand nous vous reverrons; do you remember ~ we met? te souviens-tu du jour où nous nous sommes connus?; do you know ~ he was born? savez-vous quand il est né?, connaissez-vous sa date de naissance?; I wonder ~ the shop opens je me demande à quelle heure ouvre le magasin; your contract states ~ you will be paid votre contrat spécifie quand vous serez payé; we don't agree on ~ it should be done nous ne sommes pas d'accord sur le moment où il faudrait le faire. -**2.** [at which time] quand; come back next week ~ we'll have more time revenez la semaine prochaine quand nous aurons plus de temps; he returned in the autumn, ~ the leaves were beginning to turn il est revenu à l'automne, alors que les feuilles commençaient à jaunir. -**3.** [indicating a specific point in time] quand, lorsque; he turned round ~ she called his name il s'est retourné quand OR lorsqu'elle l'a appelé; ~ she's gone, he's unhappy quand OR lorsqu'elle n'est pas là, il est malheureux; ~ I was a student lorsque j'étais OR à l'époque où j'étais étudiant; will you still love me ~ I'm old? m'aimeras-tu encore quand je serai vieux?; she's only happy ~ she's writing elle n'est heureuse que lorsqu'elle écrit; they were talking ~ he came in ils étaient en train de discuter quand il est entré; she's thinner than ~ I last saw her elle a maigri depuis la dernière fois que je l'ai vue; he left town ~ he was twenty il a quitté la ville quand il avait OR à l'âge de vingt ans; ~ she was a child quand OR lorsqu'elle était enfant; on Sunday, ~ I go to the market [this week] dimanche, quand j'irai au marché; [every week] le dimanche, quand je vais au marché; I had just walked in the door/he was about to go to bed ~ the phone rang je venais juste d'arriver/il était sur le point de se coucher quand le téléphone a sonné; we hadn't been gone five minutes ~ Susan wanted to go home ça ne faisait pas cinq minutes que nous étions partis et Susan voulait déjà rentrer. -**4.** [as soon as] quand, dès que; [after] quand, après que; put your pencils down ~ you have finished posez votre crayon quand vous avez terminé; ~ completed, the factory will employ 100 workers une fois terminée, l'usine emploiera 100 personnes; ~ he starts drinking, he can't stop une fois qu'il a commencé à boire, il ne peut plus s'arrêter; I'll answer any questions ~ the meeting is over quand la réunion sera terminée, je répondrai à toutes vos questions; ~ I had read my report, she suggested we take a break après mon exposé, elle a suggéré qu'on fasse une pause; ~ they had finished dinner, he offered to take her home quand OR après qu'ils eurent dîné, il lui proposa de la ramener; ~ you see her you'll understand quand vous la verrez vous comprendrez; ~ she had talked to him, she left après lui avoir parlé, elle est partie. -**5.** [the time that]: remember ~ a litre of milk cost 10 cents? vous souvenez-vous de l'époque où le litre de lait coûtait 10 cents?; he talked about ~ he was a soldier il parlait de l'époque où il était soldat; that's ~ it snowed so hard c'est quand il a tant neigé; that's ~ he got up and left c'est à ce moment-là OR c'est alors qu'il s'est levé et est parti; that's ~ the shops close c'est l'heure où les magasins ferment; now is ~ we should stand up and be counted c'est le moment d'avoir le courage de nos opinions. -**6.** [whenever] quand, chaque fois que; ~ it's sunny, the children play outside quand il y a du soleil, les enfants jouent dehors; ~ I hear that song, I think of her chaque fois que OR quand j'entends cette chanson, je pense à elle; I try to avoid seeing him ~ possible j'essaie de l'éviter quand c'est possible. -**7.** [since, given that] quand, étant donné que; what good is it applying ~ I don't qualify for the job? à quoi bon me porter candidat quand OR si je n'ai pas les capacités requises pour faire ce travail?; how can you treat her so badly ~ you know she loves you? comment pouvez-vous la traiter si mal quand OR alors que vous savez qu'elle vous aime?; why change jobs ~ you like what you do? pourquoi changer de travail quand OR puisque vous aimez ce que vous faites?; fancy having soup ~ you could have had caviar! pourquoi manger de la soupe quand on peut manger du caviar? -**8.** [whereas] alors que; she described him as being lax ~ in fact he's quite strict elle l'a décrit comme étant négligent alors qu'en réalité il est assez strict.
◇ *rel pron* -**1.** [at which time]: an age ~ men were men une époque où les hommes étaient des hommes; in a period ~ business was bad à une période où les affaires allaient mal; she was president until 1980, ~ she left the company elle fut président jusqu'en 1980, année où elle a quitté l'entreprise ‖ [which time]: she started her job in May, since ~ she has had no free time elle a commencé à travailler en mai et elle n'a pas eu de temps libre depuis; the new office will be ready in January, until ~ we use the old one le nouveau bureau sera prêt en janvier; jusque là OR en attendant, nous utiliserons l'ancien. -**2.** [that] où; do you remember the year ~ we went to Alaska? tu te rappelles l'année où on est allés en Alaska?; what about the time ~ she didn't show up? et la fois où elle n'est pas venue?; one day ~

he was out un jour où il était sorti OR qu'il était sorti; it was only a minute later ~ he heard a scream à peine une minute plus tard il entendait un cri; on Monday, the day ~ I was supposed to start work lundi, le jour où je devais commencer à travailler; it's one of those days ~ everything goes wrong c'est un de ces jours où tout va de travers; there were times ~ she didn't know what to do il y avait des moments où elle ne savait plus quoi faire.

whence [wens] *adv & pron fml* d'où.

whene'er [wen'eə^{r}] *lit* = **whenever**.

whenever [wen'evə^{r}] ◇ *conj* -**1.** [every time that] quand, chaque fois que; ~ we go on a picnic, it rains chaque fois qu'on part en pique-nique, il pleut; ~ it snows there's chaos on the roads chaque fois qu'il neige c'est la panique sur les routes; he can come ~ he likes il peut venir quand il veut; I go to visit her ~ I can je vais la voir dès que je peux; ~ there is an eclipse à chaque éclipse. -**2.** [at whatever time] quand; call me ~ you need me appelez-moi si vous avez besoin de moi; you can leave ~ you're ready vous pouvez partir dès que vous serez prêt; they try to help ~ possible ils essaient de se rendre utiles quand c'est possible.
◇ *adv* -**1.** [expressing surprise] quand; ~ did you find the time? mais quand donc avez-vous trouvé le temps? -**2.** [referring to an unknown or unspecified time]: I'll pick you up at 6 o'clock or ~ is convenient je te prendrai à 6 h ou quand ça te convient ❑ let's assume he started work in April or ~ *inf* supposons qu'il ait commencé à travailler en avril ou quelque chose comme ça; we could have lunch on Thursday or Friday or ~ *inf* on pourrait déjeuner ensemble jeudi, vendredi ou un autre jour.

whensoever [ˌwensəʊ'evə^{r}] *lit* = **whenever**.

where [weə^{r}] ◇ *adv* -**1.** [at, in, to what place] où; ~ is the restaurant? où est le restaurant?; ~ are we going? où allons-nous?; ~ are you from? d'où est-ce que vous venez?, d'où êtes-vous?; ~ did you put them? où les avez-vous mis?; ~ is the entrance? où est l'entrée?; the school is near ~? l'école est près d'où?; ~ does this road lead? où va cette route? -**2.** [at what stage, position]: ~ are you in your work/in the book? où en êtes-vous dans votre travail/dans votre lecture?; ~ were we? où en étions-nous?; ~ do you stand on this issue? quelle est votre position OR opinion sur cette question?; ~ do you stand with the boss? quels sont vos rapports avec le patron?; ~ do I come into it? qu'est-ce que j'ai à faire là-dedans, moi?; ~ would I be without you? que serais-je devenu sans toi?
◇ *conj* -**1.** [the place at or in which] (là) où; it rains a lot ~ we live il pleut beaucoup là où nous habitons; she told me ~ to go [gave me directions] elle m'a dit où (il fallait) aller; [was rude] elle m'a envoyé promener; there is a factory ~ I used to go to school il y a une usine là où OR à l'endroit où j'allais autrefois à l'école; how did you know ~ to find me? comment avez-vous su où me trouver?; I wonder ~ my keys are je me demande où sont mes clés; you'll find your key ~ you left it tu trouveras ta clé (là) où tu l'as laissée; sit ~ you like asseyez-vous où vous voulez OR voudrez; turn left ~ the two roads meet tournez à gauche au croisement; fishing is best ~ the Doubs meets the Saône c'est au confluent du Doubs et de la Saône que l'on fait la meilleure pêche || *fig*: I just don't know ~ to begin je ne sais vraiment pas par où commencer. -**2.** [the place that] là que, là où; this is ~ I work c'est là que je travaille; so that's ~ I left my coat! voilà où j'ai laissé mon manteau!; he showed me ~ the students live il m'a montré l'endroit où habitent les étudiants; this is ~ we get off the bus c'est là que nous descendons; the child ran up to ~ her mother was sitting l'enfant a couru jusqu'à l'endroit où sa mère était assise; we can't see well from ~ we're sitting nous ne voyons pas bien d'où OR de là où nous sommes assis || *fig*: I see ~ I went wrong je vois où je me suis trompé; that's ~ she's mistaken c'est là qu'elle se trompe, voilà son erreur; this is ~ you have to make up your mind là, il faut que tu te décides. -**3.** [whenever, wherever] quand, là où; the judge is uncompromising ~ drugs are concerned le juge est intraitable lorsqu'il OR quand il s'agit de drogue; the situation is hopeless ~ defence is concerned pour la défense, la situation est sans espoir; he can't be objective ~ she's concerned il ne peut pas être objectif lorsqu'il s'agit d'elle; ~ x equals y MATH où x égale y; ~ possible là où OR quand c'est possible ❑ ~ there's life, there's hope *prov* tant qu'il y a de la vie, il y a de l'espoir *prov*. -**4.** [whereas, while] là où, alors que; ~ others see a horrid brat, I see a shy little boy là où les autres voient un affreux moutard, je vois un petit garçon timide. -**5.** *phr*: ~ it's at *inf* là où ça bouge.
◇ *rel pron* -**1.** [in which, at which] où; the place ~ we went on holiday l'endroit où nous sommes allés en vacances; the room ~ he was working la pièce où OR dans laquelle il travaillait; the table ~ they were sitting la table où OR à laquelle ils étaient assis; it was the kind of restaurant ~ tourists go c'était le genre de restaurant que fréquentent les touristes || *fig*: I'm at the part ~ they discover the murder j'en suis au moment où ils découvrent le meurtre; it's reached a stage ~ I'm finding it difficult to work ça en est au point où travailler me devient pénible. -**2.** [in or at which place]: Boston, ~ I was born Boston, où je suis né OR ma ville natale; sign at the bottom, ~ I've put a cross signez en bas, là où j'ai mis une croix.
◇ *n*: they discussed the ~ and how of his accident ils ont parlé en détail des circonstances de son accident; you can find that any old ~ vous pouvez trouver cela n'importe où.

whereabouts [*adv* ˌweərə'baʊts, *n* 'weərəbaʊts] ◇ *adv* où; ~ are you from? d'où êtes-vous?; I used to live in Cumbria – oh, really, ~? j'habitais dans le Cumbria – vraiment? où ça OR dans quel coin?
◇ *npl*: to know the ~ of sb/sthg savoir où se trouve qqn/qqch; her exact ~ are unknown personne ne sait exactement où elle se trouve.

whereafter [weər'ɑːftə^{r}] *conj arch* OR *fml* après quoi.

whereas [weər'æz] *conj* -**1.** [gen] alors que, tandis que. -**2.** JUR OR *fml* attendu que, considérant que.

whereat [weər'æt] *arch* OR *fml* ◇ *conj* = **whereupon**.
◇ *adv* où.

whereby [weə'baɪ] *rel pron fml* par lequel, au moyen duquel; there's a new system ~ everyone gets one day off a month il y a un nouveau système qui permet à tout le monde d'avoir un jour de congé par mois.

wherefore ['weəfɔː^{r}] ◇ *adv arch* OR *fml* pourquoi, pour quelle raison.
◇ *conj arch* OR *fml* pour cette raison, donc.
◇ *n* → **why**.

wherein [weər'ɪn] *arch* OR *fml* ◇ *adv & conj* en quoi, dans quoi.
◇ *rel pron* où, dans lequel.

whereof [weər'ɒv] *arch* OR *fml* ◇ *rel pron* [person] dont, de qui; [thing] dont, duquel.
◇ *adv* de quoi.

whereon [weər'ɒn] *arch* OR *fml* ◇ *rel pron* sur quoi, sur lequel.
◇ *adv* sur quoi.

wheresoever [ˌweəsəʊ'evə^{r}] = **wherever**.

whereto [weə'tuː] *arch* OR *fml* ◇ *adv* (vers) où.
◇ *rel pron* vers quoi.

whereupon [ˌweərə'pɒn] ◇ *conj* sur OR après quoi, sur ce.
◇ *adv arch* sur quoi.

wherever [weər'evə^{r}] ◇ *conj* -**1.** [every place] partout où; [no matter what place] où que; ~ you go in Europe, you meet other tourists où que vous alliez en Europe, vous rencontrez d'autres touristes; ~ you go it's the same thing où que vous alliez c'est la même chose, c'est partout pareil; ~ we went, he complained about the food partout où on est allés, il s'est plaint de la nourriture. -**2.** [anywhere, in whatever place] (là) où; he can sleep ~ he likes il peut dormir (là) où il veut; we'll have to sit ~ there's room il faudra s'asseoir là où il y aura de la place; she works ~ she's needed elle travaille là où on a besoin d'elle; he takes on work ~ he can find it il accepte du travail où il en trouve; we can go ~ we please nous pouvons aller où bon nous semble; ~ there is poverty there are social problems là où il y a de la misère il y a des problèmes sociaux; they're from Little Pucklington, ~ that is ils viennent d'un endroit qui s'appelle Little Pucklington. -**3.** [in any situation] quand; I wish, ~ possible, to avoid job losses je souhaite éviter toute perte d'emploi quand c'est possible; grants are given ~ needed des bourses sont accordées à chaque fois que c'est nécessaire.
◇ *adv inf* -**1.** [indicating surprise] mais où donc; ~ did you get that idea? mais d'où sors-tu cette idée?; ~ have you been? où étais-tu donc passé? -**2.** [indicating unknown or unspecified place]: they're holidaying in Marbella or Málaga or ~ ils passent leurs vacances à Marbella ou Malaga ou Dieu sait où.

wherewith [weə'wɪθ] *conj fml & lit* avec quoi, avec lequel.

wherewithal ['weəwɪðɔːl] *n Br*: the ~ les moyens *mpl*; I don't have the ~ to buy a new coat je n'ai pas les moyens de me payer un manteau neuf.

wherry ['werɪ] (*pl* wherries) *n* esquif *m*; [fishing] canot *m*.

whet [wet] (*pt & pp* whetted, *cont* whetting) *vt* [cutting tool] affûter, aiguiser; [appetite] aiguiser, ouvrir; to ~ sb's appetite ouvrir l'appétit à qqn; her few days in Spain only whetted her appetite for more *fig* ces quelques jours passés en Espagne n'ont fait que lui donner envie d'y revenir.

whether ['weðə^{r}] *conj* -**1.** [if] si; I asked ~ I could come j'ai demandé si je pouvais venir; I don't know ~ she's ready or not je ne sais pas si elle est prête ou non; I don't know now ~ it's such a good idea je ne suis plus sûr que ce soit une tellement OR si bonne idée; the question now is ~ you want the job or not la question est maintenant de savoir si tu veux cet emploi ou pas. -**2.** [no matter if]: ~ it rains or not qu'il pleuve ou non; ~ you want to or not que tu le veuilles ou non; ~ they open it now or later, it doesn't matter qu'ils l'ouvrent maintenant ou plus tard, cela n'a pas d'importance; ~ by accident or design que ce soit par hasard ou fait exprès.

whetstone ['wetstəʊn] *n* pierre *f* à aiguiser.

whew [hwjuː] *interj* [relief] ouf; [admiration] oh la la; ~! I'm glad that's over! ouf! je suis bien content que ça soit fini!

whey [weɪ] *n* petit-lait *m*.

whey-faced *adj* pâle.

which [wɪtʃ] ◇ *det* -**1.** [indicating choice] quel *m*, quelle *f*, quels *mpl*, quelles *fpl*; ~ book did you buy? quel livre as-tu acheté?; ~ candidate are you voting for? pour quel candidat allez-vous voter?; ~ one? lequel?, laquelle?; ~ ones? lesquels?/lesquelles?; ~ one of you spoke? lequel de vous a parlé?; ~ one of the twins got married? lequel des jumeaux s'est marié?; I saw several films – ~ ones? j'ai vu plusieurs films – lesquels?; I wonder ~ route would be best je me demande quel serait le meilleur chemin; ~ way should we go? par où devrions-nous aller?; keep track of ~ employees come in late notez le nom des employés qui arrivent en retard. -**2.** [referring back to preceding noun or statement]: he may miss his plane, in ~ case he'll have to wait until tomorrow il est possible qu'il rate son avion, auquel cas il devra attendre demain; she arrives at 5 p.m., at ~ time I'll still be at the office elle arrive à 17 h, heure à laquelle je serai encore au bureau; they lived in Madrid for one year, during ~ time their daughter was born ils ont habité Madrid pendant un an, et c'est à cette époque que leur fille est née.

◇ *pron* -**1.** [what one or ones] lequel *m*, laquelle *f*, lesquels *mpl*, lesquelles *fpl*; **~ of the houses do you live in?** dans quelle maison habitez-vous?; **~ of these books is yours?** lequel de ces livres est le tien?; **~ is the freshest?** quel est le plus frais?; **~ is the more interesting of the two films?** lequel des deux films est le plus intéressant?; **~ of you saw the accident?** qui de vous a vu l'accident?; **~ of you three is the oldest?** lequel de vous trois est le plus âgé?, qui est le plus âgé de vous trois?; **she's from Chicago or Boston, I don't remember ~** elle vient de Chicago ou de Boston, je ne sais plus lequel des deux; **we can play bridge or poker, I don't care ~** on peut jouer au bridge ou au poker, peu m'importe; **I can't tell ~ is ~** je n'arrive pas à les distinguer (l'un de l'autre); **~ is ~?** lequel est-ce? -**2.** [the one or ones that - as subject] celui qui *m*, celle qui *f*, ceux qui *mpl*, celles qui *fpl*; [- as object] celui que *m*, celle que *f*, ceux que *mpl*, celles que *fpl*; **show me ~ you prefer** montrez-moi celui que vous préférez; **tell her ~ is yours** dites-lui lequel est le vôtre.

◇ *rel pron* -**1.** [adding further information - as subject] qui; [- as object] que; **the house, ~ is very old, needs urgent repairs** la maison, qui est très vieille, a besoin d'être réparée sans plus attendre; **the vases, each of ~ held white roses, were made of crystal** les vases, qui contenaient chacun des roses blanches, étaient en cristal; **the hand with ~ I write** la main avec laquelle j'écris; **the office in ~ she works** le bureau dans lequel OR où elle travaille; **the hotels at ~ they stayed** les hôtels où ils sont allés OR descendus. -**2.** [commenting on previous statement - as subject] ce qui; [- as object] ce que; **it took her an hour, ~ isn't bad really** elle a mis une heure, ce qui n'est pas mal en fait; **he looked like a military man, ~ in fact he was** il avait l'air d'un militaire, et en fait c'en était un; **he says it was an accident, ~ I don't believe for an instant** il dit que c'était un accident, ce que je ne crois absolument pas OR mais je ne le crois pas un seul instant; **I don't like it when rents go up, ~ they often do** je n'aime pas que les loyers augmentent, ce qui arrive souvent; **then they arrived, after ~ things got better** puis ils sont arrivés, après quoi tout est allé mieux; **she lied about the letter, from ~ I guessed she was up to something** elle a menti au sujet de la lettre, d'où j'ai deviné qu'elle combinait quelque chose; **he started shouting, upon ~ I left the room** il s'est mis à crier, sur quoi OR et sur ce j'ai quitté la pièce.

◆ **Which?** *pr n magazine de l'Union des consommateurs britanniques connu pour ses essais comparatifs.*

whichever [wɪtʃ'evəʳ] ◇ *pron* -**1.** [the one that - as subject] celui qui *m*, celle qui *f*, ceux qui *mpl*, celles qui *pl*; [- as object] celui que *m*, celle que *f*, ceux que *mpl*, celles que *fpl*; **choose ~ most appeals to you** choisissez celui/celle qui vous plaît le plus; **choose ~ most appeal to you** choisissez ceux/celles qui vous plaisent le plus; **will ~ of you arrives first turn on the heating?** celui d'entre vous qui arrivera le premier pourra-t-il allumer le chauffage?; **take ~ is (the) cheapest** prenez (celui qui est) le moins cher; **shall we go to the cinema or the theatre? — ~ you prefer** on va au cinéma ou au théâtre? — choisis ce que tu préfères; **let's meet at 3.30 or 4, ~ is best for you** donnons-nous rendez-vous à 3 h 30 ou à 4 h, comme cela vous arrange le mieux; **we will reimburse half the value or $1,000, ~ is the greater** nous vous rembourserons la moitié de la valeur ou 1 000 dollars, soit la somme la plus avantageuse. -**2.** [no matter which one]: **~ of the routes you choose, allow about two hours** quel que soit le chemin que vous choisissiez, comptez environ deux heures; **~ of the houses you buy it will be a good investment** quelle que soit la maison que vous achetiez, ce sera un bon investissement; **~ of the computers you buy will be installed free of charge** quel que soit l'ordinateur que vous achetiez, l'installation sera gratuite; **I'd like to speak either to Mr Brown or Mr Jones, ~ is available** j'aimerais parler à M. Brown ou à M. Jones, celui des deux qui est disponible.

◇ *det* -**1.** [indicating the specified choice or preference]: **grants will be given to ~ students most need them** des bourses seront accordées à ceux des étudiants qui en ont le plus besoin; **I'll buy ~ car does the best mileage** je prendrai la voiture qui consomme le moins (d'essence) (, peu importe laquelle); **take ~ seat you like** asseyez-vous où vous voulez; **we'll travel by ~ train is fastest** nous prendrons le train le plus rapide (, peu importe lequel); **keep ~ one appeals to you most** gardez celui qui vous plaît le plus. -**2.** [no matter what - as subject] quel que soit... qui; [- as object] quel que soit... que; **~ job you take, it will mean a lot of travelling** quel que soit le poste que vous preniez, vous serez obligé de beaucoup voyager; **~ party is in power** quel que soit le parti au pouvoir; **we'll still be late ~ way we go** nous serons en retard de toute façon quel que soit le chemin que nous prenions; **~ way you look at it, it's not fair** peu importe la façon dont on considère la question, c'est vraiment injuste.

whichsoever [ˌwɪtʃsəʊ'evəʳ] = **whichever**.

whichways ['wɪtʃweɪz] *adv Am* où; **she left the papers lying every ~** elle a laissé les papiers traîner partout.

whiff [wɪf] ◇ *n* -**1.** [gust, puff] bouffée *f*; **one ~ of this gas and you'd be out cold** *inf* une seule bouffée de ce gaz et vous tombez dans les pommes. -**2.** [smell] odeur *f*; **he got a sudden ~ of her perfume/of rotten eggs** il sentit soudain l'odeur de son parfum/une odeur d'œufs pourris; **get a ~ of this!** *inf* sens-moi un peu ça!; **a ~ of scandal** *fig* une odeur de scandale.

◇ *vi inf* sentir mauvais, puer.

whiffle ['wɪfl] *vi* -**1.** [blow] souffler par bouffées légères OR soudaines. -**2.** *fig* [person] se conduire capricieusement.

whiffy *inf* ['wɪfɪ] (*compar* **whiffier**, *superl* **whiffiest**) *adj* qui pue.

Whig [wɪg] ◇ *adj* whig.

◇ *n* whig *m*.

while [waɪl] ◇ *conj* -**1.** [as] pendant que; **he read the paper ~ he waited** il lisait le journal en attendant; **~ (you're) in London you should visit the British Museum** pendant que vous serez à Londres OR pendant votre séjour à Londres, il faut visiter le British Museum; **she fell asleep ~ on duty** elle s'est endormie pendant le service; **he cut himself ~ (he was) shaving** il s'est coupé en se rasant; **~ this was going on** pendant ce temps-là; **'heels repaired/keys cut ~ you wait'** 'talons/clés minute'; **~ you're up could you fetch me some water?** puisque tu es debout, peux-tu aller me chercher de l'eau?; **and ~ I'm about OR at it...** et pendant que j'y suis... -**2.** [although] bien que, quoique; **~ I admit it's difficult, it's not impossible** j'admets que c'est difficile, mais ce n'est pas impossible; **~ comprehensive, the report lacked clarity** bien que détaillé le rapport manquait de clarté. -**3.** [whereas] alors que, tandis que; **~ he loves opera, I prefer jazz** il adore l'opéra alors que moi je préfère le jazz; **she's left-wing, ~ he's rather conservative** elle est de gauche tandis que lui est plutôt conservateur.

◇ *n*: **to wait a ~** attendre (un peu); **after a ~** au bout de quelque temps; **for a ~/a long ~ I believed her** pendant un certain temps/pendant assez longtemps je l'ai crue; **I was in the States a short ~ ago** j'étais aux États-Unis il y a peu (de temps); **she was in the garden a short ~ ago** elle était dans le jardin il y a un instant; **it's been a good ~ since I've seen her** ça fait pas mal de temps que je ne l'ai pas vue; **it takes quite a ~ to get there** il faut un certain temps pour y aller; **all the ~ (pendant)** tout ce temps; **once in a ~** de temps en temps OR à autre.

◆ **while away** *vt sep* faire passer; **she ~d away the hours reading until he returned** elle passa le temps à lire jusqu'à son retour.

while-you-wait *adj*: **'~ heel repairs'** 'talons minute'; **'~ film development'** 'développement en une heure'.

whilst [waɪlst] *Br* = **while** *conj*.

whim [wɪm] *n* caprice *m*, fantaisie *f*; **it's just one of his little ~s** ce n'est qu'une de ses petites lubies; **arrangements are altered at the ~ of the King** les préparatifs sont changés sur un simple caprice du roi; **she indulges his every ~** elle lui passe tous ses caprices; **whenever the ~ takes him** chaque fois que l'idée lui prend; **on a sudden ~ I telephoned her mother** tout à coup l'idée m'a pris de téléphoner à sa mère.

whimper ['wɪmpəʳ] ◇ *vi* [person] gémir, geindre; *pej* pleurnicher; [dog] gémir, pousser des cris plaintifs.

◇ *vt* gémir.

◇ *n* gémissement *m*, geignement *m*; **"don't" he said with a ~** «non» dit-il d'un ton larmoyant OR gémit-il; **I don't want to hear a ~ out of you** je ne veux pas t'entendre te plaindre; **she did it without a ~** elle l'a fait sans se plaindre.

whimpering ['wɪmpərɪŋ] ◇ *n (U)* gémissements *mpl*, plaintes *fpl*; **stop your ~!** arrête de pleurnicher!

◇ *adj* [voice] larmoyant; [person] qui pleurniche.

whimsical ['wɪmzɪkl] *adj* -**1.** [capricious] capricieux, fantasque. -**2.** [unusual] étrange, insolite; **he said, with a ~ smile** dit-il avec un sourire étrange; **what a ~ idea!** quelle idée saugrenue!

whimsicality [ˌwɪmzɪ'kælətɪ] (*pl* **whimsicalities**) *n* caractère *m* fantasque OR curieux.

whimsically ['wɪmzɪklɪ] *adv* étrangement, curieusement.

whimsy ['wɪmsɪ] (*pl* **whimsies**) *n* -**1.** [whimsicality] caractère *m* fantasque OR fantaisiste; **a piece of pure ~** de la pure fantaisie; **full of ~** plein de fantaisie OR de malice. -**2.** [idea] caprice *m*, fantaisie *f*.

whin [wɪn] *n* ajonc *m*.

whine [waɪn] ◇ *vi* -**1.** [in pain, discomfort - person] gémir, geindre; [- dog] gémir, pousser des gémissements. -**2.** [complain] se lamenter, se plaindre; **do stop whining about your job!** arrête de te plaindre de ton travail!; **don't come whining to me about it** ne viens pas t'en plaindre à moi.

◇ *vt* dire en gémissant; **"I'm hungry" she ~d** «j'ai faim» dit-elle d'une voix plaintive.

◇ *n* -**1.** [from pain, discomfort] gémissement *m*. -**2.** [complaint] plainte *f*.

whiner *inf* ['waɪnəʳ] *n pej* pleurnichard *m*, -e *f*.

whinge *inf* [wɪndʒ] (*cont* **whingeing**) *Br* & *Austr pej* ◇ *vi* geindre, pleurnicher; **he's always whingeing (about something)** il est toujours à pleurnicher (à propos de quelque chose); **don't come ~ing to me about your problems** ne venez pas vous plaindre à moi de vos problèmes.

◇ *n* plainte *f*, pleurnicherie *f*.

whingeing *inf* ['wɪndʒɪŋ] *Br* & *Austr* ◇ *n* gémissement *m*; *pej* pleurnicherie *f*, plainte *f*.

◇ *adj* [person] pleurnicheur; [voice] plaintif.

whining ['waɪnɪŋ] ◇ *n (U)* -**1.** [of person] gémissements *mpl*; *pej* pleurnicheries *fpl*; [of dog] gémissements *mpl*; **I've had enough of your ~!** j'en ai assez de tes pleurnicheries OR jérémiades! -**2.** [of machinery, shells] gémissement *m*.

◇ *adj* [person] *pej* geignard, pleurnicheur; [voice] geignard; [dog] qui gémit.

whinny ['wɪnɪ] (*pt* & *pp* **whinnied**, *pl* **whinnies**)

◇ *vi* hennir.

◇ *n* hennissement *m*.

whip [wɪp] (*pt* & *pp* **whipped**, *cont* **whipping**)

◇ *vt* -**1.** [person, animal] fouetter; **the cold wind whipped her face** le vent glacial lui fouettait le visage; the wind whipped her hair about le vent agitait sa chevelure. -**2.** *inf* [defeat] vaincre, battre. -**3.** CULIN fouetter, battre au fouet; ~ the cream fouettez la crème; ~ the egg whites battez les blancs en neige. -**4.** *fig*: his speech whipped them all into a frenzy son discours les a tous rendus frénétiques; I'll soon ~ the team into shape j'aurai bientôt fait de mettre l'équipe en forme; I need time to ~ the project into shape il me faut du temps pour donner forme au projet; to ~ sb into line mettre qqn au pas. -**5.** *inf Br* [steal] faucher, piquer. -**6.** SEW surfiler. -**7.** [cable, rope] surlier.

◇ *vi* -**1.** [lash] fouetter; the rain whipped against the windows la pluie fouettait OR cinglait les vitres; the flags whipped about in the wind les drapeaux claquaient au vent. -**2.** [move quickly] aller vite, filer; the car whipped along the road la voiture filait sur la route; she whipped around the corner elle a pris le virage sur les chapeaux de roue; the sound of bullets whipping through the air le bruit des balles qui sifflaient; the ball whipped past him into the net la balle est passée devant lui comme un éclair pour finir au fond du filet; I'll just ~ down to the shop je vais juste faire un saut au magasin; can you ~ round to the library for me? pouvez-vous faire un saut à la bibliothèque pour moi?

◇ *n* -**1.** [lash] fouet *m*; [for riding] cravache *f*. -**2.** POL [MP] *parlementaire chargé de la discipline de son parti et qui veille à ce que ses députés participent aux votes*. -**3.** *Br* POL [summons] convocation *f*. -**4.** *Br* POL [paper] *calendrier des travaux parlementaires envoyé par le «whip» aux députés de son parti*. -**5.** [dessert]: pineapple ~ crème *f* à l'ananas.

◆ **whip away** *vt sep* [subj: wind] emporter brusquement; a sudden gust whipped my hat away une rafale de vent a emporté mon chapeau.

◆ **whip in** ◇ *vt sep* -**1.** HUNT ramener, rassembler. -**2.** *Br* POL [in parliament] battre le rappel de *(pour voter)*. -**3.** [supporters] rallier.
◇ *vi insep* -**1.** [rush in] entrer précipitamment. -**2.** HUNT être piqueur.

◆ **whip off** *vt sep* [take off - jacket, shoes] se débarrasser de; [write quickly - letter, memo] écrire en vitesse.

◆ **whip on** *vt sep* [horse] cravacher.

◆ **whip out** ◇ *vt sep* -**1.** [take out] sortir vivement; he whipped a notebook out of his pocket il a vite sorti un carnet de sa poche; she whipped out a gun elle a soudain sorti un pistolet. -**2.** [grab]: someone whipped my bag out of my hand quelqu'un m'a arraché mon sac des mains.
◇ *vi insep* sortir précipitamment.

◆ **whip round** *vi insep* [person] se retourner vivement, faire volte-face.

◆ **whip through** *inf vt insep* [book] parcourir en vitesse; [task] expédier, faire en quatrième vitesse.

◆ **whip up** *vt sep* -**1.** [curiosity, emotion] attiser; [support] obtenir. -**2.** [typhoon] susciter, provoquer; [dust] soulever (des nuages de). -**3.** CULIN battre au fouet, fouetter; I'll ~ up some lunch *inf* je vais préparer de quoi déjeuner en vitesse.

whipcord ['wɪpkɔːd] ◇ *n* whipcord *m*.
◇ *comp* en whipcord.

whip hand *n*: to have the ~ être le maître; to have the ~ over sb avoir le dessus sur qqn.

whiplash ['wɪplæʃ] *n* -**1.** [stroke of whip] coup *m* de fouet. -**2.** MED: ~ effect effet *m* du coup du lapin; ~ injury coup *m* du lapin, syndrome *m* cervical traumatique *spec*.

whipped [wɪpt] *adj* [cream] fouetté.

whipper-in [ˌwɪpəʳ-] (*pl* whippers-in) *n* HUNT piqueur *m*.

whippersnapper ['wɪpəˌsnæpəʳ] *n dated* freluquet *m*.

whippet ['wɪpɪt] *n* whippet *m*.

whipping ['wɪpɪŋ] *n* -**1.** [as punishment - child] correction *f*; [- prisoner] coups *mpl* de fouet; his father gave him a good ~ son père lui a donné une bonne correction. -**2.** *inf* [defeat]: the team received a ~ l'équipe a été battue à plate couture.

whipping boy *n* bouc *m* émissaire.

whipping cream *n* crème *f* fraîche (à fouetter), crème *f* fleurette.

whipping post *n* poteau *m (auquel étaient attachés les condamnés au fouet)*.

whipping top *n* toupie *f*.

whippoorwill ['wɪpˌpʊəˌwɪl] *n* engoulevent *m* d'Amérique du Nord.

whip-round *inf n Br* collecte *f*; they had a ~ for her ils ont fait une collecte pour elle.

whipsaw ['wɪpsɔː] ◇ *n* scie *f* à chantourner.
◇ *vt* chantourner; the candidate ~ed his opponent *Am fig* le candidat a battu son adversaire sur un double plan.

whir [wɜːʳ] = **whirr**.

whirl [wɜːl] ◇ *vi* -**1.** [person, skater] tourner, tournoyer; she ~ed round the ice rink elle a fait le tour de la piste en tourbillonnant. -**2.** [leaves, smoke] tourbillonner, tournoyer; [dust, water] tourbillonner; [spindle, top] tournoyer; snowflakes ~ed past the window des flocons de neige passaient devant la fenêtre en tourbillonnant; the water ~ed away down the sink l'eau s'est écoulée en tourbillonnant dans l'évier. -**3.** [head, ideas] tourner; my head is ~ing (j'ai) la tête (qui) me tourne; the news made her mind ~ les nouvelles lui ont fait tourner la tête. -**4.** [move quickly] aller à toute vitesse; the horses ~ed past us les chevaux sont passés devant nous à toute allure.
◇ *vt* -**1.** [dancer, skater] faire tourner; he ~ed his partner around the floor il faisait tournoyer sa partenaire autour de la piste. -**2.** [leaves, smoke] faire tourbillonner OR tournoyer; [dust, sand] faire tourbillonner; the wind ~ed the leaves about le vent faisait tourbillonner les feuilles. -**3.** [take rapidly]: she ~ed us off on a trip round Europe elle nous a embarqués pour un tour d'Europe.
◇ *n* -**1.** [of dancers, leaves, events] tourbillon *m*; *fig*: my head is in a ~ la tête me tourne; her thoughts were in a ~ tout tourbillonnait dans sa tête; the mad social ~ *hum* la folle vie mondaine; the kitchen was a ~ of activity la cuisine bourdonnait d'activité. -**2.** [try]: to give sthg a ~ *inf* s'essayer à qqch; why don't you give it a ~? pourquoi n'essayez-vous pas? -**3.** *inf* [trip] promenade *f*, tour *m*.

whirligig ['wɜːlɪɡɪɡ] *n Br* -**1.** [top] toupie *f*; [toy windmill] moulin *m* à vent *(jouet)*. -**2.** [merry-go-round] manège *m*. -**3.** [of activity, events] tourbillon *m*. -**4.** [beetle] tourniquet *m*, gyrin *m*.

whirlpool ['wɜːlpuːl] *n literal* & *fig* tourbillon *m*.

whirlpool bath *n* bain *m* à remous, Jacuzzi® *m*.

whirlwind ['wɜːlwɪnd] ◇ *n* tornade *f*, trombe *f*; he went through the office accounts like a ~ *fig* il a passé les comptes de la société en revue en un rien de temps.
◇ *adj* [trip, romance] éclair *(inv)*.

whirlybird *inf* ['wɜːlɪbɜːd] *n* hélico *m*.

whirr [wɜːʳ] ◇ *n* [of wings] bruissement *m*; [of camera, machinery] bruit *m*, ronronnement *m*; [of helicopter, propeller] bruit *m*, vrombissement *m*; we could hear the ~ of the cameras on entendait le ronronnement des caméras.
◇ *vi* [wings] bruire; [camera, machinery] ronronner; [propeller] vrombir.

whish [wɪʃ] = **swish** *vi* & *n*.

whisk [wɪsk] ◇ *vt* -**1.** [put or take quickly]: we ~ed the money into the tin/off the counter nous avons vite fait disparaître l'argent dans la boîte/du comptoir; she ~ed the gun back into her bag elle remit vivement le pistolet dans son sac; the car ~ed us to the embassy la voiture nous emmena à l'ambassade à toute allure; she ~ed the children out of the room elle emmena rapidement les enfants hors de la pièce. -**2.** CULIN [cream, eggs] battre; [eggwhites] battre en neige; ~ in the cream incorporer la crème avec un fouet. -**3.** [flick]: the horse/cow ~ed its tail le cheval/la vache agitait la queue.
◇ *vi* [move quickly] aller vite; she just ~ed in and out elle n'a fait qu'entrer et sortir; the train ~ed through the countryside le train filait OR roulait à vive allure à travers la campagne.
◇ *n* -**1.** [of tail, stick, duster] coup *m*; the horse gave a ~ of its tail le cheval agita la queue OR donna un coup de queue; give the bedroom a quick ~ with a duster passez un coup de chiffon dans la chambre. -**2.** [for sweeping] époussette *f*; [for flies] chasse-mouches *m inv*. -**3.** CULIN fouet *m*; [electric] batteur *m*; give the batter a good ~ bien travailler la pâte au fouet.

◆ **whisk away** *vt sep* -**1.** [dust] enlever, chasser; [dishes, tablecloth] faire disparaître; [flies - with fly swatter] chasser à coups de chasse-mouches; [- with tail] chasser d'un coup de queue. -**2.** [take off]: a car ~ed us away to the embassy [immediately] une voiture nous emmena sur-le-champ à l'ambassade; [quickly] une voiture nous emmena à toute allure à l'ambassade.

◆ **whisk off** *vt sep* [quickly] emporter OR emmener à vive allure; [suddenly, immediately] conduire sur-le-champ; the bus ~ed us off to the airport le bus nous emmena rapidement jusqu'à l'aéroport; we were ~ed off to the police station on nous emmena sur-le-champ au poste de police.

whisker ['wɪskəʳ] *n* poil *m*; she won the contest by a ~ *inf* elle a gagné le concours de justesse; he came within a ~ of discovering the truth *inf* il s'en est fallu d'un cheveu OR d'un poil qu'il apprenne la vérité.

◆ **whiskers** *npl* [beard] barbe *f*; [moustache] moustache *f*; [on animal] moustaches *fpl*.

whiskered ['wɪskəd] *adj* [bearded] qui a une barbe; [with moustache] qui a une moustache; [animal] qui a des moustaches.

whiskery ['wɪskərɪ] = **whiskered**.

whisky *Br*, **whiskey** *Am* & *Ir* ['wɪskɪ] (*pl* whiskies) *n* whisky *m*, scotch *m*; *Am* bourbon *m*; a ~ and soda un whisky soda; a ~ on the rocks un whisky avec des glaçons.

whisky mac *n boisson qui se compose de whisky et de vin au gingembre*.

whisky sour *n cocktail avec du whisky et du jus de citron*.

whisper ['wɪspəʳ] ◇ *vi* -**1.** [person] chuchoter, parler à voix basse; to ~ to sb parler OR chuchoter à l'oreille de qqn; stop ~ing! arrêtez de chuchoter!; what are you ~ing about? qu'est-ce que vous avez à chuchoter? -**2.** [leaves] bruire; [water, wind] murmurer.
◇ *vt* -**1.** [person] chuchoter, dire à voix basse; to ~ sthg to sb chuchoter qqch à qqn; I ~ed the answer to her je lui ai soufflé la réponse; to ~ sweet nothings to sb susurrer des mots doux à l'oreille de qqn. -**2.** *Br* [rumour]: it's ~ed that her husband's left her le bruit court OR on dit que son mari l'a quittée; I've heard it ~ed that he's lost his fortune j'ai entendu dire qu'il avait perdu toute sa fortune.
◇ *n* -**1.** [of voice] chuchotement *m*; to speak in a ~ parler tout bas OR à voix basse; we never raised our voices above a ~ nous n'avons fait que murmurer; not a ~ of this to anyone! *fig* n'en soufflez mot à personne! -**2.** [of leaves] bruissement *m*; [of water, wind] murmure *m*. -**3.** *Br* [rumour] rumeur *f*, bruit *m*; there are ~s of his leaving le bruit court OR on dit qu'il va partir; I've heard ~s that they're getting married j'ai entendu dire qu'ils allaient se marier.

whispering ['wɪspərɪŋ] ◇ *n* -**1.** [of voices] chuchotement *m*, chuchotements *mpl*. -**2.** [of leaves] bruissement *m*; [of water, wind] murmure *m*. -**3.** *(usu pl) Br* [rumour] rumeur; I've heard ~s about the new president's private life j'ai entendu toutes sortes de rumeurs sur la vie privée du nouveau président.
◇ *adj* -**1.** [voice] qui chuchote. -**2.** [leaves, tree] qui frémit OR murmure; [water, wind] qui murmure.

whispering campaign *n* campagne *f* insidieuse OR diffamatoire.

whispering gallery *n* galerie *f* à écho.
whist ['wɪst] *n* whist *m*.
whist drive *n* tournoi *m* de whist.
whistle ['wɪsl] ◇ *vi* -**1.** [person - using lips] siffler; [- using whistle] donner un coup de sifflet, siffler; **he walked in whistling happily** il est entré en sifflant joyeusement; **to ~ to sb** siffler qqn; **I ~d to my dog** j'ai sifflé mon chien; **the porter ~d for a taxi** le portier a sifflé un taxi; **he ~s at all the girls** il siffle toutes les filles; **the audience booed and ~d** le public a hué et sifflé ❑ **you can ~ for it!** *inf Br* tu peux toujours courir OR te brosser!; **let him ~ for his lunch!** *Br* il peut toujours l'attendre, son repas!; **to ~ in the dark** essayer de se donner du courage. -**2.** [bird, kettle, train] siffler; **bullets ~d past him** des balles passaient près de lui en sifflant; **the wind ~d through the trees** le vent gémissait dans les arbres.
◇ *vt* [tune] siffler, siffloter; **the coach ~d them off the field** l'entraîneur a sifflé pour qu'ils quittent le terrain; **the players were ~d off the field by the crowd** les joueurs ont quitté le terrain sous les sifflements de la foule.
◇ *n* -**1.** [whistling - through lips] sifflement *m*; [- from whistle] coup *m* de sifflet; **the cheers and ~s of the crowd** les acclamations et les sifflements de la foule; **if you need me, just give a ~** tu n'as qu'à siffler si tu as besoin de moi. -**2.** [of bird, kettle, train] sifflement *m*. -**3.** [instrument - of person, on train] sifflet *m*; **to blow a ~** donner un coup de sifflet; **the ~ blew for the end of the shift** le sifflet a signalé la fin du service; **the referee blew his ~ for half-time** l'arbitre a sifflé la mi-temps ❑ **to be as clean as a ~** briller comme un sou neuf; **it's got all the bells and ~s** il a tous les accessoires possibles et imaginables. -**4.** MUS: **(penny** OR **tin) ~** flûtiau *m*, pipeau *m*.
◆ **whistle up** *inf vt sep Br* -**1.** [by whistling] siffler; **I'll ~ up a cab** je vais siffler un taxi. -**2.** [find] dénicher, dégoter; **I managed to ~ up a van for the move** j'ai réussi à dégoter un camion pour le déménagement; **I can't ~ up a sofa just like that!** je ne peux pas faire apparaître un canapé comme par enchantement!
whistle-blower *inf n personne qui vend la mèche.*
whistle-stop ◇ *n Am* RAIL arrêt *m* facultatif; **~ (town)** village *m* perdu.
◇ *vi Am* POL *faire une tournée électorale en passant par des petites villes.*
◇ *adj*: **he made a ~ tour of the West** il a fait une tournée rapide dans l'Ouest.
whit [wɪt] *n lit* petit peu *m*; **he hasn't changed a ~** il n'a absolument pas changé; **I care not a ~ what people think** je me moque éperdument de ce que les gens pensent.
Whit [wɪt] ◇ *n* Pentecôte *f*.
◇ *comp* [holidays, week] de Pentecôte; **~ Sunday/Monday** dimanche *m*/lundi *m* de Pentecôte.
white [waɪt] ◇ *adj* -**1.** [colour] blanc; **he painted his house ~** il a peint sa maison en blanc; **she wore a dazzling ~ dress** elle portait une robe d'un blanc éclatant; **his hair has turned ~** ses cheveux ont blanchi ‖ [pale]: **she was ~ with fear/rage** elle était verte de peur/blanche de colère; **his face suddenly went ~** il a blêmi tout d'un coup ❑ **whiter than ~** *literal* plus blanc que blanc; *fig* sans tache; **you're as ~ as a ghost/sheet** vous êtes pâle comme la mort/un linge; **as ~ as snow** blanc comme neige; **'White Fang'** *London* 'Croc-Blanc'. -**2.** [flour, rice] blanc; **(a loaf of) ~ bread** du pain blanc; **~ coffee** *Br* café *m* au lait; **~ wine** vin *m* blanc. -**3.** [race] blanc; **a ~ man** un Blanc; **a ~ woman** une Blanche; **~ man's justice** la justice des Blancs; **an all-~ neighbourhood** un quartier blanc; **~ schools** écoles *fpl* pour les Blancs; **~ supremacy** la suprématie des Blancs.
◇ *n* -**1.** [colour] blanc *m*; **the bride wore ~** la mariée était en blanc; **he was dressed all in ~** il était tout en blanc; **dazzling ~** blanc éclatant. -**2.** ANAT [of an eye] blanc *m*; **don't shoot until you see the ~s of their eyes** *fig* ne tirez qu'au dernier moment. -**3.** CULIN: **(egg) ~** blanc *m* (d'œuf). -**4.** [Caucasian] Blanc *m*, Blanche *f*; **'~s only'** réservé aux Blancs; **they're trying to set ~ against black** ils essaient de monter les Blancs contre les Noirs.
◇ *vi & vt arch* blanchir.
◆ **whites** *npl* [sportswear] tenue *f* de sport blanche *(tennis, cricket)*; [linen] blanc *m*.
◆ **white out** *vt sep* effacer (au correcteur liquide); **can you ~ out this word?** peux-tu effacer ce mot?
white admiral *n papillon aux ailes marron marquées de blanc.*
whitebait ['waɪtbeɪt] *n* [for fishermen] blanchaille *f*; CULIN petite friture *f*.
white blood cell *n* globule *m* blanc.
whitecaps ['waɪtkæps] *npl* [waves] moutons *mpl*.
white Christmas *n* Noël *m* blanc.
white-collar *adj*: **~ job** poste *m* d'employé de bureau; **~ workers** les employés *mpl* de bureau, les cols *mpl* blancs.
whited sepulchre ['waɪtɪd-] *n* hypocrite *mf*.
white dwarf *n* naine *f* blanche.
white elephant *n* [useless object] *objet coûteux dont l'utilité ne justifie pas le coût*; **the new submarine has turned out to be a complete ~** le nouveau sous-marin s'est révélé être un luxe tout à fait superflu.
white elephant stall *n Br* étalage *m* d'objets inutiles.
White Ensign *n pavillon de la marine royale britannique.*
white-faced *adj* au visage pâle.
white feather *n*: **to show the ~** se dégonfler.
whitefish ['waɪtfɪʃ] (*pl inv* OR **whitefishes**) *n* corégone *m*.
white fish *n Br* poisson *m* blanc.
white flag *n* drapeau *m* blanc.
whitefly ['waɪtflaɪ] (*pl* **whiteflies**) *n* aleurode *m*.
white gold *n* or *m* blanc.
white goods *npl* [household equipment] appareils *mpl* ménagers; [linen] linge *m* de maison, blanc *m*.
white-haired *adj* [person] aux cheveux blancs; [animal] aux poils blancs; **his ~ old mother** sa vieille mère aux cheveux blancs.
Whitehall ['waɪthɔːl] *pr n rue du centre de Londres.*

WHITEHALL:
Cette rue réunit de nombreux services gouvernementaux et le nom est souvent employé pour désigner le gouvernement lui-même.

---

white-headed *adj* [person] aux cheveux blancs; [animal, bird] à la tête blanche.
white heat *n* PHYS & *fig* chaleur *f* incandescente; **in the ~ of passion** au plus fort de la passion; **anti-war feelings have reached ~** les sentiments d'hostilité par rapport à la guerre ont atteint un paroxysme.
white hope *n* espoir *m*; **he's the (great) ~ of British athletics** c'est le grand espoir de l'athlétisme britannique.
white horses *npl* [waves] moutons *mpl*.
white-hot *adj* PHYS & *fig* chauffé à blanc.
White House *pr n*: **the ~** la Maison-Blanche.
white knight *n fig* sauveur *m*.
white lead *n* blanc *m* de céruse OR de plomb.
white lie *n* pieux mensonge *m*.
white light *n* lumière *f* blanche.
white magic *n* magie *f* blanche.
white meat *n* viande *f* blanche; [of poultry] blanc *m*.
white metal *n* métal *m* blanc.
white meter *n système économique de chauffage qui utilise l'électricité pendant les heures où elle coûte moins cher.*
whiten ['waɪtn] *vi & vt* blanchir.
whiteness ['waɪtnɪs] *n* blancheur *f*; [of skin] blancheur *f*, pâleur *f*.
White Nile *pr n*: **the ~** le Nil Blanc.
whitening ['waɪtnɪŋ] *n* -**1.** [substance] blanc *m*. -**2.** [process - of walls] blanchiment *m*; [- of linen] blanchissage *m*.
white noise *n* bruit *m* blanc.
whiteout ['waɪtaʊt] *n* brouillard *m* blanc.
white owl *n* harfang *m*, chouette *f* blanche.
white paper *n Br* [government report] livre *m* blanc.
white pepper *n* poivre *m* blanc.
White Russia *pr n* Russie *f* Blanche.
White Russian ◇ *adj* biélorusse.
◇ *n* -**1.** [person] Biélorusse *mf*. -**2.** LING biélorusse *m*.
white sale *n* promotion *f* sur le blanc.
white sauce *n* sauce *f* blanche, béchamel *f*.
White Sea *pr n*: **the ~** la mer Blanche.
white slavery, white slave trade *n* traite *f* des blanches.
white spirit *n* white-spirit *m*.
white tie *n* [formal clothes] habit *m*; **'white tie'** [on invitation] ≃ 'tenue de soirée exigée'.
◆ **white-tie** *adj* habillé; **it was a ~ dinner** c'était un dîner habillé.
white trash *n pej* pauvres blancs *mpl*.
whitewall ['waɪtwɔːl] *n* pneu *m* à flanc blanc.
whitewash ['waɪtwɒʃ] ◇ *n* -**1.** [substance] lait *m* de chaux. -**2.** *fig* [cover-up]: **the police report was simply a ~** le rapport de police visait seulement à étouffer l'affaire. -**3.** SPORT [crushing defeat] défaite *f* cuisante.
◇ *vt* -**1.** [building, wall] blanchir à la chaux. -**2.** *fig* [cover up] blanchir, étouffer; **the minister tried to ~ the affair** le ministre essaya d'étouffer l'affaire. -**3.** SPORT [defeat] écraser.
white water *n* eau *f* vive.
whitewater rafting ['waɪt,wɔːtəʳ-] *n* descente *f* en eau vive.
white wedding *n* mariage *m* en blanc.
white witch *n sorcière qui a recours à la magie blanche.*
whitewood ['waɪtwʊd] *n* bois *m* blanc.
whitey▽ ['waɪtɪ] *n Am pej* Blanc *m*, Blanche *f*.
whither ['wɪðəʳ] *adv & conj arch* OR *lit* (vers) où; **~ Christianity?** [in headlines, titles] où va le christianisme?
whiting ['waɪtɪŋ] *n* -**1.** ZOOL merlan *m*. -**2.** [colouring agent] blanc *m*.
whitish ['waɪtɪʃ] *adj* blanchâtre; **her hair was ~ blond** ses cheveux étaient d'un blond presque blanc.
whitlow ['wɪtləʊ] *n* panaris *m*.
Whitsun(tide) ['wɪtsn(taɪd)] *n* Pentecôte *f*; **at ~** à la Pentecôte.
whitter ['wɪtəʳ] = **witter**.
whittle ['wɪtl] *vi & vt* tailler (au couteau); **he ~d an arrow from an old stick, he ~d an old stick into an arrow** il a taillé une flèche dans un vieux bâton.
◆ **whittle away** ◇ *vt sep fig* amoindrir, diminuer; **they ~d away his resistance** ils ont amoindri sa résistance.
◇ *vi insep* [with a knife] tailler; **he sat there whittling away at a piece of wood** il était assis à tailler un morceau de bois avec un couteau; **their constant teasing ~d away at his patience** *fig* leurs moqueries constantes ont mis sa patience à bout.
◆ **whittle down** *vt sep* [with a knife] tailler (au couteau); *fig* amenuiser, amoindrir; **rising fuel costs have ~d down our profits** l'augmentation du prix du pétrole a fait baisser nos bénéfices.
whity ['waɪtɪ] *Am* = **whitey**.
whiz(z) [wɪz] (*pt & pp* **whizzed**, *cont* **whizzing**)
◇ *vi* -**1.** [rush] filer; **a car whizzed past** une voiture est passée à toute allure; **I'll ~ down to the shops** je vais faire un saut dans les magasins. -**2.** [hiss]: **bullets whizzed around** OR **past him** des balles sifflaient tout autour OR passaient près de lui en sifflant.
◇ *n* -**1.** [hissing sound] sifflement *m*. -**2.** *inf* [swift movement]: **I'll just have a (quick) ~ round**

with the Hoover®/duster je vais juste passer un petit coup d'aspirateur/de chiffon. -**3.** *inf* [bright person] as *m*; she's a ~ at chemistry c'est un as en chimie; he's a real computer ~ c'est vraiment un as de l'informatique.

whiz(z)-bang *inf* ◇ *n* -**1.** MIL [shell] obus *m* *(utilisé pendant la Première Guerre mondiale)*. -**2.** [fireworks] pétard *m*.
◇ *adj* [first-rate] champion.

whiz(z)-kid *inf n* jeune prodige *m*; she's a computer ~ c'est un vrai génie de l'informatique.

who [huː] ◇ *pron* [what person or persons - as subject] (qui est-ce) qui; [- as object] qui est-ce que, qui; ~ are you? qui êtes-vous?; ~ is it? [at door] qui est-ce?, qui est là?; ~ is speaking? [on telephone] qui est à l'appareil?; [asking for third person] c'est de la part de qui?; ~'s going with you? qui est-ce qui OR qui t'accompagne?; it's Michael — ~? c'est Michael – qui ça?; John's here — ~? John est là – qui ça?; I told him ~ I was je lui ai dit qui j'étais; find out ~ they are voyez qui c'est OR qui sont ces gens; bring ~ you want amenez qui vous voulez; ~ do you think you are? vous vous prenez pour qui?; ~ do you think you are, giving me orders? de quel droit est-ce que vous me donnez des ordres?; ~ did you say was coming to the party? qui avez-vous dit qui viendrait à la soirée?; ~ did they invite? qui est-ce qu'ils ont invité?, qui ont-ils invité?; you'll have to tell me ~'s ~ il faudra que tu me dises qui est qui; ~ is the film by? de qui est le film?; ~ is the letter from? la lettre est de qui?, de qui est la lettre?; ~ did he go with? avec qui y est-il allé?.
◇ *rel pron* qui; the family ~ lived here moved away la famille qui habitait ici a déménagé; those of you ~ were late ceux d'entre vous qui sont arrivés en retard; anyone ~ so wishes may leave ceux qui le souhaitent peuvent partir; any reader ~ finds the story lacks imagination... les lecteurs qui trouvent que l'histoire n'est pas très originale...; Charles, ~ is a policeman, lives upstairs Charles, qui est policier, vit en haut; my mother, ~ I believe you've met,... ma mère, que vous avez déjà rencontrée je crois,...

WHO (*abbr of* World Health Organization) *pr n* OMS *f*.

whoa [wəʊ] *interj*: ~! ho!, holà!

who'd [huːd] = **who had, who would.**

whodunit *inf* [ˌhuːˈdʌnɪt] *n* série *f* noire; to read/to write ~s lire/écrire des romans de série noire.

whoe'er [huˈeəʳ] *pron lit* celui qui, quiconque.

whoever [huːˈevəʳ] -**1.** [any person who] qui; ~ wants it can have it celui qui le veut peut le prendre; I'll give it to ~ needs it je le donnerai à qui en a besoin; invite ~ you like invitez qui vous voulez. -**2.** [the person who] celui qui *m*, celle qui *f*, ceux qui *mpl*, celles qui *fpl*; ~ answered the phone had a nice voice la personne qui a répondu au téléphone avait une voix agréable; contact ~ found the body contactez celui qui OR la personne qui a trouvé le corps. -**3.** [no matter who]: come out, ~ you are! montrez-vous, qui que vous soyez!; ~ gets the job will find it a real challenge celui qui obtiendra cet emploi n'aura pas la tâche facile; ~ you vote for, make sure he's honest quel que soit celui pour qui vous votez, assurez-vous qu'il est honnête; it's from John Smith, ~ he is c'est de la part d'un certain John Smith, si ça te dit quelque chose. -**4.** [emphatic use] qui donc; ~ can that be? qui cela peut-il bien être?

whole [həʊl] ◇ *adj* -**1.** [entire, complete] *(with singular nouns)* entier, tout; it took me a ~ day to paint the kitchen j'ai mis une journée entière OR toute une journée pour peindre la cuisine; I didn't read the ~ book je n'ai pas lu tout le livre OR le livre en entier; I've never seen anything like it in my ~ life je n'ai jamais vu une chose pareille de toute ma vie; that was the ~ point of going there c'est uniquement pour ça que j'y suis allé; she said nothing the ~ time we were there elle n'a rien dit tout le temps que nous étions là; he spent the ~ time watching television il a passé tout son temps à regarder la télévision; the ~ truth toute la vérité; the ~ world was watching le monde entier regardait ‖ *(with plural nouns)* entier; ~ cities were devastated des villes entières furent dévastées; there are two ~ months still to go il reste deux mois entiers ❑ she won the ~ lot elle a gagné le tout; the ~ thing OR business was a farce ce fut un véritable fiasco; I had to start the ~ thing over again j'ai dû tout recommencer; forget the ~ thing n'en parlons plus. -**2.** [as intensifier] tout; a ~ pile of records *inf* tout un tas de disques; he's got a ~ collection of old photographs il a toute une collection de vieilles photographies; there's a ~ lot of things that need explaining il y a beaucoup de choses qui doivent être expliquées ‖ *(with adjectives)*: a ~ new way of living une façon de vivre tout à fait nouvelle. -**3.** [unbroken - china, egg yolk] intact; [unhurt - person] indemne, sain et sauf; the cups were still ~ les tasses étaient toujours intactes ‖ *arch* OR BIBLE: to make ~ sauver; thy faith hath made thee ~ ta foi t'a sauvé. -**4.** CULIN [milk] entier; [grain] complet. -**5.** [brother, sister]: ~ brothers des frères qui ont les mêmes parents.
◇ *n* -**1.** [complete thing, unit] ensemble *m*; the ~ of which this is just a part l'ensemble dont ceci n'est qu'une partie. -**2.** [as quantifier]: the ~ of tout; it will be cold over the ~ of England il fera froid sur toute l'Angleterre; we spent the ~ of August at the seaside nous avons passé tout le mois d'août au bord de la mer; she spent the ~ of her fortune on paintings elle a dépensé toute sa fortune OR sa fortune toute entière en tableaux; can you pay the ~ of the amount? pouvez-vous payer toute la somme OR l'intégralité de la somme?
◇ *adv*: to swallow sthg ~ avaler qqch en entier; he swallowed her story ~ *inf fig* il a gobé tout ce qu'elle lui a dit.
◆ **as a whole** *adv phr* -**1.** [as a unit] entièrement; as a ~ or in part entièrement ou en partie. -**2.** [overall] dans son ensemble; is it true of America as a ~? est-ce vrai pour toute l'Amérique OR l'Amérique en général?; considered as a ~, the festival was a remarkable success dans son ensemble, le festival a été un vrai succès.
◆ **a whole lot** *inf adv phr (with comparative adjectives)* beaucoup; he's a ~ lot younger than his wife il est beaucoup plus jeune que sa femme.
◆ **on the whole** *adv phr* dans l'ensemble; on the ~ he made a good impression dans l'ensemble il a fait bonne impression; I agree with that on the ~ je suis d'accord dans l'ensemble.

wholefood [ˈhəʊlfuːd] *n* aliment *m* complet; the ~ section of the supermarket le rayon diététique du supermarché; ~ shop magasin *m* diététique.

wholehearted [ˌhəʊlˈhɑːtɪd] *adj* [unreserved] sans réserve; she gave them her ~ support elle leur a donné un soutien sans réserve OR sans faille; you have my ~ sympathy je compatis de tout mon cœur à votre peine; he is a ~ supporter of our cause [devoted] il est dévoué corps et âme à notre cause.

wholeheartedly [ˌhəʊlˈhɑːtɪdlɪ] *adv* [unreservedly] de tout cœur; I agree ~ j'accepte de tout (mon) cœur; he flung himself ~ into his new job il s'est jeté corps et âme dans son nouveau travail.

wholemeal [ˈhəʊlmiːl] *adj Br* [bread, flour] complet.

wholeness [ˈhəʊlnɪs] *n* [indivisibility] intégrité *f*, intégralité *f*.

whole note *n Am* [semibreve] ronde *f*.

whole number *n* [integer] nombre *m* entier.

wholesale [ˈhəʊlseɪl] ◇ *n* (vente *f* en) gros *m*.
◇ *adj* -**1.** COMM [business, price, shop] de gros; ~ dealer OR trader grossiste *mf*. -**2.** *fig* [indiscriminate] en masse; there was a ~ massacre of civilians il y a eu un massacre en masse de civils.
◇ *adv* -**1.** COMM en gros; they only sell ~ ils vendent uniquement en gros; I can get it for you ~ je peux vous le procurer au prix de gros. -**2.** *fig* [in entirety]: her suggestions were rejected ~ ses suggestions ont été rejetées en bloc.

wholesaler [ˈhəʊlˌseɪləʳ] *n* grossiste *mf*.

wholesome [ˈhəʊlsəm] *adj* [healthy - food, attitude, image] sain; [- air, climate, environment] salubre, salutaire; [advice] salutaire; she leads a ~ life elle mène une vie saine; a ~-looking boy un garçon sain d'aspect.

wholewheat [ˈhəʊlwiːt] *adj Am*: ~ bread pain *m* complet; ~ flour farine *f* complète.

who'll [huːl] = **who will, who shall.**

wholly [ˈhəʊlɪ] *adv* entièrement; you will be ~ compensated for the damage les dommages vous seront intégralement remboursés; the firm has two ~-owned subsidiaries COMM la société a deux filiales à cent pour cent.

whom [huːm] *fml* ◇ *pron* [in questions] qui; ~ did you contact? qui avez-vous contacté?; ~ did she see? qui a-t-elle vu?; for ~ was the book written? pour qui le livre a-t-il été écrit?
◇ *rel pron* [as object of verb] que; she's the person ~ I most admire c'est la personne que j'admire le plus ‖ [after preposition]: the person to ~ I am writing la personne à qui OR à laquelle j'écris; she saw two men, neither of ~ she recognized elle a vu deux hommes mais elle n'a reconnu ni l'un ni l'autre; a composer about ~ little is known un compositeur sur qui OR sur lequel on sait peu de choses.

whomever [huːmˈevəʳ] *fml* OR *lit* ◇ *pron* [in questions]: ~ did you get that from? qui donc vous a donné cela?
◇ *rel pron*: you may go with ~ you like vous pouvez y aller avec qui vous voudrez; he greeted ~ he met il saluait tous ceux qu'il rencontrait.

whomsoever [ˌhuːmsəʊˈevəʳ] *fml* OR *lit* = **whomever** *rel pron*.

whoop [wuːp] ◇ *n* -**1.** [yell] cri *m*; ~s of delight came from the nursery il y avait des cris de joie venant de la garderie. -**2.** MED quinte *f* de toux.
◇ *vi* -**1.** [yell]: she ~ed with joy elle poussa un cri de joie. -**2.** MED avoir un accès de toux coquelucheuse.
◆ **whoop up** *inf vt sep*: to ~ it up [celebrate] faire la noce bruyamment.

whoopee *inf* [*interj* wʊˈpiː, *n* ˈwʊpiː] ◇ *interj*: ~! youpi!
◇ *n*: to make ~ [celebrate] faire la noce bruyamment; [have sex] faire l'amour.

whooping cough [ˈhuːpɪŋ-] *n* MED coqueluche *f*.

whoops *inf* [wʊps], **whoops-a-daisy** *inf interj*: ~! houp-là!

whoosh *inf* [wʊʃ] ◇ *n*: a ~ of air une bouffée d'air; with a ~ he was off il est parti comme une flèche.
◇ *vi*: fighter planes ~ed by overhead des avions de combat passèrent en trombe au-dessus de nous; the car ~ed through the puddles la voiture passa en trombe dans les flaques.
◇ *interj*: ~! zoum!

whop *inf* [wɒp] (*pt* & *pp* whopped, *cont* whopping) ◇ *vt* [beat] rosser; [defeat] écraser.
◇ *n* [blow] coup.

whopper *inf* [ˈwɒpəʳ] *n* -**1.** [large object]: he caught a real ~ [fish] il a attrapé un poisson super géant; he's got a ~ of a nose il a un nez énorme; that sandwich is a real ~ c'est un énorme sandwich OR un sandwich gigantesque; what a ~! il est gigantesque! -**2.** [lie] gros mensonge *m*, mensonge *m* énorme; to tell a ~ dire un mensonge gros comme une maison.

whopping *inf* [ˈwɒpɪŋ] ◇ *adj* énorme, géant; inflation increased to a ~ 360 % l'inflation a atteint le taux colossal de 360 %.

◇ *adv*: a ~ great lie un mensonge énorme; a ~ great fish un poisson super géant.

whore [hɔːʳ] *pej* ◇ *n* putain *f*; BIBLE [sinner] pécheresse *f*; 'Tis Pity She's a Whore' *Ford* 'Dommage qu'elle soit une putain'.
◇ *vi* -**1.** *literal*: to go whoring [prostitute o.s.] se prostituer; [frequent prostitutes] fréquenter les prostituées, courir la gueuse. -**2.** *fig*: to ~ after sthg se prostituer pour obtenir qqch.
◆ **whore around** *inf vi insep pej* se conduire comme une putain.

who're ['huːəʳ] = **who are**.

whorehouse *inf* ['hɔːhaʊs, *pl* -haʊzɪz] *n* maison *f* close.

whoremonger ['hɔːˌmʌŋgəʳ] *n arch* OR BIBLE vicieux *m*, fornicateur *m arch*.

whorish ['hɔːrɪʃ] *adj pej* dissolu, dépravé.

whorl [wɜːl] *n* [on a shell] spire *f*; [on a finger] sillon *m*; BOT verticille *m*; **~s of smoke rose from the chimney** la fumée montait en spirale de la cheminée, des volutes de fumée s'échappaient de la cheminée.

whortleberry ['wɜːtlˌberɪ] *n* myrtille *f*.

who's [huːz] = **who is, who has**.

whose [huːz] ◇ *poss pron* à qui; **~ is it?** à qui est-ce?; **~ could it be?** à qui pourrait-il bien être?; **~ was the winning number?** à qui était le numéro gagnant?
◇ *poss adj* -**1.** [in a question] à qui, de qui; **~ car was he driving?** à qui était la voiture qu'il conduisait?; **~ child is she?** de qui est-elle l'enfant?; **~ side are you on?** de quel côté êtes-vous?; **~ fault is it?** à qui la faute?; **on ~ authority are you acting?** au nom de quelle autorité agissez-vous? -**2.** [in a relative clause] dont; **isn't that the man ~ photograph was in the newspaper?** n'est-ce pas l'homme qui était en photo dans le journal?; **the girl, both of ~ parents had died, lived with her aunt** la fille, dont les deux parents étaient morts, vivait avec sa tante; **they had twins neither of ~ names I can remember** ils avaient des jumeaux mais je ne me souviens pas de leurs prénoms.

whosoever [ˌhuːsəʊ'evəʳ] *pers pron fml* OR *lit* celui qui, quiconque.

Who's Who *pr n*: the ~ ≃ le Bottin mondain.

who've [huːv] = **who have**.

WH question *n en anglais, question commençant par un «WH word»*.

why [waɪ] ◇ *adv* pourquoi; **~ am I telling you this?** pourquoi est-ce que je vous dis ça?; **~ is it that he never phones?** pourquoi est-ce qu'il ne téléphone jamais?; **~ continue the war at all?** pourquoi OR à quoi bon continuer la guerre?; **~ pay more?** pourquoi payer davantage?; **~ the sudden panic?** pourquoi toute cette agitation?; **~ not?** pourquoi pas?; **~ not join us?** pourquoi ne pas vous joindre à nous?; **~ me?** pourquoi moi?
◇ *conj* pourquoi; **I can't imagine ~ she isn't here** je ne comprends pas pourquoi elle n'est pas ici; **I wonder ~ he left** je me demande pourquoi il est parti; **that's ~ he dislikes you** c'est pour ça qu'il OR voilà pourquoi il ne vous aime pas; **is that ~ she hasn't written?** est-ce pour ça qu'elle n'a pas écrit?; **they've gone, I can't think ~** ils sont partis, je ne sais pas pourquoi.
◇ *rel pron* [after 'reason']: **the reason ~ I lied was that I was scared** j'ai menti parce que j'avais peur; **he didn't tell me the reason ~** il ne m'a pas dit pourquoi; **this is the reason ~ I lied** voilà pourquoi j'ai menti; **there is no (good) reason ~ she shouldn't come** il n'y a pas de raison qu'elle ne vienne pas.
◇ *interj* [expressing surprise, indignation etc]: **~, it's your sister!** tiens, c'est ta sœur!; **~, Mr Ricks, how kind of you to call!** M. Ricks! comme c'est gentil à vous de téléphoner!; **~, there's nothing to it!** c'est comme ça, on n'y peut rien!; **~, he's an impostor!** mais enfin, c'est un imposteur!
◇ *n*: **the ~s and wherefores** le pourquoi et le comment.

WH word *n en anglais, mot commençant par les lettres «wh» et servant à demander un renseignement (what, when, where, who, why)*.

WI ◇ *pr n abbr of* Women's Institute.
◇ -**1.** *written abbr of* West Indies. -**2.** *written abbr of* Wisconsin.

wick [wɪk] *n* -**1.** [for a candle, lamp] mèche *f*. -**2.** *Br phr*: **to get on sb's ~** *inf* taper sur les nerfs à OR casser les pieds à qqn.

wicked ['wɪkɪd] ◇ *adj* -**1.** [evil - person, action, thought] mauvais, méchant; [immoral, indecent] vicieux; **he's a ~ man** c'est un méchant OR mauvais homme; **it was a ~ thing to do** ce n'était pas gentil; **she confessed to having ~ thoughts** elle a confessé qu'elle avait de vilaines pensées; **what a ~ thing to say!** quelle méchanceté!; **she felt as if she had done something very ~** elle avait le sentiment d'avoir fait quelque chose de très mal; **it's a ~ waste of natural resources** *fig* c'est un gâchis scandaleux de ressources naturelles ❑ **to have one's ~ way with sb** *hum* séduire qqn. -**2.** [very bad - weather] épouvantable; [- temper] mauvais, épouvantable; **there are some ~ bends on those mountain roads** il y a quelques méchants virages sur ces routes de montagne; **prices have gone up something ~** *inf* les prix ont augmenté quelque chose de bien. -**3.** [mischievous - person] malicieux; [- smile, look, sense of humour] malicieux, coquin; **you're a ~ little boy** tu es un petit coquin; **a ~ remark** une réflexion malicieuse OR espiègle. -**4.** *inf* [very good] formidable; **she has a ~ forehand** elle a un sacré coup droit.
◇ *adv inf Am* vachement; **this bed is ~ comfortable** il est vachement confortable, ce lit.

wickedly ['wɪkɪdlɪ] *adv* -**1.** [with evil intent] méchamment, avec méchanceté. -**2.** [mischievously] malicieusement.

wickedness ['wɪkɪdnɪs] *n* -**1.** RELIG [sin, evil] iniquité *f*, vilenie *f*; [cruelty - of action, crime] méchanceté *f*; [- of thought] méchanceté *f*, vilenie *f*; **he spoke of the ~ in the world** il parla du mal qui règne dans le monde. -**2.** [mischievousness - of look, sense of humour, smile] caractère *m* malicieux OR espiègle, malice *f*.

wicker ['wɪkəʳ] ◇ *n* osier *m*; **made of ~** en osier.
◇ *adj* [furniture] en osier; **~ basket** panier *m* en osier.

wickerwork ['wɪkəwɜːk] ◇ *n* [material] osier *m*; [objects] vannerie *f*; **is the chair made of ~?** est-ce que la chaise est en osier?; **they sell ~** ils vendent de la vannerie.
◇ *adj* [furniture] en osier; [shop] de vannerie.

wicket ['wɪkɪt] *n* -**1.** *Am* [window] guichet *m*. -**2.** [gate] (petite) porte *f*, portillon *m*. -**3.** [in cricket - stumps] guichet *m*; [- area of grass] terrain *m* (entre les guichets); **to take a ~** éliminer un batteur; **they were 275 for six ~s** ils étaient 275 pour six guichets.

wicket keeper *n* gardien *m* de guichet.

wide [waɪd] ◇ *adj* -**1.** [broad] large; **how ~ is it?** cela fait combien (de mètres) de large?, quelle largeur ça fait?; **do you know how ~ it is?** en connaissez-vous la largeur?; **the road is thirty metres ~** la route fait trente mètres de large; **they're making the street wider** ils élargissent la route; **~ hips/shoulders** hanches/épaules larges; **a ~ forehead** un large front; **he gave a ~ grin** il a fait un large sourire; **a ~ screen** CIN un grand écran, un écran panoramique; **there are wider issues at stake here** des problèmes plus vastes sont ici en jeu; **we need to see the problem in a wider context** il faut que nous envisagions le problème dans un contexte plus général; **I'm using the word in its widest sense** j'emploie ce mot au sens le plus large ‖ [fully open - eyes] grand ouvert; **she watched with ~ eyes** elle regardait les yeux grands ouverts; **his eyes were ~ with terror** ses yeux étaient agrandis par l'épouvante. -**2.** [extensive, vast] étendu, vaste; **a ~ plain** une vaste plaine; **to travel the ~ world** parcourir le vaste monde; **she has ~ experience in this area** elle a une longue OR grande expérience dans ce domaine; **he has very ~ interests** il a des centres d'intérêt très larges; **he has a ~ knowledge of music** il a de vastes connaissances OR des connaissances approfondies en musique; **there are ~ gaps in her knowledge** il y a des lacunes importantes dans ses connaissances; **the incident received ~ publicity** l'événement a été largement couvert par les médias; **a ~ range of products** COMM une gamme importante de produits; **a ~ range of views was expressed** des points de vue très différents furent exprimés; **a ~ variety of colours** un grand choix de couleurs. -**3.** [large - difference]: **the gap between rich and poor remains ~** l'écart (existant) entre les riches et les pauvres demeure considérable. -**4.** SPORT: **the ball was ~** la balle est passée à côté; **the shot was ~** le coup est passé à côté ❑ **to be ~ of the mark** *Br literal* rater OR être passé loin de la cible; *fig* être loin de la vérité OR du compte.
◇ *adv* -**1.** [to full extent]: **open (your mouth) ~** ouvrez grand votre bouche; **she opened the windows ~** elle ouvrit les fenêtres en grand; **he flung his arms ~** il a ouvert grand les bras; **place your feet ~ apart** écartez bien les pieds. -**2.** [away from target] à côté; **the missile went ~** le missile est tombé à côté.

-wide *in cpds*: **state~** à travers tout l'État, dans l'ensemble de l'État; **world~** à travers le monde (entier).

wide-angle lens *n* grand-angle *m*, grand-angulaire *m*.

wide area network *n* réseau *m* étendu.

wide-awake *adj* tout éveillé; *fig* [alert] éveillé, vif.

wide-body *adj*: **a ~ aircraft** avion *m* à fuselage élargi, gros-porteur *m*.

wide boy *inf n Br pej personnage frimeur, bluffeur et sans scrupule*.

wide-eyed *adj* -**1.** [with fear, surprise] les yeux agrandis OR écarquillés; **he looked at me in ~ astonishment** il me regarda les yeux écarquillés d'étonnement; **she watched ~** elle regardait, les yeux écarquillés. -**2.** [naive] candide, ingénu *lit*; **he listened with ~ innocence** il écoutait avec une innocence (toute) ingénue.

widely ['waɪdlɪ] *adv* -**1.** [broadly]: **to smile ~** faire un grand sourire; **to yawn ~** bâiller profondément; **the houses were ~ scattered/spaced** les maisons étaient très dispersées/espacées. -**2.** [extensively]: **she has travelled ~** elle a beaucoup voyagé; **the talk ranged ~ over a variety of topics** la discussion embrassa un nombre de sujets très variés; **the drug is now ~ available/used** le médicament est maintenant largement répandu/utilisé; **it was ~ believed that war was inevitable** il était largement OR communément admis que la guerre était inévitable; **the truth about the incident is not ~ known** la vérité sur l'incident n'est pas connue du grand public; **~ held beliefs/opinions** des croyances/opinions très répandues; **~ held views** des points de vue très répandus; **to be ~ read** [writer, book] être très lu, avoir un grand public; [person] avoir beaucoup lu, être très cultivé; **she is ~ read in history** elle a beaucoup lu en histoire. -**3.** *fig* [significantly]: **prices vary ~** les prix varient très sensiblement; **the two versions differed ~** les deux versions étaient sensiblement différentes; **the students came from ~ differing backgrounds** les étudiants venaient d'horizons très différents.

widen ['waɪdn] ◇ *vt* élargir, agrandir; *fig* [experience, influence, knowledge] accroître, étendre; **the tax reform will ~ the gap between rich and poor** la réforme fiscale va accentuer OR agrandir l'écart entre les riches et les pauvres; **I've ~ed my study to include recent events** j'ai développé mon étude afin d'y inclure les derniers événements.
◇ *vi* s'élargir; [eyes] s'agrandir; [smile] s'accentuer; **the gulf between skilled and unskilled workers is ~ing** l'écart entre les travailleurs qualifiés et non qualifiés va en s'accentuant; **turn left where the road ~s out** tournez à gauche à l'endroit où la route s'élargit.

wide-open *adj* -**1.** [extensive] grand ouvert; the ~ spaces of Australia les grands espaces de l'Australie. -**2.** [fully open]: she stood there with her eyes/mouth wide open elle était là, les yeux écarquillés/bouche bée. -**3.** *fig* [vulnerable] exposé; he left himself wide open to attack/criticism il prêtait ainsi le flanc aux attaques/critiques. -**4.** *Am* [town] ouvert.

wide-ranging [-'reɪndʒɪŋ] *adj* -**1.** [extensive] large, d'une grande ampleur; she has ~ interests elle a des intérêts variés; a ~ cross-section of public opinion un échantillon très large de l'opinion publique; a ~ report/survey un rapport/une étude de grande envergure. -**2.** [far-reaching - effect] de grande portée; the opposition called for ~ reforms l'opposition réclama des réformes de grande portée OR de grande envergure.

wide-screen *adj* grand écran *(inv)*; a ~ epic un film à grand spectacle.

widespread ['waɪdspred] *adj* -**1.** [arms] en croix; [wings] déployé; she stood there arms ~ elle se tenait là, les bras en croix. -**2.** [extensive] (très) répandu; there has been ~ public concern l'opinion publique se montre extrêmement préoccupée.

widgeon ['wɪdʒən] = **wigeon**.

widget *inf* ['wɪdʒɪt] *n* truc *m*, machin *m*.

widow ['wɪdəʊ] ◇ *n* -**1.** [woman] veuve *f*; she's a ~ elle est veuve; Widow Thomas *arch* Madame veuve Thomas; a golf ~ *inf Br hum une femme que son mari délaisse pour le golf*; ~'s pension allocation *f* veuvage; the ~'s mite BIBLE le denier de la veuve. -**2.** TYPO *dernière ligne d'un paragraphe se trouvant à la première ligne d'une page ou d'une colonne*. -**3.** CARDS *main de cartes placée sur la table la face en dessous*.

◇ *vt (usu pass)*: he was ~ed last year il a perdu sa femme l'année dernière; she was ~ed last year elle a perdu son mari l'année dernière; she is recently ~ed elle est veuve depuis peu, elle a perdu son mari il n'y a pas longtemps; he is twice ~ed il est deux fois veuf; she supports her ~ed mother elle fait vivre sa mère qui est veuve.

widower ['wɪdəʊə^r] *n* veuf *m*.

widowhood ['wɪdəʊhʊd] *n* veuvage *m*.

widow's peak *n ligne de cheveux sur le front en forme de v*.

width [wɪdθ] *n* -**1.** [breadth] largeur *f*; the room was ten metres in ~ la pièce faisait dix mètres de largeur; she swam the entire ~ of the river elle a parcouru toute la largeur du fleuve à la nage || [of swimming pool] largeur *f*; she swam two ~s elle a fait deux largeurs de piscine. -**2.** TEX laize *f*, lé *m*; half a ~ of cloth une demi-laize OR un demi-lé de tissu.

widthways ['wɪdθweɪz], **widthwise** ['wɪdθwaɪz] *adv* dans le sens de la largeur.

wield [wiːld] *vt* -**1.** [weapon] brandir; [pen, tool] manier. -**2.** [influence, power] exercer, user de *lit*.

wiener ['wiːnə^r] *n Am* saucisse *f* de Francfort.

wife [waɪf] (*pl* wives [waɪvz]) *n* -**1.** [spouse] femme *f*, épouse *f*; ADMIN conjointe *f*; to take a ~ *arch* prendre femme; do you take this woman to be your lawful, wedded ~? *fml* prenez-vous cette femme pour épouse légitime?; to take sb to ~ *arch* prendre qqn pour femme; she's his second ~ elle est sa deuxième femme, il l'a épousée en secondes noces; she's been a good ~ to him elle a été une bonne épouse pour lui; the farmer's ~ la fermière. -**2.** *arch* OR *dial* [woman] femme *f*.

wifely ['waɪflɪ] *adj* de bonne épouse.

wife-swapping [-'swɒpɪŋ] *n* échangisme *m*.

wig [wɪg] *n* perruque *f*; [hairpiece] postiche *m*.

wigeon ['wɪdʒən] *n* canard *m* siffleur.

wigged [wɪgd] *adj* à perruque.

wigging *inf* ['wɪgɪŋ] *n Br* [scolding] savon *m*; to get a (good) ~ se faire disputer, se faire passer un savon; to give sb a (good) ~ passer un savon à qqn.

wiggle ['wɪgl] ◇ *vt* remuer; [hips] remuer, tortiller.

◇ *vi* [person] (se) remuer, frétiller; [loose object] branler.

◇ *n* -**1.** [movement] tortillement *m*; he gave his toes a ~ il remua ses orteils. -**2.** [wavy line] trait *m* ondulé.

wiggly ['wɪglɪ] *adj* frétillant, qui remue; a ~ line un trait ondulé.

wight [waɪt] *n arch* être *m*.

wigmaker ['wɪg,meɪkə^r] *n* perruquier *m*.

wigwam ['wɪgwæm] *n* wigwam *m*.

wilco ['wɪlkəʊ] *interj* TELEC j'exécute.

wild [waɪld] ◇ *adj* -**1.** [undomesticated] sauvage; [untamed] farouche; a ~ beast une bête sauvage; *fig* une bête féroce; a pack of ~ dogs une meute de chiens féroces OR sauvages; a ~ rabbit un lapin de garenne; a ~ horse un cheval sauvage ❑ 'The Wild Duck' *Ibsen* 'le Canard sauvage'. -**2.** [uncultivated - fruit] sauvage; [- flower, plant] sauvage, des champs; ~ strawberries fraises des bois; many parts of the country are still ~ beaucoup de régions du pays sont encore à l'état sauvage. -**3.** [violent - weather]: ~ weather du gros temps; a ~ wind un vent violent OR de tempête; a ~ sea une mer très agitée; it was a ~ night ce fut une nuit de tempête. -**4.** [mad] fou, furieux; to be ~ with grief/happiness/jealousy être fou de douleur/joie/jalousie; that noise is driving me ~ ce bruit me rend fou; he had ~ eyes OR a ~ look in his eyes il avait une lueur de folie dans le regard. -**5.** [dishevelled - appearance] débraillé; [- hair] en bataille, ébouriffé; a ~-looking young man un jeune homme à l'air farouche. -**6.** [enthusiastic]: the speaker received ~ applause l'orateur reçut des applaudissements frénétiques; to be ~ about sb *inf* être dingue de qqn; to be ~ about sthg *inf* être dingue de OR emballé par qqch; I'm not really ~ about modern art l'art moderne ne m'emballe pas vraiment. -**7.** [outrageous - idea, imagination] insensé, fantaisiste; [- promise, talk] insensé; [- rumour] délirant; [- plan] extravagant; he has some ~ scheme for getting rich quick il a un projet farfelu OR abracadabrant pour devenir riche en peu de temps; the book's success was beyond his ~est dreams le succès de son livre dépassait ses rêves les plus fous || [reckless] fou; they're always having ~ parties ils organisent toujours des soirées démentes; that was in my ~ youth c'était au temps de ma folle jeunesse; we had some ~ times together nous en avons fait des folies ensemble. -**8.** [random]: to take a ~ swing at sthg lancer le poing au hasard pour atteindre qqch; at a ~ guess, I'd say he was twenty je dirais, à tout hasard, qu'il avait vingt ans; aces are ~ CARDS les as sont libres ❑ to play a ~ card prendre un risque. -**9.** *inf phr*: ~ and woolly [idea, plan] peu réfléchi; [place] sauvage, primitif.

◇ *n*: in the ~ en liberté; the call of the ~ l'appel *m* de la nature; he spent a year living in the ~ OR ~s il a passé un an dans la brousse; the ~s of northern Canada le fin fond du nord du Canada.

◇ *adv* -**1.** [grow, live] en liberté; strawberries grow ~ in the forest des fraises poussent à l'état sauvage dans la forêt; the deer live ~ in the hills les cerfs vivent en liberté dans les collines. -**2.** [emotionally]: to go ~ with joy/rage devenir fou de joie/colère; when he came on stage the audience went ~ les spectateurs hurlèrent d'enthousiasme quand il arriva sur le plateau. -**3.** [unconstrained]: to run ~ [animals] courir en liberté; [children] être déchaîné; they let their children run ~ *literal* ils laissent leurs enfants traîner dans la rue; *fig* ils ne disciplinent pas du tout leurs enfants; they've left the garden to run ~ ils ont laissé le jardin à l'abandon OR revenir à l'état sauvage.

wild boar *n* sanglier *m*.

wildcard ['waɪldkɑːd] *n* COMPUT joker *m*; ~ character caractère *m* joker.

wildcat ['waɪldkæt] (*pl inv* OR wildcats) ◇ *n* ZOOL chat *m* sauvage; she's a real ~ *fig* c'est une vraie tigresse.

◇ *adj* [imprudent, ill-considered] aléatoire, hasardeux.

wildcat strike *n* grève *f* sauvage.

wild cherry *n* [fruit] merise *f*; [tree] merisier *m*.

wildebeest ['wɪldɪbiːst] (*pl inv* OR wildebeests) *n* gnou *m*.

wilderness ['wɪldənɪs] ◇ *n* -**1.** [uninhabited area] pays *m* désert, région *f* sauvage; BIBLE désert *m*; a ~ of snow and ice une région OR une étendue de neige et de glace; his warnings came like a voice in the ~ ses avertissements étaient comme une voix dans le désert || *fig*: she's been relegated to the political ~ elle en est réduite à une traversée du désert sur le plan politique; a concrete ~ un désert de béton; a cultural ~ un désert culturel. -**2.** [overgrown piece of land] jungle *f*; the garden's like a ~ le jardin est une véritable jungle.

◇ *adj* [region] reculé; the ~ years *fig* la traversée du désert.

wilderness permit *n dans les parcs naturels américains, autorisation de se rendre dans les parties les plus sauvages*.

wild-eyed *adj* -**1.** [crazed] au regard fou; she watched in ~ terror elle regardait, les yeux remplis de terreur. -**2.** [impractical] extravagant.

wildfire ['waɪld,faɪə^r] *n*: to spread like ~ se répandre comme une traînée de poudre; news of the attack spread like ~ la nouvelle de l'attaque s'est répandue comme une traînée de poudre.

wildfowl ['waɪldfaʊl] *n* oiseau *m* sauvage; HUNT [collectively] sauvagine *f*, gibier *m* à plume.

wild-goose chase *n*: you're on a ~ tu es sur une fausse piste, tu perds ton temps; I was sent on a ~ on m'a envoyé courir au diable pour rien.

wild hyacinth *n* [bluebell] jacinthe *f* des bois.

wildlife ['waɪldlaɪf] ◇ *n* [wild animals] faune *f*; [wild animals and plants] la faune et la flore.

◇ *comp* de la vie sauvage; [photographer] de la nature; [programme] sur la nature OR la vie sauvage; [expert, enthusiast] de la faune et de la flore.

wildlife park *n* réserve *f* naturelle.

wildly ['waɪldlɪ] *adv* -**1.** [violently] violemment, furieusement; waves beat ~ against the rocks les vagues venaient se heurter furieusement contre les rochers; she struggled ~ to free herself elle se débattait furieusement pour tenter de se libérer. -**2.** [enthusiastically]: the crowd applauded ~ la foule applaudissait frénétiquement. -**3.** [randomly] au hasard; "you're a Scorpio, aren't you" I said, guessing ~ «tu es Scorpion, non?» ai-je demandé, au hasard; to swing ~ at sb/sthg lancer le poing au hasard en direction de qqn/qqch; he dashed about ~ il s'agitait frénétiquement; exchange rates fluctuated ~ les taux de change fluctuaient de façon aberrante. -**4.** [extremely] excessivement; the reports are ~ inaccurate les comptes rendus sont complètement faux; ~ expensive/funny follement cher/drôle; he is ~ funny! il est d'un drôle!; his stories are ~ funny ses histoires sont à mourir de rire; to be ~ jealous/happy être fou de jalousie/bonheur; I'm not ~ happy about the decision cette décision ne m'enchante pas spécialement. -**5.** [recklessly] avec témérité; he talked ~ of joining the foreign legion il parlait avec témérité de s'engager dans la légion étrangère.

wild man *n* [savage] sauvage *m*.

wild oats *npl*: to sow one's ~ *inf euph* jeter sa gourme.

wild rice *n* zizania *f*.

wild rose *n* [dog rose] églantine *f*, églantier *m*; [sweetbrier] églantier *m* odorant.

wild silk *n* soie *f* sauvage.

wild thyme *n* serpolet *m*.

wild west ◇ *n*: the ~ le Far West.

◇ *comp*: ~ show *spectacle sur le thème du Far West*.

wile [waɪl] *n* ruse *f*; he fell victim to her feminine ~s il se laissa prendre à ses ruses de femme.

wilful *Br*, **willful** *Am* [ˈwɪlfʊl] *adj* -**1.** [action] délibéré; [damage] volontaire, délibéré; he rebuked her for ~ disobedience il l'a réprimandée pour avoir désobéi délibérément OR à dessein. -**2.** [person] entêté, obstiné.

wilfully *Br*, **willfully** *Am* [ˈwɪlfʊlɪ] *adv* -**1.** [deliberately] délibérément; he ~ disregarded my advice il n'a, délibérément OR sciemment, tenu aucun compte de mes conseils. -**2.** [obstinately] obstinément, avec entêtement.

wilfulness *Br*, **willfulness** *Am* [ˈwɪlfʊlnɪs] *n* -**1.** [of action] caractère *m* délibéré; [of damage] caractère *m* intentionnel. -**2.** [of character, person] obstination *f*, entêtement *m*.

will[1] [wɪl] *modal vb* -**1.** [indicating the future]: what time ~ you be home tonight? à quelle heure rentrez-vous ce soir?; the next meeting ~ be held in July la prochaine réunion aura lieu en juillet; I ~ be there before ten o'clock je serai là avant dix heures; I don't think he ~ OR he'll come today je ne pense pas qu'il vienne OR je ne crois pas qu'il viendra aujourd'hui; do you think she'll marry him? – I'm sure she ~/won't est-ce que tu crois qu'elle va se marier avec lui? – je suis sûr que oui/non; he doesn't think he'll be able to fix it il ne pense pas pouvoir OR il ne croit pas qu'il pourra le réparer; she's sure she'll have to work next weekend elle est sûre qu'elle devra OR elle est sûre de devoir travailler le week-end prochain; while he's on holiday his wife ~ be working pendant qu'il sera en vacances sa femme travaillera; when they come home the children ~ be sleeping quand ils rentreront, les enfants dormiront OR seront endormis. -**2.** [indicating probability]: that'll be the postman ça doit être OR c'est sans doute le facteur; they'll be wanting their dinner ils doivent attendre OR ils attendent sans doute leur dîner; she'll be grown up by now elle doit être grande maintenant; it won't be ready yet ce n'est sûrement pas prêt. -**3.** [indicating resolution, determination]: I'll steal the money if I have to je volerai l'argent s'il le faut; I won't go! je n'irai pas!; I won't have it! je ne supporterai OR n'admettrai pas ça!; you must come! – I won't! il faut que vous veniez! – je ne viendrai pas!; I won't go – oh yes you ~! je n'irai pas – oh (que) si!; he can't possibly win – he ~! il ne peut pas gagner – mais si! -**4.** [indicating willingness]: I'll carry your suitcase/drive you to the airport je vais porter votre valise/vous conduire à l'aéroport; who'll volunteer? – I ~! qui se porte volontaire? – moi!; ~ you marry me? – yes, I ~/no, I won't veux-tu m'épouser? – oui/non; my secretary ~ answer your questions ma secrétaire répondra à vos questions; our counsellors ~ help you to solve your financial difficulties nos conseillers vous aideront à résoudre vos difficultés financières ❑ ~ do! *inf* d'accord! -**5.** [in requests, invitations]: ~ you please stop smoking? pouvez-vous éteindre votre cigarette, s'il vous plaît?; you won't forget, ~ you? tu n'oublieras pas, n'est-ce pas?; won't you join us for lunch? vous déjeunerez bien avec nous?; if you ~ come with me si vous voulez bien venir avec moi ‖ [in orders]: stop complaining, ~ you! arrête de te plaindre, tu veux!; he'll do as he's told il fera ce qu'on lui dira; you'll stop arguing this minute! vous allez arrêter de vous disputer tout de suite!; ~ you be quiet! vous allez vous taire! -**6.** [indicating basic ability, capacity]: the machine ~ wash up to 5 kilos of laundry la machine peut laver jusqu'à 5 kilos de linge; this car won't do more than 75 miles per hour cette voiture ne peut pas faire plus de 120 kilomètres à l'heure ‖ [indicating temporary state or capacity]: the car won't start la voiture ne veut pas démarrer; it ~ start, but it dies after a couple of seconds elle démarre, mais elle s'arrête tout de suite; the television won't switch on la télévision ne veut pas s'allumer. -**7.** [indicating habitual action]: she'll play in her sandpit for hours elle peut jouer des heures dans son bac à sable ‖ [indicating obstinacy]: she WILL insist on calling me Uncle Roger elle insiste pour OR elle tient à m'appeler Oncle Roger; it WILL keep on doing that ça n'arrête pas de faire ça; she WILL have the last word il faut toujours qu'elle ait le dernier mot. -**8.** [used with 'have']: another ten years ~ have gone by dix autres années auront passé ‖ [expressing probability]: she'll have finished by now elle doit avoir fini maintenant.

will[2] [wɪl] ◇ *n* -**1.** [desire, determination] volonté *f*; he has a weak/strong ~ il a peu/beaucoup de volonté; she succeeded by force of ~ elle a réussi à force de volonté; every cabinet meeting is a battle of ~s chaque conseil des ministres est une lutte où chacun cherche à imposer sa volonté aux autres; she no longer has the ~ to live elle n'a plus envie de vivre; you must have the ~ to win/succeed il faut avoir envie de gagner/de réussir; it is the ~ of the people that... le peuple veut que...; his death was the ~ of God sa mort était la volonté de Dieu; thy ~ be done BIBLE que ta volonté soit faite ❑ to have a ~ of iron OR an iron ~ avoir une volonté de fer; to have a ~ of one's own n'en faire qu'à sa tête, être très indépendant; with the best ~ in the world avec la meilleure volonté du monde; where there's a ~ there's a way *prov* quand on veut on peut *prov*. -**2.** JUR testament *m*; last ~ and testament dernières volontés *fpl*; to make a ~ faire un testament; did he leave me anything in his ~? m'a-t-il laissé quelque chose dans son testament?

◇ *vt* -**1.** [using willpower]: I was ~ing her to say yes j'espérais qu'elle allait dire oui; she ~ed herself to keep walking elle s'est forcée à poursuivre sa marche; I could feel the crowd ~ing me on je sentais que la foule me soutenait. -**2.** [bequeath] léguer; she ~ed her entire fortune to charity elle a légué toute sa fortune à des œuvres de charité. -**3.** *lit* [wish, intend] vouloir; the Lord so ~ed it le Seigneur a voulu qu'il en soit ainsi; you can ~ the struggle, but you cannot ~ the outcome vous pouvez décider de vous battre, mais il ne vous appartient pas de décider qui va gagner.

◇ *vi arch* OR *lit* [wish] vouloir; as you ~ comme vous voulez.

◆ **against one's will** *adv phr* contre sa volonté; he left home against his father's ~ il est parti de chez lui contre la volonté de son père.

◆ **at will** *adv phr* à sa guise; they can come and go at ~ here ils peuvent aller et venir à leur guise ici; fire at ~! feu à volonté!

◆ **with a will** *adv phr* avec ardeur OR acharnement; we set to with a ~ and soon had the job done nous nous attelâmes à la tâche avec ardeur et le travail fut bientôt fini.

-willed [wɪld] *in cpds*: a strong~ woman une femme qui a beaucoup de volonté OR très volontaire; a weak~ boy un garçon qui manque de volonté.

willful *etc Am* = **wilful**.

William [ˈwɪljəm] *pr n*: ~ of Orange Guillaume d'Orange; ~ Rufus Guillaume le Roux; ~ Tell Guillaume Tell; ~ the Conqueror Guillaume le Conquérant.

willie [ˈwɪlɪ] *Br* = **willy**.

willies *inf* [ˈwɪlɪz] *npl*: he OR it gives me the ~ il me fiche la trouille.

willing [ˈwɪlɪŋ] *adj* -**1.** [ready, prepared]: are you ~ to cooperate with us? êtes-vous prêt à collaborer avec nous?; he isn't even ~ to try il ne veut même pas essayer; to be ~ and able (to do sthg) avoir l'envie et les moyens (de faire qqch); he's more than ~ to change jobs il ne demande pas mieux que de changer d'emploi; ~ or not, they must lend a hand qu'ils le veuillent ou non, ils devront nous aider. -**2.** [compliant]: he's a ~ victim c'est une victime complaisante. -**3.** [eager, enthusiastic – helper] bien disposé, de bonne volonté; she's a ~ pupil c'est une élève de bonne volonté. -**4.** *phr*: to show ~ faire preuve de bonne volonté.

willingly [ˈwɪlɪŋlɪ] *adv* -**1.** [eagerly, gladly] de bon cœur, volontiers; they ~ gave up their time ils n'ont pas été avares de leur temps; I'll do it ~, I'll ~ do it je le ferai volontiers. -**2.** [voluntarily] volontairement, de plein gré; I bet he didn't do it ~ je parie qu'il ne l'a pas fait de bon cœur.

willingness [ˈwɪlɪŋnɪs] *n* -**1.** [enthusiasm]: he set to with great ~ il s'est attelé à la tâche avec un grand enthousiasme. -**2.** [readiness]: the soldiers were surprised at the enemy's ~ to fight les soldats furent surpris que l'ennemi veuille se battre; he admired her ~ to sacrifice her own happiness il admirait le fait qu'elle soit prête à sacrifier son propre bonheur.

will-o'-the-wisp [ˌwɪləðəˈwɪsp] *n literal* & *fig* feu *m* follet.

willow [ˈwɪləʊ] *n* -**1.** BOT saule *m*. -**2.** *inf* CRICKET batte *f*.

willow pattern *n motif de céramique très répandu en Grande-Bretagne*; ~ plates des assiettes à motif chinois.

WILLOW PATTERN:
Ce motif de céramique, généralement bleu sur fond blanc, représente une scène chinoise avec des personnages, un saule et un pont sur une rivière.

willow warbler *n* pouillot *m* fitis.

willowy [ˈwɪləʊɪ] *adj* [figure, person] élancé, svelte; [object] souple, flexible.

willpower [ˈwɪlˌpaʊəʳ] *n* volonté *f*; he lacks the ~ to diet il n'a pas suffisamment de volonté pour se mettre au régime; he gave up smoking through sheer ~ il a arrêté de fumer par la seule force de sa volonté.

willy *inf* [ˈwɪlɪ] (*pl* willies) *n Br* zizi *m*.

willy-nilly [ˌwɪlɪˈnɪlɪ] *adv* bon gré mal gré.

wilt[1] [wɪlt] *arch* OR *dial 2nd pers sg* → **will** *aux vb*.

wilt[2] [wɪlt] ◇ *vi* [droop – flower, plant] se faner, se flétrir; [– person] languir, s'alanguir; to ~ under pressure fléchir sous la pression; he ~ed under her fierce gaze il perdit contenance sous son regard furieux.

◇ *vt* [cause to droop – flower, plant] faner, flétrir.

Wilts *written abbr of* Wiltshire.

wily [ˈwaɪlɪ] *adj* [person] rusé, malin; [scheme, trick] habile, astucieux; a ~ old devil OR fox un vieux malin OR rusé.

wimble [ˈwɪmbl] ◇ *n* vrille *f*.

◇ *vt* vriller.

wimp *inf* [wɪmp] *n pej* [person – physically weak] mauviette *f*; [– morally weak, irresolute] mou *m*, molle *f*, pâte *f* molle; don't be such a ~! ne sois pas aussi mollasson!

wimpish *inf* [ˈwɪmpɪʃ] *adj pej* mollasson.

wimple [ˈwɪmpl] *n* guimpe *f*.

wimpy *inf* [ˈwɪmpɪ] *adj pej* [physically weak] malingre; [morally weak] poule mouillée *(inv)*.

win [wɪn] (*pt* & *pp* won [wʌn], *cont* winning)

◇ *vi* [in competition] gagner; she always ~s at tennis elle gagne toujours au tennis; they're winning three nil ils gagnent trois à zéro; he won by only one point il a gagné d'un point seulement; did you ~ at cards? avez-vous gagné aux cartes?; who do you think will ~? à votre avis qui va gagner OR l'emporter?; he won by a length [in horseracing] il a gagné d'une longueur; to let sb ~ laisser gagner qqn; OK, you ~! bon, d'accord!; I (just) can't ~! j'ai toujours tort! ❑ to ~ hands down gagner haut la main.

◇ *vt* -**1.** [in competition – award, prize] gagner; [– scholarship] obtenir; [– contract] gagner, remporter; he won first prize il a gagné OR eu le premier prix; he won £100 at poker il a gagné 100 livres au poker; ~ yourself a dream holiday! gagnez des vacances de rêve!; she won a gold medal in the Olympics elle a obtenu une médaille d'or aux jeux Olympiques; his superior finishing speed won him the race il a gagné la course grâce à sa vitesse supérieure dans la dernière ligne OR au finish; to ~ a place at university *Br* obtenir une place à l'université; he has won his place in history *fig* il s'est fait un nom dans l'histoire || [in war]: we have won a great victory nous avons remporté une grande victoire; this offensive could ~ them the war cette offensive pourrait leur faire gagner la guerre. -**2.** [obtain, secure - friendship, love] gagner; [- sympathy] s'attirer; to ~ sb's heart gagner OR conquérir le cœur de qqn; to ~ sb's hand *arch* obtenir la main de qqn; his intransigence has won him many enemies son intransigeance lui a valu de nombreux ennemis; his impartiality has won him the respect of his colleagues son impartialité lui a valu OR fait gagner le respect de ses collègues. -**3.** MIN extraire. -**4.** *fml* OR *lit* [reach]: we finally won the shore after three days at sea nous avons fini par gagner le rivage après trois jours en mer.

◇ *n* -**1.** SPORT victoire *f*; they've had an unprecedented run of ~s ils ont eu une série de victoires sans précédent; we haven't had one ~ all season nous n'avons pas remporté une seule victoire de toute la saison. -**2.** *Am* [in horseracing]: ~, place, show gagnant, placé et troisième.

◆ **win back** *vt sep* [money, trophy] reprendre, recouvrer; [land] reprendre, reconquérir; [loved one] reconquérir; [esteem, respect, support] retrouver, recouvrer; POL [votes, voters, seats] récupérer, recouvrer; they were determined to ~ back the Cup from the Australians ils étaient décidés à reprendre la Coupe aux Australiens; I won every penny back from him je lui ai repris jusqu'au dernier centime; you won't ~ back your wife with threats tu ne vas pas reconquérir OR retrouver l'amour de ta femme avec des menaces.

◆ **win out** *vi insep* triompher; the need for peace won out over the desire for revenge le besoin de paix triompha du désir de revanche OR l'emporta sur le désir de revanche.

◆ **win over** *vt sep* [convert, convince] rallier; he has won several of his former opponents over to his ideas il a rallié plusieurs de ses anciens adversaires à ses idées; the report won her over to the protesters' cause le rapport l'a gagnée à la cause des protestataires; we won him round in the end nous avons fini par le convaincre.

◆ **win round** *Br* = **win over**.

◆ **win through** *vi insep* remporter; the striking rail workers won through in the end les cheminots en grève ont fini par obtenir gain de cause.

wince [wɪns] ◇ *vi* [from pain] crisper le visage, grimacer; she didn't even ~ elle n'a pas fait la moindre grimace; the blow to his stomach made him ~ with pain le coup qu'il a reçu à l'estomac l'a fait grimacer de douleur || *fig* grimacer (de dégoût); she winced at the thought cette pensée l'a fait grimacer de dégoût.

◇ *n* grimace *f*.

winceyette [ˌwɪnsɪ'et] *Br* ◇ *n* flanelle *f* de coton.

◇ *adj* [nightdress, pyjamas, sheets] en flanelle de coton.

winch [wɪntʃ] ◇ *n* treuil *m*.

◇ *vt*: to ~ sb/sthg up/down monter/descendre qqn/qqch au treuil; the survivors were ~ed to safety à l'aide d'un treuil on a hissé les rescapés hors de danger.

wind[1] [wɪnd] ◇ *n* -**1.** METEOR vent *m*; the ~ has risen/dropped le vent s'est levé/est tombé; the ~ is changing le vent tourne || NAUT: into the ~ contre le vent; off the ~ dans le sens du vent; before the ~ le vent en poupe || *fig*: the ~s of change are blowing il y a du changement dans l'air; the cold ~ of recession le vent glacial de la récession ❑ to get ~ of sthg avoir vent de qqch; to run like the ~ courir comme le vent; to be scattered to the four ~s être éparpillés aux quatre vents; there's something in the ~ il se prépare quelque chose; to take the ~ out of sb's sails couper l'herbe sous le pied à qqn; let's wait and see which way the ~ is blowing attendons de voir quelle tournure les événements vont prendre. -**2.** [breath] souffle *m*; I haven't got my ~ back yet je n'ai pas encore repris haleine OR mon souffle; to get one's second ~ reprendre haleine OR son souffle; he had the ~ knocked out of him SPORT on lui a coupé le souffle, on l'a mis hors d'haleine ❑ to put the ~ up sb *inf* flanquer la frousse à qqn. -**3.** *inf* [empty talk] vent *m*; his speech was just a lot of ~ son discours n'était que du vent. -**4.** *(U)* [air in stomach] vents *mpl*, gaz *mpl*; broad beans give me ~ les fèves me donnent des vents OR des gaz; I've got terrible ~ j'ai de terribles vents; to break ~ lâcher des vents; to get a baby's ~ up faire faire son renvoi à un bébé. -**5.** MUS: the ~ (section) les instruments *mpl* à vent, les vents *mpl*; the ~ is OR are too loud les instruments à vent sont trop forts.

◇ *vt* -**1.** [make breathless]: to ~ sb couper le souffle à qqn; the blow ~ed him le coup l'a mis hors d'haleine OR lui a coupé le souffle; she was quite ~ed by the walk uphill la montée de la côte l'a essoufflée OR lui a coupé le souffle; don't worry, I'm only ~ed ne t'inquiète pas, j'ai la respiration coupée, c'est tout. -**2.** [horse] laisser souffler. -**3.** [baby] faire faire son renvoi. -**4.** HUNT [prey] avoir vent de.

wind[2] [waɪnd] (*pt* & *pp* wound [waʊnd])

◇ *vi* [bend - procession, road] serpenter; [coil - thread] s'enrouler; the river ~s through the valley le fleuve décrit des méandres dans la vallée OR traverse la vallée en serpentant.

◇ *vt* -**1.** [wrap - bandage, rope] enrouler; I wound a scarf round my neck j'ai enroulé une écharpe autour de mon cou; ~ the string into a ball enrouler la ficelle pour en faire une pelote; the snake had wound itself around the man's arm le serpent s'était enroulé autour du bras de l'homme; to ~ sb in one's arms *lit* enlacer qqn ❑ to ~ sb round OR around one's little finger mener qqn par le bout du nez. -**2.** [clock, watch, clockwork device] remonter; [handle] tourner, donner un tour de; have you wound your watch? avez-vous remonté votre montre? -**3.** *arch* [travel]: to ~ one's way home prendre le chemin du retour.

◇ *n* -**1.** MECH: give the clock/watch a ~ remontez l'horloge/la montre; she gave the handle another ~ elle tourna la manivelle encore une fois, elle donna un tour de manivelle de plus. -**2.** [bend - of road] tournant *m*, courbe *f*; [- of river] coude *m*.

◆ **wind back** *vt sep* rembobiner.

◆ **wind down** ◇ *vi insep* -**1.** [relax] se détendre, décompresser. -**2.** MECH [clock, watch] ralentir.

◇ *vt sep* -**1.** MECH [lower] faire descendre; [car window] baisser. -**2.** [bring to an end - business] mener (doucement) vers sa fin.

◆ **wind forward** *vt sep* (faire) avancer.

◆ **wind off** *vt sep* dérouler; [from a spool or reel] dévider.

◆ **wind on** *vt sep* enrouler.

◆ **wind up** ◇ *vt sep* -**1.** [conclude - meeting] terminer; [- account, business] liquider; the chairman wound up the debate le président a clos le OR mis fin au débat; the business will be wound up by the end of the year l'entreprise sera liquidée avant la fin de l'année. -**2.** [raise] monter, faire monter; [car window] remonter, fermer. -**3.** [string, thread] enrouler; [on a spool] dévider. -**4.** MECH [clock, watch, toy] remonter; to be wound up (about sthg) *inf fig* être à cran (à cause de qqch). -**5.** *inf Br* [annoy] asticoter; [tease] faire marcher; he's just trying to ~ you up il essaie tout simplement de te faire craquer.

◇ *vi insep inf* [end up] finir; he wound up in jail il a fini OR s'est retrouvé en prison; she'll ~ up begging in the streets elle finira par mendier dans la rue; he wound up with a broken nose il a fini avec le nez cassé.

windbag *inf* ['wɪndbæg] *n pej* moulin *m* à paroles, jaseur *m*, -euse *f*.

windblown ['wɪndbləʊn] *adj* [hair] ébouriffé par le vent; [trees] fouetté OR cinglé par le vent.

wind-borne [wɪnd] *adj* transporté par le vent.

windbreak ['wɪndbreɪk] *n* [brise] abri-vent *m*, coupe-vent *m inv*.

windbreaker® ['wɪndˌbreɪkəʳ] *n Am* anorak *m*, coupe-vent *m inv*.

windbroken ['wɪndˌbrəʊkn] *adj* [horse] poussif.

windburn ['wɪndbɜːn] *n* rougeurs *fpl* cutanées *(occasionnées par l'exposition au vent)*.

windcheater ['wɪndˌtʃiːtəʳ] *n Br* anorak *m*, coupe-vent *m inv*.

windchill factor ['wɪndtʃɪl] *n facteur d'abaissement de la température provoqué par le vent.*

wind chimes [wɪnd-] *npl* carillon *m* éolien.

wind cone [wɪnd-] *n* manche *f* à air.

wind-down [waɪnd-] *n* mise *f* en sommeil, ralentissement *m*.

winder ['waɪndəʳ] *n* [for clock] remontoir *m*; [for car window] lève-vitre *m*, lève-glace *m*; [for thread, yarn] dévidoir *m*.

windfall ['wɪndfɔːl] ◇ *n* -**1.** [unexpected gain] (bonne) aubaine *f*. -**2.** [fruit] fruit *m* tombé.

◇ *adj* [fruit] tombé OR abattu par le vent; ~ profits/dividends profits *mpl*/dividendes *mpl* inespérés OR inattendus.

windfarm ['wɪndfɑːm] *n* champ *m* d'éoliennes.

wind gauge [wɪnd-] *n* anémomètre *m*.

Windhoek ['wɪndhʊk] *pr n* Windhoek.

winding ['waɪndɪŋ] ◇ *adj* [road, street] tortueux, sinueux; [river] sinueux; [staircase] en hélice, en colimaçon.

◇ *n* -**1.** [process] enroulement *m*; ELEC [wire] bobinage *m*, enroulement *m*. -**2.** [in a river] méandres *mpl*, coudes *mpl*; [in a road] zigzags *mpl*.

◆ **windings** *npl* = **winding** *n* **2**.

winding sheet *n* linceul *m*.

winding-up *n* [of account, meeting] clôture *f*; [of business] liquidation *f*; ~ **arrangement** [in bankruptcy] concordat *m*.

wind instrument [wɪnd-] *n* instrument *m* à vent.

windjammer ['wɪndˌdʒæməʳ] *n* -**1.** NAUT grand voilier *m* marchand. -**2.** *Br* [light jacket] anorak *m*, coupe-vent *m inv*.

windlass ['wɪndləs] ◇ *n* treuil *m*; NAUT guindeau *m*.

◇ *vt* [raise] monter au treuil; [haul] tirer au treuil.

windless ['wɪndləs] *adj lit* sans vent.

wind machine [wɪnd-] *n* THEAT machine *f* à souffler le vent.

windmill ['wɪnmɪl] ◇ *n* -**1.** [building] moulin *m* à vent; [toy] moulinet *m*. -**2.** [wind turbine] aéromoteur *m*, éolienne *f*.

◇ *vi* -**1.** [arms] tourner en moulinet. -**2.** AERON [propeller, rotor] tourner par la force du vent.

window ['wɪndəʊ] ◇ *n* -**1.** [in room] fenêtre *f*; [in car] vitre *f*, glace *f*; [in front of shop] vitrine *f*, devanture *f*; [in church] vitrail *m*; [at bank, ticket office] guichet *m*; [on envelope] fenêtre *f*; she looked out (of) OR through the ~ elle regarda par la fenêtre; he jumped/threw himself out of the ~ il a sauté/s'est jeté par la fenêtre; to break a ~ casser une vitre OR un carreau; can I try that dress in the ~? puis-je essayer cette robe (qui est) dans la OR en vitrine? ❑ all our plans have gone out (of) the ~ tous nos projets sont partis en fumée. -**2.** COMPUT fenêtre *f*. -**3.** [in diary] créneau *m*, moment *m* libre; ~ of opportunity de nouvelles possibilités. -**4.** [insight]: a ~ on the world of finance un aperçu des milieux financiers. -**5.** [opportune time]: launch ~ ASTRONAUT fenêtre *f* OR créneau *m* de lancement; weather ~ accalmie *f (permettant de mener à bien des travaux)*.

◇ *comp* de fenêtre; ~ frame châssis *m* de fenêtre; ~ ledge rebord *m* de fenêtre; ~ sash *cadre vitré d'une fenêtre à guillotine*.

window box *n* jardinière *f*.

window cleaner *n* [person] laveur *m*, -euse *f* de vitres OR carreaux; [substance] nettoyant *m* pour vitres.

window display *n* étalage *m*.
window dresser *n* étalagiste *mf*.
window dressing *n* [merchandise on display] présentation *f* de l'étalage; [activity]: they need someone to do the ~ ils ont besoin de quelqu'un pour composer OR faire l'étalage || *fig* façade *f*; that's just ~ ce n'est qu'une façade.
window envelope *n* enveloppe *f* à fenêtre.
windowpane ['wɪndəʊpeɪn] *n* carreau *m*, vitre *f*.
window roller *n Am* [in car] lève-vitre *m*.
window seat *n* [in room] banquette *f* sous la fenêtre; [in train, plane] place *f* côté fenêtre.
window-shade *n Am* store *m*.
window-shop *vi* faire du lèche-vitrines.
window-shopper [-'ʃɒpə] *n*: she's an inveterate ~ elle adore faire du lèche-vitrines, c'est une adepte acharnée du lèche-vitrines.
window-shopping *n* lèche-vitrines *m inv*; to go ~ faire du lèche-vitrines.
windowsill ['wɪndəʊsɪl] *n* rebord *m* de fenêtre.
windpipe ['wɪndpaɪp] *n* trachée *f*.
wind power [wɪnd-] *n* énergie *f* du vent OR éolienne *spec*.
windproof ['wɪndpruːf] *adj* protégeant du vent.
windscreen ['wɪndskriːn] *n Br* pare-brise *m inv*.
windscreen washer *n Br* lave-glace *m*.
windscreen wiper *n Br* essuie-glace *m*.
windshield ['wɪndʃiːld] *n Am* [of car, motorcycle] pare-brise *m inv*.
windshield wiper *n Am* essuie-glace *m*.
wind sleeve [wɪnd-], **windsock** ['wɪndsɒk] *n* manche *f* à air.
windstorm ['wɪndstɔːm] *n* (vent *m* de) tempête *f*.
windsurf ['wɪndsɜːf] *vi* faire de la planche à voile.
windsurfer ['wɪnd,sɜːfə^r] *n* [board] planche *f* à voile; [person] véliplanchiste *mf*, planchiste *mf*.
windsurfing ['wɪnd,sɜːfɪŋ] *n* planche *f* à voile; to go ~ faire de la planche à voile.
windswept ['wɪndswept] *adj* [place] balayé par le vent; [hair] ébouriffé par le vent; you're looking very ~ tu as l'air tout ébouriffé par le vent.
wind tunnel [wɪnd-] *n* tunnel *m* aérodynamique.
wind-up [waɪnd-] ◇ *adj* [mechanism]: a ~ toy/watch un jouet/une montre à remontoir.
◇ *n inf Br*: is this a ~? est-ce qu'on veut me faire marcher?
windward ['wɪndwəd] ◇ *adj* NAUT: on the ~ side du côté du vent.
◇ *n* côté *m* du vent; to ~ au vent, contre le vent.
Windward Islands *pl pr n*: the ~ les îles *fpl* du Vent; in the ~ aux îles du Vent.
windy ['wɪndɪ] *adj* -**1.** METEOR: tomorrow it will be very ~ everywhere demain il fera du vent OR le vent soufflera partout; it was terribly ~ up on deck il y avait un terrible vent OR le vent soufflait terriblement sur le pont; a cold, ~ morning un matin froid et de grand vent; it's a very wet and ~ place c'est un endroit très pluvieux et très éventé; the Windy City *surnom de Chicago*. -**2.** *inf* [pompous, verbose] ronflant, pompeux. -**3.** *inf dated* [nervous]: to be OR to get ~ about sthg paniquer à propos de qqch.
wine [waɪn] ◇ *n* vin *m*; a bottle/glass of ~ une bouteille/un verre de vin; red/white ~ vin rouge/blanc; the ~s of Spain les vins espagnols; rice ~ alcool *m* de riz.
◇ *vt*: to ~ and dine sb emmener qqn faire un bon dîner bien arrosé.
◇ *vi*: to go out wining and dining faire la fête au restaurant.
◇ *adj* [colour] lie-de-vin *(inv)*; a ~-coloured dress une robe lie-de-vin.
◇ *comp* [bottle, glass] à vin.
wine and cheese evening *n petite fête où l'on déguste du vin et du fromage*.
wine bar *n* [drinking establishment] bistrot *m*.
winebibber ['waɪn,bɪbə^r] *n lit & hum* ivrogne *mf*, grand amateur *m* de vin.
wine box *n* Cubitainer® *m*.
wine cellar *n* cave *f* (à vin), cellier *m*.
wine cooler *n* [container] seau *m* à rafraîchir (le vin).
wineglass ['waɪnglɑːs] *n* verre *m* à vin.
winegrower ['waɪn,grəʊə^r] *n* viticulteur *m*, -trice *f*, vigneron *m*, -onne *f*.
winegrowing ['waɪn,grəʊɪŋ] ◇ *n* viticulture *f*.
◇ *adj* [area, industry] vinicole, viticole.
wine list *n* carte *f* des vins.
wine merchant *n* [shopkeeper] marchand *m*, -e *f* de vin; [wholesaler] négociant *m*, -e *f* en vins.
winepress ['waɪnpres] *n* pressoir *m* à vin.
winery ['waɪnərɪ] *n Am* établissement *m* vinicole.
wineskin ['waɪnskɪn] *n* outre *f* à vin.
wine taster *n* [person] dégustateur *m*, -trice *f*; [cup] tâte-vin *m inv*, taste-vin *m inv*.
wine tasting *n* dégustation *f* (de vins).
wine vinegar *n* vinaigre *m* de vin.
wine waiter *n* sommelier *m*.
wing [wɪŋ] ◇ *n* -**1.** [on bird, poultry, insect] aile *f*; to take ~ *lit* prendre son envol OR essor; my heart took ~ mon cœur s'emplit de joie; to be on the ~ *lit* être en (plein) vol; he shot the bird on the ~ il tira l'oiseau en vol; desire gave OR lent him ~s *lit* le désir lui donnait des ailes ❑ ~ tip bout *m* de l'aile; to take sb under one's ~ prendre qqn sous son aile; 'The Wings of Desire' *Wenders* 'les Ailes du désir'; 'The Wings of the Dove' *James* 'les Ailes de la colombe'. -**2.** AERON aile *f*; [badge]: to win one's ~s faire ses preuves, prendre du galon. -**3.** *Br* AUT aile *f*. -**4.** POL [section] aile *f*; the radical ~ of the party l'aile OR la fraction radicale du parti; the left/right ~ l'aile gauche/droite. -**5.** ARCHIT aile *f*; the west ~ l'aile ouest. -**6.** [on windmill] aile *f*. -**7.** SPORT [of field] aile *f*; [player] ailier *m*.
◇ *vt* -**1.** [wound - bird] blesser, toucher à l'aile; [- person] blesser OR toucher légèrement. -**2.** [fly]: to ~ one's way *literal & fig* voler. -**3.** *lit* [cause to fly - arrow] darder, décocher. -**4.** *inf phr*: to ~ it [improvise] improviser.
◇ *vi lit* [fly]: the plane ~ed over the mountains l'avion survola les montagnes.
◆ **wings** *npl* THEAT coulisse *f*, coulisses *fpl*; to wait in the ~s *literal & fig* se tenir dans la coulisse OR les coulisses; younger politicians are waiting in the ~s to seize power *fig* les jeunes politiciens se tiennent dans la coulisse OR les coulisses en attendant de prendre le pouvoir.
wing case *n* élytre *m*.
wing chair *n* bergère *f* à oreilles.
wing collar *n* col *m* cassé.
wing commander *n* lieutenant-colonel *m*.
wingding *inf* ['wɪŋdɪŋ] *n* [party] fête *f*, bringue *f*; we had a real ~ on a vraiment fait la bringue.
winge *inf* [wɪndʒ] (*cont* wingeing) = **whinge**.
winged [wɪŋd] *adj* -**1.** [possessing wings] ailé. -**2.** [wounded - bird, animal] blessé à l'aile; [- person] blessé légèrement.
-winged *in cpds*: white~ aux ailes blanches.
winger ['wɪŋə^r] *n* SPORT ailier *m*.
wing forward *n* [in rugby] ailier *m*.
wingless ['wɪŋlɪs] *adj* sans ailes; [insect] aptère.
wing mirror *n* rétroviseur *m* extérieur.
wing nut *n* papillon *m*, écrou *m* à ailettes.
wingspan ['wɪŋspæn] *n* envergure *f*.
wingspread ['wɪŋspred] *n* envergure *f*.
wing three-quarter *n* [in rugby] trois-quarts aile *m*.
wink [wɪŋk] ◇ *vi* -**1.** [person] faire un clin d'œil; to ~ at sb faire un clin d'œil à qqn; to ~ at sthg *fig* fermer les yeux sur qqch. -**2.** *lit* [light, star] clignoter; the water sparkled and ~ed l'eau miroitait et scintillait.
◇ *vt*: to ~ an eye at sb faire un clin d'œil à qqn.
◇ *n* clin *m* d'œil; she gave them a knowing ~ elle leur a fait un clin d'œil entendu; "hello darling" he said with a big ~ «bonjour chérie» dit-il en faisant un grand clin d'œil ❑ I didn't get a ~ of sleep OR sleep a ~ last night je n'ai pas fermé l'œil de la nuit; (as) quick as a ~ en un clin d'œil.
winker ['wɪŋkə^r] *n Br* AUT clignotant *m*.
winking ['wɪŋkɪŋ] ◇ *adj* [lights] clignotant.
◇ *n* -**1.** [of an eye] clins *mpl* d'œil; it was all over in the ~ of an eye *lit* tout fut terminé en un clin d'œil. -**2.** [of lights, stars] clignotement *m*.
winkle ['wɪŋkl] *n Br* bigorneau *m*, vigneau *m*.
◆ **winkle out** *inf vt sep* [information] arracher, extirper; [person] déloger; to ~ information out of sb arracher des informations à qqn; we finally managed to ~ him out of his room nous avons finalement réussi à l'extirper de sa chambre.
winkle-pickers *inf npl Br* chaussures *fpl* pointues.
winner ['wɪnə^r] *n* -**1.** [of prize] gagnant *m*, -e *f*; [of battle, war] vainqueur *m*; SPORT [of match] vainqueur *m*, gagnant *m*; there will be neither ~s nor losers in this war il n'y aura ni vainqueurs ni vaincus dans cette guerre. -**2.** [successful person] gagneur *m*, -euse *f*; [successful thing] succès *m*; she's one of life's ~s c'est une gagneuse, elle est de celles qui gagnent; her latest book is a sure ~ son dernier livre va faire un vrai tabac; to be on to a ~ tirer le bon numéro, être parti pour gagner.
Winnie the Pooh [,wɪnɪðə'puː] *pr n* Winnie l'ourson.
winning ['wɪnɪŋ] *adj* -**1.** [successful] gagnant; SPORT [goal, stroke] décisif; to be on a ~ streak remporter victoire sur victoire. -**2.** [charming] engageant, charmant.
◆ **winnings** *npl* gains *mpl*.
winning post *n* poteau *m* d'arrivée.
winnow ['wɪnəʊ] ◇ *vt* AGR vanner; *fig* [separate] démêler, trier; to ~ out fact from fiction démêler le réel d'avec l'imaginaire.
◇ *n* [machine] tarare *m*, vanneuse *f*.
wino *inf* ['waɪnəʊ] (*pl* winos) *n* ivrogne *m*.
winsome ['wɪnsəm] *adj lit* [person] charmant, gracieux; [smile] engageant, charmeur.
winter ['wɪntə^r] ◇ *n* hiver *m*; it never snows here in (the) ~ il ne neige jamais ici en hiver; she was born in the ~ of 1913 elle est née pendant l'hiver 1913; we spent the ~ in Nice nous avons passé l'hiver à Nice; a cold ~'s day une froide journée d'hiver; a man of 75 ~s *lit* un homme qui a vu passer 75 hivers OR *hum* de 75 printemps ❑ the ~ of discontent *l'hiver 1978-79 en Grande-Bretagne*; 'The Winter's Tale' *Shakespeare* 'le Conte d'hiver'.
◇ *comp* d'hiver.
◇ *vi fml* [spend winter] passer l'hiver, hiverner.
◇ *vt* [farm animals] hiverner.

THE WINTER OF DISCONTENT:
Cette allusion à une phrase de Shakespeare désigne souvent l'hiver 1978-79 en Grande-Bretagne, marqué par de graves conflits sociaux qui amenèrent le gouvernement travailliste à tenir des élections qu'il perdit. L'expression est parfois utilisée pour désigner des hivers plus récents présentant les mêmes caractéristiques.

winterfeed ['wɪntəfiːd] (*pt & pp* winterfed [-fed]) *vt* nourrir en hiver.
wintergreen ['wɪntəgriːn] *n* gaulthérie *f*; oil of ~ essence *f* de wintergreen.
winterize, -ise ['wɪntəraɪz] *vt Am* aménager pour l'hiver.
winter solstice *n* solstice *m* d'hiver.
winter sports *npl* sports *mpl* d'hiver.
wintertime ['wɪntətaɪm] *n* hiver *m*; in (the) ~ en hiver.
winterweight ['wɪntəweɪt] *adj* [clothes] d'hiver.
wintry ['wɪntrɪ] *adj* hivernal; *fig* [look, smile] glacial.

wipe [waɪp] ◇ *vt* -**1.** [with cloth] essuyer; he ~d the plate dry il a bien essuyé l'assiette; go and ~ your hands va t'essuyer les mains; to ~ one's feet s'essuyer les pieds; to ~ one's nose se moucher; to ~ one's bottom s'essuyer; she ~d the sweat from his brow elle essuya la sueur de son front; she ~d her knife clean elle nettoya son couteau (d'un coup de torchon) ❑ to ~ the floor with sb *inf* réduire qqn en miettes; he ~d the floor with me il m'a complètement démoli; to ~ the slate clean passer l'éponge, tout effacer. -**2.** [delete - from written record, magnetic tape] effacer; the remark was ~d from the minutes l'observation fut retirée du compte-rendu.
◇ *vi* essuyer; she ~d round the sink with a wet cloth elle a essuyé l'évier avec un chiffon humide.
◇ *n*: give the table a ~ donne un coup d'éponge sur la table; he gave the plate a quick ~ il donna un coup de torchon rapide sur l'assiette.
◆ **wipe away** *vt sep* [blood, tears] essuyer; [dirt, dust] enlever; he ~d the mud away with a cloth il enleva OR ôta la boue avec un (coup de) chiffon.
◆ **wipe down** *vt sep* [paintwork, walls] lessiver.
◆ **wipe off** *vt sep* -**1.** [remove] enlever; ~ that smile OR grin off your face! *inf* enlève-moi ce sourire idiot! -**2.** [erase] effacer; the bombs ~d the town off the map les bombes effacèrent OR rayèrent la ville de la carte; he ~d off half the programme by accident RADIO & TV il a effacé la moitié de l'émission par mégarde.
◆ **wipe out** *vt sep* -**1.** [clean] nettoyer. -**2.** [erase] effacer; *fig* [insult, disgrace] effacer, laver. -**3.** [destroy] anéantir, décimer. -**4.** *inf* [exhaust] crever; I was ~d out after the match j'étais crevé après le match.
◆ **wipe up** ◇ *vt sep* éponger, essuyer.
◇ *vi insep Br* essuyer (la vaisselle).

wipeout ['waɪpaʊt] *n* [in surfing] chute *f*.

wiper ['waɪpəʳ] *n* AUT essuie-glace *m inv*.

wire ['waɪəʳ] ◇ *n* -**1.** [of metal] fil *m* (métallique OR de fer); a ~ fence un grillage; they've cut the telephone ~s ils ont coupé les fils téléphoniques ❑ cheese ~ fil à couper; he got his application in just under the ~ sa candidature est arrivée juste à temps; we got our ~s crossed *inf* nous ne nous sommes pas compris, il y a eu un malentendu. -**2.** [telegram] télégramme *m*.
◇ *vt* -**1.** [attach] relier avec du fil de fer. -**2.** ELEC [building, house] mettre l'électricité dans, faire l'installation électrique dans; [connect electrically] brancher; the lamp is ~d (up) to the switch on the wall la lampe est branchée sur OR reliée à l'interrupteur sur le mur; the room had been ~d (up) for sound la pièce avait été sonorisée. -**3.** TELEC [person] envoyer un télégramme à, télégraphier à; [money, information] envoyer par télégramme, télégraphier.
◆ **wire together** *vt sep* relier avec du fil de fer.
◆ **wire up** *vt sep* -**1.** = **wire** *vt* **2**. -**2.** *inf Am* [make nervous] rendre nerveux, provoquer la nervosité chez qqn; he gets all ~d up before exams il est à cran avant les examens.

wire brush *n* brosse *f* métallique.

wirecoated [ˌwaɪə'kəʊtɪd] *adj* à poils durs.

wire cutters *npl* cisaille *f*, pinces *fpl* coupantes.

wired ['waɪəd] *adj* -**1.** ELEC [to an alarm] relié à un système d'alarme. -**2.** [wiretapped] mis sur écoute. -**3.** [bra] à tiges métalliques. -**4.** ▽ [nervous] à cran.

wiredraw ['waɪədrɔː] (*pt* wiredrew [-druː], *pp* wiredrawn [-drɔːn]) *vt* METALL tréfiler.

wire gauge *n* calibre *m* pour fils métalliques.

wire gauze *n* toile *f* métallique.

wire glass *n* verre *m* armé.

wire-haired *adj* à poils durs.

wireless ['waɪəlɪs] ◇ *n Br dated* TSF *f*; ~ (set) poste *m* de TSF; we heard it on the ~ nous l'avons entendu à la TSF; he sent us a message by ~ il nous envoya un message par sans-fil.
◇ *comp* [broadcast, waves] de TSF.

wireless operator *n dated* opérateur *m*, -trice de TSF, radiotélégraphiste *mf*.

wireless room *n dated* cabine *f* radio *(inv)*.

wireless set *n dated* poste *m* de TSF, TSF *f*.

wireman ['waɪəmən] (*pl* wiremen [-mən]) *n Am* câbleur *m*.

wire netting, wire mesh *n* grillage *m*, treillis *m* métallique.

wire photo *n* phototélégraphie *f*, bélinogramme *m*.

wire-puller *inf n Am*: I'm not a ~ je ne suis pas un manipulateur.

wire-pulling *inf n Am* piston *m*; he did some ~ for me il m'a pistonné.

wire rope *n* câble *m* métallique.

wire service *n Am* agence *f* de presse *(envoyant des dépêches télégraphiques)*.

wiretap ['waɪətæp] ◇ *vt* mettre sur écoute.
◇ *vi* mettre un téléphone sur écoute.
◇ *n*: they put a ~ on his phone ils ont mis son téléphone sur écoute.

wiretapping ['waɪəˌtæpɪŋ] *n* mise *f* sur écoute des lignes téléphoniques.

wire wool *n* éponge *f* métallique.

wireworm ['waɪəwɜːm] *n* larve *f* de taupin.

wiring ['waɪərɪŋ] *n* installation *f* électrique; the house needs new ~ il faut refaire l'installation électrique OR l'électricité dans la maison.

wiry ['waɪərɪ] *adj* -**1.** [person] élancé et robuste; [animal] nerveux, vigoureux. -**2.** [hair] peu souple, rêche. -**3.** [grass] élastique, flexible.

Wisconsin [wɪs'kɒnsɪn] *pr n* Wisconsin *m*; in ~ dans le Wisconsin.

wisdom ['wɪzdəm] *n* -**1.** [perspicacity, judgement] sagesse *f*; I have my doubts about the ~ of moving house this year j'ai des doutes sur l'opportunité de déménager cette année. -**2.** [store of knowledge] sagesse *f*; folk ~ sagesse populaire. -**3.** [opinion] avis *m* (général), jugement *m*; (the) received OR conventional ~ les idées *fpl* reçues; Donald, in his ~, decided we should cancel *hum* Donald, toujours prudent, décida que nous devions annuler.

wisdom tooth *n* dent *f* de sagesse.

wise [waɪz] ◇ *adj* -**1.** [learned, judicious] sage; you'd be ~ to take my advice vous seriez sage de suivre mes conseils; do you think it's ~ to invite his wife? crois-tu que ce soit prudent d'inviter sa femme? -**2.** [clever, shrewd] habile, astucieux; a ~ move [in board games] un coup habile OR astucieux; the president made a ~ move in dismissing the attorney general le président a été bien avisé de renvoyer le ministre de la justice; it's always easy to be ~ after the event c'est toujours facile d'avoir raison après coup ❑ to be none the wiser ne pas être plus avancé; do it while he's out, he'll be none the wiser fais-le pendant qu'il est sorti et il n'en saura rien; to be ~ to sthg *inf* être au courant de qqch; I'm ~ to you OR to your schemes je sais ce que tu manigances; to get ~ to sthg *inf*: you'd better get ~ to what's going on vous feriez bien d'ouvrir les yeux sur ce qui se passe.
◇ *n fml*: he is in no ~ OR not in any ~ satisfied with his new position il n'est point OR aucunement satisfait de son nouveau poste.
◆ **wise up** *inf* ◇ *vi insep*: he'd better ~ up! il ferait bien de se mettre dans le coup!; she finally ~d up to the fact that she'd never be a great musician elle a enfin compris qu'elle ne serait jamais une grande musicienne.
◇ *vt sep Am* mettre dans le coup.

-wise *in cpds* -**1.** [in the direction of] dans le sens de; length~ dans le sens de la longueur. -**2.** [in the manner of] à la manière de, comme; he edged crab~ up to the bar il s'approcha du bar en marchant de côté comme un crabe. -**3.** *inf* [as regards] côté; money~ the job leaves a lot to be desired le poste laisse beaucoup à désirer côté argent.

wiseacre ['waɪzˌeɪkəʳ] *n pej* bel esprit *m iron*.

wisecrack *inf* ['waɪzkræk] *n* sarcasme *m*.

wise guy *inf n* malin *m*; don't be a ~! ne fais pas le malin!; OK, ~, what would you do? OK, gros malin, qu'est-ce que tu ferais?

wisely ['waɪzlɪ] *adv* sagement, avec sagesse.

wise man *n* sage *m*; the Three Wise Men BIBLE les (trois) Rois mages.

wish [wɪʃ] ◇ *vt* -**1.** [expressing something impossible or unlikely] souhaiter; to ~ sb dead souhaiter la mort de qqn; she ~ed herself far away elle aurait souhaité être loin; I ~ I were OR *Br inf* was somewhere else j'aimerais bien être ailleurs; ~ you were here [on postcard] j'aimerais bien que tu sois là; I ~ you didn't have to leave j'aimerais que tu ne sois pas OR ce serait bien si tu n'étais pas obligé de partir; I ~ I'd thought of that before je regrette de n'y avoir pas pensé plus tôt; why don't you come with us? – I ~ I could pourquoi ne venez-vous pas avec nous? – j'aimerais bien || [expressing criticism, reproach]: I ~ you'd be more careful j'aimerais que vous fassiez plus attention; I ~ you wouldn't talk so much! tu ne peux pas te taire un peu?; I ~ you wouldn't play that music so loud j'aimerais bien que tu ne mettes pas la musique aussi fort. -**2.** *fml* [want] souhaiter, vouloir; I don't ~ to appear rude, but... je ne voudrais pas paraître grossier mais...; he no longer ~es to discuss it il ne veut OR souhaite plus en parler; do you ~ to see me? désirez-vous me voir?; how do you ~ to pay? comment désirez-vous payer? -**3.** [in greeting, expressions of goodwill] souhaiter; I ~ed her a pleasant journey je lui ai souhaité (un) bon voyage; he ~ed them success in their future careers il leur a souhaité de réussir dans leur carrière; he ~ed us good day il nous a souhaité le bonjour; I ~ you no harm je ne vous veux pas de mal; I ~ you well j'espère que tout ira bien pour vous; I ~ you (good) luck je vous souhaite bonne chance ❑ to ~ sb joy of sthg souhaiter bien du plaisir à qqn pour qqch.
◇ *vi* -**1.** *fml* [want, like] vouloir, souhaiter; may I see you again? – if you ~ puis-je vous revoir? – si vous le voulez OR le souhaitez; do as you ~ faites comme vous voulez. -**2.** [make a wish] faire un vœu; close your eyes and ~ hard ferme les yeux et fais un vœu; to ~ upon a star *lit* faire un vœu en regardant une étoile.
◇ *n* -**1.** [act of wishing, thing wished for] souhait *m*, vœu *m*; make a ~! fais un souhait OR vœu!; to grant a ~ exaucer un vœu; he got his ~, his ~ came true son vœu s'est réalisé. -**2.** [desire] désir *m*; to express a ~ for sthg exprimer le désir de qqch; it is my (dearest) ~ that... *fml* c'est mon vœu le plus cher que...; it was his last ~ c'était sa dernière volonté; your ~ is my command *lit* OR *hum* vos désirs sont des ordres; I have no ~ to appear melodramatic, but... *fml* je ne voudrais pas avoir l'air de dramatiser, mais...; she had no great ~ to travel elle n'avait pas très envie de voyager; to respect sb's ~es respecter les vœux de qqn; she went against my ~es elle a agi contre ma volonté; he joined the navy against OR contrary to my ~es il s'est engagé dans la marine contre mon gré OR ma volonté ❑ ~ list desiderata *mpl*. -**3.** [regards]: give your wife my best ~es transmettez toutes mes amitiés à votre épouse; my parents send their best ~es mes parents vous font toutes leurs amitiés || [in card]: with every good ~ avec mes meilleurs vœux; best ~es for the coming year meilleurs vœux pour la nouvelle année; best ~es for a Merry Christmas joyeux Noël; best ~es on your graduation (day) toutes mes/nos félicitations à l'occasion de l'obtention de votre diplôme || [in letter]: (with) best ~es bien amicalement, toutes mes amitiés.
◆ **wish away** *vt sep*: you can't simply ~ away the things you don't like on ne peut pas faire comme si les choses qui nous déplaisent n'existaient pas.
◆ **wish for** *vt insep* souhaiter; what did you ~ for? quel était ton vœu?; what more could a man/woman ~ for? que peut-on souhaiter de plus?

◆ **wish on** *vt sep* **-1.** [fate, problem] souhaiter à; I wouldn't ~ this headache on anyone je ne souhaite à personne d'avoir un mal de tête pareil. **-2.** [foist on]: it's a terribly complicated system ~ed on us by head office c'est un système très compliqué dont nous a fait cadeau la direction; he'll probably ~ the children on us for the afternoon il nous fera sans doute cadeau des enfants pour l'après-midi.

wishbone ['wɪʃbəʊn] *n* bréchet *m*, fourchette *f* ANAT.

wish fulfilment *n* accomplissement *m* d'un désir.

wishful thinking ['wɪʃfʊl-] *n*: I suppose it was just ~ je prenais mes rêves pour la réalité.

wishy-washy *inf* ['wɪʃɪ,wɒʃɪ] *adj* [behaviour] mou; [person] sans personnalité; [colour] délavé; [taste] fadasse.

wisp [wɪsp] *n* **-1.** [of grass, straw] brin *m*; [of hair] petite mèche *f*; [of smoke, steam] ruban *m*; a ~ of a girl *fig* un petit bout de fillette. **-2.** *lit* [hint, trace] soupçon *m*, pointe *f*; there wasn't a ~ of a cloud il n'y avait pas le moindre nuage.

wispy ['wɪspɪ] *adj* [beard] effilé; [hair] épars; [person] (tout) menu.

wisteria [wɪ'stɪərɪə] *n* glycine *f*.

wistful ['wɪstfʊl] *adj* mélancolique, nostalgique.

wistfully ['wɪstfʊlɪ] *adv* d'un air triste et rêveur.

wit [wɪt] *n* **-1.** [humour] esprit *m*; to have a quick/ready ~ avoir de la vivacité d'esprit/ beaucoup d'esprit; her prose sparkles with ~ sa prose est pétillante d'esprit. **-2.** [humorous person]: he was a great ~ c'était un homme plein d'esprit. **-3.** [intelligence] esprit *m*, intelligence *f*; he didn't have the ~ to keep his mouth shut *inf* il n'a pas eu l'intelligence de OR il n'a pas été assez futé pour fermer son bec; she has quick ~s elle a l'esprit fin, elle est très fine; keep your ~s about you while you're travelling sois prudent OR attentif pendant que tu voyages; to live by one's ~s vivre d'expédients; he didn't have time to collect OR to gather his ~s il n'a pas eu le temps de se ressaisir OR reprendre ses esprits ❑ I was at my ~s' end je ne savais plus quoi faire; you frightened me out of my ~s OR the ~s out of me! tu m'as fait une de ces peurs! **-4.** *arch* OR *lit* sens *m*; one's five ~s les cinq sens.

◆ **to wit** *adv phr fml* à savoir.

witch [wɪtʃ] ◇ *n* [sorceress] sorcière *f*; it's that old ~ of a landlady *fig* c'est cette vieille sorcière de propriétaire; you little ~! petite garce!; ~es' Sabbath sabbat *m* (de sorcières). ◇ *vt* [bewitch] envoûter.

witchcraft ['wɪtʃkrɑːft] *n (U)* sorcellerie *f*; he claimed to have been a victim of ~ il a prétendu qu'on lui avait jeté un sort.

witchdoctor ['wɪtʃ,dɒktəʳ] *n* sorcier *m*.

witch elm *n* orme *m* blanc OR de montagne.

witchery ['wɪtʃərɪ] *n lit* [witchcraft] sorcellerie *f*; [charm, enchantment] ensorcellement *m*.

witch-hazel *n* hamamélis *m*.

witch-hunt *n* chasse *f* aux sorcières; *fig* chasse *f* aux sorcières, persécution *f* (politique).

witching hour ['wɪtʃɪŋ-] *n*: the ~ l'heure *f* fatale.

with [wɪð] *prep* **-1.** [by means of] avec; she broke it ~ her hands elle l'a cassé avec ses OR les mains; what did you fix it ~? avec quoi l'as-tu réparé?; I've got nothing/I need something to open this can ~ je n'ai rien pour/j'ai besoin de quelque chose pour ouvrir cette boîte; she painted the wall ~ a roller elle a peint le mur avec un OR au rouleau; they fought ~ swords ils se sont battus à l'épée; his eyes filled ~ tears ses yeux se remplirent de larmes; covered/ furnished/lined ~ couvert/meublé/doublé de. **-2.** [describing a feature or attribute] à; a boy ~ green eyes un garçon aux yeux verts; a woman ~ long hair une femme aux cheveux longs; which boy? – the one ~ the torn jacket quel garçon? – celui qui a la veste déchirée; a man ~ one eye/a hump/a limp un homme borgne/bossu/boiteux; the house ~ the red roof la maison au toit rouge; a table ~ three legs une table à trois pieds; an old woman ~ no teeth une vieille femme édentée; a child ~ no home un enfant sans foyer OR famille; she was left ~ nothing to eat or drink on l'a laissée sans rien à manger ni à boire. **-3.** [accompanied by, in the company of] avec; she went out ~ her brother elle est sortie avec son frère; can I go ~ you? puis-je aller avec vous OR vous accompagner?; I have no one to go ~ je n'ai personne avec qui aller; she stayed ~ him all night [gen] elle est restée avec lui toute la nuit; [sick person] elle est restée auprès de lui toute la nuit; are you ~ him? [accompanying] êtes-vous avec lui? ❑ are you ~ me? [supporting] vous êtes avec moi?; [understanding] vous me suivez?; I'm ~ you there là, je suis d'accord avec toi; I'm ~ you one hundred per cent OR all the way je suis complètement d'accord avec vous; I'm not ~ you [don't understand] je ne vous suis pas. **-4.** [in the home of] chez; I'm (staying) ~ friends je suis OR loge chez des amis; he stayed ~ a family il a logé dans une famille; she lives ~ her mother elle vit chez sa mère; I live ~ a friend je vis avec un ami. **-5.** [an employee of]: she's ~ the United Nations elle travaille à l'ONU; isn't he ~ Ford any more? ne travaille-t-il plus chez Ford? ‖ [a client of]: we're ~ the Galena Building Society nous sommes à la Galena Building Society; she's decided to stay OR stick ~ her present accountant elle a décidé de garder le même comptable. **-6.** [indicating joint action] avec; who did you dance ~? avec qui as-tu dansé?; stop fighting ~ your brother arrête de te battre avec ton frère ‖ [indicating feelings towards someone else]: angry/furious/at war ~ fâché/furieux/en guerre contre; in love/infatuated ~ amoureux/entiché de; pleased ~ content de. **-7.** [including]: does the meal come ~ wine? est-ce que le vin est compris dans le menu?; the bill came to £16 ~ the tip l'addition était de 16 livres service compris; the radio didn't come ~ batteries la radio était livrée sans piles ‖ CULIN à; coffee ~ milk café *m* au lait; duck ~ orange sauce canard *m* à l'orange; pasta ~ eggs pâtes *fpl* aux œufs. **-8.** [indicating manner] de, avec; he knocked the guard out ~ one blow il assomma le gardien d'un (seul) coup; he spoke ~ ease il s'exprima avec aisance; she hit him ~ all her might elle le frappa de toutes ses forces; "you'll be late again", she said ~ a smile «tu vas encore être en retard», dit-elle avec un sourire OR en souriant; ~ these words he left sur ces mots, il partit. **-9.** [as regards, concerning]: you never know ~ him avec lui, on ne sait jamais; it's an obsession ~ her c'est une manie chez elle; what's wrong ~ you?, what's ~ you? *inf* qu'est-ce qui te prend?; he isn't very good ~ animals il ne sait pas vraiment s'y prendre avec les bêtes. **-10.** [because of, on account of] de; white ~ fear vert de peur; sick OR ill ~ malaria atteint du paludisme; I was sick ~ worry *fig* j'étais malade d'inquiétude; ~ crime on the increase, more elderly people are afraid to go out avec l'augmentation du taux de criminalité, de plus en plus de personnes âgées ont peur de sortir; I can't draw ~ you watching je ne peux pas dessiner si tu me regardes; he'll never stop smoking ~ his friends offering him cigarettes all the time il n'arrêtera jamais de fumer si ses amis continuent à lui proposer des cigarettes. **-11.** [in spite of]: ~ all his money he's so stingy *inf* il a beau avoir beaucoup d'argent, il est vraiment radin; ~ all his bragging he's just a coward il a beau se vanter, ce n'est qu'un lâche.

withal [wɪ'ðɔːl] *adv lit* [as well, besides] de plus, en outre; [nevertheless] néanmoins.

withdraw [wɪð'drɔː] (*pt* withdrew, *pp* withdrawn) ◇ *vt* **-1.** [remove] retirer; they have withdrawn their support/offer ils ont retiré leur soutien/offre; the car has been withdrawn (from sale) la voiture a été retirée de la vente; he withdrew his hand from his pocket/ from my shoulder il a retiré la main de sa poche/de mon épaule. **-2.** [money] retirer; I withdrew £500 from my account j'ai retiré 500 livres de mon compte. **-3.** [bring out - diplomat] rappeler; [- troops] retirer. **-4.** [statement] retirer, rétracter; JUR [charge] retirer; he withdrew his previous statements il est revenu sur OR il a retiré ses déclarations antérieures.
◇ *vi* **-1.** [retire] se retirer; the waiter withdrew discreetly le serveur s'est discrètement retiré; she has decided to ~ from politics elle a décidé de se retirer de la politique. **-2.** [retreat] se retirer; [move back] reculer; the troops withdrew to a new position les troupes se sont retirées vers une nouvelle position; he tends to ~ into himself il a tendance à se replier sur lui-même; she often withdrew into a fantasy world elle se réfugiait souvent dans un monde imaginaire. **-3.** [back out - candidate, competitor] se retirer, se désister; [- partner] se rétracter, se dédire. **-4.** [after sex] se retirer.

withdrawal [wɪð'drɔːəl] ◇ *n* **-1.** [removal - of funding, support, troops] retrait *m*; [- of envoy] rappel *m*; [- of candidate] retrait *m*, désistement *m*; [- of love] privation *f*; I support ~ from NATO je soutiens notre retrait de l'OTAN. **-2.** [of statement, remark] rétraction *f*; JUR [of charge] retrait *m*, annulation *f*. **-3.** PSYCH repli *m* sur soi-même, introversion *f*. **-4.** MED [from drugs] état *m* de manque; to experience ~ être en (état de) manque. **-5.** [of money] retrait *m*; to make a ~ faire un retrait.
◇ *comp*: ~ symptoms symptômes *mpl* de manque; to have OR to suffer from ~ symptoms être en état de manque.

withdrawn [wɪð'drɔːn] ◇ *pp* → **withdraw**.
◇ *adj* [shy] renfermé, réservé.

withdrew [wɪð'druː] *pt* → **withdraw**.

wither ['wɪðəʳ] ◇ *vi* **-1.** [flower, plant] se flétrir, se faner; [body - from age] se ratatiner; [- from sickness] s'atrophier. **-2.** [beauty] se faner; [hope, optimism] s'évanouir; [memory] s'étioler.
◇ *vt* **-1.** [plant] flétrir, faner; [body - subj: age] ratatiner; [- subj: sickness] atrophier. **-2.** [beauty] altérer.

◆ **wither away** *vi insep* [flower, plant] se dessécher, se faner; [beauty] se faner, s'évanouir; [hope, optimism] s'évanouir; [memory] disparaître, s'atrophier.

withered ['wɪðəd] *adj* **-1.** [flower, plant] flétri, fané; [cheek] fané, flétri; he was old and ~ il était vieux et complètement desséché. **-2.** [arm] atrophié.

withering ['wɪðərɪŋ] ◇ *adj* [heat, sun] desséchant; [criticism, remark] cinglant, blessant; she gave me a ~ look elle m'a lancé un regard méprisant, elle m'a foudroyé du regard; she spoke of him with ~ scorn elle parlait de lui avec un mépris cinglant.
◇ *n* [of plant] flétrissure *f*; [of arm] atrophie *f*; [of beauty] déclin *m*; [of hope, optimism] évanouissement *m*.

witheringly ['wɪðərɪŋlɪ] *adv* avec un profond mépris.

withers ['wɪðəz] *npl* garrot *m* (du cheval).

withhold [wɪð'həʊld] (*pt* & *pp* withheld [-'held]) *vt* **-1.** [refuse - love, permission, support] refuser; [refuse to pay - rent, tax] refuser de payer; to ~ payment refuser de payer; he withheld his consent il a refusé son consentement. **-2.** [keep back - criticism, news] taire, cacher; to ~ the truth from sb cacher la vérité à qqn; they ~ 2 % of the profits ils retiennent 2 % des bénéfices.

withholding tax [wɪð'həʊldɪŋ-] *n Am* retenue *f* à la source.

within [wɪ'ðɪn] ◇ *prep* **-1.** [inside - place] à l'intérieur de, dans; *fig* [- group, system] à l'intérieur de, au sein de; [- person] en; he lived and worked ~ these four walls il a vécu et travaillé entre ces quatre murs; a play ~ a play une pièce dans une pièce; new forces are at work ~ our society des forces nouvelles sont à l'œuvre dans notre société; the man's role ~ the family is changing le rôle de l'homme au

sein de la famille est en train de changer; **a small voice ~ her** une petite voix intérieure OR au fond d'elle-même. -**2.** [inside the limits of] dans les limites de; **you must remain ~ the circle** tu dois rester dans le OR à l'intérieur du cercle; **to be ~ the law** être dans les limites de la loi; **~ the framework of the agreement** dans le cadre de l'accord; **it is not ~ the bounds of possibility** ça dépasse le cadre du possible; **to live ~ one's means** vivre selon ses moyens; **the car is well ~ his price range** la voiture est tout à fait dans ses prix OR ses moyens. -**3.** [before the end of a specified period of time] en moins de; **~ the hour** OR **an hour she had finished** en moins d'une heure, elle avait fini; **I'll let you know ~ a week** je vous dirai ce qu'il en est dans le courant de la semaine; **'use ~ two days of purchase'** 'à consommer dans les deux jours suivant la date d'achat'; **~ a week of taking the job, she knew it was a mistake** moins d'une semaine après avoir accepté cet emploi, elle sut qu'elle avait fait une erreur. -**4.** [indicating distance, measurement]: **they were ~ 10 km of Delhi** ils étaient à moins de 10 km de Delhi; **we are ~ walking distance of the shops** nous pouvons aller faire nos courses à pied; **accurate to ~ 0.1 of a milimetre** précis au dizième de millimètre près; **she came ~ seconds of beating the record** elle a failli battre le record à quelques secondes près. -**5.** [during]: **enormous changes have taken place ~ a single generation** de grands changements ont eu lieu en l'espace d'une seule génération; **did the accident take place ~ the period covered by the insurance?** l'accident a-t-il eu lieu pendant la période couverte par l'assurance?
◇ *adv* dedans, à l'intérieur; **'enquire ~'** 'renseignements à l'intérieur'; **from ~** de l'intérieur; **the appointment will be made from ~** la nomination se fera au sein de l'entreprise.

with it *inf adj* -**1.** [alert] réveillé; **she's not really ~ this morning** elle n'est pas très bien réveillée ce matin; **get ~!** réveille-toi!, secoue-toi! -**2.** *dated* [fashionable - shoes, idea, restaurant] dans le vent.

without [wɪð'aʊt] ◇ *prep* sans; **three nights ~ sleep** trois nuits sans dormir; **we couldn't have done it ~ you** on n'aurait pas pu le faire sans vous; **~ milk or sugar** sans lait ni sucre; **with or ~ chocolate sauce?** avec ou sans sauce au chocolat?; **to be ~ fear/shame** n'avoir pas peur/honte; **not ~ irony** non sans ironie; **he took it ~ so much as a thank you** il l'a pris sans même dire merci ‖ *(with present participle)*: **~ looking up** sans lever les yeux; **I knocked ~ getting a reply** j'ai frappé sans obtenir de réponse; **leave the house ~ anybody knowing** quittez la maison sans que personne le sache.
◇ *adv lit* au dehors, à l'extérieur; **a voice from ~** une voix de l'extérieur.
◇ *conj dial* [unless]: **~ they go themselves** à moins qu'ils y aillent eux-mêmes.

withstand [wɪð'stænd] (*pt* & *pp* **withstood** [-'stʊd]) *vt* [heat, punishment] résister à; **to ~ the test of time** résister à l'épreuve du temps.

witless ['wɪtlɪs] *adj* sot, stupide.

witness ['wɪtnɪs] ◇ *n* -**1.** [onlooker] témoin *m*; **the police are asking for ~es of** OR **to the accident** la police recherche des témoins de l'accident. -**2.** JUR [in court] témoin *m*; **to call sb as (a) ~** citer qqn comme témoin; **~ for the prosecution/defence** témoin à charge/décharge ‖ [to signature, will] témoin *m*; **two people must be ~es to my signature/will** deux personnes doivent signer comme témoins de ma signature/de mon testament. -**3.** [testimony]: **in ~ of sthg** en témoignage de qqch; **to be** OR **to bear ~ to sthg** témoigner de qqch; **to give ~ on behalf of sb** témoigner en faveur de qqn; **his vast bulk was ~ to his gluttony** *lit* son énorme corpulence témoignait de sa gourmandise. -**4.** RELIG témoignage *m*.
◇ *vt* -**1.** [see] être témoin de, témoigner de; **did she ~ the accident?** a-t-elle été témoin de l'accident?; **millions ~ed the first moon landing** des millions de gens ont vu le premier atterrissage sur la lune. -**2.** [signature] être témoin de; [will, document] signer comme témoin. -**3.** [experience - change] voir, connaître; **the 19th century ~ed many revolutions** le XIXe siècle a connu beaucoup de révolutions.
◇ *vi* [gen & JUR] témoigner, être témoin; **to ~ to sthg** témoigner de qqch; **to ~ against sb** témoigner contre qqn; **she ~ed to finding the body** elle a témoigné avoir découvert le cadavre.

witness box *n Br* barre *f* des témoins; **in the ~** à la barre.

witness stand *n Am* barre *f* des témoins; **to take the ~** venir à la barre.

-witted ['wɪtɪd] *in cpds*: **quick~** à l'esprit vif; **dim~** à l'esprit lent.

witter *inf* ['wɪtəʳ] *vi Br pej* bavarder, jacasser, parler pour ne rien dire; **they were ~ing on about diets** ils parlaient interminablement de régimes; **do stop ~ing on** arrête de parler pour ne rien dire, arrête tes jacasseries; **he's always ~ing on about the army** il n'en finit pas de parler de l'armée.

witticism ['wɪtɪsɪzm] *n* bon mot *m*, trait *m* d'esprit.

wittily ['wɪtɪlɪ] *adv* spirituellement, avec beaucoup d'esprit.

wittiness ['wɪtɪnɪs] *n* esprit *m*, humour *m*.

wittingly ['wɪtɪŋlɪ] *adv fml* en connaissance de cause, sciemment.

witty ['wɪtɪ] (*compar* **wittier**, *superl* **wittiest**) *adj* spirituel, plein d'esprit; **a ~ observation** un bon mot, une remarque spirituelle.

wives [waɪvz] *pl* → **wife**.

wiz *inf* [wɪz] *n* as *m*, crack *m*.

wizard ['wɪzəd] ◇ *n* -**1.** [magician] enchanteur *m*, sorcier *m* ❑ **'The Wizard of Oz'** *Fleming* 'le Magicien d'Oz'. -**2.** *fig* [expert] génie *m*; **she's a ~ with animals** elle sait vraiment s'y prendre avec les animaux; **she's a real ~ at drawing** en dessin, elle est vraiment douée; **he's a ~ with computers** c'est un champion de l'ordinateur; **a financial ~** un génie de la finance.
◇ *adj inf Br dated* épatant; **he's a ~ card player** il est épatant comme joueur de cartes; **she's got a ~ bike!** son vélo est génial!
◇ *interj dated*: **~!** épatant!

wizardry ['wɪzədrɪ] *n* -**1.** [magic] magie *f*, sorcellerie *f*. -**2.** *fig* [genius] génie *m*; **financial ~** le génie de la finance; **they've installed a new piece of technical ~ in the office** ils ont installé une nouvelle merveille de la technique dans le bureau.

wizened ['wɪznd] *adj* [skin, hands] desséché; [old person] desséché, ratatiné; [face, fruit, vegetables] ratatiné.

wk (*written abbr of* **week**) sem.

Wm. *written abbr of* William.

wo [wəʊ] = **whoa**.

WO *n abbr of* warrant officer.

woad [wəʊd] *n* guède *f*.

wobble ['wɒbl] ◇ *vi* -**1.** [hand, jelly, voice] trembler; [chair, table] branler, être branlant OR bancal; [compass needle] osciller; [drunkard] tituber, chanceler; [cyclist] aller de travers, aller en zigzag; **the stone ~d as I stood on it** la pierre a oscillé quand je suis monté dessus; **the pile of books ~d dangerously** la pile de livres oscilla dangereusement; **the tightrope walker ~d and almost fell** le funambule oscilla et faillit tomber; **the child ~d across the room** l'enfant traversa la pièce en chancelant; **she ~d off/past on her bike** elle partit/passa sur son vélo, en équilibre instable. -**2.** *fig* [hesitate, dither] hésiter.
◇ *vt* [table] faire basculer.
◇ *n*: **after a few ~s, he finally got going** après avoir cherché son équilibre, il se mit enfin en route.

wobbly ['wɒblɪ] (*pl* **wobblies**) ◇ *adj* -**1.** [table, chair] branlant, bancal; [pile] chancelant; [jelly] qui tremble; **that pile looks a bit ~** cette pile a l'air d'être en équilibre plutôt instable. -**2.** [hand, voice] tremblant; **I feel a bit ~** je me sens un peu faible; **she's rather ~ on her feet** elle flageole un peu OR elle ne tient pas très bien sur ses jambes. -**3.** [line] qui n'est pas droit; [handwriting] tremblé.
◇ *n Br phr*: **to throw a ~** *inf* piquer une crise.

wodge *inf* [wɒdʒ] *n Br* gros bloc *m*, gros morceau *m*; **great ~s of paper** de gros blocs de papier.

woe [wəʊ] *lit* OR *hum* ◇ *n* malheur *m*, infortune *f*; **a tale of ~** une histoire pathétique; **~ betide anyone who lies to me** malheur à celui qui me raconte des mensonges; **a cry of ~** un cri de détresse.
◇ *interj* hélas; **~ is me!** pauvre de moi!

woebegone ['wəʊbɪ,gɒn] *adj lit* OR *hum* désolé, abattu.

woeful ['wəʊfʊl] *adj* -**1.** [sad - person, look, news, situation] malheureux, très triste; [- scene, tale] affligeant, très triste. -**2.** [very poor] lamentable, épouvantable, consternant; **it shows a ~ lack of imagination** cela démontre un manque d'imagination consternant.

woefully ['wəʊfʊlɪ] *adv* -**1.** [sadly - look, smile] très tristement. -**2.** [badly - perform, behave] lamentablement; **he is ~ lacking in common sense** le bon sens lui fait cruellement défaut; **our funds are ~ inadequate** nous manquons cruellement de fonds; **the garden was ~ neglected for several years** le jardin avait été très négligé pendant plusieurs années.

wog▼ [wɒg] *n Br terme raciste désignant un Noir*, ≃ nègre *m*, négresse *f*.

woggle ['wɒgl] *n Br* bague en cuir *(pour cravate de scout)*.

wok [wɒk] *n* wok *m (poêle chinoise)*.

woke [wəʊk] *pt* → **wake**.

woken [wəʊkn] *pp* → **wake**.

wold [wəʊld] *n* haute plaine *f*, plateau *m*.

wolf [wʊlf] (*pl* **wolves** [wʊlvz]) ◇ *n* -**1.** ZOOL loup *m*; **he is a ~ in sheep's clothing** c'est un loup déguisé en brebis; **it helps keep the ~ from the door** c'est un travail purement alimentaire; **to throw sb to the wolves** sacrifier qqn. -**2.** *inf* [seducer] tombeur *m*.
◇ *vt* = **wolf down**.
◆ **wolf down** *inf vt sep* [food] engloutir, dévorer.

wolf child *n* enfant *m* sauvage.

wolf cub *n* [animal] louveteau *m*.
◆ **Wolf Cub** *n dated* [scout] louveteau *m*.

wolfhound ['wʊlfhaʊnd] *n* chien-loup *m*.

wolfish ['wʊlfɪʃ] *adj* [appearance] de loup; [appetite] vorace.

wolfishly ['wʊlfɪʃlɪ] *adv* voracement.

wolf pack *n* meute *f* de loups.

wolfram ['wʊlfrəm] *n* tungstène *m*, wolfram *m*.

wolfsbane ['wʊlfsbeɪn] *n* aconit *m* jaune.

wolf whistle *n* sifflement *m (au passage d'une femme)*.
◆ **wolf-whistle** *vt* siffler *(une femme)*.

wolverine ['wʊlvəri:n] (*pl inv* OR **wolverines**) *n* ZOOL glouton *m*.

Wolverine ['wʊlvəri:n] *n Am* habitant *m*, -e *f* du Michigan.

wolves [wʊlvz] *pl* → **wolf**.

woman ['wʊmən] (*pl* **women** ['wɪmɪn]) ◇ *n* -**1.** [gen] femme *f*; **a single/married ~** une femme célibataire/mariée; **a young ~** une jeune femme; **come here, young ~** venez-là, mademoiselle; **she's quite the young ~ now** elle fait très jeune fille maintenant; **women and children first** les femmes et les enfants d'abord; **man's perception of ~** la façon dont les hommes voient les femmes, la vision de la femme qu'a l'homme; **women live longer than men** les femmes vivent plus longtemps que les hommes; **what is a ~ supposed to do?** *hum* qu'est-ce qu'on peut faire!; **a ~'s work is never done** quand on est une femme, on a toujours quelque chose à faire; **I don't even know the ~!** *inf* je ne sais même pas qui elle est OR qui c'est!; **oh, damn the ~!** *inf* quelle idiote! ❑ a

~ of letters une femme de lettres; a ~ of the world [cultivated] une femme du monde; [worldly-wise] une femme d'expérience; she's a working/career ~ elle travaille/a une carrière; a business ~ une femme d'affaires; the women's page [in newspaper] la page des lectrices; a ~'s OR women's magazine un magazine féminin. -2. [employee] femme *f*; a ~ minds the children for me j'ai une femme qui me garde les enfants; the factory women left for work les ouvrières sont parties travailler; (cleaning) ~ femme de ménage. -3. *inf* [wife] femme *f*; [lover] maîtresse *f*; the little ~ ma OR la petite femme; the other ~ l'autre femme. -4. *inf* [patronizing term of address]: my good ~ *dated* ma petite dame; that's enough, ~! assez, femme!
◇ *comp*: ~ doctor (femme *f*) médecin *m*; ~ driver conductrice *f*; ~ friend amie *f*; ~ photographer photographe *f*; ~ police constable femme *f* agent de police; ~ teacher professeur *m* (femme); they have a ~ teacher leur professeur est une femme.

woman-hater *n* misogyne *mf*.

womanhood ['wʊmənhʊd] *n* (U) -1. [female nature] féminité *f*; to reach ~ devenir une femme. -2. [women collectively] les femmes *fpl*.

womanish ['wʊmənɪʃ] *adj pej* [man] efféminé; [characteristic] de femme, féminin.

womanize, -ise ['wʊmənaɪz] *vi* courir les femmes.

womanizer ['wʊmənaɪzəʳ] *n* coureur *m* de jupons.

womanizing ['wʊmənaɪzɪŋ] *n* ≃ donjuanisme *m*.

womankind [,wʊmən'kaɪnd] *n* les femmes *fpl*.

womanliness ['wʊmənlɪnɪs] *n* féminité *f*.

womanly ['wʊmənlɪ] *adj* [virtue, figure] féminin, de femme; [act] digne d'une femme, féminin.

womb [wuːm] *n* -1. ANAT utérus *m*; in his mother's ~ dans le ventre de sa mère. -2. *fig* sein *m*, entrailles *fpl*.

wombat ['wɒmbæt] *n* wombat *m*.

women ['wɪmɪn] *pl* → **woman**.

womenfolk ['wɪmɪnfəʊk] *npl*: the ~ les femmes *fpl*.

women's group *n* [campaigning organization] groupe *m* féministe; [social club] groupe *m* de femmes.

Women's Institute *pr n association britannique des femmes au foyer*.

Women's Lib [-lɪb] *n* MLF *m*, mouvement *m* de libération de la femme.

Women's Libber [-'lɪbə] *n* féministe *f*.

Women's Liberation *n* mouvement *m* de libération de la femme, MLF *m*.

Women's Movement *n* mouvement *m* féministe.

women's refuge *n* centre *m* d'accueil pour les femmes.

women's rights *npl* droits *mpl* de la femme.

women's room *n Am* toilettes *fpl* des femmes.

women's studies *npl discipline universitaire ayant pour objet la sociologie et l'histoire des femmes, la création littéraire féminine etc*.

won [wʌn] *pt & pp* → **win**.

wonder ['wʌndəʳ] ◇ *n* -1. [marvel] merveille *f*; the seven ~s of the world les sept merveilles du monde; the ~s of science les miracles de la science; the ~s of nature les merveilles de la nature; to work OR to do ~s [person] faire des merveilles; [action, event] faire merveille; a hot bath worked ~s for her aching body un bain chaud la soulagea à merveille de ses douleurs. -2. [amazing event or circumstances]: the ~ (of it) is that he manages to get any work done at all le plus étonnant dans tout cela, c'est qu'il arrive à travailler; it's a ~ to me that anyone can work in such awful conditions cela me semble incroyable qu'on puisse travailler dans des conditions aussi épouvantables; it's a ~ that she didn't resign on the spot c'est étonnant qu'elle n'ait pas démissionné sur-le-champ; no ~ they refused ce n'est pas étonnant qu'ils aient refusé; no ~! ce n'est pas étonnant!, cela vous étonne?; is it any ~ that he got lost? cela vous étonne qu'il se soit perdu?; it's little OR small ~ no one came ce n'est guère étonnant que personne ne soit venu; ~s will never cease! *hum* on n'a pas fini d'être étonné! -3. [awe] émerveillement *m*; the children were filled with ~ les enfants étaient émerveillés; they looked on, lost in ~ ils regardaient, totalement émerveillés OR éblouis; there was a look of ~ in his eyes il avait les yeux pleins d'étonnement. -4. [prodigy] prodige *m*, génie *m*; a boy ~ un petit prodige OR génie.
◇ *vt* -1. [ask o.s.] se demander; I ~ where she's gone je me demande où elle est allée; I ~ how he managed it je me demande comment il s'y est pris; I ~ why je me demande bien pourquoi; I often ~ that myself je me pose souvent la question; I ~ whether OR if she'll come je me demande si elle viendra || [in polite requests]: I was ~ing if you were free tomorrow est-ce que par hasard vous êtes libre demain?; I ~ if you could help me pourriez-vous m'aider s'il vous plaît? -2. [be surprised] s'étonner; I ~ that he wasn't hurt je m'étonne OR cela m'étonne qu'il n'ait pas été blessé.
◇ *vi* -1. [think, reflect] penser, réfléchir; it makes you ~ cela donne à penser OR réfléchir; his remarks set me ~ing ses remarques m'ont laissé songeur OR m'ont donné à réfléchir; I'm ~ing about going tomorrow je me demande si je ne vais pas y aller demain; I was ~ing about it too je me posais la même question; the war will be over in a few days – I ~ la guerre sera finie dans quelques jours – je n'en suis pas si sûr. -2. [marvel, be surprised] s'étonner, s'émerveiller; the people ~ed at the magnificent sight les gens s'émerveillaient de ce magnifique spectacle; I don't ~ (that) you're annoyed cela ne m'étonne pas que vous soyez contrariée; I don't ~ cela ne m'étonne pas.
◇ *comp* [drug, detergent] miracle; ~ child enfant *m* prodige.

wonderful ['wʌndəfʊl] *adj* [enjoyable] merveilleux, formidable; [beautiful] superbe, magnifique; [delicious] excellent; [astonishing] étonnant, surprenant; it was a ~ sight c'était un spectacle merveilleux OR magnifique; we had a ~ time/holiday on a passé des moments/des vacances formidables; the weather was ~ il a fait un temps superbe; what ~ news! quelle nouvelle formidable!; she has some ~ ideas elle a des idées formidables; that's ~! c'est merveilleux!; you've been ~ vous avez été formidable; you look ~ tu es superbe.

wonderfully ['wʌndəfʊlɪ] *adv* -1. *(+ adj or adv)* merveilleusement, admirablement; you look ~ well vous avez une mine superbe; she was ~ kind elle était d'une gentillesse merveilleuse. -2. *(+ verb)* merveilleusement, à merveille; they got on ~ ils s'entendirent à merveille; I slept ~ j'ai dormi à merveille, j'ai merveilleusement bien dormi; she plays ~ elle joue merveilleusement bien.

wondering ['wʌndərɪŋ] *adj* [pensive] songeur, pensif; [surprised] étonné; she looked at him with ~ eyes elle le regarda d'un air perplexe.

wonderingly ['wʌndərɪŋlɪ] *adv* [look - pensively] d'un air songeur; [- in surprise] d'un air étonné; [speak] avec étonnement.

wonderland ['wʌndəlænd] *n* pays *m* des merveilles; it's like ~ on se croirait au pays des merveilles; a winter ~ un paysage hivernal féerique.

wonderment ['wʌndəmənt] *n* [wonder] émerveillement *m*; [surprise] étonnement *m*; he looked around in ~ il regarda autour de lui émerveillé.

wonderworker ['wʌndə,wɜːkəʳ] *n*: he's a real ~ il accomplit de vrais miracles.

wondrous ['wʌndrəs] *lit* ◇ *adj* merveilleux.
◇ *adv* = **wondrously**.

wondrously ['wʌndrəslɪ] *adv lit* merveilleusement.

wonky *inf* ['wɒŋkɪ] (*compar* wonkier, *superl* wonkiest) *adj Br* [table] bancal, branlant; [bicycle] détraqué; [radio] déréglé, détraqué; [line] qui n'est pas bien droit; your tie is a bit ~ ta cravate est un peu de travers; I've got a ~ leg j'ai une jambe faible; the little girl did a rather ~ drawing of a cow la petite fille a fait un dessin maladroit d'une vache; the TV has gone ~ la télé est détraquée.

wont [wəʊnt] *lit* ◇ *n* coutume *f*, habitude *f*; he smoked a cigar after lunch, as was his ~ il fuma un cigare après le déjeuner comme de coutume.
◇ *adj*: to be ~ to do sthg avoir l'habitude OR coutume de faire qqch.

won't [wəʊnt] = **will not**.

wonted ['wəʊntɪd] *adj lit* coutumier.

woo [wuː] (*pt & pp* wooed) *vt* -1. *dated* [court] courtiser, faire la cour à. -2. [attract - customers, voters] chercher à plaire à, rechercher les faveurs de; they tried to ~ the voters with promises of lower taxes ils cherchaient à s'attirer les faveurs de l'électorat en promettant de baisser les impôts.

wood [wʊd] ◇ *n* -1. [timber] bois *m*; the stove burns ~ and coal le poêle fonctionne au bois et au charbon; a piece of ~ un bout de bois. -2. [forest, copse] bois *m*; we went for a walk in the ~s nous sommes allés nous promener dans les bois ❑ he can't see the ~ for the trees les arbres lui cachent la forêt; we're not out of the ~s yet on n'est pas encore sortis de l'auberge, on n'est pas encore tirés d'affaire. -3. VINIC tonneau *m*; matured in the ~ vieilli au tonneau; drawn from the ~ tiré au tonneau. -4. SPORT [in bowls] boule *f*; [in golf] bois *m*; a (number) 3 ~ un bois 3.
◇ *comp* -1. [wooden - floor, table, house] en bois, de bois. -2. [for burning wood - stove] à bois; [- fire] de bois.
◆ **woods** *npl* MUS bois *mpl*.

wood alcohol *n* esprit-de-bois *m*, alcool *m* méthylique.

wood anemone *n* anémone *f* des bois.

wood ant *n* fourmi *f* rouge.

woodbine ['wʊdbaɪn] *n* [honeysuckle] chèvrefeuille *m*; *Am* [Virginia creeper] vigne *f* vierge.

woodblock ['wʊdblɒk] *n* -1. [for printings] bois *m* de graveur. -2. [for floor] pavé *m* de bois.

wood-burning *adj* [stove, boiler] à bois.

woodcarving ['wʊd,kɑːvɪŋ] *n* -1. [craft] sculpture *f* sur bois. -2. [object] sculpture *f* en bois.

woodchip ['wʊdtʃɪp] *n* [composite wood] aggloméré *m*.

woodchuck ['wʊdtʃʌk] *n* marmotte *f* d'Amérique.

woodcock ['wʊdkɒk] (*pl inv* OR woodcocks) *n* bécasse *f*.

woodcraft ['wʊdkrɑːft] *n Am* -1. [in woodland] connaissance *f* des bois et forêts. -2. [artistry] art *m* de travailler le bois.

woodcut ['wʊdkʌt] *n* gravure *f* sur bois.

woodcutter ['wʊd,kʌtəʳ] *n* bûcheron *m*, -onne *f*.

woodcutting ['wʊd,kʌtɪŋ] *n* -1. [in forest] abattage *m* des arbres. -2. [engraving] gravure *f* sur bois.

wooded ['wʊdɪd] *adj* boisé; densely ~ très boisé.

wooden ['wʊdn] *adj* -1. [made of wood] en bois, de bois; a ~ leg une jambe de bois ❑ to try to sell sb ~ nickels *inf Am* essayer de rouler qqn; the Wooden Horse of Troy le cheval de Troie. -2. [stiff - gesture, manner, attitude] crispé, raide; [- performance, actor] raide, qui manque de naturel.

woodenhead *inf* ['wʊdnhed] *n* idiot *m*, -e *f*, imbécile *mf*.

woodenly ['wʊdnlɪ] *adv* [perform, move, smile, speak] avec raideur.

wooden spoon *n literal* cuillère *f* en bois; to win the ~ *Br* SPORT gagner la cuillère de bois.

woodland [ˈwʊdlənd] ◇ *n* région *f* boisée.
◇ *adj* [fauna] des bois; ~ walks promenades *fpl* à travers bois.

woodlark [ˈwʊdlɑːk] *n* alouette *f* des bois.

woodlouse [ˈwʊdlaʊs] (*pl* woodlice [-laɪs]) *n* cloporte *m*.

woodman [ˈwʊdmən] (*pl* woodmen [-mən]) *n* forestier *m*.

wood nymph *n* nymphe *f* des bois, dryade *f*.

woodpecker [ˈwʊd,pekəʳ] *n* pic *m*, pivert *m*.

woodpigeon [ˈwʊd,pɪdʒn] *n* ramier *m*.

woodpile [ˈwʊdpaɪl] *n* tas *m* de bois.

wood pulp *n* pâte *f* à papier.

wood screw *n* vis *f* à bois.

woodshed [ˈwʊdʃed] *n* bûcher *m (abri)*.

woodsman [ˈwʊdzmən] (*pl* woodsmen [-mən]) *n Am* forestier *m*.

wood spirit *n* esprit-de-bois *m*.

woodsy *inf* [ˈwʊdzɪ] (*compar* woodsier, *superl* woodsiest) *adj Am* [flowers] des bois; [smell] du bois; [area] boisé.

woodwind [ˈwʊdwɪnd] ◇ *adj* [music] pour les bois; ~ section OR instruments bois *mpl*.
◇ *n* -**1.** [single instrument] bois *m*. -**2.** *(U)* [family of instruments] bois *mpl*.

woodwork [ˈwʊdwɜːk] *n (U)* -**1.** [craft - carpentry] menuiserie *f*; [- cabinet-making] ébénisterie *f*. -**2.** [in building - doors, windows] boiseries *fpl*; [- beams] charpente *m*; to come OR to crawl out of the ~ *inf* sortir d'un peu partout. -**3.** *inf* FTBL poteaux *mpl*.

woodworm [ˈwʊdwɜːm] *n* [insect] ver *m* de bois; *(U)* [infestation]: a chair affected OR damaged by ~ une chaise vermoulue OR mangée aux vers; the sideboard has got ~ le buffet est vermoulu.

woody [ˈwʊdɪ] (*compar* woodier, *superl* woodiest) *adj* -**1.** [plant, vegetation] ligneux. -**2.** [countryside] boisé. -**3.** [taste] de bois; [smell] boisé.

wooer [ˈwuːəʳ] *n dated* prétendant *m*.

woof[1] [wuːf] *n* TEX trame *f*.

woof[2] [wʊf] ◇ *n* [bark] aboiement *m*.
◇ *vi* aboyer.
◇ *onomat* ouah ouah.

woofer [ˈwʊfəʳ] *n* haut-parleur *m* de graves, woofer *m*.

wool [wʊl] ◇ *n* laine *f*; pure new ~ pure laine vierge; a ball of ~ une pelote de laine; she can't wear ~ next to her skin elle ne peut pas porter de laine à même la peau ❑ all ~ and a yard wide *inf Am* de première classe, de premier ordre; to pull the ~ over sb's eyes berner OR duper qqn.
◇ *adj* [cloth] de laine; [socks, dress] en laine.

woolen *Am* = **woollen**.

wool fat *n* lanoline *f*.

woolgatherer [ˈwʊl,gæðərəʳ] *n* rêvasseur *m*, -euse *f*, rêveur *m*, -euse *f*.

woolgathering [ˈwʊl,gæðərɪŋ] *n*: to be OR to go ~ rêvasser.

woolgrower [ˈwʊl,grəʊəʳ] *n* éleveur *m*, -euse *f* de moutons *(à laine)*.

woollen *Br*, **woolen** *Am* [ˈwʊlən] *adj* -**1.** [fabric] de laine; [jacket, gloves, blanket] en laine; ~ cloth lainage *m*, étoffe *f* de laine. -**2.** [industry] lainière; [manufacture] de lainages.
◆ **woollens** *Br*, **woolens** *Am npl* lainages *mpl*, vêtements *mpl* de laine.

woolly *Br*, **wooly** *Am* [ˈwʊlɪ] (*Br pl* woollies, *Am pl* woolies) ◇ *adj* -**1.** [socks, hat] en laine. -**2.** [sheep] laineux. -**3.** [clouds] cotonneux; [hair] frisé. -**4.** [vague - thinking, ideas] confus, flou.
◇ *n inf Br* [pullover] tricot *m*, lainage *m*; [dress] robe *f* en laine; winter woollies lainages *mpl* d'hiver.

woolly-headed *adj* [person] écervelé; [ideas] vague, confus.

woolly-minded *adj* à l'esprit confus.

woolpack [ˈwʊlpæk] *n* balle *f* de laine.

woolsack [ˈwʊlsæk] *n* POL: the ~ *coussin rouge sur lequel s'assoit le président de la Chambre des lords*.

wooly *Am* = **woolly**.

woops [ˈwʊps] = **whoops**.

woozy *inf* [ˈwuːzɪ] (*compar* woozier, *superl* wooziest) *adj* -**1.** [dazed] hébété, dans les vapes. -**2.** [sick]: to feel ~ avoir mal au cœur. -**3.** [from drink] éméché, pompette.

wop▽ [wɒp] *n terme injurieux désignant un Italien*, ≃ macaroni *mf*.

Worcester sauce [ˈwʊstəʳ] *n sauce épicée en bouteille*.

Worcs *written abbr of* Worcestershire.

word [wɜːd] ◇ *n* -**1.** [gen, LING & COMPUT - written] mot *m*; [- spoken] mot *m*, parole *f*; the written ~ l'écrit *m*, ce qui est écrit; the spoken ~ la parole, ce qui est dit; the ~s of a song les paroles d'une chanson; (what) fine ~s! *iron* quelles belles paroles!; what is the Russian ~ for "head"?, what is the ~ for "head" in Russian? comment dit-on «tête» en russe?; the Japanese have/don't have a ~ for it les Japonais ont un mot/n'ont pas de mot pour dire cela; she can't put her ideas/feelings into ~s elle ne trouve pas les mots pour exprimer ses idées/ce qu'elle ressent; I can't find (the) ~s to tell you how glad I am! je ne saurais vous dire à quel point je suis content!; there are no ~s to describe OR ~s cannot describe how I feel aucun mot ne peut décrire ce que je ressens; they left without (saying) a ~ ils sont partis sans (dire) un mot; with these ~s they left sur ces mots OR là-dessus, ils sont partis; lazy isn't the ~ for it! paresseux, c'est peu dire!; idle would be a better ~ oisif serait plus juste; he doesn't know the meaning of the ~ "generosity" *fig* il ne sait pas ce que veut dire le mot «générosité»; he's mad, there's no other ~ for it il est fou, il n'y a pas d'autre mot; I didn't understand a ~ of the lecture je n'ai pas compris un mot de la conférence; I don't believe a ~ of it! je n'en crois pas un mot!; that's my last OR final ~ on the matter c'est mon dernier mot (sur la question); those were his dying ~s ce sont les dernières paroles qu'il a prononcées avant de mourir; she said a few ~s of welcome/thanks elle a dit quelques mots de bienvenue/de remerciement; I gave him a few ~s of advice je lui ai donné quelques conseils; I gave him a few ~s of encouragement je lui ai dit quelques mots d'encouragement; can I give you a ~ of warning/advice? puis-je vous mettre en garde/conseiller?; he didn't say a ~ il n'a rien dit, il n'a pas dit un mot; and now a ~ from our sponsors et maintenant, voici un message publicitaire de nos sponsors; or ~s to that effect ou quelque chose comme cela, ou du moins cela revenait au même; I'm a woman of few ~s je ne suis pas quelqu'un qui fait de grands discours; he's a man of few ~s c'est un homme peu loquace, c'est quelqu'un qui n'aime pas beaucoup parler; in the ~s of Shelley/Lenin comme l'a dit Shelley/Lénine; in the ~s of his boss, he's a layabout à en croire son patron OR d'après (ce que dit) son patron, c'est un fainéant; tell me in your own ~s dites-le moi à votre façon OR avec vos propres mots; he told me in so many ~s that I was a liar il m'a dit carrément OR sans mâcher ses mots que j'étais menteur; she didn't say it in so many ~s but her meaning was quite clear elle n'a pas dit exactement cela, mais c'était sous-entendu; by OR through ~ of mouth oralement; the news spread by ~ of mouth la nouvelle se répandit de bouche à oreille; too beautiful for ~s d'une beauté extraordinaire; too stupid for ~s vraiment trop bête; ~ for ~ [translate] littéralement, mot à mot; [repeat] mot pour mot ❑ from the ~ go dès le départ; (upon) my ~! ma parole!, oh la la!; to put ~s into sb's mouth: don't put ~s into my mouth ne me faites pas dire ce que je n'ai pas dit; he took the ~s out of my mouth il a dit exactement ce que j'allais dire; ~s fail me! j'en perds la parole!, je suis stupéfait!; he never has a good ~ to say about anyone personne ne trouve jamais grâce à ses yeux; to put in a (good) ~ for sb glisser un mot en faveur de qqn; to have the last ~ avoir le dernier mot; it's the last ~ in comfort *Br* c'est ce qui se fait de mieux en matière de confort; it's the last ~ in luxury *Br* c'est ce qu'on fait de plus luxueux. -**2.** [talk] mot *m*, mots *mpl*, parole *f*, paroles *fpl*; to have a ~ with sb about sthg toucher un mot OR deux mots à qqn au sujet de qqch; can I have a ~ with you about the meeting? est-ce que je peux vous dire deux mots à propos de OR vous parler de la réunion?; can I have a ~? je voudrais vous parler un instant. -**3.** *(U)* [news] nouvelle *f*, nouvelles *fpl*; [message] message *m*, mot *m*; the ~ got out that there had been a coup la nouvelle d'un coup d'État a circulé; ~ came from Tokyo that the strike was over la nouvelle arriva de Tokyo que la grève était terminée; she brought them ~ of Tom elle leur a apporté des nouvelles de Tom; have you had any ~ from him? avez-vous eu de ses nouvelles?; we have had no ~ from him nous sommes sans nouvelles de lui; she left ~ for us to follow elle nous a laissé un message pour dire que nous devions la suivre; spread the ~ that Mick's back in town faites passer la nouvelle OR faites dire que Mick est de retour en ville; he sent ~ to say he had arrived safely il a envoyé un mot pour dire qu'il était bien arrivé. -**4.** [promise] parole *f*, promesse *f*; he gave his ~ that we wouldn't be harmed il a donné sa parole qu'il ne nous ferait aucun mal; I give you my ~ on it je vous en donne ma parole; she gave her solemn ~ elle a juré OR promis solennellement; to break one's ~ manquer à sa parole; to go back on one's ~ revenir sur sa parole; we held OR kept her to her ~ nous l'avons obligée à tenir sa parole; to keep one's ~ tenir parole, tenir (sa) promesse; he was as good as his ~ il a tenu parole; she's a woman of her ~ c'est une femme de parole; I'm a man of my ~ je suis un homme de parole; ~ of honour! parole d'honneur!; we only have his ~ for it il n'y a que lui qui le dit, personne ne peut prouver le contraire; you can take my ~ for it vous pouvez me croire sur parole; we'll have to take your ~ for it nous sommes bien obligés de vous croire; take my ~ (for it), it's a bargain! croyez-moi, c'est une affaire!; I took her at her ~ je l'ai prise au mot; it's your ~ against mine c'est votre parole contre la mienne; my ~ is my bond je n'ai qu'une parole, je tiens toujours parole. -**5.** [advice] conseil *m*; a ~ to travellers, watch your luggage! un petit conseil aux voyageurs, surveillez vos bagages!; a quick ~ in your ear je vous glisse un mot à l'oreille; a ~ to the wise à bon entendeur, salut. -**6.** [rumour] bruit *m*; (the) ~ went round that he was dying le bruit a couru qu'il était sur le point de mourir. -**7.** [order] ordre *m*; he gave the ~ to march il a donné l'ordre OR le signal de se mettre en marche; his ~ is law c'est lui qui fait la loi; just give OR say the ~ and we'll be off vous n'avez qu'à donner le signal et nous partons. -**8.** [watchword] mot *m* d'ordre; the ~ now is "democracy" le mot d'ordre maintenant, c'est «démocratie» ‖ [password] mot *m* de passe.
◇ *vt* -**1.** [letter, document] rédiger, formuler; [contract] rédiger; they ~ed the petition carefully ils ont choisi les termes de la pétition avec le plus grand soin; we sent a strongly ~ed protest nous avons envoyé une lettre de protestation bien sentie. -**2.** *inf Austr* [advise] conseiller; [inform] informer.
◆ **Word** *n* RELIG: the Word le Verbe; the Word of God la parole de Dieu.
◆ **words** *inf npl Br* [argument] dispute *f*; to have ~s se disputer, avoir des mots; they had ~s about her drinking ils se sont disputés sur le fait qu'elle boit.
◆ **in a word** *adv phr* en un mot.
◆ **in other words** *adv phr* autrement dit, en d'autres termes.

word association *n* association *f* d'idées par les mots.

word-blind *adj Br* dyslexique.
word-blindness *n Br* dyslexie *f*.
wordbook [ˈwɜːdbʊk] *n* lexique *m*, vocabulaire *m*.
word class *n* LING classe *f* de mots.
word count *n* calcul *m* des mots.
word-for-word *adj* [repetition, imitation] mot pour mot; it's a ~ translation c'est une traduction littérale, c'est du mot à mot.
word game *n jeu de vocabulaire (sans support écrit)*.
wordiness [ˈwɜːdɪnɪs] *n* verbosité *f*.
wording [ˈwɜːdɪŋ] *n* *(U)* -**1.** [of letter, speech] termes *mpl*, formulation *f*; [of contract] termes *mpl*; I think you should change the ~ of the last sentence je crois que vous devriez reformuler la dernière phrase; the new ~ sounds better la nouvelle formulation sonne mieux; the ~ is rather strange c'est bizarrement formulé. -**2.** ADMIN & JUR rédaction *f*; I don't really understand the ~ of the contract je ne comprends pas vraiment les termes du contrat.
wordless [ˈwɜːdlɪs] *adj* -**1.** *lit* [silent - admiration] muet. -**2.** [without words - music] sans paroles.
wordlist [ˈwɜːdlɪst] *n* [in notebook, textbook] lexique *m*, liste *f* de mots; [in dictionary] nomenclature *f*.
word-of-mouth *adj* [account] oral, verbal.
word order *n* ordre *m* des mots.
word-perfect *adj* [recitation] que l'on connaît parfaitement OR sur le bout des doigts; she rehearsed her speech until she was ~ elle a répété son discours jusqu'à le connaître parfaitement OR sur le bout des doigts.
wordplay [ˈwɜːdpleɪ] *n* *(U)* jeu *m* de mots.
word-process ◇ *vi* faire de la saisie. ◇ *vt* [text] saisir.
word processing *n* traitement *m* de texte.
word processor *n* machine *f* de traitement de texte.
wordsmith [ˈwɜːdsmɪθ] *n* manieur *m* de mots.
word wrapping *n* COMPUT mise à la ligne *f* automatique des mots.
wordy [ˈwɜːdɪ] *adj* verbeux.
wore [wɔːʳ] *pt* → **wear**.
work [wɜːk] ◇ *n* -**1.** [effort, activity] travail *m*, œuvre *f*; computers take some of the ~ out of filing les ordinateurs facilitent le classement; this report needs more ~ il y a encore du travail à faire sur ce rapport, ce rapport demande plus de travail; she's done a lot of ~ for charity elle a beaucoup travaillé pour des associations caritatives; keep up the good ~! continuez comme ça!; nice ~! c'est du bon travail!; that's fine ~ OR a fine piece of ~ c'est du beau travail; your ~ has been useful vous avez fait du travail utile; ~ on the tunnel is to start in March [existing tunnel] les travaux sur le tunnel doivent commencer en mars; [new tunnel] la construction du tunnel doit commencer OR le tunnel doit être commencé en mars; '~ in progress' 'travaux en cours'; she put a lot of ~ into that book elle a beaucoup travaillé sur ce livre; to start ~, to set to ~ se mettre au travail; she set OR went to ~ on the contract elle a commencé à travailler sur le contrat; he set to ~ undermining their confidence il a entrepris de saper leur confiance; I set him to ~ (on) painting the kitchen je lui ai donné la cuisine à peindre; let's get (down) to ~! (mettons-nous) au travail! ❑ all ~ and no play makes Jack a dull boy *prov* beaucoup de travail et peu de loisirs ne réussissent à personne. -**2.** [duty, task] travail *m*, besogne *f*; I've got loads of ~ to do j'ai énormément de travail à faire; she gave us too much ~ elle nous a donné trop de travail; he's trying to get some ~ done il essaie de travailler un peu; they do their ~ well ils travaillent bien, ils font du bon travail; it's hard ~ c'est du travail, ce n'est pas facile; it's thirsty ~ ça donne soif ❑ to make short OR light ~ of sthg expédier qqch; to make short ~ of sb *fig* ne faire qu'une bouchée de qqn; it's nice ~ if you can get it! *inf* c'est une bonne planque, encore faut-il la trouver!; he's got his ~ cut out il a du pain sur la planche. -**3.** [paid employment] travail *m*, emploi *m*; what (kind of) ~ do you do? qu'est-ce que vous faites dans la vie?, quel travail faites-vous?; I do translation ~ je suis traducteur, je fais des traductions; to find ~ trouver du travail; to look for ~ chercher du travail OR un emploi; to be in ~ travailler, avoir un emploi; to be out of ~ être au chômage OR sans travail OR sans emploi; he had a week off ~ [holiday] il a pris une semaine de vacances; [illness] il n'est pas allé au travail pendant une semaine; to take time off ~ prendre des congés; she's off ~ today elle ne travaille pas aujourd'hui; factory/office ~ travail d'usine/de bureau; to do a full day's ~ faire une journée entière de travail; people out of ~ [gen] les chômeurs *mpl*; ADMIN & ECON les inactifs *mpl*. -**4.** [place of employment] travail *m*; ADMIN lieu *m* de travail; I go to ~ by bus je vais au travail en bus; I'm late for ~ je suis en retard pour le travail; he's a friend from ~ c'est un collègue; where is your (place of) ~? où travaillez-vous?, quel est votre lieu de travail?; on her way home from ~ en rentrant du travail. -**5.** [papers, material etc being worked on] travail *m*; to take ~ home prendre du travail à la maison; her ~ was all over the table son travail était étalé sur la table. -**6.** [creation, artefact etc] œuvre *f*; [on smaller scale] ouvrage *m*; SEW ouvrage *m*; it's all my own ~ j'ai tout fait moi-même; it's an interesting piece of ~ [gen] c'est un travail intéressant; ART, LITERAT & MUS c'est une œuvre intéressante; these formations are the ~ of the wind ces formations sont l'œuvre du vent; her life's ~ l'œuvre de sa vie; the silversmith sells much of his ~ to hotels l'orfèvre vend une grande partie de ce qu'il fait OR de son travail à des hôtels; the complete ~s of Shakespeare les œuvres complètes OR l'œuvre de Shakespeare; a new ~ on Portugal un nouvel ouvrage sur le Portugal; a ~ of art une œuvre d'art; ~s of fiction des ouvrages de fiction. -**7.** [research] travail *m*, recherches *fpl*; there hasn't been a lot of ~ done on the subject peu de travail a été fait OR peu de recherches ont été faites sur le sujet. -**8.** [deed] œuvre *f*, acte *m*; good ~s bonnes œuvres; each man will be judged by his ~s chaque homme sera jugé selon ses œuvres; charitable ~s actes de charité, actes charitables; the murder is the ~ of a madman le meurtre est l'œuvre d'un fou. -**9.** [effect] effet *m*; wait until the medicine has done its ~ attendez que le médicament ait agi OR ait produit son effet. -**10.** PHYS travail *m*.
◇ *vi* **A.** -**1.** [exert effort on a specific task, activity etc] travailler; we ~ed for hours cleaning the house nous avons passé des heures à faire le ménage; they ~ed in the garden ils ont fait du jardinage; we ~ hard nous travaillons dur; to ~ at OR on sthg: she's ~ing on a novel just now elle travaille à un roman en ce moment; he ~s at OR on keeping himself fit il fait de l'exercice pour garder la forme; we have to ~ to a deadline nous devons respecter des délais dans notre travail; we have to ~ to a budget nous devons travailler avec un certain budget; I've ~ed with the handicapped before j'ai déjà travaillé avec les handicapés; I ~ with the Spanish on that project je travaille (en collaboration) avec les Espagnols sur ce projet. -**2.** [be employed] travailler; he ~s as a teacher il a un poste d'enseignant; I ~ in advertising je travaille dans la publicité; she ~s in OR for a bank elle travaille dans OR pour une banque; I ~ a forty-hour week je travaille quarante heures par semaine, je fais une semaine de quarante heures; to ~ for a living travailler pour gagner sa vie; to ~ to rule INDUST faire la grève du zèle. -**3.** [strive for a specific goal or aim]: to ~ for sthg: they're ~ing for better international relations ils s'efforcent d'améliorer les relations internationales. -**4.** [study] travailler, étudier; you're going to have to ~ if you want to pass the exam il va falloir que tu travailles OR étudies si tu veux avoir ton examen. -**5.** [use a specified substance] travailler; this sculptor ~s in OR with copper ce sculpteur travaille avec le cuivre; she has always ~ed in OR with watercolours elle a toujours travaillé avec de la peinture à l'eau.
B. -**1.** [function, operate - machine - brain, system] fonctionner, marcher; the lift doesn't ~ at night l'ascenseur ne marche pas la nuit; the lift never ~s l'ascenseur est toujours en panne; the radio ~s off batteries la radio fonctionne avec des piles; a pump ~ed by hand une pompe actionnée à la main OR manuellement; she sat still, her brain OR mind ~ing furiously elle était assise immobile, le cerveau en ébullition ‖ *fig*: everything ~ed smoothly tout s'est déroulé comme prévu; your idea just won't ~ ton idée ne peut pas marcher; this relationship isn't ~ing cette relation ne marche pas; that argument ~s both ways ce raisonnement est à double tranchant; how does the law ~ exactly? comment la loi fonctionne-t-elle exactement? -**2.** [produce results, succeed] marcher, réussir; it ~ed brilliantly ça a très bien marché; their scheme didn't ~ leur complot a échoué. -**3.** [drug, medicine] agir, produire OR faire son effet. -**4.** [act] agir; the acid ~s as a catalyst l'acide agit comme OR sert de catalyseur; events have ~ed against us/in our favour les événements ont agi contre nous/en notre faveur; I'm ~ing on the assumption that they'll sign the contract je pars du principe qu'ils signeront le contrat.
C. -**1.** [reach a condition or state gradually]: to ~ loose se desserrer; to ~ free se libérer; the nail ~ed through the sole of my shoe le clou est passé à travers la semelle de ma chaussure. -**2.** [face, mouth] se contracter, se crisper. -**3.** [ferment] fermenter.
◇ *vt* **A.** -**1.** [worker, employee] faire travailler; the boss ~s his staff hard le patron exige beaucoup de travail de ses employés; you ~ yourself too hard tu te surmènes; to ~ o.s. to death se tuer à la tâche ❑ to ~ one's fingers to the bone s'user au travail. -**2.** [pay for with labour or service]: they ~ed their passage to India ils ont payé leur passage en Inde en travaillant; I ~ed my way through college j'ai travaillé pour payer mes études à l'université. -**3.** [carry on activity in]: he ~s the southern sales area il travaille pour le service commercial de la région sud; the pollster ~ed both sides of the street le sondeur a enquêté des deux côtés de la rue; the candidate ~ed the crowd *fig* le candidat s'efforçait de soulever l'enthousiasme de la foule. -**4.** [achieve, accomplish]: the new policy will ~ major changes la nouvelle politique opérera OR entraînera des changements importants; the story ~ed its magic OR charm on the public l'histoire a enchanté le public; to ~ a spell on sb jeter un sort à qqn; to ~ miracles faire OR accomplir des miracles; to ~ wonders faire merveille; she has ~ed wonders with the children elle a fait des merveilles avec les enfants. -**5.** [make use of, exploit - land] travailler, cultiver; [- mine, quarry] exploiter, faire valoir.
B. -**1.** [operate] faire marcher, faire fonctionner; this switch ~s the furnace ce bouton actionne OR commande la chaudière; he knows how to ~ the drill il sait se servir de la perceuse. -**2.** [manoeuvre]: I ~ed the handle up and down j'ai remué la poignée de haut en bas ‖ [progress slowly]: I ~ed my way along the ledge j'ai longé la saillie avec précaution; he ~ed his way down/up the cliff il a descendu/monté la falaise lentement; the beggar ~ed his way towards us le mendiant s'est approché de nous. -**3.** *inf* [contrive] s'arranger; she managed to ~ a few days off elle s'est arrangée OR débrouillée pour avoir quelques jours de congé; I ~ed it OR ~ed things so that she's never alone j'ai fait en sorte qu'elle OR je me suis arrangé pour qu'elle ne soit jamais seule.
C. -**1.** [shape - leather, metal, stone] travailler, façonner; [- clay, dough] travailler, pétrir; [- object, sculpture] façonner; she ~ed the silver into

earrings elle a travaillé l'argent pour en faire des boucles d'oreilles; she ~ed a figure out of the wood elle a sculpté une silhouette dans le bois; ~ the putty into the right consistency travaillez le mastic pour lui donner la consistance voulue. -**2.** [excite, provoke]: the orator ~ed the audience into a frenzy l'orateur a enflammé OR galvanisé le public; she ~ed herself into a rage elle s'est mise dans une colère noire.

◆ **works** ◇ *npl* -**1.** [mechanism] mécanisme *m*, rouages *mpl*; [of clock] mouvement *m*; to foul up OR to gum up the ~s *inf* tout foutre en l'air. -**2.** CIV ENG [construction] travaux *mpl*; [installation] installations *fpl*; road ~s travaux; 'road ~s' 'travaux'; Minister/Ministry of Works ministre *m*/ministère *m* des Travaux publics.

◇ *n (+ sing verb)* -**1.** INDUST [factory] usine *f*; a printing ~s une imprimerie; a gas ~s une usine à gaz; price ex ~s prix *m* sortie usine. -**2.** *inf* [everything]: the (whole) ~s tout le bataclan OR le tralala; to shoot the ~s *Am* jouer le grand jeu; we shot the ~s on the project *Am* nous avons mis le paquet sur le projet; to give sb the ~s [special treatment] dérouler le tapis rouge pour qqn *fig*; [beating] passer qqn à tabac.

◆ **at work** ◇ *adj phr* -**1.** [person]: to be at ~ (on sthg/doing sthg) travailler (à qqch/faire qqch); he's at ~ on a new book il travaille à un nouveau livre; they're hard at ~ painting the house ils sont en plein travail, ils repeignent la maison. -**2.** [having an effect]: there are several factors at ~ here il y a plusieurs facteurs qui entrent en jeu OR qui jouent ici; there are evil forces at ~ des forces mauvaises sont en action.

◇ *adv phr* [at place of work]: she's at ~ [gen] elle est au travail; [office] elle est au bureau; [factory] elle est à l'usine; I'll phone you at ~ je t'appellerai au travail; we met at ~ on s'est connus au travail.

◆ **work away** *vi insep* travailler; while he ~ed away at fixing the furnace tandis qu'il travaillait à réparer la chaudière; we ~ed away all evening nous avons passé la soirée à travailler.

◆ **work down** *vi insep* glisser; her socks had ~ed down around her ankles ses chaussettes étaient tombées sur ses chevilles.

◆ **work in** *vt sep* -**1.** [incorporate] incorporer; ~ the ointment in thoroughly faites bien pénétrer la pommade; ~ the butter into the flour CULIN incorporez le beurre à la farine. -**2.** [insert] faire entrer OR introduire petit à petit; he ~ed in a few sly remarks about the boss il a réussi à glisser quelques réflexions sournoises sur le patron; I'll try and ~ the translation in some time this week [into schedule] j'essayerai de (trouver le temps de) faire la traduction dans le courant de la semaine.

◆ **work off** *vt sep* -**1.** [dispose of - fat, weight] se débarrasser de, éliminer; [- anxiety, frustration] passer, assouvir; I ~ed off my excess energy chopping wood j'ai dépensé mon trop-plein d'énergie en cassant du bois; he ~ed off his tensions by running il s'est défoulé en faisant du jogging. -**2.** [debt, obligation]: it took him three months to ~ off his debt il a dû travailler trois mois pour rembourser son emprunt.

◆ **work on** *vt insep* -**1.** [person] essayer de convaincre; we've been ~ing on him but he still won't go nous avons essayé de le persuader mais il ne veut toujours pas y aller; I'll ~ on her je vais m'occuper d'elle. -**2.** [task, problem]: the police are ~ing on who stole the jewels la police s'efforce de retrouver celui qui a volé les bijoux; have you got any ideas? — I'm ~ing on it as-tu des idées? — je cherche.

◆ **work out** ◇ *vt sep* -**1.** [discharge fully] acquitter en travaillant; to ~ out one's notice faire son préavis. -**2.** [solve - calculation, problem] résoudre; [- answer, total] trouver; [- puzzle] faire, résoudre; [- code] déchiffrer; have they ~ed out their differences? est-ce qu'ils ont réglé OR résolu leurs différends?; things will ~ themselves out les choses s'arrangeront toutes seules OR d'elles-mêmes. -**3.** [formulate - idea, plan] élaborer, combiner; [- agreement, details] mettre au point; to ~ out a solution trouver une solution; have you ~ed out yet when it's due to start? est-ce que tu sais quand ça doit commencer?; she had it all ~ed out elle avait tout planifié; we ~ed out an easier route nous avons trouvé un itinéraire plus facile. -**4.** [figure out] arriver à comprendre; I finally ~ed out why he was acting so strangely j'ai enfin découvert OR compris pourquoi il se comportait si bizarrement; I can't ~ her out je n'arrive pas à la comprendre; I can't ~ their relationship out leurs rapports me dépassent. -**5.** [mine, well] épuiser.

◇ *vi insep* -**1.** [happen] se passer; it depends on how things ~ out ça dépend de la façon dont les choses se passent; the trip ~ed out as planned le voyage s'est déroulé comme prévu; I wonder how it will all ~ out je me demande comment tout cela va s'arranger; it all ~ed out for the best tout a fini par s'arranger pour le mieux. -**2.** [have a good result - job, plan] réussir; [- problem, puzzle] se résoudre; she ~ed out fine as personnel director elle s'est bien débrouillée comme directeur du personnel; did the new job ~ out? ça a marché pour le nouveau boulot?; it didn't ~ out between them les choses ont plutôt mal tourné entre eux; their project didn't ~ out leur projet est tombé à l'eau. -**3.** [amount to]: the average price for an apartment ~s out to OR at $5,000 per square metre le prix moyen d'un appartement s'élève OR revient à 5 000 dollars le mètre carré; that ~s out at three hours a week ça fait trois heures par semaine; electric heating ~s out expensive le chauffage électrique revient cher. -**4.** [exercise] faire de l'exercice; [professional athlete] s'entraîner.

◆ **work over** *vt sep* -**1.** *Am* [revise] revoir, réviser. -**2.** *inf* [beat up] tabasser, passer à tabac.

◆ **work round** ◇ *vi insep* -**1.** [turn] tourner; the wind ~ed round to the north le vent a tourné au nord petit à petit. -**2.** *fig* [in conversation]: he finally ~ed round to the subject of housing il a fini par aborder le sujet du logement; what's she ~ing round to? où veut-elle en venir?

◇ *vt sep* [bring round]: I ~ed the conversation round to my salary j'ai amené la conversation sur la question de mon salaire.

◆ **work through** ◇ *vt sep* -**1.** [insert] faire passer à travers. -**2.** [progress through with effort]: we ~ed our way through the crowd nous nous sommes frayé un chemin à travers la foule; he ~ed his way through the book il a lu le livre du début à la fin; I ~ed the problem through *fig* j'ai étudié le problème sous tous ses aspects.

◇ *vt insep* -**1.** [continue to work]: she ~ed through lunch elle a travaillé pendant l'heure du déjeuner. -**2.** [resolve]: he ~ed through his emotional problems il a réussi à assumer ses problèmes affectifs.

◆ **work up** ◇ *vt sep* -**1.** [stir up, rouse] exciter, provoquer; he ~ed up the crowd il a excité la foule; he ~s himself up OR gets himself ~ed up over nothing il s'énerve pour rien. -**2.** [develop] développer; I want to ~ these ideas up into an article je veux développer ces idées pour en faire un article; to ~ up an appetite se mettre en appétit; we ~ed up a sweat/thirst playing tennis jouer au tennis nous a donné chaud/soif; I can't ~ up any enthusiasm for this work je n'arrive pas à avoir le moindre enthousiasme pour ce travail; he tried to ~ up an interest in the cause il a essayé de s'intéresser à la cause. -**3.** *phr*: to ~ one's way up faire son chemin; she ~ed her way up from secretary to managing director elle a commencé comme secrétaire et elle a fait son chemin jusqu'au poste de P-DG; I ~ed my way up from nothing je suis parti de rien.

◇ *vi insep* -**1.** [clothing] remonter. -**2.** [build up]: the film was ~ing up to a climax le film approchait de son point culminant; things were ~ing up to a crisis une crise se préparait, on était au bord d'une crise; she's ~ing up to what she wanted to ask elle en vient à ce qu'elle voulait demander; what are you ~ing up to? où veux-tu en venir?

workability [ˌwɜːkəˈbɪlətɪ] *n* -**1.** [of plan] caractère *m* réalisable *(d'un projet)*. -**2.** [of mine] caractère *m* exploitable *(d'une mine)*.

workable [ˈwɜːkəbl] *adj* -**1.** [plan, proposal] réalisable, faisable; do you really think it's ~? croyez-vous vraiment que c'est faisable OR que ça va marcher? -**2.** [mine, field] exploitable.

workaday [ˈwɜːkədeɪ] *adj* [clothes, routine] de tous les jours; [man] ordinaire, banal; [incident] courant, banal.

workaholic *inf* [ˌwɜːkəˈhɒlɪk] *n* bourreau *m* de travail, drogué *m*, -e *f* du travail.

work area *n* [in school, home] coin *m* de travail.

workbag [ˈwɜːkbæg] *n* sac *m* à ouvrage.

workbasket [ˈwɜːkˌbɑːskɪt] *n* corbeille *f* à ouvrage.

workbench [ˈwɜːkbentʃ] *n* établi *m*.

workbook [ˈwɜːkbʊk] *n* -**1.** SCH [exercise book] cahier *m* d'exercices; [record book] cahier *m* de classe. -**2.** [manual] manuel *m*.

workbox [ˈwɜːkbɒks] *n* boîte *f* à ouvrage.

work camp *n* -**1.** [prison] camp *m* de travail. -**2.** [voluntary] chantier *m* de travail.

work coat *n Am* blouse *f*.

workday [ˈwɜːkdeɪ] ◇ *n* -**1.** [day's work] journée *f* de travail. -**2.** [working day] jour *m* ouvré OR où l'on travaille; Sunday is a ~ for some people il y a des gens qui travaillent le dimanche.

◇ *adj* = **workaday**.

worked up [wɜːkt] *adj* énervé, dans tous ses états; to get ~ s'énerver, se mettre dans tous ses états.

worker [ˈwɜːkəʳ] *n* -**1.** [INDUST - gen] travailleur *m*, -euse *f*, employé *m*, -e *f*; [- manual] ouvrier *m*, -ère *f*, travailleur *m*, -euse *f*; relations between ~s and management les relations entre les travailleurs OR les employés et la direction; farm ~ ouvrier agricole; office ~ employé de bureau; part-time ~ travailleur à temps partiel; research ~ chercheur *m*; rescue ~ sauveteur *m*; he's a fast ~! il travaille vite!; she's a good ~ elle travaille bien; she's a hard ~ elle travaille dur. -**2.** ENTOM ouvrière *f*.

worker ant *n* (fourmi) ouvrière *f*.

worker bee *n* (abeille) ouvrière *f*.

worker director *n ouvrier qui fait partie du conseil d'administration*.

worker participation *n* participation *f* des travailleurs OR des ouvriers.

worker-priest *n* prêtre-ouvrier *m*.

work ethic *n exaltation des valeurs liées au travail*.

work experience *n*: the course includes two months' ~ le programme comprend un stage en entreprise de deux mois.

workforce [ˈwɜːkfɔːs] *n* main-d'œuvre *f*, effectifs *mpl*.

workhorse [ˈwɜːkhɔːs] *n* -**1.** [horse] cheval *m* de labour. -**2.** *fig* [worker] bourreau *m* de travail; [machine, vehicle] bonne mécanique *f*.

workhouse [ˈwɜːkhaʊs] (*pl* workhouses [-haʊzɪz]) *n* -**1.** [in UK] HIST hospice *m*. -**2.** [in US - prison] maison *f* de correction.

work-in *n occupation d'une entreprise par le personnel (avec poursuite du travail)*.

working [ˈwɜːkɪŋ] ◇ *adj* -**1.** [mother, wife] qui travaille; [population] actif; ordinary ~ people les travailleurs ordinaires; the party of the ~ man le parti des travailleurs. -**2.** [day, hours] de travail; Sunday is not a ~ day le dimanche est chômé, on ne travaille pas le dimanche; during a normal ~ day pendant la journée de travail; a ~ week of 40 hours une semaine de 40 heures; he spent his entire ~ life with the firm il a travaillé toute sa vie dans l'entreprise; to be of ~ age être en âge de travailler. -**3.** [clothes, conditions] de travail; we have a close ~ relationship nous travaillons bien ensemble. -**4.** [functioning - farm, factory, model] qui marche; in (good) ~ order en (bon) état de marche.

-**5.** [theory, definition] de travail; [majority] suffisant; [agreement] de circonstance; [knowledge] adéquat, suffisant.

◇ *n* -**1.** [work] travail *m.* -**2.** [operation - of machine] fonctionnement *m.* -**3.** [of mine] exploitation *f*; [of clay, leather] travail *m.*

◆ **workings** *npl* -**1.** [mechanism] mécanisme *m*; *fig* [of government, system] rouages *mpl*; it's difficult to understand the ~s of his mind il est difficile de savoir ce qu'il a dans la tête OR ce qui se passe dans sa tête. -**2.** MIN chantier *m* d'exploitation; old mine ~s anciennes mines *fpl*.

working capital *n (U)* fonds *mpl* de roulement.

working class *n*: the ~, the ~es la classe ouvrière, le prolétariat.

◆ **working-class** *adj* [district, origins] ouvrier; [accent] des classes populaires; she's ~ elle appartient à la classe ouvrière; a ~ hero un héros de la classe ouvrière OR du prolétariat.

working group = **working party**.

working lunch *n déjeuner pendant lequel on travaille*.

working man *n Br* ouvrier *m*.

working men's club *n club d'ouvriers, comportant un bar et une scène où sont présentés des spectacles de music-hall*.

working party *n* -**1.** [committee - for study] groupe *m* de travail; [- for enquiry] commission *f* d'enquête. -**2.** [group - of prisoners, soldiers] groupe *m* de travail.

working title *n* titre *m* provisoire.

working woman *n* -**1.** [worker] ouvrière *f*, employée *f*. -**2.** [woman with job] femme *f* qui travaille.

workload ['wɜːkləʊd] *n* travail *m* à effectuer, charge *f* de travail; my ~ has eased off a bit j'ai un peu moins de travail en ce moment; I still have a heavy ~ je suis encore surchargé de travail.

workman ['wɜːkmən] (*pl* workmen [-mən]) *n* -**1.** [manual worker] ouvrier *m*; the workmen came to fix the drainpipe les ouvriers sont venus réparer la gouttière ❑ a bad ~ blames his tools *prov* les mauvais ouvriers ont toujours de mauvais outils *prov*. -**2.** [craftsman] artisan *m*; he is a good ~ il travaille bien, il fait du bon travail.

workmanlike ['wɜːkmənlaɪk] *adj* -**1.** [efficient - approach, person] professionnel; she did the job in a ~ way elle a fait du très bon travail. -**2.** [well-made - artefact] bien fait, soigné; he wrote a ~ report il a fait un compte rendu très sérieux. -**3.** [serious - attempt, effort] sérieux.

workmanship ['wɜːkmənʃɪp] *n (U)* -**1.** [skill] métier *m*, maîtrise *f*. -**2.** [quality] exécution *f*, fabrication *f*; she admired the fine ~ of the carving elle admira le ciselage délicat; it was a shoddy piece of ~ c'était du travail mal fait OR bâclé.

workmate ['wɜːkmeɪt] *n* camarade *mf* de travail.

workout ['wɜːkaʊt] *n* séance *f* d'entraînement; to have a ~ s'entraîner physiquement, faire une séance d'entraînement.

work party *n* [of soldiers] escouade *f*; [of prisoners] groupe *m* de travail.

workpeople ['wɜːkˌpiːpl] *npl* travailleurs *mpl*.

work permit *n* permis *m* de travail.

workplace ['wɜːkpleɪs] *n* lieu *m* de travail; in the ~ sur le lieu de travail.

workroom ['wɜːkrʊm] *n* salle *f* de travail.

works band *n* fanfare *m (d'une entreprise)*.

works committee, **works council** *n* comité *m* d'entreprise.

work-sharing *n* partage *m* du travail.

work sheet *n* COMPUT feuille *f* de travail.

workshop ['wɜːkʃɒp] *n* -**1.** [INDUST & gen] atelier *m*. -**2.** [study group] atelier *m*, groupe *m* de travail.

workshy ['wɜːkʃaɪ] *adj* fainéant, tire-au-flanc *(inv)*.

works manager *n* directeur *m* d'usine.

work space *n* coin-travail *m*; I need more ~ j'ai besoin de plus d'espace pour travailler.

workstation ['wɜːkˌsteɪʃn] *n* COMPUT poste *m* OR station *f* de travail.

work-study *n* INDUST étude *f* des cadences.

work surface *n* surface *f* de travail.

worktable ['wɜːkˌteɪbl] *n* table *f* de travail.

worktop ['wɜːktɒp] *n* [in kitchen] plan *m* de travail.

work-to-rule *n Br* grève *f* du zèle.

work week *n Am* semaine *f* de travail.

world [wɜːld] ◇ *n* **A.** -**1.** [earth] monde *m*; to travel round the ~ faire le tour du monde, voyager autour du monde; to see the ~ voir du pays, courir le monde; throughout the ~ dans le monde entier; in this part of the ~ dans cette région; the best in the ~ le meilleur du monde; I'm the ~'s worst photographer il n'y a pas pire photographe que moi; the ~ over, all over the ~ dans le monde entier, partout dans le monde; love is the same the ~ over l'amour, c'est la même chose partout dans le monde. -**2.** [planet] monde *m*; there may be other ~s out there il existe peut-être d'autres mondes quelque part. -**3.** [universe] monde *m*, univers *m*; since the ~ began depuis que le monde existe.
B. -**1.** [part of the world] HIST & POL monde *m*; the Arab World le monde arabe; the developing ~ les pays en voie de développement; the Gaelic-speaking ~ les régions où l'on parle le gaélique; the Spanish-speaking ~ le monde hispanophone. -**2.** [society] monde *m*; she wants to change the ~ elle veut changer le monde; in the modern ~ dans le monde moderne; to go up/down in the ~: she's gone up in the ~ elle a fait du chemin; he's gone down in the ~ il a connu de meilleurs jours; to come into the ~ venir au monde; to bring a child into the ~ mettre un enfant au monde; they hesitated to bring children into the ~ ils hésitaient à avoir des enfants; to make one's way in the ~ faire son chemin; you have to take the ~ as you find it il faut prendre les choses comme elles viennent. -**3.** [general public] monde *m*; the ~ awaits the outcome of the talks le monde entier attend le résultat des pourparlers; the news shook the ~ la nouvelle a ébranlé le monde entier || [people in general]: we don't want the whole ~ to know nous ne voulons pas que tout le monde le sache; (all) the ~ and his wife *fig* le monde entier.
C. -**1.** [existence, particular way of life] monde *m*, vie *f*; a whole new ~ opened up to me un monde nouveau s'ouvrit à moi; we live in different ~s nous ne vivons pas sur la même planète; to be ~s apart [in lifestyle] avoir des styles de vie complètement différents; [in opinions] avoir des opinions complètement différentes || [realm] monde *m*; he lives in a ~ of his own il vit dans un monde à lui; a nightmare/fantasy ~ un monde de cauchemar/de rêve; the child's ~ l'univers des enfants; they knew nothing of the ~ outside ils ignoraient tout du monde extérieur; the underwater ~ le monde sous-marin. -**2.** [field, domain] monde *m*, milieu *m*, milieux *mpl*; she is well known in the theatre ~ elle est connue dans le milieu du théâtre; the publishing ~ le monde de l'édition. -**3.** [group of living things] monde *m*; the animal/plant ~ le règne animal/végétal. -**4.** RELIG monde *m*; to renounce the ~ renoncer au monde; in this ~ and the next dans ce monde (-ci) et dans l'autre; he isn't long for this ~ il n'en a pas pour longtemps; ~ without end *arch* OR BIBLE pour les siècles des siècles. -**5.** *phr*: a holiday will do you a OR the ~ of good des vacances vous feront le plus grand bien; it made a ~ of difference ça a tout changé; there's a ~ of difference between them il y a un monde entre eux; he thinks the ~ of his daughter il a une admiration sans bornes pour sa fille; it means the ~ to me c'est quelque chose qui me tient beaucoup à cœur.

◇ *comp* [champion, record] mondial, du monde; [language, religion] universel; ~ peace la paix mondiale; the ~ population la population mondiale; a ~ power une puissance mondiale; ~ opinion l'opinion internationale; on a ~ scale à l'échelle mondiale.

◆ **for all the world** *adv phr* exactement; she behaved for all the ~ as if she owned the place elle faisait exactement comme si elle était chez elle.

◆ **for the world** *adv phr*: I wouldn't hurt her for the ~ je ne lui ferais de mal pour rien au monde.

◆ **in the world** *adv phr* -**1.** [for emphasis]: nothing in the ~ would change my mind rien au monde ne me ferait changer d'avis; I felt as if I hadn't a care in the ~ je me sentais libre de tout souci; we've got all the time in the ~ nous avons tout le OR tout notre temps; all the good intentions in the ~ won't bring her back on ne la ramènera pas, même avec les meilleures intentions du monde; I wouldn't do it for all the money in the ~! je ne le ferais pas pour tout l'or du monde! -**2.** [expressing surprise, irritation, frustration]: who in the ~ will believe you? qui donc va vous croire?; where in the ~ have you put it? où l'avez-vous donc mis?; what in the ~ made you do it? pourquoi donc avez-vous fait ça?; why in the ~ didn't you tell me? pourquoi donc ne me l'as-tu pas dit?

◆ **out of this world** *inf adj phr* extraordinaire, sensationnel.

World Bank *pr n* Banque *f* mondiale.

world-beater *inf n Br* [person] champion *m*, -onne *f*; this new car is going to be a ~ *fig* cette nouvelle voiture va faire un tabac.

world-class *adj* [player, runner] parmi les meilleurs du monde, de classe internationale.

World Cup *pr n*: the ~ la Coupe du monde.

World Fair *pr n* exposition *f* universelle.

world-famous *adj* de renommée mondiale, célèbre dans le monde entier.

World Health Organization *pr n* Organisation *f* mondiale de la santé.

worldliness ['wɜːldlɪnɪs] *n* -**1.** [materialism] matérialisme *m*. -**2.** [experience of the world] mondanité *f*.

worldly ['wɜːldlɪ] (*compar* worldlier, *superl* worldliest) *adj* -**1.** [material - possessions, pleasures, matters] matériel, de ce monde, terrestre; RELIG temporel, de ce monde; he is not interested in ~ things les choses de ce monde ne l'intéressent pas; all my ~ goods tout ce que je possède au monde. -**2.** [materialistic - person, outlook] matérialiste. -**3.** [sophisticated - person] qui a l'expérience du monde; [- attitude, manner] qui démontre une expérience du monde.

worldly-wise *adj* qui a l'expérience du monde.

world music *n* world music *f*.

world power *n* puissance *f* mondiale.

World Series *n*: the ~ *le championnat américain de base-ball*.

World Service *pr n* RADIO *service étranger de la BBC*.

world-shaking [ʃeɪkɪŋ] *adj* stupéfiant, d'une importance considérable.

world-shattering *adj* [event, news] renversant, bouleversant.

world view *n vue métaphysique du monde*.

world war *n* guerre *f* mondiale; the First/Second World War la Première/la Seconde Guerre mondiale.

world-weariness *n* dégoût *m* du monde, ennui *m*.

world-weary *adj* [person] las du monde.

worldwide ['wɜːldwaɪd] ◇ *adj* [depression, famine, reputation] mondial.

◇ *adv* partout dans le monde, dans le monde entier.

worm [wɜːm] ◇ *n* -**1.** [in earth, garden] ver *m* (de terre); [in fruit] ver *m*; [for fishing] ver *m*, asticot *m*; the ~ has turned *Br* il en a eu assez de se faire marcher dessus. -**2.** [parasite - in body] ver *m*; to have ~s avoir des vers. -**3.** *inf fig* [person] minable *mf*; what a ~! quel minable!

-**4.** *lit* [troublesome thing] tourment *m*, tourments *mpl*; the ~ of jealousy/remorse les affres de la jalousie/du remords.

◇ *vt* -**1.** [move]: to ~ one's way under sthg passer sous qqch à plat ventre OR en rampant; she ~ed her way through a gap in the fence en se tortillant elle s'est faufilée par une ouverture dans la palissade; he managed to ~ his way to the front il a réussi à se faufiler jusqu'à l'avant. -**2.** *pej* [sneak]: they have ~ed their way into our party ils se sont infiltrés OR immiscés dans notre parti; he ~ed his way into her affections il a trouvé le chemin de son cœur *(par sournoiserie)*. -**3.** [dog, sheep] débarrasser de ses vers.

◆ **worm out** *vt sep* [information] soutirer; I tried to ~ the truth out of him j'ai essayé de lui soutirer la vérité; he'll ~ it out of her eventually il finira par lui tirer les vers du nez.

worm cast *n* déjections *fpl* de ver.

worm drive *n* TECH transmission *f* par vis sans fin.

worm-eaten *adj* [apple] véreux; [furniture] vermoulu, mangé aux vers; *fig* [ancient] désuet, antédiluvien.

worm gear *n* TECH engrenage *m* de vis sans fin.

wormhole ['wɜːmhəʊl] *n* trou *m* de ver.

worm's-eye view *n* PHOT & CIN contre-plongée *f*; he presents a ~ of events *fig* il nous présente les événements vus par les humbles.

wormwood ['wɜːmwʊd] *n* -**1.** [plant] armoise *f*. -**2.** *lit* [bitterness] fiel *m*, amertume *f*.

Wormwood Scrubs ['wɜːmwʊd-] *pr n prison pour hommes faisant l'objet d'une première condamnation.*

wormy ['wɜːmɪ] (*compar* wormier, *superl* wormiest) *adj* -**1.** [apple] véreux; [furniture] vermoulu, piqué aux vers. -**2.** [soil] plein de vers. -**3.** [in shape] vermiculaire.

worn [wɔːn] ◇ *pp* → **wear**.

◇ *adj* -**1.** [shoes, rug, tyre] usé. -**2.** [weary - person] las.

worn-out *adj* -**1.** [shoes, tyre] complètement usé; [rug, dress] usé jusqu'à la corde; [battery] usé. -**2.** [person] épuisé, éreinté.

worried ['wʌrɪd] *adj* [person, look] inquiet; I'm ~ that they may get lost OR in case they get lost j'ai peur qu'ils ne se perdent; to be ~ about sthg/sb être inquiet pour qqch/qqn; she's ~ about the future elle est inquiète pour l'avenir; a ~ frown un froncement inquiet des sourcils; I'm ~ about him je suis inquiet OR je m'inquiète pour lui; to be ~ sick OR to death (about sb) être fou OR malade d'inquiétude (pour qqn); you had me ~ for a minute vous m'avez fait peur pendant une minute; I'm not ~ either way ça m'est égal.

worriedly ['wʌrɪdlɪ] *adv* [say] avec un air inquiet.

worrier ['wʌrɪə^r] *n* anxieux *m*, -euse *f*, inquiet *m*, -ète *f*; he's a born ~ c'est un éternel inquiet.

worriment *inf* ['wʌrɪmənt] *n Am* inquiétude *f*.

worrisome ['wʌrɪsəm] *adj dated* inquiétant.

worry ['wʌrɪ] (*pt & pp* worried, *pl* worries) ◇ *vt* -**1.** [make anxious] inquiéter, tracasser; you really worried me je me suis vraiment inquiété à cause de toi; he was worried by her sudden disappearance il était inquiet de sa disparition subite; I sometimes ~ that they'll never be found parfois je crains qu'on ne les retrouve jamais; she is ~ing herself to death about it elle en est malade d'inquiétude; nothing seems to ~ her rien ne semble l'inquiéter OR la tracasser; what's ~ing you? qu'est-ce qui vous tracasse?; don't ~ your head *inf* OR yourself about the details ne vous inquiétez pas pour les détails. -**2.** [disturb, bother] inquiéter, ennuyer; why ~ him with your problems? pourquoi l'ennuyer avec vos problèmes?; it doesn't ~ me if you want to waste your life cela m'est égal OR ne me gêne pas si vous voulez gâcher votre vie. -**3.** [subj: dog - bone, ball] prendre entre les dents et secouer; [- sheep] harceler.

◇ *vi* s'inquiéter, se faire du souci, se tracasser; to ~ about OR over sthg s'inquiéter pour OR au sujet de qqch; she has enough to ~ about elle a assez de soucis comme ça; there's nothing to ~ about il n'y a pas lieu de s'inquiéter; don't ~ ne vous inquiétez OR tracassez pas; they'll be found, don't you ~ on va les trouver, ne vous en faites pas; stop ~ing! ne vous inquiétez pas comme ça!, ne vous en faites donc pas!; not to ~! ce n'est pas grave!; YOU should ~ *iron* ce n'est pas votre problème, il n'y a pas de raisons de vous en faire.

◇ *n* -**1.** [anxiety] inquiétude *f*, souci *m*; money is a constant source of ~ l'argent est un perpétuel souci OR une perpétuelle source d'inquiétude; her sons are a constant ~ to her ses fils lui causent constamment des soucis OR du souci; he was sick with ~ about her il se rongeait les sangs pour elle OR à son sujet. -**2.** [concern] sujet *m* d'inquiétude, souci *m*; [problem] problème *m*; my greatest ~ is my health mon plus grand souci c'est ma santé; he doesn't seem to have any worries il n'a pas l'air d'avoir de soucis; it's a real ~ for her cela la tracasse vraiment; that's my ~ c'est mon problème; that's the least of my worries c'est le moindre OR le cadet OR le dernier de mes soucis; no worries! *inf* pas de problème!

◆ **worry at** *vt insep Br* = **worry** *vt* **3**.

◆ **worry out** *vt sep Br* [problem] résoudre à force de considérer sous tous ses aspects; [answer] trouver à force de chercher.

worry beads *npl chapelet de billes avec lequel on joue pour se relaxer.*

worryguts *inf* ['wʌrɪgʌts] *n Br* anxieux *m*, -euse *f*, éternel inquiet *m*, éternelle inquiète *f*.

worrying ['wʌrɪɪŋ] ◇ *adj* inquiétant; the ~ thing is that it could happen again ce qu'il y a d'inquiétant OR ce qui est inquiétant, c'est que cela pourrait se reproduire.

◇ *n* inquiétude *f*; ~ won't solve anything cela ne résoudra rien de se faire du souci.

worryingly ['wʌrɪɪŋlɪ] *adv*: the project is ~ late le projet a pris un retard inquiétant.

worrywart *inf* ['wʌrɪwɔːt] *Am* = **worryguts**.

worse [wɜːs] (*compar of* bad, *adv compar of* badly) ◇ *adj* -**1.** [not as good, pleasant as] pire, plus mauvais; the news is even ~ than we expected les nouvelles sont encore plus mauvaises que nous ne pensions; your writing is ~ than mine votre écriture est pire que la mienne; my writing is bad, but yours is ~ j'écris mal, mais vous, c'est pire; the rain is ~ than ever il pleut de plus en plus; things are ~ than you imagine les choses vont plus mal que vous l'imaginez; it could have been ~! ça aurait pu être pire!; I lost my money, and ~ still OR and what's ~, my passport j'ai perdu mon argent, et ce qui est plus grave, mon passeport; ~ than before/than ever pire qu'avant/que jamais; ~ than useless complètement inutile; to get OR to grow ~ empirer, s'aggraver; to get ~ and ~ aller de mal en pis; conditions got ~ les conditions se sont aggravées OR détériorées; his drug problem got ~ son problème de drogue ne s'est pas arrangé; things will get ~ before they get better les choses ne sont pas près de s'améliorer; his memory is getting ~ sa mémoire est de moins en moins bonne; she's only making things OR matters ~ for herself elle ne fait qu'aggraver son cas; and, to make matters ~, he swore at the policeman *iron* et pour tout arranger, il a insulté le policier; to make things ~, I lost my camera *iron* et pour tout arranger, j'ai perdu mon appareil photo ❑ ~ things happen at sea! on a vu pire!, ce n'est pas la fin du monde!; ~ luck! *inf* quelle poisse! -**2.** [in health] plus mal; I feel ~ je me sens encore plus mal OR encore moins bien; her headache got ~ son mal de tête s'est aggravé; you'll only get ~ if you go out in this awful weather ton état ne peut que s'aggraver si tu sors par ce temps. -**3.** *phr*: this carpet is looking rather the ~ for wear cette moquette est plutôt défraîchie; he's looking/feeling rather the ~ for wear [tired, old] il n'a pas l'air/il ne se sent pas très frais; [drunk] il a l'air/il se sent plutôt éméché; [ill] il n'a pas l'air/il ne se sent pas très bien; he was rather the ~ for drink il était plutôt éméché.

◇ *adv* -**1.** [less well] plus mal, moins bien; he behaved ~ than ever il ne s'est jamais aussi mal conduit; you could OR might do ~ than (to) marry him l'épouser, ce n'est pas ce que vous pourriez faire de pire; she doesn't think any the ~ of her for it elle ne l'en estime pas moins pour ça. -**2.** [more severely - snow, rain] plus fort.

◇ *n* pire *m*; there's ~ to come, ~ is to come [in situation] le pire est à venir; [in story] il y a pire encore; ~ was to follow le pire était encore à venir; there's been a change for the ~ les choses se sont aggravées; to take a turn for the ~ [health, situation] se détériorer, se dégrader; the economy has taken a turn for the ~ la situation économique s'est aggravée; the patient has taken a turn for the ~ l'état du patient s'est aggravé.

◆ **none the worse** *adj phr* pas plus mal; he's apparently none the ~ for his drinking session last night il n'a pas l'air de se ressentir de sa beuverie d'hier soir; the little girl is none the ~ for the experience la petite fille ne se ressent pas de son expérience.

worsen ['wɜːsn] ◇ *vi* [depression, crisis, pain, illness] empirer, s'aggraver; [weather, situation] se gâter, se détériorer.

◇ *vt* [situation] empirer, rendre pire.

worsening ['wɜːsnɪŋ] ◇ *adj* [situation] qui empire; [health] qui se détériore; [weather] qui se gâte OR se détériore.

◇ *n* aggravation *f*, détérioration *f*.

worse-off ◇ *adj* -**1.** [financially] moins riche, plus pauvre; tax increases mean we are ~ than before les augmentations d'impôts signifient que nous avons moins d'argent qu'auparavant; I am ~ than I was ma situation financière est pire OR moins bonne qu'avant. -**2.** [in worse state] dans une situation moins favorable; the country is no ~ for having a coalition government le pays ne se porte pas plus mal d'avoir un gouvernement de coalition.

◇ *npl*: the ~ les pauvres *mpl*, les moins nantis *mpl*.

worship ['wɜːʃɪp] (*Br pt & pp* worshipped, *cont* worshipping, *Am pt & pp* worshiped, *cont* worshiping) ◇ *n* -**1.** RELIG [service] culte *m*, office *m*; [liturgy] liturgie *f*; [adoration] adoration *f*; church ~ office religieux; an act of ~ [veneration] un acte de dévotion; [service] un culte, un office; freedom of ~ la liberté de culte; places of ~ les lieux du culte. -**2.** *fig* [veneration] adoration *f*, culte *m*; the rock star has become an object of ~ la rock star est devenue un véritable objet de culte; the ~ of wealth and power le culte de l'argent et du pouvoir.

◇ *vt* -**1.** RELIG adorer, vénérer; ~ the Lord! adorez OR vénérez le Seigneur!; they worshipped Venus ils rendaient un culte à Vénus, ils adoraient Vénus. -**2.** [person] adorer, vénérer; [money, possessions] vouer un culte à, avoir le culte de; he ~s his mother il adore sa mère; they worshipped the ground she walked on ils vénéraient jusqu'au sol sur lequel elle marchait.

◇ *vi* faire ses dévotions; the church where she worshipped for 10 years l'église où elle a fait ses dévotions pendant 10 ans; they worshipped at the temple of Apollo ils faisaient leurs dévotions au temple d'Apollon; to ~ at the altar of success *fig* vouer un culte au succès.

◆ **Worship** *n Br fml* [in titles]: His Worship the Mayor monsieur le Maire.

YOUR WORSHIP:

Cette expression est utilisée pour s'adresser à certains magistrats, notamment à un juge (= monsieur le Juge) ou à un maire (= monsieur le Maire).

---

worshiper *Am* = **worshipper**.

worshipful ['wɜːʃɪpfʊl] *adj* -**1.** [respectful] respectueux. -**2.** *Br fml* [in titles]: the Worshipful Mayor of Portsmouth monsieur le Maire de Portsmouth; the Worshipful Company of

Mercers l'honorable compagnie des marchands de tissus.

worshipper *Br*, **worshiper** *Am* [ˈwɜːʃɪpəʳ] *n* -**1.** RELIG adorateur *m*, -trice *f*, fidèle *mf*; **thousands of ~s came to the shrine** des milliers d'adorateurs sont venus au lieu saint; **the ~s take off their shoes** les fidèles enlèvent leurs chaussures. -**2.** *fig* [of possessions, person] adorateur *m*, -trice *f*.

worst [wɜːst] (*adj superl of* bad, *adv superl of* badly) ◇ *adj* -**1.** [least good, pleasant etc] le pire, le plus mauvais; **it's the ~ book I've ever read** c'est le plus mauvais livre que j'aie jamais lu; **this is the ~ thing that could have happened** c'est la pire chose qui pouvait arriver; **it has happened at the ~ possible time** c'est arrivé au plus mauvais moment; **and, ~ of all, I lost my keys** et le pire de tout, c'est que j'ai perdu mes clés; **we came off ~** [in deal] c'est nous qui étions perdants; [in fight] c'est nous qui avons reçu le plus de coups; **I felt ~ of all just after the operation** c'est juste après l'opération que je me suis senti le plus mal. -**2.** [most severe, serious - disaster, error] le plus grave; [- winter] le plus rude; **the fighting was ~ near the border** les combats les plus violents se sont déroulés près de la frontière.

◇ *adv* [most severely]: **the ~ affected** le plus affecté OR touché.

◇ *n* -**1.** [worst thing] pire *m*; **the ~ that can happen** le pire qui puisse arriver; **the ~ of it is she knew all along** le pire, c'est qu'elle le savait depuis le début; **money brings out the ~ in people** l'argent réveille les pires instincts (chez les gens); **to expect/to be prepared for the ~** s'attendre/être préparé au pire; **I fear the ~** je crains le pire; **the ~ is still to come** le pire est encore à venir; **the ~ was yet to come** le pire restait à venir ❑ **if the ~ comes to the ~** au pire, dans le pire des cas; **he got the ~ of it** c'est lui qui s'en est le moins bien sorti; **do your ~!** *hum* allez-y, je suis prêt; **at its ~, at their ~**: **the fever was at its ~ last night** la fièvre était à son paroxysme hier soir; **when the storm was at its ~** au plus fort de l'orage; **when the situation was at its ~** alors que la situation était désespérée; **things** OR **matters were at their ~** les affaires étaient au plus mal, les choses ne pouvaient pas aller plus mal. -**2.** [worst person] le pire de tous; **to be the ~ in the class** être le dernier de la classe; **when it comes to dancing, he's the world's ~** pour ce qui est de danser, il n'y a pas pire que lui.

◇ *vt lit* [opponent, rival] battre, avoir le dessus sur.

◆ **at (the) worst** *conj phr* au pire, dans le pire des cas.

worst- *in cpds*: **the ~dressed** le moins bien habillé; **the ~behaved** le moins sage; **to be the ~off** [financially] être le moins riche; [in situation] s'en sortir le moins bien.

worst-case *adj*: **this is the ~ scenario** voilà le scénario catastrophe.

worsted [ˈwʊstɪd] ◇ *n* worsted *m*, laine *f* peignée.

◇ *adj* [suit] en worsted, en laine peignée; **~ cloth** worsted *m*, laine *f* peignée.

worth [wɜːθ] ◇ *adj* -**1.** [financially, in value]: **to be ~ £40,000** valoir 40 000 livres; **how much is the picture ~?** combien vaut le tableau?; **it isn't ~ much** cela ne vaut pas grand'chose; **£10 isn't ~ much nowadays** 10 livres ne valent pas OR ne représentent pas grand-chose de nos jours; **his uncle is ~ several million pounds** la fortune de son oncle s'élève à plusieurs millions de livres; **it was ~ every penny** ça en valait vraiment la peine; **what's it ~ to you?** vous êtes prêt à y mettre combien?; **it isn't ~ the paper it's written on** *fig* ça ne vaut pas le papier sur lequel c'est écrit ❑ **to be ~ one's weight in gold** valoir son pesant d'or; **(to be) ~ one's salt** *Br*: **any proofreader ~ his salt would have spotted the mistake** n'importe quel correcteur digne de ce nom aurait relevé l'erreur. -**2.** [emotionally]: **it's ~ a lot to me** j'y attache beaucoup de valeur OR de prix; **the bracelet is ~ a lot to me** j'attache beaucoup de prix au bracelet; **their friendship is ~ a lot to her** leur amitié a beaucoup de prix pour elle; **it's more than my job's ~ to cause a fuss** je ne veux pas risquer ma place en faisant des histoires; **I can't do it, it's more than my life is ~** je ne peux absolument pas prendre le risque de faire cela. -**3.** [valid, deserving]: **the church is (well) ~ a visit** l'église vaut la peine d'être visitée OR vaut le détour; **it's ~ a try** OR **trying** cela vaut la peine d'essayer; **it wasn't ~ the effort** cela ne valait pas la peine de faire un tel effort, ça n'en valait pas la peine; **it's not ~ waiting for him** cela ne vaut pas la peine de l'attendre; **is the film ~ seeing?** est-ce que le film vaut la peine d'être vu?; **don't bother to phone, it isn't ~ it** inutile de téléphoner, cela n'en vaut pas la peine ❑ **if a thing is ~ doing, it's ~ doing well** *prov* si une chose vaut la peine d'être faite, elle vaut la peine d'être bien faite; **the game isn't ~ the candle** *inf Br* le jeu n'en vaut pas la chandelle. -**4.** *phr*: **it would be ~ your while to check** OR **checking** vous auriez intérêt à vérifier; **it's not ~ (my) while waiting** cela ne vaut pas la peine d'attendre OR que j'attende; **I'll make it ~ your while** je vous récompenserai de votre peine; **she was running for all she was ~** elle courait de toutes ses forces OR aussi vite qu'elle pouvait; **I tried/shouted for all I was ~** j'ai essayé du mieux/crié aussi fort que j'ai pu; **for what it's ~** pour ce que cela vaut.

◇ *n* -**1.** [in money, value] valeur *f*; **£2,000 ~ of damage** pour 2 000 livres de dégâts, des dégâts qui se montent à 2 000 livres; **he sold £50 ~ of ice cream** il a vendu pour 50 livres de glaces. -**2.** [of person] valeur *f*; **she knows her own ~** elle sait ce qu'elle vaut, elle connaît sa propre valeur. -**3.** [equivalent value] équivalent *m*; **he got a day's ~ of work out of me for nothing** j'ai travaillé pour lui l'équivalent d'une journée, pour rien; **a week's ~ of supplies** suffisamment de provisions pour une semaine.

worthily [ˈwɜːðɪlɪ] *adv* [live, behave] dignement.

worthiness [ˈwɜːðɪnɪs] *n* [dignity] caractère *m* digne; [praiseworthiness] caractère *m* louable.

worthless [ˈwɜːθlɪs] *adj* -**1.** [goods, land etc] sans valeur, qui ne vaut rien. -**2.** [useless - attempt] inutile; [- advice, suggestion] inutile, sans valeur. -**3.** [person] incapable, qui ne vaut rien; **he's a ~ wretch!** c'est un bon à rien!

worthlessness [ˈwɜːθlɪsnɪs] *n* -**1.** [of goods, land etc] absence *f* totale de valeur. -**2.** [of attempt] inutilité *f*; [of advice, suggestion] inutilité *f*. -**3.** [of person] nullité *f*.

worthwhile [ˌwɜːθˈwaɪl] *adj* -**1.** [useful - action, visit] qui vaut la peine; [- job] utile, qui a un sens; **they didn't think it was ~ buying** OR **to buy a new car** ils ne pensaient pas que ça valait la peine d'acheter une nouvelle voiture. -**2.** [deserving - cause, project, organization] louable, méritoire. -**3.** [interesting - book] qui vaut la peine d'être lu; [- film] qui vaut la peine d'être vu.

worthy [ˈwɜːðɪ] (*compar* worthier, *superl* worthiest, *pl* worthies) ◇ *adj* -**1.** [deserving - person] digne, méritant; [- cause] louable, digne; **to be ~ of sthg** être digne de OR mériter qqch; **to be ~ to do sthg** être digne OR mériter de faire qqch; **they are ~ of praise/respect** ils sont dignes d'éloges/de respect, ils méritent des éloges/le respect; **she was a ~ winner** elle méritait bien de gagner; **it is ~ of note that...** il est intéressant de remarquer OR de noter que... -**2.** *iron* excellent, brave; **the ~ captain** l'excellent OR le brave capitaine.

◇ *n* [important person] notable *mf*; *hum* brave citoyen *m*, -enne *f*.

wot [wɒt] ◇ *inf Br* = **what**.

◇ *vi & vt arch* savoir; **God ~** Dieu sait.

wotcha *inf*, **wotcher** *inf* [ˈwɒtʃə] *interj Br dial* salut!

would [wʊd] ◇ *pt* → **will**.

◇ *modal vb* **A.** -**1.** [speculating, hypothesizing]: **I'm sure they ~ come if you asked them** je suis sûr qu'ils viendraient si vous le leur demandiez; **he ~ be thirty now if he had lived** il aurait trente ans maintenant s'il avait vécu; **I wouldn't do that if I were you** je ne ferais pas ça si j'étais vous OR à votre place; **you ~ think they had better things to do** on pourrait penser qu'ils ont mieux à faire; **I thought he ~ understand** je pensais qu'il comprendrait; **they wouldn't have come if they'd known** ils ne seraient pas venus s'ils avaient su; **he wouldn't have finished without your help** il n'aurait pas terminé sans votre aide; **she ~ have been 16 by now** elle aurait 16 ans maintenant. -**2.** [making polite offers, requests]: **~ you please be quiet!** voulez-vous vous taire, s'il vous plaît!; **~ you mind driving me home?** est-ce que cela vous dérangerait de me reconduire chez moi?; **~ you like to see her?** aimeriez-vous OR voudriez-vous la voir?; **~ you like another cup?** en voulez-vous encore une tasse? -**3.** [expressing preferences, desires]: **I ~ prefer to go** OR **I ~ rather go alone** j'aimerais mieux OR je préférerais y aller seul; **I ~ have preferred to go** OR **I ~ rather have gone alone** j'aurais mieux aimé OR j'aurais préféré y aller seul; **I ~ love to go** je serais ravi d'y aller.

B. -**1.** [indicating willingness, responsiveness - subj: person, mechanism]: **they ~ give their lives for the cause** ils donneraient leur vie pour la cause; **she wouldn't touch alcohol** elle refusait de toucher à l'alcool; **I couldn't find anyone who ~ lend me a torch** je n'ai trouvé personne pour me prêter une lampe électrique; **the light wouldn't work** la lumière ne marchait pas; **the car wouldn't start** la voiture ne voulait pas démarrer. -**2.** [indicating habitual or characteristic behaviour]: **he ~ smoke a cigar after dinner** il fumait un cigare après le dîner; **she ~ often complain about the neighbours** elle se plaignait souvent des voisins; **they ~ go and break something!** il fallait qu'ils aillent casser quelque chose!; **I didn't really enjoy the fish — you wouldn't, ~ you?** je n'ai pas tellement aimé le poisson — ça m'aurait étonné!; **he ~!** c'est bien de lui!; **he ~ say that, wouldn't he** il fallait qu'il dise ça. -**3.** [expressing opinions]: **I ~ disagree there** je crains de n'être pas d'accord sur ce point; **I ~ imagine it's warmer than here** j'imagine qu'il fait plus chaud qu'ici; **I ~ think he'd be pleased** j'aurais cru que ça lui ferait plaisir. -**4.** [giving advice]: **I ~ have a word with her about it (, if I were you)** moi, je lui en parlerais (à votre place). -**5.** [expressing surprise, incredulity]: **you wouldn't think she was only 15, ~ you?** on ne dirait pas qu'elle n'a que 15 ans, n'est-ce pas?; **who ~ have thought it?** qui l'aurait cru?; **I wouldn't have thought it possible** je ne l'aurais pas cru possible; **~ you credit it!** tu te rends compte! -**6.** [indicating likelihood, probability]: **there was a woman there — that ~ be his wife** il y avait une femme — ça devait être sa femme.

C. -**1.** [in reported speech]: **it was to be the last time I ~ see him before he left** c'était la dernière fois que je le voyais avant son départ. -**2.** [used with 'have']: **they ~ have been happy if it hadn't been for the war** ils auraient vécu heureux si la guerre n'était pas survenue; **if you ~ have told the truth, this ~ never have happened** *Am* si tu m'avais dit la vérité, ça ne serait jamais arrivé. -**3.** *fml* OR *lit (subjunctive use)* [expressing wishes]: **~ that it were true!** si seulement c'était vrai!; **~ to God that I still had it!** plût à Dieu que je l'eusse encore!

would-be *adj* -**1.** [hopeful]: **a ~ writer/MP** un futur écrivain/député, une personne qui veut être écrivain/député. -**2.** *pej* [so-called] prétendu, soi-disant *(inv)*.

wouldn't [ˈwʊdnt] = **would not**.

wouldst [wʊdst] *arch 2nd pers sing* → **would**.

would've [ˈwʊdəv] = **would have**.

wound[1] [wuːnd] ◇ *n* -**1.** [physical injury] blessure *f*, plaie *f*; **a bullet ~** une blessure par balle; **she had three bullet ~s** elle avait été blessée par trois balles; **she had three knife ~s** elle avait reçu trois coups de couteau; **they had serious head ~s** ils avaient été gravement blessés à la tête; **to dress a ~** panser une blessure OR une plaie. -**2.** *fig* [emotional or moral] blessure *f*; **he was still suffering from deep psychological ~s** il souffrait encore de graves blessures psychologiques.

◇ *vt* -**1.** [physically] blesser; **the children were ~ed by flying glass** les enfants ont été blessés par des éclats de verre; **she was ~ed in the foot** elle a été blessée au pied. -**2.** *fig* [emotionally] blesser; **he was deeply ~ed by their criticism** il a été profondément blessé par leurs critiques; **to ~ sb's pride** heurter l'amour-propre de qqn, blesser qqn dans son amour-propre.

wound2 [waʊnd] *pt* & *pp* → **wind**.

wounded ['wuːndɪd] ◇ *adj* -**1.** [soldier, victim] blessé; **a ~ woman** une blessée. -**2.** *fig* [feelings, pride] blessé.

◇ *npl*: **the ~** les blessés *mpl*.

Wounded Knee *pr n* Wounded Knee *(lieu situé dans le Dakota du Sud, où, le 29 décembre 1890, 146 Indiens sioux détenus par des soldats américains furent abattus.)*.

wounding ['wuːndɪŋ] *adj fig* [hurtful] blessant.

wound-up [waʊnd] *adj* -**1.** [clock] remonté; [car window] remonté, fermé. -**2.** *inf* [tense - person] crispé, très tendu.

wove [wəʊv] *pt* → **weave**.

woven ['wəʊvn] *pp* → **weave**.

wow *inf* [waʊ] ◇ *interj* génial!, super!

◇ *n* -**1. it's a real ~!** c'est vraiment super!; **he's a ~ at hockey** c'est un super joueur de hockey. -**2.** ACOUST pleurage *m*.

◇ *vt* [impress] impressionner, emballer, subjuguer; **she ~ed them with her piano playing** elle les a emballés quand elle a joué du piano.

WP ◇ *n* (*abbr of* **word processing, word processor**) TTX *m*.

◇ *written abbr of* **weather permitting**.

WPC (*abbr of* **woman police constable**) *n Br femme agent de police*; **~ Roberts** l'agent Roberts.

wpm (*written abbr of* **words per minute**) mots/min.

WRAC (*abbr of* **Women's Royal Army Corps**) *pr n section féminine de l'armée de terre britannique*.

wrack [ræk] *n* -**1.** [seaweed] varech *m*. -**2.** = **rack 5**.

WRAF (*abbr of* **Women's Royal Air Force**) *pr n section féminine de l'armée de l'air britannique*.

wraith [reɪθ] *n lit* apparition *f*, spectre *m*.

wraithlike ['reɪθlaɪk] *adj lit* spectral.

wrangle ['ræŋgl] ◇ *vi* se disputer, se chamailler; **to ~ about** OR **over sthg** se disputer à propos de qqch; **they were wrangling over who should pay** ils se disputaient pour savoir qui devait payer; **to ~ with sb** se disputer OR se chamailler avec qqn.

◇ *vt Am* [cattle, horses] garder.

◇ *n* dispute *f*; **a long legal ~ over the amount of damages** une longue dispute juridique sur le montant des dommages-intérêts.

wrangler ['ræŋgləʳ] *n* -**1.** *Am* [cowboy] cowboy *m*. -**2.** UNIV [in UK] ≃ major *m (candidat en mathématiques à Cambridge qui reçoit une mention très bien)*.

wrangling ['ræŋglɪŋ] *n (U)* disputes *fpl*; **stop all this ~!** arrêtez toutes ces chamailleries!

wrap [ræp] (*pt* & *pp* **wrapped**) ◇ *vt* -**1.** [goods, parcel, gift, food] emballer, envelopper; **the fish was wrapped in foil** le poisson était enveloppé dans du papier d'aluminium; **shall I ~ it for you?** est-ce que je vous l'enveloppe?; **she wrapped the scarf in tissue paper** elle a emballé OR enveloppé l'écharpe dans du papier de soie. -**2.** [cocoon, envelop] envelopper, emmailloter; **the baby was wrapped in a blanket** le bébé était enveloppé dans une couverture; **her head was wrapped in a thick scarf** elle avait la tête enveloppée dans une grosse écharpe; **her visit was wrapped in mystery** *fig* sa visite était entourée de mystère. -**3.** [twist, wind]: **to ~ round** OR **around** enrouler; **she had a towel wrapped round her head** sa tête était enveloppée dans une serviette; **she had a towel wrapped round her body** elle s'était enveloppée dans une serviette; **he wrapped the bandage round her hand** il lui a enroulé la main dans une bande; **he wrapped his arms round her** il l'a prise dans ses bras; **he wrapped the car round a tree** *inf fig* il s'est payé un arbre.

◇ *n* [housecoat] peignoir *m*; [shawl] châle *m*; [blanket, rug] couverture *f*.

◆ **wraps** *npl fig*: **to keep a plan/one's feelings under ~s** garder un plan secret/ses sentiments secrets; **when the ~s eventually came off** lorsque tout a été dévoilé.

◆ **wrap up** ◇ *vt sep* -**1.** [gift, food, goods, parcel] envelopper, emballer, empaqueter; **he wrapped the sandwiches up in foil** il a enveloppé les sandwiches dans du papier d'aluminium. -**2.** [person - in clothes, blanket] envelopper; **~ him up in a blanket** enveloppez-le dans une couverture; **she was well wrapped up in a thick coat** elle était bien emmitouflée dans un épais manteau; **~ yourself up warmly** couvrez-vous bien. -**3.** *fig*: **politicians are skilled at wrapping up bad news in an acceptable form** les politiciens s'y connaissent pour présenter les mauvaises nouvelles sous un jour acceptable; **his meaning was wrapped up in diplomatic jargon** il enrobait ce qu'il disait de jargon diplomatique. -**4.** *inf* [conclude - job] terminer, conclure; [- deal, contract] conclure, régler; **that ~s up business for today** c'est fini pour aujourd'hui; **let's get this matter wrapped up** finissons-en avec cette question. -**5.** *Am* [summarize] résumer; **she wrapped up her talk with three points** elle a résumé son discours en trois points. -**6.** [engross]: **to be wrapped up in sthg** être absorbé par qqch; **he's very wrapped up in his work** il est très absorbé par son travail; **they're wrapped up in their children** ils ne vivent que pour leurs enfants; **she's very wrapped up in herself** elle est très repliée sur elle-même. -**7.** [implicate]: **he was wrapped up in some shady dealings** il a été impliqué dans des transactions louches.

◇ *vi insep* -**1.** [dress] s'habiller, se couvrir; **~ up warmly** OR **well!** couvrez-vous bien! -**2.** ▽ *Br* [shut up] se taire; **~ up!** la ferme!

wraparound ['ræpə,raʊnd] ◇ *adj* [skirt] portefeuille *(inv)*; [sunglasses] lunettes *fpl* de soleil panoramiques; **~ rear window** AUT lunette *f* arrière panoramique.

◇ *n* -**1.** [skirt] jupe *f* portefeuille. -**2.** COMPUT mise à la ligne *f* automatique des mots.

◆ **wraparounds** *npl* [sunglasses] lunettes *fpl* de soleil panoramiques.

wrapover ['ræp,əʊvəʳ] *adj* [dress, skirt] portefeuille *(inv)*.

wrapped [ræpt] *adj* [bread, cheese] préemballé.

wrapper ['ræpəʳ] *n* -**1.** [for sweet] papier *m*; [for parcel] papier *m* d'emballage. -**2.** [cover - on book] jaquette *f*; [- on magazine, newspaper] bande *f*. -**3.** [housecoat] peignoir *m*.

wrapping ['ræpɪŋ] *n* [on parcel] papier *m* d'emballage; [on sweet] papier *m*; **she tore the plastic ~ from the box** elle a déchiré OR arraché l'emballage en plastique de la boîte.

wrapping paper *n* [for gift] papier *m* cadeau; [for parcel] papier *m* d'emballage.

wrath [rɒθ] *n lit* colère *f*, courroux *m*

❑ **'Aguirre, Wrath of God'** *Herzog* 'Aguirre, la colère de Dieu'.

wrathful ['rɒθfʊl] *adj lit* en colère, courroucé.

wrathfully ['rɒθfʊlɪ] *adv lit* avec colère, avec courroux.

wreak [riːk] (*pt* & *pp sense 1* **wreaked** OR **wrought** [rɔːt]) *vt* -**1.** [cause - damage, chaos] causer, provoquer; **the damage ~ed by the explosion** les dommages provoqués par l'explosion; **to ~ havoc** faire des ravages, mettre sens dessus dessous; **the storm ~ed havoc with telephone communications** la tempête a sérieusement perturbé les communications téléphoniques; **it ~ed havoc with my holiday plans** *fig* cela a bouleversé mes projets de vacances. -**2.** [inflict - revenge, anger] assouvir; **to ~ vengeance on sb** assouvir sa vengeance sur qqn.

wreath [riːθ] (*pl* **wreaths** [riːðz]) *n* -**1.** [for funeral] couronne *f*; **the President laid a ~ at the war memorial** le Président a déposé une gerbe au monument aux morts; **the laying of ~s** MIL le dépôt *m* de gerbes. -**2.** [garland] guirlande *f*; **a holly ~** une guirlande de houx; **a laurel ~** une couronne de laurier. -**3.** *fig* [of mist] nappe *f*; [of smoke] volute *f*.

wreathe [riːð] ◇ *vt* -**1.** [shroud] envelopper; **the mountain top was ~d in mist** le sommet de la montagne était enveloppé OR disparaissait dans la brume; **he sat ~d in smoke** il était assis dans un nuage de fumée; **to be ~d in smiles** *fig* être rayonnant. -**2.** [with flowers - person] couronner; [- grave, window] orner; **a cross ~d with chrysanthemums** une croix ornée de chrysanthèmes.

◇ *vi* [smoke] monter en volutes.

wreck [rek] ◇ *n* -**1.** [wrecked remains - of ship] épave *f*; [- of plane] avion *m* accidenté, épave *f*; [- of train] train *m* accidenté; [- of car, lorry, bus] véhicule *m* accidenté, épave *f*; **the car was a ~** la voiture était une épave. -**2.** [wrecking - of ship] naufrage *m*; [- of plane] accident *m*; [- of train] déraillement *m*. -**3.** *inf* [dilapidated car] guimbarde *f*; [old bike] clou *m*. -**4.** *inf* [person] épave *f*, loque *f*; **a human ~** une loque humaine; **he's a ~** [physically] c'est une épave; [mentally] il est à bout; **I must look a ~** je dois avoir une mine de déterré. -**5.** *fig* [of hopes, of plans] effondrement *m*, anéantissement *m*.

◇ *vt* -**1.** [in accident, explosion - ship] provoquer le naufrage de; [- car, plane] détruire complètement; [- building] démolir; **the tanker was ~ed off the African coast** le pétrolier a fait naufrage au large des côtes africaines; **the car was completely ~ed in the accident** la voiture a été totalement détruite dans l'accident; **the store was ~ed by a bomb blast** une bombe a fait sauter le magasin, le magasin a été détruit par l'explosion d'une bombe. -**2.** [damage - furniture] casser, démolir; [- mechanism] détruire, détraquer; **he ~ed the room in a fit of rage** il a tout cassé dans la pièce dans un accès de rage. -**3.** [upset - marriage, relationship] briser; [- hopes, chances] anéantir; [- health] briser, ruiner; [- negotiations] faire échouer, saboter; **she's ~ed my plans** elle a ruiné mes plans.

wreckage ['rekɪdʒ] *n* -**1.** *(U)* [debris - from ship, car] débris *mpl*; [- from building] décombres *mpl*; **pieces of ~ from the building lay in the street** les décombres du bâtiment jonchaient la rue; **three bodies were found in the ~ of the plane** trois corps ont été trouvés dans les débris de l'avion; **to pull sb from the ~** tirer qqn des décombres; **~ has been washed up on the beach** la marée a déposé des débris sur la plage. -**2.** [wrecked ship] épave *f*, navire *m* naufragé; **he clung to the ~** il s'agrippa à l'épave. -**3.** *fig* [of hopes, plans, relationship] anéantissement *m*.

wrecked [rekt] *adj* -**1.** [ship] naufragé; [car, plane] complètement détruit; [house] complètement démoli; **~ remains** [of ship] épave *f*; [of train, car] débris *mpl*; [of building] décombres *mpl*; **~ cars** épaves *fpl* d'automobiles, voitures *fpl* accidentées. -**2.** *fig* [relationship, hopes] anéanti. -**3.** *inf Br* [exhausted] épuisé, crevé. -**4.** ▽ *Br* [drunk] plein, bourré.

wrecker ['rekəʳ] *n* -**1.** [destroyer] destructeur *m*, -trice *f*, démolisseur *m*, -euse *f*; **marriage-~** briseur *m*, -euse *f* de ménages. -**2.** *Am* [demolition man - for buildings] démolisseur *m*; [- for cars] ferrailleur *m*, casseur *m*. -**3.** *Am* [breakdown van] dépanneuse *f*. -**4.** [of ships] naufrageur *m*.

wrecking ['rekɪŋ] *n* -**1.** [of ship] naufrage *m*; [of train] déraillement *m*. -**2.** *fig* [of relationship, hopes] anéantissement *m*.

wrecking bar *n* pied-de-biche *m*.

wren [ren] *n* roitelet *m*.

Wren [ren] *n Br auxiliaire féminine de la marine britannique*.

wrench [rentʃ] ◇ *vt* -**1.** [pull] tirer violemment sur; **she ~ed the door open** elle a ouvert la

porte d'un geste violent; we'll have to ~ the lid off nous allons être obligés de forcer le couvercle pour l'ouvrir; someone ~ed the bag out of my hands OR from my grasp quelqu'un m'a arraché le sac des mains; to ~ o.s. free se dégager d'un mouvement violent; she ~ed herself free of my grasp elle s'est dégagée brusquement de mon étreinte. -2. [eyes, mind] arracher, détacher; I couldn't ~ my gaze (away) from the horrible sight je ne pouvais pas détacher mon regard de cet horrible spectacle. -3. [ankle, arm] se faire une entorse à; I've ~ed my shoulder je me suis foulé l'épaule; to ~ one's back se donner un tour de reins.
◇ *vi*: he ~ed free of his bonds *literal* il s'est dégagé de ses liens d'un mouvement violent; *fig* il s'est libéré de ses liens.
◇ *n* -1. [tug, twist] mouvement *m* violent *(de torsion)*; with a sudden ~ she pulled herself free elle se dégagea d'un mouvement brusque; he gave the handle a ~ il a tiré brusquement OR violemment sur la poignée; with a sudden ~, she threw the door open d'un mouvement brusque, elle ouvrit la porte. -2. [to ankle, knee] entorse *f*; I gave my ankle a ~ je me suis fait une entorse à OR je me suis foulé la cheville; I gave my back a ~ je me suis donné OR fait un tour de reins. -3. *fig* [emotional] déchirement *m*; it was a terrible ~ for me to leave home ce fut un déchirement terrible pour moi de quitter la maison. -4. TECH [spanner] clé *f*, clef *f*; [adjustable] clé *f* anglaise; [for wheels] clé *f* en croix; he threw a ~ into the works *Am* il nous a mis des bâtons dans les roues.

wrest [rest] *vt lit* -1. [grab - object] arracher violemment; he ~ed the gun from me OR from my grasp il m'a arraché violemment le fusil des mains; they ~ed the stick out of my hands ils m'ont arraché violemment le bâton des mains. -2. [extract - truth, secret] arracher; he ~ed the truth from her il lui a arraché la vérité; they just manage to ~ a living from the land ils réussissent tout juste à vivre de la terre. -3. [control, power] ravir, arracher; the Liberals ~ed two seats from the Conservatives les libéraux ont ravi OR arraché deux sièges aux conservateurs.

wrestle ['resl] ◇ *vi* -1. SPORT [Greek, Sumo] lutter, pratiquer la lutte; [freestyle] catcher, pratiquer le catch; to ~ with sb lutter (corps à corps) avec qqn, se battre avec qqn. -2. *fig* [struggle] se débattre, lutter; he died after wrestling with a long illness il mourut après avoir lutté contre une longue maladie; she ~d with her conscience elle se débattait avec sa conscience; I ~d with the problem all evening je me suis débattu avec le problème toute la soirée. -3. [try to control]: to ~ with sthg se débattre avec qqch; the woman ~d to keep control of the car la femme luttait pour garder le contrôle de la voiture.
◇ *vt* [fight - intruder, enemy] lutter contre; SPORT [Greek, Sumo] rencontrer à la lutte; [freestyle] rencontrer au catch; he ~d his attacker to the ground en luttant avec son agresseur, il réussit à le clouer au sol.
◇ *n* lutte *f*; to have a ~ with sb lutter avec OR contre qqn.

wrestler ['resləʳ] *n* SPORT [Greek, Sumo] lutteur *m*, -euse *f*; [freestyle] catcheur *m*, -euse *f*.

wrestling ['reslɪŋ] ◇ *n* SPORT [Greek, Sumo] lutte *f*; [freestyle] catch *m*.
◇ *comp* [hold, match - Greek, Sumo] de lutte; [- freestyle] de catch.

wretch [retʃ] *n* -1. [unfortunate person] pauvre diable *m*, malheureux *m*, -euse *f*; the poor ~ le pauvre malheureux. -2. *lit* OR *hum* [scoundrel] scélérat *m*, -e *f*, misérable *mf*; the ~ who stole my bag le scélérat qui m'a volé mon sac. -3. [esp child] vilain *m*, -e *f*, coquin *m*, -e *f*; you little ~! petit coquin!

wretched ['retʃɪd] ◇ *adj* -1. [awful, poor - dwelling, clothes] misérable; she had a ~ existence elle a eu une existence misérable; their living conditions are ~ leurs conditions de vie sont misérables OR épouvantables; she receives a ~ wage elle touche un salaire de misère. -2. [unhappy] malheureux; [depressed] déprimé, démoralisé; he was OR felt ~ about what he had said il se sentait coupable à cause de ce qu'il avait dit; I felt cold and ~ j'avais froid et je me sentais malheureux. -3. [ill] malade; the flu made me feel really ~ je me sentais vraiment très mal avec cette grippe. -4. *inf* [as expletive] fichu, maudit; keep your ~ money! garde-le, ton fichu argent! -5. [abominable - behaviour, performance, weather] lamentable; what ~ luck! quelle déveine!; I'm a ~ singer/writer je suis un piètre chanteur/écrivain.
◇ *npl*: the ~ les déshérités *mpl*.

wretchedly ['retʃɪdlɪ] *adv* -1. [poorly - live, dress] misérablement, pauvrement. -2. [unhappily - cry, look] pitoyablement, misérablement; he apologized ~ il a fait des excuses pitoyables. -3. [abominably - behave] abominablement; [- play, perform] très mal, lamentablement; a ~ small amount une somme absolument dérisoire.

wretchedness ['retʃɪdnɪs] *n* -1. [poverty - of living conditions] extrême pauvreté *f*, misère *f*. -2. [unhappiness] tristesse *f*, malheur *m*. -3. [meanness - of behaviour] mesquinerie *f*; [- of sum, wage] caractère *m* dérisoire. -4. [in quality - of performance, of weather, of meal] médiocrité *f*.

wrick [rɪk] *Br* = **rick** *vt* **2** & *n* **2**.

wriggle ['rɪgl] ◇ *vt* -1. [toes, fingers] tortiller. -2. [subj: person]: he ~d his way under the fence il est passé sous la clôture en se tortillant OR à plat ventre ‖ [subj: snake, worm]: the worm was wriggling its way across the grass le ver avançait dans l'herbe en se tortillant.
◇ *vi* [person] remuer, gigoter; [snake, worm] se tortiller; [fish] frétiller; the children were wriggling in their seats les enfants gigotaient sur leur siège; to ~ along [person] avancer en rampant OR à plat ventre; [snake] avancer en se tortillant; the fish/the little boy ~d from her grasp le poisson/le petit garçon réussit à s'échapper de ses mains en se tortillant; he ~d past the guards il est passé devant les gardes en se glissant à plat ventre; she ~d under the fence elle est passée sous la clôture à plat ventre OR en se tortillant; she ~d under the blankets elle s'est enfoncée sous les couvertures en se tortillant ❑ to ~ free *literal* se libérer en se tortillant; *fig* s'en sortir.
◇ *n*: to give a ~ [snake] se tortiller; [fish] frétiller; [person] se tortiller; with a ~ the rabbit shook itself free from the trap en se tortillant le lapin parvint à se dégager du piège.
◆ **wriggle about** *Br*, **wriggle around** *vi insep* [eel, worm] se tortiller; [fish] frétiller; [person] gigoter, se trémousser; stop wriggling about! arrête de gigoter comme ça!
◆ **wriggle out** *vi insep* -1. [fish, snake] sortir; the fish ~d out from under a rock le poisson est sorti en frétillant de sous un rocher; the fish ~d out of the net le poisson s'est échappé du filet en se tortillant. -2. [person] se dégager (en se tortillant); the little boy ~d out of my grasp le petit garçon s'est dégagé de mon étreinte en se tortillant; I managed to ~ out of an embarrassing situation *fig* j'ai réussi à me sortir d'une situation gênante. -3. [evade]: to ~ out of a task se dérober à OR esquiver une tâche; to ~ out of doing sthg trouver un moyen de se défiler pour éviter de faire qqch; he ~d out of paying il a trouvé un moyen d'éviter de payer.

wriggler ['rɪgləʳ] *n* -1. [person]: he's a terrible ~ il n'arrête pas de gigoter, il ne se tient jamais tranquille. -2. ENTOM larve *f* de moustique.

wriggly ['rɪglɪ] *adj* [eel, snake] qui se tortille; [fish] frétillant; [person] remuant, qui gigote.

wring [rɪŋ] (*pt* & *pp* wrung [rʌŋ]) ◇ *vt* -1. [wet cloth, clothes] essorer, tordre; he wrung the towel dry il a essoré la serviette en la tordant; she wrung the water from the sponge elle a exprimé l'eau de l'éponge. -2. [neck] tordre; she wrung the chicken's neck elle a tordu le cou au poulet; I'll ~ his neck! *fig* je vais lui tordre le cou! -3. [hand - in handshake] serrer; he wrung her hand il lui a serré la main vigoureusement; to ~ one's hands (in despair) se tordre les mains (de désespoir); it's no use sitting there ~ing your hands *fig* cela ne sert à rien de rester assis à vous désespérer. -4. [extract - confession, truth] arracher; [- money] extorquer; she wrung every last detail from him elle a réussi à lui extorquer tous les renseignements; I'll ~ the truth out of them je vais leur arracher la vérité; the blackmailer wrung £5,000 from her le maître chanteur lui a extorqué 5 000 livres; he's ~ing the maximum publicity from the situation il profite de la situation pour en tirer le maximum de publicité. -5. *fig* [heart] fendre; her efforts to cope with four children on her own wrung my heart ses efforts pour se débrouiller toute seule avec quatre enfants me fendaient le cœur.
◇ *vi* essorer; [on label]: 'do not ~' 'ne pas essorer'.
◇ *n*: give the cloth a ~ essorez la serpillière.
◆ **wring out** *vt sep* = **wring** *vt* **1**, **4**.

wringer ['rɪŋəʳ] *n* essoreuse *f* (à rouleaux); to put clothes through the ~ essorer des vêtements (à la machine); he has really been through the ~ *fig* on lui en a fait voir de toutes les couleurs.

wringing ['rɪŋɪŋ] *adj*: ~ (wet) [clothes] complètement trempé; [person] complètement trempé, trempé jusqu'aux os; the shirt was ~ with sweat la chemise était trempée de sueur.

wrinkle ['rɪŋkl] ◇ *vt* -1. [nose] froncer; [brow] plisser. -2. [skirt, carpet] faire des plis dans.
◇ *vi* -1. [skin, hands] se rider; [brow] se contracter, se plisser; [nose] se froncer, se plisser; [fruit] se ratatiner, se rider. -2. [skirt, stocking] faire des plis.
◇ *n* -1. [on skin, fruit] ride *f*. -2. [in dress, carpet] pli *m*; there are still some ~s in the plan which need ironing out *fig* il reste encore quelques difficultés à aplanir. -3. *inf Br dated* [trick] combine *f*; [hint] tuyau *m*.
◆ **wrinkle up** *vi insep* & *vt sep* = **wrinkle** *vi* & *vt*.

wrinkled ['rɪŋkld] *adj* -1. [skin, hands] ridé; [brow, nose] plissé, froncé; [fruit] ridé, ratatiné; a ~ old man un vieillard ratatiné. -2. [rug, skirt] qui fait des plis; [stocking] qui fait des plis OR l'accordéon.

wrinkly ['rɪŋklɪ] (*pl* wrinklies) ◇ *adj* -1. [skin] ridé. -2. [stockings] qui fait des plis.
◇ *n inf Br pej* vieux *m*, vieille *f*.

wrist [rɪst] *n* poignet *m*.

wristband ['rɪstbænd] *n* [on shirt, blouse] poignet *m*; [sweat band] poignet *m*; [of watch] bracelet *m*.

wristlet ['rɪstlɪt] *n* bracelet *m*.

wrist pin *n* MECH *Br* goujon *m*; *Am* goupille *f*.

wristwatch ['rɪstwɒtʃ] *n* montre-bracelet *f*.

writ [rɪt] ◇ *arch pt* & *pp* → **write**.
◇ *n* -1. JUR ordonnance *f*; to issue a ~ against sb [for arrest] lancer un mandat d'arrêt contre qqn; [for libel] assigner qqn en justice; to serve a ~ on sb, to serve sb with a ~ assigner qqn ❑ ~ of attachment ordonnance de saisie; ~ of execution titre *m* exécutoire; ~ of habeas corpus ordre *m* d'habeas corpus; ~ of subpoena assignation *f* OR citation *f* en justice. -2. POL [for elections] ordonnance *f (émanant du président de la Chambre des communes et convoquant les députés pour un vote)*.
◇ *adj phr*: astonishment was ~ large on everybody's face l'étonnement se lisait sur tous les visages.

write [raɪt] (*pt* wrote [rəʊt], *pp* written ['rɪtn], *pt* & *pp arch* writ [rɪt]) ◇ *vt* -1. [letter] écrire; [address, name] écrire, inscrire; [initials] écrire, tracer; [prescription, cheque] écrire, faire; [will] faire; [application form] compléter, rédiger; to ~ a letter to sb écrire OR envoyer une lettre à qqn; ~ her a letter envoyez-lui une lettre, écrivez-lui; I have some letters to ~ j'ai du courrier à faire; they wrote me a letter of thanks ils m'ont écrit pour me remercier; he wrote her a postcard il lui a envoyé une carte postale; to ~ sb *Am* écrire à qqn; she wrote me about her father's illness *Am* elle m'a écrit au sujet de la maladie de son père; **he can't speak Italian very well, but he can ~ it** il ne parle pas très bien l'italien, mais il peut l'écrire; **it is written in the Bible "thou shalt love thy neighbour as thyself"** il est écrit dans la bible «tu aimeras ton prochain comme toi-même»; **perplexity was written all over his face** *fig* la perplexité se lisait sur son visage; **he had success written all over him** *fig* on voyait bien qu'il avait réussi. -**2.** [book] écrire; [article, report] écrire, faire; [essay] faire; [music] écrire, composer; **well written** bien écrit; **written for brass ensemble** écrit pour ensemble de cuivres. -**3.** [send letter about] écrire; **he wrote that he was getting married** il a écrit (pour annoncer) qu'il se mariait. -**4.** [spell] écrire; **I never know how to ~ her name** je ne sais jamais comment s'écrit son nom. -**5.** COMPUT [program] écrire; [data - store] stocker, sauvegarder; [- transfer] transférer.

◇ *vi* -**1.** [gen] écrire; **to ~ in pencil/ink** écrire au crayon/à l'encre; **to learn to read and ~** apprendre à lire et à écrire; **I don't ~ very well** je n'ai pas une belle écriture. -**2.** [send letter] écrire; **to ~ to sb** écrire à qqn; **to ~ to thank/invite sb** écrire pour remercier/inviter qqn; **have you written to let her know?** lui avez-vous écrit pour l'avertir?; **she wrote and told me about it** elle m'a écrit pour me le raconter; **please ~ (again) soon** écris-moi vite (à nouveau), s'il te plaît; **at the time of writing** au moment où j'écris; **they wrote (to him) asking** OR **to ask for permission** ils (lui) ont écrit pour demander l'autorisation; **I've written for a catalogue** j'ai écrit pour demander OR pour qu'on m'envoie un catalogue. -**3.** [professionally - as author] écrire, être écrivain; [- as journalist] écrire, être journaliste; **he ~s on home affairs for "The Economist"** il fait des articles de politique intérieure dans «The Economist»; **she ~s for "The Independent"** elle écrit dans «The Independent»; **she ~s for children's television** elle fait des émissions pour les enfants à la télévision; **she ~s under a pseudonym** elle écrit sous un pseudonyme; **he ~s on** OR **about archeology** il écrit sur l'archéologie, il traite de questions d'archéologie; **they wrote about their experiences in the Amazon** ils ont décrit leurs expériences en Amazonie. -**4.** [pen, typewriter] écrire; **this pen doesn't ~ very well** ce stylo n'écrit pas OR ne marche pas très bien.

◆ **write away** *vi insep* -**1.** [correspond] écrire; **I had to ~ away to the publisher** j'ai dû écrire à la maison d'édition. -**2.** [order by post] écrire pour demander, commander par lettre; **I wrote away for a catalogue** j'ai écrit pour demander un catalogue; **I had to ~ away for spare parts** j'ai dû écrire pour commander des pièces.

◆ **write back** *vi insep* [answer] répondre (à une lettre); **please ~ back soon** réponds-moi vite, s'il te plaît; **he wrote back to say he couldn't come** il a répondu qu'il ne pouvait pas venir; **he wrote back rejecting their offer** il a renvoyé une lettre refusant leur offre.

◆ **write down** *vt sep* -**1.** [note] écrire, noter; [put in writing] mettre par écrit; **unless you ~ the number down, you'll forget it** si vous ne notez pas le numéro OR si vous ne mettez pas le numéro par écrit, vous allez l'oublier; **I had them written down as layabouts** *fig* je les considérais comme des bons à rien. -**2.** FIN & COMM [in price] réduire le prix de; [in value] réduire la valeur de; [undervalue] sous-évaluer.

◆ **write in** ◇ *vi insep* écrire; **to ~ in for a refund** écrire pour demander un remboursement; **hundreds wrote in to complain** des centaines de personnes ont écrit pour se plaindre.

◇ *vt sep* -**1.** [on list, document - word, name] ajouter, insérer. -**2.** *Am* POL [add - name] ajouter, inscrire *(sur un bulletin de vote)*; [vote for - person] voter pour *(en ajoutant le nom sur le bulletin de vote)*.

◆ **write off** ◇ *vt sep* -**1.** FIN [debt] passer aux profits et pertes. -**2.** [consider lost, useless] faire une croix sur, considérer comme perdu; [cancel] renoncer à, annuler; **the plan had to be written off** le projet a dû être abandonné; **three months' hard work was simply written off** on a perdu trois mois de travail acharné; **he was written off as a failure/an eccentric** on a considéré qu'il n'y avait rien de bon à en tirer/que c'était un excentrique. -**3.** [in accident - subj: insurance company] considérer comme irréparable, mettre à la casse; [- subj: driver] rendre inutilisable; **she wrote off her new car** *Br* elle a complètement démoli sa voiture neuve; **his car has been written off** *Br* sa voiture a été mise à la casse. -**4.** [letter, poem] écrire en vitesse.

◇ *vi insep* = **write away**.

◆ **write out** *vt sep* -**1.** [report] écrire, rédiger; [list, cheque] faire, établir; **can you ~ the amount out in full?** pouvez-vous écrire la somme en toutes lettres? -**2.** [copy up - notes] recopier, mettre au propre. -**3.** RADIO & TV [character] faire disparaître.

◆ **write up** *vt sep* -**1.** [diary, impressions] écrire, rédiger; PRESS [event] faire un compte rendu de, rendre compte de; **the demonstration was written up in the local newspaper** le journal local a fait un compte rendu de la manifestation; **he wrote up his ideas in a report** il a consigné ses idées dans un rapport. -**2.** [copy up - notes, data] recopier, mettre au propre. -**3.** FIN & COMM [in price] augmenter le prix de; [in value] augmenter la valeur de; [overvalue] surévaluer.

write head *n* TECH tête *f* d'enregistrement.

write-in *n Am* POL [on ballot paper - addition of name] inscription *f*, rajout *m*; [- name added] nom *m* rajouté.

write-off *n* -**1.** FIN [of bad debt] passage *m* par profits et pertes; [bad debt itself] perte *f* sèche. -**2.** [motor vehicle]: **to be a ~** être irréparable OR bon pour la casse.

write-protected *adj* COMPUT [disk] protégé (en écriture).

writer [ˈraɪtəʳ] *n* -**1.** [of novel, play] écrivain *m*, auteur *m*; [of letter] auteur *m*; **a well-known ~ of novels/poetry** un romancier/poète connu; **she's a fine ~** c'est un excellent écrivain ❑ **technical ~** rédacteur technique; **I'm a bad letter-~** je suis un mauvais correspondant. -**2.** [in handwriting]: **to be a good ~** avoir une belle écriture; **to be a bad ~** écrire mal.

writer's block *n* angoisse *f* de la page blanche.

writer's cramp *n* crampe *f* de l'écrivain.

write-up *n* -**1.** [review] compte rendu *m*, critique *f*; **the play got a good ~** la pièce a eu une bonne critique OR a été bien accueillie par la critique; **the guide contains ~s of several new ski resorts** le guide contient des notices descriptives sur plusieurs nouvelles stations de ski. -**2.** *Am* [of assets] surestimation *f*.

writhe [raɪð] *vi* -**1.** [in pain] se tordre, se contorsionner; **to ~ in** OR **with agony** se tordre de douleur, être en proie à d'atroces souffrances. -**2.** *fig*: **her remarks made him ~** [in disgust] ses remarques l'ont fait frémir; [in embarrassment] ses remarques lui ont fait souffrir le martyre; **they ~d under his criticism** ils ont vivement ressenti ses critiques.

◆ **writhe about** *Br*, **writhe around** *vi insep* se tortiller; **the fish ~d about in the grass** le poisson se tortillait dans l'herbe; **to ~ about in pain** se tordre de douleur.

writing [ˈraɪtɪŋ] *n* -**1.** [of books, letters] écriture *f*; **to devote one's time to ~** se consacrer à l'écriture; **~ as a career** la carrière OR le métier d'écrivain; **it's a good piece of ~** c'est bien écrit; **this is clear, concise ~** c'est un style clair et concis, c'est écrit avec clarté et concision; **the report was four years in the ~** il a fallu quatre ans pour rédiger le rapport. -**2.** [handwriting] écriture *f*; **I can't read your ~** je ne peux pas déchiffrer votre écriture OR ce que vous avez écrit. -**3.** [written text]: **there was ~ all over the board** il n'y avait plus de place pour écrire quoi que ce soit sur le tableau noir ❑ **the ~'s on the wall** l'issue est inéluctable. -**4.** SCH [spelling] orthographe *f*; [written language] écriture *f*; **to learn reading and ~** apprendre à lire et à écrire, apprendre la lecture et l'écriture; **~ materials** matériel *m* nécessaire pour écrire.

◆ **writings** *npl* [written works] œuvre *f*, écrits *mpl*.

◆ **in writing** *adv phr* par écrit; **to put sthg in ~** mettre qqch par écrit; **can we have that in ~?** pouvons-nous avoir cela par écrit?; **you need her agreement in ~** il vous faut son accord écrit.

writing block *n* bloc *m* de papier à lettres.

writing case *n* nécessaire *m* à écrire.

writing desk *n* secrétaire *m (meuble)*.

writing pad *n* bloc-notes *m*.

writing paper *n* papier *m* à lettres.

writing table *n* ≃ secrétaire *m (meuble)*.

written [ˈrɪtn] ◇ *pp* → **write**.

◇ *adj* [form, text] écrit; **to make a ~ request** faire une demande par écrit; **~ language** (langage *m*) écrit *m*; **the ~ word** l'écrit.

WRNS (*abbr of* Women's Royal Naval Service) *pr n section féminine de la marine de guerre britannique*.

wrong [rɒŋ] ◇ *adj* -**1.** [incorrect - address, answer, information] mauvais, faux, erroné; [- decision] mauvais; MUS [note] faux; TELEC [number] faux; **to get things in the ~ order** mettre les choses dans le mauvais ordre; **they came on the ~ day** ils se sont trompés de jour pour leur venue; **to take the ~ road/train** se tromper de route/de train; **she went to the ~ address** elle s'est trompée d'adresse; **you've put your shoes on the ~ feet** vous vous êtes trompé (de pied) en mettant vos chaussures; **the biscuit went down the ~ way** j'ai avalé le gâteau de travers; **it was a ~ number** c'était une erreur; **to dial the ~ number** se tromper de numéro; **I'm sorry, you've got the ~ number** désolé, vous vous êtes trompé de numéro OR vous faites erreur; **the clock/my watch is ~** le réveil/ma montre n'est pas à l'heure; **the clock has always shown the ~ time** la pendule n'a jamais été à l'heure OR n'a jamais indiqué l'heure exacte. -**2.** [mistaken - person]: **to be ~ (about sthg)** avoir tort OR se tromper (à propos de qqch); **you were ~ to lose your temper** vous avez eu tort de vous emporter; **you were ~ to accuse him, it was ~ of you to accuse him** vous avez eu tort de l'accuser, vous n'auriez pas dû l'accuser; **to be ~ about sb** se tromper sur le compte de qqn; **how ~ can you be!** comme quoi on peut se tromper!; **I hope he won't get the ~ idea about me** j'espère qu'il ne se fera pas de fausses idées sur mon compte. -**3.** [unsuitable] mauvais, mal choisi; **you've got the ~ attitude** vous n'avez pas l'attitude qu'il faut OR la bonne attitude; **it was the ~ thing to do/say** ce n'était pas la chose à faire/dire; **I said all the ~ things** j'ai dit tout ce qu'il ne fallait pas dire; **you're going about it in the ~ way** vous vous y prenez mal; **it's the ~ way to deal with the situation** ce n'est pas comme cela qu'il faut régler la situation; **he's the ~ man for the job** ce n'est pas l'homme qu'il faut pour le poste; **I think you're in the ~ job** *literal* je pense que ce n'est pas le travail qu'il vous faut; *hum* vous vous êtes trompé de métier!; **she was wearing the ~ shoes for a long walk** elle n'avait pas les chaussures qui conviennent OR elle n'avait pas les bonnes chaussures pour une randonnée. -**4.** *phr*: **he got hold of the ~ end of the stick** il a tout compris de travers; **to be caught on the ~ foot** *Br* être pris au dépourvu; **they got off on the ~ foot** ils se sont mal entendus au départ; **I'm (on) the ~ side of 50** *Br* j'ai 50 ans bien sonnés; **to get out of bed on the ~ side** se lever du pied gauche; **to get on the ~ side of sb** se faire mal voir de qqn; **to be on the ~ track** faire fausse route. -**5.** [immoral, bad] mal; [unjust] injuste; **cheating is ~** c'est mal de tricher; **slavery is ~** l'esclavage est inacceptable; **it was ~ of him to take the money** ce n'était pas bien de sa part de prendre l'argent; **what's ~ with reading comics?**

qu'est-ce qu'il y a de mal à lire des bandes dessinées?; what's ~ with that? qu'est-ce qu'il y a de mal à ça?; there's nothing ~ with it il n'y a rien à redire à cela, il n'y a pas de mal à cela; it's ~ that anyone should have to live in poverty il est injuste que des gens soient obligés de vivre dans la misère. -**6.** [amiss] *(+ something)*: something is ~ OR there's something ~ with the lamp la lampe ne marche pas bien OR a un défaut; something is ~ OR there's something ~ with my elbow j'ai quelque chose au coude; there must be something seriously ~ il doit y avoir un gros problème; there's something ~ somewhere il y a quelque chose qui ne va pas quelque part || *(+ nothing)*: there's nothing at all ~ with the clock la pendule marche parfaitement bien; there's nothing ~ with your work votre travail est très bon; there's nothing ~ with her decision/reasoning sa décision/son raisonnement est parfaitement valable; there's nothing ~ with you vous êtes en parfaite santé; there's nothing ~, thank you tout va bien, merci; there's nothing ~ with your eyes/hearing! vous avez de bons yeux/de bonnes oreilles! || *(+ what's)*: what's ~? qu'est-ce qui ne va pas?; what's ~ with the car? qu'est-ce qu'elle a, la voiture?; what's ~ with your elbow? qu'est-ce qu'il a, votre coude?; what's ~ with you? qu'est-ce que vous avez?; there's very little ~ with you dans l'ensemble vous êtes en très bonne santé; there wasn't much ~ with the car la voiture n'avait pas grand-chose ❑ to be ~ in the head *inf Br* avoir la tête fêlée OR le cerveau fêlé, être fêlé OR timbré. -**7.** TEX: the ~ side of the fabric l'envers du tissu; ~ side out à l'envers.

◇ *adv* mal; I guessed ~ je suis tombé à côté, je me suis trompé; you've spelt the word ~ vous avez mal écrit OR orthographié ce mot; to get sthg ~: I got the answer ~ je n'ai pas donné la bonne réponse; to get one's sums ~ MATH faire des erreurs dans ses opérations; *fig* se tromper dans ses calculs; she's got her facts ~ elle se trompe, ce qu'elle avance est faux; you've got it ~, I never said that vous vous trompez OR vous n'avez pas compris, je n'ai jamais dit cela; to get sb ~: don't get me ~ comprenez-moi bien; you've got her all ~ vous vous trompez complètement sur son compte; to go ~ [person] se tromper; [plan] mal marcher, mal tourner; [deal] tomber à l'eau; [machine] tomber en panne; something has gone ~ with the TV la télé est tombée en panne; something went ~ with her eyesight elle a eu des ennuis avec sa vue; we must have gone ~ somewhere nous avons dû nous tromper quelque part; you can't go ~ vous ne pouvez pas vous tromper, c'est très simple; you won't go far ~ if you follow her advice vous ne risquez guère de vous tromper si vous suivez ses conseils; you can't go ~ with a pair of jeans vous êtes tranquille avec un jean; you can't go ~ with a good book [for reading] vous ne risquez pas de vous ennuyer avec un bon livre; [as present] un bon livre, cela plaît toujours; when did things start going ~? quand est-ce que les choses ont commencé à se gâter?; everything that could go ~ went ~ tout ce qui pouvait aller de travers est allé de travers; to turn out ~ [event] mal (se) terminer; [calculation] se révéler faux; [person] mal tourner.

◇ *n* -**1.** [immorality, immoral act] mal *m*; to know the difference between right and ~ savoir distinguer le bien du mal; I did no ~ je n'ai rien fait de mal ❑ two ~s don't make a right *prov* on ne répare pas une injustice par une autre. -**2.** [harm] tort *m*, injustice *f*; to suffer ~ subir une injustice; to do sb ~ faire du tort à OR se montrer injuste envers qqn; he did them a great ~ il leur a fait subir une grave injustice, il leur a fait (un) grand tort. -**3.** [error] tort *m*, erreur *f*; he can do no ~ in her eyes tout ce qu'il fait trouve grâce à ses yeux. -**4.** JUR tort *m*.

◇ *vt* faire du tort à, traiter injustement; he ~ed his wife by accusing her of being unfaithful il a traité injustement sa femme en l'accusant d'infidélité; she felt deeply ~ed elle se sentait gravement lésée; she has been badly ~ed [by words] on a dit à tort beaucoup de mal d'elle; [by actions] on a agi de manière injuste envers elle.

◆ **in the wrong** *adj & adv phr* dans son tort; to be in the ~ être dans son tort, avoir tort; to put sb in the ~ mettre qqn dans son tort.

wrongdoer [ˌrɒŋˈduːəʳ] *n* -**1.** [delinquent] malfaiteur *m*, délinquant *m*, -e *f*. -**2.** [sinner] pécheur *m*, -eresse *f*.

wrongdoing [ˌrɒŋˈduːɪŋ] *n* mal *m*, méfait *m*; a sense of ~ le sentiment de mal faire; his many ~s ses nombreux méfaits.

wrong-foot *vt* SPORT & *fig* prendre à contre-pied.

wrongful [ˈrɒŋfʊl] *adj* [unjust] injuste; [unjustified] injustifié; [illegal] illégal, illicite; JUR: ~ arrest arrestation *f* arbitraire; ~ imprisonment emprisonnement *m* injustifié; ~ dismissal INDUST renvoi *m* injustifié.

wrongfully [ˈrɒŋfʊlɪ] *adv* à tort; I was ~ dismissed INDUST j'ai été renvoyé à tort.

wrongheaded [ˌrɒŋˈhedɪd] *adj* -**1.** [person] buté. -**2.** [idea] erroné, fou.

wrongly [ˈrɒŋlɪ] *adv* -**1.** [incorrectly] à tort, mal; to be ~ informed être mal renseigné; this word is spelt ~ ce mot est mal écrit OR orthographié; to be ~ accused être accusé à tort OR faussement accusé; I guessed ~ je suis tombé à côté; the cat was ~ described as a Siamese le chat a été décrit à tort comme un siamois. -**2.** [by mistake] par erreur, à tort; he was ~ assigned to the night shift il a été affecté par erreur OR à tort à l'équipe de nuit.

wrongness [ˈrɒŋnɪs] *n* -**1.** [error] erreur *f*. -**2.** [injustice] injustice *f*. -**3.** [immorality] immoralité *f*, mal *m*.

wrote [rəʊt] *pt* → **write**.

wrought [rɔːt] ◇ *arch pt & pp* → **work**.
◇ *adj lit*: wheels ~ by hand des roues façonnées OR fabriquées à la main; carefully ~ prose prose *f* finement ciselée ❑ ~ copper cuivre *m* martelé; ~ silk soie *f* ouvragée.

wrought iron *n* fer *m* forgé.

◆ **wrought-iron** *adj* en fer forgé.

wrought-up *adj* énervé.

wrung [rʌŋ] *pt & pp* → **wring**.

WRVS (*abbr of* Women's Royal Voluntary Service) *pr n* *association de femmes au service des déshérités*.

wry [raɪ] (*compar* wrier OR wryer, *superl* wriest OR wryest) *adj* -**1.** [expression, glance - of distaste] désabusé; she made a ~ face elle a fait la grimace. -**2.** [ironic - comment, smile] ironique, désabusé; ~ humour ironie *f*.

wryly [ˈraɪlɪ] *adv* de manière désabusée, ironiquement; he smiled back at me ~ il m'a répondu par un sourire ironique OR désabusé.

wt. (*written abbr of* weight) pds.

wurst [wɜːst] *n* *grosse saucisse allemande*.

WV *written abbr of* West Virginia.

WW *written abbr of* World War.

WWF (*abbr of* Worldwide Fund for Nature) *pr n* WWF *m*.

WY *written abbr of* Wyoming.

wych elm [wɪtʃ-] *n* orme *m*.

wynd [waɪnd] *n Scot* allée *f*.

Wyoming [waɪˈəʊmɪŋ] *pr n* Wyoming *m*; in ~ dans le Wyoming.

WYSIWYG [ˈwɪzɪwɪg] (*abbr of* what you see is what you get) *n & adj* COMPUT *tel écran, tel écrit: ce que l'on voit sur l'écran est ce que l'on obtient à l'impression*.

x (*pl* x's OR xs), **X** (*pl* X's OR Xs) [eks] *n* [letter] x *m*, X *m*.

x *n* MATH x *m*.

X (*pt* & *pp* X-ed OR X'd) ◇ *n* -**1.** [unknown factor] X *m*; X marks the spot l'endroit est marqué d'une croix; Mr X monsieur X. -**2.** CIN film *m* interdit aux moins de 18 ans *(remplacé en 1982 par «18»)*.
◇ -**1.** (*written abbr of* kiss) *formule affectueuse placée après la signature à la fin d'une lettre*. -**2.** *written abbr of* Christ.
◇ *vt* marquer d'une croix.
◆ **X out** *vt sep* biffer, rayer (avec des croix).

xanthene ['zænθiːn] *n* xanthène *m*.

x-axis *n* axe *m* des X, abscisse *f*.

X certificate *n Br signalait (jusqu'en 1982) un film interdit aux moins de 18 ans*.

X chromosome *n* chromosome *m* X.

x-coordinate *n* abscisse *f*.

xenon ['ziːnɒn] *n* xénon *m*.

xenophobe ['zenəfəʊb] *n* xénophobe *mf*.

xenophobia [ˌzenə'fəʊbjə] *n* xénophobie *f*.

xenophobic [ˌzenə'fəʊbɪk] *adj* xénophobe.

xerographic [ˌzɪərə'græfɪk] *adj* de photocopie; ~ **equipment** copieur *m*, photocopieuse *f*.

xerography [ˌzɪə'rɒgrəfɪ] *n (U)* photocopie *f*.

xerox ['zɪərɒks] *vt* photocopier.

Xerox® ['zɪərɒks] *n* -**1.** [machine] copieur *m*, photocopieuse *f*. -**2.** [process, copy] photocopie *f*.

Xerxes ['zɜːksiːz] *pr n* Xerxès.

XL (*written abbr of* extra-large) *n* XL *m*.

Xmas *written abbr of* Christmas.

X-rated [-reɪtɪd] *adj dated* [film] interdit aux mineurs OR aux moins de 18 ans.

x-ray, X-ray ◇ *vt* -**1.** MED [examine - chest, ankle] radiographier, faire une radio de; [- patient] faire une radio à. -**2.** [inspect - luggage] passer aux rayons X. -**3.** [treat] traiter aux rayons X.
◇ *comp* -**1.** MED [examination] radioscopique; [treatment] radiologique, par rayons X; ~ **diagnosis** radiodiagnostic *m*; ~ **photograph** radiographie *f*, radio *f*; ~ **therapy** radiothérapie *f*. -**2.** PHYS [astronomy, tube] à rayons X; ~ **star** *étoile émettant un rayonnement radioélectrique*.
◇ *n* -**1.** MED radio *f*; **to have an** ~ passer une radio; **to take an** ~ **of sthg** radiographier qqch, faire une radiographie de qqch. -**2.** PHYS rayon *m* X.

xylene ['zaɪliːn] *n* xylène *m*.

xylograph ['zaɪləgrɑːf] ◇ *n* xylographie *f*.
◇ *vt* [drawing, text] tirer à partir d'une gravure sur bois.

xylography [zaɪ'lɒgrəfɪ] *n (U)* xylographie *f*.

xylol ['zaɪlɒl] *n* xylol *m*.

xylophone ['zaɪləfəʊn] *n* xylophone *m*.

xylophonist [zaɪ'lɒfənɪst] *n* joueur *m*, -euse *f* de xylophone.

y (*pl* y's OR ys), **Y** (*pl* Y's OR Ys) [waɪ] *n* [letter] y *m*, Y *m*.
y *n* MATH y *m*.
Y -**1.** *written abbr of* yen (currency). -**2.** *written abbr of* yuan.
yabber *inf* ['jæbəʳ] *Austr* ◇ *vi* jacasser.
◇ *n* bavardage *m*, jacassement *m*.
yacht [jɒt] ◇ *n* [sailing boat] voilier *m*; [pleasure boat] yacht *m*.
◇ *vi* faire du yachting; to go ~ing faire de la voile OR du yachting.
◇ *comp* [race] de voiliers, de yachts; ~ club yacht-club *m*.
yachting ['jɒtɪŋ] ◇ *n* yachting *m*, navigation *f* de plaisance.
◇ *comp* [holiday] en yacht, sur l'eau; [magazine] de voile; [cap] de marin.
yachtsman ['jɒtsmən] (*pl* yachtsmen [-mən]) *n* yachtman *m*, yachtsman *m*.
yachtswoman ['jɒts,wʊmən] (*pl* yachtswomen [-,wɪmɪn]) *n* yachtwoman *f*.
yack [jæk] = **yak** *vi, n* **2**.
yackety-yak *inf* [,jækətɪ'jæk] ◇ *vi* jacasser.
◇ *n (U)* jacasserie *f*.
yah *inf* [jɑː] *interj* beurk.
yahoo [jə'huː] (*pl* yahoos) *n* rustre *m*, butor *m*.
yak [jæk] (*pt* & *pp* yakked, *cont* yakking) ◇ *n* -**1.** ZOOL yak *m*, yack *m*. -**2.** *inf (U)* jacasserie *f*.
◇ *vi inf*: to ~, to ~ on *Br* jacasser.
Yale lock® [jeɪl-] *n* serrure *f* de sécurité *(à cylindre)*.
y'all *inf* [jɑːl] *Am* = **you-all**.
Yalta ['jæltə] *pr n* Yalta; the ~ Conference la conférence de Yalta.
yam [jæm] *n* -**1.** [plant, vegetable] igname *f*. -**2.** *Am* CULIN patate *f* douce.
yammer *inf* ['jæməʳ] *vi* [person - whine] pleurnicher, geindre; [- chatter] jacasser; what are you ~ing (on *Br*) about? qu'est-ce que tu as à jacasser comme ça?
yang [jæŋ] *n* yang *m*.
Yangtze ['jæŋtsɪ] *pr n*: the ~ le Yang-tseu-kiang, le Yangzi Jiang.
yank [jæŋk] ◇ *vt* [hair, sleeve] tirer brusquement (sur), tirer d'un coup sec; he was ~ed to his feet on l'a tiré brutalement pour l'obliger à se lever; I ~ed the lever back j'ai tiré le levier en arrière d'un coup sec.
◇ *n* coup *m* sec; I gave the wire/her hair a ~ j'ai tiré d'un coup sec sur le fil/sur ses cheveux.
◆ **yank off** *vt sep* [button, cover] arracher; she ~ed the cloth off the table elle a enlevé la nappe de la table d'un coup sec.
◆ **yank out** *vt sep* [nail, tooth] arracher.
Yank *inf* [jæŋk] ◇ *n* -**1.** *Br pej* Amerloque *mf*. -**2.** *Am* Yankee *mf*.
◇ *adj* amerloque.
Yankee ['jæŋkɪ] ◇ *n* -**1.** *Am* Yankee *mf*. -**2.** *inf Br pej* Amerloque *mf*.
◇ *adj* -**1.** *Am* yankee. -**2.** *inf Br pej* amerloque.
Yaoundé [jɑː'ʊndeɪ] *pr n* Yaoundé.
yap [jæp] (*pt* & *pp* yapped, *cont* yapping) ◇ *vi* -**1.** [dog] japper. -**2.** [person] jacasser; the shop assistants were yapping away instead of serving les vendeuses jacassaient au lieu de servir la clientèle.
◇ *n* [yelp] jappement *m*.
yappy ['jæpɪ] (*compar* yappier, *superl* yappiest) *adj* -**1.** [dog] jappeur. -**2.** *inf* [person] jacasseur.
yarborough ['jɑːbərə] *n* [in bridge, whist] *main de treize cartes sans honneurs*.
yard [jɑːd] *n* -**1.** [of factory, farm, house, school] cour *f*; parked in the ~ garé dans la cour. -**2.** [work site] chantier *m*; builder's ~ chantier de construction. -**3.** [for storage] dépôt *m*. -**4.** RAIL voies *fpl* de garage. -**5.** [for animals - enclosure] enclos *m*; [- pasture] pâturage *m*. -**6.** *Br*: the Yard *inf* Scotland Yard; Murphy of the Yard Murphy de Scotland Yard. -**7.** *Am* [backyard] cour *f*; [garden] jardin *m*; ~ sale *vente de meubles, d'objets etc par un particulier devant sa maison*. -**8.** [unit of measure] yard *m (0,914 m)*; it was about ten ~s away c'était à environ dix mètres; it was ten ~s wide il avait dix mètres de large; to buy cloth by the ~ acheter le tissu au mètre; we still have ~s of green velvet *fig* nous avons toujours des quantités de velours vert; his calculations were ~s out *fig* il s'était complètement trompé dans ses calculs ❑ his face was a ~ long il en faisait une tête, il faisait une tête d'enterrement. -**9.** SPORT & *dated*: the 100 ~s, the 100 ~s' dash le cent mètres; she won the 3,000 ~s' steeple chase elle a gagné le 3 000 mètres steeple. -**10.** NAUT vergue *f*.
yardage ['jɑːdɪdʒ] *n* TEX ≃ métrage *m*.
yardarm ['jɑːdɑːm] *n* extrémité *f* d'une vergue carrée.
yardbird ['jɑːdbɜːd] *n Am mil sl* bleu *m*, bidasse *m (empoté)*.
yardstick ['jɑːdstɪk] *n* -**1.** [instrument] mètre *m (en bois ou en métal)*. -**2.** *fig* critère *m*; salary seems to be a ~ for success *fig* il semble que le salaire soit un critère de réussite.
yarmulke [jɑː'mʊlkə] *n* kippa *f*.
yarn [jɑːn] ◇ *n* -**1.** TEX *(U)* fil *m (à tricoter ou à tisser)*. -**2.** [tall story] histoire *f* (incroyable OR invraisemblable); [long story] longue histoire *f*.
◇ *vi* [tell tall stories] raconter des histoires; [tell long stories] raconter de longues histoires.
yarrow ['jærəʊ] *n* mille-feuille *f*.
yashmak ['jæʃmæk] *n* litham *m*, litsam *m*.
yaw [jɔː] ◇ *vi* -**1.** [ship] être déporté *(de sa trajectoire)*, faire une embardée. -**2.** [plane, missile] faire un mouvement de lacet.
◇ *vt* faire dévier *(de sa trajectoire)*.
◇ *n* -**1.** [of ship] écart *m*, embardée *f*. -**2.** [of plane, missile] mouvement *m* de lacet.
yawl [jɔːl] *n* -**1.** [sailing boat] yawl *m*. -**2.** [carried on ship] canot *m*.
yawn [jɔːn] ◇ *vi* -**1.** [person] bâiller. -**2.** [chasm, opening] être béant, s'ouvrir.
◇ *vt* [utter with yawn] dire en bâillant; she was ~ing her head off elle bâillait à se décrocher la mâchoire.
◇ *n* -**1.** [of person] bâillement *m*; to give a big ~ bâiller (bruyamment) la bouche grande ouverte. -**2.** *inf fig*: to be a ~ [meeting] être ennuyeux; [film, book] être rasoir; what a ~! qu'est-ce que c'est rasoir!
yawning ['jɔːnɪŋ] ◇ *adj* -**1.** [person] qui bâille. -**2.** [gap, chasm] béant.
◇ *n (U)* bâillement *m*, bâillements *mpl*.
yawp *inf* [jɔːp] *Am* ◇ *vi* -**1.** [yawn] bâiller bruyamment. -**2.** [bawl] gueuler. -**3.** [bark] aboyer.
◇ *n* -**1.** [bark] aboiement *m*. -**2.** [shout] cri *m*.
yaws [jɔːz] *n (U)* MED pian *m*.
y-axis *n* axe *m* des Y OR des ordonnées.
Y chromosome *n* chromosome *m* Y.
y-coordinate *n* ordonnée *f*.
yd *written abbr of* yard.
ye [jiː] ◇ *pron arch* OR BIBLE vous; ~ who weep vous qui versez des larmes.
◇ *def art arch*: ~ olde inne la vieille hostellerie.

YE OLDE:
Cette expression, qui représente la graphie ancienne de «the old», est souvent employée dans des dénominations pseudo-historiques: certains salons de thé dans les villes anciennes s'appellent «ye olde tea shoppe», par exemple.

yea [jeɪ] ◇ *adv* -**1.** [yes] oui; you know you can say ~ or nay to the plan vous savez bien que vous avez la faculté d'accepter ou de refuser ce projet. -**2.** *arch* OR *lit* [indeed] voire, vraiment.
◇ *n* [in vote] oui *m*; the ~s and nays les oui et les non, les voix pour et contre.
yeah *inf* [jeə] *adv* & *interj* [yes] ouais.
year [jɪəʳ] *n* -**1.** [period of time] an *m*, année *f*; this ~ cette année; last ~ l'an dernier, l'année dernière; next ~ l'année prochaine; the ~ after next dans deux ans; ~ by ~ d'année en année; ~ after ~ année après année; all (the) ~ round (pendant) toute l'année; ~ in ~ out année après année; it was five ~s last Christmas ça a fait cinq ans à Noël; we'll have been here five ~s next Christmas cela fera cinq ans à Noël que nous sommes là; after ten ~s in politics après dix ans passés dans la politique; he spent many ~s working for the same company il a passé de nombreuses années dans la même société ‖ [with 'in']: in a few ~s, in a few ~s' time dans quelques années; in ten

~s, in ten ~s' time dans dix ans; in ~s to come dans les années à venir; in all my ~s as a social worker au cours de toutes mes années d'assistante sociale || [with 'for']: I haven't seen her for ~s je ne l'ai pas vue depuis des années; for a few ~s pendant quelques années; I haven't been home for two long ~s cela fait deux longues années que je ne suis pas rentré chez moi; for ~s and ~s pendant des années; she'll be busy writing her memoirs for ~s elle en a pour des années de travail à écrire ses mémoires || [with 'ago']: two ~s ago il y a deux ans; that was many ~s ago cela remonte à bien des années || [with 'last', 'take']: the batteries last (for) ~s les piles durent des années; it took me ~s to build up the collection cela m'a demandé des années pour OR j'ai mis des années à rassembler cette collection || [with 'earn', 'cost' etc): he earns over £40,000 a ~ il gagne plus de 40 000 livres par an; it cost me a ~'s salary cela m'a coûté un an de salaire; it costs at least £5,000 a ~ to run a car rouler en voiture coûte au moins 5 000 livres par an ❑ 'The Best Years of Our Lives' *Wyler* 'les Plus Belles Années de notre vie'. -**2.** [in calendar] an *m*, année *f*; in the ~ 1607 en (l'an) 1607; in the ~ of grace 1900 en l'an de grâce 1900 ❑ since the ~ dot *Br*, since ~ one *Am* depuis une éternité, de tout temps. -**3.** [in age]: he is 15 ~s old OR of age il a 15 ans; the foundations are 4,000 ~s old les fondations sont vieilles de 4 000 ans; a man of 80 ~s un homme (âgé) de 80 ans; a man of your ~s un homme de votre âge; she died in her fiftieth ~ elle est morte dans sa cinquantième année; she's young for her ~s elle fait jeune pour son âge, elle ne fait pas son âge; I'm getting on in ~s je prends de l'âge; the experience put ~s on/took ~s off her l'expérience l'a beaucoup vieillie/rajeunie; the carpet is beginning to show its ~s la moquette commence à trahir son âge. -**4.** *Br* [as student] année *f*; he's in the first ~ [at school] ≃ il est en sixième; [at college, university] il est en première année; first-~ students les étudiants de première année; all the third ~ tous les élèves de troisième année, tous les troisième année. -**5.** [for wine, coin] année *f*; 1965 was a good ~ 1965 était une bonne année OR un bon millésime.

yearbook ['jɪəbʊk] *n* annuaire *m*, recueil *m* annuel.

YEARBOOK:
Aux États-Unis, les écoles, les universités, et certaines colonies de vacances ont un «yearbook», qui rassemble photos et adresses, mais aussi des anecdotes sur l'année ou l'été écoulé.

year-end ◇ *adj Br* de fin d'année; a ~ report un rapport annuel.
◇ *n*: at the ~ à la fin de l'année, en fin d'année.

yearling ['jɪəlɪŋ] ◇ *n* ZOOL petit *m* d'un an; EQUIT yearling *m*.
◇ *adj* ZOOL (âgé) d'un an.

yearlong [,jɪə'lɒŋ] *adj* de toute une année; a ~ drought une sécheresse qui a duré toute une année.

yearly ['jɪəlɪ] (*pl* yearlies) ◇ *adj* annuel.
◇ *adv* annuellement.
◇ *n* PRESS publication *f* annuelle.

yearn [jɜːn] *vi* -**1.** [desire, crave] languir, aspirer; [pine] languir; she ~ed for love OR to be loved elle aspirait à l'amour, elle avait très envie d'être aimée; to ~ to do sthg mourir d'envie OR brûler de faire qqch; he was ~ing to see her again il mourait d'envie de la revoir; she ~ed to see her home again, she ~ed for home elle avait la nostalgie du pays. -**2.** *lit* [be moved - person] s'attendrir, s'émouvoir; [- heart] s'attendrir.

yearning ['jɜːnɪŋ] *n* [longing] désir *m* ardent; [pining] nostalgie *f*; he feels a constant ~ to see his old friends OR for his old friends il n'aspire qu'à une chose, revoir ses vieux amis; I felt a sudden ~ for company j'ai eu un soudain désir OR besoin de compagnie.

year-round *adj* [activity] qui dure toute l'année, sur toute l'année; [facility] qui fonctionne toute l'année.

yeast [jiːst] ◇ *n* levure *f*.
◇ *vt* mousser.

yeast cake *n Am* bloc *m* de levure.

yeasty ['jiːstɪ] (*compar* yeastier, *superl* yeastiest) *adj* -**1.** [bread, rolls - in taste] qui a un goût de levure; [- in smell] à l'odeur de levure. -**2.** [frothy] écumeux, qui mousse. -**3.** *Br* [trivial, frivolous] frivole, superficiel.

yecch *inf* [jek] *interj Am* berk.

yegg▽ [jeg] *n Am* [robber] cambrioleur *m*, -euse *f*.

yell [jel] ◇ *vi* crier (à tue-tête); to ~ at sb crier après qqn; to ~ about sthg brailler au sujet de qqch; to ~ at the top of one's voice vociférer; if you need me, just ~ si vous avez besoin de moi, vous n'avez qu'à crier.
◇ *vt* [shout out] hurler, crier; [proclaim] clamer, crier; he was ~ing his head off *inf* il beuglait comme un veau.
◇ *n* -**1.** [shout] cri *m*, hurlement *m*; to give a ~ of terror pousser un cri de terreur; I heard a ~ outside j'ai entendu crier dehors. -**2.** *Am* [from students, supporters] cri *m* de ralliement; the Buffstone ~ [students] le cri de ralliement des étudiants de Buffstone; [supporters] le cri de ralliement des supporters de Buffstone.

yelling ['jelɪŋ] *n (U)* cris *mpl*, hurlements *mpl*; stop that ~! cesse de hurler comme ça!

yellow ['jeləʊ] ◇ *adj* -**1.** [in colour] jaune; the papers had gone OR turned ~ with age les papiers avaient jauni avec le temps ❑ ~ cab *taxi new-yorkais*. -**2.** *inf* [cowardly] lâche; we all have a ~ streak on est tous un peu lâches.
◇ *n* -**1.** [colour] jaune *m*. -**2.** [yolk] jaune *m* (d'œuf). -**3.** [in snooker] boule *f* jaune.
◇ *vi* jaunir; to ~ with age jaunir avec le temps; ~ing leaves des feuilles jaunissantes.
◇ *vt* jaunir; newspapers ~ed with age des journaux jaunis par le temps.

yellowback ['jeləʊbæk] *n roman bon marché et à sensation du XIXᵉ siècle*.

yellow-bellied *inf* [-'belɪd] *adj* trouillard.

yellow-belly *inf n* trouillard *m*, -e *f*.

yellow card *n* FTBL carton *m* jaune.

yellow fever *n* fièvre *f* jaune.

yellowhammer ['jeləʊ,hæməʳ] *n* -**1.** bruant *m* jaune. -**2.** *Am sorte de pivert*.

yellowish ['jeləʊɪʃ] *adj* jaunâtre, qui tire sur le jaune.

yellow jacket *n Am* guêpe *f*.

yellow line *n* bande *f* jaune; to park on a ~ ≃ se mettre en stationnement irrégulier; double ~ OR ~s double ligne *f* jaune.

YELLOW LINES:
En Grande-Bretagne, une ligne jaune parallèle au trottoir signifie «arrêt autorisé réglementé»; une double ligne jaune signifie «stationnement interdit».

yellow metal *n* -**1.** [brass] cuivre *m* jaune, laiton *m*. -**2.** [gold] métal *m* jaune, or *m*.

yellowness ['jeləʊnɪs] *n* -**1.** [colour] couleur *f* jaune. -**2.** *inf* [cowardice] lâcheté *f*, poltronnerie *f*.

yellow ochre *n* ocre *f* jaune.

Yellow Pages® *npl*: the ~ les Pages Jaunes.

yellow peril, Yellow Peril *n dated & offensive* péril *m* jaune.

yellow press *n* presse *f* à sensation.

yellow ribbon *n aux États-Unis, ruban jaune arboré en signe de patriotisme et de solidarité avec ceux qui sont au combat, prisonniers politiques etc.*

Yellow River *pr n*: the ~ le fleuve Jaune.

Yellow Sea *pr n*: the ~ la mer Jaune.

Yellowstone National Park ['jeləʊstəʊn-] *pr n* le parc national de Yellowstone.

yellowy ['jeləʊɪ] *adj* un peu jaune, qui tire sur le jaune.

yelp [jelp] ◇ *vi* [dog] japper, glapir; [person] crier, glapir; to ~ in OR with pain [dog] glapir de douleur; [person] crier de douleur.
◇ *n* [of dog] jappement *m*, glapissement *m*; [of person] cri *m*, glapissement *m*.

Yeltsin ['jeltsɪn] *pr n*: Boris ~ Boris Eltsine.

Yemen ['jemən] *pr n* Yémen *m*; in (the) ~ au Yémen; the ~ Arab Republic la République arabe du Yémen; the People's Democratic Republic of ~ la République démocratique et populaire du Yémen; the ~ Republic la République du Yémen.

Yemeni ['jemənɪ] ◇ *n* Yéménite *mf*.
◇ *adj* yéménite.

yen [jen] (*pl sense 1 inv*) *n* -**1.** [currency] yen *m*. -**2.** *inf* [desire] envie *f*; to have a ~ for sthg/to do sthg avoir très envie de OR mourir d'envie de qqch/faire qqch.

Yenisei [,jenɪ'seɪ] *pr n*: the (River) ~ l'Ienisseï *m*.

yeoman ['jəʊmən] (*pl* yeomen [-mən]) ◇ *n* -**1.** [in UK] yeoman *m*; Yeoman of the Guard yeoman de la garde. -**2.** MIL & NAUT [petty officer] quartier-maître *m*.
◇ *comp*: ~ farmer franc-tenancier *m*.

yeomanry ['jəʊmənrɪ] *n* yeomanry *f*, ensemble *m* des yeomen.

yep *inf* [jep] *interj* ouais.

yer *inf* [jəʳ] = **your**.

yes [jes] ◇ *adv* -**1.** [gen] oui; [in answer to negatives] si; [answering knock on door] oui (entrez); [answering phone] allô, oui; [encouraging a speaker to continue] oui, et puis?, oui, et alors?; to say/to vote ~ dire/voter oui; is it raining? — ~ (it is) est-ce qu'il pleut? — oui; will you tell her? — ~ (I will) le lui direz-vous? — oui (je vais le faire); ~? what do you want? oui? que voulez-vous?; did they enjoy the cruise? — oh, ~! ont-ils aimé leur croisière? — oh, oui!; oh ~? [doubtful] c'est vrai?; you don't like me, do you? — ~ I do! vous ne m'aimez pas, n'est-ce pas? — mais si (voyons)!; ~ please oui, s'il vous plaît; ~ of course, ~ certainly oui, bien sûr. -**2.** [introducing a contrary opinion]: ~ but... oui OR d'accord mais... -**3.** [in response to command or call] oui; ~, sir oui OR bien, monsieur; James! — ~? James! — oui? -**4.** [indeed] en effet, vraiment; she was rash, ~, terribly rash elle a été imprudente, vraiment très imprudente.
◇ *n* [person, vote]: to count the ~es compter les oui OR les votes pour; there are 10 ~es and 16 noes il y a 10 oui et 16 non.
◇ *comp*: ~ vote vote *m* pour; to give a ~ vote voter pour.
◆ **yes and no** *adv phr* oui et non; do you like him? — well, ~ and no vous l'aimez bien? — ben, oui et non.

yes-man *inf n* béni-oui-oui *m inv*.

yesterday ['jestədɪ] ◇ *adv* -**1.** hier; he came ~ il est venu hier; ~ morning/afternoon hier matin/après-midi; ~ week *Br*, a week ~, a week ago ~ il y a huit jours ❑ I wasn't born ~ je ne suis pas né de la dernière pluie. -**2.** [in the past] hier, naguère.
◇ *n* -**1.** [day before] hier *m*; ~ was Monday hier c'était lundi; ~'s programme le programme d'hier; the day before ~ avant-hier; it seems like (only) ~ c'est comme si c'était hier. -**2.** [former times] temps *mpl* passés OR anciens; ~'s fashions les coutumes d'hier OR d'autrefois; all our ~s tout notre passé.

yesternight ['jestənaɪt] *adv arch* la nuit dernière, hier soir.

yesteryear ['jestəjɪəʳ] *n fml* OR *lit* temps *m* jadis; fashions of ~ les coutumes d'autrefois OR d'antan.

yet [jet] ◇ *adv* -**1.** [up to now] déjà; is he here ~? est-il déjà là?; has he arrived ~? est-il déjà arrivé?; have you been to London ~? êtes-vous déjà allés à Londres?; did you go to the zoo ~? *Am* êtes-vous déjà allés au zoo? -**2.** [at the present time]: not ~ pas encore; not just ~ pas tout de suite; she isn't here ~ elle n'est pas encore là; I haven't finished ~ je n'ai pas

encore fini; **they haven't had any answer ~** ils n'ont pas encore (reçu) de réponse; **it isn't time for a break ~** il n'est pas encore l'heure de faire une pause. **-3.** [still] *(in affirmative statements)* encore, toujours; **I have ~ to meet her** je ne l'ai pas encore rencontrée; **the manuscripts have ~ to be deciphered** les manuscrits n'ont pas encore été déchiffrés; **the best is ~ to come** le meilleur est encore à venir OR reste à venir; **there are another ten miles to go ~** il reste encore seize kilomètres à faire; **I won't be ready for another hour ~** j'en ai encore pour une heure; **they won't be here for another hour ~** ils ne seront pas là avant une heure; **they may ~ be found** on peut encore les retrouver, il se peut encore qu'on les retrouve; **they may ~ be alive** ils sont peut-être encore OR toujours en vie. **-4.** [even] *(with comparatives and superlatives)* encore, même; **~ more expensive** encore plus cher; **~ more snow was expected** on prévoyait encore de la neige; **~ higher interest rates** des taux d'intérêt encore plus élevés; **a life of parties and ~ more parties** une existence qui consiste à aller de fête en fête; **he is not handsome, nor ~ well-dressed** *lit* il n'est pas beau, ni même bien habillé || [emphasizing amount, frequency etc]: **~ another bomb** encore une bombe; **~ again** encore une fois. **-5.** [so far - in present] jusqu'ici, jusque-là; [- in past] jusque-là; **it's her best play ~** c'est sa meilleure pièce jusqu'ici; **it was his best film ~** c'était son meilleur film jusque-là. **-6.** [despite everything] après tout, quand même; **she may ~ surprise you all** elle va peut-être vous surprendre tous après tout; **I'll manage it ~!** j'y arriverai quand même!
◇ *conj* [nevertheless] néanmoins, toutefois; [however] cependant, pourtant; [but] mais; **they had no income ~ they still had to pay taxes** ils n'avaient pas de revenus et pourtant ils devaient payer des impôts; **he was firm ~ kind** il était ferme et pourtant gentil.

yeti ['jetɪ] *n* yéti *m*.

yew [ju:] *n* **-1.** ~ (tree) if *m*. **-2.** [wood] (bois d') if *m*.

Y-fronts® *npl* slip *m* kangourou.

YHA *(abbr of* Youth Hostels Association) *pr n Br* *Fédération unie des Auberges de jeunesse*.

yid, Yid▼ [jɪd] *n terme antisémite désignant un juif*, ≃ youpin *m*, -e *f*.

Yiddish ['jɪdɪʃ] ◇ *n* yiddish *m*.
◇ *adj* yiddish.

yield [ji:ld] ◇ *vi* **-1.** [give in - person] céder; [surrender] se rendre; **he refused to ~** il a refusé de céder OR se laisser fléchir; **to ~ to** [argument] céder OR s'incliner devant; [criticism, force] céder devant; [blackmail, demand] céder à; [pressure, threat] céder sous; [desire, temptation] succomber à, céder à; **the city ~ed after a month-long siege** la ville a capitulé après un mois de siège; **the countryside has had to ~ to suburbia** la campagne a dû reculer au profit de la banlieue. **-2.** [break, bend - under weight, force] céder, fléchir; **the ice ~ed under his weight** la glace céda sous son poids; **the window catch eventually ~ed** le loqueteau de la fenêtre a fini par céder; **the door began to ~ under the pressure** la porte a commencé à céder sous la pression. **-3.** *Am* AUT céder le passage OR la priorité; **'yield'** 'cédez le passage'. **-4.** AGR [field] rapporter, rendre; [crop] rapporter.
◇ *vt* **-1.** [produce, bring in - gen] produire, rapporter; [land, crops] produire, rapporter, donner; **the orchard ~ed plentiful amounts of fruit** le verger a produit OR donné des fruits à profusion; **the investment bond will ~ 11 %** le bon d'épargne rapportera 11 %; **their research has ~ed some interesting results** leur recherche a fourni OR donné quelques résultats intéressants. **-2.** [relinquish, give up] céder, abandonner; **to ~ ground** MIL & *fig* céder du terrain; **he was forced to ~ control of the party** il a dû céder le contrôle du parti; **to ~ a position** MIL abandonner une position; **to ~ a point to sb** céder à qqn sur un point, concéder un point à qqn. **-3.** *Am* AUT: **to ~ right of way** céder la priorité.
◇ *n* **-1.** AGR & INDUST [output] rendement *m*, rapport *m*; [of crops] récolte *f*; **high-~ crops** récoltes à rendement élevé; **rice ~** récolte de riz; **~ per acre** ≃ rendement à l'hectare. **-2.** FIN [from investments] rapport *m*, rendement *m*; [profit] bénéfice *m*, bénéfices *mpl*; [from tax] recette *f*, rapport *m*; **an 8 % ~ on investments** des investissements qui rapportent 8 %.
◇ *comp Am*: **~ sign** panneau *m* de priorité.
◆ **yield up** *vt sep Br* **-1.** [surrender - town, prisoner] livrer; **he ~ed himself up to the police** il s'est livré à la police. **-2.** [reveal - secret] dévoiler.

yielding ['ji:ldɪŋ] ◇ *adj* **-1.** [soft - ground] mou. **-2.** [flexible - material, metal] flexible, extensible. **-3.** [person] complaisant, accommodant; [character] docile.
◇ *n* [of town] reddition *f*; [of rights, control] cession *f*.

yield point *n* limite *f* d'élasticité.

yin [jɪn] *n*: **~ and yang** le yin et le yang.

yippee *inf* [*Br* jɪ'pi:, *Am* 'jɪpɪ] *interj* hourra.

YMCA *(abbr of* Young Men's Christian Association) *pr n association chrétienne de jeunes gens (surtout connue pour ses centres d'hébergement)*.

yo *inf* [jəʊ] *interj esp Am* salut.

yob *inf* [jɒb], **yobbo** *inf* ['jɒbəʊ] *n Br* loubard *m*.

yod [jɒd] *n* yod *m*.

yodel ['jəʊdl] (*Br pt & pp* yodelled, *cont* yodelling, *Am pt & pp* yodeled, *cont* yodeling)
◇ *vi* jodler, iodler.
◇ *n* tyrolienne *f*.

yoga ['jəʊgə] *n* yoga *m*.

yoghourt, yoghurt [*Br* 'jɒgət, *Am* 'jəʊgərt] *n* yaourt *m*, yogourt *m*, yoghourt *m*.

yogi ['jəʊgɪ] *n* yogi *m*.

yogurt [*Br* 'jɒgət, *Am* 'jəʊgərt] = **yoghourt**.

yoke [jəʊk] ◇ *n* **-1.** [frame - for hitching oxen] joug *m*; [- for carrying buckets] joug *m*, palanche *f*. **-2.** *fig* [burden, domination] joug *m*; **to come under the ~ of slavery/tyranny** tomber sous le joug de l'esclavage/de la tyrannie; **a country struggling to cast off the ~ of foreign domination** un pays qui lutte pour rompre OR secouer le joug de la domination étrangère. **-3.** [pair of animals] attelage *m*, paire *f*. **-4.** [of dress, skirt, blouse] empiècement *m*. **-5.** CONSTR [for beams] moise *f*, lien *m*. **-6.** *lit*: **the ~ of marriage** les liens du mariage.
◇ *vt* **-1.** [oxen] atteler; **to ~ (up) oxen/bullocks to a plough** atteler des bouvillons/bœufs à une charrue. **-2.** [ideas, qualities] lier, joindre.

yokel ['jəʊkl] *n pej* péquenot *m*.

Yokohama [,jəʊkə'hɑ:mə] *pr n* Yokohama.

yolk [jəʊk] *n*: **(egg) ~** jaune *m* (d'œuf).

Yom Kippur [,jɒmkɪ'pʊə^r] *n* Yom Kippour *m inv*.

yomp *inf* [jɒmp] *vt Br* crapahuter, crapaüter.

yon [jɒn] *dem adj arch* OR *dial*: **~ tree** cet arbre-là, l'arbre là-bas.

yonder ['jɒndə^r] ◇ *adj lit*: **~ tree** l'arbre là-bas.
◇ *adv* là-bas; **way over ~** loin là-bas.

yonks *inf* [jɒŋks] *n Br*: **I haven't been there for ~** il y a belle lurette OR il y a une paie OR ça fait un bailque je n'y suis pas allé.

yoo-hoo [,ju:'hu:] *interj* ohé.

YOP [jɒp] *(abbr of* Youth Opportunities Programme) *n Br* **-1.** [programme] ≃ TUC *mpl*. **-2.** *inf* [worker] ≃ tuciste *mf*.

yore [jɔ:^r] *n arch* OR *lit*: **in days of ~** au temps jadis.

yorkie *inf* ['jɔ:kɪ] = **Yorkshire terrier**.

Yorks. *written abbr of* Yorkshire.

Yorkshire ['jɔ:kʃə^r] *pr n* Yorkshire *m*.

Yorkshire pudding *n crêpe épaisse salée traditionnellement servie avec du rôti de bœuf*.

Yorkshire Ripper *pr n*: **the ~** *l'éventreur du Yorkshire, accusé en 1981 du meurtre de 13 femmes*.

Yorkshire terrier *n* yorkshire-terrier *m*, yorkshire *m*.

you [ju:] *pron* **-1.** [as subject] vous *(sg or pl)*; [familiar use] tu *(sg)*, vous *(pl)*. **-2.** [as object] vous *(sg or pl)*; [familiar use] te *(sg)*, vous *(pl)*; **~ didn't ask** vous n'avez pas/tu n'as pas demandé; **don't ~ dare!** je te le déconseille!; **~ and I will go together** vous et moi/toi et moi irons ensemble; **would ~ like a drink?** voulez-vous boire quelque chose?; **~ and yours** vous et les vôtres/toi et les tiens; **all of ~** tous les tiens; **~ there!** vous ici!; **don't ~ say a word** je t'interdis de dire quoi que ce soit; **did he see ~?** est-ce qu'il vous a vu/t'a vu?; **I'll get ~ some dinner** je vais vous/te préparer à manger; **she gave ~ the keys** elle vous a donné/elle t'a donné les clés. **-3.** [after preposition] vous; [familiar use] toi; **with ~** avec vous/toi; **for ~** pour vous/toi; **that's men for ~** ah! les hommes!; **she gave the keys to ~** elle vous a donné/elle t'a donné les clés; **between ~ and me** entre nous. **-4.** [before noun or adjective]: **~ bloody fool!**▽ espèce de crétin!; **~ sweetie!** oh, le mignon/la mignonne!; **~ Americans are all the same** vous les Américains OR vous autres Américains, vous êtes tous pareils. **-5.** [emphatic use] vous; [familiar form] toi; **~ mean they chose ~** tu veux dire qu'ils t'ont choisie toi; **~ wouldn't do that, would ~?** vous ne feriez pas cela/tu ne ferais pas cela, n'est-ce pas? **-6.** [impersonal use]: **~ never know** on ne sait jamais; **a hot bath does ~ a world of good** un bon bain chaud vous fait un bien immense; **~ take the first on the left** prenez la première à droite.

you-all *inf pron Am dial* vous (tous).

you'd [ju:d] = **you had, you would**.

you-know-what *inf n euph*: **she saw his ~** elle a vu son truc; **they were doing ~** ils faisaient des choses.

you-know-who *inf n euph* qui tu sais, qui vous savez.

you'll [ju:l] = **you will**.

young [jʌŋ] (*compar* younger ['jʌŋgə^r], *superl* youngest ['jʌŋgɪst]) ◇ *adj* **-1.** [in age, style, ideas - person, clothes] jeune; **the ~ men and women of today** les jeunes gens et jeunes femmes d'aujourd'hui; **~ people** les jeunes *mpl*, la jeunesse *f*; **the ~er generation** la jeune génération; **families with ~ children** les familles qui ont des enfants en bas âge; **my ~er brother** mon frère cadet, mon petit frère; **I'm ten years ~er than she is** j'ai dix ans de moins qu'elle; **I'm not as ~ as I was!** je n'ai plus (mes) vingt ans!; **he is ~ for such responsibility** il est bien jeune pour de telles responsabilités; **you're only ~ once!** la jeunesse ne dure qu'un temps!; **in my ~er days** dans ma jeunesse, quand j'étais jeune; **the Young Conservatives/Liberals** les jeunes conservateurs/libéraux; **how is ~ Christopher?** *Br* comment va le jeune Christopher?; **the ~ Mr Ford, Mr Ford the ~er** le jeune M. Ford, M. Ford fils; **now listen here ~ man!** écoutez-moi bien, jeune homme!; **her ~ man** *dated* son petit ami, son amoureux; **his ~ lady** *dated* sa petite amie; **~ lady!** mademoiselle!; **she's quite a ~ lady now** c'est une vraie jeune fille maintenant; **what do you have to say for yourself, ~ lady?** qu'avez-vous à dire, mademoiselle? **-2.** [youthful] jeune; **he is ~ for 45** il fait jeune pour 45 ans; **she is a ~ 45** elle a 45 ans, mais elle ne les fait pas; **he's ~ for his age** il est jeune pour son âge, il ne fait pas son âge; **to be ~ at heart** avoir la jeunesse du cœur. **-3.** [recent - grass, plant] nouveau; [- wine] jeune, vert; GEOL [- rock formation] jeune, récent.
◇ *npl*: **the ~** [people] les jeunes *mpl*, la jeunesse; [animals] les petits *mpl*; **a game suitable for ~ and old alike** un jeu pour les jeunes et les moins jeunes; **to be with ~** [animal] être pleine OR grosse.

young blood *n* [new attitudes, ideas, people] sang *m* nouveau OR neuf.

youngish ['jʌŋɪʃ] *adj* plutôt jeune.

young-looking *adj* d'allure jeune.

youngster ['jʌŋstə^r] *n* **-1.** [child] garçon *m*, gamin *m*; [youth] jeune homme *m*. **-2.** EQUIT jeune cheval *m*.

Young Turk *n* POL jeune-turc *m*, jeune-turque *f*.

your [jɔːʳ] *det* **-1.** [addressing one or more people] votre *mf*, vos *mfpl*; [familiar use] ton *m*, ta *f*, tes *mfpl*; ~ **book** votre/ton livre; ~ **car** votre/ta voiture; ~ **books** vos/tes livres. **-2.** [with parts of body, clothes]: **don't put** ~ **hands in** ~ **pockets** ne mets pas tes mains dans les poches; **why are you scratching** ~ **head?** pourquoi est-ce que tu te grattes la tête?; **hold on to** ~ **hat!** tenez-bien votre chapeau!; **I think you've broken** ~ **finger** je crois que vous vous êtes cassé le doigt; **does** ~ **wrist hurt?** est-ce que tu as mal au poignet? **-3.** [emphatic form]: **is this** ~ **book or his?** est-ce que c'est votre livre ou le sien?; **oh it's YOUR book, is it?** ah, c'est à toi ce livre!; **that's YOUR problem** c'est TON problème. **-4.** [impersonal use]: **if you don't stand up for** ~ **rights, no one else will** si vous ne défendez pas vos droits vous-même, personne ne le fera à votre place; **swimming is good for** ~ **heart and lungs** la natation est un bon exercice pour le cœur et les poumons; **where are** ~ **Churchills and** ~ **De Gaulles when you need them?** où sont vos Churchill et vos De Gaulle quand vous avez besoin d'eux?; **it's not a film for** ~ **average cinema goer** ce n'est pas un film pour n'importe quel public. **-5.** [in titles]: **Your Highness** Votre Majesté *(à un roi, une reine, un prince ou une princesse)*; **Your Majesty** Votre Majesté *(à un roi ou une reine uniquement)*.

you're [jɔːʳ] = **you are**.

yours [jɔːz] *pron* **-1.** [addressing one or more people] le vôtre *m*, la vôtre *f*, les vôtres *mfpl*, le tien *m*, la tienne *f*, les tiens *mpl*, les tiennes *fpl*; **is this book** ~**?** est-ce que ce livre est à vous/toi?; **is this car** ~**?** c'est votre/ta voiture?; **are these books** ~**?** ces livres sont-ils à vous/toi?; **is he a friend of** ~**?** est-ce un de vos/tes amis?; ~ **is an unenviable task** votre tâche est peu enviable; **can't you control that wretched dog of** ~**?** vous ne pouvez pas retenir votre satané chien? **-2.** [up to you]: **it is not** ~ **to decide** ce n'est pas à vous OR il ne vous appartient pas de décider. **-3.** *inf Br* [in offering drinks]: **what's** ~**?** qu'est-ce que vous buvez?, qu'est-ce que je vous sers? **-4.** [in letter]: ~**, Peter** ≃ bien à vous OR à bientôt, Peter; ~ **sincerely** cordialement; ~ **faithfully** ≃ veuillez agréer mes salutations distinguées.

yourself [jɔːˈself] (*pl* **yourselves** [-ˈselvz]) *pron* **-1.** [personally - gen] vous-même; [- familiar use] toi-même; **do it** ~ faites-le vous-même/fais-le toi-même; **do it yourselves** faites-le vous-mêmes; **you've kept the best seats for yourselves** vous avez gardé les meilleures places pour vous; **see for** ~ tu n'as qu'à voir par toi-même; **did you come by** ~**?** vous êtes venu tout seul?; **did you mend the fuse (by)** ~**?** vous avez remplacé le fusible tout seul?; **did you make it** ~**?** l'avez-vous fait vous-même? **-2.** [reflexive use]: **did you hurt** ~**?** est-ce que vous vous êtes/tu t'es fait mal?; **did you enjoy** ~**?** est-ce que c'était bien?; **you were talking to** ~ tu parlais tout seul; **speak for** ~**!** parle pour toi!; **just look at** ~**!** regarde-toi donc! ❑ **you don't seem** ~ **today** tu n'as pas l'air d'être dans ton assiette aujourd'hui. **-3.** [emphatic use]: **you told me** ~**, you** ~ **told me** vous me l'avez dit vous-même, c'est vous-même qui me l'avez dit; **you must have known** ~ **that they wouldn't accept** vous-même, vous auriez dû savoir qu'ils n'accepteraient pas. **-4.** [impersonal use]: **you have to know how to look after** ~ **in the jungle** dans la jungle, il faut savoir se défendre tout seul OR se débrouiller soi-même; **you're supposed to help** ~ on est censé se servir soi-même.

yours truly *inf pron* bibi, mézigue.

youth [juːθ] (*pl* **youths** [juːðz]) ◇ *n* **-1.** [young age] jeunesse *f*; **in my** ~ dans ma jeunesse, quand j'étais jeune; **the optimism of** ~ l'optimisme de la jeunesse. **-2.** [young man] adolescent *m*, jeune *m*.
◇ *npl* [young people]: **the** ~ **of today** les jeunes *mpl* OR la jeunesse d'aujourd'hui; **the** ~ **of the nation** la jeunesse du pays.

youth club *n Br* ≃ maison *f* des jeunes.

youth culture *n* culture *f* des jeunes.

youth custody *n Br* détention *f* de mineurs, éducation *f* surveillée.

youth custody centre *n Br centre de détention de jeunes délinquants (jusqu'en 1988 - aujourd'hui appelé «young offenders' institution»)*.

youthful [ˈjuːθfʊl] *adj* **-1.** [young - person] jeune; [- appearance] d'allure jeune. **-2.** [typical of youth - idea] de jeunesse; [- enthusiasm, expectations, attitude] juvénile; ~ **good humour** bonne humeur juvénile OR propre à la jeunesse.

youthfulness [ˈjuːθfʊlnɪs] *n* [of person] jeunesse *f*; [of appearance] allure *f* jeune; [of mind, ideas] jeunesse *f*, fraîcheur *f*.

youth hostel *n* auberge *f* de jeunesse.

youth hosteller *n* habitué *m*, -e *f* des auberges de jeunesse.

youth hostelling *n (U)* séjour *m* OR séjours *mpl* dans les auberges de jeunesse; **to go** ~ passer ses vacances en auberges de jeunesse.

you've [juːv] = **you have**.

yowl [jaʊl] ◇ *vi* [cat] miauler (fort); [dog, person] hurler; **to** ~ **in pain** [cat] miauler de douleur; [dog, person] hurler de douleur.
◇ *n* [of cat] miaulement *m* (déchirant); [of dog, person] hurlement *m*.

yo-yo [ˈjəʊjəʊ] (*pl* **yoyos**) ◇ *n* **-1.** [toy] Yo-Yo® *m inv*. **-2.** ▽ *Am* [fool] couillon *m*.
◇ *vi inf* fluctuer.

yr *written abbr of* year.

YT *written abbr of* Yukon Territory.

YTS (*abbr of* Youth Training Scheme) *n (personne participant au) programme gouvernemental britannique d'insertion des jeunes dans la vie professionnelle*.

ytterbium [ɪˈtɜːbɪəm] *n* ytterbium *m*.

yttrium [ˈɪtrɪəm] *n* yttrium *m*.

yuan [juːˈɑːn] (*pl inv*) *n* yuan *m*.

Yucatan [ˌjʌkəˈtɑːn] *pr n* Yucatan *m*.

yucca [ˈjʌkə] *n* yucca *m*.

yuck *inf* [jʌk] *interj* berk, beurk.

yucky *inf* [ˈjʌkɪ] (*compar* **yuckier**, *superl* **yuckiest**) *adj* dégueulasse.

Yugoslav [ˌjuːgəˈslɑːv] ◇ *n* Yougoslave *mf*.
◇ *adj* yougoslave.

Yugoslavia [ˌjuːgəˈslɑːvjə] *pr n* Yougoslavie *f*; in ~ en Yougoslavie.

Yugoslavian [ˌjuːgəˈslɑːvjən] ◇ *n* Yougoslave *mf*.
◇ *adj* yougoslave.

yuk [jʌk] = **yuck**.

yukky [ˈjʌkɪ] (*compar* **yukkier**, *superl* **yukkiest**) = **yucky**.

Yukon Territory [ˈjuːkɒn-] *pr n* territoire *m* du Yukon.

yule, Yule [juːl] *n arch, lit* OR *dial* Noël *m*.

yule log, Yule log *n* bûche *f* de Noël.

yuletide, Yuletide [ˈjuːltaɪd] *lit* ◇ *n* (époque *f* de) Noël *m*; **at** ~ à Noël.
◇ *comp* [greetings, festivities] de Noël.

yummy *inf* [ˈjʌmɪ] (*compar* **yummier**, *superl* **yummiest**) ◇ *adj* [food] succulent, délicieux.
◇ *interj* miam-miam.

yum-yum *inf* [ˌjʌmˈjʌm] *interj* miam-miam.

Yunnan [juːˈnæn] *pr n* Yunnan *m*.

yuppie, yuppy [ˈjʌpɪ] (*pl* **yuppies**) ◇ *n* yuppie *mf*, ≃ jeune cadre *m* dynamique.
◇ *adj* [club] pour jeunes cadres dynamiques; [lifestyle] des yuppies.

YWCA (*abbr of* Young Women's Christian Association) *pr n association chrétienne de jeunes filles (surtout connue pour ses centres d'hébergement)*.

Z

z (*pl* z's OR zs), **Z** (*pl* Z's OR Zs) [*Br* zed, *Am* ziː] *n* z *m*, Z *m*.
Zacharias [ˌzækəˈraɪəs] *pr n* Zacharie.
Zagreb [ˈzɑːgreb] *pr n* Zagreb.
Zaïre [zɑːˈɪəʳ] *pr n* Zaïre *m*; in ~ au Zaïre.
Zaïrean [zɑːˈɪərɪən] ◇ *n* Zaïrois *m*, -e *f*.
◇ *adj* zaïrois.
Zambesi, Zambezi [zæmˈbiːzɪ] *pr n*: the ~ le Zambèze.
Zambia [ˈzæmbɪə] *pr n* Zambie *f*; in ~ en Zambie.
Zambian [ˈzæmbɪən] ◇ *n* Zambien *m*, -enne *f*.
◇ *adj* zambien.
zany *inf* [ˈzeɪnɪ] (*compar* zanier, *superl* zaniest, *pl* zanies) ◇ *adj* farfelu, dingue, dingo.
◇ *n* THEAT bouffon *m*, zani *m*, zanni *m*.
Zanzibar [ˌzænzɪˈbɑːʳ] *pr n* Zanzibar; in ~ au Zanzibar.
zap *inf* [zæp] (*pt* & *pp* zapped, *cont* zapping) ◇ *vi* -**1.** [go quickly] courir; **I'll ~ over to see her** je file la voir, je vais faire un saut chez elle. -**2.** TV zapper; **stop zapping!** arrête de zapper!
◇ *vt* -**1.** [destroy by bombing - town] ravager, bombarder; [- target] atteindre. -**2.** [kill - victim] tuer, descendre; [- in video game] éliminer. -**3.** COMPUT [display, data] effacer, supprimer.
◇ *n* [energy] pêche *f*, punch *m*.
◇ *interj* vlan.
zapper *inf* [ˈzæpəʳ] *n* [for TV] télécommande *f*.
zappy *inf* [ˈzæpɪ] (*compar* zappier, *superl* zappiest) *adj Br* qui a la pêche, plein de punch; **a ~ little car** une petite voiture nerveuse.
Zarathustra [ˌzærəˈθuːstrə] *pr n* Zarathoustra.
z-axis *n* axe *m* des z.
Z-car *n Br dated* voiture *f* pie *(de la police)*.
Z chart *n* INDUST & MATH *table statistique de données journalières, hebdomadaires et mensuelles pour une année*.
zeal [ziːl] *n* zèle *m*, ferveur *f*, ardeur *f*; **full of ~** plein de zèle; **she undertook the work with great ~** elle a entrepris le travail avec beaucoup de zèle; **political/religious ~** ferveur politique/religieuse.
zealot [ˈzelət] *n* fanatique *mf*, zélateur *m*, -trice *f*; **religious ~s** fanatiques religieux.
zealotry [ˈzelətrɪ] *n* fanatisme *m*.
zealous [ˈzeləs] *adj* [worker, partisan] zélé, actif; [opponent] zélé, acharné; **she is ~ in carrying out her duties** elle fait ce qu'elle a à faire avec beaucoup de zèle OR d'ardeur.
zealously [ˈzeləslɪ] *adv* avec zèle OR ardeur.
zebra [*Br* ˈzebrə, *Am* ˈziːbrə] (*pl inv* OR **zebras**) *n* zèbre *m*.
zebra crossing *n Br* passage *m* clouté OR pour piétons.
zebu [ˈziːbuː] *n* zébu *m*.
Zechariah [ˌzekəˈraɪə] *pr n* Zacharie.
zed [zed] *Br*, **zee** [ziː] *Am n* (lettre *f*) z *m*.
zeitgeist, Zeitgeist [ˈzaɪtgaɪst] *n* esprit *m* de l'époque.
Zen [zen] ◇ *n* zen *m*.
◇ *adj* zen *(inv)*; **~ Buddhism** les préceptes *mpl* du zen, le bouddhisme zen.
zenith [*Br* ˈzenɪθ, *Am* ˈziːnəθ] *n* zénith *m*; **she had reached the ~ of her career** *fig* elle était au sommet OR au faîte de sa carrière; **when the British Empire was at its ~** *fig* lorsque l'empire britannique était à son apogée, à l'apogée de l'empire britannique.
zeolite [ˈziːəlaɪt] *n* zéolite *f*.
zephyr [ˈzefəʳ] *n lit* & TEX zéphyr *m*.
zeppelin [ˈzepəlɪn] *n* zeppelin *m*.
zero [*Br* ˈzɪərəʊ, *Am* ˈziːrəʊ] (*pl* **zeros** OR **zeroes**) ◇ *n* -**1.** MATH zéro *m*. -**2.** [in temperature] zéro *m*; **40 below ~** 40 degrés au-dessous de zéro, moins 40. -**3.** SPORT: **to win 3 ~** gagner 3 (à) zéro. -**4.** [nothing, nought]: **our chances have been put at ~** on considère que nos chances sont nulles.
◇ *vt* [instrument] régler sur zéro.
◇ *comp* [altitude] zéro *(inv)*; [visibility] nul; **~ gravity** apesanteur *f*; **~ growth** croissance *f* zéro; **the ~ option** POL l'option *f* zéro; **the project has ~ interest for me** le projet ne présente aucun intérêt pour moi.
◆ **zero in on** *vt insep* -**1.** MIL [aim for] se diriger OR piquer droit sur; **the police ~ed in on the terrorists' hideout** *inf* la police a investi la cachette des terroristes. -**2.** *inf* [concentrate on] se concentrer sur, faire porter tous ses efforts sur. -**3.** *inf* [pinpoint] mettre le doigt sur.
zero hour *n* heure *f* H.
zero-rated [-ˌreɪtɪd] *adj*: **~ (for VAT)** exempt de TVA, non assujetti à la TVA.
zest [zest] *n* -**1.** [piquancy] piquant *m*, saveur *f*; **to add ~ to a situation** ajouter du sel OR du piquant à une situation. -**2.** [enthusiasm] enthousiasme *m*, entrain *m*; **she seems to have lost her ~ for life** il semble qu'elle ait perdu son appétit de vivre OR son goût pour la vie. -**3.** CULIN [of orange, lemon] zeste *m*.
zestful [ˈzestfʊl] *adj* [person] enthousiaste.
zeugma [ˈzjuːgmə] *n* zeugma *m*, zeugme *m*.
Zeus [zjuːs] *pr n* Zeus.
zigzag [ˈzɪgzæg] (*pt* & *pp* **zigzagged**, *cont* **zigzagging**) ◇ *vi* [walker, vehicle] avancer en zigzags, zigzaguer; [road] zigzaguer; [river] serpenter; **to ~ across/up the road** traverser/monter la rue en zigzaguant; **the road ~s through the valley** la route traverse la vallée en zigzaguant OR serpente à travers la vallée.
◇ *n* [in design] zigzag *m*; [on road] lacet *m*; [in river] boucle *f*.
◇ *adj* [path, line] en zigzag; [pattern] à zigzag OR zigzags; **the path follows a ~ course across the fields** le chemin traverse les champs en zigzaguant.
◇ *adv* en zigzag.
zilch *inf* [zɪltʃ] *n Am* que dalle.
zillion *inf* [ˈzɪljən] (*pl inv* OR **zillions**) ◇ *n* foultitude *f*; **they earn/cost ~s** ils gagnent/coûtent des milliards; **we got ~s of replies** nous avons eu des tas et des tas OR des tonnes de réponses.
◇ *adj*: **for a ~ reasons** pour des tas OR une foultitude de raisons.
Zimbabwe [zɪmˈbɑːbwɪ] *pr n* Zimbabwe *m*; **in ~** au Zimbabwe.
Zimbabwean [zɪmˈbɑːbwɪən] ◇ *n* Zimbabwéen *m*, -enne *f*.
◇ *adj* zimbabwéen.
Zimmer (frame)® [ˈzɪməʳ-] *n* déambulateur *m*.
zinc [zɪŋk] ◇ *n* zinc *m*.
◇ *comp* [chloride, sulphate, sulphide] de zinc; [ointment] à l'oxyde de zinc; **~ white** oxyde *m* de zinc *(pigment)*.
zinc blend *n* blende *f*.
zinc ointment *n* pommade *f* à l'oxyde de zinc.
zinc oxide *n* oxyde *m* de zinc.
zing *inf* [zɪŋ] ◇ *onomat* zim.
◇ *n* -**1.** [of bullet] sifflement *m*. -**2.** [of person] punch *m*.
◇ *vi* [projectile] siffler, passer dans un sifflement; **the bullet ~ed past me** la balle est passée à côté de moi dans un sifflement.
zinger *inf* [ˈzɪŋəʳ] *n Am* [pointed remark] pique *f*.
Zion [ˈzaɪən] *pr n* Sion.
Zionism [ˈzaɪənɪzm] *n* sionisme *m*.
Zionist [ˈzaɪənɪst] ◇ *n* sioniste *mf*.
◇ *adj* sioniste.
zip [zɪp] (*pt* & *pp* **zipped**) ◇ *n* -**1.** [fastener] fermeture *f* Éclair® OR à glissière. -**2.** [sound of bullet] sifflement *m*. -**3.** *inf* [liveliness] vivacité *f*, entrain *m*. -**4.** *inf Am* [nothing] rien *m*.
◇ *vi* -**1.** [with zip fastener]: **to ~ open/shut** s'ouvrir/se fermer à l'aide d'une fermeture Éclair® OR à glissière. -**2.** *inf (as verb of movement)*: **to ~ past/upstairs** passer/monter l'escalier comme une flèche; **she zipped out to get a paper** elle a filé chercher un journal; **I zipped through the book/my work** j'ai lu ce livre/fait mon travail en quatrième vitesse. -**3.** [arrow, bullet] siffler; **bullets zipped past us** des balles sifflaient à nos oreilles.
◇ *vt* -**1.** [with zip fastener]: **to ~ sthg open/shut** fermer/ouvrir la fermeture Éclair® OR à glissière de qqch; **I zipped myself into my sleeping bag** je me suis enfermé dans mon sac de couchage en tirant la fermeture. -**2.** *inf* [do quickly]: **I'll just ~ this cake into the oven** je glisse en vitesse ce gâteau dans le four.
◆ **zip on** ◇ *vt sep* attacher (avec une fermeture à glissière).
◇ *vi insep* s'attacher avec une fermeture Éclair® OR à glissière.

◆ **zip up** ◇ *vt sep* -**1.** [subj: clothing, sleeping bag] fermer avec la fermeture Éclair® OR à glissière. -**2.** [subj: person] fermer la fermeture Éclair® OR à glissière de.
◇ *vi insep* [dress] se fermer avec une fermeture Éclair® OR à glissière.

zip (code), ZIP (code) *n Am* code *m* postal.

zip fastener *n Br* fermeture *f* Éclair® OR à glissière.

zip gun *inf n Am* pistolet *m* rudimentaire *(à ressort)*.

zip-on *adj* [flap, hood] qui s'attache avec une fermeture Éclair® OR à glissière.

zipper ['zɪpəʳ] *Am* = **zip fastener**.

zippy *inf* ['zɪpɪ] (*compar* **zippier**, *superl* **zippiest**) *adj* [person] vif; [car] nerveux.

zip-up *adj* [bag, coat] à fermeture Éclair®, zippé.

zircon ['zɜːkɒn] *n* zircon *m*.

zirconium [zɜː'kəʊnɪəm] *n* zirconium *m*.

zit *inf* [zɪt] *n* bouton *m (sur la peau)*.

zither ['zɪðəʳ] *n* cithare *f*.

zizz *inf* [zɪz] *n Br*: to have a ~ faire un somme.

zodiac ['zəʊdɪæk] *n* zodiaque *m*.

zombie ['zɒmbɪ] *n* zombie *m*.

zonal ['zəʊnl] *adj* zonal.

zone [zəʊn] ◇ *n* -**1.** [area] zone *f*, secteur *m*; the occupied ~ MIL la zone occupée. -**2.** [sphere] zone *f*, domaine *m*. -**3.** GEOG & METEOR zone *f*.
◇ *vt* -**1.** [partition] diviser en zones. -**2.** [classify] désigner; to ~ an area as industrial/residential classer un secteur zone industrielle/résidentielle.

zone defence *n* SPORT défense *f* de zone.

zoning ['zəʊnɪŋ] *n* zonage *m*.

zonked▽ [zɒŋkt] *adj* -**1.** [exhausted] vanné, claqué. -**2.** [drunk] bourré; [drugged] défoncé.

zoo [zuː] (*pl* **zoos**) *n* zoo *m*, jardin *m* zoologique.

zookeeper ['zuː,kiːpəʳ] *n* gardien *m*, -enne *f* du zoo.

zoological [,zəʊə'lɒdʒɪkl] *adj* zoologique; ~ garden jardin *m* OR parc *m* zoologique.

zoologist [zəʊ'ɒlədʒɪst] *n* zoologiste *mf*.

zoology [zəʊ'ɒlədʒɪ] *n* zoologie *f*.

zoom [zuːm] ◇ *vi inf* -**1.** [verb of movement]: the car ~**ed up/down the hill** la voiture a monté/descendu la côte à toute allure; **the rocket ~ed up into the clouds** la fusée est montée en chandelle dans les nuages; **I'm just going to ~ into town to get some food** je vais faire un saut en ville pour acheter de quoi manger. -**2.** [prices, costs, sales] monter en flèche; **inflation ~ed up** OR **upwards** l'inflation est montée en flèche. -**3.** [engine] vrombir.
◇ *n* -**1.** [of engine] vrombissement *m*. -**2.** PHOT [lens, effect] zoom *m*.
◇ *onomat*: ~! vroum!

◆ **zoom in** *vi insep* PHOT faire un zoom; **the camera ~ed in on the laughing children** la caméra a fait un zoom sur les enfants en train de rire.

◆ **zoom off** *inf vi insep* filer; **they're ~ing off on holiday tomorrow** ils filent en vacances demain.

◆ **zoom out** *vi insep* PHOT faire OR produire un effet d'éloignement avec le zoom.

zoom lens *n* zoom *m*.

zoomorphism [,zəʊə'mɔːfɪzm] *n* zoomorphisme *m*.

zoophyte ['zəʊəfaɪt] *n* zoophyte *m*.

zooplankton [,zəʊə'plæŋtən] *n* zooplancton *m*.

zoot suit [zuːt-] *n* costume *m* zazou.

Zoroaster [,zɒrəʊ'æstəʳ] *pr n* Zoroastre.

Zoroastrian [,zɒrəʊ'æstrɪən] ◇ *adj* zoroastrien.
◇ *n* Zoroastrien *m*, -enne *f*.

zucchini [zuː'kiːnɪ] (*pl inv* OR **zucchinis**) *n Am* courgette *f*.

zugzwang ['zuːgzwæŋ] ◇ *n* [in chess] *situation du joueur qui ne peut déplacer une pièce qu'à son désavantage*.
◇ *vt* [opponent] *mettre dans une situation où tout déplacement entraîne un gros désavantage*.

Zulu ['zuːluː] (*pl inv* OR **Zulus**) ◇ *n* -**1.** [person] Zoulou *m*, -e *f*. -**2.** LING zoulou *m*.
◇ *adj* zoulou.

Zululand ['zuːluːlænd] *pr n* Zoulouland *m*, Zululand *m*.

Zürich ['zjʊərɪk] *pr n* Zurich.

zygote ['zaɪgəʊt] *n* zygote *m*.

CONJUGAISONS

VERBS

TABLEAU DES CONJUGAISONS

	1 avoir	**2 être**	**3 chanter**	**4 baisser**	**5 pleurer**
IND. présent	j'ai	je suis	je chante	je baisse	je pleure
	tu as	tu es	tu chantes	tu baisses	tu pleures
	il, elle a	il, elle est	il, elle chante	il, elle baisse	il, elle pleure
	nous avons	nous sommes	nous chantons	nous baissons	nous pleurons
	vous avez	vous êtes	vous chantez	vous baissez	vous pleurez
	ils, elles ont	ils, elles sont	ils, elles chantent	ils, elles baissent	ils, elles pleurent
IND. imparfait	il, elle avait	il, elle était	il, elle chantait	il, elle baissait	il, elle pleurait
IND. passé s.	il, elle eut	il, elle fut	il, elle chanta	il, elle baissa	il, elle pleura
	ils, elles eurent	ils, elles furent	ils, elles chantèrent	ils, elles baissèrent	ils, elles pleurèrent
IND. futur	j'aurai	je serai	je chanterai	je baisserai	je pleurerai
	il, elle aura	il, elle sera	il, elle chantera	il, elle baissera	il, elle pleurera
COND. présent	j'aurais	je serais	je chanterais	je baisserais	je pleurerais
	il, elle aurait	il, elle serait	il, elle chanterait	il, elle baisserait	il, elle pleurerait
SUBJ. présent	que j'aie	que je sois	que je chante	que je baisse	que je pleure
	qu'il, elle ait	qu'il, elle soit	qu'il, elle chante	qu'il, elle baisse	qu'il, elle pleure
	que nous ayons	que nous soyons	que nous chantions	que nous baissions	que nous pleurions
	qu'ils, elles aient	qu'ils, elles soient	qu'ils, elles chantent	qu'ils, elles baissent	qu'ils, elles pleurent
SUBJ. imparfait	qu'il, elle eût	qu'il, elle fût	qu'il, elle chantât	qu'il, elle baissât	qu'il, elle pleurât
	qu'ils, elles eussent	qu'ils, elles fussent	qu'ils, elles chantassent	qu'ils, elles baissassent	qu'ils, elles pleurassent
IMPÉRATIF	aie	sois	chante	baisse	pleure
	ayons	soyons	chantons	baissons	pleurons
	ayez	soyez	chantez	baissez	pleurez
PART. présent	ayant	étant	chantant	baissant	pleurant
PART. passé	eu, eue	été	chanté, e	baissé, e	pleuré, e

	6 jouer	**7 saluer**	**8 arguer**	**9 copier**	**10 prier**
IND. présent	je joue	je salue	j'argue, arguë	je copie	je prie
	tu joues	tu salues	tu argues, arguës	tu copies	tu pries
	il, elle joue	il, elle salue	il, elle argue, arguë	il, elle copie	il, elle prie
	nous jouons	nous saluons	nous arguons	nous copions	nous prions
	vous jouez	vous saluez	vous arguez	vous copiez	vous priez
	ils, elles jouent	ils, elles saluent	ils, elles arguent, arguënt	ils, elles copient	ils, elles prient
IND. imparfait	il, elle jouait	il, elle saluait	il, elle arguait	il, elle copiait	il, elle priait
IND. passé s.	il, elle joua	il, elle salua	il, elle argua	il, elle copia	il, elle pria
	ils, elles jouèrent	ils, elles saluèrent	ils, elles arguèrent	ils, elles copièrent	ils, elles prièrent
IND. futur	je jouerai	je saluerai	j'arguerai, arguërai	je copierai	je prierai
	il, elle jouera	il, elle saluera	il, elle arguera, arguëra	il, elle copiera	il, elle priera
COND. présent	je jouerais	je saluerais	j'arguerais, arguërais	je copierais	je prierais
	il, elle jouerait	il, elle saluerait	il, elle arguerait, arguërait	il, elle copierait	il, elle prierait
SUBJ. présent	que je joue	que je salue	que j'argue, arguë	que je copie	que je prie
	qu'il, elle joue	qu'il, elle salue	qu'il, elle argue, arguë	qu'il, elle copie	qu'il, elle prie
	que nous jouions	que nous saluions	que nous arguions	que nous copiions	que nous priions
	qu'ils, elles jouent	qu'ils, elles saluent	qu'ils, elles arguent, arguënt	qu'ils, elles copient	qu'ils, elles prient
SUBJ. imparfait	qu'il, elle jouât	qu'il, elle saluât	qu'il, elle arguât	qu'il, elle copiât	qu'il, elle priât
	qu'ils, elles jouassent	qu'ils, elles saluassent	qu'ils, elles arguassent	qu'ils, elles copiassent	qu'ils, elles priassent
IMPÉRATIF	joue	salue	argue, arguë	copie	prie
	jouons	saluons	arguons	copions	prions
	jouez	saluez	arguez	copiez	priez
PART. présent	jouant	saluant	arguant	copiant	priant
PART. passé	joué, e	salué, e	argué, e	copié, e	prié, e

	11 payer (1)		**12 grasseyer**	**13 ployer**	**14 essuyer**
IND. présent	je paie	je paye	je grasseye	je ploie	j'essuie
	tu paies	tu payes	tu grasseyes	tu ploies	tu essuies
	il, elle paie	il, elle paye	il, elle grasseye	il, elle ploie	il, elle essuie
	nous payons	nous payons	nous grasseyons	nous ployons	nous essuyons
	vous payez	vous payez	vous grasseyez	vous ployez	vous essuyez
	ils, elles paient	ils, elles payent	ils, elles grasseyent	ils, elles ploient	ils, elles essuient
IND. imparfait	il, elle payait	il, elle payait	il, elle grasseyait	il, elle ployait	il, elle essuyait
IND. passé s.	il, elle paya	il, elle paya	il, elle grasseya	il, elle ploya	il, elle essuya
	ils, elles payèrent	ils, elles payèrent	ils, elles grasseyèrent	ils, elles ployèrent	ils, elles essuyèrent
IND. futur	je paierai	je payerai	je grasseyerai	je ploierai	j'essuierai
	il, elle paiera	il, elle payera	il, elle grasseyera	il, elle ploiera	il, elle essuiera
COND. présent	je paierais	je payerais	je grasseyerais	je ploierais	j'essuierais
	il, elle paierait	il, elle payerait	il, elle grasseyerait	il, elle ploierait	il, elle essuierait
SUBJ. présent	que je paie	que je paye	que je grasseye	que je ploie	que j'essuie
	qu'il, elle paie	qu'il, elle paye	qu'il, elle grasseye	qu'il, elle ploie	qu'il, elle essuie
	que nous payions	que nous payions	que nous grasseyions	que nous ployions	que nous essuyions
	qu'ils, elles paient	qu'ils, elles payent	qu'ils, elles grasseyent	qu'ils, elles ploient	qu'ils, elles essuient
SUBJ. imparfait	qu'il, elle payât	qu'il, elle payât	qu'il, elle grasseyât	qu'il, elle ployât	qu'il, elle essuyât
	qu'ils, elles payassent	qu'ils, elles payassent	qu'ils, elles grasseyassent	qu'ils, elles ployassent	qu'ils, elles essuyassent
IMPÉRATIF	paie	paye	grasseye	ploie	essuie
	payons	payons	grasseyons	ployons	essuyons
	payez	payez	grasseyez	ployez	essuyez
PART. présent	payant	payant	grasseyant	ployant	essuyant
PART. passé	payé, e	payé, e	grasseyé, e	ployé, e	essuyé, e

(1) Pour certains grammairiens, le verbe *rayer* (et ses composés) garde le *y* dans toute sa conjugaison.

	15 créer	**16 avancer**	**17 manger**	**18 céder** (1)	**19 semer**
IND. présent	je crée	j’avance	je mange	je cède	je sème
	tu crées	tu avances	tu manges	tu cèdes	tu sèmes
	il, elle crée	il, elle avance	il, elle mange	il, elle cède	il, elle sème
	nous créons	nous avançons	nous mangeons	nous cédons	nous semons
	vous créez	vous avancez	vous mangez	vous cédez	vous semez
	ils, elles créent	ils, elles avancent	ils, elles mangent	ils, elles cèdent	ils, elles sèment
IND. imparfait	il, elle créait	il, elle avançait	il, elle mangeait	il, elle cédait	il, elle semait
IND. passé s.	il, elle créa	il, elle avança	il, elle mangea	il, elle céda	il, elle sema
	ils, elles créèrent	ils, elles avancèrent	ils, elles mangèrent	ils, elles cédèrent	ils, elles semèrent
IND. futur	je créerai	j’avancerai	je mangerai	je céderai	je sèmerai
	il, elle créera	il, elle avancera	il, elle mangera	il, elle cédera	il, elle sèmera
COND. présent	je créerais	j’avancerais	je mangerais	je céderais	je sèmerais
	il, elle créerait	il, elle avancerait	il, elle mangerait	il, elle céderait	il, elle sèmerait
SUBJ. présent	que je crée	que j’avance	que je mange	que je cède	que je sème
	qu’il, elle crée	qu’il, elle avance	qu’il, elle mange	qu’il, elle cède	qu’il, elle sème
	que nous créions	que nous avancions	que nous mangions	que nous cédions	que nous semions
	qu’ils, elles créent	qu’ils, elles avancent	qu’ils, elles mangent	qu’ils, elles cèdent	qu’ils, elles sèment
SUBJ. imparfait	qu’il, elle créât	qu’il, elle avançât	qu’il, elle mangeât	qu’il, elle cédât	qu’il, elle semât
	qu’ils, elles créassent	qu’ils, elles avançassent	qu’ils, elles mangeassent	qu’ils, elles cédassent	qu’ils, elles semassent
IMPÉRATIF	crée	avance	mange	cède	sème
	créons	avançons	mangeons	cédons	semons
	créez	avancez	mangez	cédez	semez
PART. présent	créant	avançant	mangeant	cédant	semant
PART. passé	créé, e	avancé, e	mangé, e	cédé, e	semé, e

(1) Dans la 9e édition de son dictionnaire (1993), l’Académie écrit au futur et au conditionnel *je cèderai, je cèderais.*

	20 rapiécer (1)	**21 acquiescer**	**22 siéger** (1 et 2)	**23 déneiger**	**24 appeler**
IND. présent	je rapièce	j’acquiesce	je siège	je déneige	j’appelle
	tu rapièces	tu acquiesces	tu sièges	tu déneiges	tu appelles
	il, elle rapièce	il, elle acquiesce	il, elle siège	il, elle déneige	il, elle appelle
	nous rapiéçons	nous acquiesçons	nous siégeons	nous déneigeons	nous appelons
	vous rapiécez	vous acquiescez	vous siégez	vous déneigez	vous appelez
	ils, elles rapiècent	ils, elles acquiescent	ils, elles siègent	ils, elles déneigent	ils, elles appellent
IND. imparfait	il, elle rapiéçait	il, elle acquiesçait	il, elle siégeait	il, elle déneigeait	il, elle appelait
IND. passé s.	il, elle rapiéça	il, elle acquiesça	il, elle siégea	il, elle déneigea	il, elle appela
	ils, elles rapiécèrent	ils, elles acquiescèrent	ils, elles siégèrent	ils, elles déneigèrent	ils, elles appelèrent
IND. futur	je rapiécerai	j’acquiescerai	je siégerai	je déneigerai	j’appellerai
	il, elle rapiécera	il, elle acquiescera	il, elle siégera	il, elle déneigera	il, elle appellera
COND. présent	je rapiécerais	j’acquiescerais	je siégerais	je déneigerais	j’appellerais
	il, elle rapiécerait	il, elle acquiescerait	il, elle siégerait	il, elle déneigerait	il, elle appellerait
SUBJ. présent	que je rapièce	que j’acquiesce	que je siège	que je déneige	que j’appelle
	qu’il, elle rapièce	qu’il, elle acquiesce	qu’il, elle siège	qu’il, elle déneige	qu’il, elle appelle
	que nous rapiécions	que nous acquiescions	que nous siégions	que nous déneigions	que nous appelions
	qu’ils, elles rapiècent	qu’ils, elles acquiescent	qu’ils, elles siègent	qu’ils, elles déneigent	qu’ils, elles appellent
SUBJ. imparfait	qu’il, elle rapiéçât	qu’il, elle acquiesçât	qu’il, elle siégeât	qu’il, elle déneigeât	qu’il, elle appelât
	qu’ils, elles rapiéçassent	qu’ils, elles acquiesçassent	qu’ils, elles siégeassent	qu’ils, elles déneigeassent	qu’ils, elles appelassent
IMPÉRATIF	rapièce	acquiesce	siège	déneige	appelle
	rapiéçons	acquiesçons	siégeons	déneigeons	appelons
	rapiécez	acquiescez	siégez	déneigez	appelez
PART. présent	rapiéçant	acquiesçant	siégeant	déneigeant	appelant
PART. passé	rapiécé, e	acquiescé	siégé	déneigé, e	appelé, e

(1) Dans la 9e édition de son dictionnaire (1993), l’Académie écrit au futur et au conditionnel *je rapiècerai, je rapiècerais* ; *je siègerai, je siègerais.* – (2) *Assiéger* se conjugue comme *siéger*, mais son participe passé est variable.

	25 peler	**26 interpeller**	**27 jeter**	**28 acheter**	**29 dépecer**
IND. présent	je pèle	j’interpelle	je jette	j’achète	je dépèce
	tu pèles	tu interpelles	tu jettes	tu achètes	tu dépèces
	il, elle pèle	il, elle interpelle	il, elle jette	il, elle achète	il, elle dépèce
	nous pelons	nous interpellons	nous jetons	nous achetons	nous dépeçons
	vous pelez	vous interpellez	vous jetez	vous achetez	vous dépecez
	ils, elles pèlent	ils, elles interpellent	ils, elles jettent	ils, elles achètent	ils, elles dépècent
IND. imparfait	il, elle pelait	il, elle interpellait	il, elle jetait	il, elle achetait	il, elle dépeçait
IND. passé s.	il, elle pela	il, elle interpella	il, elle jeta	il, elle acheta	il, elle dépeça
	ils, elles pelèrent	ils, elles interpellèrent	ils, elles jetèrent	ils, elles achetèrent	ils, elles dépecèrent
IND. futur	je pèlerai	j’interpellerai	je jetterai	j’achèterai	je dépècerai
	il, elle pèlera	il, elle interpellera	il, elle jettera	il, elle achètera	il, elle dépècera
COND. présent	je pèlerais	j’interpellerais	je jetterais	j’achèterais	je dépècerais
	il, elle pèlerait	il, elle interpellerait	il, elle jetterait	il, elle achèterait	il, elle dépècerait
SUBJ. présent	que je pèle	que j’interpelle	que je jette	que j’achète	que je dépèce
	qu’il, elle pèle	qu’il, elle interpelle	qu’il, elle jette	qu’il, elle achète	qu’il, elle dépèce
	que nous pelions	que nous interpellions	que nous jetions	que nous achetions	que nous dépecions
	qu’ils, elles pèlent	qu’ils, elles interpellent	qu’ils, elles jettent	qu’ils, elles achètent	qu’ils, elles dépècent
SUBJ. imparfait	qu’il, elle pelât	qu’il, elle interpellât	qu’il, elle jetât	qu’il, elle achetât	qu’il, elle dépeçât
	qu’ils, elles pelassent	qu’ils, elles interpellassent	qu’ils, elles jetassent	qu’ils, elles achetassent	qu’ils, elles dépeçassent
IMPÉRATIF	pèle	interpelle	jette	achète	dépèce
	pelons	interpellons	jetons	achetons	dépeçons
	pelez	interpellez	jetez	achetez	dépecez
PART. présent	pelant	interpellant	jetant	achetant	dépeçant
PART. passé	pelé, e	interpellé, e	jeté, e	acheté, e	dépecé, e

	30 **envoyer**	31 **aller** (1)	32 **finir** (2)	33 **haïr**	34 **ouvrir**
IND. présent	j'envoie	je vais	je finis	je hais	j'ouvre
	tu envoies	tu vas	tu finis	tu hais	tu ouvres
	il, elle envoie	il, elle va	il, elle finit	il, elle hait	il, elle ouvre
	nous envoyons	nous allons	nous finissons	nous haïssons	nous ouvrons
	vous envoyez	vous allez	vous finissez	vous haïssez	vous ouvrez
	ils, elles envoient	ils, elles vont	ils, elles finissent	ils, elles haïssent	ils, elles ouvrent
IND. imparfait	il, elle envoyait	il, elle allait	il, elle finissait	il, elle haïssait	il, elle ouvrait
IND. passé s.	il, elle envoya	il, elle alla	il, elle finit	il, elle haït	il, elle ouvrit
	ils, elles envoyèrent	ils, elles allèrent	ils, elles finirent	ils, elles haïrent	ils, elles ouvrirent
IND. futur	j'enverrai	j'irai	je finirai	je haïrai	j'ouvrirai
	il, elle enverra	il, elle ira	il, elle finira	il, elle haïra	il, elle ouvrira
COND. présent	j'enverrais	j'irais	je finirais	je haïrais	j'ouvrirais
	il, elle enverrait	il, elle irait	il, elle finirait	il, elle haïrait	il, elle ouvrirait
SUBJ. présent	que j'envoie	que j'aille	que je finisse	que je haïsse	que j'ouvre
	qu'il, elle envoie	qu'il, elle aille	qu'il, elle finisse	qu'il, elle haïsse	qu'il, elle ouvre
	que nous envoyions	que nous allions	que nous finissions	que nous haïssions	que nous ouvrions
	qu'ils, elles envoient	qu'ils, elles aillent	qu'ils, elles finissent	qu'ils, elles haïssent	qu'ils, elles ouvrent
SUBJ. imparfait	qu'il, elle envoyât	qu'il, elle allât	qu'il, elle finît	qu'il, elle haït	qu'il, elle ouvrît
	qu'ils, elles envoyassent	qu'ils, elles allassent	qu'ils, elles finissent	qu'ils, elles haïssent	qu'ils, elles ouvrissent
IMPÉRATIF	envoie	va	finis	hais	ouvre
	envoyons	allons	finissons	haïssons	ouvrons
	envoyez	allez	finissez	haïssez	ouvrez
PART. présent	envoyant	allant	finissant	haïssant	ouvrant
PART. passé	envoyé, e	allé, e	fini, e	haï, e	ouvert, e

(1) *Aller* fait à l'impér. *vas* dans *vas-y. S'en aller* fait à l'impér. *va-t'en, allons-nous-en, allez-vous-en*. Aux temps composés, le verbe *être* peut se substituer au verbe *aller* : *avoir été, j'ai été*, etc. Aux temps composés du pronominal *s'en aller, en* se place normalement avant l'auxiliaire : *je m'en suis allé(e)*, mais la langue courante dit de plus en plus *je me suis en allé(e)*. – (2) *Maudire* (tableau 104) et *bruire* (tableau 105) se conjuguent sur *finir*, mais le participe passé de *maudire* est *maudit, maudite*, et *bruire* est défectif.

	35 **fuir**	36 **dormir** (1)	37 **mentir** (2)	38 **servir**	39 **acquérir**
IND. présent	je fuis	je dors	je mens	je sers	j'acquiers
	tu fuis	tu dors	tu mens	tu sers	tu acquiers
	il, elle fuit	il, elle dort	il, elle ment	il, elle sert	il, elle acquiert
	nous fuyons	nous dormons	nous mentons	nous servons	nous acquérons
	vous fuyez	vous dormez	vous mentez	vous servez	vous acquérez
	ils, elles fuient	ils, elles dorment	ils, elles mentent	ils, elles servent	ils, elles acquièrent
IND. imparfait	il, elle fuyait	il, elle dormait	il, elle mentait	il, elle servait	il, elle acquérait
IND. passé s.	il, elle fuit	il, elle dormit	il, elle mentit	il, elle servit	il, elle acquit
	ils, elles fuirent	ils, elles dormirent	ils, elles mentirent	ils, elles servirent	ils, elles acquirent
IND. futur	je fuirai	je dormirai	je mentirai	je servirai	j'acquerrai
	il, elle fuira	il, elle dormira	il, elle mentira	il, elle servira	il, elle acquerra
COND. présent	je fuirais	je dormirais	je mentirais	je servirais	j'acquerrais
	il, elle fuirait	il, elle dormirait	il, elle mentirait	il, elle servirait	il, elle acquerrait
SUBJ. présent	que je fuie	que je dorme	que je mente	que je serve	que j'acquière
	qu'il, elle fuie	qu'il, elle dorme	qu'il, elle mente	qu'il, elle serve	qu'il, elle acquière
	que nous fuyions	que nous dormions	que nous mentions	que nous servions	que nous acquérions
	qu'ils, elles fuient	qu'ils, elles dorment	qu'ils, elles mentent	qu'ils, elles servent	qu'ils, elles acquièrent
SUBJ. imparfait	qu'il, elle fuît	qu'il, elle dormît	qu'il, elle mentît	qu'il, elle servît	qu'il, elle acquît
	qu'ils, elles fuissent	qu'ils, elles dormissent	qu'ils, elles mentissent	qu'ils, elles servissent	qu'ils, elles acquissent
IMPÉRATIF	fuis	dors	mens	sers	acquiers
	fuyons	dormons	mentons	servons	acquérons
	fuyez	dormez	mentez	servez	acquérez
PART. présent	fuyant	dormant	mentant	servant	acquérant
PART. passé	fui, e	dormi	menti	servi, e	acquis, e

(1) *Endormir* se conjugue comme *dormir*, mais son participe passé est variable. – (2) *Démentir* se conjugue comme *mentir*, mais son participe passé est variable.

	40 **venir**	41 **cueillir**	42 **mourir**	43 **partir**	44 **revêtir**
IND. présent	je viens	je cueille	je meurs	je pars	je revêts
	tu viens	tu cueilles	tu meurs	tu pars	tu revêts
	il, elle vient	il, elle cueille	il, elle meurt	il, elle part	il, elle revêt
	nous venons	nous cueillons	nous mourons	nous partons	nous revêtons
	vous venez	vous cueillez	vous mourez	vous partez	vous revêtez
	ils, elles viennent	ils, elles cueillent	ils, elles meurent	ils, elles partent	ils, elles revêtent
IND. imparfait	il, elle venait	il, elle cueillait	il, elle mourait	il, elle partait	il, elle revêtait
IND. passé s.	il, elle vint	il, elle cueillit	il, elle mourut	il, elle partit	il, elle revêtit
	ils, elles vinrent	ils, elles cueillirent	ils, elles moururent	ils, elles partirent	ils, elles revêtirent
IND. futur	je viendrai	je cueillerai	je mourrai	je partirai	je revêtirai
	il, elle viendra	il, elle cueillera	il, elle mourra	il, elle partira	il, elle revêtira
COND. présent	je viendrais	je cueillerais	je mourrais	je partirais	je revêtirais
	il, elle viendrait	il, elle cueillerait	il, elle mourrait	il, elle partirait	il, elle revêtirait
SUBJ. présent	que je vienne	que je cueille	que je meure	que je parte	que je revête
	qu'il, elle vienne	qu'il, elle cueille	qu'il, elle meure	qu'il, elle parte	qu'il, elle revête
	que nous venions	que nous cueillions	que nous mourions	que nous partions	que nous revêtions
	qu'ils, elles viennent	qu'ils, elles cueillent	qu'ils, elles meurent	qu'ils, elles partent	qu'ils, elles revêtent
SUBJ. imparfait	qu'il, elle vînt	qu'il, elle cueillît	qu'il, elle mourût	qu'il, elle partît	qu'il, elle revêtît
	qu'ils, elles vinssent	qu'ils, elles cueillissent	qu'ils, elles mourussent	qu'ils, elles partissent	qu'ils, elles revêtissent
IMPÉRATIF	viens	cueille	meurs	pars	revêts
	venons	cueillons	mourons	partons	revêtons
	venez	cueillez	mourez	partez	revêtez
PART. présent	venant	cueillant	mourant	partant	revêtant
PART. passé	venu, e	cueilli, e	mort, e	parti, e	revêtu, e

	45 courir	**46 faillir** (1)	**47 défaillir** (2)	**48 bouillir**	**49 gésir** (3)
IND. présent	je cours	je faillis, faux	je défaille	je bous	je gis
	tu cours	tu faillis, faux	tu défailles	tu bous	tu gis
	il, elle court	il, elle faillit, faut	il, elle défaille	il, elle bout	il, elle gît
	nous courons	nous faillissons, faillons	nous défaillons	nous bouillons	nous gisons
	vous courez	vous faillissez, faillez	vous défaillez	vous bouillez	vous gisez
	ils, elles courent	ils, elles faillissent, faillent	ils, elles défaillent	ils, elles bouillent	ils, elles gisent
IND. imparfait	il, elle courait	il, elle faillissait, faillait	il, elle défaillait	il, elle bouillait	il, elle gisait
IND. passé s.	il, elle courut	il, elle faillit	il, elle défaillit	il, elle bouillit	
	ils, elles coururent	ils, elles faillirent	ils, elles défaillirent	ils, elles bouillirent	
IND. futur	je courrai	je faillirai, faudrai	je défaillirai	je bouillirai	
	il, elle courra	il, elle faillira, faudra	il, elle défaillira	il, elle bouillira	
COND. présent	je courrais	je faillirais, faudrais	je défaillirais	je bouillirais	
	il, elle courrait	il, elle faillirait, faudrait	il, elle défaillirait	il, elle bouillirait	
SUBJ. présent	que je coure	que je faillisse, faille	que je défaille	que je bouille	
	qu'il, elle coure	qu'il, elle faillisse, faille	qu'il, elle défaille	qu'il, elle bouille	
	que nous courions	que nous faillissions, faillions	que nous défaillions	que nous bouillions	
	qu'ils, elles courent	qu'ils, elles faillissent, faillent	qu'ils, elles défaillent	qu'ils, elles bouillent	
SUBJ. imparfait	qu'il, elle courût	qu'il, elle faillît	qu'il, elle défaillît	qu'il, elle bouillît	
	qu'ils, elles courussent	qu'ils, elles faillissent	qu'ils, elles défaillissent	qu'ils, elles bouillissent	
IMPÉRATIF	cours	faillis, faux	défaille	bous	
	courons	faillissons, faillons	défaillons	bouillons	
	courez	faillissez, faillez	défaillez	bouillez	
PART. présent	courant	faillissant, faillant	défaillant	bouillant	gisant
PART. passé	couru, e	failli	défailli	bouilli, e	

(1) La conjugaison de *faillir* la plus employée est celle qui a été refaite sur *finir*. Les formes conjuguées de ce verbe sont rares. – (2) On trouve aussi *je défaillerai, tu défailleras*, etc., pour le futur, et *je défaillerais, tu défaillerais*, etc., pour le conditionnel, de même pour *tressaillir* et *assaillir*. – (3) *Gésir* est défectif aux autres temps et modes.

	50 saillir (1)	**51 ouïr** (2)	**52 recevoir**	**53 devoir**	**54 mouvoir**
IND. présent		j'ouïs, ois	je reçois	je dois	je meus
		tu ouïs, ois	tu reçois	tu dois	tu meus
	il, elle saille	il, elle ouït, oit	il, elle reçoit	il, elle doit	il, elle meut
		nous ouïssons, oyons	nous recevons	nous devons	nous mouvons
		vous ouïssez, oyez	vous recevez	vous devez	vous mouvez
	ils, elles saillent	ils, elles ouïssent, oient	ils, elles reçoivent	ils, elles doivent	ils, elles meuvent
IND. imparfait	il, elle saillait	il, elle ouïssait, oyait	il, elle recevait	il, elle devait	il, elle mouvait
IND. passé s.	il, elle saillit	il, elle ouït	il, elle reçut	il, elle dut	il, elle mut
	ils, elles saillirent	ils, elles ouïrent	ils, elles reçurent	ils, elles durent	ils, elles murent
IND. futur		j'ouïrai, orrai	je recevrai	je devrai	je mouvrai
	il, elle saillera	il, elle ouïra, orra	il, elle recevra	il, elle devra	il, elle mouvra
COND. présent		j'ouïrais, orrais	je recevrais	je devrais	je mouvrais
	il, elle saillerait	il, elle ouïrait, orrait	il, elle recevrait	il, elle devrait	il, elle mouvrait
SUBJ. présent		que j'ouïsse, oie	que je reçoive	que je doive	que je meuve
	qu'il, elle saille	qu'il, elle ouïsse, oie	qu'il, elle reçoive	qu'il, elle doive	qu'il, elle meuve
		que nous ouïssions, oyions	que nous recevions	que nous devions	que nous mouvions
	qu'ils, elles saillent	qu'ils, elles ouïssent, oient	qu'ils, elles reçoivent	qu'ils, elles doivent	qu'ils, elles meuvent
SUBJ. imparfait	qu'il, elle saillît	qu'il, elle ouït	qu'il, elle reçût	qu'il, elle dût	qu'il, elle mût
	qu'ils, elles saillissent	qu'ils, elles ouïssent	qu'ils, elles reçussent	qu'ils, elles dussent	qu'ils, elles mussent
IMPÉRATIF	*inusité*	ouïs, ois	reçois	dois	meus
		ouïssons, oyons	recevons	devons	mouvons
		ouïssez, oyez	recevez	devez	mouvez
PART. présent	saillant	oyant	recevant	devant	mouvant
PART. passé	sailli, e	ouï, e	reçu, e	dû, due, dus, dues	mû, mue, mus, mues

(1) Il s'agit ici du verbe 2. *saillir*. (V. à son ordre alphabétique.) – (2) V. REM. au verbe à son ordre alphabétique.

	55 émouvoir	**56 promouvoir**(1)	**57 vouloir**	**58 pouvoir** (2)	**59 savoir**
IND. présent	j'émeus	je promeus	je veux	je peux, puis	je sais
	tu émeus	tu promeus	tu veux	tu peux	tu sais
	il, elle émeut	il, elle promeut	il, elle veut	il, elle peut	il, elle sait
	nous émouvons	nous promouvons	nous voulons	nous pouvons	nous savons
	vous émouvez	vous promouvez	vous voulez	vous pouvez	vous savez
	ils, elles émeuvent	ils, elles promeuvent	ils, elles veulent	ils, elles peuvent	ils, elles savent
IND. imparfait	il, elle émouvait	il, elle promouvait	il, elle voulait	il, elle pouvait	il, elle savait
IND. passé s.	il, elle émut	il, elle promut	il, elle voulut	il, elle put	il, elle sut
	ils, elles émurent	ils, elles promurent	ils, elles voulurent	ils, elles purent	ils, elles surent
IND. futur	j'émouvrai	je promouvrai	je voudrai	je pourrai	je saurai
	il, elle émouvra	il, elle promouvra	il, elle voudra	il, elle pourra	il, elle saura
COND. présent	j'émouvrais	je promouvrais	je voudrais	je pourrais	je saurais
	il, elle émouvrait	il, elle promouvrait	il, elle voudrait	il, elle pourrait	il, elle saurait
SUBJ. présent	que j'émeuve	que je promeuve	que je veuille	que je puisse	que je sache
	qu'il, elle émeuve	qu'il, elle promeuve	qu'il, elle veuille	qu'il, elle puisse	qu'il, elle sache
	que nous émouvions	que nous promouvions	que nous voulions	que nous puissions	que nous sachions
	qu'ils, elles émeuvent	qu'ils, elles promeuvent	qu'ils, elles veuillent	qu'ils, elles puissent	qu'ils, elles sachent
SUBJ. imparfait	qu'il, elle émût	qu'il, elle promût	qu'il, elle voulût	qu'il, elle pût	qu'il, elle sût
	qu'ils, elles émussent	qu'ils, elles promussent	qu'ils, elles voulussent	qu'ils, elles pussent	qu'ils, elles sussent
IMPÉRATIF	émeus	promeus	veux, veuille	*inusité*	sache
	émouvons	promouvons	voulons, veuillons		sachons
	émouvez	promouvez	voulez, veuillez		sachez
PART. présent	émouvant	promouvant	voulant	pouvant	sachant
PART. passé	ému, e	promu, e	voulu, e	pu	su, e

(1) Les formes conjuguées de ce verbe sont rares. – (2) À la forme interrogative, avec inversion du sujet, on a seulement *puis-je ?*

	60 valoir	**61 prévaloir**	**62 voir**	**63 prévoir**	**64 pourvoir**
IND. présent	je vaux	je prévaux	je vois	je prévois	je pourvois
	tu vaux	tu prévaux	tu vois	tu prévois	tu pourvois
	il, elle vaut	il, elle prévaut	il, elle voit	il, elle prévoit	il, elle pourvoit
	nous valons	nous prévalons	nous voyons	nous prévoyons	nous pourvoyons
	vous valez	vous prévalez	vous voyez	vous prévoyez	vous pourvoyez
	ils, elles valent	ils, elles prévalent	ils, elles voient	ils, elles prévoient	ils, elles pourvoient
IND. imparfait	il, elle valait	il, elle prévalait	il, elle voyait	il, elle prévoyait	il, elle pourvoyait
IND. passé s.	il, elle valut	il, elle prévalut	il, elle vit	il, elle prévit	il, elle pourvut
	ils, elles valurent	ils, elles prévalurent	ils, elles virent	ils, elles prévirent	ils, elles pourvurent
IND. futur	je vaudrai	je prévaudrai	je verrai	je prévoirai	je pourvoirai
	il, elle vaudra	il, elle prévaudra	il, elle verra	il, elle prévoira	il, elle pourvoira
COND. présent	je vaudrais	je prévaudrais	je verrais	je prévoirais	je pourvoirais
	il, elle vaudrait	il, elle prévaudrait	il, elle verrait	il, elle prévoirait	il, elle pourvoirait
SUBJ. présent	que je vaille	que je prévale	que je voie	que je prévoie	que je pourvoie
	qu'il, elle vaille	qu'il, elle prévale	qu'il, elle voie	qu'il, elle prévoie	qu'il, elle pourvoie
	que nous valions	que nous prévalions	que nous voyions	que nous prévoyions	que nous pourvoyions
	qu'ils, elles vaillent	qu'ils, elles prévalent	qu'ils, elles voient	qu'ils, elles prévoient	qu'ils, elles pourvoient
SUBJ. imparfait	qu'il, elle valût	qu'il, elle prévalût	qu'il, elle vît	qu'il, elle prévît	qu'il, elle pourvût
	qu'ils, elles valussent	qu'ils, elles prévalussent	qu'ils, elles vissent	qu'ils, elles prévissent	qu'ils, elles pourvussent
IMPÉRATIF	vaux	prévaux	vois	prévois	pourvois
	valons	prévalons	voyons	prévoyons	pourvoyons
	valez	prévalez	voyez	prévoyez	pourvoyez
PART. présent	valant	prévalant	voyant	prévoyant	pourvoyant
PART. passé	valu, e	prévalu, e	vu, e	prévu, e	pourvu, e

	65 asseoir (1)		**66 surseoir**	**67 seoir** (2)	**68 pleuvoir** (3)
IND. présent	j'assieds	j'assois	je sursois		
	tu assieds	tu assois	tu sursois		
	il, elle assied	il, elle assoit	il, elle sursoit	il, elle sied	il pleut
	nous asseyons	nous assoyons	nous sursoyons		
	vous asseyez	vous assoyez	vous sursoyez		
	ils, elles asseyent	ils, elles assoient	ils, elles sursoient	ils, elles siéent	
IND. imparfait	il, elle asseyait	il, elle assoyait	il, elle sursoyait	il, elle seyait	il pleuvait
IND. passé s.	il, elle assit	il, elle assit	il, elle sursit	*inusité*	il plut
	ils, elles assirent	ils, elles assirent	ils, elles sursirent		
IND. futur	j'assiérai	j'assoirai	je surseoirai		
	il, elle assiéra	il, elle assoira	il, elle surseoira	il, elle siéra	il pleuvra
COND. présent	j'assiérais	j'assoirais	je surseoirais		
	il, elle assiérait	il, elle assoirait	il, elle surseoirait	il, elle siérait	il pleuvrait
SUBJ. présent	que j'asseye	que j'assoie	que je sursoie		
	qu'il, elle asseye	qu'il, elle assoie	qu'il, elle sursoie	qu'il, elle siée	qu'il pleuve
	que nous asseyions	que nous assoyions	que nous sursoyions		
	qu'ils, elles asseyent	qu'ils, elles assoient	qu'ils, elles sursoient	qu'ils, elles siéent	
SUBJ. imparfait	qu'il, elle assît	qu'il, elle assît	qu'il, elle sursît	*inusité*	qu'il plût
	qu'ils, elles assissent	qu'ils, elles assissent	qu'ils, elles sursissent		
IMPÉRATIF	assieds	assois	sursois	*inusité*	*inusité*
	asseyons	assoyons	sursoyons		
	asseyez	assoyez	sursoyez		
PART. présent	asseyant	assoyant	sursoyant	seyant	pleuvant
PART. passé	assis, e	assis, e	sursis	*inusité*	plu

(1) L'usage tend à écrire avec *-eoi-* les formes avec *oi* : *je m'asseois, il, elle asseoira, que tu asseoies, ils, elles asseoiraient.* – (2) *Seoir* a ici le sens de « convenir ». Aux sens de « être situé », « siéger », *seoir* a seulement un participe présent *(séant)* et un participe passé *(sis, e)*. – (3) *Pleuvoir* connaît au figuré une troisième personne du pluriel : *les injures pleuvent, pleuvaient, pleuvront, plurent, pleuvraient...*

	69 falloir	**70 échoir**	**71 déchoir**	**72 choir**	**73 vendre**
IND. présent			je déchois	je chois	je vends
			tu déchois	tu chois	tu vends
	il faut	il, elle échoit	il, elle déchoit	il, elle choit	il, elle vend
			nous déchoyons	*inusité*	nous vendons
			vous déchoyez	*inusité*	vous vendez
		ils, elles échoient	ils, elles déchoient	ils, elles choient	ils, elles vendent
IND. imparfait	il fallait	il, elle échoyait	*inusité*	*inusité*	il, elle vendait
IND. passé s.	il fallut	il, elle échut	il, elle déchut	il, elle chut	il, elle vendit
		ils, elles échurent	ils, elles déchurent	ils, elles churent	ils, elles vendirent
IND. futur			je déchoirai	je choirai, cherrai	je vendrai
	il faudra	il, elle échoira, écherra	il, elle déchoira	il, elle choira, cherra	il, elle vendra
COND. présent			je déchoirais	je choirais, cherrais	je vendrais
	il faudrait	il, elle échoirait, écherrait	il, elle déchoirait	il, elle choirait, cherrait	il, elle vendrait
SUBJ. présent			que je déchoie	*inusité*	que je vende
	qu'il faille	qu'il, elle échoie	qu'il, elle déchoie		qu'il, elle vende
			que nous déchoyions		que nous vendions
		qu'ils, elles échoient	qu'ils, elles déchoient		qu'ils, elles vendent
SUBJ. imparfait	qu'il fallût	qu'il, elle échût	qu'il, elle déchût	qu'il, elle chût	qu'il, elle vendît
		qu'ils, elles échussent	qu'ils, elles déchussent	*inusité*	qu'ils, elles vendissent
IMPÉRATIF	*inusité*	*inusité*	*inusité*	*inusité*	vends
					vendons
					vendez
PART. présent	*inusité*	échéant	*inusité*	*inusité*	vendant
PART. passé	fallu	échu, e	déchu, e	chu, e	vendu, e

	74 répandre	**75 répondre**	**76 mordre**	**77 perdre**	**78 rompre**
IND. présent	je répands	je réponds	je mords	je perds	je romps
	tu répands	tu réponds	tu mords	tu perds	tu romps
	il, elle répand	il, elle répond	il, elle mord	il, elle perd	il, elle rompt
	nous répandons	nous répondons	nous mordons	nous perdons	nous rompons
	vous répandez	vous répondez	vous mordez	vous perdez	vous rompez
	ils, elles répandent	ils, elles répondent	ils, elles mordent	ils, elles perdent	ils, elles rompent
IND. imparfait	il, elle répandait	il, elle répondait	il, elle mordait	il, elle perdait	il, elle rompait
IND. passé s.	il, elle répandit	il, elle répondit	il, elle mordit	il, elle perdit	il, elle rompit
	ils, elles répandirent	ils, elles répondirent	ils, elles mordirent	ils, elles perdirent	ils, elles rompirent
IND. futur	je répandrai	je répondrai	je mordrai	je perdrai	je romprai
	il, elle répandra	il, elle répondra	il, elle mordra	il, elle perdra	il, elle rompra
COND. présent	je répandrais	je répondrais	je mordrais	je perdrais	je romprais
	il, elle répandrait	il, elle répondrait	il, elle mordrait	il, elle perdrait	il, elle romprait
SUBJ. présent	que je répande	que je réponde	que je morde	que je perde	que je rompe
	qu’il, elle répande	qu’il, elle réponde	qu’il, elle morde	qu’il, elle perde	qu’il, elle rompe
	que nous répandions	que nous répondions	que nous mordions	que nous perdions	que nous rompions
	qu’ils, elles répandent	qu’ils, elles répondent	qu’ils, elles mordent	qu’ils, elles perdent	qu’ils, elles rompent
SUBJ. imparfait	qu’il, elle répandît	qu’il, elle répondît	qu’il, elle mordît	qu’il, elle perdît	qu’il, elle rompît
	qu’ils, elles répandissent	qu’ils, elles répondissent	qu’ils, elles mordissent	qu’ils, elles perdissent	qu’ils, elles rompissent
IMPÉRATIF	répands	réponds	mords	perds	romps
	répandons	répondons	mordons	perdons	rompons
	répandez	répondez	mordez	perdez	rompez
PART. présent	répandant	répondant	mordant	perdant	rompant
PART. passé	répandu, e	répondu, e	mordu, e	perdu, e	rompu, e

	79 prendre	**80 craindre**	**81 peindre**	**82 joindre**	**83 battre**
IND. présent	je prends	je crains	je peins	je joins	je bats
	tu prends	tu crains	tu peins	tu joins	tu bats
	il, elle prend	il, elle craint	il, elle peint	il, elle joint	il, elle bat
	nous prenons	nous craignons	nous peignons	nous joignons	nous battons
	vous prenez	vous craignez	vous peignez	vous joignez	vous battez
	ils, elles prennent	ils, elles craignent	ils, elles peignent	ils, elles joignent	ils, elles battent
IND. imparfait	il, elle prenait	il, elle craignait	il, elle peignait	il, elle joignait	il, elle battait
IND. passé s.	il, elle prit	il, elle craignit	il, elle peignit	il, elle joignit	il, elle battit
	ils, elles prirent	ils, elles craignirent	ils, elles peignirent	ils, elles joignirent	ils, elles battirent
IND. futur	je prendrai	je craindrai	je peindrai	je joindrai	je battrai
	il, elle prendra	il, elle craindra	il, elle peindra	il, elle joindra	il, elle battra
COND. présent	je prendrais	je craindrais	je peindrais	je joindrais	je battrais
	il, elle prendrait	il, elle craindrait	il, elle peindrait	il, elle joindrait	il, elle battrait
SUBJ. présent	que je prenne	que je craigne	que je peigne	que je joigne	que je batte
	qu’il, elle prenne	qu’il, elle craigne	qu’il, elle peigne	qu’il, elle joigne	qu’il, elle batte
	que nous prenions	que nous craignions	que nous peignions	que nous joignions	que nous battions
	qu’ils, elles prennent	qu’ils, elles craignent	qu’ils, elles peignent	qu’ils, elles joignent	qu’ils, elles battent
SUBJ. imparfait	qu’il, elle prît	qu’il, elle craignît	qu’il, elle peignît	qu’il, elle joignît	qu’il, elle battît
	qu’ils, elles prissent	qu’ils, elles craignissent	qu’ils, elles peignissent	qu’ils, elles joignissent	qu’ils, elles battissent
IMPÉRATIF	prends	crains	peins	joins	bats
	prenons	craignons	peignons	joignons	battons
	prenez	craignez	peignez	joignez	battez
PART. présent	prenant	craignant	peignant	joignant	battant
PART. passé	pris, e	craint, e	peint, e	joint, e	battu, e

	84 mettre	**85 moudre**	**86 coudre**	**87 absoudre** (1)	**88 résoudre** (2)
IND. présent	je mets	je mouds	je couds	j’absous	je résous
	tu mets	tu mouds	tu couds	tu absous	tu résous
	il, elle met	il, elle moud	il, elle coud	il, elle absout	il, elle résout
	nous mettons	nous moulons	nous cousons	nous absolvons	nous résolvons
	vous mettez	vous moulez	vous cousez	vous absolvez	vous résolvez
	ils, elles mettent	ils, elles moulent	ils, elles cousent	ils, elles absolvent	ils, elles résolvent
IND. imparfait	il, elle mettait	il, elle moulait	il, elle cousait	il, elle absolvait	il, elle résolvait
IND. passé s.	il, elle mit	il, elle moulut	il, elle cousit	il, elle absolut	il, elle résolut
	ils, elles mirent	ils, elles moulurent	ils, elles cousirent	ils, elles absolurent	ils, elles résolurent
IND. futur	je mettrai	je moudrai	je coudrai	j’absoudrai	je résoudrai
	il, elle mettra	il, elle moudra	il, elle coudra	il, elle absoudra	il, elle résoudra
COND. présent	je mettrais	je moudrais	je coudrais	j’absoudrais	je résoudrais
	il, elle mettrait	il, elle moudrait	il, elle coudrait	il, elle absoudrait	il, elle résoudrait
SUBJ. présent	que je mette	que je moule	que je couse	que j’absolve	que je résolve
	qu’il, elle mette	qu’il, elle moule	qu’il, elle couse	qu’il, elle absolve	qu’il, elle résolve
	que nous mettions	que nous moulions	que nous cousions	que nous absolvions	que nous résolvions
	qu’ils, elles mettent	qu’ils, elles moulent	qu’ils, elles cousent	qu’ils, elles absolvent	qu’ils, elles résolvent
SUBJ. imparfait	qu’il, elle mît	qu’il, elle moulût	qu’il, elle cousît	qu’il, elle absolût	qu’il, elle résolût
	qu’ils, elles missent	qu’ils, elles moulussent	qu’ils, elles cousissent	qu’ils, elles absolussent	qu’ils, elles résolussent
IMPÉRATIF	mets	mouds	couds	absous	résous
	mettons	moulons	cousons	absolvons	résolvons
	mettez	moulez	cousez	absolvez	résolvez
PART. présent	mettant	moulant	cousant	absolvant	résolvant
PART. passé	mis, e	moulu, e	cousu, e	absous, oute	résolu, e

(1) Le passé simple et le subjonctif imparfait, admis par Littré, sont rares. – (2) Il existe un participe passé *résous, résoute* (rare), avec le sens de « transformé » *(Un brouillard résous en pluie).*

	89 suivre	**90 vivre** (1)	**91 paraître**	**92 naître**	**93 croître** (2)
IND. présent	je suis	je vis	je parais	je nais	je croîs
	tu suis	tu vis	tu parais	tu nais	tu croîs
	il, elle suit	il, elle vit	il, elle paraît	il, elle naît	il, elle croît
	nous suivons	nous vivons	nous paraissons	nous naissons	nous croissons
	vous suivez	vous vivez	vous paraissez	vous naissez	vous croissez
	ils, elles suivent	ils, elles vivent	ils, elles paraissent	ils, elles naissent	ils, elles croissent
IND. imparfait	il, elle suivait	il, elle vivait	il, elle paraissait	il, elle naissait	il, elle croissait
IND. passé s.	il, elle suivit	il, elle vécut	il, elle parut	il, elle naquit	il, elle crût
	ils, elles suivirent	ils, elles vécurent	ils, elles parurent	ils, elles naquirent	ils, elles crûrent
IND. futur	je suivrai	je vivrai	je paraîtrai	je naîtrai	je croîtrai
	il, elle suivra	il, elle vivra	il, elle paraîtra	il, elle naîtra	il, elle croîtra
COND. présent	je suivrais	je vivrais	je paraîtrais	je naîtrais	je croîtrais
	il, elle suivrait	il, elle vivrait	il, elle paraîtrait	il, elle naîtrait	il, elle croîtrait
SUBJ. présent	que je suive	que je vive	que je paraisse	que je naisse	que je croisse
	qu'il, elle suive	qu'il, elle vive	qu'il, elle paraisse	qu'il, elle naisse	qu'il, elle croisse
	que nous suivions	que nous vivions	que nous paraissions	que nous naissions	que nous croissions
	qu'ils, elles suivent	qu'ils, elles vivent	qu'ils, elles paraissent	qu'ils, elles naissent	qu'ils, elles croissent
SUBJ. imparfait	qu'il, elle suivît	qu'il, elle vécût	qu'il, elle parût	qu'il, elle naquît	qu'il, elle crût
	qu'ils, elles suivissent	qu'ils, elles vécussent	qu'ils, elles parussent	qu'ils, elles naquissent	qu'ils, elles crûssent
IMPÉRATIF	suis	vis	parais	nais	croîs
	suivons	vivons	paraissons	naissons	croissons
	suivez	vivez	paraissez	naissez	croissez
PART. présent	suivant	vivant	paraissant	naissant	croissant
PART. passé	suivi, e	vécu, e	paru, e	né, e	crû, crue, crus, crues

(1) *Survivre* se conjugue comme *vivre*, mais son participe passé est toujours invariable. – (2) L'Académie écrit *crusse, crusses, crussions, crussiez, crussent* (sans accent circonflexe).

	94 accroître (1)	**95 rire**	**96 conclure** (2)	**97 nuire** (3)	**98 conduire**
IND. présent	j'accrois	je ris	je conclus	je nuis	je conduis
	tu accrois	tu ris	tu conclus	tu nuis	tu conduis
	il, elle accroît	il, elle rit	il, elle conclut	il, elle nuit	il, elle conduit
	nous accroissons	nous rions	nous concluons	nous nuisons	nous conduisons
	vous accroissez	vous riez	vous concluez	vous nuisez	vous conduisez
	ils, elles accroissent	ils, elles rient	ils, elles concluent	ils, elles nuisent	ils, elles conduisent
IND. imparfait	il, elle accroissait	il, elle riait	il, elle concluait	il, elle nuisait	il, elle conduisait
IND. passé s.	il, elle accrut	il, elle rit	il, elle conclut	il, elle nuisit	il, elle conduisit
	ils, elles accrurent	ils, elles rirent	ils, elles conclurent	ils, elles nuisirent	ils, elles conduisirent
IND. futur	j'accroîtrai	je rirai	je conclurai	je nuirai	je conduirai
	il, elle accroîtra	il, elle rira	il, elle conclura	il, elle nuira	il, elle conduira
COND. présent	j'accroîtrais	je rirais	je conclurais	je nuirais	je conduirais
	il, elle accroîtrait	il, elle rirait	il, elle conclurait	il, elle nuirait	il, elle conduirait
SUBJ. présent	que j'accroisse	que je rie	que je conclue	que je nuise	que je conduise
	qu'il, elle accroisse	qu'il, elle rie	qu'il, elle conclue	qu'il, elle nuise	qu'il, elle conduise
	que nous accroissions	que nous riions	que nous concluions	que nous nuisions	que nous conduisions
	qu'ils, elles accroissent	qu'ils, elles rient	qu'ils, elles concluent	qu'ils, elles nuisent	qu'ils, elles conduisent
SUBJ. imparfait	qu'il, elle accrût	qu'il, elle rît	qu'il, elle conclût	qu'il, elle nuisît	qu'il, elle conduisît
	qu'ils, elles accrussent	qu'ils, elles rissent	qu'ils, elles conclussent	qu'ils, elles nuisissent	qu'ils, elles conduisissent
IMPÉRATIF	accrois	ris	conclus	nuis	conduis
	accroissons	rions	concluons	nuisons	conduisons
	accroissez	riez	concluez	nuisez	conduisez
PART. présent	accroissant	riant	concluant	nuisant	conduisant
PART. passé	accru, e	ri	conclu, e	nui	conduit, e

(1) *Recroître* se conjugue comme *accroître*, mais son participe passé est *recrû, recrue, recrus, recrues.* – (2) *Inclure* et *occlure* se conjuguent comme *conclure*, mais leur participe passé est *inclus, incluse ; occlus, occluse.* – (3) *Luire* et *reluire* connaissent une autre forme de passé simple : *je luis, je reluis,* etc.

	99 écrire	**100 suffire**	**101 confire** (1)	**102 dire**	**103 contredire**
IND. présent	j'écris	je suffis	je confis	je dis	je contredis
	tu écris	tu suffis	tu confis	tu dis	tu contredis
	il, elle écrit	il, elle suffit	il, elle confit	il, elle dit	il, elle contredit
	nous écrivons	nous suffisons	nous confisons	nous disons	nous contredisons
	vous écrivez	vous suffisez	vous confisez	vous dites	vous contredisez
	ils, elles écrivent	ils, elles suffisent	ils, elles confisent	ils, elles disent	ils, elles contredisent
IND. imparfait	il, elle écrivait	il, elle suffisait	il, elle confisait	il, elle disait	il, elle contredisait
IND. passé s.	il, elle écrivit	il, elle suffit	il, elle confit	il, elle dit	il, elle contredit
	ils, elles écrivirent	ils, elles suffirent	ils, elles confirent	ils, elles dirent	ils, elles contredirent
IND. futur	j'écrirai	je suffirai	je confirai	je dirai	je contredirai
	il, elle écrira	il, elle suffira	il, elle confira	il, elle dira	il, elle contredira
COND. présent	j'écrirais	je suffirais	je confirais	je dirais	je contredirais
	il, elle écrirait	il, elle suffirait	il, elle confirait	il, elle dirait	il, elle contredirait
SUBJ. présent	que j'écrive	que je suffise	que je confise	que je dise	que je contredise
	qu'il, elle écrive	qu'il, elle suffise	qu'il, elle confise	qu'il, elle dise	qu'il, elle contredise
	que nous écrivions	que nous suffisions	que nous confisions	que nous disions	que nous contredisions
	qu'ils, elles écrivent	qu'ils, elles suffisent	qu'ils, elles confisent	qu'ils, elles disent	qu'ils, elles contredisent
SUBJ. imparfait	qu'il, elle écrivît	qu'il, elle suffît	qu'il, elle confît	qu'il, elle dît	qu'il, elle contredît
	qu'ils, elles écrivissent	qu'ils, elles suffissent	qu'ils, elles confissent	qu'ils, elles dissent	qu'ils, elles contredissent
IMPÉRATIF	écris	suffis	confis	dis	contredis
	écrivons	suffisons	confisons	disons	contredisons
	écrivez	suffisez	confisez	dites	contredisez
PART. présent	écrivant	suffisant	confisant	disant	contredisant
PART. passé	écrit, e	suffi	confit, e	dit, e	contredit, e

(1) *Circoncire* se conjugue comme *confire*, mais son participe passé est *circoncis, circoncise.*

	104 **maudire**	105 **bruire** (1)	106 **lire**	107 **croire**	108 **boire**
IND. présent	je maudis tu maudis il, elle maudit nous maudissons vous maudissez ils, elles maudissent	je bruis tu bruis il, elle bruit *inusité*	je lis tu lis il, elle lit nous lisons vous lisez ils, elles lisent	je crois tu crois il, elle croit nous croyons vous croyez ils, elles croient	je bois tu bois il, elle boit nous buvons vous buvez ils, elles boivent
IND. imparfait	il, elle maudissait	il, elle bruyait	il, elle lisait	il, elle croyait	il, elle buvait
IND. passé s.	il, elle maudit ils, elles maudirent	*inusité*	il, elle lut ils, elles lurent	il, elle crut ils, elles crurent	il, elle but ils, elles burent
IND. futur	je maudirai il, elle maudira	je bruirai il, elle bruira	je lirai il, elle lira	je croirai il, elle croira	je boirai il, elle boira
COND. présent	je maudirais il, elle maudirait	je bruirais il, elle bruirait	je lirais il, elle lirait	je croirais il, elle croirait	je boirais il, elle boirait
SUBJ. présent	que je maudisse qu'il, elle maudisse que nous maudissions qu'ils, elles maudissent	*inusité*	que je lise qu'il, elle lise que nous lisions qu'ils, elles lisent	que je croie qu'il, elle croie que nous croyions qu'ils, elles croient	que je boive qu'il, elle boive que nous buvions qu'ils, elles boivent
SUBJ. imparfait	qu'il, elle maudît qu'ils, elles maudissent	*inusité*	qu'il, elle lût qu'ils, elles lussent	qu'il, elle crût qu'ils, elles crussent	qu'il, elle bût qu'ils, elles bussent
IMPÉRATIF	maudis maudissons maudissez	*inusité*	lis lisons lisez	crois croyons croyez	bois buvons buvez
PART. présent	maudissant	*inusité*	lisant	croyant	buvant
PART. passé	maudit, e	bruit	lu, e	cru, e	bu, e

(1) Traditionnellement, *bruire* ne connaît que les formes de l'indicatif présent, imparfait (*je bruyais, tu bruyais,* etc.), futur, et les formes du conditionnel ; *bruisser* (conjugaison 3) tend de plus en plus à supplanter *bruire*, en particulier dans toutes les formes défectives.

	109 **faire**	110 **plaire**	111 **taire**	112 **extraire**
IND. présent	je fais tu fais il, elle fait nous faisons vous faites ils, elles font	je plais tu plais il, elle plaît nous plaisons vous plaisez ils, elles plaisent	je tais tu tais il, elle tait nous taisons vous taisez ils, elles taisent	j'extrais tu extrais il, elle extrait nous extrayons vous extrayez ils, elles extraient
IND. imparfait	il, elle faisait	il, elle plaisait	il, elle taisait	il, elle extrayait
IND. passé s.	il, elle fit ils, elles firent	il, elle plut ils, elles plurent	il, elle tut ils, elles turent	*inusité*
IND. futur	je ferai il, elle fera	je plairai il, elle plaira	je tairai il, elle taira	j'extrairai il, elle extraira
COND. présent	je ferais il, elle ferait	je plairais il, elle plairait	je tairais il, elle tairait	j'extrairais il, elle extrairait
SUBJ. présent	que je fasse qu'il, elle fasse que nous fassions qu'ils, elles fassent	que je plaise qu'il, elle plaise que nous plaisions qu'ils, elles plaisent	que je taise qu'il, elle taise que nous taisions qu'ils, elles taisent	que j'extraie qu'il, elle extraie que nous extrayions qu'ils, elles extraient
SUBJ. imparfait	qu'il, elle fît qu'ils, elles fissent	qu'il, elle plût qu'ils, elles plussent	qu'il, elle tût qu'ils, elles tussent	*inusité*
IMPÉRATIF	fais faisons faites	plais plaisons plaisez	tais taisons taisez	extrais extrayons extrayez
PART. présent	faisant	plaisant	taisant	extrayant
PART. passé	fait, e	plu	tu, e	extrait, e

	113 **clore** (1)	114 **vaincre**	115 **frire**	116 **foutre**
IND. présent	je clos tu clos il, elle clôt nous closons vous closez ils, elles closent	je vaincs tu vaincs il, elle vainc nous vainquons vous vainquez ils, elles vainquent	je fris tu fris il, elle frit *inusité*	je fous tu fous il, elle fout nous foutons vous foutez ils, elles foutent
IND. imparfait	*inusité*	il, elle vainquait	*inusité*	il, elle foutait
IND. passé s.	*inusité*	il, elle vainquit ils, elles vainquirent	*inusité*	*inusité*
IND. futur	je clorai il, elle clora	je vaincrai il, elle vaincra	je frirai il, elle frira	je foutrai il, elle foutra
COND. présent	je clorais il, elle clorait	je vaincrais il, elle vaincrait	je frirais il, elle frirait	je foutrais il, elle foutrait
SUBJ. présent	que je close qu'il, elle close que nous closions qu'ils, elles closent	que je vainque qu'il, elle vainque que nous vainquions qu'ils, elles vainquent	*inusité*	que je foute qu'il, elle foute que nous foutions qu'ils, elles foutent
SUBJ. imparfait	*inusité*	qu'il, elle vainquît qu'ils, elles vainquissent	*inusité*	*inusité*
IMPÉRATIF	clos *inusité*	vaincs vainquons vainquez	fris *inusité*	fous foutons foutez
PART. présent	closant	vainquant	*inusité*	foutant
PART. passé	clos, e	vaincu, e	frit, e	foutu, e

(1) *Déclore, éclore, enclore* se conjuguent comme *clore*, mais l'Académie préconise *il, elle éclot, il, elle enclot* (sans accent circonflexe). Le verbe *enclore* possède les formes *nous enclosons, vous enclosez* et *enclosons, enclosez.*

English Irregular Verbs

Infinitive	Past Tense	Past Participle
arise	arose	arisen
awake	awoke	awoken
be	was, were	been
bear	bore	borne
beat	beat	beaten
become	became	become
befall	befell	befallen
begin	began	begun
behold	beheld	beheld
bend	bent	bent
beseech	besought	besought
beset	beset	beset
bet	bet, betted	bet, betted
bid	bid, bade	bid, bidden
bind	bound	bound
bite	bit	bitten
bleed	bled	bled
blow	blew	blown
break	broke	broken
breed	bred	bred
bring	brought	brought
build	built	built
burn	burnt, burned	burnt, burned
burst	burst	burst
buy	bought	bought
can	could	—
cast	cast	cast
catch	caught	caught
choose	chose	chosen
cling	clung	clung
come	came	come
cost	cost	cost
creep	crept	crept
cut	cut	cut
deal	dealt	dealt
dig	dug	dug
do	did	done
draw	drew	drawn
dream	dreamed, dreamt	dreamed, dreamt
drink	drank	drunk
drive	drove	driven
dwell	dwelt, dwelled	dwelt, dwelled
eat	ate	eaten
fall	fell	fallen
feed	fed	fed
feel	felt	felt
fight	fought	fought
find	found	found
flee	fled	fled
fling	flung	flung
fly	flew	flown
forbear	forbore	forborne
forbid	forbade	forbidden
forecast	forecast	forecast
forego	forewent	foregone
foresee	foresaw	foreseen
foretell	foretold	foretold
forget	forgot	forgotten
forgive	forgave	forgiven
forsake	forsook	forsaken
freeze	froze	frozen
get	got	got (*Am* gotten)
give	gave	given
go	went	gone
grind	ground	ground
grow	grew	grown
hang	hung, hanged	hung, hanged
have	had	had
hear	heard	heard
hide	hid	hidden
hit	hit	hit
hold	held	held
hurt	hurt	hurt
keep	kept	kept
kneel	knelt, kneeled	knelt, kneeled
know	knew	known
lay	laid	laid
lead	led	led
lean	leant, leaned	leant, leaned
leap	leapt, leaped	leapt, leaped
learn	learnt, learned	learnt, learned
leave	left	left
lend	lent	lent
let	let	let
lie	lay	lain
light	lit, lighted	lit, lighted
lose	lost	lost
make	made	made
may	might	—
mean	meant	meant
meet	met	met
mistake	mistook	mistaken
mow	mowed	mown, mowed
pay	paid	paid
put	put	put
quit	quit, quitted	quit, quitted
read	read	read
rend	rent	rent
rid	rid	rid
ride	rode	ridden
ring	rang	rung
rise	rose	risen
run	ran	run
saw	sawed	sawn
say	said	said
see	saw	seen
seek	sought	sought
sell	sold	sold
send	sent	sent

INFINITIVE	PAST TENSE	PAST PARTICIPLE
set	set	set
shake	shook	shaken
shall	should	—
shear	sheared	shorn, sheared
shed	shed	shed
shine	shone	shone
shoot	shot	shot
show	showed	shown
shrink	shrank	shrunk
shut	shut	shut
sing	sang	sung
sink	sank	sunk
sit	sat	sat
slay	slew	slain
sleep	slept	slept
slide	slid	slid
sling	slung	slung
slink	slunk	slunk
slit	slit	slit
smell	smelt, smelled	smelt, smelled
sow	sowed	sown, sowed
speak	spoke	spoken
speed	sped, speeded	sped, speeded
spell	spelt, spelled	spelt, spelled
spend	spent	spent
spill	spilt, spilled	spilt, spilled
spin	spun	spun
spit	spat	spat
split	split	split
spoil	spoiled, spoilt	spoiled, spoilt
spread	spread	spread
spring	sprang	sprung
stand	stood	stood
steal	stole	stolen
stick	stuck	stuck

INFINITIVE	PAST TENSE	PAST PARTICIPLE
sting	stung	stung
stink	stank	stunk
stride	strode	stridden
strike	struck	struck, stricken
strive	strove	striven
swear	swore	sworn
sweep	swept	swept
swell	swelled	swollen, swelled
swim	swam	swum
swing	swung	swung
take	took	taken
teach	taught	taught
tear	tore	torn
tell	told	told
think	thought	thought
throw	threw	thrown
thrust	thrust	thrust
tread	trod	trodden
upset	upset	upset
wake	woke	woken
waylay	waylaid	waylaid
wear	wore	worn
weave	wove, weaved	woven, weaved
wed	wedded	wedded
weep	wept	wept
wet	wetted, wet	wetted, wet
will	would	—
win	won	won
wind	wound	wound
withdraw	withdrew	withdrawn
withhold	withheld	withheld
withstand	withstood	withstood
wring	wrung	wrung
write	wrote	written

ATLAS

Sommaire
Contents

THE ENGLISH-SPEAKING WORLD
L'ANGLOPHONIE

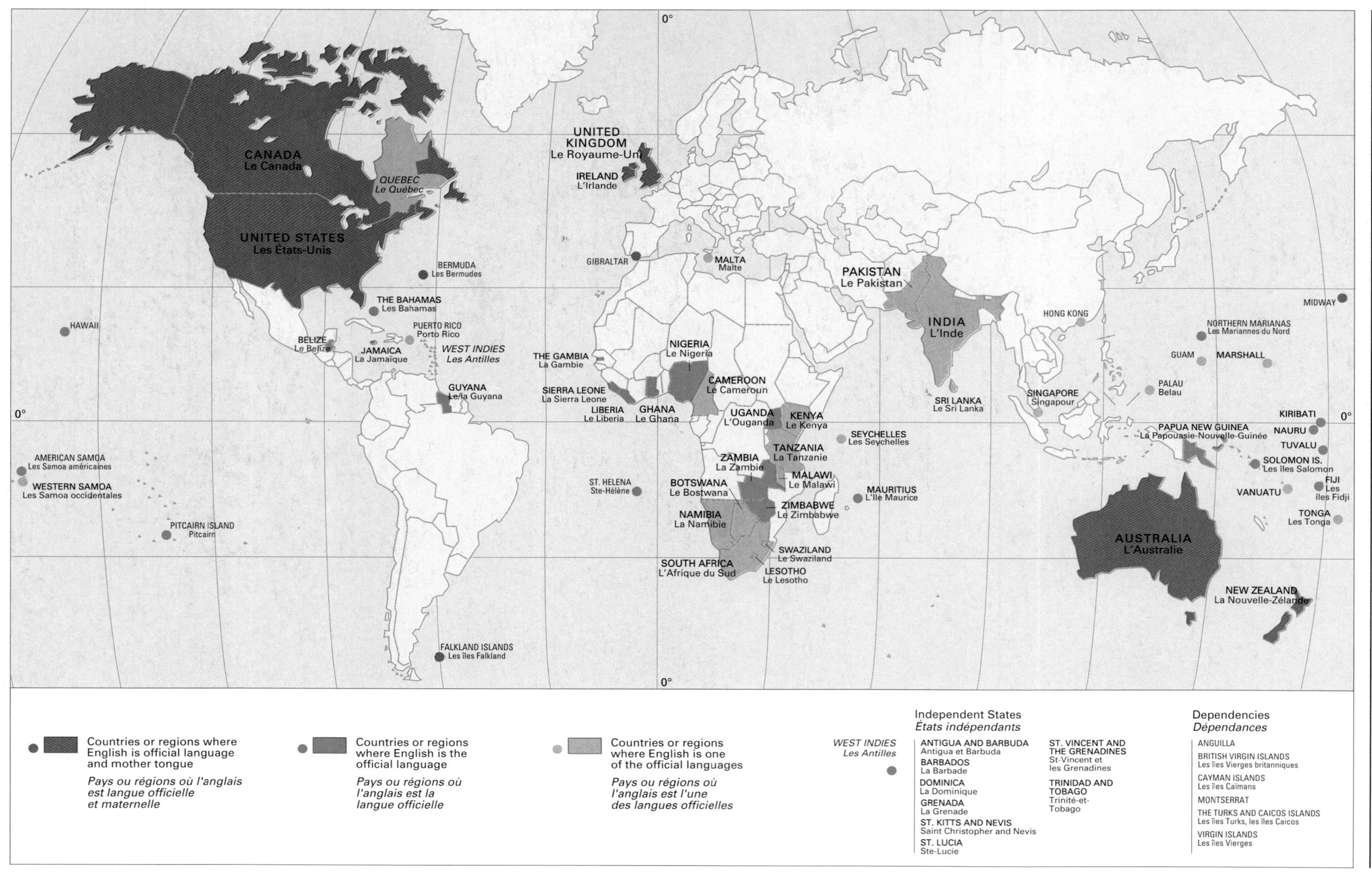

CANADA
Le Canada
QUEBEC
Le Québec
UNITED STATES
Les États-Unis
HAWAII
AMERICAN SAMOA
Les Samoa américaines
WESTERN SAMOA
Les Samoa occidentales
PITCAIRN ISLAND
Pitcairn
BERMUDA
Les Bermudes
THE BAHAMAS
Les Bahamas
PUERTO RICO
Porto Rico
BELIZE
Le Belize
JAMAICA
La Jamaïque
WEST INDIES
Les Antilles
GUYANA
Le/la Guyana
FALKLAND ISLANDS
Les îles Falkland
UNITED KINGDOM
Le Royaume-Uni
IRELAND
L'Irlande
GIBRALTAR
MALTA
Malte
THE GAMBIA
La Gambie
SIERRA LEONE
La Sierra Leone
LIBERIA
Le Liberia
GHANA
Le Ghana
NIGERIA
Le Nigeria
CAMEROON
Le Cameroun
UGANDA
L'Ouganda
KENYA
Le Kenya
TANZANIA
La Tanzanie
ZAMBIA
La Zambie
MALAWI
Le Malawi
ZIMBABWE
Le Zimbabwe
BOTSWANA
Le Botswana
NAMIBIA
La Namibie
SOUTH AFRICA
L'Afrique du Sud
SWAZILAND
Le Swaziland
LESOTHO
Le Lesotho
ST. HELENA
Ste-Hélène
SEYCHELLES
Les Seychelles
MAURITIUS
L'Ile Maurice
PAKISTAN
Le Pakistan
INDIA
L'Inde
SRI LANKA
Le Sri Lanka
HONG KONG
SINGAPORE
Singapour
PALAU
Belau
GUAM
MARSHALL
NORTHERN MARIANAS
Les Mariannes du Nord
MIDWAY
PAPUA NEW GUINEA
La Papouasie-Nouvelle-Guinée
KIRIBATI
NAURU
TUVALU
SOLOMON IS.
Les îles Salomon
FIJI
Les îles Fidji
VANUATU
TONGA
Les Tonga
AUSTRALIA
L'Australie
NEW ZEALAND
La Nouvelle-Zélande
0°
Countries or regions where English is official language and mother tongue
Pays ou régions où l'anglais est langue officielle et maternelle
Countries or regions where English is the official language
Pays ou régions où l'anglais est la langue officielle
Countries or regions where English is one of the official languages
Pays ou régions où l'anglais est l'une des langues officielles
WEST INDIES
Les Antilles
Independent States
États indépendants
ANTIGUA AND BARBUDA
Antigua et Barbuda
BARBADOS
La Barbade
DOMINICA
La Dominique
GRENADA
La Grenade
ST. KITTS AND NEVIS
Saint Christopher and Nevis
ST. LUCIA
Ste-Lucie
ST. VINCENT AND THE GRENADINES
St-Vincent et les Grenadines
TRINIDAD AND TOBAGO
Trinité-et-Tobago
Dependencies
Dépendances
ANGUILLA
BRITISH VIRGIN ISLANDS
Les îles Vierges britanniques
CAYMAN ISLANDS
Les îles Caïmans
MONTSERRAT
THE TURKS AND CAICOS ISLANDS
Les îles Turks, les îles Caicos
VIRGIN ISLANDS
Les îles Vierges

LA FRANCOPHONIE
THE FRENCH-SPEAKING WORLD

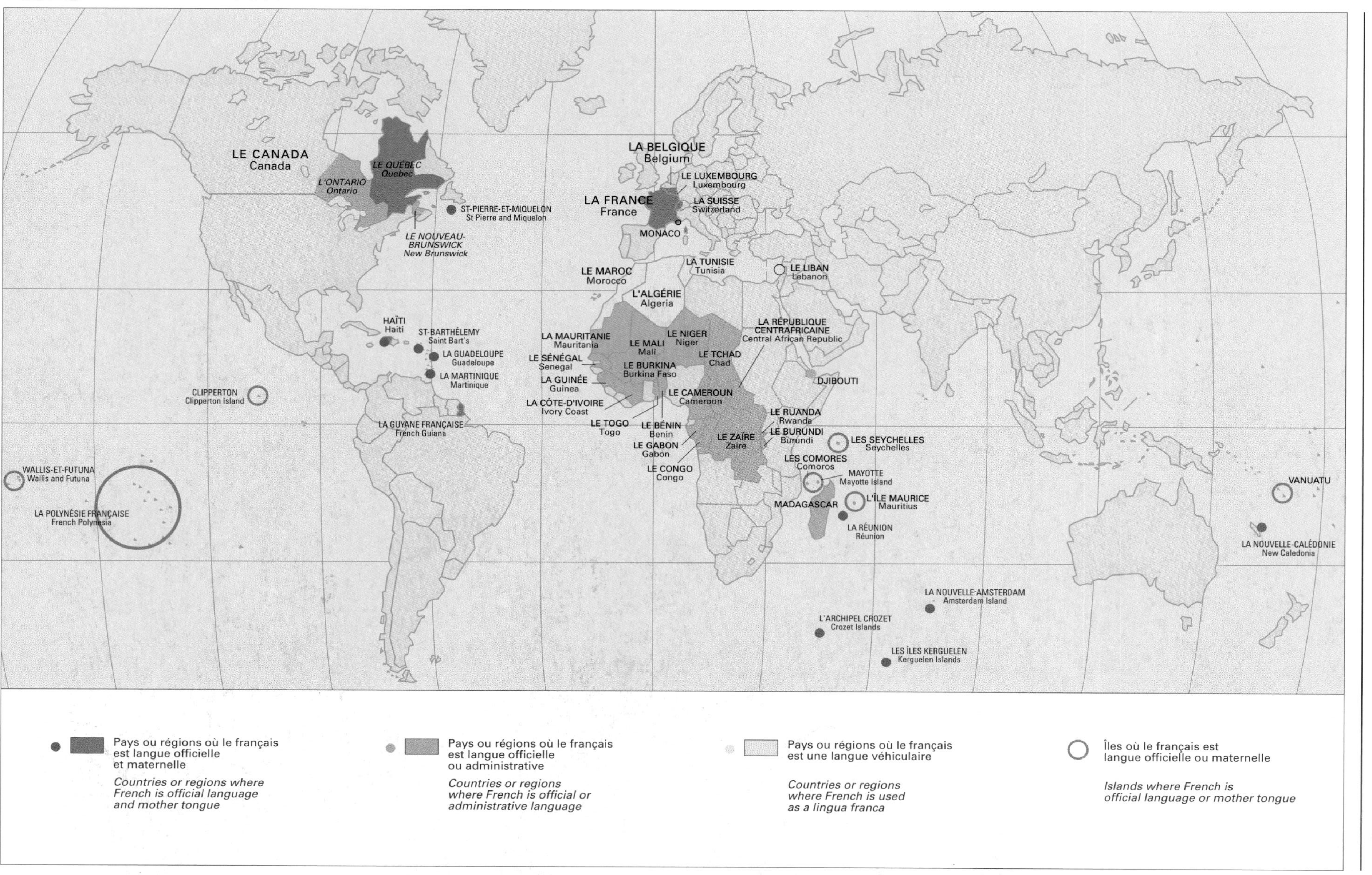

LE CANADA
Canada
L'ONTARIO
Ontario
LE QUÉBEC
Quebec
ST-PIERRE-ET-MIQUELON
St Pierre and Miquelon
LE NOUVEAU-BRUNSWICK
New Brunswick
HAÏTI
Haiti
ST-BARTHÉLEMY
Saint Bart's
LA GUADELOUPE
Guadeloupe
LA MARTINIQUE
Martinique
CLIPPERTON
Clipperton Island
LA GUYANE FRANÇAISE
French Guiana
WALLIS-ET-FUTUNA
Wallis and Futuna
LA POLYNÉSIE FRANÇAISE
French Polynesia
LA BELGIQUE
Belgium
LE LUXEMBOURG
Luxembourg
LA FRANCE
France
LA SUISSE
Switzerland
MONACO
LE MAROC
Morocco
LA TUNISIE
Tunisia
LE LIBAN
Lebanon
L'ALGÉRIE
Algeria
LA RÉPUBLIQUE CENTRAFRICAINE
Central African Republic
LA MAURITANIE
Mauritania
LE NIGER
Niger
LE MALI
Mali
LE SÉNÉGAL
Senegal
LE TCHAD
Chad
LE BURKINA
Burkina Faso
LA GUINÉE
Guinea
DJIBOUTI
LE CAMEROUN
Cameroon
LA CÔTE-D'IVOIRE
Ivory Coast
LE RUANDA
Rwanda
LE TOGO
Togo
LE BÉNIN
Benin
LE BURUNDI
Burundi
LE ZAÏRE
Zaïre
LES SEYCHELLES
Seychelles
LE GABON
Gabon
LES COMORES
Comoros
LE CONGO
Congo
MAYOTTE
Mayotte Island
VANUATU
L'ÎLE MAURICE
Mauritius
MADAGASCAR
LA RÉUNION
Réunion
LA NOUVELLE-CALÉDONIE
New Caledonia
LA NOUVELLE-AMSTERDAM
Amsterdam Island
L'ARCHIPEL CROZET
Crozet Islands
LES ÎLES KERGUELEN
Kerguelen Islands
Pays ou régions où le français est langue officielle et maternelle
Countries or regions where French is official language and mother tongue
Pays ou régions où le français est langue officielle ou administrative
Countries or regions where French is official or administrative language
Pays ou régions où le français est une langue véhiculaire
Countries or regions where French is used as a lingua franca
Îles où le français est langue officielle ou maternelle
Islands where French is official language or mother tongue

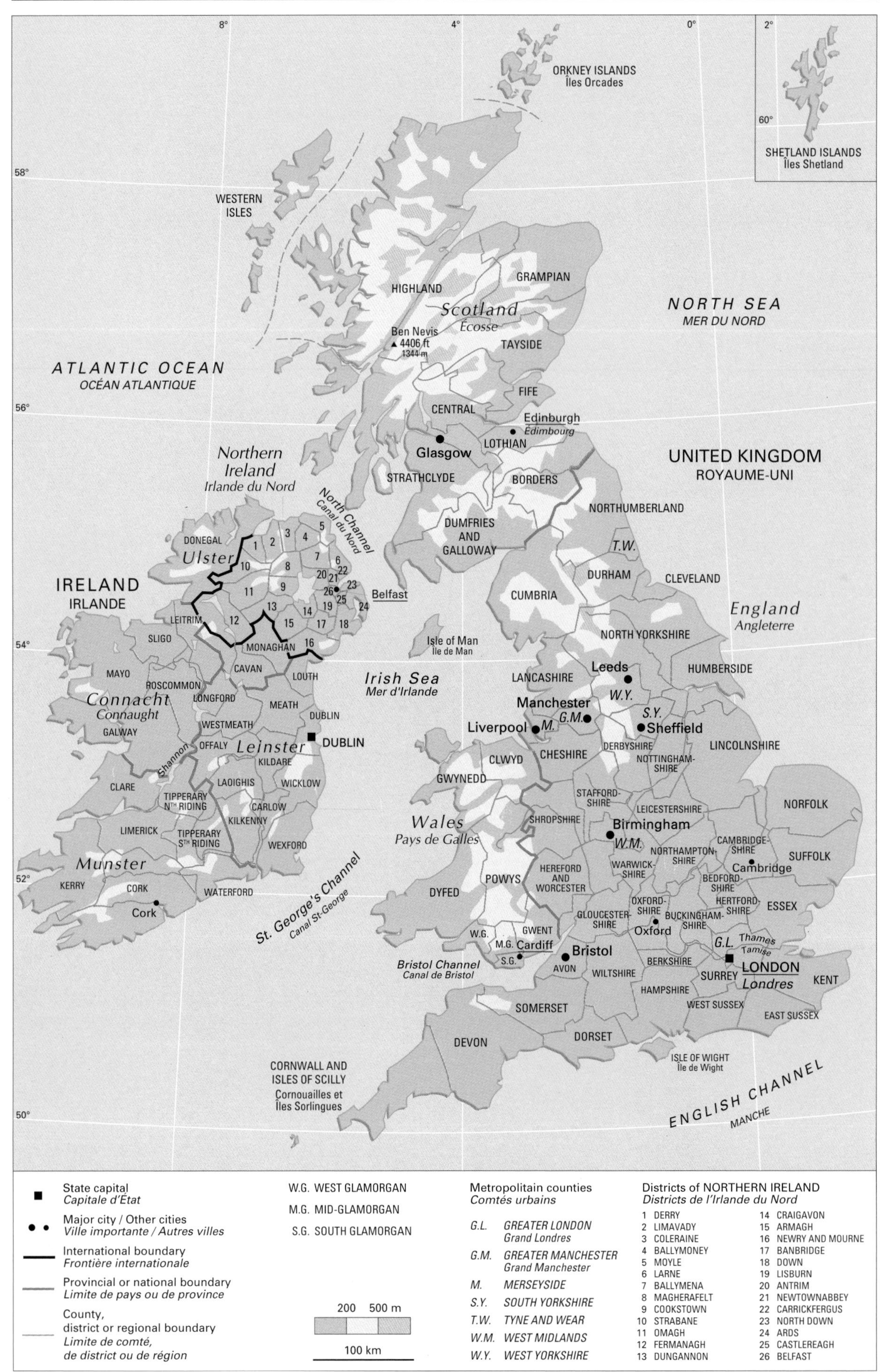

State capital / Capitale d'État

Major city / Other cities / Ville importante / Autres villes

International boundary / Frontière internationale

Provincial or national boundary / Limite de pays ou de province

County, district or regional boundary / Limite de comté, de district ou de région

W.G. WEST GLAMORGAN
M.G. MID-GLAMORGAN
S.G. SOUTH GLAMORGAN

200 500 m

100 km

Metropolitan counties / *Comtés urbains*

G.L.	GREATER LONDON / Grand Londres
G.M.	GREATER MANCHESTER / Grand Manchester
M.	MERSEYSIDE
S.Y.	SOUTH YORKSHIRE
T.W.	TYNE AND WEAR
W.M.	WEST MIDLANDS
W.Y.	WEST YORKSHIRE

Districts of NORTHERN IRELAND / *Districts de l'Irlande du Nord*

1 DERRY
2 LIMAVADY
3 COLERAINE
4 BALLYMONEY
5 MOYLE
6 LARNE
7 BALLYMENA
8 MAGHERAFELT
9 COOKSTOWN
10 STRABANE
11 OMAGH
12 FERMANAGH
13 DUNGANNON
14 CRAIGAVON
15 ARMAGH
16 NEWRY AND MOURNE
17 BANBRIDGE
18 DOWN
19 LISBURN
20 ANTRIM
21 NEWTOWNABBEY
22 CARRICKFERGUS
23 NORTH DOWN
24 ARDS
25 CASTLEREAGH
26 BELFAST

5 AUSTRALIA – ADMINISTRATIVE DIVISIONS
AUSTRALIE – DIVISIONS ADMINISTRATIVES

120° 130° 140° 150°
10° 20° 30°

ARAFURA SEA
MER D'ARAFURA
Torres Strait
Détroit de Torres
Melville Island
Île Melville
Cape York
Cap York
TIMOR SEA
MER DE TIMOR
Darwin
Gulf of Carpentaria
Golfe de Carpentarie
PACIFIC OCEAN
OCÉAN PACIFIQUE
CORAL SEA
MER DE CORAIL
Great Barrier Reef
Grande Barrière
INDIAN OCEAN
OCÉAN INDIEN
NORTHERN TERRITORY
TERRITOIRE DU NORD
Mount Isa
Great Sandy Desert
QUEENSLAND
Great Dividing Range
Alice Springs
Rockhampton
Gibson Desert
Désert de Gibson
Simpson Desert
Désert de Simpson
WESTERN AUSTRALIA
AUSTRALIE-OCCIDENTALE
Dirk Hartog Island
Île Dirk Hartog
Great Victoria Desert
Grand Désert Victoria
Lake Eyre
Lac Eyre
Brisbane
SOUTH AUSTRALIA
AUSTRALIE-MÉRIDIONALE
Nullarbor Plain
Plaine de Nullarbor
Darling
NEW SOUTH WALES
NOUVELLE-GALLES DU SUD
Perth
Fremantle
Great Australian Bight
Grande Baie Australienne
Adelaide
Adélaïde
Newcastle
Sydney
CANBERRA
Wollongong
Murray
A.C.T.
Kangaroo Island
Île Kangaroo
VICTORIA
Mount Kosciusko
7310 ft
Mont Kosciusko
2228 m
Geelong
Melbourne
Bass Strait
Détroit de Bass
Furneaux Group
Îles Furneaux
TASMANIA
TASMANIE
TASMAN SEA
MER DE TASMAN
Hobart

■ Federal capital / *Capitale fédérale*
● State or Territorial capital / *Capitale d'État ou chef-lieu de Territoire*
Perth Major city / *Ville importante*
• Other cities / *Autres villes*
— State or Territorial boundary / *Limite d'État ou de Territoire*

A.C.T. AUSTRALIAN CAPITAL TERRITORY
TERRITOIRE DE LA CAPITALE AUSTRALIENNE

200 500 m
600 km

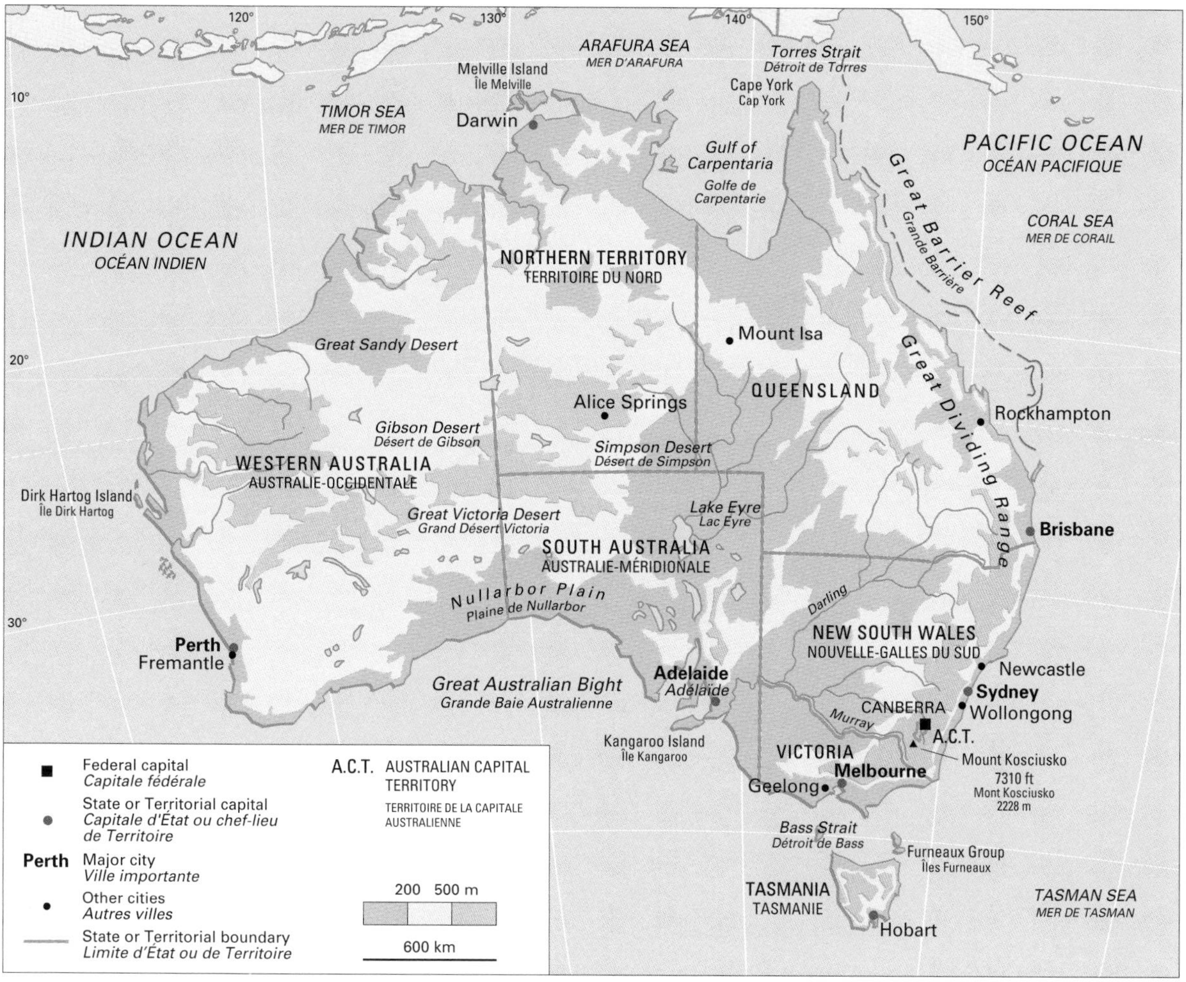

NEW ZEALAND – ADMINISTRATIVE DIVISIONS
NOUVELLE-ZÉLANDE – DIVISIONS ADMINISTRATIVES

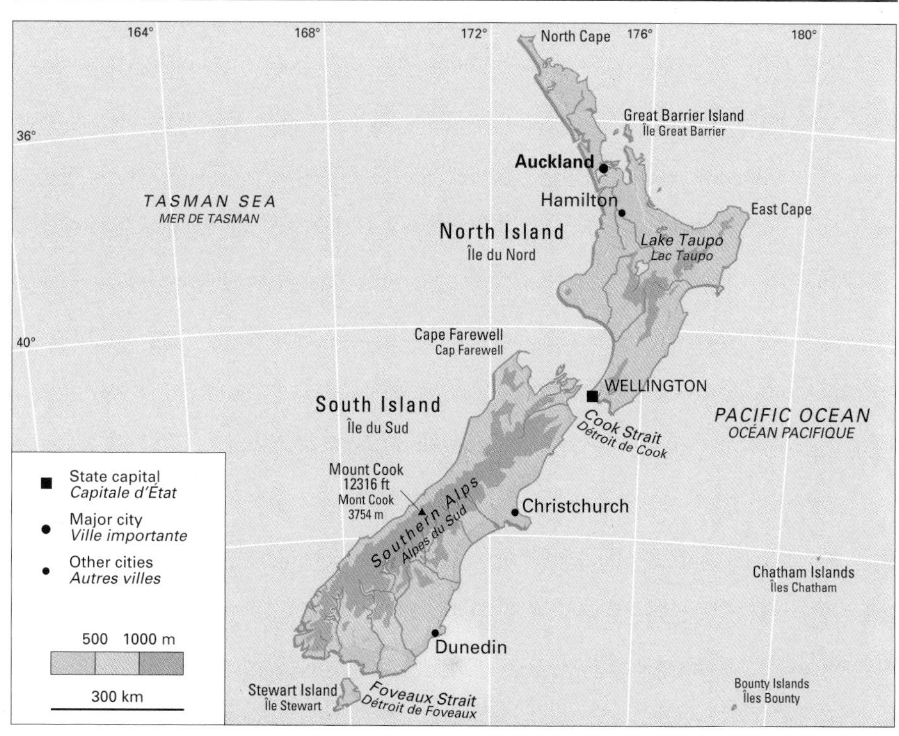

CANADA – ADMINISTRATIVE DIVISIONS
CANADA – DIVISIONS ADMINISTRATIVES

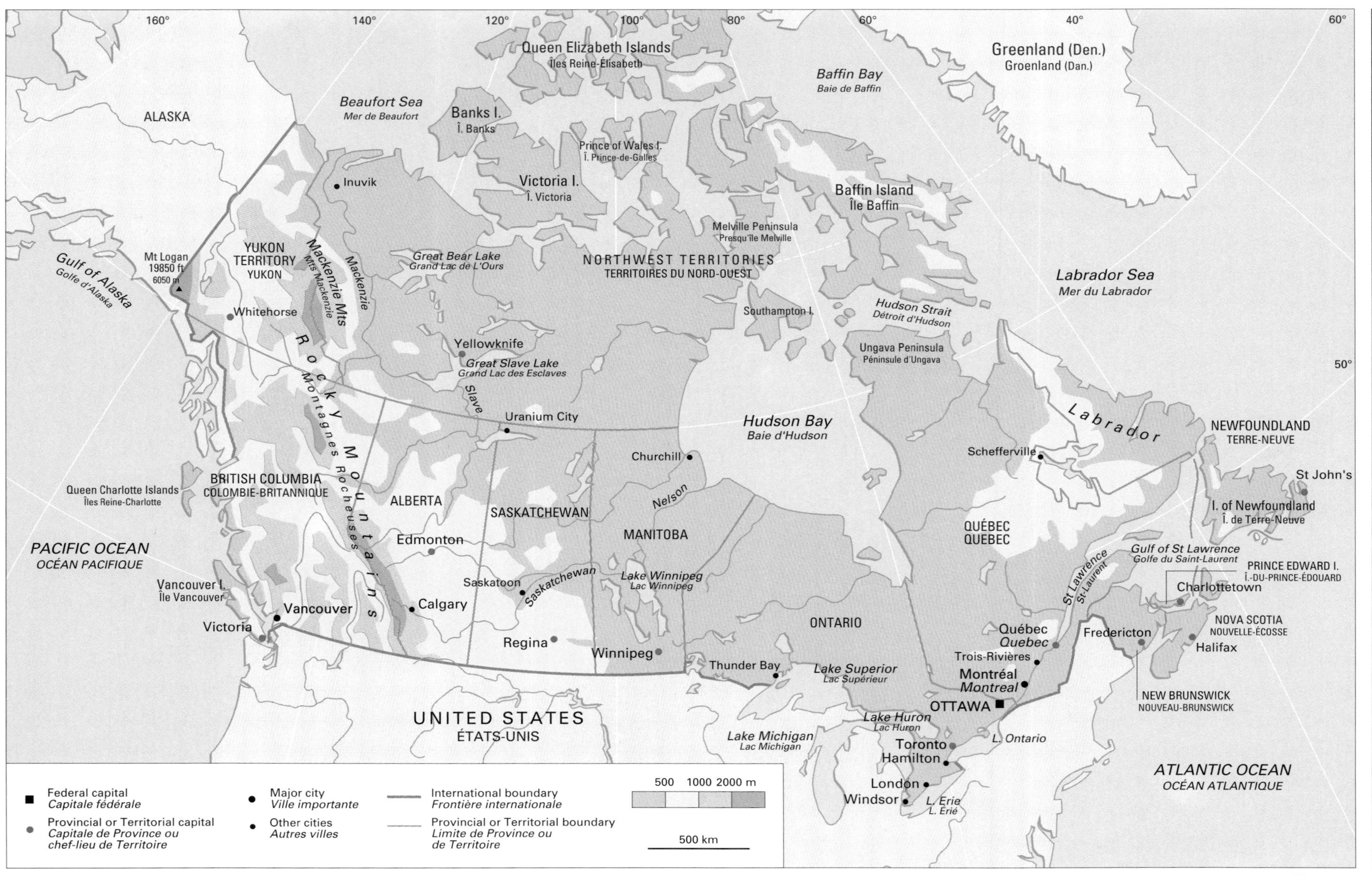

UNITED STATES OF AMERICA – ADMINISTRATIVE DIVISIONS
ÉTATS-UNIS D'AMÉRIQUE – DIVISIONS ADMINISTRATIVES

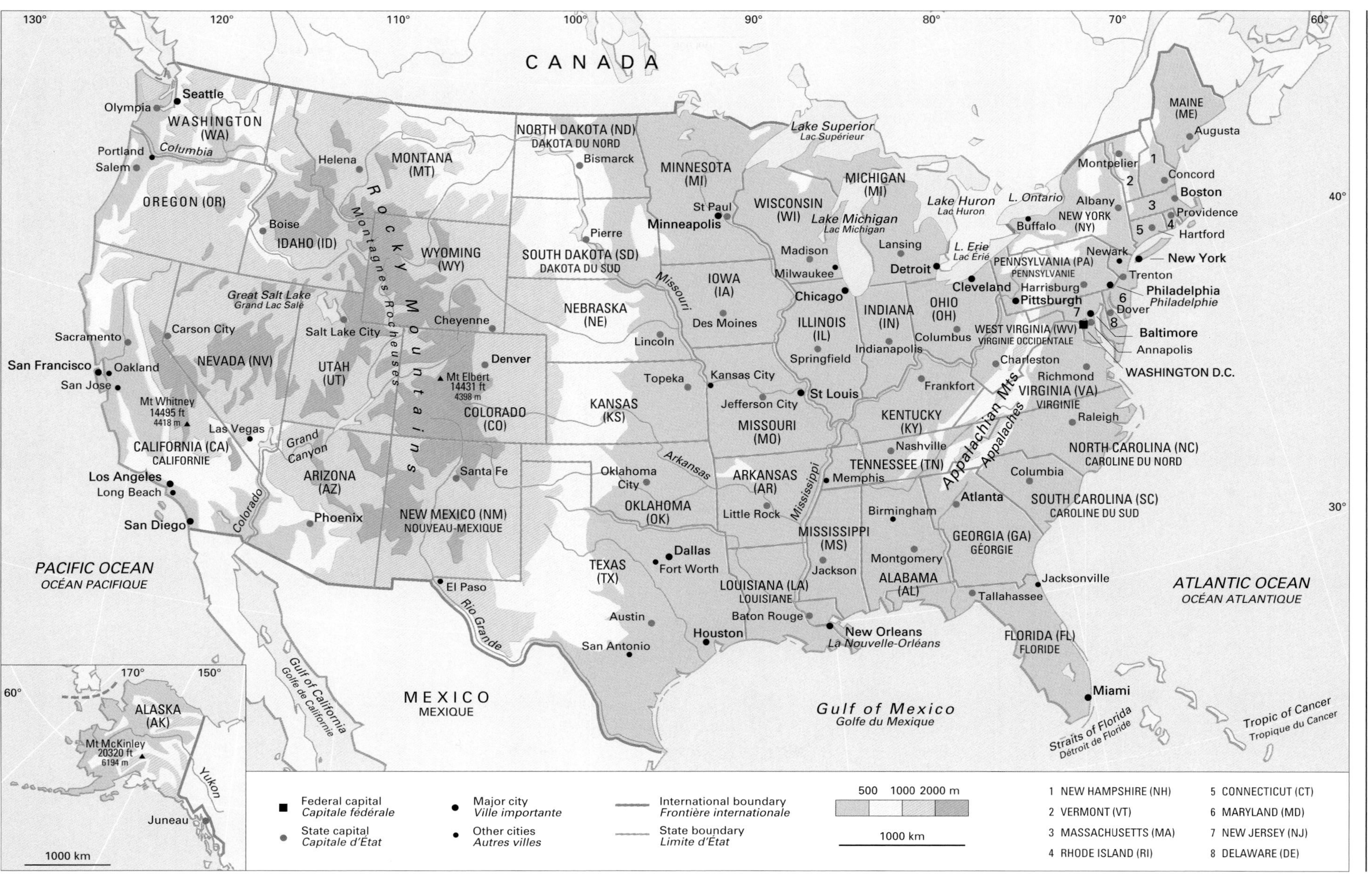

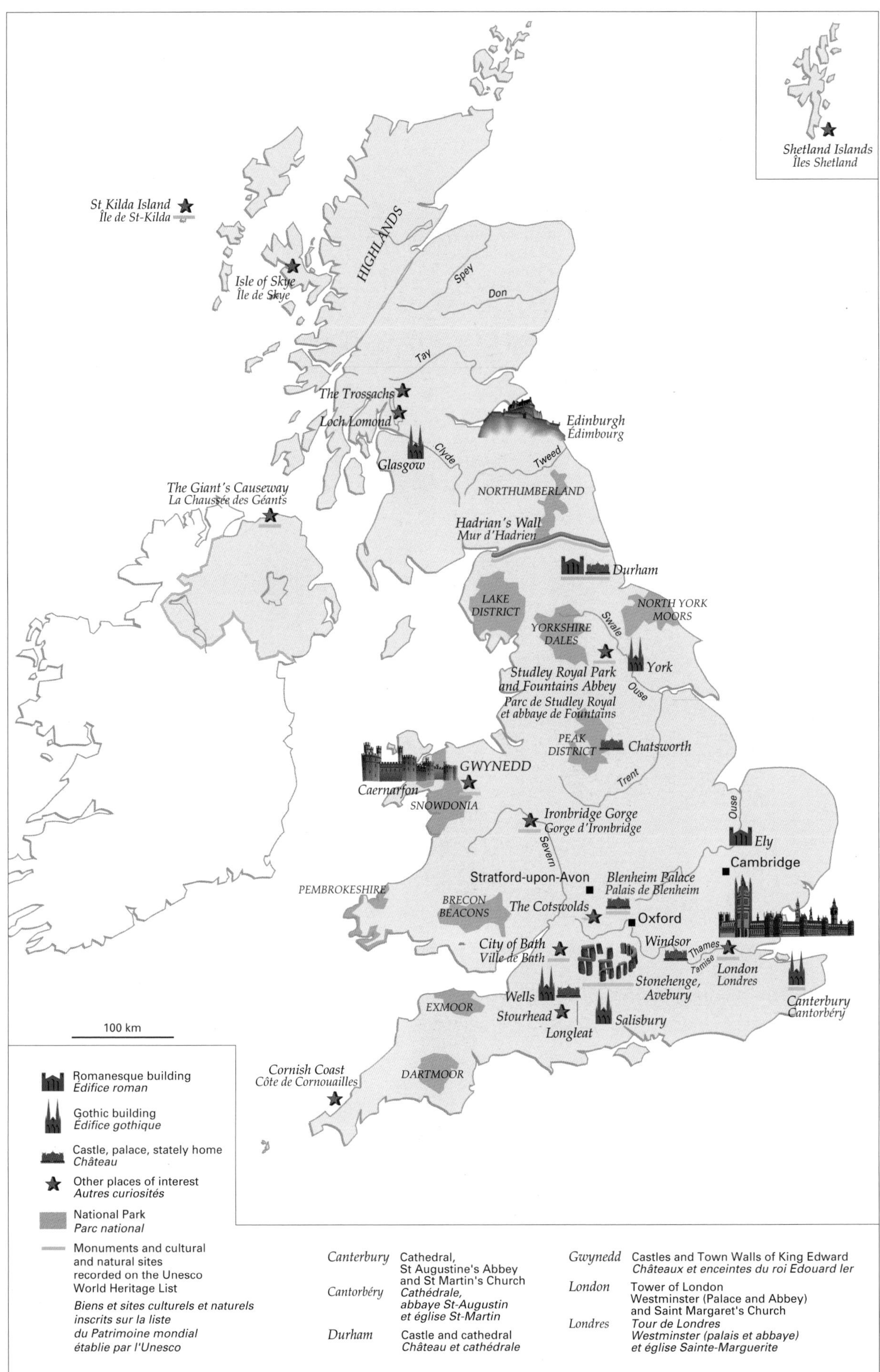
Shetland Islands
Îles Shetland
St Kilda Island
Île de St-Kilda
Isle of Skye
Île de Skye
HIGHLANDS
Spey
Don
Tay
The Trossachs
Loch Lomond
Glasgow
Clyde
Edinburgh
Édimbourg
Tweed
The Giant's Causeway
La Chaussée des Géants
NORTHUMBERLAND
Hadrian's Wall
Mur d'Hadrien
Durham
LAKE DISTRICT
NORTH YORK MOORS
YORKSHIRE DALES
Swale
York
Studley Royal Park
and Fountains Abbey
Parc de Studley Royal
et abbaye de Fountains
Ouse
PEAK DISTRICT
Chatsworth
Trent
GWYNEDD
Caernarfon
SNOWDONIA
Ironbridge Gorge
Gorge d'Ironbridge
Severn
Ouse
Ely
Cambridge
Stratford-upon-Avon
Blenheim Palace
Palais de Blenheim
PEMBROKESHIRE
BRECON BEACONS
The Cotswolds
Oxford
City of Bath
Ville de Bath
Windsor
Thames
Tamise
London
Londres
Stonehenge,
Avebury
Wells
Canterbury
Cantorbéry
EXMOOR
Stourhead
Longleat
Salisbury
100 km
Cornish Coast
Côte de Cornouailles
DARTMOOR
Romanesque building
Édifice roman
Gothic building
Édifice gothique
Castle, palace, stately home
Château
Other places of interest
Autres curiosités
National Park
Parc national
Monuments and cultural and natural sites recorded on the Unesco World Heritage List
Biens et sites culturels et naturels inscrits sur la liste du Patrimoine mondial établie par l'Unesco
Canterbury — Cathedral, St Augustine's Abbey and St Martin's Church
Cantorbéry — Cathédrale, abbaye St-Augustin et église St-Martin
Durham — Castle and cathedral
Château et cathédrale
Gwynedd — Castles and Town Walls of King Edward
Châteaux et enceintes du roi Edouard Ier
London — Tower of London
Westminster (Palace and Abbey) and Saint Margaret's Church
Londres — Tour de Londres
Westminster (palais et abbaye) et église Sainte-Marguerite

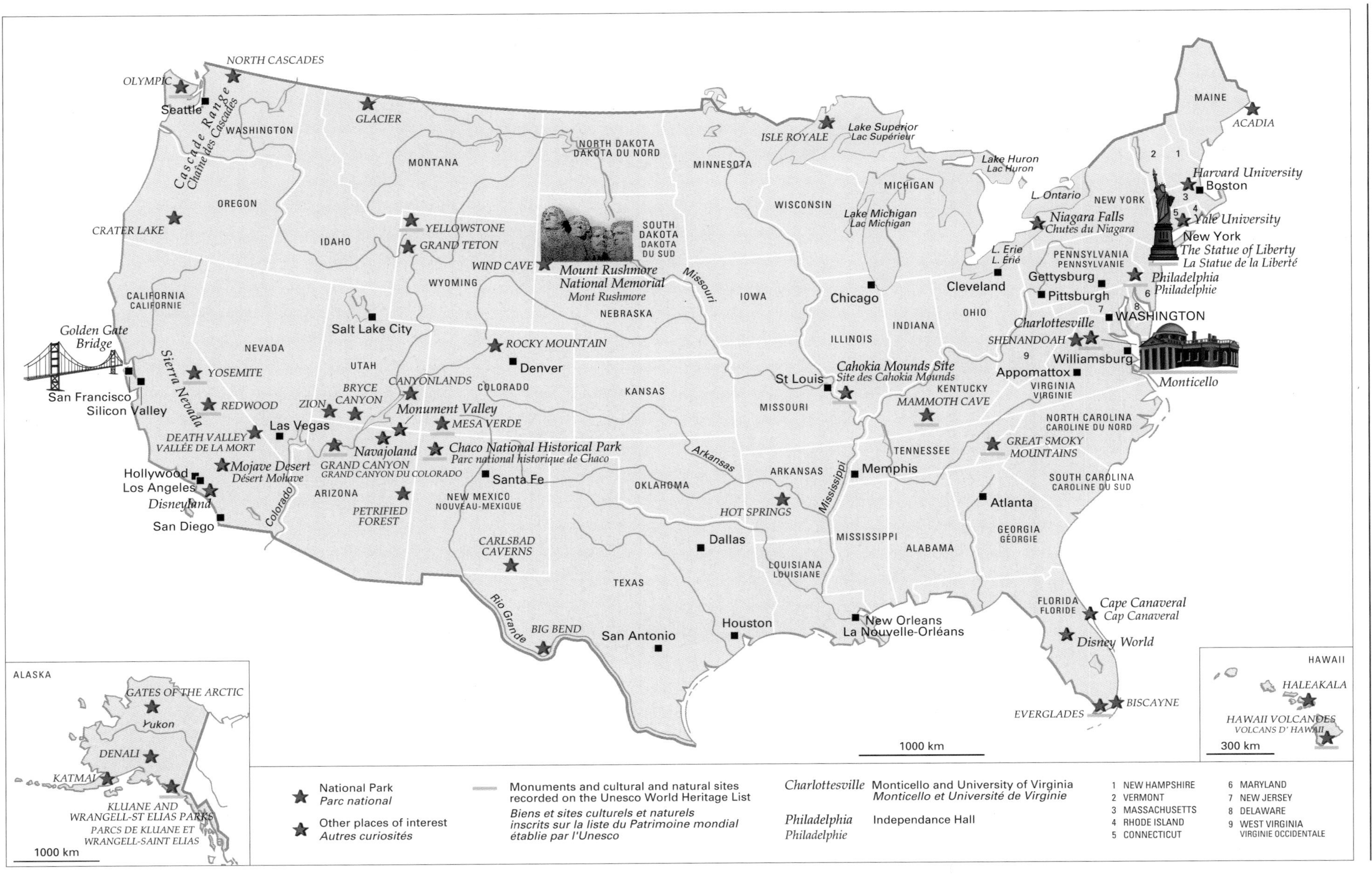
NORTH CASCADES
OLYMPIC
Seattle
Cascade Range
Chaîne des Cascades
WASHINGTON
GLACIER
MONTANA
OREGON
CRATER LAKE
IDAHO
YELLOWSTONE
GRAND TETON
WIND CAVE
WYOMING
NORTH DAKOTA
DAKOTA DU NORD
SOUTH DAKOTA
DAKOTA DU SUD
Mount Rushmore National Memorial
Mont Rushmore
NEBRASKA
Missouri
MINNESOTA
IOWA
ISLE ROYALE
Lake Superior
Lac Supérieur
WISCONSIN
MICHIGAN
Lake Michigan
Lac Michigan
Lake Huron
Lac Huron
Chicago
L. Ontario
NEW YORK
MAINE
ACADIA
Harvard University
Boston
Niagara Falls
Chutes du Niagara
Yale University
New York
The Statue of Liberty
La Statue de la Liberté
L. Erie
L. Érié
Cleveland
PENNSYLVANIA
PENNSYLVANIE
Gettysburg
Pittsburgh
Philadelphia
Philadelphie
WASHINGTON
Charlottesville
SHENANDOAH
Williamsburg
Monticello
Appomattox
VIRGINIA
VIRGINIE
OHIO
INDIANA
ILLINOIS
CALIFORNIA
CALIFORNIE
Golden Gate Bridge
San Francisco
Silicon Valley
NEVADA
Salt Lake City
UTAH
ROCKY MOUNTAIN
Denver
COLORADO
KANSAS
St Louis
Cahokia Mounds Site
Site des Cahokia Mounds
MISSOURI
KENTUCKY
MAMMOTH CAVE
Sierra Nevada
YOSEMITE
REDWOOD
ZION
BRYCE CANYON
CANYONLANDS
Monument Valley
MESA VERDE
Las Vegas
DEATH VALLEY
VALLÉE DE LA MORT
Navajoland
GRAND CANYON
GRAND CANYON DU COLORADO
Chaco National Historical Park
Parc national historique de Chaco
Santa Fe
Arkansas
ARKANSAS
Mississippi
Memphis
TENNESSEE
NORTH CAROLINA
CAROLINE DU NORD
GREAT SMOKY MOUNTAINS
Hollywood
Los Angeles
Disneyland
San Diego
Mojave Desert
Désert Mohave
Colorado
ARIZONA
PETRIFIED FOREST
NEW MEXICO
NOUVEAU-MEXIQUE
OKLAHOMA
HOT SPRINGS
SOUTH CAROLINA
CAROLINE DU SUD
Atlanta
GEORGIA
GÉORGIE
CARLSBAD CAVERNS
Dallas
MISSISSIPPI
ALABAMA
LOUISIANA
LOUISIANE
TEXAS
Rio Grande
BIG BEND
San Antonio
Houston
New Orleans
La Nouvelle-Orléans
FLORIDA
FLORIDE
Cape Canaveral
Cap Canaveral
Disney World
EVERGLADES
BISCAYNE
1000 km
ALASKA
GATES OF THE ARCTIC
Yukon
DENALI
KATMAI
KLUANE AND WRANGELL-ST ELIAS PARKS
PARCS DE KLUANE ET WRANGELL-SAINT ELIAS
1000 km
HAWAII
HALEAKALA
HAWAII VOLCANOES
VOLCANS D'HAWAII
300 km
National Park
Parc national
Other places of interest
Autres curiosités
Monuments and cultural and natural sites recorded on the Unesco World Heritage List
Biens et sites culturels et naturels inscrits sur la liste du Patrimoine mondial établie par l'Unesco
Charlottesville Monticello and University of Virginia
Monticello et Université de Virginie
Philadelphia Independance Hall
Philadelphie
1 NEW HAMPSHIRE
2 VERMONT
3 MASSACHUSETTS
4 RHODE ISLAND
5 CONNECTICUT
6 MARYLAND
7 NEW JERSEY
8 DELAWARE
9 WEST VIRGINIA
VIRGINIE OCCIDENTALE

LONDON
LONDRES

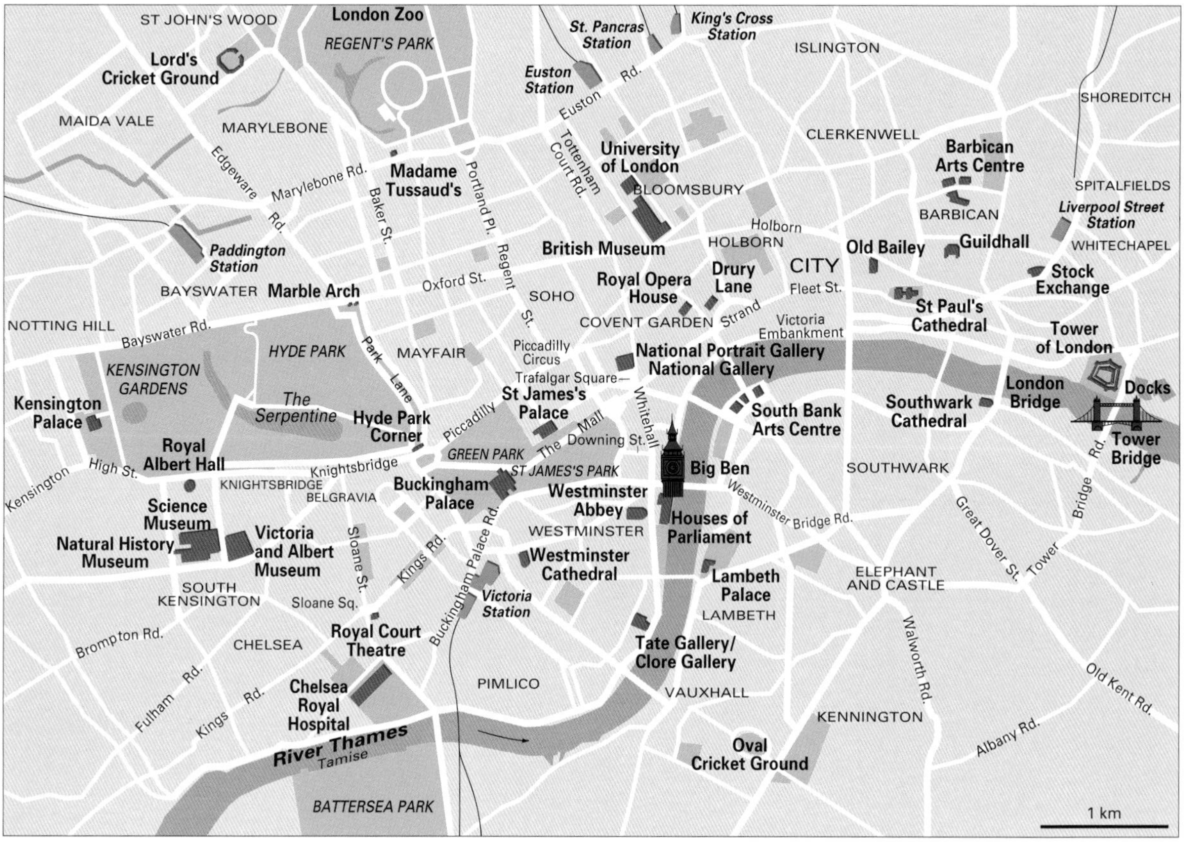

ST JOHN'S WOOD
London Zoo
REGENT'S PARK
St. Pancras Station
King's Cross Station
ISLINGTON
Lord's Cricket Ground
Euston Station
Euston Rd.
SHOREDITCH
MAIDA VALE
MARYLEBONE
CLERKENWELL
University of London
Barbican Arts Centre
Edgeware Rd.
Marylebone Rd.
Madame Tussaud's
Baker St.
Portland Pl.
Tottenham Court Rd.
BLOOMSBURY
SPITALFIELDS
Liverpool Street Station
BARBICAN
Holborn
HOLBORN
Paddington Station
British Museum
Old Bailey
Guildhall
WHITECHAPEL
Regent St.
Drury Lane
CITY
Stock Exchange
BAYSWATER
Marble Arch
Oxford St.
SOHO
Royal Opera House
Fleet St.
St Paul's Cathedral
NOTTING HILL
Bayswater Rd.
COVENT GARDEN
Strand
Victoria Embankment
Tower of London
KENSINGTON GARDENS
HYDE PARK
Park Lane
MAYFAIR
Piccadilly Circus
National Portrait Gallery
National Gallery
Trafalgar Square
Docks
Kensington Palace
The Serpentine
Hyde Park Corner
Piccadilly
St James's Palace
Whitehall
South Bank Arts Centre
Southwark Cathedral
London Bridge
Royal Albert Hall
GREEN PARK
The Mall
Downing St.
Tower Bridge
Kensington High St.
Knightsbridge
ST JAMES'S PARK
Big Ben
SOUTHWARK
KNIGHTSBRIDGE
BELGRAVIA
Buckingham Palace
Westminster Abbey
Westminster Bridge Rd.
Science Museum
Houses of Parliament
Bridge Rd.
Natural History Museum
Victoria and Albert Museum
Sloane St.
Kings Rd.
Buckingham Palace Rd.
WESTMINSTER
Westminster Cathedral
Great Dover St.
Tower
ELEPHANT AND CASTLE
SOUTH KENSINGTON
Sloane Sq.
Victoria Station
Lambeth Palace
LAMBETH
Brompton Rd.
CHELSEA
Royal Court Theatre
Tate Gallery/ Clore Gallery
Walworth Rd.
Fulham Rd.
Kings Rd.
Chelsea Royal Hospital
PIMLICO
VAUXHALL
Old Kent Rd.
River Thames
Tamise
KENNINGTON
Oval Cricket Ground
Albany Rd.
BATTERSEA PARK
1 km

NEW YORK (AND MANHATTAN)
NEW YORK (ET MANHATTAN)

YONKERS
PATERSON
Long Island Sound
Teterboro Airport
Hudson River
BRONX
NEW JERSEY
MANHATTAN
East River
La Guardia Airport
NEWARK
JERSEY CITY
QUEENS
Newark International Airport
Newark Bay
Ellis Island
Statue of Liberty
Statue de la Liberté
J.F. Kennedy International Airport
Upper Bay
BROOKLYN
Jamaica Bay
STATEN ISLAND
CONEY ISLAND
Lower Bay
ATLANTIC OCEAN
OCÉAN ATLANTIQUE
10 km

RIVERSIDE PARK
Broadway
HARLEM
Av.
Hudson River
Park Avenue
UPPER WEST SIDE
CENTRAL PARK
Guggenheim Museum
6
Metropolitan Opera House (The MET)
Metropolitan Museum of Art
Fifth Av.
UPPER EAST SIDE
First Avenue
W. 57th St.
Park Av.
Rockefeller Center
4
5
E. 57th St.
Queensboro Bridge
W. 42nd St.
THEATER DISTRICT
Twelfth Av.
W. 34th St.
TIMES SQUARE
3
E. 42nd St.
United Nations
Empire State Building
Broadway
Park Av.
E. 34th St.
W. 14th St.
West Street
WASHINGTON SQUARE PARK
E. 14th St.
GREENWICH VILLAGE
EAST VILLAGE
East River
SOHO
East Houston St.
TRIBECA
CHINATOWN
2
1
WALL STREET
Brooklyn Bridge
2 km
1 : New York Stock Exchange
2 : World Trade Center
3 : Grand Central Station
4 : Carnegie Hall
5 : Museum of Modern Art (MOMA)
6 : American Museum of Natural History

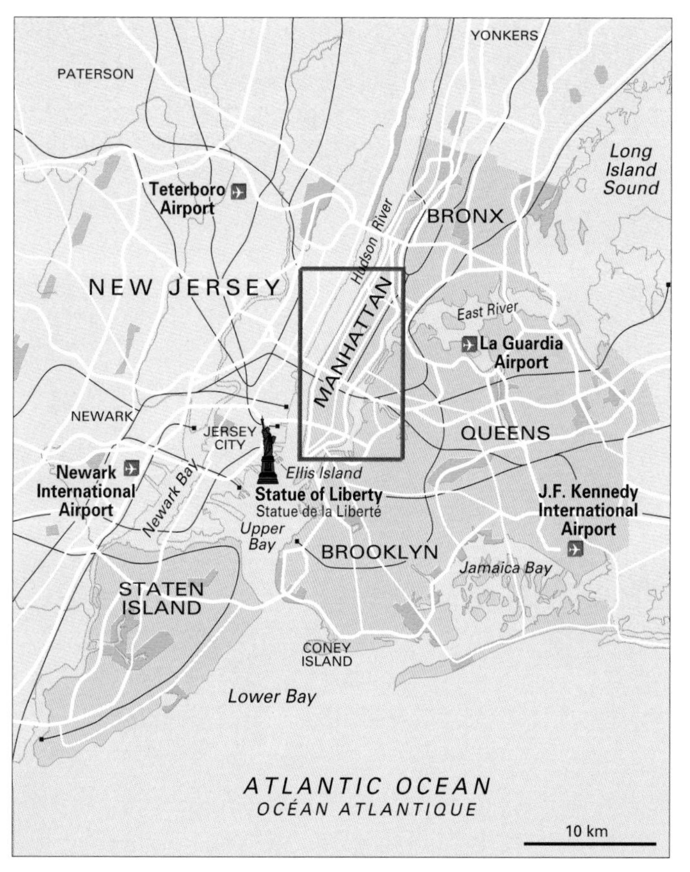

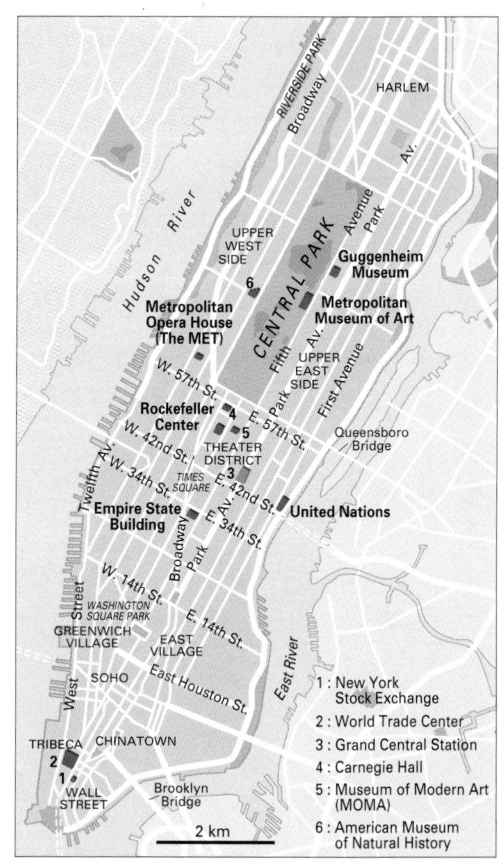

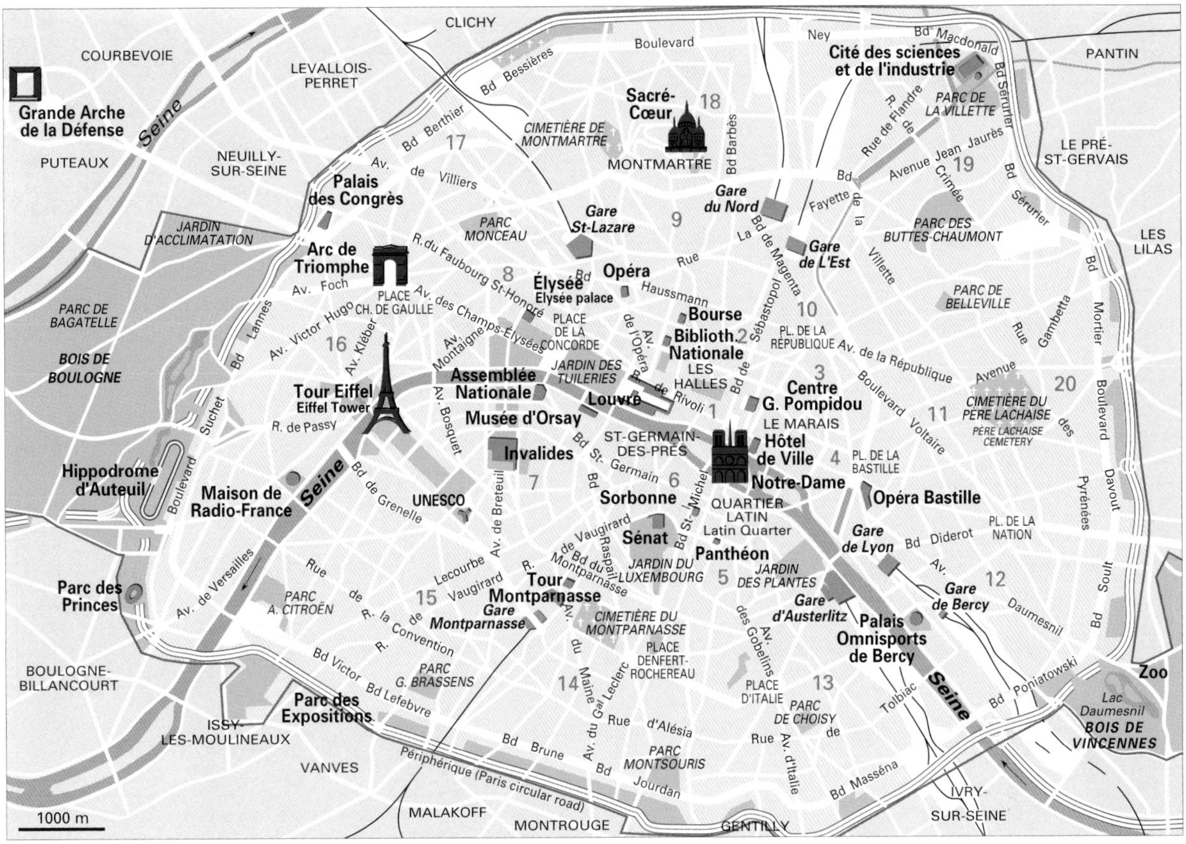

PARIS
PARIS

MONTRÉAL
MONTREAL

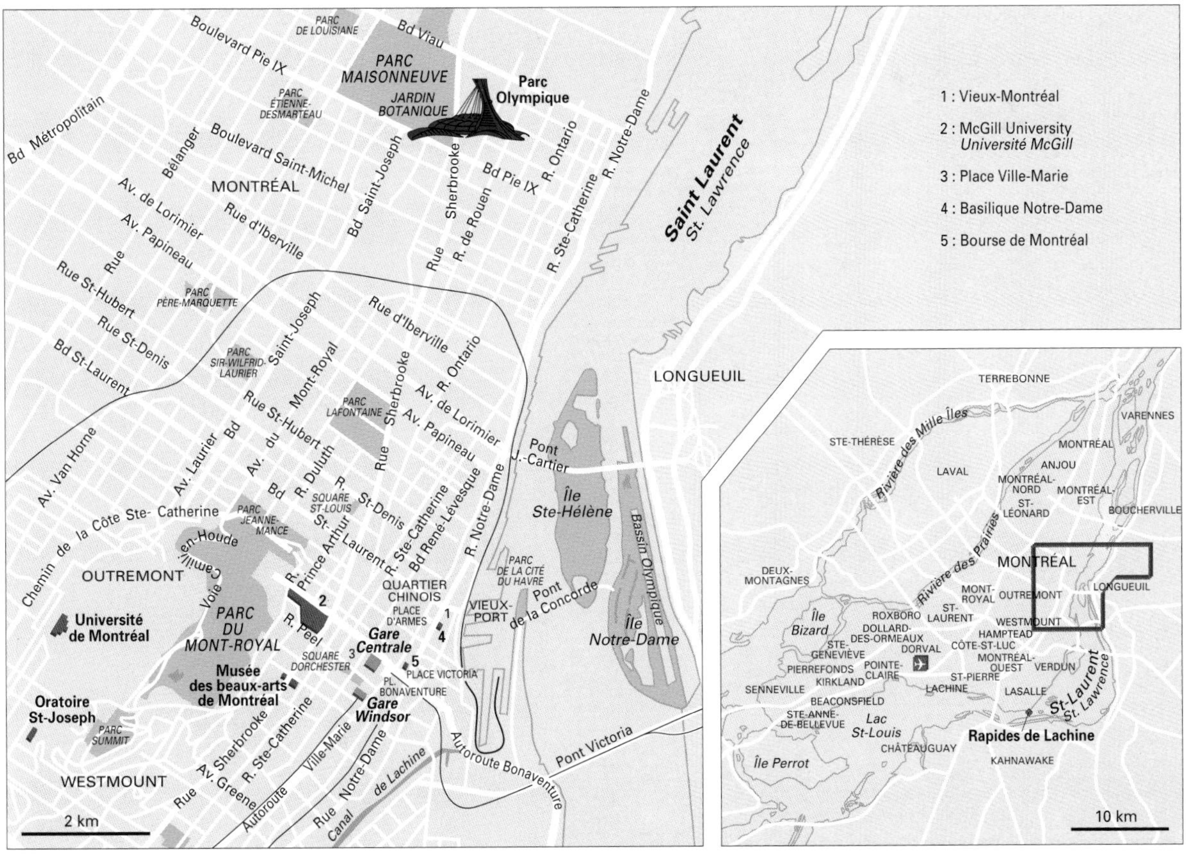

1 : Vieux-Montréal

2 : McGill University
Université McGill

3 : Place Ville-Marie

4 : Basilique Notre-Dame

5 : Bourse de Montréal

FRANCE – DIVISIONS ADMINISTRATIVES
FRANCE – ADMINISTRATIVE DIVISIONS

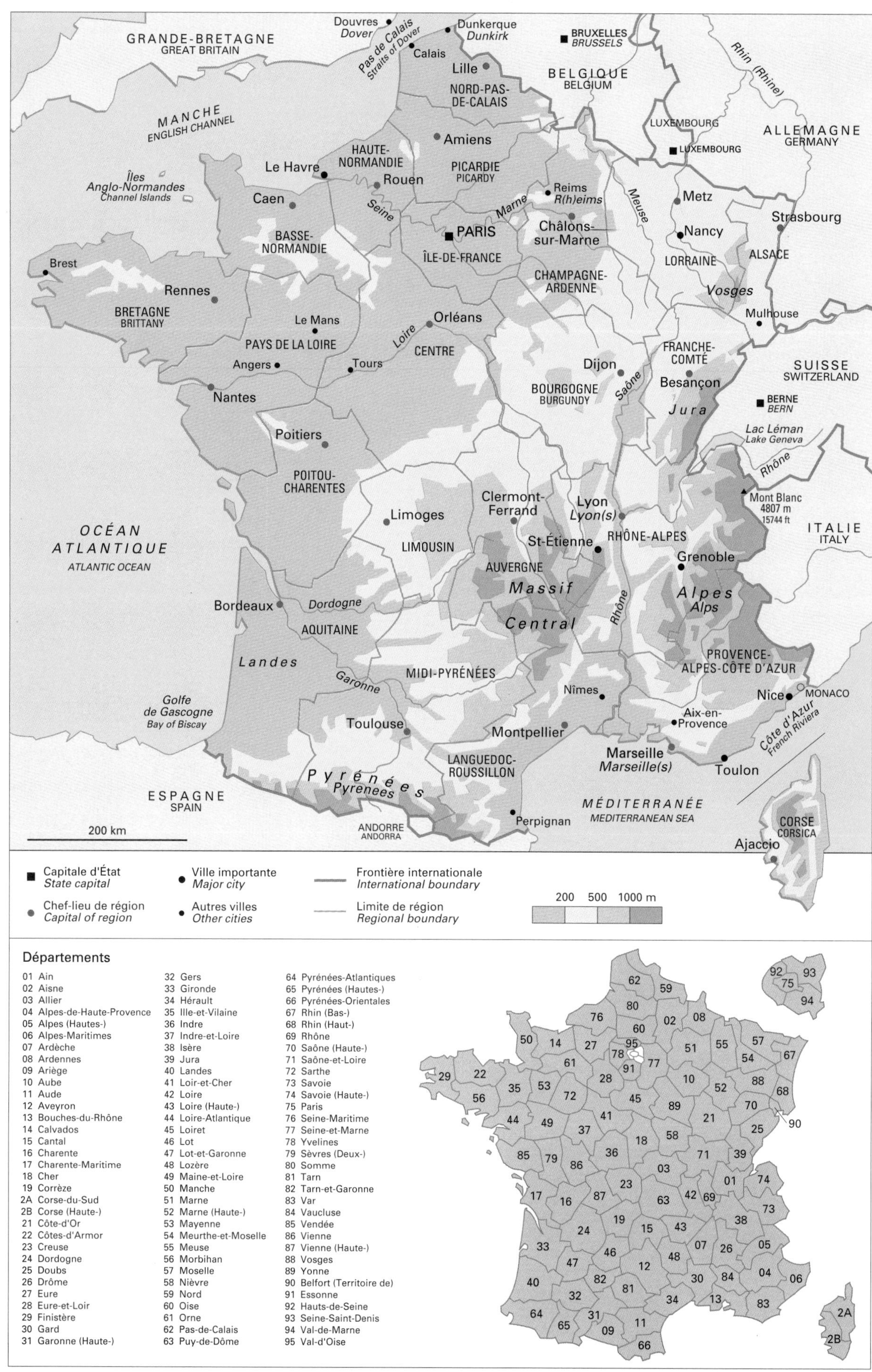

Départements

01 Ain
02 Aisne
03 Allier
04 Alpes-de-Haute-Provence
05 Alpes (Hautes-)
06 Alpes-Maritimes
07 Ardèche
08 Ardennes
09 Ariège
10 Aube
11 Aude
12 Aveyron
13 Bouches-du-Rhône
14 Calvados
15 Cantal
16 Charente
17 Charente-Maritime
18 Cher
19 Corrèze
2A Corse-du-Sud
2B Corse (Haute-)
21 Côte-d'Or
22 Côtes-d'Armor
23 Creuse
24 Dordogne
25 Doubs
26 Drôme
27 Eure
28 Eure-et-Loir
29 Finistère
30 Gard
31 Garonne (Haute-)
32 Gers
33 Gironde
34 Hérault
35 Ille-et-Vilaine
36 Indre
37 Indre-et-Loire
38 Isère
39 Jura
40 Landes
41 Loir-et-Cher
42 Loire
43 Loire (Haute-)
44 Loire-Atlantique
45 Loiret
46 Lot
47 Lot-et-Garonne
48 Lozère
49 Maine-et-Loire
50 Manche
51 Marne
52 Marne (Haute-)
53 Mayenne
54 Meurthe-et-Moselle
55 Meuse
56 Morbihan
57 Moselle
58 Nièvre
59 Nord
60 Oise
61 Orne
62 Pas-de-Calais
63 Puy-de-Dôme
64 Pyrénées-Atlantiques
65 Pyrénées (Hautes-)
66 Pyrénées-Orientales
67 Rhin (Bas-)
68 Rhin (Haut-)
69 Rhône
70 Saône (Haute-)
71 Saône-et-Loire
72 Sarthe
73 Savoie
74 Savoie (Haute-)
75 Paris
76 Seine-Maritime
77 Seine-et-Marne
78 Yvelines
79 Sèvres (Deux-)
80 Somme
81 Tarn
82 Tarn-et-Garonne
83 Var
84 Vaucluse
85 Vendée
86 Vienne
87 Vienne (Haute-)
88 Vosges
89 Yonne
90 Belfort (Territoire de)
91 Essonne
92 Hauts-de-Seine
93 Seine-Saint-Denis
94 Val-de-Marne
95 Val-d'Oise

NORD-PAS-DE-CALAIS
Amiens
Jumièges
MARAIS DU COTENTIN ET DU BESSIN
BROTONNE
Rouen
Compiègne
Reims
Le Mont-Saint-Michel
Mont St Michel
Chantilly
St-Denis
Paris
Seine
Oise
Meuse
Marne
VOSGES DU NORD
LORRAINE
Nancy
Strasbourg
Presqu'île de Crozon
Versailles
Vaux-le-Vicomte
Moselle
Colmar
Rhin
Rhine
ARMORIQUE
St-Malo
NORMANDIE-MAINE
Chartres
Fontainebleau
FORÊT D'ORIENT
BALLONS DES VOSGES
Pointe du Raz
Châteaux de la Loire
Châteaux of the Loire
Blois
Chambord
Yonne
Fontenay
BRIÈRE
Angers
Amboise
Cheverny
Vézelay
Dijon
Loire
Azay-le-Rideau
Chenonceaux
Nantes
Cher
Bourges
MORVAN
Arc-et-Senans
Creuse
BRENNE
Allier
Loire
Saône
HAUT-JURA
MARAIS POITEVIN
St-Savin-sur-Gartempe
La Rochelle
Vichy
Rhône
Annecy
Vienne
Lyon
LIVRADOIS-FOREZ
VANOISE
Vallée de la Vézère
Vézère
VOLCANS D'AUVERGNE
PILAT
Isère
ÉCRINS
Lascaux
Rhône
VERCORS
QUEYRAS
Bordeaux
Dordogne
Padirac
Rocamadour
Gorges de l'Ardèche
Lot
Conques
Gorges du Tarn
Durance
MERCANTOUR
Garonne
LANDES DE GASCOGNE
CÉVENNES
Avignon
Orange
Tarn
Moissac
Albi
Nîmes
LUBERON
Verdon
Monaco
Arles
Grand Canyon du Verdon
Nice
Cannes
Biarritz
Toulouse
HAUT-LANGUEDOC
Pau
CAMARGUE
Marseille
Pont du Gard
(Roman aquaduct)
Lourdes
Garonne
PORT-CROS
Carcassonne
PYRÉNÉES
PYRENEES
Cirque de Gavarnie
CORSE
CORSICA
Golfes de Girolata et de Porto et Réserve de Scandola
Girolata and Porto Gulfs and Scandola Reserve
200 km

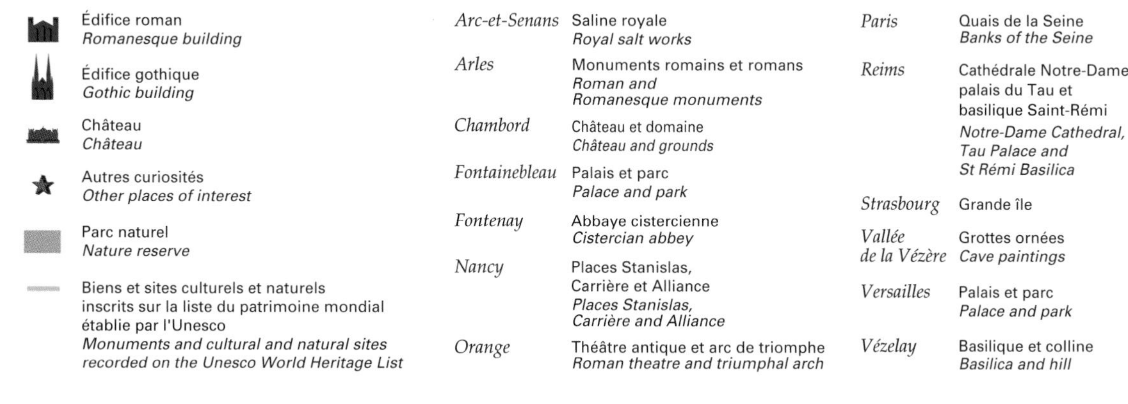

	Édifice roman *Romanesque building*
	Édifice gothique *Gothic building*
	Château *Château*
	Autres curiosités *Other places of interest*
	Parc naturel *Nature reserve*
	Biens et sites culturels et naturels inscrits sur la liste du patrimoine mondial établie par l'Unesco *Monuments and cultural and natural sites recorded on the Unesco World Heritage List*

Arc-et-Senans	Saline royale *Royal salt works*
Arles	Monuments romains et romans *Roman and Romanesque monuments*
Chambord	Château et domaine *Château and grounds*
Fontainebleau	Palais et parc *Palace and park*
Fontenay	Abbaye cistercienne *Cistercian abbey*
Nancy	Places Stanislas, Carrière et Alliance *Places Stanislas, Carrière and Alliance*
Orange	Théâtre antique et arc de triomphe *Roman theatre and triumphal arch*
Paris	Quais de la Seine *Banks of the Seine*
Reims	Cathédrale Notre-Dame, palais du Tau et basilique Saint-Rémi *Notre-Dame Cathedral, Tau Palace and St Rémi Basilica*
Strasbourg	Grande île
Vallée de la Vézère	Grottes ornées *Cave paintings*
Versailles	Palais et parc *Palace and park*
Vézelay	Basilique et colline *Basilica and hill*

BELGIQUE – PROVINCES ET RÉGIONS LINGUISTIQUES
BELGIUM – PROVINCES AND LINGUISTIC REGIONS

PAYS-BAS
NETHERLANDS
Brugge
Bruges
Bruges
Antwerpen
Anvers
Antwerp
OOST-VLAANDEREN
FLANDRE-ORIENTALE
EASTERN FLANDERS
ANTWERPEN
ANVERS
ANTWERP
LIMBURG
LIMBOURG
LIMBURG
WEST-VLAANDEREN
FLANDRE-OCCIDENTALE
WESTERN FLANDERS
Gent
Gand
Ghent
ALLEMAGNE
GERMANY
BRABANT
Leuwen
Louvain
Louvain
Hasselt
Maas
Schelde
BRUXELLES
BRUSSEL
BRUSSELS
Lys
Liège
Liege
Eupen
HAINAUT
Namur
Meuse
Mons
LIÈGE
LIEGE
Malmédy
FRANCE
Sambre
NAMUR
Ourthe
Escaut (Scheldt)
Meuse
LUXEMBOURG
LUXEMBOURG
Arlon
Semois
Luxembourg
Limites linguistiques
Linguistic boundaries
Limites de province
Provincial boundaries
50 km
Région de langue française
French-speaking region
Région de langue néerlandaise
Dutch-speaking region
Région bilingue (français-néerlandais)
Bilingual region (French-Dutch)
Région de langue allemande avec minorité de langue française protégée
German-speaking region with protected French-speaking minority
Région de langue française avec minorité de langue néerlandaise protégée
French-speaking region with protected Dutch-speaking minority
Région de langue française avec minorité de langue allemande protégée
French-speaking region with protected German-speaking minority
Région de langue néerlandaise avec minorité de langue française protégée
Dutch-speaking region with protected French-speaking minority
LUXEMBOURG
Langue nationale : luxembourgeois
National language: Luxemburgish
Langues administratives: français, allemand, luxembourgeois
Administrative languages: French, German, Luxemburgish

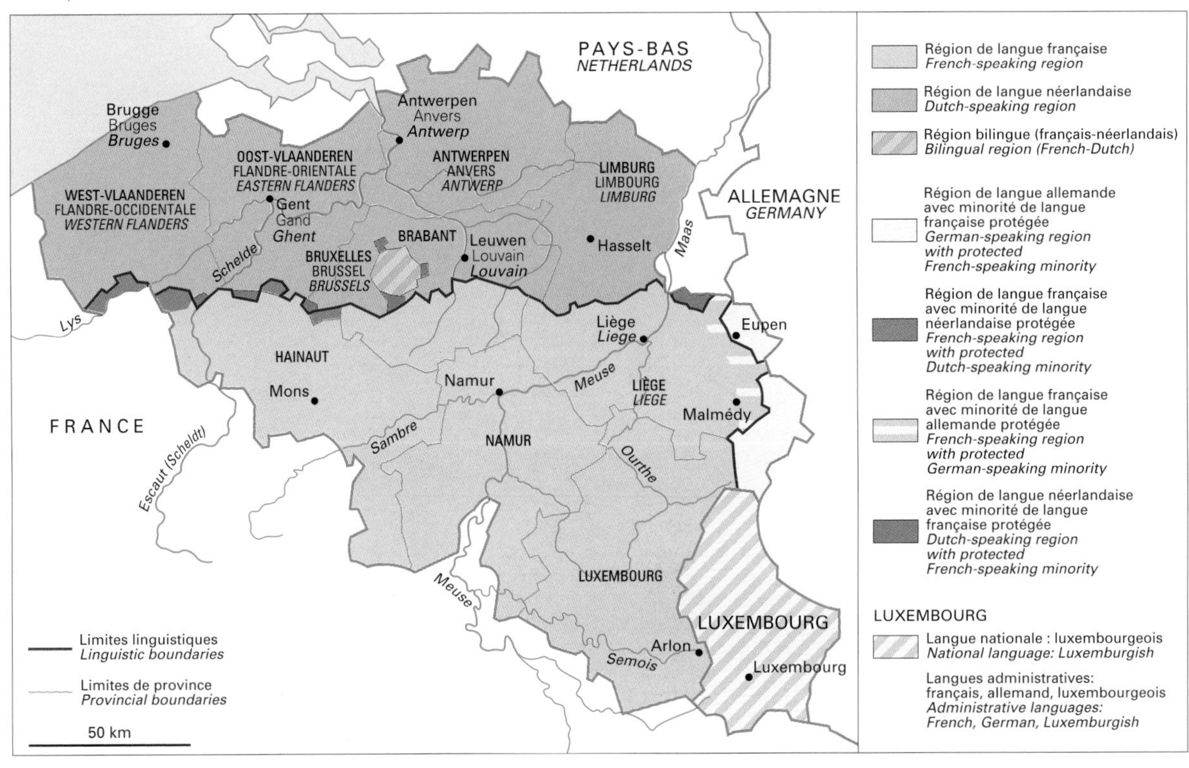

SUISSE – CANTONS ET RÉGIONS LINGUISTIQUES
SWITZERLAND – CANTONS AND LINGUISTIC REGIONS

Rhin (Rhine)
SCHAFFHAUSEN
SCHAFFHOUSE
SCHAFFHAUSEN
Schaffhausen
Bodensee
Lac de Constance
Lake Constance
ALLEMAGNE
GERMANY
BASEL-STADT
BÂLE-VILLE
BASEL-STADT
BASEL-LAND
BÂLE-CAMPAGNE
BASEL-LAND
Basel
THURGAU
THURGOVIE
THURGOVIA
Frauenfeld
AARGAU
ARGOVIE
AARGAU
ZÜRICH
ZURICH
ZÜRICH
Liestal
St-Gallen
2
Herisau
1
Appenzell
LIECHTENSTEIN
JURA
Delémont
Aarau
Zürich
Zurich
Zürich
SOLOTHURN
SOLEURE
SOLOTHURN
FRANCE
Solothurn
ST-GALLEN
ST-GALL
ST GALLEN
LUZERN
LUCERNE
LUCERNE
ZUG
Zoug
Zug
SCHWYZ
AUTRICHE
AUSTRIA
Glarus
Bern
Berne
Bern
Lucerne
Neuchâtel
NEUCHÂTEL
Schwyz
GLARUS
GLARIS
GLARUS
NIDW.
UNTERWALDEN
OBW.
Chur
Coire
Chur
BERN
BERNE
BERN
Altdorf
URI
Fribourg
Rhein
Inn
VAUD
FRIBOURG
GRAUBÜNDEN
GRISONS
THE GRISONS
Lausanne
Lac Léman
Lake Geneva
Ticino (Tessin)
(Ticino)
TICINO
TESSIN
TICINO
Genève
Geneva
Sion
VALAIS
Bellinzona
Rhône
Adda
GENÈVE
GENEVA
Lago Maggiore
Lac Majeur
Lake Maggiore
ITALIE
ITALY
Aoste
Aosta
50 km
Capitale
Capital
Chef-lieu
Capital of canton
Limites linguistiques
Linguistic boundaries
Limites de canton
Canton boundaries
Français
French
Allemand
German
Italien
Italian
Romanche
Romansh
1 AUSSERRHODEN
RHODES-EXTÉRIEURES
2 INNERRHODEN
RHODES-INTÉRIEURES

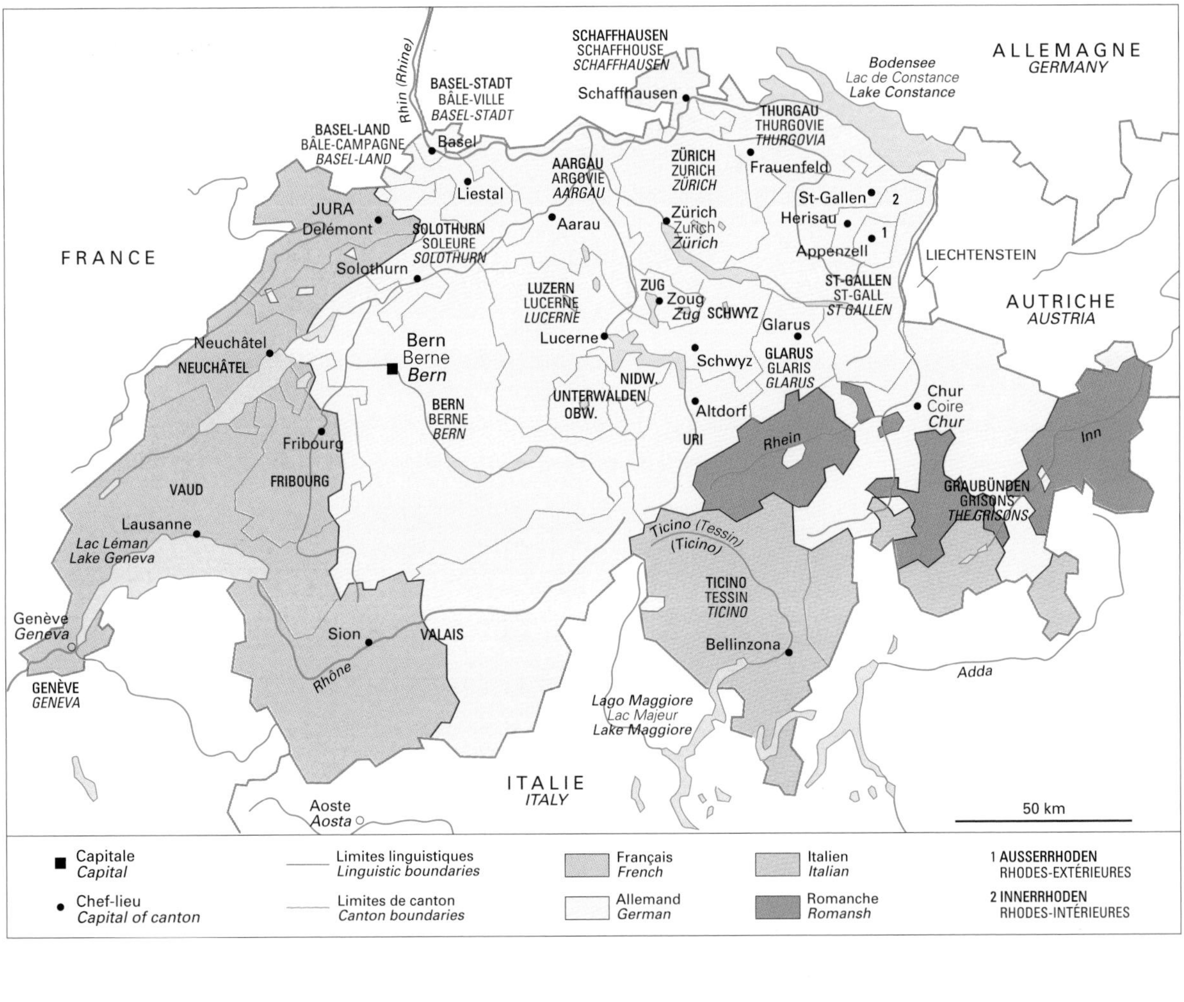

FRANCE - LANGUES, PARLERS ET DIALECTES
FRANCE - LANGUAGES AND DIALECTS

flamand
Flemish
wallon
Walloon
picard
Amiens
allemand
German
lorrain
normand
Norman French
Paris
champenois
alsacien
Alsatian
Brest
breton
Breton
francien
angevin
langue d'oïl
berrichon
franco-
provençal
poitevin
saintongeois
Limoges
Lyon
limousin
auvergnat
langue d'oc
italien
Italian
gascon
languedocien
provençal
Provençal
Toulouse
basque
Basque
béarnais
corse
Corsican
catalan
Catalan
Langue d'oïl
Langue d'oc
Franco-provençal
Autres langues romanes
Other Romance languages
Langues germaniques
Germanic languages
Autres langues
Other languages
Limites linguistiques
Linguistic boundaries
200 km

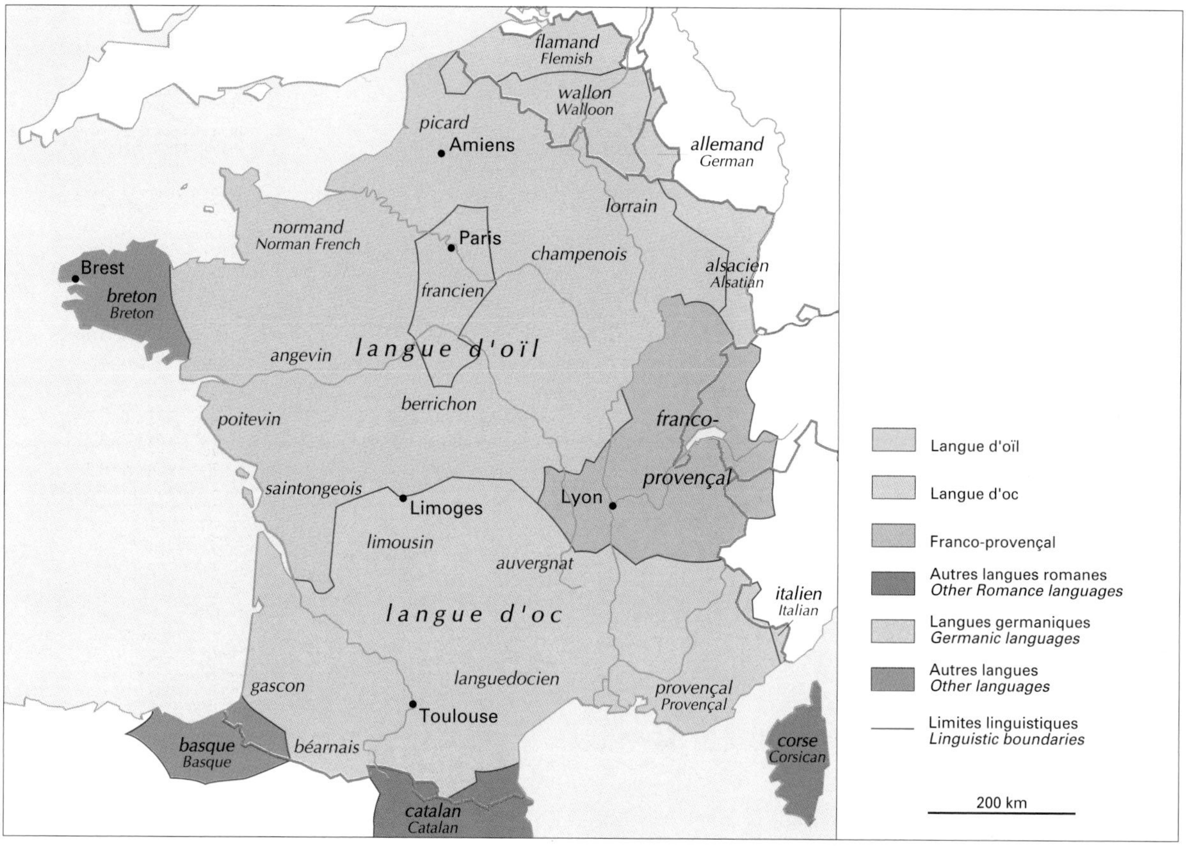

CANADA - LANGUES MATERNELLES
CANADA - MOTHER TONGUES

YUKON
TERRITORY
YUKON
NORTHWEST TERRITORIES
TERRITOIRES DU NORD-OUEST
NEWFOUNDLAND
TERRE-NEUVE
BRITISH COLUMBIA
COLOMBIE-BRITANNIQUE
ALBERTA
MANITOBA
SASKATCHEWAN
QUÉBEC
QUEBEC
PRINCE EDWARD I.
Î.-DU-PRINCE-ÉDOUARD
P
C
F
Vancouver
U
G/A
F
Winnipeg
ONTARIO
NOVA SCOTIA
NOUVELLE-ÉCOSSE
I
Montréal
Montreal
Toronto
NEW BRUNSWICK
NOUVEAU-BRUNSWICK
I
C
F
Official languages: English, French
Langues officielles: anglais, français
Total population by province and by city (in millions)
Population totale par province et par ville (en millions)
0,1 0,5 1 3 6 10 M
English / Anglais
F French / Français
Non-official languages
Langues non-officielles
C Chinese / Chinois
I Italian / Italien
G/A German / Allemand
U Ukrainian/ Ukrainien
P Punjabi / Panjabi
Others / Autres

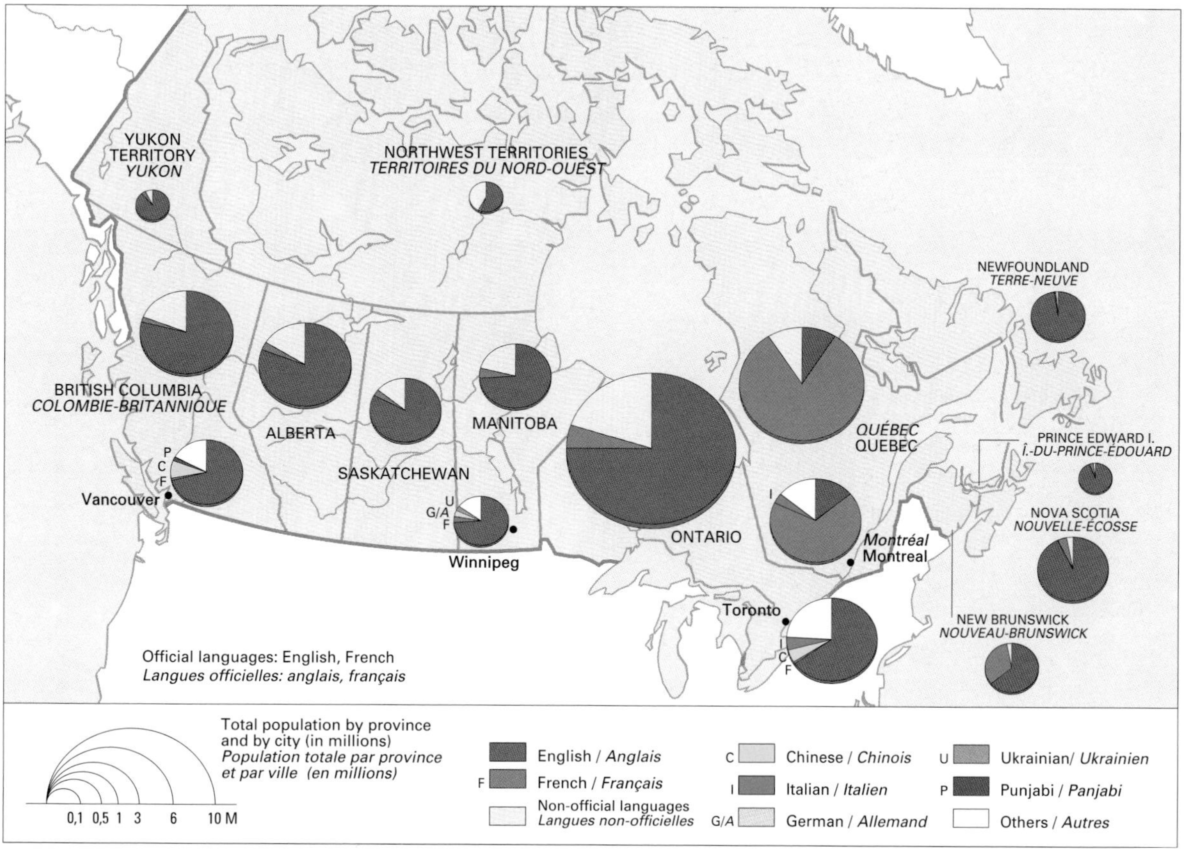

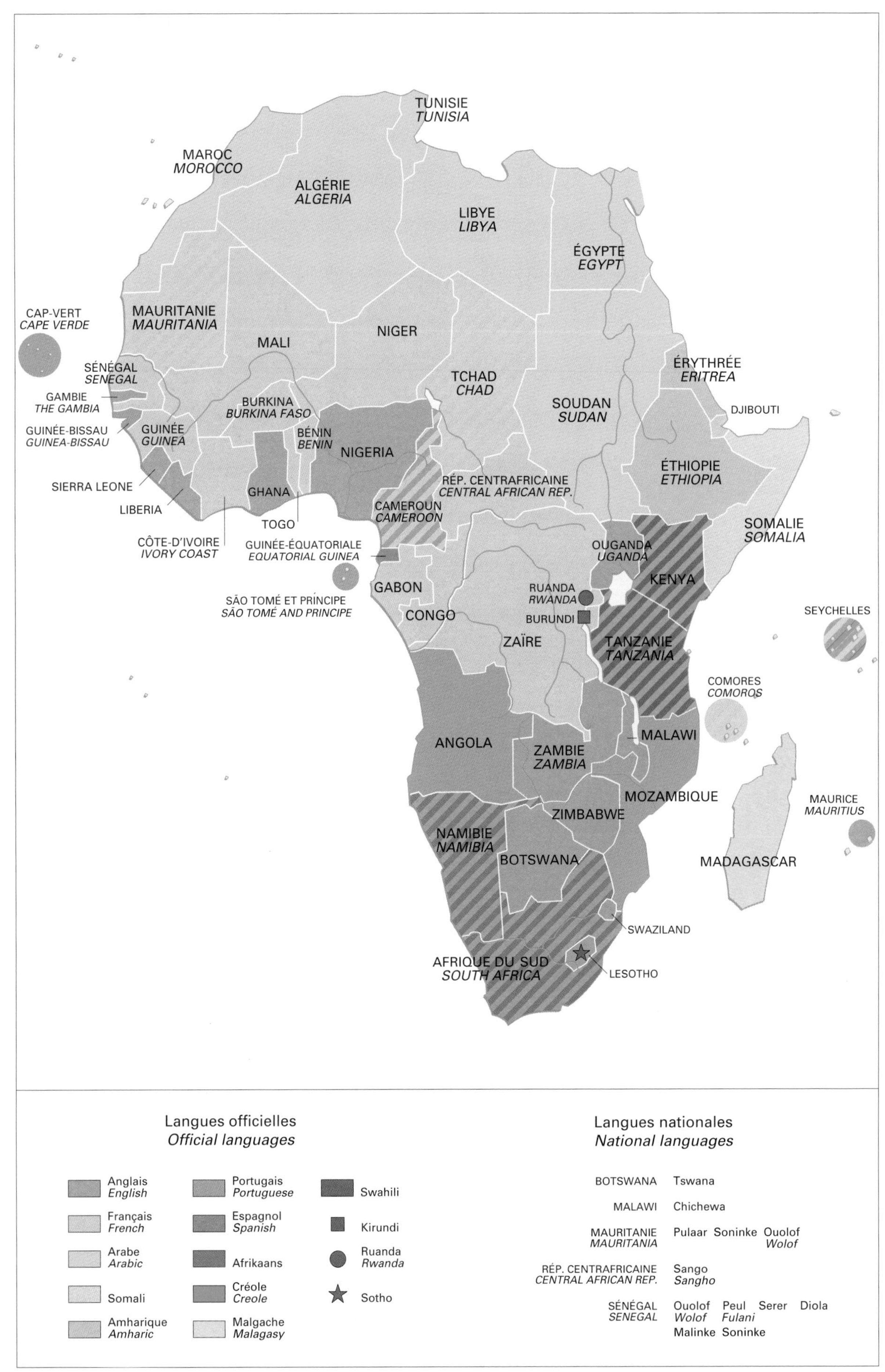
TUNISIE
TUNISIA
MAROC
MOROCCO
ALGÉRIE
ALGERIA
LIBYE
LIBYA
ÉGYPTE
EGYPT
CAP-VERT
CAPE VERDE
MAURITANIE
MAURITANIA
MALI
NIGER
TCHAD
CHAD
SOUDAN
SUDAN
ÉRYTHRÉE
ERITREA
DJIBOUTI
SÉNÉGAL
SENEGAL
GAMBIE
THE GAMBIA
GUINÉE-BISSAU
GUINEA-BISSAU
GUINÉE
GUINEA
BURKINA
BURKINA FASO
BÉNIN
BENIN
NIGERIA
SIERRA LEONE
LIBERIA
GHANA
TOGO
CÔTE-D'IVOIRE
IVORY COAST
GUINÉE-ÉQUATORIALE
EQUATORIAL GUINEA
RÉP. CENTRAFRICAINE
CENTRAL AFRICAN REP.
CAMEROUN
CAMEROON
ÉTHIOPIE
ETHIOPIA
SOMALIE
SOMALIA
OUGANDA
UGANDA
KENYA
SÃO TOMÉ ET PRÍNCIPE
SÃO TOMÉ AND PRINCIPE
GABON
CONGO
RUANDA
RWANDA
BURUNDI
ZAÏRE
TANZANIE
TANZANIA
SEYCHELLES
COMORES
COMOROS
ANGOLA
ZAMBIE
ZAMBIA
MALAWI
MOZAMBIQUE
MAURICE
MAURITIUS
ZIMBABWE
NAMIBIE
NAMIBIA
BOTSWANA
MADAGASCAR
SWAZILAND
AFRIQUE DU SUD
SOUTH AFRICA
LESOTHO
Langues officielles
Official languages
Anglais
English
Français
French
Arabe
Arabic
Somali
Amharique
Amharic
Portugais
Portuguese
Espagnol
Spanish
Afrikaans
Créole
Creole
Malgache
Malagasy
Swahili
Kirundi
Ruanda
Rwanda
Sotho
Langues nationales
National languages
BOTSWANA Tswana
MALAWI Chichewa
MAURITANIE Pulaar Soninke Ouolof
MAURITANIA Wolof
RÉP. CENTRAFRICAINE Sango
CENTRAL AFRICAN REP. Sangho
SÉNÉGAL Ouolof Peul Serer Diola
SENEGAL Wolof Fulani
Malinke Soninke